Oxford
Learner's Dictionary of Academic English

Chief Editor	Diana Lea
Senior Editor	Victoria Bull
Development Editor	Suzanne Webb
Editor	Robert Duncan

Great Clarendon Street, Oxford, OX2 6DP, United Kingdom

Oxford University Press is a department of the University of Oxford. It furthers the University's objective of excellence in research, scholarship, and education by publishing worldwide. Oxford is a registered trade mark of Oxford University Press in the UK and in certain other countries

First published in 2014
2018 2017 2016 2015 2014
10 9 8 7 6 5 4 3 2 1

ISBN: 978 0 19 433350 4 Book and CD-ROM pack
ISBN: 978 0 19 433348 1 Book in pack
ISBN: 978 0 19 433349 8 CD-ROM in pack

Printed in China

This book is printed on paper from certified and well-managed sources

ACKNOWLEDGEMENTS

Picture credits: Cover images by Corbis (Spiral staircase/Ocean), (DNA molecule/Rasieka/Science Photo Library), (Hummingbird/Ocean), (Electronic stock ticker/Tom Grill); Oxford University Press (Radcliffe Camera, Oxford/ Jenny Cundy/Image Source), (Fibre-optic cable with binary/Comstock), (Hydroelectric dam/Photodisc); SuperStock (Geometric floor mosaics/ Funkystock/age fotostock).

Contents

Acknowledgements

Advisory Board

Professor Bas Aarts
Colin Campbell
Professor Vyv Evans
Danica Gondova
Tilly Harrison
Dr Amos Paran
Dr Robert Vanderplank

Senior Lexicographers

Andrew Delahunty
Sally Wehmeier

Lexicographers

Roz Combley
Penny Hands
Alison Macaulay
Kate Mohideen
Julie Moore
Dilys Parkinson
Richard Poole
Liz Potter
Dr Martin Stark
Miranda Steel
Daryl Tayar
Jenny Watson
Donald Watt
Laura Wedgeworth

Oxford Academic Writing Tutor and iWriter

Dr Maggie Charles
Kerri Hamberg
Tilly Harrison
Dr Suganthi John
Sam McCarter
Dilys Parkinson
Dr Diane Pecorari
Suzanne Webb

Academic Writing Consultant

Dr Maggie Charles

Subject Consultants

Gloria Dawson (*cultural studies*)
Bruce Downie (*philosophy; psychology*)
Dr Elizabeth Hannon (*mathematics; statistics*)
Bob Margolis (*computer science*)
Dr James Mendelssohn (*biological sciences; earth science*)
Ruth Millership (*law*)
Dr Geoffrey Neuss (*chemistry*)
Professor Bob Reuben (*engineering*)
Fern Watson (*physics*)
Nicholas Woolley (*economics*)

Introduction

In recent years there has been an increasing focus within English Language Teaching on English for Academic Purposes (EAP). Greater numbers of international students are choosing to pursue their higher education in English-speaking countries. Additionally, universities and colleges around the world are offering courses in a whole range of academic subjects taught through the medium of English. As a result, more and more students are learning English specifically for the purposes of academic study. This dictionary has been designed to meet the particular needs of these students, with an exclusive, detailed focus on the language of academic writing.

Academic vocabulary can be divided into three broad categories. First, there is ordinary general English vocabulary. This includes all the function words such as *the*, *and*, *because*, *for*, *about*, as well as common verbs and adjectives and nouns for everyday things. At the other extreme, there is specialist subject vocabulary. This differs between different academic disciplines and can be highly technical; typically, students will need to learn these words as part of their subject studies, whether or not they are also learners of English. In between these two extremes, there is so-called 'subtechnical' or 'general academic' vocabulary. These are words that tend to be used across most or all academic disciplines; most are also used in general English. However, the way they are used in academic writing is often rather different, which is why these words deserve special study from the student of academic English. It is these 'general academic' words that are the main focus of this dictionary.

A core headword list for this dictionary was drawn up through analysis of the Oxford Corpus of Academic English (OCAE), an 85-million word corpus composed of undergraduate textbooks, academic journals, and scholarly monographs and handbooks, drawn from a range of disciplines across the four main subject areas of physical sciences, life sciences, social sciences, and arts and humanities. We also paid due attention to the work of other researchers on academic vocabulary, especially the Academic Word List (AWL) (Coxhead, 2000) and Academic Keyword List (Paquot, 2010). Detailed lexicographic analysis of these core words followed, identifying their meanings, usage patterns and collocations in different academic contexts, together with useful synonyms, opposites and defining words. All words identified as collocations, synonyms or opposites, or used in common academic phrases or idioms, were then added to the headword list, along with the words needed for explaining them. The definitions are mostly written using a controlled defining vocabulary of 2,300 words. Where it has been necessary to use a word not on this list (typically in definitions of more technical, subject-specific words), they are displayed as cross-references. The defining vocabulary, words in the AWL and four supplementary word lists for the different subject areas can be found on the CD-

ROM version of this dictionary. For further information about the word lists and treatment of collocations in the dictionary, see pages R22–23 in the reference section. Other pages in the reference section explain the treatment of nouns, verbs and adjectives in the dictionary and also survey important aspects of academic grammar

A key requirement in compiling the entries for this dictionary was that each meaning should be supported by example sentences based on authentic academic texts. In selecting examples from the corpus, we have not chosen individual, named citations, but have instead chosen to illustrate what seems to be most typical about each word across a range of texts, focusing especially on the most typical collocations and complementation patterns. Some examples have therefore been taken straight from the corpus, but many have been edited, in order to make them more accessible to students of a range of disciplines, whilst still presenting the key language.

Our research with teachers and students of EAP indicated that it is academic writing, above all, that students find most challenging. We hope that the detailed treatment given to core academic vocabulary in this dictionary will enable students to increase their knowledge of these words and the ways in which they combine with other vocabulary, and so write more fluently, more easily and more precisely. However, we also acknowledge the challenges inherent in structuring and organizing a text and in choosing appropriate language and structures for different types of academic assignments. The Oxford Academic Writing Tutor, to be found directly after the A-Z of the dictionary, on pages AWT1–48, offers guidance on many different genres of academic writing, from essays and case studies, through to all the components of a dissertation, with authentic model texts, analysed and annotated, and tips on grammar, language and presentation. The CD-ROM offers an interactive version of the Writing Tutor, the Oxford Academic iWriter, which both presents the model texts and offers frameworks for students to structure their own writing.

This dictionary draws on a long tradition of learner lexicography at Oxford University Press; it also humbly acknowledges an even longer tradition of academic excellence and scholarship. It aims to be of use to students in bridging the gap between learner resources focused on general English and academic resources that do not address the specific needs of foreign learners. As such, we believe it is the first dictionary of its kind.

Guide to the dictionary

Finding the word

Information in the dictionary is given in **entries**, arranged in alphabetical order of **headwords. Compound words** are in separate entries, also arranged alphabetically.

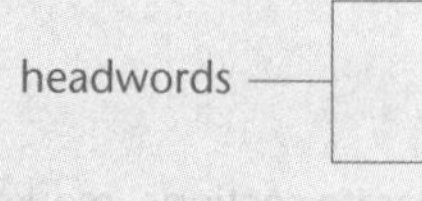

al·ler·gen /ˈælədʒən; *NAmE* ˈælərdʒən/ *noun* a substance that causes an allergy: *Shellfish, nuts, eggs and fish are examples of food allergens.*

al·ler·gic /əˈlɜːdʒɪk; *NAmE* əˈlɜːrdʒɪk/ *adj.* **1 ~ (to sth)** having an allergy to sth: *The patient was allergic to eggs.*

entry

Some headwords can have more than one part of speech.

The small **homonym number** shows that this is the first of two entries for *elite.*

elite[1] /eɪˈliːt; ɪˈliːt/ *noun* [C+sing./pl. v.] a social group that is thought to be the best or most important because of its power, money, intelligence, etc: *Economic and political elites blamed the crisis on the low skill levels of American workers.* ◇ *All organizations contain ruling elites and followers.* ◇ *In written Roman sources, a villa is usually the country estate of a wealthy member of the urban elite.*

A different part of speech is given at each headword.

elite[2] /eɪˈliːt; ɪˈliːt/ *adj.* [only before noun] better than others of the same group or type: *The pattern of advantage for graduates of elite schools is still in operation today.* ◇ *Many*

There are some words in English that have more than one possible spelling, often because of a difference between British and US English. Information about these words is usually given at the British spelling.

The US spelling is given in brackets.

col·our[1] (*US* **color**) /ˈkʌlə(r)/ *noun* **1** [C, U] the appearance that things have that results from the way in which they reflect light. Red and green are colours: *Each of the chromosomes shows a different colour when viewed with a fluorescence microscope.* ◇ *The haematite gives the rock its*

At the entry for the US spelling, a cross-reference directs you to the main entry.

color (*US*) = COLOUR[1], COLOUR[2]

Sometimes there is a difference between international academic usage and general British usage. In these cases, the main entry is placed at the preferred academic spelling, with a note to explain.

sul·fur (*BrE also* **sul·phur**) /ˈsʌlfə(r)/ *noun* [U] (*symb.* **S**) the chemical element of ATOMIC NUMBER 16. Sulfur is a pale yellow substance that produces a strong unpleasant smell when it burns and is used in medicine and industry: *All fossil fuels contain some sulfur.* **HELP** The spelling **sulfur** has been adopted by the International Union of Pure and Applied Chemistry and by the Royal Society of Chemistry in the UK. However, in non-scientific British English, **sulphur** still remains the usual spelling.

Again, there is a cross-reference from the alternative spelling.

sul·phate, **sul·phide**, **sul·phur**, **sul·phur·ic acid** (*BrE*) = SULFATE, SULFIDE, SULFUR, SULFURIC ACID

Irregular forms of verbs are treated in the same way.

Some words that are **derivatives** of other words do not have their own entry in the dictionary because they can be easily understood from the meaning of the word from which they are derived (the root word). They are given in the same entry as the root word, in a specially marked section.

The blue square shows where the derivatives section starts.

meta·phys·ics /ˌmetəˈfɪzɪks/ *noun* [U] the branch of philosophy that deals with the nature of existence, truth and knowledge: *The primary concern of metaphysics should be the investigation not of language but of reality.* ■ **meta·phys·ic·al** /ˌmetəˈfɪzɪkl/ *adj.*: *metaphysical claims/questions/principles*

You can find **idioms** and **phrasal verbs** in separate sections, marked with special symbols.

bend[1] /bend/ *verb* (**bent, bent** /bent/) [I, T] (of a person or thing) to move or change direction so they are/it is no longer straight; to make sb/sth do this: *At this point the beam is not bending at all.* ◇ **+ adv./prep.** *The pain is relieved by bending forwards.* ◇ **~ sth + adv./prep.** *The stiffness of the helix prevents it being easily bent into a circle.* ◇ **~ sth** *A massive object like the sun bends light passing near its edge.*

IDM **bend the ˈrules** to change the rules to suit a particular person or situation: *Liberal societies tend to accept the need to bend rules to suit minority groups.* ➲ *more at* BACKWARDS

PHR V **ˈbend to sth | ˈbend sb/sth to sth** to be forced to behave or act in a particular way; to force sb/sth to do this: *They bent to the intense pressure of established hierarchies.* ◇ *He exhibited the desire to bend others to his will.*

idioms section with symbol **IDM** (see page **R24**)

phrasal verbs section with symbol **PHR V** (see page **R13**)

Understanding and using the word

Words from the Academic Word List are marked with **AWL** (see page **R22**).

aban·doned **AWL** /əˈbændənd/ *adj.* [only before noun] **1** (of a person or animal) having been left: *Workhouses were meant primarily for abandoned children, the aged and the sick.* **2** (of a place) no longer in use: *Many abandoned tin mines were used as landfill sites for the city's waste.*

ab·dom·inal /æbˈdɒmɪnl; *NAmE* æbˈdɑːmɪnl/ *adj.* [only before noun] (*anatomy*) connected with the abdomen: *Patients may have fever and abdominal pain.*

pronunciation, with American pronunciation where it is different (see page **R45**)

Stress marks show stress on compounds.

the ˌ**burden of ˈproof** *noun* [sing.] (*law*) the task or responsibility of proving that sth is true: *The prosecution bears the burden of proof, and must establish guilt.*

Irregular forms of verbs, with their pronunciations. Irregular plurals of nouns are also shown.

verb codes and frames (see pages **R5–8**)

spend /spend/ *verb* (**spent, spent** /spent/) **1** [T] to use time for a particular purpose; to pass time: **~ sth + adv./prep.** *Over 70% of fathers surveyed reported a wish to spend more time with their children.* ◇ **~ sth on sth** *On average, individuals spent 2.9 hours per week on activities related to sports.* ◇ **~ sth doing sth** *He spent 20 years working in sales and marketing.* ◇ **~ sth in doing sth** *The Roman army in Britain spent long periods in establishing and maintaining frontiers.* **2** [I, T] to give money to pay for goods or services: **~ (sth)** *No business likes to spend money unless it has to.* ◇ *The need for governments to spend heavily was regarded as a priority.* ◇ **~ sth on (doing) sth** *The amount spent on foreign goods and services will increase.* ◇ **~ sth doing sth** *They spend enormous sums of money*

prepositions, adverbs and structures that can be used with this word

examples of use in *italic* type

comparatives and superlatives of adjectives

great /greɪt/ *adj.* (**great·er**, **great·est**) **1** [usually before noun] very large; much bigger than average in size or quantity: *There are a great number of regional dialects of the language.* ◇ *In the great majority of cases, a practical solution can be found.* ◇ *Waves travel great distances in deep water with little energy loss.* **2** much more than average in degree or amount: *Minerals are of great importance to microorganisms.* ◇ *The book describes in great detail the events and personalities of the period.* ◇ *Without doubt, this policy involves great risks.* ◇ **to a ~ extent** *The big supermarkets can control to a great extent which products customers buy.* **3** [only before noun] important or most important: *The great advantage of the survey data is that they include the generation born in the 1970s.* **4** extremely

information on use of adjectives (see page **R17**)

es·tab·lish·ment AWL /ɪˈstæblɪʃmənt/ *noun* **1** [U] ~ **(of sth)** the act of starting or creating sth that is meant to last for a long time: *The Directive requires the establishment of a system of strict protection for listed species.* **2** (*usually* **the Establishment**) [sing.+ sing./pl. v.] (*often disapproving*) the people in a society or a profession who have influence and power and who usually do not support change: *Many early radicals were now respected members of the Establishment they had once attacked.* ◇ *the political/religious/military establishment* **3** [C] (*formal*) a business organization or public institution: *Educational establishments should work in partnership with outside agencies to design and deliver smoking prevention activities.*

information on different types of nouns (see page **R14**)

fixed form of noun

label giving information about usage (see inside front cover)

chem·ical[1] AWL /ˈkemɪkl/ *adj.* involving atoms and MOLECULES and how they cause substances to have different structures, properties and reactions: *Many chemical reactions generate vivid colours.* ◇ *DNA and RNA are very similar in chemical composition.* HELP In non-scientific use, **chemical** is often used for describing substances that are produced in industrial processes, rather than occurring naturally. This use is best avoided in scientific writing: use **synthetic** or **artificial** instead: *Organic farming largely avoids the use of synthetic fertilizers.*

▸ CHEMICAL + NOUN **process** • **reaction** • **modification**, **shift**, **change** • **bonding** • **weathering** • **synthesis** *Chemical weathering is significant because of the high temperature and humidity.* | **nature** • **structure** • **properties** • **characteristics** • **composition** • **formula** • **energy** • **analysis** • **diversity** • **equilibrium** *The chemical nature of soils is determined by the combination of mineral and organic matter that makes up the soil.* ◇ *These zones have distinctive physical, chemical and biological properties.* | **group** • **substance** • **element** • **compound** • **bond** • **reagent** *There are several types of chemical bonds.*

word used in definition that is not in the defining vocabulary

HELP notes give extra information about usage, often concerning differences between academic and general English.

Collocations section shows words that commonly combine with the headword (see pages **R22–23**).

Build your vocabulary

The dictionary also contains a lot of information that will help you increase your vocabulary and use the language productively.

ef·fect·ive·ly /ɪˈfektɪvli/ *adv.* **1** in a way that produces the intended result or a successful result: *These risks must be effectively managed.* ◇ *The real test for a successful bridge is whether it works effectively.* ◇ *Certain skills and techniques may be needed to communicate effectively with children.* OPP INEFFECTIVELY **2** used when you are saying what the facts of a situation are SYN IN EFFECT (1): *The end of the USSR effectively removed the most serious source of organized state resistance to US power.* ◇ *The rapid increase in food prices effectively denied many poor people access to food.*

Special symbols show opposites and synonyms.

sig·nifi·cant AWL /sɪɡˈnɪfɪkənt/ *adj.* **1** large or important enough to have an effect or to be noticed: *These voters could have a significant effect on the outcome of the election.* ◇ *Although population ageing is a global phenomenon, there are significant regional differences.* ◇ **~ for sb/sth** *The contributions of Islamic civilization proved to be as significant for the West.* ◇ **it is ~ that...** *It was significant that its nearest rival only had a 5.5 per cent share of the market.* OPP INSIGNIFICANT ➲ thesaurus note *at* IMPORTANT **2** having a particular meaning: *The lighting of a candle may be symbolically significant if it denotes the bringing of light, that is, enlightenment.* ◇ **it is ~ that...** *It is particularly significant that Branagh selected Belfast for the play's United Kingdom debut.* **3** (*statistics*) having statistical significance ➲ *see also* SIGNIFICANCE (3): *After 3 years, results for breast cancer were no longer statistically significant.* ◇ *Munafo et al. (2003) found significant associations between personality and polymorphisms in three genes.*

WORD FAMILY
significant *adj.*
significantly *adv.*
signify *verb*
significance *noun*
signification *noun*
insignificant *adj.*
insignificantly *adv.*
insignificance *noun*

Word families show words related to the headword.

Notes help you choose the right word or expression, and also help with difficult grammar points. They are all listed on pages xi–xii.

WHICH WORD?

effect ◆ affect

- **effect** *noun* a result or an influence: *This section discusses the effects of information technology on strategy.*
- **affect** *verb* to have an influence on sb/sth: *A reduction of caterpillar prey has been shown to adversely affect some birds.*
- **effect** *verb* to achieve or produce a result: *To effect change does not necessarily require a great intellect as much as a brave one.*

The noun **affect** is a technical term in psychology.

Cross-references refer you to information in other parts of the dictionary.

drift[1] /drɪft/ *noun* **1** [C, usually sing., U] a slow steady movement or change, from one situation, belief or place to another: **~ towards sth** *The result was a drift towards socialism.* ◇ **~ (from sth) (to sth)** *The devastation of the land during the war had fostered the drift to the cities.* ➲ *see also* GENETIC DRIFT **2** [U] the movement of the sea or air: *Drift is almost exclusively to the east.* ◇ *Wind direction is shown by smoke drift.* ➲ *compare* CURRENT² (1) ➲ *see also* CONTINENTAL DRIFT **3** [U] **~ (from sth)** the movement of a ship, plane or bird away from its intended direction because of currents or wind: *This formula accounts for drift from the intended flight path caused by crosswinds.* **4** [U, C] a large mass of sth, for example soil, ice or snow, that has been left somewhere by the movement of water, wind, etc: *Water accumulates in depressions in glacial drift.* ◇ **~ of sth** *Winter drifts of snow contribute to streamflow in early spring.* **5** [sing.] **~ (of sth)** the general meaning of what sb says or writes: *When they were encouraged to reflect on specific problems in the past, the drift of their replies became more negative.*

See also refers you to a word with a similar or related meaning.

Compare refers you to a word with a contrasting meaning.

Notes on usage

In the dictionary, you will find many notes on various aspects of usage in academic English. These notes are listed below according to the type of note.

Which word?

These notes show the difference between words that are often confused. The word in **blue** shows you the entry where you can find the note.

actual / current / present / actually / currently / presently / at present
adverse / averse
almost / nearly
classical / classic
consent¹ / permission
continuous / continual
damage¹ / injury
disability / disabled / impairment / impaired / sighted / blind / deaf
economic / economical
effect¹ / affect
electric / electrical
especially / specially
generally / commonly
historic / historical
interesting / interested
narrow¹ / thin
old / older / oldest / elder / eldest
persuade / convince
principal¹ / principle
raise¹ / rise
strategy / tactics / strategic / tactical
subsequent / consequent / successive / consecutive
systematic / systemic
various / different
wide / broad

Grammar point

These notes help explain points of grammar that often cause problems. The word in **blue** shows you the entry where you can find the note.

can¹ / cannot / able / unable
data / bacteria / criteria / media / phenomena / strata / bacterium / criterion / datum / medium / phenomenon /stratum
despite / in spite of / although / even though / though
each / every
metre / kilometre / centimetre / millimetre / inch
might / could / may
modal¹ / can / could / may / might / must / shall / should / will / would
must / have to
none
per cent¹ / percentage
present³ / describe / examine / illustrate / reveal / show
so² / so that / in order to / to²
they / them / their / themselves / he / she
whether / if
will¹ / would

Thesaurus

These notes show the differences between groups of words with similar meanings. The word in **blue** shows you the entry where you can find the note.

argue / assert / claim / contend / maintain
carry / carry out / conduct / undertake / perform
challenge² / question / dispute / doubt
clear¹ / obvious / apparent / evident
company / business / conglomerate / corporation / firm / multinational / organization
confirm / support / verify / validate
contribute / donate / support
convincing / compelling / persuasive / strong
country / nation / state
debate¹ / controversy / disagreement / dispute
determine / establish / identify / ascertain
difficult / hard / challenging / demanding
discussion / debate / dialogue / talks / consultation

disease / illness / infection / disorder / condition
essential[1] / crucial / critical / vital
evidence[1] / proof / support / demonstration
explore / examine / investigate / analyse
feature[1] / characteristic / quality / property / trait / attribute
financial / economic / fiscal / monetary
fund[2] / finance / support / subsidize
hypothesis / thesis / proposition / premise
idea / concept / notion
important / significant / notable
indicate / suggest / imply / point to
investigation / study / research / experiment / observation / analysis
limit[2] / restriction / control / restraint / constraint / limitation
main[1] / major / key / central / principal / prime / primary
mean[1] / involve / entail / imply
money / capital / funds / income / revenue / wealth
plausible / credible / reasonable
provide / give / offer / present
record[2] / document / register / chart / enter
reference[1] / citation / quotation
reject / deny / contradict / refute
result[1] / outcome / finding / consequence
show[1] / demonstrate / illustrate / prove
situation / circumstances / position / conditions / the case
suggest / propose / put sth forward / advance
supply[2] / provide / yield / generate
target[1] / aim / objective / goal / object / end
theory / model / approach / framework
use[1] / employ / draw on/upon / utilize / deploy

Language bank

These notes show you how to express similar ideas in a variety of ways in academic writing. The word in **blue** shows you the entry where you can find the note.

about[2] — Saying what a text is about
according to — Reporting someone's opinion
addition — Adding a further point
argument — Showing your position in an argument
because — Explaining reasons
broadly — Making generalizations
cause[1] — Cause and effect
compare — Comparing and contrasting
concede — Conceding a point and making a counterargument
conclusion — Stating a conclusion
critical — Critical evaluation
define — Defining language
emphasis — Emphatic language
evaluation — Making an evaluation of your study
evidence[1] — Discussing evidence
example — Giving examples
except[1] — Making an exception
exceptionally — Adverbs of degree
hedge — Hedging language
however — Ways of saying 'but'
i.e. — Explaining what you mean
impersonal — Giving opinions using impersonal language
organize — Organizing your writing
predict — Discussing predictions
process[1] — Describing a process
proportion — Describing proportions and relative quantities
purpose — Stating purpose
reflective — Reflective writing
report[1] — Reporting verbs
research[1] — Claiming that your research is important or relevant
research[1] — Indicating a gap, problem or need in current research
research[2] — Research verbs
statistic — Describing statistics
suggestion — Giving suggestions for future research
surprising — Highlighting interesting data
table — Referring to visuals
therefore — Ways of saying 'for this reason'
time[1] — Time expressions
trend — Describing trends

A a

a /ə; *strong form* eɪ/ (*also* **an** /ən; *strong form* æn/) *indefinite article* HELP The form **a** is used before consonant sounds and the form **an** before vowel sounds. When saying abbreviations like 'FM' or 'UN', use **a** or **an** according to how the first letter is said. For example, **F** is a consonant, but begins with the sound /e/ and so you say: *an FM signal.* **U** is a vowel but begins with /j/ and so you say: *a UN agency* **1** used before countable or singular nouns referring to people or things that have not already been mentioned: *A man came to the door that morning.* ◇ *Beadle was trying to find an organism that met all these criteria.* ◇ *In 1968 President Johnson announced a halt to the bombing of North Vietnam.* ◇ *Wright was apprenticed to Archibald Hamilton, a friend of Smollett's.* **2** used before uncountable nouns when these have an adjective in front of them, or a phrase following them: *The pictures have an undeniable beauty.* ◇ *They believed that the working classes of all countries enjoyed a solidarity that cut across state boundaries.* **3** any; every: *A baby is fully and completely born when it is completely delivered from the body of its mother.* **4** used to show that sb/sth is a member of a group or profession: *Like Chiang Kai-shek before him, Rhee was a Christian.* ◇ *He was originally trained as a doctor.* ◇ *They believe it to be a Picasso and worth several million pounds.* **5** used in front of two nouns that are seen as a single unit: *The defendant in this case was driving a horse and cart negligently.* **6** used instead of *one* before some numbers: *The likelihood of this happening is less than one in a hundred.* **7** used when talking about prices, quantities and rates SYN PER: *In March 2008, the price of gold reached $1 000 an ounce for the first time ever.* ◇ *The rocket moves at 25 000 miles an hour relative to the surface of the Earth.* **8** used before the names of days of the week to talk about one particular day: *The war began on a Sunday.* **9** used before sb's name to show that nothing more is known about the person: *The author of this essay was a Mr Durand of the Royal Society.*

aban·don AWL /əˈbændən/ *verb* **1** to stop doing sth, especially before it is finished; to stop planning to do sth: **~ sth** *The Australian Museum officially abandoned the project in 2005.* ◇ *The oil company was forced to abandon its plans to sink the oil platform.* ◇ **~ sth in favour of sth** *Free trade was abandoned in favour of protectionist policies.* ◇ **~ sth for sth** *Ovid abandoned public life for poetry.* **2** to stop believing in sth or supporting a party, cause, etc: **~ sth** *He claims that the countries of Western Europe have abandoned the ideals of an open society.* ◇ **~ sth in favour of sth** *The Republican Party was increasingly abandoned by southern blacks in favour of the Democratic Party.* **3** to leave sb, especially sb you are responsible for, with no intention of returning: **~ sb** *Darius was forced to abandon his army and flee.* ◇ **~ sb to sth** *Abandoning a newborn child to its fate was not a crime at all, but rather an acceptable means of family planning.* **4 ~ sth** to leave a place or thing with no intention of returning, especially because of danger or economic problems: *Farms were abandoned as families moved in search of work.*

▸ ABANDON + NOUN **quest, search** ♦ **practice** ♦ **policy** ♦ **project** ♦ **plan** ♦ **attempt** ♦ **career** ♦ **experiment** *Peasant farmers are usually conservative and reluctant to abandon traditional practices.* | **ideal, principle** ♦ **conception, idea, notion** ♦ **assumption** ♦ **belief** ♦ **hope** ♦ **commitment** *In an effort to obtain relief from persecution, many abandoned their beliefs.*

▸ ADVERB + ABANDON **officially, formally** ♦ **progressively, gradually** ♦ **finally** ♦ **quickly** ♦ **virtually** ♦ **largely** ♦ **altogether, totally, completely** *Contemporary theorists have progressively abandoned this assumption of women's natural inferiority.* | **simply** *Normally, the slave traders would simply abandon the smallest children by the roadside to die.*

aban·doned AWL /əˈbændənd/ *adj.* [only before noun] **1** (of a person or animal) having been left: *Workhouses were meant primarily for abandoned children, the aged and the sick.* **2** (of a place) no longer in use: *Many abandoned tin mines were used as landfill sites for the city's waste.*

aban·don·ment AWL /əˈbændənmənt/ *noun* [U] **1** the act of leaving a person who depends on you SYN DESERTION (1): *Individuals may suppress anger due to fears of rejection or abandonment.* **2** the act of leaving a building, a place or a business due to a natural disaster, war or economic problems, and with no intention of returning: *These forests formed after agricultural abandonment.* ◇ **~ of sth** *The apparent widespread abandonment of villas in Italy around the end of the second century is often attributed to the plague.* **3 ~ of sth** the act of giving up an idea or stopping a course of action: *Americans felt betrayed by the abandonment of Wilsonian principles.*

ab·bre·vi·ate /əˈbriːvieɪt/ *verb* [usually passive] to make a word, phrase or text shorter: **~ sth** *There is a tendency to abbreviate the text.* ◇ **(be) abbreviated to/as sth** *Force is measured in newtons (usually abbreviated to N).* ■ **ab·bre·vi·ated** *adj.*: *The framework then poses the following questions, stated here in abbreviated form.*

ab·bre·vi·ation /əˌbriːviˈeɪʃn/ *noun* a short form of a word or phrase: *Only standard, recognized abbreviations should be used.* ◇ **~ for sth** *k is an abbreviation for kilo.* ◇ **~ of sth** *'Et al' is an abbreviation of the Latin phrase 'et alia', meaning 'and others'.*

ab·di·cate /ˈæbdɪkeɪt/ *verb* **1** [I] to give up the position of being king, queen, etc: *Charles IV had no choice but to abdicate in favour of his son, Ferdinand.* **2** [T] to fail or refuse to perform a duty: *The government was accused of abdicating its responsibility.* ■ **ab·di·ca·tion** /ˌæbdɪˈkeɪʃn/ *noun* [U, C] **~ (of sb/sth)** *The second peace followed Napoleon's abdication in April 1814 and lasted until his return from exile on Elba in March 1815.* ◇ *Sceptics would say there is an abdication of public authority in favour of unrepresentative private interests.*

ab·do·men /ˈæbdəmən/ *noun* **1** the part of the body below the chest that contains the stomach, BOWELS, etc: *The pain began in the centre of the abdomen.* ◇ *the upper/lower abdomen* **2** the end part of an insect's body that is attached to its THORAX: *Females release their larvae by pumping their abdomens.*

ab·dom·inal /æbˈdɒmɪnl; *NAmE* æbˈdɑːmɪnl/ *adj.* [only before noun] (*anatomy*) connected with the abdomen: *Patients may have fever and abdominal pain.*

abil·ity /əˈbɪləti/ *noun* (*pl.* **-ies**) **1** [sing.] the fact that sb/sth is able to do sth: **~ to do sth** *Many animals possess the ability to distinguish light of different wavelengths.* ◇ *Some of these children acquired an increased ability to cope with stress.* ◇ **~ of sb/sth to do sth** *Literacy affects the ability of target audiences to understand marketing messages.* OPP INABILITY **2** [U, C] a level of skill or intelligence: *Tests of both reading ability and non-verbal reasoning were administered.* ◇ *The all-round person possesses general abilities but is not a specialist.* ◇ **+ noun** *The pupils were taught in mixed ability classes.*

▸ ADJECTIVE + ABILITY **innate** ♦ **limited** ♦ **remarkable** *Research on newborn babies suggests an innate ability to attend to faces.* ◇ *Some animals exhibit a remarkable homing ability.* | **general** ♦ **cognitive, mental, intellectual** ♦ **academic** ♦ **verbal, linguistic** ♦ **reading** *Tests of mental abilities do not assess all important aspects of brain function.*

▸ VERB + ABILITY **have, possess** ♦ **lack** ♦ **develop** ♦ **test** *Children need opportunities to develop problem-solving abilities.* | **lose** ♦ **retain** ♦ **acquire** ♦ **demonstrate** ♦

A

A

question, doubt *Liver cells retain the ability to divide, so the liver can regrow if part of it is removed.* | **affect** ♦ **impair, limit, hinder, constrain, undermine, restrict** ♦ **enhance, improve** *Poverty impairs the ability to obtain a healthy, balanced diet.*

▸ ABILITY TO + VERB **cope** ♦ **pay** ♦ **innovate** ♦ **adapt** ♦ **communicate** ♦ **predict** ♦ **manipulate** ♦ **control** *Access to care was to be based on clinical need, not on the ability to pay.*

able /ˈeɪbl/ *adj.* **1** (used as a modal verb) **be ~ to do sth** to have the power, skill, means or opportunity to do sth: *Some families earned so little they were barely able to survive.* ◇ *The larger companies are better able to take advantage of these opportunities.* OPP UNABLE ➲ grammar note *at* CAN¹ **2** (**abler** /ˈeɪblə(r), **ablest** /ˈeɪblɪst/) intelligent; good at sth: *Hess was an able administrator as well as a brilliant scientist.*

ab·nor·mal AWL /æbˈnɔːml; *NAmE* æbˈnɔːrml/ *adj.* different from what is usual or expected, especially in a way that may be harmful or not wanted: *A patient with slightly abnormal liver function tests was referred to hospital for investigation.* ◇ *Possible causes of abnormal findings in the measurements are also discussed.* OPP NORMAL¹ ■ **ab·nor·mal·ly** AWL /æbˈnɔːməli; *NAmE* æbˈnɔːrməli/ *adv.*: *All these enzymes were abnormally high, indicating a problem with the liver.* ➲ language bank *at* EXCEPTIONALLY

ab·nor·mal·ity /ˌæbnɔːˈmæləti; *NAmE* ˌæbnɔːrˈmæləti/ *noun* (*pl.* **-ies**) [C, U] a feature in a person's body or behaviour that is not usual and may be harmful or cause illness: *The congenital heart abnormalities are seen in 40-50% of patients.* ◇ *The tests are offered to women with a family history of chromosomal abnormality.*

abol·ish /əˈbɒlɪʃ; *NAmE* əˈbɑːlɪʃ/ *verb* **~ sth** to officially end a system, practice, institution or law: *The slave trade was abolished by Act of Parliament in 1807.* ◇ *The decree completely abolished the death penalty.*

abo·li·tion /ˌæbəˈlɪʃn/ *noun* [U] **~ (of sth)** the ending of a system, practice, institution or law: *Between 1828 and 1830, some 5 000 petitions calling for the gradual abolition of slavery were submitted to Parliament.*

abor·tion /əˈbɔːʃn; *NAmE* əˈbɔːrʃn/ *noun* **1** [U] the deliberate ending of a PREGNANCY at an early stage: *In the more traditional Buddhist countries, abortion is illegal with certain limited exceptions.* **2** [C] a medical operation to end a PREGNANCY at an early stage SYN TERMINATION (2): *The court held that the girl could have an abortion.* ➲ *compare* MISCARRIAGE

about¹ /əˈbaʊt/ *prep.* **1** on the subject of sb/sth; in connection with sb/sth: *This book is all about moral philosophy.* ◇ *The courts generally obtain a social report about the young person's family.* ◇ *What was most unusual about Smith was the range of his intelligence.* ◇ *The most pressing question at the end of the war was what to do about Germany.* ◇ *Jefferson focuses on how African American soldiers felt about the army and the war.* **2** used to describe the purpose or an aspect of sth: **all ~ (doing) sth** *Politics in democracies is all about bargaining and compromise.* ◇ *These team-working and individual decision-making skills are what general practice training is all about.* **3** busy with sth; doing sth: *The state should not interfere with the right of a person to go about their legitimate business.*

about² /əˈbaʊt/ *adv.* **1** a little more or less than; a little before or after SYN APPROXIMATELY: *These in-depth interviews lasted about an hour.* ◇ *This suggestion was put in practice about ten years later.* **2** nearly; very close to: *Anti-inflammatory pain-killing agents are about the most commonly used group of drugs.*

LANGUAGE BANK

Saying what a text is about

In academic writing, there are various ways of presenting the subject matter of a text.

- a/an book/paper/article/chapter **about** sth
- a/an book/paper/article/chapter **on** sth
- a text/an author **deals with** sth
- a text/an author **discusses** sth
- a text/an author **presents an overview of** sth
- a text/an author **focuses on** sth
- a text/an author **explores** sth
- a text/an author **examines** sth
- a text/an author **considers** sth
- a text/an author **addresses** sth

– *In 2001, Cell published a paper* ***about*** *a chromosomal duplication.*
– *His book included a chapter* ***on*** *religion.*
– *The next three chapters* ***deal with*** *the data collection aspects of conducting a survey.*
– *The author* ***discusses*** *partially random machines further in Chapter 12.*
– *Our aim in this chapter is to* ***present an overview of*** *research on problem-solving.*
– *Most studies have* ***focused on*** *large organizations.*
– *This article* ***explores*** *the background to the legislation.*
– *One recent study* ***examined*** *different coping functions used to deal with daily work demands...(Daniels and Harris, 2005).*
– *Several authors* ***have considered*** *the relationships between rationality and politics.*
– *This article* ***addresses*** *both the practical and the cultural implications of bereavement in wartime.*

about³ /əˈbaʊt/ *adj.*
IDM **be about to do sth** to be close to doing sth; to be going to do sth very soon: *The material is about to become available to the public.* ◇ *The Cultural Revolution was about to begin.* **not be about to do sth** to not be willing to do sth; to not intend to do sth: *The more developed world is not about to initiate changes that would lessen its power and profits.*

above¹ /əˈbʌv/ *prep.* **1** at or to a higher place or position than sth/sb: *A light shines above the darkened stage.* ◇ *Fireflies hover above the pond.* **2** more than sth; greater in number, level or age than sb/sth: *Unemployment soared above 7 per cent nationally.* ◇ *There are mountains as high as 8 854 m (29 048 feet) above sea level.* ◇ *Only nine villages have higher secondary schools for girls above the age of 15.* **3** of greater importance or of higher quality than sb/sth: *Bacon rated Tacitus above Plato and Aristotle as a moral thinker.* **4** too good or too honest to do sth: *Everything is made to appear fair and above suspicion.* ◇ *The members of that elite were not above making major concessions to 'barbarian' rulers, as the situation required.* IDM **above ˈall** most important of all; especially: *The work shows knowledge of the major Latin poets, and above all of Cicero.*

above² /əˈbʌv/ *adv.* **1** at or to a higher place: *By contact with the atmosphere above, the river slowly accumulates oxygen again.* ◇ *In the dry season, viewed from above, Sero valley stands out as a green oasis among the brown and bare fields.* ◇ *These were reforms imposed from above.* **2** greater in number, level or age: *Success rates remained high (i.e. 80 per cent and above).* ◇ *All schools need to have at least 50 per cent of pupils achieve Level 5 or above in English, mathematics and science.* ◇ *More than 20 per cent of the population is aged 65 and above.* **3** earlier in sth written or printed: *King Malcolm of the Scots spoke English and Gaelic (see above, p. 212).* ◇ *As stated above, effective communication contributes to health outcomes in various ways.*

above[3] /ə'bʌv/ *adj.* [only before noun] mentioned or printed previously in a letter, book, etc: *For the above reasons, diagnosis often has to be based on reports by others of changes in the patient's behaviour.* ■ **the above** *noun* [sing.+ sing./pl. v.] *All the above can be expressed in the form of simple graphs.*

a,bove-'mentioned *adj.* [only before noun] mentioned or named earlier in the same letter, book, etc: *The above-mentioned studies have pointed to the critical role of family well-being in building a harmonious society.*

abroad /ə'brɔːd/ *adv.* (*especially BrE*) in or to a foreign country: *English scholars who could afford it went abroad.* ◇ *Increasingly, patients are travelling abroad in search of health care.* ◇ *US firms and workers face increasing competition from abroad.* ◇ *In 2009, bad weather in the UK increased demand for holidays abroad.*

ab·rupt /ə'brʌpt/ *adj.* **1** sudden and unexpected, often in an unpleasant way: *Canada's embrace of free trade marks an abrupt change in its strategy.* ◇ *The period of high growth came to an abrupt end.* **2** steep; not gradual or gentle: *At this point, the river makes an abrupt turn to the south.* **3** speaking or acting in a way that seems unfriendly and rude; not taking time to say more than is necessary: *He had a reputation as a bully and stories circulated about an abrupt leadership style.* ■ **ab·rupt·ly** /ə'brʌptli/ *adv.*: *The fossil insect record indicates that during the last 14 000 years, regional climates have often changed abruptly.* ◇ *These terrains consist essentially of high ridges rising abruptly from the valley floors.*

ab·sence /'æbsəns/ *noun* **1** [U] the fact of sb/sth not existing or not being available SYN LACK[1]: **~ (of sb/sth)** *The effects are difficult to measure because of the absence of reliable data.* ◇ *This theory does not explain the absence of predatory insects in the marine environment.* ◇ **in the ~ of sth** *In the absence of a reliable network of roads, markets cannot extend their reach.* OPP PRESENCE (1) **2** [U, C] the fact of sb being away from a place where they are usually expected to be; the occasion or period of time when sb is away: *This condition is a leading cause of sickness absence due to ill health.* ◇ *Truancy may be defined as a specific number of unexplained absences in a certain time period.* IDM *see* CONSPICUOUS

ab·sent *adj.* /'æbsənt/ **1** not present as part of sth: *The possibility of civil war was never totally absent.* ◇ **~ from sth** *Women were conspicuously absent from most positions of authority.* OPP PRESENT[1] (3) **2** away from a place where you are usually expected to be: *Many absent fathers made no provision for their families.* ◇ **~ from sth** *Some youths are completely absent from school for an extended period of time.* OPP PRESENT[1] (4)

ab·so·lute[1] /'æbsəluːt/ *adj.* **1** total; not limited in any way: *It is not possible to predict with absolute certainty what will happen in these cases.* ◇ *The use of abbreviations should be kept to an absolute minimum.* ◇ *The king's power was absolute.* ◇ *Absolute monarchs claimed to be accountable only to God.* **2** existing or measured independently and not in relation to sth else: *Competitiveness is a relative term which can only be interpreted in relation to a firm's competitors—it has no absolute value.* ◇ *The proportion of people living in absolute poverty, lacking such basic necessities as clean water, food and shelter, dropped significantly during this period.* OPP RELATIVE[1] (2)

▸ ABSOLUTE + NOUN **certainty** • **necessity** • **priority** • **minimum** • **monarchy** • **monarch**, **ruler** • **sovereignty** *The conservation of biodiversity today represents the absolute priority in environmental politics.* | **poverty** • **value** • **truth** • **scale** *These authors are critical of the view that there are absolute truths about the social world that it is the job of the social scientist to reveal.*

▸ PHRASES **in absolute terms** *During this period, Britain slowly advanced in absolute terms but declined relative to many other nations.*

ab·so·lute[2] /'æbsəluːt/ *noun* an idea or a principle that is believed to be true or valid in all circumstances: *In relativity theory, time and space are not absolutes.*

ab·so·lute·ly /'æbsəluːtli/ *adv.* totally; without any limitation: *The patient should not be moved unless it is absolutely necessary.* ◇ *Lawson was absolutely correct in his belief that major rift systems connect.* ◇ *The immense human population depends absolutely on these plants.* ◇ **~ no...** *Only 6% of people in the first age group have absolutely no academic qualifications.*

ab·sorb /əb'sɔːb; əb'zɔːb; *NAmE* əb'sɔːrb; əb'zɔːrb/ *verb* **1** to take in a liquid, gas or other substance from the surface or space around: **~ sth** *When immersed in water, such materials absorb water and swell.* ◇ **~ sth from sth** *Rainfall is naturally slightly acidic, absorbing small amounts of carbon dioxide from the air.* ◇ **~ sth into sth** *When the smoker inhales, nicotine is absorbed into the bloodstream.* **2 ~ sth** to take in and keep heat, light or other forms of energy, instead of reflecting it: *A black object absorbs all wavelengths of light.* ◇ *The steel bumper beam absorbed 23% more impact energy than the conventional bumper.* ➲ *compare* REFLECT (2) **3** [often passive] to take control of a smaller unit or group and make it part of sth larger: **be absorbed by sth** *Wales was absorbed by Britain in 1536, and Scotland by the Act of Union in 1707.* ◇ **be absorbed into sth** *Many of these views were absorbed into early Christian thought.* **4** to take sth into the mind and learn or understand it SYN TAKE STH IN (2): **~ sth** *Patients and relatives need time to absorb information and to adapt to bad news.* ◇ **~ sth from sth** *Edison readily absorbed ideas from every source.* **5 ~ sth** to deal with or reduce the effects of changes or costs: *Economies of scale enable firms to absorb transport costs to remain competitive in world markets.* ◇ *The low cost means that any losses can be absorbed.* **6 ~ sth** to use up a large supply of sth, especially money or time: *A large percentage of the school's income is absorbed by fixed costs.* **7 be absorbed in sth** to be so interested in sth that you pay no attention to anything else: *Young people really absorbed in classroom activity can quickly forget about a quiet observer in the corner.*

ab·sor·bance /əb'sɔːbəns; əb'zɔːbəns; *NAmE* əb'sɔːrbəns; əb'zɔːrbəns/ *noun* [U, C] (*physics*) a measure of the ability of a substance to absorb light of a particular WAVELENGTH: *The absorbance was measured at 530 and 700 nm.*

ab·sorp·tion /əb'sɔːpʃn; əb'zɔːpʃn; *NAmE* əb'sɔːrpʃn; əb'zɔːrpʃn/ *noun* [U] **1** the process of energy or a substance being absorbed: *The drug should be taken with food or milk to increase its absorption.* ◇ **~ of sth** *Tyndall measured the absorption of infrared radiation by CO_2 and water vapour.* ◇ **~ (of sth) into sth** *The skin prevents the absorption of many agents into the bloodstream.* **2** the process of a smaller unit or group becoming part of a larger unit or group: *It was claimed that western states were created by conquest, whereas Russia grew by absorption.*

ab·stract[1] AWL /'æbstrækt/ *adj.* **1** existing in thought or as an idea but not as a physical thing: *Greek culture is full of abstract notions that are personified and treated as divine beings.* **2** based on general ideas and not on any particular real person, thing or situation: *The British constitutional system is the product of experience rather than abstract theories.* **3** representing an idea, a quality or a state rather than a physical object: *In comparison with George Eliot, Jane Austen used a smaller pool of abstract nouns such as love, manners and sensibility.* ➲ *compare* CONCRETE[1] **4** (of art) not representing people or things in a realistic way, but expressing the artist's ideas about them using shapes, colours and textures: *Kandinsky was regarded as the first really abstract painter.* ➲ *compare*

REPRESENTATIONAL ■ **ab·stract·ly** AWL *adv.*: *Young children cannot think abstractly; therefore, teachers encourage them to use concrete materials such as blocks and sticks.*

ab·stract² AWL /ˈæbstrækt/ *noun* a short piece of writing containing the main ideas of a research article, book or speech SYN SUMMARY¹: *A review of dissertation titles and abstracts found approximately one hundred works on hazards research.*

IDM **in the ˈabstract** in a general way, without referring to a particular real person, thing or situation: *In the abstract, all heads of government are equal, but the fact that some have more power than others is implicitly understood by all.*

ab·stract³ AWL /æbˈstrækt/ *verb* **1** [T] **~ sth (from sth)** to remove sth from somewhere SYN EXTRACT¹: *Silicate rocks abstract CO_2 from the atmosphere.* ◇ *We abstracted soil data from the available soil surveys maps.* **2** [T, I] **~ (sth) (from sth)** to think about sth generally or separately from sth else: *To abstract science and religion from their historical context can lead to anachronism.*

ab·strac·tion AWL /æbˈstrækʃn/ *noun* **1** [C, U] a general idea not based on any real person, thing or situation: *Husserl emphasized the importance of lived experience over scientific abstractions.* ◇ *There is debate over the level of theoretical abstraction that can actually enhance empirical studies.* **2** [U] the action of removing sth from sth else; the process of being removed from sth else: *The rate of groundwater abstraction for irrigation can exceed natural recharge from rainfall.* ◇ **the ~ of sth** *The supply chain includes the abstraction of water, treatment and piping of water, and retailing to customers.* **3** [U] the quality of representing ideas using shapes, colours and textures: *Abstraction and conceptualism are pervasive in the arts of the non-western world.*

IDM **in abstraction from sth** separately from sth else: *A business cannot be studied in abstraction from its social environment.*

abun·dance /əˈbʌndəns/ *noun* **1** [U] **~ (of sth)** the quantity of sth present in a particular area or group: *Seasonal changes in the relative abundance of different species may occur.* **2** [sing.] **~ (of sth)** a large quantity of sth that is more than enough: *There was an abundance of good farmland and plenty of open pasture for animals.*

IDM **in abundance** in large quantities: *Pot fragments were found in abundance at the site.*

abun·dant /əˈbʌndənt/ *adj.* **1** existing in large quantities; more than enough: *There is abundant evidence for increased volcanic activity during the Little Ice Age.* ◇ *Calcium is the most abundant mineral in the body.* ◇ *Australia has an abundant supply of agricultural land.* **2 ~ in sth** having a lot of sth: *Low-wage countries are relatively abundant in low-skilled workers.*

abun·dant·ly /əˈbʌndəntli/ *adv.* **1** in large quantities: *Lakes and wetlands occur most abundantly where precipitation is high.* **2 ~ clear** very clear: *It was abundantly clear that reform was necessary.*

abuse¹ /əˈbjuːs/ *noun* **1** [U, C] the use of sth in a way that is wrong or harmful: *Alcohol and drug abuse are strongly associated with suicide risk.* ◇ **~ of sth** *Serious abuses of human rights have continued ever since.* ◇ **open to ~** *In Conrad's work, power is systematically open to abuse.* ➲ *compare* MISUSE¹ **2** [U] unfair, cruel or violent treatment of sb: *Women who suffer domestic abuse are often unwilling to talk about it.* ◇ *Neglect is as much a form of abuse as a violent act.* ◇ *Investigations of child abuse require professionals to work together.* ◇ *97% of this sample had experienced physical or sexual abuse.* ◇ *emotional/psychological abuse.* ◇ **+ noun** *There was no legal requirement to report suspected abuse cases.* **3** [U] rude and offensive remarks, usually made when sb is very angry: *Neighbours and other people have apparently shouted abuse from outside her house.*

abuse² /əˈbjuːz/ *verb* **1 ~ sth** to use power or knowledge unfairly or wrongly: *Managers must be monitored to make sure they do not abuse their power.* ◇ *The European Commission also found that the company had abused its dominant position by charging unfair prices.* **2 ~ sth** to make bad use of sth; to use so much of sth that it harms your health: *People who have abused drugs for a long time may need considerable help in making social relationships.* **3 ~ sb/sth** to treat a person or an animal in a cruel or violent way, especially sexually: *The four oldest children in this family have been emotionally, physically and sexually abused.* ◇ *The first refuge for abused women was set up in London in 1971.* **4 ~ sb** to make rude or offensive remarks to or about sb: *Many asylum seekers reported that they had been verbally abused by police officers.* ■ **abuser** /əˈbjuːzə(r)/ *noun*: *Some drug abusers administer drugs intravenously.* ◇ *The abuser is usually known to the child.*

abu·sive /əˈbjuːsɪv/ *adj.* **1** (of behaviour or a person) involving or using violence: *Studies have shown that women in an abusive relationship are more likely to have depression.* ◇ *The relationship was fragile; John was verbally and physically abusive with Sue and Martin.* **2** (of speech or a person) rude and offensive; criticizing in a rude and unfair way: *Yelling, cursing, raging or other forms of abusive language may indicate more serious problems with anger.*

aca·demia AWL /ˌækəˈdiːmiə/ (*also* **aca·deme** /ˈækədiːm/) *noun* [U] the world of research and education at universities, and the people involved in it: *These techniques had importance to both academia and industry.*

aca·dem·ic¹ AWL /ˌækəˈdemɪk/ *adj.* **1** [usually before noun] connected with education, especially studying in schools and universities SYN EDUCATIONAL: *This study assesses the motivational factors associated with academic achievement in high-school settings.* **2** [usually before noun] involving a lot of reading and studying rather than practical or technical skills: *There has been relatively little academic research in this area.* ➲ *compare* APPLIED, VOCATIONAL **3** not connected to a real or practical situation and therefore not important: *Questions of diversity are not merely academic: they have a real impact on people's lives.* ■ **aca·dem·ic·al·ly** AWL /ˌækəˈdemɪkli/ *adv.*: *These individuals succeeded academically despite disadvantaged backgrounds.*

aca·dem·ic² AWL /ˌækəˈdemɪk/ *noun* a person who teaches and/or does research at a university or college: *Leading academics in the field argue that the solution to health inequalities is a universalist approach.*

acad·emy AWL /əˈkædəmi/ *noun* (*pl.* **-ies**) **1** a school or college for special training: *In Sparta, boys were sent to military academy by the age of seven years.* **2** (*usually* **Academy**) a type of official organization that aims to promote standards in a particular academic field such as the arts or sciences: *The Academy of Sciences was reformed, making it a purely research body.* **3 the academy** all the established people and institutions within a field of research: *Descriptive work on plants and animals continued in the academy and at the amateur level.*

ac·cel·er·ate /əkˈseləreɪt/ *verb* **1** [I, T] to happen faster or earlier; to make sth happen faster or earlier: *Inflation was accelerating fast.* ◇ *In Alaska (Arendt et al., 2002), glaciers appear to be thinning at an accelerating rate.* ◇ **~ sth** *Enzymes vary in the degree to which they accelerate reaction rates.* ◇ *The intensity of the protest might accelerate the process of liberalization.* **2** [T] **~ sth (to sth)** (*physics*) to make an object move faster: *The electric fields accelerate electrons to a speed of about 300 000 km a* *second.* **3** [I, T] (of a vehicle) to start to go faster; to make a vehicle go faster: *When I started to cross the intersection, the car to my left unexpectedly accelerated.* ◇ **~ sth** *The power required to accelerate the vehicle is proportional to the vehicle mass.*

ac·cel·er·ation /əkˌseləˈreɪʃn/ *noun* **1** [U, C] (*physics*) the rate at which the VELOCITY (= speed in a particular direction) of an object changes: *The product of mass and acceleration is equal to the force acting on the body.* ◇ **~ of sth** *Newton decreed that the relative accelerations of two bodies per unit force is a measure of their intrinsic inertia, or 'mass'.* **2** [U, sing.] an increase in how fast sth happens: **~ in sth** *The extent of the acceleration in economic globalization is evident in the statistics of global trade.* ◇ **~ of sth** *The new century was witness to the rapid acceleration of industrialization and urbanization.*

ac·cept /əkˈsept/ *verb* **1** to take sth that is offered: **~ sth** *The shareholders accepted an offer for the purchase of their shares.* ◇ **~ sth from sb** *The company will not accept products from suppliers who use child labour.* ◇ **~ sth for sth** *Only articles that have gone through the process of peer review are accepted for publication.* OPP REJECT (3) **2** to believe or recognize that an idea is true or valid: **~ sth** *Lacan accepted the key ideas of Saussure's structural linguistics.* ◇ *This argument was accepted by the court.* ◇ **~ sth as sth** *Genocide is now accepted as an international war crime.* ◇ **~ that...** *Most scholars accept that these texts date from the first century AD.* ◇ **it is accepted that...** *It is generally accepted that early humans were genetically very similar to humans today.* OPP REJECT (1) **3** to recognize that an unpleasant situation is real: **~ sth** *The Emperor was at last forced to accept defeat.* ◇ **~ sth as sth** *Suffering was accepted as an inescapable part of human existence.* OPP DENY (2) **4 ~ sth** to agree to or approve of a suggestion, plan or practice: *They refused to accept the recommendation that compensation be paid.* ◇ *The plan was readily accepted by Germany under Chancellor Adenauer.* ◇ *He accepted the normal conventions of Chinese business in which shareholders left the operation of the business to a manager.* OPP REJECT (1) **5** to make sb/sth welcome in a particular role; to allow sb/sth to join a group: **~ sb/sth as sth** *The vast majority of church members accepted Brigham Young as leader.* ◇ **~ sb/sth for sth** *When these ten countries were accepted for membership, three others—Romania, Bulgaria and Turkey—were not considered ready to join.* OPP REJECT (2) **6 ~ sth** to admit that you are responsible for sth: *Directors were asked to accept responsibility for the crisis they had caused.* ◇ *The father accepted the obligation of raising and educating the child.*

▸ ACCEPT + NOUN **offer • invitation • proposal • job • help** *This type of poverty was characterized by low-wage jobs, two or three families sharing one apartment, and a reluctance to accept outside help.* | **argument • premise, assumption, hypothesis, thesis • view • principle • notion, idea • claim • conclusion • possibility • existence • validity** *Although the majority accepted the government view that there was a public emergency, Lord Hoffmann did not.* | **defeat • risk • criticism • the reality of sth • the fact that...** *The vast majority of scientists now accept the reality of climate change.*

▸ ADVERB + ACCEPT **readily, willingly • finally** *She did not willingly accept criticism or tolerate dissenting views.* | **widely • generally, commonly • universally • internationally • tacitly, implicitly • broadly** *The principle has come to be universally accepted by all the institutions.*

ac·cept·able /əkˈseptəbl/ *adj.* **1** that people can agree on or approve of: *Buyer and seller need to agree a mutually acceptable price.* ◇ *Divorce has become more socially acceptable.* ◇ **~ to sb** *Choosing the approach that is most acceptable to the patient improves the chances of success.* OPP UNACCEPTABLE **2** that can be allowed: *Maximum acceptable nitrate levels in water are often set at 50 mg/l.* ◇ *They conclude that it is morally acceptable to use animals in experiments, but wrong to cause unnecessary suffering.* OPP UNACCEPTABLE ■ **ac·cept·abil·ity** /əkˌseptəˈbɪləti/ *noun* [U] *The ethical acceptability of this idea is open to question.* ◇ **~ to sb** *Implementing the policy will depend on its acceptability to the public.*

▸ ACCEPTABLE + NOUN **behaviour • practice** *Attitudes towards what is acceptable behaviour in close familial relationships have varied over time and between cultures.* | **standard • level • limit** *The debates and controversies that ensued were about the acceptable limits of royal power.*

▸ ADVERB + ACCEPTABLE **perfectly • generally • universally • socially • politically • mutually** *In some countries, it would be perfectly acceptable to give a gift to an official as a token of appreciation.* | **ethically, morally** *The extent to which animal suffering is considered ethically acceptable often depends on the potential benefits that might result.*

ac·cept·ance /əkˈseptəns/ *noun* **1** [U, sing.] agreement that an idea, plan or practice is valid: *The test quickly gained widespread acceptance within the industry.* ◇ **~ of sth** *To avoid difficulties over the public acceptance of wind power, offshore development would be preferable to onshore development.* ◇ **~ by sb** *There was a growing acceptance by the political elite of the need for social improvement following the war.* OPP REJECTION (1) **2** [U] the process of being made welcome as part of a group or in a particular role: *Legal equality did not guarantee social acceptance.* ◇ **~ into sth** *Acceptance into Asia's diverse business cultures is an important advantage.* ◇ **~ as sth** *Darwin's acceptance as naturalist aboard HMS Beagle was a turning point in his life.* OPP REJECTION (2) **3** [U] **~ (of sth)** the act of accepting sth that is offered: *It is a fundamental tenet of contract law that silence cannot constitute acceptance of an offer.* ◇ *In his acceptance speech, Kennedy promised 'a new frontier'.* OPP REJECTION (1) **4** [U, sing.] willingness to accept an unpleasant or difficult situation: *The bereaved person may need help to move from denial to acceptance.* ◇ **~ of sth** *For centuries, the idea of a return to the homeland coexisted with a passive acceptance of exile.* OPP DENIAL (3)

ac·cept·ed /əkˈseptɪd/ *adj.* that most people approve of or recognize as valid: *In today's society, it is a widely accepted view that technology will increasingly dominate the future of services.*

▸ ACCEPTED + NOUN **wisdom • practice • norm, convention • standard • definition • explanation • view • principle** *People are more likely to smoke if they are socialized in a culture where smoking is an accepted norm.*

▸ ADVERB + ACCEPTED **widely • generally, commonly • universally • socially** *There is no universally accepted definition of terrorism.*

ac·cess[1] AWL /ˈækses/ *noun* **1** [U] a way of entering or reaching a place: *Measures can include installing ramps to allow wheelchair users to gain access.* ◇ **~ to sth** *Access to much of the canyon from above is limited.* **2 ~ to sth/sb** the opportunity or right to use or get sth, or to see sb/sth: *Males compete for access to females indirectly by controlling access to resources.* **3** [U, C] the process of connecting to the Internet or of opening a computer file to get or add information: *Respondents with Internet access were asked to complete the survey online.* ◇ *There was an average of 745 URL accesses per household per week throughout the study period.* ◇ **~ to sth** *The number of people with access to the Internet has grown significantly.*

▸ VERB + ACCESS **provide • allow • secure • restrict** *Restricting access to some Internet content raises questions of censorship.* | **gain, obtain, get • ensure • give, grant • facilitate • limit, control** *The raid ensured access from the Irish Sea to a route across the southern Pennines to York.* ◇ *A given level of education at one time gave access to elite jobs.* | **have • lack** *Households in Desta's village have no access to insurance companies.* | **enjoy • deny** *Social* *exclusion denies access to opportunities that most people would consider a right.*

ac·cess² AWL /ˈækses/ *verb* **1 ~ sth** to connect to the Internet or open a computer file in order to get or add information: *In 1998, just nine per cent of UK households could access the Internet.* ◇ *Technology is increasing an organization's ability to access secondary data via the web.* **2 ~ sth** to reach, enter, get or use sth: *A common consideration for most businesses is the desire to access larger markets.* ◇ *New towns emerged to access water power at locations along major rivers.*

ac·ces·si·bil·ity AWL /əkˌsesəˈbɪləti/ *noun* [U] the quality of being easy to reach, enter, use or obtain: *To improve accessibility, the document has been published in English and Spanish.* ◇ **~ of sth (to sb)** *These arrangements depended on local factors, including the accessibility of outpatient clinics to patients.*

ac·cess·ible AWL /əkˈsesəbl/ *adj.* **1** that can be reached, entered, used or obtained: *Many Australian architects have designed publicly accessible buildings which incorporate Aboriginal cultural symbolism.* ◇ **~ to sb/sth** *Services may not be equally accessible to all groups of patients.* ◇ *Some information is accessible to anyone with Internet access.* ◇ **~ by sth** *In New Urbanism, businesses are readily accessible by walking or public transit.* **2** easy to understand: *The author covers the topics in a highly accessible way.* ◇ **~ to sb** *Her work is somewhat less accessible to a general audience.*

ac·ces·sion /ækˈseʃn/ *noun* **1** [U] the act of becoming a ruler of a country: **~ to sth** *Gorbachev's accession to power in March 1985 was an event of considerable significance.* ◇ **~ of sb (to sth)** *The accession of Henri to the French throne disturbed this alliance.* **2** [U] **~ (of sth) (to sth)** the act of becoming part of an international organization: *The accession of further Member States changed the borders of Europe.* **3** [C] (*technical*) an item that is added to items that have already been collected, for example in a library or museum: **~ (of sth)** *Multiple accessions of 13 species were sampled.* ◇ **+ noun** *For museum accession numbers, see Supplementary Appendix S1.*

ac·ci·dent /ˈæksɪdənt/ *noun* **1** [C] an unpleasant event, especially in a vehicle, that happens unexpectedly and causes injury or damage: *The tree struck some telephone wires, which fell across the highway, causing an accident.* ◇ *Several serious nuclear accidents have occurred.* ◇ **car/traffic/road traffic ~** *A 30-year-old man has been involved in a road traffic accident.* ◇ **+ noun** *accident victims* **2** [C, U] something that happens by chance: **~ (of sth)** *He claimed that the human species was an accident of the evolutionary history of the earth.* ◇ *It was often a matter of historical accident that any particular piece of territory became part of any particular country.* ◇ **no ~** *It is no accident that the world's strongest software industry is found in the United States, where protection for computer programs is the strongest.*
IDM **by accident** in a way that is not planned or organized: *After the rat has pressed the lever the first time by accident, it will learn very quickly to perform this behaviour in order to become rewarded with food.* OPP DELIBERATELY, ON PURPOSE

ac·ci·den·tal /ˌæksɪˈdentl/ *adj.* happening by chance; not planned: *Accidental death ranks as the fifth leading cause of mortality in the USA.* ◇ *Many discoveries in science have been largely accidental, as a by-product of an investigation that failed in its original aim.* ➲ *compare* DELIBERATE¹ ■ **ac·ci·den·tal·ly** /ˌæksɪˈdentəli/ *adv.*: *Varying the question order can result in certain questions being accidentally omitted.* ◇ *It is not recorded whether the temples were burned accidentally or on purpose.* ➲ *compare* DELIBERATELY, ON PURPOSE

ac·com·mo·date AWL /əˈkɒmədeɪt; *NAmE* əˈkɑːmədeɪt/ *verb* **1 ~ sb** to provide sb with a room or a place to sleep, live or sit: *Classical Athens was shaped by its efforts to attract and accommodate visitors.* **2 ~ sth** to consider sb's needs or an opinion or fact and be influenced by this when you are deciding what to do: *These policies accommodated the demands of minorities who felt threatened.*

ac·com·mo·da·tion AWL /əˌkɒməˈdeɪʃn; *NAmE* əˌkɑːməˈdeɪʃn/ *noun* **1** [U] a place to live, work or stay: *The housing was to be used to provide temporary accommodation for the homeless.* **2** [C, U] **~ (with sb)** an agreement or arrangement between people or groups with different opinions which is acceptable to everyone; the process of reaching this agreement: *General Eisenhower was authorized to reach an accommodation with Admiral Darlan.* ◇ *Cooperation reflects mutual accommodation and collaboration.* **3** [U, sing.] **~ to sth** the process of adapting or adjusting to a situation: *These reforms represented a process of gradual accommodation to mass demands.* **4** [U] **~ (to sth)** (*technical*) the action of the eye adjusting its FOCUS: *Accommodation to variable light is impaired as the lens becomes inelastic.*

ac·com·pany AWL /əˈkʌmpəni/ *verb* (**ac·com·pan·ies, ac·com·pany·ing, ac·com·pan·ied, ac·com·pan·ied**) **1** to happen or appear with sth else: **be accompanied by sth** *A fall in price may be accompanied by an increase in the quantity demanded.* ◇ **~ sth** *Recent urban growth has accompanied an economic transition from agriculture to industry.* **2** to travel or go somewhere with sb: **~ sb** *Suetonius is likely to have accompanied Hadrian to Gaul.* ◇ **be accompanied by sb** *Up to the age of 18, children must be accompanied by their parents.*

ac·com·plish /əˈkʌmplɪʃ; *NAmE* əˈkɑːmplɪʃ/ *verb* to succeed in doing or completing sth SYN ACHIEVE: **~ sth** *There were minimal resources available to accomplish this task.* ◇ *A system is a collection of parts that interact to accomplish an overall goal.* ◇ **~ sth by (doing) sth** *Efficient cutting is accomplished by using a lens or mirror to concentrate the energy.*

ac·com·plish·ment /əˈkʌmplɪʃmənt; *NAmE* əˈkɑːmplɪʃmənt/ *noun* **1** [C] an impressive thing that is done or achieved after a lot of work SYN ACHIEVEMENT (1): *This was a political accomplishment of considerable magnitude.* **2** [U] the fact of successfully completing sth SYN ACHIEVEMENT (2): *Physical exertion leads to a positive sense of accomplishment.* ◇ **~ of sth** *Compensation for these employees is likely to be based on the accomplishment of specific tasks or goals.* **3** [C, U] a skill or special ability: *Students with high motivation are consistently more likely to excel across a wide range of academic accomplishments.* ◇ *In the eighteenth and nineteenth centuries, the European notion of civilization was linked to social and intellectual accomplishment.*

ac·cord¹ /əˈkɔːd; *NAmE* əˈkɔːrd/ *verb* (*formal*) to give sb/sth authority, status or a particular type of treatment SYN GRANT¹: **~ sth to sb/sth** *The USSR accorded formal sovereignty to its European satellites.* ◇ **~ sb/sth sth** *Human rights groups have pressured nations with large immigrant populations to accord them privileges formerly limited to citizens.*
PHR V **acˈcord with sth** to agree with or match sth: *This view of education accords well with Foucault's analysis of state power.*

ac·cord² /əˈkɔːd; *NAmE* əˈkɔːrd/ *noun* a formal agreement between two or more organizations or countries: *He justified US refusal to sign the Geneva accords.*
IDM **in accord (with sth/sb)** in agreement with: *There is little doubt that Kant was very much in accord with prevailing late eighteenth-century thought.* **of your own acˈcord** without being asked, forced or helped: *Democratic leaders rarely emerge of their own accord.*

ac·cord·ance /əˈkɔːdns; *NAmE* əˈkɔːrdns/ *noun*
IDM **in accordance with sth** according to a rule or the way that sb says that sth should be done: *The exchange rate fluctuates in accordance with the laws of supply and demand.* ◇ *The supplies were stored in accordance with the manufacturer's instructions.*

ac·cord·ing·ly /əˈkɔːdɪŋli; *NAmE* əˈkɔːrdɪŋli/ *adv.* **1** in a way that is appropriate to what has been done or said in a particular situation: *Human beings are creatures that respond to events, make plans and act accordingly.* **2** (used especially at the beginning of a sentence) for that reason SYN THEREFORE: *Ecosystems are shaped by environmental changes that have occurred over thousands of years. Accordingly, ecological change takes place at many timescales.*

ac·cord·ing to /əˈkɔːdɪŋ tə; *NAmE* əˈkɔːrdɪŋ tə/ *prep.* **1** as stated or reported by sb/sth: *According to this model, test scores operate as a measure of educational worth.* ◇ *According to Landes (1998), the physical geography of China facilitated the spread of a single dominant cultural group.* **2** depending on sth: *According to their energy, the charged particles penetrate to different levels in the atmosphere.*

LANGUAGE BANK

Reporting someone's opinion

In academic writing, you will often need to state another person's opinion or position; the following expressions can be used to make this clear.

- **According to** X,...
- **For** X,...
- X **takes the view that...**
- X's **view is that...**
- X **is of the view/opinion that...**
- **In** X's **view/opinion**,...
- X **believes (that)...**
- X **suggests/proposes that...**

– ***According to*** *Humphrey (1987), consciousness arose when a new form of sense organ evolved, an 'inner eye'.*
– ***For*** *Freud, that hidden cause is a neurotic psychological need;* ***for*** *Durkheim, it is society.*
– *Ben Okri* ***takes the view that*** *the suffering associated with colonial occupation may ultimately be regenerative.*
– *Hobbes's* ***view is that*** *every action is motivated by either desire or aversion.*
– *Hutchison (1989)* ***is of the opinion that*** *the Mekong has, in the past, contributed sediment to the central lowland in Thailand.*
– ***In her view****, using a policy analysis approach can help us to understand the process.*
– *Gage (2001)* ***believes*** *the long-term effects of a short-term drought are generally minimal.*
– *Wegner (2002)* ***proposes that*** *free will is an illusion created in three steps.*

ac·count[1] /əˈkaʊnt/ *noun* **1** a written or spoken description of sth that has happened: *Countless eyewitness accounts tell the story of the earthquake.* ◇ **~ of sth** *The documents provide first-person accounts of the writer's life and events within it.* **2 ~ (of sth)** an explanation or a description of an idea, a theory or a process: *The book gives a clear account of current knowledge in the field.* **3** (*abbr.* **a/c**) an arrangement with a bank or other financial institution that allows sb/sth to keep money there, pay money in, and take money out: *He was concerned that the bank might be in difficulty so he closed his accounts.* ➲ *see also* BANK ACCOUNT, CURRENT ACCOUNT (1) **4** (*business*) a regular customer; a contract to supply sth to a customer on a regular basis: *Senior marketing personnel serve important accounts.* ◇ *The account is awarded to whichever agency produces the most suitable proposal.* HELP In business, a **key account** is a customer that is considered to be very important to a business: *A small number of these key accounts have become essential for the survival of many supplying firms.* **5** [usually pl.] a written record of money that is owed to a business and of money that has been paid by it: **~ (of sb/sth)** *The National Audit Office audits the accounts of all central government departments and agencies.* ◇ **in the accounts** *The table shows overheads as they were presented in the accounts.* HELP In economics, an **account** is, more broadly, a breakdown of the state of sth into its individual parts, whether it is the financial state of a business, the business cycle or the growth rate. ➲ *see also* CAPITAL ACCOUNT, CURRENT ACCOUNT (2) **6** an arrangement with a store or business to pay bills for goods or services at a later time, for example in regular amounts every month: *It was almost impossible for a woman to open an account in a department store under her own name, even if she was a professional.* **7** an arrangement that sb has with a company that allows them to use the Internet, send and receive messages by email, order goods, etc: *With Internet-based systems, users can access their accounts from anywhere in the world.* ◇ **~ with sb/sth** *She gained access to this chat room through an account with an Internet provider.*
IDM **by/from all accounts** according to what other people say: *He was, by all accounts, a dedicated and inspired teacher.* **by your own account** according to what you say yourself: *The CEO, by his own account, is in regular contact with the firm's strategic customers.* **hold sb/sth to account** to make sb/sth take responsibility for and explain their actions or decisions: *The Assembly is responsible for holding the Mayor to account.* **on account** if you buy sth or pay **on account**, you pay nothing or only a small amount immediately and the rest later: *Having paid sums on account to cover the solicitors' fees, the trustees took no further steps.* **on account of sb/sth** because of sb/sth: *He obtained his rank on account of his family connections.* ◇ *Oil production has been flattening in recent years on account of the absence of new discoveries.* ➲ language bank *at* BECAUSE **on your own acˈcount 1** for yourself: *He found it much better to work on his own account than to work for an employer.* **2** because you want to and you have decided, not sb else: *Special advisers can commission work on their own account and not just on behalf of ministers.* **on this/that account** because of the particular thing that has been mentioned: *The Commission accepted three inability-to-pay applications, granting reductions of the fine on this account.* **take account of sth | take sth into account** to consider particular facts, circumstances, etc. when making a decision about sth: *The model has failed to take account of the fact that there are two distinct genetic groups in a population.* ◇ *GPs always took individual circumstances into account when making decisions.* ➲ *more at* CALL[1]
▸ ADJECTIVE + ACCOUNT **detailed • comprehensive, full, complete • general • good • brief, short • historical • early • popular** *This brief account explains the basis of population growth.* | **first-hand • first-person • personal • contemporary • accurate • narrative** *This book provides a remarkable first-hand account of the aftermath of the Kanto earthquake.* | **coherent • plausible • satisfactory, adequate • influential • definitive • alternative • critical • theoretical** *We can now start to give a coherent account of the role of working memory in such everyday activities as planning a shopping trip or reading a newspaper.*
▸ VERB + ACCOUNT **offer, give, provide • write • present • develop • produce • publish** *The general introduction offers an account of England in the years 1670–71.*

ac·count[2] /əˈkaʊnt/ *verb*
PHR V **acˈcount for sb/sth** to find out where sb/sth is or what has happened to them, especially after an accident: *The militia was ordered to account for all Irish families on the island.* **acˈcount for sth 1** to give an explanation for or description of sth SYN EXPLAIN (2): *The 1881 and 2001*

A

censuses cannot be compared without accounting for basic differences. ◇ *This is a problem the researchers cannot fully account for.* **2** to be the explanation or cause of sth SYN EXPLAIN (2): *Rapid droplet growth partly accounts for the increase of precipitation over hills.* ◇ *Careless methods of estimation often account for the wide discrepancies in the figures.* **3** to be a particular amount or part of sth: *Small family firms continue to be important in Japan today, accounting for 99% of all businesses (Fruin, 1980).* ◇ *It is expected that the health care of the very elderly will account for an increasing proportion of health budgets in the future.* ⊃ language bank *at* PROPORTION **ac'count for sth (to sb) | ac'count to sb (for sth)** to give a record of how the money in your care has been spent: *They should account for the profit they made on the sale of their shares.* ◇ *The director will be liable to account to the company for any profit or loss sustained.*

ac·count·abil·ity /əˌkaʊntəˈbɪləti/ *noun* [U] the fact or state of taking responsibility for your decisions or actions, so that you can explain them if necessary: **~ (of sb/sth)** *The EU is held back by the lack of democratic accountability of some of its institutions.* ◇ **~ for sth** *Consumers are curious about the practices of the company and demand accountability for its actions.* ◇ **~ to sb** *Effective boards act transparently to ensure full accountability to shareholders.*

ac·count·able /əˈkaʊntəbl/ *adj.* [not usually before noun] responsible for your decisions or actions and expected to explain them when you are asked: **~ to sb/sth** *The central bank is not directly accountable to Parliament.* ◇ **(hold sb) ~ (for sth)** *He can be held legally and morally accountable for his actions.*

ac·count·ant /əˈkaʊntənt/ *noun* a person whose job is to keep or check financial accounts: *The company's constitution is generally drafted by a professional adviser such as a lawyer or an accountant.* ■ **ac·count·ancy** /əˈkaʊntənsi/ *noun* [U] *The book is an important contribution to the history of accountancy.* ◇ **+ noun** *She works in marketing for a large accountancy firm.*

ac·count·ing /əˈkaʊntɪŋ/ *noun* [U] the process or work of keeping financial accounts: *The police brought charges against him for false accounting.* ◇ **+ noun** *The value of an organization's relationships should be acknowledged in its financial accounting systems.*

ac·credit·ation /əˌkredɪˈteɪʃn/ *noun* [U] **~ (of sth)** official approval given by an organization stating that sb/sth has achieved a required standard: *Patient satisfaction is now used in the process of accreditation of hospitals and clinics.*

ac·crue /əˈkruː/ *verb* **1** [I] to be received by sb over a period of time, so that a larger amount is built up: *People have to be convinced of the benefits that might accrue as a result of change.* ◇ **~ (to sb) (from sth)** *Benefits can also accrue to the donor.* **2** [T] to receive sth over a period of time, so that a larger amount is built up SYN ACCUMULATE (1): **~ sth (from sth)** *Older adults can accrue positive benefits from their volunteer experience.* ◇ **~ sth to sb** *Specialization will be likely to accrue some benefits to the selling firm.* ■ **ac·crual** /əˈkruːəl/ *noun* [U, sing.] **~ (of sth)** *The accrual of pension rights was not dependent on receiving pay during this period.*

ac·cu·mu·late AWL /əˈkjuːmjəleɪt/ *verb* **1** [T] **~ sth** to gradually get more and more of sth over a period of time: *During this period, churches accumulated wealth on a scale not seen before.* ◇ *Individuals accumulate knowledge through experience.* **2** [I] to gradually increase in number or quantity over a period of time SYN BUILD UP: *Evidence has steadily accumulated to show that deeply weathered granites are present all around the globe.* ◇ *Virtually no sediments have accumulated since the Cretaceous.*

ac·cu·mu·la·tion AWL /əˌkjuːmjəˈleɪʃn/ *noun* **1** [U] the act or process of getting more and more of sth over a period of time: *Capital accumulation is one of the earliest explanations for economic growth.* **2** [C, U] a mass or quantity of sth that has gradually gathered or been gathered over a period of time: *Liquid oil accumulations are rarely found deeper than 5 km.* ◇ **~ of sth** *The accumulation of Antarctic snow and ice soon led to the beginnings of the continental ice cap.*

ac·cur·acy AWL /ˈækjərəsi/ *noun* **1** [U] the state of being exact or correct: *The schools were chosen to ensure accuracy of geographic, ethnic and socio-economic representation.* OPP INACCURACY **2** [U, C] (*technical*) the degree to which the result of a measurement or calculation matches the correct value or a standard: **~ (of sth)** *Researchers have been working to improve the accuracy of radiocarbon dating at prehistoric sites.* ◇ *Accuracies of a few nanoseconds can be achieved.* ◇ **(to) an ~ of sth** *The new finding agrees with Einstein's predicted value for gamma to an accuracy of 23 parts per million.* OPP INACCURACY

▸ VERB + ACCURACY **assess • test • verify, check • improve • ensure • maximize • yield • sacrifice • question • predict sth with** *These images were used to verify the accuracy of the written descriptions.* ◇ *The speed of computation has been greatly improved without sacrificing accuracy.*

ac·cur·ate AWL /ˈækjərət/ *adj.* **1** (especially of information, measurements or predictions) correct and true in every detail: *No remotely accurate figure of Aboriginal deaths could be produced.* ◇ *These models should not be expected to produce accurate long-term forecasts.* OPP INACCURATE **2** (of an instrument or method) able to give completely correct information: *Longer periods of observation lead to more accurate models and parameters.* ◇ **~ to sth** *Harrison's clock was accurate to 39 seconds over 47 days.* **3** representing sb/sth in a way that is true and exact SYN FAITHFUL (1): *Realism dictated the need for accurate representation of textiles and furnishings.* OPP INACCURATE

▸ ACCURATE + NOUN **reporting • indication • record • information** *Accurate information is difficult to obtain.* | **measurement • measure • count • estimate • estimation • assessment • diagnosis • determination • identification** *Accurate diagnosis is necessary for effective treatment.* | **prediction • forecast** *Using such estimates may result in a less accurate yield prediction.* | **predictor • indicator, gauge** *The new scale proved to be a very accurate predictor of stroke recovery.* | **description • portrayal, depiction, representation, picture • reflection • translation** *These historians provide a much more accurate picture of the developments of the period.*

▸ ADVERB + ACCURATE **reasonably, fairly, quite • sufficiently • remarkably** *Records allowed for a reasonably accurate assessment of trends from 1984 onwards.* | **highly** *There is an increased need for highly accurate data on a global scale.* | **not entirely, not strictly** *Self-reports may not be entirely accurate.* | **historically** *The details of the plot are historically accurate.*

ac·cur·ate·ly AWL /ˈækjərətli/ *adv.* in a way that is true and exact: *Scientists have been able to accurately date African fossils.* ◇ *Only 25 per cent of the sample could accurately be described as deeply religious.* ◇ *The French word 'disponible' cannot be accurately translated into English.* OPP INACCURATELY

ac·cus·ation /ˌækjuˈzeɪʃn/ *noun* a charge or claim that sb has done sth illegal or wrong: **~ against sb** *She made serious accusations against the Trust, which have now been proven to be false.* ◇ **~ of sth** *Accusations of witchcraft often followed arguments that increased the social tensions in the community.* ◇ **~ that...** *He laid himself open to seriously damaging charges, such as the accusation that he was a racist.* ⊃ *compare* CHARGE[1] (3)

A

ac·cuse /ə'kju:z/ *verb* **1** to say formally that sb has committed a crime so there can be a trial in court: **~ sb (of sth)** *In 1681 he was accused of treason and lodged in Edinburgh castle.* ◇ **~ sb (of doing sth)** *In the play, Elizabeth Proctor is an upright woman who is accused of being a witch.* ➲ *compare* CHARGE² (2) **2** to claim that sb has done sth wrong: **~ sb (of sth)** *He had discussed many of his ideas with Wilde, whom he later accused of plagiarism.* ◇ **~ sb (of doing sth)** *Some of her own party, meanwhile, accused her of selling out and attacking the rights of workers.* ■ **ac·cuser** /ə'kju:zə(r)/ *noun*: *He should have the right to defend himself and confront his accusers.*

the ac·cused /ə'kju:zd/ *noun* (*pl.* **the ac·cused**) a person who is on trial for committing a crime: *The trial was in secret and the accused were imprisoned.* ➲ *compare* DEFENDANT

achiev·able AWL /ə'tʃi:vəbl/ *adj.* (of a goal or result) that can be reached by effort or skill SYN ATTAINABLE: *Harm reduction concentrates on achievable goals, instead of the impossible goal of a world without drugs.* ◇ *With these approaches, pain control for children is very achievable.*

achieve AWL /ə'tʃi:v/ *verb* to succeed in reaching a particular goal or result, especially by effort or skill SYN ATTAIN: **~ sth** *The index measures a country's potential to achieve sustained economic growth.* ◇ **~ sth by (doing) sth** *Substantial reductions in cervical cancer rates could be achieved by using routine Pap smears.* ◇ **~ sth through sth** *Health benefits have already been achieved through the reduced use of pesticides.*

▸ ACHIEVE + NOUN **goal, objective, aim, target, purpose, end • result, outcome • reduction • status • success • breakthrough • balance • efficiency** *The central task is to achieve a better balance between employer and employee interests at work.*

▸ ADVERB + ACHIEVE **best • finally • usually, normally • rarely, seldom • never • ever • actually • easily, readily • thereby** *Quota sampling rarely achieves a sample that is exactly representative of the target population.*

achieve·ment AWL /ə'tʃi:vmənt/ *noun* **1** [C] a thing that sb has done successfully, especially using their own effort and skill: *Laplace was not modest about his abilities and achievements.* ◇ **~ in sth** *George III's achievements in the arts remain decidedly impressive.* **2** [U] the fact or process of achieving sth: *As the authors argue forcefully, scientific achievement depends on the free flow of people and information.* ◇ **~ of sth** *After the achievement of independence, the new nation began to experiment with modern commercial banking.* **3** [U] a child's or student's progress in a course of learning, especially as measured by standard tests: *Ignoring the needs of children incurs costs in the future from increased unemployment, poor health and low educational achievement.*

▸ ADJECTIVE + ACHIEVEMENT **great, remarkable, outstanding, extraordinary • considerable** *The second half of the 1920s was a time of remarkable economic achievement.* ◇ *The greatest achievement of Rohmer's films is to make art look and feel so artless.* | **major • crowning • impressive • real** *The major achievement of this era was the work of Ptolemy.* | **intellectual • artistic • scientific • technological • personal** *The enormous altarpiece has been understood as Lorenzo Monaco's crowning artistic achievement.* | **individual** *The idea of meritocracy opens the way to success based on individual achievement.* | **academic, educational** *Chronic disease conditions lower academic achievement due to increased school absences.*

▸ VERB + ACHIEVEMENT **celebrate • undermine** *As an epic poem, it celebrates the achievements of a hero.* | **facilitate • ensure** *In order to facilitate the achievement of these aims, ...* | **assess** *Achievement was assessed with a number of measures across the years.*

acid¹ /'æsɪd/ *noun* [U, C] a chemical, usually a liquid, that contains HYDROGEN and has a PH of less than seven. The hydrogen can be replaced by a metal to form a salt. Acids can often burn holes in or damage things they touch: *The clouds on Venus are mostly sulfuric acid (H_2SO_4).* ◇ *Saliva neutralizes acids that can cause tooth decay.* ➲ *compare* ALKALI

acid² /'æsɪd/ *adj.* that contains acid or has the essential characteristics of an acid; that has a PH of less than seven: *Rye is tolerant of poor, acid soils.* ➲ *compare* ALKALINE

acid·ic /ə'sɪdɪk/ *adj.* containing acid: *The release was then tested both in neutral and acidic conditions.* ◇ *The highly acidic environment of the human stomach will usually destroy E.coli.* ➲ *compare* ALKALINE

acid·ity /ə'sɪdəti/ *noun* [U] **1** the level of acid in substances such as water, soil or wine: *More troublesome to marine habitats may be the potential impact of rising ocean acidity from fossil fuel use.* **2** the level of acid in the stomach, especially when the level is too high and causes DISCOMFORT: *High protein increases acidity while vegetables increase alkalinity.*

ac·know·ledge AWL /ək'nɒlɪdʒ; *NAmE* ək'nɑ:lɪdʒ/ *verb* **1** to accept that sth is true or exists: **~ sth** *It seems necessary for economic analyses to acknowledge the existence of social conventions.* ◇ **~ that...** *The authors acknowledge that other studies have been done on statins in children.* ◇ **it is acknowledged that...** *It must be acknowledged that DNA matching is but one part of a prosecution case.* ◇ **~ sth to be, have, etc. sth** *Most of Barker's claims are now acknowledged to be true.* **2** to accept that sb/sth has a particular quality, importance or status SYN RECOGNIZE (2): **~ sth** *Stone has acknowledged the influence of 'The Bacchae' on his films.* ◇ **~ sb/sth as sth** *Henry acknowledged Richard as his heir.* ◇ **~ sb/sth to be, have, etc. sth** *Large dams are widely acknowledged to be highly destructive of aquatic ecosystems.* **3 ~ sb/sth** to publicly express thanks for help or inspiration: *The authors acknowledge their debt to Lakoff.* **4 ~ sth** to tell sb that you have received sth that they sent to you: *Please note that we cannot acknowledge receipt of applications.*

▸ ACKNOWLEDGE + NOUN **existence • fact** *It is important to acknowledge the fact that men also now suffer from the pressure to look good.* | **importance • necessity • limitations** *This management model acknowledges the central importance of motivating and rewarding people.* | **contribution • debt • support** *Kant clearly acknowledged the contributions of both physical science and human science to the study of geography.*

▸ ADVERB + ACKNOWLEDGE **generally, widely • universally** *The value of the Kyoto protocol is not universally acknowledged.* | **readily • publicly, openly • explicitly** *Pope did not openly acknowledge authorship of the poem until 1735.* | **gratefully • formally, officially • properly** *Finally, we gratefully acknowledge the input of Dr Jane Wallis for her helpful advice in the drafting and revision of this paper.*

▸ VERB + TO ACKNOWLEDGE **refuse • fail** *Tannery refused to acknowledge the terms of this treaty.* | **would like** *I would like to acknowledge my family for their support, patience and encouragement.*

ac·know·ledge·ment AWL (*also* **ac·know·ledg·ment**) /ək'nɒlɪdʒmənt; *NAmE* ək'nɑ:lɪdʒmənt/ *noun* **1** [U, sing.] an act of accepting that is true or exists: **~ of sth** *A better understanding can form the basis of full acknowledgement of the problem.* ◇ **in ~ of sth** *In acknowledgement of the Queen's interest, Josiah Wedgwood named his new pottery 'Queen's ware' in 1763.* ◇ **~ by sb** *What is required first of all is an acknowledgement by the physician of the difficulties the parents are facing.* **2** [U, sing.] an act of accepting that sb/sth has a particular quality, importance or status

SYN RECOGNITION (2): **~ of sth** *There is a clear acknowledgement of the power of myth within Maddin's work.* ◇ **~ for sth** *Women were not given the same acknowledgement for their contribution to the war effort as male combatants.* ◇ **~ from sb** *He may gain a sense of self-worth by receiving acknowledgement from his peers.* ◇ **~ that...** *The court's official acknowledgement that the abuses constituted war crimes marks an important step forward.* **3** [C, U] an act or a statement expressing thanks for sth or giving credit to sb for sth: *A special acknowledgement and thanks also go to Davina Trent for doing the analytical work.* ◇ **~ to sb** *But these acknowledgements to Rome underestimate the originality of the works produced.* ◇ **in ~ of sth** *In public acknowledgement of this debt, the painter dedicated the treatise to his old patron.* ◇ **without ~** *Extensive borrowing from a former author, even without acknowledgement, was quite common at this period.* **4** [C, U] a letter saying that sth has been received: **~ of sth** *Apart from a formal acknowledgement of receipt of the letters, government sources remained silent.* ◇ **~ from sb** *Hope received no acknowledgement from his patron.* ◇ **in ~** *Please sign and return the attached copy in acknowledgement.* **5** [C, usually pl.] a statement, especially at the beginning of a book, in which the writer expresses thanks to the people who have helped: *In the acknowledgements, Denton expresses appreciation for his mentor's perspective.*

ac·quire AWL /əˈkwaɪə(r)/ *verb* **1 ~ sth** to learn or develop a skill, habit or quality: *Peasants who acquired skills preferred to move to work in the town.* ◇ *Behavioural habits acquired in childhood can be a cause of subsequent health problems.* ◇ *There was simply no evidence that acquired characteristics could be inherited.* **2 ~ sth** to obtain sth by buying or being given it: *Planters started to acquire land away from the original settlements.* ◇ *British citizenship is acquired by birth in the UK if the child's parents are either British or settled.* **3 ~ sth** to come to have a particular reputation: *In many poor communities people acquire status by participating in their community.*

ac·qui·si·tion AWL /ˌækwɪˈzɪʃn/ *noun* **1** [U] the act of learning or developing a skill, habit or quality: *Reading skills facilitate the independent acquisition of knowledge by the child.* **2** [U] the act of buying or obtaining sth to add to what you already have: *The company needs to divide its marketing efforts between existing customer retention and new customer acquisition.* **3** [C] (*business*) the act of one company buying another company: *The mergers and acquisitions of the 1980s and 1990s took place in two significant waves.*

acre /ˈeɪkə(r)/ *noun* a unit for measuring an area of land; 4 840 square yards or about 4 050 square metres: *3 000 acres of parkland* ◇ *a three-acre wood*

across¹ /əˈkrɒs; *NAmE* əˈkrɔːs; əˈkrɑːs/ *prep.* **1** from one side to the other side of sth: *Sperm whales can travel across entire oceans.* ◇ *In 1826 Thomas Telford had completed a suspension road bridge across the straits.* **2** on the other side of sth: *The school is next to a dry cleaner, with residences directly across the street.* **3** on or over a part of the body: *She has also noticed a red rash across her face recently.* **4** in every part of a place, group of people, etc. SYN THROUGHOUT (1): *The spending was on over 1 000 projects across the country.* ◇ *Olive oil remained a stable component of the diet across all age groups.*

across² /əˈkrɒs; *NAmE* əˈkrɔːs; əˈkrɑːs/ *adv.* from one side to the other side: *Individual crystals do not exceed a few millimetres across.*
IDM **across from sb/sth** opposite sb/sth: *He sat across from his interviewee and listened to her story.* HELP For the special uses of **across** in phrasal verbs, look at the entries for the verbs. For example, **come across** is in the phrasal verb section at **come**.

act¹ /ækt/ *verb* **1** [I] to do sth for a particular purpose or in order to deal with a situation: *In this case, the employer could not be said to have acted reasonably.* ◇ *She argued that she had been acting in self-defence.* **2** [I] to behave in a particular way: **+ adv.** *It is important that a company acts ethically.* ◇ **~ like sb/sth** *The current generates a magnetic field that causes the iron to act like a magnet.* ◇ **~ as if/though...** *As deaths from the disease soared, the president acted as though no national epidemic existed.* HELP In spoken English, people often use **like** instead of **as if** or **as though** in this meaning. This is not correct in academic English. **Like** can be used before a noun phrase (*a magnet*) but not before a clause (*no national epidemic existed*). **3** [I] **~ as sth** to perform a particular role or function: *The deep sea floor acts as a physical barrier to the sinking particles of organic matter.* ◇ *The growth of the Internet has acted as a catalyst for applied and other geographic research.* **4** [I] to have a particular effect on sth: *No one process acting alone can explain all climatic change.* ◇ **~ on sth** *If this theory holds, the forces acting on the two plates should be different.*
PHR V **ˈact for/on behalf of sb** to be employed to deal with sb's affairs for them, for example by representing them in court: *An export agent acts on behalf of the seller, undertaking to sell on a commission basis in a particular market.* **ˈact on/upon sth** to take action as a result of advice, information, etc: *The Queen acts solely on the advice of her ministers.*

act² /ækt/ *noun* **1** a thing that sb does: *People will disagree on what constitutes a violent act.* ◇ **~ of sth** *Acts of personal kindness, even to strangers, are quite common.* **2** (*also* **Act**) a law that has been made by a parliament: *Jamaica adopted a slave act in 1696 that closely followed the Barbados legislation of 1688.* ◇ *the Banking Act 2009* ◇ *On 1 May 1807 the bill became an Act of Parliament.*
IDM **ˌact of ˈGod** (*law*) an event caused by natural forces beyond human control, such as a storm, a flood or an EARTHQUAKE: *When building codes are ignored and a building collapses, this is not an act of God but of criminal negligence.*
▸ ADJECTIVE + ACT **very • final • aggressive, violent • unlawful, wrongful, criminal, illegal • negligent • terrorist • sexual** *The very act of reading draws the reader into the creative process.* ◇ *This was Nero's final act of violence against his own family.* ◇ *The unlawful act of the employee may be attributed to the employer.*
▸ ACT OF + NOUN **defiance • kindness • aggression, violence • terrorism** *This movement of the military was viewed as an act of aggression.*
▸ VERB + ACT **commit • perform • constitute** *Choosing to commit irrational acts goes against our nature.*

ac·tion /ˈækʃn/ *noun* **1** [U] the fact or process of doing sth, typically to achieve an aim: *There is a need to take urgent action to cut emissions of CO_2.* ◇ *Deciding on a course of action too quickly may result in a poor decision.* ➲ *see also* COLLECTIVE ACTION, DIRECT ACTION **2** [C] a thing that sb does: *The actions taken were reasonable in the circumstances.* ◇ *He claimed his actions were motivated by fears about his baby son's future.* **3** [C, U] **~ (for sth) (against sb)** a legal process to stop a person or company from doing sth, or to make them pay for a mistake, etc: *Mrs Donoghue brought an action for damages against the manufacturer.* ◇ *The company threatened to take legal action against anyone not buying a proper ticket.* **4** [U] fighting in a battle or war: *British troops supported the US military action.* **5** [U] the effect that one substance or chemical has on another: **~ (of sth)** *These medications act by inhibiting the action of the enzyme.* ◇ **~ (of sth) on sth** *The onset of anaesthesia is rapid due to its action on the nerve roots.*
IDM **in ˈaction** if sb/sth is **in action**, they are doing the activity or work that is typical for them: *The figures on Greek vases are portrayed in action.* **into ˈaction** if you put an idea or a plan **into action**, you start making it

happen or work: *The alternative strategy is less effective but easier to put into action.*

▸ ADJECTIVE + ACTION **appropriate • immediate • collective, joint • individual • corrective, remedial • rational • human • voluntary • political • social** *These measures are designed to ensure that appropriate action is taken.* ◇ *Human actions are different from natural processes.* | **decisive • concerted, coordinated** *The problem can be overcome only by concerted action.*

▸ VERB + ACTION **take • require • facilitate • constrain** *Problems such as climate change require effective action at a global level.* | **undertake, take, perform • guide • shape, govern • justify, defend • motivate • coordinate** *Nations increasingly seek to justify their actions in human rights terms.* | **bring, initiate, commence • take** *The company initiated an action against its former director.* | **block, inhibit • mimic** *The drug blocks the action of histamine on parietal cells in the stomach.*

▸ NOUN OF + ACTION **course • plan • mode • mechanism • freedom** *Identify a plan of action that is specific, practical and likely to succeed.* ◇ *This mode of action is referred to as parallel processing.*

▸ ACTION + NOUN **plan** *Participants identified an action plan and agreed on a timetable for the next six months.*

ac·ti·vate /ˈæktɪveɪt/ *verb* **~ sth** to make sth such as a device or chemical process start working: *Double-click the bar to activate the menu.* ◇ *The gene is activated by a specific protein.*

ac·ti·vation /ˌæktɪˈveɪʃn/ *noun* [U] **~ (of sth)** the fact or process of making sth such as a device or chemical process start working: *The activation of several target genes results in two major effects.* ◇ *to trigger/inhibit/block the activation of sth*

ac·tive[1] /ˈæktɪv/ *adj.* **1** involved in sth; making a determined effort and not leaving sth to happen by itself: *Popular demand for more active political participation is expected to grow.* ◇ *Children play an active role in growing up and are in constant negotiation with their parents.* ◇ **~ in sth** *Women became active in workhouse reform throughout this period.* **2** always busy doing things, especially physical activities: *He used to be physically active and involved in several different sports.* ◇ *Before our modern age, people had a more physical and active lifestyle.* OPP INACTIVE (1) **3** doing sth regularly: *The analysis was restricted to sexually active people.* ◇ *When students are active members of the community, a sense of responsibility is fostered.* **4** [not before noun] (of an animal) doing its usual activity at a particular place or time: *Mountain-dwelling beetles are only active during the summer months.* **5** having a chemical or biological effect on sth: *Morphine is the major active ingredient of opium.* OPP INACTIVE (3) **6** (*earth science*) (of a volcano) that is ERUPTING or has ERUPTED in historical times: *There are about 90 active volcanoes in South East Asia.* ◇ *a volcanically active region* ➲ *compare* DORMANT, EXTINCT (3) **7** (*earth science*) (of part of the earth's CRUST) that is moving or likely to move: *All of the Caribbean islands are strewn along the same active plate boundary.* ◇ *This island region is one of the most tectonically active in the world.* **8** (*grammar*) connected with a verb whose subject is the person or thing that performs the action: *In 'Table 3 shows the results', the verb is active.* OPP PASSIVE[1] (2)

ac·tive[2] /ˈæktɪv/ (*also* ˈ**active voice**) *noun* [sing.] the form of a verb in which the subject is the person or thing that performs the action: **in the ~** *In 'She drove the car', 'she' is the subject and the verb 'drove' is in the active.* ➲ *compare* PASSIVE[2]

ac·tive·ly /ˈæktɪvli/ *adv.* **1** by taking action in order to do sth, not just allowing it to happen: *Establishment of new salt marshes is being actively encouraged by flooding coastal meadows.* ◇ *In Paul's letters we find accounts of women actively engaged in church ministry.* **2** in a way

A

that has a chemical or biological effect on sth: *There may be other molecules that either assist or actively participate in the chemical reaction.* **3** actually doing sth at the present time: *When they are actively growing, crops are among the most efficient primary producers.*

ac·tiv·ist /ˈæktɪvɪst/ *noun* a person who works to achieve political or social change, especially as a member of an organization with particular aims: *The Attorney General was a former human rights activist.* ◇ **+ noun** *Activist groups are organizing using technologies such as the Internet, email and social networking sites.* ■ **ac·tiv·ism** /ˈæktɪvɪzəm/ *noun* [U] *The project aims to inspire students to greater civic engagement and political activism.*

ac·tiv·ity /ækˈtɪvəti/ *noun* (*pl.* **-ies**) **1** [U] things that are happening or being done: *There have been growing concerns about the impact of business activity on the environment.* ◇ *Human activity in and near volcanoes spans the archaeological record.* **2** [C, usually pl.] a thing that a person or group does or has done, usually in order to achieve a particular aim: *The trading companies diversified their activities.* ◇ *The patient will be asked how these symptoms have impacted on their daily activities.* ◇ *Fishing became the main economic activity in place of cereal-growing.* **3** [U] physical action or movement; the state of being active: *The patient participated in very little physical activity over the previous week.* ◇ *To record this activity, the birds were kept in an octagonal cage with radial perches.* ◇ *Electrical brain activity was first recorded in 1875.* **4** [C, usually pl.] a thing that you do for interest or pleasure: *The number and type of leisure activities pursued by audiences have increased.*

▸ ADJECTIVE + ACTIVITY **economic • entrepreneurial • innovative • promotional • political • human • daily** *Trade might stimulate economic activity and have benefits for sustainable development.* | **physical • sexual • biological • neural • volcanic** *The only current volcanic activity along this zone is within Africa.*

▸ VERB + ACTIVITY **pursue, engage in, participate in** *The percentage who engaged in political activities was very low.* | **undertake, perform • coordinate, organize** *We define labour as any activity performed by people that contributes to production.* | **regulate, control • monitor • stimulate** *In this sort of regime, groups of workers are substantially left to regulate their own activity.* | **inhibit, block** *These drugs inhibit osteoclast activity.*

actor /ˈæktə(r)/ *noun* **1 ~ (in sth)** a person or an organization that takes part in an action or a process: *The state is identified as the key actor in international politics.* **2** a person who performs on the stage, on television or in films, especially as a profession: *The brothers are identical twins and so in the film both are played by a single actor.*

ac·tress /ˈæktrəs/ *noun* a woman who performs on the stage, on television or in films, especially as a profession HELP Many women now prefer to be called **actors**, although when the context is not clear, **an actor** is usually understood to refer to a man: *Winning the Oscar revived the actress's career.*

ac·tual /ˈæktʃuəl/ *adj.* [only before noun] **1** existing in fact; real: *Comparing the budget with actual performance is the basic stage.* ◇ *This method gives a better estimate of the actual value of production in a country.* ◇ *No firm can afford to ignore actual or potential competitors.* **2** used to emphasize the most important part of sth: *The actual content of the video games, for example, is far more significant than the fact that a child plays video games.*

▸ ACTUAL + NOUN **practice • fact • performance • event • behaviour • situation • value • cost • concentration** *In actual practice, the problems raised have directed a trend towards less controversial methods.* | **practice •**

A

experience ♦ **content** *While simple in concept, the actual practice of crossdating is complicated by differences in growth rates.*

WHICH WORD?

actual ♦ **current** ♦ **present** ♦ **actually** ♦ **currently** ♦ **presently** ♦ **at present**

- **Actual** does not mean 'current' or 'present'. It means 'existing in fact; real' and is often used in contrast with sth that is not seen as real or exact: *Respondents' actual behaviour may be at variance with their answers.*
- **Current** and **present** mean 'existing or happening now': *The current economic crisis is the result of many years of irresponsibility.* ◇ *A continuation of the present situation seems the most likely short-term outcome.*
- **Current** and **present** are used in academic writing to mean 'being considered now': *the current/present study* **Present** is used with a wider range of nouns: *the present article/chapter/paper/review*
- **Current** also means 'being used or accepted by many people at the present time': *a review of current practice*
- **Actually** does not mean 'at the present time'. Use **currently**, **presently** or **at present** instead: *Vaccination is currently recommended for persons over the age of 49.* ◇ *At present, there is insufficient evidence to draw any definite conclusion.* ◇ *Table 14.1 provides a summary of presently available treatment methods.*

ac·tu·al·ity /ˌæktʃuˈæləti/ *noun* [U] (*formal*) the state of sth really existing: **in ~** *The author simply assumes a certain cause and effect to be true, when in actuality there is no basis for any such assumption.*

ac·tu·al·ly /ˈæktʃuəli/ *adv.* **1** used to emphasize a fact or the truth about a situation: *False memories are convincing 'memories' of events that never actually happened.* ◇ *It was not until the late 1970s that ozone depletion was actually observed by scientists at the British Antarctic Survey.* **2** used to show a contrast between what is true and what sb believes, and to show surprise about this contrast: *Funding per student had actually declined between 1985 and 1995.* ◇ *The defendant drank some wine, believing it to have a lower alcohol content than it actually did.*

▸ ACTUALLY + VERB **happen, occur** ♦ **exist** ♦ **mean** ♦ **do** ♦ **say** ♦ **work** ♦ **decline, fall** ♦ **observe** ♦ **perform** ♦ **benefit** *It seems probable that such growth curves never actually occur in nature.* ◇ *The courts have played a large role in determining what US legislation actually means.*

▸ ACTUALLY + ADJECTIVE **present** ♦ **responsible** ♦ **true** *It is necessary to quantify how much lead is actually present in the sample.*

acute /əˈkjuːt/ *adj.* **1** (of an illness) that has quickly become severe and dangerous: *acute illness/infection/leukaemia* ◇ *The disease can be acute or chronic and episodes can be recurrent.* ➲ *compare* CHRONIC **2** [usually before noun] designed for patients with an acute form of a disease: *The country's national patient safety goals focus on acute care.* ◇ *Acute hospitals should be places where people go when it is really necessary, not as a matter of routine.* **3** very serious or severe: *A rapid increase in students resulted in acute shortages of teachers and textbooks.* ◇ *Problems in the accuracy of government data can be particularly acute in less developed countries.* **4** (of the senses) very sensitive and well developed **SYN** KEEN (5): *His work reveals a writer with an acute ear for speech.* ◇ *The hunter's vision must be very acute.* **5** having or showing intelligence and quick understanding of things: *The essay engages in some very acute linguistic analysis.* ◇ *The entries are concise, informative and often acute.* **6** (*geometry*) (of an angle) less than 90°: *Material from comets usually approaches the Earth's surface at an acute angle.*

acute·ly /əˈkjuːtli/ *adv.* **1 ~ aware/conscious** noticing or feeling sth very strongly: *States today are more acutely aware of their legal obligations to guarantee universal rights to all.* **2** (describing unpleasant feelings or illness) very; very strongly: *Not knowing what was happening to her child was acutely distressing.* ◇ *Care must be taken with the management of acutely ill patients.* ◇ *Within these countries the adverse impact of globalization has been felt acutely.* **3** in a way that shows great understanding: *The Greeks, as Alain Schnapp (1988) acutely observed, needed images, of many different kinds.*

adapt **AWL** /əˈdæpt/ *verb* **1** [T] to change sth in order to make it suitable for a new use or situation: **~ sth** *Native Americans adapted practices involving fire and grazing.* ◇ **~ sth for sb/sth** *The test was adapted for different ages.* ◇ **~ sth to sth** *These principles can be adapted to a diversity of organizations.* ◇ **~ sth from sth** *This example is adapted from Tuggy (1988).* ◇ **~ sth to do sth** *Group models were adapted to facilitate effective decision-making in high-risk incidents.* ➲ *compare* MODIFY (1) **2** [I, T] (of a person, animal, plant, etc.) to change your/its behaviour in order to deal more successfully with a new situation: *The organisms were forced to adapt in order to survive.* ◇ **~ to sth** *Humans are adapting continuously to the environment.* ◇ **~ yourself/itself to sth** *Geological records testify that life on Earth has adapted itself to its slowly changing conditions.* ➲ *compare* ADJUST (2) **3** [T] **be adapted for sth** (of a part of the human body, an animal or a plant) to have developed for a particular purpose: *In the bat, the limb is adapted for flying.* **4** [T] **~ sth (for sth) (from sth)** to change a book or play so that it can be made into a play, film or television drama: *Many successful films have been adapted from plays.*

adapt·able **AWL** /əˈdæptəbl/ *adj.* (*approving*) able to change in order to deal successfully with new situations: *The local community provided a skilled and adaptable workforce.* ◇ **~ to sth** *In contrast to specialist species, generalist species are more adaptable to changing light conditions.* ■ **adapt·abil·ity** **AWL** /əˌdæptəˈbɪləti/ *noun* [U] *Small enterprises generally offer greater adaptability than larger firms.*

adap·ta·tion **AWL** /ˌædæpˈteɪʃn/ (*also less frequent* **adap·tion** /əˈdæpʃn/) *noun* **1** [U, C] the action or process of changing sth, or of being changed, to suit a new situation: *Thus, hunting is both learned and the outcome of an evolutionary process of adaptation.* ◇ **~ of sth** *The smaller European economies benefited from the import and adaptation of technology.* ◇ **~ to sth** *Adaptation to the global environment has been crucial.* ◇ **~ of sth (to sth)** *The precise adaptations of different wetland plants to specific degrees of waterlogging contribute to high species diversity.* **2** [C] **~ (of sth)** a play, film or television drama that is based on an original book or play: *Tate's reworking of 'King Lear' is one of the many Restoration adaptations of Shakespeare.*

adap·tive **AWL** /əˈdæptɪv/ *adj.* concerned with changing; able to change when necessary in order to deal with different situations: *Learned behaviour is often adaptive.* ◇ *Burrowing is one adaptive response to colder climates.*

add /æd/ *verb* **1** to put an extra element or part into sth: **~ sth** *The title has been added by the editors, as have all the footnotes.* ◇ **~ sth to sth** *Acid is added to the solution and the potential of the pH electrode increases by 118 mV.* ◇ *But Smith also adds some elements of his own to the theory.* **OPP** REMOVE (1) **2** to give a particular quality to a thing, event or situation: **~ sth** *The brand helps add value for consumers by conveying information about the quality of the product.* ◇ **~ sth to sth** *Air transport added a new dimension to the overall transport system.* ◇ *Model imperfections thus add another layer of complexity to the problem.* **3** to put numbers or amounts together to get a total: **~ sth** *This code adds two numbers and stores their sum in memory.* ◇ **~ A to B** *This code adds the first number to the* second and... ◇ **~ sth/A and B together** *The numbers are then added together and divided by the number of factors to give an average.* OPP SUBTRACT **4** to say sth more; to make a further comment: **~ sth (to sth)** *One caveat should be added, however...* ◇ **~ that...** *The author adds further that...*

IDM **ˈadded to this... | ˈadd to this...** used to introduce another fact that helps to emphasize a point you have already made: *Added to this is the rapidly increasing cost of fuel, which is now becoming a major factor for car buyers.*

PHR V **ˈadd to sth** to increase sth in size, number or amount: *Bulgaria, Chile, Argentina and Hungary add to the list of wine-exporting countries.* ◇ *The need to use ultra-pure H_2 for low temperature fuel cells adds significantly to the cost of the fuel.* ◇ *The civilization of ancient Rome added little to geographic knowledge, despite the expansion of the Roman Empire.* **ˌadd sthˈ up** to calculate the total of two or more numbers or amounts: *Adding up the costs and benefits gives the net benefit associated with each alternative.* **ˌadd ˈup to sth** **1** to lead to a particular result; to show sth SYN AMOUNT TO STH: *These comments do not add up to a sustained theory.* **2** to make a total amount of sth: *The sum of the angles of a triangle add up to 180°.*

added /ædɪd/ *adj.* [only before noun] in addition to what is usual SYN EXTRA: **~ bonus/advantage/benefit** *Calcium carbonate has the added bonus that it is a source of calcium.* ◇ **~ value** *The foundation looks for the added value it could deliver by investing in a particular area of service provision.*

ad·dict /ˈædɪkt/ *noun* **1** a person who is unable to stop taking harmful drugs: *The data may reveal differences between the brains of drug addicts and non-addicts.* **2** a person who is very interested in sth and spends a lot of their free time on it: *Adrenaline addicts prefer activities involving excitement and motion.*

ad·dict·ed /əˈdɪktɪd/ *adj.* [not usually before noun] **1** unable to stop taking harmful drugs, or using or doing sth as a habit: *Those who drink little are unlikely to become addicted.* ◇ **~ to sth** *She was addicted to crack cocaine.* **2 ~ to sth** spending all your free time doing sth because you are so interested in it: *Some people deprive themselves of their own freedom by becoming addicted to the web.*

ad·dic·tion /əˈdɪkʃn/ *noun* [U, C] the condition of being addicted to sth: *A concerted effort to reduce cigarette smoking and nicotine addiction is required.* ◇ *There are stigmas associated with things such as mental illnesses and drug addictions.* ◇ **~ to sth** *Alvarez has written about his addiction to risk-taking, whether in rock-climbing or poker.*

ad·dict·ive /əˈdɪktɪv/ *adj.* **1** if a drug is **addictive**, it makes people unable to stop taking it: *Nicotine is a highly addictive substance that makes people feel energized and alert.* **2** if a person's behaviour is **addictive**, they cannot stop taking drugs or doing sth else that is harmful: *There is growing evidence for a genetic component to addictive behaviour.*

add·ition /əˈdɪʃn/ *noun* **1** [U, C] the act of adding sth to sth else: **~ (of sth)** *Each of these steps requires the addition of microbes and enzymes.* ◇ **by the ~ of sth** *The solution was acidified by the addition of dilute acid.* ◇ **with the ~ of sth** *The most dramatic expansion of the EU took place in 2004 with the addition of 10 countries.* ◇ **~ of sth to sth** *Further additions of CO_2 to the atmosphere will result in...* OPP REMOVAL (1) **2** [C] **~ (to sth)** a thing that is added to sth else: *Both these works constitute significant additions to the bibliographic literature.* ◇ *The Viking grave on the island of Sanday is a recent addition to this body of evidence.* **3** [U, C] the process of adding two or more numbers together to find their total: *These mechanical computing devices could now perform addition, subtraction, multiplication and division.* ◇ *The three additions must be done before the division.* OPP SUBTRACTION

IDM **in addition (to sb/sth)** used to introduce a new fact or argument: *In addition, granites have been subdivided into two classes.* ◇ *In addition to ethical concerns, there is the issue of whether or not product placement is effective.*

LANGUAGE BANK

Adding a further point

These words and phrases may be used to introduce a further point in an argument.

- **In addition (to sth)/added to sth,...**
- **Along with sth,...**
- **Another/A further/An additional** reason/factor/example **is...**
- **Other** causes/reasons/factors/advantages **include...**
- **not only..., but also...**
- **What is more/Moreover/Furthermore,...**

– ***In addition to** this, the elderly are faced with the challenge of a life expectancy longer than ever before.*
– *Difficulty in housing his troops, **added to** the anxiety about his supply lines, forced Napoleon to quit Moscow.*
– ***Along with** all these factors, perhaps the most important are the resources available to a household.*
– ***A further** important aspect **has been** the increasing globalization of services.*
– ***Other** rarer causes of pancreatitis **include** viruses, direct trauma to the abdomen, drugs and metabolic causes.*
– *We test this theory, **not only** for Internet and mobile usage, **but also** for PCs.*
– ***What is more**, by 1970, steam locomotives had been completely replaced by diesel-electrics.*
– ***Moreover**, as cheaper ways for extracting natural resources are discovered, the extraction rate increases.*
– *There was an extensive market for sugar. **Furthermore**, sugar could be imported at prices that yielded good profits.*

add·ition·al /əˈdɪʃənl/ *adj.* more than was first mentioned or is already present or is usual SYN EXTRA: *Additional information is needed to provide a more complete assessment.* ◇ *Glass has the additional advantage of being far more resistant to scratching than plastic.* ◇ *The oil and gas industry faced additional costs as it moved into difficult new environments.* ◇ **~ to sth** *In other words, factors additional to sea surface temperature play a role.* ➲ language bank *at* ADDITION

▸ ADDITIONAL + NOUN **feature • factor • dimension • information • insight • benefit, advantage • complication, complexity • assumption • requirement • resources, funds • cost • revenue • support for sth** *Longer term data from other tropical sites could provide additional insight into this issue.* ◇ *This finding provides substantial additional support for the central hypothesis.*

add·ition·al·ly /əˈdɪʃənəli/ *adv.* **1** used to introduce a new fact or argument SYN IN ADDITION (TO SB/STH): *Additionally, researchers such as Hogarth (1981) and Connolly (1988) have pointed out that...* **2** as an extra factor SYN ALSO: *Problems additionally arise from the production of liquefied natural gas, of which Indonesia is the world's leading producer.*

addi·tive¹ /ˈædətɪv/ *noun* a substance that is added in small amounts to sth, especially food, in order to improve it, give it colour, make it last longer, etc: *There is a strong case for significant changes in food manufacturers' employment of certain food additives.*

addi·tive² /ˈædətɪv/ *adj.* [not usually before noun] connected with or produced by addition: *One simple explanation would be that the effects of the two chemicals are simply additive.*

A

ad·dress[1] /ə'dres/ *verb* **1** to think about a problem or a situation and decide how you are going to deal with it: **~ sth** *Partnerships can be developed to address local issues.* ◇ **be addressed by sb/sth** *Clearly, many of the solutions to poverty need to be addressed by the countries themselves.* ◇ **~ yourself to sth** *During the next three centuries, writers on scientific method addressed themselves to these problems.* ◇ **~ itself to sth** *Stoic philosophy addresses itself to every human being, at least in principle.* ◇ **~ sth by doing sth** *End-user demand for products and services can be partially addressed by analysing economic, technological, demographic, and social trends.* ◇ **~ sth through sth** *Issues such as education and health were addressed through public policy initiatives.* ➲ language bank *at* ABOUT[2] **2 ~ sth (to sb)** to write to sb; to write on an envelope the name and address of the person, company, etc. that you are sending it to by mail: *Ho Chi Minh addressed eight separate letters to Harry Truman on the subject.* **3 ~ sth/sb (on sth)** to make a formal speech to a group of people: *In 1965, Johnson addressed Congress on the Voting Rights Bill.* **4** to speak to sb: **~ sb** *In Godard's films, devices include characters addressing the audience directly.* ◇ **~ yourself to sb** *Addressing themselves to village audiences, the actors use Tok Pisin exclusively.*

▸ ADDRESS + NOUN **issue, question, problem • topic • concerns • challenge • need • cause** *It will be essential to address this topic in the future.*

▸ ADVERB + ADDRESS | ADDRESS + ADVERB **adequately • specifically • explicitly • directly** *However, the expansion of the education system has been at the expense of quality, which has not been adequately addressed.* ◇ *The government realized that housing issues needed to be addressed directly.*

ad·dress[2] /ə'dres; *NAmE also* 'ædres/ *noun* **1** [C] details of where sb lives or works and where letters, etc. can be sent: *The Data Protection Act regulates how an organization may store and use personal data about individuals, including their names and addresses.* **2** [C] a series of words and symbols that tells you where you can find sth using a computer, for example on the Internet: *Although the younger children tended to use a family email address, teenagers demanded greater privacy.* **3** [C] a formal speech that is made in front of an audience: *Barack Obama delivered a keynote address to the Democratic National Convention.* **4** [U] **form/mode of ~** the correct title, etc. to use when you talk to sb: *One academic examination of radio criticizes the mode of address on commercial radio.* ◇ *The terms 'brother' and 'sister' emerged as solitary forms of address.*

ad·duce /ə'dju:s; *NAmE* ə'du:s/ *verb* [often passive] **~ sth** (*formal*) to provide evidence, reasons, facts, etc. in order to explain sth or to show that sth is true SYN CITE (1): *No evidence was adduced to support this assertion.*

ad·equate AWL /'ædɪkwət/ *adj.* enough in quantity, or good enough in quality, for a particular purpose or need: *This type of damage may be caused by the patient looking at the sun without adequate eye protection.* ◇ **~ for sth** *Manual gauges were read twice per day, which was adequate for our purposes.* ◇ **~ for doing sth** *These tests are adequate for studying the impact behaviour of isotropic polymers.* ◇ **~ to do sth** *Demand was scarcely adequate to sustain production.* OPP INADEQUATE (1) ■ **ad·equacy** AWL /'ædɪkwəsi/ *noun* [U] **~ (of sth)** *The adequacy of current treatment should be established.* OPP INADEQUACY (1)

ad·equate·ly AWL /'ædɪkwətli/ *adv.* in a way that is good enough in quality for a particular purpose or need: *The speech muscles will continue to function adequately, despite the damage.* ◇ *A monetary payment might not adequately compensate the claimant.* OPP INADEQUATELY

ad·here /əd'hɪə(r); *NAmE* əd'hɪr/ *verb* [I] **~ (to sth)** to stick firmly to sth: *Platelets become 'sticky' and adhere to the vessel wall.* ◇ *These cells adhere tightly together to form a cell sheet.*

PHR V **ad'here to sth 1** to believe in and follow a particular principle or practice: *Only three countries adhered consistently to free-trade principles.* ◇ *These informal organizations do not adhere strictly to formal rules and procedures for getting things done.* **2** to closely follow or represent a particular view: *The report adhered to a traditional liberal view of the functions of education.*

ad·her·ence /əd'hɪərəns; *NAmE* əd'hɪrəns/ *noun* [U] the fact of behaving according to a particular rule, or of following a particular principle or practice: *European leaders pressed for a common electoral system, or at least adherence to a common principle.* ◇ *Given the complexity of the climate system, strict adherence to a given time framework is not practical.*

ad·her·ent /əd'hɪərənt; *NAmE* əd'hɪrənt/ *noun* a person who supports a particular party, person or set of ideas SYN SUPPORTER: *The Egyptian goddess Isis gained many adherents outside Egypt.* ◇ **~ of sth** *Adherents of this view argue that...*

ad·he·sion /əd'hi:ʒn/ *noun* [U] **~ (to sth)** the ability to stick to or become attached to sth; the action or process of sticking to a surface or an object: *Surface coatings require strong adhesion to the surface.*

ad·he·sive[1] /əd'hi:sɪv; əd'hi:zɪv/ *noun* [C, U] a substance used to make things stick together: *The composite reinforcements were bonded to the steel base structures with an epoxy adhesive.*

ad·he·sive[2] /əd'hi:sɪv; əd'hi:zɪv/ *adj.* able to stick firmly to a surface or an object: *The tentacles are adhesive and are used to catch and hold prey.* ◇ *The strength of the adhesive joint was tested.*

ad hoc /ˌæd 'hɒk; *NAmE* ˌæd 'hɑ:k/ *adj.* (*from Latin*) arranged or happening when necessary and not planned in advance: *Information may be obtained on an ad hoc basis through specialist market research projects.* ■ **ad hoc** *adv.*: *Public inquiries are set up ad hoc, as and when the government considers they are needed.*

adi·pose /'ædɪpəʊs; 'ædɪpəʊz; *NAmE* 'ædɪpoʊs; 'ædɪpoʊz/ *adj.* [only before noun] (*technical*) (of body TISSUE) used for storing fat: *Obesity is characterized as an excess of adipose tissue.*

ad·ja·cent AWL /ə'dʒeɪsnt/ *adj.* next to each other; next to sth: *The bonds between adjacent layers are relatively weak.* ◇ *Adjacent cells in some cases exchange molecules so as to coordinate the chemical activities throughout a tissue.* ◇ **~ to sth** *This is a means of disposal that can be set up in an area immediately adjacent to a population centre.*

ad·jec·tive /'ædʒɪktɪv/ *noun* (*grammar*) a word that describes a person or thing, for example *great, interesting* and *scientific* in *a great leader, interesting research* and *scientific knowledge*: *Non-gradable adjectives denote properties which are thought of as present or absent, rather than more or less.* ■ **ad·jec·tival** /ˌædʒek'taɪvl/ *adj.*: *The adjectival form of curriculum is curricular.*

ad·just AWL /ə'dʒʌst/ *verb* **1** [T] to change sth slightly to make it more suitable for a new set of conditions or to make it work better: **~ sth** *Businesses have to adjust prices to maintain margins and cover the rise in costs.* ◇ **~ sth to sth** *We adjusted the pH to 12 with 50% sodium hydroxide.* ◇ **~ sth for sth** *This figure will be adjusted for inflation every three years.* **2** [T, I] to change the way you behave and/or think in order to deal with a new situation: **~ sth** *The firms did not adjust their behaviour to respond to environmental regulations.* ◇ **~ to sth** *The first challenge concerns the way people will adjust to these technological* *changes.* ◇ **~ themselves/itself (to sth)** *A search agent may adjust itself automatically, depending on previous actions carried out by the user.* ➲ compare ADAPT (2)

ad·just·ment AWL /əˈdʒʌstmənt/ *noun* [C, U] **1** a small change made to sth in order to correct or improve it; the act of making a small change: *The law requires employers to make 'reasonable adjustments' to ensure that disabled people are not at a disadvantage in the workplace.* ◇ **~ for sth** *After adjustment for maternal age at birth, a reduction in the risk of diabetes in second- or later-born children became apparent.* ◇ **+ noun** *The adjustment mechanism for deficit countries was deflation rather than devaluation.* **2** a change in the way a person behaves or thinks: *These disorders are caused mainly by the psychological adjustments required after childbirth.* ◇ **~ to sth** *The study showed that men and women have differences in their emotional adjustment to divorce.*

ad·min·is·ter /ədˈmɪnɪstə(r)/ *verb* **1** to give or provide sth, espcecially in a way that is fair or correct: **~ sth** *The landowner administered rural justice and could send troublesome serfs into the army.* ◇ **~ sth to sb** *The questionnaire was administered to two random samples of students.* **2** [often passive] **~ sth** to manage and organize the affairs of a business, an organization, a country, etc; to manage and organize a plan SYN MANAGE (3): *Each province was administered by a governor who was usually a military commander.* ◇ *Occupational pension schemes are administered by employers.* **3** [often passive] **~ sth (to sb)** to give drugs or medicine to sb: *The insulin is administered intravenously.*

ad·min·is·tra·tion AWL /ədˌmɪnɪˈstreɪʃn/ *noun* **1** [U] **~ (of sth)** the process of organizing the way that sth is done: *Public participation in the administration of justice is central to the principle of open justice.* **2** [U] the activity of running a business, school or other organization: *University administration was placed in the hands of a council at each institution.* **3** [C] the group of people that runs a business, school or other organization: *The school's administration believed that the students were steadily growing more disruptive.* **4** (*often* **Administration**) [C, U] the government of a country; the process of governing a country: *Under the Clinton Administration, the goals of foreign policy were expanded.* ◇ *Greek cities provided the framework for Roman provincial administration.* **5** [U] **~ (of sth)** the act of giving drugs or medicine to sb: *Oral administration of drugs has several advantages.* **6** [U] (*BrE, law*) a situation in which the financial affairs of a business that cannot pay its debts are managed by an independent administrator: *The company went into administration due to the downturn in the housing market.*

ad·min·is·tra·tive AWL /ədˈmɪnɪstrətɪv; *NAmE* ədˈmɪnɪstreɪtɪv/ *adj.* **1** connected with organizing the work of a business, school or other organization: *Administrative assistants are responsible for tracking the complex schedules.* **2** connected with governing a country: *For example, much of the procedure of the courts is based on French administrative law.* ■ **ad·min·is·tra·tive·ly** AWL *adv.*: *Administratively, Wales was now assimilated to England.*

ad·min·is·tra·tor AWL /ədˈmɪnɪstreɪtə(r)/ *noun* **1** a person whose job is to organize the work of a business, school or other orgnaization: *hospital/school/university administrators* **2** (*BrE, law*) a person officially chosen to manage the financial affairs of a business that cannot pay its debts: *The company is now in the hands of the administrators.*

ad·mir·able /ˈædmərəbl/ *adj.* having qualities that you admire and respect: *Successive Thai governments have an admirable record of providing the basic conditions for private sector investment in industry.* ■ **ad·mir·ably** /ˈædmərəbli/ *adv.*: *This is a refreshingly clear text that provides an admirably concise guide to the subject.*

ad·mir·ation /ˌædməˈreɪʃn/ *noun* [U] a feeling of respect and liking for sb/sth: *Tacitus certainly regarded some powerful women as worthy of admiration.* ◇ **~ for sb/sth** *He began writing on cinema to express his admiration for film as an artistic medium.*

ad·mire /ədˈmaɪə(r)/ *verb* **1** to respect sb/sth for what they are or what they have done: **~ sb/sth** *He very much admired his father, and wanted to be like him.* ◇ *This short sample of Evans-Pritchard's analysis shows why his work has been so much admired.* ◇ **~ sb/sth for (doing) sth** *Their employees were admired for their good morale, cooperation and hard work.* **2 ~ sb/sth** to look at sb/sth and think that they are attractive and/or impressive: *They were driving along admiring the scenery.*

ad·mirer /ədˈmaɪərə(r)/ *noun* a person who admires sb/sth, especially a well-known person or thing: *He is known primarily through works written by contemporary admirers.* ◇ **~ of sb/sth** *He was a poet and literary critic and became a great admirer of Western literature.*

ad·mis·sion /ədˈmɪʃn/ *noun* **1** [U, C] the process or fact of accepting sb into an institution, organization or place: *Hospital admission is not necessary in most cases.* ◇ *There were about 8.5 million ordinary hospital admissions in the year.* ◇ **~ to sth** *Admission to higher education is by academic qualifications.* **2** [C, U] a statement in which sb admits that sth is true, especially sth wrong or bad that they have done: *On its own admission, the company's biggest technological advantage is its supply chain.* ◇ **~ of sth** *A settlement was reached without admission of liability.* ◇ **~ that...** *There was never an admission that the policy might have negative effects.*

admit /ədˈmɪt/ *verb* (-tt-) **1** [I, T] to agree that sth is true or that sth is the case: **~ sth** *In April 2003 the company finally admitted defeat.* ◇ **~ (that)...** *We often do not want to admit that we feel hurt, disappointment, sadness and other uncomfortable emotions.* ◇ **it is admitted that...** *It must be admitted that the power of public opinion is limited and hard to pin down.* ◇ **~ to sb that...** *She was too embarrassed to admit to anyone that she had made a mistake.* **2** [T, I] to state that you have made a mistake or done sth illegal: **~ (to) sth** *This finding suggests that entrepreneurs find it easy to admit past mistakes.* ◇ *Teachers are often reluctant to admit to such problems.* ◇ **~ (to) doing sth** *According to one questionnaire, 60% of Japanese doctors admitted feeling chronically tired.* ◇ *Finally, 26 per cent of study participants admitted to having used illegal drugs.* **3** [T] to accept sb/sth into an institution, an organization, a place, etc: **~ sb/sth (to sth)** *He was prepared to admit women to the ruling class.* ◇ **~ sb/sth into sth** *In 2000, Greece was admitted into the common currency.* **4** [T, often passive] **~ sb (to sth)** to take sb to a hospital, or other institution where they can receive special care: *A 63-year-old man was admitted to hospital with pneumonia.* ◇ *For example, patients admitted with surgical or medical conditions may develop a new mental health problem.* **5** [T] **~ sth** to accept sth as valid: *The courts can refuse to admit police evidence which has been illegally obtained.*

PHR V **adˈmit of sth** (*formal*) to show that sth is possible as a solution, an explanation, etc: *The partial nature of the evidence does not admit of definite conclusions.*

ad·mit·ted·ly /ədˈmɪtɪdli/ *adv.* used when you are accepting that sth is true: *Admittedly, no two economies are the same.* ◇ *The conclusions are based on interviews with an admittedly small sample of students.* ➲ language bank *at* CONCEDE

A

ado·les·cence /ˌædəˈlesns/ *noun* [U] the time in a person's life when they develop from a child into an adult: *In the transition from childhood to adolescence, teens are engaged in defining who they are.* ➲ *compare* PUBERTY

ado·les·cent /ˌædəˈlesnt/ *noun* a young person who is developing from a child into an adult: *Over nine million children and adolescents were injured in the United States in 2008.* ➲ *compare* TEENAGER ■ **ado·les·cent** *adj.*: *adolescent girls/boys* ◇ *Scientists found that adolescent problem behaviours such as aggression, illegal drug use or poor school achievement often occur together.*

adopt /əˈdɒpt; *NAmE* əˈdɑːpt/ *verb* **1** [T] **~ sth** to start to use a particular method or to show a particular attitude towards sb/sth: *These systems adopt a goal-directed approach to problem solving.* ◇ *This dispersal strategy is adopted by many freshwater species.* **2** [T] **~ sth** to formally accept a suggestion or policy by voting: *After intense discussions, the European Council adopted the Growth and Stability Pact.* **3** [T, I] **~ (sb)** to take sb else's child into your family and become its legal parent(s): *They wished to adopt a child.* ◇ *This case demonstrates the complex issues posed by step-parents wanting to adopt.* ➲ *see also* ADOPTED (1) **4** [T] **~ sth** to choose a new name or custom and begin to use it as your own; to choose and move to a country as your permanent home: *An immigrant group's culture need not disappear as its members adopt the practices associated with another society.* ➲ *see also* ADOPTED (2) **5** [T] **~ sth** to use a particular manner or way of speaking: *The advertisements adopted a slightly humorous tone.*

▸ ADOPT + NOUN **approach, strategy, policy, measures • procedure, practice • lifestyle** *The government adopted austerity measures aimed at reducing its large public sector.* ◇ *This approach seeks to encourage individuals to adopt healthy lifestyles.* | **stance • view • perspective** *Writers have adopted several different stances in relation to this issue.*

▸ NOUN + ADOPT **court • council • firm, organization** *A number of the firms had adopted work-family policies on a voluntary basis.*

▸ BE + ADVERB + ADOPTED **widely • universally** *This approach has been widely adopted*

▸ ADVERB + ADOPT **generally, commonly • increasingly • finally • subsequently, later • readily, quickly** *In Poland, managers generally adopted less harsh restructuring practices than their Western counterparts.* | **formally** *The proposal was formally adopted by the Commission.*

adopt·ed /əˈdɒptɪd; *NAmE* əˈdɑːptɪd/ *adj.* **1** an **adopted** child has legally become part of a family that is not the one in which they were born: *The parents wished to bring their adopted daughter to live with them in the UK.* ◇ *Studies of adopted children confirm the importance of genetic causes of depressive disorder.* **2** an **adopted** country is one in which sb chooses to live although it is not the one they were born in: *Many of the immigrants wished to gain employment, raise families, and live quietly in their newly adopted countries.*

adop·ter /əˈdɒptə(r); *NAmE* əˈdɑːptər/ *noun* **1** a person who adopts a child: *A full assessment of the prospective adopter's suitability to adopt a child must be completed.* **2 ~ (of sth)** a person who starts using a new technology or service: *It is common to characterize any adopter of a new technology, product or service as an innovator.* ◇ *Early adopters have more experience and capabilities in handling new media compared with late adopters.*

adop·tion /əˈdɒpʃn; *NAmE* əˈdɑːpʃn/ *noun* **1** [U] the decision to start using a particular idea, plan or name: *However, relatively few of these measures have achieved widespread adoption.* ◇ *In the case of technology adoption, most studies have found that large firms adopt any given technology early.* ◇ **~ of sth** *Critics recommend the adoption of proportional representation as a means of limiting the impact of party government.* **2** [U, C] the act of adopting a child: *Children available for adoption were abandoned, orphaned, or born as a result of an unwanted pregnancy.* ◇ *The most striking aspect of the change has been the precipitous decline in baby adoptions.*

adop·tive /əˈdɒptɪv; *NAmE* əˈdɑːptɪv/ *adj.* [usually before noun] an **adoptive** parent or family is one that has legally adopted a child: *In some cases the birth parents are involved with the selection of adoptive parents.*

ad·sorb /ədˈsɔːb; ədˈzɔːb; *NAmE* ədˈsɔːrb; ədˈzɔːrb/ *verb* **~ sth (to/onto sth)** (of a solid) to hold a liquid, gas or other substance as a thin layer on its surface: *Powdered carbon is used in some gas masks as it can adsorb many times its own volume of poisonous gases.* ◇ *Plants allow moisture adsorbed on clay soils to build up.*

adult[1] AWL /ˈædʌlt; əˈdʌlt/ *noun* **1** a fully grown person who is legally responsible for their actions: *The first group consisted of eleven young adults aged 18-25.* **2** a fully grown animal: *Adults are distinguished from juveniles by their red breast.*

adult[2] AWL /ˈædʌlt; əˈdʌlt/ *adj.* (of a person, an animal or a plant) fully grown or developed: *The average height of adult males in the UK is 178 cm.* ◇ *The males become adult when it is time to form a new nest.*

adult·hood AWL /ˈædʌlthʊd; əˈdʌlthʊd/ *noun* [U] (of a person, an animal, a fish, etc.) the state of being fully grown or developed: *When they reach adulthood, the salmon migrate back to their natal stream to reproduce.*

ad·vance[1] /ədˈvɑːns; *NAmE* ədˈvæns/ *noun* **1** [C, U] **~ (in sth)** progress or a development in a particular activity or area of understanding: *In the last decade, significant technological advances have been made in the field of radiotherapy.* ◇ *Analysis of these layers has led to major advances in our understanding of the behaviour of ice sheets.* ◇ *For two centuries economic advance has been closely tied to fossil fuel combustion.* **2** [C, U] **~ (on sth)** a forward movement of sth across an area: *The Russian army began an advance on Georgia's territory.* ◇ *There were various phases of glacial advance and retreat such as the Little Ice Age between about AD 1500 and 1850.* **3** [C] **~ (for sth)** money paid for work before it has been done; money paid earlier than expected: *In Boscawen v Bajwa (1996), a building society made an advance for the purchase of a property.* ◇ *Radcliffe ushered in a new era of publishers' advances: she was offered £500 for 'The Mysteries of Udolpho' (1794).* **4** [C] an increase in the price, value or amount of sth: *The Conservatives made a modest advance in terms of vote share.*

IDM **in advance (of sth)** **1** before sth happens: *We cannot, in advance, predict which problems will turn out to be easy and which hard.* ◇ *References can either be considered in advance of an interview, or alongside an interview.* **2** more developed than sb/sth else: *The Russian cruiser Novik was far in advance of other countries' destroyers.*

ad·vance[2] /ədˈvɑːns; *NAmE* ədˈvæns/ *verb* **1** [I] to move forward towards sb/sth or across an area: *In the northern hemisphere, ice sheets several times advanced over much of North America.* ◇ **~ on/towards sb/sth** *He ordered the cavalry corps to advance on Petrograd.* ➲ *compare* RETREAT[1] (2) **2** [I, T] (of knowledge, technology, etc.) to develop and make progress; to cause knowledge, technology, etc. to develop and make progress: *Computer technology has advanced with incredible speed.* ◇ **~ sth** *Studies of ice cores have advanced our understanding of Pleistocene climatic change.* **3** [T] **~ sth** to help sth to succeed or improve SYN FURTHER[3]: *Marx observed that groups as well as individuals may act together to advance their interests.* ◇ *Successive administrations have worked to advance the cause of human rights.* **4** [T] **~ sth** to suggest an idea, a theory or a plan for other people to discuss SYN PUT STH

FORWARD: *He advanced his theory that most unhappiness in the world had economic causes.* ◇ *The arguments advanced for justifiable killing of animals can be said to depend on three conditions.* ➲ thesaurus note *at* SUGGEST **5** [T] to give sb money before sth happens or before the time it would usually be paid: **~ sth** *Creditors included merchants who had advanced money to obtain consignments.* ◇ **~ sth to sb** *Money is advanced to a salesperson in months when commissions are low.* ◇ **~ sb sth** *He will advance her the capital at the beginning of the year.* **6** [T] **~ sth** to change the time or date of an event so that it takes place earlier: *When breeding times were either advanced or delayed by 10 days, birds experienced lower reproductive values.* OPP POSTPONE **7** [I, T] to continue forward to a later part of sth; to move sth forward to a later part: *This consensus breaks down as we advance through the teenaged years.* ◇ **~ sth (to sth)** *The rest of the companies are advanced to the next phase of the competition.*

ad·vance[3] /ədˈvɑːns; *NAmE* ədˈvæns/ *adj.* [only before noun] done, sent or given before sth is going to happen: *Given sufficient advance warning, the space technology needed to divert an asteroid could be developed.*

ad·vanced /ədˈvɑːnst; *NAmE* ədˈvænst/ *adj.* **1** having the most modern and recently developed ideas, methods, etc: *Farming in the American Midwest is characterized by larger farms, high productivity and advanced technology.* ◇ *The south and east regions are more advanced in economic development.* ◇ *Even the largest, most technologically advanced countries cannot provide strong innovation systems to all their industries.* **2** at a late stage of development: *Field trials are at an advanced stage for several other crops.* ◇ *Ovarian cancer may often remain 'silent' until the disease is advanced.* **3** (of a student or course of study) at a high or difficult level: *Monolingual dictionaries are particularly indicated for intermediate or advanced learners.* ◇ *The material requires a very advanced knowledge of English.*
IDM **advanced ˈage/ˈyears** old age: *In the wild, only a small fraction of a birth cohort will reach advanced age.*

ad·vance·ment /ədˈvɑːnsmənt; *NAmE* ədˈvænsmənt/ *noun* **1** [U, C] the process of helping sth to make progress or succeed; the progress that is made: **~ of sth** *Dissemination of work and data is essential to the advancement of science.* ◇ **~ in sth** *Advancements in molecular technology are rapidly expanding the field of genetic epidemiology.* **2** [U] progress in a job or social class: *Many of the jobs which women are doing are part-time, poorly paid, and with few prospects of career advancement.*

ad·van·tage[1] /ədˈvɑːntɪdʒ; *NAmE* ədˈvæntɪdʒ/ *noun* [C, U] **1** a thing that helps you to be better or more successful than other people: *The firm was accused of trying to gain an unfair advantage.* ◇ **~ over sb** *A few well-known institutions have advantages over other universities because of their long historical reputation.* ◇ **~ of (doing) sth** *You have the great advantage of knowing how your machine was made.* ◇ **at an ~** *Incumbent candidates are at an advantage in almost every election.* OPP DISADVANTAGE[1] **2** a quality of sth that makes it better or more useful: *Rural industry had two key advantages.* ◇ **~ of (doing) sth** *The great advantage of an MRI scan is that it can display soft tissue.* ◇ **~ to (doing) sth** *There are advantages and disadvantages to both approaches.* OPP DISADVANTAGE[1] ➲ language bank *at* CRITICAL
IDM **be/work to your adˈvantage** to give you an advantage; to change a situation in a way that gives you an advantage: *Many developing countries have long been aware of how the market dynamics of supply and demand have not worked to their advantage.* **take adˈvantage of sth/sb 1** to make use of sth well; to make use of an opportunity: *Researchers have taken advantage of many of the properties of CO_2 as a solvent.* ◇ *Firms that do not take advantage of every opportunity for growth will be left behind by firms that do.* ◇ *Within a week, Faraday had taken full advantage of this discovery.* **2** to make use of sb/sth in a way that is unfair or dishonest: *Each boy described the other as trying to control or take advantage of him.* **to (good/best) adˈvantage** in the best way possible; showing the best of sth: *We need a model of public health that uses limited resources to best advantage.* **turn sth to (your) adˈvantage** to use or change a situation so that it helps you: *Wales sought to turn its small size to advantage in the global economic crisis.*
▸ ADJECTIVE + ADVANTAGE **great • main, major • significant • important, key • considerable • comparative, relative • potential • distinct, clear • obvious • additional, further, added** *Table 4.9 summarizes the relative advantages and disadvantages of data capture methods.* | **unfair • mutual • sustainable • competitive • selective • differential • economic • strategic • military** *Competitive advantage can also be gained through increased employee productivity.*
▸ NOUN + ADVANTAGE **cost • price • location • survival** *Few new entrants will be able to match the leader's cost advantage.*
▸ VERB + ADVANTAGE **have, possess • see** *Low-cost airlines possess the competitive advantage of operating at significantly lower costs than their larger national counterparts.* ◇ *Shareholders saw the advantage of this strategy in reducing costs of production.* | **gain, obtain, secure • lose • sustain, maintain • offer, provide, give, confer, bring • enjoy • achieve, derive • create • exploit • seek** *In the modern world, where education confers many advantages, illiteracy is a severe impediment.*

ad·van·tage[2] /ədˈvɑːntɪdʒ; *NAmE* ədˈvæntɪdʒ/ *verb* [usually passive] **~ sb (over sb)** to put sb in a better position than other people or than they were in before: *Their experience will advantage them over non-diversified entrepreneurs.* ◇ *In Canada, an economically advantaged core area is surrounded by a number of relatively disadvantaged peripheries.*

ad·van·ta·geous /ˌædvənˈteɪdʒəs/ *adj.* good or helpful to sb in a particular situation SYN BENEFICIAL: *The military situation in Europe gave the Soviet Union an advantageous negotiating position.* ◇ *They had an incentive to negotiate a mutually advantageous solution.* ◇ **~ to sb** *He was empowered to act in whatever way he deemed advantageous to the Roman people.* OPP DISADVANTAGEOUS

ad·vent /ˈædvent/ *noun* [sing.] **the ~ of sth** the arrival of an important event, invention, etc: *The advent of wireless technologies, such as mobile broadband, has taken the electronic communication revolution to a new level.*

ad·verb /ˈædvɜːb; *NAmE* ˈædvɜːrb/ *noun* (*grammar*) a word that adds more information about place, time, manner, cause or degree to a verb, an adjective, a phrase or another adverb: *The suffix -ly can change an adjective into an adverb.* ■ **ad·ver·bial** /ædˈvɜːbiəl; *NAmE* ædˈvɜːrbiəl/ *adj.*: *Specifically future time is denoted by using adverbial expressions like 'tomorrow' or 'next year'.*

ad·ver·sary /ˈædvəsəri; *NAmE* ˈædvərseri/ *noun* (*pl.* **-ies**) a person that sb is opposed to and competing with in an argument or a battle SYN OPPONENT (2): *States will seek nuclear weapons both to enhance their own security and to deter potential adversaries.*

ad·verse /ˈædvɜːs; ədˈvɜːs; *NAmE* ˈædvɜːrs; ədˈvɜːrs/ *adj.* [usually before noun] negative and unpleasant; not likely to produce a good result: *The US surgeon general wrote in 1972, 'Televised violence does have an adverse effect on certain members of our society.'* ◇ *Most people believe that depression is wholly due to adverse life events.* ◇ *In the UK, the pharmaceutical industry has suffered some adverse publicity.* ➲ usage note *on* page 18

A

WHICH WORD?

adverse • averse

- **adverse** negative and unpleasant; not likely to produce a good result: *an adverse consequence/impact/outcome/reaction*
- **averse** not liking sth; not wanting to do sth: *I am certainly not averse to criticism—indeed, I welcome debate.*
- **Averse** is used in combination with the nouns *risk* and *inflation*: *Why would a central banker be more inflation-averse than the government?*

ad·verse·ly /ˈædvɜːsli; ədˈvɜːsli; *NAmE* ˈædvɜːrsli; ədˈvɜːrsli/ *adv.* in a negative or unpleasant way: *Many ordinary working people were adversely affected by the banking collapse.*

ad·ver·sity /ədˈvɜːsəti; *NAmE* ədˈvɜːrsəti/ *noun* (*pl.* **-ies**) [U, C] a difficult or unpleasant situation: *'Resilience' describes the capacity of individuals to continue functioning in the face of adversity.* ◇ *Parental neglect and other adversities are associated with the risk of early overweight (Ebbeling et al., 2002).*

ad·ver·tise /ˈædvətaɪz; *NAmE* ˈædvərtaɪz/ *verb* **1** [I, T] to tell the public about a product or a service in order to encourage people to buy or to use it: *Organizations that advertise on television are generally perceived as being more reliable and trustworthy than those that do not* ◇ **~ sth** *The Portman Group sets guidelines on how alcohol companies should advertise their products.* ◇ **~ (sth) to sb** *The different GM cars were priced differently and advertised to buyers with different incomes.* ◇ **~ sth as sth** *In 1995 the airline advertised its flights as cheaper than a pair of jeans.* **2** [I, T] to let people know that sth is going to happen, or that a job is available, by giving details about it in a newspaper, on a notice in a public place, on the Internet, etc: **~ (for sb/sth)** *In some circumstances it may be appropriate to advertise for board members.* ◇ **~ sth** *Certain posts, especially senior posts, are only advertised on a full-time basis.* ◇ *Such meetings must be advertised beforehand in the local press.* **3** [T] **~ sth** to show or tell sth about yourself to other people **SYN** PUBLICIZE: *They advertise their wealth through conspicuous and wasteful consumption.*

ad·ver·tise·ment /ədˈvɜːtɪsmənt; *NAmE* ˌædvərˈtaɪzmənt/ *noun* **1** [C] a notice, picture or film telling people about a product, job or service: *A total of ten advertisements were placed in five local papers and one magazine.* ◇ *Three quarters of food advertisements broadcast during children's viewing time promote high-calorie, low-nutrient foods.* ◇ **~ for sth** *Advertisements for nutritious foods promote selected positive attitudes and beliefs concerning these foods.* **2** [C] **~ for sth** an example of sth that shows its good qualities: *Some of the unions did not ballot members—a poor advertisement for union democracy.* **3** [U] **~ (of sth)** the act of advertising sth and making it public: *The law was amended in 2008 to restrict both the sale and advertisement of alcohol.*

ad·ver·tiser /ˈædvətaɪzə(r); *NAmE* ˈædvərtaɪzər/ *noun* a person or company that advertises: *To analyse and understand their target markets, all major advertisers carry out considerable market research.*

ad·ver·tis·ing /ˈædvətaɪzɪŋ; *NAmE* ˈædvərtaɪzɪŋ/ *noun* [U] the activity and industry of advertising things to people on television, in newspapers, on the Internet, etc: *An EU-led ban on tobacco advertising was introduced in the UK in 2003.* ◇ *television/Internet/online/radio/print advertising* ◇ **in ~** *The portrayal of elderly people in advertising is often as figures of fun or victims of tragic events.* ◇ **+ noun** *It was one of the most stunning and successful advertising campaigns in the history of American marketing.* ◇ *In 2006 the company reported a fall in advertising revenue.* ◇ *an advertising message/strategy/agency*

ad·vice /ədˈvaɪs/ *noun* [U] an opinion or a suggestion about what sb should do in a particular situation: **~ (to sb) (on sth)** *Marx gave advice and assistance to socialist parties in France and Germany.* ◇ *I am particularly grateful to Brad Astbury for his advice on methodology.* ◇ *Legal advice should be taken from a professional practitioner.* ◇ *medical/expert/specialist/professional/independent advice* ◇ *to provide/offer advice* ◇ **~ of sb** *In pregnancy, women often seek the advice of their mothers or of friends who have been pregnant.*

ad·vis·able /ədˈvaɪzəbl/ *adj.* [not usually before noun] sensible and a good idea in order to achieve sth: *The use of gloves is advisable for Containment Level 2 work.* ◇ **it is ~ to do sth** *It is advisable to continue the programme for at least a month.*

ad·vise /ədˈvaɪz/ *verb* **1** [I, T] to tell sb what you think they should do in a particular situation: **~ sb** *A ruler was usually advised and assisted by a council.* ◇ **~ sth** *The authors advised caution in interpreting this finding.* ◇ **~ (sb) against (doing) sth** *Authorities on marketing metrics advise against the use of only one measure (Ambler and Roberts, 2006, Lehmann, 2004).* ◇ **~ sb to do sth** *Her lawyer advised her to accept the settlement.* ◇ **be (well/strongly) advised to do sth** *The company would be well advised to tackle this problem urgently.* ◇ *Smokers should be strongly advised to stop before surgery.* ◇ **~ (sb) that...** *Many experts continue to advise that computer-based tests be used alongside informed professional judgement.* **2** [I, T] to give sb help and information on a subject that you know a lot about: **~ (sb) on/about (doing) sth** *There are specialist centres with experienced staff who can advise on interpretation of results.* ◇ **~ (sb) whether/how, etc...** *Doctors are sometimes asked to advise whether a patient is capable of making a will.* **3** [T] to officially tell sb sth **SYN** INFORM (1): **~ sb of/about sth** *Communication channels are developed in order for workers to advise management about issues of discontent.* ◇ **~ sb when/where, etc...** *Member states must advise the Commission when they propose to enact any such measures.* ◇ **~ sb that...** *The lawyer advised the court that his client wished to give evidence.*

ad·viser (*also* **ad·visor**) /ədˈvaɪzə(r)/ *noun* a person who gives advice, especially sb who knows a lot about a particular subject: *Applicants for asylum must have the opportunity to consult a legal adviser.* ◇ **~ to sb** *Traditionally, senior civil servants have been the main policy advisers to ministers.* ◇ **~ on sth** *Nesselrode was Nicholas's adviser on foreign affairs.*

ad·vis·ory /ədˈvaɪzəri/ *adj.* [usually before noun] having the role of giving professional advice: *Numerous parliamentary and advisory committees provide expert advice.* ◇ *The organization plays an important advisory role in the drafting of privacy related legislation.*

ad·vo·cacy **AWL** /ˈædvəkəsi/ *noun* **1** [U, sing.] the act of publicly giving support to an idea, a course of action or a belief: *Non-governmental organizations are important in human rights advocacy.* ◇ **~ of sth** *Nixon embraced Moynihan's advocacy of welfare reform.* ◇ **~ for sth** *In sub-Saharan Africa, advocacy for the abolition of school fees necessitated the search for alternative sources of resources.* **2** [U] a service that provides advice and/or support to sb: *Advocacy is available to parents in such areas as housing, education and the legal system.*

ad·vo·cate¹ **AWL** /ˈædvəkeɪt/ *verb* to support or recommend sth publicly: **~ sth** *Marx advocated democratic reforms that were considered radical at the time.* ◇ *The model advocated by radical liberals seeks to heighten regulation.* ◇ **~ doing sth** *Le Corbusier advocated increasing open space.* ◇ **~ that...** *This principle advocates that* *environmental damage should be rectified as close to its source as possible.*

ad·vo·cate² AWL /ˈædvəkət/ *noun* **1** a person who publicly supports or speaks in favour of a particular group of people, a cause or an idea: **~ for sth/sb** *Teachers need to understand the nature of children's lives in order to act as advocates for children.* ◇ **~ of sth/sb** *Mendelssohn was an ardent advocate of Jewish civil rights.* **2** a person who defends sb in court: *Experience as a barrister, an advocate or a solicitor was required.*

aer·obic /eəˈrəʊbɪk; *NAmE* eˈroʊbɪk/ *adj.* **1** (*biology*) needing, involving or connected with OXYGEN: *The process of aerobic respiration involves the breakdown of organic matter and the consumption of oxygen.* ◇ *Under aerobic conditions, nitrate is the stable nitrogen species in both water and soil.* OPP ANAEROBIC **2** (of physical exercise) especially designed to improve the function of the heart and lungs: *Adults should aim for 20–30 minutes of aerobic exercise three to five times per week.*

aero·plane /ˈeərəpleɪn; *NAmE* ˈerəpleɪn/ *noun* (*BrE*) = PLANE (1)

aes·thet·ic¹ (*NAmE also* **es·thet·ic**) /iːsˈθetɪk; esˈθetɪk; *NAmE* esˈθetɪk/ *adj.* **1** concerned with beauty and art and the understanding of beautiful things: *Party conflict and wartime paranoia often overrode literary and aesthetic judgements.* ◇ *The primary function of dictionary illustrations should not be purely aesthetic, but explanatory.* **2** beautiful to look at: *The map as an aesthetic object was explored recently in the BBC4 series 'The Beauty of Maps'.* ■ **aes·thet·ic·al·ly** (*NAmE also* **es·thet·ic·al·ly**) /iːsˈθetɪkli; esˈθetɪkli; *NAmE* esˈθetɪkli/ *adv.*: *The aim is to use these wastes to produce something more aesthetically pleasing and less of an environmental hazard.*

aes·thet·ic² (*NAmE also* **es·thet·ic**) /iːsˈθetɪk; esˈθetɪk; *NAmE* esˈθetɪk/ *noun* **1** [C] **~ (of sth)** a set of principles that express the aesthetic qualities and ideas of a particular artist or a particular group of artists, writers, etc: *These essays attempt to formulate an aesthetic of Indian English literature.* **2 aesthetics** [U] the branch of philosophy that studies the principles of beauty, especially in art: *Simmel regarded himself as a philosopher and made lasting contributions to aesthetics, ethics and the theory of knowledge.*

aeti·ology (*BrE*) (*NAmE* **eti·ology**) /ˌiːtiˈɒlədʒi; *NAmE* ˌiːtiˈɑːlədʒi/ *noun* [C, U] (*medical*) the cause of a disease or condition: *Although this is technically a stroke, it has a different aetiology.* ◇ *This is an uncommon condition of unknown aetiology.* ◇ **~ of sth** *The aetiology of this disease remains unclear.*

af·fair /əˈfeə(r); *NAmE* əˈfer/ *noun* **1 affairs** [pl.] events that are of public interest or political importance: *Central government took on a greater role in social and economic affairs.* ◇ *Both Thatcher and Reagan introduced a sharper ideological edge to domestic politics and foreign affairs.* ◇ *international/world affairs* ◇ *The Protectorate regime took over most affairs of state.* HELP The term **human affairs** is used to talk about any events that involve humans: *Some people began to believe that, contrary to traditional teaching, God did not intervene directly in human affairs.* ➲ *see also* CURRENT AFFAIRS, PUBLIC AFFAIRS **2** [C, usually sing.] an event that is talked about or can be described in a particular way: *It should be emphasized that the urbanization of Europe was a very uneven affair.* ◇ **in the ~** *He resigned as Trade and Industry Minister after vehement criticism of his role in the Westland affair.* **3 affairs** [pl.] matters connected with a person's or company's private business and financial situation: *He had deliberately arranged his financial affairs so that she would not be able to make any claim on his death.* ◇ **~ of sb/sth** *There were explicit instructions as to how the directors should conduct the affairs of the company.* **4** [C] **~ (with sb)** a sexual relationship between two people, usually when at least one of them is married to sb else: *Her husband discovered that she had been having an affair with a prominent man in the community.* IDM *see* STATE¹

af·fect¹ AWL /əˈfekt/ *verb* **1** [often passive] to make a difference to sb/sth or to what sb thinks or does: **~ sth/sb** *These differences can affect the outcome of certain experiments.* ◇ **be affected by sth** *Many countries were severely affected by the financial crisis.* ◇ **~ how/what, etc...** *The connections in a social network affect how people learn, form opinions and gather news.* ➲ *usage note at* EFFECT¹ **2 ~ sth/sb** (of a disease) to attack a part of the body; to make sb become ill: *Rheumatoid arthritis is a chronic disease that predominantly affects synovial joints.* ◇ *Affected individuals lack the enzyme to process fructose.* **3 be affected by sth** if you are affected by an event, it makes you feel very sad: *Kennedy was deeply affected by the death of his third child.*

▸ AFFECT + NOUN **outcome • process • rate • quality • ability • performance • behaviour • decision • the way...** *Research suggests that effective training does affect motivation.* ◇ *Age was also shown to affect the ability to learn.*

▸ NOUN + AFFECT **factor • decision • change** *Economic, social, academic and other environmental factors may affect school attendance.* | **condition, disease, disorder** *Skin disorders can affect all parts of the body.*

▸ ADVERB + AFFECT **adversely, negatively, badly • positively • significantly • greatly, substantially • profoundly, deeply, strongly • severely, seriously • directly • indirectly** *These molecules are significantly affected by the presence of the ion.* ◇ *Corn is severely affected by drought.* | **adversely • directly • severely • mainly, predominantly, primarily • usually, typically • commonly** *Malnutrition can adversely affect both the structure and function of skeletal muscle.* ◇ *The condition mainly affects young adults.*

af·fect² /ˈæfekt/ *noun* [U] (*psychology*) desire or emotion, especially in relation to how they influence your thoughts or behaviour: *This scale was used to measure positive and negative affect in three categories: facial display, vocalizations and body movement.*

af·fec·tion /əˈfekʃn/ *noun* **1** [U, sing.] the feeling of liking or loving sb/sth very much and caring about them: *Nalivkin received many awards and was held in great affection by his students and colleagues.* ◇ **~ for sb/sth** *Scottish writers seem to have retained an affection for their home country.* **2 affections** [pl.] a person's feelings of love: *Edward Ferrars in 'Sense and Sensibility' gains Elinor's affections while secretly engaged to Lucy Steele.*

af·fect·ive AWL /əˈfektɪv/ *adj.* [only before noun] connected with emotions and attitudes: *Values are affective because they are linked to our feelings about things.* ◇ *Some affective disorders are characterized mainly by the season in which they occur.* ■ **af·fect·ive·ly** AWL *adv.*: *Students who are affectively engaged at school hold positive attitudes towards academic activities.*

af·fili·ate¹ /əˈfɪlieɪt/ *verb* **1** [T, usually passive] **~ sb/sth (with/to sb/sth)** to link a group, a company or an organization very closely with another, larger one: *The Trades Union Congress (TUC), to which many unions are affiliated, was formed in 1868.* **2** [I, T] **~ (yourself) (with sb/sth)** to join, be connected with or support a group or organization: *Soldiers who entered the service during the Carter and Reagan years were particularly likely to affiliate with the Republican Party.* ◇ *Individuals affiliate themselves with other individuals like themselves.*

af·fili·ate² /əˈfɪliət/ *noun* **~ (of sth)** a company or an organization that is connected with or controlled by another, larger one: *Volvo Trucks North America is an affiliate of the Swedish multinational firm.*

af·fili·ated /ə'fɪlieɪtɪd/ *adj.* [only before noun] closely connected with or controlled by a group or an organization: *The London head office presided over a network of wholly owned branches and affiliated companies.*

af·fili·ation /əˌfɪli'eɪʃn/ *noun* [U, C] **1 ~ (with sb/sth)** a person's connection with a political party, religion, group of people, etc: *Teens may be attracted to gangs because of a need for affiliation with others who share similar attitudes.* ◇ *Approximately one third of interviewees could be classified as 'other', including those with no current religious affiliation.* **2 ~ (to sth)** a person or group's official connection with an organization: *Trade unions have a long history of affiliation to the Labour Party.*

af·fin·ity /ə'fɪnəti/ *noun* (*pl.* **-ies**) (*formal*) **1** [sing.] a strong feeling that you understand and like sb/sth: **~ for sb/sth** *There is a great affinity for horse racing in Hong Kong.* ◇ **~ with sb/sth** *Rochester seems to have felt a special affinity with his pet monkey.* **2** [C] a close relationship between two people or things that have similar qualities, structures or features: **~ with sb/sth** *The ideals of 20th century Communism had many affinities with ancient Spartan society.* ◇ **~ between A and B** *There is a historical affinity between American patriotism and baseball.* **3** [C] (*biochemistry*) the degree to which one substance will ASSOCIATE or combine with another: *The bacterial proteins bind to these molecules with high affinity.* ◇ **~ to sth** *One part of the molecule has an affinity to water.* ◇ **~ for sth** *Carbon monoxide has a 240 times greater affinity for Hb than oxygen.*

af·firm /ə'fɜːm; *NAmE* ə'fɜːrm/ *verb* **1** to state firmly or publicly that sth is true or that you support sth strongly: **~ sth** *Jones affirms the importance of oral history in expanding the historical record.* ◇ **~ that...** *They affirmed that policies were to be judged by their contribution to social justice.* ➲ *compare* CONFIRM (1) **2** (*law*) to accept or confirm that a judgment or agreement is valid: **~ sth** *The Court of Appeal affirmed a decision of the High Court.* ◇ **~ that...** *The court affirmed that the maintenance of the children was the primary obligation of their natural father.*

affirmation /ˌæfə'meɪʃn; *NAmE* ˌæfər'meɪʃn/ *noun* **1** [C, U] **~ (of sth)** the action or process of affirming sth: *'It's a Wonderful Life' manages a convincing and moving affirmation of the values of bourgeois family life.* **2** [U] emotional support or encouragement: *The peer group provides a milieu in which young people can attain affirmation (Rubin, 1985, pp. 109-111).*

af·firma·tive /ə'fɜːmətɪv; *NAmE* ə'fɜːrmətɪv/ *adj.* expressing agreement or the answer 'yes': *Providing affirmative responses such as 'uh huh', 'yes' or 'OK' is thought to bias interviewees' answers.* OPP NEGATIVE[1] (3) ➲ *see also* AFFIRMATIVE ACTION ■ **af·firma·tive·ly** *adv.*: *Those who replied affirmatively were asked an additional question.*

afˌfirmative 'action *noun* [U] (in the US) the practice or policy of making sure that a particular number of jobs, etc. are given to people from particular groups based on their race, sex, etc, in order to make results for all groups in society more equal: *Affirmative action programs seeking to redress racial imbalances in employment contributed to the reduction in racial earnings gaps.*

af·flu·ent /'æfluənt/ *adj.* having a lot of money and a good standard of living SYN PROSPEROUS, WEALTHY (1): *In modern, affluent societies, the average large supermarket offers shoppers about 40 000 different lines.* ◇ *Mainstream banks in most western countries have targeted relatively affluent individuals with a steady source of income.* ■ **af·flu·ence** /'æfluəns/ *noun* [U] *Since the 1960s, awareness of how global affluence and poverty are interrelated has increased.* SYN PROSPERITY

af·ford /ə'fɔːd; *NAmE* ə'fɔːrd/ *verb* **1** [no passive] (usually used with *can, could* or *be able to*, especially in negative sentences or questions) to have enough money or time to be able to buy or to do sth: **~ sth** *The Russian economy could not afford new guns.* ◇ **~ to do sth** *Low-income households cannot afford to own private vehicles.* ◇ *They cannot afford to take time from work to schedule a visit to a physician.* ◇ **~ sth to do sth** *They were the only states that could afford the military means to fight the kind of large-scale wars that were occurring.* **2** [no passive] **~ to do sth** (usually used with *can* or *could*, especially in negative sentences and questions) if you say that you **cannot afford** to do sth, you mean that you should not do it because it will cause problems for you if you do: *No firm could afford to ignore actual or potential competitors.* ◇ *Small-scale societies can ill afford to lose valuable productive group members.* **3** (*formal*) to provide sb with sth: **~ sth** *Human rights afford protection to all individuals in peace and war.* ◇ **~ sb sth** *They were not afforded the luxury of central air-conditioning.* ■ **af·ford·abil·ity** /əˌfɔːdə'bɪləti; *NAmE* əˌfɔːrdə'bɪləti/ *noun* [U] **~ (of sth)** *There is a need for improvement in the accessibility and affordability of cancer treatments.* **af·ford·able** /ə'fɔːdəbl; *NAmE* ə'fɔːrdəbl/ *adj.*: *Lack of affordable housing is having a severe impact on low-income families.* **af·ford·ably** *adv.*: *They were also able to price the product range affordably.*

afraid /ə'freɪd/ *adj.* [not before noun] **1** worried about what might happen; unwilling to do sth because of this: **~ of doing sth** *Some of the participants were afraid of appearing racist.* ◇ **~ to do sth** *The students were not afraid to express their opinions.* ◇ **~ (that)...** *Some Western countries were afraid that their economies would suffer from China's fast growth.* **2** feeling fear; frightened because you think that you might be hurt or suffer: *'All of us were afraid,' one demonstrator recalled, 'but we went and did it anyway.'* ◇ **~ of sb/sth** *She was afraid of her husband.* ◇ **~ of doing sth** *26.9% of respondents reported being very afraid of getting cervical cancer.* ◇ **~ to do sth** *The intersection was so busy and obviously dangerous that parents were afraid to send their children to school.* **3 ~ for sb/sth** worried or frightened that sth unpleasant, dangerous, etc. will happen to a particular person or thing: *Such news releases made Americans afraid for their physical and cultural security.*

after[1] /'ɑːftə(r); *NAmE* 'æftər/ *prep.* **1** later than sth; following sth in time: *The Chapelhouse Estate was built shortly after the First World War.* ◇ *A new bill was introduced and received a favourable vote soon after that.* ◇ *It was not until the day after Truman's meeting with Molotov that he was first briefed about the bomb.* ◇ *Steve James's 'Hoop Dreams' (1994) became an international hit after winning an award at the Sundance Film Festival.* **2 ... after...** used to show that sth happens many times or continuously: *The company began to lose $100 million per day, day after day.* ◇ *It was soon discovered that growing a cereal crop on the same land year after year impoverished the soil.* **3** next to and following sb/sth in order or importance: *The object is the noun phrase that comes after the verb in English.* ◇ *The Imperial Library at St Petersburg with its million titles ranked third in the world after the Bibliothèque Nationale and the British Museum.* **4** in contrast to sth: *The employees welcomed change after so many years of reckless 'entrepreneurship'.* **5** in the style of sb/sth; following the example of sb/sth: *They fashioned themselves after the Greek style.* ◇ *The gods awarded the country to Athena, who named the city Athens after herself.* **6 after-** (in adjectives) happening or done later than the time or event mentioned: *Children need to be occupied during the after-school hours.* ◇ *Simon gave an appreciative after-dinner speech about his father.* **7** trying to find or catch sb/sth: *The attraction of chasing after something new is always strong.* ◇ *The man ran from us as if the wolves were after him.*

IDM ˌafter ˈall **1** despite what has been said or expected: *The aggrieved employee may change their mind and decide to pursue a formal complaint after all.* **2** used when you are explaining sth, or giving a reason: *The Internet, after all, is the very embodiment of globalization: it is everywhere and it does everything.*

after² /ˈɑːftə(r); *NAmE* ˈæftər/ *conj.* at a time later than sth; when sth has finished: *She re-examined the data many years after the original research had been carried out.* ◇ *The Act was eventually passed after a Law Commission Report in 1989 recommended that this area of law be reformed.*

after³ /ˈɑːftə(r); *NAmE* ˈæftər/ *adv.* later in time; afterwards: *These developments were followed, soon after, by the final collapse of the agreement.*

after·math /ˈɑːftəmæθ; ˈɑːftəmɑːθ; *NAmE* ˈæftərmæθ/ *noun* [usually sing.] the situation that exists as a result of an important (and usually unpleasant) event, especially a war, an accident, etc: *The American Revolution and its immediate aftermath presented many investment opportunities for merchants.* ◇ **in the ~ of sth** *The legislation had been hurriedly passed in the aftermath of the terrorist attacks.*

after·wards /ˈɑːftəwədz; *NAmE* ˈæftərwərdz/ (*especially BrE*) (*NAmE usually* **after·ward**) *adv.* at a later time; after an event that has already been mentioned: *Afterwards, the figures increased to 11% and 21%, respectively.* ◇ *She arrived in the UK and gave birth to a child shortly afterwards.*

again /əˈɡen; əˈɡeɪn/ *adv.* **1** one more time; on another occasion: *He was very pleased to see Byron again.* ◇ *They needed to ensure that the Great Depression of the 1930s would not happen again.* ◇ **all over ~** *Each day, the schedule starts all over again.* ◇ **~ and ~** *Scientific methods have been shown to work again and again.* **2** showing that sb/sth is in the same place or state that they were in originally: *When the price of a commodity rose, consumers bought less of it, which tended to bring the price down again.* ◇ **back ~** *The swing from peak to trough and back again is called the business cycle.* **3** used to show that a comment or fact is connected with what you have just said: *American education is highly fragmented, and again, geography education is no exception.* **4 then ~** used to introduce a fact or an opinion that contrasts with what you have just said: *Employees may be inspired by a shared framework of values—but, then again, they may not.* IDM *see* ONCE¹

against /əˈɡenst; əˈɡeɪnst/ *prep.* HELP For the special uses of **against** in phrasal verbs, look at the entries for the verbs. For example **count against sb** is in the phrasal verb section at **count**. **1** opposing or disagreeing with sb/sth: *The European Council made the fight against terrorism a priority objective.* ◇ *Gender discrimination exists in society but it is against the law.* ◇ *She claimed she was forced into the marriage against her will.* ◇ *The Ministry of Education decided against publishing the report.* ◇ **for or ~** *There is no evidence for or against this proposition.* **2** not to the advantage or favour of sb/sth: *Socrates' association with such a man counted against him at the philosopher's trial.* ◇ *The packages of drugs removed from his stomach were entered in evidence against him.* ➲ *compare* FOR (10) **3** close to, touching or hitting sb/sth: *The picture showed a relaxed-looking executive, leaning against a door frame.* ◇ *A child also redirects anger when he slams an object or his hand against a wall.* **4** in order to prevent sth from happening or to reduce the damage caused by sth: *Effective vaccines against these diseases are desperately needed.* ◇ *This article considers whether leisure-time physical activity protects against shoulder pain at work.* ◇ *Most people take out some kind of insurance policy against fire, theft and so forth.* **5** with sth in the background, as a contrast: *Images of the elephants in grasslands silhouetted against Kilimanjaro presented a powerful image for raising funds.* ◇ (*figurative*) *Britain's democratic stability since 1918 has been achieved against a background of relative decline.* **6** used when you are comparing two things: *These costs must be weighed against the likely benefits.* ◇ *The scanned fingerprints are checked against police and immigration records.* ◇ *The value of the euro has increased rapidly against the dollar.* IDM *see* AS³

age¹ /eɪdʒ/ *noun* **1** [C, U] the number of years that a person has lived or a thing has existed: *Each child's exact age was used in all analyses.* ◇ *Participant age ranged from 3.67 to 17.66 years.* ◇ **~ of sb/sth** *The average age of those factories was 16 years.* ◇ **at... ~** *Women have tended to marry at younger ages than men.* ◇ **at the ~ of...** *Ronald Coase received the Nobel Prize at the age of 80.* ◇ **over/under the ~ of...** *All male citizens over the age of thirty were eligible to serve on juries.* ◇ **of... ~** *The incidence of depression has been increasing in recent years in people of all ages.* ◇ **... years/months/days of ~** *In the UK, one third of men over 75 years of age report some form of disability.* **2** [U, C] a particular period of a person's life: *Approximately half of the global deaths from smoking are expected to occur in middle age (age 35–59).* ◇ *The difficulty is that 'old age' is a relative concept, whose exact boundaries are hard to ascertain.* ◇ **of... ~** *Only women of childbearing age were tested.* ➲ *see also* MIDDLE AGE, OLD AGE **3** [U] the state of being old: *Oral cancer rates increase with age and those most affected are men in their sixth or seventh decade.* **4** [C] a particular period of history: *After the end of the last ice age, global temperatures soared by about 14 °F in a decade (Mithin, 2003).* ◇ *There is evidence of political systems that resembled sovereign states long before the modern age.* ◇ *In our digital age, virtually everything is capable of being represented in graphical form.* ➲ *see also* GOLDEN AGE, ICE AGE, MIDDLE AGES **5** [C] (*earth science*) a length of time that is a division of an EPOCH: *Two great packages of sedimentary and volcanic rocks—one of Middle Proterozoic age and one of Paleozoic age—make up most of the canyon's walls.*

IDM ˌcome of ˈage **1** (of an activity or a movement) to reach the stage of development at which people accept and value it: *Ethology, the study of animal behaviour, came of age during the early twentieth century.* **2** (of a person) to reach the age when they have an adult's legal rights and responsibilities: *Butler and Stokes (1974) show that the generation that came of age in the 1940s moved decisively to support the Labour Party.* ➲ *more at* ADVANCED

▸ ADJECTIVE + AGE **old** • **young** • **increasing** *Clearly, inequalities can be identified at all stages of the life course from pregnancy to old age.* ◇ *He was orphaned at a young age.* | **early** • **late** • **advanced** • **maximum** • **minimum** • **mean, average** • **median** • **exact** • **chronological** • **maternal** • **gestational** *Studies show that children are learning to use the Internet at earlier and earlier ages.* | **middle** • **reproductive** • **working** *At the time of this survey, only about one third of disabled adults of working age were in employment.*

▸ NOUN + AGE **school** • **childbearing** • **retirement** *Working past traditional retirement age may indicate financial insecurity.*

▸ VERB + AGE **reach, attain** • **estimate** • **determine, calculate** • **include** • **raise** *The ceremony took place when the woman reached the age of 13 or 14 (Cantarella, 2005: 246-7).*

▸ VERB + WITH AGE **increase, rise** • **decline, decrease** • **vary** • **be associated** • **correlate** *The growth and development of bones in children vary with age and sex.* ◇ *These conditions are commonly associated with old age.*

▸ AGE + NOUN **range** • **profile** • **structure** • **distribution** • **group, category, class, cohort, band, bracket** • **estimate** • **determination** • **limit** • **difference** • **discrimination** *The*

A

present results show that age differences have only a slight effect on rule-governed learning.

age² /eɪdʒ/ *verb* (**ag·ing, aged, aged**) HELP In British English the present participle can also be spelled **age·ing**. [I] to become older: *Schaie's study investigated the ways in which mental ability changes as people age.* ◇ *The sun, like all stars, is destined to grow brighter as it ages.*

aged *adj.* **1** /eɪdʒd/ [not before noun] of the age of: *12.0 per cent of girls aged 10-15 years were overweight.* ◇ *Our sample was composed of young people aged between 16 and 17 years.* ➲ *see also* MIDDLE-AGED **2 the aged** /ˈeɪdʒɪd/ *noun* [pl.] very old people: *Most synagogues organized charity for Jewish widows, orphans, the ill and the aged.*

ˈ**age group** (*also less frequent* ˈ**age bracket**) *noun* people of a similar age or within a particular range of ages: *the older/younger age group* ◇ **in an ~** *In women, the highest rates are seen in the 16-19 age group.* ◇ **across age groups** *This trend is being seen across all age groups.*

age·ing¹ (*BrE*) (*also* **aging** *NAmE, BrE*) /ˈeɪdʒɪŋ/ *noun* [U] the process of growing old: *We expect to see declines in physical health over time likely related to ageing.* ◇ *Protein changes should therefore be considered as a potential primary cause of skin ageing.* ◇ **+ noun** *In the course of the ageing process, bones tend to become less dense and therefore weaker and more likely to break.*

age·ing² (*BrE*) (*also* **aging** *NAmE, BrE*) /ˈeɪdʒɪŋ/ *adj.* [usually before noun] becoming older and usually less healthy, safe or useful: *The amount of oxidative damage generally increases in ageing cells.* ◇ *Japan has a rapidly ageing population.*

agency /ˈeɪdʒənsi/ *noun* (*pl.* **-ies**) **1** [C] a business or an organization that provides a particular service especially on behalf of other businesses or organizations: *No studies to date have explored how advertising agencies select celebrity endorsers.* ◇ **+ noun** *The maximum term for job assignments for agency workers was six months.* **2** [C] (*especially NAmE*) a government department that provides a particular service: *The National Science Foundation became the principal government agency supporting research in engineering.* **3** [U, C] a person or thing that acts to produce a particular result; action that produces a particular result: *Adams et al. (1996) detail the impact of human agency on African environments at the local, regional and continental scales.* ◇ *Forced convection occurs when the motion of the fluid is maintained by some external agency such as a fan or pump.* ◇ **through the ~ of sth/sb** *Japanese management techniques reached the West through the agency of Japanese transnational companes.*

agenda /əˈdʒendə/ *noun* **1** the most important aims that an organization, a society or a person wants to achieve; these aims considered as a list: *As the museum is publicly funded, its agenda is set by the government in terms of its educational objectives.* ◇ *The bureaucracy included many officials who were pursuing their own agendas, including taking bribes.* ◇ **on the ~** *International conferences have been very important in putting women's issues on the global agenda.* ◇ **at/to the top of the ~** *Environmental issues first rose to the top of the political agenda in the late 1960s.* **2** a list of items to be discussed at a meeting: **on the ~** *There were 172 items on the agenda of the session of the 2009-10 UN General Assembly.*

agent /ˈeɪdʒənt/ *noun* **1** a person whose job is to act for, or manage the affairs of, other people or organizations in business, politics, etc: *Universities often use agents to recruit students in overseas markets.* ◇ *The Internet has created new types of retailers, agents and other intermediaries.* **2 ~ for/of sth** a person or thing that has an important effect on a situation: *The US Secretary of State proposed that NATO should act as an agent for global stability.* ◇ *War is a profound agent of historical change.* **3** (*technical*) a chemical or a substance that produces an effect or a change or is used for a particular purpose: *Further research is needed into alternatives to the use of cytotoxic agents in the treatment of cancer.* **4** (*grammar*) the person or thing that does an action (expressed as the subject of an active verb, or in a 'by' phrase with a passive verb): *Through the use of the passive voice, the agent has been left unspecified.*

ag·glom·er·ation /əˌglɒməˈreɪʃn; *NAmE* əˌglɑːməˈreɪʃn/ *noun* [C, U] (*formal*) a group of things put together in no particular order or arrangement: *National boundaries will collapse in South America, as Rio de Janeiro, Sao Paulo, Montevideo and Buenos Aires form an urban agglomeration along the Atlantic Coast.* ◇ **~ of sth** *The larger the area became, the more the agglomeration of firms made it attractive to others as a business site.*

ag·gra·vate /ˈægrəveɪt/ *verb* **~ sth** to make an illness or a bad or unpleasant situation worse SYN WORSEN: *A minority of respondents believed that air conditioner use could aggravate health problems.* ◇ *Contemporary globalizing trends are aggravating this situation as the demand for food continues to increase.* ■ **ag·gra·vat·ing** *adj.*: *The model represents deaths due to indirect causes where pregnancy was a substantial aggravating factor.* **ag·gra·va·tion** /ˌægrəˈveɪʃn/ *noun* [U] **~ (of sth)** *Negative interactions with caregivers tended to lead to further aggravation of patients' depressive symptoms.*

ag·gre·gate¹ AWL /ˈægrɪgət/ *adj.* [only before noun] made up of several amounts that are added together to form a total number: *Aggregate data indicate that different types of social problems are often but not always connected.* ◇ *Aggregate economic growth had slowed before the crisis.* ◇ *Aggregate demand rises with the level of employment because as more people have jobs, there is more wage income to pay for the purchase of consumer goods.*

ag·gre·gate² AWL /ˈægrɪgət/ *noun* **1** [C] **~ (of sth)** a total number or amount made up of smaller amounts that are collected together; all of sth: *The amount paid is equal to the aggregate of the premiums received.* ◇ *The aggregate of these changes radically transformed the service.* **2** [C] a whole formed by combining several separate elements: *The council was an aggregate of three regional assemblies.* **3** [C, U] a material formed from a mass of separate pieces pressed together: *Magnesite usually occurs as compact granular aggregates that may appear chalky.*
IDM **in (the)** ˈ**aggregate** added together as a whole: *In the aggregate, this research suggests...*

ag·gre·gate³ AWL /ˈægrɪgeɪt/ *verb* [often passive] **1** [T] **~ sth** to put together different items or amounts into a single group or total: *The firm level data were aggregated to create regional data.* **2** [I, T] (especially of living things) to group or become grouped together: **~ into sth** *These large crustaceans aggregate into dense swarms.* ◇ **be aggregated (together/into sth)** *Soil structure reflects the way in which individual particles are aggregated together.*

ag·gre·ga·tion AWL /ˌægrɪˈgeɪʃn/ *noun* [U, C] a mass or group that has been formed: *Platelet aggregation eventually reaches a stage where clumps break off into the blood.* ◇ *By the Cretaceous period, the continental plates had separated into two aggregations, Laurasia and Gondwanaland.* ◇ **~ of sth** *Aggregation of fine particles adds to sedimentation.*

ag·gres·sion /əˈgreʃn/ *noun* [U] **1** a violent attack or threats by one person or country against another person or by one country against another country: *As students felt safer and more valued at school, levels of verbal and physical aggression decreased.* ◇ **~ against sb/sth** *Sapor I continued his father's policy of aggression against Rome.* **2** feelings of anger and hate that may result in harmful or violent behaviour: *His anger and aggression were directed at his younger brother.*

ag·gres·sive /əˈgresɪv/ *adj.* **1** angry, and behaving in a harmful or violent way; ready to attack: *Aggressive behaviour is observed in males competing for high status within the group.* ◇ *Senior generals were arguing for an aggressive policy of military expansion.* **2** acting with force and determination in order to succeed: *The company's success can be attributed to its aggressive entrepreneurial policies.* ◇ *The higher risk level of the more aggressive therapy seems to have been ignored.* **3** (*medical*) (of a disease or medical condition) quickly becoming more serious: *Obesity may promote the risk of developing aggressive disease.* ■ **ag·gres·sive·ly** *adv.*: *Sometimes parents directly encourage children to behave aggressively.* ◇ *This nocturnal rodent aggressively defends its territories.* ◇ *Japan's auto manufacturers then began to invest aggressively and directly in the US market.* **ag·gres·sive·ness** *noun* [U] *Disruption in parenting is associated strongly with subsequent aggressiveness in the child.* ◇ **~ of sth** *Decisions about surgery are usually based on the size, location and aggressiveness of the tumour.*

aging ⊃ AGEING[1], AGEING[2]

ago /əˈgəʊ; *NAmE* əˈgoʊ/ *adv.* used in expressions of time with the simple past tense to show how far in the past sth happened: *The sales transaction was completed five days ago.* ◇ *Some time ago, a group of scientists proposed a different approach.* ◇ *Around 12 000 years ago, humans began the move away from hunter-gathering towards a more settled life.*

agrar·ian /əˈgreəriən; *NAmE* əˈgreriən/ *adj.* [usually before noun] (*technical*) connected with farming and the use of land for farming: *GNP per capita can measure economic development from agrarian society, via industrial society to post-industrial society.* ◇ *The study of agrarian landscapes in transition is an integral component of the urban ecology of the region.*

agree /əˈgriː/ *verb* **1** [I, T] to have the same opinion as sb/sth; to say that you have the same opinion: *The majority of experts agreed, although a substantial minority disagreed.* ◇ **~ with sb** *The Court agreed with the Advocate General.* ◇ **~ on sth** *Both expert groups agreed on the importance of developing training programmes.* ◇ **~ about sth** *Constructivists generally agree with Max Weber about the value of interpretive understanding (Ruggie, 1998).* ◇ **~ with sth** *40% of respondents agree with the statement that being politically active takes too much effort.* ◇ **~ (that)...** *Nearly all students strongly agree that education is the key to success.* HELP If people **are agreed (on sth)** or sth **is agreed (on)**, everyone has the same opinion about sth: *Finally, the members of the committee were all agreed.* OPP DISAGREE (1) **2** [I, T] to decide with sb else to do sth or to have sth, usually after formal discussion: **~ on/upon sth** *The government was unable to agree on how to reform the wages policy.* ◇ *Each partner's share of the profits is agreed upon in advance.* ◇ **~ sth** *Timoleon agreed terms with the Carthaginians which limited them to the west of the island.* ◇ **~ to do sth** *In the Montreal Protocol, the parties agreed to phase out damaging CFCs.* ◇ **~ (that)...** *After some discussion the Committee agreed that they would provide the equipment.* **3** [I] to say 'yes'; to say that you will do what sb wants or that you will allow sth to happen: **~ to do sth** *More than 90% of the parents agreed to participate in the research.* ◇ **~ to sth** *In 1973 the British government agreed to the establishment of a Council of Ireland.* **4** [T] **~ sth** to officially accept a plan or request SYN APPROVE (1): *Work was delayed until the second round of funding was agreed in December.* **5** [I] **~ (with sth)** to be the same as sth: *The results of these two studies agreed with other experimental studies (Shaffer et al., 1996).* OPP DISAGREE (2) **6** [I] **~ (with sth)** (*grammar*) to match a word or phrase in number, GENDER or person: *In some languages, the subject can be omitted if it agrees with the verb.*

agreed /əˈgriːd/ *adv.* [only before noun] accepted by all or most people: *There is no generally agreed definition of consciousness.*

agree·ment /əˈgriːmənt/ *noun* **1** [C] an arrangement, a promise or a contract made with sb: *In March 1999, the European Council reached an agreement about the EU budget for 2000-6.* ◇ **~ with sb** *Korean auto manufacturers signed similar agreements with the EU in 1999.* ◇ **~ between A and B** *NAFTA was initially based on a free trade agreement between the US and Canada.* ◇ **~ on sth** *There are no UK-wide agreements on standards in this area.* ◇ **~ to do sth** *Enforcing patent laws was part of the Chinese agreement to join the World Trade Organization.* ◇ **under an/the ~** *Under the St Andrews agreement of 2006, the choice of First Minister became automatic.* **2** [U] the state of sharing the same opinion or feeling: **~ between A and B** *West et al. (1995) found a surprising amount of agreement between children and their parents over school selection.* ◇ **~ on/about sth** *Philosophers have still not reached agreement on what the self is.* ◇ **in ~ (with sb)** *Here Meyer (ibid, p. 319) is in agreement with Neuringer (1974b).* ◇ **~ that...** *There is widespread agreement that breast cancer screening is effective for women of certain ages.* ◇ **~ over sth** *The subcommittee negotiations reached broad inter-party agreement over most of the constitution.* OPP DISAGREEMENT (1) **3** [U] **~ (of sb/sth)** the fact of sb approving of sth and allowing it to happen: *The agreement of all member states is required.* **4** [U] the state of matching sth else and not showing it to be wrong: **~ between A and B** *There was reasonable agreement between simulation results and the manufacturer's performance data.* ◇ **in ~ (with sth/sb)** *The direction of travel was in agreement with the data of McKee and Resser.* **5** [U] **~ (with sth)** (*grammar*) (of words in a phrase) the state of having the same number, GENDER or person: *In English the subject and verb sometimes show agreement.*

agri·cul·tural /ˌægrɪˈkʌltʃərəl/ *adj.* connected with the science or practice of farming: *Egypt's wealth lay primarily in its agricultural land.* ◇ *Agricultural production is fundamental to any pre-industrial society.* ◇ *The relative importance of the agricultural sector has declined significantly.*

agri·cul·ture /ˈægrɪkʌltʃə(r)/ *noun* [U] the science or practice of farming: *In Andhra Pradesh, 70% of the population is engaged in agriculture.* ◇ *The rural poor rely on subsistence agriculture rather than cash crops.*

ahead /əˈhed/ *adv.* HELP For the special uses of **ahead** in phrasal verbs, look at the entries for the verbs. For example **press ahead (with sth)** is in the phrasal verb section at **press** *verb*. **1** further forward in time or space; in front: *There is a considerable amount of work ahead.* ◇ *These countries can hope for greater development and prosperity in the years ahead.* ◇ *The person being measured should be looking straight ahead while height is assessed.* **2** earlier: *Long-lasting business relationships allow companies to plan ahead with more confidence.*

aˈhead of *prep.* **1** further forward in time or space than sb/sth; in front of sb/sth: *The decisions and tasks ahead of the prime minister and his party were formidable.* ◇ *Younger patients received more intensive therapy because they had more years of life ahead of them.* ◇ *If a source is travelling near the speed of sound, it tends to rush ahead of the waves it emits behind.* **2** earlier than sb/sth: *The new factory was finished several months ahead of schedule.* ◇ *The customs union had been completed ahead of the deadline in 1969.* **3** further advanced than sb/sth; in front of sb, for example in a race or competition: *The United States' level of per capita income was well ahead of fast-growing nations such as Germany and Japan (Maddison, 1994: 22).*

A

aid¹ AWL /eɪd/ *noun* **1** [U] money, food, etc. that is sent to help countries in difficult situations: *The UN attempted to deliver humanitarian aid.* ◇ *Foreign aid has brought relief to millions who live in war-torn and impoverished regions.* ◇ **+ noun** *Japan remains the world's leading bilateral aid donor in Asia Pacific.* **2** [U] **~ (to sth)** financial help that is given by a government to a region, industry or group of people: *Regional aid is the largest single type of aid to manufacturing.* **3** [U] help that you need to perform a particular task: *Legal aid was made available to those who did not have enough money to obtain advice.* ◇ *Staff members are encouraged to pursue higher education and are provided with financial aid.* ◇ **with/without the ~ of sb/sth** *Messenia regained its independence with the aid of Thebes.* ➲ *see also* LEGAL AID **4** [C] a device that is used to help sb do a particular type of task: *a hearing/walking/navigational/decision aid*

aid² AWL /eɪd/ *verb* [T, I] to help sb/sth to do sth, especially by making it easier SYN ASSIST: **~ sth** *Brain imaging is commonly used to aid diagnosis of epilepsy.* ◇ **~ in sth** *A number of staining techniques were used to aid in the identification of the mineral.* ◇ **~ sb** *Several of the Slavic states aided the refugees.* ◇ **~ sb in doing sth** *Tumours may be classified by type to aid the clinician in planning treatment.*

AIDS (*BrE also* **Aids**) /eɪdz/ *noun* [U] the abbreviation for 'Acquired Immune Deficiency Syndrome' (an illness which attacks the body's ability to resist infection and which usually causes death): *Poverty is the biggest single factor contributing to the spread of AIDS.* ◇ **+ noun** *an AIDS epidemic/patient/programme*

aim¹ /eɪm/ *noun* the purpose of doing sth; what sb is trying to achieve: *Initially, the Communities were very successful in achieving the aims set out in the EEC Treaty.* ◇ *Their aim was to examine the impact of these policy changes on management structures.* ◇ **~ of sth/sb** *The main aim of this study was to assess the progress made since 2011.* ◇ **with the ~ of doing sth** *Japan has introduced financial incentives with the aim of encouraging a higher birth rate.* ➲ thesaurus note *at* TARGET¹ ➲ language bank *at* PURPOSE

IDM **take 'aim at sb/sth** to direct your criticism at sb/sth: *Locke's political writing takes aim at two arguments for absolute government.*

▸ ADJECTIVE + AIM **main, primary, principal, central, key • ultimate • overall • overarching • secondary • general • broad • stated, explicit • original • legitimate** *The key aim of the new policy is to ensure that there are always sufficient staff on duty.*

▸ VERB + AIM **achieve, fulfil, meet • pursue** *The state in Russian history has tended to pursue its own aims, with citizens' rights having low priority.*

▸ AIM OF + NOUN **study, research • article, paper • chapter, section • book • review • project • science • education** *Campbell maintained that the aim of science is the discovery and explanation of laws.*

aim² /eɪm/ *verb* **1** [T] **be aimed at (doing) sth** to have the intention of achieving sth: *Japanese customs policy was aimed at promoting the development of domestic industry.* **2** [I, T] to try or plan to achieve sth: **~ at doing sth** *Taiwan is aiming at further developing its technology-based industries.* ◇ **~ to do sth** *The project aimed to investigate Earth history by drilling the deep ocean floor.* ◇ **~ for sth** *The historian Thucydides (c. 460–395 BC) aimed above all for accuracy in his writings.* ◇ **~ at sth** *The Great Powers aimed at new forms of control over other parts of the world.* **3** [T, usually passive] **~ sth at sb** to say or do sth that is intended to influence or affect a particular person or group: *The TV series was aimed at a target audience of preschool children.* ◇ *The Commission's Report was clearly aimed at the British government.*

air¹ /eə(r); *NAmE* er/ *noun* **1** [U] the mixture of gases that surrounds the earth and that we breathe: *Around 90% of respondents agreed that the right to breathe clean air should take priority over the right to smoke.* ◇ **+ noun** *The newer power plants use advanced environmental technologies to reduce air pollution.* ◇ *Zhang et al. (1996) reported that mean annual air temperature is coldest at the coast.* **2** (*usually* **the air**) [U] the space above the ground or that is around things: *The car hit the barriers, throwing spectators about 20 feet through the air.* ◇ *When a predator begins to chase them, gazelles may leap high into the air.* **3** [U] the space above the earth where planes fly: **by ~** *She argues that the aviation industry has transformed our lives, including those who rarely travel by air.* ◇ **from the ~** *The temple is clearly visible from the air.* ◇ **+ noun** *Higher fuel prices and a drop in demand for air travel have affected the whole industry.* **4** [sing.] **~ (of sth)** the particular feeling or impression that is given by sb/sth: *There was an air of impending doom in pre-World War I Vienna.*

air² /eə(r); *NAmE* er/ *verb* **1** [T] **~ sth** to express your opinions publicly SYN VOICE²: *Angry shareholders were determined to air their grievances.* ◇ *to air your opinions/views* **2** [T, I] **~ (sth)** to broadcast a programme on the radio or on television; to be broadcast: *A content analysis of the commercials aired during the children's programmes of six Swiss stations was conducted.*

air·craft /ˈeəkrɑːft; *NAmE* ˈerkræft/ *noun* (*pl.* **air·craft**) any vehicle that can fly and carry goods or passengers: *a commercial/military/jet aircraft* ◇ *The simulation gives the trainee pilot the strong illusion of flying a real aircraft.* ◇ **+ noun** *Over 800 000 workers were laid off in the aircraft industry after VJ-Day—most of them women.*

ˈair force *noun* [C+sing./pl. v.] the part of a country's armed forces that fights using aircraft: *The US Air Force purchased large quantities of the same basic aircraft design.*

air·line /ˈeəlaɪn; *NAmE* ˈerlaɪn/ *noun* [C+sing./pl. v.] a company that provides regular flights to take passengers and goods to different places: *Competition and the potential for growth has favoured small, low-cost airlines.* ◇ **+ noun** *Rising fuel costs have badly affected the airline industry.*

air·plane /ˈeəpleɪn; *NAmE* ˈerpleɪn/ *noun* (*especially NAmE*) = PLANE (1)

air·port /ˈeəpɔːt; *NAmE* ˈerpɔːrt/ *noun* a place where planes land and take off and that has buildings for passengers to wait in: *By the 1970s, the development of international airports allowed ever greater numbers of tourists to visit the region.*

akin /əˈkɪn/ *adj.* **~ to sth** (*formal*) similar to: *This research involves concepts that are akin to those developed by Brunswik.*

alarm¹ /əˈlɑːm; *NAmE* əˈlɑːrm/ *noun* **1** [U] fear and anxiety that sb feels when sth dangerous or unpleasant might happen: *The scientific evidence shows there is no cause for alarm.* ◇ *Investors around the world reacted in alarm and began to sell their stock holdings.* ◇ *The ecologically precarious situation was noted with alarm by many observers at the time.* **2** [C, usually sing.] a loud noise or a signal that warns people of danger or of a problem: *When the alarm was raised by a passenger, a member of the Underground staff went to inspect the area.* ◇ **+ noun** *Some monkeys give alarm calls to warn others of approaching danger.* HELP A **false alarm** is a warning about a danger that does not happen: *The system was very prone to false alarms, which resulted in lost production time.* **3** [C] a device that warns people of a particular danger: *The sound of a smoke alarm likely means the presence of smoke and fire.* ◇ *The fire alarm is triggered only when two or more of the sensors indicate the presence of a fire simultaneously.* ◇ **+ noun** *an alarm bell/system*

IDM **a'larm bells ring | ring a'larm bells** if you say that **alarm bells ring** or sth **rings alarm bells**, you mean that it makes people feel worried and not sure whether they can trust sb/sth: *The fact that she has pain should ring alarm bells.*

alarm² /ə'lɑːm; *NAmE* ə'lɑːrm/ *verb* **~ sb** to make sb anxious or afraid SYN WORRY¹ (2): *The crime, which shocked and alarmed the party, was at first blamed on foreign powers.*

alarmed /ə'lɑːmd; *NAmE* ə'lɑːrmd/ *adj.* **~ (at/by sth)** anxious or afraid that sth dangerous or unpleasant might happen: *British and French leaders were clearly alarmed by this development.*

alarm·ing /ə'lɑːmɪŋ; *NAmE* ə'lɑːrmɪŋ/ *adj.* causing worry and fear: *Mexico City has grown and continues to grow at an alarming rate.* ■ **alarm·ing·ly** *adv.*: *The city suffers a rate of unemployment that is alarmingly high.* ◇ *Alarmingly, the review shows that the quality of reporting is dismal.*

al·beit AWL /ˌɔːl'biːɪt/ *conj.* although: *Globalization is occurring, albeit at a varying pace, in every domain of social activity.*

al·co·hol /'ælkəhɒl; *NAmE* 'ælkəhɔːl; 'ælkəhɑːl/ *noun* **1** [U] drinks such as beer, wine, etc. that can make people DRUNK: *Respondents were asked if they had drunk alcohol in the last 12 months.* ◇ **+ noun** *Adolescents are not always willing to acknowledge alcohol and drug use.* **2** [U, C] a COLOURLESS liquid present in drinks such as beer, wine, etc. responsible for making people DRUNK and also used in medicines, as a fuel and as a SOLVENT: *There are many different alcohols but the one found in alcoholic drinks is called ethanol or ethyl alcohol.* **3** [C] (*chemistry*) a member of a group of ORGANIC COMPOUNDS that contains -OH (a HYDROXYL group) joined directly to one of the CARBON atoms: *The three simplest alcohols are methanol, ethanol and propanol which have the formulas CH_3OH, C_2H_5OH and C_3H_7OH.*

al·co·hol·ic¹ /ˌælkə'hɒlɪk; *NAmE* ˌælkə'hɔːlɪk; ˌælkə'hɑːlɪk/ *adj.* **1** connected with or containing alcohol: *One means of reducing alcohol consumption is raising the tax on alcoholic beverages.* ➲ *see also* SOFT DRINK **2** caused by drinking alcohol: *Mortality data show that there was a threefold increase in alcoholic liver disease in the 1990s (Fisher et al., 2002).*

al·co·hol·ic² /ˌælkə'hɒlɪk; *NAmE* ˌælkə'hɔːlɪk; ˌælkə'hɑːlɪk/ *noun* a person who regularly drinks too much alcohol and cannot easily stop drinking, so that it has become an illness: *There is a strong tendency for alcoholics to deny or minimize the seriousness of their disease.*

al·co·hol·ism /'ælkəhɒlɪzəm; *NAmE* 'ælkəhɔːlɪzəm; 'ælkəhɑːlɪzəm/ *noun* [U] the medical condition caused by drinking too much alcohol regularly: *Studies of the causes of mental disorders like alcoholism and depression point to marital stress as an important factor.*

alert¹ /ə'lɜːt; *NAmE* ə'lɜːrt/ *adj.* **1 ~ to sth** aware of sth, especially a problem or danger: *The animals are constantly alert to the possibility of danger.* **2** able to think quickly; quick to notice things: *Alert viewers might have sensed the tension between some of the speakers.* ■ **alert·ness** *noun* [U] *A company's success depends on never-ending alertness to opportunities and competition.*

alert² /ə'lɜːt; *NAmE* ə'lɜːrt/ *verb* **1** to warn sb about a dangerous or urgent situation: **~ sb (to sth)** *Scientists attempted to alert local authorities to the possible arrival of a tsunami.* ◇ **~ sb that...** *He had alerted the police that the bomb would go off.* **2 ~ sb to sth** to make sb aware of sth: *This opening alerts the reader to a number of themes that will be important throughout the novel.*

al·ge·bra /'ældʒɪbrə/ *noun* [U] a type of mathematics in which letters and symbols are used to represent quantities: *Manual calculations using simple algebra are relatively easy when there is only one explanatory variable.* ■ **al·ge·bra·ic** /ˌældʒɪ'breɪɪk/ *adj.*: *ACE was a digital computer capable of performing algebraic processes at very high speeds.*

al·go·rithm /'ælgərɪðəm/ *noun* a process or set of rules to be followed when solving a particular problem, especially by a computer: *Problems are said to be computable if they can be solved by using an appropriate algorithm.* ◇ *Much effort has been devoted to the development of efficient algorithms for analysing network data*

alien¹ /'eɪliən/ *adj.* **1** [usually before noun] involving creatures, plants or diseases from another place: *Alien vegetation spread rapidly.* ◇ *Examples of invasive alien species with severe impacts range across the whole globe.* HELP Especially in non-academic English, this word also describes creatures from another planet: *The aim would be to communicate with alien beings from other worlds.* **2** [usually before noun] involving people from another country or society SYN FOREIGN (1): *Observers use their own conceptual framework to interpret alien cultures.* ◇ *They demonstrated a strong wish to throw off alien influences.* **3** very different from what you are used to, and making you feel frightened or uncomfortable: *Confused patients should be cared for by the same nurse, as this helps them orientate themselves in an alien environment.* ◇ **~ to sb/sth** *These organizations often require a creative style that is quite alien to the bureaucratic personality.*

alien² /'eɪliən/ (*NAmE also* **ˌnon-'citizen**) *noun* a person who is not a citizen of the country in which they live or work: *As illegal aliens they have few rights.* HELP In non-academic English, **alien** often refers to a creature from another planet: *He claims to have been abducted by aliens.*

alien·ate /'eɪliəneɪt/ *verb* **1 ~ sb** to make sb less friendly or sympathetic towards you: *He alienated former friends.* ◇ *The party strove to engage with first-time voters without alienating traditional voters.* **2 ~ sb (from sb/sth)** to make sb feel alone or separate from others; to make sb feel that they do not belong: *Some older people feel alienated from a society preoccupied by health, youth and beauty.* ■ **alien·ation** /ˌeɪliə'neɪʃn/ *noun* [U] **~ of sb** *Mounting resistance reflected the growing alienation of the local community.* ◇ **~ from sb/sth** *Her feelings of alienation from peers were addressed.*

align /ə'laɪn/ *verb* **1** [T, I] **~ (sth) (with sth)** to arrange sth in the correct position, or to be in the correct position, in relation to sth else, especially in a straight line: *The X-ray camera should be properly aligned with the X-ray beam.* ◇ *The proteins align over their entire length.* **2** [T] **~ sth with/to sth** to change sth slightly so that it is in the correct relationship to sth else: *Reformers attempted to reinterpret Hindu tradition to align it with their own understanding of the meaning of modernity and progress.*

PHR V **a'lign yourself with sb/sth** to publicly support an organization, a set of opinions or a person that you agree with: *Artists like Gillray were often ideologically conservative, even when they did not align themselves with one political party or another.*

align·ment /ə'laɪnmənt/ *noun* [U, C] **1** arrangement in a straight line: *The original town plan of 1692 was clearly reflected in the street alignments.* ◇ **~ of sth** *Building developments on both banks meant that the alignment of the bridge had to be skewed across the river.* ◇ **~ with sth** *The needle of a compass will settle into alignment with the earth's magnetic field.* ◇ **out of ~** *The pair of magnets were pushed slightly out of alignment.* **2** the state where things are in their correct or appropriate relative positions: **out of ~ (with sth)** *Public expectations may be out of alignment with what is actually possible.* ◇ **~ (of sth)** *Partnering is about gaining productivity improvements through alignment of supply chain members.* **3** political support given to one country or group by another: *Opportunities to create entirely new political alignments in politics are rare.* ◇ **~ (of sth) (with sth)** *This alignment of Evangelical Protestantism with the Republicans could present a dilemma for Evangelical Democrats*

alike[1] /əˈlaɪk/ *adv.* **1** in a very similar way: *As far as possible, all cases are treated alike.* **2** used after you have referred to two people or groups, to mean 'both' or 'equally': *Supporters said the switch to a single currency would benefit business and consumers alike.*

alike[2] /əˈlaɪk/ *adj.* [not before noun] very similar: *In many ways, the Korean and the US higher education systems are very much alike.* ◇ *Faces all tend to look alike in that they have similar features in similar positions.*

alive /əˈlaɪv/ *adj.* [not before noun] **1** living; not dead: *In 1995 his father was still alive and actively participating in the business.* **2** continuing to exist: *He kept alive the Romantic belief in the primacy of the imagination.* **3** full of emotion, activity or interest: **~ with sth** *The whole area is alive with commercial and industrial activity.* ◇ *The novel is vibrantly alive with suggestive possibilities.* ◇ **bring sth/come ~** *LaTour's use of oral history brings this story alive.* **4 ~ to sth** aware of sth; knowing sth exists and is important: *Providers of services to minority groups must be alive to the dangers of racism.*

IDM **a͵live and ˈwell** still existing or active: *Her parents and two older brothers are all alive and well.* ◇ *Although the McCarthy era was over, anti-communism was still alive and well.* HELP The phrase **alive and well** is often used to deny that sth has disappeared or decreased.

al·kali /ˈælkəlaɪ/ *noun* [C, U] a chemical substance that reacts with acids to form a salt and gives a SOLUTION with a PH of more than seven when it is dissolved in water: *Corrosive substances are usually strong acids or alkalis, which can attack or burn living tissues.* ◇ **+ noun** *Alkali burns tend to have more serious consequences than those caused by acid.* ➲ *compare* ACID[1]

al·ka·line /ˈælkəlaɪn/ *adj.* that contains alkali or has the essential characteristics of an alkali; that has a PH of more than seven: *The Gobi Desert is composed of wind-eroded hilly land, desert and alkaline soils.* ➲ *compare* ACID[2]
■ **al·ka·lin·ity** /͵ælkəˈlɪnəti/ *noun* [U] *Alkalosis is a clinical condition of high alkalinity in the blood and body tissues.*

all[1] /ɔːl/ *det.* **1** (used with plural nouns. The noun may have *the, these, those, my, her, his,* etc. in front of it, or a number.) the whole number of: *Almost all adults with Down's syndrome require a degree of supervision.* ◇ *All the commentators agreed.* ◇ *John had stopped working and also avoided all his friends.* ◇ *As a stepfather, he has worked hard to develop good relationships with all four boys.* **2** (used with uncountable nouns. The noun may have *the, this, that, my, her, his,* etc. in front of it.) the whole amount of: *Not all pollution is caused by man.* ◇ *So what does all this mean?* ◇ *He lost all his money in a business venture.* **3** used with singular nouns showing sth has been happening for a whole period of time: *She was unemployed for all that time.* ◇ **~ year (round)** *Where moisture is available all year round, broadleaf forest develops.* ◇ **~ day (long)** *The workers perform these repetitive tasks all day long.*

IDM **not all that good, well, etc.** not particularly good, well, etc: *Images of Asians are not all that common in American advertisements.* IDM *see* FOR

all[2] /ɔːl/ *pron.* **1** the whole number or amount: *Fortunately, they all agree.* ◇ **~ of sb/sth** *Nearly all of the participants had at least one physical symptom.* ◇ *What would happen if all of the polar ice were to melt?* **2** (followed by a relative clause, often without *that*) the only thing; everything: *At work, all he does is email.* ◇ *Less than a gram of sample is all that is needed in most cases.* ◇ *She had found all she could do was sleep all day.*

IDM **(not) at all** in any way; to any degree: *No evidence exists at all for this.* **in all** as a total SYN ALTOGETHER (2): *There were some auxiliary troops, perhaps 10 000 in all, further to the north-west.* ◇ *The females spawn some 50 eggs in all, in sequences of two or three.* ➲ *more at* ABOVE[1], AFTER[1], FOR

all[3] /ɔːl/ *adv.* **1 + adv./prep.** completely: *Some fashions, however, spread spontaneously all through Europe.* ◇ *The company has plants all over the world.* ◇ *This vegetation is found all along the western edges of the plains.* **2 ~ too...** used to emphasize that sth happens more than sb would like or than is acceptable: *All too often, parents underestimate what a child can manage.*

IDM **all aˈlong** all the time; from the beginning: *They had known the answer all along.* **all the better, harder, etc.** so much better, harder, etc: *Recently it has become all the more difficult for low-wage earners to move up the social ladder.* ◇ *The next case makes this point all the more clearly.* **all but 1** almost: *Population growth has all but ceased in developed countries, where fertility rates have fallen.* **2** everything or everyone except sth/sb: *For all but a very few wealthy people, travel beyond a short distance from home was virtually impossible.* **all ˈover** everywhere: *This shift in customer attitude that is happening all over.* **all ˈround** (*BrE*) (*NAmE* **all aˈround**) **1** in every way; in all respects: *Things are looking pretty bleak all round.* **2** for or from each person: *There were unmistakable signs of relief all round.* **be all about sb/sth** used to say what the most important aspect of sth is: *Politics in democracies is all about bargaining and compromise.*

Allah /ˈælə/ *noun* the name of God among Muslims

al·le·ga·tion /͵æləˈɡeɪʃn/ *noun* a public statement that is made without giving proof, accusing sb of doing sth that is wrong or illegal SYN ACCUSATION: **~ (of sth)** *The inquiry was investigating allegations of drug dealing.* ◇ *to make/deny an allegation* ◇ **~ (of sth) against sb** *A frequent allegation against the United Nations is that it is powerless to force states to comply with its rules.* ◇ **~ that...** *The report confirmed the allegation that he had suffered verbal abuse.*

al·lege /əˈledʒ/ *verb* [often passive] to state sth as a fact but without giving proof: **~ (that)...** *The suit alleged that workers had been made to work overtime for no pay.* ◇ **it is alleged (that)...** *It is alleged that member states have not adhered to their obligations under the treaty.* ◇ **be alleged to be/have, etc. sth** *They advocate the pursuit of charges against anyone alleged to have perpetrated war crimes.* ◇ **be alleged** *No deception is alleged.*

al·leged /əˈledʒd/ *adj.* [only before noun] stated as a fact but without giving proof: *The witnesses to the alleged crime were not credible.* ◇ *the alleged criminal/offender/perpetrator* ◇ *the alleged infringement/offence/violation*
■ **al·leged·ly** /əˈledʒɪdli/ *adv.*: *The couple were allegedly subjected to verbal abuse.*

al·le·giance /əˈliːdʒəns/ *noun* [U, C] a person's continued support for a political party, religion, ruler, etc: **~ to sb/sth** *In Japan, each citizen owed personal allegiance to the emperor.* ◇ **~ of sb/sth** *These issues are relevant to understanding changes in the political allegiances of the working class.*

al·lele /əˈliːl/ *noun* (*biology*) one of two or more possible forms of a GENE that are found at the same place on a CHROMOSOME: *One allele is inherited from the father and the other from the mother.*

al·ler·gen /ˈælədʒən; *NAmE* ˈælərdʒən/ *noun* a substance that causes an allergy: *Shellfish, nuts, eggs and fish are examples of food allergens.*

al·ler·gic /əˈlɜːdʒɪk; *NAmE* əˈlɜːrdʒɪk/ *adj.* **1 ~ (to sth)** having an allergy to sth: *The patient was allergic to eggs.*

2 caused by an allergy: *A profound allergic reaction can follow exposure to a foreign protein or drug.*

al·lergy /ˈælədʒi; *NAmE* ˈælərdʒi/ *noun* (*pl.* **-ies**) **~ (to sth)** a medical condition that causes you to react badly or feel ill when you eat or touch a particular substance: *If the patient only coughs at work, there may be an allergy to something in the workplace.* ◇ *a food/drug/penicillin allergy*

al·le·vi·ate /əˈliːvieɪt/ *verb* **~ sth** to make suffering or a problem less severe SYN EASE²(1): *New drugs can be developed to alleviate the symptoms of a disease.* ◇ *to alleviate pain/suffering/poverty* ◇ *The commission made a number of recommendations to alleviate the specific problems faced by the country.* ■ **al·le·vi·ation** /əˌliːviˈeɪʃn/ *noun* [U] **~ (of sth)** *Many of the dominant theories about the alleviation of poverty in developing countries need rethinking.*

al·li·ance /əˈlaɪəns/ *noun* **1** [C, U] an agreement between countries, political parties, etc. to work together in order to achieve sth that they all want: *The Brussels Treaty was designed to continue the alliances formed in the Second World War.* ◇ *to build/create/forge an alliance* ◇ *Since Russia's defeat in 1905, the Franco-Russian alliance had not given cause for concern.* ◇ **(in) ~ with sb/sth** *Napoleon was now in alliance with Alexander I.* ◇ **~ between A and B** *The only realistic possibility for assembling a majority coalition lay in an alliance between the Conservatives and the Liberal Democrats.* **2** [C] a group of people, political parties, etc. who work together in order to achieve sth that they all want: *NATO expansion involves integrating national armed forces into an effective military alliance.* ◇ **~ of sth** *These networks are loose alliances of government agencies, international organizations, corporations, NGOs and religious groups.*

al·lied *adj.* **1** /ˈælaɪd/ (*often* **Allied**) [only before noun] connected with countries that unite to fight a war together: *Bavaria remained under allied control for the rest of the war.* HELP **Allied** with a capital A is used especially to refer to the countries that fought together against Germany in the First and Second World Wars: *He helped to film the liberation of Paris by Allied troops in 1944.* **2** /əˈlaɪd; ˈælaɪd/ (of two or more things) similar or existing together; connected with sth: *Ten nurses, seven physicians and three allied health professionals participated.* ◇ **~ to/with sth** *These skilled jobs were closely allied to product innovation.*

al·lo·cate AWL /ˈæləkeɪt/ *verb* **1** to give sth officially to sb/sth for a particular purpose: **~ sth** *Information about the prevalence of particular conditions is vital for allocating health care resources.* ◇ **~ sth to sb/sth** *Seats are allocated to parties according to the proportion of votes gained by each.* **2 ~ sb/sth (to sth)** to put sb/sth in a group or category: *We randomly allocated patients to each group.*

al·lo·ca·tion AWL /ˌæləˈkeɪʃn/ *noun* **1** [C] **~ (of sth)** an amount of money, resources or land that is given to sb/sth for a particular purpose: *Variable costs do not include allocations of fixed costs such as factory overheads.* **2** [U, sing.] the act of giving sth to sb for a particular purpose: *Economic growth can be encouraged by efficient resource allocation.* ◇ **~ of sth** *An efficient allocation of resources in the free market may mean that there is inequality.*

allow /əˈlaʊ/ *verb* **1** [often passive] to let sb/sth do sth; to let sth happen or be done: **~ sb/sth to do sth** *Ordinary priests were allowed to marry.* ◇ *A large population of E. coli was spread on a Petri dish and allowed to grow into a thick lawn of cells.* ◇ **be (not) allowed** *Trade with non-signatory countries is not allowed.* **2** to let sb have sth: **~ sb/yourself sth** *You must allow yourself some time to read the exam paper.* ◇ **~ sth** *Ideally, the survey sponsor would allow more time to achieve a higher level of accuracy.* **3** [often passive] **~ sb/sth + adv./prep.** to let sb/sth go into, through, out of, etc. a place: *More air and fuel is allowed into the cylinder when the engine requires more power.* **4** to make sth possible SYN ENABLE(1): **~ sth** *An integrated network allows access to both subject-specific and cross-subject resources.* ◇ **~ sb to do sth** *This broader view of culture allows human geographers to consider topics beyond landscape.* **5 ~ sth (for sb/sth) (to do sth)** to make sure that you have enough of sth for a particular purpose: *Blair persuaded the US to delay invasion and allow time for diplomats to win UN approval.* **6 ~ sth** to agree that sth is true or correct SYN ACCEPT(2), ADMIT(1): *The Court of Appeal allowed her appeal and she was awarded a 65% share of the property.* IDM *see* REIN

PHR V **alˈlow for sb/sth** to consider or include sb/sth when calculating sth: *Few studies allowed for the separation of household coal use for cooking compared with heating.*

al·low·able /əˈlaʊəbl/ *adj.* that is allowed, especially by law or by a set of rules: *Maximum allowable emission rates are prescribed for a variety of pollutants.*

al·low·ance /əˈlaʊəns/ *noun* **1** an amount of money that is given to sb regularly or for a particular purpose: *The salaries are further supplemented by travel allowances.* **2** the amount of sth that is allowed in a particular situation: *The airline introduced a maximum 14 kg baggage allowance.* ◇ *The directive established a scheme for trading carbon emission allowances within the EU.* **3** (*BrE*) an amount of money that can be earned or received before you start paying tax: *The new government gave several tax allowances and exemptions.*

IDM **make allowance(s) for sth** to consider sth, for example when you are making a decision or judgement: *This chart provides a more accurate assessment as it makes allowances for the variation in body shape with age.*

al·lude /əˈluːd/ *verb*

PHR V **alˈlude to sb/sth** to mention sth in an indirect way: *In the interview, Yang alluded to the fact that his English was probably still not as good as that of a native English speaker.*

al·lu·sion /əˈluːʒn/ *noun* [C, U] **~ (to sb/sth)** something that is said or written that refers to or mentions another person or subject in an indirect way: *Keats's letters and poems are full of allusions to and quotations from other writers.* ◇ *literary/classical allusions* ◇ *Spenser, like Tasso before him, makes frequent allusion to the New World.*

ally¹ /ˈælaɪ/ *noun* (*pl.* **-ies**) **1** a country that has agreed to help and support another country, especially in case of a war: *Japan was becoming increasingly isolated from its former allies.* ◇ **~ of sth** *The Irish were seen by the English government as a potential ally of Catholic France and Spain.* HELP **The Allies** refers to a group of countries fighting together, in particular the countries that fought with Britain and the US in the First and Second World Wars: *Many people in the United States resisted support for the Allies until the Japanese bombing of Pearl Harbor.* **2 ~ (of sb)** a person who helps and supports sb who is in a difficult situation, especially a politician: *He was a close political ally of Mrs Thatcher.*

ally² /əˈlaɪ/ *verb* (**al·lies, ally·ing, al·lied, al·lied**) [T, I] **~ (yourself) with sb/sth (against sb/sth)** to give your support to another country or group: *If war was declared, Prussia would ally with France rather than Austria.* ◇ *In France, the Communists allied themselves with the Social Democrats against the conservative and radical bourgeoisie.*

al·most /ˈɔːlməʊst; *NAmE* ˈɔːlmoʊst/ *adv.* not quite SYN NEARLY: *Cable television is almost as old as commercial broadcast television.* ◇ *Eradication of marine pests appears almost impossible once they are established.* ◇ *The EU almost doubled its membership from 2004 to*

A

2007. ◇ *At times Godard seems almost to adopt a kind of radical Romanticism.*

WHICH WORD?

almost • nearly

- **Almost** and **nearly** have very similar meanings and are used in similar ways, although **almost** is much more frequent: *almost/nearly identical/perfect/complete/constant* ◇ *Wright's contribution was almost forgotten.* ◇ *Davy nearly killed himself while experimenting on carbon monoxide.* However, there is a group of adjectives, including *unchanged, unlimited, inconceivable* and *inevitable*, that are hardly ever used with **nearly**: *Post-war reforms were therefore almost inevitable.*
- Both **almost** and **nearly** are used before numbers and before verbs relating to number and size: *almost/nearly one-third/50%/30 years* ◇ *The average size of households has almost halved.* ◇ *Sales of full-sized pickup trucks have nearly doubled.*
- Both **almost** and **nearly** can be used before words like *any* and *anything*: *In Greek mythology, gods can turn themselves into almost anything.* ◇ *Recipients could choose nearly any foodstuffs they wanted.*
- **Almost** is often used before another adverb: *The earth is a planet that is almost entirely solid, yet still dynamic.* **Nearly** can only be used before a few other adverbs like *as* and *always*: *Forests are almost/nearly as dark as oceans.* ◇ *Rabies is almost/nearly always fatal.*
- **Nearly** is used in negative expressions, when it can be followed by *so* or *as*: *The situation is not nearly so simple as this.*

alone /əˈləʊn; *NAmE* əˈloʊn/ *adj.* [not before noun], *adv.* **1** without any other people: *Do not leave patients unattended or alone.* ◇ **not ~ in (doing) sth** *Winston Churchill was not alone in having a deep emotional attachment to Parliament.* **2** without the help of other people or things: *People rarely work alone. Invariably they are members of one or more teams.* **3** lonely and unhappy; without any friends: *Although she has friends, she feels alone amongst them.* **4** used to show that the person or thing mentioned is the only one: **noun + alone** *It was to Britain alone that the West Indian planters considered themselves as belonging.* ◇ **pronoun + alone** *He believed that he alone had seen how this struggle would lead to revolution.* **5 noun/pronoun + alone** used to emphasize one particular thing: *The market increased by 5% between 2006 and 2007 alone to reach €8.4 billion.*
IDM **go it aˈlone** to do sth without help from anyone: *Other distribution strategies in Asia Pacific are either to appoint a distributor or to go it alone.* **leave sb alone** to stop disturbing sb or trying to get their attention: *He is a self-sufficient man who wants to be left alone.* **let alone** used after a statement to emphasize that because the first thing is not true or possible, the next thing cannot be true or possible either: *Many people cannot afford basic necessities of life, let alone the costs of making their dwellings earthquake-safe.* **stand aˈlone** to be independent or not connected with other people, organizations or ideas: *In 2001, the United States stood almost alone in renouncing the Kyoto Protocol.* ➲ *see also* STAND-ALONE

along[1] /əˈlɒŋ; *NAmE* əˈlɔːŋ; əˈlɑːŋ/ *prep.* **1** from one end to or towards the other end of sth: *When you walk along the street, you cannot possibly look at all the detail around you.* ◇ *The fish lifts its head and uses the lower eye to look along the seabed.* **2** in a line that follows the side of sth long: *The young fish live in shallow water along the edge of the streams.* ◇ *Complete flood walls were constructed along both banks of the river.* **3** at a particular point on or beside sth long: *The nearest hand-washing facilities were in the toilet along the corridor.*

along[2] /əˈlɒŋ; *NAmE* əˈlɔːŋ; əˈlɑːŋ/ *adv.* HELP For the special uses of **along** in phrasal verbs, look at the entries for the verbs. For example **get along with sb** is in the phrasal verb section at **get**. **1** forward: *The two men were driving along admiring the scenery.* **2** with sb: *Some safari-goers brought along their personal filmmakers.*
IDM **along with sb/sth** in addition to sb/sth; in the same way as sb/sth: *The results of these investigations must be examined along with microbiological data.* ➲ language bank *at* ADDITION

along·side /əˌlɒŋˈsaɪd; *NAmE* əˌlɔːŋˈsaɪd; əˌlɑːŋˈsaɪd/ *prep.* **1** next to or at the side of sth: *There are colour diagrams and photographs alongside the text.* ◇ *A needle electrode is placed alongside the nerve using radiographic screening.* **2** together with sth/sb; at the same time as sth/sb: *Evening courses were offered alongside the normal day courses.* ◇ *British immigration officers began working alongside French border police in Calais.*

al·pha·bet /ˈælfəbet/ *noun* **1** a set of letters or symbols in a fixed order used for writing a language: *The Greek alphabet consists of twenty-four letters.* **2** the basic elements in a system which combine to form sth more complex: *Consider an alphabet consisting of a set of variables and a set of operation symbols.*

al·pha·bet·ic·al /ˌælfəˈbetɪkl/ *adj.* according to the correct order of the letters of the alphabet: *Entries are usually arranged in alphabetical order.* ■ **al·pha·bet·ic·al·ly** /ˌælfəˈbetɪkli/ *adv.*: *Entries in the dictionary are ordered strictly alphabetically from A to Z.*

al·ready /ɔːlˈredi/ *adv.* **1** before now; before a particular time in the past: *China already has a significant amount of nuclear capacity.* ◇ *As already mentioned, aquatic pests are also difficult to eradicate.* ◇ *It is already known that Bt toxin can persist in soil for several days.* ◇ *The technology already exists to tackle global warming through the greater use of biofuels and renewable energy resources.* **2** used to emphasize that a situation or problem exists: *Most teachers think that the curriculum is already too overcrowded.* ◇ *The crisis in Austria worsened an already precarious situation in Germany.*

also /ˈɔːlsəʊ; *NAmE* ˈɔːlsoʊ/ *adv.* (not used with negative verbs) in addition; too: *Many of the company's senior managers had also been part of Atari's senior management.* ◇ **not only... but ~** *California is not only famous for its earthquakes, but also for its summer fog.* ◇ **~ known as sth** *The European Economic Community (EEC) was established by the EEC Treaty, also known as the Treaty of Rome.*

alter AWL /ˈɔːltə(r)/ *verb* [T, I] to make sb/sth different; to become different: **~ (sb/sth)** *Privatization fundamentally altered the structure of the rail industry.* ◇ *Flexibility is essential as market conditions alter.* ◇ **~ sth by doing sth** *The pressure can be altered by changing the volume.*
▸ ALTER + NOUN **balance • composition • nature • structure • pattern • landscape** *Climate variability at some sites has altered tree species composition.* ◇ *Cold events did not alter temperature patterns as strongly as did warm events.*
▸ ADVERB + ALTER **radically, fundamentally, profoundly • dramatically • completely • significantly, substantially • slightly • chemically** *A very large volcanic eruption completely altered the landscape.* ◇ *Weathering occurs when rock is mechanically broken or chemically altered.*
▸ ALTER + ADVERB **significantly • radically, fundamentally • dramatically** *This situation is unlikely to alter significantly in future.* ◇ *The pattern of viral disease has been altered radically by the introduction of vaccines.*
▸ PHRASE **not alter the fact that...** *This special circumstance does not alter the fact that the field has changed greatly since this research was done.*

al·ter·ation AWL /ˌɔːltəˈreɪʃn/ *noun* **1** [C] a change to sth: *These growths are not caused by genetic alterations.* ◇ **~ in sth** *There may be alterations in personality and attitudes, such as increasing cautiousness.* ◇ **~ to sth** *The* *natural habitats had been damaged by a series of physical alterations to the river such as the construction of canals.* **2** [U] **~ (of sth)** the action of changing sth; the process of being changed: *River management refers to human alteration of natural channels.* ◇ *Snow remaining on the ground is subject to chemical alteration.*

al·ter·nate¹ AWL /ɔːlˈtɜːnət; *NAmE* ˈɔːltərnət/ *adj.* [usually before noun] **1** (of two events or things) happening or following one after the other in a repeated pattern: *The laminate contains alternate layers of fibres.* ◇ *A process of alternate flooding and draining of fields was necessary to enable the rice to grow.* **2** if sth happens on **alternate** days, etc, it happens on one day but not on the next: *Drinking water was available only for a few hours on alternate days.*

al·ter·nate² AWL /ˈɔːltəneɪt; *NAmE* ˈɔːltərneɪt/ *verb* **1** [T, I] to put two things one after the other in a repeated pattern: **~ A with/and B** *Patients alternated brief periods of activity with prolonged rest.* ◇ *Superlattices may be created by periodically alternating two different materials.* ◇ **~ between A and B** *The custom is to alternate between complete fasting on one day and one vegetarian meal on the next day.* **2** [I] (of two events or things) to happen or follow one after the other in a repeated pattern: **~ between A and B** *The summer climate alternates between periods of cold/wet and warm/dry weather.* ◇ **A alternates with B** *Periods of prosperity and stability alternate with periods of stagnation and instability.* **3** [I] (*physics*) (of an electric current, a magnetic field, etc.) to change between two states, quickly and in a repeated pattern: *Frequencies of alternating electric fields range from tens of Hz to a few GHz or more.*

al·ter·nate·ly /ɔːlˈtɜːnətli; *NAmE* ˈɔːltərnətli/ *adv.* **1** (of two actions or events) happening one after the other in a repeated pattern: *In the first experiment, we applied air pressure alternately to each of the openings.* ◇ *The lake alternately filled and drained and each emptying event caused a catastrophic flood.* **2** (*NAmE*) = ALTERNATIVELY

al·ter·na·tion /ˌɔːltəˈneɪʃn; *NAmE* ˌɔːltərˈneɪʃn/ *noun* **1** [C, U] the fact or process of two events or things happening or following one after the other in a repeated pattern: *Eight cyclic alternations, each lasting about 32 million years, can be discerned in the record since the Triassic period.* ◇ **between A and B** *The alternation between wet and dry phases would have led to the fragmentation of habitats.* ◇ **~ of A and B** *In these molecules, there is an alternation of single and double bonds along a chain of carbon atoms.* **2** [U] **~ (between/of A and B)** the action of making two things happen or follow one after the other in a repeated pattern: *In western texts, regular alternation between male and female characters creates the expectation of romance.*

al·ter·na·tive¹ AWL /ɔːlˈtɜːnətɪv; *NAmE* ɔːlˈtɜːrnətɪv/ *adj.* [only before noun] **1** (*NAmE also* **al·ter·nate**) that can be used instead of sth else: *Several alternative hypotheses have been proposed.* ◇ *An alternative approach is to analyse the circuit and eliminate all current and voltage variables.* **2** different from the usual or traditional way in which sth is done: *These groups adopted alternative lifestyles.* ◇ *The study covers four major strands of alternative medicine: acupuncture, homeopathy, chiropractic therapy and herbal medicine.* ➲ *see also* COMPLEMENTARY (2), UNCONVENTIONAL

▸ ALTERNATIVE + NOUN **hypothesis • model • explanation • interpretation • view, perspective • scenario • approach • strategy • method • mechanism • way • route • pathway • source • option • name** *These ventures offer an alternative business model to conventional charity fundraising.* ◇ *Alternative sources of vitamin C and folic acid will need to be consumed.* | **fuel • medicine • therapy • lifestyle** *By 2030, alternative fuels and new technology will have changed the dynamics of oil demand.*

al·ter·na·tive² AWL /ɔːlˈtɜːnətɪv; *NAmE* ɔːlˈtɜːrnətɪv/ *noun* a thing that you can choose to do or have out of two or more possibilities: **~ to sth** *There are several alternatives to this assumption.* ◇ **as an ~ (to sth)** *Radiotherapy may be used as an alternative or as an adjunct to surgery.*

▸ ADJECTIVE + ALTERNATIVE **viable, realistic • possible • genuine • attractive • radical • cheaper** *To extend the length of the working day was still a viable alternative to increasing productivity by mechanization.*

▸ VERB + ALTERNATIVE **offer, provide • suggest • consider • explore • find • choose** *Fuel cells offer a clean renewable energy alternative for transportation.*

▸ PHRASE **have no alternative (but to do sth)** *Women of this class had no alternative but to marry.*

al·ter·na·tive·ly AWL /ɔːlˈtɜːnətɪvli; *NAmE* ɔːlˈtɜːrnətɪvli/ *adv.* used to introduce a suggestion that is a second choice or possibility: *The arc is initiated either by means of a spark or, alternatively, by bringing together the two electrodes.*

al·though /ɔːlˈðəʊ; *NAmE* ɔːlˈðoʊ/ *conj.* **1** used for introducing a statement that makes the main statement in a sentence seem surprising SYN THOUGH¹: *Although the teenage pregnancy rate is falling, it is still not at the level experienced by other Western European countries.* ◇ *Although rare, autism is important because it is a serious disorder.* ➲ grammar note *at* DESPITE **2** used to mean 'but' or 'however' when you are commenting on a statement: *In general all children attend primary school, although not all finish because many are taken from school to work on the farm.* ➲ language bank *at* HOWEVER

al·ti·tude /ˈæltɪtjuːd; *NAmE* ˈæltɪtuːd/ *noun* **1** [C, usually sing.] the height above sea level: **at an ~ of sth** *A research balloon floating at an altitude of 50 km above sea level becomes extremely cold at night.* **2** [C, usually pl., U] a place that is high above sea level: **at an ~ (of sth)** *Tea, coffee and a wide variety of horticultural crops are grown at higher altitudes.* ◇ **at ~** *Those at risk of developing altitude-related illnesses are people who do not normally live at altitude.*

al·together /ˌɔːltəˈgeðə(r)/ *adv.* **1** (used to emphasize sth) completely; in every way: *For reasons not altogether clear, the Japanese proposal was quickly accepted.* ◇ *It is unlikely that the socio-economic and political significance of gender will disappear altogether.* **2** used to give a total number or amount: *Altogether, health care costs the USA almost three times as much as it does the UK.* **3** used to introduce a summary when you have mentioned a number of different things: *Altogether, our findings suggest that Webb's results do accurately portray the relation between repetition and learning.*

al·tru·ism /ˈæltruɪzəm/ *noun* [U] **1** the fact of caring about the needs and happiness of other people more than your own: *The sense of altruism begins to emerge as early as age two.* ◇ *Altruism is directed primarily towards one's immediate family and decreases with social distance.* **2** (*biology*) behaviour of an animal that benefits another at its own EXPENSE: *Reciprocal altruism seems restricted to few goods and services markets like feeding or grooming activities.* ■ **al·tru·is·tic** /ˌæltruˈɪstɪk/ *adj.*: *Individuals can acquire social prestige by the use of altruistic behaviour.*

alu·min·ium /ˌæljəˈmɪniəm; ˌæləˈmɪniəm/ (*BrE*) (*NAmE* **alu·mi·num** /əˈluːmɪnəm/) *noun* [U] (*symb.* **Al**) the chemical element of ATOMIC NUMBER 13. Aluminium is a light, silver-grey metal used for making aircraft, engineering parts, etc: *The body of the robot was manufactured in aluminium.* ◇ **+ noun** *A mobile phone will not work if you wrap it in aluminium foil.*

al·ways /ˈɔːlweɪz/ *adv.* **1** at all times; on every occasion: *Film by its very nature is always a representation of the*

past. ◇ *There is always the potential for different interpretations of the original text.* ◇ *Patients do not always remember what has been said completely or correctly.* ◇ *This distinction is not always clear.* **2** for a long time; since you can remember: *Resistance to this idea has always been strong.* ◇ *Language differences have always been more of a barrier to television than to movie markets.* **3** for all future time: *Unfortunately, there will always be children who come from economically disadvantaged families.*
IDM **as 'always** as usually happens or is expected: *Opinions, as always, were divided.*

am /əm; *strong form* æm/ ➲ BE[1]

am·bas·sador /æmˈbæsədə(r)/ *noun* **~ (to...)** an official who lives in a foreign country as the senior representative there of his or her own country: *Harriman served as American ambassador to Moscow after October 1943.* ◇ (*figurative*) *Existing students can be key ambassadors for the institution and play an active role as guides during open days and school visits.*

am·bi·ent /ˈæmbiənt/ *adj.* [only before noun] in the surrounding area; on all sides: *All trials were conducted in the laboratory at an ambient temperature of about 25.2°C.* ◇ *ambient air/light/conditions*

am·bi·gu·ity AWL /ˌæmbɪˈgjuːəti/ *noun* (*pl.* **-ies**) [U, C] the state of having more than one possible meaning: *Wishing to avoid ambiguity in his meaning, precision in language was important for Faraday.* ◇ **~ of sth** *These data illustrate the complexities and ambiguities of soil chemical analyses on archaeological sites.*

am·bigu·ous AWL /æmˈbɪgjuəs/ *adj.* **1** that can be understood in more than one different way SYN EQUIVOCAL (2): *The evidence is, in most cases, ambiguous and difficult to interpret.* ◇ *These studies produced ambiguous, sometimes contradictory, results.* OPP UNAMBIGUOUS **2** not clearly stated or defined SYN EQUIVOCAL (1): *There are sizeable numbers of people whose citizenship status is ambiguous.* OPP UNAMBIGUOUS ■ **am·bigu·ous·ly** *adv.*: *The term was used ambiguously for a number of different concepts.*

am·bi·tion /æmˈbɪʃn/ *noun* **1** [C] something that you want to do or achieve very much: *These developments have challenged the EU's ability to realize its ambitions.* ◇ *political/personal/literary ambitions* ◇ **~ of being/doing sth** *The company has sufficient financial resources to pursue its ambition of increasing its share of the European market.* ◇ **~ to be/do sth** *The firm's long-term ambition was to secure a slice of the organic market.* **2** [U] the desire or determination to be successful, rich or powerful: *His brilliant career can be seen as the outcome of extraordinary personal ambition.*

am·bi·tious /æmˈbɪʃəs/ *adj.* **1** determined to be successful, rich or powerful: *Alcibiades was the most politically ambitious of all the Athenians.* ◇ *Ambitious MPs would rather have a post in the Cabinet than on a committee.* **2** needing a lot of effort, money or time to succeed: *Angus embarked on a still more ambitious project, a three-volume history of the British Empire.* ◇ *an ambitious plan/programme/scheme* ◇ *an ambitious target/goal/aim* ■ **am·bi·tious·ly** *adv.*: *The book is ambitiously broad in scope.* ◇ *He states, ambitiously enough, that his aim is to lay out a 'general framework for the comparative analysis of religion'.*

am·biva·lent /æmˈbɪvələnt/ *adj.* having or showing both good and bad feelings about sb/sth: *The Left has had a very ambivalent attitude to the question of equality.* ◇ **~ about sb/sth** *These managers were also ambivalent about the continued benefits of cooperation.* ■ **am·biva·lence** /æmˈbɪvələns/ *noun* [U, sing.] **~ (about/towards sb/sth)** *In all groups there appears to be ambivalence about whether potential positive benefits outweigh negative effects.* ◇ *A much deeper ambivalence towards curricular knowledge was expressed particularly by working-class boys.*

amen·able /əˈmiːnəbl/ *adj.* **~ to (doing) sth** that you can treat in a particular way: *Smoking-related cancers tend to be less amenable to intervention.* ◇ *'Hamlet' is the least amenable of all Shakespeare's plays to being summarized.*

amend AWL /əˈmend/ *verb* **~ sth** to change a law, an agreement or a document slightly to improve or correct it or to reflect changing circumstances SYN REVISE (1): *In 1993, the Indian constitution was amended to require greater representation of women in local councils.* ◇ *An amended treaty must be ratified in all member states.*

amend·ment AWL /əˈmendmənt/ *noun* **1** [C, U] a small change or improvement that is made to a law or document; the process of changing a law or document: *Once in government, he proposed a constitutional amendment to allow his own re-election.* ◇ **~ to sth** *There have been further amendments to the legislation.* ◇ **~ of sth** *The Founding Fathers deliberately made amendment of the Constitution difficult.* **2 Amendment** [C] a statement of a change to the CONSTITUTION of the US: *The Fourteenth Amendment requires equal admission of all students to public schools.*

amen·ity /əˈmiːnəti; *NAmE* əˈmenəti/ *noun* (*pl.* **-ies**) [usually pl.] a feature that makes a place pleasant, comfortable or easy to live in: *Local government is responsible for public amenities, such as swimming pools, parks and libraries.* ◇ *Areas with higher amenities will attract more workers.*

amino acid /əˌmiːnəʊ ˈæsɪd; *NAmE* əˌmiːnoʊ ˈæsɪd/ *noun* (*biochemistry*) a chemical COMPOUND containing both an amino group (-NH_2) and an ORGANIC acid group (-COOH) which can combine with other amino acids to form the basic structure of PROTEINS: *The protein hormone insulin is formed when 51 separate specific amino acids join together.* ◇ *In bacteria and plants, all amino acids are synthesized by individual pathways using general metabolic intermediates.*

among /əˈmʌŋ/ (*also* **amongst** /əˈmʌŋst/) *prep.* **1** being included or happening in groups of things or people: *Tobacco use was higher among boys than girls.* ◇ *Among other things, senior managers have the power to decide whether people will lose their jobs.* **2** used when you are dividing or choosing sth, and three or more people or things are involved: *They argue that any tax cuts should be shared more fairly among all taxpayers.* ◇ *On his death the property was divided equally among his sons.* **3** surrounded by sb/sth; in the middle of sb/sth: *It was a delightful place among the trees on the river.*

amount[1] /əˈmaʊnt/ *noun* [C, U] **1** (used especially with uncountable nouns) **~ (of sth)** a quantity of sth: *A fair amount is known about what kinds of political activity people engage in.* ◇ *A considerable amount of time, sometimes years, may elapse until the animal returns to its home.* ◇ *Several techniques are now available for sampling large amounts of data.* **2 ~ (of sth)** a sum of money: *Governments began to reduce the vast amounts being spent on the armed forces.* ◇ *An amount of money is awarded to the innocent party as compensation for any losses sustained.*
IDM **any amount of sth** a large quantity of sth: *A good reputation is often worth more than any amount of advertising.* **no amount of sth** not even the greatest quantity of sth: *If the Vietnamese were not willing to fight, no amount of American support could win a victory.*

▸ ADJECTIVE + AMOUNT **large • significant, considerable, substantial • great • vast, huge, enormous • high • excessive • increasing • small • limited • fixed • certain • given • fair • equal • total • relative • average • maximum • minimum** *Many investors had lost substantial amounts because of poor management practices.* ◇ *Thirdly, a certain amount of subjective judgement is involved.*

▸ VERB + AMOUNT **give • provide • take • receive • reduce • limit • increase • spend • require • generate • determine • calculate • estimate • measure • show • represent • contain • include • involve** *The samples analysed in this study contain relatively small amounts of clay.* | **produce • use • consume** *Many farms produce significant amounts of waste.* | **pay** *Different groups of customers pay different amounts for airline seats.*
▸ AMOUNT OF + NOUN **time • information • data • resources • food • water • energy • heat • power • work • labour • effort • research • substance • material • product • protein • DNA • alcohol • variation • variance** *The Internet provides access to huge amounts of information.* | **money • capital • investment** *Some programmes are allocated a large amount of capital up front.*

amount[2] /əˈmaʊnt/ *verb*
PHR V **aˈmount to sth** **1** to add up to sth; to make sth as a total: *By 2003, total health expenditure amounted to £91.4 billion.* ◇ *It is estimated that war-related deaths amount to a staggering 500 000.* **2** to be equal to or the same as sth: *The defendant's conduct amounted to an offence contrary to Section 4 of the 1986 Act.* ◇ **~ to the same thing** *Planning social policy and planning public expenditure often amount to the same thing.*

amp·ere /ˈæmpeə(r); *NAmE* ˈæmpɪr; ˈæmper/ (*also rather informal* **amp** /æmp/) *noun* (*abbr.* **A**) the unit for measuring electric current: *In a current of one ampere, charge is being transferred at a rate of one coulomb per second.*

ample /ˈæmpl/ *adj.* enough or more than enough: *There is ample evidence that changes in monetary regimes produce little change in labour or financial markets.* ◇ *The company has had ample opportunity to investigate and prepare its case.* ■ **amply** *adv.*: *Researchers have amply demonstrated that 'simplified' texts are often more difficult to understand.*

amp·li·fi·ca·tion /ˌæmplɪfɪˈkeɪʃn/ *noun* [U] **1 ~ (of sth)** the process of increasing the amplitude of an electrical signal: *Care must be exercised in the amplification of a signal.* **2** (*biochemistry*) **~ (of sth)** the process by which many copies of sth, such as a GENE, are made: *The amplification of the target gene was monitored every cycle.* **3 ~ (of sth)** the action of making sth greater or easier to notice: *Inadequate leadership can give rise to the amplification of conflict within an organization.* **4** the action of adding details to a story, statement, etc; details added to a story, statement, etc: *The commentary in Levinson (1983) provides amplification and discusses some of the trickier points.* ◇ **~ of sth** *The film goes in another direction through the amplification of the book's source material.*

amp·li·fier /ˈæmplɪfaɪə(r)/ *noun* an electronic device for increasing the amplitude of electrical signals, especially one that makes sound or radio signals louder: *A powerful amplifier is needed because the signal is very weak in this area.*

amp·lify /ˈæmplɪfaɪ/ *verb* (**amp·li·fies, amp·li·fy·ing, amp·li·fied, amp·li·fied**) **1** [T] **~ sth** to increase the amplitude of an electrical signal: *Large networks require devices to amplify signals on them.* **2** [T] (*biochemistry*) to make many copies of sth such as a GENE: **~ sth** *With this technique, the DNA is amplified in two steps.* ◇ **~ sth (from sth) (to sth)** *The ribosomal RNA genes of amphibians are amplified during oocyte development from hundreds to millions.* **3** [T] **~ sth** to make sth greater or easier to notice: *This approach estimates the social and cultural factors which reduce or amplify the effects of a natural phenomenon.* **4** [I, T] to add details to a story, statement, etc: *To amplify a little, ...* ◇ **~ sth** *Such rhetorical devices are very effective in explaining and amplifying a statement.*

amp·li·tude /ˈæmplɪtjuːd; *NAmE* ˈæmplɪtuːd/ *noun* [C, U] **~ (of sth)** (*physics*) the greatest amount by which a wave, for example a sound or radio wave, OSCILLATES (= increases and decreases), measured from the middle of its range: *The amplitudes of the two waves were the same.* ◇ *At that frequency the input and output signals are equal in amplitude.*

an *indefinite article* ➲ A

an·aer·obic /ˌæneəˈrəʊbɪk; *NAmE* ˌæneˈroʊbɪk/ *adj.* (*biology*) not using or needing OXYGEN: *When livestock waste is stored in anaerobic conditions, methane is emitted.* OPP AEROBIC

an·aes·the·sia /ˌænəsˈθiːziə/ (*US* **an·es·the·sia** /ˌænəsˈθiːʒə/) *noun* [U] the use of anaesthetic during medical operations: *The operation is performed under general anaesthesia.*

an·aes·thet·ic[1] (*US* **an·es·thet·ic**) /ˌænəsˈθetɪk/ *noun* [U, C] a drug that makes a person or an animal unable to feel anything, especially pain, either in the whole body or in a part of the body: *The area of the cancer is numbed using a local anaesthetic.*

an·aes·thet·ic[2] (*US* **an·es·thet·ic**) /ˌænəsˈθetɪk/ *adj.* [only before noun] containing a substance that makes a person or an animal unable to feel pain in all or part of the body: *This is a quick procedure performed with local anaesthetic spray.* ◇ *anaesthetic agents/techniques*

an·al·gesia /ˌænəlˈdʒiːziə; *NAmE* ˌænəlˈdʒiːʒə/ *noun* [U] (*medical*) the loss of the ability to feel pain: *Patients given codeine may not receive adequate analgesia.* ◇ *to provide/administer analgesia*

an·al·gesic /ˌænəlˈdʒiːzɪk/ *noun* (*medical*) a substance that reduces pain: *The study found that more females used analgesics than males.* ■ **an·al·gesic** *adj.*: *This theory may well account for the long-term analgesic effects seen frequently in clinical practice.*

analo·gous AWL /əˈnæləgəs/ *adj.* similar in some way to another thing or situation and therefore able to be compared to it: *An exactly analogous effect occurs in atomic nuclei.* ◇ **~ to sth** *He attempts to find a cinematic style that will fulfil a creative function analogous to that of Shakespeare's verse.* HELP In biology, **analogous** is used to describe two things that perform similar functions but have different EVOLUTIONARY origins, such as the wings of insects and birds: *The two species share analogous physical traits.*

ana·logue[1] (*BrE*) (*NAmE* **ana·log**) /ˈænəlɒg; *NAmE* ˈænəlɔːg; ˈænəlɑːg/ *noun* **1 ~ (of sth)** a thing that is seen as similar to another thing: *Parts of modern machines which can be regarded as analogues of nerve cells work about a thousand times faster.* **2 ~ (of sth)** (*chemistry*) a chemical COMPOUND with a MOLECULAR structure that is very similar to that of another, often with just one ELEMENT changed: *Thiols, which contain the -SH group, are sulfur analogues of alcohols.*

ana·logue[2] (*BrE*) (*NAmE* **ana·log**) /ˈænəlɒg; *NAmE* ˈænəlɔːg; ˈænəlɑːg/ *adj.* (of an electronic process) using a continuously changing range of physical quantities to measure or store data: *Digital processing of analogue signals has several advantages.* ➲ *compare* DIGITAL (1)

ana·logy AWL /əˈnælədʒi/ *noun* (*pl.* **-ies**) [C, U] a comparison of one thing with another thing that has similar features, usually in order to explain it; a feature that is similar: **~ of sth** *The author uses the analogy of an iceberg to suggest that we ignore emotions that are uncomfortable.* ◇ **~ between A and B** *An analogy is drawn between the molecules of a gas and a swarm of particles.* ◇ **~ with sth** *A computer virus has strong analogies with biological viruses because it replicates itself, spreads, mutates, and can damage its host.* ◇ **by ~ (to/with sth)** *The term 'greenhouse effect' is derived by analogy to a garden greenhouse.* ◇ **in ~ to/with sth** *The pressure was produced with an air*

A

pump and a reservoir, in vague analogy with the hearts of living organisms.

ana·lyse AWL (*BrE*) (*NAmE* **ana·lyze**) /ˈænəlaɪz/ *verb* to examine the nature or structure of sth, especially by separating it into its parts, in order to understand or explain it: **~ sth** *Tomlinson (1999) analysed UK survey data, finding that...* ◇ *Some recent studies have analysed the impact of media on voter attitudes.* ◇ **~ sth for sth** *A 50 cm³ sample of water was analysed for its calcium content.* ◇ **~ how/what, etc...** *The authors analyse how dominant cultural values enter the classroom.* ➲ thesaurus note *at* EXPLORE

WORD FAMILY
analyse *verb*
analysis *noun*
analyst *noun*
analytical *adj.*
analytic *adj.*
analytically *adv.*

▸ ANALYSE + NOUN **data, information • sample • impact, effect • phenomenon • pattern • trend • relationship, association • dynamics • behaviour • performance • interaction** *The study analysed the relationship between colony size and variables linked to behaviour.* ◇ *Ji et al. (2010) developed a mathematical model in order to analyse the performance of a PV heat pump.*

▸ ADVERB + ANALYSE **thoroughly • carefully • systematically • critically** *Interviews were systematically analysed.*

▸ ANALYSE + ADVERB **separately • together** *We can distinguish between three main possibilities, each of which has been analysed separately.*

▸ ADVERB + ANALYSE | ANALYSE + ADVERB **statistically • thematically • qualitatively • quantitatively** *All results were statistically analysed by a two-sided t-test.*

▸ PHRASES **analyse sth in terms of sth** *Products and markets are each analysed in terms of their degree of novelty to an organization.*

an·aly·sis AWL /əˈnæləsɪs/ *noun* (*pl.* **an·aly·ses** /əˈnæləsiːz/) **1** [U, C] the detailed study or examination of sth in order to understand more about it; the result of the study: *Statistical analysis reveals an interaction between all three factors.* ◇ **~ of sth** *Detailed analysis of earthquake data suggested a subduction zone event.* ◇ *This section presents a comparative analysis of the two data sets.* ➲ thesaurus note *at* INVESTIGATION **2** [U, C] a careful examination of a substance in order to find out what it consists of: *A sample was sent for biochemical analysis.* ◇ **~ of sth** *A chemical analysis of the scents revealed they were composed of up to eighteen separate compounds.* ➲ *see also* QUANTITATIVE ANALYSIS **3** [U] = PSYCHOANALYSIS
IDM **in the ˌfinal/ˌlast aˈnalysis** used to say what is most important after everything has been discussed or considered: *In the final analysis, a computer program is simply a long stream of characters.*

▸ ADJECTIVE + ANALYSIS **present • recent • previous • further, subsequent • secondary • exploratory, preliminary • careful • detailed, in-depth • comprehensive, thorough • systematic • separate** *The measures used in the present analyses were selected based on previously published evidence.* ◇ *Our exploratory analysis found no significant correlations between the two phenomena.* | **critical • descriptive • comparative • theoretical • empirical • thematic • statistical • quantitative • qualitative • multivariate • univariate • bivariate • economic • genetic • molecular • historical • textual** *A critical analysis of the firm's business model is necessary.* ◇ *Multivariate analyses identified 12 variables which significantly differentiated the two criterion groups.*

▸ NOUN + ANALYSIS **data • factor • content • cluster • sensitivity • policy • cost-benefit • discourse** *The data analysis revealed that over half of the sample firms were involved in pyramidal arrangements.*

▸ VERB + ANALYSIS **carry out, perform, undertake, do • use** *Craddock et al. (1985) used soil P analysis along with other more traditional methods of survey.* | **conduct, run • present, offer, provide • base ~ on • focus • apply • extend • restrict, limit • simplify • facilitate • repeat • replicate** *The authors conducted econometric analysis using panel data for twenty-three nations over fifteen years.* ◇ *I decided to restrict my analysis to medium to large firms.*

▸ ANALYSIS + VERB **reveal, show, demonstrate • confirm • identify • detect • suggest, indicate** *The first analysis showed a significant and constant increase in survival rate with age.* ◇ *These results were confirmed by biochemical analysis.* | **support • highlight • yield • focus on** *Canning's analysis highlights the significance of the rural and small-town experience.*

ana·lyst AWL /ˈænəlɪst/ *noun* a person whose job involves examining facts or materials in order to give an opinion on them; a person involved in research in a particular field: *Analysts have argued that it is necessary to consider a range of factors that may influence nuclear weapons acquisition.* ◇ *a/an financial/economic/political/policy/discourse analyst*

ana·lyt·ic AWL /ˌænəˈlɪtɪk/ *adj.* **1** = ANALYTICAL **2** (*linguistics*) (of a language) that uses word order rather than the ends of words to show the function of words in a sentence: *Polysynthetic languages can develop out of more analytic languages.* ➲ *compare* SYNTHETIC (2) **3** (of a statement) that must be true: *Analytic sentences are sentences which automatically express true propositions in any context.* HELP In logic, the term **analytic** describes sth that is true by its own definition: the sentence 'John's uncle is a man' must be true because all uncles are male. ➲ *compare* SYNTHETIC (3)

ana·lyt·ic·al AWL /ˌænəˈlɪtɪkl/ (*also* **ana·lyt·ic**) *adj.* **1** using a logical method of thinking about sth in order to understand it, especially by looking at all the parts separately: *We set out an analytical framework to examine management practices.* ◇ *There are many analytical approaches to the study of culture.* **2** using scientific analysis in order to find out about sth: *A variety of analytical methods have been applied to dating soils.* ◇ *analytical tools/techniques* ■ **ana·lyt·ic·al·ly** AWL /ˌænəˈlɪtɪkli/ *adv.*: *Dimples in spherical shells have been studied both numerically and analytically.*

ana·lyze AWL (*NAmE*) = ANALYSE

an·archy /ˈænəki; *NAmE* ˈænərki/ *noun* [U] a situation in a country, an organization, etc. in which there is no government, order or control: *Meanwhile the countryside was in a state of anarchy, with the peasants organizing strikes, invading forest and farmland and burning manor houses.*

ana·tom·ical /ˌænəˈtɒmɪkl; *NAmE* ˌænəˈtɑːmɪkl/ *adj.* **1** connected with the structure of a human, animal or plant, or of a part of them: *This is the mechanism by which genes determine the anatomical structure of the resulting organism.* **2** connected with the scientific study of the structure of human or animal bodies: *Anatomical texts of the time seemed to ignore the importance of the organ.* ■ **ana·tom·ic·al·ly** /ˌænəˈtɒmɪkli; *NAmE* ˌænəˈtɑːmɪkli/ *adv.*: *About 100 000 years ago, anatomically modern humans were present in southern Africa.*

anat·omy /əˈnætəmi/ *noun* (*pl.* **-ies**) **1** [U] the scientific study of the structure of human or animal bodies: *An understanding of anatomy is essential to the accurate assessment of fractures.* **2** [C, U] **~ (of sth)** the structure of a human, animal or plant, or of a part of them: *The basic anatomy of the eye is illustrated in Fig. 1.* ◇ *The aim was to discover whether species from different environments have differences in anatomy.* **3** [C] **~ of sth** an examination of what sth is like or why it happens: *Matarazzo was among the first psychologists to study the anatomy of the clinical interview.*

an·ces·tor /ˈænsestə(r)/ *noun* **1 ~ (of sb)** a person in your family who lived a long time ago: *His ancestors had been among the earliest settlers in the colony.* ➲ *compare* DESCENDANT (1) **2 ~ (of sth)** an animal or plant that lived or grew in the past which a modern animal or plant has developed from: *The last common ancestor of apes and Old World monkeys lived around 25 million years ago.* **3 ~ (of sth)** an early form of sth which later became more developed: *Over 1 000 years ago, the Angles brought to Britain the ancestor of the modern English language.* ➲ *compare* DESCENDANT (2)

an·ces·tral /æn'sestrəl/ *adj.* connected with or belonging to earlier members of a family, race of people or species: *Limited evidence supports the idea that the ancestral population was Indo-Malay-Melanesian.* ◇ *The creation of national parks entailed the expulsion of indigenous peoples from their ancestral lands.*

an·ces·try /'ænsestri/ *noun* (*pl.* **-ies**) [C, usually sing., U] the family, the race of people or the species that sb/sth comes from: **of ... ~** *The author was a 23-year-old Guards officer of Scottish ancestry.* ◇ *According to Charles Darwin's view, the species shared a common ancestry.*

an·cient /'eɪnʃənt/ *adj.* **1** belonging to a period of history that is thousands of years in the past: *Such questions were debated by the philosophers of ancient Greece.* ◇ *The civilization of the ancient world was practically wiped out with the fall of the Roman Empire.* OPP MODERN (1) **2** very old; having existed for a very long time: *North America is made from ancient continental rocks.* **3 the ancients** *noun* [pl.] the people who lived in ancient times, especially the Egyptians, Greeks and Romans: *The ancients regarded astrology as an aspect of the science of astronomy.*

and /ənd; ən; *also* n; *especially after* /t/; /d/; *strong form* ænd/ *conj.* **1** used to connect words that are the same part of speech, clauses or sentences, that are to be taken together: *Metals such as copper and gold were not available in this region.* ◇ *The deep current is much colder and heavier than the surface current.* ◇ *War kills people and destroys property.* HELP When **and** is used in common phrases connecting two things or people that are closely linked, the determiner is not usually repeated before the second: *his mother and father* **2** added to: *What's 47 and 16?* HELP When numbers (but not dates) are spoken, **and** is used between the hundreds and the figures that follow: *one hundred and sixty-three* **3** then; following this: *He suffered a stroke whilst driving and crashed his car.* **4 go, come, try, stay, etc. ~** used before a verb instead of *to*, to show purpose: *She must go and get the tablets today and start taking them.* ◇ *Attempts are being made to try and reinstate the law.* HELP In this structure **try** can only be used in the infinitive or to tell sb what to do. ➲ *see also* AND/OR

and/or *conj.* (*rather informal*) used when you say that two situations exist together, or as an alternative to each other: *In these myths, women are very often portrayed as victims and/or deadly avengers.*

an·ec·dotal /ˌænɪk'dəʊtl; *NAmE* ˌænɪk'doʊtl/ *adj.* based on personal accounts rather than facts or research, and possibly not true or accurate: *Anecdotal evidence suggests that the bombings were designed to influence the outcome of the elections.* ■ **an·ec·dot·al·ly** /ˌænɪk'dəʊtəli; *NAmE* ˌænɪk'doʊtəli/ *adv.*: *Researchers at this site anecdotally observed fewer species of fish.*

an·ec·dote /'ænɪkdəʊt; *NAmE* 'ænɪkdoʊt/ *noun* [C, U] **1 ~ (about sb/sth)** a short, interesting or funny story about a real person or event: *The book is full of anecdotes about his meetings with many Latin American writers.* ◇ *Balint has a marvellous flair for anecdote.* **2** a personal account of an event, especially one that is considered as possibly not true or accurate: *Students build oral histories from a broad range of anecdotes.* ◇ *Opponents of the legislation relied largely on anecdote and sensationalized media stories.*

an·es·the·sia, an·es·thet·ic (*NAmE*) = ANAESTHESIA, ANAESTHETIC[1], ANAESTHETIC[2]

anger[1] /'æŋɡə(r)/ *noun* [U] the strong feeling that you have when sth has happened that you think is bad and unfair: *Only a small percentage of children and teenagers express anger through violence.* ◇ **~ at sb/sth** *De Gaulle imposed a veto in January 1963 because of his anger at a US-UK deal on nuclear weapons.* ◇ **in ~** *An email sent in anger could change the course of events in a project.* ◇ **+ noun** *Healthy anger management involves being able to let go of anger.*

anger[2] /'æŋɡə(r)/ *verb* [often passive] **~ sb** to make sb angry: *He angered some local people when he cut down a sacred pine tree.* ◇ *She is easily angered.*

angle /'æŋɡl/ *noun* **1** the space between two lines or surfaces that join, measured in degrees: *There should be a 50° angle between the planes.* ◇ **~ of sth** *The angle of inclination is small.* ◇ **at an ~ of sth to sth** *The needle is inserted at an angle of 30° to the skin.* ➲ *see also* RIGHT ANGLE **2** the direction that sth is leaning or pointing in when it is not in a vertical or horizontal line: **at an ~ (to sth)** *Waves approaching at an angle to the shoreline tend to become realigned.* **3** a position from which you look at sth: *The director's use of close-ups and unusual angles creates the same effect.* ◇ **from an ~** *It is possible to view an object from many angles.* **4** a particular way of presenting or thinking about a situation, problem, etc: *Each has taken a slightly different angle in how they approach their subject.* ◇ **from an ~** *Roberts addresses the issue from a different angle.* ◇ **~ on sth** *The media are always hungry for new stories and new angles on stories.*

angry /'æŋɡri/ *adj.* (**an·grier, an·gri·est**) (You can also use **more angry** and **most angry**.) having strong feelings about sth that you dislike very much or about an unfair situation: *Our core motivations have a major influence on what makes us angry.* ◇ **~ with/at sb** *Effective communication becomes difficult when two people are intensely angry with each other.* ◇ **~ with/at sb about/for (doing) sth** *She was angry at her father for abandoning her as a child.* ◇ **~ at/about/over sth** *A woman in this society has much to be angry about.* ◇ **~ (that)...** *The government was angry that the report was not changed following its response.* ■ **an·grily** /'æŋɡrəli/ *adv.*: *Weavers reacted angrily to worsening conditions in their trade.*

an·gu·lar /'æŋɡjələ(r)/ *adj.* **1** having angles or sharp corners: *Breakdown into angular blocks is less common in this type of rock.* **2** measured with reference to or by means of an angle: *Fluctuations over an angular range of a degree or less are relevant.*

ˌangular moˈmentum *noun* (*physics*) the MOMENTUM of a ROTATING object multiplied by its distance from the point that it is ROTATING around: *Two electrons in an atom may differ in orbital angular momentum, energy or spin direction.*

ani·mal /'ænɪml/ *noun* **1** any living thing that is not a plant or a human: *These are some of the basic arguments against keeping animals in zoos.* ◇ *Farm animals such as factory-farmed pigs, hens and turkeys are routinely denied their right to a natural life.* ◇ **+ noun** *Improvements in animal welfare are dependent on consumers being prepared to pay for them.* **2** a creature that is not a bird, a fish, a REPTILE, an insect or a human: *Some species live in soil on skin and feathers shed by animals and birds.* ◇ *Cattle, sheep and pigs were the principal domestic animals in the Roman period.* **3** any living creature, including humans: *Humans and other animals show similar reactions to pleasure, pain and fear.* ◇ *A tendency to develop cancer is a common feature of multicellular animals.* ➲ *compare* VEGETABLE **4** (used with an adjective or noun) a particular type of person, thing, organization, etc: *King is a political animal and always compromises.*

A

anion /ˈænaɪən/ *noun* (*chemistry*) an ION with a negative electrical charge: *One would expect such an oxide to dissolve in a basic solution to give a corresponding anion.* ➲ *compare* CATION

ankle /ˈæŋkl/ *noun* the joint connecting the foot to the leg: *Most patients present with what they believe is a sprained ankle.*

an·no·tate /ˈænəteɪt/ *verb* **~ sth** to add notes to a book or text, giving explanations or comments: *Hunt made a habit of annotating the margins of books that he read.* ■ **an·no·ta·tion** /ˌænəˈteɪʃn/ *noun* [C, U] *Coleridge commonly borrowed the books of friends and left annotations in them.* ◇ **~ of sth** *The next step required the selection of a range of texts, and then the annotation of these texts using our biographical scheme.* **an·no·tated** *adj.*: *An annotated bibliography is included for those interested in further reading.*

an·nounce /əˈnaʊns/ *verb* **1** to make a formal public statement about a fact, event or intention: **~ sth** *In 2008, the government announced plans for a new set of towns.* ◇ **~ sth to sb** *In February 591, he sent a letter to his fellow patriarchs announcing to them his election as pope.* ◇ **~ that...** *British Gas announced that it was increasing its prices by 14%.* ◇ **it is announced that...** *It was announced that a Data Protection Committee was to be established.* **2** to say sth in a loud and/or serious way: **+ speech** *He bluntly announced, 'I have no interest in the matter and do not care what happens.'* ◇ **~ that...** *He suddenly announced that he wanted a divorce.*

an·nounce·ment /əˈnaʊnsmənt/ *noun* **1** [C] **~ (of sth)** a spoken or written formal public statement about a fact, event or intention: *Announcements were made of spending plans for the next three years.* ◇ *A preliminary announcement of the company's results appears long before the AGM.* **2** [U] **~ (of sth)** the action of making a formal public statement about a fact, event or intention: *In response to the announcement of further industrial action, the airline applied to the High Court for an injunction.*

an·nual AWL /ˈænjuəl/ *adj.* [usually before noun] **1** covering a period of one year: *During the period, output declined at an annual rate of 0.7%.* ◇ *The average annual rainfall is 682 mm.* ◇ *These countries each have an annual per capita income below US$2 000.* **2** happening or done once every year: *Investors expect that the annual report and accounts will represent a true picture of the company's present position.* ◇ *The Applied Geography Conference continues to hold an annual meeting.*

an·nu·al·ly AWL /ˈænjuəli/ *adv.* once a year; every year: *The Committee is required to meet annually.* ◇ *The region averages 889 mm of rain annually.*

anode /ˈænəʊd; *NAmE* ˈænoʊd/ *noun* (*technical*) the ELECTRODE in an electrical device where OXIDATION happens; the positive electrode in an ELECTROLYTIC cell and the negative electrode in a battery: *Hydrogen fuel cells consist of two electrodes (anode and cathode) separated, for example, by a polymer electrolyte membrane.* ➲ *compare* CATHODE

anom·al·ous /əˈnɒmələs; *NAmE* əˈnɑːmələs/ *adj.* different from what is standard, normal or expected: *Explanations for these seemingly anomalous results are discussed below.* ■ **anom·al·ous·ly** *adv.*: *The presence of warm water on the Pacific Coast may be associated with anomalously high rainfalls over Peru and Ecuador.*

anom·aly /əˈnɒməli; *NAmE* əˈnɑːməli/ *noun* (*pl.* **-ies**) a thing or situation that is different from what is standard, normal or expected: **~ (in sth)** *He discusses anomalies in Shakespeare's texts.* ◇ *These precipitation and temperature anomalies influence ecosystem productivity throughout the Amazon.* ◇ **~ that...** *There is the unfortunate anomaly that care of emergency admissions is largely left to inexperienced junior doctors.*

ano·nym·ity /ˌænəˈnɪməti/ *noun* [U] **~ (of sb/sth)** the state of remaining unknown to most other people; a situation that allows sb to remain unknown: *It is important to safeguard the anonymity of research participants.* ◇ *The anonymity of chat rooms allows people to try out new roles.*

an·onym·ous /əˈnɒnɪməs; *NAmE* əˈnɑːnɪməs/ *adj.* **1** (of a person) with a name that is not known or that is not made public: *Most respondents wished to remain anonymous.* **2** written, given, made, etc. by sb who does not want their name to be known or made public: *An anonymous questionnaire was distributed to 54 participating teachers.* HELP The abbreviation **anon.** is often used at the end of a text, poem, etc. when the author is unknown. ■ **an·onym·ous·ly** *adv.*: *Visitors on this site usually post questions anonymously.*

an·other /əˈnʌðə(r)/ *det., pron.* **1** one more; an extra thing or person of the same type as one already mentioned or known about: *In the meantime, the couple had had another child.* ◇ *Engineers built another forty-two tanks to store an additional twenty-nine million gallons.* ◇ **~ (of sth)** *This was the starting point of another of Einstein's experiments.* ◇ *It will probably be impractical to do the laboratory analysis on one sample before deciding whether or not to take another.* HELP **Another** can be followed by a singular noun, by a number and a plural noun, or by **of** and a plural noun. ➲ *compare* OTHER ➲ language bank *at* ADDITION **2** different; a different person or thing from one already mentioned or known about: *They were not free to sell the land and move to another town.* ◇ *One form of corruption was merely exchanged for another.* ◇ **~ one** *There is the question of why the shop stocks this particular brand but not another one.* **3** a person or thing of a very similar type: *Bill Clinton could no longer aspire to be another Franklin D. Roosevelt.* ➲ *see also* ONE ANOTHER

IDM **of one kind, sort, etc. or aˈnother** used when you are referring to various types of a thing, without saying exactly what you mean: *Family firms of one kind or another were the norm until after the Second World War.* ➲ *more at* ONE[1]

ANOVA /æˈnəʊvə; *NAmE* æˈnoʊvə/ *noun* [U] (*statistics*) **analysis of variance**, a method for breaking down the VARIANCE in a set of data into those parts with causes and those due to RANDOM error: *ANOVA is a powerful statistical technique that, unlike simple t-tests, can detect interactions between variables.*

an·swer[1] /ˈɑːnsə(r); *NAmE* ˈænsər/ *noun* **1** something that you say, write or do as a reaction to a question, statement or situation: *Customers who once were happy to wait several days for an answer now want an instant response.* ◇ **~ to sth** *He was unable to give a straight answer to this question.* ◇ **in ~ to sth** *Venus, in answer to his prayers, turned the statue into a living woman.* **2** something that you write or say in reply to a question in a test, exam, exercise, etc: *The answers are marked, with 17 correct answers constituting the minimum pass mark.* ◇ **~ to sth** *Students have the option to come back later to a question they may have forgotten the answer to.* **3 ~ (to sth)** the correct solution to a question in a test, exam, exercise, etc: *One school had actually provided students with the answers to the exam beforehand.* **4** a solution to a problem: *The short answer is that it depends on the circumstances.* ◇ *to provide/find answers* ◇ **~ to sth** *There are several possible answers to this question.* ◇ *Scientists do not yet know the answer to this.* ◇ *There are no easy answers to these problems.* **5 sth's ~ to sb/sth** a person or thing from one place that may be thought to be as good as a famous person or thing from another place: *The Warsaw Pact, Moscow's answer to NATO, coordinated the armed forces of the Soviet bloc in Europe.*

an·swer² /ˈɑːnsə(r); *NAmE* ˈænsər/ *verb* **1** [T, I] to say, write or do sth as a reaction to a question or situation SYN REPLY¹: **~ sth** *He refuses to answer such questions.* ◇ *The Council summoned Leigh to answer the charges against him.* ◇ **+ speech** *The first man answered, 'No.'* ◇ **~ (that...)** *82% answered that there should be a free trade area including China, South Korea and Japan.* ◇ *Participants were reassured that all findings would be treated in confidence to encourage them to answer honestly.* **2** [T] **~ sth** to be suitable for sth; to match sth: *The development of SGML appeared to answer the need for standardization.* PHR V ˈ**answer for sth** to accept responsibility or blame for sth: *The men were expected to answer for each other's good behaviour.* ◇ *Davies argues that national systems of education have much to answer for in perpetuating such attitudes.* ˈ**answer to sb** to have to explain your actions or decisions to sb: *The constitutional position is that ministers answer to Parliament.*

ant /ænt/ *noun* a small insect that lives in highly organized groups. There are many types of ant: *Egg production in a colony of ants is delegated to one individual, the queen.*

an·tag·on·ism /ænˈtæɡənɪzəm/ *noun* [U, pl.] feelings of opposition or strong dislike SYN HOSTILITY: **~ between A and B** *Mutual antagonism between Labour and the SNP meant that the prospects for a future alliance were poor.* ◇ **~ to/towards sb/sth** *Surveys showed that many women continued to harbour antagonism towards the feminist movement as a whole.*

ante·ce·dent¹ /ˌæntɪˈsiːdnt/ *noun* a thing or an event that exists or comes before sth else and has an influence on it: *Competition law has its antecedents in the USA in the form of antitrust laws.* ◇ **~ of sth** *Life skills programmes in elementary school may reduce antecedents of adolescent risk-taking behaviour.* ◇ **~ to sth** *Characteristics that were considered potential antecedents to Internet use are presented in table 11.5.*

ante·ce·dent² /ˌæntɪˈsiːdnt/ *adj.* existing or coming before sth else, and having an influence on it: *Two particular antecedent conditions are especially significant.* ◇ **~ to sth** *Functional limitations have been shown to be antecedent to both pain and depression.*

ante·date /ˌæntiˈdeɪt/ *verb* = PREDATE

ante·natal /ˌæntiˈneɪtl/ (*BrE*) (*also* **pre·natal** *NAmE, BrE*) *adj.* [only before noun] connected with the time when a woman is pregnant and the medical care given then: *She had not received any antenatal care until very shortly before the birth of her child.* ⊃ *compare* POST-NATAL

an·ter·ior /ænˈtɪəriə(r); *NAmE* ænˈtɪriər/ *adj.* (*technical*) (of a part of the body) at or near the front; nearer to the front or the head: *Sperm enter the anterior end of the egg.* ◇ **~ to sth** *The thyroid is a midline neck organ, situated anterior to the trachea.* OPP POSTERIOR

an·thro·polo·gist /ˌænθrəˈpɒlədʒɪst; *NAmE* ˌænθrəˈpɑːlədʒɪst/ *noun* a person who studies anthropology: *The diversity of human social organization has been documented by anthropologists.*

an·thro·pol·ogy /ˌænθrəˈpɒlədʒi; *NAmE* ˌænθrəˈpɑːlədʒi/ *noun* [U] **1** (*also* **cultural anthropology** or **social anthropology**) the study of the human race by comparing human societies and cultures and how they have developed: *Anthropology, through its study of the habits of modern tribal societies, could shed light on an ancient subject.* ◇ *Evans-Pritchard became a leading figure in British social anthropology.* **2** (*also* **physical anthropology**) the study of the human race by examining how humans behave and how their bodies work and have changed during their development: *Physical anthropology and physical geography are normally classified under the natural sciences.* ■ **an·thro·po·logic·al** /ˌænθrəpəˈlɒdʒɪkl; *NAmE* ˌænθrəpəˈlɑːdʒɪkl/ *adj.*: *Durkheim's work had a profound influence on anthropological research in the twentieth century.*

anti·bi·ot·ic /ˌæntibaɪˈɒtɪk; *NAmE* ˌæntibaɪˈɑːtɪk/ *noun* [usually pl.] a substance that can destroy or prevent the growth of bacteria and cure infections: *Her GP prescribed her antibiotics and painkillers.* ■ **anti·bi·ot·ic** *adj.*: *antibiotic therapy/treatment* ◇ *Once it appears, antibiotic resistance usually increases in frequency quickly.*

anti·body /ˈæntibɒdi; *NAmE* ˈæntibɑːdi/ *noun* (*pl.* **-ies**) a substance that the body produces in the blood to fight disease, or as a reaction when particular substances are put into the body: **~ (against sth)** *The immune system recognizes the substance as a foreign compound and produces antibodies against it.* ◇ **~ (to sth)** *These methods can reliably detect serum antibodies to H. pylori with a high degree of accuracy.*

an·tici·pate AWL /ænˈtɪsɪpeɪt/ *verb* **1** to expect or predict sth: **~ sth** *The results have not been as positive as anticipated.* ◇ *The anticipated benefits outweigh the costs.* ◇ **~ that...** *The study also anticipates that wireless advertising will generate response rates two or three times higher.* ◇ **it is anticipated that...** *It is anticipated that there could be mass migrations of people from seriously affected areas.* ◇ **~ doing sth** *Our hypothesis anticipated finding that...* ⊃ *compare* UNANTICIPATED **2** to see what might happen in the future and take action to prepare for it: **~ sth** *Organizations today need to anticipate change much faster than their twentieth-century counterparts.* ◇ **~ how/what, etc...** *Every organization has to anticipate how its environment might change in the short, medium and long term.* ◇ **~ that...** *If firms anticipate that the rise in wages will lead to rising sales, they may decide to keep investment at its present level.* **3 ~ sth** to think with pleasure and excitement about sth that is going to happen: *Kennedy eagerly anticipated his election year battle, confident that he would win.* **4 ~ sth** to come before and influence sth else that is similar; to be a sign of what is going to happen: *Some argue that Shelley had anticipated the leading tenets of nineteenth-century socialist thought.* ■ **an·tici·pa·tory** /ænˌtɪsɪˈpeɪtəri; *NAmE* ænˈtɪsəpətɔːri/ *adj.*: *This type of anticipatory care forms the basis of nursing care in all clinical situations.*

an·tici·pa·tion AWL /ænˌtɪsɪˈpeɪʃn/ *noun* **1** [U] the fact of seeing that sth might happen in the future and perhaps doing sth about it now: **~ of sth** *Anticipation of danger is critical to the survival of this species.* ◇ **in ~ of sth** *Schools, churches and prisons were built in anticipation of needs.* **2** [usually sing.] **~ of sth** the fact of coming before and influencing sth that is similar; a sign of what is going to happen: *An anticipation of this method is found in a mathematical paper of 1850 by Stokes.* **3** [U] a feeling of excitement about sth (usually sth good) that is going to happen: *Some of the most outstanding artists managed to build a sense of anticipation and excitement.*

anti·depres·sant /ˌæntidɪˈpresnt/ *noun* a drug used to treat DEPRESSION: *In the past, doctors had little choice but to prescribe antidepressants if treatment was needed.* ■ **anti·depres·sant** *adj.* [only before noun] *antidepressant drugs/medication/treatment*

anti·gen /ˈæntɪdʒən/ *noun* (*medical*) a substance that enters the body and starts a process that can cause disease. The body then usually produces ANTIBODIES to fight the antigens: *When an antigen is first encountered, the immune system mounts a primary response within 5–10 days.*

ˌanti-inˈflam·ma·tory *adj.* (of a drug) used to reduce INFLAMMATION: *The treatment of acute gout is usually with non-steroidal anti-inflammatory drugs (NSAIDs) such as naproxen.* ■ **anti-inflam·ma·tory** *noun* (*pl.* **-ies**) *All*

A

participants were prescribed medication of painkillers and anti-inflammatories.

anti·oxi·dant /ˌæntiˈɒksɪdənt; *NAmE* ˌæntiˈɑːksɪdənt/ *noun* **1** (*biology*) a substance such as VITAMIN C or E that removes dangerous MOLECULES, etc, such as FREE RADICALS from the body: *Blueberries, strawberries, cranberries and cherries are rich in antioxidants.* **2** (*chemistry*) a substance that helps prevent OXIDATION, especially one used to help prevent stored food products from going bad: **+ noun** *In this research, components with strong antioxidant activity were separated from the crude nutmeg oil through chromatographic techniques.*

anti·psychot·ic /ˌæntisaɪˈkɒtɪk; *NAmE* ˌæntisaɪˈkɑːtɪk/ *adj.* [only before noun] (of a drug) used to treat PSYCHOSIS: *Antipsychotic drugs may be calming at a time of increased stress.*

an·tiquity /ænˈtɪkwəti/ *noun* (*pl.* **-ies**) **1** [U] the ancient past, especially the times of the Greeks and Romans: *The books were known to have existed in antiquity.* ◇ *This is the most comprehensive profile of any historical figure in classical antiquity.* **2** [U] the state of being very old or ancient: *All the objects are Greek and of extreme antiquity.* **3** [C, usually pl.] an object from ancient times: *He was an avid collector of antiquities.*

anti·social /ˌæntiˈsəʊʃl; *NAmE* ˌæntiˈsoʊʃl/ *adj.* not following the laws and customs of society in a way that harms or causes problems for other people: *The research found that antisocial behaviour caused by excessive drinking was the number one concern.*

anx·iety /æŋˈzaɪəti/ *noun* (*pl.* **-ies**) **1** [U] the state of feeling nervous that sth bad is going to happen; a fear about sth: *The aim is to relieve anxiety and to encourage the patient to take responsibility for their care.* ◇ **~ about sth** *In our study, anxiety about future health was more common in women.* ◇ **~ over sth** *Public anxieties over these threats to national security were seen to be increasing.* **2** [U] **~ to do sth** a strong feeling of wanting to do sth or of wanting sth to happen: *The two essays show once again Cicero's anxiety to reassure or occupy himself in times of stress and danger.*

anx·ious /ˈæŋkʃəs/ *adj.* **1 ~ (about sth)** feeling worried or nervous: *Consumers are becoming ever more anxious about the health aspects of their diet.* **2** wanting sth very much: **~ to do sth** *The king had previously been anxious to avoid military confrontation.* ◇ **~ for sth** *China had long been infiltrated by outside powers, anxious for a share of its exotic goods.* ◇ **~ for sb to do sth** *Young Jewish Americans at that time were anxious for the US to join the war against Hitler.* ■ **anx·ious·ly** *adv.*: *The British merchants anxiously waited for the completion of this railroad.*

any[1] /ˈeni/ *det., pron.* **1** used in questions and negative sentences to refer to an amount or a number of sth, however large or small: *Are there any safety issues?* ◇ *It is unclear whether any finance companies or banks would have bought the contracts.* ◇ **~ of sth** *Does the list contain any of the following:...?* ◇ *We need to know whether any of the possible treatments saves lives.* HELP Questions with **any** include indirect questions after *if* or *whether*. Negative sentences include sentences with verbs that have a negative meaning such as *prevent, ban* or *forbid*: *This effectively shuts the valve and prevents any current from flowing.* In positive sentences **some** is usually used. **2** used to refer to one of a number of things or people, when it does not matter which one: *Any attempt to resolve this issue will involve some form of compromise.* ◇ **~ of sth** *The illness may be due to any of several causes.*

any[2] /ˈeni/ *adv.* used to emphasize an adjective or adverb in negative sentences or questions, meaning 'at all': *Before proceeding any further, two points should be made.* ◇ *Does organic food taste any better than conventionally produced food?*

any·body /ˈenibɒdi; *NAmE* ˈenibɑːdi; ˈenibʌdi/ *pron.* = ANYONE

any ˈmore (*BrE*) (*also* **any·more** *NAmE, BrE*) *adv.* often used at the end of negative sentences and at the end of questions, to mean 'any longer': *Manufacturers claim they do not make money on cars any more, only on trucks.* ◇ *In what sense are we one nation and one people anymore?*

any·one /ˈeniwʌn/ (*also* **any·body**) *pron.* **1** used instead of *someone* in questions and negative sentences, and after verbs such as *prevent, forbid, avoid*, etc: *Had anyone really won the war?* ◇ *Many people protect their networks to prevent anyone from being able to access them.* ◇ **~ else** *Neither the Greeks nor anyone else understood that blood actually circulates.* HELP The difference between **anyone** and **someone** is the same as the difference between **any** and **some.** Look at the notes there. **2** any person at all, when it does not matter who: *A vehicle with this defect represents a real risk to anyone who drives it.*

any·thing /ˈeniθɪŋ/ *pron.* **1** used instead of *something* to refer to a thing in questions and negative sentences: *Does satire change anything?* ◇ **~ else** *These parasites are specific to flies and do not attack anything else.* ◇ **if/whether ~** *It is unclear whether anything has materially changed since 1999.* ◇ **do ~ (about sth)** *The design was out of date, but the company had no capital to do anything about it.* HELP The difference between **anything** and **something** is the same as the difference between **any** and **some.** Look at the notes there. **2** any thing at all, when it does not matter which: *Midas asked that anything he touched should turn to gold.* ◇ **if ~** *What, if anything, can be done to improve this situation?* ◇ **more than ~ else** *More than anything else, entrepreneurs are the creators of new economic experiments.*

IDM **anything but** definitely not: *There are many who feel that the market is anything but fair.* **(not) anything like** (not) at all like: *Most real interfaces do not transfer data at anything like an optimum speed.* IDM *see* GO, HAPPEN

any·way /ˈeniweɪ/ *adv.* **1** used when adding sth to support an idea or argument: *In small towns, where everyone knew everyone else, surnames were not particularly important anyway.* ➲ *compare* BESIDES[2] **2** despite sth; even so: *Experiments involve actively intervening in the course of nature, as opposed to observing events that would have happened anyway.*

any·where /ˈeniweə(r); *NAmE* ˈeniwer/ *adv.* **1** used in questions and negative sentences instead of *somewhere*: *Does it hurt anywhere in your chest when you swallow?* ◇ **~ else** *Immigrants who came to America found a freedom that they could not find anywhere else in the world.* **2** in, at or to any place, when it does not matter where: *Melanomas can occur anywhere on the skin.* ■ **any·where** *pron.*: *A person at a port may have arrived in the UK from anywhere.*

apart /əˈpɑːt; *NAmE* əˈpɑːrt/ *adv.* **1** separated by a distance of space or time: *Birds studied included a colony of terns, where nests were just a few centimetres apart.* ◇ *Statistics were compiled from three censuses, ten years apart.* ◇ **as far ~ as sth** *A sales network was in place across most regions of the world, including countries as far apart as Mongolia, Ghana and Venezuela.* **2** not together; separate or separately: *Austen's work stands apart from the preoccupations of many of her contemporaries.* ◇ *Priests were set apart from the laity in three ways.* **3** into pieces: *People were condemned to live in buildings that were falling apart with age.* ◇ *New democracies are easily torn apart by political controversies.* **4** used to say that sb/sth is not included in what you are talking about: *Alaska apart, much of America's energy business concentrates on producing gas.* ➲ language bank *at* EXCEPT[1]

a'part from AWL (*also* **a'side from** *especially in NAmE*) *prep.* **1** except for: *Apart from bats, New Zealand has no native mammals.* ◇ *Direct evidence is not available, apart from one report by Langan from Singapore.* **2** in addition to; as well as: *Eating, for most people, apart from being essential for survival, is also at the centre of most important events.*

apart·ment /ə'pɑːtmənt; *NAmE* ə'pɑːrtmənt/ *noun* (*especially NAmE*) a set of rooms for living in, usually on one floor of a building: *The family worked hard in order to earn enough money to rent an apartment.* ◇ **+ noun** *an apartment building/block/complex* ➲ *compare* FLAT² (1)

apex /'eɪpeks/ *noun* (*pl.* **apexes** or **apices** /'eɪpɪsiːz/) [usually sing.] the top or highest part of sth: **(at) the ~ of sth** *At the apex of the delta, the river divides into two major distributaries.* ◇ *These cities were found at or near the apex of the global economy.*

apolo·gize (*BrE also* **-ise**) /ə'pɒlədʒaɪz; *NAmE* ə'pɑːlədʒaɪz/ *verb* [I] **~ (to sb) (for sth/doing sth)** to say that you are sorry for doing sth wrong or causing a problem. *I apologize for any errors in what follows.* ◇ *Book I closes with Caroline refusing to apologize to her father.*

apol·ogy /ə'pɒlədʒi; *NAmE* ə'pɑːlədʒi/ *noun* (*pl.* **-ies**) **1** [C, U] a word or statement saying sorry for sth that has been done wrong or that causes a problem: **~ for (doing) sth** *He demanded an apology for the insults that had been directed at him.* ◇ **~ to sb** *The film-makers include an apology to any others whose work they were unable to identify.* **2** [C] **~ for sth** something that tries to defend or explain sth, especially sth that people disagree with: *Our work is not an apology for neo-liberal policies.*
IDM **make no a'pology for sth** to not feel that you have said or done anything wrong: *The book makes no apology for raising as many questions as it answers.*

ap·par·atus /ˌæpə'reɪtəs; *NAmE* ˌæpə'rætəs/ *noun* **1** [U] the tools or other pieces of equipment that are needed for a particular activity or task: *The principal apparatus used for the study is a surface film balance.* **2** [C, usually sing.] the structure of a system or an organization, particularly that of a political party or a government: *The programme included the allocation of land to all peasants and the abolition of the state apparatus.* **3** [C, usually sing.] (*technical*) a system of organs in the body: *These apes do not have the vocal apparatus needed to make the right sounds.* **4** [C, usually sing.] a collection of notes and other material that accompanies a text: *The article is printed in full, except for some of the critical apparatus.*

ap·par·ent AWL /ə'pærənt/ *adj.* **1** [not usually before noun] easy to see or understand SYN EVIDENT: *The prevalence of fantasy in Romantic literature is readily apparent.* ◇ *These advantages are immediately apparent.* ◇ **it is ~ that...** *It is apparent that some diminution in the sovereignty of nation-states has accompanied globalization.* ◇ **~ to sb** *When the Spartans' weakness became apparent to their allies, democratic revolutions broke out in many cities.* **2** [usually before noun] that seems to be true, but may not be so SYN SEEMING: *The apparent contradiction between Likert and Thurstone's conclusions can be explained.* ◇ *This apparent paradox has a twofold explanation:...* ➲ thesaurus note *at* CLEAR¹

ap·par·ent·ly AWL /ə'pærəntli/ *adv.* according to what you have heard or read; according to the way sth appears: *The structure of ancient wild rabbit populations apparently remained stable until the Middle Ages.* ◇ *The study investigated why schools in apparently similar socio-economic contexts had radically different outcomes.* ◇ *Apparently, the faults follow older planes of weaknesses in the earth's crust.*

ap·peal¹ /ə'piːl/ *noun* **1** [C, U] a formal request to a court or to sb in authority for a judgement or a decision to be changed: **~ (to sb/sth)** *His appeal to the High Court was dismissed.* ◇ *to bring/lodge/hear/allow/reject/lose an appeal* ◇ **~ against sth** *The defendant has the right of appeal against conviction and/or sentence.* ◇ **on ~ (to sb/sth)** *On final appeal to the House of Lords the decision was again reversed.* ➲ *see also* COURT OF APPEAL **2** [U] a quality that makes sb/sth attractive or interesting: *What the party defined as socialism lacked consistent and widespread popular appeal.* ◇ **~ of sth** *The prospect of multiplying the benefits per dollar spent has the appeal of good common sense.* ◇ **~ to sb/sth** *Up to the beginning of Act 3, Lear has made little appeal to our sympathy.* **3** [C] **~ (for sth)** an urgent request for money, help or information: *On the day following the earthquake, appeals were made for tents and food.*

ap·peal² /ə'piːl/ *verb* **1** [I] to make a formal request to a court or to sb in authority for a judgement or a decision to be changed: **~ (against sth)** *The defendant appealed against his conviction for murder.* ◇ **permission/leave to ~ (to sb/sth)** *The prosecution requested leave to appeal to the Supreme Court.* HELP In North American English, the form **appeal (sth) (to sb/sth)** is usually used, without a preposition: (*NAmE*) *The company appealed the decision to the General Court on a number of grounds.* **2** [I] **~ to sb** to attract or interest sb: *The products were designed to appeal to particular consumer groups.* **3** [I] to make a serious and urgent request: **~ (to sb) (for sth)** *Pilgrims visited the tomb to appeal to the saint for assistance.* ◇ **~ to sb to do sth** *Charles Nevers appealed to Louis XIII to support his claims to the inheritance.* **4** [I] **~ to sth** to try to persuade sb to do sth by suggesting that it is a fair, reasonable or honest thing to do: *We need to appeal to principles of justice to help resolve these disagreements.*

ap·peal·ing /ə'piːlɪŋ/ *adj.* attractive or interesting: *Maps can make data more visually appealing.* ◇ **~ to sb** *Buying milk in a bottle still seems appealing to many people.*

ap·pear /ə'pɪə(r); *NAmE* ə'pɪr/ *verb* **1** *linking verb* (not used in the progressive tenses) to give the impression of being or doing sth SYN SEEM (1): **+ adj.** *This rate appears likely to increase over subsequent years.* ◇ **~ to be sth** *Men and women appear to be equally at risk.* ◇ **~ to do sth** *Colony size appears to play an important role in the structure and organization of these insect colonies.* ◇ **it appears that...** *It appears that one of the earliest uses for the alphabet was to write down verses of poetry.* **2** [I] **+ adv./prep.** to start to be seen: *Radiation fog often appears shortly after dusk on a calm evening.* ◇ *An arrow will appear on the screen.* **3** [I] **+ adv./prep.** to begin to exist or be known or used for the first time: *In the twelfth century, Buddhist elements began to appear in the Angkor temples.* ◇ *When flash memories first appeared, typical capacities were 8 Mbytes.* **4** [I] **+ adv./prep.** to be published or broadcast; to be written or mentioned somewhere: *Few of Wyatt's poems appeared in print in his lifetime.* ◇ *A sample report based on a clinical interview appears at the end of the chapter.* **5** [I] **+ adv./prep.** to take part in a film, play, television programme, etc: *The minister appeared on television to announce his resignation.* **6** [I] to be present in court in order to give evidence, answer a charge or act as sb's lawyer: **+ adv./prep.** *He was issued with a notice to appear at a magistrate's court.* ◇ **~ for/on behalf of sb** *Sir Philip Miller QC appeared for the successful claimant.* ➲ *compare* DISAPPEAR ➲ *see also* APPARENT

ap·pear·ance /ə'pɪərəns; *NAmE* ə'pɪrəns/ *noun* **1** [U, C, usually sing.] the way that sb/sth looks on the outside: *Young people try to change their physical appearance to emulate models or celebrities.* ◇ *The top mineral layer of the soil has a characteristic grey ashy appearance.* ◇ **~ of (doing) sth** *As the lesions heal, they fade to give the appearance of a bruise.* **2** [U, C, usually sing.] **~ of (doing) sth** what sb/sth seems to be: *Despite the appearance of popular support, many ordinary people consider the systems to be* *unjust.* ◇ *BBC's 'Newsnight' programme was criticized for giving the appearance of being too detached.* ◇ *These canyons have the appearance of being newly formed.* **3** [C, usually sing.] the moment at which sth begins to exist or starts to be seen or used: **make its ~** *Land plants had made their appearance in the early Silurian period.* **4** [C] an act of appearing in public: *The councillor made a quick round of radio and television appearances.* ◇ *His last public appearance was in Red Square in early November 1932.* **5** [C, usually sing.] **~ (of sth)** an act of being published or broadcast: *Scholarly interest in the writer arose after the appearance of Tagore's translation.*

ap·pel·lant /əˈpelənt/ *noun* (*law*) a person who APPEALS against a decision made in court: *It was concluded that the appellant had been rightly convicted.*

ap·pend AWL /əˈpend/ *verb* **~ sth (to sth)** to add sth to the end of a piece of writing: *The results of the survey are appended to this chapter.*

ap·pen·dix AWL /əˈpendɪks/ *noun* **1** (*pl.* **ap·pen·di·ces** /əˈpendɪsiːz/ or **ap·pen·dixes** /əˈpendɪksɪz/) a section of extra information at the end of a book, article or other document: *Preparation techniques are described in Appendix E.* **2** (*pl.* **ap·pen·di·ces** /əˈpendɪsiːz/) a small bag of TISSUE that is attached to the large INTESTINE. In humans, the appendix has no clear function: *The treatment of acute appendicitis is surgical removal of the appendix.*

ap·pe·tite /ˈæpɪtaɪt/ *noun* **1** [U, C, usually sing.] physical desire for food: *Patients may complain of a loss of appetite.* ◇ **~ for sth** *Physiological factors can influence an individual's appetite for food.* **2** [C] **~ for sth** a strong desire for sth: *The more developed areas of the world are a leading cause of deforestation because of their enormous appetite for tropical timber.*

ap·pli·ance /əˈplaɪəns/ *noun* a machine that is designed to do a particular thing, especially in the home: *The coming of electrical appliances gave electricity a boost in households and offices.*

ap·plic·able /əˈplɪkəbl; ˈæplɪkəbl/ *adj.* [not usually before noun] true about or appropriate to a particular situation, group of people, etc: *Hofstede provided a universally applicable framework for classifying cultural patterns.* ◇ **~ to sb/sth** *Scholars cannot agree on whether there is a common definition applicable to all forms of Romanticism.* ➲ *compare* RELEVANT ■ **ap·plic·abil·ity** /əˌplɪkəˈbɪləti; ˌæplɪkəˈbɪləti/ *noun* [U] **~ (of sth)** *Further case studies are needed in order to test the wider applicability of these arguments.*

ap·pli·cant /ˈæplɪkənt/ *noun* a person who makes a formal request for sth such as a job: *Across all countries, these firms reported using just under five test types to evaluate job applicants.* ◇ **~ for sth** *From 2002, applicants for British citizenship were required to pass an English language test.* HELP In law, an **applicant** is sb who makes a formal request to a court.

ap·pli·ca·tion /ˌæplɪˈkeɪʃn/ *noun* **1** [U, C] the use of sth such as an idea, method, rule, etc; a use that sth has: **~ (of sth)** *The successful application of ideas has been recognized within industry as the primary source of its development.* ◇ *A variety of practical applications of these emulsions are examined.* ◇ **~ for sth** *Spatial analysis has many potential applications for political research.* ◇ **~ to sth** *Mearsheimer believes that his argument has general application to all places at all times.* **2** [C] a formal (often written) request to an organization or authority for sth, such as a job or permission to do sth, or to join a group: *Some job applications are made on standard forms, or more often online.* ◇ **~ for sth/to do sth** *Switzerland's application for EU membership was withdrawn when its people said 'no' in a referendum.* ◇ **~ to sb/sth** *There has been a rising trend in the number of applications to employment tribunals.* **3** [C] a program or piece of software designed to do a particular job: *Hundreds of software applications are now available to help implement these processes.* **4** [C, U] **~ (of sth) (to sth)** the use of sth to produce a particular physical effect: *Fatigue refers to the failure or decay of mechanical properties after repeated applications of stress.* ◇ *Application of pressure to water encourages the formation of the liquid phase.* **5** [C, U] **~ (of sth)** the action of putting or spreading sth onto a surface or object: *The application of chemical fertilizers rose from about 5 kg per acre in 1952 to 175 kg in 1985.*

▸ ADJECTIVE + APPLICATION **practical** • **successful** • **potential** • **widespread, wide** • **universal** • **general** • **specific, particular** • **straightforward** • **strict** • **uniform** • **correct** • **commercial** • **industrial** • **clinical** • **biomedical** *As described before, carbon nanotubes hold great potential for a variety of industrial applications.*

▸ NOUN + APPLICATION **job** • **grant** • **asylum** • **patent** *According to the UN, there were 2.4 million asylum applications in Europe between 1991 and 1995.*

▸ VERB + APPLICATION **limit** • **find** • **involve, entail** • **require** • **demonstrate** *Embryonic stem cells may present problems with rejection, limiting their clinical application.* | **make** • **submit, lodge, file** • **grant, accept, approve** • **oppose** • **reject, refuse, dismiss** • **withdraw** • **examine, hear** • **process, handle** *After submitting the outline planning application in 1993, the company was granted planning consent in 2001.*

▸ APPLICATION OF + NOUN **principle** • **law, legislation** • **provision** • **rule** • **theory** • **doctrine** • **method, methodology** • **approach** • **criterion** • **technique** • **knowledge** • **technology, science** • **model** • **test** • **idea** • **concept** *Research, development and application of low-carbon technologies are crucial to achieving a sustainable fuel economy.*

ap·plied /əˈplaɪd/ *adj.* [only before noun] (especially of a subject of study) used in a practical way; not THEORETICAL: *Applied research is that which is undertaken for a practical purpose.* ◇ *applied linguistics/science/mathematics* ➲ *compare* PURE (5)

apply /əˈplaɪ/ *verb* (**ap·plies, ap·ply·ing, ap·plied, ap·plied**) **1** [I] (not used in the progressive tenses) to concern or be relevant to sb/sth: *In different situations, different rules apply.* ◇ **~ to sb/sth** *The same principle could apply to other situations.* **2** [T] to use an idea, method, theory, etc: **~ sth** *Pollet and Nettle (2009) very carefully describe the data and the methods applied.* ◇ **~ sth to sth** *Difficulties have arisen when attempting to apply existing rules to new online activities.* **3** [T] to use sth in order to produce a particular physical effect: **~ sth** *Apply direct pressure with a sterile pad if there is no object embedded in the wound.* ◇ **~ sth to sth** *Minor electrical stimuli applied to the skin can relieve pain, such as in childbirth.* ◇ **~ sth to do sth** *An electronic shutter was applied to control laser pulses onto the system.* **4** [T] **~ sth (to sth)** to give a particular name to sth: *Villacorta suggested that the term 'poor' when applied to countries is perhaps no longer useful.* **5** [I, T] to make a formal (often written) request to an organization or authority for sth, such as a job or permission to do sth, or to join a group: **~ for sth** *The students apply for these jobs and are interviewed if necessary.* ◇ *When children apply for asylum in Sweden, the Migration Board's task is to take into account the best interests of the child.* ◇ **~ to sb/sth (for sth)** *Both mother and father had applied to the court for a residence order.* ◇ **~ to do sth** *Countries apply to join the EU because they think membership is in their political and economic interest.* **6** [T] **~ yourself/sth to (doing) sth** to work very hard in order to achieve sth: *Llywelyn and his successors applied themselves to the continued development of government in their lands.*

▸ APPLY + NOUN **principle** • **rule** • **law** • **idea** • **criterion** • **method, methodology** • **procedure** • **technique** • **approach** • **strategy** • **test** • **standard** • **reasoning** • **theorem** • **theory** • **model** • **formula** • **framework** •

algorithm • correction • logic • knowledge • skill *Walter Dill Scott applied psychological principles to advertising, hiring and motivation.* | **pressure • force • voltage • current • pulse • stimulus** *When a high voltage is applied across the electrodes, the neon ionizes.*

▸ NOUN + APPLY **rule • law • theorem • principle • argument • consideration • exception • provision • Act** *If light is reflected from the surface of a material, the same argument applies.*

▸ APPLY + ADVERB **only • globally • universally • generally • strictly • uniformly • differently** *Traditionally, wage levels are decided at the national level and applied uniformly across the industry.* | **equally • directly • specifically • particularly • exclusively • primarily, mainly** *The following minor treatments apply equally to adults and children.* | **systematically • successfully • consistently** *These radicals believed that guerrilla tactics could be applied successfully to the United States.*

▸ ADVERB + APPLY **also • only • currently • then • generally • actually • strictly** *Despite some exceptions, US anti-discrimination laws generally apply to foreign companies and their subsidiaries.* | **still • no longer • equally** *There is little doubt that, forty years later, Drucker's comment still applies.* | **widely • successfully • commonly • directly • usually • properly • usefully • easily, simply • now • often** *Each of these six approaches has been widely applied, but each has deficiencies.*

ap·point /ə'pɔɪnt/ *verb* **1** to choose sb for a job or position of responsibility: **~ sb** *to appoint a trustee/director/judge/minister/committee* ◇ **appointed by sb** *New members are appointed by the Selection Committee.* ◇ **~ sb to sth** *She was appointed to a post as a trainee consultant.* ◇ **~ sb + noun**| **~ sb as sth** *Roy Jenkins was appointed (as) President in 1977.* ◇ **~ sb to do sth** *A commission was appointed to investigate the accident.* **2** [usually passive] to arrange or decide on a time or place for doing sth: **be appointed** *A date for the meeting is still to be appointed.* ◇ **appointed + noun** *Thousands of people turned up on the appointed day.*

ap·point·ment /ə'pɔɪntmənt/ *noun* **1** [C] a formal arrangement to meet sb at a particular time or place: *Five of the families did not attend any clinic appointments.* ◇ *The patient should be given a follow-up appointment in a fracture clinic.* ◇ *to make/arrange/schedule/keep/miss an appointment* **2** [C, U] the act of choosing a person for a job or position of responsibility; a job, or the person chosen for a job or position of responsibility: **make an ~** *The company was making more appointments on a short-term basis.* ◇ **the ~ of sb** *Given recent concerns, there is a growing emphasis on the appointment of trustees who are experienced and capable.* ◇ **~ as/to sth** *In 1999 he accepted an appointment as Professor of Mathematics at Princeton University.*

ap·prais·al /ə'preɪzl/ *noun* [C, U] **1 ~ (of sth)** a judgement of the value, performance or nature of sb/sth: *The book provides a critical appraisal of recent developments in the law.* **2** (*BrE*) a meeting in which an employee discusses with their manager how well they have been doing their job; the system of holding such meetings: *The research evaluated the impact of the introduction of performance appraisal in British universities.*

ap·praise /ə'preɪz/ *verb* **1** to consider or examine sb/sth and form an opinion about them or it: **~ sb/sth** *Each article is critically appraised for relevance to the issue.* ◇ **~ sb/sth/yourself as sth** *They appraise themselves as unattractive, awkward, useless and a burden to others.* **2 ~ sb** (*BrE*) to make a formal judgement about the value of a person's work, usually after a discussion with them about it: *The measures for evaluating a team may differ from those used for appraising an individual member.*

ap·pre·ciable AWL /ə'priːʃəbl/ *adj.* large or important enough to be noticed SYN CONSIDERABLE: *Shared family environment has an appreciable effect when children are small.* ■ **ap·pre·ciably** AWL /ə'priːʃəbli/ *adv.*: *The room temperature did not vary appreciably between different experiments.*

ap·preci·ate AWL /ə'priːʃieɪt/ *verb* **1** [T] to understand sth to be true SYN RECOGNIZE (2): **~ sth** *Lodge and Fitzgerald could immediately appreciate the significance of what Hertz had done.* ◇ **~ that...** *It is important for managers to appreciate that the interests of workers change over time.* ◇ **~ how/what, etc...** *People in the community may not fully appreciate how difficult the job of a police officer is.* **2** [T] **~ sb/sth** to recognize the good qualities of sb/sth: *He appreciated her qualities as a writer.* ◇ *The opportunity to appreciate the arts is crucial for the development of a healthy society.* **3** [T] to be grateful for sth that sb has done; to welcome sth: **~ sth** *Russian support was appreciated by the Spanish Republicans.* ◇ **~ doing sth** *These young professionals appreciate living close to work in order to cut commuting times.* **4** [I] **~ (against sth)** to increase in value over a period of time: *The renminbi appreciated marginally against the US dollar.* OPP DEPRECIATE (1)

ap·pre·ci·ation AWL /əˌpriːʃi'eɪʃn/ *noun* **1** [U, sing.] **~ of sth** a full understanding of sth, such as a topic or problem, and of what it involves SYN AWARENESS: *The findings demonstrate increasing appreciation of the importance of health and safety.* ◇ *Western historians already had a sound appreciation of what had been happening in the Soviet Union.* **2** [U, sing.] understanding and enjoyment of the good qualities of sth: **~ of sth** *Ancient and modern reactions to Diogenes range from appreciation of his wit to dislike of his social and political values.* ◇ **~ for sth** *Also strongly evident in these narratives is a growing appreciation for landscape.* **3** [C] **~ (of sth)** a piece of writing or a speech in which the strengths and weaknesses of sb/sth, especially an artist or a work of art, are discussed and judged: *Hazlitt includes generous appreciations of the great actors he had seen.* **4** [U] **~ (for sth)** the quality of being grateful for sth: *I would like to express my appreciation to Professor Jennifer Dean for her helpful comments and advice.* **5** [U, C] increase in value over a period of time: *The question is what to do with exchange rate appreciation.* ◇ **~ of sth** *Japan intervened heavily to prevent the appreciation of the yen.* ◇ **~ in sth** *These effects generate appreciations in local real estate prices.* OPP DEPRECIATION

ap·proach[1] AWL /ə'prəʊtʃ; *NAmE* ə'proʊtʃ/ *noun* **1** [C] a way of doing or thinking about sth such as a problem or task: *The participants were interviewed using a semi-structured interview approach.* ◇ **~ to sth** *Two approaches to particle-size analysis were employed.* ◇ **~ to doing sth** *Psychologists have taken many different approaches to studying perception.* ◇ **~ for doing sth** *A common approach for adapting to the new economic environment was to globalize business activities.* ◇ **~ in sth** *Research has led to new approaches in sales training.* ◇ **according to the ... ~** *According to the ecological approach, behaviour is influenced by various facets of the environment.* ◇ **through a ... ~** *Necessary improvements could be achieved through an evolutionary approach.* ➲ thesaurus note *at* THEORY **2** [sing.] movement nearer to sb/sth in distance or time: **~ (of sb/sth) (to sb/sth)** *The approach of the negatively charged particles to the ground induces more positive charges.* ◇ **~ of sth** *With the approach of war, research and production was increased.* **3** [C] **~ (to sb/sth)** the act of speaking to sb about sth, especially when making an offer or a request: *Sun's political sympathies lay with the Western powers, but his approaches to them were rebuffed.* **4** [C] a path, sea passage, etc. that leads to a particular place: *The geographical distribution of these colonies was broad: from the western Mediterranean to the Black Sea and its approaches.* **5** [sing.] **~ to sth** a thing that is like sth else that is mentioned: *Spinning was Russia's nearest approach to the industrial revolution at this time.*

A

▸ ADJECTIVE + APPROACH **alternative, different** • **similar** • **new** • **novel** • **innovative** • **traditional, conventional** • **standard** • **common** • **general, broad** • **integrated, holistic** • **systematic** • **structured** • **flexible** • **comparative** • **qualitative** • **quantitative** • **simple** • **comprehensive** • **bottom-up** • **top-down** *There are two alternative approaches to fracture analysis.* | **theoretical** • **experimental** • **scientific** • **analytical** • **modelling** • **critical** • **strategic** • **methodological** • **multidisciplinary** • **ecological** • **evolutionary** • **behavioural** *There are a wide variety of theoretical approaches to the psychology of human reasoning.* ◇ *The section reviews the main methodological approaches.*

▸ VERB + HEADWORD **adopt, take, use, employ, apply, utilize, follow, pursue** • **implement** • **describe, outline** • **require** • **propose, suggest** • **offer** • **advocate, favour, recommend** • **develop** • **combine** *The study found that good learners tend to adopt an exploratory approach to learning.* ◇ *She advocates critical approaches borrowed from sociolinguistics.*

▸ APPROACH + VERB **be based on** • **emphasize** • **yield** • **focus on** *This approach focuses on what happens during a democratization process.*

ap·proach² AWL /ə'prəʊtʃ; *NAmE* ə'proʊtʃ/ *verb* **1** [T] to start dealing with a problem or task or considering a topic or situation in a particular way: **~ sth** *Different researchers have approached the topic in different ways.* ◇ **~ sth from sth** *Modern theories have approached the question from two perspectives.* **2** [T] **~ sth** to come close to sth in quantity or quality: *London's population approached three-quarters of a million in 1800.* ◇ *Britain began to approach European levels of spending on welfare.* ◇ *Few writers approach his richness of language.* **3** [I, T] to move near to sb/sth in distance or time: *As winter approached, post-harvest tasks were combined with preparing land for the next season's planting.* ◇ **~ sb/sth** *The Flavian army approached Rome.* **4** [T] to speak to sb about sth, especially to offer to do sth or to ask them for sth: **~ sb/sth** *In the study, twelve hospitals were approached.* ◇ **~ sb for sth** *Two major car producers approached the government for financial aid.* ◇ **~ sb about sth** *School principals are often approached by other organizations about potential partnerships.* ◇ **~ sb to do sth** *Bill Gates was approached to supply a simple operating system.*

▸ APPROACH + NOUN **topic, subject** • **question, issue, problem, matter** • **task** *They approached the task with an empirically based method.* | **zero** • **infinity** • **limit** • **value** • **level** • **significance** *After 60 years the growth rate is approaching zero.* ◇ *Today, we are approaching the limit of available land for agricultural purposes.*

▸ PHRASES **approach sth in various ways** • **approach sth from a regional/global/historical perspective** *This task can be approached in various ways.* ◇ *Military geography can be approached from a historical perspective.*

ap·pro·pri·ate¹ AWL /ə'prəʊpriət; *NAmE* ə'proʊpriət/ *adj.* suitable, acceptable or correct for the particular circumstances: *Patients receiving appropriate care should get better.* ◇ *The use of herbicides is not appropriate in wetland environments.* ◇ **~ for sth** *Pure siloxane polymers are only rarely appropriate for use in technology.* ◇ **~ to sth** *The company developed a hotel format that was appropriate to the Japanese market.* ◇ **it is ~ that...** *It was appropriate that such an important decision should be taken by heads of government.* ◇ **it is ~ to do sth** *It is appropriate to consider whether the patient is taking medication.* ◇ **as ~** *Board members may seek expert opinions as appropriate.*

▸ APPROPRIATE + NOUN **measure, course (of action), action** • **response** • **remedy** • **treatment** • **care** • **strategy** • **behaviour** • **management** • **tool** • **method** • **way** • **use** • **level** • **balance** *Appropriate measures can be taken to reduce risk.* ◇ *Almost every day, there are discussions over the appropriate balance between private and public sector.*

▸ ADVERB + APPROPRIATE **particularly** • **entirely** • **culturally** • **socially** *The programme was adapted so that it would be culturally appropriate for India.*

ap·pro·pri·ate² AWL /ə'prəʊprieɪt; *NAmE* ə'proʊprieɪt/ *verb* **1 ~ sth** to start to use sth that belongs to a different time, place or culture: *Greek thought was selectively appropriated by Christianity.* **2 ~ sth** to take sb's idea, property or money for your own use, especially without permission: *The defendant did not dishonestly appropriate property belonging to another and cannot be convicted of theft.* **3 ~ sth** to take sth from sb, legally and often by force SYN SEIZE: *Their personal assets cannot be appropriated by the firm's creditors.* **4 ~ sth** to take or give sth, especially money, for a particular purpose: *Funds have been appropriated to help local municipalities renovate municipal waste treatment plants.*

ap·pro·pri·ate·ly AWL /ə'prəʊpriətli; *NAmE* ə'proʊpriətli/ *adv.* in a way that is suitable, acceptable or correct for the particular circumstances: *Responding appropriately to cultural changes is one of the great challenges facing global marketers.* ◇ *All samples were appropriately labelled.*

ap·pro·pri·ate·ness AWL /ə'prəʊpriətnəs; *NAmE* ə'proʊpriətnəs/ *noun* [U] **~ (of sth) (for sth)** the degree to which sth is suitable, acceptable or correct for the particular circumstances: *There is a long-standing debate about the appropriateness of the natural science model for the study of society.*

ap·pro·pri·ation /əˌprəʊpri'eɪʃn; *NAmE* əˌproʊpri'eɪʃn/ *noun* **1** [U, C] **~ (of sth) (by sb)** the use of sth that belongs to a different time, place or culture: *There were many different kinds of appropriation by Romans of Greek culture.* **2** [U, sing.] **~ (of sth) (by sb)** the act of taking sb's idea, property or money for your own use, especially without permission: *The Bolsheviks did not seek to overturn the peasants' appropriation of noble land.* **3** [C] a sum of money to be used for a particular purpose, especially by a government or company: *Revenue estimates must be equal to payment appropriations.* **4** [U, sing.] **~ (of sth) (by sb)** (of a government or company) the act of keeping or saving money for a particular purpose: *the appropriation of funds by Parliament*

ap·prov·al /ə'pruːvl/ *noun* **1** [U, C] agreement to or permission for sth, especially a plan or request: **~ (for sth) (from sb)** *Ethical approval for this work was obtained from the Institute of Nutrition.* ◇ *to require/seek/grant/receive approval* ◇ *shareholder/parliamentary/board approval* ◇ **without (the) ~ (of sb/sth)** *Information should not be divulged without the approval of the users.* ◇ **seal/stamp of ~** *They waited for the chairman's seal of approval on colours, price and quality.* ◇ **subject to ~** *Deutsche Telekom's prices were subject to approval by the regulator.* **2** [U] the feeling that sb/sth is good or acceptable; a positive opinion of sb/sth: **~ from sb/sth** *By volunteering, refugees can win approval from the host community.* ◇ **with ~** *Plath spoke of this essay often and with approval.* OPP DISAPPROVAL

ap·prove /ə'pruːv/ *verb* **1** [T] **~ sth** to officially agree to a plan or request: *The minister was expected to approve plans for a fifth terminal at Heathrow.* ◇ *Congress approves the budget for one year at a time.* **2** [T, often passive] to say that sth is good enough to be used or is correct: **be approved for use** *The drug has been approved for clinical use in parts of Europe.* ◇ **be approved by sb/sth** *The research was approved by the Governing Board of the School of Psychology.* ◇ **~ sth** *The University Ethics Committee approved the study and participants provided written consent.* OPP DISAPPROVE (2) **3** [I] to think that sb/sth is good, acceptable or suitable: **~ (of sb/sth)** *Augustine did not approve of force in religious matters.* ◇ ◇ **~ of sb doing**

sth *Many colleagues did not approve of judges interviewing children.* OPP DISAPPROVE (1)

ap·prov·ing /ə'pru:vɪŋ/ *adj.* showing that you believe that sb/sth is good or acceptable: *The work drew approving reviews when it was first published.* OPP DISAPPROVING ■ **ap·prov·ing·ly** *adv.*: *This passage is quoted approvingly by Langton.*

ap·proxi·mate¹ AWL /ə'prɒksɪmət; *NAmE* ə'prɑ:ksɪmət/ *adj.* (*abbr.* **approx.**) almost correct or accurate, but not completely so: *The table below gives useful approximate values for the parameters listed.* ◇ *This calculation, however, is approximate.*

ap·proxi·mate² AWL /ə'prɒksɪmeɪt; *NAmE* ə'prɑ:ksɪmeɪt/ *verb* **1** [T, I] to be similar or close to sth in amount, quality or nature, but not exactly the same: **~ sth** *The mean length of a generation closely approximates the mean age of mothers at the birth of their daughters.* ◇ **~ to sth** *The most extreme conditions, approximating to house arrest in solitary confinement, were found unlawful.* **2** [T] **~ sth (by sth)** to calculate or estimate sth fairly accurately: *The roughness of the surface may be approximated by the following equation.*

ap·proxi·mate·ly AWL /ə'prɒksɪmətli; *NAmE* ə'prɑ:ksɪmətli/ *adv.* (*abbr.* **approx.**) in a way that is almost accurate or exact, but not completely so: *The water contains chloride at levels approximately equal to that found in river water.* ◇ *The tube is approx. 5 feet long.*

ap·proxi·ma·tion AWL /əˌprɒksɪ'meɪʃn; *NAmE* əˌprɑ:ksɪ'meɪʃn/ *noun* **1** an estimate of a number or an amount that is almost correct, but not exact: *This value differs slightly from that found in the previous calculation, because of the various approximations that were made.* **2 ~ (of/to sth)** a thing that is similar to sth else, but is not exactly the same: *Rhuddlan was the closest approximation to a town in pre-Norman Wales during its brief periods under Welsh rule.*

a pri·ori /ˌeɪ praɪ'ɔ:raɪ/ *adj.*, *adv.* (*from Latin*) using facts or principles that are known to be true in order to decide what the likely effects or results of sth will be: *A priori knowledge concerning the chemical composition of the crystal is used.* ◇ *There is no reason to assume a priori that the parent earwigs must choose either of these strategies.*

apt /æpt/ *adj.* **1** suitable or appropriate in the circumstances: *The categorization of fathers as either good providers or active carers is not an apt description of modern fatherhood.* **2 ~ to do sth** likely or having a natural tendency to do sth: *The workforce were apt to desert the factory when other work was available.* ■ **aptly** *adv.*: *The thinking behind this legislation is aptly described by Fox Harding (1991) as an 'uneasy synthesis'.*

aqua·tic /ə'kwætɪk/ *adj.* [usually before noun] **1** growing or living in, on or near water: *The loss of oxygen creates stress on many aquatic organisms including fish.* ◇ *aquatic plants/animals/species* **2** connected with water: *Water in almost all aquatic systems is moving.* ◇ *aquatic environments/ecosystems/habitats*

aque·ous /'eɪkwiəs/ *adj.* [usually before noun] (*technical*) containing or involving water: *The particles were suspended in aqueous solutions.* ◇ *This drug has poor aqueous solubility.* ◇ *Metals exist in the aqueous environment in a variety of forms.*

ar·bi·trar·ily AWL /ˌɑ:bɪ'trerəli; 'ɑ:bɪtrəli; *NAmE* ˌɑ:rbə'trerəli/ *adv.* **1** in a way that is not based on reason, rules or principles; in a way that cannot be predicted SYN RANDOMLY: *The median quality level was arbitrarily chosen for these additional analyses.* ◇ *Inflation distributes its costs very unevenly and arbitrarily.* **2** (of a ruler or power) without restriction and without considering other people: *Governors are constrained by law from acting arbitrarily.*

ar·bi·trary AWL /'ɑ:bɪtrəri; 'ɑ:bɪtri; *NAmE* 'ɑ:rbətreri/ *adj.* **1** (of a decision, rule, system, etc.) not seeming to be based on reason, and sometimes seeming unfair: *Many couples make fairly arbitrary decisions about sharing the financial burdens of home ownership.* ◇ *These recommendations appear somewhat arbitrary, and little justification is offered.* **2** using power or authority without restriction and without considering other people: *The relatively open politics of the 1990s gave way to arbitrary rule by the monarch.* **3** (*mathematics*) (of a quantity) of a value that is not stated: *In some problems, a definite value is assigned to C; in others, C is an arbitrary constant.* ■ **ar·bi·trari·ness** AWL *noun* [U, sing.] *Since it involves some arbitrariness, Stokes's interpretation is not entirely compelling.* ◇ *There is an arbitrariness in setting a minimum age for criminal responsibility.* ◇ *Yeltsin had few inhibitions against arbitrariness and the use of force.*

ar·bi·tra·tion /ˌɑ:bɪ'treɪʃn; *NAmE* ˌɑ:rbɪ'treɪʃn/ *noun* [U] the official process of settling an argument or a disagreement by sb who is not involved: *They could also refer their dispute to arbitration.*

ar·bi·tra·tor /'ɑ:bɪtreɪtə(r); *NAmE* 'ɑ:rbɪtreɪtər/ *noun* a person who is chosen to settle a disagreement: *Each party appoints an arbitrator.*

arc /ɑ:k; *NAmE* ɑ:rk/ *noun* **1 ~ (of sth)** part of a circle or a curved line; something that forms a curved shape: *AB and CD are arcs of a circle with the pumping well as centre.* ◇ *The Indonesian island arc lies on thin continental crust with ages as old as the Proterozoic.* **2 ~ (of sth)** a continuous and connected series of events: *It may be necessary to rethink the narrative arc of early American history.*

arch /ɑ:tʃ; *NAmE* ɑ:rtʃ/ *noun* a curved structure that supports the weight of sth above it, such as a bridge or the upper part of a building: *The first stone arch bridge in London was completed in 1209.*

archae·olo·gist (*NAmE also* **arche·olo·gist**) /ˌɑ:ki'ɒlədʒɪst; *NAmE* ˌɑ:rki'ɑ:lədʒɪst/ *noun* a person who studies archaeology: *Historians and archaeologists have long debated definitions of towns and town life in medieval Europe.*

archae·ology (*NAmE also* **arche·ology**) /ˌɑ:ki'ɒlədʒi; *NAmE* ˌɑ:rki'ɑ:lədʒi/ *noun* [U] the study of cultures of the past, and periods of history by examining the remains of buildings and objects found in the ground: *The notion of 'landscape' has been important in archaeology for decades (Roberts, 1987).* ■ **arch·aeo·logic·al** (*NAmE also* **arch·eo·logic·al**) /ˌɑ:kiə'lɒdʒɪkl; *NAmE* ˌɑ:rkiə'lɑ:dʒɪkl/ *adj.* [usually before noun] *Examples of everything from swords to horse harnesses have survived in the archaeological record.* ◇ *archaeological evidence/sites/research*

ar·chaic /ɑ:'keɪɪk; *NAmE* ɑ:r'keɪɪk/ *adj.* **1** old and no longer used: *The dictionary has omitted some archaic words and senses which are not in current use.* **2** from a much earlier or ancient period of history: *Many aristocrats migrated into Rome in the archaic period.* **3** very old-fashioned SYN OUTDATED: *'Variolation' was an archaic and dangerous method of preventing smallpox.*

archi·tect /'ɑ:kɪtekt; *NAmE* 'ɑ:rkɪtekt/ *noun* **1** a person whose job is designing buildings: *Greek and Roman architects sometimes used thin layers of lead instead of cement between sections of tall columns.* **2 the ~ of sth** a person who is responsible for planning or creating an idea, a system, a situation, etc: *Alfred was the architect of West Saxon survival against the Vikings.*

archi·tec·tural /ˌɑ:kɪ'tektʃərəl; *NAmE* ˌɑ:rkɪ'tektʃərəl/ *adj.* [usually before noun] **1** connected with the design or style of buildings: *Scottish nobles tended to adopt a distinctive architectural style.* **2** connected with the structure or design of sth: *Animal species richness in tropical forests and coral reefs seems linked to the architectural complexity of these systems.*

archi·tec·ture /ˈɑːkɪtektʃə(r); *NAmE* ˈɑːrkɪtektʃər/ *noun* **1** [U] the design or style of a building or buildings; the art and study of designing buildings: *Minoan art and architecture owe a large debt to the civilizations of the Near East.* ◇ *a school of architecture and design* **2** [U, C] **~ (of sth)** the structure or design of sth: *There has been a changing architecture of power both globally and within the state.* **3** [U, C] (*computing*) the structure and logical organization of a computer system: *The ideal computer architecture is rich in features and yet easy to understand.*

archival /ˌɑːˈkaɪvl; *NAmE* ˌɑːrˈkaɪvl/ *adj.* [only before noun] coming from or connected with an archive: *A good deal of archival material on the Stalinist purges and terror was unearthed and published.* ◇ *archival research/sources/records*

arch·ive¹ /ˈɑːkaɪv; *NAmE* ˈɑːrkaɪv/ *noun* (*also* **archives** [pl.]) a collection of historical documents or records of a government, a family, a place or an organization; the place where these records are stored: *The continent of Antarctica contains almost no historical archives in a traditional sense.* ◇ *In a number of cases, it was possible to check the letters against the originals in various archives and libraries.*

arch·ive² /ˈɑːkaɪv; *NAmE* ˈɑːrkaɪv/ *verb* **1 ~ sth** to put or store a document or other material in an archive: *Students are engaged in conducting and archiving complete oral histories.* **2 ~ sth** (*computing*) to move data that are not often needed to a disk or tape to store them: *Storage and retrieval systems are used to archive data.*

are /ə(r); *strong form* ɑː(r)/ ➲ BE¹, BE²

area AWL /ˈeəriə; *NAmE* ˈeriə/ *noun* **1** [C] part of a town, a country or the world: *Rural areas have less access to fast food restaurants.* ◇ *The eurozone is a common currency area.* ◇ **~ of sth** *Fever was rife in areas of rice and indigo cultivation.* **2** [C] a particular subject or activity, or an aspect of it: *The panel's report covered several areas, including law enforcement and education.* ◇ *Fluid mechanics is a very broad area.* ◇ **~ of sth** *Leadership has been an important area of research among social scientists for decades.* **3** [C, U] **~ (of sth)** the amount of space covered by a surface or piece of land, described as a measurement: *The lake covers an area of 820 km².* ◇ *The area of a black hole cannot decrease.* ◇ *Since the 1970s, sea ice in the Arctic has declined in area by about 30 per cent per decade.* ◇ *The flow per unit area is 3 m/s.* **4** [C] **~ (of sth)** a particular place on an object or a diagram: *Few areas of the body are sterile.* ◇ *On a demand curve, the total revenue is illustrated by the area under the curve*

▸ ADJECTIVE + AREA **geographical • urban, metropolitan • suburban • rural • coastal • remote • local • surrounding • wide • agricultural • industrial • residential • deprived** *Competition is likely to be more intense as more services are concentrated into a smaller geographical area.* ◇ *Resources for schools in deprived areas have been increased.* | **key, main, core • major, important • specific, particular, certain • broad • sensitive** *Three key areas of psychology are relevant to nursing the ageing patient.* ◇ *Sustainable consumption is an extremely sensitive area for governments.*

▸ NOUN + AREA **subject • policy** *The main policy areas covered were social policy, health and education.*

▸ VERB + AREA **cover • affect • occupy, inhabit • explore • identify • designate • protect • dominate** *The study was carried out in three separate coastal areas inhabited by natterjacks.* ◇ *The maps were used to identify areas of wind erosion.* | **cover, encompass • explore, address • identify • define • highlight** *Lily's quantitative research project explored areas surrounding academic life.*

arena /əˈriːnə/ *noun* **1** an area of activity, especially one where there is a lot of discussion or argument: *Many of these issues have entered the public arena through the mass media.* ◇ **in/within the... arena** *It is difficult for them to act collectively in the political arena.* **2** a place with a flat open area in the middle and seats around it where people can watch sports and entertainment: *a sports arena*

ar·gu·able /ˈɑːgjuəbl; *NAmE* ˈɑːrgjuəbl/ *adj.* **1** that you can give good reasons for: *Since there was no arguable claim for negligence, damages were not available to provide compensation.* ◇ **it is ~ that...** *It is arguable that advertisers worry rather too much about the problem of market fragmentation.* **2** not certain; that you do not accept without question SYN DEBATABLE: *The validity of this statement may be arguable.*

ar·gu·ably /ˈɑːgjuəbli; *NAmE* ˈɑːrgjuəbli/ *adv.* used when you are stating an opinion that you believe you could give reasons to support: *Asher is arguably the best medical writer of the last 100 years.* ◇ *Arguably, folk song and folk music constitute the original world music.*

argue /ˈɑːgjuː; *NAmE* ˈɑːrgjuː/ *verb* **1** [T, I] to give reasons why you think that sth is right/wrong, true/not true, etc, especially to persuade people that you are right: **~ (that) ...** *Opponents of higher education for women tried to argue that women's place was in the home.* ◇ **~ for/in favour of (doing) sth** *Morgan and Moss (1965) argued for an ecological approach that focused on the community concept.* ◇ **~ against sth** *Maxwell argues against a focus on scientific rigour in a narrow sense.* ◇ **~ sth** *In his 1940 lecture, Wilson argued the case for interpreting books in terms of their historical origins.* ◇ **it can/could be argued that...** *It can be argued that the scientific revolution began in 1643, with the publication of 'De Revolutionibus Orbium Coelestium'.* ◇ **it is possible, difficult, etc. to ~ that...** *It would be difficult to argue that states in Europe were ever more interdependent than they are today.* ◇ **as X argues...** *As Gambetta (1988) argues, trust is a means of reducing uncertainty in order that effective relationships can develop.* **2** [I] to disagree about sth: **~ (with sb) (about/over sth)** *Whilst the industry argues about the best way to sell online music, traditional CD sales continue to decline.* ◇ **~ with sb/sth** *In the context of a focus group, individuals will often argue with each other and challenge each other's views.* ◇ *It is difficult to argue with this overall analysis.* **3** [T, I] to show clearly that sth exists or is true: **~ that...** *Increasing evidence argues that climatic challenges might have shaped the rise and course of civilization in several different ways.* ◇ **~ for/against sth** *The evidence argues against this presumption.*

▸ NOUN + ARGUE **critics • authors • scholars • theorists • feminists • liberals • economists • philosophers • commentators • proponents, advocates • opponents • article, paper** *Some of Orwell's modern critics argue that he was simply wrong about the effect of technology (Huber, 1994).*

▸ ARGUE + ADVERB | ADVERB + ARGUE **persuasively, convincingly • forcefully • cogently • recently** *The philosopher John Dewey argued persuasively that the public is not just individuals added up.*

▸ ARGUE + ADVERB **strongly • at length • further • earlier • later • elsewhere • instead • above • below** *Ohmae argues further that [since] 'Information has made us all global citizens, customers' needs have globalized' (Ohmae, 1990, 1991).*

▸ ADVERB + ARGUE **famously • rightly • plausibly • successfully • reasonably • consistently • long • often • sometimes • once • explicitly** *Locke famously argued that all of our ideas originate in the impressions of external sensations upon the mind.* ◇ *It is sometimes argued that excessive price competition forces producers to cut costs.*

THESAURUS

argue ♦ **assert** ♦ **claim** ♦ **contend** ♦ **maintain** *verb*

These words can all be used to report sb's opinion.

- to argue/assert/claim/contend/maintain **that...**
- **It is** argued/asserted/claimed/contended **that...**
- **I would** argue/assert/claim/contend/maintain **that...**
- to argue/assert/maintain **a proposition/thesis**
- to argue **against/for/in favour of** an approach/a hypothesis

- **Argue** suggests that there is evidence to support a position; **assert** and **claim** are often used when no evidence is offered and/or you are reporting sb's opinion you do not agree with: *Moore (1994) argues his thesis by examining salient examples.* ◇ *It is claimed that the division of Hindu society into four castes gave stability to Indian society. However,...*
- **Maintain** is often used to defend an established point of view; **contend** is often used to put forward a position that is new or controversial: *They have consistently maintained that there is no evidence of carcinogenic hazard.* ◇ *Some researchers now contend that the cave paintings may be only 15 000 years old.*
- **Assert** and **contend** both report an opinion that is given firmly; **contend** implies that some evidence is available: *Marshall (2004) boldly asserts that public money must flow freely.* ◇ *Kupperman (2000) persuasively contends that...*

ar·gu·ment /ˈɑːgjumənt; *NAmE* ˈɑːrgjumənt/ *noun* **1** [C, U] a reason or set of reasons that sb uses to show that sth is true or correct: *Taylor makes the following argument:...* ◇ **~ for/in favour of sth** *There are strong arguments in favour of using computers for various purposes in schools.* ◇ **~ against sth** *The most persuasive argument against this idea comes from Foster (2009).* ◇ **~ that...** *The argument that improvements in knowledge are a primary source of growth is even more compelling for developing countries.* ◇ **~ about sth** *This chapter focuses on two central arguments about the effects of the end of the Cold War on international security.* ◇ **line of ~** *There are two essential problems with this line of argument.* **2** [C, U] **~ (with sb) (about/over sth)** a discussion in which two or more people disagree: *Following an argument with the local communist party, her father left the party and moved the family to Kraków.* ◇ *There remains argument about just how far this convergence in male and female values has gone.* **3** [C] **~ of a function** (*mathematics*) any of the INDEPENDENT VARIABLES that the value of a FUNCTION depends on: *Angles are the arguments of circular functions.* **4** [C] (*mathematics*) the angle formed by the line between a COMPLEX NUMBER and the ORIGIN, and the real, positive AXIS: *It is important when finding all the roots of an equation to include all possible arguments, not just the principal one.* IDM *see* SAKE

▸ ADJECTIVE + ARGUMENT **compelling, convincing, persuasive** ♦ **strong, powerful** ♦ **valid** ♦ **sound** ♦ **plausible** ♦ **cogent** ♦ **rational** ♦ **logical** ♦ **reasoned** ♦ **central, main, key** ♦ **basic** ♦ **similar** ♦ **theoretical** ♦ **philosophical** ♦ **moral** ♦ **theological** ♦ **legal** *A convincing argument can be made that the height of collectivism in Britain occurred in the late 1960s.*

▸ VERB + ARGUMENT **advance, present, put, make, deploy, adduce** ♦ **base (on)** ♦ **construct, formulate, build** ♦ **reinforce, strengthen, bolster** ♦ **counter, refute** ♦ **challenge** ♦ **undermine** ♦ **accept** ♦ **reject, dismiss** ♦ **outline** ♦ **repeat** ♦ **develop, extend** ♦ **pursue** ♦ **summarize** *Doyle based his argument on the classical liberal treatment of the subject by Immanuel Kant.*

▸ ARGUMENT + VERB **go** ♦ **run** ♦ **suggest** ♦ **assume** ♦ **imply** ♦ **seem** ♦ **fail** *As long as the diets were low in fat, one argument went, calories made little difference.*

▸ NOUN + OF + ARGUMENT **premise** ♦ **thrust** ♦ **logic** ♦ **merit** ♦ **validity** ♦ **conclusion** ♦ **implication** *The central premise of this argument is false.*

LANGUAGE BANK

Showing your position in an argument

The following words and expressions are useful when stating your own position in an argument. Some of these use *I*, *me* or *my*; others use more impersonal phrases with *it* or *there*, which are often more appropriate in academic writing.

To express degrees of certainty about your statement, see the language banks at **emphasis** and **hedge**.

- I **suggest** that...
- I **would like to suggest/propose/put forward** that...
- I **believe** that... /I **believe** X to be/have...
- In **my opinion/view**,...
- **For me**,...
- It **can be seen/noted** that...
- It **is clear/obvious** that...
- It **is/seems reasonable to suggest/conclude** that...

– ***I suggest that*** *several factors converged to strengthen this form of organization.*

– *In Tagore's case,* ***I would like to propose that*** *it is the father who plays a decisive role.*

– *I will briefly review what I* ***believe to be*** *the most sophisticated and creative attempt to model this behaviour.*

– ***In my opinion****, the interface between the two presents a serious problem.*

– *I found her argument very persuasive although there are some comparisons which,* ***for me****, did not sit easily with her central theme.*

– ***It can be seen that*** *debates about globalization provide an important context in which to approach these ideas.*

– ***It is clear that*** *societies everywhere became increasingly alike during the last decades of the twentieth century.*

– ***It is reasonable to suggest that*** *events in the French Empire played an important role in bringing about the American Civil War.*

ar·gu·men·ta·tive /ˌɑːgjuˈmentətɪv; *NAmE* ˌɑːrgjuˈmentətɪv/ *adj.* **1** using reason to make an argument: *The students were asked to write a five-paragraph argumentative essay.* **2** a person who is **argumentative** likes arguing or often starts arguing: *The patient should feel that the interviewer's response is inquiring, not argumentative or dismissive.*

arid /ˈærɪd/ *adj.* (of land or a climate) having little or no rain; very dry: *In arid regions, the main water issue concerns supply, not pollution.* ◇ *an arid environment/area/zone/climate* ■ **arid·ity** /əˈrɪdəti/ *noun* [U] *Along with the threat of increased aridity, some are predicting a major wave of extinctions in the near future.*

arise /əˈraɪz/ *verb* (**arose** /əˈrəʊz; *NAmE* əˈroʊz/, **arisen** /əˈrɪzn/) **1** [I] (of a problem, opportunity or situation) to happen and start to be noticed SYN OCCUR: *Conflict frequently arises over upbringing between parents who are separated or divorced.* ◇ *Opportunities often arise for the owners of two quite different brands to work together jointly to develop a new product.* ◇ *For investors the question arises, where and under which legal system can they bring litigation for their losses?* **2** [I] to happen as a result of a particular situation: **~ from/out of sth** *The contradiction arises from the fact that the workers (the producers) are also the potential consumers.* ◇ **~ as a result/consequence of sth** *Different outcomes and problems can arise as a consequence of the same disease.* **3** [I] (*formal*) to begin to exist or develop: *Egyptian civilization, which arose around 3200 BC, followed a trajectory similar to that of Mesopotamia.* IDM *see* OCCASION[1]

▸ NOUN + ARISE **difficulty, problem, issue** ♦ **question** ♦ **situation** ♦ **opportunity** ♦ **need** ♦ **challenge** ♦ **dispute, conflict, disagreement, tension** ♦ **duty, obligation** ♦ **liability** *Difficulties arise when research participants*

A

change their behaviour because they know they are being studied.

▸ ARISE + ADVERB **solely • mainly, primarily, largely • simply • directly** *Forces arising directly from an interaction between two bodies must always sum to zero.* | **spontaneously • naturally • independently • early • late** *Markets arise spontaneously in all cultures because people find value in trade.*

▸ ADVERB + ARISE **often, frequently, commonly • usually • never • only • probably • typically** *For some types of events, such as wars or plagues, large events often arise from small events that go wrong.* | **inevitably • naturally • immediately** *Challenges inevitably arise concerning the selection of texts to analyse.*

ar·is·toc·racy /ˌærɪˈstɒkrəsi; *NAmE* ˌærɪˈstɑːkrəsi/ *noun* (*pl.* **-ies**) [C+sing./pl. v.] (in some societies) people born in the highest social class, who have special titles SYN NOBILITY: *Paula (347–404) was a wealthy woman from the Roman aristocracy.* ◇ *The century saw the decisive shift of power from the aristocracy to the bourgeoisie.*

ar·is·to·crat /ˈærɪstəkræt; *NAmE* əˈrɪstəkræt/ *noun* a member of the aristocracy: *Toulouse-Lautrec was born in 1864 into a wealthy family of French aristocrats.*

ar·is·to·crat·ic /ˌærɪstəˈkrætɪk; *NAmE* əˌrɪstəˈkrætɪk/ *adj.* belonging to or typical of the aristocracy SYN NOBLE[1] (1): *The great aristocratic families had been replaced by a widespread class of small gentry.*

arith·met·ic[1] /əˈrɪθmətɪk/ *noun* [U] **1** the type of mathematics that deals with the use of numbers in counting and calculation: *The truths of arithmetic do not depend on the actual existence of the objects being counted.* **2** the use of numbers in counting and calculation: *We know that the brain's electrical activity is faster when we are doing mental arithmetic than when we are relaxing.*

arith·met·ic[2] /ˌærɪθˈmetɪk/ *adj.* (*mathematics*) **1 ~ progression/series** a series in which the interval between each term and the next remains CONSTANT: *Since the annual increases are the same, these numbers form an arithmetic progression or series.* ➲ *compare* GEOMETRIC (3) **2 ~ mean** = MEAN[2] (2) ➲ *compare* GEOMETRIC (4) **3** = ARITHMETICAL

arith·met·ic·al /ˌærɪθˈmetɪkl/ (*also* **arith·met·ic**) *adj.* connected with arithmetic: *the arithmetical operations of addition, subtraction, division and multiplication*

arm[1] /ɑːm; *NAmE* ɑːrm/ *noun* ➲ *see also* ARMS **1** either of the two long parts that stick out from the top of the body and connect the shoulders to the hands: *A young woman with a baby in her arms was begging from the stationary vehicles.* **2** a long narrow part of an object or a piece of machinery, especially one that moves: *A robotic arm is programmed to add oil at various time intervals after setting up the trials.* **3** [usually sing.] **~ (of sth)** a section of a large organization that deals with one particular activity: *The health sector can support other arms of government by actively assisting their policy development.* ➲ *compare* WING (4) **4 ~ (of sth)** (*medical*) any of the treatment groups in a RANDOMIZED trial of a drug or treatment: *During the study period, both the intervention and control arms of the trial experienced similar, but low, levels of exposure to incidents.*

IDM **keep sb at arm's length** to avoid having a close relationship with sb: *Unions are kept at arm's length in the modern Labour Party.* IDM *see* FOLD[1]

arm[2] /ɑːm; *NAmE* ɑːrm/ *verb* **1 ~ yourself/sb (with sth) (against sb/sth)** to provide weapons for yourself/sb in order to fight a battle or a war: *In order to be secure, states arm themselves against potential enemies.* **2 ~ yourself/sb with sth** to provide yourself/sb with information, equipment, etc. so that you/they are able to perform a task: *Corporate managers must arm themselves with long-term measures of brand performance.* ➲ *see also* ARMED

armed /ɑːmd; *NAmE* ɑːrmd/ *adj.* **1** involving the use of weapons: *He was arrested on charges of armed robbery.* ◇ **~ conflict/struggle/attack** *Whereas Gandhi never wavered from his commitment to non-violence, Mandela advocated an armed struggle.* **2** carrying a weapon, especially a gun: *Armed bands of workers and peasants were fighting heavily armed groups of the German landowners.* ◇ **~ with a gun, etc.** *The defendant had set out to commit a robbery armed with a loaded shotgun.* **3 ~ (with sth)** knowing sth or provided with sth that you need in order to help you to perform a task: *It was essential to be armed with as much biographical information as possible.* ◇ *Armed with technologies of various kinds, consumers can rewatch a film multiple times.*

the ˌarmed ˈforces (*BrE also* **the ˌarmed ˈservices**) *noun* [pl.] a country's army, navy and AIR FORCE: *They complained about the use of unnecessary force by members of the British armed forces.*

arms /ɑːmz; *NAmE* ɑːrmz/ *noun* [pl.] weapons, especially those that are used in war: *Perhaps more controversial in modern society is the right to keep and bear arms under the Second Amendment.* ◇ **+ noun** *The analysis explores ways to reduce the nuclear danger through arms control and efforts to influence policy.* ◇ *The USA and Russia began negotiating a new strategic nuclear arms reduction agreement.*

IDM **be under ˈarms** to have weapons and be ready to fight in a war: *Between 9 and 16 per cent of Roman adult males in this period were regularly under arms.* **take up arms (against sb/sth)** to prepare to fight: *In the 1880s, the farmers took up arms against high taxes and corrupt officials.* ➲ *more at* CALL[2]

army /ˈɑːmi; *NAmE* ˈɑːrmi/ *noun* (*pl.* **-ies**) **1** [C+sing./pl. v.] a large organized group of soldiers who are trained to fight on land: *The two armies finally met on October 1, 331 BC.* **2 the army** [sing.+ sing./pl. v.] the part of a country's armed forces that fights on land: *He joined the army for national service in 1949.* ◇ *Each Cossack male was required to serve in the army.* ◇ **+ noun** *At the beginning of the nineteenth century, Russia's leading officials tended to be former army officers.* **3** [C+sing./pl. v.] **~ of sb/sth** a large number of people or things, especially when they are organized in some way or involved in a particular activity: *The market research agency relies on an army of hired interviewers who carry out the interviews.*

arose *past tense of* ARISE

around[1] /əˈraʊnd/ *adv.* HELP For the special uses of **around** in phrasal verbs, look at the entries for the verbs. For example **come around** is in the phrasal verb section at **come. 1** approximately SYN ABOUT[2] (1): *The average income per person in the USA is around $46 000.* ◇ *The incubation period for most cases is around 3–10 days.* **2** in or to many places: *Lakes may be formed as a river changes course or shifts sediment around.* ◇ *The molecules are moving around at high speed.* **3** present in a place; available: *The interest in nanoscience and nanotechnology has been around for many decades.* **4** used to describe activities that have no real purpose: *The defendant was arrested after he had been seen lurking around outside a post office.* **5** (*especially NAmE*) = ROUND[2]

around[2] /əˈraʊnd/ *prep.* (*BrE also* **round**) **1** surrounding sb/sth; on each side of sth: *There is no sign of any bleeding around the wound.* ◇ *An ice shelf was beginning to form around the shore.* **2** on, to or from the other side of sb/sth: *They go to the school just around the corner.* ◇ *Several methods can be used to get around this problem.* ◇ *Lawyers found ways around the statute, however.* **3** in a circle: *Copernicus established that the earth went around the sun.* ◇ *Electrons travel around the nucleus.* **4** in or to many places in an area: *She took him all around the city.*

◇ *Email means you can communicate with people all around the world.* **5** concerning or involving sth: *The barriers to using CO_2 as a cleaning solvent have centred around two issues.* ◇ *Why is there such a debate around the subject?* ◇ *The plot hinges around the question of who will rule India once the British have been thrown out.* **6** to fit in with particular people, ideas, etc: *Some economies are organized around very long-lasting neighbourhoods and family units.* ◇ *Many Greek legends are structured around the idea of the quest for a rare or precious object or creature.*

arouse /ə'raʊz/ *verb* **1** to make sb have a particular feeling or attitude: **~ sth** *This approach has aroused much interest in recent years.* ◇ *German ambitions aroused the suspicions of both Russia and Great Britain.* ◇ **~ sth in sb** *This treatment aroused in them feelings of anger and resentment.* **2 ~ sb** to make sb feel sexually excited: *People are less likely to engage in reflective decision-making when sexually aroused.*

ar·range /ə'reɪndʒ/ *verb* **1** [T, I] to plan or organize sth in advance: **~ sth** *After the interview, a second meeting was arranged.* ◇ **~ (for sb/sth) to do sth** *Researchers arranged for different observers to attend each visit.* ◇ **~ that... | it is arranged that...** *It was arranged that they should leave the next day.* ◇ **~ with sb that.../to do sth** *He arranged with the news agencies that copyright could be suspended.* HELP An **arranged marriage** is a marriage in which the parents choose the husband or wife for their child. **2** [T] **~ sth** to put sth in a particular order; to make sth neat or attractive: *The furniture appears to have been carefully arranged for the photo shoots.* ◇ *During mathematical learning, children often arrange objects in rows or columns.* ◇ *The chapters of the Qur'an are arranged according to length, not chronology.*

ar·range·ment /ə'reɪndʒmənt/ *noun* **1** [C, usually pl.] a plan or preparation that you make so that sth can happen: **~ to do sth** *Governments will need to make financial arrangements to support a long-lived population.* ◇ **~ for (doing) sth** *Under the provisions of the Police Act 1997, new arrangements have been made for providing access to criminal records.* **2** [C, usually pl.] the way things are done or organized: *The form asks very detailed questions about children's living arrangements.* ◇ **~ for sb/sth** *There are special arrangements for children with severe learning difficulties.* **3** [C] an agreement that you make with sb that you can both accept: **~ (between A and B)** *A listing is essentially a private contractual arrangement between a public company and the stock exchange.* ◇ **~ with sb (to do sth)** *Nissan agreed an arrangement with Renault whereby the French company took a 37% stake in Nissan.* ◇ **~ that...** *There was an arrangement that he would go out to work to assist with the family finances.* **4** [C, U] the fact of a group of things being organized or placed in a particular order or position: *The seating arrangement allowed pairs of students to turn around and form groups of four.* ◇ **~ of sth** *The arrangement of atoms in this molecule has been determined by X-ray diffraction, and is shown in Fig.1.13.*

array /ə'reɪ/ *noun* **1** [usually sing.] **~ (of sth)** a group, collection or arrangement of things or people, often one that is large or impressive: *The Internet presents a bewildering array of choice to consumers.* ◇ *Computer-based retailing environments offer a wide array of products.* ◇ *a vast/broad/diverse/impressive/rich array of sth* ◇ *This light can be detected by means of large spherical mirror arrays.* **2** (*computing*) a way of organizing and storing related data in a computer memory: *The size of the array used to store the list does not have to match the length of the list exactly.* **3** (*mathematics*) a set of numbers, signs or values arranged in rows and columns: *Each element occurs exactly once in any row or column of the array.*

ar·rest[1] /ə'rest/ *verb* **1** [often passive] if the police **arrest** sb, the person is taken to a police station and kept there because the police believe they may be guilty of a crime: **~ sb** *A warrant was issued to arrest the suspect.* ◇ **~ sb for (doing) sth** *He was arrested for assaulting an officer in the execution of his duty.* **2 ~ sth** to stop a process or a development: *The question is whether the country's long economic decline can be arrested.* ◇ *Much of the research has focused on dormancy, in which insect embryos undergo a period of arrested development.*

ar·rest[2] /ə'rest/ *noun* [C, U] **1** the act of arresting sb: *It was not until 1934 that FBI agents were empowered to carry guns and make arrests.* ◇ **under ~** *He was suspended from office and placed under arrest.* **2** an act of sth stopping or being interrupted: *The patient suffered a fatal cardiac arrest.* ◇ **~ of sth** *Invasion of the root system leads to a complete arrest of root growth and ultimately to plant death.*

ar·rival /ə'raɪvl/ *noun* **1** [U, C] an act of coming or being brought to a place: *Factory masters imposed a new attitude to work, with fines for late arrival.* ◇ **~ of sb/sth** *The delayed departure or arrival of one aeroplane will affect many of the subsequent connecting flights.* ◇ **on/upon ~** *Potential participants were approached by research staff upon arrival at the clinic.* OPP DEPARTURE (1) **2** [C] a person or thing that comes to a place: *Refugees are confined to closed camps to discourage new arrivals.* ◇ **~ in...** *The sweet potato is a recent arrival in Polynesia, probably introduced directly from South America.* **3** [U] **~ of sth** the time when a new technology or idea is introduced: *The arrival of new technologies provides new opportunities for emissions reductions.*

ar·rive /ə'raɪv/ *verb* **1** [I] to get to a place, especially at the end of a journey: *Evidence suggests that the south-west monsoon arrived later than usual.* ◇ *Only about a quarter of newly arrived refugees were accepted for resettlement.* ◇ **~ at...** *After six weeks sailing across the ocean, they arrived at their destination.* ◇ **~ in...** *The majority of passengers arriving in the UK do so not for settlement but for temporary purposes.* **2** [I] (of things) to be brought to sb: *The King and Laertes are unaware of Hamlet's escape until another letter arrives from the prince.* **3** [I] (of an event or a moment) to happen or come, especially when you have been waiting for it: *The long-awaited turn in the oil market finally arrived in the third quarter of 2008.* ◇ *When the day of the march arrived, union leaders were told to moderate their position even further.*

PHR V **ar'rive at sth** to decide on or find sth, especially after discussion and thought SYN REACH[1] (1): *Different observers can arrive at different conclusions depending upon numerous factors.* ◇ *All decisions are arrived at by consensus.* ◇ *Out of the mass of such claims it is difficult to arrive at the true facts.*

arrow /'ærəʊ; *NAmE* 'æroʊ/ *noun* **1** a thin stick with a sharp point at one end, which is shot from a BOW: *No serious modern hunter would still use a bow and arrow to kill game.* **2** a mark or sign like an arrow (→), used to show direction or position: *The tariff leads to a reduction in the volume of trade, as indicated by the arrows in Figure 8.10.* ◇ **+ noun** *Use the arrow keys to position the cursor.*

art /ɑːt; *NAmE* ɑːrt/ *noun* **1** [U] the use of the imagination to express ideas or feelings, especially in painting, drawing or SCULPTURE, but also in dance, music, film, etc: *modern/contemporary/abstract art* ◇ *Chaplin's art is popular art in the best sense.* ◇ **+ noun** *Art historians and literature scholars have also confronted this issue.* ◇ *A mosaic is an ancient art form in which a picture is constructed by assembling small, differently coloured pieces of tile.* HELP **Fine art** or **fine arts** is/are forms of art, especially painting, drawing and sculpture, that are created to be beautiful rather than useful: *Kandinsky was appointed director of the new department of fine arts.* **2** [U] examples

A

of objects such as paintings, drawings or SCULPTURES: *Ancient art represents centaurs as having the upper part of a man connected to the lower part of a horse.* ◇ **+ noun** *an art exhibition/gallery* ➲ *see also* WORK OF ART **3 the arts** [pl.] art, music, theatre, literature, etc. when you think of them as a group: *State support for the arts is a highly contentious issue.* **4** [C] a type of VISUAL or performing art: *The use of models multiplied with the development of perspective in the visual arts during the Renaissance.* **5** [C, usually pl.] the subjects you can study at school or university that are not scientific, such as languages, history or literature: *She was Dean of the Faculty of Arts at the University of Wollongong, Australia.* ◇ *Foucault's analysis has achieved broad theoretical uptake throughout the arts and social sciences.* ➲ *compare* HUMANITY (4), SCIENCE (3), SOCIAL SCIENCE (2) **6** [C, U] an ability or a skill that you can develop with training and practice: *Local midwives had learned their art as apprentices to an older experienced neighbourhood midwife.* ◇ **~ of sth** *The art and science of cooking involve a large and thorough knowledge of nutritive value and of the laws of physiology and hygiene.* IDM *see* STATE[1]

arte·fact (*also* **ar·ti·fact** *especially in NAmE*) /ˈɑːtɪfækt; *NAmE* ˈɑːrtɪfækt/ *noun* **1** something that has historical or cultural importance: *Archaeological artefacts are used to date geologic strata.* ◇ *As a cultural artefact, storytelling has an ancient history.* **2** something that is created: *Opportunities to transform technological knowledge into useful artefacts vary.* **3 ~ (of sth)** something that is seen in an experiment or study that is not naturally present but occurs as a result of the method that has been followed: *The observed differences in socio-economic variables may be an artefact of the samples selected.*

ar·tery /ˈɑːtəri; *NAmE* ˈɑːrtəri/ *noun* (*pl.* **-ies**) **1** any of the tubes that carry blood from the heart to other parts of the body: *The blockage was in the arteries supplying blood to her heart and her brain.* ➲ *compare* VEIN ➲ *see also* CORONARY ARTERY **2 ~ (of sth)** a large and important road, river, railway line, etc: *The Suez Canal was perhaps the most important artery of global shipping at that time.* ■ **ar·ter·ial** /ɑːˈtɪəriəl; *NAmE* ɑːrˈtɪriəl/ *adj.* [only before noun] *Smoking is one of the most important contributing factors to arterial disease.*

art·icle /ˈɑːtɪkl; *NAmE* ˈɑːrtɪkl/ *noun* **1** a piece of writing about a particular subject in a newspaper, magazine or JOURNAL: **~ (on/about sth)** *He has written several articles on the financial system in Israel.* ◇ *The article examines the progress of US natural gas markets and their regulation.* ◇ **~ by sb (on/about sth)** *This issue also includes articles by David Bennett on shopping and the consumer unconscious.* **2** (*law*) a separate item in a legal document, agreement or contract: **(under an) ~** *His right to liberty under Article 5 of the European Convention on Human Rights had been breached.* ◇ **~ of sth** *A director may exercise the power to allot shares if he/she is authorized to do so by the company's articles of association.* **3 ~ (of sth)** (*formal*) a particular item, object or separate thing, especially one of a set SYN ITEM (1): *The consumption of choice articles of food, and frequently also of rare articles of adornment, is forbidden to the women and children.* **4** (*grammar*) the words *a* and *an* (**the indefinite article**) or *the* (**the definite article**): *It is a rule of Italian that the definite article has to agree with the noun in gender.*

IDM ˌ**article of ˈfaith** something that you believe very strongly, as if it were a religious belief: *Unrestricted cross-border flow of capital has become an article of faith for free market economists.*

▸ ADJECTIVE + ARTICLE **recent • present • original • previous • relevant • influential • seminal • published • academic, scholarly • scientific** *A recent article by Jones et al. (2000) reviewed studies of workers in the industry.* ◇ *The present article deals with mean-monthly estimates.*

▸ NOUN + ARTICLE **newspaper • news • journal • review • magazine • research** *The database comprises newspaper articles from a wide variety of newspapers.*

▸ VERB + ARTICLE **publish • write • read • review • entitle, title • submit • revise • feature • include, contain • exclude • cite • retrieve, identify** *The search retrieved 960 articles from the electronic databases.*

▸ ARTICLE + VERB **argue • explore, examine, investigate • focus on • address • demonstrate • aim, seek • conclude • appear** *The article argues that China did not see the coups as major threats to its interests.* ◇ *There is little critical appraisal of these methods and this article seeks to remedy that.*

▸ NOUN + OF + ARTICLE **aim, purpose, goal, objective • scope • focus • remainder, rest • section • series • collection • list • number • author • title • publication** *The purpose of this article is to examine the evidence more systematically.*

ar·ticu·late[1] *verb* /ɑːˈtɪkjuleɪt; *NAmE* ɑːrˈtɪkjuleɪt/ **1** [T] to express or explain your thoughts or feelings clearly in words: **~ sth** *Wessely articulated a new vision of Jewish culture.* ◇ *The international community has clearly articulated the fundamental rights and freedoms which should be guaranteed to all.* ◇ **~ sth to sb** *Social acceptance of male depression will affect the way that a man articulates his problems to his GP.* **2** [T] **~ (sth)** to speak or pronounce sth in a clear way: *When we utter a sentence we articulate one word after another.* **3** [I, T] (*technical*) to be joined to sth else by a joint, so that movement is possible; to join sth in this way: **~ (with sth)** *The femoral head is covered with a metal cap which articulates with a metal socket.* ◇ **~ sth (to sth)** *The wing is articulated to the thorax.* **4** [I] **~ (with sth)** (*formal*) to be connected with sth so that together the two parts form a whole: *The author analyses how these ethnographic findings articulate with long-standing cultural politics.*

ar·ticu·late[2] *adj.* /ɑːˈtɪkjələt; *NAmE* ɑːrˈtɪkjələt/ **1** (of a person) good at expressing ideas or feelings clearly in words: *In the summer of 1991 Clinton was only 45, handsome and articulate.* ◇ *In the post of American ambassador to the UN he was an articulate defender of Israel.* **2** (of speech or writing) clearly pronounced or expressed: *There is a large and articulate body of work regarding this subject.*

ar·ticu·la·tion /ɑːˌtɪkjuˈleɪʃn; *NAmE* ɑːrˌtɪkjuˈleɪʃn/ *noun* **1** [U, sing.] **~ (of sth)** (*formal*) the expression of an idea or a feeling in words: *The sentiments expressed in the poem seemed an eloquent articulation of national feeling.* **2** [U] **~ (of sth)** (*formal*) the act of making sounds in speech or music: *Changes in the manner of articulation of a sound to make two sounds phonetically more similar to each other are common.* **3** [C, usually sing., U] (*technical*) a joint or connection that allows movement; the state of having a joint that allows movement: *The elbow joint is a complex joint consisting of three articulations.* ◇ **~ of sth** *the articulation of the lower jaw*

ar·ti·fact (*especially NAmE*) = ARTEFACT

ar·ti·fi·cial /ˌɑːtɪˈfɪʃl; *NAmE* ˌɑːrtɪˈfɪʃl/ *adj.* **1** made or produced by humans to copy sth natural, rather than occurring naturally: *Completed in 1911, Roosevelt Dam created what was then the largest artificial lake in the world.* ◇ *artificial fertilizer/lighting/flowers* **2** created by people; not happening naturally: *Artificial selection involves humans allowing certain plants and animals to survive and breed.* ◇ *Some female monkeys reared in isolation have been impregnated by artificial insemination.* ◇ *Federal and state efforts continue to conduct policy under the artificial distinction of 'rural' and 'urban'.* ➲ *see also* ARTIFICIAL INTELLIGENCE ■ **ar·ti·fi·ci·al·ity** /ˌɑːtɪˌfɪʃiˈæləti; *NAmE* ˌɑːrtɪˌfɪʃiˈæləti/ *noun* [U] **~ (of sth)** *The play recog-*

nizes the artificiality of dramatic representation. **ar·ti·fi·cial·ly** /ˌɑːtɪˈfɪʃəli; *NAmE* ˌɑːrtɪˈfɪʃəli/ *adv.*: *Profit levels could be artificially inflated by subsidies.* ◇ *Many plant breeds, both natural and artificially created, have one or more extra sets of chromosomes.* ◇ *Surplus production is sold on world markets at artificially low prices.*

ˌartificial inˈtelligence *noun* [U] (*abbr.* **AI**) (*computing*) an area of study concerned with making computers copy intelligent human behaviour: *From a long-term perspective, the development of general artificial intelligence exceeding that of the human brain can be seen as one of the main challenges to the future of humanity.*

art·ist /ˈɑːtɪst; *NAmE* ˈɑːrtɪst/ *noun* **1** a person who creates works of art, especially paintings or drawings: *William Blake was an enormously prolific visual artist and poet.* **2** a person who performs for a profession, such as a singer, a dancer or an actor: *Umm Kulthum enjoyed success as a recording artist, making an estimated 300 recordings in her lifetime.*

art·is·tic /ɑːˈtɪstɪk; *NAmE* ɑːrˈtɪstɪk/ *adj.* **1** connected with art or artists: *The designs had significant artistic merit.* ◇ *Intellectual property law provides copyright protection for literary, musical, artistic and dramatic works.* ◇ *He replaced Eisenstein as artistic director of Mosfilm in 1944.* **2** showing a natural skill in or enjoyment of art, especially being able to paint or draw well: *Toulouse-Lautrec was born in 1864 into a family in which there was a strong tradition of artistic talent.* IDM *see* LICENCE ■ **art·is·tic·al·ly** /ɑːˈtɪstɪkli; *NAmE* ɑːrˈtɪstɪkli/ *adv.*: *During the Stalin years, the Soviet film industry was artistically limited by outside pressures.*

art·work /ˈɑːtwɜːk; *NAmE* ˈɑːrtwɜːrk/ *noun* **1** [U] photographs and pictures prepared for books, magazines, etc: *It is impossible to imagine a contemporary foreign language coursebook without numerous photographs and other kinds of artwork.* **2** [C] a work of art, especially one in a museum: *This legislation authorizes a civil action for the recovery of fine artworks that were unlawfully taken.*

as[1] /əz; *strong form* æz/ *prep.* **1** used to describe sb/sth's particular job or function: *She has a high-pressure job as a chartered accountant.* ◇ *They work as a group to uncover root causes of the conflict.* ◇ *The natural lake within this depression had been enlarged for use as a reservoir.* **2** used to describe how sb/sth is seen or considered by sb: *I value him as a colleague and count him as a friend.* ◇ *Sleep is sometimes thought of as a form of unconsciousness.* ◇ *Scores between 34 and 37 may be too small to treat as significant.* **3** used to describe sb/sth appearing to be sb/sth else: *Since 1975 she had lived and dressed as a man.* ◇ *Ravana kidnaps Sita by disguising himself as a holy man.* **4** during the time of being sth: *Seneca was brought to Rome as a child, although we know little about his early life.*

as[2] /əz; *strong form* æz/ *adv.* **1** used in comparisons to talk about the extent or degree of sth: *If there is no saving on the Internet, they are just as likely to go to a shop to make their purchase.* ◇ **as... as...** *Deflation can be just as damaging as inflation.* ◇ *Lenin embarked upon radical social change as soon as he had power.* ◇ *Breeders aimed to produce cows that made as much milk as possible every day.* **2** used to say that sth happens in the same way: *For Dickens, as for many of his contemporaries, India held a fascination.* ◇ *Nero continued to be haunted by dreams of his mother; she obsessed him in death as in life.*

as[3] /əz; *strong form* æz/ *conj.* **1** while sth else is happening: *She became distressed as she described what had happened.* ◇ *As the firm grows bigger, its unit costs will fall.* ◇ *As these marine organisms died, they formed fossil-rich beds of calcium carbonate in the shallow seas.* **2** in the way in which: *In this study, I model avian colours as they are seen by other birds.* ◇ *The essential thing, as he saw it, was that we should not forget God.* **3** used to state the reason for sth: *He prefers not to swap computer games with friends, as they return scratched.* ◇ *As he did not bother scanning older literature on his subject, he often duplicated previously known results.* ➲ language bank *at* BECAUSE **4** used to refer to a fact or to sth that you said earlier: *As everyone knows, a coal miner's job is dirty, demanding and dangerous.* ◇ *As already mentioned, mouse cells have very long telomeres.* **5** used to say that in spite of sth being true, what follows is also true SYN THOUGH[1] (1): *Strange as it seems, both the head and the deputy head appeared to find it difficult to relate to children.* ◇ *Even experienced group leaders tend to influence what the respondents say, try as they may to avoid doing so.*

IDM **as against sth** in contrast with sth: *It is predicted that by 2020, about 40% of India's population will be living in cities, as against 28% today.* **ˌas and ˈwhen** used to say that sth may happen at some time in the future, but only when sth else has happened: *Outsourcing permits organizations the opportunity to use specialist services and experts as and when required.* **as for sb/sth** used to start talking about sb/sth SYN REGARDING: *As for the OECD, its membership is no longer limited to the developed countries.* **as from.../as of...** used to show the time or date from which sth starts or is counted: *It was agreed to start the second stage of the treaty as from 1 January 2014.* ◇ *Regularly updated, this website provides (as of this writing) 1 487 links.* **as if/as though** in a way that suggests sth: *It looks as if the cost of producing fusion power will be reasonable.* ◇ *She felt as though she were a bad mother.* **ˌas it ˈis** considering the present situation; as things are: *As it is, developmental biologists have tended to focus their efforts on a relatively small number of animals.* **as to sth | as regards sth** used when you are referring to sth SYN REGARDING: *There are concerns as to costs and over-regulation.* ◇ *As regards the website itself, it is attractively and clearly presented, in the main.* ➲ *more at* WELL[1], YET[1]

as·cend /əˈsend/ *verb* [I, T] to rise; to go up; to climb up: *As the magma ascends, it cools and begins to solidify.* ◇ **~ to sth** *If humans ascend to high altitudes, they often experience high-altitude sickness.* ◇ **~ sth** (*figurative*) *She ascended the throne in 593, after her half-brother was assassinated.* OPP DESCEND

IDM **in aˌscending ˈorder** from the lowest to the highest: *The suburbs tended to be arranged in ascending order of class mobility.*

as·cent /əˈsent/ *noun* [C, usually sing., U] the act of climbing or moving up; an upward journey: *The aircraft levelled out following a rather bumpy ascent.* ◇ *Rapid ascent with breath holding can result in trauma to the diver.* OPP DESCENT (2)

as·cer·tain /ˌæsəˈteɪn; *NAmE* ˌæsərˈteɪn/ *verb* (*formal*) to find out the true or correct information about sth: **~ sth** *It will be necessary to ascertain the facts surrounding the incident.* ◇ **~ that...** *On inquiry, I ascertained that he has suffered from gastritis for three years.* ◇ **~ how/whether, etc...** *I probed deeper in order to ascertain how serious she was.* ◇ *Another way of ascertaining how customers perceive prices is by asking them.* ◇ **it is ascertained who/whether, etc...** *It must be ascertained who the beneficiaries are.* ➲ thesaurus note *at* DETERMINE ■ **as·cer·tain·able** /ˌæsəˈteɪnəbl; *NAmE* ˌæsərˈteɪnəbl/ *adj.*: *These facts are freely ascertainable from a wide number of sources.* **as·cer·tain·ment** /ˌæsəˈteɪnmənt; *NAmE* ˌæsərˈteɪnmənt/ *noun* [U, sing.] **~ (of sth)** *In breach of contract cases, first, there must be an ascertainment of the terms of the contract.*

ascribe /əˈskraɪb/ *verb*

PHR V **aˈscribe sth to sb** to consider or state that a book, work of art, etc. was produced by a particular person or belongs to a particular period SYN ATTRIBUTE[1] (2): *These scenes have not been traditionally ascribed to Shakespeare.*

A

◇ *Apart from these, there is no written legal material that can be safely ascribed to the period before 1100.* **a'scribe sth to sb/sth 1** to consider that sb/sth has or should have a particular quality: *Characteristics traditionally ascribed to males, such as aggression and discipline, are seen negatively.* **2** to consider that sth is caused by a particular thing or person SYN ATTRIBUTE¹ (1): *The decision to not participate is often ascribed to three main factors.* ■ **ascrip·tion** /ə'skrɪpʃn/ *noun* [U, C] **~ (of sth) (to sb/sth)** *This strongly supports the ascription to Sappho of the newly recovered poem.* ◇ *the ascription of moral responsibility*

ash /æʃ/ *noun* **1** [U, C] the grey or black powder that is left after sth such as wood or coal has burnt: *The eruption buried the town of Pompeii in ash.* ◇ *These soils form on volcanic ashes up to an elevation of 2 500 m.* **2 ashes** [pl.] what is left after sth has been destroyed by burning: *The town was reduced to ashes in the fighting.* ◇ (*figurative*) *Although the city rose from the ashes following the earthquake, it would never regain its former power and prestige.*

ashamed /ə'ʃeɪmd/ *adj.* [not before noun] **1 ~ (of sb/sth/yourself)** feeling SHAME or embarrassment about sb/sth or because of sth you have done: *Some patients even feel ashamed of their illness.* **2 ~ to do sth** unwilling to do sth because of SHAME or embarrassment: *She was ashamed to reveal her feelings.*

aside /ə'saɪd/ *adv.* **1** to one side; out of the way: *Teachers can take an anxious child aside and help her relax.* ◇ (*figurative*) *These wider questions will have to be put aside for now.* **2** to be used later or for a particular purpose: *Many poor communities do manage to put money aside to save for improvements.* ◇ *One week a month is set aside for committee meetings.* **3** used after nouns to say that except for one thing, sth is true: *Abstract possibility aside, however, this is not likely to happen.*

a'side from *prep.* (*especially NAmE*) = APART FROM

ask /ɑːsk; *NAmE* æsk/ *verb* **1** [I, T] to say or write sth in the form of a question, in order to get information: **~ sth** *These teachers encourage learners to ask questions.* ◇ **+ speech** *'Can any one nation,' he asked, 'have the right to prevent other nations from selling to one another?'* ◇ **~ sb + speech** *I asked him, 'What would you like to do now?'* ◇ **~ sb sth** *Some patients said they felt uncomfortable when doctors asked them questions about their personal life.* ◇ **~ (sb) (about sth)** *Respondents are frequently asked about their beliefs.* ◇ *It is important to ask about costs as well as benefits.* ◇ **~ how/where, etc...** *In logistics, it is necessary to ask how many manufacturing plants there are, and where they are located.* ◇ **~ sb why/what, etc...** *She asked him why he was crying.* **2** [T] to tell sb that you would like them to do sth or that you would like sth to happen: **~ sb to do sth** *The participants were asked to complete a survey of their attitudes towards conflict.* ◇ **~ (sb) if/what, etc...** *After class, I asked him if he could identify a quotation I had found.* ◇ **~ that...** *They were writing to ask that a police officer be sent from London to investigate the fire.* **3** [I, T] to say that you would like sb to give you sth: **~ for sth** *They were often reluctant to ask for help.* ◇ *An email was circulated to all staff asking for volunteers.* ◇ **~ sth** *Parents may ask advice about special diets and dietary supplements.* ◇ **~ sb for sth** *They decided to ask Congress for $400 million in military and economic aid.* **4** [T] to request permission to do sth: **~ sth** *Many people have asked permission to use information and pictures from the site.* ◇ **~ to do sth** *When Harriet was 16, she asked to be allowed to spend her holidays with her mother.* ◇ **~ (sb) if/whether...** *We asked if we could interview staff and students.* **5** [T] **~ sth (for sth)** to request a particular amount of money for sth that you are selling: *If a person is looking for work and is asking $20 an hour, he or she might have to look for quite a while.* **6** [T] **~ sb (to do sth)** to invite sb: *She was asked to give a paper at the conference.*

asleep /ə'sliːp/ *adj.* [not before noun] sleeping: **fall ~** *On several occasions recently, he has fallen asleep while driving.* OPP AWAKE

as·pect AWL /'æspekt/ *noun* **1** [C] a particular feature of a situation, an idea or a process; a way in which sth may be considered: **~ (of sth)** *Age is shown to have an important influence on many aspects of health.* ◇ **~ to sth** *There are two aspects to communication: verbal and non-verbal.* ◇ **~ in sth** *Branding is an important aspect in the marketing of services.* ◇ **from a... ~** *Programme effectiveness was measured from four different aspects.* **2** [C, usually sing.] **~ (of sth)** (*technical*) a particular surface or side of an object or a part of the body; the direction in which sth faces: *The muscles on the lateral aspect of the hand were affected.* ◇ *Probes were inserted into the sapwood on the north aspect of each tree.* **3** [U, C] (*grammar*) the form of a verb that shows, for example, whether the action happens once or many times, is completed or is still continuing: *Verbs are inflected for tense and aspect.* ➲ *compare* TENSE¹

▸ ADJECTIVE + ASPECT **certain, particular, specific • important, significant • key, crucial, essential • critical • fundamental • unique • interesting • relevant • positive • negative • controversial • problematic** *Language is a crucial aspect of culture.* ◇ *One negative aspect is the resulting bias in the direction of military and space expenditure.* | **practical • technical • social • cultural • political • economic • physical • emotional** *A number of technical aspects to the use of radioisotopes also pose problems.*

▸ VERB + ASPECT **cover, encompass • incorporate, include • address, consider, discuss • explore, examine, investigate, study, analyse • understand • highlight, emphasize, stress • capture • reveal • reflect • illustrate • illuminate • ignore, neglect** *This research highlighted key aspects of economic and social restructuring in Western society.*

as·pir·ation /ˌæspə'reɪʃn/ *noun* [C, usually pl., U] a strong desire to achieve a goal such as wealth or success: **~ (of sb)** *In luxury markets, the key is to position the brand so that it drives the aspirations of the wealthiest people.* ◇ **~ for sth** *Democracy reflects a human aspiration for freedom.* ◇ **~ to do sth** *Adrienne's social capital increased her chances of fulfilling her aspirations to attend college and, ultimately, law school.*

as·pire /ə'spaɪə(r)/ *verb* [I] to have a strong desire to achieve or to become sth: **~ to sth** *Those who aspired to the highest cultural status needed to gain a familiarity with Greek literature.* ◇ **~ to be/do sth** *Companies aspiring to meet the challenges of today's rapidly changing markets require a well-conceived strategy.*

as·sault¹ /ə'sɔːlt/ *noun* **1** [U, C] the crime of attacking sb physically: *These women have been victims of sexual assault.* ◇ **~ on/upon/against sb (by sb)** *Police recorded a previous assault on this particular woman by her husband.* HELP In law, **assault** is an act that threatens physical harm to sb, whether or not actual harm is done: *to commit/be charged with assault* ➲ *compare* BATTERY (3) **2** [C] (by an army, etc.) the act of attacking sb/sth SYN ATTACK¹ (1): *The castles had guns pointing out to sea to withstand enemy assaults.* ◇ **~ on/upon/against sb/sth (by sb)** *He ordered a massive assault by special forces against them.* **3** [C, usually sing., U] an act of criticizing or attacking sb/sth severely: **~ on/upon/against sb/sth** *The administration viewed the speech as an assault on their policies.* ◇ **under ~ (from sb/sth)** *Religious practice was under heavy assault from a number of quarters.*

as·sault² /ə'sɔːlt/ *verb* **~ sb** to attack sb physically: *He was convicted of assaulting a police officer in the execution of his duty.*

assay /əˈseɪ/ *noun* (*biochemistry*) a procedure for measuring the BIOCHEMICAL or IMMUNOLOGICAL activity of a sample: *All the assays were performed in duplicate.* ■ **assay** *verb* **~ sth (for sth)** *Cell contents were assayed for enzyme activity.*

as·sem·blage /əˈsemblɪdʒ/ *noun* (*technical*) a collection or group of things, animals or people: *Changes in water chemistry can have a profound effect on river species assemblages.* ◇ **~ of sth/sb** *The Cairngorm Mountains in Scotland have a rich assemblage of small-scale periglacial landforms.*

as·sem·ble AWL /əˈsembl/ *verb* **1** [I, T] to come together as a group; to bring people or things together as a group: *The Congress assembles at least once every year.* ◇ **~ sth** *They assembled a team of Irish ethnographers.* ◇ *Much can be gained by assembling data from a number of different remote sources.* **2** [T] to fit together all the separate parts of sth: **~ sth (from sth)** *The cars are assembled in the UK largely from Japanese parts.* ◇ **~ sth into sth** *The rods are assembled into carefully designed bundles which in turn are fixed in place securely within the reactor.* **3** [T] **~ sth** (*computing*) to change instructions that a human can read in an assembly language program into a code that a computer can understand and act on: *The following code is produced by assembling this program.*

as·sem·bly AWL /əˈsembli/ *noun* (*pl.* **-ies**) **1** (*also* **Assembly**) [C] a group of people who have been elected to meet together regularly and make decisions or laws for a particular region or country: *In December 1955, the constituent assembly was elected for the purpose of drafting a new constitution.* ◇ *He was briefly speaker of the National Assembly.* **2** [U, C] the meeting together of a group of people for a particular purpose; a group of people who meet together for a particular purpose: *He complained that the ban was a violation of the right to peaceful assembly.* ◇ *Fear of popular rebellion culminated in the law of 1595 prohibiting assemblies.* **3** [U] **~ (of sth)** the process of putting together the parts of sth: *My research begins with the assembly of all available data.* **4** [C] **~ (of sth)** a collection or group of things which are connected or held together in some way SYN ASSEMBLAGE: *A gas is a chaotic assembly of molecules.*

as·sert /əˈsɜːt; *NAmE* əˈsɜːrt/ *verb* **1** to state clearly and firmly that sth is true: **~ that...** *The authors assert that consumers differ from country to country.* ◇ **it is asserted that...** *It is often asserted that new technologies will equalize learning opportunities for the rich and poor.* ◇ **~ sth** *The beneficial effect of a public presence in the courts has been vigorously asserted by some senior judges.* ◇ **+ speech** *Furthermore, Clawson asserts, 'It matters not only what happened, but why it happened.'* ➲ thesaurus note *at* ARGUE **2** to make other people recognize your right or authority to do sth, by behaving firmly and confidently: **~ sth** *Other republics were asserting their independence and a break-up of the USSR seemed closer.* ◇ **~ sth over sb/sth** *The Athenian leaders arrived on the island of Melos to assert their right of conquest over the islanders.* **3 ~ yourself (as sth)** to behave in a confident and determined way so that other people pay attention to your opinions: *In the film, the gangster's whole life is an effort to assert himself as an individual.* **4 ~ itself** to start to have an effect: *The original theorists thought the need for regulation would recede as market forces asserted themselves.*

as·ser·tion /əˈsɜːʃn; *NAmE* əˈsɜːrʃn/ *noun* **1** [C] a statement saying that you strongly believe sth to be true SYN CLAIM[1] (1): *He challenged the appraisal theorists directly, making two key assertions.* **2** [U, C] the act of stating, using or claiming sth strongly: *French military assertion slowed at this prospect.* ◇ **~ of sth** *The assertion of cultural identity may be reinforced by increasing political divisions between countries.*

as·sert·ive /əˈsɜːtɪv; *NAmE* əˈsɜːrtɪv/ *adj.* (*often approving*) expressing opinions or desires strongly and with confidence, so that people take notice: *Frustration may lead to aggression or, more positively, to assertive behaviour and personal initiative.* ■ **as·sert·ive·ly** *adv.*: *Geoffrey's assertively British narrative reveals a venomous antipathy to the Saxon invaders.* **as·sert·ive·ness** *noun* [U] **~ (of sb/sth)** *This account highlights the assertiveness of Spartan women.*

as·sess AWL /əˈses/ *verb* **1** to make a judgement about the nature or quality of sb/sth: **~ sb/sth** *The patient was assessed by a team of two doctors and a social worker.* ◇ *It is by no means easy to assess the extent to which animals experience pain, distress and suffering.* ◇ **~ sth for sth** *Each month, all mounds were assessed for signs of kangaroo rat activity.* ◇ **~ sb/sth as sth** *Often parents are quick to assess such anger as just typical sibling rivalry.* ◇ **~ whether/how, etc...** *A key part of the auditor's job is to assess whether the internal controls in a business are operating properly.* ➲ language bank *at* RESEARCH[2] **2** to calculate the amount or value of sth SYN ESTIMATE[1]: **~ sth** *The objective of this review was to assess the cost-effectiveness of the different screening methods.* ◇ **~ sth at sth** *Costs were assessed at just under $5 000.* ■ **as·sess·able** AWL /əˈsesəbl; *NAmE* əˈsesəbl/ *adj.*: *Risk indicators may take many forms and the number of assessable criteria could be large.*

▸ ASSESS + NOUN **impact, effect • extent, degree • quality • effectiveness, efficacy • performance • validity • severity • reliability • significance • suitability • status • accuracy • adequacy • strength • merit • outcome • need • patient** *Respondents were asked to assess the impact this new technology is having on their lives.* ◇ *Once markets are identified, assessing customers' needs is particularly important.* | **claim • risk • damage** *There are particular difficulties in assessing this asylum claim.* | **damages** *The damages were assessed as his loss of earnings.*

▸ ADVERB + ASSESS | ASSESS + ADVERB **critically • objectively • subjectively • quantitatively • formally • carefully • systematically • independently • adequately • properly • regularly • clinically** *The company must carefully and objectively assess what its brand really means.* | **accurately** *Financial institutions are unable to accurately assess the risk of lending to small firms.*

as·sess·ment AWL /əˈsesmənt/ *noun* **1** [U, C] the act of judging or forming an opinion about sb/sth; an occasion when this is done: *Risk assessment early in pregnancy is vital to ensure high-risk women are identified.* ◇ *An environmental impact assessment must be conducted prior to the implementation of a project.* ◇ **+ noun** *A variety of assessment tools are currently used to measure a range of behaviours.* ➲ *see also* RISK ASSESSMENT, SELF-ASSESSMENT **2** [C] an opinion or a judgement about sb/sth that has been thought about very carefully SYN EVALUATION: *She was probably correct in her assessment.* ◇ **~ of sb/sth** *Consumer acceptance depends on their assessment of the brand's intrinsic features.* ◇ **~ that...** *Their assessment that future increases in lifespan are all but impossible is overly pessimistic.*

▸ ADJECTIVE + ASSESSMENT **comprehensive, thorough, full • initial, preliminary • objective • subjective • careful • accurate • detailed • rapid • overall • formal • external • specialist • critical • clinical** *Although Fairlie's judgement is harsh, it remains an essentially accurate assessment of Kennedy's first two years in office.* | **environmental • behavioural • psychological • psychiatric** *Legally, the plan must include an environmental assessment of the mining operations.*

▸ NOUN + ASSESSMENT **peer • risk • impact • quality • personality • patient** *All of the students perceived peer assessment positively.* ◇ *How should quality assessment be undertaken in a laboratory performing allergy tests?*

▸ VERB + ASSESSMENT **undertake, conduct, perform, carry out • complete • undergo • require • warrant** *The reviewing court undertook a thorough assessment of the*

A

Commission's decision. ◇ *These climatic reconstructions require the precise age assessment of each tree ring.* | **provide • offer • inform** *This paper provides an assessment of the role of the Internet within marketing strategy.*

▸ ASSESSMENT + NOUN **tool, instrument • procedure, methodology, method, protocol, technique, strategy • session • criterion • exercise • process • interview** *Interviewing generally uses fewer resources than do some other popular assessment methods.*

as·ses·sor /əˈsesə(r)/ *noun* **1 ~ (of sth)** a person who makes a judgement about the nature or quality of sb/sth: *The patient should be the prime assessor of their pain.* **2** an expert in a particular subject who is asked by a court or other official group to give advice: *The inspection process is undertaken by trained assessors.* **3** a person who judges how well sb has done in an exam, course of study, etc: *The assessor will examine the portfolio to ensure all sections have been completed.*

asset /ˈæset/ *noun* **1** a person or thing that is valuable or useful to sb/sth: *Some companies view employees as valued assets.* ◇ **~ to sb/sth** *Fear is an asset to a fighter: it makes him move faster and be quicker and more alert.* ➲ *compare* LIABILITY (3) **2** [usually pl.] a thing of value, especially property, that a person or company owns, which can be used or sold to pay debts: *40% of patients have to borrow or sell assets to meet hospital expenses.* ◇ *Most people think of their property as a home first and financial asset second.* ➲ *compare* LIABILITY (2)

as·sign AWL /əˈsaɪn/ *verb* **1** to give sb sth that they can use, or some work or a duty SYN ALLOCATE (1): **~ sth (to sb)** *She assigned tasks to different project members according to their expertise.* ◇ **~ sb sth** *Parents can assign children necessary household tasks such as cleaning or errands.* ◇ **~ sb to do sth** *Only a small number of police officers were assigned to interview more than 20 000 asylum seekers.* ◇ **~ sth for sb/sth** *Canada's Science Minister plays a key role in assigning funds for scientific research.* **2** to say that sb/sth is responsible for sth: **~ sth** *In his report, he said that it was difficult to assign responsibility for the prison escape.* ◇ **~ sth to sb/sth** *It has been difficult to assign the blame for the obesity epidemic to a single food group.* **3** to say that sth has a particular value or function, or happens at a particular time or place: **~ sth to sth** *Modern political representation assigns an important role to political parties and elections.* ◇ *There exists no rigorous scientific way of assigning a probability to the risk of a serious terrorist attack.* ◇ **~ sth sth** *Each of these eleven categories is then assigned a number.* **4** to choose sb for a particular task, position or purpose: **~ sb (to sth/as sth)** *The employer may reward a diligent worker by assigning him or her to a better shift or a more pleasant job.* ◇ **~ sb to do sth** *In this method researchers randomly assign some subjects to receive the treatment, while others receive none.* **5** [usually passive] **~ sb to sb/sth** to send a person to work or live under the authority of sb or in a particular group or place: *Prisoners should be assigned to facilities close to their home town.* **6 ~ sth to sb** (*law*) to say that your property or rights now belong to sb else: *The tenant cannot assign any interest in the property to someone else.*

as·sign·ment AWL /əˈsaɪnmənt/ *noun* **1** [C, U] a task or piece of work that sb is given to do, usually as part of their job or studies; the act of giving a task to sb: *She had failed to complete several homework assignments.* ◇ **~ of sth** *Who did what work was determined partly by markets and partly by the assignment of tasks within the family.* **2** [U] **~ (of sb/sth) (to sth)** the act of putting people or things into particular groups or categories: *The subjects' random assignment to the paper dictionary or the electronic dictionary resulted in splitting the sample into two groups.*

IDM **on (an) assignment** spending a period of time somewhere doing a particular job or task: *Helpers also learn to maintain appropriate dress and behaviour while on assignment.*

as·simi·late /əˈsɪməleɪt/ *verb* **1** [I, T] to become a part of a country or community rather than remaining in a separate group; to allow or cause people to do this: *Many individuals belonging to cultural minorities choose to assimilate.* ◇ **~ into sth** *As Chinese people assimilated into Western culture, many lost interest in their religious heritage.* ◇ **~ sb** *Earlier policies to assimilate immigrants have failed.* ◇ **be assimilated into/to sth** *Some of the invaders were assimilated into the native population.* **2** [T] **~ sth** (of the body or any biological system) to absorb or take in a substance: *The fungi contain the enzymes necessary to break down and assimilate the material.* **3** [T] **~ sth** to think deeply about sth and understand it fully, so that you can use it SYN ABSORB (4): *Participants had opportunities to reflect upon and assimilate their experiences.* ◇ *Trainees must assimilate knowledge from a range of disciplines.* **4** [T, often passive] **~ sth (into/to sth)** to accept an idea, information or activity; to make it fit into sth: *These ideas were not easily assimilated into the prevailing dogma.*

as·simi·la·tion /əˌsɪməˈleɪʃn/ *noun* [U] **1** the act or process of becoming a part of a country or community, rather than remaining in a separate group: *They do not view cultural assimilation as a prerequisite for achievement.* **2** the process by which a substance is absorbed or taken into the body or any biological system: *The chemistry of digestion and assimilation was an exciting field of study.* **3** the process by which ideas, data or activities are accepted, understood or fitted together: **~ (of sth) (into sth)** *The adoption and assimilation of a health intervention into a health system will depend on a number of factors.* ◇ **+ noun** *Data assimilation approaches have been applied in recent studies.*

as·sist AWL /əˈsɪst/ *verb* **1** [I, T] to help sb to do sth: *Peng Pai came upriver to assist.* ◇ **~ sb/sth** *The programme assists failing companies.* ◇ **~ sb/sth in/with sth** *Technology could assist clinicians with behavioural assessment.* ◇ **~ sb/sth to do sth** *Chain migration is the process whereby immigrants assist relatives to join them.* ◇ **~ sb/sth in doing sth** *The United Nations strives to assist member states in limiting conflict.* **2** [T] **~ sth** to help sth to happen more easily SYN FACILITATE: *Molecular techniques have greatly assisted the study of this phenomenon.* ◇ *This technique assists the process of linking specific bacteria with particular diseases.*

as·sist·ance AWL /əˈsɪstəns/ *noun* [U] help or support in the form of money, resources, information or practical action: *The Foundation provides humanitarian assistance.* ◇ **~ to sb/sth** *Pensions are an example of assistance to targeted groups in the community.* ◇ **~ for sb/sth** *The organization provides technical assistance and training for developing countries.* ◇ **~ in/with sth** *Mothers often needed assistance with the daily care of the child.* ◇ **~ in doing sth** *The government offered assistance in home buying.* ◇ **~ to do sth** *They provided substantial assistance to help local firms.*

as·sist·ant¹ AWL /əˈsɪstənt/ *noun* a person who helps or supports sb, usually in their job: *With the development of the welfare state, women moved into paid work as nurses, teachers and care assistants.* ◇ *a teaching/research assistant*

as·sist·ant² AWL /əˈsɪstənt/ *adj.* [only before noun] (*abbr.* **Asst**) (often in titles) having a rank below a senior person and helping them in their work: *an assistant principal/professor/teacher/manager* ◇ *Assistant Attorney General William Weld*

as·so·ci·ate¹ /əˈsəʊʃieɪt; əˈsəʊsieɪt; NAmE əˈsoʊʃieɪt; əˈsoʊsieɪt/ *verb* **1** [T] to make a connection between people or things in your mind SYN CONNECT (2), RELATE (1), LINK[1] (3): **~ sb/sth with sb/sth** *The animal learns to associate a reward with a particular behaviour.* ◇ *The firm's reputation for quality is associated in the public mind with its trademarks.* ◇ *living in rural areas was significantly associated with lower likelihood of reporting mental health problems* ◇ **~ sb/sth** *The police were able to associate the two events.* OPP DISSOCIATE (1) **2** [I] **~ with sb** to spend time with sb, especially sb that others do not approve of: *They should be discouraged from associating with other drug users.* ➲ *compare* MIX[1] **3** [T] **~ yourself with sth** to show that you support or agree with sth: *Turing never fully associated himself with this idea.* OPP DISSOCIATE (2)

as·so·ci·ate² /əˈsəʊʃiət; *NAmE* əˈsoʊʃiət/ *noun* **1** a person that you work with, do business with or spend a lot of time with: *Some of his closest associates wondered about the president's mental stability.* ◇ *In general conversation there are different ways in which we speak to business associates and close friends.* **2** (*also* **Associate**) **~ (of sth)** an associate member of an organization: *He is a foreign associate of the National Academy of Science.*

as·so·ci·ate³ /əˈsəʊʃiət; əˈsəʊsiət; *NAmE* əˈsoʊʃiət; əˈsoʊsiət/ *adj.* [only before noun] **1** (often in titles) of a lower rank; having fewer rights in a particular profession or organization: *He is an associate professor in the Department of Technology.* ◇ *Poland had been accepted as an associate member of the EU.* **2** joined or connected with a profession or an organization: *Associate professionals (doctors, teachers, nurses, etc.) may be able to fulfil the social work role just as effectively.*

as·so·ci·ated /əˈsəʊʃieɪtɪd; əˈsəʊsieɪtɪd; *NAmE* əˈsoʊʃieɪtɪd; əˈsoʊsieɪtɪd/ *adj.* **1** if one thing is **associated with** another, the two things are connected because they happen together or one thing causes the other SYN CONNECTED, RELATED (1): *The opportunities must be balanced against the associated costs and risks.* ◇ **~ with sth** *This Marxist approach is closely associated with the work of David Harvey.* ◇ *There are ethical problems associated with such research.* **2** if a person is **associated with** a person, organization or idea, they support it: *He was subsequently revealed to be associated with the human rights group Amnesty International.* **3** (of a company) connected or joined with another company or companies: *Ampol Ltd and its associated company 'Bulkships' held 55% of the shares.*

▸ ASSOCIATED + NOUN **cost • risk • problem • factor • issue • symptom • feature** *Producers are being urged to conserve energy resources and also try to reduce the associated problem of pollution.*

▸ ADVERB + ASSOCIATED **closely, strongly, intimately • significantly • commonly, frequently • generally • usually, typically, normally • independently • directly • positively • negatively, inversely • traditionally • consistently** *Living in rural areas was significantly associated with lower likelihood of reporting mental health problems.* ◇ *Parental reading practices are positively associated with children's cognitive development.*

as·so·ci·ation /əˌsəʊʃiˈeɪʃn; əˌsəʊsiˈeɪʃn; *NAmE* əˌsoʊʃiˈeɪʃn; əˌsoʊsiˈeɪʃn/ *noun* **1** [C] a connection between things where one is caused by the other: **~ with sth** *Chromosome abnormalities show a strong association with cancer.* ◇ *Maternal education had significant associations with child health.* ◇ **~ between A and B** *A causal association between TV and body weight was first reported in 1985.* ◇ **~ of A with/and B** *Many studies report an inverse association of birthweight with adult cardiovascular disease.* **2** [C, usually pl.] an idea or a memory that is suggested by sb/sth; a mental connection between ideas: *Paleness was found to carry negative associations.* ◇ **~ with sth** *Women's cultural associations with the body and materiality are obstacles to their spiritual authority.* ◇ **~ between A and B** *The idea of sponsorship is that the target audience makes positive associations between an event and the sponsor.* **3** [C, U] a connection or relationship between people or organizations: **~ with sb/sth** *The author developed his fictional style through a close association with Joseph Conrad.* ◇ **in ~ with sb/sth** *Twiggy's fame came in association with the miniskirts and small dresses of the Mod culture.* ◇ **~ between A and B** *The chapter examines the associations between age and health.* **4** [C+sing./pl. v.] (*abbr.* **Assoc.**) an official group of people who have joined together for a particular purpose: *Party leaders encouraged employers to form associations.* ◇ *the National Association of Drama Teachers*

▸ ADJECTIVE + ASSOCIATION **strong • close • significant • clear • weak, loose • direct • indirect • positive • negative, inverse • causal • independent • statistical • genetic** *Some studies have observed a direct association between supervisor support and work ability.* | **national • international • local • professional • voluntary** *Many non-profits encourage their staff to join the relevant professional association.*

▸ NOUN + ASSOCIATION **trade • business • industry • housing • neighbourhood** *Very often, formal trade associations are developed to represent the interests of a whole industry.*

▸ VERB + ASSOCIATION **find, identify, detect • show, demonstrate, reveal, indicate • examine, investigate, explore, test, analyse • assess, evaluate • explain • report • observe, see • suggest** *Several studies have examined the association of work-related factors and depressive disorders.*

as·so·cia·tive /əˈsəʊʃiətɪv; *NAmE* əˈsoʊʃiətɪv/ *adj.* **1** connected with the association of ideas or things: *These words would have associative links in the mental lexicon.* **2** (*mathematics*) giving the same result no matter what order the parts of a calculation are done, for example ($a \times b) \times c = a \times (b \times c$): *The AND and OR operators are associative so that the order in which sub-expressions are evaluated does not matter.*

as·sume AWL /əˈsjuːm; *NAmE* əˈsuːm/ *verb* **1** to think or accept that sth is true but without having proof of it: **~ sth** *The alternative model assumes the existence of an 'oscillator' within the central nervous system.* ◇ **~ (that)...** *We assume that ownership of a commodity includes the right to offer it as a gift.* ◇ *It is reasonable to assume that the problem is caused by a combinatorial process.* ◇ **it is assumed (that)...** *It is assumed that levels of employment in both regions are the same.* ◇ **be assumed to be/have sth** *In Newtonian mechanics, forces are assumed to be in equilibrium.* **2 ~ sth** to begin to have a particular quality, appearance or importance SYN TAKE ON STH: *Under strong pressures, the particles often assumed an eddying motion.* ◇ *This disease will assume increasing significance as the population ages.* **3 ~ sth** to take or begin to have power or responsibility SYN TAKE (14): *These situations can only be addressed satisfactorily if adults assume responsibility for the health of their children.* ◇ *Zhao Ziyang's associates assumed positions of power.*

▸ ASSUME + NOUN **significance, importance • role • form** *Because treatment of the disease is so limited, primary prevention has asssumed great importance.* ◇ *This area of research is assuming a prominent role in molecular biology.* | **responsibility • position, role** *The king assumed responsibility for the maintenance of justice and peace.*

▸ NOUN + ASSUMES (THAT...) **model • theory • approach • argument** *The model assumes that each market is investigated before the local marketing strategy is determined.*

▸ ADVERB + ASSUME **implicitly • simply • generally** *We implicitly assumed that the rental rate of capital was the same in the two sectors.*

▸ ADJECTIVE + TO ASSUME **reasonable, safe • wrong** *It is safe to assume that the individual household was equivalent to a family grouping.*

A

▸ PHRASES **(no) reason to assume that...** *There is no a priori reason to assume that vaccine-adapted variants will necessarily be less virulent.*

as·sumed AWL /əˈsjuːmd; *NAmE* əˈsuːmd/ *adj.* [only before noun] that you suppose to be true or to exist: *We started wth assumed initial values and readjusted them until correct present-day values were obtained.*

as·sum·ing AWL /əˈsjuːmɪŋ; *NAmE* əˈsuːmɪŋ/ *conj.* **~ (that)...** used to suppose that sth is true so that you can talk about what the results might be: *These effects will persist for the lifespan of the reservoir, assuming average sediment input remains at present levels.* ◇ *Assuming that bonds are wealth, this study compares three different methods of financing government expenditure:...*

as·sump·tion AWL /əˈsʌmpʃn/ *noun* **1** [C] a belief or feeling that sth is true or that sth will happen, although there is no proof: *Ethnographic studies strongly suggest that this assumption is false.* ◇ **~ of sth** *The explanation for this result lies in the assumption of diminishing returns to capital accumulation.* ◇ **~ about sth** *The study challenges common assumptions about free markets.* ◇ **~ behind sth** *Some historians have questioned the assumptions behind these labels.* ◇ **~ that...** *Democracy is based on the assumption that all citizens participate equally in political affairs.* ◇ **under the ~ that...** *Information and communications technologies are designed under the assumption that they will be mainly used in workplace scenarios.* ◇ **contrary to ~** *Contrary to traditional assumptions, the central role of contract in employment law is a comparatively recent phenomenon.* **2** [U, sing.] **~ of sth** the act of taking or beginning to have power or responsibility: *A truce was followed by the Bolshevik assumption of power.*

▸ ADJECTIVE + ASSUMPTION **implicit, underlying, tacit • basic, fundamental • key, core • common • traditional • initial • additional, further • reasonable, realistic • plausible • false, mistaken • questionable • unrealistic • a priori • normative • theoretical** *The underlying assumption is that markets are competitive.* ◇ *This may be a reasonable assumption but it is largely untested.*

▸ VERB + ASSUMPTION **make • question, challenge • undermine • violate • reject • accept • test • satisfy • support • share • relax • be based on • rest on, rely on** *The method we used makes no a priori assumption about relationships among species.* ◇ *This appraisal may be unrealistic and based on false assumptions.*

as·sur·ance AWL /əˈʃʊərəns; əˈʃɔːrəns; *NAmE* əˈʃʊrəns/ *noun* [C, U] a statement that sth will certainly be true or will certainly happen, particularly when there has been doubt about it; the act of giving such a statement SYN GUARANTEE[1] (1), PROMISE[1] (1): *His assurances failed to satisfy the Unionists.* ◇ **~ that...** *Brands provide assurance that an organization is worthy of trust.* ◇ **~ of sth** *He had gone to Nanjing under assurance of safe conduct.*

as·sure AWL /əˈʃʊə(r); əʃɔː(r); *NAmE* əˈʃʊr/ *verb* **1** to tell sb that sth is definitely true or is definitely going to happen, especially when they have doubts about it: **~ sb (of sth)** *The respondents were assured of confidentiality.* ◇ **~ sb (that)...** *Regulations were introduced to assure consumers that food is safe.* **2** to make sth certain to happen; to make sb/sth certain to get sth: **~ sth** *It is difficult to assure quality if grower, shipper and distributor are separate concerns.* ◇ **~ sb sth** *Companies may be assured a more prominent voice when standards are set by non-governmental bodies.* **3** to make yourself certain about sth: **~ yourself of sth** *Some shoppers assure themselves of the quality of a product by visiting a shop, before going online to get the best deal.* ◇ **~ yourself that...** *Family businesses need to assure themselves that they can attract directors and retain control.*

as·sured AWL /əˈʃʊəd; əˈʃɔːd; *NAmE* əˈʃʊrd/ *adj.* **1** certain to happen: *At this point Napoleon's success seemed assured.* **2 ~ of sth** (of a person) certain to get sth: *Investors, assured of dividends, were encouraged to put their money into railways.* **3** showing confidence in yourself and your abilities: *He gave an assured performance in the television debates.*

asthma /ˈæsmə; *NAmE* ˈæzmə/ *noun* [U] a medical condition of the chest that makes breathing difficult: **+ noun** *He had a severe asthma attack.*

astro·nom·ic·al /ˌæstrəˈnɒmɪkl; *NAmE* ˌæstrəˈnɑːmɪkl/ *adj.* connected with astronomy: *Astronomical observations can be used to measure the rate of cosmic expansion.* ■ **astro·nom·ic·al·ly** /ˌæstrəˈnɒmɪkli; *NAmE* ˌæstrəˈnɑːmɪkli/ *adv.*: *Astronomically driven changes in the intensity of the seasons might periodically trigger climate change.*

as·tron·omy /əˈstrɒnəmi; *NAmE* əˈstrɑːnəmi/ *noun* [U] the scientific study of the sun, moon, stars, planets, etc: *This method of distance estimation is widely used in astronomy, e.g. to estimate the distance of distant galaxies.*

asy·lum /əˈsaɪləm/ (*also* **poˌlitical aˈsylum**) *noun* [U] protection that a government gives to people who have left their own country, usually because they were in danger for political reasons: *They claimed asylum in the UK having travelled via Germany* ◇ *Of the 36 207 persons seeking asylum in Sweden, 18 414 were given residence permits.* ◇ **+ noun** *Although they feared persecution for their religious beliefs, their asylum claims failed.*

aˈsylum seeker *noun* a person who has been forced to leave their own country because they are in danger and who arrives in another country asking to be allowed to stay there: *Distinctions are frequently blurred between asylum seekers, economic migrants and illegal immigrants.*

asym·met·ric /ˌeɪsɪˈmetrɪk/ (*also* **asym·met·ric·al** /ˌeɪsɪˈmetrɪkl/) *adj.* **1** having two sides or parts that are not the same in size or shape: *The Earth has an asymmetric distribution of land masses, with virtually all located in or near the Northern Hemisphere.* OPP SYMMETRICAL **2** (*technical*) not equal, for example in the way each side or part behaves: *Though rich and poor countries can both gain from coordination, the relationship is decidedly asymmetric.* ■ **asym·met·ric·al·ly** /ˌeɪsɪˈmetrɪkli/ *adv.*: *A number of writers have argued that rights and duties are still asymmetrically distributed between the sexes (Walby, 1992, 1994; Yuval-Davis, 1993).*

asym·met·ry /ˌeɪˈsɪmətri/ *noun* (*pl.* **-ies**) [C, U] lack of EQUALITY or balance between parts or aspects of sth; lack of SYMMETRY: **~ between A and B** *There was an asymmetry between the right and left ears.* ◇ **~ (of sth)** *There are crucial asymmetries of power in the British political system.* ◇ *The global system is marked by great asymmetry: the most important goods are controlled by groups in a relatively small number of countries.*

asymp·tom·at·ic /ˌeɪsɪmptəˈmætɪk/ *adj.* (*medical*) (of a person or an illness) having or showing no SYMPTOMS: *Patients may be asymptomatic for years.* ◇ *A screening test may aim to detect an asymptomatic disease or a tumour.*

at /ət; *strong form* æt/ *prep.* HELP **At** is used in many idioms and phrasal verbs which are covered elsewhere in this dictionary, e.g. **at risk** is at the entry for **risk** *noun.* **1** used to say where sth/sb is or where sth happens: *Radar is used to detect aircraft, track weather patterns and control flight traffic at airports.* ◇ *Michels was the main speaker at the meeting.* ◇ *Volcanic hazards and risks at Merapi are among the highest in the world.* ◇ *Most people would choose to die at home.* **2** used to say where sb works or studies: *She is currently professor of philosophy at the University of Houston.* ◇ *He taught at Princeton from 1974 to 1981.* ◇ *He worked as a full-time assistant at the hospital.* **3** used to say when sth happens: *This was the situation at the midpoint of the twentieth century.* ◇ *It was noticed that* *certain forms occurred at regular intervals.* ◇ *At present, there is a serious problem of misuse of phones.* ◇ *Holidays were usually restricted to just three days a year at Christmas, Easter and Whitsun.* **4** used to show a rate, speed, level, etc: *The earth's ozone layer continues to disintegrate at an alarming rate.* ◇ *It oscillated at 60 cycles per minute.* ◇ *It will dissolve at room temperature.* **5** used to state the age at which sb does sth: *He entered university at the age of 18.* ◇ *The prevalence of obesity was highest at 12 years of age among boys.* **6** used to state the distance away from sth: *Birds were observed at a distance of 10–15 m with a telescope.* **7** in the direction of or towards sb/sth: *The defendant threw a stone at a group of people.* **8** used to show the situation sb/sth is in, what sb is doing or what is happening: *By late July, the two countries were at war.* ◇ *He began to feel more at ease.* ◇ *Juveniles are at a disadvantage in comparison with adult fish.* **9** used with adjectives to show how well sb/sth does sth: *What is the organization good at?* ◇ *The kidneys are less efficient at retaining potassium than sodium.* **10** used with adjectives to show the cause of sth: *The company became agitated at the delay.* ◇ *I was surprised at the results of the test.* **11** used to express the aim of an action or plan: *He made two failed attempts at poisoning the old man.* ◇ *They introduced a number of policies aimed at reducing the deficit.*

ate *past tense of* EAT

at·mos·phere /ˈætməsfɪə(r); *NAmE* ˈætməsfɪr/ *noun* **1 the atmosphere** [sing.] the mixture of gases that surrounds the earth: *Large amounts of nitrogen enter the atmosphere from the burning of fossil fuels.* ◇ *Future monitoring systems also have to consider pollution in the upper atmosphere and issues of global warming.* **2** [C] a mixture of gases that surrounds another planet or star: *The outer planets have extremely dense atmospheres made up mostly of hydrogen and helium.* **3** [C] the air in a room; the air around a place: *The patient should avoid smoky atmospheres as these damage the throat.* ◇ *Air pollutants emitted into the urban atmosphere can reach levels harmful to public health.* **4** [C, usually sing., U] the feeling or mood that exists in a particular place or situation; a feeling between two people or in a group of people: *At the end of the war there was a more relaxed atmosphere, which Russians hoped would continue.* ◇ *It is common to use background music to create atmosphere in a scene.* ◇ **~ of sth** *Rapidly shifting balances of military power may create an atmosphere of distrust.* ◇ *He found himself drawn to the intense literary and intellectual atmosphere of the writers' salons.* **5** (*abbr.* **atm**) [C] (*physics*) a unit of measurement of pressure, equal to the mean pressure at sea level: *The total pressure is 0.1 atmospheres.*

at·mos·pher·ic /ˌætməsˈferɪk/ *adj.* [only before noun] connected with or found in the earth's atmosphere: *The level of atmospheric CO_2 rose to high values during the early Triassic.* ◇ *At high altitude, the atmospheric partial pressure of oxygen is lower.*

atom /ˈætəm/ *noun* the smallest PARTICLE of a chemical element that can exist: *All of these molecules contain carbon atoms and are therefore called organic compounds.*

atom·ic /əˈtɒmɪk; *NAmE* əˈtɑːmɪk/ *adj.* [usually before noun] **1** connected with atoms or an atom: *The atomic nucleus contains most of the mass of the atom in the form of protons and neutrons.* **2** connected with or using the energy that is produced when atoms are split: *In August 1949, the Soviet Union successfully tested an atomic bomb.* **3** (*chemistry*) (of a substance) consisting of individual atoms rather than MOLECULES: *The spectrum of atomic helium is more complicated than that of atomic hydrogen.*

aˌtomic ˈnumber *noun* (*chemistry*) the number of PROTONS in the NUCLEUS of an atom, which is characteristic of a chemical element. Elements are placed in the PERIODIC TABLE according to their atomic numbers: *During radioactive decay, the atomic number changes as new elements are formed.*

ˌat-ˈrisk *adj.* [only before noun] (of a person or group) in danger of being attacked or hurt, or of getting a particular disease: *A vaccination is available for at-risk individuals.*

at·tach AWL /əˈtætʃ/ *verb* **1** [T, I] to join one thing to another; to be joined to sth; to join onto sth else: **~ sth to sth** *We attached weights to the bridge to dampen the vertical motion.* ◇ **be attached (to sth)** *In diamond, each carbon atom is attached to four other carbon atoms.* ◇ *Datasets are attached as an appendix.* ◇ **~ to sth** *Viruses enter cells by attaching to receptors.* ◇ **~ itself to sth** *Organisms that attach themselves to the river bed in rapidly flowing areas are safe from many predators.* **2** [T] **~ importance/significance/value/weight/meaning to sth** to believe that sth is important or worth thinking about: *The new regime attached importance to political as well as economic reform.* ◇ *It is arguble that insufficient weight was attached to these considerations.* **3** [I, T] to be connected with sb/sth; to connect sth to sth: **~ to sb/sth** *Preferential rights attach to preference shares.* ◇ **(be) attached to sth** *The stigma attached to divorce has eroded.* ◇ **~ yourself to sb/sth** *Women's movements had to attach themselves to existing political parties and convert them to their cause.*

at·tached AWL /əˈtætʃt/ *adj.* **1** joined or connected to sth: *Please take just 12 minutes to complete the attached questionnaire.* ◇ **~ to sth** *A lightning rod is a pointed metal rod attached to the roof of a building.* **2** [not before noun] **~ to sth** working for or forming part of an organization: *Phil is a medical student attached to the children's ward.* ◇ *Workers are attached to a team rather than a specific job.* **3 ~ to sb/sth** full of affection for sb/sth; considering sth to be part of your culture: *He did not feel very attached to his stepfather.* ◇ *They were told to be wary of becoming too attached to favourite methods.*

at·tach·ment AWL /əˈtætʃmənt/ *noun* **1** [C, U] **~ (to sth)** a strong feeling of affection for sb/sth: *The term 'homeland' suggests a strong emotional attachment to a place.* ◇ *Secure attachment formed in the first year of life permits the infant to explore from a base of safety.* **2** [U, sing.] **~ to sth** belief in and support for an idea or a set of values: *Frank had a deep attachment to the philosophy of Heidegger.* **3** [U] the act of joining one thing to another: **~ to sth** *Painful feeding may be the result of incorrect attachment to the breast.* ◇ **~ of A to B** *The attachment of an electron to an anion is invariably endothermic.* **4** [C] a document that you send to sb using email: *Files were sent backwards and forwards as email attachments.*

at·tack¹ /əˈtæk/ *noun* **1** [C, U] an act of trying to kill or injure the enemy in a war, using weapons such as guns and bombs: *Aircraft had flown low over villages to warn civilians of an imminent attack.* ◇ **~ on/against sb** *Japan launched an attack on Pearl Harbor.* ◇ **under ~** *The Roman Empire was under attack on all sides.* **2** [C] an act of using violence to try to hurt or kill sb: *He had killed a stranger in a vicious unprovoked attack.* ◇ *The terrorist attacks of September 11 also affected the entire global aviation industry.* **3** [C, U] strong criticism of sb/sth in speech or writing: *It is not a personal attack.* ◇ **~ on/against sb/sth** *Murdoch launched a scathing attack on the BBC.* ◇ **under ~** *The policy came under attack in Congress from time to time.* **4** [C] **~ (on sth)** an action that you take to try to stop or change sth that you feel is bad: *The debate shifted to the role of adult education and training in the attack on unemployment.* **5** [C] a sudden, short period of illness, usually severe, especially an illness that you have often: *a panic/an asthma attack* ◇ **~ of sth** *He has had recurrent attacks of bronchitis over 6 months.* ➲ *see also*

A

HEART ATTACK **6** [U, C] the action of sth such as a disease, insects or the weather that causes damage to sth: *Chemical fungicides are very effective at protecting plants from fungal attack.* ◇ **~ by sth** *He studied the response of cells to attacks by the leukaemia virus.*

at·tack² /əˈtæk/ *verb* **1** [I, T] to use weapons, such as guns and bombs against an enemy in a war, etc: *When Germany did attack, Finland would be Hitler's ally.* ◇ **~ sb/sth** *They sent bombers to attack military targets.* **2** [I, T, often passive] to use violence to try to hurt or kill sb: *When aggressive tendencies exceed fearful tendencies, an individual is likely to attack.* ◇ **~ sb** *She was attacked and robbed at knifepoint.* ◇ **~ sth** *Females moved before attacking prey significantly more often than males.* **3** [T] to criticize sb/sth severely: **~ sb/sth** *Those views have been attacked by neo-Marxism.* ◇ **~ sb/sth for (doing) sth** *A politician may be attacked for being ideological.* **4** [T] **~ sth** to have a harmful effect on sth: *When a fungus attacks a plant it must gain access to the interior of the plant.* ◇ *The fractured rock is first attacked by weathering.* **5** [T] **~ sth** to deal with sth with a lot of energy and determination: *Relatively little research has attacked this question.* ◇ *It offered a way to attack poverty with the lowest possible expenditure.*

at·tack·er /əˈtækə(r)/ *noun* a person who attacks sb/sth: *The attackers did not succeed in capturing the city.*

at·tain AWL /əˈteɪn/ *verb* **1 ~ sth** to succeed in achieving sth, usually after a lot of effort: *All the students attained the grades necessary to attend college.* ◇ *They sought to attain these goals through diplomacy rather than war.* **2 ~ sth** to reach a particular age, size or level: *Civil partners must have attained the age of sixteen years.* ◇ *Enormous sizes can be attained by granite boulders which have been moved by glaciers.* ◇ *The country has attained a high level of economic development.*

▸ ATTAIN + NOUN **objective, goal • grade • rank • status • freedom • equilibrium** *States may better attain their objectives if they work together with other countries.* | **age • size • height • thickness • speed • level** *Sugar cane can attain a height of six feet.*

▸ ADVERB + ATTAIN **never • eventually** *Complete self-sufficiency in shipbuilding was never attained.* ◇ *The Ottawa people eventually attained a population of approximately 1 200 people.*

at·tain·able AWL /əˈteɪnəbl/ *adj.* that you can achieve SYN ACHIEVABLE: *Specific and attainable goals should be set.* ◇ *To be effective, quotas, like goals, should be specific, measurable, and realistically attainable.*

at·tain·ment AWL /əˈteɪnmənt/ *noun* **1** [C, usually pl.] something that you have achieved, especially a qualification or skill: *The scores predicted final educational attainments at school exit.* ◇ **~ of sb/sth** *Competences are a method of detailing the attainments of the whole workforce.* **2** [U] the fact of achieving sth, usually after a lot of effort: *Low family income is strongly associated with poorer educational attainment in children (Ely et al., 1999).*

at·tempt¹ /əˈtempt/ *noun* **1** [C, U] an act of trying to do sth difficult, often with no success: **~ to do sth** *The measures Howard pursued can be seen as an attempt to restore the image of the party.* ◇ *Rats make desperate attempts to climb out when they are put in water.* ◇ **~ by sb to do sth** *There have been attempts by recent governments to push public health up the agenda.* ◇ **in an ~ to do sth** *In an attempt to provide further clarification, I have provided a description of each of these categories.* ◇ **~ at (doing) sth** *In spite of Baroody's attempts at persuasion, delegates voted against his amendment.* ◇ **suicide ~** *The patient was admitted to an inpatient psychiatric treatment unit following a suicide attempt.* **2** [C] an act of trying to kill sb: *Another assassination attempt prompted Bismarck to dissolve the Reichstag and hold fresh elections.* ◇ **~ on sb's life** *He had survived an attempt on his life.*

▸ ADJECTIVE + ATTEMPT **failed, unsuccessful • successful • deliberate, conscious • desperate • concerted • futile • misguided • ambitious • systematic • serious • early, initial • recent • previous • further • subsequent** *After five failed attempts, Chien-chen reached Japan.* ◇ *Early attempts to study culture and personality in cultural anthropology have tried to describe national characters (Barnouw, 1963).*

▸ VERB + ATTEMPT **make • represent, constitute • resist • undermine • abandon • reject • lead to** *These procedures represent a very good attempt to generate a varied sample.* ◇ *These financial pressures led to attempts to restructure public services.*

at·tempt² /əˈtempt/ *verb* to try to do or provide sth, especially sth difficult: **~ to do sth** *Numerous scholars have attempted to explain how states are created.* ◇ **~ sth** *She attempted suicide after being mocked by her schoolmates.* ◇ *To attempt an answer it is necessary to consider a range of issues.* ➲ language bank *at* PURPOSE

at·tempted /əˈtemptɪd/ *adj.* [only before noun] (of a crime, etc.) that sb has tried to do but without success: *He was charged with the attempted murder of his wife.* ◇ *The attempted coup of August 1991 was aimed at putting a stop to Gorbachev's reforms.*

at·tend /əˈtend/ *verb* **1** [I, T] to be present at an event: *The accommodation would not hold all those who wished to attend.* ◇ **~ sth** *Parents spend a lot of time attending meetings at the school.* **2** [I, T] to go regularly to a place: *She was enrolled in the class, but never attended.* ◇ **~ sth** *None of his family had attended college or held white-collar jobs.* ◇ **~ (sth) for sth** *She will have to attend a clinic regularly for blood tests.* **3** [I] (*formal*) to pay attention to sth: *Even if everyone attends closely, some will not catch the relevant information.* ◇ **~ to sb/sth** *If you do not have athlete's foot, you will not attend to advertising for an athlete's foot remedy.* **4** [T] **~ sth** (*formal*) to happen at the same time as, or as a result of, sth: *There is substantial interest in the democratization that has attended this process.* ◇ *The smallpox virus was attended by a high mortality rate.* **5** [T] **~ sb** to be with sb and help them: *The birthing mother is usually attended by midwives.*

PHR V **atˈtend to sb/sth** to deal with sb/sth; to take care of sb/sth: *The theory assumes that the leader succeeds by attending to subordinates' needs.* ◇ *To go to work, to attend to children, to look after the home, was a heavy workload.*

at·tend·ance /əˈtendəns/ *noun* [U, C] **1** the act of being present at or going regularly to a place or event: *Homelessness is a significant barrier to school attendance for many children.* ◇ *Many women reported the need for repeated attendances before their problem was accepted as genuine.* ◇ **~ at sth** *Attendance at professional development workshops is to be recommended.* ◇ **~ rate** *We started by examining student attendance rates.* **2 ~ (at sth)** the number of people present at an organized event: *The average weekly attendance at movies plummeted.* ◇ *Manchester United has been able to attract higher attendances to its fixtures than its rivals.*

IDM **in atˈtendance** present somewhere, especially at a special event or to help sb if necessary: *There were between five hundred and six hundred bishops in attendance.* ◇ *He took the precaution of having a doctor in attendance.*

at·tend·ant¹ /əˈtendənt/ *noun* **1** a person whose job is to serve or help people in a public place: *The defendants had attempted to rob an attendant at a petrol station.* ◇ *The pilot called the flight attendant into the cabin.* **2** a person who takes care of an important or sick person: *The Queen's attendants kept her at a distance from the public.* ◇ *Traditional birth attendants help African women deliver their babies.*

at·tend·ant² /əˈtendənt/ *adj.* closely connected with sth that has just been mentioned SYN ASSOCIATED (1): *Patients must understand any proposed medical treatment and its attendant risks.* ◇ **~ on/upon sth** *The Exhibition ignored the social problems attendant upon industrialization.*

at·ten·tion /əˈtenʃn/ *noun* **1** [U] the act of listening to, looking at or thinking about sth/sb carefully; interest that people show in sb/sth: **~ (of sb/sth)** *Monkeys will distract the attention of others in order to snatch food.* ◇ *Nothing escaped their attention.* ◇ *International trade organizations receive a great deal of media attention whenever they hold a large meeting.* ◇ **pay ~ (to sth)** *Some children have difficulty paying attention in school.* ◇ *Almost no attention has been paid to the role of parental influence on these students' academic outcomes.* ◇ **draw ~ to sth** *This finding draws attention to the need for understanding past climatic conditions in order to interpret current ecosystems.* ◇ **turn your ~ to sth** *Economists have turned their attention to the problem of inequality in economic behaviour.* ◇ **focus of ~** *The focus of attention has been the use of child labour by sub-contractors producing their products in overseas plant.* ◇ **centre of ~** *These cells have been the centre of attention in recent studies.* **2** [U] special care, action or treatment: *Research methods need attention if progress is to be made.* ◇ *Meningitis is an extremely serious illness and requires prompt medical attention.* ◇ **~ to sth** *Attention to detail is essential.* ◇ **care and ~** *A great deal of care and attention is devoted to the making of these programmes.* **3** [C, usually pl.] things done to try to please sb or to show an interest in them: *Sarah, the object of his attentions, died eighteen months later.*

▸ ADJECTIVE + ATTENTION **special, particular • further • considerable, great • significant • close, careful • serious • scant, insufficient, limited • sufficient • renewed • sustained • increased • widespread • public • international • critical • scholarly** *The role of play in older adults' lives has received limited attention.* ◇ *His essays have generally received less critical attention than his poetry.* | **urgent, immediate • constant • proper • particular • medical** *Their condition should be considered as acute illness requiring urgent attention.*

▸ VERB + ATTENTION **turn • pay • direct • shift, divert, switch • distract, deflect • focus, concentrate • catch, get, capture • hold • escape • draw, attract, receive, gain • command • deserve, merit, warrant • devote** *She focused her attention on helping him become calm.* ◇ *Osteoarthritis attracts little media attention, possibly because it is so common.* | **demand, require, need, be in need of • seek • get** *Marriage is something that demands constant attention.*

▸ ATTENTION + VERB **focus on • turn • shift** *In recent years much attention has focused on aggression and violence by children and teens.*

▸ PHRASES **come to sb's attention/come to the attention of sb • bring sth to sb's attention/bring sth to the attention of sb • call attention to sth • deserving/worthy of attention** *This practice had recently come to the attention of the tax authorities.* ◇ *The leadership has now accepted environmental pollution as a problem deserving of attention.*

at·tenu·ate /əˈtenjueɪt/ *verb* **~ sth** (*formal*) to reduce the force, effect or value of sth: *The drug attenuates the effects of the virus.* ■ **at·tenu·ation** /əˌtenjuˈeɪʃn/ *noun* [U] **~ (of sth)** *The attenuation of seismic waves as they travel through the Earth is the target of much research.*

at·test /əˈtest/ *verb* (*formal*) **1** [I, T, usually passive] to show or state that sth exists or is true SYN BEAR WITNESS/TESTIMONY TO STH: **~ to sth** *This finding attests to the importance of the sociopolitical context.* ◇ **(be) attested by/in sth** *The elections were not credible, as attested by reports of local and international observers.* ◇ *Artisanal work is well attested in early medieval archaeology.* ◇ **~ that...** *Rock paintings attest that humans collected honey at least 20 000 years ago.* **2** [T] **~ sth** to make an official statement that sth is true or genuine SYN WITNESS² (3): *A witness must attest the signature.*

at·ti·tude AWL /ˈætɪtjuːd; *NAmE* ˈætɪtuːd/ *noun* [C, U] a way of thinking or feeling about sb/sth; the way of behaving towards sb/sth that shows how sb thinks or feels: *It is important for teachers to encourage a positive attitude in their students.* ◇ *The situation has changed, and social and political attitudes have changed as well.* ◇ **~ of sb** *She examines the attitudes of 12 Southern writers towards Fascism.* ◇ **~ of sth** *Poor socio-economic conditions often create attitudes of apathy towards health care.* ◇ **~ to/towards/regarding sb/sth** *The study explored young people's attitudes to smoking.* ◇ **~ on/about sth** *American attitudes on firearms have to be taken into account.* ◇ **change of ~** *The election of the Labour Government in 1997 brought a huge change of attitude to industry regulating itself.*

▸ ADJECTIVE + ATTITUDE **positive, favourable • negative • critical • hostile • ambivalent • general, overall • prevailing • traditional • changing • different • differing • public • human • parental • personal • cultural • social • political • racial** *The prevailing attitude was that waste management was unimportant.* ◇ *There are differing public attitudes to GM crops.*

▸ NOUN + ATTITUDE **consumer • employee** *A major survey of consumer attitudes found that consumers did not trust food manufacturers.*

▸ VERB + ATTITUDE **hold, have • take, adopt • express • develop • change • shape, influence, affect • reinforce • reflect, reveal • explore, examine • measure** *Many Europeans held racist attitudes towards blacks.* ◇ *Did his family, which is predominantly female, shape his attitudes towards women?*

at·tract /əˈtrækt/ *verb* **1** [usually passive] if you are **attracted** by sth, it interests you and makes you want it; if you are **attracted** to sb, you like or admire them: **~ sb** *In the UK almost 4 million people, attracted by the prospect of flexible hours and improved work-life balance, work at home.* ◇ **~ sb to sb/sth** *Individuals are attracted to each other on the basis of shared characteristics.* **2** to make sb/sth come somewhere or take part in sth: **~ sb/sth** *The museum initially attracted around 500 000 visitors a year.* ◇ *They hoped this strategy would attract foreign investment by multinationals.* ◇ **~ sb/sth to sth** *Investors will only be attracted to the business if there is protection of their rights.* ◇ *Smells associated with hatching can attract predators to unhatched eggs.* **3 ~ sth** to make people have a particular reaction: *The problem of stress in the workplace continues to attract attention.* ◇ *This study is on food advertising which has recently attracted considerable interest.* ◇ *His criticism of the government attracted widespread support.* ◇ *In recent years, the institution of the monarchy has attracted criticism.* **4** (*physics*) if a MAGNET or GRAVITY **attracts** sth, it makes it move towards it: **be attracted to sth** *When a current flows through the coil, it is either attracted to the magnet or repelled.* ◇ *The oppositely charged ions are strongly attracted to one another and form a salt.* OPP REPEL (4)

at·trac·tion /əˈtrækʃn/ *noun* **1** [U, sing.] a feeling of liking sb, especially sexually; a feeling of liking sth and being interested in it: *Today we stress the desirability of sexual attraction.* ◇ **~ to sb** *Dorothea feels an attraction to Will Ladislaw though she is not yet aware of the strength of her feeling.* ◇ **~ to sth** *Wordsworth's attraction to Scotland was apparent in several poems inspired by his tour of the country.* **2** [U] the act of making an animal, etc. move nearer or be interested: *The behavioural characteristic of males are important for female attraction.* **3** [C] an interesting or enjoyable place to go or thing to do: *Both of these lakes are important tourist attractions.* ◇ *The London Eye has become the UK's most popular visitor attraction.* **4** [U, C] a

A

feature, quality or person that makes sth seem interesting and enjoyable, and worth having or doing: *For artists, the study of these texts can hold little attraction.* ◇ *Working on the land was beginning to lose its attraction.* ◇ **~ of sth (for sb)** *Many people feel the attractions of certainty, identity and membership of a community.* **5** [U, C] (*physics*) a force that pulls things towards each other: **~ of sth** *The gravitational attraction of the Earth holds the ocean firmly in its basin.* ◇ **~ to sth** *The pull of this flow is much stronger than the attraction to the anode.* ◇ **~ between A and B** *The partial charges on water molecules have a profound effect on electrical attractions between other polar molecules.* ➲ *compare* REPULSION (1)

at·tract·ive /əˈtræktɪv/ *adj.* **1** (of a person or an animal) pleasant to look at, especially in a sexual way; making an animal interested in a sexual way: *We can be drawn towards people who are physically attractive and also towards people who are like ourselves.* ◇ *Females paired with attractive males produce more male offspring.* OPP UNATTRACTIVE (2) **2** (of a thing or a place) pleasant to look at or be in: *The websites look attractive simply in terms of layout.* ◇ *'Problem' families are placed together in the least attractive housing and estates.* OPP UNATTRACTIVE (1) **3** having features or qualities that make sth seem interesting and worth having SYN APPEALING: *An increasingly attractive alternative to investment in training is to increase the use of immigrant labour.* ◇ *The government could use the tax and benefit system to make marriage more economically attractive.* OPP UNATTRACTIVE (1) **4** (*physics*) involving the force that pulls things towards each other: *A subtle but measurable attractive force starts to pull the metal plates towards one another.* ◇ *The energy due to the attractive interaction decreases as the molecules approach one another.* OPP REPULSIVE (1) ■ **at·tract·ive·ly** *adv.*: *Applications should be personalized, professional and attractively presented.* ◇ *The theory was attracitvely simple.*

at·tract·ive·ness /əˈtræktɪvnəs/ *noun* [U] **1** the fact of being pleasant to look at, especially in a sexual way; the fact of making an animal interested in a sexual way: *Images of ideal sexual attractiveness are widely circulated in the mass media.* ◇ **~ of sb/sth** *How do females judge the attractiveness of a potential mate and its mating signals?* **2** the fact of having features or qualities that make sth seem interesting and worth having SYN APPEAL[1] (2): *Assessing market attractiveness is very important when considering international market development.* ◇ **~ of sth** *Many retail outlets emphasize lifestyle themes, such as the outdoors, to increase the attractiveness of their products.*

at·trib·ut·able AWL /əˈtrɪbjətəbl/ *adj.* [not before noun] **~ to sb/sth** probably caused by the thing mentioned: *Studies estimate that 50% of the variation in human lifespan is attributable to genetic variation.*

at·tri·bute[1] AWL /əˈtrɪbjuːt/ *verb* **1 ~ sth to sth** to say or believe that sth is the result of a particular thing: *Growth in this sector was partly attributed to the use of digital technologies.* **2 ~ sth to sb** to say or believe that sb is responsible for doing sth, especially for saying, writing or painting sth: *The gospels attributed to Matthew and Luke are thought to have been written between AD 80 and 90.*

▸ ATTRIBUTE + NOUN **success • difference • meaning • significance, importance** *The business's success was attributed to its direct mail method of selling.* | **saying • speech • play • poem** *The records state that 130 plays were attributed to Plautus.*

▸ ATTRIBUTE STH TO + NOUN **the fact that... • the presence of sth • differences in sth** *The steady rise in the real wage can be attributed to the fact that during this period the unemployment rate fell from 5.5 to 3.9 per cent.*

▸ ADVERB + ATTRIBUTE **correctly • commonly • widely** *The declining relative wage of blue-collar workers was widely attributed to imports from low-wage countries.* | **largely • partly** *This massive and rapid rise in carbon dioxide levels is very largely attributed to the burning of fossil fuels.* | **falsely • mistakenly** *Literary, dramatic, artistic or musical works may not be falsely attributed to an author.*

at·tri·bute[2] AWL /ˈætrɪbjuːt/ *noun* a quality or feature of sb/sth: *This research examines how children learn to behave socially, and the personal attributes and capabilities involved.* ◇ *Malaysia's young, educated and highly productive workforce remains one of the country's key attributes.* ➲ thesaurus note *at* FEATURE[1]

at·tri·bu·tion AWL /ˌætrɪˈbjuːʃn/ *noun* [U] **1** the statement or belief that sb is responsible for saying, writing or painting sth: *Two fragments of the poem are ascribed to Nemesianus, although the attribution is doubtful.* **2** the fact of sth being the cause of sth else: *The direct effects of recruitment practices are uncertain in terms of causal attribution.*

atyp·ical /ˌeɪˈtɪpɪkl/ *adj.* not typical or usual; not representative of a type or group: *Because of the atypical nature of his pain, he was referred for tests.* ◇ *This intriguing example is not necessarily atypical.* ◇ **~ of sb/sth** *These three young men were by no means atypical of the broader population of disadvantaged white working-class men that we came across during our research.* OPP TYPICAL (1)

audi·ence /ˈɔːdiəns/ *noun* **1** [C+sing./pl. v.] the people who are watching or listening to a play, concert, sb speaking, etc: *With the use of such techniques, the audience believes that what they are seeing is true.* ◇ *A skilled presenter will make use of expert members of the audience.* ◇ **in the ~** *He noticed some people in the audience start to laugh.* ◇ **~ of sb** *One of the research group addressed an audience of 200 pre-service teachers.* **2** [C] a number of people or a particular group of people who watch, read or listen to the same thing: *By this time, cheap printed books were reaching a wider audience.* ◇ *Questions should be written in the language of the target audience.* ◇ **~ for sth** *American newspaper editors believe there is no audience for international news.* ◇ **~ of sb** *This important book appealed to an audience of general readers.* **3** [C] **~ with sb** a formal meeting with an important person: *Foucault requested a private audience with the king.*

▸ ADJECTIVE + AUDIENCE **wide, broad, large • mass • popular • general • young • international, global • intended** *Heavy emphasis is given to awareness campaigns for mass audiences.*

▸ NOUN + AUDIENCE **target • television • film, cinema** *The new media of cable and satellite have emerged to claim a small but significant share of the television audience.*

▸ VERB + AUDIENCE **reach • target • attract • appeal to • engage • persuade** *The television debates attracted large audiences.*

audio /ˈɔːdiəʊ; *NAmE* ˈɔːdioʊ/ *adj.* [only before noun] connected with sound that is recorded: *Audio recordings were made of each interview.* ■ **audio** *noun* [U] *The streaming of video and audio, via the web, has potential for use in practical lessons and classes.*

audit[1] /ˈɔːdɪt/ *noun* [C, U] **1** an official examination of business and financial records to see that they are true and correct: *Large firms must have an annual accounting audit by an external firm.* ◇ **~ of sth** *They undertook an internal audit of the firm's financial performance by customer, product line, etc.* **2** an official examination of the quality or standard of sth, or of what has happened to sth: *Conducting a marketing audit can be a very time-consuming process.* ◇ **~ of sth** *Many leading companies carry out environmental audits of their activities.* ◇ **+ noun** *It is advisable to have an audit trail outlining the path a clinical sample takes through a laboratory.*

audit[2] /ˈɔːdɪt/ *verb* **1 ~ sth** to officially examine the financial accounts of a company: *The company's accounts were audited in Singapore.* **2 ~ sth** to examine the quality or standard of sth; to find out what has happened to sth: *The quality, accuracy, timeliness and completeness of immunization data is independently audited.*

au·dit·or /ˈɔːdɪtə(r)/ *noun* **1** a person who officially examines the business and financial records of a company: *External auditors should attend the company's general shareholder meeting and answer shareholders' questions.* **2** a person who examines the quality or standard of sth, or who finds out what has happened to sth: *Hospitals are assessed by independent auditors who are themselves regulated by a national accreditation agency.*

audi·tory /ˈɔːdətri; *NAmE* ˈɔːdətɔːri/ *adj.* connected with the sense of hearing: *The link between the ear and the brain is provided by the auditory nerve.* ◇ *Schizophrenic patients tend to suffer from auditory hallucinations rather than visual hallucinations.*

aug·ment /ɔːɡˈment/ *verb* **~ sth** to add to sth, so that it increases in size, amount or value: *Evaluation can augment efficiency by making teachers more accountable to parents.* ◇ *The model can be augmented to take these effects into account.* ■ **aug·men·ta·tion** /ˌɔːɡmenˈteɪʃn/ *noun* [U, C] **~ (of sth)** *There has been substantial augmentation of the skills and experience of local labour forces.* ◇ *These augmentations were not enough.*

au·then·tic /ɔːˈθentɪk/ *adj.* **1** known to be real and genuine and not a copy SYN GENUINE (1): *The entire purpose of art museums is the display of authentic works of art, not reproductions.* **2** true and accurate; based on fact: *Early women's writing offers historians the opportunity to hear the authentic voices of seventeenth-century women.* ◇ *Vast amounts of authentic materials are now available online to help language learners build up skills.* **3** made to be exactly like the original: *Many Chinese migrants who have settled in the UK continue to buy authentic eastern-style food.* ■ **au·then·tic·al·ly** /ɔːˈθentɪkli/ *adv.*: *The music is not authentically performed unless it is performed in a domestic setting.*

au·then·ti·city /ˌɔːθenˈtɪsəti/ *noun* [U] the quality of being genuine or true, or based on fact: *It was impossible to guarantee the document's authenticity.* ◇ **~ of sth** *The paint structure could help to identify the authenticity of a painting.*

author[1] AWL /ˈɔːθə(r)/ *noun* the person who wrote a particular article, book or document: *The authors suggest that diabetic patients could benefit from a diet rich in fruits and vegetables.*

author[2] AWL /ˈɔːθə(r)/ *verb* **~ sth** to be the author of an article, a book or a document: *He has authored over ninety articles on technical change, entrepreneurship and industrial organization.*

au·thor·ial /ɔːˈθɔːriəl/ *adj.* [usually before noun] coming from or connected with the author of sth: *The authorial voice frequently intervenes to make editorial observations.* ◇ *They argued that it is not only authorial intention that determines the meaning of an artwork.*

au·thori·tar·ian /ɔːˌθɒrɪˈteəriən; *NAmE* əˌθɔːrəˈteriən; əˌθɑːrəˈteriən/ *adj.* believing that people should obey authority and rules, even if it means that people lose their personal freedom: *If such mass democracy movements grow strong enough, no authoritarian regime can resist them forever.* ◇ *Elections can be used to disguise authoritarian rule.* ◇ *The trend in Western societies is towards less authoritarian styles of parenting.* ◇ *The Soviet bloc in 1972 was resolutely authoritarian.* ■ **au·thori·tar·ian·ism** /ɔːˌθɒrɪˈteəriənɪzəm; *NAmE* əˌθɔːrəˈteriənɪzəm; əˌθɑːrəˈteriənɪzəm/ *noun* [U] *The transition from authoritarianism to democracy is always a period of high risk for any society.*

au·thori·ta·tive AWL /ɔːˈθɒrətətɪv; *NAmE* əˈθɔːrəteɪtɪv; əˈθɑːrəteɪtɪv/ *adj.* **1** that you can trust as true and accurate: *These reports are regarded as the authoritative scientific statements on climate change.* **2** (of a text) considered to be the best of its kind and not likely to be improved upon: *Ptolemy's syntheses of astronomy and geography remained authoritative for more than a millennium.* **3** showing that you expect people to obey and respect you: *The cooperative family ideal is based on the father as the authoritative figure.* ■ **au·thori·ta·tive·ly** *adv.*: *Authoritatively researched historical documentaries were expensive.* ◇ *The ethnographer was able to speak authoritatively about the workers and their lives.*

au·thor·ity AWL /ɔːˈθɒrəti; *NAmE* əˈθɔːrəti; əˈθɑːrəti/ *noun* (*pl.* **-ies**) **1** [U] the power to give orders to people or to say how things should be done: *The teacher may delegate some authority to the students.* ◇ **~ over sb** *Parents exercised considerable authority over their young adult children.* ◇ **~ to do sth** *It was accepted that the ruler of a realm had the authority to determine the religion of its people.* **2** [U] official permission or the right to do sth: **~ (to do sth)** *Supermarkets have no authority to use information about buying habits obtained from customer loyalty cards.* ◇ **with/without (the) ~ (to do sth)** *With no authority to collect taxes from their members, the society was reliant on voluntary contributions.* ◇ **with/without the ~ of sb/sth** *A person responsible for copying a work without the authority of the copyright owner will incur a liability.* **3** [C] an organization that has the power to make decisions or that has a particular area of responsibility in a country or region: *Regional representatives include local authorities, cities or regional governments.* ◇ *The Philippines monetary authority adjusted its key overnight interest rates.* **4** [U] the power to influence people because they respect your knowledge or official position: *Homer was sometimes criticized, but his authority on a range of issues was deeply rooted.* **5** [C] **~ (on sth)** a person with special knowledge SYN EXPERT[1]: *Baker became known as an authority on bridge construction.*

▸ ADJECTIVE + AUTHORITY **statutory** • **religious** • **royal** • **political** *Elaborate ceremonies were held to demonstrate the political power and religious authority of the kings.*

▸ ADJECTIVE + AUTHORITIES **local** • **national** • **public** • **regulatory** • **monetary** • **religious** • **political** *Traditionally, criminal law has been seen as the province of national authorities.*

▸ VERB + AUTHORITY **delegate** • **exercise** • **gain** • **challenge** • **lack** *Parliament may delegate to other bodies the authority to pass legislation.* ◇ *Students who challenge authority are trying to influence the world around them.* | **have** *The bishops of Rome had no effective authority in the Frankish national church.*

au·thor·iza·tion (*BrE also* **-isa·tion**) /ˌɔːθəraɪˈzeɪʃn; *NAmE* ˌɔːθərəˈzeɪʃn/ *noun* **1** [U, C] official permission or power to do sth; the act of giving permission: **~ for sth** *Caregivers also gave authorization for the release of medical information from the children's medical chart.* ◇ **without the ~ of sb/sth**| **without ~ (from sb/sth)** *A group of states decided to use force without the explicit authorization of the Security Council.* ◇ **~ to do sth** *The Secretary of Public Security obtained a judicial authorization to carry out wiretapping.* **2** [C] a document that gives sb official permission to do sth: *The King signed the authorization at the end of 1835.*

au·thor·ize (*BrE also* **-ise**) /ˈɔːθəraɪz/ *verb* [often passive] to give official permission for sth: **~ sth** *The government authorized further aircraft production.* ◇ *They undercut the prices of the authorized dealers in a market and still make a profit.* ◇ **~ sb to do sth** *The troops were authorized to use force.* ➲ *see also* UNAUTHORIZED

author·ship AWL /ˈɔːθəʃɪp; *NAmE* ˈɔːθərʃɪp/ *noun* [U] **1** the identity of the person who wrote sth, especially a

A

book: *The society studied the evidence for Francis Bacon's authorship of plays commonly ascribed to William Shakespeare.* **2** the activity or fact of writing a book: *Thackeray tended to regard authorship as an occupation rather than as a sacred or professional vocation.*

auto·biog·raphy /ˌɔːtəbaɪˈɒgrəfi; *NAmE* ˌɔːtəbaɪˈɑːgrəfi/ *noun* (*pl.* **-ies**) [C, U] the story of a person's life, written by that person; this type of writing: *Many compelling autobiographies were written and published in this period.* ◇ *This article suggests the value of autobiography for religious studies.* ➲ *compare* BIOGRAPHY ■ **auto·bio·graph·ic·al** /ˌɔːtəˌbaɪəˈgræfɪkl/ *adj.*: *This century saw an increase in autobiographical writing.* ◇ *Large sections of the novel are autobiographical.*

auto·immune /ˌɔːtəʊɪˈmjuːn; *NAmE* ˌɔːtoʊɪˈmjuːn/ *adj.* [only before noun] (*medical*) (of a disease or medical condition) caused by substances that usually prevent illness: *Interestingly, autoimmune diseases in general are less common in tropical countries.*

auto·mate AWL /ˈɔːtəmeɪt/ *verb* [often passive] **~ sth** to change a process so that it uses machines and computers instead of people: *Even when factories were automated, the workforce was rarely reduced.* ■ **auto·mated** AWL *adj.*: *A manufacturing system that was fully automated could begin making a new product without retraining or retooling.*

auto·mat·ic AWL /ˌɔːtəˈmætɪk/ *adj.* **1** (of a machine or device) having controls that work without needing a person to operate them: *The system is fully automatic and suitable for unmanned applications.* **2** done or happening without thinking: *Research shows that automatic or unconscious processes tend to be fast and efficient but inflexible.* **3** always happening as a result of a particular action or situation: *There is no automatic right for a shareholder to receive a dividend.* ◇ *In the UK, copyright is automatic and there is no registration process.*

auto·mat·ic·al·ly AWL /ˌɔːtəˈmætɪkli/ *adv.* **1** by machine or computer: *The tests were performed automatically on machines that use robotics.* ◇ *The web page is automatically updated every 15 minutes.* **2** as a result of a particular action or situation: *Tariffs automatically generate revenue for the government of the importing country.* ◇ *The statute identifies reasons for dismissal that will be automatically unfair.* **3** (of the body's physical or mental processes) not requiring thought or attention: *Thus, people seem to automatically retrieve this information from memory.*

auto·ma·tion AWL /ˌɔːtəˈmeɪʃn/ *noun* [U] the use or introduction of machines to do work that was previously done by people: *Gallie studied the impact of advanced automation on industrial workers in England and France.*

auto·mo·bile /ˈɔːtəməbiːl/ *noun* (*especially NAmE*) a car: *Railroads had already lost market share to intercity buses and private automobiles.* ◇ **+ noun** *In 2007, Toyota became the world's largest automobile manufacturer.* ◇ *the automobile industry/market* HELP In British English the term **automobile** is only used before another noun; in other cases, British English uses **car**: *Railways had already lost market share to coaches and private cars.*

auto·mo·tive /ˌɔːtəˈməʊtɪv; *NAmE* ˌɔːtəˈmoʊtɪv/ *adj.* [only before noun] connected with vehicles that are driven by engines: *The steel is recycled from waste material from the automotive industry.* ◇ *Automotive suppliers are under a constant pressure to lower their production costs.*

au·tono·mous /ɔːˈtɒnəməs; *NAmE* ɔːˈtɑːnəməs/ *adj.* **1** (of a country, a region or an organization) able to govern itself or control its own affairs: *At that time the Russian Republic had as many as fourteen autonomous republics.* ◇ *Small businesses are usually seen as independent and autonomous.* ➲ *compare* INDEPENDENT (1) **2** able to act or make decisions independently SYN INDEPENDENT (6): *The company continued to treat all employees as relatively autonomous individuals.* ◇ *In order to exploit these opportunities, learners must be largely autonomous.* ■ **au·tono·mous·ly** *adv.*: *None of the institutions of the European Union is free to act autonomously.* ◇ *Cell division proceeds autonomously.*

au·ton·omy /ɔːˈtɒnəmi; *NAmE* ɔːˈtɑːnəmi/ *noun* [U] **1** the freedom of a country, a region or an organization to govern itself independently: *In Canada the French-speaking population of Quebec began to demand greater autonomy.* ◇ *US universities retained great autonomy in their administrative policies.* ➲ *compare* INDEPENDENCE (1) **2** the ability to act and make decisions without being controlled by anyone else SYN INDEPENDENCE (4): *The obvious problem with this model is that it fails to respect patient autonomy.* ◇ *individual/personal autonomy* ◇ **~ over sth** *Teachers enjoyed great autonomy over curriculum development and decision-making.*

au·tumn /ˈɔːtəm/ (*especially BrE*) (*NAmE usually* **fall**) *noun* [U, C, usually sing.] the season of the year between summer and winter: **in ~** *Changes were made in autumn 2010.* ◇ **(in) the ~ of sth** *The financial crisis hit in the autumn of 2008.* ◇ **+ noun** *Statistical tests were performed separately for spring and autumn surveys.*

aux·il·iary[1] /ɔːgˈzɪliəri/ *adj.* **1** [usually before noun] extra; existing or being used in addition to the main one: *The working and auxiliary electrodes are arranged as symmetrically as possible.* ◇ *A second way is to accommodate the anomaly by tacking on an auxiliary hypothesis.* **2** [only before noun] working in a supporting role; not qualified to do the job mentioned, but performing some aspects of it: *Auxiliary staff should be encouraged to contribute.* ◇ *auxiliary nurses/midwives*

aux·il·iary[2] /ɔːgˈzɪliəri/ *noun* (*pl.* **-ies**) **1** (*also* **auˌxiliary ˈverb**) (*grammar*) a verb such as *be*, *do* and *have* used with main verbs to show tense, etc. and to form questions and negatives: *In the question 'Do you know where he has gone?', 'do' and 'has' are auxiliaries.* **2** a worker who gives help or support to the main group of workers: *nursing auxiliaries*

avail·abil·ity AWL /əˌveɪləˈbɪləti/ *noun* [U] the quality of being able to be used or obtained: *The least productive wetlands are limited by permanently low nutrient availability.* ◇ *Food was increasingly transported over greater and greater distances in order to ensure year-round availability.* ◇ **~ of sth** *The benefit of this approach is the ready availability of results.*

avail·able AWL /əˈveɪləbl/ *adj.* **1** (of things) that you can use or obtain: *Public health facilities were not widely available.* ◇ **~ for sth (by sb)** *A great deal of educational software is available for use both by teachers and students.* ◇ **~ for sb (to do sth)** *There are still a large number of antibiotics available for clinicians to use for the treatment of infection.* ◇ **~ to sb/sth** *In the UK, the Royal Mail service was first made available to the public in 1635.* ◇ **~ in sth** *Tap water is available in only 1 in 10 of the villages in the region.* ◇ **~ from sb/sth** *Table 7.3 illustrates data available from two case-control studies.* ◇ **~ to do sth** *There are a number of tools available to assist with the construction and simulation of models.* OPP UNAVAILABLE (1) **2 ~ (for sth)** (of a person) free or willing to do sth: *This means giving journalists and editors access to information and making senior management available for interview.* OPP UNAVAILABLE (2)

▸ AVAILABLE + NOUN **evidence • data, information • resources • supply • options** *Historically, the kinds of food consumed in various parts of the world primarily reflected available resources.*

A

▸ NOUN + BE AVAILABLE **options, alternative(s) • data, information • equipment • resources** *Therefore, little information is available on the compressive fatigue of composites.*
▸ ADVERB + AVAILABLE **commercially • publicly, widely • readily, freely, easily • immediately • currently** *Furthernore, there is a great deal of readily available information about household structure from the national census and other sources.*

av·enue /ˈævənjuː; *NAmE* ˈævənuː/ *noun* a way of approaching a problem or making progress towards sth: **~ for sth** *This is a promising avenue for future research.* ◇ **~ of sth** *This chapter will suggest new avenues of inquiry.* ➲ *compare* DIRECTION (2)

aver·age¹ /ˈævərɪdʒ/ *adj.* **1** [only before noun] calculated by adding several amounts together, finding a total, and dividing the total by the number of amounts: *The average cost of producing a product will fall as the quantity produced rises.* ◇ *Average annual temperature in the valley ranges from -16°C to -20°C.* ◇ *Niagara Falls has migrated a distance of more than 11 miles in 8 000 years, an average rate of three feet per year.* **2** typical or normal: *Someone who cannot walk as far as the average person may still be healthy.* ◇ *On an average day in March, about 100 000 motorists were paying the congestion fees.*
▸ AVERAGE + NOUN **number • amount • level • rate • concentration • value • cost • price • size • height • length • distance • time • age • temperature • income • wage • growth • increase • speed • velocity • score • consumption** *In the 1940s, the average age at marriage for Irish women was 28 and for Irish men 33.* ◇ *People in the wealthiest nations had average per capita annual incomes that were well over $20 000.* | **person • citizen • family • household • year** *The average household was 15 per cent worse off than in 2003.*

aver·age² /ˈævərɪdʒ/ *noun* [C, U] **1** a number that expresses the central or typical value of a set of data HELP The term **average** is most commonly used to mean the **mean**: the result of adding several amounts together, finding a total, and dividing the total by the number of amounts. However, the **median** and the **mode** are also types of average: *Most studies calculate an average per person by dividing the total household income by the number of people in the household.* ◇ **~ for sb/sth** *The average for the 28 nations in the OECD that year was 40.7 per cent.* ◇ **~ of sth** *Each meeting lasted an average of two hours.* ◇ *The record represents the average of December and January mean monthly temperatures for each summer.* ➲ *see also* MEAN² (2), MEDIAN², MODE (5) **2** a level that is usual: *In any given year, some companies will do better than the average and others will do worse.* ◇ *In general the East of England is less deprived than the national average.* ◇ **above/below ~** *Her mental arithmetic ability is slightly below average for her age.* ◇ **on ~** *The poorest 10% of Americans are richer on average than two-thirds of the people in the world.* ◇ *On average, 20% of the stem cells differentiate into stalk cells that die.*

aver·age³ /ˈævərɪdʒ/ *verb* **1** [no passive] **~ sth** to be equal to a particular amount as an average: *Female labour force participation rates were 63% in the USA and averaged 45% in Europe.* ◇ *Temperatures average -5°C and there are few frost-free days.* **2** [often passive] **~ sth** to calculate the average of sth: *Students are tested individually and their scores are averaged.* ◇ *Responses were averaged to create a scale of economic hardship.*
PHRV **ˌaverage ˈout (at sth)** to result in an average amount over a period of time or when several things are considered: *The company would earn US$500 million over a ten-year period, averaging out at US$50 million per annum.* **ˌaverage sth ˈout (at sth)** to calculate the average of sth: *A total score is obtained by averaging out the ratings for individual items.*

averse /əˈvɜːs; *NAmE* əˈvɜːrs/ *adj.* [not before noun] **~ to (doing) sth** not liking sth; not wanting to do sth: *Some managers are excessively averse to innovation.* HELP **Averse** is only used without 'to' if it follows a noun: *These firms tend to be less risk-averse.* ➲ *compare* OPPOSED (1) ➲ *usage note at* ADVERSE

aver·sion /əˈvɜːʃn; *NAmE* əˈvɜːrʒn/ *noun* [U, C, usually sing.] a strong feeling of not liking sth, or of not wanting to do sth: *These organizations exhibit a remarkable degree of risk aversion in their approach.* ◇ **~ to (doing) sth** *Their preferences show a strong aversion to risk.* ◇ *Their aversion to uniting into a single political unit had a profound impact.*

avert /əˈvɜːt; *NAmE* əˈvɜːrt/ *verb* **~ sth** to prevent sth bad or dangerous from happening: *Although Wilson broke off diplomatic ties with Germany, he still hoped to avert war.*

avi·ation /ˌeɪviˈeɪʃn/ *noun* [U] the activity of designing, building and flying aircraft: *In this section, the technological advances that allowed commercial aviation to emerge are outlined.* ◇ **+ noun** *The civil aviation industry has been the focus of particular controversy in the context of global climate change debates.*

avoid /əˈvɔɪd/ *verb* **1** to prevent sth bad from happening: **~ sth** *Identifying the risk factors provided the major strategy for avoiding problems in later life.* ◇ *It is hard to avoid the conclusion that oil is being consumed about one million times faster than it was made .* ◇ **~ doing sth** *This technique requires technical expertise to avoid harming the patient.* ◇ **in order to ~** *Britain was forced to ask for US support in order to avoid economic catastrophe.* ➲ *compare* PREVENT **2** to choose not to do sth; to put sb in a situation where they do not have to do sth: **~ sb/sth** *Managers have learned to take decisions instead of avoiding them.* ◇ **~ doing sth** *Casual workers in the printing industry had avoided paying income tax on their earnings* HELP Do not use **avoid** with an infinitive. Use **avoid + -ing** instead: *He avoided talking about the trauma.* ◇ ~~*He avoided to talk about the trauma.*~~ **3 ~ sb/sth** to keep away from sb/sth: *Rodents prefer living hidden away in the dark, probably because that is the best way for them to avoid predators.* ◇ *These tribes avoid contact with outsiders and little is known about them.* ◇ *She tries to avoid conflict and confrontation wherever possible.* **4 ~ sth** to prevent yourself from hitting sth: *Griffin demonstrated that plugging the bat's ears severely interfered with its ability to avoid obstacles.* ◇ *There was evidence that the defendant had swerved to avoid other vehicles.*
▸ AVOID + NOUN **need • bias • problem • conclusion • difficulty • harm • conflict • confusion • effect • risk, danger, pitfalls • error** *This may avoid the need for major surgery in patients who have a limited life expectancy.* ◇ *To avoid confusion, I shall only use this term in its strict scientific sense.* | **situation • issue • question • contact** *Young people with this condition are often anxious when attending school and avoid situations where others are present.*
▸ ADVERB + AVOID **thus • thereby • largely** *The researchers thus avoid drawing a definite conclusion, but instead make suggestions for future research.* | **generally • deliberately** *This case highlighted how the company deliberately avoided dealing with the real problem.*

avoid·able /əˈvɔɪdəbl/ *adj.* that can be prevented: *Many deaths from heart disease are actually avoidable.* ◇ *Cerebrovascular disease (stroke) was the leading cause of avoidable mortality.* OPP UNAVOIDABLE

avoid·ance /əˈvɔɪdəns/ *noun* [U] not doing sth; preventing sth from existing or happening; keeping away from sb/sth: *This is an example of tax avoidance rather than tax evasion (which is when individuals or firms act illegally).* ◇ **~ of sth** *A person's health improves with the avoidance of*

A

stress. ◇ **+ noun** *We examined predator avoidance behaviour of larval fish.*

await /əˈweɪt/ *verb* **1 ~ sth** to wait for sth: *She returned to England whilst her husband awaited immigration formalities.* ◇ *Data answering this question are eagerly awaited.* **2 ~ sth** used to say that sth still needs to happen: *Many questions await future research to clarify significant issues.* ◇ *These results await further replication and specification.* **3 ~ sb** to be going to happen to sb: *The same fate awaited others.*

awake /əˈweɪk/ *adj.* [not before noun] not sleeping: **wide/fully ~** *People are good at taking in facts about familiar objects when they are wide awake and not distracted.* ◇ **stay ~** *The nurse advises Joan to try and stay awake during the daytime, no matter how tired she feels.* OPP ASLEEP ➲ *see also* WAKE[2]

award[1] /əˈwɔːd; *NAmE* əˈwɔːrd/ *noun* **1** [C] (often in names of particular awards) a prize such as money for sth that sb has done: *She has won numerous prestigious awards.* ◇ *Liverpool will probably be the last UK city to win the European Capital of Culture award for the next 15–20 years.* ◇ **~ for sth** *The University won a major national award for the launch of a new partnership scheme with colleges.* ◇ **award-winning** *This story will be shared with the world on the authors' award-winning oral history website.* **2 ~ (of sth)** [U] the act of giving sb sth, such as a prize or contract: *I would also like to thank the Royal Society in the UK for the award of a History of Science grant that enabled me to undertake this research.* **3** [C] an increase in the amount of money sb earns: *Bonus payments, tips and performance-related pay awards may form part of the calculations.* ◇ *Everyone in each pay band received the same cash award.* **4** [C, U] the amount of money that a court decides should be given to sb who has won a case; the decision to give this money: **~ for sth** *It is difficult and costly to obtain an award for damages.* ◇ **~ of sth** *Numerous different factors will dictate the award of compensation.*

award[2] /əˈwɔːd; *NAmE* əˈwɔːrd/ *verb* to make an official decision to give a payment, prize or contract to sb: **~ sth (for sth)** *Courts are today extremely reluctant to award compensation for economic loss.* ◇ **~ sth to sb** *A contract was awarded to ICL in September 1994.* ◇ **~ sb sth** *The court awarded her a sum of £4.4 million.*

aware AWL /əˈweə(r); *NAmE* əˈwer/ *adj.* **1** [not before noun] knowing or realizing that sth is true or exists: **~ (of sth)** *The factors that motivate people to smoke are complex and most people are aware of the risks to their health.* ◇ *Obviously, people must be aware of a brand if they are going to buy it.* ◇ *Most people are aware when others are misleading them.* ◇ **~ that...** *Claudius was well aware that he would be following in the footsteps of the deified Julius Caesar.* OPP UNAWARE **2** (used with an adverb) concerned and knowing a lot about a particular situation or development: *Two of the women were long-time activists, and all were politically aware.*

▸ AWARE OF THE + NOUN **danger, risk • difficulty, problems • importance, significance • need • fact • possibility, potential • existence** *Plato was aware of the importance of law in ensuring stability.* ◇ *Rosenthal and Jacobson's subjects do not appear to have been aware of the fact that they were participating in an experiment.*

▸ VERB + AWARE **become • remain • make sb • keep sb** *One of the most common uses of marketing communications is to make potential customers aware of the features and benefits of a product or service.*

▸ ADVERB + AWARE **acutely, keenly, well • fully • increasingly • consciously** *The Jia Qing Emperor was keenly aware of the need for reform.* | **culturally • politically • socially • ecologically** *A culturally aware international firm will adopt policies to fit into the host culture.*

aware·ness AWL /əˈweənəs; *NAmE* əˈwernəs/ *noun* [U, sing.] **1** the fact of knowing that sth is true or exists: **~ (of sth)** *The patient lacked awareness of his speech difficulty.* ◇ *There are two types of brand awareness: recognition and recall.* ◇ **~ that...** *The novel shows an awareness that Afro-Americans are not the only group to be oppressed by the dominant white culture.* ➲ *see also* SELF-AWARENESS **2** concern or interest in a particular situation or development: **~ of sth** *Confronted with heightened public awareness of environmental issues, farmers sought new ways to manage their fields.* ◇ **~ about sth** *Raising awareness about tobacco is an appropriate intervention for smokers who are considering giving up smoking.* ◇ **~ (among/amongst sb) (that...)** *There is a growing awareness among practitioners that organizational learning and development are intertwined.*

▸ ADJECTIVE + AWARENESS **conscious • heightened, increased, greater** *A specific autobiographical memory is formed and can enter conscious awareness.* | **keen, acute • growing, increasing • public • cultural • moral** *Dickens' acute awareness of the inequalities of industrial England helped provoke the composition of 'A Christmas Carol'.*

▸ VERB + AWARENESS **lack** *Children often lack awareness of their emotions.* | **build, increase, raise, promote • create** *The aim of the campaign was to build greater awareness of Scotland as a diverse, exciting destination.*

▸ PHRASES **(a) lack of awareness** *Error may be introduced through lack of awareness.*

away /əˈweɪ/ *adv.* HELP For the special uses of **away** in phrasal verbs, look at the entries for the verbs. For example **get away with (doing) sth** is in the phrasal verb section at **get**. **1** to or at a distance from sb/sth in space or time: **far ~** *People who lived in or near Athens would find it easier to vote than those who lived farther away.* ◇ **~ from sb/sth** *Roman custom dictated that the dead be kept well away from the living.* **2** to a different place or in a different direction: *The underlying problem will simply not go away.* ◇ *They did not receive a reply but their letters were filed away.* ◇ **~ from sb/sth** *The student has been moved away from his group to another desk.* **3** not present SYN ABSENT (2): *Their house was burgled while they were away.* ◇ **~ from sb/sth** *He was away from home for long periods of time.* **4** until disappearing completely: *The showers will gradually die away.* ◇ *The surrounding rock mass has been eroded away.* IDM *see* RIGHT[3], STRAIGHT[2]

awk·ward /ˈɔːkwəd; *NAmE* ˈɔːkwərd/ *adj.* **1** embarrassed; making you feel embarrassed: *The stigma attached to mental illness can mean both parties feel awkward within the relationship.* ◇ *Successful conversation for many English speakers involves filling any gaps with talk; silence is regarded as awkward.* ◇ **~ with sb/sth** *Maybe he was socially awkward with boys but comfortable with girls.* **2** difficult to deal with SYN DIFFICULT (2): *Managers need to be able to answer awkward questions from company accountants.* ◇ *John can be very awkward sometimes.* **3** not convenient: *These states are in awkward locations, and lack the political foundations to be reliable members of the alliance.* **4** difficult because of its shape or design: *Manual handling involves lifting objects such as heavy boxes or awkward items of furniture.* **5** not moving in an easy way; not comfortable or elegant: *Dentists often have to sit for long periods in awkward positions while carrying out work.* ◇ *Far from conveying the author's intent, the awkward written style serves to obscure it.* ■ **awk·ward·ly** *adv.*: *At first sight, these insights seem to fit awkwardly with the points made in the preceding paragraphs.* **awk·ward·ness** *noun* [U] *The adults significantly overestimated their young people's awkwardness and lack of self-confidence.* ◇ **~ of sth** *She noted the occasional awkwardness of attempts to translate Kannada place names into English.*

axial /ˈæksiəl/ *adj.* connected with or forming an axis; around an axis: *Marked changes in the axial tilt of the earth have also taken place.* ◇ *The surface roughness was measured in the axial direction.* ◇ *The axial skeleton consists of bones that form the axis of the body.*

axiom /ˈæksiəm/ *noun* a statement or principle that is regarded as being true without proof: *Mathematics is perceived as a system that can be reduced to a set of axioms.* ◇ *Design axioms can be used to analyse why machines and processes are not working well.*

axio·mat·ic /ˌæksiəˈmætɪk/ *adj.* **1** true in such an obvious way that you do not need to prove it SYN SELF-EVIDENT: *The first axiomatic generalization is that individual members of a species vary.* ◇ **it is ~ that...** *It is axiomatic that doctors should try to do good and strive not to do harm.* **2** [usually before noun] based on statements or principles which are regarded as being true without proof: *Mathematicians have developed various axiomatic systems of geometry.*

axis /ˈæksɪs/ *noun* (*pl.* **axes** /ˈæksiːz/) **1** an imaginary line through the centre of an object, around which the object turns: **on its ~** *The Earth rotates on its axis from west to east approximately once every 24 hours.* ◇ **~ of rotation** *At a given time t, the distance of the boundary from the axis of rotation is r.* **2** (*geometry*) a line that divides a shape into two equal parts, especially in the direction of the shape's greatest length: **~ (of sth)** *This centre line is the axis of the cylinder.* ◇ **~ of symmetry** *If the 2D image is symmetrical, then the object will contain the same axis of symmetry.* **3 ~ (of sth)** a real or imaginary line that divides sth into equal or approximately equal halves: *The camera shows heavy traffic moving along the east-west axis of the town.* **4** (*technical*) a fixed line against which the positions of points are measured, especially points on a GRAPH: **horizontal/vertical ~** *The horizontal axis represents increasing time.* ◇ **on the... ~** *This graph has inflation on the vertical axis and output on the horizontal one.* **5** (*technical*) a central line in a structure, about which parts are arranged: *In plants, the main axis runs from the growing tip to the roots.* ◇ **around the ~** *The device produces a centrifugal force by spinning a sample around a central axis.* ◇ **along the... ~** *The type of cell produced is determined by positional values along the body axis.* ◇ **~ of symmetry** *The vertebrate body has three main axes of symmetry.* **6** [usually sing.] an agreement or ALLIANCE between two or more countries: *De Gaulle wanted to maintain the Franco-German axis as the key relationship within Europe.*

B b

B2B /ˌbiː tə ˈbiː/ *abbr.* BUSINESS-TO-BUSINESS

baby /ˈbeɪbi/ *noun* (*pl.* **-ies**) a very young child or animal: *A newborn baby will usually need to feed 8–12 times in a 24-hour period.* ◇ *Emily had her baby at home in Oxford in 1963.* ◇ *Her first baby was born when she was aged 23.* ◇ *When the baby turtles break through the surface of sand covering the underground nest, they are just a few centimetres long.*

back[1] /bæk/ *adv.* HELP For the special uses of **back** in phrasal verbs, look at the entries for the verbs. For example **pay sb back** is in the phrasal verb section at **pay. 1** to or into the place, condition, situation or activity where sb/sth was before: *We need to go back to the beginning of the process and conduct further analysis.* ◇ *The case was referred back to the Court of Appeal.* ◇ *After peaking early in the 1980s, permafrost temperatures fell back again.* ◇ *Darius's body was brought back to Persia and buried with full royal honours.* **2** in or into the past; ago: *An ethical code for nurses in the UK dates back to July 1983.* ◇ *The history of modern social security can be traced back to 1870s Germany.* **3** at a place previously left or mentioned: *Back at Leipzig, the geographer Goldbach was hired to design the map for the travel narrative.* ◇ *When light from the laser hits the land, the light is reflected back and can be detected by a sensor.* ◇ *A woman steel worker angrily rejected the idea that women should go back home.* **4** in return or reply: *Inevitably, banks have begun to fight back at the prospect of countries re-regulating their financial systems.* ◇ *If one of the nodes has a copy of the requested file, then it sends back a reply message to the client.* **5** at a distance away from sth: *Citizens could do little more than stand back and watch the city burn.* **6** away from the front or centre; behind you: *The piston moves back by a small distance.* OPP FORWARD[1] (1) **7** under control; prevented from being expressed or coming out: *The reformers held back privatization of the biggest state companies.*

IDM **ˌback and ˈforth** from one place to another and back again many times: *As the energy is never zero, the particle is never at rest but is always moving back and forth.* ◇ *Two ships a year went back and forth between China and Japan.*

back[2] /bæk/ *noun* **1** [usually sing.] the part or area of sth that is furthest from the front: **~ (of sth)** *The victim died from a kick to the back of his head.* ◇ **at the ~** *At the back of the classroom are two PCs, but only one of them is currently working.* **2** the part of the human body that is on the opposite side to the chest, between the neck and the tops of the legs; the part of an animal's body that CORRESPONDS to this: *She has had pain in her lower back for the past 2 weeks.* ◇ *He lay down on his back.* ◇ *Golden egg bugs (Phyllomorpha laciniata) carry their eggs on their backs.* **3** [usually sing.] **~ (of sth)** the part of sth, such as a piece of paper, that is on the opposite side to the one that has information or the most important information on it: *Health warnings must cover 30–35% of the front and 40–50% of the back of tobacco packs in all European Union states.* **4** the row of bones in the middle of the back SYN SPINE (1): *The fluid is removed using a needle from the spinal canal in the lower back.* **5** [usually sing.] **(at the) ~ (of sth)** the last few pages of sth such as a book: *The index is at the back of the book.* ◇ *There are grammar and vocabulary reference sections at the back.*

IDM **at/in the back of your mind** if a thought or idea is **at the back of your mind**, it is not what you are mainly thinking about, but you are aware of it: *Electoral politics seemed to be in the back of the President's mind throughout the 1964 Panama Crisis.* **behind sb's ˈback** without sb's knowledge or permission: *She believes she has the admiration of others, but they laugh at her behind her back.* **on the back of sth** as a result of an achievement or a success: *The business was built on the back of thirty years of manufacturing experience.* **turn your back on sb/sth** to reject sb/sth that you have previously been connected with: *Employees are turning their backs on employers with no sense of moral responsibility.* ◇ *Dixson accuses Australian intellectuals of turning their back on modernity.*

back[3] /bæk/ *adj.* [only before noun] **1** located behind or at the back of sth: *The wearing of seat belts in the front and back seats of cars is now compulsory.* ◇ *The back page of the newspaper carried a small notice of his dismissal as minister of defence.* ➲ *compare* FRONT[2] **2** of or from a past time: *Most university libraries stock back issues of newspapers on compact disc.*

back[4] /bæk/ *verb* **1** [T] **~ sb/sth** to give help or support to sb/sth: *Conclusive evidence to back his claim was lacking.* ◇ *Many were not prepared to back a full-scale invasion.* ◇ *In 1997 Labour MPs strongly backed Michael Foster's private members' bill to ban fox-hunting.* **2** [T, usually passive] (*BrE*) to be located behind sth: **be backed by sth** *The* *coastal plain is extremely narrow and over a considerable stretch is backed by rocky cliffs.*

B

PHR V **ˌback aˈway (from sb/sth)** to avoid doing sth that is unpleasant: *Even the Security Council has seemed to back away from the issue.* **ˌback ˈdown (from sth)** (*NAmE also* **ˌback ˈoff**) to take back a demand or an opinion that other people are strongly opposed to; to admit defeat: *The security forces backed down from confrontation.* ◇ *When it became evident that the Politburo majority supported Lenin, Stalin backed down.* **ˌback ˈoff (from sth)** to choose not to take action, in order to avoid a difficult situation: *The Chamber of Commerce backed off from supporting national health insurance.* ◇ *Anger serves as a signal that others should back off.* **ˌback ˈout (of sth)** to decide that you are no longer going to take part in sth that has been agreed: *If one party backs out, he or she will be in breach of contract.* **ˌback sb/sth ˈup 1** to support a particular theory, opinion or idea; to say that what sb says is true: *His assertion was backed up by strong expert evidence.* ◇ *She backed up her claim with numerous examples.* **2** to provide help or support for sb/sth: *Good communications skills are vital but need to be backed up by a sound knowledge base.* ◇ *They need rules or laws backed up by the credible threat of force.* ➲ *related noun* BACKUP (1) **ˌback sth ˈup** (*computing*) to prepare a second copy of a file or program that can be used if the main one is lost or damaged: *It is good practice to make sure that your work is saved and backed up at regular intervals.* ➲ *related noun* BACKUP (2)

back·bone /ˈbækbəʊn; *NAmE* ˈbækboʊn/ *noun* **1** [C] the row of small bones that are connected together down the middle of the back SYN SPINE (1): *Snakes have hundreds of similar vertebrae in their backbones.* **2** [sing.] **~ (of sth)** the most important part of sth such as a system or an organization that gives it support and strength: *Agriculture forms the backbone of the rural economy.* **3** [C] (*chemistry, biochemistry*) a long chain of atoms that is part of the structure of some large MOLECULES: *In polysilane polymers, the polymer backbone is made up entirely of silicon atoms.* ◇ *Phosphate molecules provide the structural 'glue' that holds the DNA backbone together.* **4** [U] the strength of character that you need to do sth difficult: *Many liberals became convinced that Clinton had no backbone at all.*

back·ground /ˈbækgraʊnd/ *noun* **1** [C, U] the details of a person's family, education and experience: *He came from a privileged military background.* ◇ **from/with a ... ~** *The challenge is how to effectively manage employees from diverse social and cultural backgrounds.* ◇ **~ in sth** *The course is unsuitable for students with no background in electronics.* **2** [C, usually sing., U] the present circumstances or past events that help to explain an event or situation; information about these: *The precise date and historical background of the poem remain uncertain.* ◇ **against a ~ of sth** *The gradual development of human culture took place against a background of changing physical environments.* ◇ **~ to sth** *First, a brief account will be given of the background to the Human Rights Act 1998.* ◇ **~ on sth** *The introduction should supply the necessary background on how the machine works.* **3** [sing.] a position in which people are not paying attention to sb/sth or not as much attention as they are paying to sb/sth else: **in the ~** *In the research, people who seemed timid tended to keep in the background and let others make decisions.* ◇ *These programs are designed to work in the background, without human interference.* ◇ **+ noun** *For hearing impaired patients, it is important to reduce background noise, e.g. by turning off the TV or radio.* ➲ *compare* FOREGROUND[1] **4** [C, usually sing., U] the part of a picture, photograph or view behind the main objects or people: **in the ~** *In the background of this photo is a hillside from which all the trees have been felled.* ◇ **against the ~** *The main figures in the painting are clearly visible against the dark background.* ➲ *compare* FOREGROUND[1]

▸ ADJECTIVE + BACKGROUND **different, diverse • similar • social • socio-economic • ethnic • cultural • linguistic • religious • educational** *Employing a mix of people from different backgrounds has led to an improvement in customer service.* | **historical • theoretical** *In this section, the theoretical background is presented along with some empirical findings.*

▸ NOUN + BACKGROUND **family • class** *All Ancient Greek citizens participated in politics, regardless of wealth or family background.*

▸ VERB + BACKGROUND **come from • have • share • reflect** *Muslims and their religious practices in North America reflect diverse backgrounds.* | **form • provide** *This atmosphere of fear and hostility formed the background against which later mob attacks took place.*

▸ BACKGROUND + NOUN **information • knowledge • material • literature, reading** *Direct intervention by senior managers may be counter-productive if they lack the necessary background information.* | **level • concentration • noise • radiation** *Nitrate levels in these waters are now many times the expected background levels.*

back·ing /ˈbækɪŋ/ *noun* [U] **~ (of sb/sth)** help or support: *Japanese businesses often exercise significant political power through financial backing of the political parties.* ◇ *Rival national groups clashed in a series of wars, with the backing of various European great powers.* ◇ *These nations have received substantial financial backing from multilateral organizations.*

back·up (*also* **back-up**) /ˈbækʌp/ *noun* [U, C] **1** extra help or support that you can get if necessary: *A range of specialized agencies can provide further backup.* ◇ **+ noun** *Aristotle has some backup arguments to strengthen his case.* **2** (*computing*) a copy of sth such as a file or program that can be used if the original is lost or damaged; the process of making these copies: **+ noun** *Since she did not have a backup copy of her work, all that she was able to submit were some notes copied from a text.* ◇ **~ of sth** *Keep backups of all work.* ◇ *Backup of all accessed files occurs at regular time intervals.* ➲ *see also* BACK STH UP

back·ward /ˈbækwəd; *NAmE* ˈbækwərd/ *adj.* **1** having made less progress than normal; developing slowly: *Backward firms should not attempt to grow, but instead seek to use their existing resources more efficiently.* ◇ *Backward countries often have a cheaper supply of labour.* ◇ *School attendance remained low in the backward regions of Europe.* **2** moving in a direction that means that no progress is being made: *The party's long-term strategy clearly took a backward step.* **3** [only before noun] directed or moving towards the back: *The rocket emits light signals in both the forward and backward directions.* ➲ *compare* FORWARD[2]

back·wards /ˈbækwədz; *NAmE* ˈbækwərdz/ (*also* **backward** *especially in NAmE*) *adv.* **1** in the opposite direction to the usual one: *Ask the patient to count backwards from 20.* ◇ *The film moves chronologically backwards in order to tell the story of their friendship.* **2** towards a place or position that is behind: *The three cups catch the wind on one side of the axle and push backwards into the wind on the other side.* OPP FORWARD[1] (1) **3** towards a worse state: *Some new democracies slide backwards while others flourish.* ◇ *Global economic integration clearly took several steps backwards during this period.* OPP FORWARD[1] (2)

IDM **ˌbackward(s) and ˈforward(s)** from one place or position to another and back again many times: *Researchers often go backwards and forwards between the literature and research question during the course of a study.* ◇ *Dickens remained with her as much as his professional commitments in London permitted, taking the train backwards and forwards.* **bend/lean over ˈbackwards (to do sth)** to make a great effort, especially in order to be helpful or fair: *In his view, the park service had leaned over backwards to accommodate the environmentalists.*

bac·teria /bækˈtɪəriə; *NAmE* bækˈtɪriə/ *noun* [pl.] (*sing.* **bac·ter·ium** /bækˈtɪəriəm; *NAmE* bækˈtɪriəm/) the simplest and smallest forms of life. Bacteria exist in large numbers in air, water and soil, and also in living and dead creatures and plants, and are often a cause of disease: *The bacteria that cause salmonella can be killed by cooking at high temperatures.* ➲ grammar note *at* DATA

bac·ter·ial /bækˈtɪəriəl; *NAmE* bækˈtɪriəl/ *adj.* connected with or caused by bacteria: *Antibiotics may be useful in controlling secondary bacterial infections following a viral disease.*

bad /bæd/ *adj.* (**worse** /wɜːs; *NAmE* wɜːrs/, **worst** /wɜːst; *NAmE* wɜːrst/) **1** unpleasant; full of problems: *Within their first year of qualifying, 79% of doctors break bad news to a patient at least once.* ◇ *Bad luck or error do not appear to explain the data.* ◇ *In 2009, bad weather in the UK increased demand for holidays abroad.* **2** of poor quality; below an acceptable standard: *The relationship had got off to a very bad start.* ◇ *He was able to avoid military service on grounds of bad health.* ◇ *These plants showed a consistently worse environmental performance than the others.* **3** [not before noun] **~ for sb/sth** harmful; causing or likely to cause damage: *Many of those who smoke know that it is extremely bad for their health.* ◇ *Currency instability is generally bad for business.* ◇ *It has been suggested that retirement is bad for mental health.* **4** serious; severe: *Raising the ankle above the level of the heart will help prevent the swelling from getting worse.* **5 ~ at sth/at doing sth** (of a person) not able to do sth well or in an acceptable way SYN POOR (3): *Geologists are notoriously bad at predicting earthquakes.* **6** [only before noun] not appropriate in a particular situation: *The summer was precisely the worst time to contact college students who were on summer vacation.* ◇ *There are many examples of bad decisions in organizations.* **7** morally wrong; behaving in a way that is morally wrong: *Economists are often portrayed as the bad guys in the environmental debate.* ◇ *Morality is primarily concerned with the inner inclinations and attitudes that motivate people to perform good or bad actions.* **8** [usually before noun] not behaving well: *Some excuse bad parental behaviour; some recognize and disapprove of it.* **9** (of food) not safe to eat because it has decayed: *The raspberries may go bad before they are sold.* **10 ~ temper/mood** the state of feeling angry: *Her crude language and bad temper reinforced this first impression.* IDM *see* FAITH

badly /ˈbædli/ *adv.* (**worse** /wɜːs; *NAmE* wɜːrs/, **worst** /wɜːst; *NAmE* wɜːrst/) **1** used to emphasize how serious a situation or an event is: *One child was killed and two others were badly injured.* ◇ *Cyclone Greg badly damaged the town of Keningau in December 1996.* ◇ *The large increases in the price of oil over the last few years have badly affected the airline industry.* ◇ *He suffered badly from smallpox as a child.* **2** used to emphasize how much you want or need sb/sth: *Western medicine badly needs to find new anti-microbial agents.* ◇ *The bill would lock up land that Alaskans badly wanted and needed for economic growth.* **3** not skilfully or not carefully: *If the sampling is done badly, the results will mislead.* ◇ *The administration had become inefficient and badly managed.* OPP WELL[1] (1) **4** not successfully: *One option might be to compare a sample of companies which have performed well with those which have performed badly.* ◇ *The war was going badly, and the government was blamed for its handling of the armed forces.* **5** not in an acceptable way: *Usually these events involve extra attention given to the child when behaving badly.* ◇ *People tend to spread negative information about others when they feel they are treated badly.* **6** in a way that makes people get a bad opinion about sth: *A minister's resignation often reflects badly on the government as a whole.*

bag /bæg/ *noun* **1** (often in compounds) a soft container that opens at the top, often used for carrying or holding sth: *Samples should only be transported to the laboratory inside a sealed plastic bag.* **2 ~ (of sth)** the amount contained in a bag: *Use ice packs, ice massages, or even a bag of frozen peas to help relieve the swelling.*

bake /beɪk/ *verb* **1** [T, I] **~ (sth)** to cook food in an OVEN without extra fat or liquid; to be cooked in this way: *to bake bread/cakes* **2** [I, T] to become or to make sth become hard by heating: *The bricks are left in the kiln to bake.* ◇ **~ sth** *The clay is baked at very high temperatures.*

bal·ance[1] /ˈbæləns/ *noun* **1** [sing., U] a situation in which all parts exist in equal or appropriate amounts: *The film clearly fails to strike a fair balance in its representation of the issues.* ◇ **~ of sth** *The research tried to ensure an even balance of the sexes.* ◇ *Higher levels of pollutants may upset the normal balance of forest life.* ◇ **~ between A and B** *The government has attempted to maintain a balance between expenditure and income.* ➲ *see also* BALANCE OF POWER, IMBALANCE **2** [C, usually sing.] the amount of money in a bank account; the amount of a bill that remains after part has been paid: *One advantage of Internet banking is that it allows customers to check their balance online.* ➲ *see also* BALANCE OF PAYMENTS, BALANCE SHEET, TRADE BALANCE **3** [U] the ability to keep steady with an equal amount of weight on each side of the body: *In his rush to get on the bus, he pushed other passengers, causing them to lose their balance.* ◇ *Many of the patients with head injuries reported difficulty in keeping their balance while walking.*
IDM **(on) a/the balance of ˈprobabilities/probaˈbility** (considering) the evidence on both sides of an argument, to find the most likely reason for or result of sth: *When something is judged on a balance of probabilities, the jury only need to be 51% sure of the facts put forward.* **be/hang in the ˈbalance** if the future or result of sb/sth important **is/hangs in the balance**, it is uncertain: *At the height of the battle, the fate of Europe hung in the balance.* **on ˈbalance** after considering all the information: *On balance, it seems that there may be very real advantages for a business in developing ethical policies.* ➲ *more at* REDRESS[1], STRIKE[1], TIP[2]

▸ ADJECTIVE + BALANCE **delicate, fine • right, appropriate, fair, proper • overall • political • ecological • work-life** *Human activities have disturbed the delicate balance which maintains the ozone layer.* ◇ *Broadcasters must be seen to be maintaining political balance in their programming.*

▸ NOUN + BALANCE **energy • water • fluid • gender** *The charts are used to monitor the patient's fluid balance.* ◇ *Equal opportunities legislation has forced many organizations to recruit workforces that reflect the racial and gender balance of the population.*

▸ VERB + BALANCE **maintain • find, achieve, strike • provide • ensure • change, affect, alter, shift, tip, upset • restore, redress** *Managers admit that they are uncertain about how to strike a balance between cost and quality.* ◇ *The function of employment law is to redress the balance between the employer and the dependent employees.*

bal·ance[2] /ˈbæləns/ *verb* **1** [T, often passive, I] to be equal in importance or amount to sth else that has the opposite effect SYN OFFSET[1]: **be balanced by sth** *In a steady thermal state, this heat influx is exactly balanced by the net heat efflux.* ◇ **~ out** *The graph shows that the supply from the producer and the demand from the consumer tend to balance out.* **2** [T] **~ A with/and B** to give equal importance to two different things or parts of sth: *Her work attempts to balance theory with experimental evidence.* **3** [T, often passive] **~ A against B** to compare the importance of two different things: *The risks are weighed and the costs are balanced against the likely benefit.* **4** [T] **~ sth** (*finance*) to show or make sure that in an account the total money spent is equal to the total money received: *The policies focused on cutting expenditure and raising taxes* *in order to balance the national budget.* **5** [I, T] **~ (sth) (on sth)** to put your body or sth else into a position where it is steady and does not fall: *It is a dynamically unstable system, like a pen precariously balanced on its tip.*

B

bal·anced /ˈbælənst/ *adj.* [usually before noun] (*approving*) **1** having all parts in equal, correct or good amounts: *A government cannot massively expand military spending, cut taxes sharply, and still have a balanced budget.* ◇ *A healthy balanced diet consists of fibre, vitamins, minerals, fresh fruit and vegetables, as well as protein, carbohydrate and fats.* ◇ *Risk-averse investors prefer a more balanced portfolio of products and services.* **2** giving careful thought to all opinions on a particular subject: *Since the 1980s, historians have taken a more balanced view of these events.* ◇ *An economic perspective alone is not enough for a balanced picture of the countryside.*

ˌbalance of ˈpayments *noun* [sing.] the difference between the amount a country pays for imports and the amount it receives for exports in a particular period of time: *There was a growing deficit in the American balance of payments.* ◇ **+ noun** *a balance of payments deficit/surplus/crisis*

ˌbalance of ˈpower *noun* [sing.] **1 ~ (between A and B)** a situation in which political or military strength is divided between two countries or groups of countries: *The rough balance of power between the two superpowers helped to secure a degree of order.* **2** the power held by a small group which can give its support to either of two larger and equally strong groups: *The party's position in holding the balance of power allowed it to negotiate with the major players.*

ˌbalance of ˈtrade *noun* = TRADE BALANCE

ˈbalance sheet *noun* (*finance*) a written statement showing the amount of money and property that a company has and listing what has been received and paid out: *The balance sheets of carbon intensive companies are likely to be negatively impacted by rising carbon prices.*

ball /bɔːl/ *noun* **1** a round object used for throwing, hitting, etc. in games and sports: *If you could throw the ball hard enough, it would escape from the Earth and carry on out into space.* **2 ~ of sth** a round object or a thing that has been formed into a round shape: *After fertilization, a mammalian egg divides to form a solid ball of cells.*

bal·lot /ˈbælət/ *noun* **1** [U, C] the system of voting in writing and usually in secret; an occasion on which a vote is held: *Jury members recorded their vote by secret ballot.* ◇ **~ of sb** *A ballot of members approved the proposals.* **2** (*BrE also* ˈ**ballot paper**) [C] the piece of paper on which sb marks who they are voting for: *Turnout is the percentage of eligible voters who cast a ballot in an election.* ◇ **~ box** *He placed his paper into the ballot box.* ➲ *see also* POLL[1] (2)

ban[1] /bæn/ *verb* (**-nn-**) **1** to decide or say officially that sth is not allowed SYN PROHIBIT (1): **~ sth** *Sweden banned the use of certain antibiotics in livestock production in 1986.* ◇ *Public protest and demonstrations are banned.* ◇ **~ sth from sth** *The government banned certain foods and drinks from schools.* **2** [often passive] to order sb not to do sth or not to go somewhere, especially officially: **~ sb from sth** *Reporters were banned from the courtroom.* ◇ **~ sb from doing sth** *He was banned from returning by the Home Secretary.*

ban[2] /bæn/ *noun* an official rule that says that sth is not allowed: *The EU refused to lift its ban.* ◇ *The costs of introducing workplace smoking bans were not assessed.* ◇ **~ on sth** *The Hunting Act 2004 imposed a ban on hunting wild animals with dogs.*

band[1] /bænd/ *noun* **1** [C] a strip or line of colour or light that appears different from what is around it: *The spectrum shows three bands coloured red, green and blue.* ◇ **~ of sth** *The Milky Way forms a band of light across the night sky.* **2** [C] a long, often narrow area or part of sth that is different from what is around it: *Mediterranean climatic zones are confined to narrow bands either side of the Equator.* ◇ **~ of sth** *Tidal channels which have strong currents may produce enriched bands of turbid water.* **3** [C] a range of sth such as numbers, ages or prices within which people or things are counted or measured: *In this table, age has been broken down into just three age bands.* ◇ *Some economists have argued for a flat rate of income tax rather than having different tax bands with increasing rates of tax.* ◇ **~ of sth** *The charts show three bands of risk: less than 10%, 10–20%, and greater than 20%.* **4** (*also* **wave·band**) [C] a certain range of FREQUENCIES of a wave, such as a light or radio wave: *Observations were made with radiometers at five frequency bands, ranging from 23 to 94 GHz.* ◇ **~ of sth** *Broadband refers to a band of frequencies available to transmit information.* **5** [C] a thin flat strip or circle of any material that is put around things, for example to hold them together or to make them stronger: *The top of each chamber was covered with aluminium foil secured with a rubber band.* ◇ *Classical architects in Greece, Rome and Gujarat held their structures together with iron bands and pegs.* **6** [C+sing./pl. v.] a group of people who do sth together or who have the same ideas: *The guerrillas are characterized as terrorists and criminal bands rather than parties to an armed conflict.* ◇ **~ of sth** *Husayn and his small band of followers were slaughtered by an Umayyad army at Karbala.*

band[2] /bænd/ *verb* **1** [usually passive] to have a band of a different material or colour around or in sth: *Of these 36 nests, 29 were attended by a female that was also colour banded.* **2** [usually passive] **~ sth** (*BrE*) to be organized into groups depending on sth such as price, income or age: *People older than 60 years were banded in one group.*
PHR V **ˌband toˈgether** to form a group in order to achieve sth: *If a local school needed a new playground, parents banded together to construct it.*

band·width /ˈbændwɪdθ/ *noun* [C, U] (*computing*) **1** a band of FREQUENCIES used for sending electronic signals: *The audio signal bandwidth is about 15 kHz.* ◇ *LEDs can be designed so as to produce coherent light with a very narrow bandwidth.* ◇ **~ of sth** *The transmission bandwidth of AM systems cannot be changed.* **2** a measurement of the amount of data that a particular computer network or Internet connection can send in a particular time. It is often measured in BITS per second: *The amount of data that can be transmitted is limited by the available bandwidth.* ◇ **~ of sth** *The provision of multiple pathways considerably increases the bandwidth of the system.*

bank /bæŋk/ *noun* **1** an organization that keeps money safely for its customers and lends money to people who want to borrow it; the local office of an organization providing these services: *People may save money by putting it in the bank.* ◇ *The interest rate is set by the central bank.* ◇ *Internet banking avoids time-consuming trips to the bank.* ➲ *see also* CENTRAL BANK **2** an amount of sth that is collected and stored; a place where sth is stored ready for use: *Blood products are collected from the blood bank in the hospital.* **3** the side of a river, CANAL, etc. and the land near it: *Erosion is visible along the steep river bank.* ◇ **~ of sth** *The cities of ancient Egypt were sited on the banks of the River Nile.*

ˈbank account *noun* an arrangement with a bank that allows sb/sth to keep money there, pay money in and take money out: *He was jailed for depositing state finances into a private bank account.*

bank·er /ˈbæŋkə(r)/ *noun* a person who works in a senior position at a bank; a person or organization that provides financial services: *European central bankers make many important policy decisions.* ◇ **~ to sb/sth** *The Bank of*

England is banker to the commercial banking system in the UK.

bank·ing /ˈbæŋkɪŋ/ *noun* [U] the business activity of banks: *With the development of Internet banking, location is becoming an irrelevant consideration for e-commerce.* ◇ **+ noun** *The banking system consists of the central bank together with the commercial banks.*

bank·note /ˈbæŋknəʊt; *NAmE* ˈbæŋknoʊt/ *noun* (*especially BrE*) = NOTE² (6)

bank·rupt /ˈbæŋkrʌpt/ *adj.* without enough money to pay what you owe: **go ~** *The firm went bankrupt in 2009.*

bank·rupt·cy /ˈbæŋkrʌptsi/ *noun* (*pl.* **-ies**) [U, C] the state of being bankrupt: *The firm filed for bankruptcy in 2009.* ◇ *There could be further bankruptcies among small farmers.*

bar¹ /bɑː(r)/ *noun* **1** [C] a place where you can buy and drink alcoholic and other drinks: *Bars and pubs had a significantly greater percentage of patrons who smoked than did cafes.* **2** [C] (especially in compounds) a place in which a particular kind of food or drink is the main thing that is served: *a coffee/wine bar* **3** [C] a piece of sth with straight sides: *Chocolate bars and magazines are typical impulse purchases.* ◇ **~ of sth** *In the bathroom, liquid soap has replaced individual bars of toilet soap.* **4** [C] a long straight piece of metal or wood: *Because concrete is strong when squashed but weak when pulled, steel bars are used to reinforce it.* **5** [C] a band or strip in sth such as a diagram or photograph, that shows information about sth: *The duration of the stimulus is indicated by the horizontal bar beneath the histogram.* ◇ *The size of the government revenue is indicated by the area with vertical bars in Figure 8.3.* **6** [C, usually sing.] **~ (to sth)** a thing that stops sb from doing sth: *The higher costs of land transport were not an absolute bar to overland trade.* ◇ *Religious belief was not necessarily a bar to party membership.* **7** [C] (*pl.* **bar** or **bars**) a unit for measuring the pressure of gas or the atmosphere: *Cylinders of compressed gas are typically filled to a pressure of 200 bar.* **8** [C] (especially in compounds) a part of the display of a computer program that is used to control sth: *Click 'Edit' on the menu bar, and select 'Column Width'.* **9 the Bar** [sing.] the profession of a lawyer, especially a lawyer that works in a higher court: *He was born in England, where he was called to the Bar in 1840.*
IDM **be͵hind ˈbars** in prison: *Infiltrators from enemy states could be sentenced to as much as seven years behind bars.* **set the ˈbar** to set a standard of quality or performance: *She has set the bar high for future scholars—those who would build on her interpretations as well as those who would challenge them.*

bar² /bɑː(r)/ *verb* (**-rr-**) to not allow sb/sth to do sth: *The illegality of the claimant's conduct might bar his claim.* ◇ *The security system bars access to the data to persons not entitled to obtain such information.* ◇ **~ sb/sth from sth** *Modernity, it seems, has not barred religion from everyday life.* ◇ **~ sb/sth from doing sth** *The holders of the shares in question are barred from voting on the resolution.*

bar³ /bɑː(r)/ *prep.* (*especially BrE*) except for sb/sth: *Travel writing became regarded as a lesser genre, the province (bar a few exceptions) of amateur writers.* ◇ *Bar anecdotal 'evidence', it is unproven that any such link is socially governed.*

ˈbar chart (*especially NAmE* **ˈbar graph**) *noun* a diagram that uses lines or narrow RECTANGLES of different heights (but equal widths) to show different amounts, so that they can be compared: *A bar chart of the data is presented in Figure 4.3.* ➲ *compare* HISTOGRAM ➲ language bank *at* TABLE

bare /beə(r); *NAmE* ber/ *adj.* (**barer**, **bar·est**) **1** [only before noun] the most basic or simple; enough, but not more: *It is advisable to keep the creative brief to the bare essentials.* ◇ *The bare facts are well known.* ◇ *They intend to do the bare minimum necessary to satisfy their obligations.* HELP **Bare** can also suggest that sth is not really enough: *Poor illiterate farmers eked out a bare living.* **2** [usually before noun] not covered with anything: *They had to sleep on the bare floor.* ◇ *The summit is largely bare rock, so there is no climatic treeline.* HELP A person with **bare** arms, feet, etc. is not wearing anything on that part of their body. **3** (of a room, cupboard, etc.) not containing anything; empty: *The room is stark and bare.*
IDM **the bare ˈbones (of sth)** the basic facts: *This gives the bare bones of the story.* **lay sth ˈbare** to make sth known or understood that was not known or understood before: *The cosy corporate culture was suddenly laid bare.* **with your bare ˈhands** without weapons or tools: *Rescuers were able to shift the pieces with their bare hands.*

bare·ly /ˈbeəli; *NAmE* ˈberli/ *adv.* **1** used to say that sth almost does not happen or exist: *The issue is barely touched upon.* ◇ *Ancient authors barely mention any of this.* ◇ *There is no systematic discussion of Christian doctrines and barely any mention of God.* **2** used to say that sth is almost impossible: *The worms are barely visible without a microscope.* ◇ *Such developments may be barely perceptible.* ◇ *These farmers are barely able to achieve a subsistence level of existence.* **3** just; certainly not more than (a particular amount, age, time, etc.): *He had left home with barely 100 dollars.* ◇ *The mobile phone sector barely existed just 20 years ago.* **4** only a very short time before: *The war had barely begun.*

bar·gain¹ /ˈbɑːɡən; *NAmE* ˈbɑːrɡən/ *noun* an agreement between two or more people or groups, to do sth for each other SYN DEAL² (1): *These two people never intended to make a bargain which could be enforced in law.* ◇ **~ with sb** *Individual companies are able to strike bargains with organized labour.* ◇ **~ between A and B** *Devolution represents a new bargain between the nations.* HELP In general English, a **bargain** is often sth that is bought for less than the normal price: *Investors have been able to snap up companies at bargain prices.* In academic writing, this is best avoided. Instead, you can use a more formal expression; for example, you can describe costs as **modest** or **relatively low**, or describe sth as **relatively inexpensive**: *At the time of writing, this service is relatively inexpensive.*
IDM *see* HARD¹, STRIKE¹

bar·gain² /ˈbɑːɡən; *NAmE* ˈbɑːrɡən/ *verb* [I, T] to talk with sb about payment, conditions, etc. in order to reach an agreement SYN NEGOTIATE: **~ for sth** *Workers were now able to bargain more effectively for better wages and conditions.* ◇ **~ over sth** *Policy stakeholders bargain over what the agenda should be.* ◇ **~ with sb** *These parents have fallen into the habit of bargaining with their children.*
PHR V **ˈbargain for sth** (usually in negative sentences) to expect sth to happen and be prepared for it: *What the Prime Minister had not bargained for, however, was the reaction of the trade unions.*

bar·gain·ing /ˈbɑːɡənɪŋ; *NAmE* ˈbɑːrɡənɪŋ/ *noun* [U] discussion of prices and conditions with the aim of reaching an agreement that is acceptable SYN NEGOTIATION: *It was difficult to coordinate annual wage bargaining.* ➲ *see also* COLLECTIVE BARGAINING

ˈbargaining power *noun* [U] the amount of control a person or group has when trying to reach an agreement with another group in a business or political situation: *Because few of them are represented by a trade union, they have little bargaining power.*

bar·rier /ˈbæriə(r)/ *noun* **1** a problem, rule or situation that prevents sb from doing sth, or that makes sth impossible: *These patients all managed to overcome barriers such as lack of time, skill and knowledge.* ◇ **~ to sth** *Environmental regulations are often seen as barriers to trade.* ◇ **~ against sth** *The largest companies often try to raise entry barriers against competitors.* **2** something that exists between one thing or person and another and keeps them separate: *Language barriers can be significant for international students.* ◇ **~ to sth** *The membrane of a cell is a barrier to virus entry.* ◇ **~ between A and B** *The cream acts as a physical barrier between the skin and the outside world.* ◇ **~ against sth** *Mass media such as television and the Internet mean that national borders are no longer effective barriers against external influences.*

▸ ADJECTIVE + BARRIER **significant • major • formidable • effective • potential • artificial • invisible • cultural • social** *Trade was significantly hampered by various invisible trade barriers, such as border controls and national technical standards for goods.* | **formidable • effective • physical • natural** *Effective natural barriers could include mountain ranges and rivers.*

▸ NOUN + BARRIER **language • trade • tariff • non-tariff • activation • energy** *Monetary controls and other non-tariff barriers have reduced total imports.*

▸ VERB + BARRIER **erect, create, raise • remove, eliminate, break down • reduce, lower • face • overcome, cross** *The court's verdict was that the company had erected significant barriers to prevent its competitors from entering the market.* | **form, constitute** *Such cells form an effective barrier between the gut and the rest of the body.*

basal /ˈbeɪsl/ *adj.* (*technical*) forming or belonging to a bottom layer or base: *The first zygotic division is unequal, with the basal cell larger than the apical cell.*

base¹ /beɪs/ *verb* [usually passive] to use a particular place as the main place for an organization or activity: **(be) based in...** *The development team, previously based in Virginia, has relocated to Florida.* ◇ **~ sb/sth/yourself in...** *Employment levels were boosted by inviting IT companies to base themselves in the city.* ➲ *see also* BASED (2)

PHR V **ˈbase sth on/upon/around sth** [usually passive] to use an idea, a fact or a situation as the point from which sth can be developed: *Idealism holds that a state should base its foreign policy on ethical principles.* ◇ **be based on sth** *Both these theories of justice are based on a principle of equality.* ◇ **be based around sth** *Such companies adopted a more strategic approach to the management of labour, based around creating a high-trust working environment.*

▸ NOUN + BE BASED ON STH **society • economy • system • relationship • decision, judgement, choice • policy, strategy • approach, method • model, theory • argument • conclusion • research, study • analysis • calculation, estimate • prediction** *All the committee's decisions were based on the welfare and best interests of the children.*

▸ BE BASED + ADVERB + ON STH **mainly, largely, primarily • only, entirely, solely, simply, purely, exclusively • more • less** *The service approach is based entirely on existing web services technology.*

▸ BE + ADVERB + BASED ON STH **often • usually • largely, mostly, mainly, primarily • broadly • typically • entirely** *All these stories of flooding are largely based on the ancient Babylonian epic Gilgamesh.* ◇ *Their conclusions were entirely based on an analysis of the results from previous studies.*

base² /beɪs/ *noun* **1** [C] an idea, a fact, a situation or a group of people from which sth can be developed or achieved: *A strong research base supports the rationale for community schools.* ◇ *The company needs to expand its knowledge base through further investment in education and training.* ◇ *The development of a loyal customer base in China will be vital to future growth.* ➲ *compare* BASIS (3) ➲ *see also* KNOWLEDGE BASE **2** [C] the main place where an organization or person operates from or stays: *Seventeen of the world's fifty largest companies had their home base in the USA in 1998.* ◇ *Russia established a new naval base in Vladivostok.* **3** [C, usually sing.] **~ (of sth)** the lowest part of sth, especially the part or surface on which it rests or stands: *The rainwater collects in a pool at the base of the cliff.* ◇ *As fewer babies are born, the base of the population pyramid narrows, producing a relative increase in the older population.* **4** [C] (*chemistry*) a chemical substance, for example an ALKALI, that can combine with an acid to form a salt: *The addition of an acid or base normally causes the pH of the solution to change.* **5** [C, usually sing.] (*mathematics*) a number on which a system of counting and expressing numbers is built up, for example 10 in the DECIMAL system and 2 in the BINARY system: *The basic algorithms of arithmetic operate with integers in base 10 notation.*

▸ ADJECTIVE + BASE **strong • large, broad • economic • industrial • legal** *The legislation was struck down on the grounds that it lacked an adequate legal base.*

▸ NOUN + BASE **tax • power • knowledge • skill • research • evidence • resource • customer • home** *With a very limited resource base, St Helena suffers from its small size and small population.*

▸ VERB + BASE **establish, build • expand, broaden • strengthen** *The king's power base in the north had been strengthened by recent victories.*

based /beɪst/ *combining form* (in compound adjectives) **1** using or developing from sth: *In the last decade the field has moved away from theoretical models and towards empirically based research.* **2** operating mainly from or staying mainly in a particular place: *The company is quickly becoming one of the largest London-based house builders.* **3** containing sth as an important part or feature: *The soldiers stationed in Germany had a predominantly beef-based diet.* ◇ *The study identified class-based differences in child-rearing practices.*

base·line /ˈbeɪslaɪn/ *noun* [C, usually sing., U] a measurement, situation or time that is used as a starting point when comparing facts: **against a ~** *The survey established a baseline against which further research can be compared.* ◇ **at ~** *General health status was measured at both baseline and follow-up.* ◇ **from ~ (to sth)** *Weight decreased significantly from baseline to 6 months.* ◇ **+ noun** *Baseline characteristics were comparable.*

bases **1** *pl. of* BASE¹ **2** *pl. of* BASIS

basic /ˈbeɪsɪk/ *adj.* **1** forming the part of sth that is most necessary and from which other things develop: *The nucleotide is the basic unit of the DNA molecule.* ◇ *Figure 1.6 illustrates the basic principle behind a digital-to-analogue converter.* ◇ **~ to sth** *The idea of moral equality is basic to Marx's thought.* **2** of the simplest kind; at the simplest level: *The PDP-11, which was introduced in 1969, would be regarded as a very basic machine by today's standards.* ◇ *Changes in meaning can be divided into four basic types:...* **3** [only before noun] necessary and important to all people: *The universality of religion suggests that it serves a basic human need.*

▸ BASIC + NOUN **principle, idea, belief, concept, premise, assumption, tenet • logic • element, feature • building block • unit • structure, framework • pattern • level • form • question, issue • problem • rule • model • skill • knowledge • information • research • emotion** *A problem and its solution are among the basic building blocks of traditional narrative.* ◇ *Islam provided the basic ideological framework for political and social life.* ◇ *It is a maths game that helps children practise basic skills.* | **need, requirement • right** *Wollstonecraft asserted that one can exercise one's duties only if one has basic human rights.*

ba·sic·ally /ˈbeɪsɪkli/ *adv.* **1** in the most important ways, without considering features that are less important SYN ESSENTIALLY: *This hypothesis, although basically correct, is generally modified in one of various ways.* **2** used when giving an opinion or stating what is important about a situation: *In this model, the workplace is basically perceived as a hostile environment.*

basics /ˈbeɪsɪks/ *noun* [pl.] **~ (of sth)** the most important and necessary ideas, facts or skills from which other things develop SYN FUNDAMENTALS: *The basics of electrochemistry are widely taught in high school.*

basin /ˈbeɪsn/ *noun* (*geography*) a place where the earth's surface is, or has been, lower than the surrounding area: *The Rhine river basin is the most industrialized region.* ◇ *Rather more important may have been the infilling of the ocean basins by sediment.* ◇ *Gas-producing sedimentary basins are characterized by shallow-water sediments.* ◇ **+ noun** *Approximately 1% of the drainage basin area is occupied by the stream channel.*

basis /ˈbeɪsɪs/ *noun* (*pl.* **bases** /ˈbeɪsiːz/) **1** [sing.] the reason why people take a particular action: **on the ~ of sth** *Businesses are obliged to make decisions on the basis of the current value of their assets.* ◇ **on the ~ that...** *Companies offer discounts on the basis that customers purchase goods in larger quantities.* **2** [sing.] **on a ... ~** the way sth is organized or arranged: *The fee was paid by members on a monthly basis.* ◇ *The industry, on a voluntary basis, should be encouraged to manufacture and market alcohol responsibly.* **3** [C, usually sing., U] the important facts, ideas or events that support sth and that it can develop from: **~ in sth** *The concept of race among humans has no basis in fact.* ◇ **~ of sth** *After 1960, Keynesian economics gradually came to form the accepted basis of government policy.* ◇ **~ for (doing) sth** *The polymers were expected to provide the basis for many future advances.*

▸ ADJECTIVE + BASIS **regular • daily, day-to-day • monthly • annual • ad hoc • individual • continuous, ongoing • worldwide • voluntary** *Monitoring is currently done on an ad hoc basis, but continuous monitoring would be preferable.* | **theoretical, conceptual • rational • sound, firm • material • legal • molecular • biological • genetic** *The literature offers a theoretical basis for distinguishing between novice and expert entrepreneurs.*

▸ VERB + BASIS **provide, form, offer, constitute • lay, establish • understand • undermine, challenge** *The claimant must first establish the basis of her claim.* ◇ *New international forces and technologies undermined the traditional basis of British society.*

bath /bɑːθ; *NAmE* bæθ/ *noun* (*pl.* **baths** /bɑːðz; *NAmE* bæðz/) **1** (*BrE*) (*also* **bath·tub** /ˈbɑːθtʌb; *NAmE* ˈbæθtʌb/ *NAmE, BrE*) a large, long container that you put water in and then get into to wash your whole body: *She fractured her arm after trying to get out of the bath unassisted.* **2** an act of washing your whole body by sitting or lying in water: *Warm baths may help relieve pain.* ◇ *to have/take a bath* **3 ~ (of sth)** a container with a liquid in it, in which sth is washed or placed for a period of time. Baths are used in industrial, chemical and medical processes: *Liquid propane is prepared by condensing gaseous propane into a tube that has been cooled in a bath of liquid nitrogen.* **4** [usually pl.] a public place where people went in the past to wash or have a bath: *The Greek settlers brought their gods and built temples, public baths and marketplaces.*

bat·tery /ˈbætri; ˈbætəri/ *noun* (*pl.* **-ies**) **1** [C] a device in which chemical energy is changed into electricity and used as a source of power: *High-energy, rechargeable batteries have been critical to the growth of laptop computers.* **2** [C] a large number or series of things of the same type: *The test battery should consist of widely used and well-known measures.* ◇ **~ of sth** *The activities of many cells are controlled by a whole battery of hormones.* HELP **Battery** farming *(BrE)* involves keeping a large number of animals, for example chickens, in small containers or spaces: *Banning battery cages is discussed in many studies.* **3** [U, C] (*law*) the crime of attacking sb physically: *The defendant was charged with battery.* ◇ *The restraint amounted to a battery.* ➲ *compare* ASSAULT[1] (1)

bat·tle[1] /ˈbætl/ *noun* **1** [C, U] a fight between armies, ships or planes, especially during a war: **the ~ of sth** *After winning the decisive battle of Jena, Napoleon triumphantly entered Berlin.* ◇ **~ with sb** *They refused to take part in battles with the Spartans.* ◇ **~ against sb** *They fought fierce battles against each other.* ◇ **~ between A and B** *The building was destroyed in a battle between government forces and rebels.* ◇ **in ~** *Decius was killed in battle in 251.* ◇ **go into ~** *Many army units refused to go into battle.* **2** [C] a competition, an argument or a struggle between people or groups of people trying to win power or control: **~ with sb/sth** *He wasted two years in battles with the Treasury.* ◇ **~ against sb/sth** *Workers are constantly urged to help the company in its battle against the competition.* ◇ **~ between A and B** *The article describes the electoral battle between John Kennedy and Hubert Humphrey.* ◇ **~ for sth** *In the late 1990s, the company lost a fierce competitive battle for market share to its main rival.* ➲ *see also* CAMPAIGN[1] (1) **3** [C, usually sing.] a determined effort that sb makes to solve a difficult problem or succeed in a difficult situation: **~ against sth** *Many factors can influence the course of the battle against AIDS.* ◇ **~ for sth** *Hopner led the battle for political reform.* ◇ **~ with sth** *Modern agriculture fights a constant battle with crop diseases.*

▸ ADJECTIVE + BATTLE **decisive • major** *Major economic battles within the regime were fought out over economic policy.* | **constant • losing** *Low-lying countries are fighting a losing battle for action on climate change.* | **competitive • political • legal** *The early 1990s witnessed major cultural and political battles in New York City over education.*

▸ VERB + BATTLE **fight, wage, do • win • lose • avoid** *The book describes how the forces of good do battle with the devil.*

bat·tle[2] /ˈbætl/ *verb* [I, T] to try very hard to deal with sth unpleasant or achieve sth difficult SYN FIGHT[1] (4): **~ with/against sb/sth** *She found herself battling with depression.* ◇ **~ for sth** *Women in the discipline continue to battle for acceptance and recognition.* ◇ **~ sb/sth** *Disability activists spent the 1960s battling what they saw as paternalism.* ◇ **~ to do sth** *They had to battle hard to secure sufficient resources.*

battle·field /ˈbætlfiːld/ *noun* **1** a place where a battle is being fought or has been fought: **on the ~** *The real difference between the armies lay in the number of troops who could be deployed on the battlefield.* **2** = BATTLEGROUND

battle·ground /ˈbætlgraʊnd/ (*also* **battle·field**) *noun* a subject that people feel strongly about and argue about: *Education has become a key political battleground.*

be[1] /bi; *strong form* biː/ *verb* HELP For irregular forms of **be**, see page R4. **1** *linking verb* **there is/are + noun** to exist; to be present: *There are no easy answers to this question.* ◇ *There were several reasons for this decision.* ◇ *In order for motion to be possible, there must be empty space into which atoms can move.* **2** [I] **+ adv./prep.** to be located; to be in a place: *The city of Jakarta is on the northern coastal plain of Java.* ◇ *Her children are all away at college.* **3** [I] **+ adv./prep.** to happen at a time or in a place: *That was before the war.* ◇ *In 2016, the Olympics will be in Rio de Janeiro.* **4** [I] **+ adv./prep.** to remain in a place: *She has been in the UK for eight years.* **5** [I] **+ adv./prep.** to attend an event; to be present in a place: *Leaders of all the G8 nations were at the summit.* ◇ *In 1913 he was in Vienna, writing a theoretical treatise.* **6** [I] (only used in the perfect tenses) **+ adv./prep.** to visit a place: *She had never been to Scotland.* **7** [I] **~ from...** used to say where sb was born or where their home is: *Richard Nixon was from California.* ◇ *He was from a Scottish landowning family.* **8** *linking verb* used when you are naming people or things, describing them or giving more information about them: **+ noun** ◇ *He wanted to be a good father.* ◇ **+ adj.** *By this time, she was 91 years old.* ◇ *The results are very encouraging.* ◇ **~ (that)...** *The fact is that US workers,* on average, saw no improvement in their living standards. ◇ **~ doing sth** *The problem is getting it all done in the time available.* ◇ **~ to do sth** *The problem is to get it all done in the time available.* ➲ *see also* WOULD-BE **9** *linking verb* **it is/was** used when you are describing a situation or saying what you think about it: **+ adj.** *It is very cold in the winter.* ◇ *In Denmark, for example, it is unusual for a woman not to work outside the home.* ◇ **+ noun** *It is a shame this evidence was not available to earlier researchers.* **10** *linking verb* **it is/was** used to talk about time: **+ noun** *It was August 1806 when Coleridge returned from Malta.* ◇ **+ adj.** *It was early on the morning of 14 April.* **11** *linking verb* [I] used to say who sth belongs to or who it is intended for: **~ mine, yours, etc.** *The money is not yours, it is John's.* ◇ **~ for me, you, etc.** *This package is for you.* **12** *linking verb* **+ noun** to cost: *The tickets were £25 each.* **13** *linking verb* **+ noun** to be equal to: *Three and three is six.* ◇ *How much is a thousand pounds in euros?* ◇ *Let x be the sum of a and b.*

IDM Most idioms containing **be** are at the entries for the nouns and adjectives in the idioms, for example **as the case may be** is at **case**. **-to-be** (in compounds) future: *The programme provides job training to young mothers and mothers-to-be.* ◇ *She became the first commoner ever to marry an emperor-to-be.*

be² /bi; *strong form* biː/ *auxiliary verb* HELP For irregular forms of **be**, see page R4. **1** used with a past participle to form the passive: *He was killed in the war.* ◇ *Fusion power is still being developed.* ◇ *Participants will be told what to do.* **2** used with a present participle to form progressive tenses: *More students are studying closer to home.* ◇ *We have been investigating two broad areas of application for this technology.* ◇ *Techniques such as these are continually being refined.* **3** used to avoid repeating the full form of a verb in the passive or a progressive tense: *Karen was not defeated in any of her games, but all the others were.* **4 ~ to do sth** used to say what must or should be done: *They could not agree on what was to be done about the problem.* **5 ~ to do sth** used to say what is arranged to happen: *Construction is to begin next summer.* **6 ~ to do sth** used to say what happened later: *He was to regret this decision for the rest of his life.* **7 ~ not, never, etc. to do sth/be done** used to say what could not or did not happen: *He was never to see England again.* ◇ *The strange blue fish was not to be found in any of the books she consulted.* **8 if sb/it were to do sth...** (*formal*) used to express a condition: *She would be ostracized both religiously and socially if she were to be divorced.*

beach /biːtʃ/ *noun* an area of sand or small stones, beside the sea or a lake: *Sea turtles, for example, lay eggs in underground nests on the beach.* ◇ *Sandy beaches stretch along the coastline.*

beam /biːm/ *noun* **1** a line of light, electric waves or PARTICLES: *The two light beams must be of exactly the same intensity.* ◇ *The finely focused electron beam is scanned over the surface.* ◇ **~ of sth** *A fine beam of ultraviolet light activates the fluorescent compound.* **2** a long piece of wood, metal, etc. used to support weight in a building or other structure: *The load-carrying capacity of the high-strength steel beam was 17.5 kN.*

bear /beə(r); *NAmE* ber/ *verb* (**bore** /bɔː(r)/, **borne** /bɔːn; *NAmE* bɔːrn/) **1 ~ sth** to have sth as a characteristic or feature; to be connected with sth: *The novel bears a passing resemblance to Shakespeare's 'King Lear'.* ◇ *He has chest pain that bears no relation to exertion.* ◇ *These phenomena bear the imprint of their times.* **2 ~ sth** to have a particular mark, word or symbol that can be seen: *Both men bore physical scars consistent with torture.* ◇ *All toys which comply with European Commission minimum safety standards must bear the CE mark.* **3 ~ sth** to have a particular name: *Kepler summarized his discoveries in three laws that now bear his name.* ◇ *Rulers bore the title 'Sultan'.* **4 ~ sth** to take responsibility for sth difficult; to be affected by or deal with sth unpleasant: *Students must bear the cost of their studies.* ◇ *Wives typically bear a greater responsibility for household duties and family care.* ◇ *The applicant should not be expected to bear the entire burden of proof.* ◇ *It was unskilled blue-collar workers who bore the brunt of redundancies.* HELP If sb **cannot bear** sth, they feel unable to deal with it or accept it: *Her jealous husband could not bear the possibility of his wife talking to another man.* The short form 'can't/couldn't bear' is not suitable in academic writing, unless you are quoting. **5** to have a feeling, especially a negative feeling: **~ sth** *She bore a grudge against them because of their role in his death.* ◇ **~ sb sth** *He bore them no ill will.* **6 ~ (doing) sth** to be suitable for sth; to be worth doing: *It bears repeating that this analysis had been firmly rejected by the Court.* HELP If sth **does not bear close inspection**, it will be found to be unacceptable when carefully examined: *This claim does not bear close inspection.* If sth **does not bear comparison** with sth else, it is not nearly as good: *Her later work does not bear comparison with her earlier novels.* **7 ~ sb/sth** (*formal*) to carry or hold sb/sth: *Relatives bearing gifts followed the couple on foot.* ◇ *The condition commonly affects weight-bearing joints (hips and knees).* ◇ *The gun lobby sought to preserve the right to bear arms.* **8** (*formal*) to give birth to a child: **~ sb** *She was not able to bear children.* ◇ **~ sb sth** *She bore him three daughters.* **9 ~ sth** (*formal*) to produce flowers or fruit: *Many species of fig trees bear fruit several times a year.*

IDM **bear ˈfruit** to have a successful result: *These efforts have finally borne fruit.* **bear witness/testimony to sth** to provide evidence of the truth of sth: *Her diary bears witness to traumatic events of the past.* ◇ *A rich fossil record bears testimony to the enormous area that was inhabited.* **bring sth to bear (on/upon sb/sth)** [often passive] to use pressure, influence or ideas to try to achieve sth or make sb do sth: *Strong pressure should be brought to bear on the child to return to school.* ◇ *The range of techniques brought to bear on the problem grew rapidly.* ➲ *more at* COMPARISON, MARK², MIND¹

PHR V **ˌbear ˈdown on sb/sth** **1** to approach or deal with sb/sth with a lot of force: *As the flood bore down on the trucks, the guides scrambled up nearby slopes to safety.* ◇ *He was determined to bear down on public debt.* **2** to press down on sth: *These three forces combine to bear down on the stone below.* **ˈbear on sb/sth** to be relevant or related to sth; to have an effect on sb/sth SYN AFFECT¹ (1): *These factors bear directly on the success or failure of the therapy.* ◇ *These policies bore most heavily on the more vulnerable elements in urban society.* **ˌbear sb/sth ˈout** [often passive] to show that sb is right or that sth is true: *This theory is not borne out by the facts.*

bear·er /ˈbeərə(r); *NAmE* ˈberər/ *noun* **1** a person or thing that carries sth, brings sth or passes sth on: *The expedition to East Africa involved trackers, porters and gun bearers.* ◇ **~ of sth** *Words are the bearers of meaning.* **2 ~ (of sth)** a person who takes responsibility for sth or who deals with sth: *The bearers of health care costs need better value for money.*

bear·ing /ˈbeərɪŋ; *NAmE* ˈberɪŋ/ *noun* **1** a part of a machine that supports a moving part, especially one that is turning: *Spinning the wheel faster will place a greater mechanical demand on the drive motor, bearings and seals.* **2** a direction measured from a fixed point using a COMPASS: *There were no steeples or bridges from which to take a bearing.* HELP The expression **get/lose your bearings** is used to talk about finding/losing your way, mainly in a figurative sense: *Faced with uncertainty, he returns to a place of familiarity to get his bearings.* ◇ *Now, he said, the country had lost its bearings.* To **take your bearings from** sth is to take it as your starting point and work out your position in relation to it: *Global constitutionalism takes its bearings from the same key themes.*

B

IDM **have (a) ˈbearing on/upon sth** to have an effect on sth; to be relevant or related to sth: *Events in France had a direct bearing on the EC.* ◇ *Disparities in party wealth had a significant bearing on how the campaigns were fought.* ◇ *Conflict of personalities may therefore have a bearing upon the result.* ◇ *This information has little bearing on the issues the report is intended to address.*

beat¹ /biːt/ *verb* (**beat**, **beaten** /ˈbiːtn/) **1** [T, often passive] to hit sb violently many times: **~ sb** *It was clear that she had been beaten.* ◇ **~ sb + adv./prep.** *He was subsequently beaten to death.* ◇ *The women had been beaten into submission.* **2** [T, I] to hit sth hard, usually more than once: **~ sth** *The drummers walk before the cart, beating their drums.* ◇ **+ adv./prep.** *The dramatic effect is heightened by the waves beating on the shore.* **3** [T] to be more successful than sb/sth else: **~ sb/sth** *To beat competitors, the service firm must continually meet or exceed customer expectation.* ◇ **~ sb/sth + adv./prep.** *The defensive strategy beat off the strategy of the market challenger.* ◇ *The Liberal Democrats were beaten into third place by the Respect party.* **HELP** In general English, **beat** is often used to talk about defeating sb in a game or war: *He beat me at chess.* In academic English, **defeat** is more common: *The French were defeated at Waterloo in 1815.* **4** [I, T] to make a regular movement; to cause sth to do this: *The heart is still beating.* ◇ *A fruit fly beats its wings around 200 times per second.*

PHR V **ˌbeat sb ˈup** to hit sb violently many times: *They were beaten up, killed or taken into custody.*

beat² /biːt/ *noun* **1** [C] a single blow or movement, or a series of blows or movements; the sound or feeling of this: *Peak heart rate was 92 beats per minute.* ◇ *These threats are accompanied by light tail beats.* ◇ *The drug is used to treat patients with an irregular heartbeat.* **2** [C] **~ (of sth)** the main rhythm, or a unit of rhythm, in a piece of music or a poem: *Reggae was inspired by the beat of the Rasta drummers.* ◇ *The regular alternation of weak and strong beats (iambic meter) is seldom disturbed.*

beau·ti·ful /ˈbjuːtɪfl/ *adj.* having beauty; pleasing to the senses or to the mind: *The dance is a beautiful art form.* ◇ *Helen of Troy is, by definition, the most beautiful woman of all time.* ■ **beau·ti·ful·ly** /ˈbjuːtɪfli/ *adv.*: *He has produced a beautifully crafted book.* ◇ *The basic idea is beautifully simple.*

beauty /ˈbjuːti/ *noun* (*pl.* **-ies**) **1** [U] the quality of being pleasing to the senses or to the mind: *Local tourism depended on the town's scenic beauty.* ◇ *The ideal of feminine beauty has changed.* ◇ **the ~ of sth** *The beauty of the natural world is seen as a divine gift.* **2** [C] **~ (of sth)** a person or thing that is beautiful: *In his mind he sees the beauties of his homeland.* **3** [C] **the ~ of sth** a pleasing feature **SYN** ADVANTAGE¹ (2): *The beauty of this model is that organizations can utilize whatever factors are relevant to their own environment.*

be·cause /bɪˈkɒz; bɪˈkəz; *NAmE* bɪˈkɔːz; bɪˈkʌz/ *conj.* for the reason that: *She is unable to sleep because she is so worried about money.* ◇ *Clearly the photographs are important because they record the events that took place.* ◇ *Because she is so well, there is no need to arrange a follow-up appointment.* ◇ **it is ~ ... that...** *It is precisely because perspectives change, and because boundaries shift, that guidance is needed.*

because of *prep.* used when giving a reason: *Many studies were eliminated because of this constraint.* ◇ *The colour of different samples may be different because of chemical variation.* ◇ **it is ~ sth that...** *It is because of these considerations that changes are not easy to interpret.* ➲ language bank *at* CAUSE¹

be·come /bɪˈkʌm/ *linking verb* (**be·came** /bɪˈkeɪm/, **be·come**) to start to be sth: **+ adj.** *She became pregnant at fifteen.* ◇ *During the last hundred years, diseases such as asthma, lung cancer and diabetes have become more common.* ◇ **it becomes + adj.** *Cable technology advanced but it soon became apparent that signals suffer distortion during transmission.* ◇ **+ noun** *Laios was buried and Kreon became king.* ◇ *The proposal eventually became law after the government accepted several amendments.*

LANGUAGE BANK

Explaining reasons

The following words and expressions are useful when giving reasons why sth is the case or for stating the cause of sth. See also the language bank at **cause**.

- **... because (of)/as a result of/on account of/due to/ owing to...**
- **X is a/the result of/is due to...**
- **X stems from...**
- **X is caused by...**
- **As/Since...**

– *English music declined, partly* ***because*** *music came to be considered less an 'art' than an 'accomplishment'.*
– *The first cities probably reflected the production of an agricultural surplus, possibly* ***as a result of*** *irrigation schemes.*
– *Liquid crystal displays provided major competition in many applications* ***on account of*** *their much lower power consumption.*
– *The Commission is regarded as the most federal institution of the EU,* ***owing largely to*** *its independence from direct national influences.*
– *These differences may* ***be due to*** *the fact that different methodologies were employed.*
– *The demotion of Malenkov* ***was the result of*** *a concentrated effort to weaken the Malenkov-Beria ascendancy.*
– *Her interest in this* ***stems from*** *her own experience of motherhood.*
– *Congenital hypothyroidism* ***is caused by*** *a deficiency of thyroid hormones at birth.*
– ***Since*** *the incubation period of smallpox is 1–2 weeks, the disease would have spread widely before it was even detected.*

bed /bed/ *noun* **1** [C, U] a piece of furniture for sleeping on: *The hospital has almost 300 beds.* ◇ *He reported difficulty getting out of bed.* ◇ *She was fine when she went to bed.* **2** [C, usually sing.] the bottom of a river, of the sea, etc: *These species live on the river bed.* **3** [C] an area of a river, sea, etc. where a particular plant or creature grows or lives: *reed/seagrass/oyster beds* **4** [C] **~ of sth** a layer of sth, especially a layer of rock or soil in the ground: *The variegated shales are interbedded with thin beds of sandstone and siltstone.*

bed·rock /ˈbedrɒk; *NAmE* ˈbedrɑːk/ *noun* **1** [C, usually sing.] **the ~ of sth** the essential ideas, facts or things on which sth is based; the people who provide essential support for sth: *These concepts form the bedrock of any study of marketing.* ◇ *Unions such as UAW or ILGWU used to be the bedrock of the Democratic Party.* **2** [U, C, usually sing.] the solid rock in the ground below the loose soil and sand: *The fragments are released from bedrock by weathering.* ◇ *In time the bedrock will be exposed.*

bee /biː/ *noun* a black and yellow flying insect. Bees live in large groups and make HONEY: *Smoking the hives reduces the risk of being stung by bees.*

been /biːn; bɪn; *NAmE* bɪn/ ➲ BE¹, BE² ➲ *see also* GO

beer /bɪə(r); *NAmE* bɪr/ *noun* [U, C] a type of alcoholic drink that is made from grain: *People might buy less beer if the price of wine suddenly dropped.* ◇ *The strengths of different beers varies.*

B

be·fore[1] /bɪˈfɔː(r)/ *prep.* **1** earlier than sth/sb SYN PRIOR TO: *The condition is uncommon before the age of 40.* ◇ *In most states individuals must register to vote thirty days before an election.* ◇ *Before doing so, it would be wise to ask some basic questions.* ◇ *He died before his father.* **2 (like sb) ~ him/her, etc.** used in comparisons with sb who did a similar thing in the past: *Like others before him, he argued that...* ◇ *They followed the same path of unstable employment that their parents had trodden before them.* **3** in a position in front of sb/sth: *The men bowed down before him.* ◇ *He keeps a copy of the Sanskrit text open before him.* **4** in or into the presence of sb who will deal with you: *His critics called a meeting of the committee and summoned him to appear before it.* ◇ *Many of these cases have now come before the courts.* **5** the task **before** you is the task that you are dealing with or that you will have to deal with: *This was perhaps the most delicate task before him.* **6** in front of sb/sth in an order or arrangement: *The company was perceived as putting profits before safety.*

be·fore[2] /bɪˈfɔː(r)/ *conj.* **1** earlier than the time when: *Males leave the group before they mature.* ◇ *He began to get in trouble even before he finished high school.* ◇ *Before the data were imported, they were checked for completeness and accuracy.* **2** until: *It may be some time before this prediction can be tested.*

be·fore[3] /bɪˈfɔː(r)/ *adv.* at an earlier time; in the past; already: *Her husband had been married three times before.* ◇ *However, as mentioned before, the results should be interpreted with caution.* ◇ **ever ~** *Women are better educated and have a greater range of jobs than ever before.* ◇ **never ~** *Never before or since have academics enjoyed positions of such prestige.*

beg /beg/ *verb* (-gg-) **1** [I, T] to ask sb for sth, especially in a way that shows you want or need it very much: **~ to do sth** *She begged to be allowed to join him.* ◇ **~ sb to do sth** *He begged the hunger strikers to give up.* ◇ **~ sth (from sb)** *The writers begged forgiveness.* ◇ **~ (sb) (for sth)** *After the battle of Pharsalus, he successfully begged Caesar for pardon.* **2** [I] to ask sb for money or food, especially in the street: *The city is full of homeless people begging in the streets.* ◇ **~ (for sth) (from sb)** *Children raised money by begging for coins from passengers on trains.* **3** [I] used to say that sth is definitely needed: **~ to do sth** *This is an area that begs to be developed.* ◇ **~ for sth** *Others pose a problem that begs for an answer.* **4** [I] **~ (for sth)** (of an animal) to sit up and wait to be given food: *The young partly beg for food and partly self-feed.*

IDM **beg the ˈquestion 1** to make sb want to ask a question that has not yet been asked: *This inevitably begs the question: by whose standards is aptness to be judged?* ◇ **~ of what/how/whether, etc...** *This begs the question of what defines space.* ◇ **~ as to whether/which, etc...** *All of these positions beg the question as to whether there is a 'male' or a 'female' set of behavioural attributes.* ◇ **~ of sth** *This then begs the question of the form that monitoring should take.* **2** to talk about sth as if it were definitely true, even though it might not be: *An argument that begs the question does not work.* **sb begs to differ** used to say that sb does not agree with sth that has just been said: *Many geographers beg to differ.*

begin /bɪˈgɪn/ *verb* (**be·gin·ning, began** /bɪˈgæn/, **begun** /bɪˈgʌn/) **1** [T, I] to start doing sth: **~ sth** *Seymour Fogel was a corn geneticist who began work on yeast in 1958.* ◇ **~ to do sth** *Fifty years ago, evidence of the harmful effects of smoking was already beginning to emerge.* ◇ **~ doing sth** *The scheme began operating in January 1999.* ◇ **~ by doing sth** *This essay will begin by surveying the traditional practices in Chinese Buddhist culture.* ◇ **~ (sth) at sth** *Sales in segment B begin at a relatively low level.* ◇ **~ (sth) with sth** *He decided to begin with a relatively low dose.* **2** [I] to start to happen or exist, especially from a particular time or in a particular way: *The work really began in the late 1970s.* ◇ *In traditional societies, childbearing begins early in life.* **3** [T, I] to be sth first, before becoming sth else: **~ sth as sth** *The European Parliament began life as a consultative assembly.* ◇ **~ as sth** *Begun as a radio network in the 1920s, the BBC became a more international service with its coverage of World War II.* **4** [I] to have sth as the first part or the point where sth starts: **~ with sth** *Use 'an' before words beginning with a vowel.* ◇ **~ at sth** *The spiral on a CD begins at the innermost track and spirals outward.*

IDM **to beˈgin with 1** at first: *Profits were slow to begin with, before the expansion overseas.* **2** used to introduce the first point you want to make: *Unfortunately, this approach presents numerous problems. To begin with, it comes at high cost and the investment of too much time.*

be·gin·ner /bɪˈgɪnə(r)/ *noun* a person who is starting to learn sth and cannot do it very well yet: *First semester courses are for complete beginners who have never taken any language classes.*

be·gin·ning /bɪˈgɪnɪŋ/ *noun* **1** [C, usually sing.] the time when sth starts; the first part of an event or story: **the ~ (of sth)** *The invention of the telephone marked the beginning of a new era in communication technology.* ◇ **at the ~ of sth** *Japanese stock and land markets collapsed at the beginning of the 1990s.* ◇ **at the ~** *Fundamentally, the key facts remained as they were at the beginning.* ◇ **from the ~ (of sth)** *From the very beginning of animal evolution, species have come into contact with each other.* ◇ **from ~ to end** *Patients are encouraged to tell their stories in their own words, from beginning to end.* HELP **At the beginning (of sth)** is used for the time and place when sth begins. **In the beginning** means **at first**, and suggests a contrast with a later situation. **2 beginnings** [pl.] the first or early ideas, signs or stages of sth: *From its humble beginnings as a small store in a Swedish village, IKEA has grown into the world's largest furniture retailer.*

IDM **the beginning of the ˈend** the first sign of sth ending: *The Alaska Highway cut through North America's last wilderness, spelling the beginning of the end of the old way of life.*

be·half AWL /bɪˈhɑːf; *NAmE* bɪˈhæf/ *noun*

IDM **on behalf of sb | on sb's behalf 1** as the representative of sb: *She accepted the prize on behalf of the committee.* ◇ *Due to illness, the defendant was unable to testify on his own behalf.* **2** in order to help sb: *Buddhist monks set up hospitals and rebuilt villages on behalf of the suffering victims of the war.*

be·have /bɪˈheɪv/ *verb* **1** [I] to function or react in a particular way: **+ adv./prep.** *The system behaves chaotically.* ◇ *The data reveal how people behave when exposed to different advertisements.* ◇ **~ as sth** *The material now behaves as an isotropic liquid.* ◇ **~ like sb/sth** *In some ways, firms behave like individuals.* ◇ **~ as if/though...** *The electrons behave as if they were tiny magnets.* HELP In spoken English, people often use **like** instead of **as if** or **as though** in this meaning. This is not correct in academic English. **Like** can be used before a noun (*individuals*) but not before a clause (*they were tiny magnets*). **2** [I] **+ adv./prep. (towards sb)** to act in a particular way, especially towards other people SYN ACT[1] (2): *The patient behaved aggressively towards medical staff.* **3 -behaved** (in adjectives) behaving in the way mentioned: *He was well-behaved at home but got into fights at school.*

▸ NOUN + BEHAVE **people • consumer • student • animal • cell • system • market • firm** *These models attempt to explain how consumers behave towards global brands.* ◇ *Zoo animals still largely behave in the ways that they would in the wild.*

▸ BEHAVE + ADVERB **differently • similarly • accordingly • rationally • opportunistically • aggressively** *The majority of people accept society's rules and behave accordingly.* | **well, responsibly • badly** *When they were given projects, the students behaved responsibly and professionally.*

▸ VERB + TO BEHAVE **tend • be expected • be likely** *These materials tend to behave as insulators.* ◇ *An unmarried retired woman is likely to behave very differently from a young, single mother.*

be·hav·iour (*US* **be·hav·ior**) /bɪˈheɪvjə(r)/ *noun* **1** [U, C] the way that sb/sth functions or reacts in a particular situation: *Ansoff et al. (1976) claimed that company behaviour reflected the changing business environment.* ◇ *It was a study into chromosome behaviour in corn.* ◇ **~ towards sth** *People's behaviour towards risk is an important factor.* ◇ (*technical*) *The young female birds exhibited complex behaviours such as nest building and nursing chicks.* **2** [U] the way that sb behaves, especially towards other people: *The study focuses on how religious belief influences behaviour.* ◇ *Aggressive behaviour occurs within and between local groups.* ◇ **~ towards sb** *Threatening behaviour towards the tenant can also breach this covenant.*

▸ ADJECTIVE + BEHAVIOUR **social • organizational • individual • parental • appropriate • acceptable • ethical • cooperative • altruistic • prosocial • inappropriate • aggressive, violent • challenging, disruptive, antisocial • criminal • unethical • rational • learned • adaptive • opportunistic • future • unusual, abnormal • risky • suicidal • sexual** *Harsh parental rejection is a major contributor to antisocial behaviour in children.* ◇ *Thus, hunting is both a learned and an evolved behaviour, essential for survival.*

▸ NOUN + BEHAVIOUR **human • animal • consumer • buying • voting** *Social and personal networks may influence the customer's buying behaviour.*

▸ VERB + BEHAVIOUR **affect, influence • change, modify, alter, adapt, adjust • shape, guide • drive, determine • underlie • control, govern, regulate • constrain • reinforce • reward • motivate • encourage, promote • produce, induce, trigger, elicit • simulate, mimic, imitate • learn • understand • analyse • consider • examine • explain • predict • describe, characterize • model • study, investigate • monitor • observe, see, view • be associated with • exhibit, show, demonstrate** *He claimed that all human social behaviour is driven by the pursuit of power and material interest.* ◇ *The machines can simulate the behaviour of the human mind very closely.*

▸ BEHAVIOUR + VERB **emerge, appear, arise, occur • develop, evolve • differ, vary • result in, lead to • affect, influence • reflect** *Intelligent insect behaviours can emerge from simple systems.*

▸ BEHAVIOUR + NOUN **pattern • change • problems • therapy • management** *Emotional distress in the child is shown to lead to unwanted behaviour patterns.*

be·hav·iour·al (*US* **be·hav·ior·al**) /bɪˈheɪvjərəl/ *adj.* [usually before noun] involving or connected with behaviour: *Self-awareness in the children is encouraged in order to aid behavioural change.* ◇ *Behavioural ecology considers behaviour as a decision-making process that involves information gathering and processing.* ■ **be·hav·iour·al·ly** (*US* **be·hav·ior·al·ly**) *adv.*: *When patients are particularly distressed and behaviourally disturbed, carefully monitored antipsychotic medication can be valuable.*

be·hind¹ /bɪˈhaɪnd/ *prep.* **1** at or towards the back of sb/sth, and often hidden by them/it: *The recording machinery was positioned behind screens.* ◇ *She cannot pick her foot up properly, but drags it behind her.* ◇ (*figurative*) *Policymakers were able to hide behind their expert scientific advisers.* ➲ *compare* IN FRONT OF **2** making less progress than sb/sth; not as far forward as expected: *Students may fall further behind their peers.* ◇ *This can result in data being released behind schedule.* **3** responsible for starting or developing sth: *The secret behind their success lies in their ability to make adjustments for local tastes.* ◇ *No economist has ever claimed that there is a single driving force behind economic growth.* ◇ *The basic idea behind this method is to use experimental conditions that reflect conditions of the world.* ◇ *The theory behind a mortgage is simple.* **4** supporting sb/sth: *They must, he insisted, unite behind the president.* ◇ *He did not have family wealth behind him.* **5 ~ sb** in sb's past: *His travelling days were largely behind him.*

be·hind² /bɪˈhaɪnd/ *adv.* **1** making less progress than sb/sth; not as far forward as expected: *The government was behind in the opinion polls.* ◇ *The UK was closing the gap with the US, although it still lagged behind.* ◇ *She felt that she was left behind in the technological age.* HELP If sb is **behind** with payments or work, he/she has not paid enough money or done enough work by a particular time: *He was behind with his mortgage payments.* **2** in the place where sb/sth is or was: *Students would stay behind after the class to continue the discussion.* **3** at or towards the back of sb/sth: *Another vehicle hit the car from behind.* OPP AHEAD (1), IN FRONT

being /ˈbiːɪŋ/ *noun* **1** [C] a real or imaginary living creature: *Buddhists believe in kindness towards all living beings.* ◇ *The capacity to feel emotion is one of the key features that distinguishes human beings from machines.* **2** [U] existence: **come into ~** *The creation myth tells the story of how the world first came into being.* ◇ **bring sth into ~** *This coalition of radical movements was brought into being by globalization.* ➲ *see also* WELL-BEING

be·lief /bɪˈliːf/ *noun* **1** [U] a strong feeling that sth/sb exists or is true; confidence that sth/sb is good or right: *Freud's personal stance was one of complete rejection of religious belief.* ◇ **~ in sth/sb** *Both men have little belief in what they are fighting for.* ◇ **~ that...** *Most of us share the fundamental belief that all people have intrinsic value.* **2** [C, usually pl.] something that you believe, often as part of your religion: *Many of the old religious beliefs and practices survived in rural areas, despite persecution.* ◇ **~ about sth** *A world view is a system of ideas and beliefs about the world.* **3** [sing., U] an opinion about sth; sth that you think is true: **~ that...** *This research has reinforced the belief that supercritical carbon dioxide can be used in future experiments.* ◇ **in the ~ that...** *Some more extreme followers forbid science and knowledge in the belief that they are safeguarding religion.* ➲ *compare* DISBELIEF IDM *see* CONTRARY¹

▸ ADJECTIVE + BELIEF **own, personal, individual • popular, mass, widespread, common, general, shared, collective • particular • strong • false, erroneous** *When she left home, she started to question her own beliefs.* | **core, fundamental • traditional, orthodox • religious** *There are ongoing tensions between traditional beliefs and values and more progressive perspectives.* | **cultural • political • superstitious • spiritual** *The study focused on students' cultural beliefs and practices.* | **mistaken** *The defendant's mistaken belief was that his action was not dangerous.*

▸ VERB + BELIEF **have • share • express, manifest • reflect • justify, defend • challenge, contradict, question • undermine, shake • reject, abandon** *According to this interpretation, if any machine has beliefs, it must therefore be conscious.* ◇ *Careful observation of the facts justifies the belief that...* | **hold, maintain • form, develop • accept • support • confirm, reinforce • revise** *Further, individuals tend to hold very strong beliefs about their capacity to exercise control over their own behaviour and the environment (Bandura, 2001).*

▸ BELIEF + NOUN **system** *Issues such as gay rights seemed to threaten the belief systems of millions of Americans.*

be·lieve /bɪˈliːv/ *verb* (not used in the progressive tenses) **1** [often passive] to think that sth is true or possible, although you are not completely certain: **~ (that)...** *Seventy per cent of biologists today believe the world is experiencing the fastest extinction of living species in the history of the planet.* ◇ **it is believed (that)...** *It is believed that the crash was caused by pilot error.* ◇ **~ sth** *Few scientists now believe the claims made in these twin studies.* ◇ **~ sb/sth to**

B

be, have, etc. sth *The painting is believed to be a fourth-century copy.* ➲ language bank *at* ACCORDING TO **2** to feel certain that sth is true or that sb is telling the truth: **~ sth** *She came to believe certain significant truths.* ◇ **~ sb** *Cassandra could foretell the future, but no one would believe her.* ◇ **~ (that)...** *Hitler came to believe that he knew better than his scientific advisers.*

PHR V **be'lieve in sb/sth** to feel certain that sb/sth exists: *They contend that the decision to believe in a God can be explained in terms of cost-benefit calculations.* **be'lieve in sb** to feel that you can trust sb and/or that they will be successful: *Teenagers need another human being to believe in them and their potential.* **be'lieve in sth** to think that sth is good, right or acceptable: *He believed in a system of trade without interference from the government.* ◇ **~ doing sth** *Edmund Burke believed in working gradually to improve the legacy of the past.*

▸ NOUN + BELIEVE **people** • **scholars** • **scientists** • **researchers** • **experts** *Most ancient people believed that preserving a correct relationship with the gods was all-important.*

▸ ADVERB + BELIEVE **also** • **now** • **still** • **previously** • **widely, commonly, generally** • **honestly, genuinely, sincerely** • **really, truly, actually** • **firmly, strongly** • **hardly** • **wrongly, mistakenly** *After the debate, only 35 per cent still believed that war was likely.* ◇ *It is widely believed that presidential democracies are more vulnerable to anti-democratic challenges.*

▸ BELIEVE + ADVERB **strongly, firmly, passionately** *They believe strongly that good design is about far more than simple functionality.*

▸ ADJECTIVE + TO BELIEVE **hard, difficult** • **impossible** • **easy** • **reasonable** *It is hard to believe that these methods could produce any measurable benefits.*

▸ VERB + TO BELIEVE **come** • **continue** • **tend** • **be inclined** • **be led** • **seem, appear** • **want** • **like** • **have** • **need** • **refuse** • **cease** *Participants were led to believe that their personal information would be kept confidential.*

▸ NOUN + TO BELIEVE **reason, grounds, cause** • **tendency** *There is every reason to believe that human beings have always been highly social creatures.*

be·liever /bɪˈliːvə(r)/ *noun* a person who believes in the existence or truth of sth, especially sb who believes in a god or religion: *The idea put forward by religious believers is that God will reward the good and punish the bad.* ◇ **~ in sth** *These students were all firm believers in the benefits of education.*

bell /bel/ *noun* **1** a hollow metal object that makes a ringing sound when hit by a small piece of metal inside it; the sound that it makes: *The bells of St Martin's church nearby were ringing.* **2** an electrical device which makes a ringing sound when a button on it is pushed; the sound that it makes, used as a signal or warning: *The students continue with their chosen work and the bell soon rings for lunch.* IDM *see* ALARM[1]

be·long /bɪˈlɒŋ; *NAmE* bɪˈlɔːŋ/ *verb* (not used in the progressive tenses) **1** [I] **+ adv./prep.** to be in the right or suitable place: *Knowledge about the breeding habits of mice properly belongs in the encyclopedia, not in the linguistic definition.* ◇ *Recovery puts the loss where it belongs, with the defendant's insurers rather than the taxpayer.* **2** [I] to be connected with or come from sth: **~ to sth** *The earliest references to her belong to the 1st century BC.* ◇ *Such instances clearly belong to the sphere of religion.* ◇ **~ together** *He reiterated that theory and research belong together.* ◇ **~ with sth** *According to Dyirbal myth, the moon goes in the class with men and husbands, while the sun belongs with females and wives.* **3** [I] to feel comfortable and happy in a particular situation or with a particular group of people: *Our most basic socio-emotional need is to belong.* ◇ **a sense of belonging (to sth)** *Through purchasing certain brands, consumers can feel that they have a sense of belonging to a large group.*

PHR V **be'long to sb** to be owned by sb: *The assets of an engineering company belong to the company and not to the official who happens to be managing director.* ◇ *These new states were largely created from land formerly belonging to Russia.* **be'long to sth** **1** to be part of a particular group, type or system; to be in the right category: *Each of these words belongs to a different syntactic category.* ◇ *The first way we classify living organisms is according to the species to which they belong.* ◇ *Claudian's poetry belongs firmly to the classical tradition.* **2** to be a member of a particular organization or group: *Only 3 per cent of Americans actually belong to a party organization.* ◇ *Individuals will often belong to more than one community.*

below[1] /bɪˈləʊ; *NAmE* bɪˈloʊ/ *prep.* **1** of a lower amount, level or standard than sb/sth: *The seasonal rainfall was 30 per cent below average.* ◇ *Mean monthly air temperatures are at or below freezing even in the summer months.* ◇ *If the frequency is below this minimum level, the likelihood is that the advertising will not work.* OPP ABOVE[1] (2) **2** of a lower rank or of less importance than sb/sth: *The supreme judicial body was the Senate; below this there were various courts of appeal.* OPP ABOVE[1] (3) **3** at or to a lower position than sb/sth: *The veins below the knee are distended.* OPP ABOVE[1] (1)

below[2] /bɪˈləʊ; *NAmE* bɪˈloʊ/ *adv.* **1** later in the text: *As discussed below, the law was extended in 2001.* ◇ *The details for each group are listed below.* ◇ *See Section 6 below.* ➲ *compare* ABOVE[2] (3), EARLY[2] (3) **2** at or to a lower level, position or place: *This air forms a warmer thermal zone on the hillside in contrast to the cooler valley floor below.* ◇ *He fell to his death in the sea below.* OPP ABOVE[2] (1)

belt /belt/ *noun* **1** a region with particular characteristics (especially a region that is also long or curved): *Convergence of tectonic plates produced large mountain belts.* ◇ *A substantial amount of the research is focused on the central Himalayan belt.* ◇ **~ of sth** *High frequencies of the trait are found in populations across a broad belt of tropical Africa.* **2** a continuous band of material that moves round and is used to carry things along or to drive machinery: *He introduced moving assembly belts into his plants.*

bench·mark[1] /ˈbentʃmɑːk; *NAmE* ˈbentʃmɑːrk/ *noun* something that provides a standard against which other things can be measured or compared: **~ for sth** *This work sets the benchmark for evidence-based practice in heath promotion.* ◇ **against a ~** *Future performance can then be measured against this benchmark.*

bench·mark[2] /ˈbentʃmɑːk; *NAmE* ˈbentʃmɑːrk/ *verb* **~ sth (against sth)** to judge the standard of sth in relation to other similar things: *This could provide valuable data against which to benchmark performance.* ■ **bench·marking** *noun* [U] *Benchmarking has become a powerful tool for increasing a company's competitiveness.* ◇ *An example of a benchmarking study is shown in Figure 10.10.*

bend[1] /bend/ *verb* (**bent, bent** /bent/) [I, T] (of a person or thing) to move or change direction so they are/it is no longer straight; to make sb/sth do this: *At this point the beam is not bending at all.* ◇ **+ adv./prep.** *The pain is relieved by bending forwards.* ◇ **~ sth + adv./prep.** *The stiffness of the helix prevents it being easily bent into a circle.* ◇ **~ sth** *A massive object like the sun bends light passing near its edge.*

IDM **bend the 'rules** to change the rules to suit a particular person or situation: *Liberal societies tend to accept the need to bend rules to suit minority groups.* ➲ *more at* BACKWARDS

PHR V **'bend to sth | 'bend sb/sth to sth** to be forced to behave or act in a particular way; to force sb/sth to do this: *They bent to the intense pressure of established hierarchies.* ◇ *He exhibited the desire to bend others to his will.*

bend² /bend/ *noun* a curve or turn, especially in a road or river: *The river runs in long straight reaches separated from each other by sharp bends.*

be·neath¹ /bɪˈniːθ/ *prep.* **1** in or to a lower position than sb/sth; under sb/sth: *What is concealed beneath the ground is not always known.* ◇ *Denser bodies of water attempt to sink beneath less dense ones.* **2** behind an appearance or feeling: *It is necessary to probe beneath the surface in order to discover what is happening.* **3** not good enough for sb: *Both women were far beneath him in status.* ◇ *They refused to undertake tasks that they considered beneath their social station.*

be·neath² /bɪˈniːθ/ *adv.* **1** in or to a lower position: *The building may settle as the ground beneath consolidates.* **2** hidden behind an appearance or feeling: *They are able to peel back the layers of obscurity, revealing the truths beneath.*

bene·fi·cial AWL /ˌbenɪˈfɪʃl/ *adj.* improving a situation; having a helpful or useful effect: *Grapefruit juice was shown to have significant beneficial effects on the reduction of blood pressure.* ◇ *The company established a mutually beneficial relationship with its suppliers.* ◇ **~ to sth/sb** *Both charities proved that they were directly beneficial to the community.* ➲ *compare* ADVANTAGEOUS, FAVOURABLE (1) OPP DETRIMENTAL

bene·fi·ciary AWL /ˌbenɪˈfɪʃəri; *NAmE* ˌbenɪˈfɪʃieri/ *noun* (*pl.* **-ies**) **~ (of sth)** a person who gains as a result of sth: *It was high-income groups that were the major beneficiaries of the urban redevelopment schemes.*

bene·fit¹ AWL /ˈbenɪfɪt/ *noun* **1** [C, U] a helpful and useful effect that sth has; an advantage that sth provides: **~ for sb/sth** *These treatments have been shown to have long-term benefits for patients.* ◇ **~ to sb/sth** *Teamwork can multiply the benefits to students.* ◇ **of ~** *Radiotherapy may be of benefit in some cases.* ◇ **~ of doing sth** *The system has the benefit of being fully automated.* ◇ **for the ~ of sb/sth** *Profits are used for the benefit of all members.* ➲ *see also* COST-BENEFIT ➲ language bank *at* CRITICAL **2** [U, C] (*BrE*) money provided by the government to people who need financial help because they are unemployed, sick, etc: *These problems were exacerbated by the increase in the number of those drawing unemployment benefit.* ◇ *housing/sickness/child benefit* ◇ *welfare benefits* ◇ **on ~** *The programme was designed to give people on benefits the help and support that they need to look for work.*

IDM **give sb the ˌbenefit of the ˈdoubt** to accept that sb has told the truth or has not done sth wrong because you cannot prove that they have not told the truth/have done sth wrong: *An asylum claimant must be given the benefit of the doubt with regards to their age.*

▸ ADJECTIVE + BENEFIT **potential, possible • key, major, main, primary • great • important, significant • substantial • real, tangible, material • full • marginal • net • positive • own • personal • mutual • expected • extra, additional • future • long-term • direct • indirect • perceived • social • economic • financial • environmental • public** *The potential benefits of modern technology for human well-being are profound.* ◇ *Social networks can facilitate collaboration and cooperation for mutual benefit among users.*

▸ NOUN + BENEFIT **health, fitness** *The health benefits of the product have been hotly contested.*

▸ VERB + BENEFIT **have, provide, bring, deliver, offer, confer • yield, generate • receive, gain, obtain, derive, reap • enjoy • outweigh, exceed • maximize • communicate, promote • share, distribute • emphasize, highlight, stress • show, demonstrate, illustrate** *Suppliers of branded goods have reaped the benefits of accessing global distribution channels.*

▸ BENEFIT + VERB **include • accrue, arise, flow • outweigh, exceed** *The benefits tend to accrue to the controlling shareholders.* ◇ *The benefits exceed the costs.*

bene·fit² AWL /ˈbenɪfɪt/ *verb* (**-t-** or **-tt-**) **1** [I] to be in a better position because of sth: *American consumers benefit when low-cost products are imported.* ◇ **~ from sth** *Shareholders benefit from the distribution of corporate assets.* ◇ **~ by doing sth** *Both countries benefited by engaging in trade.* **2** [T] **~ sb/sth** to be useful or provide an advantage to sb/sth: *The government employs people to produce goods or services intended to benefit society as a whole.* ◇ *The economic changes primarily benefited the elite.*

▸ NOUN + BENEFIT **country • society • individual • party • female • patient • consumer • shareholder • partner** *The solitary individual will usually benefit from joining the group.* ◇ *Using the win-win negotiation strategy, both parties clearly benefited.*

▸ BENEFIT + NOUN **society, the public • economy • producer • consumer • child • shareholder • partner • user** *The system was designed to benefit small producers by imposing lower taxes.*

▸ VERB + TO BENEFIT **stand • expect • tend • continue • be likely • be able** *It is the educated middle classes that stand to benefit from China's economic boom.*

▸ ADVERB + BENEFIT **also • only • still • often • ultimately • actually • undoubtedly • automatically • clearly • directly • greatly** *Ross (2006) found that capitalist democracy may not actually benefit the poor as much as this model suggests.*

▸ BENEFIT + ADVERB **greatly, enormously • most • significantly • disproportionately • directly • personally** *The labour market benefited greatly from an influx of cheap skilled labour.*

be·nign /bɪˈnaɪn/ *adj.* **1** (*medical*) not dangerous; not likely to cause death: *Benign tumours do not invade surrounding tissue.* ◇ *This is a relatively benign condition.* OPP MALIGNANT **2** not hurting anyone; not harmful: *The foregoing argument assumes a benign form of competition.* ◇ *Twenty-first century technologies could offer lifestyles that are environmentally benign.*

be·side /bɪˈsaɪd/ *prep.* next to or at the side of sb/sth: *The table beside the graph presents further descriptive statistics for the data.*

IDM **beside the ˈpoint** not important or closely connected with the main thing you are talking about SYN IRRELEVANT: *The internal arguments were beside the point.*

be·sides¹ /bɪˈsaɪdz/ *prep.* in addition to sth; apart from sth: *Besides internal networking, a company has to make alliances with outside firms.* ◇ *Today, besides the original English version, the dictionary exists in translation in several other languages.*

be·sides² /bɪˈsaɪdz/ *adv.* **1** (*rather informal*) used for introducing an extra idea: *Life cannot be measured out on a cost-benefit basis; besides, unless new techniques are tried, new cures cannot be discovered.* ◇ *Besides, there is another problem with this hypothesis.* HELP This use of **besides** is best avoided in more formal academic writing; you can use **in addition**, **furthermore** or **moreover** instead. ➲ language bank *at* ADDITION **2** in addition; also: *The organization deals with foreign policy issues, including defence and international trade, and much else besides.*

best¹ /best/ *adj.* (superlative of *good*) **1** of the highest quality or standard: *This is probably the best introduction to the life and thought of Aquinas.* ◇ *It is worth noting that the Japanese industry has had the best performance in terms of job creation.* ◇ *These figures are our best current estimate.* ◇ *It took the best scientific minds nearly 90 years to decide how the platypus should be categorized.* **2** most suitable, appropriate or effective: *Economists are divided on the best response to such uncertainty.* ◇ *Withdrawal may be a child's best strategy for coping with anger.* ◇ *Rodents prefer living hidden away in the dark, probably* *because that is the best way for them to avoid predators.* ◇ *They feel that the company's proposed strategy is not in the best interests of the current shareholders.* ◇ **it is ~ to do sth** *It is best to use a random method for assigning people to groups.* ◇ **~ for sb/sth** *The court must consider what is best for the child's welfare above all other considerations.*

best² /best/ *adv.* (superlative of *well*, often used in adjectives) **1** most; to the highest degree: *Dawkins is one of the best-known evolutionary biologists in the world.* ◇ *Many different codes exist in the world of computing and digital systems, each of which is best suited to the particular job for which it was designed.* **2** better than any other; to the highest standard: *In terms of economic growth, countries such as Thailand and China perform best.* ◇ *Portraying animated action is what cinema does best.* **3** in the most suitable, appropriate or effective way: *The method is probably best explained with an example.* ◇ *The PPP market can best be described as a developing market.* ◇ *This method works best for relatively low molecular weights.* ◇ **how ~ to do sth** *There is much debate concerning how best to eliminate poverty in the less developed world.*

best³ /best/ *noun* [sing.] (*usually* **the best**) **1** the thing or person that is of a higher quality or standard than any other: *There is no guarantee that the same design is the best at all times.* ◇ **the ~ of sth** *This is among the best of the older biographies of Lenin.* **2** something that is as close as possible to what is needed or wanted: *The simplest theory is often the best.* ◇ **the ~ of sth** *It is not always easy to decide which is the best of a number of possible choices or solutions.* ◇ **the ~ (that)...** *In this environment, the best that a national government can hope to achieve is some semblance of control over the policy network.*

ˌbest ˈpractice *noun* [U, C] a way of doing sth that is seen as a very good example of how it should be done and can be copied by other companies or organizations: *The scheme appears to fall short of full compliance with models of international best practice.* ◇ *An effective leader needs to identify and share best practices.* ◇ **+ noun** *best practice principles/standards/recommendations*

be·tray /bɪˈtreɪ/ *verb* **1** to fail to support sb/sth, by not doing what sb trusted you to do or by not doing what is right: **~ sth** *He attacked the party for betraying the ideals of its founders.* ◇ *The government betrayed the public's trust and abused its power.* ◇ **~ sb** *She betrayed the people who voted for her.* ◇ *Many felt betrayed by the president's failure to follow through.* **2** [often passive] to give information about sb/sth to an enemy: **~ sb/sth** *He was betrayed, and killed in battle.* ◇ **~ sb/sth to sb** *Russian plans had been betrayed to the enemy.* **3 ~ sth** to make sb aware of a piece of information, a feeling, etc, often without meaning to: *This remark betrays a common concern.* ◇ *The author betrayed a personal sense of frustration.* ■ **be·tray·al** /bɪˈtreɪəl/ *noun* [U, C] *His letters reveal a sense of betrayal.* ◇ *He continued the struggle until his eventual betrayal and death.* ◇ **~ of sth** *This was seen as a betrayal of trust.*

bet·ter¹ /ˈbetə(r)/ *adj.* (comparative of *good*) **1** of a higher standard or less poor quality; not as bad as sth else: *The employment of specialists can lead to better decisions and fewer mistakes being made.* ◇ *One key need is for better education facilities.* ◇ *Our estimates become more reliable as our samples get better.* ◇ **~ than sth** *Profits for the company this year were nearly $6 million, which is better than their competitors.* **2** more suitable, appropriate or effective: *The sales force will do a far better job if marketing has done a good job.* ◇ **~ than sth** *Overall, in high risk patients, warfarin is better than aspirin in preventing strokes.* ◇ **~ (for sb) to do sth** *So long as energy systems generate significant environmental costs, it is better to use less energy than more.* **3** more able or skilled: *Whether Austen is a better writer than Blyton and Constable a better painter than Picasso is largely a matter of taste.* ◇ **~ at sth** *People who are better at any one test tend to be better at all of the others.* **4** fully or partly recovered from an illness or injury; no longer painful: *Most infections get better on their own.* ➲ *see also* WELL²

IDM **the ˌbigger, ˌsmaller, ˌfaster, ˌslower, etc. the ˈbetter** used to say that sth should be as big, small, etc. as possible: *You do not have infinite time or money to apply this test—the cheaper and quicker it is, the better.*

bet·ter² /ˈbetə(r)/ *adv.* (comparative of *well*) **1** in a more excellent or effective way; not as badly: *Additional arrangements have been developed to make the procedure work better.* ◇ **do ~** *Some industries are counter-cyclical—that is, they do better in a recession.* ◇ **~ than...** *In reading, girls performed consistently and significantly better than boys.* **2** more; to a greater degree: *Acid deposition is better known by the name acid rain.* ◇ *She was interested in better understanding how the students worked in groups.* **3** used to suggest that sth would be a suitable or appropriate thing to do: *It is easy to think that time spent designing experiments would be better spent actually doing experiments.*

bet·ter³ /ˈbetə(r)/ *noun* **1** [sing.] **~ (of sth)** something that is better: *Most readers would agree that this is the better of the two sonnets.* **2 sb's betters** [pl.] people who are more intelligent or more important than sb: *Actors of lower social rank mimicked their betters.*

IDM **get the better of sb/sth** to defeat sb/sth or gain an advantage over them: *The capitalist continually tries to get the better of competition by incessantly introducing new machines.* ➲ *more at* CHANGE¹

bet·ter⁴ /ˈbetə(r)/ *verb* **1** [often passive] **~ sth** to be better or do sth better than sb/sth else: *It is widely accepted that Marx's analysis of capitalism has yet to be bettered.* **2 ~ yourself** to improve your social position through education, a better job, etc: *Huge numbers went overseas looking for new opportunities to better themselves.*

be·tween¹ /bɪˈtwiːn/ *prep.* **1** in or into the space separating two or more points, regions, objects or people: *Trading centres started to develop between the great rivers of the Loire and the Rhine.* ◇ **in ~** *The specimen is positioned in between the source and the film.* **2** in the period that separates two points in time: *Eleven volumes were published between 1965 and 1981.* ◇ *The main interview followed the screening questions with no break between the two.* ◇ **in ~** *Teachers could only be phoned in between lessons.* **3** at some point along a scale from one amount, weight, distance, etc. to another: *Informal health expenditure accounts for between 4% and 8% of total health expenditure.* ◇ *It is reasonable to aim for a weight gain of between 0.5 and 1 kg each week.* ◇ *A compromise exists between these two extremes.* **4** from one place to another: *Deutsche Bahn hopes to provide train services between London and Germany.* **5** used when mentioning how two or more things or people are similar or different: *Statistical analyses showed no difference between the two tests.* ◇ *There are a number of similarities between Christianity and Mahayana Buddhism.* ◇ *The dividing lines between the various sciences are ill-defined.* **6** used to show a connection or relationship involving two or more things, people or organizations: *Chaniotis (2005) focuses on the connections between war, culture and society during the Hellenistic period.* ◇ *Words tend to pick out concepts, though the exact relationship between them is complex.* ◇ *Three-way negotiations took place between the union, the employers and the government.* ◇ *Trade between the two countries had reached US$47 150 million the year before.* **7** used to show a choice involving two or more things or people: *Lawrence's heroine has to choose between a passionate man and one who is more cultured but not as attractive.* **8** shared by two or more people or things: *The work was shared between the Institute and Central College.* ◇ *In the Treaty of Tordesillas of 1494, Spain and*

Portugal had divided the Americas between them. **9** by putting together the efforts or actions of two or more people or groups: *China and India between them account for more than half the total increase.*

be·tween² /bɪˈtwiːn/ *adv.* (*usually* **in between**) in the space, period of time, or range separating two or more objects, dates or events, or points on a scale: *Categories have some clear members, some clear non-members, and a range of cases in between.* ◇ **somewhere/something in ~** *The annual totals for much of the rest of South East Asia lie somewhere in between.*

be·wil·der·ing /bɪˈwɪldərɪŋ/ *adj.* making you feel confused because there are too many things to choose from or because sth is difficult to understand SYN CONFUSING: *Faced with a bewildering array of choices, buyers often try to simplify the choice process.* ◇ *If you visited Rome between 100 and 200, you would have found a bewildering variety of religions.*

be·yond¹ /bɪˈjɒnd; *NAmE* bɪˈjɑːnd/ *prep.* **1** on or to the further side of sth: *Buddhism began to spread beyond its home territory to other parts of India.* ◇ *Canadian and American geographers were challenged to envision worlds beyond North America.* **2** more developed than sth; reaching further than sth: *BBC charity appeals clearly have a moral purpose beyond simple entertainment.* ◇ *Dickens developed his own art within and beyond the traditions of eighteenth-century literature.* ◇ *The later plays move beyond Noh drama into an experimental use of time and space.* **3** used to say that sth is not possible: *There are many influences beyond family control that shape children's attitudes and beliefs.* ◇ *Zen enlightenment occurs in a moment of awakening that is beyond logical comprehension.* ◇ *What is beyond doubt is that the legacies of the Second World War were a heavy burden for following generations.* **4** more than a particular amount: *This theory states that an earthquake is generated when a fault has been strained beyond its elastic strength.* **5** later than a particular time: *The plan sets out a range of targets for beyond 2014.* **6** too far or too advanced for sb/sth: *The great rebellions all began in areas far beyond the reach of foreign trade.* ◇ *The exercise was beyond the abilities of most of the class.*

be·yond² /bɪˈjɒnd; *NAmE* bɪˈjɑːnd/ *adv.* **1 (and) ~** on the other side; further on: *Humans migrated through North America, and beyond, into South America.* **2 (and) ~** afterwards or later: *Higher numbers of people are surviving into their 60s and beyond.*

bias¹ AWL /ˈbaɪəs/ *noun* **1** [U, C] the fact that the results of research or an experiment are not accurate because a particular factor has not been considered when collecting the information: *If a response rate is low, the risk of bias in the findings will be greater.* ◇ *This procedure largely eliminates bias from the selection of a sample by using a process of random selection.* **2** [U, C, usually sing.] a strong feeling in favour of or against one group of people, or one side in an argument, in a way that influences your decisions in an unfair way: *Politicians frequently express concern about political bias in the press.* ◇ **~ towards sb/sth** *The Elizabethan poor laws showed a discriminatory bias towards women.* ◇ **~ in favour of sb/sth** *There is still a bias in favour of Oxbridge graduates for certain kinds of elite jobs.* ◇ **~ against sb/sth** *Christian writers scorned Tacitus because of his supposed bias against them.* **3** [C, usually sing.] an interest in one area or subject more than others: **~ towards sth** *The book has a distinct bias towards twentieth-century material.* ◇ **~ against sth** *The firm has shown a bias against risk taking.*

▸ ADJECTIVE + BIAS **systematic • ideological • cultural • personal** *The cultural bias in testing procedures such as these has led some researchers to recommend alternative means of assessment.*

▸ NOUN + BIAS **gender, sex • selection, sampling** *Sampling bias will occur if some members of the population have little or no chance of being selected for inclusion in the sample.*

▸ VERB + BIAS **reduce, minimize • eliminate, avoid, remove • introduce • show, reflect, exhibit** *Probability sampling is a mechanism for reducing bias in the selection of samples.* ◇ *It is important to avoid bias in the wording of questionnaires.* ◇ *Even a slight degree of mismatching in the ethnicity of the cases and controls could introduce bias into the results.*

bias² AWL /ˈbaɪəs/ *verb* **1 ~ sth** to have an effect on the results of research or an experiment so that they do not show the real situation: *Excluding this category would potentially bias the results.* ◇ *Interviewers should resist varying the wording of questions, which may bias the findings.* **2 ~ sb/sth** to influence sb's opinions or decisions, sometimes in an unfair way: *Whatever evaluative framework we start from will inevitably bias our judgement one way or another.* ◇ *Experts disagree among themselves and may be biased by extraneous influences.*

biased AWL /ˈbaɪəst/ *adj.* **1** giving results that are not fair or accurate, often because of a lack of balance in the way that information has been collected: *Missing data can lead to a biased sample and incorrect conclusions.* ◇ **~ towards/in favour of sb/sth** *In the case of service quality surveys, responses are likely to be biased in favour of those who are either very happy or very unhappy with service levels.* **2** tending to show favour towards or against one group of people or one opinion for personal reasons; making unfair judgements: *The media is criticized as being sensationalistic and biased in its reporting.* ◇ *Biased attitudes among teachers may result in disengagement among students.* ◇ **~ towards/in favour of sb/sth** *In most new democracies, political reporting is biased towards particular groups, parties or ideologies.* ◇ **~ against sb/sth** *The university in question was accused of having an admissions policy that was biased against women.* OPP UNBIASED **3 ~ towards sth/sb** having a particular interest in one thing more than others: *The geographical coverage of the data is highly biased towards the USA and western Europe.*

bible /ˈbaɪbl/ *noun* **the Bible 1** [sing.] the HOLY book of the Christian religion, consisting of the Old Testament and the New Testament **2** [sing.] the holy book of the Jewish religion, consisting of the Law, the PROPHETS and the Writings

bibli·og·raphy /ˌbɪbliˈɒɡrəfi; *NAmE* ˌbɪbliˈɑːɡrəfi/ *noun* (*pl.* **-ies**) the list of books, etc. that have been used by sb writing an article, essay, etc; a list of books or articles about a particular subject or by a particular author: *Full publication details are provided in the bibliography at the end of the book.* ◇ **~ of sth** *Another very useful source is the International Bibliography of the Social Sciences.* ■ **bib·lio·graph·ic·al** /ˌbɪbliəˈɡræfɪkl/ (*also* **bib·lio·graph·ic** /ˌbɪbliəˈɡræfɪk/) *adj.*: *Online bibliographical databases that are accessible on the Internet are an invaluable source of references.*

bid¹ /bɪd/ *noun* **1 ~ (for sth)** an offer by a person or a company to pay a particular amount of money for sth: *In 2009, Kraft launched a hostile takeover bid for Cadbury.* **2 ~ (for sth)** | (*NAmE also*) **~ (on sth)** an offer to do work or provide a service for a particular price, in competition with other companies SYN TENDER³: *Three firms submitted competitive bids for the work.* **3** an effort to do sth or to obtain sth: **~ for sth** *Lord Byron supported the Greek people in their bid for national independence.* ◇ **~ to do sth** *Manchester's bid to host the 1996 Olympics did not succeed.*

bid² /bɪd/ *verb* (**bid·ding, bid, bid**) [I] to offer to do work or provide a service for a particular price, in competition with other companies, etc. SYN TENDER² (1) **~ for sth** |

B

(*NAmE also*) **~ on sth** *Three groups of companies bid for the contract to expand the Panama Canal.* ◇ **~ to do sth** *Companies anywhere in the EU are free to bid to provide services.*

bid·ding /ˈbɪdɪŋ/ *noun* [U] **~ for sth** the act of offering to do sth or to provide sth for a particular price: *Recent studies show the need for more accurate cost estimates in competitive bidding for design contracts.*

big /bɪg/ *adj.* (**big·ger**, **big·gest**) **1** (*rather informal*) large in degree, size, amount, etc: *All the power plants were situated far away from big cities.* ◇ *Unfortunately, these risks are too big and too remote for many people to take seriously.* **2** [only before noun] (*informal*) important; serious: *Up until now, Intel has been a big player in the computer industry.* ◇ *The project aims to answer some of the big questions about the origin of the universe.*
IDM **the big ˈpicture** something considered as a whole: *Employees who can see the big picture will be able to come up with suggestions as to how processes might be improved.*

bi·lat·eral /ˌbaɪˈlætərəl/ *adj.* **1** involving two groups of people or two countries: *These disputes were eventually settled fairly amicably by means of bilateral treaties.* ◇ *In December 2001, the EU concluded a bilateral agreement with the United States to combat terrorism.* ➲ *compare* MULTILATERAL, UNILATERAL (1) **2** (*medical*) involving both of two parts or sides of the body or brain: *Long-term exposure to high noise levels can result in bilateral hearing loss.* ➲ *compare* UNILATERAL (2) ■ **bi·lat·eral·ly** *adv.*: *Up until the 1980s, Japan preferred to conduct trade bilaterally with each of the EU's member states.*

bile /baɪl/ *noun* [U] the greenish brown liquid with an unpleasant taste that is produced by the LIVER to help the body to deal with the fats we eat, and that can come into your mouth when you VOMIT with an empty stomach: **+ noun** *Inflammation in the common bile duct leads to it becoming obstructed.*

bi·lin·gual /ˌbaɪˈlɪŋgwəl/ *adj.* **1** able to speak two languages equally well: *Written language difficulties in bilingual children are often explained away by teachers.* ◇ *People may acquire a new language without discarding their old one and simply become bilingual.* **2** using two languages; written in two languages: *Bilingual education really helps immigrants learn English.* ◇ *A bilingual dictionary relates the vocabularies of two languages by means of translation equivalents.*

bill /bɪl/ *noun* **1** a piece of paper that shows how much you owe sb for goods or services: *Many participants said they struggled to pay their bills, get food and keep homes clean.* ◇ *They faced a legal bill in excess of $25 000.* **2** a written suggestion for a new law that is presented to a country's parliament so that its members can discuss it: *The 2008 bill was passed by the Nigerian Senate by March 2010.* **3** (*NAmE*) = NOTE[2] (6): *The rouble lost its value daily, and huge numbers of dollar bills circulated.*

bin·ary[1] /ˈbaɪnəri/ *adj.* **1** (*computing, mathematics*) using only 0 and 1 as a system of numbers: *The internal working of the machine is entirely in the binary system.* **2** (*technical*) based on only two numbers; consisting of two parts: *The contraction of 'binary digit' to 'bit' has become an industry standard abbreviation.* ◇ *A binary variable was obtained for those babies exclusively breastfed at 3 months (yes/no).*

bin·ary[2] /ˈbaɪnəri/ *noun* (*pl.* **-ies**) **1** [C] **~ (of sth)** (*technical*) an idea or system consisting of two opposite parts: *The novel's characters are locked into a binary of black-white identity.* **2** [U] (*computing, mathematics*) a system of numbers that uses only 0 and 1: *The computer performs calculations in binary and converts the results to decimal.*

bind /baɪnd/ *verb* (**bound**, **bound** /baʊnd/) **1** [T] to unite people, organizations, etc. so that they are happier and live or work together better: *As Lippmann says, what binds the elite is cooperation in their common interest.* ◇ **~ sb/sth together** *It was these shared religious rituals that bound the French Huguenot community together.* ◇ **~ A and B together** *Mutual self-interest bound the soldier and the emperor together.* ◇ **~ A into B** *European leaders were determined to bind Germany fully into the new Europe.* ➲ *see also* BOUND TOGETHER (BY/IN STH) **2** [T, usually passive] to force sb to do sth by making them promise to do it or by making it their duty to do it: **~ sb** *Vitoria argued that laws passed by the commonwealth bind everyone, including the king.* ◇ **~ sb to do sth** *Councils were bound by the new regulations to accept the lowest bid.* ➲ *see also* BINDING[1] **3** [T, I] (*biochemistry*) to hold or combine with sth as a result of a chemical INTERACTION: **~ sth** *Apoferritin can also bind iron irreversibly within enterocytes.* ◇ **~ to sth** *These gene-regulatory proteins act by binding directly to the DNA of the control regions.* **4** [T, usually passive] **~ sth (in sth)** to fasten the pages of a book together and put them inside a cover: *two volumes bound in leather*

bind·ing[1] /ˈbaɪndɪŋ/ *adj.* that must be obeyed because it is accepted in law: *UN Resolution 1540 is a legally binding measure aimed at limiting the spread of weapons of mass destruction.* ◇ **~ on/upon sb** *However, international law is not binding upon states without their consent.*

bind·ing[2] /ˈbaɪndɪŋ/ *noun* **1 ~ (of sth) (to sth)** [U] (*biochemistry*) the process of holding or combining sth by chemical action: *Methods to study the binding of various proteins to other proteins on protein microarrays have been developed.* **2** [C, U] the cover that holds the pages of a book together; the process of putting a cover on a book: *rare books in leather bindings*

bio·chem·ical /ˌbaɪəʊˈkemɪkl; *NAmE* ˌbaɪoʊˈkemɪkl/ *noun* [U] connected with the chemical processes and substances that occur within living things: *Nitric oxide acts in many tissues, regulating different physiological and biochemical processes in plants.* ◇ *biochemical tests/analyses*

bio·chem·ist /ˌbaɪəʊˈkemɪst; *NAmE* ˌbaɪoʊˈkemɪst/ *noun* a scientist who studies biochemistry: *Biochemists have tended to concentrate on the few hundred chemicals that are commonly produced by most cells.*

bio·chem·is·try /ˌbaɪəʊˈkemɪstri; *NAmE* ˌbaɪoʊˈkemɪstri/ *noun* **1** [U] the scientific study of the chemistry of living things: *Since 1925 we have seen the rise of genetics, biochemistry and molecular biology.* **2** [U, C] **~ (of sth)** the chemical structure and behaviour of a living thing: *Much effort has been expended on studies of the biochemistry of antioxidants.*

bio·di·ver·sity /ˌbaɪəʊdaɪˈvɜːsəti; *NAmE* ˌbaɪoʊdaɪˈvɜːrsəti/ (*also less frequent* **bioˌlogical diˈversity**) *noun* [U] the existence of a large number of different kinds of animals and plants which make a balanced environment: *Rapid climate change is likely to cause major losses of biodiversity, including extinctions.*

bio·fuel /ˈbaɪəʊfjuːəl; *NAmE* ˈbaɪoʊfjuːəl/ *noun* [C, U] fuel made from plant or animal sources: *The challenge is to produce biofuels in a sustainable and economical way.* ◇ **+ noun** *There was increased demand for food and biofuel crops.*

biog·raphy /baɪˈɒgrəfi; *NAmE* baɪˈɑːgrəfi/ *noun* (*pl.* **-ies**) [C, U] **~ (of sb)** the story of a person's life written by sb else; this type of writing: *The novel was not widely known until Hemenway's biography of Hurston was published.* ◇ *He believes that biography should show the truth of the inner man or woman.* ➲ *compare* AUTOBIOGRAPHY ■ **bio·graph·ic·al** /ˌbaɪəˈgræfɪkl/ *adj.*: *The biographical details are accurate.* ◇ *He adds biographical sketches of many characters.*

bio·logic·al /ˌbaɪəˈlɒdʒɪkl; *NAmE* ˌbaɪəˈlɑːdʒɪkl/ *adj.* **1** connected with the processes that take place within living things: *Many biological processes depend on the interactions between molecules.* ◇ *Biological activity accelerates the speed of natural chemical reactions, such as rock weathering.* **2** connected with the science of biology: *The biological sciences have enjoyed huge advances during the last few decades.* **3** a child's **biological parents** are their natural parents, not the people who ADOPTED him/her: *Determining who is the natural or biological father often requires proof of paternity.* ◇ *Another factor is whether or not the stepfather has biological children of his own.* ■ **bio·logic·al·ly** /ˌbaɪəˈlɒdʒɪkli; *NAmE* ˌbaɪəˈlɑːdʒɪkli/ *adv.*: *Today, large areas of the Earth's surface have nearly ceased to be biologically productive.*

bioˌlogical diˈversity *noun* = BIODIVERSITY

biolo·gist /baɪˈɒlədʒɪst; *NAmE* baɪˈɑːlədʒɪst/ *noun* a scientist who studies biology: *Evolutionary biologists were the first to pose these questions.*

biol·ogy /baɪˈɒlədʒi; *NAmE* baɪˈɑːlədʒi/ *noun* [U] **1** the scientific study of the life and structure of plants and animals: *She has a BSc in biology and computer science.* ◇ *Genetics began to play a major role in modern biology.* ➲ *see also* MOLECULAR BIOLOGY **2** the way in which the body and cells of a living thing behave: *Human nature is seen as grounded in human biology.* ◇ *The significance of language and mental skills can be seen from looking at other aspects of our biology.* ◇ **the ~ of sth** *The second finding of importance concerns the biology of E. coli and, by extension, almost all bacteria.*

bio·mass /ˈbaɪəʊmæs; *NAmE* ˈbaɪoʊmæs/ *noun* **1** [U, sing.] (*ecology*) the total quantity or MASS of plants and animals in a particular area or volume: *Koi carp now constitute approximately 70% of total fish biomass in these waterways.* ◇ **~ of sth** *Sixty-eight plants died during the experiment, and accordingly were assigned a biomass of zero.* **2** [U] (*technical*) natural materials from living or recently dead plants, trees and animals, used as fuel and in industrial production, especially in the generation of electricity: *In low-income countries, biomass has been estimated to contribute, on average, about 40% to energy consumption.* ➲ *compare* FOSSIL FUEL

bio·med·ical /ˌbaɪəʊˈmedɪkl; *NAmE* ˌbaɪoʊˈmedɪkl/ *adj.* [usually before noun] involving biology and medicine: *They were at the forefront of research in the biomedical sciences.*

bi·opsy /ˈbaɪɒpsi; *NAmE* ˈbaɪɑːpsi/ *noun* (*pl.* **-ies**) [C, U] the act of removing and examining TISSUE from the body of sb who is ill, in order to find out more about their disease: *Every patient suspected of cirrhosis should have a liver biopsy.* ◇ *to perform/take a biopsy* ◇ *Diagnosis is confirmed by biopsy.*

bio·tech·nol·ogy /ˌbaɪəʊtekˈnɒlədʒi; *NAmE* ˌbaɪoʊtekˈnɑːlədʒi/ *noun* [U] the use of living cells and bacteria in industrial and scientific processes: *Rapid developments in biotechnology offer new perspectives for understanding how natural selection shapes adaptation.* ◇ **+ noun** *a biotechnology company/firm* ■ **bio·tech·no·logic·al** /ˌbaɪəʊteknəˈlɒdʒɪkl; *NAmE* ˌbaɪoʊteknəˈlɑːdʒɪkl/ *adj.*: *Biotechnological applications include genetically modified organisms and biomedicines.*

bird /bɜːd; *NAmE* bɜːrd/ *noun* a creature that is covered with feathers and has two wings and two legs. Most birds can fly: *In several bird species, some females may try to lay some of their eggs in another female's nest.*
IDM **a ˌbird's-ˌeye ˈview (of sth)** a view of sth from a high position looking down: *Some people often dream of seeing themselves from above, as in a bird's eye view (Blackmore, 1996b).*

birth /bɜːθ; *NAmE* bɜːrθ/ *noun* **1** [U, C] the time when a baby is born; the fact of a baby being born: *During the first year after birth, growth occurs at a rate of about 2 cm per month.* ◇ *At the beginning of the century, infant mortality was about 140 per 1 000 live births.* ◇ **at ~** *Life expectancy at birth for males is shown in the table below.* ◇ **from ~** *Babies with sickle-cell disease are anaemic from birth.* ◇ **the ~ of sb** *The birth of James's son was not received with universal rejoicing in his kingdom.* **2** [sing.] **the ~ of sth** the beginning of a new situation, idea, place, etc: *Such questions have plagued science ever since the birth of quantum theory.* ◇ *The birth of a new Germany was one of the most immediate consequences of 1989.* **3** [U] the country or social position of sb's family when they were born: *The Buddha's noble birth and high status are popular themes in Buddhist art and literature.* ◇ **by ~** *Karl Popper, an Austrian by birth, emigrated to New Zealand in 1937.*
IDM **give ˈbirth (to sb/sth) 1** to produce a baby or young animal: *Chimpanzees give birth around every 5 years.* ◇ *By this time, Elizabeth Dickens had given birth to another boy, Frederick.* **2** to make sth come into existence: *It was montage that gave birth to film as an art.* ◇ *The Maastricht Treaty gave birth to a new 'European Union'.*

ˈbirth control *noun* [U] the practice of controlling the number of children a person has, using various methods of CONTRACEPTION: *The debate led to renewed calls for greater access to be given to safe methods of birth control.*

birth·day /ˈbɜːθdeɪ; *NAmE* ˈbɜːrθdeɪ/ *noun* the day in each year which is the same date as the one on which you were born: *The twins celebrated their 21st birthday in March this year.* ◇ **+ noun** *a birthday party/cake/present*

ˈbirth rate *noun* the number of births every year for every 1 000 people in the population of a place: *a low/high birth rate* ◇ *The war resulted in a further fall in the birth rate.*

bi·sex·ual /ˌbaɪˈsekʃuəl/ *adj.* sexually attracted to both men and women: *One UK survey of 1 285 gay and bisexual men and women found that 83% reported having experienced discrimination.*

bishop /ˈbɪʃəp/ *noun* **~ (of...)** a senior priest in charge of the work of the Church in a city or district: *Augustine became bishop of Hippo in 395.*

bit /bɪt/ *noun* **1** [C] the smallest unit of information used by a computer: *Some processors clear all bits not taking part in the operation to zero.* **2 a bit** [sing.] (used as an adverb) (*especially BrE, rather informal*) rather: *The story gets a bit complicated at this point.* ◇ **~ like (doing) sth** *Learning to meditate is a bit like learning to play a musical instrument.* **3 a bit** [sing.] (used as an adverb) a small amount; a little: *She should have gone a bit further in her explanation.* ◇ **~ more/less** *Each glance provides a bit more information to add to the picture.* **4** [C] **~ of sth** (*especially BrE, rather informal*) a small piece or part of sth: *Historians must become detectives, hunting out bits of information.* ◇ *The stresses on each bit of the rope were the same.* **5** [C] **~ of sth** (*especially BrE, rather informal*) a small amount of sth: *If she lost a bit of weight, it would help with the pain in her knees.*
IDM **bit by ˈbit** (*rather informal*) a piece or part at a time; gradually: *The scriptures had been translated into Latin bit by bit by missionaries.* **every bit as good, bad, etc. (as sb/sth)** (*rather informal*) just as good, bad, etc; equally good, bad, etc: *Economic systems are every bit as chaotic as human societies.*

bite /baɪt/ *verb* (**bit** /bɪt/, **bit·ten** /ˈbɪtn/) **1** [I, T] (of a person or animal) to use the teeth to cut into or through sth or to make a small hole in sb's skin: *Most European spiders do not bite.* ◇ **~ sb/sth** *She had bitten, scratched and kicked her assailant.* **2** [I] to have an unpleasant effect: *US foreign trade declined once the depression began to bite.*

B

bit·ter /ˈbɪtə(r)/ *adj.* HELP **more bitter** and **most bitter** are the usual comparative and superlative forms, but **bitterest** can also be used. **1** [usually before noun] very serious and unpleasant, with a lot of anger or unhappiness involved: *A bitter industrial dispute raged between the miners and the government in the winter of 1890–1.* ◇ *His severity made him some bitter enemies.* ◇ *The bitter experience of religious wars in early modern Europe led to the Enlightenment's secular definition of civil society and the state.* **2** (of people) feeling angry and unhappy because you feel that you have been treated unfairly: *Though he may have been secretly frustrated about his lack of certain physical abilities, he was never bitter.* **3** (of food, etc.) having a strong, unpleasant taste; not sweet: *The drug has a bitter taste that is not fully masked by mixing it with fruit juices or syrups.* ➲ *compare* SWEET (1) **4** (of weather conditions) extremely cold and unpleasant: *The rain freezes as it falls, the waterfalls are ice-bound, and the nights are bitter.* ■ **bit·ter·ness** *noun* [U] *He expressed bitterness at the loss of fifteen years of his life under the tyranny of the regime.*

bit·ter·ly /ˈbɪtəli; *NAmE* ˈbɪtərli/ *adv.* in a way that shows feelings of anger or unhappiness: *She bitterly resented the fact that she had not attended college.* ◇ *They were bitterly opposed to the new immigration proposals.*

bi·vari·ate /baɪˈveəriət; *NAmE* baɪˈveriət/ *adj.* [only before noun] (*statistics*) involving or depending upon two VARIABLES: *Bivariate analysis is concerned with the analysis of two variables at a time in order to uncover whether the two variables are related.* ◇ *Model 1 of Table 2 presents a fixed effects model for the bivariate relationship between pain and depression.* ➲ *compare* MULTIVARIATE, UNIVARIATE

black[1] /blæk/ *adj.* (**black·er**, **black·est**) **1** having the very darkest colour, like night or coal: *Entries should be written clearly in black ink.* **2** belonging to a race of people who have dark skin; connected with black people: *Such groups demanded social and economic justice for black people.* ◇ *The Mangrove Restaurant was the informal centre for Notting Hill's black community.* HELP **Black** is the word most widely used and generally accepted in Britain. In the US the currently accepted term is **African American**. ■ **black·ness** *noun* [U, sing.] *Valerie, like many of her peers, made her blackness a central part of her identity.*

black[2] /blæk/ *noun* **1** [U] the very darkest colour, like night or coal: **in ~** *One print is drawn in black and the other in red.* **2** [C, usually pl.] a member of a race of people who have dark skin: *By 1700, some 115 000 blacks lived among a British Caribbean population of 148 000.* HELP In this meaning, **black** is more common in the plural. It can sound offensive in the singular. Instead, you can use the adjective (*a black man/woman*) or, in the US, **African American**.

IDM **(in) black and white** **1** having no colours except black, white and grey (in photographs, on television, etc.): *New technology became available, for instance the replacement of black-and-white televisions with colour sets.* ◇ *The film was shot in black and white.* **2** in a way that makes people or things seem completely bad or good, or completely right or wrong: *Youths often tend to see situations in black and white.* **3** in writing or in print: *They argued strongly that democratic rights should be laid down in black and white.*

ˌblack ˈhole *noun* **1** an area in space that nothing, not even light, can escape from, because GRAVITY is so strong there: *There is evidence for the existence of black holes as remnants of the collapse of massive stars.* **2** [usually sing.] (*rather informal*) a situation in which people or things disappear or a lot of money is wasted: *The policy can result in a legal black hole that vulnerable people will fall into.*

blad·der /ˈblædə(r)/ *noun* an organ that is shaped like a bag in which liquid waste collects before it is passed out of the body: *Patients should be encouraged to drink plenty of water and empty their bladder frequently.*

blame[1] /bleɪm/ *verb* to think or say that sb/sth is responsible for sth bad: **~ sb/sth** *Students blamed university officials who did not appear to be taking responsibility.* ◇ **~ sb/sth for (doing) sth** *Outdoor air pollution is often blamed for the increase in asthma cases in recent decades.* ◇ **~ sth on sb/sth** *Political elites blamed the economic crisis on the low skill levels of American workers.*

IDM **be to blame (for sth)** to be responsible for sth bad: *Ultimately, the committee had the unenviable task of deciding who was to blame for the failure.*

blame[2] /bleɪm/ *noun* [U] responsibility for doing sth badly or wrongly; saying that sb/sth is responsible for sth: *They continue to argue that the criminal justice system remains over-focused on punishment and blame.* ◇ **~ for sth** *Many contemporaries laid the blame for this failure on the shoulders of the leadership in Washington.* ◇ *Increasingly, doctors believe that much of the blame for health inequalities lies with diet.* ➲ *compare* CREDIT[1]

blank /blæŋk/ *adj.* (of a surface or background) empty; with no pictures, marks or decoration: *Blank spaces were provided in the online questionnaire to answer these questions.* ◇ *a blank wall/page/canvas* ◇ *Write on one side of the paper and leave the other side blank.* ◇ (*figurative*) *Human nature is basically a blank slate to be written on by society.*

bleak /bliːk/ *adj.* (**bleak·er**, **bleak·est**) **1** (of a situation) not encouraging or giving any reason to have hope: *The future looks bleak.* ◇ *Tacitus paints a bleak picture of imperial Rome.* **2** (of a place) exposed, empty or with no pleasant features: *a bleak winter landscape*

bleed /bliːd/ *verb* (**bled**, **bled** /bled/) [I] to lose blood, especially from a wound or an injury: *The wound bled profusely.*

bleed·ing /ˈbliːdɪŋ/ *noun* [U] the process of losing blood from the body: *A higher risk of major bleeding was observed with high-dose treatment.*

blew *past tense of* BLOW[1]

blind[1] /blaɪnd/ *adj.* (**blind·er**, **blind·est**) **1** not able to see: *A chip of metal entered his good eye rendering him totally blind.* ◇ **go ~** *They went blind by repeatedly staring at the sun.* ➲ *usage note at* DISABILITY **2 the blind** *noun* [pl.] people who are blind: *She taught at a school for the blind.* **3 ~ to sth** not noticing or realizing sth: *When you are a part of the mainstream culture, it is easy to be blind to the fact that you have any cultural baggage at all.* **4** [usually before noun] (of strong feelings) seeming to be unreasonable, and accepted without question: *He condemned the demand for blind obedience to the Party.* ◇ *Security could not be left to blind faith in the balance of power.* **5** [usually before noun] (of a situation or an event) that cannot be controlled by reason: *Blind chance can result in failure for even the best prepared and resourced contestant.* **6** (of a test or experiment) in which the people taking the test do not know, for example, which drug, substance, etc, they have been given: *Weston conducted a series of blind tests to find if recycled paper was comparable in quality to standard paper.* HELP A **double-blind** test is one in which neither the participants nor the researchers know which drug, substance, etc. each participant has been given.

IDM **turn a blind ˈeye (to sth)** to pretend not to notice sth bad that is happening, so you do not have to do anything about it: *International financial institutions previously turned a blind eye to corruption in projects they financed.*

blind[2] /blaɪnd/ *verb* **1** [often passive] **~ sb** to make sb unable to see, permanently or for a short time: *Fletcher* *was blinded in an industrial accident in 1999.* ◇ *She was temporarily blinded by the sun.* **2** to make sb no longer able to think clearly or behave in a sensible way: **~ sb** *Blinded by the love of power, Soto demanded permission to conquer Florida.* ◇ **~ sb to sth** *This mentality can blind people to their own weaknesses.* **3 ~ sb/sth** to make sb who is taking part in an experiment or interview unaware of what is being tested or measured: *The subject and the investigator should be blinded if possible.* ◇ *Blinding the interview process makes it much less likely that we impose our biases on the results.*

blind·ness /ˈblaɪndnəs/ *noun* [U] **1** the condition of being unable to see: *Vitamin A deficiency remains a major cause of blindness in developing countries.* **2 ~ to sth** the condition of not noticing or realizing sth: *Policy is formulated with a certain blindness to reality.*

bloc /blɒk; *NAmE* blɑːk/ *noun* a group of countries that work closely together because they have similar political interests: *The arms race put an additional strain on the economies of the Eastern bloc.* ◇ *Germany combined with other European Economic Community countries to form a single trading bloc.*

block¹ /blɒk; *NAmE* blɑːk/ *noun* **1** a large piece of a solid material that is square in shape and usually has flat sides: *The frictional force between a sliding block and a bench top is parallel to the sliding motion.* ◇ **~ of sth** *A block of iron at high temperature consists of atoms that are oscillating vigorously around their average positions.* ➲ *see also* BUILDING BLOCK **2 ~ (of sth)** (*BrE*) a tall building that contains apartments or offices: *The house was demolished in 1951 to make way for modern blocks of flats.* ◇ *Streets nearby are quiet with a mixture of apartment blocks and homes.* ◇ *High-rise blocks often lead to social segregation.* **3 ~ (of sth)** a quantity of sth that is considered as a single unit: *In each case, one firm controls the other with a large block of shares.* ◇ *Each participant performed 48 trials in blocks of 12.* **4 ~ (of sth)** (*computing*) an amount of data that is considered as a single unit for a computer program to deal with: *The program moves a block of data from one region of memory to another.* ◇ *Transmission is in 207-byte blocks.* **5** [usually sing.] **~ (to sth)** something that makes movement or progress difficult or impossible SYN OBSTACLE (1): *Politics, he believes, is a constant block to innovation and change.*

block² /blɒk; *NAmE* blɑːk/ *verb* **1 ~ sth** to stop sth from moving or flowing through a pipe, a passage, a road, etc. by putting sth in it or across it: *Volcanic rocks have poured into the gorge, temporarily blocking the Colorado River.* ◇ *One of the arteries has become partially blocked.* ◇ *The ice shelf blocked the seaward opening of the valley.* **2** to stop the movement of sth by being or putting sth in its way; to stop a process from happening: **~ sth** *As the spacecraft passes behind the planet, the radio signals will be blocked.* ◇ *The iodide blocks thyroid hormone release.* ◇ **~ sth from doing sth** *Dense algal blooms blocked light from reaching the rooted aquatic plants.* **3 ~ sth** to use your power to prevent sth from being done, developing or making progress: *European regulators blocked both deals in 2000 and 2001.*

PHR V ˌ**block sth ˈoff** to close an opening or passage by placing a barrier at one end or in front of it: *They managed to block off the main entrances to the convention centre by forming human chains.* ˌ**block sth ˈout** to stop light, sound, etc. from coming in: *As the great cloud of dust blanketed the Earth, blocking out the sun, many more animals and plants succumbed.*

block·age /ˈblɒkɪdʒ; *NAmE* ˈblɑːkɪdʒ/ *noun* **1** a thing that blocks flow or movement, for example of a liquid in a narrow place SYN OBSTRUCTION: *A rockfall formed a blockage that filled the river bed.* **2 ~ (of sth)** the state of being blocked: *Blood supply was restricted due to the blockage of an artery.*

blog /blɒg; *NAmE* blɑːg/ *noun* (*also* **web·log**) a website where a person writes regularly about recent events or topics that interest them, often including links to other websites that they find interesting: *Her current research includes a study of online blogs maintained and updated by teens.*

blood /blʌd/ *noun* **1** [U] the red liquid that flows through the bodies of humans and animals: *Before patients were given any treatment, blood was taken for tests.* ◇ **in the ~** *Cholesterol levels in the blood were very high.* ◇ **into the ~** *This protein is produced by the liver and secreted into the blood.* ◇ **+ noun** *The haemoglobin in red blood cells enables them to transport oxygen.* **2 -blooded** (in adjectives) having the type of blood mentioned: *E. coli is a bacterium commonly found in the lower intestine of warm-blooded animals.*

ˈ**blood count** *noun* **1** the number of red and white cells in sb's blood: *The object of treatment was to maintain the blood count, particularly haemoglobin and red cell volume.* **2** a medical test to count the number of red and white cells in sb's blood: *A full blood count and liver function tests were administered before treatment commenced.*

ˈ**blood group** (*also* ˈ**blood type** *especially in NAmE*) *noun* any of the different types that human blood is separated into for medical purposes: *The disorder appears to be more common in individuals with blood group A.*

ˈ**blood pressure** *noun* [U] the pressure of blood as it travels around the body: *to have high/low blood pressure* ◇ *Baseline heart rate and blood pressure were measured.*

blood·stream /ˈblʌdstriːm/ *noun* [sing.] the blood flowing through the body: *When we detect imminent danger, the hormone adrenaline is released into our bloodstream.*

ˈ**blood test** *noun* an examination of a small amount of your blood by doctors in order to make judgements about your medical condition: *All patients had a blood test for cholesterol.*

ˈ**blood transfusion** (*also* **transfusion**) *noun* [C, U] the process of putting new blood into the body of a person or an animal: *The patient required a blood transfusion.* ◇ *The possibility of blood transfusion should be discussed with the parents.*

ˈ**blood type** *noun* (*especially NAmE*) = BLOOD GROUP

ˈ**blood vessel** *noun* any of the tubes through which blood flows through the body: *These deformed cells block small blood vessels, causing damage to tissues and organs.* ➲ *see also* ARTERY, CAPILLARY, VEIN

blow¹ /bləʊ; *NAmE* bloʊ/ *verb* (**blew** /bluː/, **blown** /bləʊn; *NAmE* bloʊn/) **1** [I, T] to send out air from the mouth: **+ adv./prep.** *He has to blow into the mouthpiece hard and fast.* ◇ **~ sth + adv./prep.** *Then exhale, blowing out as much air as you can.* ◇ **~ sth out** *The patient is asked to blow as if they were blowing out a candle.* **2** [I] when the wind or a current of air **blows**, it is moving: *Renewable power is often available only intermittently (most obviously when the wind blows and the sun shines).* **3** [I, T] to be moved by the wind, sb's breath, etc; to move sth in this way: **+ adv./prep.** *Often you will see prayer flags blowing from the tops of houses.* ◇ **~ sth + adv./prep.** *Volcanic dust blown into the upper parts of the atmosphere is very effective in scattering light.*

PHR V ˌ**blow ˈup** to explode; to be destroyed by an explosion: *The Challenger space shuttle blew up on launch in 1986.* ˌ**blow sth ˈup** **1** to destroy sth by an explosion: *A scheme to blow up a St Petersburg bridge as the Tsar passed over it came to nothing.* **2** to fill sth with air or gas so that it becomes firm: *The balloon is steadily growing larger and larger as it is blown up.* **3** to make a photograph bigger SYN ENLARGE: *We can blow the images up to a larger size.*

B

blow² /bləʊ; *NAmE* bloʊ/ *noun* **1** a sudden event that has damaging effects on sb/sth, causing sadness or disappointment: *The death of Marx's wife in 1881 was a devastating blow.* ◇ **~ to sb/sth** *The outbreak of strikes in 1979 dealt a fatal blow to an already weak Labour government.* **2 ~ (to sth)** a hard hit with the hand, a weapon, etc: *Repeated minor blows to the head, such as occur in boxing, can lead to progressive deterioration in intellectual function.* IDM *see* DEAL¹

blue¹ /bluː/ *adj.* **(bluer, blu·est)** having the colour of a clear sky or the sea on a clear day: *The blue sky gets its colour from the blue light that is scattered down to us from the upper reaches of the atmosphere.* HELP **Blue** is also used to describe sb who looks slightly blue in colour because they are are cold or cannot breathe easily: *The patient was going blue and needed more oxygen.* ■ **blue·ness** *noun* [U, sing.] *The child may have pale skin with blueness around the lips.*

blue² /bluː/ *noun* [U, C] the colour of a clear sky or the sea on a clear day: **in ~** *The component waves are shown in blue.*

IDM **out of the ˈblue** unexpectedly; without warning: *The Lisbon earthquake struck out of the blue on 1 November, 1755.*

ˌblue-ˈcollar *adj.* [only before noun] connected with people who do physical work in industry: *Only 24 per cent of all employed Americans are blue-collar workers.* ➲ *compare* WHITE-COLLAR

blunt¹ /blʌnt/ *adj.* **(blunt·er, blunt·est) 1** without a sharp edge or point: *The wound had been caused by a blunt object, hit with sufficient force to penetrate the skin.* ◇ (*figurative*) *He claimed that the immigration controls introduced by the UK were a blunt instrument that do not distinguish between different classes of migrants.* OPP SHARP (3) **2** (of a person or remark) very direct; saying exactly what you think without trying to be polite: *In letters from the late 1970s he was even blunter.* ◇ *The minister said: 'To be blunt, shareholders in general do not have the ability to run a company.'*

blunt² /blʌnt/ *verb* **1 ~ sth** to make sth weaker or less effective: *The condition is managed through blunting the effect of the thyroid hormones.* **2 ~ sth** to make a point or an edge less sharp: *Abrasion and chemical weathering processes blunt particle edges.*

blunt·ly /ˈblʌntli/ *adv.* in a very direct way, without trying to be polite or kind: *To put it bluntly, how can we make sure that the State does not cheat?*

blur /blɜː(r)/ *verb* (-rr-) **1** [I, T] to become difficult to distinguish clearly; to make sth become difficult to distinguish clearly: *Since Marx's time, class divisions have blurred rather than intensified.* ◇ **~ sth** *Globalization, therefore, blurs national boundaries.* ◇ **~ the distinction between A and B** *Developments in computer technology have further blurred the distinction between hardware and software.* **2** [I, T] (of a shape) to become less clear and sharp; to make the shape of sth look less clear and sharp: *In France, advertisers must ensure tobacco brand names and logos blur during all broadcasts.* ◇ **~ sth** *Any movement of the subject blurs the image captured by the camera.*

blurred /blɜːd; *NAmE* blɜːrd/ *adj.* **1** not seeing things clearly: *The patient may complain of blurred vision.* **2** difficult to distinguish, so that differences are not clear: *The line between 'Roman' and 'barbarian' was considerably more blurred than was once thought.* **3** not clear; without a clear shape: *Processing the signals makes it possible to sharpen blurred images.*

BMI /ˌbiː em ˈaɪ/ *abbr.* BODY MASS INDEX

board /bɔːd; *NAmE* bɔːrd/ *noun* **1** [C+sing./pl. v.] **~ (of sb/sth)** a group of people who have power to make decisions and control a company or other organization: *In some companies, the board may take a larger role in routine management decisions.* ◇ **~ of directors** *The CEO (chief executive officer) is sometimes also the chairman of the board of directors.* ◇ **on the ~ (of sb/sth)** *Professor Biocca is on the editorial board of several journals.* **2** [C] used in the name of some organizations: *He helped establish the Australian National Film Board.* **3** [C] a vertical surface on which to write or attach notices: *When asked what the boards displayed, only 21% were able to give the correct answer.* ◇ **on the ~** *The students' guesses were written on the board and formed the basis of the discussion.* **4** [C] a thin, flat piece of wood or other stiff material on which to cut things, play games or perform other activities: *Participants were required to memorize the positions of chess pieces on a board.* **5** [C, U] a long thin piece of strong hard material, especially wood, used, for example, for making floors, building walls and roofs, and making boats: *Contemporary accounts describe overcrowded dormitories, bare boards and hard beds.* ◇ *The solvent has been identified in food packaging materials made from recycled board.* **6** [U] the meals that are provided when you stay in a place such as a hotel: **~ and lodging** *He performed a variety of jobs in the hostel and received free board and lodging in return.* ◇ **room and ~** *These schools provide room and board, education and clothing for thousands of boys.*

IDM **aˌcross the ˈboard** involving or applying to everyone or everything: *The UK Government announced massive decreases in public spending across the board.*

boat /bəʊt; *NAmE* boʊt/ *noun* **1** a vehicle (smaller than a ship) that travels on water: *Their means of transport was four small rowing boats.* **2** a boat or ship of any size: **by ~** *Most trade went by boat, land traffic being slow and expensive.*

bod·ily /ˈbɒdɪli; *NAmE* ˈbɑːdɪli/ *adj.* [only before noun] connected with the human body: *Patients often find it embarrassing to talk about bodily functions.* ◇ *Contagious diseases are spread by touch or close bodily contact.*

body /ˈbɒdi; *NAmE* ˈbɑːdi/ *noun* (*pl.* **-ies**) **1** [C] the whole physical structure of a human or an animal: *The heart functions as a pump, driving the blood around the body.* ◇ *In the seventeenth century, Descartes argued that the human body was a mechanism.* ◇ **+ noun** *A number of medications can increase body weight by increasing appetite.* **2** [C] the main part of a body not including the head, or not including the head, arms and legs: *He was repeatedly kicked in the head and the body.* ◇ *The sauropods had small heads, long necks and tails, and short barrel-shaped bodies.* **3** [C] the body of a dead person or animal: *Where no identifiable body has been found, family members will be unable to obtain a death certificate.* **4** [C] **~ of sth** a large amount or collection of sth, especially information or knowledge: *This theory is now supported by a large body of evidence.* ◇ *There is a large body of work that suggests that the distinction is not quite that straightforward.* **5** [sing.] **the ~ of sth** the main part of sth, especially a book, article or document: *The main body of the text revolves around Isaiah's suffering servant.* ◇ *Bacteria enter the enamel and body of the tooth.* **6** [C+sing./pl. v.] a group of people who work or act together, often for an official purpose, or who are connected in some other way: *The Chartered Institute of Marketing is a professional body for marketing professionals based in the UK.* ◇ *Irresponsible selling may result in fines from regulatory bodies.* ◇ **~ of sb** *The French responded by dispatching two large bodies of troops to reinforce Louis's army in the Netherlands.* **7** [C] (*formal*) an object: *The state of motion of a body can only* *change if there is a resultant force applied.* ◇ *This equation yields the fundamental law of dynamics for solid bodies in rotation.* **8** [C] **water ~** | **~ of water** a large area of water, such as a lake or sea: *Migrating birds die each year by drowning in oil ponds, which the birds mistake for water bodies.* ◇ *Coastal dunes are deposits of wind-blown sediment that occur next to large bodies of water.*

▸ ADJECTIVE + BODY **human** ♦ **male, female** *Gradually sculptors moved towards a more naturalistic representation of the human body.* | **large, substantial** ♦ **growing** *A substantial body of research exists on how to make writing easier for the reader to understand.* | **public** ♦ **professional** ♦ **regulatory** ♦ **decision-making** ♦ **international** ♦ **governing** *Energy advice is offered not only to individuals, but also to all companies and public bodies in the region.* | **foreign** ♦ **solid** *The immune system protects the body from invasion from foreign bodies, such as bacteria.*

▸ VERB + BODY **enter** ♦ **protect** *Anthrax can enter the body orally, or through cuts and skin lesions.* | **establish, create, form, set up** *The panel was a body established by the City of London to regulate takeovers and mergers.*

▸ BODY + NOUN **weight, size, mass** ♦ **temperature** ♦ **fat** ♦ **part** ♦ **fluid, tissue** ♦ **image** *Reptiles need external sources of heat to regulate their body temperature.*

▸ BODY OF + NOUN **work** ♦ **evidence, research** ♦ **knowledge** ♦ **literature** ♦ **opinion, theory, ideas** ♦ **law, rules** *There is an emerging body of opinion that supports these approaches.*

ˈbody language *noun* [U] **~ (of sb)** the process of communicating what you are feeling or thinking by the way you place and move your body rather than by words: *The body language of the women clearly signals grief and torment.*

ˌbody mass ˈindex *noun* (*abbr.* **BMI**) an approximate measure of whether sb weighs too much or too little, calculated by dividing their weight in kilograms by their height in metres squared: *Evidence suggests that shift workers are more likely to have a higher body mass index.*

boil /bɔɪl/ *verb* [I, T] when a liquid **boils** or when you **boil** it, it is heated to the point where it turns to steam or VAPOUR: *These solvents boil near 70°C.* ◇ **~ sth** *The solution should then be boiled gently.* HELP You can also say that you **boil** a particular type of container, meaning that you boil what is inside it: *Once the cans were filled, they were boiled and cooled.*

PHR V **ˌboil sth ˈdown (to/into sth)** to make sth, especially information, shorter by leaving out the parts that are not important: *She has managed to boil this complex text down into a one-page summary.* **ˌboil ˈdown to sth** (not used in the progressive tenses) (*rather informal*) (of a situation, problem, etc.) to have sth as a main or basic part: *Our alternatives boil down to becoming smarter or becoming extinct.* ◇ *Ultimately, the issue boils down to a problem of confidence in public policymakers.*

ˈboiling point *noun* [C, U] the temperature at which a liquid starts to boil: *The two bottles contain liquids that have different boiling points.* ◇ *The solution is then heated up to near boiling point.*

bold /bəʊld; *NAmE* boʊld/ *adj.* (**bold·er, bold·est**) **1** (of printed words, letters, etc.) thicker and darker than normal: *The more likely diagnoses are given in bold type.* ◇ *The bold page numbers in the index indicate where definitions are located.* **2** (of people or behaviour) brave and confident; not afraid to say what you feel or to take risks: *The novel's heroine, Jane Eyre, is bold and fiery.* ◇ *New Labour came to power making bold claims that they would save the welfare state.* **3** (of shapes, colour, etc.) that can be easily seen; having a strong clear appearance: *Young melons are often marked by distinct, bold stripes.*

bold·ly /ˈbəʊldli; *NAmE* ˈboʊldli/ *adv.* in a brave and confident way; without being afraid to say what you feel or to take risks: *The federal committee boldly asserted that inconsistencies between standards in different states were a problem.*

bol·ster /ˈbəʊlstə(r); *NAmE* ˈboʊlstər/ *verb* **~ sth** to improve sth or make it stronger: *They used this fact to bolster their territorial claim to the islands.* ◇ *Productivity growth increased to 2%, bolstered by the rapid growth of manufacturing productivity.*

bomb¹ /bɒm; *NAmE* bɑːm/ *noun* **1** [C] a weapon designed to explode at a particular time or when it is dropped or thrown: *A car bomb was detonated outside the headquarters of MI5 in Northern Ireland.* ◇ *The bridge collapsed because a bomb exploded nearby.* ◇ *a nuclear/an atomic bomb* ◇ **+ noun** *In the early atomic age, Americans were asked to build and stock bomb shelters.* **2 the bomb** [sing.] (*rather informal*) nuclear weapons: *The more nations get the bomb, the harder it becomes to prevent further proliferation.*

bomb² /bɒm; *NAmE* bɑːm/ *verb* **~ sb/sth** to attack sb/sth by leaving a bomb in a place or by dropping bombs from a plane: *In 1945, the Luftwaffe stopped bombing London.* ◇ *a bombed building/city*

bomb·ing /ˈbɒmɪŋ; *NAmE* ˈbɑːmɪŋ/ *noun* [C, U] an occasion when a bomb is dropped or left somewhere; the act of doing this: *Suicide bombings in crowded civilian areas are not uncommon.* ◇ **the ~ of sth** *Perhaps the most devastating of all these raids was the bombing of Dresden.*

bond¹ AWL /bɒnd; *NAmE* bɑːnd/ *noun* **1** something that forms a connection between people or groups, such as a feeling of friendship or shared ideas and experiences: *Gibbons form long-term pair bonds.* ◇ **~ between A and B** *Bonds between families in different settlements may often have been strong.* ◇ *Children make the bond between husband and wife stronger.* ◇ **~ with sb/sth** *Socially anxious and shy individuals have more difficulty forming social bonds with others.* ◇ **~ of sth** *Working effectively involves developing a bond of trust between the subjects and the researcher.* **2** the way in which atoms are held together in a chemical COMPOUND: *Collisions between molecules in solution can provide the energy required to break some chemical bonds.* ◇ **~ between A and B** *The bond between the two oxygen atoms in a peroxide is relatively weak.* ◇ **~ with sth** *Four of these electrons form covalent bonds with the neighbouring atoms.* **3** an agreement by a government or a company to pay sb interest on the money they have lent after a particular period of time; a document containing this agreement: *The company raised the finance it needed by issuing bonds.* ◇ **+ noun** *The debt was funded through government bond issues.* **4** the way in which two surfaces are joined together, often using GLUE: *Coating the nylon in this way permits a strong bond.*

▸ ADJECTIVE + BOND **strong** ♦ **weak** *The carbon-carbon bond in graphite is the strongest chemical bond known to exist.* | **emotional** *In the first year, the child forms a strong, secure emotional bond with the mother.* | **single, double** ♦ **chemical** ♦ **covalent** *The structure of these polymers is written as a sequence of alternating single and double bonds.*

▸ VERB + BOND **form, create** ♦ **be joined by, be linked by, be held together by** ♦ **break** ♦ **strengthen** ♦ **weaken** ♦ **have** ♦ **contain** *The reaction forms a new bond between carbon and hydrogen.* ◇ *Philip strengthened the bonds between the army and the king by sharing its hardships and dangers.*

bond² AWL /bɒnd; *NAmE* bɑːnd/ *verb* **1** [T, I] to join two things firmly together; to join firmly to sth else: **~ (A) to B** *A bearing housing was bonded to the arm using epoxy adhesive.* ◇ *These crystals bond poorly to one another and also form weak layers.* ◇ **~ (A and B) together** *A polymeric resin bonds the fibres together.* **2** [T] to join atoms together by a chemical bond: **~ A to B** *Each carbon atom is bonded*

B

to three others. ◇ **~ A and B together** *The number of atoms which are covalently bonded together to form a molecule can become very large.* **3** [I] **~ (with sb)** to develop or create a relationship of trust with sb: *The foster mother had bonded well with the boy but not especially with the girl.*

bond·ing AWL /ˈbɒndɪŋ; *NAmE* ˈbɑːndɪŋ/ *noun* [U] **1** the process of forming a special relationship with sb or with a group of people: *These films are full of scenes of male bonding.* ◇ **~ between A and B** *Depressive disorder can have a negative effect on bonding between mother and baby.* **2** (*chemistry*) the process of atoms joining together to form chemical COMPOUNDS: **~ of A and B** *Molecules are formed by the chemical bonding of atoms.* ◇ **~ between A and B** *The properties of liquid and solid water are dominated by the hydrogen bonding between H_2O molecules.*

bone /bəʊn; *NAmE* boʊn/ *noun* **1** [C] any of the hard parts that form the SKELETON of the body of a human or an animal: *The adult human body contains 206 bones.* ◇ **~ of sb/sth** *Darwin found bones of enormous extinct animals high in the Andes.* ◇ **+ noun** *He suffered from a rare bone disease.* **2** [U] the hard substance that bones are made of: *Magnesium in the body combines with calcium and phosphorus to form bone.* ◇ **+ noun** *A scan is indicated to determine bone mineral density in patients at high risk of osteoporosis.*

IDM **a bone of conˈtention** a subject that causes disagreement and arguments between people: *The influence of finance and the City of London has long been a bone of contention.* ➲ *more at* BARE, FEEL[1], FINGER, SKIN

ˈbone marrow (*also* **mar·row**) *noun* [U] a soft substance that fills the hollow parts of bones, and in which blood cells are produced: *The most serious side effects are those affecting the liver, bone marrow and lungs.*

bonus /ˈbəʊnəs; *NAmE* ˈboʊnəs/ *noun* (*pl.* **-es**) **1** an extra amount of money that is added to a payment, especially to sb's wages as a reward: *The company has continued to pay bonuses to its senior employees.* ◇ **+ noun** *Non-executive directors should receive fees but not options or bonus payments.* **2** an extra advantage that you were not expecting: *The new amity with Scotland had the added bonus of isolating Ulster.*

book /bʊk/ *noun* **1** [C] a set of printed pages that are fixed together inside a cover so that you can turn them and read them: *The online environment provides a more flexible way of presenting a text than does a printed book.* ◇ **+ noun** *This series of articles has been published in book form.* **2** [C] a written work published in printed or electronic form: *This book provides an introductory overview of cryptography.* ◇ **~ on/about sth** *She is the author of several books on US foreign policy.* **3** [C] a section of a large written work: *The myth provides an interesting contrast with the Book of Genesis.* ◇ *In Book 4, Medea flees to join the Argonauts and secures the golden fleece for them.* **4 the books** [pl.] **~ (of sth)** the written records of the financial affairs of a business SYN ACCOUNT[1] (5): *The books of subsidiaries are often not provided on a quarterly basis.*

- ADJECTIVE + BOOK **influential**, **important** • **classic** • **seminal** • **famous** • **popular** • **recent** • **introductory** • **scholarly** *'The Wealth of Nations' is the most influential book on economics ever written.*
- NOUN + BOOK **reference** • **history** • **travel** • **prayer** *Not all pupils have learning resources like reference books and computers at home.*
- VERB + BOOK **write** • **publish** • **read** *He has written books on language, rationality and consciousness.*

boom[1] /buːm/ *noun* [C, U] a sudden increase in trade and economic activity, in a country or region generally, or in a particular industry; a period of wealth and success: *This economic boom slowed down in the early 1970s for two principal reasons.* ◇ *In other parts of the country, a private housing boom, created many jobs.* ◇ **~ in sth** *During this period, there was a relative boom in the construction industry.* ◇ **~ and bust** *Labour appeared to have eliminated the economics of boom and bust that had characterized post-war economic policy.* ◇ **~ years** *Oil prices rose sharply during the boom years.* HELP A **baby boom** is a period when more babies are born than usual, used especially to refer to the period immediately after the Second World War: *The figures for 1970 and 1980 owe much to the effects of the baby boom.*

boom[2] /buːm/ *verb* [I] to have a period when growth is fast; to become bigger, more successful, etc: *In 2000, the US economy was booming.* ◇ *After World War II, roads and cities sprawled and timber production boomed.* ◇ *One of the fastest-growing sectors of India's economy is the booming business services sector.*

boost[1] /buːst/ *verb* **~ sth** to make sth increase, or become better or more successful: *In the past, a compound of lead was used to boost the octane number of gasoline.* ◇ *Governments would secure stable long-term growth by boosting demand through tax cuts or higher spending.* ◇ *A number of films were made that were intended to boost wartime morale.*

boost[2] /buːst/ *noun* [usually sing.] **1** something that helps or encourages sb/sth: *The movement began in 1900 and received a huge boost from a revival that started in the Chicago area in 1901.* ◇ **~ to sth** *This offensive was a great boost to Russian and foreign morale.* **2 ~ (in sth)** an increase in sth: *The deal failed to provide the expected boost in output and revenue.*

bor·der[1] /ˈbɔːdə(r); *NAmE* ˈbɔːrdər/ *noun* **1** the line that divides two countries or areas; the land near this line: *International migration is measured through information collected at borders and airports.* ◇ **cross a ~** *The first Mormon pioneers crossed the American border into the North-West Territories in 1887.* ◇ **on the ~ (between A and B)** *The Yanomamo Indians live on the border between Brazil and Venezuela.* ◇ **~ of sth** *Christianity had become the chief religion of many people living within and beyond the borders of the Roman Empire.* ◇ **~ with sth** *She moved to a town on the German border with the Netherlands.* ◇ **across/over the ~** *Refugees fled across the border to Chad.* ◇ **national/international borders** *These issues go beyond national borders.* ◇ *150 years ago, people moved freely across international borders without even the need for a passport.* **2** the point at which a quality, subject, type of object, etc. is separated from another: **~ between A and B** *Such behaviour is likely to occur in those metals that are near the border between metals and non-metals.* ◇ **on the ~ of sth** *The trial judge directed the jury to consider whether the defendant was partially insane or on the border of insanity.* **3 ~ (of sth)** the edge of sth: *The anterior border of the lower jaw is also more rounded in this species.*

bor·der[2] /ˈbɔːdə(r); *NAmE* ˈbɔːrdər/ *verb* **1 ~ sth** (of a country or an area) to be next to or share a border with another country or area: *Coffee was grown in some regions bordering the Red Sea.* ◇ *Two of NATO's member nations (Norway and Turkey) bordered the USSR.* **2 ~ sth** to form a line along or around the edge of sth: *The River Ken was bordered by an area of newly established woodland.*

PHR V **ˈborder on sth 1** to come very close to being sth, especially a strong or unpleasant emotion or quality: *She took up music with a passion that bordered on obsession.* **2** to be next to sth: *Areas bordering on the Aegean Sea appear to have suffered a briefer period of decline.*

bor·der·line /ˈbɔːdəlaɪn; *NAmE* ˈbɔːrdərlaɪn/ *adj.* not clearly belonging to a particular condition or group; not clearly acceptable: *There were borderline cases that some pathologists would call cancer and some would not.*

bore *past tense of* BEAR

bored /bɔːd; *NAmE* bɔːrd/ *adj.* feeling tired and impatient because you have lost interest in sb/sth or because you have nothing to do: **~ with sb/sth** *He says he is bored with school.* ◇ **~ with doing sth** *People quickly get bored with completing surveys.*

bor·ing /ˈbɔːrɪŋ/ *adj.* not interesting; making you feel tired and impatient: *Commentators, researchers and the public considered the campaign dull, boring, and even sad.*

born /bɔːn; *NAmE* bɔːrn/ *verb* **be born** (used only in the passive, without *by*) **1** (*abbr.* **b.**) to come out of your mother's body at the beginning of your life: *Frederic Chopin was born in Poland in 1810.* ◇ *Human babies are born with relatively underdeveloped brains.* ◇ **~ into sth** *Max Weber was born into a middle-class family in Erfurt, Germany, in 1864.* ◇ **~ of/to sb** *Rushdie, born of a Muslim family in Bombay, was educated in England.* ◇ **+ adj.** *The Declaration commences with the notion that all peoples are born free and equal in dignity and rights.* **2** (of an idea, an organization, a feeling, etc.) to start to exist: *Modern ethnography had yet to be born.* ◇ **+ adj.** *Most Internet-based companies are today born global whether or not they intend it.* ◇ **~ (out) of sth** *The class struggle, she argues, is born of economic oppression.* **3 -born** (in compounds) born in the place mentioned: *Loeb was a German-born zoologist who emigrated to the University of Chicago in 1892.*

borne *past part. of* BEAR

bor·row /ˈbɒrəʊ; *NAmE* ˈbɑːroʊ; ˈbɔːroʊ/ *verb* **1** [T, I] to take money from a person or bank and agree to pay it back to them/it at a later time: **~ sth (from sb/sth)** *In the UK, a sizeable group of people find it difficult to borrow money from these banks.* ◇ **~ (from sb/sth)** *Families are being forced to borrow to maintain their living standards.* ◇ *In 1760 the Chinese government had made it illegal for Chinese to borrow from foreigners.* ➲ *compare* LEND (1) **2** [I, T] to take a word, an idea, etc. from another language, person, etc. and use it as your own: **~ from sb/sth** *It seems likely that both authors borrowed from some unknown third source.* ◇ **~ sth (from sb/sth)** *Stonequist borrows the term from the renowned sociologist Robert E. Park.* ◇ *The term 'teenager' or 'cheenayja' has been borrowed from English but is not in widespread use.* **3** [T] to take and use sth that belongs to sb else, and return it to them at a later time: **~ sth** *The defendant had asked whether he could borrow the car for a few hours.* ◇ **~ sth from sb/sth** *She is an avid reader, always borrowing books from the library.* ➲ *compare* LEND (2)

bor·row·er /ˈbɒrəʊə(r); *NAmE* ˈbɑːroʊər; ˈbɔːroʊər/ *noun* a person or an organization that borrows money, especially from a bank: *The exact amount the borrower is to repay is clearly specified.* ➲ *compare* LENDER

bor·row·ing /ˈbɒrəʊɪŋ; *NAmE* ˈbɑːroʊɪŋ; ˈbɔːroʊɪŋ/ *noun* [C, U] **1** the money that a company, an organization or a person borrows; the act of borrowing money: *The income generated is usually sufficient to cover interest payments on borrowings.* ◇ *The interest rate rose in the US as a result of an increase in government borrowing.* **2 ~ (of sth) (from sb/sth)** a word, phrase or idea that sb has taken from another person's work or from another language and used in their own; the act of using a word, etc. taken from another source: *The word 'caveat' is a borrowing from Latin.* ◇ *Several geographers have expressed concern about the borrowing of ideas from other disciplines.*

both /bəʊθ; *NAmE* boʊθ/ *det., pron.* **1** used with plural nouns to mean 'the two' or 'the one as well as the other': *Both firms produce an identical product.* ◇ *Most people would agree that Germany and the UK are both democracies.* ◇ *The court order declared that the Californian couple should have custody of both the children at birth.* ◇ *Both his grandfathers were noted storytellers.* ◇ *The two electrons repel each other, on account of them both being negatively charged.* ◇ *Kozinets (2002) and Arnould (2007) have both asked this question and their answers differ.* ◇ **~ of sb/sth** *Divorce involves a conscious decision by one or both of the spouses to bring the marriage to an end.* ◇ *Two further estates were purchased in 1789, both of them in the south of the island.* **2 both... and...** not only... but also...: *Life in rural schools tends to be harsh for both students and teachers.* ◇ *The objective of the study is to assess the human rights impact of the policy, both now and in the future.*

bot·tom¹ /ˈbɒtəm; *NAmE* ˈbɑːtəm/ *noun* **1** [C, usually sing.] the lowest part of sth: *Between 600 and 1 200 m of relief separate the valley bottom from the ridge top.* ◇ **~ of sth** *When the spot reaches the bottom of the screen, it returns to the top again.* ◇ **at the ~ (of sth)** *Leave a space at the bottom of a page for the student to insert an answer.* ◇ **from top to ~** *In Figure 3, the timeline runs from top to bottom, each row representing one recording.* OPP TOP¹ (1) **2** [sing.] the lowest position on a scale, list, etc: **~ (of sth)** *Decision-makers tend to push such issues to the bottom of their priority list.* ◇ **at the ~ (of sth)** *'Villeins' were at the very bottom of the social hierarchy.* ◇ **from the ~ up** *They suggest that we think about security from the bottom up instead of from the top down, meaning that we start with the security of the individual rather than with that of the state.* OPP TOP¹ (2) ➲ *see also* BOTTOM-UP **3** [C, usually sing.] the lowest surface on the inside or outside of a container: **~ (of sth)** *The density of the liquid increases towards the bottom of the tube.* ◇ **at the ~ (of sth)** *Slices of the tissue were placed at the bottom of a Petri dish.* ◇ **on the ~ (of sth)** *No more salt dissolves and salt crystals remain on the bottom of the glass.* ◇ *The manufacturer's name usually appears on the bottom of the device.* **4** [sing.] the ground below the water in a sea, lake, river, etc: **(on the) ~ (of sth)** *The company abandoned its plan to dump a disused oil rig on the bottom of the Atlantic Ocean.*
IDM **at bottom** used to say what sb/sth really is: *The question for the judge is, at bottom, how this point of government policy should be interpreted.* ➲ *more at* RACE

bot·tom² /ˈbɒtəm; *NAmE* ˈbɑːtəm/ *adj.* [only before noun] in the lowest place or position: *The top and bottom surfaces are easier to cool than the centre.* ◇ *The village priest was at the bottom end of a hierarchical chain of command headed by the bishop.* ◇ **~ left/right** *Note that there is a general pattern of points flowing from the bottom left of the graph to the top right.* ➲ *compare* TOP²

ˌbottom-ˈup *adj.* **1** (of a plan, project, etc.) starting with details and then later moving on to more general principles: *They describe a bottom-up approach to constructing artificial cells, using molecular components to directly assemble them.* OPP TOP-DOWN (2) **2** starting from or involving the people who have lower positions in an organization: *Respondents were asked whether they thought the programme was driven by a top-down (management-led), or bottom-up (frontline-led) approach.* OPP TOP-DOWN (1)

bought *past tense, past part. of* BUY

bound¹ /baʊnd/ *adj.* [not before noun] **1 ~ to do/be sth** certain or likely to happen, or to do or be sth: *Without the support of the Catholic Church, the project was bound to fail.* ◇ *Any answer to such questions is bound to be speculative.* **2** forced to do sth by law, duty or a particular situation: **~ by sth** *US multinationals operating within Europe are bound by EU competition law.* ◇ **~ to do sth** *Member States are bound to comply with Security Council resolutions under the United Nations Charter.* **3** (in compounds) prevented from working normally by the conditions mentioned: *Coketown was based on the strike-bound manufacturing town of Preston.* ◇ *Vladivostok was ice-bound for much of the year.* **4** (also in compounds) travelling, or ready to travel, in a particular direction or to a particular place: *The poster was erected alongside the busy London-bound side of the M4 motorway.* ◇ *The second photograph shows a southbound train on the main peninsular railway line.* ◇ **~ for...** *On 23 September 1936, he left England on a ship bound for New York.*

IDM **bound to'gether (by/in sth)** closely connected: *Organizations are groups of individuals bound together by some common purpose.* **bound 'up in sth 1** very busy with sth; very interested or involved in sth: *In his collection of short stories, Dublin's citizens are portrayed as bound up in private concerns.* **2** (*also* **bound 'up with sth**) closely connected with sth: *Many people assume that ethical behaviour is intimately bound up with religion.*

bound² /baʊnd/ *noun* **1 bounds** [pl.] the accepted or furthest limits of sth: **within ~** *Britain entered an alliance with France to keep French ambitions within bounds.* ◇ **beyond/outside/within the ~ of sth** *This scenario is not beyond the bounds of possibility.* ◇ **know no ~** *The ancient Greeks called it hubris, an arrogance that knows no bounds.* **2** [C] **~ (of sth)** (*technical*) a limiting value, line or PLANE: *The lower bound for the natural numbers is either 0 or 1.*

IDM **out of 'bounds** not reasonable or acceptable: *Appeals to the intentions of the artist are out of bounds.* **out of 'bounds (to/for sb)** (*especially BrE*) outside the limits of where sb is allowed to be: *Certain areas of the institution's premises are declared out of bounds to outsiders.*

bound³ /baʊnd/ *verb* [usually passive] **1 ~ sth** to form the edge or limit of an area, object or quantity: *Many species inhabit a restricted region bounded by geographic barriers such as seas or mountains.* ◇ *The cell contents remain bounded by a cell membrane throughout.* **2 ~ sth** to limit sth: *The spirit of competition affects every part of life and is not bounded by class or gender.*

bound⁴ *past tense, past part. of* BIND

bound·ary /ˈbaʊndri/ *noun* (*pl.* **-ies**) **1** a line that marks the limits or edges of an area and separates it from other areas; a dividing line: **~ of sth** *A flood control dyke was constructed along the eastern boundary of the city.* ◇ **~ between A and B** *The sites of the largest earthquakes coincide with the boundaries between the tectonic plates.* ◇ **across the ~ | across boundaries** *Labour is much less mobile across national boundaries than within them.* ◇ **within/beyond the boundaries of sth** *Substantial forms of self-government can be achieved within the boundaries of a larger state.* **2** [usually pl.] a limit of sth, especially a subject or area of activity: *At the beginning of a business partnership, it is important to establish boundaries.* ◇ **~ of sth** *Nurses must be aware of the boundaries of their own knowledge and skill.* ◇ **~ between A and B** *The boundaries between work and family have been blurring steadily since the 1950s.* ◇ **across the boundaries** *Disputes may occur across the boundaries of different disciplines.* ◇ **within/beyond the boundaries of sth** *Unfortunately this activity lies beyond the boundaries of legal regulation.*

▸ ADJECTIVE + BOUNDARY **sharp, clear** *There is a sharp boundary between the soil and overlying deposits.* ◇ *This suggests the existence of clear gender boundaries in manual and low-skilled, non-manual work.* | **national • international • territorial • geographical** *Comparing statistics across national boundaries is difficult.* | **traditional • cultural • professional • disciplinary • organizational** *Geographers have responded by broadening their focus beyond traditional boundaries.*

▸ VERB + BOUNDARY **mark, form • draw • redraw • cross • respect** *It is impossible to draw a single line that marks the boundary between the two dialects.* ◇ *Many of the world's major rivers cross international boundaries.* | **cross, transcend, cut across, span • blur • define, establish, draw, set • maintain • transgress • push, extend** *Patterns of social interaction often transcend language boundaries.* ◇ *It is important to define the boundaries of the study.*

ˌbound ˈvariable *noun* = DUMMY VARIABLE (2)

bour·geois /ˈbʊəʒwɑː; ˌbʊəˈʒwɑː; *NAmE* ˌbʊrˈʒwɑː; ˈbʊrʒwɑː/ *adj.* **1** belonging to or characteristic of the middle class, especially when this involves being interested mainly in possessions and social status and supporting traditional values: *The novel ends with his assimilation into modern American bourgeois society.* ◇ *Harold is continually attempting to better himself, to adopt bourgeois attitudes.* **2** (*politics*) supporting the interests of CAPITALISM: *The new state was run by a bourgeois political class of lawyers, civil servants and landowners.* ■ **bour·geois** *noun* (*pl.* **bour·geois**)*The growing competition among the bourgeois make the wages of the workers ever more fluctuating.*

the bour·geoisie /ˌbʊəʒwɑːˈziː; *NAmE* ˌbʊrʒwɑːˈziː/ *noun* [sing.+ sing./pl. v.] **1** the middle classes in society: *This form of family exists only among the bourgeoisie.* **2** (*politics*) the CAPITALIST class: *There is inequality between social classes, especially the bourgeoisie and the proletariat.*

bow /bəʊ; *NAmE* boʊ/ *noun* a weapon used for shooting ARROWS, consisting of a long curved piece of wood with a tight string joining its ends: *No serious modern hunter would still use a bow and arrow to kill game.*

bowel /ˈbaʊəl/ *noun* the tube along which food passes after it has been through the stomach, especially the end where waste is collected before it is passed out of the body: *the small/large bowel* ◇ **+ noun** *bowel disease/cancer/obstruction/surgery* HELP In non-technical language **bowel** is often used in the plural: *a pain in the bowels.* In medical language, the singular is usually used, except in the phrase *to open/empty your bowels*, meaning 'to pass solid waste out of the body': *He describes only opening his bowels twice a week for the past 2 months.*

bowl /bəʊl; *NAmE* boʊl/ *noun* (especially in compounds) a deep round dish with a wide open top, used especially for holding food or liquid: *The pottery includes cooking jars and eating bowls.* ◇ **~ of sth** *The tube is then placed into a bowl of liquid.*

box /bɒks; *NAmE* bɑːks/ *noun* **1** a small square or RECTANGLE on a page or computer screen containing information, or for people to put information in: **in a ~** *Typing the term in the search box will display the screen for this term.* ◇ **tick/check a ~** *Customers who do not tick the box are considered to have given their consent.* **2** (especially in compounds) a container made of wood, metal, etc. with a flat stiff base and sides and often a lid, used especially for holding solid things: *A cat shut in a box might suffer intense distress, even though subjected to no physical harm.* ◇ *She checked the cash box and discovered that £100 was missing.* ◇ *The company attempted to address environmental issues by eliminating cardboard boxes when shipping materials from one plant to another.* **3 ~ (of sth)** a box and its contents: *It would be highly inconsistent to advertise a box of chocolates as 'sophisticated' if the packaging was cheap.* **4** (especially in compounds) a container that holds or protects part of a larger device: *In a switch loop, only one of the cables enters the junction box.* ◇ *The gears and shafts in a car are held together and lubricated in the gearbox.* **5** a small area in a theatre or court separated off from where other people sit: *At the opera in Paris, Americans often took boxes for six to twelve of their compatriots.* ◇ *the jury/witness box* **6** a small SHELTER used for a particular purpose: *Double-decker buses, red telephone boxes and black cabs are recurrent images of London in films of the 1960s.*

boy /bɔɪ/ *noun* a male child or a young male person: *When he was a young boy he used to watch his father working.* ◇ *Both girls and boys can be encouraged to engage in creative writing.* ◇ *Several studies focused on working-class boys who had no interest in being at school.*

bracket[1] /ˈbrækɪt/ *noun* **1** (*BrE*) (*also* **par·en·thesis** *NAmE* or *formal*) [usually pl.] either of a pair of marks, ( ), placed around extra information in a piece of writing or part of a problem in mathematics: **in brackets** *Numbers in brackets refer to the numbered paragraphs in Appendix 21.* ◇ **inside the brackets** *Calculate the sum inside the brackets before tackling those outside.* **2** (*NAmE*) = SQUARE BRACKET **3 income, tax, age, etc. ~** income, etc. within a particular range: *This response was most common in the 30–44 age bracket.* ◇ *As people earn more, they move into higher marginal tax brackets.* ◇ *Special interest and hobby magazines' circulations usually fall in the 50 000 to 100 000 bracket.* **4** a piece of metal, wood or plastic fixed to the wall to support a SHELF, etc: *The bracket and the steel fixture were joined with four bolts.*

bracket[2] /ˈbrækɪt/ *verb* **1 ~ sth** to put words or figures between brackets: *The two editions differ here, in so far as the second brackets the pronoun in its text.* HELP In mathematics, parts of an EQUATION may be **bracketed**, in order to indicate the order in which to perform calculations: *Calculate the bracketed portion of the equation before tackling the rest.* **2** to consider people or things to be similar or connected in some way: **~ A and B together** *Both Lorentz and Einstein tended to bracket Maxwell and Faraday together.* ◇ **~ A (together) with B** *Sadosky brackets the Jackson Doctrine of 1814 with the 1823 Monroe Doctrine.*

brain /breɪn/ *noun* the organ inside the head that controls movement, thought, memory and feeling: *Scientists know in some detail how colour information is processed in the human brain.* ◇ *By then our ancestors had evolved bigger brains.* ◇ **+ noun** *Brain activity creates an electromagnetic field that can be measured.*

▸ BRAIN + NOUN **damage, injury • disorder • tumour • tissue • cell • region, area • stem • size • development • function • activity • scan, imaging** *Brain damage may result in personality change.* ◇ *The hippocampus is one brain region whose functions are relatively well understood.*

brain·storm /ˈbreɪnstɔːm; *NAmE* ˈbreɪnstɔːrm/ *verb* [T, I] (of a group of people) to think about and discuss sth, often in order to solve a problem or to create good ideas: *Groups of children can be helped to brainstorm in order to identify alternative ways of responding to their anger.* ◇ **~ sth** *Members of one group brainstormed ways for staff to improve interpersonal communication.* ■ **brain·storm·ing** *noun* [U] *Facilitators may use brainstorming, scenario planning or other techniques.* ◇ **~ session** *They held a brainstorming session to prepare topics for an upcoming strategy meeting.*

branch[1] /brɑːntʃ; *NAmE* bræntʃ/ *noun* **1** a part of a government or other large organization that deals with one particular aspect of its work SYN DEPARTMENT: *Congress designs and enacts laws, which are implemented by the executive branch.* ◇ **~ of sth** *It is imperative that the judiciary is independent of the other two branches of government.* **2** a local office or shop belonging to a company or organization: *This non-profit organization also has branches in Berlin, London and Jerusalem.* ◇ **~ of sth** *He opened a number of accounts in his own name at various branches of the bank.* **3 ~ (of sth)** a division of an area of knowledge, or of a group of languages: *Like other branches of law, human rights law develops through cases.* ◇ *These languages belonging to the West Atlantic branch of the Niger-Congo linguistic family.* **4 ~ (of sth)** a group of members of a family who all have the same ANCESTORS: *Thomas belonged to a different branch of the family.* **5 ~ (of sth)** a part of a tree that grows out from the TRUNK and on which leaves, flowers and fruit grow: *The forest canopy is formed of the upper branches of mature trees.* **6 ~ (of sth)** a smaller or less important part of sth that leads away from the main part: *The two branches of the Heihe River flow to the East and West Juyan Lakes respectively.* IDM *see* ROOT[1]

branch[2] /brɑːntʃ; *NAmE* bræntʃ/ *verb* [I] to divide into two or more parts, especially smaller or less important parts: *As the spinal cord passes through the spinal column, it branches at each vertebra.* ◇ **~ into sth** *A tree starts as a single tiny stem, which then branches into two thin twigs.* ■ **branched** *adj.* *The extent of relatedness can be represented in a branched model called a phylogenetic tree.* **branch·ing** *adj.*: *Branching diagrams are a logical way to represent a hierarchical structure.*

PHR V ˌ**branch** ˈ**off (from sth)** to separate and go in a different direction: *Each kidney receives blood through a single renal artery that branches off from the abdominal aorta.* ˌ**branch** ˈ**out (into sth)** to start to do an activity that you have not done before, especially in your work or business SYN DIVERSIFY: *Its expertise in training shoes has enabled it to branch out into sportswear, sports equipment and managing sports events.*

brand[1] /brænd/ *noun* **1** a type of product with its own name made by a particular company; the name or reputation that a product has: *A strong brand is generally seen to be a huge benefit when selling online.* ◇ **~ of sth** *Many Hollywood stars of the period were paid to endorse certain brands of cigarettes as being stylish.* ◇ **+ noun** *One of the reasons high-profile grocery brands are advertised so frequently is to create brand awareness.* ◇ **own ~** (*BrE*) *Retailers' own brands are usually cheaper.* **2 ~ (of sth)** a particular type or kind of sth: *The former Yugoslavia had its own brand of socialism in place.*

brand[2] /brænd/ *verb* [often passive] **1** to describe sb/sth as being sth bad or unpleasant, especially unfairly: **~ sb as sth** *They were branded as traitors at home because they had allowed themselves to be taken prisoner.* ◇ **~ sb + noun/adj.** *He was branded a liar by Strabo because he was describing places presumed not to exist.* **2** to give a brand name and image to a product, etc: *The process of branding a non-profit organization bears many similarities to the process of developing a brand in the corporate sector.*

brand·ed /ˈbrændɪd/ *adj.* [only before noun] (of a product) made by a well-known company and having that company's name on it: *In the USA a number of large charities have introduced their own branded products.*

brand·ing /ˈbrændɪŋ/ *noun* [U] the activity of giving a particular name and image to goods and services so that people will be attracted to them and want to buy them: *Airlines and financial services organizations use corporate branding to instil trust.*

ˈ**brand name** *noun* the name given to a product or range of products by the company that produces it: *Companies such as Virgin, Microsoft, Nike and Coca-Cola all have very strong brand names.* ◇ **under a ~** *The retailer operates several chains of convenience stores under different brand names.* ◇ **+ noun** *It sells a range of brand-name products at extremely low prices.*

brave /breɪv/ *adj.* (**braver**, **brav·est**) **1** (of a person) willing to do things that are difficult, dangerous or painful; not afraid SYN COURAGEOUS: *They recorded the names of people brave enough to vote against the Bolsheviks.* **2** (of an action) requiring or showing courage: *They participated in a brave attempt to seize a Yangzi gunboat.* ■ **brave·ly** *adv.*: *The soldiers fought bravely and intelligently.* **bravery** /ˈbreɪvəri/ *noun* [U] SYN COURAGE: *He admired Christian bravery under persecution.*

B

IDM a/the ˌbrave new ˈworld a situation or society that changes in a way that is meant to improve people's lives but is often a source of extra problems: *Economic success depended on the fitness of individuals and groups to survive in the brave new world of competitive industrial society.*

breach¹ /briːtʃ/ *noun* **1** [C, U] an action that breaks a law or an agreement to behave in a particular way: **~ of sth** *The mere use of the software might constitute a breach of copyright.* ◇ *He could be sued for breach of contract.* ◇ *A breach of Article 82 of the Treaty had occurred.* ◇ *a breach of trust/confidence* ◇ **in ~ (of sth)** *The directors were in breach of their duties to the company.* **2** [C] a break in a relationship between people or countries SYN RIFT (1): **~ between A and B** *The breach between Caesar and the senate majority became irreparable.* **3** [C] **~ (in sth)** an opening in sth, especially where it is damaged or broken: *Any breach in the skin can allow the penetration of bacteria.* ◇ *The water had drained away through a breach in the dam.*

IDM **(a) breach of the ˈpeace** (*BrE*) the crime of behaving in a loud or violent way in public: *The police have the power to arrest any person who has committed or is about to commit a breach of the peace.*

breach² /briːtʃ/ *verb* **1 ~ sth** to not keep to an agreement or not keep a promise SYN BREAK¹: *Her deportation would breach Article 3 of the Convention on Human Rights.* ◇ *Confidentiality cannot be breached without the patient's permission.* **2 ~ sth** to make a gap or hole in sth so that sb/sth can go through it: *A civilian car had breached the police barrier.* ◇ *The enamel of the tooth can be breached by cariogenic bacteria.* ◇ *Sometimes, the barriers between species may be breached and interbreeding occurs.*

bread /bred/ *noun* [U] a type of food made from flour, water and YEAST mixed together and baked: *a loaf of bread* ◇ *High-fibre foods such as wholemeal bread are recommended.*

IDM **the bread and butter of sth** the main part of a company or organization's work: *Academic targets have become the bread and butter of school management.*

breadth /bredθ/ *noun* [U, C] **1** a wide range (of subjects, knowledge, interests, etc.); the fact of sth including a wide range of subjects, etc: *The book succeeds in offering detail and breadth.* ◇ **~ of sth** *The author's breadth of knowledge is evident.* ◇ **~ and depth of sth** *The computing techniques employed enhanced the breadth and depth of the investigation.* **2** the distance or measurement from one side to the other; how broad or wide sth is SYN WIDTH: *The height of the waves as well as their length and breadth varied with the dimensions of the ship.* ◇ **in ~** *Lambeth was a compact area about a mile and a half in length and half a mile in breadth.* ➲ *compare* DEPTH, LENGTH ➲ *see also* BROAD IDM *see* LENGTH

break¹ /breɪk/ *verb* (**broke** /brəʊk; *NAmE* broʊk/, **broken** /ˈbrəʊkən; *NAmE* ˈbroʊkən/) **1** [I, T] to be damaged and separated into two or more parts, as a result of force; to damage sth in this way: *As the wind increased, the vertical supports of the bridge began to break.* ◇ **~ apart** *The supercontinent of Pangaea began to break apart during the Mesozoic period.* ◇ **~ in/into sth** *The rocks crashed against other rocks, breaking into pieces.* ◇ **~ sth** *The protesters broke windows, started fires and fought with the police.* **2** [T] **~ sth** to do sth that is against the law; to not keep a promise, etc: *9 out of 10 adolescent boys admitted to behaviour that broke the law, often minor acts of stealing.* ◇ *Governments that break promises are likely to become unpopular.* **3** [T] **~ sth** to make sth end by using force or strong action: *The strike was broken by armed force and its leaders imprisoned.* ◇ *In the 1830s, the East India Company broke the Chinese monopoly on tea production by planting tea in India.* **4** [T] **~ sth** to interrupt sth so that it ends suddenly: *The attack on the city broke the two-month deadlock.* ◇ *Morley Safer's film 'Vietnam' (1967) finally broke the silence, with footage showing a war very different from the official version.* **5** [T] **~ sth** to end a connection with sth or a relationship with sb: *Mass production broke the direct link between customer and producer.* **6** [I] **~ free (from sb/sth)** (of a person, a group or an object) to get out of a situation in which they are stuck or limited: *After 200 years of British colonial rule, India broke free and became independent.* ◇ *Large multinational businesses have broken free from the constraints imposed by national planning.* **7** [T] **~ sb/sth** to destroy sth or make sb/sth weaker: *The Tribunal ruled that police actions had been intended to break the defendant's physical and moral resistance.* ◇ *The scandal broke him.* **8** [I] to change from one state to another; to end or begin: *There were signs that the drought was beginning to break.* ◇ *As dawn broke on 22 June similar conversations took place wherever officers met.* **9** [T] **~ a record** to do sth better than anyone has ever done it before: *Michael Moore's 'Fahrenheit 9/11' broke all box-office records for a documentary.* **10** [T] **~ a code** to find the meaning of sth secret: *At Bletchley Park, 10 Colossus computers worked around the clock to break German codes.* **11** [T] **~ sth** to cut the surface of the skin and make it BLEED: *This alarm substance is released only if the skin is broken after injury, for example, caused by the bite of a predator.* **12** [T] **~ the/bad news to sb** to be the first to tell sb some bad news: *Nurses have a key role in breaking bad news and caring for the family and loved ones.* **13** [I] if a piece of news **breaks**, it becomes known: *News of the Brunswick Manifesto first broke in Paris between 28 July and 1 August.* **14** [I] when waves **break**, they fall and are dissolved into FOAM, usually near land: *Waves constantly break along this same section of the shoreline.*

IDM Idioms containing **break** are at the entries for the nouns and adjectives in the idioms, for example **break new ground** is at **new**.

PHR V **ˌbreak aˈway (from sb/sth) 1** to become free of the control of a group or person, especially to form a separate group: *After the February Revolution, the Church saw an opportunity to break away from state control.* **2** to become free of the usual way of acting or thinking: *Politicians and industry are still unable to break away from dependence on coal and oil.*

ˌbreak ˈdown 1 to fail: *With the Family Law Act 1996, the single ground for divorce was that the marriage had broken down.* ◇ *The gradualist approach broke down in 1972 when the government was forced to take emergency measures.* ➲ *related noun* BREAKDOWN (1) **2** (of a machine or vehicle) to stop working because of a fault: *Participants were on a camping trip when the camp truck broke down.* ➲ *related noun* BREAKDOWN (4) **3** to lose control of your feelings and start crying: *When the survivors saw the ruins they broke down and cried.* **4** to separate into parts or change into a different form in a chemical process: *Sea level changes caused methane hydrates to break down to methane gas.* ➲ *related noun* BREAKDOWN (2) **ˌbreak sth ˈdown 1** to destroy sth or make it disappear, especially a particular feeling or attitude that sb has: *To break down barriers to women's equality in the workplace, new laws were required.* ◇ *Fox argues that King Records broke down the boundaries between genres.* **2** to divide sth into parts in order to analyse it or make it easier to do: *First, we broke down the price of the product into its various components.* ◇ *The figures are broken down into age, sex and cause of death.* ➲ *related noun* BREAKDOWN (3) **3** to make a substance separate into parts or change into a different form in a chemical process: *Dermatophytes are able to break down keratin and use it as a nutrient.* ➲ *related noun* BREAKDOWN (2)

ˌbreak ˈin to enter a building by force: *The police broke in, and Walden, still fighting, was shot down.*

ˌ**break ˈinto sth** **1** to enter a building by force; to open a car, etc. by force: *The price rises were such that citizens broke into the bakeries to steal bread.* **2** to be successful when you get involved in sth: *Many developing countries are now beginning to break into global markets for manufactured goods and services.* **3** to begin laughing, singing, etc. suddenly: *Then her rather intense expression breaks into a smile.*

ˌ**break ˈoff** **1** to become separated from sth as a result of force: *NASA managers were aware that a chunk of solid foam had broken off during launch.* **2** to end suddenly: *The narrative breaks off in 167 AD.* ˌ**break sth ˈoff** **1** to separate sth, using force: *Both arms of the statue had been broken off at the elbows.* **2** to end sth suddenly: *Darwin began studying medicine at Edinburgh in 1825 but broke off his studies in 1828.* ◇ *The French abruptly broke off the negotiations.*

ˌ**break ˈout** (of war, fighting or other unpleasant events) to start suddenly: *In 312-313, two civil wars broke out.* ➲ *related noun* OUTBREAK (1) ˌ**break ˈout (of sth)** to escape from a situation or place: *With the help of foreign investment, some poor countries have been able to break out of poverty.*

ˌ**break ˈthrough** to be successful or make new and important discoveries: *In the Netherlands, women writers did not really break through until the 1990s.* ◇ *Antoine Lavoisier broke through to a new understanding of the principle of chemical combination.* ➲ *related noun* BREAKTHROUGH ˌ**break ˈthrough** | ˌ**break ˈthrough sth** to make a way through sth using force: *The Russians broke through on the Caucasus front in November 1855.* ◇ *The hurricane broke through sea defences and left hundreds of thousands homeless.* ˌ**break ˈthrough sth** to succeed in dealing with an attitude that sb has and the difficulties it creates SYN OVERCOME (1): *Months of patient work were required to break through the fear and anger dominating the community.*

ˌ**break ˈup** **1** to separate into smaller pieces: *The ice began to break up in early January, opening the river to boats once more.* ◇ **~ into sth** *These muons are unstable, and almost immediately break up into smaller particles.* **2** to come to an end: *As the revolution progressed, it seemed that society was on the point of breaking up.* ➲ *related noun* BREAK-UP (2) ˌ**break sth ˈup** **1** to make sth separate into smaller pieces; to divide sth into smaller parts: *Various methods were tried for breaking up the largest rocks.* ◇ *The new Conservative government was determined to break up the nationalized industries.* ◇ **~ into sth** *In a fast food restaurant, tasks are broken up into small, repetitive actions.* ➲ *related noun* BREAK-UP (2) **2** to end a relationship, a company, etc: *The client was reluctant to take any action that might break up the family.* ➲ *related noun* BREAK-UP (1) **3** to make people leave sth or stop doing sth, especially by using force: *In 1914 the Colorado militia broke up a strike at a Rockefeller-owned coal mine.*

ˈ**break with sth** to end a connection with sth: *The Left Socialist Revolutionaries finally broke with the moderate wing of their party.* ◇ *Mrs Thatcher broke with the tradition of compromise in government.*

break² /breɪk/ *noun* **1** [C] a short period of time when you stop what you are doing and rest, eat, etc: *The schools commonly used the lunch break for organized physical activity.* ◇ **take breaks/a ~** *Taking regular short breaks away from the computer screen is essential.* ◇ **~ in sth** *We handed out the research questionnaire to those who agreed, during breaks in several seminars.* **2** [C] a pause or period of time when sth stops before starting again: *Now was not the time for a career break.* ◇ **~ in sth** *The city would be vulnerable to breaks in gas, water and electricity supplies in the event of an earthquake.* **3** [sing.] the fact of a situation or relationship changing, ending or being interrupted: **~ with sb/sth** *This was at the time of Henry VIII's break with the Catholic Church.* ◇ **~ in sth** *New Labour represented a major break in Labour party traditions.* ◇ **~ from sth** *We should not view the eighth century as a radical break from the past.* **4** [C] a pause for advertisements in the middle of a television or radio programme: *Many people leave the room when commercial breaks begin.* **5** [C] **~ in sth** a space or an opening between two or more things or in a surface: *There was no break in the clouds.* ◇ *Bacteria commonly gain entry via breaks in the skin surface.* **6** [C] a place where sth, especially a bone in your body, has broken: *Fractures are classified according to the nature of the break in the bone.* **7** [C] an opportunity to do sth, usually to get sth that you want or to achieve success: *His big break came when he was cast in the Broadway production of 'Picnic'.*

break·down /ˈbreɪkdaʊn/ *noun* **1** [C, U] a failure of a relationship, system or discussion: *Sufficient levels of crime could lead to social breakdown.* ◇ **~ of sth** *There is uncertainty over how much habitat can be destroyed before there is a catastrophic breakdown of the ecosystem.* ◇ *Byron left England following the breakdown of his marriage.* ◇ **~ in sth** *A breakdown in the negotiations might have suggested that the EU had failed the new democracies in the East.* **2** [U] the breaking of a substance into the parts of which it is made: *Some minerals, such as gold and platinum, are particularly resistant to chemical breakdown.* ◇ **~ of sth** *Microbial breakdown of soil organic matter is a major source of atmospheric carbon.* ◇ **~ of sth into sth** *Physical weathering results in the breakdown of massive rock materials into smaller aggregates.* **3** [C, usually sing.] detailed information that you get by studying a set of figures: *A further detailed statistical breakdown can be found in Appendix B.* ◇ **~ of sth** *The proposal shows a breakdown of direct costs and staff time.* **4** [C] an occasion when a vehicle or machine stops working: *It may be in a manager's interests to retain spare vehicles to cover for breakdowns.*

break·through /ˈbreɪkθruː/ *noun* an important development or discovery that helps people to achieve or understand sth: *The Greens achieved an electoral breakthrough in 1989.* ◇ *Although some important innovations stem from scientific breakthroughs, this is not true most of the time.* ◇ **~ in sth** *The discovery of antibiotics was one of the major breakthroughs in modern medicine.*

ˈ**break-up** *noun* [C, usually sing., U] **1** the ending of a relationship or an association: *Alvarez had just been through a difficult marriage break-up.* ◇ **~ of sth** *Apartheid led to the break-up of family and friendship networks that had built up over decades.* **2** **~ (of sth)** the division of a large organization or country into smaller parts: *Until the very end, Gorbachev resisted the break-up of the USSR.* ◇ *Break-up of such dominant companies as Boeing or Microsoft has not been contemplated.* **3** the breaking of sth into several or many pieces: *The recurring episodes of continental break-up, drift and collision have been called the Wilson cycle.* ◇ **~ of sth** *Beach materials are derived from the break-up of corals.*

breast /brest/ *noun* **1** either of the two round soft organs at the front of a woman's body that produce milk when she has had a baby; a similar but smaller organ on a man's body, which does not produce milk: *She discovered a lump in her left breast.* ◇ **+ noun** *Some drugs can pass into breast milk.* ◇ *Carcinoma of the male breast is uncommon, accounting for less than 1% of all breast cancers.* **2** the top part of the front of a person's body, below the neck: **+ noun** *Measurements of the trees' diameters were taken at breast height.* **3** the front part of a bird's body: *The female is light grey with a chestnut breast.*

breast·feed /ˈbrestfiːd/ *verb* (**breast·fed**, **breast·fed** /ˈbrestfed/) [I, T] (of a woman) to feed a baby with milk from the breast: *The current advice is that mothers should breastfeed for a minimum of one year.* ◇ **~ sb** *Some mothers are unable to breastfeed their babies at all.*

➲ compare NURSE² (2) ■ **breast·feed·ing** *noun* [U] *There may be good reasons to promote breastfeeding in certain contexts.*

B

breath /breθ/ *noun* **1** [U] the air that you take into your lungs and send out again: *His breath smelt of alcohol.* ◇ *She is able to lie flat without becoming short of breath.* **2** [C] an amount of air that enters the lungs at one time: *The pain is worse if she tries to take a deep breath.*
IDM **hold your ˈbreath 1** to stop breathing for a short time: *Hold your breath for 10 seconds.* **2** to be anxious while you are waiting for sth that you are worried about: *The UK cigarette industry held its breath awaiting the outcome of the case.*

breathe /briːð/ *verb* [I, T] to take air into your lungs and send it out again through your nose or mouth: *The victim is unable to breathe.* ◇ *Encourage the child to breathe deeply.* ◇ **~ sth** *We all breathe the same air.* ◇ **~ in/out sth** *There is mounting evidence about the harmful effects of breathing in other people's smoke.* ◇ **~ in/out** *The canister is activated only as the person breathes in.*
IDM **ˌbreathe (new) ˈlife into sth** to improve sth by introducing new ideas and making people more interested in it: *Talking with someone who participated directly in an event that students are studying breathes life into the facts.*

breath·ing /ˈbriːðɪŋ/ *noun* [U] the action of taking air into the lungs and sending it out again: *Deep breathing can help reduce feelings of anxiety.* ◇ **+ noun** *breathing difficulties/problems*

breed¹ /briːd/ *verb* (**bred**, **bred** /bred/) **1** [I] (of animals) to have sex and produce young: *In these migratory species, individuals breed on the site or patch where they were born.* ◇ **~ with sth** *Those birds that bred with the same partner as in the previous breeding season were defined as faithfuls.* **2** [T] to keep animals or plants in order to produce young ones in a controlled way: **~ sth** *Horses were bred and reared by specialist horse breeders.* ◇ *Desirable characteristics of plants are selected and then bred in traditional programmes.* ◇ **~ sth for sth** *These particular mice were bred for experimental use.* **3** [T] **~ sth** to be the cause of sth: *Inequality often breeds conflicts such as strikes and fosters hostile relationships between employers and employees.* ◇ *Success tends to breed success.*

breed² /briːd/ *noun* **1** a type of animal with a particular appearance that makes it different from others of the same species and that is the result of having been developed in a controlled way: *Dogs are a single species with many different breeds.* ◇ **~ of sth** *The thickness of a particular egg shell may also depend on the age or breed of the hen.* **2** [usually sing.] a type of person: *Company archivists are a rare breed in Britain.* ◇ **~ of sth** *The new breed of customer is less likely to take adverts at face value.*

breed·ing /ˈbriːdɪŋ/ *noun* [U] **1** the activity of keeping animals or plants in order to breed from them: *New strains of plant were produced through selective breeding.* ◇ **~ of sth** *This led to the breeding of chickens that grew faster with less feed.* **2** the production of young animals, plants, etc: *The same burrows are used in winter and during breeding.* ◇ **+ noun** *The breeding season is short, leading many females to look for a suitable breeding site at the same time.* **3** (*old-fashioned*) good manners, especially regarded as a result of the family or social background that sb comes from: *They were obviously men of good breeding and education.*

brev·ity AWL /ˈbrevəti/ *noun* [U] **1** the quality of using few words when speaking or writing: *The paper is a model of brevity and clarity.* ◇ *For the sake of brevity, I have limited myself to the Western tradition.* ◇ **for ~** *For brevity, this transformation will be identified as the C/P transformation.* **2 ~ (of sth)** the fact of lasting a short time: *Many of these epigrams deal with the brevity of human life.* ➲ *see also* BRIEF¹

brick /brɪk/ *noun* [U, C] baked CLAY used for building walls, houses and other buildings; an individual block of this: *It was a large building, built of brick.* ◇ *The early Spanish colonists built buildings with sun-dried clay bricks.* ◇ **+ noun** *a brick wall/buiilding*

bridge¹ /brɪdʒ/ *noun* **1** a structure that is built over a road, river, etc. so that people or vehicles can cross from one side to the other: *There is some doubt about the exact date the bridge was built.* **2** a thing that provides a connection or contact between two different things: **~ (between A and B)** *His writings form a bridge between the 19th century and the civil rights movement of the 1960s.* ◇ *A salt bridge provides an electrical contact between two solutions by allowing ions to flow through it.* ◇ **build bridges (between A and B)** *They are trying to build bridges between the sciences and the humanities in ways that could enrich the university as a whole.*

bridge² /brɪdʒ/ *verb* **~ sth** to build or form a bridge over sth: *The distance that can be bridged by a single slab of stone is rarely more than four metres.*
IDM **bridge the ˈgap/diˈvide (between A and B)** to reduce or get rid of the differences that exist between two things or groups of people: *This work attempts to bridge the gap between theory and practice.*

brief¹ AWL /briːf/ *adj.* (**brief·er**, **brief·est**) **1** using few words: *The following is a brief summary of the techniques most commonly used.* ◇ *A brief description of each of the methods is provided in the table below.* **2** lasting only a short time SYN SHORT¹ (1): *The death of Commodus led to a brief period of political confusion.* ◇ *Human beings have existed for only a brief moment in the universe's history.* OPP LENGTHY ➲ *see also* BREVITY, BRIEFLY
IDM **in brief** in a few words, without details: *In brief, these molecules are made of two parts, one allowed to move around or along the other one.* ◇ *The three phases are outlined in brief below.*
▸ BRIEF + NOUN **overview, summary, outline • review • survey • description, account • sketch • discussion • mention • comment • introduction • history** *This section gives a brief overview of the empirical findings.* ◇ *Two other possible contributory factors merit a brief mention.* | **period • moment • interval • episode** *Brief episodes of depression are frequent among patients with this disorder.*

brief² AWL /briːf/ *noun* **1** (*BrE*) the instructions that a person is given explaining what their job is and what their duties are: *Turing's brief was to design and develop an electronic digital computer.* ◇ *Shortlisted agencies are given a preliminary outline of the client's needs in a research brief.* **2** (*law*) a document giving the facts about a legal case: *The two sides in the dispute then prepare briefs setting out their positions.*

brief³ AWL /briːf/ *verb* to give sb information about sth so that they are prepared to deal with it: **~ sb** *Journalists are briefed twice daily by the Number 10 press secretary.* ◇ **~ sb on/about sth** *Staff should be briefed on how to handle media inquiries.*

brief·ing AWL /ˈbriːfɪŋ/ *noun* [C, U] a meeting in which people are given instructions or information; the detailed instructions or information that are given at such a meeting: *As he pointed out at a press briefing, air power alone cannot stop paramilitary action.* ◇ *Prior to the experiment, participants were given a one-hour briefing describing the task.* ◇ *Briefing promotes efficiency that in turn leads to improved effectiveness.*

brief·ly AWL /ˈbriːfli/ *adv.* **1** in few words: *The most common forms of direct marketing are briefly described below.* ◇ *Section 2 considers briefly the neuropsychology of consciousness.* ◇ *Briefly, the main institutions concerned* *are the following...* **2** for a short time: *Like the Persians, the Macedonians were to remain only briefly in India.*

▸ BRIEFLY + VERB **discuss, consider, examine, look at** ◆ **describe** ◆ **review** ◆ **summarize, outline** ◆ **mention** ◆ **introduce** ◆ **explain** *Topics only briefly mentioned here are covered in more detail later in the book.*

▸ VERB + BRIEFLY **discuss, consider, look ~ at** ◆ **describe** ◆ **mention** ◆ **explain** *Each of these five areas is discussed briefly below.*

bright /braɪt/ *adj.* (**bright·er**, **bright·est**) **1** full of light; shining strongly: *The rooms are bright and spacious.* ◇ *Proper assessment of the pupils of the eyes requires a bright light.* ◇ *bright sunshine/sunlight/stars* ◇ *The bright spots are star-forming regions in the very distant galaxy.* **2** (of a colour) strong and easy to see: *African consumers particularly liked the bright colours of Indian textiles.* ◇ **~ red, blue, green, etc.** *The colour changes to bright red and the solution has a pH of 6.0.* **3** intelligent; quick to learn: *She had the bright idea of writing the report in French.* ◇ *Einstein was one of the brightest minds of modern times.* **4** giving reason to believe that good things will happen; likely to be successful: *Lenin envisaged a bright future for Bukharin and Pyatakov.* ■ **bright·ly** *adv.*: *Smaller stars, like the Sun, are also formed in spiral arms, but do not burn so brightly.* ◇ *Colours are often paler in more brightly lit sites.* ◇ *The male is more brightly coloured than the female.* **bright·ness** *noun* [U] **~ (of sth)** *Astronomers use 'magnitudes' to refer to the brightness of stars.* ◇ *This mixing effect reduces the brightness of the colours.*

bril·liant /ˈbrɪliənt/ *adj.* **1** extremely clever, skilful or successful: *a brilliant scientist/engineer* ◇ *This war witnessed the brilliant career of the Duke of Marlborough.* ◇ *He had no doubt that natural selection, a simple but brilliant idea, could explain the origin of design in the natural world.* **2** (of light or colours) very bright: *The colours vary from purple to red to brilliant orange.*

bring /brɪŋ/ *verb* (**brought**, **brought** /brɔːt/) **1** to come to a place with sth/sb: **~ sth/sb (with you)** *Participants were encouraged to bring their families with them.* ◇ *Merchants brought with them lightweight luxuries such as spices.* ◇ **~ sth/sb to sth** *Ecosoc was intended as a forum for bringing specialist expertise to the EU.* ◇ **~ sth for sth/sb** *Students were asked to find examples in advance and bring them for discussion.* ◇ **~ sb sth** *Fellow Christians visited Peregrinus in prison and brought him fine meals.* **2** to provide sb/sth with sth: **~ sth** *Octavian's victory in 31 BCE finally brought peace and stability.* ◇ **~ sb/sth sth** *Good (1995) argues that people will not easily abandon pleasurable behaviour which brings them income or power.* ◇ **~ sth to sb/sth** *Many employers fail to recognize that older workers can bring many benefits to a business.* ◇ **~ sb/sth + adv./prep.** *In many cities the local sources are inadequate and water has to be brought in from rural areas.* **3** to cause sth: **~ sth** *Perhaps the most important change brought by the war was the employment of married middle-aged women.* ◇ **~ with it sth** *Wherever capitalism has taken root, it has brought with it unprecedented change.* **4 ~ sb/sth + adv./prep.** to cause sb/sth to be in a particular condition or place: *The disintegration of the Soviet Union in the 1990s brought the Cold War to an end.* ◇ *His anti-Prussian stance repeatedly brought him into conflict with the authorities.* **5 ~ sth (against sb)** to officially accuse sb of a crime: *Black was famous for bringing legal actions against anyone who challenged him.* ◇ *She brought a claim for damages but the hotel denied responsibility.* **6 ~ yourself to do sth** to force yourself to do sth: *Coleridge could not quite bring himself to abandon his wife and children.*

IDM Idioms containing **bring** are at the entries for the nouns and adjectives in the idioms, for example **bring sb/sth to life** is at **life**.

PHR V ˌ**bring sth aˈbout** to make sth happen **SYN** CAUSE[1]: *The publication of 'The Origin of Species' brought about a rapid change in the scientific world view.* ➲ language bank *at* CAUSE[1]

ˌ**bring sth ˈback** to make sth that existed before be introduced again: *A month later, Labour defeat in the General Election brought the Conservatives back to power.* ˌ**bring sth ˈback (for sb)** to return with sth for sb: *The quantity of food brought back to the nest did indeed increase with the number of chicks.*

ˈ**bring sth/sb before sb** to present sth/sb for discussion or judgement: *The British were successful in bringing the matter before the Beijing government itself.* ◇ *Paul was brought before the Roman governor Felix.*

ˌ**bring sb ˈdown** to make sb lose power or be defeated: *The labour unions contributed to bringing down the dictatorship.* ˌ**bring sth ˈdown** to reduce sth: *In the early 1980s, restrictive monetary policy brought down the rate of inflation.* ◇ *Immediate treatment brought the pulse rate down to normal levels.*

ˌ**bring sb/sth ˈforth** (*formal*) to produce sth: *These developments brought forth strident calls for fresh elections.*

ˌ**bring sth ˈforward** to suggest sth for discussion: *EU citizens are encouraged to bring forward new policy proposals.*

ˌ**bring sb ˈin** to ask sb to do a particular job or to be involved in sth: *Malays and Chinese were brought in as labourers to work the phosphate mine.* ◇ **~ to do sth** *Banks typically bring in their own advisers to do independent forecasts.* ˌ**bring sth ˈin 1** to introduce a new system or a new element into an existing system: *The government made an attempt to bring in a socialist market system.* **2** to introduce a new law: *Even when new Acts were brought in, they proved difficult to enforce against the weight of tradition.* **3** to introduce an idea into a piece of writing: *In the next part of the essay, Hazlitt brings in the idea of time.* **4** to give a decision in court: *The jury brought in a verdict of not guilty.* ˌ**bring sb ˈin sth** | ˌ**bring ˈin sth** to make or earn a particular amount of money: *The corporation brings in more than $5 billion in annual revenues.*

ˌ**bring sth ˈon** to make sth develop, usually sth unpleasant **SYN** CAUSE[1]: *Migraine headaches may be brought on by a number of factors such as alcohol, exercise or stress.* ˈ**bring sth on yourself/sb** to be responsible for sth unpleasant that happens to you/sb: *Acting unethically in business may bring shame on an individual, which may be an incentive to act ethically.*

ˌ**bring sth ˈout 1** to describe sth that is not obvious in such a way that you become aware of it and understand it: *The report brings out some crucial policy issues that demand immediate attention.* **2** to make sth appear: *The Asian financial crisis has brought Japan's underlying problems out into the open.* **3** to produce sth; to publish sth: *IBM brought out its 360 series of mainframe computers in 1965.*

ˌ**bring A and B toˈgether 1** to combine two things: *Beadle and Ephrussi's work brought together genetics and embryology.* **2** to help two people or groups to end a disagreement: *Agrippina brought together the warring factions of the imperial family.*

ˌ**bring sb ˈup** [often passive] to care for a child, teaching him or her how to behave, etc. **SYN** RAISE[1] (5): *Kibbutzim are Israeli collective farms where all the children are brought up communally.* ◇ **~ to do sth** *Children can be brought up to hate or to love.* ➲ *related noun* UPBRINGING ˌ**bring sth ˈup** to mention a subject **SYN** RAISE[1] (1): *The case was then brought up in Parliament.*

broad /brɔːd/ *adj.* (**broad·er**, **broad·est**) **1** wide: *In tropical moist areas, plants have broad leaves and large flowers.* ◇ *The developments include a change in skull shape from broad and flat to tall and narrow.* ◇ *The phosphor emits a broad band of red and green light.* **OPP** NARROW[1] (1) ➲ *usage note at* WIDE **2** including a great variety of things: *Owls can hear over a broad range of frequencies.* ◇ *There are two broad categories of costs: economic costs and*

B

accounting costs. ◇ *Individual employment rights emerged in two broad areas.* ◇ *A broad-spectrum antibiotic is effective against a wide variety of diseases caused by bacteria.* OPP NARROW¹ (2) ➲ *compare* WIDE (1) ➲ *usage note at* WIDE **3** [only before noun] general; not detailed: *Soils (defined in a broad sense) cover approximately 80% of the earth's land mass.* ◇ *In an environmental context, however, the term 'precipitation' has a broader definition.* ◇ **in ~ terms** *In broad terms, Marx worked to construct a body of social theory that would explain how society actually worked.* ➲ *compare* WIDE (3) ➲ *usage note at* WIDE **4** with most people agreeing about sth in a general way: *There was broad agreement between political parties about the social policies that were needed.* **5** covering a wide area: *The Little Colorado River meanders across north-eastern Arizona in a broad, open valley.* ◇ *A glance at the map of Canada reveals a broad arc of large lakes.* ➲ *compare* WIDE (2) ➲ *usage note at* WIDE

▸ BROAD + NOUN **range, spectrum, array, set • category, class • area • audience** *This herbicide is used to control a broad spectrum of weeds.* | **sense • definition • term • outline, overview • context, framework • scope • perspective, view • understanding, conception • concept • distinction • approach • theme, issue • trend • pattern** *The broad outlines of Bob Marley's life are relatively well known.* | **consensus, agreement • coalition** *There is a broad consensus that free trade will maximize welfare in the long run.*

broad·band /ˈbrɔːdbænd/ *noun* [U] **1** (*technical*) the use of a wide range of FREQUENCIES: **+ noun** *Brief audio broadband signals are used by some bat species that hunt near the ground or in an environment rich in denser vegetation.* **2** a way of connecting to the Internet which allows you to receive information, including pictures, etc, very quickly and that is always active (i.e. the user does not have to connect each time): **+ noun** *Internet users can talk with one another through their existing broadband connection.* ◇ *The UK government is working towards a nationwide high-speed broadband network by 2016.*

broad·cast¹ /ˈbrɔːdkɑːst; *NAmE* ˈbrɔːdkæst/ *verb* (**broad·cast, broad·cast** or **broad·cast, broad·casted**) **1** [T, I] to send out programmes on television or radio: *The channel began broadcasting in 1988.* ◇ **~ sth** *This study examines the children's programmes broadcast by six stations.* ◇ **~ media** *They argue that the Internet should be as highly regulated as the broadcast media.* **2** [T] **~ sth** to tell a lot of people about sth: *He broadcast his ideas in the 'Avenir' newspaper.*

broad·cast² /ˈbrɔːdkɑːst; *NAmE* ˈbrɔːdkæst/ *noun* [C, U] a radio or television programme; the sending out of a radio or television programme: **television/TV/radio ~** *The events were shown in a live television broadcast.* ◇ **~ of sth** *Many different brands are advertised during the broadcast of a football match.*

broad·cast·er /ˈbrɔːdkɑːstə(r); *NAmE* ˈbrɔːdkæstər/ *noun* **1** a company that sends out television or radio programmes: *They claim that the BBC is now a commercial broadcaster like any other.* **2** a person whose job is talking on television or radio programmes: *Wright is a writer and broadcaster with an interest in the cultural and political dimensions of modern history.*

broad·cast·ing /ˈbrɔːdkɑːstɪŋ; *NAmE* ˈbrɔːdkæstɪŋ/ *noun* [U] the business of making and sending out radio and television programmes: *His supporters began to occupy key positions in the press and broadcasting.* ◇ **television/TV/radio ~** *Developments in television broadcasting changed the role of the media in politics.*

broad·en /ˈbrɔːdn/ *verb* **1** [I, T] to include or affect more people or things; to make sth do this: **~ (out)** *The limits of earth science have broadened out.* ◇ **~ sth (out)** *They wanted to broaden the scope of their study.* ◇ *The World Bank sought to broaden its appeal through enhanced relations with governments.* **2** [T] **~ sth** to increase your experience, knowledge, etc: *Learning is about broadening understanding rather than accumulating facts.* **3** [I] to become wider: *By then the individual cloud may have broadened to several hundred metres.*

broad·ly /ˈbrɔːdli/ *adv.* generally, without considering details: *Broadly, these activities can be divided into four categories.* ◇ *The two sets of results were broadly consistent.* ◇ *Broadly speaking, there are three types of computer user.*

LANGUAGE BANK

Making generalizations

In academic writing, you sometimes need to say what the general situation is, rather than mention a specific case or talk about a situation in detail.

broadly • generally • mainly • predominantly • essentially • Broadly/Generally speaking... • In general... • tend to • to a great/large extent

- *These types of advertisements* ***generally*** *do not work.*
- *Hospitals throughout the world are* ***broadly*** *similar in the way that they deliver medical care.*
- *Bowel cancer occurs* ***mainly*** *in people of middle age or older.*
- *This viewpoint is* ***predominantly*** *a male one.*
- *The structure of the Commission has remained* ***essentially*** *unchanged for more than 40 years.*
- ***Broadly speaking****, culture heroes are of two kinds.*
- ***In general****, most drugs should be given on the day of surgery.*
- *Real incomes* ***tend to*** *rise during periods when unemployment is falling and inflation is picking up.*
- *How people view their natural environment depends* ***to a great extent*** *on their cultural background.*

bro·chure /ˈbrəʊʃə(r); *NAmE* broʊˈʃʊr/ *noun* a small magazine or book containing pictures and information about sth or advertising sth: *A travel agent uses colourful brochures of holiday destinations.* ➲ *compare* PAMPHLET (1)

broke *past tense of* BREAK¹

broken¹ *past part. of* BREAK¹

broken² /ˈbrəʊkən; *NAmE* ˈbroʊkən/ *adj.* **1** that has been damaged or injured; no longer whole or working correctly: *There was broken glass everywhere.* ◇ *The victim fell and sustained several broken bones.* **2** [usually before noun] (of a relationship) ended or destroyed: *Very excessive drinking was associated with broken marriages.* **3** [usually before noun] (of a promise or agreement) not kept: *With several broken peace agreements, the war continued.* ◇ *They became frustrated by the frequent broken promises of agents.* **4** [usually before noun] not continuous; disturbed or interrupted: *The broken lines mark the links between each word and its role.* **5** [only before noun] made weak and tired by illness or difficulties: *He returned from the voyage a broken man.* **6** [only before noun] (of a language that is not your own) spoken slowly and with a lot of mistakes: *Users found practitioners with poor or broken English difficult to understand.* OPP FLUENT (2)

brother /ˈbrʌðə(r)/ *noun* a boy or man who has the same mother and father as another person: *The film was another comedy-thriller from the creative minds of the Coen brothers.* ◇ *Desta's older brother helps him to farm the land and care for the household's livestock.* ◇ *A brother and sister in the same household can have very different experiences of social engagement outside the home.* ➲ *see also* SIBLING

brought *past tense, past part. of* BRING

brown¹ /braʊn/ *adj.* (**brown·er, brown·est**) having the colour of wood or coffee: *The soil type is a typical brown* *forest soil.* ◇ *Some people with light brown skin are labelled 'black'.*

brown² /braʊn/ *noun* [U, C] the colour of wood or coffee: *The cowboys wore different shades of brown.* ◇ *This is the reason for the dominant reds, oranges, yellows and browns of most bare rock in arid regions.*

bru·tal /ˈbruːtl/ *adj.* **1** violent and cruel: *The former Russian Empire deteriorated into a brutal civil war.* ◇ *It was a regime of savage and brutal repression.* **2** direct and clear about sth unpleasant; not thinking of people's feelings: *Samuel is utterly brutal in his choice of phrases.* ■ **bru·tal·ity** /bruːˈtæləti/ *noun* (*pl.* **-ies**) [U, C] *There have been diverse explanations for police brutality.* ◇ **~ of sth** *He pointed out the casual brutality of the language with which powerful people address the powerless.* **bru·tal·ly** /ˈbruːtəli/ *adv.*: *She was brutally murdered.* ◇ *The report offered a brutally frank assessment of the problems.*

brute /bruːt/ *adj.* [only before noun] **1** involving physical strength only and not thought or intelligence: *They can silence opposition by brute force.* **2** basic and unpleasant: *The brute fact is that many young people face unemployment when they leave school.*

bub·ble /ˈbʌbl/ *noun* **1** a ball of air or gas in a liquid; a ball of air inside a solid substance such as glass: *The gas comes out of solution to form bubbles.* ◇ *Bubbles trapped in the cement are a persistent problem.* **2** (*economics*) used to refer to a large, fast increase in ASSET prices that is soon followed by a collapse in prices, usually caused by SPECULATION and enthusiasm, not real increases in value: *Various factors have been invoked to explain the housing bubble.* ◇ **~ in sth** *There is no evidence of a bubble in prices for coffee, cotton or cocoa.* ◇ **the ~ bursts** *When the bubble burst in 1990, the banks were left with mountains of bad debt.*

bud /bʌd/ *noun* **1** a small lump that grows on a plant and from which a flower or leaf develops; a flower or leaf that is not fully open: *Seedlings of trees from northern populations produced buds three weeks earlier than those from the south (Karhu et al., 1996).* **2** a small lump on an animal that has not yet grown into a leg or other body part: *Limb buds appear on the flanks of the embryo on the third day of incubation.*

Bud·dhism /ˈbʊdɪzəm/ *noun* [U] an Asian religion based on the teaching of Siddhartha Gautama (or Buddha): *My own interest has been in the actual practice of Buddhism in Buddhist lands today.* ■ **Bud·dhist** /ˈbʊdɪst/ *noun*: *Buddhists, for instance, do not believe in a personal God like the one described in the Bible and the Qur'an.* **Bud·dhist** *adj.* [usually before noun] *a Buddhist monk/temple*

budget¹ /ˈbʌdʒɪt/ *noun* **1** [C, U] the money that is available to a person or an organization and a plan of how it will be spent over a period of time: *It is generally the woman who controls the household budget.* ◇ *Pressures to balance budgets and be more competitive have also led to reduced public expenditure.* ◇ **~ for sth** *They have a £50 000 budget for advertising.* ◇ **~ of sth** *The hospital received an annual budget of $660 000 from the Ministry of Health.* ◇ **within/on ~** *The project was completed on time and within budget.* ◇ **over ~** *The Channel Tunnel was 80% over budget.* ◇ **+ noun** *Councils in England and Wales are now confronted by radical budget cuts and the need to find substantial savings.* **2** (*BrE also* **Budget**) [C, usually sing.] an official statement by the government of a country's income from taxes, etc. and how it will be spent: *The Budget contains good and bad news for taxpayers.* ◇ **+ noun** *The budget deficit rises when activity falls and declines when activity rises.*

budget² /ˈbʌdʒɪt/ *verb* [I, T] to allow or provide a particular amount of money for a particular purpose: **~ for sth** *The company budgeted for expenditure of £300 million.* ◇ **~ sth (for sth)** *A firm may have budgeted $100 000 for a trade exhibition.* ■ **budget·ing** *noun* [U] *This is a wholly different approach to school budgeting.*

budget·ary /ˈbʌdʒɪtəri; *NAmE* ˈbʌdʒɪteri/ *adj.* connected with a budget: *Budgetary constraints limit road construction.* ◇ *India is planning to double the government budgetary allocations for health.*

buf·fer¹ /ˈbʌfə(r)/ *noun* **1** a thing or person that protects sb/sth against difficulties: **~ between A and B** *Local government may act as a buffer between citizens and central government.* ◇ **~ against sth** *The group held the majority of the firm's stock, providing a buffer against takeover.* ◇ **+ noun** *The absorption of Poland meant that there was no longer a buffer state separating Russia from Prussia.* **2** (*also* **buffer solution**) (*chemistry*) a SOLUTION that resists changes in PH when small amounts of acid or ALKALI are added to it: *The sodium phosphate buffer pH and Triton X-100 concentration requirements were determined empirically.* **3** (*computing*) an area in a computer's memory where data can be stored for a short time: *Some interfaces can deal with short bursts of high-speed data because they store data in a buffer.*

buf·fer² /ˈbʌfə(r)/ *verb* **1** to protect sb/sth from sth: **~ sb/sth (against sth)** *Here the climate was relatively buffered against the glacial cycles.* ◇ *These friends can help buffer the child against anxiety.* ◇ **~ sb/sth from sth** *The deep ocean floors are buffered from significant change.* **2 ~ sth** to reduce the harmful effects of sth: *Such social support systems buffer stressful experiences.*

build /bɪld/ *verb* (**built**, **built** /bɪlt/) **1** [T] to make sth, especially a building, structure or machine, by putting parts together: **~ sth** *The Conservative government came to power in 1951 promising to build 300 000 new homes a year.* ◇ *French engineers were busy building new canals and improving the navigability of rivers.* ◇ *Taught by its mother, the young animal learns more quickly how to fly or build its nest.* ◇ **~ sth of sth** *Before the earthquake, Tokyo was like a large, close-knit village in which most houses were built of wood.* **2** [T] **~ sth** to create sth by putting information or ideas together: *In order to try and understand these effects we built a mathematical model.* ◇ *The company uses direct marketing to build a customer database.* ◇ *There are transaction costs involved in building a portfolio of investments.* **3** [T] **~ sth** to develop a business or relationship over a period of time: *In Asia, Western firms should be aiming to build a business, not an asset (Young, 1998).* ◇ *It can take years to build a relationship with a client.* **4** [I] (of a feeling, force, etc.) to become gradually stronger: *The impetus builds relentlessly to the closing couplet, which supplies a double shock.*

PHR V ˌ**build sth aˈround sth** [usually passive] to create sth, using sth else as a basis: *A personality cult was built around the figure of Mussolini.* ◇ *Microsoft's advertising campaign was built around the strapline 'Where do you want to go today?'* ˌ**build sth ˈin** | ˌ**build sth ˈinto sth** [often passive] **1** to include sth as a permanent part of a larger structure: *More and more consumers turned to mobile phones with cameras built in.* ◇ *Computers are now built into a wide range of everyday items.* **2** to include sth as a permanent part of a system or plan: *Collective responsibility is built into the EU's institutional system.* ◇ *Scepticism is built into the refereeing process for scientific publications.* ➲ *see also* BUILT-IN ˈ**build on/upon sth** to use sth as a basis for further progress: *The models proposed by Mann and White build on this earlier work.* ◇ *These initiatives build on a history of collaboration between university and industry researchers.* ˈ**build sth on/upon sth** [usually passive] to base sth on sth: *Air traffic control systems are built on complex statistical models.* ◇ *Brands can be the keystones upon which the long-term success of companies is built.* ˌ**build ˈup** to become greater, more powerful or larger in number: *Ice built up on*

Antarctica and eventually formed an ice shelf over the sea. ◇ *Eventually the pressure may build up and affect the uninjured lung.* ➲ *related noun* BUILD-UP (1) **ˌbuild sth ˈup 1** to create or develop sth gradually: *By using such data it is possible to build up a picture of the climate.* ◇ *This scheme is intended to build up a long-term relationship with the customer.* **2** to make sth bigger or stronger than it was before: *There was time to train the conscripts properly and to build up ammunition stocks.*

build·er /ˈbɪldə(r)/ *noun* **1** a person or company whose job is to build or repair houses or other buildings: *She monitored the builders' work for the whole of the renovation project.* **2** (usually in compounds) a person who builds sth by putting parts or material together: *Historically, bridge builders have tended to think of bridges as static objects.* ◇ *Robot builders need to find out what real consciousness is and whether it can be put into a machine.* **3** (usually in compounds) a person or thing that creates or develops sth: *Knowledge builders produce knowledge that can be linked to other ideas.*

build·ing /ˈbɪldɪŋ/ *noun* **1** [C] a structure with a roof and walls, such as a house or factory: *The earthquake resulted in the collapse of numerous high-rise buildings.* ◇ *Office buildings usually have higher electricity consumption than residential buildings.* **2** [U] the process and work of building: *Constantine undertook a massive programme of church building.* ◇ **+ noun** *Sand and gravel are extracted for use in the building industry.*

ˈbuilding block *noun* [usually pl.] **~ (of sth)** a basic unit from which sth is built up: *The basic building blocks of digital systems are logic circuits and memory circuits.* ◇ *Amino acids are the building blocks of proteins.*

ˈbuild-up *noun* **1** [sing., U] an increase in the amount of sth over a period of time: *The military build-up continued.* ◇ **~ of sth** *The build-up of bilirubin causes jaundice.* **2** [C, usually sing.] **~ to sth** the time before an important event, when people are preparing for it: *Sales of many products will tend to increase in the build-up to Christmas.* **3** [C, usually sing.] a very positive and enthusiastic description of sth that is going to happen or be introduced, that is intended to make people excited about it: *The product had an aggressive promotional build-up prior to launch.*

ˌbuilt-ˈin (*also less frequent* ˌ**in-ˈbuilt**) *adj.* [only before noun] included as part of sth and not separate from it: *The word processor has a built-in dictionary.*

bulb /bʌlb/ *noun* **1** (*also* ˈ**light bulb**) the glass part that fits into an electric light, etc. to give light when it is switched on: *The light from the bulb is directed upwards.* ◇ *a fluorescent light bulb* ◇ *a low-energy bulb* **2** the round underground part of some plants, that grows into a new plant every year: *The company sells bulbs and shrubs for domestic gardeners.* **3** an object shaped like a bulb, for example the end of a THERMOMETER: **~ (of sth)** *the glass bulb of a pH electrode* ◇ **+ noun** *Ambient temperature was measured with a bulb thermometer.*

bulk AWL /bʌlk/ *noun* **1** [sing.] **the ~ (of sth)** the main part of sth; most of sth SYN MAJORITY: *People of peasant status and below constituted the vast bulk of the European population.* ◇ *On average, participants devoted the bulk of their time online to three domains: IM, visiting websites and email.* **2** [U] the large quantity of sth: **in ~** *Retailers can achieve significant economies of scale through buying in bulk more cheaply.* ◇ **+ noun** *Organizations reward customers for early payment, bulk buying, or off-season buying.* ◇ *Most freight moved by truck but bulk commodities were shipped by rail or river barge.* **3** [U] (used in compounds) **+ noun** (*technical*) a mass or quantity of a substance (as opposed to very small quantities or individual atoms): *Unlike bulk materials, semiconductor nanoparticles are made of only hundreds to thousands of atoms.* ◇ *Either a small sample is withdrawn or the bulk solution is monitored.* ◇ *For conventional dating, radiocarbon laboratories require large bulk samples (sometimes spanning several centimetres of a core).*

bulky AWL /ˈbʌlki/ *adj.* (**bulk·ier**, **bulki·est**) (*sometimes disapproving*) large and difficult to move or carry, or taking up a lot of space: *The 'mobile' phones of the 1980s were bulky and expensive.* ◇ *As a bulky commodity, cement is not predominantly an export-oriented industry.*

bul·let /ˈbʊlɪt/ *noun* a small metal object that is fired from a gun: *Bullets were fired by drunken soldiers as they roamed the streets.*

bun·dle /ˈbʌndl/ *noun* **1 ~ (of sth)** a number of things tied or wrapped together: *The carbon-fibre belt is composed of bundle of fibres.* **2 ~ (of sth)** a number of things that belong or are sold together: *In her book, firms are seen as bundles of resources.*

bur·den[1] /ˈbɜːdn; *NAmE* ˈbɜːrdn/ *noun* a duty, responsibility, etc. that causes worry, difficulty or hard work: **the ~ of (doing) sth** *The prosecution bear the burden of proving that the defendant committed the offence.* ◇ **a ~ on/to sb** *The measure was to ease the financial burden on low income families.*

bur·den[2] /ˈbɜːdn; *NAmE* ˈbɜːrdn/ *verb* to cause worry, difficulty or hard work for sb, especially by giving them a duty or responsibility: **~ sb/sth with sth** *Small organizations are not burdened with bureaucracy and high fixed costs.* ◇ **~ sb/sth** *Diseases such as TB continue to burden a large part of the world.*

the ˌburden of ˈproof *noun* [sing.] (*law*) the task or responsibility of proving that sth is true: *The prosecution bears the burden of proof, and must establish guilt.*

bur·eau·cracy /bjʊəˈrɒkrəsi; *NAmE* bjʊˈrɑːkrəsi/ *noun* (*pl.* **-ies**) **1** [U, C] a system of government in which there are a large number of state officials who are not elected; a country with such a system: *A new system of government and bureaucracy was created.* ◇ *Competing agendas within state bureaucracies often prevented the formation of coherent policy regimes.* **2** [U] (*often disapproving*) the system of official rules and ways of doing things that a government or an organization has, especially when these seem to be too complicated: *The Conservative Party pledged to reduce bureaucracy.*

bur·eau·crat /ˈbjʊərəkræt; *NAmE* ˈbjʊrəkræt/ *noun* (*often disapproving*) an official working in an organization or a government department, especially one who follows the rules of the department too strictly: *Government bureaucrats were liable to become corrupt.* ◇ *Many senior career bureaucrats know that they will outlast the president.*

bur·eau·crat·ic /ˌbjʊərəˈkrætɪk; *NAmE* ˌbjʊrəˈkrætɪk/ *adj.* (*often disapproving*) connected with a bureaucracy or bureaucrats and involving complicated official rules which may seem unnecessary: *The imperial government became more bureaucratic.* ◇ *Bureaucratic structures are not innovative and cannot cope with novelty or change.* ■ **bur·eau·crat·ic·al·ly** /ˌbjʊərəˈkrætɪkli; *NAmE* ˌbjʊrəˈkrætɪkli/ *adv.*: *The economy had been run bureaucratically.*

bur·ial /ˈberiəl/ *noun* [U, C] the act or ceremony of burying a dead body: *Christians were prevented from recovering the bodies for burial.* ◇ **+ noun** *a burial ground/place*

burn[1] /bɜːn; *NAmE* bɜːrn/ *verb* (**burnt**, **burnt** /bɜːnt; *NAmE* bɜːrnt/) or (**burned**, **burned** /bɜːnd; *NAmE* bɜːrnd/) **1** [I] to produce flames and heat while using a fuel such as wood or coal: *There may be a rise in 'copy-cat' arson incidents once large fires are already burning.* ◇ *Low-mass stars will burn for trillions of years.* **2** [I] (used especially in the progressive tenses) to be on fire: *By nightfall the whole city was* burning. ◇ *Patients who have jumped from a burning building should be assessed for other injuries.* **3** [T, I] to destroy, damage, injure or kill sb/sth by fire; to be destroyed, etc. by fire: **~ (sb/sth)** *People resorted to violence, destroying fields, burning houses, and demanding lower taxes.* ◇ *Ferns are known to colonize areas burned by fires.* ◇ *The temple of Apollo burned to the ground.* ◇ **~ (sb/sth) to sth** *The penalty for witchcraft was to be burned to death.* **4** [T, I] **~ (sth)** if you **burn** a fuel, or a fuel **burns**, it produces heat, light or energy: *The most common greenhouse gas is carbon dioxide, which is released when fossil fuels are burned.* ◇ *Most of the power plants in China burn coal, which causes acid rain and pollution.* ◇ *These compounds burn more smoothly and efficiently and are used to produce higher octane fuels.* **5** [I, T] to be damaged or injured by the sun, heat, acid, etc; to damage or injure sb/sth in this way: *People with fair skin, which tends to burn easily, are at greatest risk.* ◇ **~ sb** *A six year-old boy was badly burned by an electrified rail while trespassing on the defendant's land.* ◇ **~ sth** *Excessive ultraviolet light destroys sweat glands and burns skin.* ◇ **~ yourself** *If you burn yourself getting something out of the oven, you approach the oven with more care next time.*

PHR V **ˌburn ˈdown | ˌburn sth ˈdown** to be destroyed by fire; to destroy sth by fire: *When the palace burned down, early in the eighth century, it was not rebuilt.* ◇ *His employer had asked him to burn the property down in order to make a fraudulent insurance claim.*

ˌburn ˈout to stop working or to make sth stop working because it gets too hot or is used too much: *If the plant goes down because a machine burns out, it costs millions in repair and lost production.* **ˌburn ˈout | ˌburn itself ˈout** (of a fire) to stop burning because there is nothing more to burn: *The kind of stars that form supernovae burn out in only a few million years.* **ˌburn ˈout | be ˌburnt ˈout** to ruin your health or become very tired by working too hard or because of stress: *Many teachers burn out, especially if they are not accustomed to the challenges of teaching in urban public schools.* ➲ *related noun* BURNOUT

ˌburn ˈup to be destroyed by heat: *Most of the carbon in the product would eventually burn up.* **ˌburn sth ˈup** to get rid of or destroy sth by burning: *Mankind will burn up the vast majority of oil resources in less than 200 years.*

burn[2] /bɜːn; *NAmE* bɜːrn/ *noun* an injury or a mark caused by fire, heat, acid or FRICTION: *Prolonged skin contact with liquid propane at any temperature can cause severe burns.* ◇ *He suffered a relatively minor burn.* ◇ **+ noun** *Engineers at NASA met to discuss the escalating evidence of burn damage to the solid rocket boosters.*

burn·out /ˈbɜːnaʊt; *NAmE* ˈbɜːrnaʊt/ *noun* [U] the state of being extremely tired or ill, either physically or mentally, because of too much work or stress: *Burnout is especially common in caregiving contexts.*

burst[1] /bɜːst; *NAmE* bɜːrst/ *verb* (**burst, burst**) **1** [I, T] to break open or apart, especially because of pressure from inside; to make sth break in this way: *The dam burst after days of torrential rain.* ◇ **~ sth** *The claimant's land was flooded as a result of the stream bursting its banks.* **2** [I] **+ adv./prep.** to go or come from somewhere suddenly: *The twenty-first century burst upon us in an era of seemingly unbounded optimism about the future.*

PHR V **ˈburst into sth** to start producing sth suddenly and with great force: *The truck crashed and burst into flames.*

burst[2] /bɜːst; *NAmE* bɜːrst/ *noun* a short period of a particular activity or strong emotion that often starts suddenly: **~ of sth** *The children have short intense bursts of activity followed by longer periods of inactivity.* ◇ **in bursts** *Her breath was coming in short bursts.*

bury /ˈberi/ *verb* (**bur·ies, bury·ing, bur·ied, bur·ied**) **1 ~ sb/sth** to place sth in the ground, especially a dead body in a GRAVE: *The body is buried in a simple cloth shroud.* ◇ *The two brothers murder Lorenzo and bury him in a wood.* **2** [often passive] **~ sb/sth** to cover sth with soil, rocks, leaves, etc: *The soil has been buried under a layer of sand.* **3 ~ sth** to ignore or hide a feeling, a mistake, etc: *Many Australian families worked hard to bury any evidence of their convict connections.*

bus /bʌs/ *noun* (*pl.* **buses**, *US also* **busses**) **1** a large road vehicle that carries passengers, especially one that travels along a fixed route and stops regularly to let people get on and off: *The bus stop is 10 minutes' walk away and buses are infrequent.* **2** (*computing*) a set of connections that carry data from one part of a computer system to another: *Internal buses link devices within the computer.*

busi·ness /ˈbɪznəs/ *noun* **1** [U] the activity of making, buying, selling or supplying goods or services for money: *Many US banks were eager to do business with the Russians.* ◇ **in ~** *Marketing managers have to make hard decisions if they are to stay in business.* ◇ **+ noun** *For many companies, corruption is considered to be an everyday aspect of the global business environment.* ➲ *compare* COMMERCE, TRADE[1] **2** [C] a commercial organization such as a company, shop or factory HELP In this meaning, the word **business** often describes a small or medium-sized organization; the word **company** can be used for both small and large organizations: *The chair is responsible for the running of the board, whilst the CEO is responsible for running the business.* ◇ *Small businesses make a direct contribution to economic growth.* ◇ *The UK pharmaceutical sector is now dominated by relatively few businesses.* ◇ *Changes in the value of a currency are particularly significant now that so many businesses operate globally.* ➲ *compare* COMPANY, FIRM[1] ➲ thesaurus note *at* COMPANY **3** [U] work or another activity that is part of your job and not done for pleasure or for any other reason: **on ~** *One segment of the market is people travelling on business, often at short notice.* ◇ **+ noun** *She had recently returned from a business trip to Europe.* **4** [U] the amount of work done by a company, etc; the rate, volume, value or quality of this work: *Unions could be sued by an employer for damages for lost business resulting from industrial action.* ◇ *The firm needs to calculate the potential increase in business relative to the cost of the advertising required to secure it.* **5** [C] a particular area of commercial activity: *She had great depth of knowledge of the retail business.* ◇ *Out of the 24 largest Brazilian private groups in 2007, three had banking as their core business.* ◇ *The process attempted to define what business the company wished to be in, in the future.* ➲ *compare* INDUSTRY **6** [U] the fact of a person or people buying goods or services from a business: *Many companies enjoy high levels of repeat business without providing high levels of customer satisfaction.* ➲ *compare* CUSTOM (2) **7** [U] something that concerns a particular person or organization: *Entrepreneurs are in the business of reducing costs.* ◇ *Ed Diener has made it his business to discover where people have higher levels of personal happiness.* ➲ *compare* RESPONSIBILITY **8** [U] important matters that need to be dealt with or discussed: *There is unfinished business in areas such as the reform of the House of Lords.* **9** [sing.] (usually with an adjective) **~ (of sth/of doing sth)** a situation or a series of events: *The qualification has no relevance to the practical business of life.* ◇ *The whole business of being a successful parent is the most complex of life's challenges.*

IDM **go about your ˈbusiness** to do the things that you normally do: *Everyone should be free to go about their daily business.* **out of ˈbusiness** having stopped operating as a business because there is no more money or work available: *Some firms will move away to alternative locations while others will simply go out of business* ◇ *Some firms will succeed and achieve high profits; others will fail and be driven out of business.* ◇ *Competition from supermarkets forced many petrol retailers out of business.*

▸ ADJECTIVE + BUSINESS **big • small • international, global • local • national • private** *An understanding of international business is essential for marketers.* | **large •**

B

new • **successful** *A local community group was attempting to attract new businesses to the area.*
▸ NOUN + BUSINESS **family** *The role of women in family business is relatively under-investigated.*
▸ VERB + BUSINESS **do, conduct** *A growing number of credit card suppliers conduct business over the Internet.* | **run** • **manage** • **start** • **build** • **expand, grow** • **own** • **acquire** • **sell** *People running their own businesses tended to be working in construction and retailing.*
▸ BUSINESS + NOUN **group** • **strategy** • **cycle** • **environment** • **unit** • **owner** • **leader** • **interests** • **activity** • **practices** • **services** • **opportunities** *Business strategy will dictate how firms compete.* ◇ *Many business leaders take different stances depending on the issue under discussion.*

ˈbusiness cycle *noun* the way in which an economy repeatedly expands and contracts: *During the expansion phase of a business cycle, output and employment increase rapidly.*

busi·ness·man /ˈbɪznəsmæn; ˈbɪznəsmən/, **busi·ness·woman** /ˈbɪznəswʊmən/ *noun* (*pl.* **-men** /-men; -mən/, **-women** /-wɪmɪn/) a person who works in business, especially at a high level: *Emily's father had been a successful businessman in his home country.*

ˌbusiness-to-ˈbusiness *adj.* [usually before noun] (*abbr.* **B2B**) done between one business and another rather than between a business and its ordinary customers: *The characteristics of business-to-business marketing are very different from consumer marketing.*

bust /bʌst/ *noun* (*rather informal*) a period of economic difficulty or DEPRESSION: *The boom was followed by the present bust.* ➲ *compare* BOOM[1]

busy /ˈbɪzi/ *adj.* (**busier**, **busi·est**) **1** having a lot to do; perhaps not free to do sth else because you are working on sth: *This manager is very busy and has two production shifts running per day.* ◇ **too ~ to do sth** *They are too busy to respond to customer requests promptly.* ◇ **~ with sth/sb** *The Social Democrats in exile were too busy with their own feuds to pay full attention to what was happening in Russia.* **2 ~ (doing sth)** spending a lot of time on sth: *She is planning a second career as a non-executive director and is busy talking to headhunters and contacts.* **3** (of a place) full of people, activity, vehicles, etc: *The police officer wanted to move the cars which were blocking the busy street in front of the station.* ◇ *If an earthquake strikes at 3 o'clock in the afternoon, the freeways will still be busy.* OPP QUIET (2) ➲ *compare* CROWDED **4** (of a period of time) full of work and activity: *Farming families did industrial work during the less busy seasons of the agricultural year.* ◇ *Traditionally, the busiest time for Internet shopping is lunchtime on the second Monday in December.* OPP QUIET (2) **5** (of a machine) in use or active: *Figure 6.2 depicts the remaining process times for the busy machines.* ◇ **~ doing sth** *While the printer is busy printing the document, the CPU is idling with nothing to do.*

but[1] /bət; *strong form* bʌt/ *conj.* **1** used to introduce a word or phrase that contrasts with what was said before: *Productivity has been continuously rising but unemployment has not been continuously falling.* ◇ *Her age is uncertain, but she was most likely fourteen.* ◇ *A market is not a place, but rather a set of buying and selling activities.* **2** however; despite this: *The food is cheap but delicious.* ◇ *Along the way he was tested by God but overcame all temptation.* ◇ *This is one principle, but it is not the only one.* **3** except: *People will have little or no alternative but to move.*
IDM **but for** if it were not for: *The two women would not have been persecuted but for their gender.*

but[2] /bət; *strong form* bʌt/ *prep.* except; apart from: *All but one member of his family were killed.* ◇ *The costume covered everything but her face.*

but[3] /bət; *strong form* bʌt/ *adv.* only: *The egg itself is but a single cell.* ◇ *Formal education is but one element of a child's learning.*

but·ter /ˈbʌtə(r)/ *noun* [U] a soft yellow food made from milk, used in cooking and for spreading on bread: *Cattle provided milk which was converted to butter and cheese.*
IDM *see* BREAD

but·ton /ˈbʌtn/ *noun* **1** a small part of a machine that you press to make it work SYN SWITCH[2] (1): *The transistor is switched on when the button is pressed.* ◇ *the on/off button* **2** a small area on a computer screen that you use to make it do sth: *The page formatting can be changed by clicking the Setup button.*

buy /baɪ/ *verb* (**bought, bought** /bɔːt/) **1** to obtain sth by paying money for it SYN PURCHASE[2]: **~ sth** *When you are buying a car, you will also consider the other costs associated with running it, such as fuel, insurance and tax.* ◇ *Currencies can be bought and sold openly on the foreign exchange market in many countries.* ◇ *Foreign markets could not afford to buy American goods.* ◇ **~ sth from sb** *The strong pound means that customers can buy products from overseas competitors more cheaply.* ◇ **~ sb sth** *Mike's parents offered to buy him a car if he agreed to commit himself to his college studies.* ◇ **~ sth for sb** *Mr and Mrs Brown bought a house for their daughter.* OPP SELL (1) **2** (of money) to be enough to pay for sth: **~ sth** *Economic growth may not buy happiness, but it usually purchases a better quality of life.* ◇ *The value of the dollar is the amount of a foreign currency that a dollar will buy when exchanged in the foreign exchange market.* ◇ **~ sb sth** *Personal wealth won't buy you a better National Health Service.*
PHR V **ˌbuy sth ˈin** (*BrE*) to buy sth in large quantities: *Meals are typically bought in by airlines from local food processors.* HELP **Buy in** is often used to talk about products or services that are bought by a large company from a smaller specialist company.
ˌbuy ˈinto sth **1** to buy shares in a company, especially in order to gain some control over it: *Recent developments offer new opportunities for international firms seeking to buy into local companies.* ◇ *Foreign conglomerates were quick to buy into countries where economic growth promised profitable returns.* **2** (*rather informal*) to believe sth, especially an idea that many other people believe in: *Staff have to buy into the change if they are to make it work.* ◇ *These women entering marriage don't buy into the view of romantic love.*
ˌbuy sb ˈoff (*often disapproving*) to pay sb money, especially in a way that is dishonest, to prevent them from doing sth that you do not want them to do: *Farmers had to produce enough to buy off rulers and priests, and insure society against the ever-present risk of harvest failure.*
ˌbuy sb ˈout to pay sb for their share in a business, usually in order to get total control of it for yourself: *Rural society started to polarize, as successful farmers bought out their neighbours.*
ˌbuy sth ˈup to buy all or as much as possible of sth, often in order to control its supply, or to increase the size and power of a company: *It became possible to make fortunes by buying up raw materials at internal prices and exporting them at world prices.*

buyer /ˈbaɪə(r)/ *noun* **1** a person who buys sth, especially sth expensive: *Competitive markets consist of many potential buyers and sellers.* ◇ *Foreign buyers were initially attracted by low labour costs.* ◇ **~ for sth** *The company needs to target prospective buyers for its product.* OPP SELLER (1) ➲ *compare* PURCHASER **2** a person whose job is to choose stock or materials for a large shop or business: *Ernest Oppenheimer went to South Africa in 1902 as a diamond buyer for a London firm.*

by[1] /baɪ/ *prep.* **1** used, usually after a passive verb, to show who or what does, creates or causes sth: *Between 20% and 25% of all deaths in these countries are caused by cancer.* ◇ *a play by Ibsen* ◇ *It was a clear decision by the electorate to reject the policies of the last five years.* ◇ *What is meant by 'a fair test'?* ◇ *In 1744 Frederick became alarmed by Austrian successes and re-entered the war.* ◇ *Further support for this claim is provided by experimental studies by Fletcher (2009) and Fernandez et al. (2010).* **2** used for showing how or in what way sth is done: *This is a field that has been revolutionized by the use of computers.* ◇ *The interviewees were all contacted by email.* ◇ *to travel by boat/bus/car/plane* ◇ *to travel by air/land/sea* ◇ **~ doing sth** *Malaria can be controlled by attacking the parasite.* ◇ **~ means of sth** *They plan to provide further working capital by means of borrowing.* **3** used before particular nouns without *the*, to show how sth happens: *These results could not have occurred by chance.* ◇ *Anderson, by contrast, rejects this view.* ◇ *The first Europeans had reached Japan by accident in 1543.* **4** from what sb/sth says or shows; according to sb/sth: *He was, by all accounts, a dedicated and inspired teacher.* ◇ *The table presents a breakdown of employment figures by age and occupation.* **5** used to show the degree or amount of sth: *House prices rose by 10%.* ◇ *In 2006 it was revealed that the government had missed its target by 17%.* **6** used to state the rate at which sth happens: *The symptoms were noted day by day.* ◇ *In this sector, international financial market information is changing by the minute.* **7** used with *the* to show the period or quantity used for buying, selling or measuring sth: *In capitalist employment, labour is paid for by the hour.* ◇ *Acai is processed into vinho at small stands or shops and sold by the litre.* **8** used to show the measurements of sth: *Each plot measured 50 m by 50 m.* **9** used when multiplying or dividing: *6 multiplied by 2 equals 12.* ◇ *6 divided by 2 equals 3.* **10** not later than the time mentioned; before: *By early 1915, the Russian armies were in retreat.* ◇ **~ now/this time** *By now, France was under the control of Napoleon Bonaparte.* ◇ **~ the time of sth/that...** *By the time of his death in 1815 he owned two houses and two mills in the town.* **11** near sb/sth; at the side of sb/sth; beside sb/sth: *Waste is dumped by the roadside, in drainage channels and in other public areas.* **12** past sb/sth: *Later that morning I passed by the cafe again.* **13** during sth; in a particular situation: **~ day/night** *These animals always hunt by night.* ◇ *They had to work by candlelight.* **14** used to show the part of sb/sth that sb touches, holds, etc: *She takes him gently by the hand.* ◇ *Pick it up by the handle.* **15** used for giving more information about where sb comes from, what sb does, etc: *He was German by birth.* ◇ *She is a journalist by profession.* **16** used when swearing to mean 'in the name of': *I swear by Almighty God...*

by[2] /baɪ/ *adv.* **1** past: *As time goes by, sales start to stabilize.* ◇ *Einstein imagined a passenger on a train watching another train pass by.* **2** used to say that sth is saved so that it can be used in the future: *She has put some money by for college fees.*

ˈby-product *noun* **1** a substance that is produced during the process of making or destroying sth else: *Many modern processes have hazardous and toxic waste as their by-products.* ◇ **~ of sth** *Oxygen is released as a by-product of photosynthesis.* **2 ~ (of sth)** a thing that happens, often in an unexpected way, as the result of sth else: *One of the by-products of unemployment is an increase in crime.*

Cc

cab·inet /ˈkæbɪnət/ *noun* (*usually* **the Cabinet**) [C+sing./pl. v.] a group of chosen members of a government, which is responsible for advising and deciding on government policy HELP In the UK, Canada and some other countries, the **Cabinet** is the group of senior ministers responsible for policy; in the US, it is a group of advisers to the president: (*BrE*) *The Cabinet as a whole must carry responsibility for all major decisions.* ◇ **+ noun** *a cabinet meeting* ◇ (*BrE*) *A number of cabinet ministers resigned over the issue.*

cable /ˈkeɪbl/ *noun* [C, U] **1** a set of wires, covered in plastic or rubber, that carries electricity, telephone signals, etc: *In 1978, an agreement was made to develop the first transatlantic fibre-optic cable.* ◇ **+ noun** *The development of technology such as cable television, cell phones and Internet access has accelerated globalization.* **2** thick strong metal rope used on ships, for supporting bridges, etc: *Steel cables were used to hold the netting in place on the slope.*

cal·cium /ˈkælsiəm/ *noun* [U] (*symb.* **Ca**) the chemical element of ATOMIC NUMBER 20. Calcium is a soft silver-white metal. HELP **Calcium** COMPOUNDS occur naturally in LIMESTONE and other minerals. **Calcium** salts are an important element in bone, teeth and shells: *Deficiency of vitamin D prevents the absorption of calcium.* ◇ **+ noun** *Calcium ions control many metabolic and physiological functions in cells.*

cal·cu·late /ˈkælkjuleɪt/ *verb* **1** to use numbers or mathematics to find out a total number, amount, distance, etc. SYN WORK STH OUT (1): **~ sth** *We calculated the percentage of water in the sample.* ◇ *A variety of models can be used to calculate viscosity.* ◇ **~ that...** *The organization calculated that from 1998 to 2008 the incidence of type 2 diabetes rose by 54%.* ◇ **~ how much, what, etc.** *Calculate how many in a birth cohort survive from one census to the next.* ◇ **it is calculated that...** *It is calculated that for polio, elimination depends on virtually 100% vaccine uptake.* **2** to guess sth or form an opinion by using experience, common sense or reason SYN ESTIMATE[1]: **~ sth** *The overall size of the electorate in England and Wales in this period is impossible to calculate.* ◇ **~ that...** *One historian has calculated that five million soldiers died in the wars between 1618 and 1713.* ◇ **~ how much, what, etc...** *These students may calculate how many times they have to misbehave to achieve their aim.* **3 be calculated to do sth** (of an action) to be intended to have a particular effect: *The tone of the advertisement was calculated to appeal to its target market.*

▸ CALCULATE + NOUN **value • quantity, amount • rate • ratio • percentage, fraction • volume • distance • mass • concentration • density • probability • energy • coefficient • constant** *We calculated the concentration of sucrose within the solution.*

▸ ADVERB + CALCULATE **easily, readily • first • now • then** *The error probability is then calculated.*

▸ BE CALCULATED FROM + NOUN **data • model • equation • formula** *Death rates are calculated from data for a twelve month period.*

cal·cu·lated /ˈkælkjuleɪtɪd/ *adj.* [usually before noun] carefully planned in order to get a particular result: *Individuals acting against the law in this way were of course taking a calculated risk.*
IDM **be calculated to do sth** to be intended to do sth; to be likely to do sth: *Imperial art in general was calculated to give an impression of stability.*

cal·cu·la·tion /ˌkælkjuˈleɪʃn/ *noun* [C, U] **1** the act or process of using numbers to find out an amount: *Computers can perform complex calculations.* ◇ *There is a simple method for doing these calculations.* ◇ **by ~** *The value of n can be determined by calculation from Equation 6.1.* ◇ **+ noun** *The calculation method takes account of the population size.* **2** the process of using your judgement to decide what the results would be of doing sth: *The strategies chosen are based on rational calculation.* ◇ **~ that...** *This policy has been driven by the calculation that Labour* *had to demonstrate economic competence if it was to win a general election.*

▸ ADJECTIVE + CALCULATION **detailed • simple • numerical • mathematical • theoretical** *This conclusion is supported by detailed calculations.*

▸ VERB + CALCULATION **perform, do • simplify • repeat** *To simplify the calculations, the square roots were rounded off to one decimal place.* | **make** *The president will make many political calculations before selecting a name.*

▸ CALCULATION + VERB **indicate, show • suggest** *Calculations show that the lake behind the Prospect Dam required 22 years to fill with water.* | **be based on** *These calculations were based on an extremely limited amount of data.*

cal·cu·lus /ˈkælkjələs/ *noun* [U] the branch of mathematics that deals with rates of change, for example in the slope of a curve or the speed of a falling object: *In physics. Newton's laws of motion can be described using calculus.*

cal·en·dar /ˈkælɪndə(r)/ *noun* **1** a system by which time is divided into fixed periods, showing the beginning and end of a year: *Ramadan is the ninth month of the Islamic calendar.* **2** [usually sing.] a list of important events or dates of a particular type during the year: *Demand for male labour in agriculture is dictated by the agricultural calendar.*

ˌcalendar ˈyear *noun* (*technical*) = YEAR (1)

cali·brate /ˈkælɪbreɪt/ *verb* **1** to mark units of measurement on a scientific instrument so that it can be used for measuring sth accurately: **~ sth** *Use calibrated containers of appropriate size.* ◇ **~ sth for sth** *Flasks are calibrated for volume measurement with high levels of accuracy.* **2** to check the readings of an instrument with those of a standard in order to check how accurate the instrument is: **~ sth** *It is necessary to calibrate the instrument at regular intervals with standard reference materials.* ◇ **~ sth against sth** *The balance is calibrated against a sample of known susceptibility.* **3 ~ sth** to adjust the results of an experiment in order to take other factors into account or to allow comparison with other data: *Weighting is a way of calibrating a survey.* ◇ *Fossil data are used to calibrate the rate of molecular evolution.* ➲ *compare* ADJUST **4 ~ sth** to carefully assess, set or adjust sth abstract: *Calibrating supply and demand is not the only distinctive feature of the new strategy.* ◇ *The fines were carefully calibrated according to the status of the people involved.*

cali·bra·tion /ˌkælɪˈbreɪʃn/ *noun* **1** [U] the act of calibrating an instrument or a method: *Because it does not require calibration, the basic instrument is still the mercury-in-glass barometer.* ◇ **+ noun** *Appropriate values can be read off the calibration graphs.* HELP In chemistry, a **calibration curve** is a method used to determine the concentration of a substance in a sample by comparing it with a set of samples of known concentrations: *The data have been plotted in the form of a calibration curve.* **2** [C] the units of measurement marked on a scientific instrument: *Burettes are glass tubes with a tap at one end containing a range of volume calibrations along their length.*

call¹ /kɔːl/ *verb* **1** [T] to give sb/sth a particular name; to use a particular name or title when you are talking to sb: **~ sb/sth + noun** *Pentland calls his approach 'reality mining'.* ◇ **(be) called + noun** *The bubbles in lava are called vesicles.* ◇ *The return to equilibrium is the process called spin relaxation.* ◇ **~ sb/sth by sth** *It is important for the teacher to call students by their names.* ◇ **~ sb/sth after sb** *The agency was called after its founder, Ted Bates.* ➲ *see also* SO-CALLED **2** [T] **~ sb/sth + noun/adj.** to describe sb/sth in a particular way; to consider sb/sth to be sth: *Although it is called a documentary, many would see the film as propaganda.* **3** [T] **~ yourself + noun** to claim that you are a particular type of person, especially when other people question whether this is true: *In the modern society that emerged, even a merchant's daughter could call herself a lady.* **4** [I, T] to shout or say sth loudly to attract sb's attention: **~ (sth) out** *Jack tends to irritate teachers by calling out in class.* ◇ **~ sth** *Gao raised her hand and the teacher gave her the floor by calling her name.* **5** [T] to ask sb/sth to come to a place, by shouting, by telephoning, or as an official order or request: **~ sb/sth** *to call the police/an ambulance/a doctor* ◇ *The prosecution will present their case and call their witnesses first.* ◇ **~ sb/sth + adv./prep.** *About 7% of patients will be called back for a further diagnostic investigation.* **6** [T, I] **~ (sb/sth)** to make a telephone call: *All those whom we interviewed stated a preference for calling a friend on a mobile rather than a home phone.* **7** [I] **~ + adv./prep.** (*especially BrE*) to make a short visit to a place or person: *Ships calling at the port rarely exceeded 6 000 tons.* **8** [T] **~ sth** to order sth to happen; to announce that sth will happen: *She called a meeting with supervisors to identify possible reasons for this.* ◇ *Bismarck promptly dissolved the Reichstag and called elections.* **9** [I] (of a bird or animal) to make the cry that is typical for it: *There might be a mechanism that made animals call when they smelt odours similar to their own in urine.*

IDM **call sth into ˈquestion** to doubt sth or make others doubt sth: *This failure called into question the whole basis of postwar cooperation.* **call sb to acˈcount (for/over sth)** to make sb explain a mistake, etc. because they are responsible for it: *They believed that the people had the right to call officials to account.* ➲ *more at* MIND¹

PHR V **ˌcall ˈback** | **ˌcall sb ˈback** to telephone sb again or to telephone sb who telephoned or contacted you earlier: *Donors receiving an engaged tone or a holding message do not call back.* **ˈcall for sth 1** to publicly ask for sth to happen: *Others have called for more research into the relationships between social networks and entrepreneurship.* ◇ *The Board called for a change in the law.* **2** to need sth: *Care of older adults calls for an understanding of the features of dementia.* **ˌcall sth ˈforth** (*formal*) to produce a particular reaction: *The growth in global trade in food calls forth new kinds of responses by business.* **ˌcall sb/sth ˈin** to ask for the services of sb: *It was necessary to call in the aid of the military.* ◇ *Experts were called in to help decide whether to build it in stone or timber.* **ˌcall sth ˈin** to order or ask for the return of sth: *There are insufficient funds and assets to pay the creditors when the debts are called in.* **ˌcall sth ˈoff** to cancel sth; to decide that sth will not happen: *The plant's owners agreed to improve conditions, and the union agreed to call off the protests.* **ˈcall on/upon sb 1** to ask or demand that sb do sth: *He is calling on the Australian government to push for an international inquiry.* **2** to use or refer to sth when it is needed: *Large states can call on far more extensive administrative and technical resources.* **3** to formally invite or ask sb to speak, etc: *The teacher calls on students to read out their answers.* **ˌcall sb ˈup** to make sb join the armed forces SYN CONSCRIPT¹, DRAFT² (3): *In 1940 he was called up, and despite his degree, was not considered officer material.* **ˌcall sth ˈup** to bring sth back to your mind SYN RECALL¹ (2): *For Americans, this campaign calls up nostalgic images of a simpler life.*

call² /kɔːl/ *noun* **1** a request, an order or a demand for sb to do sth or to go somewhere: *Schnoring says that 'few governments have responded positively to this call' (2001: 157).* ◇ **~ for sth** *The riot naturally produced calls for political reform.* ◇ **~ (to sb) to do sth** *There were calls to reduce the right to trial by jury.* ◇ **~ to sth** *The book's foreword is a spirited call to action against the threat of human-induced climate change.* **2** the act of contacting sb on the telephone: *Unsolicited direct marketing messages can include direct mail, telephone calls, emails and text messages.* ◇ *Even calls made on wireless phones are still primarily carried over the traditional landline telephone network.* **3** a loud sound made by a bird or an animal, or by a person to attract attention: *A classic* *example is the alarm calls given by birds when they have detected a predator.* **4 ~ on sb/sth** a demand or pressure placed on sb/sth: *Close monitoring of the board is costly for shareholders, who may have other more pressing calls on their time.*

IDM **a ˌcall to ˈarms** a request that makes you want to take action and try to defend sth or get ready for a fight: *She made a call to arms to fight the dominance and abuses of multinationals.* **(be) on ˈcall** (of a doctor, police officer, etc.) available for work if necessary, especially in an emergency: *A call to the emergency phone number reaches the answering service, which will contact the doctor on call.* ➲ *more at* PORT

ˈcall centre (*BrE*) (*NAmE* **ˈcall center**) *noun* an office in which a large number of people work using telephones, for example arranging insurance for people, or taking customers' orders and answering questions: *The ads generated 250 000 calls to the organization's call centre.*

call·er /ˈkɔːlə(r)/ *noun* a person who is making a telephone call: *The emergency services stood to benefit from 3G's ability to pinpoint precisely a caller's location.*

call·ing /ˈkɔːlɪŋ/ *noun* **1** a strong desire or feeling of duty to do a particular job, especially one in which you help other people SYN VOCATION: *Cyprian's theme was that some bishops and presbyters were unworthy of their sacred calling.* ◇ *For many, caring for the sick is more a calling than an occupation.* **2** a profession or career: *Schiller emerges as a man dedicated to the literary calling.*

calm[1] /kɑːm/ *adj.* (**calm·er**, **calm·est**) **1** not excited, nervous or upset: *During the reply, interviewers should notice whether their patients are calm or distressed.* **2** (of the sea) without large waves: *The faintest wind can produce waves on calm water.* **3** (of the weather) without wind: *The most serious pollution episodes occur in calm or nearly calm conditions.* ■ **calm·ly** *adv.*: *It is important to assess risk calmly and fairly (McCann and McKeown, 2002).*

calm[2] /kɑːm/ *verb* **~ sb/sth** to make sb/sth become quiet and more relaxed, especially after strong emotion or excitement: *The doctor's first action will be to calm the patient and ensure the safety of others.* ◇ *The management might have calmed the situation but the police exacerbated it by arresting the leaders.*

PHR V **ˌcalm ˈdown** | **ˌcalm sb/sth ˈdown** to become calm; to make sb/sth become calm: *Telling an emotional or angry person 'Calm down' is likely to have the opposite effect.* ◇ *This was a move which some felt only exacerbated the situation rather than calming it down.*

cal·orie /ˈkæləri/ *noun* **1** (*also* **Calorie**) a unit for measuring how much energy food will produce: *School dinners account for an extra 40 calories per day, enough to cause significant weight gain.* HELP This unit is defined as the energy needed to raise the temperature of 1 kilogram of water by 1°C; it is mainly used to measure the energy value of foods. It is sometimes written as **Calorie**, with a capital C, as it is equal to one thousand times the scientific value of a **calorie**. **2** a unit of heat energy: the energy needed to raise the temperature of a gram of water by 1°C (but now usually defined as 4.1868 joules): *The ocean circulation system is currently responsible for the northward transport of some 51 021 calories of heat to the North Atlantic region annually.*

came *past tense of* COME

cam·era /ˈkæmərə/ *noun* a piece of equipment for taking photographs, moving pictures or television pictures: *She sings her lines directly into the camera.* ◇ *It has become possible for anyone with a digital video camera to make movies and distribute them over the Internet.*

IDM **on ˈcamera** being filmed or shown on television: *The Prime Minister was mocked for his awkward attempts to smile on camera.*

camp /kæmp/ *noun* **1** [C] (used in compounds) a place where people are kept in temporary buildings, especially by a government and often for long periods: *Political prisoners were sent to labour camps.* ◇ *He fled the country in 1980 and resided in a temporary refugee camp in Malaysia.* ➲ *see also* CONCENTRATION CAMP **2** [C, U] a place where people live in temporary buildings for part of the year: *Every year, semi-nomadic herders set up a base camp half-way up the mountain.* **3** [C, U] a place where young people go on holiday and take part in various activities or a particular activity: *Saturday programmes, holiday programmes and summer camps are provided for the children.* **4** [C, U] a place where soldiers live while they are training or fighting: *A military training camp was set up outside the city.* **5** [C] a group of people who have the same ideas about sth and oppose people with other ideas: *Stolypin was an outspoken politician who had enemies in every political camp.*

C

cam·paign[1] /kæmˈpeɪn/ *noun* **1** a series of planned activities that are intended to achieve a particular social, commercial or political aim: *Pepsi launched a TV advertising campaign featuring the popular Miss Vietnam, Ha Kieu Anh.* ◇ **~ against sth** *Some took part in local political campaigns against the construction of a nuclear power plant.* ◇ **~ for sth** *Non-governmental organizations (NGOs) have now become a crucial actor in campaigns for human rights.* ◇ **~ to do sth** *There is a national campaign to help people get the most out of their medications.* ◇ **+ noun** *While four out of five Americans report discussing politics, 10% or less report engaging in any form of campaign activity.* **2** a series of attacks and battles that are intended to achieve a particular military aim during a war: *Between 1940 and 1945, the Allies waged a campaign of ever-increasing intensity.* ◇ **~ against sb/sth** *Menelaus now planned a military campaign against Troy under the leadership of his brother Agamemnon.*

- ADJECTIVE + CAMPAIGN **successful • new • presidential • political • promotional • national • global • local** *The reduction in disease following a successful vaccine campaign can easily be reversed.*
- NOUN + CAMPAIGN **election • advertising, marketing • public relations, PR • media, mass media • communications • health • information • awareness • education** *Business owners can make large contributions to election campaigns and influence political agendas.*
- VERB + CAMPAIGN **launch, begin, initiate • conduct, undertake • mount, wage , organize • lead • support • plan** *Paolo Freire was a Brazilian educator who conducted a national literacy campaign in the 1960s.* ◇ *Caracalla led two campaigns in northern Scotland, with the professed intention of conquering the whole of Britain.* | **run • develop • design, create** *Most candidates for state and local offices do not have the resources to run high-profile campaigns.*
- CAMPAIGN + VERB **be aimed at • target** *A different commercial was made for each of the major markets targeted by the campaign.*
- CAMPAIGN + NOUN **activity • contribution • finance, funds • spending, expenditure • strategy • planning • manager • message, slogan • material, poster, website** *The Democrats have always received a significant minority of campaign contributions from business.*

cam·paign[2] /kæmˈpeɪn/ *verb* [I] **1** to take part in or lead a political, social or commercial campaign, for example in order to achieve change or win an election: *Organizations campaigning in the election used web tools to good effect.* ◇ *Campaigning residents have used conservationist tactics to prevent further council redevelopment.* ◇ **~ for sth/sb** *A number of Labour supporters joined the Liberal Democrats in campaigning for electoral reform.* ◇ **~ against sth/sb** *Coleridge campaigned against the employment of children in cotton factories.* ◇ **~ to do sth** *He campaigned to revive*

Magyar language and culture. ◇ **~ on sth** *Greenpeace and Friends of the Earth campaign on environmental issues.* **2** to take part in or lead a military campaign: *Louis VIII and his baronial allies were campaigning in the south.* ◇ **~ against sb/sth** *After returning from Greece, Alexander campaigned in the spring of 335 against the Thracians and Illyrians.* ■ **cam·paign·ing** *noun* [U] *Following extensive campaigning, the government was persuaded to retain the current rules.* ◇ *Military campaigning sometimes demanded the emperor's presence on the frontier.*

cam·paign·er /kæmˈpeɪnə(r)/ *noun* a person who leads or takes part in a campaign, especially one for political or social change: *Environmental campaigners have questioned the sustainability of the project.* ◇ **~ against sth** *Benezet was a printer, schoolmaster, and respected campaigner against slavery.* ◇ **~ for sth** *Groups like Charter 88 and Democratic Audit were influential campaigners for reform.*

can[1] /kən; *strong form* kæn/ *modal verb* (*negative* **can·not** /ˈkænɒt; *NAmE* ˈkænɑːt/, *short form* **can't** /kɑːnt; *NAmE* kænt/, *pt* **could** /kəd; *strong form* kʊd/, *negative* **could not**, *short form* **couldn't** /ˈkʊdnt/) HELP The short forms **can't** and **couldn't** are best avoided in academic writing, unless you are quoting or deliberately using a less formal style. **1** used to say that it is possible for sb/sth to do sth, or for sth to happen: *Organizations can take action to reduce the causes and symptoms of stress.* ◇ *The test can be interpreted by computer.* ◇ *Signs of heart disease could not be detected.* ◇ *The government was under pressure to find and deport as many of the freed prisoners as they could.* **2** used to say that sb knows how to do sth: *In general they can speak only limited English.* ◇ *Her parents can neither read nor write, but they are numerate.* **3** used with the verbs 'feel', 'hear', 'see', 'smell', 'taste': *An advertisement is revealed for shorter and shorter intervals and respondents are asked what they can see.* **4** used to show that sb is allowed to do sth: *The children can go to the library computer lab before and after school to access their email and the Internet.* **5** used to say what sb/sth is often like: *Students can become too focused on obtaining teacher approval.* ➲ grammar note *at* MODAL[1]

GRAMMAR POINT

can • cannot • be able to • be unable to

- **Can** and **be able to** can each be used to express possibility. The negatives are **cannot**, **be unable to** or **not be able to**. These expressions are all followed by the infinitive without *to*: *Although we* ***can measure*** *sea ice extent relatively easily, we* ***cannot measure*** *the volume.* ◇ *Principally, the glider* ***is able to survey*** *the head of the adjacent submarine canyon.*
- The past form of *can* is **could**; the past form of *be able* is **was/were able**: *Formerly, employers* ***could insist*** *that all sickness absence be confirmed by a certificate issued by a doctor.* ◇ *Thus, these refugees* ***were able to choose*** *where in France they would be resettled.*
- To talk about possibility in the future, use **could** and **would be able**: *In the future, the UK* ***could use*** *biomass to satisfy about 4.5% of its present total energy needs.* ◇ *Figure 6 relates to the population in Wales, but a similar graph* ***could be constructed*** *for Scotland, England or Ireland.* ◇ *Some politicians optimistically predicted that the country* ***would be able to free*** *itself from aid and donor influence.*

can[2] /kæn/ (*BrE also* **tin**) *noun* a metal container in which food and drink is sold: *Cardboard, food tins, aluminium drink cans, milk cartons and plastic bottles can all be recycled.* ◇ **~ of sth** *a can of cola* HELP In American English, **can** is the usual word for both food and drink. In British English, **can** is always used for drink, but **tin** or **can** can be used for food, paint, etc.

canal /kəˈnæl/ *noun* **1** a long straight passage dug in the ground and filled with water for boats and ships to travel along; a smaller passage used for carrying water to fields, crops, etc: *In 1772 the River Mersey was joined to the Severn by the Staffordshire and Worcestershire canal.* ◇ *Reservoirs were dug and irrigation canals constructed.* **2** a tube inside the body through which liquid, food or air can pass: *Discharge from the ear canal may indicate infection.* ◇ *Head size is ultimately constrained by limits on the size of the birth canal.*

can·cel /ˈkænsl/ *verb* (**-ll-**, *US* **-l-**) **1 ~ sth** to decide that sth that has been arranged will not now take place: *The new military government cancelled the elections and banned all political parties.* ◇ *Several flights were cancelled due to poor visibility.* ➲ *compare* POSTPONE **2 ~ sth** to say that you no longer want to continue with an agreement, especially one that has been legally arranged: *Gonzalez cancelled the company's contract and ordered all company officials to leave the country.* ◇ *After the revolution, the majority of foreign debts were cancelled.*

PHR V **ˌcancel ˈout | ˌcancel sth ˈout** if two or more things **cancel out** or one **cancels out** the other, they are equally important but have an opposite effect on a situation so that the situation does not change: *Boyne (1998) shows that rising transaction costs of privatization tend to cancel out short-term efficiency gains.* ◇ **~ each other out** *The two signals cancelled each other out.* HELP In mathematics, equal factors on either side of an EQUATION can **cancel** each other **out**: *'Divide by 9' cancels out 'multiply by 9'.*

can·cel·la·tion /ˌkænsəˈleɪʃn/ *noun* [U, C] **~ (of sth)** a decision to stop sth that has already been arranged from happening: *The Alternative Declaration called for immediate cancellation of all debt.* ◇ *The report detailed the number of contract cancellations and reasons why customers had cancelled.*

can·cer /ˈkænsə(r)/ *noun* [U, C] a serious disease in which GROWTHS of cells, also called cancers, form in the body and kill normal body cells. The disease often causes death: *Currently in the UK, one in four people dies of cancer.* ◇ *Ultraviolet radiation can cause cancer.* ◇ *60% of all cancers are diagnosed in those aged over 65 years.* ◇ *breast/lung/prostate cancer* ◇ **~ of sth** *People who have cancer of the larynx may have to have a laryngectomy.* ■ **can·cer·ous** /ˈkænsərəs/ *adj.*: *Radiotherapy Involves the use of high-energy ionizing radiation directed at cancerous cells.*

can·di·date /ˈkændɪdət; ˈkændɪdeɪt/ *noun* **1** a person who is trying to be elected or is applying for a job: *Citizens have the right to vote and to stand as candidates in elections.* ◇ *The committee recommended her as the most suitable candidate.* ◇ **~ for sth** *Candidates for senior posts need to demonstrate solid management experience.* **2 ~ (for sth)** a person or thing that is considered suitable for sth or that is likely to be sth or get sth: *Even in those patients who are suitable candidates for this surgery, 5-year survival is less than 10%.* ◇ *There are unfortunately a number of viruses that at present do not seem promising candidates for vaccines.* ◇ *The outer core is an iron alloy with about 10 per cent of lighter elements, the most likely candidates being oxygen, sulfur, nickel and silicon.* HELP In biochemistry, **candidate gene** is a GENE that is suspected of being involved in the expression of a TRAIT such as a disease: *The first candidate genes for Huntington's disease had features that made them seem plausible.* **3** (*BrE*) a person taking an exam: *For Task 1, candidates write a report of around 150 words based on a table or diagram.*

can·not /ˈkænɒt; *NAmE* ˈkænɑːt/ can not: *The timing of the largest earthquakes cannot be predicted precisely.*

canon /ˈkænən/ *noun* **1** a list of the books or other works that are generally accepted as being important or as being the genuine work of a particular writer: *These postcolonial texts refer to classics of the English literary canon such as 'The Tempest', 'Robinson Crusoe', and 'Heart of Darkness'.* ◇ *Various first quarto editions of plays from the Shakespeare canon were published before 1600.* **2** **~ (of sth)** a generally accepted rule, standard or principle by which sth is judged: *Plays in performance were subject to new theatrical fashions, new styles of acting and new canons of taste.*

ca·non·ic·al /kəˈnɒnɪkl; *NAmE* kəˈnɑːnɪkl/ *adj.* **1** connected with or included in a list of highly respected texts or works of literature: *Descartes's 'Meditations' is perhaps the most closely studied of all the canonical texts in Western philosophy.* ◇ *The New York Trilogy is packed full of references to canonical writers: Hawthorne, Melville, Thoreau, Poe, Milton.* **2** included in a list of HOLY books that are accepted as genuine: *In the four canonical gospels, Jesus was never depicted as attacking the Roman state.* **3** (*mathematics*) in the simplest accepted form in mathematics: *the canonical form for a matrix*

can·opy /ˈkænəpi/ *noun* (*pl.* **-ies**) **1** a layer of sth that spreads over an area like a roof, especially branches of trees in a forest: *Invasive trees will rapidly colonize open areas and exploit gaps in the forest canopy.* ◇ **+ noun** *Average percentage canopy cover did not differ significantly between the territories.* **2** a cover that is fixed or hangs above sth, especially a bed, seat, etc: *At their meeting, she sat in state under a canopy, with a robe on her shoulders and a crown upon her head.*

cap[1] /kæp/ *noun* **1** something that covers the top or end of sth: *These volcanic flows formed a cap covering the older rocks.* ◇ *A thick metal test tube closed by a screw cap was heated under pressure.* **2** an upper limit placed on spending or borrowing, or on the number or amount of sth that is allowed: *The government introduced price caps and wage controls in the effort to control inflation.* ◇ **~ on sth** *There is no cap on the amount of damages that may be awarded in this type of case.* ◇ *They plan to impose a cap on new immigration from outside the EU.* ➲ *see also* ICE CAP

cap[2] /kæp/ *verb* (**-pp-**) [often passive] **1** **~ sth (with sth)** to cover the top or end of sth with sth: *A large body of ice capped the Sierra Nevada de Santa Marta in Colombia.* ◇ *The cylinder had both ends capped with copper.* **2** **~ sth** (*especially BrE*) to place an upper limit on spending or borrowing, or on the number of amount of sth that is allowed: *Central government has made repeated efforts since the 1980s to cap local government spending.* ◇ *Tradable permits are one method of capping emissions of greenhouse gases.* ◇ **~ sth at sth** *The VAT base was capped at 55 per cent of GNP in all member states.*

cap·abil·ity **AWL** /ˌkeɪpəˈbɪləti/ *noun* (*pl.* **-ies**) **1** [C, U] the ability or qualities necessary to do sth: *There are differences in the way employers utilize the skills and capabilities of their workforce.* ◇ **~ of doing sth** *Television has the capability of influencing the behaviour of children in a positive direction.* ◇ **~ to do sth** *Technological competence will enhance our capability to protect the environment.* **2** [C] the power or weapons that a country has for war or for military action: *States will inevitably develop offensive military capabilities to defend themselves.* ◇ *More countries are in a position to acquire a nuclear capability.*

▸ ADJECTIVE + CAPABILITY **technological** • **technical** • **innovative** • **organizational** • **managerial** • **industrial** • **manufacturing** • **strategic** *Government policies help local firms to acquire sufficient technological capabilities to compete in the international economy.*

▸ VERB + CAPABILITY **possess** • **acquire** • **build** • **accumulate** • **enhance**, **improve** • **develop** • **demonstrate** *The firm must possess the capability to manufacture or distribute goods.* ◇ *There was a tendency for firms to begin with simple tasks and accumulate capabilities gradually.*

cap·able **AWL** /ˈkeɪpəbl/ *adj.* **1** having the ability or qualities necessary for doing sth: **~ of sth** *Crows are capable of highly intelligent behaviour.* ◇ **~ of doing sth** *Ms Pierce believes investors are quite capable of making their own judgements of value.* **HELP** Note that **capable** is never followed by an infinitive. So, you can say *Korea is capable of developing its own applications software* or *The technology is capable of being improved* but NOT ~~*capable to develop*~~ or ~~*capable to be improved*~~. **OPP** INCAPABLE (1) **2** having the ability to do things well **SYN** SKILLED (1), COMPETENT (2): *She is well read and a highly capable student.*

cap·aci·tance /kəˈpæsɪtəns/ *noun* [U, C] (*physics*) the ability of a system to store an electrical charge: *The total capacitance was kept to a minimum.* ◇ *We did not account for the finite time required to charge and discharge the various internal capacitances.*

cap·acity **AWL** /kəˈpæsəti/ *noun* (*pl.* **-ies**) **1** [C, U] the ability to understand or to do sth: *There are important variations in learning capacities among individuals.* ◇ **~ to do sth** *The river has the capacity to erode through any rock type.* ◇ **~ for sth** *Humans have greater capacity for happiness than most other species.* ◇ **~ for doing sth** *Vico argued that all human beings have a capacity for understanding history.* **2** [U, C, usually sing.] the number of things or people that a container or space can hold: *An airline with excess capacity would lose sales opportunities if there were no customers.* ◇ **~ of sth** *The total capacity of the drainage pumps installed for the city is 692 m^3.* ➲ *see also* CARRYING CAPACITY **3** [sing., U] the quantity that a factory, machine, etc. can produce: *Korea has expanded its shipbuilding capacity a great deal in recent years.* ◇ *If demand is strong, the plant will need to build additional capacity quickly.* **4** [C, usually sing.] the official position or function that sb has **SYN** ROLE: **in a... ~** *This rule applies whether the individual was acting in a professional or a personal capacity.* ◇ *to act in an official capacity* ◇ **in sb's ~ as sth** *He kept paying off the mortgage in his capacity as solicitor to the mortgagor.* **5** [C, U] the size or power of a piece of equipment, especially the engine of a vehicle: *Turbine farms with a total capacity of 3.3 GW may be foreseen.* ◇ *The design called for a memory of roughly the same capacity as an early Apple Macintosh computer.* ➲ *see also* HEAT CAPACITY

▸ ADJECTIVE + CAPACITY **remarkable** • **great** • **innate** • **mental**, **intellectual**, **cognitive** • **reproductive** *Sea urchin embryos have a remarkable capacity for regulation.* ◇ *Malnutrition reduces mental capacity.* | **limited** • **full** *The brain has a limited capacity for detailed processing.* | **excess**, **spare** • **maximum**, **total** *Some firms have excess capacity and can therefore meet an increase in demand.* | **productive** • **unused** *Businesses are likely to have unused productive capacity: they will have machinery idle for lack of demand.*

▸ NOUN + CAPACITY **storage** *The computer must have an adequate storage capacity.* | **production**, **manufacturing** *When orders exceeded his production capacity, he outsourced from other potters.*

▸ VERB + CAPACITY **possess**, **have** • **lack** • **lose** • **retain** • **strengthen**, **enhance**, **develop** • **exercise** • **assess** *The teacher has an important role in helping students develop their capacity to be responsible.* | **exceed** • **build**, **expand**, **increase** • **reduce** • **limit** *The volume of water that must be pumped out may exceed the capacity of the system.*

ca·pil·lary /kəˈpɪləri; *NAmE* ˈkæpəleri/ *noun* (*pl.* **-ies**) **1** (*anatomy*) any of the smallest tubes in the body that carry blood: **+ noun** *Free flowing capillary blood was collected on filter paper.* **2** (*technical*) a tube which is as thin as a hair: **+ noun** *A glass capillary tube of internal radius 0.320 mm was used.*

C

cap·ital /ˈkæpɪtl/ *noun* **1** [U] wealth or property that is owned by a business or a person and is available to invest or be used to start a business: *The average return on capital invested in land was only about 5 per cent.* ◇ *Amazon's share capital was seventeen times greater than that of the world's largest 'bricks and mortar' book chain-store.* ◇ **+ noun** *The individual resources of the firm include items of capital equipment.* ➲ *see also* VENTURE CAPITAL ➲ thesaurus note *at* MONEY **2** [U] people who use their money to control a society's economic activity, considered as a group: *The division of social wealth between capital and labour has become still more unequal.* HELP Although this meaning of **capital** is fairly common in history and sociology, it is not used in economics. Economists only use the term **capital** to refer to the capital itself, not the people who own it. **3** [U] (used in compounds) a valuable resource of a particular kind: *Investment in human capital has become more critical than ever.* ➲ *see also* CULTURAL CAPITAL, HUMAN CAPITAL, SOCIAL CAPITAL **4** [U] (*economics*) used as a general term to describe anything other than labour and land that can be used in the production process, usually with the property that it can be used repeatedly: *As countries develop, their production methods become more capital-based.* **5** (*also* ˌ**capital** ˈ**city**) [C] the most important town or city of a country or region, usually where the central government operates from: *Beijing, the nation's capital, represents the culture of North China.* ◇ *There were demonstrations in several provincial capitals.* ◇ *Seven of the world's ten largest capital cities are built on estuaries.* ◇ (*figurative*) *Mumbai is the financial capital and richest city in India.* HELP In this use, **capital** describes a place that is associated more than any other place with a particular activity or product. **6** (*also* ˌ**capital** ˈ**letter**) [C] a letter of the form and size that is used at the beginning of a sentence or a name (= A, B, C rather than a, b, c): *They presented participants with target words written in capitals.* ◇ *Sets are usually denoted by capital letters such as S, A, B, X, etc.*

▸ ADJECTIVE + CAPITAL **foreign, international • private • working** *The government relied on foreign capital for economic development.* | **human • cultural • social • intellectual • natural** *Language is a form of social and cultural capital that can be converted into economic capital.* | **national • regional, provincial** *Decisions on whether to support the war were almost entirely made in national EU capitals, not Brussels.*

▸ VERB + CAPITAL **invest • raise • attract • accumulate** *Producers need time to attract new capital.*

▸ CAPITAL + NOUN **mobility • investment • goods, stock • asset • equipment** *Market controls were lifted in Europe and capital mobility increased.* ◇ *Investment may include the purchase of necessary capital equipment.*

ˈ**capital account** *noun* (*economics*) one of the two main parts that make up a country's BALANCE OF PAYMENTS (along with the CURRENT ACCOUNT) HELP A country's **current account** reflects the country's net income; the **capital account** reflects changes in ownership of ASSETS: *The capital account records changes in the stock of various types of foreign assets owned by home residents and home assets owned by overseas residents.*

ˈ**capital goods** *noun* [pl.] (*business*) goods such as factory machines that are used for producing other goods: *The income of employers derives mainly from their ownership of the capital goods used in production and their control over the labour of others.* ➲ *compare* CONSUMER GOODS

cap·it·al·ism /ˈkæpɪtəlɪzəm/ *noun* [U] an economic system in which a country's businesses and industry are controlled and run for profit by private owners rather than by the government: *The protesters do not really have an alternative to global capitalism.* ◇ *A feature of paid work under capitalism is that the nature of jobs and skills changes.* ➲ *compare* COMMUNISM, SOCIALISM

cap·it·al·ist[1] /ˈkæpɪtəlɪst/ (*also less frequent* **cap·it·al·is·tic** /ˌkæpɪtəˈlɪstɪk/) *adj.* based on the principles of capitalism: *Unemployment is a chronic problem in a capitalist economy.* ◇ *Women do more unpaid domestic work than men in advanced capitalist societies.* ◇ *The capitalistic system is essentially an international system.*

▸ CAPITALIST + NOUN **economy • society • democracy • country • system • class • world • development** *The power of the capitalist class over the working class has grown.* ◇ *The region provides an interesting exception to much of the rest of the capitalist world.*

cap·it·al·ist[2] /ˈkæpɪtəlɪst/ *noun* **1** a person who supports capitalism: *Traditional Marxism divided society into three classes: capitalists, workers and the petty bourgeoisie.* ➲ *compare* COMMUNIST[1], SOCIALIST **2** a person who owns or controls a lot of wealth and uses it to produce more wealth, for example by investing in trade and industry: *In the 1860s, German banks effectively displaced foreign capitalists in Rhineland-Westphalia.*

cap·it·al·ize (*BrE also* **-ise**) /ˈkæpɪtəlaɪz/ *verb* **1 ~ sth** to write or print a letter of the alphabet as a capital; to begin a word with a capital letter: *The term may be capitalized when used in this specific context.* **2** [usually passive] **~ sth** (*business, finance*) to provide a company, etc. with the money it needs to function: *Many banks were insufficiently capitalized to support their lending.*

PHR V ˈ**capitalize on/upon sth** to gain a further advantage for yourself from a situation SYN TAKE ADVANTAGE OF STH/SB (1): *Labour was able to capitalize on the extension of the vote to the working class.* ◇ *Coca-Cola are able to capitalize upon the brand value that they have established across cultures.*

ˌ**capital** ˈ**letter** *noun* = CAPITAL (6)

ˌ**capital** ˈ**punishment** *noun* [U] punishment by death: *The member states have reaffirmed the Union's opposition to capital punishment.*

cap·sule /ˈkæpsjuːl; *NAmE also* ˈkæpsl/ *noun* **1** a small container which has a measured amount of a medicine inside and which dissolves when you swallow it: *The medicine can be taken as tablets or capsules.* **2** (*anatomy*) a covering of an organ or other structure in the body, for example a KIDNEY: *The tough capsule surrounding each kidney offers protection against trauma and prevents the entry of bacteria.* **3** (*biology*) a layer that forms the outer surface of some BACTERIAL cells: *When stressed, certain bacteria form protective capsules that are heat stable.* ◇ *These capsules are secreted by the cells and account for the virulence of the bacterium.*

cap·tion /ˈkæpʃn/ *noun* words that are printed under a picture, diagram, etc. that explain or describe it: *Brief captions explain events depicted in the paintings.* ◇ **~ for/to/under sth** *The caption for Fig. 15.6 provides the details of layer thicknesses in each configuration.*

cap·ture[1] /ˈkæptʃə(r)/ *verb* **1 ~ sb's attention/imagination/interest** to make sb interested in sth: *The spiritual wisdom of India captured his imagination.* ◇ *Vivid or dramatic events or discoveries have played an important role in capturing political attention.* **2** to record sth accurately in words or pictures: **~ sth** *The advent of sound and colour transformed the way that filmmakers could capture reality.* ◇ **~ sb/sth on film/tape/canvas, etc.** *The revolution was witnessed by an international audience thanks to images captured on mobile telephones.* **3** to catch or take control of sb/sth using physical force: **~ sth** *These spiders do not build webs, but capture prey by jumping onto them.* ◇ *The fighting continued until 30 April 1975, when communist troops captured Saigon and reunified the country.* ◇ **~ sb** *Ali Pasha was captured by the Turks and executed in February 1822.* **4** to succeed in getting control of sth that other people are also trying to control: **~ sth** *Initially, the product was a huge success, capturing 40% of the market.* ◇ **~ sth from sb/sth** *The company has been successful in capturing market share from its nearest rivals.* **5 ~ sth** to collect and record data using a computer: *Table 4.8 presents the remaining demographic data captured in the survey.* ➲ *see also* DATA CAPTURE **6 ~ sth** to collect a natural supply of sth and either make use of it, or store it where it can do no harm: *Chloroplasts capture the energy from light and use it to drive a series of reactions.* ◇ *After the CO_2 is captured, the remaining H_2 can be used for running a gas turbine.* **7 ~ sth** (*physics*) to absorb a very small piece of matter, for example an ELECTRON: *At least two photons must be captured to supply the reaction energy.*

▸ CAPTURE + NOUN **essence, nature • complexity, richness • aspect • idea • meaning • spirit • moment • image** *For each of the datasets, I have chosen one or more illustrations that capture some important aspect of the results.* ◇ *As a poet, he captures vivid moments of visual perception.*

▸ ADVERB + CAPTURE **nicely • accurately • adequately • fully** *The spirit of the movement is nicely captured in this quotation from Catherine Booth:...*

cap·ture² /ˈkæptʃə(r)/ *noun* [U] the act of capturing sb/sth or of being captured: *In 1812 he records in his logbook his capture by pirates off the coast of Jamaica.* ◇ **the ~ of sth** *The one success of the 1544 campaign was the capture of Boulogne.* ◇ *The first of these processes involves the capture of an electron by the nucleus.* ➲ *see also* DATA CAPTURE

car /kɑː(r)/ *noun* **1** (*NAmE also* **auto·mo·bile**) a road vehicle with an engine and four wheels that can carry a small number of passengers: *The use of mobile telephones while driving a car has been identified as dangerous.* ◇ **by ~** *In 2008, with rising oil prices, the distances people travelled by car began to fall.* ◇ **+ noun** *The film star Montgomery Clift was involved in a car accident in 1956.* **2** (*NAmE*) a separate section of a train, for carrying passengers, animals or goods; a COACH or TRUCK: *Several cars went off the rails.*

carbo·hy·drate /ˌkɑːbəʊˈhaɪdreɪt; *NAmE* ˌkɑːrboʊˈhaɪdreɪt/ *noun* [C, U] a substance such as sugar or STARCH that consists of carbon, HYDROGEN and OXYGEN: *The wider availability of foods that are high in fats and simple carbohydrates is a primary cause of obesity.* ◇ *After eating, most of the carbohydrate in food is broken down by the body into glucose.*

car·bon /ˈkɑːbən; *NAmE* ˈkɑːrbən/ *noun* [U] **1** (*symb.* **C**) the chemical element of ATOMIC NUMBER 6. Carbon is found in all living things, existing in a pure state in several different forms, including diamond and GRAPHITE: **+ noun** *Two hydrogen atoms are attached to each carbon atom by its remaining two bonds.* **2** used when referring to the gas carbon dioxide in terms of the effect it has on the earth's climate in causing CLIMATE CHANGE: **+ noun** *Tropical deforestation and forest degradation are major sources of carbon emissions.*

car·bon·ate /ˈkɑːbəneɪt; *NAmE* ˈkɑːrbənət/ *noun* (*chemistry*) a salt that contains carbon and OXYGEN together with another chemical: *Adding calcium carbonate to an acid lake should improve the quality of water by reducing its acidity.*

ˈcarbon cycle *noun* [U, C] the processes by which carbon is changed from one form to another within the environment, for example in plants and when wood or oil is burned: *Human activities have a significant impact on the global carbon cycle.*

ˌcarbon diˈoxide *noun* [U] (*symb.* **CO_2**) a gas breathed out by people and animals from the lungs or produced by burning carbon: *Water trickling through soil thus becomes enriched in carbon dioxide.* ◇ **+ noun** *Emissions from fossil fuel burning are virtually certain to drive the upward trend in atmospheric carbon dioxide levels.*

card /kɑːd; *NAmE* kɑːrd/ *noun* **1** a small piece of stiff paper or plastic with information on it, especially information about sb's identity: *Every citizen was issued with an identity card.* ◇ *The teacher gave each student a card with two pieces of information on it* **2** a small piece of plastic, especially one given by a bank or shop, used for buying things or obtaining money: *A much smaller proportion of Chinese customers used credit cards.* **3** (*computing*) a small device containing an electronic CIRCUIT that is part of a computer or added to it, enabling it to perform particular functions: *These differences have all but vanished with the introduction of high-speed graphics cards.*

car·diac /ˈkɑːdiæk; *NAmE* ˈkɑːrdiæk/ *adj.* [only before noun] (*medical*) connected with the heart or heart disease: *cardiac disease/failure/surgery* ◇ *Heart attacks, in some cases, may lead to cardiac arrest.* **HELP** If sb has a **cardiac arrest**, their heart suddenly stops temporarily or permanently.

car·dio·vas·cu·lar /ˌkɑːdiəʊˈvæskjələ(r); *NAmE* ˌkɑːrdioʊˈvæskjələr/ *adj.* (*medical*) connected with the heart and the BLOOD VESSELS: *The role of diet on cardiovascular risk is well established.* ◇ *cardiovascular disease/factors/events*

care¹ /keə(r); *NAmE* ker/ *noun* [U] **1** the process of caring for sb/sth and providing what they need for their health or protection: *Many women feel an obligation to undertake unpaid social care.* ◇ **~ of sb** *Women are usually those responsible for the care of children.* ◇ **~ for sb** *Rowles et al. (1996) addressed the issue of long-term care for the rural elderly population.* ➲ *see also* CHILDCARE, DAY CARE, HEALTH CARE, INTENSIVE CARE, PRIMARY CARE **2** attention or thought that you give to sth that you are doing so that you will do it well and avoid mistakes or damage: **with ~** *These figures need to be interpreted with care.* ◇ **take ~ to do sth** *The government has taken great care to protect freshwater supplies.* ◇ **take ~ that...** *Advertisers need to take care that they do not infringe a culture's aesthetic codes.*

IDM **in ˈcare** (*BrE*) (of children) living in an institution run by the local authority rather than with their parents: *The child and two siblings were placed in care and subsequently adopted.* **in the care of sb | in sb's care** being cared for by sb: *The boy was placed in the care of foster parents acting on behalf of the local authority.* **take care of sb/sth/yourself** **1** to care for sb/sth/yourself: *Leo has volunteered to take care of all four children.* **2** to be responsible for or to deal with a situation or task: *There are no simple technological fixes that can take care of the problem.* **under the care of sb** receiving medical care from sb: *He is thought to be safe to go back to university under the care of a community psychiatric nurse.*

▸ ADJECTIVE + CARE **medical • social • personal • parental • primary • secondary • palliative • post-operative • long-term • intensive • residential** *A good system of primary care is an essential component of an efficient and equitable health care system.* | **great • special • reasonable • proper** *The event would not have occurred if the defendant had exercised proper care and attention.*

▸ NOUN + CARE **health • nursing • community • emergency** *Nursing care should focus on vigilant monitoring of the patient's condition and on patient comfort.*

▸ VERB + CARE **provide, deliver, give • receive • access • require, need** *The nursing role in relation to patients with alcohol-related problems is to deliver care in a non-judgemental way.* | **take, exercise** *Care must be exercised when interpreting these data.*

care² /keə(r); *NAmE* ker/ *verb* (not used in the progressive tenses) **1** [I, T] to feel that sth is important and worth being concerned about: **~ about sth** *Consumers do not care about price increases as much as they did in the past.* ◇ **~ whether/what, etc.** *Predators do not care whether it is sunny or not.* **2** [I] **~ (about sb)** to like or love sb and be concerned about what happens to them: *Teachers show* *that they care about students by listening to them, trusting and respecting them.* **3** [T] **~ to do sth** to make the effort to do sth: *Once this idea took hold, historians found further evidence for it wherever they cared to look.* HELP To **not care to do sth** means to not do sth because you do not want to: *The company which owned the oil rig did not care to publicize the accident.*

PHR V ˈ**care for sb** to look after sb, for example because they are sick, very old or very young: *When parents grow old and can no longer care for their disabled son or daughter, special accommodation is required.*

car·eer /kəˈrɪə(r); *NAmE* kəˈrɪr/ *noun* **1** the period of time that you spend in your life working or doing a particular thing: *He began his academic career at Imperial College.* **2** the series of jobs that a person has in a particular area of work, usually involving more responsibility as time passes: **~ in sth** *She came to teaching from a brief career in journalism.* ◇ **~ as sth** *Marx had hoped for a career as a university professor.* ◇ **+ noun** *Approximately 25 per cent of senior technical staff have left the company for career advancement elsewhere.*

care·ful /ˈkeəfl; *NAmE* ˈkerfl/ *adj.* **1** giving a lot of attention to details: *Careful consideration should be given to how these resources will be obtained.* **2** [not before noun] giving attention or thought to what you are doing so that you avoid doing sth wrong or damaging sth: **~ to do sth** *Weber was careful to distinguish capitalism of the early modern centuries from capitalism of his own day.* ◇ **~ not to do sth** *When reducing costs, they must be careful not to reduce the quality of the product.* ◇ **~ about/with sth** *Some service providers are careful about how they make their services available globally through the Internet.* ◇ **~ that...** *The questions were pre-prepared but we were careful that they should naturally fit with the general flow of conversation.* ◇ **~ when/how, etc...** *Patients taking these drugs must be careful when out in the sun.*

care·ful·ly /ˈkeəfəli; *NAmE* ˈkerfəli/ *adv.* in a careful way: *It is important that nurses listen carefully to their clients.* ◇ *Their carefully designed project focused on managerial processes in three industries.*

care·giver /ˈkeəgɪvə(r); *NAmE* ˈkergɪvər/ *noun* (*NAmE*) = CARER

care·less /ˈkeələs; *NAmE* ˈkerləs/ *adj.* **1** not giving enough attention and thought to what you are doing, so that you make mistakes: **~ about sth** *The minister was revealed to have been careless about his financial dealings.* ◇ **~ in sth** *The authorities were found to have been careless and insensitive in their handling of the case.* OPP CAREFUL (2) **2** resulting from a lack of attention and thought: *The schoolwork produced by children with these disorders contains many careless errors.* ◇ *The defendant was liable for all the damage directly resulting from his careless behaviour.* **3 ~ of sth** not showing interest or effort SYN CASUAL (2): *The emperor seemed to his officers to be increasingly careless of the empire's real needs.* ■ **care·less·ly** *adv.*: *Police had handled the evidence carelessly.* ◇ *The terms religion and spirituality are often used inconsistently and carelessly.* **care·less·ness** *noun* [U] *There was no proof of carelessness by the defendant.*

carer /ˈkeərə(r); *NAmE* ˈkerər/ (*BrE*) (*NAmE* **care·giver**) *noun* a person who takes care of a sick, old or DISABLED person at home: *Assessments were conducted in the families' homes, where the primary carer—usually the mother—completed questionnaires.*

car·ing /ˈkeərɪŋ; *NAmE* ˈkerɪŋ/ *adj.* [usually before noun] **1** (*especially BrE*) connected with work that involves looking after other people: *Many young carers enjoy and are proud of their caring role.* ◇ *Women are disproportionately represented in the caring professions, such as nursing.* **2** kind, helpful and showing that you care about other people: *She had several very caring friends.* ◇ *The aim was to develop a learning environment that was welcoming and caring.*

car·rier /ˈkæriə(r)/ *noun* **1 ~ (of sth)** a person or an animal that passes a disease to other people or animals but does not suffer from it: *There is some evidence that carriers of Tay-Sachs disease have increased immunity to tuberculosis.* HELP A **carrier** may carry bacteria or a virus that can be passed to other people/animals; or they may possess a particular GENE that can result in a medical condition in their own children/young. **2** a company that carries goods or passengers from one place to another, especially by air: *In fact, as the main air carriers struggled, the cut-price airlines experienced a boom in travel.* **3** a substance that supports or carries another substance or PARTICLE: **~ for sth** *Ethanol functions as a carrier for the perfume oils.* ◇ **+ noun** *Argon is also an ideal carrier gas, a propellant with no propensity to react.* **4** (*biochemistry*) a MOLECULE that makes possible the transfer of a particular molecule or ION into or within a living ORGANISM: *Most of the water-soluble vitamins are transported across the small intestinal membrane by mechanisms mediated by a carrier.*

carry /ˈkæri/ *verb* (**car·ries, carry·ing, car·ried, car·ried**) **1** to support the weight of sb/sth and take them/it from place to place; to take sb/sth from one place to another: **~ sb/sth** *The birchbark canoe was able to carry heavy loads, and yet was light enough to be carried when necessary.* ◇ **~ sb/sth + adv./prep.** *Soil particles are carried away in the runoff water.* **2 ~ sth** to have sth with you and take it wherever you go: *They believed the message was clear: the way to stop crime was for citizens to carry weapons.* **3** to contain and direct the flow of water, electricity, etc: **~ sth** *Current is carried by free electrons travelling from source to drain.* ◇ **~ sth + adv./prep.** *They built an 8 000-mile pipeline system to carry the crude oil to the port.* **4 ~ sth** to contain sth such as information, a message or a signal and be able to pass it from one place, person, etc. to another: *Well after 1953, he opposed the notion that DNA actually carries genetic information.* ◇ *AM signals carry a message with their varying amplitude.* **5 ~ sth** if a person, an animal, etc. **carries** a disease, they are infected with it and might spread it to others although they might not become ill themselves: *Deaths from malaria, carried by mosquitoes, were only 6 per million population in England and Wales.* **6 ~ sth** to support the weight of sth: *Footbridges, highway bridges and railway bridges carry pedestrians, road traffic and trains.* **7 ~ sth** to have sth as a quality, feature or possible result: *The educated elite held high positions in government, and their opinions carried great weight.* ◇ *This offence carries a maximum sentence of 14 years' imprisonment.* **8 ~ sth** to accept responsibility for sth; to suffer the results of sth: *Her guardian believes that C is too young to carry the burden of decisions about her own future.* **9 ~ sth/sb + adv./prep.** to take sth/sb to a particular point or in a particular direction: *This hope appears to have carried many people through dark times.* ◇ *Policymakers became convinced of the need to carry the war to the North.* **10** [usually passive] to approve of sth by more people voting for it than against it: **be carried** *A Conservative motion of no confidence was carried by one vote.* **11 ~ sth** (of a newspaper or broadcast) to publish or broadcast a particular story: *It was reported on by a Toronto community paper and by Radio Canada International; no other media outlet carried the story.* IDM *see* DAY, MARK[2]

PHR V ˌ**carry sth ˈforward 1** to develop sth or cause it to progress: *This work has been carried forward by Coriat and Weinstein (2002).* **2** to cause sth to continue into a later period: *These inequalities had been carried forward from colonial times.* **3** (*also* ˌ**carry sth ˈover**) to move a total amount from one column, page or calculation to the next: *At each step a number x is carried forward from the previous working.* ˌ**carry sb/sth ˈoff** to take sb/sth away from the place where they belong by force: *Sidonius writes of a woman carried off by 'local bandits' (Epistles 6.4.1).* **ˌcarry ˈon** (*especially BrE*) to continue moving: *If we then carry on in the same direction for the same distance, we end up at an equivalent position.* **ˌcarry ˈon (with sth)** | **ˌcarry sth ˈon** to continue doing sth: *They carried on as before, hoping that the passage of time would solve their problems.* ◇ *Ministers were determined to carry on with this approach.* ◇ **~ doing sth** *People who genuinely could not work would carry on receiving the same level of benefits.* **ˌcarry sth ˈout 1** to do and complete a task: *We carry out a detailed analysis of these internal layers.* ◇ *Redundancy is when the genome has duplicate genes carrying out the same functions.* **2** to do sth that you have said you will do or have been asked to do: *They lacked the resources to carry out these plans.* ◇ *The threats could not be carried out.* **ˌcarry ˈover** to continue to exist in a different situation: *Certain cinematic values carry over from the silent to the sound film.* **ˌcarry sth ˈover 1** to keep sth from one situation and use it or deal with it in a different situation: *Typically, people carry over features from their first language into another language that they learn later in life.* **2** = CARRY STH FORWARD **ˌcarry sth ˈthrough** to continue with or complete sth successfully: *In Part II, we set out some ways to ensure these principles are carried through.*

THESAURUS

carry sth out • conduct • undertake • perform *verb*

These words all mean to do a task or an activity.

- to carry out/conduct/undertake/perform a/an **study/analysis/survey/experiment/test/activity**
- to carry out/conduct/undertake/perform **work**
- to carry out/perform a **role/duty/function**
- to carry out/conduct/undertake/perform sth **to assess/determine/identify** sth
- **typically/usually/regularly** carry out/conduct/undertake/perform sth

- **Carry out** places emphasis on work done over a period of time according to a plan; **undertake** often refers to the responsibility involved in completing a project; **perform** often emphasizes the skill involved in a task: *The actual engineering work was being carried out at the National Physical Laboratory.* ◇ *Traditionally, manufacturers were only able to undertake projects for companies wanting high volumes.* ◇ *Such transplantation procedures should only be performed in centres with the necessary expertise.*
- **Conduct** is often used with words like *interview, survey* and *focus group* in which people are trying to get answers to questions; it is also used with words like *investigation, assessment* and *evaluation* in which people are checking or testing sb/sth: *We conducted in-depth interviews with a sample of 42 men.* ◇ *The lab conducted environmental audits of its manufacturing plants.*
- **Carry out** and **perform** can be used to talk about a role or responsibility; **conduct** and **undertake** are used about a task or an activity: *The account manager has to perform several roles.* ◇ *They may even undertake practical tasks in the classroom like mixing paints.*

ˈcarrying caˌpacity *noun* [U, C] **~ (of sth)** (*ecology*) the maximum population of a species that an area can support continuously without environmental damage to the area: *Ecological critics would argue that there is still a fundamental tension between economic growth and the carrying capacity of the planet.* ◇ *Small islands with a small carrying capacity can only support small populations.*

car·tel /kɑːˈtel; *NAmE* kɑːrˈtel/ *noun* [C+sing./pl. v.] a group of separate companies that agree to increase profits by fixing prices and not competing with each other: *Any business found to be a member of a cartel can be fined up to 10 per cent of its UK turnover.*

cas·cade¹ /kæˈskeɪd/ *noun* **~ (of sth)** a series of stages in a process, each of which causes the next to happen: *Thus, even a few degrees of global warming could provoke a cascade of devastating climatic changes.*

cas·cade² /kæˈskeɪd/ *verb* **1** [I] to happen as part of a process, each stage of which causes the next: *Problems began to cascade during the New Orleans emergency.* ◇ **+ adv./prep.** *These toxic effects can cascade down the food chain.* **2** [T] **+ adv./prep.** (*formal*) to communicate information to a series of people or groups, each passing it on to the next: *The learning targets are cascaded from the education authority to schools, students and parents.* **3** [I] **+ adv./prep.** to flow downwards in large amounts: *Molten rock cascaded into the valley from the east.*

C

case /keɪs/ *noun* **1** [C] a particular situation or a situation of a particular type: **~ of sth** *Sachs sees the Asian financial crisis as a classic case of financial panic.* ◇ **in this ~** *In this case, any solution to the problem would require drastic reductions in carbon dioxide emissions in the rich countries.* ◇ **in some cases** *In some cases, Asian applicants were treated more favourably than those of African-Caribbean origin.* ◇ **in cases of sth** *A clause in the agreement allows patents to be set aside in cases of national emergency.* ➲ *see also* WORST-CASE **2 the case** [sing.] **~ (that...)** the true situation: *It is often the case that symptoms have been present for some time before the patient seeks medical advice.* **SYN** SITUATION **3** [C] a legal matter that is investigated by an authority such as the police or a court of law: *Recent cases investigated have highlighted illegal behaviour by many well-known companies.* ◇ *Each case brought before the court must be considered according to its special circumstances.* **4** [C, usually sing.] a set of facts or arguments that support one side in a discussion or trial: **~ for (doing) sth** *There is a case for suspension when a student's behaviour threatens the educational opportunity of others.* ◇ *A strong case can be made for ensuring universal access to this inexpensive treatment.* ◇ **~ against sth** *The case against such research appeals to several ethical arguments.* **5** [C] **~ (of sth)** the fact of sb having a disease or an injury; a person suffering from a disease or an injury: *Antibiotics are indicated for severe cases of salmonella.* ◇ *There are over 40 000 new cases of skin cancer annually in the UK.* **6** [C] (often in compounds) a container or covering used to protect or store things: *The machine's case was fitted with three small windows.*

IDM **as the case may be** used to say that one of two or more possibilities is true, but which one is true depends on the circumstances: *Parents or, as the case may be, legal guardians, have the primary responsibility for the upbringing of the child.* **a case in point** a clear example of the situation or problem that is being discussed: *Industrialization was less advanced or on a smaller scale in a number of countries. Australia is a case in point.* **in any case** whatever happens or may have happened: *Price is, in any case, a sensitive issue in international markets.* ◇ *None of these explanations has proved adequate, although each probably contains some truth. In any case, different archaeologists are trying to explain different things.*

▸ ADJECTIVE + CASE **special, exceptional • extreme • rare • particular, certain, specific • present • simple • interesting** *Seven special cases of interest are illustrated in Fig.16.* ◇ *In the present case, a more direct approach is possible.* | **individual • present • recent, earlier, previous** *The tribunal is not bound by decisions made in previous cases.*

▸ VERB + CASE **consider, take, discuss, examine • cite, mention • illustrate** *Section 3 discusses the particular case of election turnout.* ◇ *Menard (1991) cites the case of a study of adolescent drug use in the USA.* | **bring • hear • decide • refer • review • handle • win • lose • cite** *The Attorney General referred the case to the Court of Appeal.* | **make, present, argue • prove • strengthen • overstate** *In* *his philosophical work he argued the case for complete separation of Church and State.* ◇ *However, philosophers of science are in general agreement that Mill failed to prove his case.*

C

ˈcase law *noun* [U] law based on decisions made by judges in earlier cases: *The Commission's position stands on firm ground since it is based on previous case law.* ➲ *compare* COMMON LAW

ˈcase study *noun* **1** a detailed account of the development of a person, a group of people or a situation over a period of time: *The case study was undertaken over a period of two months through a series of visits to the school.* ◇ **~ of sb/sth** *The syndrome can be illustrated by a brief case study of a typical patient.* **2** an example of sth, usually provided in order to explain an idea or a theory: *Detailed case studies may provide an answer to this question.* ◇ **~ of sth** *Airline deregulation provides a case study of the effects of the internal market.*

cash /kæʃ/ *noun* [U] **1** money in the form of coins or notes: **in ~** *All workers were paid in cash.* ◇ **+ noun** *One important innovation has been direct cash payments to disabled people..* **2** (*rather informal*) money in any form: *In the early 1990s, these finance companies had plenty of cash and were simply looking for quick gains.*

ˈcash flow *noun* [C, U] the movement of money into and out of a business as goods are bought and sold: *Some of the conglomerates survived and grew by maintaining a positive cash flow, not by making a profit.* ◇ *Value ultimately depends upon the ability of the business to generate long-term sustainable cash flow.*

cast¹ /kɑːst; *NAmE* kæst/ *verb* (**cast**, **cast**) **1 ~ doubt (on/upon sb/sth)** to say, do or suggest sth that makes people doubt sth or think that sb is less honest or good: *However, some studies cast doubt on this explanation.* ◇ *Only extreme radicals such as Thomas Paine publicly cast doubt on the Bible's reliability.* ◇ *The financial crisis of the late 1990s cast some doubt on the country's economic stability.* **2 ~ a/your vote/ballot (for sb/sth)** to vote for sb/sth: *59% of electors cast their vote for the Labour Party candidate.* ◇ *In 1983 the United States cast the sole vote against a UN motion to restrict the trade in hazardous substances.* **3** to describe or present sb/sth/yourself in a particular way: **~ sb/sth/yourself (as sth)** *Socrates may be fairly cast as a champion of democratic values.* ◇ **~ sb/sth/yourself (in sth)** *Historians generally cast these events in colonialist terms.* ◇ *She often laughs at him when he attempts to cast himself in the role of her defender.* **4 ~ sth (over/on sth)** to make light or a shadow appear in a particular place: *Shadows of people walking past are cast on the walls of the cave.* **5 ~ an/your eye over/on sth** to examine and analyse sth: *Wharton (2012) casts a critical eye over recent attempts to reduce sexual discrimination.*

IDM **cast your net wide/widely** to consider a lot of different people, activities, possibilities, etc. when you are looking for sth: *In his search for data, Freeborg casts his net widely and includes a wide range of oral sources.* **cast a (long) ˈshadow (over sb/sth)** (of sth negative, such as a war) to have a negative effect that lasts a long time, especially by making people feel that sth is less good than they believed before: *Military rule ended in 1989 but its legacy continued to cast a long shadow over the country for decades.* **cast a ˈspell (on/over sb/sth)** to use words that are thought to be magic and have the power to change sb/sth; to have a powerful influence over sb/sth: *The portrayal of Sparta as an egalitarian society continues to cast a spell over historians and philosophers.* ➲ *more at* LIGHT¹

PHR V **ˌcast sth aˈside** to get rid of sth or stop thinking in a particular way because it is no longer useful **SYN** DISCARD: *The Liberal Democrats finally cast aside their doubts and formed a coalition with the Conservatives.* **ˌcast sth ˈoff** to get rid of sth because you no longer want or need it: *She argues that women took up physical training as a way of casting off Victorian restrictions on dress and behaviour.* **ˌcast sb/sth ˈout** (*literary*) to get rid of sb/sth, especially by using force: *Some healers claimed to be able to cast out or expel evil spirits from people.*

cast² /kɑːst; *NAmE* kæst/ *noun* **1** [C+sing./pl. v.] all the people who act in a play or film; all the characters who appear in a story: *The film had a very strong cast, with Jude Law in the lead role.* ◇ **~ of sb/sth** *Both novels are populated by a large cast of colourful characters.* **2** [sing.] **~ (of sth)** the way that a person or thing is or appears: *Those of a more authoritarian cast of mind wished to destroy the rebels.* **3** [C] a case that covers a broken bone and protects it: *The leg is immobilized by placing it in a cast.*

caste /kɑːst; *NAmE* kæst/ *noun* **1** [C] any of the four main divisions of Hindu society, originally those made according to functions in society: **+ noun** *In India, the caste system divided local rural society.* ◇ *These government policies have enraged high-caste Hindus.* **2** [C] a social class, especially one whose members do not allow others to join it: *The Norman Conquest fixed a division between a privileged ruling caste and the alienated mass of the population.* **3** [U] the system of dividing society into classes based on differences in family rank or wealth: *These women became involved in shaping the debates on gender and caste.*

cas·ual /ˈkæʒuəl/ *adj.* **1** [usually before noun] without paying attention to detail: *Even casual observation suggests that human behaviour is also controlled by informal rules.* ◇ *The elements of religion appear in Nuer culture in an almost hidden way, so that the casual observer could easily miss them.* **2** [usually before noun] not showing much care or thought: *These comments are more than just casual reminiscences.* ◇ *People in casual conversation may make ethical judgements that would not be considered valid by a philosopher.* **3** [usually before noun] (of a relationship) without deep affection: *Members of this group were more likely to have engaged in casual sex.* **HELP** **Casual sex** is sex with sb with whom you do not have a steady relationship. **4** [usually before noun] (*BrE*) (of work) not permanent; not regular: *The growth of flexible and casual work has affected not only the unskilled but also professional workers.* ◇ *casual workers/labour/jobs* **5** not formal: *Staff at the company had a reputation for casual dress.* ◇ *These features are much more frequent in formal speech than in everyday casual conversation.* **6** [only before noun] happening by chance; doing sth by chance: *a casual encounter/meeting* ◇ *HIV is not transmitted by casual contact such as shaking hands or sharing a fork.* ■ **cas·ual·ly** *adv.*: *Modernism in English historiography attacked what we now rather casually refer to as the 'whig' view of history.*

casu·alty /ˈkæʒuəlti/ *noun* (*pl.* **-ies**) **1** a person who is killed or injured in war or in an accident: *Modern warfare is characterized by increasing numbers of civilian casualties.* ◇ *The thickest ash layers fall close to the volcano and cause casualties.* **2 ~ (of sth)** a person who suffers or a thing that is destroyed when sth else takes place: *Gender equality was an unintended casualty of the restructuring process.* ◇ *Some believe the first casualty of war is truth.* ➲ *compare* VICTIM (2)

cata·logue (*NAmE also* **cata·log**) /ˈkætəlɒɡ; *NAmE* ˈkætəlɔːɡ; ˈkætəlɑːɡ/ *noun* a complete list of items, for example of all the books or resources in a library, or of items for sale: *Access to this catalogue can be obtained by going to the Data Archive home page.*

cata·lyse (*BrE*) (*NAmE* **cata·lyze**) /ˈkætəlaɪz/ *verb* **~ sth** to make a chemical reaction happen faster: *Enzymes are soluble proteins that catalyse biochemical reactions.*

ca·taly·sis /kəˈtæləsɪs/ *noun* [U] an increase in the rate of a chemical reaction that is caused by a substance called a catalyst: *The rate of catalysis is dependent on the pH.*

cata·lyst /ˈkætəlɪst/ *noun* **1** a substance that makes a chemical reaction happen faster without being changed itself: *This reaction will occur quickly only if the surface is hot enough and the proper catalyst is used.* **2 ~ (for sth)** a person or thing that causes a change: *Developments in the economic base act as a catalyst for the broader transformation of society as a whole.*

cata·lyt·ic /ˌkætəˈlɪtɪk/ *adj.* connected with the action of a catalyst: *The catalytic activity was strongly influenced by the structure of the catalyst and the reaction conditions.*

ca·tas·trophe /kəˈtæstrəfi/ *noun* **1** a sudden very serious event that causes great suffering for many people SYN DISASTER: *The threat of a global nuclear catastrophe has hung over the world for over half a century.* **2** an event that has a very bad effect on sb/sth or makes very serious difficulties: *Many believed that Johnson's re-election would be a catastrophe for the country.*

cata·stroph·ic /ˌkætəˈstrɒfɪk; *NAmE* ˌkætəˈstrɑːfɪk/ *adj.* **1** connected with a sudden very serious event that causes great suffering for many people: *Recent catastrophic events, such as Hurricane Katrina, highlight the critical role of the public health system.* ◇ **~ for sb/sth** *Of course, a nuclear war would be catastrophic for all mankind.* **2** having a very bad effect on sb/sth, or making very serious difficulties SYN DISASTROUS: *A fairly financed system would protect all individuals against catastrophic financial loss due to illness.* ◇ **~ for sb/sth** *A number of studies indicate how major illness can be catastrophic for household finances (Russell, 2004; McIntyre et al., 2006).* ■ **cata·stroph·ic·al·ly** /ˌkætəˈstrɒfɪkli; *NAmE* ˌkætəˈstrɑːfɪkli/ *adv.*: *Mount Pinatubo erupted catastrophically in 1991.*

catch[1] /kætʃ/ *verb* (**caught, caught** /kɔːt/) **1 ~ sb/sth** to capture a person or an animal that tries or would try to escape: *The workers catch fish by throwing nets out from the ship.* **2 ~ sth** to stop and hold a moving object, especially in your hands: *Each time the ball was thrown up in the air and caught, reaction times were measured.* **3** [often passive] to cause sb to be in a dificult and usually unexpected situation: **~ sb (+ adv./prep.)** *Arguably, the declarations of war in September 1939 caught Hitler by surprise.* ◇ *The Council was caught in a trap as a result of its own disorganization.* ◇ **be caught between A and B** *Front-line employees are caught between customer demands and management demands (Bowen and Schneider, 1985).* **4** to find or discover sb doing sth, especially sth wrong: **~ sb doing sth** *Several traders were caught breaking international rules.* ◇ **~ sb + adv./prep.** *Two junior managers were caught in the act of placing recording equipment in the meeting room.* **5 ~ sb's attention, imagination, etc.** if sth **catches** your attention, imagination, etc, you notice it and feel interested in it SYN CAPTURE[1] (1): *The growing presence of Chinese goods in world markets caught the attention of many observers.* ◇ *Scientific approaches to religion first caught the imagination of scholars in the nineteenth century.* **6 ~ sth** to show or describe sth accurately SYN CAPTURE[1] (2): *The procedure was filmed from six angles in order to catch every detail.* **7 ~ sight/a glimpse of sb/sth** to notice sb/sth, if only for a moment: *There is a pause when Ismene enters and the figures on the stage first catch sight of her.* ◇ (*figurative*) *He was arguably the first modern Muslim to catch a glimpse of the character of the age that was coming.* **8 ~ sth (from sb/sth)** to get an illness: *Stage three of the model represents people who have caught a disease but who are not yet infectious.* **9 ~ fire** to begin to burn: *In 1986 a warehouse at a chemical factory near Basel, Switzerland caught fire.* **10 ~ sth** to be in time for a bus, train, plane, etc. and get on it: *The patient got up early and rushed to catch the train to university.*

IDM **catch sb's/the ˈeye** to attract sb's attention: *Of course, advertising is designed to catch the eye.* ➲ *more at* SURPRISE[1]

PHR V **ˌcatch ˈon** to become popular or fashionable: *The idea of producing coins soon caught on in ancient Greece.* **be/get ˌcaught ˈup in sth** to become involved in sth, especially when you do not want to be: *Churches in tenth-century England were occasionally caught up in this political violence.* **ˌcatch ˈup (with sb)** to reach the same level or standard as sb who was better or more advanced: *The fact that India is catching up with the rich countries has little to do with international investment.*

catch[2] /kætʃ/ *noun* **1 ~ (of sth)** an act of catching sth: *Since 2004, ICES has recommended that there should be no commercial catch of Norwegian coastal cod north of 62°N.* **2** an amount of fish that are caught: *The global fish catch grew more than six times between 1950 and 1997.* ◇ **+ noun** *The total catch is estimated to have considerably exceeded the 2008 Scottish catch quota.*

cat·egor·ic·al /ˌkætəˈgɒrɪkl; *NAmE* ˌkætəˈgɔːrɪkl/ *adj.* [usually before noun] **1** expressed clearly and in a way that shows that you are very sure about what you are saying: *The report argues that it is not possible to give categorical answers to such ethical questions.* **2** connected with a category or categories: *An example of categorical data is the number of people who fall into only one of a small number of well-defined categories, such as being male or female.* ➲ *see also* CATEGORICAL VARIABLE ■ **cat·egor·ic·al·ly** /ˌkætəˈgɒrɪkli; *NAmE* ˌkætəˈgɔːrɪkli/ *adv.*: *The Court of Appeal categorically rejected these arguments.*

cateˌgorical ˈvariable (*also* **disˌcrete ˈvariable**) *noun* (*statistics*) a VARIABLE that can only be one of a limited number of items: *Comparisons of categorical variables (e.g. current smoking—yes or no; sex—male or female) between groups were performed.* ➲ *compare* CONTINUOUS VARIABLE

cat·egor·iza·tion (*BrE also* **-isa·tion**) AWL /ˌkætəgəraɪˈzeɪʃn; *NAmE* ˌkætəgərəˈzeɪʃn/ *noun* [U, C] the activity or action of putting sth into one or more categories: *The EU defies simple categorization.* ◇ *Table 26.2 uses the categorizations developed by Schneider and Guillen.*

cat·egor·ize (*BrE also* **-ise**) AWL /ˈkætəgəraɪz/ *verb* to put people or things into groups according to what type they are SYN CLASSIFY: **~ sb/sth** *Different people do not necessarily categorize things in the same way.* ◇ **~ sb/sth according to sth** *Countries are categorized according to their income.* ◇ **~ sb/sth as sth** *The majority of members of society can be categorized as opinion followers.* ◇ **~ sb/sth into sth** *This approach to personality categorizes people into different personality types.* ➲ language bank *at* RESEARCH[2]

cat·egory AWL /ˈkætəgəri; *NAmE* ˈkætəgɔːri/ *noun* (*pl.* **-ies**) a group of people or things with particular features in common SYN CLASS[1]: *These criticisms fall into three broad categories.* ◇ **~ of sb/sth** *Fault rocks are a texturally distinct category of rocks.*

▸ ADJECTIVE + CATEGORY **broad, general, basic • main, major • different • distinct, separate • certain, particular, specific • special** *There are many different categories of donor that a charity can target.*

▸ VERB + CATEGORY **identify, distinguish • define, specify • create** *The Town Planning Department identified three categories of residential property—good, medium and poor.*

cater /ˈkeɪtə(r)/ *verb* **1** [I] to provide the things that a particular person or situation needs or wants: **~ for sb/sth** *Many companies are becoming more customer-driven in catering for the needs of consumers.* ◇ **~ to sb/sth** *Attractions have been skilfully tailored and packaged to cater to Japanese taste.* **2** [I, T] to provide food and drinks for a social event: **~ for sb/sth** (*BrE*) *Women's groups were involved in decorating the sanctuary for festivals and*

C

catering for synagogue events. ◇ **~ sth** (*NAmE*) *They were involved in catering synagogue events.*

cath·ode /ˈkæθəʊd; *NAmE* ˈkæθoʊd/ *noun* (*technical*) the ELECTRODE in an electrical device where REDUCTION happens; the negative electrode in an ELECTROLYTIC cell and the positive electrode in a battery: *Hydrogen is formed at the cathode during the electrolysis of seawater.* ➲ *compare* ANODE

Cath·olic /ˈkæθlɪk/ *noun* = ROMAN CATHOLIC ■ **Cath·olic** *adj.* = ROMAN CATHOLIC **Cath·oli·cism** /kəˈθɒləsɪzəm; *NAmE* kəˈθɑːləsɪzəm/ *noun* [U] = ROMAN CATHOLICISM

cat·ion /ˈkætaɪən/ *noun* (*chemistry*) an ION with a positive electrical CHARGE: *When electricity is passed through copper sulfate solution, the copper cations gain electrons and form metallic copper.* ➲ *compare* ANION

caught *past tense, past part. of* CATCH[1]

causal /ˈkɔːzl/ *adj.* connected with the relationship between two things, where one causes the other to happen: *Research findings have established a causal link between smoking and lung cancer.* ◇ *DNA damage has drawn ample attention in the past because of its causal relationship with cancer.* ◇ *The great contribution of Darwin was to realize the causal mechanism for adaptive evolution.* ■ **caus·al·ly** /ˈkɔːzəli/ *adv.*: *The ensuing reaction was causally related to the prescription of penicillin.*

caus·al·ity /kɔːˈzæləti/ *noun* [U] **1** (*also* **caus·ation**) **~ (between A and B)** the relationship between sth that happens and the reason for it happening: *The assumption of causality between poverty and lack of education may be mistaken.* **2** the principle that nothing can happen without a cause: *Four distinctive preoccupations can be discerned in quantitative research: measurement, causality, generalization and replication.*

caus·ation /kɔːˈzeɪʃn/ *noun* [U] **1** the process of one event causing or producing another event: *The most common risk factors for cancer causation are tobacco use, dietary factors, infective causes and UV light.* ◇ **~ of sth** *Excess cholesterol is a risk factor in causation of heart attacks.* HELP In law, a **chain of causation** is a linked series of events leading from cause to effect, typically considered when examining a claim for DAMAGES: *There are circumstances in which the conduct of the victim may break the chain of causation.* **2** = CAUSALITY (1)

causa·tive /ˈkɔːzətɪv/ *adj.* acting as the cause of sth: *Smoking is a causative factor for lung cancer.*

cause[1] /kɔːz/ *verb* to make sth happen, especially sth bad or unpleasant: **~ sth** *If inhaled, the gas can cause damage to the lungs.* ◇ **~ sth for sb** *Personality disorder may cause difficulties for elderly patients and their families.* ◇ **~ sth to do sth** *High elevation of mountain ranges causes them to erode rapidly.* ◇ **~ sb sth** *He is reluctant to cough as this causes him considerable pain.* ➲ language bank *at* BECAUSE

▸ CAUSE + NOUN **damage, harm, injury • problems, difficulties • disruption • confusion • anxiety, concern • distress** *These processes cause significant engineering problems for roads, buildings and other structures.* | **disease, infection, illness, syndrome, disorder • cancer • death • pain** *There are several types of infection caused by fungi.* | **increase • reduction • change • delay • loss** *Invasive GM plants might cause changes in communities of other plants.*

▸ ADVERB + CAUSE **usually • often, frequently • commonly, generally • typically • rarely • directly • mainly, largely, primarily • partly • thus, thereby • probably • actually** *CO_2 and other greenhouse gases may trap the outgoing thermal radiation from the earth, thereby causing global warming.*

LANGUAGE BANK

Cause and effect

In academic writing, you often need to show a link between two or more actions or events, or link a cause X to an effect Y.

- X **causes/produces/leads to/brings about/results in** Y.
- Y **is caused by/is due to** X.
- X **has/exerts an influence on** Y.
- X **has an effect/impact on** Y.
- **As a result of** X,...
- **... because...**
- **... consequently/therefore...**

– *There is no scientific evidence that magnetic fields in that range* ***produce*** *harmful effects in humans.*
– *Higher levels of employment* ***bring about*** *higher rates of capacity utilization.*
– *Application of the points system has* ***resulted in*** *an increase in the number of qualified professionals.*
– *The majority of air pollutants* ***are caused by*** *industry or transport.*
– *Only about half of the permafrost warming* ***is due to*** *an increase in air temperature.*
– *The first of these factors* ***has*** *a powerful* ***influence on*** *the melting point of a polymer.*
– *Legislative protection can* ***have*** *a direct* ***effect on*** *health.*
– ***As a result of*** *these technologies, televisual viewing changed radically.*
– *Age at weaning is younger in humans than chimpanzees and the interbirth interval is* ***consequently*** *50% shorter (Kaplan et al., 2000; Hawkes and Paine, 2006).*

cause[2] /kɔːz/ *noun* **1** [C] **~ (of sth)** a person or thing that makes sth happen: *The western Allies failed to understand the underlying causes of Russian resentment.* ◇ *Malthus saw population growth as the primary cause of poverty.* ◇ *Tuberculosis was a major cause of death in Europe, and remains so in the developing world.* **2** [U] a reason for having particular feelings or behaving in a particular way: **~ for sth** *The scientific evidence shows there is no cause for alarm.* ◇ **without ~** *The symptoms can appear without apparent cause in some people.* **3** [C] an organization or idea that people support or fight for: *Orwell left for Spain to fight for the Republican cause.* ◇ *Governments want to encourage charitable causes to be more active in seeking donations.* ◇ **the ~ of sth** *These global forces sometimes use their power to further the cause of democracy.* IDM *see* COMMON[1]

▸ ADJECTIVE + CAUSE **major, main, principal, primary, prime • underlying, root • possible, potential • likely, probable • immediate • common • proximate • sole • physical • unknown • contributory • ultimate • multiple** *In reality, the root causes of such problems often lie much deeper.*

▸ VERB + CAUSE **identify, determine • understand • exclude • treat** *Clearly, additional studies are required to identify the exact cause of this problem.* | **tackle, address • investigate, examine** *The Japanese economy grew very suddenly, prompting many countries to examine the causes of Japan's success.* | **further, advance • champion, espouse, support • promote** *Orwell's '1984' described how new technologies would advance the cause of totalitarianism.*

cau·tion[1] /ˈkɔːʃn/ *noun* [U] **1** care that you take in order to avoid mistakes or danger: *Caution must be exercised when attempting to transfer sales methods from one culture to another.* ◇ **with ~** *These drugs should be used with caution in patients at risk of developing diabetes.* **2** a warning or a piece of advice about a possible danger or risk: **a note/word of ~** *Some have sounded a note of caution in connection with the practical application of this technique.*

cau·tion[2] /ˈkɔːʃn/ *verb* [I, T] to warn sb about the possible dangers or problems of sth: **~ (sb) against sth** *Other environmentalists caution against abandoning Enlightenment* *values (Hayward, 1995).* ◇ **~ (sb) that...** *The authors caution, however, that these conclusions are based on a relatively small number of studies.* ◇ **~ sb to do sth** *Whitty cautions us not to mistake rhetoric for reality.*

cau·tion·ary /ˈkɔːʃənəri; *NAmE* ˈkɔːʃəneri/ *adj.* giving advice or a warning: *However, Twidale and Bourne (1993) have sounded a cautionary note, arguing that these relationships are more complicated than they might seem.* ◇ *The French case offers a cautionary tale about the limits of industry influence.*

cau·tious /ˈkɔːʃəs/ *adj.* being careful about what you say or do, especially in order to avoid danger or mistakes; not taking any risks: *These results are cause for cautious optimism.* ◇ **~ about (doing) sth** *Although we are cautious about generalizing from our small scale study, our key findings do seem highly significant.* ■ **cau·tious·ly** *adv.*: *Philip's senior commanders urged the young king to proceed cautiously.* ◇ *Most interviewees were cautiously optimistic about their financial future.*

cave /keɪv/ *noun* a large hole in the side of a hill or under the ground: *The five longest and deepest caves are listed in Table 1.* ◇ **+ noun** *The landscape is underlain by extensive cave systems.*

cav·ity /ˈkævəti/ *noun* (*pl.* **-ies**) a hole or empty space inside a solid object: *This mineral may occur in voids or cavities in volcanic rocks.*

CD /ˌsiː ˈdiː/ (*also* **disc**) *noun* [C, U] the abbreviation for 'compact disc' (a small disc on which sound or data is recorded): *The cost of purchasing blank CDs in bulk was minimal.* ◇ **on ~** *Initially, the data were only available on CD.*

CD-ROM /ˌsiː diː ˈrɒm; *NAmE* ˈrɑːm/ *noun* [C, U] the abbreviation for 'compact disc read-only memory' (a CD on which large amounts of data, sound and pictures can be stored, for use on a computer): *The photographs were reissued as a CD-ROM by NASA.* ◇ **on ~** *The listings were sold on CD-ROM.*

cease AWL /siːs/ *verb* **1** [I] to stop happening or existing: *In Iceland, corn-growing decreased greatly not long after 1300 and ceased altogether in the sixteenth century.* ◇ **~ to do sth** *Unrestrained nineteenth-century capitalism, with its dreadful conditions for the working class, has largely ceased to exist in the West.* **2** [T] to stop doing sth: **~ sth** *Chronic use of cocaine can lead to psychiatric disorders when use is ceased.* ◇ **~ doing sth** *In 2008, the furniture retailer MFI ceased trading, with the loss of 1 400 jobs.* ➲ *see also* CESSATION

ceil·ing /ˈsiːlɪŋ/ *noun* **1** the top inside surface of a room: *The house had fallen into a state of disrepair, with peeling paint on the walls and ceilings.* **2** the highest limit or amount of sth: *A five per cent ceiling was imposed on wage increases in 1978.* ◇ *OPEC's role is not to prevent oil prices from rising above certain levels or to set a price ceiling.* ➲ *compare* FLOOR (6)

cele·brate /ˈselɪbreɪt/ *verb* **1** [I, T] to show that a day or an event is important by doing sth special on it: *After performing a sacrifice, the Trojans celebrated with a feast.* ◇ **~ sth** *Titus built a triumphal arch at Rome to celebrate his victory.* **2** [T] to praise sb/sth: **~ sb/sth** *Many early European epic poems celebrated some kind of military success.* ◇ **~ sb/sth as sth** *Alan Turing is celebrated as a genius, both for his mathematical work in 1936 and later for his codebreaking skill.* **3 ~ sth** [T] (*religion*) to perform a religious ceremony, especially the Christian COMMUNION service: *Bishop Wulfstan celebrated communion, preached and performed mass confirmations during journeys round his diocese.*

cele·brated /ˈselɪbreɪtɪd/ *adj.* famous for having good qualities: *Sean Wilentz is the celebrated author of numerous books on the nineteenth century.* ◇ *Cut into the stone are words from Winston Churchill's most celebrated wartime speech.*

cele·bra·tion /ˌselɪˈbreɪʃn/ *noun* **1** [C] a special event that people organize in order to celebrate sth: *Rewards may be distributed on special occasions such as during the Chinese New Year celebration.* **2** [U] the act of celebrating sth: *Rather than being a cause for celebration, this shortening of working life is seen as a major problem in many European societies.* ◇ **in ~ of sth** *Expensive gifts may be given in celebration of significant milestones, like high school or college graduation.* **3** [C, usually sing.] **~ of sb/sth** an act that shows how much you admire sb/sth: *Delinquency was seen by some as a rejection of middle-class values and a celebration of working-class values.*

ce·leb·rity /səˈlebrəti/ *noun* (*pl.* **-ies**) **1** [C] a famous person: *It was from that moment that Einstein became a celebrity.* **2** [U] the state of being famous SYN FAME: *It was only after his death that Aubrey achieved celebrity as a biographer.* ◇ **+ noun** *Celebrity is increasingly associated with a wide range of jobs—for example, celebrity chefs, celebrity historians and celebrity doctors.*

cell /sel/ *noun* **1** the smallest unit of living matter that can exist on its own. All plants and animals are made up of cells: *Plant and animal cells share many common internal features, but there are some crucial differences.* ◇ *Each time a cell divides, its DNA must be duplicated or the chromosomes must be replicated.* ◇ *blood/brain/liver/muscle cells* ➲ *see also* GERM CELL, STEM CELL **2** a device for producing an electric current, for example by the action of chemicals or light: *Extensive research is still taking place to improve the electrodes and electrolyte performance in fuel cells.* ◇ *Individual cells can be wired together to produce greater voltages or higher currents.* **3** each of the small sections that together form a larger structure, for example a HONEYCOMB: *The unit cell has the same dimension along all three crystallographic axes.* **4** one of the small squares in a SPREADSHEET computer program in which you enter a single item of data: *The test works by calculating for each cell in the table an expected frequency or value.* **5** a small group of people who work as part of a larger political organization, especially secretly: *These new technologies have enabled terrorist cells to mount coordinated attacks in different countries.* **6** a room for one or more prisoners in a prison or police station: *The dialogue is set in Socrates' prison cell.* **7** (*informal, especially NAmE*) = MOBILE PHONE

ˈcell phone /ˈselfəʊn; *NAmE* ˈselfoʊn/ (*also* **ˌcellular ˈphone**, *informal* **cell**) *noun* (*especially NAmE*) = MOBILE PHONE

cel·lu·lar /ˈseljələ(r)/ *adj.* [usually before noun] **1** connected with or consisting of the cells of plants or animals: *Blood plasma is blood with its cellular components removed.* **2** connected with a telephone system that works by radio instead of wires: *Japan provides a huge market for new products in high technology industries such as personal computers and cellular phones.* **3** connected with or consisting of small sections that together form a larger structure: *The machines are arranged in a cellular structure and the worker moves in a loop opposite to the flow of the work piece.*

cel·lu·lose /ˈseljuləʊs; *NAmE* ˈseljuloʊs/ *noun* [U] a natural substance that forms the cell walls of all plants and trees and is used in making plastics, paper, etc: **+ noun** *Such work has been done using cellulose fibres and silica as the substrates.*

Cel·sius /ˈselsiəs/ (*also* **centi·grade**) *adj.* (*abbr.* **C**) of or using a scale of temperature in which water freezes at 0° and boils at 100°: *The average temperature is 25.3 degrees Celsius.* ■ **Cel·sius** *noun* [U] *temperatures in Celsius and Fahrenheit*

C

cen·sus /ˈsensəs/ *noun* (*pl.* **cen·suses**) the process of officially counting sth, especially a country's population, and recording various facts: *Since 1801, the UK government has conducted a census every ten years of every household in the country.* ◇ **+ noun** *The 2000 census data show a ratio of 118 males to 100 females.*

cen·ter (*US*) ➲ CENTRE[1], CENTRE[2]

centi·grade /ˈsentɪgreɪd/ *adj.* = CELSIUS ■ **centi·grade** *noun* [U] *temperatures in centigrade and Fahrenheit*

centi·metre (*US* **centi·meter**) /ˈsentɪmiːtə(r)/ *noun* (*abbr.* **cm**) a unit for measuring length. There are 100 centimetres in a metre: *The individual is 180 centimetres tall.*

cen·tral /ˈsentrəl/ *adj.* **1** in the centre of an area or object: *Within central Europe, the most abundant species of toad is the common toad.* ◇ *A water molecule consists of a central oxygen atom, bonded to two hydrogen atoms.* **2** very important or essential: *The holiness of the body and its desires is a central theme of Blake's later work.* ◇ *National governments play a central role in the EU's policy process.* ◇ *Glutamic acid is an amino acid of central importance in metabolism.* ◇ **~ to sth** *As the Christian church became more central to Graeco-Roman society, its important buildings became more prominent.* ◇ **~ in sth** *Religion has always been central in human affairs.* ➲ thesaurus note *at* MAIN[1] **3** [only before noun] having power or control over other parts, countries or organizations: *The Onin War (1467–1478) brought an end to central government control in Japan.* ➲ *see also* CENTRAL NERVOUS SYSTEM

▸ CENTRAL + NOUN **district** • **location** • **point** *Retail shops were concentrated in the central business district.* | **role** • **theme** • **issue, concern, question** • **concept, idea** • **tenet** • **feature** • **part** • **place** • **focus** • **point** • **figure** *Global climate change is a central issue facing the world today.* ◇ *Some schools of social theory accord a more central place to political questions than others.* | **bank** • **government** • **authority** • **office** • **planning** *The threat of family vendetta was of vital importance in a society lacking a central political authority.*

▸ ADVERB + CENTRAL **absolutely** • **increasingly** *Greek religion is absolutely central to our understanding of Greek culture and society.*

ˌcentral ˈbank *noun* a national bank that does business with the government and other banks, and issues the country's coins and paper money: *As inflation comes down, the central bank steps in and cuts the interest rate.*

ˌcentral ˈgovernment *noun* [C, U] the government of a whole country rather than a region; the work that this government does: *The central government lays down the framework and minimum standards for services.* ◇ *Decision-making governance at the local level, however, requires the support and cooperation of central government.* ➲ *compare* LOCAL GOVERNMENT

cen·tral·ity /senˈtræləti/ *noun* [U] the fact of being very important or essential: *Customer centrality means that anticipating and satisfying customer needs can be a competitive advantage.* ◇ **~ of sth (in sth)** *The centrality of food in the family budget and the mother's responsibility for it were dominant features of working class life.* ◇ **~ of sth (to sth)** *The centrality of Alexander the Great to the study of imperialism and cultural transfer can scarcely be in doubt.*

cen·tral·ize (*BrE also* **-ise**) /ˈsentrəlaɪz/ *verb* to give the control of a country or an organization to a group of people in one particular place: *The conduct of war compelled governments to centralize power in order to mobilize the resources necessary for victory.* OPP DECENTRALIZE ■ **cen·tral·iza·tion, -isa·tion** /ˌsentrəlaɪˈzeɪʃn; *NAmE* ˌsentrələˈzeɪʃn/ *noun* [U] **~ (of sth)** *For many parts of Greece, the eighth century was a period of increasing political centralization.* OPP DECENTRALIZATION

cen·tral·ized (*BrE also* **-ised**) /ˈsentrəlaɪzd/ *adj.* done or controlled by one main organization or group of people: *Many people found change to a market-based system difficult to cope with after 40 years of centralized planning.* ◇ *A large shareholding body makes centralized management a necessity for the efficient conduct of its business.*

cen·tral·ly /ˈsentrəli/ *adv.* **1** in the centre of an area or object: *Later settlers favoured homes that had large rooms and a centrally located kitchen.* ◇ *First, the empty weighing container should be placed centrally on the pan.* **2** from one main place or by one main organization: *Efficiencies could be created if all of their separate activities were centrally coordinated.* ◇ *The Beveridge Report in 1942 recommended the establishment of a centrally organized and funded health service.* **3** mainly or in the most important part: *Marx and Durkheim were both centrally concerned with the emergence of modern capitalism.*

ˌcentral ˈnervous system *noun* the part of the system of NERVES in the body that consists of the brain and the SPINAL CORD: *Multiple sclerosis is a chronic disease of the central nervous system.* ➲ *see also* NERVOUS SYSTEM

centre[1] (*US* **cen·ter**) /ˈsentə(r)/ *noun* **1** [C] the middle point or part of sth: *It is now believed that most galaxies have a black hole at their centre.* ◇ **in the ~** *Many grains are thinner at their edges than in the centre.* ◇ **~ of sth** *The positive charge is concentrated at the very centre of the atom.* **2** [C] a place or an area where a lot of people live; a place where a lot of business or cultural activity takes place: *Eventually a large earthquake will strike in the heart of an urban centre and claim a million lives.* ◇ *Nairobi has long had a good reputation as an administrative centre.* ◇ *A properly sited landfill should not be located in the immediate vicinity of population centres.* ◇ **~ of sth** *The core area north of the Thames remained the centre of commerce.* **3** [C] a building or place used for a particular purpose or activity: *The use of overseas call centres is growing in the UK.* ◇ *After serving 12 years in a juvenile detention centre, she was released.* ➲ *see also* CALL CENTRE, HEALTH CENTRE **4** [C] a place that is important for a particular activity or where sth happens a lot: **~ of sth** *Birmingham was the centre of the gunmaking trade in Britain.* ◇ **~ for sth** *Poland can now be regarded as the centre for motor vehicle production in Eastern Europe.* **5** [sing.] the most important part of sth: **~ of sth** *The centre of her interest was the Holy Land.* ◇ **~ of attention** *These cells have been the centre of attention in recent studies.* ◇ **at the ~ of sth** *Bhutan is the only country in the world that puts happiness at the centre of government policy.* **6** [C] **~ of excellence** a place where a particular kind of work is done extremely well: *The Hadley Centre for Climate Change Prediction and Research is widely acknowledged to be among the world's leading centres of excellence.* **7 -centred** (in adjectives) having the thing mentioned as the most important feature: *Teaching methods are now proliferating far beyond simple distinctions between traditional and child-centred methods.* ◇ *These developments in geology were part of a larger shift away from a human-centred worldview.* **8** (*usually* **the centre**) [sing.] a MODERATE (= middle) political position or party, between the extremes of LEFT-WING and RIGHT-WING parties: *Under the new leader, the policies shifted to the centre.* ◇ *Voters tend not to have extreme ideological preferences and will align themselves near the centre.* IDM *see* FRONT[1]

▸ ADJECTIVE + CENTRE **regional** • **local** *Regional cancer centres serve a population of at least one million.* | **major** • **urban** • **metropolitan** • **cultural** • **industrial** • **administrative** • **financial** • **commercial** *At several major centres, including Athens, occupation continued without interruption.* ◇ *The city of Dubai is the trading and financial centre for much of the larger Middle East region.*

▸ NOUN + CENTRE **call** • **shopping** • **leisure** • **health** • **community** • **detention** • **research** • **distribution** *Firms want to establish efficient distribution centres with good links to other parts of Europe.*

▸ NOUN + -CENTRED **client, customer • patient • family • student • teacher • person, people • state • sun • earth** *Patient-centred medicine seeks an integrated understanding of the patient's world.*

centre[2] (*US* cen·ter) /ˈsentə(r)/ *verb* [often passive] **~ sth** to move sth so that it is in the centre of sth else: *Every element within the lens must be accurately centred.*
PHR V **ˈcentre around/on/round/upon sb/sth | ˈcentre sth around/on/round/upon sb/sth** to be or make sb/sth become the person or thing around which most activity takes place: *Much of the early competition between film and television centred around screen size and format.* ◇ *In Ukraine, industry is centred on coal but the region also has access to supplies of iron, manganese, salt and gas.* **be ˈcentred in...** [usually passive] to taken place mainly in or around a particular place: *Social and economic life at the end of the ninth century was centred in the local communities.* **be ˈcentred on/upon sth** to have a particular place or feature as the middle point: *The glacial mass appears to have been centred upon Saharan Africa.*

ˌcentre of ˈgravity *noun* (*US* **center of gravity**) (*pl.* **centres of gravity**, *US* **centers of gravity**) **1** the point in an object at which its weight is considered to act: *If a rod is hanging from a point a little above its centre of gravity it will be in stable equilibrium.* **2** the place where the most important developments in a particular situation or activity are happening: *There was much talk in the late 1980s of the centre of gravity of the world economy shifting from the US to Asia.*

ˌcentre ˈstage (*US* **ˌcenter ˈstage**) *noun* [U] an important position where sb/sth can easily get people's attention: *Education has taken centre stage in policymaking.* ■ **ˌcentre ˈstage** *adv.*: *It now seemed that concerns about child protection had, again, moved centre stage.*

cen·tri·fu·gal /ˌsentrɪˈfjuːgl; senˈtrɪfjəgl/ *adj.* (*technical*) moving or tending to move away from a centre: *Polar flattening is the result of a balance between gravity and the centrifugal effect of rotation.* OPP CENTRIPETAL

ˌcentriˌfugal ˈforce (*also* **cenˈtrifugal force**) *noun* (*physics*) a force that appears to cause an object travelling around a centre to fly away from the centre and off its CIRCULAR path: *The centrifugal force arising from rotation distorts the molecule.*

cen·tri·fuge[1] /ˈsentrɪfjuːdʒ/ *noun* a machine with a part that turns around very quickly to separate substances, for example liquids from solids, by forcing the heavier substance to the outer edge: *The digested material can be spun in a centrifuge, so that the cellular debris sinks to the bottom of the sample.*

cen·tri·fuge[2] /ˈsentrɪfjuːdʒ/ *verb* [usually passive] to use a centrifuge to make substances turn around very quickly so that the different parts separate by forcing the heavier substance to the outer edge: **be centrifuged** *After 1 hour, the tissue samples were centrifuged for 20 minutes at 20 000 g at 4°C.*

centri·pet·al /senˈtrɪpɪtl; ˌsentrɪˈpiːtl/ *adj.* (*technical*) moving or tending to move towards a centre: *The centrifuge creates centripetal force perpendicular to the rotation axis.* OPP CENTRIFUGAL

cen·tury /ˈsentʃəri/ *noun* (*pl.* **-ies**) **1** (*abbr.* **c, cent.**) any of the periods of 100 years before or after the birth of Christ: *The eighteenth century brought important changes in both western and eastern hemispheres.* ◇ **in the... ~** *In the US in the early 21st century, one child in six is growing up in poverty.* ◇ **during the ~** *The Spanish explored what is now Arizona during the 16th century.* ◇ **throughout the ~** *Two economies, England throughout the century and the Netherlands before 1650, did improve their agriculture.* ◇ **(not) until the... ~** *It was not until the mid-nineteenth century that the term came into common use.* ◇ **since the... ~** *Apart from a brief period (1649-60), England has had a monarchy since the 10th century.* **2** a period of 100 years: *The Hellenistic period spans the three centuries from the death of Alexander to the death of Cleopatra VII of Egypt.* ◇ **~ of sth** *The empire provided about two centuries of peace.* ◇ **~ ago** *Until half a century ago, the country was almost entirely cut off from the outside world.* ◇ **over the... ~** *Over the last five centuries, capitalism has traced a steady rise to dominance.* ➲ language bank *at* TIME[1]
IDM *see* TURN[2]

▸ ADJECTIVE + CENTURY **past • preceding, previous** *Over the past century, the economic importance of the government has grown dramatically.* | **early • mid • late • twentieth, nineteenth, eighteenth, etc. • mid-sixteenth, mid-tenth, etc.** *By the mid-seventeenth century, chocolate had become fashionable among the rich in Paris.*
▸ NOUN + CENTURY **half • quarter** *There has been a phenomenal growth of scientific knowledge over the last half century.*
▸ VERB + CENTURY **begin, enter • mark, characterize • dominate** *The growth of population that marked these centuries is significant.*
▸ CENTURY + VERB **witness, see** *The eighteenth century witnessed the birth of the Enlightenment.*
▸ CENTURY + ABBREVIATION **AD, CE • BC, BCE** *Aristotle lived in the fourth century BCE.*

CEO /ˌsiː iː ˈəʊ; *NAmE* ˌsiː iː ˈoʊ/ *abbr.* **chief executive officer** (the person with the highest rank in a business company): *Klaus Kleinfeld was the company's CEO from 2005 to mid-2007.*

cere·bral /ˈserəbrəl; *NAmE* səˈriːbrəl/ *adj.* connected with the brain: *Various factors affect cerebral blood flow.*

cere·monial /ˌserɪˈməʊniəl; *NAmE* ˌserɪˈmoʊniəl/ *adj.* connected with or used in a ceremony: *In a constitutional monarchy, the monarch plays a largely ceremonial role.* ◇ *The nomadic Turkmen people used woven textiles to make both practical and ceremonial artefacts.*

cere·mony /ˈserəməni; *NAmE* ˈserəmoʊni/ *noun* (*pl.* **-ies**) **1** [C] a public or religious occasion that includes a series of formal or traditional actions: *The official marriage ceremony is quite simple.* **2** [U] formal behaviour; traditional actions and words used on particular formal occasions: *Prizes were given out with due ceremony.* ◇ *More than 30 individuals, including women and children, were buried without apparent ceremony in a large pit.*

cer·tain[1] /ˈsɜːtn; *NAmE* ˈsɜːrtn/ *adj.* **1** that you can rely on to happen or be true: *In the wild, parapox means certain death for red squirrels.* ◇ **it is/seems ~ (that)...** *Although exact figures are rarely available, it is certain that the Church owned very high proportions of the land.* ◇ **it is ~ how, what etc...** *It is not certain how effective such measures would be.* ◇ **~ to do sth** *Emissions from fossil fuel burning are virtually certain to drive the upward trend in atmospheric carbon dioxide levels.* ◇ **~ of doing sth** *In these conditions, the person who sells most cheaply is certain of securing the greatest sales.* **2** [not before noun] firmly believing sth; having no doubts: **~ (that)...** *He could not be certain he made the right decision.* ◇ **~ of/about sth** *Sometimes customers are certain about what they want, but often they are not.* ◇ **~ what/where, etc...** *Wegener was not certain what drove the continents apart.* OPP UNCERTAIN (1) **3** [only before noun] used to mention a particular thing, person or group without giving any more details about it/them: *Certain groups of people are much more at risk than others.* ◇ *Forests can be severely damaged by unusual or sustained low temperatures during certain times of the year.* **4 a certain...** [only before noun] slight; that can be seen but is difficult to describe: *Thus, there will be a certain amount of change in genotype over time in a population.*

IDM **for ˈcertain** without doubt: *It is impossible to say for certain if earthquakes were responsible for destroying the Mississippian temples.* **make certain (that...)** to do sth in order to be sure that sth happens or is definitely true: *The courts make certain that laws and policies are consistent with the Constitution.* **to a certain extent** in some ways but not completely: *While this is clearly true to a certain extent, there are three important exceptions.*

▸ CERTAIN + NOUN **kind, type • category, class • group • aspect, characteristic, feature, property, trait • way, respects • circumstance, condition • situation • things • cases • area • point • limit • level • period • assumption** *Human survival is dependent on certain kinds of behaviour.* ◇ *Sometimes, tradition or religion may mean that people will dress in a certain way.* ◇ *Current begins to flow through the valve once the grid voltage reaches a certain level.*

▸ ADVERB + CERTAIN **virtually, almost • absolutely, quite • reasonably, fairly** *It is impossible to be absolutely certain that a finding based on a sample will also be found in the population.*

cer·tain² /ˈsɜːtn; *NAmE* ˈsɜːrtn/ *pron.* **certain of...** (*formal*) used for talking about some particular members of a group of people or things without giving their names or any more details about them: *Russia never had a real Renaissance, although certain of her rulers tried to impose one.* ◇ *Possible biases were dealt with by repeating the experiments with certain of the environmental conditions changed.*

cer·tain·ly /ˈsɜːtnli; *NAmE* ˈsɜːrtnli/ *adv.* without doubt SYN DEFINITELY (1): *He almost certainly had a rare bone disease as a result of his parents being first cousins.* ◇ *It is certainly true that very high interest rates discourage investment.* ◇ *Certainly, there is a lot of evidence that boys talk more in the classroom and get more attention from teachers than girls.*

▸ CERTAINLY + VERB **hope • seem • help • exist • contribute, play a part/role** *A demand for printed plays certainly existed.*

▸ CERTAINLY + ADJECTIVE **true • possible • important** *It is certainly important for the consumer to have a clear idea of what the product stands for.*

cer·tainty /ˈsɜːtnti; *NAmE* ˈsɜːrtnti/ *noun* (*pl.* **-ies**) **1** [U] the strong belief that sth is true: **with ... ~** *Archaeologists can say with a fair degree of certainty that people were living in this area 40 000 years ago.* ◇ **~ that...** *There can be no certainty that the trends identified from this data are likely to continue in the future.* ➲ *compare* CONVICTION (3) **2** [C] something that you know is completely true or reliable; an event that is definitely going to happen: *The communist party promised a return to the old certainties of punctual wages and pensions.* ◇ *A more federal European structure is a certainty in the long run.* **3** [U] the quality of being definitely true or reliable: *The Court has restored legal certainty after a period of incoherent case law.* ◇ **the ~ of sth** *These arguments are persuasive, but do not offer the certainty of mathematical proof.*

cer·tifi·cate *noun* /səˈtɪfɪkət; *NAmE* sərˈtɪfɪkət/ (*abbr.* **cert.**) **1** an official document that may be used to prove that the facts it states are true: *a birth/marriage/death certificate* ◇ *It is up to the GP to issue a medical certificate if appropriate.* **2** an official document proving that you have completed a course of study or passed an exam; a qualification obtained after a course of study or an exam: *All students in the class were working towards obtaining a language proficiency certificate.*

cer·tify /ˈsɜːtɪfaɪ; *NAmE* ˈsɜːrtɪfaɪ/ *verb* (**cer·ti·fies, cer·ti·fy·ing, cer·ti·fied, cer·ti·fied**) **1** to state officially, especially in writing, that sth is true: **~ (that)...** *The Secretary of State certified that the two men were suspected of international terrorist connections.* ◇ **~ sb/sth (as) sth** *The ship had been certified as seaworthy.* ◇ **certified + noun** *By that time there were 360 Fairtrade certified producer groups in 40 producer countries.* **2** [usually passive] **~ sb (as) + adj.** (*BrE, law*) to officially state that sb is mentally ill, so that they can be given medical treatment: *Many members of the opposition were imprisoned, exiled or certified insane.*

ces·sa·tion /seˈseɪʃn/ *noun* [U, C] (*formal*) the stopping of sth; a pause in sth: *The smoker may decide that the costs of smoking cessation outweigh the benefits.* ◇ **~ of sth** *They were repatriated only three years after the cessation of hostilities.*

cf. *abbr.* (in writing) compare: *Dennett's position here is similar to Quine's (cf. Chapter 4).* ◇ *Maintaining differences in culture is indeed an independent goal, cf. Article 128 of the Amsterdam Treaty.*

chain /tʃeɪn/ *noun* **1** [C] a series of connected things or people: *The products are sold through a supply chain.* ◇ **~ of sth/sb** *These islands form a chain of over 300 reef platforms.* ◇ *The offices are arranged in a clear hierarchy with unambiguous chains of command.* ➲ *see also* FOOD CHAIN, SUPPLY CHAIN **2** [C] a group of shops or hotels owned by the same company: *More high-tech supermarket chains use loyalty cards to track individuals' purchases.* ◇ **~ of sth** *The organization has a chain of hotels in Mediterranean destinations.* **3** [C, U] a series of connected metal rings, used for pulling or fastening things; a length of chain used for a particular purpose: *Chains were suspended across a nearby gorge.* ◇ *She wore enormous gold earrings and heavy gold chains around her neck.* IDM *see* LINK², WEAK

ˌchain reˈaction *noun* **1** (*chemistry, physics*) a chemical or nuclear change that forms products which themselves cause more changes and new products: *Nuclear reactors and nuclear weapons differ in their management of the nuclear chain reaction and the energy produced.* **2** a series of events, each of which causes the next: *Stock market fluctuations in the major industrialized countries set off a chain reaction throughout the industrialized world.*

chair¹ /tʃeə(r); *NAmE* tʃer/ *noun* **1** a piece of furniture for one person to sit on, with a back, a seat and four legs: *He realized he found it difficult getting out of a chair.* **2** [usually sing.] **~ (of sth)** the position of being in charge of a meeting or committee; the person who holds this position: *The Secretary of State has the power to appoint the chair and directors of the trusts.* ◇ *Although not chair of the audit committee, he is a member of it.* **3 ~ (of sth)** the position of being in charge of a department in a university: *He held the chair of moral philosophy at the University of Glasgow.*

chair² /tʃeə(r); *NAmE* tʃer/ *verb* **~ sth** to act as the chairperson of a meeting, discussion, etc: *The most important committees are chaired by the Prime Minister.* ◇ *One decision the teacher needs to make is who will chair the meeting.*

chair·man /ˈtʃeəmən; *NAmE* ˈtʃermən/, **chair·woman** /ˈtʃeəwʊmən; *NAmE* ˈtʃerwʊmən/ *noun* (*pl.* **-men** /-mən/, **-women** /-wɪmɪn/) **1 ~ (of sth)** the person in charge of a meeting, who tells people when they can speak, etc. SYN CHAIR¹ (2), CHAIRPERSON: *The chairman of the meeting should be impartial.* **2 ~ (of sth)** the person in charge of a committee, a company, etc: *After Stalin died, Malenkov became chairman of the Council of Ministers.*

chair·per·son /ˈtʃeəpɜːsn; *NAmE* ˈtʃerpɜːrsn/ *noun* (*pl.* **-per·sons**) the man or woman in charge of a meeting, who tells people when they can speak, etc. SYN CHAIR¹ (2), CHAIRMAN, CHAIRWOMAN

chal·lenge¹ AWL /ˈtʃælɪndʒ/ *noun* **1** [C, U] a new or difficult task or situation that tests sb's ability and skill: *Children with poor self-esteem are often quick to give up when* *facing a new challenge.* ◇ **~ for sb** *Some chronic diseases are a great challenge for vaccine developers.* ◇ **~ for sb to do sth** *The company issued a public challenge for hackers to attack its system in order to test its security.* ◇ **~ of sth** *It may take decades to change lifestyles in response to the challenge of climate change.* ◇ **~ of doing sth** *The challenges of running a successful business are enormous.* ◇ **~ to sb/sth** *The rapidly spreading virus posed a unique challenge to global health care systems.* **2** [C] a statement or an action that shows that sb refuses to accept sth and questions whether it is right, legal, etc: **~ to sth** *There are two main challenges to this theory.* ◇ **~ (from sb)** *In America, corporations are very vulnerable to legal challenges from consumers.* **3** [C] **~ to sth** something that is likely to cause trouble or danger to sb/sth SYN THREAT (3): *We become aroused and ready to respond when we think something is a challenge to our safety.* ◇ *The UN Secretary General created a panel to examine the major threats and challenges to global peace.* **4** [C] an attempt to defeat sb/sth in a competition or fight: **~ (of sb/sth)** *The company has maintained its top position, despite the challenges of newer rivals.* ◇ **~ to sb/sth** *Henry VII's main priority was to stifle any challenge to his position.*

IDM **rise to the challenge (of sth)** to be successful in dealing with a new or difficult task or situation: *Global marketers will only be successful if they rise to the challenge of understanding local cultures.*

▸ ADJECTIVE + CHALLENGE **major • serious • significant • formidable** *Enlargement was a major challenge for the new EU.* ◇ *Meeting the costs of oil demand presents a significant challenge to the global economy.* | **new • great, big • main • key • unique • real • future** *Perhaps the biggest challenge for researchers is to bridge the wide gulf between theory and practice.* | **environmental • economic • intellectual • political** *As with many environmental challenges, it is developing countries that bear the brunt of the problems.* | **direct • legal • political** *The king could not ignore so direct a challenge to his authority.*

▸ VERB + CHALLENGE **face • pose, present • meet, address • represent** *Significant work has been done to address these new challenges.* | **raise • offer** *One of the biggest challenges raised by Internet shopping is how to overcome the customers' perceptions of risk.* | **confront • overcome** *Successfully confronting this challenge will require a change in gender roles.* | **mount** *He lost the election in South Carolina and never again mounted a strong challenge to the front-runner.*

▸ CHALLENGE + VERB **face, confront** *Perhaps the greatest challenge facing Mexico City is that it is sinking at a rate of up to 38 cm a year.*

chal·lenge² AWL /ˈtʃælɪndʒ/ *verb* **1 ~ sth** to question whether sth is right, legal or true; to refuse to accept or believe sth: *The women campaigned to challenge social injustices.* ◇ *If the defendant pleads not guilty, he may challenge the prosecution case in one of three ways.* ◇ *The belief in some countries that obesity represents wealth and prosperity may need to be challenged.* ➲ *compare* DISPUTE² (1) **2 ~ sb/sth** to refuse to accept, or present a threat to, sb/sth's authority or position of power: *The percentage of students who consistently challenge authority is small.* ◇ *Hereditary rulers were challenged by the American and French Revolutions of the 18th century.* ◇ *The English never seriously challenged the Dutch in the spice trade, despite considerable effort.* **3 ~ sb** to invite sb to enter a competition or fight or to attempt to do sth new or difficult: *A weak successor will be challenged by rivals eager to replace him as head chief.* ◇ **~ sb to sth** *He challenged them to a singing contest.* ◇ **~ sb to do sth** *The film challenges the viewer to ask questions about reality.* **4 ~ sb** to test sb's ability and skills: *People need to feel that they are challenged by their work.* ◇ *The process of globalization has challenged national governments, as it makes them more interdependent.*

▸ CHALLENGE + NOUN **assumption • view • belief • idea, notion • decision • validity • legality • wisdom • status quo** *He wanted to challenge the assumption that quality and productivity are incompatible.* | **authority • order • dominance, hegemony** *The 1960s was an era in which authority and the existing order were increasingly challenged.*

▸ ADVERB + CHALLENGE **seriously • successfully • increasingly • directly** *The claimant successfully challenged the refusal to allow him a hearing.*

THESAURUS

challenge • question • dispute • doubt *verb*

These words all mean to have or express uncertainty about sth.

- to question/dispute/doubt **whether...**
- to dispute/doubt **that...**
- to challenge/question/dispute a/an **claim/view/idea**
- to challenge/question a/an **belief/assumption/approach**
- to challenge/question/doubt the **validity** of sth
- to question/doubt the **ability/existence/value** of sb/sth
- to **seriously** challenge/question/doubt sth

- **Challenge** and **dispute** are used when sb expresses uncertainty about sth quite strongly, especially publicly; **question** and **doubt** can be used to talk about an opinion expressed more tentatively or a feeling of uncertainty: *This approach is now increasingly challenged by competing theories.* ◇ *The impact of these measures was hotly disputed at the time.* ◇ *Researchers are beginning to doubt whether burnout is confined to the helping professions.*
- **Question** and **doubt** are used especially to express uncertainty about how good, important, effective, etc. sth is: *Dodd and Anderson (2001) question the effectiveness of government-sponsored enterprise initiatives.* ◇ *There are, however, reasons to doubt the adequacy of the existing framework.*

chal·len·ger AWL /ˈtʃælɪndʒə(r)/ *noun* a person, company, etc. that competes with another in business or politics for an important position that the other one already holds: *Currently, with no real challengers, the USA dominates the global economic scene.* ◇ *Candidates who already hold their seats usually attract more votes than challengers do.*

chal·len·ging AWL /ˈtʃælɪndʒɪŋ/ *adj.* difficult in an interesting way that tests your ability: *Managing the euro will continue to be a challenging task for the EU.* ◇ *About 16% of people with learning disabilities have challenging behaviour.* ◇ *The management of these symptoms can be very challenging.* ➲ thesaurus note *at* DIFFICULT

cham·ber /ˈtʃeɪmbə(r)/ *noun* **1** [C] a space inside the body, a plant, a machine, etc. which is separated from the rest: *Pacemakers can have electrodes that stimulate both chambers of the heart.* ◇ *Temperatures in the combustion chamber range from 1 000 to 1 400°C.* ◇ *When gas from the magma chamber has been exhausted, the lava erupts more quietly.* **2** [C] (in compounds) a room used for the particular purpose that is mentioned: *The walls of the burial chamber were decorated with paintings and inscriptions.* **3** [C] a large room in a public building that is used for formal meetings: *It was not unusual for a palace to have royal apartments alongside council chambers.* **4** [C+sing./pl. v.] one of the parts of a parliament; the people who belong to that part: *The Polish Sejm had an upper chamber, the senate, composed of the ecclesiastical, military and royal officials.* ◇ *Less than half the chamber exercised their right to vote.*

cham·pion¹ /ˈtʃæmpiən/ *noun* **1** a person, team, etc. that has won a competition, especially in a sport: *Simon and Newell predicted that within ten years, the world chess champion would be a computer.* **2** a person who fights for, or speaks in support of, a group of people or a belief: *Try to get the support of someone within the organization who will act as your champion.* ◇ **~ of sth** *He was a fierce champion of democracy.*

C

cham·pion² /ˈtʃæmpiən/ *verb* **~ sth** to fight for or speak in support of a group of people or a belief: *Wiessner's article robustly champions the cause of indigenous peoples.* ◇ *He championed the rights of the working class and the poor.*

chance /tʃɑːns; *NAmE* tʃæns/ *noun* **1** [C, U] a possibility of sth happening, especially sth that you want: *The damage to his reputation ruined his chances as a politician.* ◇ **~ of sth** *Another significant problem is that the use of several eggs increases the chances of multiple births.* ◇ **~ of doing sth** *Staying in groups lowers each individual animal's chance of being captured by a predator.* ◇ *Until the law changed in the 1960s, couples had very little chance of obtaining a divorce.* ◇ **~ of sth doing sth** *If there are more molecules present, the chances of them colliding must increase.* ◇ **~ that...** *The protocol aims to maximize the chances that a dispute can be resolved without resort to a full legal hearing.* **2** [C] a suitable time or situation when you have the opportunity to do sth: **~ to do sth** *The young males are regularly chased away by the dominant males and have few chances to mate.* ◇ **~ for sb/sth to do sth** *Every time DNA is copied, there is a chance for copy errors to occur.* ◇ **~ for sth** *The chance for a productive alliance between the two most powerful states in Greece was lost.* **3** [C, usually pl.] used to refer to the opportunities that sb has in their life: *It still seems that occupation, gender and race have a major impact on our life chances.* **4** [U] the way that some things happen without any cause that you can see or understand: *These similarities must be due to more than pure chance.* ◇ *Chance also plays a role in determining which of these mutations persist and which are lost.* ◇ **by ~** *Sometimes a disease dies out because, just by chance, its earliest victims happen not to pass the disease on to others.*

IDM **the chances ˈare (that)...** (*rather informal*) it is likely that...: *If a pedagogical tool is popular with the students, the chances are that it will also be beneficial for learning.* **stand a ˈchance (of doing sth)** to have the possibility of succeeding or achieving sth: *Surgery must take place within two months of birth to stand any chance of success.* **take a ˈchance (on sth/sb) | take (any) chances** to decide to do sth, knowing that it might be the wrong choice or a risk: *The bank was prepared to take a chance and lend him 40% of the purchase price.* ◇ *It was probably safe, but she was taking no chances.* ➲ *more at* EVEN²

change¹ /tʃeɪndʒ/ *noun* **1** [C, U] the act or process of sth becoming different; the result of this: *The changes associated with technological innovation demand different skills.* ◇ *Change has been very slow.* ◇ **~ in sth** *Longitudinal studies are more likely to detect changes in social interaction over time.* ◇ **~ of sth** *This sudden change of direction has not yet been explained.* ◇ **~ to sth** *The Act made radical changes to the way in which courts dealt with children.* ◇ **~ from sth** *This situation represents a significant change from the mid-twentieth century.* ➲ *compare* ADJUSTMENT, ALTERATION ➲ *see also* CLIMATE CHANGE **2** [C, U] the act or process of sth passing from one state or form into another; the result of this: **~ of sth** *When a substance undergoes a change of state, energy is involved.* ◇ **~ from A to B** *The change from grassland to shrubland over the last 150 years is an interesting example.* ◇ **~ to sth** *The company was keen to reduce its overheads and therefore made the change to a 'stockless warehouse' system.* ◇ **~ towards sth** *There has also been a change towards more cohabitation before marriage.* ➲ *compare* MOVE² (2) **3** [C, U] **~ (of sth)** the act or process of replacing sth with sth else: *There have been changes of government in the meantime.* ◇ *There is a huge literature on regime change.*

IDM **change(s) for the ˈbetter** improvement(s): *They believed that market forces would drive change for the better.* **a ˌchange of ˈheart** a new attitude towards sth: *Unless there is a radical change of heart by the Court of Justice, the previous requirements will apply.* ➲ *more at* WIND¹

▸ ADJECTIVE + CHANGE **rapid • abrupt, sudden • future • long-term • permanent • gradual** *The last twenty years have been a period of rapid technological change.* | **significant, important • major, substantial • dramatic, revolutionary • radical, fundamental, profound • drastic • global • small, minor • incremental • further • positive** *Fundamental changes have taken place in the labour market.* | **social • cultural • economic • political • historical • constitutional • demographic • structural • strategic • organizational, institutional • technological, technical** *The economy had undergone a major structural change.* | **evolutionary • environmental • climatic • genetic • behavioural • chemical** *These environmental changes had economic implications.*

▸ NOUN + CHANGE **colour • temperature • energy • price • population • policy • regime** *This lack of colour change indicates a positive reaction.*

▸ VERB + CHANGE **make • cause, bring, produce • bring about, induce, effect • promote, facilitate • drive • initiate • achieve • manage • force ~ (upon/on sb/sth)** *Sometimes the repair process causes a permanent change to the DNA sequence.* ◇ *These attempts to induce cultural change were largely unsuccessful.* | **undergo, experience • resist, oppose • predict, anticipate • involve, entail • be caused by • see, observe, witness • reflect, represent, mark • explain • understand** *The meatpacking industry was undergoing structural change.* ◇ *All the key steps in development reflect changes in gene activity.* | **show, indicate, reveal • detect, identify, notice • be characterized by** *The glacial period was characterized by significant changes in average temperature.* | **monitor, track • examine, study • analyse • measure • calculate** *The researcher is well placed to monitor changes over time.*

▸ CHANGE + VERB **occur, happen, take place • affect** *A dramatic change occurred late in the eighteenth century.* | **result from • result in, lead to** *Changes may also result from neurological disorders.*

change² /tʃeɪndʒ/ *verb* **1** [T] **~ sth** to make sth different SYN ALTER (1): *Technology is changing the way children learn.* ◇ *Difficulties arise when research participants change their behaviour because they know they are being studied.* ◇ *The operating speed of the engine can be changed by altering the air/fuel ratio.* **2** [I] to become different SYN ALTER (1): *The political balance has changed substantially.* ◇ *And, of course, the existing technologies are constantly changing.* **3** [T] to make sth pass from one state or form into another SYN CONVERT¹ (1): **~ A to/into B** *The hydrogen and the oxygen molecules are changed to water molecules.* ◇ *Glacial erosion may change V-shaped fluvial valleys into U-shaped glacial valleys.* ◇ **~ sth from A to/into B** *There had been severe restrictions on the amount of currency that could be changed from roubles to other currencies.* **4** [I] to pass from one state or form into another: **~ from A to B** *The solution changed from a deep brown colour to clear.* ◇ **~ to sth** *After 1953, the agenda changed to the study of DNA.* ➲ *compare* BECOME (1), TURN¹ (7) **5** [T] **~ sth** to start having a different colour, form or direction: *Non-specific binding may also cause the crystal to change colour.* ◇ *Unless we change course now, these people will be left in a world where energy is a scarce resource.* **6** [T, I] to replace sth with sth else: **~ sth (to sth)** *We changed the name of the zoo to ZSL in order to reflect the conservation work of the Zoological Society of London.* ◇ **~ to sth** *There is no doubt that changing to new, simpler architectures made many more developments possible.* ➲ *see also* UNCHANGING

IDM **change ˈhands** to pass to a different owner: *Nuclear assets could change hands, for example because of a coup.* **change your/sb's ˈmind** to change a decision or an opinion: *Mr Lipman then changed his mind and did not want to complete the sale.*

PHR V **ˌchange ˈback (into/to sth)** to return to a previous state or form: *The diamonds have changed back to the low-temperature form of carbon, which is graphite.* **ˌchange sth ˈback (into/to sth)** to make sth return to a previous state or form: *The court ordered that the contract be changed back to the previous draft.*

▸ CHANGE + NOUN **the way... • the course of sth • the situation • the conditions • the world, the landscape • the nature of sth, the character of sth, the face of sth • the meaning of sth** *E-commerce has changed the way in which business can be done and has opened up whole new markets.* ◇ *The demise of state socialism changed the nature of geographic research in this region.* | **behaviour, practices • mind • attitude, position • view, perception • focus** *It can be very difficult to change cultural attitudes within an organization.* | **shape • structure • composition • pattern • the parameters • the rules • the law • policy • value • price** *Normally, the lens changes its shape to help the eye focus.* | **shape • colour • position • course, direction • state • sex** *The researcher can change direction in the course of his or her investigation much more easily than in quantitative research.*

▸ NOUN + CHANGE **things, the situation, circumstances, the picture • conditions, the climate • the environment • technology • attitudes** *Things have changed, but history has left its legacy.* ◇ *Societal conditions have changed in a fundamental way over the last two decades.*

▸ CHANGING + NOUN **nature of sth, character of sth, pattern • conditions, circumstances, situation • context • environment • world • landscape • climate • pattern • role • needs • attitudes** *Bacteria live in continually changing environments to which they must adapt for survival.*

▸ ADVERB + CHANGE **significantly, substantially • completely • fundamentally • slightly, subtly • hardly • never • rapidly • undoubtedly, certainly, inevitably** *The Asian crisis has significantly changed the business environment in the region.* ◇ *Rapidly changing family roles make social support less readily available than in the past.* | **dramatically, drastically • radically, profoundly • permanently • thus, thereby** *It is also possible to exchange the magnetic ions, thus changing the magnetic properties without modifying the structure.* | **suddenly • slowly, gradually • constantly, continually, continuously** *Lifestyles are constantly changing and consumers are constantly shifting their preferences over time.*

▸ CHANGE + ADVERB **dramatically, drastically • radically, fundamentally • significantly, considerably, markedly, greatly, substantially, appreciably • completely • rapidly, quickly, fast • abruptly • slowly, gradually • frequently • constantly, continuously • forever • accordingly** *All this would change dramatically with the advent of industrialization.* ◇ *Economic policy in Britain has changed considerably since the 19th century, yet a number of themes remain constant.*

chan·nel[1] AWL /ˈtʃænl/ *noun* **1** [usually pl.] a way of sending and receiving information or goods: *The Internet is reshaping distribution channels.* ◇ **~ of sth** *It is important to keep channels of communication open.* ◇ **~ for sth** *Different people have different views and need channels for the exchange of ideas.* ◇ **through ... ~** *The issue had been discussed first through diplomatic channels.* **2** a way of achieving sth: **through a/the ~** *These people cannot afford to buy houses through the usual channels.* ◇ **~ for sth** *Grammar schools opened up new channels for social mobility.* **3** a passage along which water flows: *In arid zones, river channels may be common, but water flows only rarely.* ◇ *Erosion may widen the channel.* ◇ *The floodwater is managed using drainage channels and sluices.* **4** [usually sing.] a passage of water that connects two areas of water, especially two seas: *Depending on tidal conditions, this channel can be of varying depth.* HELP **The Channel** or **The English Channel** is the sea between England and France: *The Channel Tunnel between France and England cost £5 billion to construct.* **5** a television station: *Today there are hundreds of television channels.* **6** a band of radio waves used for sending signals: *Several signals are transmitted simultaneously on the same channel.* **7** a path for a current or signal: *The voltage at every point along the channel is zero.*

C

chan·nel[2] AWL /ˈtʃænl/ *verb* (-ll-, *US* -l-) **1** to send money, information or other resources to a particular place or using a particular route: **~ sth into/to sth** *The banks then channelled funds into speculative investments.* ◇ *The findings are already being channelled to country managers.* ◇ **~ sth through sth** *Much of the EU's development aid is channelled through the European Development Fund.* **2** to use thoughts, feelings and attitudes for a particular purpose or in a particular way: **~ sth** *This initiative was seen as a way of channelling conflict constructively.* ◇ **~ sth into sth** *Energies were channelled into a cross-party campaign for devolution.* ◇ **~ sth towards sth** *Much of their energy is channelled towards trying to maintain positive self-esteem.* ➲ *compare* HARNESS (1) **3 ~ sth (+ adv./prep.)** to carry water, a current, etc. in a particular direction: *Drainage is channelled away from potential source areas.* ◇ *These components channel the electrically charged ions to create the rhythmic activity.*

chaos /ˈkeɪɒs; *NAmE* ˈkeɪɑːs/ *noun* [U] a state of complete confusion and lack of order: *The change created so much chaos that the benefits were never realized.* ◇ *As Europe descended into chaos in the 1930s and 1940s, social theory found a flourishing home in the US.* HELP In physics, **chaos** is the property of a complex system whose behaviour is so UNPREDICTABLE that it appears RANDOM, especially because small changes in conditions can have very large effects. **Chaos theory** is the branch of mathematics that deals with these complex systems: *The study of chaos and complexity has become a subculture within science.*

cha·ot·ic /keɪˈɒtɪk; *NAmE* keɪˈɑːtɪk/ *adj.* **1** in a state of complete confusion and lack of order: *The collapse of communism in the Soviet Union had produced a somewhat chaotic situation.* **2** (*physics*) connected with systems that show chaos: *Chaotic systems are extremely sensitive to small variations in some of their parameters.*

chap·ter AWL /ˈtʃæptə(r)/ *noun* **1** (*abbr.* **chap.**) a separate section of a book, usually with a number or title: *The following five chapters will provide a more detailed analysis of the factors that influence health status.* ◇ *Chapter 4 focuses on Mahayana Buddhism.* ◇ **~ on sth** *Four themes provide the organizational framework for this chapter on Dickens.* **2** a period of time in history or a person's life: **~ in sth** *The reign of Edward I opened a new chapter in the history of the British Isles.* ◇ **~ of sth** *The collapse of the USSR ended that chapter of human history.*

▸ ADJECTIVE + CHAPTER **opening, introductory • early • late • concluding, closing, final** *In this opening chapter I will sketch the major developments to be discussed.* | **previous • present • following, subsequent • first, second, third, etc.** *As outlined in the previous chapter, the significance of these developments may not have been apparent at the time.*

▸ VERB + CHAPTER **read • write • begin, start • conclude, end** *The fifth section concludes the chapter by making remarks on future research agendas.*

▸ CHAPTER + VERB **focus on, be devoted to, concentrate on • discuss, consider, address, deal with, examine, explore, cover • outline • argue • conclude** *The next three chapters are devoted to the behaviour of electrons in atoms.*

char·ac·ter /ˈkærəktə(r)/ *noun* **1** [C, usually sing., U] the way that sth/sb is; one or more qualities or features that cause sth/sb to be a particular way SYN NATURE (3): *The seasonal cycle gives this area its distinctive character.* ◇ **the ~ of sth** *Lenin argued that the character of capitalism had changed.* ◇ **the… ~ of sth** *The government emphasized the strictly humanitarian character of the operation.* ◇ **… in ~** *These data sets are clearly very different in character.* ◇ *River flow may become more uniform in character.* ◇ **of (a)… ~** *The results are mainly of a negative character.* **2** [U] (*approving*) strong personal qualities such as the ability to deal with difficult situations: *Gergen (2001) argued that character, vision and political capacity are three essential traits for leadership.* ◇ *Her fragile appearance belied her formidable strength of character.* **3** [C, U] the opinion that people have of you, particularly of whether you can be trusted or relied on SYN REPUTATION: *The play constitutes a frontal attack on Shaftesbury's character and the motives of his party.* ◇ **of… ~** *They were chosen from men of good character.* **4** [C] a person or an animal in a story, play or film: *These outsiders are the central characters in his novels.* **5** [C] a letter, sign, mark or symbol used in writing, printing or computers: *A maximum number of characters can be specified.* ◇ *They transmit data as ASCII characters.* **6** [C] (*biology*) a characteristic, especially one that helps you identify a species: *The females chose mates that possessed these characters.* ◇ *In some species, males show obvious secondary sexual characters.*

IDM ˌ**out of** ˈ**character** not typical of a person's character: *I do not think the action was wholly out of character.*

▸ ADJECTIVE + CHARACTER **different • distinctive • unique • moral** *Each segment has its own unique character.* ◇ *A person might have great moral character yet never really do anything of great significance.* | **fictional • central, principal, main • minor • male • female** *When we read a novel, we typically take the perspective of the principal character.*

▸ VERB + CHARACTER **reflect • emphasize • shape • give sth/sb ~ • alter, change • possess, have • acquire • retain • lose** *The voluntary sector has to be capable of retaining its distinctive character.*

char·ac·ter·is·tic¹ /ˌkærəktəˈrɪstɪk/ *noun* **~ (of sth/sb)** a typical feature or quality that sth/sb has: *A key characteristic of the American political system is its dominance by the two major parties.* ◇ *He agrees that multinationals display the characteristics of their economy of origin.* ◇ *Characteristics associated with pre-term birth include multiple pregnancy and smoking.* ➲ thesaurus note *at* FEATURE¹

▸ ADJECTIVE + CHARACTERISTIC **distinctive, defining, distinguishing • unique • individual • certain, specific, particular • key, main, principal • important • essential • common** *Alpine regions have their own distinctive characteristics.* | **demographic • cultural • personal • behavioural • sexual • physical • structural • chemical** *The tests were designed to assess the personal characteristics of applicants.*

▸ VERB + CHARACTERISTICS **exhibit, display, show • possess, have • share • acquire • retain** *We are developing carbon-based materials that exhibit these characteristics.* ◇ *These hormones share common characteristics.* | **identify • determine • describe • examine • assess • study** *Childe (1951) identified 10 characteristics of civilization.*

char·ac·ter·is·tic² /ˌkærəktəˈrɪstɪk/ *adj.* very typical of sth/sb: *These winds are a characteristic feature of the Antarctic interior.* ◇ *The top mineral layer has a characteristic grey ashy appearance.* ◇ **~ of sth/sb** *This method is characteristic of modern mathematics.* ■ **char·ac·ter·is·tic·al·ly** /ˌkærəktəˈrɪstɪkli/ *adv.*: *The soil is characteristically shallow and easily eroded.*

char·ac·ter·iza·tion (*BrE also* **-isa·tion**) /ˌkærəktəraɪˈzeɪʃn; *NAmE* ˌkærəktərəˈzeɪʃn/ *noun* [U, C] **1 ~ (of sth)** the process of discovering or describing the qualities or features of sth; the result of this process: *Further characterization of the polymer is in progress.* ◇ *Such characterizations are quite simply not accurate.* ➲ *compare* CATEGORIZATION **2** the way in which the characters in a story, play or film are made to seem real: *It is a tale told with a comic sensibility and witty characterization.* ➲ *compare* PORTRAYAL

char·ac·ter·ize (*BrE also* **-ise**) /ˈkærəktəraɪz/ *verb* **1** [usually passive] **~ sth** to be the most typical or most obvious quality or feature of sth SYN TYPIFY (2): *The economy was characterized by high wages and high unemployment.* ◇ *Tourette's syndrome is a neurological disorder characterized by repetitive and involuntary tics.* **2** [usually passive] **~ sth** to be the feature or quality that makes sth different from similar things SYN DISTINGUISH (2): *Each chemical element is characterized by its number of protons.* **3** [often passive] **~ sb/sth (as sth)** to describe sth/sb in a particular way: *The people were typically characterized as passive and effeminate.* ◇ *Freud characterized unconscious mental activity as 'primary process thinking'.*

▸ NOUN+ (BE) CHARACTERIZED BY **disorder, syndrome, condition, disease • environment • landscape • economy • industry • society** *The disease is characterized by increased numbers of plasma cells in the bone marrow.* ◇ *The US and UK are most competitive in industries characterized by science-based innovative activities.*

▸ BE CHARACTERIZED BY + NOUN **the presence of • the onset of • a lack of • a… degree of** *Corporate ownership in Chile is characterized by a high degree of ownership concentration.*

▸ BE + ADVERB + CHARACTERIZED **generally • typically • usually, normally • often, frequently • increasingly** *The higher education sector is too often characterized by conservatism.*

charge¹ /tʃɑːdʒ; *NAmE* tʃɑːrdʒ/ *noun* **1** [C, U] **~ (for sth)** the amount of money that sb asks for goods and services: *The company is currently considering introducing charges for all of its websites.* ◇ *The most prominent green tax in the UK is the congestion charge levied on vehicles entering central London.* ◇ *People with diabetes are also exempt from prescription charges.* ◇ *In the US local telephone calls are generally free of charge.* **2** [C, U] an official claim made by the police that sb has committed a crime: *At trial, the judge dismissed the charge.* ◇ *He was acquitted of the theft charge but convicted of the assault charges.* ◇ *She was released without charge.* ◇ **~ of sth** *The vice-president and several others were arrested on charges of treason.* ◇ **~ of doing sth** *He faced charges of kidnapping, torturing and killing political opponents.* **3** [C] a statement accusing sb of doing sth wrong or bad SYN ALLEGATION: *Voyeurism is a charge often levelled against reality television.* ◇ **~ that…** *Labour law is open to the charge that it is confusing and costly for employers to apply.* **4** [C, U] the amount of electricity that is put into a battery or carried by a substance: *Since the ions carry a charge, they may be accelerated and focused into a beam by an electric field.* ◇ *It is this field that controls the amount of charge in the channel.* ◇ **a positive/negative ~** *As the electron leaves its parent atom, it leaves behind a net positive charge.* **5** [U] responsibility for the care or control of sb/sth: **~ (of sb/sth)** *They are eager to take charge of their own lives.* ◇ **in ~ of (doing) sth** *In Nicholas's many absences, Alexander was left in charge of routine state affairs.* ◇ *Life at home after the war was, in effect, no different, with women still in charge of running the home.* **6** [C] (*formal*) a person that you have responsibility for and care for: *The relationship between nurses and their charges could develop as the child grew.* **7** [C] a sudden attack where sb/sth runs straight at sb/sth else: *He disrupted the front line with a cavalry charge from the right.*

IDM **bring/press** ˈ**charges (against sb)** (*law*) to accuse sb formally of a crime so that there can be a trial in court: *Charges were brought under Section 3 of the 1990 Act.*

charge² /tʃɑːdʒ; *NAmE* tʃɑːrdʒ/ *verb* **1** [T, I] to ask an amount of money for goods or a service: *The company is charging lower prices in order to gain market share.* ◇ **~ sth for sth** *A higher rate is charged for telephone calls during the daytime.* ◇ **~ sb for sth** *There is a growing pressure to charge farmers for water used for irrigation.* ◇ **~ sb sth (for sth)** *Chinese property developers are able to charge buyers a premium for a flat on the eighth floor.* ◇ **~ for sth** *They have started charging for previously free services.* ◇ **~ sth to sb/sth** *The majority of BAA's income is derived from charging landing fees to airlines.* **2** [T] to accuse sb formally of a crime so that there can be a trial in court: **~ sb** *Although the president was not formally charged, he was indicted as an accomplice.* ◇ **~ sb with (doing) sth** *Reginald was charged with her murder.* ◇ *They were both charged with assaulting an officer in the execution of his duty.* **3** [T, usually passive] to give sb a responsibility or task: **be charged with sth** *The NGO is charged with the task of identifying and cleaning contaminated water sources.* ◇ **be charged with doing sth** *Overseers were charged with disciplining the field workers.* **4** [T] **~ sth (up)** to pass electricity through sth so that it is stored there: *It takes 16 hours to charge the batteries from a 13-amp electricity supply.*

cha·risma /kəˈrɪzmə/ *noun* [U] the powerful personal quality that some people have to attract and impress other people: *First, leaders must possess charisma and engender trust and respect.*

cha·ris·mat·ic /ˌkærɪzˈmætɪk/ *adj.* having charisma: *Ali was a charismatic figure who inspired fierce loyalty and commitment.*

char·it·able /ˈtʃærətəbl/ *adj.* **1** connected with a charity or charities: *The museum was constituted a charitable trust in 1989.* ◇ *Many fee-paying public schools enjoy charitable status.* HELP In British English, to have **charitable status** means to be an official charity. **2** helping people who are poor or in need: *In 2004, charitable giving reached a record $248.52 billion.* ◇ *Married women of the middle classes busied themselves with charitable works visiting hospitals, prisons and poor houses.* **3** kind in your attitude to other people, especially when you are judging them: *Emma's private judgement on the new Mrs Elton is less charitable: 'self-important, presuming, familiar, ignorant and ill-bred.'*

char·ity /ˈtʃærəti/ *noun* (*pl.* **-ies**) **1** [C] an organization for helping people in need: *There has been a significant fall in public giving to charities.* ◇ *About 60% of registered charities have incomes of less than £10 000 per annum.* **2** [U] charities considered as a group: *He has given $5 billion in donations to charity.* ◇ *The ball was auctioned off for charity at the end of the match.* **3** [U] money, food, help, etc. that is given to people who are in need: *Sickness reduced people to helplessness and dependence on charity.* ◇ **+ noun** *Muslim charity work includes both mutual support to members of the congregation and social work in the local community.* **4** [U] kindness and sympathy towards other people, especially when you are judging them: *The protection of human rights is emphatically not a matter of charity but rather an entitlement of all human beings.*

chart¹ AWL /tʃɑːt; *NAmE* tʃɑːrt/ *noun* **1** a page or sheet of information in the form of diagrams, lists of figures, etc: *The pie chart shows the relative percentage of the cell mass contributed by each class of molecules.* ◇ **on/in a/the ~** *The number of people in each position is indicated on the chart.* ◇ *The frequencies are displayed in the bar chart in Fig. 5.3.* ➲ *see also* BAR CHART, PIE CHART **2** a detailed map of the sea: *Mercator's map replaced all earlier charts used at sea.*

chart² AWL /tʃɑːt; *NAmE* tʃɑːrt/ *verb* **1 ~ sth** to record or follow the progress or development of sb/sth: *Because the data are compiled over many years, it is possible to chart trends over time.* ◇ *Both historians share an interest in charting the rise and fall of power.* ➲ *compare* TRACK² (1) ➲ thesaurus note *at* RECORD² **2 ~ sth** to plan a course of action: *She insisted on charting her own course, and enrolled at the college.* ◇ *The party claimed to have charted a new path to revolution.* **3 ~ sth** to make a map of an area SYN MAP² (3): *The expedition embarked on charting the newly acquired territory.* **4 ~ sth** to discuss or deal with a topic or area of study SYN COVER¹ (2): *Philosophers and neurobiologists have already charted some of this terrain.* ◇ *His poetry seemed to chart quite new territory.*

cheap /tʃiːp/ *adj.* (**cheap·er**, **cheap·est**) **1** costing little money or less money than you expected SYN INEXPENSIVE: *The combination of cheap imports and domestic over-supply led to a collapse in the price of beef.* ◇ *In order to participate in the global capitalist economy, these countries must sell their raw materials at cheap prices.* ◇ *Both countries have a huge supply of relatively cheap labour.* HELP **Cheap labour** refers to people who are paid very little in comparison with people from other countries or areas. **it is ~ (for sb/sth) to do sth** *With lower interest rates, it is cheaper for households to borrow money.* ◇ *There are abundant world reserves of gas and it is cheaper to produce than oil.* OPP EXPENSIVE **2** charging low prices: *Thousands of jobs have been lost as jobs have moved to cheaper countries.* ◇ *The film's main action takes place in cheap hotels and squalid gyms.* OPP EXPENSIVE **3** (*often disapproving*) low in price and quality: *One publisher introduced cheap editions of Russian classics, printing at least 100 000 copies of each volume.* ■ **cheap·ness** *noun* [U] **~ (of sth)** *The relative cheapness of fossil fuel energy is a product of years of investment in infrastructure systems.*

cheap·ly /ˈtʃiːpli/ *adv.* without spending or costing much money: *Deuterium can be easily and cheaply extracted from water.* ◇ *Branded fashion clothing is sold more cheaply in Malaysia than in Europe.*

check¹ /tʃek/ *verb* **1** [T, I] to examine sth to make sure it is correct or acceptable, or to see if sth is present or as you think it is: **~ sth** *The experiment was designed to check the validity of this hypothesis.* ◇ *The sample must be checked to ensure it is sputum, not saliva.* ◇ **~ for sth** *Check for signs of bleeding.* ◇ **~ sth for sth** *Blood test results are checked for high levels of protein.* ◇ **~ sth against/with sth** *The scanned fingerprints are checked against police records.* ◇ **~ sth by doing sth** *Therefore, inheritance patterns could only be checked by conducting breeding experiments.* ◇ **~ that...** *We checked that the crystals were not cracked or dissolved by looking at them under a microscope.* ◇ **~ whether/how, etc...** *To check whether the catalysis is photo-induced, the experiment was repeated in complete darkness.* **2** [T] **~ sth** to control sth; to stop sth from increasing or getting worse: *Population growth was checked by a shortage of prey species.* **3** [T] **~ sth** (*NAmE*) = TICK¹ (1)

PHR V ˈ**check on sb/sth** to make sure that there is nothing wrong with sb/sth: *Procedures exist to check on the quality of the work done by the technicians.*

check² /tʃek/ *noun* **1** an act of making sure that sth is safe, correct or in good condition by examining it: *The clinic provides annual health checks.* ◇ **~ on sth** *External regulators could make checks on financial markets.* ◇ **~ for sth** *The procedure includes a check for bruising and signs of bleeding.* **2** something that delays the progress of sth else or stops it from getting worse: **~ on sth** *The only practical checks on the government's power were a lack of resources and its own inefficiency.* ◇ *The new constitution was intended to serve as a check on corruption and abuse of power.* ◇ **~ to sth** *Once climatic conditions permitted, there were few checks to a rapid spread of tree species across Europe.* **3** (*US*) = CHEQUE **4** (*NAmE*) = TICK² (1)

IDM **hold/keep sth in ˈcheck** to keep sth under control so that it does not spread or get worse: *Such diseases are present in the body all the time but are kept in check by the immune system.*

C

check·list /ˈtʃeklɪst/ *noun* **~ (of sth)** a list of the things that you must remember to do, to take with you or to find out: *She had a checklist of things to ask when someone reported a crime.*

cheese /tʃiːz/ *noun* [U, C] a type of food made from milk that can be either soft or hard and is usually white or yellow in colour; a particular type of this food: *Denmark found new markets for its bacon, eggs, butter and cheese in urban Britain.* ◇ *Until the mid-nineteenth century, Camembert, like most other cheeses, was sold in only a few local markets.*

chem·ical[1] AWL /ˈkemɪkl/ *adj.* involving atoms and MOLECULES and how they cause substances to have different structures, properties and reactions: *Many chemical reactions generate vivid colours.* ◇ *DNA and RNA are very similar in chemical composition.* HELP In non-scientific use, **chemical** is often used for describing substances that are produced in industrial processes, rather than occurring naturally. This use is best avoided in scientific writing: use **synthetic** or **artificial** instead: *Organic farming largely avoids the use of synthetic fertilizers.*

▸ CHEMICAL + NOUN **process • reaction • modification, shift, change • bonding • weathering • synthesis** *Chemical weathering is significant because of the high temperature and humidity.* | **nature • structure • properties • characteristics • composition • formula • energy • analysis • diversity • equilibrium** *The chemical nature of soils is determined by the combination of mineral and organic matter that makes up the soil.* ◇ *These zones have distinctive physical, chemical and biological properties.* | **group • substance • element • compound • bond • reagent** *There are several types of chemical bonds.*

chem·ical[2] AWL /ˈkemɪkl/ *noun* a substance obtained by or used in a chemical process: *The main chemicals in these oils are triglycerides.* ◇ *Cellulose is the most abundant organic chemical on earth.* ◇ **+ noun** *The chemical industry focused on ways to reduce pollution.*

▸ ADJECTIVE + CHEMICALS **synthetic • organic • toxic • industrial** *Synthetic chemicals were increasingly used in perfume production.*

▸ CHEMICAL + NOUN **weapons, warfare** *The use of chemical and biological weapons is proscribed.*

chem·ic·al·ly AWL /ˈkemɪkli/ *adv.* involving chemical reactions, properties or structures: *The heated water will react chemically with the rocks.* ◇ *The liquid phase must be chemically inert.*

chem·ist /ˈkemɪst/ *noun* a scientist who studies chemistry: *Our reliance on analytical chemists will increase.* ◇ *Other organic chemists were fascinated by the structures.* HELP In non-academic British English, a **chemist** is also a PHARMACIST working in a shop where you can buy medicines.

chem·is·try /ˈkemɪstri/ *noun* (*pl.* **-ies**) **1** [U] the scientific study of substances, including the study of their chemical structures, properties and reactions: *His interests are in inorganic chemistry and bioenergetics.* ◇ *The more complicated the molecule being made, the more difficult synthetic organic chemistry becomes.* ◇ *physical/analytical/environmental/green chemistry* ➲ *see also* BIOCHEMISTRY **2** [C] (*technical*) the chemical structure or properties of a particular substance, process or site: *The patient's blood chemistry was monitored regularly.* ◇ **the ~ of sth** *The chemistry of the molecule is relatively simple.* ◇ *The chemistry of this reduction is given below.*

cheque (*BrE*) (*US* **check**) /tʃek/ *noun* **~ (for sth)** a printed form that you can write on and sign as a way of paying for sth instead of using money: *They presented him with a cheque for £4 000.*

chest /tʃest/ *noun* the top part of the front of the body, between the neck and the stomach: **+ noun** *The hallmark of the disease is chest pain, which can often be intense.*

chief[1] /tʃiːf/ *adj.* **1** [usually before noun] most important: *The chief advantage of a digital recording is that the recording is far superior.* ◇ *However, oil continues to be the chief source of industrial energy.* ◇ *Chief among the honourable employments in any feudal community is warfare.* **2** (*often* **Chief**) [only before noun] highest in rank: *The deployment of police resources was within the discretion of the Chief Constable.* ◇ *In 1833 he was appointed chief engineer of the London and Birmingham line.* **3 -in-ˈchief** (in nouns) of the highest rank: *Paskevich rose to be commander-in-chief, even though better generals were available.* ➲ *see also* CHIEFLY

chief[2] /tʃiːf/ *noun* **1** a person with a high rank or the highest rank in a company or an organization: *Most Cabinet ministers see themselves firstly as departmental chiefs.* ◇ **~ of sth** *The new chief of the general staff was Zhukov.* **2** (often as a title) a leader or ruler of a people or community: *The most successful of the barbarian tribal chiefs was Arminius.* ◇ *Many disputes could be resolved by the local chief and the simple court of the village elders.*

ˌchief eˈxecutive *noun* the person with the highest rank in a company or an organization: *The company's chief executive said that the business was fighting for survival after a downturn in demand.*

chief·ly /ˈtʃiːfli/ *adv.* not completely, but as a most important part SYN MAINLY, PRIMARILY: *Savannah, steppe and prairie are composed chiefly of grasses.* ◇ *His study is chiefly concerned with literature written in English.*

child /tʃaɪld/ *noun* (*pl.* **chil·dren** /ˈtʃɪldrən/) **1** a young human who is not yet an adult: *Newborns and young children are particularly vulnerable to infectious diseases.* ◇ *Children learn through observation as well as through discussion.* **2** a son or daughter of any age, belonging to a particular family: *She has four children, all of whom are in their thirties.* ◇ *There was evidence that awards were being made to children from poor homes.* ◇ **~ of sb** *Children of working-class parents have a much higher chance of themselves ending up in manual work.* HELP In non-technical language, you are likely to talk about **children from** a particular type of family. In academic writing, **(the) children of** is more common: *The children of families with high incomes are more likely to have high incomes when they grow up.*

child·bear·ing /ˈtʃaɪldbeərɪŋ; *NAmE* ˈtʃaɪldberɪŋ/ *noun* [U] the process of being pregnant and giving birth to children: *Women were delaying marriage and childbearing.* ◇ **+ noun** *The drug also has certain advantages, particularly in women of childbearing age.*

child·birth /ˈtʃaɪldbɜːθ; *NAmE* ˈtʃaɪldbɜːrθ/ *noun* [U] the process of giving birth to a baby: *These women are more likely to require medical intervention during childbirth.*

child·care /ˈtʃaɪldkeə(r); *NAmE* ˈtʃaɪldker/ *noun* [U] the care of children, especially while parents are at work: *The researchers noted a class difference in fathers' participation in housework and childcare.*

child·hood /ˈtʃaɪldhʊd/ *noun* [U, C] the period of sb's life when they are a child: *Gauguin spent his childhood in Peru.* ◇ *Poverty during childhood has been shown to be related to adult health and socio-economic status.* ◇ **+ noun** *The second new area of interest was the rising rate of childhood obesity.*

chip /tʃɪp/ *noun* = MICROCHIP

chi-square test /ˌkaɪ ˈskweə test; *NAmE* ˌkaɪ ˈskwer test/ *noun* (*statistics*) a calculation that is used to test how well a set of data fits the results that were expected according to a theory: *Chi square tests were performed to evaluate differences for quantitative and categorical variables, respectively.*

chlor·ide /ˈklɔːraɪd/ *noun* [U, C] (*chemistry*) a COMPOUND of chlorine and another chemical element: *Two samples of potassium chloride were weighed and were recorded as being 34.5645 g and 35.5664 g, respectively.*

chlor·ine /ˈklɔːriːn/ *noun* [U] (*symb.* **Cl**) the chemical element of ATOMIC NUMBER 17. Chlorine is a poisonous, light green gas with a strong smell: **+ noun** *The two reactions form a chain in which a single chlorine atom can destroy many ozone molecules.*

choice /tʃɔɪs/ *noun* **1** [C, U] an act of choosing between two or more possibilities: *Habitat choice affects breeding choices.* ◇ **~ of sth** *The outcome of the experiment was determined by the initial choice of methodology.* ◇ **~ about sth** *Patients were able to make educated choices about treatment options.* ◇ **~ between A and B** *Managers face a difficult choice between conflicting goals.* **2** [C] something that you can choose: *The villagers had two choices: emigration or armed resistance.* ◇ *Participants were given a list of five possible choices.* **3** [U, sing.] the possibility of choosing; the right to choose: *There are financial constraints on managers' freedom of choice in pursuing preferred strategies.* ◇ *Consumer choice will be compromised if GM foods are not adequately labelled.* ◇ **~ about** *Researchers had no choice about the materials used.* ◇ *The child may not be considered capable of exercising a choice about complex matters.* ◇ **have no/little ~ (but to do sth)** *Each business owner has no choice but to engage in a never-ending race to avoid falling behind.* **4** [C] a person or thing that is chosen: **~ for sth** *Area detectors are thus the best choice for any kind of diffraction data collection.* ◇ **~ as sth** *Palmerston was a popular choice as prime minister.* **5** [U, sing.] the number or range of different things to choose from: *Supermarkets offer customers greater choice and convenience.* ◇ **~ of sth** *Participants were given a wider choice of tasks.*

IDM **by ˈchoice** because you have chosen: *Most students who attend this programme do so not by choice but because they are compelled to by the school board.* **of ˈchoice (for sb/sth)** (used after a noun) that is chosen by a particular group of people or for a particular purpose: *Gas liquid chromatography is the method of choice for separating volatile compounds.* **of your ˈchoice** that you choose yourself: *Explain, for a country of your choice, the role that the voluntary sector plays in society.*

▸ ADJECTIVE + CHOICE **actual** *The survey focuses on the reasons for the actual choices made by customers.* | **good** *Radiotherapy is a good choice for a patient who would not be keen or fit for surgery.* | **obvious • rational • appropriate • suitable • healthy • optimal** *These findings may help to explain why poorer people are less likely to make healthy choices.* | **stark** *Politicians are faced with stark choices about how to allocate scarce resources.* | **free • real • individual, personal, own • parental** *She argues that the state of one's health is largely dependent on individual choices rather than social factors.* | **random, arbitrary • careful • informed • conscious • difficult • moral** *Information must be available for parents to make informed choices about the schools they select for their children.* | **wide • great • more • limited** *The more choice the buyer has to purchase goods and services, the more the balance of power is in his/her favour.*

▸ NOUN + CHOICE **habitat • breeding • policy • lifestyle • brand • career** *Increasing globalization is making policy choices harder for democratically elected leaders.*

▸ VERB + CHOICE **make • face** *Every individual must make a choice for herself or himself.* | **influence, affect, shape, inform • determine, dictate • explain • justify** *The experiment demonstrates clearly that female mate choice is directly influenced by this trait.* | **have • offer, give** *Ultimately, the film is offering a choice between two lifestyles within bourgeois democracy.* | **restrict, limit, constrain** *Limited access to material also constrains the choices of historical documentarians.* | **exercise** *There are few local schools, making it difficult for parents to exercise genuine chioce.*

chol·es·terol /kəˈlestərɒl; *NAmE* kəˈlestərɔːl/ *noun* [U] a substance found in blood, fat and most TISSUE of the body. Too much cholesterol can cause heart disease: *Jon suffers from high cholesterol and chronic fatigue.* ◇ *Lowering total cholesterol by 25% reduces cardiovascular risk significantly.*

choose /tʃuːz/ *verb* (**chose** /tʃəʊz; *NAmE* tʃoʊz/, **chosen** /ˈtʃəʊzn; *NAmE* ˈtʃoʊzn/) **1** [I, T] to decide which thing or person you want out of the ones that are available: **~ between A and/or B** *Soon the independent producers had to choose between surviving or falling behind.* ◇ **~ among sth** *Firms already find it hard to choose among the available strategic options.* ◇ **~ A over B** *Historically, the people of the United States have tended to choose personal freedom over public order.* ◇ **~ sth** *One member from each family was randomly chosen.* ◇ **~ sb/sth from sth** *The research sites were chosen from four different regions.* ◇ **~ sb/sth as sth** *The interesting question is why a pagan emperor would choose Christianity as the official religion.* ◇ **~ sb/sth for sth** *The new state held free elections to choose political leaders for national and local levels of government.* ◇ **~ whether/what, etc...** *However, viewers can choose whether to accept the director's version of reality or not.* ◇ *In the early experiments, subjects were allowed to choose what to draw.* ◇ **~ sb/sth to be/do sth** *He believed God had chosen him to be a spiritual leader.* **2** [I, T] to prefer or decide to do sth: *Customers will be able to block direct marketing if they choose.* ◇ **~ to do sth** *They chose to wait and see what would happen.* ⊃ *see also* CHOICE

IDM **there is little to choose between A and B** there is very little difference between two or more things or people: *There is little to choose between these technologies, in terms of fuel efficiency.* ⊃ *more at* PICK

▸ CHOOSE + NOUN **option, alternative • item • the one • method, strategy • path, course • value • name • site, location • candidate • mate** *When the choices appear on the screen, participants are asked to choose the one they would like to receive.* ◇ *Many in the rural areas are choosing a different path from the one chosen by their ancestors.*

▸ NOUN + CHOOSE **people • person, individual • female • company, firm • employer • policy maker • researcher • consumer** *It thus appears that females may choose a mate based on the size of his song repertoire.*

▸ ADVERB + CHOOSE **randomly • arbitrarily • suitably, appropriately •** *Suitably chosen books can reinforce the therapist's advice.* | **carefully • deliberately, consciously • actively • freely • simply** *The site location was carefully chosen in order to avoid flooding.*

▸ CHOOSE + ADVERB **at random • instead** *Five numbers were chosen at random.* ◇ *Wordsworth avoids most of these conventions, choosing instead to present a starkly realistic portrait of rural life.*

▸ CHOOOSE TO + VERB **do • focus on • study • pursue • ignore • withdraw • live • satisfy • perform** *Other authors such as George (1990) have chosen to focus on the role of internal marketing.*

Chris·tian[1] /ˈkrɪstʃən/ *adj.* **1** based on or believing the teachings of Jesus Christ: *the Christian Church/faith/religion* ◇ *She had a Christian upbringing.* **2** connected with Christians: *the Christian sector of the city*

Chris·tian² /ˈkrɪstʃən/ *noun* a person who believes in the teachings of Jesus Christ: *Only 10% of the population are now practising Christians.*

Chris·tian·ity /ˌkrɪstiˈænəti/ *noun* [U] the religion that is based on the teachings of Jesus Christ and the belief that he was the son of God: *the spread of Christianity in the first century*

C

chromo·some /ˈkrəʊməsəʊm; *NAmE* ˈkroʊməsoʊm/ *noun* (*biology*) one of the very small structures like threads in the NUCLEI of animal and plant cells, that carry the GENES: *In most cells, chromosomes are visible via microscopy only during the process of cell division.* ◇ *A single chromosome contains many genes embedded within a single DNA molecule.* ■ **chromo·somal** /ˌkrəʊməˈsəʊməl; *NAmE* ˌkroʊməˈsoʊməl/ *adj.* [only before noun] *Chromosomal abnormalities occur in 10–20% of spermatozoa.*

chron·ic /ˈkrɒnɪk; *NAmE* ˈkrɑːnɪk/ *adj.* (especially of a disease) lasting for a long time; difficult to cure or get rid of: *Asthma is a common chronic disease of childhood.* ◇ *These symptoms are associated with chronic hepatitis.* ◇ *The treatment of severe chronic pain is difficult.* ◇ *a chronic illness/condition/infection/disorder* ◇ *The financial crash had created chronic unemployment and poverty.* OPP ACUTE (1) ■ **chron·ic·al·ly** /ˈkrɒnɪkli; *NAmE* ˈkrɑːnɪkli/ *adv.*: *Rousseau was by now chronically ill.*

chrono·logic·al /ˌkrɒnəˈlɒdʒɪkl; *NAmE* ˌkrɑːnəˈlɑːdʒɪkl/ *adj.* **1** (of a number of events) arranged in the order in which they happened: *The method involved listing the incidents in chronological order from 1900 onwards.* **2 ~ age** the number of years a person or animal has lived as opposed to their level of physical, mental or emotional development: *The results suggest that the level of mutations in the rats reflected their biological rather than their chronological age.* ■ **chrono·logic·al·ly** /ˌkrɒnəˈlɒdʒɪkli; *NAmE* ˌkrɑːnəˈlɑːdʒɪkli/ *adv.*: *The next play in the sequence to be written, Richard III, was chronologically the last in terms of the events that it portrays.*

chron·ology /krəˈnɒlədʒi; *NAmE* krəˈnɑːlədʒi/ *noun* (*pl.* -ies) [U, C] **~ (of sth)** the order in which a series of events happened; a list of these events in order: *It is in fact exceedingly hard to establish the chronology of these developments in government.* ◇ *Other relative chronologies were based on the succession of climatic phases during the Ice Age.*

church /tʃɜːtʃ; *NAmE* tʃɜːrtʃ/ *noun* **1** [C] a building where Christians go to worship: *They married in her parish church.* ◇ *During religious holidays, crowds gather in or near the mosques and churches.* **2** [U] a service or services in a church: *I grew up going to church.* ◇ *Attending church was one way for them to socialize and be active in their community.* ◇ **in ~** *They wanted to be married in church.* ◇ **+ noun** *There has been a significant decline in church attendance in Italy.* **3** (*often* **Church**) [C] a particular group of Christians: *There is a lot of opposition to family planning, particularly from the Catholic Church.* ◇ *People in closed network religious groups tend to be suspicious of people outside the church.* **4** (*also* **(the) Church**) [sing.] the ministers of the Christian religion; the institution of the Christian religion: *Despite the separation of Church and State, the USA retains a Judaeo-Christian ethos.*

cig·ar·ette /ˌsɪɡəˈret; *NAmE* ˈsɪɡəret/ *noun* a thin tube of paper filled with TOBACCO, for smoking: *He smokes about 10 cigarettes each day and drinks about 20 units of alcohol each week.* ◇ **+ noun** *Cigarette smoking is a major risk factor for several cancers.*

cin·ema /ˈsɪnəmə/ *noun* **1** (*BrE*) (*NAmE* ˈ**movie theater, theater**) [C] a building in which films are shown: *Working women preferred to spend their leisure hours at the cinema or dance-hall.* **2 the cinema** [sing.] (*BrE*) (*NAmE* **the movies** [pl.]) when you go to **the cinema**, you go to a cinema to see a film: *Will people still go to the cinema to watch films if they can download them direct to their PCs?* ◇ *How frequently do you usually visit the cinema?* **3** [U, sing.] (*especially BrE*) (*NAmE usually* **the movies** [pl.]) films as an art or an industry: *Even in silent cinema, someone is always speaking.* ◇ *During British cinema's postwar heyday, female supporting players were very important.*

cine·mat·ic /ˌsɪnəˈmætɪk/ *adj.* (*technical*) connected with films and how they are made: *In this study, he examines the use of expressionist cinematic techniques.* ◇ *cinematic images/styles* ◇ *This book deploys a distinctive non-linear, even cinematic, structure.*

cir·ca·dian /sɜːˈkeɪdiən; *NAmE* sɜːrˈkeɪdiən/ *adj.* [only before noun] (*biology*) connected with the changes in the bodies of people or animals over each period of 24 hours: *Shift work can disrupt the circadian rhythm.*

cir·cle¹ /ˈsɜːkl; *NAmE* ˈsɜːrkl/ *noun* **1** a completely round flat shape: *In Fig. 3 the triangles and circles represent boys and girls respectively.* **2** the line that forms the edge of a circle: *The circle formed by the equator has the North Pole as its centre.* **3** a thing or a group of people or things shaped like a circle: *A very short length of tubing is bent into a circle.* **4** a group of people who are connected because they have the same interests, jobs, etc: *These ideas found a receptive hearing in some Christian circles.* ◇ **~ of sb** *She was described as a strong-minded and outgoing person with a large circle of friends.* ➲ *see also* VICIOUS CIRCLE

IDM **come full ˈcircle** to return to the situation in which you started, after a series of events or experiences: *The argument has now come full circle.* ◇ *A reduction in the profit rate will tend to discourage investment, and the process may then come full circle.*

cir·cle² /ˈsɜːkl; *NAmE* ˈsɜːrkl/ *verb* **1** [I, T] to move in a circle, especially in the air: **~ sth** *A GPS involves a group of satellites circling the earth in precisely known orbits.* ◇ **~ adv./prep.** *In a sense, the poem circles back to its title.* **2** [T] **~ sth** to draw a circle around sth: *They were asked to circle the answer that best represented the meaning.*

cir·cuit /ˈsɜːkɪt; *NAmE* ˈsɜːrkɪt/ *noun* the complete path of wires and equipment along which an electric current flows: *Ohm's law accurately describes the behaviour of electrical circuits.* ◇ **+ noun** *This operation is illustrated in the circuit diagram in Fig. 4.2.* ➲ *see also* INTEGRATED CIRCUIT

cir·cu·lar /ˈsɜːkjələ(r); *NAmE* ˈsɜːrkjələr/ *adj.* **1** shaped like a circle; round: *The standard manual gauge has a circular mouth with internal diameter 127 mm.* **2** moving around in a circle: *The ions follow a circular path.* ◇ *He believed that the planets Venus and Mercury moved in circular orbits around the sun.* **3** (of an argument or a theory) using an idea or a statement to prove sth which is then used to prove the idea or statement at the beginning: *Their reasoning amounts to little more than a circular argument.*

cir·cu·late /ˈsɜːkjəleɪt; *NAmE* ˈsɜːrkjəleɪt/ *verb* **1** [I, T] to move continuously or freely around a system or area; to cause sth to move in this way: *Infancy marks a period during which circulating sex hormone levels are very low.* ◇ **~ through/throughout/around sth** *Once imported, the goods circulate freely throughout the countries of the customs union.* ◇ **~ sth (through/throughout/around sth)** *Cold water is circulated through the engine.* **2** [I, T] (of ideas or information) to pass from place to place or person to person; to pass on ideas or information, especially to all the members of a group: *Rumours circulated that the factory would close.* ◇ **~ sth (among sb/sth)** *The technical plans for the computer were widely circulated among US research institutes.* ◇ **~ sth to sb/sth** *The draft proposal was circulated to all departments for comments.*

cir·cu·la·tion /ˌsɜːkjəˈleɪʃn; *NAmE* ˌsɜːrkjəˈleɪʃn/ *noun* **1** [U] the movement of blood around the body: *The patient was suffering from poor circulation.* ◇ *Iodide is rapidly removed from circulation by the thyroid and kidney.* ◇ **~ of the blood** *It was Harvey who discovered the circulation of the blood.* **2** [U] the movement of sth (for example air, water or gas) around an area or inside a system or machine: *These changes in atmospheric circulation led to increased ice age aridity over most areas of Africa.* ◇ **~ of sth** *The circulation of ocean currents is influenced by ocean basin topography and by climate.* ◇ **~ around sth** *Lanchester discovered that air circulation around wings was the main cause of lift.* **3** [U] the fact of goods, information or ideas passing from one person or place to another: **~ of sth** *They believed in a common market for the free circulation of goods.* ◇ **in ~** *At any given time, many different versions of the traditional stories would be in circulation around the ancient Greek world.* ◇ **into ~** *The euro came into circulation in 2002.* ◇ **out of ~** *The manufacturer must either repair the product or take it out of circulation.* **4** [C, usually sing.] the usual number of copies of a newspaper or magazine that are sold each day, week, etc: *Over this period, the magazine increased its circulation by over 70 per cent.* ◇ **a ~ of 10 000, etc.** *Chambers' Edinburgh Journal had a circulation of 50 000 in Scotland in the 1830s.*

cir·cu·la·tory /ˌsɜːkjəˈleɪtəri; *NAmE* ˈsɜːrkjələtɔːri/ *adj.* connected with the circulation of the blood: *The lung interacts with the outside environment and the circulatory system.* ◇ *circulatory arrest/disease/failure*

cir·cum·fer·ence /səˈkʌmfərəns; *NAmE* sərˈkʌmfərəns/ *noun* [C, U] a line that goes around a circle or any other curved shape; the length of this line: *This group also had larger waist circumferences and higher percentage body fat.* ◇ **~ of sth** *The mathematician Eratosthenes produced a strikingly accurate estimate of the circumference of the earth.* ◇ **in ~** *Boys had to cut down a tree at least nine inches in circumference and build a bridge.*

cir·cum·stance AWL /ˈsɜːkəmstəns; ˈsɜːkəmstɑːns; ˈsɜːkəmstæns; *NAmE* ˈsɜːrkəmstæns/ *noun* **1** [C, usually pl., U] the conditions and facts that are connected with and affect a situation, an event or an action: *The circumstances surrounding the crisis will be examined.* ◇ **in... circumstances** *Unaccompanied minors may only be detained in very exceptional circumstances.* ◇ **in circumstances where...** *Offering choice in circumstances where users are not able to exercise it could simply increase inequalities.* ◇ **under... circumstances** *Under normal circumstances, the body's immune system will protect the patient from infection.* ◇ **according to... circumstance(s)** *The legal duty of the licensee differs according to the different circumstances.* ◇ *Relationships in politics vary according to circumstance and the tactics of the various politicial parties.* **2 circumstances** [pl.] the conditions of a person's life, especially the money they have: *The judge failed to take sufficiently into account the personal circumstances of the claimant.* ➲ thesaurus note *at* SITUATION

IDM **in/under the ˈcircumstances** used before or after a statement to show that you have thought about the conditions that affect a situation before making a decision or a statement: *In the circumstances, the decision to abandon the case was a reasonable one.* **in/under no circumstances** used to emphasize that sth should never happen or be allowed: *Reith genuinely believed that the General Strike could under no circumstances be justified.*

▸ ADJECTIVE + CIRCUMSTANCES **certain, particular, individual, specific, such** ◆ **different** ◆ **changing** ◆ **exceptional, special** ◆ **extreme** ◆ **normal** ◆ **favourable** ◆ **the right** ◆ **adverse** ◆ **local** ◆ **economic** ◆ **historical** ◆ **social** ◆ **political** *The reform happened under extreme political circumstances that empowered government reformers and discredited business elites.* | **personal** ◆ **financial, material** ◆ **family** *Arguably, it will not be enough simply to wait for economic growth to improve the material circumstances of people in poverty.*

▸ VERB + CIRCUMSTANCES **describe** ◆ **specify** ◆ **reflect** ◆ **imagine, envisage** ◆ **suit, fit** *It would have been difficult for anyone to envisage the particular circumstances that led to the global financial crisis.* ◇ *The aim was to design a template that could be modified to suit the actual circumstances.*

▸ PHRASE **circumstances beyond sb's control** *Costs may also be incurred through circumstances beyond the control of the licensing firm.*

cir·cum·vent /ˌsɜːkəmˈvent; *NAmE* ˌsɜːrkəmˈvent/ *verb* **~ sth** (*formal*) to find a way of avoiding a difficulty or a rule: *Javelosa (1994) has circumvented the problem by attaching a numerical score to each category.* ◇ *Their underlying aim was to discover a way to reduce or circumvent their tax obligations.* ■ **cir·cum·ven·tion** /ˌsɜːkəmˈvenʃn; *NAmE* ˌsɜːrkəmˈvenʃn/ *noun* [U] **~ (of sth)** *The new legislation reduced the scope for circumvention of the regulations.*

cit·ation AWL /saɪˈteɪʃn/ *noun* **1** [C] words taken from a piece of writing or a speech; a reference, usually consisting of a name and a date, that identifies the original writer or speaker of these words: **~ to sth/sb** *Before the 1950s, writings on classroom management were limited and few of the works included citations to previous research.* ◇ **~ from sth/sb** *Legal arguments and conclusions are justified or supported by citations from the Qur'an and traditions.* ➲ *compare* QUOTATION (1) **2** [U, C] **~ (of sth)** an act of citing or being cited: *The citation of web pages soon became generally accepted.* ◇ *There were disappointingly few citations of recent articles.* ➲ thesaurus note *at* REFERENCE[1]

cite AWL /saɪt/ *verb* **1 ~ sth (as sth)** to mention sth as a reason or an example, or in order to support what you are saying: *Most respondents cite convenience as a principal benefit of accessing health care information online.* ◇ *Foley cites some evidence in support of this view.* ➲ *compare* QUOTE[1] (2) **2** to speak or write words taken from another writer or speaker; to give a reference, usually consisting of a name and date, that identifies the original writer or speaker of these words: **~ sth** *She cites several influential papers, such as Boxall and Dowling (1990).* ◇ *To back up this claim, he cites a passage from Kant's 'Physical Geography', which goes as follows:...* ◇ **~ sb** *He became one of the authors most cited in the revolutionary press.* ➲ *compare* QUOTE[1] (1)

▸ CITE + NOUN **example, case** ◆ **evidence** ◆ **reason** *The most commonly cited reason for relocation was high labour costs.* | **passage** ◆ **paper, article, study, work** ◆ **author, source, authority** ◆ **reference** *In the article cited, he disputes this claim.* ◇ *Primary sources cited in Ludlum (1963) were consulted wherever possible.*

▸ ADVERB + CITE **often, widely, frequently, commonly** *One of Simmel's most often cited essays is his essay of 1903 'The Metropolis and Mental Life'.*

▸ CITE + ADVERB **above, earlier** ◆ **here** *As the few examples cited here show,...*

citi·zen /ˈsɪtɪzn/ *noun* **1** a person who has the legal right to belong to a particular country: *States have primary responsibility for protecting their own citizens.* ◇ *They could register as a British citizen after five years' lawful residence in the UK.* ◇ **+ noun** *Most freeborn Romans had full citizen status.* ➲ *compare* SUBJECT[1] (5) **2** a person who lives in a particular place: *Ordinary citizens often found it safer to be politically passive.* ◇ *This attitude reduced women to the status of second-class citizens.*

▸ ADJECTIVE + CITIZEN **ordinary, private, average** ◆ **individual** ◆ **fellow** ◆ **wealthy** ◆ **poor** ◆ **good, responsible, active** ◆ **global** *This approach fails to develop students to be active citizens and problem solvers when they leave school.* ◇ *Ohmae (1991) argues further that information has made us all global citizens.*

▸ VERB + CITIZEN **become • allow, permit • enable • entitle** *Most importantly, having a free media allows citizens to make informed political choices.*
▸ CITIZEN + VERB **enjoy • vote • participate** *Irish citizens also enjoy full rights of British citizenship when they are resident in the UK.*
▸ NOUN + CITIZEN **participation, involvement** *Arguably, successful citizen participation in a free and democratic society requires a common language and common values.*

citi·zen·ship /ˈsɪtɪzənʃɪp/ *noun* [U] **1** the legal right to belong to a particular country: *In 2002, more than 100 000 people acquired British citizenship.* **2** the state of being a citizen and accepting the responsibilities of it: *What appears to be missing from economic rationalism is any notion of active citizenship.*

city /ˈsɪti/ *noun* (*pl.* **-ies**) **1** [C] a large and important town: *Some major cities are located close to active volcanoes.* ◇ **+ noun** *The evidence showed that women and the elderly are often reluctant to use the city centre at night.* ➲ *see also* INNER CITY **2 the City** [sing.] Britain's financial and business centre, in the oldest part of London: *One of the main elements in Labour's economic policy was the need to reassure the City that it could run the economy.*

civic /ˈsɪvɪk/ *adj.* [usually before noun] **1** officially connected with a town or city: *These two countries do a better job integrating immigrants into common civic and political institutions.* **2** connected with the activities of people in relation to their town, city or local area: *Democracy depends on civic engagement.* ◇ *The less relatively deprived people feel, the more likely they are to participate in civic life.* ◇ *civic duty/responsibility*

civil AWL /ˈsɪvl/ *adj.* [only before noun] **1** connected with the people who live in a country rather than with the state: *Post-war Italy was characterized by a weak state and a strong civil society.* ◇ *It remains among the world's most corrupt countries and recently has faced increasing civil unrest.* ➲ *see also* CIVIL LIBERTY, CIVIL RIGHTS, CIVIL WAR **2** connected with the state rather than with religion or with the armed forces: *The civil aviation industry has been the focus of particular controversy in the context of global climate change debates.* ◇ *If a civil authority has broken down, this is the responsibility of that state's citizens and its political leaders.* ◇ *Diocletian began an important reform, separating military from civil power in frontier provinces.* ➲ *see also* CIVIL SERVANT, CIVIL SERVICE **3** involving personal legal matters and not criminal law: *In civil law, the innocent party instigates the claim against the defendant.* ◇ *In the United Kingdom, defamation is almost entirely a matter for the civil courts.* ➲ *compare* CRIMINAL[1] ➲ *see also* CIVIL LAW

▸ CIVIL + NOUN **society • war, conflict • unrest, strife, disobedience, disturbance • rights, liberties** *Gandhi mobilized a mass campaign of civil disobedience against British rule.* | **servant • service • authority • administration • aviation • engineering • engineer** *The army, navy and civil administration grew in size and power.* | **partnership • partner • proceedings, action, case • law, regulation • liability • court** *Different terminology is used in criminal proceedings to that which is used in civil proceedings.* ◇ *There are a number of treaties which establish rules on civil liability for environmental damage.*

ˌcivil engiˈneering *noun* [U] the design, building and repair of roads, bridges, CANALS, etc; the study of this as a subject: *The Construction Group carries out various construction, civil engineering, and land development projects.* ■ **ˌcivil engiˈneer** *noun*: *Developing nations are hiring American civil engineers to advise on building roads and dams.*

ci·vil·ian[1] /səˈvɪliən/ *noun* a person who is not a member of the armed forces or the police: *This resulted in a number of attacks in which innocent civilians were killed.* ◇ *After initial failures, peacekeeping forces have succeeded in protecting civilians.* ➲ *compare* MILITARY[2]

ci·vil·ian[2] /səˈvɪliən/ *adj.* [usually before noun] connected with people who are not members of the armed forces or the police: *The number of military abuses against the civilian population is said to be high.* ◇ *The share of civilian casualties in armed conflict has increased.* ➲ *compare* MILITARY[1]

civ·il·iza·tion (*BrE also* **-isa·tion**) /ˌsɪvəlaɪˈzeɪʃn; *NAmE* ˌsɪvələˈzeɪʃn/ *noun* **1** [U] a state of human society that is very developed and organized: *Modern civilization has changed our activity patterns and our diet.* ◇ *The potential benefits of modern technology for improving human civilization are profound in every sphere.* ◇ *Even those who seek to get away from it all maintain contact with civilization by mobile phone.* **2** [U, C] a society, its culture and its way of life during a particular period of time or in a particular part of the world: *The Mediterranean Basin was the cradle of Western civilization.* ◇ *The pyramids of Egypt are monuments to an ancient civilization.* **3** [U] all the people in the world and the societies they live in, considered as a whole: *These considerations suggest that volcanic super-eruptions pose a real threat to civilization.*

civ·il·ize (*BrE also* **-ise**) /ˈsɪvəlaɪz/ *verb* **~ sb/sth** to educate and improve a person or a society; to make sb's behaviour or manners better: *Literature was seen as a special kind of writing which, it was argued, could civilize the lower classes.* ◇ *The Romans' view of their 'civilizing mission' emphasized their political and military contributions to a chaotic and corrupt world.*

civ·il·ized (*BrE also* **-ised**) /ˈsɪvəlaɪzd/ *adj.* **1** well-organized socially with a very developed culture and way of life: *The discovery revealed the sudden demise of an early Greek settlement of a highly civilized people.* ◇ *The contrast between civilized Greeks and uncultured barbarians is a familiar feature of the literary tradition from an early period.* **2** having laws and customs that are fair and morally acceptable: *A concern for the health of others could be considered as one of the hallmarks of a civilized society.*

ˌcivil ˈlaw *noun* [U] **1** law that deals with the rights of private citizens rather than with crime: **in/under ~** *The divorce becomes effective in civil law after a period allowed for reconciliation.* **2** the system of law that is common on the European continent, historically based on the law of ancient Rome: **in/under ~** *They contend that property rights are better protected under British common law than under French civil law.*

ˌcivil ˈliberty *noun* [C, usually pl., U] the right of people to be free to say or do what they want while respecting others and staying within the law: *In July 2003 the first election was held under the new constitution, guaranteeing political rights and civil liberties.* ◇ *By the end of the year, a revolution that had promised freedom and civil liberty was waging a bloody civil war against its own citizens.*

ˌcivil ˈpartnership *noun* [C, U] a relationship between two people of the same sex, recognized as having the same legal status as a marriage between a man and a woman: *The couple entered into a civil partnership one year ago.* ◇ *Marriage or civil partnership remain the only legal means of establishing a stable relationship.*

ˌcivil ˈrights *noun* [pl.] the rights that every person in a society has, for example to be treated equally, to be able to vote, work, etc. whatever their sex, race or religion: *Some nations have responded to the inequities facing immigrants by granting them political and civil rights.* ◇ **+ noun** *In the 1960s, the civil rights movement changed the political climate in the southern states.*

ˌcivil ˈservant *noun* a person who works in the civil service: *Traditionally, senior civil servants have been the main policy advisers to ministers.*

the ˌ**civil** ˈ**service** *noun* [sing.] the government departments in a country, except the armed forces, and the people who work for them: *He had a long career in the civil service.* ◇ *The role of the civil service was to advise ministers on policy.*

ˌ**civil** ˈ**war** *noun* [C, U] a war between groups of people in the same country: *There was a general understanding that both sides were responsible for plunging Spain into a brutal civil war.* ◇ *In the wake of independence, civil war erupted across the country.* HELP **The Civil War** may be used to refer to a particular war, especially the one fought in the US in the 1860s: *Any study of the causes of the Civil War cannot end with the outbreak of fighting in April 1861.* ◇ *the English/Spanish Civil War*

claim[1] /kleɪm/ *noun* **1** a statement that sth is true although it has not been proved and other people may not agree with or believe it: *Despite the similarities in the arguments, they involve some very different claims and assumptions.* ◇ **~ that...** *In general, participants reject the claim that globalization is inevitable.* ◇ *The authors refrain from making strong claims that the models describe underlying processes.* ◇ **~ to do sth** *The EU's claim to represent the peoples of Europe is seriously undermined by low and declining turnouts in European elections.* **2** a right that sb believes they have to be given sth, treated in a particular way, or credited with a particular quality: *The ongoing land claims by Native Canadians mean that Canada's political geography is still far from settled.* ◇ **~ to sth** *Henry was anxious to strengthen his doubtful claim to the throne.* ◇ *Many of these traditions have very strong claims to authenticity.* ◇ **~ on sth** *She failed to recognize her children's claims on her attention.* ◇ **~ for sth** *The intertribal conflict was fuelled by competing claims for the land and the bison that grazed on it.* ◇ **~ (of sb) to be/do/have sth** *Utilitarianism is a theory of how to respect the moral claim of each individual to be treated as an equal.* **3** an official request for sth that you believe you have a legal right to: *Where an asylum claim is made at a UK port of entry there is an obligation to consider it.* ◇ *Following a successful claim, the court is empowered to issue a remedy within its jurisdiction.* ◇ **~ for sth** *She brought a claim for damages but the hotel denied responsibility.* ◇
IDM **lay claim to sth** to state that you have a right to own sth or be credited with sth: *The Portuguese laid claim to the eastern part of South America.* ◇ *It is the classical Athenians who can probably lay claim to the invention of commercial advertising as we know it today.* **make no claim (to sth)** used to say that sb/sth obviously does not have a particular characteristic, but should be judged on other qualities: *As a drama, it makes no claim to documentary truth.* ➲ *more at* STAKE[2]
▸ ADJECTIVE + CLAIM **strong • central • general • competing • theoretical** *The general claim is that 'no one seems now to be in control' (Bauman, 1998).* | **strong • legitimate • moral • competing, rival • territorial** *Technical expertise may be the basis for a legitimate claim to professional status.*
▸ NOUN + CLAIM **asylum, refugee • human rights • wage** *The freer atmosphere had encouraged many strikes, usually in support of wage claims or better conditions.*
▸ VERB + CLAIM **make, advance • support • undermine • challenge • justify • evaluate • accept • reject, dismiss • refute** *There is much evidence to support the claim that a process of political globalization has been underway for quite some time.* ◇ *It is easy to dismiss such claims as ideologically motivated, rather than empirically drawn.* | **make, assert • have • support** *Vienna supported the claims of Germans against Italians in Trentino and Trieste.* | **establish • base a ~ on • bring, pursue • hear • allow • settle • defeat • reject, dismiss, deny, refuse** *In order to establish a successful claim of negligence, three tests must be satisfied.*

claim[2] /kleɪm/ *verb* **1** to say that sth is true although it has not been proved and other people may not agree with or believe it: ◇ **~ (that)...** *Some reports claim that the military bases on the island lost all communications with the mainland.* ◇ **~ to be/do sth** *Absolute monarchs claimed to be accountable only to God.* ◇ **~ sth** *He was a fierce fighter and reformer who claimed direct descent from the Prophet Muhammad.* ◇ **it is claimed that...** *It is claimed that the climate in certain buildings produces unhealthy symptoms.* ◇ **be claimed to be/do sth** *These products are claimed to repel insects and other pests through high-frequency sound.* ➲ thesaurus note *at* ARGUE **2 ~ sth** to say that you own or have earned sth, especially because you believe it is your legal right: *Many regimes have claimed the entitlement to ignore human rights.* ◇ *She left her home country to claim asylum in the US.* ◇ *Canada claimed sovereignty over the entire Arctic Archipelago of North America in 1895.* ◇ *The communist party, since it claimed credit for all technical successes, could logically be blamed for the failures too.* ➲ thesaurus note *at* ARGUE **3** [T, I] to ask officially for money because you believe you have a legal right to it: **~ sth** *Some unemployed people are not entitled to claim benefits.* ◇ **~ sth (from sb/sth) (for sth)** *She claimed damages from the defendants for the economic loss resulting from the cost of bringing up the child.* ◇ **~ for sth** *Four police officers, who were present at the disaster, claimed for their psychiatric injuries as primary victims.* **4 ~ sth/sb** (of a disaster, an accident, etc.) to cause sb's death: *Many of the diseases and illnesses which claimed the lives of people in the last century have been eradicated.* ◇ *The monsoon claimed ten victims.* **5 ~ sth** to gain, win or achieve sth: *The father had held the house on trust for the daughter, so she could claim her share of it.* IDM *see* LIFE, MORAL[1]
PHR V ˌ**claim sth** ˈ**back (from sb)** to ask or demand to have sth returned because you have a right to it: *There has to be some point at which a landowner is too late to claim his or her land back from someone who has been in possession of it for a long time.*
▸ CLAIM + NOUN **right, entitlement • asylum • sovereignty • status • authority • credit** *The priests claimed the authority to interpret the Law.* | **damages, compensation • benefits** *She was paid at a substantially lower rate than her male colleagues and claimed compensation for the damage suffered.*
▸ ADVERB + CLAIM **legitimately • plausibly • later** *The manager could legitimately claim that he was only doing his job.*

claim·ant /ˈkleɪmənt/ *noun* a person who makes an official request or demand for sth because they believe they have a right to it: *The claimant must prove that the defendant acted in bad faith.* ◇ *The House of Lords held that detention of asylum claimants was lawful 'to prevent unauthorized entry'.* ◇ **~ to sth** *There had been a long-running succession dispute between rival claimants to the throne.* ➲ *compare* PLAINTIFF

clar·ify AWL /ˈklærəfaɪ/ *verb* (**clari·fies**, **clari·fy·ing**, **clari·fied**, **clari·fied**) to make sth clearer or easier to understand: **~ sth** *Appealing to ethical frameworks may help to clarify the issues.* ◇ *Firstly, it is necessary to clarify the meaning of the term 'business groups'.* ◇ **~ what/why, etc...** *Let me clarify what I mean by service work.* ◇ *It is necessary to clarify why low inflation targets have been adopted.* ■ **clari·fi·ca·tion** AWL /ˌklærəfɪˈkeɪʃn/ *noun* [U, C] *As the circumstances are very different in these cases, there is a need for further clarification by the higher courts.* ◇ *I would like to thank my supervisor, Mary Reno, who suggested several revisions and clarifications.*

clar·ity AWL /ˈklærəti/ *noun* [U] **1** the quality of being expressed clearly: *The merits of this approach are that it provides greater clarity and control over spending.* ◇ *The difficulty with many accounts of planned change is their lack of conceptual clarity.* **2** the ability to think about or understand sth clearly: *The Buddha saw with such clarity how different states of mind and courses of action lead to different results.* ◇ **~ of sth** *Dealing with climate change urgently requires a shared clarity of vision and purpose at all levels.* **3** if a picture, substance or sound has **clarity**, you can see or hear it very clearly, or see through it easily: *This lack of clarity results from the main sound being partly smothered by slightly later echoes.*

class[1] /klɑːs; *NAmE* klæs/ *noun* **1** [C+sing./pl. v.] one of the groups of people in a society that are thought of as being at the same social or economic level: *The Labour Party was broadly seen as the party of the working class.* ◇ *Young people from the upper and middle classes are still far more likely to go to unversity.* ➲ *see also* LOWER CLASSES, MIDDLE-CLASS, MIDDLE CLASS **2** [U] the way that people are divided into different social and economic groups: *The definition of social class has varied over time.* ◇ **+ noun** *For Marx, revolution involved overthrowing the class system.* **3** [C] a group of things that have similar characteristics or qualities: *The chemical compounds are separated into classes based on their chemical or physical properties.* ◇ **~ of sth** *Ewert and his group identified at least ten different classes of neuron.* ◇ *There are two main classes of muscles: striated and smooth.* ➲ language bank *at* DEFINE **4** [C, U] an occasion when a group of students meets to be taught SYN LESSON (1): *Some youths periodically skip classes or miss school altogether for a day.* ◇ *The Council announced that funding for English classes would be ended for asylum seekers.* **5** [C+sing./pl. v.] a group of students who are taught together: *The class began to brainstorm ways that they could increase class activities.* ◇ *To complete the project, the class is divided into small groups of five students.* **6** [C] (*biology*) a group into which animals, plants or other life forms are divided, below a PHYLUM: *The phylum Echinodermata has five classes and about 6 000 living species.* ➲ *compare* FAMILY[1] (5), GENUS, KINGDOM (3), ORDER[1] (9), SPECIES **7** [C] (especially in compounds) one of the levels of achievement in a British university degree: *He obtained a first-class honours degree.* **8** [C] (especially in compounds) each of several different levels of comfort that are available to people who travel on public transport: *The company had been particularly hit by a fall in business-class and first-class passengers.*

▸ ADJECTIVE + CLASS **social • socio-economic • middle • working, lower • upper • ruling, dominant • capitalist • privileged • elite • professional • educated** *A dominant class typically favours maintaining things as they are.* ◇ *In medieval times, the language of the educated class was Latin.* | **main • broad • certain • different • distinct • special** *There are two broad classes of abnormal cell growth in the body.* ◇ *Some level of certain classes of mild pathogens may be acceptable in irrigation water.*

▸ VERB + CLASS **define • denote, represent, describe • constitute • identify** *Lipids represent a wide-ranging class of compounds.* | **take • attend • skip • teach** *One mother reports that her son was failing in school because he would not attend classes.*

▸ CLASS + NOUN **struggle, conflict • antagonism • structure • background • differences, inequality • divisions • relations • identity** *The interviews show that people's sense of class identity is weak.*

class[2] /klɑːs; *NAmE* klæs/ *verb* [often passive] to think or decide that sb/sth is a particular type of person or thing SYN CLASSIFY (2): **~ sb/sth as sth** *Only 14 per cent of the adult population were classed as belonging to professional or managerial groups.* ◇ **~ A and B together** *These groups share important properties that justify their being classed together.*

clas·sic[1] AWL /ˈklæsɪk/ *adj.* [usually before noun] **1** accepted or deserving to be accepted as one of the best or most important of its kind: *His book, first published in 1924, became a classic text.* ◇ *There have been several classic studies demonstrating the relationship between the environment and health.* ◇ *In her classic experiment, Perky asked subjects to look at a blank screen and to imagine an object on it.* **2** (*also* **clas·sic·al**) having all the typical features of sth that you would expect to find: *South Korea and Taiwan are classic examples of countries pursuing a strategy of export-led development.* ◇ *Classic symptoms of the disease are weight loss, fatigue, diarrhoea and anaemia.* ➲ *usage note at* CLASSICAL

clas·sic[2] AWL /ˈklæsɪk/ *noun* **1** [C] a book, film or song which is well known and considered to be of very high quality: *Today the book is recognized as a classic that was far ahead of its time.* ◇ *The films became classics among film students for their bold artistic experiment.* **2 Classics** [U] the study of ancient Greek and Roman culture, especially their languages and literature: *She studied Classics, ancient history and philosophy at Oxford University.*

clas·sic·al AWL /ˈklæsɪkl/ *adj.* [usually before noun] **1** widely accepted and used for a long time: *In classical physics, light is described as electromagnetic radiation.* ◇ *The classical approach has been frequently criticized.* ◇ *Classical Freudian theory describes human behaviour in terms of 'drives' or 'instincts'.* **2** connected with or influenced by the culture of ancient Greece and Rome: *In classical mythology, the roles of hero and trickster can be combined in a single character.* ◇ *In his studies of classical antiquity, he turned instinctively to the Greeks, rather than the Romans.* **3** (of music) written in a Western musical tradition, usually using an established form (for example, a SYMPHONY) and not played on electronic instruments. Classical music is generally considered to be serious and to have a lasting value: *It is a story about a rainy day, set to a piece of classical music.* **4** = CLASSIC[1] (2)

WHICH WORD?

classical • classic

- **Classical** refers to ideas and fields of study that are widely accepted and have formed the basis of later study: *classical liberalism/logic/physics/thermodynamics*. It also refers to things that are connected with the culture of Ancient Greece and Rome: *classical antiquity/mythology*
- **Classic** describes sth that is accepted as being one of the best or most important of its kind: *a classic essay/experiment/paper/study/text/textbook*. It also refers to expressions of ideas that are accepted as being strong and accurate: *a classic account/definition/formulation/justification/statement*
- Both words, but especially **classic**, can be used to describe things that have all the typical features of sth: *The classic example of an emerging infectious disease is HIV/AIDS.*
- A **classic** work of literature is considered to be serious and have lasting value.
- **Classical** music is written in a Western tradition and is considered to be serious and have lasting value.

clas·sic·al·ly /ˈklæsɪkli/ *adv.* **1** in a way that is widely accepted as being true or valid: *The term 'class' is classically defined by Karl Marx and Max Weber.* **2** used to say that sth is typical of sb/sth: *The books' cover photographs often show classically American cultural images (such as the Statue of Liberty).* **3** used to describe what usually or typically happens: *Classically, the affected limb is shortened and the hip is externally rotated.* **4** according to the traditional standard: *Geographers must continue to collaborate with classically trained oceanographers, ocean engineers and marine policy specialists.*

clas·si·fi·ca·tion /ˌklæsɪfɪˈkeɪʃn/ *noun* **1** [U] the act or process of putting animals, people or things into a group or category: *She argues that black identity has been influenced by the practice of racial classification in America.* ◇ **+ noun** *The Dewey decimal classification system is* *commonly used in educational libraries throughout the world.* ◇ **2** [C] a group or category into which sb/sth is put: *Classifications based on appearances alone can be misleading.* ◇ *Many of these classifications are simplistic and do not capture the characteristics and diversity of markets.*

clas·sify /ˈklæsɪfaɪ/ *verb* (**clas·si·fies, clas·si·fy·ing, clas·si·fied, clas·si·fied**) **1** to arrange sb/sth in groups according to features that they have in common: **~ sb/sth** *The first way of classifying consumer products is to consider them in terms of their durability.* ◇ **~ sb/sth according to sth** *Population members can be classified according to multiple criteria.* ◇ **~ sb/sth into sth** *It is common to use some form of diagnostic test that classifies individuals into categories.* **2** to decide which type or group sb/sth belongs to: **be classified as sth** *Crustal rocks can be broadly classified as igneous, metamorphic or sedimentary.* ◇ *216 students were classified as English learners, all of whom spoke Spanish as their first language.* ◇ **~ sb/sth (as sth)** *His verse has always been difficult to classify.*

class·room /ˈklɑːsruːm; ˈklɑːsrʊm; *NAmE* ˈklæsruːm; ˈklæsrʊm/ *noun* a room where a class of children or students is taught **HELP** The word **classroom** is often used to talk about the practice and methods of teaching: **in the ~** *If students are to grow as responsible citizens, then they need to learn responsibility in the classroom.* ◇ **outside the ~** *Learning does not stop outside the classroom.* ◇ **+ noun** *Effective classroom management is more than quick-fix strategies.* ◇ *classroom practice/activities*

ˌclass ˈstruggle (*also* ˌclass ˈwar) *noun* [U, sing.] (*politics*) opposition between the different social classes in society, especially that described in Marxist theory: *Their study can teach us a lot about the role of literacy and media in class struggle.*

clause **AWL** /klɔːz/ *noun* **1** an item in a legal document that says that a particular thing must or must not be done: *This contract contained a clause that laid down in which courts any disputes were to be settled.* **2** (*grammar*) a group of words that includes a subject and a verb, and forms a sentence or part of a sentence: *Some clauses may be complex and may include several embedded clauses.* ◇ *The main clause always contains a finite verb.*

clay /kleɪ/ *noun* [U] a type of heavy, sticky earth that becomes hard when it is baked and is used to make things such as POTS and bricks: *The soil was composed mainly of sand, with approximately 15% silt and 9% clay.*

clean[1] /kliːn/ *adj.* (**clean·er, clean·est**) **1** not dirty: *The wound was kept clean and dry.* ◇ *Guests expect a hotel room to be clean and comfortable.* ◇ *One prisoner complained that the authorities had not provided him with shoes or clean clothes.* **2** not containing or producing harmful or unpleasant substances: *The organizations worked together to supply clean drinking water to the village.* ◇ *Hydrogen is viewed as a clean energy alternative that could one day replace fossil fuels.*

clean[2] /kliːn/ *verb* [T, I] **~ (sth)** to make sth free from dirt or dust: *The hotel room had not been adequately cleaned.* ◇ *A low-sugar diet and regular teeth cleaning are both essential for dental health.* ◇ *She has written about her experiences cooking and cleaning with Mexican American women in New Mexico.*

PHR V **ˌclean sth ˈup** | **ˌclean ˈup** to remove dirt or pollution from somewhere or sth: *The city council spent millions cleaning up the abandoned mines.* ◇ *Two mechanisms were used to clean up the water supply.* ◇ *All staff were expected to work tidily and clean up after themselves.*

WORD FAMILY
clear *adj.*, *verb*
unclear *adj.*
clearly *adv.*
clarity *noun*
clarify *verb*

clear[1] /klɪə(r); *NAmE* klɪr/ *adj.* (**clear·er, clear·est**) **1** obvious and leaving no doubt at all: *There is clear evidence of several ice ages in the Permian and Carboniferous periods.* ◇ *The clearest example of how individual behaviour can affect health is smoking.* ◇ **it is ~ that...** *After a little investigation, it became clear that many of the stories were recycled.* ◇ **it is ~ to sb that...** *It was quite clear to everyone except Lenin that Malinovsky was a police informer.* ◇ **it is ~ from sth that...** *It is clear from these data that the world population is no longer growing at an increasing rate.* ◇ **it is ~ what/how, etc...** *It is not clear what the benefits of this method are.* ◇ **make ~ that...** *Early on, he made clear that he was an atheist.* ◇ **make it ~ that...** *The Buddha made it clear that women could attain all the goals of his religion.* **2** easy to understand or read: *The diagrams are very clear and informative.* ◇ *The law needs to be kept as clear and simple as possible.* ◇ *A strong brand identity will send a clear message to the consumer.* **3** having or feeling no doubt or confusion: *It is important to have a clear understanding of the issues.* ◇ **~ about/on sth** *She was not clear about what the question was actually asking.* ◇ *Ecologists are quite clear on what to do when it comes to wilderness: protect it.* ◇ **~ who/what, etc...** *At twelve he was not clear who he was yet.* **4** easy to see or hear: *A VCR could not deliver the same clear image and high-quality sound as a DVD.* ◇ *Headphones can make listening to the TV or radio easier by making sounds louder and clearer.* **5** that you can see through: *In clear waters, blue-green light penetrates to the greatest depth.* ◇ *Formaldehyde is a poisonous, clear, colourless liquid with a pungent odour.* ◇ *Termites collected from logs were placed in clear plastic boxes.* **6** without cloud or rain, etc: *Clear skies are often associated with descending air.* ◇ *On cloudy days, there is a considerable reduction in solar insolation compared with clear days.* **7** **~ (of sth)** free from things that are blocking the way or covering the surface of sth: *For most of this period the waters around Iceland were largely clear of ice.* ◇ *A large area of forest was bulldozed clear of all vegetation.* **8** **~ of sth** free from sth that is unpleasant: *Pathology confirmed that the area was fully clear of tumour.* ◇ *It takes about two years for the farm to become completely clear of pesticides.* **9** [not before noun] **~ (of sb/sth)** not touching sb/sth; a distance away from sb/sth: *She decided to keep well clear of him.* ◇ *They use their tentacles to attach to the sea floor so that they float just clear of the bottom.*

▸ CLEAR + NOUN **evidence • example, illustration • case • distinction • difference • indication, sign • implication • link • majority • consensus • intention** *There was no clear distinction between philosophy and science in Aristotle's day.* ◇ *American culture draws a clear link between romantic love and marriage.* ◇ *A clear majority of voters supported devolution.* | **instruction • guidelines • meaning • message • statement • definition • picture • answer • explanation** *The instructions were very clear.* ◇ *Clear definitions are important at the outset.* ◇ *They needed to gain a clearer picture of local markets and conditions.* | **understanding • sense • idea** *It is difficult to get a clear sense of how widespread these practices are.*

▸ VERB + CLEAR **become • seem • remain** *It seems clear that poverty is the biggest single factor contributing to the spread of AIDS.*

▸ ADVERB + CLEAR **very • quite • fairly • relatively • reasonably • sufficiently • not entirely** *The situation is not entirely clear.* | **increasingly • abundantly • immediately • perfectly, absolutely • not always** *The deleterious effects of misguided human modification of our environment have become abundantly clear.*

clear[2] /klɪə(r); *NAmE* klɪr/ *verb* **1** [T] to remove sth that is not wanted or needed from a place: **~ sth/sb** *Humans have cleared forests to make way for their crops.* ◇ **~ sth for sth** *Fire was a key method of clearing land for agriculture.* ◇ **~ A of B** *The patient is not breathing out deeply enough to clear his lungs of mucus.* ◇ **~ B from A** *Mucus is continually cleared from the respiratory tract by cilia.* **2** [I] to gradually go away or disappear: *The infection can clear*

THESAURUS

clear ♦ **obvious** ♦ **apparent** ♦ **evident** *adj.*

These words can all be used to say that sth is easy to see or understand.

- **It is** clear/obvious/apparent/evident **that...**
- **It is** clear/obvious/apparent/evident **what/how, etc...**
- to **make** sth clear/obvious/apparent/evident
- to **make it** clear/obvious/apparent **that...**
- to **become/seem** clear/obvious/apparent/evident
- clear/obvious/apparent/evident **to** sb
- clear/obvious/apparent/evident **from/in** sth
- **immediately** clear/obvious/apparent/evident
- a clear/an obvious **example/reason**

- These words all have almost exactly the same meaning; however, there are slight differences in how they are used. If you *make sth clear*, you do so deliberately because you want people to understand sth: *The review made clear the important role of the audit committee.* However, if sth *becomes clear/obvious/evident/apparent* or *makes it obvious/apparent that...*, it is facts or circumstances that make people realize sth: *It became evident to city leaders that a more formal approach would be beneficial.*
- When **apparent** is used before a noun, it often suggests that sth may not be true; the other words in this group do not change their meaning in this way: *He resolved the apparent contradiction* (= it was not really a contradiction). ◇ *There is an obvious contradiction here* (= it really is a contradiction).

spontaneously in 20% of cases. ◇ *Fortunately, during the two-week period, to a large extent the smog cleared.* **3** [T] **~ sth** to give or get official approval for sth to be done: *The second merger was also cleared by the competition authorities.* **4** [T] to prove that sb is not guilty of a crime: **~ sb** *They were convicted of the hijacking and served prison sentences, though later cleared by the Court of Appeal.* ◇ **~ sb of sth** *He was fortunate to escape a more serious charge of tax evasion and was cleared of eight other charges.* **5** [I, T] **~ (sth)** if a payment made to sb **clears**, or a bank **clears** it, the money is available for them to use: *Sales include only those transactions for which payment has been cleared.*

IDM **clear the ground/way (for sth/for sth to happen)** to remove things that are stopping the progress or movement of sth: *The Labour leader's announcement that he would stand down in September cleared the way for formal discussions to take place.*

PHR V ˌ**clear sth aˈway** to remove sth because it is not wanted or needed, or in order to leave a clear space: *By the spring, however, the last of the ruined buildings were cleared away.* ˌ**clear sth ˈout** to make sth empty and clean by removing things or throwing things away: *Her father cleared out the family home once the two children were at college.* ˌ**clear ˈup** (of an illness or infection) to disappear: *In many cases, the rash will clear up with no treatment.* ˌ**clear sth ˈup** to solve or explain sth: *Piloting or pre-testing may clear up problems in question formulation.*

clear·ance /ˈklɪərəns; *NAmE* ˈklɪrəns/ *noun* **1** [U, C] the act of removing things that are not wanted: *The impact of such large-scale forest clearance on river systems is evident.* ◇ **~ of sth** *The clearance of a drug is the irreversible elimination of the drug from the body.* ◇ **+ noun** *The massive slum clearance programme of the 1950s and 1960s created space for further building of council houses and flats.* **2** [U, C] official permission that is given to sb before they can work somewhere, have particular information, or do sth they want to do: *Ethical clearance was not required for this observational study.* ◇ *Access to the data and the computer equipment are limited to persons with appropriate security clearances.* **3** [U] official permission for a person or vehicle to enter or leave a country: *The usual immigration application made abroad is for entry clearance.* ◇ **+ noun** *The paperless customs clearance system has resulted in cost savings.*

ˌ**clear-ˈcut** *adj.* definite and easy to see or identify: *The distinction between the focus group method and the group interview is by no means clear-cut.* ◇ *Here we have a clear-cut case of film trying to measure up to a literary work.*

clear·ly /ˈklɪəli; *NAmE* ˈklɪrli/ *adv.* **1** used to emphasize that what you are saying is obvious and true SYN OBVIOUSLY: *The patient was clearly in severe pain.* ◇ *Inflation clearly has negative effects on real incomes.* ◇ *Clearly, low-wage countries are relatively abundant in low-skilled workers.* **2** in a way that is easy to see, hear or understand: *All packages must be clearly labelled with hazard information.* ◇ *The division of the exoskeleton into three parts is clearly seen in most of these species.* **3** in a normal way and without difficulty: *After the accident she was confused and had difficulty thinking clearly.*

- CLEARLY + VERB | VERB + CLEARLY **show, demonstrate, indicate** ♦ **define** ♦ **state** ♦ **identify** ♦ **distinguish** ♦ **illustrate** ♦ **establish** *The graph shows clearly that whales have the smallest relative brain size among all mammals.* ◇ *The evidence clearly indicated that women are often reluctant to enter the city centre at night.*
- VERB + CLEARLY **see** ♦ **speak** ♦ **think** ♦ **hear** *On waking, he could not see clearly out of either eye.*
- CLEARLY + ADJECTIVE **related** ♦ **important** ♦ **different** ♦ **impossible** ♦ **relevant** *Understanding how markets work is clearly important to managers.* | **evident** ♦ **present** ♦ **visible** ♦ **identifiable, recognizable** ♦ **distinct** *The effects of the 1988 drought were still clearly evident in 1993.* ◇ *Most bacteria are clearly visible in a light microscope.*

clergy /ˈklɜːdʒi; *NAmE* ˈklɜːrdʒi/ *noun* (*often* **the clergy**) [pl.] the priests or ministers of a religion, especially of the Christian Church: *After the revolution, Catholic clergy were required to take an oath of loyalty to the state.*

cler·ic·al /ˈklerɪkl/ *adj.* **1** connected with office work: *Increasingly, such employees as clerical workers, draftsmen and sales personnel have seen their jobs computerized and deskilled.* **2** connected with the clergy: *Papal reformers had condemned clerical marriage since the mid-eleventh century.*

clever /ˈklevə(r)/ *adj.* (**clever·er**, **clever·est**) (You can also use **more clever** and **most clever**.) **1** (*especially BrE*) quick at learning and understanding things SYN INTELLIGENT: *The idea that clever people are somehow mentally faster is an old and vague one.* **2 ~ (at sth/doing sth)** (*especially BrE*) skilful: *Some people are very clever at concealing their real feelings.* **3** showing intelligence or skill, for example in the design of an object, in an idea or sb's actions: *Church buildings like Westminster Abbey are clever pieces of medieval structural engineering.* ◇ *Many farmers were clever enough to invest their earnings in the modernization of their farms.* ■ **clev·er·ly** *adv.*: *The doors are cleverly designed so that they cannot open directly outwards.*

click /klɪk/ *verb* [T, I] to press a button on a mouse, etc. to choose a function or item on a computer screen: **~ sth** *Selecting the required text and then clicking the right mouse button will provide access to the relevant menu.* ◇ **~ on sth** *Click on the company's website to find recipes and tips about nutrition.*

cli·ent /ˈklaɪənt/ *noun* **1** a person who uses the services or advice of a professional person or organization: *Agencies provided their clients with a wide range of varied marketing services.* ◇ *All of these organizations are potential clients for social research.* ◇ *It is hoped that the health facilities will become more responsive to the needs of the clients.* **2** (*computing*) a computer that is linked to a SERVER: *The operating system is distributed between the client and the server.*

cli·mate /ˈklaɪmət/ *noun* **1** [C, U] the regular pattern of weather conditions of a particular place: *The mild climate results in a long growing season.* ◇ *Small variations in climate can have a significant impact on ecosystems.* ◇ **+ noun** *Climate variability refers to shorter term variations in climate.* **2** [C] an area with particular weather conditions: *These soils are found only in drier climates.* ◇ *Inuit children are leaner, not fatter, than children from warmer climates.* **3** [C] a general attitude or feeling; an atmosphere or a situation that exists in a particular place: *In today's political climate, countries increasingly work together in the interests of national security.* ◇ **~ of sth** *Education can promote a climate of ethnic tolerance.* ◇ *The climate of opinion in China changed overnight.* ◇ **~ for sth** *Government support would create a favourable climate for research.*

▸ ADJECTIVE + CLIMATE **warm • hot • cold • dry • wet • tropical • humid • temperate • arid • harsh • prevailing** *In general, Vietnam has a humid tropical climate.* ◇ *Warm-blooded organisms are larger in colder climates than in warmer ones.* | **global • regional • local** *Volcanic eruptions have had measurable effects on global climate.* | **favourable • current • political • economic • moral • cultural • intellectual • social** *An exceptionally harsh economic climate prevailed in the 1590s, with poor harvests, low wages and high taxation.*

▸ VERB + CLIMATE **affect • influence • change** *Altitude affects climate.* ◇ *Since 2005, there has been a broad consensus that human activity is influencing our climate.* ◇ *The civil rights movement changed the political climate in the southern states.* | **create, foster** *Their aim was to foster a climate of understanding and respect.*

▸ CLIMATE + NOUN **change • variability • variation • system • model • event • record** *Severe climate events, such as major droughts, present severe challenges.*

ˈclimate change *noun* [U] changes in the earth's weather, including changes in temperature, wind patterns and RAINFALL, especially the increase in the temperature of the earth's atmosphere that is caused by the increase of particular gases, especially CARBON DIOXIDE: *Developing and commercializing clean energy is one of the basic strategies to combat global climate change.* ➲ *compare* GLOBAL WARMING

cli·mat·ic /klaɪˈmætɪk/ *adj.* [only before noun] connected with the climate of a particular area: *Tree ring data point to a sudden climatic change in 536–545 AD.* ◇ *climatic variation/variability* ◇ *climatic fluctuations/oscillations* ◇ *Some varieties of rocks can be deposited only under specific climatic conditions.* ■ **cli·mat·ic·al·ly** /klaɪˈmætɪkli/ *adv.*: *South-western Michigan was climatically well suited for wheat production.*

climb /klaɪm/ *verb* **1** [T, I] **~ (up) (sth)** to go up sth towards the top: *Overall, normal-weight workers were more likely to climb the stairs than the overweight.* ◇ *People climbed up on the roofs of buildings to watch.* **2** [I] **~ (to sth)** to increase in value or amount: *By 1966, however, that figure had climbed to 85 per cent.* **3** [I] **~ (to sth)** to move to a higher level of importance in a society, organization, etc, by your own effort: *Eight years later he had climbed to the position of Secretary of State.* **4** [I] **+ adv./prep.** to move somewhere, especially with difficulty or effort: *Rats make desperate attempts to climb out when they are put in water.* ◇ *The emergency team climbed into a helicopter.*

clin·ic /ˈklɪnɪk/ *noun* **1** a building or part of a hospital where people can go for special medical treatment or advice: *Only 2.5% of all pregnant women fail to attend an antenatal clinic.* ◇ **in a ~** *These patients are usually treated in outpatient clinics as day cases.* ◇ **at a ~** *All children have a routine check-up at the child health clinic.* ◇ **+ noun** *Many injury patients return for clinic visits to check progress two weeks following treatment.* **2** (*especially BrE*) a period of time during which doctors or nurses give special medical treatment or advice: *Monthly diabetic clinics were held.* **3** (*especially BrE*) a private hospital or one that treats health problems of a particular kind: *Private clinics tend to have longer consultation times than those in the public sector.*

clin·ic·al /ˈklɪnɪkl/ *adj.* [only before noun] connected with the examination and treatment of patients and their illnesses: *This test is not yet used in routine clinical practice.* ◇ *There is, however, insufficient evidence from clinical trials on which to evaluate these treatments.*

▸ CLINICAL + NOUN **practice • trial • study, research • laboratory • setting • guidelines • assessment, examination • interview • diagnosis • outcome • feature, sign • sample • data, findings • decision, judgement** *The clinical features of each of these syndromes are similar.*

clin·ic·al·ly /ˈklɪnɪkli/ *adv.* in a way that is connected with the examination and treatment of patients and their illnesses: *Clinically, the symptoms of lung cancer and tuberculosis are often similar.* ◇ *Some newer strains are resistant to almost all clinically available antibiotics.* ◇ *An effective treatment for the clinically diagnosed condition is available.*

clin·ician /klɪˈnɪʃn/ *noun* a doctor, PSYCHOLOGIST, etc. who has direct contact with patients: *The Internet is also increasingly being used by clinicians to acquire health information.*

clock /klɒk; *NAmE* klɑːk/ *noun* an instrument for measuring and showing time, in a room or on the wall of a building (not worn or carried like a watch): *The time measured by the clock was 12.10* ◇ *Both clocks were set to zero.* ◇ *The first clock was running slower.* HELP A **biological clock** is a natural system in living things that controls regular physical activities such as sleeping: *The movements of the leaves are triggered by the plant's biological clock.*

IDM **around/round the ˈclock** all day and all night without stopping: *Satellite technology meant that Al-Jazeera broadcasts could be watched around the clock on all five continents.* **turn/put the ˈclock back** (*often disapproving*) to return to a situation that existed in the past, or to old-fashioned methods or ideas: *After the war's end, various policies attempted to turn the clock back for female war workers.*

clone[1] /kləʊn; *NAmE* kloʊn/ *noun* (*biology*) a plant or an animal that is produced naturally or artificially from the cells of another plant or animal and is therefore exactly the same as it: *A population of plants derived from a single clone will have no genetic variability at all.* ◇ **~ of sth** *The body contains many different clones of plasma cells.*

clone[2] /kləʊn; *NAmE* kloʊn/ *verb* (*biology*) **~ sth** to produce an exact copy of an animal or a plant from its cells: *Scientists have cloned a gene that helps brain cells communicate.* ◇ *The long-term effects of this genomic mixing are unknown, but cloned animals develop a range of health problems.*

close[1] /kləʊz; *NAmE* kloʊz/ *verb* **1** [T, I] **~ (sth)** to put sth into a position so that it covers an opening; to get into this position SYN SHUT: *to close a door/window* ◇ *The patient may be encouraged to close their eyes and listen.* ◇ *The valve begins to close and the flow of steam is reduced.* OPP OPEN[2] (1) **2** [T] to move the parts of sth together so that it is no longer open SYN SHUT: *She closes the book and puts it on her lap.* ◇ *These immensely strong muscles close the jaws.* OPP OPEN[2] (1) **3** [T, often passive, I] to make the work of a shop, etc. stop for a period of time; to not be open for people to use: **~ sth (to sb/sth)** *On January 18 the river was closed to all fishing activities.* ◇ **~ (for sth)** *Airports would have to close if the strikes were to go ahead.* ◇ *Business and government offices close for Friday prayer.* OPP OPEN[2] (2) **4** (*also* ˌ**close ˈdown**, ˌ**close sth ˈdown**) [T, I]

C

~ (sth) (of a company, shop, etc.) it stop operating as a business; to stop operating a company, shop, etc. as a business: *The town's population has declined since the factory closed.* ◇ *His newspaper, 'Rheinische Zeitung', was closed down by the government.* OPP OPEN²(2) **5** [I, T] to end; to make sth end: **~ with sth** *This dramatic book closes with the murder of the disgraced Vitellius.* ◇ **~ sth (with sth)** *Evans-Pritchard closes his discussion with a short account of prophets and priests.* ◇ *He closed his bank account.* OPP OPEN²(5) **6** [T, I] **~ (sth)** to make the distance or difference between two people or things smaller; to become smaller or narrower: *Researchers will be able to close further gaps in our knowledge.* ◇ *The gap between male and female wages began to close during the 1980s.*

PHR V **ˌclose ˈdown** | **ˌclose sth ˈdown** = CLOSE¹(4) **ˌclose ˈin (on sb/sth)** to move nearer to sb/sth, especially in order to attack them: *The rebels were closing in on the city.* **ˌclose sth ˈoff** to separate sth from other parts so that people cannot use it: *After closing off the enemy's harbour, he overcame long resistance and captured Carthage.*

close² /kləʊz; *NAmE* kloʊz/ *noun* [sing.] the end of a period of time, an activity or a text: *The Cold War was coming to a close.* ◇ *As the century drew to a close, scientists did not have any way to gauge the overall size of an earthquake.* ◇ **~ of sth** *He took British citizenship only at the close of his life.* ◇ *Karas's claim had been refused shortly before the close of business on 11 October.* ◇ *I often write a sentence such as 'Thank you in advance for your time and attention' prior to the close of the email.*

close³ /kləʊs; *NAmE* kloʊs/ *adj.* (**closer, clos·est**) **1** near in space or time: *Animals that graze in the open need to sense a predator before it gets too close.* ◇ *The area's climate is controlled by its close proximity to the Pacific Ocean.* ◇ **~ to sb/sth** *During an inversion, cooler air remains close to the surface of the earth.* ◇ **~ together** *The earthquakes occurred very close together.* **2** [not before noun] almost in a particular state; likely to do sth soon: **~ to sth** *He seemed close to death.* ◇ **~ to doing sth** *The party has yet to come close to winning a seat in parliament.* **3** very similar to sth else or to an amount: *The food provided to males in our experiment is a very close match to their natural food supply.* ◇ **~ to sth** *She was treated with something close to veneration.* ◇ *Poverty levels for black Americans are close to double the rate for whites.* **4** [only before noun] careful and thorough: *After 2008, banks began taking a closer look at their loans.* ◇ *Only after his second book did people begin to pay close attention to his views.* **5** used to describe a connection with sb/sth that is very strong: *In many countries, there is a close relationship between business and politics.* ◇ *There is a close link between health and housing.* **6** near in family relationship: *In the past, marriages between close relatives such as first cousins were common.* ◇ *He wrote various poems about his close family.* OPP DISTANT(2) **7** belonging to the same group of plants or animals: *Our close relatives the chimpanzees also live in highly complex social groups.* OPP DISTANT(2) **8** very involved in the work or activities of sb else, usually seeing and talking to them regularly: *In Europe, there is close cooperation between national governments.* ◇ *Antibiotics may be needed by those who have had close contact with the patient.* **9** knowing sb very well and liking them very much: *Her once close relationship with her mother had deteriorated.* ◇ *Hugh had few close friends.* ◇ **~ to sb** *Girls are often considered to be closer to their mothers than boys.* **10** won by only a small amount or distance: *Manchester was the most popular film location, with London a close second.*

IDM **at/from ˌclose ˈquarters** very near: *The fighting was at very close quarters.* **keep a close ˈeye/ˈwatch on sb/sth** to watch sb/sth carefully: *It is important to keep a close eye on electrolyte levels and replace where necessary.* ◇ *The government is keeping a close watch on the economy.*

▸ CLOSE + NOUN **approximation • match** *This is a close approximation of the optimum performance attainable.* | **look • observation • examination, inspection • analysis • attention • scrutiny • reading • supervision • monitoring** *On closer inspection, it appears that state aid has increased.* ◇ *The church came under close supervision by the tsar.* | **relationship, link, association, tie, relations, connection • integration** *Traditionally, there is a close association between geography, mapping and exploration.* ◇ *Kuwait maintains close ties with the West.* | **relative, relation** *Some cultures regard it as preferable to marry a close relation.* | **contact, touch • cooperation, collaboration • associate** *The president's closest associates advised him against the plan.*

▸ ADVERB + CLOSE **very • fairly, quite, reasonably • relatively • sufficiently • remarkably** *If the molecules are sufficiently close to one another, the energy emitted by the donor can be absorbed by the acceptor.* | **geographically • physically** *Geographically close lakes will share a common pool of species.* | **dangerously • uncomfortably** *In business, gift-giving and hospitality can come dangerously close to bribery.* ◇ *His actions brought the country dangerously close to disaster.*

▸ PHRASES **in close proximity to sb/sth • at close range** *Most people were farmers and lived in close proximity to the water.* ◇ *At close range, dolphins utilize vision for hunting.*

close⁴ /kləʊs; *NAmE* kloʊs/ *adv.* (**closer, clos·est**) near; not far away: *The Christmas Island population is largely composed of people living close together whose families know each other.* ◇ *Small galaxies that come too close to our own galaxy get broken up by the gravitational forces they encounter.* ◇ *Significant progress has been made toward getting closer to this goal.* ◇ *The London exchange is close behind the NASDAQ and Tokyo exchanges in size.*

IDM **close at ˈhand** near; in a place where sb/sth can be reached easily: *The need for mutual support in a potentially hostile environment made it desirable to have neighbours close at hand.* **close ˈby (sb/sth)** at a short distance (from sb/sth): *Attending meetings was easier for those who lived close by.* **close to** almost; nearly: *Job dissatisfaction among nurses was close to 20% in most countries.* **come close (to sth/to doing sth)** to almost reach or do sth: *None of them came close to discovering what was really going on.*

closed /kləʊzd; *NAmE* kloʊzd/ *adj.* **1** [not before noun] not open: *The windows are kept closed.* ◇ *The patient loses balance with his/her eyes closed.* OPP OPEN¹(1) **2** [not before noun] not open, especially of a shop or public building that is not open for a period of time: *Government offices are closed on some days.* ◇ **~ to sb/sth** *The defendant was found in an area of the building which was closed to the public.* OPP OPEN¹(7) **3** not willing to accept outside influences or new ideas: *Only North Korea still maintains a traditional hard-line, secretive, closed system.* ◇ *The perception of the Soviet Union as a closed society had changed.* HELP A **closed economy** is one in which all the goods and services people need are produced within that economy, and there is no trade with other economies. OPP OPEN¹(14) **4** [usually before noun] limited to a particular group of people or things; not open to everyone: *The committee meets in closed session.* ◇ *Prepositions largely constitute a closed set (unlike nouns and verbs).* OPP OPEN¹(9) **5** (*geometry*) (of a curve or figure) formed from a single line without end : *The curves join smoothly at these two points so that the phase paths are closed curves.*

IDM **behind closed ˈdoors** without the public being allowed to attend or know what is happening; in private: *These meetings take place behind closed doors.*

ˌclosed ˈquestion *noun* a question to which the answer is either 'yes' or 'no' or one of a very limited set of possible answers: *With a closed question, respondents are presented* *with a set of fixed alternatives from which they have to choose an appropriate answer.* ➲ *compare* OPEN QUESTION (2)

closely /ˈkləʊsli; *NAmE* ˈkloʊsli/ *adv.* **1** in a way that has a strong connection with sb/sth: *Vegetation is closely linked to climate.* ◇ *The histories of the Cold War and of the bomb are very closely connected.* **2** in a careful or thorough way: *The patients are closely monitored.* ◇ *After looking closely at a number of studies, I came to this conclusion.* **3** in a way that is very similar to sb/sth: *Cordierite closely resembles quartz.* ◇ *One day, machines may simulate the human mind very closely.* **4** in a way that involves working or being with sb/sth a lot: *In Japan, schools and families collaborate closely on behavioural issues.* ◇ *Central government is closely involved in overseeing the provision of many services.* ◇ **~ together** *They worked closely together to come up with a design.* **5** if people, animals or plants are **closely** related, they are near in their family relationship: *Closely related species often have many characteristics in common.* **6** with little time or space between one person or thing and another: **~ to sth** *The Yellow River shifted course in the 12th century and flowed more closely to the Shangqui area.* ◇ **~ together** *The molecules are packed closely together in the crystal.* **7** used to describe a situation in which there is very little difference between one person, thing or amount and another: *He lost in a closely fought contest.*

▸ CLOSELY + VERB + -ED **related, connected, linked, correlated, coupled, interrelated, bound up with** ♦ **associated with** ♦ **aligned, allied** ♦ **tied to, affiliated** ♦ **intertwined** ♦ **integrated** *Type 2 diabetes is closely associated with obesity.* ◇ *A person's self-esteem can be closely tied to having a job.* | **packed** ♦ **spaced** *An atoll usually consists of a string of closely spaced coral islets.*

▸ CLOSELY + VERB **monitor** ♦ **examine** ♦ **scrutinize** *Alleged infringements of economic and social rights are closely scrutinized by the court.* | **resemble** ♦ **match** ♦ **parallel** ♦ **follow** ♦ **approximate** ♦ **mimic** ♦ **mirror, reflect** *The sample closely matched the ethnic distribution of the US population.* ◇ *This Nordic myth closely parallels a Roman tale.* | **follow** *Spaniards in particular (closely followed by the Greek and the Italians) exhibit clearly above-average values.*

▸ VERB + CLOSELY **monitor** ♦ **look** ♦ **examine** ♦ **follow** *Her novels examine the role of women in history closely.* | **correspond** *The results correspond closely to those reported for osteoarthritis of the knee.* | **work** ♦ **cooperate** ♦ **collaborate** *The organizations cooperate closely on many matters.* | **follow** *Her best work followed closely after the success of 'Lady Audley's Secret'.*

close·ness /ˈkləʊsnəs; *NAmE* ˈkloʊsnəs/ *noun* [U] **1** the fact of knowing sb very well and liking them very much: *She regretted the lack of emotional closeness in their relationship.* ◇ **~ to sb** *Closeness to high-school and college friends declines with time.* ◇ **~ with sb** *She wanted closeness with her dad.* **2 ~ (to sb)** the fact of being very involved in the work or activities of sb else: *His authority and closeness to Blair led to him being called 'the real deputy Prime Minister'.* **3 ~ (to sth)** the fact of having a strong connection with sb/sth: *The dying person is placed on the floor, symbolizing closeness to 'mother earth'.* **4 ~ (to sth)** the fact of being near in time or space: *The closeness of some of the active large volcanoes and densely populated centres is a serious hazard in Java.* **5** the fact of being very similar to sth else: *There is no simple correlation between semantic closeness and degree of synonymy.*

clos·ing¹ /ˈkləʊzɪŋ; *NAmE* ˈkloʊzɪŋ/ *adj.* [only before noun] coming at the end of a speech, a period of time or an activity: *What followed was a series of formal closing remarks.* ◇ *Douglas's design team's extensive experience with jets began in the closing days of World War II.* ◇ *the closing chapters/pages/lines* OPP OPENING²

clos·ing² /ˈkləʊzɪŋ; *NAmE* ˈkloʊzɪŋ/ *noun* [U] **~ (of sth)** the act of shutting sth such as a factory, hospital, school, etc. permanently: *Halliburton announced the closing of the Dover plant on October 13, 2000.*

clos·ure /ˈkləʊʒə(r); *NAmE* ˈkloʊʒər/ *noun* **1** [C, U] **~ (of sth)** the situation when a factory, school, hospital, etc. shuts permanently: *The new president initiated the closure of one-third of the company's factories.* ◇ *They complain that hospital closures or job losses are more prominently reported than the opening of a new hospital or factory.* ◇ *Texas schools that receive low ratings face sanctions, including possible closure.* **2** [C, U] **~ (of sth)** the temporary closing of a business, public place, etc: *The Richmond River was reopened to normal fishing activities after a closure of some six weeks.* ◇ *The closure of UK airports was due to an ash cloud caused by a volcanic eruption in Iceland.* **3** [U] the act of blocking up a hole or opening: *Repair is usually achieved by surgical closure.* ◇ **~ of sth** *With the closure of Glen Canyon Dam in 1963, major floods were eliminated.* **4** [U] a sense of conclusion at the end of a work of art, piece of music, etc: *The plots generate a desire for narrative closure, which the endings do indeed offer the reader.*

clot¹ /klɒt; *NAmE* klɑːt/ *noun* a lump that is formed when a liquid, especially blood, dries or becomes thicker: *When blood becomes too thick, the risk of blood clots rises.*

clot² /klɒt; *NAmE* klɑːt/ *verb* (-tt-) [I] when blood **clots**, it forms thick lumps: *The ability of the blood to clot is a vital part of the body's natural defence.*

cloth /klɒθ; *NAmE* klɔːθ/ *noun* (*pl.* **cloths** /klɒθs; *NAmE* klɔːðz/) **1** [U] material made by WEAVING or KNITTING cotton, wool, etc: *The production of cotton cloth was China's greatest industry.* ◇ *Cover the food with a piece of cloth.* ◇ **+ noun** *The fruit was collected and stored in cloth bags.* ◇ *The Wiltshire village of Castle Combe became a centre of cloth production.* **2** [C] a piece of cloth, often used for a special purpose, especially cleaning things or covering a table: *Never apply ice directly onto the skin: wrap in a cloth or towel before applying.*

clothes /kləʊðz; kləʊz; *NAmE* kloʊðz; kloʊz/ *noun* [pl.] the things that you wear: *Community nurses wear their own clothes, not uniforms.* ◇ **+ noun** *'The Look' is a high-street clothes retailer mainly based in the UK.*

cloth·ing /ˈkləʊðɪŋ; *NAmE* ˈkloʊðɪŋ/ *noun* [U] clothes, especially a particular type of clothes: *Removal of containers must be done by staff wearing suitable protective clothing.* ◇ *These items of clothing have a symbolic function within the Muslim community itself.* ◇ **+ noun** *It was a difficult time for the clothing industry.*

cloud¹ /klaʊd/ *noun* **1** [C, U] a grey or white mass made of very small drops of water, that floats in the sky: *As the air cools, water vapour condenses to form clouds.* ◇ *Lightning almost always originates within cloud.* **2** [C] **~ (of sth)** a large mass of sth in the air, for example dust or smoke: *The explosion would produce a cloud of radioactive dust.* ◇ *An industrial accident at a chemical plant released a cloud of poisonous gas that killed thousands of people.* **3** (*often* **the cloud**) [sing.] a system of software and other computer resources that are stored on the Internet and to which computer users have access: *Data are uploaded and analysed in a shared cloud.* ◇ *In this model, providers install and operate application software in the cloud.* ◇ **~ computing** *Cloud computing offers an attractive solution to customers keen to acquire computing infrastructure without large upfront investment.*

cloud² /klaʊd/ *verb* to make sth become less clear or certain: **~ sth** *His concern for order and decency clouds his judgement.* ◇ *Uncertainty also clouded the economy.* ◇ **~ the issue** *Variation in anatomical structure clouded the issue of what was a distinct species and what was merely a variety.*

cloudy /ˈklaʊdi/ *adj.* **(cloud·ier, cloudi·est)** **1** (of the sky or the weather) covered with clouds; with a lot of clouds: *Dry seasons tend to be warmer, being less cloudy.* ◇ *The figure shows the hourly average values of solar radiation for typical clear and cloudy days.* OPP CLEAR[1] (6) **2** (of liquids) not clear or transparent: *Cloudy fluids indicate a raised white cell count and possible infection.* ■ **cloudi·ness** /ˈklaʊdinəs/ *noun* [U] *Increasing cloudiness is a factor often invoked to explain changes in vegetation.*

club /klʌb/ *noun* **1** [C+sing./pl. v.] (especially in compounds) a group of people who meet together regularly, for a particular activity, sport, etc: *After-school sports clubs such as football, netball and rugby were established.* **2** [C+sing./pl. v.] (*BrE*) a professional sports organization that includes the players, managers, owners and members: *Premier League clubs spent 1.3 billion on player wages in 2008–09.* **3** [C] a group of people or countries that share characteristics and aims: *As Kenneth Waltz argued, 'Nuclear weapons will nevertheless spread, with a new member occasionally joining the club.'*

clue /kluː/ *noun* a fact or a piece of evidence that helps you discover the answer to a problem: **~ to sth** *The cosmic microwave background provides clues to the origin of galaxies.* ◇ **~ about sth** *Climate data over previous decades may offer clues about environmental impacts on breeding success.* ◇ **~ as to sth** *Routine biochemical tests can give clues as to the presence of cancer.* ◇ **~ that...** *These soil characteristics provide valuable clues that a soil was affected by frost during its formation.*

clus·ter[1] /ˈklʌstə(r)/ *noun* **1** a group of things of the same type that appear or are found close together: *In South Africa, diamonds are found as clusters in funnel-shaped pipes.* ◇ *The industrial clusters within Harare comprise firms that are located in an easily defined physical area.* ◇ **in clusters** *Most galaxies occur in clusters.* ◇ **~ of sth** *a cluster of atoms/cells/galaxies* ◇ *Prior to the 1970s, American professional football players came primarily from a cluster of southern states.* **2** a small group of people who are chosen to represent a larger group, used in research: *It would be better to choose respondents from small, geographically local clusters.* ◇ **+ noun** *Cluster analysis was used to classify the adolescents.*

clus·ter[2] /ˈklʌstə(r)/ *verb* [I, T, usually passive] **1** [I, T] to come or be together in a small group or groups: **~ together** *The women clustered together, listening intently.* ◇ **be clustered together** *Groups of firms in different industries can be clustered together geographically.* ◇ **be clustered around/round sb/sth** *Most of the electron density is clustered around the atomic nuclei.* **2** [T] **be clustered around/round sth** (of data points) to have a similar value: *The data are mostly clustered around the mean with few extremely high or low values.* **3** [T] **be clustered (+ adv./prep.)** to happen at about the same time or in the same place: *Individual hurricanes tended to be clustered in time.*

coach /kəʊtʃ; *NAmE* koʊtʃ/ *noun* **1** a person who trains a person or team in sport: *The school soccer club needs an experienced football coach.* **2** a person who gives sb extra teaching or training, especially in professional skills: *The company used coaches and mentors for career development and advice.* **3** (*BrE*) a comfortable bus for carrying passengers over long distances: **+ noun** *The coach operator had a long history of safe operation.* **4** (*BrE*) (*NAmE* car) a separate section of a train for carrying passengers: *Several coaches went off the rails.* ➲ *compare* TRUCK (3)

coal /kəʊl; *NAmE* koʊl/ *noun* **1** [U] a hard black mineral that is found below the ground and burnt to produce heat: *Most of the power plants burn coal, which causes acid rain and pollution.* ◇ *In 2000 about 200 million people used coal for household cooking in East Asia.* ◇ **+ noun** *Methane and coal dust in coal mines cause explosions.* **2** [C] a type of coal: *Western coals generally have a low mineral and sulfur content.*

co·ali·tion /ˌkəʊəˈlɪʃn; *NAmE* ˌkoʊəˈlɪʃn/ *noun* **1** [C+sing./pl. v.] a government formed by two or more political parties working together: **~ (with sth)** *The Conservatives formed a coalition with the Liberal Democrats.* ◇ **+ noun** *Coalition governments composed of many minority parties—as in Mali and Niger—are rare.* ◇ *Diverse views of coalition partners can lead to political instability.* **2** [C+sing./pl. v.] **~ (of sth)** a group formed by people from several different groups, especially political ones, agreeing to work together for a particular purpose: *Government ministers have refused to meet a coalition of ten environmental groups to discuss their current policy.* **3** [U] **(in) ~ (with sth)** the act of two or more groups joining together: *Some community organizations work in coalition with traditional unions.*

coarse /kɔːs; *NAmE* kɔːrs/ *adj.* **(coars·er, coars·est)** **1** consisting of fairly large pieces: *Coarser sediment derived from river mouths is trapped close to the shoreline by waves.* OPP FINE[1] (3) **2** (of skin, hair, cloth or other material) rough: *Symptoms include fatigue, weight gain, coarse dry hair and dry skin.* OPP SMOOTH[1] (1)

coast /kəʊst; *NAmE* koʊst/ *noun* the land beside or near to the sea or ocean: *Property damage along the US coast from storms at sea occurs each year.* ◇ **~ of sth** *the south/southern coast of France* ◇ **on the ~ (of sth)** *It is the largest estuary on the Atlantic coast of the USA.* ◇ **off the ~ (of sth)** *The Canaries lie off the west coast of Africa.*

coast·al /ˈkəʊstl; *NAmE* ˈkoʊstl/ *adj.* [usually before noun] of or near a coast: *Most of the population live in highly urbanized areas along the coastal plains.* ◇ *A number of minerals are mined in the coastal zone of South East Asia.* ◇ *Much of Thailand's coastal erosion is on the western coast of the Thai Peninsula.*

coast·line /ˈkəʊstlaɪn; *NAmE* ˈkoʊstlaɪn/ *noun* the land along a coast, especially when you are thinking of its shape or appearance: *Until the age of oceanic trade, China's long coastline was almost a closed frontier.* ◇ *a rugged/rocky coastline* ◇ **~ of...** *The Greeks began founding colonies along the southern coastline of Italy and most of Sicily.*

coat[1] /kəʊt; *NAmE* koʊt/ *noun* **1** a piece of outdoor clothing that is worn over other clothes to keep you warm or dry : *They dress in long dark coats and large-rimmed black hats.* **2** a piece of clothing that is worn by doctors and scientists over other clothes for protection at work: *Laboratory coats are worn to protect everyday clothing and skin from exposure to hazardous substances.* **3** the fur, hair or wool that covers an animal's body: *The animal has white spots on its coat.* **4** an outer layer or covering: *A virus is a microscopic organism, consisting mainly of nucleic acid in a protein coat.* ◇ *The unfertilized egg is surrounded by a protective external coat.*

coat[2] /kəʊt; *NAmE* koʊt/ *verb* [often passive] **~ sth (with/in sth)** to cover sth with a layer of a substance: *The original floppy disk was made of plastic coated with a magnetic material.* ◇ *Cave walls are frequently coated in organic mud.*

coat·ing /ˈkəʊtɪŋ; *NAmE* ˈkoʊtɪŋ/ *noun* **~ (of sth)** a thin layer of a substance covering a surface: *In many soils, coatings of iron oxides or other compounds mask the colour of the primary particles.* ◇ *Spores are individual cells wrapped in a tough outer coating, which are dispersed to other locations.*

code[1] AWL /kəʊd; *NAmE* koʊd/ *noun* **1** [C] a series of letters, numbers or symbols that are used to identify, sort or represent sth: *In this code, 'a' stands for 'age', 's' stands for 'sex' and 'l' stands for 'location'.* **2** [C, U] (often in compounds) a system of words, letters, numbers or symbols that represent a message or record information secretly:

At Bletchley Park, 10 Colossus computers worked around the clock to break German codes. ◇ **in ~** *He had to write in code in order to confuse the prison censor.* ◇ **+ noun** *The Navy used three alternative code words for 'very, very urgent'.* **3** [U] a word, phrase or symbol that is used to represent an idea in an indirect way: **~ (for sth)** *The Confederate flag may still be seen by some as code for white supremacy.* ◇ **+ noun** *Gender is often used as a code word for women.* **4** [U] (*computing*) a system of computer programming instructions: *NT and Windows 2000 used underlying 32-bit binary code rather than the 16-bit code of DOS.* **5** [C] a set of moral principles or rules of behaviour that are generally accepted by society or a social group: *The samurai lived by a rigorous ethical code.* ◇ **~ of sth** *a code of practice/conduct/ethics* **6** [C] a system of laws or rules that state how people in an institution or a country should behave: *South Africa arguably has the most comprehensive corporate governance code in the world.* ◇ *In the UK, there are a number of voluntary codes which set standards for responsible advertising.* **7** [C] (*biology*) = GENETIC CODE

code² AWL /kəʊd; *NAmE* koʊd/ *verb* **1** [T, often passive] **~ sth** to write or print words, letters, numbers, etc. on sth so that you know what it is, what group it belongs to, etc: *Text can be coded according to who is speaking and reflect gender, income and age.* ◇ *Blood tubes are generally colour coded.* **2** [T, often passive] **~ sth** to put a message into code so that it can be understood by only a few people: *A message can be coded to protect it from unauthorized readers.* **3** [T, often passive] **~ sth (as sth)** (*computing*) to write a computer program by putting one system of numbers, words and symbols into another system SYN ENCODE: *Instructions can be stored in memory coded as numbers.* **4** [T, usually passive] **be coded (into sb/sth)** (*biology*) to be contained in a person's GENETIC CODE: *There is an assumption that behaviours are genetically coded into humans and are therefore beyond change.* **5** [I] **~ for sth** (*biology*) to be the GENETIC CODE for sth: *The alleles code for a long tail in males.*

coded /ˈkəʊdɪd; *NAmE* ˈkoʊdɪd/ *adj.* [only before noun] **1** written in or marked with information, often in the form of letters or numbers, that are used to identify, sort or represent sth: *Coded data are input into a computer manually or scanned.* ◇ *DNA carries chemically coded instructions for development.* **2** written or sent using a secret system of words, letters, numbers, etc. that can only be understood by a few other people: *He deciphered coded messages exchanged between Mary and others conspiring to overthrow the queen.*

ˌcode of ˈpractice *noun* (*pl.* **codes of practice**) a set of standards that members of a particular profession agree to follow in their work: *Codes of practice issued by professional bodies may constitute significant evidence of what constitutes reasonable care.*

co·dify /ˈkəʊdɪfaɪ; *NAmE* ˈkɑːdɪfaɪ/ *verb* (**co·di·fies, co·di·fy·ing, co·di·fied, co·di·fied**) **~ sth** to arrange laws, rules, information, etc. into a system: *The Compensation Act 2006 was passed to codify existing common law.* ◇ *The Hebrew prayers were first codified in the ninth century.* ■ **co·difi·ca·tion** /ˌkəʊdɪfɪˈkeɪʃn; *NAmE* ˌkɑːdɪfɪˈkeɪʃn/ *noun* [U, sing.] **~ of sth** *Codification of knowledge is the outcome of a conscious effort.* ◇ *The 1893 Act was a codification of various rights into one Act of Parliament.*

cod·ing /ˈkəʊdɪŋ; *NAmE* ˈkoʊdɪŋ/ *noun* [U] **1** the process of using a code to CLASSIFY or identify items: **~ (of sth)** *The two authors undertook independent coding of participants' interview transcripts.* ◇ **+ noun** *Interviews were read and coding schemes were developed around emerging themes.* **2** (*biochemistry*) the means by which the cells of the body form PROTEINS and GENERATE characteristics from information carried in GENETIC material: **~ for sth** *Genetic coding for six toes is rare in humans, though apparently not in cats.* ◇ **+ noun** *This type of mutation is highly disruptive and usually lethal if it occurs within coding regions.*

co·ef·fi·cient /ˌkəʊɪˈfɪʃnt; *NAmE* ˌkoʊɪˈfɪʃnt/ *noun* **1** (*mathematics*) a number that is placed before another quantity and that multiplies it, for example 3 in the quantity 3*x*: *In order to calculate any given coefficient, it is necessary to consider only a finite number of factors.* ➲ *see also* CORRELATION COEFFICIENT **2** (*physics*) a number that measures a particular property of a substance: *The moisture diffusion coefficient strongly depends on temperature.*

co·erce /kəʊˈɜːs; *NAmE* koʊˈɜːrs/ *verb* to make sb do sth by using force or threats: **~ sb into (doing) sth** *Henry subsequently attempted to coerce the Scots into accepting the treaty.* ◇ **~ sb (to do sth)** *The party in power determines the agenda and coerces its members to support it.*

co·er·cion /kəʊˈɜːʃn; *NAmE* koʊˈɜːrʒn/ *noun* [U] the action or practice of making sb do sth by using force or threats: *The greater the legitimacy of the regime, the less the need for government to use coercion.*

co·er·cive /kəʊˈɜːsɪv; *NAmE* koʊˈɜːrsɪv/ *adj.* connected with or using force or threats: *The police have more armed officers and coercive powers than ever before.*

co·ex·ist /ˌkəʊɪɡˈzɪst; *NAmE* ˌkoʊɪɡˈzɪst/ *verb* **1** [I] to exist together in the same place or at the same time: *If this resource is abundant, the two species may coexist.* ◇ **~ with sb/sth** *Malaria has coexisted with the human population for millennia.* ◇ **~ in sb/sth** *The disease is conventionally divided up into three types, although features of each may coexist in the same patient.* **2** [I] (of different countries or groups) to exist together in a peaceful way, despite having different interests or ways of thinking: *The task of diplomacy was to help different states to coexist.* ■ **co·ex·ist·ence** /ˌkəʊɪɡˈzɪstəns; *NAmE* ˌkoʊɪɡˈzɪstəns/ *noun* [U] *Peaceful coexistence requires acceptance by the diverse populations involved.* ◇ **~ of sth** *The coexistence of different species that depend on, and compete for, the same resources at the same time is commonly observed.*

cof·fee /ˈkɒfi; *NAmE* ˈkɔːfi; ˈkɑːfi/ *noun* **1** [U, C] the cooked seeds (called **coffee beans**) of a tropical plant; a powder made from them: *The value of the raw beans contained in a jar of instant coffee may be no more than a few pence.* **2** [U, C] a hot drink made from coffee powder and boiling water. It may be drunk with milk and/or sugar added: *For this advertising to work, the reader must already drink coffee.* ◇ *The appointment is negotiated over a cup of coffee.* ◇ *I'd like a strong black coffee.* **3** [U] a tropical plant that produces **coffee beans**: *Arabica coffee is grown throughout Latin America, Central and East Africa, India and Indonesia.* ◇ **+ noun** *Fairtrade labelling was created in 1986 in response to the request of coffee farmers in southern Mexico.*

cog·ni·tion /kɒɡˈnɪʃn; *NAmE* kɑːɡˈnɪʃn/ *noun* [U] (*psychology*) the process by which knowledge and understanding are developed in the mind: *Much of human cognition occurs at a subconscious level.*

cog·ni·tive /ˈkɒɡnətɪv; *NAmE* ˈkɑːɡnətɪv/ *adj.* [usually before noun] (*psychology*) connected with the mental processes of understanding: *Many younger children do not have the cognitive ability to describe their emotions at length.* ◇ *Everyday behaviour involves multiple cognitive processes.* ◇ *Even minor head injuries can cause cognitive impairments.*

co·habit /kəʊˈhæbɪt; *NAmE* koʊˈhæbɪt/ *verb* [I] (usually of a man and a woman) to live together and have a sexual relationship without being married: *The parents had cohabited for some 50 years and had seven children.* ◇ *There has been a rise in the percentage of children born to cohabiting couples.* ◇ **~ with sb** *She had never cohabited*

C

with the father of her child. ■ **co·hab·it·ation** /ˌkəʊˌhæbɪˈteɪʃn; *NAmE* ˌkoʊˌhæbɪˈteɪʃn/ *noun* [U] *Premarital cohabitation is increasingly common.*

co·her·ence AWL /kəʊˈhɪərəns; *NAmE* koʊˈhɪrəns/ *noun* [U] **1** the quality of being logical and well organized: *The current law lacks coherence and is in need of reform.* ◇ **~ of sth** *These elements threaten the overall coherence of the text.* OPP INCOHERENCE **2** the situation in which all the parts of sth fit or work well together: **~ between sth** *The aim is to achieve maximum coherence between the various components.* ◇ **~ of sth** *The addition of new member states has not affected the coherence of existing groups in the EU.* OPP INCOHERENCE

co·her·ent AWL /kəʊˈhɪərənt; *NAmE* koʊˈhɪrənt/ *adj.* **1** (of an argument, theory, statement or policy) logical and well organized; easy to understand and clear: *These ideas have yet to be developed into a coherent theory.* ◇ *a coherent account/narrative* ◇ *a coherent strategy/approach* ◇ *The aim is to synthesize the existing research into a coherent framework.* OPP INCOHERENT (1) **2** (of a person) able to talk and express yourself clearly; showing this: *Anxious people become more coherent when put at ease.* ◇ *The stroke left him incapable of coherent speech.* OPP INCOHERENT (2) **3** made up of different parts that fit or work well together: *She organized the different parts of the story into a coherent whole.* ◇ *Under Constantine, the scattered and often unmarked places were reshaped into a coherent 'holy land'.* **4** (*physics*) (of waves) in PHASE with each other: *Light from a laser is coherent and all the waves are synchronized: they go up and down together.* OPP INCOHERENT (3)

co·her·ent·ly AWL /kəʊˈhɪərəntli; *NAmE* koʊˈhɪrəntli/ *adv.* **1** in a logical and well organized way that is clear and easy to understand: *In Ancient Greece, the ability to speak coherently and persuasively was an important key to political influence.* **2** in a way that involves different parts fitting or working well together: *Teams of workers need to act coherently during a crisis.*

co·he·sion /kəʊˈhiːʒn; *NAmE* koʊˈhiːʒn/ *noun* [U] **1** the act or state of keeping together SYN UNITY: *Governments frequently call on culture as a source of social cohesion.* ◇ *There is evidence of high levels of group cohesion, with members eager to find agreement with their colleagues.* **2** (*physics, chemistry*) the force causing MOLECULES of the same substance to stick together: *Cohesion is a force of attraction between like molecules.*

co·he·sive /kəʊˈhiːsɪv; *NAmE* koʊˈhiːsɪv/ *adj.* **1** forming a united whole: *Indian Muslims constitute arguably one of the largest cohesive groups in India.* ◇ *Sections 1 to 6 of the Theft Act 1968 should be read as a cohesive whole.* **2** causing people or things to become united: *Unless societies can find a cohesive force to bring people together, they confront an unending war of 'all-against-all'.* ■ **co·he·sive·ness** *noun* [U] *Group cohesiveness can be built on members' similarity and liking for each other.*

co·hort /ˈkəʊhɔːt; *NAmE* ˈkoʊhɔːrt/ *noun* [C+sing./pl. v.] **~ (of sb)** a group of people who share a common feature or aspect of behaviour: *The drafting of government legislation is carried out by a small cohort of legally qualified senior civil servants.* ◇ *In 2009 the same virus was identified in a cohort of patients with chronic fatigue syndrome (CFS).* ◇ *This is a longitudinal study of health and mortality that has followed an original cohort of 6 928 adults since 1965.*

coin¹ /kɔɪn/ *noun* **1** [C] a small flat piece of metal used as money: *Euro notes and coins came into circulation in January 2002.* ◇ *He issued a commemorative gold coin with his portrait.* **2** [U] money made of metal: *Enormous sums were collected, in coin, and paid to Viking raiders of England in the late tenth and early eleventh centuries.* IDM *see* SIDE¹

coin² /kɔɪn/ *verb* **~ sth** to invent a new word or phrase that other people then begin to use: *'Sarvodaya' is a term first coined by Mahatma Gandhi to mean 'the well-being of all'.* ◇ *Sinn (2007) coined the phrase the 'Green Paradox'.*

co·in·cide AWL /ˌkəʊɪnˈsaɪd; *NAmE* ˌkoʊɪnˈsaɪd/ *verb* **1** [I] (of two or more events) to take place at the same time: *Patterns of boom and recession do not always coincide in different countries.* ◇ **~ with sth** *The reign of Alexander coincided almost exactly with the golden age of Russian literature.* **2** [I] (of ideas or opinions) to be the same or very similar: *The two men only remained friends so long as their views coincided.* ◇ **~ with sth** *People listen best to advice when it coincides with their own opinions.* **3** [I] (of objects or places) to meet; to share the same space: *Before the nineteenth century, the boundaries between states and languages rarely coincided.* ◇ *The two curves coincide at high frequencies.* ◇ **~ with sth** *The axis may coincide with the plane of cleavage or be at right angles to it.*

co·in·ci·dence AWL /kəʊˈɪnsɪdəns; *NAmE* koʊˈɪnsɪdəns/ *noun* **1** [C, U] the fact of two things happening at the same time by chance, often in a surprising way: *Only a series of remarkable coincidences have made earth habitable for humans.* ◇ **by ~** *It was by sheer coincidence that the two artists met.* ◇ **It is a/no ~ that...** *It is no coincidence that sites such as Babylon and Thebes were sited on the banks of major rivers.* **2** [sing., U] **~ of A with/and B** the fact of things being present in the same place at the same time: *The coincidence of industrialization with urbanization means that cities generate most of East Asia's pollution.* **3** [sing., U] **~ of sth** the fact of two or more opinions, etc. being the same: *The barter system relies on a double coincidence of wants.*

co·in·ci·dent AWL /kəʊˈɪnsɪdənt; *NAmE* koʊˈɪnsɪdənt/ *adj.* **~ (with sth)** happening or found in the same place or at the same time: *The tundra zone is broadly coincident with permafrost.*

co·in·ci·dent·al AWL /kəʊˌɪnsɪˈdentl; *NAmE* koʊˌɪnsɪˈdentl/ *adj.* [not usually before noun] happening by chance; not planned: *There is a 5% probability that the difference could be coincidental, that is due to chance.* ◇ *Similar features encountered in different manuscripts sometimes turn out to be purely coincidental.* ■ **co·in·ci·den·tal·ly** /kəʊˌɪnsɪˈdentəli; *NAmE* koʊˌɪnsɪˈdentəli/ *adv.*: *Many tumours of this type are found coincidentally during surgery for other conditions.*

cold¹ /kəʊld; *NAmE* koʊld/ *adj.* (**cold·er**, **cold·est**) **1** having a lower than usual temperature; having a temperature lower than the human body: *Joyce was complaining of feeling cold.* ◇ *This cold air remains close to the surface of the earth.* ◇ *Hold the patient's affected eye under gently running cold water for at least 10 minutes.* ◇ *The Natufian peoples deserted much of the area as the climate became colder.* **2** (of food or drink) served, eaten or drunk without being heated, or after cooling: *Innocent is a business that produces and sells cold drinks made from fruit.* **3** (of a person) without emotion; unfriendly: *He could sometimes act in a stern, cold, distant way.* ◇ *Premodern families are no longer seen as emotionally cold.*

cold² /kəʊld; *NAmE* koʊld/ *noun* **1** [U] a lack of heat; a low temperature, especially in the atmosphere: *The livestock died of cold and hunger.* ◇ *The child shivered in the cold.* ◇ *This is a period of extreme cold in the Tatra mountains.* **2** [C] (*also less frequent* **the ˌcommon ˈcold**) a common illness that affects the nose and/or throat, making it difficult to breathe through the nose and causing a sore throat: *He has had a cold and fever for the past couple of days.* ◇ *Even minor illnesses of short duration, notably the common cold, have a major economic impact through absences from work.*

ˌ**cold ˈwar** *noun* [sing., U] (*often* **Cold War**) a very unfriendly relationship between two countries who are not actually fighting each other, usually used about the situation between the US and the Soviet Union after the Second World War: *The end of the Cold War had major implications for defence, foreign and security policy.*

col·lab·or·ate /kəˈlæbəreɪt/ *verb* **1** [I] to work together with sb in order to produce or achieve sth: *Organizations collaborate to reduce the costs of developing innovation.* ◇ **~ (with sb) (on sth)** *The company collaborates closely with its suppliers to increase access to the best product design skills.* ◇ *Mulvey collaborated on a number of films with her husband, film theorist Peter Wollen.* ◇ **~ (with sb) (in sth/in doing sth)** *His vision was to have universities and government collaborate in their research efforts.* **2** [I] **~ (with sb)** to help the enemy who has taken control of your country during a war: *During the Second World War the Vichy regime collaborated with the Nazis.*

col·lab·or·ation /kəˌlæbəˈreɪʃn/ *noun* **1** [U, C] the act of working with another person or group of people to create or produce sth: **~ with sb** *Francis Crick is best known for his collaboration with James D. Watson in their discovery of the structure of DNA.* ◇ **~ (with sb) (on sth)** *The collaboration on the integrated circuit illustrates that innovation is rarely the product of a single mind.* ◇ **in ~ with sb** *These fields of US university research frequently developed in close collaboration with industry.* ◇ **~ between A and B** *The opera was the result of a collaboration between Hofmannsthal, Reinhardt and Strauss.* **2** [C] a piece of work produced by two or more people or groups of people working together: *The book was a collaboration from three scientists who spent their lives trying to understand how genes influence behaviour.*

col·lab·ora·tive /kəˈlæbərətɪv; *NAmE* kəˈlæbəreɪtɪv/ *adj.* [only before noun] involving, or done by, several people or groups of people working together: *Trust is an important factor in creating a collaborative relationship among workers.* ◇ *A key to success was the establishment of a collaborative research group.* ■ **col·lab·ora·tive·ly** *adv.*: *Most environmental historians need to work collaboratively with scientists or other specialists.*

col·lab·or·ator /kəˈlæbəreɪtə(r)/ *noun* **1** a person who works with another person to create or produce sth such as a book: *Smith was able to enlist the help of her long-time collaborator, script editor Tony Holland.* **2 ~ (with sb/sth)** a person who helps the enemy in a war, when they have taken control of the person's country: *Some rival sects perceived the Sadducees as collaborators with the Romans.*

col·lapse¹ AWL /kəˈlæps/ *noun* **1** [U, C, usually sing.] a sudden failure of sth, such as a system, an institution, a business or a course of action: *A natural disaster on this scale would lead to social collapse.* ◇ *An economic collapse in 2001 triggered a brief upsurge in social protests.* ◇ **the ~ of sth** *Popular revolts hastened but did not cause the collapse of the empire.* ◇ **on the verge of ~** *The bank was on the verge of collapse.* **2** [U, C] the action of a building or part of a hill, etc. suddenly falling down: *The bridge collapse was caused by a fracture within a joint.* ◇ *It is argued that such catastrophic slope collapses were triggered by powerful earthquakes.* **3** [C, usually sing.] a sudden fall in value: *The stock market suffered a major collapse.* ◇ **~ of sth** *A sudden loss of investor confidence led to a dramatic collapse of the rupiah.* ◇ **~ in sth** *The IMF acted to prevent a collapse in the value of the pound.* **4** [U] a medical condition when sb suddenly becomes very ill, or when sb falls because they are ill or weak: *The risks are complete cardiovascular collapse and death.*

col·lapse² AWL /kəˈlæps/ *verb* **1** [I] (of a system, an institution, a business or a course of action) to fail suddenly or completely: *The regime quickly collapsed after the defeat.* ◇ *The evidence suggests that such high CO_2 levels would quickly cause major fisheries to collapse.* ➲ compare BREAK DOWN (1) **2** [I] to fall down or fall in suddenly, often after breaking apart: *The inquiry concluded that the bridge collapsed as a result of poor design.* ◇ *Eventually the weak continental crust begins to collapse under its own weight.* ➲ compare GIVE WAY **3** [I] (of prices or a CURRENCY) to decrease suddenly in amount or value: *Exports fell and commodity prices collapsed.* **4** [I] to fall down, and usually become unconscious, especially because you are very ill: *A 63-year-old man collapsed while running across the road and lost consciousness for a short period.* **5** [T] to make a system simpler by removing or ignoring differences between categories: **~ sth** *A broader definition would collapse the distinction between these two categories.* ◇ **~ sth into sth** *The main proposal was to collapse the two-tier system of immigration appeals into one.* ◇ **be collapsed into sth** *These complex descriptions are interconnected but cannot be collapsed into each other.*

col·lat·eral /kəˈlætərəl/ *adj.* connected with sth else, but in addition to it and less important: *The collateral benefits of increased energy efficiency include improved air quality and reduced greenhouse gas emissions.* ◇ *US General Stanley McChrystal issued instructions that collateral damage in the form of civilian casualties should be minimized.*

col·league AWL /ˈkɒliːg; *NAmE* ˈkɑːliːg/ *noun* a person that you work with, especially in a profession or business: *Mrs Thatcher had to persuade her Cabinet colleagues to agree to her economic strategy.* ◇ *Khanna and colleagues argued that there are three factors underlying the process.*

col·lect /kəˈlekt/ *verb* **1** [T] to bring things together from different people or places: **~ sth** *All information collected in the survey will be kept confidential.* ◇ *Steno travelled around Italy looking at rock strata and collecting fossils.* ◇ **~ sth from sb/sth** *The first year was spent collecting data from both reading and primary sources.* ◇ **~ sth together** *Hills (1994) collected together the preliminary findings of this research.* ➲ compare GATHER (1) **2** [T] to obtain sth, especially for use in tests: **~ sth** *A urine sample was collected by nursing staff and sent to the laboratory.* ◇ **~ sth from sb/sth** *It was easy to collect a soil sample from the local hillside.* **3** [T] **~ sth** to obtain the money that sb owes: *Local leaders were appointed by the sultan to collect the taxes due to the royal household.* **4** [I, T] to gradually increase in amount in a place; to gradually obtain more and more of sth in a place SYN ACCUMULATE: *Water that collects in these hollows supports a specialized community of microorganisms.* ◇ **~ sth** *The new reservoir collects enough rainwater for the whole village.* ◇ *The solar cells collected light and converted it into electricity.* **5** [T] **~ sth (from...)** to go somewhere in order to take sth away: *The patient had to collect her tablets from the pharmacy.*

▸ COLLECT + NOUN **data, information • statistics • evidence • material • fossils** *The advent of computers enabled companies to collect statistics on almost every aspect of performance.* | **sample • specimen • blood • urine** *A tissue specimen may be collected from virtually any part of the body.* | **tax • money • revenue • rent • fees** *There was no monitoring of the money collected in taxation by the government.*

col·lec·tion /kəˈlekʃn/ *noun* **1** [U] the action or process of bringing information or things together into one place: *The most successful method of data collection turned out to be the structured questionnaires.* ◇ **the ~ of sth** *In addition, the soil acts as a medium for the collection and movement of rainwater.* **2** [C] **~ (of sth)** a group of things or an amount of liquid gathered in one place: *A complex organism is not merely a collection of cells.* ◇ *A collection of 13 varied mental tests was given to over 2 000 adult Americans.* ◇ *What exists on the Web at the present time is information, essentially a large collection of facts.* **3** [C] **~ (of sth)** a group of pieces of writing on one topic published together in one book; many pieces of information on one topic gathered in one place: *It is a comprehensive collection of essays on global citizenship.* ◇ *The database contains a rich collection of linguistic data drawn from around 550 of the world's languages.* **4** [C] **~ (of sth)** a group of objects, often of the same type, that have been brought together in one place: *The museum possesses an extensive collection of mid-nineteenth century photographs.* **5** [U] an act of taking sth away from a place: *Local authorities are obliged to provide refuse collection.*

col·lect·ive[1] /kəˈlektɪv/ *adj.* [usually before noun] **1** done or shared by all members of a group of people; involving a whole group or society: *The church was governed by the collective decisions of bishops.* ◇ *Nurses have an individual and collective responsibility to protect the patient.* ◇ *It is through dialogue that understandings are reached and collective identities constructed (Miller, 1992).* **2** used to refer to all members of a group: *Respiration is a collective term that refers to several functions:...*

col·lect·ive[2] /kəˈlektɪv/ *noun* a group of people who own a business or a farm and run it together; the business that they run: *Urban communists sent to supervise the new collectives were ignorant of agriculture.*

colˌlective ˈaction *noun* [U, pl.] activities of a group working together to achieve a shared goal: *Future wars were to be deterred by the League of Nations, which would take collective action against aggressor states.* ◇ *The treaty provides an international legal framework that allows for collective actions to address pressing global security issues.*

colˌlective ˈbargaining *noun* [U] discussions between a trade union and an employer about the pay and working conditions of the union members: *The level of payment at each point was determined through collective bargaining.* ◇ **+ noun** *Many people benefited from prevailing wage rates established in collective bargaining agreements.*

col·lect·ive·ly /kəˈlektɪvli/ *adv.* (of all members of a group) together: *In fact, small- and medium-sized firms collectively employ more people than do large business firms.* ◇ *These theorems are collectively called the central limit theorem.*

col·lege /ˈkɒlɪdʒ; *NAmE* ˈkɑːlɪdʒ/ *noun* **1** [C, U] (often in names) (in the US) a university where students can study for a degree after they have left school: *She was the first in her family to attend college.* ◇ *In 1990, an average of 15.9 per cent of the adult population had a college degree.* ◇ *Carleton College* ◇ **at ~** *Black female students at many elite colleges and universities personify this statistic.* ◇ *Her children are now away at college.* ◇ **+ noun** *The survey was sent to a sample of American college students.* **2** [C, U] (often in names) (in Britain) a place where students go to study or to receive training after they have left school: *The role of further education colleges expanded.* **3** [C, U] (often in names) one of the separate institutions that some British universities, such as Oxford and Cambridge, are divided into: *She graduated from Trinity College, Cambridge.* **4** [C, U] (often in names) (in the US) one of the main divisions of some large universities: *He was Professor of Public Health at Cornell University Medical College.* ◇ **5** [C +sing./pl. v.] (usually in names) an organized group of professional people with special interests, duties or powers: *The research was published by the Royal College of Physicians.*

col·lide /kəˈlaɪd/ *verb* **1** [I] if two people, vehicles, land masses, etc. **collide**, they CRASH into each other; if a person, vehicle, land mass, etc. **collides** with another, or with sth that is not moving, they crash into it: *When cars and light trucks collide, car occupants account for 80% of deaths.* ◇ *When continents collide, mountain chains are thrust upwards.* ◇ *Even if two galaxies do collide head-on, there is very little chance of stellar collisions.* ◇ **~ with sth/sb** *As the molecules collide with each other, energy is constantly being passed about.* **2** [I] **~ (with sb/sth)** (of people, their opinions, etc.) to disagree strongly: *These ideas collided head-on with Christian orthodoxy.*

col·li·sion /kəˈlɪʒn/ *noun* [C, U] **1** an accident in which two vehicles or people CRASH into each other: **in a ~ (with sb/sth)** *The mother and newborn baby were killed in a head-on collision.* ◇ **in ~ with sb/sth** *The cyclist was in collision with a car.* ◇ **~ between A and B** *There was a collision between two ships due to the negligent navigation.* ◇ **~ of A and/with B** *In a two-vehicle collision of vehicles of unequal mass, the lighter vehicle absorbs more than its own kinetic energy.* **2** an occasion when two objects hit each other by chance: **~ between A and B** *Collisions between molecules in solution can provide the energy required to break some chemical bonds.* ◇ **~ of A and/with B** *The Himalayas formed as a result of the collision of India with Asia.* **3** a strong disagreement between two people or between opposing ideas, opinions, etc; the meeting of two things that are very different: **~ between A and B** *There is a collision between voters' demands for better public services and their resistance to paying higher taxes.* ◇ **~ of A and/with B** *His films intentionally set up collisions of cultures and meanings.*

IDM **be set/be on a colˈlision course (with sb/sth)** to be in a situation which is almost certain to cause a disagreement or argument: *The trade union leaders and the government were set on a collision course.*

col·lo·cate[1] /ˈkɒləkət; *NAmE* ˈkɑːləkət/ *noun* (*linguistics*) a word that is often used together with another word in a language: *Typical collocates are printed in bold type.* ◇ **~ of sth** *It is instructive to consider the collocates of 'web' in 1990–94 compared with 2005–09.*

col·lo·cate[2] /ˈkɒləkeɪt; *NAmE* ˈkɑːləkeɪt/ *verb* [I] **~ (with sth)** (*linguistics*) (of words) to be often used together in a language: *'Heavy' collocates with 'drinker' and 'smoker', but not with 'eater' or 'spender'.* ◇ *There are many ways in which words collocate.*

col·lo·ca·tion /ˌkɒləˈkeɪʃn; *NAmE* ˌkɑːləˈkeɪʃn/ *noun* (*linguistics*) **1** [C] a combination of words in a language that happens very often and more frequently than would happen by chance: *The results show that the use of a dictionary significantly increased the number of correct collocations in a fill-in task.* **2** [U] the fact of two or more words often being used together, in a way that happens more frequently than would happen by chance: *It was found that knowledge of collocation lagged far behind that of general vocabulary knowledge.*

colon /ˈkəʊlən; *NAmE* ˈkoʊlən/ *noun* **1** the mark (:) used to introduce a list, a summary, an explanation, etc. or before reporting what sb has said: *You can use a colon to introduce a quotation.* ➲ *compare* SEMICOLON **2** (*anatomy*) the main part of the large INTESTINE (= part of the BOWEL): **+ noun** *These data indicate that tomatoes may help to prevent colon cancer.*

co·lo·nial /kəˈləʊniəl; *NAmE* kəˈloʊniəl/ *adj.* connected with or belonging to a country that controls another country: *The earliest colonial powers were Spain and Portugal.* ◇ *Liberation came with the end of colonial rule.* ◇ *During the colonial period, the British authorities adopted a system of indirect rule.* ➲ *see also* COLONY (1)

co·lo·ni·al·ism /kəˈləʊniəlɪzəm; *NAmE* kəˈloʊniəlɪzəm/ *noun* [U] the practice by which a powerful country controls another country or other countries: *European colonialism was at its height in the Victorian era.* ■ **co·lo·ni·al·ist** /kəˈləʊniəlɪst; *NAmE* kəˈloʊniəlɪst/ *adj.*: *Colonialist attitudes were formed in response to the culture and also the struggles of the colonized.*

col·on·ist /ˈkɒlənɪst; *NAmE* ˈkɑːlənɪst/ *noun* a person who settles in an area that has become a COLONY: *Many of the early American colonists had been persecuted for their religious beliefs in the European states they had left.*

col·on·iza·tion (*BrE also* **-isa·tion**) /ˌkɒlənaɪˈzeɪʃn; *NAmE* ˌkɑːlənəˈzeɪʃn/ *noun* [U] **1 ~ (of sth)** the practice of a country taking control of another country or area, especially by force, and sending people to live there: *The nineteenth-century colonization of these countries was followed eventually by independence.* ◇ *Countries such as Japan that escaped colonization were still obliged to accept the rules of the Western state system.* **2 ~ (of sth) (by sth)** (*biology*) the fact of an animal or plant living or growing in large numbers in a particular area: *The moderate climate encourages colonization by species which cannot tolerate more extreme conditions.*

col·on·ize (*BrE also* **-ise**) /ˈkɒlənaɪz; *NAmE* ˈkɑːlənaɪz/ *verb* **1 ~ sth** to take control of an area or a country that is not your own, especially by force, and send people from your own country to live there: *European nations colonized and exploited North and South America.* ◇ *Empire building usually involved a fair amount of fighting with colonized peoples.* **2 ~ sth** (*biology*) (of animals or plants) to live or grow in large numbers in a particular area: *Some crustaceans, such as woodlice, have colonized damp terrestrial habitats.* ■ **col·on·izer, -iser** *noun*: *This theory applies to the USA, where the European colonizers largely wiped out the indigenous cultures.* ◇ **~ (of sth)** *Marram (Ammophila arenaria) is a colonizer of shifting coastal sands.*

col·ony /ˈkɒləni; *NAmE* ˈkɑːləni/ *noun* (*pl.* **-ies**) **1** [C] a country or an area that is governed by people from another, more powerful, country: *Most of the former British colonies experienced a relatively smooth transition to independence.* **2** [C+sing./pl. v.] **~ (of sth)** (*biology*) a group of plants or animals that live together or grow in the same place: *Egg production in a colony of ants is delegated to one individual, the queen.* ◇ *Penguin breeding colonies are located on coastal sites that offer the best foraging and nesting habitats.*

color (*US*) = COLOUR[1], COLOUR[2]

col·or·ation (*BrE also* **col·our·ation**) /ˌkʌləˈreɪʃn/ *noun* [U] **~ (of sth)** the natural colours and patterns on a plant or an animal: *Weismann's special interest was in the coloration of caterpillars and butterflies.*

col·ored, col·or·ful, col·or·ing, col·or·less (*US*) = COLOURED, COLOURFUL, COLOURING, COLOURLESS

col·our[1] (*US* **color**) /ˈkʌlə(r)/ *noun* **1** [C, U] the appearance that things have that results from the way in which they reflect light. Red and green are colours: *Each of the chromosomes shows a different colour when viewed with a fluorescence microscope.* ◇ *The haematite gives the rock its characteristic red colour.* ◇ *For drinking water, requirements relate to toxicity, colour, odour and taste.* ◇ **~ of sth** *The eye colour of each subject was recorded.* ◇ *The program enables the precise original colours of photographs to be reconstructed.* ◇ **in ~** *The mudstone is usually dark reddish brown in colour.* **2** [U] (usually before another noun) the use of all the colours, not only black and white: **in ~** *The photographs were in colour.* ◇ **+ noun** *It was one of the five main companies manufacturing colour televisions.* ◇ *The patient's colour vision appeared to be intact.* **3** [U, C] the colour of a person's skin, when it shows the race they belong to: *The research strongly suggests that it is colour rather than being a member of an ethnic minority as such that causes discrimination.* ◇ *No standard scale has been adopted to classify skin colour, posing a challenge to the present study.* HELP Especially in American English, a **person/man/woman of colour** is sb who is not white: *Some sixty whites and sixty free people of colour lost their lives in the conflict.*

col·our[2] (*US* **color**) /ˈkʌlə(r)/ *verb* **1 ~ sth** to affect sth, especially in a negative way: *The experience of economic development gained in this situation coloured the views of those leaders involved.* **2** to put colour on sth or change the colour of sth: **~ sth** *It is possible to colour the vertices with three colours so that adjacent vertices are in different colours.* ◇ *Patients should not perm or colour the hair for 3-6 months after treatment is finished.* ◇ **~ sth + adj.** *The setting sun coloured the sea red.*

col·our·ation (*BrE*) = COLORATION

col·oured (*US* **col·ored**) /ˈkʌləd; *NAmE* ˈkʌlərd/ *adj.* **1** (often in compounds) having a particular colour or different colours: *It is conventional to introduce contrast into specimens by staining them with coloured dyes.* ◇ **brightly ~** *Females of these species are generally larger and more brightly coloured than males.* ◇ **light-/dark-coloured** *This deposit consists mainly of light-coloured very fine-grained sand.* **2** (*offensive* or *old-fashioned*) (of a person) from a race that does not have white skin: *Some wealthy coloured people and Jewish merchants also inhabited these areas.* HELP The term **coloured** to mean 'black' or 'African American' is now considered offensive, except in historical contexts. However, in South Africa, it is used to mean 'mixed race' and this is not generally considered offensive. **3 Coloured** (in South Africa) having parents who are of different races: *Western (1981) analyses the impact of apartheid on Coloured populations in the Cape Town area.*

col·our·ful (*US* **col·or·ful**) /ˈkʌləfl; *NAmE* ˈkʌlərfl/ *adj.* **1** full of bright colours or having a lot of different colours: *Colourful murals were painted on the walls of the main entrance.* **2** interesting or exciting; full of variety, sometimes in a way that is slightly shocking: *Some of these spiritual leaders have been controversial and colourful characters.*

col·our·ing (*US* **col·or·ing**) /ˈkʌlərɪŋ/ *noun* **1** [C, U] a substance that is used to give a particular colour to food: *Food colourings are still tested on animals.* ◇ *The drink was said to contain a vast amount of artificial colouring.* **2** [U] the colours that exist in sth, especially a plant or an animal: *Piebald colouring is also seen in domestic cats, horses, cows, sheep and goats.*

col·our·less (*US* **col·or·less**) /ˈkʌləlǝs; *NAmE* ˈkʌlərləs/ *adj.* without colour: *The ingredients are all colourless fluids.*

col·umn /ˈkɒləm; *NAmE* ˈkɑːləm/ *noun* **1** (*abbr.* **col.**) one of the vertical sections into which a table, or the printed page of a book or newspaper is divided: *The first column shows the proportion of respondents who reported having had an accident at work.* ◇ **in the... ~** *Some typical examples are listed in the right-hand column of Figure 6.6.* ◇ *The figures in the first two columns seem less significant.* ➲ *compare* ROW (1) **2** a thing with a tall, narrow shape: **~ of sth** *The result depends on the amount of ozone present in the column of air.* ◇ **in a... ~** *The hot humid air rises in a vertical column.*

com·bat[1] /ˈkɒmbæt; *NAmE* ˈkɑːmbæt/ *noun* [U, C] fighting or a fight, especially during a time of war: *For the majority of the Royal Marines, this was their first experience of combat.* ◇ **in ~** *Those whose fathers or sons had been killed in combat were exempted from the April 1933 law.* ◇ **~ between A and B** *The highlight of the games would be the individual combats between professional gladiators.*

com·bat[2] /ˈkɒmbæt; *NAmE* ˈkɑːmbæt/ *verb* (**-t-** or **-tt-**) **~ sth** to stop sth unpleasant or harmful from happening or from getting worse: *Immediately after the Madrid attacks, the European Council adopted a declaration on combating terrorism.* ◇ *There is an urgent need to find new agents to combat disease caused by resistant bacteria.*

com·bat·ant /ˈkɒmbətənt; *NAmE* ˈkɑːmbətənt/ *noun* a person or group involved in fighting in a war or battle: *Captured combatants must be treated humanely.*

com·bin·ation /ˌkɒmbɪˈneɪʃn; *NAmE* ˌkɑːmbɪˈneɪʃn/ *noun* **1** [C] **~ (of sth)** two or more things joined or mixed together to form a single unit: *Treatment may involve a combination of surgery, radiotherapy and drugs.* ◇ *The same level of output can be produced using many different combinations of capital and labour.* **2** [U] the act of joining or mixing together two or more things to form a single unit: **in ~** *The effects of these genes, alone and in combination, were modelled in the laboratory.* ◇ **in ~ with sth** *The treatment may be used on its own or in combination with chemotherapy.*

com·bine *verb* /kəmˈbaɪn/ **1** [T, I] to join two or more things or groups together to form a single one; to come together to form a single thing or group: **~ sth** *In the second approach, the two polymers are combined.* ◇ *Fewer than one in five Americans now work in agriculture, mining, and manufacturing combined.* ◇ **~ A with B** *A suitable drug can be combined with a second active substance by salt formation.* ◇ **~ with sth** *Leptin is carried to the brain in the blood and combines with receptors.* ◇ **~ (sth) together** *Different proteins may combine together.* ◇ **~ to do sth** *Water and the carbon dioxide in plant leaves combine to form carbohydrate molecules.* **2** [T] to have two or more different features or characteristics; to put two or more different things, features or qualities together: **~ sth** *Nearly all the creatures from classical myth combine body parts from two or more creatures.* ◇ **~ A and/with B** *His work successfully combines descriptive narrative and insightful analysis.* **3** [T] **~ A and/with B** to do two or more things at the same time: *The measures were designed to help parents combine paid work with family responsibilities.* **4** [T, I] to put two things or groups together so that they work or act together; to come together in order to work or act together: **combined + noun** *Risk-taking is an area where there has been some investigation of the combined effects of age and gender.* ◇ **~ A and/with B** *This information, combined with earlier data, provides a few more specifics on the nature of the lowland streams.* ◇ **~ (to do sth)** *Various factors combined to persuade these European states to start the process of European integration.* ◇ *In March 1979, virtually all non-Labour MPs finally combined and voted against the government.*

com·bus·tion /kəmˈbʌstʃən/ *noun* [U] the process of burning sth **HELP** In technical terms, **combustion** is a chemical process in which substances combine with the OXYGEN in the air to produce heat and light: *For two centuries, economic advance has been closely tied to fossil fuel combustion.* ◇ **~ of sth** *Indoor emissions from household combustion of coal have been deemed carcinogenic to humans.* ◇ **+ noun** *The air and fuel mixture is ignited to begin the combustion process.* **HELP** An **internal-combustion engine** is a type of engine where the power is produced when a mixture of fuel and air is burned inside the **combustion chamber**.

come /kʌm/ *verb* (**came** /keɪm/, **come**) **1** [I] **(+ adv./prep.)** to move to or towards a person or place: *Many immigrants came to America, fleeing from religious intolerance and oppression.* ◇ *Indian and African soldiers had come home from the war inspired by the new radical movements abroad.* **2** [I] **~ (to sth)** to arrive at or reach a place: *Children come to school with an array of issues that limit their capacity to learn.* **3** [I] to arrive somewhere in order to do sth or get sth: **~ to do sth** *More than sixty thousand people come each day to buy and sell goods.* ◇ **~ doing sth** *Others might come seeking business advice or legal opinions.* ◇ **~ for sth** *Many young people coming for a first appointment may not even acknowledge that a problem exists for them at all.* **4** [I] (of a point in time) to arrive: *By February 1965 the administration concluded that the time had come to act.* **5** [I] to happen: *The biggest improvements in speed and sensitivity came in the 1980s.* ◇ *The ultimate impact of the women's movement would come later.* ◇ **~ with sth** *The most dramatic changes came with the Industrial Revolution.* ◇ **~ as sth** *This result came as no surprise.* ◇ **there comes + noun** *There will come a point where the costs start to outweigh the benefits.* **6** [I] **~ to do sth** used to talk about how or why sth happened: *Samuel explains how he came to adopt Celie's children.* ◇ *We do not know exactly who wrote these books or why they came to be hidden.* **7** [I] **+ adv./prep.** (not used in the progressive tenses) to be in a particular position in an order: *The subject is the noun that comes before the verb.* ◇ *Even though the headline in this advert comes first, the eye is still drawn initially to the picture.* ◇ *As it was, he came second with 17 per cent of the votes cast.* **8** [I] **~ to/into sth** used in many expressions to show that sth has reached a particular state: *The East India Company's monopoly was coming to an end in 1833.* ◇ *The Democrats came to power in March 1933.* ◇ *The ethics of embryo research came to prominence in the 1980s.* ◇ *Such bureaucratic organizations came into existence at the end of the nineteenth century.* **9** [I] (not used in the progressive tenses) to be available or to exist in a particular way: **~ in sth** *Their thin shells come in a variety of shapes, with lengths from 0.3 to 10 mm.* ◇ *Genetic information comes in different forms.* ◇ **+ adj.** *Often the courses come free of charge with the installation of newly purchased equipment.* **10** [I] **~ (to do sth)** to start to do or achieve sth: *In reality, however, some firms may come to dominate their markets.* ◇ *Popular culture is coming to play an increasingly important part in the lives of the young.* **11** [I] **~ to do sth** to reach a point where you realize, understand or believe sth: *Many are coming to recognize the benefits that older workers can bring.*

IDM Most idioms containing **come** are at the entries for the nouns or adjectives in the idioms, for example **come to light** is at **light**. **ˌcome and ˈgo 1** to arrive and leave; to move freely: *In EU law, EU citizens have freedom to come and go.* **2** to be present for a short time and then go away: *Fashions might come and go very quickly, whereas some brands have endured for decades.* **come ˈeasily, ˈnaturally, etc. to sb** (of an activity, a skill, etc.) to be easy, natural, etc. for sb to do: *What comes naturally to a young child is often considered socially unacceptable.* ◇ *Regardless of method, systemic change in a school never comes easily.* **come to ˈnothing** to fail; to have no successful result: *The negotiations came to nothing.* **to ˈcome** (used after a noun) in the future: *Fossil fuels will continue to supply three-quarters of global primary energy for decades to come.* ◇ *These steps are crucial to ensure the legitimacy of water law in years to come.* **when it comes to (doing) sth** when it is a question of sth: *The family-tree model breaks down when it comes to creole languages.* ◇ *Visual perception is not so useful when it comes to judging the weight of an object.*

PHR V **ˌcome aˈbout (that...)** to happen: *The change has come about because of greater public concern.*

ˌcome aˈcross (*also* **ˌcome ˈover**) to make a particular impression: **~ as sth** *The investigator's questions may come across as patronizing.* **ˈcome across sb/sth** [no passive] to meet or find sb/sth, especially by chance: *We come across very few examples of this kind of motor in our everyday lives.*

ˌcome aˈlong to arrive; to appear: *Unfortunately, the recession of 1937 came along and the bridge company ran out of work.*

ˌcome aˈpart to break into pieces: (*figurative*) *The tight-knit fabric of Cold War social order was coming apart.*

ˌcome aˈround/ˈround 1 (*also* **ˌcome ˈto**) to become CONSCIOUS again: *Encourage parents to stay with the child when they come round from the anaesthetic.* **2** (of a date or a regular event) to happen again: *When election time comes round, inter-gang rivalries are set aside.* **ˌcome aˈround/ˈround (to sth)** to change your mood or your

opinion: *Gradually Boeing came around to their way of thinking.*
ˌ**come aˈway (with sth)** [no passive] to leave a place with a particular feeling or impression: *I came away from the course informed and inspired to research further.*
ˌ**come ˈback (from...)** to return: *Veterans came back from World War II to demand their citizenship rights.* ˌ**come ˈback to sth** [no passive] to return to a subject or an idea: *I will come back to the question of how this exchange rate is determined.*
ˈ**come before sb/sth** [no passive] (*formal*) to be presented to sb/sth for discussion or a decision: *In most of the cases which have come before the courts, the dispute has centred on the interpretation of a specific contract between the parties.*
ˈ**come by sth** to manage to get sth: *Exact figures are impossible to come by.* ◇ *Hard evidence on alternative arguments is hard to come by.*
ˌ**come ˈdown** **1** (of a price, temperature, rate, etc.) to get lower SYN FALL[1] (1): *Set prices will come down as demand increases.* ◇ *The minimum size of an efficient plant is coming down, thanks to automation.* **2** to break and fall to the ground: (*figurative*) *When trade barriers come down, consumers can buy goods more cheaply.* **3** to decide and say publicly that you support or oppose sb: *The House of Lords came down in favour of the council.* ˌ**come ˈdown (to sb)** to have come from a long time in the past: *The majority of texts that have come down to us under his name are brief.* ˌ**come ˈdown to sth** [no passive] to be able to be explained by a single important point: *The key challenges come down to cost, performance and durability.*
ˌ**come ˈforward** to offer or ask for help, services, etc: *Cultural factors also inhibit some victims from coming forward.*
ˈ**come from...** (not used in the progressive tenses) to have as your place of birth or the place where you live: *The participants came from thirteen different countries.* ˈ**come from sth** **1** to start in a particular place or be produced from a particular thing: *The images come from a variety of digital sources.* ◇ *Most evidence for these arguments comes from individual case studies.* ◇ *Child tax benefits come directly from the federal government.* **2** = COME OF/FROM STH
ˌ**come ˈin** **1** to have a part in sth: *Hence, individual behaviour comes in as part of an explanation of the larger picture.* **2** to arrive somewhere; to be received: *Donations came in from diverse sources.* ˌ**come ˈin for sth** [no passive] to receive sth, especially sth unpleasant: *The Act has come in for much criticism for the speed with which it was pushed through Parliament.*
ˈ**come of/from sth** to be the result of sth: *Nothing came of these proposals.* ◇ *Another source of discrepancy comes from the fact that the theory is based on an approximation.*
ˌ**come ˈoff (sth)** to become separated from sth: *Pieces of foam had been coming off the fuel tank for years.* ˌ**come ˈoff sth** [no passive] to stop taking medicine or a drug: *After she developed heart failure she was told she would have to come off the drug.*
ˌ**come ˈon** **1** (of an illness) to begin: *The pain comes on with exercise and is relieved slowly by rest.* **2** to begin to operate: *When the target light comes on, a timer starts immediately.* ˈ**come on/upon sb/sth** [no passive] (*formal*) to meet or find sb/sth by chance: *Explorers hoped to come upon the lost tribes.*
ˌ**come ˈout** **1** to be produced or published: *The book's first edition came out in 1874.* ◇ *There are studies coming out on how ageing affects the speed of processing information.* **2** (of news, the truth, etc.) to become known: *Bond traders began selling their clients' bonds as soon as the employment news came out.* **3** to be shown clearly: *This tendency comes out clearly in the second half of the article.* **4** (of research or a calculation) to produce a particular result: **+ adv./prep.** *Using Hubble's own value for the constant, the age of the Universe comes out as about two billion years.* ◇ **~ to be sth** *That the final result comes out to be so close to the critical value requires explanation.* **5** to say publicly whether you agree or disagree with sth: **~ against/in favour of sth** *The German finance minister is the latest to come out in favour of a directly imposed EU tax.* **6** to no longer hide the fact that you are HOMOSEXUAL: *Part II highlights two women involved in the anti-war movement who then came out as lesbians.* ˌ**come ˈout (of sth)** (of an object) to be removed from a place where it is fixed: *A small balloon on the end of the catheter is then inflated to prevent it from coming out.*
ˌ**come ˈover** = COME ACROSS (1)
ˌ**come ˈround** | ˌ**come ˈround (to sth)** (*BrE*) = COME AROUND/ROUND
ˌ**come ˈthrough** to arrive, especially by telephone, radio, etc. or through an official organization: *Local employees initially handle all these tasks as the orders come through.*
ˌ**come ˈto** = COME AROUND/ROUND (1) ˈ**come to sth** [no passive] to add up to sth: *Pretax profits on ships came to $56.8 million.*
ˌ**come toˈgether** (of two or more different people or things) to form a united group: *Partnerships are two or more persons who come together to form a business.*
ˈ**come under sth** [no passive] **1** to be included in a particular group: *Many other compounds come under the broad term of 'plant hormone'.* **2** to be a person or idea that others are attacking or criticizing: *This policy came under attack in Congress from time to time.* ◇ *Local producers are coming under increasing pressure to become more competitive.* **3** to be controlled or influenced by sth: *The central parts of Sudan came under British control after the battle of Omdurman in 1898.*
ˌ**come ˈup** **1** (of the sun) to rise: *When the sun comes up, the surface is warmed by absorption of solar radiation.* **2** to happen: *If your brand is not in the consumer's mind when the problem comes up, it has very little likelihood of being purchased.* **3** to be mentioned or discussed: *This question comes up repeatedly when researching this topic.* **4** (of an event or a time) to be going to happen very soon: *When an election was coming up, for example, the pressure was on to reduce the interest rate.* ˌ**come ˈup against sb/sth** [no passive] to be faced with or opposed by sb/sth: *In pursuing this line of research, however, we came up against a major problem.* ˌ**come ˈup for sth** [no passive] **1** to be considered for a job or an important position: *Judges came up for reappointment every five years.* **2** to be reaching the time when sth must be done: *The Bilingual Education Act came up for renewal in 1978.* ˌ**come ˈup to sth** [no passive] to reach an acceptable level or standard: *There is an implied threat that, if the work completed does not come up to expectation, employment is not guaranteed.* ˌ**come ˈup with sth** [no passive] to find or produce an answer, an idea, a result, etc: *It is better to come up with a design that avoids this kind of problem.* ◇ *A social entrepreneur comes up with new solutions to social problems.*
ˈ**come upon sb/sth** = COME ON/UPON SB/STH

com·edy /ˈkɒmədi; *NAmE* ˈkɑːmədi/ *noun* (*pl.* **-ies**) [C, U] a play or film that is intended to be funny, usually with a happy ending; plays and films of this type: *The Hollywood romantic comedy hit its own high renaissance in the 1930s.* ◇ *Greek tragedy and comedy have been adapted in a variety of cinematic genres and traditions.* ➲ *compare* TRAGEDY

com·fort[1] /ˈkʌmfət; *NAmE* ˈkʌmfərt/ *noun* **1** [U] the state of being physically relaxed and free from pain: *Mass-produced cars offer acceptable levels of comfort and reliability.* ◇ **the ~ of sth** *Some patients prefer to take their blood pressure in the comfort of their own home.* **2** [U] the state of having a pleasant life, with everything that you need: *She appears to be tempted by the life of comfort Grover offers.* **3** [U] a feeling of not suffering or worrying so much; a feeling of being less unhappy: *For many people, prayer is a source of comfort and strength.* ◇ **take ~ from/in sth** *It is possible to take comfort in the fact that* some societies have coped well with large-scale population growth. ◇ **it is some/little/no ~ to sb (that...)** *It was no comfort to the company that their accusers were proved wrong.* **4** [sing.] **~ (to sb)** a person or thing that helps you when you are suffering, worried or unhappy: *He was a great comfort to her.* ◇ *The knowledge that he had been affected would be a comfort and inspiration to others suffering from the syndrome.* **5** [C, usually pl.] **~ (of sth)** a thing that makes your life easier or more comfortable: *Those interviewed desired the comforts and security of middle-class America.*

C

com·fort² /ˈkʌmfət; *NAmE* ˈkʌmfərt/ *verb* **~ sb** to make sb who is worried or unhappy feel better by being kind and sympathetic towards them: *Guidance is given to caregivers on ways to comfort children who have been victims of hate.*

com·fort·able /ˈkʌmftəbl; ˈkʌmfətəbl; *NAmE* ˈkʌmfərtəbl/ *adj.* **1 ~ (with sb/sth)** confident and not worried or afraid: *Younger people tend to be more comfortable with the latest technology.* OPP UNCOMFORTABLE **2** feeling physically relaxed in a pleasant way; warm enough, without pain, etc: *If the child is comfortable (often on a parent's knee), the child and parent will be more relaxed.* ◇ *The patient should be placed in a comfortable position.* OPP UNCOMFORTABLE **3** (of clothes, furniture, etc.) making you feel physically relaxed; pleasant to wear, sit on, etc: *Comfortable shoes can help but are not acceptable for some patients.* ◇ *Improvements were made to the rooms, including more comfortable chairs and beds.* OPP UNCOMFORTABLE **4** having enough money to buy what you want without worrying too much about the cost: *Teachers' salaries are seldom sufficient for them to have comfortable lives.* **5** quite large; allowing you to win easily: *They believe that Labour will have a comfortable majority over the Conservatives.*

com·fort·ably /ˈkʌmftəbli; ˈkʌmfətəbli; *NAmE* ˈkʌmfərtəbli/ *adv.* **1** with no problem SYN EASILY: *One of these new reactors would be small enough to fit comfortably inside a modestly sized house.* **2** in a way that feels physically relaxed and pleasant: *With their subjects sitting comfortably, they record the electrical activity of the brain.* **3** with enough money to buy what you want without worrying too much about the cost: *Others lived comfortably in retirement as country squires.* **4** in a confident way without being worried or afraid: *Some health topics may be too embarrassing for them to comfortably discuss with parents and medical professionals.*

IDM **ˌcomfortably ˈoff** having enough money to buy what you want without worrying too much about the cost: *It seems sensible to assume that those with rich graves were comfortably off in life too.*

comic /ˈkɒmɪk; *NAmE* ˈkɑːmɪk/ *adj.* **1** funny and making you laugh: *The comic effect of the scene derives from Harold's embarrassment in front of the doctor.* ◇ *Don DeLillo's 'End Zone' is a first-person comic novel set in west Texas.* **2** [only before noun] connected with COMEDY (= entertainment that is funny and makes people laugh): *These comic poets were making a satirical point.* ◇ *Both contributed to the development of the European comic tradition.*

com·ing /ˈkʌmɪŋ/ *noun* [sing.] **the ~ of sb/sth** the time when sb/sth arrives or sth happens, or when sth new begins: *John is a prophetic figure who baptizes in water in order to prepare the way for the coming of Jesus.* ◇ *Until the coming of the Industrial Revolution, environmental degradation was slow, occurring over thousands of years.*

comma /ˈkɒmə; *NAmE* ˈkɑːmə/ *noun* the mark (,) used to separate the items in a list or to show where there is a slight pause in a sentence: *A comma may also be used before a short quotation.*

com·mand¹ /kəˈmɑːnd; *NAmE* kəˈmænd/ *noun* **1** [U] **~ (of sb/sth)** control and authority over a situation or a group of people: *In the eighteenth century, the French, Spanish and British navies fought for command of sea lanes to the Caribbean.* ◇ **have ~ of sb/sth** *Under the constitution, the emperor alone had supreme command of the military forces.* ◇ **take ~ (of sb/sth)** *He took virtual command of foreign policy soon after he became Prime Minister in 1937.* ◇ **in ~ (of sb/sth)** *Mao Zedong was put in command of a force to invade Hunan and Hubei.* ◇ **under the ~ of sb** *The troops were under the command of the Duke of Wellington.* **2** [sing., U] **~ (of sth)** your knowledge of sth; your ability to do or use sth, especially a language: *Such jobs required good command of the Russian language.* ◇ *Nobody can hope to understand these economic phenomena without an adequate command of historical facts.* **3** [C] an order given to a person or an animal: *Robinson was court-martialled for disobeying a lawful command given by an officer.* **4** [C] an instruction causing a computer to perform a function: *If a particular command results in an error, the user is informed of this by the operating system.*

IDM **at your comˈmand** if you have a skill or an amount of sth **at your command**, you are able to use it well and completely: *These writers have gifts at their command that allow us to see the past in new ways.* ◇ *The authority will have to decide how the resources at its command are to be employed.*

com·mand² /kəˈmɑːnd; *NAmE* kəˈmænd/ *verb* **1** [T] (of sb in a position of authority) to tell sb to do sth SYN ORDER²: **~ sb to do sth** *Abraham was commanded by God to sacrifice his only son, Isaac.* ◇ **~ that...** *Caesar commanded that they be put to death.* ◇ (*BrE also*) *Caesar commanded that they should be put to death.* **2** [T, I] **~ (sb/sth)** to be in charge of a group of people in the army, navy, etc: *General Wesley Clark commanded NATO forces during the conflict.* **3** [T, no passive] (not used in the progressive tenses) **~ sth** to deserve and get sth because of the special qualities you have: *His opinions commanded the attention of many when he first expressed them.* ◇ *The legislation will not be passed unless it can command widespread support.* **4** [T, no passive] (not used in the progressive tenses) **~ sth** to be in a strong enough position to have or get sth: *No one party could command a majority in the House of Commons.* **5** [T, no passive] (not used in the progressive tenses) **~ sth** to have sth available for use: *The state commanded large-scale resources such as publicly owned industries.* **6** [T, no passive] (not used in the progressive tenses) **~ sth** to be in a position from where you can see or control sth: *The site was located on top of a hill commanding a panoramic view.*

com·mand·er /kəˈmɑːndə(r); *NAmE* kəˈmændər/ *noun* **~ (of sb/sth)** a person who is in charge of sth, especially an officer in charge of a particular group of soldiers or a military operation: *This plan was submitted by the commander of the south-western armies, Brusilov.*

com·mence AWL /kəˈmens/ *verb* [T, I] (*formal*) to begin sth; to begin to happen: **~ (sth)** *The bank commenced proceedings to sell the property.* ◇ *A public inquiry is due to commence on the 16th.* ◇ **~ with sth** *The chapter commences with a brief consideration of communication theory.* ◇ **~ doing sth** *She commenced working on the project in 1980.*

com·mence·ment AWL /kəˈmensmənt/ *noun* [U, C, usually sing.] **~ (of sth)** (*formal*) beginning: *The length of time between disease onset and the commencement of treatment was crucial.*

com·ment¹ AWL /ˈkɒment; *NAmE* ˈkɑːment/ *noun* [C, U] something that you say or write that gives an opinion on or explains sb/sth: *Comments posted on the website indicated widespread public dissatisfaction.* ◇ *Government policy in this area has attracted adverse comment.* ◇ **~ on sb/sth** *I would like to thank Eileen Abbott for her helpful* *comments on the first draft.* ◇ *For further comment on this issue, see Clarke (2011).* ◇ **~ about sb/sth** *One soldier was imprisoned for making a critical comment about the president.*

com·ment² AWL /ˈkɒment; *NAmE* ˈkɑːment/ *verb* [I, T] to express an opinion about sth: **~ on/upon sth** *The unions demanded an opportunity to comment on the proposals.* ◇ **~ that...** *This point is made very clearly by Campbell (1999), who comments that there are still serious concerns among managers.* ◇ **+ speech** *One factory owner commented sadly: 'We suffer from the legacy of the colonial days.'*

com·men·tary AWL /ˈkɒməntri; *NAmE* ˈkɑːmənteri/ *noun* (*pl.* **-ies**) **1** [C] **~ (on sth)** a written explanation or discussion of sth such as a theory or book: *She has written numerous commentaries on biblical texts.* ◇ *Mitchell (1996) presents a critical commentary on the power of capital to shape the agricultural landscape.* **2** [C, U] **~ (on sth)** a criticism or discussion of sth: *'Ozymandias' is most often read as an ironic commentary on the vanity of political ambition.* ◇ *As social commentary, the film only partly succeeds.*

com·men·ta·tor AWL /ˈkɒmənteɪtə(r); *NAmE* ˈkɑːmənteɪtər/ *noun* a person who is an expert on a particular subject and talks or writes about it, especially on television or radio, or in a newspaper: **~ on sth** *He is one of the UK's foremost expert commentators on climate change.* ◇ **according to ~** *According to many commentators, later this century the oil will run out.*

com·merce /ˈkɒmɜːs; *NAmE* ˈkɑːmɜːrs/ *noun* [U] trade, especially between countries; the buying and selling of goods and services: *Good links with industry and commerce are important for finding work placements for students.* ◇ *Today, Lisbon is a vibrant city and an important centre of commerce.*

com·mer·cial¹ /kəˈmɜːʃl; *NAmE* kəˈmɜːrʃl/ *adj.* **1** [usually before noun] connected with the buying and selling of goods and services: *There seemed to be no limits to the potential growth of commercial activities on the Internet.* ◇ *When students view themselves as consumers, they are more likely to view the act of learning as a commercial transaction.* **2** [only before noun] making or intended to make a profit: *Defence spending has fostered the development of many commercial products.* ◇ *Sadly, the company was not a commercial success.* **3** (of television or radio) paid for by the money charged for broadcasting advertisements: *Commercial television and radio stations are now dominant in the market.* **4** more concerned with profit and being popular than with quality: *He acknowledged that their work was very commercial.*

com·mer·cial² /kəˈmɜːʃl; *NAmE* kəˈmɜːrʃl/ *noun* **~ (for sth)** an advertisement on the radio or on television: *The government ensures that commercials for certain products will not be transmitted at times it deems inappropriate.*

com·mer·cial·ize (*BrE also* **-ise**) /kəˈmɜːʃəlaɪz; *NAmE* kəˈmɜːrʃlaɪz/ *verb* [often passive] **~ sth** to use sth to try to make a profit, especially in a way that other people do not approve of: *In Japan, universities for the most part do not do research that could quickly be commercialized.* ■ **com·mer·cial·iza·tion, -isa·tion** /kəˌmɜːʃəlaɪˈzeɪʃn; *NAmE* kəˌmɜːrʃləˈzeɪʃn/ *noun* [U] **~ (of sth)** *The commercialization of knowledge has assumed greater importance in economic growth.*

com·mer·cial·ly /kəˈmɜːʃəli; *NAmE* kəˈmɜːrʃəli/ *adv.* **1** in a way that is intended to make a profit for a business: *New ideas are then developed into commercially viable products.* **2** in order to be sold: *Most commercially available psychological tests are copyrighted.* ◇ *Teaching materials may be teacher-made or commercially produced.*

com·mis·sion¹ AWL /kəˈmɪʃn/ *noun* **1** (*often* **Commission**) [C] an official group of people who have been given responsibility to control sth, or to find out about sth, usually for the government: *The European Commission can ban all trade in a particular foodstuff.* ◇ *An independent commission assesses the impact of this type of project.* ◇ **+ noun** *Barroso took office as Commission President in late 2004.* **2** [U, C] an amount of money that is paid to sb for selling goods and which increases with the amount of goods that are sold: *The more people you persuade to sign up, the more commission you will be paid.* ◇ *Relatively high commissions are paid for sales of the most profitable products.* ➲ *compare* FEE (1) **3** [U] an amount of money that is charged by a bank or other business for providing a particular service: *The supply of available housing is affected by the commission charged by estate agents.* ➲ *compare* FEE (1), CHARGE¹ (1) **4** [C] a formal request to sb to design or make a piece of work such as a building or a painting: *Shipyards were receiving sufficient commissions to double the world's fleet.* ➲ *compare* ORDER¹ (6) **5** [U] **~ of sth** the act of doing sth wrong or illegal: *The maximum sentence for commission of the offence is five years' imprisonment.* **6** [C] an officer's position in the armed forces: *Trotsky offered commissions to former officers of the tsarist army.*

- ADJECTIVE + COMMISSION **regulatory** • **international** • **independent** *The FTC (Federal Trade Commission) was created in 1915 as an independent regulatory commission.*
- VERB + COMMISSION **notify** • **establish, create** • **empower** • **request** • **appoint** *Member States must notify the Commission in advance of aid projects.* ◇ *In 1990 a Press Complaints Commission was established.*
- COMMISSION + VERB **recommend** • **propose** • **publish** *The Law Commission recommended the abolition of the current law.*
- COMMISSION + NOUN **president** • **official** • **proposal** • **report** • **representative** • **decision** *The Jenkins Commission proposals attracted a fair amount of comment.*

com·mis·sion² AWL /kəˈmɪʃn/ *verb* [often passive] to officially ask sb to write, make or create sth or to do a task for you: **~ sb to do sth** *The government commissioned Lord Beveridge to look at the problems affecting Britain.* ◇ **~ sth** *The company now wishes to commission research to help decision-making.* ◇ *In 1997, a report was commissioned by the Chief Medical Officer of England.*

com·mis·sion·er AWL /kəˈmɪʃənə(r)/ *noun* **1** (*usually* **Commissioner**) a member of a commission: *There were fears that the Irish voice would be lost in the Commission if Ireland no longer had its own Commissioner.* **2** (*usually* **Commissioner**) the head of a government department in some countries: *In the United Kingdom, the Information Commissioner has commissioned annual surveys of public opinion.* **3** (*also* **poˈlice commissioner**) the head of a particular police force in some countries: *There is disagreement within the coalition on the proposed election of local police commissioners.* ◇ **~ of sth** *Sir John Stevens, then Commissioner of the Metropolitan Police, was the keynote speaker.*

com·mit AWL /kəˈmɪt/ *verb* (**-tt-**) **1** [T] **~ a crime, etc.** to do sth wrong or illegal: *Problems may exist where an employer cannot identify which of the employees has committed an offence.* ◇ *A murder may be committed without any planning or premeditation.* ◇ *Statistics show that the majority of crimes committed in England and Wales are property related.* **2** [T] **~ suicide** to kill yourself deliberately: *Many people who commit suicide have contacted their doctors shortly beforehand.* **3** [T, often passive] to promise that you will definitely do sth or keep to an agreement or arrangement: **be committed to (doing) sth** *The Prime Minister is committed to holding a referendum.* ◇ **~ yourself to (doing) sth** *The European Union has committed itself to the eventual membership of Turkey.*

◇ **~ yourself to do sth** *The government committed itself to respond to wage restraint with tax cuts.* ◇ **be committed to do sth** *The Thatcher governments were committed to shift the balance from the state to market forces.* **4** [T] **~ yourself (to sth)** to give an opinion or make a decision publicly so that it is then difficult to change it: *Evans-Pritchard does not completely commit himself to this last view.* ◇ *The research will show whether the communications encourage respondents to buy or commit themselves.* **5** [I] **~ (to sb/sth)** to be completely loyal to one person or organization or give all your time and effort to your work or an activity: *It is unclear whether trust develops from the decision to commit to one supplier.* ➲ *see also* COMMITTED **6** [T] **~ sb/sth (to sth)** to spend resources such as money, people or time on sth/sb: *The Clinton administration committed troops to Bosnia in 1999.* ◇ *Risk can be minimized by gradually committing more resources to a market.* **7** [T, usually passive] **~ sb to sth** to order sb to be sent to a hospital, prison, etc: *Mrs Greenhill was committed to prison for contempt of court.* ◇ *He was committed to a state psychiatric facility.* **8** [T] **~ sth to memory** to learn sth well enough to remember it exactly: *One category of idioms consists of chunks of language which speakers have committed to memory.*

com·mit·ment AWL /kəˈmɪtmənt/ *noun* **1** [sing., U] a strong belief in a cause or activity and a promise to support it: **~ to sb/sth** *The company has maintained a strong commitment to excellence in the arts.* ◇ *The school was selected because of its commitment to community involvement.* ◇ **~ to doing sth** *The World Bank requires borrowing governments to demonstrate their commitment to reducing poverty.* **2** [C, U] a promise to do sth or to behave in a particular way: **~ on sth** *The summit addressed the need for long-term commitments on carbon emissions.* ◇ **~ to doing sth** *The government made an explicit commitment to increasing public expenditure.* ◇ **~ to do sth** *A characteristic of a strong research university is its commitment to provide a quality education for its students.* ➲ *compare* PLEDGE[1] (1) **3** [U] the willingness to work hard and give your energy and time to a job or an activity: *High-performance work systems require a degree of employee commitment.* ◇ *Successful performance is dependent on the level of commitment demonstrated by the workforce.* ◇ **~ to sb/sth** *Respondents' commitment to work varied according to whether they were still unemployed at the time of the interview.* ➲ *compare* DEDICATION (1) **4** [C] (used in compounds) a thing that you have promised or agreed to do, or that you have to do: *Not wanting to fall behind with her work commitments, she went to her office in the city.* ◇ *If revenue falls, they may struggle to meet their loan commitments.* ➲ *compare* DUTY (1), RESPONSIBILITY (1) **5** [C, U] agreeing to use money, time or people in order to achieve sth: **~ of sth** *Global expansion often requires a serious commitment of financial and human resources.* ◇ **~ (of sth) to sth** *A deep commitment of United States forces to a land war would be a catastrophic error.*

▸ ADJECTIVE + COMMITMENT **strong, deep • ideological • emotional** *The alliance has integrated education into a wider set of ideological commitments.* ◇ *His views emerged from an emotional commitment to the underclasses of the world.* | **long-term • political • religious • ethical • personal** *Austen's novels ostensibly suggest little active political commitment.* | **long-term • credible • personal** *Parties in a multi-party system are more likely to make credible commitments to their long-term voters.* | **long-term • professional • organizational • emotional** *Recent research has shown that professional and organizational commitment are positively correlated.* ◇ *The customer contributes their money, time and emotional commitment.* | **financial • professional • prior** *The industry provides goods and services that help people to fulfil their financial commitments.* | **long-term • financial • prior** *Government must support efforts that involve long-term commitment of resources.*

▸ VERB + COMMITMENT **require • share • maintain • demonstrate** *Ecological modernization requires political commitment.* | **reaffirm • strengthen** *The UN General Assembly has reaffirmed its strong commitment to linguistic diversity.* | **require • make • implement • meet • fulfil** *International aid can increase countries' capacity to implement their commitments.* | **meet • fulfil** *Often, the male partner meets the mortgage commitments, and the female partner meets other expenses.*

com·mit·ted AWL /kəˈmɪtɪd/ *adj.* (*approving*) willing to work hard and give your time and energy to sth; believing strongly in sth SYN DEDICATED (1): *Matilda had a group of strongly committed supporters.* ◇ *Durkheim was a deeply committed defender of individual liberty.* ◇ **~ to sth** *A study of engineers suggests that high performers may be more committed to their profession.*

com·mit·tee /kəˈmɪti/ *noun* [C+sing./pl. v.] a group of people who are chosen, usually by a larger group, to make decisions or deal with a particular subject. A committee typically consists of members of the larger group: *A scientific committee chaired by Sir Richard Southwood was appointed.* ◇ *The remuneration committee is comprised of independent non-executive directors.* ◇ **+ noun** *All committee meetings are held in public.*

com·mod·ity AWL /kəˈmɒdəti; *NAmE* kəˈmɑːdəti/ *noun* (*pl.* **-ies**) **1** a product or a raw material that can be bought and sold: *The majority of Michigan's agricultural commodities were consumed domestically.* ◇ **+ noun** *Higher commodity prices would make government support unnecessary.* **2** a thing that is useful or has a useful quality: *Information is a valuable commodity in an increasingly commercial media environment.*

com·mon[1] /ˈkɒmən; *NAmE* ˈkɑːmən/ *adj.* (**com·mon·er, com·mon·est**) (**more common** and **most common** are more frequent) **1** happening often; existing in large numbers or in many places: *The most common feature of asthma in the very young is a persistent night-time cough.* ◇ *Extra-pair matings are quite common in many pair-bonding species.* ◇ **it is ~ (for sb/sth) (to do sth)** *It is increasingly common for countries to be affected by migration.* OPP RARE (1), UNCOMMON (1) ➲ *compare* UNUSUAL (1) **2** [usually before noun] shared by or belonging to two or more people, groups or things, or by the people or things in a group: *Humans and monkeys share a more recent common ancestor than humans and rabbits.* ◇ **~ to sb/sth** *While many of the problems are city-specific, a number are common to cities all over the region.* ◇ *There are some needs which are common to all living organisms.* ➲ *see also* COMMON DENOMINATOR, COMMON GROUND **3** [only before noun] not unusual or special SYN ORDINARY (1): *Russia's gentry regarded Russian as the language of the common people.* ➲ *see also* COMMON LAW, COMMON SENSE

IDM **make common ˈcause with sb** to be united with sb about sth that you both agree on, believe in or wish to achieve: *Vlasov decided to make common cause with the Germans after he and his troops were captured.* **the common ˈgood** the benefit or interests of everyone: *Central government is not a unified organization with ministers working together for the common good.* ◇ *These adolescents thought about how schools might promote the common good.* ➲ *more at* KNOWLEDGE

▸ COMMON + NOUN **cause • feature • type • form • example • theme • practice • method • approach • problem • disease, disorder • symptom • use** *In developing countries, liver cancer is the third most common type of cancer.* ◇ *These terms are all in common use.* | **element • characteristic • factor • interest • intention, purpose • goal • identity • humanity • language • culture • ancestor • currency • policy • market** *Organizations are able to set up chat rooms for groups of users who share a common interest.*

▸ ADVERB + COMMON **increasingly • quite, fairly • relatively • particularly • very • extremely** *Alunite is a relatively common mineral in volcanic rocks.*

com·mon² /ˈkɒmən; *NAmE* ˈkɑːmən/ *noun*
IDM **have sth in common** (of things, places, etc.) to have the same features or characteristics: *What these works have in common is their portrayal of life in a secular society.* ◇ *Macedonian and Greek culture had little in common.* ◇ *Organisms grouped together at the lowest levels have more in common than those grouped further up.* **have, etc. sth in common (with sb)** (of people) to have the same interests and ideas as sb else: *I could see that the younger people and the older people had a lot in common.* **in common** shared by everyone in a group: *Meals in common were central to the social and religious life of some Jewish sects.*

the ˌ**common ˈcold** *noun* [sing.] = COLD² (2)

ˌ**common deˈnominator** *noun* **1 ~ (in sth)** an idea, attitude or experience that is shared by all the members of a group: *The common denominator in all of the plans is the commitment to end child labour.* **2** a number that can be divided exactly by all the numbers below the line in a set of FRACTIONS: *One obtains simpler numbers by writing the given fractions with a large common denominator.* ➲ *compare* DENOMINATOR

ˌ**common ˈground** *noun* [U] **~ (with sb)** an opinion, interest or aim that you share with sb, although you may not agree with them about other things: *During the debate his opponent had sought to find common ground with him so as to appear reasonable.*

ˌ**common ˈlaw** *noun* [U] a system of laws that have been developed from customs and from decisions made by judges, not created by a parliament: **under/in (the) ~** *Under common law, parents cannot legally compel their children to look after them.* ➲ *compare* CASE LAW

com·mon·ly /ˈkɒmənli; *NAmE* ˈkɑːmənli/ *adv.* usually; very often; by most people: *It is possible to carry out these steps using commonly available materials.* ◇ *This type of asthma is commonly known as allergic asthma.* ➲ *usage note at* GENERALLY

▸ COMMONLY + VERB **occur • found, encountered • observed • used, employed • known as, referred to as, called • associated with • affected** *Type 1 diabetes commonly occurs in childhood.* ◇ *Brucite is most commonly found in marble.*

ˌ**common ˈmarket** *noun* [C, usually sing.] a group of countries that have agreed on low or no taxes on goods traded between countries in the group, and higher fixed taxes on goods imported from countries outside the group: *The treaty sought to create a common market with free movement of goods, persons, services and capital.* HELP **The Common Market** is a former name of the European Union, used especially in the 1960s and 1970s.

the **Com·mons** /ˈkɒmənz; *NAmE* ˈkɑːmənz/ *noun* [pl.] = HOUSE OF COMMONS

ˌ**common ˈsense** *noun* [U] the ability to think about things in a practical way and make sensible decisions: *Jurors will be expected to use their common sense in deciding whether such a defence is valid.* ◇ *The common-sense view is that language just provides names for thoughts that exist independently.* ◇ **it is ~ to do sth** *It is common sense to recognize that knowledge of what is wrong is required before steps can be taken to put it right.*

com·mu·nal /kəˈmjuːnl; *BrE also* ˈkɒmjənl/ *adj.* **1** shared by, or for the use of, a number of people, especially people who live together SYN SHARED: *As average incomes are very low, household benefits from communal ownership are large.* ◇ *The infection may spread from person to person in communal showers.* **2** involving different groups of people in a community, especially those having different religions or ETHNIC background: *Communal violence ensued in Indian cities, and both Muslims and Hindus died.* ◇ *Early post-independence writers tended to endorse the need for communal solidarity.* ■ **com·mu·nal·ly** /kəˈmjuːnəli; ˈkɒmjənəli; *NAmE* kəˈmjuːnəli/ *adv.*: *Alpine marmots live communally in family groups.*

C

com·mune /ˈkɒmjuːn; *NAmE* ˈkɑːmjuːn/ *noun* [C+sing./pl. v.] **1** the smallest division of local government in France and some other countries: *In 1833, the Education Minister, Guizot, required every commune to set up and fund one elementary school.* **2** a group of people who live together and share responsibilities, possessions, etc: *Either standards of privacy, space, job rotas, etc. are introduced or the commune breaks up.*

com·mu·nic·able AWL /kəˈmjuːnɪkəbl/ *adj.* (of a disease) that can be passed from one person to another: *The problems posed by communicable diseases are increasingly significant.* ◇ **~ through sth** *AIDS is not communicable through normal social contact.* ➲ *compare* CONTAGIOUS, INFECTIOUS

com·mu·ni·cate AWL /kəˈmjuːnɪkeɪt/ *verb* **1** [I, T] to exchange information, news, ideas, etc. with sb: **~ with sb/sth** *The role of marketing in communicating effectively with customers will become increasingly crucial.* ◇ *Computers communicate with each other to share resources such as printers.* ◇ **~ (by sth)** *The server enables graduates to communicate by email.* ◇ **~ sth to sb/sth** *Disease outbreaks are detected and communicated to the proper authorities.* ◇ *Field bees communicate information about new food sources to other worker bees.* ◇ **~ sth (by sth)** *Complaints may be communicated by telephone or mail.* **2** [I, T] to make your ideas, feelings, thoughts, etc. known to other people so that they understand them: *A Spaniard can go to Italy and communicate well.* ◇ **~ sth (to sb)** *When we communicate anger, we are being open and vulnerable.* ◇ **~ what/how, etc...** *You need to communicate what you have learned to other people.* ◇ *Peacocks communicate how beautiful they are by flashing their enormous tails.* ➲ *compare* EXPRESS¹ (1) **3** [I] to have a good relationship because you are able to understand and talk about your own and other people's thoughts, feelings, etc: *Family conflicts may increase with some members finding it difficult to communicate easily.* **4** [T, usually passive] **~ sth** to pass a disease from one person or animal to another: *Contagious diseases and parasites can be communicated when people touch.* ➲ *compare* INFECT (1)

▸ COMMUNICATE + NOUN **information, message • benefits • results, findings** *The primary purpose of the maps was to communicate information.* ◇ *Results can be communicated in real time.*

▸ ADVERB + COMMUNICATE | COMMUNICATE + ADVERB **directly** *The secretary at one factory appears to communicate directly with the secretary at the other factory.* | **clearly** *Biomedical scientists are required to communicate clearly and precisely.* | **successfully • effectively** *Staff should be trained to be able to communicate effectively.*

com·mu·ni·ca·tion AWL /kəˌmjuːnɪˈkeɪʃn/ *noun* **1** [U] the activity or process of expressing ideas and feelings or of giving people information: *The patient's non-verbal communication can reveal the emotional impact of their illness.* ◇ **+ noun** *Effective communication skills are essential for the constructive management of anger.* HELP In business, **communication** often describes the activity or process of giving information to the public, for example in commercials: *Without a link between the message and the brand, there is no chance for effective marketing communication.* **2** [U] (*also* **communications** [pl.]) methods of sending information, especially telephones, radio, computers, etc: *Computer technologies are improving with increased use of wireless communication.* ◇ **+ noun** *Wind* *turbines can have an adverse effect on communication systems.* ◇ *A tsunami warning system could utilize existing radio communications systems.* **3 communications** [pl.] methods of travelling or transporting goods, such as roads and railways: *The distribution of aid is often made difficult by poor communications.* ◇ **+ noun** *Royal Mail has a communications network of postmen and vans.* **4** [C] a message, letter, email or telephone call: *I am indebted to Suzanne Webb for her account of this matter (personal communication, 9 January 2012).* HELP In business, a **communication** is a way of contacting potential customers, such as a commercial or a letter: *In developing markets, radio still remains the main channel for marketing communications.*

▸ ADJECTIVE + COMMUNICATION **effective • poor • verbal • non-verbal • interpersonal • face-to-face • two-way • mass** *Interpersonal communication is one of the most frequent uses of new technologies.* ◇ *An integrated planning approach is important to effective mass communication.* | **global, international • mass • electronic • wireless • online • digital • mobile** *Global communications such as the Internet have made it possible for organizations to reach a wider audience.*

▸ NOUN + COMMUNICATION **marketing • brand** *Marketing communications play an important role in communicating a brand's personality.* | **Internet • email • satellite • phone, telephone • radio** *Pioneering research in the 1980s examined the effects of email communication within the workplace.* | **personal • email** *Incentives can be offered through an email communication.*

▸ VERB + COMMUNICATION **facilitate, enable • improve • maintain** *A common language facilitates communication.* | **receive** *The number of communications received by the Court has continued to increase.*

▸ COMMUNICATION + NOUN **objective • skills • strategy • campaign • tool • effect • system** *Brand recall is a more difficult communication objective to achieve than brand recognition.* | **technology • channel** *Modern communications technology has made it possible for some people to work at home.* | **infrastructure • network • system** *Hong Kong's strategic location and its excellent communications network have made it a hub for trade.*

com·mu·ni·ca·tive AWL /kə'mju:nɪkətɪv; *NAmE* kə'mju:nɪkeɪtɪv/ *adj.* **1** connected with the ability to communicate: *Many students can develop communicative skills in a new language within two years.* ◇ *Karl von Frisch studied the communicative dances of bees.* **2** willing or able to talk or give information: *This technique can work with adolescents who have a history of not being very communicative.* ◇ *Dolphins and whales are extremely intelligent and communicative creatures.*

com·mu·nion /kə'mju:niən/ *noun* [U] **1** (*also* **Communion**) a ceremony in the Christian Church during which people eat bread and drink wine in memory of the last meal that Christ had with his DISCIPLES; the bread and wine that are given and received at Communion: *Frequent and regular communion was the common custom of the early Church.* ◇ *As a consequence, most Christians received communion only once a year.* **2 (in) ~ (with sb/sth)** the state of sharing or exchanging thoughts and feelings; the feeling of being part of sth: *The experience offers an impression of being in real communion with God.*

com·mun·ism /'kɒmjunɪzəm; *NAmE* 'kɑ:mjunɪzəm/ *noun* [U] **1** a political movement that believes in an economic system in which the state controls the means of producing everything on behalf of the people. It aims to create a society in which everyone is treated equally: *Marxism became the official form of communism following Marx's death.* **2 Communism** the system of government by a ruling communist party, such as in the former Soviet Union: *After the collapse of Soviet Communism in 1991, the USSR disintegrated along national lines.* ➲ *compare* CAPITALISM

com·mun·ist[1] /'kɒmjənɪst; *NAmE* 'kɑ:mjənɪst/ *noun* **1** a person who believes in or supports communism: *Marx's writings are sacred to some communists.* **2 Communist** a member of a communist party: *This period of 42 years commenced with the arrival of the totalitarian political leadership of the Communists.*

com·mun·ist[2] /'kɒmjənɪst; *NAmE* 'kɑ:mjənɪst/ *adj.* (*also* **Communist**) connected with communism: *In the early 1970s, the eastern half of Europe was ruled by communist parties.*

com·mu·nity AWL /kə'mju:nəti/ *noun* (*pl.* **-ies**) **1** (*often* **the community**) [sing.] all the people who live in a particular area, country, etc. when considered as a group: **in the ~** *Health and illness in the community have been studied in a number of ways.* ◇ *The husband has lived in the local community for the last 14 years.* ◇ **+ noun** *Our survey asked participants about their community involvement.* **2** [C] (used in compounds) a group of people who share the same religion, race, job, etc: *The company works with the academic community, sponsoring research projects and university symposia.* ◇ *The immigrants expanded the number of Jewish communities in France.* **3** [U] (*approving*) the feeling of sharing things and belonging to a group in the place where you live: *People's health is strongly linked to where they live and their sense of community.* ◇ **+ noun** *They promote their property developments as a return to old-fashioned family and community values.* **4** [C] (*biology*) a group of plants and animals growing or living in the same place or environment: *Corals are keystone species upon which whole marine communities depend.* ◇ **~ of sth** *The streams support communities of bacteria.*

IDM **the ˌglobal/interˌnational comˈmunity** the countries of the world, considered as a group: *This is one of the most difficult and dangerous problems facing the international community.*

▸ ADJECTIVE + COMMUNITY **local • wider, broader • diverse • rural • urban** *The network should embrace teachers, students, families and the wider community.* | **academic • scientific • political • ethnic • black • indigenous • religious • monastic • online, virtual** *Climate research remains a major focus in the scientific community.* ◇ *People from minority ethnic communities are more likely than others to live in poor areas.* | **ecological • microbial • bacterial • coastal • marine** *Most ecological communities are adapted to nutrient shortages.*

▸ NOUN + COMMUNITY **minority • business • farming** *The central bank's tight monetary policy has presented severe problems for the business community.* | **plant • animal** *As the density of the plant community increases, the ability to trap sand also increases.*

▸ VERB + COMMUNITY **create, build, establish • form • constitute** *Organizations can create online communities where customers can share ideas.* | **serve** *Today, it seems natural to compensate people for time spent serving the community.*

▸ COMMUNITY + NOUN **involvement, participation, engagement • initiative • development • setting • school • nurse** *Community participation in education has been receiving increased attention in Malawi.* | **leader • member • organization** *The project aimed to turn the building into a workspace for community organizations.*

com·pact /kəm'pækt; 'kɒmpækt; *NAmE* 'kɑ:mpækt/ *adj.* **1** closely and firmly packed together: *Most proteins have a compact globular shape.* ◇ *Some rocks that are compact and hard resist being worn down, even by the action of glaciers.* ➲ *compare* DENSE (2) **2** smaller than is usual for things of the same kind: *All compact cameras have a fixed lens.* ◇ *Sales of full-sized pickup trucks have nearly doubled since 1991, while sales of compact pickups have fallen.* **3** using or filling only a small amount of space: *In traditional societies, residential units were not compact.* ◇ *Sales* *territories that are geographically compact make it easier for salespeople to be responsive to customer needs.* **4** (of speech or writing) giving the information that is important using few words or symbols: *This program can be expressed in a more compact way.* ◇ *The system of Arabic numerals is beautifully compact and efficient.* ➲ *compare* CONCISE (1)

ˌcompact ˈdisc *noun* = CD

com·pan·ion /kəmˈpæniən/ *noun* **1** a person or an animal that goes somewhere with you or spends a lot of time with you: *Dickens and his companions were seriously shaken but unhurt.* ◇ *a travelling/drinking companion* **2** one of a pair of things that go together or can be used together: **+ noun** *Additional exercises can be found on the book's companion website.*

THESAURUS

company ◆ **business** ◆ **conglomerate** ◆ **corporation** ◆ **firm** ◆ **multinational** ◆ **organization** *noun*

These words can all be used to describe an organization that makes money by producing or selling goods or services.

- **an insurance/a limited/a pharmaceutical** company
- a **family/local** business
- an **entertainment/industrial** conglomerate
- a **multinational** company/conglomerate/corporation/firm
- **an accounting/a consulting/a manufacturing** firm
- **a foreign/a European/an oil** multinational
- a **non-governmental/non-profit/voluntary** organization

- **Company** refers to a business organization that is recognized in law and that exists independently of its owners and employees. The term **corporation** is also often used, especially in American English: *Company law enables a company to own its own assets.* ◇ *Pertamina became a corporation established by law.*
- **Business** is often used to refer to a small company that is owned by an individual or a family; whereas **firm** is often used to mean a company that provides a particular professional service: *Family businesses have been the basis of entrepreneurship...* ◇ *Accounting firms should limit their services to audit and closely related services.*
- **Conglomerate** refers to an organization formed of a group of companies that have different business activities: *The OCBC acquired numerous commercial and industrial concerns to form a highly diversified conglomerate.*
- **Multinational** and **corporation** are both used to mean a company that operates in more than one country: *Foreign multinationals are increasingly setting up operations in this country.* ◇ *The corporations that are headquartered in these cities reach around the world.*
- **Organization** can be used to mean a company that exists to make a profit, but it can also mean a non-profit organization: *Business organizations should understand the processes of gradual cultural change.* ◇ *This voluntary organization provides emergency provisions to refugees.*

com·pany /ˈkʌmpəni/ *noun* (*pl.* **-ies**) **1** [C] (*abbr.* **Co.**) (often in names) a business organization that makes money by producing or selling goods or services: *Companies operating in foreign countries need to be aware of employment legislation.* ◇ *Tata bought Land Rover and Jaguar from the Ford Motor Company.* ◇ *Hershey Co. had to raise the wholesale prices of its confectionery line by 4–5 per cent.* ◇ **+ noun** *Dell sells computer equipment through the company website.* ➲ *see also* HOLDING COMPANY, LIMITED COMPANY, PRIVATE COMPANY, PUBLIC COMPANY **2** (often in names) [C+sing./pl. v.] a group of people, especially actors or dancers, who work or perform together: *Stuart (2006) studied a series of successful theatre companies.* ◇ *The theatre now attracts top touring companies such as the Royal Shakespeare Company.* **3** [U] the fact of being with sb else and not alone, especially in a way that provides friendship or enjoyment: *A husband may neglect his wife because he does not enjoy her company.* ◇ **in the ~ of sb** *Coleridge spent much of his time in the company of William and Dorothy Wordsworth.* ◇ **in ~** *These people are ill at ease in company and fearful of disapproval.*

com·par·able /ˈkɒmpərəbl; *NAmE* ˈkɑːmpərəbl/ *adj.* similar to sth else and able to be compared: *Even if measures of output were available, they would not be directly comparable.* ◇ *In 1950, only 8% was exported; now the comparable figure is almost 30%.* ◇ **~ to sth** *These animals swam in a way that is comparable to that of modern sea lions.* ◇ **~ with sth** *Buck's results are broadly comparable with those of other large-scale surveys.* ◇ **~ across sth** *The intensification of work seemed to be comparable across each of the groups.* ◇ **~ in sth** *This task is comparable in scale to the sequencing of human DNA.* ■ **com·par·abil·ity** /ˌkɒmpərəˈbɪləti; *NAmE* ˌkɑːmpərəˈbɪləti/ *noun* [U] **~ (between/across sth)** *It is essential to ensure comparability between and across cultures.*

com·para·tive¹ /kəmˈpærətɪv/ *adj.* [usually before noun] **1** connected with studying things to discover how they are similar or different: *There is a need for more comparative research.* ◇ *He devoted his life to the comparative study of religion.* ◇ *The field of comparative anatomy has revealed remarkable similarities between these groups.* **2** measured or judged by how similar or different sth is to sth else SYN RELATIVE¹ (1): *In London Marx lived a life of comparative poverty.* **3** (*grammar*) connected with adjectives or adverbs that express more in amount, degree or quality, for example *higher, better, more frequently* and *more clearly* ➲ *compare* SUPERLATIVE¹ (2)

▸ COMPARATIVE + NOUN **research** ◆ **study** ◆ **analysis** ◆ **assessment** ◆ **data** ◆ **perspective** ◆ **approach** ◆ **methodology** ◆ **method** *He was convinced of the importance of the comparative approach.* | **politics** ◆ **literature** ◆ **psychology** ◆ **anatomy** ◆ **genomics** *Some scholars of comparative politics have expressed similar ideas.*

com·para·tive² /kəmˈpærətɪv/ *noun* (*grammar*) the form of an adjective or adverb that expresses more in amount, degree or quality ➲ *compare* SUPERLATIVE²

com·para·tive·ly /kəmˈpærətɪvli/ *adv.* **1** when measured or judged by how similar or different sth is to sth else SYN RELATIVELY: *These cases are comparatively rare.* ◇ *There are comparatively few results from longitudinal studies.* ➲ language bank *at* EXCEPTIONALLY **2** connected with studying things to discover how they are similar or different: *It is useful to think comparatively about these developments.* ◇ *This section comparatively analyses the role of advocacy networks.*

com·pare /kəmˈpeə(r); *NAmE* kəmˈper/ *verb* **1** [T] to examine people or things to see how they are similar and how they are different: **~ A and B** *The channel widened by 10–15 metres (compare Figs. 16.11c and 16.11d).* ◇ *When we compared the various findings across populations, the results were encouraging.* ◇ **~ A with B** *The validity of this law is established by comparing its predictions with experimental observations.* HELP **Compare** is sometimes abbreviated to **cf.** but only when it is an instruction: *Cf. Burke (1995) for a brief discussion of this topic.* **2** [T, often passive] to measure or judge sb/sth by how similar or different they are to sb/sth else: **~ A with/to B** *This information allows individual plants to compare their performance with firm-wide performance targets.* ◇ **compared with sb/sth** *Imports rose by 5.2 per cent compared with the previous month.* ◇ **compared to sb/sth** *Only 6% of people in the first age group have no academic qualifications, compared to 22% of the older group.* ◇ **as compared with/to sb/sth** *Their study uncovered a decreased willingness for men to seek psychotherapy, as compared with women.* **3** [I] **how A and B ~**

how two things **compare** is the extent to which they are similar or different: *How the two compared, either in terms of funding or in terms of priorities, is difficult to say.* **4** [I] **A compares well, etc. with B** to be as good as, or better than, sth else: *The results compare well with those of Gartling (2009).* ◇ *Their environmental performance compares favourably with other plants.* **5** [T] **~ A to B** to show or state that sth is similar to sth else SYN LIKEN: *Seth's work has been compared to that of Dickens, Tolstoy and Jane Austen.*

IDM **compare 'notes (with sb)** if people **compare notes**, they each say what they think about the same event, situation, etc: *Comparing notes with the groups' other teachers can provide quite different data.*

▸ COMPARE + NOUN **predictions** • **models** • **approaches** • **results, outcomes** • **findings** • **readings** • **scores** • **data** • **efficiency, effectiveness** *There are currently no trial results directly comparing these approaches.* | **rate** • **level** • **profile** • **groups** • **sequences** • **performance** • **values** • **costs** • **prices** *The growth of the Internet has made it easier to compare prices.*

LANGUAGE BANK

Comparing and contrasting

In your academic writing, you may need to compare two theories, arguments, ideas, etc, pointing out the similarities between them. You may also need to contrast them, pointing out the differences between them.

- X is **as... as** Y.
- X is **(not) the same as** Y.
- X is **similar/equivalent/identical to** X.
- **In a similar way** to X, Y.../**Similarly** (to)...
- X..., **as do/does** Y.
- **compared/in comparison with** X, Y...
- X... **much/far more/less... than** Y.
- X... **potentially/perhaps more/less... than** Y.
- **in contrast to** X, Y...
- **The main difference(s) between** X and Y is/are...
- X..., **whereas/while** Y...
- X, **unlike** Y...
- X **differs from** Y **in that...**
- X... **On the other hand**, Y...

– *Political factors perhaps were **as important as** cultural attitudes in explaining this.*
– *Correlation is **not the same as** causation.*
– *This approach yields an **identical** result **to** that found in Example 12.4.*
– *Frequency curves present data **in a similar way to** histograms.*
– *Men and women face different constraints, **as do** members of different classes and ethnic groups.*
– *This rate is high **in comparison with** current rates of plate movements.*
– *Educated women today are **much more** likely to work for pay **than** before.*
– *Bulb pipettes are simple to use and **potentially more** accurate **than** a graduated pipette.*
– *Teens sent approximately 70 emails a month **in contrast to** 30 for the slightly older set.*
– ***The main difference between** trees and networks is that nodes in a tree can only have one parent, **while** this is not true for networks.*
– *Today, **unlike** in the recent past, more children are driven to school than walk or cycle.*
– *The tropics **differ from** other parts of the world **in that** their seasonality is determined by water availability, not by temperature.*
– *The Royal African Company relied on chartered ships sent out at set intervals. Private traders, **on the other hand**, had no such rigid schedule.*

com·pari·son /kəm'pærɪsn/ *noun* [U, C] the process of examining people or things to see how they are similar; an occasion when people or things are compared: *There was a failure to conduct cross-cultural comparison.* ◇ **~ with sb/sth** *Table 22.3 summarizes these developments and enables comparison with Table 22.2.* ◇ **through ~ with sb/sth** *Information was also collected through comparison with data from related settings.* ◇ **~ between A and B** *Where relevant, comparisons are drawn between Muslim, Jewish and Christian teachings.* ◇ **~ to sb/sth** *Comparisons to smaller but more precise surveys indicate...* ◇ **~ across sth** *The use of different definitions prevents meaningful comparisons across studies.* ◇ **~ of A and B** *Table 12.6 provides a comparison of traditional and digital media.* ◇ **~ of A with/to B** *A comparison of domestic policies with similar arrangements elsewhere will be used as a form of evaluation.* ◇ **~ of sth between A and B** *Registration data allow comparison of cancer survival rates between countries (Berrino et al.,1995).* ◇ **by way of ~** *The EU modified its basic treaties five times in fifteen years. By way of comparison, the US Constitution has been subject to fewer than thirty amendments over 200 years.* ◇ **+ noun** *Price comparison websites are having a dramatic impact on business.* ◇ *For comparison purposes, we included one household consisting of an unmarried male to provide contrast.*

IDM **bear/stand com'parison (with sth)** to be as good (as sth else): *British television stands comparison with that of any other country.* **by/in comparison (with/to sb/sth)** when compared with sb/sth: *Foreign investment in Africa has been minimal by comparison with Asia or Latin America.* ◇ *The noise is small in comparison to the signal.* ◇ *Demand for budget items increased. Organic food, by comparison, was seen as an unnecessary luxury, and demand fell.* ➲ language bank *at* COMPARE

▸ ADJECTIVE + COMPARISON **direct** • **simple** • **systematic** • **constant** • **post hoc** • **detailed** • **interesting** • **valid, meaningful** • **statistical** • **quantitative** • **cross-cultural** • **international, cross-national, cross-country** *Further statistical comparisons between the different population groups are summarized in Table 5.*

▸ VERB + COMPARISON **draw, make** • **perform, conduct** • **permit, allow (for), enable** • **facilitate** • **invite** *The importance of this is that international comparisons can be made.* ◇ *The aim is to develop high-quality data that allows for systematic comparison across projects.*

▸ COMPARISON + NOUN **group** • **purposes** • **website, site** *Students showed improvement, but no more so than the comparison group.*

com·part·ment /kəm'pɑːtmənt; *NAmE* kəm'pɑːrtmənt/ *noun* **1** one of the separate sections in sth such as a piece of equipment: *Containers should have separate compartments for the drugs to be taken at each time of day.* **2** (*technical*) one of the separate parts of an area or system: *Current research focuses on the processes that operate within and between various environmental compartments.* HELP In biology, a **compartment** is a section within a cell or another structure.

com·pass /'kʌmpəs/ *noun* **1** (*also* **mag,netic 'compass**) [C] an instrument for finding direction, with a needle that always points to the north: *Samples are oriented using a magnetic compass.* ◇ **+ noun** *a compass needle/direction/bearing* HELP The **points of the compass** are north, south, east, west, etc. **2** [usually sing.] used to refer to sb's ability to know what is right: *Everyone loses their moral compass when terror is the dominant psychological register.* **3** [C] (*also* **compasses** [pl.]) an instrument for drawing circles and measuring distances, consisting of two long thin parts joined at the top: *The aspect of the slope was measured using a pair of compasses.* **4** [sing.] the range or limits of sth, especially of what can be achieved in a particular situation: **within/beyond the ~ of sth** *Also included are publications which lie beyond the compass of this relatively short study.*

com·pati·bil·ity AWL /kəm,pætəˈbɪləti/ *noun* [U] **1** the fact that things can exist together or be used together, despite differences: **~ of sth** *The aim was to achieve compatibility of systems up and down the supply chain.* ◇ **~ with sth** *The scientists assured the public of their work's compatibility with Christian belief.* ◇ **~ between A and B** *The software enables compatibility between different operating systems.* OPP INCOMPATIBILITY **2 ~ (between A and B)** the fact that people or groups can live or work together without problems: *Cultural compatibility between the partners is an important factor.* OPP INCOMPATIBILITY **3** (*biology*) the fact of having similar blood or GENETIC properties; the fact of being useful because of this: *Tissue compatibility is needed for successful transplant surgery.* ◇ *Genetic compatibility can be the basis for selection.* OPP INCOMPATIBILITY

com·pat·ible AWL /kəmˈpætəbl/ *adj.* **1** (of ideas, policies or methods) able to exist together or be used together, despite differences: **A and B are ~** *Not all of the theories are mutually compatible.* ◇ **A is ~ with B** *Economic growth is compatible with sustainable development.* ◇ *Regional priorities are not always compatible with national ones.* OPP INCOMPATIBLE (1) **2** (of computers, software, etc.) able to be used together: *All software would be compatible across all platforms.* ◇ **~ with sth** *The computers in the network must be compatible with each other.* OPP INCOMPATIBLE (2) **3 ~ with sth** suggesting the existence of sth; not CONTRADICTING sth SYN CONSISTENT (1): *These results would be compatible with an infection from the lungs.* **4** (*medical*) having similar blood or GENETIC properties; useful because of this: *Stem cells would be obtained from a compatible donor.*

com·pel /kəmˈpel/ *verb* (-ll-) **1** to force sb to do sth: **~ sb to do sth** *By early 1955 Khrushchev and his followers were able to compel Malenkov to resign.* ◇ **feel compelled to do sth** *Such people often feel compelled to agree with others in order to avoid conflict.* **2 ~ sth** to make sth happen through the use of force or pressure: *To compel restitution now would be unfair to the creditors of the bankrupts.* **3 ~ sth** (not used in the progressive tenses) to cause a particular reaction: *The theory is, nevertheless, one that compels attention.* ➲ *see also* COMPULSION

com·pel·ling /kəmˈpelɪŋ/ *adj.* **1** that makes you think it is true or valid: *Unless there are compelling reasons to do otherwise, humans do what they have done before.* ◇ *There is little compelling evidence to support this hypothesis.* ➲ thesaurus note *at* CONVINCING **2** making you pay attention through being so interesting and exciting: *Desai creates engaging characters and compelling stories of sibling rivalry.* **3** that cannot be resisted: *Often there is no compelling need to adapt to local consumer tastes.*

com·pel·ling·ly /kəmˈpelɪŋli/ *adv.* in a way that convinces you: *This position is compellingly argued by Jackendoff (1983).*

com·pen·sate AWL /ˈkɒmpenseɪt; *NAmE* ˈkɑːmpenseɪt/ *verb* **1** [T, often passive] to pay sb money because they have been hurt or have suffered loss or damage: **~ sb for sth** *The idea was to partially compensate individuals for the loss of state benefits.* ◇ **~ sb** *A scheme for compensating the victims of crime was established.* ◇ **be compensated for sth** *The claimant should be fully compensated for his loss.* ◇ **be compensated (for sth) by sb** *This may involve the applicant being financially compensated by the state.* **2** [I, T, usually passive] to reduce, balance or remove the negative effect of sth: **~ for sth** *Abundant labour compensated for poor technology.* ◇ *A rise in kinetic energy compensates for a loss of potential energy.* ◇ **be compensated for by sth** *This lack of certainty is compensated for by flexibility and adaptability.* ◇ **be compensated by sth** *The drop in profits at home is only partially compensated by an increase in profits abroad.* HELP If sth **more than compensates for** sth else, it not only reduces the impact, but also reverses it: *The higher price per item will more than compensate for the smaller number of products sold.* **3** [T, often passive] to give sb sth, usually money, in return for doing sth: **~ sb for sth** *The interest rate has to increase to compensate savers for the higher risk involved.* ◇ **be compensated (for sth)** *The inventor expects to be compensated for his innovation accordingly.*

com·pen·sa·tion AWL /ˌkɒmpenˈseɪʃn; *NAmE* ˌkɑːmpenˈseɪʃn/ *noun* [U] **1** money that sb receives because they have been hurt or have suffered loss or damage: **~ for sth** *She must receive full compensation for her loss.* ◇ **~ to sb** *Compensation to individual beneficiaries is generally impracticable.* ◇ **~ from sb** *The company sought compensation from the government.* ◇ **in ~ (for sth)** *The Commission granted him $1.2 million in compensation.* ◇ **+ noun** *The compensation payments are too low to provide a significant deterrent.* **2** something that reduces, balances or removes the negative effect of sth: **~ for sth** *An insect can make some compensation for its small size by beating its wings faster.* ◇ **by way of ~** *The government demanded wage restraint and had little to offer by way of compensation.* **3 ~ (for sth/doing sth)** a reward or benefit that sb receives in return for doing sth: *Investors will demand financial compensation for running the risks.*

com·pen·sa·tory AWL /ˌkɒmpenˈseɪtəri; *NAmE* kəmˈpensətɔːri/ *adj.* [usually before noun] **1** reducing, balancing or removing the negative effect of sth; intended to do this: *An increase in the respiratory rate is a compensatory mechanism.* ◇ *Successive governments provided compensatory measures to assist children from disadvantaged backgrounds.* **2** (of money) paid because sb has been hurt or has suffered loss or damage: *She was entitled to a significant award of compensatory damages.*

com·pete /kəmˈpiːt/ *verb* **1** [I] to try to be more successful than others: *Global economic integration has altered the way firms compete.* ◇ *Customers do not perceive a difference in quality between competing brands.* ◇ **~ with sb/sth** *All animals compete with other members of their species.* ◇ **~ against sb/sth** *Firms may decide to compete against each other, in which case prices are likely to go down.* ◇ **~ in sth** *Being able to compete successfully in the global marketplace is now a critical factor for survival.* ◇ **~ on sth** *Firms have traditionally competed on low price or high quality.* HELP If sb/sth **cannot compete** with/against sb/sth else, they are not as successful: *Local producers could not compete against foreign businesses.* **2** [I] to try to get sth or do sth, rather than letting sb/sth else get it or do it: **~ for sth** *Inboxes and mobile phone displays are full of messages competing for attention.* ◇ **~ with sb/sth for sth** *Predators compete with each other for prey.* ◇ **~ against sb/sth for sth** *Organizations are forced to compete against each other for the right to provide services.* ◇ **~ to do sth** *Individual producers will compete to sell energy to consumers.* ◇ **~ with/against sb/sth to do sth** *Suppliers can then compete against each other to win the business.* **3** [I] **~ (with sb/sth)** to oppose sb/sth: *The various techniques are designed to work together, rather than compete with one another.* ➲ *see also* COMPETING **4** [I] to take part in an election, sports event or other contest: *She was not allowed to compete.* ◇ **~ in sth** *Candidates from different political parties competed in the elections.* ◇ **~ against sb** *The rule is that women do not compete against men.*

com·pe·tence /ˈkɒmpɪtəns; *NAmE* ˈkɑːmpɪtəns/ *noun* **1** (*also less frequent* **com·pe·ten·cy**) [U, C] the ability to do sth well: **~ in sth** *All trainees will be expected to show that they have competence in these areas.* ◇ **~ in doing sth** *Labour's competence in managing the economy was now seen as superior to the Conservatives'.* ◇ **~ to do sth** *Managers need to develop the strategic competence to develop global marketing strategies to ensure successful market entry.* OPP INCOMPETENCE **2** [U] **~ (of sth)** the legal authority of a court or other institution or organization to deal with a particular matter: *The definition of this term is a matter for the competence of the national courts.* ◇ **~ (of sth) to do sth** *Some delegates attempted to restrict the competence of the Committee to examine State policies.* **3** (*also* **com·pe·ten·cy**) [C] **~ (to do sth)** a skill needed in a particular job or for a particular task: *Japanese companies were not lacking in the necessary competences to design either software or microprocessors.*

com·pe·tency /ˈkɒmpɪtənsi; *NAmE* ˈkɑːmpɪtənsi/ *noun* (*pl.* **-ies**) = COMPETENCE (1), COMPETENCE (3)

com·pe·tent /ˈkɒmpɪtənt; *NAmE* ˈkɑːmpɪtənt/ *adj.* **1** accepted as having legal authority to deal with a particular matter: *His right to have his case reviewed by the competent authority was breached.* ◇ **~ to do sth** *The International Court of Justice is not competent to adjudicate on disputes raised by individuals.* **2** having enough ability, skill or knowledge to do sth well or to the necessary standard: *Sick children should have access to trained and competent professionals and high-quality treatment.* ◇ **~ to do sth** *He is receiving instruction, and is not yet considered competent to work alone.* ◇ **~ in sth** *This group are better educated and more competent in English.* ◇ **~ in doing sth** *High-status parents are more competent in positively affecting the academic performance of their offspring.* **OPP** INCOMPETENT **3** of a good standard but not very good: *Skills are what distinguish an excellent doctor from a merely competent one.*

com·pe·tent·ly /ˈkɒmpɪtəntli; *NAmE* ˈkɑːmpɪtəntli/ *adv.* with enough ability, skill or knowledge to do sth well or to the necessary standard: *The minister had selected an official of such inexperience that he could not be expected to perform the work competently.*

com·pet·ing /kəmˈpiːtɪŋ/ *adj.* [only before noun] **1** (of different ideas, explanations, interests, etc.) unable to exist together easily or be true at the same time: *These competing hypotheses need to be investigated.* ◇ *Balancing competing priorities proved difficult.* ◇ *Finding common ground between competing claims is a serious challenge to policy development.* **2** (of different products, services or businesses) each trying to get the attention of possible customers and be more successful than the others: *A final variable is the price of a competing product.*

com·pe·ti·tion /ˌkɒmpəˈtɪʃn; *NAmE* ˌkɑːmpəˈtɪʃn/ *noun* **1** [U] (used especially about the world of business) a situation in which sb/sth tries to be more successful than sb/sth else, or tries to get sth rather than let sb/sth else get it: *As business owners search for profits, competition drives them to change their operations.* ◇ *In the past, the economy was not characterized by the intense global competition that exists today.* ◇ **~ for sth** *The fierce competition for jobs in professional sports prevents them from realizing their aspirations.* ◇ **~ (between A and B) (for sth)** *The first chapter focuses on the competition between French and German universities for American students.* ◇ **~ between/among sb/sth** *There is strong competition among all schools.* ◇ **~ with sb/sth** *Countries have to engage in greater competition with each other in order to attract foreign investment.* ◇ **~ in sth** *The lack of competition in a market may reduce the pressure on firms to innovate and be efficient.* ◇ **in ~ with sb/sth** *Imported products are in competition with the domestic products.* ◇ **~ to do sth** *The competition to attract investments intensified.* ◇ **+ noun** *Such schemes may be incompatible with EU competition law.* **2 the competition** [sing.] a person or business that is trying to be more successful than others; goods or services that are intended to be more successful than others: *The design of the product may be enhanced in some way to distinguish it from the competition.* ◇ **ahead of the ~** *He is looking for ways to stay ahead of the competition.* ◇ **against the ~** *The company positions itself against the competition by producing specialist high-quality goods.* **3** [U, C] (*ecology*) a situation in which animals, plants or other living things try to get resources, with the result that other animals, plants, etc. may not be able to get them: *The organisms have evolved to reduce competition.* ◇ *In most competitions there was no predictable outcome.* **4** [C] a contest to find out who is the best at sth: *In many league competitions, teams are awarded a fixed number of points for a win or a draw.* ◇ *to win/lose a competition* ◇ **~ to do sth** *The council organized a competition to design a new footbridge across the river.*

▸ ADJECTIVE + COMPETITION **fierce, intense, strong, stiff • increasing, greater • direct • effective • free • unfair • global • international, foreign • local • monopolistic • economic • electoral** *The organization is divided in its approach to unfair competition.* | **direct • fierce, intense, strong • interspecific • intraspecific** *The larvae are not in direct competition with each other.*

▸ VERB + COMPETITION **face • engage in • avoid • stimulate, promote, encourage, foster • enhance • intensify • restrict, limit • reduce • harm • prevent • exclude • eliminate • be characterized by** *They are currently facing intense competition from other developing countries.* ◇ *Increased international trade stimulates competition and entrepreneurship.* | **face • avoid • reduce** *African wild dogs try to avoid competition with hyenas.*

▸ COMPETITION + NOUN **law • legislation • rules • policy • authority** *It is widely accepted that competition policy remains necessary.*

com·peti·tive /kəmˈpetətɪv/ *adj.* **1** connected with competition, especially in the world of business: *To stay ahead in this highly competitive market, it is vital to invest in innovation.* ◇ *Advertising can enhance the firm's competitive positioning in the market.* **2** (used especially about the world of business) as good as, or better than, others: *Established companies could sell their products at competitive prices.* ◇ **~ with sth** *The price of wind power is almost competitive with conventional means of generating electricity.* **3** competing to be the best: *If a market is shrinking, firms are likely to be very competitive as they struggle to survive.* ◇ *In every area of interaction with peers, he became extremely competitive and felt compelled to be the best.* **4** (*ecology*) connected with a situation in which animals, plants or other living things compete to get resources: *It is clear that the competitive ability of a species is very important during early growth stages.* ■ **com·peti·tive·ly** *adv.*: *Their products are priced very competitively.* ◇ *He plays sports, teaches karate and swims competitively.*

▸ COMPETITIVE + NOUN **advantage, edge • disadvantage • pressure • environment • market, marketplace • industry • economy • position • positioning • equilibrium • capabilities • strategy • bidding, tendering • election** *They will have a competitive advantage over their rivals.* ◇ *High levels of investment in technology gave the country a competitive edge.* ◇ *Competitive multi-party elections have become an established norm of African politics.*

▸ ADVERB + COMPETITIVE **highly, intensely, very • internationally • perfectly • purely • economically • increasingly** *The company sought to maintain itself in an increasingly competitive market.* ◇ *There exists scope for the government to step in to restore perfectly competitive conditions.*

com·peti·tive·ness /kəmˈpetətɪvnəs/ *noun* [U] **1** (used especially about the world of business) **~ (of sth)** the ability to compete; the fact that people or things compete: *Technological upgrading may enhance competitiveness.* ◇ *A related issue is that of changing patterns of competitiveness.* **2 ~ (of sth)** the ability to compete based on price: *As prices rose within the US economy, the competitiveness of US goods and services in the world economy dropped.* **3 ~ (of sth)** (*ecology*) the fact that animals, plants, etc. compete for resources; their ability to do this: *This will decrease the nutrient status of the soil and reduce the competitiveness of grasses.*

com·peti·tor /kəmˈpetɪtə(r)/ *noun* **1** a person or business that is competing to be more successful than another person or business: *Enterprises with a supportive corporate culture tend to outperform their competitors.* ◇ *They will have an advantage over potential competitors.* **2 ~ for sth** a person, animal or organization that is competing to get sth, with the result that sb/sth else may not be able to get it: *Larger offspring are better competitors for resources and have a higher probability of survival.* ◇ *Its main competitor for funds is Human Rights Watch.*

com·pil·ation AWL /ˌkɒmpɪˈleɪʃn; *NAmE* ˌkɑːmpɪˈleɪʃn/ *noun* **1** [C] **~ (of sth)** a collection of items, especially pieces of writing, taken from different places and put together: *The text is a compilation of several ancient stories.* **2** [U] the process of compiling sth: *Questions have been raised concerning the methods of compilation.* ◇ **~ of sth** *GIS software can be useful for speeding the compilation of transportation data.*

com·pile AWL /kəmˈpaɪl/ *verb* **1** to produce a book, list, report, etc. by bringing together information from different places: **~ sth** *Parish priests in London were required to compile weekly lists of deaths from plague.* ◇ *This important collection of medieval Welsh verse was probably compiled in the early 13th century.* ◇ **~ sth from sth** *Official crime statistics are compiled from police records.* **2 ~ sth (into sth)** (*computing*) to translate instructions from one computer language into another so that a particular computer can understand them: *Before a program can be executed, the instructions must be compiled into the form required by the computer.*

com·plain /kəmˈpleɪn/ *verb* [I, T] to say that you are unhappy or not satisfied about sb/sth: **~ (to sb) (about/of sth)** *After she had complained to the bank manager, the charges were refunded.* ◇ *He complained about the lack of reliable information.* ◇ **~ (that)...** *Reviewers often complain that the website does not give enough information.* ◇ **+ speech** *One patient complained, 'When I see your glasses, I cannot see your face.'*

PHR V **comˈplain of sth** to say that you feel ill or are suffering from a pain: *He went to his local hospital complaining of a shortness of breath.*

com·plain·ant /kəmˈpleɪnənt/ *noun* (*BrE*, *law*) = PLAINTIFF

com·plaint /kəmˈpleɪnt/ *noun* **1** [C] a statement that sb makes saying that they are not satisfied: *The patient subsequently made a formal complaint.* ◇ *to lodge/file a complaint* ◇ **~ about sb/sth** *The first Advertising Standards Authority was set up to handle consumer complaints about advertising.* ◇ **~ against sb/sth** *There were no official complaints against her.* ◇ **~ that...** *Many people are sympathetic to road hauliers' complaints that the price of fuel is too high.* **2** [C] a reason for not being satisfied: **~ about sb/sth** *One of the main complaints about Kant's ethics is that he downplays feeling and focuses exclusively on action.* ◇ **~ against sb/sth** *It is a common complaint against markets that they harbour vast inequalities in wealth.* **3** [U] the act of complaining: *He felt that he had been treated unfairly and wrote a formal letter of complaint to the company.* ◇ *This narrow focus has been a cause for complaint.* ◇ **without ~** *Stoicism is the idea that we should accept whatever happens without complaint.* **4** [C] an illness, especially one that is not serious, and often one that affects a particular part of the body: *Heartburn is a very common complaint.*

com·ple·ment¹ AWL *noun* /ˈkɒmplɪmənt; *NAmE* ˈkɑːmplɪmənt/ **1** something that provides extra qualities, so that it improves or completes sth else: *The two approaches may be complements rather than substitutes.* ◇ **~ to sth** *This new book provides an excellent complement to another recently published book.* **2** [usually sing.] the complete number or quantity that is possible or normal: *It was essential that a full working complement was available to carry out these tasks.* ◇ **~ of sth** *Humans and chimpanzees have the same complement of genes.* ◇ *At the surface, the atoms do not have their full complement of four neighbouring atoms.* **3** (*grammar*) a word or phrase, especially an adjective or a noun phrase, that is used after a linking verb such as *be* or *become*, and describes the subject of the verb. In the following sentences, the **complements** are *happy* and *a teacher*: *She was happy.* ◇ *He became a teacher.* HELP In some descriptions of grammar, a **complement** is any word or phrase which is GOVERNED by a verb, usually coming after the verb in a sentence. **4 ~ (of sth)** (*mathematics*) the members of a set that are not members of a particular SUBSET: *For example, the complement of the set of odd numbers is the set of even numbers.*

com·ple·ment² AWL *verb* /ˈkɒmplɪment; *NAmE* ˈkɑːmplɪment/ to add to sth in a way that improves it or completes it: **~ sth** *This generalized model usefully complements detailed empirical studies.* ◇ **~ each other** *The different experimental approaches complement each other to provide a more complete understanding of the process.*

com·ple·men·tary AWL /ˌkɒmplɪˈmentri; *NAmE* ˌkɑːmplɪˈmentri/ *adj.* **1** having or adding qualities that are suitable together, or that improve or complete sth: *The purpose is to ensure that teams possess the complementary skills required for effective performance.* ◇ **~ to sth** *The brands are seen as complementary to each other, rather than as directly competitive.* **2** (*BrE*) connected with medical treatment that is not part of the usual scientific treatment used in Western countries: *complementary medicine/therapies* ➲ *compare* ALTERNATIVE¹ (2)

com·ple·men·ta·tion /ˌkɒmplɪmenˈteɪʃn; *NAmE* ˌkɑːmplɪmenˈteɪʃn/ *noun* [U] (*grammar*) the types of complements of a verb in a clause: **+ noun** *The book gives a review of the main complementation patterns in English.*

com·plete¹ /kəmˈpliːt/ *adj.* **1** including all of the parts of sth: *The declaration must be complete and accurate.* ◇ *See Westhead et al. (2006) for a complete set of results.* ◇ **not be ~ without sth** *No account of African soccer would be complete without reference to the players themselves.* OPP INCOMPLETE **2** [usually before noun] used when you are emphasizing sth, to mean 'to the greatest degree possible' SYN TOTAL¹: *Their ambition was to secure complete freedom of trade.* ◇ *It is hard to draw any conclusions in the almost complete absence of evidence outside these texts.* **3** [not before noun] finished: *He continued to work on a 'History of Religious Ideas', which was almost complete at his death.* OPP INCOMPLETE **4** [not before noun] **~ with sth** including sth as an important part or feature: *The case received extensive coverage in the press, including court transcripts complete with eyewitness accounts.*

▸ COMPLETE + NOUN **set • list • sequence • data, information • account • picture, description • record • solution, answer • understanding • cycle, revolution** *Complete genome sequences are available for all these organisms.* ◇ *Such data cannot provide a complete picture of symptoms, illness or disease occurring in society.* ◇ *A complete understanding of the mechanism is difficult.* | **absence, lack • loss • removal • elimination • control • ban • freedom • recovery • revolution** *The complete removal of the rat population released the mice from their competitors.* ◇ *The past decade has witnessed an almost complete revolution in the way these data are recorded.*

▸ ADVERB + COMPLETE **almost • nearly, virtually • essentially • largely** *In more developed countries, registration of births and deaths is virtually complete.*

com·plete² /kəmˈpliːt/ *verb* **1 ~ sth** to finish doing sth: *To complete the task, the class is divided into small groups.* ◇ *She had recently completed her doctorate.* ◇ *In March he completed the purchase of a detached house.* **2 ~ sth** to write all the information you are asked for on a form SYN FILL STH IN (1): *60% completed the survey online.* ◇ *Questionnaires were completed by a whole class under the supervision of a researcher.* **3 ~ sth** to make sth whole: *All this information can be used to complete the diagnostic picture.* ◇ *Annual plants complete their life cycle within a year.*

com·plete·ly /kəm'pliːtli/ *adv.* (used to emphasize the following word or phrase) in every way possible SYN TOTALLY: *The model completely ignores exposure to predators.* ◇ *In the real world we are not completely independent.* ➲ language bank *at* EXCEPTIONALLY

▸ COMPLETELY + ADJECTIVE **unknown • unexpected • different • novel, new • independent • free • separate • unrelated • absent • random, arbitrary • irrelevant • useless • wrong • satisfactory • not ~ accurate, not ~ reliable** *This book was almost completely unknown until 1945.* ◇ *Some youths are completely absent from school for an extended period.* ◇ *The predictions of Newtonian theory are not completely accurate.*

▸ COMPLETELY + VERB **eliminate, remove • destroy • change, transform • fill • cover • lack • ignore • block, inhibit • absorb • surround • abolish • disappear • be ~ lost • be ~ understood • be ~ determined (by)** *These policies cannot completely eliminate unemployment.* ◇ *The original plant cover can be partially or completely removed.*

▸ VERB + COMPLETELY **disappear • change • remove • fail** *Lynx and wolf disappeared completely from the Netherlands before the end of the 19th century.*

com·plete·ness /kəm'pliːtnəs/ *noun* [U] the fact that sth has all of its parts: *For the sake of completeness, the main equations are presented here.* ◇ **for ~** *This method, which is now used rarely, is mentioned for completeness.* ◇ **~ of sth** *Our selling point was the completeness of our analysis.*

com·ple·tion /kəm'pliːʃn/ *noun* [U] the act or process of finishing sth; the state of being finished and having all of the necessary parts: *The book was nearing completion.* ◇ **~ of sth** *Some barriers remain to successful completion of the research.* ◇ **after/following ~ (of sth)** *After completion of the Arizona Canal, the first railroad reached Phoenix.* ◇ **upon/on ~ (of sth)** *Upon completion of his doctorate, he taught at the University of Wyoming.* ◇ **+ noun** *Many projects end up over budget and past the planned completion date.*

com·plex¹ AWL /'kɒmpleks; *NAmE* kəm'pleks; 'kɑːmpleks/ *adj.* **1** made of many different things or parts that are connected SYN COMPLICATED: *The immune system is a complex system of organs, tissues, cells and cell products.* ◇ *Wine is a chemically complex mixture.* ◇ *Earthquakes radiate seismic energy in a complex pattern.* **2** difficult to understand or deal with: *The answer to this question is complex.* ◇ *Managing a larger business is a more complex process than running a small business.* ◇ *Models allow us to think about complex problems in simple ways.* ➲ *see also* COMPLEX NUMBER

▸ COMPLEX + NOUN **structure • system • pattern • picture • mixture • phenomenon • organism** *A human hair strand has a complex structure, made of bundles of intertwined fibres.* | **relationship • web, network • interplay, interaction, dynamics** *There is a complex relationship between politics and economics.* | **issue, problem • process • task • situation** *The interaction between long-term economic growth and migration is a complex issue.*

▸ ADVERB + COMPLEX **very, highly • extremely, immensely • increasingly • rather, quite, fairly, somewhat • inherently • technically** *Merging multiple lists can be a highly complex task.* | **structurally • chemically** *A structurally complex reef will provide more habitats than a mobile sand bank.*

com·plex² AWL /'kɒmpleks; *NAmE* 'kɑːmpleks/ *noun* **1 ~ of sth** a large number of things that are connected, often in a way that is confusing or difficult to understand: *Tourism involves a complex of industries.* ◇ *The Great Barrier Reef is a huge complex of many individual reefs, coral masses and some islands.* **2** a group of buildings of a similar type together in one place: *Billions of dollars were committed to build residential complexes in central Tokyo.* ◇ *Large office complexes were built as quickly as smaller buildings could be knocked down.* **3** (*chemistry*) an ION or MOLECULE in which one or more groups are BONDED to a metal atom by shared pairs of ELECTRONS provided by atoms in the group: *Transition metal complexes show many characteristic properties such as the ability to act as good catalysts.*

com·plex·ity AWL /kəm'pleksəti/ *noun* **1** [U] the state of being formed of many parts; the state of being difficult to understand: *Computers vary enormously in their complexity and in the operations they perform.* ◇ **a level/degree of ~** *These fundamental properties are shared among all living organisms, regardless of their level of complexity.* ◇ **~ of sth** *No simple model can capture the complexity of relationships between employers and employees.* **2 complexities** [pl.] **~ of sth** the features of a problem or situation that are difficult to understand: *Western companies need to be well advised when negotiating the cultural complexities of South East Asia.* ◇ *These studies have played a huge part in unravelling the complexities of the immune system.*

▸ ADJECTIVE + COMPLEXITY **great, considerable • enormous, extraordinary • increasing, growing • additional, further • sheer • inherent • computational • technical • structural • mathematical • biological • linguistic** *The UK's immigration law on children is an area of increasing complexity.*

▸ VERB + COMPLEXITY **understand • appreciate, recognize • illustrate, demonstrate • reveal • reflect • explain • highlight • capture • reduce • increase • deal with, cope with** *This case illustrates the complexity of ethical decision-making.*

▸ COMPLEXITY OF + NOUN **system • process • situation • issue • problem • relationship • task • organism** *Because of the complexity of the atmospheric system, it is difficult to quantify the role that humans have played.*

ˌcomplex ˈnumber *noun* (*mathematics*) a number that can be put into the form $x + iy$, where x and y are REAL NUMBERS and i is an imaginary unit equal to the SQUARE ROOT of -1: *Each of these vectors may be represented by a complex number.*

com·pli·ance /kəm'plaɪəns/ *noun* [U] the practice of obeying rules or requests made by people in authority: **~ with sth** *In order to ensure compliance with emission standards, furnace design must be carefully evaluated.* ◇ **in ~ with sth** *The UK is currently not in compliance with clause 5.* OPP NON-COMPLIANCE ➲ *see also* COMPLY

com·pli·ant /kəm'plaɪənt/ *adj.* **1** willing to agree with other people or to obey rules: *A business owner can move his plant to a place where employees will be more compliant.* OPP REBELLIOUS (1) **2** in agreement with a set of rules: *Most of their existing products were not EU compliant.* ◇ **~ with sth** *The study was fully compliant with research guidelines.* ➲ *compare* CONSISTENT (1) ➲ *see also* COMPLY

com·pli·cate /'kɒmplɪkeɪt; *NAmE* 'kɑːmplɪkeɪt/ *verb* **~ sth** to make sth more difficult to do, understand or deal with: *More recent developments may complicate matters.* ◇ *The situation is complicated by the fact that not all websites are commercial.*

com·pli·cated /'kɒmplɪkeɪtɪd; *NAmE* 'kɑːmplɪkeɪtɪd/ *adj.* **1** made of many different things or parts that are connected; difficult to understand SYN COMPLEX¹: *The right of a country to engage in military action is a complicated matter.* ◇ *The embryo has undergone a complicated turning* *process around day 9.* ◇ *This approach makes a relatively simple problem unnecessarily complicated.* OPP UNCOMPLICATED (1) **2** (of a medical condition) involving complications: *With complicated infections, response to antibiotics is less.* OPP UNCOMPLICATED (2)

com·pli·ca·tion /ˌkɒmplɪˈkeɪʃn; *NAmE* ˌkɑːmplɪˈkeɪʃn/ *noun* **1** [C, U] a thing that makes a situation more complicated or difficult SYN DIFFICULTY (1): *The content of the book avoids unnecessary complications.* ◇ *The operation was performed two weeks later without complication.* **2** [C, usually pl.] (*medical*) a new problem or illness that makes treatment of a previous one more complicated or difficult: *It is a comparatively mild infection and serious complications are rare.*

com·ply /kəmˈplaɪ/ *verb* (**com·plies, com·ply·ing, com·plied, com·plied**) [I] to obey a rule, an order, etc: *There are strict penalties for those who fail to comply.* ◇ **~ with sth** *Companies have to comply with the requirements in the contract.* ➲ *see also* COMPLIANCE

com·pon·ent AWL /kəmˈpəʊnənt; *NAmE* kəmˈpoʊnənt/ *noun* **1** one of several parts that combine together to make a system, machine or substance: *In the mid-1990s, Japan held more than 50% of the market for computer components.* ◇ *Enzymes produced by the digestive system completely digest the food into its components.* ◇ **~ of sth** *The most important components of sand are usually primary minerals such as quartz and feldspars.* ◇ **~ in sth** *Pyrite, a compound of iron and sulfur, is found as a minor component in many rocks.* **2** a necessary feature or part of sth: **~ of sth** *Training is an essential component of raising competitiveness.* ◇ **~ in/to sth** *There are two principal components to current economic change.* ■ **com·pon·ent** *adj.* [only before noun] *Sending an electric current through water splits it into its component parts of hydrogen and oxygen.*

▸ ADJECTIVE + COMPONENT **important, major, significant** • **key** • **principal, main** • **essential, critical, crucial** • **necessary** • **core, central, basic, fundamental** • **integral** *Fish are a major component of marine ecosystems.* ◇ *Statistical literacy is considered a key component of being numerate in an information society.* | **individual** • **different** • **small** • **large** • **cellular** • **genetic** • **structural** • **chemical** *All the cellular components of the immune system are derived ultimately from the bone marrow.*

▸ VERB + COMPONENT **have** • **include, incorporate** • **contain** • **identify** • **form, constitute, comprise** • **add** • **remove** • **separate, isolate** *Our analysis includes three main components.*

com·pose /kəmˈpəʊz; *NAmE* kəmˈpoʊz/ *verb* **1 be composed of sth** to be made or formed from several substances, parts or people: *Grape juice is composed mainly of sugars, organic acids and pectin.* ◇ *Insect compound eyes are composed of hundreds of individual photoreceptor organs.* ◇ *These committees are composed of experts from the member states.* **2** (not used in the progressive tenses) **~ sth** to combine together to form a whole SYN MAKE STH UP (1): *In the 1990s, women composed half the labour force.* ◇ *The ancient Greek city states together composed the cultural-linguistic civilization known as Hellas.* **3** to write a piece of music: *Chaplin also composed the music for his films.* ◇ *Haydn composed the 'Emperor's Hymn' as a movement of a string quartet.* **4** to write sth, especially a poem: *Coleridge claimed to have composed the poem while asleep.*

com·poser /kəmˈpəʊzə(r); *NAmE* kəmˈpoʊzər/ *noun* a person who writes music, especially CLASSICAL music: *Other composers have used recordings of the wind and the sea as elements in composition.*

com·pos·ite¹ /ˈkɒmpəzɪt; *NAmE* kəmˈpɑːzət/ *adj.* **1** [only before noun] (of a material) made of different materials: *Composite materials can be tailored to meet the specific demands of each particular application.* ◇ *There are many different kinds of composite structures and many different fabrication techniques.* **2** [only before noun] made of different parts or elements: *The Chimaera is a composite being having the body and head of a lion, the tail of a serpent and a goat's head.*

com·pos·ite² /ˈkɒmpəzɪt; *NAmE* kəmˈpɑːzət/ *noun* **1** a material made of different materials: *Composites are widely used in constructing aeroplanes.* **2 ~ (of sth)** something that consists of different parts or elements SYN COMBINATION (1), MIXTURE (1): *Personality is a composite of a large number of traits.*

com·pos·ition /ˌkɒmpəˈzɪʃn; *NAmE* ˌkɑːmpəˈzɪʃn/ *noun* **1** [U] the different parts that sth is made of; the way in which the different parts are organized: **~ of sth** *The chemical composition of rain is highly variable.* ◇ *The social composition of Kingston was rather different from that of Jamaica as a whole.* ◇ *The composition of the management board became a point of contention.* ◇ **in ~** *Lavas vary in composition.* **2** [C] a piece of music or a poem: *In folk and blues traditions, most compositions are generated from a very few chord progressions.* **3** [U] the act of writing a piece of music or a poem: *Whether Tacitus completed the Annals is not known; nor do we know the date of composition.* **4** [U] (*art*) the arrangement of people or objects in a painting, photograph or scene of a film: *Griffith's style favoured elements such as composition and lighting.*

com·pound¹ AWL /ˈkɒmpaʊnd; *NAmE* ˈkɑːmpaʊnd/ *noun* **1 ~ (of A and B)** a substance formed by a chemical reaction of two or more elements in fixed amounts relative to each other: *Salt is a compound of sodium and chlorine.* ◇ *A protein is a complex organic compound, typically of high molecular mass.* ◇ *Carbon dioxide and other chemical compounds lock in heat close to the surface of the earth.* ➲ *compare* ELEMENT (2), MIXTURE (3) **2 ~ (of A and B)** a thing consisting of two or more separate things combined together: *His book is a compound of history and morality.* **3** (*grammar*) a noun, an adjective or a verb made of two or more words or parts of words, written as one or more words, or joined by a hyphen. *Climate change, far-reaching* and *breakthrough* are all compounds.

com·pound² AWL /ˈkɒmpaʊnd; *NAmE* ˈkɑːmpaʊnd/ *adj.* [only before noun] formed of two or more parts: *The writer of book 4 is notable for his many new compound nouns and adjectives.* ◇ *Elementary propositions can be combined together to form compound propositions.*

com·pound³ AWL /kəmˈpaʊnd/ *verb* **1** [often passive] **~ sth** to make a problem or difficult situation become even worse by causing further damage or problems: *The increasing number of elderly people is compounding this health care problem.* ◇ *The onset of another economic recession in 1866–8 was compounded by bad harvests in the same years.* **2 be compounded of sth** (*formal*) to be formed from two or more things: *The test is compounded of two elements: the size of the risk and the severity of impact.* ◇ *Each of us is compounded of mixed and frequently contradictory elements and desires.* **3** [usually passive] to mix two or more things together: **(be) compounded with sth** *Kelly has the energy of Buster Keaton, compounded with the glee of Douglas Fairbanks.* **4** [often passive] **~ sth** (*finance*) to pay or charge interest on an amount of money that includes any interest already earned or charged: *Simple interest is compounded annually, while compound interest is compounded continuously.*

com·pre·hend /ˌkɒmprɪˈhend; *NAmE* ˌkɑːmprɪˈhend/ *verb* (often used in negative sentences) to understand sth fully: **~ sth** *Globalization is a complex phenomenon that is difficult to comprehend.* ◇ *Many people do not fully comprehend the implications of a life-threatening illness at the time of diagnosis.* ◇ **~ how/why, etc...** *Examination of*

C

these questions is essential in order to comprehend how the Cold War evolved. ◇ **~ that...** *All of these students comprehended that education is critical to success.*

com·pre·hen·sible /ˌkɒmprɪˈhensəbl; *NAmE* ˌkɑːmprɪˈhensəbl/ *adj.* that can be understood by sb: *Grammar is required to construct comprehensible sentences.* ◇ **~ to sb** *Reform would make the law more comprehensible to juries, especially in serious fraud trials.* OPP INCOMPREHENSIBLE ■ **com·pre·hen·sib·il·ity** /ˌkɒmprɪˌhensəˈbɪləti; *NAmE* ˌkɑːmprɪˌhensəˈbɪləti/ *noun* [U] **~ (of sth)** *A lack of cohesion undermines the comprehensibility of the text.*

com·pre·hen·sion /ˌkɒmprɪˈhenʃn; *NAmE* ˌkɑːmprɪˈhenʃn/ *noun* [U] the ability to understand: *Affected individuals have trouble with language comprehension.* ◇ *This story has been used in New Zealand to test reading comprehension.* ◇ **~ of sth** *Young children's comprehension of an array of cinematic techniques was explored in a recent study.*

com·pre·hen·sive AWL /ˌkɒmprɪˈhensɪv; *NAmE* ˌkɑːmprɪˈhensɪv/ *adj.* **1** including all, or almost all, the items or information that may be concerned SYN COMPLETE[1] (1), FULL (1): *Fischer (1997) provides a comprehensive review of the many types of neural networks.* ◇ *The bibliography gives a comprehensive list of critical studies in the field.* ◇ *It is beyond the scope of this essay to offer a comprehensive account of these events.* **2** (*BrE*) (of education) designed for students of all abilities in the same school: *The local authority refused to accept the government's policy on comprehensive education.* ◇ *She was educated at a comprehensive school and then at Oxford.* ■ **com·pre·hen·sive·ness** /ˌkɒmprɪˈhensɪvnəs; *NAmE* ˌkɑːmprɪˈhensɪvnəs/ *noun* [U] **~ (of sth)** *The scale and comprehensiveness of the welfare state varies between countries.*

▸ COMPREHENSIVE + NOUN **review, overview, survey** ◆ **account, description** ◆ **study** ◆ **assessment, analysis** ◆ **approach** ◆ **guide** ◆ **coverage** ◆ **programme** ◆ **framework** ◆ **list** ◆ **understanding** ◆ **picture** *McCormick (2001) delivers a comprehensive overview of environmental policy.*

com·pre·hen·sive·ly AWL /ˌkɒmprɪˈhensɪvli; *NAmE* ˌkɑːmprɪˈhensɪvli/ *adv.* completely; thoroughly: *These organisms have not been comprehensively studied.* ◇ *The Internet is an ideal tool through which to gather these data quickly and comprehensively.*

com·press *verb* /kəmˈpres/ **1** [T, I] to press sth together or into a smaller space; to be pressed in this way: **~ (sth)** *The air and the fuel are compressed within the mixing cylinder by the piston.* ◇ *Unmodified starch has poor flow properties and does not compress very well.* ◇ **~ sth into sth** *At depths of tens of thousands of kilometres, pressure is sufficient to compress hydrogen into a metallic state.* **2** [T] **~ sth (into sth)** to reduce sth and fit it into a smaller space or amount of time SYN CONDENSE (3): *An overview of the economic consequences of the Hanoverian victory is compressed into a brief chapter.* ◇ *Globalization compresses the time and space aspects of social relations.* **3** [T] **~ sth** (*computing*) to make computer files, etc. smaller so that they use less space on a disk, etc: *There are techniques for compressing the amount of storage required by a picture.*

com·pres·sion /kəmˈpreʃn/ *noun* [U] **1** the process of pressing sth together or into a smaller space: **under ~** *Rocks are relatively strong when placed under compression.* ◇ **~ of sth** *Neurological complications may occur due to compression of cranial nerves in the skull.* **2** (*computing*) a method of making computer files, etc. smaller so that they use less space on a disk, etc: **+ noun** *MP3 is an audio compression format for storing and transferring audio files on a computer with a relatively small file size.*

com·prise AWL /kəmˈpraɪz/ *verb* (not used in the progressive tenses) **1** (*also* **be comprised of**) to have sb/sth as parts or members SYN COMPOSE (1), CONSIST OF SB/STH: **~ sth** *Each individual language may comprise several dialects.* ◇ *The solar radiation approaching the earth comprises a wide band of wavelengths.* ◇ *Book 1 comprises Satires 1–5.* ◇ **be comprised of sth** *The committee should be comprised of at least three non-executive directors.* ◇ *These sediments are comprised of calcium carbonate.* **2 ~ sth** to be the parts or members that form sth SYN MAKE STH UP (1): *The three plays comprise one grand and complex drama.* ◇ *Oceanic crust comprises 59% of the total crust by area.* ➲ language bank *at* PROPORTION

com·prom·ise[1] /ˈkɒmprəmaɪz; *NAmE* ˈkɑːmprəmaɪz/ *noun* **1** [C] **~ (between A and B)** a solution to a problem in which two or more things cannot exist together as they are, in which each thing is reduced or changed slightly so that they can exist together: *The design may have been the result of a conscious compromise between cost and safety.* ◇ *The process represents a compromise between using wastes exclusively for fuel or exclusively as a soil additive.* ◇ **+ noun** *In practice, most commercial devices employ the compromise solution illustrated in Figure 7.3.* **2** [C] an agreement that is reached between two people or groups in which each side gets part, but not all, of what they wanted: *In the end a compromise was reached.* ◇ *This provisional constitution was a compromise, the result of negotiation between Yuan and the revolutionaries.* ◇ *The government needed to make compromises, which included giving some land back to the landowners.* ◇ **+ noun** *These discussions finally resulted in a compromise agreement.* **3** [U] the act of reaching a compromise: *All these decisions involve an element of compromise.* ◇ *Compromise is a means of allowing all parties in a situation to save face.*

com·prom·ise[2] /ˈkɒmprəmaɪz; *NAmE* ˈkɑːmprəmaɪz/ *verb* **1** [T] **~ sth** to risk harming sth: *Researchers' objectivity might be compromised if they become too involved with the people they study.* ◇ *As soon as the immune system is compromised in some way, the risk of infection increases.* ◇ *There is a limit to the period of continuous use before operator fatigue begins to compromise performance.* **2** [T, I] to do sth that is against your principles or does not reach standards that you have set: **~ sth** *Religious groups such as these have sought to invest their funds without compromising their principles.* ◇ **~ on sth** *The electric car must not compromise on performance, looks or handling.* **3** [I] to accept less than you want or are aiming for, especially in order to reach an agreement: *Presidents must be prepared to compromise as well as persuade.* ◇ **~ with sb** *The government had to negotiate and compromise with a broad coalition of interests.* ◇ **~ on sth** *Reagan would not compromise on SDI, and nor would Gorbachev.*

com·pul·sion /kəmˈpʌlʃn/ *noun* **1** [U, C] strong pressure that makes sb do sth that they do not want to do: **~ to do sth** *There is no compulsion to attend the meetings.* ◇ **under ~ (of sth)** *Disclosure is required under compulsion of law.* ➲ *compare* OBLIGATION (1) **2** [C] **~ to do sth** a strong desire to do sth, especially sth that is dangerous or wrong SYN URGE[2]: *Addicts feel an overwhelming compulsion to continue destructive behaviours.* ➲ *see also* COMPEL

com·pul·sive /kəmˈpʌlsɪv/ *adj.* **1** (of behaviour) that is difficult to stop or control: *She says her compulsive eating has nothing to do with hunger.* ◇ *Such addictive behaviours include drug abuse and compulsive gambling.* **2** (of people) not being able to control their behaviour: *The successful entrepreneur is not a compulsive competitor, but a person who chooses whom to compete against.* ◇ *An individual with indications of an obsessive-compulsive personality style could be a compulsive handwasher.*

com·pul·sory /kəmˈpʌlsəri/ *adj.* that must be done because of a law or rule SYN MANDATORY: *The 'public good' argument is relatively easy to make for compulsory education.* ◇ **~ for sb** *Wearing a crash helmet is* *compulsory for all motorbike riders.* ◇ **it is ~ (for sb) to do sth** *In Sparta, it was compulsory to keep in good physical condition.* OPP VOLUNTARY ■ **com·pul·sor·ily** /kəm'pʌlsərəli/ *adv.*: *The judge ordered that she be compulsorily detained for a period of seven days.*

com·pu·ta·tion AWL /ˌkɒmpju'teɪʃn; *NAmE* ˌkɑːmpju'teɪʃn/ *noun* **1** [C, U] **~ (of sth)** an act or the process of calculating sth: *This research led to the first testable numerical computations of the earth's magnetic field.* ◇ *The program is capable of performing computations with reasonable accuracy within a reasonable amount of time.* ◇ *Different methods of computation have been employed to prepare the presentations.* **2** [U] the use of computers, especially as a subject of study: *Logic has found radically new roles in computation and information processing.*

com·pu·ta·tion·al AWL /ˌkɒmpju'teɪʃənl; *NAmE* ˌkɑːmpju'teɪʃənl/ *adj.* [usually before noun] using or connected with computers: *A computational approach works well for DNA.* ◇ *computational methods/models* ◇ *At present the scope of these simulations is limited by computational speed.* ■ **com·pu·ta·tion·al·ly** *adv.*: *Computationally, this is a very complex task.*

com·pute AWL /kəm'pjuːt/ *verb* **~ sth (for sb/sth)** to calculate sth, especially using a computer program: *A score was computed for each participant.* ◇ *The probabilities can easily be computed for small values of n.* ■ **com·put·able** AWL /kəm'pjuːtəbl/ *adj.*: *This analysis was applied to games of chance with known or computable probabilities.*

> **WORD FAMILY**
> compute *verb*
> computer *noun*
> computing *noun*
> computable *adj.*
> computational *adj.*
> computationally *adv.*
> computerize *verb*

com·puter AWL /kəm'pjuːtə(r)/ *noun* an electronic machine that can store, organize and find data, do calculations and control other machines: *Computers have allowed rapid and elaborate analysis of biological systems.* ◇ **by ~** *Images of the grids are digitized and manipulated by computer.* ◇ **+ noun** *Spam filters are computer programs that scan incoming email messages and decide which are likely to be spam.* ➲ *see also* PERSONAL COMPUTER

com·pu·ter·ize (*BrE also* **-ise**) /kəm'pjuːtəraɪz/ *verb* **1 ~ sth** to use computers to control a system, process or machine: *The water treatment plants are now computerized.* ◇ *Today, car assembly lines employ computerized design and manufacturing systems.* **2 ~ sth** to store data on a computer: *The Swedes eventually computerized these records into one large national registry.* ◇ *The secure storage of data in computerized databases is intrinsically difficult.* ■ **com·pu·ter·iza·tion, -isa·tion** /kəmˌpjuːtəraɪ'zeɪʃn; *NAmE* kəmˌpjuːtərə'zeɪʃn/ *noun* [U] **~ (of sth)** *The computerization of many traditional craft skills provided opportunities for deskilling or reskilling jobs.*

comˌputer 'science *noun* [U] the study of computers and how they can be used: *She received a PhD in Computer Science at Virginia Tech in 2005.* ■ **comˌputer 'scientist** *noun*: *Computer scientists have long talked about intelligent systems.*

com·put·ing AWL /kəm'pjuːtɪŋ/ *noun* [U] the use of computers: *These figures demonstrate how rapidly the face of computing changed in the 1990s.* ◇ **+ noun** *PCs brought computing power to people in offices and in their own homes.* ◇ *Advances in computing capacity have enabled large quantities of data to be handled more easily.*

con·ceal /kən'siːl/ *verb* to hide sth: **~ sth** *She had concealed the fact that she was engaged to another man.* ◇ **~ sth from sb** *The company was accused of concealing information from customers.* ■ **con·ceal·ment** *noun* [U] *Their footsteps betrayed their place of concealment.*

con·cede /kən'siːd/ *verb* **1** [T] to admit that sth is true or logical: *As the authors readily concede, it is a work in progress.* ◇ **~ that...** *Patten (2001) concedes that Europe lacks a single foreign policy.* ◇ **~ sth** *Ryan reluctantly concedes the point.* **2** [T] to give sth away, especially unwillingly; to allow sb to have sth: **~ sth to sb** *Britain was forced to concede independence to its thirteen rebel American colonies.* ◇ **~ sb sth** *Women were only conceded full voting rights in the 1950s.* ➲ *see also* CONCESSION (1) **3** [T, I] **~ (defeat)** to admit that you have lost a battle, an election, etc: *By 142 BCE, the Syrian rulers were forced to concede defeat.* ◇ *After losing this decisive battle, the general was forced to concede.*

> **LANGUAGE BANK**
>
> **Conceding a point and making a counterargument**
>
> In academic writing, it it is often good practice to acknowledge a possible criticism, exception or difficulty, before going on to show why your point is still valid.
>
> ▸ **While/Although it is true/possible that...**
> ▸ **While/Although it can be argued that...**
> ▸ **Certainly/Of course/Admittedly,... but...**
> ▸ **Nevertheless,...**
> ▸ **Still,...**
>
> – ***While it is true that*** *many brands have dominated their markets for years, it is also true that new products are being developed each year.*
> – ***Although is is possible that*** *the GL hypothesis is correct, the data do not enable us to infer this at the present time.*
> – ***Although it can be argued that*** *behavioural observations are unnecessary, translating such a principle into practice is difficult.*
> – ***Of course****, calculations of this type are interesting* ***but*** *not conclusive proof of the conformational preferences of a polymer.*
> – ***Admittedly****, no two economies are the same,* ***but*** *modern economists work on the commonality in the human experience.*
> – *The extent of this activity has been the topic of debate;* ***nevertheless****, there is no argument that the Grand Canyon region is seismically active.*
> – *Other groups have disputed these estimates as being too low.* ***Still****, it is useful to compare the effects.*

con·ceiv·able AWL /kən'siːvəbl/ *adj.* that you can imagine or believe SYN POSSIBLE (2): *Even very detailed laws cannot specify how they are to be applied in every conceivable case.* ◇ **it is ~ that...** *It is conceivable that human beings will some day contain artificially synthesized chromosomes in their cells.* OPP INCONCEIVABLE ■ **con·ceiv·ably** AWL /kən'siːvəbli/ *adv.*: *A land impact of this order could conceivably exterminate humanity.* ◇ *Conceivably, we might claim that memory puts us in direct touch with the past.*

con·ceive AWL /kən'siːv/ *verb* **1** [T] to form an idea or plan in your mind: **~ sth** *By 1796 Smith had conceived the idea of identifying the rock units by the fossils they contain.* ◇ *The Deep Sea Drilling Project was conceived by scientists from American oceanographic research centres.* ◇ **~ sth as sth** *Many Greek texts were originally conceived as scripts for performance, rather than as literature for reading.* ◇ **~ that...** *Helmholtz conceived that discontinuous motion played an important role in atmospheric phenomena.* **2** [T, I] to think of sth in a particular way; to imagine sth: **~ sth as sth** *Working memory can be conceived as a workspace with a limited capacity.* ◇ **~ of sth** *It is very difficult to conceive of modern life without digital systems.* ◇ **~ of sth as sth** *The boreal region is often*

> **WORD FAMILY**
> conceive *verb*
> conceivable *adj.*
> conceivably *adv.*
> concept *noun*
> conception *noun*
> conceptual *adj.*
> conceptualize *verb*
> inconceivable *adj.*
> misconception *noun*

C

conceived of as a zone of relatively homogeneous climate. ◇ **broadly/narrowly conceived** *Modernism has hitherto been too narrowly conceived: as an aesthetic but not a social phenomenon.* **3** [I, T] (of a woman) to become pregnant: *This procedure has been of great help to couples who have difficulty in conceiving.* ◇ **~ sth** *Two children were conceived by donor insemination.* ➲ *see also* CONCEPTION

C

con·cen·trate¹ AWL /ˈkɒnsntreɪt; *NAmE* ˈkɑːnsntreɪt/ *verb* **1** [T, often passive] **~ sth + adv./prep.** to bring sth together in one place: *The company concentrated its marketing efforts on one narrowly defined segment.* ◇ *All the signal power is concentrated at the highest frequency.* ◇ *The view is that power is concentrated in the hands of a narrow range of organizations.* **2** [I, T] to give all your attention to sth and not think about anything else: **~ (on sth)** *The patient was unable to relax or concentrate on anything.* ◇ **~ sth** *Having to provide justification tends to concentrate the mind of the decision-maker.* ◇ **~ sth on sth** *Kennedy found it easier to concentrate his attention on streamlining the economy.* **3** [T] **~ sth** to increase the strength of a substance by reducing its volume, for example by boiling it: *A protein sample was concentrated using an ultrafiltration centrifugal device.*

PHR V **ˈconcentrate on sth** to spend more time doing one particular thing than others: *Mansfield worked determinedly on a small scale, concentrating on short stories rather than novels.* ◇ *The older manufacturers changed their product mix to concentrate on more basic, cheaper models.* ◇ *Health promotion targets have been set, but concentrate on 'high risk' groups, ignoring other groups such as the elderly.*

▸ CONCENTRATE + NOUN **effort** • **resources** • **production** • **power** *Hospitals should concentrate their resources in those areas most likely to enhance the overall experience of their patients.*

▸ ADVERB + CONCENTRATE **heavily**, **highly** • **mostly** • **increasingly** • **more** • **disproportionately** • **geographically**, **spatially** *Women have been heavily concentrated in low-paid and low-status employment in the UK.*

▸ CONCENTRATE + ADVERB + ON **solely**, **only**, **entirely** • **mainly**, **primarily** • **instead** *Delivering the best possible quality of life means more than concentrating solely on economic growth.*

con·cen·trate² AWL /ˈkɒnsntreɪt; *NAmE* ˈkɑːnsntreɪt/ *noun* [C, U] **~ (of sth)** a substance that is made stronger because water or other substances have been removed: *These supplements consist of a concentrate of vitamins and other potential growth factors.* ◇ *Red cell concentrate is the usual form in which blood is issued.*

con·cen·trated AWL /ˈkɒnsntreɪtɪd; *NAmE* ˈkɑːnsntreɪtɪd/ *adj.* **1** if sth exists or happens in a **concentrated** way, there is a lot of it in one place or at one time: *The population coalesced into larger, more concentrated settlements, or in other words, cities.* ◇ *The people's voice carried little weight against the concentrated power of the rich.* ◇ *A concentrated force was applied.* **2** (of a substance) made stronger because water or other substances have been removed: *A strip of copper metal is added to a concentrated solution of sulfuric acid.* **3** showing determination to do sth: *A new understanding had emerged from over a decade of concentrated scientific effort.*

con·cen·tra·tion AWL /ˌkɒnsnˈtreɪʃn; *NAmE* ˌkɑːnsnˈtreɪʃn/ *noun* **1** [C, U] the amount of a substance in a liquid or in another substance: **~ (of sth)** *This procedure enables lower concentrations of the drug to be used.* ◇ **~ of A in B** *The graph shows the concentration of chemical elements in soils and stream sediments.* **2** [C] **~ (of sth)** a lot of sth in one place: *The concentration of economic power is also evident in the US, where 1 200 corporations produce about half the nation's output.* ◇ *It was mistakenly believed that globalization would lead to a concentration of knowledge work in the developed economies.* **3** [U] the process of people directing effort and attention on a particular thing: **~ on sth** *This public misperception could be because of media concentration on violent events (Fountain, 1995).* ◇ **~ of sth on sth** *The concentration of attention on synthetic chemicals is partly due to the need to fulfil regulatory requirements.* **4** [U] the ability to direct all your effort and attention on one thing, without thinking of other things: *The patient reported a loss of self-confidence and poor concentration.*

concenˈtration camp *noun* a type of prison, often consisting of a number of buildings inside a fence, where political prisoners, etc. are kept in extremely bad conditions: *Dachau was the first Nazi concentration camp, established in 1933.*

con·cept AWL /ˈkɒnsept; *NAmE* ˈkɑːnsept/ *noun* an idea; a basic principle: *Health is a complex concept, which is perhaps easier to define by its absence than its presence.* ◇ **~ in sth** *Structure and agency are key concepts in social theory.* ◇ **~ of sth** *The second problem with the concept of sustainability is that there may appear to be no sustainable actions.* ◇ **~ behind sth** *The first chapters deal with the concepts behind modern cancer treatment.* ◇ **~ that...** *The principle of proportionality embodies the concept that the punishment should fit the crime.* ➲ thesaurus note *at* IDEA

▸ ADJECTIVE + CONCEPT **key**, **core**, **central**, **fundamental** • **basic** • **underlying** • **very** • **abstract** • **theoretical** • **complex** • **broad** • **general** • **related** • **underlying** • **traditional** • **new** • **modern** • **important** • **useful** • **scientific** • **mathematical** • **legal** • **philosophical** *The very concept of murder seems to include the idea of wrongness.* ◇ *I use the term 'ethnicity', which is a broader concept than 'race', to analyse this diversity.*

▸ VERB + CONCEPT **introduce** • **define** • **explain** • **clarify** • **explore**, **examine** • **discuss** • **illustrate** • **understand**, **grasp** • **use**, **employ**, **apply** • **embrace** • **develop** • **extend** *Gomart and Hennion (1999) introduce the concept of 'subject networks'.* ◇ *Few scholars using the concept of culture have rigorously defined it.*

con·cep·tion AWL /kənˈsepʃn/ *noun* **1** [C, U] an understanding or a belief of what sth is or what sth should be: **~ of sth** *Traditional conceptions of an organization's hierarchy imply a single chief executive, the CEO.* ◇ **no ~ of sth** *Rogers had no conception of how far Kissinger and Nixon would go to accomplish that goal.* ◇ **~ that...** *Here we find expression of the conception that there exist three types of knowledge about the world.* ➲ *see also* CONCEIVE (2) **2** [U] the process of forming an idea or a plan: *Although grand in scale, the experiment was poor in its conception.* ◇ **~ of sth** *It was a skilled job involving the conception and carrying out of complex tasks.* ➲ *see also* CONCEIVE (1) **3** [U, C] the process of an egg being FERTILIZED inside a woman's body so that she becomes pregnant: *These changes take place at the moment of conception.* ➲ *see also* CONCEIVE (3)

con·cep·tual AWL /kənˈseptʃuəl/ *adj.* connected with or based on ideas: *The conceptual framework for the current research is based on contemporary social theories.* ◇ *a conceptual model/scheme* ◇ *The lack of conceptual clarity complicates attempts at systematic comparisons of case studies.* ■ **con·cep·tu·al·ly** AWL /kənˈseptʃuəli/ *adv.*: *The potential model is conceptually similar to the gravity model.* ◇ *This is a very important area of disagreement, both conceptually and empirically.*

con·cep·tu·al·ize (*BrE also* -ise) AWL /kənˈseptʃuəlaɪz/ *verb* to form an idea of sth in your mind: **~ sth** *Researchers have conceptualized culture in numerous different ways.* ◇ **~ sth as sth** *Stress has been conceptualized as a mismatch between the individual and their particular environment (Cumings and Cooper, 1979).*

con·cern¹ /kənˈsɜːn; *NAmE* kənˈsɜːrn/ *verb* **1** [often passive] to affect sb/sth; to involve sb/sth: **~ sb/sth** *The study* *concerned adult workers only.* ◇ *The data did not show whether the person concerned was a worker or self-employed.* ◇ *Such negative outcomes reduce the gains for all concerned.* ◇ **be concerned in sth** *The evidence showed he was concerned in a variety of fraudulent dealings.* ➲ *see also* CONCERNING **2** to be about sth: **be concerned with sth** *This analysis is mainly concerned with changes in the routine operation of the economic system.* ◇ **~ sth** *The article concerns his search for exactly the right form of artistic expression.* **3** to take an interest in sth; to cause sb to take an interest in sth: **be concerned with sth** *These Chinese factory managers were less concerned with efficiency than with welfare considerations.* ◇ **~ yourself with/about sth** *Few researchers had previously concerned themselves with managerial misbehaviour.* ◇ **~ sb** *Ordinary voters may not be interested in many of the issues which deeply concern political activists.* **4** [usually passive] to make sb anxious: **be concerned about sth** *Many industry observers are deeply concerned about these developments.* ◇ **be concerned that...** *The company is concerned that the cold may cause problems.* **5 be concerned to do sth** to think it is important to do sth: *What Parsons is concerned to establish here is that the coercive aspects of power do not define its essential features.* IDM *see* FAR[1]

▸ CONCERN + NOUN **extent • nature • status • relationship • issue, matter • question • case • meaning • interpretation • application** *The debate concerns the extent to which these changes are caused by human activity.*

▸ NOUN + CONCERN **debate, argument • question, issue • case** *The key question concerns whether or not the gap between rich and poor parts of the world is widening.*

▸ NOUN + CONCERNED WITH **issue, matter, question • case** *Issues concerned with class struggle have received far less positive commentaries.*

▸ ADVERB + CONCERN/CONCERNED WITH **primarily, mainly, largely, principally, chiefly, especially, particularly • increasingly • directly • centrally • essentially, fundamentally • specifically • explicitly • only, solely, exclusively • more, most • less** *While these battles primarily concerned editorial freedoms, they also involved advertising freedoms.* ◇ *Marx and Durkheim were both centrally concerned with the emergence of modern capitalism.*

▸ CONCERNED + ADVERB + WITH **primarily, mainly • only, solely • here** *He felt that society was concerned only with the pursuit of profit.*

con·cern[2] /kənˈsɜːn; *NAmE* kənˈsɜːrn/ *noun* **1** [C, U] a feeling of being anxious, especially a feeling that is shared by many people: *Media reports about food safety concerns are relatively common.* ◇ *Salespeople are given ample opportunity to voice their concerns.* ◇ **~ about sth/sb** *The patient had concerns about her mother's health.* ◇ **~ for sth/sb** *Engineers once again showed more concern for safety than did managers.* ◇ **~ over sth/sb** *The Labour government shared its predecessor's concern over quality of service.* ◇ **~ that...** *If there is a major concern that a nurse may be a danger to the public, the committee can suspend the individual at once.* **2** [C] something that is important to a person, an organization, etc: *Three main concerns are central to existentialism.* ◇ **~ with sth** *All three writers share a postmodern concern with multiculturalism.* ◇ **~ for sth** *To overcome the human tendency to act out of a concern for profit, Confucius proposed 'doing for nothing'.* ◇ **~ to do sth** *The Japanese approach has been characterized by their concern to achieve the highest possible quality in manufacture.* **3** [sing., U] **~ (for sth/sb)** a desire to protect and help sb/sth: *Team leaders need to demonstrate a deep concern for the interests of team members.* ◇ *The deciding factor is whether or not the act is motivated by concern for others.* **4** [C, usually sing.] **~ (of sth/sb)** something that is your responsibility or that you have a right to know about: *Most schools were the direct concern of the Ministry of Education.*

▸ ADJECTIVE + CONCERN **primary, main, principal, central, key • overriding • fundamental • particular, specific • immediate • real • practical** *Malthus's central concern was imbalance between population and food.* ◇ *Of particular concern are tactical nuclear weapons, since they are not covered by formal arms control accords.* | **serious, major, great, considerable, deep • widespread • pressing • growing, increasing • public • genuine • legitimate • ethical, moral • humanitarian • environmental** *There is a tension here between commercial objectives and ethical concerns over food safety.* | **broad • traditional • theoretical** *The traditional concerns of socialist geography no longer dominate the agenda.*

▸ NOUN + CONCERN **safety • security • health** *There continue to be major health concerns associated with the spreading of animal manure.*

▸ VERB + CONCERN **have • share • discuss • cause • reflect • show • reveal** *The growth of CO_2 has been causing increasing concern since the 1950s.* ◇ *Romantic poetry reveals a creative concern with form.* | **express, raise, voice • articulate • report • highlight • echo • address • alleviate** *Within small communities, patients may express concerns about confidentiality (Robinson, 1998).*

▸ PHRASES **a matter of concern (to sb) • cause for concern** *Millions of white Americans believed that racial discrimination had disappeared as a matter of public concern.* ◇ *The researchers did not regard the error as a cause for concern.*

con·cerned /kənˈsɜːnd; *NAmE* kənˈsɜːrnd/ *adj.* **1** worried and feeling concern about sth: **~ about/for sth** *Tom was getting increasingly concerned about the situation.* ◇ **~ (that)...** *Her GP was concerned she might have appendicitis.* **2** interested in sth: **~ about/with sth** *Ashby was particularly concerned with anti-aircraft systems.* ◇ **~ to do sth** *City planners became increasingly concerned to improve public health through more effective sewage systems.* IDM *see* FAR[1]

con·cern·ing /kənˈsɜːnɪŋ; *NAmE* kənˈsɜːrnɪŋ/ *prep.* about sth; involving sb/sth: *They differ in their conclusions concerning the nature of power in Britain.* ◇ *A regulation concerning procedural issues was passed.*

con·cert /ˈkɒnsət; *NAmE* ˈkɑːnsərt/ *noun* a public performance of music: *There is often a black market for tickets for rock concerts.*

IDM **in concert (with sb/sth)** doing sth together with sb/sth: *He worked in concert with a journalist from the 'Brooklyn Daily Eagle'.* ◇ *For much of the earth's surface, however, physical and chemical weathering act in concert.*

con·cert·ed /kənˈsɜːtɪd; *NAmE* kənˈsɜːrtɪd/ *adj.* [only before noun] done by a group of people, organizations or countries working together: *All the countries involved need to make a concerted effort to use their shared water resources more effectively.*

con·ces·sion /kənˈseʃn/ *noun* **1** [C] something that you allow or do, or allow sb to have, in order to end an argument or to make a situation less difficult: *They refused to make any political concessions.* ◇ **~ to sb** *The government had to accept hostile amendments and make concessions to party rebels.* ◇ **~ from sb** *In the 1980s, indigenous groups became more vocal and won some concessions from the government.* ➲ *see also* CONCEDE (2) **2** [U] **~ of sth** the act of giving sth or allowing sth; the act of CONCEDING: *Following this principle entails concession of relatively greater control to employees.* **3** [C, usually pl.] (*BrE*) a reduction in an amount of money that has to be paid: *Cutting established subsidies and tax concessions is always a political challenge.* ◇ *They made tariff concessions on British exports.* **4** [C] a right to do sth or an advantage that is given to a group of people, an organization, etc, especially by a government: *Oil concessions were the most important international contracts at the time.* ◇ **~ to do sth** *The government granted concessions to foreign investors to build and operate railroad lines.*

C

con·cise /kən'saɪs/ *adj.* giving only the information that is necessary and important, using few words: *This project will begin with a concise overview of the literature.* ◇ *A concise way of putting this is to say that scientists need to engage more with the public.* ■ **con·cise·ly** *adv.*: *The theoretical concepts are explained clearly and concisely.*

con·clude AWL /kən'klu:d/ *verb* **1** [T] (not used in the progressive tenses) to decide or believe sth as a result of what you have heard or seen: **~ (that)...** *These authors concluded that most sedimentation occurred below the beach zone.* ◇ *The WHO report concludes that it is possible for quite poor countries to achieve considerable health equality.* ◇ **~ from sth that...** *Many scientists concluded from this that light must really be a wave.* ◇ **it is concluded that...** *For these reasons, it was concluded that questionnaires would be the most practicable research tool.* ◇ **+ speech** *Brown (1992) concludes: 'The addition of international capital flows suggests... welfare gains for Mexico of 4 to 7 per cent.'* ➲ language bank *at* ARGUMENT ➲ language bank *at* CONCLUSION **2** [I, T] to come to an end; to bring sth to an end: *The concluding remarks discuss the significance of this advancement.* ◇ *the concluding paragraph/section/chapter* ◇ **~ with sth** *The discussion concludes with suggestions for further research.* ◇ **~ by doing sth** *Finally, we conclude by discussing the implications of our analysis.* ◇ **~ sth** *To conclude this brief overview of the literature, practical applications for the current research will be considered.* ◇ **~ sth with sth** *I will conclude this section with a summary of the evidence.* ◇ **~ sth by doing sth** *McHale concludes his essay by suggesting that the two approaches are incompatible.* **3** [T] (*formal*) to arrange or agree sth with sb formally and finally: **~ sth with sb** *In 314, Messana concluded a peace treaty with Agathocles.* ◇ **~ sth** *An alliance was concluded between the Tsarist regime and the conservative upper class of Poland.*

WORD FAMILY
conclude *verb*
conclusion *noun*
conclusive *adj.*
conclusively *adv.*
inconclusive *adj.*

▸ CONCLUDE + NOUN **chapter • section • discussion • study • paper • essay • book** *I want to conclude this chapter with a note on the validity of the initial results.* | **alliance • treaty • agreement • contract** *As a result of an agreement concluded by the Benelux countries, the duty levied on the goods increased.*

▸ ADVERB + CONCLUDE **therefore, thus • then • reasonably • tentatively** *McHugh therefore concluded that the carrying capacity of the plains lay close to 32 million bison.*

▸ ADJECTIVE + TO CONCLUDE **tempting • safe • reasonable • fair • entitled • wrong** *In our fast-changing societies, it is tempting to conclude that history has few lessons to teach us.* ◇ *The court was entitled to conclude that the child was not competent to make the decision on her own behalf.*

con·clu·sion AWL /kən'klu:ʒn/ *noun* **1** [C] an opinion that you reach after thinking about all the information connected with a situation: *The report's conclusions formed the basis for the subsequent Treaty on European Union.* ◇ **~ that...** *After many years of experimentation, he came to the conclusion that the motion was essentially unstable.* ◇ **~ of sth** *Section 5.6 reviews the main conclusions of the first part of the research.* ◇ **~ about sth/sb** *Atkins arrives at a different conclusion about the same texts.* **2** [C, usually sing.] the end of sth such as a piece of writing or a process: **~ to sth** *In the conclusion to her article, she produces a powerful summary of the arguments against independence.* ◇ **~ (of sth)** *At the conclusion of this initial assessment, the social services make a determination of the child's needs.* ◇ *The same train of thought is followed to its logical conclusion in Hesiod's Pandora myth.* ◇ **in conclusion, ...** *In conclusion, the arguments for being proactive in knowledge management are strong and compelling.* **3** [U] **~ (of sth)** the formal and final arrangement of sth official SYN COMPLETION: *There were major issues preventing the successful conclusion of the treaty negotiations.* IDM **jump to con'clusions | jump to the con'clusion that...** to make a decision about sb/sth too quickly, before you know or have thought about all the facts: *However suggestive the evidence, one should not jump to conclusions.* ➲ *more at* FOREGONE

▸ ADJECTIVE + CONCLUSION **main • general • overall • following • similar • same • opposite • firm, definite • final • definitive • inescapable, inevitable • obvious • tentative • false, erroneous • logical • reasonable • important** *The overall conclusion reached by the authors is that the birth rate is likely to continue to fall.* ◇ *Saleh (2008) drew the following conclusion:...*

▸ VERB + CONCLUSION **draw, reach, arrive at, come to, derive • yield • support • confirm, reinforce • accept • justify • summarize** *A large and growing literature supports this conclusion.*

▸ CONCLUSION + VERB **(be) based on • follow** *From these premises, two or three conclusions follow:...*

▸ PHRASE + CONCLUSION **be hard/dificult/impossible to escape/avoid the conclusion** *Despite the protests of the European Commission, it is difficult to escape the conclusion that there is an element of truth in the company's argument.*

LANGUAGE BANK

Stating a conclusion

The following words and expressions are useful when stating your conclusions at the end of a piece of academic writing, or when saying what conclusions can be drawn from an experiment, analysis or piece of evidence.

- **In conclusion/To conclude/To sum up,...**
- **Overall/in general,...**
- **It can be concluded that...**
- This **leads to/supports the conclusion that** ...
- **Thus/Therefore,...**
- **It is reasonable to conclude that...**
- **The basic/main/general conclusion (to be drawn) is...**
- **This** study/work/essay, etc. **shows/has shown that...**
- From this, **it is clear/obvious that...**

– ***To conclude***, *established firms pursue investment in new ventures for various reasons.*
– ***Overall***, *this evidence supports the argument in favour of introducing more marketplace competition into education.*
– *Based on this distribution,* ***it can be concluded that*** *women go to pharmacies more frequently than men.*
– *The US evidence strongly* ***supports the conclusion that*** *parents value freedom of choice (Peterson and Hassel, 1998).*
– ***Thus***, *we believe that* ***it is reasonable to conclude that*** *the concentration differences reflect differences in how our study plants absorb, utilize and store N and P.*
– ***The general conclusion*** *from this* ***is*** *that language can be treated as an evolving system.*
– *The present analysis* ***shows that*** *single indicators can potentially misrepresent the attitudes of some survey respondents.*
– *From these figures,* ***it is clear that*** *the implementation of the project does affect the growth rate of the economy.*

con·clu·sive AWL /kən'klu:sɪv/ *adj.* proving sth, and allowing no doubt or confusion: *To sum up, the evidence for these changes is suggestive, but not conclusive.* ◇ *There seems to be no definitive or conclusive answer possible to this question.* OPP INCONCLUSIVE ■ **con·clu·sive·ly** AWL *adv.*: *It is difficult to prove conclusively, but all the data point in this direction.*

con·crete¹ /ˈkɒŋkriːt; *NAmE* ˈkɑːŋkriːt/ *adj.* **1** made of concrete: *These acid producers can also cause considerable damage to underground concrete pipes.* **2** based on facts or actions, not on ideas, guesses or intentions: *In the next section I will give two concrete examples of how the theory has been applied in the UK.* ◇ *By collecting a petition, community groups are taking a concrete step towards achieving their vision.* ➲ *compare* ABSTRACT¹ (2) **3** a **concrete** object is one that you can see and feel: *Her point is that unicorns and dragons are supposed to be concrete objects which, if they existed, would exist 'in' space and time.* OPP ABSTRACT¹ (1) ■ **con·crete·ly** *adv.*: *The case studies that are the focus of this research will be described as concretely as possible, avoiding generalities.*

con·crete² /ˈkɒŋkriːt; *NAmE* ˈkɑːŋkriːt/ *noun* [U] building material that is made by mixing together CEMENT, sand, small stones and water: *The walls are made of reinforced concrete.*

con·cur /kənˈkɜː(r)/ *verb* (-rr-) [I, T] to agree with sb/sth: **~ with sb/sth** *Their data concur with previous findings.* ◇ **~ (that...)** *Stolp (1994) concurs that school culture and student motivation are powerfully intertwined.* ◇ **~ in (doing) sth** *The court concurred in affirming that they could not interfere.*

con·cur·rent AWL /kənˈkʌrənt; *NAmE* kənˈkɜːrənt/ *adj.* existing or happening at the same time: *The region experienced increased temperatures without a concurrent increase in precipitation.* ◇ **~ with sth** *The emergence of social theory is concurrent with the rise of modernity.* ■ **con·cur·rent·ly** AWL *adv.*: *Using five computers, it was possible to have all of the processes running concurrently.*

con·demn /kənˈdem/ *verb* **1 ~ sb/sth** to express very strong disapproval of sb/sth, usually for moral reasons: *The international community also condemns such practices.* ◇ *Bribery is almost universally condemned around the world.* ◇ **~ sb/sth as sth** *He was condemned as a vicious racist in editorials.* ◇ **~ sb for (doing) sth** *They generally condemn protesters for trying to disrupt meetings.* **2** [usually passive] **~ sb (to sth)** to say what sb's punishment will be SYN SENTENCE²: *He was tried and condemned to death.* **3** [usually passive] **~ sb to sth** to force sb to accept a difficult or unpleasant situation: *These categories of race, class and gender condemn Celie to a life of deprivation and exclusion.* ◇ *He was inevitably condemned to a certain political isolation.* **4** [usually passive] **~ sth (as sth)** to say officially that sth is not safe enough to be used: *He died in conditions condemned by an official inspection of 1843 as 'foul and disgusting'.*

con·dem·na·tion /ˌkɒndemˈneɪʃn; *NAmE* ˌkɑːndemˈneɪʃn/ *noun* [U, C] an expression of very strong disapproval: *Widespread international condemnation followed the attacks.* ◇ **~ of sb/sth** *Local and international observers were unanimous in their outright condemnation of the elections.*

con·den·sa·tion /ˌkɒndenˈseɪʃn; *NAmE* ˌkɑːndenˈseɪʃn/ *noun* **1** [U] the process of a gas changing to a liquid: *Condensation led to latent heat release.* ◇ **~ of sth** *The sulfides act as nuclei for the condensation of water droplets.* **2** [U] drops of water that form on a cold surface when warm water VAPOUR becomes cool: *Condensation was prevented by warming the apparatus to room temperature before starting the experiment.*

con·dense /kənˈdens/ *verb* **1** [I, T] to change from a gas into a liquid; to make a gas change into a liquid: *Water vapour had condensed on the inside of the bottle.* ◇ **~ into sth** *The water vapour condensed into water droplets.* ◇ **~ sth into sth** *The steam is condensed into water in a condenser.* **2** [I, T] to fill a smaller amount of space; to put sth into a smaller amount of space : **~ (from sth)** *The planets condensed and aggregated from the nebular material.* ◇ **~ sth (into sth)** *These proteins help to condense the DNA into a relatively tiny volume of space.* **3** [T] to put sth such as a piece of writing into fewer words; to put a lot of information into a small space: **~ sth** *This section is based on Koch (1996), but I have condensed his discussion.* ◇ **~ sth into sth** *By eliminating, these two equations can be condensed into a single linear partial differential equation.*

con·di·tion¹ /kənˈdɪʃn/ *noun* **1** [C] a situation that must exist in order for sth else to happen: *All applicants must satisfy certain conditions before their right of access to the court will be recognized.* ◇ **~ for sth** *Innovation is a condition for success in creative industries such as publishing.* ◇ *Governance is concerned with creating the conditions for ordered rule.* ◇ **~ of (doing) sth** *A high level of economic development is not a necessary condition of being an accountable democracy.* **2** [C] a rule or decision that you must agree to, sometimes forming part of a contract or an official agreement: *The Act empowers the police to impose conditions on a demonstration.* ◇ **terms and conditions** *The consumer needs to be aware of the terms and conditions associated with the contract.* **3 conditions** [pl.] the physical situation that affects how sth happens: *The climatic conditions in winter are mild.* ◇ *Access to offshore wind turbines is restricted by poor weather conditions at sea.* ◇ **under... ~** *Measurements made under standard conditions can act as reference values.* ◇ **under the ~ of sth** *The film chronicles the seasonal struggle of penguins to reproduce under the conditions of the Antarctic.* ➲ thesaurus note *at* SITUATION **4 conditions** [pl.] the circumstances or situation in which people live, work or do things: *Working conditions are a crucial aspect of motivation.* ◇ *The project was set up in 2003 to improve conditions for small agricultural producers in Kenya.* ◇ **in... ~** *The labourers work long days and live in wretched conditions.* ➲ thesaurus note *at* SITUATION **5** [C] an illness or a medical problem that sb has for a long time: *Her infant daughter has a rare condition known as Turner syndrome.* ◇ *Chronic illness and medical conditions can obviously impact a child's school attendance.* ◇ *The drug has been used to treat conditions such as hypertension and angina.* ◇ *Some skin conditions are long-term and extremely difficult to cure.* ➲ thesaurus note *at* DISEASE **6** [U] the state of sb's health or how fit they are: *While waiting for treatment, her condition was deteriorating quite badly.* ◇ **in... ~** *The variety of tasks that characterize police work highlights the importance of police officers being in good physical condition.* **7** [sing.] the state of a particular group of people because of their situation in life: *Self-interest is a basic fact of the human condition.* ◇ **the ~ of sb** *The condition of the urban poor had not materially improved.* **8** [U, sing.] the state that sth is in: **in... ~** *The vans are frequently noisy and in poor condition.* ◇ **in a... ~** *The premises had been left in a dangerous condition.* ◇ **the ~ of sth** *The purchaser will usually have a survey completed in order to establish the condition of the property.*

▸ ADJECTIVE + CONDITION **necessary • sufficient** *Having delocalized electrons is a necessary, but not sufficient, condition for a material to be a metallic conductor.* | **poor • adverse • favourable • normal, standard • prevailing • natural • changing • extreme • dry • wet • acidic • certain • local • environmental, climatic • economic • social • physical • experimental** *The stable form of beryllium under normal conditions is a metallic solid.* ◇ *Local conditions shape and define what customers will need and require from suppliers.* | **poor • working • living • social • material** *Overactivity is more frequent among children living in poor social conditions.* | **long-term, chronic • rare • medical, clinical** *Common chronic conditions include cystic fibrosis, coeliac disease and diabetes.*

▸ VERB + CONDITION **satisfy, meet, fulfil • violate • specify** *Unions will need to develop strategies that fulfil the necessary conditions of cooperation.* | **impose • attach • set • set out** *The Marshall Plan directed massive financial aid to Europe and permitted the US to set conditions on it.* |

C

create • provide • require • reflect *Slopes facing the sun provide warmer conditions that are beneficial to vines.* | **have • cause • affect • diagnose • treat** *Newborn surveys indicate that this condition affects approximately 1 in 1 000 males.*

C

con·di·tion² /kən'dɪʃn/ *verb* **1** [usually passive] to train sb/sth to think or behave in a particular way or to become used to a particular situation: **be conditioned** *Most people's perceptions of health and disease are socially conditioned to a large degree.* ◇ **be conditioned to sth** *Patients can become conditioned to particular forms of treatment.* ◇ **be conditioned to do sth** *Young people can be conditioned to behave in certain ways by our society.* **2** [usually passive] to have an important effect on sb/sth; to influence the way that sth happens: **be conditioned by sth** *The current lake ecosystem is strongly conditioned by past climatic events.* ◇ *Consumers' purchase behaviour is conditioned by culture and social values.*

con·di·tion·al /kən'dɪʃənl/ *adj.* **1** depending on sth: *The conditional nature of loyalty may be one of the most important trends affecting modern political communities.* ◇ **~ on/upon sth** *All international agreements are conditional on the willingness of states to observe them.* ◇ *The World Bank offers funds to developing countries conditional upon their satisfying certain demands.* OPP UNCONDITIONAL **2** [only before noun] (*grammar*) expressing sth that must happen or be true if another thing is to happen or be true: *a conditional sentence/clause* ■ **con·di·tion·al·ly** /kən'dɪʃənəli/ *adv.*: *The boulders are only conditionally stable and may be forced to move if external force is applied.*

con·di·tion·ing /kən'dɪʃənɪŋ/ *noun* [U] the training or experience that an animal or a person has that makes them behave in a particular way in a particular situation: *This theory states that all behaviours are acquired through conditioning.*

con·du·cive /kən'djuːsɪv; *NAmE* kən'duːsɪv/ *adj.* **~ to sth** making it easy, possible or likely for sth to happen: *The location is carefully chosen to create an atmosphere conducive to open discussion.* ◇ *A climate of general macroeconomic stability is conducive to business development.*

con·duct¹ AWL /kən'dʌkt/ *verb* **1 ~ sth** to organize and/or do a particular activity: *Raine and his colleagues conducted a series of studies.* ◇ *Interviews were conducted by telephone rather than face-to-face.* ◇ *They conducted a vigorous campaign for a shorter working week.* ➲ thesaurus note *at* CARRY **2 ~ sth** (of a substance) to allow heat or electricity to pass along or through it: *The diode conducted a DC current.* **3 ~ yourself + adv./prep.** (*formal*) to behave in a particular way: *The concept assumes that consumers conduct themselves as rational agents.*

▸ CONDUCT + NOUN **research, study • experiment • observation • fieldwork • investigation, inquiry • survey • search • review • analysis • audit • evaluation, assessment • examination • test • trial • interview • campaign • operation • work • business • affairs** *In conclusion, more research needs to be conducted on these apparent similarities.* ◇ *Much of the work in this field has been conducted in the UK.* | **heat • electricity • current** *The solid form was not used since it does not conduct electricity.*

con·duct² AWL /'kɒndʌkt; *NAmE* 'kɑːndʌkt/ *noun* [U] (*formal*) **1** a person's behaviour: *The Mosaic Law directed not just religious ritual but also moral conduct.* ◇ *Defining what constitutes criminal conduct in such a situation can be difficult.* **2 ~ of sth** the way in which a business or an activity is organized and managed: *Flexibility in the conduct of the interviews was maintained.* ◇ *Voluntary industry sector codes of conduct may help to raise standards.*

con·duct·ance /kən'dʌktəns/ *noun* [U] (*physics*) the degree to which an object allows heat or electricity to pass along or through it: *Thermal conductance is greater during heating than in cooling.* OPP RESISTANCE (5) ➲ *compare* CONDUCTIVITY

con·duc·tion /kən'dʌkʃn/ *noun* [U] (*physics*) the process by which heat or electricity passes along or through a material: *The heat transfer between the two end walls is mainly by heat conduction.* ➲ *compare* CONVECTION (1), RADIATION (2)

con·duct·ive /kən'dʌktɪv/ *adj.* (*physics*) able to CONDUCT electricity, heat, etc: *The glass and frame of a window are highly conductive.*

con·duct·iv·ity /ˌkɒndʌk'tɪvəti; *NAmE* ˌkɑːndʌk'tɪvəti/ *noun* [U, C] (*physics*) the degree to which a particular material CONDUCTS electricity; the rate at which heat passes through a particular material: *electrical/thermal conductivity* ◇ **~ of sth** *The conductivity of a solution depends on the number of ions present.* ➲ *compare* CONDUCTANCE

con·duct·or /kən'dʌktə(r)/ *noun* (*physics*) a substance that allows electricity or heat to pass along it or through it: *Aluminium nitride is both a good thermal conductor and a good electrical insulator.*

con·duit /'kɒndjuɪt; *NAmE* 'kɑːnduɪt/ *noun* **1** a pipe, channel or tube which liquid, gas or electrical wire can pass through: *A system of conduits and drains provided many of the rooms with running water and waste disposal.* ◇ **~ for sth** *A number of volcanic vents occur near the fault, which may have served as a conduit for the ascending lava.* **2** a person, an organization or a country that is used to pass things or information to other people or places: **~ of sth** *Their offices act as a conduit of information from the EU to the subnational level within the member states.* ◇ **~ for sth** *NGOs provide a conduit for the spread of policies across the country.*

cone /kəʊn; *NAmE* koʊn/ *noun* **1** a shape with a round flat base and sides that slope up to a point; an object that has this shape: *The light produced by the lamp is focused into a cone.* ➲ *see also* CONICAL **2** the hard dry fruit of a tree such as a PINE tree: *Black rats living in pine forests strip the scales from pine cones in order to access the nutritious seeds within.* **3** the top part of a VOLCANO: *A typical volcanic cone also contains lava flows and larger pieces of volcanic material.* **4** (*anatomy*) a type of light-sensitive cell that is found in the part of the eye called the RETINA, reacting mainly to bright light and colour: *In the visual system, rods and cones of the retina transduce light energy.* ➲ *compare* ROD (2)

con·fer AWL /kən'fɜː(r)/ *verb* (-rr-) **1** [T] to give sb a particular power, right or honour: **~ sth** *EU citizenship confers the right to move and reside freely.* ◇ *Parliament confers powers and can amend or withdraw them.* ◇ **~ sth on/upon sb** *A decree conferred the title of baron on all the brothers and their legitimate descendants.* **2** [T] to give sb/sth a particular advantage: **~ sth on sb/sth** *Proponents of NATO expansion claim that it will confer benefits on Russia too.* ◇ **~ sth** *Being able to see above the grass is likely to confer considerable advantage in finding food and avoiding predators.* ◇ *Resistance to this infection is conferred by a single dominant gene.* **3** [I] **~ (with sb) (on/about sth)** to discuss sth with sb, in order to exchange opinions or get advice: *In the days preceding the crisis, Gorbachev went to London to confer with western leaders about possible economic aid.*

con·fer·ence AWL /'kɒnfərəns; *NAmE* 'kɑːnfərəns/ *noun* **1** a large official meeting, usually lasting for a few days, at which people with the same work or interests come together to discuss their views: *The French Foreign Minister invited officials throughout Europe to attend a conference in Paris.* ◇ *to organize/hold/host a conference* **2** a formal meeting for discussion: *There was no suggestion* *at the case conference that the child should be removed from the care of the parents.*

con·fi·dence /ˈkɒnfɪdəns; *NAmE* ˈkɑːnfɪdəns/ *noun* [U] **1** the feeling that you can trust, believe in and be sure about the abilities or good qualities of sb/sth: *Transparency should be improved to help restore investor confidence.* ◇ **~ in sb/sth** *A series of medical scandals had undermined public confidence in the medical profession.* ◇ **~ of sb/sth** *To gain the confidence of the local population was not easy.* **2** a belief in your own ability to do things and be successful: *Visually impaired people may lack confidence out of their normal environment.* ◇ *The parents need advice on how to help the child to gain confidence and overcome fears.* ◇ **~ in sth/yourself** *Her experiences at school had undermined her confidence in her friendships.* **3** the feeling that you are certain about sth: **with ~** *It is possible to predict secondary structural elements with some confidence.* ◇ **~ that...** *The participants must have absolute confidence that the data will remain confidential.* ◇ **~ in sth** *Although subjects typically expressed high confidence in their guesses, only 21% of them guessed correctly.* **4 (in) ~** a feeling of trust that sb will keep information private: *Their findings were reported back in confidence to the Home Secretary.* IDM *see* VOTE[1]

ˈ**confidence interval** *noun* (*statistics*) a range of values that are defined such that there is a particular chance that the value of a PARAMETER lies within it: *Upper and lower lines represent the 95% confidence interval for the mean.*

con·fi·dent /ˈkɒnfɪdənt; *NAmE* ˈkɑːnfɪdənt/ *adj.* **1** feeling sure about your own ability to do things and be successful: *On leaving university I felt confident, motivated and ready to provide excellent nursing care.* ◇ **~ in (doing) sth** *Fewer respondents were confident in the identification of species from tracks.* ◇ **~ about (doing) sth** *As unemployment falls, workers begin to feel more confident about finding new jobs.* **2** feeling certain that sth will happen in the way that you want or expect: *It is impossible to make any confident predictions about what would have happened.* ◇ **~ of (doing) sth** *While I am fairly confident of the conclusions presented here, many problems remain to be explored.* ◇ **~ that...** *He was reasonably confident that the design he had proposed was correct and would work.* ■ **con·fi·dent·ly** *adv.*: *For the remaining 12 cases, we could not confidently assign the error to either method.*

con·fi·den·tial /ˌkɒnfɪˈdenʃl; *NAmE* ˌkɑːnfɪˈdenʃl/ *adj.* intended to be kept secret: *Competitors' bids usually remain highly confidential.* ◇ *Confidential information must only be given to certain groups of users.* ■ **con·fi·den·tial·ly** /ˌkɒnfɪˈdenʃəli; *NAmE* ˌkɑːnfɪˈdenʃəli/ *adv.*: *All data will be treated confidentially.*

con·fi·den·tial·ity /ˌkɒnfɪˌdenʃiˈæləti; *NAmE* ˌkɑːnfɪˌdenʃiˈæləti/ *noun* [U] a situation in which important information is expected to be kept secret: *Patient confidentiality must be maintained at all times.* ◇ *Inadvertent breaches of confidentiality can occur through corridor conversations.*

con·fig·ur·ation /kənˌfɪgəˈreɪʃn; *NAmE* kənˌfɪgjəˈreɪʃn/ *noun* **1 ~ (of sth)** an arrangement of the parts of sth or a group of things: *The configurations of older supercontinents cannot be easily determined.* ◇ *Over the last two decades, new configurations of inequality have emerged within as well as between social groups.* ◇ *The availability of complementary devices makes many powerful circuit configurations possible.* **2** (*chemistry, physics*) a particular arrangement of atoms in a MOLECULE; a particular arrangement of ELECTRONS in an atom: *In a diamond, carbon atoms are arranged in a three-dimensional configuration with little structural flexibility.* ◇ *The chemical properties of an element are largely determined by its electronic configuration.*

con·fig·ure /kənˈfɪgə(r); *NAmE* kənˈfɪgjər/ *verb* [usually passive] **~ sth (for sth)** to arrange sth in a particular way, especially equipment or computer SOFTWARE: *The circuit can be configured for a variety of applications.* ◇ *The machines are mounted on wheels so that they can be moved around and configured as required.*

C

con·fine AWL /kənˈfaɪn/ *verb* **1** [usually passive] **~ sb/sth (in/within sth)** to keep sb/sth in a small or closed space: *250 cm^3 of the gas was confined in a glass vessel.* ◇ *As the Internet is not confined within national boundaries, it is becoming a medium for international trade.* **2 be confined to bed, a wheelchair, etc.** to have to stay in a bed, a WHEELCHAIR or a particular place because of illness or injury: *The onset of symptoms leads to 40% of patients being confined to a wheelchair within 6 months.* ◇ *The accident permanently crippled her and she was confined to her home.*
PHR V **confine sb/sth to sth** [often passive] to keep sb/sth inside the limits of a particular activity, subject or area SYN RESTRICT (1): *Remarks here are confined to aerial and chemical pollutants.* ◇ *By 1939, illiteracy was increasingly confined to the elderly.*

con·fined AWL /kənˈfaɪnd/ *adj.* [usually before noun] small in area and surrounded by walls or sides: *More severe injuries usually occur when a blast occurs in a confined space.*

con·fine·ment /kənˈfaɪnmənt/ *noun* [U] the state of being forced to stay in a closed space; the act of putting sb/sth there: *Prisoners were assigned to more restrictive conditions of confinement than necessary.* ◇ **solitary ~** *He was placed in solitary confinement for 29 days.*

con·fines /ˈkɒnfaɪnz; *NAmE* ˈkɑːnfaɪnz/ *noun* [pl.] limits or borders: **within the ~ of sth** *Most ancient travellers stayed within the familiar confines of the Mediterranean.* ◇ **beyond/outside the ~ of sth** *Pollen from the corn is likely to spread beyond the confines of crop fields.* ◇ *Faraday became a public figure beyond the narrow confines of the scientific community.*

con·firm AWL /kənˈfɜːm; *NAmE* kənˈfɜːrm/ *verb* **1** to state or show that sth is definitely true or correct, especially by providing evidence: **~ sth** *Further genetic tests are required to confirm the diagnosis.* ◇ *The procedure can confirm the presence of a clinically suspected heart condition.* ◇ *The hypothesis was confirmed by the new data.* ◇ **~ (that)...** *Research has confirmed that schools in poor urban communities have higher percentages of troubled students.* ◇ **~ which/when, etc...** *An examination of the DNA sequences will confirm which species the various meat products came from.* ◇ **~ sth as sth** *Breathing other people's smoke has been confirmed as a cause of lung cancer and other diseases.* **2 ~ sth** to make sb's feeling or belief about sth even stronger: *Subsequent events confirmed his belief in the possibility of Anatolian Greek independence.* ◇ *Reports of mass famine served only to confirm the perception that communism no longer offered a viable alternative.* **3** to make a position or an agreement more definite or official: **~ sth (as sth)** *The appointments confirmed his position as the most respected British philosopher of the post-war period.* ◇ **~ sb/sth as sth** *These events appeared to confirm Britain's role as a leading imperial nation.*

▸ CONFIRM + NOUN **results, findings • conclusion • observation • diagnosis • hypothesis • prediction • view • suspicion • presence • existence • identity • validity • importance** *The theory's predictions have been confirmed by experiments at CERN in recent years.* ◇ *Tests that used to take weeks to confirm the identity of a microorganism can now be done in days.*

▸ NOUN + CONFIRM **experiment • study • observation • results • analysis** *These measurements have been confirmed by numerous subsequent studies.*

▸ ADVERB + CONFIRM **subsequently • further • thus • experimentally** *The existence of this particle was then experimentally confirmed.*

C

THESAURUS

confirm • support • verify • validate *verb*

These words all mean to provide evidence to prove that sth is true or correct.

- to confirm/support/verify/validate sth **by** sth
- to confirm/verify **that/whether...**
- to confirm/support/validate the **findings**
- to confirm/support/verify a **hypothesis**
- to confirm/verify/validate the **results**
- to support/verify/validate a **claim**
- a **study** confirms/supports/validates sth
- an **analysis/experiment** confirms/supports/verifies sth

- **Confirm** suggests that there is definite proof that sth is true; **support** is used when there is some evidence that helps to show sth, but it may not be definitive: *Diagnosis is confirmed by laboratory tests.* ◇ *These results further support the claim that the impact of lower-quality jobs is greater for women compared with men.*
- **Verify** and **validate** are used to talk about carrying out extra checks or research to provide clear proof for sth already put forward; **verify** is used to talk about sth that is clearly either true or false; **validate** can be used to talk about evidence of how effective or valid sth is: *In this way, it is possible to verify the identity of the molecules.* ◇ *When validating the model, the modeller needs to show that the model reflects biological reality.*

con·firm·ation AWL /ˌkɒnfəˈmeɪʃn; *NAmE* ˌkɑːnfərˈmeɪʃn/ *noun* [U, C] evidence that shows that sth is true, correct or definite: **~ (of sth)** *Archaeological excavations have provided confirmation of a Roman assault on the hill fort.* ◇ *Final confirmation of meteorite impact came from the discovery of a crater more than 200 km wide.* ◇ **~ that...** *High unemployment figures were a further confirmation that the economy was in recession.*

con·flict¹ AWL /ˈkɒnflɪkt; *NAmE* ˈkɑːnflɪkt/ *noun* [C, U] **1** a situation in which people, groups or countries are involved in a serious disagreement or argument: *Staff members meet with families to work on resolving family conflicts.* ◇ **~ between A and B** *Conflicts between employees and employers are widespread in most highly developed economies today.* ◇ **~ with sb/sth** *The human desire for power inevitably brings men and women into conflict with each other.* ◇ **~ over sth** *Conflict over resources is central to several ongoing or recent civil wars.* ◇ **+ noun** *Clear communication is critical to conflict resolution.* **2** a violent situation or period of fighting between countries or groups of people: *Humanity has not yet found a means of preventing violent conflict and enabling people to live in peace.* ◇ **~ between A and B** *Elsewhere in North America, there were similar conflicts between Native Americans and white settlers.* ◇ **~ with sb/sth** *However, from the eleventh century onwards, conflict arose with the rising powers of Europe.* **3** a situation in which there are opposing ideas, opinions, feelings or wishes: **~ (between A and B)** *There is potential conflict between the interests of informal carers and disabled people.* ◇ **~ over sth** *Conflict over the content of economic policy occurs in all market democracies.* ◇ **~ with sth** *Revivalist Islam identified a cultural conflict with the West.* ◇ **in ~ with sth** *To some extent, these findings are in conflict with results obtained by Imam et al. (2003).*

IDM **conflict of ˈinterest(s)** **1** a situation in which sb has a role or responsibility that may prevent them from treating another role or responsibility equally and fairly: *Any conflict of interest should be disclosed to the supervisory board.* **2** a situation in which sb's aims or needs are in opposition to the aims or needs of another person or group: *A solution must be found for the conflict of interests between employers and workers in the labour market.*

▸ ADJECTIVE + CONFLICT **ongoing • unresolved • intense • serious • international • marital • interpersonal • internal • political • social** *The case sheds light on the internal conflicts underlying power struggles among elites.* ◇ *Education will always be a source of political and social conflict.* | **armed • violent • deadly • military • international • civil, internal • ethnic** *Since the end of the Cold War, the vast majority of armed conflicts have taken place within states rather than between states.* | **inherent • potential • direct • ideological • cultural** *The teaching of English literature was seen as a way to disseminate English values without coming into direct conflict with native religious beliefs.*

▸ NOUN + CONFLICT **class • family** *After the intense class conflict of the 1930s and 1940s, corporations and unions developed an uneasy working relationship.*

▸ VERB + CONFLICT **resolve • avoid, prevent • reduce • experience** *Group therapy may be indicated for patients experiencing interpersonal conflicts.* | **solve • generate, cause, create** *Attempts to solve the conflict through the courts have failed.*

con·flict² AWL /kənˈflɪkt/ *verb* [I] if two ideas, opinions, reports, etc. **conflict**, it is not possible for them to exist together or for both of them to be true : **~ (with sth)** *These results conflict with earlier findings.* ◇ *These humanitarian principles often conflict with principles of sovereignty and non-intervention.* ◇ **conflicting interests/results** *International politics is an arena of conflicting state interests.*

con·form AWL /kənˈfɔːm; *NAmE* kənˈfɔːrm/ *verb* **1** [I] to behave and think in the same way as most other people in a group or society: *There is considerable pressure on teenagers to conform.* ◇ **~ to sth** *Members of groups tend to conform to a group norm, increasing the feeling of group identity.* ◇ **~ with sth** *Drug users may be under pressure to conform with a group ethos of criminal activity.* **2** [I] to obey a rule or law SYN COMPLY: *Arbitrary corporal punishment was officially forbidden in the army, but not all officers conformed.* ◇ **~ to sth** *Products must conform to these minimum requirements to be marketed in France.* ◇ **~ with sth** *The site must conform with all Health and Safety regulations.*

PHR V **conform to sth** to agree with or match sth: *Two of these results clearly conform to expectations.* ◇ *Marriage had to conform to religious views about sexual relationships.* ◇ *All three plots give very straight lines, indicating that the experimental data conform well to the equation.*

con·form·ation AWL /ˌkɒnfɔːˈmeɪʃn; *NAmE* ˌkɑːnfɔːrˈmeɪʃn/ *noun* [U, C] the particular shape and structure of sth HELP In chemistry, a **conformation** is any of the SPATIAL arrangements that atoms in a MOLECULE can take and freely change between, especially by ROTATION around individual single BONDS: *A protein's conformation dictates the physical interactions it can have with other molecules.* ◇ *Prions are protein molecules that adopt toxic conformations and cause infectious diseases.*

con·form·ist AWL /kənˈfɔːmɪst; *NAmE* kənˈfɔːrmɪst/ *adj.* (*often disapproving*) behaving and thinking in the same way as most other people: *It is a welfare state in which the young are taught to be conformist and respectful.* ◇ *Young believes that large cities liberate people from conformist pressures.*

con·form·ity AWL /kənˈfɔːməti; *NAmE* kənˈfɔːrməti/ *noun* [U] behaviour or actions that follow accepted rules or laws: *Religious conformity was a requirement for most forms of office-holding.* ◇ **~ to sth** *All member States pledge conformity to the rule of law.* ◇ **~ with sth** *The customer was given 30 days to test the software to ensure its conformity with the specifications.*

IDM in con'formity with sth following the rules of sth; conforming to sth: *English law must be interpreted in conformity with EU laws and decisions of the ECJ.*

con·found /kən'faʊnd/ *verb* (*formal*) **1** to prove sth wrong; to appear to prove sth wrong: **~ sth** *The rise in prices confounded expectations.* ◇ *Bias may confound the results in one direction or another.* ◇ **confounding + noun** *After controlling for the potentially confounding factors, the association between job demand and work stress was equally strong.* ◇ *confounding variables/effects* **2 ~ sb** to confuse and surprise sb: *What confounded the reformers was that the existing state managers managed to stay in control.*

con·front /kən'frʌnt/ *verb* **1** (of problems or a difficult situation) to appear and need to be dealt with by sb SYN FACE¹: **~ sb/sth** *There are many challenges confronting the legal profession.* ◇ **be confronted with/by sth** *Historians are constantly confronted with the dilemma of prioritizing some events over others.* **2 ~ sth** to deal with a problem or difficult situation SYN FACE UP TO STH: *There was a reluctance in the 1950s and 1960s to confront the realities of Nazi mass extermination.* **3 ~ sb** to face sb so that they cannot avoid seeing and hearing you, especially in an unfriendly or dangerous situation: *300 police officers confronted an equal number of union supporters.* **4 ~ sb with sb/sth** to make sb face or deal with an unpleasant or difficult person or situation: *When the police confronted him with the evidence against him, he changed his story several times.*

con·fron·ta·tion /ˌkɒnfrʌn'teɪʃn; *NAmE* ˌkɑːnfrən'teɪʃn/ *noun* [U, C] a situation in which there is an angry disagreement between people or groups who have different opinions: **~ between A and B** *There were violent confrontations between rival groups.* ◇ **~ with sb** *This brought Germany into direct confrontation with Russia.*

con·fron·ta·tion·al /ˌkɒnfrʌn'teɪʃnl; *NAmE* ˌkɑːnfrən'teɪʃnl/ *adj.* tending to deal with people in an aggressive way that is likely to cause arguments, rather than discussing things: *He was committed to a more confrontational approach with the Soviets on arms control.*

con·fuse /kən'fjuːz/ *verb* **1 ~ sb** to make sb unable to think clearly or understand sth: *Poor sentence construction just confuses the reader.* **2** to think wrongly that sb/sth is sb/sth else SYN MIX STH UP (WITH STH) (2): **~ A with B** *Adolescence should not be confused with puberty.* ◇ **~ A and B** *It is easy to confuse ideologies and political doctrines.* **3 ~ sth** to make a subject more difficult to understand SYN COMPLICATE (1): *His comments simply confuse the real issue.*

con·fused /kən'fjuːzd/ *adj.* **1** unable to think clearly or to understand what is happening or what sb is saying: *The patient may feel very confused and frightened after a fit.* **2** not clear or easy to understand: *The process of globalization has been a contradictory and confused one.*

con·fus·ing /kən'fjuːzɪŋ/ *adj.* difficult to understand; not clear: *'Common law' can be a confusing term because it carries at least three distinct meanings.* ◇ *The pH scale is potentially confusing to the non-chemist.* ■ **con·fus·ing·ly** *adv.*: *Some find this area of the subject confusingly academic.* ◇ *Confusingly, a food calorie is the same unit as the chemists' kilocalorie.*

con·fu·sion /kən'fjuːʒn/ *noun* **1** [U] a state of not being certain about what is happening, what you should do, what sth means, etc: **~ about/over sth** *Employees may feel confusion over their roles and responsibilities.* ◇ **~ as to sth** *This led to some confusion as to the nature of the disease.* **2** [U, C] the fact of making a mistake about who sb is or what sth is: *Their children were deported because of some confusion during the selection process.* ◇ **~ with sth** *There are numerous causes of abdominal pain that may cause confusion with appendicitis.* ◇ **~ between A and B** *There has been considerable confusion between the terms 'marketing' and 'market research'.* **3** [U] a feeling of not knowing where you are, or of not understanding sth and not being sure what to do in a situation: *Most people experience drowsiness and confusion when they wake up from an operation.* ◇ **in ~** *People were running around in confusion.* **4** [U] a confused situation in which people do not know what action to take: *Normal trade patterns were disrupted, and economic life thrown into confusion.* ◇ *After the Revolution, the political landscape was characterized by chaos and confusion.*

con·geni·tal /kən'dʒenɪtl/ *adj.* (of a disease or medical condition) existing since or before birth: *Congenital heart defects are a common and serious birth anomaly.* ■ **con·geni·tal·ly** /kən'dʒenɪtəli/ *adv.*: *a congenitally blind woman*

con·ges·tion /kən'dʒestʃən/ *noun* [U] **1** the state of being full of TRAFFIC or people: **+ noun** *The primary objective of a congestion charge is to reduce traffic congestion.* **2** (*medical*) the state of part of the body being blocked with blood or MUCUS: *Symptoms include nasal congestion, sneezing, sore throat and cough.*

con·glom·er·ate /kən'glɒmərət; *NAmE* kən'glɑːmərət/ *noun* **1** [C] a large company formed by joining together different firms: *A small number of multinational cement conglomerates have been buying up cement plants around the world.* ➲ thesaurus note *at* COMPANY **2** [U] (*earth science*) a type of rock made of small stones held together by dried CLAY: *Sparse outcrops of quartz conglomerate indicate local exposure to erosion.*

con·gre·ga·tion /ˌkɒŋgrɪ'geɪʃn; *NAmE* ˌkɑːŋgrɪ'geɪʃn/ *noun* [C+sing./pl. v.] the group of people who attend a particular place of worship, especially regularly: *This study is based on a nationwide survey of local Muslim congregations.* ◇ *A member of the congregation, not the clergy, led the services.* ■ **con·gre·ga·tion·al** /ˌkɒŋgrɪ'geɪʃənl; *NAmE* ˌkɑːŋgrɪ'geɪʃənl/ *adj.*: *Religious worship services, youth groups, Bible studies and other congregational meetings were observed.*

con·gress /'kɒŋgres; *NAmE* 'kɑːŋgrəs/ *noun* **1** [C] **~ (of sth)** a large formal meeting or series of meetings where representatives from different groups discuss ideas, make decisions, etc: *He attended the party congresses of 1903, 1904 and 1905 as a delegate.* ◇ *The two papers were presented in 1967 at the Brussels world congress of the International Political Science Association.* **2** [C+sing./pl. v.] **Congress** (in the US and some other countries) the name of the group of people who are elected to make laws HELP In the US, **Congress** consists of the Senate and the House of Representatives: *In 1924 the US Congress reversed its open-door immigration policy.* ◇ *Support for gun control measures in Congress is not uniform.* ◇ *Even among Republican members of Congress, there was no consensus.* ➲ *compare* PARLIAMENT (2)

con·gres·sion·al /kən'greʃənl/ *adj.* [only before noun] connected with or belonging to a congress or the Congress in the US: *Congressional elections are held every two years, in even-numbered years.* ◇ *a congressional committee/hearing*

con·ic·al /'kɒnɪkl; *NAmE* 'kɑːnɪkl/ *adj.* shaped like a CONE: *Sharp conical teeth in the jaws indicate that this animal was a predator.*

con·junc·tion /kən'dʒʌŋkʃn/ *noun* **1** (*grammar*) a word that joins words, phrases or sentences, for example 'and', 'but', 'or': *The authors focus on items such as adjacency pairs and cohesive devices (pronouns and conjunctions).* **2 ~ of A and B** (*formal*) a combination of events, etc, that causes a particular result: *The film is striking specifically because of its conjunction of sound and image.*

C

IDM in conˈjunction with together with: *Interpretative data should be used in conjunction with data from other sources.*

con·nect /kəˈnekt/ *verb* **1** [T, I] to join together two or more things; to be joined together: **~ sth (with sth)** *The Brooklyn Bridge connects Manhattan with Brooklyn over the East River.* ◇ **~ sth to sth** *Ancient art represents centaurs as having the upper part of a man connected to the lower part of a horse.* ◇ **~ A and B** *These vessels connect the arterial and venous systems.* ◇ **~ sth together** *Many fuel cells can be connected together to provide the necessary power.* ◇ **~ (with sth)** *The Gulf of Aden connects with the Indian Ocean ridge system.* **2** [T] to notice or make a link between people, things, events, etc. SYN ASSOCIATE[1] (1): **~ A to B** *A myth may connect suitable imaginary events to the lives of legendary or historical figures.* ◇ **~ A with B** *There is no direct evidence to connect this story, set in 1780, with the riots of the early 1840s.* ◇ **~ A and B** *My aim was to try and connect the economic and cultural dimensions.* **3** [I] to form a good relationship with sb so that you like and understand each other: *The need is to connect and build relationships.* ◇ **~ with sb** *The Internet enables people to connect with others who share their interests.* **4** [I, T] **~ (sb) (to sth)** to join a computer to the Internet or a computer network: *Currently, only a small minority of the world's population can connect to the Internet.* **5** [T] **~ sth (to sth)** to join sth to the main supply of electricity, gas, water, etc. or to another piece of equipment: *All properties are connected to the water, sewage and electricity systems.*

PHR V con̩nect sth ˈup (to sth) | con̩nect ˈup (to/with sth) to join sth to a supply of electricity, gas, etc. or to another piece of equipment; to be joined in this way: *Metal wires connect up the different parts of the circuit.* ◇ *The vessels connect up with those of the embryo to provide a circulation with a beating heart.*

con·nect·ed /kəˈnektɪd/ *adj.* (of two or more things, people or events) having a link between them: *These apparently unrelated events were, in fact, very closely connected.* ◇ *Loosely connected groups of firms come into association to reach common objectives.* ◇ **~ with sb/sth** *Economies are always connected with wider aspects of human society.* ◇ *When people mask their feelings, they become less hopeful about feeling connected with others.* OPP UNCONNECTED

▸ ADVERB + CONNECTED **closely, intimately • strongly • highly • directly • loosely • causally • politically** *Neurons are generally highly locally connected, making synaptic connections with many of their neighbours.* ◇ *Research shows that politically connected groups were more diversified than non-connected groups.*

con·nec·tion (*BrE also old-fashioned* **con·nex·ion**) /kəˈnekʃn/ *noun* **1** [C] something that connects two facts or ideas SYN LINK[2] (1): **~ with sth** *Sociolinguistics has close connections with the social sciences.* ◇ **~ between A and B** *Locke makes an important connection between ethics and politics.* **2** [C] a relationship between people or groups of people, often for a particular purpose: **~ with sb/sth** *Children, and especially teens, need connections with peers.* ◇ **~ between A and B** *In Thailand, the connections between business leaders and the government have always been strong.* **3** [U, C] the action of connecting sth to a supply of water, electricity, etc. or to a computer or telephone network; the fact of being connected in this way: *Even where piped connection exists, water supplies are not available round the clock.* ◇ *In the 1950s, there was rapidly increasing demand for efficient long-distance telephone connections.* ◇ **~ to sth** *Today, high-speed connections to the Internet are commonplace.* **4** [C] a point, especially in an electrical system, where two parts connect: *Current is passed through the cylinder for heating via electrical connections at either end.* ◇ *The pipes were fed through a T-shaped connection.* **5** [C, usually pl.] a means of travelling to another place: *Railway connections became essential for ports, the most successful of which developed shipbuilding industries.* **6** [C, usually pl.] people that you know, who can help or advise you in your professional or social life: *Wedgwood used his English aristocratic connections to court international royalty.* ◇ *Personal connections are a key element of doing business in Hong Kong.* ➲ *compare* CONTACT[1] (4)

IDM in connection with sb/sth for reasons connected with sb/sth: *A dramatic change occurred in connection with the industrial revolution.* **in this/that connection** for reasons connected with sth recently mentioned: *A further key difference in this connection is that unlike sociology, psychology retains close links with the natural sciences.*

▸ ADJECTIVE + CONNECTION **close, intimate • direct • clear, obvious • strong, powerful • causal • logical • necessary • historical** *The data point overwhelmingly to a causal connection between media violence and aggressive behaviour in some children.* | **close • direct • strong, powerful • emotional • personal • political** *The Labour Party had strong connections with the trade unions.* | **physical • electrical • synaptic** *Fibre optic links require a single fibre, whereas radio links do not need a physical connection.*

▸ NOUN + CONNECTION **Internet, broadband • telephone** *In 2006, just 23 per cent of European households had a broadband connection.*

▸ VERB + CONNECTION **have • make, establish • see, draw • show • explore, examine • understand** *The following section explores the connections between the insurance industry and global catastrophic risk.* | **have • create, establish, forge • maintain • strengthen • sever** *The Association of South East Asian Nations is strengthening trading connections with Japan and India.*

con·nect·ive /kəˈnektɪv/ *adj.* that connects things: *Cellulitis is an inflammation of the connective tissue under the skin.* ◇ *They were interested in using friendship networks as a connective device.*

con·nec·tiv·ity /ˌkɒnekˈtɪvəti; *NAmE* ˌkɑːnekˈtɪvəti/ *noun* [U] the state of being connected; the degree to which two things are connected: *First-generation PCs suffered from poor connectivity.* ◇ **~ of sth** *The connectivity of the atoms is different in each case.*

con·no·ta·tion /ˌkɒnəˈteɪʃn; *NAmE* ˌkɑːnəˈteɪʃn/ *noun* [usually pl.] an idea suggested by a word in addition to its main meaning: **~ (of sth)** *Describing migrants as 'illegal' carries connotations of criminality that are often quite inappropriate.* ◇ **negative/positive connotations** *The term 'cartel' has negative connotations, as in drug or economic cartels.* ➲ *compare* DENOTATION

con·quer /ˈkɒŋkə(r); *NAmE* ˈkɑːŋkər/ *verb* **1 ~ sb/sth** to take control of a country or city and its people by force: *The British conquered Kandy in 1815 to rule the whole island.* ◇ *His forces were devoted to pacifying the newly conquered territory.* **2 ~ sth** to succeed in dealing with or controlling sth: *Conquering the high level of inflation remained the priority.*

con·quest /ˈkɒŋkwest; *NAmE* ˈkɑːŋkwest/ *noun* **1** [U, C] the act of taking control of a country, city, etc. by force: *In the sixth century, they systematically expanded their territory by military conquest.* ◇ *At least forty major languages were spoken in Italy prior to the Roman conquest.* ◇ **~ of sth** *In the early spring of 324, Alexander celebrated the conquest of India.* **2** [C] an area of land taken by force: *There was a vast influx of goods from Europe's overseas conquests in Asia, Africa and the Americas.* **3** [U] **~ of sth** the act of gaining control over sth that is difficult or dangerous: *The conquest of major epidemic diseases such as the plague and smallpox was an important contribution.*

con·science /ˈkɒnʃəns; *NAmE* ˈkɑːnʃəns/ *noun* **1** [C, U] a person's moral sense of right and wrong, which guides their behaviour: *Most biographers accept that he had a guilty conscience.* ◇ *Christians in public roles may be required at times to act against their conscience.* ◇ *It was a matter of personal conscience.* **2** [U] the fact of behaving in a way that you feel is right even though this may cause problems: *Amnesty International was created to demand the release of prisoners of conscience.* ◇ *An individual's right to freedom of conscience should be respected.*
IDM **on your ˈconscience** making you feel guilty for doing or failing to do sth: *Anyone who starts a war has a lot on their conscience.*

con·scien·tious /ˌkɒnʃiˈenʃəs; *NAmE* ˌkɑːnʃiˈenʃəs/ *adj.* **1** taking care to do things carefully and correctly: *Nightingale was conscientious and careful in her written representation of the poor.* **2** connected with a person's conscience: *A student's conscientious objection to killing or using animals needs to be taken seriously.* ■ **con·scien·tious·ly** *adv.*: *All the issues have been conscientiously addressed.* ◇ *Some people conscientiously object to military service.*

con·scious /ˈkɒnʃəs; *NAmE* ˈkɑːnʃəs/ *adj.* **1** [not before noun] aware of sth; noticing sth: **~ of sth** *Kissinger was acutely conscious of his rivals in the administration.* ◇ **~ of doing sth** *She was always very conscious of being an outsider.* ◇ **~ that...** *Conscious that it was getting dark, they decided to return home.* OPP UNCONSCIOUS[1] (3) ➲ *see also* SELF-CONSCIOUS **2** able to use your senses and mental powers to understand what is happening: *He was now fully conscious.* ◇ *The patient is likely to remain conscious for many hours after an overdose.* OPP UNCONSCIOUS[1] (1) **3** (of actions, feelings, etc.) deliberate or controlled: *It is difficult to learn a language without some conscious effort.* ◇ *African film-makers have made a conscious attempt to draw on the traditional African arts in film-making.* ◇ *All these people had made conscious decisions not to smoke.* OPP UNCONSCIOUS[1] (2) **4** being particularly interested in sth: *Socially conscious investment funds have grown 15-fold.* ◇ *Some social groups are not class conscious in any traditional sense.*

con·scious·ly /ˈkɒnʃəsli; *NAmE* ˈkɑːnʃəsli/ *adv.* **1** if sb does sth **consciously**, they are aware of doing it: *Through words and behaviour, consciously and unconsciously, parents greatly influence how their child handles anger.* OPP UNCONSCIOUSLY **2** deliberately: *The British Crime Survey was consciously devised to provide an alternative measure of levels of crime.*

con·scious·ness /ˈkɒnʃəsnəs; *NAmE* ˈkɑːnʃəsnəs/ *noun* [U] **1** the state of being able to use your senses and mental powers to understand what is happening: *The patient started to show signs of regaining consciousness.* ◇ *What she sees causes her to lose consciousness from sheer terror.* **2** the state of being aware of sth SYN AWARENESS: *There is little class consciousness in Japan.* ◇ **~ of sth** *The consciousness of being an exile was central to his identity.* **3** the ideas and opinions of a person or group: *War and religion were the main factors in creating a British national consciousness.* ◇ *Green conciousness focuses on the way people experience and regard the world in which they live.*

con·script[1] /kənˈskrɪpt/ *verb* (*especially BrE*) (*US usually* **draft**) [usually passive] to make sb join the armed forces SYN CALL SB UP: **be conscripted (into sth)** *Young men were conscripted into the army and were slaughtered by the million.*

con·script[2] /ˈkɒnskrɪpt; *NAmE* ˈkɑːnskrɪpt/ *noun* (*especially BrE*) (*US usually* **draft·ee**) a person who has been made to join the armed forces: *The new soldiers were mainly conscripts from the cities.* ◇ **+ noun** *Garibaldi's volunteers were replaced in 1861 by a conscript army.* ➲ *compare* VOLUNTEER[1] (3)

con·scrip·tion /kənˈskrɪpʃn/ *noun* [U] (*especially BrE*) (*US usually* **the draft**) the practice of ordering people by law to serve in the armed forces: *The introduction of mass conscription was arguably the innovation of a democratic age.* ◇ **~ of sb (into sth)** *Finnish nationalists were outraged at the conscription of Finns into the Russian army in 1901.*

con·secu·tive /kənˈsekjətɪv/ *adj.* [usually before noun] following one after another in a series, without interruption SYN SUCCESSIVE: *We should expect averages over a sufficient number of consecutive years to be virtually static.* ◇ *consecutive days/months/weeks* ◇ *Under his leadership, the party has won two consecutive elections.* ➲ *usage note at* SUBSEQUENT ■ **con·secu·tive·ly** *adv.*: *Each page of a patient's notes should be numbered consecutively.*

con·sen·su·al /kənˈsenʃuəl/ *adj.* involving agreement by everyone concerned: *Decision-making within the groups is mainly consensual, with much effort put into building trust.*

con·sen·sus AWL /kənˈsensəs/ *noun* [sing., U] an opinion that all members of a group agree with: *The consensus today is that famine relief does not provide a long-term solution.* ◇ **~ on sth** *Reaching consensus on what constitutes terrorism is difficult.* ◇ *Up until the middle of the 1970s, there was a broad political consensus on the role of the welfare state.* ◇ **~ about sth** *An emerging consensus about the form of matter in the universe suggests that a complete understanding of it may be within reach.* ◇ **~ among sb (about/on sth)** *There was a lack of consensus among educators on whether commercial broadcasters could be trusted in schools.* ◇ **~ that...** *There was a general global consensus that torture was illegitimate.*

con·sent[1] AWL /kənˈsent/ *noun* [U] **1** permission that you give for sth, especially sth that affects you personally: *Before a doctor treats a patient, they need to obtain the patient's consent.* ◇ **~ to sth** *The parents refused consent to the child's medical treatment.* ◇ **~ to do sth** *The subjects had given their informed consent to take part in the experiments.* **2** agreement about sth: **~ (of sb)** *No change may be made without the consent of all the partners.* ◇ **by common ~** *Child marriages, by common consent, are believed to be bad for the participants and for the institution of marriage.* ◇ **by mutual ~** *The transfer of power took place almost by mutual consent.*

▸ ADJECTIVE + CONSENT **informed** • **valid** • **verbal** • **written** • **prior** • **explicit** • **parental** *In order to conduct an HIV test, explicit consent is required.*

▸ VERB + CONSENT **give** • **refuse**, **withhold** • **withdraw** • **obtain**, **gain** • **seek** • **require** • **have** *Once consent has been gained for the intervention, it is recorded in the client's medical file.*

WHICH WORD?

consent • **permission**

Both these words mean the action of allowing sb to do sth.

- **Consent** is used especially about sb agreeing personally to allow sth to be done to or for them, especially medical treatment or legal actions: *Consent is required of all those with parental responsibility.* ◇ *Wherever possible, consent should be obtained before the proposed procedure.*
- **Permission** is used about sb giving another person the right to have or use sth that belongs to them; or about an authority officially agreeing to allow sb to do sth: *Image reproduced by permission of M. Franx.* ◇ *The High Court granted permission to appeal to the Court of Appeal.*
- **Informed consent** means that the person who is agreeing to sth understands all the possible risks and consequences: *Counselling and informed consent are essential before genetic testing.*

C

con·sent² AWL /kən'sent/ *verb* [I] to give your permission for sth, especially sth that affects you personally: *Blood samples may be collected from the patient if they consent.* ◇ *Her husband cannot consent on her behalf.* ◇ **~ to sth** *All information about the patient is confidential and the patient must consent to its release.*

con·se·quence AWL /'kɒnsɪkwəns; *NAmE* 'kɑːnsəkwens/ *noun* **1** [C] (often plural) a result of sth that has happened: *This series of changes has had many consequences.* ◇ **~ of sth** *The most important consequence of unexpected inflation is redistribution of wealth.* ◇ **~ (of sth) for sb/sth** *The consequences for the patient could be significant.* ◇ **with... consequences** *Large earthquakes strike, sometimes with devastating consequences.* ◇ **as a ~** *Unemployment is relatively high and, as a consequence, the labour market position of workers is rather weak.* ➲ thesaurus note *at* RESULT¹ **2** [U] importance: **(not) without ~ (for sb/sth)** *These decisions, with their associated resource implications, were not without consequence for Britain.* ◇ **of no ~ (to sth)** *This detail, however, is of no consequence to the present study.*

IDM **in consequence (of sth)** as a result of sth: *Polar sea ice became permanent. In consequence, world sea level began to fall.* ◇ *In consequence of the delay, Harvey suffered a loss of £5 000 in production.*

▸ ADJECTIVE + CONSEQUENCE(S) **serious, profound** • **important, significant** • **negative, adverse** • **unfortunate** • **disastrous, dire, devastating, catastrophic** • **fatal** • **direct** • **immediate** • **long-term** • **far-reaching** • **possible** • **likely, probable** • **inevitable, necessary** • **obvious** • **unintended** • **natural** • **logical** *The crisis over the succession had ended, it seemed, without serious consequences.* ◇ *Political uncertainty is a direct consequence of the democratic process.* | **practical** • **legal** • **political** • **economic** • **social** • **environmental** • **ecological** • **evolutionary** *The environmental consequences of economic growth are rarely assessed.*

▸ VERB + CONSEQUENCE(S) **have** • **suffer** • **predict, foresee** • **avoid** • **explore, consider, analyse, assess** • **understand** *The downturn in the Japanese economy soon affected the Korean economy, which suffered similar consequences.*

con·se·quent AWL /'kɒnsɪkwənt; *NAmE* 'kɑːnsəkwənt/ *adj.* happening as a result of sth SYN RESULTANT: *This can lead to the release of lethal enzymes and consequent cell death.* ◇ **~ on/upon sth** *The shift from close-knit to loose-knit networks consequent upon industrial change was significant.* ➲ *usage note at* SUBSEQUENT

con·se·quen·tial /ˌkɒnsɪ'kwenʃl; *NAmE* ˌkɑːnsə'kwenʃl/ *adj.* **1** (*formal*) happening as a result or an effect of sth SYN RESULTANT: *The judge held that the company had negligently caused the oil spill and was liable for the consequential damage.* **2** (*law*) resulting from an act for which sb is responsible and not so distant from the act that it could not have been FORESEEN: *The terms and conditions excluded all liability for consequential loss and limited liability for other losses.* **3** (*formal*) important; that will have important results: *The court rulings that have been most consequential are the sovereign immunity decisions.* ◇ **~ for sth/sb** *Student choice of upper-secondary school subjects is highly consequential for their subsequent educational career.*

con·se·quent·ly AWL /'kɒnsɪkwəntli; *NAmE* 'kɑːnsəkwentli/ *adv.* as a result SYN THEREFORE: *The Internet is accessible almost anywhere in the world. Consequently, even minority political interests can access supporters.* ◇ *Some gave out land to gain loyalty, but consequently had ever less to give.* ➲ language bank *at* CAUSE¹

con·ser·va·tion /ˌkɒnsə'veɪʃn; *NAmE* ˌkɑːnsər'veɪʃn/ *noun* [U] **1** the protection of the natural environment: *Tourism can provide a strong incentive for conservation.* ◇ *These countries developed strategies to promote wildlife conservation.* ◇ **~ of sth** *The conservation of local woodlands was no longer an economic necessity.* **2** the act of preventing a resource from being wasted: *The programme aimed to encourage energy conservation and efficiency.* ◇ **~ of sth** *Here, conservation of water has become vital.* **3 ~ (of sth)** the protection of works of art, buildings, etc. from damage by light or pollution: *He provided advice on the conservation of paintings in the National Gallery.* **4 ~ (of sth)** the official protection of buildings or sites that have historical or other importance: *The association was formed for the conservation of the whole area rather than just the individual buildings.* **5 ~ (of sth)** (*physics*) the principle by which the total value of a physical quantity, such as energy, remains at the same level within a system: *Conservation of angular momentum keeps a spinning top upright.*

con·ser·va·tism /kən'sɜːvətɪzəm; *NAmE* kən'sɜːrvətɪzəm/ *noun* [U] **1** the tendency to resist great or sudden change: *For the rest of his career, he repeatedly denounced British conservatism in matters of ship design.* ◇ **~ of sb/sth** *They noted the traditional innate conservatism of the farming community.* **2** the belief that society should change as little as possible: *Their political conservatism meant that they were reluctant to abandon traditional institutions like the monarchy.* **3** (*also* **Conservatism**) the beliefs of a political party that has traditional ideas about society and that favours businesses that are privately owned and that operate with little government control: *The great philosopher of British Conservatism is the statesman and writer Edmund Burke.*

con·ser·va·tive¹ /kən'sɜːvətɪv; *NAmE* kən'sɜːrvətɪv/ *adj.* **1** opposed to great or sudden social change; showing that you prefer traditional styles and values: *Consumers here are relatively conservative, yet are still open to new product ideas.* ◇ *Initially, the movement aimed to restructure society but gradually it became more socially conservative.* ◇ *He outraged half the electorate by airing his conservative views on women.* **2** (*also* **Conservative**) (of a political system or party) favouring businesses that are privately owned and operate with little government control, and having traditional social ideas SYN RIGHT-WING: *Authoritarian regimes and conservative parties tended to oppose the extension of voting rights.* ◇ *In the UK, the Conservative Party was the most electorally successful right-wing party anywhere in the 20th century.* ◇ *Conservative political principles insisted on the value of existing institutions.* **3** (of an estimate) lower than what is probably the real amount or number: *Even conservative estimates suggest that one-fifth of the population has done some form of voluntary work.* **4** not taking or involving unnecessary risk: *Many companies take a conservative approach to financing.* **5** (of medical treatment) intended to control rather than cure a condition, and to preserve the affected part of the body: *The surgeon carried out the conservative treatment, which averted the threat of imminent death, but was concerned that the gangrene could develop again.* ■ **con·ser·va·tive·ly** *adv.*: *The ratio of unexposed to exposed patients has been conservatively estimated as 4:1.* ◇ *Some cancers can be treated conservatively by excision of the tumour and a rim of normal tissue.*

con·ser·va·tive² /kən'sɜːvətɪv; *NAmE* kən'sɜːrvətɪv/ *noun* **1** (*also* **Conservative**) (*abbr.* **Con.**) a member or supporter of a conservative political party or system: *The Conservatives, like the Republicans, have generally tried to project an image of being the more patriotic party.* ◇ *During this period, Gorbachev oscillated between trying to satisfy conservatives and liberals.* **2** a person who is opposed to great or sudden social change; a person who prefers traditional styles and values: *Jenner first had to allay the suspicions of metropolitan conservatives.*

con·serve /kən'sɜːv; *NAmE* kən'sɜːrv/ *verb* **1 ~ sth** to use as little of sth as possible so that it lasts a long time: *In a* *drought, plants have to conserve water.* ◇ *These business strategies frequently fall short in terms of conserving natural resources.* ➲ *see also* CONSERVATION (2) **2** ~ **sth** to protect the natural environment and prevent it from being changed or destroyed: *Conserving a species in the wild means conserving its habitat.* ➲ *see also* CONSERVATION (1) **3** [often passive] ~ **sth** (*physics*) to keep a physical quantity, such as energy, at the same overall total: *It is a fundamental law that energy is conserved in any process.* **4** [often passive] ~ **sth** (*biochemistry*) to preserve a sequence of AMINO ACIDS, etc. in a different PROTEIN or in NUCLEIC ACID: *These functional rRNA sequences are highly conserved among widely divergent taxonomic groups.*

con·sider /kən'sɪdə(r)/ *verb* **1** [T] (often used in orders) to think about or give attention to sth that you are discussing or studying: ~ **sth** *Consider, for example, the case of a coin tossed twice in succession.* ◇ *It is important when considering cultural aspects of disability not to fall into stereotypes of cultural reactions.* ◇ ~ **how/what, etc...** *Consider how long bacteria survive outside the body.* ◇ *This project will then consider what limited the growth of the early settlement.* ➲ language bank *at* ABOUT² **2** [T, often passive] to think of sb/sth in a particular way: ~ **sb/sth + noun** *Education is considered a basic right.* ◇ ~ **sb/sth + adj.** *The communists considered money 'bourgeois'.* ◇ **be considered to be sth** *The large population of Pacific rats is considered to be the main threat by local farmers.* ◇ *Tomato fruits were initially considered to be poisonous when introduced to Europe.* ◇ **be considered as sth** *Protein changes are considered as a potential primary cause of skin ageing.* ◇ **be considered to do sth** *Nation states were historically considered to have exclusive jurisdiction in these areas.* ◇ ~ **(that)...** *Lord Denning considered that rules of natural justice did apply to some extent.* ◇ **it is considered that...** *It is considered that the strict legal approach typical of a court of law is unsuitable for some cases.* **3** [T, I] to think about sth carefully, especially in order to make a decision: ~ **sth** *Several alternative designs were considered.* ◇ ~ **doing sth** *The claimant and her husband considered moving away from the area.* ◇ ~ **(how/what, etc...)** *Applicants should consider how they will demonstrate their suitability for the post.* ◇ *Participants were encouraged to consider carefully before making their decision.* **4** [T] ~ **sb/sth** to think about sth, especially the needs and feelings of other people, and be influenced by this when making a decision or taking action: *They argue that traditional economists fail to consider people's real needs.* ◇ *The state has a duty to consider the effect of any such legislation on the environment.*

IDM **all things con'sidered** thinking carefully about all the facts of a situation, especially the problems or difficulties: *Perhaps the system of national implementation of international human rights, all things considered, is not such a bad thing.*

▸ CONSIDER + NOUN **possibility • alternative, option • way • approach • factors • evidence, facts • aspect • extent • implications, consequences • effect, impact • needs** *For countries that are economically volatile, firms also need to consider the possibility of dramatic policy shifts.* ◇ *All dam and reservoir projects will have to consider their impacts on communities and wildlife.* | **case • situation, scenario • example • question • issue, matter • problem • role • relationship • nature • type • model** *I shall start by considering a very simple example of isometry, the rolling of a plane into a cylinder.*

▸ ADVERB + CONSIDER **now • first • then, next • already • previously, once • carefully • fully • seriously** *Let us now consider the electrons injected from the emitter into the base.* | **generally, widely • normally, usually • often • traditionally** *US television markets are generally considered to be highly competitive in comparison with their European counterparts.*

▸ CONSIDER + ADVERB **first • here • above • below • next • later • carefully, in detail • briefly • separately, individually • further** *Perhaps a more interesting state to consider here is anaesthesia.* ◇ *This geometrical problem is considered in some detail below.*

▸ VERB + TO CONSIDER **need • want • fail • refuse** *Teachers need to consider what kinds of working groups best enhance the process of learning.*

▸ IT IS + ADJECTIVE + TO CONSIDER **necessary • important • appropriate • helpful, useful • interesting, instructive** *It was necessary to consider the implications of the new data.*

con·sid·er·able AWL /kən'sɪdərəbl/ *adj.* great in amount, size or importance: *The company spent a considerable amount of money buying new safety equipment.* ◇ *There has been considerable debate over whether school quality can be easily codified and quantified.* ◇ *Discontent in Ionia was considerable.* ➲ *compare* SIGNIFICANT (1)

▸ CONSIDERABLE + NOUN **amount, number • extent, degree • scope • variation, variability • diversity • difference • overlap • importance, significance • influence • effort • attention, interest • debate, controversy • uncertainty • difficulty • progress • success • potential • distance • time, period • evidence • detail** *Studies have shown considerable variation in the frequency of these antibodies among patients.* ◇ *The economy took a considerable time to recover from the impact of the war.*

con·sid·er·ably AWL /kən'sɪdərəbli/ *adv.* much; a lot: *The results were considerably higher in the first test group.* ◇ *Standards of care vary considerably.* ◇ *Interest rates increased considerably over the period.* ➲ *compare* SIGNIFICANTLY

con·sid·er·ation /kənˌsɪdə'reɪʃn/ *noun* **1** [C] something that must be thought about when you are planning, deciding or studying sth: *Climate is clearly a key consideration in many human decisions.* ◇ *Practical considerations determined the technique to be used.* **2** [U, C] the act of thinking carefully about sth: *Careful consideration was given to the design of the questionnaire.* ◇ *Each group, after due consideration, chose its own method.* ◇ ~ **by sb/sth** *The government brought forward alternative legislative solutions for consideration by Parliament.* ◇ ~ **of sth** *These are some of the issues that are raised by a consideration of the organizational dimension.* ◇ **under** ~ *Many other strategies are under consideration.*

IDM **take sth into consideration** to think about and include a particular thing or fact when you are forming an opinion or making a decision: *Leigh (2001) discussed several factors that must be taken into consideration in addressing the issue.* ◇ *The actual price was then selected, taking into consideration distributor margins and users.*

▸ ADJECTIVE + CONSIDERATION **important • key, paramount, overriding • practical, pragmatic • theoretical • strategic • irrelevant • relevant • ethical • environmental • economic, financial • political** *Targeting was the single most important consideration in creating the recruitment campaign.* ◇ *Ethical considerations confront business organizations on many occasions.* | **further • brief • careful, detailed • serious • special • equal • explicit • proper • due** *This is a conceptually rich area that merits further consideration.* ◇ *This case is worthy of special consideration.*

▸ VERB + CONSIDERATION **give • receive • require, need • deserve, merit, warrant, be worthy of** *An exceptional case was mentioned above that deserves brief consideration.* | **include • involve** *The study includes a consideration of both verbal and non-verbal forms of communication.*

con·sider·ing /kən'sɪdərɪŋ/ *prep., conj.* used to show that you are thinking about a particular fact, and are influenced by it, when you make a statement about sth: *This research area has great promise, especially considering the federal funds available.* ◇ *Considering the important role played by myelin, it is not surprising that damage to or loss* *of this substance has devastating effects.* ◇ **~ that...** *Considering that these findings derive from small samples, it would be highly desirable to replicate the study with larger samples.*

C

con·sist AWL /kən'sɪst/ *verb* (not used in the progressive tenses)
PHR V **con'sist in sth** to have sth as the main or only part or feature: *Human fulfilment consists in activity, not in mere passive enjoyment.* ◇ **~ doing sth** *Intuition consists in making spontaneous judgements which are not the result of conscious trains of reasoning.* **con'sist of sb/sth** to be formed from the people or things mentioned: *Each committee consists of three judges.* ◇ *The country's exports consist mainly of clothing goods.* ◇ *Fatty acid molecules usually consist of an even-numbered chain of carbon atoms that terminates with a carboxyl group.* HELP Although **consist** is not used in the progressive tenses, **consisting of** is common after a noun: ~~*Each committee is consisting of three judges.*~~ ◇ *a committee consisting of three judges*

con·sist·ency AWL /kən'sɪstənsi/ *noun* (*pl.* -ies) **1** [U] (*often approving*) the quality of always behaving in the same way or of having the same opinions or standards; the quality of being consistent: *The data was evaluated in terms of consistency, reliability and completeness.* ◇ **~ in (doing) sth** *An essential attribute of a leader is his or her consistency in applying moral standards to organizational life.* ◇ **~ of sth** *Automation has produced improved consistency of analysis.* ◇ **~ between A and B** *The management has maintained a high consistency between the long-term strategy and HR practices.* **2** [C, U] the **consistency** of a mixture or a substance, especiallly a liquid, is how thick, firm or smooth it is: *The lump had a smooth surface and a rubbery consistency.* ◇ **~ of sth** *Under these conditions, water would take on the consistency of thick soup.*

con·sist·ent AWL /kən'sɪstənt/ *adj.* **1 ~ with sth** in agreement with sth; not CONTRADICTING sth: *These results are entirely consistent with the hypothesis.* ◇ *Political appointees, on the whole, act in ways they believe are consistent with the president's wishes.* OPP INCONSISTENT (1) **2** happening in the same way and continuing for a period of time: *The distribution of population densities is remarkably consistent for all urban areas.* ◇ *The results did not show a consistent pattern and might well be due to chance.* ◇ *Consistent errors were made by both researchers.* OPP INCONSISTENT (3) **3** always behaving in the same way, or having the same opinions or standards: *There is a need to establish a consistent approach.* ◇ **~ about sth** *Government departments must be clear and consistent about how and what they communicate.* ◇ **~ in (doing) sth** *One weakness of the research was that interviewers were not consistent in the way they asked questions.* OPP INCONSISTENT (2) **4** (of an argument or a set of ideas) having different parts that all agree with each other: *The ideology of segregation was not even internally consistent when subjected to analysis.* OPP INCONSISTENT (1)

con·sist·ent·ly AWL /kən'sɪstəntli/ *adv.* always in the same way; following the same pattern or standard: *As predicted, feeding rates were consistently higher at shallow depths.* ◇ *Studies have consistently shown that women have a higher risk for depression than men do.* ◇ *The notion of 'users' is clearly not being applied consistently across all these previous studies.*

con·soli·date /kən'sɒlɪdeɪt; *NAmE* kən'sɑːlɪdeɪt/ *verb* **1 ~ sth** to make a position of power or success stronger so that it is more likely to continue: *Over the next months, he consolidated his position as leader.* ◇ *He consolidated his power in the eastern coastal districts.* ◇ *The great political challenge today is consolidating existing democracies.* **2** (*technical*) to join things together into a single more effective whole; to join financial accounts or sums of money into a single overall account or sum: **~ sth** *All the debts have been consolidated.* ◇ **consolidated + noun** *The government proposes a consolidated and redrafted set of rules.* ◇ *In 2008, the group had consolidated sales over US $5 600 million.* ■ **con·soli·da·tion** /kənˌsɒlɪ'deɪʃn; *NAmE* kənˌsɑːlɪ'deɪʃn/ *noun* [U] **~ (of sth)** *Colonialism involves the consolidation of imperial power.* ◇ *During the late 1990s, the world motor manufacturing industry was engaged in a process of industrial consolidation.*

con·son·ant /'kɒnsənənt; *NAmE* 'kɑːnsənənt/ *noun* **1** (*phonetics*) a speech sound made by completely or partly stopping the flow of air being breathed out through the mouth: *In many languages of the Pacific, for example, final consonants are regularly dropped.* **2** a letter of the alphabet that represents a consonant sound, for example 'b', 'c', 'd', 'f', etc. ➲ *compare* VOWEL

con·spicu·ous /kən'spɪkjuəs/ *adj.* easy to see or notice; likely to attract attention: *Some of these movements make the males more conspicuous and more vulnerable to predators.* ◇ *Thai business people tend to avoid conspicuous displays of wealth.* ◇ **~ consumption** *The elite spent heavily on conspicuous consumption to maintain their social standing.* ■ **con·spicu·ous·ly** *adv.*: *Over time, female literacy levels rose conspicuously.* ◇ *Environmental considerations are conspicuously absent from Wallerstein's analysis.* HELP **Conspicuously absent** is used to refer to the fact that sth/sb is obviously not present when it/they should be. **con·spicu·ous·ness** *noun* [U] *Conspicuousness can make prey individuals more vulnerable to attacks by predators.*
IDM **conˌspicuous by your 'absence** not present in a situation or place, when it is obvious that you should be there: *At the final meeting, the UK MEPs were conspicuous by their absence.*

con·stancy AWL /'kɒnstənsi; *NAmE* 'kɑːnstənsi/ *noun* [U] the quality of staying the same and not changing: *Many insects show little constancy in their population size.*

con·stant¹ AWL /'kɒnstənt; *NAmE* 'kɑːnstənt/ *adj.* **1** [only before noun] happening all the time or repeatedly: *The colonia were a constant reminder to the Britons of Roman rule and military dominance.* ◇ *Language and culture are in constant flux.* ◇ *Biological pest control calls for constant vigilance.* ➲ *compare* CONTINUAL, CONTINUAL **2** that does not change SYN FIXED: *Most systems expand when heated at constant pressure.* ◇ *constant volume/temperature/velocity* ◇ *In a fixed exchange rate economy, inflation will be constant at the 'world' inflation rate.*

con·stant² AWL /'kɒnstənt; *NAmE* 'kɑːnstənt/ *noun* **1** a situation that does not change: *Warfare was a constant in these years, but fighting styles changed.* **2** (*mathematics*) a quantity or measure that does not change its value: *The constants calculated were comparable to previously reported values.* OPP VARIABLE¹

con·stant·ly AWL /'kɒnstəntli; *NAmE* 'kɑːnstəntli/ *adv.* all the time: *Technology is constantly evolving.* ◇ *The chemistry of the atmosphere has been changing constantly since the beginning of Earth's history.* ◇ *Western children are constantly reminded to say thank you at every appropriate opportunity.* ➲ *compare* CONTINUALLY, CONTINUOUSLY

con·stitu·ency AWL /kən'stɪtjuənsi; *NAmE* kən'stɪtʃuənsi/ (*pl.* -ies) *noun* **1** [C+sing./pl. v.] a particular group of people in society who are likely to support a person, an idea or a product: *The liberal democrats had a strong constituency among nationalists.* ◇ *The government was responding to pressures from a number of domestic constituencies.* **2** [C] (*especially BrE*) a district that elects its own representative to parliament: *MPs divide their time between Westminster and their home constituencies.*

con·stitu·ent¹ AWL /kən'stɪtjuənt; *NAmE* kən'stɪtʃuənt/ *noun* **1** one of the parts of sth that combine to form the whole: *Tar preparations can contain up to 10 000 constituents.* ◇ **~ of sth** *Lactose is a major constituent of milk.* **2** a person who lives in a constituency and can vote in elections: *These reforms would give MPs more time to help their constituents.*

con·stitu·ent² AWL /kən'stɪtjuənt; *NAmE* kən'stɪtʃuənt/ *adj.* [only before noun] forming or helping to make a whole: *The nucleus is broken up into its constituent parts.* ◇ *Taylor further recommended that each task be broken down into its constituent elements.*

con·sti·tute AWL /'kɒnstɪtju:t; *NAmE* 'kɑ:nstətu:t/ *verb* **1** *linking verb* (not used in the progressive tenses) **+ noun** to be considered to be sth: *His message constituted a direct challenge to traditional polytheistic religion.* ◇ *This failure constituted professional negligence.* **2** *linking verb* (not used in the progressive tenses) **+ noun** to be the parts that together form sth SYN MAKE STH UP: *In 1870, these social classes together constituted about three fifths of the population.* ◇ *Chimpanzees do hunt and consume meat, but it constitutes a small proportion of their diets.* **3** [T, usually passive] **(be)... constituted** to form a group legally or officially SYN ESTABLISH (1), SET STH UP (1): *The task was assigned to a specially constituted Constitutional Court.*

▸ CONSTITUTE + NOUN **offence • nuisance • breach, infringement, violation • negligence • abuse • threat • barrier • basis** *She argues that Russia did not constitute a military threat to the United States at the time.* | **part, proportion • majority • minority • ... per cent** *In all these countries, women now constitute a majority of students in education.* ◇ *Migrants to Portugal constitute at least 5 per cent of the resident population.*

con·sti·tu·tion AWL /ˌkɒnstɪ'tju:ʃn; *NAmE* ˌkɑ:nstə'tu:ʃn/ *noun* **1** the system of laws and basic principles that a state, a country or an organization is governed by: *Wales is one of the few nations with sustainable development enshrined in its constitution.* ◇ *Montesquieu's theory of the separation of powers had a very significant influence on the US Constitution.* ◇ **under the ~** *Judicial independence is guaranteed under the constitution.* **2** [usually sing.] **~ (of sth)** the way sth is formed or organized SYN STRUCTURE¹ (1), COMPOSITION (1): *These elements can generate changes in the genetic constitution of their host cells.* ◇ *Organizational theory will be used to analyse the constitution of society.*

con·sti·tu·tion·al AWL /ˌkɒnstɪ'tju:ʃənl; *NAmE* ˌkɑ:nstə'tu:ʃənl/ *adj.* **1** [only before noun] connected with the constitution of a country or an organization: *He had no plans for basic social, economic or constitutional reforms.* ◇ *In 1919, a constitutional amendment banned the manufacture, sale and transport of intoxicating liquors.* **2** allowed or limited by the constitution of a country or an organization: *It would hardly be democratic for the government to decide for itself what is or is not constitutional.* ◇ *Constitutional monarchies survive in some countries such as Britain and the Netherlands.* OPP UNCONSTITUTIONAL ■ **con·sti·tu·tion·al·ly** AWL /ˌkɒnstɪ'tju:ʃənəli; *NAmE* ˌkɑ:nstə'tu:ʃənəli/ *adv.*: *Constitutionally, legally and educationally, Pakistan relied heavily on Western models of development.* ◇ *Individual liberty is constitutionally guaranteed.*

con·sti·tu·tion·al·ism /ˌkɒnstɪ'tju:ʃənəlɪzəm; *NAmE* ˌkɑ:nstə'tu:ʃənəlɪzəm/ *noun* [U] belief in constitutional government: *Advocates of constitutionalism tend to argue that vulnerable minorities should be constitutionally protected.*

con·sti·tu·tive AWL /'kɒnstɪtju:tɪv; *NAmE* 'kɑ:nstətu:tɪv/ *adj.* (*formal*) forming a part of sth, often an essential part: *There are three constitutive elements to the concept of sustainable development.* ◇ **~ of sth** *Jacobs is concerned with institutions whose racism is more or less constitutive of their identity.*

con·strain AWL /kən'streɪn/ *verb* **1** to restrict or limit sb/sth: **~ sth** *Her choices as a film-maker were constrained by the commercial environment.* ◇ **~ what/who, etc...** *Environmental regulations constrain what firms are able to do with their waste products.* ◇ **~ sb (from doing sth)** *One factor that constrains these groups from fabricating a nuclear weapon is the difficulty of enriching uranium.* **2 ~ sb to do sth** (*formal*) to force sb to do sth or behave in a particular way: *These external limitations constrained senior managers to act more cautiously.*

con·straint AWL /kən'streɪnt/ *noun* **1** [C, usually pl.] a thing that limits or restricts sth, or your freedom to do sth: *Funding and time constraints determine that data are often only collected for species with economic value.* ◇ **~ on sth** *There were severe budget constraints on the new central government.* ◇ **~ of sth** *The e-company can operate internationally without the physical constraint of geographical boundaries.* **2** [U] **~ (on sth)** (*formal*) strict control over the way that you behave or are allowed to behave: *In the UK, there is little constraint on political organizations.* ⊃ thesaurus note *at* LIMIT²

con·strict /kən'strɪkt/ *verb* **1** [I, T] to become tighter or narrower; to make sth tighter or narrower: *The pupils of the eyes constrict as the light increases.* ◇ **~ sth** *Large boulders tightly constricted the river channel.* **2** [T] **~ sb/sth** to limit or restrict what sb is able to do: *The tendency to keep land in the family constricted social mobility in ancient Greece.* ■ **con·stric·tion** /kən'strɪkʃn/ *noun* [U, C] *The water gets shallower and faster as the constriction in the channel gets tighter.* ◇ *Dickens had never really liked the constrictions imposed upon him by weekly publication in 'All the Year Round'.*

con·struct¹ AWL /kən'strʌkt/ *verb* **1 ~ sth** to form sth such as a story, system or idea, especially by putting different things together: *She constructed a narrative of events using contemporary texts.* ◇ *Education is seen as the key to constructing a better society.* ◇ *Caplan (1987) argued that human sexuality is socially and culturally constructed.* ⊃ *compare* PUT STH TOGETHER **2** [often passive] to build or make sth such as a road, building or machine: **(be)... constructed** *High winds destroyed many poorly constructed buildings.* ◇ **be constructed from/out of sth** *The semiconductors are constructed from pure silicon.* ◇ **be constructed of sth** *The palaces were constructed of stone and mud brick.* **3 ~ sth** (*geometry*) to draw a line or shape according to the rules of mathematics: *The problem is to construct a square whose area is equal to that of a circle of unit radius.* ◇ *We can construct an angle of 30° by bisecting the angle of an equilateral triangle.*

▸ CONSTRUCT + NOUN **argument • theory • model • story, plot, narrative, scenario • representation • meaning • reality • identity • code • map • diagram • graph • table** *The argument is constructed from three apparently independent generalizations.* ◇ *Reader response critics insist that meaning is constructed by the reader who receives the text.* | **building, dwelling • dam • machine, device** *She contends that machines can be constructed which will simulate the behaviour of the human mind very closely.*

▸ ADVERB + CONSTRUCT **carefully • specially • poorly** *The Liberals proposed a carefully constructed system of constitutional checks and balances.*

con·struct² AWL /'kɒnstrʌkt; *NAmE* 'kɑ:nstrʌkt/ *noun* a way of explaining sth, sometimes based more on a particular idea or attitude than on evidence: *A useful construct here is the notion of a mental space (Fauconnier, 1994).* ◇ *Gender is arguably a social construct influenced by social conditioning.*

con·struc·tion AWL /kən'strʌkʃn/ *noun* **1** [U] the process or method of building or making sth, especially roads, bridges, buildings or machines: *Brick was used for construction in the southern towns.* ◇ *Dam construction came under stricter scrutiny.* ◇ **the ~ of sth** *In the 1940s, he was involved in the construction of an electronic digital computer.* ◇ **under ~** *Two more hospitals are currently under construction.* ◇ **+ noun** *Housing was in short supply and the construction industry was booming.* **2** [U, C] **~ (of sth)** the act or process of creating sth from ideas, opinions and knowledge; something created in this way: *Hitchcock played an active role in the construction of his reputation as a significant film-maker.* ◇ *Maps are social constructions whose form, content and meaning vary with the intentions of their makers.* **3** [U] the way that sth has been built or made: **of... ~** *Buildings were of brick or stone construction.* ◇ **the ~ of sth** *The defendants were negligent in the design and construction of the ferry terminal.* **4** [C] the way in which words are used together and arranged to form a sentence or a phrase: *We have tried to avoid difficult grammatical constructions, such as conditionals or passives.* **5** [C] (*formal*) the way in which words, statements or actions are understood by sb SYN INTERPRETATION (1): **put a... ~ on/upon sth** *It is hard to put an honest construction on their conduct.*

con·struct·ive AWL /kən'strʌktɪv/ *adj.* having a useful and helpful effect rather than being negative or with no purpose: *The suggestions were constructive and forward-looking.* ◇ *The course teaches the teenagers constructive ways of dealing with anger.* ◇ *Business too can play a constructive role in environmental decisions.* ➲ *compare* DESTRUCTIVE ■ **con·struct·ive·ly** *adv.*: *The aim is to resolve future conflicts more constructively.* ◇ *The patients received help in using their time constructively.*

con·strue /kən'stru:/ *verb* [usually passive] (*formal*) to understand the meaning of a word, a sentence or an action in a particular way; to understand sth to be sth SYN INTERPRET (2): **~ sth** *The term may be construed in different ways.* ◇ **broadly/narrowly construed** *In this paper, legislation will be broadly construed to include not only domestic statutes but also international treaties.* ◇ **~ sth as sth** *Some writers construe modern workplaces as intrinsically attractive environments to which people are drawn.*

con·sult AWL /kən'sʌlt/ *verb* **1** [T, I] to discuss sth with sb to get their permission for sth, or to help you make a decision: **~ sb** *The 1973 War Powers Resolution required presidents to consult Congress before committing troops.* ◇ **~ sb about/on sth** *The Committee must be consulted on proposals affecting regional interests.* ◇ **~ with sb (about/on/over sth)** *There is a statutory duty to consult with the Commissioner before making use of regulatory powers.* **2** [T, I] to go to sb for information or advice, especially an expert such as a doctor or lawyer: **~ sb** *Women are known to consult the doctor more frequently than men.* ◇ **~ sb about sth** *Forty per cent of those surveyed consulted a qualified professional about their decision before buying.* **3** [T] **~ sth** to look in or at sth to get information SYN REFER TO STH (2): *For more information concerning these relationships, consult the references listed in the appendix.*

con·sult·ancy AWL /kən'sʌltənsi/ *noun* (*pl.* **-ies**) **1** [U] expert advice that a company or person is paid to provide on a particular subject: *The company provided a range of computer consultancy and training services.* ◇ *management/marketing consultancy* **2** [C] a company that gives expert advice on a particular subject to other companies or organizations: *The group's secretariat is usually provided by an outside body, either an NGO or a consultancy.*

con·sult·ant AWL /kən'sʌltənt/ *noun* **1** a person who has a lot of knowledge about a particular subject and is employed to give advice about it to other people: *He has worked as a management consultant for leading global consulting firms.* ◇ **~ to sth** *She has served as an independent consultant to various international organizations.* ◇ **~ on sth** *He is an international consultant on corporate governance.* **2** (*BrE*) a hospital doctor of the highest rank who is a specialist in a particular area of medicine: *Hospital consultants remain powerful despite the creation of professional management functions.* ◇ **+ noun** *Only a consultant ophthalmologist can register a patient as 'partially sighted' or 'blind'.* ➲ *compare* REGISTRAR (1)

con·sult·ation AWL /ˌkɒnsl'teɪʃn; *NAmE* ˌkɑ:nsl'teɪʃn/ *noun* **1** [U] the act of discussing sth with sb or with a group of people before making a decision about it: *Trade union rights were removed without any prior consultation.* ◇ **~ with sb** *Such changes require consultation with employee representatives.* ◇ **in ~ with sb** *The Health and Safety Executive published these guidelines in consultation with the police.* ◇ **+ noun** *Following a consultation process, the Royal Commission produced its report in January 2000.* **2** [C] a meeting with an expert, especially a doctor, to get advice or treatment: *Most medical consultations begin with the patient describing their complaint.* ◇ *The aim of the study was to find out how GPs use their computer during consultations.* **3** [C] a formal meeting to discuss sth: *The outcomes of these consultations are fed into the democratic decision-making process.* ➲ thesaurus note *at* DISCUSSION

con·sulta·tive AWL /kən'sʌltətɪv/ *adj.* giving advice or making suggestions SYN ADVISORY: *In a number of important areas, the European Parliament only plays a consultative role.*

con·sume AWL /kən'sju:m; *NAmE* kən'su:m/ *verb* **1 ~ sth** to eat or drink sth: *She consumes 6–8 units of alcohol per week.* ◇ *Any increase in the predator population must mean that more prey are consumed.* ◇ *Seed-eaters, for example, consume a food rich in stored carbohydrates and oils.* **2 ~ sth** to use sth, especially resources or energy: *Older people are more likely to become ill, and so can be expected to consume more health service resources.* ◇ *Uganda consumes about ten times less energy per head of population than the United States.* ◇ *The conventional dyeing of textiles consumes large quantities of water.* **3 ~ sth** to buy goods or use services: *Wages pay for the goods people consume.* ◇ *A service is consumed at the point where it is produced.* ➲ *see also* CONSUMPTION, TIME-CONSUMING

con·sumer AWL /kən'sju:mə(r); *NAmE* kən'su:mər/ *noun* **1** a person who buys goods or uses services: *Companies cannot employ people unless consumers buy the goods and services those people produce.* ◇ *The Internet has given consumers more control and record companies less.* ◇ **+ noun** *External forces, such as severely depressed consumer demand, can have a devastating effect on suppliers.* **2 ~ (of sth)** a country, machine, process, etc. that uses sth, especially resources or energy: *The United States is the world's leading consumer of oil.* ◇ *Buildings are major consumers of energy.* ◇ *Methane and carbon monoxide are the two principal consumers of hydroxyl radicals.* ➲ *compare* PRODUCER (1)

con'sumer goods *noun* [pl.] goods such as food, clothing, etc. bought by individual customers: *Higher wages will increase workers' incomes, and this will tend to result in an increase in the demand for consumer goods.* ➲ *compare* CAPITAL GOODS

con·sumer·ism /kən'sju:mərɪzəm; *NAmE* kən'su:mərɪzəm/ *noun* [U] **1** (*sometimes disapproving*) the fact of buying and using goods and services; the belief that it is good for a society or an individual person to buy and use a large quantity of goods and services: *Industrialization was characterized by mass production and mass consumerism.* ◇ *It can be claimed that Buddhism offers an alternative to today's materialism and consumerism.* **2** the protection of the rights of people who buy goods and services: *From the 1960s onwards, consumerism—consumers lobbying for* *better trading standards and for consumer protection—grew apace.* ■ **con·sumer·ist** /kən'sjuːmərɪst; *NAmE* kən'suːmərɪst/ *adj.*: *Cahill argues that our increasingly consumerist society has led to profound inequalities.*

con,sumer 'surplus *noun* [U] (*economics*) the difference between the actual price that sth costs and the higher price that sb would be willing to pay for it: *Price discrimination boosts the profits of the business by reducing consumer surplus.*

con·sump·tion AWL /kən'sʌmpʃn/ *noun* [U] **1** the act of using energy, food or materials; the amount used: *Traditional regulatory measures have done little to reduce energy consumption.* ◇ *For any class of car, the typical fuel consumption has fallen over the past decade or so.* ◇ *To make the water suitable for human consumption, further purification is needed.* ◇ **~ of sth** *Lower-income households tend to have higher consumption of fats and sugars.* ➲ *see also* CONSUME (1), CONSUME (2) **2 ~ (of sth)** the act of buying and using products: *Families increased their consumption of market goods.* ◇ *Spain has seen a fall in domestic consumption due to a change in consumer habits.* ◇ *Spending on non-durable goods and services comprises about 70% of UK consumption.* ➲ *see also* CONSUME (3)

▸ ADJECTIVE + CONSUMPTION **high** ◆ **excessive** ◆ **increased** ◆ **low** ◆ **total** ◆ **average** ◆ **current** ◆ **domestic** ◆ **global** ◆ **per capita** ◆ **daily** *This is the percentage of the population who live in households with per capita consumption below the poverty line.*

▸ NOUN + CONSUMPTION **energy** ◆ **power, electricity** ◆ **fuel** ◆ **alcohol** ◆ **cigarette, tobacco** ◆ **food** *Light-emitting diodes provide substantial savings in terms of power consumption compared with conventional lighting.*

▸ VERB + CONSUMPTION **reduce, decrease** ◆ **increase** *Development activities in many of these countries are increasing their consumption of fossil fuels.*

▸ CONSUMPTION + VERB **increase, grow, rise** ◆ **fall** *Global alcohol consumption has increased in recent decades.*

▸ NOUN + IN CONSUMPTION **increase, growth** ◆ **reduction, drop, fall, decrease** ◆ **change** *Depression may also be the result of an increase in alcohol consumption.*

con·tact¹ AWL /'kɒntækt; *NAmE* 'kɑːntækt/ *noun* **1** [U] the act of communicating with sb, especially regularly: **~ between A and B** *The Internet allows more direct contact between voters and politicians.* ◇ **~ (with sb)** *She has no contact with the children's father.* ◇ *In some cultures, sustained eye contact is perceived as disrespectful.* ◇ **in ~ with sb** *Participation in chat rooms can put teens in contact with strangers.* **2** [U] the state of touching sth/sb: *Head lice are transmitted by close contact and are more common in children.* ◇ **~ with sth/sb** *Scabies is highly contagious and is acquired from physical contact with infected persons.* ◇ **in ~ with sth** *The sphere coloured red is in direct contact with eight spheres coloured grey.* ◇ **come into ~ (with sth)** *When the enzyme comes into contact with its substrate, a light-emitting fluorescent product is formed.* ◇ **on ~ (with sth)** *Corrosives cause destruction of body tissues on contact.* **3** [U] the state of meeting sb or experiencing sth: **~ with sb/sth** *The isolation-reared chimpanzees avoided social contact with other chimpanzees, including sexual contact.* ◇ **come into ~ with sb/sth** *Carlzon calculated that each airline customer came into contact with approximately five employees.* ◇ **bring sb into ~ with sb/sth** *The increasing globalization of business has brought more companies into contact with human rights issues.* **4** [C, usually pl.] a person that you know, especially sb who can be helpful to you in your work; a meeting, communication or relationship with sb: *The entrepreneur needs to create a network of social contacts.* ◇ *Archaeologists determined that there were cultural contacts between the two groups in the past.* **5** [C] an electrical connection: *Electrical contacts for the heating element are made at either end of the tube.* **6** [C] a person who may be infectious because they have recently been near to sb with an infectious disease: *Infected people and close physical contacts should be treated whether or not they are symptomatic.* ◇ *Measles, rubella and chickenpox infect a high proportion of contacts.* IDM *see* POINT¹

▸ ADJECTIVE + CONTACT **direct** ◆ **close** ◆ **regular, frequent** *Although some of the children had regular contact with their fathers, none resided together.* | **physical** *Cells that are in physical contact with each other are often very active in signalling to each other.* | **social** ◆ **personal** *The engine of Asian business is built largely on personal contacts.*

▸ VERB + CONTACT **have** ◆ **make, establish** ◆ **maintain** ◆ **provide** ◆ **require** ◆ **avoid** ◆ **lose** *The company wants its salespeople to maintain close contact with the customer.* ◇ *Some groups like the Amish seek to avoid any contact with members of other faiths.*

con·tact² AWL /'kɒntækt; *NAmE* 'kɑːntækt/ *verb* to communicate with sb, for example by telephone, letter or email: **~ sb (by sth)** *Of those initially contacted by telephone, 43% agreed to participate.* ◇ **~ sb with sth** *Customers will only be contacted with marketing information that they have said will be of interest to them.*

'contact lens *noun* [usually pl.] a small round piece of thin plastic that you put on your eye to help you see better: *to wear contact lenses*

con·ta·gious /kən'teɪdʒəs/ *adj.* **1** (of a disease) that spreads by people or animals being in close physical contact with each other: *Globalized travel and trade means that a highly contagious disease could spread to virtually all parts of the world within weeks.* **2** [not usually before noun] (of a person or animal) having a disease that can be spread to others by touch or body contact: *Patients with Norwegian scabies are highly contagious.* **3** (of an idea or feeling) that spreads quickly to other people: *These ideas proved remarkably contagious, bringing about the plate tectonics revolution.* ◇ *This was not a classic contagious banking panic.* ➲ *compare* INFECTIOUS

con·tain /kən'teɪn/ *verb* (not used in the progressive tenses) **1 ~ sth** if sth **contains** sth else, it has that thing inside it or as part of it: *Sea water contains a higher concentration of dissolved oxygen.* ◇ *The site contains information designed to help parents care for children.* ◇ *Both poems contain elements of satire and mythology.* **2 ~ sth** to prevent sth harmful from spreading or getting worse: *Patients can be given drugs to contain the severity and spread of the disease.* ◇ *NATO governments were worried that if they failed to contain the crisis, it could spread and engulf the region.* ➲ *see also* SELF-CONTAINED

con·tain·er /kən'teɪnə(r)/ *noun* **1** an object for holding or transporting sth: *The fluid was placed in a sterile container and transported to the laboratory for analysis.* ◇ *A gas is a form of matter that immediately fills any container it occupies.* ◇ *Plastic containers tend to be used now, as glass containers can pose a safety hazard if they break.* **2** a large metal box of a standard design and size used for transporting goods on ships, trains and lorries: *Some container ships can carry over 14 000 20-foot containers with a crew of fewer than 15 people.*

con·tain·ment /kən'teɪnmənt/ *noun* [U] **1** the act of keeping sth under control so that it cannot spread in a harmful way: *The pollution caused by oil spills is often best treated by containment, leaving nature to restore itself.* ◇ **~ of sth** *The rapid containment of a disease outbreak requires identification of the area that is contaminated.* **2** the act of keeping another country's power within limits so that the country does not become too powerful: *Along the Danube, Claudius pursued a policy of containment.* ◇ **~ of sth** *The USA made its first priority the containment of the Soviet Union.*

C

C

con·tam·in·ant /kən'tæmɪnənt/ *noun* (*technical*) a substance that makes sth dirty or no longer pure: *Processing the collected blood involves filtering and washing to remove contaminants.*

con·tam·in·ate /kən'tæmɪneɪt/ *verb* **1** [usually passive] to make a substance or place dirty or no longer pure by adding a substance that is dangerous or carries disease: **be contaminated with sth** *Antibiotics may be required if the water was contaminated with sewage or other waste.* ◇ **be contaminated by sth** *As many ports are sites of polluting discharges, the natural sediment may be contaminated by pollutants.* **2 ~ sth** to influence people's ideas or attitudes in a bad way: *The leadership struggles eventually limited the Caliph's power and contaminated his authority.*

con·tam·in·ation /kənˌtæmɪ'neɪʃn/ *noun* [U] the act or process of making sth dirty or no longer pure: *Agricultural fertilizers and pesticides are a common source of groundwater contamination.* ◇ *The site should be cleaned with 70% alcohol to reduce bacterial contamination.* ◇ **~ of sth** *Potential contamination of drinking water is a serious issue.*

con·tem·plate /'kɒntəmpleɪt; *NAmE* 'kɑːntəmpleɪt/ *verb* **1** to think about whether you should do sth, or how you should do sth SYN CONSIDER (3): **~ sth** *The percentage of couples contemplating divorce who enter into marriage counselling is unknown.* ◇ **~ doing sth** *An international investor is contemplating starting up an IT software business.* ◇ **~ how/what, etc...** *He spent hours alone in his study contemplating how he could transform the world.* **2** to think carefully about and accept the possibility of sth happening: **~ sth** *They failed to contemplate the possibility of radical changes in markets and prices.* ◇ **~ how/what, etc...** *The researcher must contemplate how the solution will affect related areas.* ◇ **~ that...** *The legislation clearly contemplates that employers may negotiate for agreements with unions.* **3 ~ sth** (*formal*) to think deeply about sth for a long time: *As we contemplate the far future of the universe, there are many speculations that could be made.*

con·tem·pla·tion /ˌkɒntəm'pleɪʃn; *NAmE* ˌkɑːntəm'pleɪʃn/ *noun* [U] the act of thinking deeply about sth; the act of looking at sth in a calm and careful way: *The monks were dedicated to a life of prayer and contemplation.* ◇ **~ of sth** *The sublime could be experienced in the contemplation of nature.*

IDM **in contem'plation** (*formal*) being considered: *No specific proposal was in contemplation.*

con·tem·por·ary¹ AWL /kən'temprəri; *NAmE* kən'tempəreri/ *adj.* **1** belonging to the present time SYN MODERN (1): *Wight illustrated his argument with historical and contemporary examples.* ◇ *Contemporary literature for young people reflects a different set of values.* **2** (especially of people and society) belonging to the same time as sb/sth else: *Jean-Philippe Rameau was the major contemporary writer on musical theory.* ◇ **~ with sb/sth** *Paul was contemporary with the Jewish Christians at Jerusalem.* ◇ *Other developments in physics were contemporary with the events described here.*

▸ CONTEMPORARY + NOUN **writer • philosopher • politics • culture • reader • theorist • theory • literature • life** *The role of international law in contemporary world politics is more complex than at first appears.* ◇ *Milton's opening lines would have startled his contemporary readers.* | **society • world • debate, discourse • issue • research • art • film** *Words and images provide an important means of communication in contemporary society.*

con·tem·por·ary² AWL /kən'temprəri; *NAmE* kən'tempəreri/ *noun* (*pl.* **-ies**) a person or thing living or existing at the same time as sb/sth else, especially sb who is about the same age as sb else: *Thackeray was recognized by his contemporaries as a moralist.* ◇ *The computer was about three times faster than its contemporaries.* ◇ **~ of sb/sth** *Lamb was a friend and contemporary of Coleridge and Wordsworth.*

con·tempt /kən'tempt/ *noun* [U] **1** the feeling that sb/sth is without value and deserves no respect at all: *The Jews regarded Greek and Roman gods with contempt.* ◇ **~ for sb/sth** *In 19th century Vienna, Metternich had nothing but contempt for the middle classes.* **2 ~ for sth** a lack of worry or fear about rules, danger, etc: *Kerouac's novel celebrated individualism and the search for identity, displaying contempt for security and stability.* **3** (*also* **conˌtempt of 'court**) the crime of refusing to obey or show respect for a court or a judge: *The defendant refused to be searched and was imprisoned for contempt of court.*

con·tend /kən'tend/ *verb* **1** [T] **~ (that...)** to say that sth is true, especially in an argument SYN MAINTAIN: *Previous authors, he contended, had failed to derive correct equations.* ◇ *She contended that more regulation could fracture the global financial system.* ➲ thesaurus note *at* ARGUE **2** [I] **~ (for sth)** to compete against sb in order to gain sth; to be in opposition to sb/sth: *Similarly, in twelfth-century Ireland, there were numerous rulers contending for power.* ◇ *In this article, I introduce and discuss two contending definitions of the term 'institution'.*

PHR V **con'tend with sth/sb** to have to deal with a problem or with a difficult situation or person: *This research finds that US activists contend with substantial political and cultural obstacles.*

con·tent¹ /'kɒntent; *NAmE* 'kɑːntent/ *noun* **1 contents** [pl.] **~ (of sth)** the things that are contained in sth: *Often, the patient is not warned of the exact contents of the medicine.* ◇ *The contents of the tube were mixed by centrifuging the mixture in a microcentrifuge.* ➲ *see also* INFORMATION CONTENT **2 contents** [pl.] the different sections that are contained in a book, magazine, JOURNAL or website; a list of these sections: *The handbook is well structured and the contents are assembled logically.* ◇ **+ noun** *Each chapter begins with a brief contents list and finishes with a summary.* **3** [sing.] the subject matter of a book, speech, programme, etc: *His poetry was novel in both form and content.* ◇ **~ of sth** *There are now a number of computer programs which analyse the content of discussions.* **4** [sing.] (following a noun or an adjective) the amount of a substance that is contained in sth else: *Typically, highly fertile soils have a high organic content.* ◇ **~ of sth** *A variety of factors influence the mineral content of a sediment.* **5** [U] the information or other material contained on a website, CD-ROM, etc: *Uploading content and making it accessible to all was already possible before the advent of the Web 2.0.* ◇ *The policy restricts the streaming video and audio many museum websites use to deliver content.* ◇ *The amount of non-English media content on the World Wide Web has been steadily increasing.*

▸ ADJECTIVE + CONTENT **high • low** *Most aquatic plants have a very high water content.*

▸ NOUN + CONTENT **water • moisture • fat • protein • iron • carbon • nitrogen • oxygen** *The steel had quite a high carbon content so that it was stronger.*

▸ VERB + CONTENT **determine • influence** *The moisture content was determined by drying overnight at 100°C, then reweighing the sample.* ◇ *Corporate media giants deny that consolidation of the industry influences news content.* | **increase • reduce** *The US reached an agreement with the Alliance of Auto Manufacturers to reduce sulfur content in gasoline.*

▸ CONTENTS + NOUN **page • list** *The approach is not entirely transparent from the contents page.*

▸ CONTENT + NOUN **analysis** *A content analysis of 'The Daily Show' found that the news media were targets 15% of the time.* | **provider • services** *The website is created and hosted by the content provider.*

con·tent² /kən'tent/ *adj.* [not before noun] satisfied and happy with what you have; willing to do or accept sth: **~ with sth** *He is content with his new life in New York.* ◇ *Many victims of negligence are not content with mere financial compensation.* ◇ **~ to do/be sth** *King Frederick knew that, unless he was content to be the client of powerful neighbours, he needed a military force of his own.*

con·tent³ /kən'tent/ *verb* **~ yourself with sth** to accept and be satisfied with sth and not try to have or do sth better: *Poisson performed no experiments and contented himself with calling for others to confirm his theory.*

con·ten·tion /kən'tenʃn/ *noun* **1** [C] a belief or an opinion that is expressed, especially in an argument: *Our results did not support these contentions.* ◇ *This contention was rejected by the court.* ◇ **~ that...** *He cites Reinhold Niebuhr to support his contention that democracy requires virtue.* **2** [U] disagreement between people or groups SYN DISPUTE¹: *This was a phase of heightened conflict and contention.* ◇ *The new restrictions became a point of contention between the Commission and environmentalists.* ◇ *an area/a matter/a source of contention* IDM *see* BONE

con·ten·tious /kən'tenʃəs/ *adj.* **1** likely to cause disagreement between people: *A critical and highly contentious issue is the distinction between freedom fighters and terrorists.* ◇ *Whether the onset of the Cold War after 1945 was inevitable remains contentious.* **2** involving a lot of arguing or disagreement: *A series of contentious negotiations took place over pricing issues.*

con·test¹ /kən'test/ *verb* **1 ~ sth** to formally disagree with a decision, statement or theory because you think it is wrong: *Participants must have the opportunity to contest the claims or ideas of others.* ◇ *Such research attempts to capture the contested nature of 'citizenship'.* **2** [usually passive] to enter an argument or fight about sth: **be contested** *The introduction of Western civilization in the region was fiercely contested.* ◇ **hotly/highly contested** *The relationship between firearms ownership rates and violent death rates is one of the most hotly contested issues under discussion.* **3 ~ sth** to take part in a competition, election, etc. and try to win it: *Two oppostion parties were banned from contesting the 2011 election.*

con·test² /'kɒntest; *NAmE* 'kɑːntest/ *noun* **1** a struggle to gain control or power: **~ between A and B** *In 2008, for the first time, the US presidential election became a contest between a non-white and a white candidate.* ◇ **~ for sth** *The confrontation was essentially a contest for supremacy between president and parliament.* ◇ **~ over sth** *The war then developed into a costly contest over the possession of Sevastopol.* ◇ **win/lose a ~** *D. basalis females were more aggressive and won most contests.* **2** a competition in which people's skill is tested: *Marsyas found a flute and challenged the god Apollo to a musical contest.*

con·text AWL /'kɒntekst; *NAmE* 'kɑːntekst/ *noun* [C, U] **1** the situation or set of circumstances in which sth happens and that helps you to understand it: *The first section sets the context by briefly reviewing the federalism literature.* ◇ **in/within a ~** *Interpretations of this phenomenon have varied in different cultural contexts and eras.* ◇ **the ~ in which...** *It is important to understand the larger context in which much of this research has taken place.* ◇ **in the ~ of sth** *Beliefs about health are rooted in the wider context of people's lives.* ◇ **in ~** *This decision can only be understood in context.* ◇ **out of ~** *This quotation has been taken out of context.* ◇ **out of its (...) ~** *The building should not be viewed out of its social context.* ◇ **~ for sth** *Arabian tribal society provided the context for the rise of Islam.* **2** the words that come just before and after a word, phrase or statement and help you to understand its meaning: *Which meaning of the word is intended has to be inferred from the context.* ◇ *Depending on the context, the word could stand in for 'clan', 'tribe', 'extended family' or 'nation'.* ◇ **in ~** *Pronunciation changes when words are spoken in isolation compared with when they are spoken in context.* ◇ **out of ~** *Carter claimed that the local newspaper story took his words out of context.*

▸ ADJECTIVE + CONTEXT **different, other • specific, particular • present • wider, broader, larger • global, international • national • local • social • historical • cultural • institutional • organizational • political • environmental • economic** *Today, popular culture is usually discussed in the broader context of globalization processes.*

▸ VERB + CONTEXT **provide, create, set • understand • examine, consider** *Three important factors set the context for research in disease ecology.*

▸ VERB + STH IN CONTEXT **understand • consider, view, examine, discuss, see • place, set** *Specific purchasing decisions are best understood in the long-term context of the relationship.*

con·text·ual AWL /kən'tekstʃuəl/ *adj.* connected with a particular context: *These case studies highlight that a variety of contextual factors can have a positive impact on outcomes.* ◇ *The practice of recruitment may be influenced by several contextual variables.* ◇ *Contextual information is required to make good strategic decisions about potential markets.*

con·text·ual·ize (*BrE also* **-ise**) AWL /kən'tekstʃuəlaɪz/ *verb* to consider sth in relation to the situation in which it happens or exists: **~ sth** *The novel contextualizes her life in a way which shows that nothing happens in isolation.* ◇ **~ sth within sth** *Demographic development needs to be properly contextualized within the wider sphere of environmental history.*

con·tin·ent /'kɒntɪnənt; *NAmE* 'kɑːntɪnənt/ *noun* **1** [C] one of the seven main continuous land masses of the earth (Africa, Asia, Australia, Antarctica, Europe and North and South America): *SARS demonstrated the speed at which infectious diseases can spread across continents.* ◇ **on the... ~** *A handful of new democracies emerged on the African continent during the 1990s.* ◇ **~ of sth** *In his famous speech in March 1946, Churchill spoke of an 'iron curtain' across the continent of Europe.* **2 the Continent** [sing.] (*BrE*) the main part of the continent of Europe, not including Britain or Ireland: **on the ~** *By 700 AD, numerous monasteries had been founded in England as well as on the Continent.*

con·tin·en·tal /ˌkɒntɪ'nentl; *NAmE* ˌkɑːntɪ'nentl/ *adj.* **1** forming part of or connected with any of the seven main land masses of the earth: *In these cases, the continental crust becomes thinner toward the oceans.* ◇ *Japan's location just off the coast of continental Asia would have a monumental influence on the country's history.* ◇ *Northern Greece has a more continental climate, with much colder and wetter winters, than the south.* **2** (*also* **Continental**) [only before noun] (*BrE*) of or in the continent of Europe, not including Britain and Ireland: *Pennington (1969, p.1) points out the comparative poverty of British flora, compared with that of continental Europe.*

ˌcontinental 'drift *noun* [U] (*earth science*) the slow movement of the continents towards and away from each other during the history of the earth: *Before the acceptance of continental drift, some geologists devised elaborate explanations for movement of fossils around the earth.* ⊃ *see also* PLATE TECTONICS

ˌcontinental 'shelf *noun* [usually sing.] (*earth science*) the area of land on the edge of a continent that slopes into the ocean: *The continental shelf of the Western Antarctic Peninsula extends some 200 km offshore.*

con·tin·gency /kən'tɪndʒənsi/ *noun* (*pl.* **-ies**) **1** [C] an event that may happen but that is not certain to happen: *It is mothers who are responsible for allocating family* resources, including reserves for unexpected contingencies. ◇ ~ **plan** *Each department has developed a contingency plan in case of gas or electricity failure.* **2** [C] ~ **(for sth)** something that is done or provided in case sth bad happens: *The airline saw its revenues fall by some 20% and the company made contingencies for total closure if the trend continued.* **3** [U] the fact of sth being uncertain, or of things in general being uncertain: *In the film we see not how identities are fixed, but their terrifying contingency.*

C

con·tin·gent¹ /kənˈtɪndʒənt/ *noun* [C+sing./pl. v.] **1** a group of soldiers that are part of a larger force: *Napoleon's invasion force was a multinational army that included contingents from Prussia and Austria.* **2** a group of people at a meeting or an event who have sth in common, especially the place they come from, that is not shared by the other groups: *The Japanese contingent at the G5 meeting was/were surprised by the way negotiations developed.*

con·tin·gent² /kənˈtɪndʒənt/ *adj.* **1** depending on sth that may or may not happen: ~ **on/upon sth** *Implementation of the reforms was contingent on the availability of sufficient funds.* ◇ *Bonuses were contingent upon performance.* **2** influenced by particular factors or by chance: *This review has shown the context dependence and contingent nature of recruitment practices.* ◇ *Arguably, almost all judgements on Saenger's work have been highly contingent and influenced by social, medical and political forces.* **3** ~ **worker/work** (*business*) a person who does not have a permanent contract with a company; work done by such a person: *Savings were achieved through the employment of increasing numbers of contingent workers.*

con·tin·ual /kənˈtɪnjuəl/ *adj.* [only before noun] **1** repeated many times SYN CONSTANT¹ (1): *There were continual efforts to render the sector more economically effective.* **2** continuing without interruption SYN CONTINUOUS (1): *The process of continual improvement is a never-ending cycle.* ◇ *Decision-making is viewed as a continual process which is reflected upon, learned and socially constructed.* ➲ *usage note at* CONTINUOUS

con·tinu·al·ly /kənˈtɪnjuəli/ *adv.* happening very often or all the time SYN CONSTANTLY: *Bacteria live in continually changing environments to which they must adapt for survival.* ◇ *Information collection, processing and storage technologies are continually improving.*

con·tinu·ation /kənˌtɪnjuˈeɪʃn/ *noun* **1** [U, sing.] an act or the state of continuing: ~ **of sth** *Political circumstances in Ethiopia have made continuation of this analysis difficult.* ◇ *Throughout the reign there was steady economic progress and a continuation of railway-building.* ◇ ~ **in sth** *Education is an important predictor of continuation in full-time employment.* **2** [C] ~ **of sth** something that continues or follows sth else: *War has become a continuation of economics by other means.* ◇ *In some respects, the thought of Emmanuel Levinas can be seen as a continuation of Buber's.* **3** [C] ~ **of sth** something that is joined on to sth else and forms a part of it: *The region was viewed as either a northern continuation of the Great American Desert or a southern continuation of the Arctic.*

con·tinue /kənˈtɪnjuː/ *verb* **1** [I, T] to keep existing or happening without stopping: *This situation is expected to continue for many years to come.* ◇ *The process will continue until the temperatures of the two systems are equal.* ◇ ~ **to do sth** *While the number of people in the world continues to grow, the pace of growth is slowing.* ◇ ~ **doing sth** *The children most likely to continue living in poverty included those from ethnic minority families.* **2** [T, I] to keep doing sth without stopping: ~ **sth** *After Pierre's death, Marie continued her work on the chemistry of radium.* ◇ ~ **doing sth** *The employer is obliged to consider the employee's request to continue working.* ◇ ~ **to do sth** *Despite growing awareness of the dangers of sunbeds, many men and women continue to use them regularly.* ◇ ~ **(with sth)** *The Czech Republic continued with its programme of privatization.* **3** [I] + **adv./prep.** to go or develop further in the same direction: *Both men continued down parallel paths of opposition to racism, poverty and war.* ◇ *Nothing was done for a year, during which the economy continued on its downward course.* ◇ *Europe continues along the path of integration.*

▸ CONTINUE + NOUN **work** • **studies** • **research** • **discussion** • **tradition** • **efforts** • **war** *He began working in the Vienna General Hospital, where he continued his brain research.*

▸ NOUN + CONTINUE **trend** • **process** • **debate** • **work** *If trends continue, there will be 71 million people living in the UK by 2031.*

▸ CONTINUE + ADVERB **indefinitely** *If caring is likely to continue indefinitely, a review date should be set.*

con·tinued /kənˈtɪnjuːd/ (*also* **con·tinu·ing** /kənˈtɪnjuɪŋ/) *adj.* [only before noun] existing in the same state without change or interruption; happening regularly: *The reforms were too few to halt the continued decline of the dynasty.* ◇ *The continued presence of visitors can adversely affect wildlife populations such as bats.* ◇ *Continuing developments in this field will almost certainly improve the safety of the treatment.*

con·tinu·ity /ˌkɒntɪˈnjuːəti; *NAmE* ˌkɑːntəˈnuːəti/ *noun* (*pl.* **-ies**) **1** [U] the fact of not stopping or not changing over a long period of time: *Institutions provide continuity and a sense of stability.* ◇ ~ **of sth** *Good written communication is essential in ensuring continuity of patient care.* OPP DISCONTINUITY (2) **2** [U, C] a logical connection between the parts of sth, or between two things: ~ **between A and B** *Marx emphasized the continuity between humans and nature.* ◇ ~ **of sth** *Darwin proposed a continuity of morphological and behavioural characteristics within the living world.* OPP DISCONTINUITY (1)

con·tinu·ous /kənˈtɪnjuəs/ *adj.* **1** happening or existing for a period of time without interruption SYN CONTINUAL (2): *Continuous monitoring of gases at volcanoes might help to predict volcanic eruptions.* ◇ *These standards provide a framework for continuous improvement in the quality of care patients receive.* ◇ *Reconciling conflicting interests within the Council is achieved through a continuous process of negotiation.* **2** forming a line or covering an area without any spaces: *Wastes are fed into the incinerator in batches or in a continuous stream.* ◇ *These DNA fragments will be eventually joined to form a continuous DNA strand.* **3** (*grammar*) = PROGRESSIVE¹ (5) **4** (*mathematics*) (of a function) of which the GRAPH is a smooth curve without any breaks: *A continuous function cannot go from negative to positive values without passing through zero.*

WHICH WORD?

continuous • continual

- **continuous** happening or existing for a period of time without interruption: *The brain generates a seemingly continuous stream of consciousness.* ◇ *continuous improvement/monitoring*
- **continual** repeated many times: *Clean energy policies require continual adjustment.*
- The difference between these two words is now disappearing. In particular, **continual** can mean the same as **continuous**: *He demanded continual improvement in innovations from his employees.* However, **continuous** is much more frequent in this meaning.

con·tinu·ous·ly /kənˈtɪnjuəsli/ *adv.* in a way that continues without change or interruption: *Life expectancy has increased continuously in Western countries.* ◇ *Both the birth rate and the death rate vary continuously.* ◇ *Heraclitus saw everything that exists in the world as part of some continuously changing process.*

con͵tinuous ˈvariable *noun* (*statistics*) a VARIABLE for which any value within a set range is possible: *Age was reported as a continuous variable.* ➲ *compare* CATEGORICAL VARIABLE

con·tinuum /kənˈtɪnjuəm/ *noun* (*pl.* **con·tinua** /kənˈtɪnjuə/) a series of similar items in which each is almost the same as the ones next to it but the last is very different from the first: *At one end of the continuum, the teacher had all the power and the student had none.* ◇ **on/along a ~** *The descriptive scale consists of a range of words on a continuum ranging from 'no pain' to 'severe pain'.* ◇ **~ of sth** *There is a continuum of different strengths of hydrogen bonding interactions throughout the sample.*

con·tour /ˈkɒntʊə(r); *NAmE* ˈkɑːntʊr/ *noun* **1 ~ (of sth)** the outer edges of sth; an outline representing the shape of sth: *Eighteenth-century roads were winding because they followed the contours of the landscape.* **2** a line on a map that joins points that are the same height; a line on a diagram that joins points that have the same value: *On a standard geographical map, each contour links all of the locations with the same altitude.* ◇ **+ noun** *In a contour plot, lines are drawn between points which have the same value.*

con·tra·cep·tion /͵kɒntrəˈsepʃn; *NAmE* ͵kɑːntrəˈsepʃn/ *noun* [U] the practice of preventing a woman from becoming pregnant; the methods of doing this SYN BIRTH CONTROL: *Attitudes towards contraception and abortion often reflect religious beliefs.* ◇ *There are over 215 million women worldwide who lack effective methods of contraception.*

con·tra·cep·tive /͵kɒntrəˈseptɪv; *NAmE* ͵kɑːntrəˈseptɪv/ *noun* a drug, device or practice used to prevent a woman from becoming pregnant: *Column 3 shows the numbers of women taking oral contraceptives.* ■ **con·tra·cep·tive** *adj.* [only before noun] *contraceptive use/methods/advice/services* ◇ *Much research has been conducted into the side effects of the combined oral contraceptive pill.*

con·tract¹ AWL /ˈkɒntrækt; *NAmE* ˈkɑːntrækt/ *noun* an official written agreement, especially one concerned with employment or selling sth: *The company admitted it had paid bribes to win contracts.* ◇ **~ with sb** *The book was withdrawn from sale and the author's contract with the publisher cancelled.* ◇ **~ between A and B** *A lease is essentially a contract between landlord and tenant.* ◇ **~ for sth** *Peter signed a contract for the purchase of the freezer.* ◇ **~ to do sth** *Firms compete against each other for short-term contracts to provide government services.* ◇ **on a... ~** *As chief executive he is employed on a fixed-term contract.* ◇ **+ noun** *There are more temporary and contract workers than there used to be.* ➲ *see also* SOCIAL CONTRACT

▸ ADJECTIVE + CONTRACT **permanent • long-term • fixed-term • temporary • short-term • valid • binding • enforceable • standard • formal • written** *When the parties enter into a lease, they are entering into a binding contract.*

▸ NOUN + CONTRACT **employment • marriage** *Those benefits are not part of a normal employment contract, but are provided by the employer.*

▸ VERB + CONTRACT **sign • conclude • enforce • negotiate • win, secure • award • enter • establish • make • terminate, cancel • breach, break** *The fundamental principle is that courts will not enforce an illegal contract.* ◇ *Two directors were dismissed from the board and their service contracts were terminated.*

▸ CONTRACT + NOUN **law • term • worker** *Cultures in the West rely on contract law to ensure that firms honour their obligations.*

con·tract² AWL /kənˈtrækt/ *verb* **1** [I, T] to become less or smaller; to make sth become less or smaller: *Changes in the temperature of the ocean cause the water to expand or contract.* ◇ *When companies are forced to contract, they often reduce costs by cutting staff.* ◇ **~ sth** *Electrical stimulation can be used if the patient cannot contract these muscles.* ◇ **~ sth to sth** *'Going to' tis often contracted to 'gonna'.* OPP EXPAND (1) **2** [T] to get an illness: **~ sth** *Homeless people are more at risk of contracting infectious diseases.* ◇ **~ sth from (doing) sth** *She contracted food poisoning from eating pork.* **3** [T, often passive, I] to make a legal agreement with sb for them to work for you or provide you with a service: **be contracted (by sb) (to do sth)** *The architects will be contracted to design a house type.* ◇ *She is currently part of a team contracted by the Home Office to evaluate the project.* ◇ *A Polish provider of building services was contracted in Germany.* ◇ **~ with sb (for sth)** *She would regularly contract with suppliers for the purchase of stock.* ◇ **~ with sb to do sth** *The defendants contracted with him to provide holiday accommodation for his family.* **4** [I] **~ to do sth** to make a legal agreement to work for sb or provide them with a service: *The labourers contracted to work for a certain period.* ◇ *Farmers contract to use government-owned land.* **5** [T] **~ a marriage/an alliance (with sb)** to formally agree to marry sb or form an ALLIANCE with sb: *At the end of the 20th century, marriages were still contracted at a relatively young age.* ◇ *Athens had probably contracted alliances with several Sicilian cities.*

PHR V **con͵tract ˈout (of sth)** (*BrE*) to formally agree that you will not take part in sth: *Employees have been encouraged to contract out of state pensions in favour of private schemes.* **con͵tract sth ˈout (to sb)** to arrange for work to be done by another company rather than your own: *Firms are increasingly contracting out services.* ◇ *The delivery of many public services has been contracted out to private firms.*

con·trac·tion /kənˈtrækʃn/ *noun* **1** [U, C] the process of becoming smaller: **~ of sth** *Subsidence may be caused by the gradual contraction of the sea floor.* ◇ **~ in sth** *An increase in price will usually lead to a contraction in demand.* OPP EXPANSION ➲ *compare* REDUCTION (1) **2** [C, U] **~ (of sth)** the process in which a muscle becomes or is made shorter and tighter: *Pain is likely to be due to abnormal contractions of the oesophagus.* ◇ *Raising the head from the floor will result in contraction of the abdominal muscles.* **3** [C] (*often* **contractions** [pl.]) a regular and painful contracting of the muscles around a woman's UTERUS that happens when she is giving birth to a child: *The hormone oxytocin triggers uterine contractions during childbirth.*

con·tract·or AWL /kənˈtræktə(r)/ *noun* a person or company that has a contract to do work or provide goods or services for another company: *Some companies outsource major parts of their manufacturing to independent contractors.* ◇ *The damage was due to the negligence of the electrical contractor.*

con·tract·ual /kənˈtræktʃuəl/ *adj.* connected with the conditions of a legal written agreement; agreed in a contract: *The court ruled that the agency had failed to fulfill its contractual obligations to the client.* ■ **con·trac·tu·al·ly** *adv.*: *The agreement was contractually binding between the members and the company.*

con·tra·dict AWL /͵kɒntrəˈdɪkt; *NAmE* ͵kɑːntrəˈdɪkt/ *verb* **1** (of statements or pieces of evidence) to be so different from each other that one of them must be wrong: **~ sth** *This finding contradicts the main hypothesis underlying the research.* ◇ **~ each other** *Some of the rules seem to contradict each other.* ◇ **~ what...** *Political candidates make a variety of claims that often contradict what they have said to another group.* OPP REINFORCE (1) **2** to say that sth that sb else has said is wrong, and that the opposite is true: **~ sth** *He had not been given the opportunity of correcting or contradicting any of the information.* ◇ *National policy was ignored or contradicted by politicians.* ◇ **~ sb/yourself** *I have said this problem has no available* *solution and will not contradict myself by proposing one.* ➲ thesaurus note *at* REJECT

con·tra·dic·tion AWL /ˌkɒntrəˈdɪkʃn; *NAmE* ˌkɑːntrəˈdɪkʃn/ *noun* **1** [C, U] a lack of agreement between facts, opinions or actions: *Women achieve a better education but earn less. Part of the explanation for this apparent contradiction is that more women hold part-time jobs.* ◇ **~ of sth** *The reform programme fell apart under the contradictions of Liberal policy.* ◇ **in ~ to sth** *The two approaches are in direct contradiction to each other.* ◇ **~ between A and B** *If there are contradictions between sources, then the historian has to decide which ones to believe.* **2** [U, C] the act of saying that sth that sb else has said is wrong or not true; an example of this: *That piece of information is not available for contradiction or confirmation.* ◇ *It may seem to be a contradiction to say that a thing can be both the same and different.*

IDM **a ˌcontradiction in ˈterms** a statement containing two words or phrases that contradict each other's meaning: *Higher education for the masses, Nietzsche says, is a contradiction in terms.*

con·tra·dict·ory AWL /ˌkɒntrəˈdɪktəri; *NAmE* ˌkɑːntrəˈdɪktəri/ *adj.* containing or showing a contradiction: *The initial studies led to conflicting and apparently contradictory conclusions.* ◇ *The relationship between the overuse of resources and globalization is complex and sometimes contradictory.*

con·trary[1] AWL /ˈkɒntrəri; *NAmE* ˈkɑːntreri/ *adj.* **1** different from sth; against sth: **~ to sth** *Contrary to expectations, a majority of recent immigrants do not live in concentrated ethnic zones.* ◇ *Contrary to what you might expect, it is the absolute size of a sample that is important, not its relative size.* ◇ **it is ~ to sth (to do sth)** *It is contrary to European Union law to require women to resign from the armed forces upon becoming pregnant.* **2** [only before noun] completely different in nature or direction: *A number of historians have taken the contrary view.* ◇ *He could override anyone who attempted to present contrary evidence.* ➲ *compare* OPPOSITE[1] (1)

IDM **ˌcontrary to popular beˈlief** opposite to what most people believe: *Contrary to popular belief, the Tasmanians did not become extinct.*

con·trary[2] AWL /ˈkɒntrəri; *NAmE* ˈkɑːntreri/ *noun* **the contrary** [sing.] the opposite fact, event or situation: *It should be assumed that public authorities will always act reasonably unless the contrary is proved.*

IDM **on the ˈcontrary** used to introduce a statement that says the opposite of the last one: *Most Greeks and Romans did not believe that their gods were the only gods. On the contrary, they were sure that all peoples had their own gods.* **ˌquite the ˈcontrary** used to emphasize that the opposite of what has been said is true: *This does not mean that women were absent from Jesus's ministry. Quite the contrary: women feature in the Gospel stories on a regular basis.* **to the ˈcontrary** showing or proving the opposite: *Delusions are held firmly despite evidence to the contrary.* ◇ *Despite advice to the contrary, Eisenhower refused to initiate tax cuts in the midst of the recession.*

con·trast[1] AWL /ˈkɒntrɑːst; *NAmE* ˈkɑːntræst/ *noun* **1** [C, U] a difference between two or more people or things that you can see clearly when they are compared or put close together; the fact of comparing two or more things in order to show the differences between them: **~ between A and B** *Striking contrasts were observed between the two populations.* ◇ **~ in sth** *The boundary between the sea and land air can be very sharp, with marked contrasts in temperature and humidity.* ◇ **~ with sb/sth** *The contrast with Malthus is clear: Malthus saw population as dependent on food supply; Boserup reversed this relationship.* ◇ **by ~** *Having two or more children decreases a woman's time in employment. By contrast, fathers' employment does not decline.* ◇ **in ~** *Negative feedback may lead to the student abandoning the task altogether. In contrast, positive feedback contributes to successful task performance.* ◇ **in ~ to/with sb/sth** *In contrast to the situation in poor countries, agricultural output is a small fraction of national income in the rich world.* ➲ language bank *at* COMPARE **2** [C, usually sing.] a person or thing that is clearly different from sb/sth else: **~ to sb/sth** *Their case studies are a contrast to previous research.* ◇ **~ with sb/sth** *This situation represents a dramatic contrast with the policy stances of 80 years ago.* **3** [U] the amount of difference between light and dark in a photograph or the picture on a screen: *Closing the aperture diaphragm increases the contrast in the image seen through the microscope.* **4** [C, U] differences in colour or in light and dark, used in photographs and paintings to create a special effect: *Wetting of exposures with a fine spray of water can help bring out colour contrasts.* ◇ *The artist's use of contrast is masterly.*

▸ ADJECTIVE + CONTRAST **stark, sharp, marked, strong** • **striking, dramatic** • **clear** • **direct** *The US model's potential for job creation stands in stark contrast to Europe's struggle to create jobs.*

▸ VERB + CONTRAST **draw** • **emphasize** *The speaker draws a clear contrast between Europe and his own country.* | **provide, offer, present** *The post-1990 Japanese economy provides a dramatic contrast to that of the United States.*

▸ IN CONTRAST TO + NOUN **situation** • **finding** • **view** • **study** *Technically trained personnel moved into management positions within German industry, in contrast to the situation in Great Britain.*

con·trast[2] AWL /kənˈtrɑːst; *NAmE* kənˈtræst/ *verb* **1** [T, often passive] to compare two things in order to show the differences between them: **A is contrasted with B** *The social market economy can be contrasted with the free market economy.* ◇ **A and B are contrasted** *To illustrate this point, two well-known cases can be contrasted.* **2** [I] to show a clear difference when close together or when compared: *The impact of the Afghani and Peruvian reports contrasted strongly.* ◇ **~ with sth** *The agency's stance on organics contrasted sharply with its more positive stance on GM food.* ◇ *to contrast starkly/markedly with sth*

con·trast·ing AWL /kənˈtrɑːstɪŋ; *NAmE* kənˈtræstɪŋ/ *adj.* [usually before noun] very different in style, colour or attitude: *Differences in teaching style reflected contrasting views about teaching.* ◇ *Successful advertising comes from two contrasting styles of problem-solving.*

con·trast·ive AWL /kənˈtrɑːstɪv; *NAmE* kənˈtræstɪv/ *adj.* showing the differences clearly, especially the differences between languages: *This approach allows more detailed contrastive analysis of specific language situations.*

con·tra·vene /ˌkɒntrəˈviːn; *NAmE* ˌkɑːntrəˈviːn/ *verb* **~ sth** to do sth that is not allowed by a law or rule; to go against a right or principle SYN INFRINGE: *The Commission considered that the restrictions contravened Article 28.* ◇ *The Court of Appeal held that the government decision contravened residents' human rights.* ■ **con·tra·ven·tion** /ˌkɒntrəˈvenʃn; *NAmE* ˌkɑːntrəˈvenʃn/ *noun* [U, C] SYN INFRINGEMENT: **~ of sth** *Breach of this requirement will constitute a contravention of the Data Protection Act 1998.* ◇ **in ~ (of sth)** *Regulations which removed benefit for asylum seekers were ruled to be in contravention of the Immigration Appeals Act 1993.*

con·trib·ute AWL /kənˈtrɪbjuːt; *BrE also* ˈkɒntrɪbjuːt/ *verb* **1** [I] **~ (to sth)** to be one of the causes of sth: *Poor care was felt to have contributed to the patient's death.* ◇ *It seems clear that poverty is the biggest single factor contributing to the spread of AIDS.* ◇ *Overuse of antibiotics has been a major contributing factor to the development of resistant bacteria.* **2** [I, T] to help to improve or achieve sth, especially by adding new ideas: **~ to sth** *Geographers have contributed to an improved understanding of African rural systems.* ◇ **~ sth to sth** *What historians can best* *contribute to modern politics is a cautionary note.* **3** [T, I] to give sth, especially money or goods, to help sb/sth: **~ sth (to/towards sth)** *19 million people a year visit Liverpool, contributing £381.5 million to the local economy.* ◇ **~ (to/towards sth)** *Even poor communities are often willing to contribute towards the cost of education.* ➲ *compare* DONATE (1) **4** [T, I] to write sth for a newspaper, magazine, website, or a radio or television programme; to speak during a meeting or conversation, especially to give your opinion: **~ sth** *The discussion was open and all the participants actively contributed their ideas.* ◇ **~ sth to sth** *Several researchers contributed chapters to the first edition of the book.* ◇ **~ (to sth)** *The facilitator is free to ensure that each individual has the opportunity to contribute.* ➲ *compare* PARTICIPATE

THESAURUS

contribute • donate • support *verb*

These words all mean to give money or goods to help sb/sth.

- to contribute/donate (sth) **to** sth
- to contribute/donate **money**
- to contribute/donate **$5 million, etc.**
- to support (a) **development/programme**
- to contribute/support (sth) **financially**

- **Contribute** suggests that a number of people or groups are giving money to a charity or a fund; **donate** places the emphasis on an individual person or organization that has given sth: *Even poor communities are often willing to contribute towards the cost of education.* ◇ *The developer pledged to donate 1% of gross revenues to support on-site research.*
- You **contribute** or **donate** an amount of money to a charity or a fund; you **support** a charity, a cause, a programme, etc. by giving money or other help, especially over a period of time: *The company provides funds for these works by donating a percentage of a product's sales to the cause.* ◇ *Immunization programmes in developing countries, supported by the WHO, have had a major impact on infant mortality rates.*

See also the Thesaurus note at **fund**.

con·tri·bu·tion AWL /ˌkɒntrɪˈbjuːʃn; *NAmE* ˌkɑːntrɪˈbjuːʃn/ *noun* **1** [usually sing.] the part played by a person or thing in achieving, improving or causing sth: *This is a case where publicity can make an important contribution.* ◇ **~ of sth** *Figure 8.13 indicates the relative contribution of emissions of different greenhouse gases.* ◇ **~ to sth** *Fast-growing small businesses make a direct contribution to economic growth.* ◇ **~ towards (doing) sth** *The case made a considerable contribution towards clarifying the situation concerning professional sport.* **2** a sum of money that is given to a person or an organization in order to help pay for sth SYN DONATION: *Even 'public' radio and TV now depend heavily on corporate contributions.* ◇ **~ to sth** *Corporations attempt to cultivate a good image by making contributions to charities.* ◇ **~ towards (doing) sth** *Over half a million people in the UK make a regular financial contribution towards Oxfam's work.* **3 ~ (to sth)** an item that forms part of a book, magazine, broadcast, discussion, etc: *His paper is an interesting contribution to the debate.* **4** a sum of money that you pay regularly to your employer or the government in order to pay for benefits such as health insurance or a PENSION: **~ (to sth)** *Households save for their retirement by making contributions to a fund that consists of bonds and equities.* ◇ **+ noun** *In these schemes, contribution rates are fixed at a level that should not be exceeded.*

▸ ADJECTIVE + CONTRIBUTION **important, significant • major, key • valuable • positive • great, substantial, large • small • direct • main • potential • unique • original • relative** *Biomass could make a significant contribution to global energy demand.* ◇ *Entrepreneurs and small businesses make a positive contribution to job generation.*

▸ VERB + CONTRIBUTION **make** *Screening could make a major contribution to population health.* ◇ *People in health promotion can continue to make contributions to scholarly journals.* | **recognize, acknowledge, identify • assess • examine • represent** *Young carers often feel that their contribution is not recognized or respected.*

▸ CONTRIBUTION TO + NOUN **understanding, knowledge • literature • scholarship • field • theory • development** *His study represents a qualitative contribution to our understanding of German society.*

con·tribu·tor AWL /kənˈtrɪbjətə(r)/ *noun* **1 ~ (to sth)** something that helps to cause sth: *Environmental and lifestyle factors are major contributors to gastric cancer.* ◇ *Polluted water is a very important contributor to the world water crisis.* **2 ~ (to sth)** a person or thing that provides money to help pay for sth or support sth: *The UK remains a large net contributor to the EU budget.* ◇ *Information technology is an important contributor to economic growth in modern economies.* ◇ *Both companies were major contributors to the Conservative Party.* ➲ *compare* DONOR (1), SUPPORTER (1) **3 ~ (to sth)** a person who writes articles for a magazine, book or website, or who talks on a radio or television programme or at a meeting: *He became a regular contributor to the influential liberal newspaper the 'Morning Chronicle'.*

con·tribu·tory /kənˈtrɪbjətəri; *NAmE* kənˈtrɪbjətɔːri/ *adj.* [usually before noun] **1** helping to cause sth: *Contributory factors for weight increase include age and lower income.* ◇ *Hypertension is a likely contributory cause in any stroke.* ◇ *The report stressed that genes play only a contributory role in human behaviour.* HELP In law, **contributory negligence** refers to NEGLIGENCE that helped to cause an accident: *In contributory negligence, the claimant is referred to as having 'contributed to his/her own misfortune'.* **2** involving payments from the people who will benefit: *EU citizens will have equal rights to the full spectrum of contributory and non-contributory social benefits.*

con·trol¹ /kənˈtrəʊl; *NAmE* kənˈtroʊl/ *noun* **1** [U] the power to direct how a company, a country, etc. is run or to influence a process or a course of events: *When the Spanish authorities finally lost control, a republic was declared.* ◇ **~ of sth** *Many sea battles were fought to win control of the spice trade.* ◇ **~ over sth** *Freedom in the economic realm meant control over productive resources.* ◇ *Earthquakes are governed by the forces of plate tectonics, over which human beings currently have no control.* ◇ **under sb/sth's ~** *For much of the post-war period, the economy was under tight government control.* ◇ **subject to sth's/... ~** *Local government is subject to central control.* ◇ **beyond sb/sth's ~** *In most cases of restructuring, these changes in work will be beyond the control of most employees.* ➲ thesaurus note *at* LIMIT² **2** [U, C] (often in compounds) the act of restricting, limiting or managing sth; a method of doing this: *The next section deals with the system of immigration control.* ◇ *Stringent air pollution controls have been implemented in recent decades.* ◇ **~ of sth** *Herbicides are used for the control of weeds where other methods are difficult or impractical.* ◇ **~ on sth** *Strict controls on immigration were introduced between 1962 and 1971.* ➲ *see also* BIRTH CONTROL, QUALITY CONTROL ➲ thesaurus note *at* LIMIT² **3** [U] the ability to manage your emotions or actions: *High scorers reported emotional turmoil and fear of losing control.* ◇ **~ of/over sth/yourself** *An enraged child needs help in gaining control over the physical reactions that accompany anger.* ➲ *see also* SELF-CONTROL **4** [C] (often in compounds) a person, group or thing used as a standard of comparison for checking the results of a survey or an experiment; an experiment whose result is known, used for checking working methods: *For both tests, positive and negative controls are essential and must give expected reactions before interpretation is made.* ◇

C

+ noun *The volunteers were divided into an untreated control group and a study group treated with injections of the antibody.* **5** [U, C] a place where checks are made; the people who make these checks: *On arrival at Heathrow airport, she passed through immigration control on her own passport.* ◇ *As the EU's internal border controls are removed, cooperation between the judicial authorities beomes much more important.* **6** [C, usually pl.] the switches and buttons, etc. that you use to operate a machine or a vehicle: *Pilots may choose to operate the aircraft's manual flight controls.* **7** [U] (*also* **con'trol key** [sing.]) (on a computer keyboard) a key that you press when you want to perform a particular operation: *Important keys like enter, shift, control and space are often made larger than other keys to make it easy to hit them.*

IDM **be in control (of sth)** to direct or manage a situation, an area or an organization: *You are in control, taking the lead and making decisions.* **be in control (of sth/ of yourself)** to be able to keep calm: *She was in control of herself at all times.* **be out of con'trol** to be impossible to manage or control: *There may be times when your child is completely out of control.* **be under con'trol** to be being dealt with successfully: *Unemployment was under control in Sweden.* **bring/get/keep sth under con'trol** to succeed in dealing with sth so that it does not cause any damage or hurt anyone: *Smallpox was brought under control in the early nineteenth-century Caribbean.* ◇ *UN peacekeeping has arguably helped keep crises under control and prevent recurrence of conflict.*

▸ ADJECTIVE + CONTROL **tight, strict • internal • external • financial** *Chilean business groups exercise tight control of all companies.* ◇ *Concerns were raised about the company's internal financial controls.* | **effective • greater • complete • direct • central • local • social • political • managerial • corporate** *Another aspect of informal social control was that people often felt secure because they knew each other.* ◇ *Managerial control over technology can lead to surveillance and control of employees.* | **positive • negative • healthy • matched** *The group also included healthy control participants.*

▸ NOUN + CONTROL **government, state • management** *By the late 1980s, state control of industry in Hungary was being eroded.* | **government • quality • pollution • immigration • birth • gun • arms • tobacco • infection** *Policies included an end to government controls on incomes, prices and dividends.*

▸ VERB + CONTROL **gain • lose** *Greeks from the mainland gained control of Crete.* ◇ *An adolescent may fear losing control of his anger.* | **take, seize, assume • assert • have • exercise, exert • achieve • regain, reestablish • retain, maintain • relinquish • escape • tighten** *Students may start to take control of their own learning.* ◇ *In 1630, the Dutch seized control of the area around Pernambuco.* | **impose • implement, introduce • tighten** *The aim was to protect endangered species by imposing controls on international trade in those species.*

▸ CONTROL + NOUN **group • participant • variable • measure** *The control group consisted of 248 subjects.*

con·trol² /kən'trəʊl; *NAmE* kən'troʊl/ *verb* (-ll-) **1** to have power over a person, company, country, process, etc. so that you are able to decide what they must do or how it is run: **~ sb/sth** *Technically, the people who control the company are the shareholders.* ◇ *This cartel controlled production and prices of crude oil.* ◇ *This mating system depends on the ability of the males to control access to essential resources.* ◇ **~ what/how, etc...** *Increasingly, the non-farm sector of the food supply system is controlling what people are able to consume and eat.* **2 ~ sth** to limit the number, level or strength of sth, usually sth negative: *The government was committed to controlling inflation.* ◇ *Treatment can delay or control symptoms.* ◇ *Tools to control vertebrate pests include snares, traps and toxins.* **3** to make sth, such as a machine or system, work in a particular way SYN REGULATE (1): **~ sth (by sth)** *We controlled the water flow by a valve at the lower end of the tube.* ◇ **~ sth (through sth)** *Many endocrine functions are controlled through neurotransmitters.* ◇ **~ where/when, etc...** *Genes control cell behaviour by controlling where and when proteins are synthesized.* **4 ~ sth/yourself** to manage to make yourself remain calm, even though you are upset or angry: *Withdrawal controls anger by avoiding the situation.*

PHR V **con'trol for sth** to consider factors which are not important in your research but which may influence the results of an experiment or survey: *We control for the age difference in the couple.* ◇ *Researchers found that, controlling for size, small firms innovated more.*

▸ CONTROL + NOUN **company • access • production • operation • movement** *This section addresses the key issues involved in managing and controlling global marketing operations.* | **level • number • rate • symptoms • disease • pain • emissions • pests • population** *In order to control CO_2 emissions, policy makers can use taxes or permits.* | **behaviour • activity • process • development • rate • flow • level** *Living organisms need to be able to control the rates of different chemical processes.*

▸ NOUN + CONTROL **genes • proteins • hormones • factors** *This process of cell division is highly controlled by several genes.*

▸ ADVERB + CONTROL **tightly, strictly • easily • effectively** *Iron levels must be tightly controlled as high levels can be toxic.* | **carefully • closely • directly • centrally • largely** *The reaction is carefully controlled.* ◇ *Male elders closely control life within and outside the family.* | **well • precisely** *By gathering participants in a dedicated room, the experiment precisely controls the decision-making environment.* | **poorly • adequately** *Fertility may be impaired in poorly controlled diabetes.*

con·trolled /kən'trəʊld; *NAmE* kən'troʊld/ *adj.* **1** (of a survey method) that uses a group of people who are not given the treatment that is being studied, so that the results may be compared with the group receiving treatment: *Twelve randomized controlled trials were reviewed by Wilk et al.* HELP A **controlled trial** tests how effective a drug or treatment is. A control group of people is given either a PLACEBO, standard treatment or no treatment. The results are compared with the group that receives the treatment being tested. **2** that considers factors that are not important to the research but which may influence the results of an experiment or survey: *We conducted two controlled experiments.* HELP In a **controlled experiment**, VARIABLES that are not important to the study, but which may influence the DEPENDENT VARIABLE, are controlled. **3** done or arranged in a very careful way: *It is a carefully controlled environment in which the seeds get uniform illumination and uniform nutrient solution.* **4** managed by sth: *Reproductive function in both sexes is a controlled process involving hormones.* **5 -controlled** (in compounds) managed in a particular way: *a British-controlled company* ◇ *computer-controlled systems* ◇ *Remotely controlled machines enable tunnels below man-entry size to be constructed.*

con·trol·ler /kən'trəʊlə(r); *NAmE* kən'troʊlər/ *noun* **1** a person or thing that manages or directs sth: *Air traffic controllers work in a highly programmed context.* ◇ *The data controller is responsible for determining how personal data will be used.* ◇ **~ of sth** *The state still holds the dominant position as the controller of business groups in China.* **2** a device that controls a machine or process: *The temperature of the heating chamber was regulated by a temperature controller.* ◇ *The controller reads and controls the flow of gases.* **3** a person who is in charge of the financial accounts of a business or an organization: *Financial management is the responsibility of the financial controllers.*

con·trol·ling /kən'trəʊlɪŋ; *NAmE* kən'troʊlɪŋ/ *adj.* [only before noun] having power over a company so that you are able to decide how it is run: *Table 14.7 shows that* *controlling shareholders hold more equity than is needed for control.* ◇ *The group purchased a controlling interest in the company.*

conˈtrol variable *noun* (*statistics*) a VARIABLE that remains the same in an experiment in order to test the relative effects of INDEPENDENT VARIABLES: *Smoking and body mass index (BMI) were considered as control variables.*

con·tro·ver·sial AWL /ˌkɒntrəˈvɜːʃl; *NAmE* ˌkɑːntrəˈvɜːrʃl/ *adj.* causing a lot of angry public discussion and disagreement SYN CONTENTIOUS (1): *Nuclear power is a controversial issue in South Africa and remains politically unpopular.* ◇ *Treatment with this drug remains highly controversial.* OPP UNCONTROVERSIAL ■ **con·tro·ver·sial·ly** AWL /ˌkɒntrəˈvɜːʃəli; *NAmE* ˌkɑːntrəˈvɜːrʃəli/ *adv.*: *More controversially, DNA analysis is increasingly being used to define species.*

con·tro·versy AWL /ˈkɒntrəvɜːsi; kənˈtrɒvəsi; *NAmE* ˈkɑːntrəvɜːrsi/ *noun* (*pl.* **-ies**) [U, C] public discussion and argument about sth that many people strongly disagree about, disapprove of, or are shocked by: *His work generated considerable controversy in the 1970s and 1980s.* ◇ *Chomsky's early work sparked intense controversies in academic linguistics.* ◇ **~ over/about sb/sth** *There is controversy over how long a patient should stay on an antidepressant for.* ◇ **~ surrounding sb/sth** *The aim of this paper is to summarize the issues and controversies surrounding these questions.* ➲ *compare* DISAGREEMENT, DISPUTE[1] ➲ thesaurus note *at* DEBATE[1]

con·vec·tion /kənˈvekʃn/ *noun* [U] (*physics*) the process in which heat moves through a gas or a liquid as the hotter part rises and the cooler, heavier part sinks: *As the water is cooled, it will undergo thermal convection and descend, forcing deeper warmer water to the surface.* ◇ **+ noun** *Heating can increase the diffusion of molecules in the sample and may also cause convection currents.*

con·vene AWL /kənˈviːn/ *verb* **1** [T] to arrange for people to come together for a meeting or an activity SYN SUMMON: **~ sth/sb** *The court convened a meeting of the company's creditors.* ◇ *The inquest was convened by the coroner.* ◇ **~ sth/sb to do sth** *Johnson convened congressional leaders to discuss the crisis.* **2** [I] to come together for a formal meeting SYN ASSEMBLE: *The groups convene regularly in Brussels.*

con·veni·ence /kənˈviːniəns/ *noun* **1** [U] the quality of being useful, easy or suitable for sb: *Consumers typically purchase products on the basis of price, convenience and quality.* ◇ *Current practice may still be shaped around administrative convenience.* ◇ **for ~** *Responses to these questions may be divided for convenience into three rough groups.* ◇ **+ noun** *A convenience sample is one that is simply available to the researcher by virtue of its accessibility.* **2** [C] something that is useful and can make things easier or quicker to do, or more comfortable: *XML namespaces are a convenience that prevents us from having to repeatedly type a lengthy URI.*

con·veni·ent /kənˈviːniənt/ *adj.* useful, easy or quick to do; not causing problems: *Tables are a convenient way of listing a large amount of numerical data.* ◇ *a convenient method/means* ◇ *Voters benefit from voting at a convenient time and place.* ◇ **~ for sb/sth** *Self-completion questionnaires are more convenient for respondents.* ◇ **~ to do** *Those with digital displays are easier and more convenient to use.* ◇ **it is ~ to do sth** *It is convenient to divide the instructions into two types.* ■ **con·veni·ent·ly** *adv.*: *The atmosphere can be conveniently divided into four sections.* ◇ *Conveniently, cells for cloning can be moved long distances, and even frozen for later use.*

con·ven·tion AWL /kənˈvenʃn/ *noun* **1** [C, U] a particular system for analysing or calculating sth; the accepted way of doing sth: *I have adopted the WHO convention in categorizing age into bands.* ◇ *Their disregard for social convention seemed to threaten the fabric of society.* ◇ **by ~** *By convention, the term 'tremolite' is applied to samples having greater than 90 per cent Mg.* **2** [C] an official agreement between countries or leaders SYN AGREEMENT: *In 1973, an international convention was agreed to prevent intentional oil pollution from ships.* **3** [C] **~ (of sb/sth)** a large meeting of the members of a particular group, political party or profession SYN CONFERENCE: *The European Council held a convention of national and EU-level politicians to draft a new treaty.* **4 Convention** [C] an official group that is set up for a particular purpose: *The Annapolis Convention recommended that...* **5** [C, U] **~ (of sth)** a traditional style or method in literature, art or the theatre: *In his poetry and essays, Yeats draws on the conventions of English pastoral.* ◇ *In 'Canada: A Descriptive Poem' (1806), Bayley's diction followed British poetic convention.*

con·ven·tion·al AWL /kənˈvenʃənl/ *adj.* **1** [usually before noun] based on what is generally believed; following the way sth is usually done: *This paper challenges the conventional wisdom about how useful the product life-cycle is.* ◇ *In the conventional sense of leadership in foreign affairs, the EU is politically weak.* ◇ *conventional methods/approaches* ◇ *conventional medicine/treatment* ◇ **~ in sth** *The methodology used here is conventional in the field of economics.* ◇ **it is ~ to do sth** *It is conventional to classify semiconductors with low electrical conductivities as insulators.* **2** (*often disapproving*) tending to follow what is done or considered acceptable by society in general; normal and ordinary, and perhaps not very interesting: *These women refused to be confined to the conventional roles of wife and mother.* ◇ *Their attitude is very conventional.* OPP UNCONVENTIONAL **3** [usually before noun] (especially of weapons) not nuclear: *This strategy relied heavily on nuclear weapons, without the need to maintain large conventional military forces.* **4** (of literature, art or the theatre) using a traditional style or method: *Wollstonecraft pointedly alters the conventional romance plot.*

con·ven·tion·al·ly AWL /kənˌvenʃənəli/ *adv.* according to what is generally believed or usually done: *There are two main sources of acids, conventionally defined as metabolic acids or respiratory acids.* ◇ *Conventionally, population density is arithmetic density: the total number of people in a unit area.*

con·verge /kənˈvɜːdʒ; *NAmE* kənˈvɜːrdʒ/ *verb* **1** [I] (of two or more lines or paths) to move towards each other and meet at a point: *Lines of longitude converge at the poles and are farthest apart at the equator.* OPP DIVERGE (1) **2** [I] **~ (on...)** (of people, animals or vehicles) to move towards a place from different directions and meet: *Female turtles converge on particular beaches to deposit their eggs.* **3** [I] (of ideas, policies or aims) to become very similar or the same: *National interests might converge and become the basis for cooperation.* ◇ *The market for detergents in different European countries has gradually converged.* OPP DIVERGE (3)

con·ver·gence /kənˈvɜːdʒəns; *NAmE* kənˈvɜːrdʒəns/ *noun* **1** [U, sing.] the state or process of moving together or becoming similar: **~ of A and B** *The narrow peninsula is formed by the convergence of the two rivers.* ◇ **~ towards sth** *A global society will develop with an increasing convergence towards one type of welfare policy.* HELP In biology, **convergence** refers to the tendency of animals or plants that are not related to EVOLVE similar characteristics if they have experienced similar environmental conditions: *There has been evolutionary convergence in the body colour of penguins.* HELP In economics, **convergence** refers to the tendency of poorer economies to grow faster than richer economies, so that, in theory, poorer and richer economies will eventually converge to the same level of OUTPUT per worker: *The hypothesis of absolute*

C

C

convergence is that countries with lower levels of output per worker grow faster than those with higher levels, and therefore converge to the same living standards. OPP DIVERGENCE **2** [U] a place where ocean CURRENTS or air flows meet: **~ (of sth)** *Precipitation associated with this convergence and uplift of the air is called cyclonic precipitation.* ◇ **+ noun** *The convergence zone in the East Pacific remains close to the equator throughout the year.* HELP In earth science, **convergence** also refers to the COLLISION of two TECTONIC plates: *During convergence between two tectonic plates, the plate bearing denser oceanic crust is liable to be forced below the one bearing less-dense continental crust.*

con·ver·gent /kənˈvɜːdʒənt; *NAmE* kənˈvɜːrdʒənt/ *adj.* coming closer together: *Three smaller studies showed convergent results.* ◇ *We were able to vary the degree by which the electrons are focused, allowing the beam to be convergent or divergent.* ◇ *Responses to similar factors occur in very distantly related animals, suggesting convergent evolution.* HELP In biology, **convergent** EVOLUTION occurs when animals or plants that are not related but have experienced similar environmental conditions EVOLVE similar characteristics: *There are difficulties in determining which similarities are the result of shared ancestry and which are merely superficial cases of convergent evolution.* HELP In earth science, **convergent** describes TECTONIC plates that COLLIDE with each other: *Mountains are thought to be created along convergent plate boundaries in at least four major ways.* OPP DIVERGENT

con·ver·sa·tion /ˌkɒnvəˈseɪʃn; *NAmE* ˌkɑːnvərˈseɪʃn/ *noun* [C, U] an informal talk involving a small group of people or only two; the activity of talking in this way: *a phone/telephone conversation* ◇ **~ (with sb) (about sth)** *I had informal conversations with parents about their hopes and aspirations for their children.* ◇ *For many English speakers, making conversation involves filling any gaps with talk in order to avoid silences.* ◇ *Even today the major topics of conversation between both men and women can be classified as 'gossip'.* ◇ **in ~ (with sb)** *In conversation with Gorbachev, Zhao had revealed the existence of the secret agreement.*

con·ver·sa·tion·al /ˌkɒnvəˈseɪʃənl; *NAmE* ˌkɑːnvərˈseɪʃənl/ *adj.* **1** not formal; as used in conversation: *Collins is noted for his conversational style and personal choice of subject matter.* **2** [only before noun] connected with conversation; consisting of conversation: *The book is aimed at students interested in improving their conversational skills.* ◇ *Plato's works are in conversational form.*

the **con·verse** AWL /ˈkɒnvɜːs; *NAmE* ˈkɑːnvɜːrs/ *noun* **1 ~ (of sth)** the opposite of a fact or statement: *This section has focused on the effects of hormones on behaviour. However, the converse is also is true: behaviour affects hormone secretions.* **2 ~ (of sth)** (*mathematics*) a THEOREM whose HYPOTHESIS and conclusion are the conclusion and hypothesis of another theorem: *The statement 'Q implies P' is the converse of the statement 'P implies Q'.* ■ **converse** *adj.*: *There were effects of agricultural transformation on ecosystems, and converse effects of ecosystems on agricultural transformation.*

con·verse·ly AWL /ˈkɒnvɜːsli; *NAmE* ˈkɑːnvɜːrsli/ *adv.* in a way that is the opposite of sth: *Figure 3.2 shows how the pH changes as a strong acid is slowly added to a strong base; or, conversely, if a strong base is added to a strong acid.* ◇ *A physically large system is not necessarily complex. Conversely, even a small system can be complex.*

con·ver·sion AWL /kənˈvɜːʃn; *NAmE* kənˈvɜːrʒn; kənˈvɜːrʃn/ *noun* **1** [U, C] the process or act of changing sth from one form, use or system to another: **~ of sth (into/to sth)** *Photosynthesis is the mechanism of conversion of light energy into useful chemical energy.* ◇ **~ from sth (into/to sth)** *The greatest obstacle to conversion from traditional schools to extended-service schools is funding.* ◇ **~ (to sth)** *We report results using local currency units, but also make conversions to US dollars.* **2** [U, C] the process or experience of changing your religion, beliefs or way of life: *Religious conversion put women in a place of intensely divided loyalties.* ◇ **~ to sth** *Even leading communists had begun announcing their conversion to nationalism.* ◇ *The number of conversions to Christianity drastically decreased.*

con·vert¹ AWL /kənˈvɜːt; *NAmE* kənˈvɜːrt/ *verb* **1** [T, I] to change the form, use or character of sth; to change from one form, purpose or system to another: **~ sth into sth** *A fuel cell converts chemical energy into electrical energy.* ◇ **~ sth to sth** *Low coastal wetlands, usually converted to farming, were eroded.* ◇ **~ sth from sth (into/to sth)** *Land is increasingly being converted from forests and pasture into cropland.* ◇ **~ sth back into/to sth** *During rest, the lactic acid is converted back to glycogen.* ◇ **~ to sth** *The networks were faced with steadily eroding audiences and the heavy costs of converting to digital TV.* **2** [I] **~ into/to sth** to be able to change or be changed from one form or purpose to another: *A neutron converts into a proton with the emission of an electron.* **3** [I, T] to change or make sb change their religion, beliefs or way of life: **~ (from sth) (to sth)** *Protestant Henry IV converted to Catholicism in 1598 to assume the crown of France.* ◇ *The last ruler from the Constantinian dynasty converted from Christianity to paganism.* ◇ **~ sb (from sth) (to sth)** *Among the preachers who cared about converting slaves to Christianity, no one was more effective than George Whitefield.*
PHR V **convert sb to sth** to persuade sb to support a particular idea: *He sought to convert professionals, bureaucrats and intellectuals to his cause.*

con·vert² AWL /ˈkɒnvɜːt; *NAmE* ˈkɑːnvɜːrt/ *noun* a person who has changed their religion, beliefs or way of life: *Vegetarians in western cultures, in most instances, are not life-long practitioners but converts.* ◇ **~ to sth** *He was a young Chinook convert to Christianity.* ◇ **~ from sth (to sth)** *Barlaam of Calabria was a convert from eastern to western Christianity.*

con·vert·er /kənˈvɜːtə(r); *NAmE* kənˈvɜːrtər/ *noun* a device that changes sth into a different form: *After the onset of agriculture, new forms of energy converter were developed, for example the watermill.* ◇ *Catalytic converters were first fitted to cars in the 1970s in order to reduce air pollution in Los Angeles (Kendall, 2004).*

con·vert·ible AWL /kənˈvɜːtəbl; *NAmE* kənˈvɜːrtəbl/ *adj.* **1** that can be changed to a different form, use or character: *Commerce requires a set of common or at least consistently convertible weights and measures.* ◇ **~ to sth** *Buildings suitable for future modification include office blocks convertible to apartment blocks.* ◇ **~ into sth** *Romer's work (1990) implies that all knowledge is accessible and convertible into economic knowledge.* **2** (of a currency) that can be freely changed into another currency or gold: *As there are many countries with convertible currencies, there are many exchange rates.* ◇ **~ into sth** *Each national currency was freely convertible into gold at a pre-determined and fixed rate.* ➲ *compare* LIQUID² (3)
■ **con·vert·ibil·ity** /kənˌvɜːtəˈbɪləti; *NAmE* kənˌvɜːrtəˈbɪləti/ *noun* [U] **~ (of sth) (between/to sth)** *The convertibility of buildings between residential and other uses is limited.* ◇ *On 15 August 1971, Nixon formally ended the convertibility of US dollars to gold until an agreement was reached.*

con·vey /kənˈveɪ/ *verb* **1** to communicate information, a message, an idea or a feeling: **~ sth** *This single diagram conveys much information.* ◇ *The aim here is to convey the general idea rather than to set out every step of the argument.* ◇ *These monuments convey a vivid impression of wealth and power.* ◇ *Facial expression, eye movements and body posture also help convey meaning.* ◇ **~ sth to sb** *Advertising uses paid-for media to convey messages to the target audiences.* ◇ *High expectations are about conveying* *hope to the students.* ◇ **~ what/how, etc...** *The contributors aim to convey what it means to be a parent in the everyday context of domestic life.* ◇ **~ that...** *Talking with a youth first also conveys that his viewpoint will be taken seriously.* ◇ **~ to sb that...** *Parents must convey to their children that school attendance is expected* **2** to take, carry or transport sb/sth from one place to another: **~ sb to sth** *The Mycenaeans employed chariots to convey elite warriors to and from the fighting.* ◇ **~ sth to sb/sth** *A network of organic producers conveys products to local stores and restaurants.* ◇ *This conveys sensory information to the brain.* **3** (*law*) to change the legal owner of a property or piece of land SYN TRANSFER² (5): **~ sth to sb** *Bleak House, which is unregistered land, was conveyed to Anna in 1925.* ◇ **~ sth into sb's name** *The legal title of the property was conveyed into the joint names of the couple.*

con·vey·ance /kən'veɪəns/ *noun* **1** [U] **~ (of sb/sth)** (*formal*) the process of taking sb/sth from one place to another: *It is the responsibility of the owner to arrange for proper conveyance of the grain that is to be shipped out.* **2** [U] **~ (of sth) (to sb)** (*formal*) the process of making an idea or a feeling known to sb: *One of the important aspects of the doctor-patient relationship is the conveyance of clear information to the patient.* **3** [U, C] **~ (of sth)** (*law*) the act or process of transferring property from one owner to another; the document in which this is recorded: *The conveyance is made under the powers conferred by the Settled Land Act 1925.*

con·vict /kən'vɪkt/ *verb* [often passive] to decide and state officially in court that sb is guilty of a crime: **~ sb** *He was convicted and sentenced to one year in prison.* ◇ **~ sb of sth** *The jury convicted the defendant of murder.* ➲ *compare* PROSECUTE (1), SENTENCE²

con·vic·tion /kən'vɪkʃn/ *noun* **1** [C, U] the act of finding sb guilty of a crime in court; the fact of having been found guilty: *The Court of Appeal quashed his conviction.* ◇ *The prosecution carries a heavy burden of proof so as to minimize the risk of wrongful conviction.* ◇ **~ for sth** *The defendant appealed against his conviction for murder.* ➲ *compare* PROSECUTION (1) **2** [C, U] a strong opinion or belief: *Their religious convictions helped to form their personalities, as well as their political beliefs.* ◇ *moral/political/philosophical convictions* ◇ **~ that...** *There is an increasingly widespread conviction that being able to speak to consumers on a one-to-one basis will be crucial.* ◇ **~ about sth** *This may articulate many people's deeper convictions about the ethical use of animals.* **3** [U] the feeling of believing sth strongly and of being sure about it: *Smokers may be aware of the dangers of their habit, but they may lack the necessary conviction to quit.* ◇ **with ~** *We certainly can no longer say with conviction that no link exists between these two phenomena.*

con·vince AWL /kən'vɪns/ *verb* **1** [T, I] to make sb/yourself believe that sth is true: **~ sb/yourself (of sth)** *Steinmann's paper was the first to convince geologists of the tectonic significance of a sequence of rocks.* ◇ **~ sb/yourself (that...)** *Each side tried to convince the public that its view was best.* ◇ *An adolescent may convince himself that he does not care, as a way of denying his needs.* ◇ **fail to ~** *As a study of the relationship between Maoism and major French intellectuals, the work fails to convince.* **2 ~ sb to do sth** to persuade sb to do sth: *The government may find it difficult to convince foreign lenders to let it borrow at a low interest rate.* ➲ *usage note at* PERSUADE

con·vinced AWL /kən'vɪnst/ *adj.* **1** [not before noun] completely sure about sth: ◇ **~ of sth** *In the 1960s, development economists were not convinced of the importance of measuring small-scale peasant production.* ◇ **~ (that)...** *In the late 1880s, Thomson became convinced that vortex rings were unstable.* ◇ **~ by sb/sth** *Convinced by FBI arguments, Kennedy complied with their request.* **2** [only before noun] strongly believing in and supporting a particular set of ideas: *A convinced evolutionist, Giard did not dismiss natural selection.* ◇ *Dennis was a convinced admirer of Milton.*

con·vin·cing AWL /kən'vɪnsɪŋ/ *adj.* that makes sb believe that sth is true: *There is no convincing evidence that any of these treatments are generally effective.* ◇ *Yet this analysis may not be entirely convincing.* ◇ *A convincing argument can be made that...* ■ **con·vin·cing·ly** AWL *adv.*: *Mulvey convincingly argues that new image technologies have dramatically impacted on film aesthetics.* ◇ *Worley demonstrates convincingly that party members came from a wide variety of backgrounds.*

THESAURUS

convincing • compelling • persuasive • strong *adj.*

These words all describe an argument or evidence that makes sb believes it is true.

- (a) convincing/compelling/persuasive/strong **argument/case/evidence**
- a convincing/compelling/persuasive **account/reason**
- a convincing/compelling **explanation/example**
- **very/particularly** convincing/compelling/persuasive/strong

- If an argument or evidence is **persuasive**, you are inclined to believe it; if it is **convincing**, you do believe it; if it is **compelling**, there is no room for any doubt that it is true. However, **convincing** is often used in negative sentences to say that sth is *not entirely convincing*; **compelling** is usually used in positive sentences before a noun; **persuasive** is slightly more subjective and emphasizes that sb is trying to persuade people of a particular argument or point of view: *There should be compelling reasons for continuing treatment for more than 5 years.* ◇ *The appearance of H. erectus has been linked to climatic shifts in eastern Africa, but the evidence is not entirely convincing.* ◇ *Cost-effectiveness arguments were highly persuasive in a context of financial stringency.*
- **Strong** is only used in this meaning with certain nouns, including *evidence*, *argument* and *case*; it suggests that the evidence or argument has a good basis which is difficult to criticize: *Thornton's results (Thornton and McAuliffe 2006) provide the strongest evidence so far of teaching in non-human animals.* ◇ *There are strong arguments for improving learning and development in organizations.*

cook /kʊk/ *verb* [I, T] to prepare food by heating it, for example by boiling or baking it: *She had never learned to cook.* ◇ **~ sth** *In those days, it was usually the wife who cooked the meals.*

cook·ing /'kʊkɪŋ/ *noun* [U] the process of preparing food: *It was still the women who did most of the cooking and cleaning.*

cool¹ /kuːl/ *adj.* (**cool·er, cool·est**) **1** fairly cold; not hot or warm: *In Los Angeles, the geographical conditions tend to trap cool air under a layer of warm air.* ◇ *The Holocene period experienced significant global warming after over 100 000 years of cooler temperatures.* ◇ *Patients with severe eczema should keep cool and wear cotton clothing.* **2** calm; not excited, angry or emotional: *In 'The Matrix' (1999), Agent Smith initially appears utterly cool and collected, his face unemotional.* ◇ *The stereotype of the scholar is of a solitary, dispassionate, cool and objectively methodical researcher.* **3** (*informal*) used to show that you admire or approve of sb/sth because they are or it is fashionable and attractive: *Many students expressed the idea that speaking English makes you cool.*

cool² /kuːl/ *verb* **1** [I, T] to become or to make sth/sb become cool or cooler: **~ (to sth)** *As the Southern Ocean cooled to the freezing point of seawater, temperate fish became largely extinct.* ◇ **~ sth/sb** *Before mass production,* *cans were filled by hand and then boiled and cooled several times.* ◇ **~ sth to sth** *The solution was cooled to 0°C in an ice bath.* **2** [I] to become calmer, less excited or less enthusiastic: *Mann's advice to the president was, 'We need to give time for tempers to cool.'*

C

PHR V ˌ**cool ˈdown 1** to become cool or cooler: *As the air expanded and cooled down, so this water was condensed.* **2** to become calm, less excited or less enthusiastic: *After a violent incident, a child takes time to cool down and work with an adult to understand their behaviour.* ˌ**cool sth ˈdown** to make sth cool or cooler: *After being attached, the shaft was cooled down to room temperature.*

cool·ing /ˈkuːlɪŋ/ *noun* [U] the action of becoming or making sth become less warm or hot: *Energy for heating and cooling are the main reasons for the associated CO_2 emissions.* ◇ **~ of sth** *Cooling of the air to produce clouds can occur in a variety of ways.* ◇ **+ noun** *The wet heat exchangers used in the buildings' cooling systems have usually low cooling capacity.*

co·oper·ate AWL (*BrE also* **co-operate**) /kəʊˈɒpəreɪt; *NAmE* koʊˈɑːpəreɪt/ *verb* **1** [I] to work together with sb in order to achieve sth: **~ with sb** *Colleagues need to cooperate with each other.* ◇ **~ on sth** *Member states agreed to cooperate on issues of foreign policy.* ◇ **~ in sth** *Many employees cooperate in a complex production process such as car manufacture.* ◇ **~ in doing sth** *States cooperate in providing disaster relief in times of emergency.* **2** [I] to be helpful by doing what sb asks you to do: *In covert observation, participants are not given the opportunity to refuse to cooperate.* ◇ **~ with sb** *Some people fail to cooperate with police as a way of expressing their right to challenge policies and laws.* ◇ **~ in sth** *Protection is frequently available if a victim cooperates in criminal investigations.* ■ **co·oper·ator** (*BrE also* **co-operator**) /kəʊˈɒpəreɪtə(r)/ *Most people are conditional cooperators; that is, most people prefer to cooperate.*

co·oper·ation AWL (*BrE also* **co-operation**) /kəʊˌɒpəˈreɪʃn; *NAmE* koʊˌɑːpəˈreɪʃn/ *noun* [U] **1** the action or process of working together towards a shared aim SYN COLLABORATION: *The Fund promotes international monetary cooperation.* ◇ **~ between A and B** *Cooperation between states occurs, but it is difficult to sustain.* ◇ **~ with sb/sth** *Parental cooperation with the local authority throughout the investigation has a significant impact on the outcome.* ◇ **~ in sth** *Regional cooperation in trade, investment and finance should be intensified.* ◇ **~ among sb/sth** *An awareness campaign would encourage cooperation among the relevant stakeholders.* ◇ **in ~ with sb/sth** *The survey was administered in cooperation with China's State Environmental Protection Administration.* **2** willingness to be helpful and do as you are asked: **~ (of sb)** *The scheme depended on the voluntary cooperation of farmers.* ◇ **~ in doing sth** *Programme directors showed high levels of cooperation in distributing and collecting the surveys.* **3** the action of forming and running a cooperative: *The small scale of the Welsh family farm is not a sufficient explanation for the historical aversion to cooperation and cooperatives.*

▸ ADJECTIVE + COOPERATION **close** • **peaceful** • **mutual** • **bilateral** • **multilateral** • **international** • **intergovernmental** • **inter-agency** • **regional** • **economic** • **political** • **social** • **judicial** *In some world regions, close cooperation has led to common rights for citizens of different countries.* ◇ *Interdependence did not produce peaceful cooperation.*

▸ VERB + COOPERATION **require** • **facilitate, promote, encourage, foster** • **ensure** • **enhance** *To facilitate cooperation, states create international institutions.*

co·opera·tive¹ AWL (*BrE also* **co-operative**) /kəʊˈɒpərətɪv; *NAmE* koʊˈɑːpərətɪv/ *adj.* **1** [usually before noun] involving working together with others towards a shared aim: *A concerted and cooperative international effort is needed.* ◇ *Several different models have been proposed to account for cooperative behaviour in animals.* **2** helpful by doing what you are asked to do: *He was a cooperative member of the team.* ◇ *The suspect was cooperative and non-combative.* **3** [usually before noun] (of a business) owned and run by the people involved, with the profits shared by them: *a cooperative farm* ◇ *I will examine the role played by the cooperative movement within the labour movement.* ■ **co·opera·tive·ly** AWL (*BrE also* **co-operatively**) *adv.*: *Small groups worked cooperatively together towards shared goals.*

co·opera·tive² AWL (*BrE also* **co-operative**) /kəʊˈɒpərətɪv; *NAmE* koʊˈɑːpərətɪv/ *noun* a farm, business or other organization which is owned and run jointly by its members, who share the profits or benefits: *Marketing cooperatives are common for organic farming.*

co·ord·in·ate¹ AWL (*BrE also* **co-ordinate**) /kəʊˈɔːdɪneɪt; *NAmE* koʊˈɔːrdɪneɪt/ *verb* to organize the different parts of an activity and the people involved in it so that it works well: **~ sth** *The company uses account managers to coordinate sales activity.* ◇ *Local, state and federal policies should be coordinated.* ◇ *The work of the team is coordinated by an experienced team leader.* ◇ **~ sth with sth** *Public relations should be coordinated with advertising strategy.*

PHR V **coˈordinate with sb** to reach an agreement with other people about how to work together effectively: *It is important that staff members coordinate with each other and share information.*

co·ord·in·ate² AWL (*BrE also* **co-ordinate**) /kəʊˈɔːdɪnət; *NAmE* koʊˈɔːrdɪnət/ *noun* one of the numbers or letters used to fix the position of a point on a map or GRAPH: *I shall use x and y coordinates to express the position of each of the balls.* ◇ **~ of sth** *The coordinates of any point of intersection of the planes is the solution of the equations.*

co·ord·in·ation AWL (*BrE also* **co-ordination**) /kəʊˌɔːdɪˈneɪʃn; *NAmE* koʊˌɔːrdɪˈneɪʃn/ *noun* [U] **1** the process of making the parts of sth or groups of people work together in an efficient and organized way: **~ of sth** *The proposed plan required the coordination of resources across state boundaries.* ◇ **~ among sb/sth** *Lack of coordination among salespeople who dealt with the same accounts frustrated customers.* ◇ **~ between A and B** *Cooperation and coordination between countries is facilitated by the WHO's Global Outbreak and Response Network.* ◇ **in ~ with sb/sth** *The procurement of these devices is managed by the clinical laboratory in coordination with the supplies department.* **2** the ability to control your movements well: *Alcohol impairs attention, coordination and judgement.* ◇ *Some affected boys show muscle weakness with poor coordination.*

co·ord·in·ator AWL (*BrE also* **co-ordinator**) /kəʊˈɔːdɪneɪtə(r); *NAmE* koʊˈɔːrdɪneɪtər/ *noun* a person whose job is to organize the different parts of an activity and the people involved in it so that it works well: *Project coordinators are responsible for coordinating the work of their groups, and reporting back on it.*

cope /kəʊp; *NAmE* koʊp/ *verb* [I] to deal successfully with sth difficult; to be successful in particular conditions SYN MANAGE: *Most ex-smokers said that they were enjoying life more and coping better than when they were smoking.* ◇ **~ with sth** *The smaller firms were not able to cope with international competition and many went bankrupt.* ◇ *To cope with the problem of seasonal flooding, a new drainage project has been completed.* ◇ *Organisms will have evolved to cope with the chemical environment in which they have lived.*

cop·per /ˈkɒpə(r); *NAmE* ˈkɑːpər/ *noun* [U] (*symb.* **Cu**) the chemical element of ATOMIC NUMBER 29. Copper is a soft red-brown metal used for making electric wires, pipes and coins: *Heavy metals such as lead, zinc, copper and* *cadmium have been detected.* ◇ **+ noun** *A coil is made of 150 turns of copper wire wound on a cylindrical core.*

cop·ula /ˈkɒpjələ; *NAmE* ˈkɑːpjələ/ *noun* (*grammar*) = LINKING VERB

copy[1] /ˈkɒpi; *NAmE* ˈkɑːpi/ *noun* (*pl.* -ies) **1** [C] **~ (of sth)** a thing that is made to be the same as sth else, especially a document or a computer file: *Click 'Print' to print a copy of the chart.* ◇ *A copy of the software may be made for backup purposes only.* ◇ *Gametes can carry only one copy of a given gene.* **2** [C] a single example of a book, newspaper, CD, etc. of which many have been made: *The book, published in an edition of 6 000 copies, sold out in a few days.* ◇ **~ of sth** *A DVD is included with every copy of the textbook.* **3** [U] written material that is to be printed in a newspaper, magazine, etc. or published on a website: *The content of the magazine blurred the distinction between editorial copy, written by journalists, and advertising.*

copy[2] /ˈkɒpi; *NAmE* ˈkɑːpi/ *verb* (cop·ies, copy·ing, cop·ied, cop·ied) **1** to make sth that is the same as or similar to sth else: **~ sth (to sth)** *To enable changes to be saved, first copy the files to the computer's hard drive.* ◇ **~ sth (from sth)** *Many other words have been copied from forms that were found in ancient Latin.* ◇ **~ sth from sth to sth** *Genetic information is encoded in DNA, and copied from generation to generation.* **2** to write sth exactly as it is written somewhere else: **~ sth** *Every text had to be copied by hand, a time-consuming and expensive proposition.* ◇ **~ sth out** *Keats copied out his 'Bright star' sonnet on a blank page of his 1806 Shakespeare.* **3 ~ sb/sth** to behave or do sth in the same way as sb else SYN IMITATE: *Children will tend to copy the behaviour of older and more powerful peers.* ◇ *This idea has been copied by a number of different retailers and marketers.*

copy·right /ˈkɒpiraɪt; *NAmE* ˈkɑːpiraɪt/ *noun* [U, C] if a person or an organization holds the **copyright** in a piece of writing, music, etc, they are the only people who have the legal right to publish, broadcast, perform it, etc, and other people must ask their permission to use it or any part of it: *The court ruled that mere use of the software did not constitute a breach of copyright.* ◇ **~ in sth** *The originator of any literary work automatically holds a copyright in it, even without registering it.* ◇ **+ noun** *The owner of the song threatened to sue for copyright infringement.*

coral /ˈkɒrəl; *NAmE* ˈkɔːrəl; ˈkɑːrəl/ *noun* [C, usually pl., U] any of a group of very small creatures that live in warm seas and have a SKELETON that they SECRETE, which forms a hard red, pink or white substance on the bottom of the sea, also called **coral**: *Corals flourish where water movement is moderate.* ◇ **+ noun** *Pollution may play a role in coral reef degradation.*

cord /kɔːd; *NAmE* kɔːrd/ *noun* **1** [U, C] strong thick string or thin rope; a piece of this: *Cord may be made water-resistant with a plastic coating.* ◇ *to tie sth with a cord* **2** [C] (in compounds) a structure of the body that looks like a piece of cord: *In insects, the main nerve cord lies ventrally, rather than dorsally as in vertebrates.* ◇ *Voiced sounds are those made while the vocal cords are vibrating.* ➲ *see also* SPINAL CORD **3** [C] a piece of wire that is covered with plastic, used for carrying electricity to a piece of equipment: *a telephone/power cord*

core[1] AWL /kɔː(r)/ *noun* **1** [usually sing.] the most important or central part of sth: **~ of sth** *These two propositions form the core of her argument.* ◇ *All these myths express the same core of ideas.* ◇ **at the ~ of sth** *Waste is at the core of urban environmental problems.* ◇ **at its ~** *Building bridges is, at its core, about practical problem-solving.* **2 ~ (of sth)** the central part of an object: *the core of a nuclear reactor* ◇ *Concentric zoning is common with the core of crystals usually having lower alkali content than the rim.* **3 ~ (of sth)** a small group of people who take part in a particular activity: *The consultancy has a small core of permanent staff but a large network of associates.* ◇ *Greek mercenaries formed the core of the Persian army.* **4** the central inner part of a planet or star: *Earth scientists realized that the magnetic field is almost certainly generated by rotation of the earth's core.* ◇ **~ of sth** *Most of the energy generated in our universe arises from nuclear fusion that takes place in the cores of ordinary stars.* **5** a piece of rock, ice or other material that is obtained using a hollow DRILL: *Abrupt climatic shifts were clearly revealed in Greenland ice cores.*

core[2] AWL /kɔː(r)/ *adj.* [usually before noun] most important; main or essential: *D&S is a group of companies whose core business is food retail.* ◇ *The findings show significant subsets within the population in terms of core beliefs about advertising.* ◇ *Organizations have to develop their core employees continuously to remain competitive and innovative.* ◇ **~ to sth** *What is peripheral to one firm may be core to another.*

▸ CORE + NOUN **feature, element, component** • **concept, idea** • **theme** • **area, subject** • **issue** • **value, principle** • **belief** • **business** • **activity** • **competence, skill** • **curriculum** • **product** • **vocabulary** *Nightingale proposed five core concepts for nursing education and practice.* ◇ *The exchange of commodities constitutes the core activity of all market societies.*

corn /kɔːn; *NAmE* kɔːrn/ *noun* [U] **1** (*BrE*) any plant that is grown for its grain, such as WHEAT; the grain of these plants: *The corn harvest was gathered in.* **2** (*NAmE*) = MAIZE: *High-yielding varieties of corn (maize) require large amounts of fertilizer.*

cor·ner /ˈkɔːnə(r); *NAmE* ˈkɔːrnər/ *noun* **1** a part of sth where two or more sides, lines or edges join: *The three atoms lie at the corners of an equilateral triangle.* ◇ **in the/a ~ (of sth)** *The search box is in the lower-left corner of the screen.* ◇ *the left-hand/right-hand corner* **2** the area inside a room or other space near the place where two walls or other surfaces meet: **in the/a ~** *Having an observer sitting in the corner of a school classroom almost inevitably means that the class dynamics will alter.* **3** the part at the end of the mouth or an eye: *On inspection it was noted that the left corner of his mouth was drooping.* **4** a place where two streets or roads join: **the ~ (of sth)** *Turning the corner of a street, Dickens found himself on Landport Terrace.* ◇ **on/at the (street) ~** *His father remembered unemployed men standing on the street corner hoping to be offered work during the Great Depression.* **5 ~ of sth** a region or an area of a place (sometimes used for one that is far away or difficult to reach): *Significant gains have been made in restoring peace and prosperity to all corners of the country.* ◇ *In 25 years, the human immunodeficiency virus (HIV) had reached virtually every corner of the world (Fauci, 2006).*

IDM **(just) around the ˈcorner** (*rather informal*) coming soon: *The next major development in genetic screening may be around the corner.* **cut ˈcorners** (*disapproving*) to do sth in the easiest, cheapest or quickest way, often by ignoring rules or leaving sth out: *From the interviews, it seemed that managers had cut corners with safety in order to reach performance targets.* **turn the ˈcorner** (*rather informal*) to pass a very important point in a difficult situation and begin to improve: *The 2010 UN Report on AIDS claims that 'the world has turned the corner—it has halted and begun to reverse the spread of HIV.'*

cor·ner·stone /ˈkɔːnəstəʊn; *NAmE* ˈkɔːrnərstoʊn/ *noun* an important part of sth that the rest depends on: *This book is a cornerstone in European refugee literature.* ◇ **~ of sth** *The idea of the struggle for existence forms one of the cornerstones of the theory of evolution.*

cor·on·ary /ˈkɒrənri; *NAmE* ˈkɔːrəneri; ˈkɑːrəneri/ *adj.* [only before noun] connected with the heart, particularly with the ARTERIES that take blood to the heart: *An increase* *in oxygen demand must be met by an increase in coronary blood flow.* ◇ *This has been associated with an increased risk of coronary heart disease.*

ˌcoronary ˈartery *noun* either of the two ARTERIES that supply blood to the heart: **+ noun** *Those with a past history of coronary artery disease are at highest risk.*

cor·pora *pl. of* CORPUS

cor·por·ate AWL /ˈkɔːpərət; *NAmE* ˈkɔːrpərət/ *adj.* [only before noun] **1** connected with large business companies or a particular large company: *Assessing and preparing for the future lies at the heart of corporate strategy.* ◇ *The appearance of the staff can help reinforce the corporate image that the organization is looking to project.* **2** forming a single unit as a CORPORATION: *Japan relies less on government agencies than on corporate organizations for lifelong support systems.*

▸ CORPORATE + NOUN **governance • strategy, objectives • responsibility • structure • management, practice • finance • culture • image, identity • headquarters** *The report highlighted failures in corporate governance as one of the most important causes of the financial crisis.* ◇ *A common issue of corporate responsibility is the preservation of the environment.*

cor·por·ation AWL /ˌkɔːpəˈreɪʃn; *NAmE* ˌkɔːrpəˈreɪʃn/ *noun* (*abbr.* **Corp.**) a large business company, or a group of companies that is recognized by law as a single unit: *The company sells to customers ranging from huge multinational corporations to small businesses.* ◇ *The average salary of a CEO employed in a large corporation has risen dramatically.* ◇ *In 2005, News Corporation bought MySpace for $580 million.* ➲ thesaurus note *at* COMPANY

cor·pus /ˈkɔːpəs; *NAmE* ˈkɔːrpəs/ *noun* (*pl.* **cor·pora** /ˈkɔːpərə; *NAmE* ˈkɔːrpərə/ or **cor·puses** /ˈkɔːpəsɪz; *NAmE* ˈkɔːrpəsɪz/) **1** a collection of written texts, especially all the works of a particular author, or writing on a particular subject: *By 1270, the extensive Aristotelian corpus had been translated into Latin.* ◇ **~ of sth** *Today there exists a clear corpus of international law governing internal armed conflict.* **2** a collection of written or spoken material in electronic form, that can be used for language research: *Studies of collocations based on the analysis of large text corpora often throw up interesting and unexpected results.* ◇ **~ of sth** *This study is based on a corpus of tagged Sanskrit texts that has been compiled during the last 10 years.* ◇ **+ noun** *Her research interests lie mainly in the areas of corpus linguistics, discourse analysis, and English for Academic Purposes.*

cor·rect[1] /kəˈrekt/ *adj.* **1** accurate or true, without any mistakes SYN RIGHT²: *On this point of independent activity of different genes, Mendel was not entirely correct.* ◇ *If Einstein's special theory of relativity is correct, then it would appear that this 'speed' is indeed variable.* ◇ **~ in (doing) sth** *Ball and Thompson were, of course, correct in their analysis.* ◇ **~ for sth** *This prediction was correct for two out of nine sites sampled.* ◇ **it is ~ to do sth** *It would not be correct to say that every moral obligation involves a legal duty.* OPP INCORRECT **2** right and suitable, so that sth is done as it should be done: *It is important to follow the correct laboratory procedures.* ◇ *Gloves must be of the correct size to ensure safe handling of the substance.* ■ **cor·rect·ness** /kəˈrektnəs/ *noun* [U] **~ (of sth)** *Later work demonstrated the essential correctness of this hypothesis.*

▸ CORRECT + NOUN **answer, solution • response • interpretation • diagnosis • identification • decision, choice • sequence** *There is no correct answer to this question.* | **position, placement, orientation • procedure** *This is the correct procedure in all but exceptional cases.*

▸ ADVERB + CORRECT **basically • (not) entirely, (not) quite • certainly, undoubtedly • partially • technically** *She is certainly correct in asserting that very little research has been done on this topic.* ◇ *It turned out that most students could write correct or at least partially correct sentences.*

cor·rect[2] /kəˈrekt/ *verb* **1** [T] **~ sth** to make sth right or accurate, for example by changing it or removing mistakes: *Another element in robust organizations is an ability to recognize and correct errors.* ◇ *Such educational material aims to correct misconceptions about eating and weight control.* **2** [T] **~ sth** to deal with a problem so that sth works in the way that it should: *Phosphate supplements may be required to correct phosphate deficiency.* ◇ *These economic imbalances should be corrected swiftly by market forces.* **3** [T, I] to change a calculation, measurement or amount in order to make it more accurate: **~ sth for sth** *The US average real wage (corrected for changes in the cost of living) fell 9.7% between 1975 and 1995.* ◇ **~ for sth** *Two frequencies are needed to correct for the delay introduced by the ionosphere.* ◇ **~ sth** *Real income refers to income corrected to take account of the effects of inflation.*

cor·rec·tion /kəˈrekʃn/ *noun* **1** [C] a change, for example in a piece of writing, that makes sth more accurate than it was before: *Where misinformation is published, corrections of equal prominence should be published.* **2** [U] the act or process of correcting sth, especially by putting a problem right: *Few people now see left-handedness as a problem needing correction.* ◇ **~ of sth** *This condition has become relatively rare in the UK due to early surgical correction of cardiac defects.* **3** [U, C] a change that makes a calculation, measurement or amount more accurate: *Temperature correction is often needed since conductivity varies considerably with temperature.* ◇ **~ for sth** *For accurate calculations, a correction for partial pressure of water can be made.*

cor·rect·ive[1] /kəˈrektɪv/ *adj.* designed to improve or put right sth that was wrong before: *If the process starts to go wrong, then corrective action needs to be taken.* ◇ *Corrective surgery may be required where joints are damaged.*

cor·rect·ive[2] /kəˈrektɪv/ *noun* **~ (to sth)** something that corrects sth or that helps to give a more accurate or fairer view of sb/sth: *Rutlidge's writings provide a useful corrective to the idea that the French simply endorsed the actions of their government.*

cor·rect·ly /kəˈrektli/ *adv.* **1** in a way that is accurate or true, without any mistakes: *Berkeley correctly observed that the motion of water in the bucket is not a truly circular motion.* ◇ *Treatment of infections relies on the ability to correctly identify the infective agent.* ◇ *The basic function of a mass spectrometer is to measure the mass of a molecule or, more correctly, an ion.* ◇ *Lorentz and Fitzgerald supposed, correctly, that the forces holding solids together are electromagnetic.* **2** in a way that is right and suitable, so that sth is done as it should be done: *Facial hair may prevent face masks from fitting correctly.* ◇ *The patient's head must be correctly positioned and supported to prevent unnecessary movement.*

cor·rel·ate[1] /ˈkɒrəleɪt; *NAmE* ˈkɔːrəleɪt; ˈkɑːrəleɪt/ *verb* **1** [I, T, usually passive] (of two or more facts or figures) to be closely connected and affect or depend on each other: **~ with sth** *The breakdown rate of leaf litter was found to correlate strongly with fungal activity.* ◇ **be correlated** *Earnings and occupational status are, unsurprisingly, highly correlated.* ◇ *Factors may be significantly correlated because they have a mutual cause, rather than because they are in a cause-and-effect relationship.* ◇ **be positively/negatively correlated** *Height and weight in humans are positively correlated: taller people tend to be heavier.* ◇ **be correlated to sth** *The activity of certain enzymes is correlated to the intensity of sound.* **2** [T] to show that there is a close connection between two or more facts or figures: **~ sth** *Attempts were made to correlate peat layers of similar humification across north-west Europe.* ◇ **~ sth with sth** *Functions of the protein family have been* *correlated with particular structural features in the amino acid sequence.*

cor·rel·ate² /ˈkɒrələt; *NAmE* ˈkɔːrələt; ˈkɑːrələt/ *noun* **~ (of sth)** one of two or more facts or figures that are closely connected and affect or depend on each other: *Age is a powerful correlate of cancer risk in humans.* ◇ *This study aimed to identify correlates of physical activity and sedentary behaviour among 7-year-old children in England.*

cor·rel·ation /ˌkɒrəˈleɪʃn; *NAmE* ˌkɔːrəˈleɪʃn; ˌkɑːrəˈleɪʃn/ *noun* [C, U] a connection between two things in which one thing changes as the other does: **~ between A and B** *No significant correlation between the age of the sea and tectonic activity appears to exist.* ◇ **~ with sth** *Enzyme activity shows a correlation with toxicity and efficacy.* ◇ **~ of A with/and B** *Various epidemiological studies have demonstrated the correlation of tea consumption and cancer prevention.* HELP In statistics, **correlation** is a measure of the extent to which one VARIABLE changes as another variable changes: *Bivariate correlations were conducted to examine if child risk-taking related significantly to maternal supervision.* ◇ *Canonical correlation is a technique to analyse the relationship between two sets of variables.* ➲ language bank *at* STATISTIC

▸ ADJECTIVE + CORRELATION **strong, close • significant • simple, direct • partial • weak • positive • negative, inverse • canonical • bivariate** *There may be a positive correlation between the amount of income that people have and the amount that they spend.*

▸ VERB + CORRELATION **find, observe • detect • report • show, reveal • demonstrate • compute, calculate • examine, investigate** *The study found a strong correlation between income and expenditure on a range of leisure activities.*

corre̩lation coeˈfficient *noun* (*symb.* **r**) **~ (of sth)** (*statistics*) a number between -1 and +1 that represents the extent to which two VARIABLES or sets of data vary in direct PROPORTION to one another: *The two versions of the carbon dioxide rankings have a high correlation coefficient of 0.71.*

cor·res·pond AWL /ˌkɒrəˈspɒnd; *NAmE* ˌkɔːrəˈspɑːnd; ˌkɑːrəˈspɑːnd/ *verb* **1** [I] to be the same as or match sth else SYN AGREE (5): ◇ **~ with sth** *These findings correspond with those of McKinlay.* ◇ *Simulations have been shown to correspond well with actual measurements.* ◇ **~ to sth** *The very notion of 'democracy' in the 19th century does not correspond to present-day definitions.* **2** [I] **~ (to sth)** to be equal to or similar to sth else; to be the EQUIVALENT of sth: *In this analogy, thermal resistance corresponds to electrical resistance.* **3** [I] **~ with sth** to be connected with or related to sth: *The successful eradication of rats corresponded with a dramatic increase in mouse numbers.* **4** [I] **~ (with sb)** (*formal*) to write letters and emails to sb and receive letters and emails from them: *Although he continued to read and correspond with friends, all of his major writing was by then behind him.*

▸ ADVERB + CORRESPOND **roughly • closely** *Shrublands and grasslands occur in elevations below about 1 678m, which roughly corresponds to 330 mm annual rainfall.*

▸ CORRESPOND + ADVERB **exactly, precisely, directly • closely, well • roughly** *These predictions do not correspond exactly to the results from experiments.*

▸ CORRESPOND TO + NOUN **value • fact • situation • increase • decrease** *The point where the two curves cross corresponds to the only values of n that satisfy both equations.*

cor·res·pond·ence AWL /ˌkɒrəˈspɒndəns; *NAmE* ˌkɔːrəˈspɑːndəns; ˌkɑːrəˈspɑːndəns/ *noun* (*formal*) **1** [C, U] a connection between two things; the fact of two things being similar: **~ (between A and B)** *There is a remarkably close correspondence between seismic upheaval and cultural upheaval.* ◇ **in ~ with sth** *Real-time pricing allows prices to change in close correspondence with costs.* **2** [U] the letters and emails that a person sends and receives: **~ (with sb)** *Prison officers had opened his correspondence with his legal adviser in breach of prison rules.* ◇ **in sb's ~** *Lord Salisbury referred to France in his private correspondence as Britain's 'faithful ally'.* **3** [U, C] the activity of writing letters and emails: **in ~ with sb** *Bjorkman was in regular correspondence with Marsden.* ◇ **~ (with sb)** *Durrell embarked on a long correspondence with the novelist Henry Miller.*

cor·res·pond·ent /ˌkɒrəˈspɒndənt; *NAmE* ˌkɔːrəˈspɑːndənt; ˌkɑːrəˈspɑːndənt/ *noun* **1** a person who reports news from a particular country or on a particular subject for a newspaper or a television or radio station: *War correspondents saw it as their duty to censor their reports, highlighting the good and glossing over the bad.* ◇ *She became America's first female foreign correspondent.* **2** a person who writes letters or emails to another person: *Many of Darwin's correspondents were scientists of great distinction.*

cor·res·pond·ing AWL /ˌkɒrəˈspɒndɪŋ; *NAmE* ˌkɔːrəˈspɑːndɪŋ; ˌkɑːrəˈspɑːndɪŋ/ *adj.* matching or connected with sth that you have just mentioned SYN EQUIVALENT¹: *Current increases rapidly with a small corresponding increase in voltage.* ◇ *A total of 65 insured patients had chronic ailments; the corresponding figure for uninsured patients was 18.* ◇ **~ to sth** *The new system provided the opposition with a share of the seats corresponding to its share of the votes.*

cor·res·pond·ing·ly AWL /ˌkɒrəˈspɒndɪŋli; *NAmE* ˌkɔːrəˈspɑːndɪŋli; ˌkɑːrəˈspɑːndɪŋli/ *adv.* in a way that matches or is connected with sth that you have just mentioned: *If fewer firms seek a public listing, investment options for market participants will be correspondingly reduced.* ◇ *The Scandinavians have tended to favour high rates of taxation with correspondingly high levels of social provision.* ◇ *The risk of low birth weight was higher in laboratory workers than in teachers. Correspondingly, the prevalence of high birth weight (4 000 g) was lower in newborns of laboratory workers.*

cor·ri·dor /ˈkɒrɪdɔː(r); *NAmE* ˈkɔːrɪdɔːr; ˈkɑːrɪdɔːr/ *noun* **1** a long narrow passage in a building, with doors that open into rooms on either side: **in the ~** *All her students were forced to wait in the corridor until the room became free.* ◇ *Hospital patients are sometimes left on trolleys in corridors for hours.* ➲ *compare* PASSAGE (3) **2** a long narrow strip of land that links two areas or that follows a river or a road: *These deposits are well developed where the river corridor is at least 200–400 m wide.* **3** a route that is followed by people travelling between countries, especially for economic reasons: *The evidence enables the authors to identify the most important migration corridors.* ◇ **~ (from...) (to...)** *The two largest corridors to the United States were from Mexico and the Philippines.*

cor·rob·or·ate /kəˈrɒbəreɪt; *NAmE* kəˈrɑːbəreɪt/ [often passive] to provide evidence or information that supports sth such as a statement or theory SYN CONFIRM (1): **~ sth** *Other research has corroborated these findings.* ◇ **~ sth by (doing) sth** *Evidence of commercially important discoveries has to be corroborated by data from different sources.* ■ **cor·rob·or·ation** /kəˌrɒbəˈreɪʃn; *NAmE* kəˌrɑːbəˈreɪʃn/ *noun* [U] **~ (of sth)** *Marsh's systematic collecting provided direct corroboration of Darwin's theory of evolution.*

cor·rupt¹ /kəˈrʌpt/ *adj.* **1** (of people) willing to use their power to do dishonest or illegal things in return for money or to get an advantage: *These payments are often squandered by corrupt government officials.* ◇ *In this part of the world, governments continue to be viewed as inefficient and largely corrupt.* **2** (of behaviour) dishonest or immoral: *It is a non-governmental organization dedicated to combating all forms of corrupt practice.* ◇ *Ethics and* *notions of corrupt behaviour are known to vary across cultures.*

cor·rupt² /kə'rʌpt/ *verb* **1** ~ **sb** to have a bad effect on sb and make them behave in an immoral or dishonest way: *He was corrupted by power and ambition.* **2** [often passive] ~ **sth** to change the original form of sth, so that it is damaged or spoiled in some way: *The transmitted signal is corrupted by an additive channel noise.* **3** ~ **sth** (*computing*) to cause mistakes to appear in a computer file, etc. with the result that the data in it is no longer correct: *Computers can crash and lose or corrupt files.*

cor·rup·tion /kə'rʌpʃn/ *noun* **1** [U] dishonest or illegal behaviour, especially of people in authority: *This was a case related to police corruption and fabrication of evidence.* ◇ *There is no shortage of examples of corporate complicity in political corruption.* ◇ ~ **in sth** *This finding could be due to widespread corruption in local governments.* **2** [U] ~ **(of sth)** the act or effect of making sb change from moral to immoral standards of behaviour: *The equation of money and sex in the play suggests the corruption of urban society.* **3** [C, usually sing.] ~ **of sth** the form of a word or phrase that has become changed from its original form in some way: *The term 'hobgoblin' is thought to be a corruption of 'Robgoblin'.*

cor·tex /'kɔːteks; *NAmE* 'kɔːrteks/ *noun* (*pl.* **cor·ti·ces** /'kɔːtɪsiːz; *NAmE* 'kɔːrtɪsiːz/) (*anatomy*) the outer layer of an organ in the body, especially the brain: *Lashley attempted to analyse the function of the cortex in the brain.* ◇ *Other neurons then convey the signals to the visual cortex.* ■ **cor·tic·al** /'kɔːtɪkl; *NAmE* 'kɔːrtɪkl/ *adj.*: *In the brains of rodents, over 70% of cortical structures are responsible for processing olfactory information.*

co·sine /'kəʊsaɪn; *NAmE* 'koʊsaɪn/ *noun* (*abbr.* **cos**) (*mathematics*) the RATIO of the length of the side next to one of the angles in a RIGHT-ANGLED triangle that are less than 90° to the length of the longest side: *The mathematics of navigation uses trigonometry, which requires an accurate knowledge of the sine, cosine and tangent of an angle.* ➲ *compare* SINE, TANGENT

cos·met·ic¹ /kɒz'metɪk; *NAmE* kɑːz'metɪk/ *noun* [usually pl.] a substance that sb puts on their face or body to make it more attractive: *Hollywood encouraged women to use cosmetics.*

cos·met·ic² /kɒz'metɪk; *NAmE* kɑːz'metɪk/ *adj.* **1** connected with medical treatment that is intended to improve a person's appearance: *Cosmetic surgery has always been controversial among doctors and the larger public.* **2** improving only the outside appearance of sth and not its basic character: *The second edition made only cosmetic changes, leaving the seven main chapters untouched.*

cos·mic /'kɒzmɪk; *NAmE* 'kɑːzmɪk/ *adj.* [usually before noun] connected with the universe and space; not from the earth: *This cosmic microwave background radiation is the residue of energy released during the Big Bang.*

cosmo·pol·itan /ˌkɒzmə'pɒlɪtən; *NAmE* ˌkɑːzmə'pɑːlɪtən/ *adj.* (*approving*) **1** containing people of different types or from different countries, and influenced by their culture: *The company recently moved to the cosmopolitan city of Amsterdam, in order to attract high-quality international personnel.* **2** having or showing a wide experience of people and things from many different countries: *Cosmopolitan lifestyles have seen a shift away from traditional beers towards European and New World wines.*

cos·mos /'kɒzmɒs; *NAmE* 'kɑːzmoʊs; 'kɑːzməs/ *noun* **the cosmos** [sing.] the universe, especially when it is thought of as an ordered system: *The Buddha taught that the cosmos is uncreated and dynamic.* ◇ *He sought to exploit this new theoretical framework to explain the large-scale behaviour of the entire cosmos.*

cost¹ /kɒst; *NAmE* kɔːst/ *noun* **1** [C, U] the amount of money that you need in order to buy, make or do sth: *No additional cost is involved if this option is chosen.* ◇ ~ **of sth** *Renewable energy projects are designed to minimize the unit cost of production.* ◇ **at a (...)** ~ *These products provide better performance, but at a higher cost.* ◇ **at a ~ of sth** *The bridge was renovated in 2005 at a cost of $500 000.* ◇ ~ **to sth/sb** *The overall cost of this to the cattle industry in 2001 was estimated to be AU $18.3 million.* **2** [C, U] the effort, loss or damage that is involved in order to do or achieve sth: *The negative social and environmental costs associated with energy production were ignored.* ◇ ~ **in sth (of doing sth)** *In this system, the cost in time and energy of moving from a waiting line to another is almost non-existent.* ◇ ~ **in doing sth** *Women bear the far greater cost in having and rearing children.* ◇ **at...** ~ *Victory in the war was achieved at terrible social and economic cost.* ◇ **at the ~ of sth** *Government policies favoured lower unemployment, even at the cost of higher inflation.* ◇ ~ **to sth/sb (of doing sth)** *Thus, the overall cost to society of fighting inflation with more unemployment may be high.* ◇ **+ noun** *A standardized brand can generate substantial cost reductions.* ➲ *see also* OPPORTUNITY COST **3 costs** [pl.] the total amount of money that needs to be spent by a business: *Costs were reduced by greater concentration on core products.* ➲ *see also* FIXED COSTS **4 costs** [pl.] the sum of money that sb is ordered by a court to pay for a legal case: *Legal costs incurred in the action are usually awarded to the successful party.*

IDM **at 'all costs/at 'any cost** under any circumstances and without considering the amount of effort or money that may be used: *In conditions of stress and shortage, social differences are a threat that must be eliminated at all costs.* ◇ *The meat industry was prepared to exploit rural poverty and to minimize expenses at any cost.*

▸ ADJECTIVE + COST/COSTS **low • high • average • rising • variable • fixed • annual • total, overall • net • relative • marginal • initial • direct • indirect • financial • operating** *Labour costs ranged from 65 to 85 per cent of total costs (Rose, 1995).* ◇ *She observes that a programme with a low financial cost may come with a high social cost.* | **high • direct • indirect • economic • social** *There are also indirect costs, such as the loss of organizational reputation.*

▸ NOUN + COST/COSTS **capital • production • transaction • labour • transport • trade** *The funding issue is dominated by the capital cost of computer processors and human personnel.* ◇ *Research has been firmly centred upon new technology for reducing production costs.*

▸ VERB + COST/COSTS **incur • involve, entail • impose • pay, bear • minimize • avoid • outweigh • exceed • offset • reflect** *The firm's total costs incurred in 2009 were significantly lower.* ◇ *Natural selection will favour a strategy if the benefits outweigh the costs.* | **estimate • calculate • underestimate • face • cover • meet • save • raise, increase • reduce, lower, cut • discount • recover, recoup • equal** *Customer payments cover the cost of cement and other materials.* ◇ *The business recovered its initial costs within three years.*

▸ COST/COSTS + VERB **rise, increase • fall • exceed • vary** *As labour and materials costs rose, profits fell.*

▸ COST + NOUN **saving • reduction, minimization, cutting • advantage** *Major cost savings were achieved through computerization.*

cost² /kɒst; *NAmE* kɔːst/ *verb* (**cost, cost**) HELP In sense 3 **costed** is used for the past tense and past participle. **1** if sth **costs** a particular amount of money, you need to pay that amount in order to buy, make or do it: ~ **sth** *The optical scanner usually costs $3 000.* ◇ *The same holiday can cost up to 100% more in summer than in winter.* ◇ *Ideas cost nothing; hence, in a society where money is everything, ideas seem unimpressive.* ◇ **it costs sth (for**

sb) (to do sth) *It costs money for people to move around the city.* ◇ **~ sb sth** *The entire programme cost the Singapore government some $S200 million.* **2 ~ sb/sth sth** to cause the loss of sth that is valuable: *These factors have cost the tourism industry millions of jobs worldwide.* ◇ *Lactose utilization is a more complex process and therefore costs the cell more energy.* **3** (**costed, costed**) [usually passive] to estimate how much money will be needed for sth; to estimate the price that should be charged for sth: **be costed (into sth)** *The installation of the computer system was costed into the total price.* ◇ **be costed at sth** *The contract was costed at some $3.6 million.*

ˈcost-benefit *noun* [U] the relationship between the cost of doing sth and the value of the benefit that results from it: **+ noun** *The commission undertook a cost-benefit analysis when examining the proposed sites for the new runway.*

ˌcost-efˈfective *adj.* giving the best possible profit or benefits in comparison with the money that is spent: *A ROM provides the most cost-effective way of storing this type of software.* ■ **ˌcost-efˈfect·ive·ness** *noun* [U] **~ (of sth)** *Evidence on cost-effectiveness of preventive measures is increasingly becoming available.*

cost·ly /ˈkɒstli; *NAmE* ˈkɔːstli/ *adj.* (**cost·lier, cost·li·est**) (**more costly** and **most costly** are more frequent.) **1** costing a lot of money, especially more than you want to pay **SYN** EXPENSIVE: *It can be costly and time-consuming to redesign these products.* ◇ *More frequent censuses would be more costly and would not yield extra information of any great importance.* ◇ *In many situations, determining exactly how much work each employee has done can be a difficult and costly process.* ◇ **~ for sb/sth** *Clinical negligence cases are financially very costly for both the complainant and the hospital involved.* **2** causing problems, disadvantages or the loss of sth **SYN** EXPENSIVE: *Incubation and nest building are energetically costly processes.* ◇ **~ for sb/sth** *For both groups of animals, activity is always costly at high temperatures.* ◇ **~ in terms of sth** *It is essential that all the technology works perfectly, as problems could be very costly in terms of lost sales and lost reputation.*

cot·ton /ˈkɒtn; *NAmE* ˈkɑːtn/ *noun* [U] **1** a plant grown in warm countries for the soft white hairs around its seeds that are used to make cloth and thread: **+ noun** *Cotton fibres are widely used in the textile industry.* ◇ *American planters increasingly devoted land to cotton production from the 1790s onwards.* **2** the cloth made from the cotton plant: *The earliest evidence of using cotton is from India.* ◇ **+ noun** *The cotton industry of Lancashire was the cutting edge of the first Industrial Revolution.* ◇ *Keep the environment cool and instruct patients to wear loose cotton clothing.* ◇ *The price of cotton cloth has risen at least tenfold since the beginning of the 20th century.* **3** (*NAmE*) (*BrE* **ˌcotton ˈwool**) a soft mass of white cotton material that is used for cleaning the skin or a wound: **+ noun** *Use gauze or cotton wool balls and wipe from inner to outer eye.*

cough[1] /kɒf; *NAmE* kɔːf/ *noun* [C, U] an illness or infection that makes you cough often; an act of sound of coughing: *If a patient has a cough and fever, then infection is the likely cause.* ◇ *a dry/productive/chronic/persistent cough* ◇ *In asthma patients, objective signs of losing control include waking at night with wheeze, cough or chest pain.* ◇ **+ noun** *Women have a more sensitive cough reflex than men.*

cough[2] /kɒf; *NAmE* kɔːf/ *verb* **1** [I] to force out air suddenly and noisily through your throat, for example when you have a cold: *Encourage the patient to cough deeply.* ◇ *An urge to cough can normally be suppressed.* **2** [T] **~ sth (up)** to force sth out of your throat or lungs by coughing: *He is not coughing up any blood at present and appears well.*

could /kəd; *strong form* kʊd/ *modal verb* (*negative* **could not**, *short form* **couldn't** /ˈkʊdnt/) **HELP** The short form **couldn't** is best avoided in academic writing, unless you are quoting or deliberately using a less formal style. **1** used to show that sth is, was or might be possible: *On several points, the analysis could have gone deeper.* ◇ *Figure 16.4 relates to the population in Wales, but a similar graph could be constructed for Scotland, England or Ireland.* ◇ **~ easily** *There may be changes that could easily be made to existing services.* ◇ **~ always** *The town was impossible to besiege by land, as supplies could always be brought in by boat.* ➲ grammar note *at* MIGHT **2** used as the past tense of 'can': *British industry could not supply the extra production and so goods had to be imported.* ◇ *He could speak English, French, Dutch, Danish and Portuguese.* **3** used to politely ask sb to do sth for you: *Could we have a meeting sometime this week?* ➲ grammar note *at* MODAL[1]

coun·cil /ˈkaʊnsl/ *noun* [C+sing./pl. v.] (*often* **Council**) **1** a group of people who are elected to govern an area such as a city or county: *The Council meets/meet every two months.* ◇ **+ noun** *The city council elections of summer 1917 registered a swing toward the Bolsheviks.* ◇ *If the minutes of General Council meetings are published, council members might be inhibited from stating their true opinions.* **2** (*BrE*) the organization that provides services in a city or county, for example education, houses and libraries: *In the UK, non-profit housing is provided by local councils and by housing associations.* ◇ **+ noun** *The way households get access to council housing depends on council allocation policies.* **3** a group of people chosen to be responsible for sth such as giving advice, making rules, doing research or providing money: *Each of these university councils supervised teaching and degree awards.* ◇ *the Council for Economic Planning and Development* ◇ **~ of sb** *He referred the matter to a council of bishops at Rome.* **4** (especially in the past) a formal meeting to discuss what action to take in a particular situation: *King Edwin of Northumbria held a council to discuss whether or not to accept Christianity.*

coun·sel[1] /ˈkaʊnsl/ *noun* [U, C] **1** (*formal*) advice, especially given by older people or experts; a piece of advice: *The first Parliament was assembled in 1265 to provide counsel to Henry III.* ◇ *The teachers began to interpret these sayings as advice or counsels that did not bind every Christian.* **2** a lawyer or group of lawyers representing sb in court: **~ (for sb)** *Counsel for the appellant submitted that the Court of Appeal decision was wrong.* ◇ *In-house lawyers are bound by the same rules as external counsels.* ◇ **prosecuting/defence ~** *The job of defence counsel is to undermine the prosecution's case and to put forward his/her client's defence.*

coun·sel[2] /ˈkaʊnsl/ *verb* (**-ll-**, *US* **-l-**) (*formal*) **1 ~ sb** to listen to and give support or professional advice to sb who needs help: *The GP has a pivotal role in counselling patients and their families.* **2** to advise a particular course of action; to advise sb to do sth: **~ sth** *While President Kennedy counselled patience, Baldwin, Clark and others vented their rage at the administration's inaction.* ◇ **~ sb to do sth** *In this early work, Wollstonecraft counsels women to seek happiness through reason and self-discipline.*

coun·sel·ling (*US* **coun·sel·ing**) /ˈkaʊnsəlɪŋ/ *noun* [U] professional advice about a problem, especially a personal problem: *Local agencies can provide counselling and support to help with these issues.* ◇ **+ noun** *Each clinic counselling session lasted for 30 minutes.*

coun·sel·lor (*US* **coun·sel·or**) /ˈkaʊnsələ(r)/ *noun* a person who has been trained to advise people with problems, especially personal problems: *His parents and guidance counsellor have grown increasingly worried about him.*

count¹ /kaʊnt/ *verb* **1** [T] to calculate the total number of items in a particular group: **~ sth (up)** *The program can count the keywords on a page.* ◇ *The number of flowers counted in July 2000 correlated well with temperature data.* ◇ **~ (up) how many...** *Husbands were asked to count up how many hours they spent on housework.* ◇ **~ sth from... (to...)** *Years were counted from the foundation of the Republic.* **2** [T] **~ sth/sb** to include sth/sb when you calculate a total: *Our difficulty was deciding which types of small businesses we would count in the survey.* **3** [I] (not used in the progressive tenses) to be important: *For capitalist firms, what counts is profitability, not efficiency.* ◇ **~ for sth** *In any struggle for succession, charisma and military skill always count for a great deal.* **4** [T, I] to be considered in a particular way; to consider sb/sth in a particular way: **~ as sb/sth** *Experts differ concerning what counts as 'arthritis'.* ◇ **~ sb/sth as sb/sth** *Twenty minutes' lateness was counted as absence.* ◇ **~ sb/sth/yourself + adv./prep.** *By the end of the century, tenant farmers could no longer be counted among the peasantry.* ◇ **~ sb/sth/yourself + adj.** *Nobles who could claim the labour services of a single serf family could count themselves lucky.* ◇ **~ sb/sth/yourself + noun** *A failure to choose correctly may be counted a failure of rationality.* **5** [I, T] to be officially accepted; to accept sth officially: *In France until quite recently, bakers' wives who sold bread all day long were classified as 'unemployed' since their labour did not officially count.* ◇ **~ sth** *These official statistics are almost certainly underestimates because uncertain cases are not counted.* **6** [I] **~ (from sth) (to/up to sth)** to say numbers in the correct order: *The experiment involved counting repeatedly from one to six.*

PHR V **ˌcount aˈgainst sb/sth | ˌcount sth aˈgainst sb/sth** to be considered a disadvantage in sb/sth; to consider sth a disadvantage in sb/sth: *Descartes ignored experimental evidence that counted against his analogy.* **ˈcount on sb/sth** to trust sb to do sth; to be sure that sth will happen: *In his campaign against corruption he could count on the gratitude of the majority of Soviet citizens.* ◇ **~ sb/sth to do sth** *Neither church nor state could be counted on to improve women's position in society.* ◇ **~ (sb/sth) doing sth** *Only the factory owner can count on owning the profits.*

count² /kaʊnt/ *noun* **1 ~ (of sth)** an act of counting to find the total number of sth; the total number that you find: *We made daily counts of the number of larvae in each pool.* ◇ *Votes are then further transferred to other candidates at subsequent counts.* ◇ *For birds of prey, the final count was much lower than expected.* **2** [usually sing.] (*technical*) a measurement of the amount of sth contained in a particular substance or area: *Hay fever sufferers are advised to stay indoors when the pollen count is high.* ➲ *see also* BLOOD COUNT **3** [usually pl.] **on... counts** used to refer to a point made during a discussion or an argument: *Overall, the occupational ranking of Norway is notable on two counts.* ◇ *Some economists argue that mass unemployment will tend to force wages down and thus create new employment but this approach is wrong on both counts.*

count·able /ˈkaʊntəbl/ *adj.* (*grammar*) a noun that is **countable** can be used in the plural or with *a* or *an*, for example *table, animal* and *idea*: *In French, 'smoking' is a countable noun, with the meaning which in English is expressed by 'dinner jacket'.* OPP UNCOUNTABLE

coun·ter¹ /ˈkaʊntə(r)/ *verb* **1** [T, I] to reply to an argument or criticism by trying to prove that it is not true: **~ sth** *His work counters the common notion that globalization is both inevitable and necessary.* ◇ **~ that...** *Opponents counter that the new curriculum is as distorted as the old.* ◇ **~ with sth** *Neo-liberals counter with claims that all states have mutual interests and can gain from cooperation.* **2** [T] **~ sth** to do sth to reduce or prevent the bad effects of sth SYN COUNTERACT: *Practices may need to import better business skills to counter the threats of competition.* ◇ *Sea level rise would normally be countered by the saltmarsh migrating inland.*

coun·ter² /ˈkaʊntə(r)/ *noun* **1** [usually sing.] **~ (to sth)** a response to an argument or criticism that tries to prove that it is not true: *The film provided a counter to the mythology surrounding the revolutionary leader.* **2** [usually sing.] **~ (to sth)** an action that you take to reduce or prevent the bad effects of sth: *Opponents lacking counters to these technologies could not stand up to US military power.* **3** (especially in compounds) an electronic device for counting sth: *We used a diffractometer equipped with a photon counter.* **4** a long flat surface over which goods are sold or business is done in a shop, bank, etc: *Studies illuminate the importance of oral information at the pharmacy counter.*

IDM **over the ˈcounter** goods, especially medicines, for sale **over the counter** can be bought without a PRESCRIPTION or special licence: *The problem is compounded by easy availability of medications containing codeine obtainable over the counter.*

coun·ter³ /ˈkaʊntə(r)/ *adv.*

IDM **run ˈcounter to sth** (of evidence or an opinion) to show or be the opposite of other evidence or opinions: *This finding runs counter to the expectations raised by other studies.* ◇ *This view ran counter to the departmental line that prison did not work as a deterrent.*

coun·ter·act /ˌkaʊntərˈækt/ *verb* **~ sth** to do sth to reduce or prevent the effects of sth SYN COUNTER¹ (2): *Vitamin K, which is found in some vegetables, will counteract the effect of warfarin.* ◇ *With competition, direct and indirect effects may counteract each other.*

coun·ter·ar·gu·ment /ˌkaʊntərˈɑːgjumənt/ *noun* **~ (to sth)** an argument or set of reasons put forward to oppose an idea or theory developed in another argument: *Leys (2007) offers a timely counterargument to such ideas.* ➲ language bank *at* CONCEDE

coun·ter·fac·tual /ˌkaʊntəˈfæktʃuəl; *NAmE* ˌkaʊntərˈfæktʃuəl/ *adj.* connected with what did not happen or what is not the case: *In counterfactual history, history is 'overwritten' with an alternative version.* ◇ *All 26 countries analysed would have displayed lower economic growth under the counterfactual scenario.* ■ **coun·ter·fac·tual** *noun*: *A counterfactual is any statement that is untrue in that it typically queries, 'What would have happened if...?'*

coun·ter·part /ˈkaʊntəpɑːt; *NAmE* ˈkaʊntərpɑːrt/ *noun* a person or thing that has the same position or function as sb/sth else in a different place or situation: *There are about 10 genes on the Y chromosome that do not have a counterpart on the X.* ◇ *The authors suggest that enslaved women faced additional dangers compared with their male counterparts.* ◇ **sb's ~ in...** *National policy officials work together with each other and their counterparts in the EU institutions.*

coun·ter·pro·duct·ive /ˌkaʊntəprəˈdʌktɪv; *NAmE* ˌkaʊntərprəˈdʌktɪv/ *adj.* [not usually before noun] having the opposite effect to the one that was intended: *Henry's attempts to coerce the Scots into accepting the treaty simply proved counterproductive.* ◇ **it is ~ to do sth** *It would be counterproductive to try to address every possible ethical concern.*

count·less /ˈkaʊntləs/ *adj.* [usually before noun] very many; too many to be counted or mentioned: *History provides countless examples of such attacks on groups of people.* ◇ *Gender-based discrimination persists in the workplace, housing, education, health care and countless other areas.*

coun·try /ˈkʌntri/ *noun* (*pl.* **-ies**) **1** [C] an area of land that has or used to have its own government and laws:

The European countries that had experienced the Industrial Revolution needed to develop new markets. ◇ *Intriguingly, the rise in the incidence of obesity is even more pronounced in developing countries (WHO, 2003).* ◇ *Participation in these programmes varies markedly across countries.* ◇ *In some parts of the country, however, Democrats largely agreed with their Republican opponents.* ➲ *see also* CROSS-COUNTRY (1) **2** [U] (often following an adjective) an area of land, especially with particular physical features: *Wind farms must be sited in open country avoiding inhabited buildings and roads.* **3** (*often* **the country**) [U] any area outside towns and cities, with fields, woods, farms, etc: *Feelings of alienation were reported more commonly among residents in the city than among those in the country.* ➲ *see also* CROSS-COUNTRY (2)

▸ ADJECTIVE + COUNTRY **foreign** • **home** • **neighbouring** • **developed, industrialized, industrial, advanced** • **developing** • **rich, wealthy** • **poor** *The risks were significantly higher for selling in a foreign country.*

▸ NOUN + COUNTRY **host** • **destination** • **member** • **high-income** • **low-income** • **middle-income** *The USA remained the main destination country for immigrants.*

▸ VERB + COUNTRY **enter** • **leave** • **flee** • **classify** • **list** • **rank** • **compare** *The Aliens Office issued an order directing him to leave the country.*

▸ COUNTRY + VERB **experience** • **face** • **develop** • **produce** • **adopt** *These programmes could be adopted by other countries around the world.*

▸ PHRASES **vary across/between countries** *Views of the role of government vary between countries and over time.*

THESAURUS

country • **nation** • **state** *noun*

These are all words for an area of land that has its own government and laws.

- **in** a country/nation
- a **European/Western/African/Asian** country/nation/state
- a **different/member** country/nation/state
- a **foreign** country/state
- a **developed/developing/poor/industrialized** country/nation
- a **new/modern/sovereign** nation/state

- To refer to a country as a political unit or to its government, you can use **country**, **nation** or **state**: *NATO has expanded from its original 12 member countries.* ◇ *Less than one third of the political systems in the world today are fully democratic states.*
- **Country** and **nation** can also refer to an area where people live, its economy, culture, etc: *In developed countries, cancer is now a leading cause of death.* ◇ *Today, the wealthy, industrialized nations typically dominate research and development.*
- **Country** is the only word which can be used to refer to a country as a geographical area: *Features such as dustproof keypads were crucial in dry, hot countries.*

coun·try·side /ˈkʌntrisaɪd/ *noun* [U] the land outside or around towns and cities, with fields, woods, etc: *Commercial centres are usually several degrees warmer than the surrounding countryside.* ◇ *Drystone walling is a well-known feature of the English countryside.* ◇ **in the ~** *A wind turbine, or even a wind farm, is becoming an increasingly familiar sight in the countryside today.*

county /ˈkaʊnti/ *noun* (*pl.* **-ies**) (*abbr.* **Co.**) an area of Britain, Ireland or the US that has its own local government: *The Poor Law allowed parishes with exceptional levels of distress to appeal to other parishes in the same county.* ◇ **~ of sth** *The area includes major conurbations along the rivers Tyne and Wear, plus the large rural county of Northumberland.*

coup /kuː/ *noun* (*pl.* **coups** /kuːz/) **1** a sudden change of government that is illegal and often violent: *The project dissolved when a military coup overthrew Allende.* ◇ **+ noun** *The country has seen a series of unsuccessful coup attempts and mass protests.* **2** the fact of achieving sth that was difficult to do: *It was a major coup to get such a prestigious contract.*

couple¹ AWL /ˈkʌpl/ *noun* HELP In *BrE* a plural verb is usually used in both meanings. **1** [C+sing./pl. v.] two people who are married or in a romantic or sexual relationship: *It was claimed that the couple seldom lived together for long periods of time.* ◇ *Transferable tax allowances were introduced for married couples.* ◇ *Same-sex couples in a 'significant relationship' are permitted to adopt a child.* **2** [sing.+ sing./pl. v.] **~ of sth** two or approximately two things or people of the same sort: *Some workers had already developed symptoms after a couple of months.* ◇ *So far, only a couple of studies have been done on the question.*

couple² AWL /ˈkʌpl/ *verb* [usually passive] to link together two or more things or parts of sth: **be coupled together** *All these models have to be coupled together in order to simulate the climate.* ◇ **be coupled to sth** *Most modifications that are added to proteins are coupled to nucleotide carriers.* ◇ **(be) coupled with sth** *State control was coupled with the relentless persecution of religious minorities.* ◇ *Poor agricultural practices and dry soil, coupled with wind, can erode soils.* ◇ *The small number of studies, coupled with the fact that in one case evidence was of low quality, means that no firm conclusions can be drawn.*

coup·ling AWL /ˈkʌplɪŋ/ *noun* [U, usually sing.] a combination or joining of two things; an act of combining or joining: **~ between A and B** *There is strong electrotonic coupling between the relay cells and the pacemaker cells.* ◇ **~ of A with B** *The main thyroid hormones are produced by a coupling of iodide with tyrosine.*

cour·age /ˈkʌrɪdʒ; *NAmE* ˈkɜːrɪdʒ/ *noun* [U] the ability to do sth dangerous, or to face pain or opposition, without showing fear SYN BRAVERY: *Marshall's courage in the face of constant danger became legendary.* ◇ **with ~** *The Dacians resisted with great determination and courage.* ◇ **have the ~ (to do sth)** *It has been a gradual process to persuade staff to have the courage to accept failings and address problems.*

cour·age·ous /kəˈreɪdʒəs/ *adj.* showing courage SYN BRAVE: *To oppose white masters was a courageous act, for the penalties could be severe.* ■ **cour·age·ous·ly** *adv.* SYN BRAVELY: *The crew acted courageously in staying with the ship until all the passengers had been taken to safety.*

course /kɔːs; *NAmE* kɔːrs/ *noun* **1** [C] a series of classes or lectures on a particular subject: *Some students take these new bioethics courses as part of bioscience degree programmes.* ◇ *a short/an introductory course* ◇ **~ in sth** *Universities are already offering specialist training courses in geothermal energy.* ◇ **~ on sth** *She teaches courses on African-American history.* **2** [C] (*especially BrE*) a period of study at a college or university that leads to an exam or a qualification: *Most first degree courses in education are concerned primarily with producing professional practitioners.* ➲ *compare* PROGRAMME¹ (4) **3** [sing.] the way that sth develops or should develop: *The two revolts followed a similar course and both ended in failure.* ◇ **~ of sth** *The gods are shown intervening directly in human affairs and determining the course of events.* ◇ *Marx's writings soon became controversial and had a great impact on the course of history.* ➲ *see also* LIFE COURSE **4** (*also* ˌ**course of** ˈ**action**) [C] a way of acting in or dealing with a particular situation: *The report made a strong recommendation as to the best course for the department to follow.* ◇ **~ of sth** *All team*

C

members had to agree on a course of conduct that would achieve the project goals. ◇ *The client decided to refuse his lawyer's advice and take another course of action.* **5** [C, usually sing.] the general direction in which sb's ideas or actions are moving: *After the election, however, Obama changed course, and was willing to negotiate with the Republicans.* ◇ *Steering a middle course between these two unacceptable positions involves a pragmatic approach.* **6** [U, C, usually sing.] a direction or route followed by a ship or an aircraft, or by another moving object: *Only knowledge of the current course, heading, altitude or airspeed to be flown is necessary.* ◇ **on/off ~** *Initially it was assumed that what was keeping each star on course was the gravitational attraction of all the closer stars.* **7** [C] **~ (of sth)** a series of medical treatments: *The infection required repeated courses of intravenous antibiotics.*

IDM **during/in/over the course of...** during: *During the course of the nineteenth century, a remarkable development of transport networks took place.* ◇ *If an employee does commit a criminal offence in the course of his or her duties, the company will cooperate with the public authorities.* ◇ *Expectations on both sides changed over the course of time.* **the normal, ordinary, etc. course of events, things, etc.** the way that things usually happen: *If such a finding leads to the suspicion of an abscess, then the normal course of events is to try and find its location* **of course** used to show that what you are saying is not surprising or is generally known or accepted: *I am, of course, responsible for the final text of the paper.* ◇ *Of course, there are other methods that could be tried.* **on 'course (for sth/to do sth)** likely to achieve or do sth: *In the first five years, the democratization process seemed to be on course.* **run/take its 'course** to develop in the usual way and come to the usual end: *Few people would prefer to live in a society that leaves epidemics to run their course and devastate the population.* ➲ *more at* COLLISION, DUE¹, MIDDLE¹

course·work /ˈkɔːswɜːk; *NAmE* ˈkɔːrswɜːrk/ *noun* [U] work that students do during a course of study, not in exams, that is included in their final grade: *Coursework accounts for 40% of the final marks.*

court¹ /kɔːt; *NAmE* kɔːrt/ *noun* **1** [C, U] the place where legal trials take place and where crimes and legal cases are judged; the process of taking legal action against sb: *People or firms who ignore these standards are punished in the civil or criminal courts.* ◇ *There were two threats of court action when the book was published.* ◇ *Several hundred of these cases have come before the courts.* ◇ **in ~** *It might be a difficult case to prove in court.* ◇ **take sb/sth to ~** *She threatened to take the company to court.* ◇ **+ noun** *The group ultimately fought a court case against their employer.* **2 the court** [sing.] the people in a court, especially those who make the decisions, such as the judge and JURY: *This allows the court to act on behalf of the young person.* **3** [C, U] the official place where kings and queens live: *Shen-hsiu was called to the imperial court.* ◇ **at ~** *She served at court as a maid of honour.*

court² /kɔːt; *NAmE* kɔːrt/ *verb* **1** [T] **~ sb** to try to please sb in order to get sth you want, especially the support of a person or an organization: *Leading business figures have been courted by Labour politicians.* ◇ *It was not until the 1930s that firms began to consider West Africans as consumers worth courting through advertising.* **2** [T] **~ sth** to try to obtain sth: *Celebrities may court and value a greater degree of attention than the average person would find tolerable.* ◇ *He was aggressively courting the youth vote in 1992.* **3** [T] **~ sth** to do sth that might result in sth unpleasant happening: *No firm can afford to cut itself off from local knowledge sources. To do so would be to court disaster.* ◇ *She judges that Heath deliberately courted discord between Britain and the USA, because of his favour for British relations with Europe.* **4** [T, I] (*biology*) (of an animal) to try to attract another animal of the same species, and the opposite sex, in order to MATE: *In this species, large males do not court but defend territories to monopolize females.* ◇ *The daily energy expense of vigorously courting males was twice that of non-courting males.* ◇ **~ sth** *Females can benefit from breeding near a more attractive male in order to court him as a mate for a subsequent breeding attempt (Wagner, 1999).* **5** [T] **~ sb** (*old-fashioned*) if a man **courts** sb, he spends time with them and tries to make them love him: *By the latter half of 1831, he was also courting the first great love of his life, Maria Beadnell, the daughter of a City banker.*

ˌcourt of apˈpeal *noun* (*pl.* **courts of appeal**) a court that people can go to in order to try and change decisions that have been made by a lower court: *The European Court of Justice is the final court of appeal for such cases.* HELP In the UK and some other countries, the **Court of Appeal** is the highest court (apart from the Supreme Court) that can change decisions made by a lower court: *The Court of Appeal upheld the original judgment.* In the US, a **Court of Appeals** is one of the courts that can change decisions made by a lower court: *In Hendersen v. Hendersen, the Ohio Court of Appeals upheld the decision of the trial judge to award custody to the father.*

court·ship /ˈkɔːtʃɪp; *NAmE* ˈkɔːrtʃɪp/ *noun* **1** [U] (*biology*) the special way animals behave in order to attract a MATE; the time when this behaviour occurs: *These three species are closely related and have a similar breeding cycle of courtship, egg laying, incubation, brooding and fledging.* ◇ **+ noun** *Courtship behaviour often differs greatly between close species.* **2** [C, U] (*old-fashioned*) the time when two people have a romantic relationship before they get married; the process of developing this relationship: *Their families insisted on following the tradition of a long courtship.* ◇ *The dislocations of wartime meant that courtship was less likely to be supervised by family or neighbours.*

co·va·lent /ˌkəʊˈveɪlənt; *NAmE* ˌkoʊˈveɪlənt/ *adj.* (*chemistry*) (of a chemical BOND) sharing a pair of ELECTRONS: *The basic types of bonding are covalent, ionic and metallic.* ◇ *In a crystal of intrinsic or pure silicon, the atoms are held in position by covalent bonds.* ➲ *compare* IONIC

cov·en·ant /ˈkʌvənənt/ *noun* a promise to sb, or a legal agreement, especially one to pay a regular amount of money to sb/sth: *The reference in Jeremiah is to the new covenant which God promised to make with his people.* ◇ (*law*) *Any party to the deed can enforce the covenant against the person who made the promise.*

cover¹ /ˈkʌvə(r)/ *verb* **1** [often passive] to lie or spread over the surface of sth: **~ sth** *The lake covers an area of 820 square kilometres.* ◇ **be covered by sth** *In northern regions the land has been periodically covered by thick sheets of glacial ice.* ◇ **be covered with sth** *The rolling foothills at the site are covered with low tundra vegetation.* ◇ **be covered in sth** *Large areas of seasonal uplands are now covered in open woodlands or savannahs.* **2 ~ sth** to include sth; to deal with sth: *The word 'nanotechnology' covers a broad range of scientific and technical disciplines.* ◇ *The trading agreement mainly covers agricultural products.* ◇ *This issue will be covered in detail in Chapter 7.* **3** [often passive] to place sth over or in front of sth in order to protect or decorate it: **~ sth (with sth)** *Cover the wound with a sterile pad to stop air from entering.* ◇ **be covered with sth** *The disk is covered with a transparent plastic protective layer.* ◇ *Some of the architectural and sculptural features were covered with gold leaf.* **4 ~ sb/sth** (of an agreement or law) to apply to a particular situation or type of person: *Public-sector workers are usually covered by collective bargaining agreements.* **5 ~ sth** to be or provide enough money for sth: *There is usually a delivery charge to cover the cost of packing, postage and insurance.* ◇ *Most local governments have difficulty getting sufficient revenue to cover their operating expenses.* **6** [often passive] (of insurance) to protect sb against loss or injury: **be covered (by sth)** *Around 10 per cent of the population is covered by private health insurance.* ◇ **be covered for/against sth** *Self-employed people would probably not be covered against unemployment.* **7 ~ sth** to travel or fill the distance or area mentioned: *The growth of suburbs often requires commuters to cover greater distances.* ◇ *Stretching from east to west, Indonesia covers a distance of around 5 000 km.*

PHR V **ˌcover sth ˈup** (*disapproving*) to try to stop people from knowing the truth about sth such as a mistake or a crime: *British government is highly secretive and ministers and civil servants have exploited this to cover up mistakes.* ◇ *This appears to be a guilty response, as if the person is trying to cover up something she knows is wrong.*

▸ COVER + NOUN **area • surface** *The cells multiply and spread out to cover the surface of the plate in a single layer.* | **range, variety • area, aspect, issue, topic • period • year • material • case, situation** *This book covers fundamental aspects of the mechanics of solids.* ◇ *Lees-Milne's published diaries, covering the years from 1942 to 1947, offer a unique account of this period.*

▸ NOUN + COVER **survey • study • paper • book • chapter** *Our study covers a much larger set of countries and respondents than any previous work.*

cover[2] /ˈkʌvə(r)/ *noun* **1** [U] a layer of sth, such as trees, ice or clouds, that exists on or over a part of the earth's surface: *The world lost one-fifth of its tropical forest cover between 1960 and 1990.* ◇ *vegetation/plant cover* ◇ *The Weddell Sea is one of the few areas of the Antarctic to retain a permanent ice cover.* ◇ *Cloud cover can be predicted quite reliably a day in advance.* **2** (*BrE*) (*NAmE* **cov·er·age**) [U] protection that an insurance company provides by promising to pay you money if a particular event happens: *A person applying for insurance cover might be required to supply details relating to the health of parents, grandparents or siblings.* ◇ **~ against sth** *The agreement provides cover against any possible trade actions from customers.* ◇ **~ for sth** *An estimated 1.8 million employees have no cover for workplace injuries or illnesses.* **3** [C] the outside of a book or magazine: *The front cover of the second edition has a different photograph.* ◇ **+ noun** *The magazine carried a cover story on the economic crisis.* **4** [C] a thing that is put over or on another thing, usually to protect it: *The steel cover protects the inside of the bar from being scratched.* ◇ **+ noun** *A cover slip is placed on the slides, which are then examined using a microscope.* **5** [C, usually sing.] activities or behaviour that hide sb's real identity or feelings, or that hide sth bad or illegal: **~ for sth** *Marx saw civil society as little more than a cover for the interests of the bourgeoisie.* ◇ **~ for sb to do sth** *Events in Asia provided a convenient cover for Hitler to begin the process of German rearmament.*

cov·er·age /ˈkʌvərɪdʒ/ *noun* **1** [U, C, usually sing.] the amount of sth that sth provides; the extent to which sth covers an area or group of people: *As in other European countries with universal health coverage, access to a GP in Italy is rapid and free.* ◇ **~ of sth** *Vaccination coverage of high-risk groups remains low despite efforts to reach these groups.* ◇ **high/low ~** *The advertiser will look at ways of achieving a higher coverage of the target market.* ◇ **+ noun** *The model assumed an 80% vaccination coverage rate.* **2** [U] the reporting of news and issues in the MEDIA: *Studies show that media coverage influences demand for products.* ◇ *Newspaper coverage was analysed to quantify the proportion of articles providing public health information.* ◇ **~ of sth** *Press coverage of this issue was overwhelmingly critical and negative.* **3** [U, C, usually sing.] **~ (of sth)** the range or quality of information about a subject that is given by sth such as a book or course of study: *The following texts provide useful coverage of the principles discussed in this article:..* ◇ *Most of these books contain a good coverage of the topics of structural mechanics.* **4** [U] the area that can be covered by a particular volume or weight of a substance: *Coverage is 6.5 square metres per litre.* ◇ **~ of sth** *The uniform coverage of chromium from the electroplating process produces a layer which is approximately 1.3 µm thick.* **5** [U] (*NAmE*) = COVER[2] (2)

cov·er·ing /ˈkʌvərɪŋ/ *noun* **1** [usually sing.] **~ (of sth)** a layer of sth that covers sth else: *The sky was obscured by a covering of cloud.* **2** a piece of material that covers sb/sth: *An amniote egg has a hard outer covering.* ◇ *The paranji is the traditional covering for Uzbek women.*

cov·ert /ˈkʌvət; ˈkəʊvɜːt; *NAmE* ˈkoʊvɜːrt/ *adj.* secret or hidden, making it difficult to notice: *Covert observation methods may pose certain kinds of problems regarding the invasion of privacy.* ◇ *Resistance to a community school initiative can come in many forms, both overt and covert.* ➲ *compare* OVERT ■ **cov·ert·ly** *adv.*: *A cartel exists when companies covertly agree to share markets between themselves and not to undercut each other's prices.*

cow /kaʊ/ *noun* a large animal kept on farms to produce milk or beef: *Since the mid 1940s, the number of dairy cows in the region has declined continuously up to the present.*

ˈco-worker *noun* a person who works on the same project as sb; a person who works with sb, doing the same kind of job: *Tomas Santos and his co-workers have shown that woodland habitats regenerate more slowly in drier areas.* ◇ **+ noun** *The results of this present study showed that stress levels reduced with better supervisor and co-worker support.* ➲ *compare* COLLEAGUE

crack[1] /kræk/ *noun* a line on the surface of sth where it has broken but not split into separate parts: *The crack widens due to further accumulation of ice within it.* ◇ **~ in sth** *Seasonal wetting and drying results in significant cracks in the clay.* ◇ (*figurative*) *Just as the popularity of the movement reached its peak, cracks began to appear within the party.*

crack[2] /kræk/ *verb* **1** [I, T] to break without dividing into separate parts; to break sth in this way: *The surface of the ground cracked and fractured in every direction.* ◇ **~ sth** *As the inside expands, it cracks the outer shell of the lava block.* **2** [I] to no longer be able to function normally because of pressure: *Clearly, the backbone of the Democratic alignment of 1932–68 was starting to crack.* **3** [T] **~ sth** to find the solution to a problem, etc: *Supercomputers are also used by the security services to crack codes and to monitor telecommunications traffic.*

PHR V **ˌcrack ˈdown on sb/sth** to try harder to prevent an illegal activity and deal more severely with those who are caught doing it: *The government claims success in cracking down on tax fraud.*

craft[1] /krɑːft; *NAmE* kræft/ *noun* **1** [C, U] an activity involving a special skill at making things with your hands: *They found their traditional crafts made obsolete by the new factories.* ◇ *At this time there were almost no small enterprises outside agriculture or craft.* **2** [sing.] all the skills needed for a particular activity: *Many molecular biologists learned their craft before these techniques were in widespread use.* **3** (*pl.* **craft**) [C] a boat or ship: *It was unusual for such craft to be found in South East Asian waters.*

craft[2] /krɑːft; *NAmE* kræft/ *verb* [usually passive] **~ sth** to make sth using a special skill SYN FASHION[2] (1): *Most of his writing was carefully crafted.*

crafts·man /ˈkrɑːftsmən; *NAmE* ˈkræftsmən/ *noun* (*pl.* **-men** /-mən/) a skilled worker, especially one who makes things by hand: *When the industrial age began, many skilled craftsmen rapidly lost their livelihood.*

crash[1] /kræʃ/ *noun* **1** an accident in which a vehicle hits sth, for example another vehicle, causing damage and often injury or death: *He was tragically killed in a car crash.* **2** a sudden serious fall in the price or value of sth; the occasion when a business suddenly fails SYN COLLAPSE[1] (3): *There was a worldwide depression following the Wall Street stock market crash of 1929.* ◇ *Through the East Asian financial crash of 1997–8, China developed rapidly as a major trading nation.* **3** a sudden failure of a machine, especially of a computer system: *No matter how good the network is, system crashes and data loss are inevitable.*

crash[2] /kræʃ/ *verb* **1** [I, T] to hit sth hard while moving, causing noise and/or damage; to make sth hit sb/sth in this way: *The aeroplane crashed a few minutes before landing, leaving no survivors.* ◇ **+ adv./prep.** *Furniture rattled and fell as the earth shook, and chimneys crashed to the ground.* ◇ **~ sth (into sth)** *She crashed her father's car into a tree.* **2** [I] (of prices, shares, a business, etc.) to lose value or fail suddenly and quickly: *During Mexico's economic crisis in 1994, the value of the peso crashed.* **3** [I] (of a computer) to stop working suddenly: *When a user program crashes, the operating system mounts a rescue attempt.*

cre·ate AWL /kriˈeɪt/ *verb* **~ sth** to make sth happen or exist: *The revolution in computing technologies in the 1980s created a demand for new skills.* ◇ *Most such sedimentation problems are created by human activities, especially mining.* ◇ *Governments can do a great deal to create the right business environment.* ◇ *According to Aquinas, God created nature and this is the reason we should try to live in accordance with it.*

> **WORD FAMILY**
> create *verb*
> creation *noun*
> creative *adj.*
> creatively *adv.*
> creativity *noun*
> creator *noun*
> recreate *verb*
> recreation *noun*

▸ CREATE + NOUN **situation • problem • opportunity • value • system • model • conditions, environment • atmosphere, climate • awareness • sense • space • market • jobs • demand • incentive** *Technology has created opportunities for the movement of information, goods and services as never before.* ◇ *Loyalty programmes create a sense of belonging amongst customers.*

cre·ation AWL /kriˈeɪʃn/ *noun* **1** [U] the act or process of making sth that is new, or of causing sth to exist that did not exist before: *These forests are in regions where agriculture is still the principal means of wealth creation.* ◇ *The idea is to promote job creation and capital investment throughout the EU.* ◇ **~ of sth** *Globalization involves the creation of new social networks and activities that overcome traditional boundaries.* ◇ *The Bretton Woods agreement led to the creation of the International Monetary Fund and the World Bank.* **2** [C] a thing that sb has made, especially sth that shows ability or imagination: *Shakespeare took existing materials from various sources and crafted them into new artistic creations.* ◇ **~ of sth** *The states of contemporary Africa are not products of a long African history but creations of colonialism.*

cre·ative AWL /kriˈeɪtɪv/ *adj.* **1** [only before noun] involving the use of skill and imagination to produce sth new: *Marketing is a blend of scientific analysis and creative thinking.* ◇ *A creative idea of some kind is obviously needed before advertising can be developed.* ◇ *The organization has to support the creative aspects of engineering that will be important to the nation.* **2** having the skill and ability to produce sth new: *Teachers reported feeling creative, enthusiastic, and even inspired about the work.* ◇ *Highly creative people are different from other people in certain specific ways.* ■ **cre·ative·ly** AWL *adv.*: *The study examines the competences that can be developed to respond creatively to the changing global environment.*

cre·ativ·ity AWL /ˌkriːeɪˈtɪvəti/ *noun* [U] the ability to produce sth new, using skill and imagination: *Innovation requires creativity and a culture to support it.* ◇ *The optimists believe that human creativity can find technological solutions to the challenges of environmental sustainability.*

cre·ator AWL /kriˈeɪtə(r)/ *noun* **1** [C] a person, organization or quality that makes or produces a particular thing: *It is doubtful that any of the Internet's creators could have predicted the meteoric rise of the Web.* ◇ **~ of sth** *Private enterprises are the country's biggest creators of new jobs.* **2 the Creator** [sing.] God: *The world was perceived as God's creation, following a historical course mapped out from the beginning in the mind of the Creator.*

crea·ture /ˈkriːtʃə(r)/ *noun* **1** a living thing, real or imaginary, that can move around, such as an animal: *It has been estimated that there are more species of virus than of all other creatures put together.* ◇ **living ~** *Throughout history, the study of living creatures in their natural environment has been a source of fascination for people.* **2** a person, considered in a particular way: *There is every reason to believe that human beings have always been highly social creatures.* **3 ~ of sth/sb** a person or organization that is considered to be under the complete control of another: *They argued that the European Union was no longer a creature of its member states.*

cre·dence /ˈkriːdns/ *noun* [U] (*formal*) **1** the fact of an idea or a story being likely to be true: **lend ~ (to sth)** *The results lend further credence to the hypothesis that climate change can force volcanism.* ◇ **gain ~** *A theory which has gained much credence recently is that of Schwartz and Bilsky, who maintain that all humans share a set of seven motivational values.* **2** belief in sth as true: **give ~ to sth** *It is difficult to know how much historical credence can be given to any of these stories.*

cre·den·tials /krəˈdenʃlz/ *noun* [pl.] **1** the qualities, training or experience that make sb/sth suitable to do or be sth: *The company announced an advertising campaign designed to demonstrate its environmental credentials.* ◇ **~ as sth** *His 1986 book further establishes his credentials as a non-mainstream economist.* ◇ **~ of sb/sth** *People want to know about the ethical credentials of potential employers.* **2** documents that prove who you are or what you have done: *There were long queues at airports as the migrants' credentials were checked.*

cred·ibil·ity /ˌkredəˈbɪləti/ *noun* [U] the quality that sb/sth has that makes people believe or trust them/it: *The government wanted the legislation to have human rights credibility.* ◇ *The prime minister lost credibility by reversing his earlier decision.* ◇ *Her work tends to lend credibility to these claims.* ◇ *to lack/gain credibility* ◇ **~ of sb/sth** *This has been a major factor undermining the credibility of reformers in the eyes of traditionalists.*

cred·ible /ˈkredəbl/ *adj.* **1** that can be believed or trusted SYN CONVINCING (1): *The federal government has not demonstrated credible commitment to economic growth.* ◇ *They need rules or laws backed up by the credible threat of force.* ◇ *No credible scientific evidence exists to support this view.* ◇ *Trade press magazines are often perceived as credible sources of information.* ➲ thesaurus note at PLAUSIBLE **2** that can be accepted, because it seems possible that it could be successful SYN VIABLE (1): *The apparent lack of a credible alternative to capitalism may have led to a crisis in Marxism.* ■ **cred·ibly** /ˈkredəbli/ *adv.*: *These findings could not be credibly explained by the existing theory.* ◇ *Specialization based on small firms might credibly offer a challenge to the dominance of mass production.*

credit[1] AWL /ˈkredɪt/ *noun* **1** [U] praise or approval that is given to sb because they are responsible for sth: **take (the) ~ (for sth)** *They took credit for the creation of a* *million new jobs.* ◇ **~ for sth** *Russian scientists deserve credit for laying the world's first practical electric telegraph.* ◇ *His quickness to claim credit for his achievements played into the hands of his enemies.* ➲ *compare* BLAME² **2** [U] the act of stating who sb is and the work that they have done: *An appendix to the work gives credit to all the individuals who were interviewed in the course of the study.* **3** [U, C] money that is borrowed from a bank or another financial institution; a loan: *If the interest rate increases, it becomes more attractive for the bank to extend credit.* ◇ *The International Development Association provides interest-free credits and grants to the world's poorest countries.* **4** [U] the status of being trusted to pay back money to sb who lends it to you: *Individuals or countries with bad credit must pay a higher interest rate than those with good credit.* ◇ *Poor peasants were often debt-free for the reason that, having no credit, they could not borrow.* ◇ **+ noun** *Favourable credit ratings enable large firms to take on long-term development projects.* **5** [C, U] (*technical*) payment that sb has a right to receive for a particular reason: *Educational vouchers and tuition tax credits apply to a very small proportion of school populations in the US.* ◇ *In March 1914, the Russian Duma voted massive credits for a three-year military programme.* **6** [U] an arrangement that you make, for example with a shop, to pay later for sth that you buy: *People living in these neighbourhoods found it difficult to get credit at stores.* ◇ **on ~** *These policies will make it more difficult for families to borrow in order to buy cars, houses or other goods on credit.* ◇ **+ noun** *Information is required to ensure that credit facilities are not extended to those under the age of eighteen.* **7** [U] if you or your bank account are **in credit**, there is money in the account: *The bank had the right to stop the company making withdrawals even when the account was temporarily in credit.* **8** [C, U] a unit of study at a college or university (or, in the US, also at a school); the fact of having successfully completed a unit of study: *A minimum of 50 credits is required per year (where one credit equates to 1 hour of educational activity).* ◇ *Undergraduates received extra credit in psychology courses as compensation for their participation in the study.*

IDM **to sb's credit** making sb deserve praise or respect: *To his credit, Carter confronted the issue directly.*

credit² AWL /ˈkredɪt/ *verb* [usually passive] to believe or say that sb/sth is responsible for doing sth, especially sth good: **be credited for sth** *Globalization, it seems, is variously blamed and credited for an incredibly wide range of phenomena.* ◇ **be credited as (doing) sth** *Mill is credited as introducing the word 'entrepreneur' into English economics.* ◇ **A is credited with B** *Guglielmo Marconi is credited with the first use of radio to span the Atlantic in 1901.* ◇ **B is credited to A** *The first use of radio to span the Atlantic is credited to Marconi.*

cred·it·or AWL /ˈkredɪtə(r)/ *noun* a person, a country or an organization that sb/sth owes money to: *Eventually, the bank's creditors were paid in full.* ◇ *The policy is aimed at safeguarding the interests of creditors.* ◇ *All foreign creditors, whether private or public, would be treated on an equal basis.* ➲ *compare* DEBTOR

cried *past tense, past part. of* CRY¹

crime /kraɪm/ *noun* **1** [U] activities that involve breaking the law: *The research highlighted the organizational similarities between organized crime and large businesses.* ◇ *It could be argued that the current concern with crime prevention has created a 'culture of fear'.* ◇ **+ noun** *The crime rate was declining rapidly in the 1990s.* **2** [C] an illegal act or activity that can be punished by law: *The authors believed that violent crimes are typically committed by those whose anger is overcontrolled.* ◇ **~ against sb** *The UN report concluded that crimes against humanity, including genocide, had occurred.* ➲ *see also* WAR CRIME

crim·inal¹ /ˈkrɪmɪnl/ *adj.* **1** [usually before noun] connected with or involving crime: *Any breach of the injunction is a criminal offence.* ◇ *The lack of reporting of this criminal behaviour makes it especially difficult to assess the true nature of the problem.* ◇ *These acts would not be considered criminal in the national law of Member States.* **2** [only before noun] connected with the laws that deal with crime: *These are fundamental questions in criminal law.* ◇ *Criminal charges were brought against both men.* ◇ *These measures are essential to improving the effectiveness of the criminal justice system.* ➲ *compare* CIVIL (3)

crim·inal² /ˈkrɪmɪnl/ *noun* a person who commits a crime: *False or stolen identities are the means by which serious criminals often go undetected.* ◇ *The aim was to bring all war criminals to just and swift punishment.*

cri·sis /ˈkraɪsɪs/ *noun* (*pl.* **cri·ses** /ˈkraɪsiːz/) [C, U] a time of great danger, difficulty or confusion when problems must be solved or important decisions must be made: *The world is facing a major ecological crisis.* ◇ *It is at times of crisis that opportunities for change arise.* ◇ **~ of sth** *Local stock exchanges were failing due to a crisis of confidence amongst investors.* ◇ **in ~** *The public security situation is in crisis: homicides have increased by approximately 75 per cent in the last six years.* ◇ **+ noun** *Many organizations now have crisis management plans to cope with, say, a serious health and safety incident.* ➲ *see also* CRITICAL (6)

▸ ADJECTIVE + CRISIS **severe** • **current** • **recent** • **global** • **financial, economic, fiscal** • **banking** • **humanitarian** • **ecological** *She describes how the global financial crisis of 2008 precipitated a deep recession.* ◇ *At times of severe economic crisis, the demands for greater democracy increase significantly.*

▸ VERB + CRISIS **precipitate, trigger** • **face** • **experience** • **prevent, avert** • **resolve, solve** *All these wars precipitated humanitarian crises.* ◇ *The crisis was resolved when the two men were released.*

cri·ter·ion AWL /kraɪˈtɪəriən; *NAmE* kraɪˈtɪriən/ *noun* (*pl.* **cri·teria** /kraɪˈtɪəriə; *NAmE* kraɪˈtɪriə/) a standard or principle by which sth is judged, or with the help of which a decision is made: *His classification is based on the following criteria:...* ◇ *As many as 78% of adult prisoners meet the diagnostic criteria for personality disorder.* ◇ *Organizational control systems specify the criteria by which employees are evaluated and rewarded.* ◇ **~ of sth** *It appears that there is no single criterion of beauty common to all human cultures.* ◇ **~ for (doing) sth** *They developed two criteria for measuring the strength of composite materials.* ◇ **according to ~** *This approach entails the classification of consumers according to criteria other than age, residence, income and such.* ➲ grammar note *at* DATA

▸ ADJECTIVE + CRITERION **important** • **key, main** • **different** • **certain** • **specific** • **standard** • **objective** • **strict** • **diagnostic** • **environmental** • **economic** *The directive did not establish any specific criteria for the amount of benefit payable to this group.*

▸ NOUN + CRITERION **inclusion** • **exclusion** • **selection** • **eligibility** • **performance** • **quality** • **assessment, evaluation** *Only clients who were psychologically stable and met the inclusion criteria were invited to participate.*

▸ VERB + CRITERION **define, identify, specify** • **establish, provide, set** • **develop** • **use, employ, apply** • **meet, satisfy, fulfil** *The company introduced its own labelling system to identify healthier products, using criteria set by an independent board of health experts.* ◇ *To qualify for a patent, a product must satisfy certain criteria.*

▸ PHRASES **set of criteria** *They established a set of criteria to be used when evaluating screening programmes.*

crit·ic /ˈkrɪtɪk/ *noun* **1** a person who expresses disapproval of sb/sth and talks about their/its bad qualities, especially publicly: *Many critics have pointed out that navigating the Internet on a tiny screen can be extremely difficult.* ◇ *Of course, the plan was not without its critics; some of the party argued strongly against it.* ◇ **~ of sth**

Martin Luther King became an outspoken critic of America's involvement in Vietnam. **2** a person whose work challenges traditional ideas, especially in subjects such as literature, history and philosophy: *He was one of the major literary and cultural critics of the mid-twentieth century.* ◇ *Feminist critics have developed a number of arguments against classical social theory.* **3** a person whose job is to write or broadcast their opinions about the good and bad qualities of books, art, music, plays and films: *European-American theories of cinema have had a powerful influence on Latin American film critics.*

LANGUAGE BANK

Critical evaluation

In academic writing, it is often necessary to give an evaluation of what is good or bad about a particular method, piece of research, argument, etc.

- **The strength/weakness** of X **is...**
- **The advantage/disadvantage** of X **is...**
- **A particular strength/advantage** of X **is...**
- **One of the/Among the advantages/disadvantages/limitations** of X **is...**
- X **has its advantages/disadvantages/strengths/weaknesses/limitations.**
- **There are a number of benefits/advantages/limitations to...**
- X **offers the advantage/benefit of...**
- X **has/suffers the disadvantage of...**
- **The benefits/advantages outweigh the drawbacks/disadvantages.**
- X **does not account for/fails to account for...**

– ***The strength of*** *this approach was that it did not appear to require any major transfer of budgetary resources.*
– ***The main disadvantage is*** *that exploiting secondary data may require a compromise between what is wanted and what is available.*
– ***One particular advantage of*** *this approach is the possibility of controlling the density of sugar ligands.*
– ***Among the disadvantages of*** *a bipolar signal is the requirement for twice as much power.*
– *All research* ***has its weaknesses****, however.*
– ***There are a number of limitations to*** *this study.*
– *The LED sources* ***offer the advantage of*** *longevity, up to 10 000 hours usage compared with xenon and mercury.*
– *DC machines* ***suffer the disadvantage of*** *needing brushes and a commutator which require frequent maintenance.*
– *Risks from surgery may* ***outweigh benefits*** *in older people.*
– *This approach* ***fails to account for*** *unsuccessful transitions.*

crit·ic·al /ˈkrɪtɪkl/ *adj.* **1** extremely important, for example because a future situation will be affected by it SYN CRUCIAL: *The choice of methodology is critical.* ◇ *Careful quality control for new products will be of critical importance.* ◇ *Pressure on water resources is one of the most critical environmental issues of the twenty-first century.* ◇ **~ to sth** *Understanding the role of chance is critical to understanding patterns of molecular evolution.* ◇ *Relatives and carers of such people are critical to the success of pain management.* ◇ **it is ~ to do sth** *It is critical to develop and strengthen community-based support systems for such vulnerable adults.* ◇ **~ for sth** *Farmer cooperation is seen as critical for the continued expansion of organic farming.* ◇ **~ in (doing) sth** *Fertility rates are critical in determining the future size of the global population.* ◇ **it is ~ that...** *It is critical that the sales force are very clear about what the firm is offering.* ➲ thesaurus note *at* ESSENTIAL[1] **2** involving making fair, careful judgements about the good and bad qualities of sb/sth: *The article provides a critical analysis of Greene's achievements.* OPP UNCRITICAL ➲ *see also* CRITICAL THINKING **3** challenging traditional ideas in the study of society, literature, etc: *However, the critical perspective argues that culture should not be regarded as a management tool.* **4** (of a text) containing detailed notes and analysis by an expert: *In spite of the lack of a modern critical edition of this work, the evidence is solid.* **5 ~ (of sb/sth)** expressing disapproval of sb/sth and saying what you think is bad about them/it: *The new chief accountant was highly critical of the Commission's book-keeping standards.* **6** used to describe a situation that is serious and uncertain and in which bad things could happen: *In the winter of 1940 the food situation became critical.* **7** [only before noun] according to the judgement of people whose job is to write or broadcast their opinions about art, music, plays, etc: *The previous year had seen the publication, to great critical acclaim, of his deeply moving autobiography.*

▸ CRITICAL + NOUN **role • factor • question • issue • incident • point, moment • importance** *Both these hormones play a critical role in pregnancy.* ◇ *When the critical moment in a confrontation arrives, instant decisions must be made.* | **approach • analysis • reflection • thinking • scrutiny, examination • appraisal • review • study** *This essay has presented a critical appraisal of the effectiveness of the international law of internal armed conflict.*

▸ ADVERB + CRITICAL **especially, particularly • increasingly** *Corporate branding becomes particularly critical when the company needs to present itself as a good corporate citizen.*

crit·ic·al·ly /ˈkrɪtɪkli/ *adv.* **1** in a way that carefully analyses what is good or bad about sth: *I intend to discuss critically the different theories of market entry strategies.* ◇ *The notion of semantic prosody will be critically examined below.* **2** extremely; in a way that is important: *Two factors were critically important for this conclusion to be reached.* ◇ *The accuracy of prediction will depend critically on how well the model fits the data.* ◇ *Critically, the work was not carried out according to the operating instructions.* **3** seriously: *These patients are often critically ill and require rapid assessment and intervention.*

ˌcritical ˈmass *noun* [sing., U] **1** the smallest number of people or things that is necessary to make sth happen or be successful: *This was the historical moment when female readers for the first time entered British print culture in numbers large enough to form a critical mass.* ◇ *An attempt at direct action failed to achieve critical mass and received no support from responsible social elements.* ◇ **~ of sb/sth** *By the late 1970s, a critical mass of member governments was persuaded that the Commission should be led by a political figure.* **2** (*physics*) the smallest amount of a substance that is needed for a nuclear CHAIN REACTION to take place: *When the mass of the white dwarf exceeds a critical mass, its outer parts explode while its central parts collapse.*

ˌcritical ˈtheory *noun* [U] a way of thinking about and examining culture and literature by considering the social, historical and IDEOLOGICAL forces that affect it and make it the way it is: *Some themes in postmodernism seem to be very much informed by critical theory.*

ˌcritical ˈthinking *noun* [U] the process of analysing information in order to reach a logical decision about the extent to which you believe sth to be true or false: *Access to an education that promotes and develops critical thinking is also essential.* ◇ **+ noun** *The students improved their problem-solving and critical thinking skills.*

criti·cism /ˈkrɪtɪsɪzəm/ *noun* **1** [U, C] the act of expressing disapproval of sb/sth and opinions about their faults or bad qualities; a statement showing disapproval: *Two aspects of this code have attracted particular criticism from the farming unions.* ◇ *Mining companies faced sharp public criticism over pollution of groundwater.* ◇ *It is important to know how to give and receive constructive criticism.* ◇ *The main criticism levelled at this thesis is that it is simply incorrect.* ◇ **~ of sb/sth** *A potential criticism of e-relationships is impersonality, because the customer sees* *only a screen and never talks to a real human being.* ◇ **~ that...** *The criticism that a machine cannot have much diversity of behaviour is just a way of saying that it cannot have much storage capacity.* ◇ **open to ~** *Their argument is open to criticism on a number of fronts.* ➲ *compare* PRAISE² (1) **2** [U] the work or activity of analysing and making fair, careful judgements about sb/sth, especially books, music, etc: *This approach has fundamentally altered the kinds of questions posed by literary criticism.* ◇ *Derrida's textual criticism involves discovering, recognizing and understanding underlying assumptions and ideas.*

criti·cize (*BrE also* **-ise**) /ˈkrɪtɪsaɪz/ *verb* to say what you do not like or what you think is wrong about sb/sth: **~ sb/sth** *The new law has been heavily criticized by senior judges.* ◇ **~ sb/sth as sth** *Thomas Paine famously criticized Burke as an enemy of the natural right to self-legislate.* ◇ **~ sb/sth for (doing) sth** *From the onset of the Great Depression in 1929, corporations were widely criticized for their role in the financial catastrophe.* ➲ *compare* PRAISE¹ (1)

cri·tique¹ /krɪˈtiːk/ *noun* a detailed and usually critical examination and analysis of a system, a situation, a set of ideas or a work of art: *In his devastating critique, Marx examines every aspect of the capitalist system.* ◇ **~ of sth** *She produced a feminist critique of the sexual revolution of the 1960s and 1970s.*

cri·tique² /krɪˈtiːk/ *verb* **~ sth** to write or give an opinion about sth by considering it in detail; to give a negative opinion about sb/sth: *The authors critique the methods and practices used in the research.* ◇ *Globalization is often critiqued as promoting one dominant set of cultural practices and values.*

crop¹ /krɒp; *NAmE* krɑːp/ *noun* **1** [C] a plant that is grown in large quantities, especially as food: *Currently, approximately 24% of Earth's land area has been converted into land for growing crops or rearing livestock.* ◇ *These small family farms grow tobacco as a major cash crop.* ◇ *Sugar was the staple crop that dominated the West Indian economy.* ◇ *They cultivated root crops, as well as rice and millet.* ◇ *Wheat is an important cereal crop widely grown all over the world.* ◇ **+ noun** *Argentina, Brazil, India and China all are increasing GM crop production.* ◇ *Other strategies to prevent soil impoverishment included crop rotation and leaving land fallow for a season.* **2** [C] the amount of grain, fruit or other parts of a plant that are grown and collected at a particular time: *This factor often limits rice production to one crop per year.* ◇ **~ of sth** *In these conditions, market gardeners are able to grow four to six crops of vegetables a year.* ◇ **+ noun** *Many experiments have shown that loss of soil leads to lower crop yields.* **3** [sing.] **~ of sb/sth** a group of people who do sth at the same time; a number of things that happen at the same time: *Each year brings its crop of new ideas about the philosophy and practices of marketing.*

crop² /krɒp; *NAmE* krɑːp/ *verb* **(-pp-)** [T, usually passive, I] **~ (sth)** to use land for growing plants for food: *The Corn Belt has been cropped intensively since the discovery of its rich soil base and a climate conducive to the production of row crops.* ◇ *Farmers attempted cropping in the uplands, but it was exceedingly difficult to subsist as an upland farmer.*

PHR V **ˌcrop ˈup** to appear or happen, especially in a way that is sudden or unexpected SYN COME UP (2): *This type of problem can crop up in any number of situations.* ◇ *The same underlying themes crop up again and again.*

cross¹ /krɒs; *NAmE* krɔːs/ *verb* **1** [I, T] to go across or through sth; to pass or stretch from one side of sth to the other: **~ (over) (from...) (to/into...)** *The Air Force bombed Helsinki and the Red Army crossed into Finland.* ◇ **~ sth** *Toxins can cross cerebral membranes and cause cerebral dysfunction.* ◇ *The ability to cross international borders and immigrate has been made far easier in the modern world.* ◇ *At that time, London could still be crossed on foot from west to east in a little over an hour.* ◇ **~ a/the road/river** *He had been hit by a car while attempting to cross the road.* ◇ **~ over sth** *Taking the cattle, he crossed back over the river.* ◇ **~ a line/boundary** *With his growing celebrity, Jordan crossed all boundaries of race, age and gender and essentially appealed to everyone.* **2** [I, T] to pass across each other; to pass in an opposite or different direction: *It is useful to know whether the circuit can be redrawn so that no wires cross.* ◇ **~ sth** *Paths cross the x axis at right angles.* **3** [T] **~ sth** to put or place sth across or over sth else: *Sitting with legs crossed and arms folded may convey lack of interest and defensiveness.* **4** [T] to breed two types of plants or animals to make a new one with a new combination of GENES: *Mendel systematically crossed 34 different pure-bred strains of peas.* ◇ **~ A with B** *When these tall offspring were crossed with each other, their offspring varied in height in predictable ratios.*

PHR V **ˌcross sth ˈout/ˈthrough** to draw a line through a word, usually because it is wrong: *Mistakes were neatly crossed out, leaving the original material still visible.* **ˌcross ˈover (from sth) (to/into sth)** to move or change from one group or type to another: *From time to time, social policy analysts have crossed over and changed their ideological position.* ◇ *At the time, few songs and few performers crossed over from country to popular charts.*

cross² /krɒs; *NAmE* krɔːs/ *noun* **1** a mark or an object formed by two lines crossing each other (X or +) HELP The mark (X) is often used to show sth, for example that you have chosen sth, or that an answer is wrong: *Highlight the passage to be uncoded, and press the button with a red cross on it.* ◇ *Voters have to mark a cross within a box placed opposite the name of the candidate they wished to see elected.* ➲ *compare* TICK² (1) **2** a long vertical piece of wood with a shorter piece across it near the top. In the past people were hung on crosses and left to die as a punishment: *Death on a cross was considered the worst kind of execution a person could suffer.* **3** an object, a design, etc. in the shape of a cross, used as a symbol of Christianity: *Muslim women often favour the wearing of veils or burkas, while some Christians choose to wear crosses.* ◇ *Soldiers were usually buried on or near the battlefield and the spot was marked with a simple wooden cross.* **4** [usually sing.] **~ (between A and B)** a mixture of two different things, breeds of animal or types of plant: *A mule is a hybrid resulting from a cross between a horse and a donkey.* ◇ *The building looks like a cross between a prison and an art gallery.* ➲ *see also* HYBRID²

cross- /krɒs; *NAmE* krɔːs/ *combining form* (in nouns, verbs, adjectives and adverbs) involving movement or action from one thing to another or between two things: *It is important that hand washing is strictly observed to minimize cross-infection.* ◇ *Mendel cross-fertilized plants grown from green seeds with plants grown from yellow seeds.* ◇ *The effects of cooperative learning may lead to close cross-ethnic friendships.* ◇ *The ensuing data may then be analysed cross-culturally.*

ˌcross-ˈcountry *adj.* [usually before noun], *adv.* **1** involving or between two or more countries: *A cross-country comparison shows that most East Asian economies have exceptionally high levels of imports.* ◇ *Knowledge of pricing law and regulation for advertising and marketing research activities differs cross-country.* ➲ *compare* INTERNATIONAL HELP Note that while **international research** may involve work by people from two or more countries, **cross-country research** usually involves simply the analysis of information about more than one country. **2** from one part of a country to the other, especially not using main roads or routes: *They commandeered freight trains for cross-country transit.* ◇ *Cross-country mail services allowed the national postal system to develop into a reliable and swift service.*

ˌcross-ˈcultural *adj.* involving two or more different countries or cultures: *The analysis of comparable data* *from two or more countries provides one possible model for conducting cross-cultural research.*

cross·ing /ˈkrɒsɪŋ; *NAmE* ˈkrɔːsɪŋ/ *noun* **1** [C] a place where you can safely cross a road, a river, etc, or where you can cross from one country to another: *The major railway junctions and the main river crossings were the objects of attack.* ◇ *There are difficulties that hinder access, such as lack of pedestrian crossings and quality of pavements.* ◇ **+ noun** *She was being transported with other Greek-Cypriots to a crossing point in Nicosia.* **2** [C] a journey across a sea or a wide river: *Perhaps as many as half of the captives did not survive the crossing.* ◇ **~ of sth** *He won the prize for the first plane crossing of the English Channel.* **3** [C, U] the act of going across sth or from one place to another: *They were trying to combat the rise in illegal border crossings.* ◇ **~ of sth** *Some of the most promising areas of research involve the crossing of boundaries between ancient history and other fields.* **4** [C, U] the act of making two different types of animal breed together, or of breeding two types of plant to form a new one: **+ noun** *Many of these rare species are unsuited to genetic crossing experiments in the laboratory.*

ˌcross ˈreference *noun* **~ (to sth)** a note that tells the person who is reading sth to look for further information in another book or document, or in another part of the same book or document: *Each chapter features numerous cross-references to other chapters in the book.*

ˈcross section (*also* **ˈcross-section**) *noun* **1** [C, U] the surface or shape that you see when you cut through the middle of sth; a drawing of this view: *Apatite usually forms elongate crystals with hexagonal cross sections.* ◇ **~ of sth** *In the CT scanner, X-rays are used to form three-dimensional images of cross sections of the body.* ◇ **in ~** *Many fish are not cylindrical in cross section.* **2** [C] a piece cut from body TISSUE or other material by making two straight PARALLEL cuts: *Thin freehand cross sections were cut every 5 mm with a razor blade.* **3** [C, usually sing.] **~ (of sb/sth)** a group of people or things that are typical of a larger group: *The party's leadership and members were drawn from a cross section of society.* ◇ *The report polled 2 052 people chosen at random on the streets in a cross section of British cities.* ➲ *see also* CROSS-SECTIONAL

ˌcross-ˈsectional *adj.* involving or connected with a typical or representative sample of a larger group: *A cross-sectional study of 470 workers revealed that 21% of respondents were in the high job strain group.* HELP A **cross-sectional** study or survey typically looks at a large, representative sample at a particular point in time; a **longitudinal** study follows its subjects over a period of time, but may take a smaller, more focused sample. ➲ *compare* LONGITUDINAL (1)

crowd¹ /kraʊd/ *noun* **1** [C+sing./pl. v.] a large number of people gathered together in a public place: *The nine African American teenagers walked through a hostile crowd to the school.* ◇ *Several people in the crowd said the police opened fire with live ammunition.* ◇ **~ of sb** *A crowd of 100 or more had gathered to hear the speech.* **2 the crowd** [sing.] ordinary people, who are not special or unusual in any way: *Even within a group there are those who experiment, take risks and refrain from joining the crowd.*

crowd² /kraʊd/ *verb* **~ sth** to fill a place so there is little room to move: *Poor working people crowded the industrial districts of the city.*

PHR V **ˌcrowd sb/sth ˈout** to become stronger, more successful or more important than sb/sth else so that they/it cannot compete: *Some evidence shows that increased public spending merely crowds out private spending, leaving overall resources for health unchanged.* ◇ *The organization must avoid crowding out entrepreneurs and businesses in the local sector.*

crowd·ed /ˈkraʊdɪd/ *adj.* **1** having a lot of people or too many people: *The planet is becoming more and more crowded.* ◇ *Tokyo is a crowded city with a constant demand for more space.* ◇ **~ with sb** *On the day of the protest, the streets were crowded with strikers and demonstrators.* **2** full of sth: *Unfortunately, the engineering curriculum is so crowded that there is no room for a course on ethics.*

crown¹ /kraʊn/ *noun* **1 the Crown** [sing.] the government of a country, thought of as being represented by a king or queen: *There are still many large tracts of land which belong to the Crown.* **2 the crown** [sing.] the position or power of a king or queen: *James had forfeited his right to the crown.* ◇ **~ of sth** *In 1485, at the Battle of Bosworth, Henry Tudor seized the crown of England from Richard III.* **3** [C] an object in the shape of a circle, usually made of gold, that a ruler, especially a king or queen, wears on his or her head on official occasions: *Otto set his own crown on Boleslaw's head.*

crown² /kraʊn/ *verb* **1** [often passive] to put a crown on the head of a new king or queen as a sign of royal power: **~ sb** *The nine-year-old Henry III was crowned at Gloucester on 18 October 1216.* ◇ **~ sb + noun** *Franz Josef was crowned King of Hungary in 1867.* **2** [often passive] **~ sth (with sth)** to make sth complete or perfect, especially by adding an achievement or a success: *By and large, this enterprise had been crowned with success.*

cru·cial AWL /ˈkruːʃl/ *adj.* extremely important, because it will affect other things SYN CRITICAL (1), ESSENTIAL¹ (1): *The consideration of culture has become crucial in international marketing.* ◇ *Metaphors play a crucial role in enabling us to understand the world.* ◇ **it is ~ to do sth** *It is crucial to listen to the patient and document their concerns.* ◇ **~ to/for sth** *Earning respect and trust is absolutely crucial to the success of the programme.* ◇ **it is ~ that...** *In order for the central bank to be able to control the interest rate, it is crucial that its announcements are credible.* ➲ thesaurus note *at* ESSENTIAL¹

▸ CRUCIAL + NOUN **point • question, issue • part, aspect, element, component • factor • role • importance • difference, distinction • step** *The crucial importance of bioethics is increasingly being recognized.* ◇ *There are crucial differences between EU member states and ordinary nation states in international politics.*

cru·cial·ly AWL /ˈkruːʃəli/ *adv.* in a way that is very important or essential for sth: *Defective economies often depend crucially on the world market, because they are based on the export of a few primary goods.* ◇ *A crucially important property of all polymers is their molecular weight distribution.* ◇ *Crucially, all parties had to agree to 'democratic and exclusively peaceful means of resolving political issues'.*

crude /kruːd/ *adj.* (**cruder**, **cru·dest**) **1** [usually before noun] (of oil or another natural substance) in its natural state, before it has been treated with chemicals: *About 37% of commercial energy consumed throughout the world is produced from crude oil.* **2** (of figures) not adjusted or corrected: *In 2001, the United Kingdom's crude death rate was 11 per thousand.* **3** (of an estimate or guess) simple and not very accurate but giving a general idea of sth: *A crude estimate of the number of pages on the Web puts that number at over 25 billion.* **4** (of an object, machine, etc.) simple and basic; not showing much skill or attention to detail: *One study concluded that it was possible for a terrorist group to build a crude nuclear device.* **5** (of people or the way they behave) offensive or rude, especially about sex: *Patients may use crude language.*

cruel /ˈkruːəl/ *adj.* (**cruel·ler**, **cruel·lest**) **1** having a desire to cause pain and suffering: *He hoped to help those innocent people who were suffering under the cruel oppressors.* ◇ **~ to sb/sth** *Kant wrote that it is wrong for a person to be cruel to animals.* OPP KIND² **2** causing pain or suffering

SYN HARSH (1): *Roman society saw nothing wrong with cruel public punishments.* ◇ *The distinction between treatment that constitutes torture and treatment that is considered cruel, inhuman or degrading is not clear.* ◇ *She described the decision as 'a cruel blow for women and their families'.* ■ **cruel·ly** /ˈkruːəli/ *adv.*: *Parents are not morally free, and should not be legally free, to treat their children cruelly.*

cruelty /ˈkruːəlti/ *noun* (*pl.* **-ies**) **1** [U] behaviour that causes pain or suffering to others, especially deliberately: *Troops were not only killing the local populations, but doing so with unnecessary cruelty.* ◇ **~ to sb/sth** *The charity's mission is to end cruelty to children.* **2** [C, usually pl.] a cruel action: *There was no excuse for the cruelties inflicted on innocent citizens by an institution which was intended to protect them.* **3** [C, U] something that happens that seems unfair: *It seems a further cruelty that refugees might be represented as a problem by the country of settlement.*

crush /krʌʃ/ *verb* **1** to break sth into small pieces or into a powder by pressing hard: **~ sth** *These fish crush the whole shell in their jaws.* ◇ **~ sth into sth** *The seeds can also be crushed into oil and used for cooking.* **2 ~ sb/sth** to use violent methods to defeat people who are opposing you: *Sejanus attempted to crush all opposition by means of threats, violence, fear and murder.* ◇ *The mighty Hittite empire fell apart around 1200 BC, crushed by invaders from the north.*

crust /krʌst/ *noun* [C, U] **1** the outer layer of rock of which a planet consists, especially that of the earth: *Much of the earth's crust is covered by water.* ◇ *Fragments of the lower continental crust are brought to the surface during volcanic eruptions.* **2** a hard layer that forms on the surface of sth soft: *The supply of excessive water through irrigation systems can draw salts to the surface where they crystallize as a saline crust.*

cry[1] /kraɪ/ *verb* (**cries, cry·ing, cried, cried**) [I] to produce tears from your eyes because you are unhappy or hurt: *Olivia often cries before entering school.*
PHR V **ˌcry ˈout | ˌcry ˈout sth** to make a loud sound or shout sth loudly: **+ speech** *Macduff cries out, 'Bleed, bleed, poor country!'* **ˌcry ˈout for sth** (*rather informal*) to need sth very much: *Compulsory treatment schemes cry out for proper evaluation.*

cry[2] /kraɪ/ *noun* (*pl.* **cries**) **1 ~ (of sth)** a loud sound without words that expresses a strong feeling; a loud shout: *cries of pain/distress/grief/joy* ◇ *There was a cry of 'Silence!'* **2 ~ for sth** an urgent demand or request for sth: *Cries for social justice challenge the wisdom of the conservative culture.* ◇ *These events are immediately followed by cries for gun control.* **3** (especially in compounds) a word or phrase that expresses a group's beliefs and calls people to action: *This was the rallying cry of the French Revolution—'liberté, égalité, fraternité'.* IDM *see* FAR[2]

crys·tal /ˈkrɪstl/ *noun* **1** [C] a small piece of a substance with many even sides, that is formed naturally when the substance becomes solid: *Certain conditions can cause the protein to form crystals.* ◇ **~ of sth** *High-quality single crystals of germanium and silicon were essential to scientific progress.* ◇ **+ noun** *The optical properties of minerals reflect their crystal structure and symmetry.* ◇ *It is clear that ice crystal concentrations in clouds increase with height.* ◇ *The properties of quartz are what makes quartz crystal watches tell the time so accurately.* HELP In chemistry, a **crystal** is any solid that has its atoms, IONS or MOLECULES arranged in an ordered, SYMMETRICAL way: *The pattern of the diffracted X-rays is determined by the arrangement of the atoms and the distances between them in the crystal.* **2** [U] a clear mineral, such as QUARTZ, used in making DECORATIVE objects: *Graves dated to the fifth century include silver earrings and buckles made of rock crystal.*

crys·tal·line /ˈkrɪstəlaɪn/ *adj.* having the structure or form of a crystal; made of crystals: *Cellulose is highly crystalline as a result of an extensive hydrogen bonding network.* ◇ *Aggregates are typically produced from limestone, crystalline rocks and sandstones.*

crys·tal·lize (*BrE also* **-ise**) /ˈkrɪstəlaɪz/ *verb* **1** [I, T] to form into crystals; to make sth form into crystals: *The salt crystallizes as the solution cools.* ◇ **~ sth** *This method has been successful in crystallizing problematic target proteins (e.g. Mandelman et al., 2002; Isupov et al., 2004).* **2** [I, T] (of thoughts, plans, etc.) to become clear and fixed; to make thoughts, etc. clear and fixed: *The office is a place where organizational tensions can crystallize and have to be carefully managed.* ◇ **~ sth** *The book skilfully crystallizes key ideas from complex scholarship on conflict and identity.* ■ **crys·tal·lization, -isa·tion** /ˌkrɪstəlaɪˈzeɪʃn; *NAmE* ˌkrɪstələˈzeɪʃn/ *noun* [U] *Too quick a cooling rate will not allow crystallization to occur.* ◇ **~ of sth** *Rocks that result from the crystallization of molten magma within the earth's crust are called 'igneous'.*

cube /kjuːb/ *noun* **1** a solid or hollow figure with six equal square sides: *The volume of a cube is equal to the length of one side to the power of three.* ◇ *Crystals are octahedra, dodecahedra and cubes, often crude or rounded.* **2 ~ (of sth)** (*mathematics*) the number that you get when you multiply a number by itself twice: *The cube of 5 (5^3) is 125 ($5 \times 5 \times 5$).*

cubic /ˈkjuːbɪk/ *adj.* **1** (*abbr.* **cu**) [only before noun] used to show that a measurement is the volume of sth, that is the height multiplied by the length and the width: *Some 419 cubic kilometres of water are evaporated from the oceans every year.* **2** having the shape of a cube: *Metals with cubic close-packed structures, like copper, are malleable.* ◇ *Ilmenite usually forms tiny cubic or octahedral crystals.*

cue /kjuː/ *noun* an action or situation that is a signal for sb/sth to do sth: *In both insects and amphibians, environmental cues such as nutrition, temperature and light control metamorphosis.* ◇ **~ from sb/sth** *Doctors should be alert to verbal and non-verbal cues from the patient.* ◇ **~ for sth** *Females could use the proportion of unhatched eggs in their nest as a cue for their decision on how far to move.* ◇ **~ to do sth** *Some embryos develop at a consistent rate, and then wait for a cue to hatch.*
IDM **take your ˈcue from sb/sth** to follow or copy what sb else does as an example of how to behave or what to do: *Taking her cue from Bill Clinton, she also used the talk show format successfully at the Republican convention.*

cul·min·ate /ˈkʌlmɪneɪt/ *verb* [I] to end with a particular result, or at a particular point: **~ in sth** *The rapid development of international criminal law in the 1990s culminated in the establishment of the International Criminal Court.* ◇ **~ with sth** *A significant degree of liberalization took place, culminating with the election of the pro-reform candidate to the presidency.*

cul·min·ation /ˌkʌlmɪˈneɪʃn/ *noun* [sing.] **~ (of sth)** the highest point or end of sth, usually happening after a long time: *The restructuring can be seen as the culmination of a process of change initiated in 1953.*

cult /kʌlt/ *noun* **1 ~ (of sb/sth)** a system of religious beliefs and practices connected with a particular figure or object: *Apuleius wrote a description of initiation into the cult of Isis.* **2** a small group of people who have extreme religious beliefs and who are not part of any established religion: *The study by Festinger et al. (1956) focused on a religious cult whose members believed that the end of the world was about to happen.* **3** [usually sing.] a person or thing that has become very popular among a particular group or section of society: **+ noun** *cult films such as 'Rocky Horror' or 'Star Wars'* ◇ *The picture* *achieved cult status as an icon of wartime endeavour.* HELP A **personality cult** happens when people are encouraged to show extreme love and admiration for a famous person, especially a political leader: *An extraordinary personality cult had been created around the leader.*

C

cul·ti·vate /ˈkʌltɪveɪt/ *verb* **1 ~ sth** to prepare and use land for growing plants or crops: *The settlers began to cultivate the more fertile land.* ◇ *Using capital-intensive technologies, some farmers cultivate 1 000 acres or more.* **2 ~ sth** to grow plants or crops SYN GROW: *Demand for biofuels has increased competition for land and water resources that would otherwise be used for cultivating edible crops.* ◇ *Wheat was extensively cultivated here, both as a commercial crop and as a bread corn for peasant consumption.* **3 ~ sth** (*biology*) to grow or keep living cells, etc. in CULTURE[1] (5): *The E. coli bacterium is small and easily cultivated and replicates in 20 minutes.* **4 ~ sb/sth** (*sometimes disapproving*) to try to get sb's friendship or support, often because you want sth in return: *The PR team carefully cultivated a strong relationship with key sports journalists.* ◇ *He spent most of his retirement cultivating literary friendships and writing poems.* **5 ~ sth** to develop an attitude, a way of talking or behaving, etc: *Violence in movies, TV and video games helps to cultivate a taste for violence in some children.* ◇ *Corporations attempt to cultivate a good image by making contributions to charities.*

cul·ti·vated /ˈkʌltɪveɪtɪd/ *adj.* **1** (of people) having a high level of education and showing good manners SYN CULTURED: *That summer, Marx married Jenny von Westphalen, an intelligent and cultivated woman whose own father was a socialist.* **2** (of land) used to grow crops: *In parts of the country, the amount of cultivated land has declined by 68 per cent.* **3** (of plants) grown on farms, etc. in order to be eaten or sold: *The forest was cut and burned as rapidly as possible to make way for cultivated crops.* ◇ *Wild and cultivated raspberries are in the genus Rubus.* OPP WILD[1]

cul·ti·va·tion /ˌkʌltɪˈveɪʃn/ *noun* [U] **1** the preparation and use of land for growing plants or crops: **~ (of sth)** *Declining yields were associated with continuous cultivation of the same land.* ◇ **under ~** *In North Africa the area under cultivation has expanded with the rapid growth of its population.* **2** the process of growing crops or plants: *sugar/rice/tobacco cultivation* ◇ **~ of sth** *Cattle farming required more intensive cultivation of fodder crops such as maize, potatoes and turnips.* **3** the deliberate development of a particular relationship, quality or skill: *Excellent customer service needs careful cultivation and management.* ◇ **~ of sth** *Money, political power and cultural capital enables the cultivation of social networks.*

cul·tural AWL /ˈkʌltʃərəl/ *adj.* [usually before noun] **1** connected with the customs, beliefs, art, way of life or social organization of a particular country or group: *The students came from differing cultural backgrounds.* ◇ *Bridges are not just physical objects; they are embedded in a technical, aesthetic, social and cultural context.* ◇ *Thus it seems that cultural traditions are also widespread in the animal kingdom.* ➲ *see also* CROSS-CULTURAL **2** connected with activities such as film, literature, music and art, thought of as a group: *The city has an impressively rich cultural life.*

▸ CULTURAL + NOUN **identity • context • background • difference, diversity • tradition • practice • norm • trait • belief • value • factor • influence • change • evolution • history • politics • landscape • awareness, sensitivity** *His expression of affection is framed within the cultural norms of his society.* ◇ *The impacts of humans on physical geography result in what may be called the cultural landscape.*

ˈ**cultural capital** *noun* [U] the non-financial aspects of a person, such as education, intelligence, skills, etc, that may allow them to improve their position in society: *A degree from an internationally renowned university brings the student a level of cultural capital necessary for a competitive job market.*

cul·tur·al·ly AWL /ˈkʌltʃərəli/ *adv.* in a way that is connected with the customs, beliefs, art, way of life or social organization of a particular country or group: *The definitions of these terms are highly culturally specific.* ◇ *Drunkenness is not a culturally acceptable behaviour in Mediterranean countries.* ◇ *Legally available methods of birth control appear to be culturally determined in most countries.* ◇ *Some images were changed to make them culturally appropriate for particular groups.*

cul·ture[1] AWL /ˈkʌltʃə(r)/ *noun* **1** [U] the customs, beliefs, art, way of life or social organization of a particular country or group: *Immigrants were convinced that they could only prosper in the United States by conforming with the dominant culture.* ◇ *All these researchers believed that the educational system would inevitably reflect the local culture.* **2** [C] a country or group with its own customs and beliefs, art, way of life and social organization: *According to Hofstede, most Western cultures tend to be more individualistic, while Asian and Latin American cultures are more collectivist.* ◇ *Weber argues that religions can play a role in constituting and preserving different cultures and civilizations.* **3** [C, U] the typical beliefs, attitudes and behaviour that people in a particular group or organization share: *Thus, organizations should foster a corporate culture that encourages creativity and innovation.* ◇ *There is increasing 'sexualization' of youth culture.* ◇ **~ of sth** *Classical republicanism influenced the political cultures of both early modern Britain and France.* ◇ *The new director's strategy was to promote a culture of openness and a platform for workers to express their views.* ◇ **+ noun** *This innovation required a culture change in the ways government departments viewed each other.* **4** [U] **~ (of sth)** activities such as literature, music, art and film, thought of as a group: *The propaganda draws on the American popular culture of newspapers, radio and film of the time.* ◇ *Sentiment and love—traditional female concerns—were now prevailing in mainstream literary culture.* **5** [U] the process of growing cells or bacteria in an artificial substance for medical or scientific study; the substance in which they are grown: *Cells are removed from the culture medium by centrifugation.* ◇ *Yeast cells can be grown in liquid culture or on agar plates.* ◇ **+ noun** *The eggs are sucked into tubes containing culture medium.* **6** [C] a group of cells or bacteria grown for medical or scientific study: *Skin swabs and blood cultures are taken to identify the pathogen.*

▸ ADJECTIVE + CULTURE **modern • contemporary • ancient • traditional • folk • local • indigenous, native • national • global • dominant, prevailing • black** *The interaction of local and international black cultures warrants further research.* ◇ *The interview is embedded in contemporary culture and it has been said that we live in 'an interview society'.* | **commercial • political • organizational • corporate** *Enterprises that have highly skilled employees and a supportive corporate culture tend to outperform their competitors.* | **popular • mass • oral • visual • literary** *The emergence of a standardized mass culture appeared in the consolidation of TV networks and the media in general.*

▸ NOUN + CULTURE **school • youth • consumer** *I shall explore the environmental impact of modern consumer culture.*

▸ VERB + CULTURE **study • explore • understand • view • define • preserve • adopt • embrace • share • reflect • influence • be based on • change, transform** *Kim's situation allows him the freedom to understand Indian culture both as a native and as a detached European observer.* ◇ *The most important and the most difficult job* *of an instructional leader is to change the prevailing culture of a school.*

cul·ture² AWL /ˈkʌltʃə(r)/ *verb* **~ sth** to keep cells or bacteria in conditions that are suitable for growth, for medical or scientific study: *Pathogenic infection was detected by culturing and identifying bacteria present in the sample.*

cul·tured AWL /ˈkʌltʃəd; *NAmE* ˈkʌltʃərd/ *adj.* **1** (of cells or bacteria) grown in artificial conditions for medical or scientific study: *DNA is mixed with calcium phosphate to form a fine precipitate which is dispersed in the cultured cells.* **2** (of people) well educated and able to understand and enjoy activities such as literature, music, art and film SYN CULTIVATED (1): *These films were capable of pleasing a worldwide public, as well as a cultured elite.*

cu·mu·la·tive /ˈkjuːmjələtɪv; *NAmE* ˈkjuːmjəleɪtɪv/ *adj.* **1** having a result that increases in strength or importance each time more of sth is added: *The cumulative impact of a series of scandals finally brought the government down.* ◇ *An organism's adaptation to its environment is the result of the cumulative effects of natural selection in the past.* **2** including all the amounts that have been added previously: *Her cumulative absences from school totalled more than three months.* ■ **cu·mu·la·tive·ly** *adv.*: *The incidence of an individual rare disease may be small; however, cumulatively, the 6 000 known rare diseases affect about 25 million Americans.*

cup /kʌp/ *noun* **1** a small container shaped like a bowl, usually with a handle, used for drinking out of; the contents of a cup: *a coffee cup* ◇ **~ of sth** *He drinks about six cups of coffee a day and rarely exercises.* **2** a thing shaped like a cup: *A waterproof thermometer with a suction cup was attached to the inside surface of the apparatus to monitor water temperature.*

cura·tive /ˈkjʊərətɪv; *NAmE* ˈkjʊrətɪv/ *adj.* able to cure illness: *The service provided preventive and curative health care for all.* ◇ *Palliative treatment aims to prolong survival and maintain quality of life in patients who can no longer be offered curative treatment.* ➲ *compare* PALLIATIVE, PREVENTIVE

curb /kɜːb; *NAmE* kɜːrb/ *verb* **~ sth** to control or limit sth, especially sth bad: *If nothing is done to curb fossil fuel emissions, there will be a likely rise in mean temperatures of 2.4–6.4°C by 2099.* ◇ *A consistent theme of central government interventions has been to curb the growth of spending by local authorities.*

cure¹ /kjʊə(r); *NAmE* kjʊr/ *noun* **1** [C] a medicine or medical treatment that cures a disease or medical condition: *Although HIV still has no known cure, treatment can now increase length and quality of life.* ◇ **~ for sth** *It is envisaged that research with stem cells will lead to the development of cures for conditions such as Alzheimer's disease.* **2** [C, U] the act of curing sb of an illness or the process of being cured: *Once the disease reaches this stage, it may be impossible to effect a cure.* ◇ *Government health policy is starting to focus on prevention rather than cure.* ◇ **+ noun** *Early detection and treatment can result in a higher cure rate for some cancer types.* **3** [C] something that will solve a problem or improve a bad situation: *Keynes suggested that the cure might be to raise rather than cut wages.* ◇ **~ for sth** *Motherhood was also seen as a cure for uncertainty and solitude.*

cure² /kjʊə(r); *NAmE* kjʊr/ *verb* **1 ~ sth** to make a disease stop affecting a person, animal or plant: *The study described how the two chemicals cured bacterial infections in cattle.* ◇ *This paper will argue that an evolutionary approach can enhance our ability to cure disease.* **2** to make a person, animal or plant healthy again: **~ sb/sth** *Increasingly, it is becoming clear that patients cured by chemotherapy are at risk of long-term toxicity arising from their treatment.* ◇ **~ sb of sth** *Freud claimed success in curing her of hysteria.* **3 ~ sth** to deal with a problem successfully: *It seems that GM crops have failed to deliver on their promise to cure world hunger.* **4 ~ sth** to make a material or substance hard using a chemical process: *The best solution was to cure the adhesive at an elevated temperature.*

curi·os·ity /ˌkjʊəriˈɒsəti; *NAmE* ˌkjʊriˈɑːsəti/ *noun* (*pl.* -ies) **1** [U, sing.] a strong desire to know about sth: *Children need an environment in which they can learn and develop their intellectual curiosity.* ◇ **~ about sth** *The work requires a keen interest in international issues and a curiosity about other cultures.* ◇ **out of ~** *Patients may test themselves for cholesterol as a routine check or out of curiosity.* **2** [C] **~ (of sth)** an unusual and interesting thing: *Many at that time believed that the curiosities of the Orient were worth crossing deserts to see.*

curi·ous /ˈkjʊəriəs; *NAmE* ˈkjʊriəs/ *adj.* **1** having a strong desire to know about sth: *Muller's writings on language and on mythology appealed greatly to curious Victorian readers.* ◇ **~ about sth** *Humans have always been curious about the traces left by their predecessors.* ◇ **~ to do sth** *I was curious to find out about these individuals' experiences of interacting in English.* **2** strange and unusual: *Millard notes the curious fact that the Assyrians adopted Aramaic as their language.* ◇ **it is ~ that...** *It is curious that few other plant products are medically established for the treatment of infection.* ■ **curi·ous·ly** *adv.*: *For such a clear thinker on other matters, this is a curiously illogical statement to make.* ◇ *Curiously, Smith's own survey apparently did not include these data.* ◇ **~ enough** *Curiously enough, the first parts of Europe really to profit from free trade were the Danubian Principalities.*

cur·rency AWL /ˈkʌrənsi; *NAmE* ˈkɜːrənsi/ *noun* (*pl.* -ies) **1** [U, C] the system of money that a country uses: *Thai investors became nervous about holding local currency and rushed to convert to US dollars.* ◇ *Some of the most loyal state functionaries obtained part of their pay in western currencies.* ◇ **+ noun** *Problems associated with currency fluctuations are prevalent in less developed countries.* HELP **hard currency** is money that is easy to exchange for money from another country, because it is not likely to lose its value: *In the early 1990s, China strictly regulated the amount of hard currency that foreign investors were allowed to send home.* ➲ *see also* SINGLE CURRENCY **2** [U, sing.] the fact that sth such as an idea, a word or a book is accepted or used by many people at a particular time: *The concept of postmodernism first gained currency among architects.* ◇ *Whether the book will have a wider currency is questionable, however, given its concentration on such limited themes.*

▸ ADJECTIVE + CURRENCY **foreign** • **local**, **home**, **domestic**, **national** • **common**, **single** • **hard** *Glick and Rose conclude that if two countries use a common currency, their trade flows tend to double.*

▸ VERB + CURRENCY **buy** • **sell** • **devalue** *The UK devalued its currency in the 1960s when the pound was strong against other currencies.*

▸ CURRENCY + NOUN **area** • **market** • **union** • **fluctuation** • **depreciation** • **crisis** *Speculation may mount about likely future depreciation of the exchange rate, which could spark a currency crisis.*

cur·rent¹ /ˈkʌrənt; *NAmE* ˈkɜːrənt/ *adj.* **1** [only before noun] existing, happening or being used now; of the present time: *Nearly half of the respondents in the current study reported neck pain.* ◇ *Table 4.2 summarizes the current demographic situation in Canada.* ◇ *This has implications for current and future trends in cirrhosis among women.* ◇ *None of the women over the age of 80 years were current smokers.* **2** being used by or accepted by many people at the present time: *There are phrases in English* *that are still current but that do not really make sense unless we investigate their origin.* ➲ *usage note at* ACTUAL ▸ CURRENT + NOUN **study • research • debate • understanding • knowledge • thinking • literature • evidence • situation • climate • state • status • trend • level** *Most current research on these matters stresses that gender, class, ethnicity and sexuality are often interwoven.* ◇ *The Institute for European Politics website features a round-up of current thinking on EU policies and issues.* | **position • policy • guidelines • recommendations • practice • affairs • crisis • regime • price • technology** *Current treatment guidelines recommend aspirin or no treatment for those at low risk of stroke.* ◇ *In these ways current technology limits how an employer can organize work.*

C

cur·rent² /ˈkʌrənt; *NAmE* ˈkɜːrənt/ *noun* **1** an area of water or air moving in a definite direction, especially through a surrounding area of water or air in which there is less movement: *Warm ocean currents bring heat to the seas surrounding the Greenland ice sheet.* ◇ **~ of sth** *A thermal is a rising current of air which develops over parts of the earth's surface that are warmer than their surroundings.* **2** the rate of flow of electric CHARGE through a wire, etc, measured in units of AMPERES: *A wire carries the electrical current out of the fuel cell.* ◇ *Sometimes it requires a much higher current to turn the motor that rotates the solar panel because of the increased resistance to turning.* **3** the fact of particular ideas, opinions or feelings being present in a group of people: *In Chapters 8 and 9, the authors look into different methodological currents in International Relations.* ◇ **~ of thought** *Durkheim criticizes those currents of thought typified by Marx which reduce religion to ideology or to metaphysical nonsense.*

ˈcurrent account *noun* **1** (*BrE*) a type of bank account that you can take money out of at any time: *Financial innovation and deregulation were dramatic in the 1980s and 1990s, with the introduction of interest-bearing current accounts, credit cards, debit cards and cash machines.* **2** (*economics*) one of the two main parts that make up a country's BALANCE OF PAYMENTS (along with the CAPITAL ACCOUNT) HELP A country's **current account** consists of earnings from exports and foreign investments, and cash transfers, minus payments for imports and to foreign investors: *In the early 1990s, the country's current account was virtually in balance and the large government deficit was matched by a large private sector surplus.*

ˌcurrent afˈfairs *noun* [pl.] events of political or social importance that are happening now: *After the tsar's death, journals were at last allowed openly to discuss current affairs.*

cur·rent·ly /ˈkʌrəntli; *NAmE* ˈkɜːrəntli/ *adv.* at the present time: *Vaccination is currently recommended for infants aged from 6 to 23 months.* ◇ *This is the best book on Austen's fiction currently available.* ◇ *Currently, no genetic predisposition to lower vitamin D status in these groups has been established.* ➲ *usage note at* ACTUAL

cur·ricu·lum /kəˈrɪkjələm/ *noun* (*pl.* **cur·ric·ula** /kəˈrɪkjələ/) the subjects that are included in a course of study or taught in a school, college or university: *General study skills are taught as part of the school curriculum.* ◇ **in the ~** *Professional development has a place in the curriculum of most, if not all, medical schools.* ➲ *compare* SYLLABUS

curs·ory /ˈkɜːsəri; *NAmE* ˈkɜːrsəri/ *adj.* (*often disapproving*) done quickly and without giving enough attention to details SYN BRIEF¹: *Even a cursory glance at European history will reveal just how long Europeans have been fighting and killing each other.*

cur·tail /kɜːˈteɪl; *NAmE* kɜːrˈteɪl/ *verb* **~ sth** to limit sth, especially sth good, or make it last for a shorter time SYN LIMIT¹ (1), RESTRICT (1): *'Illiberal democracy' refers to political systems where the rule of law is weak and civil liberties are severely curtailed.* ◇ *Integration may be seen as an attempt to curtail competition by denying other firms access to these sources and markets.* ■ **cur·tail·ment** *noun* [U, C, usually sing.] **~ (of sth)** *The USA refused to accept any curtailment of their right to intervene in the internal affairs of other states in their hemisphere until 1933.*

curv·ature /ˈkɜːvətʃə(r); *NAmE* ˈkɜːrvətʃər/ *noun* [U, C] **~ (of sth)** the fact of being curved; the degree to which sth is curved: *Fig. 8.11 shows the effect of the curvature of space on angular measurements of distant objects.* ◇ *Kyphosis is abnormal curvature of the spine.* ◇ *Any curve of this type with constant curvatures and twist is therefore a helix.*

curve¹ /kɜːv; *NAmE* kɜːrv/ *noun* **1** (*statistics*) a line on a graph (either straight or curved) showing how one quantity varies with respect to another: *A decrease in supply shifts the supply curve to the left: less is supplied at each and every price.* ◇ *The spreadsheet plots a curve through these three points to obtain values for the other years.* ◇ *The curve shows a large drop in CO_2 during the Palaeozoic.* ◇ **~ of sth** *Figure 4.3 shows a moisture characteristic curve of a sandy soil.* ◇ **~ for sth** *Fig.11.2 shows an ideal performance curve for a fuel cell running on hydrogen and oxygen.* ➲ *see also* CALIBRATION (1), DEMAND CURVE **2 ~ (of sth)** a line or surface that bends gradually; a smooth bend: *The ruler bent quite easily and you could see the curve of the bent shape.*

curve² /kɜːv; *NAmE* kɜːrv/ *verb* [I, T] to form the shape of a curve; to make sth form the shape of a curve: **~ sth** *As this film creeps up the inside wall it has the effect of curving the surface of the liquid.* ◇ **~ sth + adv./prep.** *These forces can be resisted by making a concrete dam very heavy, or by curving the dam in the horizontal plane.* ◇ **~ + adv./prep** *The barrel is formed by a sheet curving round to form a cylinder.*

curved /kɜːvd; *NAmE* kɜːrvd/ *adj.* having a round shape; having the form of a curve: *Viewed from the air, most beaches are curved in outline.* ◇ *He was the first person to tackle a problem that remains with us today: how to map the curved surface of the earth on a flat surface.*

cus·tom /ˈkʌstəm/ *noun* ➲ *see also* CUSTOMS **1** [C, U] an accepted way of behaving or of doing things in a society or a community: *Even global marketing campaigns are adapted to match local customs and laws.* ◇ **~ of sb/sth** *An identity is imposed on them by the language, nation and customs of the place where they were born.* ◇ **~ of doing sth** *They describe the traditional custom of having a Buddhist priest conduct a funeral ceremony.* ◇ **be the ~ of/for sb to do sth** *Some gifts would also be brought the following day, when it was the custom of the bride's friends to visit her in her new residence.* **2** [U] (*BrE*) the fact of a person or people buying goods or services SYN BUSINESS (6): *Industries have to find new products to attract more custom.*

cus·tom·ary /ˈkʌstəməri; *NAmE* ˈkʌstəmeri/ *adj.* **1** if sth is **customary**, it is what people usually do in a particular place or situation: *These customary practices proved resilient in Ireland.* ◇ **it is ~ (for sb) to do sth** *It is still customary to divide the labour force into two major groups: the low-skilled and the high-skilled.* ◇ *In many government offices in Canada, it is customary for employees to answer the telephone by saying 'Bonjour, hello'.* HELP In law, sth that is **customary** is based on custom rather than on COMMON LAW or STATUTE: *They admit that there is no legal basis for unilateral humanitarian intervention in the UN Charter, but argue that it is permitted by customary international law.* **2** typical of a particular person SYN HABITUAL: *She translated the text with her customary skill and her poet's ear for the two languages.* ■ **cus·tom·ar·ily** /ˈkʌstəmərəli; *NAmE* ˌkʌstəˈmerəli/ *adv.*: *Greeks customarily drank their wine diluted with water.*

cus·tom·er /ˈkʌstəmə(r)/ *noun* a person or an organization that buys goods and services: *In the 1970s, academics emphasized the importance of understanding customers' needs and wants.* ◇ **+ noun** *It was her responsibility to maintain good customer relations with all corporate customers.*

▸ ADJECTIVE + CUSTOMER **potential, prospective • new • existing, current • regular • individual • final • satisfied • dissatisfied • loyal • profitable • key, important • large, major • internal • external • industrial • corporate** *A leaflet was produced to make potential customers aware of the new service.*

▸ NOUN + CUSTOMER **target • business • retail** *The vast majority of their customers are business customers.*

▸ VERB + CUSTOMER **identify • target • reach • attract, win, acquire, get • serve • satisfy • reassure • persuade • encourage • help • keep, retain • lose • charge** *Regional offices were maintained in order to serve nearby customers.* ◇ *Of course, it is far more expensive to win new customers than maintain existing ones.*

▸ CUSTOMER + VERB **want, demand • value • perceive • buy, purchase • pay • receive** *The table shows which benefits are most valued by customers.*

▸ CUSTOMER + NOUN **relationship(s) • acquisition • loyalty • retention • perception(s) • satisfaction • needs, requirements • demand(s), expectations • experience • service • base • contact • focus, orientation** *Customer satisfaction increased as a result of better after-sales service.*

cus·tom·ize (*BrE also* **-ise**) /ˈkʌstəmaɪz/ *verb* **~ sth** to make or change sth to suit the needs of the owner: *The company designs and customizes products and services to the requirements of the organizations purchasing them.* ■ **cus·tom·ized, -ised** *adj.*: *There is a demand for customized business software packages.*

cus·toms /ˈkʌstəmz/ *noun* [pl.] ➲ *see also* CUSTOM **1** (*also* **Customs**) the government department that collects taxes on goods bought and sold and on goods brought into the country, and that checks what is brought in: *He was a former Commissioner of Trade and Customs for the state of Victoria.* ◇ *Chinese customs seized more than 11 200 smuggled antiquities.* ◇ **+ noun** *When the customs officers asked to search the applicant again, she refused, claiming that she had already been searched.* HELP American English uses a singular verb with **customs** in this meaning. *Singapore Customs is responsible for processing applications for permits in relation to import/export of strategic goods.* **2** the taxes that must be paid to the government when goods are brought in from other countries: **+ noun** *Customs duty must be paid on the goods at the point of entry into the country.* **3** the place at a port or an AIRPORT where your bags are checked as you come into a country: *The reporting of a case where a suspect was arrested at customs was of concern.*

ˈcustoms union *noun* a group of states that agree to have the same taxes on imported goods: *An external tariff was imposed on goods and services entering the customs union.*

cut[1] /kʌt/ *verb* (**cut·ting, cut, cut**) **1** [T] to reduce sth by removing a part of it: **~ sth** *Managers were under constant pressure to cut costs.* ◇ *IMF structural adjustment programmes forced governments to cut spending drastically.* ◇ *For the film, Shakespeare's text was drastically cut and rearranged.* ◇ **~ sth by...** *Hood et al. (1999) contend that Civil Service numbers were cut by about 30% between 1976 and 1995.* ◇ **~ sth from... to...** *The number of public-sector inspectorates was cut from eleven to four.* ◇ **~ sth off sth** *Shopkeepers typically cut 10% off their prices as a result.* **2** [T] to remove sth from sth: **~ sth** *By the end of the year, 1 900 jobs had been cut.* ◇ **~ sth from sth** *The final scene in the book was cut from the film adaptation.* **3** [T, I] **~ (sth) (from sth)** to remove part of a text on a computer screen in order to place it somewhere else: *The key skill was being able to cut data from the database and paste it into reports.* **4** [T] to remove sth or a part of sth, using a knife, etc: *51 per cent of coal was cut by machine in the United States in 1913.* **5** [T] to divide sth into two or more pieces with a knife, etc: **~ sth** *Sections of the frozen sample were cut and stained for microscopic observation* ◇ **~ sth in/into sth** *The blocks were each cut into eight identical pieces.* **6** [T] **~ sth (in/into sth)** to make or form sth by removing material: *These are grooves cut into sloping and vertical rock surfaces.* **7** [T, I] to make an opening or a wound in sth, especially with a sharp tool such as a knife: **~ sth/sb/yourself** *He cut himself on the glass.* ◇ **~ through sth** *A sharp knife is used to cut through the tough, outer layers.* **8** [T] **~ sth** (of a line) to cross another line: *The LM curve cuts the line at Z in the diagram.*

IDM Idioms containing **cut** are at the entries for the nouns and adjectives in the idioms, for example **cut your losses** is at **loss**.

PHR V **ˌcut aˈcross sth** to affect or be true for different groups that usually remain separate: *The resistance movement created a new sense of community identity that cut across class divisions.* ◇ *Catholicism has tended to be a religion that cuts across national boundaries.* **cut ˈback (on sth)** (*also* **ˌcut sth ˈbackˌ**) to reduce sth: *Businesses cut back on travel budgets as the recession began to bite.* ◇ *The great powers cut back their military budgets.* **ˌcut sth ˈdown** to make sth fall down by cutting it at the base: *As agriculture expanded, settlers altered the landscape by cutting down trees and draining wetlands.* **ˌcut ˈdown (on sth)** | **ˌcut sth ˈdown (to...)** to reduce the size, amount or number of sth: *Providing regular balanced meals at home helps children cut down on unhealthy snacks.* **ˌcut sb/sth ˈoff** to stop the supply of sth to sb: *Members of the Resistance cut off the power supply to the building where Henriot was speaking.* ◇ **ˌcut sth ˈoff** to remove sth from sth larger by cutting: *The surplus rock was cut off with a diamond trim saw.* ➲ *see also* CUT-OFF **ˌcut sb/sth/yourself ˈoff (from sb/sth)** [often passive] to prevent sb/sth/yourself from leaving or reaching a place or communicating with particular people: *The early Christians consciously cut themselves off from ordinary life.* **ˌcut sb/sth ˈout (of sth)** to stop sb/sth's involvement in sth: *Experts predicted that the Internet would cut out intermediaries, as people bought products directly from the producer.* **ˌcut sth ˈout** to block sth, especially light: *The filters cut out most of the available light.* **ˌcut sth ˈout (of sth)** to stop doing, using or eating sth: *Increasingly, doctors recommended that pregnant women should cut out alcohol entirely.* **ˌcut ˈthrough sth** **1** to deal with sth complicated or difficult in a very efficient way: *Tsar Nicholas's reforms aimed to cut through the mass of complex army laws.* **2** (*also* **ˌcut sth ˈthrough sth**) to make a path or passage through sth by cutting: *Streams cut deep channels through the clay.* **ˌcut sth ˈup (into sth)** to divide sth into small pieces with a knife, etc: *The sets of microchips are then cut up into individual disks and sent for testing.*

cut[2] /kʌt/ *noun* **1** a reduction in amount, size, supply, etc: *There can be real conflict and tension between managers and academics, especially at a time of cuts.* ◇ **tax, pay, wage, price, etc. ~** *A tax cut may not lead to an increase in spending if households decide to save the extra disposable income.* ◇ *Business operations have been restructured, with workers across the board accepting wage cuts and layoffs.* ◇ **~ in sth** *Without deep cuts in emissions, average temperatures could rise by about 3°C by 2100.* ◇ *A cut in interest rates makes borrowing cheaper, and can boost demand from consumers and businesses.* HELP Note that a **cut in sth** describes what is cut, while a **cut of sth** describes how large the cut is: *Salary cuts of 10–20 per* *cent were planned for the public sector.* **2** a wound caused by sth sharp: *The organism is believed to enter the skin through cuts and abrasions.* **3** a hole or an opening in sth, made with sth sharp: *The head of the insect was removed using sharp scissors and a cut made along the full length of the body.* **4** an act of removing part of a film, play, piece of writing, etc: *One version was unedited; the other featured 14 cuts with frequent alterations of close-ups, long shots and zooms.* ◇ **~ in sth** *He was obliged to make substantial cuts both in the dialogue and in the plot.*

D

ˈcut-off (*also* ˈ**cutoff**) *noun* **1** a point or limit when you stop sth: *Both measures have different cut-offs based on ethnicity.* ◇ **~ point/value** *There is no single cut-off point for determining what age is actually old.* ◇ **low/high ~** *A lower cut-off will dilute the effect in the morbidity analysis.* ◇ **~ of sth** *We state in the paper which of the studies included had a weight cut-off of 2 000 g.* **2** an act of stopping the supply of sth: *They were marching to protest against the massive unemployment, lack of essential services and water and electricity cut-offs.* HELP In engineering, a **cut-off** is a device for stopping the flow of a power or fuel supply: *Modern cars are fitted with a fuel cut-off to prevent fires in the event of an accident.*

cut·ting /ˈkʌtɪŋ/ *noun* **1** [U] (often in compounds) the action of cutting sth: *Most of the energy spent in cutting was converted into heat.* ◇ *Marketing activities can be used to boost demand whilst cost-cutting can reduce waste.* ◇ *Timber cutting continues in the national parks but it is closely managed.* **2** [C] a piece that has been cut off from sth, or out of sth: *He sent her a newspaper cutting giving details of the inheritance.* HELP In biology, a **cutting** is a piece cut off a plant that will be used to grow a new plant: *The cuttings were left to grow in the greenhouse for 5 months before sectioning.* **3** [C] (*BrE*) a narrow open passage that is dug through high ground for a road, railway or CANAL: *This was the first railway into London and involved solving some difficult engineering problems including cuttings and tunnels.*

cycle AWL /ˈsaɪkl/ *noun* **1** the fact of a series of events being repeated many times, always in the same order: *Large birds have longer production cycles, and might therefore be more susceptible to poultry diseases.* ◇ **~ of sth** *The seasonal cycle of work began in the autumn with the planting of new sugar cane.* HELP In biology, a **cycle** is a series of events or processes in the life of a plant or animal: *The chromosomes of a cell undergo a variety of changes in the course of the cell cycle.* ➲ *see also* BUSINESS CYCLE, CARBON CYCLE, LIFE CYCLE **2** a complete set or series of movements in a machine or part of the body: *The amount of fuel burned per cycle is lowered by reducing the engine pressure.* ◇ **~ of sth** *We allowed another 90 minutes for another complete cycle of rotation.*

▸ ADJECTIVE + CYCLE **complete** • **natural** • **seasonal** • **annual** • **long-term** • **regular** • **economic** *Expenditure and income have to balance out over the economic cycle.*

▸ VERB + CYCLE **enter** • **go through** • **complete** • **repeat** • **break** • **halt, arrest** • **control** • **drive** *The Grameen Bank aimed to break the cycle of poverty by providing the poor with micro-credit.*

▸ PHRASES **a stage/phase/part of the cycle** • **a point in the cycle** *Each phase of the cycle must be completed before the next phase is initiated.*

cyc·lic AWL /ˈsaɪklɪk; ˈsɪklɪk/ (*also* **cyc·lic·al** /ˈsaɪklɪkl; ˈsɪklɪkl/) *adj.* [usually before noun] **1** repeated many times and always happening in the same order: *The collection of data will be an ongoing, cyclic process.* ◇ *These were the industries that suffered most in cyclical downturns.* **2** (*chemistry*) (of a COMPOUND) with a structure that contains one or more closed rings of atoms: *Borazines are very stable cyclic molecules.* ■ **cyc·lic·al·ly** *adv.*: *This tide varies cyclically due to the oscillations of the sun as it orbits the galaxy.*

cy·lin·der /ˈsɪlɪndə(r)/ *noun* **1** a solid or hollow shape with round ends and long straight sides: *Spheres or cylinders are, however, not very good approximations for the shape of most real crystals.* **2** the tube in an engine, shaped like a cylinder, inside which the PISTON moves: *During this intake process, the fuel and vapour are mixed in the cylinder.* **3** an object shaped like a cylinder, especially one used as a container for gas: *During critical-care transportation, oxygen is commonly supplied from gas cylinders.*

cy·lin·dric·al /səˈlɪndrɪkl/ *adj.* shaped like a cylinder: *These plant stems and roots have cylindrical structures that are completely symmetrical around a central axis.*

cy·to·plasm /ˈsaɪtəʊplæzəm; *NAmE* ˈsaɪtoʊplæzəm/ *noun* [U] (*biology*) all the living material in a cell, not including the NUCLEUS: *In some animals, many sperm penetrate the egg but all but one are destroyed in the cytoplasm.* ■ **cy·to·plas·mic** /ˌsaɪtəʊˈplæzmɪk; *NAmE* ˌsaɪtoʊˈplæzmɪk/ *adj.*: *Cytoplasmic and nuclear proteins were extracted with a commercially available kit.*

Dd

daily[1] /ˈdeɪli/ *adj.* [only before noun] happening, done or produced every day: *The film brings viewers into the daily life of a village near Madrid.* ◇ *Daily newspapers tend to have a high degree of reader loyalty.* ◇ *The average daily energy requirements of an adult male human are 10 000 kJ.*

daily[2] /ˈdeɪli/ *adv.* every day: *Temperature was monitored using an alcohol thermometer that was checked daily.* ◇ **once, twice, etc. ~** *She takes insulin twice daily but is on no other medications.*

dairy[1] /ˈdeəri; *NAmE* ˈderi/ *noun* (*pl.* **-ies**) **1** [C] a company that sells milk, and makes and sells food made from milk, such as butter and cheese: *The supermarkets restructured their milk supply chains, with consequences for the three biggest dairies and the producers who supplied them.* ◇ *In the 1880s, the number of cooperatively owned dairies grew from 3 to 700.* **2** [C] a place on a farm where milk is kept and where butter and other milk products are made: *To separate the fat from the milk, the 'separator' was developed in Sweden, but it was first brought into use in Danish dairies.* **3** [U] milk, eggs, cheese and other milk products thought of as a group: *There appeared to be no major differences by income group in consumption of the major food groups—meat, dairy or grains.*

dairy[2] /ˈdeəri; *NAmE* ˈderi/ *adj.* [only before noun] **1** made from milk: *For infants, milk and dairy products need to be full-fat until at least the age of 2 years.* **2** connected with the production of milk rather than meat: *The raw milk produced by UK dairy farmers is processed into a number of different products.* ◇ *From 1925 to 1940, the number of farms with dairy cattle decreased by 12.0%.*

dam[1] /dæm/ *noun* **1** a barrier that is built across a river in order to stop the water from flowing, used especially to make a RESERVOIR (= a lake for storing water) or to produce electricity: *There are plans to build a series of seven dams across the upper Mekong.* ◇ *Where a reservoir is formed behind a dam, aquatic and terrestrial ecosystems are greatly altered.* **2** a natural barrier of rock or other material that forms across a river: *Glaciers may also advance across fjords to form a glacier dam.*

dam[2] /dæm/ *verb* (**-mm-**) to build a dam across a river, especially in order to make a RESERVOIR (= a lake for storing water) or to produce electricity: **~ sth** *The Burnett River* *was dammed in 2005.* ◇ **~ sth up** *Damming up more rivers is encountering increasing public resistance.*

dam·age¹ /ˈdæmɪdʒ/ *noun* **1** [U] **~ (to sth)** physical harm caused to sth: *Hurricanes can cause serious damage to populated land areas.* ◇ *Tumours are primarily the result of DNA damage.* ◇ *People with diabetes are at increased risk of long-term damage to various organs and systems.* **2 ~ (to sb/sth)** harmful effects on sb/sth: *A failure of food safety control can do serious damage to the reputation of a business.* **3 damages** [pl.] an amount of money that a court decides should be paid to sb by sb/sth that has caused them harm or injury: *The Court awarded the company damages.* ◇ *The defendant was ordered to pay damages of £5000 and legal costs of £13500.*

▸ ADJECTIVE + DAMAGE **serious, severe • extensive • significant • irreversible, permanent • potential • physical • environmental • criminal • cellular • neurological • collateral** *The defendants were both convicted of criminal damage.* ◇ *Collateral damage in the form of civilian casualties should be minimized.*

▸ NOUN + DAMAGE **DNA • tissue • muscle • nerve • cell • organ • brain • liver • kidney** *Cirrhosis is the end result of long-term liver damage.*

▸ VERB + DAMAGE **cause, do, inflict, induce • suffer, sustain • avoid • prevent • reduce • minimize • limit • repair** *Unfortunately, his stern policies initially did more damage than good.* ◇ *Radiotherapy requires meticulous planning to avoid damage to the upper spinal cord.*

▸ VERB + DAMAGES **award • claim, seek • pay • recover** *Due to the employer's failure to provide the correct safety equipment, he was entitled to claim damages for his injury.* ◇ *Britain and France sought punitive damages from Germany in the form of reparations.*

WHICH WORD?

damage • injury

- **Damage** and **injury** can both refer to physical harm to sb's body, or harm to sb's mind: *Inflammation may be defined as the reaction or response of the body to tissue injury or damage.* ◇ *psychological damage/injury*
- **Injury** generally refers to the event or act of being physically harmed; **damage** is more to do with the results or effects of this harm: *He suffered a brain injury after falling off a balcony.* ◇ *Fatal liver damage can be prevented by giving an antidote within 10–12 hours of ingestion.*
- **Injury** is usually the result of deliberate or accidental actions by a person; **damage** can be the result of natural physical processes: *It was found that non-accidental injuries had been caused to the child.* ◇ *... the various forms of cell damage observed to occur during ageing.*
- In law, **injury** refers to damage to a person's feelings, while **damages** are an amount of money that has to be paid to sb who has been harmed in some way.

dam·age² /ˈdæmɪdʒ/ *verb* **1 ~ sth** to cause physical harm to sth: *Unfortunately the bridge was badly damaged by fire in 1993.* ◇ *The earthquake created tsunami waves which severely damaged villages on the south coast of Java.* ◇ *DNA can be damaged through its interaction with a variety of reactive chemicals or radiation.* **2 ~ sth** to have a harmful effect on sth: *Once the markets discovered these errors, the companies' reputations were irreparably damaged.*

dam·aging /ˈdæmɪdʒɪŋ/ *adj.* having a harmful effect on sb/sth; causing damage: *Unpopular legislation can have a very damaging effect upon a government.* ◇ *The region was rocked by several large and damaging earthquakes.* ◇ **~ to sb/sth** *Conflicts between civil and military authority were frequent and damaging to the war effort.*

dance¹ /dɑːns; *NAmE* dæns/ *noun* **1** [C] a series of movements and steps that are usually performed to music: *Daughters learn the dances by watching and imitating their elders.* ◇ **+ noun** *The dance routine was carefully choreographed and the work of intensive training.* **2** [U] the art of dancing, especially for entertainment: *Thailand's traditional art forms, from dance to painting, provide the world with recognized cultural treasures.* ◇ *Kelly often includes ballet and modern dance in his films.*

D

dance² /dɑːns; *NAmE* dæns/ *verb* [I] to move your body to the sound and rhythm of music: *People dance to folk music played in parks or community centres.* ◇ **~ with sb** *She politely refuses Darcy's offer to dance with her.*

dan·cer /ˈdɑːnsə(r); *NAmE* ˈdænsər/ *noun* a person who dances or whose job is dancing: *The first group targeted by the regime was the intelligentsia, including artists and ballet dancers.*

dan·cing /ˈdɑːnsɪŋ; *NAmE* ˈdænsɪŋ/ *noun* [U] the activity or skill of moving your body to music, for pleasure or in order to entertain other people: *Kandy had become an influential cultural centre with its distinctive arts, architecture, crafts, dancing and music.*

dan·ger /ˈdeɪndʒə(r)/ *noun* **1** [U, C] the possibilty of sth happening that will injure, harm or kill sb, or damage or destroy sth: **~ (of sth)** *It is almost impossible to exaggerate the danger of climate change.* ◇ *Nuclear physicists had long recognized the dangers of radiation exposure to the human body.* ◇ **in ~** *Although their lives may not be in danger, basic human rights are lacking.* **2** [C, U] the possibility that sth bad might happen: **~ (of sth)** *Grave concern was expressed about the danger of a renewed boycott.* ◇ **in ~ of (doing) sth** *Many languages are in danger of disappearing.* ◇ **~ that...** *There is a danger that some wars will occur as democracies attempt to overthrow non-democratic regimes.* **3** [C] **~ (to sb/sth)** a person or thing that may harm sb or cause damage: *Unused drugs are a danger to children.* ◇ *Education about the potential dangers around the home is now part of the national UK school curriculum.* ➲ *see also* ENDANGER

dan·ger·ous /ˈdeɪndʒərəs/ *adj.* likely to injure, harm or kill sb, or to damage or destroy sth: *Only a very small minority of patients are potentially dangerous.* ◇ *Many organizations operate in dangerous situations with high levels of uncertainty and risk.* ◇ **~ for sb** *It would be dangerous for the observer if this light were to fall directly onto the eye.* ◇ **is is ~ (for sb) to do sth** *It can be dangerous for academics to stray too far from their home discipline.* ◇ **~ to sb/sth** *This fungus is potentially dangerous to human health.*

dan·ger·ous·ly /ˈdeɪndʒərəsli/ *adv.* **1** to a degree that might result in harm, death or damage: *The ships were blown dangerously close to the rocky coastline.* ◇ **~ high/low** *The CO concentration in the flue gas rose to dangerously high levels.* **2** in a way that is likely to harm or kill sb or damage sth: *She was found guilty of causing death by driving dangerously under the influence of drink.*

dark¹ /dɑːk; *NAmE* dɑːrk/ *adj.* (**dark·er**, **dark·est**) **1** with no or very little light, especially because it is night: *People living alone may be reluctant to answer the door when it is dark because of fear of crime.* ◇ *The cages were placed in a dark room so that the birds were less aware of the observer.* OPP LIGHT² **2** not light; nearer black than white: *After a few minutes of microwave heating, the samples turned dark brown.* ◇ *Mineral matter becomes more concentrated in the snow, giving it a darker colour.* OPP LIGHT², PALE **3** having a colour that is close to black: *Unstained samples thus appear bright against a dark background.* ◇ *Highly humified peat is dark in colour.* **4** brown or black in colour: *He is described as 'tall and broad with dark hair and dark eyes'.* ◇ *It is always optimal to have a darker skin where the sunlight is stronger and a paler one where it is* *less strong.* **5** evil or frightening, and usually hidden: *If Livy held up examples of virtue, Tacitus looks at the dark side of public life.* ◇ *The unconscious was a prey to dark forces over which the individual had no control.* ◇ *Delegates testified and debated the dark secrets of national history.* **6** without any hope that sth good will happen: *Many contemporary observers did not share Orwell's dark vision.*

D

dark² /dɑːk; *NAmE* dɑːrk/ *noun* **1 the dark** [sing.] the lack of light in a place, especially because it is night: **in the ~** *The solution should be prepared freshly and kept refrigerated in the dark.* **2** [U] an amount of sth that is dark in colour: *The appearance of interference patterns of alternating light and dark signals the presence of waves.*
IDM **after/before dark** after/before the sun goes down and it is night: *They are nocturnal, inhabiting burrows in the daytime and emerging only after dark to graze.* **in the ˈdark (about sth)** knowing nothing about sth: *All the children we interviewed took measures to keep parents in the dark about the content of their email and calls.*

dark·en /ˈdɑːkən; *NAmE* ˈdɑːrkən/ *verb* [I, T] to become dark; to make sth dark: *Distant thunder was heard, the air darkened and some drops of rain fell.* ◇ **~ sth** *The ash cloud covered 200 000 square kilometres, darkening the sky.* ◇ *The simulator was located in a quiet, darkened room kept at a comfortable temperature.*

ˌdark ˈmatter *noun* [U] according to some theories, material which exists in space that does not produce any light: *The main evidence for dark matter comes from studies of the rotation of galaxies.*

dark·ness /ˈdɑːknəs; *NAmE* ˈdɑːrknəs/ *noun* [U] **1** the state of being dark, without any light: **(in) ~** *The experiment was repeated in complete darkness.* ◇ *Clear skies during the hours of darkness can lead to very cold nights.* **2 ~ (of sth)** the quality or state of being dark in colour: *The vividness of lightning is accentuated by the brooding darkness of the clouds in which it occurs.*

dash /dæʃ/ *noun* the mark (—) used to separate parts of a sentence, often instead of a colon or in pairs instead of brackets : *She breaks up her sentences with dashes at this point in the poem.* ➲ *compare* HYPHEN

data AWL /ˈdeɪtə; ˈdɑːtə; *NAmE* ˈdætə/ *noun* **1** [pl.] facts or figures, especially when examined and used to find out things or to make decisions: *These data were collected from more than 25 000 respondents in 12 countries.* ◇ *These data clearly show the desired decrease in water content.* ◇ *The available empirical data do not point to any consistent pattern.* HELP In general English, **data** is often treated as uncountable and used with singular forms: *This data shows...* In academic English, however, it should almost always be used with plural forms: *These data are...*; the exception is in computer science, where it is sometimes used with singular forms (see sense 2, below): *Data is extracted using SQL queries.* The singular is **datum**; you can also use **data point.** **2** [pl., U] facts that are stored by a computer or transferred between computers: *Instructions and data can be stored using the same kinds of symbols.* ◇ *The telephone network was not originally designed to handle high-speed transfer of digital data.*
▸ ADJECTIVE + DATA **available • new • relevant • reliable • raw • empirical • primary • secondary • qualitative • quantitative • personal • experimental • demographic • administrative • clinical • molecular • historical** *To achieve the most accurate forecasts, managers should attempt to use both secondary and primary data sources.* ◇ *The assessor gathered qualitative data on parent-child interactions.*
▸ VERB + DATA **use • collect, obtain, gather • extract • record • provide, present, report, show • include • analyse, examine • interpret • generate, produce • compare • share** *Each publication was reviewed and data were extracted.* ◇ *A major challenge in epidemiological research is ensuring the quality of the raw data generated for analysis.*
▸ DATA + VERB **suggest, indicate, show • support** *The most recent data suggest that obesity rates are continuing to climb in men.* ◇ *This prediction is not supported by the data.*

GRAMMAR POINT

data • bacteria • criteria • media • phenomena • strata

- In general English, these words are often used with the singular form of the verb: ***Bacteria is** killed by thorough cooking.* ◇ In academic English, this usage is considered incorrect and it is important to use the correct plural form of the verb: ***Bacteria enter** the skin through ulcers or cracks.* ◇ *Based on **these criteria**,...* ◇ *No **data are** available on the mineralogy of the local sediment, however.* ◇ *Contemporary screen **media are** typically the result of numerous processes, only one of which involves actual filming.* ◇ *Many atmospheric **phenomena are...*** ◇ *Younger Precambrian **strata are** widely exposed across central and southern Arizona.*
- The singular forms are **bacterium**, **criterion**, **datum**, **medium**, **phenomenon** and **stratum**: *The **bacterium is** rich in virulence factors.* ◇ *The **criterion** of fairness **is** controversial.* ◇ ***Every** reference **datum makes** it possible for third persons to match data.* ◇ *Downloading music rather than listening to the radio merely swaps **one medium** for another.* ◇ *Flooding is **a natural phenomenon** in the Lower Central Plain* ◇ *In **each** age **stratum**, four gender-ethnicity groups were defined.*

data·base /ˈdeɪtəbeɪs; *NAmE also* ˈdætəbeɪs/ *noun* an organized set of data that is stored in a computer and can be looked at and used in various ways: *With direct marketing, a company can use its database to develop a profile of who its best customers are.* ◇ **in/on a ~** *Each record in the database identifies the establishment at which an individual is employed.* ◇ **~ of sth** *The associated gene can be identified by searching the databases of genome sequences.*

ˈdata capture *noun* [U] the action or process of collecting data, especially using computers: *Different methods of data capture can be used to look at a problem in different ways.*

ˈdata point *noun* an item in a set of data: *A gross error usually causes one data point to lie significantly away from the rest of the data.*

ˌdata ˈprocessing *noun* [U] a series of actions that a computer performs on data to produce an OUTPUT: *For data processing, scientists should have access to analytical tools such as statistical and modelling software.*

ˌdata proˈtection *noun* [U] legal restrictions that keep information stored on computers private and that control who can read it or use it: **+ noun** *data protection laws/legislation* ◇ *The processing must be carried out in accordance with the data protection principles.*

ˈdata set *noun* (*computing*) a collection of data which is treated as a single unit by a computer: *Large data sets can frequently yield quite large nationally representative samples.*

date¹ /deɪt/ *noun* **1** [C] a particular day of the month, sometimes in a particular year, given in numbers and words; a particular year when sth happens: *Johnson's birth date is given as 7 September 1709.* ◇ *There is some doubt about the exact date the bridge was built.* ◇ **~ of sth** *Details held include full name, date of birth, sex and address.* ◇ *All sources cited in this book are referenced according to their first historical dates of publication.* **2** [sing., U] a time in the past or future that is not a particular day: *The municipal government decided to*

postpone the election to a later date. ◇ *Arabs established themselves in southern India from an early date.* ◇ *At some future date, the supply of oil will be unable to meet demand in an economically feasible way.*
IDM **to ˈdate** until now: *To date, the principal technology for generating renewable energy has involved the damming of rivers.* ◇ *The majority of studies conducted to date have found little support for the hypothesis.*

date[2] /deɪt/ *verb* **1** to say or find out when sth old existed or was made: **~ sth** *These poems are hard to date.* ◇ **~ sth at sth** *The grave has been dated at around 550 BC.* ◇ **~ sth to sth** *The shape of these skulls is very similar to that of the African finds dated to the same period.* ◇ **~ sth between A and B** *The consecration of King Asoka can be plausibly dated anywhere between 280 and 267 BCE.* **2 ~ sth** to write or print the date on sth: *Ensure each partner has signed and dated the agreement.* ◇ *Turing's reaction is described in a letter by Birch dated 20 October 1940.*
PHR V **ˌdate ˈback (to...)** | **ˈdate from...** to have existed since a particular time in the past or for the length of time mentioned: *The floppy disk drive is an IBM invention dating back to the 1960s.* ◇ *The use of wind to provide mechanical power dates from ancient times.*

date·book /ˈdeɪtbʊk/ *noun* (*NAmE*) = DIARY (2)

datum /ˈdeɪtəm/ *noun* (*pl.* **data**) a fact or piece of information: *The median is defined as the central datum when all of the data are arranged in numerical order.* ◇ *Each datum comprises an x-y pair of values represented by a dot or other symbol on the plot.* ➲ *see also* DATA ➲ grammar note *at* DATA

daugh·ter /ˈdɔːtə(r)/ *noun* **~ (of sb)** a person's female child: *Born in London, he married the daughter of a wine merchant.* ◇ *Since her husband's death, Mrs Crabbe has been living with her eldest daughter and her family.* ◇ *Sons and daughters in the same family were often treated differently.*

day /deɪ/ *noun* **1** [C] a period of 24 hours: *These wounds can take 10–21 days to heal.* ◇ *They died on the same day, July 4, 1826.* ◇ **per ~** *Russia produces 10 million barrels of oil per day.* **2** [C, usually sing.] the hours of the day when you are awake or working: *A worker is entitled to a 20-minute rest break if the working day is longer than 6 hours.* ◇ *During her depressive episodes, she would sometimes spend the entire day watching television.* ◇ **during the ~** *Students claimed that it was very easy to go off campus during the school day.* ➲ *see also* WORKING DAY **3** [U] the part of the day when it is light: *In and around cities, heavy traffic can be a serious problem at almost any time of the day or night.* ◇ **during the ~** *Nocturnal owls and nightjars stay hidden during the day.* ◇ **by ~** *Without evaporation, the Earth's surface would be considerably warmer by day and colder by night.* **4** [C, usually pl.] a particular period of time or history: *She had access to a computer, rare in those days.* ◇ **~ of sth** *Even simple domestic products use electronics that are far more powerful than those used in the early days of space travel.* ➲ *see also* NOWADAYS, PRESENT DAY
IDM **carry/win the ˈday** to be successful against sb/sth: *The anti-slave trade cause needed to win the votes of the majority of independent MPs to carry the day.* **day after ˈday** every day for a long period of time: *Day after day, people waited to be rescued.* **day by ˈday** every day; a little at a time and gradually: *The symptoms were noted day by day.* ◇ *Napoleon's forces were disintegrating day by day.* **from day to ˈday 1** if a situation changes **from day to day**, it changes often: *In healthy people, mood varies from day to day and hour to hour.* **2** with no thoughts or plans for the future: *Farmers had to consume their meagre stores of grain, just to keep themselves alive from day to day.* **in/of sb's ˈday** during a particular period of time in the past when sb lived: *Science in Hobbes's day was materialistic and did not leave much room for anything supernatural.* ◇ *The book places Austen in the context of the revolutionary politics of her day.* **of the ˈday** during a particular period of time: *The moral code of the day stressed devotion to the church.* ◇ *Many of the political issues of the day were a response to the impact of the Second World War.* **ˈone day** at some time in the future; on a particular day in the past: *Hydrogen is viewed as a clean energy alternative that could one day replace fossil fuels.* ◇ *Vera confronted him one day after she had discovered he had lost most of their life savings.* **ˈsome day** at an unknown time in the future: *Eighty per cent of the girls' mothers believed that their daughters would some day have a well-paying job.* **ˈthese days** used to talk about the present, especially when you are comparing it with the past: *These days, short-term expectations are high among shareholders.* **to this ˈday** even now, when a lot of time has passed: *The debate between liberalism and realism continues to this day.* ➲ *more at* END[2]

ˈday care *noun* [U] care for small children, or for old or sick people, away from home, during the day: *Japan had only 13% of three-year-olds in day care compared with 54% in the US and 34% in the UK.* ◇ **~ center** (*US*) *More children are now taken care of in day care centers.*

day·light /ˈdeɪlaɪt/ *noun* [U] the light that comes from the sun during the day: *The individual will secrete melatonin during the hours of natural daylight.* ◇ *In daylight, the only human artefact visible from space was a portion of the Great Wall of China.* ◇ **+ noun** *Algae can photosynthesize throughout daylight hours.*

day·time /ˈdeɪtaɪm/ *noun* [U, sing.] the period during the day between the time when it gets light and the time when it gets dark: **in/during the ~** *Fruit flies are active in the daytime.* ◇ **+ noun** *Research shows that daytime sleepiness impacts school performance.*

ˌday-to-ˈday *adj.* [only before noun] involving the usual events or tasks of each day; happening every day in a regular way: *The management board is responsible for the day-to-day running of the company.* ◇ *Many people live with a condition that limits their ability to cope with day-to-day activities.* ◇ *Different agencies have different names for those who handle contact with their clients on a day-to-day basis.*

dead[1] /ded/ *adj.* **1** no longer alive: *The police had no way of knowing if Jakob was dead or alive.* ◇ *King was shot dead as he stood on the balcony of his hotel.* ◇ *Lear comes on to the stage for the last time, carrying the dead body of his daughter.* ◇ *Most of these dead trees are still standing.* ◇ *Once cell death has been completed, the remains of the dead cell need to be removed.* **2** [not before noun] no longer believed in or aimed for; belonging to the past: *Geopolitics may be dead, but history is not.* ◇ *Nash has argued that video art is dead because the conditions that gave rise to its funding have been destroyed.*

dead[2] /ded/ *noun* **the dead 1** [pl.] people who have died: *Africans in Jamaica often had their own burial grounds where they observed their own practices to honour the dead.* **2** [sing.] the state of being dead: *Jesus lived in Palestine, taught, died, and, his followers believed, rose from the dead.*

dead·line /ˈdedlaɪn/ *noun* a point in time by which sth must be done: *If these deadlines are not met, they may affect delivery of other results.* ◇ **~ for sth** *The company has to set a clear deadline for payment.*

dead·ly /ˈdedli/ *adj.* (**dead·lier**, **dead·li·est**) (**More deadly** and **deadliest** are the usual forms. You can also use **most deadly**.) causing or likely to cause death SYN LETHAL (1): *European explorers brought with them deadly foreign diseases.* ◇ *Plants contain some of the deadliest chemicals known.* ◇ *He was held on charges of aggravated assault with a deadly weapon.*

deaf /def/ *adj.* (**deaf·er, deaf·est**) **1** unable to hear anything or unable to hear very well: *She was born deaf.* ➲ *usage note at* DISABILITY **2 the deaf** *noun* [pl.] people who cannot hear: *Slowly, the use of signs became part of the education models used at schools for the deaf.* ➲ *usage note at* DISABILITY **3** [not before noun] **~ to sth** not willing to listen or pay attention to sth: *Sumner and his allies were deaf to the appeal of these arguments.* ■ **deaf·ness** *noun* [U] *Despite deafness and other disabilities, she was a spirited actor on the political scene.*

IDM **fall on deaf 'ears** to be ignored or not noticed by other people: *Lincoln's pleas fell on deaf ears.*

deal¹ /diːl/ *verb* (**dealt, dealt** /delt/)

IDM **deal a 'blow to sb/sth** to be very shocking or harmful to sb/sth: *The Protestant Reformation dealt a devastating blow to the Catholic Church's claim to supreme authority.*

PHR V **'deal in sth** to buy and sell a particular product SYN TRADE² (1): *The case concerned an alleged conspiracy to deal in stolen motor vehicles.* ◇ *If a company deals in products that can be delivered electronically, then all business can be done electronically.* **'deal with sb** to take appropriate action, according to who you are talking to, managing or looking after SYN HANDLE (1): *Nurses should adopt a calm and understanding approach when dealing with patients with such symptoms.* **'deal with sb/sth** to do business with a person, a company or an organization: *The company deals with its customers mainly through its website.* **'deal with sth 1** to take action in order to solve a problem or complete a task: *Alternative ways of dealing with these situations should be discussed.* ◇ *Teachers have a large role to play in helping children deal with the challenges of the digital world.* **2** to be about a particular subject: *Levinson's work deals extensively with philosophical questions.* ◇ *The first two sections deal with the academic study of social policy.* ➲ language bank *at* ABOUT²

▸ DEAL WITH + NOUN **situation • case • problem • change • conflict • challenge • crisis • complexity • range • uncertainty • consequence** *The first step in dealing with the problem is to recognize that it exists.* | **issue • question • matter • aspect • topic, subject** *The website deals with all aspects of infectious disease.*

▸ DEAL + ADVERB + WITH | ADVERB + DEAL WITH **effectively** *An in-house lawyer is less able to deal effectively with conflicts between his professional obligations and the aims of his client.* | **specifically • mainly, primarily • directly** *The book specifically deals with the southern part of Alberta and Saskatchewan.*

deal² /diːl/ *noun* **1** [C] an agreement, especially in business, on particular conditions for buying or doing sth: *After extended discussion, the deal was made.* ◇ *The next stage of the buying process is negotiating with the supplier for the best deal.* ◇ *The two countries have recently signed a deal to work in partnership on a range of research projects.* ◇ *Union bosses struck a deal whereby they agreed to make lower wage demands.* **2** [sing.] **a good/great ~ (of sth)** much; a lot: *A good deal of what we think and feel follows from our behaviour.* ◇ *A great deal of knowledge has been accumulated by microbiologists regarding the growth requirements of bacteria.* IDM *see* STRIKE¹

deal·er /ˈdiːlə(r)/ *noun* **1** a person or company whose business is buying and selling a particular product: *Car dealers and manufacturers account for a huge portion of media ad revenues.* ◇ *Sony distributes its computers via authorized dealers and its own network of retail centres.* ◇ **~ in sth** *The company sells to hospitals and to dealers in health care equipment.* **2** a person who sells illegal drugs: *The defendant voluntarily associated with a man he knew to be a drug dealer.*

deal·ing /ˈdiːlɪŋ/ *noun* **1 dealings** [pl.] business activities; the relations that you have with sb in business: *In our business dealings, we expect our partners to adhere to business principles consistent with our own.* ◇ **~ with sb/sth** *The business that can bring a 'human touch' to its dealings with customers will often gain the advantage.* **2** [U, C] buying and selling: *Worldwide trading and foreign exchange dealing complicate the issue further.* ◇ *The tablets list dealings in goods such as grain and livestock.* **3** [U] **~ (between A and B)** a way of doing business or making agreements with sb: *The purpose of the Act is to ensure fair dealing between employer and Union.*

dealt *past tense, past part. of* DEAL¹

dear /dɪə(r); *NAmE* dɪr/ *adj.* (**dear·er, dear·est**) **1** loved by or important to sb: *Tennyson lost his dear friend Arthur Henry Hallam when he was 24 years old.* ◇ **~ to sb** *They lost everything that was dear to them.* **2 Dear** used at the beginning of a letter before the name or title of the person that you are writing to: *Dear Sir or Madam* ◇ *Dear Dr Jones*

death /deθ/ *noun* **1** [U] the end of life; the state of being dead: *The major poisons causing death in England and Wales in 2005 are listed below.* ◇ *Rigor mortis occurs 2–4 hours following death.* ◇ *There is a significant amount of cell death in all growing tissues.* ◇ **~ of sb/sth** *The death of a loved one is often a shattering and bewildering experience.* **2** [C] the fact of sb dying or being killed: *World War II caused at least 50 million deaths.* ◇ *Most traffic deaths occur in small accidents involving one or two vehicles.* ◇ **+ noun** *Russia's high death rate and low birth rate have led to a shrinking population since the early 1990s.* **3** [U] **~ of sth** the permanent end of sth: *This essay opposes the notion that the advent of the digital image has been accompanied by the death of cinema.*

IDM **put sb to death** to kill sb as a punishment SYN EXECUTE (1): *Socrates was put to death for his teachings in 399BC.* **to the death** until sb is dead: *The Spartan soldiers surrendered rather than fight to the death.* ➲ *more at* FIGHT¹, LIFE

de·bat·able AWL /dɪˈbeɪtəbl/ *adj.* not certain because people can have different ideas and opinions about the thing being discussed SYN ARGUABLE (2), QUESTIONABLE (1): *The value of summit diplomacy has been historically debatable.* ◇ **it is ~ whether...** *It is debatable whether people are today more secure economically than they were 100 years ago.*

de·bate¹ AWL /dɪˈbeɪt/ *noun* **1** [U, C] an argument or discussion expressing different opinions: *Euthanasia is currently the subject of much debate.* ◇ **~ on/about/over sth** *Recent debate about the origin of modern humans has focused on two competing hypotheses.* ◇ **~ between** *The old debate between science and faith has been rekindled.* **2** [C] a formal discussion of an issue at a public meeting or in a parliament: *The candidates appeared in live televised debates.* ◇ **~ on sth** *The final debates on emancipation began in Parliament on 14 May 1833.* HELP In a **debate**, two or more speakers express opposing views and then there is often a vote on the issue. ➲ thesaurus note *at* DISCUSSION

▸ ADJECTIVE + DEBATE **heated, fierce • vigorous, intense • lively** *Abortion has often become a focus of heated debate.* ◇ *There were fierce debates in the Lords and in the Commons.* | **ongoing • current • wide, broad** *The Internet's role in people's social lives remains a topic of ongoing debate.* ◇ *This has been part of a wider debate about the future of banking.* | **public • political • parliamentary** *The decision was made without any proper parliamentary and public debate.* ◇ *They decided to arrange a proper public debate on the matter.* | **philosophical • theological • academic • theoretical • intellectual** *This is an issue that has attracted much academic debate.*

▸ VERB + DEBATE **spark, provoke, fuel, stimulate, ignite, generate, trigger • inform • frame • shape** *His new book should spark some debate.* ◇ *Three questions have framed* *this debate.* | **open** ◆ **close** ◆ **hold** *She opened the debate by insulting her opponent.*

▸ DEBATE + VERB **rage** ◆ **surround** ◆ **concern** ◆ **continue** *For more than a century now, a debate has raged over the origins of this literature.*

THESAURUS

debate ◆ **controversy** ◆ **disagreement** ◆ **dispute** *noun*

These are all words for an argument between people or groups.

- (a) debate/controversy/disagreement/dispute **about/over** sth
- (a) debate/controversy/disagreement/dispute **between/within/among** sb
- (a) **political** debate/controversy/disagreement/dispute
- **considerable** debate/controversy/disagreement
- **public/academic** debate/controversy
- a/an **recent/current/ongoing** debate/controversy
- to **generate/provoke/spark/cause** debate/controversy
- to **resolve** a controversy/disagreement/dispute
- (a) debate/controversy **surrounds sth/concerns sth/rages**
- a disagreement/dispute **arises**
- a **subject of/matter of/area of** debate/controversy/dispute

- **Debate** is the most positive of these words; it describes a situation where people discuss different ideas and opinions in order to reach a better understanding of a subject: *We hope that the papers in this issue will help to stimulate debate over what shape future research might take.*
- **Controversy** is general discussion and argument on a subject that people feel strongly about; **disagreement** usually involves opposite opinions about a particular point: *The redevelopment plans have been a source of some controversy.* ◇ *There is considerable disagreement about who should be granted access to these documents.*
- **Disagreement**, like **controversy**, can involve a public discussion; a **disagreement** can also be directly between two people or groups; a **dispute** is usually a direct argument over a particular issue between two people, groups or countries: *There is considerable disagreement over the risks to human health.* ◇ *There are major disagreements between the parties on public expenditure.* ◇ *Voluntary codes of conduct can offer a cheaper means of resolving disputes compared with more formal legal channels.*

de·bate² AWL /dɪˈbeɪt/ *verb* [T, I] to discuss sth, especially in a formal way or at a public meeting: **~ sth** *Usually, the Council debates an issue and then votes.* ◇ *The cause of the extinction of these birds is still hotly debated.* ◇ **~ whether/what, etc...** *They debated whether men and women viewed issues differently.* ◇ **~ with sb (on sth)** *Elizabeth debates with Darcy on a whole range of subjects.*

deb·ris /ˈdebriː; ˈdeɪbriː; *NAmE* dəˈbriː/ *noun* [U] **1** broken pieces of wood, rock or other materials that are left somewhere as part of a natural process, or after sth has been destroyed: *The woody debris and fallen logs replenish the soil and provide nutrients for many species.* ◇ *Much of the gas is debris expelled from early generations of very massive stars.* **2** pieces of material that are separated or removed from sth because they are not wanted: *After air drying, the soil samples were sieved to remove debris.*

debt /det/ *noun* **1** [C] a sum of money that sb owes: *The group could not pay its debts and had to surrender the enterprise.* ◇ *The US was on the brink of defaulting on its debts.* HELP A **bad debt** is a debt that is unlikely to be paid: *Most of this bad debt has now been written off.* **2** [U] the situation of owing money, especially when you cannot pay: **in ~** *The project turned out to be far more expensive than estimated and so Darby was in debt for the rest of his life.* ◇ **into ~** *Many families went into debt to pay for treatment for their children.* ◇ **+ noun** *The Greek debt crisis triggered serious concern among EU institutions.* **3** [C] **~ to sb/sth** the fact that sb's ideas or work have been influenced by sb/sth: *The book owes a considerable debt to previous work, as the author acknowledges.* ◇ *Many of the great medieval Christian philosophers acknowledged an intellectual debt to their Muslim predecessors.* **4** [C, usually sing., U] **~ to sb** the fact that you should feel grateful to sb because they have helped you or been kind to you: *Modern scientists owe a tremendous debt to the individuals who witnessed the New Madrid earthquakes and documented their effects.* ◇ **~ of sth** *I owe a debt of gratitude to many people for their help in the development of the ideas contained in this paper.* ◇ **in ~ to sb** | **in sb's ~** *There are many people I am in debt to for their assistance over these past six years.*

debt·or /ˈdetə(r)/ *noun* a person, a country or an organization that owes money: *She argues that the crisis is due to both the debtors and the creditors.* ◇ **+ noun** *The IMF aided economic development in the country, but in the process made it into a debtor nation.* OPP CREDITOR

dec·ade AWL /ˈdekeɪd; dɪˈkeɪd/ *noun* a period of ten years, especially one beginning with a year ending in 0: *Over the past two decades, per capita income in South Korea has quadrupled.* ◇ *His career spanned nearly seven decades.* ◇ **~ of sth** *Nepal emerged in 2006 from a decade of civil war.* ➲ language bank *at* TIME¹

decay¹ /dɪˈkeɪ/ *noun* [U] **1 ~ (of sth)** the process or result of being broken down or destroyed by natural processes: *Disease accompanies the decay of incompletely buried bodies.* ◇ *This chapter examines the influence of diet and fluoride on the prevention of tooth decay.* **2** (*physics*) the change of a RADIOACTIVE substance, PARTICLE, etc. into another as it gives out RADIATION: **~ (of sth) (to sth)** *The gas radon is produced by the decay of uranium in rocks and soil.* ◇ *Potassium-argon (K-Ar) dating utilizes the radioactive decay of potassium isotopes (^{40}K) to argon isotopes (^{40}Ar) in a rock sample.* ◇ **+ noun** *Uranium-235 has the fastest decay rate (or shortest half-life).* **3** the gradual process in which a society, an institution, etc. is destroyed or becomes weaker: *Slums are the most visible sign of urban decay and poverty.* ◇ **~ of sth** *Mellors, the gamekeeper, expresses Lawrence's own views on the decay of society when it abandons true values.* **4** (*technical*) gradual decrease in the MAGNITUDE (= size) of a physical quantity: *The required time constant for current decay is 1 ms.*

decay² /dɪˈkeɪ/ *verb* **1** [I] to be destroyed gradually by natural processes: *When the leaves on deciduous trees die at the end of the summer, the chlorophyll decays.* ◇ *Microorganisms that live on decaying organic matter are called saprophytes.* **2** [I] (of a RADIOACTIVE substance) to change into another substance as it gives out RADIATION: *The radiocarbon is trapped and then begins to decay.* ◇ **~ to sth** *^{40}K decayed radioactively to ^{40}Ar to produce the third major component of the present atmosphere.* **3** [I] **~ (into sth)** if a building or an area **decays**, its condition slowly becomes worse: *The densely populated old town during the later 19th century had decayed into a classic ghetto for the poor.* ◇ *Today, many urban areas are experiencing problems related to decaying infrastructures.* **4** [I] **~ (to sth)** (*technical*) (of a quantity or an amount) to gradually decrease: *the time taken for the current to decay to zero*

de·ceive /dɪˈsiːv/ *verb* [T] **1 ~ sb** to deliberately make sb believe sth that is not true: *For Chinese people, a company should be honest and not deceive customers.* ◇ *She realized too late that she had been badly deceived.* ◇ **~ sb into doing sth** *Consumers might be deceived into paying more for a perceived, but unrealistic, health benefit.* **2 ~ sb/sth** (of a thing) to make sb have a false idea about sb/sth: *He* *thought his senses were deceiving him.* ◇ *Some butterflies have an eye pattern on their wings to deceive predators.* ➲ *see also* DECEPTION

de·cency /'di:snsi/ *noun* [U] honest, polite behaviour that follows accepted moral standards and shows respect for others: *Rights to free expression needed to be balanced with other considerations of taste and decency.* ◇ *Forster's narrative insists on the virtues of tolerance and human decency.*

D

de·cent /'di:snt/ *adj.* **1** of a good enough standard or quality: *They choose to go to college because it is their only hope for getting a decent job.* **2** (of people or behaviour) honest and fair; treating people with respect: *Jurors should apply the current standards of ordinary decent people.* **3** acceptable according to the moral or social rules of a particular group: *Sick people were not abandoned, and when they died they were given a decent burial.*

de·cen·tral·ize (*BrE also* **-ise**) /ˌdi:'sentrəlaɪz/ *verb* [T, I] to give some of the power of a central government, organization, etc. to smaller parts or organizations around the country: *Some of the most centralized countries such as the UK, Italy and Spain have deliberately decentralized.* ◇ **~ sth** *Rather than having a central laboratory, other firms decentralize their R&D organization structures.* OPP CENTRALIZE ■ **de·cen·tral·iza·tion, -isa·tion** /ˌdi:ˌsentrəlaɪ'zeɪʃn; *NAmE* ˌdi:ˌsentrələ'zeɪʃn/ *noun* [U, sing.] *Fiscal decentralization may lead to greater overall economic efficiency.*

de·cep·tion /dɪ'sepʃn/ *noun* **1** [U] the act of deliberately making sb believe sth that is not true: *Chat rooms are a place in which deception is commonplace.* ◇ **by ~** *She was charged with obtaining property by deception.* **2** [C] something that you say or do that is intended to make sb believe sth that is not true: *Prometheus's deceptions of Zeus have far-reaching consequences.*

de·cide /dɪ'saɪd/ *verb* **1** [I, T] to think carefully about the different possibilities that are available and choose one of them: **~ to do sth** *A company may decide to adopt different strategies in different regions of the world.* ◇ **~ between A and B** *Based on the results, it is difficult to decide between these two hypotheses.* ◇ **~ against (doing) sth** *There are many situations in which mothers decide against breastfeeding.* ◇ **~ in favour of (doing) sth** *Beginning a job and marriage are the most important triggers for deciding in favour of leaving the city.* ◇ **~ what/whether, etc...** *Customers have choices when it comes to deciding what to buy.* ◇ **~ (that)...** *She decided that she did not want to accept the offer.* ◇ **it is decided (that)...** *In the end it was decided that all the Athenian prisoners should be put to death.* ◇ **~ for sb/yourself (what/whether, etc...)** *She was in a fit state to decide for herself whether she should be admitted to hospital.* **2** [T, I] (*law*) to make an official or legal judgement: **~ sth** *Each case must be decided on its facts.* ◇ **~ (sth) for/in favour of sb** *The cases were decided in favour of the applicants.* ◇ **~ (sth) in sb's favour** *The court decided in his favour* ◇ **~ (sth) against sb** *The Supreme Court decided against them.* ◇ **it is decided (that)...** *It was decided that he did not qualify for asylum.* **3** [T] **~ sth** to affect the result of sth: *Future research will no doubt decide this matter.* ◇ *In the US, abortion is an issue that could decide close elections.* IDM *see* ISSUE[1]

PHR V **de'cide on/upon sth** to choose sth from a number of possibilities: *It will be important to decide on an appropriate name for the brand.* ◇ *The policy was decided upon at cabinet level.*

de·cided /dɪ'saɪdɪd/ *adj.* [only before noun] obvious and definite: *Among reptiles and amphibians, there is a decided leaning towards female supremacy.* ◇ *Attitudes underwent a decided shift at the end of World War II.*

de·cided·ly /dɪ'saɪdɪdli/ *adv.* (used with an adjective or adverb) in an obvious way that you cannot doubt: *Attitudes to older workers are still decidedly mixed.*

deci·mal[1] /'desɪml/ *adj.* [only before noun] based on or counted in tens or tenths: *The system converts decimal numbers into binary form and stores them.*

deci·mal[2] /'desɪml/ *noun* **1** (*also* ˌ**decimal 'fraction**) [C] a FRACTION (= a number less than one) that is shown as a dot or point followed by the number of 10ths, 100ths, etc: *The decimal 0.61 stands for 61 hundredths.* **2** [U] the system of decimal numbers: *The computer converts the initial data from decimal to binary.*

de·ci·sion /dɪ'sɪʒn/ *noun* **1** [C] a choice or judgement that you make after thinking and talking about what is the best thing to do: *They worried whether or not they had made the right decision.* ◇ *A decision was reached after long deliberation.* ◇ *Basing a decision on specimens from a single area can be misleading.* ◇ **~ about/on sth** *Because of her illness, Joyce was unable to make decisions about her life.* ◇ **~ to do sth** *Before his decision to abandon worldly life, Gregory was the governor of Rome.* **2** [U] the process of deciding sth: *It was the moment of decision.* ◇ *The Commission was given an autonomous power of decision.*

▸ ADJECTIVE + DECISION **key, important, major • difficult • rational • informed • strategic • final** *International pricing is a key strategic decision.* ◇ *They lacked some of the facts they needed to make an informed decision.*

▸ VERB + DECISION **make, take, reach, come to, arrive at • influence, affect, guide, inform, shape • implement • justify • challenge • reverse • uphold** *They took the decision to go to war.* ◇ *In some industries unionists can influence managerial decisions.*

de'cision-maker (*also* **decision maker**) *noun* a person or institution that decides sth, especially on behalf of a group of people or an organization: *In the United States, courts are the final decision-makers in competition cases.* ◇ *During the ancien regime, the decision-maker in each diocese was the local bishop.*

de'cision-making (*also* **decision making**) *noun* [U] the process of deciding about sth important, especially in a group of people or in an organization: **~ (about sth)** *Local communities should be able to participate in decision-making about local services.* ◇ **+ noun** *Market research can be used to help inform the decision-making process.*

de·cisive /dɪ'saɪsɪv/ *adj.* **1** making the result of sth final or certain: *On election day, Kennedy scored a decisive victory.* ◇ *His education had a decisive influence on his career.* ◇ *Voters who are not firmly attached to any party may prove decisive in marginal seats.* **2** having or showing the ability to make clear decisions quickly: *The people demanded more decisive leadership.* ◇ *Decisive action must be taken to sustain our rural landscapes.* ■ **de·cisive·ly** *adv.*: *The Athenian fleet was decisively defeated at the Battle of Amorgus.* ◇ *A market leader must be able to act decisively and swiftly to defend its position.*

dec·lar·ation /ˌdeklə'reɪʃn/ *noun* **1** [C, U] an official or formal statement, especially about the plans of a government or an organization: **~ (of sth)** *The white minority in Southern Rhodesia issued a unilateral declaration of independence in November 1965.* ◇ *The ostensible reason for Russia's declaration of war was the protection of Balkan Christians.* ◇ **in a ~** *In a joint declaration, Roosevelt and Churchill called for the 'final destruction of Nazi tyranny'.* **2** [C] **~ (that...)** an official written statement giving information: *They require taxpayers to make a formal declaration that they have paid enough tax to cover the amount the charity will reclaim.* **3** [C] **~ (of sth)** a written or spoken statement, especially about what people feel or believe: *Salmon (pp. 194–5) points out that such an assumption is 'no more than a declaration of faith'.*

de·clare /dɪˈkleə(r); *NAmE* dɪˈkler/ *verb* **1** to say sth officially or publicly: **~ sth** *Georgia shortly declared its independence under a nationalist coalition government.* ◇ *When, in September 1939, Hitler invaded Poland, the western allies declared war on Germany.* ◇ **~ that...** *The minister declared that students had the right to wear discreet religious symbols.* ◇ **~ sth + noun** *The city was declared a world cultural heritage site by UNESCO in 1988.* ◇ **~ sth to be sth** *The Act did not however declare child marriages to be illegal.* ◇ **~ sth + adj.** *The constitutional court declared the proposed referendum invalid.* **2** to state sth clearly and in public: **+ speech** *'Our purpose,' one New Right leader declared, 'is to organize discontent.'* ◇ **~ that...** *Odysseus declared that he was the second best archer of his generation, after Philoktetes.* ◇ **~ sth** *By carving their initials on trees and stone tablets, colonists declared their intention to make a home.* ◇ **~ yourself + adj./noun** *Until quite recently, it was shocking, even foolhardy, to declare oneself not a Christian.* **3 ~ sth (to sb/sth)** to tell the tax authorities about money you have earned or valuable goods that you have: *In some countries, there is a culture of not declaring earnings to the government.*

de·cline[1] AWL /dɪˈklaɪn/ *noun* [C, usually sing., U] a continuous decrease in the number, strength, value, etc. of sth: *In a period of a few months, food prices doubled, followed by a very sharp decline.* ◇ **~ in sth** *At the last elections there was a decline in the number of women elected to parliament.* ◇ **~ of sth** *The decline of Communism brought an end to the Cold War.* ◇ **in ~** *Theatre audience numbers are in decline.* ◇ **fall/go into (a) ~** *Following a national shift from coal to oil in 1959, Japan's mining industry went into decline.* ➲ language bank *at* TREND

▸ ADJECTIVE + DECLINE **gradual, slow • steady • slight, modest • sharp, steep, precipitous • rapid • dramatic, drastic • marked, significant • long-term • terminal** *In the early 2000s, US gas production was in slow but steady decline.* ◇ *Oil pollution is driving many reefs to the point of terminal decline.* | **economic • moral** *In the 1970s, Britain was in the grip of economic decline.*

▸ VERB + DECLINE **experience, suffer, undergo • witness, see • cause • show • reverse** *Most rural counties have experienced some population decline since 1900.*

de·cline[2] AWL /dɪˈklaɪn/ *verb* **1** [I] to become smaller, fewer or weaker: *Agricultural industries such as dairy farming continue to decline.* ◇ *Investment levels declined sharply after the stock crash of 1987.* ◇ *Infant and child mortality rates have declined over the past two decades.* ◇ *He retired because of declining health.* ➲ language bank *at* TREND **2** [I, T] to refuse politely to accept or to do sth SYN REFUSE (2): *He asked her to marry him, but she declined.* ◇ **~ sth** *The Home Secretary declined an invitation to be interviewed on radio.* ◇ **~ to do sth** *She wisely declined to enter into the debate.*

de·code /ˌdiːˈkəʊd; *NAmE* ˌdiːˈkoʊd/ *verb* **~ sth** to find the meaning of sth, especially by changing a code of letters, symbols or signals into ordinary language: *The two parties wishing to exchange messages share a key that they use to encode and decode the messages.* ◇ *With early telecommunications systems, human operators were required to decode the signals.* ➲ *compare* ENCODE

de·com·pose /ˌdiːkəmˈpəʊz; *NAmE* ˌdiːkəmˈpoʊz/ *verb* **1** [I] to be destroyed gradually by natural chemical processes SYN DECAY[2] (1): *Once leafy green vegetables are torn or chopped, they decompose more rapidly.* ◇ *Potassium can be incorporated into soils from decomposing animal remains.* **2** [I, T] to separate into smaller or simpler parts; to make sth do this: *The mixture partially decomposes with time.* ◇ **~ (sth) into sth** *Any signal can be decomposed into a series of sine waves and cosine waves of different frequencies.*

de·com·pos·ition /ˌdiːkɒmpəˈzɪʃn; *NAmE* ˌdiːkɑːmpəˈzɪʃn/ *noun* [U] **1 ~ (of sth)** the process of being destroyed by natural chemicals and bacteria: *The decomposition of organic matter releases organic acids and generates carbon dioxide.* **2 ~ (of sth) (into sth)** the act of separating or being separated into smaller or simpler parts: *Heat leads to formamide decomposition into carbon monoxide and ammonia.*

de·con·struc·tion /ˌdiːkənˈstrʌkʃn/ *noun* [U] (*technical*) (in literature and philosophy) a theory that states that it is impossible for a text to have one fixed meaning, and emphasizes the role of the person reading the text in the production of meaning: *'Postmodernism and deconstruction question the implicit or explicit rationality of all academic discourse.' (Dear, 1988: 271).* ➲ *compare* POSTMODERNISM, STRUCTURALISM

dec·or·ate /ˈdekəreɪt/ *verb* **1** [T] **~ sth (with sth)** to make sth look more attractive by putting things on it; to be put on sth to make it look more attractive: *There is a set of ceremonial tables decorated with flowers and candles.* **2** [I, T] (*especially BrE*) to put paint, paper, etc. on the walls and ceilings of a room or house: *They feature a wide range of activities and products tied to gardening, decorating and home care.* ◇ **~ sth** *Culturally, home furnishings are not regarded as important and little time is spent on decorating the home.* **3** [T, usually passive] **~ sb (for sth)** to give sb an award as a sign of respect for sth they have done: *Policemen were decorated for saving the lives of some of these people.*

dec·or·ation /ˌdekəˈreɪʃn/ *noun* **1** [U, C] a pattern, etc. that is added to sth and that stops it from being plain: *The bowls underwent gradual changes in style and decoration.* ◇ *A stele is a stone slab inscribed with a text or a decoration.* **2** [C, usually pl.] a thing that makes sth look more attractive on special occasions: *It is estimated that 80% of the world's Christmas decorations are made in China.* **3** [U] the style in which sth is decorated: *Dublin's eighteenth-century architecture and interior decoration reflected Italian and German influences.* **4** [C] an award that is given to sb as a sign of respect for sth they have done: *He received a military decoration from the Kaiser.*

dec·ora·tive /ˈdekərətɪv; *NAmE* ˈdekəreɪtɪv/ *adj.* connected with the decoration of an object or place; intended to be attractive or pleasant to look at, especially as opposed to being useful: *In the late 19th and early 20th centuries, design and the decorative arts were also known as 'applied arts'.*

de·couple /diːˈkʌpl/ *verb* [T, I] to end the connection or relationship between two things; to become separate: **~ sth** *This assumption does not completely decouple the manual and cognitive aspects of the modelling.* ◇ **~ (sth) (from sth)** *Japan has aimed to decouple economic growth from environmental stress in terms of pollution (Barrett and Fisher, 2005).* ◇ *Particles may also decouple if they are massive.*

de·crease[1] /dɪˈkriːs/ *verb* [I, T] to become smaller in size, number, etc; to make sth smaller in size, number, etc: *Temperatures decrease as we go from low to high elevation.* ◇ *Poverty rates decreased sharply up to the late 1960s.* ◇ **~ sth** *Another way of decreasing the risks of reproductive cancers would be to use hormonal treatments.* ◇ **~ (sth) by sth** *At 35% O_2, plant growth decreased by about 20%.* ◇ **~ (sth) (from sth) (to sth)** *The rate of union membership has decreased from 10.1% in 1990 to 8.3% in 2003 (OECD, 2004).* ◇ **~ (sth) in sth** *Because of this, the lakes began to decrease in salinity.* OPP INCREASE[1] ➲ language bank *at* TREND

▸ DECREASE + NOUN **rate • level • number, amount • size • risk, likelihood, probability • incidence, frequency • cost, price • value • concentration • content • activity • performance • temperature • time • demand • consumption** *If the concentration of important nutrients decreases, cells respond by decreasing their growth rate.*

▸ NOUN + DECREASE **rate, level • value • size • percentage, ratio • intensity • temperature • concentration, density • pressure • mortality • population • content • cost, price** *As explained by Boyle's law, as the aircraft climbs, the cabin pressure decreases compared with sea level.*
▸ ADVERB + DECREASE | DECREASE + ADVERB **significantly, substantially • dramatically, drastically • sharply • markedly • considerably • greatly • rapidly • slightly • gradually, steadily • progressively • exponentially • linearly** *The findings provide evidence that the vaccination programme significantly decreased hepatitis in infants.* ◇ *Energy expenditure has decreased markedly because of changes in the urban environment.*

D

de·crease² /ˈdiːkriːs/ *noun* [C, U] the process of reducing sth; the amount that sth is reduced by SYN REDUCTION: *55–64 is the only age group among which volunteering has shown an overall decrease.* ◇ *Height does undergo some decrease with age.* ◇ **~ in sth** *Social explanations include a decrease in the birth rate and the financial independence of women.* ◇ *An improved security situation has enabled a marked decrease in the number of police deployed.* ◇ **~ of sth** *Results showed an increase of 15% in turnover but a decrease of 46% in profit.* OPP INCREASE² ➲ language bank *at* TREND

de·cree¹ /dɪˈkriː/ *noun* **1** [C, U] an official order from a ruler or government that becomes the law: *The president issued decrees approving the contract and granting the company an exploration licence.* ◇ *a royal/presidential decree* ◇ **by ~** *In Austria, the monarch had emergency powers to rule by decree.* **2** [C] a decision that is made in court: *Before the court grants the decree, it must be satisfied that appropriate arrangements have been made for any children.*

de·cree² /dɪˈkriː/ *verb* (**de·cree·ing, de·creed, de·creed**) to decide, judge or order sth officially: **~ sth** *In July 1959, President Sukarno decreed the dissolution of the constituent assembly.* ◇ **~ that...** *The government decreed that cases of political violence would be tried henceforth by military courts.*

dedi·cate /ˈdedɪkeɪt/ *verb* **1** to give time and effort to a particular activity or purpose because you think it is important SYN DEVOTE: **~ sth to sth** *Kennedy continued: 'Martin Luther King dedicated his life to love and to justice for his fellow human beings.'* ◇ **~ sth to doing sth** *Mediterranean countries dedicate a smaller percentage of GDP to funding education in comparison with Nordic countries.* ◇ **~ yourself to (doing) sth** *He turned to politics early in his career and dedicated himself to revolutionary action.* **2 ~ sth to sth** to use all or part of a piece of writing to discuss a particular subject: *Habermas dedicates a whole chapter to this question.* **3 ~ sth to sb** to say at the beginning of a book, a piece of music or a performance that you are doing it for sb, as a way of thanking them or showing respect: *He dedicated his book, 'Principles of Stratigraphy', published in 1913, to Walter.* **4 ~ sth (to sb/sth)** to officially say that a building or an object has a special purpose, especially a religious one: *Small bronze figurines of men were also dedicated to deities.*

dedi·cated /ˈdedɪkeɪtɪd/ *adj.* **1** working hard at sth because it is very important to you SYN COMMITTED: *'Amateurs' can often be far more dedicated than those who see archaeology as merely a career.* ◇ **~ to sth** *While we are dedicated to this approach, it can be tricky to implement in practice.* **2** [only before noun] designed to do only one particular type of work; used for one particular purpose only: *Immediate recovery from anaesthesia and surgery should take place in a dedicated area with specialist staff and equipment.*

ded·ica·tion /ˌdedɪˈkeɪʃn/ *noun* **1** [U] the hard work and effort that sb puts into an activity or purpose because they think it is important SYN COMMITMENT: *Loyalty, dedication, and team spirit are more important than current job skills.* ◇ **~ to sb/sth** *His life was characterized by absolute dedication to whatever he did.* ◇ *The company clearly states its dedication to social goals in its mission statement.* **2** [C] a ceremony that is held to show that a building or an object has a special purpose, especially a religious one: **~ (of sth)** *A grand procession occurred at the dedication of the monument in 13 BCE.* ◇ **~ to sb/sth** *Egyptian priestly families spent large sums on lavish tomb furnishings and dedications to the gods.* **3** [C] the words that are used at the beginning of a book, piece of music, a performance, etc. to offer it to sb as a sign of thanks or respect: **~ (of sth)** *In the dedication of the translated work, Bruni addressed Pope Innocent VII.* ◇ **~ to sb/sth** *The dutiful dedication to the young Earl of Southampton was signed with the poet's full name.*

de·duce AWL /dɪˈdjuːs; *NAmE* dɪˈduːs/ *verb* to form an opinion about sth based on the information or evidence that is available SYN INFER (1): **~ sth** *Plant fossils may be used to deduce ancient levels of atmospheric O_2.* ◇ **~ sth from sth** *Weakness of the upper limbs may be deduced from general inspection.* ◇ **~ that...** *Epicurus deduced that gods exist because people saw their images in dreams.* ◇ **~ where/how, etc...** *We can use this logic to deduce where the disease-causing gene is located in the genome.* ➲ *see also* DEDUCTION

de·duct /dɪˈdʌkt/ *verb* **~ sth (from sth)** to take away money, points, etc. from a total amount SYN SUBTRACT: *The procedural costs awarded were deducted from the legal aid payable.*

de·duc·tion AWL /dɪˈdʌkʃn/ *noun* **1** [C] **~ (about sb/sth) (from sth)** something that you know or find out from the information you already have SYN INFERENCE (1): *It is possible to make deductions about an object's thermal properties from our perception of whether it feels hot or cold.* **2** [U] the process of using the information you have in order to find sth out SYN INFERENCE (2): *They worked out, through a process of deduction, that he was of Eastern European origin.* ➲ *compare* INDUCTION (1) ➲ *see also* DEDUCE **3** [U, C] **~ (of sth) (from sth)** the process of taking an amount of sth, especially money, away from a total; the amount that is taken away: *The Soviet system of automatic deduction of taxes ended as more and more enterprises left the state system.* ◇ *Taiwan offers tax deductions to adult children supporting an elderly parent.*

de·duct·ive /dɪˈdʌktɪv/ *adj.* [usually before noun] using knowledge about things that are generally true in order to understand particular situations or problems: *Deductive reasoning can be applied where a choice must be made between multiple competing plans.* ➲ *compare* INDUCTIVE

deed /diːd/ *noun* **1** [C] a thing that sb does, especially sth that is very good or very bad: *Mill recognizes that getting into heaven is what motivates some people to do good deeds.* **2** [C] (often plural in British English) **~ (of sth)** a legal document that you sign, especially one that proves that you own a house or building: *The lender holds the deeds of the house as long as the occupier has an outstanding loan.* **3** [U] action or performance: *The bishop decided that the penitent had shown sincere repentance in word and deed.*

deem /diːm/ *verb* (not usually used in the progressive tenses) to have a particular opinion about sth SYN CONSIDER (2): **~ sth + noun/adj.** *The experiment was deemed a failure.* ◇ *They did not deem it necessary to conduct a more thorough investigation.* ◇ **~ sth to be sth** *The experiment was deemed to be a failure.* ◇ **~ that...** *The court has deemed that the circumstances are such that parental consent can be dispensed with.*

deep¹ /diːp/ *adj.* (**deep·er, deep·est**) **1** going or being a long way down from the surface or top of sth: *The valleys here are deep and narrow.* ◇ *Lake Baikal is the world's deepest lake.* ◇ *Some mammals remain active even when* *there is deep snow cover but many hibernate for the winter.* ◇ *Deep ocean species are unaffected by surface climate.* ◇ *Large and dominant trees tend to have deep roots.* ◇ *In this area, the water table is very deep beneath the surface.* ◇ *Large or deep wounds require suturing.* OPP SHALLOW (1) **2** going or being a long way from the front or outer edge of sth: *He was brought up in a log cabin deep in the woods.* ◇ *Unconscious intentions start out somewhere deep in the brain.* **3** used to describe or talk about the depth of sth: *The snow lay six inches deep.* ◇ *Spawning areas are located in saline waters deeper than 20 m.* ◇ *The study involved the excavation of a metre-deep trench.* **4** showing great knowledge or understanding: *It can take years for a company to establish a deep understanding of Japanese consumers.* ◇ *By visiting Afghanistan, she gained a deep insight into family life there.* OPP SHALLOW (2) **5** extreme or serious: *The economy has plunged into a deep recession.* ◇ *Conversion to Judaism is a subject that has exposed deep divisions among Jews.* **6** (of a feeling or connection) very strong: *The refugees all suffer from a deep sense of alienation.* ◇ *As a leader, he had a deep concern for the plight of the common person.* ◇ *This is another example of the deep connection between elasticity and geometry.* **7** difficult to understand SYN PROFOUND: *There are deeper meanings embedded within this play.* **8** **~ in sth** fully involved in an activity or a state: *He spent some time in a sanatorium, sunk deep in depression.* **9** taking in or giving out a lot of air: *His breathing became deep and regular.* ◇ *Patients with a chest injury may reveal that they are unable to take a deep breath due to pain.* OPP SHALLOW (3) **10** a person in a **deep** sleep is difficult to wake: *Sleepwalking occurs during deep non-REM sleep.* ◇ *Hypoxia and carbon dioxide retention are common in deep coma.* **11** (of colour) strong and dark: *Cinnabar is deep red.* ◇ *The best emeralds are deep in colour.* OPP PALE (2) **12** (of sound) low: *When speech is slowed down, the voice tends to get deeper.* **13** (in adjectives) as far up or down as the point mentioned: *They stood knee-deep in mud.* ◇ *The ground was covered, nearly ankle-deep, with filth.* **14** (in adjectives) in the number of rows mentioned, one behind the other: *A phalanx was a tactical formation consisting of ranks of heavy infantry, usually eight deep.* ➲ *see also* DEPTH

deep² /diːp/ *adv.* (**deep·er, deep·est**) **(+ adv./prep.)** a long way below the surface of sth; a long way inside or into sth: *Mantle plumes originate deep in the earth.* ◇ *Many of the aerosol particles are able to penetrate deep into the respiratory passages.* ◇ (*figurative*) *Investigators dug deep and found out about a surname change early in his life.*

IDM **deep ˈdown** (*rather informal*) if sb feels sth or if sth is true **deep down**, those are sb's true feelings or the true facts, although they may not be admitted or obvious: *Johnson said, 'Deep down, I knew that the American people loved me.'* **go/run ˈdeep** (of emotions, beliefs, etc.) to be felt in a strong way that is difficult to change: *These resentments run deep and operate on numerous levels.*

deep·en /ˈdiːpən/ *verb* **1** [I, T] (of a feeling or connection) to become stronger; to make a feeling or connection stronger: *Her love for him deepens the more she endures the pain of separation.* ◇ *Recent decades have seen deepening East Asian economic integration.* ◇ **~ sth** *Kennedy deepened American involvement in Vietnam.* **2** [I, T] to become worse; to make sth worse: *As the Great Depression deepened, in many countries the Communist Party gained credibility.* ◇ **~ sth** *A series of natural disasters further deepened the economic crisis.* **3** [I, T] to become greater in size; to make sth greater in size: *Democracy must expand and deepen if it is to incorporate the political claims of all women.* ◇ **~ sth** *Wealthy consumers broadened and deepened the markets for sugar, coffee and chocolate from the Caribbean.* **4** [T] **~ sth** to improve your knowledge or understanding of sth: *Many movies reinforce stereotypes rather than deepen our understanding of human nature.* **5** [I, T] to become deeper; to make sth deeper: *The gullies widen and deepen as they collect more and more water.* ◇ **~ sth** *Due to rising sea levels, shallow harbours became deepened.*

deep·ly /ˈdiːpli/ *adv.* **1** very; very much: *The Spartans were deeply religious.* ◇ *Humans are deeply social beings.* ◇ *Le Brun began to develop a personal style that was nevertheless still deeply indebted to Poussin.* **2** in a very strong way that is difficult to change: *The term 'hypothesis' is deeply rooted in the history of scientific thought.* ◇ *The bridge metaphor is deeply embedded in our thinking.* ◇ *His many odes share a deeply held belief in an old-fashioned heroism.* **3** in a serious and thorough way: *The questions are designed to make children think more deeply.* **4** a long way into or below the surface of sth: *The surgeon was careful not to cut too deeply.* ◇ *Coal is found buried deeply in the ground, or under the seabed, or close to the surface.* **5** with a dark or strong colour: *Some deeply coloured samples may be practically opaque.* **6** (of breathing) in a way that takes in and lets out a lot of air: *The most common symptom is sharp chest pain that is made worse by inhaling deeply.*

de facto /ˌdeɪ ˈfæktəʊ; *NAmE* ˌdeɪ ˈfæktoʊ/ *adj.* [usually before noun] (*from Latin*) existing, although not officially accepted as existing: *A de facto director is one who has not been formally appointed as such, but has nevertheless acted as a director.* ■ **de facto** *adv.*: *The country formally or de facto pegs its currency at a fixed rate to another currency.*

de·fault¹ /dɪˈfɔːlt; ˈdiːfɔːlt/ *noun* **1** [U, C] failure to do sth that must be done by law, especially paying a debt: **in ~ (on sth)** *The hotel chain was in default on a loan for $70 million.* ◇ **~ on sth** *The slump in property sales increased defaults on interest payments.* **2** [C, usually sing.] what happens, appears or is done if you do not make any other choice or change: *The default is to search from 1970 to date.* ◇ **+ noun** *The default position is that, for a British degree, standard English varieties are the only acceptable forms of language.*

IDM **by deˈfault** if sth happens **by default**, it happens because you have not made any other decision or choices which would make things happen in a different way: *Everyone in hospital in the UK, by default, receives CPR in the event of cardiac or respiratory arrest.* **in deˈfault of sth** because of a lack of sth: *An arbitrator would impose a settlement in default of agreement.*

de·fault² /dɪˈfɔːlt; ˈdiːfɔːlt/ *verb* **1** [I] **~ (on sth)** to fail to do sth that you legally have to do, especially by not paying a debt: *Different households present different risks of defaulting on loans.* **2** [I] **~ (to sth)** (of a computer program, system, machine, etc.) to cause an option chosen in advance to happen or appear, if no other choice or change is made: *The program defaults to a simple keyword search.*

de·feat¹ /dɪˈfiːt/ *verb* **1** **~ sb/sth** to win against sb in a battle, election or other contest SYN BEAT¹ (3): *The Athenian fleet was decisively defeated at the Battle of Amorgus.* ◇ *Narrowly defeated by John Adams, he became vice president.* **2** **~ sth** to stop an aim from being achieved: *The amendment was defeated in the Senate.* ◇ *The only really secure form of Internet banking is a system that is not accessible from outside a bank's offices: of course, this would defeat the whole purpose of Internet banking.*

de·feat² /dɪˈfiːt/ *noun* **1** [C, U] failure to win or be successful: *In the general election of 1983, Labour suffered its heaviest defeat in modern times.* ◇ *The Nazi regime became increasingly violent and irrational as military defeat loomed.* ◇ *In 1988, Sony finally had to accept defeat and switch to their rival's system.* OPP VICTORY

2 [C, usually sing.] **~ (of sb/sth)** the act of winning a victory over sb/sth: *the defeat of tyranny*

de·fect¹ /ˈdi:fekt/ *noun* something that is wrong with or missing from sb/sth: *There is uncertainty over whether maternal smoking is associated with birth defects.* ◇ *a congenital/genetic/visual/skeletal defect* ◇ *a heart/gene/growth defect* ◇ **~ in sb/sth** *A structural survey should discover any defects in the building.*

D

de·fect² /dɪˈfekt/ *verb* **1** [I] **~ (from sth) (to sth)** to leave a political party, country, etc. to join another that is considered to be an enemy: *Other literary figures who either defected or emigrated included V. Nekrasov, A. Sinyavsky, and I. Brodsky.* **2** [I] **~ (from sth) (to sth)** to leave a group, an arrangement or a relationship and join or start another: *Some customers defect to competitors, no matter how hard the firm tries to retain them.* ■ **de·fec·tion** /dɪˈfekʃn/ *noun* [U, C] **~ (of sb/sth) (from sth) (to sth)** *Green parties can rarely make a credible threat of defection to a coalition with larger right-wing parties.* ◇ *Reducing customer defections will require a proactive approach from a high level within the organization.* **de·fect·or** *noun* **~ (from sth) (to sth)** *Of the several defectors from the secret service, W. G. Krivitsky was sufficiently important to be murdered by his former colleagues.*

de·fect·ive /dɪˈfektɪv/ *adj.* having sth wrong or missing; not perfect or complete SYN FAULTY (1): *Consumers injured by defective products tend to receive extremely low compensation.* ◇ *The baby's brain, heart and lungs were defective.*

de·fence (*US* **de·fense**) /dɪˈfens/ *noun* **1** [C, U] support for sb/sth that has been criticized: *Hooker provided the Church with a clearly argued philosophical defence.* ◇ **~ of sb/sth** *He led the planters' defence of slavery and the slave trade.* ◇ **in ~ of sb/sth** *The argument in defence of monopolies also highlights that their profits are often generated by offering a better service or product.* ◇ **in sb/sth's ~** *In his defence, he argued that he was responsible for policy but not for operational matters.* OPP ATTACK¹ (3) **2** [U, C] the action of protecting sb/sth from attack: *The Persians were unable to mount an effective defence in Anatolia.* ◇ **~ of sb/sth** *Defence of the long frontiers demanded more men and equipment.* ◇ **in ~ of sb/sth** *The defendant shot his father whilst acting in defence of his mother.* OPP ATTACK¹ (2) ➲ *see also* SELF-DEFENCE **3** [C, U] something that provides protection against attack from enemies, the weather, illness, etc: *Planners need to start thinking more deliberately about coastal defences and flood protection.* ◇ **~ against sth** *White blood cells also provide defence against infection.* ◇ *The communities they established served as a first line of defence against alien peoples, notably the Turks.* ◇ **~ mechanism** *However, this defence mechanism is not found in all of the mussel species.* **4** [U] military measures or resources for protecting a country from attack: *Member states agreed to consult and cooperate on issues of foreign policy, but not on defence.* ◇ **+ noun** *Partly because of the end of the Cold War, defence spending has been shrinking.* **5** [C] a set of facts or arguments presented in court to support a person who has been accused of committing a crime, or who is being SUED: **~ of sth** *The jury rejected the defence of insanity and convicted the defendant of murder.* ◇ **as a ~** *They would not be able to use this fact as a defence.* ➲ *compare* PROSECUTION (1) **6 the defence** [sing.+ sing./pl. v.] the lawyer or lawyers whose job is to represent in court a person who has been accused of committing a crime, or who is being SUED: *The defence argued that the prosecution had failed to prove its case.* ➲ *compare* PROSECUTION (2)

de·fend /dɪˈfend/ *verb* **1** to speak or write in support of sb/sth that has been criticized: **~ sb/sth/yourself** *Helvidius defended the view that marriage and celibacy were equally good and spiritual.* ◇ **~ sb/sth/yourself from sb/sth** *He defended himself from critics by describing his hard life.* ◇ **~ sb/sth/yourself against sb/sth** *James defended Carmichael vigorously against press allegations that he was preaching racial hatred.* OPP ATTACK² (3) **2** to protect sb/sth from attack: **~ sb/sth** *Smaller males are unable to defend a territory successfully.* ◇ **~ yourself** *The body defends itself by destroying the infected cells.* ◇ **~ sb/sth/yourself from sb/sth** *National security involves more than simply defending the state from external military attack.* ◇ **~ sb/sth/yourself against sb/sth** *In 279, he fell in battle, defending Macedon against the Gauls.* ◇ **~ against sb/sth** *They exhibit aggressive behaviour in defending against potential predators.* OPP ATTACK² (2) **3 ~ sth** to take part in a competition that you won the last time and try to win it again: *The Liberal Democrats were also defending a number of seats with small majorities.* **4** to act as a lawyer for sb who has been accused of committing a crime, or who is being SUED: **~ sb** *He made a reputation defending left-wing activists facing trial on political charges.* ◇ **~ yourself** *Christians were stripped of legal rights, such as that of defending themselves in court.*

de·fend·ant /dɪˈfendənt/ *noun* the person, company or institution in a trial that is accused of committing a crime, or that is being SUED by another person, etc: *The trial judge directed the jury to convict the defendant of assault.* ➲ *compare* ACCUSED, PLAINTIFF

de·fend·er /dɪˈfendə(r)/ *noun* a person who speaks or writes in support of sb/sth that has been criticized: *Huxley was a grandson of Darwin's defender, Thomas Henry Huxley.* ◇ **~ of sb/sth** *The Constitutional Court has built up a strong reputation as a defender of human rights.*

de·fense (*US*) = DEFENCE

de·fen·sive /dɪˈfensɪv/ *adj.* **1** used or intended to protect sb/sth against attack: *Tolerance is another defensive strategy that plants have evolved.* ◇ *Important settlements were established, with substantial defensive walls.* ➲ *compare* OFFENSIVE¹ (2) **2** behaving in a way that shows that you feel that people are criticizing you in an unfair way: *Sometimes people react badly to feedback, becoming defensive and hostile.*

de·fi·ance /dɪˈfaɪəns/ *noun* [U] open refusal to obey sb/sth: *Slaves frequently engaged in acts of defiance.* ◇ **in ~ of sb/sth** *The company continued its business relationship with the regime, in defiance of an international boycott.*

de·fi·ciency /dɪˈfɪʃnsi/ *noun* (*pl.* **-ies**) **1** [U, C] the state of not having enough of sth that is essential: *Vitamin D deficiency is commonly associated with obesity.* ◇ **~ of sth** *A deficiency of electrons on an object makes the static charge positive.* ◇ **~ in sth** *The boy's shortness was caused by a deficiency in growth hormone.* ➲ *compare* SHORTAGE **2** [C] a fault or weakness in sth/sb that makes it/them less successful: **~ (of sth)** *Despite the deficiencies of his literary style, he wrote a great deal.* ◇ **~ in sth** *The company's declining sales and profits were due to deficiencies in its supply chain.*

de·fi·cient /dɪˈfɪʃnt/ *adj.* **1** not having enough of sth, especially sth that is essential: *Vitamin B_2 is not present in plants so vegan diets are often deficient.* ◇ **~ in sth** *These soils are deficient in phosphorus.* **2** not good enough: *The bridge was structurally deficient but not dangerous.* ◇ *Some types of virus cause disease only when the immune system is deficient in some way.*

def·icit /ˈdefɪsɪt/ *noun* **1** (*economics*) the amount by which money spent or owed is greater than money earned in a particular period of time: *If the deficit is already high, then further borrowing could lead to extremely high interest rates.* ◇ *a budget/fiscal/trade/current account deficit* ➲ *compare* SURPLUS¹ **2** a lack of sth, especially sb's physical or mental abilities: *That there is a democratic deficit in the*

EU is a frequently heard complaint. ◇ *a neurological/sensory/cognitive/motor deficit*

de·fied past tense, past part. of DEFY

LANGUAGE BANK

Defining language

In academic writing, it is important to define what you mean when you use a particular term or expression.

- **X can/may be defined as...**
- **X is also known as/is referred to as...**
- **X includes/consists of/comprises...**
- **X involves/concerns/is related to...**
- **X is a kind/type/class of...**
- **X is a term referring to...**
- **I use the term X to refer to/to mean...**
- **The term X refers to/is used to refer to...**
- **This is what is meant by...**

– *'Economic distance'* ***can be defined as*** *the cost incurred to overcome physical distance.*
– *Propaganda,* ***also known as*** *disinformation, continues to be...*
– *Culture* ***includes*** *codes of behaviour, dress, language, rituals and beliefs.*
– *The third dimension of economic systems is called 'change', which* ***concerns*** *the passage of time.*
– *Salmonella* ***is a type of*** *bacteria.*
– *Postmodernism* ***is a term referring to*** *cultural phenomena which...*
– *I have* ***used the term to refer to*** *all languages descended from a protolanguage.*
– *Nuclear medicine* ***is a term used to*** *describe the use of radioactive compounds in diagnostic tests or treatment of diseases.*
– *This is what* ***is meant by*** *'commodity production'.*

de·fine AWL /dɪˈfaɪn/ *verb* **1** to describe or show exactly the nature or extent of sth: **~ sth** *Both thinkers are adept at defining the problems they wish to solve.* ◇ **~ sth as sth** *Nationalism, which at times could better be defined as chauvinism, was on the rise.* ◇ **~ what/how, etc...** *The first thing that Plato tries to do is to define what it means to be good.* ➲ *see also* WELL DEFINED **2** to say or explain what the meaning of a word or phrase is: **~ sth** *'Insight' is a difficult term to define.* ◇ **~ sth as sth** *Durkheim defined sociology as the study of 'social facts'.* **3** to form or establish the essential character of sth: **~ sb/sth/yourself** *Like Kipling's Kim, Jim is concerned to define his own identity.* ◇ **~ sb/sth/yourself as sth** *About 35% defined themselves as completely secular.* **4 ~ sth** to show clearly the outline or position of sth: *Taylor Glacier is the largest glacier in the valley, defining its western boundary.*

WORD FAMILY
define *verb*
definition *noun*
redefine *verb*
redefinition *noun*
undefined *adj.*

▸ DEFINE + NOUN **identity, nature** ◆ **role** ◆ **relationship** ◆ **group** *Each of these religions defines America's global role differently.* ◇ *Religion was important in understanding the character of groups defined by their social, ethnic or regional identity.* | **boundary** ◆ **limit** *Business networks are not formal affiliations with clearly defined boundaries.* ◇ *It is the path of the electron that defines the outer limit of the atom.* | **scope** ◆ **objective, goal** ◆ **category, class, set** ◆ **function** ◆ **criterion** ◆ **standard** ◆ **parameter** ◆ **variable** ◆ **market** ◆ **region, area** ◆ **problem** *It was left to the courts to define the scope of the legislation.* | **term, word** ◆ **phrase** ◆ **vocabulary** ◆ **concept** ◆ **meaning** *The concept of 'strategy' was first introduced and defined in ancient military dictionaries.*

▸ ADVERB + DEFINE | DEFINE + ADVERB **broadly** ◆ **narrowly** ◆ **precisely** *Education, broadly defined, has a responsibility to provide understanding and insight as well as applied knowledge.* ◇ *Defined narrowly, sprawl refers to the rapid and unplanned expansion of a metropolitan area.*

▸ ADVERB + DEFINE **well** ◆ **poorly** ◆ **clearly** *The socially sanctioned roles of men and women within these institutions were well defined.* ◇ *The clearly defined borders of this lump are consistent with those of a cyst.* | **strictly** ◆ **explicitly** ◆ **specifically** ◆ **uniquely** ◆ **loosely** ◆ **vaguely** ◆ **properly** ◆ **formally** ◆ **conventionally** ◆ **traditionally** ◆ **usually, generally** ◆ **variously** ◆ **geographically** ◆ **culturally** *Ethnic groups are often loosely defined.* ◇ *Finkl and Catt specifically define the term to refer to closely spaced buried soils with no 'overlap'.* | **sharply** *Most galaxies do not have sharply defined outer edges.*

▸ DEFINE + ADVERB **above** ◆ **below** ◆ **here** *Over-confidence, as defined above, leads to incorrect estimates of risks faced.*

deˈfining vocabulary *noun* a set of carefully chosen words used to write the explanations in some dictionaries: *Those words do not belong to the approved defining vocabulary for that level.*

def·in·ite AWL /ˈdefɪnət/ *adj.* **1** clearly stated or decided; sure or certain: *The novel, as one might expect, provides no definite answers.* **2** clearly true or real; having a clear meaning: *It is difficult to draw any definite conclusions in the absence of complete lifespan studies.* **3** having an exact outline or form that can be recognized easily: *Proteins have definite structures and shapes.*

ˌdefinite ˈarticle *noun* the word *the* in English, or a similar word in another language: *In languages such as French, Spanish and Italian, the definite article has to agree with the noun in gender and number.* ➲ *compare* INDEFINITE ARTICLE

def·in·ite·ly AWL /ˈdefɪnətli/ *adv.* **1** without doubt: *The interview definitely had a more formal feel than the other interviews thus far.* ◇ *The categories in the questionnaire ranged from 1 (not true at all) to 5 (definitely true).* ◇ *This was definitely not the case for the respondents in the low-income group.* **2** in a way that is certain or that shows that you are certain: *The cause of the outbreak is not definitely known.*

def·in·ition AWL /ˌdefɪˈnɪʃn/ *noun* **1** [C] an exact statement or description of the nature, extent or meaning of sth: *Studies of urban populations sometimes adopt a definition based on a minimum size, such as centres with 5 000 inhabitants.* ◇ **~ of sth** *Broader definitions of democracy emphasize multiple forms of participation in politics.* **2** [C] a statement of the exact meaning of a word or phrase, especially in a dictionary: *Up-to-date definitions can usually be found on these websites.* ◇ **~ of sth** *The trial judge made reference to dictionary definitions of the term.* **3** [U] the action or process of stating the exact meaning of a word or phrase: *A similar problem of definition occurs when one considers the word 'tool' to describe a software application, interface, etc.*

IDM **by defiˈnition** as a result of what sth is: *Most non-profits are, by definition, little concerned with profit.*

▸ ADJECTIVE + DEFINITION **broad, general** ◆ **narrow** ◆ **clear** ◆ **simple** ◆ **precise, exact** ◆ **explicit** ◆ **strict** ◆ **very** ◆ **standard, accepted** ◆ **formal** ◆ **traditional** *No precise definition of this term is offered.* ◇ *In the European Union, the very definition of social policy is closely related to employment issues.* | **legal** ◆ **statutory** ◆ **working, operational** *Although legal definitions vary, refugees are generally considered to be people fleeing life-threatening circumstances.* ◇ *One good working definition of statistics might be that it is the technology of extracting meaning from data.*

▸ VERB + DEFINITION **provide, give, offer, propose** ◆ **use, employ, adopt** ◆ **meet, fit** ◆ **extend, expand, broaden** *Dennett's view neatly fits the definition of 'illusion' used here.*

▸ DEFINITION OF + NOUN **term, word • concept** *Different definitions of the concepts of efficiency and productivity may lead to confusion among team members.* | **terrorism • crime • culture • democracy** *There is no universally accepted definition of terrorism.*

de·fini·tive AWL /dɪˈfɪnətɪv/ *adj.* **1** final; that cannot be changed: *In the case of these viruses, the mere presence of the antibody is sufficient to make a definitive diagnosis.* ◇ *a definitive conclusion/answer* **2** [usually before noun] considered to be the best of its kind and almost impossible to improve: *This is the definitive study in any Western language of Japanese cinema.* ■ **de·fini·tive·ly** *adv.*: *However, this study cannot definitively answer these questions.*

D

de·flate *verb* **1** /dɪˈfleɪt; ˌdiːˈfleɪt/ [T, I] **~ (sth)** to let air or gas out of sth; to become smaller because of air or gas coming out: *He deflated one of the tyres.* ◇ *The balloon deflated.* **2** /ˌdiːˈfleɪt/ [T, I] (*economics*) to reduce the amount of money being used in a country so that prices fall or stay steady; to be reduced in this way: *Germany was forced to deflate, even though already in the early stages of a depression.* ◇ **~ sth** *Weak member states were forced to deflate their economies.* **3** /dɪˈfleɪt/ [T, often passive] **~ sb/sth** to make sb feel less confident; to make sb/sth feel or seem less important: *Marlowe impels his dramas forwards by evoking the power of dreams and then deflating them.* ➲ *compare* INFLATE

de·fla·tion /ˌdiːˈfleɪʃn/ *noun* [U] (*economics*) a general fall in the prices of services and goods in a particular country: *When a country faces the risk of deflation, demand reduces as people wait for prices to fall.* OPP INFLATION ■ **de·fla·tion·ary** /ˌdiːˈfleɪʃənri; *NAmE* ˌdiːˈfleɪʃəneri/ *adj.*: *Keynes opposes both deflationary and inflationary remedies to unemployment.*

de·flect /dɪˈflekt/ *verb* **1 ~ sth** to make sth change direction: *Alpha and beta particles are deflected by an electric field, but gamma rays are not.* **2 ~ sth (away) from sth** to succeed in preventing sth from being directed towards you SYN DIVERT (3): *Throughout the election campaign, Nixon successfully deflected attention from the Watergate break-in.*

de·flec·tion /dɪˈflekʃn/ *noun* [U, C, usually sing.] **~ (of sth)** a sudden change in the direction that sth is moving in, usually after it has hit sth; the act of causing sth to change direction: *The gravitational deflection of light implies that massive objects may act as gravitational lenses.*

de·form /dɪˈfɔːm; *NAmE* dɪˈfɔːrm/ *verb* **1** [T] **~ sth** to change or spoil the usual or natural shape or form of sth: *Actively intruding rocks deform the rocks around them to create a space for themselves.* **2** [I] to be changed or spoiled in shape or form: *The sphere deforms when subjected to stress.*

de·form·ation /ˌdiːfɔːˈmeɪʃn; *NAmE* ˌdiːfɔːrˈmeɪʃn/ *noun* [U] **~ (of sth)** the process or result of changing or spoiling the usual or natural shape or form of sth: *Newton maintained that deformation of the water surface indicates that a force is acting on it.* ◇ *A sample subjected to a small stress typically undergoes elastic deformation but recovers its original shape when the stress is removed.*

defy /dɪˈfaɪ/ *verb* (**de·fies, defy·ing, de·fied, de·fied**) **1 ~ sb/sth** to refuse to obey sb/sth: *Some clergy defied the authorities and were imprisoned, tortured or even killed.* ◇ *He defied a court order to return his sons to their mother.* **2 ~ belief, explanation, description, etc.** to be impossible to believe, explain, describe, etc: *Southey's epic poem almost defies description.* ◇ *For more than three centuries, this group of Panamanian orchids defied all attempts at classification.* **3** to not be affected by sth in the usual way: **~ sth** *Some animal behaviour may appear to defy logic at first.* ◇ **it defies sth (to do sth)** *It defies all common sense to imagine that future death tolls from earthquakes will not be larger.*

de·gen·er·ate /dɪˈdʒenəreɪt/ *verb* [I] to become worse, for example by becoming lower in quality or weaker SYN DETERIORATE: *In 1884 Brabazon declared that 'physically, the population of our large towns was degenerating'.* ◇ **~ into sth** *Conflict can actually have beneficial results provided it does not degenerate into violence.*

de·gen·er·ation /dɪˌdʒenəˈreɪʃn/ *noun* [U, sing.] **~ (of sth)** the process of becoming worse or less acceptable in quality or condition: *Motor neuron disease is an uncommon disease that causes progressive degeneration of the motor system.* ◇ *They have argued that the centralization of power led to a degeneration of local culture and life.*

de·gen·era·tive /dɪˈdʒenərətɪv/ *adj.* (of an illness) getting or likely to get worse as time passes: *Inflammation plays an important role in many chronic degenerative diseases associated with ageing.*

deg·rad·ation /ˌdeɡrəˈdeɪʃn/ *noun* [U] **1** the process of being made worse, especially in quality: *Environmental degradation resulting from pollution is now commonplace in industrial societies.* ◇ **~ of sth** *Whether criminal organizations were a factor in the degradation of the market economy is an interesting question.* **2** the process of being changed to a simpler chemical form: *Such polymers can be dissolved in strong acids, frequently without degradation.* ◇ **~ of sth** *An extremely important mechanism used for the control of cellular function is the degradation of proteins.* **3** a situation in which sb has lost all SELF-RESPECT and the respect of other people: *The shame these women feel at the degradation they have suffered may be as painful as the assault itself.* ◇ **~ of sb** *Colonial writing is important for revealing the ways in which the degradation of other human beings was perceived as natural.*

de·grade /dɪˈɡreɪd/ *verb* **1** [T, I] **~ (sth)** to make sth worse, especially in quality; to become worse: *Discharge of untreated waste water degrades the quality of the rivers and canals.* ◇ *Mountain environments are more susceptible to adverse impacts than lowlands and are degrading accordingly.* **2** [I, T] to change to a simpler chemical form; to make sth change to a simpler chemical form: *The material is inert and does not degrade.* ◇ **~ sth** *Soluble protein is rapidly degraded by these microbes.* **3** [T] **~ sb/yourself** to treat sb in a way that makes them seem not worth any respect or not worth taking seriously: *The social effects of colonialism are to degrade and dehumanize the people of the colonized countries.*

de·grad·ing /dɪˈɡreɪdɪŋ/ *adj.* treating sb as if they have no value, so that they lose respect for themselves and the respect of other people: *People have, by virtue of the Human Rights Act 1998, a right to life and a right not to undergo degrading treatment.*

de·gree /dɪˈɡriː/ *noun* **1** [C, U] the amount, level or extent to which sth happens or is present: **~ (of sth)** *Many countries are developing legislation to reduce tobacco consumption, with varying degrees of success.* ◇ *The differences are typically more a matter of degree than kind.* ◇ **to a… ~** *To a large degree, the local ethnic groups continued to use their own languages.* ◇ *In the USA (and to a lesser degree, the UK), companies argue that these massive pay packages are needed in order to maintain competitiveness.* **2** [C] a qualification obtained by a student who successfully completes a university or college course: *Candidates are expected to have a degree.* ◇ **~ in sth** *Moon had graduated from Ohio State in 1924 with a degree in journalism.* ◇ **+ noun** *A total of 197 Japanese intermediate EFL learners on a first-year English degree course participated in this study.* **3** [C] (*BrE*) a university or college course, normally lasting three years or more: *This information is aimed at students thinking about coming to the UK to do a degree.* ◇ **~ in sth** *She was in the first year of a bachelor's degree in environmental science.* **4** [C] (*symb.* °) a unit for measuring angles: *In this technique, the electron beam is tilted by a small angle, typically 1–3 degrees (1–3°).* **5** [C] (*abbr.* **deg.**) (*symb.* °) a unit for measuring temperature: *These winds can raise air temperatures by 10 degrees within 15–20 minutes.* ◇ *degrees Celsius/centigrade/Fahrenheit* **6** [C] (*symb.* °) a unit for measuring LATITUDE and LONGITUDE: *To fly from London at 55 degrees north to Los Angeles at nearer 30, you might expect to head in a south-westerly direction.* **7** [C] **~ (of sth)** a unit for measuring how strong or hard sth is: *The strength of beer can be measured in degrees of alcohol.* ◇ *Rubber which is vulcanized to a very high degree forms a hard, glassy material known as ebonite.* **8** [C] a legal category of crime, especially murder: *first-degree murder* ◇ **in the first/second/third ~** *Comparatively serious reckless killings would be regarded as murder in the second degree, if the recommendation is implemented.* **9** [U, C] (*mathematics*) the category to which an EQUATION belongs according to the highest POWER of the UNKNOWNS or VARIABLES in it: *There is no formula for the solution of most polynomials of degree 5 or greater.* ◇ *The zero polynomial is either given a negative degree or is not defined.*

IDM **by deˈgrees** slowly and gradually: *A squire was able to rise by degrees to the dignity of knighthood.* **to a/some degree** to some extent: *The movement had been successful to a degree in alleviating poverty and exploitation.* ◇ *Even here judges are bound to some degree by precedent and certain rules of procedure.*

▸ ADJECTIVE + DEGREE **high, great, large, significant, considerable, substantial • low, small • lesser • certain • sufficient • reasonable • same • varying, different, differing, various** *We can predict with a high degree of certainty how many radioactive events will be observed over a given period of time.* | **doctoral • advanced • honorary** *She holds a doctoral degree from Yale University.*

▸ NOUN + DEGREE **college, university • undergraduate • graduate, postgraduate** *College graduates, when compared with students without college degrees, showed more interest in international news events.*

▸ VERB + DEGREE **have, possess • require** *If individuals believe they have some degree of control over their lives, they may be more likely to take action in difficult situations.* ◇ *More and more members possessed advanced degrees such as an MBA from a top American business school.* | **show, indicate, demonstrate, exhibit, reflect • suggest • assess • measure • determine • involve • offer • achieve • enjoy** *If you enjoy a high degree of brand loyalty, it makes little sense to spend much money on promotion.* | **obtain, get, earn • receive • hold • award** *The study shows that 21 per cent went on to get degrees.* | **do, pursue, take • complete • offer** *Three decades ago, students taking a degree in electronics had to study electrodynamics.*

▸ DEGREE + NOUN **programme, course • level • student** *Candidates must have completed studies in English to at least degree level.*

▸ DEGREE OF + NOUN **freedom, autonomy • control • certainty • uncertainty • confidence • success • accuracy • risk • similarity • overlap** *It seems self-evident that human individuals retain a degree of freedom to act as they wish or intend.*

deity /ˈdeɪəti; ˈdiːəti/ *noun* (*pl.* **-ies**) **1** [C] a god or GODDESS: *Zeus presided over the other deities on Mount Olympus.* **2 the Deity** [sing.] God: *Weber was interested in the way different religions conceive of the Deity.*

delay¹ /dɪˈleɪ/ *noun* **1** [C] a period of time by which sth is slow or late; the period of time between two things happening: *The claimant must bring his/her claim in a reasonable time, with no unreasonably long delays.* ◇ **~ of sth** *Cases were interviewed with a median delay of 15 days from the onset of symptoms.* ◇ **~ in (doing) sth** *The delay in legislating for a strengthened UK competition policy is explored in Wilks (1999: 308–25).* ◇ **~ between A and B**

Measuring the time delay between transmission and reception of each GPS microwave signal gives the distance to each satellite. **2** [U] a situation in which sth does not happen when it should: **without ~** *Diagnosis of meningitis is a medical emergency and samples must be processed without delay.*

delay² /dɪˈleɪ/ *verb* **1** [T] to not do sth until a later time: **~ sth** *Economic hardship in the wake of the war encouraged couples to delay marriage.* ◇ **~ doing sth** *The Roman authorities in Judea delayed carrying out the emperor's order.* **2** [T, usually passive] if an event is **delayed**, it happens at a later time than is normal or expected: **~ sth** *Many plants exhibit a reproductive strategy in which reproduction is delayed as long as possible.* ◇ **~ sth for sth** *The actual outbreak of hostilities was delayed for another year.* ◇ **delayed + noun** *The delayed departure or arrival of one aeroplane will affect many of the subsequent connecting flights and arrival times.*

dele·gate¹ /ˈdelɪɡeɪt/ *verb* [I, T] to give part of your work, power or authority to sb, especially sb in a lower position than you: *In order to work effectively, managers must delegate.* ◇ **~ (sth) (to sb)** *The board may delegate power to the chairman.* ◇ *to delegate authority/responsibility/a task*

dele·gate² /ˈdelɪɡət/ *noun* a person who is chosen or elected to represent the views of a group of people and vote and make decisions for them: *Originally 55 non-governmental organizations were invited to send a single delegate each to the World Forum.*

dele·ga·tion /ˌdelɪˈɡeɪʃn/ *noun* **1** [C+sing./pl. v.] **~ (of sb)** a group of people chosen or elected to represent the views of an organization, country, etc: *In these conferences, each country was represented by a delegation of government officials.* ◇ *Gaius disdainfully ignored the delegations sent to Rome by both groups.* **2** [U] **~ (of sth) (to sb)** the process of giving part of your work, power or authority to sb, especially sb in a lower position than you: *Numerous management committees were set up to supervise the delegation of power to the Commission.*

de·lete /dɪˈliːt/ *verb* **1 ~ sth (from sth)** to remove sth that has been written or printed: *In the excerpts that follow, I use bracketed ellipses ([. . .]) to indicate that I have deleted portions of the conversation.* **2 ~ sth (from sth)** to remove data from a computer's memory: *In a computer system, everything is recorded and nothing is deleted.* **3** [usually passive] **be deleted (from sth)** (*biochemistry*) (of a section of GENETIC code) to be lost or removed from a GENETIC SEQUENCE: *If one important gene is deleted from an animal's DNA, other genes can stand in.*

dele·teri·ous /ˌdeləˈtɪəriəs; *NAmE* ˌdeləˈtɪriəs/ *adj.* (*formal*) harmful and damaging: *Many studies have shown deleterious effects of prenatal maternal stress on offspring.*

de·le·tion /dɪˈliːʃn/ *noun* [U, C] **~ (of sth)** **1** the act of removing sth that has been written or printed; sth that has been removed in this way: *Participants could make any deletions, changes or additions to the interview transcripts as they saw fit.* **2** (*biochemistry*) the loss or REMOVAL of a section of GENETIC code; code that is lost or removed: *Insertion, deletion and rearrangement of DNA sequences are major drivers of genomic evolution.*

de·lib·er·ate¹ /dɪˈlɪbərət/ *adj.* done on purpose rather than by accident SYN INTENTIONAL: *The attack was deliberate and unjustified.* ◇ *This occurs when the government makes a deliberate attempt to change the level of economic activity.* OPP UNINTENTIONAL

de·lib·er·ate² /dɪˈlɪbəreɪt/ *verb* [I, T] to think very carefully about sth, usually before making a decision: *Having deliberated, some people may decide to act in ways that the majority of others consider unethical.* ◇ **~ about/on sth** *At* the Warsaw meeting, officials from 107 countries deliberated on issues of international democracy. ◇ **~ sth** Participants are brought together for two days or more to deliberate the issue in question.

de·lib·er·ate·ly /dɪˈlɪbərətli/ adv. on purpose rather than by accident SYN INTENTIONALLY: *I have deliberately chosen not to correct the spelling of the original text.* ◇ *Mesolithic humans may have utilized fire deliberately for clearing woodland.*

D

de·lib·er·ation /dɪˌlɪbəˈreɪʃn/ noun [U, C, usually pl.] the process of carefully considering or discussing sth; the result of this process: *Educational values are always a matter of debate and deliberation.* ◇ *The council's deliberations were then presented to an assembly of the people.*

deli·cate /ˈdelɪkət/ adj. **1** (of a state or condition) easily affected, even by slight changes: *There is a delicate balance to be achieved between personal privacy and the interests of the government.* **2** showing or needing careful or sensitive treatment in order to avoid offending people: *The author deals with some very delicate legal issues.* **3** easily damaged SYN FRAGILE (1): *The conjunctiva is a delicate transparent membrane that lines the eyelids.*

de·lin·eate /dɪˈlɪnieɪt/ verb **1 ~ sth** to decide on or show the limits of sth: *Rumours, Newcomb asserts, can delineate the boundaries of a particular social group.* ◇ *The work is organized into clearly delineated areas.* **2 ~ sth** to describe, draw or explain sth in detail: *Solomon clearly delineates the problems that narrative film-making posed for Houdini.* ◇ *In Constable's paintings, we are expected to study and reflect upon the carefully delineated details of the natural world.* ■ **de·lin·ea·tion** /dɪˌlɪniˈeɪʃn/ noun [C, usually sing., U] **~ between A and B** *There is a clear delineation between the Conservative and Liberal Democrat positions on this issue.* ◇ **~ of sth** *These detailed extracts concern not only the composition of the scene but also the delineation of the characters.*

de·liver /dɪˈlɪvə(r)/ verb **1** [T, I] to take sth to the place where it is wanted or needed; to take sb somewhere: **~ sth** *The amount of oxygen delivered depends upon the patient's breathing pattern.* ◇ **~ (sth/sb) to sb/sth** *Packaging is needed to ensure that goods are delivered to customers in a sound condition.* **2** [I, T] to do what you promised to do or what you are expected to do; to produce or provide what people expect you to: *The policy failed to deliver in terms of votes.* ◇ **~ on sth** *So far, the Junta appears to be delivering on its promise to return the country to democratic rule.* ◇ **~ sth** *The new hospitals will have even more control over how they use funds and deliver services.* **3** [T] **~ sth** to give a speech, talk, etc. or other official statement; to communicate sth: *On 15 November, he delivered a speech in which he demanded that King Louis XVI be brought to trial.* ◇ *In the fifty years from its first judgment in 1954, the European Court of Justice delivered 6 465 judgments.* ◇ *Adults need to deliver consistent messages to children about the importance of education.* **4** [T] **~ a baby** to help a woman to give birth to a baby: *A baby girl was delivered by Caesarean section and was admitted to the neonatal unit.* **5** [T] **~ sth (to sth)** to throw or aim sth: *Satellite-guided missiles can deliver deadly blows with pinpoint accuracy.* ◇ (*figurative*) *This event delivered a savage blow to American prestige.* **6** [T] **~ sb/yourself (from sth)** (*formal*) to save sb/yourself from sth bad SYN SAVE (1): *Mbeki called on Africans to deliver themselves from the legacy of colonialism.*

IDM **deliver the ˈgoods** (*rather informal*) to do what you have said you would do or are expected to do: *The units are selling and the original marketing strategy is still delivering the goods.*

de·liv·ery /dɪˈlɪvəri/ noun (pl. -ies) **1** [U, C] the act or process of moving sth to the place where it is wanted or needed: *Reliable on-time delivery means that a retailer can reduce the need to carry safety stock.* ◇ *The need for more frequent deliveries can be problematic.* ◇ **~ of sth** *Effective storage and delivery of hydrogen gas is key to the commercial development of devices that use it as a fuel.* ◇ **+ noun** *Polymers are used in a variety of targeted, controlled drug delivery devices.* **2** [U, C] **~ (of sth)** the act or process of providing a service: *The delivery of many public services, from schools to prisons, has been contracted out to private firms.* ◇ *Pharmacists are expected to play a greater role in health care delivery in the future.* **3** [C, U] **~ (of sb)** the process of giving birth to a baby: *The delivery of a healthy baby who survives to adulthood is one of the most valuable assets a community can enjoy.*

delta /ˈdeltə/ noun an area of land, shaped like a triangle, where a river has split into several smaller rivers before entering the sea: *The Niger delta has tidal channels that penetrate onto the delta plain.*

de·mand¹ /dɪˈmɑːnd; NAmE dɪˈmænd/ noun **1** [U, C] the desire or need of customers or employers for goods or services that they want to buy or use: *Demand has been falling for the past couple of years.* ◇ **~ for sth/sb** *Stable market conditions are required so that businesses can count on an adequate demand for their products in the future.* ◇ *Men have been hardest hit by a decline in the demand for low-skilled workers in manufacturing.* ➲ see also SUPPLY AND DEMAND **2** [C] a very firm request for sth which you think you have a right to have: *Some patients with personality disorder may threaten self-harm if their demands are not met.* ◇ **~ for sth** *There have been demands for the formal repeal of these laws.* ◇ **~ that...** *They rejected the military's demand that certain candidates and parties be banned from the election.* **3 demands** [pl.] things that sb/sth makes you do, especially things that are difficult or make you tired or anxious: *Life at sea imposes additional demands compared with life ashore.* ◇ **~ of sth** *Couples have to juggle the demands of work and family life.* ◇ **~ on sb/sth** *Even with all those demands on his time and energy, he was a copious writer.*

IDM **in deˈmand** wanted by a lot of people: *Some firms and individuals may earn very high incomes if they have products or skills that are in demand.* **on deˈmand** as soon as or whenever sth is required: *As the Internet merges with television, any kind of film will be readily available on demand.*

▸ ADJECTIVE + DEMAND **increasing, growing, rising** *These policy interventions led to increasing demands by firms for technology upgrading.* ◇ *The rapidly growing demand means the country's energy sector must urgently provide additional capacity.* | **high, great • low • increased • total, aggregate • excess • elastic • inelastic • global • domestic** *Singapore provides the extreme example of high demand driven by the size and prosperity of its population.*

▸ ADJECTIVE + DEMANDS **great • increasing, growing • increased • excessive • competing, conflicting** *The findings also demonstrate the influence of competing demands and busy schedules on family food practices.*

▸ NOUN + DEMAND **consumer, customer** *Direct communications with customers via sales promotions are mechanisms to stimulate consumer demand.* ◇ *By contrast, development projects aim at commercializing products to fit customer demands.* | **market • world • labour • energy • oil • electricity • water** *Fast technological development and fluctuating market demand often combine to cause great instability in the computer supply chain.*

▸ VERB + DEMAND **meet, satisfy • face** *Tractors were not being produced in sufficient quantities to meet demand.* ◇ *The aim of the moderate right in Turkey has always been to satisfy demands for social justice in this way.* | **boost, stimulate, raise, increase • reduce, decrease • fulfil • create, generate • affect, influence, manage • shift • exceed** *A decision to expand the business may require an increased marketing effort to boost demand.* | **make** *Union* *bosses struck a deal whereby they agreed to make lower wage demands.*

▸ VERB + DEMANDS **make • impose, place ~ on • increase • face • meet, satisfy • balance** *Any form of curricular innovation places new demands on teachers.*

▸ DEMAND + VERB **fall • increase, grow, rise • exceed, outstrip** *By the time the former Spanish colonies became independent, demand was outstripping supply.*

▸ DEMAND FOR + NOUN **product • goods • exports • imports • services • money, currency • loans • labour, workers • resources • oil • energy • water • food • quality** *One of the main influences on the level of demand for goods and services is the distribution of income between profits and wages.*

▸ NOUN + OF DEMAND **level • lack • elasticity • indicator • determinant** *The ability of firms to set prices is limited by the level of demand and supply within the market they serve.*

de·mand² /dɪˈmɑːnd; *NAmE* dɪˈmænd/ *verb* **1** to ask for sth very firmly: **~ sth** *Their aim was to demand change in Conservative policy on immigration.* ◇ **~ sth of sb** *As competition for good education increases, parents demand more of their children.* ◇ **~ sth from sb** *They could easily demand higher wages from their employers by threatening to strike just at harvest time.* ◇ **~ that...** *Japan's press turned jingoistic, demanding that China be challenged.* ◇ **~ to do sth** *People will demand to know what is being done to manage the risks.* **2 ~ sth** to need sth in order to be done successfully: *Weaving is an activity that demands considerable skill and time.* IDM *see* OCCASION¹

deˈmand curve *noun* a GRAPH showing how the demand for a product, service, etc. varies with changes in its price: *The demand curve for beverages in general may be fairly inelastic, on the basis that people will always want to buy drinks of some description (Figure 9.11).*

de·mand·ing /dɪˈmɑːndɪŋ; *NAmE* dɪˈmændɪŋ/ *adj.* **1** (of a task) needing a lot of skill, care or effort: *Nearly 30% of the women were employed in physically demanding work.* ➲ thesaurus note *at* DIFFICULT **2** (of a person) expecting a lot of work or attention from others; not easily satisfied: *The more demanding customers become, the more companies will need to be able to adjust their supply to meet demand.*

de·men·tia /dɪˈmenʃə/ *noun* [U] (*medical*) a serious mental DISORDER caused by brain disease or injury, that affects the ability to think, remember and behave normally: *Two studies indicate that the risk of dementia is higher in diabetic subjects treated with insulin.*

dem·oc·racy /dɪˈmɒkrəsi; *NAmE* dɪˈmɑːkrəsi/ *noun* (*pl.* -ies) **1** [U] a system of government in which all the people of a country can vote to elect their representatives: *Since the termination of the Cold War, the principles of liberal democracy are increasingly accepted around the world.* ◇ *They argue that industrial capitalism promotes democracy by empowering the urban working class.* ◇ *constitutional/representative/electoral/parliamentary democracy* **2** [C] a country which has this system of government: *In some cases, Western democracies have used their power to install democracy by military intervention.* ◇ *Inglehart and Welzel (2005) present strong evidence that economic development does help new democracies to emerge.* **3** [U] fair and equal treatment of everyone and their right to take part in making decisions: *Freedom and democracy are the core values for liberals.*

demo·crat /ˈdeməkræt/ *noun* **1** a person who believes in or supports democracy: *As an Athenian democrat, Sophocles certainly saw the need to uphold the rule of law.* **2 Democrat** (*abbr.* **D, Dem.**) a member or supporter of the Democratic Party of the US: *John F. Kennedy, a Democrat elected in 1960, is considered to have been the first Keynesian president.* ➲ *compare* REPUBLICAN¹

demo·crat·ic /ˌdeməˈkrætɪk/ *adj.* **1** (of a country or system) controlled by representatives who are elected by the people of a country; connected with this system: *The country's first democratic government was elected in 1994.* ◇ *Democratic institutions are the most secure protectors of human rights.* **2** (of an organization or society) based on the principle that everyone has an equal right to be involved in making decisions: *She argues that schools need to educate students to live in a democratic society.* ◇ *Democratic decision-making is encouraged at all levels of the organization.* **3 Democratic** (*abbr.* **Dem., D**) connected with the Democratic Party in the US: *The Democratic candidate Hubert Humphrey was the only candidate to address crime as a social problem.* ■ **demo·crat·ic·al·ly** /ˌdeməˈkrætɪkli/ *adv.*: *Wahid later became the first democratically elected president in Indonesian history (1999–2001).* ◇ *The economic advantages of a worker-owned and democratically run firm are clear.*

D

dem·oc·ra·tize (*BrE also* **-ise**) /dɪˈmɒkrətaɪz; *NAmE* dɪˈmɑːkrətaɪz/ *verb* **~ sth** to make a country or an institution more democratic: *Just as Romantic literature, visual art and politics worked to democratize society and its attitudes, so did music.* ■ **dem·oc·ra·tiza·tion, -isa·tion** /dɪˌmɒkrətaɪˈzeɪʃn; *NAmE* dɪˌmɑːkrətəˈzeɪʃn/ *noun* [U] *Demands for democratization usually began with condemnations of corruption in high places.*

demo·graph·ic¹ /ˌdeməˈɡræfɪk/ *adj.* connected with the population and different groups within it: *Important data about population and demographic change are presented.* ◇ *The following demographic characteristics were recorded from the participants: level of education, marital status, presence of children and religious belief.* ◇ *demographic variables/factors* ◇ *demographic data/information* ■ **demo·graph·ic·al·ly** /deməˈɡræfɪkli/ *adv.*: *The country continued to be dominated, politically as well as demographically, by whites of European descent.*

demo·graph·ic² /ˌdeməˈɡræfɪk/ *noun* **1 demographics** [pl.] data about the population and different groups within it: *Changing demographics have introduced far greater diversity in schools.* ◇ **~ of sth** *At this time, the demographics of the school population were shifting.* **2** [sing.] a particular group of people within the population who have a common characteristic: *The nominal target demographic for the marketing campaign was young adults.*

dem·og·raphy /dɪˈmɒɡrəfi; *NAmE* dɪˈmɑːɡrəfi/ *noun* [U] **~ (of sth)** the changing number of births, deaths, diseases, etc. in a community over a period of time; the scientific study of these changes: *Changes in the demography of a society can also change patterns of social need.* ■ **dem·og·raph·er** /dɪˈmɒɡrəfə(r); *NAmE* dɪˈmɑːɡrəfər/ *noun*: *Demographers have noted that educated women are among the first to make the move towards smaller families.*

dem·on·strable AWL /dɪˈmɒnstrəbl; ˈdemənstrəbl; *NAmE* dɪˈmɑːnstrəbl/ *adj.* that can be shown or proved: *Consumers generally favour organizations that have demonstrable links to good causes.* ■ **dem·on·strably** AWL /dɪˈmɒnstrəbli; ˈdemənstrəbli; *NAmE* dɪˈmɑːnstrəbli/ *adv.*: *The accused's version of events was demonstrably false.*

dem·on·strate AWL /ˈdemənstreɪt/ *verb* **1** [T] to show sth clearly by giving proof or evidence: **~ sth** *This example clearly demonstrates the importance of regular safety inspections.* ◇ **~ that...** *This study demonstrates that the type of fastening can affect a helmet's effectiveness in preventing head injuries.* ◇ **~ how/what, etc...** *Our findings demonstrate how young people are using the Internet to ask and respond to highly personal questions.* ◇ **be demonstrated to be sth** *Income level has been demonstrated to be an important factor affecting physical health.* ◇ **it is demonstrated that...** *In this study, it was demonstrated*

D

that low morale at work was associated with exhaustion in both men and women. ➲ thesaurus note *at* SHOW[1] **2** [T] **~ sth** to show by your actions that you have a particular quality, feeling or opinion SYN DISPLAY[1] (2): *Gibbons' novels demonstrate an acute awareness of the power of modern technology to aid social mobility.* ◇ *He repeatedly demonstrated his willingness to agree to the president's demands.* **3** [T] **~ sth** to show and explain how sth works or how to do sth: *The procedure is demonstrated in the following example...* **4** [I] **~ (against sb/sth)** to take part in a public meeting or march, usually as a protest or to show support for sth: *The Petrograd workers were demonstrating against the Bolsheviks on several grounds.* ➲ *compare* MARCH[1]

▸ DEMONSTRATE + NOUN **importance, significance • existence • extent • relevance • validity • reliability • efficacy, effectiveness • effect • improvement • link, association • benefit • utility • feasibility • potential** *One study demonstrated a strong link between deprivation and obesity.* ◇ *Previous trials have demonstrated important clinical benefits with statin therapy.* | **awareness • understanding • competence, ability • willingness • commitment** *Research has indicated that girls need to demonstrate competence before boys allow them to play.*

▸ NOUN + DEMONSTRATE **study, research • experiment, trial • findings, results • researcher, author • article, paper** *Our results demonstrated a significant relationship between marital status and income.* ◇ *This article demonstrates that historians must take a longer history of local circumstances into consideration.*

▸ ADVERB + DEMONSTRATE | DEMONSTRATE + ADVERB **clearly • convincingly • empirically, experimentally** *Geographic research has clearly demonstrated that where a voter lives is crucial.* ◇ *The feasibility of this approach has been demonstrated experimentally.*

▸ ADVERB + DEMONSTRATE **amply • conclusively • effectively, successfully • vividly • repeatedly, consistently • recently • previously** *This history vividly demonstrates the human capacity to do immense harm in extreme circumstances.*

de·mon·stra·tion AWL /ˌdemənˈstreɪʃn/ *noun* **1** [C, U] **~ (of sth)** an act of giving proof or evidence for sth: *A convincing demonstration of the effect was provided by the following experiment.* ◇ *His contributions to biology include the demonstration of colour vision in bees.* ➲ thesaurus note *at* EVIDENCE[1] **2** [C] a public meeting or march at which people show that they are protesting against or supporting sb/sth: *Some of the protesters organized peaceful street demonstrations.* ◇ **~ against sb/sth** *The workers immediately staged a demonstration against the agreement.* ➲ *compare* MARCH[2] (2), PROTEST[1] **3** [C] an act of showing or explaining how sth works or is done: *When designing a training programme, it is useful to include practical demonstrations wherever possible.*

dem·on·stra·tor AWL /ˈdemənstreɪtə(r)/ *noun* a person who takes part in a public meeting or march in order to protest against sb/sth or to show support for sb/sth: *Workers attacked student anti-war demonstrators.*

de·nial AWL /dɪˈnaɪəl/ *noun* **1** [C, U] **~ of sth** the act of refusing to allow sb to have sth that they have a right to expect: *The basis of the decision was that not to do so would amount to a denial of justice.* ◇ *Denial of fundamental rights would be unconstitutional in the EU.* **2** [C, U] a statement that says that sth is not true or does not exist; the act of making such a statement: *The Minister of Foreign Affairs issued a categorical denial.* ◇ **~ of sth** *Gore had stood by Clinton, defending his denials of an affair and praising his leadership.* ◇ **in ~ of sth** *In denial of this, it is first alleged that she is economically independent.* ◇ **~ that...** *Citizens were angered by government denial that any problem existed.* **3** [U] the act of refusing to accept that sth unpleasant or painful is true: *Denial is usually the first reaction to the news of fatal illness.* ◇ **in ~** *Even now, too many MPs are still in denial, reluctant to see the need for change.* ◇ **in ~ about sth** *Not to think about this question is to be in denial about the reality of the severe problems that lie ahead.*

de·nom·in·ator /dɪˈnɒmɪneɪtə(r); *NAmE* dɪˈnɑːmɪneɪtər/ *noun* **~ (of sth)** (*mathematics*) the value below the line in a FRACTION, representing the number of parts the whole has been divided into, for example 4 in ¾: *Assuming the numerator remains constant, the larger the denominator, the smaller the fraction of cake each child will receive.* HELP In statistics, a **denominator** is a figure representing the total population in terms of which statistical values are expressed: *It is not enough to calculate risk to know only that 1 356 people suffered cardiac problems having taken the drug; we also need to know the denominator.* ➲ *compare* NUMERATOR ➲ *see also* COMMON DENOMINATOR

de·nota·tion AWL /ˌdiːnəʊˈteɪʃn; *NAmE* ˌdiːnoʊˈteɪʃn/ *noun* [C, U] (*technical*) the actual object or idea to which a word refers; the act of naming sth with a word: *In its specific denotation, plague is an acute infection caused by the bacterium Yersinia pestis.* ◇ *Moreover, Metz says, we should study denotation before connotation.* ➲ *compare* CONNOTATION

de·note AWL /dɪˈnəʊt; *NAmE* dɪˈnoʊt/ *verb* to be a sign of sth SYN INDICATE (2): **~ sth** *The speed of light is conventionally denoted by the symbol c.* ◇ *Let Y denote the set of natural numbers for which all the digits are 7.* ◇ **~ that...** *The arrow is pointing in both directions to denote that this is a reversible reaction.*

dense /dens/ *adj.* **(dens·er, dens·est) 1** containing a lot of people, things, plants, etc. with little space between them: *Dense tropical forests are one of the least attractive environments for human subsistence.* ◇ *The city has a dense network of canals which drain into the Gulf of Thailand.* **2** (*technical*) (of a substance) heavy in relation to its size: *Salt water is marginally denser than tap water.* **3** (of clouds, smoke, etc.) thick and difficult to see through: *A dense fog covered the Greater London area during 5–8 December 1952.*

dense·ly /densli/ *adv.* in a way that includes a lot of people, things, plants, etc, with little space between them: *Rwanda is situated in one of the most densely populated regions in Africa.*

dens·ity /ˈdensəti/ *noun* (*pl.* **-ies**) [U, C] **1** the number of people or things in a particular area or space: *The Netherlands is a smaller country, with a greater population density.* ◇ **~ of sth** *The density of population was striking in the smaller West Indian islands.* ◇ **at high/low densities** *When flies were reared at high densities, they were less likely to engage in aggressive behaviours.* **2** (*physics*) the mass per unit volume of a solid, liquid or gas: *The therapy has been shown to increase bone density.* ◇ *Both aluminium and titanium have low densities.* ◇ **~ of sth** *The density of water at 20°C is 0.998 g/cm³.* ◇ **at high/low densities** *At high liquid densities, carbon dioxide exhibits improved solvent performance.* **3** (*technical*) the amount of any physical property, such as energy or charge, per unit volume, in a substance or field: *In molecules, most of the electron density is clustered around the atomic nuclei.* ◇ **~ of sth** *The chemical energy density of hydrogen is significantly higher than that found in electric battery materials.* **4 ~ (of sth)** (*computing*) the number of things that can be stored per unit of area or volume, especially on a disk: *The density of a memory system is a measure of how much data can be stored per unit area or per unit volume.*

▸ ADJECTIVE + DENSITY **high • low** *The highest density orchards have more than 500 trees per acre.*

▸ NOUN + DENSITY **population** *There is a high population density of 328 people per square kilometre.* | **air • bone, bone mineral • breast • fluid, liquid • bulk** *Air density* *falls by over 10% for each kilometre height rise.* ◇ *Soil bulk density was determined by the core method.* | **electron • current • charge • energy • power** *Modern power connectors must transmit high electrical current density to meet increasing system power requirements.*

▸ VERB + DENSITY **have • increase • reduce • estimate** *By simply cooling the system from 25°C to 8°C, it is possible to increase the solvent density by nearly 50%.* | **reach** *In the absence of strong predation pressure from fish, zooplankton reached high densities.* | **calculate, determine • measure** *We calculated the density of electricity at an arbitrary point in space.*

den·tist /ˈdentɪst/ *noun* a person whose job is to take care of people's teeth: *Less than a third of the population of Serbia had visited a dentist in the previous year as reported in 2006.*

deny AWL /dɪˈnaɪ/ *verb* (**de·nies, deny·ing, de·nied, de·nied**) **1** to say that sth is not true: **~ sth** *Some doctors have denied the existence of the syndrome.* ◇ **~ (that)...** *Both companies again denied they were subject to the jurisdiction of the court.* ◇ **it cannot be denied that...** *Clearly, it cannot be denied that nationalism and national identity invoke powerful emotions for most people.* ◇ **~ doing sth** *He denies taking any illicit drugs.* ➲ thesaurus note *at* REJECT **2 ~ sth** to refuse to admit or accept sth: *The company denied all responsibility for the incident.* ◇ *Patients sometimes deny any knowledge of their previous life or personal identity.* **3** to refuse to allow sb to have sth that they want or ask for: **~ sth** *Others have highlighted the effects of social exclusion in denying access to opportunities that most people would consider to be a right.* ◇ **~ sb sth** *No woman should be denied maternity services because she is unable to pay.* ◇ **~ sth to sb** *However, they denied this right to non-Russian peoples inside the Empire.* **4** to refuse to let yourself have sth that you would like to have, especially for moral or religious reasons: **~ yourself** *The worldly ascetic denies himself in the service of God.* ◇ **~ yourself sth** *The Council denied itself this form of voting.*

IDM **there is no deˈnying sth/that...** used to say that it is impossible to refuse to accept that sth is true: *There is no denying the inherent complexity of ecological problems.* ◇ *There is no denying that the poem is a brilliant accomplishment.*

de·part /dɪˈpɑːt; *NAmE* dɪˈpɑːrt/ *verb* [I, T] to leave a place, especially to start a journey: **~ (from...) (for...)** *More than 50 million migrants departed from Europe for the USA, Canada, South America and Australia.* ◇ **~ sth (for...)** (*NAmE*) *He voluntarily departed Australia for India on 28 July 2007.* OPP ARRIVE (1)

PHR V **deˈpart from sth** to behave in a way that is different from what is usual or expected: *Canadian tribunals have been known to depart from this approach.*

de·part·ment /dɪˈpɑːtmənt; *NAmE* dɪˈpɑːrtmənt/ *noun* (*abbr.* **Dept**) a section of a large organization such as a government, business or university: *Fig.11 shows patterns of collaboration between scientists in a university department.* ◇ *The Treasury reduced expenditure in all government departments.* ◇ *the marketing/IT/HR/personnel department*

de·part·ment·al /ˌdiːpɑːtˈmentl; *NAmE* ˌdiːpɑːrtˈmentl/ *adj.* [only before noun] connected with a department rather than with the whole organization: *The majority of policy decisions are made at departmental level.*

de·part·ure /dɪˈpɑːtʃə(r); *NAmE* dɪˈpɑːrtʃər/ *noun* **1** [C, U] **~ (for...) (from...)** the act of leaving a place, especially to start a journey: *He preached a sermon at Lincoln's Inn before his departure for Germany.* ◇ *Her departure from Egypt was her own decision.* ◇ *Every flight is issued a flight route prior to departure.* OPP ARRIVAL (1) **2** [C] a plane, train, etc. leaving a place at a particular time: *Migration statistics are obtained from records of international arrivals and departures.* OPP ARRIVAL (2) **3** [C] **~ (from sth)** an action that is different from what is usual or expected: *This represents a significant departure from standard practice.* ◇ *'Hyperion' marked a radical departure in style for Keats.* ◇ *a new/major/dramatic departure from sth* IDM *see* POINT[1]

de·pend /dɪˈpend/ *verb*

PHR V **deˈpend on/upon sth** (not used in the progressive tenses) to be affected or decided by sth: *The velocity of light depends on the nature of the material that it travels through and the wavelength of the light.* ◇ **~ doing sth** *The firm's success depends on providing value to customers.* ◇ **~ how/what, etc...** *The slope of a supply curve will depend on how sensitive it is to changes in price.* **deˈpend on/upon sb/sth (for sth)** (not used in the progressive tenses) to need money or help from sb/sth else for a particular purpose: *Most people in low-income countries depend on agriculture for their livelihood.* ◇ *Human beings are social animals: they depend on others.*

▸ DEPEND ON/UPON + NOUN **nature, type • size, number • extent, degree • circumstances, context • factor, parameter, condition • ability • location • temperature • orientation • strength** *Motivation is likely to depend on factors such as the management style and whether employees get feedback.*

▸ DEPEND + ADVERB + ON/UPON **only, entirely, solely • largely, primarily, mainly, essentially, mostly • crucially, critically • strongly, greatly, substantially, significantly • partly** *People's propensity to purchase certain categories of products depends primarily on their level of income.* ◇ *How the molecule reacts depends crucially on its shape.* | **heavily • primarily • solely** *All industrialized countries depend heavily on small business as a source of innovation and employment.*

▸ ADVERB + DEPEND ON/UPON **crucially, critically • ultimately • largely • strongly • obviously** *Success largely depends on forming a good relationship with the patient.*

de·pend·ant /dɪˈpendənt/ (*BrE*) (*also* **de·pend·ent** *NAmE, BrE*) *noun* a person who depends on another person for a home, food, money, etc: *Boys were educated to become husbands and fathers, providing for their dependants, and working full time in a man's job.*

de·pend·ence /dɪˈpendəns/ *noun* [U] **1** the state of needing sb/sth in order to survive or be successful: **~ on/upon sb/sth** *It is clear that the current dependence on oil cannot be sustained.* ◇ *Industrial growth would reduce dependence on overseas markets.* ◇ **~ (of sb/sth)** *The economic dependence of women has kept them back from their share in human progress.* ➲ *compare* INDEPENDENCE (4) **2** (*also* **de·pend·ency**) the state of being ADDICTED to sth: *The patient's symptoms may reflect substance abuse or dependence.* **3 ~ of A and B** the fact of one thing being affected by another: *Figure 12.6 shows the mutual dependence of transport and land use in a simplified form.*

de·pend·ency /dɪˈpendənsi/ *noun* (*pl.* **-ies**) **1** [U] the state of relying on sb/sth for sth, especially when this is not normal or necessary: *Encampment creates dependency by disempowering refugees.* ◇ **~ on/upon sb/sth** *Diversification may help to manage risk by reducing dependency on a narrow product area.* HELP In economics and geography, the **dependency ratio** is the number of children under the age of 18 and adults over the age of 64 (i.e. people not in the labour force) per hundred workers: *Owing to the enormous rise in life expectancy, India's old-age dependency ratio is expected to increase by 13.4 percentage points by 2050.* **2** [C] a country or area that is controlled by another country: *This methodology significantly underpredicts the numbers of migrants from US dependencies.* **3** = DEPENDENCE (2)

de·pend·ent¹ /dɪˈpendənt/ *adj.* **1** needing sb/sth in order to survive or be successful: *There has been growing concern about the provision of financial support for dependent children.* ◇ **~ on/upon sb/sth** *The principal consuming countries are likely to become increasingly dependent on imports.* ◇ **~ on/upon sb/sth for sth** *Most of us are dependent on others for food, housing and health.* ➲ *compare* INDEPENDENT (6) **2 ~ (on/upon sth)** ADDICTED to sth: *When the patient is dependent on alcohol, a sudden cessation of drinking may cause severe withdrawal symptoms.* ◇ *Nicotine dependence level was classified into three levels: low, moderate and severe, and 37% were severely dependent.* **3 ~ on/upon sth** affected or decided by sth: *The quality of the results is heavily dependent on the quality of the data.* ◇ *The ability of lone parents to go out to work is dependent upon a range of factors.* ➲ *compare* INDEPENDENT (3)

▸ DEPENDENT + NOUN **relative • child • adult • person** *Many dependent older people have limited access to family resources (e.g. if childless or widowed).*

▸ DEPENDENT ON/UPON + NOUN **each other, one another • others • adult • agriculture • imports • resources • industry • technology • aid, help, assistance, cooperation, support** *As social beings we are dependent on each other.* ◇ *Almost two thirds of the population live below the poverty line, and the country remains highly dependent on external assistance.* | **factors • size • presence, existence • conditions, context, circumstances • number, amount • level • type • nature • state • concentration • quality • temperature • availability** *Clearly, this technique is dependent on the availability of the necessary equipment.*

▸ ADVERB + DEPENDENT **heavily, highly • mutually** *What began as a choice to outsource can become a deep, mutually dependent collaboration.*

▸ ADVERB + DEPENDENT ON/UPON SB/STH **entirely, completely, totally, wholly • heavily, highly • financially, economically • increasingly** *In some cases, one twin is completely dependent on the other for survival.* | **critically, crucially • highly, strongly • largely, primarily • partly, partially** *The profitability of GM crops seems to be highly dependent on public attitudes to GM food.*

de·pend·ent² /dɪˈpendənt/ *noun* (*especially NAmE*) = DEPENDANT

de,pendent ˈvariable *noun* (*mathematics*) a VARIABLE whose value depends on another variable: *The model used obesity status as the dependent variable, while controlling for race, gender and age group.* ➲ *compare* INDEPENDENT VARIABLE

deˈpending on *prep.* according to: *People react to pain in differing ways, depending on their own circumstances, situation and abilities.* ◇ **~ whether/how, etc...** *The effect of an intense rainstorm will be different, depending on whether the soil is already saturated.*

de·pict /dɪˈpɪkt/ *verb* **1** to show an image of sb/sth in a picture: **~ sb/sth** *The cartoon depicts a street scene in contemporary Manhattan.* ◇ **~ sb/sth as sb/sth** *In mythological art, Argos is depicted as a humanoid male with eyes distributed over his body.* ◇ **~ sb/sth doing sth** *The earlier photographic images depict a girl holding a balloon.* ◇ **~ sb/sth as doing sth** *Sea deities are sometimes depicted as riding on sea horses.* **2** to describe sb/sth in words; to give an impression of sb/sth in words or with a picture: **~ sb/sth** *I would like to address the question of how the film depicts gender.* ◇ **~ sb/sth as sb/sth** *Carol seems to be depicted as the alluring yet shy and inhibited femme fatale.* **3 ~ sth** (of a chart or diagram) to show or describe sth: *Figure 6.3 depicts the key steps in the method.*

de·pic·tion /dɪˈpɪkʃn/ *noun* **1 ~ (of sth)** a description of sb/sth using words or pictures: *Reviewers were positive about the film's depiction of war.* ◇ *The most common depiction of refugees was as frauds.* **2 ~ (of sth)** a description in the form of a drawing or diagram: *Figure 3.2 provides a graphical depiction of the lens model that was created.*

de·plete /dɪˈpliːt/ *verb* [usually passive] **~ sth** to reduce sth by a large amount so that there is not enough left: *Rapid population growth depletes key natural resources such as water, fuel and soil fertility.* ◇ *If the world's current consumption rate continued at the same rate, gas reserves would be depleted in about 60–65 years.* ■ **de·ple·tion** /dɪˈpliːʃn/ *noun* [U] **~ (of sth)** *The successful international effort to reverse the depletion of the ozone layer is an example of the kind of cooperation that is needed.*

de·ploy /dɪˈplɔɪ/ *verb* **1** [T] to use sth/sb effectively: *Small states can often deploy resources more freely.* ◇ *A sales force needs to be deployed effectively across customers and prospects in order to achieve maximal productivity.* ➲ thesaurus note *at* USE¹ **2** [T, I] **~ (sb/sth) (to sth)** to move soldiers or weapons into a position where they are ready for military action; to move in this way: *Parliamentary approval is not needed if troops are deployed to NATO or EU missions.* ◇ *The air force began to deploy forward.*

de·ploy·ment /dɪˈplɔɪmənt/ *noun* [U, C] **1 ~ (of sth)** the effective use of sth: *Defending interests requires resources and the skilful deployment of resources.* **2** the movement of soldiers or weapons into a position where they are ready for military action: *In Austria, it is parliament's 'main committee' that discusses and decides on military deployments.*

de·posit¹ /dɪˈpɒzɪt; *NAmE* dɪˈpɑːzɪt/ *noun* **1** a layer of a substance that has been left somewhere, especially by a river or flood, or is found at the bottom of a liquid: *These elements gradually settle to form a sedimentary deposit.* ◇ *Extensive alluvial deposits have been interpreted to indicate a drier, more seasonal climate during glacial times.* **2** a layer of a substance that has formed naturally underground: *gold/diamond/mineral/ore deposits* **3** [usually sing.] **a ~ (on sth)** a sum of money that is given as the first part of a larger payment: *The claimant paid a deposit on the house, and was allowed to go into occupation of the property with immediate effect.* **4** (in the British political system) the amount of money that a candidate in an election to Parliament has to pay, and that is returned if they get enough votes: *The party lost 267 deposits (after contesting 339 seats).*

de·posit² /dɪˈpɒzɪt; *NAmE* dɪˈpɑːzɪt/ *verb* **1** (especially of a river) to leave a layer of sth on a surface, especially gradually and over a period of time: **~ sth** *The sediment deposited by the rivers of South East Asia resulted in the building of deltas of various sizes.* ◇ **~ sth into sth** *Each tributary transports and deposits this material into the lake.* **2 ~ sth + adv./prep.** (of an animal) to put or lay eggs in a particular place: *The females deposit their eggs inside the cavity of a mussel, where development occurs.* **3 ~ sth (in sth)** to put money into a bank account: *When money is deposited in banks, the financial institutions lend it out or invest it.* **4 ~ sth (on/onto sth)** (*engineering*) to apply a very thin layer of a substance to a surface: *The spraying process makes it possible to deposit very thin films onto a surface.*

de·pos·ition /ˌdepəˈzɪʃn/ *noun* **1** [U] **~ (of sth)** the natural process of leaving a layer of a substance on rocks or soil or in the body: *Estuaries are generally zones of deposition of sediment, and are therefore structurally dynamic.* ◇ *Glucagon and insulin are involved in regulating fat deposition.* **2** [C] (*law*) a formal statement, taken from sb and used in court: *This was not mentioned in any trial depositions.*

de·pre·ci·ate /dɪˈpriːʃieɪt/ *verb* **1** [I, T] to become less valuable over a period of time; to cause sth to become less valuable over a period of time: **~ (by sth) (against sth)**

In 2003–4, the dollar depreciated by over 30% against the euro. ◇ **~ sth** *The government may reduce interest rates and take other steps designed to depreciate its currency.* OPP APPRECIATE (4) **2** [T] **~ sth** (*business*) to reduce the value, as stated in a company's accounts, of a particular ASSET over a particular period of time: *Watch out for changes in the total asset figure as you depreciate your assets.*

de·pre·ci·ation /dɪˌpriːʃiˈeɪʃn/ *noun* [U, C] the process by which sth, especially a CURRENCY, becomes less valuable; an example of this: *Exchange rate depreciation has increased the real cost of imports and cut real wages.* ◇ **~ of sth** *The domestic interest rate fell below the foreign interest rate, causing a depreciation of the domestic currency.*

de·press AWL /dɪˈpres/ *verb* **1 ~ sth** to make the value of prices or wages lower: *Food aid tends to depress food prices in the receiving country.* **2 ~ sth** to make trade or business less active: *Sales promotions may actually depress demand for the product in future periods.* **3 ~ sth** to press or push sth down, especially part of a machine: *An incorrect volume may be delivered if the plunger is not fully depressed.*

de·pressed AWL /dɪˈprest/ *adj.* **1** suffering from the medical condition of depression: *Clearly, he was depressed.* ◇ *A severely depressed mother may neglect her children.* HELP In non-academic English, **depressed** is often used to refer to a less serious feeling of sadness, which is not considered to be a medical condition: *Now I won't get so depressed about all the small mistakes I make.* **2** [usually before noun] (of a place or an industry) without enough economic activity or jobs for people: *The principal policy has been simply to provide funds to depressed regions.* ◇ *The recovery had its biggest impact in some of the most depressed industries.* **3** having a lower amount or level than usual: *The price remained depressed for a number of months.* ◇ *Countries with high levels of corruption generally have depressed rates of investment.*

de·press·ing AWL /dɪˈpresɪŋ/ *adj.* making you feel sad; making you feel that you have no enthusiasm or hope: *The data make depressing reading.*

de·pres·sion AWL /dɪˈpreʃn/ *noun* **1** [U, C] a medical condition in which sb feels very sad and anxious and often has physical SYMPTOMS such as being unable to sleep: *Depression was diagnosed.* ◇ *These children may experience depression or alienation.* ◇ *A large proportion of adult depressions had their first appearance in adolescence.* **2** [U, C] a period when there is little economic activity and many people are poor or without jobs: *Britain began to face a prolonged period of depression.* ◇ *During the Great Depression of the 1930s, stable employment disappeared.* ◇ *Despite major trade depressions, these firms survived.* **3** [C] a part of a surface that is lower than the parts around it SYN HOLLOW² (1): *Though dry now, many large depressions in this desert were filled with lakes at various times.* **4** [C] (*technical*) a weather condition in which the pressure of the air becomes lower, often causing rain: *These events were associated with hurricanes, tropical storms or tropical depressions.* **5** [U, C] **~ of sth** the action of pressing sth; the fact of sth becoming lower: *The addition of meltwater to the oceans causes depression of the ocean floor.* ◇ *This can lead to a significant depression of the global temperature.*

de·pres·sive /dɪˈpresɪv/ *adj.* connected with the medical condition of depression: *These patients are frequently diagnosed with depressive disorders.* ◇ *Participants who used the Internet more showed higher levels of loneliness, stress and depressive symptoms.*

de·priv·ation /ˌdeprɪˈveɪʃn/ *noun* [U] **1** the fact of not having the things that are necessary to live a happy and comfortable life; the process that causes this: *For many rural dwellers, the countryside is actually a place of poverty and deprivation.* **2** the fact of not having sth that you need or want: *Sleep deprivation may have negative effects on motivation, attention and alertness.*

de·prive /dɪˈpraɪv/ *verb*
PHR V **deˈprive sb/sth of sth** to prevent sb from having or doing sth, especially sth important: *These people have been deprived of the support that they have a right to expect.* ◇ *Children may be deprived of their liberty on suspicion of committing a crime.*

D

de·prived /dɪˈpraɪvd/ *adj.* without all the things that are necessary for people to live a happy and comfortable life: *Research suggests that the most deprived groups typically lack confidence in themselves.* ◇ *There is evidence that living in a materially deprived neighbourhood contributes to worse health for individuals.*

depth /depθ/ *noun* **1** [C, U] the distance from the top or surface to the bottom of sth; how deep sth is: **at a ~ of sth** *The ground temperature at a depth of 27 m is approximately equal to local annual average air temperature.* ◇ **to a ~ of sth** *Sperm whales can travel across entire oceans and can dive to a depth of a kilometre.* ◇ **at/to depths of sth** *Such basins are found at depths of 800 m or deeper.* ◇ **in ~** *In each enclosure, 2 tubs were 13.5 cm in depth, and the other 2 were 4.5 cm in depth.* ◇ **~ of sth** *The depths of soils on the deforested areas were significantly less and there were larger patches of exposed bedrock.* **2** [U] **~ (of sth)** the fact of having or providing a lot of information or knowledge: *Firms producing complex products require both breadth and depth of knowledge.* ◇ *The novel lacks any real psychological depth.* **3** [U] **~ (of sth)** the fact of being very important or serious: *Banking crises contributed crucially to the length, depth and spread of the Great Depression.* **4** [U] the quality in an image that makes it appear not to be flat: *Texture in a picture gives it depth.*
IDM **ˌin ˈdepth** in a detailed and thorough way: *This principle has not previously been analysed in depth.* ◇ *This area will be explored in greater depth in the next chapter.* ⊃ *compare* IN-DEPTH **ˌthe ˈdepths of sth 1** the deepest part of sth: *The water temperature immediately beneath the ice is 0°C and warms to 3–4°C in the depths of the lake.* **2** the most serious or extreme part of sth: *Griffin somehow manages to explore the depths of these complex debates without becoming dry and boring.*

de·regu·lation AWL /ˌdiːˌreɡjuˈleɪʃn/ *noun* [U, C] the process of freeing a trade or business activity from rules and controls; an example of this: *Deregulation and privatization vastly reduced public interest obligations.* ◇ **~ of sth** *Following the deregulation of the dairy industry, only 50 per cent of milk producers stayed with the cooperative structure.* ■ **de·regu·la·te** AWL /ˌdiːˈreɡjuleɪt/ *verb* [I, T] *California, the first major state to deregulate, experienced serious market disruptions.* ◇ **~ sth** *Some countries started to deregulate their domestic oil markets.* **de·regu·la·tory** /ˌdiːˈreɡjələtəri; *NAmE* ˌdiːˈreɡjələtɔːri/ *adj.* [only before noun] *Congress had to abandon its deregulatory ambitions.*

der·iv·ation AWL /ˌderɪˈveɪʃn/ *noun* **1** [C, U] **~ (of sth)** a calculation that shows how an idea or quantity is developed or obtained from existing information; the process of developing an idea or obtaining a quantity in this way: *Mathematical derivations of the end results are presented in Appendix B.* ◇ *The equation was quoted without derivation.* **2** [U, C] **~ (from sth)** the fact that sth develops from sth else; something that has been developed from sth else: *Some rocks, like Kimberlites, contain diamonds, showing their derivation from a depth of more than 100 km.* ◇ *The study will examine how learners acquire knowledge of word inflections and derivations.*

de·riva·tive¹ AWL /dɪˈrɪvətɪv/ *noun* **1** a substance that has developed or been produced from another substance: *Among cellulose derivatives, cellulose esters (CEs) have found the widest variety of uses.* ◇ **+ noun** *The derivative* *polymers possess a broad range of useful properties.* **2** a word that has developed from another word: *The word 'translate' and its derivatives occur frequently in the texts.* ◇ **~ of sth** *The dictionary includes the term 'localization' as a derivative of 'localize'.* **3** (*finance*) a financial product involving the transfer of money based on the value of an ASSET, where the OWNERSHIP of the asset itself is not included in the product: *The use of financial derivatives clearly added to recent extraordinary financial results.* ◇ **derivatives + noun** *Derivatives trading is a primary business focus.* **4** (*mathematics*) an expression representing a rate of change of some quantity: *One can compute the derivative and see that it is positive.* ◇ *The acceleration of the element is the time derivative of v.*

D

de·riva·tive² AWL /dɪˈrɪvətɪv/ *adj.* **1** (*often disapproving*) copied from sth else; not having new or original ideas: *Within the film world, video games are often dismissed as purely derivative works.* **2 ~ (of sth)** based on or developing from sth else: *He accepted the view that human geography was derivative of physical geography.*

de·rive AWL /dɪˈraɪv/ *verb* **1** to calculate, discover or establish sth, using information that is available: **~ sth** *Both theories can be used to derive the same formula.* ◇ **(be) derived by (doing) sth** *The overall score was derived by computing the mean of all of the responses.* ◇ **~ sth from sth** *Previous authors failed to derive correct equations of motion from the general laws of mechanics.* ◇ *Original data were mainly derived from cross-sectional designs.* **2 adv. + derived** used after an adverb and before a noun, to indicate how sth develops or is obtained: *A number of culturally derived factors were identified.* ◇ *Against the backdrop of these theoretically derived claims, this article reports some preliminary results.*

PHR V **be deˈrived from sth | deˈrive from sth** to come or develop from sth: *These names were all derived from local geographic features.* ◇ *The English word 'giants' derives ultimately from the Greek 'Gigantes'.* ◇ *Their influence derived from two sources.* HELP **Derived from** is often used after a noun or pronoun, without *that are/were*, etc: *Hypotheses generated using molecular data should be compared with those derived from other sources of information.* **deˈrive sth from sth** to get sth from sth: *Both spouses derive benefit from the home.* ◇ *He derived great enjoyment from the endless ceremonies and parades.*

▸ DERIVE + NOUN **prediction • hypothesis • estimates • data • statistics • result • score • curve • equation, formula, expression • parameters • benefit • solution • conclusion** *This problem was dealt with in the early literature: see, for example, Thomas et al. (1964), who derived the following expressions...*

▸ DERIVE + NOUN + FROM STH **utility • advantage • profit • revenue • satisfaction • pleasure, enjoyment • inspiration • insight • knowledge • evidence • name** *They derive decreasing marginal utility from wealth.* ◇ *The knowledge and insights derived from these processes can be invaluable in the design and evaluation of public policy.*

▸ (BE) DERIVED + ADVERB (+ FROM) **originally • directly • ultimately • entirely • mainly, primarily, mostly, largely • analytically** *The evidence for their effectiveness is derived mainly from several controlled studies.* ◇ *The design parameters for the optimal performances were derived analytically.*

▸ DERIVE + ADVERB + FROM **directly • ultimately • exclusively, entirely • mainly, primarily, largely** *Written evidence derives primarily from police and military records.*

▸ ADVERB + DERIVED + NOUN **locally • theoretically • experimentally, empirically • culturally • maternally • paternally** *The low levels of maternally derived antibodies are thought to play a role in the development of disease.*

des·cend /dɪˈsend/ *verb* [I, T] to come or go down from a higher to a lower level: *As the Macedonian army descended through the Khyber Pass, it encountered some of the fiercest resistance in the campaign.* ◇ **~ sth** *As he descended the stairs, he suddenly lost consciousness.* ◇ **~ (from sth) (to sth)** *Many insects are confined to the canopy or subcanopy, rarely descending to the ground.* OPP ASCEND

IDM **in deˌscending ˈorder** from the highest to the lowest: *In descending order of importance, these workers valued pay, promotion prospects and job security as the three most important aspects.*

PHR V **be desˈcended from sb** to be related to sb who lived a long time ago: *He was from a distinguished family, descended from the Duke of Marlborough.* **be desˈcended from sth** to develop from sth similar in the past: *French is descended from Latin, and Samoan is descended from Proto-Polynesian.* **desˈcend into sth** [no passive] to gradually get into a bad state: *As Europe descended into chaos in the 1930s and 1940s, sociology found a flourishing home in the USA.*

des·cend·ant /dɪˈsendənt/ *noun* **1 ~ (of sb)** a person's **descendants** are their children, their children's children, and all the people who live after them who are related to them: *Alexander believed himself the descendant of Heracles, Perseus, and ultimately Zeus.* **2 ~ (of sth)** something that has developed from sth similar in the past: *Gustav Kirchhoff's diffraction theory is a direct descendant of Helmholtz's paper on organ pipes.*

des·cent /dɪˈsent/ *noun* **1** [U] a person's family background SYN ANCESTRY: *Most people have come to accept that humans share a common descent with all other creatures on Earth.* ◇ **~ from sb** *The 'clans' were associations of aristocratic households claiming descent from a common ancestor.* ◇ **of... ~** *The Hubbard family was typical of most families of European descent then living in North America.* **2** [C, usually sing.] an action of coming or going down: *Descent is often very slow, of the order of a few centimetres per hour.* ◇ **~ (from sth)** *Traditional epic involves at some stage a descent into the underworld, the world of the past.* OPP ASCENT **3** [C, usually sing.] **~ (into/to sth)** the process of gradually getting into a bad state: *Even in highly innovative organizations, some maintenance of hierarchy may help to avoid a descent into chaos.*

de·scribe /dɪˈskraɪb/ *verb* **1** [often passive] to give an account of sth in words: **~ sth** *Unfortunately, they do not describe their methods.* ◇ *Participants were asked to describe their experience of being off work.* ◇ **be described (by sb)** *Several new procedures will be described briefly below.* ◇ *The design is similar to that described by Moinet and Peltier [68].* ◇ **~ doing sth** *A number of participants described feeling uncomfortable.* ◇ **~ how/what, etc...** *I will not attempt to describe how it works.* ◇ **be described in sth** *Some of this work is described in Chapter 8.* ◇ **as described (in sth)** *All data refer to a temperature of 25°C and other standard conditions as described in the text.* HELP **Described** is often used after a noun phrase, without *that is/was*, etc: *The effect of aspirin on an enzyme, described below, is one such case.* ➲ grammar note *at* PRESENT³ ➲ language bank *at* REPORT¹ **2** [often passive] to say what sb/sth is like; to say what sb/sth is: **~ sth/sb** *I cannot even begin to describe them.* ◇ **~ sth/sb as sth** *It would be an exaggeration to describe him as anti-democratic.* ◇ **~ sth/sb as doing sth** *The activities are described as providing opportunities for children to learn useful skills.* ◇ **be described in terms of sth** *This process can be described in terms of a progression from transcript to script.* **3 ~ sth** to make a movement which has a particular shape; to form a particular shape: *The net result is a trajectory that describes a spiral around the fixed point.* **4 ~ sth** (*technical*) (of a diagram or calculation) to represent sth: *The relationship is described by a linear regression line.* ■ **de·scrib·able** *adj.*: *These processes cannot be computed using describable procedures.* ◇ **~ as sth** *This distinction is more accurately describable as a liberal than a feminist one.* ◇ **~**

by sth *The motion of microscopic molecules is not describable by Newtonian mechanics.*

▸ DESCRIBE + NOUN **way, manner • strategy • approach • method, methodology, technique • system • model • mechanism • principle • operation • process • procedure • protocol • activity • experiment** *Terms such as 'green chemistry' have been coined to describe this approach.* | **situation • phenomenon • experience • structure • development • relationship • effect • motion • event** *Using software solutions would provide precise information about each of the phenomena described in this study.* | **type, kind • characteristics, properties, features • condition • aspect • pattern • symptoms • behaviour • role • feeling • reaction • interaction • distribution** *The four behaviours described were not assumed to be equal in any way.* | **work • case • study • scenario • example • findings**

▸ NOUN + DESCRIBE **scholar • historian • linguist • journalist • commentator • narrator • author • colleague** *In Chapter 8, the authors describe how 'neural network mapping' can be applied to investigation.* | **participant • respondent • interviewee • witness** *Many respondents described extreme situations for which they did not feel appropriately prepared.* | **report • paper • article • chapter • section** *The Committee's report also describes the practical and legal complexities.*

▸ ADVERB + DESCRIBE **better, best • aptly • accurately • precisely • properly • correctly • completely • explicitly • clearly • vividly • adequately • simply, merely • only • briefly • once • first, initially • now • later • then • typically • further • repeatedly • famously • thus** *Section 2 briefly describes the minimal regulation of internal armed conflict up to the 1990s.*

▸ (AS) DESCRIBED + ADVERB **above • previously, earlier, before • here, herein • elsewhere • below • next • later, subsequently • briefly • at length • more fully • in (more/greater) detail** *As described earlier, some salespeople are now being called upon to fill more challenging strategic roles.*

▸ BE + ADVERB + DESCRIBED **well • fully • extensively • formally** *The conditions that differentiate Antarctica from other environments have been well described (Knox; Arnaud; Hempel; Dayton et al).*

▸ BE + ADVERB + DESCRIBED AS STH **better, best • appropriately • sometimes • usually, generally • variously • recently • often • commonly • frequently • originally • loosely** *This phenomenon would be better described as nationalization.*

de·scrip·tion /dɪˈskrɪpʃn/ *noun* **1** [C, U] writing or speech that gives an account of sth or that says what sth/sb is like: *'Things could be better' would probably be an accurate description.* ◇ **~ of sth/sb** *Brunswik's lens model offers a classic description of the process (1943,1956).* ◇ *Very little space is devoted to description of landscape.* ◇ **~ of sth/sb as sth/sb** *The description of the men as 'hard-liners' was not helpful.* ◇ **as a ~ of sth/sb** *This model has been interpreted as a description of emerging trends.* ◇ **from... ~** *From this description, it follows that social competence is achieved.* ◇ **in... ~** *According to quantum physics, particles have a degree of freedom called spin, which does not exist in a classical description.* **2** [U] the process of giving an account of sth or of saying what sth/sb is like; the fact that this happens: *The goal became explanation rather than description.* ◇ *The Third Industrial Revolution defies summary description.* ◇ **beyond ~ (of sth)** *This will entail moving beyond basic description of data, to a richer, more in-depth analysis.* **3** [C, usually sing.] **fit/match/satisfy a ~ (of sb/sth)** used to say that sb/sth is the way that they have been described: *The clinician can then indicate the extent to which a patient matches this description.* ◇ *The witness saw a man fitting the description of the killer getting into a car.* **4** [U, pl.] in the following patterns **description** means 'type' or 'category': **of any/every/some ~** *The text does not mention authorities of any description.* ◇ **of this/that ~** *Workers of that description have a different type of contract.* ◇ **of all descriptions** *The Act covers public authorities of all descriptions.*

▸ ADJECTIVE + DESCRIPTION **clear • vivid, graphic • realistic • accurate • apt • precise • detailed, thorough, in-depth • elaborate • rich • full, comprehensive, complete • definite • brief, short • simple • basic • adequate • vague** *This categorization is not an apt description of modern fatherhood.* ◇ *Smith presents detailed descriptions for a sample of individuals in each category.* | **general • theoretical • formal • classic, classical • qualitative • quantitive • mathematical • physical • anatomical • verbal • linguistic** *A computer model was developed based on the mathematical description above.*

▸ NOUN + DESCRIPTION **job • product • case • summary** *The job description should explain what the purpose of the role will be.*

▸ VERB + DESCRIPTION **contain, include • provide, give, offer, present** *The article provides a rich description of how teenagers use online conversation to cope with adolescent concerns.*

de·scrip·tive /dɪˈskrɪptɪv/ *adj.* **1** describing what sth is like, rather than saying what it should be like or what category it belongs to: *Survey data were analysed using descriptive statistics and significance tests.* ◇ *Descriptive analyses were performed.* ◇ *The approach was mostly descriptive and non-mathematical.* ➲ *compare* NORMATIVE, PRESCRIPTIVE **2** saying or showing clearly what sth is like; giving a clear account of sth: *Morgan is a talented writer with a gift for descriptive prose.* ◇ *Edgington presents a richly descriptive account of the urban planning aspects of the region's recovery.*

des·ert[1] /ˈdezət; *NAmE* ˈdezərt/ *noun* [U, C] a large area of land that has very little water and very few plants growing on it. Many desert areas are covered by sand: *The soil, left untended, became desert.* ◇ *The valleys are among the driest and coldest deserts on the planet.* ◇ *desert terrain/vegetation* ◇ **in the ~** *Despite being in the desert, Dubai is home to the first ski resort in the Middle East.* ◇ **+ noun** *desert sands/landscapes/areas*

des·ert[2] /dɪˈzɜːt; *NAmE* dɪˈzɜːrt/ *verb* **1** [T, often passive] **~ sb** to leave sb without help or support SYN ABANDON (3): *Brutus was defeated, deserted by his soldiers, and committed suicide.* **2** [T, often passive] **~ sth** to go away from a place and leave it empty SYN ABANDON (4): *The Thebans fled, deserting the city and relocating elsewhere.* ◇ **deserted + noun** *Kineton itself is surrounded by deserted medieval villages.* **3** [I, T] **~ (sth)** to leave the armed forces without permission: *Italian troops serving in the Austrian army deserted, and the Piedmontese entered the city.* **4** [T] **~ (sth) (for sth)** to stop using, buying or supporting sth: *One by one, companies started to desert the coalition.*

de·serve /dɪˈzɜːv; *NAmE* dɪˈzɜːrv/ *verb* (not used in the progressive tenses) to make a particular action or reaction appropriate; to have qualities that do this SYN MERIT[2]: **~ sth** *The complexities of this case deserve further attention.* ◇ *One other element of environmental policy deserves mention.* ◇ *to deserve careful consideration/closer scrutiny/further investigation* ◇ **~ sth for doing sth** *He deserves credit for taking the correct decisions.* ◇ **~ sth for sth** *This book deserves praise for its balanced assessment of a wide range of conflicting sources.* ◇ **~ to do sth** *This provocative study deserves to become required reading.*

de·serv·ing /dɪˈzɜːvɪŋ; *NAmE* dɪˈzɜːrvɪŋ/ *adj.* **~ (of sth)** (*formal*) that deserves help, praise, a reward, etc: *The hero is a great man, sympathetic, deserving of our pity, who engages in action that involves some sort of fatal mistake.* ◇ *The drafters of the Poor Laws of 1834 drew a firm distinction between the deserving and the undeserving poor.*

de·sign[1] AWL /dɪˈzaɪn/ *noun* **1** [U, C] the way that sth works, looks or is used; the process of planning how sth will work, look or be used HELP In non-academic English, **design** is used mainly about physical objects and places. In academic English, **design** is used in this way, but more often is used about a system or process: *The studies were similar in design.* ◇ *They each conducted fieldwork using the same basic research design.* ◇ **~ of sth** *Her most recent work was the design and implementation of a new information system.* ◇ *As a young engineer, he worked on the design of the Sydney Harbour Bridge.* ◇ **+ noun** *The six design principles are relatively straightforward.* **2** [C] a drawing, diagram or proposal that shows how sth will work or be used, or what sth will look like: *Without detailed designs, this can be only speculation.* ◇ **~ for sth** *They were invited to submit designs for the new playground.* **3** [C] **~ (for/of sth)** an arrangement of lines and shapes as a decoration SYN PATTERN[1] (2): *One of the buildings had been painted over with designs for imaginary flags.* **4** [C] **grand ~** an overall plan, idea or intention: *Agricultural policy remained patchy and did not follow a grand design.* **5** [pl.] **designs on sth** (*usually disapproving*) a desire or plan to get sth: *When corporations have designs on economically depressed areas, there is a power mismatch.*

IDM **by design** according to sb's plan or intention SYN DELIBERATELY: *New technologies are producing, whether by design or by accident, new ways to succeed.*

▸ ADJECTIVE + DESIGN **original, initial • basic • simple • detailed • new • innovative • good • optimal • robust • careful • poor** *The shrubs and greenery form an essential part of the original design.* | **standard • traditional • experimental • quasi-experimental • randomized • cross-sectional • longitudinal • prospective • structural • organizational • institutional • architectural • graphic** *The cross-sectional design of the study does not allow us to draw conclusions about causality.*

▸ NOUN + DESIGN **research • study • survey • questionnaire • sampling • cohort** *It was not possible to provide information about prevalence due to study design and data collection methods.* | **product • computer • circuit • software • engine • engineering • aircraft • building • interior • fashion • drug** *The company has invested heavily in product design.*

▸ VERB + DESIGN **work on • influence, inform • guide • propose • employ, use, utilize • adopt • incorporate • alter, modify • simplify** *Using a longitudinal design, we obtained multiple measures of Internet use.* ◇ *The initial design had to be modified to compensate for unforeseen data-collection issues.*

▸ DESIGN + NOUN **principles • parameters • specification • matrix • solutions • features • flaws • goals • team • engineer** *The vehicle design parameters affecting vehicle fuel efficiency are vehicle mass, aerodynamic drag and rolling friction.*

de·sign[2] AWL /dɪˈzaɪn/ *verb* [often passive] to plan how sth will work, look or be used HELP In academic English, **design** is often used about a system or process: **~ sth** *He has designed and implemented educational and social service programmes.* ◇ **(be) designed for sb/sth** *Both curricula were specifically designed for use in after-school settings.* ◇ **(be) designed as sth** *The building is designed as two schools and a community centre within a single building.* ◇ **(be) designed around sb/sth** *Nursing care needs to be designed around the patient.* ◇ **(be) designed with sth** *Much of our research is designed with an open-ended structure.* ◇ **(be) designed to do sth** *There are provisions designed to protect minorities.*

▸ DESIGN + NOUN **system • policy • strategy • plan • project • scheme, programme, initiative • intervention • measures • campaign • instrument, tool • questionnaire, survey • experiment** *Manufacturing systems must be designed so as to minimize their complexity.* ◇ *The framework is an analytic tool designed to help researchers to consider the ethical issues.* | **product • machine • engine • device • building • bridge** *The company had sufficient expertise to design aircraft engines.*

▸ (BE) + ADVERB + DESIGNED **carefully • deliberately • specially • especially • specifically, expressly, explicitly • originally, initially • primarily • well • properly • poorly** *These influences can be strengthened by specially designed school programmes.*

▸ (BE) DESIGNED TO + VERB **protect • ensure • prevent • address • help, assist • encourage • improve • maximize • minimize • promote • assess • test • measure • capture • achieve • meet • appeal • elicit** *There are provisions designed to protect minorities.* ◇ *The research is designed to assess the relative roles of climate and grazing.*

des·ig·nate /ˈdezɪgneɪt/ *verb* [often passive] **1** to say officially that sb/sth has a particular character, name or purpose; to describe sb/sth in a particular way: **~ sb/sth** *The government has designated areas where agriculture runs alongside wildlife management.* ◇ **~ sb/sth (as) sth** *This applies only to states designated by the State Department as sponsors of terrorism.* ◇ *Type 2 diabetes has been designated an epidemic.* ◇ **~ sb/sth as doing sth** *Certain areas were designated as being smoking or non-smoking.* ◇ **~ sb/sth for sb/sth** *This facility is specifically designated for survivors of domestic violence.* **2** to choose or name sb/sth for a particular job or position: **~ sb/sth** *The board might designate a person who would be responsible for this function.* ◇ *They have to buy from the supplier, or from companies designated by the supplier.* ◇ **~ sb/sth as sth** *He had designated his son as his successor.* ◇ **~ sb to do sth** *A new ministry designated to coordinate land affairs began developing a national land policy.* **3** (of a symbol) to identify or show sth: **~ sth** *There is also a Roman numeral designating the order of discovery.* ◇ **(be) designated (by/with) sth** *These mutations are called 'cold-sensitive', designated by 'cs'.*

des·ig·na·tion /ˌdezɪgˈneɪʃn/ *noun* **1** [U, C] the fact of describing sb/sth as having a particular character, status or purpose: *These symptoms do not warrant a high-risk designation.* ◇ **~ as sth** *Low tax rates are not in themselves a sufficient criterion for designation as a tax haven.* ◇ **~ of sth (as sth)** *The designation of states as 'safe' is made by UK statute.* **2** [C] a way of naming or describing sb/sth; a name or label: *The following discussion uses standard designations to describe the incidence of side effects.*

de·sign·er AWL /dɪˈzaɪnə(r)/ *noun* a person whose job is to plan how products or places will work, look or be used: *She is a web page designer.* ◇ **~ of sth** *The principal designer of the bridge was Benjamin Baker.* HELP In academic English, a **designer** is also a person who designs a system or process: *Respondents must comprehend the questions as intended by the survey designer.*

de·sir·abil·ity /dɪˌzaɪərəˈbɪləti/ *noun* [U] **~ (of sth/doing sth)** the quality of being worth having or doing: *Arguments over the desirability of grand public works projects can reveal much about a society's priorities.* HELP The **social desirability bias** or **effect** refers to the fact that people will give answers to questions according to what they think is socially acceptable rather than what they really do or think.

de·sir·able /dɪˈzaɪərəbl/ *adj.* that you would like to have or do; worth having or doing: *These measures do not always produce desirable outcomes.* ◇ *While health care for all may be socially desirable, it is not necessarily economically efficient.* ◇ **it is ~ (for sb/sth) that...** *It is highly desirable for the global economy that students are enabled to pursue their studies abroad.* ◇ **it is ~ (for sb/sth) (to do sth)** *It would not be desirable for a certain pupil in a school classroom always to be observed at the end of the day.* OPP UNDESIRABLE

de·sire[1] /dɪˈzaɪə(r)/ *noun* **1** [C, U] a strong wish to have or do sth: **~ for sth** *Only 11% of respondents expressed a* *desire for compensation.* ◇ **~ (to do sth)** *In the free market, it is assumed that decisions are driven by individual desires to maximize personal welfare.* ◇ *In Hobbes's view, human life is a constant struggle to satisfy desire.* **2** [U] **~ (for sb)** a strong wish to have sex with sb: *Clearly, Austen shares Wollstonecraft's view that sexual desire is not a solid foundation for a good marriage.*

de·sire² /dɪˈzaɪə(r)/ *verb* (not used in the progressive tenses) (*formal*) to want sth: **~ sth** *Ultimately the person knows what is best for them and they have the ability to make the changes they desire.* ◇ **~ to do sth** *After the Dutch War, the Sun King desired only to protect his new frontiers.* ◇ **desired + noun** *Individuals base their choices on their understanding about how certain actions may bring about the desired outcomes.*

IDM **as deˈsired** in the way that sb wants: *If a design was successful, it could be manufactured immediately in as many copies as desired.* **if deˈsired** if sb wants to do it: *The cycle may be repeated several times if desired.* **leave a lot, much, something, etc. to be deˈsired** to be bad or unacceptable; to be less good than it should be: *The efficiency of the administrative system also leaves much to be desired.*

des·per·ate /ˈdespərət/ *adj.* **1** feeling or showing that you have little hope and are ready to do anything without worrying about danger to yourself or others: *The prisoners grew increasingly desperate.* **2** [usually before noun] (of an action) giving little hope of success; tried when everything else has failed: *Their reaction to economic distress was to produce more in a desperate attempt to raise total income.* ◇ *Bedie made desperate efforts to consolidate power and gain support.* ◇ *The economic situation, despite desperate measures, remained dire.* **3** (of a situation) extremely serious or dangerous: *The economy was in desperate need of massive capital investment.* ◇ *They seek to provide a calm and reassuring voice of hope in a desperate situation.* ■ **des·per·ate·ly** *adv.*: *Effective vaccines against these diseases are desperately needed.*

des·pite AWL /dɪˈspaɪt/ *prep.* without being affected by sth SYN IN SPITE OF STH HELP **Despite** is used to introduce the thing that might be expected to affect sth else, but does not; the other thing happens anyway: **~ sth** *Despite my disability, I could hold a job like other people.* ◇ *The Welsh language is threatened, despite vigorous local efforts to preserve it.* ◇ **~ doing sth** *Despite being a young company, Google™ is now a household name.* ◇ **~ the fact that...** *Their leader, despite the fact that he was not present at this protest, was arrested.* ➲ language bank *at* HOWEVER

GRAMMAR POINT

despite • in spite of • although • even though • though

- Use **despite** and **in spite of** with the *-ing* form of the verb or a noun or pronoun: ***Despite being*** *common, heart failure is difficult to diagnose.* ◇ ***Despite the wide effect*** *of agriculture on the landscape, the evidence for past agriculture is not always immediately obvious (Sandor, 1995).* ◇ *Ecosystem services provide benefits... **In spite of this**, ecosystem services are continually undervalued.*
- Use **although**, **even though** and **though** with a main clause (= with a subject and verb): ***Although*** *some questions have been answered, new ones are raised.* ◇ *Many of the transferred employees wanted to remain in London, **even though** their commute had been increased.*
- Note the use of the comma. The clause with *despite*, *in spite of*, *although*, *even though* or *though* may come after the other clause: *Bamboo is another natural composite that grows very tall due to its reinforcing fibres, **in spite of** its slender shape.*

de·sta·bil·ize (*BrE also* **-ise**) /ˌdiːˈsteɪbəlaɪz/ *verb* **1 ~ sth** to make a system, country, government, etc. become less firmly established or successful: *Terrorist attacks were threatening to destabilize the government.* ➲ *compare* STABILIZE (1) **2 ~ sth** to cause the different parts of a substance to WEAKEN or separate: *This temperature is not so high that it destabilizes the native protein, but high enough that an already slightly destabilized protein becomes non-functional.* ■ **de·sta·bil·iza·tion**, **-isa·tion** /ˌdiːˌsteɪbəlaɪˈzeɪʃn; *NAmE* ˌdiːˌsteɪbələˈzeɪʃn/ *noun* [U] *In both controversies, the top political leadership was paralysed, leaving both states on the brink of destabilization.* ◇ **~ of sth** *Sedimentation is frequently observed in the estuary due to destabilization of the river colloids as they encounter the high-salt sea water.*

des·tin·ation /ˌdestɪˈneɪʃn/ *noun* a place to which sb/sth is going or being sent: *Unforeseen circumstances prevented them from reaching their destination.* ◇ **to a ~** *The data set defines the movement of general freight from Santiago to destinations throughout Chile.*

des·tined /ˈdestɪnd/ *adj.* [not before noun] **1** certain to experience or do a particular thing: **~ for sth** *The brand is destined for success.* ◇ **~ to do sth** *The situation seemed destined to become worse.* HELP In everyday English, **destined** often suggests that sth has been decided by FATE. This is less usual in academic English. However, when discussing literature, beliefs, etc, it may be an important part of the meaning: *Kronos had learned that he was destined to be overthrown by one of his own sons.* Nevertheless, saying that sth **was destined to** happen is often simply a way of reporting that it later happened: *Many of these translations were destined to survive.* **2 ~ for sth** going to, or intended for, a particular place SYN BOUND¹ (4): *Many of these ships were destined for the markets in Cuba.*

des·tiny /ˈdestəni/ *noun* (*pl.* **-ies**) **1** [C, U] what happens to sb or what will happen to them in the future, especially things that they cannot change or avoid SYN FATE (1): *The hero has to come to terms with his past before he can fulfil his destiny.* ◇ *Progress depended on a strong sense of national destiny.* **2** [U] the power believed to control events SYN FATE (2): *They believed in some form of destiny.* ◇ *He avoids the notion of destiny in favour of a belief in personal responsibility.*

des·troy /dɪˈstrɔɪ/ *verb* **~ sth** to damage sth so badly that it no longer exists or can no longer be used: *Militias destroyed every village in the west of the region.* ◇ *Some of the cells are damaged or destroyed.* ◇ *The store was destroyed by fire.*

de·struc·tion /dɪˈstrʌkʃn/ *noun* [U, C] the act of destroying sth; the process of being destroyed: *The rhino population was severely affected by habitat destruction.* ◇ **~ of sth** *He ordered the destruction of a vast number of temples.*

de·struc·tive /dɪˈstrʌktɪv/ *adj.* causing destruction or damage: *We should think carefully about the destructive consequences of human activity.* ➲ *compare* CONSTRUCTIVE ■ **de·struc·tive·ly** *adv.*: *The syndrome progresses steadily and destructively.* **de·struc·tive·ness** *noun* [U] *The report explains the sheer destructiveness of the civil war.*

de·tail¹ AWL /ˈdiːteɪl; *NAmE also* dɪˈteɪl/ *noun* **1** [U] exact information about sth: *More detail is provided in the next section about the UK case.* ◇ *For further detail, see Bass (2002).* ◇ *Six studies contained sufficient detail to be included in a meta-analysis.* **2** [C, usually pl.] a small individual fact or item of information: *The managers had to consult the ministries about quite minor details.* ◇ **~ of sth** *The details of the analysis performed above are illustrated in Fig. 6.23.* ◇ *The purpose of a model is to represent what is important for the task at hand, not to represent every detail of the problem.* ◇ **~ on sth** *Please see Appendix A for exact details on survey methodology.* ◇ **~ about sth** *For more details about the various models of strategic* *planning, see Mintzberg (1994a).* **3** [C, U] a small part of sth that can be looked at; one or more of these taken together: *The Corinthians invented a technique called 'black figure', which permitted the rendition of minute details.* ◇ **~ of sth** *The main goal of scanning this statuette was to reveal greater surface detail of the corrosion.* **4** [pl.] information about sb such as their name, address, age, etc: *Customers are asked to provide their personal details, which are then entered into a database.* ◇ *44 of a possible 54 (82%) individuals provided their contact details and agreed to future contact.*

IDM **go into 'detail(s)** to explain sth fully: *It is not possible here to go into detail about the relations between landforms and climate.* ◇ *Plato goes into considerable detail about the kind of education he envisages.* **go into more/greater/further, etc. 'detail** to explain sth more fully: *Below, I will go into more detail about the nature of the stages in the research chain.* **in 'detail** including exact information: *These cases will be discussed in detail in 6.1.5.* ◇ *The phenomenon he explored in great detail was operant conditioning, also called instrumental conditioning.* **in more/further, etc. 'detail** including more exact information: *I will describe in more detail how this work illuminated the nature of the genetic code below.*

▸ ADJECTIVE + DETAIL **full • considerable • sufficient • more, further • additional • precise, exact • specific • technical • methodological • biographical • demographic • historical** *When I transcribed the interviews, I altered specific details that could make a participant identifiable.* ◇ *Little biographical detail is available concerning the latter half of the Buddha's life.* | **minute • fine** *The fine detail of exactly how the objectives will be achieved is provided.* ◇ *There are worms whose delicate hairy bodies are preserved in astoundingly fine detail.*

▸ VERB + DETAIL **reveal, disclose** *Electronic spectra can reveal additional details of molecular structure when experiments are conducted with polarized light.* ◇ *The resident parent must disclose details of the non-resident parent as a condition of receiving benefit.* | **provide, give, supply • include • add • contain • capture • omit** *Box 5.13 provides details on an area of the world that is regularly subject to devastating floods.* ◇ *A series of publications arose from this, of which more detail is given below.*

▸ VERB + IN DETAIL **describe • explain • outline • discuss, consider • explore, examine, investigate, look at • study • analyse** *The deflation trap is explored in more detail in section 4.*

de·tail² AWL /ˈdiːteɪl; *NAmE also* dɪˈteɪl/ *verb* **1** to give full information about a subject: **~ sth** *Parents were given written information that detailed their role in addressing the problem.* ◇ **~ how/what, etc.** *She details how raw meat extracts were suggested as a cure for tuberculosis by French physiologist Charles Richet.* ◇ **detailed above/below** *In Mulcahy and Call's experiments detailed above, the motivation of the subjects is likely to have been constant.* **2 ~ sth** to give a list of facts or items: *Assessment formats often include a checklist, detailing the patient's main long-term conditions.* ◇ *The table details the top 20 of the 186 products surveyed.*

de·tailed /ˈdiːteɪld; *NAmE also* dɪˈteɪld/ *adj.* giving many details; paying great attention to details: *A detailed analysis of these results is not the goal of this paper.* ◇ *The MRI gives very detailed images, which is particularly useful when imaging the brain and cervical spine.*

▸ DETAILED + NOUN **description • picture • account • explanation • review • overview • look • scrutiny • examination, investigation, exploration • study • analysis • discussion • consideration • assessment • knowledge • understanding • specifications • information • notes • calculation • guidance • instructions • plan • map** *Turing offered a detailed description of the memory device.* ◇ *A much more detailed discussion of systems of the type shown in Figure 1.1 can be found in Xu et al.*

▸ ADVERB + DETAILED **very • extremely • highly • richly • sufficiently • fairly • quite • relatively** *Relatively detailed accounts describe damage to military fortifications along much of the island's north shore.*

de·tain /dɪˈteɪn/ *verb* **~ sb** to keep sb in a police station, a prison or a hospital, and prevent them from leaving: *He had been arrested and detained without trial and he fled into exile.* ◇ *The European Court of Human Rights agreed with the Appeal Court that he was unlawfully detained.* ◇ **~ sb under sth** *Patients detained under the Mental Health Act can refuse treatment.* HELP In general English, **detain** also means to delay sb. Academic authors sometimes use phrases such as *X need not detain us here* to show that they are aware of an issue but do not intend to discuss it. ➲ *see also* DETENTION

de·tect AWL /dɪˈtekt/ *verb* to discover or notice sth that is difficult to discover or notice: **~ sth** *The screening test failed to detect the cancer.* ◇ **~ whether/which, etc.** *It is difficult to detect whether these measures have been effective.* ◇ *Further research is needed to detect which style is best for GPs and patients.* ■ **de·tect·able** AWL *adj.*: *The toxin was detectable in both body tissues and faeces.* ◇ *No detectable differences existed.*

▸ DETECT + NOUN **change • difference • effect • association • error • the presence of sth** *The changes are hard to detect.* ◇ *The sample sizes reduced our ability to detect significant differences.* | **disease • abnormalities • mutations • cancer • tumour • antibodies • radiation • signal • pulse • protein • predator** *The analysis could be used to detect abnormalities in the subjects with diabetes.*

▸ ADVERB + DETECT **easily, readily • reliably • accurately** *The protein is readily detected by eye using a UV light source.*

de·tec·tion AWL /dɪˈtekʃn/ *noun* [U] **1** the process of detecting sth; the fact of being detected: *The species escaped detection for a long time.* ◇ **~ of sth** *These screening programmes lead to earlier detection of the cancer.* **2** the action of finding sb who does not wish to be found: *Runaways stood a better chance of escaping detection in an urban setting.*

de·tect·or AWL /dɪˈtektə(r)/ *noun* a device used for finding or recording the presence of a particular object, substance or type of RADIATION: *The use of metal detectors in schools may reduce violence.* ◇ *Infrared detectors monitor the absorption of organic molecules.*

de·ten·tion /dɪˈtenʃn/ *noun* [U] the state of being kept in a place, especially a prison, by sb in authority, and prevented from leaving: *Indefinite detention without trial was found unlawful by the House of Lords.* ◇ **~ of** *Singh and Burns (2006) argued that high rates of detention of black patients in mental hospitals are not a result of racism.* ➲ *see also* DETAIN

deter /dɪˈtɜː(r)/ *verb* (-rr-) to make sb decide not to do sth or continue doing sth, especially by making them understand the difficulties and unpleasant results of their actions: **~ sb (from sth/from doing sth)** *The high price of the service could deter people from seeking advice.* ◇ **~ sth** *Unanticipated inflation is likely to deter investment because of the uncertainty that it brings.* ➲ *see also* DETERRENT

de·teri·or·ate /dɪˈtɪəriəreɪt; *NAmE* dɪˈtɪriəreɪt/ *verb* [I] to become worse: *His condition deteriorated and he died.* ◇ **~ into sth** *The areas of small, terraced houses where workers lived quickly deteriorated into slums.* ■ **de·teri·or·ation** /dɪˌtɪəriəˈreɪʃn; *NAmE* dɪˌtɪriəˈreɪʃn/ *noun* [U, C] **~ (of sth)** *The main obstacles to implementing policies that might halt the deterioration of the environment are political.* ◇ **~ in sth** *The city has experienced a noticeable deterioration in its air quality in recent years.*

de·ter·min·ant /dɪˈtɜːmɪnənt; *NAmE* dɪˈtɜːrmɪnənt/ *noun* **1** a thing that decides whether or how sth happens: *For road transport, the key determinants include traffic volumes, fuel efficiency, and the location and time of day of travel.* ◇ **~ of sth** *The social determinants of health are by nature not completely divorced from the individual's personal choices.* **2** (*biology*) a GENE or other factor that determines the character and development of a cell or cells in an animal, plant, etc: *In many animals, the future germ cells are specified by localized cytoplasmic determinants in the egg.* **3** (*mathematics*) a quantity obtained by the addition of products of the elements of a square MATRIX according to a given rule: *A determinant with a row or column of zeros has a value of zero.*

de·ter·min·ation /dɪˌtɜːmɪˈneɪʃn; *NAmE* dɪˌtɜːrmɪˈneɪʃn/ *noun* **1** [U, C] (*formal*) the act of finding out or calculating sth: *The primary signal for sex determination is set by the number of X chromosomes.* ◇ **~ of sth** *The determination of blood glucose levels has been greatly simplified since the 1960s due to the development of glucose biosensors.* **2** [C, U] (*formal*) the process of deciding sth officially: *It is not enough that the court makes a determination; what matters is that resident parents comply with the order.* ◇ **~ of sth** *The determination of whether non-regulars can become regular employees is mainly based on the employee's work experience.* ➲ *see also* SELF-DETERMINATION **3** [U] **~ (to do sth)** the quality that makes you continue trying to do sth even when this is difficult: *The doctor's determination to get at the truth typifies the passion for knowledge that drove Japan's intellectuals.*

de·ter·mine /dɪˈtɜːmɪn; *NAmE* dɪˈtɜːrmɪn/ *verb* **1** [T] to make sth happen in a particular way or be of a particular type: **~ sth** *The mass of a rocket determines the amount of energy needed to place it in an orbit around the Earth.* ◇ *This has been shown to be a critical factor in determining the success or failure of an enterprise.* ◇ **~ what/whether, etc...** *The genotype determines what proteins a cell contains, and the proteins in turn determine the cell's properties.* ◇ *We live in a world in which money determines whether or not a person can eat.* **2** [T] to discover the facts about sth SYN ESTABLISH (3): **~ sth** *Further research is necessary to determine the likely cause of this phenomenon.* ◇ **be determined by (doing) sth** *The nature of candidate genes may be determined by searching the relevant DNA sequences.* ◇ **as determined by sth** *The coprolites ranged in age (as determined by carbon dating) from more than 28 000 years to around 11 000 years old.* ◇ **~ what/whether, etc...** *The first step was to determine what information each participant had when they made a judgement.* ◇ **~ that...** *Prior to approving a new drug application, the FDA must determine that the drug is safe.* ◇ **it is determined that...** *Finally, by 1826, it was determined that sensory nerves were of five distinct types.* ◇ **in order to ~ sth/if/what, etc...** *In order to determine if the species was adapted to saline environments, a field investigation was carried out in September 2007.* **3** [T] to calculate sth exactly SYN ESTABLISH (3): **~ sth** *A downward-pointing radar is used to determine the height of the satellite above the ground.* ◇ **be determined by (doing) sth** *The refraction of the ordinary ray can be determined by applying Snell's law.* ◇ **it is determined that...** *It was determined that 120 seconds per reading would be sufficient.* **4** [T] to officially decide and/or arrange sth: **~ sth** *To determine the basic amount of the fine, the Commission first calculates the value of sales.* ◇ **~ that...** *Once a court has determined that procedures should be stayed, the focus of attention switches to the Commissioner.* ◇ **it is determined that...** *It was determined that the Polytechnique would be reorganized.* **5** [T, I] (*formal*) to decide definitely to do sth: **~ to do sth** *The Reds determined to hold Tsaritsyn at all costs.* ◇ **~ that...** *Companies might determine that social benefits to keep employees happy would be a boon for productivity.* ◇ **~ on sth** *Most of the original wording determined on by Cranmer remained unaltered.*

▸ DETERMINE + NOUN **amount** • **extent** • **direction** • **size** • **composition** • **content** • **level** • **degree** • **rate** • **distribution** *From the calibration curve, Fig. 6.3, we can determine the amount of protein present in each sample.* ◇ *Engaged learners are highly motivated to learn and determine the direction of the learning.* | **price** • **status** *The company determines a price that yields a target return on investment (ROI).* | **outcome** • **behaviour** • **effectiveness** • **shape** • **structure** • **nature** • **location** *In any war, the outcome will be largely determined by the relative power of the combatants.* | **fate** • **success** *Ultimately, events in England determined the political fate of both Scotland and Ireland.* | **value** • **parameter** *Another important factor in determining the value of an estate was planters' residency.* | **cause** • **sequence** *Mass spectrometry helps determine the exact sequence of components.* | **constant** • **velocity** • **concentration** *A flame photometer was used to determine the Ca_2 concentration of the water sample.*

▸ ADVERB + DETERMINE | DETERMINE + ADVERB **fully**, **completely**, **entirely** *The significance of these findings has yet to be fully determined.* | **largely**, **mainly** • **primarily** • **partially**, **partly** • **solely**, **uniquely** • **genetically** • **culturally** • **biologically** • **endogenously** *Prices were partly determined by the efficiency of merchants, traders and peddlers.* ◇ *According to Ferns (2005), the extent to which we value independence is culturally determined.* | **accurately** • **exactly**, **precisely** • **experimentally** • **empirically** *In many situations, determining exactly how much work each employee has done can be a costly process.*

▸ ADJECTIVE + TO DETERMINE **difficult**, **hard** • **impossible** • **possible** • **easy** • **able** • **unable** • **necessary** • **sufficient** *It is difficult to determine exactly how far the canoe can be tipped before it will flip over.*

▸ VERB + TO DETERMINE **try**, **attempt** • **aim**, **seek** • **need** • **wish** • **help** *This project aimed to determine the environmental parameters that affect the distribution of ticks along the Tamsin trail.*

THESAURUS

determine • **establish** • **identify** • **ascertain** *verb*

These words all mean to find out or calculate the facts about sth by researching or studying.

- to determine/establish/identify/ascertain **what/how/when/whether/why...**
- to establish/ascertain **that...**
- to determine/establish/identify/ascertain the **extent/cause** of sth
- to determine/identify/ascertain the **impact/effect**
- to establish/ascertain the **facts**
- to determine/identify **factors**

- **Determine** can be used to talk about finding facts and calculating figures; **establish** and **identify** are used mostly about finding and proving facts: *First, we must determine the value of the parameter VZ.* ◇ *Crawford (1989), Whalley (1986b) and Zussman (1985) established three important facts.* ◇ *The researchers identified 14 further factors, including...*
- **Identify** is used especially to talk about searching for connections, problems and causes: *SWOT analysis serves to identify the key issues.*
- **Ascertain** is often used to talk about understanding people's feelings and intentions: *The GPs should ascertain whether patients were motivated to change their habits.*

de·ter·mined /dɪˈtɜːmɪnd; *NAmE* dɪˈtɜːrmɪnd/ *adj.* **1** [not before noun] **~ to do sth** if you are **determined** to do sth, you have made a decision to do it and you will not let anyone prevent you: *China is determined to balance the power of the USA.* **2** [only before noun] showing determination to do sth: *Determined opposition from a very few* *governments can block such a move.* ◇ *Many Japanese companies are making determined efforts to eliminate the seniority principle completely.* ■ **de·ter·mined·ly** *adv.*: *Mansfield worked determinedly on a small scale.*

de·ter·miner /dɪˈtɜːmɪnə(r); *NAmE* dɪˈtɜːrmɪnər/ *noun* (*grammar*) (abbreviation *det.* in this dictionary) a word such as *the, some, my,* etc. that comes before a noun to show how the noun is being used: *Countable nouns cannot occur in the singular without a determiner.*

D

de·ter·min·ism /dɪˈtɜːmɪnɪzəm; *NAmE* dɪˈtɜːrmɪnɪzəm/ *noun* [U] (*philosophy*) the belief that people are not free to choose what they are like or how they behave, because these things are decided by causes they cannot control: *Nietzsche sees no comfort in determinism and seems almost to embrace determinism for this reason alone.* ■ **de·ter·min·ist** /dɪˈtɜːmɪnɪst; *NAmE* dɪˈtɜːrmɪnɪst/ *adj., noun*: *The apparent logic of the environmental determinist argument was attractive in itself.* ◇ *The determinists argued that to attribute free will to human beings limited an omnipotent God.* **de·ter·min·is·tic** /dɪˌtɜːmɪˈnɪstɪk; *NAmE* dɪˌtɜːrmɪˈnɪstɪk/ *adj.*: *If the universe is deterministic, then free will must be an illusion.*

de·ter·rent /dɪˈterənt; *NAmE* dɪˈtɜːrənt/ *noun* **1** a thing that makes sb less likely to do sth: *The criminal law is punitive and seeks to act as a deterrent.* ◇ **~ to sb/sth** *Mental health problems in children are a major deterrent to learning.* ◇ **~ against sb/sth** *An additional deterrent against speculative claims is, of course, costs.* **2 ~ (against sb/sth)** a weapon or weapons system that makes others less likely to attack you: *In some security situations, landmines may be the only effective deterrent against a neighbouring state with superior land forces.* ■ **de·ter·rence** /dɪˈterəns; *NAmE* dɪˈtɜːrəns/ *noun* [U] *Bull points out that mutual nuclear deterrence is a special case of general deterrence, which has always been a defence policy of states.* ◇ **+ noun** *In general, any legal prohibition should have a deterrence effect.* **de·ter·rent** *adj.*: *The sanctions are quite tough and could be expected to have a deterrent effect.*

det·ri·ment /ˈdetrɪmənt/ *noun* (*formal*) **1** [C, usually sing.] **~ (to sth)** something that causes harm or damage: *His argument is that old-age benefits are a major detriment to the health of the economy.* **2** [U] **~ (to sth)** the act of causing harm or damage: *The students need to become proficient in both languages, without any detriment to the acquisition of academic knowledge.*
IDM **to the detriment of sb/sth | to sb/sth's detriment** causing harm or damage to sb/sth: *In these conditions, growth of invasive species can increase unchecked to the detriment of native flora.*

det·ri·ment·al /ˌdetrɪˈmentl/ *adj.* (*formal*) harmful SYN DAMAGING: *This development had a detrimental effect on decision-making.* ◇ **~ to sb/sth** *Caring can be very stressful and thus may be detrimental to health.*

de·valu·ation /ˌdiːˌvæljuˈeɪʃn/ *noun* [C, U] **1** the process of reducing the official value of the money of one country when it is exchanged for the money of another country: *Policymakers were concerned that devaluation might lead to inflation.* ◇ **~ of sth** *Such a move would have implied a devaluation of their currencies against the pound.* **2 ~ (of sb/sth)** the process of giving less or not enough value or importance to sb/sth: *Wollstonecraft rejects this type of romance and its intrinsic devaluation of women.* ◇ *A devaluation of educational qualifications is the likely result.*

de·value /ˌdiːˈvæljuː/ *verb* **1** [T, I] **~ (sth) (against sth)** to reduce the official value of the money of one country when it is exchanged for the money of another country: *The member state must not have devalued its currency against the currencies of any other member state.* ◇ *Labour governments were forced to devalue in 1949 and 1967.* **2** [T] **~ sb/sth** to give less or not enough value or importance to sb/sth: *It has been suggested that globalization may devalue the significance of existing national communities.*

dev·as·tat·ing /ˈdevəsteɪtɪŋ/ *adj.* **1** causing a lot of damage and destruction SYN DISASTROUS: *The devastating effects of the Lisbon earthquake stretched far beyond the city.* **2** extremely shocking to a person: *The death of his wife in 1881 was a devastating blow.*

dev·as·ta·tion /ˌdevəˈsteɪʃn/ *noun* [U] great destruction or damage, especially over a wide area: *Asteroids might crash into the Earth and cause massive devastation as they have in the past.*

de·velop /dɪˈveləp/ *verb* **1** [I, T] to gradually grow or become bigger, more advanced or stronger; to make sth do this: *Severe tropical cyclones develop only over extensive warm sea surfaces.* ◇ **~ (from sth) (into sth)** *Mendel found that the peas developing from the artificially fertilized flowers were all yellow.* ◇ **~ sth** *The challenge will be how to compete and yet help to develop these economies.* ◇ **~ sth (from sth) (into sth)** *Singapore and Hong Kong have developed themselves into leading centres for private wealth management.* **2** [T] to think of or produce a new method, system, product, etc. and make it successful: **~ sth** *A number of promising methods have been developed, some of which are discussed in the next section.* ◇ **~ sth (from sth) (into sth)** *Nike developed Jordan's products into a sub-brand: Brand Jordan.* **3** [T] to make an idea or a theory clearer and more useful by explaining it further SYN ELABORATE² (2): **~ sth** *Montesquieu analysed the forms of government and developed his theory of the separation of powers.* ◇ **~ sth into sth** *Nelson and Winter (1982) developed these ideas into a framework of 'evolutionary economics'.* **4** [T] **~ sth** to start to have a skill, ability, quality, etc. that becomes better and stronger: *The opportunity to develop new skills should not be overlooked.* ◇ *Many felt that the process had helped them develop a sense of community.* ◇ *Children need to be helped to develop relationships with others around their own age.* **5** [I, T] **~ (sth)** to begin to have sth such as a disease or a problem; (of a disease or problem) to start to affect sb/sth: *Occasionally patients can develop tuberculosis and require careful monitoring.* ◇ *It is far better not to let such problems develop in the first place.* **6** [T] **~ sth** to build new houses, factories, etc. on an area of land, especially land that was not actively being used before: *The plan involved developing an area of wetland at the mouth of the Yangtze River.* **7** [T] **~ sth** to treat film which has been used to take photographs with chemicals so that the pictures can be seen: *An X-ray film was exposed to the membrane and the film was developed.*

▸ DEVELOP + NOUN **strategy, plan, scheme • model, approach • framework • system • method, methodology, technique • tool • policy • programme • measures • guidelines • standard • procedure • solution • questionnaire • product** *Industrialized countries such as Ireland and the UK have developed poverty reduction strategies.* | **idea, concept, notion • theory • argument • theme** *Once he had developed the basic ideas of psychoanalysis, Freud found religion a most promising subject of study.* | **skill, competence • expertise • capability, capacity, ability • understanding • knowledge • awareness • sense • relationship** *There is a need to develop clearer understanding of the type of information required by decision-makers.* | **disease • cancer • symptom** *Only about 5% of humans infected with tuberculosis develop the disease.*

▸ NOUN + DEVELOP **embryo • larva • egg • cell • child** *The thorax and abdomen become divided into segments as the embryo develops.* | **researcher • author • scientist • scholar • theorist • team • company, firm • organization •**

manufacturer *An interview guide was developed by the authors consulting existing literature.*

▸ ADVERB + DEVELOP **subsequently, later, then** *New theories were later developed, according to which these different groups came from different origins.* | **gradually** ♦ **eventually** ♦ **quickly** *Through the domestic network, the organization eventually develops business relationships in other countries.* | **typically, normally** *Aneurysms typically develop at points of bifurcation of the blood vessels.* | **further** *The theorist Michael Saward has further developed this line of thinking.* | **originally, initially, first** ♦ **recently** ♦ **previously, already** ♦ **currently** *The method was originally developed in China from the sixth century onward.* | **specifically** ♦ **independently** ♦ **jointly** *The study reported here was jointly developed by Chinese and Australian researchers.*

▸ DEVELOP + ADVERB **independently** ♦ **primarily, largely, mainly** ♦ **originally, initially** ♦ **further** ♦ **later** ♦ **early** *The gas turbine engine was developed initially for aircraft propulsion.* ◇ *Pygmy stature seems to have developed independently many different times.* | **rapidly** ♦ **slowly, gradually** *Historical study of disability is developing rapidly.* | **normally** *The embryos developed normally if incubated in water rather than their usual terrestrial habitat.* | **jointly, collaboratively** ♦ **specifically** *The checklist was developed specifically for use in this study.*

de·veloped /dɪˈveləpt/ *adj.* **1** a **developed** country, region or society has many industries and a complicated economic system: *Children in more developed countries grow up surrounded by media.* HELP The phrase **the developed world** is used to refer to the rich countries of the world as a group. Poorer/richer countries may be referred to as **the less/more developed world**: *Urban growth in some parts of the less developed world appears to be slowing down.* ➲ *compare* DEVELOPING (1), UNDERDEVELOPED (1) **2** in an advanced state; at a high level: *Measuring toxicity is a complex and highly developed science.* ➲ *compare* DEVELOPING (2), UNDERDEVELOPED (2)

▸ DEVELOPED + NOUN **country, state, nation** ♦ **economy** ♦ **society** ♦ **region** *Conflicts between employees and employers are widespread in most highly developed economies today.*

▸ ADVERB + DEVELOPED **less** ♦ **more** ♦ **highly** ♦ **newly** *As shown in Figure 3.4, rainforests are located primarily in less developed areas of the world* | **poorly** ♦ **highly** ♦ **well, fully** ♦ **newly** *Regeneration is the ability of a fully developed organism to replace lost parts.*

de·vel·op·er /dɪˈveləpə(r)/ *noun* **1** a person or company that designs and creates new products or systems: *Software developers, engineers and technicians are responsible for designing almost every technology that we use.* **2** a person or company whose business is buying land or buildings in order to build new houses, shops, etc, or to improve the old ones: *Developers should recognize that firm foundations are far more important in the long term than good views.*

de·vel·op·ing /dɪˈveləpɪŋ/ *adj.* [only before noun] **1** a **developing** country, region or society is poor, and trying to make its industry and economic system more advanced: *There is currently a flood of foreign investment into rapidly growing developing countries.* ➲ *compare* DEVELOPED (1), UNDERDEVELOPED (1) **2** becoming bigger, stronger or more advanced: *This is a rapidly developing area of research.* ◇ *The fuel economy goal was judged to be attainable using current or developing technologies.* ➲ *compare* DEVELOPED (2), UNDERDEVELOPED (2)

de·vel·op·ment /dɪˈveləpmənt/ *noun* **1** [U] the process of creating a new method, system, product or theory: *The major costs of drug development are safety testing, preclinical trials and clinical trials.* ◇ **~ of sth** *The ideas of Max Black have been influential in the development of modern theories of metaphor.* ➲ *see also* RESEARCH AND DEVELOPMENT **2** [C] a new or advanced method, system, product or theory: *The bar code is a relatively recent development.* ◇ **developments in sth** *Newspapers were the main driving force in developments in print technology.* **3** [U] the process of making a country or area richer and more successful: *The EU has increasingly deployed trade instruments and political dialogue to promote development.* **4** [U] the way in which a child or other living creature grows before and after birth: *Exposure of the embryo to specific combinations of hormones is not constant during development.* ◇ **~ from sth (to/into sth)** *The notion of development from carefree child to disciplined adult is an ideal, not a template.* **5** [U] gradual growth or changes that make sb/sth more advanced, more skilled or stronger: *Older GPs have limited opportunity or incentive for professional development.* ◇ **~ of sth** *Little is known about the actual development of the Spartan system.* ◇ **~ (of sth) into sth** *Key to understanding the development of the slum into the ghetto is the growth of Kingston's population.* **6** [C] a new event or stage that is likely to affect what happens in a continuing situation: *Expectations about future developments are incorporated into today's exchange rate.* ◇ **~ in/within sth** *Developments within nursing have led to a blurring of professional boundaries.* **7** [U] **~ of sth** the fact of starting to have sth such as an illness or a problem: *Development of cancer involves loss of control of a number of processes.* **8** [C] a piece of land with new buildings on it: *The valley was being converted into new housing developments.* **9** [U] the process of using an area of land, especially to make a profit by building on it: *Vast areas of farmland are being destroyed by urban development.*

▸ ADJECTIVE + DEVELOPMENT **subsequent** ♦ **later** ♦ **early** ♦ **rapid** *Early development, especially nutrition, has an important effect on health in later life.* ◇ *Rapid economic development has significantly affected the role of law for business.* | **new** ♦ **recent** ♦ **further** ♦ **future** ♦ **significant** *This seems to be a very fruitful idea worthy of further development.* ◇ *A recent development is that even white-collar work has been subjected to deskilling.* | **technological** ♦ **technical** ♦ **commercial** *Technological developments consisted primarily of tractors, sprayers and new pesticides.* | **sustainable** ♦ **international** ♦ **regional** ♦ **local** ♦ **urban** ♦ **rural** ♦ **economic** ♦ **industrial** ♦ **technological** *In retrospect, it is clear that what Russia needed was industrial development.* | **normal** ♦ **abnormal** ♦ **healthy** ♦ **sexual** ♦ **cognitive** ♦ **human** ♦ **embryonic** ♦ **fetal** *The abnormal behaviour starts in early childhood after a period of normal development.* | **personal** ♦ **professional** ♦ **intellectual** ♦ **social** ♦ **political** ♦ **historical** ♦ **human** *The global pattern of gender-related human development is mapped in Figure 7.4.*

▸ NOUN + DEVELOPMENT **product** ♦ **software** ♦ **drug** ♦ **vaccine** *Drug development is complicated, time-consuming and expensive.* | **skill/skills** ♦ **career** *The firm has invested extensively in training and skills development.*

▸ VERB + DEVELOPMENT **inform** ♦ **shape, guide, influence** *Strategy development should be informed by the market environment.* | **promote** ♦ **stimulate** ♦ **accelerate** ♦ **impede, hinder** *Aid intended to promote development has served to encourage increased dependence.* | **encourage, facilitate, foster** ♦ **support, aid, further** *Governments in Japan and France have successfully supported the development of high-speed trains.* | **prevent** ♦ **favour** *It is extremely difficult to prevent the development of any new technology for which there is market demand.* | **study** ♦ **describe** ♦ **understand** *Section 2 describes developments in the voluntary sector.* | **affect** ♦ **inhibit** ♦ **control** *The role of the genes in controlling development has only been fully appreciated in the past 30 years.* | **trace, chart** ♦ **review** ♦ **examine** ♦ **discuss** *Crookes traces the development over 600 years of key beliefs about education.*

▸ DEVELOPMENT + NOUN **process** ♦ **project** ♦ **stage** ♦ **work** ♦ **effort** ♦ **cost** *Early development work was performed primarily in Japan.* | **project** ♦ **aid, assistance** ♦ **policy** ♦

goal • trajectory, path • strategy, plan, programme, initiative • efforts • economics *The urban explosion began around 1900 as a result of development policies favouring industrialization.*

de·vel·op·men·tal /dɪˌveləp'mentl/ *adj.* [usually before noun] **1** developing or being developed: *Rapid prototyping enables developmental processes to be considerably shortened.* **2** connected with the development of sb/sth: *Achieving autonomy is a key developmental milestone of adolescence.* **3** connected with way a child or other living creature grows before and after birth: *One of the goals of developmental biology is to understand how gene families and signalling pathways interact.* ◇ *All the hatchlings were similar in size and developmental stage.*

de·vel·op·men·tal·ly /dɪˌveləp'mentəli/ *adv.* **1** connected with the development of a child or other living creature before and after birth: *The developmentally more advanced hatchlings are better able to escape from the flatworms.* **2** connected with the way sb/sth develops: *Middle school is a developmentally challenging time for all students.*

de·vi·ant /'di:viənt/ *adj.* **1** behaving differently from what most people consider to be normal and acceptable: *Deviant behaviour in adolescence is strongly correlated with deviant behaviour in early adulthood.* **2** different from what was expected or what is usual: *We actively sought contradictory data and deviant cases.* ■ **de·vi·ance** /'di:viəns/, **de·vi·ancy** /'di:viənsi/ *noun* [U] *Are acts of terrorism the product of mental deviance, or rational political acts?* ◇ *Performing this calculation yielded a change in deviance between the two models.*

de·vi·ate AWL /'di:vieɪt/ *verb* **1** [I] **~ (from sth)** to do sth in a different way from what most people consider to be normal and acceptable: *It is reasonable to believe that girls had a difficult time deviating from the norms of their family environment.* ◇ *Everyone had to conform to the anti-communist line; no one dared deviate.* **2** [I] **~ (from sth)** to be different from what is usual or expected: *Of the 134 markers, 77 did not show any distortion, while 33 deviated slightly from the expected ratio.*

de·vi·ation AWL /ˌdi:vi'eɪʃn/ *noun* **1** [U, C] **~ (from sth)** a difference from what is expected or usual: *As Holes notes, the deviations from classical Arabic norms arise from the writer's dialect.* ◇ *The system notes and corrects any deviation from the desired temperature (see Figure 6.1).* **2** [C] **~ (from sth)** (*statistics*) the amount by which a single measurement is different from a fixed value such as the MEAN: *Robeson and Shein (1997) have examined the spatial coherence of wind data using mean absolute deviations.* ➲ *see also* STANDARD DEVIATION ➲ language bank *at* STATISTIC **3** [U] **~ (from sth)** behaviour that is different from what most people consider normal or acceptable: *According to this philosophy, the presence of a strong state, one that will crush any threat of deviation, is absolutely essential.*

de·vice AWL /dɪ'vaɪs/ *noun* **1** an object or a piece of equipment that has been designed for a particular purpose: *Participants wore the device for two days and were unaware of when it was recording.* ◇ **~ for (doing) sth** *According to Steele, 'Huge mechanical devices for shovelling and loading were invented and set to work.'* ◇ **~ to do sth** *An inverter is a device to convert direct current into AC.* **2** a bomb or weapon that will explode: *The act of detonating the device would be relatively straightforward.* **3** a plan or method with a particular purpose: **~ for (doing) sth** *'High Anxiety' (1977) parodied the use of the fall as a device for creating suspense in classical film.* ◇ **~ to do sth** *In the non-profit context, a brand is a device to allow members of the public to recognize a particular non-profit.* **4** speech or writing that produces a particular result or effect: *Hedley shows how Brooks employed sophisticated rhetorical devices in poems like 'We Real Cool'.* ◇ **~ to do sth** *Scott used the minstrel as a framing device to dramatize Anglo-Scottish history.*

▸ ADJECTIVE + DEVICE **practical • useful • electronic • mechanical • digital • mobile • portable • hand-held • medical • contraceptive** *Radioactivity is detectable only with the aid of mechanical or electronic devices.* | **explosive • nuclear** *A state does not need to test a nuclear device to be in possession of a nuclear stockpile.* | **useful • legal • constitutional • pedagogic • heuristic** *Questioning the legitimacy of an action by the executive is a useful device for the opposition.* | **rhetorical • narrative • stylistic** *In Roland Barthes' terms, specific narrative devices and techniques can give us a 'reality effect'.*

▸ NOUN + DEVICE **storage, recording, measuring** *Cell design is the other important factor for energy storage devices.*

▸ VERB + DEVICE **use, employ, utilize** *Even those with no fixed address can still own and use mobile devices.* | **fabricate, construct, build • design • operate** *Several other countries have the capability to construct nuclear devices.*

de·vise /dɪ'vaɪz/ *verb* **~ sth** to plan or invent a procedure, system or method, especially one that is new or complicated, by using careful thought SYN THINK STH UP: *The political establishment seems unable to devise new strategies for economic development.* ◇ *Devising an appropriate method of control has proved difficult.* ◇ *to devise a system/scheme/plan/policy/procedure*

de·void /dɪ'vɔɪd/ *adj.* **~ of sth** completely lacking in sth: *Written text is devoid of many of the qualities of spoken text that facilitate effective communication.*

de·vote AWL /dɪ'vəʊt; *NAmE* dɪ'voʊt/ *verb*

PHRV **de'vote yourself to sb/sth** to give most of your time, energy or attention to sb/sth SYN DEDICATE (1): *The nuns devoted themselves to prayer and meditation.* **de'vote sth to sth** to give an amount of time, attention or resources to sth: *The authors devote an entire chapter to the consumer decision process.* ◇ *Cells devote significant resources to the repair of DNA double-strand breaks.* ◇ *Much attention has been devoted to addressing physical activity and obesity among youth.*

de·vo·tion AWL /dɪ'vəʊʃn; *NAmE* dɪ'voʊʃn/ *noun* [U, sing.] **1 ~ (of sb) (to sb/sth)** great love, care and support for sb/sth: *Those who knew her say that she lived by the principles she taught, with kindness and devotion to others.* ◇ *The devotion of the patient's family was highlighted as a significant factor.* **2 ~ (to sb/sth)** the action of spending a lot of time or energy on sth SYN DEDICATION (1): *Romans were attracted to Stoicism because it emphasized devotion to duty.* **3** great religious feeling: *The song reflects her interest in history and her religious devotion.* ◇ **~ to sb/sth** *Christianity calls for selfless devotion to God and to others.*

dia·betes /ˌdaɪə'bi:ti:z/ *noun* [U] a medical condition which makes the patient produce a lot of URINE and want to drink a lot. There are several types of diabetes: *Over 2 million people in the United Kingdom have diabetes.*

dia·bet·ic[1] /ˌdaɪə'betɪk/ *adj.* **1** having or connected with diabetes: *Diabetic patients are also more prone to infection after surgery.* ◇ *Risks of diabetic complications should not be overstated.* **2** suitable for or used by sb who has diabetes: *Patients are referred to dietitians for advice on diabetic diets.*

dia·bet·ic[2] /ˌdaɪə'betɪk/ *noun* a person who suffers from diabetes: *Most diabetics are able to identify the early signs of low blood sugar and take remedial action.*

diag·nose /'daɪəgnəʊz; ˌdaɪəg'nəʊz; *NAmE* ˌdaɪəg'noʊs/ *verb* [often passive] to say exactly what an illness or the cause of a problem is: **~ sth** *This group of diseases can be particularly difficult to diagnose.* ◇ *Different studies used* *different ways of diagnosing type 2 diabetes.* ◇ *Only 25% of the faults were diagnosed correctly.* ◇ **~ sb with sth** *Each year, 37 000 patients are diagnosed with lung cancer.* ◇ **~ sth as sth** *Two-thirds of fever cases were systematically diagnosed as malaria.* ◇ **~ sb (as) sth** *He was diagnosed as epileptic.* ◇ *This man is a newly diagnosed diabetic.*

diag·no·sis /ˌdaɪəɡˈnəʊsɪs; *NAmE* ˌdaɪəɡˈnoʊsɪs/ *noun* (*pl.* **diag·noses** /ˌdaɪəɡˈnəʊsiːz; *NAmE* ˌdaɪəɡˈnoʊsiːz/) [C, U] **~ (of sth)** the act of discovering or identifying the exact cause of an illness or a problem: *Various investigations can help confirm a clinical diagnosis of multiple sclerosis.* ◇ *Fast and accurate diagnosis is essential to ensure the most effective approach to managing cancer.*

▸ ADJECTIVE + DIAGNOSIS **likely • accurate, correct • definitive • early • initial • alternative • final • clinical • medical • primary • secondary • prenatal, antenatal • psychiatric** *To make the definitive diagnosis, a biopsy is required.* ◇ *Prenatal diagnosis is an emotive topic and many prospective parents struggle with the difficult ethical issues that it generates.*

▸ NOUN + DIAGNOSIS **cancer • dementia** *Five cancers—lung, colorectal, breast, skin and prostate—account for more than 50% of cancer diagnoses in the UK.*

▸ VERB + DIAGNOSIS **make • confirm • establish • support • suggest • aid • exclude • receive** *Two tests are commonly used to support a diagnosis of pernicious anaemia.*

diag·nos·tic /ˌdaɪəɡˈnɒstɪk; *NAmE* ˌdaɪəɡˈnɑːstɪk/ *adj.* [usually before noun] connected with identifying sth, especially an illness: *Treatments are tested on patients who meet formal diagnostic criteria.* ◇ *This has been the most widely used diagnostic test for cystic fibrosis.* ◇ *The problem with these measures is that they are descriptive, not diagnostic.* ➲ *compare* INDICATIVE (1), SYMPTOMATIC

diag·nos·tics /ˌdaɪəɡˈnɒstɪks; *NAmE* ˌdaɪəɡˈnɑːstɪks/ *noun* [U] the practice or methods of diagnosis: *This approach is frequently used in medical diagnostics.*

di·ag·onal[1] /daɪˈæɡənl/ *adj.* (of a straight line) at an angle; joining two opposite sides of sth at an angle: *The graph shows that most cars lie on a diagonal line between the high-comfort/high-price position and the low-price/low-comfort position.*

di·ag·onal[2] /daɪˈæɡənl/ *noun* **~ (of sth)** a straight line that joins two opposite sides of sth at an angle; a straight line that is at an angle: *In the conventional cubic cell, the four axes are parallel to the principal diagonals of a cube.*

dia·gram /ˈdaɪəɡræm/ *noun* a simple drawing using lines to explain where sth is, how sth works, etc: *The diagram in Figure 15.5 illustrates this situation.* ◇ *a diagram shows/represents sth* ◇ **~ of sth** *A diagram of the test apparatus is shown in figure 7.24.* ◇ **in a/the ~** *The analysis is shown in the diagram (Fig.12.2).* ◇ **on a/the ~** *The Lorenz curve is plotted on a scatter diagram.* ➲ *compare* CHART[1] (1), GRAPH, TABLE (1) ■ **dia·gram·mat·ic** /ˌdaɪəɡrəˈmætɪk/ *adj.*: *Figure 2.7 gives a diagrammatic representation of the double-helix structure of DNA.* **dia·gram·mat·ic·al·ly** /ˌdaɪəɡrəˈmætɪkli/ *adv.*: *The strategy is shown diagrammatically in Figure 4.7.*

dia·logue (*US also* **dia·log**) /ˈdaɪəlɒɡ; *NAmE* ˈdaɪəlɑːɡ; ˈdaɪəlɔːɡ/ *noun* [U, C] **1** a formal discussion between two or more people, groups or countries, especially in order to solve a problem or end a disagreement: **~ (between A and B) (about sth)** *He wanted to facilitate dialogue between the two countries.* ◇ **~ (with sb) (about sth)** *Recognizing this problem, the government of Alberta initiated a dialogue with local community groups and industry.* ◇ *They acknowledge the problem and seek to engage in a constructive dialogue about solutions.* ➲ thesaurus note *at* DISCUSSION **2** conversations in a book, play or film: *It is a fragment of dialogue from the closing scene of the first episode of the series.* ◇ **~ on sth** *The work is a series of dialogues on various subjects.*

diam·eter /daɪˈæmɪtə(r)/ *noun* [C, U] a straight line going from one side of a circle or any other round object to the other side, passing through the centre: **~ of sth** *If the diameter of the caecum is greater than 10 cm, then the patient should be considered for urgent surgery.* ◇ **~ of 20 mm, 5 cm, etc.** *These are plastic pipes with an outer diameter of 25 mm, and an inner diameter of 20.4 mm.* ◇ **in ~** *The rods are typically 10–15 cm in length and 5–6 mm in diameter.* ➲ *compare* CIRCUMFERENCE, RADIUS (1)

dia·met·ric·al·ly /ˌdaɪəˈmetrɪkli/ *adv.* completely; directly: **~ opposed/opposite** *These two perspectives reflect views that are diametrically opposed to each other.*

dia·mond /ˈdaɪəmənd/ *noun* **1** [C, U] a clear, rare valuable stone of pure CARBON, the hardest substance known: *Diamonds have been prized since antiquity.* ◇ *In diamond, each carbon atom is attached to four other carbon atoms.* ◇ **+ noun** *diamond mining/production* **2** [C] a shape with four straight sides of equal length and with angles that are not RIGHT ANGLES: *Arthur Wynne's first printed crossword puzzle from 1913 appeared as a diamond.*

diary /ˈdaɪəri/ *noun* (*pl.* **-ies**) **1** a book in which you can write down the experiences you have each day, your private thoughts, etc: *Diaries and letters have been used a great deal by historians.* ◇ *While Secretary of the Navy, he kept a diary, which was published in three volumes in 1911.* ◇ **+ noun** *The following diary entry is from 9 October 1978:...* ➲ *compare* JOURNAL (2) **2** (*BrE*) (*NAmE* **date·book**) a book with spaces for each day of the year in which you can write down things you have to do in the future: *They are the sort of people who cram their diaries full of appointments.*

dias·pora /daɪˈæspərə/ *noun* [sing.] **1 the diaspora** the movement of the Jewish people away from their own country to live and work in other countries: *Idelsohn documented the various ways in which music could represent the diaspora.* **2** the movement of people from any group away from their own country: *This area of philosophical research addresses the problems faced and raised by the African diaspora.*

di·chot·omy /daɪˈkɒtəmi; *NAmE* daɪˈkɑːtəmi/ *noun* (*pl.* **-ies**) [usually sing.] the division that exists between two groups or things that are completely opposite to and different from each other: **~ (of A and B)** *the dichotomy of good and evil* ◇ **~ between A and B** *A false dichotomy has been created between biological and psychosocial psychiatry.*

dic·tate[1] /dɪkˈteɪt; *NAmE* ˈdɪkteɪt/ *verb* **1** [I, T] to control how sth happens SYN DETERMINE (1): *They want flexible contracts that enable them to increase or decrease supply as demand dictates.* ◇ **~ sth** *His choice of reading was dictated by availability.* ◇ **~ what/whether, etc...** *In many societies, a person's gender dictates what direction their life will take.* ◇ **~ that...** *Necessity often dictates that friends of the patient or members of their family act as interpreters.* **2** [T] to tell sb what to do, especially when you have more power than them: **~ sth** *The NFL could dictate the terms on which football games would be broadcast.* ◇ **~ sth to sb** *The Ministry dictates many things to universities, both public and private.* ◇ **~ how/what, etc...** *The checklist did not dictate how these actions were to be done.* ◇ **~ to sb how/what, etc...** *In the past, the music industry has been able to dictate to the public what it can buy.* ◇ **~ (to sb) that...** *Government policy dictates that all refugees must stay in one of the two camps.* **3** [T] to say words for sb else to write down: **~ sth** *Writing or dictating the letter is a separate and distinct activity from sending it.* ◇ **~ sth to sb** *The assistant dictates a letter to a secretary who, in turn, types the letter and hands it to a courier.*

PHR V **dic'tate to sb** [often passive] to give orders to sb, often in a rude or aggressive way: *Smaller states were less* *willing to be dictated to by the great powers.* ◇ *One purpose of federalism is to prevent one level of government from dictating to another.*

dic·tate² /ˈdɪkteɪt/ *noun* [usually pl.] **~ (of sb/sth)** an order, rule or principle that you must obey: *They are free to worship according to the dictates of their consciences.*

dic·ta·tor /dɪkˈteɪtə(r); *NAmE* ˈdɪkteɪtər/ *noun* (*disapproving*) a ruler of a country who uses force to gain and keep power over the country: *By Constantine's day, emperors were military dictators who had no effective legal limits on their power.*

dic·ta·tor·ship /ˌdɪkˈteɪtəʃɪp; *NAmE* ˌdɪkˈteɪtərʃɪp/ *noun* **1** [C, U] government by a dictator: *The mid-1970s saw the breakdown of dictatorships in Portugal, Greece and Spain.* ◇ *The country now faces the legacy of 48 years of dictatorship.* **2** [C] a country that is ruled by a dictator: *In 1961, South Korea became a military dictatorship.*

dic·tion·ary /ˈdɪkʃənri; *NAmE* ˈdɪkʃəneri/ *noun* (*pl.* **-ies**) a book or electronic resource that gives a list of the words of a language or subject in alphabetical order and explains what they mean, or gives a word for them in a foreign language: *a bilingual/monolingual dictionary* ◇ *an English-Portuguese dictionary* ◇ *This article presents some methods of using online dictionaries.* ◇ **~ of sth** *This hypothesis is validated in several dictionaries of Business English.* ➲ *compare* THESAURUS, LEXICON

did /dɪd/ ➲ DO¹, DO²

die /daɪ/ *verb* (**dies, dying, died, died**) **1** [I, T] to stop living: *The Mogul emperor Aurangzeb Alamgir died in 1707.* ◇ **~ of sth** *He died of cancer on 8 January 1975.* ◇ **~ from sth** *Only 2–3% of those who got sick died from the disease.* ◇ **~ for sth** *Both men ultimately died for their beliefs.* ◇ **~ a... death** *Monarchs who died a natural death lived to an average age of 53.3 years.* ◇ **+ adj.** *Many of the new generation of poets died young.* ◇ **+ noun** *Beau Brummell died a beggar.* **2** [I] to stop existing; to disappear: *Some discussion of what causes a language to die is necessary.* ◇ **~ with sb** *The remarkable stories her parents' generation had to tell about China's modern history were dying with them.*
PHR V **ˌdie aˈway** to become gradually weaker and finally disappear: *The showers will gradually die away.* ◇ *The mournful strings of the soundtrack die away.* **ˌdie ˈback** (of a plant) to die in the part above the ground but remain alive in the roots: *The grasses die back in the dry season.* **ˌdie ˈdown** to become gradually less strong, loud or easy to notice: *Four months later, the fuss had died down.* **ˌdie ˈoff** to die one after the other until there are none left: *By this time, the apostles themselves had begun to die off.* **ˌdie ˈout** to stop existing: *Towards the end of the period, the dinosaurs and giant marine reptiles died out.*

diesel /ˈdiːzl/ (*also* **ˈdiesel fuel, ˈdiesel oil**) *noun* [U] a type of heavy oil used as a fuel instead of petrol: **+ noun** *Diesel engines are used more commonly for larger vehicles such as buses, trucks, locomotives and ships.* ➲ *compare* PETROL

diet /ˈdaɪət/ *noun* **1** [C, U] **~ (of sth)** the food that you eat regularly: *She argues that eating a balanced diet of fresh fruit, low-fat spreads and lean meat is expensive.* ◇ *The importance of diet in promoting health is hardly a new discovery.* **2** [C] a limited variety or amount of food that you eat for medical reasons or because you want to lose weight; a time when you only eat this limited variety or amount: *Patients should maintain a high-fibre diet for life.* ◇ **be/go on a ~** *Respondents were asked: 'How often have you thought about going on a diet in the past year?'*

diet·ary /ˈdaɪətəri; *NAmE* ˈdaɪəteri/ *adj.* [usually before noun] connected with or provided by your diet: *Another limitation of this study was lack of data regarding dietary habits.* ◇ *The child's dietary intake was observed, and physical activity levels were measured.*

dif·fer /ˈdɪfə(r)/ *verb* **1** [I] to be different from sb/sth: **A differs from B** *This type of research differs greatly from traditional marketing research.* ◇ **A and B ~ (from each other)** *The groups did not significantly differ from each other.* ◇ **~ between A and B** *The rate of ageing can differ considerably between individuals.* ◇ **~ in sth** *Males and females differed in the way they captured prey.* ➲ language bank *at* COMPARE **2** [I] to disagree with sb: **~ about sth** *Christians differed about the way churches should be organized.* ◇ **~ over sth** *Writers often differ quite widely over what is ethically acceptable.* ◇ **~ on sth** *The two groups differed, however, on how the changes should be implemented.* ◇ **~ as to sth** *Opinions differ as to when the peak in oil production will occur.* IDM *see* BEG

▸ DIFFER + ADVERB/ADVERB + DIFFER **substantially • widely • greatly • fundamentally** *All five countries differ substantially in terms of their water use.* ◇ *Theorists differ fundamentally in their responses to such questions.* | **significantly • markedly • dramatically • radically • slightly • systematically** *People differ markedly in their readiness to try new products.*

▸ DIFFER + ADVERB **considerably • sharply • somewhat • little** *The situation differs sharply in the breeding colonies of vertebrates.*

▸ DIFFER IN + NOUN **respect • size • the way that • the degree to which, the extent to which** *The two countries differ in several respects.* ◇ *Individuals in any country differ greatly in the extent to which they share beliefs and values.*

▸ PHRASES **differ with regard to, differ with respect to, differ in terms of** *China's cities differ greatly with respect to their winter temperatures.*

dif·fer·ence /ˈdɪfrəns/ *noun* **1** [C, U] the way in which two people or things are not like each other; the state of being different: *Although population ageing is a global phenomenon, there are significant regional differences.* ◇ **~ between A and B** *There are very few real differences between the two groups.* ◇ **~ in sth** *There is no difference in what each producer is offering.* ◇ **~ in sth between A and B** *Numerous studies have indicated that there is a difference in life chances between social classes.* ◇ **~ from sth** *According to Hazlitt, poetry is defined by its difference from other kinds of writing.* OPP SIMILARITY ➲ *compare* DISPARITY ➲ language bank *at* COMPARE **2** [U, C, usually sing.] the amount by which sth is greater or smaller than sth else: *Photosensors were used to measure the time difference.* ◇ **~ between A and B** *The difference between biofuel prices and gasoline and diesel prices varies.* ◇ **~ in sth (between A and B)** *The professor found no difference in the size of plants from the two groups.* ◇ **~ of sth (between A and B)** *There is a difference of 25 per cent between US and EU GHG emissions from new cars.* ➲ *see also* POTENTIAL DIFFERENCE **3** [C] a disagreement between people SYN DISAGREEMENT: *Differences were resolved through consultation.* ◇ **~ of opinion** *The conference exposed substantial differences of opinion on the matter of new forms of family structure.*
IDM **make a, no, some, etc. difference (to/in sb/sth)** to have an effect/no effect on sb/sth: *Improving the gas mileage of cars could certainly make a difference.* ◇ *It makes no difference whether they have a few workers running many machines or many workers and few machines.* ◇ *Government action made little difference to these events.* ➲ *more at* WORLD

▸ ADJECTIVE + DIFFERENCE **significant, substantial, important, major, considerable • fundamental** *The research found no significant difference between the weights of the two types of female.* ◇ *There are significant differences of opinion about how these answers should be given.* | **key, crucial • main • real • essential • clear, obvious, marked • striking • subtle • slight • systematic** *There are some key differences between the two cases.* |

individual • regional • cultural • racial • ethnic • genetic • sexual • behavioural • socio-economic *Understanding the effects of cultural differences on buyer behaviour is crucial to successful overseas marketing.* | **mean • absolute • statistical** *The mean differences between the groups on all the outcome measures were not significant.*

▸ NOUN + DIFFERENCE **gender, sex • age** *Information about age and gender differences is important for the planning of services.*

▸ VERB + DIFFERENCE **find, detect • identify • observe • note • report • reveal • show, indicate • exhibit • reflect • highlight • examine, investigate • understand • explain • demonstrate • illustrate • compare** *Worker bees can detect the difference between eggs of fellow workers and the queen.* ◇ *The shapes of the beaks reflected differences in the birds' diets and how they got their food.* | **explore • recognize • emphasize** *The aim of this study was to explore differences between children's and adolescents' perceptions of influences on their food choices.* | **calculate • measure** *The temperature difference calculated from the heat extraction rate from the ground is 55 W/m.*

▸ DIFFERENCE + VERB **exist • arise • remain • explain** *Significant differences exist between the United States and European systems of data and privacy protection.* ◇ *This disparity can be explained by differences in sample size.*

dif·fer·ent /ˈdɪfrənt/ *adj.* **1** not the same as sb/sth; not like sb/sth else: *In Switzerland, he discovered a different type of industrial organization.* ◇ **~ from sth** *Islamic banking systems are quite different from those of the West.* ◇ *Reported intentions are different from actual behaviour.* ◇ **~ from each other/one another** *These explanations are all so different from each other that it is hard to assess their relative merit.* HELP In British English, **different to** is sometimes used instead of **different from**; in American English, **different than** is sometimes used. However, these expressions are slightly more informal; in academic writing it is better to use **different from.** OPP SIMILAR **2** [only before noun] (of things of the same kind) separate and individual: *Research was used to determine different types of people in the market.* ◇ *The drugs all have slightly different effects on the brain and the immune system.* ➲ *usage note at* VARIOUS IDM *see* MATTER[1], PULL[1]

> **WORD FAMILY**
> different *adj.*
> differently *adv.*
> difference *noun*
> differ *verb*
> differentiate *verb*
> differentiation *noun*

▸ DIFFERENT + NOUN **type, kind • group, set • class, category • form • level • stage • position • time • value** *Half the world's population is exposed to a different form of indoor air pollution, resulting from burning solid fuels for cooking and heating.* ◇ *Shares in companies take a number of different forms.* | **context • perspective, view • aspect • approach • method • strategy • pattern • direction • source • meaning • interpretation** *The Observational Method requires a different approach from the one normally used.* ◇ *There are many different approaches to improving group relations.* | **country • region, area • location • setting, environment • culture • population • species • gene** *By the 1970s, Germany was becoming a different country.* ◇ *There are dozens of different species of mosquitoes that can transmit the parasite.*

▸ VERB + DIFFERENT **look, appear • sound • feel • become** *Children with chronic illness may feel different from their peers.*

▸ ADVERB + DIFFERENT **very • significantly, substantially • radically • fundamentally • dramatically • vastly • completely, entirely, totally, altogether • distinctly, markedly • strikingly • essentially • somewhat, rather • slightly** *The two cases are strikingly different.* ◇ *Different land uses are likely to have significantly different impacts on biodiversity.* ◇ *Many fundamentally different kinds of animals appear in the fossil record.*

dif·fer·en·tial[1] /ˌdɪfəˈrenʃl/ *adj.* [only before noun] showing or depending on a difference: *Differential treatment of boys and girls is a nearly universal, cross-cultural circumstance.* ◇ *Differences between individuals may be caused solely by the differential effects of the environment during development.* ◇ *The company has been transformed by having a clear differential advantage over its competitors.*

dif·fer·en·tial[2] /ˌdɪfəˈrenʃl/ *noun* a difference in the amount, value or size of sth: **~ in sth** *A growing body of evidence indicates differentials in both socio-economic status and in health, by gender and ethnicity.* ◇ **~ (between A and B)** *A large temperature differential may exist between the lower surface temperature and the higher air temperature.* ◇ **wage ~** *International offshoring of services is driven by large wage differentials between developed and developing countries.* HELP In mathematics, a **differential** is a very small difference between those values of a VARIABLE that follow straight after each other.

diffe͵rential eˈquation *noun* (*mathematics*) an EQUATION that involves FUNCTIONS (= quantities that can vary) and their rates of change: *The corresponding functions are genuine solutions of the differential equation.*

dif·fer·en·ti·ate AWL /ˌdɪfəˈrenʃieɪt/ *verb* **1** [I, T] to recognize or show what makes sb/sth different SYN DISTINGUISH (1): **~ between A and B** *It is important that the organization differentiates between different types of customer.* ◇ *Weiser (2001) differentiated between using the Internet for social reasons and for information purposes.* ◇ **~ A from B** *These symptoms are less useful in differentiating appendicitis from other abdominal conditions.* ◇ **~ A and B** *People need to be able to differentiate good and bad instruction so as to have a true impact on their children's education.* **2** [T] to make sth different or seem different from other similar things: **~ sth** *Branding is an important way for manufacturers to differentiate their brands in crowded marketplaces.* ◇ **~ A (from B)** *The traditional role of a brand has been to differentiate a product from competing products.* ◇ *To differentiate itself from its competitors, the airline offers more space and excellent-quality food.* **3** [T] **~ sb/sth (from sb/sth)** to be the particular thing that shows that things or people are not the same SYN DISTINGUISH (2): *There is no consensus on what it is that differentiates the employee from the self-employed.* ◇ *The grasshoppers in France were genetically differentiated from those in both the Iberian and Italian peninsulas.* **4** [I] **~ between A and B** to treat people or things in a different way: *Hard-line policies do not differentiate between different types of crimes.* ◇ *In differentiating between married and unmarried parents, the Act seemed to confirm the value attached to traditional family forms.* **5** [I, T] (*biology*) (of cells) to become different in the process of growth or development; to make cells become different: **~ (into sth)** *Bone marrow stem cells differentiate into many types of blood cells.* ◇ **~ sth** *Some long-lived cells, such as neurons, do not divide once they are differentiated.*

dif·fer·en·ti·ation AWL /ˌdɪfəˌrenʃiˈeɪʃn/ *noun* **1** [U, sing.] the fact of two or more things being different; the act or process of showing that two or more things are not the same: **~ among sth** *There is little genetic differentiation among populations from south-east Europe and western Anatolia.* ◇ **~ (between A and B)** *In early modern Spain, there was a strict differentiation between academic and popular medicine.* ◇ *Advertising and sales promotion were used to emphasize product differentiation.* ◇ **+ noun** *To succeed with a differentiation strategy, an organization has to understand what buyers regard as important.* **2** [U] **~ between A and B** the act of treating people or things in a different way: *The Court found that differentiation between permanent residents and citizens was not acceptable.* **3** [U] (*biology*) the process of a cell becoming different during growth and development: *The proteins of* *a cell may change during differentiation.* ◇ *Cancer can result from mutations in genes that control cell multiplication and differentiation.* ◇ **~ of sth (into sth)** *Sexual reproduction requires the differentiation of simple cells into cells called gametes.*

dif·fer·ent·ly /ˈdɪfrəntli/ *adv.* **1** in various different ways: *Different types of tumours may respond differently to therapy.* ◇ *The plant produces differently sized leaves according to the season.* **2** in a different way from sb/sth else: *Research of this kind has shown that parents do treat their children differently.* ◇ **~ from sth** *The results suggest that manufacturing firms may behave differently from other sectors of the economy.*

IDM **put/stated ˈdifferently** in other words; used to introduce an explanation of sth: *Many patients will know precisely how to take their medicine. Put differently, every customer does not need information every time they visit the pharmacy to collect their prescription.* HELP Note that this expression is usually used at the start of a sentence.

dif·fer·ing /ˈdɪfərɪŋ/ *adj.* [only before noun] different from sb/sth: *Policy makers, academics, charities and campaigning organizations have differing opinions on what causes health inequality.*

dif·fi·cult /ˈdɪfɪkəlt/ *adj.* **1** not easy; needing effort or skill to do or to understand SYN HARD[1] (1): *This was the first railway into London and involved solving some difficult engineering problems.* ◇ **~ to do** *The diffraction pattern is difficult to interpret without appropriate analytical software.* ◇ **it is ~ to do sth** *It is difficult to determine exactly how many people die of hunger in any particular year.* ◇ **~ for sb** *The religious situation of American Muslims can be especially difficult for the younger generation.* ◇ **~ for sb to do** *No question seemed too difficult for them to answer.* ◇ **it is ~ for sb to do sth** *Global economic considerations make it increasingly difficult for people in the less developed world to purchase food.* OPP EASY (1) ➔ *compare* CHALLENGING, DEMANDING (1) **2** [only before noun] full of problems; causing a lot of trouble SYN HARD[1] (5): *The new republican government in France faced a difficult situation.* ◇ *People in the river valley already live in difficult circumstances, and their lives may become much worse.* **3** (of people) not easy to please; not helpful SYN AWKWARD (2), DEMANDING (2): *Cynthia likes dealing with difficult children.* ◇ *It is important to remember that the person being cared for is not deliberately being difficult.* IDM *see* LIFE

▸ DIFFICULT + NOUN **task • challenge • question • issue • problem • decision • choice • case** *A particularly difficult task in global marketing is how to coordinate prices across subsidiaries.* | **situation • circumstances, condition • time** *The cost of sickness absence was £16.8 billion in 2009—a significant burden in these difficult economic times.*

▸ VERB + DIFFICULT **prove • become • seem • remain • find sth** *Despite the successes in a few cases, gene therapy has unfortunately proved more difficult than was anticipated.* ◇ *The task may become even more difficult in the future with further city expansion.*

▸ ADVERB + DIFFICULT **extremely, exceedingly • very • particularly, especially • increasingly • quite, rather, somewhat** *It is extremely difficult to win a customer back once the business has a reputation for poor service.* ◇ *His resignation came at a particularly difficult moment.* | **notoriously** *The term 'terrorist' has been notoriously difficult to define.*

▸ BE DIFFICULT TO + VERB **distinguish • determine, establish • interpret • define • quantify • measure • discern • detect • identify • assess • understand • explain • predict • imagine • prove • reconcile • achieve • obtain • implement** *It is difficult to determine the specific cause of any human tumour.* ◇ *The data provided by organisms and plants can be difficult to interpret.*

THESAURUS

difficult • hard • challenging • demanding *adj.*

These words all describe sth that is not easy and requires a lot of effort or skill to do.

- difficult/hard **for** sb
- difficult/hard **to see/find/imagine/understand**
- hard/challenging/demanding **work**
- a difficult/challenging/demanding **task**
- a difficult/hard **time/decision**
- a difficult/challenging **question/problem/issue**
- **increasingly/particularly** difficult/hard/challenging/demanding

- **Hard** is slightly less formal than **difficult**; it is used particularly in the structure *hard to see/find/imagine/understand* and in the common phrases *hard work, hard times, have a hard time doing*: *It is hard to see any practical and viable alternative to the state at present.* ◇ *People have a much harder time adapting to uncertainty than to one-time shocks.*
- A **challenging** or a **demanding** task, problem or situation is difficult to deal with; **challenging** can be used in an approving way to describe sth that is difficult but which you hope to achieve or overcome; a **demanding** standard is high and difficult to achieve: *All of these issues serve to ensure an exciting and intellectually challenging environment for human resource practitioners.* ◇ *Only the larger firms are able to meet these increasingly demanding criteria.*

dif·fi·culty /ˈdɪfɪkəlti/ *noun* (*pl.* **-ies**) **1** [C, usually pl., U] a problem; a thing or situation that causes problems: *The opportunity for a buy-out may arise when the firm encounters difficulties.* ◇ **~ for sb/sth** *Difficulties can arise for all the family when one member has memory problems.* ◇ **in ~** *Creditors may protect themselves from severe losses when the company is in financial difficulty.* **2** [U] the state or quality of being hard to do or to understand; the effort that sth involves: **~ of sth** *James did not underestimate the difficulty of the task.* ◇ **~ of doing sth** *The controversy stems from the difficulty of distinguishing between the two species.* ◇ **~ doing sth** *The patient had difficulty sleeping through the night.* ◇ **~ in doing sth** *The person may have difficulty in trusting others.* ◇ **with ~** *Larger groups tend to reach decisions only with great difficulty.* **3** [U] a measure of how difficult sth is: *The total score was 0–8, with a higher score indicating a higher level of difficulty.*

▸ ADJECTIVE + DIFFICULTY **considerable • great • particular** *Once unemployed, older workers often experience considerable difficulties in finding work.* | **severe, serious • main, major • current • inherent • practical • technical • methodological • financial, economic** *These changes often cause serious difficulties for the patient and his family.* ◇ *Childhood economic difficulties can be associated with poorer adult health.*

▸ NOUN + DIFFICULTY **learning • breathing • comprehension** *Even on medication, he continues to experience learning difficulties.*

▸ VERB + DIFFICULTY **encounter, experience, face • have • cause, pose, lead to, present • raise • involve • report • highlight • illustrate • overcome • resolve** *Parts of the health service are facing serious financial difficulties.* ◇ *This graph illustrates the difficulties in trying to assess the effectiveness of sales promotion activities.* | **have** *The social services department considered that her parents would have great difficulty in looking after her.*

▸ DIFFICULTY + VERB **arise • associated with • confronting, facing** *There may be practical difficulties associated with mixed methods research.* ◇ *There are two difficulties confronting this undertaking.*

dif·fract /dɪˈfrækt/ *verb* **~ sth** (*physics*) to make light or other waves bend or spread out when they pass through a narrow opening or across an edge HELP In light, this process causes the light to break into a series of dark and light bands or into the different colours of the SPECTRUM: *Experiments found that a beam of electrons could be diffracted like light.*

dif·frac·tion /dɪˈfrækʃn/ *noun* [U] (*physics*) the process by which light or other waves bend or spread out when they pass through a narrow opening or across an edge: **+ noun** *A number of different structures could produce the same diffraction pattern.* ◇ *Large numbers of proteins have had their three-dimensional structure determined by X-ray diffraction studies.*

dif·fuse[1] /dɪˈfjuːz/ *verb* **1** [I, T] to spread widely in all directions; to spread sth in this way: *Over the next 50 years the technology diffused across Europe.* ◇ **~ sth** *A lack of incentives for diffusing new knowledge generally leads markets to under-invest in research and development.* **2** [I, T] (of a gas or liquid) to become slowly mixed with a substance; to make a gas or liquid become slowly mixed with a substance: **~ through sth** *The rate of reaction is governed by the rate at which the molecules diffuse through the solvent.* ◇ **~ (across sth) (into sth)** *Carbon dioxide from the blood sample diffuses across the membrane into the solution.* ◇ **~ sth (into sth)** *The evaporation rate is controlled by the energy needed to diffuse water vapour into the atmosphere.* **3** [T] **~ sth** to make light shine less brightly by spreading it in many directions: *At all times, the light should be diffused by reflecting it off the ceiling.*

dif·fuse[2] /dɪˈfjuːs/ *adj.* **1** spread over a wide area: *85% of the farmers surveyed thought that diffuse pollution was not a significant problem.* ◇ *As organizations mature they become increasingly diffuse.* ◇ *The distinction between beam and diffuse radiation is important to the design of solar energy collection systems.* **2** not clearly defined: *If a definition is too broad then it becomes simply a diffuse collection of ideas.* ◇ *They managed to translate diffuse concern over social issues into direct political action.* ➲ *compare* VAGUE (1) **3** (*medical*) (of a disease or medical condition) not limited to one part of the body: *He complains of diffuse abdominal pains and cramps.* OPP LOCALIZED

dif·fu·sion /dɪˈfjuːʒn/ *noun* [U] **1** the spreading of sth more widely: *The rate at which a market adopts an innovation is referred to as the process of diffusion.* ◇ **~ of sth** *Environmental policies can accelerate diffusion of specific types of clean energy.* **2** the mixing of substances by the natural movement of their PARTICLES: *The architecture of membranes enhances oxygen diffusion.* ◇ **~ of sth** *The lung has the very large surface area needed for the diffusion of gases between blood and air.* ◇ *Data for the rates of diffusion of various gases from polystyrene pellets at room temperature are shown in Figure 11.2.* **3** the spreading of elements of culture from one region or group to another: *Contemporary challenges to the UN include widespread cultural diffusion resulting in higher expectations.* ◇ **~ of sth** *The diffusion of both people and culture traits has made a significant contribution to the material landscape of much of North America.*

dig /dɪg/ *verb* (**dig·ging, dug, dug** /dʌg/) **1** [T, I] to make a hole in the ground or to move soil from one place to another using your hands, a tool or a machine: **~ sth** *The women would plant the seeds in clusters of six or seven after digging small holes with sticks.* ◇ *During the next 20 years, settlers dug new canals and rapidly established farmlands.* ◇ **~ for sth** *As Commander of the Upper Rhine army, Tiberias employed his troops with digging for silver in the territory.* **2** [T] to remove sth from the ground with a tool: **~ sth (out of/from sth)** *This type of mining uses a huge drill to dig the coal out of the seams.* ◇ **~ sth up** *The jewel may have been dug up within the grounds of Middleham Castle.* **3** [I] **+ adv./prep.** to search in sth in order to find sth: *Large green crabs dig into the sediment in search of food.* ◇ (*figurative*) *Journalists may dig deep into a company's past in the hope of exposing bad practice.*

di·gest /daɪˈdʒest; dɪˈdʒest/ *verb* **1 ~ sth** to break down food in the stomach into substances that the body can use: *The inability to digest lactose is due to reduced activity of the enzyme LPH.* ◇ *Partly digested food leaves the stomach and enters the duodenum.* **2** to apply heat, ENZYMES or a chemical to a substance in order to change its structure or obtain a particular substance: **~ sth** *A protease is added to digest cellular proteins.* ◇ **~ sth with sth** *The separated proteins were digested with trypsin and analysed by mass spectrometry.* **3 ~ sth** to think about a piece of information until you fully understand it and can use it SYN ASSIMILATE (3): *Entrepreneurs need to collect and digest information about business opportunities.*

di·ges·tion /daɪˈdʒestʃən; dɪˈdʒestʃən/ *noun* **1** [U] **~ (of sth)** the body's process of changing food into substances that can be used by the body: *The main digestion of fat occurs in the small intestine.* **2** [C] a person's or an animal's ability to digest food: *Invalids of the period would have received poor advice from their doctors about their digestions.* **3** [U, C] the process of applying heat, ENZYMES or chemicals to a substance in order to change its structure or obtain a particular substance: *Anaerobic digestion can be used to create renewable energy from livestock wastes.* ◇ *The digestions yield comparable results, but both methods may underestimate total phosphorous.*

di·gest·ive /daɪˈdʒestɪv; dɪˈdʒestɪv/ *adj.* [only before noun] connected with the digestion of food: *Digestive enzymes are released from the pancreas when food enters the gut.* ◇ *Changes in the digestive system during ageing are relatively minor.*

digit /ˈdɪdʒɪt/ *noun* **1** any of the numbers from 0 to 9 SYN FIGURE[1] (2): *A sequence of binary digits is transmitted over this channel.* ◇ *Individual differences were found in how people grouped a six-digit telephone number.* ◇ **double ~** *The market saw double digit decline at 18%.* ◇ *In Sweden, inflation went into double digits.* **2** a person's finger, thumb or toe: **+ noun** *Digit anomalies include missing, fused or extra fingers or toes.* **3 ~ (of sth)** a structure like a finger, thumb or toe at the end of the limbs of an animal: *In bats, the digits of the forelimb grow extremely long and support a leathery wing membrane.*

digit·al /ˈdɪdʒɪtl/ *adj.* **1** using a system of receiving and sending information as a series of the numbers one and zero, showing that an electronic signal is there or is not there; connected with computer technology: *Digital technology has shifted photography from a chemical process to an electronic process.* ◇ *The simplest digital signals are obtained when the binary system is used.* ◇ *a digital computer/camera/image* ◇ *the digital age/era/world* ➲ *see also* ANALOGUE[2] (1) **2** (of clocks, watches, etc.) displaying only the appropriate numbers, rather than pointing to numbers from a larger set of numbers; other information displayed in this way: *Many young people tell the time from the digital display on their mobile phone.* **3** connected with a finger or the fingers of the hand: *Apply direct digital pressure to the dressed wound.* ■ **digit·al·ly** /ˈdɪdʒɪtəli/ *adv.*: *The interviews were digitally recorded and professionally transcribed.*

dig·nity /ˈdɪgnəti/ *noun* [U] **1** the fact of being given honour and respect by people: *Make your patients' care your first concern, treating them as individuals and respecting their dignity.* ◇ *Human rights are primarily about human dignity.* **2** a sense of your own importance and value: *The sermons offered words of encouragement that instilled a sense of pride and dignity in the parishioners.* **3** a calm and serious manner that deserves respect: *We all have limitations, many of which we can learn to accept with dignity.*

di·lemma /dɪˈlemə; daɪˈlemə/ *noun* **1** a situation in which a difficult choice has to be made between two options, often when you do not like either option: *Advances in medical science often pose ethical dilemmas for doctors.* ◇ *The International Court of Justice has taken a pragmatic approach in resolving this dilemma.* ◇ **~ of sth** *Marketers face the dilemma of whether to segment the market on a country-by-country basis or a global segment basis.* **2** a difficult situation or problem: *The following discussion explores the practical dilemma of control in greater detail.*

di·lute[1] /daɪˈluːt; *BrE also* daɪˈljuːt/ *verb* **1** [often passive] to make a liquid weaker by adding water or another liquid: **be diluted (with sth)** *The solution was diluted with acetone.* ◇ **be diluted in sth** *The compounds were diluted in 95% ethanol.* ◇ **be diluted by sth** *The two product gases are both combustible, but are diluted by nitrogen.* ◇ **be diluted to sth** *An aliquot of the filtrate was diluted to 10 ml with pure water.* ◇ **be diluted by a factor of sth** *The concentrations were diluted by a factor of 10.* **2 ~ sth** to make sth weaker in force or value by changing it or adding sth SYN DIMINISH (1): *Although the increased risk persisted, the effect was diluted when studies were pooled.* **3** (*business*) to reduce the value of the shares that a particular SHAREHOLDER owns by issuing more shares without increasing the company's ASSETS: *Banks discussed the process of raising fresh funds without diluting existing investors' holdings.*

di·lute[2] /daɪˈluːt; *BrE also* daɪˈljuːt/ *adj.* **1** (*also* **di·luted**) (of a liquid or solution) made weaker by adding water or another liquid: *Very dilute fruit juice is a good alternative to fizzy drinks.* ◇ *Body fluids are relatively dilute.* ◇ *Reagent was added to each diluted protein solution.* **2** (of light, colour or RADIATION) weak: *The solar system is bathed in the very dilute remnants of black-body radiation.*

di·lu·tion /daɪˈluːʃn; *BrE also* daɪˈljuːʃn/ *noun* **1** [U, C] the action or process of making a liquid or solution weaker by adding water or another liquid: *Dilution must be performed before crystals are visible.* ◇ *Successive dilutions halved the concentration each time.* **2** [C] **~ (of sth)** a liquid or solution that has been made weaker by adding water or another liquid: *Serial dilutions of extracts were prepared.* **3** [C] the degree to which a solution has been made weaker by adding water or another liquid: **at a ~ of sth** *The membrane was incubated with antibodies at a dilution of 1:10 000 for one hour.* **4** [U, C] **~ of sth** the action of making sth weaker in force or value: *Under its Brezhnev Doctrine, the Soviet Union would not permit any dilution of Communist rule.* ◇ *The extension of Russia's war front down to the Black Sea was a dilution of troops she could ill afford.* **5** [C, U] **~ of sth** (*business*) a reduction in the value of the shares that a particular SHAREHOLDER owns: *Investors were concerned that the proposed deal would result in a dilution of their shareholdings.*

dim /dɪm/ *adj.* (**dim·mer**, **dim·mest**) **1** not bright: *Even our own naked eyes are very efficient detectors of very dim light.* **2** (of a situation) not giving any reason to have hope; not good: *The prospects of stable democracy in many poorer countries looked dim.* **3** not remembered or imagined clearly SYN VAGUE: *He still retained a dim recollection of the vision.* **4** (of a room or other space) difficult to see in because there is not much light: *Usually the subjects sit in a quiet, dim room in a psychology laboratory.* **5** (of an object or shape) difficult to see because there is not much light: *The flying bird is now a dim speck.*

di·men·sion AWL /daɪˈmenʃn; dɪˈmenʃn/ *noun* **1** [usually pl.] a measurement such as length or height; the size or extent of sth: *Precision measuring instruments measure dimensions to an accuracy of tens of microns.* ◇ *The majesty of the Grand Canyon emanates from the magnitude of its impressive dimensions.* **2** a direction in space that is at an angle of 90° to each of two other directions: *In three dimensions we have latitude, longitude and height above the ground.* **3** a particular feature of sth; a way of thinking about sth SYN ASPECT (1): *Employee safety and health have ethical dimensions.* ◇ **~ of sth** *Delivery time is often an important dimension of quality.* ◇ **~ to sth** *There was a regional dimension to the outbreaks against oppression.* **4** (*technical*) the combination of FUNDAMENTAL quantities, such as mass, length and time, which make up any physical quantity: *Speed has the dimension length divided by time.* ◇ *Width and distance have the same dimension.* ➲ *see also* THREE-DIMENSIONAL, TWO-DIMENSIONAL

▸ ADJECTIVE + DIMENSION **physical** *Table 4.1 lists selective physical dimensions of the large rivers of South East Asia.* | **extra • multiple • spatial • vertical • horizontal** *Incorporating a spatial dimension is important in the analysis of agricultural markets.* ◇ *These two categories are depicted along the horizontal dimension of the grid.* | **key, important • additional • international • ethical • temporal • spiritual • historical • cultural • social • political • normative • affective** *Four key dimensions of risk perceptions were explored:...* ◇ *Emphasis is on the historical dimension of international relations.*

▸ VERB + DIMENSION **have • measure** *The reactor had dimensions 9 m wide, 9.5 m long and 6 m high.* | **add • explore • examine • assess • identify • capture • ignore • represent** *Televised debates added a new dimension to electoral campaigns.* ◇ *The study identified six different dimensions of family well-being, including spending quality time with family members.*

-dimensional AWL /daɪˈmenʃənl; dɪˈmenʃənl/ *combining form* (in adjectives) having the number of dimensions mentioned: *A three-dimensional model is used to simulate temperature and pressure inside the vortex tube.* ➲ *see also* MULTIDIMENSIONAL, THREE-DIMENSIONAL, TWO-DIMENSIONAL

di·min·ish AWL /dɪˈmɪnɪʃ/ *verb* [I, T] to become weaker or less; to make sth become weaker or less SYN REDUCE (1): *With continued treatment, the effects of the disease may diminish.* ◇ **~ in sth** *Rules and regulations may diminish in importance as complex issues call for flexibility and careful judgement.* ◇ **~ sth** *However, this oversight does not diminish the importance of Ingman's study.* ◇ **be diminished by sth** *Coverage of elections was regularly diminished by intensified coverage of other issues.* HELP The law of **diminishing returns** is used to refer to a point at which the level of profits or benefits gained is less than the amount of money or energy spent on sth: *For mammals and birds, providing care for offspring has diminishing returns; selection will favour stopping at the point where the marginal costs start to outweigh the marginal benefits.*

dim·in·ution AWL /ˌdɪmɪˈnjuːʃn; *NAmE* ˌdɪmɪˈnuːʃn/ *noun* **1** [U] the act of reducing sth or of being reduced: **~ (of sth)** *One of the factors that led to some diminution of the independence of nation-states was immigration.* ◇ **~ in sth** *He would be unable to recover damages for diminution in the value of his property.* **2** [C, usually sing.] **~ (of sth)** a reduction; an amount reduced: *The lowest point was probably in the sixth century, with an average diminution of temperature of 1.5°C.* ◇ *The researchers found no evidence of a diminution in the level of racial discrimination.*

diode /ˈdaɪəʊd; *NAmE* ˈdaɪoʊd/ *noun* (*technical*) an electronic device with two TERMINALS, in which the electric current passes in one direction only: *Second-generation optical mouse technology uses a light-emitting diode to illuminate the surface underneath the mouse.*

di·ox·ide /daɪˈɒksaɪd; *NAmE* daɪˈɑːksaɪd/ *noun* [U, C] a substance formed by combining two atoms of OXYGEN and one atom of another chemical element: *Titanium dioxide is a cheap and abundant material that is widely used as a pigment in white paint.* ◇ *As for the remaining elements of the group, the dioxides are all well known.* ➲ *see also* CARBON DIOXIDE

diph·thong /ˈdɪfθɒŋ; ˈdɪpθɒŋ; *NAmE* ˈdɪfθɑːŋ; ˈdɪfθɔːŋ; ˈdɪpθɑːŋ; ˈdɪpθɔːŋ/ *noun* (*phonetics*) a combination of two vowel sounds or vowel letters, for example the sounds /aɪ/ in *pipe* /paɪp/ or the letters *ou* in *doubt*: *The core of the syllable is a vowel or a diphthong.*

dip·loid /ˈdɪplɔɪd/ *adj.* (*biology*) **1** (of a cell) containing two complete sets of CHROMOSOMES, one from each parent: *The egg and sperm nuclei then fuse to form the diploid zygote nucleus.* **2** consisting of diploid cells: *In diploid organisms, two alleles of each gene are present (one on each chromosome of a homologous pair).* ➲ *compare* HAPLOID

dip·lo·macy /dɪˈpləʊməsi; *NAmE* dɪˈploʊməsi/ *noun* [U] the activity of managing relations between different countries; the skill in doing this: *In the eleventh century, the western waterways were the scene of trade, diplomacy and war.* ◇ *Nazzal's essay tells us a great deal about the place of technology in international diplomacy.* ◇ *Skill in diplomacy could not replace skill in war, but the former was essential to final success.*

dip·lo·mat /ˈdɪpləmæt/ *noun* an official whose job is to represent their country in a foreign country: *This strategy was first publicly espoused by an American diplomat, George Kennan, in 1947.*

dip·lo·mat·ic /ˌdɪpləˈmætɪk/ *adj.* connected with managing relations between countries: *Kigali immediately broke off diplomatic relations with France.* ◇ *In August 1922, a formal diplomatic mission from Moscow arrived in Beijing.*

di·pole /ˈdaɪpəʊl; *NAmE* ˈdaɪpoʊl/ *noun* **1** (*physics*) a pair of separated POLES, one positive and one negative: *The North and South poles of a bar magnet form a magnetic dipole.* **2** (*chemistry*) a MOLECULE in which a CONCENTRATION of positive electric charge is separated from a concentration of negative charge: *Water heats up in a microwave oven as the dipoles in the molecules continually realign with the changing electric field.*

dire /ˈdaɪə(r)/ *adj.* (**direr**, **dir·est**) **1** [usually before noun] very serious or urgent: *DNA damage has potentially dire consequences.* ◇ *These agencies make billions of dollars available to nations in dire need of loans.* **2** stating that sth very bad will happen: *More dire warnings were issued the following year.*

dir·ect¹ /dəˈrekt; dɪˈrekt; daɪˈrekt/ *adj.* **1** [usually before noun] happening or done without involving other people or factors; having no one or nothing in between: *The weathering of carbonates has no direct effect on atmospheric CO_2.* ◇ *Many adolescents feel uncomfortable with direct eye contact.* ◇ *China's policy is to augment domestic savings by attracting foreign direct investment.* HELP **Direct cost** describes the costs involved in producing a product, such as raw materials and wages: *In many manufacturing operations, the cost of labour is less than 10% of the total direct manufacturing cost.* HELP **Direct taxation** describes tax that is paid on a person's income or a company's profits, rather than on the goods and services they buy: *The government will earn less from direct taxation because people are not earning.* OPP INDIRECT (1) ➲ *see also* DIRECT ACTION **2** [only before noun] with nothing between sth/sb and the source of light or heat: *In this climate, the best window design is one that minimizes direct sunlight.* **3** [usually before noun] clear and able to be understood in only one way: *There is direct empirical evidence for our common ancestry with other animals.* OPP INDIRECT (3) **4** (*sometimes disapproving*) (of a person or their behaviour) saying what you mean in a way that is honest and that can be understood in only one way SYN FRANK: *The Conservatives were direct in the way they confronted some of the established policy networks.* OPP INDIRECT (4) **5** going in the straightest line between two places without stopping or changing direction: *As shown in Fig. 15.2, the data bit can have a direct path to the output bit.* OPP INDIRECT (5) **6** [only before noun] related through parents and children rather than brothers or sisters: *Mary, Queen of Scots, was also a direct descendant of the first of the Tudors.* **7** [only before noun] **~ quotation** taken from sb's words without being changed: *Direct quotations from interview transcripts highlight particular aspects of these themes.* ■ **direct** *adv.* **~ from/to sb/sth** *The Internet has enabled customers to obtain products and services direct from the producer.*

▸ DIRECT + NOUN **contact** • **access** • **effect, consequence, impact, result** • **influence** • **benefit** • **link, connection, relationship** • **bearing** • **comparison** • **observation** • **measurement** • **involvement** • **interaction** • **experience** • **control** • **discrimination** • **investment** • **cost** • **sale** • **marketing** • **mail** • **election** *The direct economic benefits of industrial heritage tourism may be overstated.* ◇ *Breslow proposed a direct link between the prevalence of obesity and rates of cardiovascular disease.* ◇ *Events in France had a direct bearing on the EU.*

dir·ect² /dəˈrekt; dɪˈrekt; daɪˈrekt/ *verb* **1** [T] to give attention or effort to sth: **~ sth at sth** *So far, little academic attention has been directed at this event.* ◇ **~ sth to/towards sth/sb** *Effort is directed towards places where the invasive species is least abundant.* ◇ **~ attention away from sth/sb** *This focus on language directs attention away from biographical understanding.* **2** [T] to aim sth in a particular direction or at a particular person or object: **~ sth at sb/sth** *A laser pulse directed at the dried protein results in ion formation (Fig. 8.17).* ◇ **~ sth against sb/sth** *The immune attack is directed against intracellular antigens.* ◇ **~ sth to/towards sb/sth** *Blood flow is directed towards the legs.* **3** [T] **~ sth at sb/sth** to aim a comment or criticism at sb/sth: *Deary and Johnson direct three criticisms at this conclusion.* **4** [T] **~ sth** to control or manage sth: *The essence of voluntary action is that it is not directed or controlled by the state.* **5** [T, I] **~ (sb/sth)** to be in charge of actors in a play or film, a group of musicians, etc: *Roome worked on silent films directed by Alfred Hitchcock.* ◇ *Langton directed for the BBC.* **6** [T] **~ sb to sth** to tell or show sb how to reach a place or access sth: *Sir Gawain is finally directed to the Green Chapel.* ◇ *Potential respondents need to be directed to the website containing the questionnaire.* **7** [T] to give an official order or instruction: **~ sb to do sth** *The court directed the trustees not to take steps to enforce the covenant.* ◇ **~ sb that...** *The trial judge directed the jury that a duty of care existed.* ◇ **~ sth** *If the judge directs an acquittal, the trial is over.*

diˌrect ˈaction *noun* [U, C] the use of strikes and protests instead of discussion in order to get what you want: *There have been occasions when groups have felt it necessary to resort to direct action against a law.* ◇ *Most of the people present had never before participated in a non-violent direct action.*

dir·ec·tion /dəˈrekʃn; dɪˈrekʃn; daɪˈrekʃn/ *noun* **1** [C, U] the general position that sb/sth moves or points towards: *Tectonic plates can and do change directions.* ◇ *Wind direction and speed were also recorded.* ◇ **in a/the... ~** *These crystals are all oriented in the same direction.* ◇ **in the ~ of sth** *The sand beds increase in number in the direction of the river.* **2** [C, U] the general way in which sb/sth develops: **~ in sth** *New directions in research have shown how positive and fulfilling life can be for older people.* ◇ **~ for sth** *Finally, we draw implications and suggest directions for future research.* ◇ **~ of sth** *Governors have the capacity to shape the future direction of the school.* ◇ **a step/move in the ~ of sth** *This legislation was a step in the direction of governmental support for working families.* **3** [C] the general position a person or thing comes or develops from: **from... ~** *They approached the issue from opposite directions.* ◇ **from the ~ of sth** *In fact, no evidence has been found for an extra flux of high-energy neutrinos from the direction of the sun.* **4** [U] a purpose; an aim:

Mission statements can provide a sense of direction for employees. **5 directions** [pl.] instructions on how to do sth or how to reach a place: *The duty of the advocate is to investigate the issues and give directions to the client.* **6** [U] the art of managing or guiding sb/sth: *The mayor is expected to provide strategic direction.* ◇ **under the ~ of sb/sth** *These new forms of agriculture required that people work cooperatively, under the direction of some central authority.* IDM *see* PULL[1]

D

dir·ec·tion·al /də'rekʃənl; dɪ'rekʃənl; daɪ'rekʃənl/ *adj.* **1** moving, facing or developing in a particular direction; connected with movement in a particular direction: *This difference in predator behaviour should cause directional selection towards darker red hind wings.* ◇ *Hydrogen bonding is highly directional.* **2** [only before noun] sending or receiving light, radio or sound waves in or from a particular direction or directions: *Although directional microphones are now very efficient, usually much of the sound is lost.*

dir·ect·ive /də'rektɪv; dɪ'rektɪv; daɪ'rektɪv/ *noun* **~ (on sth)** an official instruction: *The government has reserved the right to opt out of aspects of the EU directives on human rights.*

dir·ect·ly /də'rektli; dɪ'rektli; daɪ'rektli/ *adv.* **1** with nothing or no one in between: *The vast majority of drugs interact directly with molecules that are part of cells.* ◇ *In Sweden, county councils are directly elected, but county governors are appointed by the central government.* ◇ *The UN has estimated that transnational companies are directly responsible for half of all emissions of greenhouse gases.* OPP INDIRECTLY (1) **2** immediately SYN STRAIGHT[2] (2): *67% of patients stated that they would have gone directly to hospital if a home visit were not available.* ◇ *I shall proceed directly to an analysis of the results.* **3** exactly: *The reflectivity of charcoal is directly proportional to the temperature at which the charcoal formed.* **4** in a manner that is honest, especially when other people may dislike what you say SYN FRANKLY: *This research directly challenges many previously accepted ideas.* ◇ *The poems deal directly with the Western Front, treating death as the ultimate destroyer.* ◇ *Schrag's image directly addresses the phenomenon of mass death in wartime.* **5** without changing direction or stopping SYN STRAIGHT[2] (2): *The pulse travels directly upwards.* ◇ *Atoms moving directly towards the detector emit radiation observed as being of a shorter wavelength.*

▸ VERB + DIRECTLY **speak • communicate • interact • participate ~ in • relate ~ to • bear ~ on • connect ~ to/with, link ~ to/with • intervene • compete • lead ~ to • measure • obtain • derive (sth) ~ from • act ~ on • feed (sth) ~ into • inject sth ~ into** *These factors bear directly on the success or failure of the therapy.* ◇ *All the power from the PV array is fed directly into the grid.*

▸ DIRECTLY + VERB **affect, impact • influence • link, connect • relate to • interact (with) • involve, concern • benefit • target • observe • test • measure • compare • be ~ correlated with • be ~ elected** *Members of the community who are directly involved with students have a positive view of young people.*

▸ DIRECTLY + ADJECTIVE **related to, connected to • applicable, relevant (to) • proportional to • comparable • observable • attributable to • responsible (for)** *The density of CO_2 is directly related to its solvent power.*

di͵rect 'marketing *noun* [U] the business of selling products or services directly to customers who order by mail, telephone or the Internet instead of going to a shop: *The manager should consider whether or not to use direct marketing as part of the brand's marketing communication.*

di͵rect 'object *noun* **~ (of sth)** (*grammar*) a noun, noun phrase or pronoun that refers to a person or thing that is directly affected by the action of a verb: *A noun can take a determiner, it can be modified by adjectives, and it can function as the subject or direct object of a verb.*

dir·ect·or /də'rektə(r); dɪ'rektə(r); daɪ'rektə(r)/ *noun* **1** one of a group of senior managers who are involved in running a company: *The board should include non-executive directors.* ➲ *see also* MANAGING DIRECTOR **2** a person who is in charge of a particular activity or department in a company, a college, etc: *The marketing director and his team undertook an in-depth analysis of implementation.* ◇ *The community school director oversees the after-school programme.* **3** a person in charge of a film or play who tells the actors and staff what to do: *The Indian film director Ritwik Ghatak focused on important issues related to the Indian public sphere.* ➲ *compare* PRODUCER (3)

dir·ec·tory /də'rektəri; dɪ'rektəri; daɪ'rektəri/ *noun* (*pl.* **-ies**) **1** a book or website containing lists of information, usually in alphabetical order, for example people's telephone numbers or the names and addresses of businesses in a particular area: *The telephone directory was used to locate the telephone numbers of selected households.* **2** (*computing*) a file containing a group of other files or programs in a computer: *The 'LS' command lists all the files in the current directory.*

dirt /dɜːt; *NAmE* dɜːrt/ *noun* [U] **1** any substance that makes sth dirty, for example dust, soil or mud: *First remove any grease or dirt from the surface.* **2** (*especially NAmE*) loose earth or soil: *Pack the dirt firmly round the plants.*

dirty /'dɜːti; *NAmE* 'dɜːrti/ *adj.* (**dirt·ier, dirti·est**) not clean: *Many women worked outside of their homes and they often worked in hot and dirty factories.*

IDM **(do sb's) 'dirty work** (*rather informal*) (to do) the unpleasant or dishonest jobs that sb else does not want to do: *Through much of Ike's presidency, Nixon did the president's political dirty work.*

dis·abil·ity /͵dɪsə'bɪləti/ *noun* (*pl.* **-ies**) **1** [C] a physical or mental condition that means sb cannot use a part of their body completely or easily, or that they cannot learn easily: *Positive legislation can help prevent discrimination against people with disabilities.* ◇ **a physical/mental ~** *The women participating in the study have a physical disability that limits mobility.* **2** [U] the state of not being able to use a part of the body completely or easily; the state of not being able to learn easily: *The prevalence of disability was higher in older Americans than in older Britons.*

dis·able /dɪs'eɪbl/ *verb* **1 ~ sb** to injure or affect sb permanently so that, for example, they cannot walk or cannot use a part of their body: *There are smaller-scale accidents and illnesses that kill or disable individuals.* **2 ~ sth** to make sth unable to work so that it cannot be used: *Global Internet breaches can disable a system infrastructure.*

dis·abled /dɪs'eɪbld/ *adj.* **1** unable to use a part of the body completely or easily because of a physical condition, illness, injury, etc; unable to learn easily: *The provision of social care for disabled people has been a feature of the welfare state.* **2 the disabled** *noun* [pl.] people who are disabled: *Research was conducted on different eligible groups such as the disabled and the elderly.* ➲ *usage note at* DISABILITY

dis·ad·van·tage[1] /͵dɪsəd'vɑːntɪdʒ; *NAmE* ͵dɪsəd'væntɪdʒ/ *noun* [C, U] a factor that makes sb/sth less effective or less likely to succeed; a circumstance that makes a situation difficult: *These disadvantages can be overcome by proper selection and storage of the chemical.* ◇ *The advantages outweigh the disadvantages.* ◇ *Socio-economic disadvantage has been associated with high smoking rates.* ◇ **~ of sth** *A disadvantage of this method is that it relies on an even distribution.* ◇ *However, the fibre has*

WHICH WORD?

Talking about disabilities

- The term **disability** is generally used when referring to a long-term condition which makes it difficult for a person to use part of their body completely or easily: *Interviews with young adults who have grown up with disability focused on their achievement of employment and independent households.* You can also say **physical disability**, **mental disability** or **learning disability**: *Children with dyslexia or other learning disabilities need more attention at school to have the same learning opportunities as others.*
- The expression **disabled people** is often preferred to **the disabled** because it sounds more personal: *The Act requires employers to make 'reasonable adjustments' to ensure that disabled people are not at a disadvantage in the workplace.*
- **Visual impairment** is the term used to refer to conditions which result in a person being either **partially sighted** or **blind**, and which cannot be corrected with glasses or contact lenses. You can also use the term **visually impaired**: *Clinical data included hearing and visual impairments.* ◇ *Visually impaired people may lack confidence out of their normal environment.*
- **Hearing impairment** is the term used to refer to conditions which result in a person having a degree of hearing loss, which in some cases may be improved with a device such as a hearing aid: *An association was made between work as a diver and greater prevalence of significant hearing impairment.* Some people with hearing loss, especially if it is severe and/or they were born with it, prefer the term **deaf** or **Deaf** because they do not consider deafness an impairment: *Members of the Deaf community use Sign Language as their first or preferred language.*

disadvantages of low thermal conductivity and short life span. ◇ **at a ~** *Slow decision-making may put a firm at a competitive disadvantage in a fast-moving market.* ◇ **to sb's ~ | to the ~ of sb** *Children's rights were used to the disadvantage of women.* OPP ADVANTAGE¹ ➲ language bank *at* CRITICAL

dis·ad·van·tage² /ˌdɪsədˈvɑːntɪdʒ; *NAmE* ˌdɪsədˈvæntɪdʒ/ *verb* [T, usually passive] to put sb/sth in a position that is likely to be difficult and that is worse than the position of other people or things: **be disadvantaged (by sth)** *The government claims that the Omo people will not be disadvantaged by the construction of the dam.*

dis·ad·van·taged /ˌdɪsədˈvɑːntɪdʒd; *NAmE* ˌdɪsədˈvæntɪdʒd/ *adj.* **1** not having the things, such as education, or enough money, that people need in order to succeed in life SYN DEPRIVED: *Children from disadvantaged backgrounds succeeded in making up lost ground in arithmetic.* ◇ *A number of specific interventions were identified as most likely to help disadvantaged groups.* ◇ *In most societies of the world, women are economically disadvantaged relative to men.* **2 the disadvantaged** *noun* [pl.] people who are disadvantaged: *Economic inequalities can generate resentment among the disadvantaged.*

dis·ad·van·ta·geous /ˌdɪsædvænˈteɪdʒəs/ *adj.* **~ (to/for sb)** causing sb to be in a worse situation in comparison with other people: *The fall in value of the minimum wage was particularly disadvantageous to women at the bottom of the labour market.* OPP ADVANTAGEOUS

dis·agree /ˌdɪsəˈɡriː/ *verb* **1** [I] to have or express a different opinion from sb else: *Caution is necessary in any case where the medical experts disagree.* ◇ **~ with sth** *We asked respondents to agree or disagree with three statements.* ◇ **~ on sth** *Historians disagree on whether revolution was inevitable.* ◇ **~ about sth** *These are questions about which scholars disagree.* ◇ **~ over sth** *Trainees and consultants disagreed over whether named consultant supervision was required.* ◇ **~ with sb (on/about/over sth)** *They disagree with each other on a number of important issues.* ◇ **~ that...** *Few readers would disagree that 'Don Juan' is a brilliant poetic achievement.* OPP AGREE (1) **2** [I] (of two results or reports) to give different information about the same thing SYN CONFLICT²: **~ (about sth)** *The ancient sources sometimes disagree about the parentage of deities.* ◇ **~ with sth** *Results for the Eocene disagree with those based on the plankton fractionation and boron isotope methods.* OPP AGREE (5)
PHR V **disagree with sth** to disapprove of sth: *The Chinese government may disagree with US management culture.*

dis·agree·ment /ˌdɪsəˈɡriːmənt/ *noun* [U, C] **1** a situation in which people have different opinions about sth and may argue: *Disagreement was resolved through discussion.* ◇ **~ with sb** *Despite major disagreements with Thatcher, Lawson was unassailable.* ◇ **~ between A and B** *Disagreements arose between engineers and managers.* ◇ **~ among sb** *Disagreements among the reviewers were discussed until consensus was reached.* ◇ **~ about sth** *However, there was no disagreement about these general principles themselves.* ◇ **~ as to sth** *There is considerable disagreement as to whether performance pay enhances motivation.* ◇ **~ on sth** *There remains much disagreement on these details.* ◇ **~ over sth** *There has been persistent disagreement over the nature of American frontier settlement.* ◇ **in ~ with sb** *The outgoing head of state had been in disagreement with Brezhnev at this time.* OPP AGREEMENT (2) ➲ thesaurus note *at* DEBATE¹ **2 ~ between A and B** a difference between two or more things, especially when they are expected to be the same: *There is strong disagreement between the two sets of results.* ◇ *The disagreements between the two studies can be explained by the following factors:...*

dis·ap·pear /ˌdɪsəˈpɪə(r); *NAmE* ˌdɪsəˈpɪr/ *verb* **1** [I] to stop existing SYN VANISH: *With this approach, the problem usually disappears.* ◇ *In the Cretaceous period, many species disappeared, including the dinosaurs.* **2** [I] to become impossible to see SYN VANISH: *Images appear and disappear, often flashing across the screen for an instant.* ◇ **+ adv./prep.** *All six men had left the path and disappeared into the forest.* ◇ **~ from view/sight** *He crossed the bridge and disappeared from view.* **3** [I] to become lost or impossible to find SYN VANISH: *Thousands of people disappeared without trace during periods of military rule.* ◇ **~ from sth** *Large numbers of coins and other objects were disappearing from the museum's storerooms.*

dis·ap·pear·ance /ˌdɪsəˈpɪərəns; *NAmE* ˌdɪsəˈpɪrəns/ *noun* [U, C] **1 ~ (of sth)** the process of sth stopping existing: *There are at least two ways of thinking about the disappearance of a traditional way of life.* ◇ *When languages disappear, their disappearances are usually related to the demise of particular groups of people.* **2 ~ (of sb/sth)** the act or the fact of sb/sth becoming lost or impossible to find: *A key sequence of the film involves the early stages of Yumisaka's investigation into the disappearance of Inukai.* ◇ *From 1919 to 2005, there were 1 511 disappearances at sea involving seafarers employed in UK merchant shipping.*

dis·ap·point /ˌdɪsəˈpɔɪnt/ *verb* **1 ~ sb** to make sb feel sad because sth that they hope for or expect to happen does not happen or is not as good as they hoped: *The measure, however, has disappointed reformers.* **2 ~ sth** to prevent sth that sb hopes for from becoming real or true: *The expectations raised by the Wilson Government were quickly disappointed.*

dis·ap·point·ed /ˌdɪsəˈpɔɪntɪd/ *adj.* upset because sth you hoped for has not happened or been as good, successful, etc. as you expected: **~ at/by sth** *Liberals were* *disappointed at the slow pace of social reform.* ◇ **~ with sb/sth** *Some reformers have been disappointed with the progress so far.* ◇ **~ that...** *They were deeply disappointed that the government chose to reject their findings.*

dis·ap·point·ing /ˌdɪsəˈpɔɪntɪŋ/ *adj.* not as good, successful, etc. as you had hoped; making you feel disappointed: *In the 1960s, many experiments were carried out but with disappointing results.* ◇ **~ for sb** *The Liberal Democrat performance in the 2010 election was disappointing for the party.* ◇ **it is ~ (for sb) to do sth** *It is disappointing for authors to receive a rejection letter.* ◇ **it is ~ that...** *It is disappointing that the family as a unit is not questioned or redefined more penetratingly.* ■ **dis·ap·point·ing·ly** /ˌdɪsəˈpɔɪntɪŋli/ *adv.*: *The response rate from the groups targeted was disappointingly low.* ◇ *Disappointingly, the author does not even attempt an answer.*

dis·ap·point·ment /ˌdɪsəˈpɔɪntmənt/ *noun* **1** [U] sadness because sth has not happened or been as good, successful, etc. as you expected or hoped: **~ (with sb/sth)** *Disappointment with the organization can destroy an employee's commitment.* ◇ **~ at sth** *Law enforcement personnel expressed disappointment at the results of previous financial investigations.* ◇ **to sb's ~** *To his disappointment, he found that Whitehead had by then lost interest in studying logic.* **2** [C] a person or thing that is disappointing: *In this respect he was a disappointment.* ◇ **~ to/for sb** *Yeltsin's period of office was a great disappointment to many.*

dis·ap·proval /ˌdɪsəˈpruːvl/ *noun* [U] **~ (of sb/sth)** a feeling that you do not like an idea, an action or sb's behaviour because you think it is bad, not suitable or going to have a bad effect on sb else: *The report expresses clear disapproval of the reporting framework.* OPP APPROVAL (2)

dis·ap·prove /ˌdɪsəˈpruːv/ *verb* **1** [I, T] to have or express the opinion that sb/sth is not good or suitable: **~ of sb/sth** *There were many critics who strongly disapproved of these private negotiations.* ◇ **~ of sb doing sth** *North American Quakers disapproved of their members owning slaves.* ◇ **~ sth** *People often disapprove the change of wording in well-known sacred texts.* OPP APPROVE (3) **2** [T] **sth ~** (*formal*) to officially refuse to agree to a course of action, especially when this prevents it from happening: *Only three applications were disapproved.* OPP APPROVE (1)

dis·ap·prov·ing /ˌdɪsəˈpruːvɪŋ/ *adj.* showing that you do not approve of sb/sth: *Critical reactions ranged from sceptical to openly disapproving.* OPP APPROVING

dis·as·so·ci·ate /ˌdɪsəˈsəʊʃieɪt; ˌdɪsəˈsəʊsieɪt; *NAmE* ˌdɪsəˈsoʊʃieɪt; ˌdɪsəˈsoʊsieɪt/ *verb* = DISSOCIATE (2)

dis·as·so·ci·ation /ˌdɪsəsəʊʃiˈeɪʃn; *NAmE* ˌdɪsəˌsoʊʃiˈeɪʃn/ = DISSOCIATION (2)

dis·as·ter /dɪˈzɑːstə(r); *NAmE* dɪˈzæstər/ *noun* **1** [C] an unexpected event that kills a lot of people or causes a lot of damage SYN CATASTROPHE: *When natural disasters strike, women survivors often suffer the most.* ◇ *The oil spill was a major environmental disaster in which hundreds of miles of coastline were polluted.* ➲ *see also* NATURAL DISASTER **2** [C, U] **~ (for sb/sth)** a very bad situation that causes problems: *Economically, the Revolution was a disaster for France.* ◇ *An unexpected downturn in the business cycle can spell financial disaster.* ◇ *The Egyptian campaign ended in disaster, with the loss of forty thousand men and two hundred ships.*

dis·as·trous /dɪˈzɑːstrəs; *NAmE* dɪˈzæstrəs/ *adj.* very bad, harmful or UNSUCCESSFUL SYN DEVASTATING: *For poorer families, even a small loss in income can have disastrous consequences.* ◇ *The conflict led to a disastrous war that lasted 17 years.*

dis·be·lief /ˌdɪsbɪˈliːf/ *noun* [U] the feeling of not being able to believe sth: *Many among the local population expressed disbelief when the election results were announced.* ◇ **suspend (your) ~** *With this film, there are spectators who refuse to suspend their disbelief.* ➲ *compare* BELIEF

disc (*also* **disk** *especially in NAmE*) /dɪsk/ *noun* **1** a thin flat round object or shape: *About 0.15 ml of this infusion was loaded onto sterile discs, 13 mm in diameter.* ◇ **~ of sth** *The particles of matter form a swirling disc of hot material known as an accretion disc.* **2** = CD, CD-ROM, DVD: **(on) ~** *However, the cost of storing information on disc is very low indeed.* **3** a part of the body that resembles a disc in appearance or shape: *Swelling of the optic disc usually indicates severe hypertension.*

dis·card /dɪsˈkɑːd; *NAmE* dɪsˈkɑːrd/ *verb* to get rid of sth that you no longer want or need: **~ sth** *The weight of discarded fish has been estimated at 25% of total worldwide catches.* ◇ (*figurative*) *Descartes was the first to discard the ancient notion that motion was some type of process.* ◇ **~ sb/sth as sth** *For most radical critics, aesthetics still tends to be discarded as part of the problem rather than part of the solution.*

dis·cern /dɪˈsɜːn; *NAmE* dɪˈsɜːrn/ *verb* (not used in the progressive tenses) **1** to know, recognize or understand sth, especially sth that is not obvious SYN DETECT: **~ sth** *Kant, Hegel and Marx each claimed to discern an overall pattern in human history.* ◇ **~ what/how, etc...** *Scholars today are trying to discern what exactly was involved in this debate.* ◇ **~ that...** *Werner discerned that the time at which a rock had been formed was more important than its composition.* **2 ~ sth** to see or hear sth, but not very clearly SYN MAKE SB/STH OUT: *The organic matter is well decomposed and original plant structures cannot be discerned.*

dis·cern·ible /dɪˈsɜːnəbl; *NAmE* dɪˈsɜːrnəbl/ *adj.* **1** that can be known, recognized or understood, especially despite not being obvious SYN PERCEPTIBLE: *There was no discernible difference in hospital admission rates between the two categories.* **2** that can be seen or heard, but not very clearly SYN PERCEPTIBLE: *The figures on the dial were barely discernible.*

dis·charge¹ /ˈdɪstʃɑːdʒ; *NAmE* ˈdɪstʃɑːrdʒ/ *noun* **1** [U, C] the action of releasing a substance such as a liquid or gas: **~ (of sth) (from sth) (into sth)** *The 1874 Act was designed to prevent the discharge of poisonous gases from the factories into the atmosphere.* ◇ **~ of sth** *Microbial infections of the eyes can lead to a discharge of pus or other fluid.* **2** [U, C] a thick liquid that comes out of a person's body when they are ill: *Symptoms include muscle pains, sore throat, cough and nasal discharge.* ◇ **~ from sth** *A discharge from the ear canal may indicate infection.* **3** [U, C] **~ (from sth)** the act of officially allowing or forcing sb to leave somewhere, especially a hospital or the army: *The patient died soon after discharge from hospital.* ◇ *Delayed discharges are particularly associated with older people with complex needs.* **4** [U] **~ of sth** the act of performing a task or duty: *Trusteeship requires the proper discharge of a number of fundamental duties.*

dis·charge² /dɪsˈtʃɑːdʒ; *NAmE* dɪsˈtʃɑːrdʒ/ *verb* **1** [T, usually passive] **be discharged from sth** to allow or force sb officially to leave a place or organization such as a hospital, prison, army or business: *The patient responded well and was discharged from hospital three days after her operation.* ◇ *Many of those who were discharged from prison soon became homeless.* **2** [T, usually passive, I] to allow a gas or liquid to flow somewhere; (of a gas or liquid) to flow somewhere: **be discharged (by sb/sth) (into sth)** *Pollutants were discharged by chemical companies into the waters of Minamata Bay.* ◇ **~ into sth** *The Amazon discharges directly into the Atlantic Ocean.* **3** [I, T] to release electricity: *At these times the capacitor is discharging, and energy is being transferred to the rest of the circuit.* ◇ **~ sth** *When electric charges build up in clouds past a critical limit, they are discharged to the Earth during* *a thunderstorm.* **4** [T] **~ sth** to do everything that is necessary to perform a particular duty: *President Bush claimed the United States would discharge all its international obligations.* ◇ *Directors should have the knowledge and information to discharge their responsibilities effectively.*

dis·ciple /dɪˈsaɪpl/ *noun* **1** (according to the Bible) one of the people who followed Jesus Christ and his teachings when he was living on earth, especially one of the original group of twelve: *Jesus and his disciples normally kept the sabbath and attended the synagogue.* **2 ~ (of sb)** a person who believes in and follows the teachings of a leader in politics, religion, philosophy, etc. SYN FOLLOWER: *Feuerbach was at first a disciple of Hegel.*

dis·cip·lin·ary /ˈdɪsəplɪnəri; ˌdɪsəˈplɪnəri; *NAmE* ˈdɪsəpləneri/ *adj.* **1** connected with the punishment of people who break rules: *Disciplinary action had been taken against two soldiers.* ◇ *She was dismissed on the ground of gross misconduct following a disciplinary hearing.* **2** connected with a subject of study, especially in a university: *Globalization studies is emerging as a new field that cuts across traditional disciplinary boundaries.*

dis·cip·line[1] /ˈdɪsəplɪn/ *noun* **1** [C] a subject of study, especially in a university: *Scholars from a variety of academic disciplines have commented on these developments.* ◇ **~ of sth** *Of course, Darwin's work sits within the discipline of biology.* **2** [U] the practice of training people to obey rules and behave well: *Most parents prefer schools to impose fairly strict discipline on the students.* ◇ *Lack of fiscal discipline at the federal level is reflected in the federal government's own recurring budget deficits.* **3** [U] the practice of training your mind or body or of controlling your behaviour: *Ramadan is a time for reflection and spiritual discipline.*

dis·cip·line[2] /ˈdɪsəplɪn/ *verb* **1 ~ sb (for sth)** to punish sb for sth they have done: *Workers who consistently fall behind are disciplined or fired.* **2 ~ sb** to train sb, especially a child, to obey particular rules and control the way they behave: *Many parents seem uncertain about how to monitor, guide and discipline their own children.*

dis·cip·lined /ˈdɪsəplɪnd/ *adj.* showing control in the way you behave or work: *They perform their task in a disciplined manner.* ◇ *His themes and style are highly disciplined and often traditional.*

dis·close /dɪsˈkləʊz; *NAmE* dɪsˈkloʊz/ *verb* to give sb information about sth, especially sth that was previously secret SYN REVEAL: **~ sth (to sb)** *There will also be a legal duty on a solicitor to disclose relevant information to his client.* ◇ **~ that...** *He failed to disclose that he had a criminal conviction.* ◇ **~ whether/what, etc...** *The Act requires a statement disclosing whether the audit committee includes a 'financial expert'.*

dis·clo·sure /dɪsˈkləʊʒə(r); *NAmE* dɪsˈkloʊʒər/ *noun* **1** [U] **~ (of sth) (to sb)** the act of making sth known or public that was previously secret or private SYN REVELATION (2): *It is not just disclosure of data to third parties that customers may be concerned about.* **2** [C] **~ (about sb/sth)** information or a fact that is made known or public that was previously secret or private SYN REVELATION (1): *The entire Commission resigned in March 1999 after embarrassing disclosures about mismanagement.*

dis·com·fort /dɪsˈkʌmfət; *NAmE* dɪsˈkʌmfərt/ *noun* **1** [U] a feeling of slight pain or of being physically uncomfortable: *The patient reported no abdominal pain or discomfort.* **2** [U] a feeling of being anxious or embarrassed SYN UNEASE: *If eye contact promotes too much discomfort, it is not empathic.* ◇ **~ with (doing) sth** *A significant proportion of parents said they experienced discomfort with displaying strong emotion.* **3** [C, usually pl.] something that makes you feel uncomfortable or causes you a slight feeling of pain: *He had to live with the tensions and discomforts that his new beliefs produced in him.*

dis·con·tent /ˌdɪskənˈtent/ (*also* **dis·con·tent·ment** /ˌdɪskənˈtentmənt/) *noun* **1** [U] a feeling of being unhappy because you are not satisfied with a particular situation SYN DISSATISFACTION: **~ at/over sth** *There is national discontent over the government's plans for radical cuts in public expenditure.* ◇ **~ with sth** *Doctors' poor communication skills are often at the root of patients' discontent with health care.* **2** [C] **~ (of sb)** a thing that makes you feel unhappy and not satisfied with a particular situation SYN DISSATISFACTION: *The very real discontents of millions of Chinese were not heard.*

dis·con·tinue /ˌdɪskənˈtɪnjuː/ *verb* **~ sth** to stop doing, using or providing sth: *The prosecutor decided to discontinue the case and drop all charges.* ◇ *Drugs that contain dopamine should not be abruptly discontinued or withdrawn.* ◇ *The production of chlorofluorocarbons (CFCs) was discontinued in the early 1990s.*

dis·con·tinu·ity /ˌdɪsˌkɒntɪˈnjuːəti; *NAmE* ˌdɪsˌkɑːntəˈnuːəti/ *noun* (*pl.* **-ies**) **1** [C] a break or change in a continuous process: **~ in sth** *Changes in government have resulted in discontinuities in policy.* ◇ **~ between A and B** *The presence of colluvium above weathered rock creates a discontinuity between the two types of material.* OPP CONTINUITY (2) **2** [U] the state of not being continuous: **~ in sth** *discontinuity in the children's education.* ◇ **~ between A and B** *There is no significant discontinuity between modern and primitive societies.* OPP CONTINUITY (1)

dis·con·tinu·ous /ˌdɪskənˈtɪnjuəs/ *adj.* not continuous; stopping and starting again SYN INTERMITTENT: *Wars, civil strife and political intransigence are but a few reasons why records may be discontinuous.*

dis·count[1] /ˈdɪskaʊnt/ *noun* [C, U] **~ (on/off sth)** an amount of money that is taken off the usual cost of sth SYN REDUCTION (3): *Similarly, mobile phone companies offer discounts on long-term contracts.* ◇ *The effective price that a rival needs to sell at is equivalent to a 40% discount off the list price.* ◇ *A dissatisfied shareholder can sell his shares at a fair price and without discount.*

dis·count[2] /dɪsˈkaʊnt; *NAmE also* ˈdɪskaʊnt/ *verb* **1** to regard a possibility or fact as not worth considering because it is not important or not true SYN DISMISS (2): **~ sth** *It is not possible to discount the possibility that smoking is a causal factor.* ◇ **~ sth as sth** *Such patients discount any success as a chance happening for which they can take no credit.* **2 ~ sth** to take an amount of money off the usual cost of sth; to sell sth at a DISCOUNT SYN REDUCE (1): *Managers will need to consider discounting their prices to promote sales.* ◇ *Shoppers assume that because these items are discounted, all other items must be too.*

ˈ**discount rate** *noun* (*finance*) the minimum interest rate set by the US Federal Reserve (and some other national banks) for lending to other banks: *To fight the recession, Fed Chairman Greenspan brought down the discount rate from 6.5% to 1.75% within the course of a single year.*

dis·cour·age /dɪsˈkʌrɪdʒ; *NAmE* dɪsˈkɜːrɪdʒ/ *verb* **1** to try to prevent sth from happening or to prevent sb from doing sth, especially by making it difficult to do or by showing that you do not approve of it: **~ sth** *The plan is designed to discourage the use of private cars.* ◇ *It is true that advertising has helped discourage drunken driving.* ◇ **~ sb (from doing sth)** *Corporations did these things to discourage their workers from joining unions.* OPP ENCOURAGE (2) **2** to make sb feel less confident or enthusiastic about doing sth: **~ sb** *Economic and political risks have discouraged foreign investors.* ◇ **~ sth** *Higher interest rates will discourage borrowing and spending.* ◇ **~ sb from doing sth** *These drugs may have adverse effects that discourage patients from continuing treatment.* OPP ENCOURAGE (1) ■ **dis·cour·aged** *adj.* [not usually before

D

noun] *Teachers became discouraged, and returned to more conventional methods.* **dis·cour·aging** *adj.*: *The government's attitude is highly discouraging.* OPP ENCOURAGING

dis·course /ˈdɪskɔːs; *NAmE* ˈdɪskɔːrs/ *noun* **1** [U, C] written or spoken communication, especially a discussion within society about a serious subject: **in... ~** *McPherson observes that in Australian discourse 'otherness' is perceived negatively.* ◇ **~ about/on sth** *Parents in this study had concerns that related closely to the public discourse about the dangers of childhood.* ◇ **~ of sth** *Taylor explores several themes within the new discourses of identity and multiculturalism.* **2** [U, C] a point of view shared by a group, expressed through writing, speech or art: **in... ~** *Schreiber demonstrates how counter-feminism exploits the weaknesses in feminist discourse.* ◇ **~ about sth** *Painters provided images of peasants that shaped competing discourses about the nature of rural life.* **3** [C] a long, serious talk or piece of writing that discusses a subject: *The book looks more like an extended PowerPoint presentation than an academic discourse.* ◇ **~ on/about sth** *The many recent discourses on sexuality share a common focus on 'truth-telling'.* **4** [U] (*linguistics*) the use of language in speech and writing in order to produce meaning: *Research suggests that up to 70% of language (spoken and written discourse) is comprised of fixed expressions.* HELP In linguistics, spoken and written **discourse** is studied, usually in order to see how the different parts of a text are connected.

▸ ADJECTIVE + DISCOURSE **critical** • **academic, scholarly** • **theoretical** • **scientific** • **religious** • **political** *Modern critical discourses on ancient Greece have also been influenced by cinema.* | **contemporary** • **prevailing** • **dominant** • **official** • **public** • **popular** • **rational** • **democratic** • **colonial** • **nationalist** • **feminist** *The dominant Western discourse that sees third-world women as passive has been challenged by feminists.*

▸ VERB + DISCOURSE **shape** • **dominate** • **challenge** • **analyse** *These organizations have played a major role in shaping global policy discourse on Africa.*

dis·cover /dɪˈskʌvə(r)/ *verb* **1** to find some new information about sth: **~ sth** *From the data, they discovered evidence of sex discrimination.* ◇ **~ (that)...** *The police discovered that bribes had been paid to top officials.* ◇ **~ how/what, etc...** *Much research has aimed at discovering how using the Internet affects our social interactions.* ◇ **it is discovered that...** *It was discovered that he had defrauded the company.* ◇ **sb/sth is discovered to be/have...** *Many people were discovered to be practising the old religion in secret.* **2 ~ sth** to be the first person to realize that a particular thing or place exists: *In 1985, Kroto and Smalley discovered a new form of carbon.* ◇ *At this time, Europeans began to 'discover' what they called the 'New World'.* **3 ~ sb/sth** to find sb/sth that was hidden or that you did not expect to find: *The data shows that only 40% of these impact craters may have been discovered.* ◇ *The latest writing of Maslow, discovered after his death, counters this claim.* ■ **dis·cov·er·er** *noun*: *This whole process, known as the Calvin cycle after its discoverer, is shown in Fig.18.10.*

dis·cov·ery /dɪˈskʌvəri/ *noun* (*pl.* **-ies**) **1** [C, U] an act or the process of finding sb/sth, or learning about sth that was not known about before: **~ of sth** *Crick and Watson are best known for their discovery of the structure of DNA.* ◇ *Chiasson claims the Chinese established a colony on Cape Breton Island following the discovery of gold.* ◇ **~ (that...)** *This led to the groundbreaking discovery that human somatic cells can be reprogrammed.* ◇ **~ about sth/sb** *They have used genetics to make discoveries about the biology of behaviour.* **2** [C] a thing, fact or person that is found or learned about for the first time: *New discoveries and advances are usually published first in journals.* ◇ *Important discoveries have arisen from visualizing information in map form.*

dis·credit /dɪsˈkredɪt/ *verb* **1 ~ sb/sth** to make people stop respecting sb/sth: *He quietly took every opportunity to discredit rivals.* ◇ *Reimarus was not the first to attempt to discredit orthodox Christianity.* **2 ~ sth** to make people stop believing that sth is true; to make sth appear unlikely to be true: *Both industries have sought to discredit evidence about the harm caused by their products.*

dis·crep·ancy /dɪsˈkrepənsi/ *noun* (*pl.* **-ies**) a difference between two or more things that should be the same: **~ between A and B** *This research aims to explain the discrepancies between economic results and accountancy results.* ◇ **~ in sth** *To understand the apparent discrepancy in the results, it is necessary to consider the techniques used to create the models.*

dis·crete AWL /dɪˈskriːt/ *adj.* independent of other things of the same type SYN SEPARATE[1]: *It is usual to divide resources into two discrete categories: stock resources and renewable resources.* ◇ *The code is written as a series of discrete units, the genes, down the length of the chromosome.* ◇ *DNA replication can be described as a series of discrete steps.* ■ **dis·crete·ly** AWL *adv.*: *Qualitative data from the first questionnaire were analysed and similar data were categorized and discretely grouped.*

disˌcrete ˈvariable *noun* = CATEGORICAL VARIABLE

dis·cre·tion AWL /dɪˈskreʃn/ *noun* **1** [U, sing.] the freedom or power to decide what should be done in a particular situation: *Employees need the skills and motivation to use their discretion to make decisions.* ◇ *In the decisions relating to leave to appeal, the courts have exercised their discretion on a case by case basis.* ◇ *Trustees have a wide discretion to act as they think fit.* ◇ **~ of sb** *In Russia, the education of serfs was left to the discretion of serf-owners.* **2** [U] **~ (of sb)** care in what you say or do, in order to keep sth secret or to avoid causing EMBARRASSMENT to or difficulty for sb: *Politicians used to rely on the discretion of elite society to prevent the disclosure of their affairs.*

IDM **at sb's disˈcretion** according to what sb decides or wishes to do: *The period may be extended at the court's discretion.*

dis·cre·tion·ary AWL /dɪˈskreʃənəri; *NAmE* dɪˈskreʃəneri/ *adj.* [usually before noun] decided according to the judgement of a person in authority about what is necessary in each particular situation; not decided by rules: *Statutes often confer wide discretionary powers on ministers and officials.*

dis·crim·in·ate AWL /dɪˈskrɪmɪneɪt/ *verb* **1** [I, T] to recognize that there is a difference between people or things; to show a difference between people or things SYN DIFFERENTIATE (1), DISTINGUISH (1): **~ between A and B** *After a training phase, the bats were able to discriminate between an oscillating and a motionless target.* ◇ **~ among sb/sth** *The real test of a model is whether it discriminates among alternative explanations of a phenomenon.* ◇ **~ A from B** *The technique can discriminate disease from a healthy state.* ◇ **~ sth** *These parent birds are able to discriminate and reject parasitic eggs.* **2** [I] to treat one person or group worse/better than another in an unfair way: **~ against sb** *Welfare rules discriminated against those who had a husband present.* ◇ **~ in favour of sb** *The legislation discriminates in favour of women by requiring women-only shortlists.* ◇ **~ (against sb) on the grounds/basis of sth** *The applicant claimed to have been discriminated against on the grounds of her disability.*

dis·crim·in·at·ing AWL /dɪˈskrɪmɪneɪtɪŋ/ *adj.* (*approving*) able to judge the good quality of sth: *These plays were written to entertain a wide, largely uneducated though discriminating audience.*

dis·crim·in·ation AWL /dɪˌskrɪmɪˈneɪʃn/ *noun* **1** [U] the practice of treating sb or a particular group in society less fairly than others: *Respondents were asked whether they had experienced any racial discrimination.* ◇ **~ against sb** *There is compelling evidence that discrimination against Asian Americans is not uncommon in US society.* ◇ **~ in favour of sb** *Discrimination in favour of deprived groups can reduce these health inequalities.* ◇ **~ on the grounds of sth** *She claimed discrimination on the grounds of disability.* HELP **Positive discrimination** is discrimination in favour of a particular group, defined by their race, sex, age, etc, in order to make results for all groups in society more equal. In the US this policy is called **affirmative action**: *A commitment to equal opportunities and positive discrimination offers virtually the only chance of breaking the cycle of disadvantage.* **2** [U, C] the ability to recognize a difference between one thing and another; a difference that is recognized: **~ of sth** *These functions of the eye aid in discrimination of closely spaced objects.* ◇ **~ between A and B** *It is a sacred text that emphasizes discriminations between wholesome and unwholesome things.*

dis·crim·in·atory /dɪˈskrɪmɪnətəri; *NAmE* dɪˈskrɪmɪnətɔːri/ *adj.* treating sb or one group of people worse than others in an unfair way: *Discriminatory practices based on religion and ethnicity tend to correlate with violent conflicts.* ◇ *Both countries enacted racially discriminatory immigration laws.*

dis·cur·sive /dɪsˈkɜːsɪv; *NAmE* dɪsˈkɜːrsɪv/ *adj.* **1** (of a style of writing or speaking) moving from one point or subject to another without any strict structure: *The discipline of statistics was characterized by discursive explorations of data before becoming more mathematical in the early 20th century.* **2** connected with written or spoken communication: *Ideology can never be absent from literature, any more than it can be absent from any discursive practice.*

dis·cuss /dɪˈskʌs/ *verb* **1** to write or talk about sth in detail, showing the different ideas and opinions about it: **~ sth** *Chapter 7 will discuss two important ethical issues.* ◇ *Segmentation of fan surfaces is discussed by Cooke et al. (1993, pp.19–184).* ◇ **~ how/what, etc...** *Brown's article critically discusses how marketing theory has developed over the last fifty years.* ➲ language bank *at* ABOUT² **2** to talk about sth with sb, especially in order to decide sth or in order to increase knowledge or understanding: **~ sth with sb** *His family did not discuss his sister's illness with him.* ◇ **~ sth** *The students were hesitant about discussing personal issues in groups.* ◇ **~ how/why, etc...** *The focus group participants discussed how people view media reporting of social science research.* HELP You cannot say 'discuss about sth'. Look also at **discussion**.

▸ DISCUSS + NOUN **issue, topic, matter, subject • problem** *This topic is discussed in greater detail in Chapter 14.* ◇ *The committee met fortnightly to discuss financial matters.* | **question • theme • idea, concept • principle • aspect • option • way • method • strategy, approach • mechanism • example • case • role • reasons • result, findings • implications • possibility • importance** *We conclude by discussing the implications of our findings.*

▸ ADVERB + DISCUSS **previously, already, just • much, extensively • widely • frequently, often • never • further • fully • openly • explicitly** *The theme of the decline of ideology was much discussed in the late 1950s and 1960s.* ◇ *Ageing is often discussed in the context of increasing vulnerability to disease.*

▸ DISCUSS + ADVERB **above, earlier, before, previously • below, next, later, shortly • here • elsewhere • in detail, further, more fully, at length, extensively • briefly** *The research findings discussed above have a number of messages about effective teacher practices.*

dis·cus·sion /dɪˈskʌʃn/ *noun* [C, U] **1** a speech or a piece of writing that discusses many different aspects of a subject: **~ of sth** *See Section 4.6 for a critical discussion of the most recent theories.* ◇ **~ on/about sth** *There has been considerable discussion in the literature on the possible effects of IV iron.* **2** a conversation about sb/sth; the process of discussing sb/sth: **~ (with sb) (about/on sb/sth)** *Researchers conducted group discussions with teachers and students.* ◇ *The doctor had a second discussion with him about the need to change his diet.* ◇ **~ between people** *Disagreements were resolved by discussion between the authors.* ◇ **~ of sth** *The management meeting began with an open and honest discussion of the problems facing the company.* ◇ **for ~** *These are both important issues for discussion.* HELP If sth is **under discussion**, it is being talked about so that a decision can be made: *The proposal is still under discussion, as the deadline is not until next month.*

▸ ADJECTIVE + DISCUSSION **earlier, previous, preceding, foregoing • recent • present • ongoing • following, subsequent, ensuing • detailed, in-depth, thorough, comprehensive, full • broad • lengthy, extensive, extended • much • further • brief • little • interesting • excellent • online • public • theoretical • philosophical** *As the preceding discussion suggests, some groups have developed very successful innovations.* ◇ *He provides little discussion of how his findings might extend the theory.* | **open, frank • heated • informal** *His lab mates were engaged in a heated discussion in another corner of the lab.*

▸ VERB + DISCUSSION **stimulate, encourage, prompt, promote, generate • facilitate • start, initiate • participate in, engage in, be involved in • present, provide • continue • conclude • recall • inform • include • focus • limit, confine, restrict • frame • see • dominate** *The authors hope these suggestions will stimulate further discussion about the dangers of the new tests.* ◇ *Two conceptual frameworks will inform the discussion of the findings.* | **have, conduct, hold** *She conducted group discussion with community members to gauge reactions to draft research reports.*

THESAURUS

discussion • debate • dialogue • talks • consultation *noun*
These words all refer to the fact that sth is being discussed.

- discussion/debate/dialogue/talks/consultation **on/about** sth
- discussion **of** sth
- discussions/dialogue/talks **with** sb/**between** A and B
- to **hold** discussions/consultations/talks
- sb is **in** consultation **with** sb
- sth is **under** discussion

- **Discussion**, **debate**, **consultation** and **dialogue** can involve discussing sth on more than one occasion; **talks** are a specific event: *The last decade has seen much public discussion of immigration policy.* ◇ *There is ongoing debate on the extent of these challenges.* ◇ *The government offered to hold talks about the constitution.*
- **Dialogue** is often used when only two groups of people are involved: *There are no formal mechanisms by which a dialogue between the two institutions can be initiated.*
- **Consultation** and **debate** can both refer to an organized process or meeting; **consultation** implies that information is shared, whereas a **debate** involves presenting opposing opinions: *Guidelines were drafted in consultation with experts in the US.* ◇ *This point was also highlighted in Parliamentary debates.*

dis·ease /dɪˈziːz/ *noun* [U, C] an illness of the body in humans, animals or plants: *Natural disasters are frequently followed by the spread of infectious disease.* ◇ *Many serious diseases affected the chances of infant survival.* ◇ **with... ~** *The risks are significantly higher for patients with*

cardiovascular disease. ◇ **+ noun** *The emphasis is on disease prevention and health promotion.*
▸ ADJECTIVE + DISEASE **rare • common • chronic • severe, serious • advanced • underlying • infectious, communicable • sexually transmitted • non-communicable • genetic • congenital • degenerative • occupational • autoimmune • inflammatory • respiratory • coronary, cardiovascular, cardiac • renal • pulmonary • human** *In the past, many chronic diseases were managed mainly by the hospital sector.* ◇ *A complete physical examination failed to detect any underlying disease.*
▸ NOUN + DISEASE **heart • lung • liver • kidney • bowel • thyroid** *Chronic anger has been shown to be strongly associated with certain forms of heart disease.*
▸ VERB + DISEASE **cause • spread, transmit • contract, catch, get • have • inherit • develop • diagnose, detect • suspect • indicate, suggest • treat • cure • combat • eradicate, eliminate • control • manage • prevent** *There was a 70 per cent chance of dying within six months of contracting the disease.* ◇ *In terms of the dengue virus, more research is necessary to effectively control, diagnose and treat the disease.*
▸ DISEASE + VERB **progress • spread • affect • cause • be characterized by • be associated with** *His disease gradually progressed and he died in hospital a year later.*
▸ DISEASE + NOUN **susceptibility • prevention • incidence • outbreak • onset • progression • transmission • severity • burden • surveillance • management** *Early intervention has been shown to delay disease progression.*

THESAURUS

disease • illness • infection • disorder • condition *noun*

These are all words for a medical problem.

- a **chronic/serious** disease/illness/infection/disorder/condition
- a **mental/psychiatric** illness/disorder
- a **medical/health/physical** condition
- to **cause/have/develop** a/an disease/illness/infection/disorder/condition
- to **prevent/diagnose/treat** a/an disease/illness/infection
- the **symptoms/treatment of** a/an disease/illness/infection/disorder/condition

- **Disease** is used to talk about more severe physical medical problems, especially those that affect the organs; **illness** is used to talk about both severe and more minor medical problems; a **condition** is a medical problem you have for a long time because it is not possible to cure it: *heart/kidney/liver disease* ◇ *Even minor illnesses, notably the common cold, have a major economic impact through absences from work.* ◇ *The number of people living with long-term health conditions has risen.*
- **Illness** and **disorder** are used to talk about mental health problems as well as physical problems: *Some of these women have a history of psychiatric illness.* ◇ *Depression is one of the most common mental disorders in Western societies.*
- An **infection** is caused by bacteria or a virus; a **disease** is often caused by an **infection**; a **disorder** is usually not infectious: *Viral infections may be acquired from health care settings.* ◇ *This is a rare disorder caused by adrenocortical insufficiency.*

dis·eased /dɪˈziːzd/ *adj.* suffering from a disease: *One cell has been taken from healthy tissue, and one from diseased tissue.*

dis·equi·lib·rium /ˌdɪsˌiːkwɪˈlɪbriəm; ˌdɪsˌekwɪˈlɪbriəm/ *noun* [U] a loss or lack of balance in a situation: *The increase in the value of money in the hands of the public creates disequilibrium in the money market.*

dis·guise¹ /dɪsˈɡaɪz/ *verb* **1** to hide the true nature of sth so that it cannot be recognized SYN CONCEAL: **~ sth** *This generalized overview disguises significant differences between countries.* ◇ **~ the fact that...** *Some travel authors made no attempt to disguise the fact that their stories were invented.* ◇ **thinly disguised** *The novel has thinly disguised autobiographical elements.* **2 ~ sb/yourself (as sb/sth)** to change your appearance so that people cannot recognize you: *The king would disguise himself as a beggar in order to discover what his subjects were thinking.*

dis·guise² /dɪsˈɡaɪz/ *noun* [C, U] a thing that you wear or use to change your appearance so that people do not recognize you: *He immediately threw off his disguise and seized the weapons nearest to hand.* ◇ **in ~** *He is helped by a strange bearded man who turns out to be his daughter Edwina in disguise.*

dish /dɪʃ/ *noun* **1** a flat shallow container used for cooking food or serving it from: *a baking/serving dish* **2** a flat shallow container used in laboratories for growing CULTURES: *Nematodes are usually cultivated on solid agar medium in plastic Petri dishes.* ◇ *The cells were collected from the culture dish with a cell scraper.*

dis·hon·est /dɪsˈɒnɪst; *NAmE* dɪsˈɑːnɪst/ *adj.* not honest; intending to deceive people: *There are, very rarely, dishonest scientists who cheat and make up their data.* ◇ *Different people have different views of what constitutes dishonest conduct.* OPP HONEST ■ **dis·hon·est·ly** *adv.*: *He was accused of dishonestly obtaining a benefit by giving false information.* **dis·hon·esty** *noun* [U] *In fact, cases of dishonesty are not unknown in the biosciences.*

dis·in·ter·est·ed /dɪsˈɪntrəstɪd; dɪsˈɪntrestɪd/ *adj.* not influenced by personal feelings or by the chance of getting some advantage for yourself SYN IMPARTIAL, OBJECTIVE², UNBIASED: *Valuations should be checked by disinterested third parties.*

disk /dɪsk/ *noun* **1** a device for storing data on a computer, with a MAGNETIC surface that records data in electronic form: *In just two decades, the capacity of hard disks in PCs has increased by a factor of 40 000.* ◇ *Physically smaller disk drives were initially inferior in performance.* ◇ **onto/on ~** *Some video cameras record directly onto disk.* ◇ **+ noun** *Digital video files require a lot of disk space for storage.* **2** (*especially NAmE*) = DISC

ˈdisk drive (*also* **drive**) *noun* a part of a computer that reads and stores data in a form so that it is kept even when the power is turned off: *Smaller disk drives soon surpassed the larger ones.*

dis·like¹ /dɪsˈlaɪk/ *verb* to not like sb/sth: **~ sb/sth** *When participants were finished with the experiment, we asked them what they liked or disliked about the game.* ◇ **~ doing sth** *One view is that humans are naturally lazy, and therefore dislike doing things that require effort.*

dis·like² /dɪsˈlaɪk/ *noun* **1** [U, sing.] a feeling of not liking sb/sth: **~ (of sb/sth)** *We do not know if Martial attempted a legal career: he certainly expressed dislike of the idea.* ◇ **~ for sb/sth** *Nixon had developed a strong dislike for Kissinger, and was planning to replace him as National Security Adviser.* **2** [C, usually pl.] a thing that you do not like: *Ensure that dietitians are in regular contact to determine the patient's likes and dislikes.*

dis·miss /dɪsˈmɪs/ *verb* **1** to officially remove sb from their job, especially because of bad work or bad behaviour SYN FIRE² (2): **~ sb** *Before the Industrial Relations Act of 1971, an employer could dismiss a worker for any reason.* ◇ **~ sb from sth** *What are the rights of an employee who is unfairly dismissed from a company that then goes out of business?* **2** to decide that sb/sth is not important and not worth thinking or talking about: **~ sth** *Frank dismissed the claim that Jews should embrace the American melting pot theory.* ◇ **~ sb/sth as sth** *Some retailers have dismissed loyalty programmes as an expensive gimmick.*

3 ~ sth to put thoughts or feelings out of your mind: *We cannot dismiss these concerns entirely.* **4 ~ sth** (*law*) to say that a trial or legal case should not continue, often because there is not enough evidence: *The magistrate dismissed the case.* ◇ *The defendant's appeal was dismissed.*

dis·missal /dɪsˈmɪsl/ *noun* **1** [U, C] the act of dismissing sb from their job; an example of this: *The Court of Session held that the claimant was entitled to claim unfair dismissal.* ◇ *Economic, technical or organizational reasons enable the employer to justify a dismissal as being 'potentially' fair.* **2** [U] **~ (of sth) (as sth)** the failure to consider sth as important or worth considering: *The government's immediate dismissal of the report as biased demonstrates that there is no chance of a serious reversal of policy.* **3** [U, C] **~ (of sth)** (*law*) the act of not allowing a trial or legal case to continue, usually because there is not enough evidence: *The appeals court upheld the dismissal of the case by the lower court.*

dis·obedi·ence /ˌdɪsəˈbiːdiəns/ *noun* [U] **~ (to sb/sth)** the act of refusing or failing to obey rules or sb in authority: *Parliament could have decided to have him executed for disobedience to the king.*

dis·order /dɪsˈɔːdə(r); *NAmE* dɪsˈɔːrdər/ *noun* **1** [C, U] an illness that causes the body or the mind to stop working correctly: *One in five of these teenagers has an eating disorder* ◇ *Younger homeless women had the highest risk of mental disorder.* ➲ *see also* PERSONALITY DISORDER ➲ thesaurus note *at* DISEASE **2** [U] violent behaviour of large groups of people: *This essay will evaluate a variety of strategies to reduce crime and disorder.* ◇ *The Chief Constable believed that the assembly might lead to serious public disorder.* ➲ *compare* ORDER[1] (3) **3** [U] confusion; a lack of order or organization: **in ~** *Much of China was still in disorder in the aftermath of the Cultural Revolution.* OPP ORDER[1]

dis·ordered /dɪsˈɔːdəd; *NAmE* dɪsˈɔːrdərd/ *adj.* **1** showing a lack of order or control; not arranged in an organized way: *His symptoms are only one aspect of a disordered family life.* ◇ *The tendency of things to become more disordered represents a fundamental physical law—the second law of thermodynamics.* OPP ORDERED **2** (*medical*) suffering from a mental or physical illness: *Most shoplifters act for gain but a minority do so when mentally disordered.*

dis·or·gan·ized (*BrE also* **-ised**) /dɪsˈɔːɡənaɪzd; *NAmE* dɪsˈɔːrɡənaɪzd/ *adj.* not organized or controlled well; not able to plan or organize well: *Her school work is disorganized and contains many careless errors.* ◇ *Other symptoms include disorganized thinking and incoherent speech.* ➲ *compare* ORGANIZED ■ **dis·or·gan·iza·tion, -isa·tion** /dɪsˌɔːɡənaɪˈzeɪʃn; *NAmE* dɪsˌɔːrɡənəˈzeɪʃn/ *noun* [U] *Residents were frustrated by delays and perceived disorganization.*

dis·par·ate /ˈdɪspərət/ *adj.* **1** [usually before noun] (of two or more things or people) completely different from others that are being mentioned, considered or dealt with: *A vast amount of seemingly disparate data is brought together.* ◇ *Coordinating the system's disparate elements is a complex task.* ◇ *Religion was a unifying force, bringing together previously disparate tribes.* ◇ *This will affect policy in areas as disparate as trade, development and immigration.* **2** [only before noun] made up of parts or people that are very different from each other: *The residents had become a disparate group of isolated individuals.*

dis·par·ity /dɪˈspærəti/ *noun* (*pl.* **-ies**) [U, C] a difference, especially one that is considered unfair: *Reducing health disparities is a goal of the project.* ◇ **~ of sth** *He reported disparities of income and living conditions across the city.* ◇ **~ between A and B** *There is no disparity between the two groups of households in their level of education and their ethnicity.* ◇ **~ in sth** *Significant racial disparities in pregnancy outcomes persist.* ◇ **~ among sb** *There is great racial and ethnic disparity among prisoners.*

dis·pel /dɪˈspel/ *verb* (**-ll-**) **~ sth** to get rid of a false belief or bad feeling: *This study sets out to dispel two common misconceptions.* ◇ *This should dispel doubts and encourage greater support.*

dis·pense /dɪˈspens/ *verb* **1** to provide sth, usually sth that is intended to help people: **~ sth** *The courts must retain public confidence in their ability to dispense justice.* ◇ **~ sth to sb** *Their duty was to dispense advice to clients.* **2 ~ sth** to prepare medicine and give it to people: *The regulations allow private clinics to dispense prescriptions.* ◇ *They keep a record of the drugs dispensed.* **3 ~ sth** (of a machine) to provide money, food, drink, etc: *If the customer is sufficiently in funds, cash will be dispensed.* ◇ *The machine dispenses a range of drinks and snacks.*
PHR V **diˈspense with sb/sth** to not use or stop using sb/sth; to get rid of sb/sth: *The court can dispense with the consent of parents if the welfare of the child requires it.*

dis·pers·al /dɪˈspɜːsl; *NAmE* dɪˈspɜːrsl/ *noun* [U, C] the process of sending sb/sth in different directions or spreading sth over a wide area: **~ (of sb/sth)** *Chaos followed the forced dispersal of the refugee population.* ◇ **+ noun** *In this case, seed dispersal distances are short.*

dis·perse /dɪˈspɜːs; *NAmE* dɪˈspɜːrs/ *verb* **1** [I, T] to move apart and go away in different directions; to make sb/sth do this: *The Achaean army destroyed Troy and then dispersed, each group returning to its own homeland.* ◇ **~ sb/sth** *A wind arose which dispersed the smoke.* ◇ *The massed force of Swiss soldiers succeeded in dispersing the knights.* **2** [I, T] **~ (sth)** to spread over a wide area; to make sth spread over a wide area SYN SCATTER[1] (4): *Indo-European language and culture dispersed widely from its likely origins north of the Black Sea.* ◇ *Trade and colonization dispersed Greek goods far beyond the limits known to the Bronze Age traders.*

dis·persed /dɪˈspɜːst; *NAmE* dɪˈspɜːrst/ *adj.* spread over a wide area SYN SCATTERED: *The traders are in dispersed locations around the world.* ◇ *Most gene families are not clustered but are instead dispersed throughout the genome.* ◇ *Today's workforce is often geographically dispersed.*

dis·per·sion /dɪˈspɜːʃn; *NAmE* dɪˈspɜːrʒn/ *noun* (*technical*) **1** [U] **~ (of sth)** the process by which people or things are spread over a wide area; the fact of being spread over a wide area: *The effects of turbulence include the unsteady dispersion of smoke plumes.* ◇ *Due to the wide geographical dispersion of affected farms, it was difficult to gather information.* **2** [C] a mixture of one substance evenly mixed into another: *The solid dispersions we investigated were prepared by solvent evaporation and co-precipitation using several techniques.* ◇ **~ of sth** *The dispersion of sulfur dioxide from coal burning power stations from one country to other countries was increased by strong winds.*

dis·place AWL /dɪsˈpleɪs/ *verb* [often passive] **1 ~ sb/sth** to take the place of sb/sth SYN REPLACE (1): *There were extensive areas of Russia where grain had been displaced by beans and clover.* ◇ *They measured the volume of gas displaced by the piston.* ◇ *European institutions are increasingly displacing national institutions as the principal drivers of policy change.* **2 ~ sb** to force people to move away from their home to another place: *Half a million people were displaced by the war.* ◇ *In 2008, there were some 42 million forcibly displaced people in the world.* **3** to remove sb from a job or position: **~ sb** *New technology not only displaced workers but also replaced their skills.* ◇ **~ sb as sth** *In 1975, Edward Heath was displaced as leader of the Conservative Party by Margaret Thatcher.* **4 ~ sth (+ adv./prep.)** to move sth from its usual position: *In five billion years, the sun will have been displaced into an orbit four times further from the centre of the Milky Way.*

D

dis·place·ment AWL /dɪsˈpleɪsmənt/ *noun* **1** [U] the act of displacing sb/sth; the process of being displaced: *The article describes these refugees' experience of displacement and resettlement.* ◇ **~ of sb/sth** *Material then flowed from beneath the ocean to beneath the continents, causing upward displacement of the continents.* **2** [U, sing.] **~ (of sth)** (*physics*) the distance between the final and INITIAL (= first) positions of an object which has moved: *The displacement of a particle that experienced a force was five metres.*

D

dis·play¹ AWL /dɪˈspleɪ/ *verb* **1** [T] to put sth in a place where people can see it easily; to show sth to people SYN EXHIBIT¹ (2): **~ sth** *Cigarette cartons are required by law to display the notice that 'Smoking Kills'.* ◇ *The university prominently displays its quality rankings on its website.* ◇ **~ sth to sb** *The film aimed to display a positive face of Japan to the rest of the world.* **2** [T] **~ sth** to show signs of sth, especially a quality, characteristic or feeling: *The patient displayed no signs of life.* ◇ *The statistics for beef consumption in the UK display a similar pattern.* **3** [T] **~ sth** (of a computer, notice, table, etc.) to show information: *The web interface allows multiple 3D images to be displayed at the same time.* ◇ *CO_2 emissions for global and Indian conditions are displayed in Table 3.* **4** [I] (of male birds and animals) to show a special pattern of behaviour that is intended to attract a female bird or animal: *The male birds spent several hours each day displaying.*

dis·play² AWL /dɪˈspleɪ/ *noun* **1** [C] an arrangement of things in a public place to give information or entertain people or advertise sth for sale: *Attractive window displays helped to increase sales.* ◇ **~ of sth** *The government organized a stunning display of modern technology at the exhibition.* ◇ **~ about sth** *The exhibits will include interactive displays about energy efficient heating.* HELP Things that are **on display** are put in a place where people can look at them: *The manuscripts were brought back to Britain and put on public display.* ➲ *compare* SHOW² (3) **2** [C, U] **~ of sth** behaviour that shows a particular quality, feeling or ability: *He attempts to dazzle his readers with displays of cleverness.* ◇ *Sutton and Rafaeli (1988) found a surprising relationship between sales and the display of positive emotion by staff.* **3** [U] **~ of sth** the act of placing sth in a public place for people to see: *The court ruled that the display of a crucifix in classrooms was illegal.* **4** [C] **~ (of sth)** an act of performing a skill or of showing sth happening, in order to entertain: *Displays of horsemanship were part of Kababish culture.* **5** [C, U] **~ (of sth)** a special pattern of behaviour that a male bird or animal shows in order to attract a female bird or animal: *The complex courtship displays of different bird species were much described at the time.*

dis·pos·able AWL /dɪˈspəʊzəbl; *NAmE* dɪˈspoʊzəbl/ *adj.* [usually before noun] **1** made to be thrown away after use: *Disposable gloves must be worn when handling fluid samples.* **2** (of income) available for use: *As children grow up and leave home, so the needs of the parents change and their disposable income increases.*

dis·posal AWL /dɪˈspəʊzl; *NAmE* dɪˈspoʊzl/ *noun* [U] **1** the act of getting rid of sth: *The use of estuaries for human waste disposal has led to many environmental problems.* ◇ **~ (of sth)** *Citizens can be expected to ask questions about plans for safe disposal of nuclear waste.* ◇ **+ noun** *Disposal sites for solid waste material now occupy thousands of hectares of land.* **2 ~ (of sth)** the sale or transfer of sth that belongs to sb/sth, such as property: *He left no will regarding the disposal of his property.* ◇ *Capital gains tax is charged on gains arising from the disposal of assets by individuals and trustees.*
IDM **at your/sb's disposal | at the disposal of sb** available to be used: *The parliamentary opposition has a number of resources at its disposal.* ◇ *There is now a computerized database at the disposal of police and customs officers in the Schengen area.*

dis·pose AWL /dɪˈspəʊz; *NAmE* dɪˈspoʊz/ *verb*
PHR V **diˈspose of sb/sth** **1** to get rid of sb/sth that you do not want or cannot keep: *Unsold stocks of an older model become more difficult to dispose of after the launch of a new one.* ◇ *Disposing of mixed waste in a landfill is one means by which urban garbage is handled.* **2** to sell or transfer control of sth that belongs to sb/sth: *If the loan is unpaid, the lender will be able to dispose of the property.* ◇ *The company's assets may not be disposed of unless a court authorizes such actions.*

dis·posed AWL /dɪˈspəʊzd; *NAmE* dɪˈspoʊzd/ *adj.* [not before noun] **1 ~ to do sth** likely or willing to do sth: *Clients are now more disposed to switch service firms in search of savings or better service.* ◇ *Courts are not generally disposed to order an 'out of court' settlement.* **2** (following an adverb) having a particular opinion of a person or thing: **~ to sb/sth** *The European Parliament is generally well disposed to environmental initiatives.* ◇ **~ towards sb/sth** *The assumption is that people will be more favourably disposed towards those with a similar personality profile.*

dis·pos·ition /ˌdɪspəˈzɪʃn/ *noun* **1** [C, U] the natural qualities of a person's character: *This permits fairly good assessments of individual dispositions and preferences.* ◇ *Psychological disposition has limited bearing on disease outcome.* **2** [C] a tendency to behave in a particular way, or to have a particular opinion: **~ to do sth** *Conservatives have a generalized disposition to dislike change.* ◇ **~ towards/to sth** *There was generally a favourable disposition towards presidential legislative initiatives.* **3** [C, U] **~ (of sth)** (*technical*) the way sth is placed or arranged; the fact of sth being placed somewhere: *The geologist records the structural disposition of the rock layers.* ◇ *The disposition of muscles and tendons is more intricate.* **4** [C, U] (*law*) a formal act of giving property or money to sb: *The law demands that charitable dispositions be for the public benefit.* ◇ *The land was inspected at the time of disposition.* ◇ **~ of sth** *This is a tax which affects the disposition of assets on death.*

dis·pro·por·tion·ate AWL /ˌdɪsprəˈpɔːʃənət; *NAmE* ˌdɪsprəˈpɔːrʃənət/ *adj.* too large or too small when compared with sth else: *A disproportionate amount of the nation's poor live in rural areas.* ◇ **~ to sth** *The damage to civilian objects was clearly disproportionate to the military advantage gained.* ➲ *compare* PROPORTIONATE
■ **dis·pro·por·tion·ately** AWL *adv.*: *Minority groups are disproportionately affected by obesity at all ages.*

dis·prove /ˌdɪsˈpruːv/ *verb* **~ sth** to show that sth is false or that sth does not exist: *It is not easy to see how a claim like this could be either proved or disproved.* ◇ *This hypothesis was quickly disproved by experiment.* OPP PROVE (1)

dis·pute¹ /dɪˈspjuːt; ˈdɪspjuːt/ *noun* [C, U] an argument or a disagreement between two people, groups or countries; discussion about a subject where there is disagreement: *China has developed new structures and processes for resolving commercial disputes.* ◇ *a trade/family dispute* ◇ *a legal/political/industrial/territorial dispute* ◇ *Inevitably, disputes will arise between parties subject to the regulations.* ◇ **~ between A and B** *Students and adults may work together to settle disputes between students and teachers.* ◇ **~ over/about sth** *By the eighteenth century, rulers were becoming involved in disputes over land, population and commerce.* ◇ **in ~** *If both parties are still in dispute, they may seek to use a mediator.* ◇ **+ noun** *The second part of the article deals with dispute resolution.* ➲ thesaurus note *at* DEBATE¹

dis·pute² /dɪˈspjuːt/ *verb* **1** to question whether sth is true and valid: **~ sth** *Few observers would dispute the fact that public services have improved radically in recent years.* ◇ *The evidence from Canada strongly disputes the* *claim that multiculturalism promotes political instability.* ◇ **~ that...** *No one would dispute that flexibility is needed.* ◇ **~ whether/how, etc...** *Many have disputed how widely such power laws apply (Bilham, 2004).* ◇ **it is disputed whether/how, etc...** *It is disputed whether moral theory should guide legislation.* ➲ thesaurus note *at* CHALLENGE[2] **2** [often passive] to argue or disagree strongly with sb about sth, especially about who owns sth: **be disputed** *The impact of these measures was hotly disputed at the time.* ◇ **be disputed between A and B** *Northwards was territory that would be disputed between the Scots and the English for many centuries to come.*

dis·qual·ify /dɪsˈkwɒlɪfaɪ; *NAmE* dɪsˈkwɑːlɪfaɪ/ *verb* (**dis·quali·fies, dis·quali·fy·ing, dis·quali·fied, dis·quali·fied**) **1** to prevent sb from being or doing sth because they have broken a rule or are not suitable SYN BAR[2]: **~ sb** *The court must disqualify a director if his conduct renders him unfit.* ◇ **~ sb from (doing) sth** *Certain persons are disqualified from acting as trustees of charitable trusts.* **2 ~ sth (from sth/from being sth)** to cause sth not to belong in a particular group: *An inability to fly does not automatically disqualify a creature from membership in the category of birds.* ■ **dis·quali·fi·ca·tion** /dɪsˌkwɒlɪfɪˈkeɪʃn; *NAmE* dɪsˌkwɑːlɪfɪˈkeɪʃn/ *noun* [U, C] *The minimum period of disqualification is two years.* ◇ **~ to (doing) sth** *There are few formal disqualifications to taking a seat in the House of Commons.*

dis·re·gard[1] /ˌdɪsrɪˈɡɑːd; *NAmE* ˌdɪsrɪˈɡɑːrd/ *verb* **~ sth** to not consider sth; to treat sth as unimportant SYN IGNORE: *These studies confirmed the importance of behavioural differences that were previously disregarded.* ◇ *In general, such warnings were either disregarded or dismissed.* ◇ *One cannot simply disregard the fact that...* ◇ *Previous studies have focused on consent in clinical trials, disregarding other types of research.*

dis·re·gard[2] /ˌdɪsrɪˈɡɑːd; *NAmE* ˌdɪsrɪˈɡɑːrd/ *noun* [sing., U] the act of treating sb/sth as unimportant and not caring about them or it; the act of ignoring sth: **~ for sb/sth** *His actions show a callous disregard for her life and welfare.* ◇ **(in) ~ of sth** *They made copies of protected works in disregard of the rights of the copyright owners.*

dis·rupt /dɪsˈrʌpt/ *verb* **1 ~ sth** to make it difficult for sth to act or continue in the normal way: *The beginning of war between Holland and Britain severely disrupted trade.* ◇ *Demographic growth was disrupted by wars, famine and epidemics.* **2 ~ sth** to change or destroy the structure of sth: *A mutation disrupts the normal function of a gene.*

dis·rup·tion /dɪsˈrʌpʃn/ *noun* [U, C] a situation when it is difficult for sth to continue in the normal way; the act of stopping sth from continuing in the normal way: **~ to sth/sb** *Chance events can cause disruption to an existing thriving business environment.* ◇ *There is a need to make provision for these pupils while minimizing disruption to others.* ◇ *Participants expressed concerns about how they would get to work if there were disruptions to public transport.* ◇ **~ of sth** *Protracted disruption of economic activity will cause long-term losses.*

dis·rup·tive /dɪsˈrʌptɪv/ *adj.* **1** causing problems so that sth cannot continue in the normal way: *Some students were sent home early for disruptive behaviour.* ◇ *He drew attention to the disruptive effects of rapid urbanization.* ◇ *Army Intelligence deployed over a thousand agents to gather information on potentially disruptive groups.* **2** new, and changing the way that people do things: *The fuel cell is widely described as a disruptive technology.*

dis·sat·is·fac·tion /ˌdɪsˌsætɪsˈfækʃn/ *noun* [U, C] a feeling that you are not pleased or satisfied, because sth is not as good as you expected: *Causes of job dissatisfaction need to be addressed.* ◇ *Any concerns or dissatisfactions were noted to be discussed later.* ◇ **~ with sth** *She expressed dissatisfaction with the level of detail.* ◇ **~ at sth** *There was widespread dissatisfaction at the slow pace of change.* OPP SATISFACTION (1)

dis·sat·is·fied /dɪsˈsætɪsfaɪd; dɪˈsætɪsfaɪd/ *adj.* not pleased or satisfied with sb/sth because they are/it is not as good as you expected: *Dissatisfied customers are unlikely to come back.* ◇ **~ with sth** *Employers are increasingly dissatisfied with the quality of graduates.* OPP SATISFIED (1)

D

dis·sem·in·ate /dɪˈsemɪneɪt/ *verb* **~ sth** to spread information or knowledge so that it reaches many people: *These organizations disseminate useful information and provide expert advice on international issues and problems.* ◇ *English is the means to access, produce and disseminate knowledge in US research communities.* ◇ *There seemed to be a lot of support for Putnam's ideas, which were widely disseminated.*

dis·sem·in·ation /dɪˌsemɪˈneɪʃn/ *noun* [U] the act of spreading knowledge or information: **~ (of sth)** *The major mode of dissemination of research throughout the sciences is the refereed journal article.* ◇ **+ noun** *Social networking proved to be an effective information dissemination tool during the crisis.*

dis·sent[1] /dɪˈsent/ *noun* [U] the fact of having or expressing opinions that are different from those that are officially accepted or given: *Sometimes political dissent was violently suppressed.* ◇ *A judgment issued without dissent increases the weight of the judicial decision.* ◇ **~ from sth** *Of course a member may express his dissent from any decision by voting against the resolution in question.* HELP In law, a **dissent** is a statement by a judge giving reasons as to why he or she disagrees with a decision made by the other judges in a legal case: *Justice Kerr, in a further separate dissent, held that moral guilt and harm caused were two separate considerations.*

dis·sent[2] /dɪˈsent/ *verb* [I] **~ (from sth)** to have or express opinions that are different from those that are officially accepted or given: *Seven of the committee's 16 members dissented from this view.* HELP In law, judges **dissent** when they state formally that they disagree with a decision made by the other judges in a legal case: *The Supreme Court handed down a 7-2 decision, with only Justices Scalia and Thomas dissenting.* ■ **dis·sent·ing** *adj.*: *There have been occasional dissenting voices over the years.* ◇ *a dissenting judge/judgment*

dis·ser·ta·tion /ˌdɪsəˈteɪʃn; *NAmE* dɪsərˈteɪʃn/ *noun* a long piece of writing on a particular subject, especially one written for a university degree: *She recently completed a doctoral dissertation at the University of Toronto.* ◇ **~ on sth** *He wrote his dissertation on the effects of sunlight on animals.*

dis·simi·lar AWL /dɪˈsɪmɪlə(r)/ *adj.* not the same as sb/sth else: **~ to sb/sth** *Market conditions abroad are often dissimilar to those in the home country.* ◇ *Birds are physiologically dissimilar to mammals.* ◇ **~ from sb/sth** *Many invertebrates are so dissimilar from humans that there is no real identification with them.* OPP SIMILAR ■ **dis·simi·lar·ity** /ˌdɪsɪmɪˈlærəti/ *noun* (*pl.* **-ies**) [U, C] *An increasing number of studies point to the role of genetic dissimilarity.* ◇ **~ between A and B** *There are similarities and dissimilarities between electric and magnetic fields.*

dis·si·pate /ˈdɪsɪpeɪt/ *verb* **1** [I, T] to become weaker and then disappear; to make this happen: *The dust storm formed and dissipated quickly.* ◇ *The effects of many health interventions dissipate over time.* ◇ **~ sth** *This particular worry has since been dissipated.* **2** [T] (*physics*) to cause energy to be lost or changed to a form that is not useful: **~ sth** *Heat was dissipated by convection and radiation.* ◇ *The topography influences how the wave energy is dissipated along the shoreline.* ◇ **~ sth as sth** *Computers dissipate energy as heat.* **3** [T] **~ sth** (*usually disapproving*) to use up or waste money or resources: *War and internal conflict are dissipating resources that ought to be invested elswhere.*

dis·si·pa·tion /ˌdɪsɪˈpeɪʃn/ *noun* [U] **1** the fact or process of becoming weaker or more spread out, or of disappearing: *Cloud formation and dissipation is rapid and widespread in the troposphere.* **2** (*physics*) the changing of energy into a different form that is not useful, in a way that cannot be REVERSED: *Thermal inertia is based upon the physical properties of heat dissipation whereby larger objects retain heat for longer than smaller objects.* ◇ **~ of sth** *They studied the dissipation of wave, tidal and current energy across the broad, gently dipping sea floor.*

D

dis·so·ci·ate /dɪˈsəʊʃieɪt; dɪˈsəʊsieɪt; *NAmE* dɪˈsoʊʃieɪt; dɪˈsoʊsieɪt/ *verb* **1** [T] **~ sth (from sth)** to think of two things as separate and not connected with each other: *This holistic framework of analysis does not dissociate behaviour from its context.* OPP ASSOCIATE[1] (1) **2** (*also* **dis·as·so·ci·ate**) [T] **~ yourself/sb from sb/sth** to say or show that you, or other people, are not involved with or do not support sb/sth: *He explicitly dissociates himself from their ideas.* OPP ASSOCIATE[1] (3) **3** [I, T] (*chemistry*) (of a MOLECULE) to split into separate smaller atoms, IONS or molecules, especially when this process can be REVERSED; to make a molecule do this: *Weak acids are only slightly dissociated into their ions in solution.* ◇ **~ from sth** *In the liver, bilirubin dissociates from albumin.* ◇ **~ sth** *The salt can be considered to be fully dissociated in solution.*

dis·so·ci·ation /dɪˌsəʊʃiˈeɪʃn; *NAmE* dɪˌsoʊʃiˈeɪʃn/ *noun* **1** [U] **~ (to sth)** (*chemistry*) the process of a MOLECULE dissociating: *At sufficiently high temperatures, dissociation to atomic H occurs.* **2** (*also* **dis·as·so·ci·ation**) [U, C] the fact or feeling of being separate or not related: **~ from sth** *The drug induces feelings of dissociation from the surroundings.* ◇ **~ between A and B** *A dissociation was found between conscious and unconscious perception.*

dis·sol·ution /ˌdɪsəˈluːʃn/ *noun* [U] **1** the act of officially ending an agreeement or organization: *The feud persisted right up to the Soviet Union's dissolution in 1991.* ◇ **~ of sth** *This led to the dissolution of the marriage.* ◇ *A general election in the UK is preceded by the dissolution of Parliament.* ◇ *Three main patterns for the dissolution of business groups were observed.* **2** the process in which sth is removed or destroyed, or disappears: **~ of sth** *Dissolution of calcium carbonate under these conditions is slow.* ◇ **+ noun** *Mineral dissolution rates are typically fastest at higher temperatures.* **3** the process in which a solid mixes with a liquid and becomes part of it; the process of dissolving or being dissolved: *Some polymers are subject to dissolution or swelling when in contact with solvents or fluids in commercial applications.* ◇ **~ in sth** *The sample should ideally be prepared by dissolution in methanol.*

dis·solve /dɪˈzɒlv; *NAmE* dɪˈzɑːlv/ *verb* **1** [I] (of a solid or a gas) to mix with a liquid and become part of it: *Reactions were run until the cellulose had dissolved completely.* ◇ **~ in sth** *Carbon dioxide dissolves in water to form carbonic acid.* **2** [T] to make a solid or a gas become part of a liquid: **~ sth** *It is generally more difficult to find a solvent that will dissolve a polymer than it is to find a solvent for a small molecule.* ◇ **~ sth in sth** *The sample for analysis was dissolved in a solvent, such as acetone or methanol.* **3** [T] **~ sth** to officially end a marriage or other legal agreement, or a parliament or similar organization: *The marriage was dissolved in 1921.* ◇ *Upon his May 1981 presidential victory, he dissolved the National Assembly.*

dis·tal /ˈdɪstl/ *adj.* (*anatomy, technical*) located away from the centre of the body; at the far end of sth: *The distal end of a structure such as a limb is furthest away from the point of attachment to the body.* ◇ **~ to sth** *Patients usually complain of immediate severe discomfort distal to the site of injection.* OPP PROXIMAL

dis·tance[1] /ˈdɪstəns/ *noun* **1** [C, U] the amount of space between two places or things: *Waves travel great distances in deep water with little energy loss.* ◇ **~ between A and B** *The shortest distance between two points on a flat surface is a straight line.* ◇ **~ from sth** *Population decline was most evident in areas at greater distances from urban centres.* ◇ *The electron probability, or density, varies with distance from the nucleus.* ◇ **~ to sth** *By determining the distance to at least three satellites, the receiver can compute its position using triangulation.* ◇ **~ of sth** *The rift extends from the Alpine front at Basle for a distance of 440 km.* ➲ *see also* LONG-DISTANCE **2** [C, usually sing., U] **~ (between A and B)** a difference or lack of a connection between two things or people: *Hierarchy creates a relational distance between people.* ◇ *The genetic distance between species represents a measure of the time elapsed since these species diverged.* **3** [U, C] **~ (from sb/sth)** a situation in which there is a lack of friendly feelings or of a close relationship between two people or groups of people: *Steroids and hormonal therapy can cause patients to experience emotional distance from others.* ◇ *In these years, Scotland's sense of distance from England probably increased.*

IDM **at/from a ˈdistance** from a place or time that is not near; from far away: *The location of the boundary between the formations can be difficult to determine, both from a distance and from close range.* ◇ *Telecommunications technologies can allow people to maintain friendships at a distance.* **in/into the ˈdistance** far away but still able to be seen or heard: *The hillside is covered with tea estates and low buildings in the distance.* ◇ *The camera movement finishes on a close-up of Bradbury gazing into the distance.*

▸ ADJECTIVE + DISTANCE **long, great, large, considerable** • **short** • **maximum** • **minimum** • **average** • **horizontal** • **vertical** • **perpendicular** • **geographic, geographical** • **physical** *The average annual distance travelled by a car in the EU is 15 000 km.*

▸ VERB + DISTANCE **travel, move, cover** • **measure** • **estimate** • **calculate** *Long legs may allow ants to cover greater distances more efficiently.*

dis·tance[2] /ˈdɪstəns/ *verb* **~ yourself/sb/sth (from sb/sth)** to become less involved or connected with sb/sth; to make sb become less involved or connected with sb/sth: *Labour was keen to distance itself from the tax and spend policies that were seen as the core of the welfare state.* ◇ *As medical students become absorbed into the profession, they become more distanced from the people that they are meant to be serving.*

dis·tant /ˈdɪstənt/ *adj.* **1** far away in space or time SYN REMOTE (2): *In astronomy, distant objects are very faint.* ◇ *The Internet allowed geographically distant people to collaborate with people unknown to them.* ◇ **the ~ past** *At some point in the distant past, there must have been a transition from a mixture of reactive molecules to the formation of life.* ◇ **the ~ future** *Nuclear fusion holds promise as a commercially viable source of power in the distant future.* ◇ **the not too ~ future** *There seems little doubt that the law will be reformed in the not too distant future.* **2** [only before noun] not closely related: *At about this time Weber became engaged to Marianne Schnitger, a distant cousin.* ◇ *Most bacteria are capable of acquiring novel genes by horizontal transfer from close or distant relatives.* ◇ *Mitochondria are descended from free-living bacteria that became incorporated within the cells of a very distant ancestor.* **3** not like sth else; different from what is usual: *The more culturally distant two firms are, the greater the differences in their organizational and administrative practices.* ◇ *Global environmental problems, especially climate change, no longer seem distant or 'foreign' to most US citizens.* ◇ **~ from sth** *Simultaneous listening and reading may be especially suited to learners whose L1 is distant from English.* **4 ~ (with sb)** not friendly; not wanting a close relationship with sb: *There may be problems with* *motivation when managers become more distant with their staff.* ◇ *Wives struggled to overcome the emotionally distant behaviour of their returning husbands as they adjusted to civilian life after the war.*

dis·tinct AWL /dɪ'stɪŋkt/ *adj.* **1** clearly different or of a different kind: *The paper identifies four distinct forms of customer complaints.* ◇ *Insects and crustaceans are distinct groups of arthropods that have evolved from a common ancestor.* ◇ **~ from sth** *The study of sales management has remained quite distinct from the study of consumer behaviour.* ◇ **as ~ from sth** *Each employee has agreed to act in the furtherance of the corporation's interests, as distinct from their own.* **2** [only before noun] used to emphasize that you think an idea or situation definitely exists and is important SYN DEFINITE (1): *A hill was a distinct advantage to a city-state.* ◇ *Gilbert and Mulkay noticed a distinct difference between the ways in which the scientists presented their work in formal and informal contexts.* ◇ *If she had gone into hospital two weeks earlier, there was a distinct possibility that they might have saved her.* **3** easily or clearly heard, seen or felt: *The flowers appear white, without any distinct pattern.* ◇ *This paper seeks to draw a clear and distinct line between the requirements for marketing products and services.*

▸ DISTINCT + NOUN **group, set, category • type, form, kind • phase, stage • way • identity • area, region • entity • part** *The study was conducted in two distinct phases.* ◇ *A dialect is a distinct way of using a given language that is not always comprehensible to other speakers of that language.* | **advantage • difference • possibility • lack** *There has been a distinct lack of research into aspects of corporate governance in small companies.*

▸ ADVERB + DISTINCT **quite, entirely • clearly • functionally • physically** *These two fields of study are quite distinct.*

dis·tinc·tion AWL /dɪ'stɪŋkʃn/ *noun* **1** [C] a clear difference, especially between people or things that are similar or related: *These distinctions are often blurred in the literature.* ◇ **~ between A and B** *The Companies Act 2006 recognizes a distinction between two different types of company.* ◇ *Jaworski makes a fundamental distinction between formal and informal control systems.* ◇ *There is an important distinction between internal energy on the one hand, and heat and work on the other.* **2** [U] the division of people or things into different groups: **~ (of sth)** *This method allowed the distinction of different development strategies of the root systems adopted by neighbour species.* ◇ **~ between A and B** *Soldiers made no distinction between the wounded based on nationality, and many Germans donated money for both French and German prisoners of war.* ◇ **without ~ (of sth)** *The captain of every vessel at sea has the duty to provide aid to all people in distress without distinction of status or conditions.* **3** [sing.] **~ of being/doing sth** the quality of being sth that is special: *The Puerto Rico Trench holds the distinction of being the deepest part of the Atlantic Ocean.* ◇ *The Iberian Lynx has the dubious distinction of being the most critically endangered cat species.* ◇ *The only Spartans who earned the distinction of having their names inscribed on tombstones were those who had died in childbirth or in battle.* **4** [U, C] a special mark, grade or award that is given to sb, especially a student, for excellent work: **(with) ~** *He has just finished a mathematics degree from the University of York, graduating with first class honours with distinction.*

▸ ADJECTIVE + DISTINCTION **important • key, crucial • clear, sharp • fundamental, basic • fine • traditional • useful • conceptual** *Table 10.2 indicates the key distinctions between the supervisory board and the management board.* ◇ *Professionals draw fairly clear distinctions between traditional and modern irrigation systems.*

▸ VERB + DISTINCTION **make, draw • note • blur • maintain • introduce • recognize • emphasize** *Gronroos (1981) draws a distinction between what he sees as the strategic and tactical levels of internal marketing.* ◇ *Developments in computer technology in the late 1990s further blurred the distinction between hardware and software.*

dis·tinct·ive AWL /dɪ'stɪŋktɪv/ *adj.* having a quality or characteristic that makes sth different and easily noticed SYN CHARACTERISTIC²: *Ancient China, India and Rome all had their own distinctive international societies.* ◇ *A distinctive feature of genetic modification is that it can rapidly produce qualitatively major genetic changes.* ◇ **~ about sb/sth** *The authors examine the question of what is distinctive about theatre as an art form.* ■ **dis·tinct·ive·ly** AWL *adv.*: *In Jamaica, decolonization in the realms of politics and government has followed a distinctively Jamaican path.*

▸ DISTINCTIVE + NOUN **feature, characteristic • character • type • form • nature • pattern • way • approach • contribution • culture** *Both sets of stem cells have distinctive patterns of gene expression.* ◇ *Baron, Hannan and Burton (2001) identify five distinctive approaches to organizing work and motivating employees.*

dis·tinct·ly AWL /dɪ'stɪŋktli/ *adv.* in a way that is clear and easily noticed; showing a clear difference: *Baumann (1996) discusses the idea that societies comprise distinctly different groups of people.* ◇ *Public spending tends to be distinctly higher amongst the rich countries of Western Europe and distinctly lower in the United States.*

dis·tin·guish /dɪ'stɪŋgwɪʃ/ *verb* **1** [I, T] to recognize or show the difference between two people or things SYN DIFFERENTIATE (1): **~ between A and B** *The FDA regulations distinguished between safe drugs that could be sold and dangerous ones that could not.* ◇ *Because of the small rural sample size, it was impossible to distinguish clearly between different types of rural areas.* ◇ **~ A from B** *Depressive symptoms have to be distinguished from a depressive disorder, such as major depression.* ◇ **~ A and B** *Edelman and Tononi distinguish two types of consciousness.* ◇ *Featherstone (1995) distinguishes local folk cultures and a global popular culture.* **2** [T] (not used in the progressive tenses) to be a characteristic that makes two people, animals or things different SYN DIFFERENTIATE (3): **~ (A from B)** *Competition between parties clearly distinguishes democracy from dictatorship.* ◇ *Prokaryotes are distinguished from all other organisms by their lack of a cell nucleus.* ◇ *A unique distinguishing feature of the EU is that it possesses the power to make and enforce laws.* ◇ **~ on the basis of sth** *Most urban areas contain residential districts distinguished on the basis of income, class, ethnicity, religion or some other economic or cultural variable.* **3** [T] **~ A (from B)** to make sth different or seem different from other similar things SYN DIFFERENTIATE (2): *Logistics service firms are constantly looking for ways to distinguish themselves from other firms providing similar services.* **4** [T] to do sth so well that people notice and admire you: **~ yourself** *Artillery had always been a strong point in the Russian army, but in the war against Japan it had not distinguished itself.* ◇ **~ yourself as sth** *Poliziano distinguished himself as the best philologist of the fifteenth century.* **5** [T] (not used in the progressive tenses) **~ sth** to be able to see or hear sth SYN MAKE SB/STH OUT (2): *These arrangements were diverse and no evident pattern could be distinguished.* ◇ *When an earthquake is large, distinguishing any sounds from the earth itself can be difficult.*

▸ DISTINGUISH + NOUN **type, form, kind • case • group • effects • approach** *Bull distinguishes three kinds of order in world politics (Bull, 1995).*

▸ ADVERB + DISTINGUISH | DISTINGUISH + ADVERB **clearly • sharply • carefully • adequately • correctly** *Schumpeter distinguished sharply between the entrepreneur and the capitalist.*

▸ ADVERB + DISTINGUISH **easily, readily • reliably • explicitly** *Males and females of the species are easily distinguished.*

D

▸ ADJECTIVE + TO DISTINGUISH **possible** ◆ **impossible** ◆ **difficult** ◆ **easy** ◆ **important** ◆ **necessary** ◆ **useful, helpful** *The earliest feature of dementia is usually minor forgetfulness, which may be difficult to distinguish from the effects of normal ageing.*

dis·tin·guish·able /dɪˈstɪŋɡwɪʃəbl/ *adj.* **~ (from sb/sth)** that can be recognized as different from sb/sth else: *In this particular magazine, advertisements are often barely distinguishable from editorial content.*

D

dis·tin·guished /dɪˈstɪŋɡwɪʃt/ *adj.* very successful and admired by other people: *The British Antarctic Survey has a long and distinguished history of scientific research in Antarctica.* ◇ *distinguished scholars in the field*

dis·tort AWL /dɪˈstɔːt; *NAmE* dɪˈstɔːrt/ *verb* **1 ~ sth** to change or have an effect on sth so that it gives a false impression of what is true, or so that it shows sth in a different way: *The low number of respondents distorted the results of the survey.* ◇ *In these works, ordinary reality is deliberately distorted so that we will see it differently.* ◇ *Competition is further distorted by subsidies to state-owned airlines.* **2 ~ sth** to change the shape, appearance or sound of sth so that it is no longer the same shape, etc: *The galaxies pass right through each other, with gravity distorting the shapes of the galaxies as it changes the orbits of their stars.*

dis·tort·ion AWL /dɪˈstɔːʃn; *NAmE* dɪˈstɔːrʃn/ *noun* **1** [U, C] a change in the way sth works or appears that makes it a different shape or not clear, or affects it in a negative way: *Low frequency sounds are less sensitive to distortion.* ◇ **~ in sth** *Massive objects such as galaxies or clusters can cause systematic distortions in images of more distant objects.* ◇ *Globalization can lead to distortions in the rational workings of the labour market.* ◇ **~ of sth** *The swelling that occurs causes distortion of the face or neck.* **2** [C, U] a change in facts or ideas that makes them no longer correct or true: **~ (of sth)** *The corruptions and distortions of language became a particular concern of Orwell's last years.* ◇ *He sought an apology from the publishers for what he saw as a distortion of his views.* ◇ **without ~** *Tufte emphasizes the need to represent statistics faithfully, without distortion.*

dis·tress /dɪˈstres/ *noun* [U] **1** a feeling of being extremely anxious or unhappy: *Some people tend to withdraw completely from situations that might cause them psychological distress.* ◇ **in ~** *It is normal to have empathy for other people when we see them crying or in distress.* **2** great pain; a situation in which the body is having difficulty functioning correctly: *Medication may be prescribed to alleviate psychological and physical distress.* ◇ *One of the symptoms is acute respiratory distress.* **3** suffering and problems caused by not having enough money, food or other basic things SYN HARDSHIP: *This paper will highlight ways of protecting the poor from hardship and economic distress.* ◇ **in ~** *At that time, local governments were in severe financial distress.*

dis·tressed /dɪˈstrest/ *adj.* **1** upset and anxious: *Many patients sleep poorly at night, waking disorientated and distressed.* ◇ **~ about sth** *The child was extremely distressed about school and showed physical signs of anxiety.* **2** having problems caused by lack of money: *During the recession, national governments took measures to help distressed banks.* ◇ *They located new businesses in distressed areas and encouraged labour mobility.*

dis·tress·ing /dɪˈstresɪŋ/ *adj.* making you feel anxious or upset: *The HDI data in Table 5.9 paint a distressing picture of global inequalities.* ◇ **~ for/to sb** *Memory loss is generally extremely distressing for the individual and the family.* ■ **dis·tress·ing·ly** *adv.*: *These symptoms are sometimes distressingly mistaken for drunkenness.*

dis·trib·ute AWL /dɪˈstrɪbjuːt; ˈdɪstrɪbjuːt/ *verb* **1** [T, often passive] to give sth, or a share of sth, to a large number of people: **~ sth** *Most open-source software is distributed free of charge.* ◇ *An economic system that distributes its burdens and benefits more equitably may also be a better economic system.* ◇ **~ sth to sb/sth** *The postal questionnaires were distributed at random to 30 local doctors.* ◇ **~ sth among sb/sth** *The property of the deceased was distributed equally among her children.* **2** [T] **~ sth** to send goods to shops and businesses so that they can be sold: *The company has a global sales network that distributes its products in around 130 countries.* **3** [I, T] to spread or spread sth in a particular way: **+ adv./prep.** *As all the cells are nucleated nearly at the same time, the gas distributes more or less evenly among all these cells.* ◇ **~ sth + adv./prep.** *The suspension was distributed uniformly over the surface of the plate and allowed to dry.*

dis·trib·u·ted AWL /dɪˈstrɪbjuːtɪd; ˈdɪstrɪbjuːtɪd/ *adj.* **(+ adv./prep.)** spread over a particular area; existing in a particular way: *The weight of the rope was uniformly distributed along its length.* ◇ *This beetle is widely distributed throughout the major and minor islands of Japan.* HELP In computing, a **distributed system** is any system in which a number of individual computers are linked into a network and can work together: *Some modern operating systems use a client-server architecture and run on distributed systems.*

▸ ADVERB + DISTRIBUTED | DISTRIBUTED + ADVERB **uniformly** ◆ **normally** ◆ **evenly** ◆ **equally** ◆ **unequally** ◆ **randomly** ◆ **widely** *Barnes and Marshall (1951) established that plankton were not distributed randomly, but often occurred in dense blooms.*

dis·tri·bu·tion AWL /ˌdɪstrɪˈbjuːʃn/ *noun* **1** [C, U] the way that sth exists or is shared over a particular area or among a particular group of people: *Exposed limestone has a very patchy distribution in the region.* ◇ **~ (of sth) (between A and B)** *Figure 4.1 shows the age distribution of PC ownership.* ◇ *This research focuses on the unequal distribution of power between women and men.* ◇ **+ noun** *Different species have different distribution ranges.* ➲ *see also* NORMAL DISTRIBUTION ➲ language bank *at* STATISTIC **2** [U, C] **~ (of sth) (to sb/sth)** the act of giving or delivering sth to a number of people: *A warehouse was built to store food and clothing for distribution to the poor.* ◇ *Methods of privatization involving the free distribution of shares were not favoured by the government.* ◇ *Ethnic monitoring was introduced to ensure an equitable distribution of locally delivered services.* **3** [U] (*business*) the system of transporting and delivering goods: **+ noun** *As a small family firm, they lack a corporate marketing and distribution network.* ■ **dis·tri·bu·tion·al** AWL /ˌdɪstrɪˈbjuːʃənl/ *adj.*: *A random distributional pattern is more likely to be found.*

▸ ADJECTIVE + DISTRIBUTION **uniform, even** ◆ **equal** ◆ **uneven** ◆ **unequal** ◆ **random** ◆ **wide** ◆ **narrow** ◆ **geographical, geographic** ◆ **spatial** ◆ **temporal** *Von Thunen theory is inadequate to explain the spatial distribution of agricultural activities today.*

▸ NOUN + DISTRIBUTION **size** ◆ **age** ◆ **species** ◆ **population** ◆ **income** ◆ **temperature** *A detailed study of boulder size distributions at different places along the Colorado river could be used to infer flood histories.*

▸ VERB + DISTRIBUTION **show** ◆ **reflect** ◆ **affect, influence** ◆ **govern, control, determine** ◆ **ensure** ◆ **produce** ◆ **predict** ◆ **analyse, examine** ◆ **describe** ◆ **compare** ◆ **map** *Variations in the temperature of the oceans strongly affect the distribution of marine life.* ◇ *I started by examining the geographic distribution of shoe manufacturing plants across the United States.*

▸ DISTRIBUTION + NOUN **pattern** ◆ **curve** ◆ **range** *Dietary factors may explain the different distribution patterns found between adult and juvenile fish.* | **network** ◆ **system** ◆ **channel** ◆ **centre** ◆ **facilities** ◆ **chain** *This was an affluent* *market characterized by mass consumerism, served by mass distribution channels and fuelled by mass media.*

dis·tribu·tive AWL /dɪˈstrɪbjətɪv/ *adj.* [usually before noun] **1** connected with the way that things are shared between people: *Distributive justice is the idea that the poor and weak deserve special treatment, such as development aid.* **2** (*business*) connected with the way that goods are supplied or delivered: *Other technologies are used in distributive services.* **3** (*mathematics*) (of an operation) fulfilling the condition that $x(y + z) = xy + xz$

dis·tribu·tor AWL /dɪˈstrɪbjətə(r)/ *noun* a person or company that supplies goods to shops or other businesses: *It is important for a firm to maintain good relationships with suppliers, distributors and retailers.* ◇ *Both films had won numerous awards in Asia but had not found a distributor in the UK.* ◇ **~ of sth** *Tata Tea became the second largest global distributor of tea.*

dis·trict /ˈdɪstrɪkt/ *noun* **1** an area of a country or town, especially one that has particular features: *Larger urban areas tend to have both residential and industrial districts.* ◇ *Their research examines many of the late twentieth-century changes that cities experienced, especially the decline of central business districts.* ◇ **~ of sth** *Life expectancy in the working-class districts of the city was much lower.* **2** one of the areas which a country, town or state is divided into for purposes of organization, with official BOUNDARIES (= borders): *The students involved in the studies were from inner-city school districts in the United States.* ◇ *The table reveals substantial variation across the different police districts.* ◇ **~ of sth** *The governors of the administrative districts of the Persian Empire were known as satraps.*

dis·trust[1] /dɪsˈtrʌst/ *noun* [U, sing.] a feeling of not being able to trust or believe sb/sth: *Their relationship is marked by mutual distrust and even hostility.* ◇ **~ of sb/sth** *There is widespread distrust of government.* ◇ *This led to a general public distrust of large companies.* ■ **dis·trust·ful** /dɪsˈtrʌstfl/ *adj.* [not usually before noun] **~ of sb/sth** *People have grown distrustful of politicians.*

dis·trust[2] /dɪsˈtrʌst/ *verb* **~ sb/sth** to feel that you cannot trust or believe sb/sth: *People in this group may distrust their doctors.* ◇ *He had good reason to distrust the political system.*

dis·turb /dɪˈstɜːb; *NAmE* dɪˈstɜːrb/ *verb* **1 ~ sth** to change the arrangement of sth, or affect how sth functions: *When the price level changes, it disturbs the equilibrium in the money markets.* ◇ *Such plants mostly occupy habitats that have been disturbed, such as roadsides.* **2 ~ sb/sth** to interrupt sb and prevent them from continuing with what they are doing: *Caller ID may be used by an individual to avoid being disturbed by unwanted calls.* **3 ~ sb** to make sb feel anxious or upset: *The racism they encountered disturbed them but they did not feel that they were in danger.* ◇ *People in affluent areas are often disturbed by images of suffering in poorer regions.*

dis·turb·ance /dɪˈstɜːbəns; *NAmE* dɪˈstɜːrbəns/ *noun* **1** [U, C, usually sing.] the act of moving sth; a change in the normal arrangement or state that sth is in: *This study aims to measure the impact of habitat disturbance on bat fertility.* ◇ **~ in sth** *The slightest movement produces a disturbance in the fluid.* ◇ **~ to sth** *Any disturbance to the economy will have an effect on inflation.* **2** [U] **~ (to sb/sth)** the act of interrupting a peaceful situation: *The chicks were measured as quickly as possible in order to minimize disturbance to the parents.* **3** [U, C] a state in which sb's mind or a function of the body is not working normally: *Violence and aggression have been linked with emotional disturbance.* ◇ *The patient had a history of headaches and visual disturbance.* ◇ *Symptoms include gastrointestinal disturbances such as nausea, vomiting and abdominal pain.* **4** [C] a situation in which people behave violently in a public place: *The defendant admitted to causing a disturbance while under the influence of alcohol.*

dis·turbed /dɪˈstɜːbd; *NAmE* dɪˈstɜːrbd/ *adj.* **1** having or caused by emotional and mental problems: *The teachers spoke about the very disturbed behaviour of a minority of pupils.* **2** having had the normal arrangement or functioning changed: *Both children had problems, perhaps as a result of a disturbed family background.* ◇ *Functional root systems are particularly important in disturbed areas that are prone to the loss of nutrients during heavy rainfall.* ◇ *These patients may also experience disturbed sleep and feel constantly tired.* ➲ *compare* UNDISTURBED (1) **3** very upset about sth that you disagree with or that has made you unhappy: *The company was so disturbed to learn that its traditional view of the market was wrong that it refused to complete the project.*

dis·turb·ing /dɪˈstɜːbɪŋ; *NAmE* dɪˈstɜːrbɪŋ/ *adj.* **1** making you feel anxious and upset or shocked: *The revelation that bullying was so widespread was disturbing.* **2** changing the way sth functions or is arranged: *The external disturbing forces on the bridge came from the wind.* ■ **dis·turb·ing·ly** *adv.*: *Disturbingly, 14% of the junior doctors reported making mistakes of this kind.*

di·ur·nal /daɪˈɜːnl; *NAmE* daɪˈɜːrnl/ *adj.* **1** (*technical*) happening over a period of one day: *Patients should be questioned about symptoms such as loss of appetite and diurnal variation in mood.* ◇ *Rotation imposes a diurnal cycle on much of the life on earth.* **2** (*biology*) (of animals) active during the day: *The eastern chipmunk is a small diurnal rodent of eastern North America.* OPP NOCTURNAL

di·verge /daɪˈvɜːdʒ; *NAmE* daɪˈvɜːrdʒ/ *verb* **1** [I] to separate and go in different directions: *This phenomenon occurs where surface ocean currents diverge, forcing deep water to rise.* OPP CONVERGE (1) **2** [I] to develop in a different way, after being the same: *The 'natural' price and the 'market' price began to diverge significantly.* ◇ **~ from sth** *Both populations slowly diverged genetically from each other and eventually evolved into separate species.* OPP CONVERGE (3) **3** [I] **~ (from sth)** (of opinions or views) to be different: *His theory diverges from that of Marx on this issue.* OPP CONVERGE (3) **4** [I] **~ from sth** to do sth in a way that is different from what is expected or planned: *Only a very small number of companies have so far diverged from the traditional model of corporate governance.* **5** [I] (*mathematics*) (of a series) to increase forever as more of its terms are added: *The impact velocities diverge exponentially away from the limit point.*

di·ver·gence /daɪˈvɜːdʒəns; *NAmE* daɪˈvɜːrdʒəns/ *noun* **1** [U] the process or fact of becoming different: **~ of sth** *It is estimated that the time of divergence of Neanderthal and modern humans was less than 440 000 years.* ◇ **~ in sth** *Pandit and Bagchi-sen (1993) established growing divergence in regional fertility rates between 1970 and 1990.* OPP CONVERGENCE (1) **2** [C, U] a difference in things, attitudes or opinions: **~ between A and B** *We observed very few divergences between the predictions of our model and our experimental results.* ◇ **~ of sth** *There seems likely to be a divergence of opinion amongst senior judges on this fundamental question.* ◇ **~ in sth** *These recent studies reveal noticeable divergence in body shape among stickleback populations.*

di·ver·gent /daɪˈvɜːdʒənt; *NAmE* daɪˈvɜːrdʒənt/ *adj.* different; developing or moving in different directions: *Japan's industrial organization has moved down two divergent paths.* ◇ *Interviews amongst managers have revealed widely divergent views about what constitutes customer satisfaction.* ◇ *In this condition, fast divergent eye movements are followed by slow convergent eye movements.* ◇ **~ from sth** *In this respect, the US approach is* *often quite divergent from those of other states.* OPP CONVERGENT

di·verse AWL /daɪˈvɜːs; *NAmE* daɪˈvɜːrs/ *adj.* very different from each other; containing people or things of various kinds: *The mechanisms are similar across a diverse range of organisms, from bacteria to fungi.* ◇ *The labour force became increasingly diverse with the influx of immigrant workers.* ◇ **as ~ as sth** *The ethical policy covers issues as diverse as the arms trade, the environment and genetic modification.*

D

▸ DIVERSE + NOUN **range • group, set, sample, array • population • community • audience • background • settings • traditions • cultures • perspectives** *Participants in the study came from diverse ethnic backgrounds.* ◇ *Our aim was to identify diverse perspectives on what doctors and primary care should do for patients with depression.*

▸ ADVERB + DIVERSE **very, highly • extremely • increasingly • quite • culturally • religiously • racially • socially • geographically • structurally** *The eight Indian schemes we identified are very diverse in terms of design, size and target populations.* ◇ *Future studies need to include culturally diverse samples.*

di·ver·sify AWL /daɪˈvɜːsɪfaɪ; *NAmE* daɪˈvɜːrsɪfaɪ/ *verb* (**diver·si·fies, di·ver·si·fy·ing, di·ver·si·fied, di·ver·si·fied**) **1** [I, T] (especially of a business or company) to develop a wider range of products, investments or skills in order to be more successful or reduce risk: **~ (into sth)** *Producing paper and pulp since the 1920s, Suzano Group diversified into petrochemicals in 1974.* ◇ **~ sth (by doing sth)** *Unilever's German subsidiaries diversifed their business portfolio by investing in the frozen food industry.* **2** [I, T] to change or to make sth change so that there is greater variety: *65 million years ago, mammals and birds flourished and diversified, filling the ecological gaps left by the dinosaurs.* ◇ **~ sth** *Immigration since the 1960s has increasingly diversified the previously ethnically homogeneous Swedish population.* ■ **di·ver·si·fi·ca·tion** AWL /daɪˌvɜːsɪfɪˈkeɪʃn; *NAmE* daɪˌvɜːrsɪfɪˈkeɪʃn/ *noun* [U] **~ into sth** *These companies have not engaged in indiscriminate diversification into unrelated technologies and markets.* ◇ **~ of sth** *Its global expansion has encouraged the diversification of the English language.*

di·ver·sion /daɪˈvɜːʃn; *NAmE* daɪˈvɜːrʒn/ *noun* [C, U] **~ (of sth) (from sth) (to sth)** the act of changing the direction that sb/sth is following, or what sth is used for: *The debate concerning globalization is a diversion from some deeper conflicts.* ◇ *Diversion of water from mountain streams for irrigation is relatively easy.* ◇ *Molotov and Kaganovich resented the diversion of resources from heavy to light industry.*

di·ver·sity AWL /daɪˈvɜːsəti; *NAmE* daɪˈvɜːrsəti/ *noun* [C, usually sing., U] a range of things or people that are very different from each other; the fact of including such a range: **~ (of sth)** *Researching social facts almost always produces a diversity of points of view.* ◇ *The Sonoran Desert offers the greatest diversity of plant life of any desert in the world.* ◇ *Mechanized industrial monocultures show low species diversity compared with natural vegetation.* ◇ **~ in/within sth** *There is considerable ethnic diversity in the student community.*

▸ ADJECTIVE + DIVERSITY **great, high, considerable • enormous • sheer • increasing, growing, increased • wide, broad • rich • structural • regional • cultural • ethnic • racial • religious • genetic • biological** *Once again, the sheer diversity of opinion is striking.* ◇ *Females increase the genetic diversity of their offspring by mating with several males.*

▸ VERB + DIVERSITY **recognize • reveal • reflect • explain • generate • maintain, preserve • enhance • respect** *Darwin used the mechanism of natural selection to explain the diversity of life.*

di·vert /daɪˈvɜːt; *NAmE* daɪˈvɜːrt/ *verb* **1** to make sth change direction: **~ sth** *Rivers were diverted to irrigate fields.* ◇ **~ sth to sth** *Noise levels in town may fall as traffic is diverted to the new road.* ◇ **~ sth +adv./prep.** *Most of the meltwater was diverted southwards into the Black Sea.* **2** to use money, materials, etc. for a purpose that is different from their original purpose: **~ sth from sth** *The campaign diverted resources from other important programmes.* ◇ **~ sth to sth** *This will lead to cash shortages as funds are diverted to other organizations.* ◇ **~ sth into sth** *Land will therefore be diverted into new uses.* ◇ **~ sth** *Much of the foreign aid money was diverted.* **3 ~ sth from sth** to take sb's thoughts or attention away from sth: *The current focus on gender diverts attention from the way that class affects educational outcomes.*

div·ide¹ /dɪˈvaɪd/ *verb* **1** [T, usually passive, I] to separate into parts or groups; to make sth separate into parts or groups: *This stage in the life-cycle involves the cells dividing.* ◇ **~ (up) into sth** *After the death of the dominant male, the group divided into two subgroups.* ◇ **~ sth (up) into sth** *The book is divided into three parts.* ◇ *The farms were divided up into smaller holdings.* **2** [T] **~ sth (up) between/among sb** to give a share of sth to each of a number of different people or organizations SYN SHARE¹ (6): *In 387, the two great powers divided Armenia between them.* ◇ *These resources are then divided between the institutions on the basis of a politically determined allocation.* **3** [T] to be the real or imaginary line or barrier that separates two areas, things or people SYN SEPARATE² (3): **~ sth (off)** *The Annamite mountains divide the lowlands of Vietnam.* ◇ **~ A from B** *National boundaries served merely to divide Muslims from each other.* **4** [T] **~ sth (between A and B)** to use different parts of your time or energy for different activities: *Other planters were genuine transatlantic figures, who divided their time between the West Indies and Britain.* **5** [T] to cause two or more people to disagree SYN SPLIT¹ (2): **~ sb/sth** *The problem of slavery deeply divided the public in the northern states.* ◇ **be divided (on/over sth)** *Academics were sharply divided on the issue.* **6** [T] **~ sth by sth** to calculate sth by finding out how many times one number or amount is contained in another: *Embryo survival is the number of normally developed embryos divided by the number of eggs initially received.* ◇ *The profit rate is defined as the amount of profit divided by the value of the capital goods owned.*

IDM **diˌvide and ˈrule** to keep control over people by making them disagree with and fight each other, therefore not giving them the chance to join together and oppose you: *The divide and rule approach used by the British in Trinidad created distrust between Africans and Indians.*

▸ DIVIDE/BE DIVIDED INTO + NOUN **groups • sections • parts • categories • types • classes • regions • phases • stages • chapters** *These genes can be broadly divided into three basic categories.* ◇ *One type of medieval map divided the world into a number of climatic regions.*

▸ ADVERB + DIVIDE **further • broadly, roughly • equally, evenly • randomly • traditionally** *The provinces are divided into districts, and these are further divided into municipalities.*

div·ide² /dɪˈvaɪd/ *noun* [usually sing.] **1** a difference between two groups of people that separates them from each other; a difference between two sets of ideas or areas of activity: *The digital divide means that many people, even in North America, still do not have regular access to the Internet.* ◇ *The work was badly received by both sides of the political divide.* ◇ **~ between A and B** *The linguistic and cultural divide between the French conquerors and the Anglo-Saxon natives was deep and long-lasting.* ◇ **across the ~** *The gap in attitudes between users and non-users is far greater than the gap across the gender divide.* **2 ~ (between A and B)** (*especially NAmE*) a line of high land that separates two VALLEYS or systems of rivers SYN WATERSHED: *The Central Range of Hills forms the* *divide between the drainage westward to the Bay of Bengal and that flowing eastward.* IDM see BRIDGE[2]

div·ided /dɪˈvaɪdɪd/ *adj.* (of a group or an organization) having a lot of disagreements or different opinions: *Spain after the civil war was a deeply divided society.* ◇ *to be sharply/bitterly/internally divided* ◇ **~ about/over/as to sth** *The parties remained divided over the appropriate level of state intervention.*

divi·dend /ˈdɪvɪdend/ *noun* **1** an amount of the profits that a company pays to people who own shares in the company: *Profitable US corporations generally paid ample dividends to shareholders.* ◇ **+ noun** *Table 2.2 shows that dividend payments to shareholders are much higher in the UK than in other large, developed economies.* **2** an advantage or benefit: *They implemented an alternative fuels programme that is yielding substantial environmental dividends.* IDM see PAY[1]

diˈviding line *noun* [usually sing.] **~ (between A and B)** something that marks the difference between two things or ideas, or where one thing stops and another starts: *Modern political science has challenged traditional analyses based on a crude dividing line between capital and labour.* ◇ *Extreme cases are easy to define but the dividing line between normal and abnormal behaviour is sometimes difficult to draw.*

di·vine /dɪˈvaɪn/ *adj.* [usually before noun] coming from or connected with God or a god; being a god: *Christians believed that the emperors were chosen by God and that they carried out the divine will on Earth.* ◇ *The demigods of Greek mythology were half human and half divine.* ■ **div·ine·ly** *adv.*: *They believed that they were governed by a divinely appointed ruler.*

div·in·ity /dɪˈvɪnəti/ *noun* (*pl.* **-ies**) **1** [U] the state of being God or a god: *Alexander the Great encouraged belief in his own divinity and was worshipped as a god after his death.* **2** [C] a god or GODDESS: *The political value of sculpture is obvious in the images of kings in the company of local divinities.* **3** [U] the study of the nature of God and religious belief SYN THEOLOGY: *Renaissance intellectuals broke free of the restrictions of medieval science and divinity.*

div·is·ible /dɪˈvɪzəbl/ *adj.* **1** [not usually before noun] **~ (by sth)** (*mathematics*) that can be divided, usually with nothing remaining: *In Godel's system, each symbol was associated with a prime number (that is, a number that is divisible only by itself or by 1).* **2** [not before noun] **~ (into sth)** that can be divided: *Roman aristocrats were roughly divisible into four overlapping categories.* ➲ *compare* INDIVISIBLE

div·ision /dɪˈvɪʒn/ *noun* **1** [U, C, usually sing.] the process or result of dividing into separate parts; the process or result of dividing sth or sharing it out: *During cell division the entire DNA of the cell is copied.* ◇ **~ into sth** *One of the most basic divisions in the world today is the division into political states.* ◇ **~ of sth (into sth)** *For Marx, the division of classes into rich and poor determined all other issues.* ◇ **~ (of sth) between A and B** *The division of housework between men and women is more unequal in these countries.* **2** [U] the process of dividing one number by another: *The arithmetic operations of subtraction and division do not exist in Boolean algebra.* ➲ *compare* MULTIPLICATION **3** [C, usually pl., U] a disagreement or difference in people's opinions or ways of life, especially between members of a society or an organization: **~ in/within sth** *He admits that the army was an organization that reinforced the class divisions in British society.* ◇ **~ between A and B** *The length of the discussion reflected the bitter divisions between those for and against the legislation.* ◇ **~ among sb/sth** *The Commission aimed at overcoming deep divisions among Protestant churches.* **4** [C] **~ (of sth)** a part of sth into which it is divided: *Patients complain of facial pain involving one or more of the divisions of the trigeminal nerve.* **5** [C+sing./pl. v.] (*abbr.* **Div.**) a large and important unit or section of an organization: *The company created a specialist division to meet the challenges of the global market.*

diˌvision of ˈlabour *noun* the way in which work is divided among different people: *Adam Smith explained the economic benefits derived from the efficiency of the division of labour.* ◇ **~ between A and B** *The more conservative Christian sects emphasize a traditional division of labour between a husband and wife.*

div·isive /dɪˈvaɪsɪv/ *adj.* (*disapproving*) causing people to divide into groups that disagree with or oppose each other: *This topic remains a highly divisive issue among academics.* ◇ *She argued that this policy was socially divisive.* ■ **div·isive·ness** *noun* [U] *They developed strategies for addressing the divisiveness in national politics.*

di·vorce[1] /dɪˈvɔːs; *NAmE* dɪˈvɔːrs/ *noun* **1** [C, U] the legal ending of a marriage: *The new regulations made it easier to obtain a divorce.* ◇ *This second marriage also ended in divorce.* ◇ **+ noun** *The divorce rate climbed by almost 100 per cent in the US during the 1960s.* ➲ *compare* SEPARATION (2) **2** [C, usually sing.] **~ (between A and B)** the ending of a relationship between two things SYN SEPARATION (1): *The relationship between investors and managers is interesting because there is a divorce between ownership and control.*

di·vorce[2] /dɪˈvɔːs; *NAmE* dɪˈvɔːrs/ *verb* **1** [T, I] to end your marriage to sb legally: *They divorced eight years later.* ◇ **~ sb** *She divorced him in 1965.* **2** [T, often passive] **~ sth from sth** to separate an idea, a subject, etc. from sth else: *Religion cannot be divorced from morality.*

di·vorced /dɪˈvɔːst; *NAmE* dɪˈvɔːrst/ *adj.* **1** no longer married: *One study found that women with divorced parents were more likely to have a child before age 21.* ◇ *Participants who were widowed, separated or divorced were more likely to use mental health services.* **2 ~ from sth** appearing not to be affected by sth; separate from sth: *People cannot make choices that are wholly divorced from their environment.* ◇ *By the early fourteenth century, this theory was becoming somewhat divorced from social reality.*

DNA /ˌdiː en ˈeɪ/ *noun* [U] (*biochemistry*) the chemical in the cells of animals and plants that carries GENETIC information and is a type of NUCLEIC ACID HELP **DNA** is short for 'deoxyribonucleic acid': *Humans share 98% of their DNA with other higher primates.* ◇ **+ noun** *DNA damage and genome instability have long since been implicated in Alzheimer's disease.*

do[1] /də; du; *strong form* duː/ *verb* HELP For irregular forms of **do**, see page R4. **1** [T] **~ sth** used to refer to actions that you do not mention by name or do not know about: *The technicians admitted that they had no idea what to do.* ◇ *To the vice-chairman, the decision appeared to be both legitimate and the right thing to do.* ◇ *There was only a partial recognition by the hospital that they should have done more to improve the situation.* **2** [T] **~ sth** to work at or perform an activity or a task: *The study compared the salaries of men and women doing similar work for the same employer.* ◇ *The research was done by a group from Columbia University.* ◇ *The two methods do the same thing in different ways.* **3** [I] to act or behave in the way mentioned: **~ as...** *The court's decision supports the view that people should be free to do as they wish with their money.* ◇ **+ adv./prep.** *Arguably, bioscientists would do well to consider Maxwell's concept of the philosophy of wisdom.* **4** [I, T] used to talk about the success or progress of sb/sth: **+ adv./prep.** *History shows that single-issue candidates usualy do badly in general elections.* ◇ *Potatoes became an important subsistence crop, doing well in poor* *acidic soils.* ◇ **~ sth (to sb/sth)** *The area committee concluded that closing the road had done no harm to local businesses.* **5** [T] to perform the activity or task mentioned: **~ more, some, a little, etc. fighting, cooking, writing, etc.** *By the second century BCE, Roman allies were doing more of the fighting for less of the reward.* ◇ **~ the/your cooking, shopping, etc.** *Buying online is increasingly seen as a highly convenient way of doing one's shopping.* **6** [T] **~ sth** to produce or make sth: *Students were asked to do an essay every week for homework.* **7** [T] **get sth done** to finish sth: *The aim was to find lower-cost ways of getting the necessary work done.*

D

IDM Most idioms containing **do** are at the entries for the nouns and adjectives in the idioms, for example **do sb good** is at **good** *noun*. **be/have to do with sb/sth** to be about or connected with sb/sth: *The explanation for the Conservative defeat in 1997 is partly to do with tactical voting.* **have (got) something, nothing, a little, etc. to do with sb/sth** used to talk about how much sb/sth is connected with sb/sth: *These issues have little directly to do with health care provision.*

PHR V **ˌdo aˈway with sth** to stop doing or having sth; to make sth end SYN ABOLISH: *The East African Community common market also aims to do away with all internal barriers to trade.* **ˈdo sth with sb/sth** used in negative sentences and questions with *what*: *The officials debated what to do with the prisoners.* **ˌdo withˈout (sth/sb)** to manage without sth/sb: *A poor family can do without air conditioning or a car, but not without heat in winter.*

do² /də; du; *strong form* duː/ *auxiliary verb* HELP For irregular forms of **do**, see page R4. **1** used before a full verb to form negative sentences and questions: *The tumour was benign and did not require further follow-up.* ◇ *What about non-Western values? Where do they fit into this emerging global world?* **2** used to avoid repeating a full verb: *As landscapes evolve, so do the human activities associated with them.* ◇ *The Buddha belongs to the category 'exemplary prophet', as does Confucius.* ◇ *US workers in 2000 actually worked more hours than they did 20 years earlier.* **3** used to emphasize what you are saying: *The study found no genetic influence on life span prior to 60, but did find a very significant effect thereafter (Hjelmborg et al., 2006).* **4** used to change the order of the subject and verb when an adverb is moved to the front: *McKendall argues that not only does planned change involve the desire to control organizations, but that it unethically reduces personal freedom.* ◇ *Although other animals apart from Homo sapiens live in houses, rarely do they build such precarious structures.*

doc·tor /ˈdɒktə(r); *NAmE* ˈdɑːktər/ *noun* (*abbr.* **Dr**) **1** a person who has been trained in medical science, whose job is to treat people who are ill or injured: *Self-tests can be done at home without involving a doctor, nurse or other health professional.* ◇ *The median patient delay before seeing a doctor was 2 months.* ◇ *to go to/visit/ask/consult the doctor* ◇ *It is not uncommon for junior doctors to have to break bad news.* **2 ~ (of sth)** a person who has received the highest university degree: *He attended courses at several universities, graduating as a doctor of philosophy at Erlangen and as a doctor of medicine at Munich.*

doc·tor·al /ˈdɒktərəl; *NAmE* ˈdɑːktərəl/ *adj.* [only before noun] connected with a doctorate: *Davis (1850–1934) was the subject of a doctoral dissertation by Rigdon (1933).* ◇ *a doctoral student/candidate/adviser/degree/programme/thesis*

doc·trine /ˈdɒktrɪn; *NAmE* ˈdɑːktrɪn/ *noun* **1** [C, U] **~ (of sth)** a belief or principle, or set of beliefs or principles, held by a religion, a political party or a legal system: *He describes the faith and doctrines of Islam.* ◇ *This is a relatively recent change in international legal doctrine.* **2 Doctrine** [C] (*US*) a statement of government policy, especially foreign policy: *the Truman Doctrine*

docu·ment¹ AWL /ˈdɒkjumənt; *NAmE* ˈdɑːkjumənt/ *noun* **1** an official paper, book, etc. that gives information about sth, or that can be used as evidence or proof of sth: *Scribes wrote the ancient documents by hand.* ◇ *He signed a document promising political union between Russia and Belarus.* ◇ *The Application Registration Card is the official identity document issued to asylum seekers.* ◇ *The government produced a discussion document that outlined 120 different indicators to assess if Britain was on a sustainable track.* ◇ *a policy/consultation/planning document* **2** a computer file that contains text and that has a name that identifies it: *Some documents had been deleted.* ◇ *The full tables are available as electronic documents, illustrating in greater detail the studies reviewed.* ◇ *In a standard index search, one typically types in a set of keywords and gets back a list of documents containing those words.*

docu·ment² AWL /ˈdɒkjument; *NAmE* ˈdɑːkjument/ *verb* [often passive] to record the details of sth; to prove or support sth with documents: **~ sth (in sth)** *This study is the first to document the massive population changes among certain groups in the area.* ◇ *The phenomenon has been widely documented in the literature.* ◇ *clearly/extensively/poorly documented* ◇ **well documented** *Life in the countryside during this period is not well documented and there are few sources available.* ◇ **documented + noun** *There are several documented cases of comets whose activity has died.* ◇ *Potential participants were excluded if they had documented evidence of significant developmental disabilities.* ⊃ *see also* WELL DOCUMENTED ⊃ thesaurus note *at* RECORD²

docu·men·tary¹ /ˌdɒkjuˈmentri; *NAmE* ˌdɑːkjuˈmentri/ *noun* (*pl.* **-ies**) **~ (on/about sb/sth)** a film or a radio or television programme that gives facts about real people and events: *He made several documentaries on poverty and inequality in the area.*

docu·men·tary² /ˌdɒkjuˈmentri; *NAmE* ˌdɑːkjuˈmentri/ *adj.* [only before noun] **1** consisting of documents: *Ownership of the land has to be proven by documentary evidence.* ◇ *She based her arguments on reliable documentary sources.* **2** giving a record of or report on the facts about sth, especially by using pictures, recordings, etc. of people involved: *The article examines documentary films made in the post-war years.*

docu·men·ta·tion AWL /ˌdɒkjumenˈteɪʃn; *NAmE* ˌdɑːkjumenˈteɪʃn/ *noun* [U] **1** the documents that are required for sth, or that give evidence or proof of sth, or information about it: *These applicants often lacked official documentation, such as birth or marriage certificates, to prove their status.* ◇ **~ of sth** *He failed to provide full documentation of his recordings to validate his original source material.* **2 ~ (of sth)** the act of recording sth in a document: *Preservation of evidence and careful documentation of facts is of the utmost importance.*

does /dʌz/ ⊃ DO¹, DO²

dol·lar /ˈdɒlə(r); *NAmE* ˈdɑːlər/ *noun* **1** [C] (*symb.* **$**) the unit of money in the US, Canada, Australia and several other countries: **~ (of sth)** *It turned out that millions of dollars of debt had been hidden from investors.* ◇ **+ noun** *Between 2000 and 2006 the dollar value of global trade leapt from US$8.6 trillion to US$11.8 trillion.* **2 the dollar** [sing.] (*finance*) the value of the US dollar compared with the value of the money of other countries: *Eventually, the dollar would reach its maximum real value in February 1985.*

do·main AWL /dəˈmeɪn; dəʊˈmeɪn; *NAmE* doʊˈmeɪn/ *noun* **1** an area of knowledge or activity: *The spread of English into the family domain is seen as a threat to indigenous languages.* ◇ **~ of sth** *The study of most leisure activities falls within the domains of psychology, physical education* *and sociology.* ◇ **~ of sb** *Household tasks are no longer exclusively the domain of the woman.* ➲ *see also* PUBLIC DOMAIN **2** (*computing*) a set of websites on the Internet that end with the same group of letters, for example '.com', '.org': *Additionally, the domains .edu, .gov, and .mil are reserved for United States users, and the domain .int for recognized international agencies.* ➲ *see also* DOMAIN NAME **3 ~ (of sth)** (*mathematics*) the range of possible values of a particular VARIABLE in a FUNCTION: *Ignoring complex numbers, the domain of cosine is the set of all the real numbers.* **4 ~ (of sth)** (*biochemistry*) a particular region of a complex MOLECULE or structure: *Many proteins with similar function share a core domain of amino acids.* **5** lands owned or ruled by a particular person, government, etc, especially in the past: *Hoping to add Naxos to his domain, Aristagoras persuaded the Persians to join him.*

do'main name *noun* (*computing*) a name that identifies a website or group of websites on the Internet: *A company does not need to be established in a particular country in order to register a domain name in that location.*

do·mes·tic AWL /də'mestɪk/ *adj.* **1** [usually before noun] of or inside a particular country; not foreign or international: *Even companies that only compete in domestic markets are affected by globalization.* ◇ *To protect its domestic industry, the Indian government raised import tariffs.* ◇ *The same rights should generally apply in both domestic and international law.* **2** [only before noun] connected with or happening in the home; used in the home: *During the 1930s, the majority of employed black women in the US worked as domestic servants.* ◇ *Studies show that pregnant women are at increased risk of domestic violence.* ◇ *Domestic hot water in the UK accounts for 7.5% of all energy use.* **3** (of animals and plants) kept or produced by people; not wild: *The ticks affect both wild and domestic animals.* ◇ *There is a concern that herbicide-resistance genes from domestic plants could spread into wild species.*

do·mes·tic·al·ly AWL /də'mestɪkli/ *adv.* inside a particular country; not abroad or internationally: *If a country devalues its currency, then domestically produced goods become cheaper.* ◇ *This can cause problems, both domestically and internationally.*

do·mes·ti·cate AWL /də'mestɪkeɪt/ *verb* **1 ~ sth** to make a wild animal used to living with or working for humans: *In the high Andes of Peru, llama, alpaca and guinea pigs were domesticated.* **2 ~ sth** to grow plants or crops for human use SYN CULTIVATE (2): *Three regions of the Americas independently domesticated corn, squashes, potatoes and sunflowers.* ■ **do·mes·ti·cated** AWL *adj.* [usually before noun] *The earliest domesticated animal was the dog.* ◇ *domesticated crops* **do·mes·ti·ca·tion** /dəˌmestɪ'keɪʃn/ *noun* [U] **~ (of sth)** *The domestication of cattle led to an increase in beef eating.* ◇ *The timing for the domestication of crops in this region is comparable with that of the Levant.*

dom·in·ance AWL /'dɒmɪnəns; *NAmE* 'dɑːmɪnəns/ *noun* [U] **1** the fact of having power or influence over sb/sth SYN PREDOMINANCE (2): *Feminists revolted against male dominance in the family.* ◇ *The magazine faced a crisis when its 50-year market dominance was challenged.* ◇ **~ (of sb/sth) (in/over sb/sth)** *They documented the dominance of the company over the UK supermarket sector.* **2 ~ (of sb/sth)** the fact of being more common in a place than other people, animals or things SYN PREDOMINANCE (1): *The relative dominance of the two types of penguin has changed in response to cooling and warming periods.* ◇ *Low-cost land and ease of construction led to the dominance of the ranch house in rural America.* **3** (*biology*) (of GENES) the ability to cause a person, animal or plant to have a particular characteristic, even if only one of their parents has passed on this GENE: *The yellow colour of the peas reflects the dominance of the yellow allele over the recessive, green allele.*

dom·in·ant AWL /'dɒmɪnənt; *NAmE* 'dɑːmɪnənt/ *adj.* **1** stronger, and having more power and influence than other things or people SYN PREDOMINANT (2): *The females benefit from being mated to dominant males.* ◇ *The desire for a dominant position is why firms are continually fighting for market share.* ◇ *In the early 20th century, the Conservative and Liberal Parties were dominant.* ◇ **~ in sth** *British Airways was found to be dominant in the market for air travel agency services.* **2** more common, easier to notice, or more important than other things SYN PREDOMINANT (1): *In Spain, the married couple with children remains the dominant form of family life.* ◇ *Throughout his career, a concern with appearing tough and manly had been a dominant theme.* ◇ *The most dominant feature of the conflict is the struggle between the guerrilla groups and the government.* ◇ **~ in sth** *These ideas became dominant in the political discussion of the day.* **3** (*ecology*) (of a type of plant or animal) more common in a place than other types of plant or animal: *Longleaf pine was the dominant tree, making up 86% of the forest.* ◇ *Cod and sprat are the dominant fish species in the central Baltic.* **4** (*biology*) connected with a characteristic that appears in an individual even if it only has one GENE for this characteristic, passed on by only one of its parents: *The lack of tail in the Manx cat is caused by a dominant allele of a single gene.* ➲ *compare* RECESSIVE

▸ DOMINANT + NOUN **male • female • figure • group • class • firm • position • role • force • culture • language** *A dominant firm may have a near-monopoly share of its market.* ◇ *Many non-Greeks assimilated to the dominant culture by learning Greek.* | **theme • ideology • feature • form • model • mode • theory** *Liberalism remained the dominant ideology of nineteenth-century social thought.*

dom·in·ate AWL /'dɒmɪneɪt; *NAmE* 'dɑːmɪneɪt/ *verb* **1** [T, I] **~ (sth/sb)** to control or have a lot of influence over sth/sb, especially in a negative way: *At the retailing level, a few large organizations tend to dominate the market.* ◇ *There is an inherent appeal of a united Europe in a world dominated before 1991 by the US and USSR and now by the US alone.* ◇ *It was a civilization with religion as its unifying and dominating factor.* **2** [T] **~ sth** to be the most important or obvious feature of sth: *In the election campaign, the economy and public finances dominated the agenda.* ◇ *Climate change dominates the discourse on future food production.* **3** [T, I] **~ (sth)** to be the largest, highest or most common thing in a place: *Reptiles dominated much of the earth for about 135 million years.* ◇ *During this period, coniferous forests dominated across France.*

> **WORD FAMILY**
> dominate *verb*
> domination *noun*
> dominant *adj.*
> dominance *noun*

▸ DOMINATE + NOUN **market • politics • industry • economy • world** *Today, the worldwide steel-making industry is dominated by China.* | **the agenda • the scene • thinking • discourse • discussion • debate • the literature • the field** *The threat of bioterrorism has dominated recent national security discussions.* | **landscape • forest • area** *Slender volcanic cones dominate the landscape.*

▸ VERB + TO DOMINATE **come • tend • continue** *It was a rich civilization that came to dominate much of Europe.*

domination AWL /ˌdɒmɪ'neɪʃn; *NAmE* dɑːmɪ'neɪʃn/ *noun* [U] power or control over sb/sth; the fact of being most powerful or common in a particular area: *Many societies are patriarchal, based on male domination and female subordination.* ◇ **~ of sb/sth** *The domination of the foreign species S. lespedeza has the potential for transforming the prairie ecosystem.* ◇ **~ (of sb/sth) by sb/sth** *He criticized the domination of the market by a small number of giant companies.* ◇ **~ over sb/sth** *The United States insisted on retaining total domination over the Western hemisphere.*

D

do·min·ion /dəˈmɪniən/ *noun* **1** [U] authority to rule; control: *The World Trade Organization is seeking to extend its dominion into the domestic affairs of member countries.* ◇ **~ over sb/sth** *The Bible talks of men and women being given dominion over the rest of creation by God (Genesis 1:27–28).* **2** [C, usually pl.] (*formal*) an area controlled by one ruler or government: *The treaty extended to all Ottoman dominions.*

do·nate /dəʊˈneɪt; *NAmE* ˈdoʊneɪt/ *verb* **1** [T, I] to give money, food, clothes, etc. to sb/sth, especially a charity: **~ sth** *Over 800 people donated significant amounts of money and time.* ◇ **~ sth to sb/sth** *Local families and businesses have donated food and clothing to the refugees.* ◇ **~ to sth** *It is possible that many of those who donated to the appeal were already supporting charities on a regular or informal basis.* ➲ thesaurus note *at* CONTRIBUTE **2** [T, I] to allow doctors to remove blood, a body organ, etc. in order to help sb who needs it, or so that it can be used for research: **~ sth** *She finally conceived when her sister donated some eggs.* ◇ **~ (sth to sb)** *People with an O Rhesus negative blood group can donate blood to any recipient.* ◇ *Not all potential donors are able to donate if the dying process is prolonged.* **3** [T] **~ sth (to sth)** (*chemistry, physics*) to provide one or more ELECTRONS or a PROTONS to another atom, MOLECULE or ION: *Each phosphorus atom donates a free electron to the silicon crystal.* ◇ *Water acts as a Lewis base when it donates a pair of electrons to a proton in solution.*

do·na·tion /dəʊˈneɪʃn; *NAmE* doʊˈneɪʃn/ *noun* **1** [C] something that is given to a person or an organization such as a charity, in order to help them: **~ (of sth)** *The women of her church helped young pregnant girls with donations of clothing.* ◇ **~ to sb/sth** *He made substantial donations to organizations in Ukraine.* **2** [U] **~ of sth (to sb/sth)** the act of giving sth to a person or an organization such as a charity, in order to help them: *She organizes the donation of food to soup kitchens.* **3** [U] the act of giving blood, a body organ, etc. to be used by doctors in medical treatment: **+ noun** *The UK has one of the lowest organ donation rates in Europe.*

done /dʌn/ ➲ DO[1], DO[2]

donor /ˈdəʊnə(r); *NAmE* ˈdoʊnər/ *noun* **1** a person or an organization that makes a gift of money, clothes, food, etc. to a charity, etc: *Most of their financing comes from individual donors.* ◇ **~ to sth** *He was a major donor to Richard Nixon's presidential campaign.* ◇ **+ noun** *The abolition of school fees in these regions was only possible with the help of donor countries.* **2** a person who gives blood, SPERM, a body organ, etc. to be used by doctors in medical treatment: *Generally, there is a scarcity of suitable organ donors.* ◇ **+ noun** *Their two children were conceived by donor insemination.* **3** (*chemistry, physics*) an atom, MOLECULE or ION that provides one or more ELECTRONS or PROTONS to another atom, molecule or ion: *Acids are proton donors when they come into contact with water.*

door /dɔː(r)/ *noun* **1** a piece of wood, glass, etc. that is opened and closed so that people can get in and out of a room, building, car, etc: *to open/shut/close/lock/unlock the door* ◇ **at/on the ~** *The patient had knocked on the door of a neighbour for help.* ◇ **front ~** *Soldiers stood guard at his front door.* ◇ **~ of sth** *The centre-reinforced impact beam was also manufactured and mounted on the side door of a compact passenger car.* **2** the space when a door is open: *All visitors have to walk through the door into reception.*
IDM **(from) ˌdoor to ˈdoor** from one house or building to the next in an area: *New donors are also solicited by trained recruiters going door to door in selected neighbourhoods.* ◇ *In 19th-century America, door-to-door salesmen sold everything from health tonics to encyclopedias.* **(open) the door to sth** (to provide) the means of getting or reaching sth; (to create) the opportunity for sth: *When earthquakes disrupt water supply systems, it opens the door to water-borne infections.* **lay sth at sb's/sth's ˈdoor** to say that sb is responsible for sth that has gone wrong: *The problem of teenage crime was often laid at the door of mothers who worked rather than staying at home.* **leave the door ˈopen (for sth)** to make sure that there is still the possibility of doing sth: *The court's decision leaves the door open for expansion of trading programmes by other states.* ➲ *more at* CLOSED, OPEN[2]

dor·mant /ˈdɔːmənt; *NAmE* ˈdɔːrmənt/ *adj.* not active or growing now but able to become active or to grow in the future SYN INACTIVE: *The cells are maintained in a dormant state.* ◇ *The tetanus bacteria may lie dormant in the soil for years until the conditions for growth reappear.* ◇ *The plan remained dormant for a year, before being taken up by the next administration.* ➲ *compare* ACTIVE[1]
■ **dor·mancy** /ˈdɔːmənsi; *NAmE* ˈdɔːrmənsi/ *noun* [U] **~ (of sth)** *We concluded that dormancy of L. chinensis seeds is not mainly controlled by endogenous hormones.*

dor·sal /ˈdɔːsl; *NAmE* ˈdɔːrsl/ *adj.* [only before noun] (*biology*) on or connected with the back of a fish or an animal: *Some elongate fishes have dorsal fins that run the full length of the body.* ➲ *compare* VENTRAL

dos·age /ˈdəʊsɪdʒ; *NAmE* ˈdoʊsɪdʒ/ *noun* [C, U] the amount of a medicine or drug that is taken or used: **~ (of sth)** *A dosage of 7.5 mg/day or more is associated with increased cardiovascular risk.* ◇ *Tolerance to the drug develops rapidly, leading to increasing dosage.* ◇ **high/low ~** *When the drugs are combined they should be started together, both at low dosage.*

dose[1] /dəʊs; *NAmE* doʊs/ *noun* **1** an amount of a medicine or a drug that is taken, or recommended to be taken: **~ (of sth)** *The starting dose of methadone is usually 10–20 mg daily.* ◇ **high/low ~** *Prolonged treatment with high doses of steroids can cause major medical problems.* **2 ~ (of sth)** an amount of RADIATION that is given at one time, or over a period of time: *He received a dose of 30 Gy in 15 fractions over 3 weeks.*

dose[2] /dəʊs; *NAmE* doʊs/ *verb* **~ sb/sth (with sth)** to give a person or animal a medicine or drug: *Dosing female alligators with a cocktail of pesticides at ovulation reduced hatching rates of their eggs.*

dot[1] /dɒt; *NAmE* dɑːt/ *noun* a small round mark, especially one that is printed: *On the map, each dot represents a single village.* ◇ **~ of sth** *Each inch of the canvas is covered by tiny dots of colour.*

dot[2] /dɒt; *NAmE* dɑːt/ *verb* (**-tt-**) [often passive] to spread things or people over an area; to be spread over an area: **~ sth** *Numerous small lakes and ponds dot the landscape.* ◇ **be dotted with sth** *By 1500 the country was dotted with rudimentary castle towns.*

double[1] /ˈdʌbl/ *adj.* [usually before noun] **1** having or made of two things or parts that are equal or similar: *Our study found that double-layer latex gloves provided better protection than single-layer gloves.* HELP In chemistry, a **double bond** is a chemical bond in which two pairs of ELECTRONS are shared between two atoms: *There is a double bond between the third and fourth carbon atoms.* **2** twice as big, or as much or many, as usual: *Studies have shown that physical activity reduces stress; a double effect was observed when this took place outdoors.* **3** combining two things or qualities: *According to Derrida (1978), all texts carry double or multiple meanings.* **4** made for two people or things: *The renovations provided the hospital with more double rooms for patients.* ➲ *compare* SINGLE[1]

double[2] /ˈdʌbl/ *det.* twice as much or as many as: *By 1999 the value of business-to-business e-commerce was double the amount of business-to-consumer e-commerce.* ◇ *The* *fuel efficiency of the Toyota Prius Hybrid is about double that of conventional vehicles.*

double[3] /ˈdʌbl/ *verb* [I, T] to become, or make sth become, twice as big, or twice as much or as many: *From 1998 to 2001, Internet adoption rates in UK households more than doubled from 24% to 51%.* ◇ *Alley et al. (1993) showed that the rate of ice accumulation doubled in just three years.* ◇ **~ in size** *During this time the cell doubles in size and its DNA is replicated.* ◇ **~ sth** *Men whose alcohol intake is at the higher level double their risk of stroke.*
PHR V **ˈdouble as sth** to have another use or function as well as the main one: *The school's playground doubles as a community gathering place in the evenings.*

doubly /ˈdʌbli/ *adv.* (used before adjectives) **1** in two ways; for two reasons: *Mobility for the urban poor is doubly constrained by lack of vehicles and fear of violence.* **2** to twice the normal extent or degree: *The high budget made the initial choice of software doubly important.* ◇ *Two doubly charged ions interact four times more strongly than two singly charged ions at the same separation.*

doubt[1] /daʊt/ *noun* [U, C] a feeling of not being sure about sth or not believing sth: *She continued to struggle with feelings of doubt.* ◇ **~ about sth** *Foreign investors had doubts about Russian financial stability.* ◇ *Laboratory tests raised doubts about safety, and development of the product was stopped.* ◇ **cast/throw ~ on sth** *The results of the study cast doubt on the effectiveness of imprisonment as a sanction.* ◇ **~ that...** *There is little doubt that shift work is associated with a number of health problems.* ◇ **~ as to sth** *There is some doubt as to whether screening for prostate cancer improves patient outcome.*
IDM **beyond (any) ˈdoubt** in a way that shows that sth is completely certain: *His wishes and feelings are clear beyond any doubt.* ◇ *The prosecution must prove beyond reasonable doubt that the defendant is guilty.* **be in ˈdoubt** to be uncertain: *The success of the project is currently in doubt.* **have your ˈdoubts (about sth)** to have reasons why you are not certain about whether sth is good or whether sth good will happen: *Though Alison tried to be the supportive wife, she secretly had her doubts about his ability to achieve his career goals.* **if in ˈdoubt** used to give advice to sb who cannot decide what to do: *If in doubt, you should consult the manufacturer.* **ˌno ˈdoubt 1** used when you are saying that sth is probable: *Some of the sources that did not survive were no doubt destroyed by Christians who found their teachings to be offensive.* **2** used when you are saying that sth is certainly true: *There can be no doubt that the air temperature has warmed over the past 15 years in northern Alaska.* **without/beyond (a) ˈdoubt** used when you are giving your opinion and emphasizing the point that you are making: *Adapting literary works to film is, without a doubt, a creative undertaking.* ➲ *more at* BENEFIT[1]

doubt[2] /daʊt/ *verb* **1** to not feel sure about sth; to feel that sth is not true or will probably not happen: **~ sth** *Few experts doubt the importance of population in relation to climate change.* ◇ *Evidence suggests that there are grounds for doubting this presumption.* ◇ **~ (that)...** *It cannot be doubted that the opportunities available to women now are much greater than 50 years ago.* ◇ **~ whether/if...** *Some ecologists doubt whether stability is really a property of ecological systems over the longer term.* ➲ thesaurus note *at* CHALLENGE[2] **2 ~ sb/sth** to not trust sb/sth; to not believe sb: *Provided there is no clear reason to doubt them, a patient's account is the single most reliable indicator of pain.*

doubt·ful /ˈdaʊtfl/ *adj.* **1** [not usually before noun] unlikely: *Any quick solution to current difficulties is doubtful.* ◇ **it is ~ whether/if...** *It is doubtful whether anyone could have done better in the circumstances.* ◇ **it is ~ (that)...** *It is doubtful that this experiment can tell us anything relevant.* **2** [not before noun] (of a person) not sure; feeling doubt SYN DUBIOUS (3): **~ about (doing) sth** *Other scientists are more doubtful about these claims.* ◇ **~ as to sth** *Many commentators remain doubtful as to whether the government can meet its targets.* ◇ **~ of (doing) sth** *One might be doubtful of accepting discoveries from a study that could not replicate large known effects.* **3** (of a thing) not certain; that can be doubted: *In doubtful cases, a liver biopsy may be required.* ◇ *All the readings were doubtful or negative.* **4** [only before noun] not of a quality that you can rely on SYN DUBIOUS (1): *It was a country with a doubtful human rights record.* ◇ *Many Russian officers were former officer-cadets of noble birth and doubtful education.*

doubt·less /ˈdaʊtləs/ *adv.* almost certainly SYN WITHOUT/BEYOND (A) DOUBT: *Some of these stories are doubtless exaggerated.* ◇ *Reductions in running costs have meant that customers can now afford a bigger car that will doubtless use more fuel.*

down[1] /daʊn/ *adv.* HELP For the special uses of **down** in phrasal verbs, look at the entries for the verbs. For example **break down** is in the phrasal verb section at **break**. **1** to a lower level or rate: *The concentration fluctuates from a low level to a higher level, and back down again.* ◇ *This situation is unsustainable, and will require costly increases in unemployment to bring the associated inflation down.* **2** used to show that the amount or strength of sth is lower, or that there is less activity: *Economic crises can slow down and even temporarily reverse this type of industrial development.* ◇ *Banks were forced to scale down their business.* **3** to a lower place or position: *The knowledge of how to assemble a structure so that it will not fall down has been around for decades.* ◇ *Ask the patient to look down and away from the affected side.* **4** from a standing or vertical position to a sitting or horizontal one: *Instead of walking off the job to go on strike, the workers simply sat down inside the factory.* ◇ *Pain that is not relieved when the patient lies down suggests malignancy or infection.* **5** on paper: *In this task, the participants read the passages and wrote down what they thought the words meant.*

down[2] /daʊn/ *prep.* **1** from a high or higher point on sth to a lower one: *These base surges rush down the slope of the volcano at hurricane speed and are absolutely deadly.* ◇ *Obstruction of the blood supply will result in chest pain, often radiating down the left arm.* **2** along; towards the direction in which you are facing: *The president walked down Pennsylvania Avenue on inauguration day in a business suit.*

down·load[1] /ˌdaʊnˈləʊd; *NAmE* ˌdaʊnˈloʊd/ *verb* **~ sth (from sth) (to sth)** to move data to a smaller computer system, TABLET or similar device, from a larger computer system: *Downloading music and video from the Internet had become the most common legal offence among young people in the UK.* ◇ *The department provided revision files for students to download to their computers or smart phones.* OPP UPLOAD ➲ *compare* LOAD[2] (4) ■ **down·load·able** /ˌdaʊnˈləʊdəbl; *NAmE* ˌdaʊnˈloʊdəbl/ *adj.*: *The Prelinger Archives also make government films available in a free, downloadable digital form off the Internet.* ◇ *All images are downloadable for research and teaching purposes.*

down·load[2] /ˈdaʊnləʊd; *NAmE* ˈdaʊnloʊd/ *noun* [C, U] data that are downloaded from a computer system; the act of downloading data: *By 2006, video downloads occupied perhaps half the total traffic on the Internet.* ◇ *The website provides additional material that is available for download.*

down·stream /ˌdaʊnˈstriːm/ *adv.*, /ˈdaʊnstriːm/ *adj.* **1** in or towards a position along a river that is nearer the sea: *The adults spawn in fresh waters and the developing embryos drift downstream.* ◇ *Developments upstream are significant for all downstream fisheries.* ◇ **~ of/from sth**

Some of these pollution-sensitive species returned to the river downstream of a tributary. OPP UPSTREAM (1) **2 ~ (of/ from sth)** at or towards a later point in a process or series: *Genes can be placed downstream of different regulatory regions that allow controlled expression.* HELP In economics, **upstream** markets contribute to your supplies and **downstream** markets are the people who use your goods: *These price changes are not immediately passed downstream to consumers.* OPP UPSTREAM (2)

D

down·turn /ˈdaʊntɜːn; *NAmE* ˈdaʊntɜːrn/ *noun* [C, usually sing., U] a fall in the amount of business that is done; a time when the economy becomes weaker: *Many feared a deep and prolonged economic downturn.* ◇ *These developments coincided with a period of economic downturn.* ◇ **~ in sth** *The downturn in the economy is partly to blame.* ◇ *A sharp downturn in business investment pushed the country further into recession.*

down·ward /ˈdaʊnwəd; *NAmE* ˈdaʊnwərd/ *adj.* [usually before noun] moving or leading towards a lower place or level: *The downward movement of water may be insufficient to leach out all the salts that accumulate near the soil surface.* ◇ *The upward spiral turns into a downward spiral of decline, damage and loss.* ◇ *There is a downward trend in the proportion of men holding long-tenure jobs.* ◇ *All these factors put further downward pressure on wages.* OPP UPWARD

down·wards /ˈdaʊnwədz; *NAmE* ˈdaʊnwərdz/ (*also* **down·ward** *especially in NAmE*) *adv.* towards a lower place or level: *Precipitation moves downwards through the soil.* ◇ *The demand curve is downward sloping.* ◇ *Interest rates were adjusted downwards.* OPP UPWARDS

draft[1] AWL /drɑːft; *NAmE* dræft/ *noun* **1** [C] a rough written version of sth that is not yet in its final form: *This is just a first draft that needs more work.* ◇ **~ of sth** *The original draft of Eliot's poem was severely edited by Ezra Pound.* ◇ *Final drafts of the policy and law were approved by the Cabinet.* ◇ **+ noun** *The draft budget was sent to the European Parliament for approval.* **2 the draft** [sing.] (*US*) = CONSCRIPTION

draft[2] AWL (*also* **draught** *especially in BrE*) /drɑːft; *NAmE* dræft/ *verb* **1 ~ sth** to write the first rough version of sth such as a letter, speech or book: *The constitution was hastily drafted in twenty days and was intended to be provisional only.* ◇ *The committee was charged with drafting a document that would outlaw war.* **2** [usually passive] **be drafted + adv./prep.** to choose people and send them somewhere for a special task: *State peasants could be drafted to factory work.* ◇ *School-leavers were drafted to certain key jobs where there was a labour shortage.* ◇ *She was drafted in to help.* **3** [usually passive] **be drafted (into sth)** (*US*) = CONSCRIPT[1]: *He was drafted into the army in November 1942.*

draft·ee /ˌdrɑːfˈtiː; *NAmE* ˌdræfˈtiː/ *noun* (*US*) = CONSCRIPT[2]

drain[1] /dreɪn/ *noun* **1** [C] a pipe that carries away dirty water or other liquid waste: *Drains choked with sediment are common features of building sites in the city.* **2 the drains** [pl.] a system of pipes that carry away dirty water or other liquid waste: *The drains became blocked.* **3** [C] a tube for removing liquid from a part of the body where it could be harmful: *A chest drain may be used to drain the cavity.* **4** [sing.] **a ~ on sb/sth** a person or thing that uses a lot of the time, money, etc. that could be used for sb/sth else: *Asylum seekers are more likely to be perceived as a drain on resources than as contributors to economic growth.*

drain[2] /dreɪn/ *verb* **1** [I] (of a liquid) to flow away: **+ adv./ prep.** *The river drains north-eastwards.* ◇ **~ from/out of sth** *When the ice shelf receded, the lake waters drained from the valley.* ◇ **~ away/off** *She tilted his head to the injured side to allow blood to drain away.* ◇ **~ into sth** *Temperatures stabilized as the great North American ice cap continued to melt and drain into the Gulf of Mexico.* **2** [T] to make sth empty or drier by removing all the liquid from it: **~ sth (from sth)** *Excess water is drained from the substrate to maintain a constant water level.* ◇ **~ sth of sth** *The accident at the power plant occurred because the reactor was completely drained of its coolant.* **3** [I] to become completely empty or drier because liquid has been removed or flows away: *Very wet soils may never drain properly.* ◇ *An ice sheet retreat about 9500 years ago caused the lake to drain.* **4** [T] **~ sth** to make land drier by making water flow away from it: *The settlers had to drain swamps and clear dense forests.* ◇ *Flat basin floors are often marshy and poorly drained.* **5** [T] (of a river or CANAL) to carry water away from an area: **~ sth** *The Chao Phraya originates as four rivers that drain the hills of northern Thailand.* ◇ **~ sth from sth** *Canals drain water from the eastern suburban areas.* **6** [T] to make sb/sth weaker or poorer by using up their/its strength, money, etc: **~ sb/sth** *She felt emotionally drained by her work.* ◇ **~ sth from sb/sth** *American consumption, especially of energy, drains natural resources from the world.* ◇ **~ sb/ sth of sth** *Sugar can drain the soil of its fertility if planted repeatedly on the same ground.*

drain·age /ˈdreɪnɪdʒ/ *noun* [U] **1** the process by which water or liquid waste material flows or is taken away from an area: *The frozen ground impedes drainage.* ◇ **~ of sth** *The first stage in drainage of a wetland is normally creation of open water drainage channels.* ◇ **+ noun** *The geologists could find no evidence for an older drainage system that could be called the Colorado.* **2** a system of drains: *The persistent rain overloaded the local drainage, causing localized flooding.*

drama AWL /ˈdrɑːmə/ *noun* **1** [C] a play for the theatre, television or radio SYN PLAY[2] (2): *Several members of the cast have appeared regularly in period dramas.* ◇ *Below the Acropolis, dramas were staged in honour of the god Dionysus.* **2** [U] plays considered as a form of literature: *Romantic drama tends to focus on the psychological.* ◇ **+ noun** *The idea for the book came from the Australian drama teachers' association.* **3** [U] the fact of being exciting SYN EXCITEMENT (2): *Most of the time, states cooperate with each other without much political drama.* ◇ *Full of drama and intriguing individuals, the history of geography is a fascinating subject.* **4** [C] an exciting event: *The country watched obsessively as the courtroom drama unfolded on live TV.*

dra·mat·ic AWL /drəˈmætɪk/ *adj.* **1** (of a change or an event) sudden, very great and often surprising: *A dramatic change occurred late in the 18th century when nationalism became a powerful force in Europe.* ◇ *The past 100 years have seen a dramatic improvement in the ability of media to target messages.* ◇ *The increase in life expectancy among older adults has been particularly dramatic.* **2** exciting and impressive: *These parks cover some of Scotland's most dramatic landscape and varied habitats.* ◇ *The opening line of this poem is brilliantly dramatic.* ◇ *The research programme culminated in the dramatic announcement of the birth of Dolly the cloned sheep.* **3** [usually before noun] connected with the theatre or plays: *The programme incorporates the visual and dramatic arts.* ◇ *The form is closer to that of a diary than a dramatic text.*

▸ DRAMATIC + NOUN **change, shift, swing** • **increase, rise** • **improvement** • **decrease, decline, fall, reduction** • **expansion** • **impact** *There has been a dramatic rise in the new treatment options for rare diseases.* ◇ *Performance-related pay can have a dramatic impact on service output.* | **effect** • **transformation** • **event** *The recession had dramatic effects in a range of countries and industries.* ◇ *Light from a candle, reflected by an ornate mirror, gives a dramatic effect to the scene.* | **contrast** • **example** • **demonstration** *Marsh used dramatic examples of ruined Mediterranean landscapes in support of his argument.*

dra·mat·ic·al·ly AWL /drəˈmætɪkli/ *adv.* **1** in a very sudden or extreme way; to a very great degree: *In the next two years the situation changed dramatically.* ◇ *The population increased dramatically, growing from about 11 000 in 1860 to nearly 200 000 in 1900.* ◇ *State schools in more affluent areas have dramatically different results from those in poorer areas.* ➲ *compare* SIGNIFICANTLY (1) **2** in a way that is exciting or impressive: *Figure 16.12 dramatically illustrates the large swings in economic prosperity.* ◇ *Marshall dramatically announced his proposal at Harvard University.* **3** using the style of a play in telling a story or giving an account of an event: *These authors show how the events unfold dramatically rather than simply recounting them.*

drama·tist AWL /ˈdræmətɪst/ *noun* a person who writes plays for the theatre, television or radio SYN PLAYWRIGHT: *Beckett came to be recognized as the most important dramatist writing in English in the latter half of the 20th century.*

drama·tize (*BrE also* -ise) AWL /ˈdræmətaɪz/ *verb* **1** to present a book or an event as a play or film: **~ sth** *There are popular plays that dramatize the lives of Romantic writers.* ◇ **~ sth for sth** *Hollywood studios turned in the 1930s to adapting novels that had not yet been dramatized for the stage.* **2 ~ sth** to make sth seem more exciting or important than it really is: *Matters were dramatized further by the energy crisis that arrived suddenly in 1973.* ■ **drama·tiza·tion, -isation** AWL /ˌdræmətaɪˈzeɪʃn; ˌdræmətəˈzeɪʃn/ *noun* [C, U] **~ (of sth) (for sth)** *There have been over 100 dramatizations of 'Frankenstein' for stage or screen.* ◇ *The process of dramatization for screen of a long and weighty novel inevitably means selection and condensation.*

drank *past tense of* DRINK[2]

dras·tic /ˈdræstɪk; *BrE also* ˈdrɑːstɪk/ *adj.* extreme in a way that has a sudden, serious or violent effect on sth: *This target can only be achieved through a drastic reduction of fossil fuel use.* ◇ *Sales dropped by one third in a year, forcing the company to take drastic action to save the business.* ■ **dras·tic·al·ly** /ˈdræstɪkli; *BrE also* ˈdrɑːstɪkli/ *adv.*: *Vietnam's mangrove forests have decreased drastically, both in area and quality.* ◇ *E-commerce has drastically reduced some costs and delays associated with marketing.*

draught *verb* (*especially BrE*) = DRAFT[2]

draw /drɔː/ *verb* (**drew** /druː/, **drawn** /drɔːn/) **1** [I, T] to make pictures, or a picture of sth, with a pencil or pen (but not paint): *The children are encouraged to express themselves through drawing and painting.* ◇ **~ sth** *This can be confirmed graphically by drawing a Venn diagram.* ◇ (*figurative*) *Further studies are needed to draw the whole picture of the emergency referral system.* **2** [T] **~ sth/sb (+ adv./prep.)** to move sth/sb by pulling it/them: *The pressure is changed by drawing out a piston.* ◇ *Except for the affluent who could afford horse-drawn carriages, most workers walked from home to their place of employment.* **3** [I] **+ adv./prep.** to move towards a point in time or a process: *The time for McDonald's resignation drew closer.* ◇ *As the nineteenth century drew to a close, increasing numbers of political refugees were beginning to settle in Britain.* **4** [T] to attract or interest sb: **~ sb** *The demonstration reportedly drew crowds of 400 000.* ◇ **~ sb + adv./prep.** *The snippets of oral history in the text draw the readers deeper into the story.* ◇ **~ sth to sth** *Her comments also draw attention to the issues of age and generation.* **5** [T] to produce a reaction or response SYN ATTRACT (3): **~ sth** *The administration drew major international criticism for its imprisonment of suspects without the protections of the Geneva Convention.* ◇ **~ sth from sb** *Attempts by the rebels to draw support from Canada, the West Indies and Ireland failed.* **6** [T] to have a particular idea after you have studied sth or thought about it: **~ sth** *In the absence of independent confirmation of these results, it is difficult to draw conclusions.* ◇ **~ sth from sth** *Managers must draw lessons from past strategic mistakes and failure.* **7** [T] **~ sth** to express a comparison or a contrast: *He draws an important parallel between ethnicity and gender.* ◇ *A clear distinction was drawn between retirement and pensions.* **8** [T] to take money or payments from a bank account SYN WITHDRAW (4): **~ sth out (from/of sth)** *Definitions focus on liquid assets, such as accounts from which you can draw your money out quickly.* ◇ **~ sth from sth** *States draw federal grants from a common revenue pool.* ◇ **~ sth on sth** *The defendant drew forged cheques on his employer's bank accounts.* OPP DEPOSIT[2] (3) **9** [T] **~ sth (+adv./prep.)** to take or pull liquid or gas from somewhere: *Due to the intense cold and the Earth's rotation, a stream of air is drawn towards the South Pole.* ◇ *Blood is drawn into a syringe, which contains the anticoagulant.*

IDM **draw the ˈline (between sth and sth)** to distinguish between two closely related ideas; to set a balance between two opposite things: *The difficulty of drawing the line between ethical and unethical practices can be revealed in several ways.*

PHR V **ˌdraw ˈback (from sth/from doing sth)** to choose not to take action, especially because you feel nervous: *He drew back from supporting the government.* **ˈdraw sth from sb/sth 1** to take or obtain sth from a particular source: *French and American revolutionaries drew inspiration from him.* ◇ *A wide range of insights drawn from the work of literary critics has been applied to these texts.* **2** to choose sth/sb from a group of people or things: *A random sample of telephone numbers was drawn from a computerized list of subscribers.* ◇ *The committee drew its membership from the local community.* **ˈdraw sb into (doing) sth | ˌdraw sb ˈin** to involve sb or make sb take part in sth, although they may not want to take part at first: *At the onset of war, people who would otherwise be in the civilian labour force are drawn into military service.* ◇ *The controversial but accessible nature of the pieces drew participants in.* **ˈdraw on/upon sth** to use a supply of sth that is available to you: *She draws on her personal experience as a professional musician.* ◇ *They drew upon his technical expertise to help in the negotiations.* ➲ thesaurus note *at* USE[1] **ˌdraw sb/sth ˈout** to encourage sb to talk or express themselves freely: *The silence led her to reformulate her questions in order to draw out responses.* **ˌdraw sth ˈout** to make sth last longer than usual or necessary: *The whole process was very drawn out with much waiting around.* **ˌdraw sth ˈup** to make or write sth that needs careful thought or planning: *Plans are being drawn up to fit all cars with a microchip which will monitor driving behaviour.*

draw·back /ˈdrɔːbæk/ *noun* a disadvantage or problem that makes sth a less attractive idea SYN DISADVANTAGE[1]: *Each theory has some serious drawbacks in terms of practical application.* ◇ **~ of (doing) sth** *The only drawback of working in this way comes when more detailed investigations are required.* ◇ **~ to sth** *A drawback to this technique is that sample size has to be increased.*

draw·ing /ˈdrɔːɪŋ/ *noun* **1** [C] a picture made using a pencil or pen rather than paint: *Numerous original drawings and photographs are provided.* ◇ **~ of sth** *A schematic drawing of this mechanism is given in Fig. 21.41.* **2** [U] the art or skill of making pictures, plans, etc. using a pen or pencil: *He developed an early fondness for drawing and painting.*

dream[1] /driːm/ *noun* **1** a series of images, events and feelings that happen in your mind while you are sleeping: *Constantine had a dream in which he was told to inscribe a special sign on his men's shields.* ◇ *A 'lucid dream' is defined as a dream in which you know, at the time, that you are dreaming.* **2 ~ (of sth/doing sth)** a wish to have, do or be sth, especially one that seems difficult to achieve:

He knew he would have to work hard to realize his dream of launching a company. ◇ *The interviewees fill their recollections with good times, hard times, love, laughter, hopes and dreams.*

dream² /driːm/ *verb* (**dreamt**, **dreamt** /dremt/) or (**dreamed**, **dreamed**) **1** [I, T] to imagine and think about sth that you would like to happen: **~ of/about sth** *After the revolution, many dreamed of a future in free America.* ◇ *Agriculture has delivered something that previous generations could only dream about, namely a ready supply of cheap food.* ◇ **~ of/about doing sth** *The Housing Act of 1968 removed the last legal obstacle to black citizens who dreamed of moving to a better neighbourhood.* **2** [I, T] to experience a series of images, events and feelings in your mind while you are sleeping: **~ of/about sb/sth** *Many people have the experience of dreaming about a bell ringing, only to wake to the sound of their alarm clock.* ◇ **~ (that)...** *That night he dreamt that Christ came to him with a sign.*

dress¹ /dres/ *noun* **1** [C] a piece of women's clothing that is made in one piece and covers the body down to the legs: *Typically, the bride wore her best dress to marry, which generally was not white and was worn again after the wedding.* **2** [U] clothes for either men or women: *It is the responsibility of the employer to determine appropriate dress.*

dress² /dres/ *verb* **1** [I, T] to put clothes on yourself/sb: **get dressed** *She had an episode of chest pain while getting dressed.* ◇ **~ sb/yourself** *He is no longer able to dress himself.* **2** [I, T] to wear a particular type or style of clothes: *A doctor should always dress professionally and conservatively when meeting patients.* ◇ **~ for/in/as sth** *Many teens who dress in an unusual manner resent the fact that others stare at them.* ◇ **be dressed (for/in/as sth)** *All three were dressed in black suits and white shirts.* **3** [T] **~ sth** to clean, treat and cover a wound: *It is appropriate for these wounds to be cleaned and dressed.*

drew *past tense of* DRAW

dried *past tense, past part. of* DRY²

dri·est ➲ DRY¹

drift¹ /drɪft/ *noun* **1** [C, usually sing., U] a slow steady movement or change, from one situation, belief or place to another: **~ towards sth** *The result was a drift towards socialism.* ◇ **~ (from sth) (to sth)** *The devastation of the land during the war had fostered the drift to the cities.* ➲ *see also* GENETIC DRIFT **2** [U] the movement of the sea or air: *Drift is almost exclusively to the east.* ◇ *Wind direction is shown by smoke drift.* ➲ *compare* CURRENT² (1) ➲ *see also* CONTINENTAL DRIFT **3** [U] **~ (from sth)** the movement of a ship, plane or bird away from its intended direction because of currents or wind: *This formula accounts for drift from the intended flight path caused by crosswinds.* **4** [U, C] a large mass of sth, for example soil, ice or snow, that has been left somewhere by the movement of water, wind, etc: *Water accumulates in depressions in glacial drift.* ◇ **~ of sth** *Winter drifts of snow contribute to streamflow in early spring.* **5** [sing.] **~ (of sth)** the general meaning of what sb says or writes: *When they were encouraged to reflect on specific problems in the past, the drift of their replies became more negative.*

drift² /drɪft/ *verb* **1** [I] to be carried somewhere in air or water: *Spores and pollen do not fly; they drift.* ◇ **+ adv./prep.** *New species could reach the site by drifting from upstream.* **2** [I] **(+ adv./prep.)** to act, happen or change without a particular plan or purpose: *With less competitive pressure on firms, costs will drift upwards.* ◇ *The government just appeared to drift from crisis to crisis.*

drill¹ /drɪl/ *verb* **1** [T, I] to make a hole in the ground in order to find oil, gas or water: **~ sth** *The first well was drilled in Indonesia in 1872.* ◇ **~ for sth** *The global recession caused a big reduction in the number of rigs actively drilling for gas.* **2** [T] **~ sth (+ adv./prep.)** to make a hole in sth, using, or as though using, a DRILL: *Thaid snails typically drill a hole in the shell of their prey.* ◇ *The cylinder has a hole drilled though the middle.*

PHR V ˌ**drill** ˈ**down** to find out more detail or information about sb/sth in order to understand them/it better: **~ into/to sth** *I took each issue and drilled down into more detail than before.*

drill² /drɪl/ *noun* **1** [C] a tool or machine with a pointed end for making holes: *Auger mining uses a huge drill to dig the coal out of the seams.* **2** [C, U] a practice of what to do in an emergency, for example if there is a fire: *There was no staff training in fire drill or evacuation procedures.* ◇ *The Chinese health authority conducted an emergency drill to test the response to a possible avian influenza outbreak.* **3** [C, U] military training in marching, the use of weapons, etc: *In the Hitler Youth, military drills took precedence over sports, hiking and camping.* ◇ *Drill and field training were neglected with the result that the men were not prepared for attack.* **4** [C, U] a way of learning sth by means of repeated exercises: *Traditional methods of teaching mathematics have been fundamentally drill and practice.*

drink¹ /drɪŋk/ *noun* [C, U] **1** a liquid for drinking; an amount of a liquid that you drink: *These patients should avoid caffeinated drinks.* ◇ *Coconut palms were a source of food and drink.* ◇ **~ of sth** *The child was not even allowed a drink of water.* ➲ *see also* SOFT DRINK **2** alcohol or an alcoholic drink; sth that you drink on a social occasion: *The findings showed differences in attitudes towards designer drinks and other forms of alcoholic drink.*

drink² /drɪŋk/ *verb* (**drank** /dræŋk/, **drunk** /drʌŋk/) **1** [T, I] to take liquid into your mouth and swallow it: *The patient can be allowed to eat and drink normally after 8 hours.* ◇ **~ sth** *An estimated 600 million people drink contaminated water daily (Economy, 2004).* **2** [I, T] to drink alcohol, especially regularly: *He enjoys wine but does not drink heavily.* ◇ **~ sth** *It is recommended that pregnant women should avoid drinking alcohol.* ➲ *see also* DRUNK¹

drink·er /ˈdrɪŋkə(r)/ *noun* **1** a person who drinks alcohol regularly: *Heavy drinkers are up to four times as likely to report an accident in the previous year compared with non-drinkers.* **2** (after a noun) a person who regularly drinks the particular drink mentioned: *It is often said that American beer drinkers prefer lighter beers.*

drink·ing /ˈdrɪŋkɪŋ/ *noun* [U] **1** the act of drinking alcohol: *Binge drinking is a particular problem in this age group.* ◇ *hazardous/excessive/heavy drinking* ◇ **+ noun** *Drinking and smoking patterns in adulthood are often established in childhood.* **2** (after a noun) the act of drinking the particular drink mentioned: *The Europeans encountered tea drinking, sampled the drink, and, being businessmen, they wondered if there was a market for the product back home.*

drive¹ /draɪv/ *verb* (**drove** /drəʊv/; *NAmE* droʊv/, **driven** /ˈdrɪvn/) **1** [I, T] to operate a car, train, bus, etc. so that it goes in a particular direction: *He was driving home from work when he noticed that the vision in his left eye was becoming blurred.* ◇ **~ sth** *The use of mobile telephones while driving a car has been identified as dangerous.* **2** [T] **~ sb (+ adv./prep.)** to take sb somewhere in a car, etc: *Her husband had to drive her to the hospital in the middle of the night.* **3** [T, often passive] to provide the power that makes a machine work **SYN** POWER² (1): **be driven by sth** *The amplifier is driven by a voltage source with a resistance of 500 Ohms.* ◇ **~ sth** *The steam drives a turbine that drives the electric generator.* **4** [T] to cause sth to happen or develop: **be driven by sth** *The company's actions were driven by a desire to reduce risk and get rid of unprofitable* *customers.* ◇ *Climate change is driven more by consumer behaviour than simply by population numbers.* ◇ **~ sth** *Research is needed to determine which factors are driving the risk of lung cancer associated with coal use.* ➲ *compare* MOTIVATE (1) **5** [T, often passive] to force sb to act in a particular way, especially in a way that is bad or extreme: **(be) driven by sth** *He plunges into this tragedy, driven by paranoid desire for power.* ◇ **~ sb to do sth** *These symptoms cause great distress, which drives the person to seek further supplies of the drug.* ◇ **~ sb to (doing) sth** *Evicted villagers were driven to begging and stealing.* **6** [T] to make sb very angry, anxious, etc. or bring them to a particular state: **~ sb + adj.** *The documentation needed to prepare for the report drives clinicians mad.* ◇ **~ sb to sth** *Typically, these characters are depicted as having a selfish or greedy motive that drives them to the point of destruction.* **7** [T] **~ sb/sth + adv./prep.** to force people or animals to move in a particular direction: *Their approach is to drive people to their website and use the FAQs to answer customer queries.* ◇ *The Texas ranchers drove cattle north in increasing numbers.* **8** [T] **~ sth + adv./prep.** to force sth to go in a particular direction or into a particular position by pushing or hitting it: *A tube was driven into the soil to a depth of 10 cm.* ◇ *The combusting air and fuel mixture drives the piston downwards.* **9** [T] **~ sth (+ adv./prep.)** (of wind or water) to carry sth along: *Strong offshore wind drives air over the ocean surface.* ◇ *100 000 tonnes of oil were being driven towards the coast by strong winds.*

IDM **drive sth ˈhome (to sb)** to make sb understand or accept sth by saying it often, loudly, angrily, etc: *A few final examples will drive this point home.* ➲ *more at* HARD[1]

PHR V **ˌdrive sb aˈway** to make sb not want to stay or not want to go somewhere: *Bad publicity can drive away investors and consumers.* ◇ *Mammals such as deer are driven away by rising water levels.* **ˌdrive sb/sth ˈoff** to force sb/sth to go back or away: *Heating to drive off water and alcohol will complete the condensation process.* ◇ *In some species, the host drives off the parasite.* **ˌdrive sb/sth ˈout (of sth)** to make sb/sth disappear or stop doing sth: *Large corporate plantation owners have driven out smaller farmers.* ◇ *Inefficient and uncompetitive firms might be driven out of business.* **ˌdrive sth ˈup/ˈdown** to make sth such as prices rise or fall quickly: *Car use drives up food prices through its influence on the price of oil.* ◇ *The initiative comes in an effort to drive up standards in the industry.* ◇ *An increase in supply is likely to drive the price down and reduce the profits of individual firms.*

drive[2] /draɪv/ *noun* **1** [C] an organized effort by a group of people to achieve sth: **~ for sth** *They embarked on a drive for modernization.* ◇ **~ to do sth** *The drive to increase community participation is laudable.* ◇ **~ towards sth** *This shift reflects a global drive towards primary health care as an approach to achieving health for all.* **2** [C] **~ (to do sth)** a strong desire or need that is a natural part of a person or animal: *These parents have a drive to succeed and they value education.* ◇ *Testosterone levels decrease, resulting in fewer sperm and a decreased sexual drive.* **3** [U] energy and determination: *The position calls for a combination of intelligence, drive and tact.* **4** [C] = DISK DRIVE **5** [U] the transfer of power to machinery or to the wheels of a motor vehicle: *Huge blades supply the drive for a wind turbine.* ◇ **+ noun** *The traction motor is geared to the drive wheels at a fixed speed ratio.* ◇ *The officials always use big four-wheel drive vehicles.* **6** [C] an act of driving a car or other vehicle; a journey made in a car or other vehicle: *They undertook a pilot study in the remote village of Ruhoko, Tanzania, which is reachable only after a two-hour drive on a rough road.*

driver /ˈdraɪvə(r)/ *noun* **1** a person who drives a vehicle: *He has been working as a driver for a rental car company.* ◇ *a car/taxi/cab/bus/lorry/truck driver* ◇ **~ of sth** *Drivers of smaller cars are at much greater risk.* **2** one of the main things that cause sth to happen or to make progress: *Many different drivers have been associated with the emergence of diseases.* ◇ **~ of sth** *External funding was a driver of change.* ◇ **~ for sth** *This poverty creates a driver for activities that have put pressure on the forest.* ◇ **~ behind sth** *One of the drivers behind this is a desire for reform of public services.* ◇ *the key/important/principal/major driver behind sth* ◇ *The main driver behind this dramatic shift was the ever-increasing population.* IDM *see* SEAT[1]

driv·ing[1] /ˈdraɪvɪŋ/ *noun* [U] the way that sb drives a vehicle; the act of driving: *Building safer cars can induce faster and less careful driving.* ◇ *He was charged with causing death by dangerous driving.* ◇ **drunk/drunken ~** *Alcohol poisonings and drunk driving are by definition alcohol-related.* ◇ **~ of sth** *The careless driving of a motor vehicle, for example, would be the subject of a common law action.* ◇ **+ noun** *We then compared participants' recorded driving behaviour over the course of one week.* IDM *see* SEAT[1]

driv·ing[2] /ˈdraɪvɪŋ/ *adj.* [only before noun] strong and powerful; having a strong influence in making sth happen: **~ force (behind/for sth)** *One of the major driving factors in developing AIMS was improving patient safety.* ◇ *An important driving force for these processes has been the end of the Cold War.*

drop[1] /drɒp; *NAmE* drɑːp/ *verb* (**-pp-**) **1** [I, T] to become or make sth weaker, lower or less: **~ (from sth) (to sth)** *Infection rates dropped from 16.9 to 9.0%.* ◇ *Fifteen minutes later his blood pressure had dropped to an acceptable level.* ◇ **~ sth** *Making price changes for products and services often invokes a response from competitors, who may also drop their prices.* ◇ **~ by sth** *Land temperatures globally dropped by 5–15°C.* ◇ **~ dramatically/sharply/significantly** *In the current economic downturn, car sales have dropped dramatically.* ➲ language bank *at* TREND **2** [I, T] to fall or make sth fall deliberately: **+ adv./prep.** *It is certainly easier to gain speed by dropping from a tree than running along the ground.* ◇ **~ sth (+ adv./prep.)** *These waves travel from the source like the waves generated when a stone is dropped into a quiet pond.* **3** [I, T] to fall or allow sth to fall by accident: **+ adv./prep.** *The seeds drop on the ground, near the parent plant.* ◇ **~ sth (+ adv./prep.)** *When you drop a glass on the floor, one type of outcome is overwhelmingly likely.* **4** [T] **~ sb/sth (from sth)** to leave sb/sth out by accident or deliberately: *The actress was dropped from the advertising campaign after she was seen taking illegal drugs.* ◇ *Our preliminary analyses determined that our groups did not differ significantly by gender, so gender was dropped from subsequent analyses.* **5** [T] **~ sth** to stop doing or discussing sth; to not continue with sth: *The proposal was eventually dropped following objections from Parliament.* ◇ *The prosecutor may choose to drop the case.* **6** [I] **~ (from sth) (to/down to sth)** to slope steeply downwards: *Between Lees Ferry and Diamond Creek, the Colorado River drops from 3 116 feet in elevation down to 1 336 feet.* **7** [T] **~ sb/sth (off)** to stop so that sb can get out of a car, etc; to deliver sth on the way to somewhere else: *At these times, parents were picking up or dropping off their children at school.* ◇ *The package was dropped off by a courier at the television company's office.*

PHR V **ˌdrop ˈby/ˈin | ˌdrop ˈin on sb** to pay a short informal visit to a person or place: *He invites constituents to drop by and have a chat.* ◇ *Neighbours regularly drop in on each other to ask a favour or share a problem.* **ˌdrop ˈoff** to become fewer or less: *Numbers of births dropped off in February and increased again in March.* **ˌdrop ˈout (of sth)** **1** to no longer take part in or be part of sth: *Thirty-five participants (6.5%) dropped out.* ◇ *It is not uncommon for patients to drop out of clinical trials of medicines.* **2** to leave school, college, etc. without finishing your studies: *These schools are more successful in keeping students from dropping out.*

drop[2] /drɒp; *NAmE* drɑːp/ *noun* **1** [C, usually sing.] a fall or reduction in the amount, level or number of sth:

D

Speculators were forced to sell more, causing a further price drop. ◇ *A turbine's efficiency is also determined by the pressure drop across the blades.* ◇ **~ in sth** *A slight drop in blood pressure is often seen in such cases.* ◇ *The economic decline caused a significant drop in sugar prices in the late 1820s.* ◇ *A sharp drop in the demand for US exports could slow economic growth.* ➲ language bank *at* TREND **2** [C] a very small amount of liquid that forms a round shape: *Cloud drops are formed by water vapour condensing around minute particles in the air.* ◇ **~ of sth** *A single drop of blood obtained by a pin prick from a finger is placed onto a sensor.* **3 drops** [pl.] a liquid medicine that is put in small amounts into the eyes, ears or nose: *Antibiotic eye drops are usually prescribed for bacterial and viral infections.*

drop·let /ˈdrɒplət; *NAmE* ˈdrɑːplət/ *noun* a small drop of a liquid: *Water droplets reach the surface with diameters ranging from about 0.1 mm to about 3 mm.* ◇ **~ of sth** *The little droplets of oil start to coalesce to make bigger ones.*

drought /draʊt/ *noun* [C, U] a long period of time when there is little or no rain: *A severe drought occurred during the period 1985–1988.* ◇ **+ noun** *Long-term drought conditions could lead to changes in species composition.*

drove *past tense of* DRIVE¹

drug /drʌg/ *noun* **1** a substance used as a medicine: *Tolerance can develop when drugs are prescribed continuously for a long period.* ◇ *Treatment with four antituberculous drugs led to a gradual complete recovery.* ◇ **+ noun** *Long-term drug treatment can substantially reduce the risk of relapse.* **2** a substance that some people use to give them pleasant and exciting feelings. Many drugs are illegal: *Dependencies on alcohol and illicit drugs are major public health problems in Western societies.* ◇ **+ noun** *He died of a drug overdose.*

▸ ADJECTIVE + DRUG **anti-inflammatory • antipsychotic • antidepressant** *Recently new classes of anti-inflammatory drugs have been developed.* | **recreational • illicit, illegal** *Recreational drug use in the UK is common.*

▸ NOUN + DRUG **prescription** *Four prescription drugs are currently approved by the US Food and Drug Administration to treat the condition.*

▸ VERB + DRUG **prescribe • administer • dispense • take, be on • stop • metabolize • absorb • test • license** *The patient should remain upright for at least 30 minutes after taking the drug.* ◇ *Features of withdrawal syndrome usually occur within a few hours of stopping the drug responsible.* | **inject • abuse • use • take, be on • sell • supply** *People abuse drugs or alcohol for a variety of reasons.* ◇ *The defendant was convicted of supplying a Class A drug.*

▸ DRUG + NOUN **therapy, treatment • delivery • resistance • allergy** *It was decided to postpone surgery in favour of a course of drug therapy.* | **user • addict • dealer • abuse • use • addiction • overdose** *Intravenous drug users are at high risk of blood-borne infections.*

drum /drʌm/ *noun* **1** a musical instrument that you play by hitting it with sticks or your hands. It has plastic or skin stretched across a round frame: *Drums and drummers were an integral part of their culture.* **2** a container for oil or chemicals, in the shape of a CYLINDER: *The oxide is packed into 200-litre drums for shipment.* **3** a thing shaped like a CYLINDER or like a musical drum, especially a part of a machine: *a rotating drum*

drunk¹ /drʌŋk/ *adj.* [not usually before noun] having drunk so much alcohol that it is impossible to think or speak clearly: **be/get ~** *Compared with boys, girls get drunk less often.* ◇ **~ driving** *In this age group, no increase was found in violent assaults and drunk driving.*

drunk² *past tense, past part. of* DRINK²

dry¹ /draɪ/ *adj.* (**drier, dri·est**) **1** not wet; without water or MOISTURE: *The drug's side effects include dry mouth, blurred vision and abnormal heartbeat.* ◇ *When water is added to a dry soil, the smaller pores will be the first to suck in the water.* ◇ *Dry air that ascends in the atmosphere expands and cools down at a fixed rate of 1°C for every 100 m it rises.* OPP WET (1) **2** (of weather) with very little rain: *Eastern regions of the UK have a relatively dry and mild climate in summer seasons.* ◇ *Pollen is indicative of cooler, drier conditions.* ◇ *Rivers in regions with clearly defined wet and dry seasons may be seasonal and intermittent.* OPP WET (2) **3** (of skin or hair) without the natural oils that makes it soft and healthy: *Emollients can help reduce itching, particularly in patients with dry skin.* **4** (of a cough) that does not produce any MUCUS: *The patient has a persistent dry cough, which started soon after he commenced the treatment.* ■ **dry·ness** *noun* [U] **~ (of sth)** *Avoid dehydration as it causes dryness of skin.* ◇ *The extreme dryness of the stratosphere means that there is little opportunity for these gases to be rained out.*

dry² /draɪ/ *verb* (**dries, dry·ing, dried, dried**) [I, T] to become dry; to make sth dry: *As the water table falls and the soil dries, the iron and manganese may be leached from the soil.* ◇ **~ sth** *Samples were dried under vacuum at 60°C for 12 hours.*

PHR V **ˌdry ˈout | ˌdry sth ˈout** to become or to allow sth to become dry, often in a way that is not wanted: *A plant starts to wilt and die when a soil dries out or 'desiccates'.* ◇ *Electrodes that have been dried out may normally be revitalized by soaking in distilled water.* **ˌdry ˈup** **1** (of rivers, lakes, etc.) to become completely dry: *During the 1998 drought, streams dried up and agricultural fields became barren.* **2** if a supply of sth **dries up**, there is gradually less of it until there is none left: *Many health promotion campaigns rely on volunteer time to sustain them, especially after funding dries up.* ◇ *In 2001, demand for the company's products dried up and sales collapsed.*

dual /ˈdjuːəl; *NAmE* ˈduːəl/ *adj.* [only before noun] having two parts or aspects: *The project managers have the dual role of keeping the teams reporting to them motivated and ensuring that the organization continues to support the project with resources.* ◇ *It was not until the 1920s that the dual nature of light as both particle and wave was finally made clear.*

dual·ism /ˈdjuːəlɪzəm; *NAmE* ˈduːəlɪzəm/ *noun* [U, C] the state of having two parts, often very different or opposite from each other: *Many economic liberals take note of a dualism in developing countries, that is a traditional sector still rooted in the countryside and an emerging modern sector concentrated in the cities.* ◇ **~ between A and B** *There was a dualism between government statement and action.* HELP In philosophy, **dualism** is a system of thought based upon any two radically different concepts, such as good and evil, fact and value, FINITE and INFINITE and, especially, mind and matter: *He rejects dualism, claiming that the experienced world and the physical world are the same thing.* ■ **dual·ist·ic** /ˌdjuːəˈlɪstɪk; *NAmE* ˌduːəˈlɪstɪk/, **dual·ist** /ˈdjuːəlɪst; *NAmE* ˈduːəlɪst/ *adj.* [usually before noun] *He carried the dualistic tradition further by theorizing a distinction between voluntary and involuntary behaviour.* **dual·ist** *noun*: *He is not a dualist and believes that 'our brains are completely controlled by physics of some kind' (Penrose, 1994b: 243).*

dual·ity /djuːˈæləti; *NAmE* duːˈæləti/ *noun* (*pl.* **-ies**) [U, C] **~ (of sth)** the state of having two parts or aspects; a contrast between two ideas or two aspects of sth: *The Commission has an unusual duality of roles.* ◇ *Descartes' idea of the duality of mind and brain then descended into a whole set of simple dualities: mind/spirit, art/science, intellectual/physical.*

du·bi·ous /ˈdju:biəs; *NAmE* ˈdu:biəs/ *adj.* **1** that you cannot be sure about; that is probably not good: *Much of the data is of dubious quality.* ◇ *The value of these resolutions was dubious.* HELP **Dubious** is also used when you are stating that sth is the opposite of a particular good quality: *The country has the dubious distinction of having the world's highest adult HIV rate.* **2** [usually before noun] probably not honest SYN SUSPICIOUS (2): *Power lay in the hands of organized crime bosses and other dubious characters.* ◇ *They are likely to engage in ethically dubious practices.* **3** [not usually before noun] **~ about sth** feeling uncertain about sth; not knowing whether sth is good or bad SYN DOUBTFUL (2): *Clinicians are dubious about using treatments that are not officially approved.*

duct /dʌkt/ *noun* **1** a pipe or tube carrying liquid, gas, electric or telephone wires, etc: *An exhaust fan blows the air out of the system through the central air duct.* **2** a tube in the body through which liquid passes: *Inflammation in the liver could be due to obstruction of the common bile duct.*

due[1] /dju:; *NAmE* du:/ *adj.* **1** [not before noun] caused by sb/sth: **~ to sth/sb** *The fall towards the end of period was due to a lack of demand in the economy.* ◇ **partly/mainly/largely/probably/possibly ~ to sth** *The failure of development in the area is partly due to poor implementation of policy in most countries.* ◇ **~ in part to sth** *These symptoms are due in part to the parasite's direct effect of obstructing capillaries in the brain.* ➲ language bank *at* BECAUSE, CAUSE[1] **2** [only before noun] suitable or right in the circumstances: *This important point has not been given due recognition by the government in its rush to move wind farms offshore.* ◇ **~ attention/consideration/regard/respect** *Due consideration should be given to likely impacts on the child's health and welfare.* ➲ *compare* UNDUE **3** [not before noun] arranged or expected: *The report was due in autumn 2012.* ◇ **~ to do sth** *Airports would have to close, because key staff were due to take part in the strike.* ◇ **~ for sth** *For example, insurance companies use their databases to remind customers that their policies are due for renewal.* **4** [not usually before noun] when a sum of money is **due**, it must be paid immediately: *The agreement will usually state how much rent is to be paid and when it is due.* **5** [not before noun] **~ (to sb)** owed to sb as a debt, because it is their right or because they have done sth to deserve it: *The directors had not paid money due to the tax authorities.* ◇ *Those individuals and institutions treated him with courtesy and the respect due to him.*
IDM **in ˌdue ˈcourse** at a later or the right time and not before: *Analysts forecast that the steel market would recover in due course.*

due[2] /dju:; *NAmE* du:/ *noun* **1 your/sb's/sth's due** [U] something that should be given to sb/sth by right: *Some people flourish by depriving others of their due.* ◇ *Unfortunately, this short review cannot give these texts their due.* **2 dues** [pl.] charges, for example to be a member of a club: *They are encouraged to become party members, paying dues and attending party meetings.*

ˈdue to *prep.* **~ sth/sb** because of sth/sb SYN BECAUSE OF, OWING TO: *Sales also fell due to competition from rivals.* ◇ *Consultations by phone were often difficult due to a lack of time.* ◇ *Due to the difficulties involved in measuring evaporation directly, it is generally estimated from meteorological data.*

dug *past tense, past part. of* DIG

dull /dʌl/ *adj.* (**dull·er**, **dull·est**) **1** (of pain) not very severe, but continuous: *The patient may have a dull ache in the lower abdomen.* **2** not interesting or exciting: *His writing is rather dull and mechanical.* **3** not bright: *The owls' dull coloration probably results from natural selection.* **4** (of sound) not clear or loud: *The sound of these waves is rather dull and very low in pitch.* **5** slow to understand things; not intelligent: *She contrasts the 'bright' working-class students with the 'dull' middle-class ones.* ■ **dull·ness** *noun* [U] **~ (of sb/sth)** *Many young refugees are trying to escape the dullness of camp life by immersing themselves in their studies.*

duly /ˈdju:li; *NAmE* ˈdu:li/ *adv.* **1** in the correct or expected manner: *Transactions were duly noted and recorded by specially trained officials.* **2** at the expected and correct time: *This publication duly came out in the course of December.* ➲ *compare* UNDULY

D

dummy /ˈdʌmi/ *noun* (*pl.* **-ies**) an object designed to look like and act as a substitute for the real or usual one; sth that can take the place of sth else: *David Lack confirmed this hypothesis by placing dummies of various types in the territory of wild male robins.* ◇ **+ noun** *Some of the larger supermarkets have dummy stores, where manufacturers are invited to carry out tests of their packaging.*

ˌdummy ˈvariable *noun* **1** (*statistics*) a VARIABLE that is given to data in order to create a SUBSET of that data, usually given the value of zero or one: *For 'church attendance', a simple dummy variable was created, where 1 indicates regular church attendance 'at least once a month' and 0 'less often/never'.* **2** (*also* **ˌbound ˈvariable**) (*mathematics*) a VARIABLE in an EQUATION that does not feature in the final result: *The domain, but not the value, of a dummy variable is required to establish the truth of a statement.*

du·pli·cate[1] /ˈdju:plɪkeɪt; *NAmE* ˈdu:plɪkeɪt/ *verb* **1 ~ sth** to make an exact copy of sth; to create a situation that is exactly like another one: *The ease with which software can be illegally duplicated often makes copyrights meaningless.* ◇ *They have not been able to duplicate his successes.* **2 ~ sth** to multiply sth by two; to double sth: *Chromosomes are duplicated and distributed to daughter cells in the course of the cell cycle.* **3 ~ sth** to do sth again, especially when it is unnecessary: *The work was complementary and did not duplicate previous work.*

du·pli·cate[2] /ˈdju:plɪkət; *NAmE* ˈdu:plɪkət/ *noun* one of two or more things that are the same in every detail: *After excluding duplicates, the updated search of these bibliographic databases yielded a total of 261 references.* ◇ **~ of sth** *It is possible for an organism to make duplicates of each chromosome as cells grow and divide.* ■ **du·pli·cate** *adj.* [only before noun] *Duplicate records were removed from the data.*
IDM **in duplicate** **1** twice in exactly the same way: *The measurements were performed in duplicate.* **2** (of documents, etc.) as two copies that are exactly the same in every detail: *The questionnaire may exist in duplicate when data files are backed up.*

du·pli·ca·tion /ˌdju:plɪˈkeɪʃn; *NAmE* ˌdu:plɪˈkeɪʃn/ *noun* [U, C] **1 ~ (of sth)** the act of making an exact copy of sth; sth that is exactly the same as sth else: *Production, duplication and delivery of reports changed radically with presentation software and electronic data file transfer.* ◇ *The statement could not be added to the list if it was an exact duplication of another.* **2 ~ (of sth)** the act of multiplying sth by two; the act of doubling sth: *An essential part of cell division is the duplication of certain cellular components.* ◇ *It is generally accepted that large-scale duplications of the genome have occurred during vertebrate evolution.* **3 ~ (of sth)** the act of doing sth again, especially when it is unnecessary: *He wanted to avoid duplication of effort in individual research programmes.* ◇ *Difficulties in coordinating resources may result in delays or duplications of services.*

dur·ation AWL /djuˈreɪʃn; *NAmE* duˈreɪʃn/ *noun* [U] **~ (of sth)** the length of time that sth lasts or continues: *They lived with host families for the duration of their stay.* ◇ *Vertigo attacks vary in duration from a few minutes to* hours. ◇ *The next phase is relatively short, with an average duration of 2–4 hours.*

dur·ing /ˈdjʊərɪŋ; *NAmE* ˈdʊrɪŋ/ *prep.* **1** all through a period of time: *She provides a vivid description of what life was like during the Civil War.* ◇ *We checked the nests every 2-3 hours during daylight hours.* ➲ language bank *at* TIME[1] **2** at some point in a period of time: *During the trial, a photograph of the man was shown to the jury and his name was mentioned.* ◇ *The study was limited to patients with diabetes who visited the hospital once or more during 2004.* HELP **During** is used to say when sth happens; **for** answers the question 'how long?': *The average American household has its television set on for six hours a day.* ◇ ~~*The average American household has its television set on during six hours a day.*~~

E

dust /dʌst/ *noun* [U] **1** a fine powder that consists of very small pieces of sand, earth, etc: *We see a long line of trucks, raising clouds of dust on the unmade road.* ◇*NAmE* **+ noun** *Changes in temperature and precipitation have had an influence on the development of dust storms.* **2** the fine powder of dirt that forms in buildings, on furniture, floors, etc: *She is allergic to house dust.* **3** a fine powder that consists of very small pieces of a particular substance: *Volcanic dust blown into the upper parts of the atmosphere might reduce sunshine totals by promoting cloudiness.* ◇ *coal/gold/asbestos dust*

duty /ˈdjuːti; *NAmE* ˈduːti/ *noun* (*pl.* **-ies**) **1** [C, U] something that you have to do because people expect you to do it or because you think it is right: **~ (to do sth)** *This man had a moral and legal duty to provide for his children.* ◇ **under a ~ to do sth** *The council was under a statutory duty to increase the average rents charged for its dwellings.* ◇ **a sense of ~ (towards sb)** *Many children do not find their parents lovable and feel no special sense of duty towards them.* HELP In law, a **duty of care** is a legal duty that a person has to use a reasonable standard of care while performing acts which might be harmful to others: *The test establishes that the doctor owed a duty of care to the patient.* ➲ *compare* RESPONSIBILITY (1) **2** [U] the work that is your job: *The next day, he reported for duty in the Army.* **3 duties** [pl.] tasks that are part of your job: *A small administration team handles invoicing and general office duties.* ◇ *The project conducted a survey to see how local government officials use the Internet in the course of their duties.* **4** [C, U] a tax that you pay on things that you buy, especially those that you bring into a country: *The government announced that it was imposing a 10 per cent surcharge on import duties.* ◇ **~ on sth** *The UK imposed a higher duty on table wines than on beer.*
IDM **on/off duty** (of nurses, police officers, etc.) working/not working at a particular time: *GPs take turns being on duty during out-of-office hours.*

DVD /ˌdiː viː ˈdiː/ *noun* [C, U] a disk on which data, especially photographs and video, can be stored, for use on a computer or **DVD player** (the abbreviation for 'digital versatile disc' or, originally, 'digital videodisc'): *The class were asked to jot down ideas and observations as they watched the DVD.* ◇ **~ of sth** *DVDs of the campaign material were also distributed.* ◇ **on ~** *Films in this category have done extraordinarily well on DVD.*

dwell /dwel/ *verb* (**dwelt**, **dwelt** /dwelt; *NAmE* dwelt/) or (**dwelled**, **dwelled**) [I] **+ adv./prep.** (*formal* or *literary*) to live somewhere: *Hermits in the strict sense dwelt alone, although some lived with a brother or a servant.*
PHR V ˈ**dwell on/upon sth** **1** to think or talk a lot about sth, especially sth it would be better to forget: *One reason given by families who declined to participate in the study was not wanting to dwell on the cancer experience.* **2** (of sb's eyes or attention) to focus on sth for a long time: *The summer schedules featured many programmes that dwelt on landscape imagery.*

dwell·er /ˈdwelə(r)/ *noun* (especially in compounds) a person who lives in the particular place that is mentioned: *In 1800, urban dwellers comprised only 3 per cent of the world population.* ◇ *city/slum/rural/forest dwellers*

dwell·ing /ˈdwelɪŋ/ *noun* (*formal*) a house, flat, etc. where a person lives: *The target population included persons aged 15 and older who lived in private dwellings.*

dy·nam·ic[1] AWL /daɪˈnæmɪk/ *noun* **1 dynamics** [pl.] the way in which people or things behave, develop or react to each other in a particular situation: **~ (of sth)** *I also consider teenagers' perspectives to understand better the complex dynamics of parenting.* ◇ *Population dynamics affect both climate change and societal development (Stephenson et al., 2010).* ◇ **~ between A and B** *It is clear that the dynamics between consumers, employees and firms in the service economy have changed in important ways over the past few decades.* **2 dynamics** [U] the science of the forces involved in movement: *The diffusion of chemical compounds follows the characteristics of fluid dynamics.* ◇ **~ of sth** *Newton used Kepler's insights to explore mathematically the dynamics of planetary motion.* **3** [sing.] **~ (of sth)** a force that produces change, action or effects: *For ancient Greeks, the basic dynamic of love was attraction.* ◇ *These concepts are all interrelated in a complex dynamic that influences how people cope under stress.*

dy·nam·ic[2] AWL /daɪˈnæmɪk/ *adj.* **1** (of a process) always active, changing or making progress: *Globalization is a dynamic process that governments and other actors continuously influence.* ◇ *The climate is in dynamic equilibrium, that is, over a sufficient period of time the incoming and outgoing radiation are in global balance.* OPP STATIC (1) **2** (*physics*) (of a force) producing movement: *The wind creates a dynamic force on the whole bridge.* **3** (*approving*) (of a person) full of energy and ideas: *As the more dynamic managers who set up the changes moved on, the organization settled once more into its familiar culture.* ■ **dy·nam·ic·al·ly** AWL /daɪˈnæmɪkli/ *adv.*: *Social systems do not resemble static equilibria but dynamically evolving 'organisms' subject to constant change.*

dyˌnamic equiˈlibrium *noun* (*chemistry*) = EQUILIBRIUM (2)

dyna·mism /ˈdaɪnəmɪzəm/ *noun* [U] the quality of changing and developing in an exciting way: *For these thinkers, inequality is a sign of economic dynamism and growth.* ◇ **~ of sth** *It is difficult to deny the power of accounts that recognize the dynamism of ethnic identity in modern Britain.*

dys·func·tion /dɪsˈfʌŋkʃn/ *noun* [U, C] (*medical*) the fact of a part of the body not working normally: *Renal dysfunction after surgery is often associated with multiple organ dysfunction syndrome.*

dys·func·tion·al /dɪsˈfʌŋkʃənl/ *adj.* **1** (of relationships within a society, family, etc.) not working normally; not happy or successful: *Many of these women need to escape from dysfunctional family relationships.* **2** not working normally: *Films and TV programmes all too frequently portray a dysfunctional political system.*

each /iːtʃ/ *det., pron.* used to refer to every one of two or more people or things, when you are thinking about them separately: *It was argued that in each case severe problems flowed from the misdiagnosis.* ◇ *The four largest states, Germany, France, Italy and the UK, have 10 votes each.* ◇ *Respondents were asked which daily newspaper they each* *read most frequently.* ◇ **~ of sb/sth** *Each of the main types of customer is described below.* ◇ **~ one (of sb/sth)** *At each one of these sampling points, we estimated 1) the total number of trees, and 2) the number of different species.* ◇ **one ~** *The hospitals were located in five cities, one each from the North, West, South, East and Central zones of the country.*

GRAMMAR POINT

each • every

- **Each** is used to refer to every one of two or more people or things, when you are thinking about them separately; **every** is used to refer to all the members of a group of people or things: ***Each boy*** *thought the other was selfish and inconsiderate.* ◇ ***Every system*** *has shortcomings.*
- **Each** is used before a singular noun and is followed by a singular verb, but it can also be used after a plural subject, with a plural verb; **every** is always followed by a singular verb: ***Each student has*** *different learning needs.* ◇ *They each have different learning needs.* ◇ ***Every student*** *in the class* ***is*** *capable of passing the exam.*
- **Each** is a pronoun as well as a determiner and so can be used without a following noun; **every** is only a determiner and so always has to be followed by a noun: *The panel of experts then reviewed the list of behaviours, rating the severity of* ***each***. ◇ *One common feature is apparent in* ***every one*** *of these theories.* ◇ ~~*One common feature is apparent in every of these theories.*~~

each ˈother *pron.* used as the object of a verb or preposition to show that each member of a group does sth to or for the other members: *After a couple of weeks of working together, the students really trusted each other.* ◇ *In drawing upon each other's strengths, volunteers became close to one another.*

eager /ˈiːɡə(r)/ *adj.* very interested and excited by sth that is going to happen or about sth that you want to do SYN KEEN (1): *Today's children are generally eager users of technology.* ◇ **~ for sth** *The young are eager for change, but grow more conservative as they age.* ◇ **~ to do sth** *Many US banks were eager to do business with the Russians.* ■ **eager·ly** *adv.*: *The promise of a new national public health service offers much in principle, and further details in the autumn will be eagerly awaited.* **eager·ness** *noun* [U, sing.] **~ (to do sth)** *Many female participants expressed eagerness to utilize any opportunities to claim a better life for themselves and their families.*

ear /ɪə(r); *NAmE* ɪr/ *noun* **1** [C] either of the organs on the sides of the head that you hear with: *The sound wave that reaches our ears does not inherently contain words: our minds impose words on signals we hear.* ◇ *The middle ear and inner ear cannot be sampled using a swab.* ◇ **+ noun** *Discharge from the ear canal may indicate bacterial or fungal infection.* **2** [sing.] **~ (for sth)** an ability to recognize and copy sounds well: *Coleridge also has an acute ear for how phrases sound.* IDM *see* DEAF

early[1] /ˈɜːli; *NAmE* ˈɜːrli/ *adj.* (**earl·ier**, **earli·est**) **1** [usually before noun] near the beginning of a period of time or an event: *Malnutrition was common in Europe during the early twentieth century.* ◇ *An estimated 540 million people used the Internet daily in early 2002.* ◇ *This earlier work had only been conducted on a single species.* ◇ *It is too early to tell whether the measures being implemented will ultimately be successful.* OPP LATE[1] (1) **2** arriving or done before the usual, expected or planned time: *Since there are no bonuses for being early, all contractors will complete either on time or late.* ◇ *Cigarette smoking is associated with a risk of an earlier onset of menopause.* OPP LATE[1] (2) **3** happening soon enough to avoid or deal with difficulties or problems: *Early detection of tumours raises the possibility of intervention and cure.* ◇ *Patients with type II diabetes may show few early signs or symptoms.* OPP LATE[1] (2)

IDM **at the earliest opportunity** as soon as possible: *The publisher will undertake to rectify any errors or omissions at the earliest opportunity.* ➲ *more at* HOUR

▸ EARLY + NOUN **stage, phase • part • years • days • decades • period • era • times • date • history • development** *In the early days of computing, it seemed a great challenge to build a computer that could play chess.* | **work, study • research • paper • chapter • text • version • example • discussion • writing • edition • finding** *Levi-Strauss does not attempt to search for the earliest version of a particular myth.* | **age • life • childhood • adulthood • pregnancy • earlier generations** *Students who are at risk are consistently disengaged in school from early childhood.* | **film • cinema • literature** *He has pieced together the surviving fragments of an early film.* | **attempt • intention • experience** *These early experiences affected his subsequent character and career.* | **retirement • onset • death** *His early death brought an end to this experiment.* | **detection • warning • sign • intervention • diagnosis** *Early intervention with antifungal drugs can increase survival rates.*

▸ EARLY + ADJECTIVE (+ NOUN) **modern • eighteenth-century, nineteenth-century, twentieth-century, twenty-first century • medieval • postwar • colonial** *Territorial states in early modern Europe were ruled by absolute monarchs.*

early[2] /ˈɜːli; *NAmE* ˈɜːrli/ *adv.* (**earl·ier**, **earli·est**) **1** near the beginning of a period of time, an event or a piece of work: *The English Electric Company became interested in computers as early as 1949.* ◇ **~ in sth** *It is a remarkably simple device that uses a technology discovered early in the twentieth century.* OPP LATE[2] (1) **2** before the usual, expected or planned time: *Those who have retired early are more likely to be financially secure.* ◇ *Embryos can hatch early in response to predators of eggs.* OPP LATE[2] (2) **3 earlier** before the present time or the time mentioned: *As mentioned earlier, the smallest stars will shine for trillions of years.* ◇ *Participants were recalling events that had happened several weeks earlier.* HELP Several words can be used instead of **mention** in the first example, in order to refer to sth that has already been discussed in a piece of writing. **Note, discuss, describe, state** and **outline** can all be used in this way: *As discussed earlier, one consequence is the difficulty of transferring local knowledge for use in other contexts.* OPP LATER[1] (1) **4** soon enough to avoid difficulties SYN QUICKLY (2): *Provided that treatment is started early, the patient should have a normal lifespan.*

IDM **early ˈon** at an early stage of a situation, relationship or period of time: *He was influenced early on by Marxist theory.* ◇ *Public health information should encourage more women to quit smoking before or early on in pregnancy.* ➲ *compare* LATER ON

earn /ɜːn; *NAmE* ɜːrn/ *verb* **1** [T, I] to get money for work that you do: **~ (sth)** *The farm workers earn their income by working for the farmers in their region.* ◇ *Jeff runs his own business and earns $60 000 a year.* ◇ *She reared her children on her own and turned to writing in order to earn.* ◇ **~ a living** *A good chair-maker could not make the chairs quickly enough to earn a living.* ◇ **~ sb sth** *The photographs were sold by him to the tabloid press, allegedly earning him a small fortune.* **2** [T] **~ sth** to get money as profit from business or interest on money you lend or have in a bank: *A firm will reinvest profits only if it expects to earn more profits.* ◇ *Interest earned on savings is usually automatically taxed at the basic rate of 20%.* ➲ *compare* GAIN[1] (4) **3** [T] to get sth that you deserve, usually because of sth good you have done or because of the good qualities you have SYN WIN (3) HELP Note that you can only use the word **win** instead of **earn** in this meaning: **~ sth** *Although new to politics, Edwards soon earned the respect*

E

of his fellow senators. ◇ *The MSc programme has earned a reputation as one of the best in the country.* ◇ **~ sb sth** *Koch's work on infectious diseases earned him a Nobel Prize in 1905.*

earn·er /ˈɜːnə(r); *NAmE* ˈɜːrnər/ *noun* **1** a person who earns money for a job that they do: *The number of wage earners in manufacturing fell by 40 per cent.* **2** an activity or a business that makes a profit: *The outsourcing industry is one of the country's biggest export earners.*

E

earn·ings /ˈɜːnɪŋz; *NAmE* ˈɜːrnɪŋz/ *noun* [pl.] **1** the money that you earn for the work that you do: *On average, women working part-time have hourly earnings that are 22 per cent less than women working full-time.* ◇ **~ from sth** *The sample was divided into three categories based on annual earnings from work.* ➲ *compare* INCOME, SALARY, WAGE[1] **2** the profit that a company, industry or economy makes in a particular period: *Energy savings would be beneficial to Russian export earnings.* ◇ *Financial risk impacts on the firm's earnings but lies outside the domain of managerial control.* ◇ **~ from sth** *Earnings from agriculture grew more rapidly in metropolitan than non-metropolitan counties.* OPP EXPENDITURE ➲ *compare* INCOME

earth /ɜːθ; *NAmE* ɜːrθ/ *noun* **1** (*also* **Earth, the Earth**) [U, sing.] the world; the planet that we live on: *Only a series of quite remarkable coincidences have made earth habitable for humans.* ◇ *More than twice as many people inhabit the earth today as when the post-war era began.* ◇ *The warming effect on the earth's surface by certain gases in the atmosphere was first recognized in 1827.* ◇ **on ~** *Darwin had come to believe that all life on Earth evolved over millions of years from a few common ancestors.* **2** [U] the substance that plants grow in: *The eggs are laid in a mound of earth, plant litter, twigs and branches.* ◇ *The rice plantation contained more than 55 miles of bank, covering 6 million cubic feet of earth.* **3** [U, sing.] land; the hard surface of the world that is not the sea or the sky SYN GROUND (2): *The journey home required careful navigation around fallen trees and cracks in the earth.* ◇ **to the ~** *Precipitation starts when large water droplets or ice crystals fall to the earth due to gravity.* ◇ **to ~** *Even in still air, a feather only sinks to earth slowly while a rock falls rapidly.* **4** (*BrE*) (*NAmE* **ground**) [U, C, usually sing.] electrical connection to the ground; a wire that connects an electric CIRCUIT with the ground and makes it safe: *The gate is connected to earth and the source to +5 V.*

earth·quake /ˈɜːθkweɪk; *NAmE* ˈɜːrθkweɪk/ (*also* **quake**) *noun* a sudden, violent shaking of the earth's surface: *Most earthquakes occur at the margins of tectonic plates.* ◇ *Future catastrophes will be severe when large earthquakes strike increasingly densely populated urban centres.*

ˈ**earth science** *noun* [C, U] a science concerned with studying the earth or part of it. Geography and GEOLOGY are both earth sciences: *One of the most important applications of the earth sciences today is the evaluation of earthquake hazards.* ➲ *compare* LIFE SCIENCES, NATURAL SCIENCE, PHYSICAL SCIENCE

ease[1] /iːz/ *noun* [U] **1** lack of difficulty or effort: **~ of sth** *A vast amount of data can be stored, allowing greater ease of access to information.* ◇ **~ of doing sth** *The state of the economy will affect the ease of doing business and the likelihood of success.* ◇ **with ~** *Transnational corporations can relocate production and other facilities with relative ease.* ◇ **the ~ with which...** *It is the ease with which the sheets slide past one another that leads to the softness of graphite.* OPP DIFFICULTY (2) **2** the state of feeling relaxed or comfortable, without anxiety, problems or pain: *In his retirement, he lived a life of wealth and ease.*

IDM **at (your) ˈease** relaxed and confident and not nervous or embarrassed: *They feel at ease in social situations and may be well liked by others.* ◇ *There are no open spaces where they can sit down and talk at their ease.* **put sb at (their) ˈease** to make sb feel relaxed and confident, not nervous or embarrassed: *It is essential to take time to put patients at their ease.* ➲ *more at* ILL[1]

ease[2] /iːz/ *verb* **1** [I, T] to become less unpleasant, painful, severe, etc; to make sth less unpleasant, etc: *He has noticed that the pain eases the more activity he does.* ◇ **~ sth** *This was a measure to ease the financial burden on low-income families.* ◇ *The Commission plays a vital role in easing tension between the Member States.* ➲ *compare* ALLEVIATE **2** [T] **~ sth** to make sth easier SYN FACILITATE: *Home visits can help reassure children and ease their transition back to school.* **3** [T] **~ sb/sth + adv./prep.** to slowly and carefully make sb/sth reach a particular state or condition: *The government undertook a number of measures to ease Britain out of the recession.* ◇ *This policy requires frequent readjustment to ease the economy towards a sustainable position.* **4** [I, T] to become lower in price or value; to make sth lower in price or value: *The UK new car market has eased in recent years.* ◇ *The oil price would ease back as gas competition intensified.* ◇ **~ sth** *Critics ask how corporate social responsibility has eased corporate tax burdens.*

eas·ily /ˈiːzəli/ *adv.* **1** without problems or difficulty SYN READILY (1): *The website provides easily accessible information on acute poisoning and its management* ◇ *This is a complex concept which is not easily understood.* ◇ *The adverts show flight attendants walking through an airport, easily recognizable in their bright red uniforms.* ◇ *With this readout, the various peaks in the sample can be easily identified.* **2** very probably; very likely: *X-ray abnormalities are easily missed and diagnosis can be difficult.* ◇ *An acquittal in court might easily be mistaken for a verdict of innocence.* ◇ **all too ~** *Under-nutrition in pregnant women and infants can all too easily become irreversible.* **3 ~ the best, largest, etc.** without doubt; definitely: *Jamaica was easily the largest West Indian island to come into British possession.* ◇ *Sugar was easily the most valuable commodity imported from anywhere.* ◇ *Insects are easily the most diverse group of animals.* **4** quickly; more quickly than is usual: *He is seen as a leader by his peers but teachers find him easily distracted.* ◇ *Lipids do not usually dissolve easily in water.*

▸ EASILY + VERB **understand** • **recognize, identify, distinguish** • **verify** • **detect** • **visualize** • **manipulate** • **accommodate** • **access** • **imagine** • **explain** • **calculate** *Children are often on their computers and can therefore easily access the Internet.* | **miss** • **forget** • **confuse** • **overlook** *As consumers tend not to be well organized, their interests can be easily overlooked by governments.*

▸ EASILY + ADJECTIVE **accessible** • **available** • **recognizable, identifiable, distinguishable** • **detectable** • **visible, observable** • **measurable** • **understandable** *Behavioural loyalty is based on easily measurable factors such as market share or repeat purchase.*

east[1] /iːst/ *noun* [U, sing.] (*abbr.* **E**) **1** (*usually* **the east**) the direction that you look towards to see the sun rise; one of the four main points of the COMPASS: *The wind was blowing from the east.* ◇ **to the ~ (of...)** *a town to the east of Chicago* ➲ *compare* NORTH[1], SOUTH[1], WEST[1] **2 the East** the countries of Asia, especially China, Japan and India: *the protection of trade routes to the East* **3 the East** (in the past) the Communist countries of Central and Eastern Europe: *East-West relations*

east[2] /iːst/ *adj.* [only before noun] (*also* **East**) (*abbr.* **E**) in or towards the east: *East Africa* ◇ *They live on the east coast.* ■ **east** *adv.*: *The house faces east.*

east·ern /ˈiːstən; *NAmE* ˈiːstərn/ *adj.* **1** (*also* **Eastern**) (*abbr.* **E**) [only before noun] located in the east or facing east: *eastern Spain* ◇ *Eastern Europe* ◇ *the eastern slopes of the mountain* **2** (*usually* **Eastern**) connected with the part of the world that is to the east of Europe: *Eastern cultures*

easy /ˈiːzi/ *adj.* (**eas·ier, easi·est**) **1** not difficult; done or obtained without a lot of effort or problems: *Defining global marketing is not an easy task.* ◇ *A dramatic reduction in overseas transport costs gave Russia and the US easier access to other markets.* ◇ **~ to do** *This problem is relatively easy to understand.* ◇ **it is ~ to do sth** *It is easy to imagine the urban poor in the less developed world as some anonymous mass.* OPP HARD[1] (1) **2** simple to do, but possibly not the correct or best thing to do: *Evolutionary biology is not going to provide easy answers to medical dilemmas.* ◇ **it is ~ to do sth** *It would be too easy to dismiss what he is saying as nonsense.* ◇ **it is ~ for sb to do sth** *It is very easy for people to think they know far more about AI than they actually do.* **3** [only before noun] open to attack; not able to defend yourself: *Advertising spending is seen as an easy target for reducing expenditure in bad times.* ◇ *His placid nature made him an easy prey for bullying.* **4** comfortable, relaxed and not anxious: *She tends to go along with the crowd just for an easy life.* OPP UNEASY **5** [only before noun] pleasant and friendly: *The poems all retain an easy familiarity between addresser and addressee.* OPP AWKWARD (1) ➲ *see also* EASILY IDM *see* REACH[2]

eat /iːt/ *verb* (**ate** /et; eɪt/, **eaten** /ˈiːtn/) [I, T] to put food in your mouth, then bite and swallow it: *Patients with this condition will lose weight due to the inability to eat comfortably.* ◇ **~ sth** *Because of the belief in the sacredness of all living creatures, many Hindus do not eat meat.* ◇ *All infant mammals make a transition from suckling milk to eating solid foods.*

PHR V ˈ**eat into sth** to use up a part of sth, especially sb's money or time: *The rapidly rising demand for chilled convenience foods is eating into the market share and growth of frozen products.*

eat·ing /ˈiːtɪŋ/ *noun* [U] the act of eating sth: *The primary care setting provides an ideal setting for nurses to promote healthy eating and exercise.* ◇ **+ noun** *Poor eating habits established during adolescence may affect long-term health outcomes.* ◇ *Eating disorders can produce a wide array of physiological derangement.*

echo[1] /ˈekəʊ; *NAmE* ˈekoʊ/ *verb* (**echoes, echo·ing, echoed, echoed**) **1** [I, T] (of a sound) to be reflected off a wall, the side of a mountain, etc. so that you can hear it again; to send back and repeat a sound: *A strange noise echoed throughout the whole building.* ◇ **~ sth** *A rotating radar antenna sends out a radio signal that is echoed back from a target.* **2** [T, I] **~ (sth)** (of an object or event) to have similar characteristics to sth; to remind you of sth similar: *The research echoes findings from other studies.* ◇ *Biblical language echoed throughout the religious poetry of the seventeenth and eighteenth centuries.* **3** [T] **~ sth** to repeat an idea or opinion because you agree with it: *Sometimes women echoed the sentiments of the advice manuals.*

echo[2] /ˈekəʊ; *NAmE* ˈekoʊ/ *noun* (*pl.* **-oes**) **1** the reflecting of sound off a surface so that a noise appears to be repeated; a sound that is reflected back in this way: *The echoes from distant objects take longer to come back and therefore sound higher than the echoes from nearer objects.* **2 ~ of sth** the fact of an idea, event, etc. being like another and reminding you of it; sth that reminds you of sth else: *Yeltsin's form of government did have echoes of the old tsarist autocracy.* ◇ *Perhaps Larkin heard an echo of his own work in Patten's poem.* **3** an opinion or attitude that agrees with or repeats one already expressed or thought: **find an ~ in sth** *Cole's (1959) thesis found echoes in the new academic discipline of development economics.*

eco·logic·al /ˌiːkəˈlɒdʒɪkl; *NAmE* ˌiːkəˈlɑːdʒɪkl/ *adj.* connected with the relation of plants and living creatures to each other and to their environment: *Coastal subsidence and loss of land has resulted in destruction of the ecological system.* ◇ *Sustainable development provides a framework through which to address rural social and ecological decline.* ◇ *The novel's anti-industrialism and ecological concerns seem remarkably up to date.* ■ **eco·logic·al·ly** /ˌiːkəˈlɒdʒɪkli; *NAmE* ˌiːkəˈlɑːdʒɪkli/ *adv.*: *More food is being grown in ecologically sustainable ways.* ◇ *Littoral zones are ecologically important because they contain diversity and abundant marine life.*

ecolo·gist /iˈkɒlədʒɪst; *NAmE* iˈkɑːlədʒɪst/ *noun* a scientist who studies ecology: *Ecologists have used a variety of measures of ecosystem stability.* ◇ *There is general opposition by marine ecologists to disposing of anything in the ocean.*

ecol·ogy /iˈkɒlədʒi; *NAmE* iˈkɑːlədʒi/ *noun* **1** [C, usually sing.] **~ (of sth)** the relation of plants and living creatures to each other and to their environment: *Any process occurring upstream can potentially affect the ecology of the river further downstream.* ◇ *Massive upheavals in the ecology of the planet have led to both the extinction and the evolution of species.* **2** [U] the study of the relation of plants and living creatures to each other and to their environment: *Ecology is based on the premise that things cannot be studied except in context.*

eco·nom·ic AWL /ˌiːkəˈnɒmɪk; ˌekəˈnɒmɪk; *NAmE* ˌiːkəˈnɑːmɪk; ˌekəˈnɑːmɪk/ *adj.* **1** [only before noun] connected with the trade, industry and development of wealth of a country, an area or a society: *Africa's economic development will be a significant step in overcoming the North-South divide.* ◇ *No economist has ever claimed that there is a single driving force behind economic growth.* ◇ *The later Roman Empire had severe economic problems and an insatiable need for income.* ➲ thesaurus note *at* FINANCIAL **2** producing enough profit to continue; not costing much money SYN PROFITABLE (1): *The most economic way of extracting the ore is from open surface mines.* ◇ *A suspension bridge was, from a structural point of view, unlikely to be the most economic solution.* ◇ **~ (for sb/sth) to do sth** *Niche markets often arise because it is not economic for the leading competitors to enter this segment.*

> **WORD FAMILY**
> economic *adj.*
> economical *adj.*
> economically *adv.*
> economy *noun*
> economics *noun*
> economist *noun*

▸ ECONOMIC + NOUN **growth • development, change • activity • policy • system • theory • performance • conditions, circumstances • factors • interests • benefits • efficiency • success • problems, difficulties • inequalities • downturn • decline • crisis • recovery • power • analysis • reform • integration • globalization** *A major social and economic change was the collapse of feudal societies and the rise of capitalism.*

▸ ADVERB + ECONOMIC **purely, strictly • primarily** *In purely economic terms, the results of these changes were striking.* ◇ *Justification for the military colonies was primarily economic.*

WHICH WORD?

economic • economical

- **Economic** means connected with the economy of a country or area, or with the money that a society or an individual has: *Mitterrand had promised to bring about economic recovery through large injections of government spending into the economy.* ◇ *the economic aspects of having children*
- **Economic** also means 'profitable': *Older workers can compensate for a reduced ability to meet job demands by drawing upon experience and applying their resources in a more economic way.*
- **Economical** means spending money or using resources in a careful way that avoids waste: *Running the plant at full load is more economical.*

E

eco·nom·ic·al AWL /ˌiːkəˈnɒmɪkl; ˌekəˈnɒmɪkl; *NAmE* ˌiːkəˈnɑːmɪkl; ˌekəˈnɑːmɪkl/ *adj.* **1** providing good service or value in relation to the amount of time or money spent: *The challenge is to produce large quantities of biofuels in a sustainable and economical way.* ◇ **it is ~ to do sth** *The reduction of transportation costs has made it more economical to ship goods over long distances.* **2** using no more of sth than is necessary: *This triangular lattice represents the most economical use of space.* ➲ *usage note at* ECONOMIC

E

eco·nom·ic·al·ly AWL /ˌiːkəˈnɒmɪkli; ˌekəˈnɒmɪkli; *NAmE* ˌiːkəˈnɑːmɪkli; ˌekəˈnɑːmɪkli/ *adv.* **1** in a way that is connected with the trade, industry and development of wealth of a country, an area or a society: *Economically disadvantaged areas would be the first to benefit from this plan.* ◇ *There are currently no economically viable technologies to reduce CO_2 emissions from carbon-based fuels.* ◇ *Underemployment remained at about 60% of the economically active population.* ◇ *If the isolation is too complete, the country is likely to fall far behind economically and militarily.* **2** in a way that provides good service or value in relation to the amount of time or money spent: *Concentrating fruit juice products allows them to be transported more economically by reducing the water content.*

eco·nom·ics AWL /ˌiːkəˈnɒmɪks; ˌekəˈnɒmɪks; *NAmE* ˌiːkəˈnɑːmɪks; ˌekəˈnɑːmɪks/ *noun* **1** [U] the study of how a society organizes its money, trade and industry: *He studied economics in Germany before returning to the University of Stockholm.* ◇ *Neoclassical economics presents a simple model of individuals and their basic behaviour.* **2** [pl.] **the ~ of sth** the way in which money affects, or is organized within, an area of business or society: *Digital video may change the economics of film production.* ◇ *Their strategy reflects a sophisticated understanding of the economics of an online business.*

econo·mist AWL /ɪˈkɒnəmɪst; *NAmE* ɪˈkɑːnəmɪst/ *noun* a person who studies or writes about economics: *Many economists argue that inflation does not impede growth as long as it does not rise above about 8–10%.* ◇ *Liberals draw from the economic analysis of Adam Smith and other classical liberal economists.*

econ·omy AWL /ɪˈkɒnəmi; *NAmE* ɪˈkɑːnəmi/ *noun* (*pl.* -ies) **1** (*often* **the economy**) [C] the relationship between production, trade and the supply of money in a particular country or region: *The US economy grew by 4.2% between 1999 and 2000.* ◇ *Each of these innovations had an almost immeasurable impact on the economy.* ◇ *He developed the country's economy rapidly by promoting export industries.* ➲ *see also* KNOWLEDGE ECONOMY **2** [C] a country, when you are thinking about its economic system: *Despite its being one of the fastest growing economies in the world, poverty and ill-health persist.* ◇ *The majority of the world's economies were linked to each other by the gold standard.* ◇ *Many Asian economies were badly hit and barely avoided a collapse of most of their industries.* **3** [U, C] the use of time, money or other resources in a way that avoids waste: *The car performs at similar speeds to a traditional car, but with greater fuel economy.* ◇ **economies of scale/scope** *Lower costs may be achieved by economies of scale, reducing the cost of each unit through volume production.*

▸ ADJECTIVE + ECONOMY **global, international** ◆ **national** ◆ **local** ◆ **capitalist** ◆ **emerging, developing** ◆ **developed, advanced** ◆ **new** ◆ **political** *Far more consumer goods were available and many rural people were eager to take part in the new economy.* ◇ *The Japanese political economy remained unchanged throughout the 1990s and the first decade of the new millennium.*

▸ NOUN + ECONOMY **world** ◆ **market** *In market economies, the role of the state has been increasing steadily since the Second World War.*

▸ VERB + ECONOMY **manage, run** ◆ **regulate** ◆ **transform** ◆ **stabilize** ◆ **modernize** ◆ **stimulate** ◆ **create** ◆ **affect** ◆ **dominate** *The Irish Government has published statements outlining strategies for creating a smart green economy.*

▸ ECONOMY + VERB **grow** ◆ **be booming** ◆ **slow** ◆ **shrink** ◆ **recover** ◆ **adjust** *In the mid- to late 1980s, the British economy was booming.* ◇ *By 1936, the European economy had apparently recovered from the Great Depression.*

eco·sys·tem /ˈiːkəʊsɪstəm; *NAmE* ˈiːkoʊsɪstəm/ *noun* all the plants and living creatures in a particular area considered in relation to their physical environment: *Australia is targeting several major invasive plants that affect natural ecosystems.* ◇ *aquatic/marine/terrestrial/forest ecosystems*

edge /edʒ/ *noun* **1** [C] the outside limit of an object, a surface or an area; the part furthest from the centre: *A polygon is a closed figure with straight edges.* ◇ **the ~ of sth** *Much of the western edge of North America will have higher temperatures and a reduction in summer rainfall.* ◇ *The length of a track close to the centre of a disc is less than that of a track near to the outer edge of the disc.* ◇ **on/at the ~ of sth** *Hanging Spring Post was located about sixty kilometres from Dunhuang, on the edge of the Gobi Desert.* **2** (*usually* **the edge**) [sing.] the point at which sth unpleasant or important may begin to happen: **on the ~ of sth** *The novel explores a society on the edge of change.* ◇ **to the ~ of sth** *France itself was brought to the edge of civil war.* **3** [sing.] a slight advantage over sb/sth: *The pressure to outperform competition enables forward-looking organizations to maintain a competitive edge.* ◇ **~ over sb/sth** *Muslims in Tanzania have a slight numerical edge over Christians.* **4** [sing.] a strong, often exciting, quality: *Many of Paley's stories have a political edge to them.*

edit AWL /ˈedɪt/ *verb* **1 ~ sth** to prepare a book to be published by collecting together and arranging pieces of writing by one or more authors: *He has written or edited more than twenty books on aerospace history.* ◇ *Map-making and map use among native peoples were the subjects of a collection edited by Malcolm Lewis (1998).* **2 ~ sth (for sth)** to prepare a piece of writing to be published by correcting the mistakes and making improvements to it: *The text of the interview has been edited for web publication.* ◇ *This is an edited version of a paper presented at the tenth annual conference of the Global Philanthropy Forum.* **3 ~ sth** when sb **edits** a film or television programme, they take what has been filmed or recorded and decide which parts to include and in which order: *The DVD includes edited video versions of the interviews and short profiles of the people featured.*

PHR V ˌ**edit sth ˈout (of sth)** to remove words, phrases or scenes from a book or programme before it is published or shown: *All identifying comments were edited out in order to maintain confidentiality.*

edi·tion AWL /ɪˈdɪʃn/ *noun* **1** (*abbr.* **ed.**) **~ (of sth)** the total number of copies of a book, newspaper or magazine published at one time: *The first edition of the book was enthusiastically received by reviewers.* ◇ *This new edition includes an additional chapter on the psychiatric interview.* **2** the form in which a book is published: *The paperback edition has not been updated since the appearance of the original hardcover in 1978.* ◇ *In the digital edition, a transcription and translation are presented along with facsimile images of the original manuscript.*

edi·tor AWL /ˈedɪtə(r)/ *noun* (*abbr.* **ed.**) **1 ~ (of sth)** a person who chooses texts written by one or by several writers and prepares them to be published in a book or JOURNAL: *She is the author or editor of thirty books in the field.* **2** a person who is in charge of a newspaper or magazine, or part of one, and who decides what should be included: *American newspaper editors believe there is no audience for international news (Hoge, 1997).* **3 ~ (of sth)** a person who prepares a book to be published, for example by checking and correcting the text and making improvements: *In 1879 Murray became the principal editor of the 'Oxford English Dictionary'.*

edi·tor·ial[1] AWL /ˌedɪˈtɔːriəl/ *adj.* [usually before noun] connected with the task of preparing sth such as a newspaper, a book, or a television or radio programme, to be published or broadcast: *He serves on the editorial board of 'Strategic Management Journal'.* ◇ *The author was fully responsible for all content and editorial decisions.*

edi·tor·ial[2] AWL /ˌedɪˈtɔːriəl/ *noun* an important article in a JOURNAL or a newspaper, that expresses the editor's opinion about an issue: *In the survey we included 7 scientific editorials and 23 narrative reviews.* ◇ *A 'New York Times' editorial judged that the accused in this case were bound 'to answer at the bar of moral justice'.*

edu·cate /ˈedʒukeɪt/ *verb* **1** [often passive] **~ sb** to teach sb over a period of time at a school, university, etc: *Traditional systems of educating children and teenagers changed.* ◇ *Like most upper-class girls, she was educated at home.* **2** to teach sb about sth or how to do sth: **~ sb (about/in/on sth)** *The findings reinforce the importance of educating the public about the dangers of cigarette smoke exposure.* ◇ **~ sb to do sth** *All health professionals should be educated to deliver patient-centred care as members of an interdisciplinary team.*

edu·cated /ˈedʒukeɪtɪd/ *adj.* **1** having had a high standard of education: *The educated elite held high positions in the empire's government.* ◇ *Leaders are highly educated, with a bachelor's degree in nursing or another field of health care.* **2** (*often* **-educated**) having had a particular kind or standard of education; having been to the school, college or university mentioned: *People became better educated, with male literacy passing the 90% mark at the turn of the century.* ◇ *It is increasingly the case that MPs are middle class and university educated.* ◇ *Russian born, Princeton-educated, Kagolovsky was a senior vice president at the company's main office in New York.*
IDM **an ˌeducated ˈguess** a guess that is based on some degree of knowledge and is therefore likely to be correct: *The researcher will not know in advance how much of an effect the treatment will have, so they have to make an educated guess.*

edu·ca·tion /ˌedʒuˈkeɪʃn/ *noun* **1** [U, sing.] a process of teaching, training and learning, especially in schools or colleges, to improve knowledge and develop skills: *The majority have little or no formal education, especially among the rural population.* ◇ *Parents have a duty to ensure that the child receives an education.* ◇ *Since 2003, every Kenyan child has been able to access free primary education.* ◇ **+ noun** *The higher education system in the United States has been a model for many nations.* ➲ *see also* HIGHER EDUCATION **2** [U] a particular kind of teaching or training: *Crookes traces the development of key beliefs about language education.* ◇ *Health education is provided as part of screening and routine health services.* ◇ *Traditionally, most medical education has taken place in hospitals.* **3** (*also* **Education**) [U] the institutions or people involved in teaching and training: *The Ministry of Education agreed that he would be permitted to take university examinations.* ◇ **+ noun** *Education departments throughout Europe are working hard on ways to improve foreign language learning in schools.* **4** (*usually* **Education**) [U] the subject of study that deals with how to teach: *Most first degree courses in Education are concerned primarily with producing professional practitioners, not researchers.*

edu·ca·tion·al /ˌedʒuˈkeɪʃənl/ *adj.* connected with education; providing education: *The educational level of participants was divided into three categories.* ◇ *Low educational attainment does not always occur because children are taken out of school.* ◇ *educational policy/reforms* ◇ *All of the students in these educational institutions were given the opportunity to participate in the survey.* ■ **edu·ca·tion·al·ly** /ˌedʒuˈkeɪʃənəli/ *adv.*: *The classrooms are designed to provide an educationally rich environment.*

edu·ca·tor /ˈedʒukeɪtə(r)/ *noun* (*formal*) **1** a person whose job is to teach or educate people: *During the training period, educators keep trainees' performance under review.* **2** (*especially NAmE*) a person who is an expert in the theories and methods of education: *Leading educators and psychologists were consulted on the creation of the program.*

ef·fect[1] /ɪˈfekt/ *noun* **1** [C, U] a change that sb/sth causes in sb/sth else: *The higher the dose, the more severe the effect.* ◇ *International protests had little effect, and the scheduled elections took place as planned in October.* ◇ **~ on/upon sb/sth** *Wind turbines can have an adverse effect on communication systems through electromagnetic interference.* ◇ *The Second World War had a very significant effect upon patterns of immigration to the UK.* ◇ **~ of sth** *There is evidence of growing collective resistance to the negative effects of globalization.* ◇ **cause and ~** *Changes in climate bring about changes in atmospheric composition, so it is frequently difficult to identify cause and effect.* ➲ *see also* FIXED EFFECT, RANDOM EFFECT, SIDE EFFECT ➲ language bank *at* CAUSE[1] **2** [C] a physical fact or situation that is OBSERVED to happen, typically named after the person who discovered it: *Astronomers can study the way stars move through space using the Doppler effect.* ◇ *The neighbourhood effect occurs in those circumstances where an individual's behaviour is strongly conditioned by the local social environment.* ➲ *see also* GREENHOUSE EFFECT **3** [C, U] a particular look, sound or impression that sb, such as an artist or a writer, wants to create: *From its very silence, film received the power to achieve excellent artistic effects.* ◇ **for ~** *Sometimes fierceness is exaggerated for effect.*
IDM **bring/put sth into efˈfect** to cause sth to come into use: *The legislation was first brought into effect in 1981.* ◇ *EU Directives establish laws that the Member State must put into effect in its own legal system.* **come into efˈfect** to come into use; to begin to apply: *On 7 June 2006, new powers came into effect connected with the introduction of identity cards.* **give efˈfect (to sth)** to cause sth to happen or exist by applying a law, policy or decision: *Even before a new government assumes office, civil servants have drafted proposals to give effect to the party's manifesto promises.* **in efˈfect** **1** used when you are stating what the facts of a situation are: *Together, these men, in effect, ran the government.* ◇ *In effect, education establishes desirable goals and develops a system for achieving those goals.* **2** (of a law or rule) in use: *Laws requiring immunization are now in effect in most US states.* **take efˈfect** **1** to come into use; to begin to apply: *Most influential of all was a new constitution, which took effect in 1947.* ◇ *The policy change took effect on 30 August 2005.* **2** to start to produce the results that are intended: *The drugs take about 30–60 minutes to take effect.* ◇ *Unemployment should put downward pressure on wages, but this may take time to take effect.* **to the effect that... | to this/that efˈfect** used to show that you are giving the general meaning of what sb has said or written rather than the exact words: *The envelope bears a legend to the effect that opening it signifies acceptance of a licence agreement.* **to good, great, dramatic, etc. efˈfect** producing a good or successful result or impression: *Fear is an emotion often evoked to good effect by social marketers.* ◇ *Text messaging is being used to great effect in fundraising.* **with immediate effect | with effect from...** starting now; starting from...: *Later that month, she was sacked by the council without compensation and with immediate effect.* ◇ *The fee was reduced, and finally abolished, with effect from 15 May 2002.*

▸ ADJECTIVE + EFFECT **significant • strong, large, great, profound, major • dramatic • small • marginal •**

long-term • cumulative • overall, net • main • immediate • direct • indirect • opposite • negative, adverse, detrimental, deleterious, harmful • positive, beneficial • protective • potential, possible • the desired • unwanted • causal • inhibitory • genetic • environmental *Hurricanes have a profound effect on many coastal ecosystems. ◇ The vast majority of these complications are minor with no long-term effects.*

▸ VERB + EFFECT **have • exert • show • produce • cause • estimate • predict • see, observe • demonstrate • find • detect • identify • examine, investigate, study, explore • analyse • test • measure • report • reveal • consider, assess, evaluate • describe • illustrate • capture • understand • explain • reduce, limit • moderate • minimize • eliminate • mitigate • counteract, offset • mediate** *The gravity field of a planet can be measured by observing its effect on a satellite in low orbit. ◇ Only one other study has experimentally investigated the effects of relative size on mating patterns.*

WHICH WORD?

effect • affect

- **effect** *noun* a result or an influence: *This section discusses the effects of information technology on strategy.*
- **affect** *verb* to have an influence on sb/sth: *A reduction of caterpillar prey has been shown to adversely affect some birds.*
- **effect** *verb* to achieve or produce a result: *To effect change does not necessarily require a great intellect as much as a brave one.*

The noun **affect** is a technical term in psychology.

ef·fect² /ɪˈfekt/ *verb* **~ sth** to make sth happen, especially a change in sth: *Interventions need not be perfect to effect an improvement in economic performance. ◇ The overall logic of the reforms was undoubtedly to effect a change in the political control of public services.* ➲ *usage note at* EFFECT¹

ef·fect·ive /ɪˈfektɪv/ *adj.* **1** producing the result that is wanted or intended; producing a successful result: *This treatment is effective in 70–90% of cases. ◇ This process allows organizations to focus on specific customers' needs in the most effective way.* ◇ **~ for sb/sth** *Bone marrow transplantation has proved to be extremely effective for the treatment of several genetic disorders.* ◇ **~ in doing sth** *Low cost, simple interventions can be highly effective in improving health care quality.* ◇ **~ at doing sth** *In contrast, Bombus queens were equally effective at pollinating both types of plants.* OPP INEFFECTIVE ➲ *see also* COST-EFFECTIVE **2** [only before noun] real or actual, although not officially intended: *Brides got most marriage gifts from their husbands, who kept effective control of these gifts until their deaths.* **3** (of laws and rules) in use: *This policy became effective in 1991.*

▸ EFFECTIVE + NOUN **way, means, method • strategy, policy • communication • management, control • treatment • remedy • intervention • use • implementation • system • tool • mechanism • protection • prevention** *Effective communication and genuine understanding become extremely difficult when two people are intensely angry with each other. ◇ Effective pain control is dependent upon good assessment.*

▸ ADVERB + EFFECTIVE **very, highly, particularly, especially • extremely • truly • equally • potentially • fully** *It has been shown that smaller doses may be equally effective.*

ef·fect·ive·ly /ɪˈfektɪvli/ *adv.* **1** in a way that produces the intended result or a successful result: *These risks must be effectively managed. ◇ The real test for a successful bridge is whether it works effectively. ◇ Certain skills and techniques may be needed to communicate effectively with children.* OPP INEFFECTIVELY **2** used when you are saying what the facts of a situation are SYN IN EFFECT (1): *The end of the USSR effectively removed the most serious source of organized state resistance to US power. ◇ The rapid increase in food prices effectively denied many poor people access to food.*

ef·fect·ive·ness /ɪˈfektɪvnəs/ *noun* [U] the degree to which sth produces a successful result: *By researching other companies, marketing managers can learn a lot about how to improve their own marketing effectiveness. ◇ This research stream is focused on adding value by enhancing organizational effectiveness and performance.* ◇ **~ of sth** *There is good evidence for the effectiveness of psychological interventions with older people. ◇ There have been massive advances in the efficiency and effectiveness of distribution systems.*

▸ ADJECTIVE + EFFECTIVENESS **relative • overall • increasing • limited • organizational • clinical** *For high-cost drugs with limited proven effectiveness, it is not unfair to deny funding.*

▸ VERB + EFFECTIVENESS **evaluate, assess • test • determine, measure • examine, investigate • monitor • demonstrate • improve, increase, enhance • reduce • ensure** *The best way to determine the effectiveness of the programme is through long-term research.*

eˈffect size *noun* (*statistics*) a measure of the difference between two groups in terms of how they have been affected by sth; an estimate of this: *Effect sizes for each variable studied were large (above 0.80).* ◇ **~ of sth** *It is not uncommon for pilot studies to be performed to assess the effect size of new treatments before progressing to evaluate their use in randomized controlled clinical trials.*

ef·fi·cacy /ˈefɪkəsi/ *noun* [U] the ability of sth, especially a drug or a medical treatment, to produce the results that are wanted SYN EFFECTIVENESS: *There are no differences in efficacy between the classes of drugs.* ◇ **~ of sth** *The efficacy of the vaccine was assumed to be 90 per cent, with 10 years' duration of protection. ◇ to evaluate/assess/test/demonstrate the efficacy of sth*

ef·fi·ciency /ɪˈfɪʃnsi/ *noun* **1** [U] the quality of doing sth well with no waste of time or money: *For these writers, organizational efficiency was achieved through the rational design of organizations.* ◇ **~ of sth** *Strategies that improve the overall economic efficiency of firms can also yield important environmental benefits.* **2** [U, C] (*technical*) the relationship between the amount of energy that goes into a machine or an engine, and the amount that it produces: **~ of sth** *Combined cycle power plants can achieve an efficiency of about 45%. ◇ The aerodynamic efficiencies of the compressor and turbine both need to be high.* ◇ **+ noun** *Comparing fuel efficiency standards across countries is not simple.* **3 efficiencies** [pl.] ways of wasting less time and money or of saving time or money: *A key strategic objective is to optimize the return to shareholders through improved margins and efficiencies.* ◇ **~ of sth** *The efficiencies of mass production seemed to require a new social organization emphasizing mass consumption.*

▸ ADJECTIVE + EFFICIENCY **greater, improved, increased • economic • technical • productive** *The development of process innovations leads to greater efficiency of production. ◇ Emissions may be reduced in parallel with improving technical efficiency and productivity.* | **high • low • maximum • average • overall** *Two-stroke engines have lower fuel efficiency and higher exhaust pollutant emissions. ◇ The overall efficiency of the photosynthetic process is around 5%.*

▸ NOUN + EFFICIENCY **energy • fuel** *It is estimated that for every one-third drop in average vehicle speed, fuel efficiency drops by 30%.*

▸ VERB + EFFICIENCY **improve, increase, promote • achieve • enhance • maximize • reduce • compare • measure • evaluate** *In order to reduce costs and increase efficiency, the general manager decided to create work teams.*

ef·fi·cient /ɪˈfɪʃnt/ *adj.* doing sth well and with no waste of time, money or energy: *The system is intended to ensure effective and efficient use of resources.* ◇ *As a means of removing sulfur dioxide, this is a highly efficient process.* ◇ **~ at (doing) sth** *The kidneys are less efficient at retaining potassium than sodium.* OPP INEFFICIENT

ef·fi·cient·ly /ɪˈfɪʃntli/ *adv.* in a way that does not waste time, money or energy: *Resources must be used efficiently to avoid waste.* ◇ *If markets fail or do not work efficiently, government has a role to play.*

ef·fort /ˈefət; *NAmE* ˈefərt/ *noun* **1** [U, C] the physical or mental energy that you need to do sth; sth that takes a lot of energy: *The effort involved in performing such an analysis is too great to be justified in practice.* ◇ *Internet shopping requires relatively little effort on the part of the purchaser.* ◇ *Developmental biologists have tended to focus their efforts on a relatively small number of animals.* ◇ **with (an) ~** *With effort, a logical analysis could reduce the unknowns and confidence could be increased.* **2** [C] an attempt to do sth, especially when it is difficult to do: **~ (to do sth)** *She made a concerted effort to improve her language skills.* ◇ *Norway has made strenuous efforts to incorporate environmental values into policymaking.* ◇ **in an ~ to do sth** *Streets are intentionally narrow in an effort to reduce traffic speed.* **3** [C] (usually after a noun) a particular activity that a group of people organizes in order to achieve sth: *The government refused to allow international aid efforts access to these areas.* ◇ *Bureaucracies and tax burdens increased in size to support the war effort.* ◇ *Their research effort has centred on the South American and Central American tropics.*

▸ ADJECTIVE + EFFORT **considerable, much, great** ♦ **little** *Considerable effort is still to be expended on improving fuel cell technology in terms of cost and performance.* | **concerted** ♦ **joint, collective** ♦ **conscious** ♦ **sustained** ♦ **strenuous** ♦ **major** *A concerted effort to reduce cigarette smoking and nicotine addiction is required.*

▸ VERB + EFFORT **focus, concentrate, direct** ♦ **require, take, need** ♦ **put, devote, expend** ♦ **increase** *The government has not put any effort into measuring poverty or social exclusion.* | **make** ♦ **support** ♦ **undertake** *Immigrants undertook new efforts to improve the appearance of the area.*

e.g. /ˌiː ˈdʒiː/ *abbr.* **for example** (from Latin 'exempli gratia'): *Most research shows that people strongly prefer visiting and conversing with friends to watching television (e.g., Kubey & Csikszentmihalyi, 1990).* ◇ *'Confusion' is a very vague term that can refer to various medical syndromes, e.g. dementia, psychosis, etc.*

egali·tar·ian /iˌɡælɪˈteəriən; *NAmE* iˌɡælɪˈteriən/ *adj.* based on or holding the belief that everyone is equal and should have the same rights and opportunities: *They looked to the gradual transformation of capitalism into a classless egalitarian society.* ■ **egali·tar·ian** *noun*: *Some liberal egalitarians have gradually lost confidence in the ability of the state to achieve justice.* **egali·tar·ian·ism** /iˌɡælɪˈteəriənɪzəm; *NAmE* iˌɡælɪˈteriənɪzəm/ *noun* [U] *Theatre-going enacted a kind of egalitarianism, all classes gathered in one place, engaging in the same activity.*

egg /eɡ/ *noun* **1** an almost round object with a thin hard shell produced by a female bird and containing a young bird; a similar object produced by a female fish, insect, etc: *A butterfly lays its eggs on leaves selected according to the plant species and their nutrient status.* ◇ *to fertilize/incubate/hatch the eggs* **2** (in women and female animals) a cell that combines with a SPERM to create a baby or young animal: *Whether the right or left ovary provides the egg each month is relatively random.*

eight /eɪt/ *number* 8 HELP There are examples of how to use numbers at the entry for **five**.

ei·ther[1] /ˈaɪðə(r); ˈiːðə(r)/ *det., pron.* **1** one or the other of two; it does not matter which: *If circumstances alter for either party, they can renegotiate prices and other details.* ◇ *Britton (2010) proposed two possible explanations, but experimental evidence to validate either is still scarce.* ◇ **~ of sb/sth** *A path exists from input to output if either of the two switches is closed.* **2** each of two: *No improvement was found in either age group.*

ei·ther[2] /ˈaɪðə(r); ˈiːðə(r)/ *adv.* **1 either... or...** used to show a choice of two things: *High wage jobs either disappeared or moved overseas.* ◇ *The fundamental need either to find or to grow food meant that the majority of people lived in rural rather than urban settings.* **2** used after negative phrases to show that one statement is similar to or connected with another that has already been made: *If costs are not rising and aggregate demand is weak, prices are not likely to rise either.* **3** used at the end of a negative phrase that adds extra information to a statement, often to make what you said clearer: *They were not forced immigrants, but they were not quite voluntary either.* ➲ *compare* OR

elab·or·ate[1] /ɪˈlæbərət/ *adj.* [usually before noun] very complicated and detailed; carefully prepared and organized: *For over 3 000 years, an elaborate system of competitive examinations was used in China.* ◇ *Darwin made elaborate arrangements for the publication of the 1844 essay in the event of his early death.* ■ **elab·or·ate·ly** *adv.*: *The chapel's walls were elaborately decorated with scenes from the life of St James.* ◇ *These networks were more elaborately organized in the later Middle Ages.*

elab·or·ate[2] /ɪˈlæbəreɪt/ *verb* **1** [I, T] to explain or describe sth in a more detailed way: **~ on/upon sth** *It is regrettable that the Court's decision does not elaborate on this point.* ◇ **~ sth** *This point was elaborated further by Allen (1995).* **2** [T] **~ sth** to develop a plan, an idea, etc. and make it complicated or detailed: *Later, more emphasis was placed on elaborating the basic model and extending its application.* **3** [T] (*biology*) (of a natural process) to produce a substance or structure from its elements or simpler CONSTITUENTS: *Many peptide hormones are elaborated by neural tissue.*

elab·or·ation /ɪˌlæbəˈreɪʃn/ *noun* [U, C] **1** the act of explaining or describing sth in a more detailed way: *This statement requires some elaboration.* ◇ **~ of sth** *These brief elaborations of the implications of the changes highlight the complexity of the situation.* **2** the process of developing a plan, an idea, etc. and making it complicated or detailed: *There is a need for further theoretical elaboration.* ◇ **~ of sth** *Further elaborations of these ideas look at how both sets of hypotheses might be combined.* **3 ~ (of sth)** (*biology*) the production of a substance or structure from elements or simpler CONSTITUENTS in a natural process: *His work focused on the interaction of organism and environment in the elaboration of the phenotype.*

elas·tic /ɪˈlæstɪk/ *adj.* **1** able to stretch and return to its original size and shape: *Hooke's law describes the relation between stress and strain for a perfectly elastic material.* ◇ *As people age, the skin tends to become thinner, less elastic, drier and finely wrinkled.* ➲ *compare* INELASTIC (2) **2** (*economics*) (of demand or supply) affected by changes in prices or incomes: *Demand for any one garage's fuel is likely to be more price elastic than for fuel as a whole; this is because drivers can switch to a competitor's garage if there is a noticeable price difference.* ➲ *compare* INELASTIC (1) **3** that can change or be changed: *Only Sweden and Germany seem to have an elastic response to changes in unemployment.* **4** (*physics*) (of a COLLISION) involving no decrease of KINETIC energy: *The process can be described in terms of an elastic collision between a photon and a free electron.*

elas·ti·city /ˌiːlæˈstɪsəti; ˌelæˈstɪsəti; ɪˌlæˈstɪsəti/ *noun* **1** [U] the quality that sth has of being able to stretch and

E

return to its original size and shape: *Such materials are used in technology because of their flexibility and elasticity at low temperatures.* ◇ **~ of sth** *In this section, I shall look at a simple model for the elasticity of a single human hair.* **2** [U, C] (*economics*) the way in which two measures, such as demand for a product and its price, change PROPORTIONALLY in relation to each other HELP For example, if there is a *constant elasticity of demand*, a particular percentage change in price will lead to a fixed percentage change in the quantity demanded: **~ (of sth)** *Studies have found that the elasticity of demand for fuel is, on the whole, rather low.* ◇ **price/income/demand ~** *The price elasticity of demand for UK products will depend on factors such as how unique they are, the power of the brand, the quality and the reliability.*

E

elder[1] /ˈeldə(r)/ *adj.* **1** [only before noun] (of people, especially two members of the same family) older: *He succeeded to the throne as a young man, after the assassination of his elder brother.* ➲ *usage note at* OLD **2 the elder, the Elder** used before or after sb's name to show that they are the older of two people who have the same name: *He lacked the drive and decisiveness of the elder Pitt as a war leader.* ◇ *The use of 'magnifying glasses' was recorded in the first century AD by Pliny the Elder.* **3** [only before noun] connected with older people: *It is most often women who take responsibility for child and elder care.*

elder[2] /ˈeldə(r)/ *noun* **1 elders** [pl.] people of greater age, often thought of as having greater experience and authority: *According to Confucianism, one of the most important values is respect for elders.* ◇ *The elders of the village had chosen to stay behind.* ◇ **your, etc. elders** *In these cultures, younger people are expected to defer to their elders.* **2 your, sb's, etc. elder** [sing.] a person who is older than you or another person: *Justus Lipsius was just as famous in his day as Erasmus, his elder by several decades.* **3** [C] an official in some Christian churches: *He was an elder in the local church.*

eld·er·ly /ˈeldəli; *NAmE* ˈeldərli/ *adj.* **1** (of people) used as a polite word for 'old': *Doses should be reduced for elderly patients.* ◇ *With an increasing elderly population the number of patients with cancer is likely to increase.* **2 the elderly** *noun* [pl.] people who are old: *In Japan, there was a 600 per cent increase in government spending on the elderly during the 1990s.*

eld·est /ˈeldɪst/ *adj.* **1** (of people, especially of three or more members of the same family) oldest: *His eldest son, Hugh, succeeded him as Earl of Shrewsbury.* **2 the eldest (of sb)** used to show who is the oldest of three or more people: *William James was born in New York, the eldest of five children.*

elect /ɪˈlekt/ *verb* **1** to choose sb to do a particular job by voting for them: **~ sb/sth** *The members of the supervisory board are elected by the shareholders.* ◇ *Democratically elected governments are more likely to pursue policies that address problems of poverty.* ◇ **~ sb to sth** *Roosevelt was first elected to office in 1932.* ◇ **~ sb + noun | ~ sb as sth** *The Belgian Herman van Rompuy was elected (as) the first President in January 2010.* **2 ~ to do sth** to choose to do sth: *Some writers elect to use a theoretical framework, while others favour a more explicitly empirical focus.*

elec·tion /ɪˈlekʃn/ *noun* **1** [C, U] the process of choosing a person or a group of people for a position, especially a political position, by voting: *Elections are held every five years.* ◇ *Political parties at all levels win elections by finding issues on which to campaign.* ◇ **in an ~** *The party won a smaller vote share than in any election between 1857 and 1997.* ◇ **for ~** (*especially BrE*) *Over 98 per cent of countries in the world have granted women the formal right to vote and to stand for election.* ◇ (*especially NAmE*) *to run for election* ◇ **+ noun** *The election result was not accepted by significant numbers of citizens.* ➲ *see also* GENERAL ELECTION **2** [U] the fact of having been chosen by election: *In the end, Nixon had won election by securing the votes of only 27% of all those eligible to vote.* ◇ **~ to sth** *Europe was a key issue in Cameron's election to the Conservative leadership.* ◇ **~ as sth** *Reagan's election as the next US president promised new anxieties.*

elect·ive /ɪˈlektɪv/ *adj.* [usually before noun] **1** (of medical treatment) that you choose to have; not required urgently SYN OPTIONAL: *Private health insurance is used mainly for elective surgery.* **2** chosen or filled by people voting: *This trend towards party government has been referred to as elective dictatorship.* ◇ *Singapore's presidency was transformed in 1991 from a ceremonial into an elective office.* **3** (of a course or subject) chosen by the student SYN OPTIONAL: *Some Italian Law Schools have introduced elective courses in immigration law.* ➲ *compare* COMPULSORY

elect·or·al /ɪˈlektərəl/ *adj.* [only before noun] connected with elections: *The choice of electoral system is one of the most important institutional decisions for any democracy.* ◇ *Electoral reform would fundamentally alter the relationships between the main political parties.* ■ **elect·or·al·ly** /ɪˈlektərəli/ *adv.*: *The Conservative Party was the most electorally successful right-wing party anywhere in the 20th century.*

elect·or·ate /ɪˈlektərət/ *noun* [C+sing./pl. v., usually sing.] the people in a country or an area who have the right to vote, thought of as a group: *The turnout was low with only 25% of the electorate bothering to vote.* ◇ *The Norwegian electorate once again chose to reject membership in a referendum.*

elec·tric /ɪˈlektrɪk/ *adj.* [usually before noun] connected with electricity; using, produced by or producing electricity: *Electric fields can also be produced by chemical or electromagnetic means.* ◇ *Electric motors and generators must be cooled when operating to prevent the overheating of internal parts.* ➲ *see also* ELECTRIC SHOCK

WHICH WORD?

electric • electrical

- **Electric** is usually used to describe sth that uses or produces electricity: *an electric car/motor/organ* ◇ *an electric discharge/field/generator*
- **Electrical** is usually used with more general nouns, and things that are concerned with electricity: *electrical equipment/appliances* ◇ *electrical conductivity/energy* ◇ *an electrical engineer*
- However, this distinction is not always made clearly: *an electric/electrical charge/circuit/current*

elec·tric·al /ɪˈlektrɪkl/ *adj.* connected with electricity; using or producing electricity: *A solar cell converts light to electrical energy.* ◇ *Several companies in the industry were convicted of fixing the prices of electrical equipment.* ➲ *usage note at* ELECTRIC ■ **elec·tric·al·ly** /ɪˈlektrɪkli/ *adv.*: *Atoms are electrically neutral overall.* ◇ *Magnetic fields are generated by the movement of electrically charged particles.*

elec·tri·city /ɪˌlekˈtrɪsəti/ *noun* [U] a form of energy from charged ELEMENTARY PARTICLES, usually supplied as electric current through CABLES, wires, etc. for lighting, heating, driving machines, etc: *Semiconductors do conduct electricity, but not nearly as well as metals.* ◇ *Currently about two thirds of the world's electricity is generated from fossil fuels.* ◇ **+ noun** *On a commercial scale, electricity generation using geothermal energy is now over 100 years old.*

eˌlectric ˈshock (*also* **shock**) *noun* a sudden flow of electricity passing through a person's body and causing pain and possibly death: *Any electrical equipment has the potential to cause an electric shock.*

elec·tro·chem·ical /ɪˌlektrəʊˈkemɪkl; *NAmE* ɪˌlektroʊˈkemɪkl/ *adj.* [only before noun] involving both electricity and chemistry: *A battery is in fact an example of an electrochemical cell.* ◇ *A fuel cell generates electricity by the electrochemical reaction of hydrogen and oxygen.*

elec·trode /ɪˈlektrəʊd; *NAmE* ɪˈlektroʊd/ *noun* either of two points (or TERMINALS) by which an electric current enters or leaves a battery, device, object, substance or region: *Silver and copper electrodes are sometimes used when these elements cannot interfere with the analysis.* ◇ *Electrodes are placed on the patient's scalp.* ◇ *Further metal ions are drawn to the electrode and accumulate over a period of time.* ➲ *see also* ANODE, CATHODE

elec·tro·lyte /ɪˈlektrəlaɪt/ *noun* **1** (*chemistry*) a liquid that an electric current can pass through, especially in an electric cell or battery: *As for the fuel cell and all other electrochemically based devices, two electrodes and an electrolyte are present.* **2** (*medical*) dissolved salts and minerals in the body that carry an electric charge and that cells need to control the balance of liquid in the body: *Dissolved oral rehydration salts are much better than water because they also contain the electrolytes lost in the diarrhoea.* ■ **elec·tro·ly·tic** /ɪˌlektrəˈlɪtɪk/ *adj.*: *In an electrolytic cell, however, the electrochemical reactions are not spontaneous.*

elec·tro·mag·net·ic /ɪˌlektrəʊmægˈnetɪk; *NAmE* ɪˌlektroʊmægˈnetɪk/ *adj.* (*physics*) in which the electrical and MAGNETIC properties of sth are related: *Electromagnetic radiation occurs naturally at a variety of wavelengths.* ◇ *When current flows in a wire, an electromagnetic field is created.*

elec·tro·mag·net·ism /ɪˌlektrəʊˈmægnətɪzəm; *NAmE* ɪˌlektroʊˈmægnətɪzəm/ *noun* [U] (*physics*) the production of a MAGNETIC FIELD by means of an electric current, or of an electric current by means of a MAGNETIC FIELD; the branch of physics concerned with this: *Einstein knew from Maxwell's laws of electromagnetism that light had to be seen as travelling at speed.* ◇ *Michael Faraday made breakthrough experiments in electromagnetism.*

elec·tron /ɪˈlektrɒn; *NAmE* ɪˈlektrɑːn/ *noun* (*physics*) a very small piece of matter with a negative electric charge, found in all atoms HELP An **electron** is a **subatomic particle**. Electrons are the main carriers of electricity in solids: *Each hydrogen atom has a single electron.* ◇ *The free electrons interact strongly with all electromagnetic radiation.* ◇ **+ noun** *In transmission electron microscopy, the electron beam passes through the specimen and the image is collected on a screen.* ➲ *compare* NEUTRON, PROTON

elec·tron·ic /ɪˌlekˈtrɒnɪk; *NAmE* ɪˌlekˈtrɑːnɪk/ *adj.* [usually before noun] **1** (of a device) having or using many small parts, such as MICROCHIPS, that control and direct a small electric current: *The lithium ion battery is commonly used in portable electronic equipment.* ◇ *Each memory cell is an electronic circuit capable of storing one bit.* **2** done by means of a computer or other electronic device, especially over a network: *Knowledge and human relationships have been restructured as a result of electronic communication.* ◇ *The sources included printed and electronic data on total deaths and causes of death.* ◇ *With the emergence of multiple new electronic media, marketers face complicated choices about how to engage most effectively with customers.* **3** connected with electronic equipment: *The development of electronic technologies has facilitated the rapid growth in the collection of consumer purchase data.* **4** connected with ELECTRONS: *This means that the electronic state of the atoms or molecules is affected; their energy is increased from a ground state to an excited one.* **5** connected with electronics: *These topics belong to the realm of electronic engineering.*

elec·tron·ic·al·ly /ɪˌlekˈtrɒnɪkli; *NAmE* ɪˌlekˈtrɑːnɪkli/ *adv.* in an electronic way; using a device that works in an electronic way: *These forms are also available electronically.* ◇ *Images such as X-rays are stored electronically and viewed on screens.*

ˌelectronic ˈmail *noun* [U] (*formal*) = EMAIL¹ (1)

elec·tron·ics /ɪˌlekˈtrɒnɪks; *NAmE* ɪˌlekˈtrɑːnɪks/ *noun* **1** [U] the branch of science and technology that studies electric currents in electronic equipment: *The invention of this transistor represented a critical turning point in electronics.* **2** [U] the use of electronic technology; the making of electronic products: *Thomas's own background was in industrial electronics.* ◇ **+ noun** *Electronics industries tend to employ immigrants in the lowest-paying assembly jobs.* ◇ *He wrote a study of a Japanese-owned consumer electronics plant operating in the UK.* **3** [pl.] the electronic CIRCUITS and COMPONENTS used in electronic equipment: *A lightning strike had wrecked the electronics in the control room.*

eˌlectron ˈmicroscope *noun* a very powerful MICROSCOPE that uses ELECTRONS instead of light: *An electron microscope can obtain a magnification of up to 2 million times.*

elec·tro·stat·ic /ɪˌlektrəʊˈstætɪk; *NAmE* ɪˌlektroʊˈstætɪk/ *adj.* connected with electric charges that are not moving, rather than electric currents: *The electrostatic field of a fully charged atom extends at equal strength in all directions.* ◇ **~ interaction/attraction/repulsion** *In such solids there are strong electrostatic interactions between the ions.*

ele·gant /ˈelɪgənt/ *adj.* **1** (of people or their behaviour) attractive and showing a good sense of style: *In Vienna, the elegant ladies who presided over aristocratic salons organized recitals and benefit concerts.* **2** (of clothes, places and things) attractive and designed well: *Elegant clothes, fine jewels and rich ornaments were in demand as money circulated more freely in certain circles.* **3** (of a plan or an idea) clever but simple: *Coltheart (1980) offered an elegant solution to this problem.* ■ **ele·gance** /ˈelɪgəns/ *noun* [U] *She is dark-haired, not blonde, and devoid of royal elegance or rich costume.* ◇ *The elegance with which these ideas fit together makes the theory very attractive.* **ele·gant·ly** *adv.*: *The young man was seated, talking to a very attractive young woman; she was elegantly dressed.* ◇ *Kepler derived elegantly simple rules to predict the motions of the planets.*

elem·ent AWL /ˈelɪmənt/ *noun* **1** [C] a necessary or typical part of sth: *The design axioms were created by identifying common elements that are present in all good designs.* ◇ **~ of (doing) sth** *Lifelong learning is a key element of a new view of education.* ◇ *Negotiations are an important element of forming a contract.* ◇ **~ in sth** *He argued that the development of social policy was an essential element in the functioning of modern industrialism.* **2** [C] a simple chemical substance that consists of atoms of only one type and cannot be split by chemical means into a simpler substance. Gold, OXYGEN and CARBON are all elements: *Masks must be worn to prevent inhalation of mining dust, which can contain radioactive elements.* ◇ *The Earth is a constantly changing system, and chemical elements within and on its surface are always on the move.* ➲ *compare* COMPOUND¹ (1) ➲ *see also* TRACE ELEMENT **3** [C, usually sing.] **~ of risk, truth, surprise, etc.** a small amount of a quality or feeling: *Investment decisions inevitably have an element of risk and uncertainty.* ◇ *There was an element of truth in his assertion.* **4** [C, usually pl.] **~ (of sth)** a group of people who form a part of a larger group or society: *The Nixon administration felt besieged by radical elements of the civil rights movement.* ◇ *The socialist state mobilized new elements of society to support it.* **5** [C] (*mathematics*) a member of a set or group: *The number of elements in a set is its cardinality.* **6** [C] the part of a piece of electrical equipment that gives out heat: *The currents flowing into the two heating elements are adjusted to keep the*

E

temperature difference at zero. **7** [C] one of the four substances (earth, air, fire and water) which people used to believe everything else was made of: *Each of Aristotle's four elements, fire, earth, air and water, possessed two basic properties.* **8 the elements** [pl.] the weather, especially bad weather: *Like the skin, most parts of the respiratory tract are exposed to the elements.*

IDM **in your ˈelement** doing what you are good at and enjoy: *The president was clearly in his element, rising to the occasion with a memorable address.*

E

elem·en·tal /ˌelɪˈmentl/ *adj.* [usually before noun] **1** (*chemistry*) connected with the chemical elements that are contained in sth: *This is one of the most powerful techniques for the elemental analysis of complicated samples.* **2** wild and powerful; like the forces of nature: *Watching the weather and the seasons, Hutton concluded that the elemental forces operating around him had shaped the landscape.* **3** basic and important: *The apprehension of beauty is, at its most elemental level, a visceral response to form.*

elem·en·tary /ˌelɪˈmentri/ *adj.* **1** connected with the first stages of a course of study, or the first years at school: *The students in these two classes were at an elementary level.* ◇ *We assessed paternal and maternal education separately as: elementary school, high school, first university degree and second university degree.* ➲ *compare* PRIMARY, SECONDARY (4) **2** of the most basic kind: *It is an elementary principle of international law that a state is entitled to protect its subjects.* **3** very simple and easy: *He set out the argument in elementary terms in 1949.*

ˌelementary ˈparticle *noun* = PARTICLE (1)

ele·vate /ˈelɪveɪt/ *verb* **1 ~ sth** (*technical*) to make the level of sth increase: *The secretion of cortisol elevates the levels of sugar and other nutrients in the blood.* ◇ *His blood pressure is quite elevated and needs to be reduced.* **2 ~ sth** (*technical*) to lift sth up or put sth in a higher position: *If appropriate, elevate limbs to reduce swelling, inflammation and pain.* **3 ~ sb/sth (to/into sth)** to give sb/sth a higher position or rank: *Women writers elevated the genre of the novel to the highest status.* ◇ *Scientists claiming to have developed revolutionary Soviet theories were elevated into high positions.* **4 ~ sth** to improve a person's mood, so that they feel happy: *Antidepressants relieve the symptoms of depressive disorders but do not elevate the mood of healthy people.*

ele·vated /ˈelɪveɪtɪd/ *adj.* [usually before noun] **1** higher than normal: *The blood shows elevated levels of long chain fatty acids.* ◇ *They may be at an elevated risk for heart disease due to the strain under which they live.* ◇ *an elevated temperature/pressure/concentration* ◇ *The antibodies were only significantly elevated in women with Stage II disease.* **2** high in rank: *Rulers wanted to display and distribute symbols of their elevated status.* **3** higher than the area around; above the level of the ground: *In the most elevated mountain ranges on Earth, steep, almost vertical, rock slopes dominate.* **4** having a high moral or INTELLECTUAL level: *They wanted to abolish traditional popular theatre, and establish instead more elevated forms of drama.*

ele·va·tion /ˌelɪˈveɪʃn/ *noun* **1** [C, usually sing.] (*technical*) the height of a place, especially its height above sea level: *As it courses through the canyon, the Colorado River drops about 2 000 feet in elevation.* ◇ **at an ~ of sth** *The top of the barrier was at an elevation of 840 m, or 339 m above river level.* **2** [C] (*technical*) a piece of ground that is higher than the area around: *The highest elevations in southern Africa are found along or near the rim of the Great Escarpment.* **3** [sing., U] (*technical*) an increase in the level or amount of sth: **~ (of sth)** *These drugs produce an elevation of mood, overactivity and insomnia.* ◇ **~ in sth** *This elevation in body temperature is seen as a dysfunction of the body that must be corrected.* **4** [U] **~ (of sth)** (*technical*) the act of raising sth; an increase in the height of sth: *Pain is relieved by rest and relief is speeded by elevation of the limb.* **5** [U] **~ (of sb) (to sth)** the process of sb getting a higher or more important rank: *He was one more example of Nicholas's crucial failing, the elevation of men who were loyal and hard-working, regardless of competence.* ◇ *Following his elevation to government, Henriot embarked on an intensive schedule of twice-daily broadcasts.* **6** [C] (*architecture*) one side of a building; a drawing of this by an ARCHITECT: *A comprehensive study requires an accurate survey of the masonry, producing stone-by-stone drawings of each elevation.* ➲ *compare* PLAN[1] (3)

ele·va·tor /ˈelɪveɪtə(r)/ *noun* (*NAmE*) = LIFT[2] (2)

elicit /iˈlɪsɪt/ *verb* to get information or a reaction from sb/sth: *With the development of interactive television, advertising can be used to elicit an immediate response.* ◇ *This use of closed questions elicited specific information concerning the participant's prior research experiences.* ◇ **~ sth from sb/sth** *Adult males elicit aggressive behaviour from the owner of a territory, while juveniles are not attacked.* ■ **elicit·ation** /iˌlɪsɪˈteɪʃn/ *noun* [U] **~ (of sth)** *The expression and elicitation of emotion in film is a central element of the film experience.*

eli·gible /ˈelɪdʒəbl/ *adj.* a person who is **eligible** for sth or to do sth is able to have or do it because they have the right qualifications, are the right age, etc: *Vitamin supplements are available free of charge to eligible families.* ◇ **~ for sth** *All patients with diabetes were eligible for inclusion in the study.* ◇ **~ to do sth** *Workers who are dismissed for taking lawful industrial action will become eligible to claim unfair dismissal.* OPP INELIGIBLE ■ **eli·gi·bil·ity** /ˌelɪdʒəˈbɪləti/ *noun* [U] **~ (for sth)** *Affected workers were advised regarding eligibility for compensation.* ◇ **+ noun** *Other eligibility criteria included age, ability to understand English, and willingness to participate in the study for 24 months.*

elim·in·ate AWL /ɪˈlɪmɪneɪt/ *verb* **1** to remove or get rid of sth/sb: **~ sth/sb** *Dominance by multinational corporations eliminates the need for local skills and production.* ◇ *Slow careful withdrawal from a medication can decrease or eliminate the risk of side effects.* ◇ *Natural predator-prey dynamics mean that a predatory species is unlikely to completely eliminate its prey.* ◇ **~ sth/sb from sth** *The hormones are quickly eliminated from the blood.* **2 ~ sb** to kill sb, especially an enemy or opponent: *He established a bandit-like regime, using special troops to eliminate political opponents.* **3 ~ sth** (*mathematics*) to remove a VARIABLE from an EQUATION, typically by substituting another which is shown by another equation to have the same value: *This eliminates the variable y, so that the final result is a definite number.* **4 ~ sth** (*chemistry*) to produce a simple substance such as water in addition to a more complex substance as a result of a chemical reaction involving larger ORGANIC MOLECULES: *When two amino acids molecules combine to form a dipeptide a molecule of water is eliminated.*

elim·in·ation AWL /ɪˌlɪmɪˈneɪʃn/ *noun* [U] **1** the act or process of removing or getting rid of sb/sth: **~ (of sth)** *Many businessmen and professionals profited from the elimination of their competition.* **2 ~ (of sth)** (*chemistry*) the process of producing a simple substance such as water in addition to a more complex substance as a result of a chemical reaction involving larger ORGANIC MOLECULES: *Sulfuric acid is often used as the catalyst to help remove the water in the elimination reaction of alcohols to form alkenes.*

elite[1] /eɪˈliːt; ɪˈliːt/ *noun* [C+sing./pl. v.] a social group that is thought to be the best or most important because of its power, money, intelligence, etc: *Economic and political elites blamed the crisis on the low skill levels of American workers.* ◇ *All organizations contain ruling elites and* *followers.* ◇ *In written Roman sources, a villa is usually the country estate of a wealthy member of the urban elite.*

elite² /eɪˈliːt; ɪˈliːt/ *adj.* [only before noun] better than others of the same group or type: *The pattern of advantage for graduates of elite schools is still in operation today.* ◇ *Many in this elite group are top executives of multinational corporations.*

el·lip·sis /ɪˈlɪpsɪs/ *noun* (*pl.* **el·lip·ses** /ɪˈlɪpsiːz/) [C, U] **1** (*grammar*) the act of leaving out a word or words from a sentence deliberately, when the meaning can be understood without them: *Many forms of spoken language appeared in Luther's writing, including free word order, ellipsis, modal particles and idioms.* **2** three dots (...) used to show that a word or words have been left out: *The final line of the poem does not end in a period, but with an ellipsis that indicates the possibility of change or additions.*

elong·ate /ˈiːlɒŋgeɪt; *NAmE* ɪˈlɔːŋgeɪt; ɪˈlɑːŋgeɪt/ *verb* [I, T] to become longer; to make sth longer SYN LENGTHEN: *About 5 hours after fertilization, the embryo begins to elongate rapidly.* ◇ **~ sth** *By elongating the bubble in the barrel, the area-to-volume ratio of the gas bubble is increased.* ■ **elonga·tion** /ˌiːlɒŋˈgeɪʃn; *NAmE* ˌiːlɔːŋˈgeɪʃn; ˌiːlɑːŋˈgeɪʃn/ *noun* [U] *Cotton fibre provides an excellent system for studying cell elongation and cell wall biosynthesis.*

elong·ated /ˈiːlɒŋgeɪtɪd; *NAmE* ɪˈlɔːŋgeɪtɪd; ɪˈlɑːŋgeɪtɪd/ *adj.* long and thin, often in a way that is not normal: *Fibrinogen is a highly elongated molecule.*

else /els/ *adv.* (used in questions or after *nothing*, *nobody*, *something*, *anything*, etc.) **1** in addition to sth already mentioned: *Apart from the price, what else can affect the demand for products?* ◇ *Vigorous activity was defined as running, aerobics, heavy yard work or anything else that causes large increases in breathing or heart rate.* ◇ *Studies of work, politics and practically everything else focused on men.* **2** different: *Its new product was very different from anything else on the market.* ◇ *More wide-ranging reforms could enable schools in poor areas to work as well as schools anywhere else.* ◇ *The annexe did not belong to the vendor, but to someone else.*
IDM **or else 1** used for saying that sth bad will happen, if sth is not done SYN OTHERWISE: *There are some parallel processes that must be addressed, or else they will become potential risks.* **2** used to introduce the second of two possibilities: *Each individual is faced with a choice between either searching for food or else looking for a companion that has already found food.*

else·where /ˌelsˈweə(r); *NAmE* ˌelsˈwer/ *adv.* in, at or to another place: *The purpose of the research was to compare these samples with samples found elsewhere.* ◇ *If a firm tried to sell at a price above the market level, consumers would simply go elsewhere.* ◇ *This idea is not mentioned elsewhere in his writings.*

elu·ci·date /iˈluːsɪdeɪt/ *verb* (*formal*) to make sth clear; to explain sth more fully SYN EXPLAIN: **~ sth** *More studies are needed in order to elucidate the role of these cells.* ◇ **~ how/what, etc...** *Knowledge of the components of the genome has been crucial in elucidating how genes work.* ■ **elu·ci·da·tion** /iˌluːsɪˈdeɪʃn/ *noun* [U, C, usually sing.] *This is an interesting point that requires further elucidation.* ◇ **~ of sth** *Major advances in science include Watson and Crick's elucidation of the structure of DNA.*

email¹ (*also* **e-mail**) /ˈiːmeɪl/ *noun* **1** (*also formal* ˌ**electronic** ˈ**mail**) [U] a way of sending messages and data to other people by means of computers connected together in a network: *Most non-manual workers are likely to be familiar with the details of using email and the Internet.* ◇ **by ~** *A questionnaire was administered by telephone, email or post to all participants.* ◇ **+ noun** *In order to enter the competition, the customer has to register their email address online.* **2** [C, U] a message sent by email: *Online users who sent an email to the company to resolve a problem would typically wait 48 hours for a reply.* ◇ *Some users regularly receive email, but do not have a computer at home.*

email² (*also* **e-mail**) /ˈiːmeɪl/ *verb* to send a message to sb by email: **~ sth (to sb)** *Questionnaires were emailed to respondents prior to interviews.* ◇ **~ sb** *The senior manager emailed all members of the department to inform them of the decision.*

em·an·ate /ˈeməneɪt/ *verb*
PHR V ˈ**emanate from sth** to come from sth or somewhere SYN ISSUE FROM STH: *Before and during a film's production, all publicity emanates from Hollywood.* ◇ *The idea of a policy of protectionism emanating from Brussels went against national policies.*

em·bark /ɪmˈbɑːk; *NAmE* ɪmˈbɑːrk/ *verb* [I] to get onto a ship: *He embarked for India in 1817.*
PHR V **emˈbark on/upon sth** to start to do sth new or difficult: *China has in recent years embarked upon an intensive programme to modernize every aspect of its economy and society.* ◇ *Many of the authors are junior researchers just embarking on their academic careers.*

em·bar·rassed /ɪmˈbærəst/ *adj.* (of a person or their behaviour) uncomfortable or ashamed, usually because of what other people might think: **~ about sth** *She feels very embarrassed about these episodes and does not want her children to know about them.* ◇ **~ at sth** *They were a little embarrassed at the roughness and lack of sophistication of their place of worship.* ◇ **~ to do sth** *Teens may be too embarrassed to seek information on sex from parents or friends.*

em·bar·rass·ing /ɪmˈbærəsɪŋ/ *adj.* **1** making you feel uncomfortable or ashamed: *Indirect language is also employed to avoid confrontation, embarrassing situations and direct rejections.* ◇ **~ to do sth** *Patients often find it embarrassing to talk about bodily functions.* **2** causing sb to look stupid, dishonest, etc; causing a problem for sb: *This could have been an embarrassing moment for Cameron as he had written an open letter promising to hold a referendum.* ◇ **~ to do sth** *It will be deeply embarrassing to publish something that turns out later to be wrong.*

em·bar·rass·ment /ɪmˈbærəsmənt/ *noun* **1** [U] uncomfortable or guilty feelings; a feeling of being embarrassed: *Interviewees may also be reluctant to talk due to feelings of embarrassment.* ◇ *The publication by the Bolsheviks of the secret treaties of the Tsarist government caused embarrassment in London and Paris.* **2** [C] **~ (to/for sb)** a situation that causes problems for sb: *The minister's blunders had become an embarrassment to the government.* **3** [C] **~ (to sb)** a person who causes problems for another person or other people and makes them feel embarrassed: *He was encouraged to leave rather hastily when he became a political embarrassment to the government.*

embed (*also* **imbed**) /ɪmˈbed/ *verb* (**-dd-**) [usually passive] **1** to make sth a fixed and important part of sth else, that is difficult to change or remove: **~ sth (in sth)** *This desire for continuous change is deeply embedded in the company's corporate culture.* ◇ **~ itself in sth** *Poverty and income redistribution have firmly embedded themselves in the Japanese policy agenda.* **2 ~ sth (in sth)** to fix sth firmly into a substance or solid object: *CD-ROM technology uses a laser beam to read tiny dots embedded in a layer within the disk.* **3 ~ sth (in sth)** to make images, sound, software, etc. part of a computer program: *A single CD could contain the text of some 300 volumes, although this figure would drop if pictures were embedded in the text.* **4 ~ sth** (*linguistics*) to place a sentence inside another sentence. In the sentence 'I'm aware that she knows', *she knows* is an embedded

E

sentence: *'John thinks Mary left Montreal yesterday' is a complex clause that contains a main clause and an embedded clause.*

em·bodi·ment /ɪmˈbɒdimənt; *NAmE* ɪmˈbɑːdimənt/ *noun* [usually sing.] **~ of sth** a person or thing that represents or is a typical example of an idea or a quality: *In Cecil John Rhodes, Kipling found an embodiment of his own colonial ideals.* ◇ *The Internet, after all, is the very embodiment of globalization: it is everywhere and it does everything.*

E

em·body /ɪmˈbɒdi; *NAmE* ɪmˈbɑːdi/ *verb* (**em·bodies, em·body·ing, em·bodied, em·bodied**) **1** to express or represent an idea or a quality SYN REPRESENT (2): **~ sth** *Canadian education embodies the principles of comprehensive schooling.* ◇ **be embodied in sth** *The oil and gas industry is physically embodied in oil rigs, pipelines, refineries and retail filling stations.* **2 ~ sth** (*formal*) to include or contain sth: *The rules governing transactions in the marketplace are embodied in the law of contracts.*

em·brace /ɪmˈbreɪs/ *verb* **1 ~ sth** to accept an idea, a proposal, a set of beliefs, etc, especially when it is done with enthusiasm: *Traditional disciplines must embrace new ideas from other fields to deal with future challenges.* ◇ *Despite the benefits, the Higher Education sector has been slow to fully embrace the concept.* ◇ **~ sth as sth** *The adoption of a Western lifestyle, once enthusiastically embraced as a symbol of progress and modernity, was now increasingly criticized.* **2 ~ sth** to include sth: *His reading embraced a wide range of knowledge—history, poetry, philosophy and the natural sciences.* ◇ *'Validation' is a generic term embracing various procedures and concepts.* **3 ~ sb** to put your arms around sb as a sign of love or friendship: *Martin was presented to Cavaignac, who embraced him enthusiastically.* ■ **em·brace** *noun* [C, U] **~ (of sth)** *He made clear his discomfort with Margaret Thatcher's embrace of market forces.* ◇ *Intimacy includes a physical embrace, engaging in activities together, and sharing feelings.*

em·bryo /ˈembriəʊ; *NAmE* ˈembrioʊ/ *noun* (*pl.* **-os**) a young animal or plant in the very early stages of development before birth, or before coming out of its egg or seed, especially a human egg in the first eight weeks after FERTILIZATION: *It is possible to generate genetically modified mice by manipulating the genes in mouse embryos.* ◇ **+ noun** *More information is required to determine the impact on human embryo development.* ➲ *compare* FETUS

em·bry·on·ic /ˌembriˈɒnɪk; *NAmE* ˌembriˈɑːnɪk/ *adj.* [usually before noun] **1** connected with an embryo: *All the information for embryonic development is contained within the fertilized egg.* ◇ *Embryonic stem cells are derived from blastocyst, a stage of embryo 5–6 days after fertilization.* **2** in an early stage of development: *Although it is well established in Europe, wind power is still embryonic in the UK.* ◇ *The reform process in general is slow, and in some sectors at its infancy or even embryonic stage.*

emerge AWL /iˈmɜːdʒ; *NAmE* iˈmɜːrdʒ/ *verb* **1** [I, T] (of facts or ideas) to become known: *Evidence has emerged of extensive labour exploitation in the industry.* ◇ *Latent periods for each symptom varied widely, although certain patterns emerged.* ◇ **~ from sth** *Three major themes emerged from this research.* ◇ **it emerges that...** *It emerged that there were several kinds of these elements, which decayed at different rates.* **2** [I] to start to exist or appear: *Questions about the eligibility of computer programs for copyright protection began to emerge in the 1960s.* ◇ *In emerging economies, regulatory bodies are poorly developed.* ◇ *There is an emerging market for specialized food processing machinery.* ◇ **~ into sth** *When the Internet first emerged into public consciousness, about 95% of its US users were male.* ◇ **~ as sth** *He quickly emerged as a major Muslim religious leader internationally and at home.* **3** [I] **~ (from sth) (into sth)** to come out of a dark or hidden place: *The shoot has leaves that are capable of photosynthetic activity as soon as they emerge from the seed.* **4** [I] **~ (from sth)** to survive a difficult situation or experience: *China paid an appalling price, but she emerged from the war as an acknowledged great power.*

emer·gence AWL /iˈmɜːdʒəns; *NAmE* iˈmɜːrdʒəns/ *noun* [U] **1 ~ (of sth)** the fact of appearing or beginning to exist: *Lee and Jin (2009) discuss three alternative theories to explain the emergence of business groups in China.* ◇ *Liberal thinking is closely connected with the emergence of the modern constitutional state.* **2 ~ (of sth)** the process of starting to become known: *The last decade has seen an emergence of research on the link between law and finance.* ◇ *The 1970s and 1980s witnessed the emergence of a series of important anti-physicalist arguments.* **3** the process of coming out of a dark or hidden place: *Seedling emergence strongly depends on environmental conditions and varies among species.*

emer·gency /iˈmɜːdʒənsi; *NAmE* iˈmɜːrdʒənsi/ *noun* (*pl.* **-ies**) [C, U] a sudden serious and dangerous event or situation which needs immediate action to deal with it: *Caring for patients with medical emergencies requires careful assessment and referral to appropriate services.* ◇ **in an ~** *Except in an emergency, oxygen therapy requires a prescription.* ◇ **a state of ~** *The king immediately declared a state of emergency and martial law.* ◇ **+ noun** *It is essential that all emergency department medical staff are competent to assess risk.*

emer·gent AWL /iˈmɜːdʒənt; *NAmE* iˈmɜːrdʒənt/ *adj.* [usually before noun] **1** new and still developing: *The cost of keeping up with emergent new technologies was proving too expensive for the company.* ◇ *At the end of the nineteenth century, the newly emergent profession of social work instructed working-class women how to be 'good' mothers.* **2** (*philosophy*) an **emergent** property of sth happens as the result of complex causes and is greater than the sum of their effects: *Social action has emergent properties which exceed the consciousness of the individual.* ◇ **~ from sth** *Language is emergent from interactions at all levels from brain to society.* **3** (*ecology*) (of a plant) taller than the surrounding plants, especially a tall tree in a forest; (of a water plant) with leaves and flowers that appear above the water surface: *Large emergent trees uprooted most often.* ◇ *Here the water is shallow enough to allow emergent species to grow.*

emi·grate /ˈemɪɡreɪt/ *verb* [I] to leave your own country to go and live permanently in another country: *Kaba details the reasons why many African professionals choose to emigrate.* ◇ **~ (from...) (to...)** *Herbert Spiegelberg was a Jewish philosophy professor who emigrated to America in 1938.* ➲ *compare* IMMIGRATE ■ **emi·gra·tion** /ˌemɪˈɡreɪʃn/ *noun* [U, C] **~ (of sb) (from...) (to...)** *At this time there was mass emigration of Germans to America.* ◇ *Their ability to support themselves is so limited in their native country that they may perceive emigration as the only solution.* ◇ *Following the breakup of empires, widespread emigrations and immigrations occur.* ➲ *compare* IMMIGRATION

emi·nent /ˈemɪnənt/ *adj.* [usually before noun] **1** (of people) famous and respected, especially in a particular profession: *He was then one of the most eminent scholars writing in English on Islamic family law.* **2** (of good qualities) unusual; excellent: *His careful approach made eminent sense.*

emis·sion /iˈmɪʃn/ *noun* **1** [C, usually pl.] an amount of sth, especially gas or light, that is sent out into the air: *The electric-drive vehicles have very low emissions.* ◇ *The Kyoto Protocol of 1997 aimed to reduce annual global greenhouse gas emissions by an average of 55% below 1990 levels.* **2** [U] the production or sending out of sth, especially gas or light: **~ of sth** *Some of this excess energy is* *dissipated by the emission of a photon, that is, the emission of light.* ◇ **+ noun** *The Clean Air Act required power companies to install emission controls.*

▸ ADJECTIVE + EMISSIONS **net • total • annual • industrial** *'Zero carbon' means that, over a year, the net carbon emissions from energy use in a building would be zero.*

▸ NOUN + EMISSION **air pollutant • greenhouse gas, GHG • carbon dioxide, carbon, CO_2 • methane • sulfur • vehicle • exhaust** *The major news story was that of human-induced climate change produced by carbon emissions.*

▸ VERB + EMISSION **calculate • estimate • reduce, cut • minimize • limit, curb • generate** *These developing countries were under no immediate pressure to limit their emissions.*

▸ EMISSION + NOUN **standards • control • reduction • trading • allowance • tax** *A new engine was designed to satisfy stricter emission standards.*

emit /i'mɪt/ *verb* (**-tt-**) **~ sth** to send out sth such as light, heat, sound or gas: *We see the object at the instant when the light was emitted.* ◇ *Magnetic resonance imaging measures the radio signals emitted by some atomic nuclei.*

emo·tion /ɪ'məʊʃn; *NAmE* ɪ'moʊʃn/ *noun* **1** [C, U] a strong feeling such as love, fear or anger; these feelings considered together: *Tears are interesting because they can express almost any emotion at all.* ◇ *Fear and horror, as well as other intense negative emotions, were experienced by those involved in the accident.* ◇ *He was overcome with emotion at the thought of his daughter being taken into hospital against her will.* **2** [U] the part of a person's nature that consists of feelings rather than thought or knowledge: *Historically, cognition and emotion have tended to be seen as competing explanations.*

emo·tion·al /ɪ'məʊʃənl; *NAmE* ɪ'moʊʃənl/ *adj.* **1** [usually before noun] connected with people's feelings: *It is harder to estimate a person's emotional state when speaking on the phone.* ◇ *The emotional response to separation or loss is usually depression.* ◇ *The study explored the correlation between emotional distress and smoking.* **2** causing people to feel strong emotions SYN EMOTIVE: *Academic writing strives to be as objective as possible and avoid emotional language.* ◇ *Bread prices had long been an emotional issue.*

emo·tion·al·ly /ɪ'məʊʃənəli; *NAmE* ɪ'moʊʃənəli/ *adv.* **1** in a way that is connected with people's feelings: *The common image is of nursing as being incredibly hard work, both physically and emotionally.* ◇ *Affective empathy is a tendency to react emotionally to the emotions of others.* **2** in a way that causes people to feel strong emotions: *The protagonist calmly faces a series of emotionally charged situations.*

emo·tive /i'məʊtɪv; *NAmE* i'moʊtɪv/ *adj.* causing people to feel strong emotions: *Slavery is an emotive subject but has to be addressed.* ◇ *The language used by the newspaper was highly emotive.*

em·pathy /'empəθi/ *noun* [U, sing.] the ability to understand another person's feelings or experience: *Some teens experience little or no guilt regarding aggression or violence, which is very much related to their lack of empathy.* ◇ **~ with sb/sth** *Mary Day went on to marry a farmer and demonstrated a real empathy with farm women and country life.* ◇ **~ for sb/sth** *Our ability to experience empathy for another person allows us to be sensitive to that person's feelings.*

em·peror /'empərə(r)/ *noun* the ruler of an EMPIRE: *He was captured during a battle in 1041 against the Byzantine emperor, Michael IV.* ◇ *Gosanjo became emperor in 1068.* ◇ *the reign of Emperor Tiberius*

em·phasis AWL /'emfəsɪs/ *noun* (*pl.* **em·phases** /'emfəsi:z/) [U, C] **1** special importance that is given to sth SYN STRESS¹ (5): *Kane gives great emphasis to this second point.* ◇ **~ (is) on/upon sth** *In these alternative primary schools, the emphasis is on teaching children to be independent learners.* ◇ *The more recent texts place great emphasis on global human rights.* ◇ **with ~ on sth** *The first part of this essay will provide an overview of urban planning, with emphasis on recent British examples.* **2** a way of marking a word in a text to show that it is important SYN STRESS¹: *To signify enthusiasm, titles of articles sometimes carried exclamation marks for added emphasis.* HELP When you are quoting a text with words marked in it, you can show whether these words were marked by you, or by the original author of the text, by using **(emphasis added)** or **(original emphasis)**: *In 'Computing Machinery and Intelligence', Turing claimed to be offering only a 'criterion for "thinking"' (emphasis added).*

> **WORD FAMILY**
> emphasis *noun*
> emphasize *verb*
> emphatic *adj.*
> emphatically *adv.*

▸ ADJECTIVE + EMPHASIS **great, considerable, strong, heavy, special, particular • increasing, growing • new • renewed** *This renewed emphasis on citizenship raises important questions.*

▸ VERB + EMPHASIS **place ~ on, put ~ on, lay ~ on • give ~ to • shift** *Romantic women poets tend to lay more emphasis on female experience.* ◇ *Nations are shifting the emphasis away from social towards individual responsibility.*

▸ NOUN + OF EMPHASIS **shift, change** *The Act marked a shift of emphasis from parental rights to parental responsibilities.*

LANGUAGE BANK

Emphatic language

In academic writing, you may want to emphasize that you are stating a definite fact or that you are very confident of the truth of sth.

- It is **clear/evident/certain** that...
- **There is no doubt** that...
- This **clearly** shows/demonstrates/indicates...
- a **firm/strong/clear** conclusion
- a/an **definite/clear/obvious** advantage
- a/an **clear/obvious** difference/example

– ***It is clear that*** *further significant improvements could be made.*
– *In seeking to protect children's safety,* ***it is evident that*** *we risk undermining their privacy.*
– ***There is no doubt that*** *sounds can elicit very definite emotional responses.*
– *These studies* ***clearly demonstrate*** *the positive value of silence as showing appropriate listening behaviour.*
– *Whether free will is an illusion or not, we may draw one* ***firm conclusion****:...*
– *Noise is not allowed to propagate further through the system, a* ***definite advantage*** *of digital over analogue circuits.*
– *The household is the most* ***obvious example*** *of an institution based on affection.*

em·pha·size (*BrE also* **-ise**) AWL /'emfəsaɪz/ *verb* to give special importance to sth SYN STRESS² (1): **~ sth** *All these studies emphasize the importance of antibiotic-resistant bacteria.* ◇ *Recent discussions in the literature emphasize the need for further research.* ◇ **~ that...** *She emphasizes that smokers use cigarettes to reduce feelings of stress and anxiety.* ◇ **~ how/what, etc...** *Blenkinsopp emphasizes how language has always been an important ingredient of national identity.* ◇ **it must/should be emphasized that...** *It must be emphasized here that the above definition does not apply to small family farms.*

▸ EMPHASIZE + NOUN **the fact that • the importance of, the significance of, the centrality of • the need to/for • the role of • the aspect of • the nature of • the distinction**

E

between • difference • similarities • connection between/to • continuity • theme • point *The authors emphasize the role of chance in determining the outcomes.* ◇ *The findings emphasize the fact that biological potential is available in these cells.*
▸ ADVERB + EMPHASIZE **also • further • again • increasingly • often • strongly, clearly • thus** *Her inflexibility is further emphasized when contrasted with the other parents' more accepting attitude.* ◇ *The article thus emphasizes welfare rather than rights.*

E

em·phat·ic AWL /ɪm'fætɪk/ *adj.* **1** (of a statement or answer) given with force to show that it is important: *Marxist theory has had an emphatic rejection in the last decade.* ◇ *Spofford gave emphatic support to women's struggle for equality.* **2** (of a person) making it very clear what you mean by writing or speaking with force: **~ that...** *Students were emphatic that they wanted teachers who were able to maintain order in the classroom.* ◇ **~ about sth** *Moore is emphatic about the importance of the family resource centre.* ■ **em·phat·ic·al·ly** AWL /ɪm'fætɪkli/ *adv.*: *These Asian nations emphatically reject Western values.* ◇ *Rousseau proclaimed himself emphatically an ancient, not a modern, political thinker.*

em·pire /'empaɪə(r)/ *noun* **1** a group of countries or states that are controlled by one ruler or government: *Within a decade, Ismail had conquered the rest of Iran, rapidly building an empire east of the Ottoman frontier.* ◇ *The end of the Cold War and the disintegration of the Soviet empire produced a radical change in world politics.* ◇ *the Roman/British Empire* **2** a group of commercial organizations controlled by one person or company: *Sir Tom Farmer built a £1bn business empire before he eventually sold the business to Ford in 1999.*

em·pir·ic·al AWL /ɪm'pɪrɪkl/ *adj.* [usually before noun] based on experiments or experience rather than ideas or theories: *There is direct empirical evidence for our common ancestry with other animals.* ◇ *Empirical and theoretical research in this field has revealed the complexity of different mating systems.* OPP THEORETICAL (1)
▸ EMPIRICAL + NOUN **research, work, study • literature • science • investigation, inquiry • evidence, data, fact • phenomenon • grounds, basis, foundation • findings, results • analysis • observation • question • test, testing • estimate • generalization • formula • reality • regularity • validity • approach, method** *Recent empirical studies have challenged the assumptions underlying the model.* ◇ *He argued on empirical grounds that there was simply no evidence that acquired characteristics could be inherited.*

em·pir·ic·al·ly AWL /ɪm'pɪrɪkli/ *adv.* by using experiments or experience rather than ideas or theories: *This hypothesis has never been tested empirically.* ◇ *Empirically, it has been shown that an object is no longer visible when the contrast against the background is less than 2%.*

em·piri·cism AWL /ɪm'pɪrɪsɪzəm/ *noun* [U] (*philosophy*) the belief that knowledge is based on the evidence of experience or experiments, rather than ideas or theories: *Hume built on the empiricism founded by Locke and Berkeley.* ■ **em·piri·cist** /ɪm'pɪrɪsɪst/ *adj.*: *He employed an empiricist approach, attempting to allow the facts to speak for themselves.* **em·piri·cist** *noun*: *Like Hume, Bentham was an empiricist, believing that knowledge is based on experience.*

em·ploy /ɪm'plɔɪ/ *verb* **1** to use sth such as a skill, method, device or word for a particular purpose: **~ sth** *My feminist background influenced my decision to employ feminist research methods.* ◇ **~ sth to do sth** *They employ a sophisticated control system to maximize energy capture.* ◇ **~ sth in sth** *Many political movements have employed documentary films in their campaigns.* ➲ thesaurus note at USE[1] **2** to give sb a job to do for payment: **~ sb** *The business is based in Beijing, where it employs 1 500 people.* ◇ **~ sb in sth** *In the 1950s, only a small proportion of Koreans were employed in middle class jobs.* ◇ **~ sb as sth** *He is currently employed as a youth worker.* ◇ **~ sb to do sth** *The defendant was a railway gate keeper, who was employed to operate a level crossing.* ➲ *see also* SELF-EMPLOYED, UNEMPLOYED
▸ EMPLOY + NOUN **method, methodology, approach • procedure, technique • tactic • measure • concept • design • tool, device • technology • language, word, terminology, rhetoric** *This article employs two theoretical approaches: the economic approach and the cultural approach.* ◇ *There has been a shift in the language employed to describe welfare provision.* | **people, person, worker, workforce, staff, labour** *Fewer than one in seven UK workers was employed in manufacturing.*
▸ ADVERB + EMPLOY **frequently, commonly, widely, often • usually, normally • typically • sometimes • first • increasingly • still • successfully, usefully** *Enzymes commonly employ more than one strategy to catalyze a reaction* | **gainfully • currently • still** *By 1921, almost 40 per cent of the gainfully employed females in Kingston were domestic servants.*

em·ploy·ee /ɪm'plɔɪiː/ *noun* a person who is paid to work for sb: *The Honhai Group hired 469 906 employees in 2006.* ◇ *Full-time employees working in large companies had the lowest risk of redundancy.* ◇ **~ of sth** *The evidence comes from a French study of nearly 10 000 employees of GAZEL.*

em·ploy·er /ɪm'plɔɪə(r)/ *noun* a person or company that pays people to work for them: *The evidence suggests that employers are paying higher wages to married men.* ◇ *Eighty-three per cent of employees said their employer was helpful.* ◇ *EU law in this case makes no distinction between public and private employers.*

em·ploy·ment /ɪm'plɔɪmənt/ *noun* [U] **1** work, especially when it is done to earn money; the state of being employed: *More and more American workers were forced to seek employment in low-wage service industries.* ◇ *She hopes to find employment with an animal welfare charity.* ◇ **in (...) ~** *The statistics include only people in full-time paid employment.* ◇ **+ noun** *There was no significant relationship between patient characteristics such as age, gender and employment status.* **2** the situation in which people have work; the number of people who have work in a country or area: *Policymakers were aiming to achieve full employment.* ◇ *Employment rose from 35% to 37% for women.* OPP UNEMPLOYMENT (1) **3 ~ (of sb)** the act of employing sb: *The pay structure encouraged the employment of part-timers.* **4 ~ (of sth)** the use of sth: *Methodologically, the employment of both quantitative and qualitative approaches has helped enrich the subfield.*

em·power /ɪm'paʊə(r)/ *verb* [often passive] **1** to give sb more control over their own life or the situation they are in: **~ sb** *Their goal is to empower women economically, socially and politically.* ◇ **~ sb to do sth** *The syllabus aims to empower students to become independent learners.* **2 ~ sb to do sth** to give sb the power or authority to do sth SYN AUTHORIZE: *The law empowered the police to make arrests on the grounds of reasonable suspicion.*

em·power·ment /ɪm'paʊəmənt; *NAmE* ɪm'paʊərmənt/ *noun* [U] a positive feeling that you have some control over your life or the situation you are in: *Human resource management aimed to increase employee motivation and empowerment.* ◇ **~ of sb** *They seek the empowerment of women, to be achieved through participation in decisions that affect their own lives.*

emp·ti·ness /'emptinəs/ *noun* [U, sing.] **1 ~ (of sth)** a feeling of being sad because nothing seems to have any value: *Feeding her son gave her a kind of self-importance that masked the emptiness of her life.* **2 ~ (of sth)** the fact that there is nothing or no one in a place: *In the first scene,* *the emptiness of the car suggests that the important action occurs inside the house.*

empty[1] /ˈempti/ *adj.* (**emp·tier**, **emp·ti·est**) **1** with no people or things inside: *In 2001, it was estimated that in Great Britain there were 750 000 empty dwellings.* ◇ *The plane was half empty.* ◇ *The antibiotics must be taken on an empty stomach.* ◇ *Atoms, in particle terms, are mostly empty space.* ◇ **~ of sth** *Thought blocking refers to an experience in which the mind is suddenly empty of thoughts.* **2** [usually before noun] (of sth that sb says or does) with no meaning; not meaning what is said: *These are not empty questions and therefore deserve serious consideration.* ◇ *Politicians, as a class, were mistrusted for 'not giving straight answers and making empty promises'.* ➲ *compare* HOLLOW[1] (2) **3** (of a person or their life) unhappy because life does not seem to have a purpose, usually after sth sad has happened: *When he found out that he had failed the exam, he felt hopeless and empty.* ◇ *Life may feel very empty without caring tasks to do.*

empty[2] /ˈempti/ *verb* (**emp·ties**, **empty·ing**, **emp·tied**, **emp·tied**) **1** [T] to remove everything that is in sth: **~ sth** *Each chamber can be filled or emptied via a suitably drilled channel.* ◇ **~ sth of sth** *Sampling tubes were emptied of soil.* **2** [I] to become empty: *The rate at which the stomach emptied was measured.* **3** [I] **~ into sth** to flow or move out from one place to another: *The Mekong River empties into the South China Sea.*

en·able AWL /ɪˈneɪbl/ *verb* **1 ~ sb to do sth** to make it possible for sb to do sth SYN ALLOW (1): *Video conferencing technology has enabled many people to work from home.* **2** to make it possible for sth to happen or exist by creating the necessary conditions SYN ALLOW (4): **~ sth to do sth** *These business systems are used to enable the organization to function smoothly.* ◇ **~ sth** *The political unity of the Roman Empire enabled the creation of wider trade networks.*

enact /ɪˈnækt/ *verb* **1** to pass a law; to make sth legal by passing a law: **~ sth** *Many countries have enacted legislation to control trade in these species.* ◇ *A national insurance system was enacted in 1963 to subsidize the costs of medication and health care for everyone in need.* **2 ~ sth** (*formal*) to act according to a suggestion, policy, etc; to make a suggestion, policy, etc. happen in practice: *If the nurse believes that enacting a policy may endanger the patient's safety, then they must report and record their decision not to enact the policy.* **3 ~ sth** to perform a play or act a part: *In psychodrama, problems are enacted (as in a play) rather than merely talked about.*

en·act·ment /ɪˈnæktmənt/ *noun* [U, C] **1 ~ (of sth)** the process of a law becoming official; a law that has been made official: *Since the enactment of the Domestic Violence, Crime and Victims Act 2004, the term 'cohabitants' includes both gay and heterosexual partners.* ◇ *The function of the court is to interpret and apply the enactments of Parliament.* **2 ~ (of sth)** the process of performing in a play or acting a part; an event or part that is performed by actors: *On the stage, tragedy was reinforced by explicit enactments of the death of kings.*

en·cap·su·late /ɪnˈkæpsjuleɪt/ *verb* **1 ~ sth (in/within sth)** to express the most important parts of sth in a few words or a single object SYN SUM STH UP: *The poem encapsulates many of the central themes of her writing.* ◇ *Conclusions reached are encapsulated in a final document.* **2 ~ sth (in/within sth)** to surround sth in an outer covering: *The company would encapsulate the asbestos waste in concrete pellets.* ■ **en·cap·su·la·tion** *noun* [U, C] **~ (of sth) (in/within sth)** *Fowler's (1985) account provides a helpful encapsulation of the history of its application to the field.* ◇ *This is a valuable approach for the encapsulation of cells and proteins.*

en·close /ɪnˈkləʊz; *NAmE* ɪnˈkloʊz/ *verb* **1** [usually passive] to build a wall, fence, etc. around sth: **~ sth (in sth)** *Infrared radiation warms the Earth as if the planet were enclosed in a huge greenhouse.* ◇ (*figurative*) *The disputed words are enclosed in square brackets.* ◇ **~ sth with sth** *Areas of native vegetation are enclosed with fences that restrict immigration of all alien mammals.* ◇ **an enclosed area/space** *Grazing and cultivation takes place in enclosed areas around the settlement.* **2 ~ sth** (especially of a wall, fence, etc.) to surround sth: *The typical native settlement across Wales and Cornwall was enclosed by an earth or stone bank and a ditch.* **3 ~ sth (with sth)** to put sth in the same envelope or package as sth else: *Each questionnaire was enclosed with an invitation letter explaining the project and a prepaid envelope.*

E

en·clos·ure /ɪnˈkləʊʒə(r); *NAmE* ɪnˈkloʊʒər/ *noun* **1** [C] a piece of land that is surrounded by a fence or wall and is used for a particular purpose: *Two wooden boxes were placed in each enclosure as feeding sites for the rabbits.* **2** [U, C] the act of placing a fence or wall around a piece of land HELP In British history, **enclosure** refers especially to the practice of enclosing common land (= land owned jointly by a whole village) and making it private property, as happened between the 16th and early 19th centuries: *The unrest was caused by the desire for an end to new farming practices such as enclosure.* ◇ *When James I passed through Northamptonshire in 1603, crowds protested against the recent enclosures by Sir John Spencer.* **3** [C] something that is placed in an envelope with a letter: *The paper number was written on the covering letter only and omitted from any enclosures.*

en·code /ɪnˈkəʊd; *NAmE* ɪnˈkoʊd/ *verb* **1 ~ sth** (*biochemistry*) (of a GENE) to produce a substance or behaviour: *It was discovered that genes encode proteins.* **2 ~ sth** to change ordinary language into letters or symbols in order to send secret messages: *Binary digits may be used to encode these messages.* OPP DECODE (1) **3 be encoded in/within sth** to exist within sth, especially in a form that is not easily noticed but can be studied: *Modleski's work is concerned with the gender and power relationships encoded within mass media.*

en·com·pass /ɪnˈkʌmpəs/ *verb* (*formal*) **1 ~ sth** to include a large number or range of things: *Marine environments encompass a diverse range of habitats and ecosystems.* ◇ *No one narrative can encompass all aspects of German history.* ◇ *This concept could be extended to encompass information associated with multiple cancer types.* **2 ~ sth** to surround or cover sth completely: *The Coweeta Basin encompasses 1 626 hectares and has been a primary site for watershed experimentation.*

en·coun·ter[1] AWL /ɪnˈkaʊntə(r)/ *verb* **1 ~ sth** to experience sth, especially sth unpleasant or difficult, while you are trying to do sth else SYN RUN INTO STH (1): *One problem commonly encountered by customers ordering products over the Internet is difficulty with delivery.* ◇ *Kinnock's administrative reform programme encountered bitter resistance.* ◇ *to encounter difficulties/obstacles/opposition* **2 ~ sth/sb** to discover or experience sth, or meet sb, especially sth/sb new, unusual or unexpected SYN COME ACROSS SB/STH: *Evans-Pritchard travelled to East Africa, where he encountered a number of tribal communities.* ◇ *The study aimed to investigate the strategies of learners when they encounter unknown words.*

en·coun·ter[2] AWL /ɪnˈkaʊntə(r)/ *noun* a meeting, especially one that is sudden or unexpected: *47.5% of single UK visitors to Spain reported a casual sexual encounter during a 2-week holiday.* ◇ **~ with sb/sth** *In this sample, mothers of colour reported more encounters with the police than did other mothers.* ◇ **~ between A and B** *There have been a number of face-to-face encounters between members of the two groups.*

en·cour·age /ɪnˈkʌrɪdʒ; *NAmE* ɪnˈkɜːrɪdʒ/ *verb* **1** to make sth more likely to happen or develop: **~ sth** *Lower borrowing costs may encourage new investment.* ◇ *Research suggests current work environments actually encourage obesity among workers.* ◇ *There are a number of social factors that encourage dieting.* ◇ **~ sb to do sth** *Businesses used discounts to encourage shoppers to make purchases.* OPP DISCOURAGE (1) **2** to persuade sb to do sth by making it easier for them and making them believe it is a good thing to do: *Collaboration between different departments should be actively encouraged and facilitated.* ◇ **~ sb to do sth** *The NHS ran a national campaign encouraging young people to give blood.* OPP DISCOURAGE (1) **3 ~ sb** to give sb support or hope: *Boys experience great satisfaction in creative writing, especially when they are supported and encouraged.* OPP DISCOURAGE (2)

en·cour·age·ment /ɪnˈkʌrɪdʒmənt; *NAmE* ɪnˈkɜːrɪdʒmənt/ *noun* [U] **1** the act of encouraging sb to do sth: *With Turing's encouragement, Strachey finally got his programme working.* ◇ **~ of sth** *A positive factor has been local authority encouragement of cooperation between schools.* ◇ **~ to do sth** *The patient needed encouragement to continue with treatment.* **2** something that encourages sb: **~ that...** *Preliminary results gave encouragement that the tests would be successful.* ◇ **~ to/for sb/sth (to do sth)** *The government provided significant encouragement for companies to invest in alternative energies.* **3 ~ of sth** the act of making sth more likely to happen or develop: *The encouragement of business activity in the single market inevitably creates increased pressures on the environment.*

en·cour·aging /ɪnˈkʌrɪdʒɪŋ; *NAmE* ɪnˈkɜːrɪdʒɪŋ/ *adj.* positive and giving hope, especially by suggesting that sth/sb is correct: *The results of the first tests are encouraging and would seem to justify further research.* ◇ *In 2010, there were encouraging signs of attempts to reduce the role of nuclear weapons in world politics.* ◇ **it is ~ that...** *It is encouraging that funding agencies are willing to provide additional resources.* ■ **en·cour·aging·ly** *adv.*: *Encouragingly, only about 5% of exposed individuals develop disease.*

end¹ /end/ *noun* **1** the final part of a period of time, an event, an activity or a story: **at the ~ (of sth)** *The reforms only came into effect at the very end of the 1930s.* ◇ *References and appendices are at the end.* ◇ **by the ~ (of sth)** *By the end of 2008, there were an estimated 4 billion mobile phone subscribers worldwide.* ◇ **following the ~ of sth** *Following the end of the Cold War, many countries redrew their political boundaries.* **2** the part of sth that is the furthest away from its centre: **at the ~ (of sth)** *Colonnata is a small village located at the end of a long winding road.* ◇ *Perfect competition and monopoly are market structures at the opposite ends of the competitive spectrum.* ◇ **~ (of sth)** *The higher end of these values are within the climatic averages reported for tropical regions.* ◇ **+ noun** *The end points of the earth's axis of rotation are the north and south poles.* **3** a situation in which sth does not exist any more: **the ~ of sth** *The existing class system had been abolished, but this did not mean the end of class distinctions.* ◇ **an ~ to sth** *Scientists calling for an end to the arms race pointed to the dire consequences of an atomic explosion.* ◇ **come to an ~** *The decline in economic activity across the world came to an end in 1932–3.* ◇ **put an ~ to sth** *Growing scandal within his administration put an end to his political career.* ◇ **bring an ~ to sth/bring sth to an ~** *The allied offensive finally achieved the rapid advances that helped bring an end to the fighting.* ◇ **at an ~** *Western European dominance of the world was clearly at an end.* **4** [usually pl.] an aim or a purpose: *The main disagreement between Marxists and other socialists is over means rather than ends.* ◇ *The view that animals were created solely to serve human ends became increasingly untenable.* ◇ **for... ends** *William knew how to use the papacy for his own ends, and was prepared to pay a price.* ◇ *In the past, biology has often been exploited for political ends.* ◇ **to this ~** *Reversing the decline in physical activity could confer health benefits. To this end, the government set targets to increase levels of participation in sport.* ➲ thesaurus note *at* TARGET¹

IDM **an ˌend in itˈself** an aim that is itself worth achieving, not because it helps you achieve sth more important: *Employment should be seen not as an end in itself, but as a means to achieving a better quality of life.* **the ˌend justifies the ˈmeans** used to say that bad or unfair methods of doing sth are acceptable if the result of that action is good or positive: *Machiavelli is associated with the view that, in politics, the end justifies the means.* **ˌend to ˈend** in a line, with the ends touching: *Each macromolecule typically contains from 100 to 15 000 or more repeating units linked end to end.* **in the ˈend** **1** after a long period of time or series of events: *In the end, they broke up just eleven large companies instead of the 300 originally intended.* **2** after everything has been considered: *In the end, archaeology cannot prove that the Trojan War as Homer described it actually occurred.* **make (both) ends ˈmeet** to earn just enough money to be able to buy the things you need: *Despite working full-time, many individuals found that they could not make ends meet.* **on ˈend** **1** for the stated length of time, without stopping: *The scandal relating to MPs' expenses made headlines for weeks on end.* **2** in a vertical position: *Heart rate increases, breathing is shallower, pupils dilate and hair stands on end.* ➲ *more at* BEGINNING, MEANS

end² /end/ *verb* [I, T] to finish; to make sth finish: *When the war ended, at least 25 million Russians were homeless.* ◇ **~ with sth** *The article ends with an overall discussion.* ◇ **~ sth** *The president pledged to end the war.* ◇ **~ sth by doing sth** *Punch ends the book by setting out what an anti-corruption strategy might look like.* ◇ **~ sth with sth** *Turing ends the chapter with a comment on the significance of what he has shown.*

IDM **ˌend your ˈdays/ˈlife (in sth)** to spend the last part of your life in a particular state or place: *He ended his life as a Saint-Dominguan refugee in France.* **ˌend your ˈlife** to kill yourself: *Almost half who end their life by suicide have previously self-harmed.*

PHR V **ˈend in sth** [no passive] to have sth as a result: *Like his previous tries, this one ended in failure.* **ˌend ˈup** to find yourself in a place or situation that you did not intend or expect to be in: **~ doing sth** *When a child is not allowed to discuss her vulnerability, she ends up feeling even more emotionally isolated.* ◇ **+ adv./prep.** *Millions of old PCs end up in landfill sites each year.* ◇ *Women with multiple roles end up with more duties, time pressures and life stresses than their male counterparts.* ◇ **+ adj.** *Development projects cause the displacement of 15 million people each year, and many of these people end up impoverished.*

en·dan·ger /ɪnˈdeɪndʒə(r)/ *verb* **~ sb/sth** to put sb/sth in a situation in which they could be harmed or damaged: *Sometimes, poor performance at work may endanger other people.* ◇ *Arson is setting fire to property, an act that may also endanger life.* ◇ *The animals that were dependent on this habitat have become endangered or are extinct.* ◇ **endangered species** *Captive breeding programmes for endangered species must also take account of inbreeding problems.*

en·deav·our¹ (*US* **en·deavor**) /ɪnˈdevə(r)/ *noun* (*formal*) **1** [U, C] serious effort to achieve sth; an attempt to do sth, especially sth new or difficult: *Time seems to control every aspect of human endeavour.* ◇ *scientific/intellectual/artistic endeavour* ◇ *The new era brought new ideas, new discoveries, new methods and new machines in every field of endeavour.* ◇ **in an/the/sb's ~ to do sth** *An art history department had launched a degree in 'Communication Studies' in an endeavour to bring in more students.* **2** [C, usually pl.] something that sb does: *Because of their success in educational and occupational endeavours,*

Asian Americans are widely perceived as being insulated from racial discrimination and prejudice.

en·deav·our[2] (*US* en·deavor) /ɪnˈdevə(r)/ *verb* **~ to do sth** (*formal*) to try hard to do or achieve sth SYN STRIVE: *The present study has endeavoured to address concerns about subjectivity.*

en·dem·ic /enˈdemɪk/ *adj.* **1** regularly in a particular place or among a particular group of people and difficult to get rid of: **~ (in...)** *Typhoid fever was endemic in Europe in the Middle Ages.* ◇ **~ (among...)** *In the sixteenth century, cattle raiding and feuding were endemic among the Irish nobility.* ◇ *Throughout its history, the country has experienced endemic corruption in government.* ➲ *compare* PANDEMIC **2** (of a particular place or a particular group of people) in which a particular disease is regularly found: *In these endemic areas, the pattern of disease is determined by numerous factors:...* **3** (of a plant or animal) only found in a particular place: *A relatively high proportion of endemic species is a feature of many islands.* ◇ **~ to...** *This beetle is endemic to Japan and is widely distributed throughout the major and minor islands.*

end·ing /ˈendɪŋ/ *noun* **1** the last part of a story, film, etc: *This is the same commercial, but with two different endings.* ◇ **happy ~** *The most striking and persistent of all classical Hollywood phenomena is the happy ending.* ◇ **~ of sth** *The article compares the endings of two of Paterson's most famous ballads.* ➲ *compare* OPENING[1] **2** the act of finishing sth or the fact of sth not continuing; the last part of sth: *These issues do not have a precise beginning or a precise ending.* ◇ **~ of sth** *The virtual ending of public building in the early fifth century speaks of an uncertain economic climate.* ◇ *With the ending of the Cold War, neo-liberal philosophy came to dominate development thinking.* ➲ *compare* BEGINNING **3** the tip or end part of a long object: *As people age, the number of nerve endings in the skin decreases.* **4** the last part of a word, that is added to a main part: *Her brother's name is the same—but without the feminine -a ending.*

end·less /ˈendləs/ *adj.* **1** very large in size or amount and seeming to have no end: *An endless stream of organizations provide free news.* ◇ *The list of biological materials that have been used as sources of DNA now seems almost endless.* **2** continuing for a long time and seeming to have no end: *The seemingly endless cycle of war and conflict confirms the aggressive impulses in human nature.* ◇ *There were endless debates about Japan's role in the world.* ■ **end·less·ly** *adv.*: *Debate still rages endlessly about who was or were responsible for this prank.*

end·note /ˈendnəʊt; *NAmE* ˈendnoʊt/ *noun* a note printed at the end of a book or section of a book: *As well as being used to refer to sources, footnotes and endnotes are often used to provide additional detail.* ➲ *compare* FOOTNOTE (1)

en·dogen·ous /enˈdɒdʒənəs; *NAmE* enˈdɑːdʒənəs/ *adj.* (*technical*) caused or created by sth within a body, system, etc, as opposed to having a cause that is outside it: *It is difficult to distinguish changes associated with use of a technology from changes that are endogenous.* ◇ *The first complete model of endogenous economic growth was originally published in 1962 by Marvin Frankel.* ◇ *It was soon accepted that these chemicals were endogenous plant hormones.* ◇ **~ to sth** *They regarded these problems as endogenous to the country concerned.* ➲ *compare* EXOGENOUS ■ **en·dogen·ous·ly** *adv.*: *We view preferences as endogenously determined, that is, determined mostly by processes internal to the economy.* ◇ *Creatinine is endogenously produced and released into body fluids at a constant rate.*

en·dorse /ɪnˈdɔːs; *NAmE* ɪnˈdɔːrs/ *verb* **1 ~ sth** to say publicly that you support a statement or course of action: *Yinger strongly endorses Durkheim's claim that religion is too well integrated into social life ever to disappear.* ◇ *Today, this view is endorsed by a number of scholars including Lubell himself.* **2 ~ sth** to say in an advertisement that you use and like a particular product so that other people will want to buy it: *Companies have managed to get through to children by paying celebrities to endorse their products.*

en·dorse·ment /ɪnˈdɔːsmənt; *NAmE* ɪnˈdɔːrsmənt/ *noun* [C, U] **1** a public statement or action showing that you support sb/sth; the fact of supporting sb/sth: **~ for sth** *The May 1999 elections could not be regarded as an endorsement for devolution.* ◇ **~ (of sth)** *The president had offered a ringing endorsement of almost every basic demand pressed by civil rights activists.* **2** a statement made in an advertisement, usually by sb famous or important, saying that they use and like a particular product; the act of making such a statement: *Firms spend enormous sums of money obtaining celebrity endorsements.*

E

ˈend product *noun* **~ (of sth)** something that is produced by a particular activity or process: *CO_2 is an end product of most combustion processes.* ◇ *Component parts (e.g. steering wheels) are then manufactured into the end product (e.g. cars).*

ˌend reˈsult *noun* [usually sing.] **~ (of sth)** the final result of a particular activity or process: *The end result is a mixture of gases containing methane and carbon dioxide as major components.* ◇ *Note that these two sequences of steps achieve the same end result.*

en·dur·ance /ɪnˈdjʊərəns; *NAmE* ɪnˈdʊrəns/ *noun* [U] the ability to continue doing sth painful or difficult for a long period of time without complaining: *Both individual and team sports are associated with increased muscular strength, endurance and power.*

en·dure /ɪnˈdjʊə(r); *NAmE* ɪnˈdʊr/ *verb* **1** [T] **~ sth** to experience and deal with sth that is painful or unpleasant, especially without complaining: *The book describes the hardships endured by these immigrants.* ◇ *They will have to endure more years of poor health.* **2** [I] (*formal*) to continue to exist for a long time SYN LAST[4] (1): *The fragility of this unity would place limits on how long Greek civilization could endure.*

en·dur·ing /ɪnˈdjʊərɪŋ; *NAmE* ɪnˈdʊrɪŋ/ *adj.* lasting for a long time: *The parent-child relationship is one of the most enduring relationships of all.* ◇ *A poor start in life can leave an enduring legacy of impairment.*

ˌend-ˈuser (*also* **end user**) *noun* a person who actually uses a product rather than one who makes or sells it, especially a person who uses a product connected with computers: *Client/Server Piracy occurs when a program is accessed by more end-users than the company has bought licences for.* ◇ *In business-to-business markets, firms sell products and services to one another rather than to end users.*

enemy /ˈenəmi/ *noun* (*pl.* -ies) **1** [C+sing./pl. v.] a country that you are fighting a war against; the soldiers, etc. of this country: *A realist may advise bombing a neutral state if it will serve the military goals of defeating the enemy.* ◇ *The USA and Soviet Union found a common enemy in Nazi Germany.* ◇ **+ noun** *enemy combatants/forces/soldiers/troops* **2** [C] a person who hates sb or who acts or speaks against sb/sth: *He had been a US Senator for many years, and had made enemies across the political spectrum.* ◇ **~ of sth/sb** *He showed himself as an implacable enemy of the deep-seated corruption he found in Moscow.* **3** [C] anything that harms sth or prevents it from being successful: *There are risks associated with the introduction of natural enemies to control invasive species.* ◇ **~ of sth** *The regulatory state can be simultaneously a friend and an enemy of business.*

en·er·get·ic AWL /ˌenəˈdʒetɪk; *NAmE* ˌenərˈdʒetɪk/ *adj.* **1** (*physics*) connected with the energy that sth contains, needs or produces: *Nuclear reactions are much more energetic than molecular ones.* ◇ *Most organisms cannot afford the energetic cost of splitting molecular nitrogen.* **2** having or showing a lot of energy or enthusiasm: *They were energetic, passionate about their kids, and eager to get involved.* ◇ *Victor is an energetic student who does his best in most activities.* ■ **en·er·get·ic·al·ly** AWL /ˌenəˈdʒetɪkli; *NAmE* ˌenərˈdʒetɪkli/ *adv.*: *Both incubation and nest-building are energetically costly processes.* ◇ *The government energetically pushed through reforms.*

en·ergy AWL /ˈenədʒi; *NAmE* ˈenərdʒi/ *noun* **1** [U, C] the ability of matter or RADIATION to perform work because of its mass, movement, electrical charge, etc: *Radiation is the energy released when an unstable atom decays to a stable form.* ◇ *The rise in kinetic energy is compensated for by the loss of potential energy.* ◇ **~ (of sth)** *The internal energy of an isolated system is constant.* ◇ *The electrons emitted will have a range of energies; the values shown are the maximum energies observed in each case.* ➲ *see also* FREE ENERGY, POTENTIAL ENERGY **2** [U] a source of power that can be used by sb/sth, for example to provide light and heat, or to work machines: *Turn off all non-essential equipment to conserve energy.* ◇ *The average energy consumed in a three-bedroom, two-storey house is 58.2 kWh/day.* ◇ **+ noun** *Solar energy and wind energy are the two main renewable energy sources.* **3** [U] the effort needed to do work or other physical or mental activities: *Managers on projects spend significant energy defining processes.* ◇ *These studies suggest that married men devote more time and energy to their job.* ◇ *Living standards also depend on having enough energy left after finishing one's work to enjoy life.* ◇ **+ noun** *Requirements for food vary according to energy expenditure.* **4 energies** [pl.] the physical and mental effort that you use to do sth: *Governments directed their humanitarian energies to crises in other parts of the world.* ◇ *They next turned their military energies towards the Byzantine and Persian Empires.*

▸ ADJECTIVE + ENERGY **high • low • internal • potential • kinetic • thermal • elastic • electrical • mechanical** *A small amount of thermal energy is required to free the electron.* ◇ *To convert the mechanical energy of the turbine to electricity, an alternator is also needed.* | **renewable • clean • global • solar • electrical • nuclear** *Developing and commercializing clean energy is one of the basic strategies to combat climate change.* ◇ *About 85% of the total global energy consumed at present comes from burning fossil fuels.*

▸ VERB + ENERGY **use • generate, produce • conserve** *The sun generates its energy from the conversion of hydrogen to helium in thermonuclear fusion reactions.* ◇ *This rapid rise in carbon dioxide levels is largely attributed to the burning of fossil fuels to generate energy.* ◇ *The First Law of thermodynamics states that energy is conserved in any process.* | **require, need • store • release • produce • supply, provide • lose • convert • absorb • transfer** *Energy is needed to break a stable nucleus up into its constituent parts.* ◇ *Any hot body loses its energy through thermal radiation.*

▸ ENERGY + NOUN **source • resources • consumption, use • efficiency • supply • demand • production • prices • sector • market • policy** *These measures have the potential to yield a 30% improvement in energy efficiency.*

ˈenergy level *noun* (*physics*) the fixed amount of energy that a system described by QUANTUM MECHANICS, such as a MOLECULE, atom, ELECTRON or NUCLEUS, can have: *When excited by a photon, one of the electrons is excited to a higher energy level.* ➲ *see also* GROUND STATE

en·force AWL /ɪnˈfɔːs; *NAmE* ɪnˈfɔːrs/ *verb* **1** to make sure that people obey a particular law or rule: **~ sth** *Enforcing traffic laws poses a particular challenge for public trust in police.* ◇ *Unfortunately, the law was not generally followed or strictly enforced.* ◇ **~ sth on/against sb/sth** *Rents are high, and tenants cannot always enforce their rights against landlords.* **2** to make sth happen; to force sb to do sth: **~ sth** *Women viewed their increased responsibilities as a temporary arrangement that was enforced by the war.* ◇ **~ sth on sb** *The administration, one union official charged, was attempting to enforce economic servitude on the miners.*

en·force·able /ɪnˈfɔːsəbl; *NAmE* ɪnˈfɔːrsəbl/ *adj.* (of a rule, law or contract) that people can be made to obey: *The document did not constitute an enforceable contract.* ◇ *Legally enforceable property rights depend upon the state being able to exercise sufficient authority.*

en·forced AWL /ɪnˈfɔːst; *NAmE* ɪnˈfɔːrst/ *adj.* that sb is forced to do or experience without being able to control it: *After the Nazis came to power, journalists conformed to the enforced optimism of the new regime.* ◇ *As one of the few countries without any form of enforced film censorship, the country largely maintained a liberal film policy.*

en·force·ment AWL /ɪnˈfɔːsmənt; *NAmE* ɪnˈfɔːrsmənt/ *noun* [U] the process of making sb/sth obey sth, such as a rule or the law: **~ (of sth)** *The high incidence of road crashes is due, in part, to poor enforcement of traffic safety regulations.* ◇ **+ noun** *Law enforcement agencies, guided by the FBI, have identified a wide range of dissident groups.* ◇ *An effective enforcement mechanism is a core part of a successful data protection system.*

en·gage /ɪnˈɡeɪdʒ/ *verb* **1 ~ sb/sth** to succeed in attracting and keeping sb's attention and interest: *The role of advertising is to engage audiences.* ◇ *It is essential to engage the interest of the local community.* ◇ *Students are more likely to be engaged when the set task matches their ability.* **2** to employ sb to do a particular job: **~ sb (as sth)** *Captain Powell engaged Cutter as part of his crew in a voyage from Jamaica to Liverpool.* ◇ **~ sb to do sth** *If the projection of sales is high, more staff members need to be engaged to deliver the service.*

PHR V **enˈgage in sth | be enˈgaged in sth** to take part in an activity: *Positive relations with teachers should influence students' willingness to engage in classroom activities.* ◇ *Only 5 per cent of the population is actively engaged in agriculture.* **enˈgage with sth/sb** to become involved with and try to understand sth/sb: *Despite having fewer MPs, Liberal Democrats engaged more fully with the issue than the larger parties.* ◇ *Campuses provide opportunities for students to engage with people from different parts of the world.*

en·gaged /ɪnˈɡeɪdʒd/ *adj.* involved with sb/sth in an active and interested way: *Engaged learners are highly motivated to learn and determine the direction of the learning.* ◇ *The flourishing of NGOs across the globe is often considered to be an indicator of a politically engaged citizenry.* ◇ **~ on sth** *The Security Council remains engaged on the issue of children and armed conflict.*

en·gage·ment /ɪnˈɡeɪdʒmənt/ *noun* [U] being involved with sb/sth in an attempt to understand them or achieve sth: *Festivals and other arts organizations have a long history of political engagement.* ◇ *community/civic/social engagement* ◇ **~ with sb/sth** *Students learn through active engagement with their physical environment.* ◇ *A critical engagement with history is essential for a better understanding of contemporary issues.* ◇ **~ in sth** *The students reported higher levels of engagement in group activities compared with lectures.*

en·gen·der /ɪnˈdʒendə(r)/ *verb* **~ sth** to make a feeling or situation exist: *Aaker (1997) found that these companies were successful in engendering loyalty as well as profitability.* ◇ *There is no simple solution to the problems engendered by fossil fuel usage.*

en·gine /ˈendʒɪn/ *noun* **1** the part of a vehicle that produces power to make the vehicle move: *Heavy cars will require more powerful engines and will consume more fuel.* ◇ *Fuel cells could, eventually, replace the internal combustion engine.* ◇ *a steam/petrol/diesel engine* ◇ **+ noun** *The maximum engine power available to a vehicle is shown in Figure 9.6.* **2 ~ (of/for sth)** a thing that causes a process to happen or causes sth to develop: *Education is accepted as one of the prime engines of long-term economic growth.* ◇ *Design can be a powerful engine for the evolution of communities.* ➲ *see also* SEARCH ENGINE

en·gin·eer¹ /ˌendʒɪˈnɪə(r); *NAmE* ˌendʒɪˈnɪr/ *noun* a person whose job involves designing or building engines, machines or structures: *The world's first large-scale electronic digital computer was built by Thomas H. Flowers and his team of engineers.* ◇ *a/an civil/electrical/mechanical/software engineer* ➲ *see also* CIVIL ENGINEER

en·gin·eer² /ˌendʒɪˈnɪə(r); *NAmE* ˌendʒɪˈnɪr/ *verb* **1 ~ sth** to design and build sth: *King Bhumipol played an important role in engineering the current flood protection system of Bangkok.* ◇ *The principal problem was to engineer diodes that emitted at the appropriate wavelength.* **2 ~ sth (to do sth)** to change the GENETIC structure of sth: *The second strain was genetically engineered to be incapable of sexual function.* ➲ *see also* GENETIC ENGINEERING **3 ~ sth** to arrange for sth to happen or take place, especially when this is done secretly in order to give yourself an advantage: *The disturbance was engineered by intellectuals and young officers.* ◇ *Khrushchev's rivals and critics were able to engineer his downfall.*

en·gin·eer·ing /ˌendʒɪˈnɪərɪŋ; *NAmE* ˌendʒɪˈnɪrɪŋ/ *noun* [U] the activity of using scientific knowledge to design and build things: *This remarkable feat of Roman engineering is the most complete surviving pagan temple.* ◇ *electrical/mechanical engineering* ◇ **+ noun** *Planning and engineering projects require the information provided by geological maps.* ◇ *These methods were the direct result of interdisciplinary work overlapping chemistry and engineering science.* ➲ *see also* CIVIL ENGINEERING, GENETIC ENGINEERING

en·hance AWL /ɪnˈhɑːns; *NAmE* ɪnˈhæns/ *verb* **~ sth** to increase or further improve the good quality, value or status of sb/sth: *Until recently, this additive was widely used to enhance engine performance.* ◇ *This research should enhance our understanding of the nature of economic development.* ◇ *The Internet has greatly enhanced distance-learning opportunities.*

▸ ENHANCE + NOUN **understanding • learning • skills • ability, capability • capacity • power • efficiency, effectiveness • effect • performance • productivity • quality • value • reputation • rate • activity** *Sales training attempts to teach and enhance critical selling skills.* ◇ *The newer types of combustion processes enhance efficiency.*

▸ ADVERB + ENHANCE **greatly • further • significantly** *The Romans further enhanced security by enclosing the city in a semicircular wall.* ◇ *It was found that physical activity significantly enhanced children's self-esteem.*

en·hance·ment AWL /ɪnˈhɑːnsmənt; *NAmE* ɪnˈhænsmənt/ *noun* [U, C] **~ (of sth)** an increase or further improvement in the good quality, value or status of sb/sth: *Enhancement of quality of life is a goal for all people, regardless of health status or disability.* ◇ *Lessons learned from the programme have resulted in a number of enhancements.*

enjoy /ɪnˈdʒɔɪ/ *verb* **1 ~ sth** to have sth good that is an advantage to you: *All permanent adult residents must enjoy full rights of citizenship.* ◇ *Hollywood movies enjoyed growing popularity with European audiences.* **2** to get pleasure from sth: **~ sth** *A common reason cited for early retirement is being able to enjoy life while still young and fit enough.* ◇ **~ doing sth** *Anyone interested in Darwin's thoughts will enjoy reading this compelling study.* **3 ~ yourself** to be happy and get pleasure from what you are doing: *It is clear that some people do not enjoy themselves while visiting the theme park.*

▸ ENJOY + NOUN **right • privilege • advantage • benefit • success • popularity • support • status • reputation • freedom, autonomy • power • access to sth • protection • monopoly • a degree of sth, a level of sth** *The debate has focused on whether or not business has enjoyed unfair advantages in politics.* ◇ *Heads of State have always enjoyed a degree of freedom.*

E

en·joy·able /ɪnˈdʒɔɪəbl/ *adj.* giving pleasure: *The firm that offers the most enjoyable service experience for their customers will stay ahead of the competition.* ◇ *The concepts have been adapted to make them developmentally appropriate as well as enjoyable for students.*

en·joy·ment /ɪnˈdʒɔɪmənt/ *noun* [U] **1 ~ of sth** the fact of having and using sth: *The effects of climate change have implications for the full enjoyment of human rights.* ◇ *To ensure the effective enjoyment of the right to education, there is often a need for enhancing school services.* **2 ~ (of sth)** the pleasure that you get from sth: *Consumers increasingly regarded health as the key to active enjoyment of life.* ◇ *As a young officer in Paris, he derived great enjoyment from the endless ceremonies and parades.*

en·large /ɪnˈlɑːdʒ; *NAmE* ɪnˈlɑːrdʒ/ *verb* [T, I] **~ (sth)** to make sth bigger; to become bigger: *The process of modernization enlarges the scope for cooperation across international boundaries.* ◇ *Legislators forced the university to enlarge its class size from 150 to 200 students.* ◇ *Other symptoms include raised white cell count and enlarged spleen.* ◇ *A greatly enlarged EU implies a much greater diversity of national needs, preferences and resources.* PHR V **enˈlarge on/upon sth** to say or write more about sth that has been mentioned SYN ELABORATE² (1): *To enlarge on these remarks would lead beyond the scope of this note.*

en·large·ment /ɪnˈlɑːdʒmənt; *NAmE* ɪnˈlɑːrdʒmənt/ *noun* [U, sing.] **~ (of sth)** the process or result of sth becoming or being made larger: *Iodine deficiency commonly causes enlargement of the thyroid gland.* ◇ *Growth can occur by cell enlargement, which is an increase in cell size without division.* ◇ *The countries of Western Europe were not well placed to meet the financial challenges of EU enlargement.*

en·light·en /ɪnˈlaɪtn/ *verb* **~ sb** (*formal*) to give sb information so that they understand sth better: *Health literacy is an educational tool that can be used to 'inform, enlighten and empower individuals and communities' (Sparks, 2009: 201).* ■ **en·light·en·ing** *adj.*: *The interviews were enlightening and enlivening, providing new perspectives on several key issues within the research.*

en·light·ened /ɪnˈlaɪtnd/ *adj.* [usually before noun] (*approving*) having or showing an understanding of people's needs, a situation, etc. that is not based on old-fashioned attitudes and PREJUDICE: *Shakespeare provided an enlightened vision of female independence and strength of character.*

en·light·en·ment /ɪnˈlaɪtnmənt/ *noun* **1** [U] knowledge about and understanding of sth; the process of understanding sth or making sb understand it: *Benjamin (1934) argued that theatre and film should be a forum for political enlightenment.* **2 the Enlightenment** [sing.] the period in the 18th century when many writers and scientists began to argue that science and reason were more important than religion and tradition: *Reason was the central value of the Enlightenment.*

en·list /ɪnˈlɪst/ *verb* **1** [T] to persuade sb to help you or to join you in doing sth: **~ sth/sb (in sth/in doing sth)** *The violence prevention programmes enlist the support of the* *community in preventing youth violence.* ◇ **~ sb (as sth)** *Plataea tried to enlist Athens as a protector against its large neighbour Thebes.* ◇ **~ sb to do sth** *The federal education department enlisted a group of peer reviewers to rate the proposals.* **2** [I, T] to join or to make sb join the armed forces SYN CALL SB UP, CONSCRIPT[1], DRAFT[2] (3): **~ (in sth)** *Wu enlisted in the army partly to earn a living and partly for patriotic reasons.* ◇ **~ sb** *Hundreds of thousands of recruits were enlisted.*

E

enor·mous AWL /ɪˈnɔːməs; NAmE ɪˈnɔːrməs/ *adj.* extremely large SYN HUGE, IMMENSE: *Natural clouds have an enormous effect on global climate.* ◇ *The paper attracted an enormous amount of attention.* ◇ *The nurses work long hours and see an enormous number of patients—approximately 100 per day.* ◇ *A centralized health database offers enormous potential for research.*

enor·mous·ly AWL /ɪˈnɔːməsli; NAmE ɪˈnɔːrməsli/ *adv.* very; very much: *Like his father, he was enormously popular with the people.* ◇ *Eggs vary enormously in size among different animals.* ◇ *The company has benefited enormously from its monopoly position.* ➲ language bank *at* EXCEPTIONALLY

enough[1] /ɪˈnʌf/ *det.* used before plural or uncountable nouns to mean 'as many or as much as is needed or wanted' SYN SUFFICIENT: *Participants questioned whether there would be enough police to enforce the law.* ◇ *We do not have enough data to weigh up the social costs and benefits of this kind of finance.* ◇ *Overall there was enough food for everybody.* ◇ *Given enough time, our planet's biosphere can recover and regain its former diversity.*

enough[2] /ɪˈnʌf/ *pron.* as many or as much as is needed or wanted: *These problems suggest that just asking customers for information is not really enough.* ◇ *The energy would have been enough for particles of matter and antimatter to have emerged.* ◇ **~ of sth** *Marx and Engels had seen enough of the history of capitalism to have a different view.* IDM **have had eˈnough (of sth/sb)** used when you do not like sth/sb and you no longer want to do, have or see it/them: *Diaries can suffer from a process of attrition, as people decide they have had enough of the task of completing a diary.*

enough[3] /ɪˈnʌf/ *adv.* (used after verbs, adjectives and adverbs) **1** to the necessary degree: *If a firm is large enough to control the whole market for a product, it is a monopoly.* ◇ *In real world situations, a procedure has to be able to solve the problem quickly enough.* ◇ *The banks were not regulated enough.* **2** to a reasonable degree, but not to a very great degree: *On the surface, it is a notion easy enough to grasp.* **3** to a degree that you do not wish to get any greater: *Trying to understand the universe is hard enough without adding further questions.*
IDM **ˌcuriously/ˌstrangely, etc. eˈnough** used to show that sth is surprising: *Strangely enough, in most tortoises, sex determination can be influenced by the temperature at which the eggs are incubated.* ➲ *more at* FAR[1]

en·quire, en·quir·ing, en·quiry = INQUIRE, INQUIRING, INQUIRY

en·rich /ɪnˈrɪtʃ/ *verb* **1** [often passive] to add a substance or more of a substance to sth, especially in a way that makes it more concentrated, more valuable, etc: *Animal manure was then the only fertilizer which could enrich the soil and increase the yield of grain.* ◇ *Generally, these reactors are fuelled by natural or enriched uranium.* ◇ **~ sth with sth** *Here the groundwater is enriched with nutrients supporting a greater diversity of plants.* **2** to improve the quality of sth, often by adding sth to it: **~ sth** *More collaborative work between US and South East Asian geographers will enrich our understanding of this dynamic, diverse part of the world.* ◇ **~ sth with sth** *This book is enriched with a range of learning tools to help you navigate the text.* **3 ~ sb/sth/yourself** to make sb/sth/yourself rich or richer: *Individuals and communities were certainly enriched greatly by overseas trade.* ◇ *The leader and his family were enriching themselves through open and widespread corruption.*

en·rich·ment /ɪnˈrɪtʃmənt/ *noun* **1** [U, C] **~ (of sth)** the process of adding a substance to sth, especially in a way that makes it more concentrated, more valuable, etc: *The recent history of warming is the result of human enrichment of the atmosphere with carbon dioxide.* ◇ *Producing a nuclear bomb involves uranium enrichment or plutonium production.* ◇ *These deposits represent enrichments of ore minerals caused by surface waters that percolate downwards.* **2** [U] **~ (of sth)** the process of improving the quality of sb's life, education, understanding, etc, often by adding different things to it: *One can argue that state support is simply not necessary for the artistic and cultural enrichment of society.* ◇ *Staff turnover is an obstacle to providing high-quality academic enrichment, particularly in after-school programmes.* **3** [U] **~ (of sb/sth)** the process of making sb/sth rich or richer: *The regime was marked by the spectacular personal enrichment of the ruler and his family.*

enrol (*US* **en·roll**) /ɪnˈrəʊl; NAmE ɪnˈroʊl/ *verb* (-ll-) [I, T] to arrange for yourself or for sb else to officially join a course, school, etc: **~ on sth** (*BrE*) *The teachers who participated in the project enrolled on a 10-hour course covering the study objectives and procedures.* ◇ **~ in sth** (*NAmE*) *to enroll in a program* ◇ **~ sb (on/in sth)** *The patients enrolled in the study were selected from 427 who had undergone coronary artery angiography.*

en·rol·ment (*US* **en·roll·ment**) /ɪnˈrəʊlmənt; NAmE ɪnˈroʊlmənt/ *noun* [U, C] **~ (on/in sth)** the act of officially joining a course, school, etc; the number of people who do this: *Automatic enrolment in the American 401(k) employee saving plans is thought to benefit employees.* ◇ *Statistics on school enrolments can provide up-to-date information about younger age groups.*

en·shrine /ɪnˈʃraɪn/ *verb* [usually passive] **~ sth (in sth)** to make a law, right, etc. respected or official, especially by stating it in an important written document: *The right to freedom of expression is enshrined in English law.*

en·slave /ɪnˈsleɪv/ *verb* [usually passive] **1 ~ sb** to make sb a SLAVE: *At Eretria the Persians burned temples, sacked the city and enslaved the inhabitants.* ◇ *Enslaved people were perennially hungry and ill-clothed.* **2 ~ sb/sth (to sth)** [usually passive] to make sb/sth completely depend on sth so that they cannot manage without it: *They elaborated the idea that the individual is an egoistic, irrational being, enslaved to his appetites.* ■ **en·slave·ment** *noun* [U] **~ (of sb)** *The Qur'an forbade the enslavement of co-religionists.* ◇ **~ to sth** *Blake suggests we do not notice our mental enslavement to ideas and systems imposed by others.*

ensue /ɪnˈsjuː; NAmE ɪnˈsuː/ *verb* [I] to happen after or as a result of another event SYN FOLLOW (1): *A national debate ensued concerning the form this legislation should take.* ◇ *Liver function is compromised, and in rare cases death may ensue from multi-organ failure.* ■ **en·su·ing** *adj.*: *The ensuing war was to last for over four years.* ◇ *In the ensuing decades, numerous studies confirmed these results.*

en·sure AWL (*also* **in·sure** *especially in NAmE*) /ɪnˈʃʊə(r); ɪnˈʃɔː(r); NAmE ɪnˈʃʊr/ *verb* to make sure that sth happens or is definite: **~ sth** *Appropriate assessment and investigation must be performed in order to ensure patient safety.* ◇ *Irrigation schemes need to ensure a reliable supply of water for rice cultivation.* ◇ **~ (that)...** *Ensure patients have the opportunity to make informed choices at every stage.* ◇ *Particle filters are used to ensure that the airflow in the processing area is free from dust.*

▸ ENSURE + NOUN **compliance • access • quality • accuracy • success • effectiveness • safety • security • protection • stability • consistency • continuity • survival • supply • support • accountability • equality • a level of sth** *As the world runs out of resources, the most powerful military alliances will use their might to ensure access.* ◇ *It is critical to ensure a high level of job satisfaction in the sales force.*

en·tail /ɪnˈteɪl/ *verb* **1** to have sth as a necessary part of a process or plan SYN INVOLVE (1): **~ sth** *Health care reform entailed major subsidies.* ◇ **~ doing sth** *Our approach entailed determining the likelihood that an individual would be a crime victim.* ◇ **(be) entailed in sth** *There are serious drawbacks entailed in state intervention.* ➲ thesaurus note *at* MEAN¹ **2** to have sth as a necessary result, according to the laws of LOGIC: **~ sth** *This idea logically entails the view that ageing is adaptive.* ◇ **~ (that)...** *This entails that such a world may exist, but it does not entail that it is our world.*

enter /ˈentə(r)/ *verb* **1** [I, T] (not usually used in the passive) **~ sth** to come or go into sth: *He had entered the UK, but did not find work.* ◇ *A judge entered the room and was seated.* ◇ *The earth had entered a new phase in its history.* ◇ *This image repeatedly enters the patient's mind.* **2** [T, no passive] **~ sth** to start taking part in an activity or start working in an organization or profession; to become part of sth: *Students had been learning English for about six years before entering university.* ◇ *Both men became successful lawyers before entering politics.* ◇ *Women have entered the workforce in greater numbers.* ◇ **~ sth through sth** *The issue entered popular culture through a television series entitled 'Monster Parent'.* **3** [T, usually passive] to put data into a computer program, list or other record: **~ sth** *Until data are entered, each column simply has 'var' as its heading.* ◇ **~ sth into sth** *The results can be entered directly into an electronic database.* ◇ *The crime may not be entered into the crime statistics.* ◇ **~ sth in sth** *Recordings were transcribed and entered in the qualitative data analysis program.* ◇ **~ sth on sth** *Data were entered on a laptop or PC during the consultation.* ◇ **~ sth as sth** *All the independent variables were entered as dummy variables.* ➲ thesaurus note *at* RECORD² **4** [T] **~ sth** (*law*) to say sth officially so that it can be recorded: *Summary judgment may be entered where the petition has no realistic prospect of success.* **5** [T, I] to say officially that sb will take part in an exam or contest; to take part in an exam or contest: **~ sb (for/in sth)** *These pupils cannot attain the required level because they are entered for too few subjects.* ◇ **~ sth** *Females are more willing to enter contests in which their side has a numerical advantage.* ➲ *see also* ENTRANCE, ENTRY IDM *see* FORCE¹

PHR V **ˈenter into sth** **1** to begin to discuss or deal with sth: *I will not enter too deeply into the details.* **2** to take an active part in sth: *We are grateful to her for entering into and furthering this conversation.* ◇ *He enters into the spirit of things with his mock-solemn criticism of their theories.* **3** [no passive] to form part of sth or have an influence on sth: *Seed capital did not seem to enter into his calculations.* **ˈenter into sth (with sb)** to begin sth or become involved in sth: *The parties have entered into a contract with each other.* ◇ *Government authorities have entered into arrangements with private investors to finance toll roads.* **ˈenter on/upon sth** to start to do sth or become involved in sth: *No one would desire to enter upon such a comparison.*

en·ter·prise /ˈentəpraɪz; *NAmE* ˈentərpraɪz/ *noun* **1** [C] a company or business: *They had little experience of running a successful retail enterprise.* ◇ *She is a water and sanitation specialist working with governments, NGOs and private enterprises.* ◇ *They supply software to small and medium-sized enterprises (SMEs).* **2** [C, U] a project or attempt, especially one that is difficult SYN VENTURE¹: *The Trojan War was the last great enterprise of the heroic age.* ◇ *These groups are informally bound together by shared experience and commitment to a joint enterprise.* ◇ *To Dickens's mind, most scientific enterprise was impractical, esoteric and effectively useless.* **3** [U] the development of businesses by the people of a country rather than by the government: *The role of government in the early 19th century was to encourage private enterprise, not regulate or constrain it.* ◇ **+ noun** *We need to do more to create an enterprise culture, where success is admired and new business ideas flourish.* **4** [U] the ability to think of new projects and make them successful SYN INITIATIVE (2): *Lord Young stated that the problems of the British economy have largely stemmed from a lack of enterprise.*

E

en·ter·pris·ing /ˈentəpraɪzɪŋ; *NAmE* ˈentərpraɪzɪŋ/ *adj.* having or showing the ability to think of new projects or new ways of doing things and make them successful: *Growing urban markets created openings for enterprising farmers to accelerate production.* ◇ *Many of these initiatives are focused on making small businesses more enterprising.*

en·ter·tain /ˌentəˈteɪn; *NAmE* ˌentərˈteɪn/ *verb* **1** [T, I] to interest and be enjoyed by sb: *Are the displays designed to sell products or to inform and entertain?* ◇ **~ sb** *Most Hollywood movies are created with the intention of entertaining the widest audience possible.* ◇ **~ sb with sth** *He began writing the popular histories with which he entertained his readers for thirty years.* **2** [T] (not used in the progressive tenses) **~ sth** to consider an idea, a hope, a feeling, etc: *As a governor, he entertained comparatively radical ideas.* ◇ *We must entertain the possibility that low educational aspirations are the root of poor grades.* **3** [I, T] to invite people to eat or drink with you as your guests, especially in your home: *The USA has a strong tradition of entertaining at home.* ◇ **~ sb** *In this room, guests were entertained at banquets and drinking-parties (symposia).*

en·ter·tain·ing /ˌentəˈteɪnɪŋ; *NAmE* ˌentərˈteɪnɪŋ/ *adj.* interesting and enjoyable: *This is a wonderfully entertaining and informative book that looks at the evolutionary tree of life.* ◇ *While to us mythological tales are merely entertaining, to archaic peoples they meant a great deal more.*

en·ter·tain·ment /ˌentəˈteɪnmənt; *NAmE* ˌentərˈteɪnmənt/ *noun* **1** [U, C] films, music, etc. used to entertain people; an example of this: *The majority of viewers use television passively, as a form of entertainment.* ◇ *Shakespeare was popular entertainment in nineteenth-century America.* ◇ *Theatres put on plays and musical entertainments.* ◇ **+ noun** *Three of the most important forms of the global entertainment industry are recorded music, movies and television.* **2** [U] **~ (of sb)** the act of entertaining sb: *The guests 'performed' for the entertainment of their fellow guests.*

en·thu·si·asm /ɪnˈθjuːziæzəm; *NAmE* ɪnˈθuːziæzəm/ *noun* [U, C] a feeling of excitement about or interest in sth, or of wanting to be involved in sth: *The author's enthusiasm and commitment are impressive.* ◇ *The time-lag between policy enthusiasms and more sober analyses is not unusual.* ◇ **~ for sth** *Following the initial enthusiasm for biofuels, there has been increased awareness of their limitations.* ◇ **~ for doing sth** *He had no enthusiasm for repeating the experience.*

en·thu·si·ast /ɪnˈθjuːziæst; *NAmE* ɪnˈθuːziæst/ *noun* a person who is very interested in or very excited about sth, or who strongly approves of sth: *Internet enthusiasts claim that this interactivity is revolutionizing marketing.* ◇ **~ for sth** *He is an enthusiast for innovation and change.* ◇ **~ of sth** *She was one of the strongest enthusiasts of the plan.*

en·thu·si·ast·ic /ɪnˌθjuːziˈæstɪk; *NAmE* ɪnˌθuːziˈæstɪk/ *adj.* feeling or showing a lot of interest in and excitement about sth: *British governments have tended to be enthusiastic advocates of economic liberalization.* ◇ **~ about sth** *Staff were highly enthusiastic about their projects.* ◇ **~ about doing sth** *The general public was enthusiastic about participating in the programme.* ■ **en·thu·si·as·tic·al·ly** /ɪnˌθjuːziˈæstɪkli; *NAmE* ɪnˌθuːziˈæstɪkli/ *adv.*: *This concept of globalization was enthusiastically embraced by a number of developing nations.* ◇ *Big business responded enthusiastically to the prospect of a fully integrated European marketplace.*

E

en·tire /ɪnˈtaɪə(r)/ *adj.* [only before noun] (used when you are emphasizing that the whole of sth is involved) including everything, everyone or every part SYN WHOLE[1]: *By 1960, one quarter of the entire population lived in suburban areas.* ◇ *If any one of the links fails, the entire system fails.*
▸ ENTIRE + NOUN **universe • world • nation • city • population • community** *Entire communities were obliterated.* | **system • process • period • course • range • spectrum • network • body • sample** *The aim is consistency across the entire spectrum of education.*

en·tire·ly /ɪnˈtaɪəli; *NAmE* ɪnˈtaɪərli/ *adv.* in every way possible SYN COMPLETELY: *The question of who pays is an entirely different issue.* ◇ *The reasons for the failure are not entirely clear.* ◇ *These theories rely entirely on third-person data and validation.* ◇ *This simple explanation entirely ignores any detailed understanding of degradation mechanisms.* ➲ language bank *at* EXCEPTIONALLY

en·tir·ety /ɪnˈtaɪərəti/ *noun* [sing.] **the ~ of sth** the whole of sth: *It is not possible to condense the entirety of the medical and surgical syllabus into one book.* ◇ *Universal norms that aspire to cover the entirety of the human race are problematic.*
IDM **in its/their enˈtirety** as a whole; considering or including all of sth: *In his view, religion in its entirety can be reduced to little more than a by-product of psychological distress.* ◇ *Once complete genome sequences were available, it became possible to compare them in their entirety.*

en·title /ɪnˈtaɪtl/ *verb* **1** [often passive] to give sb the right to have or to do sth: **~ sb to sth/to do sth** *Shareholders buy shares in the company which entitle them to certain rights.* ◇ **(be) entitled to sth** *The applicant was entitled to assistance with legal costs.* ◇ **(be) entitled to do sth** *Some unemployed people are not entitled to claim benefits.* **2** [usually passive] to give a title to a book, document, film, etc: **(be) entitled sth** *Section 4, entitled 'Coming of Age', contains interviews with older subjects.*

en·title·ment /ɪnˈtaɪtlmənt/ *noun* **1** [U] the official right to have or do sth: *Holiday entitlement is usually written into a contract of employment.* ◇ **~ to sth** *Entitlement to welfare benefits is restricted.* **2** [C] something that you have an official right to; the amount that you have the right to receive: *Consumers are generally unaware of their entitlements under the Health Insurance Law.* ◇ *They enjoy excessively generous pension entitlements.* **3** [C, U] (*NAmE*) a government system that provides financial support to a particular group of people: **+ noun** *The strategy would be to create a new entitlement program.*

en·tity AWL /ˈentəti/ *noun* (*pl.* **-ies**) something that exists separately from other things and has its own identity: *It has typically been assumed that nature and culture are separate entities.* ◇ *The court treated the group of companies as a single legal entity.*

en·trance /ˈentrəns/ *noun* **1** [C] a way in to a place: *The photograph shows the main entrance.* ◇ **~ to sth** *Along the coast, wide entrances to sea caves are numerous.* ◇ **~ of sth** *The family resource centre should be located close to the entrance of the school.* ➲ *compare* EXIT[1] (1) **2** [U, C] the process of sb becoming part of a group or institution, such as a university or parliament; the act of becoming involved in sth: **~ into sth** *The first woman made her entrance into the Swedish Parliament after the election of 1921.* ◇ **~ of sb into sth** *Family factors, especially children, help to explain the entrance of women into non-professional self-employment.* ◇ **+ noun** *Few students met university entrance requirements.* HELP In writing about literature or the theatre, a person's **entrance** is the act of them coming onto the stage: *The scene opens with the entrance of the guests into the ballroom.* ➲ *compare* ENTRY

en·trant /ˈentrənt/ *noun* **1** a company, product, etc. that joins or enters a market or area of business activity: *The set-up costs for some industries can be so high that it will deter entrants.* ◇ **~ to sth** *The onset of digital technology brought a raft of new entrants to the camera market.* **2** a person who joins a profession, university, school, etc: *Investigators examine the immunization records of new school entrants.* ◇ **~ to sth** *Professional enclaves may seek to restrict the number of entrants to a given profession by raising entry requirements.* **3** a person who enters a country or place: *New entrants should be identified from Port of Arrival Reports.* ◇ **~ to sth** *The aim is to ensure that illegal entrants to the EU can be repatriated.* **4** a person or an animal that enters a race or a competition: *Recent innovations include a national awards competition where entrants can win over £10 000.*

entre·pre·neur /ˌɒntrəprəˈnɜː(r); *NAmE* ˌɑːntrəprəˈnɜːr/ *noun* a person who makes money by starting or running businesses, especially when this involves taking financial risks: *Opportunities to attract talented entrepreneurs are few.* ■ **entre·pre·neur·ship** *noun* [U] *Students of entrepreneurship typically focus on young firms.*

en·tre·pre·neur·ial /ˌɒntrəprəˈnɜːriəl; *NAmE* ˌɑːntrəprəˈnɜːriəl/ *adj.* [usually before noun] making money by starting or running businesses, especially when this involves taking financial risks: *Economic development requires entrepreneurial activity and innovation.* ◇ *They were entrepreneurial firms that pioneered new industries.*

en·tropy /ˈentrəpi/ *noun* [U] **1** (*symb.* **S**) (*physics*) **~ (of sth)** a measurement PROPORTIONAL to the energy that is present in a system which is not available to do work: *The entropy of a system always increases over time.* ◇ *If water molecules have very little energy, they will tend to adopt a very organized, low-energy structure—namely, ice, which has low entropy.* **2** (*technical*) a way of measuring the lack of order that exists in a system: *An increase in entropy represents a decrease of organization within the system.*

en·trust /ɪnˈtrʌst/ *verb* to make sb responsible for doing sth or taking care of sth: **~ B with A** *Inspectors were entrusted with the task of applying the regulations.* ◇ **~ A to B** *He entrusted authority to men of his own choice.*

entry /ˈentri/ *noun* (*pl.* **-ies**) **1** [U, sing.] the act or process of coming or going into a place; the fact that sb/sth can do this: *The defendant had the weapon with him at the time of entry.* ◇ **~ of sb/sth** *A state has the right to control the entry of non-nationals.* ◇ **~ (of sb/sth) into sth** *The legal system may prohibit the entry of certain goods and services into a country.* ◇ **~ via/through sth** *Bacteria commonly gain entry via breaks in the skin surface.* **2** [U, C, usually sing.] the act or process of becoming involved in sth or of becoming part of sth; the fact that sb/sth can do this: *Such agreements can facilitate market entry.* ◇ **~ into sth** *Pregnancy was a requisite for entry into the study.* ◇ **~ to sth** *Exams are the most common way for high school students to gain entry to university.* ◇ **on/upon ~** *A counsellor made contact with families upon entry into the programme.* ◇ **after ~** *Family background continues to be relevant long after entry to school.* ◇ **+ noun** *The entry qualifications were relatively high.* **3** [C] a piece of information or data that is put into a computer program, list, book or other record: *diary/journal/dictionary entries* ◇ **~ in sth** *At present there are over 360 000 entries in the database.* **4** [U] the act or process of recording information in a computer, list, book, etc: *Staff spent valuable time on data entry.* **5** [C] something that you do, write or make, in order to take part in a competition: *Over 5 200 entries were received.* **6** [U] **~ (into sth)** the act of taking part in a competition, race, etc: *It can be argued that, to encourage entry into scientific contests, losers ought to be rewarded too.* **IDM** *see* PORT

en·vel·ope /ˈenvələʊp; ˈɒnvələʊp; *NAmE* ˈenvəloʊp; ˈɑːnvəloʊp/ *noun* **1** a flat paper container used for sending letters in: *Questionnaires were returned in sealed envelopes collected by the research coordinator.* **2** (*technical*) a covering or containing structure or layer: *The switch itself is a glass envelope filled with rare gases and containing two contacts.*

en·vir·on·ment **AWL** /ɪnˈvaɪrənmənt/ *noun* **1** [C, U] the conditions that affect the behaviour and development of sb/sth; the conditions in which sb/sth exists: *They had taken steps to improve the working environment.* ◇ *Surviving in these different environments would demand adaptability and ingenuity.* **2 the environment** [sing.] the natural world (used in discussing ways in which the natural world is damaged or protected, especially by humans): *68% thought the government was working to protect the environment.* ◇ *The escape of mercury into the local environment is another cause for concern.* **HELP** **Environment** is sometimes used without 'the' to refer generally to the protection and/or destruction of the natural world: *There are many views on sustainability in relation to environment and development.* **3** [C] (*computing*) the complete structure within which a user, computer or program operates: *The effect depends on the particular operating environment.*

WORD FAMILY
environment *noun*
environmental *adj.*
environmentally *adv.*
environmentalist *noun*

▸ ADJECTIVE + ENVIRONMENT **natural • local • global • marine** *The qualitative researcher confronts members of a social setting in their natural environments.* ◇ *Continued consumption of fossil fuel presents an increasing threat to the global environment.* | **external • wider • immediate • social • political • institutional • economic • physical • built • urban** *Policy and practice are influenced by the wider environment.* ◇ *The design of the built environment is often a cause for concern.* | **safe • supportive • controlled • competitive • dynamic • different • changing • shared** *This procedure must be carried out in a controlled environment.*

▸ NOUN + ENVIRONMENT **work, working • business • learning • school • classroom • home • family** *A great deal is known about the health risks that may be present in the work environment.*

▸ VERB + ENVIRONMENT **create , provide • foster • shape • alter, change, modify • improve • maintain • monitor, scan** *Teachers create classroom environments that support conflict resolution.* ◇ *Firms can actively shape their institutional environments through their strategic actions (Oliver, 1991).* | **be present in • inhabit • occur in/within • operate in/within • function in • work in • survive in • thrive in • be reared in** *Local government operates within an environment which is the product of social, historical, political and economic conditions.* | **protect • improve • pollute • damage, harm** *The volatile organic solvent pollutes the environment.*

▸ ENVIRONMENT + VERB **affect • influence • change • play a role in** *The family environment plays a key role in the development of eating behaviours among children.*

en·vir·on·men·tal **AWL** /ɪnˌvaɪrənˈmentl/ *adj.* [usually before noun] **1** connected with the natural world; connected with the ways in which the natural world is damaged or protected, especially by humans: *As can be seen, environmental quality improves, with particular gains in the reduction of SO_2 emissions.* ◇ *Environmental groups will seek to ensure that companies operate to international environmental standards.* **2** connected with the conditions that affect the behaviour and development of sb/sth; connected with the conditions in which sb/sth exists: *These differences cannot be attributed to either genetic or environmental influences.* ◇ *Cultural and environmental factors influence each other.* ■ **en·vir·on·men·tal·ly** **AWL** /ɪnˌvaɪrənˈmentəli/ *adv.*: *The objective should be to promote agriculture which is sustainable economically, environmentally and socially.* ◇ *Past failures have led to wasteful and environmentally damaging uses of water.*

▸ ENVIRONMENTAL + NOUN **quality • conditions • exposure • influences • change • variables • factors • cues • effects** *A wind farm can only be placed where the environmental conditions support such a development.* ◇ *Both social and environmental cues are promotive of youth smoking.* | **impact • damage, degradation, pollution • issues, concerns, problems • sustainability • protection • standards • policy • performance • regulation, legislation, law • organizations, groups • movement • agency** *Businesses must take responsibility for their economic, social and environmental impacts.* ◇ *The scope of environmental policy and regulation has expanded.*

en·vir·on·men·tal·ist **AWL** /ɪnˌvaɪrənˈmentəlɪst/ *noun* a person who is concerned about the natural world and wants to improve and protect it: *Many environmentalists realized that the best defence was pollution prevention.* ■ **en·vir·on·men·tal·ist** *adj.* [only before noun] *The global environmentalist movement has Green Parties around the world.* **en·vir·on·ment·al·ism** /ɪnˌvaɪrənˈmentəlɪzəm/ *noun* [U] *She had strong views on environmentalism and political engagement.*

en·vis·age /ɪnˈvɪzɪdʒ/ (*especially BrE*) (*NAmE usually* **en·vi·sion** /ɪnˈvɪʒn/) *verb* **1** to imagine sth as a future possibility or aim: **~ sth** *We can envisage a situation where firms attempt to influence policy.* ◇ *Their obligations were different from those envisaged by the parties when the contract was made.* ◇ **~ doing sth** *The government envisaged making payments to some of the affected persons.* ◇ **~ sb/sth doing sth** *It is difficult to envision policy integration working in such environments.* ◇ **it is envisaged that...** *It was originally envisaged that proposals would be considered by a new Planning Commission.* ◇ **~ that...** *Many envisage that this information will eventually lead to new treatments.* ◇ **~ how/what...** *It is difficult to envisage how this approach would succeed.* **2** (of a plan, rule or agreement) to include sth that is expected to happen: **~ sth** *The strategy also envisaged the deployment of 25 000 solar water heating systems.* ◇ *The data reveal a widespread failure to give effect to the protections envisioned by international refugee law.* ◇ **~ (sb) doing sth** *The original proposal did not envisage the Commissioner's role extending to disability services generally.* **3** to think of sb/sth in a particular way: **~ sb as sb** *She envisions herself as a 'self-made individual'.* ◇ **~ sth as (doing) sth** *We have envisaged the two integrations as being linked.*

en·zyme /ˈenzaɪm/ *noun* (*biochemistry*) a substance, produced by all living things, which helps a chemical change happen or happen more quickly, without being changed itself: *Enzymes generally catalyse just one type of chemical reaction.* ◇ *The enzyme urease, which destroys urea, increases the reaction rate 1 014 times.* ◇ *In this disease, a mutation in a gene encoding a specific liver enzyme can lead to severe mental retardation.* ■ **en·zym·at·ic** /enzaɪˈmætɪk/ *adv.*: *The maximal enzymatic activity was observed at pH 4.5 and 65°C respectively.*

epic[1] /ˈepɪk/ *noun* [C, U] a long poem about the actions of great men and women or about a country's history; this style of poetry: *This is yet another difference between Athens and the world depicted in the Homeric epics.* ◇ *The issue of oral composition thus became central to the study of Greek epic.* ➲ *compare* LYRIC[2] (1)

E

epic² /ˈepɪk/ *adj.* [usually before noun] **1** having the features of an epic: *Virgil's epic poem the 'Aeneid' recounted the quest of Aeneas to found the Roman people.* ➲ *compare* LYRIC¹ **2** taking place over a long period of time and involving a lot of difficulties: *In 1869, John Wesley Powell led a party of ten men on an epic journey by boat down a thousand miles of the Colorado River.* **3** (*rather informal*) very great and impressive: *Environmental pressure on the industry has reached epic proportions.*

E

epi·centre (*US* **epi·cen·ter**) /ˈepɪsentə(r)/ *noun* **1** the point on the earth's surface where the effects of an EARTHQUAKE are felt most strongly: *Mallet posited that earthquakes generate longitudinal waves that radiate in all directions away from the epicentre.* **2 ~ (of sth)** (*formal*) the central point of sth: *It is a small town of great significance in the political history of the region, so often the epicentre of demonstrations and revolts.*

epi·dem·ic /ˌepɪˈdemɪk/ *noun* **1** a large number of cases of a particular disease happening at the same time in a particular community: *Julia Chinn died in the cholera epidemic of 1833.* ◇ *The AIDS epidemic has caused a resurgence of tuberculosis in the tropics.* ◇ **~ of sth** *The study is investigating the epidemic of obesity in developed countries.* ➲ *compare* PANDEMIC **2 ~ (of sth)** a sudden increase in how often sth bad happens: *By mid 1936, an epidemic of world lawlessness was spreading.* ◇ *The region is still at an early stage of the tobacco epidemic where smoking prevalence is very high.*

epi·demi·ology /ˌepɪˌdiːmiˈɒlədʒi; *NAmE* ˌepɪˌdiːmiˈɑːlədʒi/ *noun* [U] the branch of medicine that deals with the spread and control of diseases; the spread of diseases within a society: *Epidemiology will continue to guide the provision of appropriate and effective health care services in our society.* ◇ **~ of sth** *It is important to understand how the epidemiology of our society is changing.* ■ **epi·demi·ologic·al** /ˌepɪˌdiːmiəˈlɒdʒɪkl; *NAmE* ˌepɪˌdiːmiəˈlɑːdʒɪkl/ *adj.*: *Epidemiological studies demonstrate that diabetes is related to the increased risk of many cancers.* **epi·demi·olo·gist** /ˌepɪˌdiːmiˈɒlədʒɪst; *NAmE* ˌepɪˌdiːmiˈɑːlədʒɪst/ *noun*: *Epidemiologists estimate that measles will remain active within a population of more than 200 000 individuals.*

epi·sode /ˈepɪsəʊd; *NAmE* ˈepɪsoʊd/ *noun* **1** an event, a situation or a period of time that is important or interesting in some way SYN INCIDENT¹: *There was a distressing episode when, as a child, she was shut in a cupboard and forgotten.* ◇ *Depending on climatic conditions, smog episodes were frequent.* ◇ **~ of sth** *Episodes of violent state intervention pushed the country towards its dissolution.* **2** a period of illness; an attack of illness: *The effect is to reduce the onset of manic episodes.* ◇ *depressive/psychotic episodes* ◇ **~ of sth** *He experienced recurrent episodes of chest pain.* **3** one of the parts of a television or radio show that are broadcast separately: *Viewers will recall the first episode of Season 6.*

epi·sod·ic /ˌepɪˈsɒdɪk; *NAmE* ˌepɪˈsɑːdɪk/ *adj.* **1** happening for limited periods of time and not regularly: *This would explain the episodic nature of his illness.* ◇ *Episodic storm events may have contributed to sediment transport.* **2** involving or consisting of a series of separate and different events, situations or periods: *His episodic memory was almost completely destroyed.* ◇ *The book is episodic, flitting from example to example without weaving disparate people, ideas and places together.* ■ **epi·sod·ic·al·ly** /ˌepɪˈsɒdɪkli; *NAmE* ˌepɪˈsɑːdɪkli/ *Volcanic sediment reaches the rivers episodically.* ◇ *The story is narrated episodically.*

epi·stem·ic /ˌepɪˈstiːmɪk; ˌepɪˈstemɪk/ *adj.* (*formal*) connected with knowledge: *To back up the epistemic authority of their arguments, parties often make use of experts.*

epis·te·mol·ogy /ɪˌpɪstəˈmɒlədʒi; *NAmE* ɪˌpɪstəˈmɑːlədʒi/ *noun* [U, sing.] (*philosophy*) the branch of philosophy that deals with knowledge; the theory of knowledge: *What Europe achieved during the Age of Enlightenment was a revolution in epistemology.*

epoch /ˈiːpɒk; *NAmE* ˈepək/ *noun* **1** a period of time in history, especially one during which important events or changes happen SYN ERA (1): *The capitalist epoch began in some parts of Europe around AD 1500.* ◇ *Mann argues that different sources of social power have been more significant in different historical epochs.* **2** (*earth science*) a length of time that is a division of a PERIOD: *This date marks the end of the Pleistocene geological epoch and the beginning of the Holocene.*

equal¹ /ˈiːkwəl/ *adj.* **1** the same in size, quantity, value, etc. as sth else: *Everyone has an equal share.* ◇ *Their decisions have equal weight.* ◇ *Newton's third law of motion says that action and reaction are equal and opposite.* ◇ **~ to sth** *The woman's social status was equal to the man's.* ◇ *We set this variable equal to zero.* ◇ **~ in sth** *The two groups were not equal in size.* HELP Some people think that it is wrong to use combinations such as **more equal** and **nearly equal**. However, these combinations are used in this meaning, unless an exact quantity, size, etc. is being discussed: *Many pastures now have a cover of grass nearly equal to that before the dry years.* When talking about an exact quantity, size, etc, **exactly equal** may be used: *It was impossible to start with three samples of exactly equal mass.* **2** (of people) having the same rights or being treated in the same way as other people: *Everyone is equal before the law.* ◇ *Women were recognized as equal citizens.* HELP **More equal** is used in this meaning: *In this way, they felt themselves to be more equal partners sitting round the table together.* **3** [usually before noun] based on the idea that people have, or should have, the same rights or treatment: *They are committed to securing equal rights.* ◇ *Equal pay legislation requires that women receive the same rates of pay as men.* **4 ~ to sth** having the necessary strength, courage or ability to deal with sth successfully: *The council has not proved equal to the task.* ➲ *see also* EQUALLY

IDM **ˌall/ˌother things being ˈequal | all ˌelse being ˈequal** if everything, or everything else, stays the same: *Each of these would, other things being equal, reduce unit labour costs and raise the profit rate.* **on ˌequal ˈterms (with sb) | on (an) equal footing (with sb)** having the same advantages and disadvantages as sb else: *Competition has become more intense as women are encouraged to compete on equal terms with men.* ◇ *Non-compliant agreements could be revised to put all airlines on an equal footing.*

▸ EQUAL + NOUN **amount • number • share, proportion • division, distribution • importance, weight • probability, chance** *Each contribution is matched by an equal amount of money from the treasury.* ◇ *All children have an equal probability of being selected.* | **rights • opportunity • access • status, standing • treatment • protection • bargaining power • worth • pay** *A commitment to equal opportunities offers a chance of breaking the cycle of disadvantage.* ◇ *There must be equal access to education, the media and so on.*

▸ ADVERB + EQUAL **approximately, roughly, about, almost, nearly • virtually • exactly • numerically** *These two parameters are generally assumed to be approximately equal.*

equal² /ˈiːkwəl/ *noun* a person or thing that has the same rights, quality, etc. as another person or thing: *People should be treated as equals.* ◇ *Part of the idea of being moral equals is the claim that none of us is inherently subordinate to the will of others.* ◇ **be the ~ of sb/sth** *In diction and technique, Claudian is the equal of Lucan and Statius.* IDM *see* FIRST³

equal[3] /ˈiːkwəl/ *verb* (-ll-, *US* -l-) **1** *linking verb* **+ noun** to be the same in size, quantity, value, etc. as sth else: *When demand for goods and services equals supply, there will generally be some unemployment.* ◇ *In aqueous solutions, the sum of all the positive ions in any compartment must equal the sum of all negative charged ions.* **2 ~ sth** to be as good as sth else; to do sth to the same standard as sb else: *This achievement is unlikely ever to be equalled.*

equal·ity /iˈkwɒləti; *NAmE* iˈkwɑːləti/ *noun* **1** [U, C] the fact of being equal in rights, advantages, etc; an example of this: *Governments have been proactive in seeking to promote racial equality.* ◇ **~ (of sth)** *Equality of aspiration is not matched by equality of opportunity.* ◇ *People may depict the equalities and inequalities in their relationships differently.* OPP INEQUALITY **2** [U, C] **~ (of sth)** the fact of being equal in size, quantity, value, etc; an example of this: *The unions have not achieved greater equality of incomes.* ◇ *We formally test for the equality of the coefficients.* **3** [C] (*mathematics*) a statement showing that two values are equal SYN EQUATION (1): *The same equality also holds here.* ◇ *The set A is specified through linear equalities and inequalities.*

equal·ize (*BrE also* -ise) /ˈiːkwəlaɪz/ *verb* **~ sth** to make things equal in size, quantity, value, rights, etc: *The density of seeds per pot was equalized.* ◇ *Additional seaborne trade tends to equalize prices in different areas.* ■ **equal·iza·tion, -isa·tion** /ˌiːkwəlaɪˈzeɪʃn; *NAmE* ˌiːkwələˈzeɪʃn/ *noun* [U] **~ (of sth)** *Changes that moved towards a near equalization of the rights of cohabitants and spouses were made in the 1990s.*

equal·ly /ˈiːkwəli/ *adv.* **1** to the same degree; in the same way: *The audio and written formats yield equally valid results.* ◇ *All persons matter equally.* ◇ *Why people smoke is an important question. Equally important is why people resist smoking.* ◇ *Leibniz's thought experiment applies equally well to the human brain.* HELP **Almost equally** means to a similar degree or in a similar way: *Both analyses are almost equally powerful and give similar results.* 'Equally as' is sometimes used, but is best avoided in academic writing; **as** and **equally** mean the same and you do not need to use both: ~~*Both analyses are equally as powerful.*~~ **2** in equal parts or amounts: *Financial costs were divided equally between the two interventions.* **3** used when adding a sentence or phrase, to show that it is as important as what you have just said: *It is right to celebrate achievements. Equally, it is right to acknowledge the difficulties associated with some of these achievements.*

equate AWL /iˈkweɪt/ *verb* **1** to think that sth is the same as sth else or is as important: **~ A and B** *These writers saw women as mothers and even began to equate the two roles.* ◇ **~ sth with sth** *Research for too many years equated culture with ethnic minority.* ◇ **~ sth to sth** *A woman's contribution to a marriage cannot be equated to any sum of money.* **2** to cause two or more things to be the same in quantity or value: **~ sth** *Interest rates are equated internationally.* ◇ **~ sth to sth** *In this model, marginal revenue is equated to marginal cost.* ◇ **~ A and B** *Prices are adjusted to equate supply and demand.*
PHR V **eˈquate to/with sth** to be the same as or equal to sth else: *Modernization does not necessarily equate to progress or improvement.* ◇ *A day equated to a minimum of seven hours' work.* ◇ *Robustness equates with the ability to adapt and evolve.*

equa·tion AWL /ɪˈkweɪʒn/ *noun* **1** [C] (*mathematics*) a statement showing that two amounts or values are equal, for example $2x + y = 54$: *To solve these equations, we used a standard numerical approach.* ➲ *see also* DIFFERENTIAL EQUATION, SIMULTANEOUS EQUATIONS **2** [C] (*chemistry*) a statement using symbols to show the changes that happen in a chemical reaction: *From the equation, it can be seen that when one molecule of benzene burns, six molecules of carbon dioxide are produced.* **3** [U, sing.] the act of making sth equal or considering sth as equal: **~ of A with/and B** *They were critical of what they saw as a growing equation of the American idea of progress with material progress.* ◇ *He underlines his opposition to the equation of Nazism and Stalinism.* ◇ **~ between A and B** *He was seeking here to draw an equation between Lincoln's manipulation of public opinion in the 1860s and the Cold War rhetoric of a hundred years later.* **4** [C, usually sing.] a situation in which several factors must be considered and dealt with: **into the ~** *The war in South East Asia introduced new complex dynamics into the equation.* ◇ **~ (of sth)** *With this, the whole equation of ancient religion is significantly altered.*
▸ VERB + EQUATION **solve** • **derive, obtain** • **yield, give** • **satisfy** • **write** • **rewrite, rearrange** • **simplify** • **estimate** • **integrate** • **use** *Newton derived equations to model the effects of gravity.* | **enter, enter into, come into, be part of** • **introduce sth into, bring sth into, factor sth into** *Let us hope that by then democracy is still part of the equation.*

equa·tor /ɪˈkweɪtə(r)/ *noun* (*usually* **the equator**) [sing.] an imaginary line around the earth at an equal distance from the North and South Poles: *Air at the equator is warmer and less dense than the colder air at the poles.*

equa·tor·ial /ˌekwəˈtɔːriəl/ *adj.* of, at or near the equator: *Tropical rainforests lie mainly in equatorial regions.*

equi·lib·rium /ˌiːkwɪˈlɪbriəm; ˌekwɪˈlɪbriəm/ *noun* [U, sing.] **1** a state in which opposing forces or influences are balanced: *It is essential to maintain an equilibrium in which people live in harmony with nature.* ◇ **in ~** *In Newtonian mechanics, forces are assumed to be in equilibrium.* HELP A **stable equilibrium** is a state in which sth tends to return to its original position after being disturbed. **2** (*also* **dyˌnamic equiˈlibrium**) (*chemistry*) a state in which a process and its opposite are happening at equal rates so that no overall change is taking place: *Fig. 5.69 represents a solid-liquid equilibrium.* ◇ **in ~** *Both gas and liquid are present in equilibrium.* ◇ **in ~ with sth** *This is the pH of pure water in equilibrium with atmospheric carbon dioxide.* ◇ **~ between A and B** *An equilibrium between iron and helium nuclei is set up.* HELP In a **dynamic equilibrium**, continuous opposing processes combine to produce a steady state. **3** (*economics*) a situation in which supply and demand are matched and prices stay the same: *The market will adjust to reach a new equilibrium.* ◇ **in ~** *Markets are assumed to be 'perfectly' competitive and in equilibrium.* ➲ *see also* GENERAL EQUILIBRIUM

equip AWL /ɪˈkwɪp/ *verb* (-pp-) **1** to provide yourself/sb/sth with the necessary items for a particular purpose or activity: **~ sth** *The proposal was to build and equip interplanetary space vehicles.* ◇ **~ yourself/sb/sth (with sth) (for sth)** *By the 1970s, 50 per cent of UK homes were equipped with a telephone.* ◇ *At that time, only those who could afford to equip themselves for army service became soldiers.* ◇ **well/fully/poorly equipped** *Hospitals in the country are generally very poorly equipped.* **2** to prepare sb for a particular activity or task, especially by teaching them what they need to know: **~ sb (with sth) (for sth/to do sth)** *The curriculum must equip students with the skills to enable them to practise as competent doctors.* ◇ **~ sb to do sth** *Nurses will need to be equipped to take on leadership roles in many areas of care.* ◇ **well/fully/poorly equipped** *Historians are particularly well equipped for this kind of research.*

equip·ment AWL /ɪˈkwɪpmənt/ *noun* [U] the necessary items for a particular purpose or activity: *The fishermen were trained in how to use the equipment.* ◇ *The truck had not been designed to carry such a large piece of equipment.*

equit·able /ˈekwɪtəbl/ *adj.* **1** fair and reasonable; treating everyone in an equal way SYN FAIR[1] (2): *The government implemented a scheme to finance equitable access to health care.* ◇ *Where food is short, resources, in the form of food and labour, are moved to give a more equitable*

E

distribution. OPP INEQUITABLE **2** (*especially BrE, law*) connected with a system of natural JUSTICE, which allows a fair judgement in a situation which is not covered by the existing laws: *The beneficiaries have an equitable interest in the property.* ■ **equit·ably** /ˈekwɪtəbli/ *adv.*: *It is important that these facilities are equitably distributed geographically with regard to accessibility.* ◇ *The company should ensure that all shareholders are treated equitably.*

equity /ˈekwəti/ *noun* **1** [U] a situation in which everyone is treated equally SYN FAIRNESS: *In order to protect the most vulnerable and ensure equity, there will always be a role for the state in providing some services.* OPP INEQUITY **2** [U] (*especially BrE, law*) a system of natural JUSTICE, which allows a fair judgement in a situation which is not covered by the existing laws: *The rules of common law and equity are both, in essence, systems of private law.* **3** [U] (*finance*) the value of a company's shares; the value of a property after all charges and debts have been paid: *He owns 62% of the group's equity.* ◇ *The company earned very low profits and only a 3–4 per cent return on equity from 2010 to 2012.* ◇ *They discussed selling the house but decided to wait because of the negative equity in the property.* **4 equities** [pl.] (*finance*) shares in a company which do not pay a fixed amount of interest: *The same sum invested in equities might produce a much higher return, but might equally produce a significantly lower return.*

equiva·lence AWL /ɪˈkwɪvələns/ *noun* [U, C] the fact of being equal or equivalent in value, amount, meaning or importance: **~ (of sth)** *They proposed a system for ensuring equivalence of university diplomas.* ◇ *A table of equivalences has been provided in an appendix.* ◇ **~ between A and B** *These regulations will establish complete equivalence between domestic and imported products.*

equiva·lent¹ AWL /ɪˈkwɪvələnt/ *adj.* **1** equal in value, amount, meaning or importance: *The farmers were allowed to exchange their land for an equivalent amount of land elsewhere.* ◇ **~ to sth** *China's share is roughly equivalent to that of a large European country.* **2 ~ to sth** having the same or a similar effect as sth else: *The government has denied the claim that civil partnership is equivalent to same-sex marriage.*

equiva·lent² AWL /ɪˈkwɪvələnt/ *noun* **1** a person or thing that is equal in value, amount, meaning or importance to another: **~ of sth** *Martinez used to earn the equivalent of 55 cents an hour at a plant in El Salvador.* ◇ **~ to sth** *The nearest equivalent to this in English is the word 'creature'.* **2** sth that has the same or a similar effect as sth else: **~ of sth** *Any criticism of the government would be considered the equivalent of treason.* ◇ **~ to sth** *The poem is Hazlitt's equivalent to Wordsworth's 'Ode'.*

era /ˈɪərə; *NAmE* ˈɪrə; ˈerə/ *noun* **1** a period of time, usually in history, that is different from other periods because of particular characteristics or events: *the postwar/modern/Victorian era* ◇ **~ of sth** *We have entered an era of globalization.* ◇ **during/in ~** *During the apartheid era, certain beaches were designated for 'whites only'.* ◇ **the beginning/end of an ~** *The death of Catherine de Bourbon, only sister of Henri IV, in 1605, marked the end of an era.* **2** (*earth science*) a MAJOR division of time that can itself be divided into periods: *The Alpine-Himalayan mountain belt formed mainly during the Cenozoic era.*

eradi·cate /ɪˈrædɪkeɪt/ *verb* to destroy or get rid of sth completely, especially sth bad: **~ sth** *Developed countries are working to help the Third World eradicate poverty.* ◇ **~ sth from sth** *Fortunately, smallpox has been eradicated from the natural world.* ■ **eradi·ca·tion** /ɪˌrædɪˈkeɪʃn/ *noun* [U] **~ (of sth)** *The introduction of a Hib vaccination has led to a virtual eradication of Hib meningitis.*

erase /ɪˈreɪz; *NAmE* ɪˈreɪs/ *verb* **1** to remove sth completely: **~ sth** *Three decades have not been enough time to erase bad memories of the past.* ◇ **~ sth from sth** *Their exceptional lives having been either unrecorded or erased from public record.* **2 ~ sth** to remove a mark or sth you have written, especially in order to correct it: *She erased the name in the notebook.* **3 ~ sth** to remove a recording from a tape or disk or data from a computer's memory: *The interviews were taped; recordings were erased immediately after transcription.*

erect /ɪˈrekt/ *verb* **1 ~ sth** to build sth: *A monument was subsequently erected on the site.* **2 ~ sth** to create or establish sth: *The most powerful companies have erected barriers to entry into the markets they control.*

erode AWL /ɪˈrəʊd; *NAmE* ɪˈroʊd/ *verb* **1** [T, often passive, I] to gradually destroy the surface of sth through the action of wind, rain, etc; to be gradually destroyed in this way: **~ sth (away)** *At the southernmost end of the island, the cliffs were being eroded by the sea.* ◇ **~ (away)** *In most cases, the loose deposits erode away.* **2** [T, often passive, I] **~ (sth)** to gradually destroy sth or make it weaker over a period of time; to be destroyed or made weaker in this way: *They will react when their wages are eroded by inflation.* ◇ *Research suggests that the traditional family structure may be eroding.*

ero·sion AWL /ɪˈrəʊʒn; *NAmE* ɪˈroʊʒn/ *noun* [U] **1** the process of gradually destroying the surface of sth through the action of wind, rain, etc: *Ploughing can be a major cause of soil erosion.* ◇ **~ of sth** *Erosion of the bare soil led to an increase in drainage density.* **2 ~ (of sth)** the process of gradually destroying sth or making it weaker over a period of time: *Globalization is gradually leading to the erosion of national traditions and cultures.*

err /ɜː(r); *NAmE* er/ *verb* [I] to make a mistake: **~ in (doing) sth** *The Court of Appeal held that the Tribunal had erred in considering each relationship separately.*

IDM **err on the side of sth** to show too much of a good quality: *Afraid of making the mistakes of past Labour administrations, Blair erred on the side of caution.*

er·ro·ne·ous AWL /ɪˈrəʊniəs; *NAmE* ɪˈroʊniəs/ *adj.* (*formal*) not correct; based on wrong information: *A simple direct comparison between species can lead to erroneous conclusions.* ■ **er·ro·ne·ous·ly** AWL *adv.*: *It was erroneously believed that the population of the world had been steadily falling since classical times.*

error AWL /ˈerə(r)/ *noun* [C, U] a mistake, especially one that causes problems or affects the result of sth: *Measurement errors may have biased the results.* ◇ *Most railway accidents could be attributed to human error.* ◇ **~ of sth** *He admitted he had made a serious error of judgement.* ◇ **~ in sth** *Errors in the data have been left uncorrected.* ◇ **~ in doing sth** *This mechanism may help to prevent errors in copying the repeated DNA sequences.* ◇ **in ~** *Wilkinson is in error when he gives 1950 as the date of the reforms.* ◇ **+ noun** *The final round of classroom observations focused on error correction.* ➲ *see also* SAMPLING ERROR, STANDARD ERROR

IDM **see, realize, etc. the ˌerror of your ˈways** to realize or admit that you have done sth wrong and decide to change your behaviour: *They believed Soviet leaders might in time see the error of their ways.* IDM *see* MARGIN, TRIAL¹

▸ ADJECTIVE + ERROR **large • small • common • possible • serious • factual • experimental • systematic • medical • grammatical • human** *The book contains a few small factual errors.*

▸ VERB + ERROR **make, commit • contain • detect, discover • correct, rectify • reduce, minimize • eliminate • avoid, prevent • introduce • cause • calculate** *This approach required the least experimental data and could minimize the errors caused by measurement.* ◇ *Unfortunately, in this methodology statistical errors are introduced.*

▸ ERROR + VERB **occur • cause • affect** *Errors may occur in the decision-making process.*

▸ ERROR + NOUN **rate • probability • variance • correction** *Data on the Police National Computer was subject to an 86 per cent error rate.*
▸ NOUN + OF ERROR **source • probability • possibility, risk • type, kind • magnitude • margin** *There are several potential sources of error arising from the nature of the data.* ◇ *This measure yields a margin of error that is under 6 per cent.*

erupt /ɪˈrʌpt/ *verb* **1** [I, T] (of a VOLCANO) to become active and throw out burning rocks, gases, etc; (of burning rocks, etc.) to be thrown out from a VOLCANO: *Since 1826 the volcano has reportedly erupted seventeen times.* ◇ **~ from sth** *The lava erupting from Kilauea volcano spread over a wide area.* ◇ **~ sth** *Small amounts of magma were periodically erupted.* **2** [I] to start happening, suddenly and violently SYN BREAK OUT: *Conflict erupted in the region in 1994.* ◇ **~ into sth** *It is widely feared that these tensions could erupt into war.*

erup·tion /ɪˈrʌpʃn/ *noun* **1** [C, U] an occasion when burning rocks, gases, etc. are thrown out from a volcano: *Large volcanic eruptions might lead to longer-term climatic change.* ◇ *This mountain has been in continuous eruption for over twenty years.* **2** [C] **~ (of sth)** the sudden start of sth unpleasant: *The president had appointed a commission to assess the eruption of racial violence in America's cities.*

es·cal·ate /ˈeskəleɪt/ *verb* [I, T] to become or make sth greater, worse, more serious, etc: *Power companies tend not to favour nuclear precisely because of concerns of escalating costs.* ◇ **~ into sth** *The end of the Cold War removed the threat of regional conflict escalating into nuclear war.* ◇ **~ sth** *Their efforts at control have often escalated tensions.* ■ **es·cal·ation** /ˌeskəˈleɪʃn/ *noun* [C, usually sing., U] **~ (of sth)** *An escalation of conflict can progress into actual physical violence.*

es·cape¹ /ɪˈskeɪp/ *verb* **1** [I] to get away from a place where you have been kept as a prisoner or not allowed to leave: *If they try to escape, they are usually captured by local police and returned to the work camp.* ◇ **~ from sb/sth** *The police are entitled to enter premises in order to recapture a person who has escaped from prison.* **2** [I, T] to get away from an unpleasant or dangerous situation: **~ (from sth)** *Hatching early can allow embryos to escape from predators of eggs.* ◇ **~ (into sth)** (*figurative*) *In these novels of provincial life, Eliot was not escaping into a rural idyll.* ◇ **~ sth** *The article emphasizes the institutional barriers to escaping poverty through education.* **3** [T, no passive] to avoid sth unpleasant or dangerous: **~ sth** *In Homer's 'Iliad', Aeneas escapes death in battle at the hands of Diomedes.* ◇ *It is difficult to escape the conclusion that we are living in an economy that is becoming more competitive.* ◇ **~ doing sth** *Few thinkers on culture can have escaped being accused of bias of some sort.* **4** [I] to suffer no harm or less harm than you would expect: **~ (with sth)** *Mayaguez was farther from the earthquake origin than other towns that escaped with less damage.* ◇ **+ adj.** *Only a small percentage of buildings escaped unscathed.* **5** [T, no passive] **~ sb/sth** to be forgotten or not noticed: *It is hard for any global brands to escape notice.* ◇ *This assumption is so widely accepted that it has largely escaped critical attention.* **6** [I] (of gases, liquids, etc.) to get out of a container, especially through a hole or crack: *If the seal is loose or damaged, it allows heat to escape.* ◇ **~ into sth** *CFCs are volatile compounds, used as refrigerants, which have escaped into the atmosphere.*

es·cape² /ɪˈskeɪp/ *noun* **1** [U, C] the act or a method of escaping from a place or an unpleasant or dangerous situation: **~ (from sth)** *A principal theme of Aeneas's life is close escape from danger.* ◇ *They were in Naples when they heard the news of Napoleon's escape from Elba.* ◇ *Groups of captive monkeys will kill a newcomer who has no means of escape.* ◇ **+ noun** *The Church became an escape route for peasants with a little Latin.* **2** [sing., U] **~ (for sb) (from sth)** a way of forgetting sth unpleasant or difficult for a short time: *The luxury hotel industry provides an escape for their consumers from their everyday lives.* **3** [C] **~ (of sth) (from sth) (into sth)** the fact of a liquid, gas, etc. coming out of a pipe or container by accident; the amount that comes out: *These systems involve sealing the landfill to prevent an escape of the gas into the surrounding soil.*

es·pe·cial·ly /ɪˈspeʃəli/ *adv.* (*abbr.* **esp.**) **1** very much; to a particular degree: *The last point the author makes is especially important.* ◇ *This essay will focus especially on India.* ◇ *Much criminal behaviour is unreported and this is especially true of violence within the home.* **2** more with one person or thing than with others; more in particular circumstances than in others SYN PARTICULARLY: *Much of the work involves caring for family members, especially young children.* ◇ *Feminist ideas have contributed to widespread social change, especially in the Western world.* **3** for a particular purpose, person, etc: *The book has maps made especially for it.*

E

WHICH WORD?

especially • specially

- **Especially** is more formal than **specially** and is very much more frequent in academic writing.
- **Especially** usually means particularly': *A professional appearance by staff is especially important in service industries such as health care.* ◇ *Especially in the east, the clergy began to wear special garments during the liturgy.* **Specially** is sometimes used with this meaning, but it is rather informal and should be avoided in academic writing.
- **Especially** and **specially** can both mean for a particular person, purpose, etc.', but **specially** is more frequent in this meaning: *a specially designed machine* ◇ *an instrument especially designed for use in younger age groups*

es·pouse /ɪˈspaʊz/ *verb* **~ sth** (*formal*) to give your support to a belief, policy or way of life: *The idea that most Americans espouse the same values and views is unsustainable.* ■ **es·pousal** /ɪˈspaʊzl/ *noun* [U, sing.] **~ of sth** *The activity for which Shotoku was best known was his espousal of Buddhism.*

essay /ˈeseɪ/ *noun* **1 ~ (on sth)** a short piece of writing by a student as part of a course of study: *Students wrote essays on such themes as comparison/contrast and persuasion.* **2 ~ (on sth)** a short piece of writing on a particular subject, written in order to be published: *He alludes to Herder's famous essay on the Scottish poet Ossian.* ◇ *In his essay 'On Liberty', John Stuart Mill provides a strong argument in defense of individual freedom against government intervention.* **3 ~ (in sth)** an attempt to do sth: *Johnson's various essays in poetry span his career.*

es·sence /ˈesns/ *noun* [U] **~ (of sth)** the most important quality or feature of sth, that makes it what it is: *The summary manages to capture the essence of the book.* ◇ *Values represent the very essence of any culture and society.* ◇ *That argument says that it is God's nature or essence to contain all perfect qualities.*
IDM **in ˈessence** in the most important and basic ways, without considering things that are less important: *The Bill was, in essence, the same as that of 1909.* **of the ˈessence** necessary and very important: *Time is of the essence in police investigations.*

es·sen·tial¹ /ɪˈsenʃl/ *adj.* **1** completely necessary; extremely important in a particular situation or for a particular activity SYN VITAL (1): *Making mistakes is an essential part of the learning process.* ◇ **~ to sth** *The well-being* of the family is still perceived as essential to the well-being of society. ◇ **~ for sth** *Most companies have a small number of customers who are essential for their survival.* ◇ **it is ~ to do sth** *It is essential to know exactly where and when particular genes are active.* ◇ **it is ~ that...** *It is essential that every member of the team is aware of their own responsibilities.* **2** [only before noun] connected with the most important aspect or basic nature of sb/sth SYN FUNDAMENTAL (1): *The form of war might change, but the essential nature of war could not.* ◇ *The argument is that there is no essential difference between humans and other kinds of animal.* **3** (of an AMINO ACID or FATTY ACID) required for normal growth but not produced in the body, and therefore necessary in the diet: *Essential amino acids and fatty acids, minerals and vitamins are also vital for health.*

▸ ESSENTIAL + NOUN **part, component • ingredient, element • property, feature, characteristic • aspect • factor • point • role, function • requirement, condition, prerequisite • information • tool • step • skill • nutrient • services** *Water is an essential ingredient for life.* ◇ *Fluency in English is an essential requirement of some high-profile jobs.*

▸ ADVERB + ESSENTIAL **absolutely** *It is absolutely essential that a good understanding of these concepts is achieved.*

▸ ESSENTIAL FOR + NOUN **development, growth • life • survival • viability • success** *Improved social and communications skills are essential for their future career development.*

THESAURUS

essential • crucial • critical • vital *adj.*

These words all describe sth that is extremely important and completely necessary because a particular situation or activity depends on it.

- to be essential/crucial/critical/vital **for/to/in** sth
- it is essential/crucial/critical/vital **that...**
- to be essential/crucial/critical/vital **to do sth**
- an essential/a crucial/a critical/a vital **role/point**
- an essential/a crucial/a vital **part/element/component/factor**
- a crucial/critical/vital **question/issue**
- **absolutely** essential/crucial/critical/vital

- **Essential** and **vital** can often be used in the same way; **essential** is typically used to state a fact or an opinion with authority; **vital** is used to try to persuade sb that a fact or an opinion is important; **vital** is less often used in negative statements: *Nitrates form an essential component within the nitrogen cycle.* ◇ *Sharing a common language is not always essential to a sense of ethnic community.* ◇ *Food is relatively 'culture bound', so local knowledge is vital to market success.*
- **Crucial** and **critical** can both be used to describe sth that is necessary to avoid a bad outcome; **critical** is often used to talk about more objective, technical matters in science or business; **crucial** can be used in more subjective contexts, especially when talking about an important time or stage in a process: *Mangrove trees are critical to the functioning of mangrove swamps as they stabilize sediments and filter the water.* ◇ *Many historians have suggested this was a crucial moment in the emancipation of women.*

es·sen·tial² /ɪˈsenʃl/ *noun* [usually pl.] **1** something that is needed in a particular situation or in order to do a particular thing: *They store food and other essentials that they require to survive.* **2 ~ (of sth)** an important basic fact or piece of knowledge about a subject: *Pudovkin enrolled in the State Cinema School where he learned the essentials of film-making.*

es·sen·tial·ly /ɪˈsenʃəli/ *adv.* used to emphasize the basic or true nature of a person or thing SYN BASICALLY, FUNDAMENTALLY: *Urban society is still considered essentially different from rural society.* ◇ *Gene frequencies remain essentially unchanged from one generation to the next.* ◇ *Essentially, this means that everyone should have equal access to health services.* ➲ language bank *at* BROADLY

es·tab·lish AWL /ɪˈstæblɪʃ/ *verb* **1 ~ sth** to start or create an organization, system or practice that will last for a long time SYN SET STH UP (1): *A coordinating committee was established to oversee the policy.* ◇ *The Australian Constitution of 1901 established a federal system of government.* ◇ *These experiments established the foundations of modern molecular genetics.* **2 ~ sth** to start having a relationship, especially a formal one, with another person, group or country: *Hawks and Grant had established a solid working relationship.* **3** to discover or find proof of the facts of a situation SYN ASCERTAIN: **~ sth** *A Board of Inquiry was convened to establish the facts of the case.* ◇ **~ that...** *Copernicus established that the earth went around the sun.* ◇ **~ what/how, etc...** *The incident must be investigated to establish what went wrong.* ◇ **it is established that...** *It had been established that all the claims were false.* ➲ thesaurus note *at* DETERMINE **4 ~ sth** to make people accept a principle, claim or custom: *Article 119 of the Treaty establishes the principle that men and women should receive equal pay for equal work.* **5 ~ sb/sth/yourself (in sth) (as sth)** to succeed in sth well enough to make people accept or respect you or make your future safe: *He had established himself as a scholar of exceptional promise.* ◇ *The fish is now firmly established in the south-eastern USA.*

▸ ESTABLISH + NOUN **system, procedure, mechanism • rules • standards • rights • conditions • framework • foundation • pattern • precedent • committee • network • programme • regime • institution • base • contract** *The UK was one of the first nations to establish rules for the operation of companies.* ◇ *Karamanlis moved rapidly to establish a new democratic regime.* | **relationship, connection, link, relations • rapport • trust** *Indian nationalists began to establish links with their Irish counterparts.* ◇ *It was important to establish a rapport with each interviewee.* | **relationship, connection, link, relation • facts • the truth • diagnosis • existence • validity • identity • cause • liability** *Her recent work has helped to establish the connection between personality and memory.* ◇ *A clinical examination will be required to establish a definitive diagnosis.* | **principle • criterion • reputation** *Businesses invest a great deal of time and resources establishing a reputation.*

▸ ADVERB + ESTABLISH **already, previously • long • quickly** *Several universities had already established ambitious research programmes of their own.* ◇ *Under these circumstances, previously established data may be used.* ◇ *The newly independent Ukrainian state quickly established good relations with Israel.* | **firmly • well • fully • successfully • clearly** *Soon this idea was firmly established within the major European states.* ◇ *In Britain, about 10 per cent of introduced species have successfully established themselves.* | **newly, recently • formally** *The recent increase in crime poses a threat to the stability of newly established democracies in Latin America.*

es·tab·lished AWL /ɪˈstæblɪʃt/ *adj.* [only before noun] **1** respected or given official status because of having existed or been used for a long time: *The post-1945 Federal Republic of Germany has succeeded in becoming an established democracy.* ➲ *see also* WELL ESTABLISHED **2** (of a Church or religion) recognized by the state as the national Church or religion: *The influence of a religion upon a state does not depend on whether it is an established religion or not.* ◇ *At that time 90 per cent of the British people belonged to the established Church.* **3** (of a person) well known and respected in a job that they have been doing for a long time: *Hubble was by now an established astronomer.*

es·tab·lish·ment AWL /ɪˈstæblɪʃmənt/ *noun* **1** [U] **~ (of sth)** the act of starting or creating sth that is meant to last for a long time: *The Directive requires the establishment of a system of strict protection for listed species.* **2** (*usually* **the Establishment**) [sing.+ sing./pl. v.] (*often disapproving*) the people in a society or a profession who have influence and power and who usually do not support change: *Many early radicals were now respected members of the Establishment they had once attacked.* ◇ *the political/religious/military establishment* **3** [C] (*formal*) a business organization or public institution: *Educational establishments should work in partnership with outside agencies to design and deliver smoking prevention activities.*

es·tate AWL /ɪˈsteɪt/ *noun* **1** a large area of land in the country, usually with a large house, owned by one person, family or organization: *He died some weeks later at his country estate.* **2** an area of land where coffee, rubber, GRAPES or other crops are grown: *He owned two estates producing coffee and cotton.* **3** all the money and property owned by a particular person, especially everything that is left when they die: *She left her estate to her nieces and nephews.* **4** (*BrE*) an area of land with a lot of modern houses of the same type on it: *The study was conducted in a Catholic housing estate in West Belfast.* ➲ *see also* REAL ESTATE

es·teem¹ /ɪˈstiːm/ *noun* [U] (*formal*) great respect and admiration; a good opinion of sb: *She was held in high esteem by her colleagues.* ➲ *see also* SELF-ESTEEM

es·teem² /ɪˈstiːm/ *verb* [usually passive] (not used in the progressive tenses) (*formal*) to respect and admire sb/sth very much: **be esteemed (by sb)** *Many of these qualities are esteemed by managers.* ◇ **highly ~** *a highly esteemed scientist*

ester /ˈestə(r)/ *noun* (*chemistry*) a sweet-smelling substance that is formed when an ORGANIC acid reacts with an alcohol with the loss of water: **+ noun** *Ester hydrolysis occurs when animal fat is heated with alkali to form soap.*

es·thet·ic (*NAmE*) = AESTHETIC¹, AESTHETIC²

es·ti·mate¹ AWL /ˈestɪmeɪt/ *verb* [often passive] to approximately calculate or judge the value, number, quantity or extent of sth: **~ sth** *Often it is not possible to estimate the probability of a possible catastrophe.* ◇ **~ sth at sth** *The world population was estimated at 500 million in 1650.* ◇ **~ sth to do sth** *The London 2012 Olympics was estimated to cost £24 billion.* ◇ **~ (that)...** *Friends of the Earth has estimated that half a billion tonnes of carbon dioxide were emitted by aircraft into the atmosphere in 2006.* ◇ **it is estimated (that)...** *It is estimated that over 40% of 15- and 16-year-olds have used illicit drugs.* ◇ **~ how many/long, etc...** *Such monitoring can estimate how many people see an advertisement.*

> **WORD FAMILY**
> estimate *verb, noun*
> estimation *noun*
> overestimate *verb, noun*
> overestimation *noun*
> underestimate *verb, noun*
> underestimation *noun*

▸ ESTIMATE + NOUN **number • rate • size, magnitude • cost • value • time • age • distance • length • frequency • prevalence • ratio, proportion • parameters • probability, risk • effect • impact • model • equation • coefficient** *For example, in Beijing, we estimate the car ownership rate to be 23%.* ◇ *They could not estimate the effect of reductions in risky behaviours on transmission rates of the virus.*

▸ ADVERB + ESTIMATE **accurately, precisely • reliably • roughly • directly • simultaneously • separately • jointly • empirically • subjectively** *The molecular mass of proteins in the samples can be roughly estimated.*

▸ ESTIMATE + ADVERB **accurately • directly • separately, independently • simultaneously** *One can always discuss the extent to which the structural models have been estimated accurately.*

es·ti·mate² AWL /ˈestɪmət/ *noun* an approximate calculation or judgement of the value, number, quantity or extent of sth: *These numbers are at best very rough estimates.* ◇ **~ of sth** *Participants in the study were asked to provide estimates of time spent on various activities.* ◇ *The rise in temperatures is likely to be in the range 2–4.5°C with a best estimate of 3°C.*

▸ ADJECTIVE + ESTIMATE **good • best • accurate, precise • reliable • reasonable • realistic • unbiased • biased • rough • high • low • conservative • initial • recent • current • empirical • quantitative** *The Quick Test gives a reliable estimate of intelligence.* ◇ *Even a conservative estimate suggests that the numbers are likely to rise considerably.*

▸ NOUN + ESTIMATE **parameter • prevalence • coefficient** *Prevalence estimates were higher in children of mothers who were heavy smokers during pregnancy.*

▸ VERB + ESTIMATE **provide, present, give • yield • produce, generate • obtain, derive • make, calculate • use • base ~ on • report, show • bias • compare** *This approach yields dramatically lower estimates.* ◇ *More accurate estimates could have been obtained using these more advanced techniques.*

▸ ESTIMATE + VERB **vary • range • suggest** *Current estimates of when this happened range from 35 million years to just 30 000 years ago.* ◇ *Estimates suggest that about 1 million out of a total population of 2.1 million were killed.*

▸ ESTIMATE OF + NOUN **number • rate • size, magnitude • cost • value • age • prevalence • incidence, frequency • ratio, proportion • parameters • probability, risk • variance • effect • impact** *Estimates of the number of American Muslims vary significantly.*

es·ti·ma·tion AWL /ˌestɪˈmeɪʃn/ *noun* **1** [C, U] **~ (of sth)** an approximate calculation of the value, number, quantity or extent of sth: *A rough estimation can be made of the effect of a national campaign.* ◇ *There are insufficient cases in either Scotland or Wales to allow estimation of possible regional variations.* **2** [sing.] a judgement or opinion about the value or quality of sb/sth: *According to his estimation, the level of inequality in England was high.* ◇ **in sb's ~** *She also identified two locations where, in her estimation, the effects were greatest.*

es·tu·ary /ˈestʃuəri/ *noun* (*pl.* **-ies**) the wide part of a river where it flows into the sea: *Estuaries have an ecology that is very different from the adjacent freshwater or coastal systems.*

et al. /ˌet ˈæl/ *abbr.* and others (used especially in referring to academic books and articles that have more than one author) (from Latin 'et alii/alia'): *They used an example given by Bahl et al.*

etc. /ˌet ˈsetərə; ˌɪt ˈsetərə/ *abbr.* used at the end of a list to show that there are other things that you could have mentioned (the abbreviation for 'et cetera'): *The data are used in statistics, medical research, direct mailing, etc.*

eter·nal /ɪˈtɜːnl; *NAmE* ɪˈtɜːrnl/ *adj.* without an end; existing or continuing forever: *Eos forgot to ask that Tithonus be given eternal youth.* ◇ *They claim that the morals they preach are eternal truths.* ■ **eter·nal·ly** *adv.*: *According to Plato, the soul will exist eternally after death.*

etha·nol /ˈeθənɒl; *NAmE* ˈeθənɔːl; ˈeθənɑːl/ *noun* [U] (*chemistry*) the type of alcohol in alcoholic drinks, also used as a fuel or SOLVENT: *The yeast cells were observed and fixed in 70% ethanol for 1 hour.* ◇ **+ noun** *World ethanol production is dominated by the USA and Brazil.*

ethic AWL /ˈeθɪk/ *noun* **1 ethics** [pl.] moral principles that control or influence a person's behaviour: *Much of the discussion of public health ethics has focused on the*

E

distribution of scarce resources. ◇ *Many global businesses have a code of ethics under which they do business.* ◇ **the ~ of (doing) sth** *The NHS reforms raised issues about the ethics of charging high prices within a public health care system.* ◇ **+ noun** *The study was approved by the research ethics committee at the University Hospitals of Geneva.* **2** [sing.] a system of moral principles or rules of behaviour: *The Puritans established a colony with a coherent social, economic and religious ethic.* ◇ *High levels of productivity were maintained through a strong work ethic among members.* **3 ethics** [U] the branch of philosophy that deals with moral principles: *This research has been guided by the relevant literature in theoretical and applied ethics.*

eth·ic·al AWL /ˈeθɪkl/ *adj.* **1** connected with beliefs and principles about what is right and wrong: *Doctors have an ethical and legal responsibility to avoid gender discrimination.* ◇ *Rapid advances in technology and science have given rise to ethical dilemmas in health care.* **2** morally correct or acceptable: *The bank limits its investments to a list of companies selected for their ethical behaviour.* ◇ **~ to do sth** *There is no consensus on whether it is ethical to enrol adolescents in clinical trials.*

▸ ETHICAL + NOUN **issue, question, consideration • dimension, perspective • concern, dilemma, challenge • implications • reasoning • justification • judgement • approval, clearance • standing • responsibility, obligation • imperative • principles, values • standards, norms, guidelines • framework, code** *Ethical issues are nowadays more central to discussions about research than ever before.* ◇ *A coherent ethical framework is needed as a foundation for policymaking in public health.* | **conduct, behaviour • investment** *Procedures were laid down for ensuring the ethical conduct of all biomedical research.*

eth·ic·al·ly AWL /ˈeθɪkli/ *adv.* **1** in a way that is connected with beliefs and principles about what is right and wrong: *The research was conducted in an ethically sensitive manner.* ◇ *Of course, it is ethically unacceptable to deny life-sustaining treatment to elderly people.* **2** in a way that is morally correct or acceptable: *In 2000, the UN appealed to businesses to act ethically in the new global economy.*

eth·nic AWL /ˈeθnɪk/ *adj.* connected with or belonging to a race or people that shares a cultural tradition: *The Roman elite believed that every ethnic group had its own gods who were worthy of honour.* ◇ *ethnic background/origin/identity/diversity* ◇ *minority ethnic communities/populations* ◇ *84% of the population are ethnic Vietnamese.* ◇ *The community was split by sectarian and ethnic violence.* ■ **eth·nic·al·ly** /ˈeθnɪkli/ *adv.*: *In Brent, the most ethnically diverse area in the UK, non-white ethnic groups make up 55% of the population.* ◇ *Most Hong Kong residents were ethnically Chinese and therefore obtained Chinese nationality.*

eth·ni·city AWL /eθˈnɪsəti/ *noun* (*pl.* **-ies**) [U, C] the fact or state of belonging to a social group that has a shared national or cultural tradition: *Identities such as race, ethnicity and class significantly influence how individuals approach these problems.* ◇ *Teens of all races and ethnicities idolize pop stars.*

ˌethnic miˈnority *noun* a group of people from a particular culture or race living in a country where the main group is of a different culture or race: *Besides this large cultural diversity among ethnic minorities, Brussels is also composed of two mainstream groups.* ◇ **+ noun** *an ethnic minority background/community/group*

eth·nog·raph·er /eθˈnɒɡrəfə(r); *NAmE* eθˈnɑːɡrəfər/ *noun* a person who studies different races and cultures: *Ethnographers are typically immersed in a social setting for a long time.*

eth·nog·raphy /eθˈnɒɡrəfi; *NAmE* eθˈnɑːɡrəfi/ *noun* (*pl.* **-ies**) [U, C] the scientific description of different peoples and cultures; a particular study of a different people or culture: *It is a classic piece of what anthropologists call scientific ethnography.* ◇ **~ of sth** *Markham's (1998) approach to an ethnography of life on the Internet involved interviews.* ■ **ethno·graph·ic** /ˌeθnəˈɡræfɪk/ *adj.*: *Europeans commonly used ethnographic labels that oversimplified African identity groups.*

ethos /ˈiːθɒs; *NAmE* ˈiːθɑːs/ *noun* [sing.] **~ (of sth)** the moral ideas and attitudes that belong to a particular group, society or activity: *Traditionally, the ethos of academic research has been different from that of industrial research.* ◇ *The general opinion was that the volunteer ethos was not something that could be taught.*

eti·ology (*NAmE*) = AETIOLOGY

eu·kary·ote /juːˈkæriəʊt *NAmE* juːˈkærioʊt/ *noun* (*biology*) any ORGANISM consisting of cells in which the GENETIC material is contained within a NUCLEUS: *Multicellular eukaryotes evolved at the beginning of the Cambrian period 570 million years ago.* ■ **eu·kary·ot·ic** /juːkæriˈɒtɪk/ *adj.*: *The nucleus, as in other eukaryotic cells, contains the DNA and its associated proteins.*

euro /ˈjʊərəʊ; *NAmE* ˈjʊroʊ/ *noun* (*symb.* **€**) (*pl.* **euros** or **euro**) the unit of money of many countries in the European Union: *The transaction involves billions of euros.* ◇ *Fears were raised that the euro could collapse.*

evade /ɪˈveɪd/ *verb* **1 ~ sth** to escape or avoid sb/sth: *The ability to evade predators is important for many animals.* ◇ *Small groups of intellectuals mastered the art of evading censorship.* **2 ~ sth** to find a way of not doing sth, especially sth that legally or morally you should do: *There was evidence that the defendant had tried to evade payment.* ◇ *Self-employment is sometimes used by employers to evade legal obligations.* **3 ~ sth** to avoid dealing with or talking about sth: *He exaggerated and lied, and evaded difficult issues.* ➲ *see also* EVASION

evalu·ate AWL /ɪˈvæljueɪt/ *verb* to form an opinion of the amount, value or quality of sth after thinking about it carefully SYN ASSESS (1): **~ sth** *A study by Allan (2010) evaluated the effectiveness of the traffic safety campaign.* ◇ **~ whether/how, etc...** *The framework helped in evaluating whether cash flow problems could be safely addressed by increasing borrowing.* ■ **evalu·ative** AWL /ɪˈvæljuətɪv/ *adj.*: *In consumer markets, evaluative criteria are thought to be based on social issues and level of usefulness of the product.* **evalu·ative·ly** *adv.*: *Students need to learn to think evaluatively.*

▸ EVALUATE + NOUN **effect, impact • outcome • consequences • progress • potential • option • evidence • programme • significance • effectiveness, efficacy • efficiency • performance • quality • validity • accuracy • extent** *A few studies have evaluated the effect of iron depletion on metabolic parameters.* ◇ *Statistical indicators were used to evaluate the performance of the two chosen models.*

evalu·ation AWL /ɪˌvæljuˈeɪʃn/ *noun* [U, C] the act of forming an opinion of the amount, value or quality of sth after thinking about it carefully: *However, the technique is not practised widely and requires further evaluation.* ◇ **~ of sth** *A systematic and rigorous evaluation of the theory was carried out.*

▸ ADJECTIVE + EVALUATION **careful • rigorous, thorough, detailed • comprehensive, full • systematic • proper • initial • formal • external • subjective • positive • negative • overall • comparative • critical • diagnostic • formative • economic** *They claim literary criticism should be based on scientific methods rather than on subjective evaluations.* ◇ *The discussion includes a critical evaluation of the documentary sources.*

▸ NOUN + EVALUATION **impact • performance • job** *All employees are subject to performance evaluation and monitoring.*
▸ VERB + EVALUATION **conduct, undertake, perform, carry out • require** *One year after the start-up of the project, an evaluation was conducted.*
▸ EVALUATION + NOUN **criteria • method, methodology, procedure** *The project assessment was based on three main evaluation criteria.*

LANGUAGE BANK

RESEARCH STUDY

Making an evaluation of your study

- **Achievements** of the study (positive markers):
– *This study **provides evidence** that...*
– *This work has **contributed to a number of key issues** in the field.*
- **Limitations** of the study (negative markers):
– *The present study is a **small scale exploratory** work...*
– ***Several limitations** should be noted...*
- **Combine negative and positive** markers in one sentence to give a balanced assessment:
– *Although this research is **somewhat limited in scope**, its findings can **provide a basis for** future studies.*
– ***Despite the limitations**, findings from the present study can help us understand...*

evap·or·ate /ɪˈvæpəreɪt/ *verb* **1** [I, T] to change from a liquid into a gas, especially steam; to change a liquid into a gas: *A comparable change in volume occurs when any liquid evaporates.* ◇ **~ sth** *The energy originally used to evaporate the water is released as latent heat.* **2** [I] to stop existing: *The threat to essential services largely evaporated as soon as the oil tanker drivers' dispute was resolved.*

evap·or·ation /ɪˌvæpəˈreɪʃn/ *noun* [U] **1** the process of changing from a liquid into a gas, especially steam: *Lids were placed on each bucket to prevent evaporation.* ◇ **~ of sth** *Evaporation of the solvent leaves a thin film of protein molecules.* **2 ~ (of sth)** the act of stopping existing: *The sudden evaporation of support for the Liberal Democrats is one of the mysteries of the election.*

eva·sion /ɪˈveɪʒn/ *noun* **1** [U] the act of not doing sth, especially sth that legally or morally you should do: *He was fortunate to escape a more serious charge of tax evasion.* ◇ **~ of sth** *Evasion of the call-up for military service was widespread.* **2** [C] a statement that sb makes that avoids dealing with sth or talking about sth honestly and directly: *The interviewer needs to be alert to evasions and vague replies.* **3** [U] **~ (of sth)** the act of escaping or avoiding sb/sth: *The fish's body shape improves its evasion of predators.* ➲ *see also* EVADE

even¹ /ˈiːvn/ *adv.* **1** used to emphasize sth unexpected or surprising: *No one cared or even noticed.* ◇ *However, even the US system can be improved.* ◇ *The accounts of children are ambiguous, at times even contradictory.* ◇ *Southern white politicians refused even to recognize the existence of blacks.* **2** used when you are comparing things, to make the comparison stronger: *He accepted a post with even greater prestige.* ◇ *Mobile phone use grew even faster.* ◇ *This may cause staff even more stress.* **3** used to introduce a more exact description of sb/sth: *The reforms place an enormous challenge, or burden even, on primary care providers.*
IDM **even as** just at the same time as sb does sth or as sth else happens: *Even as the Roman Empire declined in Europe, the taste for spices continued.* **even if** despite the possibility, fact or belief that; no matter whether: *Even if you do not succeed, trying is empowering.* ◇ *Many American politicians were isolationists, even if President Wilson was not.* **ˌeven ˈnow/ˈthen 1** despite what has/had happened: *Even now we may be doing irreversible damage to our environment.* ◇ *The problem was not solved until later, and even then not completely.* **2** at this or that exact moment: *A new report is even now in preparation.* **ˌeven ˈso** despite that: *They may not ever meet an English-speaking person, but even so, they take English classes.*

even² /ˈiːvn/ *adj.* **1** equal in number, amount or value; shared equally: *There was a relatively even balance of power between the government and the opposition.* ◇ *In the US, increases in unemployment have typically led to a less even distribution of income.* ◇ *The Liberal Democrats had a relatively even spread of support across the country.* OPP UNEVEN **2** that can be divided exactly by two: *Between successive pulses of the same polarity, an even number of 0s must occur.* ◇ *A sum of odd numbers can only be even if there is an even number of them.* OPP ODD (1)
IDM **break ˈeven** to complete a piece of business without either losing money or making a profit: *A bookseller would normally have to sell about 60 per cent of a first edition of a play to break even.* **have an even ˈchance (of doing sth)** to be equally likely to do or not do sth: *If a fair coin is thrown without bias, then it has an even chance of landing on heads or tails.*

even·ly /ˈiːvnli/ *adv.* **1** in a smooth or regular way: *Apply adequate padding smoothly and evenly.* ◇ *The hydrogen atoms are all evenly spaced.* **2** with equal amounts for each person or in each place: *If wealth were exactly evenly distributed, then each 10% of the population would possess exactly 10% of the total wealth.* ◇ *The effects of cuts are not likely to be spread evenly across the sector.*

event /ɪˈvent/ *noun* a thing that happens, especially sth important: *The patients tended to experience these traumatic events as very frightening and threatening.* ◇ *Schaefer's study focuses on extreme rainfall events.* ◇ **~ of sth** *In his diary, he recorded the events of the day.* ◇ **a sequence/series/chain of events** *Gene action sets in motion an important sequence of events within the embryo.* ◇ **the course of events** *The assassination of the king changed the course of events dramatically.*
IDM **after the eˈvent** (*BrE*) after sth has happened: *Most accounts of the revolution were collected long after the event and could not be directly verified.* **in ˈany event | at ˈall events** used to emphasize or show that sth is true or will happen despite other circumstances SYN IN ANY CASE: *Contesting a petition is costly and, in any event, is unlikely to succeed.* **in the eˈvent** when a situation actually happened: *The ACE computer had serious problems in development but in the event it proved to be a commercial success.* **in the event of sth | in the event that sth happens** if sth happens: *The father stated he did not want resuscitation in the event of heart failure.* ➲ *more at* TURN²

ˌeven ˈthough *conj.* despite the fact that SYN ALTHOUGH (1): *He was sentenced to a year in prison even though he was 78 years old.* ◇ *Even though there is no government, the EU undertakes the sort of activities that governments traditionally have done.* ➲ grammar note *at* DESPITE

even·tual AWL /ɪˈventʃuəl/ *adj.* [only before noun] happening at the end of a period of time or of a process: *A paper produced by Amnesty International significantly influenced the eventual outcome of the negotiations.* ◇ *Such a bomb would cause 500 000 immediate fatalities, plus an eventual 200 000 cancer deaths due to radiation.*

even·tu·al·ity AWL /ɪˌventʃuˈæləti/ *noun* (*pl.* -ies) something that may possibly happen, especially sth unpleasant: *The instructions must cover every possible eventuality.* ◇ *They knew the town was likely to be destroyed, so plans were drawn up in preparation for such an eventuality.*

even·tu·al·ly AWL /ɪˈventʃuəli/ *adv.* at the end of a period of time or a series of events: *He received a 30-year sentence and eventually died in prison.* ◇ *For patients with HIV, continued damage to the immune system eventually leads to the development of AIDS.* ◇ *Eventually, the investment paid off.* HELP Use **finally** for the last in a list of things: *Finally, it should be noted that these findings are largely exploratory.* ◇ ~~*Eventually, it should be noted that...*~~

ever /ˈevə(r)/ *adv.* **1** used in negative sentences and questions, or sentences with *if* to mean 'at any time': *The truth could be very unsettling if it ever got out.* ◇ *Is it possible for teachers ever to really 'know' their students?* ◇ **hardly ~** *Peter hardly ever goes to the doctor himself.* ◇ **if ~** *The chapter focused on children who rarely, if ever, lose control.* **2** used for emphasis when you are comparing things: *Far more couples divorce than ever before.* ◇ *The country was experiencing its worst ever economic crisis.* **3** all the time or every time; always: *The need for funding has become ever greater.* ◇ *Horsten, ever the prudent businessman, ceased all political engagement.* ◇ *To cope with today's ever-changing environment, firms are becoming more flexible and adaptable.* ◇ *Farmers had to produce enough to insure society against the ever-present risk of harvest failure.* ➲ *see also* FOREVER (1)

IDM **ever since (...)** continuously since the time mentioned: *Lawrence had experienced tension with his stepfather ever since his mother married him.* ◇ *Ever since the Industrial Revolution, many approaches have been tried to maximize industrial productivity.* ◇ *This observation, first made in 1965, seems to have held ever since.* **only ever** used for saying that sth only happens in a particular situation: *Learning only ever occurs in a particular sociocultural context.*

every /ˈevri/ *det.* **1** used with singular nouns to refer to all the members of a group of things or people: *Every child deserves a decent education.* ◇ *Neil checks his email every time he goes on the Internet.* ◇ *Their every move is recorded on film.* ◇ **~ single** *Now she meditates every single day.* ◇ **~ one (of sth)** *Every one of the 13 villages was destroyed.* **2** all possible: *Every effort was made to make it a reality.* ◇ *He had every reason to be proud.* ◇ *Students are given every opportunity to show their creativity.* **3** used to say how often sth happens or is done or how common sth is: *Women are screened for cervical cancer every 3 years.* ◇ *Cuba has about 1 car for every 29 people.* ➲ grammar note *at* EACH

IDM **every other** if sth happens **every other** day, night, etc. it happens on one day, etc. but not the next SYN ALTERNATE[1] (2): *He trained in the gym every other day.*

every·day /ˈevrideɪ/ *adj.* [only before noun] used or happening every day or regularly; ordinary: *In some societies, alcohol is part of everyday life.* ◇ *Linguistic theory was becoming far removed from people's everyday experience of what language is.*

every·one /ˈevriwʌn/ (*also* **every·body** /ˈevribɒdi; *NAmE* ˈevribɑːdi; ˈevribʌdi/) *pron.* every person; all people: *Everyone has to live somewhere.* ◇ *Not everyone agrees.* ◇ *The events of September 11, 2001 affected everyone's views.* ◇ **~ else** *Roman citizens enjoyed the same wide religious choices as everyone else.*

every·thing /ˈevriθɪŋ/ *pron.* (with a singular verb) **1** all things: *Everything had to be kept in its proper place.* ◇ *He could not tell them everything.* ◇ *It is unrealistic to think that everything will always go well.* ◇ **~ else** *It is a standard against which everything else is judged.* **2** the situation at a particular time; life generally: *Everything is going well.* ◇ *Then, in May 1940, everything changed.* **3** (*rather informal*) the most important thing: *Money isn't everything.* ◇ *Her children are everything to her.*

every·where /ˈevriweə(r); *NAmE* ˈevriwer/ *adv., pron., conj.* in, to or at every place; all places: *We see these images everywhere.* ◇ *People everywhere should be encouraged to make low-carbon choices.* ◇ *Everywhere they went people recognized them.* ◇ **~ else** *The figures show a gap in incomes between Europe and everywhere else.*

LANGUAGE BANK

Discussing evidence

In academic writing, it is often necessary to say what evidence there is to support your point or to support a theory.

- **There is clear evidence** that...
- **There is little/no evidence** that...
- **It is clear from** the data/research/results **that...**
- **Evidence suggests** that...
- the study/research/experiment **demonstrates** that...
- the study/evidence/model **proves** that...
- the data/findings/results **reveal/show...**
- the data/findings/results **support...**
- the findings/results **contradict...**

– *There is clear evidence that, for many students, adolescence is a period of declining motivation.*
– *There is little evidence to support the use of compression bandages in the acute phase.*
– *It is clear from the data that a man who applied to the university was more likely to be accepted than a woman.*
– *Available evidence suggests that smaller sections of the fault can rupture as well.*
– *Epidemiological studies have demonstrated that migrants tend to display cancer rates specific to their new adopted country.*
– *They published a rigorous study that proved that the mutations to resistance were spontaneous.*
– *Research has revealed the dropout rate to be much higher than the official one.*
– *The indirect and direct effects model was supported by the data.*
– *The thesis has clear theoretical limitations and is contradicted by the empirical evidence.*

THESAURUS

evidence ◆ **proof** ◆ **support** ◆ **demonstration** *noun*
These are all words for the facts or signs that make you believe that sth is true.

- evidence/proof/a demonstration **of** sth
- support **for** sth
- (a) **further/clear** evidence/proof/support/demonstration
- (a) **scientific/convincing** evidence/proof/demonstration
- **little/strong/empirical** evidence/support
- to **provide** evidence/proof/support/a demonstration
- to **find/have/give/offer** evidence/proof/support

- **Proof** shows that sth is true in a way that no one can argue against; **evidence** makes you believe that sth is true, but can be open to debate: *Current studies fall far short of definitive proof.* ◇ *Some areas show relatively little evidence of a downward trend.*
- **Support** helps to show that an argument or a theory is true or valid, in the form of research findings, facts or arguments: *These findings offer support for the idea that decreased performance is due to a threat to social identity.*
- A **demonstration** is the act of giving proof or evidence of sth, sometimes in a practical way: *This classic experiment is often cited as a demonstration of how priming works.*

evi·dence[1] AWL /ˈevɪdəns/ *noun* **1** [U, C] the facts, signs or objects that make you believe that sth is true: **~ (of sth)** *There is clear evidence of culture in chimpanzees.* ◇ **~ for sth** *These studies have been widely cited as evidence for the*

WORD FAMILY
evidence *noun, verb*
evident *adj.*
evidently *adv.*
evidential *adj.*

existence of intelligence in pigeons. ◇ **~ against sth** *They wanted to find evidence against a purely materialist view of human nature.* ◇ **on... ~** *On the available evidence, it seems reasonable to conclude that...* ◇ **~ (that)...** *Owens found no evidence that banning the sale of alcohol increased the rate of violence in the United States.* ◇ **~-based** *The advice on adult nutrition provided at the centre was not evidence-based.* **2** [U] the information that is used in court to try to prove sth: *Due to a lack of evidence, the case against her was dropped.* ◇ **give ~ (against sb)** *By 1830, slaves were allowed to give evidence in court.* IDM **(be) in ˈevidence** present and clearly seen: *There is little brand loyalty from customers in evidence in the market today.*

▸ ADJECTIVE + EVIDENCE **recent • current, existing • available • preliminary • considerable, substantial • increasing, growing, mounting • ample, abundant • further, additional • conflicting • strong, good, robust, solid, clear • conclusive, overwhelming • convincing, compelling • direct • indirect • sufficient • insufficient** *These results provide strong evidence for relative decline in benefits accruing to workers.* ◇ *In his view, there is no convincing evidence for consciousness in other species.* | **empirical, experimental • scientific • statistical • anecdotal • documentary • archaeological • historical** *There is no firm empirical evidence available on how monetary union has affected unemployment in Europe.* ◇ *It is only relatively recently that we have clear scientific evidence of the unity of the human race.* | **sufficient • insufficient • incriminating • circumstantial • expert** *There was sufficient evidence for the jury to find that the golf balls belonged to the golf club.* ◇ *The courts place heavy reliance on expert evidence which is usually crucial to the outcome of an action.*

▸ VERB + EVIDENCE **have • provide • present • submit, offer • cite, adduce • contain • produce, yield • show, reveal • constitute • gather, collect • find • obtain • summarize • consider, examine, discuss, review • evaluate, assess • interpret • need, require • lack** *The Nordhaus study produced solid evidence that energy consumption was driven by the desire for energy services.* ◇ *In this paper, we review the evidence that non-human vertebrates choose mates based on their cognitive ability.*

▸ EVIDENCE + VERB **exist • emerge • come from • accumulate • be lacking • show, demonstrate • suggest, indicate, point to** *The little evidence regarding historical trends in national culture suggests that cultural change is very slow (Schwartz et al., 2000).*

▸ EVIDENCE TO + VERB **suggest, indicate • support • show, prove, demonstrate** *There is no textual evidence to support this interpretation of Turing's work.*

evi·dence² AWL /ˈevɪdəns/ *verb* [usually passive] to prove or show sth; to be evidence of sth: **be evidenced by sth** *The low cancer risk in these organisms is evidenced by the fact that...* ◇ **as evidenced by sth** *Disasters can also have devastating impacts in the more developed world, as evidenced by the hurricane that hit New Orleans in 2005.*

evi·dent AWL /ˈevɪdənt/ *adj.* clear; easily seen SYN OBVIOUS (1): *The spherical symmetry of the wave function was immediately evident.* ◇ **~ (that)...** *It has become evident that the provision of irrigation alone does not necessarily guarantee results.* ◇ **~ to sb (that)...** *It seems that the underlying purpose of the questionnaire was not evident to many respondents.* ◇ **~ in/from sth** *The Hellenization of Egyptian religion is evident in an inscription from the city of Cyme.* ➲ *see also* SELF-EVIDENT ➲ thesaurus note *at* CLEAR¹

evi·den·tial AWL /ˌevɪˈdenʃl/ *adj.* [usually before noun] providing or connected with evidence: *There is no evidential basis for this assumption.*

evi·dent·ly AWL /ˈevɪdəntli/ *adv.* **1** in a way that can be clearly seen or understood SYN OBVIOUSLY (2): *The authorial commentary of 'Middlemarch' evidently presents the personal views of George Eliot throughout.* ◇ *Nowadays, apart from examples of evidently erroneous use, two meanings of the term persist.* **2** based on the available evidence: *Infections, tumours and other symptoms were noted. Evidently, a new form of immunodeficiency had appeared.* ◇ *Evidently, extreme life events have health consequences, which may last for a prolonged period of time.*

evil¹ /ˈiːvl; ˈiːvɪl/ *noun* **1** [U] a force that causes bad things to happen; morally bad behaviour: *Much of the poem is framed around the idea of a vast struggle between the principles of good and evil.* ◇ *They believed that God was soon to overthrow the forces of evil to bring in his kingdom.* OPP GOOD² (2) **2** [C, usually pl.] a bad or harmful thing; the bad effect of sth: *Education is seen as a means to eliminate such social evils as child marriage.* ◇ **~ of sth** *He felt obliged to deplore the evils of capitalism.* IDM *see* LESSER, NECESSARY

E

evil² /ˈiːvl; ˈiːvɪl/ *adj.* **1** (of people) enjoying harming others; morally bad and cruel: *He was portrayed as the innocent victim of evil men.* **2** having a harmful effect on people; morally bad: *Belief in evil spirits and witchcraft was widespread.*

evoca·tive /ɪˈvɒkətɪv; *NAmE* ɪˈvɑːkətɪv/ *adj.* making you think of or remember a strong image or feeling, in a pleasant way: *Many words have evocative power.* ◇ **~ of sth** *The building's interiors are highly evocative of past centuries.*

evoke /ɪˈvəʊk; *NAmE* ɪˈvoʊk/ *verb* **~ sth** to bring a feeling, a memory or an image into your mind: *The word 'home' evokes extraordinarily strong emotions.* ◇ *The mall is filled with street furniture and vendors evoking the feel of a European marketplace.* ■ **evo·ca·tion** /ˌiːvəʊˈkeɪʃn; *NAmE* ˌiːvoʊˈkeɪʃn/ *noun* [C, U] **~ (of sth)** *'Machine Dreams' is devoted to the vivid evocation of small town life in West Virginia.*

evo·lu·tion AWL /ˌiːvəˈluːʃn; ˌevəˈluːʃn/ *noun* [U] **1** (*biology*) the gradual development of living things over many years as they adapt to changes in their environment: *Darwinian evolution is the single most important idea in the study of living things.* ◇ *Organisms carry in themselves the reflection of the whole biological evolution of which they are the end product.* ◇ **the ~ of sth** *The evolution of breeding strategies is directly linked to that of gene flow among populations.* **2** the gradual development of sth: *In the sequence of cultural evolution, the emergence of a leisure class coincides with the beginning of ownership.* ◇ *The field evidence can be used as the basis of a model of landscape evolution.* ◇ **the ~ of sth** *Pakistan offers the most sustained example of the evolution of a modern Islamic republic.*

▸ ADJECTIVE + EVOLUTION **gradual • rapid • progressive • recent • long-term • future** *There has been a gradual evolution of issues in the area of ageing, work and retirement.* | **adaptive • convergent • biological • human • organic • molecular** *The evolution of gene families is a key mechanism for the adaptive evolution of organisms.* ◇ *Throughout human evolution, social relationships have provided the fundamental basis for human adaptation.* | **cultural • historical** *Hudson (1994) traced the historical evolution of one of the world's pre-eminent agricultural regions.*

▸ VERB + EVOLUTION **undergo • shape, drive • influence • study, investigate, examine • trace, track • understand • explain** *The concept has undergone considerable evolution since Lovelock first introduced it.*

evo·lu·tion·ary AWL /ˌiːvəˈluːʃənri; ˌevəˈluːʃənri; *NAmE* ˌiːvəˈluːʃəneri; ˌevəˈluːʃəneri/ *adj.* connected with evolution; connected with gradual development and change: *Contemporary single-celled organisms have undergone hundreds of millions of years of evolutionary change.* ◇ *The evolutionary design innovations in South Korea's nuclear plants are a significant factor in the analysis.*

■ **evo·lu·tion·ar·ily** *adv.*: *Drosophila belongs to an evolutionarily advanced group of insects.*

▸ EVOLUTIONARY + NOUN **theory • thinking • perspective • approach • explanation • origin • past • history • process • change • force • dynamics • consequences • biology • psychology** *A key issue for evolutionary theory is how cooperation is maintained within social groups.* ◇ *Traditionally, the development of the UK constitution has been regarded as an incremental evolutionary process.*

E

evolve AWL /iˈvɒlv; *NAmE* iˈvɑːlv/ *verb* **1** [I, T] to develop gradually, especially from a simple to a more complicated form; to develop sth in this way: *As landscapes evolve, so do human activities and so do sites.* ◇ *The meaning of the term 'liturgy' has evolved over time.* ◇ **~ from sth** *Modern commercial banks evolved from safe houses that simply looked after valuables.* ◇ **~ into/to sth** *China has evolved into a highly differentiated economy.* ◇ **~ from sth into/to sth** *Durkheim assumes human societies evolve from the elementary to the complex.* ◇ **~ sth** *Internet language has evolved a number of ways, such as the use of emoticons, to mark utterances.* **2** [I, T] (*biology*) (of living things) to develop over time, often many generations, into forms that are better adapted to survive changes in their environment: **~ from sth** *This hypothesis proposes that modern humans evolved from a group of hominid ancestors in a single place in Africa.* ◇ **~ sth** *All biological organisms have evolved sophisticated and diverse DNA repair mechanisms.*

WORD FAMILY
evolve *verb*
evolution *noun*
evolutionary *adj.*
evolutionarily *adv.*

▸ EVOLVE + ADVERB **rapidly • slowly, gradually** *Wind turbine technology has evolved rapidly over the last twenty years.* | **independently** *It is now thought that eyes have evolved independently more than 40 times on planet earth.*

▸ BE + ADVERB + EVOLVING **rapidly • slowly, gradually • still • constantly, continually** *A common European approach to science and technology is still evolving.*

ex·acer·bate /ɪɡˈzæsəbeɪt; *NAmE* ɪɡˈzæsərbeɪt/ *verb* **~ sth** to make sth worse, especially a disease or problem SYN AGGRAVATE: *Air pollution exacerbates asthma.* ◇ *Problems have been further exacerbated by the introduction of a new computing system.* ■ **ex·acer·ba·tion** *noun* [U, C] **~ (of sth)** *the exacerbation of chronic illness*

exact /ɪɡˈzækt/ *adj.* correct in every detail SYN PRECISE (1): *There is no exact match between the values in the two tables.* ◇ *Interview excerpts retain the exact wording of our informants.* ◇ *Although we do not have an exact number, perhaps forty or fifty Christians were killed.* ◇ *The exact nature of these substances may vary among species.* IDM **the ˌexact ˈopposite** a person or thing that is as different as possible from sb/sth else: *For Mitford, Aristophanic comedy was a reaction against democracy; for Grote, it was the exact opposite.* **not an ˌexact ˈscience** used to describe an activity that is based partly on guessing and opinions, not only on accurate measurements and set rules: *Organizational analysis is not an exact science, since to some extent it relies on personal judgement.*

exact·ly /ɪɡˈzæktli/ *adv.* used to emphasize that sth is correct in every way or in every detail SYN PRECISELY (1): *The market value of the bond is exactly equal to its face value.* ◇ *Predictions from these simple models do not correspond exactly to the experimental results.* ◇ **~ what/how, etc...** *Benson agrees that it seems very difficult to specify exactly what autonomy consists of.* ◇ *Exactly how cell division and DNA replication are coordinated is not understood.* ◇ **~ the same** *A carrier was used of exactly the same frequency as the carrier used for modulation.*

▸ EXACTLY + ADJECTIVE **equal • similar • analogous • equivalent** *An exactly analogous situation exists in the case of a signal spectrum.*

▸ VERB + EXACTLY **correspond • coincide • say • know** *Even in its lowest energy state, we cannot say exactly where the particle is.*

▸ EXACTLY + VERB **match • balance • coincide** *In the steady state, this absorbed energy is exactly balanced by the average energy emitted.*

ex·ag·ger·ate /ɪɡˈzædʒəreɪt/ *verb* **~ sth** to make sth seem larger, better, worse or more important than it really is: *The power shift in the direction of knowledge workers has been greatly exaggerated.* ◇ *The chapter counters exaggerated claims about economic globalization by emphasizing some of its limits.* ■ **ex·ag·ger·ation** /ɪɡˌzædʒəˈreɪʃn/ *noun* [C, usually sing., U] *It is not an exaggeration to state that telecommunications helped shape the very world we live in today.* ◇ *The urgency should be clearly and accurately explained to the patient without exaggeration.*

exam /ɪɡˈzæm/ (*also* **exam·in·ation**) *noun* **1** a formal written, spoken or practical test, especially at school or college, to see how much you know about a subject, or what you can do: *He took the civil service exam for a job in the US postal service.* ◇ *By passing exams and gaining credentials, young people can gain an advantage in the labour market.* ◇ *Entrance exams are the most common way for high school students in Japan to gain entry to university.* ◇ **in an ~** (*BrE*) *She cheated in her law exam.* ◇ **on an ~** (*NAmE*) *She cheated on her law exam.* ◇ **+ noun** *In terms of exam results the two schools are very similar.* **2** (*NAmE*) a medical test of a particular part of the body: *He has an annual exam with his physician.* ◇ *Dental care includes a full dental exam and preventive and restorative treatment as necessary.*

exam·in·ation /ɪɡˌzæmɪˈneɪʃn/ *noun* **1** [U, C] the act of looking at or considering sth very carefully: *The situation merits examination since habits acquired early in one's career are likely to persist.* ◇ **~ of sth** *Even a cursory examination of Table 4.2 reveals profound differences between the two groups.* ◇ **on/upon ~** *However, on closer examination, these claims are actually more limited in their scope.* ◇ **under ~** *It is important to analyse the main sources of mortality in each country under examination.* **2** [C] a close look at sb/sth, especially to see if there is anything wrong or to find the cause of a problem: *Only 38.2% of patients had an eye examination at least once a year.* ◇ **~ of sth** *A complete examination of the bridge was made in 1951.* ◇ **on/upon ~** *On examination, the patient is thin but there is no abdominal tenderness.* ◇ **+ noun** *The examination findings suggest that a clot may have developed in veins of the leg.* **3** [C] = EXAM: *Admission to universities is determined by scores in the national entrance examination.* HELP Note that when you **pass an examination**, you succeed in achieving the required standard. You **take, do** or **sit an examination** when you answer the questions: *He completed his studies in Australia before returning to take his final examinations.* ⊃ *compare* TEST[1]

▸ ADJECTIVE + EXAMINATION **thorough, detailed, in-depth • further • comprehensive • systematic • critical** *After a thorough clinical examination, I could not find much to explain his tiredness.* | **careful • close • cursory** *A closer examination of trends and developments around work suggests a more complex picture.* | **full, complete • routine • physical • medical • clinical • forensic • neurological • abdominal • radiological** *Blood samples were taken during routine veterinary examinations.*

▸ VERB + EXAMINATION **perform, conduct, carry out • undergo, have • undertake** *Doctors, airline pilots and applicants to many other occupations must expect to undergo a screening examination.* | **pass • sit, take • fail** *Some students had taken more than one attempt to pass the highly competitive entry examination.*

exam·ine /ɪɡˈzæmɪn/ *verb* **1** to consider or study an idea or subject very carefully: **~ sth** *This paper examines the effects of population ageing on economic growth.* ◇ **~ how/what, etc...** *The study aims to examine how fluctuations in* *capital affect the volunteer process.* ➲ grammar note *at* PRESENT³ ➲ thesaurus note *at* EXPLORE ➲ language bank *at* ABOUT² **2** to look at sb/sth closely, to see if there is anything wrong or to find the cause of a problem: **~ sb/sth** *She is interested in the analytical processes involved in examining patients.* ◇ *Potentially invasive organisms need to be examined in a secure area.* ◇ **~ sth/sb for sth** *It is important to examine the abdomen for scars.* **3 ~ sb** to give sb a test to see how much they know about a subject or what they can do: *This type of summary is often used in teaching and in examining students.* ➲ *compare* TEST² (4)

▸ EXAMINE + NOUN **association, relationship, relation, link, correlation • interaction, interplay • difference** *Three recent studies examined the association between obesity and prostate cancer risk.* |**impact, effect • influence • implication • effectiveness • consequence • outcome** *A series of recent studies examine the direct impact of media on social behaviour and public attitudes.* |**trend • pattern • nature • way** *This article examines long-term trends and challenges related to the road transport sector.* |**role • issue, question • hypothesis • concept • aspect • factor • characteristic • variable • data • evidence • extent • determinant • validity • inequality • attitude • variation** *This study examined the role of health insurance in access to health care among older immigrants.*

▸ NOUN + EXAMINE **research • study • article • paper • essay • chapter • section** *This chapter will examine the debate concerning the impact of globalization on economic policymaking.* |**researcher • author • colleague** *Researchers are examining the impacts of climate change.*

▸ ADVERB + EXAMINE | EXAMINE + ADVERB **closely • thoroughly • further** *The EU's preferences for greener policies should be closely examined.* ◇ *The whole leg and foot should be thoroughly examined.* |**briefly • carefully • critically • empirically • specifically • separately** *He identifies and carefully examines many of the difficult questions raised by the issue.* ◇ *Lessons from the US experience should be examined critically.*

▸ ADVERB + EXAMINE **systematically** *Previous research has not systematically examined the factors that drive public preferences in this area.*

▸ EXAMINE + ADVERB **in detail, in depth** *This question will be examined in more detail in the next section.*

exam·in·er /ɪɡˈzæmɪnə(r)/ *noun* **1** a person who writes the questions for, or marks, a test of knowledge or ability: *Examiners look for evidence that the candidate uses the literature to develop an argument.* **2** a person whose job is to examine sth and find out information about it: *The initial examination was made by an experienced fingerprint examiner.*

ex·ample /ɪɡˈzɑːmpl; *NAmE* ɪɡˈzæmpl/ *noun* **1** something such as a fact or a situation that shows, explains or supports what you say: *The use of microwaves has greatly expanded; examples include telecommunications, radio astronomy, land surveying and radar.* ◇ *These examples illustrate a couple of things about the diffusion of innovations.* ◇ **~ of sth** *Examples of goods and services that are not commodities are public education, police protection and other government services.* **2** a thing that is typical of or represents a particular group or set: *Request forms come in many shapes and sizes. Figure 1.3 shows a typical example.* ◇ **~ of sth** *The classic example of an emerging infectious disease is HIV/AIDS.* ◇ **as an ~** *Denmark is often hailed as the prime example of the successful development of wind energy.* **3** a person or thing that is a good or bad model for others to copy: *Support agencies could try to identify successful role models to encourage others to follow their example.* ◇ *Many of their officers set bad examples of drunkenness and violence.* ◇ **~ to sb** *The writing in this book is a fine example to other feminist writers.* ◇ **~ of sth** *The UK needs to persuade other governments by setting an example of good practice.* ◇ **by ~** *Children learn best by example.* ➲ *compare* ROLE MODEL

IDM **for example** (*abbr.* **e.g.**) **by way of example** used to emphasize sth that explains or supports what you are saying; used to give an example of what you are saying SYN FOR INSTANCE: *Some adolescents may be disruptive in a passive way. For example, your fourteen-year-old may challenge you by his appearance.* ◇ *Trainees are assessed using a combination of tools. By way of example, the system in the UK is illustrated in Table 3.*

▸ ADJECTIVE + EXAMPLE **good • excellent** *Perhaps the best example of supply chain exploitation is that taking place between supermarkets and their suppliers.* |**numerous • recent • early • obvious • clear • interesting** *The household is the most obvious example of an institution based on affection.* |**simple • illustrative • concrete, specific, particular • following • further • final • previous • hypothetical • practical** *Surgery and burial rites are further examples of good things that often bring no pleasure.* |**classic • typical • prime • striking, dramatic • notable • extreme • famous, well-known • best-known • prominent • familiar, common • important • useful** *Tourism can do enormous damage to cultural monuments; Venice is a striking example.*

▸ VERB + EXAMPLE **cite (sth as) • provide, give, offer • consider, discuss • present, show, illustrate • see • take (sth as) • serve as • represent • find • use • describe • include** *A number of scholars have cited such laws as examples of environmental protection.* ◇ *These data present the clearest example of the importance of sample preparation.* |**set • follow** *The US is setting the worst example for energy use on the globe.*

▸ EXAMPLE + VERB **illustrate • show, demonstrate • include • concern** *There is a trend in the retailing industry towards instant delivery, which the following example illustrates.*

▸ EXAMPLE OF + NOUN **the latter, the former • kind, type • application • phenomenon • use • approach • way** *Plates*

LANGUAGE BANK

Giving examples

In academic writing, it is important to support your points with examples.

- ..., **e.g./such as...**
- **For example/For instance,...**
- ..., **including...**
- ..., **typically/usually/most often...**
- ..., **particularly/especially...**
- **To take one example,...**
- Consider, **as an example,...**
- **A good example/One example of this is...**
- X **is one example.**
- X **is a case in point.**
- ..., as **exemplified/illustrated/shown** by...

– *Non-invasive tests,* ***such as*** *ultrasound, often add little to the diagnosis of abdominal pain.*
– ***For example****, a wind speed of 20 knots (10.29 m/s) will generate an energy density of 3.13 kJ/m^2.*
– *Biomaterials can be used in many applications,* ***including*** *artificial transplants and drug delivery implants.*
– *Primary defects are genetic abnormalities,* ***usually*** *single recessive mutations.*
– *Modern bacteria,* ***particularly*** *the primitive Archaea, can live in cold Antarctic lakes and water boiling in geysers.*
– *Cocteau's film,* ***to take one example****, derives its style from Welles's use of interior shooting.*
– *Consider,* ***as an example****, the market for beer in Iowa City.*
– *Here, I shall focus on socially influential behaviour. Conformity* ***is one example****.*
– *The large flood of 1996 is* ***a case in point****.*
– *The classic vampire myth of popular fiction,* ***as exemplified by*** *Bram Stoker's 'Dracula', is based on...*

E

17.4 and 17.5 provide examples of the kinds of photograph that were taken.

ex·ceed AWL /ɪk'siːd/ *verb* **1 ~ sth** to be greater than a particular number or amount: *The ice thickness may locally have exceeded 400 m.* ◇ *One cannot accelerate a real object so that its final speed exceeds the speed of light.* **2 ~ sth** to go beyond what the law, an order or a rule says you are allowed to do: *A sensor within the exhaust pipe determines whether or not the levels of CO exceed a legal threshold.* ◇ *It appears that exceeding speed limits is still not seen as a crime by many.* ◇ *If a local authority exceeds its powers, then its actions will lack legal validity.* **3 ~ sth** to be better than sth SYN SURPASS: *If expectations are exceeded, then customers are delighted.* ◇ *Their achievements have exceeded most people's wildest dreams.* ➲ *see also* EXCESS[1]

E

excel /ɪk'sel/ *verb* (-ll-) [I] to be very good at doing sth: *He was a bright young man who had excelled academically.* ◇ **~ in/at sth** *The Germans excelled at gymnastics.* ◇ **~ at doing sth** *They excelled at winning elections.*

ex·cel·lence /'eksələns/ *noun* [U] the quality of being extremely good: *She was awarded the University Prize for academic excellence.* ◇ **~ in sth** *The aim is to achieve excellence in standards of education and levels of skills.* ➲ *see also* CENTRE[1] (6)

ex·cel·lent /'eksələnt/ *adj.* extremely good: *Tesco.com is an excellent example of an e-commerce success.* ◇ *Plants offer excellent opportunities for studying the genetic basis of adaptive variation.* ◇ *The French wine harvest was a disaster and the harvest in the rest of the world was excellent.*

LANGUAGE BANK

Making an exception

The following words and expressions are useful in academic writing when mentioning one or more things that you want to exclude from a general statement.

- **except (for)...**
- **... apart/aside,...**
- **apart/aside** from...
- **excluding...**
- **with the exception of** ...
- **with some/one or two exceptions**
- **with few/minor/rare exceptions**
- **the main/notable exception being...**

– *Neoclassical economics eclipsed its rivals,* ***except*** *in Communist countries, where Marxian economics dominated the curriculum.*
– ***Except for*** *Newfoundland, slave labour was eventually used in all of these colonies.*
– ***These cases aside****, wind erosion is most effective in deserts.*
– ***Apart from*** *some intrigues in Bulgaria and Romania, the government concentrated its attention on the east.*
– *For full-time male workers (****excluding*** *the United States), average weekly earnings rose 22.6 per cent.*
– *Tidal energy is predictable, offering an advantage over other forms of renewable energy,* ***with the exception of*** *geothermal energy.*
– ***With some*** *well-known* ***exceptions****, the Norman aristocracy did not contract marriages with the English.*
– *These are diseases for which,* ***with very few exceptions****, no genetic tests are available.*
– *Less is known on this topic for low- and middle-income countries—* ***the notable exceptions being*** *Brazil and South Africa.*

ex·cept[1] /ɪk'sept/ (*also* **ex'cept for**) *prep.* used before you mention the only thing or person about which a statement is not true SYN APART FROM: *Except for the USA, the most important German export markets are Germany's immediate neighbours.* ◇ *All other environmental factors except day length change as one ascends a mountain.*

ex·cept[2] /ɪk'sept/ *conj.* used before you mention sth that makes a statement not completely true: **~ (that)...** *The circuit is similar to that in Fig. 4.31 except that the diode is reversed.* ◇ **~ where/when etc...** *Notice must be given 15 days in advance, except where either party is seriously ill.*

ex·cep·tion /ɪk'sepʃn/ *noun* a person or thing that is not included in a general statement, or that does not follow a rule: *With very few exceptions, the issue of religious tolerance did not feature in their political agenda.* ◇ **~ to sth** *There are many exceptions to the generalizations in Table 2.2.* ◇ **be no ~** *The communications sector has always been regulated and the Internet is no exception.* ➲ language bank *at* EXCEPT[1]
IDM **make an ex'ception (for sb)** to allow sb not to follow the usual rule on one occasion: *In formulating this proposition, Dicey was prepared to make an exception for soldiers and clergymen.* **with the ex'ception of** except; not including: *With the exception of the relatively small areas of upland rice, rice fields are flooded for part of the year.* ➲ language bank *at* EXCEPT[1] **without ex'ception** used to emphasize that the statement you are making is always true and everyone or everything is included: *Almost without exception, studies of economic growth show a close relation between economic performance and schooling.*

ex·cep·tion·al /ɪk'sepʃənl/ *adj.* **1** very unusual; not typical: *In exceptional circumstances, asylum seekers may seek permission to work from the Home Office.* ◇ *The pollution was wholly exceptional in terms of the seriousness of its impact on the environment.* **2** unusually good SYN OUTSTANDING (1): *The work calls for men and women who combine exceptional interpersonal skills with a strong intellect.* ◇ *James had been exceptional in his behaviour since the last case conference was called.*

ex·cep·tion·al·ly /ɪk'sepʃənəli/ *adv.* **1** used before an adjective or adverb to emphasize how strong or unusual the quality is: *The data do not show exceptionally high temperatures during the summer.* ◇ *Working together exceptionally well as a team, they have produced a scientifically informed and rigorous treatment of the topic.* ➲ *compare* ABNORMALLY **2** only in unusual circumstances: *Only exceptionally does a minister resign or suffer dismissal because of a policy mistake.* ◇ *Exceptionally, a board may agree to a chief executive becoming chairman.*

ex·cerpt /'eksɜːpt; *NAmE* 'eksɜːrpt/ *noun* **~ (from sth)** a short piece of writing, music, film, etc. taken from a longer whole: *The film ends with an excerpt from President Kennedy's American University speech of June 1963.* ◇ *The following excerpt is from the same poem that is quoted in chapter 3.* ■ **ex·cerpt** *verb* **~ sth (from sth)** *Portions of this chapter were excerpted from two prior papers.*

ex·cess[1] /ɪk'ses/ *noun* **1** [U, sing.] more than is necessary, reasonable or acceptable: **in ~** *Meat-eating in excess can have serious adverse health implications.* ◇ **~ of sth** *The patient is producing an excess of thyroxine.* ◇ **to ~** *Individuals who misuse other substances often also drink alcohol to excess.* **2** [C, U] an amount by which sth is larger than sth else: *In humans, there is always a slight excess in the number of male births.* ◇ **in ~** *It is evident from these data that certain symptom categories were reported in significant excess by hairdressers.* ◇ **~ of sth (over sth)** *His excess of expenditure over income of £1 298 a year was brought about by his extravagant expenditure on car maintenance.* **3 excesses (of sth)** [pl.] extreme behaviour that is unacceptable, illegal or immoral: *In an attempt to address some of the worst excesses of the tabloid press, the UK has a system of self-regulation for the press.* ◇ *The central character keeps his youthful appearance despite the excesses of his life.*

LANGUAGE BANK

Adverbs of degree

These adverbs are used with an adjective to describe the strength of a particular quality.

A HIGH DEGREE

enormously • exceptionally • extremely • immensely • remarkably

– *The study reveals **exceptionally high** levels of imports.*

– *Low-denomination coins minted in the third century are **extremely rare**.*

– *Although woodblock prints were not respected as genuine art at the time, they were **immensely popular**.*

• The adverbs **enormously, immensely** and **remarkably** may also be used with a verb in this meaning:

– *The content of soluble salts **varies enormously** between rock types.*

– *Furthermore, male and female fig wasps **differ remarkably** in their morphology.*

A MODERATE DEGREE

fairly • moderately • sufficiently

– *The temperatures of ocean surfaces remain **fairly constant**.*

– *The headaches are **moderately severe** but not disabling.*

Note that **sufficiently** is used to express a level of need: *Once a **sufficiently large** bubble is formed, it could expand.*

• The adverbs **moderately** and **sufficiently** may also be used with a verb in this meaning:

– *The CAS Planning scale has been shown to **correlate moderately** with IQ.*

– *By the 1970s, these economies had **recovered sufficiently** to compete on a global scale.*

AN ABSOLUTE DEGREE

completely • entirely

• These adverbs may be used with *not* or *almost* to make your assertion less strong:

– *Some bacteria are considered to be **completely independent** of photosynthesis.*

– *This evidence is **not entirely consistent** across studies.*

– *Although econometric evidence is **almost entirely absent**, historical evidence suggests...*

– *Evidently, myth had been too entrenched in Greek life to **disappear completely.***

OTHER ADVERBS OF DEGREE

abnormally • extraordinarily • surprisingly • unusually

• These adverbs emphasize how **unusual** a particular quality is, especially an amount or the level of sth:

– *Despite the interest in market-oriented conservation, **surprisingly little** research has focused on peasant farmer incomes in rainforest areas.*

– *Less frequent events, such as **unusually high** tides, have an impact on erosion (Wong, 1991).*

comparatively • relatively

• These adverbs may be used when **comparing** sets of data, objects, techniques, etc.:

– *Even in eras of **comparatively high** literacy, ancient cultures remained oral to a considerable degree.*

– *The mass exchange of these polar glaciers is **relatively small**, compared with temperate glaciers.*

IDM **in exˈcess of sth** of more than a particular amount: *The husband was a successful fund manager with an annual income in excess of £1 million.* ◇ *Temperatures in excess of 150°C can be used for electricity generation.*

ex·cess² /ˈekses/ *adj.* [only before noun] in addition to an amount that is necessary, usual or legal: *Firms will hire more people, increasing supply, and this will tend to reduce the excess demand.*

ex·ces·sive /ɪkˈsesɪv/ *adj.* **1** greater than what seems reasonable or appropriate: *Excessive alcohol drinking is second only to tobacco smoking as the cause of overall damage to health.* ◇ *The allegations included a claim that the directors had awarded themselves excessive remuneration.* ◇ *These precautions do not seem excessive.* **2** much greater than what is usual: *Excessive daytime sleepiness may result in accidents.* ◇ *Farmers often face production risks that are created by weather conditions, such as drought or excessive rainfall.* ■ **ex·ces·sive·ly** *adv.*: *Public statements regarding food safety have on occasion been excessively optimistic.*

E

ex·change¹ /ɪksˈtʃeɪndʒ/ *noun* **1** [C, U] an act of giving sth to sb or doing sth for sb and receiving sth in return: **~ of sth** *First there was the exchange of gifts.* ◇ *Consider the following exchange of information between a control tower and an aircraft:...* ◇ **~ of sth for sth** *Markets involve exchanges of commodities for money.* ◇ **in ~ for sth** *There are schemes for providing clean needles in exchange for used ones.* ◇ **in ~** *He makes sacrifices for his family and, in exchange, expects his family to be there for him.* **2** [C] a conversation or an argument: **~ with sb** *In an angry exchange with Peter, she called him 'a liar'.* ◇ **~ between A and B** *He overheard the following exchange between an older and younger academic.* **3** [U] the process of changing the money of one country into that of another: *The lower diagram shows the possible rates of exchange between the two countries.* ◇ **+ noun** *US policymakers have grown concerned about the exchange rate between the US dollar and the Chinese yuan.* ◇ *Some countries have strict foreign exchange controls.* **4** [C] an arrangement when two people or groups from different countries visit each other's homes or do each other's jobs for a short time: **+ noun** *JIC invited a delegation of 19 trainees from all over Europe to the UK for an exchange visit.* ➲ *see also* STOCK EXCHANGE

ex·change² /ɪksˈtʃeɪndʒ/ *verb* **1** to give sth to sb and at the same time receive the same type of thing from them: **~ sth** *Weekly meetings are a forum for exchanging information.* ◇ *The term 'market' has traditionally been used to describe a place where buyers and sellers gather to exchange goods and services.* ◇ **~ sth with sb** *Over a three-week period, they exchanged emails with the supplier.* **2** to give or return sth that you have and get sth different or better instead SYN CHANGE²: **~ sth** *The company has a reputation for exchanging goods without question.* ◇ **~ A for B** *The costs associated with exchanging one currency for another disappear if the countries involved use a single currency.*

ex·cite /ɪkˈsaɪt/ *verb* **1** to make sb feel a particular emotion or react in a particular way SYN AROUSE (1): **~ sth** *His abilities excited the interest of his teachers.* ◇ **~ sth in/among sb** *Corruption was blatant, and it excited disapproval and envy among those who witnessed it.* **2 ~ sb** to make sb feel very pleased, interested or enthusiastic, especially about sth that is going to happen: *His moderate policies and calm demeanour failed to excite voters.* ◇ *An increase in profits could so excite investors that it stimulates an increase in investment.* **3 ~ sb/sth** to make sb/sth nervous, upset or active and unable to relax: *She had shaken the nerve of the regime and excited the revolutionaries.* ◇ *The dance excites other bees, which begin to follow the dancing bee.* **4 ~ sth** to produce a state of increased energy or activity in a physical or biological system SYN STIMULATE (3): *He cites midwives who excite or relieve the pains of childbirth.* **5 ~ sth** (*physics*) to bring sth to a state of higher energy: *The energy of light is used to excite an electron to a state of higher energy.* ◇ *The internal energy increases as the various modes of motion are excited.*

ex·cited /ɪk'saɪtɪd/ *adj.* **1** feeling or showing happiness and enthusiasm: *The marketing department became very excited.* ◇ **~ about sth** *The Production Manager is not excited about this new order, as it will affect the smooth operation of the factory.* ◇ **~ at sth** *The archaeologist in charge was quite excited at the find.* ◇ **~ by sth** *She chose this job because she was excited by the prospect of overseas travel.* ◇ **~ to do sth** *I was excited to find old maps and thousands of photographs.* HELP Note that in this meaning, **excited** describes how sb feels. To describe things or events that make you feel excited, use **exciting.** ➲ *compare* EXCITING **2** nervous or upset and unable to relax: *If the patient is very excited or abnormally aggressive, drug treatment may be needed.* ◇ *The capital's population became excited and shots were fired.* **3** (*physics*) of or in an energy state that is higher than the normal state: *A molecule in an excited state must either decay to the ground state or form a photochemical product.*

ex·cite·ment /ɪk'saɪtmənt/ *noun* **1** [U] the state of feeling excited: *These approaches have generated great excitement in all areas of biology.* ◇ **~ about sth** *Games and contests have the ability to help create excitement about a brand.* **2** [U, pl.] **~ (of sth)** something that you find exciting: *The excitement of extreme sports or roller-coaster rides combines pleasure with fear.* ◇ *I have tried to convey a sense of the principal developments, complexities and excitements of this period.*

ex·cit·ing /ɪk'saɪtɪŋ/ *adj.* causing great interest or excitement: *Electromagnetic energy offers many new and exciting possibilities in agriculture.* ◇ *exciting discoveries/developments/opportunities* ◇ *The story is fast, gripping and exciting.*

ex·clude AWL /ɪk'skluːd/ *verb* **1** to deliberately not include sth in what you are doing or considering: **~ sth** *Data on ethnic differences were excluded for reasons of incomparability.* ◇ **~ sth from sth** *Those who had been infected with the hepatitis B virus were excluded from the analyses.* OPP INCLUDE (2) ➲ *compare* OMIT **2** to prevent sb/sth from entering a place or taking part in sth: **~ sb/sth** *The results show that those with low levels of educational attainment are more likely to be socially excluded.* ◇ **~ sb/sth from sth** *Large segments of the workforce are excluded from skilled jobs.* ◇ *Employers have the right to exclude others from entering the property they own.* HELP In British English, if a school **excludes** a student, it does not allow the student to attend because of bad behaviour: *We have seen a massive growth in the number of students excluded from school in the UK since 1991.* **3 ~ sth** to decide that sth is not possible or is not the cause of sth: *It is not possible to exclude the possibility that the disease was already present in some patients before exposure.* ◇ *The chest and abdomen should be examined to exclude other possible causes of chest pain.* OPP INCLUDE (2)

> **WORD FAMILY**
> exclude *verb*
> excluding *prep.*
> exclusion *noun*
> exclusionary *adj.*
> exclusive *adj.*
> exclusively *adv.*
> exclusivity *noun*

ex·clud·ing AWL /ɪk'skluːdɪŋ/ *prep.* not including: *A marketing budget may be between 5 and 7 per cent of sales revenues (excluding salaries).* ◇ *Excluding squirrels, all of the above species were detected by tracks and signs.* OPP INCLUDING ➲ language bank *at* EXCEPT[1]

ex·clu·sion AWL /ɪk'skluːʒn/ *noun* **1** [U] the act of preventing sb/sth from entering a place or taking part in sth: *The prime minister created a cabinet post specifically to tackle social exclusion.* ◇ **~ of sb/sth (from sth)** *She highlights the traditional exclusion of women from international relations.* ◇ **~ from sth** *Exclusion from access to health care can influence the decision to intervene.* OPP INCLUSION (1) **2** [C] a person or thing that is not included in sth: *Further exclusions for missing data reduced the sample to 7531 participants.* OPP INCLUSION (2) **3** [U] **~ of sth** the act of deciding that sth is not possible: *Diagnosis depends partly on the exclusion of physical causes, but also on psychological assessment.* **4** [U, C] (*BrE*) a situation in which a child is not allowed to attend school because of bad behaviour or because they have an infectious disease: *Recent policy measures have focused on tackling truancy and school exclusions.* ◇ **~ of sb (from sth)** *Exclusion of challenging students does not increase the time on academic tasks in classrooms.* ◇ **~ from sth** *New Dutch guidelines on bacterial skin infection no longer recommend exclusion from school.*
IDM **to the ex'clusion of sth** with the result that other things cannot be included: *Perception was limited by relying on technical solutions to the exclusion of anything else.*

ex·clu·sion·ary AWL /ɪk'skluːʒənri/ *adj.* designed to prevent a particular person or group of people from taking part in sth or doing sth: *The company's pricing practices had an exclusionary effect on competitors.* ◇ *The location of the meeting, a local pub, was potentially exclusionary.*

ex·clu·sive AWL /ɪk'skluːsɪv/ *adj.* **1** limited to one particular person, group or area; only given to one particular person, group or area: *The patent acts as an exclusive right to stop others from making commercial use of the invention.* ◇ *The governments of states had exclusive jurisdiction within their own frontiers.* ◇ **~ to sth/sb** *The importance of the distribution business is not exclusive to the retail sector.* **2** not including or allowing other things; complete: *Some members of the left wing rejected exclusive reliance on parliamentary methods to achieve reforms.* ◇ *Scholars need to turn from an exclusive focus on inequality between men and women to a broader focus on new contexts of inequality.* **3** (of a group or society) not very willing to allow new people to become members, especially if they are from a lower social class: *Until 1994, the South African government was racially exclusive.* ◇ *Noble status was becoming less exclusive.* OPP INCLUSIVE (1) **4** that cannot exist or be a true statement at the same time as sth else: *The four theories are difficult to distinguish and are not mutually exclusive.* ◇ *These are not exclusive statements.* **5** of a high quality and expensive and therefore not often bought or used by most people: *Passengers can choose to fly in the very exclusive first-class cabin.* **6 ~ of sth** not including: *The fees quoted below are exclusive of VAT.* ■ **ex·clu·sive·ness** *noun* [U] *They protected their economic and social exclusiveness by marrying only among themselves.* HELP **Exclusiveness** is related to meaning 3 of **exclusive** above. For other meanings, **exclusivity** is generally used.

ex·clu·sive·ly AWL /ɪk'skluːsɪvli/ *adv.* used to say that sth is limited to one person, group or thing: *The discussion here focuses exclusively on the political factors.* ◇ *Scholars have often treated some activities as exclusively male.*

ex·clu·siv·ity /ˌekskluː'sɪvəti/ *noun* [U] the quality of being EXCLUSIVE: *The wealthy consumer values exclusivity and uniqueness.*

ex·cuse[1] /ɪk'skjuːs/ *noun* a reason, either true or invented, that you give to explain or defend your behaviour: **~ for sth** *They made excuses for their poor performance.* ◇ **~ for doing sth** *There are few legitimate excuses for not responding to emails.*

ex·cuse[2] /ɪk'skjuːz/ *verb* **1 ~ sth** to make your or sb else's behaviour seem less bad by finding reasons for it SYN JUSTIFY: *She does not seek to excuse her failures.* **2** [usually passive] to allow sb to not do sth that they should normally do: **~ sb from (doing) sth** *They were excused from participation in many daily chores.* ◇ **~ sb sth** *The young and old were usually excused military duties.* **3 ~ yourself** to say in a polite way that you are leaving: *He excused himself and left.*

exe·cute /ˈeksɪkjuːt/ *verb* **1** [usually passive] to kill sb, especially as a legal punishment: **~ sb** *Some former leaders were executed.* ◇ **~ sb for sth** *Thomas More was tried and executed for treason in 1535.* **2 ~ sth** to do a piece of work, perform a duty, put a plan into action, etc: *First they had to identify the resources required to execute the plan.* **3 ~ sth** (*computing*) carry out an instruction or program: *Programs not currently being executed have to be stored somewhere.* **4 ~ sth** (*law*) to follow the instructions in a legal document; to make a document legally valid: *The time limit for executing a search warrant was originally one month.*

exe·cu·tion /ˌeksɪˈkjuːʃn/ *noun* **1** [U, C] the act of killing sb, especially as a legal punishment: *3 701 prisoners were awaiting execution.* ◇ *Public executions took place before eager crowds.* **2** [U] the act of doing a piece of work, performing a duty or putting a plan into action: *Successful project execution relies on effective management.* ◇ **~ of sth** *He was convicted of assaulting a police officer in the execution of his duty.* **3** [U] **~ (of sth)** (*law*) the act of following the instructions in a legal document: *The letter had been written before the execution of the will.* IDM *see* STAY²

ex·ecu·tive¹ /ɪɡˈzekjətɪv/ *noun* **1** [C] a person who has an important job as a manager of a company or an organization: *The script was rejected by several studio executives.* ◇ *Quinn's research examines how senior executives in large companies develop strategy.* ➲ *see also* CHIEF EXECUTIVE (1) **2 the executive** [sing.+ sing./pl. v.] the part of a government responsible for putting laws into effect: *Parliament does not make policy—that is a matter for the executive.* ➲ *compare* JUDICIARY, LEGISLATURE

ex·ecu·tive² /ɪɡˈzekjətɪv/ *adj.* [only before noun] **1** connected with managing a business or an organization, and with making plans and decisions: *At the age of 34 he became an executive director.* ◇ *Each business has an executive committee headed by the business chief executive.* ◇ *executive power/authority* ◇ *executive pay/renumeration* **2** having the power to put important laws and decisions into effect: *The head of the executive branch of government is the Prime Minister.* ➲ *compare* LEGISLATIVE (1)

ex·em·plar /ɪɡˈzemplɑː(r)/ *noun* (*formal*) a person or thing that is a good or typical example of sth SYN MODEL¹: *These cases were chosen to provide exemplars.* ◇ **as an ~ of sth** *This chapter investigates the issues of climate change with respect to London as an exemplar of a major world city.*

ex·em·plary /ɪɡˈzempləri/ *adj.* **1** providing a good example for people to copy: *A business should try to maintain existing customers through exemplary service.* ◇ *Finland provides an exemplary case of developing practices within its schools that prevent some students from falling behind others.* **2** [usually before noun] (*law* or *formal*) (of punishment) severe; used especially as a warning to others: *Exemplary damages are intended not to compensate the claimant, but to punish the defendant.*

ex·em·plify /ɪɡˈzemplɪfaɪ/ *verb* (**ex·em·pli·fies**, **ex·em·pli·fy·ing**, **ex·em·pli·fied**, **ex·em·pli·fied**) **1** [usually passive] **be exemplified by/in sth** to be a typical example of sth: *Recent critical shifts are perhaps best exemplified in the developing work of Judith Butler.* **2 ~ sth** to give an example in order to make sth clearer SYN ILLUSTRATE (1): *They quote a focus group participant to exemplify their point.* ■ **ex·em·pli·fi·ca·tion** /ɪɡˌzemplɪfɪˈkeɪʃn/ *noun* [U, C] *I shall not provide further exemplification here.* ◇ **~ of sth** *Photography and film are the most useful exemplifications of this new function.* ➲ language bank *at* EXAMPLE

ex·empt¹ /ɪɡˈzempt/ *adj.* [not before noun] **~ (from sth)** if sb/sth is **exempt** from sth, they are not affected by it, do not have to do it, pay it, etc: *Foods are usually exempt from value added tax.* ◇ *Infant mortality was extremely high and the upper classes were not exempt.*

ex·empt² /ɪɡˈzempt/ *verb* **~ sb/sth (from sth/from doing sth)** to give or get sb's official permission not to do sth or not to pay sth they would normally have to do or pay: *The Qur'an specifically exempts the sick from the duty of fasting.*

ex·emp·tion /ɪɡˈzempʃn/ *noun* [U, C] **~ (from sth)** official permission not to do sth or pay sth that you would normally have to do or pay: *This money could not qualify as income for which they could claim exemption from income tax.* ◇ *The state still lacks an alternative military service law that grants religious exemptions.*

ex·er·cise¹ /ˈeksəsaɪz; *NAmE* ˈeksərsaɪz/ *noun* **1** [U] physical or mental activity that you do to stay healthy or become stronger: *The heart is a muscle and benefits from regular exercise.* ◇ *Child obesity could also be linked to inactive lifestyles and a lack of exercise in general.* **2** [C] a set of movements or activities that you do to stay healthy or develop a skill: *Patients should be encouraged to perform exercises to ensure that they retain movement of the elbow.* ◇ *These team-building exercises were helping the groups to get to know each other.* **3** [C] a set of questions in a book that tests your knowledge or practises a skill: *Some of these methods are illustrated in the examples and exercises that follow.* ◇ *The following background information is provided as an aid in solving this exercise.* **4** [U] **~ of sth** the use of power, a skill, a quality or a right to make sth happen: *The exercise of managerial power may lead to unethical practice.* ◇ *Immigration control was the very visible exercise of sovereignty by an island nation.* **5** [C] an activity that is designed to achieve a particular result: *The proposal was the subject of a public consultation exercise.* ◇ **~ in sth** *The election campaign ended up more as an exercise in media manipulation than serious dialogue.* **6** [C, usually pl.] a set of activities for training soldiers: *Several military exercises and scientific expeditions have been conducted in recent years.*

ex·er·cise² /ˈeksəsaɪz; *NAmE* ˈeksərsaɪz/ *verb* **1** [T] **~ sth** to use your power, rights or personal qualities in order to achieve sth: *The Commission is answerable to the Parliament for the way it exercises its powers.* ◇ *Asylum seekers are exercising a legal right to seek refuge from persecution.* ◇ *Civil servants could be trusted to exercise considerable discretion.* **2** [I] to do sports or other physical activities in order to stay healthy or become stronger: *People who exercise regularly are less likely to develop colorectal cancer.* **3** [T] **~ sth** to give a part of the body the movement and activity it needs to keep strong and healthy: *Encourage the patient to exercise their neck.*

▸ EXERCISE + NOUN **power** • **authority** • **jurisdiction** • **control** • **influence** • **right** • **prerogative** • **freedom** • **autonomy** • **choice, option** • **care** • **caution** • **discretion** • **judgement** • **restraint** • **tolerance** *Some aristocratic women exercised political influence through their husbands or sons.* ◇ *The law would protect the minorities' rights to exercise their religious freedom.* ◇ *Caution must be exercised in drawing conclusions about causality.*

exert /ɪɡˈzɜːt; *NAmE* ɪɡˈzɜːrt/ *verb* **1** to use your influence or power to affect sb/sth: **~ sth on/over sb/sth** *Women can exert great influence on the development of family businesses.* ◇ **~ sth over sb/sth** *New laws enable local authorities to exert greater control over the management of construction sites.* ◇ **~ sth** *A country may limit exports to another country as a result of pressure exerted by the government of the importing country.* **2** to have an effect on sb/sth: **~ sth on sb/sth** *Normally, the weather exerted the greatest influence on the quality of the harvest in a particular locality.* ◇ **~ sth** *Evidence suggests that early quality care continues to exert positive results throughout childhood.* **3 ~ yourself** to make a great physical or mental effort: *The patient felt as if she might faint, especially when exerting herself.*

ex·er·tion /ɪɡˈzɜːʃn; *NAmE* ɪɡˈzɜːrʃn/ *noun* **1** [U] physical or mental effort: *The patient showed increasing breathlessness on exertion.* ◇ *Some teenagers engage in physical exertion as a way of coping with anger.* **2 exertions** [pl.] **~ (of sb)** actions that involve physical or mental effort: *The author records a barbarian attack on Britain in 410 which was repulsed by the exertions of the islanders themselves.* **3** [sing.] **~ of sth** the use of power or influence: *The book examines political narratives that involve the exertion of power by one state or group over another.*

E

ex·haust¹ /ɪɡˈzɔːst/ *noun* **1** [U] waste gases that come out of a vehicle, an engine or a machine: *These standards limit the emissions in vehicle exhaust.* ◇ **+ noun** *The other important constituent of exhaust gas is nitric oxide.* ◇ *Motor exhaust fumes are an important cause of poisoning.* **2** (*also* **exˈhaust pipe**) [C] a pipe through which exhaust gases come out: *Unburned fuel remains in the engine and can leak to the atmosphere from the air intake or exhaust.*

ex·haust² /ɪɡˈzɔːst/ *verb* **1 ~ sth** to use all of sth so that there is none left: *When stars have exhausted their nuclear fuel resources, they implode.* ◇ *The two repertoires discussed by Gilbert and Mulkay by no means exhaust the range of possibilities.* ◇ *They have exhausted all reasonable efforts to reach a peaceful resolution.* **2 ~ sb** to make sb feel very tired: *Multiple complex physical and psychological problems can completely exhaust even the most caring family.*

ex·haust·ed /ɪɡˈzɔːstɪd/ *adj.* **1** completely used or finished: *A very severe winter can decimate squirrel populations if their food stocks become exhausted.* ◇ *Embryos delaying hatching for too long lose their ability to hatch due to exhausted energy reserves.* **2** very tired: *Some volunteers find themselves physically and psychologically exhausted by their role.*

ex·haus·tion /ɪɡˈzɔːstʃən/ *noun* [U] **1** the state of being very tired: *Exhaustion and despair threatened these struggling mothers.* ◇ *Emotional exhaustion, considered a key to job burnout, is characterized by a shortness of energy.* **2 ~ of sth** the act of using sth until it is completely finished: *The lower layer becomes anoxic due to the exhaustion of oxygen.*

ex·haust·ive /ɪɡˈzɔːstɪv/ *adj.* including everything possible; very thorough or complete: *This review represents an exhaustive search of a diverse array of databases.* ◇ *This section does not intend to be an exhaustive list of the legislation.* ◇ *an exhaustive study/analysis/account/review* ■ **ex·haust·ive·ly** *adv.*: *This claim is discussed exhaustively in the industrial relations literature.* ◇ *The words can be exhaustively analysed into their component morphemes.*

ex·hibit¹ AWL /ɪɡˈzɪbɪt/ *verb* **1** [T] **~ sth** to show a particular sign, quality or type of behaviour SYN DISPLAY¹ (2): *Teachers were vigilant for students exhibiting signs of boredom.* ◇ *Cancer cells tend to exhibit an abnormal number of chromosomes.* ◇ *Young fish exhibited a strong preference for mud and fine sand, unlike older fish.* **2** [T, I] to show sth in a public place for people to enjoy or to give them information SYN DISPLAY¹ (1): **~ sth (at/in...)** *Her work has been widely exhibited in exhibitions in London and Paris.* ◇ **~ (at/in...)** *Many of the artists who exhibit at Kettle Art also live in the area.*

▸ EXHIBIT + NOUN **behaviour • characteristic, feature, property • pattern • sign • symptom • variation • similarity • preference • tendency • bias** *The study involved children who were recognized as exhibiting aggressive behaviour at school.* ◇ *The species exhibits a unique growth pattern, in which the shell remains thin.*

▸ ADVERB + EXHIBIT **typically • commonly** *Successful bids typically exhibit low labour costs, tight profit margins and quick project turnaround times.*

ex·hibit² AWL /ɪɡˈzɪbɪt/ *noun* **1** an object or a work of art put in a public place, for example a museum, so that people can see it: *Observers noted how visitors to the museum handled the exhibits.* **2 ~ (of sth)** (*NAmE*) = EXHIBITION (1): *The first exhibit of African art in the US was held at the Brooklyn Museum in 1923.*

ex·hib·ition AWL /ˌeksɪˈbɪʃn/ *noun* **1** (*especially BrE*) (*NAmE usually* **ex·hibit**) [C] a collection of things, such as works of art or interesting objects, that are shown to the public, for example in a museum: **~ of sth (in/at...)** *The international exhibition of the work of the Surrealists was held in London in 1936.* ◇ **~ on sth (in/at...)** *He organized the exhibition on Faraday and electrification.* **2** [U] **~ of sth** the act of showing sth, for example works of art, to the public: *Film music was first used in the exhibition of silent films to hide the noise of the projector.* **3** [sing.] **an ~ of sth** the act of showing a skill, a feeling, a quality or a type of behaviour: *The play rapidly turns into an exhibition of white male vulnerability.*

exile¹ /ˈeksaɪl; ˈegzaɪl/ *noun* **1** [U] the state of being sent to live in another country that is not your own, especially for political reasons or as a punishment: **in/into ~** *They were forced into exile by the Nazis' rise to power in the early 1930s.* **2** [C] a person who chooses or is forced to live away from their own country: *Industrialists, professionals and landowners who fled the country at this time considered themselves political exiles.*

exile² /ˈeksaɪl; ˈegzaɪl/ *verb* [usually passive] **~ sb (from...)** to force sb to leave their country, especially for political reasons or as a punishment; to send sb into exile: *The Jews had been exiled from England in 1290.* ◇ *The two risings in support of the exiled Stuarts provoked a more determined policy of repression.*

exist /ɪɡˈzɪst/ *verb* **1** [I] (not used in the progressive tenses) to happen or be found in a particular place, time or situation; to be: *The Sun is the source of all the energy that enables life to exist on the Earth.* ◇ *A wide literature exists on the subject.* ◇ *The report argued that the technology already exists to tackle global warming.* ◇ *A company ceases to exist when it is dissolved.* **2** [I] (not used in the progressive tenses) to be real: *According to Aristotle, God exists and should be imitated as far as possible.* **3** [I] **~ (on sth)** to live, especially in a difficult situation or with very little money SYN SURVIVE (1): *Over two thirds of the world's population exist on only a few dollars per day.*

▸ NOUN + EXIST **opportunity • possibility • evidence • uncertainty, doubt • tension • difference, distinction • relationship, correlation • gap** *Historically, few opportunities existed for women to pursue higher levels of religious studies.* ◇ *Sufficient evidence exists to link diet, cholesterol and heart disease.*

▸ ADVERB + EXIST **already • still • always • currently, now • previously • actually • only • certainly** *Smallpox is a virus that now only exists in laboratory cultures.* | **only • never • actually, really** *The book questions whether globalization really exists as anything more than a buzzword.*

▸ EXIST + ADVERB **only • simultaneously • independently** *For Kant, material objects exist independently of being perceived by anyone.*

▸ VERB + TO EXIST **cease • continue • seem, appear** *There are many varieties of shift work and a legal definition does not appear to exist.*

ex·ist·ence /ɪɡˈzɪstəns/ *noun* **1** [U, C, usually sing.] the state or fact of happening or being found in a particular place, time or situation; the state of being alive: *Bacteria are capable of fully independent existence.* ◇ *States do not have an existence separate from the human beings who compose them.* ◇ **in ~** *Photography had been in existence for about sixty years, but cinema was a new invention.* ◇ **the ~ of sth** *Huge mergers have threatened the continued existence of many smaller firms.* **2** [U] **~ (of sth)** the fact of being real: *The experimental evidence for the existence of black holes is convincing.* **3** [C, usually sing.] a way of living, especially when this is difficult: *After some commercial activity in the fourteenth century, the town's tenants returned to an agricultural existence.*

▸ ADJECTIVE + EXISTENCE **very • mere • continued • human • independent, separate** *Historically, the very existence of an urban centre depended on the surrounding rural areas as farmers came to the town to buy goods and services.*

▸ VERB + EXISTENCE **come into • bring sth into • go out of • indicate • threaten • owe** *The International Monetary Fund came into existence in December 1945.* | **deny • accept, acknowledge • assume, presuppose • imply • demonstrate • prove • reveal** *The philosopher Berkeley famously denied the existence of matter.*

ex·ist·ing /ɪɡˈzɪstɪŋ/ *adj.* [only before noun] found or used now or at the time being discussed: *This chapter reviews the existing literature on sales leadership in business.* ◇ *The main purpose of the study was to provide information on the benefits, risks and costs of both new and existing technologies.* ◇ *The Conquest of England by the French did little to alter the existing social structure of the kingdom.*

exit¹ /ˈeksɪt; ˈeɡzɪt/ *noun* **1** a way out of a public building or vehicle: *Employees must be familiar with the location of fire exits and evacuation routes.* ➲ *compare* ENTRANCE (1) **2** an process of stopping being part of a group or institution; the act of stopping being involved in sth: **~ from sth** *Both parties advocate Britain's exit from the EU.* ◇ **+ noun** *Many literatures have examined modes to enter to a foreign market, while few consider the exit strategy.* HELP In writing about literature or the theatre, a person's **exit** is the act of them leaving the stage: *The scene is built around a series of exits and entrances by different characters.* OPP ENTRANCE (2)

exit² /ˈeksɪt; ˈeɡzɪt/ *verb* **1** [I, T] to go out; to leave a place, situation, etc: **(+ adv./prep.)** *Figure 5.4 shows a water-filled reservoir with water exiting through a lower opening in the dam.* ◇ **~ sth** *Motorists pay a charge not only to enter or exit a zone but also to travel within it.* OPP ENTER (1) **2** [I, T] to finish using a computer program: **~ (from sth)** *Exit by using the Q (quit) command.* ◇ **~ sth** *Exit the Template Editor and close the macro.*

ex·ogen·ous /ekˈsɒdʒənəs; ɪkˈsɒdʒənəs; *NAmE* ekˈsɑːdʒənəs/ *adj.* caused or created by sth outside a body, system, etc. as opposed to having a cause that is within it: *Technology is usually seen as an exogenous factor, determined by developments outside the country concerned.* ◇ *Various demographic and other individual factors are considered as exogenous variables.* ◇ *Many years ago, insulin isolated from beef (bovine) or pork (porcine) were the only forms of exogenous insulin.* OPP ENDOGENOUS ■ **ex·ogen·ous·ly** *adv.*: *Prices are completely fixed and exogenously given throughout the analysis.*

exot·ic /ɪɡˈzɒtɪk; *NAmE* ɪɡˈzɑːtɪk/ *adj.* **1** from, typical of or connected with a distant foreign country, especially a hot one: *A multitude of trading links brought exotic goods into European households.* ◇ *All these novels involve travel to exotic lands.* **2** from another region or country, often with a different climate or environment: *Many examples exist of the public being directly responsible for the introduction of exotic species that turn invasive.*

ex·pand AWL /ɪkˈspænd/ *verb* **1** [I, T] to become greater in size, number or importance; to make sth greater in size, number or importance: *During the 1960s, social welfare programmes in the United States expanded rapidly.* ◇ *Over thousands of years, the lakes in the African Rift Valley have expanded and contracted considerably.* ◇ *As time passed, the universe expanded and the same amount of matter occupied an increasing volume of space.* ◇ *There was increasing pressure on resources from an expanding population.* ◇ **~ beyond/into/to sth** *The company expanded into Europe and profits soared.* ◇ **~ sth** *The company is seeking to expand the market share of four key products.* ◇ **~ sth to do sth** *The study was subsequently expanded to cover a wide range of maternal and child health issues.* ◇ **~ sth beyond/into/to sth** *There has been an increase in regional trade agreements in which free trading areas have been expanded beyond national boundaries.* OPP CONTRACT² (1) **2** [T] **~ sth** to write sth such as a scientific formula in a longer form: *The formula can be expanded as shown in Fig. 2.*

PHR V **exˈpand on/upon sth** to add more details and give more information about sth: *Participants were encouraged to expand on topics, experiences and feelings of interest to them.* ◇ *These results have been studied and expanded upon by several authors.*

▸ EXPAND + NOUN **scope, range, coverage • reach • horizon • capacity • operations • output, production** *Physicists in this century have sought to expand the scope of science to describe all aspects of the natural world.* ◇ *Toll revenues can be used to expand road capacity or invest in public transport.*

▸ ADVERB + EXPAND | EXPAND + ADVERB **further • greatly, considerably • rapidly • significantly • dramatically** *The Indonesian spinning industry is expected to further expand production over the next five years.* ◇ *Since then, the road network has expanded dramatically and freight costs have declined sharply.*

▸ ADVERB + EXPAND **vastly • gradually** *The production of the first 'browser' in 1994 vastly expanded use of the Internet.*

ex·pan·sion AWL /ɪkˈspænʃn/ *noun* **1** [U, C] the process of increasing in size, number or importance: **~ (of sth)** *The rapid expansion of urban industrial areas resulted in high-density housing areas of poor quality.* ◇ *The interior lakes of Australia have shown major expansions and contractions.* ◇ **~ in sth** *The new regulations did not lead to a significant expansion in part-time work.* ◇ **+ noun** *The authors studied the expansion strategies of several well-known companies.* OPP CONTRACTION (1), REDUCTION (1) **2** [C] **~ of sth** something such as a book or a talk that gives more details and information about a subject than sth done before: *The book is an expansion of an earlier magazine article.*

ex·pan·sive AWL /ɪkˈspænsɪv/ *adj.* **1** covering a wide subject area or a large number of different areas: *The research reported in this book has a deep and expansive coverage of business groups.* ◇ *The school had an expansive programme of careers education from Year 7.* **2** covering a large area SYN EXTENSIVE (3): *Most common species found in the area could only have existed if there were expansive grasslands over most of the region.* **3** (of a country, government, policy or business) growing in political or economic influence: *Cell phone usage is expansive and global.* ◇ *Small boats were of no use in an expansive foreign policy; it was battleships that were needed.* **4** tending to grow or increase in size, number or amount: *Smectite is often expansive; it swells when it absorbs water.*

ex·pect /ɪkˈspekt/ *verb* **1** to think or believe that sth will happen or that sb will do sth: **~ sth** *By the end of the century, we can expect a sea level rise of 300 mm.* ◇ **~ sth from sb/sth** *As might be expected from the data, the size and diversity of the non-British-born population is most marked in London and the South-East.* ◇ **~ sth of sb/sth** *These results were as expected of the plants in a reduced light environment.* ◇ **~ to do sth** *Most of us expect to get a cold or flu once or twice a year.* ◇ *By 1980, almost all women expected to be employed for most of their lives.* ◇ *One might expect to find the purest water in far northern or southern latitudes, remote from human activity.* ◇ **~ sb/sth to do sth** *In 1997, 28 000 visitors came to Phong Nha and this can be expected to increase substantially.* ◇ **~ that...** *Rome expected that British rulers should recognize its authority like client kings elsewhere.* ◇ **it is expected that...** *It might be expected that more companies' records would be available for the postwar period, but this does*

E

not appear to be the case. **2** to demand that sb will do sth because it is their duty: **~ sth from sb** *Students in this study perceived that teachers did not expect much from them.* ◇ **~ sth of sb** *The standard of behaviour expected of a minor is not that of an adult.* ◇ **~ sb to do sth** *The court expects you to do what is best for your child.* ◇ **~ to do sth** *At the minimum, most employees expect to be managed and treated fairly.* ➲ *compare* UNEXPECTED

IDM **be (only) to be ex'pected** to be likely to happen; to be quite normal: *Unbalanced growth is to be expected in a developing country.*

E

ex·pect·ancy /ɪk'spektənsi/ *noun (pl.* -ies) [U, C] **~ (of sth)** the state of expecting or hoping that sth, especially sth good, will happen: *Expectancy of success and perceptions of value will influence a person's willingness to overcome challenges.* ◇ *Research has identified a number of self-beliefs that govern outcome expectancies.* ➲ *see also* LIFE EXPECTANCY

ex·pect·ation /ˌekspek'teɪʃn/ *noun* **1** [C, usually pl., U] the belief that sth will happen or is likely to happen: *The differences in knowledge levels were consistent with our expectations.* ◇ **contrary to ~** *Contrary to expectation, rock coasts are not bare of vegetation.* ◇ **~ of sth** *The increase in exports was higher than analysts' expectations of a rise of between 35 per cent and 40 per cent.* ◇ *A lottery ticket is not an investment as there is no expectation of any return.* ◇ **in ~ of sth** *The system could bank water in expectation of wintertime demands.* ◇ **~ about sth** *Expectations about future development are incorporated into today's exchange rate.* ◇ **~ that...** *The expectation that inequality would increase within global cities was based on these factors.* **2** [C, usually pl.] a belief about the particular way sth should happen or how sb should behave: *Patients had high expectations regarding therapy.* ◇ *The success of the project exceeded expectations.* ◇ *More than 50 suppliers failed to meet expectations on product price, quality or delivery.* ◇ *Universities are recognizing that they need to understand and manage student expectations.* ◇ **~ that...** *There is an expectation that both boys and girls in the culture will attend schools.*

ˌexpectation of 'life *noun* [U] = LIFE EXPECTANCY

ex·pect·ed /ɪk'spektɪd/ *adj.* that you think is likely to happen: *The expected outcomes of treatment were discussed with the patient.* ◇ *Merged companies frequently fail to deliver the expected benefits.* ◇ *The study suggests that pesticide users may have higher than expected numbers of some types of cancer.* ➲ *compare* UNEXPECTED

exˌpected 'value *noun (mathematics)* a predicted value of a VARIABLE, calculated as the sum of all possible values each multiplied by the PROBABILITY that it will occur: *These results are close to the expected values.* ◇ **~ of sth** *The expected value of any new idea is highly uncertain.*

ex·ped·ition /ˌekspə'dɪʃn/ *noun* **1** an organized journey with a particular purpose, especially to find out about a place that is not well known: **~ to...** *The same year Napoleon led an expedition to Egypt.* ◇ *In 1915, the British government considered mounting a full-scale military expedition in order to capture Constantinople.* ◇ **on ~** *The ship later took Charles Darwin on his famous expedition.* **2 ~ (to...)** the people who go on an expedition: *Thomas Moran was a member of a government expedition to the Yellowstone Valley in the early 1870s.*

expel /ɪk'spel/ *verb* (-ll-) **1 ~ sb (from sth)** to officially make sb leave a school or an organization: *One youth was expelled from 15 different schools before ending up at Free LA High School.* ◇ *In 1972, a Politburo member was expelled for recommending precisely this course of action.* **2 ~ sb (from sth)** to force sb to leave a country: *In 1290, Edward I expelled all Jews from England.* **3 ~ sth (from sth)** *(technical)* to force air, water, etc. out of a part of the body or from a container: *Both mammals and amphibians produce sounds by expelling air from the lungs.* ◇ *Coals are rich in organic matter and rarely expel any generated oil.* ➲ *see also* EXPULSION

ex·pend /ɪk'spend/ *verb* to use or spend time, money, energy, etc: **~ sth** *The fixed cost of recruiting, training and maintaining specialist staff is considerable, as is the effort expended.* ◇ **~ sth in/on sth** *In humans and other mammals, mothers expend resources on gestation and lactation.* ◇ *Organizations expend large amounts of time and resources on creativity training.* ◇ **~ sth in/on doing sth** *In an agricultural society, additional energy is expended in growing, reaping and storing food.*

ex·pend·iture /ɪk'spendɪtʃə(r)/ *noun* [U, C] **1** the act of spending or using money; an amount of money spent: *The government was forced to cut public expenditure.* ◇ *In 2007 total health expenditure in China reached 984.3 billion yuan.* ◇ *After 1950 social expenditure began an even more marked rise in absolute terms and relative to GDP.* ◇ *average/per-capita expenditure* ◇ *daily/monthly/annual expenditure* ◇ **~ on sth** *Expenditure on tertiary education is relatively low.* ◇ **~ for sth/sb** *Hospitalization represents a major expenditure for most households.* **2** the use of energy, time, materials, etc: *Requirements for food vary according to energy expenditure and habit.* ◇ **~ of sth** *The expenditure of effort is also linked to rewards.* ➲ *compare* INCOME

ex·pense /ɪk'spens/ *noun* **1** [U] the money that you spend on sth: *The amount of time and expense incurred in undertaking research must be compared with the benefits that will result from it.* ◇ *The prosecution served no useful purpose yet involved considerable expense.* ◇ **at... ~** *Marginal land was brought into cultivation at great expense.* ◇ **~ of (doing) sth** *The expense of purchasing new equipment may force an organization to persist with obsolete technology.* **2 expenses** [pl.] money spent in doing a particular job, or for a particular purpose: *Most of the household expenses were paid for out of the joint account.* ◇ *Helpfully, living expenses overseas can often be less than in the UK.* **3 expenses** [pl.] money that you spend while you are working and that your employer will pay back to you later: *He has to provide his own car when he has to travel, although he can claim expenses.* **4** [C, usually sing.] something that makes you spend money: *Spot advertising is now a huge expense for media firms themselves.*

IDM **at sb's expense** paid for by sb: *Citizens have to acquire the vaccine at their own expense.* ◇ *Legal representation is available at public expense for their initial asylum claim.* **at the expense of sb/sth** with loss or damage to sb/sth: *Including this information would come at the expense of a greatly reduced sample size.* ◇ *Beneficial advances in science, medicine and telecommunications have been gained at the expense of the natural world.*

ex·pen·sive /ɪk'spensɪv/ *adj.* costing a lot of money: *Customers feel confident that the more expensive products must be better quality.* ◇ *The extraction of bitumen from the oil sands is an expensive process.* ◇ *Imported goods were becoming more expensive.* ◇ *Building customized software had proved too expensive.* ◇ **~ to do sth** *The enormous number of doses that would be required would be difficult and expensive to produce.* OPP INEXPENSIVE ■ **ex·pen·sive·ly** *adv.*: *'Flexible production' means that manufacturers are able to produce specific goods less expensively in small quantities.*

ex·peri·ence¹ /ɪk'spɪəriəns; *NAmE* ɪk'spɪriəns/ *noun* **1** [U] the knowledge and skill that you have gained through doing sth for a period of time; the process of gaining this: *52% of participants had teaching experience of over ten years.* ◇ **~ in sth** *The factory started with 5 000 employees who had no prior experience in automobile production.* ◇ **~ as sth** *The author has experience as a social* *worker and family therapist.* ◇ **~ with sth/sb** *One of the researchers had extensive experience with the experimental task.* ◇ **~ in doing sth** *Many doctors described lack of experience in dealing with addiction.* ◇ **~ of doing sth** *The focus group leaders all had experience of conducting interviews, but they varied in their research experience.* ➲ *see also* WORK EXPERIENCE **2** [U] the things that have happened to you that affect the way you think and behave: *Past experience shows that refugees will return to their country of origin at the first opportunity.* ◇ **~ of sth** *All the participants in the study had direct experience of illness in the past or currently.* ◇ **from ~** *We know from experience that gases mix unconditionally and completely.* **3** [C] an event or activity that affects you in some way: *Generally, retirement was seen as a positive experience.* ◇ **~ of sth** *Some enjoyable experiences of exercise were reported, but it was often viewed as unpleasant.* ◇ **~ of doing sth** *Class members reflected on their own experiences of living with a disability.* **4 the... experience** [sing.] events or knowledge shared by all the members of a particular group in society, that affects the way they think and behave: *Business is an important part of the American experience.* ◇ *One feature of the human experience, especially in the Western world, has been the quest for greater control over the natural world.*

▸ ADJECTIVE + EXPERIENCE **previous, prior** • **extensive, considerable, long** • **practical** • **clinical** • **international** *The study found that entrepreneurs often have high education levels and previous management experience.* ◇ *The surveys allow students to gain practical experience of the use of graphs, tables and charts.* | **previous, prior, past** • **early** • **direct, first-hand** • **lived** • **everyday** • **personal** • **individual** • **shared** • **human** • **subjective** • **religious** • **historical** *A few studies have discussed retirement in the light of earlier experiences in different areas of life.* ◇ *All four plays are based on the lived experiences of ordinary South Africans.* | **first** • **positive, good** • **negative, bad** • **traumatic** • **stressful** *These are the children's first experiences in a classroom in which parents are not present.*

▸ NOUN + EXPERIENCE **life** • **childhood** • **patient** • **customer** *Two childhood experiences shaped the economist's career.*

▸ VERB + EXPERIENCE **have** *Some patients may have had bad experiences with side effects of the drugs in the past.* | **gain** • **lack** *The engineers wanted to produce a trial machine quickly to gain experience.* | **share** • **recall** • **report** • **describe** • **explore** • **understand** • **shape** • **enhance** • **reflect** • **capture** *The changes introduced served to enhance the experience for both new and existing customers.* ◇ *The movie successfully reflects the experience of adolescence.*

▸ EXPERIENCE + VERB **show** • **suggest** • **teach** *Experience shows that even large office buildings can be cooled using natural cooling resources.*

ex·peri·ence[2] /ɪkˈspɪəriəns; *NAmE* ɪkˈspɪriəns/ *verb* **1 ~ sth** to have a particular situation affect you or happen to you: *At that time, traditional cities outside Europe began to experience substantial change.* ◇ *Men may also experience domestic violence.* ◇ *The discussion paper examined the problems experienced by all those who share homes.* ➲ *compare* UNDERGO **2 ~ sth** to have a particular emotion or physical feeling: *Anger is a perfectly natural emotion experienced by children, teens and adults.* ◇ *After 22 years, four out of five patients still experienced low back pain.*

▸ EXPERIENCE + NOUN **event** • **change** • **increase** • **growth** • **decline** • **loss** • **problem, difficulty** • **crisis** • **discrimination** • **violence** • **abuse** • **conflict** *The tourism industry has experienced dramatic growth since about 1960.* | **symptom** • **pain** • **emotion, feeling** • **anger** • **frustration** • **anxiety** • **stress** *Salespeople who experience job stress tend to be less involved in their jobs.*

ex·peri·enced /ɪkˈspɪəriənst; *NAmE* ɪkˈspɪriənst/ *adj.* having knowledge or skill in a particular job or activity, usually as a result of doing it for a long time: *Interviews were conducted by trained and experienced interviewers.* ◇ *The judges in the study were selected as they were highly experienced judges in family law disputes.* ◇ *7 of the volunteers had more than 10 years' clinical experience and were considered 'very experienced'.* OPP INEXPERIENCED

ex·peri·en·tial /ɪkˌspɪəriˈenʃl; *NAmE* ɪkˌspɪriˈenʃl/ *adj.* based on or involving experience or observation: *Experiential learning and workplace knowledge were incorporated into the curriculum.* ◇ *Doctors often rely on experiential knowledge gained from their training and personal clinical experience.* ■ **ex·peri·en·tial·ly** /ɪkˌspɪəriˈenʃəli; *NAmE* ɪkˌspɪriˈenʃəli/ *adv.*: *The use of new technology was learned experientially.*

E

ex·peri·ment[1] /ɪkˈsperɪmənt/ *noun* **1** [C] a scientific test that is done in order to study what happens and to gain new knowledge: *A second experiment was conducted to confirm the previous finding.* ◇ *We performed two separate field experiments to test our hypotheses.* ◇ *Experiments have shown that the birds' appearance and body condition are affected by the intake of nutrients.* ◇ *The results of these experiments demonstrated that the bat's detection system is extremely sensitive.* ◇ **~ on sb/sth** *This study expands upon previous experiments on food safety.* ➲ *see also* THOUGHT EXPERIMENT ➲ thesaurus note *at* INVESTIGATION **2** [C] a new activity, idea or method that you try out to see what happens or what effect it has: **~ in sth/in doing sth** *'Sesame Street' began in 1969 as an experiment in children's educational television.* ◇ **~ with sth** *In the electricity sector, there have been experiments with privatization and deregulation.* **3** [U] the process of testing sth to study what happens or to see what effect it has: **(by) ~** *This hypothesis was quickly disproved by experiment.*

▸ ADJECTIVE + EXPERIMENT **early** • **previous** • **recent** • **classic** • **preliminary** • **simple** • **independent** • **randomized** • **controlled** • **natural** *Plant decay has been subjected to controlled experiments both in the laboratory and under natural conditions.* ◇ *Twins provide a fascinating natural experiment in human variability.*

▸ NOUN + EXPERIMENT **laboratory** • **field** • **animal** *Field observations are supported by laboratory experiments.*

▸ VERB + EXPERIMENT **conduct, perform, do, carry out, undertake** • **design** • **repeat** • **describe** • **run** *Experiments were run between January and April 2010.*

▸ EXPERIMENT + VERB **show, demonstrate, reveal** • **suggest** • **confirm** • **test** *Experiments on captive birds have revealed that the memory of seed hiding places can last for several weeks.*

ex·peri·ment[2] /ɪkˈsperɪmənt/ *verb* **1** [I] to try or test new ideas or methods to find out what effect they have: *The job of the salesperson is to experiment, take risks and explore possibilities.* ◇ **~ with sth** *Painters have always experimented with light.* ◇ **~ with doing sth** *Normal adolescent developmental needs include experimenting with adopting adult behaviours.* **2** [I] to do a scientific experiment or experiments: *The solution the electricians found would probably have worked if they had had a few more months experimenting.* ◇ **~ on sb/sth** *Some people feel that experimenting on animals is wrong.* ◇ **~ with sth** *Under the direction of two biologists, the lab experimented with a number of fish species.*

ex·peri·men·tal /ɪkˌsperɪˈmentl/ *adj.* **1** [usually before noun] connected with scientific experiments: *There are very few experimental studies comparing the parental behaviour of young and old animals.* ◇ *The software used for the present analysis has been tested and verified under experimental conditions.* ◇ *In the experimental group, each word list contained a word related to the concept of old age.* **2** based on new ideas, forms or methods that are used to find out what effect they have: *The non-story film can be broken down into the experimental film and the* *film of fact.* ◇ *The therapy he needs is both costly and experimental.*

▸ EXPERIMENTAL + NOUN **design** ♦ **study** ♦ **research** ♦ **work** ♦ **approach** ♦ **technique, method, procedure** ♦ **condition** ♦ **set-up** ♦ **data, evidence, result** ♦ **observation** ♦ **investigation** ♦ **measurement** ♦ **manipulation** ♦ **error** *No experimental data are yet available to test this assumption.* ◇ *In this paper, a brief description of the experimental set-up that was constructed and a description of the experimental procedure that was followed will be given.*

E

ex·peri·men·tal·ly /ɪkˌsperɪˈmentəli/ *adv.* by using a scientific test or tests: *These reactions have been studied experimentally.* ◇ *The aim of this study was to test experimentally whether the size of the nest opening acts as a defence against aggressive males.*

ex·peri·men·ta·tion /ɪkˌsperɪmenˈteɪʃn/ *noun* [U] **1** the process of trying a new activity, idea or method to see what effect it has: *Ancient Greek art is characterized by variety and experimentation.* ◇ **~ in sth** *The seventh century was the greatest period for experimentation in design in China.* ◇ **~ with sth** *While first experimentation with cigarettes typically occurs earlier in life, regular smoking is usually established in early adulthood.* **2** the process of using scientific tests in order to study what happens or to gain new knowledge: *The website provides information on the law concerning animal experimentation.* ◇ *Whether the female's behaviour is learned through experience is unclear and requires further experimentation.* ◇ **~ on sb/sth** *There have been campaigns against scientific or commercial experimentation on animals.*

ex·peri·men·ter /ɪkˈsperɪməntə(r)/ *noun* a person who conducts a scientific test: *Eight undergraduate research assistants served as experimenters.* ◇ *The experimenter measures the time that the subject takes to respond to the letters on the screen.*

ex·pert[1] AWL /ˈekspɜːt; *NAmE* ˈekspɜːrt/ *noun* a person with special knowledge, skill or training in sth: *The company's 5 000 sales engineers liaise with technical experts inside their own business.* ◇ *The Delphi technique involves asking a panel of experts to take part in a series of questionnaires.* ◇ **~ in sth** *The analysis of the drawings was carried out by an expert in children's art.* ◇ **~ on sth** *He is a leading expert on the international monetary system.* ◇ **~ at/in doing sth** *Specialist speech and language therapists are experts at assessing whether a patient is safe to swallow food without choking.*

ex·pert[2] AWL /ˈekspɜːt; *NAmE* ˈekspɜːrt/ *adj.* **1** done or provided by sb with special knowledge or skill in a particular area: *Published data and expert opinion support the effectiveness of this technique for pain control.* ◇ *An expert assessment of the child found him to be unhappy and confused.* **2** having special knowledge, skill or training in sth: *The expert panel was composed of health care providers from various settings.* ◇ *An analysis of an airplane crash by expert investigators can lead to changes in aircraft design.* ◇ **~ at/in sth** *The users of these web tools are not expert in computer science.* ◇ **~ at/in doing sth** *The artist was expert at portraying psychological intensity and extreme behaviours.* ■ **ex·pert·ly** AWL *adv.*: *Techniques for sea level studies are expertly analysed in the article.* ◇ *Bureaucracy demands expertly trained technicians and clerks.*

ex·pert·ise AWL /ˌekspɜːˈtiːz; *NAmE* ˌekspɜːrˈtiːz/ *noun* [U] special knowledge or skill in a particular subject, activity or job: *This technique requires a high level of technical expertise to avoid harming the patient.* ◇ **~ in sth** *The ancient Greek maps had been drawn by scholars with expertise in astronomy, geometry and mathematics.* ◇ **~ in doing sth** *These workers brought expertise in implementing health projects and services specifically for Arabic speakers.*

ex·plain /ɪkˈspleɪn/ *verb* **1** [T, I] to tell sb about sth in a way that makes it easy to understand: **~ sth** *The legislators must explain and justify these laws* ◇ **~ (sth) (to sb)** *It is important to explain the risks to parents.* ◇ **~ that...** *He explained that the man had been taken into custody.* ◇ **~ how/what, etc...** *The article explains how the research was conducted.* ◇ **~ to sb how/what, etc...** *Explain to the patients what each food is.* ◇ **+ speech** *'They had to steal food to survive,' the priest explained.* **2** [I, T] to give a reason for sth; to be a reason for sth: **~ that...** *In English she explained that she lacked the vocabulary to describe the image.* ◇ **~ why/how, etc...** *This theory does not explain why the illness occurs.* ◇ *This explains how genes can be 'selfish'.* ◇ **~ sth (to sb)**| **~ to sb why/how, etc...** *Kelly has to explain to her friend why she is leaving the party early.* HELP You cannot say 'explain me, him, her, etc.': ~~*Kelly has to explain her friend why...*~~

PHR V **exˌplain sth aˈway** to give reasons why sth is not important or is not your fault: *Not all the discrepancies have been explained away.*

▸ EXPLAIN + NOUN **meaning** ♦ **concept** ♦ **nature** ♦ **relationship** ♦ **role** ♦ **process** *We explained the nature, purpose and process of our study to the participants.* | **difference** ♦ **variation** ♦ **variance** ♦ **discrepancy** ♦ **disparity** ♦ **change** ♦ **behaviour** ♦ **effect** ♦ **phenomenon** ♦ **result** ♦ **finding** ♦ **observation** ♦ **fact** ♦ **pattern** ♦ **reason** ♦ **choice** ♦ **origin** ♦ **evolution** ♦ **success** *It is beyond the scope of this paper to try and explain this phenomenon.* ◇ *Several possibilities have been proposed to explain these inconsistent findings.*

▸ NOUN + EXPLAIN **factor** ♦ **theory, hypothesis** *These factors may explain the differences in prices that were observed.*

▸ BE EXPLAINED BY + NOUN **the fact that** ♦ **reference to** ♦ **differences** *Late marriage and non-marriage are usually explained by reference to social organization and economic aspirations.*

▸ ADVERB + EXPLAIN | EXPLAIN + ADVERB **fully** ♦ **well** ♦ **adequately** ♦ **clearly** ♦ **briefly** ♦ **further** *Age and gender did not fully explain the variance in the data.*

▸ ADVERB + EXPLAIN **partially, partly** ♦ **largely** ♦ **easily, readily** *Water content may partially explain the behaviour of the fish.*

▸ EXPLAIN + ADVERB **below, above** ♦ **later, earlier** *The results are explained later.*

ex·plan·ation /ˌekspləˈneɪʃn/ *noun* **1** [C, U] a statement, fact or situation that tells you why sth happened: *An alternative explanation is that potatoes were cheaper than fresh fruit.* ◇ *These differences require some explanation.* ◇ **~ for sth** *This model is less successful in providing an explanation for what happened.* ◇ ◇ **~ of sth** *One possible explanation of this finding is that participants did not process the raw data accurately.* ◇ **~ as to how/why...** *Barnes offers no explanation as to why the king made this decision.* **2** [C] **~ (of sth)** a statement or piece of writing that tells you how sth works or makes sth easier to understand: *The briefing covered detailed explanations of every process to be undertaken.* ◇ *The author provides a brief explanation of his oral history process.*

▸ ADJECTIVE + EXPLANATION **detailed** ♦ **full, complete** ♦ **simple** ♦ **clear** *The patient's anxiety can be reduced by a clear explanation of the operation and its likely consequences.* | **possible, potential** ♦ **plausible** ♦ **convincing** ♦ **good** ♦ **adequate, satisfactory** ♦ **reasonable** ♦ **rational** ♦ **likely** ♦ **obvious** ♦ **alternative** ♦ **partial** ♦ **causal** ♦ **scientific** ♦ **theoretical** ♦ **sociological** ♦ **historical** ♦ **economic** ♦ **pyschological** ♦ **evolutionary** *There is, as yet, no satisfactory explanation for this result.* ◇ *Palissy offered scientific explanations for the growth of plants and fruits and their dependence on nutrients in the soil.*

▸ VERB + EXPLANATION **provide, offer, give** *Linnaeus described the pattern of similarities between species without giving an explanation of why biological diversity* *was organized that way.* | **require, need • demand • seek • find • suggest • propose, advance** *Our results suggest two explanations for this decline.*

ex·plana·tory /ɪk'splænətri; *NAmE* ɪk'splænətɔːri/ *adj.* [usually before noun] intended to describe how sth works or to make sth easier to understand: *Brief explanatory notes are provided in appendix 21.1.* ◇ *The explanatory power of transition theory is quite limited.* ◇ *an explanatory model/framework* HELP In statistics, an **explanatory variable** is one that helps explain differences in a set of data: *The key explanatory variable of our analysis was marital status.*

ex·plic·able /ɪk'splɪkəbl; 'eksplɪkəbl/ *adj.* [not usually before noun] that can be explained or understood: **~ by sth** *The signs and symptoms may be explicable by a number of disorders.* ◇ **~ in terms of sth** *Species diversity in tropical rainforest could be explicable in terms of existing ecological factors.*

ex·pli·cit AWL /ɪk'splɪsɪt/ *adj.* **1** saying sth clearly and exactly: *This was the first UN statement to make an explicit reference to gender identity.* ◇ **~ about sth** *Robbins was explicit about her research questions.* ◇ **~ that...** *He is quite explicit that what he is doing is making a supposition.* ◇ **~ in doing sth** *Bradbury is far more explicit in presenting his view.* ➲ *compare* IMPLICIT (2) **2** showing or referring to sex in a very obvious or detailed way: *In the changed climate of the late 1970s, it was possible to include more sexually explicit material.* ◇ *Hawks and his screenwriters had to tone down much of the novel's explicit content.*

ex·pli·cit·ly AWL /ɪk'splɪsɪtli/ *adv.* **1** used to say that sth is mentioned or explained or in a way that is clear and easy to understand: *The initial judgement states explicitly that some of the responsibility lay with the trade unions.* ◇ *For much of his information, Brown was dependent on an earlier book, which he explicitly mentions in his novel.* **2** used to say that an aspect of sth is presented or shown in a way that is very clear or obvious: *The novels are not explicitly political.* ◇ *Much of the art and iconography has explicitly sexual content.*

ex·plode /ɪk'spləʊd; *NAmE* ɪk'sploʊd/ *verb* **1** [I, T] to burst or make sth burst loudly and violently, causing damage SYN BLOW UP: *Because of the high reactivity, dry iron nanoparticles tend to explode in contact with air.* ◇ **~ sth** *Britain had not yet exploded her first nuclear weapon.* **2** [I] **~ (into sth)** (of a situation) to suddenly become very violent or dangerous: *The tension, first provoked by Vasco da Gama, now exploded into violence.* **3** [I] to increase suddenly and very quickly in number or amount: *The world's population really exploded in the 20th century with the development of modern medicine.*

ex·ploit AWL *verb* /ɪk'splɔɪt/ **1 ~ sth** to use sth well in order to gain as much from it as possible: *In order to exploit these opportunities, organizations need to adopt a new approach.* ◇ *Alternative approaches have been explored, although their potential has not yet been fully exploited.* **2** to develop or use sth for business or industry: **~ sth** *The government hopes that these mineral resources will eventually be fully exploited.* ◇ **~ sth for sth** *Certain features of coactivator action can be exploited for clinical use.* **3 ~ sb/sth (for sth)** (*disapproving*) to treat a person or situation as an opportunity to gain an advantage for yourself: *She tackles the question of whether patients were exploited for commercial gain.* **4 ~ sb** (*disapproving*) to treat sb unfairly by making them work and not giving them much in return: *The company was accused of exploiting workers, including children, who worked for long hours for little pay.*

ex·ploit·ation AWL /ˌeksplɔɪ'teɪʃn/ *noun* [U] **1** the use of land, oil, minerals or other resources: *The company maintains control over domestic natural gas exploration and exploitation.* ◇ **~ of sth** *Fishing permits are used as a means of managing the exploitation of fishing grounds.* ◇ *There is evidence of ruthless exploitation of nature in this region.* **2 ~ of sth** the fact of using sth in order to gain as much from it as possible: *Commercial exploitation of the Internet proceeded most rapidly in the United States during the 1990s.* ◇ *A new trend is the party's efficient and cynical exploitation of international feelings of guilt and ineptitude.* **3** (*disapproving*) a situation in which sb treats sb else unfairly, especially in order to make money from their work: *Immigrants are often vulnerable to exploitation.* ◇ *The Convention on the Rights of the Child strives to protect children from economic and sexual exploitation.*

E

ex·ploit·ative /ɪk'splɔɪtətɪv/ (*NAmE also* **ex·ploit·ive** /ɪk'splɔɪtɪv/) *adj.* treating sb unfairly in order to gain an advantage or to make money: *There are large numbers of women who are subject to particularly exploitative conditions of work.* ◇ *There has been a history of research being carried out on Aboriginal peoples in insensitive and exploitative ways.*

ex·plor·ation /ˌekspləˈreɪʃn/ *noun* **1** [U, C] an examination of sth in order to find out about it: *This theory deserves further exploration.* ◇ **~ (of sth)** *This result allows exploration of thermoelectric energy conversion at the molecular scale.* ◇ *Historical explorations in urban geography include Cobban's work on public housing.* **2** [U, C] the act of travelling through a place in order to find out about it: *The Mariner is portrayed as a sixteenth-century sailor on a voyage of exploration.* ◇ *Contending with this extreme environment is the core problem of human space exploration.* ◇ *Different constructions of Africa emerged as a result of travels, explorations and conquest.* **3** [U] the action of searching an area for natural resources: *Relative political stability and economic development have sparked African oil exploration and production.* ◇ *gas/petroleum/geochemical exploration*

ex·plora·tory /ɪk'splɒrətri; *NAmE* ɪk'splɔːrətɔːri/ *adj.* [usually before noun] done with the intention of examining sth in order to find out more about it: *The present investigation is an exploratory study aimed at gaining new insights into the allocation of processing resources.* ◇ *Exploratory analysis of the data found a high proportion of missing values in the outcome variables.*

ex·plore /ɪk'splɔː(r)/ *verb* **1** [T] to examine sth completely or carefully in order to find out more about it SYN ANALYSE: **~ sth** *The film explores the relationship between a young girl and her five-year-old brother.* ◇ *Unfortunately, he fails to fully explore this issue.* ◇ *This concept is worth exploring further.* ◇ **~ what/who, etc...** *Future research should explore what is likely to happen when the new industries begin to decline.* ➲ thesaurus note *on* page 304 ➲ language bank *at* ABOUT² **2** [T, I] to travel to or around an area or a country in order to learn about it: **~ sth (for sth)** *This is the main reason America continues to explore space.* ◇ **~ (for sth)** *The Libyan Government granted Hunt permission to explore for oil.* ➲ *see also* UNEXPLORED

▸ EXPLORE + NOUN **issue • question • idea, concept • theme • topic • aspect • way • nature • extent • range • role • relationship • link • effect • consequence • possibility • meaning • implication • difference • reason** *Further research is needed to explore these possibilities.* ◇ *There is a strong case for exploring the effects of management change on employees.*

▸ ADVERB + EXPLORE | EXPLORE + ADVERB **further • fully • briefly** *The findings thus need to be explored further in future studies.* ◇ *In this section I shall briefly explore why this should be so.*

ex·plorer /ɪk'splɔːrə(r)/ *noun* a person who travels to unknown places in order to find out more about them: *Early map-makers obtained their data from explorers and travellers.* ◇ **~ to...** *Most of the early European explorers to the New World noted the curious local habit of smoking.*

THESAURUS

explore • examine • investigate • analyse *verb*

These words are all used to describe the aims of a piece of academic work; they all mean to study, research or discuss sth carefully in order to find out or understand more.

- to explore/examine/investigate/analyse the **effect/role/impact** of sth
- to explore/examine/investigate/analyse the **relationship/difference/factors**
- to explore/examine/investigate/analyse a/an **question/issue**
- a **study/article/chapter/author** explores/examines/investigates/analyses sth
- to explore/examine/investigate/analyse sth **in depth/in detail**
- to explore/examine/investigate/analyse sth **in terms of/in relation to** sth

- **Explore** and **examine** are the most general of these words; they can involve discussing a topic, considering existing evidence or conducting research; **investigate** typically involves conducting research in order to find out more about sth: *This chapter will explore the complex issues impacting on international marketing communications in today's global marketplace.* ◇ *This section examines the relationship between age and attitudes toward ICTs.* ◇ *Many studies have investigated the association between birth order and childhood onset diabetes.*
- **Analyse** is used to talk about a more structured analysis of a problem, evidence, etc.: *to analyse data/information/samples* ◇ *The report analyses health services in terms of efficiency of delivery of health care.*

E

ex·plo·sion /ɪkˈspləʊʒn; *NAmE* ɪkˈsploʊʒn/ *noun* [C, U] **1** the sudden violent bursting and loud noise of sth such as a bomb exploding; the act of deliberately causing sth to explode: *Unlike conventional weapons, a nuclear explosion also produces lethal radiation.* ◇ **~ of sth** *Many of the scientists who had seen the first explosion of the bomb in New Mexico were in awe of its destructive potential.* **2** a large or sudden increase in the amount or number of sth: *Combined with economic growth, population explosion was going to exhaust stocks of energy, cropland, clean water and minerals.* ◇ **~ of sth** *In the last fifty years, there has been an explosion of interest in climate change.*

ex·plo·sive /ɪkˈspləʊsɪv; ɪkˈspləʊzɪv; *NAmE* ɪkˈsploʊsɪv; ɪkˈsploʊzɪv/ *adj.* **1** exploding; easily able or likely to explode: *Major explosive volcanic eruptions often result in cooling of global climate.* ◇ *A state does not actually need to test a nuclear explosive device to be in possession of a nuclear stockpile.* **2** likely to cause violence or strong feelings of anger: *Abortion is still an explosive issue in American politics.* ◇ *Economic reform produced massive and potentially explosive social changes.* **3** increasing suddenly and quickly: *The explosive growth and use of the Internet has been at the heart of global development.*

ex·po·nent /ɪkˈspəʊnənt; *NAmE* ɪkˈspoʊnənt/ *noun* **1 ~ (of sth)** a person who supports an idea or theory and persuades others that it is good SYN PROPONENT: *Turing was a leading early exponent of the theory that the brain is in effect a digital computer.* **2 ~ (of sth)** a person who is able to perform a particular activity with skill: *He was well regarded by the swimming community, both as an exponent and a teacher of the sport.* **3** (*mathematics*) a small number written above another number that shows how many times a quantity must be multiplied by itself, for example the figure 4 in a^4: *This exponent can take values both greater than and less than two.* **4 ~ (of sth)** (*linguistics*) a feature of language that allows speakers or writers to change tense, mood, etc: *The word looks plural; it ends in 's', which is a typical exponent of plurality.*

ex·po·nen·tial /ˌekspəˈnenʃl/ *adj.* [usually before noun] **1** (of a rate of increase) becoming faster and faster: *The exponential growth of the Internet provides opportunities for improving public health.* ◇ *The aftermath of these events witnessed an exponential increase in multifaith initiatives.* **2** (*mathematics*) of or shown by an exponent: *This equation indicates that solubility is an exponential function of temperature.* ◇ *Many system failures have an exponential curve, as shown in Figure 5.6.*

ex·po·nen·tial·ly /ekspəˈnenʃəli/ *adv.* **1** used to say that a rate of increase is getting faster and faster: *The city's coal consumption had grown exponentially over a forty-year period.* ◇ *Oil demand is clearly rising exponentially.* **2** (*mathematics*) in a way that is shown or caused by an exponent: *A population growing exponentially at 2 per cent per annum increases by a constant ratio in each interval.*

ex·port[1] AWL *noun* /ˈekspɔːt; *NAmE* ˈekspɔːrt/ **1** [U, C] the process of sending goods or services to another country for sale: **~ (of sth)** *A ban on the export of wine in bulk was held to breach Article 29.* ◇ *The Chinese government increased the VAT rebates for exports of certain products.* ◇ **+ noun** *Canada is the fourth largest export market for Greek virgin olive oil.* OPP IMPORT[1] (1) **2** [C, usually pl.] a product or service that is sold to another country: *The worldwide economic slowdown reduced demand for Russia's chief exports: oil and gas.* ◇ *Exports were promoted as a way to earn foreign exchange and pay off foreign debt.* ◇ *A higher interest rate may have an impact on net exports.* OPP IMPORT[1] (2)

ex·port[2] AWL *verb* /ɪkˈspɔːt; *NAmE* ɪkˈspɔːrt/ **1** [T, I] to send goods or services to another country for sale: **~ sth (to...)** *The volume of Australian beef exported to Japan has more than doubled.* ◇ **~ to...** *Exporting directly to China has been encouraged by the lowering of trade barriers.* ◇ **~ (sth) (from...) (to...)** *Ground-nut oil and palm oil were exported from Senegal.* OPP IMPORT[2] (1) **2** [T] **~ sth (+ adv./prep.)** to introduce an idea or activity to another country or area: *Rome exported this model of political organization to its non-Mediterranean territories.* ◇ *The format of this TV show is so successful that it has been exported around the world.* OPP IMPORT[2] (2) **3** [T, often passive] **~ sth (to sth)** (*computing*) to send data to another program, changing its form so that the other program can read it: *The data were exported to a spreadsheet for statistical analysis.* OPP IMPORT[2] (3) **4** [T, usually passive] **be exported + adv./prep.** (*biology*) (of a substance) to be moved out of a cell and used in another part of the plant or animal: *The fat is not stored but is exported and taken up by cells of adipose and other tissues.*

ex·port·er AWL /ekˈspɔːtə(r); *NAmE* ekˈspɔːrtər/ *noun* **~ (of sth)** a person, company or country that sells goods or services to another country: *The USA and the UK are the largest net exporters of business services.* OPP IMPORTER

ex·pose AWL /ɪkˈspəʊz; *NAmE* ɪkˈspoʊz/ *verb* **1 ~ sth** to show sth that is usually hidden SYN REVEAL (2): *Adult tamarins helped their offspring to eat by exposing the hidden food.* ◇ *Rocks may be exposed both by naturally occurring and by artificial means.* **2** to tell the true facts about a person or a situation, and show them/it to be immoral, illegal, etc: **~ sb/sth** *A succession of royalist intrigues had already been exposed.* ◇ **~ sb/sth as sth** *He feared that his handlers would expose him as a Communist agent.* **3** to allow light onto the film inside a camera when taking a photograph: *Film was exposed for 1 minute, then developed for 5 minutes, washed and fixed.* ➲ *see also* EXPOSURE

PHR V **be exposed to sth** to be in a place or situation where you are/it is not protected from sth harmful or unpleasant: *Children are more exposed to marketing than* *ever before.* ◇ *Many polymers degrade when exposed to ultraviolet or gamma radiation.* ◇ *Tungara frog males are exposed to predation risk from a number of animals.* **expose sb to sth** to let sb find out about sth by giving them experience of it or showing them what it is like: *The workshops empowered women by exposing them to new ideas on gender relations.*

ex·posed AWL /ɪk'spəʊzd; *NAmE* ɪk'spoʊzd/ *adj.* **1** (of a place) not protected from the weather by trees, buildings or high ground: *Plants growing in exposed positions exhibit symptoms of leaf drop.* ◇ *This phenomenon occurs on exposed rock surfaces in equatorial rainforest in Surinam (Bakker, 1960).* **2** (*finance*) likely to experience financial losses: *The interests of large firms in the exposed manufacturing sector will diverge substantially from those of small firms in the sheltered sector.* **3** **~ (to sth)** (of a person) not protected from attack or criticism: *Perhaps the reason for these resignations lies in the pressures to which scientists feel exposed.*

ex·pos·ition /ˌekspə'zɪʃn/ *noun* [C, U] (*formal*) a full explanation of a theory, plan, etc: *There are still many areas in need of greater exposition and clarification.* ◇ **~ of sth** *Cadbury gives an excellent exposition of corporate governance and chairmanship.*

ex·pos·ure AWL /ɪk'spəʊʒə(r); *NAmE* ɪk'spoʊʒər/ *noun* **1** [U, C] **~ (to sth)** the state of being in a place or situation where there is no protection from sth harmful or unpleasant: *Prolonged exposure to stress can lead to exhaustion.* ◇ *These recommendations should reduce worker exposure to radiation to a tolerable level.* ◇ *Environmental exposures during childhood are also a key influence in determining adult height.* **2** [U] **~ (of sth)** the fact of being discussed or mentioned on television, in newspapers, etc. SYN PUBLICITY (1): *The refugees were also helped by the positive effects of media exposure of their ordeal.* ◇ *These organizations are gaining exposure through being listed in the Clubcard brochure.* **3** [U] **~ (of sth)** the state of having the true facts about sb/sth told after they have been hidden because they are bad, immoral or illegal: *The exposure of very poor working conditions in some of the company's overseas operations led to a fall in market share.* **4** [U] a medical condition caused by being out in very cold weather for too long without protection: *The victim died from exposure.* **5** [U] **~ (of sth)** the act of showing sth that is usually hidden: *Exposure of the granite masses is due to the work of rivers flowing over them.*

ex·press[1] /ɪk'spres/ *verb* **1** to make a feeling or an opinion known by words, looks or actions: **~ sth** *Patients expressed concern about taking medications long term.* ◇ *Trade unions have expressed the view that employees lost out during the reform process.* ◇ *Doubts are occasionally expressed concerning the relevance of this theory.* ◇ **~ how/what, etc.** *This view undoubtedly expresses what many people feel about work.* **2** to speak, write or communicate in some other way what you think or feel: **~ yourself** *Her only way to express herself was by drawing pictures.* ◇ **~ yourself + adv./prep.** *Grattius does not always express himself lucidly in his historical accounts.* **3** [often passive] (*mathematics*) to represent sth in a particular way, for example by symbols: **~ sth as sth** *The figures are expressed as percentages.* ◇ **~ sth in terms of sth** *Signals are expressed in terms of the relative amplitudes and phases of their frequency components.* **4** **~ sth (+ adv./prep.)** (*biochemistry*) (in plants and animals) to show a feature due to the presence of a GENE: *The genes are expressed in a variety of cell lines.*

ex·press[2] /ɪk'spres/ *adj.* [only before noun] **1** (*formal*) (of a wish or an aim) clearly stated SYN DEFINITE, EXPLICIT (1): *Information will not be passed to a third party without the express permission of the confider.* ◇ *Both parties need to sign a written contract containing all of the express terms of the agreement.* **2** done for a definite reason SYN SPECIFIC: **with the ~ purpose of** *A conference was held with the express purpose of increasing awareness among Anglophone scholars.*

ex·pres·sion /ɪk'spreʃn/ *noun* **1** [C, U] things that people say, write or do in order to show their feelings, opinions and ideas: **~ of sth** *For most teenagers, running away is clearly an expression of anger and frustration.* ◇ **freedom of ~** *Arcticle 8 of the European Convention of Human Rights guarantees the right to freedom of expression.* ◇ **give ~ to sth** *In this scene, the Duchess gives expression to the struggle between her passions and her reason.* ◇ **find ~ in sth** *This new cinematic version of the city found expression in Patrick Keiller's remarkable film 'London'.* **2** [C, U] a look on a person's face that shows their thoughts or feelings: *Facial expressions are used to reinforce the verbal message.* ◇ *Balazs sees facial expression as far more individual and personal than spoken language.* **3** [C] a word or phrase: *The expression 'therapeutic range' can be misleading.* **4** [C] (*mathematics*) a group of signs that represent an idea or a quantity: *The expression for the circumference of a circle is 2πr.* **5** [U] (*biochemistry*) the presence of a GENE product in a cell, which shows the gene is there: *These molecules are very important in regulating gene expression.*

ex·pres·sive /ɪk'spresɪv/ *adj.* **1** showing or able to show thoughts and feelings: *Political leaders exploited the expressive power of art.* ◇ *Greek is an exceptionally rich and expressive language.* **2** [not before noun] **~ of sth** (*formal*) showing sth; existing as an expression of sth: *Her face and gestures are so vividly expressive of inner life.* ■ **ex·pres·sive·ness** *noun* [U] **~ (of sth)** *The term 'melodrama' referred to the use of music to enhance the emotional expressiveness of key dramatic moments in a play.*

ex·press·ly /ɪk'spresli/ *adv.* **1** clearly; definitely: *The article expressly states that persons are born free and equal in dignity and rights.* **2** for a special and deliberate purpose SYN ESPECIALLY: *A survey designed expressly to identify ancient arable farms was carried out.*

ex·pul·sion /ɪk'spʌlʃn/ *noun* **1** [U, C] **~ (of sb) (from...)** the act of forcing sb to leave a place; the act of EXPELLING sb: *In 1844, Marx and Engels moved to Brussels on their expulsion from France.* ◇ *Post-independence expulsions of Asians from Kenya and Uganda resulted in another wave of migration to Britain.* **2** [U, C] **~ (of sb) (from...)** the act of sending sb away from a school or an organization, so that they can no longer belong to it; the act of EXPELLING sb: *The dispute ended with Nekrich's expulsion from the party.* ◇ *The programme may lead to positive outcomes such as a reduction in the number of detentions, suspensions or expulsions.* **3** [U] **~ (of sth) (from...)** (*formal*) the act of sending or driving a substance out of your body or a container: *Vomiting is the forceful expulsion of gastric contents through the mouth.*

ex·tant /ek'stænt; 'ekstənt/ *adj.* still in existence: *Of the world's 18 extant species of penguin, the Adélie penguin is one of only two true Antarctic species.* ◇ *Some of Crates' satirical verse is still extant.*

ex·tend /ɪk'stend/ *verb* **1** [T] to make a piece of research or an idea or theory cover more areas or subjects: **~ sth (by doing sth)** *The aim of this study was to extend our previous findings by examining the narrative-based intervention method.* ◇ **~ sth + adv./prep.** *There are several problems associated with extending the scope of research beyond a single country's borders.* ◇ *Over the last decade this idea has been extended in a number of directions.* ◇ **~ sth to do sth** *The model has been extended to include exports and imports and international financial markets.* **2** [T] to make sb/sth have more powers or rights: **~ sth** *A number of regional human rights treaties have extended the reach of human rights law.* ◇ **~ sth to sb/sth** *The Reform Bill extended the franchise to all male*

E

householders. **3** [T] to make a business or an organization operate in more places: **~ sth** *The organization is extending the range of markets into which its services will be delivered.* ◇ **~ sth to sth** *The company is also extending its market coverage to the private sector.* **4** [T] **~ sth** to make sth last longer: *The phenomenon of extending lifespan through calorie restriction has been known since the 1930s.* **5** [I] **+ adv./prep.** to include sth: *The analysis extends to the cases where I and J are both double integrals.* ◇ *This construction of nationhood extends beyond boundaries of race.* **6** [I] **+ adv./prep.** to cover a particular area, distance or length of time: *Scientific study of Rorschach assessment extends far beyond American borders.* ◇ *These fluctuations in the economic cycle may extend over periods of 30 to 50 years.* **7** [T] to agree to lend sb money or to give them credit: **~ sth** *As the interest rate increases, it becomes more attractive for the bank to extend credit.* ◇ **~ sth to sb** *Banks extend loans to more marginal borrowers during periods of economic expansion.* **8** [T] **~ sth** to stretch part of your body, especially an arm or a leg, away from yourself: *Ask the patient to flex and extend each elbow.* ➲ *see also* EXTENSION, EXTENSIVE

ex͵tended ˈfamily *noun* a family group that includes not only parents and children but also grandparents and other relatives: *Most of the orphans are cared for by extended family members.* ➲ *compare* NUCLEAR FAMILY

ex·ten·sion /ɪkˈstenʃn/ *noun* **1** [U, C] the act of making an idea or activity cover more areas or subjects: **~ of sth** *This research is a natural extension of the work begun by Zhao and Zobel.* ◇ **~ of sth to do sth** *The extension of the model to include imports and exports raises a second issue.* ◇ **~ to sth** *This idea is capable of extension to the study of relations between governments and contractors.* **2** [U, C] an increase in the powers or rights that sb/sth has: **~ of sth** *With the extension of police powers, human rights groups have warned that the country could become a police state.* ◇ **~ to sth** *A further extension to the employee's rights has been the introduction of 'parental leave' days.* **3** [C] an extra period of time allowed for sth: *The department's powers include the issuing of work permit extensions.* ◇ **~ of sth** *Married partners will be granted an extension of stay for two years in the first instance.* **4** [C] a part that develops or spreads from a central point: *The New York City–Philadelphia axis, with extensions north to Boston and south to Baltimore, remained the core area.* **5** [U] the act of stretching a part of your body, especially an arm or a leg, away from yourself: *If a patient has normal extension and flexion, they do not require emergency elbow radiographs.*

IDM **by exˈtension** taking the argument or situation one stage further: *The emergence of the Methodist Church had an immense impact on English culture, and, by extension, other English-speaking cultures.*

ex·ten·sive /ɪkˈstensɪv/ *adj.* **1** including or dealing with a wide range of information: *There is an extensive literature on the relationship that consumers develop with a brand.* ◇ *Following extensive research, the company developed a format that was appropriate to the Japanese market.* **2** great in amount or degree: *Many modern appliances make extensive use of microprocessors to control their functioning.* ◇ *This procedure is performed when there is extensive middle-ear damage.* **3** covering a large area: *The northern hemisphere has the most extensive temperate forests and grasslands.* ◇ *Underlying the karst is an extensive network of caves.*

▸ EXTENSIVE + NOUN **research, study • work • analysis • discussion • review • literature • body of sth • range • coverage • data, information** *The extensive study of 2 149 doctors provides worrying evidence that trainees lack confidence in managing diabetes.* ◇ *An extensive body of empirical research establishes that large cities have relatively high levels of earnings.* | **use • experience • training • power • consultation • damage** *Two senior researchers with extensive experience in qualitative research conducted all interviews.* ◇ *The legislation had been hurriedly passed because the government claimed that it needed extensive new powers.* | **network • system • area** *Indonesia and the Philippines support the most extensive areas of coral reef in the region.*

ex·ten·sive·ly /ɪkˈstensɪvli/ *adv.* **1** in a way that includes or deals with a wide range of information: *Doniger has written extensively on the myths, rituals and religions of India.* ◇ *The development of marketing strategy has been discussed extensively in the marketing literature.* ◇ *In this interpretive work, the author draws extensively on oral histories conducted in the field.* **2** in a way that covers a large area: *Dewey also travelled extensively, including trips to China, Mexico, Russia, South Africa and Turkey.* **3** to a great extent; in a wide range of ways: *Glass fibre composites are used extensively in the automotive and chemical industries.*

ex·tent /ɪkˈstent/ *noun* [sing., U] **1 ~ of sth** how large, important or serious sth is: *It may be difficult to determine the full extent of the problem.* ◇ *It is important to define the extent of the infection.* ◇ *There is disagreement over the role and the extent of family involvement in the decision-making process.* **2** the physical size of an area: *Sea ice varies considerably in extent and duration from year to year.* ◇ **~ of sth** *Calculation of the worldwide extent of wetlands is difficult because they are so widely scattered.*

IDM **to a/an... extent** used to show how far sth is true or how great an effect it has: *They communicate with their friends via IM, and, to a lesser extent, by phone.* ◇ *To a large extent, the distribution of dominant tree species in Interior Alaska has been shaped by fire.* ◇ *The company has grown to such an extent that it is now responsible for processing half of all lamb and beef produced in Wales.* ◇ *The size of the market itself depends on the extent to which modern techniques are adopted.* IDM *see* CERTAIN[1]

▸ ADJECTIVE + EXTENT **full** *The syllabus should take into account learners' needs to the fullest possible extent.* | **lesser • greater • large, great, significant, considerable • certain • limited • small** *To a limited extent, these relationships allow the prediction of the properties of polymers not yet synthesized.*

▸ VERB + EXTENT **determine, establish, define • measure • assess, evaluate • examine, consider, explore, investigate • indicate, reveal, show, demonstrate • reflect • limit • influence** *'Relative poverty' measures the extent to which a household's income falls below the average income.* ◇ *The judge limited the extent of the fine because of the company's outstanding conservation record.*

ex·ter·ior[1] /ɪkˈstɪəriə(r); *NAmE* ɪkˈstɪriər/ *noun* the outside of sth, especially a building SYN OUTSIDE[1] (1): *The churches' exteriors were usually plain, but the interiors were artistically magnificent.* ◇ **~ of sth** *The landlord has to keep the structure and exterior of the building in repair.* OPP INTERIOR[1]

ex·ter·ior[2] /ɪkˈstɪəriə(r); *NAmE* ɪkˈstɪriər/ *adj.* [usually before noun] on the outside of sth; done or happening outdoors SYN OUTSIDE[2] (1), EXTERNAL (1): *The exterior walls of the building are made of 20-mm-thick cement mortar.* ◇ *Laboratory conditions shut out, as far as possible, all potentially disruptive exterior factors.* OPP INTERIOR[2]

ex·ter·nal AWL /ɪkˈstɜːnl; *NAmE* ɪkˈstɜːrnl/ *adj.* **1** coming from outside the place, organization or situation that is affected: *For the expansion to take place, the external pressure has to be less than the internal pressure.* ◇ *The external forces that drive change can be grouped into a number of categories.* HELP The **external validity** of a study is the degree to which its findings apply beyond its own research context: *External validity is strong when the sample from which data are collected has been randomly* selected. OPP INTERNAL (5) **2** existing outside a place, an organization or a particular situation; connected with the outside of sth: *Where the external environment is changing fast, employees of the organization may feel threatened.* ◇ *The directive applies to the external borders of the EU, and not to borders between EU countries.* OPP INTERNAL (3) **3** connected with foreign countries: *China has increased its level of external trade from almost zero in 1978 to the point where it is now the third largest trading nation in the world.* OPP INTERNAL (4)

▸ EXTERNAL + NOUN **pressure, force • influence, stimulus • shock • threat • constraint • control • factor • source • assessment • support • funding, finance** *Bacterial genes are able to adapt rapidly to external threats.* ◇ *In looking for external influences on behaviour, it is also necessary to look beyond the immediate family group.* | **environment, world, reality • conditions • borders** *Living beings are robust, and survive for relatively long periods of time, even when the external conditions continuously vary.* | **trade • market • debt • enemy** *Technology-oriented human resources are difficult to obtain from external markets in emerging economies.*

ex·ter·nal·ity AWL /ˌekstɜːˈnæləti; *NAmE* ˌekstɜːrˈnæləti/ *noun* (*pl.* **-ies**) (*also* **exˌternal ˈcost**) (*economics*) a result of an industrial or commercial activity that affects other people or things without this being reflected in market prices: *Incentive payments encourage farmers to reduce negative externalities associated with agricultural activities.* ◇ **~ of sth** *The cost of emission reduction is borne by the polluter, thereby internalizing the externality of pollution into the production process.*

ex·ter·nal·iza·tion (*BrE also* **-isation**) AWL /ɪkˌstɜːnəlaɪˈzeɪʃn; *NAmE* ɪkˌstɜːrnəlaɪˈzeɪʃn/ *noun* [U] **1 ~ (of sth)** the process of changing a way that a company operates so that more of its work is done by outside organizations: *We have seen major reductions in the size of corporate departments, and the externalization of services to call centres, consultants and independent contractors.* **2** (*psychology*) the act of blaming your problems on causes outside yourself, rather than taking personal responsibility for them: *These patients were more prone to utilize projection and externalization.*

ex·ter·nal·ize (*BrE also* **-ise**) AWL /ɪkˈstɜːnəlaɪz; *NAmE* ɪkˈstɜːrnəlaɪz/ *verb* **~ sth** (*psychology*) to blame your problems on causes outside yourself, rather than taking personal responsibility for them: *The person may tend to externalize blame, and become defensive when criticized.* ➲ *compare* INTERNALIZE HELP In psychology, **externalizing** is used to describe any situation in which sth internal is MANIFESTED or PROJECTED onto the external world. **Externalizing behaviour** is behaviour that shows what sb is thinking and feeling, especially ANTISOCIAL behaviour that does not consider the thoughts and feelings of others: *In the analysis, no association was found between cortisol reactivity and externalizing behaviour.* ➲ *compare* INTERNALIZE (1)

ex·ter·nal·ly AWL /ɪkˈstɜːnəli; *NAmE* ɪkˈstɜːrnəli/ *adv.* **1** in a way that comes from the outside: *The child may understand his anger only as it relates to externally imposed punishment.* **2** on the outside: *Radiotherapy is applied externally or internally.* OPP INTERNALLY (1) **3** coming from a foreign country: *The country is likely to fall far behind economically, making itself vulnerable to externally imposed regime change.* OPP INTERNALLY (4) **4** in a way that is directed towards the outside: *HR professionals need to be more externally focused and skilled at building networks.* OPP INTERNALLY (3)

ex·tinct /ɪkˈstɪŋkt/ *adj.* **1** (of a type of plant, animal, etc.) no longer in existence: *After Europeans arrived in New Zealand, all moa species became extinct.* ◇ *He found bones of enormous extinct animals and fossilized remains of sea creatures high in the Andes Mountains.* **2** (of a type of person, job or way of life) no longer in existence in society: *By 1580, the traditional industry was virtually extinct.* **3** (of a VOLCANO) no longer active: *These hills also include several extinct volcanoes.* OPP ACTIVE¹ (6)

ex·tinc·tion /ɪkˈstɪŋkʃn/ *noun* [U, C] a situation in which a plant, an animal, a way of life, etc. stops existing: *Environmental change in many cases has resulted in species extinction.* ◇ **~ of sth** *This was triggered largely by concerns about the possible extinction of tigers in the wild.* ◇ *The Chicxulub meteorite has become famous for its likely role in the mass extinction of living species, including the dinosaurs.*

extra /ˈekstrə/ *adj.* more than is usual, expected, or than exists already SYN ADDITIONAL: *For parents in the study, these extra costs add worry.* ◇ *The firm's conduct has led to extra benefits for the firm and its customers.* ◇ *An added 10 kcal per day of extra calories can result in an extra pound (0.45 kg) of weight gained per year.*

ex·tract¹ AWL /ɪkˈstrækt/ *verb* **1** to remove or obtain a substance from sth, for example by using an industrial or chemical process: **~ sth** *Acidification is often used to extract valuable ores.* ◇ **~ sth from sb/sth** *DNA was extracted from the tissue samples and sequenced.* ◇ *Different plants extract different amounts of phosphate from the same soil.* **2 ~ sth (from sb/sth)** to choose information, etc. from a book, a computer, etc. to be used for a particular purpose: *The program extracts data from a file or a database and produces a list or report.* ◇ *Animals can extract information by observing others.* **3 ~ sth (from sb/sth)** to obtain information, money, etc, often by taking it from sb who does not wish to give it: *Western liberal democracies debated whether torture could be justified to extract information from terrorist suspects.* ◇ *Employers reason that paying higher wages will enable them to extract more work from their employees.*

ex·tract² AWL /ˈekstrækt/ *noun* **1 ~ (from/of sth)** a short passage taken from a text, film or piece of music: *The booklet is short collection of extracts from the writings of western and Soviet historians.* **2** a substance that has been obtained from sth else using a particular process: *Traditional medicines were mainly just plant extracts.* ◇ **~ of sth** *Many of the early studies of catalysis were performed using extracts of yeast.*

ex·trac·tion AWL /ɪkˈstrækʃn/ *noun* [U, C] the act or process of removing or obtaining sth from sth else: *The data extraction and analysis were carried out by four members of the research team.* ◇ *Extractions were performed with blank controls to test for contamination.* ◇ **the ~ of sth** *The extraction of fossil fuel led to the destruction of tribal lands.*

extra·or·din·ar·ily /ɪkˈstrɔːdnrəli; *NAmE* ɪkˌstrɔːrdəˈnerəli/ *adv.* extremely: *Chambers is an extraordinarily gifted writer.* ◇ *These factors do not account for the extraordinarily high rates of school dropout.* ➲ language bank *at* EXCEPTIONALLY

extra·or·din·ary /ɪkˈstrɔːdnri; *NAmE* ɪkˈstrɔːrdəneri/ *adj.* **1** unexpected, surprising or strange: *Halliday exercised a quite extraordinary influence over all those who knew him.* ◇ *These developments suggested something that at the time seemed extraordinary.* **2** not normal or ordinary; greater or better than usual: *Dubai is a truly extraordinary city where almost anything has seemed possible.* ◇ *The work is an extraordinary achievement.* ➲ *compare* ORDINARY **3** [only before noun] (of a meeting, etc.) arranged for a special purpose and happening in addition to what normally or regularly happens: *The council meets four times a year with the possibility of extraordinary meetings in exceptional circumstances.*

ex·treme¹ /ɪkˈstriːm/ *adj.* **1** not ordinary or usual; serious or severe SYN EXCEPTIONAL (1): *In some extreme cases,*

E

people have felt obliged to seek refuge in a country other than their own. ◇ *Military force should only be used in extreme circumstances.* ◇ *Some species are adapted to life in poor, highly stressed environments, where conditions are extreme.* ◇ *The frequency of extreme weather events, such as severe floods, is more likely to increase than decrease.* **2** [usually before noun] very great in degree: *Worldwide, there are an estimated one billion people living in extreme poverty.* ◇ *The police must exercise extreme caution before releasing information which suggests that a person has committed a criminal offence.* **3** (of people, political organizations, opinions, etc.) far from what most people consider to be normal, reasonable or acceptable: *Knox's ideas were still too extreme for most people.* ◇ *Depressions resulted in extremist political movements gaining strength, many of which were of an extreme right-wing nature.* OPP MODERATE[1] (2) ➲ *compare* RADICAL[1] (3) **4** [only before noun] as far as possible from the centre, the beginning or in the direction mentioned SYN FAR[2] (2): *The area lies at the extreme southern end of Thailand.* ◇ *On the extreme left of Figure 61.1 is the secondary school system.*

ex·treme[2] /ɪk'striːm/ *noun* **1** a feeling, situation, way of behaving, etc. that is as different as possible from another or is opposite to it: **(at one ~)... (at the other/opposite ~)** *At one extreme, a city might be at the centre of its nation. At the opposite extreme, a city might be of little significance to its nation.* ◇ **~ of A and B** *Some economists suggest a compromise between the extremes of economic autonomy and full integration into the global capitalist economy.* **2** the greatest or highest degree of sth: **~ (of sth)** *The nurse needs to assess the patient's ability to cope with extremes of temperature.* ◇ **~ of A and B** *These cities are characterized by extremes of wealth and poverty.*
IDM **go, etc. to ex'tremes/to the ex'treme | take sth to ex'tremes/to the ex'treme** to act or be forced to act in a way that is far from normal or reasonable: *People went to the extreme of separating babies from their parents to see what language they would speak naturally if they were not taught.* ◇ *Taken to its logical extreme, consumption of the vast majority of goods and services can result in some form of ecological harm.* **in the ex'treme** to a great degree: *His account of his family is sentimental in the extreme.*

ex·treme·ly /ɪk'striːmli/ *adv.* (usually with adjectives and adverbs) to a very high degree: *It is extremely difficult to win a customer back once the business has a reputation for poor service.* ◇ *European cultural influence in Africa before the twentieth century was extremely limited.* ◇ *The International Division has performed extremely well in growing sales in the past few years.* ➲ language bank *at* EXCEPTIONALLY

ex·trin·sic /eks'trɪnsɪk; eks'trɪnzɪk/ *adj.* not belonging naturally to sb/sth; coming from or existing outside sb/sth rather than within them: *The learners were very aware of the extrinsic motivation for learning a language, but none of them mentioned any intrinsic motivation.* ◇ **~ to sb/sth** *Other reasons for infant abandonment would have been extrinsic to the infant, such as older children competing for maternal care.* ➲ *compare* INTRINSIC

eye /aɪ/ *noun* **1** [C] either of the two organs on the face that you see with: *Care should be taken to see that the mouth and eyes are closed.* ◇ *If the eye perceives the colour red, it is responding to red light entering the iris of the eye and striking the retina.* HELP **Eye** is also used to describe the organ of vision in many INVERTEBRATES: *Insect compound eyes are composed of hundreds of individual photoreceptor organs.* **2 -eyed** (in adjectives) having the type or number of eyes mentioned: *Melanoma is most common in fair-skinned blue-eyed people.* ◇ *According to Homer, the huge, one-eyed Cyclopes dwell somewhere on the shores of the Mediterranean Sea.* **3** [C] used to refer to sb's opinion or attitude towards sth: **in the eyes of sb** *Existing firms will try to make their products different, in the eyes of the consumer, from competitors' products.* ◇ **to... eyes** *To modern eyes, some of the disputes appear very childish.* **4** [sing.] **~ (for sth)** the ability to see: *He writes well and generally has a good eye for detail.*
IDM **before/in front of sb's (very) eyes** in front of sb: *What is occurring before his very eyes is causing him to doubt his conclusion.* **keep an eye on sb/sth** to keep sb/sth under careful observation: *The Migration Policy Group in Brussels keeps a close eye on migration in Europe.* **look at, see, etc. sth through sb's eyes** to think about or see sth the way that another person sees it: *The 'New Oxford World History' gives an overview of world events seen through the eyes of ordinary people.* ➲ *more at* BIRD, BLIND[1], CATCH[1], CLOSE[3], MEET, NAKED, OPEN[2], PUBLIC[1]

eye·lid /'aɪlɪd/ *noun* either of the pieces of skin above and below the eye that cover it when you close the eye: *The whole of the eyelid may be affected.* ◇ *the upper/lower eyelid*

eye·wit·ness /'aɪwɪtnəs/ *noun* = WITNESS[1] (1)

Ff

fab·ric /'fæbrɪk/ *noun* **1** [U, C] cloth used for for making clothes, covering furniture, etc. SYN MATERIAL[1] (4): *Lyons replaced northern Italy as Europe's premier producer of the finest silk fabrics.* ◇ **+ noun** *Fabric suppliers have proved willing to invest in physical assets, such as specialized equipment for manufacturing.* **2** [sing.] the basic structure of a society, an organization, etc. that enables it to function successfully: *These conflicts were the result of the collapse of state structures and the disintegration of the social fabric.* ◇ **~ of sth** *Many Americans felt that the very fabric of their society was coming unravelled.* **3** [U] the basic structure of a building, such as the walls, floor and roof: *The amount of heat lost through building fabric will be reduced.* ◇ **~ of sth** *His position involved overseeing the fabric of the building, from leaking roofs to drains.*

fab·ri·cate /'fæbrɪkeɪt/ *verb* [often passive] **1 ~ sth** (*technical*) to make or produce goods, equipment, etc. from various different materials SYN MANUFACTURE[2]: *Figure 5.10 illustrates how the transistors are fabricated.* **2 ~ sth** to invent false information in order to deceive people SYN MAKE STH UP (3): *The biomedical community was shocked by the revelation that a high profile researcher had fabricated scientific data.* ■ **fab·ri·ca·tion** /ˌfæbrɪ'keɪʃn/ *noun* [U, C] *The process makes it possible to generate the narrow features desired in modern microchip fabrication.* ◇ **+ noun** *The capital cost of a semiconductor fabrication plant is huge.* ◇ **~ by sb** *The original reporting was found later to be based on fabrications by witnesses.*

face[1] /feɪs/ *verb* **1** [T] if you **face** a particular situation, or it **faces** you, you have to deal with it: **~ sth** *People in lower socio-economic groups face higher risks of unemployment.* ◇ *Schiemann described the difficulties faced by asylum claimants in dealing with visa regimes.* ◇ *The biggest problem facing the energy supply sector is the large seasonal variation in electricity consumption.* ◇ **be faced with sth** *The world is faced with two major dilemmas: climate change and security of energy supplies.* **2** [T] **~ sth** to accept that a difficult situation exists, although you would prefer not to: *He was reluctant to face the fact that they had failed.* **3** [I] **+ adv./prep.** to have part of your body pointing in a particular direction: *Ask the patient to hold both arms outstretched with the palms facing upwards.*
PHR V **ˌface 'up to sth** to accept and deal with sth that is difficult or unpleasant: *They refuse to face up to the fact that they are not achieving.*

▸ FACE + NOUN **challenge • difficulty, problem, dilemma • obstacle, barrier, hurdle • constraint • prospect • situation • uncertainty • competition • threat, risk, danger • crisis • criticism • opposition • pressure •**

persecution, discrimination *Multinational firms face the challenge of managing employees from diverse cultural backgrounds.* ◇ *Small businesses from transition economies face major obstacles in accessing global markets.* | **fact, truth** *Herrington thinks we should face the truth of our situation, even if it is unpleasant.*

▸ NOUN + FACE **firm • entrepreneur • manager • investor, marketer • farmer • applicant, claimant • researcher • practitioner • refugee, migrant** *These firms will face increased competition from elsewhere in the single market.* ◇ *The key issue faced by international researchers is to ensure comparable data are collected.* | **challenge, dilemma, problem** *Globalization is the greatest challenge facing humans at the present time.*

face[2] /feɪs/ *noun* **1** the front part of sb's head: *Her vision was normal except that she could not recognize people's faces.* **2 ~ (of sth)** a side or surface of sth: *The case of surface forces acting on the faces of a cube is sketched in Fig.10.10.* **3 ~ of sth** the particular character of sth: *The Second World War changed the face of Jewish demography.*

IDM **in the face of 'sth 1** despite problems or difficulties: *Their beliefs gave them comfort in the face of suffering and death.* **2** as a result of sth: *She was forced to adjust this theory in the face of new evidence.* **lose 'face** to be less respected or look stupid because of sth you have done: *The teachers were afraid of losing face by making mistakes in front of their students.* **on the 'face of it** used to say that sth seems to be true, but that this opinion may need to be changed when you know more about it: *On the face of it, these findings appear contradictory.* ➲ *more at* FLY[1], HUMAN[1], SAVE

facet /ˈfæsɪt/ *noun* a particular part or aspect of sth: *The concept of mind has many facets and some of these may exist in non-human primates.* ◇ **~ of sth** *These elements represent different facets of Asian culture.*

ˌface-to-ˈface *adj.* involving people who are close together and looking at each other: *The format for the assessment is usually a face-to-face interview.* ■ **face-to-face** *adv.*: *Future research should take into account what happens when chat partners meet face-to-face.*

ˌface ˈvalue *noun* [U, C, usually sing.] the value of a coin, ticket, etc. that is shown on the front of it: *Generally, the face value of a coupon is not large because the retail price of the product is not high.* ◇ *Two dice are rolled until the sum of the face values is 7.*

IDM **take sth at face 'value** to believe that sth is what it appears to be, without questioning it: *These sources can rarely be taken at face value but must be read deeply and creatively.* HELP Note that the reader expects a statement beginning **Taken at face value** to be followed by a word like 'but' or 'however', giving a reason why the facts are not true or reliable: *Taken at face value, her opinion is of course valid. However, she does not include any empirical evidence to endorse her comments.*

fa·cial /ˈfeɪʃl/ *adj.* [usually before noun] connected with a person's face; on a person's face: *Non-verbal communications like facial expression, eye movements and body posture also help convey meaning.* ◇ *Race is generally defined in terms of physical characteristics such as skin colour, facial features or hair type.*

fa·cili·tate AWL /fəˈsɪlɪteɪt/ *verb* **~ sth** to make an action or a process possible or easier: *The committee has a genuine interest in facilitating access to medication for the poor.* ◇ *In mathematics, children's capacity for learning has been greatly facilitated by the use of technology.* ■ **fa·cili·ta·tion** AWL /fəˌsɪlɪˈteɪʃn/ *noun* [U, sing.] **~ (of sth)** *The facilitation of cross-border cooperation between national authorities is a priority.*

▸ FACILITATE + NOUN **cooperation • coordination • identification • comparison • access • entry • dialogue, communication, exchange, discussion • learning, acquisition, understanding • decision-making • implementation • spread • transfer** *Academies in Paris, Rome and Berlin were established in order to facilitate the exchange of scientific knowledge.*

▸ ADVERB + FACILITATE **greatly • thereby, thus** *Significant technological advances greatly facilitated communications over large areas.*

fa·cili·ta·tor AWL /fəˈsɪlɪteɪtə(r)/ *noun* **1** a person who manages a discussion or activity by guiding people and giving advice rather than telling them what to do: *The role of the facilitator is critical— how you talk to them, and the manner of approach.* ◇ **as a ~** *Acting as a facilitator, the researcher helped them to overcome their anxieties by creating a friendly atmosphere.* **2** a thing that helps a process take place: **(as a) ~** *Perceived social norms can serve as a facilitator of behaviour change.*

fa·cil·ity AWL /fəˈsɪləti/ *noun* (*pl.* **-ies**) **1 facilities** [pl.] buildings, services and equipment that are provided for a particular purpose: *Public health care facilities are available in less than one-tenth of the villages in the region.* ◇ *Companies moved production facilities to formerly non-industrial countries because labour costs were much lower there.* **2** [C] a place, usually including buildings, used for a particular purpose or activity: *This study was carried out in a UK research facility.* **3** [C] a special feature of a machine, service, etc. that makes it possible to do sth extra: *The program includes a facility that allows the analyst to produce simple word frequency counts.* ◇ *The bank granted the organization a £200 000 overdraft facility.*

fact /fækt/ *noun* **1** [C] a thing that is known to be true, especially when it can be proved: *The historical facts are beyond dispute.* ◇ **the ~ that...** *Galileo used the fact that hot air rises to show that air has weight.* ◇ *The mere fact that a source is ancient does not necessarily make it reliable.* ◇ **~ about sth** *These long-term studies have revealed many interesting facts about breeding success.* ◇ **the facts of sth** *There must always be an exercise of judgement based on the actual facts of the case.* ◇ **the ~ remains (that...)** *The fact remains that the fires, not the earthquake, caused most of the property damage.* ➲ language bank *at* HOWEVER **2** [sing.] used to refer to a particular situation that exists: **the ~ that...** *Linguists in the past have ignored the fact that linguistic systems tend to be fuzzy.* ◇ *Such figures highlight the fact that online media is growing in significance in its own right.* ◇ **despite the ~ that...** *The council maintained its wage levels, despite the fact that comparable wages in the private sector were lower.* ◇ **owing to the ~ that...** *This discrepancy may be owing to the fact that different methodologies were employed.* ◇ **the ~ of sth** *The mere fact of human evolution does not imply that the human species lacks any goal external to its own biological nature.* **3** [U] things that are true rather than things that have been invented: *In the aftermath of any damaging earthquake, it can be hard to separate fact from fiction.* ◇ *Statements of fact are sometimes difficult to separate and distinguish from opinions.* ◇ *It now seemed that every argument used to justify the war had no basis in fact.*

IDM **ˌafter the 'fact** after sth has happened or been done, when it is too late to prevent it or change it: *Truly convincing evaluation may remain impossible even long after the fact.* ◇ *Sometimes, a person may see after the fact that he was mistaken in his moral judgment and really did act wrongly.* **the fact (of the matter) is (that)...** used to emphasize a statement, especially one that is the opposite of what has just been mentioned: *The fact is that getting a good grade requires more than knowledge of the subject.* **a ˌfact of 'life** a situation that cannot be changed, especially one that is unpleasant: *Mistakes and failure are facts of life that most organizations cannot escape.* ◇ *Risk is an inescapable fact of life.* **ˌfacts and 'figures** accurate and detailed information: *A sports section of a newspaper will*

F

not just contain facts and figures; it will also include commentary, analysis and speculation. **in (actual) fact** **1** used to give extra details about sth that has just been mentioned: *The large intestine has a huge population of bacteria. In fact, the number of bacterial cells in the colon exceeds the total number of other cells in the body.* **2** used to emphasize a statement, especially one that is the opposite of what has just been mentioned: *Corporations that sell stock to outside investors are said to be selling shares to 'the public'. In fact, 'public' corporations are in no way accountable to the public.* ➲ language bank *at* HOWEVER ➲ *more at* POINT[1]

F

▸ ADJECTIVE + FACT **mere • very • simple • brute • basic • relevant • actual • particular • obvious • well-established • well-known • remarkable • inescapable** *The very fact that he was released is because they did not have a case against him.* ◇ *These writers were simply responding to the brute fact of colonialism.* | **objective • empirical • historical • material • contingent** *Judgements of value are not empirical facts.*

▸ VERB + FACT **reflect • illustrate • highlight, emphasize, underline, underscore, stress • ignore, overlook, neglect • obscure, disguise, conceal, hide • ascertain, establish • acknowledge, recognize • accept • know • use • exploit • explain • consider • express • present • lament** *International trade flows reflect the fact that goods and services can sometimes be imported at lower cost from abroad.* ◇ *The state overlooked the fact that it needed—even depended on—forced and economic migrants.* | **be explained by • be supported by • be illustrated by • be compounded by • be justified by** *This phenomenon can be explained by the fact that the viscosity and surface tension of the adhesive were too high.*

▸ PHRASES **the fact remains (that...) • fit the facts • does not alter the fact that...** *This theory does not fit the facts.*

ˈfact-finding *adj.* [only before noun] done in order to find out information about a country, an organization, a situation, etc: *The UN sent a fact-finding mission to the region to investigate alleged human rights abuses.*

fac·tion /ˈfækʃn/ *noun* **~ (of sb/sth)** a small group of people within a larger one whose members have some different aims and beliefs from those of the larger group: *Religious conflicts between warring factions of Christians displaced the wars with the Turks.*

fac·tor[1] **AWL** /ˈfæktə(r)/ *noun* **1** one of several things that cause or affect sth: *Many factors can influence blood pressure, especially emotions and stress.* ◇ *Political, social, institutional and historical factors affect the long-term performance of an economy.* ◇ **~ in sth** *Trust is a key factor in the success of this approach.* ◇ **~ for sth** *Physical inactivity is a risk factor for many chronic diseases.* **2 by a ~ of sth** the amount by which sth increases or decreases **HELP** The **factor** is the number you multiply or divide by to show the amount of the increase or decrease: *The analyses show that worldwide geothermal use could increase by a factor of more than 100.* ◇ *The output resistance of the circuit decreases by a factor of 5.5.* **3** (*mathematics*) a number that divides into another number exactly: *A prime number has no factors except one and itself.* **4** (*also* ˌ**factor of proˈduction**) (*economics*) any of the resources that are used to produce goods and services. The main **factors of production** are land, labour and capital: *The more easily the factors of production can move from one sector of production to another, the easier it will be for the economy to adapt to changes in demand.* ◇ **+ noun** *Firms that cluster in an area will experience increased local factor prices, which must be compensated by economies of scale.* **5** (*biology*) a substance that has a function in a particular biological process, for example growth or blood CLOTTING: *A growth factor is a specific compound that is required for growth of a particular organism.* ◇ *He has never received any blood transfusions or clotting factors.*

▸ ADJECTIVE + FACTOR **important, major • key, critical, crucial • the main • significant • different, other • various • multiple • individual • external • additional • contributing, contributory • limiting • relevant • common • potential** *This research demonstrated that for most working Americans the economy was still the most significant factor in their lives.* | **contextual • structural • causal • situational • social • cultural • institutional • economic • socio-economic • demographic • environmental • psychological • genetic** *There are deeper cultural and social factors influencing the adoption process.*

▸ NOUN + FACTOR **risk • lifestyle** *There are multiple genetic and lifestyle factors that contribute to the development of the disease.*

▸ VERB + FACTOR **identify, determine • list • consider, assess, discuss • examine, investigate, explore, analyse • understand • include • highlight • address • ignore** *The analysis was conducted to identify the factors associated with high job strain.* ◇ *Schmidlin et al. (1998) have examined risk factors for death during tornadoes.*

▸ FACTOR + VERB **influence, affect, contribute to, play a role (in sth), impact (on sth) • drive • determine, shape • control • limit • account for, explain • be associated with • be involved • interact** *Several other factors played a role in the decision-making.* ◇ *Collectively, these factors account for the negative effect of visual impairment on quality of life.*

fac·tor[2] **AWL** /ˈfæktə(r)/ *verb*

PHRV ˌ**factor sth ˈin | factor sth into sth** to include a particular fact or situation when you are thinking about or planning sth: *There was a difference in the pattern of responses when age was factored in.* ◇ *The importance of domestic politics needs to be factored into the analysis.*

fac·tory /ˈfæktri; ˈfæktəri/ *noun* (*pl.* **-ies**) a building or group of buildings where goods are made: *By building larger factories, business leaders were able to reduce the cost of production per unit of their goods.* ◇ *a shoe/car/chemical factory* ◇ **+ noun** *Deafness in certain groups of factory workers is a clear example of occupational disease.*

fac·tual /ˈfæktʃuəl/ *adj.* based on or containing facts: *factual knowledge/information* ◇ *The evidence is scrutinized by the court in order to determine its factual basis.* ◇ *Too many factual errors remain in this otherwise well-written book.* ■ **fac·tual·ly** /ˈfæktʃuəli/ *adv.*: *factually accurate/correct* ◇ *This statement is factually incorrect.*

fac·ulty /ˈfæklti/ *noun* (*pl.* **-ies**) **1** [C] a physical or mental ability, especially one that people are born with: *The ultimate goal is an understanding of the human language faculty.* ◇ *There is evidence that undernourishment in early childhood affects the development of cognitive faculties.* ◇ **~ of/for (doing) sth** *Plato says that we can, by the proper use of our faculty of reason, actually become good.* **2** [C] **~ (of sth)** a department or group of related departments in a college or university: *She is a professor of public law at Bielefeld University, faculty of law.* ◇ *The dean of the medical faculty had little doubt that Schonenberger was a competent clinician.* **3** [C+sing./pl. v.] all the teachers in a faculty of a college or university: *Included among the faculty are developers and other experts in the use of computer programs.* ◇ **+ noun** *In faculty meetings, we talked with English teachers who wanted to participate in the study.* **4** [C, U] (*NAmE*) all the teachers of a particular university or college: **~ (of sth)** *In 1906 Jennings joined the faculty of Johns Hopkins University.* ◇ *The mediation program provides both students and faculty with an alternative forum for problem solving.* ◇ **on the ~** *Arjun Kalyanpur is a doctor who had been on the faculty at Yale.*

Fahr·en·heit /ˈfærənhaɪt/ *adj.* (*abbr.* F) of or using a scale of temperature in which water freezes at 32° and boils at 212°: *fifty degrees Fahrenheit* ■ **Fahr·en·heit** *noun* [U] *to give the temperature in Fahrenheit*

fail /feɪl/ *verb* **1** [I] to not do sth: **~ to do sth** *Local councils may fail to provide adequate services for all city residents.* ◇ **~ in sth** *The Belgian authorities had failed in their obligations under Articles 2 and 3 of the Convention.* **2** [I, T] to not be successful in achieving sth; to end without success: *Diocletian tried to arrange an orderly succession to the emperorship, but his plan failed.* ◇ **~ to do sth** *Captain Scott and his party failed to reach the South Pole before Amundsen.* ◇ **~ in sth** *The airline failed in its attempts to enter the North American market.* **3** [I] to be unable to continue operating as a business or company: *Younger firms are more likely to fail than older ones.* ◇ *These organizations had US$5 trillion of home loans and could not be allowed to fail.* **4** [I] to stop working correctly: *There are instances where the market mechanism fails and governments may be compelled to intervene.* ◇ *Should the cooling circuit fail completely, the temperature would peak well below the temperature at which the structure could melt.* **5** [T, I] to not pass a test or an exam; to decide that sb/sth has not passed a test or an exam: **~ (sth)** *The majority of children (61%) failed the test.* ◇ *The majority of children failed.* ◇ *Although Luke is fairly bright, his grades have declined to the point that he may fail the academic year.* ◇ **~ sb** *Academic institutions are there to pass students, rather than fail them.* OPP PASS[1] (11) **6** [I] (used especially in the progressive tenses) to become weak: *Poor health and failing sight forced her to resign.* ◇ *In the 1850s his health failed and he died in 1855.* **7** [T] **~ sb** to disappoint sb; to be unable to help when needed: *When the courts failed them, they went back to their communities and started all over again.* ◇ *Tacitus the politician was not a hero; he admits that his courage failed him.* **8** [I] to not be enough when needed or expected: *By September, the first crops had largely failed and the colony began to suffer from serious food shortages.* ◇ *In 1992, the rains failed, rendering the grain reserve inadequate to cope with the crisis.*

▸ ADVERB + FAIL **largely** • **ultimately, eventually** • **frequently** • **consistently** • **completely** *The family consistently failed to keep hospital or doctors' appointments.*

▸ FAIL TO + VERB **provide** • **meet** • **do** • **act, take action** • **recognize** • **make** • **comply** • **find** • **address** • **show** • **capture** • **achieve** • **respond to** • **reach** • **produce** • **account for** • **take into account, take account of** • **understand** *If managers fail to take account of such developments, their strategies will be inappropriate.*

failed /feɪld/ *adj.* [only before noun] not successful: *Most clients reported a desire to quit smoking and had made multiple failed attempts to quit in the past.* ◇ *The proposal was that welfare support should be withdrawn from failed asylum seekers with families.*

fail·ing[1] /ˈfeɪlɪŋ/ *noun* [usually pl.] a weakness or fault in sb/sth: *Political leaders are liable to moral failings.* ◇ **~ in sth** *The case revealed failings in the capacity of agencies to share information effectively.* ◇ **~ of sth** *A major failing of capitalism, according to Marx, is that it has a dehumanizing effect on individuals living within it.*

fail·ing[2] /ˈfeɪlɪŋ/ *prep.* used to introduce a suggestion that could be considered if the one just mentioned is not possible: *The typical response to these critics has been to ignore them or, failing that, to attempt to discredit them.*

fail·ure /ˈfeɪljə(r)/ *noun* **1** [U, C] the state of not working correctly or as expected; an occasion when this happens: *A combination of these drugs has been shown to be beneficial in patients with chronic heart failure.* ◇ *acute renal/respiratory/liver failure* ◇ *As the components of the circuit are only 100 nm wide, the tiniest speck of dust can cause a failure.* **2** [U, C] **~ to do sth** an act of not doing sth, especially sth that you are expected to do: *Failure to comply with an enforcement notice can result in imprisonment for up to 6 months.* ◇ *Past failure to recognize the economic value of water has led to wasteful uses of the resource.* ◇ *A failure to understand the economic environment leaves managers without a clear view of what is happening in their markets.* **3** [U] lack of success in doing or achieving sth: *Like his previous tries, this one ended in failure.* ◇ *Students were significantly more likely to attribute both success and failure to luck than were teachers.* OPP SUCCESS (1) **4** [C] a person or thing that is not successful: *Feeling depressed and a failure, he swam out to the middle of the lagoon with the intention of drowning.* ◇ *The experiment was deemed to be a failure and was not repeated.* OPP SUCCESS (3) **5** [C, U] a situation in which a business has to close because it is not successful: *Between 1930 and 1933, there were about 2 000 bank failures per year.* ◇ *In emerging economies, credit constraints are one of the leading causes of small business failure.* ◇ **~ of sth** *A 'rescue' is a major intervention necessary to avert eventual failure of the company.* **6** [C, U] **crop/harvest ~** a situation in which crops do not grow correctly and do not produce food: *The crisis began with the harvest failures and plague epidemics of the 1590s.* ◇ *During extended dry seasons, crop failure may become widespread.*

fair[1] /feə(r); *NAmE* fer/ *adj.* **(fair·er, fair·est) 1** acceptable and appropriate in a particular situation: *Farmers are assured of a reliable market for their livestock at fair prices.* ◇ *The fair trade movement aims to guarantee a better deal for producers in the developing world.* ◇ **it is ~ to do sth** *It is fair to say that China is still in an early stage of political liberalization.* ◇ **it is ~ that...** *It is only fair that all students should have the opportunity to achieve the jobs that carry the higher rewards in society.* OPP UNFAIR **2** treating everyone equally and according to the rules or law: *Every person has a right to a fair trial.* ◇ *While the 2009 elections were generally free and fair, concerns remain relating to media freedom.* ◇ *Many of the propaganda films made by the government emphasized the need to build a better, fairer society after the war.* ◇ **~ to sb** *The chief argument in favour of proportional government is that it is fair to all citizens.* OPP UNFAIR **3** [only before noun] quite large in number, size or amount: *The idea worked well and generated a fair amount of money.* ◇ *The model predicts periodic trends with a fair degree of accuracy.* ◇ *In a fair number of cases, it was possible to check the letters against the originals in various archives and libraries.* **4** (of hair or skin) pale in colour: *Melanoma is most common in fair-skinned, blue-eyed people.* OPP DARK[1] (4)

IDM **(give sb) a fair ˈhearing** (to allow sb) the opportunity to give an opinion of sth before sb decides if they have done sth wrong, often in court: *Both sides in the dispute should be given a fair hearing.* **(more than) your fair share of sth** (more than) the usual or expected amount of sth: *Study after study has found that husbands do not do their 'fair share' of housework and childcare.* ◇ *While Edison enjoyed great commercial successes, he had his fair share of failures.*

fair[2] /feə(r); *NAmE* fer/ *noun* **1** an event at which people, businesses, etc. show and sell their goods: *International trade fairs or exhibitions can be an effective channel through which small companies develop relationships with foreign buyers.* **2** a type of entertainment in a field or other open space at which people can go on large machines and play games to win prizes: *Celebrations would be observed with foods, fairs and parades.* HELP In American English, a **fair** also refers to a type of entertainment at which farm animals and products are shown and take part in competitions: *Annual pumpkin weigh-offs began in produce contests at county and state agricultural fairs.*

fair·ly /ˈfeəli; *NAmE* ˈferli/ *adv.* **1** (before adjectives and adverbs) quite but not very: *The two reasons are fairly straightforward...* ◇ *In 1980, the Korean economy was* *fairly simple and small.* ◇ *The options available to the Commissioner are fairly limited.* ◇ *Symptoms such as nausea and vomiting are fairly common in patients with cardiac disorders.* ◇ *There are some fairly clear distinctions between the newspaper-run blogs and the independent blogs surveyed here.* ⊃ language bank *at* EXCEPTIONALLY **2** in a fair way; in a way that treats people equally and according to the rules or law: *The company should ensure that all shareholders are treated fairly.*

fair·ness /ˈfeənəs; *NAmE* ˈfernəs/ *noun* [U] the quality of treating people equally or according to the law or rules: *The law is founded on fundamental principles of fairness.* ◇ *Certain procedures are required to ensure fairness and efficiency in the process.*

faith /feɪθ/ *noun* **1** [U] **~ (in sb/sth)** trust in sb's ability or knowledge; trust that sb/sth will do what has been promised: *There were those who had great faith in technology as a solution for all social problems.* ◇ *It could be a mistake to put too much faith in this strategy.* ◇ *Most lower-class Americans had lost faith in the political process.* **2** [U, sing.] strong religious belief: *Religious faith and practice served as a source of continuity in their lives.* ◇ *For some, a deep spiritual faith can bring healing and should be supported.* ◇ **~ in sb/sth** *Belief in science has replaced faith in God, not necessarily for the better.* **3** [C] a particular religion: *Constantine converted to the Christian faith.* ◇ *Like followers of other faiths, Muslims are engaged in an ongoing debate over religious reform.* **4** [U] **good ~** the intention to behave in an honest way: *In the civil law tradition, there is a broad recognition of the place of good faith in contracts.*

IDM **in bad ˈfaith** knowing that what you are doing is wrong: *Although much of this kind of criticism is malicious and made in bad faith, it can nevertheless stick.* **in good ˈfaith** believing that what you are doing is right and honest: *The export company was not responsible for the breach of rules and had acted in good faith.* ⊃ *more at* ARTICLE

faith·ful /ˈfeɪθfl/ *adj.* **1** true and accurate; not changing anything: *On the surface, the film is a faithful adaptation of the novel.* ◇ *Before cells divide, they must make a complete and faithful copy of the DNA in their chromosomes.* ◇ **~ to sth** *The film remains faithful to the original text, merely rearranging a few scenes.* **2** staying with or supporting a particular person, organization or belief SYN LOYAL: *He gathered a small band of faithful followers.* ◇ **~ to sb/sth** *Reiner remains faithful to his social democratic roots.* **3 the faithful** *noun* [pl.] people who believe in a religion; the loyal supporters of a political party: *On Palm Sunday, the faithful processed bearing palms in imitation of the people of Jerusalem.* ◇ *The conventions provide an opportunity to rally the party faithful on behalf of the presidential candidates.* **4 ~ (to sb)** (of a wife, husband or partner) not having a sexual relationship with anyone else: *The lovers remain faithful to each other until they are finally reunited.*

faith·ful·ly /ˈfeɪθfəli/ *adv.* **1** accurately; carefully: *Theatre managers felt no obligation to adhere faithfully to Shakespeare's scripts.* ◇ *A hallmark of cancers is the reduction in their ability to faithfully replicate their genome.* **2** in a loyal way; in a way that you can rely on: *She had served the family faithfully from youth to old age.*

fall[1] /fɔːl/ *verb* (**fell** /fel/, **fall·en** /ˈfɔːlən/) **1** [I] to decrease in amount, number or strength SYN DECREASE[1]: *As temperatures fall, there is less and less vapour to condense.* ◇ **+ adv.** *Sales have been falling steadily for a number of years now.* ◇ *Domestic gas prices in the US fell sharply.* ◇ **falling + noun** *The prison population has continued to rise, despite falling crime rates.* OPP RISE[2] (1) ⊃ language bank *at* TREND **2** [I] to drop down from a higher level to a lower level: *Heavy rain normally falls during the north-east monsoon.* ◇ **+ adv./prep.** *The bulk of this material falls to the sea floor and accumulates as thick layers of sediment.* OPP RISE[2] (2) **3** [I] to suddenly stop standing: *They claimed that Mrs Parker had slipped and fallen.* ◇ **~ over** *The victim fell over and banged his head on the ground.* ◇ **~ down** *Somebody must be responsible for maintaining the premises: otherwise the building might eventually fall down.* **4** [I] to pass into a particular state; to begin to be sth: **+ adj.** *One fifth of children aged between 1 and 2 years of age take at least an hour to fall asleep.* ◇ *With interest rates low and falling, critics fell silent.* ◇ **~ into sth** *Some existing words are used more frequently and other existing words fall into disuse.* ◇ **+ noun** *Consumers run the risk of falling victim to fraud in every aspect of life.* **5** [I] **+ adv./prep.** to belong to a particular class, group or area of responsibility: *Several possible reasons have been mentioned in the literature, but they generally fall into two categories.* ◇ *There are a number of interesting examples which fall under this heading.* ◇ *Indigenous Australians in rural and remote areas naturally fall outside the scope of this research.* **6** [I] to be defeated or captured: *Dynasties rise and fall, but life for the peasant changes little.* ◇ **~ to sb** *Jerusalem fell to the Romans in AD70.* **7** [I] **+ adv./prep.** (of light or a shadow) to show on a surface: *When light falls on the stone, every sphere reflects some of the light.*

IDM Idioms containing **fall** are at the entries for the nouns and adjectives in the idioms, for example **fall into place** is at **place**.

PHR V **ˌfall aˈpart 1** to have so many problems that it is no longer possible to exist or function: *Their relationship fell apart as Mark's brain damage led to violent outbursts.* ◇ *The administration ran deficits, largely because the economy was falling apart.* **2** to break into pieces: *In certain parasitic wasps, the egg forms a ball of cells, which then falls apart.*

ˌfall aˈway to become gradually fewer or smaller SYN DISAPPEAR (1): *Even when the ratings are high, there remains a perpetual fear that they might start to fall away.*

ˌfall ˈback 1 to move or turn back SYN RETREAT[1] (1): *In Lower Germany, Roman forces fell back permanently to the line of the Rhine.* **2** to decrease in value or amount: *In the 1983 general election, the two parties gained over 25% of the vote, but fell back slightly in the 1987 election.*

ˌfall ˈback on sb/sth [no passive] to go to sb for support; to have sth to use when you are in difficulty: *Measures tend to fall back on customer satisfaction as an indicator of loyalty.*

ˌfall beˈhind (sb/sth) to fail to keep level with sb/sth: *Even as some firms fall behind or drop out of the race, new firms will enter.* **ˌfall beˈhind with sth** (*also* **ˌfall beˈhind on sth** *especially in NAmE*) to not pay or do sth at the right time: *Not wanting to fall behind with her work commitments, she went to her office in the city.*

ˌfall ˈdown to be shown to be not true or not good enough: *This argument falls down in three places.* ⊃ *see also* FALL[1] (3)

ˌfall ˈoff to decrease in quantity or quality: *Five firms have market shares of more than 11 per cent each, after which market share falls off sharply.*

ˈfall on/upon sb/sth [no passive] (*especially BrE*) to be the responsibility of sb: *The burden will fall on the existing members of the EU to support the transformation of the financial services sector.*

ˌfall ˈout to become loose and drop: *Her hair fell out, but had regrown by the end of the treatment.* **ˌfall ˈout (with sb)** (*BrE*) to have an argument with sb so that you are no longer friendly with them: *After falling out with his son, the father sold the property at a fraction of its true price.*

ˌfall ˈthrough to not be completed, or not happen: *The deal fell through when the company failed to make payments.*

ˈfall to sb to become the duty or responsibility of sb: *The task of providing a remedy fell to the Chancellor.* ◇ **it falls to sb to do sth** *It falls to the government either to introduce changes or to coordinate them proactively.*

fall² /fɔːl/ *noun* **1** [C] an act of falling: *Work-related falls have been identified as a high priority area by health care employers and unions.* ◇ **+ noun** *Fall prevention programmes have been shown to reduce the number of falls.* **2** [C] a decrease in an amount, number or level: *As the squeeze on international lending affected the economy, production and trade experienced sharp falls.* ◇ **~ in sth** *A 10 per cent increase in the value of a currency leads to a 5 per cent fall in export sales.* ◇ **~ of sth** *The donation represented only 0.17% of national income, which was a fall of 20% in real terms from the previous year.* HELP Note that you use a **fall in sth** to talk about the thing that falls, and a **fall of sth** to talk about how large or small the fall is. OPP RISE¹ (1) ➲ language bank *at* TREND **3** [C] an amount of snow, rocks, etc. that falls or has fallen; the fact of sth falling: *Very large rock falls can trap enough air to create a cushion, enabling a landslide to travel great distances.* ◇ **~ of sth** *Since the fall of the Berlin Wall in 1989, there have been huge changes in gender divisions of paid work.* **4 falls** [pl.] (especially in names) a large amount of water falling down from a height: *They visited the Niagara Falls at the end of April.* ◇ *Mills had to be located near river falls so that water could be diverted and fed to a water wheel.* **5** [sing.] a loss of political, economic, etc. power or success; the loss or defeat of a city, country, etc. in war: *He escaped from the city, but was dismissed from office in the aftermath of its fall.* ◇ **~ of sth** *The risks of doing business in Russia and Eastern Europe have changed since the fall of communism.* ◇ *The rise and fall of farming in New England is a familiar story.* ➲ *compare* DEFEAT² **6** [sing.] a situation in which a person, an organization, etc. loses the respect of other people because they have done sth wrong: *His reluctance to split the party was one of the basic reasons for his fall.* ◇ **~ from sth** *The company had a century of success prior to its fall from grace in the 1990s.* **7** [C, usually sing.] (*NAmE*) = AUTUMN: **in the ~ (of sth)** *The school opened in the fall of 2000.* ◇ **+ noun** *Twenty-two surveys were sent to veterans interviewed during the summer and fall semesters of 2006.*

false /fɔːls/ *adj.* **1** wrong; not correct or true: *This may encourage carers to exaggerate or provide false information if applying for support services.* ◇ *Reason is a faculty of determining what is true and what is false.* OPP TRUE (1) **2** wrong, because it is based on sth that is not true or correct: *Ethnographic studies strongly suggest that this assumption is false.* ◇ *The false belief that the vaccine can cause influenza persisted among 35% of our cohort.* ◇ *Such policies create a false impression that regulators are making progress on environmental problems.* ◇ *People often feel a false sense of security in their cars.* **3** not genuine, but made to look real to deceive people: *Asylum seekers may travel on false documents as this may be the only way to leave their country.* **4 ~ positive/negative** a result of a test or an experiment that wrongly shows that a substance or condition is present/not present: *A survey found that women viewed false positives as acceptable consequences of screening.* ■ **false·ly** *adv.*: *They were falsely accused of wrongdoing.* ◇ *A poor trace may give a falsely low reading.* ◇ *Popular views falsely assume that the family is a contained space, with relatively few outside influences.*

fame /feɪm/ *noun* [U] the state of being known and talked about by many people: *He achieved international fame as an abolitionist, editor, orator, and the author of three autobiographies.* ◇ *In 1533, he had gained fame and fortune by helping Francisco Pizarro conquer the Inca Empire in Peru.* ◇ *Dietrich rose to fame through the theatre and then film in Berlin in the 1920s.* ➲ *see also* FAMOUS

fa·mil·ial /fəˈmɪliəl/ *adj.* [only before noun] **1** connected with or typical of a family: *The major contributor to familial resemblance is the genes.* **2** (*medical*) (of diseases or conditions) affecting several members of a family: *Evidence suggested the presence of a familial cancer syndrome.*

fa·mil·iar /fəˈmɪliə(r)/ *adj.* **1 ~ with sth** knowing sth well: *All staff members are familiar with the performance standards.* ◇ *Students rapidly became familiar with the new ways of working.* OPP UNFAMILIAR (2) **2** well known to you; often seen or heard and therefore easy to recognize: *The World Wide Web provides a familiar example of the importance of robustness.* ◇ *For Spanish speakers, many of these French words would sound quite familiar.* ◇ **~ to sb** *The topics discussed by al-Mubārak would have been familiar to most scholars at the time.* OPP UNFAMILIAR (1)

fa·mil·iar·ity /fəˌmɪliˈærəti/ *noun* **1** [U, sing.] **~ with sth** the state of knowing sb/sth well; the state of recognizing sb/sth: *Participants chose pictures of the technology they had most familiiarity with.* ◇ *The book draws upon extensive archival research, as well as a thorough familiarity with the work of other historians.* **2** [U] the fact of being well known to you: **~ (of sth)** *The very familiarity of the concept of attention can make it hard to think about clearly.* ◇ **~ to sb** *At the dedication of Shakespeare's statue in Central Park in 1872, his familiarity to Americans was taken for granted.*

fam·ily¹ /ˈfæməli/ *noun* (*pl.* **-ies**) **1** [C+sing./pl. v.] a group consisting of one or two parents and their children: *In most cases, children from single-parent families spent the weekend visiting their absent biological parent.* ◇ *Price inflation poses a grave financial burden to many local families.* ➲ *see also* NUCLEAR FAMILY **2** [C+sing./pl. v., U] a group consisting of one or two parents, their children and close relations: *The support of family, friends and neighbours was very valuable for the patient.* ◇ *Her family are all from Poland.* ◇ *She published a study of family and community on the Isle of Man.* ➲ *see also* EXTENDED FAMILY **3** [C+sing./pl. v.] all the people who are related to each other, including those who are now dead: *Figure 3.1 shows five generations of an American family who have Huntington's disease.* **4** [C+sing./pl. v.] a couple's or a person's children, especially young children: *Married men anticipate they will have higher expenditures after starting a family.* **5** [C] a group of related animals and plants; a group of related things, especially languages: *Studies suggest that these changes are likely to evolve in the sunflower family.* ◇ **~ of sth** *The Hox genes are members of the large family of homeobox genes.* ◇ *There are subgroups of languages within each larger family of related languages.* HELP In biology, a **family** is a group into which animals, plants or other life forms are divided, smaller than an ORDER and larger than a GENUS. ➲ *see also* CLASS¹ (6), KINGDOM (3), PHYLUM, SPECIES

▸ ADJECTIVE + FAMILY **large • whole, entire** *Financial allowances were granted for large families.* ◇ *Ordinarily, we can assume that languages, or entire language families, will occupy contiguous areas.* | **immediate • close • adoptive • birth • ideal • happy • traditional • average • rural • middle-class • working-class • poor, low-income • single-parent, lone-parent • two-parent** *Fragmentation of services makes it difficult for low-income families to access the services they need.* | **royal • aristocratic, noble • wealthy** *Alexander was the first member of the royal family to visit Siberia.*

▸ VERB + FAMILY **feed • support • help • protect • visit** *The film showed how young children raised money to feed their families by begging.* | **come from, belong to • be born into** *Long came from a family associated with Jamaica since the 1660s.* | **start • raise, bring up** *Women tended to stay at home to raise their large families.*

fam·ily² /ˈfæməli/ *adj.* [only before noun] **1** connected with the family or a particular family: *None of her family members had attended college or held white-collar jobs.* ◇ *No aspect of family life has changed more strikingly than the role of adolescents.* ◇ *Screening tests can be performed* on those with a family history of a reaction. ◇ An ongoing longitudinal investigation originally focused on family relationships. ◇ family size/groups/units **2** owned by a family: *The family home has become a source of wealth which can be passed on, by inheritance, from parent to child.* ◇ *Her research also showed that women are often involved in founding and running family businesses.* ◇ *a family firm/farm*

ˌfamily ˈdoctor *noun* (*informal, especially BrE*) = GENERAL PRACTITIONER

ˌfamily ˈplanning *noun* [U] the process of controlling the number of children you have by using CONTRACEPTION: *These are local women employed by the family planning and reproductive health clinics.* ◇ **+ noun** *a family planning programme/service*

fam·ine /ˈfæmɪn/ *noun* [C, U] a lack of food in a region during a long period of time: *Scotland was hit by a serious famine in 1697–9, and again in 1739–41 and 1782.* ◇ *In general, floods cause less loss of life than earthquakes, drought and famine, and high winds (Fig. 2a).*

fam·ous /ˈfeɪməs/ *adj.* known about by many people SYN WELL KNOWN (1): *A famous example of an adoption study was carried out by Heston (1966).* ◇ *Her most famous work, 'A New England Girlhood' (1889), is still read today.* ◇ *The discovery that made Pavlov famous was the phenomenon of the conditioned reflex.* ◇ **~ for sth** *King Asoka became famous for his public works.* ◇ **~ as sth** *In his time he was famous as a teacher of geology at the Freiberg Mining Academy in Germany.* ➲ *see also* FAME, NOTORIOUS

fam·ous·ly /ˈfeɪməsli/ *adv.* in a way that is famous: *Locke famously argued that all of our ideas originate in the impressions of external sensations upon the mind.* ◇ *Famously, Aristotle identifies two forms of justice.*

fan /fæn/ *noun* **1** a person who admires sb/sth or enjoys watching or listening to sb/sth very much: *Movie stars are available for fantasy and appropriation by fans.* ◇ *a football/sports/movie fan* ◇ **~ of sb/sth** *Freud was, as it happens, a fan of the work of John Galsworthy.* **2** a machine with parts that turn around very quickly to create a current of air: *In winter, the heated air was circulated into the house by a fan.* ◇ *Use tepid sponging and electric fans to keep the patient cool.* **3** (*earth science*) a layer of material that has been left by a river, flood, current, etc. that starts narrow at one end and becomes wide with a curved edge at the other: *In map view, these alluvial deposits encircle the debris fans, outlining the fanlike shape.*

fan·tasy /ˈfæntəsi/ *noun* (*pl.* **-ies**) **1** [C] an idea, image or situation that a person imagines, but that is not real or is not likely to happen: *In dreams and fantasies, all sorts of illogical things can happen.* ◇ **~ about sth** *In this poem, Southey projected his contemporaries' prejudices and fantasies about the East.* ◇ **~ of sth** *Frankenstein's project of creating a living being is a fantasy of omnipotence.* **2** [U] the act of imagining things; a person's imagination: *They tend to confuse the boundary between fantasy and reality.* ◇ *Hollywood was a locus of fantasy and desire where anybody could become a star.* ◇ **~ world** *Each of the characters is locked in a separate fantasy world.*

far[1] /fɑː(r)/ *adv.* (**far·ther, far·thest** or **fur·ther, fur·thest**) **1** a long distance away: **+ adv./prep.** *Dust from the Gobi Desert in north-western China and Mongolia is carried far to the south and east.* ◇ *The molecules are far apart relative to their size.* ◇ **~ from sth** *Many volunteers may not be willing to travel far from their home.* ◇ *The writing may have originated in Syria, not far from Antioch.* ◇ **~ away (from sth)** *This allows families to move to unexploited food patches less far away.* **2** used when you are asking or talking about the distance between two places or the distance that has been travelled or is to be travelled: *How far can the patient walk on the flat without breathlessness?* ◇ *We could deduce from this pattern how far apart the atoms were.* **3** a long time from the present: **~ back** *This association was first alluded to as far back as 1932.* ◇ *The roots of lyric poetry extend far back in time to folk songs.* ◇ **~ ahead** *They were unable to plan any further ahead.* **4** very much; to a great degree: *Boys typically enjoyed far greater freedom than girls did.* ◇ *The Internet can provide far more information than the average shop.* ◇ *Party recruitment fell far short of the targets.* **5** used when you are asking or talking about the degree to which sth is true or possible: *Poortinga et al. (2004) were interested in how far the public trusted the information the government was supplying* ◇ **as ~ as possible** *English merchants tried, as far as possible, to cultivate trade with certain parts of the African coast.* **6** used to talk about how much progress has been made in doing or achieving sth: *The American dream means that how far you get in life is determined not by who your parents are but rather by how hard you work.* ◇ *Broadly, they seek to outline how far social policy has come and where it might be going.*

IDM **as far as I ˈknow | as far as I can reˈmember, ˈsee, ˈtell, etc.** used to say that you think you know, remember, understand, etc. sth but you cannot be completely sure, especially because you do not know all the facts: *This approach is, as far as I can see, innovatory.* ◇ *However, as far as we are aware, this approach has not been implemented elsewhere at this level of the health sector.* **as/so far as sb/sth is concerned | as/so far as sb/sth goes** used to give facts or an opinion about a particular aspect of sth: *Wetland areas have had a chequered past so far as human activity is concerned.* **as/so far as it ˈgoes** to a limited degree, usually not enough: *This is a fair point as far as it goes, but its true significance is easily overstated.* **far and ˈwide** over a large area: *The mammals became the dominant tetrapods, spreading rapidly far and wide and evolving many large species.* **far from sth/from doing sth** almost the opposite of sth or of what is expected: *The relationship among all these factors is far from clear.* ◇ *The legal aid system in the United Kingdom is far from perfect.* ◇ *Programmed cell death in animals is far from being a rare phenomenon.* **far ˈfrom it** (*rather informal*) used to say that the opposite of what sb says is true: *Disagreement has not disappeared—far from it—but its range appears to have narrowed.* **go far enough** (used in questions and negative sentences) to achieve all that is wanted: *The government did legislate to improve conditions and reduce hours for women and children, but it never went far enough.* **go so/as far as to...** to be willing to go beyond usual limits in dealing with or describing sth: *Some observers have gone as far as to argue that the office of AG may be more powerful than governor.* **go too ˈfar (in sth/doing sth)** to behave in an extreme way that is not acceptable: *Some argue that 'family policy' has gone too far and has created a culture of dependency.* ◇ *His book suggests that government went too far in limiting such rights during wartime.* **in so/as ˈfar as** to the degree that: *In so far as building relationships based on trust and satisfaction is desirable, there are limits to which salespeople can go in their behaviour.* **ˈso far | ˈthus far** until now; up to this point: *Approximately two million species have so far been described and given scientific names.* ◇ *Apart from the arguments discussed so far, other considerations have been put forward in the debate.* **take sth too ˈfar** to continue doing sth beyond reasonable limits: *Persuasive as the notion of cultural centralization appears, it should not be taken too far.* ➲ *more at* FEW[1], NEAR[3]

far[2] /fɑː(r)/ *adj.* (**far·ther, far·thest** or **fur·ther, fur·thest**) [only before noun] **1** at a greater distance away from you: *The connecting pipes are protected at the far end by a sheet metal cover.* ◇ *The slave trade shattered entire cultures within Africa, and created new ones on the far side of the Atlantic.* **2** at the furthest point in a particular direction: *Despite their isolation in the far north, it seems that the bears may be affected by our industrial activity.* ◇ *The term*

'Nationalist parties' is now normally used to define the anti-immigrant parties of the far right. ◇ *Radiometers sensitive to wavelengths in the far infrared operate beyond the solar spectrum.*

IDM **a far cry from sth** a very different experience from sth: *Contemporary Sri Lanka is a far cry from the tropical Indian Ocean island called 'Serendip' by the first Arab visitors.*

farm[1] /fɑːm; *NAmE* fɑːrm/ *noun* **1** an area of land, and the buildings on it, used for growing crops and/or keeping animals: *People are most willing to pay for organic foods if they believe doing so supports small family farms.* ◇ **on a/the ~** *Butter and cheese were produced on the farms.* ◇ **+ noun** *Several surveys show that consumers are concerned about the welfare of farm animals.* **2** (used especially in compounds) a place where particular fish or animals are bred: *The fish were sampled randomly from a fish farm off the coast of Scotland.* ◇ *The number of poultry farms in the region decreased by about 75%.* ➲ *see also* DAIRY[1], WIND FARM

farm[2] /fɑːm; *NAmE* fɑːrm/ *verb* [I, T] to use land for growing crops and/or keeping animals: *Pima Indians continued to farm along the Gila River.* ◇ **~ sth** *The men of the village farmed the land and tended to their livestock.* ◇ *In 2009, almost 20 000 tons of farmed Atlantic cod were produced in Norway.*

farm·er /ˈfɑːmə(r); *NAmE* ˈfɑːrmər/ *noun* a person who owns or manages a farm: *Small farmers responded to the loss of farm income from beef and sheep by turning to poultry.*

farm·ing /ˈfɑːmɪŋ; *NAmE* ˈfɑːrmɪŋ/ *noun* [U] the business of managing or working on a farm: *Farming, logging and mining have altered more than 90% of this landscape.* ◇ *The most prominent system of sustainable farming is organic farming.* ◇ *In Atlantic Canada, salmon farming established itself as a viable industry.* ◇ **+ noun** *Better farming methods mean that more can be produced from the same amount of land.*

ˌfar-ˈreaching *adj.* likely to have a lot of influence or many effects: *The policy has potentially far-reaching consequences for neighbouring countries.* ◇ *All of these changes had far-reaching implications that were not fully understood at the time.* ◇ *There was a widespread awareness that far-reaching economic reforms were needed.*

far·ther /ˈfɑːðə(r); *NAmE* ˈfɑːrðər/ *adv.* (comparative of *far*) at or to a greater distance in space or time; at a more advanced point: *When water transport was available, it allowed people to transport bulk goods much farther.* ◇ *During regional haze periods, occasionally one cannot see objects farther than hundreds of metres away.* ◇ **~ adv./prep.** *The sites chosen for the intervention were located substantially farther apart than would normally be the case.* ◇ *Jupiter is farther from the Sun than we are, so it moves more slowly in its orbit than the Earth.* ◇ *Following that event, the regime shifted even farther towards the right.* ◇ *Farther east, the Urals area is a source of many raw materials.*

far·thest[1] /ˈfɑːðɪst; *NAmE* ˈfɑːrðɪst/ (*also* **fur·thest**) *adv.* (superlative of *far*) **(+ adv./prep.)** at or to the greatest distance in space or time: *Lines of longitude converge at the poles and are farthest apart at the equator.* ◇ *The particles of largest velocity will have travelled the farthest from the origin.*

far·thest[2] /ˈfɑːðɪst; *NAmE* ˈfɑːrðɪst/ (*also* **fur·thest**) *adj.* (superlative of *far*) at the greatest distance in space, direction or time: *Solstice occurs twice each year when the sun is vertically overhead at the farthest distance from the equator.*

fas·cin·ate /ˈfæsɪneɪt/ *verb* [T, I] to attract or interest sb very much: *Crimes of passion gripped the 19th-century imagination, and they continue to fascinate.* ◇ **~ sb** *The study of the mechanisms of migration has fascinated researchers for a long time.*

fas·cin·ated /ˈfæsɪneɪtɪd/ *adj.* very interested: **~ by/with sth** *He was absolutely fascinated with murders that seemed to lack motivating factors.* ◇ **~ to do sth** *Members of the community were fascinated to see and hear about what the students had learned.*

fas·cin·at·ing /ˈfæsɪneɪtɪŋ/ *adj.* extremely interesting: *In a fascinating study, Moss explores two Christian sources from late antiquity.* ◇ *The details of the arguments are often fascinating.*

fas·cin·ation /ˌfæsɪˈneɪʃn/ *noun* **1** [C, usually sing.] a very strong attraction, that makes sth very interesting: *For Dickens, as for many of his contemporaries, India held a fascination.* ◇ *This elusiveness has been intrinsic to cinema's fascination and its beauty.* **2** [U, sing.] the state of being very attracted to and interested in sb/sth: *Most readers will respond with either horrified fascination or scepticism.* ◇ **~ for/with sb/sth** *Hamlet and Lear are used as ciphers for the Romantic period's fascination with madness and death.*

fash·ion[1] /ˈfæʃn/ *noun* **1** [U] the business of making or selling clothes in new and different styles: *The Continental domination of fashion was seen as a threat.* ◇ **+ noun** *The fashion industry has finally decided not to use models younger than 16.* **2** [C] a popular style of clothes, hair, etc. at a particular time or place: *In these elegant boutiques, they shop for the latest fashions from New York, Milan and Paris.* **3** [U] the state of being popular at a particular time or place: **in ~** *Long hair was back in fashion at the court of William Rufus.* ◇ **come into ~** *Shortly after tombs of this type came into fashion, Greeks from the mainland gained control of Crete.* ◇ **out of ~** *Today such arguments are out of fashion with both scientists and theologians.* ◇ **go out of ~** *It was not simply that certain opinions had gone out of fashion or been discredited,* **4** [C] a popular way of behaving, doing an activity, etc: **~ for sth** *The even larger number of people now in their 30s and 40s is a result of the fashion for large families in the 1960s.* ◇ **~ in sth** *Abrahamson is internationally recognized for his research on fashions in management techniques.*

IDM **after a ˈfashion** to some extent, but not very well: *This view would seem to explain, after a fashion, time's fundamental difference from space.* **in (a)... ˈfashion** in a particular way: *All clinical waste is disposed of in a similar fashion.* ◇ *A society organized in this fashion would be highly efficient.*

fash·ion[2] /ˈfæʃn/ *verb* **1** **~ sth** to create or invent sth: *The hero of the novel seeks to fashion a new identity for himself in a changed world.* **2** to make or shape sth, especially with your hands; to use a particular material to make or shape an object: **~ sth (from/out of sth)** *Hesiod relates how the first woman was fashioned from clay by Hephaistos.* ◇ **~ sth into sth** *Much more iron was being produced and fashioned into tools, weapons and ornaments.*

fash·ion·able /ˈfæʃnəbl/ *adj.* **1** popular; in a popular style at a particular time: *An increasing proportion of income was spent on leisure activities and fashionable clothing.* ◇ **it is ~ to do sth** *It is fashionable to deride the idea that the scientific method guarantees truth.* ◇ **~ among sb** *By the mid-seventeenth century, chocolate had become fashionable among the rich in Paris.* **2** (of a person) dressing or behaving according to the current fashion: *His screen image was of a charming, handsome and fashionable man.* **3** (of a place) used or visited by people following a current fashion, especially by rich people: *These schools clustered around London and fashionable county towns.* ➲ *compare* OLD-FASHIONED

fast¹ /fɑːst; *NAmE* fæst/ *adj.* (**fast·er, fast·est**) **1** happening in a short time or without delay: *Between 1750 and 1950 the population grew at a faster rate.* ◇ *Higher rates of entrepreneurial activity were strongly associated with faster growth of local economies.* OPP SLOW¹ (1) **2** able to do sth quickly: *It was the fastest computer of its day.* **3** moving or able to move quickly: *The fluids find the fractures and keep them open to maintain sufficiently fast flow.* HELP There is no noun related to **fast**. Use **speed** in connection with vehicles, actions, etc; **quickness** is used about thinking. IDM *see* HARD¹

F

fast² /fɑːst; *NAmE* fæst/ *adv.* (**fast·er, fast·est**) **1** quickly; at a high speed: *It is not possible to accelerate particles to move faster than the speed of light.* **2** in a short time; without delay: *Wage costs have been rising fast.* ◇ *In North America, overall energy production and consumption did not grow as fast as in Asia.* HELP There is no noun related to **fast**. Use **speed** in connection with vehicles, actions, etc; **quickness** is used about thinking.
IDM **hold ˈfast to sth** to continue to believe in an idea, etc. despite difficulties: *America would remain strong as long as its citizens held fast to the principles of the Declaration of Independence.* **stand ˈfast/ˈfirm 1** to refuse to change your opinions: *Although the dissident movement had seemed to stand fast, it had diminished in influence.* **2** to refuse to move back: *The regiments stood firm until they were overwhelmed by the enemy's greater numbers.*

fast³ /fɑːst; *NAmE* fæst/ *verb* [I] to eat little or no food for a period of time, especially for religious or health reasons: *During the holy month of Ramadan, Muslims are required to fast from dawn until dusk.*

fas·ten /ˈfɑːsn; *NAmE* ˈfæsn/ *verb* **1 ~ sth** to close sth firmly so that it will not open; to close or join together the two parts of sth: *Fasten doors and windows securely.* ◇ *She finds it difficult to fasten buttons.* **2 ~ sth + adv./prep.** to fix or place sth in a particular position, so that it will not move: *The spider constructs a sort of cocoon fastened to the vegetation by two to eight threads.*

fat¹ /fæt/ *adj.* (**fat·ter, fat·test**) (of a person's or an animal's body) weighing too much; covered with too much fat: *One respondent commented: 'I feel so fat compared to some of my friends.'* ◇ *Comparative data are limited but suggest human babies are fatter than neonates of most other mammals.* HELP **Fat** is not a polite word; in academic English, use **overweight** or **obese** instead. OPP THIN¹ (2)

fat² /fæt/ *noun* **1** [U] a white or yellow substance in the bodies of animals and humans, stored under the skin: *Obesity may be defined as a medical condition characterized by excess body fat.* **2** [U, C] animal and vegetable fat, when considered as part of what a person eats: *Patients were encouraged to eat a balanced healthy diet that was low in fat.* ◇ *Data indicate that lower income households tend to have higher consumption of fats and sugars in the diet.* **3** [C] (*chemistry*) any of a group of natural ESTERS, mainly found in animals, which are solid at room temperature: *Some 40 per cent of our daily calories are derived from dietary fats.* ➲ *compare* OIL (4)

fatal /ˈfeɪtl/ *adj.* **1** causing or ending in death: *Almost 43% of all fatal injuries among women occurred in the manufacturing and mining sector.* ◇ *Both wounds were potentially fatal.* ◇ *For those over 85 years of age, a fall may prove fatal.* ◇ **~ to/for sb** *The collapse of single-storey dwellings is seldom fatal to their occupants.* ➲ *compare* MORTAL (2) **2** causing disaster or failure: *This lack of fiscal stability could be the fatal flaw in the deficit reduction programme.* ◇ **~ to/for sth** *The consequences of poor governance may be fatal to an organization.* ■ **fa·tal·ly** /ˈfeɪtəli/ *adv.*: *The victims were playing in the roadway when they were knocked down and fatally injured.* ◇ *The tourism policy was fatally flawed.*

fa·tal·ity /fəˈtæləti/ *noun* (*pl.* **-ies**) **1** [C] a death that is caused in an accident or a war, or by violence or disease: *The graph shows numbers of fatalities resulting from industrial accidents 1999–2011.* **2** [U] the fact that a particular disease or injury will cause death: *Even within rural areas, pedestrian fatality is more than three times higher than that of car occupants.* ◇ **+ noun** *Colorectal cancer has a high fatality rate.*

fate /feɪt/ *noun* **1** [C] **~ (of sb/sth)** the things, especially bad things, that will happen or have happened to sb/sth: *The success or failure of these repair processes determines the fate of the cell.* ◇ *This report suffered the same fate as its predecessor: publication was limited and its results were disputed.* ◇ **seal the ~ of sb/sth** *The findings of audience research can effectively seal the fate of particular television series or of individual characters within them.* **2** [U] the power that is believed to control everything that happens and that cannot be stopped or changed: *Philip intended to invade but fate intervened and he was assassinated by a member of his own bodyguard.*

father /ˈfɑːðə(r)/ *noun* **1** a male parent of a child or an animal; a person who is acting as the father to a child: *He had recently become a father.* ◇ *Not all biological fathers have parental responsibility for their children.* **2 ~ (of sth)** the first man to introduce a new way of thinking about sth or of doing sth: *Francis Bacon is regarded as the father of the scientific method of inquiry.*
IDM **from ˌfather to ˈson** from one generation of a family to the next: *Membership in these groups is passed on from father to son.*

fa·tigue /fəˈtiːɡ/ *noun* **1** [U] a feeling of being extremely tired, because of hard work, exercise or illness SYN EXHAUSTION (1), TIREDNESS: *Working women experience fatigue, strain, guilt and anxiety because they 'choose' to be employed.* ◇ *There are many who present with symptoms of chronic fatigue in whom no diagnosis is possible.* **2** [U] (usually after another noun) a feeling of not wanting to do a particular activity any longer because you have done too much of it: *There was a decline in the number of volunteers due to a combination of factors including donor fatigue.* ◇ *Might the increase in the number of elections and referendums have induced election fatigue?* **3** [U] weakness in metal or wood caused by repeated bending or stretching: *The bridge's life may have been curtailed due to metal fatigue.*

fatty /ˈfæti/ *adj.* (**fat·tier, fat·ti·est**) containing a lot of fat; consisting of fat: *The taste for sweet or fatty foods seems universal.* ◇ *Human fatty tissue comprises some 40 billion adipose cells.*

ˌfatty ˈacid *noun* an acid that is found in fats and oils: *The cells release reserves of fat into the blood as fatty acids for the rest of the body to use.*

fau·cet /ˈfɔːsɪt/ *noun* (*NAmE*) = TAP²

fault¹ /fɔːlt/ *noun* **1** [U] the responsibility for sth wrong that has happened or been done: *She claimed that the accident was not her fault.* ◇ **it is sb's ~ that...** *It is neither party's fault that this has occurred.* ◇ **it is sb's ~ for doing sth** *It was assumed to be the buyer's fault for buying the wrong item.* ◇ **at ~** *In an attempt to avoid a claim against themselves, the employers stated that the contractors were at fault.* ◇ **through no ~ of your own** *Through no fault of their own, they were unable to support themselves.* **2** [C] a bad or weak aspect of sth, especially in a piece of work or in a person's character SYN SHORTCOMING: *If he did have a fault, it was that he trusted others too much.* ◇ *The book is not without its faults.* ◇ **for all sb/sth's faults** *Marx, for all his faults, provides a social and historical dimension.* **3** [C] something that is wrong with a machine or system that stops it from working correctly SYN DEFECT¹: *An unexpected drop in electricity supply might arise from a fault.* ◇ **~ in sth** *A fault in the software meant that the client made an overpayment of $36 800.* **4** [C] a place where there is a break that is longer than usual in the layers of rock in the earth's CRUST: *The San Andreas fault crosses San Francisco Bay a few miles west of the Golden Gate Bridge.* ◇ *The terrain itself also complicates efforts to investigate faults in Puerto Rico.* ◇ **+ noun** *The state is marked by a number of long fault lines running along the foothills of the high mountain ranges.* IDM *see* FIND[1]

fault[2] /fɔːlt/ *verb* (often used in negative sentences with *can* and *could*) to find a mistake or a weakness in sb/sth SYN CRITICIZE: **~ sb/sth (for sth)** *It is easy to fault a book for what it does not cover.* ◇ **~ sb/sth for doing sth** *One cannot fault the politicians for seeking to bring their constituents some of the benefits of modernity.*

faulty /ˈfɔːlti/ *adj.* **1** not perfect; not working or made correctly SYN DEFECTIVE: *Faulty electrical wiring can cause a fire.* ◇ *The Court hears claims including breach of contract, faulty goods and personal injury.* **2** (of a way of thinking) wrong or containing mistakes: *The argument fails because of its faulty logic.*

fauna /ˈfɔːnə/ *noun* [U, C] all the animals living in an area or in a particular period of history: *Much of the mammal and bird fauna of Madagascar was devastated following large-scale human settlement.* ◇ (*technical*) *These soils and their faunas are indicative of cold conditions, including permafrost.* HELP **Fauna** is often used in the phrase **fauna and flora**, to mean plants and animals: *Canals functioned as ecosystems analogous to rivers, supporting fauna and flora of their own.*

fa·vour[1] (*US* favor) /ˈfeɪvə(r)/ *noun* **1** [C] a thing that you do to help sb: *Some member countries granted special favours, such as lower customs rates, to other WTO members.* ◇ *The customer had no money and offered to do the shopkeeper a favour instead of paying.* **2** [U] approval or support for sb/sth: *In the late '60s, his ideas were considered radical to the left, but in the '80s they found favour with the radical right.* ◇ *Malthus's theory lost favour in the mid-nineteenth century.* ◇ *Both writers have fallen from favour in recent years.*

IDM **in favour (of sb/sth) 1** supporting and agreeing with sth/sb: *This essay will examine the main arguments in favour of establishing a single institution to promote human rights.* ◇ *The wealthier socio-economic groups were most in favour of an expanded welfare system.* **2** likely to produce a particular result, often in an unfair way: *The voting rule should not be biased in favour of any candidate.* ◇ *The answers are loaded in favour of a positive rather than a negative reply.* **3** in exchange for another thing (because the other thing is better or you want it more): *Free trade was abandoned in favour of protectionist policies.* **in sb's favour 1** if sth is **in sb's favour**, it gives them an advantage or helps them: *The evidence seemed to be in the prosecution's favour at the pre-trial stage.* **2** a decision or judgement that is **in sb's favour** benefits that person or says that they were right: *The ruling of the court was in our favour on all the main points.* IDM *see* FIND[1]

fa·vour[2] (*US* favor) /ˈfeɪvə(r)/ *verb* **1** to prefer one thing to another, especially a particular system, plan or way of doing sth: **~ sth** *Empirical evidence shows that the majority of citizens favour democracy as an ideal form of government.* ◇ *This was a tactic particularly favoured by Voltaire.* ◇ **~ (sb) doing sth** *Workers with secure jobs and people living on fixed incomes often favour fighting inflation.* ◇ **~ sth over sth** *Under normal conditions, most religious believers favour peace over extremism.* **2** to treat sb/sth better than others, especially in an unfair way: **~ sb/sth** *Females presumably favour males who are good at defending their territory.* ◇ *Such investment policies favour the largest cities.* ◇ **~ sb/sth over sb/sth** *The gender hierarchy in society has historically favoured men over women.* **3 ~ sth** to provide suitable conditions for sth; to make it easier for sth to happen: *The findings suggest that malaria vaccines could favour the spread of more virulent malaria parasites.*

fa·vour·able (*US* fa·vor·able) /ˈfeɪvərəbl/ *adj.* **1** good for sth and making it likely to be successful or have an advantage SYN ADVANTAGEOUS: *Hence, the most favourable conditions for building nation-states existed in north-west Europe.* ◇ *There is no guarantee of a favourable outcome when a new application for a grant is made.* ◇ **~ to sth/sb** *The legislation was altered so as to be more favourable to state interests.* ◇ **~ for sth/sb (to do sth)** *Conditions in the region are favourable for the mangroves to develop fully.* OPP UNFAVOURABLE (1) **2** positive and showing your good opinion of sb/sth: *The reviews of 'The Bad Seed' were generally favourable.* ◇ *For purchase to occur, you must have a favourable attitude towards the brand.* ◇ **~ to sth/sb** *A surprisingly large amount of press coverage was favourable to annexation.* OPP UNFAVOURABLE (2) **3** making people have a good opinion of sb/sth: *These scores do not indicate deception, but rather an attempt to make a favourable impression.* ◇ *Of course, all governments seek to present their policies in a favourable light.* OPP UNFAVOURABLE (2)

fa·vour·ably (*US* fa·vor·ably) /ˈfeɪvərəbli/ *adv.* **1** in a way that gives an advantage to sb/sth or shows that sb/sth has an advantage: *Fig. 2 shows that life expectancy in the USA does not compare favourably with that in Europe.* **2** with approval: *The government responded favourably to several of these recommendations.*

fa·voured (*US* favored) /ˈfeɪvəd; *NAmE* ˈfeɪvərd/ *adj.* **1** treated in a special way or receiving special help or advantages in a way that may seem unfair: *It is not uncommon for a particular proposal or idea to be leaked to a favoured newspaper.* ◇ *All Latin American countries were required to apply 'most favoured nation' tariff rates to India.* **2** preferred or chosen by sb: *The machine enabled voters to punch holes in a ballot paper next to the names of their favoured candidates.* ◇ *Among these farmers, the favoured solution to impoverished soil was to plant legumes along with the cereal crops.*

fa·vour·ite[1] (*US* fa·vor·ite) /ˈfeɪvərɪt/ *adj.* liked more than others of the same kind: *Children were asked, 'What are your favourite television programmes?'* ◇ *Hills have always been favourite places to build defensive settlements.*

fa·vour·ite[2] (*US* fa·vor·ite) /ˈfeɪvərɪt/ *noun* **1** a person or thing that is liked more than others of the same type: *'The Last Chronicle of Barset' was Trollope's personal favourite amongst his books.* **2 ~ (of sb)** a person who is liked better by sb and receives better treatment than others: *In Greek myth, Paris is the favourite of the goddess Aphrodite.* ◇ *Livia had her favourites and protected them from the emperor and even from the law.* **3 ~ (for sth)** the person who is expected by most people to get a particular job or position: *For the Russian presidency, Yeltsin was the favourite.*

fear[1] /fɪə(r); *NAmE* fɪr/ *noun* [U, C] the bad feeling that you have when you are in danger, when sth bad might happen, or when a particular thing frightens you: *The power of the ruling party was regarded by many with fear and suspicion.* ◇ **~ of sb/sth** *Fear of crime prompts the public to favour repressive measures.* ◇ **~ for sb/sth** *The discussion covered topics such as their relationships with friends and loved ones, and their hopes and fears for the future.* ◇ **~ that...** *Some MEPs expressed fears that the decision would permit member states to suppress legitimate forms of public protest.* ◇ **in ~ (of sb/sth)** *The majority of the population no longer lives in fear of police brutality.*

IDM **for fear of sth/of doing sth | for fear that...** to avoid the danger of sth happening: *Asylum is provided to a foreigner who is unable to stay in their country of citizenship/residence for fear of persecution.* ◇ *Students often refrain from asking questions for fear of appearing foolish.*

F

◇ *Governments are reluctant to raise taxes for fear that higher taxes will induce businesses to relocate abroad.*

fear² /fɪə(r); *NAmE* fɪr/ *verb* **1** to be frightened of sb/sth or frightened of doing sth: **~ sb/sth** *Millions feared Hitler and millions were enthralled by him.* ◇ *The Greek philosopher Epicurus argued that death should not be feared.* ◇ **have nothing to ~ (from sb/sth)** *Müller believed that the truth of his faith had nothing to fear from science.* ◇ **~ to do sth** *Research shows that minorities fear to act in ways that confirm a stereotype.* ◇ **~ doing sth** *Women were most likely to fear becoming a victim of crime.* **2** to feel that sth bad might have happened or might happen in the future: **~ sth** *They feared persecution for their religious beliefs.* ◇ **~ the worst** *The Emperor, fearing the worst, left for Innsbruck.* ◇ **be feared to do sth** *Ethnic political parties are feared to lead to ethnic conflict.* ◇ **it is feared that...** *It is feared that getting 27 heads of state to agree will prove very difficult.* ◇ **~ that...** *France and Britain feared that Russia would make peace with Germany.*

PHR V **ˈfear for sb/sth** to be worried about sb/sth: *Victims fear for their lives if they speak to investigators.*

feasi·bil·ity /ˌfiːzəˈbɪləti/ *noun* [U] how possible or likely sth is to be achieved: **~ of (doing) sth** *Johnston et al. (2006) tested the feasibility of using EMA to study work-related stress in nurses.* ◇ **+ noun** *A feasibility study was done to examine the practical possibility of conducting a large-scale study.*

feas·ible /ˈfiːzəbl/ *adj.* that is possible and likely to be achieved SYN PRACTICABLE: *Sustained control may be the only feasible option to manage such species.* ◇ *The domestic market is too small to make industrial production economically feasible.* ◇ **~ to do sth** *It may not be technically feasible to carry out the experiment.*

fea·ther /ˈfeðə(r)/ *noun* one of the many soft light parts covering a bird's body: *The outermost tail feathers are longer.*

fea·ture¹ AWL /ˈfiːtʃə(r)/ *noun* [C] **1** something important, interesting or typical of sth such as a system, structure or place: *While democracies share common features, there is no single model of democracy.* ◇ *The device should incorporate design features that will minimize potential later complications.* ◇ **~ of sth** *Provision of social care for disabled people has been a key feature of the welfare state.* **2** [usually pl.] a part of sb's face such as the nose, mouth and eyes: *Biometric technology allows measurements of eye retinas and facial features to be taken and stored digitally.*

▸ ADJECTIVE + FEATURE **important, significant • key, crucial • salient • basic , fundamental • essential • central, principal, main, major • special • unique • unusual • distinctive, striking, remarkable, notable, prominent • distinguishing, defining • typical, characteristic • common • general • permanent • interesting • attractive, desirable • additional • certain, particular, specific • peculiar • architectural** *Religious meeting houses became characteristic features of the village landscape.* ◇ *After World War II, a high level of military spending became a permanent feature of the US economy.*

▸ VERB + FEATURE **have, possess • contain, include • incorporate • combine • share • retain • exhibit, display, show, reveal • illustrate • become** *By the end of the fifth century AD, the landscape of Britain no longer contained the distinctive features that had made it Roman.* ◇ *This formation displays several unique features.* | **describe • explain • highlight • summarize • outline • capture • identify • recognize** *This paper will describe the key features, causes and mechanisms of neuropathic pain.* ◇ *In what follows, I identify four salient features exhibited in the two judicial decisions.*

THESAURUS

feature • characteristic • quality • property • trait • attribute *noun*

These are all words for sth that is typical of sb/sth, especially making them different from others.

- a/an feature/characteristic/quality/property/trait/attribute **of** sb/sth
- a/an **important/essential/key** feature/characteristic/property/attribute
- **different** characteristics/qualities/properties/traits/attributes
- a **personal** characteristic/quality/trait/attribute
- a **physical** characteristic/property/trait/attribute
- to **have** a/an feature/characteristic/quality/property/trait/attribute
- to **share/identify/associate** a/an feature/characteristic/trait/attribute
- to **show/exhibit** a feature/characteristic/property/trait
- to **possess** a/an quality/property/trait/attribute

- Several of these words can be used to talk about a person; a **characteristic** can refer to sb's character, behaviour or appearance; a **quality** can refer to sb's character or ability: *Individual socio-demographic characteristics considered were age, sex, household income and work status.* ◇ *Results-based leadership seeks to balance personal qualities with appropriate knowledge.*
- **Attribute** and **trait** are slightly more formal and are often used in life sciences to describe what can be observed or measured about people or animals; **trait** is used especially to talk about typical behaviour: *Certain physical attributes, such as height, are not easily modified.* ◇ *The patterns of behavioural traits in different populations throughout tropical Africa reveal surprising variation.*
- **Feature** and **characteristic** can be used to talk about sth important or typical of a place or thing; **property** is used especially to talk about the features of a material or substance: *The absence of clear boundaries between rural and urban areas is a distinctive feature of contemporary land use.* ◇ *The product of the radioactive decay can possess very different chemical properties.*

fea·ture² AWL /ˈfiːtʃə(r)/ *verb* **1** [T] to include a particular person or thing as a special feature: **~ sb/sth** *The latest issue of 'Bioscience Horizons' features 12 articles by undergraduate researchers.* ◇ *Even the comedy series 'South Park' regularly features a disabled character, called Timmy.* ◇ **~ sb/sth as sb/sth** *Paula Cole's 'I Don't Wanna Wait' became a top-ten single after being featured as the show's theme song.* **2** [I] to have an important part in sth: **~ in sth** *Corruption and targeted killings are two key themes that feature prominently in many of his reports.* ◇ **~ as sth** *Water will certainly feature as an important issue of development in the region in the decades ahead.*

fed *past tense, past part. of* FEED¹

fed·eral AWL /ˈfedərəl/ *adj.* **1** having a system of government in which the individual states of a country have control over their own affairs, but are controlled by a central government for national decisions: *Public responsiveness to government policy may be weaker in federal regimes.* **2** (within a federal system, for example the US and Canada) connected with national government rather than the local government of an individual state: *The budget of the US federal government is roughly thirty times as large as the European Union's budget.* ◇ *Increased federal spending has produced large federal deficits.* ■ **fed·er·al·ly** *adv.*: *Analysis was conducted on three federally funded database projects.*

fed·er·ation AWL /ˌfedəˈreɪʃn/ *noun* **1** [C] a country consisting of a group of individual states that have control over their own affairs but are controlled by a central government for national decisions: *Some federations, such as*

Australia, Austria and the United States, record higher per pupil spending. ◇ *The Russian Federation ratified the treaty on 3 June 2008.* ◇ **~ of sth** *The philosophers of the European Enlightenment looked towards a universal federation of free republics.* **2** [C] an organization that represents and works on behalf of the groups that are its members: *The International Diabetes Federation estimated that, in 2006, 246 million people were living with diabetes worldwide.* ◇ **~ of sth** *The National Federation of Small Business represents hundreds of thousands of small firms.* **3** [U] **~ (of sth)** the act of forming a federation: *The Schuman declaration was one step in the federation of Europe.*

fee AWL /fiː/ *noun* **1** an amount of money that you pay for professional advice or services: *Many advertising agencies charge a fee for services in addition to their commission.* ◇ *Each student makes an application, enrols onto a course, and pays their fees.* **2** an amount of money that you pay to join an organization, or to do sth: *Community Partners introduced a system in which all members pay a low annual membership fee.* ◇ *Entrance fees could vary by season to encourage off-peak demand.*

feed[1] /fiːd/ *verb* (**fed**, **fed** /fed/) **1** [T] to give food to a person or an animal: **~ sb/sth/yourself** *Experiments showed that parents preferentially feed the chicks with the brightest colours.* ◇ **~ sb/sth (on) sth** *They were fed on a diet of mainly grain or vegetables.* ◇ **~ sth to sb/sth** *Crushed cane is fed to the pigs to fatten them.* ◇ **~ sb/sth with sth** *In the experiment, the beetle was fed with spiders that had previously eaten aphids.* **2** [I] (of a baby or an animal) to eat food: *A newborn baby will usually need to feed 8-12 times in a 24-hour period.* ➲ *see also* FEED ON/OFF STH **3** [T] **~ sb/sth** to provide enough food for a family or group of people or animals: *Young children raised money to feed their families by begging for coins.* ◇ *Feeding the growing world population is a significant challenge.* **4** [T] to give advice or information to sb/sth: **~ sb sth** *He held secret consultations with the president, feeding him ideas.* ◇ **~ sth to sb** *False information was fed to editors of underground journals, who could then be charged with spreading false reports.* **5** [T] to supply sth to sb/sth: **~ sth** *The streams are fed by glacial meltwater.* ◇ **~ sb/sth with sth** *Celtic mythology fed Romantic writers with an exciting alternative to the familiar legends of Greece and Rome.* ◇ **~ sth to/into sth** *The plantations of Virginia and Georgia fed raw cotton to the textile mills of Manchester.* **6** [T] to put or push sth into or through a machine: **~ sth (with sth)** *The engines were fed with pulverized coal.* ◇ **~ sth into/through sth** *The data are fed into a central database.*
PHR V **ˌfeed ˈback (into/to sth)** to have an influence on the development of sth by reacting to it in some way: *It is hoped that their research will feed back into the study of Sophocles' Theban plays.* **ˌfeed (sth) ˈback (to sb)** to give information or opinions about sth, especially so that it can be improved: *Staff regularly have the opportunity to feed back their views to management.* **ˈfeed into sth** to have an influence on the development of sth: *The hardship caused by the war fed into the anti-imperialist upsurge.* **ˈfeed on/off sth** (of an animal) to eat sth: *Sperm whales feed mainly on squid.* ◇ *Migrating buffalo feed off the abundant grasses.* **ˌfeed ˈthrough (to sb/sth)** to reach sb/sth after going through a process or system: *It takes time for a change in the interest rate to feed through to consumption and investment decisions.*

feed[2] /fiːd/ *noun* **1** [C] a meal of milk for a young baby; a meal for an animal: *A baby may suddenly start demanding more feeds than he or she had done previously.* **2** [U, C] food for animals or plants: *Approximately two thirds of corn was used as livestock feed.* ◇ *In Kampala, farmers pay market vendors for vegetable peelings to be used as animal feeds.* **3** [U] a supply of sth, especially material supplied to a machine: **+ noun** *In this boiler, feed water is boiled into steam, which powers a steam turbine.* **4** [C] a pipe or other device that supplies a machine with sth: **+ noun** *The condensed water is recycled into the boiler by means of a feed pump.* **5** [C] a system for providing the user of a BLOG or other website with new information as it is added: *The live video feed provided a unique continuity to the story of the oil spill.*

feed·back /ˈfiːdbæk/ *noun* [U] **1** advice, criticism or information about how good or useful sth or sb's work is: *Overall, feedback has been positive.* ◇ *Experience provides feedback that allows people to assess their true ability.* ◇ **~ on sth** *Companies will often pay to get consumer feedback on their items.* **2** (*technical*) the way in which the results or effects of a process or system increase or decrease its activity: *There are many examples of positive feedback within the climate system.* ◇ **+ noun** *Feedback mechanisms, both negative and positive, regulate release of hormones.* ➲ *see also* NEGATIVE FEEDBACK, POSITIVE FEEDBACK

feed·ing /ˈfiːdɪŋ/ *noun* [U] **1** the act of giving food to a person, an animal or a plant: *In the study, inappropriate feeding was a major factor in infant mortality.* **2** (of animals) the act of eating food: **+ noun** *The feeding habits of the Eurasian otter have been extensively researched.*

feel[1] /fiːl/ *verb* (**felt**, **felt** /felt/) **1** *linking verb* to experience a particular feeling or emotion: **+ adj.** *Women who are unable to breastfeed are often made to feel guilty.* ◇ *A third of cyclists do not feel safe from accidents during the day.* ◇ **+ adv./prep.** *The adolescents were asked to rate how they would feel if they became pregnant in the next year.* ◇ **~ sth** *When challenged, he said he felt no need to apologize.* ◇ **~ like sth** *She said she felt like an outsider.* **2** [T] (not usually used in the progressive tenses) to notice or be aware of sth because it is touching you or having a physical effect on you: **~ sth** *She felt a sharp pain when she coughed.* ◇ **~ sb/sth/yourself do sth** *The attacks last 2-3 min and she feels her finger twitch before they start.* ◇ **~ sb/sth/yourself doing sth** *He could feel his heart pounding.* **3** *linking verb* (not used in the progressive tenses) to give you a particular feeling or impression: **+ adj.** *It felt strange to be back in my old school.* ◇ **~ like sth** *In this exercise, five minutes felt like an eternity.* ◇ **~ as if/though...** *To the health professionals, it felt as if she made no attempt to gain control over her life.* HELP In spoken English, people often use **like** instead of **as if** or **as though** in this meaning. This is not correct in academic English. **Like** can be used before a noun phrase (*an eternity*) but not before a clause (*she made no attempt...*). **4** [T, I] (not usually used in the progressive tenses) to think or believe that sth is the case; to have a particular opinion or attitude: **~ (that)...** *For the good of all involved, they felt that the war must end as soon as possible.* ◇ **~ it + adj.** *Most students felt it important to study abroad during their educational careers.* ◇ **+ adv./prep.** *They feel strongly about the implications of having their children labelled 'at risk'.* **5** [T, often passive] to experience the effects or results of sth, often strongly: **be felt (by sb)** *Across the whole of the capitalist world, the shock waves of the financial crash were keenly felt.* ◇ *The impact of this new policy will be felt most acutely by the very poor.* ◇ **~ sth** *The government clearly felt the force of this argument.* **6** *linking verb* (not used in the progressive tenses) to have a particular physical quality which you become aware of by touching: **+ adj.** *At times the joints can feel warm to touch.* ◇ **~ like sth** *The skin rash is light pink and feels like sandpaper.* **7** [T, I] to move your fingers over sth in order to find out what it is like, or in order to find sth: **~ sth** *I checked the patient's colour and felt his skin temperature.* ◇ **~ for sth** *The doctor felt for tenderness on the bridge of the nose.*
IDM **feel ˈgood (about sth/yourself)** to feel happy, confident, etc: *Self-esteem is present when workers feel good about themselves.* **feel like doing sth** (*rather informal*) to want to have or do sth: *At some point, most people with*

F

severe depression will feel like ending it all. **feel 'sick** (*especially BrE*) to feel as though you will VOMIT soon: *The patient says he has been feeling sick, although he has not actually vomited.*

feel² /fiːl/ *noun* [sing.] **1** the impression that is created by a place, situation, etc. SYN ATMOSPHERE (4): *It is essential that all aspects of a marketing campaign have a consistent look and feel.* ◇ **a... ~ to it** *The story has a Shakespearian feel to it.* ◇ **the ~ of sth** *The mall is filled with street furniture and vendors, evoking the feel of a European marketplace.* **2** the way that sth feels when you touch it or are touched by it: *These rocks are characterized by a curiously slippery feel.* ◇ **the ~ of sth** *One of the joys of reading books lies in the feel of the paper.* **3 ~ (of sth)** an act of feeling or touching: *A feel of the radial pulse may give an early clue as to why someone fainted.*
IDM **get/be given a feel for sth** to gain an understanding of sth: *It is difficult to get a feel for the case from the very sparse information supplied.* **have a feel for sth** to have an understanding of sth or be naturally good at doing it: *He had an instinctive feel for figures.*

feel·ing /ˈfiːlɪŋ/ *noun* **1** [C] **~ (of sth)** something that you feel through the mind or the senses: *At the age of 32, he began to notice a feeling of weakness when climbing the stairs.* ◇ *A child may mask feelings of anger.* ◇ *The ordinary view is that our subjective feelings and conscious volitions cause our actions.* **2** [sing.] the idea or belief that a particular thing is true or a particular situation is likely to happen: **~ (of sth)** *For many people, having a job is essential to the feeling of being a part of a society.* ◇ **~ that...** *Despite the feeling that everyone was being watched, it is probably true that police repression was accepted as a necessary evil.* ➲ *compare* IMPRESSION (3) **3** [C, U] an attitude or opinion about sth: **~ (about/on sth)** *All three groups had mixed feelings about the benefits of education.* ◇ **~ that...** *There is a strong feeling that countries should govern themselves and should not be governed by foreigners.* ◇ **~ towards sth** *It has been claimed that media coverage had a significant impact on public feeling towards the Asian crisis.* **4 feelings** [pl.] a person's emotions rather than their thoughts or ideas: *He worried terribly about having hurt his mother's feelings.* ◇ *Writing a letter can be an easier way for teens to express their feelings.* **5** [U] **~ for sb/sth** the ability to understand sb/sth or to do sth in a sensitive way: *In Korea, 'kibun' is a sort of intuitive feeling for social balance and correct behaviour.* ◇ *These quotations give us a feeling for Carr's writing.* **6** [pl., U] **~ (for sb/sth)** sympathy or love for sb/sth: *Wordsworth's feelings for Dorothy are clearly present in the image of the companionable glow-worms.* ◇ *Foreign travel often heightens the homecomer's feeling for their own country.* **7** [U] strong emotion: *She spoke slowly and with great feeling.* **8** [U] the ability to feel physically SYN SENSATION (2): *The patient says he has lost feeling in the lower part of his leg.* **9** [sing.] **~ (of sth)** the atmosphere of a place or situation: *The town was lacking in any feeling of warmth.* ◇ *Despite the sheer volume of adults and children in the school, it manages to retain an intimate feeling.*

feet *pl. of* FOOT

fell *past tense of* FALL¹

fel·low¹ /ˈfeləʊ; *NAmE* ˈfeloʊ/ *noun* **1** [usually pl.] a person that you work with or that is like you; a thing that is similar to the one mentioned: *She has a very good reputation among her fellows.* ◇ *Many caged birds live longer than their fellows in the wild.* **2** (*BrE*) a senior member of some colleges or universities: *Eventually he became a fellow of Trinity College, Cambridge.* **3** a member of an academic or professional organization: *He is a fellow of the American Psychological Society.* **4** (*especially NAmE*) a GRADUATE student who holds a FELLOWSHIP: *Fink worked on Salmonella as a postdoctoral fellow.*

fel·low² /ˈfeləʊ; *NAmE* ˈfeloʊ/ *adj.* [only before noun] used to describe sb who is the same as you in some way, or in the same situation: *The Roman authorities generally protected the Jews from their pagan fellow citizens.* ◇ *Online tools can help patients to find and talk to fellow sufferers.*

fel·low·ship /ˈfeləʊʃɪp; *NAmE* ˈfeloʊʃɪp/ *noun* **1** [U] a feeling of friendship between people who do things together or share an interest: *Such societies offered a sense of friendship and fellowship.* **2** [C] an award of money to a GRADUATE student to allow them to continue their studies or to do research: *The Council funds fellowships for research into cancer.* **3** [C] (*especially BrE*) the position of being a senior member of a college or university: *Miller had a fellowship at St. John's College, Cambridge.* **4** [C] an organized group of people who share an interest, aim or belief: *The Buddhist Churches of America have over sixty churches and fellowships around the country.*

felt *past tense, past part. of* FEEL¹

fe·male¹ /ˈfiːmeɪl/ *adj.* **1** belonging to the sex that can give birth to babies or lay eggs: *The pay gap between male and female workers increased in the late 1950s.* ◇ *In many primates, female offspring inherit the territory or social rank of their mothers.* OPP MALE¹ (1) **2** connected with women or female animals: *Younger women tend to be concentrated in traditionally female sectors of employment.* OPP MALE¹ (1) ➲ *compare* FEMININE (1) **3** (*biology*) (of plants and flowers) that can produce fruit: *In maize, male and female flowers develop at particular sites on the shoot.* OPP MALE¹ (3)

fe·male² /ˈfiːmeɪl/ *noun* **1** an animal that can give birth to babies or lay eggs; a plant that can produce fruit: *The males acquire a breeding site and then display on it to attract a female.* ◇ *Most male mammals are relieved from parental duties because females feed the offspring with their own milk.* OPP MALE² (2) **2** (*formal*) a woman or girl: *Male teachers outnumbered females in urban senior schools by 2:1.* HELP In this meaning, **female** is used mainly in formal and official language to talk about women or girls as a group. OPP MALE² (2)

femi·nine /ˈfemənɪn/ *adj.* **1** having the qualities or appearance considered to be typical of women; connected with women: *They may want their brand's image to make customers feel more masculine, or more feminine, or more healthy.* ◇ *In Greek thought, these two aspects of feminine sexuality were normally kept distinct from one another.* ➲ *compare* FEMALE¹, MASCULINE **2** (in some languages) belonging to a class of nouns, pronouns or adjectives that have feminine GENDER, not MASCULINE or NEUTER: *'Wisdom' is a feminine noun in Hebrew.*

femi·nin·ity /ˌfeməˈnɪnəti/ *noun* [U] the fact of being a woman; the qualities that are considered to be typical of women: *Historically and conventionally, femininity has been equated with conformity, docility and acceptance.* ◇ *The film demonstrates just how much ideals of femininity have changed.*

femi·nism /ˈfemənɪzəm/ *noun* [U] the belief and aim that women should have the same rights and opportunities as men; the struggle to achieve this aim: *Feminism pervades Woolf's novels.* ◇ *One of the goals of feminism is to produce knowledge that can help improve women's lives.*

femi·nist¹ /ˈfemənɪst/ *noun* a person who supports the belief that women should have the same rights and opportunities as men: *Feminists have long complained about the male domination of the British political system.*

femi·nist² /ˈfemənɪst/ *adj.* [usually before noun] connected with or supporting the belief that women should have the same rights and opportunities as men: *In the late 1960s and early 1970s, feminist theory began to make its mark* *within sociology.* ◇ *The success of the feminist movement enabled more women to pursue career paths and postpone having children.*

fence /fens/ *noun* a structure made of wood or wire supported with posts that is put between two areas of land as a BOUNDARY, or around a garden, field, etc. to keep animals in, or to keep people and animals out: *A barbed-wire fence surrounded the camp.*

fer·tile /ˈfɜːtaɪl; *NAmE* ˈfɜːrtl/ *adj.* **1** (of land or soil) that plants grow well in: *A huge construction project transformed the marsh into well-drained, fertile agricultural land.* OPP INFERTILE (2) **2** (of people, animals or plants) that can produce babies, young animals, fruit or new plants: *There is fierce competition between males for access to the most fertile females.* OPP INFERTILE (1) ➲ *compare* STERILE (1) **3** [usually before noun] that encourages activity; that produces results: *The socio-economic conditions of the depression provided fertile soil for right-wing extremism.*

fer·til·ity /fəˈtɪləti; *NAmE* fərˈtɪləti/ *noun* [U] **1** the ability of a person, animal or plant to produce babies, young animals, fruit or new plants: *Men do not undergo the same abrupt decline in fertility observed during menopause.* ◇ **+ noun** *Fertility rates have been relatively stable since the 1970s.* OPP INFERTILITY **2** the ability of land or soil to grow plants successfully: *Soil fertility needs to be maintained if regular cropping is practised.*

fer·til·ization (*BrE also* **-isation**) /ˌfɜːtəlaɪˈzeɪʃn; *NAmE* ˌfɜːrtələˈzeɪʃn/ *noun* [U] **1** the act of putting POLLEN into a plant so that a seed develops, or of joining SPERM with an egg so that a baby or young animal develops: *Most fish species show external fertilization, and females have limited control over mating.* ◇ *Following fertilization, the pistil develops into a specialized seedpod which may hold 50–100 seeds.* **2** the act or practice of adding a substance to soil to make plants grow more successfully: *Productivity was increased by daily fertilization with phosphorus.*

fer·til·ize (*BrE also* **-ise**) /ˈfɜːtəlaɪz; *NAmE* ˈfɜːrtəlaɪz/ *verb* **1 ~ sth** to put POLLEN into a plant so that a seed develops; to join SPERM with an egg so that a baby or young animal develops: *In each nest, the female lays 500–1 000 eggs, which are fertilized by the male.* ◇ *All cells of the body arise from a single fertilized egg cell.* **2 ~ sth** to add a substance to soil to make plants grow more successfully: *Many grasslands have been artificially fertilized and treated with herbicides to increase productivity.*

fer·til·izer (*BrE also* **-iser**) /ˈfɜːtəlaɪzə(r); *NAmE* ˈfɜːrtəlaɪzər/ *noun* [C, U] a substance that is added to soil to make plants grow more successfully: *Nitrogen fertilizers were used widely by the 1950s.* ◇ *The addition of fertilizer can alter soil chemistry.*

fes·ti·val /ˈfestɪvl/ *noun* **1** a series of performances of music, plays, films, etc, usually organized in the same place once a year; a series of public events connected with a particular activity or idea: *The city hosts one of the world's premier international film festivals every September.* ◇ *Bluegrass spread regionally through fiddle contests, music festivals, radio broadcasts and recordings.* **2** a day or period of the year when people stop working to celebrate a special event, often a religious one: *In the 1770s, there was a general move by the secular authorities to reduce the number of religious festivals.*

fetal (*BrE also* **foe·tal**) /ˈfiːtl/ HELP The spelling **foetal** is only used in non-technical contexts; in scientific writing use **fetal**. *adj.* [only before noun] connected with a fetus: *Pregnancy in older age increases the risk of fetal abnormality.*

fetus (*BrE also* **foe·tus**) /ˈfiːtəs/ HELP The spelling **foetus** is only used in non-technical contexts; in scientific writing use **fetus**. *noun* a young human or animal before it is born, especially a human more than eight weeks after FERTILIZATION: *Women pregnant with male fetuses exhibited a 10% greater caloric intake (Tamimi et al., 2003).* ➲ *compare* EMBRYO

feu·dal /ˈfjuːdl/ *adj.* [usually before noun] connected with or similar to feudalism: *Under the feudal system, all land was owned by the king, who effectively delegated control of it to his warrior lords.* ◇ *The feudal lord and serf replaced the ancient master and slave.*

feu·dal·ism /ˈfjuːdəlɪzəm/ *noun* [U] the social system that existed during the Middle Ages in Europe in which people were given land and protection by a LORD, and had to work and fight for him in return: *There were two principal classes in feudalism, the lords (either church officials or members of the 'noble' class) and the serfs (or peasants).*

F

fever /ˈfiːvə(r)/ *noun* **1** [C, U] a medical condition in which a person has a temperature that is higher than normal: *On examination, he was jaundiced and had a fever.* ◇ *Symptoms include fever, lethargy and weight loss.* ➲ *compare* TEMPERATURE (2) **2** [U, C] (used mainly in compounds) a particular type of disease in which sb has a high temperature: *The spread of yellow fever, again by mosquitoes, was another major killer of white folk in early South Carolina.* **3** [sing., U] **~ (of sth)** great interest or excitement about sth: *Returning soldiers were swept up in a fever of revolutionary Bolshevist ideas.*

few[1] /fjuː/ *det., adj.* **(fewer, few·est) 1** used with plural nouns and a plural verb to mean 'not many': *Few studies have been conducted on this subject.* ◇ *In the agricultural sector, fewer people were required to produce the same or greater amounts of food.* ◇ **very ~** *Very few items cost less today than they did 10 or 20 years ago.* HELP In spoken English, people often use **less** with plural nouns. This is not considered correct in academic writing, and **fewer** should be used instead: *There has been a trend for women to have fewer children.* ◇ ~~*less children*~~ **2** (*usually* **a few**) used with plural nouns and a plural verb to mean 'a small number', 'some': *These products are traded locally, regionally and, in a few cases, internationally.* ◇ *Only a few plants and animals have adapted to this environment.* ◇ **quite a ~** *The Russian government has since nationalized quite a few companies.* ◇ **every ~ minutes/days/years etc.** *Most citizens' political involvement is restricted to voting at an election every few years.*

IDM ˌ**few and** ˌ**far be'tween** not many; not done, seen, happening, etc. often: *Potential customers for a new product may be few and far between.* ◇ *Shareholder revolts were few and far between.*

few[2] /fjuː/ *pron.* **1** not many people, things or places: *Few would argue that these measures are inappropriate.* ◇ **~ of sb/sth** *Thus few of the recommendations found their way into public policy.* ◇ **as ~ as...** *As few as 100 individuals may have initially colonized some islands.* **2 a few (of sb/sth)** a small number of people, things or places; some: *A few, including Bellairs, Beauchamp and Craig, had personal experience of life in the Royal Navy.* ◇ *Health, education and defence are a few of the areas that require public investment.* ◇ **quite a ~** *While many business groups are now specialized, quite a few have remained diversified.* **3 fewer** not as many as: *Between 1934 and 1981, on average there were fewer than 15 bank failures per year.* ◇ **no fewer than...** *No fewer than four different experimental research groups claimed success within a matter of weeks of one another.* **4 the few** used with a plural verb to mean 'a small group of people': *With democratic governance, political power is held by the many and not the few.*

fibre (*US* **fiber**) /ˈfaɪbə(r)/ *noun* **1** [C] one of the many thin threads that form body TISSUE, such as muscle: *The number of muscle fibres considerably decreases with ageing.* **2** one of the many thin threads that form natural materials, such as wood and cotton: *The task of separating* *cotton fibres from seeds was so labour-intensive that supplies were limited.* **3** [C, U] a material such as cloth or rope that is made from a mass of natural or artificial threads: *Cotton clothing is often more comfortable than clothing made from synthetic fibres.* ◇ *The high electrical and thermal conductivity of carbon fibre makes it useful in a wide variety of products.* **4** [U] the part of food that helps to keep a person healthy by keeping the BOWELS working and moving other food quickly through the body: *The study found no significant independent link between dietary fibre and the risk of colorectal cancer.*

F

fi·brous /ˈfaɪbrəs/ *adj.* [usually before noun] made of many fibres; looking like fibres: *As people age, the layer of fat under the skin thins and is replaced by more fibrous tissue.* ◇ *Cirrus are detached, white, fibrous clouds, often with a silky sheen in direct sunlight.*

fic·tion /ˈfɪkʃn/ *noun* **1** [U] a type of literature that describes people and events that are not real: *Behn wrote fiction for easy domestic consumption.* ◇ *'Moby Dick' by Herman Melville is often proposed as the greatest American work of fiction.* **2** [C, U] **~ (that...)** a thing that is invented or imagined and is not true: *The large size of Athenian juries facilitated the legal fiction that a decision of a jury was a decision of the people.*

fic·tion·al /ˈfɪkʃənl/ *adj.* not real or true; connected with or happening in fiction: *Fictional characters in novels may have conversations about real plays.* ◇ *The stories about his heroic military exploits are almost certainly fictional.* **OPP** REAL-LIFE

fi·del·ity /fɪˈdeləti/ *noun* [U] **1 ~ (of sth) (to sth)** the quality of being accurate: *They argue that judging film on the basis of its fidelity to historical or literary sources is misguided.* ◇ *Fidelity of implementation is important to the efficacy of the programme.* **2 ~ (to sth)** the quality of being loyal to sb/sth: *Ultimately, what counts is membership of the Jewish people, rather than fidelity to any particular creed or praxis.* **3 ~ (to sb)** the quality of being FAITHFUL to your husband, wife or partner by not having a sexual relationship with anyone else: *Other key HIV control strategies include promoting mutual fidelity.*

field /fiːld/ *noun* **1** [C] a particular subject or activity that sb works in or is interested in **SYN** AREA (2): *Post-colonialism as an academic field was heavily influenced by research trends in India.* ◇ **~ of sth** *Hilgard won numerous awards for scientific contributions to nearly every field of psychology.* ◇ *Feedback inhibition was an important discovery in the field of biochemistry.* **2** [C] an area of land in the country used for growing crops or keeping animals in, usually surrounded by a fence, etc: *In poor regions, children were required to work in the fields.* ◇ **~ of sth** *They started to clear patches of forest to plant crops, mainly paddy, as well as smaller fields of maize.* **3** [C] (usually in compounds) a large area of land covered with the thing mentioned; an area from which the thing mentioned is obtained: *Most, if not all, of these ice fields are currently experiencing rapid retreat (Hastenrath and Greischer, 1997; Thompson et al., 2000).* ◇ *Over time, more oil and gas fields will be depleted.* **4** [C] (usually in compounds) an area of land used for the purpose mentioned: *Many taller, healthier redwoods can be found lining the city's parks and playing fields.* ◇ **the ~ of sth** *Wild women fought the Roman legionaries alongside men on the field of battle.* ➲ *see also* BATTLEFIELD **5** [C] (usually used as an adjective) the fact of people doing practical work or study, rather than working in a library or laboratory: **in the ~** *Where sampling takes place in the field, duplicate interviews must be avoided by careful record keeping.* ◇ **+ noun** *GM varieties resistant to the virus are currently undergoing field trials.* ➲ *see also* FIELDWORK **6** [sing.+ sing./pl. v.] all the people or products competing in a particular area of business or activity: *Ben & Jerry's led the field in the use of natural ingredients in ice cream.* ◇ *Both firms have dominated their fields: Microsoft in operating systems and Google in search engines.* **7** [C] (usually in compounds) an area within which the force mentioned has an effect: *The spinning motion of the electron gives rise to a magnetic field.* ◇ *The vapour pressure of a liquid in a gravitational field varies with the depth below the surface.* ◇ **+ noun** *The electric breakdown of the insulation will depend on the electric field strength around the wire.* ◇ *electric/magnetic field intensity* ➲ *see also* MAGNETIC FIELD **8** [C] the area within which objects can be seen from a particular point: **~ of view/vision** *The intensity of the light should be adjusted so that the field of view is well illuminated but not uncomfortably bright.* ◇ **visual ~** *She has a large permanent blind area to the left of her visual field.* **9** [C] part of a record that is a separate item of data: *Two students did not fill in the field for gender.* ◇ *The search can be further constrained to specific fields and cross-references.*

IDM **leave the field open to sb/sth** to enable sb/sth to be successful in a particular area of activity because other people or groups have given up competing with them: *After this first success, Williams withdrew from computer research, leaving the field open to Tom Kilburn.*

▸ ADJECTIVE + FIELD **new, emerging • related • academic** *The emerging field of work psychology was enormously enriched by the contribution of German researchers.* | **magnetic • electric • gravitational • electromagnetic • electrostatic** *Under fair weather conditions, the electric field measured near the surface is generally about 120 volts/metre.*

▸ VERB + FIELD **advance • broaden • open • revolutionize • work in • enter • dominate • cover** *Some studies advanced the field by including fathers, who are often under-represented in paediatric psychology research.* ◇ *Quantitative techniques have dominated the field of marketing research.* | **generate • produce • apply** *The ultracentrifuge can generate gravitational fields of the order of several hundred thousand times gravity.*

▸ FIELD + NOUN **research • trial, test • experiment • investigation • observation • trip • notes • journal • survey • worker • officer • staff** *In one observational session, our field notes record the following:...*

▸ FIELD OF + NOUN **study, research, inquiry • interest • endeavour** *Mountain geography as a distinct field of study is thriving and growing.*

field·work /ˈfiːldwɜːk; *NAmE* ˈfiːldwɜːrk/ *noun* [U] research or study that is done in the real world rather than in a library or laboratory: *He conducted his fieldwork in the interior of Brazil.* ■ **field·worker** *noun*: *The work of the German fieldworker Carl von Strehlow helped to provide a detailed portrait of social life in these communities.*

fierce /fɪəs; *NAmE* fɪrs/ *adj.* **(fier·cer, fier·cest)** **1** showing strong feelings or emotions or a lot of activity, often in a way that is violent: *Few thinkers in modern times have stirred more fierce debate than Sigmund Freud.* ◇ *Fierce domestic competition has allowed Chilean retail companies to build strong competitive capabilities.* ◇ *Despite fierce opposition, Caesar succeeded in fulfilling Pompey's aims.* **2** (especially of people or animals) angry and aggressive in a way that is frightening: *The Huns were skilled horsemen and fierce warriors who terrified their enemies.* ◇ *A few generations can turn a thoroughly domesticated breed into a fierce feral animal.* ■ **fierce·ly** *adv.*: *The company entered the fiercely competitive tourism market with little apparent competitive advantage.* ◇ *The introduction of Western civilization in the region was fiercely contested.*

fig. *abbr.* (*also* **Fig.**) (in writing) FIGURE: *See Fig. 3.*

fight[1] /faɪt/ *verb* **(fought, fought** /fɔːt/**)** **1** [I, T] to take part in a war or battle against an enemy: *In general, it is wrong to fight in a war that lacks a just cause.* ◇ **~ against sb/sth** *The Czechs volunteered to fight against Austria for an* *expected independent Czech state after the war.* ◇ **~ sb** *Asians who had fought the occupying Japanese were not always eager to have their former European rulers back.* ◇ **~ sth (against sb/sth)** *For centuries, the Roman Empire had fought wars on its eastern frontier against the Persian Empire.* **2** [I, T] to use physical strength against another person or animal: *Several young men spoke of situations where they had stopped their friends from fighting.* ◇ **~ with sb** *In many species, males fight with each other much more than females do.* ◇ **~ over sth** *Herring and black-blacked gulls were observed fighting over scraps of fish.* ◇ **~ sb** *They were willing to fight and kill those whom they considered to be threatening their social and economic position.* **3** [T] **~ sth** to try hard to stop or deal with sth bad: *A conference on avian influenza was held to raise money to fight the disease.* ◇ *Monetary authorities generally try to fight inflation and unemployment and promote stability and economic growth.* ◇ *The UN Development Programme has been at the forefront of fighting poverty.* **4** [I] to try very hard to get or achieve sth: **~ for sth** *Although women fought for the right to vote, they did not achieve it quickly.* ◇ **~ to do sth** *Existing institutions, communities and owners of resources fought to protect their rights and property.* **5** [T] **~ sth** to take part in a contest against sb: *Elections cannot be fought without significant sums of money being spent.* ◇ *The party that fought the 2010 campaign was a shadow of its former self.* **6** [I] **~ (with sb) (about/over sth)** (*rather informal*) to have an argument with sb about sth: *Gisela has been fighting with her parents about her school attendance and is in danger of failing her grade.* ◇ *The doctors are unable to find a cure, fighting over both the cause of his illness and the best treatment.*

IDM **fight to the ˈdeath/ˈfinish** to fight until one of the two people or groups is dead, or until one person or group defeats the other: *The Spartan soldiers surrendered rather than fight to the death.*

PHR V **ˌfight ˈback (against sb/sth)** to protect yourself with actions or words by attacking sb who has attacked you: *Female chimpanzees routinely fight back against bullying behaviour by group males.* **ˌfight sb/sth ˈoff** to resist sb/sth by fighting against them/it: *Her body was unable to fight off a disease that she contracted.* ◇ *Clinton successfully fought off efforts to impose a budget that, in his view, would have destroyed many essential programmes.* **ˌfight ˈout sth | ˌfight it ˈout** to fight or argue until an agreement or result has been achieved: *The matter was fought out in the courts for months.*

fight[2] /faɪt/ *noun* **1** [sing.] the work of trying to destroy, prevent or achieve sth: **~ against sth** *The European Council made the fight against terrorism a priority objective.* ◇ *Along with education, peer support is an important part of the fight against AIDS.* ◇ **~ for sth** *The fight for the formal representation of women in politics was long, difficult, and occasionally bloody.* ◇ **~ to do sth** *In nearly every case, the broadcasters had a hard fight to assert the right of access on behalf of their audiences.* **2** [C] the act of using physical force against another person or animal: *British participants were involved in fights more often than Germans or Spanish participants.* ◇ **~ with sb/sth** *During a police interview, it became apparent that the petrol bombs were intended to be used in a fight with a rival gang.* ◇ **~ between A and B** *Females that had observed fights between two males preferred the winner (Doutrelant and McGregor, 2000).* **3** [C] **~ (with sb) (over/about sth)** an argument about sth: *Stein is at her best in her analysis of intragovernmental fights over economic policy.* ◇ *Blair would appeal to voters by disagreeing with his party, and even picking fights with sections of it.*

fight·er /ˈfaɪtə(r)/ *noun* **1** a person who fights: *Spartan boys were brought up to become brave fighters.* **2** (*also* **ˈfighter plane**) a fast military plane designed to attack other aircraft: *Women have qualified to fly combat aircraft, including fighters, for the Royal Air Force.* ◇ **+ noun** *Yeltsin's running mate for vice-president was the fighter pilot and Afghanistan veteran Aleksandr Rutskoi.*

fight·ing /ˈfaɪtɪŋ/ *noun* [U] an occasion when people use weapons or physical strength against each other: *Fighting broke out in 1775 and in 1776 the American colonies declared their independence.*

fig·ura·tive /ˈfɪɡərətɪv; *NAmE also* ˈfɪɡjərətɪv/ *adj.* [usually before noun] **1** (of language, words, phrases, etc.) used in a way that is different from the usual meaning, in order to create a particular mental picture. For example, 'He exploded with rage' shows a figurative use of the verb 'explode': *Tagore was a poet who was renowned for his dexterity with figurative language.* ➲ *compare* LITERAL, METAPHORICAL **2** (of paintings, art, artists, etc.) showing people, animals and objects as they really look: *Figurative art lies at the centre of the grand tradition of painting, as well as of sculpture.* ➲ *compare* ABSTRACT[1] ■ **fig·ura·tive·ly** *adv.*: *The hero of the poem goes on a voyage of discovery, both literally and figuratively.* ➲ *compare* LITERALLY, METAPHORICALLY

F

fig·ure[1] /ˈfɪɡə(r); *NAmE* ˈfɪɡjər/ *noun* **1** a number representing a particular amount, especially one given in official information: *In 1986, 52% reported skill increases over the previous five years, but in 1992 that figure had risen to 63%.* ◇ **~ of sb/sth** *Realistic estimates put the figure of trained soldiers at under 10 000.* ◇ **~ for sb/sth** *While only 44% of uninsured patients were admitted, the corresponding figure for the insured was 65%.* **2** a symbol rather than a word representing one of the numbers between 0 and 9: *Inflation had been in double figures for five months.* ◇ *The data are quoted with the same number of significant figures as the original data.* **3** a person of the type mentioned, especially sb who is important in some way: *The company's investors included prominent public figures such as the philosopher John Locke.* ◇ **~ in sth** *Descartes was a key figure in the emergence of modern philosophical and scientific thinking.* ◇ **~ of sth** *Iris Murdoch was one of the great literary figures of the twentieth century.* **4** (*abbr.* **fig.**) a picture or diagram in a book, that is often referred to by a number: *Figures 2.1 and 2.2 show the increases in the overall number of Internet users from mid-2012 to the end of 2012.* ◇ *The initial distribution of the molecules is uniform, but over time the system forms wave-like patterns (see figure).* ◇ *Fig. 14.1 summarizes the distribution of data in these four categories.* **5** a person or an animal in a drawing or painting; a statue of a person or an animal: *The sign features a drawing of a human figure walking up the stairs.* ◇ *The statue was immediately hailed as the finest example of a nude female figure to survive from Greek antiquity.* **6** the shape of a person seen from a distance or not clearly: *On the ground lay the shadowy figure of a man, crippled in pain.* **7** a particular shape formed by lines or surfaces: *Triangles are geometric figures with sides consisting of perfectly straight lines meeting at vertices whose angles add up to 180°.*

IDM **cut a... ˈfigure** (of a person) to have a particular appearance: *Over six feet tall, Franz cut an imposing figure at the national conference of German historians in Erfurt in 1937.* ➲ *more at* FACT

▸ ADJECTIVE + FIGURE **corresponding, comparable** • **high** • **low** • **exact** *The haematology analyser had revealed abnormally high figures for the red and white cell counts.* | **key, central** • **leading, major, important, great** • **public, well-known, prominent** • **iconic** • **historical** • **political** • **literary** *He is a central figure in twentieth and twenty-first century British poetry.*

▸ VERB + FIGURE **use** • **obtain** • **give, provide, produce** • **calculate** • **report** *It is difficult to obtain accurate figures, but in 2006, Internet sales rose by 29% in the UK.* | **become** • **remain** • **include** *Throughout her term of office, Supari remained a popular political figure.*

F

fig·ure² /ˈfɪgə(r); *NAmE* ˈfɪgjər/ *verb* [I] to be included as part of a process or situation, especially a large or important part: **~ in sth** *The prospect of facing trial did not figure at all in their calculations.* ◇ *Both earthquakes and volcanoes have figured prominently in human history since the dawn of recorded time.* ◇ **~ on sth** *The issue of Korean car imports figured high on the US administration's agenda.* ◇ **~ among sth** *Working-class youth figure disproportionately among the unemployed.* ◇ **~ as sth** *In any discussion of social equity and justice, illness and health must figure as a major concern.*

PHR V ˌ**figure sth ˈout** to think about sth until you understand it SYN WORK STH OUT: *In all environments, humans have to figure out a good way of getting resources.* ◇ **~ how/what, etc...** *All that Newton needed to do was to figure out how to describe the force of gravity.*

fila·ment /ˈfɪləmənt/ *noun* **1** a long thin piece of sth that looks like a thread: *The result of the many thick and thin filaments in the muscle moving over each other is to make the muscle contract.* ◇ **~ of sth** *Filaments of cloud emerge from the main mass and evaporate within a few tens of seconds.* **2** a thin wire in a LIGHT BULB that produces light when electricity is passed through it: *In a conventional incandescent light bulb, electricity is used to heat up a filament which then glows.* ◇ **+ noun** *The luminous efficiencies now being obtained from LEDs have outstripped tungsten filament lamps.*

file¹ AWL /faɪl/ *noun* **1** a collection of data stored together in a computer, under a particular name: *A large computer system may have thousands of programs and millions of data files.* ◇ *As time passes and files are created, modified and deleted, files on a disk may become very fragmented.* ◇ *It is becoming common among electronic dictionaries to include audio files in the entries of some terms.* **2** a collection of information about a particular person or subject, especially one kept by an official organization: *The letter was placed in the case file, which was available to the sentencing judge.* ◇ *Data were extracted from patient files by an independent researcher and verified by a second researcher.* ◇ **~ on sb** *Operation Chaos, started by the CIA in 1967, eventually collected files on 7 200 Americans.*

IDM **on ˈfile** kept in a file, to be used later: *The customer's details were kept on file, together with details about their recent purchases.*

file² AWL /faɪl/ *verb* **1** [I, T] (*law*) to present sth so that it can be officially recorded and dealt with: **~ for sth** *The American-based airline filed for bankruptcy in December 2007.* ◇ **~ sth** *Upon his release, he filed a claim for refugee status.* ◇ *In 2006, 13.6 million civil cases were filed in state courts in the United States.* **2** [T] to put and keep documents or information in a particular place and in a particular order so that you can find them easily; to put a document into a file: **~ sth + adv./prep.** *All US public companies are required to file registration statements, periodic reports and other forms electronically.* ◇ **~ sth away** *They did not receive a reply but their letters were filed away, to be unearthed by later generations.*

fill /fɪl/ *verb* **1** [T, I] to make sth full of sth; to become full of sth: **~ sth** *A gas expands to fill the available volume.* ◇ *Vapour from the liquid filled the space at the top of the tube.* ◇ **~ sth with sth** *We filled the bottom of each chamber with paraffin oil.* ◇ **be filled with sth** *Cartesians believed that the universe was completely filled with matter.* ◇ **~ (with sth)** *The largest channel filled with water in 17.5 days and was silted up completely in 6.5 years.* **2** [T] **~ sth** to make information about sth more complete; to provide sth that is required in a particular situation: *This article aims to fill a gap in existing literature.* ◇ *In the absence of a fair trade system, the Fairtrade label helped to fill the vacuum.* ◇ *Immigrants routinely fill niches left vacant by natives.* **3 -filled** (in adjectives) full of the thing mentioned: *They struggled through the swamps and climbed snow-filled mountain passes.* ◇ *Gaseous detectors consist of a gas-filled chamber that contains two electrodes across which a voltage is applied.* **4** [T] **~ sth** to have a job or position in a company or an organization: *By the late 1920s, almost one-third of all executive positions in business were filled by college graduates.* ◇ *Simply finding people to fill vacancies has become a major challenge in some industries.* ◇ *Most soldiers in support roles are also trained to fill combat roles, and will do so if necessary.* **5** [T] **~ sth** to choose sb for a job: *The pressure to fill new positions must necessarily lead to the hiring of many who are not qualified to teach or do research.* ◇ *Care organizations typically filled internal vacancies for paid staff from their pool of volunteers.* **6** [T] to block a hole with a substance: **~ sth** *Filler clays are so called because they fill the gaps between wood fibres in the papermaking process.* ◇ **~ sth with sth** *Natural fractures in diamonds and other gems can be filled with a glassy material.* **7** [T] **~ sth** if sb **fills** an order or a PRESCRIPTION, they give the customer what they have asked for: *Foreign machine manufacturers were happy to fill the orders.* **8** [T] **~ sth** to stop people from continuing to want or need sth: *The administration emphasized the importance of filling labour needs as quickly as possible.* **9** [T] **~ sth (up)** to use up a particular period of time doing sth: *Work filled up six days of the week.*

PHR V ˌ**fill sth ˈin 1** (*BrE*) (*also* ˌ**fill sth ˈout**) to complete a form by writing information on it: *Participants were asked to fill in a questionnaire regarding their status of vaccination.* **2** to fill sth completely: *In Western cultures, there is a tendency to feel uncomfortable with silences and to try to fill in gaps in conversations.* ˌ**fill ˈup (with sth)** | ˌ**fill sth ˈup (with sth)** to become completely full; to make sth completely full: *In the 19th century, southern Manchuria rapidly filled up with Chinese peasant immigrants.* ◇ *A driver who fills her car up with petrol at the same garage every week is not necessarily demonstrating loyalty.*

film¹ /fɪlm/ *noun* **1** [C] (*especially BrE*) (*NAmE usually* **movie**) a series of moving pictures recorded with sound that tells a story, shown on television or at the cinema: *The critic can never assume that a bad director will always make a bad film.* ◇ *Watching a film from the 1950s, it is apparent how class distinctions in accents have softened.* ◇ *The studios located in Los Angeles produce the most feature films of anywhere in the world outside of Asia.* **2** [U] (*especially BrE*) (*NAmE usually* **the movies** [pl.]) (*BrE also* **the cin·ema**) the art or business of making films: *In film, the voiceover is quite often dissociated from any specific figure.* ◇ **+ noun** *The film industry has increasingly relied on big stars to draw audiences.* ➲ *compare* CINEMA (3) **3** [U] moving pictures of real events, shown for example on television SYN FOOTAGE: **~ (of sth)** *If a captive monkey sees film of a wild monkey making a fear reaction to a snake, it learns to avoid snakes.* ◇ **on ~** *The film team captured the death on film, to some amount of criticism.* **4** [C, usually sing.] **~ (of sth)** a thin layer of sth, usually on the surface of sth else: *The sands often become cloaked by a thin film of mud.* ◇ *One of the most widely used methods for depositing thin films is chemical vapour deposition.* ➲ *compare* COATING

film² /fɪlm/ *verb* to make a film of a story or a real event: **~ sth** *Every scene was filmed on the actual location depicted.* ◇ *Encounters between predators and caterpillars were filmed at 30 frames per second.* ◇ **~ sb/sth doing sth** *The leaders were usually depicted as soldiers and filmed holding weapons in outdoor locations.*

fil·ter¹ /ˈfɪltə(r)/ *noun* **1** a device containing paper, sand, chemicals, etc. that a liquid or gas is passed through in order to remove any materials that are not wanted: *The second stage of water treatment is to pass the water through a filter, typically a sand bed.* ◇ **+ noun** *Seeds were germinated in a Petri dish lined with moist filter paper.* **2** a device that allows only particular types of light or sound to pass through it: *The polarizing filters stop light from passing through them.* **3** (*computing*) a program that stops particular types of data, email, etc. being sent to a computer: *The government encouraged investment in a new generation of Internet filters.*

fil·ter² /ˈfɪltə(r)/ *verb* **1** [T] to pass liquid, gas, light or sound through a special device, especially to remove sth that is not wanted: **~ sth** *To some extent, the ecosystem can filter pollutants.* ◇ *These sound engineers try to capture a world carefully filtered to eliminate all insignificant sounds.* ◇ **~ sth through sth** *The solution was filtered through a 0.22 μm membrane.* ➲ *see also* FILTRATION **2** [T] **~ sth (from sth)** to use a special program to check the content of emails or websites before they are sent to your computer: *The service filters malicious messages from email traffic.* **3** [I] **+ adv./prep.** to move slowly in a particular direction: *Sandsheets and small dune fields may filter into adjacent environments* ◇ *The $400 billion in oil revenues earned since 1970 has not filtered into the larger economy.* **4** [I] **+ adv./prep.** (of information, news or ideas) to slowly spread and become known: *African beliefs filtered through to America via the slave trade.* ◇ *News of these events filtered back to England.* **5** [T] **+ adv./prep.** to understand sth in a particular way: *Many Latinos filter most of their interactions with whites through the lens of their racial and ethnic identities.* ◇ *Consciousness, according to Marxists, filters the world according to the shape of its particular ideology.* **6** [I] **+ adv./prep.** (of light or sound) to come into a place slowly or in small amounts: *He had a memory of sunlight filtering gently through green curtains in an empty room.*

PHR V **ˌfilter sth ˈout** **1** to remove sth that you do not want from a liquid, gas, light or sound, using a special device or substance: *The main reason is that the ozone layer filters out harmful ultraviolet radiation from the sunlight.* ◇ *The sound is passed through a bandpass filter, which filters out the irrelevant noise.* **2** to remove sth/sb that you do not want from a large number of things or people, often using a special system or device: *A password system was set up to filter out people for whom the questionnaire was not appropriate.*

fil·tra·tion /fɪlˈtreɪʃn/ *noun* [U] the process of FILTERING a liquid or gas: *The samples required careful filtration to remove suspended particulates.*

fin /fɪn/ *noun* **1** a thin flat part that sticks out from the body of a fish, used for swimming and keeping balance: *The limbs of the first land vertebrates evolved from the fins of their fish-like ancestors.* **2** a thin flat part that sticks out from the body of a vehicle, an aircraft, etc, used for improving its balance and movement: *An aircraft manufacturer wishes to reduce the weight of the tail fin of a large commercial airliner.*

final AWL /ˈfaɪnl/ *adj.* **1** [only before noun] being or happening at the end of a series of events, actions or statements: *One final point is worth making.* ◇ *The final stage of the buying process is the post-purchase evaluation.* ◇ *In the final chapter, Milne et al. use dendrochronology to analyse drought cycles in New Mexico.* **2** [only before noun] being the result of a particular process: *Therefore, these conditions were excluded from the final model.* ◇ *High hydrostatic pressure was used to preserve the components of the final product.* **3** that cannot be argued with or changed: *The committee's decision is final and there is no right of appeal.* ◇ *The board of directors has the final say in decision-making.* IDM *see* ANALYSIS, WORD¹

▸ FINAL + NOUN **act • step • stage, phase • part • chapter, section • volume • scene • column • paragraph • sentence • point • remark • destination • year • decade** *Disinfection by chlorine was the final step in the treatment of the water.* | **result, outcome • conclusion • report • version • draft • model • product** *It is questionable whether the debates contributed to the final outcome of the election.* | **decision, say • judgement/judgment • word • approval • answer** *It was the captain who made the final decisions and also controlled the aircraft.*

fi·nal·ize (*BrE also* **-ise**) AWL /ˈfaɪnəlaɪz/ *verb* **~ sth** to put sth such as a plan or an agreement into its final form: *By late January, the WFL had finalized its arrangements for the protest.* ◇ *Some details of the contract are still being finalized.*

fi·nal·ly AWL /ˈfaɪnəli/ *adv.* **1** after a long time, especially when there has been some difficulty or delay SYN EVENTUALLY: *Agamemnon rejects the idea of a sacrifice at first, but he finally agrees.* ◇ *The long-awaited turn in the oil market finally arrived in the third quarter of 2008.* **2** used to introduce the last in a list of things or the final point that you want to make SYN LASTLY: *Thirdly and finally, Comte describes a 'scientific stage' in society's evolution.* ◇ *Finally, it should be noted that these findings are largely exploratory.* ➲ language bank *at* ORGANIZE **3** in a way that ends all discussion about sth: *It is the national court that finally decides the case.*

fi·nance¹ AWL /ˈfaɪnæns; faɪˈnæns; fəˈnæns/ *noun* **1** (*especially BrE*) (*NAmE usually* **fi·nan·cing**) [U] money used to run a business, an activity or a project: *Sales volumes, prices, and availability of finance can all change dramatically in a short time.* ◇ **~ for sth** *Finance for the project was raised from domestic and foreign investors.* **2** [U] the activity of managing money, especially by a government or commercial organization: *Global finance had become increasingly self-regulated.* ◇ **+ noun** *G8 finance ministers meet regularly to analyse the world's economic situation.* **3 finances** [pl.] the money available to a person, an organization or a country; the way this money is managed: *Most developing countries have fragile public finances.* ◇ *The costs of home ownership then became a heavy burden on household finances.*

> **WORD FAMILY**
> finance *noun, verb*
> finances *noun*
> financial *adj.*
> financially *adv.*

fi·nance² AWL /ˈfaɪnæns; faɪˈnæns; fəˈnæns/ *verb* **~ sth** to provide money for a project SYN FUND²: *They took out a loan of $100 000 to finance the purchase of a home.* ◇ *Opponents to the minimum wage quoted a study financed by the restaurant industry.* ◇ *Today in the US, more than 90% of new investment in corporations is financed by debt.* ➲ thesaurus note *at* FUND²

fi·nan·cial AWL /faɪˈnænʃl; fəˈnænʃl/ *adj.* [usually before noun] connected with money and finance: *The Asian and Latin American financial crises of the late 1990s demonstrated the downside of globalization.* ◇ *Protesters believe that the global financial institutions and agreements undermine local decision-making.* ➲ thesaurus note *on* page 326

▸ FINANCIAL + NOUN **system • sector • centre • institutions • services • markets • management • analyst • statement • position, situation • transaction • instrument • regulation • constraints • penalty • burden • risk • cost • loss • difficulties • hardship, distress • crisis • collapse • stability • support, assistance, aid • contribution • investment • incentive • interest • reward • returns • capital • assets • resources** *A family friend was willing to provide financial support.* ◇ *Federal government created a range of powerful financial incentives to stimulate the ailing economy.*

fi·nan·cial·ly AWL /faɪˈnænʃəli; fəˈnænʃəli/ *adv.* in a way that is connected with money and finance: *In earlier periods, women were financially dependent on their husbands.* ◇ *The shipyard would need to find additional business in order to remain financially viable.* ◇ *The Australian Research Council supported the research programme financially.*

THESAURUS

financial • economic • fiscal • monetary *adj.*
These words can all be used to refer to money.
- financial/economic **performance**
- financial/monetary **stability**
- (a/the) financial **institution/markets/sector/support**
- economic/fiscal/monetary **policy**
- economic **activity/development/growth**
- fiscal **expansion/deficit**

- **Financial** is used generally to refer to money; **economic** refers specifically to the amount of money a country, a region, etc. gets from trade in goods and services: *World cities are key centres for financial institutions and producer services such as banking and advertising.* ◇ *Many Pennsylvanians believed that the anthracite trade would lead to personal, regional and national economic growth.*
- **Fiscal** is used to refer to the money that a government spends or that it gets, for example through taxation; **monetary** relates to the government's regulation of the money supply of a country: *Singapore announced a fiscal policy aimed at boosting economic activity.* ◇ *One of the difficulties of monetary policy is that the timing of interest rate changes is not an exact science.*

fi·nan·cing AWL /ˈfaɪnænsɪŋ; faɪˈnænsɪŋ; fəˈnænsɪŋ/ *noun* [U] (*NAmE*) = FINANCE[1]

find[1] /faɪnd/ *verb* (**found, found** /faʊnd/) **1** [T] to discover or learn that sth is true after you have tried it, tested it or experienced it: **~ (that)...** *Khanna and Palepu (1999c) found that the performance of groups increased after economic reforms were implemented.* ◇ **it is found that...** *It was found that the system worked better at a heating power input above 900 W.* ◇ **~ sb/sth + adj./noun** *He is seen as a leader by his peers but teachers find him rather loud and difficult.* ◇ **~ sb/sth to be sth** *On examination, the patient was found to be slightly confused.* ◇ **~ sb/sth to do sth** *City mills in poor countries have been found to employ high numbers of workers from the same village.* ➲ language bank *at* RESEARCH[2] **2** [T] **~ sth/sb** to discover sth/sb by searching, studying or thinking carefully: *West (1948) found no convincing evidence for telepathy.* ◇ *Our aim was to find support for our initial hypothesis.* ◇ *The hope is to find new uses for the existing drugs.* ◇ *Trade therefore enables businesses to find new resources and export markets.* ➲ *see also* FACT-FINDING **3** [T] to discover sb/sth by chance or when you do not expect to: **~ sb/sth** *In 1362, Boccaccio found a manuscript of Tacitus's Annals in a monastery library.* ◇ **~ sb/sth doing sth** *Many of the cases of children supposedly found living in the forest like wild animals were hoaxes.* **4** [T] **~ sb/sth** to get back sth/sb that was lost after searching for it/them: *Macpherson claimed he had found the lost epics of the third-century Celtic poet Ossian.* ◇ *Eleven workers on the rig evidently died, because their bodies were never found.* **5** [T, often passive] **~ sth + adv./prep.** used to say that sth exists or grows somewhere: *The flood narrative is found in both the Greek and Roman traditions.* ◇ *The Eastern Cape habitat includes plants found nowhere else in the world.* **6** [T] to have a particular feeling or opinion about sth: **~ sth + adj.** *We often find it hard to explain the cognitive processes behind our decisions.* ◇ **~ sth + noun** *After losing his job and his family, he found his life a burden.* **7** [T] to discover sb/sth/yourself doing sth or in a particular situation, especially when this is unexpected: **~ sb/sth/yourself + adv./prep.** *Nekrich eventually found himself in exile for his political beliefs.* ◇ **~ sb/sth/yourself + adj.** *When he read these arguments of Feuerbach, Marx found himself completely convinced.* ◇ **~ sb/sth/yourself doing sth** *At one point in the dream, he finds himself approaching some sort of barrier or border.* ◇ **~ (that)...** *Small independent producers who succeeded in expanding found that they had become capitalists.* **8** [T, I] to make a particular decision in a court case: **~ (that)...** *The court found that the policy was rational.* ◇ **~ sb + adj.** *The jury found Dr Hadleson guilty.* ◇ **~ in sb's favour** *The Court of Appeal found in the plaintiff's favour.* **9** [T] **~ sth** to have or make sth available for use: *Western governments were reluctant to find the necessary money.* **10** [T] **~ sth** to arrive at sth naturally; to achieve or begin to have sth: *The metal finds the easiest way to move as a result of the pressure.* ◇ *The proposal has found widespread support in the bioscience community.*

IDM **find fault (with sb/sth)** to look for and discover mistakes in sb/sth; to complain about sb/sth: *The Court found no fault with the previous judgment.* **find favour (with sb/sth)** to become accepted and popular: *This compromise position has found favour with some Australian politicians.* **find your ˈvoice** to be able to express your opinion: *It was at the Cancun negotiations that developing countries found their voice.* **find your way (to...)** to discover the right route (to a place): *A large number of studies have investigated the precision with which salmon find their way home.* **find its ˈway into...** to come to a place or a situation, especially after many stages, and often by chance: *The phosphorus pollution eventually finds its way into the local lakes and rivers.*

PHR V **ˌfind ˈout (about sth/sb)** | **ˌfind ˈout sth (about sth/sb)** to get some information about sth/sb by looking, asking, reading, etc: *As Edison found out, employees will work extraordinarily hard when given interesting, rewarding jobs.* ◇ *The aim of the questionnaire was to find out more about these patients and their dietary preferences.* ◇ **~ what/when, etc...** *Young rats observe what older rats eat in order to find out what is safe to eat.* ◇ **~ that...** *Hamlet finds out that the sealed message contains an order to have him executed.*

- FIND + NOUN **evidence • information • solution • answer • example • way, method • pattern • balance • relationship, association, correlation • difference • variation • expression • meaning • reason • application • effect • result • value • increase • place • partner • employment, work, job** *First of all, the company had to find ways to reduce its unit labour costs.* ◇ *Immigrants are more likely to find employment in the low status end of the service sector.* | **expression • support • common ground** *The generally repressed rage of the alienated can find expression in deviant subcultural forms.*
- NOUN + FIND **study • research • researchers • survey • trial** *One study found large differences in reporting errors between The Netherlands, Italy and North America.* | **court • commission • tribunal** *As a result of its investigation, the Commission found that the 17 producers had indeed been operating a cartel.*
- ADVERB + FIND **commonly, often, frequently • usually, generally, normally • typically • always • still • sometimes • rarely • never** *There are 20 different amino acids commonly found in proteins.*
- VERB + TO FIND **need • want, wish, aim, seek • expect • hope • be likely • try • fail, be unable • be able** *People sometimes suggest that researchers find what they expect to find.*
- ADJECTIVE + TO FIND **hard, difficult • impossible • easy • possible** *It is difficult to find evidence to support this hypothesis.*
- FIND IT/NOUN + ADJECTIVE **difficult, hard • impossible • easy • useful, helpful • necessary** *These immigrant workers found it difficult, if not impossible, to formulate plans for the future.* ◇ *Persons with colour blindness have found this method particularly useful.*

find[2] /faɪnd/ *noun* a thing or person that has been found, especially one that is interesting, valuable or useful: *A number of significant archaelogical finds were made at the site on the island.*

find·ing /ˈfaɪndɪŋ/ *noun* **1** [usually pl.] information that is discovered as the result of research into sth: *These findings suggest that age differences may have been overestimated in the literature.* ◇ **~ of sth** *Table 18.1 presents the key findings of the study.* ◇ **~ from sth** *This confirms findings from other research that e-learning has positive effects on learning outcomes.* ➲ thesaurus note *at* RESULT[1] **2** (*law*) a decision made by the judge or JURY in a court case: **~ (of sth)** *A finding of parental neglect was made and the children were taken into care.* ◇ **~ against/in favour of sb/sth** *Italy had already failed to respond appropriately to the Committee's previous finding against it.*

▸ ADJECTIVE + FINDINGS **previous • recent • present • preliminary, initial • early • main, key • important, significant • similar** *This result is consistent with previous findings.* ◇ *Further research was conducted in order to confirm the preliminary findings.* ◇ *Table 2.3 shows the main findings.* | **interesting • striking • surprising, unexpected • inconsistent • abnormal • negative • null • incidental • mixed • consistent • positive • empirical • experimental • clinical • quantitative • qualitative** *However, there are also some unexpected findings from within the studied region.* ◇ *In the light of our empirical findings, it is clear that the existing models need revision.*

▸ VERB + FINDINGS **support, confirm, corroborate • be in line with, be consistent with • yield • extend** *Statistical evidence supporting the findings is provided in tables and graphs.* | **present • report, communicate • publish • reveal • discuss • review • summarize • explain • interpret • generalize • relate • compare • replicate** *The researchers attempted to generalize their findings to a larger population.*

▸ FINDINGS + VERB **suggest, indicate, imply • show, demonstrate, reveal • provide • support, confirm • be consistent with, be in line with • highlight • be based on** *Overall, our findings indicate that Internet use has no adverse psychological impact on children.* ◇ *This assumption is supported by the findings of another study.*

▸ NOUN + OF FINDINGS **significance • implications • interpretation • generalizability • validity • summary • presentation • report** *These limitations may severely restrict the generalizability of our findings.*

fine[1] /faɪn/ *adj.* (**finer, fin·est**) **1** [usually before noun] difficult to see or describe SYN SUBTLE: *The resolution of a lens is a measure of its ability to reveal fine detail.* ◇ *They have not made sufficiently fine distinctions between types of engineers.* ◇ **a ~ line between A and B** *It is said that there is a fine line between genius and insanity.* **2** very small: *The fine particles of the ash are released into the atmosphere.* **3** made of very small grains: *Flooding may leave thin layers of fine sand, silt and clay.* OPP COARSE (1) **4** very thin or narrow: *Acupuncture involves the placement of fine needles in the skin at specific points on the body.* **5** [usually before noun] of high quality; good: *This is a fine example of the way that academia should ideally operate.* **6** (*especially BrE*) (of weather) bright and not raining: *This sea fog affects the eastern coasts of Britain, particularly in fine weather.* **7** [usually before noun] pleasing to look at: *The next year Shakespeare bought New Place, a fine old house built by Sir Hugh Clopton.* **8** [usually before noun] attractive and DELICATE: *The quality of the cheaply imported fine china forced European potteries to innovate in order to compete.* **9** sounding important and impressive but unlikely to have any effect: *Fine words, however, could not solve the problem.*

fine[2] /faɪn/ *noun* a sum of money that must be paid as an official punishment for breaking a law or rule: *The Commission can impose fines on the offending Member State.* ◇ **~ for sth** *Fines for infringements of competition law are calculated on the basis of turnover.* ◇ **~ of sth** *The supermarkets and dairies agreed to pay fines of £116 million.*

fine[3] /faɪn/ *verb* [often passive] to make sb pay money as an official punishment for breaking a law or rule: **~ sb (for sth/for doing sth)** *Six of the leading hotels in Paris were fined for sharing commercial information that helped to keep prices artificially high.* ◇ **~ sb sth (for sth/for doing sth)** *The Commission fined the software giant €780 million for anti-competitive behaviour.*

fine·ly /ˈfaɪnli/ *adv.* **1** in a very DELICATE or exact way: *The above arguments are finely balanced.* ◇ *The traders needed a finely tuned knowledge of the consumer goods of different Africans.* **2** into very small grains or pieces: *The result of the weathering of rocks is the production of a finely divided material that is classified as a soil.*

fin·ger /ˈfɪŋɡə(r)/ *noun* one of the four long thin parts that stick out from the hand (or five, if the thumb is included): *The children were counting on their fingers.*

IDM **put your finger on sth** (*rather informal*) to identify what is different or wrong about a particular situation: *Wittgenstein put his finger on the problem.* ➲ *more at* POINT[2]

fin·ger·print /ˈfɪŋɡəprɪnt; *NAmE* ˈfɪŋɡərprɪnt/ *noun* a mark made on a surface by the pattern of lines on the tip of a person's finger, often used by the police to identify criminals: *The scanned fingerprints are checked against police and immigration records.* ◇ **take sb's fingerprints** *The applicant entered the European Union through Greece, where his fingerprints were taken.*

fin·ish[1] /ˈfɪnɪʃ/ *verb* **1** [T, I] to stop doing sth or making sth because it is complete: **~ (sth)** *She finished her studies in 2007.* ◇ *The participants were given as much time as they needed to finish the task.* ◇ *Looking back on it when he had finished, Frazer described his book as a great 'voyage of discovery'.* ◇ **~ doing sth** *A quarter of the time, doctors interrupted patients before they had finished speaking.* **2** [I, T] to come to an end; to bring sth to an end: *By the time work finished in June 2001, the tower had been returned to its position in 1838.* ◇ **~ with sth** *Each chapter begins with a brief contents list and finishes with a summary.* ◇ **~ sth (by doing sth)** *It is crucial to finish the consultation by making a clear plan for what will happen next.*

PHR V ˌ**finish sb/sth ˈoff** (*informal*) to destroy sb/sth, especially sb/sth that is badly injured or damaged: *The Japanese finished off the British motorcycle industry in the space of little more than a decade.* ˌ**finish sth ˈoff** to do the last part of sth; to make sth end by doing one last thing: *Jasmine returned to the front of the class to finish off a table she was drawing on the board.* ˌ**finish ˈup...** (*BrE*) to be in a particular state or at a particular place after a series of events: *Not all migrants who arrived finished up at the bottom of the pile.*

fin·ish[2] /ˈfɪnɪʃ/ *noun* [usually sing.] **1** the last part or the end of sth: **from start to ~** *The whole process from start to finish relies on adequate communications between all the groups involved.* **2** the last covering of paint, etc. that is put onto the surface of sth; the condition of the surface: *The specimens were polished with diamond paste to produce a smooth surface finish.* IDM *see* FIGHT[1]

fin·ished /ˈfɪnɪʃt/ *adj.* **1** [usually before noun] brought to an end; completed: *Canals, railways and roads were essential for moving raw materials to factories and finished products to markets.* ◇ *At this point the photo processing is finished.* **2** [not before noun] no longer doing sth or dealing with sb/sth: *When participants were finished, they met individually with a research assistant to provide feedback.* ◇ **~ with sb/sth** *However, we are not finished with E. coli gene transcription for there is still the question of gene control.* **3** [not before noun] no longer powerful, effective or useful: *In 413 Athens seemed to be finished, but by 410 the Spartans were suing for peace.* **4** [usually before noun] (of a person's work) showing a lot of skill: *The very finished tone of much of the text somehow makes one rather too conscious of the artist at work here.*

fi·nite AWL /ˈfaɪnaɪt/ *adj.* **1** having a definite limit or fixed size: *There is a finite number of sounds that each language makes use of.* ◇ *Correct policy is surely a matter of recognizing that energy resources are finite.* OPP INFINITE (2) **2** (*grammar*) a **finite** verb form or clause shows a particular tense, person and number: *In languages like Italian, the subject of a finite clause can be dropped.*

fire¹ /ˈfaɪə(r)/ *noun* **1** [U] the flames, light and heat that are produced when sth burns: *Fire can be an effective weed management tool.* ◇ *Early evidence for the controlled use of fire comes from Kooba Fori, Kenya.* **2** [U, C] flames that are out of control and destroy sth: *The houses were destroyed by fire in 1955.* ◇ **on ~** *Large parts of the city were soon on fire.* ◇ **in a ~** *She died in a forest fire.* ◇ **catch ~** *In 1986 a warehouse near Basel, Switzerland caught fire.* ◇ **set ~ to sth** *Other protesters set fire to a bank building.* **3** [C] a PILE of burning fuel, such as wood or coal, used for cooking food or heating a room: *They lit a fire to keep warm.* ◇ *The study focused on the change from smoky coal fires to stoves with chimneys.* **4** [U] shooting from guns: *13.7 per cent of casualties in the battle were the result of artillery fire.* ◇ **open ~** *Suddenly, the National Guardsmen opened fire and shot four students dead.*

IDM **be/come under ˈfire** (*rather informal*) to be strongly criticized for sth you have done: *Car manufacturers have come under fire from environmentalists for continuing to manufacture inefficient 'gas guzzlers'.*

fire² /ˈfaɪə(r)/ *verb* **1** [I, T] to shoot bullets, etc. from a gun or other weapon: **~ on sb/sth** *Soldiers fired on rioters in London.* ◇ *A North Vietnamese boat fired on the American destroyer.* ◇ **~ sth** *The soldier fired four shots.* ◇ **~ (sth) (into sth)** *He fired the gun twice into the rear of the car.* ◇ **~ (sth) (at sb/sth)** *On July 7 1937, shots fired at Japanese troops south-west of Beijing led to full-scale war.* **2** [T] **~ sb (for doing sth)** to tell an employee that they can no longer work for you (because of bad work or bad behaviour): *Several employees were fired for failing to achieve sales targets.* **3** [T] to make sb feel very excited about sth or interested in sth: **~ sth** *The displays of Graeco-Roman sculpture fired the imaginations of Romantic writers.* ◇ **~ sb with sth** *Around 372, fired with ascetic zeal, Jerome set out for the east.* **4** [T] to supply an engine or a power station with fuel: **~ sth** *Smaller rockets are fired in order to change the course of the spacecraft.* ◇ **-fired** *The construction of coal-fired power stations continued.* **5** [I] (*biology*) (of a cell, especially a NEURON) to generate an electrical signal that can cause an effect elsewhere in the body: *Neurons fire when threshold stimulation is reached.*

firm¹ /fɜːm; *NAmE* fɜːrm/ *noun* a business or company, especially one involving a PARTNERSHIP of two or more people: *The role that multinational firms play in the global economy makes them extremely powerful.* ➲ thesaurus note *at* COMPANY

▸ ADJECTIVE + FIRM **large • small • new • established • entrepreneurial • innovative • dominant • major** *Corporations based in Japan and western Europe are challenging the market dominance of large American firms.* | **private • local • domestic • foreign • international • multinational • global • transnational • manufacturing • industrial** *The delivery of many public services, from schools to prisons, has been contracted out to private firms.*

▸ NOUN + FIRM **family • service • group • member • business • law** *In South and East Asia, family firms are the norm and include firms such as Samsung.*

▸ VERB + FIRM **start • establish • run • attract • encourage • enable • allow** *Joint ventures enabled local firms to advance into newly growing industries and markets.*

▸ FIRM + VERB **be located • be based • operate • supply • produce • sell • earn • invest in • adopt • face • dominate • compete** *Global networks operated by global firms are under increasing scrutiny.* ◇ *At an international level, firms will face different labour market conditions and a different range of labour costs.*

▸ FIRM'S + NOUN **ability • capability • strategy • performance • resources • portfolio** *These centres were set up to increase a firm's ability to develop products that suited local customer needs.*

firm² /fɜːm; *NAmE* fɜːrm/ *adj.* (**firm·er, firm·est**) **1** fairly hard; not easy to press into a different shape: *The mixture forms a paste which sets to a firm rubbery solid.* ◇ *This disc of tissue is firm and mobile.* OPP SOFT (1) **2** [usually before noun] not likely to change; that you can rely on: *This study did not include a control group and therefore it is difficult to draw any firm conclusions.* ◇ *There is now a firm basis for believing that human activities are warming the planet.* ◇ *Firm evidence of an association between coal use and lung cancer was observed in 17 of the 20 studies.* **3** strongly fixed in place: *Firm foundations are especially critical for traditional structures such as arches.* OPP UNSTABLE (4) **4** showing that you are strong and in control of a situation: *The new leaders feared that a strong state would be a threat to their firm grip on power.* ◇ *Teachers must be firm yet responsive in their management of the classroom.* **5** (of sb's voice or hand movements) strong and steady: *It is important to present the comments in a calm, firm voice to help the child feel that you are in control.* ➲ *see also* FIRMLY IDM *see* FAST²

firm·ly /ˈfɜːmli; *NAmE* ˈfɜːrmli/ *adv.* **1** in a strong or definite way, that is unlikely to change: *By the 1880s, it was obvious that capitalism was firmly entrenched in Russia.* ◇ *Research has firmly established that families living on low incomes have a lower health status than those with higher incomes.* **2** in a way that makes it difficult for sth/sb to move or be moved: *Some proteins have groups such as ions or non-protein molecules firmly attached to them.*

first¹ /fɜːst; *NAmE* fɜːrst/ *det., ordinal number* **1** happening or coming before all other similar things or people; 1st: *Diagnosis is the first step in the treatment process.* ◇ *This legislation established, for the first time, the legal right of workers to come together in unions.* ◇ *Notification of acceptance will be communicated by January 1st, 2015.* ◇ *The battle occurred during the reign of Queen Elizabeth I.* HELP In this example, **Elizabeth I** is pronounced 'Elizabeth the first'. OPP LAST¹ (1) **2** most important: *Simonds observed that the 'first duty' of the judge was 'to administer justice according to the law'.*

IDM Idioms containing **first** are at the entries for the nouns in the idioms, for example **at first sight** is at **sight**.

first² /fɜːst; *NAmE* fɜːrst/ *adv.* **1** before anyone or anything else; at the beginning: *I intend to answer the question by first considering the purpose of the analysis.* ◇ *Depending on which part of the robot moves first, the subsequent operations will be affected.* OPP LAST² (1) **2** for the first time: *Edward Said's 'Orientalism', first published in 1978, is often regarded as the founding text of postcolonial criticism.* ◇ *Since 1976, when Ebola first appeared in Zaire, there have been intermittent outbreaks of the disease.* OPP LAST² (2) **3** used to introduce the first of a list of points you want to make in a piece of writing or a speech SYN FIRSTLY (1): *There are two things about this chart that I would like to draw attention to. First, Japan and Sweden, though less rich than the US, have somewhat better health. Second,...* OPP LASTLY (1) ➲ language bank *at* ORGANIZE

IDM **at ˈfirst** at or in the beginning: *At first, agricultural groups grew crops in small areas close to their home.* ◇ *This result seemed at first to be rather implausible.* **come ˈfirst** **1** to be considered more important than anything else: *The Child Support Agency stressed that the child must come first.* **2** to happen before sth or anything else: *Despite the usual word order ('thunder and lightning'), lightning always comes first.* **ˌfirst and ˈforemost** more than anything else: *Wallerstein's focus is first and foremost on* *economic power and capability.* **ˌfirst of ˈall 1** before doing anything else; at the beginning: *She was told that she should first of all be tested for AIDS status.* ◇ *Three comments need to be made. First of all,...* **2** as the most important thing: *Advertising must first of all be able to present the brand as it will be seen by the customer at the point of purchase.* **ˌput sb/sth ˈfirst** to consider sb/sth to be more important than anyone/anything else: *He insisted that committee members put duty first.*

first³ /fɜːst; *NAmE* fɜːrst/ *pron.* **the first** (*pl.* **the first**) the first person or thing mentioned; the first person or thing to do a particular thing: *The second implication arises inevitably from the first.* ◇ **~ of sth** *The work is divided into four sections. The first of these outlines the political and economic background.* ◇ **~ to do sth** *Birch (1979) was the first to demonstrate that smaller businesses were responsible for a high proportion of the new jobs in the US economy.* ◇ **~ of sb/sth to do sth** *These fossils were the first of their kind to be found in the Grand Canyon (Breed, 1968).* OPP LAST³
IDM **ˌfirst among ˈequals** the person or thing with the highest status in a group: *Khrushchev's opinion was increasingly first among equals, for his was the voice of the party.* **from the (very) ˈfirst** from the beginning: *From the very first, there were tensions among the different leaders.*

ˌfirst-ˈhand *adj.* [only before noun] obtained or experienced yourself: *Many senior executives entered agencies in this way and gained first-hand experience in production.* ■ **ˌfirst-ˈhand** *adv.*: *Most of these startling new revelations were witnessed first-hand by millions of Americans glued to their TV sets.*

ˌfirst ˈlanguage *noun* the language that you learn to speak first as a child; the language that you speak best: *Translated versions of the survey were made available for families whose first language was Somali or Spanish.* ⊃ *compare* SECOND LANGUAGE

first·ly /ˈfɜːstli; *NAmE* ˈfɜːrstli/ *adv.* **1** used to introduce the first of a list of points you want to make in a piece of writing or a speech SYN FIRST² (3): *Carer support groups can be therapeutic in several ways. Firstly, the couple can see that they are not alone.* ⊃ language bank *at* ORGANIZE **2** used to say what happens or happened first: *Firstly, the sample was heated to evaporate off the solvent in the normal way.* ◇ *The paper firstly describes an experimental system that has been used to demonstrate the new technology.*

the ˌfirst ˈperson *noun* [sing.] **1** (*grammar*) a set of pronouns and verb forms used by a speaker to refer to himself or herself, or to a group including himself or herself: *'I' and 'me' are both first person singular pronouns.* **2** a way of writing a novel, etc. as if one of the characters is telling the story using the word *I*: *The text is written in the first person.* ⊃ *compare* SECOND PERSON, THIRD PERSON

ˌfirst ˈprinciples *noun* [pl.] the basic ideas on which a theory, system or method is based: *Ptolemy started from first principles and used carefully selected observations to develop his theories.* ◇ *It is often useful, when doing a problem in thermodynamics, to go back to first principles.*

fis·cal /ˈfɪskl/ *adj.* connected with government or public money, especially taxes: *Radical monetary and fiscal policies were pursued.* ◇ *According to the World Bank, East Asian economies generally limited fiscal deficits.* ⊃ thesaurus note *at* FINANCIAL ■ **fis·cal·ly** /ˈfɪskəli/ *adv.*: *The most fiscally decentralized countries are Switzerland, Germany and Canada.*

fish /fɪʃ/ *noun* (*pl.* **fish** or **fishes**) HELP **Fish** is the usual plural form. The older form, **fishes**, can be used to refer to different kinds of fish. **1** [C] a creature that lives and breathes in water, and swims: *If fishermen catch immature and breeding fish, it impacts on fish stocks.* ◇ *Taxonomic identification of some fishes may be difficult even for experts.* ◇ **+ noun** *Some fish species behave like true parasites.* **2** [U] fish as food: *The monks were not permitted to eat meat or fish.*

fish·ery /ˈfɪʃəri/ *noun* (*pl.* **-ies**) **1** a part of the sea or a river where fish are caught in large quantities: *A proportion of the catch from commercial fisheries is thrown overboard at sea.* **2** a place where fish are bred as a business: *In China, this system is in place for professional small-scale inland fisheries.*

fish·ing /ˈfɪʃɪŋ/ *noun* [U] the business or sport of catching fish: *The Sea Fish Order 1982 prohibited fishing in UK waters by Danish vessels.* ◇ *Recreational fishing as a tourist activity has become an increasingly important part of the Norwegian travel industry.*

fis·sion /ˈfɪʃn/ *noun* [U] **1** (*also* ˌnuclear ˈfission) (*physics*) the act or process of splitting the NUCLEUS (= central part) of an atom, when a large amount of energy is released: *In the process of fission and fusion, there is a conversion of mass to energy.* ◇ *Leakage is a problem that continues to limit enthusiasm for nuclear fission as a major power source.* ⊃ *compare* FUSION (2) **2** (*biology*) the process of cells dividing into new cells: *Tuberculosis bacteria divide by fission.*

fit¹ /fɪt/ *verb* (**fit·ting, fit·ted, fit·ted**) (*NAmE usually* **fit·ting, fit, fit** except in the passive) **1** [I, T] (not used in the progressive tenses) to be of the right size or shape for sb/sth, or to go somewhere: *Components for assembly can be designed so that only the correct positioning will fit.* ◇ **+ adv./prep.** *Phones became smaller, slimmer and fitted into the pocket.* ◇ **~ sb/sth** *The website does not fit the computer screen and the user has to scroll down.* **2** [T] to put or fix sth somewhere: **~ sth + adv./prep.** *As the vehicles moved along the production line, workers recorded details of the components fitted to a particular vehicle.* ◇ **~ sth with sth** *Many large aircraft have been fitted with automatic sensors that transmit pressure, temperature and wind data.* **3** [I, T] to join in the right place; to join sth in the right place: **~ together** *He observed that the Atlantic coasts of South America and Africa fitted together like pieces of a jigsaw puzzle.* ◇ **~ sth together** *Each part had to be individually made and fitted together by a skilled craftsman* **4** [I, T] (not used in the progressive tenses) to agree with or match sth or be suitable to be included in a group; to make sth do this: **~ into sth** *There are some methods that do not fit neatly into these categories.* ◇ **~ sth** *All growth models fitted the data well.* ◇ *The witness saw a man fitting the description of the killer getting into a car.* ◇ *The content of the email was tailored to fit the recipient's age, lifestyle and other factors.* ◇ **~ sth into sth** *New facts and information were fitted into this framework.* ◇ **~ sth to sth** *Policymakers must fit technologies to local conditions.* **5** [T] (*especially BrE*) **~ sb/sth for sth** to make sb/sth suitable for a particular job: *These apprenticeships fitted young working-class men for manual jobs.* IDM *see* SIZE¹
PHRV **ˌfit sb/sth ˈin | ˌfit sb/sth ˈin/ˈinto sth 1** to find time to see sb or to do sth: *Fathers tend to participate in those tasks that they can fit in at convenient times.* ◇ *Teachers faced the challenge of fitting extra lessons into the already-crowded school curriculum.* **2** to find or have enough space for sb/sth in a place: *Cutting down on packaging enables the company to fit more goods into each delivery truck.* **ˌfit ˈin (with sb/sth)** to live, work, etc. in an easy and natural way with sb/sth: *Young people need to feel that they fit in with their peers.* **ˌfit ˈin with sth** to match or agree with sth; to belong to a group: *Not all the observations that were made seemed to fit in with this simple description.* **ˌfit sb/sth ˈout/ˈup (with sth)** to supply sb/sth with all the equipment, clothes, food, etc. they need SYN EQUIP (1): *The organization not only fitted out*

hospitals, but they organized new industries to provide hospital supplies and other items.

fit² /fɪt/ *noun* **1** [C] a sudden attack of an illness, in which sb becomes unconscious and their body may make violent movements SYN SEIZURE (1): *There is a risk of epileptic fits and medication is appropriate following the first fit.* **2** [C] a sudden short period of coughing or of laughing, that you cannot control: *His parliamentary performances were widely ridiculed and undermined by coughing fits.* ◇ **~ of sth** *Patients develop fits of prolonged coughing ending with a characteristic 'whoop'.* **3** [C] **~ of sth** a short period of a very strong feeling: *Cowper was a man naturally subject to fits of depression.* **4** [C, usually sing.] the way that two things match each other or are suitable for each other: **~ for sb/sth** *She was able to recognize that this peer group was not a good fit for her.* ◇ **~ between A and B** *Figure 9.1 highlights reasons for a lack of fit between the UK policy framework and that of other EU member states.* **5** [C, usually sing., U] **~ (of sth)** the relationship between data that you collect and the values expected by a theory: *A method of improving the fit of the model by adjusting the parameters is needed.* ◇ *A small value indicates good fit, and a large one indicates poor fit.* **6** [C] the way that sth fits into a space, or on a person: *All the components are carefully measured to ensure a perfect fit.*

F

fit³ /fɪt/ *adj.* (**fit·ter, fit·test**) **1** healthy and strong; in good physical or mental condition: *She is fit and healthy and a non-smoker.* ◇ **~ to do sth** *Only those fit enough to pass the medical examination were permitted to work on the ship.* ◇ *The judge must decide whether the defendant is fit to plead.* OPP UNFIT (3) **2** suitable; of the right quality; with the right qualities or skills: *These issues became a fit subject for public debate.* ◇ *Natural selection favours the fittest individuals, those best suited to survive in their environment.* ◇ **~ for sb/sth** *The software supplied was not to be considered fit for its intended purpose.* ◇ *It is fairly easy to work out when a property is not fit for human habitation.* ◇ **~ to do sth** *If the home is not fit to live in, the person is technically homeless.* OPP UNFIT (1)
IDM **see/think 'fit (to do sth)** to consider it right or acceptable to do sth; to decide or choose to do sth: *The company is able to move workers to other jobs and teams as it sees fit.* **fit for 'purpose** suitable for what it is intended to do: *I trialled the questionnaire to ensure that it was fit for purpose.* ➲ *more at* SURVIVAL

fit·ness /ˈfɪtnəs/ *noun* [U] **1** the state of being physically healthy and strong: *Although physical fitness can be measured through laboratory tests, this is quite an expensive procedure.* ◇ **+ noun** *Graduate volunteers were assigned to two different fitness training regimes.* **2** the state of being suitable or good enough for sth: **~ for sth** *The product was acceptable in terms of quality and fitness for purpose.* ◇ **~ to do sth** *Questions about fitness to drive arise quite often in relation to psychiatric disorder.*

five /faɪv/ *number* 5: *There are five main steps in the process.* ◇ *five of Sweden's top financial experts* ◇ *Of these countries, only five fulfil all the criteria.* ◇ *a five-month contract* ◇ *Look at page five.* ◇ *Five and four is nine.* ◇ *Three fives are fifteen.*

fix¹ /fɪks/ *verb* **1 ~ sth + adv./prep.** (*especially BrE*) to put sth firmly in a place so that it will not move: *Self-adhesive electrodes are fixed to the skin of the patient's chest.* ◇ (*figurative*) *This connection is firmly fixed in the minds of most investigators.* ◇ (*figurative*) *Inflation was only stabilized after 1991, when the Argentine peso was fixed to the US dollar.* **2 ~ sth** to decide on a date or time for sth SYN SET¹ (4): *They must decide whether it is appropriate to review the case, and then to fix a date for that review.* **3** to decide on sth and not change it SYN SET¹ (4): **~ sth** *Fixing the exchange rate has immediate consequences for the inflation rates.* ◇ **~ sth at sth** *The US government fixed the price of gold at $35 per ounce.* **4 ~ sth** to repair or correct sth: *Customers rightly believe the firm should fix the problem.* ◇ *The underlying code of the software is available to everyone, so anyone can have a go at fixing a bug.* **5 ~ sth** (*biology*) to preserve sth with a chemical substance before studying it with a MICROSCOPE, etc: *Colonies were fixed with methanol, treated with stain and counted using microscopy.* ◇ *The organisms are fixed on a slide to which serum is added.* **6 ~ sth (from sth)** (*biology*) (of a MICROORGANISM or plant) to take in and TRANSFORM NITROGEN or CARBON DIOXIDE: *Blue-green algae are capable of fixing nitrogen from the atmosphere.* ◇ *Many laboratory experiments have shown that plants fix more carbon if growth is not limited by water, nutrients or light.* **7 ~ sth** to arrange the result of sth in a way that is not honest or fair: *The Radicals fixed the elections to give themselves a majority.*
PHRV **'fix sth on sb/sth** [often passive] if you **fix** your eyes or your mind **on** sth, or they are **fixed on** sth, you are looking at or thinking about sth with great attention: *The judge's gaze was fixed on the attorney for the prosecution.*

fix² /fɪks/ *noun* (*informal*) a solution to a problem, especially an easy or temporary one: *A peaceful solution to the conflict depends on sustained efforts because there is no quick fix or ready-made solution.*

fix·ation /fɪkˈseɪʃn/ *noun* **1** [C] **~ (with/on sth/sb)** an extreme interest or belief in sth/sb, that does not match the truth or is not normal or natural: *The fixation with work is part of the consumerism that pervades American society (Schor, 1992).* **2** [U] (*biology*) the process by which a MICROORGANISM or plant takes in and TRANSFORMS NITROGEN or CARBON DIOXIDE: *The graph below shows the change in nitrogen fixation in three different soil communities with bacterial species richness.*

fixed /fɪkst/ *adj.* **1** staying the same; that cannot be changed: *Because radio waves travel at a fixed speed, radar can be used to measure the distance of each aircraft.* ◇ *A fixed amount of timber was removed without damaging the ecosystem within which the trees were growing.* **2** (of ideas) not easily changed: *One should abandon the fixed idea that school refusal occurs only among specific types of children.* **3** put in place so that it does not move: *The processes were recorded using fixed cameras.*

fixed 'costs *noun* [pl.] (*business*) the costs that a business must pay that do not change even if the amount of work produced changes: *The fixed costs of production will be lower if rents and overheads are lower.*

fixed e'ffect *noun* (*statistics*) the treatment of VARIABLES within a study as though they are not RANDOM and so the differences between them are not of interest: **fixed effects + noun** *Fixed effects models were used to control for time-stable influences.*

'fixed point *noun* (in compounds) **+ noun** (*computing*) a way of representing a number by a single series of numbers whose values depend on their location relative to a reference point, such as a DECIMAL point: *The fixed point representation of fractional numbers is very useful in some circumstances, particularly for financial calculations.*

flame /fleɪm/ *noun* [C, U] a hot bright stream of burning gas that comes from sth that is on fire: *The flames spread in all directions, even against a fresh north wind.* ◇ *The car had a major design flaw, which meant that it burst into flames if another car hit it from behind.* ◇ *Atomic emission spectroscopy is further affected by the temperature of the flame.* ◇ **+ noun** *Phosphorus-containing polymers are extensively used as flame retardants for fabrics.*

flash¹ /flæʃ/ *noun* **1 ~ (of sth)** a sudden bright light that shines for a moment and then disappears: *The device converts the flashes of light into an electronic signal.* ◇ *Lightning flashes can be several kilometres long.* **2 ~ of sth** a particular feeling or idea that suddenly comes into your mind or shows in your face: *The answer arrived in a flash of insight.*

flash[2] /flæʃ/ *verb* **1** [I, T] **~ (sth)** to shine very brightly for a short time; to make sth shine in this way: *The light begins to flash and the countdown is displayed.* **2** [I, T] to appear on a television screen, computer screen, etc. for a short time; to make sth do this: **+ adv./prep.** *Images appear and disappear, often flashing across the screen for an instant.* ◇ **~ (sth) (up)** *The web will flash up thousands of references within seconds.*

flat[1] /flæt/ *adj.* (**flat·ter, flat·test**) **1** having a level surface, not curved or sloping: *For millennia, people were utterly convinced that the earth was flat.* ◇ *The shortest distance between two points on a flat surface is a straight line.* **2** (of land) without any hills or slopes: *A large number of the rivers flow through flat coastal plains.* ◇ *Most of the region's sea floor is characterized by a relatively flat continental shelf.* **3** (of surfaces) smooth and level: *Leaves are flat and green so they can photosynthesize efficiently.* **4** wide and not very deep: *These mammals have flat flippers instead of legs.* **5** (of a business organization) without many different levels of employees: *The company has a very flat organizational structure and staff are flexible in their roles.* ◇ *Organizations have become flatter and more decentralized.* **6** (of business or an economic trend) not showing much activity; not changing much: *The new car market was expected to be flat in 2012.* ◇ *Earnings have remained flat as companies have struggled to maintain their interest payments.* **7** [only before noun] (of a price or charge) the same in all cases; not varying with changed conditions or in particular cases: *The company charges a flat rate of $9.99 for most of its e-books in the US.* ◇ *Instead of being charged a flat fee, customers are charged according to how much water they use.* **8** dull; lacking interest or enthusiasm: *Many patients with frontal lobe damage have lost normal emotional responses and become emotionally flat.* ◇ *The rather flat monologue threatens to dominate the final part of the book.* **9** [only before noun] not allowing discussion or argument; definite: *They claim that the results are in flat contradiction to the conclusions that an impartial scientist would draw.* ■ **flat·ness** *noun* [U] *There were slight, but significant, differences in shell flatness among sites within each species.* ◇ **~ of sth** *The flatness of the terrain has resulted in large swamps.*

flat[2] /flæt/ *noun* **1** (*BrE*) a set of rooms that is used as a home, usually on one floor of a building: *Many of the interviewees live in rented high-rise flats within the inner city.* ◇ **block of flats** *New and better-planned blocks of flats were built to give people a better chance of a decent life.* ➲ *compare* APARTMENT (1) **2** [usually pl.] an area of low flat land, especially near water: *Estuaries often contain a high diversity of habitats, including rocky shores, sand flats, mud flats, saltmarshes and lagoons.*

flat·ten /ˈflætn/ *verb* **1** [T, I] to make sth flat or flatter; to become flat or flatter;: **~ sth** *These buried logs have become flattened from their original round shape to a more oval form.* ◇ **~ (sth) (out)** *The gradient flattens out near the summit.* ◇ (*figurative*) *Over the centuries, the social hierarchy flattened, until today, when it comprises just the people and their government.* **2** [T] **~ sth** to destroy a building, town, tree, etc: *Tens of thousands of homes were flattened by the bombing.*
PHR V ˌ**flatten** ˈ**out** (of an increasing rate or quantity) to stop increasing so fast; to slow down: *Export growth has started to flatten out.*

flat·ter /ˈflætə(r)/ *verb* **~ sb** to say nice things about sb, often in a way that is not sincere, because you want them to do sth for you or you want to please them: *Herod wished to flatter his Roman masters.*

fla·vour (*US* **fla·vor**) /ˈfleɪvə(r)/ *noun* **1** [U] **~ (of sth)** how food or drink tastes SYN TASTE[1] (1): *A blend was prepared with apple juice in order to modify the strong flavour of pure blueberry juice.* **2** [C] a particular type of taste: *Volatiles found in fruits are diverse, giving unique flavours to different fruits.* **3** [sing.] a particular quality or atmosphere: *Used in this sense nowadays, the word has a somewhat old-fashioned flavour.* ◇ *Communitarianism involves two separate lines of argument, and each has a rather different political flavour.* **4** [sing.] **a/the ~ of sth** an idea of what sth is like: *The material covered here gives a flavour of the kinds of calculations that are possible.*

flaw /flɔː/ *noun* **1** **~ (in sth)** a mistake or weakness in sth that means that it is not correct or does not work correctly SYN DEFECT[1], FAULT[1]: *The review uncovered serious flaws in the original calculations.* ◇ *Despite its flaws, the multicultural programme is highly valued by the local community.* **2** **~ (in/of sb/sth)** a weakness in sb's character: *Johnson exhibited fatal flaws of personality and political philosophy that contributed to his downfall.*

flawed /flɔːd/ *adj.* having a flaw; damaged or spoiled: *Alexander, however, regards this view as flawed in a number of ways.* ◇ *But the nationalist endeavour was fundamentally flawed.* ◇ *The flawed design was abandoned and the design process was re-started.*

flee /fliː/ *verb* (**fled, fled** /fled/) [I, T, no passive] to leave a place very quickly, especially because you are afraid of possible danger, or because the situation that you are in is difficult: *Each of them described their desire to return to the families they left behind when they fled.* ◇ **~ from sb/sth** *Many sought refuge after fleeing from oppressive regimes.* ◇ **~ to...** *The president of the local NAACP branch was driven from his home and forced to flee to Atlanta for safety.* ◇ **~ sth** *The United States was well known as a haven for revolutionaries fleeing persecution in Europe.*

fleet /fliːt/ *noun* **1** [C] **~ (of sth)** a group of military ships that sail together: *A combined fleet of Russian, French and British ships attacked at Navarino.* **2** [C] a group of ships that catch fish together: *Technological advances made it possible for fishing fleets to harvest ever-greater proportions of global fish stocks.* **3 the fleet** [sing.] all the military ships of a particular country: *Cimon attacked the Persians in southern Anatolia and destroyed the entire Persian fleet.* **4** [C] **~ (of sth)** a group of planes, buses, taxis, etc. travelling together or owned by the same organization: *Toyota supplied fleets of trucks to help with food deliveries.*

flew *past tense of* FLY[1]

flexi·bil·ity AWL /ˌfleksəˈbɪləti/ *noun* [U, C] **1** the ability to change to suit new conditions or situations: **~ in sth** *The use of raw data allows greater flexibility in downstream analysis.* ◇ **~ of sth** *The flexibility of the manufacturing system has been an important factor.* **2** the ability to bend easily: *The flippers are highly mobile at the shoulder and exhibit some flexibility along their length.*

flex·ible AWL /ˈfleksəbl/ *adj.* **1** able to change to suit new conditions or situations: *Flexible working practices are increasing.* ◇ *Successful companies must be flexible and adaptable.* OPP INFLEXIBLE (1) HELP In economics, **flexible** is used to describe prices, wages, exchange rates, etc. that are quick to change or react to change: *When prices are flexible, people become less worried about anticipating price changes for their decisions.* OPP STICKY (2) **2** able to bend easily: *The wings are made of a flexible polymer.* ■ **flex·ibly** /ˈfleksəbli/ *adv.*: *The company was not able to respond flexibly to unforeseen developments.*

flight /flaɪt/ *noun* **1** [U] the act of flying: *Larger flocks tended to take flight when the predator was further away.* **2** [C] a journey made by air, especially in a plane; a plane making a particular journey: *Increasing numbers of travellers were taking cheap flights to Europe.* ◇ **on a ~** *She recently returned from Australia on a 26-hour flight.* ◇ **+ noun** *Manual control allows the flight crew to respond* *quickly to emergencies.* **3** [U, sing.] the act of running away from a dangerous or difficult situation: *We noted similar themes in the stories of flight and exile told by our refugee informants.* ◇ **~ from sth/sb** *The significance of the Prophet Mohammad's flight from persecution in Mecca was often cited.* **4** [C] **~ (of stairs/steps)** a series of steps between two floors or levels: *He had fallen down a flight of stairs.*

float /fləʊt; *NAmE* floʊt/ *verb* **1** [I] **+ adv./prep.** to move slowly on or in water or in the air: *These planktonic species float freely in the upper 50 m of ocean.* ◇ *There are abundant salt particles floating in the air above the ocean.* ◇ *Icebergs break off and float away in ocean currents.* ◇ *In solution, ions do not float around free, but instead have strong interactions with the solvent.* **2** [I] to stay on or near the surface of a liquid and not sink: **~ (in/on sth)** *The lighter coal particles float on top, and the heavier minerals sink to the bottom.* ◇ *Floating rafts of seaweed to some extent reduce light penetration.* **3** [T] **~ sth (+ adv./prep.)** to make sth move on or near the surface of a liquid: *We had to float equipment and supplies 180 miles downstream.* ◇ *Two 138.7-m bridge spans were built on the shore then floated into position on pontoons.* **4** [T] **~ sth** to suggest an idea or a plan for other people to consider: *Some commentators have floated the idea of voluntary donations as a useful supplement to the BBC's income.* **5** [T] **~ sth** to sell shares in a company or business to the public for the first time: *The reform process involved privatizing many nationalized industries through floating the companies on the stock market.* **6** [T, I] (*economics*) if a government **floats** its country's money or allows it to **float**, it allows its value to change freely according to the value of the money of other countries: *Thailand's newly appointed finance minister allowed the Thai baht to float freely against the world's currencies.* ◇ **~ sth** *Emerging economies that float their currency experience sharp exchange rate appreciation.*

flood¹ /flʌd/ *noun* **1** a large amount of water covering an area that is usually dry: *Floods caused by torrential monsoon rains affected more than three million people.* ◇ **+ noun** *The project is another flood protection scheme for the suburban areas surrounding Bangkok.* **2** a large amount of sth, or a large number of things or people that appear at the same time: **~ of sth** *The authors have managed to distilll the flood of information on developments in Europe, the USA, Australia and Japan.* ◇ **in a ~** *European settlers began arriving, initially in small numbers, and then in an increasing flood.*

flood² /flʌd/ *verb* **1** [I, T] (of a place) to become filled or covered with water; to fill or cover a place with water: *As a result of the earthquake, the harbour at Port Blair began to sink, and the town slowly flooded.* ◇ **~ sth** *In 1864 the Dale Dyke Dam burst, flooding the town and killing 250 people.* ◇ *They flooded the rice paddies in the spring.* **2** [I] (of a river) to become so full that it spreads out onto the land around it: *The river always flooded in late spring and early summer.* **3** [I] **~ in/into/out of sth** to arrive or go somewhere in large numbers or amounts SYN POUR (3): *Cheap North American grain flooded into Europe.* ◇ *Billions of dollars can flood into or out of a country overnight.* **4** [T, usually passive] to send sth somewhere in large numbers or amounts: **be flooded with sth** *The local newspaper was flooded with letters on the subject.* **5** [T, often passive] to become or make sth become available in a place in large numbers or amounts: **~ sth** *Foreign-manufactured televisions flooded the European market.* ◇ **be flooded with sth** *In the late 1980s, tariff barriers were reduced and the Jamaican market was flooded with imports.* ◇ *Households were flooded with information through hundreds of television channels, Internet access, newspapers and radio.* ■ **flood·ed** *adj.*: *The flooded forests and plain provide habitat for a multitude of fish.*

flood·ing /ˈflʌdɪŋ/ *noun* [U] the situation when rain or water from a river, etc. covers a large area of land that is usually dry: *Frequent flooding poses severe health hazards in low-lying areas.*

floor /flɔː(r)/ *noun* **1** [C] the lower surface of a room that you walk on: *They were basic apartments with bare walls and concrete floors.* ◇ **on the ~** *There are big plastic tubs on the floor to store teaching equipment.* **2** [C, usually sing.] the ground at the bottom of the sea, a forest, etc: *The residual organic matter sinks to the lake or ocean floor.* ◇ *Rainfall passes through the canopy to the forest floor.* ◇ **~ of sth** *One of the expeditions reached the floor of the canyon in 1858.* **3** [C] **~ (of sth)** all the rooms that are on the same level of a building: *The entire organization occupied the downstairs floor of a small suburban house.* ◇ *He went to work on the top floor of Whiteley's department store in London.* **4 the floor** [sing.] the part of a building where discussions or debates are held, especially in a parliament; the people who attend a discussion or debate: *Controversial aspects are debated on the floor of the House of Commons.* ◇ *The nomination failed on the Senate floor.* ◇ *Authors discuss one of their key works and take questions from the floor.* **5** [C, usually sing.] **~ (of sth)** an area in a building that is used for a particular activity: *The computerized system connected brokers across the USA instantly to the trading floor of the New York Stock Exchange.* ◇ *Historically, the shop floor in an assembly factory was organized in islands.* **6** [C] the lowest level that is allowed or that can be reached: *State and federal agencies have produced measures that are meant to establish floors for nursing home quality.* ➲ *compare* CEILING (2)

flora /ˈflɔːrə/ *noun* **1** [U, C] **~ (of sth)** the plants of a particular area, type of environment or period of time: *The rich flora of the Mediterranean Basin could suffer major species loss.* HELP **Flora** is often used in the phrase **flora and fauna**, to mean plants and animals: *The native non-coastal flora and fauna are largely adapted to forest.* **2** [U, pl.] **~ (of sth)** the bacteria or other MICROORGANISMS in a particular part of the body: *E. coli forms part of the normal gut flora of man.* ◇ *The skin's normal bacterial flora helps prevent colonization by pathogenic organisms.* HELP In both meanings, **flora** is sometimes used as a plural noun: *Woodland ground flora are found not to inhabit these areas.* In sense 1, the plural form **floras** is also used: *Land floras were remarkably uniform everywhere.*

flour /ˈflaʊə(r)/ *noun* [U] a fine white or brown powder made from grain, used in cooking for making bread and other products: *It is reported that the protein content of buckwheat flour is significantly higher than that of rice, wheat and maize.*

flour·ish /ˈflʌrɪʃ; *NAmE* ˈflɜːrɪʃ/ *verb* **1** [I] to develop quickly and be successful or common SYN THRIVE: *During these two centuries poetry, philosophy and the visual arts flourished.* ◇ *The International Monetary Fund was established after 1945 to promote an environment where trade could flourish.* **2** [I] to grow well; to be healthy and strong SYN THRIVE: *Some trees flourish by depriving others of nutrients or light.* ◇ *The system should be changed so that people everywhere can flourish.*

flow¹ /fləʊ; *NAmE* floʊ/ *noun* **1** [U, C, usually sing.] the continuous movement in one direction of a liquid, gas or electric current; the liquid, gas or current that moves: *The aim is to restore blood flow.* ◇ **~ of sth** *This flow of moist air picks up further quantities of water vapour.* ◇ **~ through/across, etc. sth** *The flow through the compressor remains unchanged.* ◇ *Current flow across the junction is not uniform.* ◇ (*technical*) *The flows around the fixed point will look similar to those of Fig. 18.1.* ◇ **+ noun** *Oxygen was given at a high flow rate.* **2** [C, U] the movement or supply of people or things, especially in large or continuous amounts; the people or things involved: *Global capital flows have become increasingly dynamic and complex.* ◇ **~ of sb/sth** *Media organizations offer a steady flow of news.* ◇ **~ between A and B** *Researchers measured the potential gene flow between populations.* ◇ **~ of sb/sth between A and B** *These devices control the flow of information between the computer and peripheral.* ◇ **~ (of sb/sth) across/from, etc. sth** *These mechanisms regulate the flows of people, finance and arms across borders.* HELP In economics, **flow** is the rate of change of sth, or a VARIABLE used to describe this change. ➲ *see also* CASH FLOW **3** [sing.] the way in which words, ideas or activities follow one another, especially when this is good: *The visual material interrupts the narrative flow.* ◇ **~ of sth** *This technique discourages comments that inhibit the flow of thought.*

▸ ADJECTIVE + FLOW **steady, continuous, constant** • **high** • **low** • **maximum, peak** • **net** *This belief is the reason for the constant flow of new initiatives.* ◇ *There is no net flow of current.* | **free** • **global** • **international** • **financial** *International flows of students follow well-defined routes.*

▸ NOUN + FLOW **fluid** • **water** • **groundwater** • **blood** • **debris** • **lava** • **gas** • **air** • **heat** • **current** • **electron** *The device measured the rate of electron flow from the glucose to the electrode surface.* | **information** • **trade** • **revenue** • **capital** *Imbalances in trade flows affect transport prices.*

▸ VERB + FLOW **stop** • **impede, inhibit** • **interrupt** • **influence** • **enhance, improve** *The bureaucracy impeded the flow of information.* ◇ *The drug decreases blood viscosity, improving blood flow to tissues.* | **control** • **regulate** • **direct** • **restrict** • **reduce** • **prevent** • **block** • **stem** • **facilitate** • **enable** • **stimulate** • **generate, produce** • **maintain** • **increase** *We controlled the water flow by a valve at the lower end of the tube.* ◇ *Bridges enable the flow of people, traffic, trains, water, oil and many other goods and materials.* | **alter** • **divert** • **restore** *It may become more efficient to divert flow through a shorter route to the sea.*

▸ FLOW + NOUN **pattern** • **regime** • **rate** • **velocity** • **path** *Flow patterns are determined by the volume of water and its velocity.*

flow² /fləʊ; *NAmE* floʊ/ *verb* **1** [I] (of a liquid, a gas or electricity) to move continuously in one direction: *The meltwater supply ceases and the streams stop flowing.* ◇ **+ adv./prep.** *Current cannot flow in the other direction.* ◇ *Cold polar air flowing southwards follows a path along the eastern part of the continent.* **2** [I] **+ adv./prep.** (of people or things) to move or be supplied from one place to another, especially in large or continuous amounts: *Goods and services flow freely between countries.* ◇ *People, information and ideas flow in multiple directions.* ◇ *Gold started flowing out of the country.* **3** [I] **(+ adv./prep.)** to develop or be produced in an easy and natural way: *The moderator has to allow the discussion to flow freely.* ◇ *Her use of narrative is effective, flowing from one chapter to the next.*

PHR V ˈ**flow from sth** to come or result from sth: *There are many insights flowing from this work.*

flower¹ /ˈflaʊə(r)/ *noun* **1** the coloured part of a plant from which the seed or fruit develops. Flowers usually grow at the end of a STEM and last only a short time: *Some individuals produce red flowers, but some carry a mutation that means they have dark pink flowers.* **2** a flower with its STEM that has been picked as a decoration: *Flowers are not only bought as gifts but also as a way of enhancing one's own home.* **3** a plant grown for the beauty of its flowers: *A wide range of vegetables, fruits and flowers are grown in the valley.*

flower² /ˈflaʊə(r)/ *verb* **1** [I] (of a plant or tree) to produce flowers: *In their natural habitat they flower in spring to early summer.* ◇ *Most flowering plants are hermaphrodites, which means that they have both male and female parts.* **2** [I] (*literary*) to develop and become successful: *Modern humanism flowered in the nineteenth century.*

flown *past part. of* FLY¹

fluc·tu·ate AWL /ˈflʌktʃueɪt/ *verb* [I] to change frequently in amount, size or quality SYN VARY (2): *People's mood and energy levels fluctuate.* ◇ *These rock deposits may have been caused by fluctuating sea levels.* ◇ **+ adv./prep.** *The quality of output fluctuated wildly.* ◇ *The population size fluctuates over time.* ◇ **~ between A and B** *Social welfare expenditures fluctuated between 3 and 4 per cent of GDP.* ◇ **~ around sth** *The actual number can fluctuate around this figure.*

fluc·tu·ation AWL /ˌflʌktʃuˈeɪʃn/ *noun* [C, usually pl., U] one of a series of changes in amount, size or quality; the fact that these changes happen: **~ in sth** *There are marked seasonal fluctuations in concentration.* ◇ **~ of sth** *The fluctuation of the air temperature has no effect on underground soil temperature.*

flu·ency /ˈfluːənsi/ *noun* [U, sing.] **~ (in sth)** the quality of being able to speak or write a language, especially a foreign language, easily and well: *Practice is vital to developing fluency in any language.*

flu·ent /ˈfluːənt/ *adj.* **1 ~ (in sth)** able to speak, read or write a language, especially a foreign language, easily and well: *She is fluent in Polish.* ◇ *a fluent speaker/reader* **2** (of a language, especially a foreign language) expressed easily and well: *He speaks fluent Italian.* ■ **flu·ent·ly** *adv.*: *She speaks German fluently.* ◇ *Most of the children are just beginning to read fluently.*

fluid¹ /ˈfluːɪd/ *noun* [C, U] **1** a liquid or gas; a substance that can flow: *The wash fluid is pumped out of the tank.* ◇ **+ noun** *Excessive fluid input is a risk in unconscious patients.* HELP **Fluid** is frequently used before another noun: *fluid overload/intake* ◇ *fluid mechanics/dynamics* **2** a liquid in a person's body: *Minute quantities of bodily fluids, such as blood and saliva, will contain DNA that could link a person to a crime.*

fluid² /ˈfluːɪd/ *adj.* **1** (of a situation) likely to change; not fixed: *Politically, socially and culturally, the situation is still fluid.* ◇ *Labour markets were relatively fluid, with high labour turnover and short unemployment durations.* **2** able to flow easily, as liquids and gases do: *The liquids are so fluid that they have viscosities only slightly higher than water.*

flu·id·ity /fluˈɪdəti/ *noun* [U] **1** the quality of being likely to change, rather than being fixed: *There is a trend towards greater social fluidity.* **2** the quality of being able to flow easily, as liquids and gases do: *This will depend on the fluidity of the migrating liquid.*

fluor·es·cence /ˌflɔːˈresns; ˌflʊəˈresns; *NAmE* ˌflʊˈresns/ *noun* [U] visible or invisible RADIATION produced from certain substances as a result of radiation of a shorter WAVELENGTH such as X-RAYS or ULTRAVIOLET light: **+ noun** *However, there are a number of limitations and disadvantages associated with X-ray fluorescence spectroscopy.*

fluor·es·cent /ˌflɔːˈresnt; ˌflʊəˈresnt; *NAmE* ˌflʊˈresnt/ *adj.* (of substances) having, showing or using fluorescence: *The chromosomes were stained with a fluorescent dye.* ◇ *All lighting in the building was converted from incandescent to compact fluorescent bulbs.*

flux /flʌks/ *noun* **1** [C, U] **~ (of sth)** (*technical*) a flow; an act of flowing: *It was possible to calculate the emitted flux of atoms.* HELP In physics, **flux** can be the rate of flow of a liquid, a gas, energy or PARTICLES across a particular area; or the total electric or MAGNETIC field passing through a surface: *The temperature difference was related to the size of heat flux.* ◇ *When a current flows in the coil, a magnetic flux is created within the ring.* **2** [U] continuous movement and change: **in ~** *Language is in constant flux.* ◇ **in**

F

a state of ~ *The legal definition of food additives is in a state of flux.*

fly[1] /flaɪ/ *verb* (**flies, fly·ing, flew** /fluː/, **flown** /fləʊn; *NAmE* floʊn/) **1** [I] **(+ adv./prep.)** to travel in an aircraft: *Statistics show that it is more dangerous to drive on a highway than to fly.* ◇ *After the meeting, the Civil Secretary flew back to Khartoum.* **2** [I, T] **~ (sth)** (of an aircraft) to move through the air: **(+ adv./prep.)** *The majority of enemy aircraft were flying at speeds above 600 knots.* ◇ **~ sth** *The cost of flying each route is calculated precisely.* **3** [I] **(+ adv./prep.)** to move through the air, using wings: *As the sea ice retreated, the Icelandic birds had to fly over larger distances for food.* ◇ *The film starts with footage of a gull flying serenely over the sea.* ◇ *Athena turned herself into a vulture and flew away.* **4** [T, I] **~ (sth) (+ adv./prep.)** to control an aircraft, etc. in the air: *First generation aircraft were harder to fly at high speeds.* **5** [T] **~ sb/sth (+ adv./prep.)** to transport goods or passengers in a plane: *Hamilton contracted malaria in the Congo and was flown back to Britain.* **6** [I] **(+ adv./prep.)** to move suddenly and with force: *When the larger rocks crashed against other rocks, the fragments flew into the air.*

IDM **fly in the face of 'sth** to oppose or be the opposite of sth that is usual or expected: *They assume that production costs rise with output but this assumption flies in the face of the facts.*

fly[2] /flaɪ/ *noun* (*pl.* **flies**) a small flying insect with two wings. There are many different types of fly: *Studies have shown that fruit flies can be trained to learn and remember particular smells and sights.*

fly·ing[1] /ˈflaɪɪŋ/ *adj.* [only before noun] able to fly: *Many species of flying insects, such as dragonflies, were also present.*

fly·ing[2] /ˈflaɪɪŋ/ *noun* [U] flight, especially in a aircraft: *A few people experience such intense fear that flying is impossible.*

foam /fəʊm; *NAmE* foʊm/ *noun* **1** [U] a thick liquid that contains a mass of very small BUBBLES: *The water surface is now largely free of spray and foam.* **2** [U, C] a chemical substance that forms or produces a mass of very small BUBBLES; a light form of rubber or plastic made by SOLIDIFYING liquid foam: *The fire extinguisher directs foam onto the fire.* ◇ *Polyurethane foam was used for the core of the structure.*

focal /ˈfəʊkl; *NAmE* ˈfoʊkl/ *adj.* [only before noun] **1** connected with the main thing that people are interested in or are working on: *Equity and access to health care is the focal theme in part three.* ◇ *Additional focal observations were made.* **2** (*physics*) connected with the focus of a LENS: *Figure 5.7 shows the simulated irradiance distribution on the lens focal plane.* **3** (*medical*) happening in one part of the body, rather than in several parts: *Focal neurological deficits are uncommon.*

ˈfocal point *noun* **1** a thing that is the centre of interest or activity SYN FOCUS[2] (2): **~ for sth** *The programme will serve as a focal point for global scholarship in a variety of fields.* ◇ **~ of sth** *Such towns were the focal points of regional identities.* **2** (*also* **focus**) (*physics*) a point at which waves of light, sound, etc. meet after REFLECTION or REFRACTION; the point from which waves of light, sound, etc. seem to come: *Chromatic aberration is the inability of a lens to bring electromagnetic rays of different wavelengths to a common focal point.*

focus[1] AWL /ˈfəʊkəs; *NAmE* ˈfoʊkəs/ *verb* (**-s-** or **-ss-**) **1** [I, T] to give attention or effort to a particular thing (or to just a few things), rather than to many things: **~ on/upon (doing) sth** *Studies have primarily focused on the nature, extent and magnitude of the problem.* ◇ **~ sth on/upon (doing) sth** *She now focuses her efforts on promoting the use of public bioscience resources.* ◇ **~ (sth) on/upon how/what, etc.** *This book focuses on how beliefs about God map onto other beliefs and attitudes.* HELP Although **focus** is most commonly used with **on** in this meaning, it is sometimes used without **on** or **upon**: *Changes to social security benefits were focused around two main problems.* ◇ *Listeners felt better able to focus.* ➲ language bank *at* ABOUT[2] **2** [I, T] (of a person or their eyes, or a camera, etc.) to adjust or be adjusted, so that things can be seen clearly: *Patients have reduced ability to focus and perceive colour.* ◇ **~ on sb/sth** *The camera focuses on her face.* ◇ **~ sth** *To help focus the microscope, a drop is placed on the slide.* ◇ **~ sth on sb/sth** *His eyes have been focused on his meal throughout the scene.* **3** [T] (*physics*) to CONDENSE a BEAM of light or other energy: **~ sth** *A carefully designed electromagnet can focus an electron beam.* ◇ **~ sth + adv./prep.** *The light is then focused by another lens towards an exit slit.*

▸ FOCUS + NOUN + ON/UPON **attention • interest • effort • discussion • mind • study, research • investigation • analysis** *Geographers have not focused much attention on this important topic.*

▸ FOCUS (STH) ON/UPON + NOUN **area • theme • issue, topic, question • impact • nature • way • role • aspect, dimension • factor • relationship • development • implication • outcome** *Research focused on two areas:...* ◇ *At present, much interest is focused on dietary factors.*

▸ NOUN + FOCUS ON/UPON **study • book • paper • article • essay • section • chapter • research • discussion, debate • attention • literature • researchers** *Discussions tend to focus on issues rather than on people.*

▸ FOCUS + ADVERB + ON/UPON | ADVERB + FOCUS ON/UPON **mainly, mostly, largely, predominantly, primarily • initially • increasingly • particularly, especially, specifically • solely, only, exclusively • explicitly** *The project predominantly focuses upon a certain type of photography.* ◇ *The study focused exclusively on women.*

▸ FOCUS + ADVERB + ON/UPON **entirely • heavily • in particular** *He focuses in particular on the issue of positive introspection.*

▸ ADVERB + FOCUS ON/UPON **traditionally • typically** *Such arguments typically focus on the role of state policy and practice.*

focus[2] AWL /ˈfəʊkəs; *NAmE* ˈfoʊkəs/ *noun* (*pl.* **fo·cuses** or **foci** /ˈfəʊsaɪ; *NAmE* ˈfoʊsaɪ/) **1** [U, C, usually sing.] attention or effort that is given to a particular thing (or to just a few things), rather than to lots of things: *This led many researchers to narrow their focus to specific practice.* ◇ *The literature suffers from a lack of focus.* ◇ **~ on sth** *A focus on immediate outcomes is essential.* HELP **Shift** and **change** are used as a verb and noun with **focus**: *This approach shifts the focus from the text to the actors.* ◇ *The focus has shifted from growth to sustainable development.* ◇ *She remarks on the shift of/in focus from teacher to learner.* **2** [C, usually sing.] the main thing that people are interested in or are working on: **~ of sth** *Five cities have become the main focus of investigation.* ◇ **~ for sth** *International culture was the focus for a growing field of analysis.* **3** [U, C, usually sing.] the quality or state of being seen with clear edges; a device (for example, on a MICROSCOPE) that allows this: *This procedure allows the sample to be brought into focus without damaging it against the lens.* ◇ *By carefully adjusting the focus, it is possible to determine the position of the fibres.* ◇ **in ~** *The image is no longer in focus.* ◇ **out of ~** *A page of text appears, but the words are out of focus.* **4** [C] (*physics*) = FOCAL POINT (2): *The receiver plane was placed 4 cm in front of the focus.* **5** [C] (*earth science*) the point below the earth's surface where an EARTHQUAKE starts: *His research into locating the foci of earthquakes was well known.* ➲ *compare* EPICENTRE (1) **6** [C] **~ (for sth)** (*medical*) the part of sb's body in which a disease starts or is most developed: *Haematomas can provide a focus for infection.*

IDM **bring sth into focus** to make sth very clear SYN HIGHLIGHT[1] (1): *This brings into focus the need for a* *more vigorous risk assessment process.* **come into focus** to become very clear: *The issues come into even sharper focus when dealing with people who are ill.*

▸ ADJECTIVE + FOCUS **major, key, main, primary • central • traditional • initial • sole, exclusive • particular, specific** *Comedy was never her primary focus as a writer.* ◇ *Her research interests include EU law, with a particular focus on environmental law.* | **clear • sharp • strong • special • greater • narrow • broad • excessive** *The authors move beyond this narrow focus to address other issues.*

▸ VERB + FOCUS **shift • place the ~ on • keep the ~ on • maintain • broaden, widen • narrow • sharpen • lack** *This approach keeps the focus on learning.* ◇ *This study has broadened the focus of research into these products.* | **become • emerge as • have sth as • provide • remain** *Globalization has emerged as a new focus of historical social theory.* ◇ *The meetings have as their main focus the modernization of the European economy.*

▸ FOCUS OF + NOUN **interest • attention • concern • investigation, enquiry • research • debate • analysis** *Human social relations are the focus of much attention.* | **paper • article • review • chapter** *These will be the focus of later chapters.*

fo·cused AWL (*also* **fo·cussed**) /ˈfəʊkəst; *NAmE* ˈfoʊkəst/ *adj.* with your attention directed to what you want to do; with very clear aims: *This difficult task requires the focused attention of both theoreticians and practitioners.* ◇ **~ on sth** *These interventions attempt to help parents stay focused on their children's needs.* ◇ *The need for social workers to participate in research was not recognized by managers who were very focused on service delivery goals.*

ˈ**focus group** *noun* a small group of people, specially chosen to represent different social classes, etc, who are asked to discuss and give their opinions about a particular subject. The information obtained is used by people doing MARKET RESEARCH, for example about new products or for a political party: *One focus group was conducted with adolescents from a local youth centre.* ◇ **+ noun** *a focus group discussion/participant/session*

foe·tal, foe·tus (*BrE*) = FETAL, FETUS

fold[1] /fəʊld; *NAmE* foʊld/ *verb* [T, I] to bend sth so that one part lies on top of another part and it becomes smaller or flatter; to bend or be able to bend in this way: **~ (up)** *Collisions will tend to cause the molecule to bend and fold up.* ◇ **~ sth (up)** *He will then fold the paper, stamp it with the national seal and put it in a closed box.* ➲ *compare* UNFOLD (2)

IDM **fold your ˈarms** to put one of your arms over the other one and hold them against your body: *Avoid sitting with legs crossed and arms folded as this may convey defensiveness and lack of interest.*

fold[2] /fəʊld; *NAmE* foʊld/ *noun* **1** [C] **~ (of sth)** a part of sth that is folded or hangs as if it had been folded: *The thickness of a fold of skin can be used to give an estimate of total body fat.* **2** [C] (*earth science*) a curve or bend in the line of the layers of rock in the earth's CRUST: *Almost all folds in rocks form in the subsurface region at depths in the crust of about 1 to 45 km.* **3 the fold** [sing.] a group of people who share the same ideas or beliefs and who feel they belong together: *Campaigns were mounted to bring the working classes into the fold of religion.*

folk /fəʊk; *NAmE* foʊk/ *adj.* [only before noun] **1** (of art, culture, etc.) traditional and typical of the ordinary people of a country or community: *Irish folk music centres on the local pub where groups of musicians gather to perform.* **2** based on the beliefs of ordinary people: *These plants have been used as folk medicines for centuries in China and India.*

folk·lore /ˈfəʊklɔː(r); *NAmE* ˈfoʊklɔːr/ *noun* [U] the traditions and stories of a country or community: *In Northern European folklore, the raven was closely associated with war.* ◇ *These ideas became part of the general folklore about television at the time.*

fol·low /ˈfɒləʊ; *NAmE* ˈfɑːloʊ/ *verb* **1** [T, I] to come after sth/sb else in time or order; to happen as a result of sth else: **~ (sth/sb)** *Both workers and employers prospered in the decades that followed the Second World War.* ◇ *Whether a withdrawal from the eurozone is voluntary or enforced, certain consequences will inevitably follow.* ◇ **there follows/followed...** *There followed debates about which experiments should have been included.* ◇ **as follows...** *The procedure to be used is as follows:...* ◇ **~ on from sth** *Each stage is linked to and follows on from its predecessor.* **2** [I, T] (not usually used in the progressive tenses) to be the logical result of sth: **~ from sth** *An interesting observation follows from the table above.* ◇ **it follows that...** *If character is largely determined by a person's genes, it follows logically that education and upbringing will have little influence.* ◇ **~ sth** *Following this logic, Jordan and Kaups (1989) proposed that the American backwoods culture had significant Northern European roots.* **3** [T] **~ sth** to develop or happen in a particular way or according to a particular pattern: *There are four technologies that do not follow the general trend.* ◇ *The spread of invasive fish typically follows the same pattern as for other invasive organisms.* **4** [T] **~ sth** to take a particular course of action: *Both parties have generally followed strategies of widening their electoral base.* **5** [T] **~ sth** to act according to advice, instructions or rules: *Patients often fail to follow the advice that is given to them by their doctor.* ◇ *They did not generally follow Jewish dietary rules.* **6** [T] to act according to the example of sb; to do sth in the same way as sb/sth else: **~ sth** *Belgium has attempted to follow the example of Switzerland, but without success.* ◇ *He follows the work of A. Tal in accounting for the differences between the various versions.* ◇ **~ sb** *In his own 'Critique of Hegel', written a year after Feuerbach's book, he followed Feuerbach almost to the letter.* **7** [T] to understand the meaning of an argument, or what sb is saying: **~ sth** *Many ordinary Christians probably could not follow the subtle theological arguments.* ◇ **easy/difficult to ~** *Her reasoning is not always easy to follow.* **8** [T] **~ sth** to take an active interest in sth and be aware of what is happening: *The Court asked the Greek government to follow developments in the applicant's case closely.* ◇ *The journal enables scholars to follow ongoing work.* **9** [T] **~ sb/sth** (of a book, film, programme, etc.) to be concerned with the life or development of sb/sth: *This project aims to follow settlers and their descendants over five generations.* **10** [T] **~ sth** to go along a road, path, etc: *Light follows the shortest path between any two points.* ◇ *The flight crew must follow planned routes.* **11** [T] **~ sth** (of a road, path, etc.) to go in the same direction as sth: *Before 800, the Germanic-Slavic linguistic border roughly followed the line of the Elbe and Saale rivers.* **12** [T] to come or go after or behind sb/sth: **~ sb/sth** *Merchants cut off credit, cars followed civil rights workers at night, and beatings occurred constantly.* ◇ **~ sb/sth + adv./prep.** (*figurative*) *He followed his father into the medical profession.*

IDM **follow in sb's ˈfootsteps 1** to use the work or example of sb as a basis for further progress: *Following in the footsteps of Benjamin Franklin, Michael Faraday studied the nature of electricity.* **2** to do the same job, have the same style of life, etc. as sb else, especially sb in your family: *For generations, daughters followed in their mothers' footsteps.* **follow ˈsuit** to act or behave in the way that sb else has just done: *India and Canada immediately offered help and many other countries followed suit.*

PHR V ˌ**follow ˈthrough (with/on sth)** to finish what you have started: *No one deserved more censure for the failure to follow through than the president himself.* ◇ *Congress, however, followed through on other Republican promises.* ˌ**follow sth ˈthrough** to finish sth that you have started:

Committees will only be more effective if they systematically follow through their work. ˌ**follow sb** ˈ**up** to make a further medical examination of sb in order to check the success of earlier treatment: *It is also important to follow these patients up for at least 6 months.* ˌ**follow sth** ˈ**up** to find out more about sth that sb has told you or suggested to you SYN INVESTIGATE (2): *News stories are frequently not covered or not followed up.* ˌ**follow sth** ˈ**up (with sth)** to take further action in addition to sth that you have already done: *It is vital to identify success and be clear about the way to follow it up.* ◇ *The Law Commission followed up its earlier work with the publication of a consultative report.* ➲ *related noun* FOLLOW-UP ˈ**follow sth with sth** to do or produce sth after sth else: *Dodge followed this first paper with a series of more detailed studies.*

▸ FOLLOW + NOUN **period • event • end • death • war • decision • publication** *The high inflation of the 1970s followed the decision of oil producers to cut production.* | **path • line • route • course** *In the USSR, politicians claimed to be following the Marxist-Leninist line even when they manifestly were not.* ◇ *The president was surprised when events did not follow the course he expected.* | **pattern • sequence • trend • distribution • trajectory** *In this instance the data follow a normal distribution.* | **strategy, policy • approach, method • model • procedure , process • practice • steps** *The same procedures were followed at each stage for consistent results.* | **rule • guidelines • protocol • principle • advice • recommendation • instructions** *The laboratories are publicly funded, and are therefore required to follow governmental guidelines.* | **example • model • lead • tradition** *The international community, following the lead of France, threw its support behind the new regime.*

▸ ADVERB + FOLLOW | FOLLOW + ADVERB **immediately, directly • closely • quickly, rapidly, soon** *The method closely follows that of Weideman &. Reddy (2000).* ◇ *Historically, when market economies have been successful over a period of time, pressure for democratization has often followed soon after.*

▸ ADVERB + FOLLOW **necessarily, inevitably • typically • largely, broadly • usually, generally • simply** *People in organizations do not simply follow orders.*

fol·low·er /ˈfɒləʊə(r); *NAmE* ˈfɑːloʊər/ *noun* **1 ~ (of sb/sth)** a person who supports and admires a particular person or set of ideas: *The followers of Marx were regarded as the most impressive thinkers of the age.* **2 ~ (of sth)** a person who is very interested in a particular activity and follows all the recent news about it: *These changes are of great interest to followers of British politics.* **3** a person, company, etc. that does things after another has done them first: *Once one of the world's leading high-tech companies, it has been reduced to the role of a follower.*

fol·low·ing[1] /ˈfɒləʊɪŋ; *NAmE* ˈfɑːloʊɪŋ/ *adj.* **the following... 1** next in time or order: *The Prussian authorities soon forced the paper to close, and in the following year Marx emigrated to Paris.* ◇ *The following three sections then explore the impact of this principle on social research.* **2** that will be mentioned next in a piece of writing or a speech: *The study aims to answer the following questions:...*

fol·low·ing[2] /ˈfɒləʊɪŋ; *NAmE* ˈfɑːloʊɪŋ/ *noun* **1 the following** (used with either a singular or a plural verb, depending on whether you are talking about one thing or person or several things or people) the thing or things that you will mention next; the people that you will mention next: *The following is a brief summary of the techniques that were used.* ◇ *The following are some specific examples that have been widely discussed in the international media:...* ◇ *I should like to thank the following for their support during the writing of this thesis:...* ◇ *Businesses fail for a number of reasons, including the following:...* **2** [usually sing.] a group of supporters: *He was able to command a substantial following among Ghana's intellectuals.*

fol·low·ing[3] /ˈfɒləʊɪŋ; *NAmE* ˈfɑːloʊɪŋ/ *prep.* after or as a result of a particular event: *This situation changed following the events of 2010.* ◇ *The patients were asked to sign an informed consent agreement. Following this, they completed an in-depth interview.*

ˈ**follow-up** *noun* [U, C] an action or a thing that continues sth that has already started or comes after sth similar that was done earlier: *A lack of long-term follow-up makes it difficult to assess the effectiveness of these interventions.* ◇ **at ~** *It can be seen that the intervention group showed fewer depressive symptoms at follow-up.* ◇ **(as) a ~ to sth** *The project was a follow-up to earlier developmental research at Purdue University.* ◇ **+ noun** *Patients' satisfaction was evaluated over an 18-month follow-up period.*

food /fuːd/ *noun* **1** [U] things that people or animals eat: *When food is scarce, the birds lay fewer eggs than they do when food is abundant.* ◇ *2.4 million people were in need of food, shelter or medical care.* ◇ **+ noun** *Food safety policy developed slowly in the EU.* **2** [C, U] a particular type of food: *There has been an increasing interest in healthy foods and fitness.* ◇ *The government took action to control salt in processed food.*

IDM **food for** ˈ**thought** an idea that makes you think seriously and carefully: *While these results should be viewed with caution, they do provide interesting food for thought.*

ˈ**food chain** *noun* (*usually* **the food chain**) **1** a series of living creatures in which each type of creature feeds on the one below it in the series: *Photosynthetic organisms must have been the base of the oceanic food chain throughout the history of the earth.* **2** the series of processes by which food is grown or produced, sold and then eaten: *A few very powerful companies control most of the food chain from 'field to fork'.*

food·stuff /ˈfuːdstʌf/ *noun* [usually pl.] any substance that is used as food: *In Venezuela, the government provides basic foodstuffs at low prices in state-run markets.*

ˈ**food web** *noun* a system of FOOD CHAINS that are related to and depend on each other: *The Antarctic oceanic food web is centred on krill, which is consumed by baleen whales, seals, penguins, fish and squid.*

foot /fʊt/ *noun* (*pl.* **feet** /fiːt/) **1** [C] the lowest part of the leg, on which a person or an animal stands: *Symptoms include numbness and tingling in the hands and feet.* ◇ *Dickens was troubled with gout in his left foot.* ◇ **on ~** *In Britain in 1950, the average person travelled about 8 km a day, mostly on foot.* **2** [sing.] **the ~ of sth** the lowest part of sth; the base or bottom of sth: *There are usually shore platforms or beaches at the foot of cliffs, but some plunge directly into deep water.* ◇ *Venous return can be improved by elevating the legs (usually by raising the foot of the bed).* **3** (*pl.* **feet** or **foot**) (*abbr.* **ft**) a unit for measuring length equal to 12 inches or 30.48 centimetres: *This plant could produce timbers up to 150 feet in length.* ◇ *His analysis of Fortune 500 companies found that almost 60% of CEOs were six foot or taller.* ◇ *Large international firms often require hundreds of thousands of square feet of office space.* ➲ grammar note *at* METRE

IDM **set** ˈ**foot in/on sth** to enter or visit a place: *The first Europeans set foot in Australia in the 1600s and 1700s.* ➲ *more at* VOTE[2]

foot·age /ˈfʊtɪdʒ/ *noun* [U] part of a film showing a particular event: *Historical documentaries using extensive archival footage not in the public domain have become more and more expensive.* ◇ **~ of sth/sb** *The findings derive from 900 minutes of video footage of children at play during school breaks.*

foot·ing /ˈfʊtɪŋ/ *noun* [sing.] **1** a SECURE or well established position: *Business groups strived to find their footing in an increasingly regulated environment.* ◇ *Latin learning* *had established a firm footing in Ireland.* ◇ *The policy aimed to rationalize production so that farms could be placed on a sound economic footing.* **2** the basis on which sth is organized or its position or status in relation to others: *The government intended to bring forward legislation to put the civil service on a statutory footing.* ◇ *The company was not ready to compete with other global car producers on an equal footing.* **3** the position of your feet when they are safely on the ground or some other surface: *He struggled to keep his footing as a series of jolts threw him backwards and forwards.* IDM *see* EQUAL[1]

foot·note /ˈfʊtnəʊt; *NAmE* ˈfʊtnoʊt/ *noun* **1** an extra piece of information that is printed at the bottom of a page in a book: *Significant differences between the draft and the published version are mentioned in footnotes.* ➲ *compare* ENDNOTE **2** an event or a person that may be remembered but only as sth/sb that is not important: *The incident was destined to become a mere footnote in history.*

foot·print /ˈfʊtprɪnt/ *noun* **1** [usually pl.] a mark left on a surface by a person's foot or shoe or by an animal's foot: *If the burglar had broken in through the kitchen window, there would be footprints outside.* ◇ *Fossil footprints were found preserved in volcanic ash.* **2** the amount of space that sth fills: *A house with this footprint is calculated to have a south facing surface area of 44.3 m².* ◇ *The land area occupied by each turbine, called its footprint, is proportional to the square of its diameter.* **3** damage to the environment because of human activity: *Carbon footprints measure how much carbon dioxide is pumped into the atmosphere in the making of a particular product.* ◇ *These programmes are designed to reduce the environmental footprint of cement manufacture.*

foot·step /ˈfʊtstep/ *noun* [usually pl.] the sound or mark made each time your foot touches the ground when you are walking or running: *the sound of footsteps* ◇ *footsteps in the snow* IDM *see* FOLLOW

for /fə(r); *strong form* fɔː(r)/ *prep.* HELP For the special uses of **for** in phrasal verbs, look at the entries for the verbs. For example, **account for sth** is in the phrasal verb section at **account** *verb*. **1** concerning sb/sth: *For women, the estimate is 0.08 and not significant.* ◇ *The aim has been to explore how these firms developed the technological expertise necessary for success.* ➲ language bank *at* ACCORDING TO **2** used to show what or who is intended to have or use sth: *International resources for HIV/AIDS increased to over $10 billion in 2007.* ◇ *He was writing for the political and intellectual elite of the period.* ◇ *These characteristics make this circuit suitable for applications involving very small signals.* **3** in order to help sb/sth: *Peer emotional support for children with diabetes helped them feel more accepted.* ◇ *Increasing the income of poor households may do more for their health than increasing the health care budget.* **4** in order to obtain or achieve sth: *He relied on trusted aides for advice and support.* ◇ *The model appears to be a useful tool for understanding ecosystem functioning.* **5** used to show a length of time: *This paper will evaluate the success of the national health reform programme for 2006–2010.* ◇ *Many of the families had lived in the area for a number of generations.* ◇ *Company regulations require that such data be retained for a period of twelve months.* ➲ language bank *at* TIME[1] **6** used to show a distance: *The Central Valley runs north-south for 450 miles.* **7** used to show purpose or function: *The company set up a coconut oil production plant for soap production (Tongzon, 1998: 145).* **8** used to show a reason or cause: *It seems from the World Values Survey that trust is good for economic growth.* ◇ *For these reasons, biosensors are continuing to be the focus of much research.* **9** used to say how necessary, difficult, pleasant, etc. sth is that sb might do or has done: *Rapid technological change increases the need for a more skilled and better-educated workforce.* ◇ *It is very important for an economy to be stable and to maintain a steady growth rate.* **10** in support of sb/sth: *There is increasing evidence for the hypothesis that lack of vitamin D increases Multiple Sclerosis risk.* ➲ *compare* AGAINST (2) **11** in exchange for sth: *Later, the emperors abandoned Rome for places more strategically significant.* **12** in relation to a particular aspect of sth: *Hawaii's teachers are paid the lowest salaries in the USA, adjusted for cost of living.* ◇ *68.4% of the sample were considered normal weight for their age and sex.* **13** as a representative of sb/sth: *It is important to remember that the press in India speaks for an elite minority.* **14** employed by sb/sth: *She worked for the same employer for 27 years.* **15** meaning sth: *The term 'MATLAB' is an abbreviation for 'Matrix Laboratory'.* **16** used to show where sb/sth is going: *After spending three years in the United States, Bankole Awoonor-Renner left for Moscow.* **17** used to show that sth is arranged or intended to happen at a particular time: *Her departure was scheduled for 27 June.* **18** used to show the occasion when sth happens: *After 1990, state enterprises in Eastern Europe faced the prospect of bankruptcy for the first time since 1939.* **19 to be ~ sb/sth to do sth** used to show who can or should do sth: *Ultimately, it is for the patient to decide on the type of treatment plan.*

IDM **for ˈall (that...)** despite: *The novel does in fact contain, for all its solid realism, plenty of poetry and passion.* ◇ *The Emperor's word was no less powerful for all that he could act only through messengers.*

F

for·age /ˈfɒrɪdʒ; *NAmE* ˈfɔːrɪdʒ; ˈfɑːrɪdʒ/ *verb* [I] **~ (for sth)** (especially of an animal) to search for food: *Wild Mediterranean rock doves nest on cliffs and forage for food on nearby fields.* ◇ *Different phenotypes within the same population may adopt different foraging strategies.*

for·bid /fəˈbɪd; *NAmE* fərˈbɪd/ *verb* (**for·bade** /fəˈbæd; fəˈbeɪd; *NAmE* fərˈbæd; fərˈbeɪd/, **for·bid·den** /fəˈbɪdn; *NAmE* fərˈbɪdn/) **1** to order sb not to do sth; to order that sth must not be done: **~ sb (from doing sth)** *Her mother forbade her from using the bus.* ◇ **~ sth** *All alcoholic drinks are forbidden.* ◇ *To avoid pollution, pagan legislation forbade the burial of the dead within a city's sacred boundary.* ◇ **~ sb to do sth** *Christians were forbidden to assemble for worship.* ◇ **~ sb sth** *A Virginian law of 1640 forbade slaves the right to bear weapons.* OPP ALLOW (1), PERMIT[1] (1) **2 ~ sth** to make it difficult or impossible to do sth: *Limitations of space forbid the discussion of macroeconomic fluctuations.*

for·bid·den /fəˈbɪdn; *NAmE* fərˈbɪdn/ *adj.* not allowed: *The book was placed on the Catholic Church's Index of Forbidden Books.* ◇ *He imposed heavy fines on imperial officials who practiced forbidden rituals.* ◇ *Building a settlement inside a so-called Reserved Forest is strictly forbidden without the consent of the Forest Department.*

force[1] /fɔːs; *NAmE* fɔːrs/ *noun* **1** [C] a person or thing that has a lot of power or influence: *Global economic forces pushed oil prices up.* ◇ *These changes are all driven by market forces.* ◇ **the forces of sth** *Believers were expected to struggle against the forces of evil and unbelief.* ◇ **a ~ for sth** *International law is a force for good.* ➲ *see also* MARKET FORCES **2** [U] power or influence that sb/sth has: *Larger firms are able to exert more force on pricing.* ◇ **the ~ of sth** *Despite the force of the arguments, little attention was paid to these recommendations.* ◇ *The sheer force of his personality led to some weaker ideas being accepted.* HELP **Legal force** or **the force of the law** is the power or authority of the law: *The Protocols have the same legal force as the Treaties.* ◇ *This activity was met with the full force of the law.* **3** [C, U] (*physics*) an effect that causes things to move, change direction or change shape: *Newton was able to determine the gravitational force acting between two masses.* ◇ **~ on sth** *Non-conducting fibres exert force on the copper wire.* ➲ *see also* CENTRIFUGAL FORCE **4** [U] violent physical action used to obtain or achieve sth: *Military force was deployed.* ◇ **by ~** *They sought to mobilize the* *militia in order to seize power by force.* **5** [C+sing./pl. v., usually pl.] soldiers or others whose job is to fight or to protect people: *Many of them were killed by security forces.* ◇ *The Security Council has been unwilling to deploy UN forces.* ◇ *He mobilized forces loyal to the old regime.* **HELP** **Forces** can also refer to both people and weapons, considered together: *Nuclear forces moved to unprecedented states of alert.* ➲ *see also* AIR FORCE, ARMED FORCES, POLICE FORCE, TASK FORCE **6** [C+sing./pl. v.] a group of people who have been organized for a particular purpose: *The sales force will do a better job if marketing has done a good job.* ◇ **+ noun** *Women's labour force participation has increased.* ➲ *see also* LABOUR FORCE, TASK FORCE (1), WORKFORCE **7** [U] the physical strength of sth as it hits sth else: **~ of sth** *The enormous force of the waves tore the ship from its anchor.* ◇ **with ~** *If a ball hits with sufficient force a sufficiently brittle object, that object will shatter.* **8** [C, usually sing.] a unit for measuring the strength of the wind: *Winds often reach gale force.*

IDM **bring sth into 'force** to cause a law or rule to start being used: *The legislation had not yet been brought into force.* **by force of sth** as a result of sth; under the influence of sth: *He was wholly driven by force of circumstances into doing what he did.* **come/enter into 'force** (of a law or rule) to start being used: *The Protocol came into force in 2005.* **the forces of 'nature** the power of the wind, rain, etc, especially when it causes damage or harm: *The threat to human survival does not come from predators or dangerous forces of nature, but from other humans.* **in 'force** **1** (of a law or rule) being used: *The statute has been in force for almost 30 years.* **2** (of people) in large numbers: *A year later the exiles returned in force.* ➲ *more at* JOIN

▸ ADJECTIVE + FORCE **strong** • **opposing** • **external** • **internal** *Their atoms are held together by strong forces that resist rearrangement of the atoms.* ◇ *The opposing forces of secularization and religiosity have shaped our political culture.* | **main, major** • **powerful** • **dominant** • **driving** • **evolutionary** • **social** • **political** • **economic** • **competitive** • **creative** *The main driving force was the discovery of electromagnetic waves.* ◇ *They were a formidable political force.* | **net** • **weak** • **repulsive** • **attractive** • **magnetic** • **electromagnetic** • **intermolecular** • **nuclear** • **frictional** • **centripetal** • **centrifugal** • **gravitational** • **tidal** *Gravitational, magnetic or centrifugal forces can also act on the body.* | **lethal** • **brute** • **excessive** • **military** *The Supreme Court requires agents to refrain from using lethal force if less harmful means are available.*

▸ ADJECTIVE + FORCES **military** • **peacekeeping** *UN peacekeeping forces withdrew in 2008.*

▸ NOUN + FORCES **security** • **government** • **rebel** *Government forces are fighting insurgents.*

▸ VERB + FORCE **become** • **unleash** • **defeat** *One of the major economic forces unleashed by globalization has been an intensification of competition.* | **exert** • **experience** • **balance** • **weaken** • **resist** • **overcome** *Increasing the temperature weakens the forces holding the molecules together.* | **generate** • **transmit** • **apply** *The force generated by the gravitational interaction of two nanoscale particles is negligible.* | **deploy** • **use, employ** *He had employed excessive force.*

▸ VERB + FORCES **deploy** • **use, employ** • **command** • **gather** • **mobilize** • **withdraw** *He commanded NATO forces during the conflict.*

▸ FORCE + VERB **operate** • **act (on)** • **govern** • **drive** *Marketing in the public sector is governed by three main forces: social, economic and political.*

force[2] /fɔːs; *NAmE* fɔːrs/ *verb* **1** [often passive] to make sb do sth that they do not want to do, or go somewhere that they do not want to go: **~ sb to do sth** *He was forced to resign from his post.* ◇ **~ sb into sth** *They were forced into exile.* ◇ **~ sb into doing sth** *The publicity forced the company into making a statement.* ◇ **~ sb + adv./prep.** *He was forced out of office.* ◇ *Farmers forced peasants off the land.* ➲ *compare* COMPEL (1) **2** to make sth happen, especially before people are ready: **~ sth** *Neither partner has the power to force the decision.* ◇ *There is no reason to force the issue.* ◇ **~ sth + adv./prep.** *They will be able to force up the price of the land.* **3** **~ sth + adv./prep.** to make sth move in a particular direction: *The gas is forced through the column at a rate of 40–80 cm³ per minute.* ◇ *The net pressure difference must be sufficient to force the filtrate along the tubules.*

IDM **force sb's 'hand** to make sb do sth, especially before they have decided that they want to do it: *Lenin had initially expected to proceed very cautiously, but events forced his hand.* **force the 'pace** to make sth happen more quickly than expected or wanted: *Technology is forcing the pace of liberalization in many markets.*

PHR V **'force sb/sth on/upon sb** to make sb accept sth that they do not want: *Usually, the more powerful groups in society are able to force their language upon the less powerful.*

forced /fɔːst; *NAmE* fɔːrst/ *adj.* happening or done against sb's will: *Actions should be taken to fight against forced labour.* ◇ *It is difficult for both the man and the woman to accept this forced change in gender roles.* ◇ *The term 'refugee' was coined for the Protestants fleeing France to avoid forced conversion.*

force·ful /'fɔːsfl; *NAmE* 'fɔːrsfl/ *adj.* **1** (of people) expressing opinions firmly and clearly in a way that persuades other people to believe them **SYN** ASSERTIVE: *Su Shun was a man of severe and forceful personality.* ◇ *Hallstein was both a political heavyweight and a forceful leader.* **2** (of opinions, etc.) expressed firmly and clearly so that other people believe them: *He brought his forceful, fluid writing style to bear on a wide range of topics.* ◇ *These works present a forceful argument for the introduction of appropriate technologies.* **3** using force: *The government of Sudan launched a forceful counter-offensive.* ◇ *Vomiting is the forceful expulsion of gastric contents through the mouth.* **4** (of action) strong and effective: *The 1998 Insider Trading Act enabled the Financial Services Board to take more forceful action against illegal transactions.* ■ **force·ful·ly** /'fɔːsfəli; *NAmE* 'fɔːrsfəli/ *adv.*: *Westphal (2001) argues this most forcefully and convincingly.* **force·ful·ness** *noun* [U] *By this time there seemed little hope of resisting Stalin's forcefulness.*

fore·cast[1] /'fɔːkɑːst; *NAmE* 'fɔːrkæst/ *noun* a statement about what will happen in the future, based on information that is available now: *On 15 October 1987, Britain's TV weather forecasts predicted strong winds, but nothing more.* ◇ *These techniques do not improve the accuracy of sales forecasts.* ◇ **~ of sth** *Climate is now monitored globally to feed developing forecasts of climate change.*

fore·cast[2] /'fɔːkɑːst; *NAmE* 'fɔːrkæst/ *verb* (**fore·cast, fore·cast** or **fore·cast·ed, fore·cast·ed**) to say what you expect to happen in the future, based on information that is available now **SYN** PREDICT: **~ sth** *It is difficult to forecast sales.* ◇ **be forecast to do sth** *The world's population is forecast to rise to 9 billion by 2050.* ◇ **~ that...** *They forecast that there would be an end to the war.* ◇ **~ how/what, etc...** *Results from patient satisfaction surveys are useful in forecasting how patients will behave in the future.* ➲ language bank *at* PREDICT

fore·going /'fɔːgəʊɪŋ; *NAmE* 'fɔːrgoʊɪŋ/ *adj.* [only before noun] **1** used to refer to sth that has just been mentioned: *As much of the foregoing discussion has implied, coding is a crucial stage in the process of doing a content analysis.* ◇ *It may be helpful to set out the foregoing argument in a rather more formal fashion.* **OPP** FOLLOWING[1] (2) **2 the foregoing** *noun* [sing.+ sing./pl. v.] what has just been mentioned: *In truth, however, despite the foregoing, it may be unwise to overstate the role of the monarchy in the UK constitution.*

fore·gone /ˈfɔːɡɒn; *NAmE* ˈfɔːrɡɔːn/ *adj.*
IDM **a ˌforegone conˈclusion** if you say that sth is **a foregone conclusion**, you mean that it is a result that is certain to happen: *Given Russia's overwhelming military superiority, the outcome of the conflict was a foregone conclusion.* ◇ *A Labour victory in the election was by no means a foregone conclusion.*

fore·ground[1] /ˈfɔːɡraʊnd; *NAmE* ˈfɔːrɡraʊnd/ *noun* **the foreground 1** [C, usually sing.] the part of a view, picture, etc. that is nearest to you when you look at it: **in the ~** *The figure in the foreground is the artist's mother.* ➲ *compare* BACKGROUND (4) **2** [sing.] an important position that is noticed by people: **in the ~** *The economy was very much in the foreground of all political discussion.* ➲ *compare* BACKGROUND (3)

fore·ground[2] /ˈfɔːɡraʊnd; *NAmE* ˈfɔːrɡraʊnd/ *verb* **~ sth** to give particular importance to sth: *Her writing foregrounds themes of change and renewal.*

for·eign /ˈfɒrən; *NAmE* ˈfɔːrən; ˈfɑːrən/ *adj.* **1** in or from a country that is not your own: *Over the next few years, foreign firms cut back on their purchases of Japanese goods.* ◇ *More and more European schools and universities are offering courses taught in a foreign language.* **2** [only before noun] dealing with or involving other countries: *It has been a central element of British foreign policy to retain a close relationship with the US.* OPP DOMESTIC (1) **3** [only before noun] coming or introduced from outside sth, for example the body: *Airway obstruction may be due to a foreign body, trauma or infection.* ◇ **~ to sth** *Organic biocides include many types of synthetic compounds foreign to the soil/water environment.* **4 ~ to sb/sth** not familiar to sb/sth and therefore seeming strange: *Many of these practices would have seemed quite foreign to Buddhists.* **5 ~ to sb/sth** not belonging to or characteristic of sb/sth: *Such behaviour is not foreign to human nature.*
▸ FOREIGN + NOUN **language • country, state, land, power • government • market • firm, company • subsidiary • partner • affiliate • operation • ownership • producer • goods • product • bank • currency • investor • national • resident • official • student • worker** *Small companies had previously seen their access to foreign markets restricted.* ◇ *Foreign nationals made up just under 12 per cent of the male and 21 per cent of the female populations.* | **policy • minister • ministry • affairs • relations • investment • aid • trade • sales • debt** *The US economy was heavily dependent on foreign trade in 1914.* | **body • object • material • matter** *Antibodies recognize foreign material that enters the body, and are part of the immune response.*

for·eign·er /ˈfɒrənə(r); *NAmE* ˈfɔːrənər; ˈfɑːrənər/ *noun* a person who comes from a different country: *The Athenians, like other Greeks, excluded foreigners from citizenship.*

fore·most[1] /ˈfɔːməʊst; *NAmE* ˈfɔːrmoʊst/ *adj.* the most important or famous; in a position at the front: *He is the world's foremost authority on the subject.* ◇ **~ among sb/sth** *Foremost among mountains as divine residences is Mount Olympus.*

fore·most[2] /ˈfɔːməʊst; *NAmE* ˈfɔːrmoʊst/ *adv.* IDM *see* FIRST[2]

fo·ren·sic /fəˈrensɪk; fəˈrenzɪk/ *adj.* [only before noun] connected with the scientific tests used by the police and courts when trying to solve a crime: *Forensic scientists may be called upon to interpret evidence in relation to a particular investigation.* ◇ *Despite the absence of forensic evidence to support the accusation, a court returned a guilty verdict.* ◇ *He went on to become a very distinguished forensic psychiatrist.*

fore·see /fɔːˈsiː; *NAmE* fɔːrˈsiː/ *verb* (**fore·saw** /fɔːˈsɔː; *NAmE* fɔːrˈsɔː/, **fore·seen** /fɔːˈsiːn; *NAmE* fɔːrˈsiːn/) to know about sth before it happens: **~ sth** *The shareholders cannot foresee the future.* ◇ **~ that...** *The defendant had not foreseen that some harm might occur.* ◇ **~ how/what, etc...** *Orwell foresaw how the manipulation of terror would deprive the world of many freedoms.* ➲ *compare* UNFORESEEN

fore·see·able /fɔːˈsiːəbl; *NAmE* fɔːrˈsiːəbl/ *adj.* that you can predict will happen; that can be foreseen: *This was not a foreseeable risk.* ◇ *Professionals are normally liable for the foreseeable consequences of their negligence.*
IDM **for/in the foreseeable ˈfuture** for/in the period of time when you can predict what is going to happen, based on the present circumstances: *There is little sign that the poor world will catch up with the rich world in the foreseeable future.*

for·est /ˈfɒrɪst; *NAmE* ˈfɔːrɪst; ˈfɑːrɪst/ *noun* **1** [C, U] a large area of land that is covered with trees: *Temperate forests have considerably fewer tree species than their tropical counterparts.* ◇ *Large areas of forest had been cleared over most areas of Britain.* ◇ **+ noun** *Rapid clearing drove forest cover to a low of perhaps no more than 25% across the region by mid-century.* ➲ *see also* RAINFOREST **2** [C] **~ (of sth)** a mass of tall narrow objects that are close together: *A forest of limestone towers stands above a comparatively flat surface.*

for·ever (*BrE also* **for ever**) /fərˈevə(r)/ *adv.* for all future time; for always: *Even particles as fundamental as protons will not last forever.*

for·gave *past tense of* FORGIVE

forge /fɔːdʒ; *NAmE* fɔːrdʒ/ *verb* **1** to put a lot of effort into making sth successful or strong: **~ sth** *Attempts to forge a political compromise failed.* ◇ *New relationships were forged between the academic and commercial worlds.* ◇ **~ sth from/out of sth** *Networks forged out of strategic purposes can lead to more personal ties.* **2 ~ sth** to make an illegal copy of sth: *He was in possession of three forged passports.* **3 ~ sth (from sth)** to shape metal by heating it in a fire and hitting it with a heavy tool; to make an object in this way: *In forging the head of the nail, he is obliged to change his tools.*
PHR V **ˌforge aˈhead (with sth)** to continue in a determined way and make a lot of progress quickly: *The town forged ahead with developing itself as a site for dairy production.*

for·get /fəˈɡet; *NAmE* fərˈɡet/ *verb* (**for·got** /fəˈɡɒt; *NAmE* fərˈɡɑːt/, **for·got·ten** /fəˈɡɒtn; *NAmE* fərˈɡɑːtn/) **1** [I, T] (not usually used in the progressive tenses) to be unable to remember sth that has happened in the past or information that you knew in the past: **~ (about sth)** *Studies constantly show how quickly people forget about a brand once its advertising stops.* ◇ **~ sth** *Impaired memory usually takes the form of everyday lapses such as forgetting well-known names.* ◇ *Individual decision-makers or the organization as a whole may well forget the lessons learned over several years.* ◇ **~ (that)...** *Agrippina never forgot that it was Narcissus who had opposed her selection as empress.* ◇ **~ how/where, etc...** *It is easy to forget how diverse Europe is.* ◇ **it is forgotten that...** *It must not be forgotten that access to the Internet is still not universal.* **2** [I, T] to not remember to do sth that you ought to do: **~ to do sth** *Patients with memory impairment may forget to take medication.* ◇ **~ sth/sb** *Eisenhower appeared to forget his promise.* **3** [I, T] to deliberately stop thinking about sb/sth: **~ (about sb/sth)** *Alcohol may be used to try to improve mood or forget about troubles.* ◇ **~ sb/sth** *They were finally able to forget their differences and work together.*

for·give /fəˈɡɪv; *NAmE* fərˈɡɪv/ *verb* (**for·gave** /fəˈɡeɪv; *NAmE* fərˈɡeɪv/, **for·given** /fəˈɡɪvn; *NAmE* fərˈɡɪvn/) [T, I] to stop feeling angry with sb who has done sth to harm or

F

upset you; to stop feeling angry with yourself: **~ (sth)** *They believed that God had forgiven their sins.* ◇ *They had to learn to forgive.* ◇ **~ sb/yourself (for sth/for doing sth)** *Some people find it very hard to forgive others for their mistakes.*

IDM **sb could/might/would be forgiven for doing sth** used to say that it is easy to understand why sb does or thinks sth, although they are wrong: *The reader would be forgiven for thinking that there is nothing new here.*

for·give·ness /fəˈɡɪvnəs; *NAmE* fərˈɡɪvnəs/ *noun* [U] the act of forgiving sb; willingness to forgive sb: *They wished to seek forgiveness and reconciliation.* ◇ **~ of sth** *the forgiveness of sins*

F

forgo (*also* **forego**) /fɔːˈɡəʊ; *NAmE* fɔːrˈɡoʊ/ *verb* (**for·went** /fɔːˈwent; *NAmE* fɔːrˈwent/, **for·gone** /fɔːˈɡɒn; *NAmE* fɔːrˈɡɔːn/) **~ sth** to decide not to have or do sth that you would like to have or do: *The authors show that employees are willing to forgo financial benefits to work for a socially responsible employer.*

for·got *past tense of* FORGET

for·got·ten *past part. of* FORGET

form¹ /fɔːm; *NAmE* fɔːrm/ *noun* **1** [C] **~ (of sth)** a type or variety of sth: *There has been a lively debate about the best form of government for new democracies.* ◇ *Our sense organs are able to detect various forms of energy (such as light or sound waves).* ◇ *All of these former Communist nations adopted some form of capitalist economic system.* ◇ *Carbon exists in two distinct forms—graphite and diamond—which have identical compositions but different structures.* ➲ *see also* LIFE FORM **2** [C, U] a particular way in which a thing exists or appears: *Antagonism between social classes assumed different forms at different epochs.* ◇ **in the ~ of sb/sth** *Performance bonuses, often in the form of stock options, are common in large corporations.* ◇ **take the ~ of sth** *This payment sometimes took the form of crops.* ◇ **in some ~ or other** *Party politics, in some form or other, has long been a feature of local government.* ◇ **in... ~** *The data is held in electronic form.* **3** [C, U] the visible shape or arrangement of parts of sth: *The cells continue to change shape and adopt a wedge-shaped form.* ◇ **in ~** *The finely made, hand-crafted bowls are broad and flat in form.* ◇ **~ of sth** *During the early development of the worm, there is little change in shape from the ovoid form of the fertilized egg.* **4** [C] an official document containing spaces for information to be put in: *Those who agreed to take part in the survey were asked to sign a form to confirm their consent.* **5** [C] a style or category of art, music or literature: *For Perez, the history of film is the history of an art form.* ◇ *The sonnet virtually disappeared as a literary form for a hundred years.* ◇ **~ of sth** *The 1940s and 1950s also witnessed the emergence of a new form of jazz.* **6** [U] style, design and arrangement in a work of art or literature, as opposed to its content: *Her poetry is distinctive in both form and content.* ◇ *His essay attacks a recent exhibition of nineteenth-century French painting for its focus on form.* **7** [C] a way of spelling or pronouncing a word that shows, for example, if it is plural or in a particular tense: *'Mice' is an example of an irregular plural form.* ◇ *Only working-class speakers use these forms with any great frequency.* ◇ **+ noun** *In this study, word form production was defined as the ability to recall and spell target word forms correctly.* **8** [C] the body or shape of a person or animal: *The Minoans of Ancient Crete adapted Egyptian conventions for depicting the human form.* **9** [U, C] (*especially BrE*) the usual or correct method for doing sth: *The request was made more for form's sake than out of any real hope or expectation of its being granted.* ◇ *The film is set in an eighteenth-century Spanish Roman Catholic country with all its elaborate social forms.* **10** [C] **~ (of sth)** a fixed order of words: *Both parties have agreed the form of words they wish to be inserted into the settlement.*

IDM **take ˈform** to gradually develop: *The book also provides an analysis of the global context in which US feminism took form.*

▸ ADJECTIVE + FORM **other • different, alternative • various • certain • particular, specific • general • common • standard • popular • dominant • distinctive • distinct • new • modern • early** *Younger women were ahead of the younger men in their adoption of a more standard form of English.* ◇ *In its earliest form, Christianity was a movement within Judaism.* | **simple • basic • traditional • original • pure • extreme • complex** *In its simplest form, the cycle consists of two phases.*

▸ VERB + FORM **adopt • determine • develop • create, produce** *These factors combined to create a peculiarly British form of Judaism and Jewish identity.* | **represent • constitute • introduce • describe • identify** *At the end of World War II, radio and movies constituted the principal form of entertainment.* | **take, assume • give** *Both kings gave form and substance to the idea that Wales should be regarded as a single political unit.* | **complete, fill in/out • sign** *Then the GP is sent a form to fill in to confirm the patient's disability.*

▸ FORM OF + NOUN **organization • government • governance • regulation • communication • expression • representation • life • knowledge • control • cooperation • engagement, participation • behaviour • discrimination • violence • resistance • energy • power • activity** *Some behaviourists claimed that any form of behaviour was learned.*

form² /fɔːm; *NAmE* fɔːrm/ *verb* **1** *linking verb* **+ noun** to be sth: *Each person is not an isolated individual, but forms part of a wider group.* ◇ *Agriculture formed the basis of the economy.* **2** [I, T] (especially of natural things) to gradually appear or develop; to make sth gradually appear or develop: *A small blood clot may have formed.* ◇ **~ sth** *Granite is a plutonic rock formed deep in the Earth.* ◇ **~ sth from sth** *Each of these structures is formed from many individual molecules.* ◇ **~ sth of sth** *The planets in the solar system are formed of heavy elements created in the interior of a star.* **3** [T, I] **~ (sth)** to think of an idea in your mind; to be thought of in the mind: *She argues that human beings should be free to form opinions, and to express their opinions without reserve.* ◇ *In later adulthood, these attitudes may be less flexible than in earlier years when attitudes and beliefs are still forming.* **4** [T, I] **~ (sth)** to establish a relationship between people; (of a relationship) to be established between people: *Some researchers have argued that the Internet improves people's ability to form new close relationships.* ◇ *A bond does form and they often feel closer to each other after the experience.* **5** [T, I] **~ (sth)** to start a group of people, such as an organization, a committee, etc; to come together in a group of this kind: *The rebels attempted to form an alliance with the Scots.* ◇ *Disabled veterans groups formed after World War I and World War II.* ◇ *Team-building exercises were helping the newly formed groups to get to know each other.* **6** [I, T] to make sth with a particular shape; to make sth have a particular shape: *There were reports of long queues forming at some polling stations.* ◇ **~ sth** *Deep clouds form a broad line from the central Pacific to the horizon.* ◇ **~ sth into sth** *The moth collects the pollen and forms it into a ball.* **7** [T, I] to move or arrange people or objects so that they are in a group with a particular shape; to become arranged in a group like this: **~ sb/sth** *I asked the students to form groups of four.* ◇ **~ (sth) into sth** *Clusters of galaxies are still forming into superclusters.* **8** [T] to make a word or a particular form of a word: **~ sth** *Initially children are very good at forming the past tense correctly.* ◇ **~ sth from sth** *The word laser is an acronym formed from 'light amplification by stimulated emission of radiation'.* **9** [T] **~ sth** to have an influence on the way that sth develops SYN MOULD² (1): *He offers an* *account of how character may be formed as a result of early experiences.*

▸ FORM + NOUN **group • unit • barrier** *Thomson concluded that the Chinese in Thailand do not form a distinct political group.* ◇ *The mineral usually forms groups of needle-shaped crystals.* | **part, component • basis, foundation • core** *Many of these skills have formed the foundation of mental health nursing for a long time.* | **structure • network • rock • deposit • soil • ring, band • layer • compound • cluster • complex • bond • ion • molecule** *Earth washed down from the hills has formed deep deposits.* | **intention • belief • opinion • judgement • expectation** *Advertising is meant to contribute to the target audience forming a positive intention to buy a brand.* | **relationship • friendship • partnership • alliance • bond** *He also formed close friendships with political radicals.* | **alliance • coalition • partnership • union • committee • company • government • group • unit** *A special unit was formed within the Cabinet Office.*

▸ PHRASE **newly formed** *Seawater, driven by convection, circulates within the newly formed rock.*

for·mal /ˈfɔːml; *NAmE* ˈfɔːrml/ *adj.* **1** following strict rules of how to do sth; suitable for an official occasion: *Venice issued the first set of formal rules relating to diplomacy in the thirteenth century.* ◇ *For this reason, Koreans are very formal in business relations.* ◇ *In Western culture, a firm handshake is the expected formal way of greeting somebody.* OPP INFORMAL (1) **2** (of speech or writing) suitable for official or serious situations: *The judges tended to use the more formal term 'judicial interview'.* ◇ *Slang terms are expressions not used in formal speech.* OPP INFORMAL (5) **3** (of education or training) received in a school, college or university rather than gained just through practical experience: *Khrushchev was a self-made man with little formal education.* OPP INFORMAL (4) **4** concerned with the form or structure of sth rather than its content: *The essay examines the formal structure of tragedy.* **5** concerned only with following rules: *Many such cases go undefended, or are defended only in a formal manner.*

▸ FORMAL + NOUN **rules • requirement • procedure • mechanism • institution • notice • charge • agreement • approval • recognition** *They often have little confidence in their country's formal institutions.* ◇ *He was arrested and detained without any formal charges for almost a year.* | **education • training • schooling • qualifications** *People now spend longer in full-time education and many more obtain formal qualifications.*

for·mal·ity /fɔːˈmæləti; *NAmE* fɔːrˈmæləti/ *noun* (*pl.* **-ies**) **1** [C, usually pl.] a thing that you must do as a formal or official part of a legal process, a social situation, etc: *Asylum seekers may not be in a position to comply with the legal formalities for entry.* ◇ **~ of sth** *the formalities of business etiquette* **2** [C, usually sing.] a thing that you must do as part of an official process, but which has little meaning and will not affect what happens: *The granting of a licence is automatic and a mere formality.* **3** [U] **~ (of sth)** correct and formal behaviour: *In choosing which speech forms to use, speakers assess the relative formality or informality of the context.* ◇ *Levels of formality varied according to the relationships between interviewer and interviewee.*

for·mal·ize (*BrE also* **-ise**) /ˈfɔːməlaɪz; *NAmE* ˈfɔːrməlaɪz/ *verb* **1 ~ sth** to make an arrangement, a plan or a relationship official: *The 1924 Constitution formalized the creation of the federal Union of Soviet Socialist Republics.* **2 ~ sth** to give sth a fixed structure or form by introducing rules: *The emphasis in 'Syntactic Structures' (Chomsky, 1957) was on the development of a formalized grammar.* ■ **for·mal·iza·tion, -isa·tion** /ˌfɔːməlaɪˈzeɪʃn; *NAmE* ˌfɔːrmələˈzeɪʃn/ *noun* [U] **~ (of sth)** *A further summit in Paris in 1974 led to the formalization of the previously informal European Council Summit meetings.*

for·mal·ly /ˈfɔːməli; *NAmE* ˈfɔːrməli/ *adv.* **1** officially: *In April 1744, Louis XV formally declared war on Austria.* ◇ *The supremacy of the House of Commons over the House of Lords was formally recognized in the Parliament Act of 1911.* OPP INFORMALLY (1) **2** in the way that sth appears or is presented: *Formally, the distinction between town and country workers was clear, but in practice there was some overlap.* ◇ *His analysis was also formally identical to the account by the political philosopher, Thomas Hobbes.* **3 ~ trained/educated/taught** trained, etc. in a school, college or other institution: *Never formally trained in science, Faraday developed his own methodology.*

for·mat¹ AWL /ˈfɔːmæt; *NAmE* ˈfɔːrmæt/ *noun* [C, U] **1** the general arrangement, plan or design of sth: **~ (of sth)** *The format of the show is so successful that it has been exported around the world.* ◇ **~ for sth** *The format for the assessment is usually a face-to-face interview.* ◇ **in ~** *This is a method that has changed little in format since 1989.* **2** a particular way in which data is processed, stored or displayed; the form in which information or recordings are made available: *The library archives materials in many formats, ranging from paper to film to a wide range of digital formats.* ◇ **in... ~** *Simply providing information in electronic format does not guarantee uptake in routine clinical care.* **3 ~ (of sth)** the shape, size and appearance of a book, magazine, etc: *The format, content and style of the two publications are entirely different.*

for·mat² AWL /ˈfɔːmæt; *NAmE* ˈfɔːrmæt/ *verb* (**-tt-**) **1 ~ sth** to prepare a computer disk so that data can be recorded on it: *Floppy disks had to be formatted before they could be used.* **2 ~ sth (to do sth)** to arrange text, etc. in a particular way on a page or screen: *There are also special advertising supplements that are formatted to look like feature journalism.*

for·ma·tion /fɔːˈmeɪʃn; *NAmE* fɔːrˈmeɪʃn/ *noun* **1** [U] the action of forming sth; the process of being formed: *Soil formation usually takes at least a century.* ◇ **~ of sth** *The presence of contaminants can often prevent the formation of crystals suitable for X-ray analysis.* **2** [C] a thing that has been formed, especially in a particular place or in a particular way: *The rock is one of the most conspicuous formations in the Grand Canyon.* ◇ *Vast amounts of hydrocarbons are distributed in various geological formations, such as oil shales and oil sands.* **3** [C, U] a particular arrangement or pattern of people or things: *It took a great deal of training to hold together such an extremely tight formation in battle.* ◇ **in ~** *In order to stay in formation, soldiers tried not to run until they came within the reach of enemy missiles.*

▸ NOUN + FORMATION **cloud • rock** *He made innumerable sketches in order to capture phenomena like changing cloud formations with absolute fidelity.* | **soil • star • bone • clot • tumour • synapse • bond • identity** *Bone formation is an essential process for skeletal development.*

▸ VERB + FORMATION **cause, induce • trigger, initiate • stimulate • favour, promote, facilitate, encourage • catalyse • inhibit, block • prevent • suppress** *Increased precipitation caused the formation of a shallow lake in Death Valley.* ◇ *The government actively encouraged the formation of business groups in China.*

▸ FORMATION OF + NOUN **alliance • clot • ice • deposit • aggregate • compound • bond** *The start of the Cold War was not simply the formation of military alliances.*

for·ma·tive /ˈfɔːmətɪv; *NAmE* ˈfɔːrmətɪv/ *adj.* [only before noun] **1** having an important and lasting influence on the development of sth or of sb's character: *In these formative years, Marx encountered the other great intellectual influences of his life.* ◇ *Mahler had been a formative influence on Soviet composers like Shostakovich and Schnittke.* ◇ *a formative stage/period/phase* **2** connected with a person's development: *Formative assessment is the regular and ongoing assessment during a course of study.*

F

for·mer¹ /ˈfɔːmə(r); *NAmE* ˈfɔːrmər/ *adj.* [only before noun] **1** that used to exist in earlier times: *Most of the former British colonies experienced a relatively smooth transition to independence.* ◇ *Within the countries of the former Soviet Union, the Kyrgyz Republic has been a pioneer in reforming the system of health care finance.* **2** that used to have a particular position or status in the past: *The film features former vice president Al Gore performing a vividly illustrated lecture on global warming.* **3 the former...** used to refer to the first of two things or people mentioned: *The former option would be much more sensible.* ➲ *compare* LATTER¹ (2)

F

for·mer² /ˈfɔːmə(r); *NAmE* ˈfɔːrmər/ *pron.* **the former** (*pl.* **the former**) the first of two things or people mentioned: *Influencers can be internal or external to the client firm. An example of the former could be an engineer with specialist knowledge of competitive offers.* ➲ *compare* LATTER²

for·mer·ly /ˈfɔːməli; *NAmE* ˈfɔːrmərli/ *adv.* in earlier times: *Fjords are found in many formerly glaciated coastlines across both hemispheres.* ◇ *By this time, large populations of cyanobacteria (formerly known as blue-green algae) were growing in colonies.*

for·mid·able /ˈfɔːmɪdəbl; fəˈmɪdəbl; *NAmE* ˈfɔːrmɪdəbl; fərˈmɪdəbl/ *adj.* if people, things or situations are **formidable**, you feel fear and/or respect for them, because they are impressive or powerful, or because they seem very difficult: *Large multicellular parasites represent a formidable challenge to the immune system.* ◇ *a formidable obstacle/barrier/task* ◇ *This degree of national commitment made Britain a formidable opponent in the second half of the eighteenth century.*

for·mula AWL /ˈfɔːmjələ; *NAmE* ˈfɔːrmjələ/ *noun* (*pl.* **for·mu·lae** /ˈfɔːmjəliː; *NAmE* ˈfɔːrmjəliː/ or **for·mu·las**) HELP The plural **formulae** used to be preferred in scientific writing, but **formulas** is now used just as frequently. **1** (*mathematics*) a series of letters, numbers or symbols that represent a rule or law: *Balmer discovered that these frequencies could be described by some rather simple mathematical formulae.* ◇ *The following formula is used to calculate the PPP exchange rate:...* ◇ **~ for sth** *The formula for heat conduction is given below.* **2 ~ (of/for sth)** (*chemistry*) letters and symbols that show the parts of a chemical COMPOUND: *The alkanes are a class of compounds all with the general formula C_nH_{2n+2}.* **3** a particular method of doing or achieving sth: **~ for doing sth** *The president addressed the nation, proposing a new formula for ending the war.* ◇ **~ (for sth)** *These students subscribe to the conventional formula for success: obtain a high-school degree, a college diploma, and then a good job.* ◇ *The international mediators were too wedded to the traditional peace formula that had been employed in other countries.* **4** a list of the things that sth is made from, giving the amount of each substance to use: *The number of herbs in a herbal formula can range from 1 to over 20.*

for·mu·la·ic /ˌfɔːmjuˈleɪɪk; *NAmE* ˌfɔːrmjuˈleɪɪk/ *adj.* made up of fixed patterns of words or ideas: *O'Keeffe et al. argue that formulaic sequences improve fluency, since they have phonological unity.* ◇ *Formulaic TV films and documentaries often subsidize more creative independent work.*

for·mu·late AWL /ˈfɔːmjuleɪt; *NAmE* ˈfɔːrmjuleɪt/ *verb* **1 ~ sth** to create or prepare sth carefully, giving particular attention to the details: *The Governing Council is responsible for formulating monetary policy.* ◇ *The concept of Third Cinema was originally formulated by Fernando Solanas and Octavio Getino.* ◇ *to formulate a hypothesis/theory/principle* **2 ~ sth** to express your ideas in carefully chosen words: *The information was used to formulate questions for the questionnaire.*

for·mu·la·tion AWL /ˌfɔːmjuˈleɪʃn; *NAmE* ˌfɔːrmjuˈleɪʃn/ *noun* **1** [U, C] the act of creating or preparing sth carefully, giving particular attention to the details; something that has been created in this way: *The chief executive officer has a role to play in strategy formulation.* ◇ **~ of sth** *These qualitative studies are intended to assist the formulation of research hypotheses.* ◇ *Recent formulations of the theory suggest that friendship and its attendant positive emotions do much to shape peer norms.* **2** [C] a medical drug that has been prepared in a particular way: *This substance is widely used in pharmaceutical formulations as a disintegrant for capsules and tablets.*

forth /fɔːθ; *NAmE* fɔːrθ/ *adv.* (*literary* except in particular idioms) **1** away from a place; out: *An enormous explosion of creativity burst forth in the city.* ◇ *On February 1, 1960, four young black freshmen in Greensboro set forth on a historic journey.* **2** so as to be known or brought into view; out: *At the heart of Burke's thinking was a rejection of the idea set forth by Rousseau and others.* IDM *see* BACK¹

forth·com·ing AWL /ˌfɔːθˈkʌmɪŋ; *NAmE* ˌfɔːrθˈkʌmɪŋ/ *adj.* **1** [only before noun] going to happen, be published, etc. very soon: *The goal of the campaign is to encourage voter turnout at the forthcoming elections.* ◇ *Oqvist is the author of the forthcoming book, 'Virtual Shadows: Your Privacy in the Information Society'.* **2** [not before noun] ready or made available when needed: *Training will be provided, although none will be forthcoming until the organization is formally accredited.* ◇ *Such cooperation may not readily be forthcoming.* **3** [not before noun] willing to give information about sth: *It may be that GPs are less forthcoming in consultations where they have reservations about their own ability.*

for·tu·nate /ˈfɔːtʃənət; *NAmE* ˈfɔːrtʃənət/ *adj.* having or bringing an advantage, an opportunity or a piece of good luck: *With such material to hand, the historian studying the time of Alexander is in a very fortunate position.* ◇ **~ to do sth** *He was fortunate to escape a more serious charge of tax evasion.* ◇ **~ in sth** *Dickens proved to be fortunate in his choice of journal.* ◇ **it is ~ (for sb) (that...)** *It is fortunate that many museum specimens are stored in ethanol, an ideal preservative for DNA.* OPP UNFORTUNATE

for·tu·nate·ly /ˈfɔːtʃənətli; *NAmE* ˈfɔːrtʃənətli/ *adv.* by good luck: *Fortunately, papyrus endures well in a hot, dry environment, as in the desert sands of Egypt.* ◇ *Fortunately for Elizabeth, however, Mary Stuart's reign in Scotland turned out to be almost as short as Mary Tudor's.* OPP UNFORTUNATELY

for·tune /ˈfɔːtʃuːn; *NAmE* ˈfɔːrtʃən/ *noun* **1** [U] chance or luck, especially in the way it affects people's lives: *He was arrested but had the good fortune to be acquitted of all charges in court.* **2** [C] a large amount of money: *The wealthier planters had made sufficient fortunes to enable them to retire home.* ◇ *He sustained their operations with millions of dollars from his own family fortune.* **3** [C, usually pl., U] the good and bad things that happen to a person, family, country, etc: *Dramatic shifts in military and political fortunes had taken place on the battlefields of Europe.* ◇ *Aristotle identified reversals of fortune as a basic plot element in tragedy.* IDM *see* SEEK

forum /ˈfɔːrəm/ *noun* (*pl.* **forums** or **fora** /ˈfɔːrə/) **1** a place where people can exchange opinions and ideas on a particular issue; a meeting organized for this purpose: *In international forums such as the WTO, the US strikes a neo-liberal posture.* ◇ **~ for sth** *Schools offer a forum for discussions about civil responsibilities.* ◇ **~ for doing sth** *It is debatable as to whether the courts are the most appropriate forum for deciding questions of the public interest.* **2** an Internet group or website for discussing a particular issue: *There are online forums that can be helpful, particularly for mothers in full-time employment.* ◇ *The sample was sought by posting a notice on a bodybuilding Internet forum.* **3** (in ancient Rome) a public place where meetings were held: *In the middle of this forum is a stone statue of Mercury.*

for·ward¹ /ˈfɔːwəd; *NAmE* ˈfɔːrwərd/ *adv.* **1** (*also* **for·wards** *especially in BrE*) towards a place or position that is in front: *He took several steps forward.* ◇ *A bicycle can stay upright only if it is moving forwards.* OPP BACK¹, BACKWARDS **2** towards a good result: *Recently, an important step forward has been achieved.* ◇ *Greater investment in public health care is the most efficient way forward.* OPP BACKWARDS **3** towards the future: *Tennyson's poems are almost always happier looking back than looking forward.* ◇ *The central motor which drives the story forward is Darcy's sexual attraction to Elizabeth.* **4** earlier; sooner: *The general election, originally scheduled for 2002, was brought forward to 1999.*
IDM **ˌgoing/ˌmoving ˈforward** (*rather informal*) in the future, starting from now: *Going forward, we need continuing studies of individual risks.* ◇ *It is the key piece of policy for the energy sector moving forward.* ➲ *more at* BACKWARDS

for·ward² /ˈfɔːwəd; *NAmE* ˈfɔːrwərd/ *adj.* **1** [only before noun] directed or moving towards the front: *The rocket emits light signals in both the forward and backward directions.* ◇ *It might seem that wheels should present little or no resistance to forward motion.* **2** connected with the future: *Part of a successful pain management programme is forward planning.* ◇ *The British economy is further forward in the processes of change than many other countries.* ◇ *Forward projections indicated an ever-growing development fund gap.* ➲ *compare* BACKWARD

for·ward³ /ˈfɔːwəd; *NAmE* ˈfɔːrwərd/ *verb* **1 ~ sth (to sb)** to send or pass goods or information to sb: *He immediately forwarded the report to all state departments of health.* **2 ~ sth (to sb)** to send a letter or email on to another place: *They seemed to have forwarded the email to everyone they knew.* **3 ~ sth** to help sth to succeed SYN FURTHER³: *German humanists and English Puritans used Tacitus to forward their own agendas.* **4 ~ sth** to provide sth in support of an argument: *A more nuanced argument is forwarded by Robinson (2001).*

ˈforward-looking *adj.* planning for the future; willing to consider modern ideas and methods: *Investors display forward-looking behaviour.* ◇ *Innovation is more likely to occur in organizations that are forward-looking.*

for·went *past tense of* FORGO

fos·sil /ˈfɒsl; *NAmE* ˈfɑːsl/ *noun* part of an animal or plant that lived thousands of years ago that has turned into rock: *Marine rocks commonly contain plant fossils.* ◇ **+ noun** *The fossil record does not provide a complete or continuous record of evolutionary history.*

ˈfossil fuel *noun* [C, U] fuel such as coal or oil, that was formed over millions of years from dead animals or plants in the ground: *The burning of fossil fuels has caused enormous damage to the environment.* ◇ *Fossil fuel is the most easily and cheaply exploitable form of energy.* ◇ **+ noun** *fossil fuel consumption/energy/reserves* ➲ *compare* BIOMASS (2)

fos·ter¹ /ˈfɒstə(r); *NAmE* ˈfɔːstər; ˈfɑːstər/ *verb* **1 ~ sth** to encourage sth to develop SYN PROMOTE (1): *This approach is intended to foster a sense of community among members.* ◇ *An increased ability to communicate helps to foster collaboration in activities such as research and knowledge sharing.* **2 ~ sb** (*especially BrE*) to take another person's child into your home for a period of time, without becoming the child's legal parent: *Tizard's (1977) research on children adopted from care reported good outcomes compared with those for children who were fostered.* ➲ *compare* ADOPT (3)

fos·ter² /ˈfɒstə(r); *NAmE* ˈfɔːstər; ˈfɑːstər/ *adj.* [only before noun] used with some nouns in connection with the fostering of a child: *Child neglect is a common reason for foster care.* ◇ *The local authority found that the foster mother could not meet the children's long-term needs.*

fought *past tense, past part. of* FIGHT¹

found¹ *past tense, past part. of* FIND¹

found² AWL /faʊnd/ *verb* **1 ~ sth** to start sth, such as an organization or an institution, especially by providing money SYN ESTABLISH (1): *Universal Studios was founded in 1912 in Chicago.* ◇ *After his studies in the West, Hanh returned to Vietnam and founded the School of Youth for Social Service.* **2 ~ sth** to be the first to start building and living in a town or country: *Sao Paulo, founded in 1554 by Jesuits, remained relatively unimportant until the late nineteenth century.* **3** [usually passive] **be founded (on sth)** to be based on sth: *The Union is founded on the principles of liberty, democracy and respect for human rights.* HELP If sth is **well founded**, it is based on good reasons or evidence: *These criticisms are well founded.* ◇ *The refugees need to prove a well-founded fear of persecution.* ➲ *see also* UNFOUNDED

foun·da·tion AWL /faʊnˈdeɪʃn/ *noun* **1** [C] a principle, an idea or a fact that sth is based on and that it grows from: **~ for sth** *This study provides a solid theoretical foundation for further research and development.* ◇ **~ of sth** *Confucianism regarded the family as the foundation of society.* ◇ **lay the ~ (for sth)** *Humanist scholarship laid the foundations for modern philology and the later stages of classical studies.* **2** [U] **~ (of sth)** the act of starting a new organization or institution SYN ESTABLISHMENT (1): *The meeting in Udine led to the foundation of the International Society for Quality Assurance.* **3** [U] **~ (of sth)** the act of being the first to start living in a town or country: *The continued demand to settle in Britain is evidenced by the foundation of two new colonies at the end of the first century AD.* **4** [C] an organization that is established to provide money for a particular purpose, for example for scientific research or charity: *Financial support for much of this work was provided by grants from the National Science Foundation.* **5** [C, usually pl.] **~ (of sth)** a layer of bricks, etc. that forms the solid underground base of a building: *Archaeologists uncovered the foundations of thirteen buildings of diverse function and construction.*
IDM **have no ˈfoundation (in fact) | be without ˈfoundation** to not be based on any facts: *Brock's argument would appear to be without foundation.* ➲ *more at* SHAKE

foun·der AWL /ˈfaʊndə(r)/ *noun* **~ (of sth)** a person who starts an organization, institution, etc. or causes sth to be built: *Murchison was a founder of the Royal Geographical Society.*

four /fɔː(r)/ *number* 4 HELP There are examples of how to use numbers at the entry for **five**.

fourth /fɔːθ; *NAmE* fɔːrθ/ *noun* (*especially NAmE*) = QUARTER (1)

frac·tion /ˈfrækʃn/ *noun* **1 ~ (of sth)** a small part or amount of sth: *Only a tiny fraction of this information flow reaches our brain, and even less is consciously perceived.* HELP If **fraction** is used with a plural noun, the verb is usually plural: *Only a fraction of the individuals have been vaccinated against the disease.* If it is used with a singular noun that represents a group of people, the verb can be singular or plural in British English, but is usually singular in American English: *This small fraction of the population (5%) is able to grow, process and serve enough food to meet the needs of the whole country.* **2** a division of a number, for example ⅝: *A rational number is any number that can be expressed as a fraction having the form p/q, where p and q are integers.* ➲ *compare* INTEGER **3** (*chemistry*) a quantity of liquid that has been collected as a result of a process that separates the parts of a liquid mixture: *The*

F

solution was centrifuged at 18 000 rpm for 20 min, and the supernatant (soluble fraction) was stored.

frac·tion·al /ˈfrækʃənl/ *adj.* **1** (*chemistry*) connected with the process in which a liquid mixture separates or is separated into its different parts: *Fractional distillation can be used to separate the different hydrocarbons in crude oil according to their boiling points.* **2** (*mathematics*) of or in fractions: *For gases that make up a large proportion of the atmosphere, fractional or percentage concentrations are used.*

frac·ture¹ /ˈfræktʃə(r)/ *noun* [C, U] a break or crack in a bone or other hard substance; the fact of sth breaking: *A combination of risk factors multiplies the risk of sustaining a fracture.* ◇ *a hip/vertebral/skull/pelvic/rib fracture* ◇ **~ of sth** *Ground movements could cause fracture of the pipe.*

frac·ture² /ˈfræktʃə(r)/ *verb* **1** [T, I] **~ (sth)** to cause a break or crack in a bone or other hard substance; to break or crack in this way: *Some life events, such as fracturing a hip, have the potential to change one's mobility profile suddenly and substantially.* ◇ *These thick rods can fracture spontaneously when a crack in the rod reaches a critical length.* **2** [T, I] **~ (sth)** to split a society, group or organization into several parts so that it no longer functions or exists; to split in this way: *The pre-war global Jewish community had been fractured by many divisions.* ◇ *By the early 1960s, the broad Cold War consensus was beginning to fracture.*

frac·tured /ˈfræktʃəd; *NAmE* ˈfræktʃərd/ *adj.* [usually before noun] **1** broken or CRACKED: *Deposition of salts in fractured rocks may occur.* ◇ *A fractured rib can be the cause of the lacerated vessel.* **2** (of a society, group or organization) split into several parts so that it no longer functions or exists: *The venture was almost immediately a source of rivalries among the fractured elite of the city.*

fra·gile /ˈfrædʒaɪl; *NAmE* ˈfrædʒl/ *adj.* **1** easily broken or damaged: *The elderly have fragile skin and veins which may rupture on injection.* ◇ *These are some of the most fragile ecosystems because sandy soils are more vulnerable to wind erosion.* **2** weak and uncertain; easily destroyed or spoilt: *The corporatist economy is a fragile balance between competing interests.* ◇ *The priority was to maintain the fragile peace between colonists and Indians.* ■ **fra·gil·ity** /frəˈdʒɪləti/ *noun* [U] *Osteoporosis leads to bone fragility and increased fracture risk.* ◇ **~ of sth** *This was precautionary behaviour, triggered by the increased fragility of the global financial system.*

frag·ment¹ /ˈfrægmənt/ *noun* **1** a small part of sth that has broken off: *City dust contains vegetative plant fragments, cement, and tyre and brake-lining particles.* ◇ **~ of sth** *During flooding, streams can transport large fragments of rock from their banks.* **2 ~ (of sth)** a small part of sth that comes from sth larger: *We have fragments of his poems in which he attacks conventional religious and ethical beliefs.* HELP In biochemistry, a **fragment** can be a biologically interesting short piece of DNA or other MOLECULE: *The DNA fragments may be complete genes, although they more usually comprise only a portion of one.*

frag·ment² /frægˈment/ *verb* [I, T] to separate into smaller parts; to make sth separate into smaller parts: **~ (into sth)** *Around this time, large estates started to fragment into individual manors.* ◇ **~ sth** *Globalization tends to fragment existing political communities and national identities.*

frag·men·tary /ˈfrægməntri; *NAmE* ˈfrægmənteri/ *adj.* **1** made up of small, separate parts that are not connected: *Although people have known this for centuries, knowledge remained fragmentary until comparatively recently.* **2** made up of small pieces that do not form a complete whole: *Fragmentary diaries survive for the years 1838–41.* ◇ *Some of these writings have survived only in very fragmentary form.*

frag·men·ta·tion /ˌfrægmenˈteɪʃn/ *noun* [U] the process by which sth separates or is separated into smaller parts: *There is clear evidence that globalization and fragmentation are transforming political communities across the world.* ◇ **~ of sth** *Belts of the same age are now scattered all over the earth's land surface because of fragmentation of supercontinents.*

frag·ment·ed /frægˈmentɪd/ *adj.* separated into smaller parts: *Most automobile factories involve highly fragmented jobs on assembly lines.* ◇ *The application of reason and science to politics has highlighted the fragmented nature of the political community.*

frame¹ /freɪm/ *noun* **1** [C] a strong border or structure of wood, metal, etc. that holds a picture, door, piece of glass, etc. in position: *The window frames and the door were painted white.* **2** [C] the supporting structure of a piece of furniture, a building, a vehicle, etc. that gives it its shape: *Most houses were built of wood, with light frames but often heavy roofs.* ◇ *All combatants carried large shields made of ox hide stretched over a wooden frame.* **3** [sing.] **~ (of sth)** the general ideas or structure that form the background to sth: *He makes his argument using a theoretical frame of cognitive linguistics.* ➲ *see also* SAMPLING FRAME, TIME FRAME **4** [C] one of the single photographs that a film or video is made of: *Film is usually projected at a rate of 24 frames per second.* **5** [C] = FRAME OF REFERENCE (2)

IDM ˌ**frame of** ˈ**mind** a particular state or condition of your feelings: *It is important to adopt a frame of mind that is aware of any personal bias that might influence one's results.*

frame² /freɪm/ *verb* **1** [usually passive] to put or make a frame or border around sth: **be framed** *Clark is also concerned with the various ways in which a painting is framed.* ◇ *He's framed off-centre, at the top of the picture.* **2 ~ sth** to create and develop sth such as a plan, a system or a set of rules: *He framed a plan for the establishment of an industrial college for African Americans.* **3 ~ sth** to use a set of ideas or beliefs as the background to a discussion or examination of a subject: *She frames her discussion in the vocabulary of Freudian psychoanalysis.* **4 ~ sth** to express sth in a particular way: *The questions should be very precisely framed and carefully worded.* ■ **framed** *adj.* (often in compounds)*There were framed prints and photographs on the wall.* ◇ *A row of timber-framed shops fronting on to Watling Street was replaced in the third century.*

ˌ**frame of** ˈ**reference** *noun* (*pl.* **frames of reference**) (*also* ˈ**reference frame**) **1** a particular set of beliefs, ideas or experiences that affects how a person understands or judges sth: *The problem with questions that are very general is that they lack a frame of reference.* ◇ **~ for doing sth** *Other writers, however, argue for the development of a single frame of reference for studying organizations (Pfeffer, 1993; Donaldson, 2001).* **2** (*also* **frame**) (*physics*) a system of GEOMETRIC AXES which can be used for defining the size, position or movement of sth: *The astronaut was in an inertial frame of reference while cruising at steady speed to the distant planet.*

frame·work AWL /ˈfreɪmwɜːk; *NAmE* ˈfreɪmwɜːrk/ *noun* **1** a set of beliefs, ideas or principles that is used as the basis for examining or understanding sth: *Using a comprehensive analytical framework, this article presents a review of the literature on the topic.* ◇ **~ for sth** *Several attempts have been made to provide theoretical frameworks for making strategic choices.* ◇ **~ of sth** *His framework of cultural analysis draws strength from its ability to offer insights into the way in which different cultures communicate.* **2** a system of rules, laws or agreements that controls the way that sth works in business, politics or society: **~ (for sth)** *A legal framework for corporations* *had been established and property rights were well protected.* ◇ **~ of sth** *Capitalism requires trust in order for cooperation and competition to develop within a framework of rules.* ➲ thesaurus note *at* THEORY

▸ ADJECTIVE + FRAMEWORK **general** ◆ **new** ◆ **broad** ◆ **existing** ◆ **basic** ◆ **common** ◆ **comprehensive** *The 1995 Directive established a general framework for regulating how personal data are processed by organizations.* | **useful** ◆ **theoretical** ◆ **conceptual** ◆ **analytical** *Scientists began to establish a conceptual framework that would organize scientific thinking about the earth's tectonic processes.* | **national** ◆ **international** ◆ **legal** ◆ **legislative** ◆ **regulatory** ◆ **institutional** ◆ **ethical** *An existing international framework is already available with regard to the fight against terrorism.*

▸ VERB + FRAMEWORK **provide, present, propose** ◆ **offer** ◆ **develop** ◆ **establish, create** ◆ **use, apply, adopt** *The Mayo Clinic has developed a conceptual framework of how patients and health care workers interact to reduce risk.*

fran·chise /ˈfræntʃaɪz/ *noun* **1** [sing., U] the right to vote in a country's elections: *Neither Gladstone nor Disraeli believed in a fully democratic franchise.* ◇ *Whilst Britain was introducing the secret ballot and extending the franchise at home, it was imposing colonial rule abroad.* **2** [C, U] formal permission given by a company to sb who wants to sell its goods or services in a particular area; formal permission given by a government to sb who wants to operate a public service as a business: *In the UK, the government grants franchises to run railway services.* ◇ **+ noun** *However, franchise agreements are not just used in the fast food sector.* **3** [C] a business or service run under franchise: *The company has over 25 000 restaurants in over 100 countries and about 80% are franchises.*

frank /fræŋk/ *adj.* **1** (**frank·er, frank·est**) (**more frank** is also common) honest and direct in what you say, sometimes in a way that other people might not like: *The report offered a brutally frank assessment of the nature of the problems.* ◇ *Public authorities need to be able to obtain full and frank legal advice in confidence.* ◇ **~ about sth** *Cultural issues may prevent patients from being frank about their complaints.* **2** (*medical*) that cannot be confused with sth else; obvious: *The oesophagus may show evidence of frank ulceration.* ■ **frank·ness** *noun* [U] *He speaks with admirable frankness about the shortcomings of the programme.*

frank·ly /ˈfræŋkli/ *adv.* **1** in an honest and direct way that people might not like: *Patients need to feel that they can talk openly and frankly with you.* ◇ *In his 'Critique of Dialectical Reason', he presented a frankly materialist view of human nature.* **2** used to show that you are being honest about sth, even though people might not like what you are saying: *Quite frankly, it is not a significant issue.*

fraud /frɔːd/ *noun* **1** [U, C] the crime of deceiving sb in order to get money or goods illegally: *The rise in online fraud and identity theft has left many customers feeling vulnerable.* ◇ *Consent is invalid if it is obtained by fraud.* ◇ *He committed a cheque fraud for which he was sentenced to six years' imprisonment.* **2** [C] a person who pretends to have qualities, abilities, etc. that they do not really have in order to deceive other people: *She denounces her sister as a fraud.*

free¹ /friː/ *adj.* (**freer** /ˈfriːə(r)/, **freest** /ˈfriːɪst/) **1** not restricted or controlled: *The right to free speech is the cornerstone of any democratic society.* ◇ *The first free elections took place in the country in 1991.* ◇ *The Single European Act of 1986 sought to eliminate barriers to the free movement of goods, services and capital.* HELP If sb/sth is in **free fall**, it is falling without anything to stop or slow its fall: *In Figure 1.3, the body is in free fall, so throughout the motion its speed is increasing.* **2** not under the control or in the power of sb else; able to do what you want: *Fundamental human rights are founded upon recognition of the principle that all persons are free.* ◇ *Appiah notes: 'We had adopted Pan-African socialism and pledged to set our countries free as quickly as possible.'* ◇ *Diversity of academic inquiry should permit free choice of research partners—including industrial partners.* ◇ **~ to do sth** *The majority decision supported the view that people should be free to do as they wish with their money and property.* **3** (of a person) not a prisoner or SLAVE: *We know that in some communities there existed more than one slave for every two free men.* **4** costing nothing: *The Scottish government decided in 2001 that personal care should be free at the point of use.* **5** clear; not blocked: *During the past fifty years, society has changed dramatically because of the free flow of information across all boundaries.* **6 ~ from/of sth** not containing or affected by sth harmful or unpleasant: *The current study included only participants who were free from pre-existing diseases.* ◇ *This is an important aspect of ethics, but it is not completely free of problems.* **7 -free** (in adjectives) without the thing mentioned: *The average ice-free period is roughly two weeks longer than it was five decades ago.* ◇ *The review's objective was to quantify the effect of smoke-free workplaces.* **8** (*physics, chemistry*) not contained in an atom, a MOLECULE or a COMPOUND: *The electric fields in wires cause the free electrons to move.* ◇ *In acid oils, the amount of free fatty acid (FFA) could vary from 3 to 40%.* **9** (of a translation) not exact but giving the general meaning: *The poem is a free translation of an anonymous poem that influenced his early work.* ➲ *compare* LITERAL (2), LOOSE (4)

IDM **get, have, etc. a free ˈhand** to get, have, etc. the opportunity to do what you want to do and to make your own decisions: *The nobles had a generally free hand in supervising their serfs so long as they did not abuse their privileges too notoriously.* ➲ *more at* REIN

free² /friː/ *verb* **~ sb** to allow sb to leave somewhere they have been kept against their will SYN RELEASE¹ (1): *Slaves were freed in the Danish and French colonies between 1848 and 1849.* ◇ *Karamanlis quickly freed political prisoners and legalized all political parties.*

PHR V **ˈfree sb/sth from sth** to remove sth that is unpleasant or not wanted from sb/sth SYN RID STH/SB OF STH/SB: *Improvements in farming technologies freed some people from the need to produce food.* ◇ *In these novels, we often see women freed from traditional gender constraints.*

free³ /friː/ *adv.* **1** (*also* ˌ**free of ˈcharge**) without payment: *Instances where medical services were provided free by an employer were not considered in this analysis.* ◇ *Employees have the opportunity to use the company's holiday homes free of charge.* **2** away from or out of a position in which sb/sth is stuck or trapped: *Large multinational businesses have broken free from the constraints imposed by national planning.* **3** (of an animal) without being stopped from going where it likes; not tied to anything or kept in a cage: *The defendant allowed an untrained Alsatian dog to roam free in his scrapyard at night as a guard dog.*

free·dom /ˈfriːdəm/ *noun* **1** [U, C] **~ (of sth)** the right to do or say what you want without anyone stopping you: *The constitutional right to freedom of speech guarantees that people can say whatever they please.* ◇ *They reaffirmed their belief in those fundamental freedoms which are the foundation of justice and peace in the world.* **2** [U] the state of being able to do what you want, without anything stopping you: **~ of sth** *The UK's harmonization with the rest of Europe brings freedom of movement on the one hand, and security on the other.* ◇ **~ to do sth** *It is feared that escalating tuition fees will infringe on students' freedom to choose tertiary education.* ◇ **~ in doing sth** *The subsidiary company has a certain degree of freedom in shaping its own destiny.* **3** [U] the state of not being a prisoner or SLAVE: *Some slaves had a greater chance of achieving freedom than others.* **4** [U] **~ (from sth)** the state of not being ruled by a foreign country: *In 1947 India* *won its freedom from the British Crown.* **5** [U] **~ from sth** the state of not being affected by the thing mentioned: *For the first time in American history, the government tried to guarantee freedom from fear and want.* IDM *see* MANOEUVRE[1]

▸ ADJECTIVE + FREEDOM **fundamental • individual, personal • democratic, civic • political • religious • academic • artistic** *Strong social bonds, while enabling social interactions, carry the potential of limiting individual freedom.* ◇ *Religious freedom has been enshrined in the American Constitution since the early days of the state.* | **complete, absolute, perfect • economic • sexual** *Independence cannot mean that the supervisory agency has complete freedom to act.* ◇ *Sisters and girlfriends perceived that the boys had more sexual freedom.*

▸ VERB + FREEDOM **constrict, constrain, limit, curtail • guarantee • grant • preserve, protect, defend • respect • threaten • win, secure, gain • exercise • value** *Article 24 of the 1982 Turkish Constitution guarantees freedom of religious expression.* ◇ *To advance democracy, people have to value the freedoms that define it.* | **enjoy, have • allow** *She is now enjoying the freedom of being able to choose when and how she wants to work.*

▸ FREEDOM OF + NOUN **speech, expression • will • thought • conscience • religion • the press** *The court held that any restraints on freedom of expression called for the most careful scrutiny.* | **movement • choice • action** *In the absence of benefits, and assuming they have freedom of choice, workers are unlikely to maintain their trade union membership.*

ˌfreedom of inforˈmation *noun* [U] the right to see any information that a government has about people and organizations: **+ noun** *A Freedom of Information Act came into effect in 2005.* ◇ *Freedom of information legislation allows journalists to view any information held by public bodies that affect the public interest.*

ˌfree ˈenergy *noun* [U] (*physics*) a measure of the amount of energy that is available to perform work in a system: *In order to drive the engine, the reaction must produce sufficient free energy.*

free·ly /ˈfriːli/ *adv.* **1** without anyone trying to prevent or control sth: *What is most important in Odysseus's case is whether he acts freely or voluntarily.* ◇ *Consumers freely choose between the various options on offer.* ◇ *Sayle made the program's source code freely available on the web.* **2** without anything stopping the movement or flow of sth: *Whilst most species move freely between reefs, the corals themselves are often relatively immobile.* ◇ *The idea is that goods and services will flow freely between countries.* **3** in an honest way without worrying about what people will say or do: *The members were encouraged to talk freely about their beliefs and doubts.* **4** in a willing and generous way: *De Tocqueville was impressed by the willingness of the people to give freely of their own funds for social improvements (Probst, 1962).*

ˌfree ˈmarket *noun* an economic system in which the price of goods and services is affected by supply and demand rather than controlled by a government: *Changes in supply and demand conditions in the free market can lead to major changes in the price level.* ◇ **+ noun** *a free market economy/system*

ˌfree ˈradical *noun* (*chemistry*) an atom or group of atoms that has an ELECTRON that is not part of a pair, allowing it to take part easily in chemical reactions. Free radicals in the body are thought to be one of the causes of diseases such as cancer: *An important cause of damage is oxygen free radicals generated in cells.* ⊃ *see also* ANTIOXIDANT

ˌfree ˈtrade *noun* [U] a system of international trade in which there are no limits or taxes on imports and exports: *It was suggested that British politicians and traders wished to see a move away from protectionism towards free trade.* ◇ **+ noun** *36% of respondents also object to the notion of a regional free trade area.*

ˌfree ˈwill *noun* [U] the power to make your own decisions without being controlled by God or FATE: *Positivist theories of crime focus on the offender as determined rather than possessing free will.*

IDM **of your own free ˈwill** because you want to do sth rather than because sb has told or forced you to do it: *A person should be morally responsible for what he does of his own free will.*

freeze /friːz/ *verb* (**froze** /frəʊz; *NAmE* froʊz/, **fro·zen** /ˈfrəʊzn; *NAmE* ˈfroʊzn/) **1** [I, T] to become hard, and often turn to ice, as a result of extreme cold; to make sth do this: *Mercury freezes at about -40°C.* ◇ *Water freezes and thaws seasonally, creating stresses within the upper layer of permafrost.* ◇ **~ sth** *A cold spell settled into the Mississippi River Valley in January, freezing the river.* **2** [I] to be very cold; to be so cold that you die: *During the siege, about 700 000 of the population starved or froze to death.* **3** [T] **~ sth** to keep sth at a very low temperature in order to preserve it: *Plasma samples may, unlike whole blood samples, be frozen for long-term storage.* **4** [T] **~ sth** to prevent money, a bank account, etc. from being used by getting a court order: *The activities of 18 NGOs were suspended, their assets frozen, and their equipment impounded.* **5** [T] **~ sth** to hold wages, prices, etc. at a fixed level for a period of time: *Price controls were reimposed and wages were frozen.* **6** [T] **~ sth** to stop a film or video in order to look at a particular image: *Lopes now freezes the shot when Alvaro enters the room.* **7** [T] **~ sth** to stop a process or make it seem to stop: *The static approach of conventional economics freezes time at a moment.* ◇ *Jumping to a conclusion too quickly temporarily freezes the learning process.*

PHR V **ˌfreeze sb ˈout (of sth)** to deliberately make it difficult for sb to take part in sth or join a group: *New entrants may be frozen out of an industry because of the capital requirements necessary to set up business.* **ˌfreeze ˈover** to become completely covered by ice: *When, in 1281, the Thames froze over, five of the arches collapsed under the pressure of the ice.*

freez·ing /ˈfriːzɪŋ/ *adj.* **1** [only before noun] having temperatures that are below 0° Celsius: *Freezing temperatures before pollination did have a negative effect on ovule fertilization.* ◇ *The plant must maintain water transport during freezing conditions to support its evergreen foliage.* **2** extremely cold: *For these unfortunates, Christmas promised only another freezing night in a doorway.*

fre·quency /ˈfriːkwənsi/ *noun* (*pl.* **-ies**) **1** [U, C] **~ (of sth)** the rate at which sth happens or is found: *Climate change may increase the frequency of storms.* ◇ *When dams and levees are built, they reduce the frequency of floods.* ◇ *In a small population, large changes in gene frequency can occur within a few generations.* ◇ *The words have a relatively high frequency in academic texts.* **2** [U] the fact of sth happening often: *The disease occurred with disturbing frequency in military trainees in the 1960s.* **3** [C, U] the rate at which a sound or ELECTROMAGNETIC wave VIBRATES: *The signal has relatively less power at high frequencies.* ◇ **at a ~** *The modulator, transmitter and receiver operated at a carrier frequency of 15 MHz.*

▸ ADJECTIVE + FREQUENCY **high • low** *While large disasters are less likely, their enormous damage more than makes up for their low frequency.* | **increased, increasing • greater • relative • observed • expected** *One of the distinctive features of the past three decades has been the increased frequency of financial crises.*

▸ VERB + FREQUENCY **have • use** *Today, communication satellites use frequencies near 14 GHz.* | **increase • reduce • report • predict • estimate • measure • determine • compare** *Participants were asked to report the frequency of various emotions felt during the previous week.*

fre·quent /ˈfriːkwənt/ *adj.* happening or doing sth often: *Hurricanes are expected to become more frequent, with more intense precipitation.* ◇ *Until 1953, the term Marxism-Leninism-Stalinism was in frequent use.* ◇ *The very young and very old are also frequent attenders at GP surgeries.* ◇ **~ in sb/sth** *Falls are very frequent in older people.* OPP INFREQUENT

fre·quent·ly /ˈfriːkwəntli/ *adv.* often: *Statistical methods are frequently used for data handling and processing.* ◇ *In clinical trials, the most frequently reported side effects include soreness at the injection site and headache.* ◇ *Disagreements between the overseers and the gang labourers occurred frequently.* OPP INFREQUENTLY

fresh /freʃ/ *adj.* (**fresh·er**, **fresh·est**) **1** (usually of food) recently produced or picked and not frozen, dried or preserved in tins or cans: *Eating a balanced diet of fresh fruit and lean meat is expensive.* ◇ *The amount of fresh produce in US supermarkets has expanded dramatically.* ◇ *Highly perishable products, such as meats and fresh flowers, have a much shorter shelf life.* **2** made or experienced recently: *The horrors of post-war hyperinflation were fresh in the memory of the German public and policymakers.* **3** [usually before noun] new or different in a way that adds to or replaces sth: *A fresh approach is required.* ◇ *There is genuine fresh evidence to be considered.* ◇ *Ongoing research can be expected to bring fresh insights.* ◇ *Recently, Chang (2002) has taken a fresh look at the evidence on this issue.* **4** [usually before noun] pleasantly clean, pure or cool: *The hospital environment should smell fresh and have no unpleasant odours.* ◇ *He was kept in bed but getting gradually more fresh air and exercise.* **5** [usually before noun] (of water) containing no salt: *Such a membrane can be used to remove salt from sea water to yield drinkable fresh water.* ➲ *see also* FRESHWATER **6 ~ from sth** having just come from a particular place; having just had a particular experience: *Joseph Rauh began his political career in the summer of 1935, fresh from Harvard Law School.* ■ **fresh·ness** *noun* [U] *The company introduced a foil wrap for its cereals to improve freshness.* ◇ *Their work is hailed through the festival circuit as bringing a freshness to film language.*

fresh·ly /ˈfreʃli/ *adv.* (usually followed by a past participle) used to show that sth has been made, prepared, etc. recently: *The company uses its successful brand name to promote freshly baked food products.*

fresh·water /ˈfreʃwɔːtə(r)/ *adj.* [only before noun] **1** living in water that is not the sea and does not contain salt: *Most people in the Mekong Basin depend on freshwater fish.* **2** having water that does not contain salt: *Lake Victoria in East Africa is the world's second largest freshwater lake.*

fric·tion /ˈfrɪkʃn/ *noun* **1** [U] (*physics*) the RESISTANCE (= the physical force that opposes movement) between surfaces or substances moving against or through each other: *The barrel is coated in oil, which reduces the internal friction.* ◇ *Surface ocean currents are generated by wind friction on the sea surface.* **2** [U, C] disagreement or a lack of friendship among people who have different opinions about sth SYN TENSION (1): **~ between A and B** *The globalization of European regulation may cause friction between the European system and non-EU countries.* ◇ **~ within sth** *The drive for worker control largely bypassed traditional unions, setting off frictions within the labour movement.* ■ **fric·tion·al** /ˈfrɪkʃnl/ *adj.* [only before noun] (*physics*) *Smaller ions experience a lower frictional resistance and so migrate through the gel faster and travel further than larger ones for a given time.*

friend /frend/ *noun* **1** a person you know well and like, and who is not usually a member of your family: *Hannah would rather sit and chat with her friends than do schoolwork.* ◇ *She felt she could not talk about her husband's problems, even to a close friend.* **2 ~ (of sth)** a person or group that supports a particular organization, cause or idea: *Known widely as an 'anti-communist', Orwell was, at the same time, a socialist and no friend of capitalism.* **3 ~ (of sb/sth)** a country that has a good relationship with and supports another country: *Russia was a traditional friend of the Greeks and traditional enemy of the Turks.*

IDM **be/make ˈfriends (with sb)** to be/become a friend of sb: *The Chinese trait of making friends before doing business is again alien to the attitude of Western businessmen.*

friend·ly /ˈfrendli/ *adj.* (**friend·lier**, **friend·li·est**) **1** behaving in a kind and pleasant way; treating sb as a friend: *At that time he was a relatively young man, with a serious yet friendly manner.* ◇ **~ towards sb** *It is possible to try to see the good side of someone and to make an effort to be friendlier towards him or her.* OPP UNFRIENDLY **2** (often in compound adjectives) that helps sb/sth or does not harm them/it: *It is important to explain procedures to children in child-friendly language.* ◇ *Various barriers may prevent the widespread adoption of cost-effective environmentally friendly technologies.* ➲ *see also* USER-FRIENDLY **3** (especially of the relationship between countries) not treating sb/sth as an enemy: *War between states with contrasting political and economic systems may be unthinkable because they have a history of friendly relations.* OPP HOSTILE (4), UNFRIENDLY **4** in which the people, teams or sides taking part are not seriously competing against each other: *Research staff shared information among the teams regarding goal achievement to spur friendly competition.* ■ **friend·li·ness** *noun* [U] *The speed and friendliness with which a restaurant processes its customers may be just as important as the meal itself.*

friend·ship /ˈfrendʃɪp/ *noun* **1** [C] a relationship between friends: *His close personal friendships contributed to his innovations throughout his career.* ◇ **~ with sb** *He met and began a lifelong friendship with Friedrich Engels.* ◇ **~ between A and B** *The friendship between Byron and Shelley is celebrated as one of the closest in English literary history.* **2** [U] the feeling or relationship that friends have; the state of being friends: *They meet socially on a regular basis to provide friendship and support to one another.* ◇ **~ with sb| ~ between A and B** *Throughout most of the nineteenth century the foundation of Russian foreign policy was friendship with Austria and Prussia.*

fright·en /ˈfraɪtn/ *verb* **~ sb** to make sb feel afraid: *The document was intended to frighten the government in the hope that they might back down.*

fright·ened /ˈfraɪtnd/ *adj.* afraid; feeling fear: *This misuse of power in a relationship can leave a person feeling frightened or powerless.* ◇ **~ of sth** *In many cases, victims are too frightened of reprisals to acknowledge their situation.*

fright·en·ing /ˈfraɪtnɪŋ/ *adj.* making you feel afraid: *Simple phobias often develop after a very frightening experience.*

fringe /frɪndʒ/ *noun* **1** the outer edge of an area: *To survive, farmers on the urban fringe have adapted to new forms of urban farming.* **2** [usually pl.] **~ (of sth)** the part of a society consisting of people who do not take an active part in their society, especially because they lack money, education and other advantages SYN MARGIN (4): *These people often live in severely disadvantaged conditions, on the fringes of society.*

from /frəm; *strong form* frɒm; *NAmE* frʌm; frɑːm/ *prep.* HELP For the special uses of **from** in phrasal verbs, look at the entries for the verbs. For example **keep sth from sb** is in the phrasal verb section at **keep**. **1** used to show what the origin of sb/sth is: *Grain, timber and wool were exported to Great Britain from Danzig.* ◇ *Evidence from the*

F

UK suggests that more than a fifth of these deaths are preventable. ◇ *Between August and October 2007, a total of 2339 participants from 15 schools were recruited.* ◇ *Numerous accounts were collected from eyewitnesses.* **2** used to show sb's position or point of view: *We photographed the entire canyon wall from viewpoints on the opposite side of the river.* ◇ *From an economic perspective, investments in the transport of coal far outweighed the costs of mining it.* **3 ~ A (to B)** used to show where sb/sth starts: *London could still be crossed on foot from west to east in a little over an hour.* ◇ *The final host depends on the vector that carries the parasite from one host to another.* **4** used to show when sth starts: *From a very early point, the central religious ritual of the Christians was the meal of bread and wine.* ◇ **~ the beginning/start** *From the beginning, feminists have differed among themselves, sometimes hotly.* **5 ~ sth (to sth)** used to show the range of sth: *The rate of unemployment for young men increased from 0.33 per cent in 1951 to 2.02 per cent in 1970.* ◇ *The 7-point response scale to each question ranges from 'never' to 'several times a week'.* **6** used to show how far apart two places are: *The city of Tours, on the Loire River, is about seven hundred miles from Rome.* **7** used to show the reason for sth or the cause of sth: *In 2003, 934 men and 832 women died from melanoma in the UK.* ◇ *Learning from experience must involve linking the doing and the thinking.* **8** used to show the reason or basis for making a judgement: *From the evidence, it is clear that very few family business groups in Thailand separated ownership and management.* ◇ *It is clear from the graph that being older is the key determinant in this distribution.* ◇ *What can we conclude from this?* **9** used to show what sth is made of: *In order to supplement their household income, she brews a local drink made from maize.* **10 ~ A (to B)** used to show the state or form of sth/sb before a change: *The government aims to transform agriculture from subsistence to commercial production.* **11** used when distinguishing between two people or things: *The way in which a doctor defines or conceives health may be different from that of the patient.* ◇ *The deviations vary greatly from embryo to embryo within a species.* **12** used to show that sb/sth is separated or removed: *Some bacteria could be removed from infected animals and subjected to microscopic study.* ◇ *The judge accepted that a committee of the council was not separate from but an integral part of the authority.* **13** used to show that sth is prevented: *Cicero never wavered in his belief that he had acted rightly and had saved Rome from catastrophe.*

IDM **from... on/onward(s)** starting at the time mentioned and continuously after that: *The economy of Korea grew very rapidly from 1980 onwards.* ◇ *British governments from then on acted on the assumption that little would be gained by any further opening up of China.*

front[1] /frʌnt/ *noun* **1** [C, usually sing.] (*usually* **the front**) the side or surface of sth that faces forward: **on the ~** *Cigarette packs must carry a health warning on the front.* ◇ **on the ~ of sth** *They have an organ on the front of the head which is probably used for detection of prey.* ◇ **at the ~ (of sth)** *Parking lots and garages are not located at the front of dwellings but at the rear.* OPP BACK[2] (1), REAR[2] (1) **2 the front** [sing.] the part or area of sth that is furthest forward: *Species living close to the ice front included woolly mammoth, rhinoceros and caribou.* ◇ **the ~ of sth** *The ornithopods included the hadrosaurs or duck-billed dinosaurs, in which the front of the mouth was enlarged to form a broad flat beak.* ◇ **in the ~ (of sth)** *Swelling is likely to occur in the front of the knee.* OPP BACK[2] (1) **3** [C, usually sing.] an area where fighting takes place during a war: *His regiment was immediately sent to the front.* ◇ **on the ... ~** *They no longer faced any major obstacles in their effort to defeat Germany on the eastern front.* ◇ *Women on the home front were usually completely unaware of the exact moment that their son, brother or husband had been killed.* ➲ *see also* FRONT LINE **4** [C] **(on the...) ~** a particular area of activity: *On the economic front, the government committed itself to providing full employment.* ◇ *Specific responses to globalization have been produced on multiple academic fronts.* **5** [C] the place where a mass of cold air meets a mass of warm air, shown as a line on a weather map: **a cold/warm ~** *The cold front behind the depression moves faster than the warm front and eventually catches up with it.* **6** [sing.] behaviour that is intended to give a particular impression to other people, sometimes in order to hide true feelings or opinions: *Despite internal differences, the EU usually manages to present a united front with respect to its external trade diplomacy.* **7** [C, usually sing.] **~ (for sth)** a person or an organization that is used to hide an illegal or secret activity: *Some accuse the organization of being a front for corporate interests, especially influential transnationals.* **8 Front** [sing.] used in the names of some political organizations: *Fielding (1982) conducted research on the extreme right-wing organization, the National Front.*

IDM **ˌfront and ˈcentre** (*NAmE* **ˌfront and ˈcenter**) (*especially NAmE*) in or into the most important position: *A review of current global famine areas confirms that famine seems to have six principal causes, with bad government front and centre.* **in ˈfront** *adv.* in a position that is further forward than sb/sth, or that faces forward: *In mammals, the brain dominates the back half of the skull, and the sense organs are concentrated in front.* ◇ *The village chieftain's house had a large courtyard in front.* **in ˈfront of** *prep.* **1** in a position that is further forward than sb/sth but not very far away: *Most of the work involves sitting in front of a computer screen all day.* ◇ *The pen and paper was placed centrally on the table, directly in front of where the subject was asked to sit.* **2** if you do sth **in front of** sb, you do it when they are there: *Students are often nervous about speaking in class in front of classmates.* ➲ *more at* EYE, UNITED

front[2] /frʌnt/ *adj.* [only before noun] on or at the front of sth: *About a week later, a follow-up article appeared on the front page of the 'Washington Post'.* ◇ *A light signal is emitted from the front end of the rocket.* ◇ *The patient was a young woman who was a passenger in the front seat of a car in a head-on collision.* OPP BACK[3] (1)

fron·tier /ˈfrʌntɪə(r); *NAmE* frʌnˈtɪr/ *noun* **1** [C] a line that separates two countries, etc; the land near this line SYN BORDER[1]: **~ between A and B** *Barbed wire and minefields sealed the frontiers between the USSR and its allies.* ◇ **beyond the ~ (of sth)** *In some cases a national group extended beyond the frontiers of the Habsburg Monarchy.* ◇ **+ noun** *The highly militarized frontier zone between England and Wales meant that territorial control fluctuated dramatically.* **2 the frontier** [sing.] the edge of land where people live and have built towns, beyond which the country is wild and unknown, especially in the western US in the 19th century: **on the ~** *These settlers were adapted well to life on the American frontier because of their previous experience in Europe.* **3** [C, usually pl.] **(at the) ~ of sth** the limit of sth, especially the limit of what is known about a particular subject or activity: *When working at the frontiers of knowledge, there are bound to be areas of uncertainty.*

the ˌfront ˈline *noun* [sing.] an area where the enemies are facing each other in a war and where fighting takes place: *Soldiers in the front line fought essentially as individuals against individuals.*

IDM **at/in/on the front line (of sth)** doing the most important or practical work: *Doctors and nurses are at the front line of patient care.*

froze *past tense of* FREEZE

fro·zen[1] *past part. of* FREEZE

fro·zen[2] /ˈfrəʊzn; *NAmE* ˈfroʊzn/ *adj.* **1** [usually before noun] (of food, blood, etc.) kept at a very low temperature in order to preserve it: *The frozen convenience foods category within the UK retail market is fiercely competitive.* ◇ *The frozen samples were analysed for cell wall nitrogen as described by Hikosaka and Shigeno (2009).* **2** (of rivers, lakes, etc.) with a layer of ice on the surface: *Edison walked eighty miles to the US border and crossed the frozen St Clair River.* **3** (of ground) so cold that it has become very hard: *Permanently frozen ground imposes a broad array of problems for engineering.*

fruit /fru:t/ *noun* **1** [U, C] the part of a plant or tree that contains seeds and that we eat: *Evidence suggests that diets rich in fruit and vegetables protect against the development of colon cancer.* ◇ *In Europe, the post-glacial forests would have been a rich source for edible berries, fruits, nuts and fungi.* ➲ *compare* VEGETABLE (1) **2** [U, C] (*biology*) a part of a plant or tree that is formed after the flowers have died and in which seeds develop: *Flowering plants usually require fertilization to produce fruit.*
IDM **the fruit/fruits of sth** the good results of an activity or a situation: *The fruits of much of this research are drawn together in Algra et al. (1999).* ➲ *more at* BEAR

fruit·ful /ˈfru:tfl/ *adj.* producing many useful results SYN PRODUCTIVE (2): *The relationship between politics and the press is a particularly fruitful area for research.* ■ **fruit·ful·ly** /ˈfru:tfəli/ *adv.*: *The goal is to provide methods that can be fruitfully applied to solving problems in human-technology interaction.* **fruit·ful·ness** /ˈfru:tfəlnəs/ *noun* [U] **~ (of sth)** *The fruitfulness of this type of abstract approach has long been established.*

frus·trate /frʌˈstreɪt; *NAmE* ˈfrʌstreɪt/ *verb* **~ sth** to prevent sth from happening or succeeding SYN THWART: *The wording of the document is so obscure as to frustrate attempts to examine its contents.*

frus·trated /frʌˈstreɪtɪd; *NAmE* ˈfrʌstreɪtɪd/ *adj.* **1** feeling impatient and slightly angry because you cannot do or achieve what you want: *The prosecution argued that the defendant had become frustrated and angry, and had struck out in the heat of the moment.* ◇ **~ at/with sth** *Managers were frustrated at the lack of enthusiasm from some general practice staff.* **2** (of an emotion) having no effect; not being satisfied: *Violence often seems to be stimulated by frustrated ambitions and missed opportunities.*

frus·trat·ing /frʌˈstreɪtɪŋ; *NAmE* ˈfrʌstreɪtɪŋ/ *adj.* causing you to feel impatient and slightly angry because you cannot do or achieve what you want: *Bus travel can be time-consuming, frustrating and difficult for visually-impaired people.* ■ **frus·trat·ing·ly** *adv.*: *Implementation of new policies is often frustratingly slow.*

frus·tra·tion /frʌˈstreɪʃn/ *noun* **1** [U] **~ (at/with sb/sth)** the feeling of being frustrated: *Successive governments have expressed their frustration with the Senate when legislative programmes have been delayed.* **2** [C, usually pl.] something that causes you to feel frustrated: *The patient is unable to cope successfully with everyday stresses, frustrations and setbacks.* **3** [U] **~ of sth** the fact that sth is preventing sth/sb from succeeding: *In spite of the frustration of her policies, Elizabeth's international reputation soared in the last decades of her reign.*

fuel[1] /ˈfju:əl/ *noun* **1** [U, C] any material that produces heat or power, usually when it is burnt: *Wood provided fuel for domestic heat and cooking.* ◇ *The costs for storage and transportation of liquid fuels are much lower than for gaseous ones.* ◇ **+ noun** *The fuel consumption of a car will vary with the speed of the car.* ➲ *see also* FOSSIL FUEL **2** [U] a thing that is said or done that makes sth, especially an argument, continue or get worse: *The reforms added fuel to the already smouldering social tension in the countryside.* ◇ **~ for (doing) sth** *Empirical research methods provide abundant fuel for continuing conversations about ethics.*

fuel[2] /ˈfju:əl/ *verb* (-ll-, *US* -l-) **1 ~ sth** to increase sth; to make sth stronger: *The criticisms have fuelled ongoing debates about the benefits of these policies.* ◇ *The growth of direct marketing has been fuelled by advances in technology.* **2 ~ sth** to supply sth with material that can be burnt to produce heat or power: *These reactors are fuelled by natural or enriched uranium.*

ˈfuel cell *noun* (*chemistry, engineering*) a device that produces electricity directly from a fuel, such as HYDROGEN, by its reaction with another chemical, such as OXYGEN, without any burning, in order to supply power to a vehicle or machine: *A fuel cell can convert hydrogen into electricity two or three times more efficiently than internal combustion engines or turbines.*

ful·fil (*BrE*) (*NAmE* **ful·fill**) /fʊlˈfɪl/ *verb* (**ful·fill·ing, ful·filled, ful·filled**) **1 ~ sth** to do or have what is required or necessary: *The State concerned has failed to fulfil its obligations under the Treaty.* ◇ *Some officials were dismissed because they could not fulfil their duties.* ◇ *Studies that fulfilled these criteria were reviewed and data were extracted by two reviewers.* ◇ *to fulfil the conditions/requirements/needs* **2 ~ sth** to have a particular role or purpose: *A biological system fulfils many functions at the same time.* ◇ *Many of these species are known to fulfil important roles in coral reef ecosystems.* **3 ~ sth** to do or achieve what was hoped for or expected: *To fulfil the aims of the study, a controlled experiment and two surveys were conducted* ◇ *The data suggest we are fulfilling our goal in this area.* ◇ *He never fulfilled his early promise as a painter.*

ful·fil·ment /fʊlˈfɪlmənt/ (*BrE*) (*NAmE* **ful·fill·ment**) *noun* [U] **1 ~ (of sth)** the fact of doing or having what is required or necessary: *Member states must take all appropriate measures to ensure the fulfilment of their EU obligations.* **2** the feeling of being happy or satisfied with what you are doing or have done: *The pleasure and sense of fulfilment in seeing students develop over time should not be underestimated.* **3 ~ (of sth)** the fact of doing or achieving what was hoped for or expected: *These young people should have greater opportunity to seek fulfilment of personal goals.*

full /fʊl/ *adj.* (**full·er, fullest**) **1** [usually before noun] complete; with nothing missing: *Most medical practices offer the full range of services to their patients.* ◇ *The full details of the policy are yet to emerge but the principles are relatively clear.* ◇ *Potentially relevant papers were accessed in order to review the full text.* ◇ *A full understanding of individual and community needs must be acquired.* **2** [usually before noun] to the highest level or greatest amount possible SYN MAXIMUM[1]: *All these drugs are slow to act, taking up to 6 weeks to reach their full effect.* ◇ *Firms should use their range of marketing communication facilities to their fullest extent.* ◇ *Few governments have made long-lasting commitments to the goal of full employment.* ◇ *There are many children on earth not developing to their full potential because of malnutrition and starvation.* **3 ~ of sth** having or containing a large number or amount of sth: *Very often qualitative studies seem to be full of apparently trivial details.* ◇ *Ancient history is full of many examples of states and empires, small and large, that were destroyed.* **4 ~ (of sth)** containing or holding as much or as many as possible; having no empty space: *Within 162 years, the lake was full of sediment.* ◇ *If a pipe is full of fluid flowing one way, then there is no room for fluid flowing the other way at the same time*
IDM Most idioms containing **full** are at the entries for the nouns in the idioms, for example **come full circle** is at **circle** *noun.* **in full** including the whole of sth: *The yearly total of this sum can be paid in full.* ◇ *The experimental study examined here has been previously documented in full (Pritchett, 2000).* **to the full** (*NAmE usually* **to the fullest**) to the greatest possible degree; as much as possible:

Students should be encouraged to use their creative energies to the full.

ˌfull-ˈlength *adj.* [only before noun] of a standard or complete length: *a full-length study/biography/book* ◇ *In a genome with tens of thousands of genes, it is extremely laborious to isolate a full-length cDNA for each gene.*

ˈfull professor *noun* (*NAmE*) = PROFESSOR (1)

ˌfull-ˈscale *adj.* [only before noun] **1** complete and not limited in any way: *By 1937, Japan was involved in full-scale war with China.* **2** that is the same size as sth that is being copied: *After the measurements, a correction factor was used to compare the full-scale mock-up with the scale models.*

ˌfull ˈstop (*also* **ˌfull ˈpoint**) (*both BrE*) (*NAmE* **period**) *noun* the mark (.) used at the end of a sentence and in some abbreviations, for example *e.g.*: *The text contains 88 commas, 35 full stops, six semicolons and four colons.*

ˌfull-ˈtime *adj.* for all the hours of a week during which people normally work or study, rather than just for a part of it: *Women's participation in full-time paid employment also has an effect on domestic divisions of labour.* ◇ *full-time jobs/workers/work/education/students* ➲ *compare* PART-TIME ■ **ˌfull-ˈtime** *adv.*: *Women who continue to work full-time and women without children are the best paid in relation to men.*

fully /ˈfʊli/ *adv.* completely; as much as possible: *Clearly, much more research will be needed before these complex links can be fully understood.* ◇ *Members of Congress are expected to participate fully in the national policymaking process.* ◇ *By the time the landings took place, Castro was fully aware of the invasion plan.* ◇ **never ~** *The nation has never fully or honestly dealt with its race problem.*

▸ FULLY + ADJECTIVE **aware • conscious • prepared • developed • integrated • functional • operational • functioning • automated** *Heinroth became convinced that instinctive behaviour is perfect and fully functional from the outset (Lorenz, 1977).*

▸ FULLY + VERB **understand • explain • explore • appreciate • realize • determine • recognize • specify • describe • inform • implement • exploit • accept** *Scholarship has fully explored the contribution of working-class power to social policy outcomes.*

func·tion¹ AWL /ˈfʌŋkʃn/ *noun* **1** [C, U] the action or purpose that sb/sth has in a particular situation; the ability that sb/sth has to perform a particular job or role: *Proteins serve many vital functions in living organisms.* ◇ *Paracetamol should not be given until liver function has returned to normal.* ◇ **~ of sb/sth** *Most of these mutations by themselves will not affect the function of the gene.* ◇ **~ as sth** *UNHCR is described and analysed in its function as an international organization.* **2** [C] **~ (of sth)** (*mathematics*) a quantity whose value depends on the varying values of others. In the statement $2x = y$, x is a function of y: *In this case, the simplest method of specifying a function is by means of a formula.* **3** [C] a part of a computer program or system that performs a basic operation: *The index function is used to select information from the data spreadsheet.* **4** [C] a social event or official ceremony: *The monarch plays a largely ceremonial role, representing Britain on overseas tours, attending public functions, and so on.*

> **WORD FAMILY**
> function *noun, verb*
> functional *adj.*
> functionally *adv.*
> functionality *noun*
> functioning *noun*

IDM **be a function of sth** to be sth that depends on sth else: *What makes an organization distinctive may be a function of its values, the actions it will take, or the manner in which these actions will be undertaken.*

▸ ADJECTIVE + FUNCTION **normal • different • important • main, primary • specific • similar • cognitive • biological • ecological • physiological • social • executive** *Protecting citizens from attack is a compelling state interest; it is in fact the state's primary function.*

▸ VERB + FUNCTION **have, serve, fulfil • perform, exercise • describe • assess • understand • affect • interfere with • impair • disrupt • restore • improve** *Increasingly, companies are developing sales technology departments that perform various functions for the sales organization.*

func·tion² AWL /ˈfʌŋkʃn/ *verb* [I] to work in the correct way; to work in a particular way SYN OPERATE (1): **(+ adv./prep.)** *To function properly, markets require the existence of law, regulation and property rights.* ◇ *Children need to acquire the appropriate skills and knowledge to be able to function in the adult world.* ◇ **fully functioning** *At this stage, the embryo at last becomes a fully functioning organism, capable of independent survival.*

PHR V **ˈfunction as sb/sth** to perform the action or the job of the thing or person mentioned: *The city continued to function as a significant urban centre throughout the Middle Ages.*

func·tion·al AWL /ˈfʌŋkʃənl/ *adj.* **1** connected with the way in which sth works or operates: *The door should have been designed differently to satisfy these two functional requirements.* ◇ *Functional equivalence relates to whether a concept has a similar function in different countries.* ◇ **fully ~** *The primary sequence of a protein may need to be altered before the protein can adopt its final, fully functional form.* ➲ *see also* FUNCTIONAL GROUP **2** connected with people's health and ability to live, work and look after themselves without help: *The impact of ageing populations on health systems is dependent on the health and functional ability of older people.* ◇ *functional limitations/impairment/decline/disability* **3** useful and having a special purpose: *Packaging has a functional role to protect and preserve products during transit.*

ˌfunctional ˈgroup *noun* **1** (*chemistry*) a group of atoms responsible for the characteristic reactions of a particular COMPOUND or series of compounds: *The presence of highly polar functional groups like carboxylic acids or alcohols increases the solubility in water.* **2** (*ecology*) a group of ORGANISMS (= living things) that are similar in their form, structure, behaviour, chemical processes or physical functions, or their position in the FOOD CHAIN: *Aquatic organisms can be classified into ecological groups, either on the basis of habitat or by functional group.*

func·tion·al·ity /ˌfʌŋkʃəˈnæləti/ *noun* (*pl.* **-ies**) **1** [U, C] the range of functions that a computer or other system can perform: *Consumers are quite happy to switch brands in order to get the level of functionality they need from a phone.* ◇ *They are working on integrating new functionalities into the operating system.* **2** [U] **~ (of sth)** the purpose that sth is designed for or expected to perform: *It is important that the name of the brand reflects the functionality of the product itself.*

func·tion·al·ly AWL /ˈfʌŋkʃənəli/ *adv.* in a way that is connected with the purpose or use of sth: *From the beginning, cities have been functionally distinct from surrounding rural areas.*

func·tion·ing AWL /ˈfʌŋkʃnɪŋ/ *noun* [U] **~ (of sth)** the way in which sb/sth functions: *Potassium is essential to the normal functioning of the heart and muscles.* ◇ *The study has formed the basis for a decade of reform efforts designed to improve the functioning of labour markets.* ◇ *There was considerable variation in the group in terms of cognitive ability, physical functioning, health and disease status.* ◇ *family/social/cognitive/everyday functioning*

fund¹ AWL /fʌnd/ *noun* **1 funds** [pl.] money that is available to be spent: *The advertisement was designed both to raise funds for the charity and to communicate the organization's brand personality.* ◇ *Some rulers, like Peter the*

Great and Catherine, had allocated substantial funds for opening schools in Russia. ◇ *For every dollar of public funds given to public transportation, the automobile industry receives $7.* ➲ thesaurus note *at* MONEY **2** [C] an amount of money that has been saved or has been made available for a particular purpose: *Some enterprises maintained a fund from which such fines could be paid.* **3** [C] a financial organization that invests money in a range of shares, etc. for a large number of people: *Large pension funds and other institutional investors are active participants on the foreign exchange market.* ◇ *The company's shares are included in many ethical investment funds because of its good record on social, environmental and ethical issues.* **4** [sing.] **~ of sth** a supply of sth: *Every year new discoveries are made that continue to enlarge our fund of information.*

fund² AWL /fʌnd/ *verb* [often passive] to provide money for sth, usually sth official SYN FINANCE²: **(be) funded (by sb/sth)** *This article is based on research undertaken for a project funded by the European Commission.* ◇ **funded + noun** *In Japanese universities, ownership of intellectual property rights resulting from publicly funded research is determined by a committee.*

THESAURUS

fund • finance • support • subsidize *verb*

These words all mean to provide money for sth in order to help it function or be successful.

- to fund/finance/support/subsidize a/an **project/programme/activity**
- to fund/support **research**
- to finance **investment/expenditure**
- to subsidize a/an **business/industry**
- **publicly** funded/financed/subsidized
- **privately** funded/financed

- **Fund** is often used to describe continued support for a project or programme over a period of time; **finance** is used more for one-off financial support: *All four countries have nationally funded vaccination programmes for the elderly.* ◇ *Corporations are able to finance new investments by borrowing from the financial sector or by issuing bonds.*
- **Fund** and **subsidize** are often used to talk about money from an official source; **finance** and **support** can be used to talk about public or private sources: *The clinic is publicly funded and there is access for all eligible patients.* ◇ *The authors wish to thank the Nissan Motor Company for supporting this research.*
- If sth is **subsidized**, it receives part of the money it needs in order to reduce its costs: *The production and use of this bioethanol has been heavily subsidized.*

See also the Thesaurus note at **contribute**.

fun·da·men·tal AWL /ˌfʌndəˈmentl/ *adj.* **1** serious and very important; affecting the most central and important parts of sth SYN BASIC (1): *Enlargement of the EU also poses fundamental questions for existing members.* ◇ *Microbial ecology is a subject of fundamental importance in biology.* **2** forming the necessary basis of sth SYN ESSENTIAL¹: *The right to vote is one of the fundamental rights which define a truly democratic society.* ◇ **~ to sth** *The concept is seen to be fundamental to his theory.* HELP In physics, **fundamental particle** is another term for **elementary particle**.

▸ FUNDAMENTAL + NOUN **question, issue • problem • change, shift • difference, distinction • aspect • role • value • flaw • error** *This UNICEF study emphasized that fundamental changes must occur in education at every level.* ◇ *This approach suffers from a fundamental flaw.* | **right • freedom • component • property • principle, tenet • law** *The states reaffirmed their belief in those fundamental freedoms that are the foundation of justice and peace in the world.*

fun·da·men·tal·ly AWL /ˌfʌndəˈmentəli/ *adv.* **1** in an important and basic way: *A fundamentally different view has been offered by Palmer and Neilson.* ◇ *Bacteria differ fundamentally from all other cellular organisms.* ◇ *Some of these assumptions were rejected as being fundamentally flawed.* **2** used for stating the basic facts about sth, or what is the most important feature of sth SYN BASICALLY (2): *Fundamentally, obesity results from an energy imbalance that occurs when energy consumption exceeds energy expenditure.*

fun·da·men·tals AWL /ˌfʌndəˈmentlz/ *noun* [pl.] **~ (of sth)** the basic and most important parts of sth: *The fundamentals of modern genetics were discovered in the nineteenth century.*

F

fun·der AWL /ˈfʌndə(r)/ *noun* an organization that provides money for a particular purpose: *The need for a broader research approach is being increasingly accepted by academic bodies and major research funders.*

fund·ing AWL /ˈfʌndɪŋ/ *noun* [U] money provided by an organization or government for a particular purpose; the act of providing such money: *public/government/federal/state funding* ◇ **~ for sth** *The Centre provides funding for new projects in the community.* ◇ **~ of sth** *Better funding of these services is badly needed.* ◇ **+ noun** *The funding agency did not play any role in the conception, design or execution of this study.*

fung·al /ˈfʌŋgl/ *adj.* **1** connected with a fungus: *Fungal spores enter through stomata in the pine leaves (needles) and germinate to cause bright yellow spots.* **2** (of an infection) caused by a fungus: *Thrush is a fungal infection caused by a yeast, usually Candida albicans.*

fun·gus /ˈfʌŋgəs/ *noun* (*pl.* **fungi** /ˈfʌŋgiː; ˈfʌŋgaɪ; ˈfʌndʒaɪ/) **1** any plant without leaves, flowers or green colouring, usually growing on other plants or on decaying matter. MUSHROOMS and MOULD are both fungi: *These are the two main fungi causing the decay of berry fruits.* **2** a type of fungus that causes infection: *Fungi cause skin conditions such as athlete's foot.*

funny /ˈfʌni/ *adj.* **(fun·nier, fun·ni·est) 1** making you laugh: *He claims that Pinter has written 'many of the funniest lines and the funniest scenes in modern drama'.* **2** (*rather informal*) strange or unusual SYN STRANGE (1): *They led a funny kind of existence.*

fur /fɜː(r)/ *noun* **1** [U] the soft thick mass of hair that grows on the body of some animals: *The house mouse is a small rodent with grey-brown fur.* **2** [C, U] the skin of an animal with the fur still on it, used especially for making clothes: *In North America, Europeans conducted a huge trade in furs through native peoples.* ◇ *Overhunting of animals for their fur, shells, tusks or skins is a threat to biodiversity.*

fur·ni·ture /ˈfɜːnɪtʃə(r); *NAmE* ˈfɜːrnɪtʃər/ *noun* [U] objects that can be moved, such as tables, chairs and beds, that are put into a house or an office to make it suitable for living or working in: *Mrs Rowe sold her own home and stored her furniture.* ◇ *They sell office furniture and equipment to small and medium-sized businesses.*

fur·ther¹ /ˈfɜːðə(r); *NAmE* ˈfɜːrðər/ *adv.* **1** (comparative of **far**) (*especially BrE*) at or to a greater distance SYN FARTHER: **~ from sb/sth** *Because they were formed further from the sun, comets are mostly ice of various sorts.* ◇ **~ away (from sb/sth)** *If the proteins are further away from each other, no such energy transfer occurs.* ◇ **~ than...** *She had never travelled further than Italy.* ◇ **~ afield** *Countries from the EU were represented, as well as countries from further afield, such as Mexico or Japan.* ◇ **further and further** *As part of the rehabilitation process, the rescued monkeys are successively moved further and further from humans, both geographically and in terms of human contact.* **2** beyond the point already reached or the distance already covered: **(+ adv./prep.)** *China is attempting to move even further along the road of trade liberalization.* ◇ **~ on** *Shakespeare states this more clearly in the speech Hamlet makes a few lines further on.* **3** to a greater extent or degree; beyond or in addition to what has already happened or been done: *These findings will be discussed further in the next section.* ◇ *Most ethical issues are further complicated by the legal questions they raise.* **4** a longer way in the past or the future: *This tradition can be traced back even further, to ancient and medieval times.* ◇ *Other damage may occur further in the future.* **5** in addition to what has just been stated SYN FURTHERMORE, MOREOVER: *Further, a substantial body of literature was ignored.* **6** used to emphasize the difference between a supposed or suggested fact or state of mind and the truth: **can/could not be ~ from sth** *However, the reality could not be further from these preconceived ideas.* ◇ **nothing could be ~ from sth** *It is argued that the strikes showed the power of the unions, but nothing could be further from the truth.* **7** at or to a more advanced, successful or better stage: *He never got further than outlining the hypothesis.* ◇ **~ forward** *They were no further forward in finding a solution to the problem.*

IDM **go ˈfurther 1** to say more about sth, or make a more extreme point about it: *Schein goes further and attempts to offer an explanation of how culture comes into being.* ◇ *The author goes further, suggesting that Stalin consciously followed in the footsteps of Ivan the Terrible.* **2** to take more action, especially more extreme action, about sth: *The Council of Europe went further and delivered a ruling banning smacking in the home.* **take sth ˈfurther 1** to explain or describe sth in a more detailed way: *Several recent studies have taken these general arguments further.* **2** to take more serious action about sth or speak to sb at a higher level about it: *The original six member states resolved to take matters further.*

fur·ther² /ˈfɜːðə(r); *NAmE* ˈfɜːrðər/ *adj.* (comparative of **far**) more SYN ADDITIONAL: *Further investigations are needed to address these issues.* ◇ *See Berner (1994) for further details.* ➲ language bank *at* ADDITION

▸ FURTHER + NOUN **research • investigation, examination, exploration • analysis • testing • consideration • discussion • details, information • evidence • reading • development • increase • reduction • example • complication** *The European Commission proposed a further increase in the budget to 1.37 per cent.* ◇ *A further example comes from the Lawrence and Philips article discussed above.*

fur·ther³ /ˈfɜːðə(r); *NAmE* ˈfɜːrðər/ *verb* **~ sth** to help the progress or development of sth SYN PROMOTE (1): *The fundamental purpose of American foreign policy is to further the interests of the United States in the wider world.* ◇ *More broadly, the study is intended to further our understanding of cultural forms of speech styles and communication.*

fur·ther·more AWL /ˌfɜːðəˈmɔː(r); *NAmE* ˌfɜːrðərˈmɔːr/ *adv.* (*formal*) in addition to what has just been stated. Furthermore is used especially to add a point to an argument. SYN FURTHER¹ (5), MOREOVER: *Furthermore, air transport is responsible for around 11% of the total CO_2 emissions from UK food transport.* ◇ *The invention, furthermore, confers a technical benefit, namely a substantial increase in processing speed.* ➲ language bank *at* ADDITION

fur·thest /ˈfɜːðɪst; *NAmE* ˈfɜːrðɪst/ *adj., adv.* = FARTHEST¹, FARTHEST²

fuse /fjuːz/ *verb* [I, T] (of two things) to join together to form a single thing; to join two things in this way: *The egg and sperm nuclei then fuse to form the diploid zygotic genome.* ◇ **~ sth (together) (into sth)** *Sadosky fuses two approaches that add new vitality to the study of early American diplomacy.* ◇ *The material of the satellite and meteorite are fused together into a solid whole.* ◇ **~ sth with sth** *It was noted that if malignant cells were fused with normal cells, they lost their malignant properties.*

fu·sion /ˈfjuːʒn/ *noun* **1** [U, sing.] **~ (of sth)** the process or result of joining two or more things together to form one: *This arrangement of muscle fibre is a consequence of the fusion of many embryonic cells.* **2** (*also* ˌ**nuclear ˈfusion**) [U] (*physics*) the act or process of combining the NUCLEI (= central parts) of atoms to form a heavier NUCLEUS, with energy being released: *The cases are presented for the two different types of nuclear energy: fission and fusion.* ➲ *compare* FISSION (1) **3** [U] **~ (of sth)** a mixture of different styles or ideas: *Droysen believed that it was the fusion of Greek and Oriental cultures that made possible the introduction of Christianity.*

fu·ture¹ /ˈfjuːtʃə(r)/ *adj.* [only before noun] **1** taking place or existing at a time after the present: *The environment must be safeguarded for future generations.* ◇ *This will remain a key area for future research.* **2** (of a person) planned or intended to hold the position mentioned: *Appiah was living in London amongst a group of intellectuals and future political leaders.* **3** (*grammar*) expressing an event that has not yet happened: *Canudo uses the future tense in most of his essay.*

▸ FUTURE NOUN **generations • research • study • investigation • work • development • direction • trend • event • change • health • prospects** *Finding the right people to serve on the board and thus shape the future direction of an organization is a far from easy task.*

fu·ture² /ˈfjuːtʃə(r)/ *noun* **1 the future** [sing.] the time that will come after the present: *The arrangement allows the firm to wait and see what the future holds.* ◇ **in the ~** *She believes that the situation will not improve in the future.* ◇ **in the near/distant ~** *African countries will probably move towards some form of integration in the near future.* **2 the future** [sing.] events that will or are likely to happen in time to come: *Understanding current circumstances may help to predict the future.* **3** [C] what will happen to sb/sth in time to come: *The Buddha remained there for seven weeks pondering his future.* ◇ **~ of sth** *In the early 1970s, many people were extremely pessimistic about the future of democracy in the world.* **4** [sing.] the possibility of being successful or surviving at a later time: *There was some doubt about whether European integration actually had a future.* ◇ *They could see no future for themselves.* **5 futures** [pl.] (*finance*) contracts for goods or shares that are bought at agreed prices but that will be delivered and paid for later: *Most institutions are barred from directly trading futures.* **6 the future** (*also* **the ˌfuture ˈtense**) [sing.] the form of a verb that expresses events that have not yet happened: *The use of the future in the first clause ('we shall see') indicates that he planned to discuss the subject more fully in text that is now missing.*

IDM **in future** (*BrE*) (*NAmE* **in the future**) from now on: *Only less dangerous pesticides would be permitted in future.* ➲ *more at* FORESEEABLE

Gg

gage (*US*) = GAUGE¹, GAUGE²

gain¹ /ɡeɪn/ *verb* **1** [T] to obtain sth, especially sth that is needed or wanted: **~ sth** *The defendant was a computer hacker who gained unauthorized access to a computer network.* ◇ **~ sth from sth** *The insights gained from the survey can be summarized as follows:...* ◇ **~ sth by doing sth** *No real advantage is gained by making such modifications to the system.* ◇ **~ sth through sth** *They ensured that they benefited from the knowledge gained through past failures.* ◇ **~ sb sth** *His job as a miner gained him exemption from military service.* **2** [I] to get a benefit from sth: *Investors may gain if the business is in a protected market.* ◇ **~ from**

sth *Participants also felt that they had gained from the training courses.* ◇ ~ **by doing sth** *Their research suggests that the region would gain by adopting this technology.* ◇ **stand to ~** *That company stood to gain most from a change in consumers' habits.* **3** [T] ~ **sth** to increase the amount or rate of sth: *The opposition movement against martial law gradually gained momentum.* ◇ *She stopped taking her medication after a month as she had started to gain weight and felt self-conscious.* ◇ *Female rats rapidly gain 15–20 g during pregnancy.* OPP LOSE (2) **4** [T, I] to increase in value: *Some companies' stocks gained on the news of the takeover.* ◇ ~ **sth** *The corporation gained 4.5 points when it introduced its performance guarantee.*

IDM **gain 'ground** to become more successful or popular: *That view is gaining ground in the United States but it is still more likely to be found among British and continental European scholars.*

PHR V **'gain in sth** to get more of a particular quality: *These methods have gained considerably in popularity in recent years.*

▸ GAIN + NOUN **access • entry • insight, understanding • knowledge • experience • information • advantage, benefit • control • power • influence • recognition • acceptance, approval** *All states seek to gain more power and influence to secure their national interests.* ◇ *His Latin version of the New Testament began to gain acceptance.*

gain² /geɪn/ *noun* **1** [C, U] an increase or improvement in sth: ~ **of sth** *Entirely replacing coal with renewable energy by 2030 will give a net gain of 10 000 jobs in the Australian economy.* ◇ ~ **in sth** *Any form of parent involvement appears to produce measurable gains in student achievement.* ◇ ~ **(for sb)** *These markets can generate substantial gains for buyers and sellers.* ◇ *Side effects of the medication may include weight gain.* OPP LOSS (1) **2** [C, U] an advantage or benefit: ~ **for sb** *The increase in the amount of training appears to be a genuine gain for employees.* ◇ ~ **from sth** *The gains from increased freedom of choice in a market may be limited for some groups.* ◇ *In some cases there will be little or no gain from collaboration.* OPP LOSS (1) **3** [U] (*often disapproving*) financial profit: *The aim is to target individuals who leak information for gain.* ◇ *Personal gain is a primary motivation for much criminal behaviour.* **4** [C, U] ~ **(of sth)** the factor by which power or VOLTAGE is increased in an electronic device using an AMPLIFIER: *The output voltage, plotted in Fig. 8.7, corresponds to the gain of the amplifier.* ◇ *When a channel has high gain, it is able to boost the power of its input much more effectively than a channel with low gain.*

▸ ADJECTIVE + GAIN **large • overall • net • potential • relative** *Other textile producers experience large gains because of the relative decrease in prices.* ◇ *The potential gains from successful gene therapy are enormous.* | **personal • private • economic • financial • political** *The directors clearly abused their position for financial gain.*

▸ NOUN + GAIN **weight • health • welfare • efficiency • heat** *There would be efficiency gains if governments increasingly modelled themselves on firms.*

▸ VERB + GAIN **make • achieve • provide • produce, lead to** *Those companies have achieved gains in productivity and market share.* | **increase • maximize • reduce** *They remain aware of the need to maximize their gains in a competitive and uncertain international environment.*

gain·ful /ˈgeɪnfl/ *adj.* (*formal*) used to describe useful work that you are paid for: *Sweden is a highly work-oriented society, where both women and men are expected to have gainful employment.* ■ **gain·ful·ly** /ˈgeɪnfəli/ *adv.*: *According to the 1959 census, two thirds of females over 14 years old were gainfully employed.*

gal·axy /ˈgæləksi/ *noun* (*pl.* **-ies**) any of the very large systems of stars, planets, gas and dust in space: *The light from a distant galaxy is old, in the sense that it has been a long time on its journey.* HELP **The Galaxy** refers to our own galaxy, containing our sun and its planets, seen as a bright band in the night sky, and also known as **the Milky Way**: *The Solar System is located far out towards the edge of the Galaxy.*

gal·lon /ˈgælən/ *noun* (*abbr.* **gal.**) a unit for measuring liquid. In the UK, Canada and other countries it is equal to about 4.5 litres; in the US it is equal to about 3.8 litres: *The plant was designed to process 30 million gallons of seawater a day.*

game /geɪm/ *noun* **1** [C] an activity or a sport with rules that you play for entertainment and that you can win or lose: *Research has indicated that boys often actively exclude girls from football games.* ◇ *Television viewing and solitary playing of computer and video games are linked with inappropriate snacking and obesity.* ◇ ~ **of sth** *It should be fairly easy to program a computer to play a game of chess against a beginner.* **2** [C] (*especially NAmE*) an event where a team sport is played: *Anyone who has been to a baseball game in both Japan and America will have noticed differences in how fans in the two countries cheer their teams.* **3** [C] a children's activity when they play with TOYS, pretend to be sb else, etc: *Many children's games, such as dressing up, have no statable rules.* **4** [C] ~ **(of sth)** (*rather informal*) a type of activity or business: *The significance of these institutions as players in the game of international politics is likely to increase substantially.* **5 games** [pl.] a large organized sports event: *The Olympic Games became the biggest event in the calendar for families from all over the Greek world.* **6** [U] wild animals or birds that people hunt for sport or food: *Von Wissmann valued wild animals as game, not as endangered species.*
IDM *see* RULE¹

gam·ete /ˈgæmiːt/ *noun* (*biology*) a cell that has the single, HAPLOID, number of CHROMOSOMES, that FUSES (= combines) with another haploid cell to produce a DIPLOID ZYGOTE: *When the gametes fuse at fertilization, the full chromosome number is restored.* ◇ *The embryos of sexually reproducing organisms develop from a single cell, formed by the fusion of a male and a female gamete at fertilization.*

ˈgame theory *noun* [U] the branch of mathematics and economics concerned with strategies, where the OUTCOME of a particular choice depends critically on the actions of other players: *Juul's book offers a useful account of game theory as it applies to contemporary digital game worlds.*

gap /gæp/ *noun* **1** ~ **(between A and B)** a difference, especially one that is not wanted, between two views or situations: *It is possible that the gap between theory and practice may in fact not be as great as has been suggested.* ◇ *By the 1930s, there was a wide gap between party officials and party members.* **2** ~ **(in sth)** a space where sth is missing: *Trainees may try to hide gaps in their knowledge.* ◇ *The two airlines spotted a gap in the market for a low-cost service.* **3** a space between two things or in the middle of sth, especially because there is a part missing: ~ **in sth** *He had obtained access through a gap in a fence.* ◇ ~ **between A and B** *The gap between one neuron and another is called a nerve synapse.* **4** a period of time when sth stops, or between two events: ~ **of sth** *Border talks with China were reopened after a gap of nine years.* ◇ ~ **(of sth) between A and B** *There was a gap of one week between the two phases.* IDM *see* BRIDGE²

▸ ADJECTIVE + GAP **large • wide • narrow, small • important, significant** *Legislation was passed in 1908, 1929, 1948 and, after a slightly larger gap, 1980.* ◇ *Important gaps in key areas render reliable estimates impossible.*

▸ NOUN + GAP **knowledge • technology • achievement • income, pay, wage • gender • poverty** *The gender gap in life expectancy between men and women is caused by many factors.*

▸ VERB + GAP **create • be separated by • address • explain • identify, highlight** *Natural forests contain gaps created by* *the death of individual trees.* ◇ *The financial crisis of 2008 highlighted serious gaps in financial regulation.* | **bridge, close • reduce, narrow • increase, widen** *The Equality Bill aimed to reduce the gap between rich and poor through legislative means.* | **fill (in) • leave** *Gaps were left in three places to allow boats to pass in or out of the Black Sea.*

▸ GAP + VERB **exist • remain** *A gap exists between urban and rural pension provisions.* | **narrow • widen** *Men were more likely to get ulcers than women, but the gap is narrowing.*

▸ GAP IN + NOUN **knowledge, understanding • literature • record • data • system • coverage • law • market** *The paper has also identified big gaps in the literature.*

G

gar·bage /ˈɡɑːbɪdʒ; *NAmE* ˈɡɑːrbɪdʒ/ *noun* [U] (*especially NAmE*) waste food, paper, etc. that you throw away; a place or container where waste food, paper, etc. can be placed SYN RUBBISH: *In industrial societies, many people do happily sort and recycle their garbage.* ◇ **+ noun** *These mongooses had access to garbage dumps in their territory.*

gar·den /ˈɡɑːdn; *NAmE* ˈɡɑːrdn/ *noun* **1** [C] (*BrE*) (*NAmE* **yard**) a piece of land next to or around your house, with grass on it, and where you can grow flowers, fruit, vegetables, etc: *Farm women cultivated vegetable gardens that were crucial to the family's survival.* **2** (*usually* **gardens**) [pl.] an area of land in a town or city planted with grass, trees, flowers, etc. where people go to walk, play and relax: *Nearly all German towns had suburban pleasure gardens where all classes of people could afford to listen to the orchestra.*

gas /ɡæs/ *noun* (*pl.* **gases**) **1** [C, U] any substance like air that is not a solid or a liquid, for example HYDROGEN or OXYGEN: *Being a gas, it readily mixes with air.* ◇ *The large quantities of gas and ash emitted by volcanoes often result in violent rainstorms.* ➲ *see also* GREENHOUSE GAS **2** [U] a particular type of gas or mixture of gases used as fuel for heating and cooking: *It is predicted that coal will outlast oil and gas by a few hundred years.* ◇ **+ noun** *This body regulates the privatized gas and electricity industries in the UK.* ➲ *see also* NATURAL GAS **3** [U] a particular type of gas used during a medical operation, to make the patient unconscious or to reduce pain: *They altered the blend of helium and oxygen when administering gas to patients.* **4** [U] a particular type of gas used in war to kill or injure people, or used by the police to control people: *Gas was one of the most dreaded weapons of the war.* ◇ **+ noun** *a gas attack* **5** (*also* **gasoline**) (*both NAmE*) (*BrE* **petrol**) [U] a liquid obtained from PETROLEUM, used as fuel in car engines, etc: *The price of gas rose from $0.39 a gallon for unleaded gasoline in 1973 to $1.31 eight years later.*

gas·eous /ˈɡæsiəs; ˈɡeɪsiəs/ *adj.* [usually before noun] like or containing gas: *Considerable energy is required to convert the carbon atoms from solid to gaseous form.* ◇ *The only practical fuel cell for vehicle use requires gaseous hydrogen fuel.*

gas·oline (*also* **gas·olene**) /ˈɡæsəliːn/ *noun* [U] (*NAmE*) = GAS (5): *In this relatively wealthy city, 77% of households are consuming zero gasoline.*

gas·tric /ˈɡæstrɪk/ *adj.* [only before noun] (*medical*) connected with the stomach: *Over the last 100 years, gastric cancer has shown a dramatic decrease in incidence.*

gate /ɡeɪt/ *noun* **1** a barrier like a door that is used to close an opening in a fence or a wall outside a building; an opening that can be closed by a gate: *In 1667, the cities of Flanders opened their gates to the French after little more than token resistance.* ◇ (*figurative*) *The Internet opened the gates for businesses to sell direct to consumers across national borders.* **2** (*also* ˈ**logic gate**) (*computing*) an electronic switch that reacts in one of two ways to data that is put into it: *The output of an AND gate is true if and only if each of its inputs is also in a true state.* HELP A computer performs operations by passing data through a very large number of **logic gates**.

gather /ˈɡæðə(r)/ *verb* **1** [T] **~ sth** to collect information from different sources: *The purpose of the study is to gather data about life in the United States.* ◇ *It must be clear how the evidence was gathered, selected and collated, and by whom.* ◇ **~ sth from sth** *In the absence of survey data, we gathered information from newspaper articles.* **2** [I, T] **+ adv./prep.** to come together in one place to form a group; to bring people together in this way: *More than a million people gathered in Washington for Obama's inauguration.* ◇ *Aboriginal people were gathered together and the children were separated from their parents.* **3** [T] **~ sth (together/up)** to bring things together: *The raw materials arrive packaged, sorted and frozen so as to minimize the time it takes to gather the materials together for production.* **4** [T] **~ sth** to collect plants, fruit, etc. from a wide area: *They continued to hunt wild animals and gather herbs, nuts and mountain plants.* **5** [T] **~ sth (up)** to pick or cut and collect crops to be stored: *Women do the entire work of gathering up, binding and stacking the wheat.* **6** [T] **~ sth** to increase in speed, force, etc. SYN GAIN[1] (3): *Rolling down a steep hill we gather speed faster than on a gentle slope.* ◇ *Nationalism was gathering momentum in eastern Europe.* **7** [T] (not used in the progressive tenses) to believe or understand that sth is true because of information or evidence that you have, although you have not been told directly: **~ (that)...** *He gathered that the drug treatment was having a great beneficial effect.* ◇ **from what sb can gather...** *From what she could gather, the girl had been living largely with her grandmother for several years.*

gath·er·ing /ˈɡæðərɪŋ/ *noun* **1** [C] a meeting of people for a particular purpose: *Archaeological evidence indicates that large groups came together for social gatherings.* ◇ **~ of sb** *He spoke at a gathering of about 30 eminent scientists.* **2** [U] the process of collecting sth: *Behaviour is a decision-making process that involves information gathering.* ◇ *Today only a minority of human societies depend on hunting and gathering.* ◇ **~ of sth** *The authors advocate the gathering of data to test this hypothesis.*

gauge[1] (*US also* **gage**) /ɡeɪdʒ/ *noun* **1** (often in compounds) an instrument for measuring the amount or level of sth: *The chamber was fitted with a sensitive pressure gauge.* ◇ *The device used for testing the patient's breathing is a small tube with a mouthpiece and a gauge.* **2** [usually sing.] **~ (of sth)** a fact, an action or an event that can be used to estimate or judge sth: *The treatment that police accord to minority groups is used as a gauge of police neutrality.* **3 ~ (of sth)** the width, thickness, size or volume of sth, especially as a standard measure: *An engineer would not use just one gauge of metal to build an entire bridge structure.*

gauge[2] (*US also* **gage**) /ɡeɪdʒ/ *verb* **1** to make a judgement about about sth, especially people's feelings or attitudes, or the likely effect of sth: **~ sth** *The study sets out to gauge the extent to which central government is becoming involved in local government decision-making.* ◇ **~ what/how, etc...** *This tool identifies possible or likely errors, and gauges what their effect may be.* ◇ *Respondents were asked a number of questions to gauge how far they approved of the measures.* **2 ~ sth** to measure sth accurately using a special instrument: *The highest ever gauged flow for the river was recorded on 20 July 2007.*

gave *past tense of* GIVE

gay[1] /ɡeɪ/ *adj.* **1** (of people, especially men) sexually attracted to people of the same sex SYN HOMOSEXUAL: *In many parts of the world, lesbians and gay men continue to experience discrimination and prejudice.* **2** [only before noun] connected with people who are gay: *The progress of gay rights has followed on the heels of the feminist revolution.*

gay² /geɪ/ *noun* [usually pl.] a person, especially a man, who is sexually attracted to people of the same sex: *It is clear that while many problems remain, gays and lesbians are now able to be more open about who they are.* HELP As a noun, **gay** is more common in the plural. It can sound offensive in the singular. Instead, you can use the adjective (*a gay man*).

GDP /ˌdʒiː diː ˈpiː/ *noun* [U, C, usually sing.] the abbreviation for **'gross domestic product'** (the total value of all the goods and services produced by a country in one year): *The question is: is growth in real GDP compatible with sustainable economic development?* ◇ *GDP per capita would double every 35 years if it were to grow at an annual rate of 2%.* ◇ **~ of sth** *In 1997, the block had a population of 220 million people and a GDP of US$1.3 billion.* ➲ *compare* GNP

gel /dʒel/ *noun* [U, C] a soft substance like JELLY, especially one used in scientific experiments: *This technique separates proteins and other chemicals using an electrical current passing through agar gel.* ◇ *Gels are prepared with different pore sizes depending on the range of sizes of molecules to be separated.*

gen·der AWL /ˈdʒendə(r)/ *noun* **1** [U] the fact of being male or female, especially when considered with reference to social and cultural differences, not differences in biology: *Such characteristics as ethnicity, gender and social background may influence the answers that respondents provide.* ◇ **~ of sb** *The social position of a household is based on the occupation of the main breadwinner, regardless of their gender.* ◇ **+ noun** *Her parents had always maintained strong traditional gender stereotypes.* ◇ *gender identity/differences/relations/roles/equality/inequality/bias* ➲ *compare* SEX (2) **2** [C] male people as a group or female people as a group: *The people did more than merely treat both genders equally; they chose women as leaders.* **3** [C, U] (*grammar*) (in some languages) each of the classes (MASCULINE, FEMININE and sometimes NEUTER) into which nouns, pronouns and adjectives are divided; the division of nouns, pronouns and adjectives into these different genders. Different genders may have different endings, etc: *As is well known, nouns in German are assigned to one of three genders: masculine, feminine and neuter.* ◇ *An article or adjective agrees with the noun in gender and number.*

gene /dʒiːn/ *noun* a unit inside a cell that controls a particular quality in a living thing that has been passed on from its parents: *Scientists are still far from clearly understanding how genes influence behaviour.* ◇ **~ for sth** *The method was successful in isolating the genes for cystic fibrosis.* ◇ **+ noun** *Less fit individuals fail to reproduce and their genes are lost from the gene pool.* HELP In technical use in biochemistry, a **gene** is that section of DNA that carries the code to make a particular PROTEIN. ➲ *see also* GENETIC

▸ ADJECTIVE + GENE **maternal • developmental • ancestral • mitochondrial • eukaryotic • zygotic • nuclear • functional** *The expression of maternal genes during egg formation creates differences in the egg even before it is fertilized.*

▸ VERB + GENE **involve • contain • carry • express • clone • transcribe • activate • inactivate • regulate • encode • mutate • identify • locate, find • isolate • sequence • map • target • insert • delete • amplify** *Various tests are being developed to identify genes liable to cause certain diseases.* ◇ *The nucleus is given the signal to activate genes leading to cell division.*

▸ GENE + VERB **encode • code • influence • control • affect** *Some genes can encode dozens or even hundreds of related but different proteins.*

▸ GENE + NOUN **expression • flow • cluster • frequency • activity • function • product • duplication • transcription • conversion • mutation • regulation • coding • mapping • sequence • family • pool • therapy** *The extent to which genes exist in gene families was not widely appreciated until genomes were sequenced.*

gen·era *pl. of* GENUS

gen·eral¹ /ˈdʒenrəl/ *adj.* **1** affecting or including all or most people, places or things: *The general level of interest was low.* ◇ *The general consensus is that the Internet's advertising growth will continue for many years.* ◇ *In contrast to the general population (68.1%), almost all students (91.7%) report that they send over five emails a day.* **2** [usually before noun] normal; usual; true in most cases: *As a general principle, it is recommended that organizations review their own activities.* **3** including the most important aspects of sth; not exact or detailed SYN BROAD (3): *This approach is too general and fails to accommodate different buyer needs.* ◇ *It is difficult to define when a contract will breach competition rules because competition laws are written in very general terms.* OPP SPECIFIC (3) **4 the ~ direction/area** used to describe the approximate, but not exact, direction or area mentioned: *There is a question about the general direction of change in the British economy.* ◇ *Cotton cloth from the general area of Nanjing provided the first great export from China to the West.* **5** not limited to a particular subject, use or activity: *The discussion has been general and applies to all reactions.* ◇ *A sufficiently general manufacturing technology could in theory displace almost all manufacturing and transportation jobs.* **6** not limited to one part or aspect of a person or thing: *Children may need a general anaesthetic for this procedure.* ◇ *It is important to monitor the patient's general condition.* **7** [only before noun] highest in rank: *The general manager has no directorial responsibilities and so is not accountable to shareholders.* HELP In some titles, **General** comes after the noun: *The Inspector General of the Police denied the allegations.*

IDM **as a general ˈrule** usually: *As a general rule, poor people tend on average to be less healthy than richer people.* **of general ˈinterest** of interest to most people: *Two points of general interest emerge from the speech.*

▸ GENERAL + NOUN **agreement, consensus, acceptance • lack • perception • circulation • population • meeting** *There is general agreement that the world is a changing place.* | **principle • rule • solution • strategy • tendency** *The general solution to this equation contains two parts.* | **theory • model, framework • trend, pattern • sense, idea • feature, characteristic • conclusion • approach • way • process • form • problem • issue • term • statement • question • point • information** *The study produced four general conclusions:...* | **hospital • practitioner • education • law • duty • strike** *In a world of limited resources, general education should be prioritized.*

gen·eral² /ˈdʒenrəl/ *noun* (*abbr.* **Gen.**) an officer of very high rank in the army or the US AIR FORCE; the COMMANDER of an army: *Sulla marched against Rome, the first Roman general to lead an army against the Republic.*

IDM **in ˈgeneral 1** usually; mainly: *In general, decisions for or against investing depend on investors' optimism or pessimism about the future.* ➲ language bank *at* BROADLY **2** as a whole: *Antibiotics are used at very high rates in hospitals in general and in intensive care units in particular.*

ˌgeneral eˈlection *noun* an election in which all the people of a country vote to choose a government: *As the next general election approached, support flowed back to the governing party.* ◇ **+ noun** *Cameron hoped to enter the 2010 general election campaign with a much more convincing set of strengths.*

ˌgeneral equiˈlibrium *noun* (in economic theory) a situation in which prices are at exactly the right level to ensure a steady balance of supply and demand across a whole economy: **+ noun** *The general equilibrium* *approach permits us to capture the implications of changes in national commodity and factor prices.*

gen·er·al·ist /ˈdʒenrəlɪst/ *noun* a person who has knowledge of several different subjects or activities: *Nurses in primary care can be generalists or specialists.* OPP SPECIALIST[1]

gen·er·al·ity /ˌdʒenəˈræləti/ *noun* (*pl.* **-ies**) **1** [U] **~ (of sth)** the quality of a theory or model that can be applied being across a wide range of cases and situations: *He saw an opportunity to demonstrate the powerful generality of physical laws.* ◇ *The result of Theorem 21.4 is applicable in much greater generality.* HELP The phrase **without loss of generality** means that a statement about one particular case can be easily applied to all other cases: *Lagrange believed he could restrict his analysis to potential flows without loss of generality.* **2** [C, usually pl.] a statement that makes general points rather than giving details or particular examples: *Many rejection letters either contained no reasons at all, or were filled with generalities.* **3 the generality** [sing.+ sing./pl. v.] **~ (of sb/sth)** (*formal*) the greater part of a group of people or things SYN MAJORITY (1): *This spoken form of the language is used by the generality of speakers in most situations.*

gen·er·al·iz·able (*BrE also* **-is·able**) /ˈdʒenrəlaɪzəbl/ *adj.* **~ (to sth)** that can be applied to a wide range of people, situations, etc: *As with all industry-specific research, the findings may not be generalizable to other environments.* ■ **gen·er·al·iz·abil·ity, -is·abil·ity** /ˌdʒenrəlaɪzəˈbɪləti/ *noun* [U] **~ (of sth)** *The relatively small sample size limits the generalizability of the findings.*

gen·er·al·iza·tion (*BrE also* **-isa·tion**) /ˌdʒenrəlaɪˈzeɪʃn; *NAmE* ˌdʒenrələˈzeɪʃn/ *noun* **1** [C] a general statement that is true in most situations: *It is difficult to formulate generalizations or rules from the evidence.* ◇ **~ about sth** *The exercise may produce some useful generalizations about regional identity.* **2** [C] **~ (about sth)** (*disapproving*) a general statement that seems to be true, but that is based on too few facts or examples: *The situation is a complex one about which it would be unwise to make sweeping generalizations.* **3** [U] the act of making general statements based on only a few facts or examples: **~ of sth** *The small sample size does not allow generalization of the findings.* ◇ **~ to sth** *The geographical spread of the databases also allows for broad generalization to the UK population.*

gen·er·al·ize (*BrE also* **-ise**) /ˈdʒenrəlaɪz/ *verb* **1** [I] **~ (from sth)** to use a particular set of facts or ideas in order to form an opinion that is considered valid for a different situation: *It is difficult to generalize from the samples utilized in these studies, but the pattern of findings is striking.* **2** [I] to make a general statement about sth and not look at the details: *Positivists seek to generalize, whereas humanists focus on the individual and specific.* ◇ **~ about sth** *As these examples show, it is difficult to generalize about consumer behaviour because consumption patterns vary.* **3** [T, often passive] to apply a theory, idea, etc. to a wider group or situation than the original one: **~ sth** *The results should be generalized with care.* ◇ **~ sth to sth** *We cannot generalize our findings to all Albanian youth since we targeted university students only.*

gen·er·al·ized (*BrE also* **-ised**) /ˈdʒenrəlaɪzd/ *adj.* [usually before noun] **1** (of a theory, an idea, etc.) developed in order to apply to a wide group or situation: *This generalized model usefully complements detailed empirical studies.* **2** (*medical*) (of a disease or condition) affecting much or all of the body: *He has generalized abdominal pain that has never really improved since its onset.*

ˌgeneral ˈknowledge *noun* [U] knowledge of facts about a lot of different subjects: *Children who had viewed the show regularly performed better on tests of general knowledge, numbers, letters and word skills.*

gen·er·al·ly /ˈdʒenrəli/ *adv.* **1** by or to most people SYN WIDELY (1): *Globally, it is generally accepted that there are about 101 males for each 100 females.* ◇ *The work he did on volcanic rocks is generally regarded as his most important contribution.* ◇ *to be generally agreed/acknowledged/recognized/assumed/considered/thought/believed* **2** in most cases SYN USUALLY: *As yet, it is unclear whether this model is generally applicable.* ◇ *He generally remains cautious in his approach to proposed takeovers.* **3** without discussing the details of sth: *She has felt generally unwell but has no clear symptoms.* ◇ *Generally speaking, most companies have specific goals of one sort or another when they put together their marketing plan.* ➲ language bank *at* BROADLY

WHICH WORD?

generally • commonly

- Both **generally** and **commonly** are used to say what most people think or know: *Currently, it is generally agreed that genetic influence probably accounts for 30 to 70 per cent of behaviour.* ◇ *There is no commonly accepted definition of turbulence.*
- **Generally** is used when talking about what happens in most cases; **commonly** is used to say that sth is usual or frequent: *As yet, it is unclear whether this model is generally applicable.* ◇ *Type I diabetes commonly occurs in childhood, but can occur at any age.*
- **Commonly** is also used to say what ordinary people say: *Members of the Church of Jesus Christ of Latterday Saints are commonly known as Mormons.*
- **Generally** is used, especially in the phrase **generally speaking**, to indicate that you are not going to discuss details: *Hereditary peers have, generally speaking, inherited the title that they hold.*

ˌgeneral ˈpractice *noun* [U, C] (*especially BrE*) the work of a doctor who treats people in the community rather than at a hospital and who is not a specialist in one particular area of medicine; a place where a doctor like this works: *The assessment focuses on managing patients in general practice and not in a hospital environment.*

ˌgeneral pracˈtitioner (*abbr.* **GP**) (*also informal* ˌ**family ˈdoctor**) (*especially BrE*) *noun* a doctor who is trained in general medicine and who treats patients in a local community rather than at a hospital: *It is generally not possible for a patient to see a specialist without first consulting a general practitioner.*

the ˌgeneral ˈpublic *noun* [sing.+ sing./pl. v.] ordinary people who are not members of a particular group or organization: *Typically, this information is not available to the general public.*

gen·er·ate AWL /ˈdʒenəreɪt/ *verb* **1 ~ sth** to create feelings, opinions or situations: *His work generated considerable controversy in the 1970s and 1980s.* ◇ *National and international media have also been used to generate negative publicity.* **2 ~ sth** to produce a physical effect: *Mallet suggested that earthquakes generate longitudinal waves that radiate in all directions away from an epicentre.* ◇ *The engine needs to be heavily constructed to withstand the pressures generated within the cylinders.* **3 ~ sth** to produce sth by performing a particular operation, for example using a computer: *The calculations are entered into a spreadsheet to generate the data required.* ◇ *Zaniewski and Rosen (1998) published a computer-generated atlas of ethnic diversity in Wisconsin.* **4 ~ sth** to make money or create work; to increase business: *Shares may be issued to generate revenue for the company.* ◇ *The company is able to generate high total profits because it has such a high level of sales overall.* ➲ thesaurus note *at* SUPPLY[2] **5 ~ sth** to produce energy, especially electricity: *The* *dam's turbines will generate as much electricity as 18 nuclear power plants.* ➲ thesaurus note *at* SUPPLY²

▸ GENERATE + NOUN **interest • knowledge • insight • hypothesis • debate • controversy • publicity • problem • pressure • effect** *Public interest generated through the media also helped to maintain focus on the problem.* ◇ *The purpose of theory is to generate hypotheses that can be tested.* | **list • estimate • data • pattern • sequence • model** *An initial search generated a list of 432 publications.* | **revenue • profit • return • income • output • sales • growth** *Arts organizations will typically generate income through a number of streams:...* | **electricity • heat • signal • current • power • force** *Wood can be used to generate heat, electricity, biogas and other biofuels.*

gen·er·ation AWL /ˌdʒenəˈreɪʃn/ *noun* **1** [C+sing./pl. v.] all the people who were born at about the same time: *The aim is to enable people to improve their quality of life without compromising that of future generations.* ◇ **the younger/older ~** *The older generation tend to observe religious practices a lot more closely.* **2** [C] the average time in which children grow up, become adults and have children of their own (usually considered to be about 30 years): *Some family firms have survived for many generations.* ◇ *Within a generation, Japan was transformed from a medieval to a modern state.* **3** [C, U] a single stage in the history of a family: *The condition can actually appear to skip a generation.* ◇ **from ~ to ~** *Some stories that are passed on from generation to generation are myths that reflect the social system of a community.* ◇ *A significant number of participants were second-generation Americans.* HELP a **first-generation** American, etc. is a person whose family has lived in America, etc. for one generation. A **second-generation** American, etc. is a person whose family has lived in America, etc. for two generations. **4** [C, usually sing.] **~ (of sb)** a group of people involved in a particular activity at a particular time: *His research inspired a subsequent generation of economists.* ◇ *This new generation of entrepreneurs had access to considerable business knowledge.* **5** [C, usually sing.] a stage in the development of a product, usually one that is an improvement on the one before, because, for example, it uses more advanced technology: *First-generation microprocessors had truly tiny cache memories.* ◇ **~ of sth** *The company has developed an IT network that represents the next generation of airline IT technology.* **6** [U] the production of sth: *It is likely that in the future nuclear power will increase its share of the world's electricity generation.* ◇ *Research identified revenue generation and sales effectiveness as the top priorities of senior executives.* ◇ **~ of sth** *The generation of liquid water on a glacier surface is determined by very small changes in surface temperature.*

gen·er·ator /ˈdʒenəreɪtə(r)/ *noun* **1** a machine for producing electricity: *In the United States almost all utility electric power is generated by steam, gas, hydro or wind turbines driving an electric generator.* ◇ *Most farms were without electricity, although some had their own diesel generators.* **2** (*BrE*) a company that produces electricity to sell to the public: *Union Fenosa was the third largest electricity generator and supplier in Spain.* **3** a machine, an organization, etc. that produces sth: *Fuel is gasified in gas generators.* ◇ *The second biggest royalty generator was Germany, with £15 million.*

gen·er·ic /dʒəˈnerɪk/ *adj.* **1** shared by, including or typical of a whole group of things: *Nylon is the generic name for all synthetic polyamides.* ◇ *The generic term bronchopneumonia tends to be used for most non-specific pneumonias.* OPP SPECIFIC (1) **2** (of a product, especially a drug) not using the name of the company that made it; not having a BRAND NAME or TRADEMARK: *Some people felt that generic medicines were inferior or fake, mainly because these medicines were cheaper.* OPP BRANDED **3** connected with a GENUS: *Confusion resulted, as Linnaeus used the same generic name for too many species.* ■ **gen·er·ic·al·ly** /dʒəˈnerɪkli/ *adv.*: *The term 'polity' refers generically to any unit of politically organized power.*

gen·er·os·ity /ˌdʒenəˈrɒsəti; *NAmE* ˌdʒenəˈrɑːsəti/ *noun* [U] the quality of being kind and generous: *Generosity was everywhere recognized as a kingly virtue.*

gen·er·ous /ˈdʒenərəs/ *adj.* (*approving*) **1** giving or willing to give time, money, etc. freely; given freely: *Americans are very generous: in 2004, charitable giving reached a record $248.52 billion (Giving USA Foundation, 2006).* ◇ *Wealthy men and women made generous gifts to their cities, including aqueducts, feasts, schools and various types of charities.* **2** more than is necessary; large: *Generous provision was made for the children of his first marriage.* **3** kind in the way you treat people; willing to see what is good about sb/sth: *She wrote a very generous assessment of his work.* ■ **gen·er·ous·ly** *adv.*: *Our database contains 391 analyses from Iceland (unpublished data generously made available to us by K. Gronvold).* ◇ *As Mrs Cooper points out, her flat is well designed and generously proportioned.*

G

gen·et·ic /dʒəˈnetɪk/ *adj.* connected with GENES or GENETICS: *Mutation is the ultimate cause of all the genetic variation found in nature.* ◇ *Genetic analysis begins with parents that differ in one or more obvious ways.* ■ **gen·et·ic·al·ly** /dʒəˈnetɪkli/ *adv.*: *Individuals may be genetically predisposed to developing autoimmune disease.* ◇ *The second strain was genetically engineered to be incapable of sexual function.*

▸ GENETIC + NOUN **variation, diversity • variance, variability • variant • difference • differentiation • change • drift • mutation • modification, manipulation • engineering** *South African cheetahs show almost no genetic diversity across a wide range of different genes.* | **material • code • marker • data • make-up, constitution • map** *Evolution depends on the fact that genetic material does not replicate precisely.* | **factor • effect • predisposition, susceptibility • basis • information • background • association • correlation • influence** *Type 2 diabetes has increased rapidly in the developed world within a single generation, so this increase cannot be due to genetic factors alone.* | **disease • defect • disorder • risk • condition** *Genetic diseases vary among populations of different geographical origin and ethnicity.* | **study, research • analysis • test • testing • screen • screening** *Genetic studies to date have been limited by small sample sizes.*

geˌnetically ˈmodified *adj.* (*abbr.* **GM**) (of a plant, etc.) having had its genetic structure changed artificially, for example so that it will produce more fruit or not be affected by disease: *A series of food scares and concern over genetically modified organisms (GMOs) have propelled this issue up the EU's agenda.*

geˌnetic ˈcode *noun* (*biology*) the means by which DNA and RNA MOLECULES carry genetic information in living cells: *The genetic code is almost identical across all living things.*

geˌnetic ˈdrift *noun* [U] (*biology*) variation in the relative frequency of different GENOTYPES in a small population, as particular GENES disappear by chance as individuals die or do not produce young: *It can be difficult to distinguish between natural selection and random genetic drift.*

geˌnetic ˌengiˈneering *noun* [U] the science of changing how a living creature or plant develops by changing the information in its GENES: *There has been much speculation about the effects of genetic engineering on the future of our species.*

gen·eti·cist /dʒəˈnetɪsɪst/ *noun* a scientist who studies genetics: *Many developmental mutations studied by geneticists lie in the nucleus.*

gen·et·ics /dʒəˈnetɪks/ *noun* **1** [U] the scientific study of the ways in which different characteristics are passed from each generation of living things to the next through their GENES: *The ability of population genetics to tell us about the history of the human population is improving all the time.* ◇ *Molecular genetics is now integral to all aspects of biomedical science.* **2** [sing.+ sing./pl. v.] **~ (of sth)** the genetic features of a particular living thing or being: *The third preoccupation of many Neurospora investigators after 1945 was the basic genetics of Neurospora.*

ge·nius /ˈdʒiːniəs/ *noun* (*pl.* **ge·niuses**) **1** [U] **~ (of sb)** unusually great intelligence, skill or ARTISTIC ability: *The genius of Einstein lay in extending this principle to all the laws of physics.* **2** [C] a person who is unusually intelligent, or who has a very high level of skill, especially in one area: *By the 1550s, regarding composers as musical geniuses was a well-established practice.*

G

geno·cide /ˈdʒenəsaɪd/ *noun* [U, C] the murder of a whole race or group of people: *He was indicted for genocide and other crimes against humanity.* ◇ *News of genocides went unreported.* ■ **geno·cidal** /ˌdʒenəˈsaɪdl/ *adj.*: *genocidal policies/violence*

gen·ome /ˈdʒiːnəʊm; *NAmE* ˈdʒiːnoʊm/ *noun* the complete set of GENES in a cell or living thing: *It has been predicted that about 10 years from now it will be possible to sequence an entire human genome in 30 minutes.* ◇ *Establishing the whole genome sequence for a pathogen is very expensive and time-consuming.* ◇ **~ of sth** *Mycoplasmas have the smallest genomes of any non-virus organism.*

gen·om·ics /dʒiːˈnəʊmɪks; dʒiːˈnɒmɪks; *NAmE* dʒiːˈnoʊmɪks; dʒiːˈnɑːmɪks/ *noun* [U] the scientific study of the structure, function and development of genomes: *Comparative genomics examines the genomes of closely related species to identify sequences that could be significant.*

geno·type /ˈdʒenətaɪp; ˈdʒiːnətaɪp/ *noun* (*biology*) the combination of GENES that a particular living thing carries, some of which may not be noticed from its appearance: *These tissues are composed of cells of two different genotypes.* ◇ **~ of sth** *The process of defining the genotype of an individual uses laboratory techniques such as DNA sequencing and PCR.* ➲ *compare* PHENOTYPE ■ **geno·typic** /ˌdʒenəˈtɪpɪk; ˌdʒiːnəˈtɪpɪk/ *adj.*: *Phenotypic variation is much more extensive than genotypic variation.*

genre /ˈʒɒ̃rə; ˈʒɒnrə; *NAmE* ˈʒɑːnrə/ *noun* a particular type or style of literature, art, film or music that you can recognize because of its special features: *These poets assumed that poetry was the highest of the literary genres.* ◇ *Greek tragedy and comedy have been adapted in a variety of cinematic genres and traditions.*

gen·tle /ˈdʒentl/ *adj.* (**gent·ler** /ˈdʒentlə(r)/, **gent·lest** /ˈdʒentlɪst/) **1** having only a small effect; not strong or violent: *The beads were washed three times for 10 minutes by gentle agitation in a tube rotator.* **2** not steep or sharp: *The long, gentle slopes of the uplands allow for easy extension of agricultural land.* **3** calm and kind; doing things in a quiet and careful way: *It is essential that the child's induction is managed in a gentle and sympathetic manner.* **4** (of weather, temperature, etc.) not strong or extreme: *Winter storms originate in the North Pacific and bring relatively gentle rains.* ➲ *see also* GENTLY

gentle·man /ˈdʒentlmən/ *noun* (*pl.* **-men** /-mən/) **1** (*formal*) a polite or formal way of referring to a man: *Mr Bell is a 62-year-old gentleman who presented to his GP complaining of chest pain.* ➲ *compare* LADY (1) **2** (in the past) a man from a high social class, especially one who did not need to work: *After serving in the Peninsular War, he returned to the life of an English country gentleman.* ➲ *compare* LADY (3)

gen·tly /ˈdʒentli/ *adv.* **1** in a way that only has a small effect, and that is not strong or violent: *The mixture was then heated gently until the initial reaction subsided.* ◇ *The bottles should be mixed gently by inversion and sent to the laboratory.* **2** in a way that is not steep or sharp: *Flat or gently sloping land composes less than 5% of the southern Appalachian landscape.* **3** in a way that is calm and kind: *The film seems particularly well suited to Hepburn's style with its gently comic scenes.*

genu·ine /ˈdʒenjuɪn/ *adj.* **1** real; exactly what it appears/they appear to be: *None of them was in possession of a genuine passport.* ◇ *The Act had the effect of criminalizing genuine asylum seekers who often can only leave their own country using a false passport.* ◇ *The main question is whether or not the marriage was genuine.* ➲ *compare* AUTHENTIC **2** honest; that can be trusted SYN SINCERE: *Most of the respondents had a genuine desire to be able to teach in the UK.* ◇ *It is important for patients to sense that the nurse is honest and genuine in his or her intentions.* ■ **genu·ine·ly** *adv.*: *The first genuinely democratic South African government was elected in 1994.*

genus /ˈdʒiːnəs/ *noun* (*pl.* **gen·era** /ˈdʒenərə/) (*biology*) a group into which animals, plants, etc. that are related are divided, smaller than a FAMILY and larger than a SPECIES: *Plants or animals belonging to the same genus share more characteristics than others in the same order or class.* ◇ *The genus Homo, appearing first in Africa, spread rapidly into Eurasia.* ➲ *compare* CLASS[1] (6), KINGDOM (2), ORDER[1] (9), PHYLUM ➲ *see also* GENERIC (3)

geog·raph·er /dʒiˈɒgrəfə(r); *NAmE* dʒiˈɑːgrəfər/ *noun* a person who studies geography; an expert in geography: *Cultural geographers have long been interested in the movement of cultural groups and how this affects the related landscape.* ◇ *Human geographers recognize that any one area changes through time.*

geo·graph·ic·al /ˌdʒiːəˈgræfɪkl/ (*also* **geo·graph·ic** /ˌdʒiːəˈgræfɪk/) *adj.* connected with an area or a place, or its geography: *The prevalence of chronic conditions varies with age, social class and geographical location.* ◇ *The geographical distribution of Roman Catholicism in the British Isles was dramatically uneven.* ■ **geo·graph·ic·al·ly** /ˌdʒiːəˈgræfɪkli/ *The region is also geographically distant from the clusters of powerful democracies in the West.*

geog·raphy /dʒiˈɒgrəfi; *NAmE* dʒiˈɑːgrəfi/ *noun* (*pl.* **-ies**) **1** [U] the scientific study of the earth's surface, physical features, divisions, products, population, etc: *In this article I shall examine the links between physical and human geography.* ◇ *The relevance of economic geography for carbon market operation has important policy implications.* ◇ *regional/cultural/historical/political/feminist geography* ➲ *see also* PHYSICAL GEOGRAPHY (2) **2** [C, usually sing.] **the ~ of sth** the way in which the physical features of a place are arranged: *Europeans had little knowledge of the geography of Africa beyond fifty or a hundred miles from the coast.* ◇ *The behaviour of the bears is largely defined by the geography of the landscape through which they move.* ➲ *see also* PHYSICAL GEOGRAPHY (1) **3** [C, usually sing.] **~ of sth** the way in which a particular aspect of life or society is found in an area: *Globalization exhibits a distinctive geography of inclusion and exclusion, resulting in clear winners and losers.*

geo·logic·al /ˌdʒiːəˈlɒdʒɪkl; *NAmE* ˌdʒiːəˈlɑːdʒɪkl/ (*also less frequent* **geo·logic** /ˌdʒiːəˈlɒdʒɪk; *NAmE* ˌdʒiːəˈlɑːdʒɪk/) *adj.* connected with the scientific study of the earth, including the ORIGIN and history of the rocks and soil of which the earth is made: *Soil is formed over periods of geological time by a combination of physical and chemical processes.* ◇ *There is evidence in the geological record to support the notion of extensive glaciation.* ■ **geo·logic·al·ly** /ˌdʒiːəˈlɒdʒɪkli; *NAmE* ˌdʒiːəˈlɑːdʒɪkli/ *adv.*: *The earth evolved into a planet with many of its present properties* *in a very short time, geologically speaking: about 500 million years.*

geolo·gist /dʒiˈɒlədʒɪst; *NAmE* dʒiˈɑːlədʒɪst/ *noun* a scientist who studies geology: *Based on bedding types, geologists can recognize three kinds of sandstone.*

geol·ogy /dʒiˈɒlədʒi; *NAmE* dʒiˈɑːlədʒi/ *noun* **1** [U] the scientific study of the earth, including the ORIGIN and history of the rocks and soil of which the earth is made: *Shepard was author of many scientific papers, mainly concerned with marine geology and research.* **2** [sing.] **~ (of sth)** the ORIGIN and history of the rocks and soil of a particular area: *The four largest rivers in Africa are all affected by rapids and waterfalls because of the geology of the continent.*

geo·met·ric /ˌdʒiːəˈmetrɪk/ (*also less frequent* **geo·met·ric·al** /ˌdʒiːəˈmetrɪkl/) *adj.* **1** connected with GEOMETRY: *Pythagoras was credited for the geometric theorem to which he gives his name.* **2** of or like the lines, shapes, etc. used in geometry, especially because of having regular shapes or lines: *To completely cover an area without any overlap, the ideal shape is the hexagon—the nearest geometric figure to a circle.* **3 ~ progression/series** (*mathematics*) a series in which the RATIO of each term and the next remains CONSTANT, for example 1, 3, 9, 27, 81: *A savings account with a fixed compound interest rate will grow by geometric progression.* ⊃ *compare* ARITHMETIC² (1) **4 ~ mean** (*mathematics*) an average arrived at through calculating the *n*th root of the product of *n* numbers: *The geometric mean can be used to average proportional increases in wages.* ⊃ *compare* MEAN² (2)

geo·met·ric·al·ly /ˌdʒiːəˈmetrɪkli/ *adv.* **1** in a way that uses geometric lines and shapes: *Integrals can be represented geometrically, as the area under the curve on a graph.* **2** (of the way a figure increases) in a regular way, multiplying by the same amount over the same period: *Population, Malthus argued, had a constant tendency to increase geometrically, doubling in size every 25 years.*

geom·etry /dʒiˈɒmətri; *NAmE* dʒiˈɑːmətri/ *noun* **1** [U] the branch of mathematics that deals with the measurements and relationships of lines, angles, surfaces and solids: *Using some simple geometry and a geological map, it is possible to get an idea of the three-dimensional geology beneath the surface of the land.* **2** [sing.] **~ (of sth)** the measurements and relationships of lines, angles, etc. in a particular object or shape: *The field of plate kinematics aims to describe the movements of plates and the changing geometry of their boundaries.*

germ /dʒɜːm; *NAmE* dʒɜːrm/ *noun* **1** [usually pl.] a MICRO-ORGANISM (= a very small living thing) that can cause disease: *The worldwide spread of germs became possible only after all the inhabited continents were connected by travel routes.* **2** (*biology*) the part of a plant or animal that can develop into a new one or part of one: **+ noun** *The concept of germ layers is useful to distinguish between regions of the early embryo that give rise to quite distinct types of tissues.*

ˈgerm cell *noun* (*biology*) a cell that has the POTENTIAL (= possibility) to develop into a GAMETE: *An important property of germ cells is that they remain totipotent—able to give rise to all the different types of cells in the body.* HELP In more informal use, **germ cell** may be used to refer to eggs, SPERM or gametes, i.e. any cell that can join one of the opposite sex to form a new individual; however, this is not correct scientific usage.

ges·ta·tion /dʒeˈsteɪʃn/ *noun* **1** [U, sing.] the time that the young of a person or an animal develops inside its mother's body until it is born; the process of developing inside the mother's body: **during ~** *Changes in physical body size during gestation were monitored.* ◇ **at ... weeks' ~** *Babies born at less than 32 weeks' gestation may need some oxygen.* ◇ **+ noun** *The gestation period in the African elephant is relatively long (22 months).* **2** [U] the process by which an idea or a plan develops: *Many international business projects are of very long gestation.*

ges·ture /ˈdʒestʃə(r)/ *noun* **1** [C, U] **~ (of sth)** something that you do or say to show a particular feeling or intention: *German Chancellor Willy Brandt went down on his knees at the death camp and this gesture of atonement was widely reported.* **2** [C, U] a movement that you make with your hands, your head or your face to show a particular meaning: *the stylized gestures of the silent cinema* ◇ *The use of gesture and facial expression are vital elements of non-verbal communication.*

get /get/ *verb* (**getting, got, got** /gɒt; *NAmE* gɑːt/) HELP In spoken American English, the past participle **gotten** /ˈgɑːtn/ is almost always used. HELP **Get** is one of the most common words in English, but people often try to avoid it in formal writing and use alternative words such as **obtain** or **receive**. **1** [T, no passive] **~ sth** to obtain sth: *When we repeated the procedure, we got the same results.* ◇ *The central issue here is that 800 million people still do not get enough food (UNDP, 1996: 20).* ◇ *Studies show that to get good grades one also has to develop certain personality traits.* **2** [T, no passive] **~ sth** to receive sth: *Surprisingly, Switzerland gets more US investment than all of South America.* ◇ *Individuals might get the impression that good health can be maintained by regular health checks only.* **3** *linking verb* to reach a particular state or condition; to make sb/sth/yourself reach a particular state or condition: **+ adj.** *Of course, most species in the wild tend to die long before they get old.* ◇ *In conclusion, it seems that the world food crisis can only get worse, regardless of technological change.* ◇ **~ sb/sth/yourself + adj.** *Grace is a student who always wants to get things right and is reluctant to take risks.* **4** [T] to help, persuade or force sb/sth to do sth: **~ sb/sth + adv./prep.** *In the 1980s, self-employment seemed a positive mechanism for getting people back to work (Birch, 1979).* ◇ **~ sb/sth to do sth** *There are many pricing techniques used by companies to get people to try out a product.* ◇ **~ sb/sth doing sth** *Timebank is a national charity that aims to get more people volunteering across the country.* **5** [I, T] to move to or from a particular place or in a particular direction, sometimes with difficulty; to make sb/sth do this: **+ adv./prep.** *Nevertheless, most people in the city still rely on public transport to get to work.* ◇ **~ sb/sth + adv./prep.** *The main problem was getting a message to every node in the network.* **6** [I] **+ adv./prep.** to arrive at or reach a place or point: *In the novel, an elderly man crosses the English Channel, but then only gets as far as Paris.* ◇ *The legislation never got far in the Senate.* **7** [I] **~ to do/be sth** to reach the point at which you feel, know, are, etc. sth: *It took a few weeks for most of the students to get to know each other.* **8** [I] **~ to do sth** to have the opportunity to do sth: *Only the alpha male gets to mate with visiting females.* **9** [T] **~ sth done** to cause sth to happen or be done: *The office lacked any standardized procedures for getting things done.* **10** [T, no passive] **~ sth** to become infected with an illness; to suffer from a pain, etc: *Patients with coeliac disease are twice as likely to get cancer as the general population.* **11** [T, no passive] **~ sth** to receive sth as a punishment: *According to studies, African American murderers were almost three times as likely to get the death sentence as white murderers.*
IDM Most idioms containing **get** are at the entries for the nouns and adjectives in the idioms, for example **get hold of sth** is at **hold** *noun.* **ˈget there** to achieve an aim or complete a task: *The company aimed to produce a luxury watch, but it took a few decades to get there.*
PHR V **ˌget sth aˈcross (to sb)** to succeed in communicating sth: *She uses analogies to get her point across to the reader.*
ˌget aˈhead to make progress or become more successful, especially in comparison with other people: *Membership*

of the Communist Party was almost essential for anybody wishing to get ahead.

ˌget aˈlong = GET ON WITH SB, GET ON (TOGETHER)

ˌget aˈround ➲ GET ROUND/AROUND STH

ˈget at sth **1** to find out and understand sth: *Delamont (1976) used semi-structured interviews to get at some of the reasons for differences in teaching styles.* **2** to try to express or explain sth: *This sense of homelessness is what the novel is getting at.*

ˌget aˈway from sth to stop thinking and talking about sth in the usual way: *It is important to get away from the idea that commercial advertising is part of a sustainable system.*

ˌget aˈway with (doing) sth to do sth wrong and not be punished for it: *Several cabinet members were clearly angry that Bush had got away with the deception.*

ˌget ˈback to/into sth to start doing an activity again that you previously stopped: *Disability advisers can assist patients with bipolar disorder to get back into employment.* **ˌget sth ˈback** to obtain sth again after having spent it or lost it: *Advertisers naturally want to get back the money they have spent on their campaign fairly quickly.*

ˌget ˈby (on/in/with sth) to manage to live or do a particular thing using the money, knowledge, equipment, etc. that you have: *A sea hare gets by with a nervous system of only about 20 000 neurons.*

ˌget ˈinto sth | ˌget sb/yourself ˈinto sth to reach a particular state or condition; to make sb reach a particular state or condition: *As the crisis deepened, investment projects were halted, and industrial firms got into difficulties.* ◇ *His outspoken views got him into trouble with the authorities.*

ˌget ˌon **1** used to talk about how well sb is doing in a particular situation: *According to Kvande and Rasmussen (1995), both women and men get on better in gender balanced organizations.* **2** to be successful in your career, etc: *The policy rested on the assumption that employment is the means by which people get on in life.* **ˌget ˈon with sb | ˌget ˈon (together)** (*both BrE*) (*also* **ˌget aˈlong with sb, ˌget aˈlong (together)** *NAmE, BrE*) to have a friendly relationship with sb: *Although Tyndall and Faraday got on well at a personal level, their ideological positions were quite different.* ◇ *Peace education would help nations to get along with each other through communication and mutual respect.* **ˌget ˈon with sth** to continue doing sth, especially after an interruption: *When Bohr went on holiday, Heisenberg took the opportunity to get on with his own work.*

ˌget ˈout (of sth) to leave or go out of a place: *After the operation, these patients were fully mobile, able to get out and meet people.*

ˌget ˈover sth to deal with or gain control of sth SYN OVERCOME (1): *Covert research methods were used to get over the difficulties in gaining access.*

ˌget ˈround/aˈround sth to deal with a problem successfully SYN OVERCOME (1): *Designers can get round the problem by providing audio feedback.*

ˈget through sth to survive a difficult period or task: *Getting through this global crisis requires an understanding of our own ethical systems.* **ˌget ˈthrough (sth) | ˌget sth ˈthrough (sth)** to be officially accepted; to make sth be officially accepted: *Cooperation is usually essential to get a policy through Congress.* **ˌget ˈthrough (to sb)** to reach sb; to communicate with sb and make them understand what you say: *By the late 1990s, it seemed that public health messages about sexually transmitted infections were not getting through.*

ˌget toˈgether (with sb) to meet with sb socially or in order to discuss sth: *The group gets together once a year to share experiences.*

ˌget ˈup **1** to stand up after sitting, lying, etc: *Seated black passengers were supposed to get up and let white passengers sit down.* **2** to get out of bed: *Risk is accepted as part of most day-to-day activities, even getting up in the morning and travelling to work.*

GHG /ˌdʒiː eɪtʃ ˈdʒiː/ *abbr.* GREENHOUSE GAS

giant[1] /ˈdʒaɪənt/ *adj.* [only before noun] very large; much larger or more important than similar things usually are: *Engwall (2006) looked generally at the role of giant firms in global governance.* ◇ *All four giant planets have ring systems, made of dust and icy debris.*

giant[2] /ˈdʒaɪənt/ *noun* **1** (*rather informal*) a very large and powerful organization: *They were unable to compete with the global media giants.* **2** (*rather informal*) a person who is very good at sth: *Avicenna (d.1037) and Averroes (d.1198) were among the intellectual giants of their times.* **3** an unusually large person, animal or plant: *Most ostracods are small, generally 0.3 to 3 mm long, although a few giants are as much as 30 mm in length.* **4** (in stories) a very large strong person who is often cruel and stupid: *The blinded giant cursed Odysseus, asking his father to punish him.*

gift /ɡɪft/ *noun* **1** something that you give to sb without payment SYN PRESENT[2] (2): *In Saudi Arabia diamonds are an important wedding gift.* ◇ **~ to sb/sth** *He had made several large gifts to charity.* **2** a natural ability ➲ *compare* TALENT (1): **~ for sth** *Morgan is a talented writer with a gift for descriptive prose.* ◇ **~ for doing sth** *She had a gift for capturing people's attention and getting them to listen.* **3 ~ (of sth)** something that is freely available to sb and is good to have: *Unlike other creatures on earth, we have the wonderful gifts of language and culture, art and science.* ◇ *The beauty of the natural world is seen by some as a divine gift.* **4** [usually sing.] **~ (to/for sb)** a thing that is very easy to do or an opportunity that sb should not miss, for example because it gives them an advantage: *This was a gift to the Conservatives who wanted to make defence an issue in the campaign.*

gift·ed /ˈɡɪftɪd/ *adj.* [usually before noun] having a lot of natural ability or intelligence: *These intellectually gifted children were compared with their peer group.* ◇ *He was acknowledged as one of the most gifted writers of his generation.*

girl /ɡɜːl; *NAmE* ɡɜːrl/ *noun* **1** a female child: *Both girls and boys can be encouraged to engage in creative writing.* ◇ *young/adolescent/teenage girls* **2** (*sometimes offensive*) a young woman: *In the interwar period, there was anxiety that the modern 'career girl' would undermine the values of marriage and motherhood.* HELP This use of **girl** is considered offensive by many people; it is better to use 'young woman', unless you are quoting.

give /ɡɪv/ *verb* (**gave** /ɡeɪv/, **given** /ˈɡɪvn/) **1** [T] to provide sb/sth with sth; to provide sth: **~ sb/sth sth** *These activities give students opportunities to work on public speaking skills.* ◇ *Participants were given a one-hour briefing.* ◇ **~ sth to sb/sth** *He gave advice to the British government before and during World War II.* ◇ *The treatment is given directly to the inflamed area.* ◇ **~ sth** *The website gives information about this.* ◇ *All participants gave written informed consent.* ◇ **(be) given + adv./prep.** *Two examples are given below.* ◇ *The results are given in Table 8.1.* ◇ *For the reasons given above, these specific environmental effects can be difficult to quantify.* HELP **Give** is often used with a noun, forming an expression that has the same meaning as the related verb. For example, 'to give advice' means 'to advise'. ➲ thesaurus note *at* PROVIDE **2** [T] to hand sth to sb: **~ sth to sb** *A single ticket is given to each participant.* ◇ **~ sb sth** *Research assistants gave the children an introduction letter and consent form to take home to their parents.* **3** [T, I] to hand sth to sb as a present; to allow sb to have sth as a present: **~ sb sth** *It was common practice to give medical personnel gifts of chocolates or flowers.* ◇ **~ sth to sb/sth** *Among those who do give money to religious or charitable causes, the distribution of giving is not spread evenly.* ◇ **~ sth** *No employee* *may offer, give or receive any gift or payment which may be construed as a bribe.* ◇ **~ (to sb/sth)** *This system makes it possible for employees to give to any charity of their choice.* **4** [T, often passive] to say that sb should have sth, for example a score, prize or punishment: **~ sth** *32.7% of respondents gave the maximum number of points.* ◇ **~ sth for sth** *This was an award given for academic excellence.* ◇ **~ sb sth** *She was given a suspended prison sentence.* ◇ **~ sth to sb/sth** *Officials give priority to those individuals who are most in need of protection.* ➲ *compare* AWARD² (1) **5** [T] to produce a particular feeling or effect SYN CREATE: **~ sth** *Political leaders try to give the impression that they are in control of events.* ◇ **~ sb/sth sth** *This produces patches of star formation around the galaxy, giving it an irregular, patchy appearance.* **6** [T] **~ sth** to produce a particular value or result: *5 multiplied by itself gives 25.* ◇ *The balanced concentration of positive and negatively charged species gives a net ionic charge of zero.* **7** [T] to use time, energy, etc. for sb/sth: **~ sth to sb/sth** *Little attention is given to their emotional problems.* ◇ **~ sb/sth sth** *Certain decisions are made automatically, seemingly without giving them much thought.* **8** to speak in a formal situation, usually in public SYN DELIVER (3): **~ sth** *She was there to give a paper at the conference.* ◇ **~ sth to sb/sth** *Victims may give a statement to the court.* HELP Idioms containing **give** are at the entries for the nouns and adjectives in the idioms, for example **give rise to sth** is at **rise** *noun.*

PHR V **ˌgive sth aˈway** to hand sth to sb; to allow sb to have sth: *The company may give away free gifts as a sales incentive.* ◇ *Lear gives away his kingdom to his daughters in a show of power and bravado.*

ˌgive ˈback (to sb/sth) to do sth in order to help sb/sth, because you are grateful: *Ten respondents (40%) expressed aspirations to give back to their community and society as a whole.* **ˌgive sth ˈback (to sb)** to return sth to its owner; to allow sb to have sth again: *Many companies were given back to their original owners.* ◇ *It was right to give the money back.* HELP In general English, **give sb back sth** is often used: *The gods gave him back his sight.* This is more informal, and is therefore best avoided in academic writing: instead, use **return sth (to sb)** or **give sth back (to sb).**

ˌgive ˈin to sth/sb to agree to do sth that you do not want to do: *Discomfort leads some parents to give in to a child's demands.* ◇ *He criticized the men for giving in to their wives.*

ˌgive ˈoff sth to produce sth such as gas or energy: *Carbon dioxide is given off during the combustion of every carbon-based fuel.* ◇ *It can split into two smaller atoms, giving off energy in the process.*

ˌgive sth ˈout (to sb) to hand sth to a lot of people: *Questionnaires were given out to first-year undergraduate students.* **ˌgive ˈout sth** to produce sth such as gas or energy, rather than taking it in: *Such a process gives out energy rather than requiring energy to be supplied.*

ˌgive sth ˈover to sth [usually passive] to use sth for one particular purpose: *Land was cleared of forest and given over to arable fields.*

ˌgive ˈup to stop trying to do sth; to stop doing sth: *These people give up easily when they encounter difficulties.* ◇ *Two thirds of cigarette smokers said that they wanted to give up.* **ˌgive ˈup sth** [no passive] to stop doing or having sth: *Helena gave up work to care for the baby.* ◇ *Many people who give up smoking relapse.* ◇ *He had never given up hope that they would one day get back together.* ◇ *They were prepared to give up everything for the sake of a political ideology.* **ˌgive sb/sth ˈup** to hand or pass sb/sth over to sb/sth else: *She had given her child up for adoption.* ◇ *When a photon collides with an electron, it gives up all its energy.* **ˌgive ˈup on sb/sth** to stop believing that sb/sth is good, valuable or worth working for: *Divorced individuals generally do not give up on marriage.* ◇ *These teachers do not give up on their students.*

given¹ *past part. of* GIVE

given² /ˈgɪvn/ *prep.* when sth is considered: *Given these difficulties, it is unsurprising that the issue came before the Supreme Court.* ◇ *Coronary artery disease was the most likely diagnosis, given the patient's history of myocardial infarction.*

given³ /ˈgɪvn/ *adj.* [usually before noun] **1** that you have stated or are discussing; particular: *A temporary shortage of resources at a given location can be overcome in two ways.* ◇ **any ~** *This is invaluable for deciding on the best e-marketing strategy in any given situation.* ◇ **at a/any ~ time/moment** *The supply of shares in a company at any given moment is fixed.* **2** already decided or known: *Those wishing to participate were asked to respond within a given time.* ◇ *We also assume that the total number of people seeking work is given, that prices are constant, and that wages do not vary with the level of employment.*

G

given⁴ /ˈgɪvn/ *noun* something that is accepted as true or that already exists: *Many scholars have accepted as a given his argument that...* ◇ **~ of sth** *Borders were often drawn arbitrarily, ignoring actual givens of the land, patterns of settlement and centuries old trading ties.* ◇ **take it/sth as a ~ (that...)** *Virtually every commentator in the country took it as a given that Clinton would be nominated.*

ˈgiven that *conj.* considering the stated facts: *Given that management time is finite, an interesting question is why particular issues seem to take priority.*

giver /ˈgɪvə(r)/ *noun* a person or an organization that gives sth, especially money: *Five per cent of givers contribute 60 per cent of the total amount.* ◇ **~ of sth** *God is seen as the only legitimate giver and taker of life.*

gla·cial /ˈgleɪʃl; ˈgleɪsiəl/ *adj.* [usually before noun] **1** (*earth science*) connected with an Ice Age: *During the most recent glacial period, ice covered an area approximately three times greater than that covered today.* ◇ *Over the last million years, there have been four major glacial advances and retreats.* **2** caused or made by glaciers; connected with glaciers: *Elias notes that glacial ice has been the dominant force in shaping alpine landscapes.*

gla·ci·ation /ˌgleɪsiˈeɪʃn/ *noun* [U, C] (*earth science*) the process or result of land being covered by glaciers; a period when this happens: *The South Pole was centred in north-western Africa, causing widespread glaciation in that region.* ◇ *Evidence of former extensive glaciations is recorded in high-latitude ice cores and in ocean sediments.*

gla·cier /ˈglæsiə(r); *NAmE* ˈgleɪʃər/ *noun* a large mass of ice, formed by snow on mountains, that moves very slowly down a VALLEY: *Explanations for the advance or retreat of glaciers rely on both climatic variables and landscape characteristics.*

glance /glɑːns; *NAmE* glæns/ *noun* **~ (at sb/sth)** a quick look: *A first glance at the results reveals two key findings.* IDM **at a (single) ˈglance** immediately; with only a quick look: *Potential supporters and clients should be able to see at a glance what the organization is trying to achieve.* **at first ˈglance** when you first look at or think about sth, often rather quickly: *At first glance, the EU's policy process seems hopelessly complicated.*

gland /glænd/ *noun* an organ in the body that produces a substance for the body to use. There are many different glands in the body: *The commonest causes of swellings of the salivary glands are stones, tumours or infection.* ◇ *the pituitary/thyroid gland* ◇ *the adrenal/endocrine/sweat glands* ■ **glan·du·lar** /ˈglændjʊlə(r); *NAmE* ˈglændʒələr/ *adj.* [usually before noun] *There was no evidence of glandular tissue swelling.*

glass /glɑːs; *NAmE* glæs/ *noun* **1** [U] a hard, usually transparent substance used, for example, for making windows: *The cover slip is a piece of 0.17-mm-thick glass.* ◇ **+ noun**

glass slides/jars/beakers/tubes **2** [U, C] (*technical*) a clear substance usually made from heating sand with SODIUM CARBONATE and LIME that becomes solid after cooling from the liquid state without forming CRYSTALS: *Volcanic glass older than the Cenozoic era is extremely rare.* ◇ *At this temperature the polymer changes from a glass to a rubbery material.* **3 glasses** (*also* **spec·tacles**) [pl.] an object consisting of a pair of LENSES or pieces of glass that sb wears in front of their eyes in order to see better or to protect the eyes: *Distance glasses should be worn as the test is of the best corrected visual acuity.* ◇ *There are personal safety protocols to be observed that include wearing ear plugs and safety glasses.* **4** [C] a container made of glass, used for drinking out of; the contents of a glass: *a wine glass* ◇ **~ of sth** *He was offered a glass of water.*

G

glean /gliːn/ *verb* [often passive] **~ sth (from sb/sth)** to collect or obtain information or knowledge: *The knowledge gleaned from these studies is important and needs to be built on.* ◇ *There will also be information gleaned from liaison with other professionals.*

global AWL /ˈgləʊbl; *NAmE* ˈgloʊbl/ *adj.* [usually before noun] **1** covering or affecting the whole world: *Global weather patterns can be affected by airborne pollution from volcanic eruptions.* ◇ *Thus, to a significant extent, the economy is now global while government is still local.* ◇ *Many non-profit organizations are now truly global in scope.* **2** considering or including all parts of sth: *This review will attempt to integrate these trends into a global picture.* ◇ *The new ICT solutions gave executives a global view of operations and efficiencies across all departments.* IDM *see* COMMUNITY

▸ GLOBAL + NOUN **scale • context • standard • level • change • trend • phenomenon • issue • crisis • perspective • communication • strategy • system • network • reach** *On a global scale, the largest 1 000 corporations produce about four-fifths of the world's output.* ◇ *The global financial crisis of the early twenty-first century recalled the lessons of the Great Depression.* | **industry • production • trade • competition • market, marketplace • marketing • brand • economy • finance • capitalism • recession** *Consumers are more demanding in this age of global competition.* ◇ *The demands of global markets appear able to erode cultural traditions.* | **society • culture • institution • politics • governance • security • environment • climate • temperature • warming** *An increase in global temperatures is expected to increase the intensity of extreme weather events.*

glob·al·iza·tion (*BrE also* **-isa·tion**) AWL /ˌgləʊbəlaɪˈzeɪʃn; *NAmE* ˌgloʊbələˈzeɪʃn/ *noun* [U] the fact that different cultures and economic systems around the world are becoming connected and similar to each other because of the influence of large MULTINATIONAL companies and of improved communication: *There is a continuing trend towards globalization in businesses and markets.* ◇ *Globalization has therefore turned what were once local, or at most national, problems into international ones.*

glob·al·ize (*BrE also* **-ise**) /ˈgləʊbəlaɪz; *NAmE* ˈgloʊbəlaɪz/ *verb* [I, T] to involve countries all around the world; to create connections with organizations, businesses, etc. in different countries: *This is occurring largely because of the improved communications associated with the globalizing economy.* ◇ **~ sth** *In a globalized world, power is no longer organized according to a national or territorial logic.* ◇ *Retailers are looking to globalize their activities as part of their growth strategy.*

glob·al·ly AWL /ˈgləʊbəli; *NAmE* ˈgloʊbəli/ *adv.* in a way that involves the whole world: *The fact that populations are increasingly elderly has implications locally, nationally and globally.*

ˌglobal ˈwarming *noun* [U] the increase in temperature of the earth's atmosphere, that is caused by the increase of particular gases, especially CARBON DIOXIDE: *Because of their very long lifetimes in the atmosphere, CFCs will contribute to global warming for many decades to come.* ➲ *compare* CLIMATE CHANGE ➲ *see also* GREENHOUSE EFFECT

globe AWL /gləʊb; *NAmE* gloʊb/ *noun* **1 the globe** [sing.] the world (used especially to emphasize its size): **(across/around) the ~** *Across the globe, women's education reflects both serious inequality and significant change.* ◇ **every corner/all corners of the ~** *The human immunodeficiency virus had reached virtually every corner of the globe, infecting over 65 million people.* **2** [C] an object shaped like a ball with a map of the world on its surface: *If we imagine a globe, we can draw a grid on it with lines radiating from any point.*

glu·cose /ˈgluːkəʊs; ˈgluːkəʊz; *NAmE* ˈgluːkoʊs; ˈgluːkoʊz/ *noun* [U] a simple type of sugar that is an important energy source in living things and that is a part of many CARBOHYDRATES: *Her body is unable to metabolize glucose.* ◇ *As the blood sugar levels fall, glucagon levels in the blood rise, telling the liver to release glucose.* ◇ **+ noun** *They monitored their blood glucose levels on a regular basis.* HELP **Glucose** is a member of a class of simple sugars whose MOLECULES contain six CARBON atoms. Its chemical formula is $C_6H_{12}O_6$: *The condensation reaction between two glucose molecules produces sucrose, $C_{12}H_{22}O_{11}$, with the elimination of water.*

glue /gluː/ *noun* **1** [U, C] a sticky substance that is used for joining things together: *In Greek myth, Icarus flew so high that the sun melted the glue in his wings.* **2** [U] something that forms a connection between people or groups: *Durkheim claims that the glue holding society together is ritual.*

GM /ˌdʒiː ˈem/ *abbr.* (*BrE*) GENETICALLY MODIFIED

GNP /ˌdʒiː en ˈpiː/ *noun* [U, C, usually sing.] the abbreviation for **'gross national product'** (the total value of all the goods and services produced by a country in one year, including the total income from foreign countries): *The two countries had similar levels of per capita GNP.* ◇ **~ of sth** *Namibia is a lower-middle income country with a GNP per capita of US$6 960.* ➲ *compare* GDP

go /gəʊ; *NAmE* goʊ/ *verb* (**goes** /gəʊz; *NAmE* goʊz/, **went** /went/, **gone** /gɒn; *NAmE* gɔːn/) **1** [I] to move or travel somewhere: **~ to sth** *Park went to Africa in 1794 and returned in 1799.* ◇ **+ adv./prep.** *Patients go home within 24 hours.* ◇ *The electron is going at a speed which is very close to the speed of light.* ◇ *The shockwaves of these events went around the world.* HELP If sb/sth has returned, the past participle is **been**: *He has been abroad only twice.* **2** [I] to move or travel somewhere and stay there for a particular purpose or activity: **~ to sth** *Settlers went to North America in their thousands.* ◇ *to go to work/school/church/prison/bed* ◇ **(+ adv./prep.) (to do sth)** *The girls had gone abroad to study.* ◇ **~ shopping/swimming, etc.** *When they go shopping, they use a list.* ◇ **~ for sth** *Older participants were most likely to go for a check-up with their family doctor.* ◇ **~ on sth** *The children in the study did not go on school trips with any regularity.* HELP If sb has returned, the past participle is **been**: *Anyone who has been to a baseball game in both Japan and America will have noticed differences.* **3** *linking verb* **+ adj.** to become different, especially in a bad way: *There are cases where things have simply gone wrong.* ◇ *Many farmers went bankrupt as prices collapsed.* ◇ *After ten years the company went public.* **4** *linking verb* **+ adj.** to be or remain as described: *These subtle expressions of anger may go unnoticed.* ◇ *to go unrecognized/undetected/unchallenged* ◇ *Ten per cent of children said they had gone hungry in the preceding month.* **5** [I] to reach a particular state; to stop being in a particular state: **~ to sth** *He shut his eyes and went to sleep.* ◇ **~ into sth** *The company went into liquidation.* ◇ *Patients with cancer may go into remission with* treatment. ◇ **~ out of sth** *Several operators have gone out of business.* ◇ *Older authoritarian standards have gone out of fashion.* **6** [I] **+ adv./prep.** to reach or pass a particular level: *They argue that industrial progress can go further without damage to the environment.* ◇ *Many similar tasks have gone over budget.* ◇ *Production went from 305 000 barrels per day in 2005 to 480 000 by 2008.* **7** [I] **~ (that...)** used when stating what others have said or thought: *The argument goes that two negatives make a positive.* ◇ *The usual explanation goes like this:...* **8** [I] to stop existing or working in the same way; to stop or disappear altogether: *His narrative seeks to recover an innocence that has gone forever.* ◇ *His fine mind went as his illness progressed.* **9** [I] **~ to sb/sth** to be sent or passed somewhere: *Thanks go to the many colleagues and students who...* ◇ *If the Cabinet agrees, the proposal goes to its Future Legislation Committee.* **10** [I] (of money, energy or other resources) to be used for sth or given to sb/sth: **~ to sb/sth** *If there is any money left, it goes to shareholders.* ◇ **~ on sth** *Too much donor money goes on administration.* **11** [I] **+ adv.** used to talk about how successful sth is or about how sth develops: *The court case was going badly for the defendant.* ◇ *Not everything went smoothly.* ◇ *They seek to outline how far social policy has come and where it might be going.* **12** [I] used to say that sth shows or deals with what is important: **~ to sth** *This question actually goes to the heart of the matter.* ◇ **~ to do sth** *All this goes to show how very sensitive human rights are.*

IDM Most idioms containing **go** are at the entries for the nouns or adjectives in the idioms. For example, **go it alone** is at **alone**. **anything goes** (*informal*) used to say that anything is accepted or allowed, however unusual or shocking it is. This expression is rather informal, and so it is often written in inverted commas: *The century saw rapid change from a society in which people shared similar values to a modern society where it seems 'anything goes'.* **as people, things, etc. go** in comparison with the average person, thing, etc: *As militarists go, he was a man who preferred peace to war.* ◇ *The US Constitution is not, as constitutions go, very long.* **be going to do sth** used to say that sth will happen or that sb will do sth: *Investors believe that demand is going to be high in the future.* ◇ *It is essential that patients understand what is going to happen.*

PHR V **ˌgo aˈbout sth** to begin or continue doing sth **SYN** TACKLE: *One might go about this task by undertaking in-depth case studies.* ◇ *They went about their business as usual.* ◇ **~ doing sth** *It is important to understand how consumers go about making decisions.*

ˌgo ˈafter sb/sth to try to get sb/sth: *Once the company's assets are exhausted, the creditors cannot go after the members' assets.*

ˌgo aˈgainst sb/sth to resist or oppose sb/sth: *This goes against basic principles of the law.* ◇ *This proposal went against the interests of the ruling class.*

ˌgo aˈhead (with sth) to happen or to make sth happen, especially after discussion or thought **SYN** PROCEED (1): *The sale went ahead.* ◇ *The decision was made to go ahead.* ◇ *In the event the trustees went ahead with the investment.*

ˌgo aˈlong to continue with an activity: *They adjusted the plans as they went along.* **ˌgo aˈlong with sb/sth** to not oppose or resist sb/sth: *This policy goes along with a requirement to declare any overriding interests.* ◇ *She tends to go along with the crowd just for an easy life.*

ˌgo aˈround/ˈround to be enough for everyone to have sth: *There are simply not enough good jobs to go around.*

ˌgo aˈway to disappear: *They thought that the problem would go away.*

ˌgo ˈback (to sth) **1** to have existed since a particular time or for a particular period: *Most of today's human diseases probably go back to prehistoric times.* ◇ *This collaboration goes back a long way.* **2** to think about sth or do sth that was said or done earlier **SYN** RETURN[1] (4): *It was essential to go back and investigate this question.* ◇ *The company will have to go back to transactional marketing tactics to hold on to its market share.*

ˌgo beˈfore to exist or happen in an earlier time: *The new model differed radically from what had gone before.* **ˈgo before sb/sth** to be presented to sb/sth for discussion, decision or judgement: *The judge was right to allow the case to go before the jury.*

ˌgo beˈyond sth (to sth) to be or do more than sth; to be or do not just one thing, but another as well: *These questions go beyond the scope of the present article.* ◇ **~ what...** *The action should not go beyond what is necessary to achieve the objectives of the Treaties.* ◇ **~ doing sth (to doing sth)** *This means going beyond designing individual products to developing whole systems.*

ˌgo ˈby (of time) to pass: *As the months went by, she began to suspect the worst.*

ˌgo ˈdown (to sth) to become lower or less; to decrease to the level or amount mentioned **SYN** FALL[1] (1): *Prices are going down fast due to increased competition.* ◇ *Spending on arms has gone down.* ◇ *The rate goes down as the concentration of oxygen goes up.* ◇ *This proportion went down to 19.2% after 12 months.* **OPP** GO UP (TO STH) **ˌgo ˈdown (in sth)** to be written in sth; to be recorded or remembered in sth: *This letter will go down in the annals of history as a lasting appeal to humanity's conscience.*

ˈgo for sb/sth to apply to sb/sth: *The more attractive the prospects of a deal, the more willing governments are in making generous concessions. The same goes for multinational companies.* **ˈgo for sth** to choose sth: *The book goes for breadth rather than depth.*

ˌgo ˈin for sth to do or use sth frequently: *He goes in for meticulous and skilful stylization.*

ˌgo ˈinto sth **1** to join an organization or area of activity, in order to have a career: *The younger sons went into the Church or the army.* **2** to examine or discuss sth: *It is not necessary to go into details here.* **3** (of money, time, effort, etc.) to be spent on sth or used to do sth: *A great deal of money goes into research projects.* ◇ **~ doing sth** *Considerable resources went into making sure that poverty did not interfere with the core curriculum.*

ˌgo ˈoff **1** to leave a place, especially in order to do sth: **~ to do sth** *When men go off to fight, women are left behind as family providers and caregivers.* **2** (of a bomb, gun or alarm) to explode, be fired or make a noise: *The gun went off accidentally.*

ˌgo ˈon **1** (of time) to pass: *As time went on, a pattern emerged.* **2** to happen or continue: *There is a lot of hard work going on behind the scenes.* ◇ *The debate has been going on for over fifty years.* **3** to continue saying sth: **+ speech** *'Theory,' Helmholtz went on, 'allows us to recognize that...'* **ˌgo ˈon (with sth)** to continue an activity: *They enter English-medium schools to go on with their secondary education.* **ˌgo ˈon to do sth | ˌgo ˈon to sth** to do sth after doing sth else: *Many people diet, but only a minority go on to develop an eating disorder.* ◇ *She goes on to argue that...* ◇ *The report goes on to discuss the recommendation in further detail.* ◇ *to go on to consider/describe/explain/show/suggest sth* ◇ *Young people from the middle classes are more likely to go on to university than their working-class peers.*

ˌgo ˈout to be sent, broadcast, announced or published: *A bimonthly newsletter goes out to all school staff and parents.* ◇ *All articles go out for peer review.* **ˌgo ˈout (into sth) to do sth | ˌgo ˈout (to sth) (with sb)** to leave somewhere in order to do sth: *The children go out into the community to research a topic that arises from the week's learning.* ◇ *Husbands went out to work and earned a wage.* ◇ *Respondents were asked how frequently they went out with friends.*

ˌgo ˈover sth to deal with sth by examining it carefully: *It is impossible here to go over all the ground that has been covered in the debate.* **ˌgo ˈover to sb/sth** to move to a different place, side, opinion or activity: *These soldiers* have broken their oath and gone over to the opposite camp. ◇ Northern Europe was going over to 'industrial' crops.

ˌ**go ˈround** = GO AROUND/ROUND

go through sth **1** to reach and pass different stages of a process, especially when this requires effort or is unpleasant; to experience sth difficult or unpleasant: *Only articles that have gone through the process of peer review are accepted for publication.* ◇ *Brian went through a period of mourning.* **2** to examine sth carefully: *The committee then went through each document and selected elements that were useful.* ˌ**go ˈthrough with sth** to do what is necessary to complete a course of action, especially one that is difficult or unpleasant: *If she refused to go through with the ceremony, she would not be permitted to return.*

ˌ**go toˈgether** = GO WITH STH

ˈ**go towards sth** to be used as part of the payment for sth: *Any discretionary income may go towards medical expenses.* ◇ **~ doing sth** *Much of the initial investment would go towards acquiring new software.*

ˌ**go ˈup (to sth)** to become higher or greater; to increase to the level or amount mentioned SYN RISE[2] (1): *Inflation has gone up.* ◇ *The unemployment rate went up to about 18 per cent in the 1890s.* OPP GO DOWN (TO STH)

ˈ**go with sth** (*also* ˌ**go toˈgether**) to exist at the same time or in the same place as sth; to be found together: *In general, poverty goes with high infant mortality rates.* ◇ *These two preoccupations frequently go together and inform each other.*

ˌ**go wiˈthout sth** | ˌ**go wiˈthout** to not have sth that you usually have or need: *Children are less likely to go without food because they are protected by their mothers.* ◇ *She did not have the means to buy her medications and went without.*

goal AWL /gəʊl; *NAmE* goʊl/ *noun* something that you hope to achieve SYN AIM[1] (1): *She set herself ambitious personal goals.* ◇ **~ of sth** *The ultimate goal of the war was to weaken and eventually absorb the other tribes.* ◇ **towards a/your ~** *Small groups of students were working cooperatively towards shared goals.* ➲ thesaurus note *at* TARGET[1]

▸ ADJECTIVE + GOAL **stated • explicit • specific • desired • common, shared, collective • main, major, primary • short-term • ultimate, long-term • overarching, overall • broad • strategic • ambitious • realistic • conflicting** *When the National Health Service was formed in 1948, a stated goal was 'Health for all by the year 2000'.* ◇ *She argues that people are being manipulated to believe that material growth is the ultimate goal in life.* | **national • societal • educational • corporate • personal** *Several studies have shown that educational goals are linked to adolescents' sexual behaviour and attitudes.*

▸ VERB + GOAL **define • set, establish • share • pursue • achieve, accomplish, attain, realize, fulfil, reach, meet • advance, serve, promote, further** *Care was taken to set goals that were both realistic and shared by all staff involved.* ◇ *By working together, the two corporations were able to jointly realize their goals.*

▸ GOAL + NOUN **setting • attainment • orientation** *Students had a workshop on study skills such as goal setting and time management.*

god /gɒd; *NAmE* gɑːd/ *noun* **1 God** [sing.] (not used with *the*) (in Christianity, Islam and Judaism) the BEING or spirit that is worshipped and is believed to have created the universe: *Because Jews believed that God should not be represented in art, there were no statues in the Temple.* **2** [C] (in some religions) a BEING or spirit who is believed to have power over a particular part of nature or who is believed to represent a particular quality: *They worshipped many gods.* ◇ *Greek/Roman/Egyptian gods* ◇ **~ of sth** *In ancient India, the community of priests promoted Varuna and Mitra, the gods of cosmic law and order, against Rudra, the chaotic god of storms.* IDM see ACT[2]

god·dess /ˈgɒdes; ˈgɒdəs; *NAmE* ˈgɑːdəs/ *noun* a female god: *They were revered as living incarnations of Hindu goddesses.* ◇ **~ of sth** *Nike, the Greek goddess of victory*

gold[1] /gəʊld; *NAmE* goʊld/ *noun* [U] (*symb.* **Au**) the chemical element of ATOMIC NUMBER 79. Gold is a valuable yellow metal that is used for making jewellery and other DECORATIVE objects, and as a measurement of wealth: *The value of gold and silver fell in relation to other commodities.* ◇ **+ noun** *Gold reserves stayed high.* ◇ *He issued a commemorative gold coin.*

gold[2] /gəʊld; *NAmE* goʊld/ *adj.* [only before noun] bright yellow in colour, like gold: *His name was written on the board in large gold letters.*

gold·en /ˈgəʊldən; *NAmE* ˈgoʊldən/ *adj.* [usually before noun] **1** special and wonderful; successful or likely to be successful: *The present had not kept the promises of a glorious, golden past.* ◇ *Trade fairs provide a golden opportunity for low-cost market research.* **2** bright yellow in colour like gold: *Its golden metallic colour has led it to be mistaken for gold.* HELP In traditional stories, **golden** is also used to say that sth is made of gold: *the golden chariots of the gods*

ˈ**golden age** *noun* [usually sing.] **~ (of sth)** a period, especially in the past, of great success in a particular activity: *Many historians describe this period as 'the golden age of journalism'.*

ˈ**gold standard** *noun* **1** (*usually* **the gold standard**) [sing.] an economic system in which the value of money is based on the value of gold: *In this world view, maintenance of the gold standard was the primary prerequisite for prosperity.* ◇ *In August 1931, Germany abandoned the gold standard.* **2** [usually sing.] a high level of quality that others try to copy; something with this high level of quality: *Wales did not have a native royal court or university to set and maintain the linguistic gold standard.* ◇ **~ for sth** *The gold standard for an experimental study is the randomized controlled trial (RCT).*

gone *past part. of* GO

good[1] /gʊd/ *adj.* (**bet·ter** /ˈbetə(r); *NAmE* ˈbetər/, **best** /best/) **1** of high quality or an acceptable standard: *Good teachers help develop a feeling of self-worth among students.* ◇ *Meat-packing was considered a good job, with relatively high wages.* ◇ *The algorithm gave better results for the second experiment.* ◇ *The measurements were repeated several times and averaged to obtain a best estimate.* **2** sensible, logical or strongly supporting what is being discussed: *A good point is made by Williams (2000).* ◇ *Their success provides a good example of how to expand overseas.* ◇ *There is good reason to believe that the new approach will significantly advance psychopathology research.* ◇ *The best way to help children manage their reactions is to allow them to express their feelings.* **3** [only before noun] great in number, amount or degree: *Urban dust has been the subject of a good number of studies.* ◇ *These facts enable us to construct a solid history that has a good chance of being correct.* ◇ *Today, Fuller is best known for her treatise, 'Woman in the Nineteenth Century'.* **4** suitable or appropriate: *Wordsworth's poetry posed a radical challenge to contemporary principles of good taste.* ◇ **~ (for sb/sth) to do sth** *A period of high economic activity is a good time for a company to enter a market.* **5 ~ (for sb/sth)** having a useful or helpful effect on sb/sth: *As humans are social beings, what is good for the community or state is also good for the individual.* **6** able to do sth well: **~ at doing sth** *The project leader was particularly good at explaining how to use statistics effectively.* ◇ **~ at sth** *Several students declared that they were not good at sport.* **7 ~ with sth/sb** able to use sth or deal with people well: *She chose her bank because she said* they were 'good with money'. ◇ *They ascribed their success to 'feminine' qualities of caring and being good with people.* **8** morally right; behaving in a way that is morally right: *According to their beliefs, a 'good' man should honour the gods, keep oaths and be loyal to fellow warriors.* **9** following strictly a set of rules or principles: *A daily check of all medicines was undertaken, in line with good practice.* **10** showing or getting approval or respect: *In East Africa, Nairobi had a good reputation as an administrative centre.* **11** pleasant; that you enjoy or want: *The good news is that school culture can be changed in positive directions.* IDM *see* FAITH, FEEL[1]

good² /gʊd/ *noun* ➲ *see also* GOODS **1** [U, sing.] something that helps sb/sth: *Privacy is not an absolute good because it imposes real costs on society.* ◇ **for ~** *In Bond's plays, anger is seen as the engine of social change, both for good and for ill.* ◇ **for the common ~** *There are many examples of species where individuals cooperate for the common good.* ◇ **for sb's own ~** *The government misled the population into believing that the welfare reforms were for their own good.* ➲ *see also* PUBLIC GOOD **2** behaviour that is morally right or acceptable: *The Reagan administration tried to portray the Cold War in terms of a battle between good and evil.*

IDM **do 'good | do sb 'good** to have a useful effect; to help sb: *Whether vitamin pills really do any good has never been critically established.* ◇ *Doing good, in a Christian sense, might involve tackling global injustice and poverty.* **for 'good** forever; permanently: *Once a tropical rainforest has been cleared, it is effectively lost for good.* ➲ *more at* DELIVER

good·ness /ˈgʊdnəs/ *noun* [U] the quality of being good: *Stories about the Buddha's life show the capacity to find goodness in those who are different from us.* ◇ **~ of sth/sb** *Jean-Jacques Rousseau (1755) argued for the essential goodness of human nature.*

goods /gʊdz/ *noun* [pl.] **1** things that are produced to be sold: *Few luxury goods made their way into the houses of common people.* ◇ *The bureaucratic machine enabled the mass production of goods and services.* ➲ *see also* CAPITAL GOODS, CONSUMER GOODS **2** possessions that can be moved: *He was convicted of handling stolen goods.*

good·will /ˌgʊdˈwɪl/ *noun* [U] **1** friendly or helpful feelings towards other people, organizations or countries: *Being flexible was key to maintaining feelings of goodwill among all parties.* ◇ **~ of sb** *Our ability to continue depends on the goodwill of the government.* **2** the good relationship between a business and its customers that is calculated as part of its value when it is sold: *Financially, brands consist of their physical assets plus a sum that represents their reputation or goodwill.*

got *past tense, past part. of* GET

got·ten (*NAmE*) *past part. of* GET

gov·ern /ˈgʌvn; *NAmE* ˈgʌvərn/ *verb* **1** [T, I] **~ (sth)** to control a country or its people and be responsible for introducing new laws and for organizing public services and the economy: *Empires have usually been governed by military elites.* ◇ *The EU has altered the policy framework within which the member state governments govern.* **2** [T, often passive] **~ sth** to control or influence how sth happens or functions; to control or influence sb's actions or behaviour: *We examined the rules governing air quality in theatres.* ◇ *A sociopath may be defined as a person whose behaviour is governed entirely by self-interest.* ◇ *The laws of chemistry and physics govern all that goes on in an organism as fully as they govern all other processes in the universe.*

gov·ern·ance /ˈgʌvənəns; *NAmE* ˈgʌvərnəns/ *noun* [U] (*technical*) the way in which a country is governed or a company or an organization is controlled; the activity of governing a country or controlling a company or an organization: *The shareholders want to improve corporate governance at all levels within the group.* ◇ *She suggests that good governance is based on several factors, including an efficient public service and an independent judicial system.* ◇ **~ of sth** *Ownership of a share of stock confers a legal right to participate in the governance of a corporation.* ◇ **+ noun** *Braithwaite and Drahos (2000) show how a global governance structure has been created that regulates business beyond the level of the nation state.*

gov·ern·ing /ˈgʌvənɪŋ; *NAmE* ˈgʌvərnɪŋ/ *adj.* [only before noun] **1** having the right and authority to control sth such as a country or an institution: *The governing party and the opposition competed in a free and fair election.* ◇ *These targets are set by the school's governing body and the head teacher.* **2** used to describe an idea or a rule that controls a situation or process: *The law of contract has been considered as the governing principle of the employment relationship.*

gov·ern·ment /ˈgʌvənmənt; *NAmE* ˈgʌvərnmənt/ *noun* **1** [C+sing./pl. v., U] (*often* **the Government**) (*abbr.* **govt**) the group of people and the institutions connected with them that are responsible for controlling a country or state: *They found that democratically elected governments were more likely to pursue policies that address problems of poverty.* ◇ *The new Conservative government proposed drastic cuts to the welfare budget.* ◇ *Much policymaking in central government is not through formal institutions but through contacts of informal networks.* ◇ **~ of sth** *The governments of the USA and the EU reached opposing decisions on the acceptability of licensing the drug.* ◇ **+ noun** *Changes in government policy had raised the significance of overseas recruitment for the universities.* ➲ *see also* CENTRAL GOVERNMENT, LOCAL GOVERNMENT, SELF-GOVERNMENT **2** [U] a particular system or method of controlling a country: *Democratic government maximizes the extent to which people attain individual autonomy.* ◇ *A constitution can be defined as a body of rules which regulates the system of government within a state.* **3** [U] the activity or manner of controlling a country: *Good government, at national and local level, could increase the chances of individuals living a long and healthy life.* ◇ **in ~** *Both parties when in government have used central funding to reward their geographical areas of political support.*

▸ ADJECTIVE + GOVERNMENT **democratic • representative • authoritarian • military** *She gives examples of authoritarian governments that have been overthrown as a result of student protest.* ◇ *Representative government had never existed in Russia.* | **national • foreign • federal • central • state • provincial • regional • local • municipal** *Financial support for the associations came primarily from the national and state governments.*

▸ NOUN + GOVERNMENT **coalition • minority • majority** *There were some 13 years of coalition government between 1915 and 1945.*

▸ VERB + GOVERNMENT **elect • establish • form • support • advise • influence • persuade • encourage • urge • commit • lobby • pressure • force, compel • criticize • overthrow** *The Conservative Party, having won the most votes and seats, had a mandate to form the government.*

▸ GOVERNMENT + VERB **decide • choose to • seek to • intervene • adopt • announce • pursue • introduce • issue • appoint • encourage • set • impose • regulate • fund • subsidize** *The union believed that the government should intervene and subsidize the industry.* ◇ *Factories exceeding the pollution standard set by the government received stiff fines.*

▸ GOVERNMENT + NOUN **policy • regulation(s) • intervention • action • programme • support • funding • subsidy • budget • deficit • debt • revenue • spending, expenditure • department, agency • office • minister • official** *A health care market without a suitable level of* *government intervention can have problems of market failure and inequity.*

gov·ern·men·tal /ˌɡʌvnˈmentl; *NAmE* ˌɡʌvərnˈmentl/ *adj.* connected with government: *The project required the involvement of a range of governmental and non-governmental agencies.* ◇ *governmental organizations/institutions/responsibility/authority/power*

gov·ern·or /ˈɡʌvənə(r); *NAmE* ˈɡʌvərnər/ *noun* **1** (*also* **Governor**) **~ (of sth)** a person who is elected to be in charge of the government of a state in the US: *State governors are aware of the need to increase minority participation in education.* ◇ *Republican/Democratic governors* **2** (*also* **Governor**) **~ (of sth)** a person who is chosen as the official head of a country or region that is governed by another country: *In the Roman Empire, ultimate political authority rested with provincial governors and their superiors at Rome.* **3 ~ (of sth)** (*especially BrE*) a member of a group of people who are responsible for controlling an institution such as a school, college or hospital: *The 1988 Education Reform Act gave the board of governors for each school responsibility for managing the budget.* **4** (*BrE*) a person who is in charge of an institution: *The prisoner was denied access to his solicitor by the prison governor.* ◇ **~ of sth** *She was appointed governor of the central bank.*

G

GP /ˌdʒiː ˈpiː/ *noun* (*BrE*) the abbreviation for 'general practitioner' (a doctor who is trained in general medicine and who works in the local community, not in a hospital): *The sample was from a 50-year-old man who had seen his GP to report problems with tiredness.* ◇ *to visit/consult your GP* ◇ *Care may be carried out by the GP and primary care team in the community or in an outpatient clinic at a hospital.*

grade¹ AWL /ɡreɪd/ *noun* **1** the level of quality of a particular product or material: **~ of sth** *It is considered the highest grade of pulp because it has the highest percentage of solids.* ◇ **of (a)... ~** *This mineral is common in regional metamorphic rocks, usually of fairly high grade.* ➲ *see also* LOW-GRADE **2 ~ (of sth)** a level of ability or rank that sb has in an organization: *The aim of the policy was to increase the number of women in the higher grades of the profession.* **3** a mark given in an exam or for a piece of school work: **~ in sth** *Results indicated that high school students who had attended a preschool on average had higher grades in mathematics, science and English.* ◇ (*BrE*) *She got good grades in her exams.* ◇ **~ on sth** (*NAmE*) *She got good grades on her exams.* **4** (in some countries, including the US) one of the levels in a school with children of similar age: *He was unable to finish the 10th grade.* **5** (*NAmE*) = GRADIENT (1)

grade² AWL /ɡreɪd/ *verb* **1** [T, usually passive] to put things or people into categories according to their qualities or abilities: **be graded (by/according to sth)** *The extent of inflammation was graded according to the Hinchey classification.* ◇ **be graded from A to B** *There is no single scale along which animals can be graded from 'higher' to 'lower'.* ◇ **be graded in sth** *The ritual objects had been carefully graded in size and colour.* **2** [T] (*especially NAmE*) to give a mark to a student or to a piece of their written work: **~ sb/yourself** *The students graded themselves by reflecting on the quality of their own work.* ◇ **~ sth** *The teacher evaluated and graded written work based on each student's academic level.* ➲ *compare* MARK¹ (6) **3** [I] **~ into sth**| **~ from A to B** to change gradually from one type or level to another: *Towards the top, the shale grades into red mudstones.*

graded AWL /ˈɡreɪdɪd/ *adj.* arranged in order or in categories according to difficulty, size, etc: *The patients were asked to complete a set of graded tasks.*

gra·di·ent /ˈɡreɪdiənt/ *noun* **1** (*also* **grade** *especially in NAmE*) the degree to which the ground slopes: *This steep gradient allows the river to continue its erosion of the chasm's floor.* **2** (*physics*) the rate at which any physical quantity, such as temperature or pressure, increases or decreases from one place to another: **~ between A and B** *The graph shows the temperature gradient between Iceland and the Azores.* ◇ **~ across sth** *The steep concentration gradient across the membranes means that there is an instant delivery of Ca^{2+} to the cytoplasm.* **3 ~ (in sth)** (*technical*) the degree to which a value changes between one person, group or region and another: *There is evidence of a socio-economic gradient in diet, whereby people in higher socio-economic groups tend to have a healthier diet.* **4 ~ (of sth)** (*mathematics*) how steep a GRAPH is: *The gradient of a curve can be determined by dividing the change in height by the change in horizontal distance.* **5** (*mathematics*) a VECTOR that is PERPENDICULAR to a SCALAR field: *The negative gradient of electric potential is the electric field.*

grad·ual /ˈɡrædʒuəl/ *adj.* happening slowly over a long period: *The increase in fish numbers in the lake was very gradual at first.* ◇ *In the early modern period, there were great but gradual changes in the ways that physicians viewed diet.* OPP SUDDEN

grad·ual·ly /ˈɡrædʒuəli/ *adv.* slowly, over a long period of time: *Our sun will continue to evolve, gradually becoming hotter and eventually entering a red giant phase.* ◇ *Gradually, the health innovations were accepted by the medical community.* OPP SUDDENLY

gradu·ate¹ /ˈɡrædʒuət/ *noun* **1** a person who has successfully completed a course of study, especially a person who has a first university degree: **~ (from/of sth)** *To oversee production, the company hired new graduates from Japanese engineering faculties.* ◇ **~ in sth** *Many members of the organization are university graduates in medicine or law.* ◇ **+ noun** *a graduate student/school/programme* ➲ *compare* UNDERGRADUATE **2** (*NAmE*) a person who has completed their high school studies: *The number of high-school graduates without job offers is indicative of the youth unemployment problem.*

gradu·ate² /ˈɡrædʒueɪt/ *verb* **1** [I, T] to get a degree, especially your first degree, from a university or college: **~ from...** *Both her parents had graduated from college.* ◇ **~ in sth** *In the USA, one out of six students graduates in natural sciences or engineering.* ◇ **~ as sth** *Louis Agassiz graduated as a doctor of philosophy at Erlangen University.* **2** [I, T] (*NAmE*) to complete a course in education, especially at HIGH SCHOOL: **~ from...** *By 1920, more than half of the children graduating from elementary school proceeded to secondary schools.* ◇ **~ sth** *People who have not graduated high school are less likely to participate in education in later life.* **3** [I] **~ (from sth) to sth** to start doing sth more difficult or important than what you were doing before: *His autobiography describes how he graduated from manual labour to management roles.*

grain /ɡreɪn/ *noun* **1** [U, C] the small hard seeds of food plants such as WHEAT, rice, etc; a single seed of such a plant: *These were the areas where little grain was grown.* ◇ **+ noun** *Grain production has increased.* ◇ **~ of sth** *In this religious ritual, a cup of water and a few grains of rice are offered to other types of living beings.* **2** [C] **~ (of sth)** a small piece of a particular substance, usually a hard substance: *This method is effective for grains of sand and smaller particles.* ◇ *Pollen grains from a different plant were used.* ◇ *A few dozen grains of the mineral are sprinkled on a microscope slide.* **3** [C, usually sing.] **~ of sth** a very small amount: **~ of truth** *There is, of course, a grain of truth in this view.* **4** [C] an individual PARTICLE or CRYSTAL in metal, rock, etc, usually examined with a LENS or MICROSCOPE: *The grain size of an igneous rock depends upon the rate of cooling.*

IDM **go against the 'grain (of sth)** to be or do sth different from what is normal or natural: *The organization floundered as it went against the grain of economic trends.*

gram /græm/ *noun* (*abbr.* g) **~ (of sth)** a unit for measuring mass. There are 1 000 grams in one kilogram: *Less than a gram of sample is all that is needed in most cases.* ◇ *The amount of water that can be stored per gram of organic matter was calculated.*

gram·mar /'græmə(r)/ *noun* **1** [U] the whole system and structure of a language or of languages in general: *Poets change the rules of grammar to achieve a certain aesthetic result.* ◇ *The Qur'an provided the basis for the development of Arabic grammar, vocabulary and syntax.* **2** [U] a person's knowledge and use of the rules of a language: *He has problems with his grammar but his pronunciation is very good.* **3** [C] a book containing a description of the whole system and structure of a language: *Speakers of new varieties of English began to produce their own dictionaries and grammars.* **4** [C] **~ (of sth)** the basic elements of an area of knowledge or skill: *The grammar of science helps bridge engineers understand the nature of these internal forces.*

gram·mat·ical /grə'mætɪkl/ *adj.* **1** connected with grammar: *Difficult grammatical constructions, which are taught at advanced levels, have been avoided.* **2** correctly following the rules of grammar: *Participants were asked to decide whether each sentence was grammatical or ungrammatical.* ■ **gram·mat·ical·ly** /grə'mætɪkli/ *adv.*: *Although grammatically correct, the sentence could be phrased more helpfully.*

grand /grænd/ *adj.* (**grand·er**, **grand·est**) **1** large and impressive or important: *They built grand houses and became men of influence.* ◇ *The Emperor had celebrated a grand triumph.* ◇ *This way of thinking encouraged risk-taking on a grand scale.* **2** (of ideas) intended to achieve impressive results: *His mind was habitually drawn to grand schemes and narratives.* ◇ *The founder members had much grander aspirations.* ◇ *Merton argues that grand theories are of limited use in connection with social research.* HELP **Grand** is often used when, in fact, sth is not likely to be impressive: *He has a tendency to make grand claims that cannot be adequately supported.* ■ **grand·ly** *adv.*: *The houses were grandly decorated, with fine furniture, wallpaper and curtains.* ◇ *This is rather grandly called the principle of microscopic reversibility.*

grand·par·ent /'grænpeərənt; *NAmE* 'grænperənt/ *noun* the father or mother of your father or mother: *He was raised by his grandparents.*

grant[1] AWL /grɑːnt; *NAmE* grænt/ *verb* **1** [often passive] to agree to give sb what they ask for, especially formal or legal permission to do sth: **~ sth** *He had expected that his application would be granted.* ◇ **~ sb sth** *Over 98 per cent of countries in the world have granted women the right to vote.* ◇ **~ sth to sb/sth** *Aid granted to the company by the German government was found to be unlawful by the court.* **2 ~ (that)...** to admit that sth is true, although you may not like or agree with it: *Addison grants that greatness in nature may inspire greatness in art, but goes on to express a preference for nature over art.*

grant[2] AWL /grɑːnt; *NAmE* grænt/ *noun* **1** [C] a sum of money given by a government or other organization for a particular purpose: *Services were originally provided for free, through grants received from federal, state and local sources.* ◇ **~ to do sth** *The government made available improvement grants to cover part of the cost of modernization.* **2** [U] **~ (of sth) (to sb)** the action of granting sth: *One of the results of the reconquest of Spain from the Moors was the grant of vast estates to the Church.*

grant·ed[1] AWL /'grɑːntɪd; *NAmE* 'græntɪd/ *adv.* it is true HELP **Granted** is used to introduce a factor that is opposed to the main line of argument but is not regarded as so strong as to prove it wrong: *Granted, national governments continue to play a role in this, but increasingly international networks are taking the lead.*

grant·ed[2] AWL /'grɑːntɪd; *NAmE* 'græntɪd/ *conj.* **~ (that...)** if it is accepted that sth is true: *Granted that resources for law enforcement are limited, we need to ask how priorities should be determined.*

grape /greɪp/ *noun* a small fruit that grows in CLUSTERS on a climbing plant. Wine is made from grapes: *Bunches of purple grapes were hanging from the vine.* ◇ *These wines are produced from grapes grown in registered vineyards.*

graph /græf; *BrE also* grɑːf/ *noun* a diagram, consisting of a line or lines, showing the relation between two or more sets of numbers: *In a line graph, the bars are replaced by points or symbols joined together by a straight line.* ◇ *The graph shows the carbon dioxide concentration profile (solid line) and saturation curve (dashed line).* ◇ **on a ~** *It is possible to plot the change in the population size on a graph.* ➲ language bank *at* TABLE

G

graph·ic /'græfɪk/ *adj.* **1** (of descriptions, etc.) very clear and full of details, especially about sth unpleasant SYN VIVID (1): *Graphic images of animals in laboratories are used to bring the issue to the public's attention.* ◇ *The historian Barbara Ehrenreich described in graphic detail the stories of such women.* **2** [only before noun] connected with drawings and design, especially in the production of books, magazines, etc: *The graphic style of advertisements that have run in these publications is highly original.*

graph·ic·al /'græfɪkl/ *adj.* **1** in the form of a graph: *Graphical representations of data are useful in identifying patterns in the data.* **2** [only before noun] connected with art or computer graphics: *This interface is an enhanced graphical display.*

graph·ic·al·ly /'græfɪkli/ *adv.* **1** in the form of a graph: *These results are shown graphically in Fig. 13.5.* **2** very clearly and in great detail SYN VIVIDLY: *The experience of countries such as Uganda graphically illustrates this problem.*

graph·ics /'græfɪks/ *noun* **1** [pl.] the pictures or diagrams used in a document, book, magazine, etc. or on a website etc: *Multimedia presentations are a versatile medium that can incorporate video, sound, motion and graphics.* ◇ **~ of sth** *His lecture was illustrated with intricate computer graphics of ladders, cubes and knots made out of DNA.* HELP An individual picture is a **graphic**: *The viewer can click on the graphic to pause the clip.* **2** (*also* **computer graphics**) [U] the use of computers to create and change images: *The future in high-powered graphics is no longer scientific workstations, but computer games.* ◇ **+ noun** *This is an image synthesized in a 3-D graphics package.*

graph·ite /'græfaɪt/ *noun* [U] a soft black substance that is a form of CARBON which conducts electricity HELP **Graphite** is used to make the parts of a machine move smoothly against each other, in pencils, as ELECTRODES in ELECTROCHEMICAL cells and as a control material in some nuclear REACTORS: *Solid carbon is abundant in the rock in the form of either graphite or diamond.* ◇ **+ noun** *Porous graphite electrodes are also used for the uptake of liquid samples.*

grasp[1] /grɑːsp; *NAmE* græsp/ *verb* **1** to understand sth completely: **~ sth** *In order to make the concept easier for the students to grasp, a simple example was given.* ◇ *It is only in recent years that it has been possible to fully grasp the significance of this process of social evolution.* ◇ **~ how/why, etc...** *Campbell fails to grasp how weak the evidence is for his later arguments.* **2 ~ an opportunity** to take an opportunity without hesitating and use it: *Without education or technical skills, victims of poverty had no chance of* *grasping new employment opportunities.* **3 ~ sb/sth** to take a firm hold of sb/sth SYN GRIP² (1): *The lizards attempt to grasp each other by the mouth, often locking jaws*

grasp² /grɑːsp; *NAmE* græsp/ *noun* [usually sing.] **1** a person's understanding of a subject: **~ of sth** *Nearly half of the respondents indicated that they had a reasonable grasp of another language.* ◇ *Panati (2012) displays a firmer grasp of immigration patterns.* ◇ **beyond the ~ of sth** *Gregory described God as beyond the grasp of the human mind.* **2** a firm hold of sb/sth or control over sb/sth: *Control of public opinion began to slip from the president's grasp.* ◇ **in sb's ~** *With Moscow in his grasp, Napoleon thought that victory would be his.* **3** the ability to get or achieve sth: **in/within sb's ~** *Victory, which had been within their grasp, had been taken away.*

G

grass /grɑːs; *NAmE* græs/ *noun* **1** [U] a common wild plant with narrow green leaves and STEMS that are eaten by animals: *The farms were mostly given over to grass for pasture.* **2** [C] any type of grass: *This pesticide is used to control a broad spectrum of weeds including deep-rooted grasses and woody plants.*

grass·land /ˈgrɑːslænd; *NAmE* ˈgræslænd/ *noun* [U] (*also* **grasslands** [pl.]) a large area of open land covered with wild grass: *Areas that had formerly been covered by forests opened up and became grasslands.*

grate·ful /ˈgreɪtfl/ *adj.* **1** feeling or showing thanks because sb has done sth kind for you or has done as you asked: **~ (to sb) (for sth)** *These European immigrants were grateful to the US for asylum and the opportunities it offered them.* ◇ **~ to do sth** *Many patients are relieved and grateful to be told the truth.* ◇ **~ (that)...** *They were grateful that she had agreed to help.* **2** used to make a request, especially in a letter or in a formal situation: *I would be grateful if you could offer an urgent assessment of this case.* ■ **grate·ful·ly** /ˈgreɪtfəli/ *adv.*: *The authors gratefully acknowledge funding support from the Canadian Institutes of Health Research.*

grati·tude /ˈgrætɪtjuːd; *NAmE* ˈgrætɪtuːd/ *noun* [U] the feeling of being grateful and wanting to express your thanks: **~ (to sb) (for sth)** *I owe a debt of gratitude to many people for their help with this paper.* ◇ **in ~ (to sb) (for sth)** *In gratitude for their generosity, Athens rewarded them with citizenship.*

grave¹ /greɪv/ *noun* **1** a place in the ground where a dead person is buried: *He often visited his brother's grave.* ◇ *The individuals buried in such graves typically wore gold neck rings and other ring jewellery.* **2** [sing.] (*often* **the grave**) death; a person's death: *For many, there is faith in a spiritual life beyond the grave.*

grave² /greɪv/ *adj.* [usually before noun] (**graver**, **grav·est**) very serious; causing great worry: *The charge was grave human rights violations.* ◇ *They saw grave danger in the relaxation of control.* ◇ *This is a serious crime involving a grave threat to life.* ➲ *see also* GRAVITY ■ **grave·ly** *adv.*: *Senior management gravely underestimated the competition.* ◇ *He was gravely ill with cancer.*

gravi·ta·tion /ˌgrævɪˈteɪʃn/ *noun* [U] (*physics*) the movement towards a CENTRE OF GRAVITY, as when objects fall to the ground when they are dropped; the force that is responsible for this: *According to Newton's theory of gravitation, the Sun and Earth attract each other.* ◇ *Gravitation explained not just the fall of objects to the ground but also the rhythm of the tides and the movements of the planets.*

gravi·ta·tion·al /ˌgrævɪˈteɪʃənl/ *adj.* (*physics*) connected with or caused by the force of gravity: *Einstein predicted that starlight would be deflected by the sun's gravitational field.* ◇ *gravitational attraction/pull/force/energy*

grav·ity /ˈgrævəti/ *noun* [U] **1** (*abbr.* g) (*physics*) the force that attracts objects in space towards each other, and that on the earth pulls them towards the centre of the planet, so that things fall to the ground when they are dropped: *Under the force of gravity, the natural motion is to fall downhill.* ◇ *Most galaxies occur in clusters that are held together by gravity.* ➲ *see also* CENTRE OF GRAVITY **2 ~ (of sth)** extreme importance and a cause for worry SYN SERIOUSNESS (1): *He has failed to appreciate the gravity of the situation.* ◇ *Judges can be expected to pass heavy sentences to mark the gravity of the offence.* ➲ *see also* GRAVE² (1) **3** serious behaviour, speech or appearance: *Charles's court was characterized by what Clarendon calls 'gravity and reverence in all mention of religion'.*

gray (*especially NAmE*) = GREY¹, GREY²

great /greɪt/ *adj.* (**great·er**, **great·est**) **1** [usually before noun] very large; much bigger than average in size or quantity: *There are a great number of regional dialects of the language.* ◇ *In the great majority of cases, a practical solution can be found.* ◇ *Waves travel great distances in deep water with little energy loss.* **2** much more than average in degree or amount: *Minerals are of great importance to microorganisms.* ◇ *The book describes in great detail the events and personalities of the period.* ◇ *Without doubt, this policy involves great risks.* ◇ **to a ~ extent** *The big supermarkets can control to a great extent which products customers buy.* **3** [only before noun] important or most important: *The great advantage of the survey data is that they include the generation born in the 1970s.* **4** extremely good in ability or quality and therefore admired by many people: *The great European poets of the past had all excelled in the sonnet.* ◇ *The great city was utterly destroyed, and its population enslaved.* ◇ *This is one of their great cultural achievements.* **5** [only before noun] used to emphasize a particular description of sb/sth: *Over 1 000 letters survive from Wedgwood to his great friend and business partner Thomas Bentley.* ◇ *Aquinas was a great admirer of Aristotle's work.* **6** having an important position and a lot of influence: *According to Wight, the UN Charter is based on the interests of the great powers.* **7 the Great** used as a title to mean the most important person of the name: *Alexander the Great conquered much of the world in the fourth century BC.* **8 great-** added to words for family members to show a further stage in relationship: *His great-grandfather had invented the Gatling gun.* **9** [only before noun] (*also* **greater**) used in the names of some types of animals, birds or plants that are larger than similar kinds: *A laboratory experiment showed that great tits can discriminate between orange and red wings.* ◇ *An example of this type of signal is the sound of the greater horseshoe bat.* **10 Greater** [only before noun] (of a city) including the centre and a large area all around it: *The population of Greater London at this time was roughly eight million.*

IDM **ˌgreat and ˈsmall** of all sizes or types: *It is the right of nations great and small to choose their way of life.* **the greater part of sth** most of sth; more than half of sth: *Women form the greater part of the elderly population.* ➲ *more at* SUM¹

great·ly /ˈgreɪtli/ *adv.* very much HELP **greatly** is usually used with a verb or participle: *Unemployment rates vary greatly among advanced capitalist nations.* ◇ *Medical advances have resulted in greatly increased lifespans.*

great·ness /ˈgreɪtnəs/ *noun* [U] **~ (of sb/sth)** the quality of being extremely good and therefore admired by many people: *The greatness of his work was soon recognized.*

green¹ /griːn/ *adj.* (**green·er**, **green·est**) **1** having the colour of grass or the leaves of most plants and trees: *Patients are advised to eat a healthy diet rich in fruit and green vegetables.* ◇ *These minerals are white, becoming green with increasing iron.* **2** covered with grass or other plants: *They argued that green spaces influence how people feel about the quality of their surroundings.* **3** concerned with the protection of the environment; supporting the protection of the environment as a political principle: *The most prominent green tax is the congestion charge levied on vehicles entering central London.* ◇ *Green parties have emerged as a significant electoral force.*

green[2] /griːn/ *noun* **1** [U, C] the colour of grass and the leaves of most plants and trees: *After an hour, the solution had changed colour from transparent yellow to a deep transparent green.* ◇ **in ~** *Carbon atoms are shown in green, nitrogen in blue and oxygen in red.* **2** (*usually* **Green**) [usually pl.] a person who is concerned with the protection of the environment; a member or supporter of a Green Party (= a party whose main aim is the protection of the environment): *If nothing else, green comedy would help prevent Greens from becoming like their opponents: serious, calculating and grey.* ◇ **the Greens** *In the Italian national election of 1996, the Greens formed part of the victorious Olive Tree alliance.*

green·house /ˈgriːnhaʊs/ *noun* a building with glass sides and a glass roof for growing plants in: *Plants were grown in a greenhouse and the anatomical features of stems and leaves were examined using light microscopy.*

the ˈgreenhouse effect *noun* [sing.] the problem of the gradual rise in temperature of the earth's atmosphere, caused by an increase of gases such as CARBON DIOXIDE in the air: *CO_2 contributes to the greenhouse effect.* ➲ *see also* GLOBAL WARMING

ˌgreenhouse ˈgas *noun* (*abbr.* **GHG**) any of the gases that are thought to cause the greenhouse effect, especially CARBON DIOXIDE: *Concentrations of greenhouse gases are now higher than at any point in the past 800 000 years.* ◇ **+ noun** *Many scientists advocate a worldwide reduction in greenhouse gas emissions.*

greet /griːt/ *verb* **1** to say sth to sb when you first meet them; to welcome sb: **~ sb** *The nurse should greet the patient in a calm and welcoming manner.* ◇ **~ sb with sth** *Refugees were greeted with hospitality at their destinations.* **2** [usually passive] to react to sb/sth in a particular way: **be greeted (by sb)** *The release of the survey was not greeted warmly by military officials.* ◇ **be greeted with sth** *Deming and Juran's lectures on quality control had been greeted with enthusiasm in Japan.* **3 ~ sb** (of sights, sounds or smells) to be the first thing that you see, hear or smell at a particular time: *The sight that greets the visitor is remarkable.*

greet·ing /ˈgriːtɪŋ/ *noun* [C, U] something that you say or do to greet sb: *They exchanged greetings before starting the session.* ◇ *She raised her hand in greeting.* HELP In a letter or an email to sb, the **greeting** is how you begin, often by writing 'Dear John/Dr Smith/Sir'.

grew *past tense of* GROW

grey[1] (*especially BrE*) (*NAmE usually* **gray**) /greɪ/ *adj.* having a colour between black and white that is the colour of smoke or the sky on a dull day: *Organic soils and peats tend to be black, dark grey, dark brown or dark reddish-brown.*

grey[2] (*especially BrE*) (*NAmE usually* **gray**) /greɪ/ *noun* [U, C] a colour between black and white that is the colour of smoke or the sky on a dull day: *These minerals have colours in reflected light that range from nearly pure white to various shades of grey.*

grid /grɪd/ *noun* **1 ~ (of sth)** a pattern of straight lines that cross each other to form squares or RECTANGLES: *Various large civic and cultural buildings are set in a grid of streets and open, grassy areas.* **2** a system of electric wires or pipes carrying gas, for sending power over a large area: *A significant percentage of the plant's electricity output is available for dispatch to the grid.* ◇ *a power/an electricity grid* HELP The **national grid** is the electricity supply of a country: *Local small-scale hydropower resources can play an important role in providing electricity to areas remote from the national grid.* **3** a pattern of squares on a map that are marked with letters or numbers to help you find the exact position of a place: **+ noun** *The majority of the samples were collected at grid reference ST 449, 397.* **4** (*often* **the Grid**) [sing.] a number of computers that are connected together using the Internet so that they can share power, data, etc. in order to work on difficult problems: **+ noun** *Grid computing over the Internet will probably become prevalent.*

grief /griːf/ *noun* [U, sing.] **~ (over/at sth)** a feeling of great sadness, especially when sb dies: *She found it hard to express her sense of loss and grief.*

griev·ance /ˈgriːvəns/ *noun* **~ (against sb)** something that you think is unfair and that you complain or protest about: *The worker believes that he or she has a legitimate grievance against the company.* ◇ *International organizations can help groups to address grievances effectively without violence.*

grim /grɪm/ *adj.* (**grim·mer, grim·mest**) serious, unpleasant and DEPRESSING: *Both countries continue to suffer from the grim economic outlook.* ◇ *Much of the discussion of the less developed world paints a grim picture.* ■ **grim·ly** *adv.*: *The film grimly exposes the harsh realities of life in the camp.*

grip[1] /grɪp/ *noun* **1** [C, usually sing.] an act of holding sb/sth tightly; a particular way of doing this: *I forcefully removed my right arm from his grip.* **2** [sing.] control or power over sb/sth: *After the Kornilov affair, Kerensky and his government began to lose their grip.* ◇ *Where French Revolutionary armies had passed before, Napoleonic rule had a firmer grip.* ◇ **~ on sb/sth** *These East Asian economies have generally maintained a tight grip on inflation.* **3** [sing.] **~ (on sth)** an understanding of sth SYN GRASP[2] (1): *Without this principle we effectively lose all real grip on the notion of identity.*

IDM **come/get to ˈgrips with sth** to begin to understand and deal with sth difficult: *A number of academic writers have attempted to get to grips with this issue.* **in the ˈgrip of sth** experiencing or controlled by sth unpleasant and powerful: *In the grip of strong emotion such as anger, people may act impulsively.*

grip[2] /grɪp/ *verb* (**-pp-**) **1 ~ sth** to hold sth firmly SYN GRASP[1]: *An anxious patient typically sits upright, with head erect and hands gripping the chair.* **2** (of an emotion or a situation) to have a powerful effect on sb/sth: **~ sb/sth** *In the 1960s Cold War hysteria gripped the US.* ◇ **be gripped by sth** *King's family was gripped by the fear that he would never emerge alive.* **3** [often passive] to interest or excite sb; to hold sb's attention: **be gripped by sth** *No enthusiast for the lyric poem will fail to be gripped by every chapter in this book.*

gross /grəʊs; *NAmE* groʊs/ *adj.* (**gross·er, gross·est**) [only before noun] **1** being the total amount of sth before anything is taken away: *The company's gross profit margin continued to decrease, and revenue declined.* ➲ *compare* NET[1] **2** (of a crime or bad act) very obvious and unacceptable: *Unlike in Kosovo, the gross violation of human rights was not given as a main justification for the invasion until later.* **3** extreme: *Even the most sophisticated theories invariably represent a gross simplification of processes at play in the real world.* ◇ *These estimates are probably a gross underestimation of the actual occurrence of the disease.* **4** not detailed: *The cause may be immediately apparent even on gross inspection.*

ˌgross doˌmestic ˈproduct *noun* [U, C, usually sing.] = GDP

gross·ly /ˈgrəʊsli; *NAmE* ˈgroʊsli/ *adv.* **1** (used to describe negative qualities) extremely: *The UK guidelines for vitamin*

D consumption appear grossly inadequate. ◇ *In this condition, the abdomen is usually grossly distended.* **2** to a very large and unacceptable degree: *People grossly overestimated both their own and others' ability to detect change (Levin, 2002).*

ˌgross ˌnational ˈproduct *noun* [U, C, usually sing.] = GNP

ground /graʊnd/ *noun* **1** [C, usually pl.] a good or true reason for saying, doing or believing sth: **~ for (doing) sth** *There are strong economic grounds for favouring democratic firms.* ◇ *The police cannot act without reasonable grounds for suspicion.* ◇ **on (the) grounds of sth** *The Court of Justice accepted there could be objective reasons justifying compulsory retirement on grounds of age.* ◇ **on the grounds that...** *The Romans granted Judaism a special status on the grounds that it was an ancient national religion to which its members owed allegiance.* ◇ **on political/economic, etc. grounds** *The war did not involve any British interest but was fought on humanitarian grounds.* **2** (*often* **the ground**) [U] the solid surface of the earth: *In winter, snow covers the ground to a depth of only 3-29 mm.* ◇ **on the ~** *To express humility or repentance, the person praying might kneel or lie prostrate on the ground.* ◇ **above/below (the) ~** *A downward-pointing radar is used to determine the height of the satellite above the ground.* ◇ **+ noun** *Temperatures at and under the ground surface are important for road transport and agriculture.* **3** [U] soil on the surface of the earth: *The ground needed to be tilled regularly until August, when the tobacco harvest began.* **4** [U, C, usually sing.] an area of interest, knowledge or ideas; a situation in which ideas are examined or can be developed: *Sandbrook's work covers much of the same ground but gives more attention to cultural developments.* ◇ **on... ~** *Immediately as we read Plutarch, we feel ourselves to be on familiar ground.* ◇ **testing ~ (for sth)** *Northern Europe has proved an important testing ground for the geographical theory of epidemics.* ◇ **fertile ~ (for sth)** *In the 1990s, bars, clubs and discos increasingly became fertile ground for cigarette promotions.* ➲ *see also* COMMON GROUND, MIDDLE GROUND **5** [C, usually pl., U] (usually in compounds) a large area of land or sea that is of a particular type or used for a particular purpose, or where a particular thing happens: *Every year, migrating birds make long seasonal journeys from their breeding grounds to their wintering grounds and back.* ◇ *fishing/hunting grounds* ◇ **open ~** *Walking on two feet is a more efficient way of moving over open ground.* **6** [C] (usually in compounds) (*BrE*) an area of public land that is used for a particular purpose, activity or sport: *Larkin writes of an England of false cheer, cheap fashions, joyless wedding parties and drab recreation grounds.* **7** [U, C, usually sing.] (*NAmE*) = EARTH (4)

IDM **get (sth) off the ˈground** to start happening successfully; to make sth start happening successfully: *Analysts believe that the pipeline project will not get off the ground in the absence of state support.* **give/lose ˈground (to sb/sth)** to allow sb to have an advantage; to lose an advantage for yourself: *Bristol lost ground to its north-western rival in the war years of the 1740s.* ◇ *Reagan was not prepared to give ground unilaterally or put American security at risk.* **on the ˈground** in the place where sth is happening and among the people who are in the situation: *A management system that looks good on paper is of little value if not effectively implemented on the ground.* ➲ *more at* CLEAR[2], GAIN[1], MORAL[1], NEW, PREPARE, SHIFT[2]

ground·ed /ˈgraʊndɪd/ *adj.* [not usually before noun] **~ (in/on sth)** having a firm basis in sth; based on sth: *The story lines of Aristophanes were firmly grounded in the culture and politics of his day.* ◇ *Such theoretically informed and empirically grounded research is especially useful in analysing the actual effects of new institutional arrangements.*

ground·ing /ˈgraʊndɪŋ/ *noun* [sing., U] knowledge and understanding of the basic parts of a subject; a basis for sth: **~ in sth** *Henken's book provides a thorough grounding in Cuba's geography, history and institutions.* ◇ **~ for sth** *The authors provide historical grounding for contemporary issues.*

ˈground state *noun* (*physics*) the lowest energy state of an atom, other PARTICLE, or system of particles: *When an excited molecule returns to its ground state, energy is emitted.* ➲ *see also* ENERGY LEVEL

ground·water /ˈgraʊndwɔːtə(r)/ *noun* [U, pl.] water that is found under the ground in soil, rocks, etc: *An excess of nitrogen contaminates groundwater.* ◇ *Pollutants in groundwaters, surface waters and the atmosphere are introduced into the environment as a result of many industrial activities.*

group[1] /gruːp/ *noun* [C+sing./pl. v.] **1** a number of people or things that are similar in some way so that they can be considered together: *The homeless, women, and children appear to be those groups in society exposed to the greatest risk.* ◇ **~ of sth** *There is another group of genes in which mutations can also lead to cancer.* ◇ **into groups** *These verbs can be classified into five groups.* ➲ *see also* AGE GROUP, BLOOD GROUP, FUNCTIONAL GROUP, PEER GROUP, SUBGROUP **2** a number of people who do an activity together or share particular beliefs: *The police consult widely with local community groups in developing operational priorities.* ◇ *Dialogue has been initiated with armed groups in several countries.* ➲ *see also* FOCUS GROUP, INTEREST GROUP, PRESSURE GROUP, SUPPORT GROUP, WORKING GROUP **3** a business organization consisting of several companies that have the same owner: *The group has multiple affiliated companies, each acting independently.* ◇ *Business groups can also press legislatures to stop regulation that business does not like.* **4** a number of people or things that are found or put together in the same place: **~ of sth** *Davidson (1974) studied a small group of islands, the Bay Islands, off Honduras.* ◇ *The class was divided into six groups of five students.* ◇ **in groups** *When animals live in groups, they all have an interest in making the predator leave the area.* **5** (*chemistry*) a set of chemical elements in a particular column in the PERIODIC TABLE that have similar chemical properties and whose atoms contain the same number of outer ELECTRONS: *Boron stands apart from the rest of the elements in the group.* ➲ *compare* PERIOD (6)

▸ ADJECTIVE + GROUP **small • large** *Work was carried out by individuals or by small groups working together.* | **major • main** *There is pressure on the major supermarket groups to compete with the discount stores.* | **religious • professional** *Religious groups are one of the primary avenues through which people give service.* | **diverse • distinct • dominant • vulnerable • high-risk • disadvantaged, marginalized • ethnic • racial • cultural • social • socio-economic • occupational** *Planters in South Carolina were the wealthiest social group in eighteenth-century North America.*

▸ NOUN + GROUP **target • control, comparison, reference • intervention • treatment • minority • immigrant** *Boys in the intervention group reported a difference of approximately 20 min in weekend screen time compared with boys in the control group.*

▸ VERB + GROUP **form** *The Greens have since then formed a group of their own in the Parliament.* | **comprise • constitute • represent • identify • define • target • study • compare • distinguish • characterize • include • exclude** *Ethnicity is often used instead of language or religion to identify a group.* | **join • organize** *Many parents find it helpful to join a group of other parents of autistic children.*

▸ GROUP + VERB **consist of, (be) composed of, comprise • (be) based on • differ • experience • face • dominate** *The fourth group consists of low-income economies in East Asia.*

▸ VERB + INTO GROUPS **be divided, fall ◆ be classifed, be categorized** *Aquatic systems are divided into two separate groups: marine and freshwater systems.*
▸ GROUP + NOUN **size ◆ member** *Optimal group size for this sort of activity is thought to be between 5 and 10.* | **membership ◆ identity** *The importance of religion for individual and group identity today varies considerably.* | **participant ◆ leader ◆ interaction ◆ dynamics** *Fifteen focus group participants enrolled in one of two initial focus groups in June 2008.* | **meeting ◆ cohesion ◆ solidarity ◆ affiliation ◆ living** *In highly collectivistic countries such as Japan, group cohesion is a central value.* | **discussion ◆ interview ◆ session** *A range of methods is used, for example, group discussions, workshop sessions and one-to-one counselling.*
▸ GROUP OF + NOUN **people, individuals ◆ men ◆ women ◆ children ◆ friends ◆ students ◆ workers, employees ◆ patients ◆ experts ◆ scholars ◆ researchers ◆ stakeholders ◆ customers ◆ organisms ◆ cells ◆ countries** *The study explores employers' perceptions of particular groups of migrant workers.* ◇ *A group of these countries has agreed the need to tackle climate change.*

group² /gru:p/ *verb* **1** [usually passive] to make people or things form a group or groups: **(be) grouped (in sth) (round/around sb/sth)** *Students, grouped in four- to five-member teams, work on mathematics problems.* ◇ *Each plot was occupied by several houses grouped around a yard.* ◇ **(be) grouped together** *In the first book, related poems are grouped together in three groups of three.* **2** to divide people or things into groups that are similar in some way: **~ sb/sth (together)** *These are the possible ways of grouping together the languages in the family.* ◇ **~ sb/sth into sth** *Data were grouped into categories via the following process:...* ◇ **~ sb/sth according to sth** *In the Greek and Turkish censuses, people were grouped according to religion or schooling or both.*

group·ing /ˈgru:pɪŋ/ *noun* **1** [C] a set of people acting together, especially within a larger organization: *These small nations consitute an important grouping within the EU.* ◇ **~ of sb/sth** *There is also a large centrist grouping of MPs who help resolve differences between the two wings of the party.* **2** [U] the action of putting people or things into a group or groups: **~ of sb/sth** *The process involves subjective decisions about the grouping of data.* ◇ **~ of sb/sth into sth** *The grouping of these patients into one category is too general.*

grow /grəʊ; *NAmE* groʊ/ *verb* (**grew** /gru:/, **grown** /grəʊn; *NAmE* groʊn/) **1** [I] to increase in size, number, strength or quality: *Many smaller towns and cities are growing even faster.* ◇ **~ in sth** *The European Union has grown in importance for social policy over the last 25 years.* ◇ **~ by sth** *The US economy grew by 4.2% between 1999 and 2000.* ◇ **+ adj.** *The proportion of older people in the population is growing larger.* ➲ language bank *at* TREND **2** [I, T] (of a plant) to exist and develop; to cause a plant to develop by taking care of it: *The plant only grows in tropical climates.* ◇ **~ sth** *In south-western Uganda, the range of crops grown has decreased significantly.* **3** [I] (especially of a living thing) to increase in size and change physically through a process of natural development; to cause sth to do this: *Boys and girls grow at different rates.* ◇ **+ adj.** *The insect then goes through two more stages, growing bigger each time.* ◇ **~ sth** *It generally takes 48 hours to grow the organism.* **4** [I, T] (of a part of the body) to become longer or develop; to allow or cause sth to become longer or develop: *She decided to let her hair grow.* ◇ **~ sth** *If a newt's leg is amputated, it will grow a new one.* **5** *linking verb* **+ adj.** to gradually become sth: *There is evidence that the richest groups in the UK have grown richer.* ◇ *The American tax system has grown more and more complex.* **6** [I] **~ to do sth** to gradually begin to do sth: *Consumers have grown to trust the information provided.* **7** [I] (of a person) to develop and improve particular qualities or skills: *In this way teachers help the students to grow and develop in ways beyond the normal classroom education.* ◇ **~ as sth** *The book shows how President Lincoln grew as a leader in office.* **8** [T] **~ sth** (*business*) to increase the size, quality or number of sth: *Selling abroad can be a means of growing a business.* **HELP** Although this use of **grow** with a direct object is common in everyday business contexts, it is not correct in the context of academic economics.
PHR V ˌ**grow** ˈ**back** to begin growing again after being cut off or damaged: *Up to 70% of the liver can be removed, and the liver will grow back to a normal size.* ˌ**grow** ˈ**into sth** [no passive] **1** to become sth as a result of natural development or gradual increase: *The American film business grew into a multimillion-dollar industry in the first decade of the twentieth century.* **2** to gradually develop into a particular type of person over a period of time: *The child grew into a handsome youth.* ˌ**grow** ˈ**out of sth** to develop from sth: *The book grew out of a series of lectures that she gave at Harvard in 2007.* ◇ *Film festivals notably grew out of a European film tradition focused upon art and artists.* ˌ**grow** ˈ**up 1** (of a person) to develop into an adult: *He had grown up in a council flat in the area.* ◇ **~ to do sth** *She grew up to become a famous mathematician.* **2** to develop gradually: *A new popular non-political culture has grown up.*
▸ GROW + NOUN **plants ◆ crops ◆ food ◆ vegetables ◆ corn ◆ wheat ◆ grain ◆ rice ◆ coffee** *Too little was done to help small farmers grow food in sustainable and organic ways.* | **organism ◆ cells ◆ bacteria ◆ culture ◆ crystals ◆ film ◆ layer** *There appeared to be no way to grow the cells in the laboratory.*
▸ NOUN + GROW **population ◆ city ◆ economy ◆ market ◆ industry ◆ firm ◆ number ◆ demand** *Through time, populations grew, resources were limited, and conflict occurred.* | **organism ◆ cell ◆ bacteria** *Sugary solutions are excellent media in which bacteria can grow and multiply.*
▸ GROW + ADVERB **rapidly, quickly ◆ slowly** *In the eastern parts of the empire, Christianity was growing rapidly.* | **fast ◆ exponentially ◆ dramatically ◆ significantly ◆ substantially, considerably ◆ enormously ◆ steadily ◆ indefinitely** *The city's coal consumption had grown exponentially.* | **well** *Unfortunately, the cultures did not grow well.*
▸ GROW IN + NOUN **size ◆ importance, significance ◆ number ◆ popularity ◆ strength** *American firms grew in size during this period.*

grow·er /ˈgrəʊə(r); *NAmE* ˈgroʊər/ *noun* a person or company that grows plants, fruit or vegetables to sell: *Kenya, which is Africa's largest grower of tea, will probably produce 328 million kg of the crop this year.*

grow·ing /ˈgrəʊɪŋ; *NAmE* ˈgroʊɪŋ/ *adj.* [only before noun] increasing in size, amount or degree: *Many cities struggle to cope with growing numbers of people living on the street.* ◇ *There is a growing awareness of online privacy issues.* ◇ *Mental health disorders are a rapidly growing public health problem.*

ˈ**growing season** *noun* [usually sing.] the period of the year during which the weather conditions are right for plants to grow: *In contrast to other regions of the world, the growing season in the study area is extremely short (2 months).* ◇ *In the growing season, deciduous species require large amounts of nitrogen for leaf expansion.*

grown *past part. of* GROW

growth /grəʊθ; *NAmE* groʊθ/ *noun* **1** [U, sing.] an increase in the size, amount or degree of sth: *In Canada, during this five-year period, the rate of urban growth was five per cent.* ◇ **~ in sth** *There has been a rapid growth in the number of immigrants coming from Latin America and Asia.* ◇ **~ of sth** *The growth of the global economy has diminished the significance of national boundaries.*

G

➲ language bank *at* TREND **2** [U] an increase in economic activity or value: *Regional policy has a role to play in encouraging growth and employment.* **3** [U] (of people, animals or plants) the process of growing physically, mentally or emotionally: *Inadequate nutrition has direct effects on fetal growth.* ◇ *Learning is seen as a vital form of personal growth.* **4** [C] a lump caused by a disease that forms on or inside a person, an animal or a plant: *The continued uncontrolled division of the cell can lead to the development of a cancerous growth.* **5** [U, C] **~ (of sth)** something that has grown or is growing: *Parnell wears a day's growth of beard.* ◇ *The waters here generally contain dense growths of algae.*

▸ ADJECTIVE + GROWTH **rapid, fast • slow • new • average** *There follows a period of slow growth until puberty.* | **high • low • annual • future** *By the 1990s, organic produce witnessed a 20 per cent annual growth in sales.* | **economic • continued • continuing • regional • endogenous** *The environmental consequences of economic growth are rarely assessed.*

▸ NOUN + GROWTH **population • productivity • income • employment** *English population growth was stagnant in the last half of the seventeenth century.* | **plant • cell** *Phosphorus is important in plant growth.*

▸ VERB + GROWTH **promote • stimulate • support • limit • reduce • affect, influence** *High levels of the protein promote the uncontrolled growth of infected cells.* | **encourage, foster • facilitate • generate • drive • sustain • accelerate • slow • hinder • show • explain • see, witness • experience, enjoy** *Buddhism in Asia is today experiencing new growth.* | **achieve • boost** *Growth is achieved by capturing a larger share of the market with the same products.* | **inhibit • regulate** *These additives are crucially important in inhibiting the growth of bacteria in the food product.*

▸ GROWTH + NOUN **rate • model • curve • process** *The growth rate of a stable population is based only on the population's birth and death rates.* | **theory • strategy** *The two companies briefly shared similar successful growth strategies.* | **factor • hormone** *Stem cells numbers are dramatically increased using growth factors.*

▸ GROWTH IN + NOUN **number • population • size • volume • demand • productivity • output • production • income • trade • sales • spending • use** *Some had predicted that continued growth in the volume of email would render the Internet unusable by 2008.*

▸ GROWTH OF + NOUN **population • economy • trade • market • sector • industry • firm • group • output • productivity • production • city • movement** *The mobile phone industry failed to predict the spectacular growth of the market in Africa.* | **plant • organism • cell • bacteria** *It contains antibiotics to suppress the growth of bacteria.*

guar·an·tee¹ AWL /ˌɡærənˈtiː/ *noun* **1** a firm promise that sth will be done or that sth will happen SYN ASSURANCE: *Today many of us are able to live our lives taking for granted the guarantees provided by the welfare state and social policy.* ◇ **~ of sth** *Even the Human Rights Act does not give a constitutional guarantee of the right to family life of Commonwealth citizens living in the UK.* ◇ **~ that...** *He made a guarantee that total taxation as a share of GDP would fall over the lifetime of a Conservative government.* ◇ **~ against sth** *One credit card provider offers its customers a guarantee against the risk of loss of money through fraud.* **2** something that makes sth else certain to happen: **(no) ~ of sth** *Glucose-lowering per se is not a guarantee of long-term benefit in terms of outcome.* ◇ **(no) ~ that...** *There is no guarantee that a rerun of evolution would produce anything like a human species.* **3** a written promise given by a company that sth you buy will be replaced or repaired without payment if it goes wrong within a particular period: *The company offered a money-back guarantee to persuade customers that they would be completely satisfied.* **4** a written promise to pay back money that sb else owes, or do sth that sb else promised to do, if they cannot do it themselves: **+ noun** *Since 1981, the UK 's loan guarantee scheme has been evaluated five times.*

guar·an·tee² AWL /ˌɡærənˈtiː/ *verb* **1** to promise to do or keep sth; to promise sth will happen or exist: **~ sth** *It should be recalled that the principal obligations to guarantee human rights lie with the national states.* ◇ *These guaranteed minimum prices for agricultural products are maintained through EU-financed intervention buying.* ◇ **~ (that)...** *The ANEP guaranteed that only national data would be made available to the public.* ◇ **~ to do sth** *Supermarkets seek a continuity of supplies from large growers who can guarantee to deliver a specified quantity at a specified time and place.* ◇ **~ sb sth** *Most people see the state as designed to guarantee individuals the freedom to pursue their private goals.* **2** to make sth certain to happen: **~ sth** *Some companies hope that simply putting a popular name on an average product or service will guarantee success.* ◇ **~ (that)...** *The existence of laws governing animal experiments in no way guarantees that ethical questions are adequately addressed.* **3** to agree to be legally responsible for sth or for doing sth, especially for paying back money that sb else owes if they cannot pay it back themselves: **~ sth** *Foreign banks were willing to provide loans because the government guaranteed these loans.*
IDM **be guaranˈteed to do sth** to be certain to have a particular result: *No single one of these methods was guaranteed to identify all of the genes in the region.*

guard¹ /ɡɑːd; *NAmE* ɡɑːrd/ *noun* **1** [C] a person, such as a soldier, a police officer or a prison officer, who protects a place or people, or prevents prisoners from escaping: *Elite neighbourhoods often advertise that they are protected by armed guards supplied by security firms.* ◇ *a security/prison/border guard* **2** [sing.+ sing./pl. v.] a group of people, such as soldiers or police officers, who protect sb/sth: *the captain of the palace guard* **3** [U] the act or duty of protecting property, places or people from attack or danger; the act or duty of preventing prisoners from escaping: **under ~** *Kerensky was placed under guard for his own protection.* ◇ **~ duty** *Most of these troops were on guard duty outside banks, prisons or railway stations.*
IDM **be on (your) ˈguard (against sb/sth)** to be very careful and prepared for sth difficult or dangerous: *Security staff are permanently on guard.* ◇ *Those who trade in brand products are aware of the need to be on guard against counterfeit goods.*

guard² /ɡɑːd; *NAmE* ɡɑːrd/ *verb* **1 ~ sb/sth** to watch a place in order to protect the people or things in it, or to prevent people from leaving: *Both parents collaborate in digging a burrow, guarding the nest and collecting food for their offspring.* **2 ~ sb/sth** to protect sb/sth from damage or harm: *The law in these courts was concerned with guarding the sexual morals of the nation.* ◇ *Senior managers often jealously guard their own departmental budgets.*
PHR V **ˈguard against (doing) sth** to take care to prevent sth or to protect yourself from sth: *There is a need for constitutional checks and balances to guard against exploitation or tyranny.*

guard·ian /ˈɡɑːdiən; *NAmE* ˈɡɑːrdiən/ *noun* **1** a person who is legally responsible for the care of another person, especially a child whose parents have died: *Although fathers and other legal guardians also sent in responses, roughly 90% of survey participants were mothers.* **2 ~ (of sth)** a person who protects sth: *Many criticisms are directed at the World Trade Organization in its capacity as guardian of world trade.*

guer·rilla (*also* **guer·illa**) /ɡəˈrɪlə/ *noun* a member of a small group of soldiers who are not part of an official army and who fight against official soldiers, usually to try to change the government: *He joined an expeditionary force* *that landed in Cuba to fight nationalist guerrillas.* ◇ **+ noun** *In the rest of Ireland, Home Rule was rejected, and a guerrilla war launched against British rule.*

guess[1] /ges/ *verb* **1** [T] to find the truth or the right answer to a question without knowing all the facts: **~ sth** *Although subjects typically expressed high confidence in their guesses, only 21% guessed the experimenter's rule.* ◇ **~ (that)...** *Darwin guessed correctly that Africa would yield the earliest fossils ancestral to apes.* **2** [I, T] to try and give an answer or make a judgement about sth without being sure of all the facts: **~ at sth** *It is not possible to define or even guess at all the possible actions someone might take.* ◇ **~ how/what, etc...** *He said that archaeology was basically just looking at dead people's leftovers and trying to guess how they lived their lives.* ◇ **~ sth** *We cannot confidently guess lifestyles, attitudes, social structures or population sizes a century from now.*

guess[2] /ges/ *noun* an attempt to give an answer or an opinion when you cannot be certain if you are right: *We tried to make an intelligent guess based on similar studies.* ◇ **~ about/as to sth** *We can assume that Saussure would regard any guesses about the future changes a language might undergo as being irrelevant.* ◇ **~ at sth** *There are not enough data even to make a guess at the total number of species.* ◇ **~ that...** *Over the long run, our guess is that there will probably be few major cultural centres that are not also economic centres.* ◇ **best ~** *Our best guess is that thousands of schools fall into the first category.* IDM *see* EDUCATED

guest /gest/ *noun* **1** a person that you have invited to your house or to a particular event that you are paying for: *They did not generally invite guests to their houses, but socialized outside the home.* ◇ *wedding/dinner guests* **2** a person who is staying at a hotel, etc: *The hotel will want to encourage guests to come for a return visit, as well as attracting new guests.* **3** a person who is invited to a particular place or organization, or to speak at a meeting: **+ noun** *Teacher A, one of the three guest speakers, underlined the pivotal role played by teacher education.*

guid·ance /ˈgaɪdns/ *noun* [U] **1** help or advice that is given to sb, especially by sb in authority: **~ on sth** *The British National Formulary gives reliable guidance on which drugs are safe and recommended in pregnancy.* ◇ **~ in (doing) sth** *The book provides practical guidance in actually carrying out statistical tests.* ◇ **~ as to sth** *Some patients do ask for guidance as to how best to proceed.* ◇ **under the ~ of** *Commissioners are each appointed for five years and work under the guidance of the President.* **2** the process of controlling the direction or position of sth using special equipment: *Egg collection takes place either by ultrasound guidance or laparoscopy.*

guide[1] /gaɪd/ *verb* **1** [often passive] to direct or influence the way sth is done, what sb thinks, etc: **be guided (by sth)** *It is evident that human rights work is now guided by a reasonably well-defined set of core values.* ◇ **guiding principle/philosophy, etc.** *Schwartz asked 60 000 respondents from 63 countries to assess 57 values as 'guiding principles of one's life'.* **2 ~ sb (through sth)** to explain sth to sb, especially sth complicated or difficult: *Part I of the book seeks to guide the reader through the fundamental principles which underlie company law.* **3 ~ sb (through sth)** to help sb do sth, especially sth complicated or difficult: *Knowledge was vital for the Roman paterfamilias in guiding his family through the trials of life.* **4 ~ sb/sth (+ adv./prep.)** to help or encourage sb/sth to move in a particular direction; to move sth in a particular direction: *Foraging bees are guided to the centre where the nectar is by the honey guides—the radiating lines on the petals of many flowers.*

guide[2] /gaɪd/ *noun* **1** something that gives you enough information to be able to make a decision about sth or form an opinion: **~ (to sth)** *The openness of elections serves as a reliable shorthand guide to the quality of democracy.* ◇ **~ for sb/sth** *The holistic approach viewed Islam as a comprehensive guide for private as well as public life.* ◇ **as a ~** *Further research should also consider testing various analytic models using a conceptual/theoretical framework as a guide.* **2** a book, article, etc. that gives you information, help or instructions about sth: *Following the guidelines for conducting focus groups, we used an interview guide to direct the discussion and to fulfil the research aims.* ◇ **~ to (doing) sth** *'5 Steps to Risk Assessment' (HSE Books, Bootle, 1998) is an essential guide to performing risk assessments.* **3** (*also* **guide·book** /ˈgaɪdbʊk/) **~ (to sth)** a book that gives information about a place for TRAVELLERS or tourists: *Despite the availability of free hotel review sites, paid-for hotel guides continue to prosper.* **4 (as a) ~** a person who shows other people where to go or how to do sth: *Marx also visited England, with Engels as a guide.* ◇ *Learners have to trust that their teachers will act as reliable guides in the process of discovery.* **5** a structure or marking that directs where sth can move or be positioned: *The tool was inserted into a guide to ensure that it only moved in one direction.*

guide·line AWL /ˈgaɪdlaɪn/ *noun* **1** [usually pl.] a rule or instruction that is given by an official organization telling you how to do sth: *Codes of practice, circulars and guidelines play an important part in the administration of government.* ◇ **~ for sb/sth** *The organization has issued guidelines for people working with prisoners.* ◇ **in accordance with/according to the ~** *The whole investigation was performed according to local guidelines and the Data Protection Act 1998 was followed.* **2** something that can be used to help you decide or form an opinion about sth: *The following is a simple guideline to understanding the interpretation of acid-base data.*

▸ ADJECTIVE + GUIDELINES **national • local • new • current • clear • general • clinical • ethical** *They all took on a key role in implementing national guidelines and regulations.*

▸ NOUN + GUIDELINES **practice • policy • treatment** *These screening tools have been recommended in several best practice guidelines.*

▸ VERB + GUIDELINES **provide, issue, produce, publish • develop • establish, set • follow, use, implement, adopt, adhere to • meet** *The Code provides guidelines for the responsible introduction, production and management of fish species under managed conditions.*

▸ GUIDELINES + VERB **recommend • state** *Both international and national guidelines recommend that all adults should be physically active for at least 30 min per day.*

guilt /gɪlt/ *noun* [U] **1** the fact that sb has done sth illegal: *Criminal defendants are presumed innocent and their guilt must be proved beyond reasonable doubt.* OPP INNOCENCE (1) **2** the unhappy feelings caused by knowing or thinking that you have done sth wrong: *Failure to lose weight often leads to feelings of guilt and loss of self-confidence.* ◇ **~ about sth** *Shame and guilt about anger may also motivate a child to withdraw.*

guilty /ˈgɪlti/ *adj.* (**guilt·ier**, **guilti·est**) (**more guilty** and **most guilty** are more frequent.) **1** having done sth illegal: **~ (of sth)** *Corrupt judges can let people off, or find them guilty of much lesser offences.* ◇ **plead ~ to (doing) sth** *The defendant denied murder but pleaded guilty to manslaughter.* ◇ **not ~** *If the jury or magistrates return a not guilty verdict, the defendant is acquitted and is free to leave court.* OPP INNOCENT (1) **2 ~ of (doing) sth** having done sth wrong: *Darcy too is guilty of pride and prejudice, and he too must mature in the course of the novel.* ◇ *Unfortunately, health care professionals are often guilty of stereotyping older people.* OPP INNOCENT (1) **3** feeling ashamed because you have done sth that you know is wrong or have not done sth that you should have done: **~ (that...)** *Many bereaved people feel guilty that they failed to do* enough for the deceased. ◇ **~ about (doing) sth** *She felt guilty about disappointing others.*

gun /gʌn/ *noun* a weapon that is used for firing bullets, etc: *Walden bolted himself inside his farmhouse and fired a gun, wounding several policemen.* ◇ *King Charles's ships by 1640 carried almost 1 200 heavy guns.* ◇ **+ noun** *Most Americans support tougher gun control.*

gut /gʌt/ *noun* **1** [C] the tube in the body through which food passes when it leaves the stomach **SYN** INTESTINE: *The cells lining the gut secrete specialized digestive enzymes.* ◇ **+ noun** *E. coli forms part of the normal gut flora of man as well as many animals and birds.* **2 guts** [pl.] **~ (of sth)** the organs in and around the stomach, especially in an animal: *The virus infects the guts of pigs and is a common source of mortality in piglets.*

H h

habit /ˈhæbɪt/ *noun* **1** [C, U] something that you do often and almost without thinking about it, especially sth that is difficult to change or stop; a person's usual behaviour: *Factors such as poverty appear to be associated with poor dietary habits.* ◇ *Half of all regular cigarette smokers will eventually be killed by their habit.* ◇ *Trade association membership is more a matter of habit than of calculation.* **2** [C] a typical way of behaving that sth has; the fact that sth tends to happen in a particular way: **~ (of sth)** *The feeding habits of the Eurasian otter have been extensively researched.* ◇ **have a ~ of doing sth** *Films have a habit of dwelling on the sensational much longer than any moral purpose would seem to justify.*

habi·tat /ˈhæbɪtæt/ *noun* [C, U] the natural environment of a particular type of animal or plant: *In their natural habitat in South America, the insects' breeding season coincides with the tropical rainy season.* ◇ *The data implied substantial migration of individuals between habitats, especially from deeper ponds into shallower pools.* ◇ *The alga is found across a wide range of habitats, ranging from exposed coastline to calm, sheltered bays.* ◇ **~ for sth** *Such areas may provide an important habitat for wildlife.* ◇ **~ of sth** *This type of grass is the preferred habitat of the introduced ship rat (Rattus rattus).* ◇ **+ noun** *Species of all kinds are threatened by habitat destruction.*

ha·bit·ual /həˈbɪtʃuəl/ *adj.* [only before noun] usual or typical of sb/sth: *Saudi Arabia was his country of habitual residence.* ◇ *The biggest difficulty in achieving change, he observed, was the resistance caused by habitual behaviours.* ■ **ha·bit·ual·ly** /həˈbɪtʃuəli/ *adv.*: *Moose is another deer species which habitually feeds upon aquatic plants.*

had /həd; əd; *strong form* hæd/ ➲ HAVE[1], HAVE[2]

hair /heə(r); *NAmE* her/ *noun* **1** [U, C] the mass of material like thin threads growing on the bodies of people and some animals (in people especially on the head); one of these threads: *Both men and women have long hair and wear gold bracelets and necklaces.* ◇ **body/facial ~** *Partial loss of body hair is seen in 60% of patients.* ◇ *The adult moths have a large number of hairs covering each segment.* **2** [C] a piece of material like a thin thread growing on the leaves and STEMS of some plants, or as part of a living cell: *Fine hairs, sometimes with sticky secretions, can prevent small insects from getting close to the leaf surface.* ◇ *It damages the cilia, tiny hairs that clear invading bacteria from the lung.*

half[1] /hɑːf; *NAmE* hæf/ *noun* (*pl.* **halves** /hɑːvz; *NAmE* hævz/) either of two equal parts into which sth is or can be divided: **~ of sth** *Patients experience visual loss in the upper or lower half of the visual field.* ◇ **the other ~** *Half of the males were provided with water, 20% sucrose solution, and pollen, whereas the other half were provided only with water.* ◇ **the first/second ~ of sth** *The first half of the 19th century is generally regarded as the era of classic liberalism.* ◇ **in ~** *The fruit was rinsed with deodorized distilled water and then cut in half.* ◇ **into halves** *The ball was cut into two halves and then one piece was slowly pushed against a flat plane.* ◇ **by ~** *One recent success is the case of measles, with the number of deaths globally falling by half between 1999 and 2004.*

half[2] /hɑːf; *NAmE* hæf/ *det., pron.* an amount equal to half, or approximately half, of sth/sb: *For half a century, many countries have achieved impressive progress in their health conditions.* ◇ *The World Health Organization has estimated that over half a billion individuals (1 in 10 of the world 's population) have a disability.* ◇ **~ an hour** *Within half an hour of its first appearance as a little cloudlet, a cumulonimbus may fill a thousand cubic kilometres of troposphere.* ◇ **~ of sth** *By the 1990s, it was expected that half of all new marriages would end in divorce.*

half[3] /hɑːf; *NAmE* hæf/ *adv.* to the extent of half: *The cells were half filled with 0.05 ml of normal saline.* ◇ **~ as sth** *Lone mothers were half as likely as married mothers to be in paid employment (McRae, 1999a: 15).* ◇ *Growth in Japan has been half as fast as that of the USA.* ➲ language bank *at* PROPORTION

ˈhalf-life *noun* **1 ~ (of sth)** (*physics*) the time taken for the RADIOACTIVITY of a substance to fall to half its original value: *Carbon-14 decays to nitrogen-14, with a half-life of 5 730 years.* **2 ~ (of sth)** (*chemistry*) the time taken for the CONCENTRATION of a substance to fall to half its original value: *Unlike a first-order reaction, the half-life of a substance in a second-order reaction varies with the initial concentration.*

half·way /ˌhɑːfˈweɪ; *NAmE* ˌhæfˈweɪ/ *adv.* **~ + adv./prep.** at an equal distance between two points; in the middle of a period of time: *Other animals, including some insects, fly halfway across the world to mate and lay their eggs.* ◇ *Halfway between the spring tides, at the time of the first and last quarters of the moon's monthly cycle, the solar effect is least.* ■ **half·way** *adj.* **~ mark/point** *The two equinoxes, vernal and autumnal (spring and fall), are the halfway points between the solstices.* **IDM** *see* MEET

halt[1] /hɔːlt; *BrE also* hɒlt/ *verb* [I, T] to stop; to make sb/sth stop, especially suddenly or for a short time: *In the month following the disaster, business activity in the region largely halted.* ◇ **~ sb/sth** *Wordsworth's poem was written during the precarious Peace of Amiens, which had temporarily halted the war with France.* **IDM** *see* TRACK[1]

halt[2] /hɔːlt; *BrE also* hɒlt/ *noun* [sing.] an act of stopping the movement or progress of sb/sth: **~ in sth** *Although vaccination resumed in 2004, the halt in the programme caused a polio outbreak that spread through the country.* ◇ **~ to sth** *This was a call to the nations of the world to gather together and discuss a halt to the arms race.* ◇ **bring sth to a ~** *By the time the First World War brought immigration to a halt, the Jewish community in Britain had quadrupled in size.* ◇ **come/grind to a ~** *Ricardo believed that because the country was running out of land, its economic growth would grind to a halt.*

halve /hɑːv; *NAmE* hæv/ *verb* [I, T] to reduce by a half; to make sth reduce by a half: *World illiteracy halved between 1970 and 2005, according to UNESCO's most recent statistics.* ◇ *Japan currently has about three workers to every pensioner, but this number is expected to halve by 2050.* ◇ **~ sth** *The opening of the world's longest sea-crossing bridge has halved the travel time between Ningbo and Shanghai.*

halves *pl. of* HALF[1]

ham·per /ˈhæmpə(r)/ *verb* [often passive] to prevent sth from being achieved easily or happening normally; to prevent sb from easily doing sth **SYN** HINDER, IMPEDE: **be**

hampered (by sth) *Efforts to restrain illegal timber cutting have been hampered by lack of resources.* ◇ **~ sb/sth** *Wyla did not feel that either her low-income background or her race would hamper her.*

hand[1] /hænd/ *noun* **1** [C] the part of the body at the end of the arm, including the fingers and thumb: *A student raised his hand to pose a question.* ◇ *Standing alongside her in the picture, holding her hand, is a crying child.* ◇ *They eat with their right hand and consider it rude to be handed anything in the left hand.* ➲ *see also* LEFT-HAND, RIGHT-HAND **2 -handed** (in adjectives) using the hand or number of hands mentioned: *The controller was attached to a desk via Velcro to stabilize it for one-handed use.* **3** [sing.] the part or role that sb/sth plays in a particular situation; sb's influence in a situation: *The vast majority of these posters and journals supported Deng Xiaoping; their purpose was to strengthen his hand.* ◇ **~ in sth** *The many scholars who thought Shakespeare had a hand in 'Edward III' could well be right.* **4** (in compounds) done or used by a person rather than a machine: *These earlier techniques all relied on hand-painted or hand-drawn images.* ◇ *Humans using hand tools were replaced by complex machines powered by steam.*

IDM **at hand** being considered or dealt with at the present time: *In the case at hand, the Court of Justice found that the General Court had not erred in law.* **(close/near) at ˈhand** close to you in time or distance: *Miller begins by teasingly announcing that 'the end of literature is at hand'.* ◇ *The need for mutual support made it desirable to have neighbours close at hand.* **at the hands of sb | at sb's hands** if you experience sth **at the hands of sb**, they are the cause of it: *They observed the death of Romanian President Nicolae Ceausescu at the hands of his own citizens.* **by ˈhand** by a person rather than a machine: *Virtually all of these tasks were carried out by hand, although some threshing machinery had appeared in South Carolina by the 1760s.* **fall into sb's ˈhands/the ˈhands of sb** to become controlled by sb: *There is wide recognition of the need to prevent fissile material from falling into the wrong hands.* **(at) first ˈhand** by experiencing, seeing, etc. sth yourself rather than being told about it by sb else: *The work was begun with a view to discovering the problems of classification at first hand.* **ˌhand in ˈhand** if things **go hand in hand**, they are closely connected and are always found together: *Popularity and moral goodness do not always go hand in hand.* **in ˈhand 1** being done or dealt with at the present time: *If the room is too small, people may begin to feel uncomfortable and not really be interested in the task in hand.* **2** being successfully controlled or dealt with: *With the airborne problem apparently well in hand, the major focus of environmental managers was on the river.* **in the hands of sb | in sb's ˈhands** if sth is **in the hands of** sb, they control it or have the power to deal with it: *Ownership of capital goods is concentrated in the hands of relatively few people.* ◇ *Such strategies target individuals and imply that the solution is in their hands.* **on ˈhand** available to be used or to help: *The company had the right fabric on hand and was able to fulfil the order.* ◇ *It is essential that competent technical support be on hand at all times.* **on your ˈhands** if you have sb/sth **on your hands**, you are responsible for them/it: *He warned that if Japan responded harshly, 'We may find ourselves with a full-scale war on our hands.'* **(on the ˈone hand...) on the ˈother (hand)...** used to introduce different points of view, ideas, etc, especially when they are opposites: *Negative conduct should not be taken into account unless it is of an extreme nature; positive conduct, on the other hand, could be taken into account.* ◇ *The close association between Western ideas about exploration and discovery on the one hand, and geography on the other hand, cannot be denied.* **ˌplay into sb's ˈhands** to do exactly what an enemy, opponent, etc. wants so that they gain the advantage in a particular situation: *His quickness to claim credit for his achievements played into the hands of his enemies.* **(at) second, third, etc. ˈhand** by being told about sth by sb else who has seen it or heard about it, not by experiencing, seeing, etc. it yourself: *His quotations from classical authors are taken mostly at second hand.* **take sth into your own ˈhands** to deal with a particular situation yourself because others cannot or will not help you: *When Pope Gregory was threatened by invaders and had no effective support from the emperor, he took matters into his own hands.* **to ˈhand** that you can reach or get easily: *The equipment should be arranged in an effective manner with centrifuge, refrigerators or freezers readily to hand.* ➲ *more at* BARE, CHANGE[2], CLOSE[4], FORCE[2], FREE[1], INVISIBLE, SHOW[2], TRY, UPPER

hand[2] /hænd/ *verb* to pass or give sth to sb: **~ sth to sb** *Financial control would be handed to the headteacher and governors of a school.* ◇ **~ sb sth** *The operator of the Enigma machine would be handed a message in plain text.*

PHR V **ˌhand sth ˈback (to sb)** to give or return sth to the person who owns it or to where it belongs: *The doctor who had been awarded the Order of Lenin handed back her decoration.* **ˌhand sth ˈdown (from sb) (to sb) 1** [usually passive] to give or leave sth to sb who is alive after you die SYN PASS STH DOWN: *His vision was kept alive and handed down to another generation.* **2** to officially give a decision, statement, etc. SYN ANNOUNCE (1): *In a judgment handed down on 1 July 2010, the European Court of Justice confirmed the €85.8 million fine.* **ˌhand sth ˈin (to sb)** to give sth to a person in authority: *He had not progressed much in his assignment, and asked if he could hand it in next week.* ◇ *Substantial numbers of unlicensed firearms were handed in during the amnesty.* **ˌhand sth ˈon (to sb)** to give or leave sth for another person to use or deal with SYN PASS STH ON (TO SB) (1): *He still works on the sheep farm that he has handed on to his son.* **ˌhand sth ˈout (to sb)** to give a number of things to people in a group or place SYN DISTRIBUTE (1): *Two protesters were handing out leaflets in the street.* ◇ *The Arts Councils have the power to hand out money to arts bodies and institutions.* **ˌhand ˈover (to sb) | ˌhand sth ˈover (to sb)** to give sb else your position of power or the responsibility for sth: *He won some successes, but had to hand over to Lucius Mummius and returned to Rome.* ◇ *The coup makers handed over power to democratically elected leaders after a nine-month transition.* ➲ *related noun* HANDOVER **ˌhand sb/sth ˈover (to sb)** to give sth/sb officially or formally to another person: *Poor farmers who had fallen into debt to wealthy landowners had to hand over to them a sixth of their produce.*

hand·book /ˈhændbʊk/ *noun* a book giving information such as facts on a particular subject or instructions on how to use sth: *This will be an excellent handbook for teachers, teacher educators and researchers.* ➲ *compare* MANUAL[2]

hand·ful /ˈhændfʊl/ *noun* **1** [sing.] **~ (of sb/sth)** a small number of people or things: *To date, only a handful of studies have assessed the impact of pollination on mating patterns.* ◇ *It is difficult to observe more than a handful of selected people at the same time.* **2** [C] **~ (of sth)** the amount of sth that can be held in one hand: *Handfuls of mixed sand and wheat grains were cast upon the sea.*

han·dle /ˈhændl/ *verb* **1 ~ sth/sb** to deal with a situation, a problem, a strong emotion, etc: *In the traditional myth of masculinity, men are characterized by their ability to handle stressful situations.* ◇ *Handling customers who are frequent complainers can be a big draw on the organization's time and resources.* **2 ~ sth** to touch, hold or move sth with your hands: *Automating laboratory processes reduces the number of occasions an individual may need to handle specimens.* **3 ~ sth** to control a vehicle, an animal, a tool, etc: *Learning to handle a gun remains as much a rite of passage for boys in rural Alabama or Idaho as learning to drive or fish.*

hand·ling /ˈhændlɪŋ/ *noun* [U] **1** the way that sb deals with or treats a situation, a problem, a person, etc: *People have differing attitudes to receiving bad news and this needs sensitive handling.* ◇ **~ of sth/sb** *Through constructive handling of conflicts, relationships between students can be enhanced.* **2** the action of touching, using or dealing with physical objects or substances: *Improvements in food handling, storage and preparation helped reduce infectious disease mortality.* ◇ **~ of sth** *The handling of compressed gas requires suitable high-pressure equipment.* **3** the action of organizing or controlling sth: **~ of sth** *The numerical handling of data is intended to add clarity to complex issues.* ◇ **+ noun** *Mower (1996) lists a number of spatial data-handling problems that have been addressed with parallel processing.*

hand·over /ˈhændəʊvə(r); *NAmE* ˈhændoʊvər/ *noun* [C, U] the act of moving power or responsibility from one person or group to another; the period during which this is done: *There have to be systems for effective handovers between shifts to protect patient safety.* ◇ **~ (of sth) (to sb)** *The aim of these talks was to ensure the peaceful, non-violent and orderly handover of power.*

hang /hæŋ/ *verb* (**hung**, **hung** /hʌŋ/) HELP In sense 2, **hanged** is used for the past tense and past participle. **1** [T, I] to attach sth, or to be attached, at the top so that the lower part is free or loose: **~ sth + adv./prep.** *Greenpeace International hung a banner from one of the cooling towers at the power station.* ◇ **~ adv./prep.** *Stalactites hang down from the ceilings of caves, while stalagmites grow up from the floor.* ◇ *On the walls hung the portraits of Jefferson Davis, Robert E. Lee and other prominent Southern generals.* **2** (**hanged**, **hanged**) [T, I] **~ (sb/yourself)** to kill sb, usually as a punishment, by tying a rope around their neck and allowing them to drop; to be killed in this way: *Found guilty and sentenced to die, John Brown was hanged in Charlestown, Virginia on December 2, 1859.* **3** [I] **+ adv./prep.** to stay in the air: *The satellite hangs vertically above a fixed point on the Equator.* ◇ *The heavy smoky haze hangs over cities and the surrounding countryside.* IDM *see* BALANCE[1]

PHR V ˌ**hang ˈon to sth** (*rather informal*) to keep sth, not sell it, lose it or give it away: *Many lucky enough to hang on to their jobs worked fewer hours and experienced pay cuts.* ˌ**hang ˈout** (*informal*) to spend a lot of time in a place; to spend a lot of time with a particular person or group of people: *She cut class frequently, hanging out in the cafeteria or hallways and playing cards with friends.* ˌ**hang ˈover sb** if sth bad or unpleasant is **hanging over** you, you think about it and worry about it a lot because it is happening or might happen: *For now, uncertainty still hangs over the military's political plan.* ˌ**hang toˈgether** **1** to fit together well; to be the same as or CONSISTENT with each other: *Delap considers the logic by which these ideas hang together.* ◇ *In times of economic crisis, it usually becomes clearer that politics and economics hang together.* **2** (of people) to support or help one another: *Norms functioned as rallying posts around which conversations revolved and communities hung together.*

hap·loid /ˈhæplɔɪd/ *adj.* (*biology*) **1** (of a cell) containing a single set of CHROMOSOMES: *The net result of meiosis is that every gamete is haploid, having only one copy of a particular chromosome, whereas the diploid parent has two.* **2** consisting of haploid cells: *Yeast can survive indefinitely as a haploid organism, carrying a single copy of its genome.* ➲ *compare* DIPLOID

hap·pen /ˈhæpən/ *verb* **1** [I] to take place, especially without being planned; to take place as the result of sth: *Events happening in one part of the world are able to produce effects in other parts of it.* ◇ *The aim of the investigation was not to accuse individuals, but to establish the truth about what happened.* ◇ *Newton was interested primarily in how things happened in nature, not in philosophical arguments as to why they happened.* ◇ *Innovation is what happens when new thinking is successfully introduced in and valued by organizations.* **2** *linking verb* to do or be sth by chance: **~ to be/do sth** *If a surge happens to coincide with a high tide, there is a serious risk of sea defences being breached.* ◇ *The assets of an engineering company belong to the company and not to the official who happens to be managing director.* ◇ **it happens that...** *It happened that the trigger for the conflict came from Bohemia, where the elites had struggled to limit the authority of the king.*

IDM **anything can ˈhappen** used to say that it is not possible to know what the result of sth will be: *One cannot predict that this tendency will not be halted or even reversed: anything can happen in a dictatorship.* **as it happens/happened** used when you say sth that is connected with what has just been said and may be surprising: *As it happens, both these perceptions are correct.* **it (just) so happens that...** by chance: *It so happens that the enhancement of human capabilities also tends to go with an expansion of productivities and earning power.*

PHR V ˈ**happen to sb/sth** to have an effect on sb/sth: *As the body changes, support from nurses may need to increase to help patients deal with and accept what is happening to them.*

hap·pily /ˈhæpɪli/ *adv.* **1** in a happy way: *The novel ends happily, with Rae and Sammar planning to marry and travel to Egypt.* **2** by good luck SYN FORTUNATELY: *Happily, clams and mussels are just the sorts of creatures that fossilize well.* **3** willingly: *Visitors to African protected areas happily pay more for a wildlife experience (Moran, 1994).* **4** in a suitable or appropriate way: *This fact does not tie in too happily with the theory of progressive sea level decline during the Pleistocene.*

hap·pi·ness /ˈhæpinəs/ *noun* [U] the quality or state of being happy: *Most people find the greatest happiness in their family life, work, religion or leisure, not in politics.* ◇ *He views human happiness and social well-being as the sole purpose of existence.*

happy /ˈhæpi/ *adj.* (**hap·pier**, **hap·pi·est**) **1** satisfied that sth is good or right; not anxious: **~ with sb/sth** *International observers seemed to be happy with the way in which the election was conducted.* ◇ **~ about sb/sth** *Most teachers were not entirely happy about the situation.* ◇ **~ that...** *Almost all patients were happy that their records were stored on the computer.* ◇ **~ for sb to do sth** *If a patient is conscious, you should always ask them whether they are happy for you to talk to their relatives.* **2** **~ to do sth** willing or pleased to do sth: *By and large, patients were happy to accept their doctor's recommendations.* **3** giving or causing pleasure: *Charles I's famously happy, faithful and fruitful marriage was not mirrored by that of his eldest son.* ◇ *Nahum Tate's 1681 reworking of 'King Lear' with a happy ending is one of many Restoration adaptations of Shakespeare.* **4** feeling or showing pleasure: *Understanding what makes people happy and why may help us understand some of the fundamental questions in economics.* ◇ **~ for sb** *The majority of girls believed that having a baby would be a positive event and that their friends would be happy for them.*

hard[1] /hɑːd; *NAmE* hɑːrd/ *adj.* (**hard·er**, **hard·est**) **1** difficult to do, understand or answer: *These events raise some hard questions about the way science is done.* ◇ *In times of crisis, hard choices have to be made.* ◇ **it is ~ to do sth** *It is hard to see how the dispute might be settled satisfactorily.* ◇ *It is not hard to find cases where policies or institutions are in desperate need of reform.* ◇ **~ to do** *As oil reserves become harder to locate, the industry is also exploiting new markets for natural gas.* ◇ **it is ~ for sb (to do sth)** *The male peacock's tail reduces his chances for survival by making it harder for him to fly.* OPP EASY (1) ➲ thesaurus note *at* DIFFICULT **2** needing or using a lot of physical strength or mental effort; putting a lot of effort into an activity: *Having children involves both expense and hard work.* ◇ *Enslaved men and women soon found themselves hard at work.* ➲ thesaurus note *at* DIFFICULT **3** not soft to touch; difficult to bend or break: *The victim died having hit his head against a hard surface.* ◇ *Diamond is the hardest mineral known.* OPP SOFT (1) **4** [only before noun] definitely true and based on information that can be proved: *All too frequently these arguments have not been based on hard evidence.* ◇ *The situation was compounded by Knox's biographer presenting completely erroneous information as hard fact.* ◇ *The databases used by the organizations vary from hard data to expert and executive opinions.* ➲ *compare* SOFT (6) **5** full of difficulty and problems, especially because of a lack of money SYN TOUGH (2): *The company may have fallen on hard times.* ◇ *They had few illusions about how hard life would be after resettlement.* ◇ *Most schools are having a hard time funding new technology initiatives.* ➲ thesaurus note *at* DIFFICULT **6** strict; not sympathetic; preferring to criticize or punish sb/sth SYN TOUGH (3): *Stalin decided that a hard line should be taken with the peasantry.* ◇ **~ on sb/sth** *Students tend to be very hard on their own performance.* OPP SOFT (5) **7** [only before noun] used to describe strong alcoholic drinks or powerful illegal drugs: *Between 1986 and 2003, members of the cohort decreased their intake of beer and hard liquor but increased wine consumption.* ◇ *About 95 per cent of the world's hard drugs are produced in countries experiencing civil war.* ➲ *compare* SOFT DRINK **8** (of winter weather) very cold and severe: *The best harvests seem to have followed dry autumns, hard winters and dry summers.* ➲ *compare* MILD (2)

IDM **drive/strike a hard ˈbargain** to argue in an aggressive way and force sb to agree on the best possible price or arrangement for you: *French negotiators drove a hard bargain in the negotiations in Brussels.* **ˌhard and ˈfast** (especially after a negative) (*rather informal*) that cannot be changed in any circumstances: *There are no hard and fast rules about which approach is best.* **the ˈhard way** (*rather informal*) by having an unpleasant experience or by making mistakes: *Owners and managers have learned the hard way that the 'free market' does not have all the answers.*

hard² /hɑːd; *NAmE* hɑːrd/ *adv.* (**hard·er, hard·est**) **1** with great effort; with difficulty: *She worked hard to pay off her debts.* ◇ *Governments of Asian countries are trying hard to build stronger financial systems.* **2** with great force; in a way that has a powerful effect: *At first there is some resistance but if you push hard enough eventually it slides as you overcome the friction.* ◇ *The companies pressed hard to abolish the State monopoly.* ◇ *President Truman proposed that federal spending be directed to those areas hardest hit by unemployment.* **3** very carefully and thoroughly: *These firms need to think hard about their marketing strategy.*

IDM **be ˌhard ˈpressed/ˈput to do sth** to find it very difficult to do sth: *Companies spend billions of dollars on training, yet managers are often hard pressed to identify the long-term benefits.*

hard·en /ˈhɑːdn; *NAmE* ˈhɑːrdn/ *verb* **1** [I, T] to become firm, stiff or solid; to make sth firm, stiff or solid: *After the epoxy resin hardened, the cover slip was removed from it.* ◇ **~ sth** *Walls covered with plaster are painted to get rid of the dust and to harden their surface.* **2** [I, T] (of feelings or attitudes) to become more fixed and determined; to make feelings or attitudes more fixed and determined: *As attitudes harden on both sides of the divide, the situation becomes more and more complex.* ◇ **~ sth** *Duncan Smith hardened the position on the single currency to one of opposing membership in principle.* **3** [T, usually passive] **~ sb/sth/yourself** to make sb less kind or less affected by extreme situations: *They were intelligent types hardened by circumstance.* ■ **hard·en·ing** *noun* [U, sing.] **~ (of sth)** *These problems included hardening of arteries, diabetes and liver disease.* ◇ *This centralized orthodoxy was mirrored by a corresponding hardening of attitudes towards outsiders.*

hard·ly /ˈhɑːdli; *NAmE* ˈhɑːrdli/ *adv.* **1** used to suggest that sth is not likely or not reasonable: *It is hardly surprising that food scares often have dramatic economic effects.* ◇ *A customer is hardly likely to return for more if he or she is not satisfied.* ◇ *This type of fiction is hardly a recent introduction to Australia.* **2** almost no; almost not; almost none: *Although access to television broadcasting in English is much easier now, most Spanish students hardly ever use it.* ◇ *Hardly any of the biggest companies listed on the Paris Bourse were founded during the last fifty years.* ◇ *The basic methods of acquiring human capital have hardly changed since the time of Socrates.* **3** used especially after 'can' or 'could' and before the main verb, to emphasize that it is difficult to do sth: *He was so fat that he could hardly walk.* ◇ *Some tiny island microstates in the Pacific Ocean are so small that they can hardly afford to have a government at all.*

H

hard·ness /hɑːdnəs; *NAmE* hɑːrdnəs/ *noun* [U] the quality of being difficult to bend or break and not soft to touch: *In terms of hardness, both copper and aluminium are suitable for this purpose.*

hard·ship /ˈhɑːdʃɪp; *NAmE* ˈhɑːrdʃɪp/ *noun* [U, C] a situation that is difficult and unpleasant because you do not have enough money, food, clothes, etc: *Economic hardship in childhood has potentially very negative effects on later life chances.* ◇ *Children who have endured such hardships are more prone to violence.*

hard·ware /ˈhɑːdweə(r); *NAmE* ˈhɑːrdwer/ *noun* [U] **1** the machinery and electronic parts of a computer system: *Established producers of computer hardware were severely affected by the rise of desktop systems.* ◇ **+ noun** *Technological developments have enabled the integration of previously incompatible hardware components.* ➲ *compare* SOFTWARE **2** the equipment, machinery and vehicles used to do sth: *The US extended its lead in the application of new technologies to military hardware.* **3** tools and equipment that are used in the house and garden: **+ noun** *A bomb could be built using materials and equipment that could be purchased at a hardware store.*

harm¹ /hɑːm; *NAmE* hɑːrm/ *noun* [U] damage or injury that is caused by sb/sth: *Many viruses cause no harm or disease whatever.* ◇ *Granting a government the right to interfere with the workings of markets may do more harm than good.* ◇ **~ to sb/sth** *Care orders are made where the court believes this is necessary to prevent significant harm to the child.* ➲ *see also* SELF-HARM

harm² /hɑːm; *NAmE* hɑːrm/ *verb* **~ sb/sth** to hurt or injure sb; to damage sth: *They claimed that they acted out of fear that they would be seriously harmed or killed.* ◇ *Smoking harms nearly every organ in the body.* ◇ *This bad publicity could harm the reputation of the central bank.* ➲ *see also* SELF-HARM

harm·ful /ˈhɑːmfl; *NAmE* ˈhɑːrmfl/ *adj.* causing damage or injury to sb/sth, especially to a person's health or to the environment: *There is evidence that chronic levels of stress have a harmful effect on a person's mental and physical health.* ◇ *Ozone protects the earth's surface from harmful ultraviolet radiation from the sun.* ◇ **~ to sb/sth** *During children's television, 73.4% of advertising time was devoted to foods potentially harmful to teeth.* OPP HARMLESS

harm·less /ˈhɑːmləs; *NAmE* ˈhɑːrmləs/ *adj.* unable or unlikely to cause damage or harm: *In the river water, microorganisms break down organic matter into relatively harmless substances.* ◇ **~ to sb/sth** *A major advantage of MRI is that it is harmless to the patient.* OPP HARMFUL

har·mony /ˈhɑːməni; *NAmE* ˈhɑːrməni/ *noun* [U] a state of peaceful existence and agreement: *Confucius asserted that to maintain social harmony, the community's well-being must supersede that of the individual.* ◇ **in ~ (with sb/sth)** *Tribal peoples use deceptively simple technologies to live in close harmony with their physical environment.*

har·ness /ˈhɑːnɪs; *NAmE* ˈhɑːrnɪs/ *verb* **~ sth** to control and use the force or strength of sth to produce power or to achieve sth: *Tidal current turbines harness the kinetic energy of freely flowing water.* ◇ *Teachers should try to harness the skills and knowledge that their students bring to their classes.*

harsh /hɑːʃ; *NAmE* hɑːrʃ/ *adj.* **(harsh·er, harsh·est)** **1** very strict: *Plato and Aristotle subjected democracy to harsh criticism.* ◇ *Calls for law and order led to harsher punishment for offenders.* **2** (of weather or living conditions) very difficult and unpleasant to live in: *Winters are extremely harsh over a wide area.* ◇ *He led a happy and indulgent childhood, protected from the harsh realities of life.* ■ **harsh·ly** *adv.*: *The Roman authorities dealt harshly with those cults that encouraged resistance to Roman rule.* **harsh·ness** *noun* [U] *The lay brethren, in particular, were treated with great harshness.*

H

har·vest[1] /ˈhɑːvɪst; *NAmE* ˈhɑːrvɪst/ *noun* **1** [C] the crops, or the amount of crops, cut and gathered: *Poor harvests occurred on average every third year.* ◇ *Even when the harvest failed in one region, food was usually available somewhere.* **2** [C, U] the time of year when the crops are gathered in on a farm; the act of cutting and gathering crops: *In bad years, the grain they store at home gets depleted well before the next harvest.* ◇ *The fruit samples were taken to the laboratory immediately after harvest.* ◇ **+ noun** *There were annual celebrations at harvest time and other key points of the agricultural year.*

har·vest[2] /ˈhɑːvɪst; *NAmE* ˈhɑːrvɪst/ *verb* **1 ~ sth** to cut and gather a crop; to catch a number of animals or fish to eat: *For approximately 6 to 8 weeks, they helped farmers to harvest crops.* ◇ *At the end of the 10-week treatment period, the plants were harvested and growth was recorded.* **2** (*biology*) to collect cells or TISSUE from sb/sth for use in medical experiments or operations: **~ sth** *Cultures were harvested by centrifugation at 10 000 g for 30 min at 4°C.* ◇ **~ sth from sth** *Using stem cells harvested from umbilical cord blood, the company has treated over 5 000 patients to date.* **3 ~ sth** to collect or obtain a resource for future use: *There are substantial differences in how energy is harvested by various organisms.* ◇ *These cells fare 20–40% better than conventional devices in harvesting solar energy under real outdoor conditions.*

has /həz; əz; *strong form* hæz/ ➲ HAVE[1], HAVE[2]

hatch /hætʃ/ *verb* **1** [I] (of a young bird, fish, insect, etc.) to come out of an egg: *Embryos hatch at different developmental stages in response to changing risks or opportunities.* **2** [I] (of an egg) to break open so that a young bird, fish, insect, etc. can come out: *The female moth oviposits on the leaves, the eggs hatching about 10 days later.* **3** [T] **~ sth** to make a young bird, fish, insect, etc. come out of an egg: *In Finland, goshawks hatch their eggs in late May.* **4** [T] **~ sth** to create a plan or an idea, especially in secret: *He hatched a plot to substitute Demetrius for Philip as king.*

hate[1] /heɪt/ *verb* (not used in the progressive tenses) **1** to dislike sth very much: **~ sth** *He hated school because he was made to feel dumb.* ◇ **~ doing sth** *One salesman said: 'I hate having to sell something which I know is rubbish.'* ◇ **~ to do sth** *She hates to be away from her family.* **2** to dislike sb very much: **~ sb/yourself** *The two men hated each other.* ◇ *The university inspectors were hated by everyone.* ◇ **~ sb/yourself for (doing) sth** *He hated Churchill for siding with Stalin in the war against Hitler.*

hate[2] /heɪt/ *noun* [U] a very strong feeling of dislike for sb: *Love and hate seem to be fundamental elements of normal mental lives.* ◇ **+ noun** *Research suggests that most incidents of homophobic hate crime go unreported.*

hat·red /ˈheɪtrɪd/ *noun* [U, C] a very strong feeling of dislike for sb/sth: *Harsh economic conditions also facilitate hatred and violence.* ◇ *He was arrested for inciting racial hatred.* ◇ **~ of/for sb/sth** *They were motivated by a profound hatred of war.* ◇ *Tiberius concealed a deep hatred for his adopted son.*

have[1] /həv; əv; *strong form* hæv/ *verb* **HELP** For irregular forms of **have**, see page R4. **1 ~ sth** to produce a particular effect: *Changes in the climate can have a significant effect on the sales of some products.* ◇ *In a number of areas, direct action seems to have considerable impact on government policy.* **2** **HELP** In meanings 2–9, **have got** is also used in informal British English, but is best avoided in academic writing. **~ sth** (not used in the progressive tenses) to show a quality, feature or ability: *Males have entirely black plumage and a yellow-orange beak.* ◇ *Films have the potential to teach important lessons.* ◇ *Bricks cut from wet clay and stacked to dry in the sun have the advantage of being free.* ◇ *The politicians should have the nerve to argue their positions.* **3 ~ sth** (not used in the progressive tenses) to hold or own sth: *The patient has a history of cardiac failure.* ◇ *At that time, Europeans had little knowledge of the geography of inland Africa.* ◇ *Investors usually do not have a personal interest in the corporation in which they invest.* **4 ~ sth** (not used in the progressive tenses) to be able to make use of sth because it is available: *As illegal aliens they have few rights.* ◇ *Economic growth has allowed more people to have access to clean drinking water.* ◇ *A significant number of males do not have a single opportunity to mate during a season.* ◇ *I have unfortunately not had the time to carry out this experiment.* **5 ~ sth** (not used in the progressive tenses) to be made up of sth; to contain sth: *In this study, the selected team had 10 members.* ◇ *Most of the websites have an FAQ section.* **6 ~ sb/sth** (not used in the progressive tenses) used to show a particular relationship: *They had been married for 35 years and had no children.* ◇ *He had a difficult relationship with his father.* **7 ~ sth** (not used in the progressive tenses) to suffer from a disease, an illness or negative feelings: *Her mother had breast cancer.* ◇ *He has low self-esteem.* **8 ~ sth** (not used in the progressive tenses) to feel or experience a particular emotion or thought: *Men in online dating seemed to have fewer reservations than women.* ◇ *Severely depressed patients may have delusional ideas.* **9** (not used in the progressive tenses) to be in a position where you ought or need to do sth: **~ sth** *Doctors have a general duty to maintain confidentiality.* ◇ **~ sth to do** *All candidate countries still have a great deal of work to do in order to qualify.* **10 ~ sth** to experience a particular problem: *He has particular difficulty with mathematical tasks.* ◇ *The later Roman Empire had severe economic problems.* **11 ~ sth** to receive particular treatment: *A few patients are not fit to have surgical treatment.* **12** [no passive] **~ sb** to employ sb in a particular role: *Private companies are no longer required to have a company secretary.* **13 ~ sth** to perform a particular action: *They had had an argument.* ◇ *The tingling often seems to come on after she has had a hot bath.* **HELP** **have** + noun is often used in place of a more specific verb. **14 ~ sth** to organize or hold an event: *They have a staff meeting at 8:00 every Friday.* **15 ~ sth** to eat, drink or smoke sth: *Many Malay children have rice for breakfast.* **16 ~ sb/sth** to give birth to sb/sth: *The risk of having a baby with Downs Syndrome increases with maternal age.* **17 ~ sth done** to suffer the effects of what sb else does to you: *She had her car seized for driving without insurance.* **18 ~ sth done** to cause sth to be done for you by sb else: *He had his stepbrother, Britannicus, murdered.* **19** to tell or order sb to do sth: **~ sb do sth**

She planned to have the students build models. ◇ **~ sb/sth doing sth** *The teacher also rethinks how she has her groups working together.* **20 ~ sb/sth + adj.** to cause sb/sth to be in a particular state: *Anderson had a draft ready by late August and finalized the play in late September.*
IDM ˈ**have it (that...)** to claim that it is a fact that...: *Tradition has it that, around 250 BCE, he sent his own daughter and son to Sri Lanka.*

have² /həv; əv; *strong form* hæv/ *auxiliary verb* HELP For irregular forms of **have**, see page R4. Used with the past participle to form perfect tenses: *Diseases such as asthma, lung cancer and diabetes have become more common.* ◇ *Marine invertebrate and vertebrate fossils have been studied by many authors.* ◇ *The price of West Indian sugar had been falling since 1815.*

have to /ˈhæv tə; ˈhæf tə/ *modal verb* (*also* **have got to**) (**has to** /ˈhæz tə; ˈhæs tə/**had to, had to** /ˈhæd tə; ˈhæt tə/) used to show that you must do sth or that sth must happen or is necessary: *This emergency procedure has to be performed rapidly.* ◇ *For very sick patients, information may have to be obtained from a relative or friend.* ◇ *The irresistible pressure of global forces demands that everyone will have to make sacrifices.* ➲ grammar note *at* MUST

haz·ard /ˈhæzəd; *NAmE* ˈhæzərd/ *noun* a thing that can be dangerous or cause damage: *Frequent flooding poses severe health hazards in low-lying areas.* ◇ **~ to sb/sth** *Of the three large predators, bears pose the greatest potential hazard to human safety.* ◇ **~ of (doing) sth** *The hazard of smoking is generally well acknowledged by society.*

haz·ard·ous /ˈhæzədəs; *NAmE* ˈhæzərdəs/ *adj.* involving risk or danger, especially to sb's health or safety: *Hazardous wastes include solids and liquids that are corrosive, flammable, reactive or toxic.* ◇ *Microbiology samples are potentially hazardous and must be handled and transported safely at all times.* ◇ **~ to sb/sth** *Evidence supports the view that environmental tobacco smoke is hazardous to the respiratory health of children.*

he /hi; iː; i; *strong form* hiː/ *pron.* (used as the subject of a verb) **1** a male person or animal that has already been mentioned or is easily identified: *If Schrödinger had been more confident in his work, he could have published it earlier.* ◇ *The radicals feared that he was planning a coup and assassinated him.* ➲ *compare* HIM **2** a person, male or female, whose sex is not stated or known, especially when referring to sb mentioned earlier or to a group in general: *A defendant would be reckless if he recognizes that there is some risk involved and, nonetheless, goes on to do it.* HELP This use is considered by many people to be sexist. To avoid this, use 'they' or 'he or she' instead. ➲ grammar note *at* THEY

head¹ /hed/ *noun* **1** [C] the part of the body on top of the neck containing the eyes, nose, mouth and brain: *Each time the owls turn their heads in response to a sound stimulus, they are rewarded with a small piece of meat.* ◇ **+ noun** *Major head injury has both immediate effects and longer term consequences.* **2** [C] the mind or brain: *People are asked to say or write down the word that first comes into their heads.* **3** [C, U] the person in charge of a group of people or an organization: **~ (of sth)** *Heads of government meet three times a year as the European Council.* ◇ *The head of the household, whether male or female, was likely to be economically active.* ◇ *The mechanical engineering department had a new department head.* ◇ **+ noun** *This system was abolished by the new head teacher.* ➲ *see also* HEAD OF STATE **4 heads** [U] the side of a coin that has a picture of the head of a person on it: *We cannot predict whether each toss of the coin will land heads or tails.* ➲ *compare* TAIL (5) **5** [sing.] **~ of sth** the top or highest part of sth: *Ice may have been as much as 450 m thick near the heads of the glaciers.* ◇ *Great Britain remained at the head of the league, though its share of European exports fell.* **6** [C, usually sing.] **~ (of sth)** the end of a long narrow object that is larger or wider than the rest of it: *The plasma membrane on the head of the sperm contains various specialized proteins.* **7** [C] **~ (of sth)** the place where a river or section of a river begins: *The Thunder Springs section is at the head of Thunder River.* ◇ *In most Grand Canyon rapids, the largest boulders are at the head.* **8** [sing.] **~ of sth** the position at the front of a line of people: *He marched at the head of a column clearing a path for the candidate.* **9** [C] the mass of leaves or flowers at the end of a STEM: *The number of flower heads in one plant was recorded for 40 randomly chosen plants.* **10** [C] **~ (of sth)** (*linguistics*) the central part of a phrase, which has the same GRAMMATICAL function as the whole phrase. In the phrase 'the tall man in a suit', *man* is the head: *Apart from its semantics, there are other ways of identifying the head of a construction.*
IDM **a/per** ˈ**head** for each person: *Table 8.2 shows health care expenditure per head of the population.* **bring sth to a** ˈ**head | come to a** ˈ**head** if you **bring** a situation **to a head** or if a situation **comes to a head**, you are forced to deal with it quickly because it suddenly becomes very bad: *Further military difficulties brought to a head the differences within this uneasy coalition.* ◇ *The conflict came to a head during the IMF's July 2010 two-week visit to the country.* **over sb's** ˈ**head 1** to a higher position of authority than sb: *He made an appeal over the heads of members of Congress directly to the public.* **2** too difficult or complicated for sb to understand: *The full text might be over the heads of many high school students.* **stand/turn sth on its** ˈ**head** to make people think about sth in a completely different way: *Bruner turns much conventional thinking on its head.* ➲ *more at* REAR¹

head² /hed/ *verb* **1** [T] **~ sth** to lead or be in charge of sth: *The minister heads a department and is responsible for all policy and actions.* **2** [I] (*also* **be headed** *especially in NAmE*) **+ adv./prep.** to move in a particular direction: *They visited the Niagara Falls at the end of April, then headed north to Canada.* ◇ *The debate appeared to be headed toward a showdown over morality.* **3** [T] **~ sth** to be at the top of a list of names or at the front of a line of people: *Influenza currently heads the list of pandemic threats.* **4** [T, usually passive] to put a word or words at the top of a page or section of a book as a title: **(be) headed sth** *The paper contains a section headed 'Migration and International Development'.*
PHR V **be** ˈ**heading for sth** (*also* **be** ˈ**headed for sth** *especially in NAmE*) to be likely to experience sth bad: *Economists cannot agree on whether the economy is heading for a recession.* ˌ**head sth** ˈ**off** to take action in order to prevent sth from happening: *Some organizations attempt to head off criticism by setting up discussion sites where controversial issues can be discussed.* ˌ**head sth** ˈ**up** to lead or be in charge of a department or part of an organization: *The head of internal audit may also head up the internal control system.*

head·ache /ˈhedeɪk/ *noun* a continuous pain in the head: *She had a severe headache and felt generally tired and miserable.*

head·ing /ˈhedɪŋ/ *noun* **1** a category of information or knowledge about sth; the subject of each section of a piece of writing or a speech: *The subject headings that are most commonly used are described below.* ◇ **under a ~** *These theories can broadly be classified under two headings: classical and modern.* ◇ **under the ~ of sth** *Part 4 deals with topics which are normally held to fall under the heading of pragmatics.* **2** a title printed at the top of a page or at the beginning of a section of a book: *The chapter headings give an idea of the area covered.* ◇ *Note that there are no column headings at the start of the table.*

ˌ**head of** ˈ**state** *noun* (*pl.* **heads of state**) the official leader of a country who is sometimes also the leader of

H

the government: *Pakistan's constitution required that the head of state be a Muslim.*

head·quar·ters /ˌhedˈkwɔːtəz; *NAmE* ˈhedkwɔːrtərz/ *noun* [U+sing./pl. v., C] (*pl.* **head·quar·ters**) (*abbr.* **HQ**) a place from which an organization or a military operation is controlled: *Eventually the company's headquarters moved to Paris.* ◇ *Asylum applications must be made in person to the Border Police or at a local police headquarters.*

ˌhead ˈteacher *noun* (*BrE*) (*NAmE* **prin·ci·pal**) a teacher who is in charge of a school: *A letter was sent to school head teachers, informing them of the study and asking for their cooperation.*

head·word /ˈhedwɜːd; *NAmE* ˈhedwɜːrd/ *noun* (*technical*) a word that forms a HEADING in a dictionary, under which its meaning is explained: *Headwords are followed by an indication of part of speech.*

H

heal /hiːl/ *verb* **1** [I, T] to become healthy again; to make sth healthy again: *After the wound has healed, risk of infection decreases and continues to do so with time.* ◇ **~ (sth)** *These patients have a reduced ability to heal skin breaks and fight infection.* ◇ (*figurative*) *Not all of the wounds healed, especially not for families and friends of those who had lost their lives.* **2** [T] **~ sb** (*old use* or *formal*) to cure sb who is ill: *Hospital personnel feel that they have a mandate to heal the sick and to relieve suffering.*

heal·ing /ˈhiːlɪŋ/ *noun* [U] the process of becoming or making sb/sth healthy again; the process of getting better after an emotional shock: *Inadequate nutrition impairs wound healing.* ◇ *There is little or nothing that medical providers can do to speed the process of emotional healing.*

health /helθ/ *noun* [U] **1** the condition of a person's body or mind: *Many of today's older people have good health.* ◇ *Work is generally good for physical and mental health.* ◇ **in good/poor ~** *All three children were in poor health, with persistent coughs and colds.* ➲ *see also* ILL HEALTH **2** the work of providing medical services and care: *Government expenditure on health was 9% of the total government budget in 2006.* ◇ **+ noun** *Over 400 firms offered on-site health care to their workers by 1926.* ◇ *All the patients in the study were approached by health professionals known to them.* ➲ *see also* PUBLIC HEALTH **3** the state of being physically and mentally healthy: *Amateur sport is bound up with health, teamwork and fair play.* **4 ~ (of sth)** how successful sth is: *The focus of the government in the 1990s was firmly on the health of the economy.* ◇ *The task of monitoring the financial health of borrowers usually falls to banks.* **5 ~ (of sth)** the condition of living things or a particular area of land or water: *There is a rapidly growing body of scientific data about the health of the oceans.*

▸ ADJECTIVE + HEALTH **good** • **better** • **poor** • **ill** • **worse** • **general, overall** • **mental** • **phsyical** • **sexual** • **reproductive** • **human** • **global** *Side effects of the treatment will vary depending on the general health of the patient.* ◇ *Water pollution has severe impacts on human health.* | **public** • **international** • **national** • **occupational** • **environmental** *The study involved 276 professionals working in occupational health, human resources and counselling.*

▸ NOUN + HEALTH **child** • **population** • **community** *The role of screening in individual and population health has grown dramatically over the past 50 years.*

▸ VERB + HEALTH **affect, influence** • **monitor** • **improve** • **endanger, threaten** • **harm, damage** *There is evidence indicating that high job stress adversely affects health.* ◇ *The report suggested that people can improve their own health through physical activity and better diet.* | **promote** • **protect** • **maintain** • **restore** *Another participant uses exercise as a tool to maintain mental health.*

▸ HEALTH + VERB **improve** • **deteriorate** • **suffer** *Some studies show that health deteriorates after retirement.*

▸ HEALTH + NOUN **problem, issue** • **benefit** • **status** • **inequalities** • **behaviour** • **need** • **outcome** • **information, education** • **research** *Added ingredients in pesticides may cause health problems for children and older adults.* ◇ *Health status was assessed by questions on general health and the presence of long-term illness or disability.* | **care** • **service** • **system** • **sector** • **organization** • **authority** • **provider** • **policy** • **programme, plan** • **intervention** • **centre** • **facility** • **professional, worker, practitioner** • **insurance** • **expenditure** • **cost** *In the health sector, four-fifths of the workers were women.* ◇ *Half of the health facilities in the survey had fewer than 100 beds and were non-teaching.* ◇ *In the USA, most employed adults have health insurance through their employers.* | **promotion** • **risk** *Nurses have more opportunities for health promotion with patients than any other health professionals.*

ˌhealth and ˈsafety *noun* [U] ways of preventing accidents or injury at work: *The company won a national award in Thailand for its excellence in occupational health and safety.* ◇ *Less than 10% of workers in the country are covered by existing health and safety legislation.*

ˈhealth care *noun* [U] the service of providing medical care: *A programme launched in the country in 2004 provides free health care for all children under the age of 6.* ◇ **+ noun** *a health care professional/provider/system* ➲ *see also* PRIMARY CARE

ˈhealth centre (*BrE*) (*US* **ˈhealth ˌcenter**) *noun* a building where a group of doctors see their patients and where some local medical services have their offices: *Nursing care is given in the home when the person is unable to receive care at a clinic in the community health centre.*

ˈhealth service *noun* **1** [C] a service providing medical care: *In the last half century, health services have made fantastic advances due to scientific developments.* ◇ **+ noun** *Community nurses liaise with family doctors, practice nurses, hospitals and other health service providers.* **2 the health service** [sing.] the public health services in a particular country considered as one organization: *Alcohol has a substantial economic cost through its impact on the health service.*

healthy /ˈhelθi/ *adj.* (**health·ier**, **healthi·est**) **1** having good health; in good physical or mental condition: *Samples from 30 cancer patients and 30 healthy individuals were used.* ◇ *People with stronger social networks tend to be both healthier and happier.* ◇ *Health care services play a central role in helping people live healthy lives.* OPP UNHEALTHY (2) **2** [usually before noun] good for your health: *Consumer trends towards healthy eating have resulted in poor chocolate sales.* ◇ *In the study, higher scores meant healthier lifestyles.* ◇ *Maintaining healthy weight in children is critical in improving their health.* OPP UNHEALTHY (1) **3** free from disease: *One cell has been taken from healthy tissue and one from diseased tissue.* OPP UNHEALTHY (2) ➲ *compare* DISEASED (1) **4** normal and sensible: *There are healthy and unhealthy ways to express anger.* OPP UNHEALTHY (3) **5** successful and working well: *The enterprise is suffering relative decline within a generally healthy industry.* **6** [usually before noun] large and showing success: *The company's published accounts for the year showed a seemingly healthy profit of US $979 million.*

hear /hɪə(r); *NAmE* hɪr/ *verb* (**heard**, **heard** /hɜːd; *NAmE* hɜːrd/) **1** [I, T] (not used in the progressive tenses) to receive sounds with your ears: *More than a quarter of the respondents had problems seeing or hearing.* ◇ **~ sth/sb** *The highest frequency that the human ear can hear is 20 kHz.* ◇ *Heart murmurs caused by faulty blood flow through damaged valves can be heard.* ◇ **~ sb/sth doing sth** *The patient said that he had heard voices commenting on his actions.* ◇ **~ sb/sth do sth** *One interviewee said: 'When I* *hear somebody's mobile phone go off on a train, it bothers me.'* ◇ **~ what...** *When patients appear to be sleeping, it is very easy to forget that they might still be able to hear what is going on around them.* **2** [T] (not used in the progressive tenses) to listen or pay attention to sb/sth: **~ sth** *A total of 65.5% of respondents reported watching or hearing drug advertisements in the media several times a day.* ◇ **~ sb/sth/yourself do sth** *Towards the end of the story, young Miles invites the governess to hear him play the piano.* ◇ **~ what...** *The author says that professionals may listen to children, but seem to have great difficulty in hearing what they say.* **3** [I, T] (not usually used in the progressive tenses) to be told or receive information about sth: **~ about sb/sth** *Almost half of those mailed claimed that they first heard about the brand from a 'leaflet through the post'.* ◇ **~ from sb** *The Committee heard from 197 witnesses over a period of almost two years.* ◇ **~ sth (from sb)** *A patient has a right to hear bad news and it should be delivered in a sensitive way.* ◇ **~ from sb that...** *Later in the play, we hear from her husband that he has not danced since before his wife was born.* ◇ **~ that...** *Hearing that there is heavy traffic on one road, the commuter chooses an alternative route.* **4** [T] **~ sth** to listen to and judge a case in court: *The case will be heard by a High Court Judge.* ◇ *The opinion of one judge was not shared by the other judges who heard the appeal.* IDM see VOICE[1]

PHR V **'hear from sb** to receive a letter, email, phone call, etc. from sb: *As long as the product works properly, the customer will not expect to hear from the manufacturer.*
'hear of sb/sth | 'hear sth of sb/sth to know about sb/sth because you have been told about them: *Examples in the book chosen to illustrate points often involved languages that students had never heard of.* ◇ *Nothing had been heard of him for several years.*

hear·ing /ˈhɪərɪŋ; *NAmE* ˈhɪrɪŋ/ *noun* **1** [U] the ability to hear: *An age-related decline in hearing is estimated to affect 7–15% of the population.* ◇ **+ noun** *One to two per 1000 babies are born with a hearing loss.* **2** [C] an official meeting at which the facts about a crime or complaint are presented to the person or group of people who will have to decide what action to take: *Article 6 requires a fair and public hearing in the determination of civil rights and obligations.* ◇ *The applicant's appeal against deportation was dismissed without a hearing.* **3** [sing.] an opportunity to explain your actions, ideas or opinions: *Many politicians feel they cannot get a fair hearing in much of the print media.* ◇ *His views may be unfashionable but he deserves a hearing.* IDM see FAIR[1]

heart /hɑːt; *NAmE* hɑːrt/ *noun* **1** [C] the organ in the chest that sends blood around the body: *There are a number of changes in the heart and blood vessels that occur with age.* ◇ *In normal functioning, the heart beats at a steady rate.* ◇ **+ noun** *Lung cancer, heart disease and other illnesses are closely linked to smoking.* ◇ *A diagnosis of heart failure has serious implications.* ➲ *see also* CORONARY **2** [sing.] **~ (of sth)** the most important part of sth: *New product development lies at the heart of a company's survival and growth.* ◇ *The heart of the author's argument is the importance of equal education.* **3** [C, usually sing.] **~ (of sth)** the part that is in the centre of sth: *Tourists have become an integral part of daily life in the heart of the leading global cities.* ◇ *Today the crocodile is found in pools in the Tibesti Massif in the heart of the Sahara.* **4** [C] the place in a person where the feelings and emotions are thought to be, especially those connected with love: *The book is a remarkable window into the hearts and minds of ordinary Chinese people.*

IDM **at 'heart** used to say what sb is really like even though they may seem to be sth different: *Many studies have shown that, at heart, most consumers are loyal to a core of products and services in most markets.* **by 'heart** using only your memory: *Roman civilian aristocrats had to know Virgil's poems by heart.* ➲ *more at* CHANGE[1]

'heart attack *noun* a sudden serious medical condition in which the heart stops working normally, sometimes causing death: *Elevated cholesterol increases the risk of having a heart attack.*

heat[1] /hiːt/ *noun* **1** [U, C, usually sing.] the quality of being hot; high temperature: *The animal maintains a steady environment through its own body heat.* ◇ *The signs of inflammation are heat, redness, swelling and pain.* ◇ *Clothing had to be changed following treatment and washed at a high heat.* ◇ **~ of sth** *The intense heat of the lava flow causes trees to catch fire.* HELP In physics, **heat** is considered as a form of energy that is transferred from one object or substance to another as a result of a difference in temperature: *The efficiency of converting solar heat to electric energy is 35%.* ◇ *Conduction is the result of heat transfer between metal parts of the turbine.* ➲ *see also* LATENT HEAT **2** [U] the hot conditions in a building or vehicle; hot weather: *Dangerous machinery, intense heat and long hours made factory work dangerous and exhausting.* ◇ **+ noun** *Heat stroke is very common in tropical or semitropical climates, during heat waves and in hot buildings.* **3** [U] (*especially NAmE*) = HEATING: *Some suppliers provide consumables (e.g. heat, light, water and stationery).* ◇ **+ noun** *In recent years, heat demand for new buildings was reduced significantly by technical measures.* **4** [U] strong feelings, especially of anger or excitement: **in the ~ of sth** *The prosecution argued that the defendants became frustrated and angry and hit out in the heat of the moment.*

▸ ADJECTIVE + HEAT **extreme, intense** *Extreme ambient heat is a serious public health threat.* | **high • low • solar • waste** *Large quantities of energy are used in industry and released into the environment as waste heat.*

▸ VERB + HEAT **generate, produce • release • transfer • transport • conduct • absorb • dissipate • extract • remove • exchange • supply • apply • lose** *Laptops can generate significant heat when used for prolonged periods.* ◇ *A ground source heat pump is an energy efficient method of supplying heat to a building.*

▸ HEAT + NOUN **energy • capacity • source • loss • gain • generation • transfer • transport • flow • input • conduction • dissipation • leakage • pump • reservoir** *The low thermal conductivity of moss reduces the heat flow into the soil layer.*

heat[2] /hiːt/ *verb* to make sth hot or warm: **~ sth** *The reaction can be accelerated by heating the mixture at 70°C.* ◇ *The improvement in the carbon emissions for electrically heated houses is found to be marginal.* ◇ **~ sth to sth** *Cement production is a process in which raw materials are heated to over 2 000 degrees in a kiln.*

PHR V **,heat 'up | ,heat sth 'up** to become hot or warm; to make sth hot or warm: *The incubator will carry on heating up even after the heater is switched off.* ◇ *The mixture was heated up for 20 mins at 70°C.*

'heat capacity *noun* **~ (of sth)** the amount of energy required to raise the temperature of sth by one degree: *The heat capacity of the apparatus needs to be taken into account when measuring the energy released by burning alcohol.*

heat·ed /ˈhiːtɪd/ *adj.* **1** (of a discussion) full of anger and excitement: *After weeks of heated debate, the city council voted for a minimum wage of $8.50.* ◇ *Next day, the steering committee members met, and discussion became heated.* **2** made warmer, for example by using a heater: *A heated metal bar glowing red hot becomes white hot when heated further.* ◇ *Hypothermia most commonly occurs due to environmental conditions, such as poorly heated housing in winter.*

heat·er /ˈhiːtə(r)/ *noun* a machine used for making air or water warmer: *Tests were performed on 31 commercially*

H

available solar water heaters. ◇ *The incubator will carry on heating up even after the heater is switched off.*

heat·ing /ˈhiːtɪŋ/ *noun* [U] (*especially BrE*) (*also* **heat** *especially in NAmE*) the process of supplying heat to a room or building; a system used to do this: *Manure is used as fuel for heating and cooking.* ◇ *Damp housing, poor heating and traffic pollution are among the problems people face.* ◇ **+ noun** *When the temperature falls below the set point a relay switches the heating system on.*

heav·ily /ˈhevɪli/ *adv.* **1** to a great degree; in large amounts: *Large European companies in the coal and steel industry relied heavily on unskilled workers.* ◇ *The development of germ cells is normally heavily influenced by the environment in which they find themselves.* ◇ *A number of towns, regions and even whole countries have become very heavily dependent on archaeological tourism.* ◇ *Lincoln's own words feature heavily in the play.* **2** in a way that is difficult to accept and deal with: *The costs of overcoming such problems as air pollution weigh heavily on the emerging economies of the region.*

▸ HEAVILY + ADJECTIVE **dependent, reliant • indebted • involved • biased • weighted towards/in favour of** *Third and fourth graders were selected for the study because at that stage parents are still heavily involved in children's lives.*

▸ VERB + HEAVILY **rely ~ on, depend ~ on • invest • borrow • draw ~ on • focus ~ on • feature • drink** *As well as manufacturing industries, some service industries invest heavily in research and development.*

▸ HEAVILY + VERB **influenced by • criticized • concentrated in • subsidized • regulated • populated** *The company was heavily criticized for its loosely regulated supply chain, which regularly used child labour.*

heavy /ˈhevi/ *adj.* (**heav·ier, heavi·est**) **1** weighing a lot; difficult to lift or move: *During an earthquake, heavy buildings will sink and light structures will rise from the ground.* ◇ *Male animals are often larger and heavier than their mates.* ◇ *In the thirteenth century, large boats, known as shouts, were used for carrying heavy loads on the Thames.* OPP LIGHT² (3) **2** more or worse than usual in amount, size or degree: *The students thought the overall workload was too heavy.* ◇ *The monsoon season is from May to October each year, with the heaviest rain occurring between September and October.* ◇ *In 101 AD, the Dacians inflicted heavy losses on the Romans in battle.* OPP LIGHT² (5) **3** [usually before noun] used to describe large, powerful machines, vehicles or weapons, or sth that uses these: *The large-scale production of timber requires heavy machinery and large areas of forest for economic returns.* ◇ *In developed countries, manufacturing and heavy industry have been declining with a loss of traditionally 'male jobs.'* OPP LIGHT² (4) **4** (of work) hard, especially because it requires a lot of physical strength: *Research suggests that the heavy physical activity associated with farming is the primary cause of knee problems.* ◇ *Physical factors such as heavy lifting have been reported to increase the risk of sick leave due to back pain.* OPP LIGHT² (8) **5** (of a duty) hard to carry out, especially because it requires a lot of money to be paid: *Home ownership became a heavy burden on household finances.* ◇ *Much of the industry's loss was at that time also the result of the heavy welfare responsibilities which the firms carried.* **6** [only before noun] used to describe sb who does the thing mentioned more than usual: *Customers may be classified according to whether they are heavy, medium or light users of the product.* ◇ *a heavy drinker/smoker* OPP LIGHT² (10) **7** (*physics, chemistry*) used to describe ISOTOPES that have a higher atomic mass than other isotopes of the same element: *Each atom of hydrogen in heavy water contains a neutron as well as a proton in its nucleus.* OPP LIGHT² (11)

ˌheavy ˈmetal *noun* (*technical*) a metal that has a very high DENSITY (= the relation of its mass to its volume), such as gold or LEAD: *The levels of heavy metals in the air, soil and water of the town far exceeded the maximum permitted levels.*

hec·tare /ˈhekteə(r); ˈhektɑː(r); NAmE ˈhekter/ *noun* (*abbr.* **ha**) a unit for measuring an area of land; 10 000 square metres or about 2.5 ACRES: *A third of all farms in the area had only two hectares of land or less.*

LANGUAGE BANK

Hedging language

In academic writing, it is important to use language to show that you are presenting your opinion and not a proven fact.

- data/evidence/findings/research/results **(would) suggest that...**
- **There is some evidence to suggest that...**
- **There appears/seems to be...**
- **It would appear/seem that ...**
- data/evidence/findings/research/results **appear/seem to be...**
- analysis **seems/would seem to suggest that...**
- data **appear to suggest that...**
- **It seems reasonable to suggest that...**
- **It seems possible/probable that...**
- findings/results **might/may/could** indicate (that)/suggest (that)/reflect...
- **I/We tentatively (conclude) that...**
- a **tentative** conclusion

– *Overall, the data* ***suggest that*** *cell fusion occurred.*
– ***There is some evidence to suggest that*** *self-pollinations are common in some milkweeds.*
– ***There appears to be*** *a range of factors that influence students' decisions.*
– ***It would appear that*** *a major change began to take place 200 000 years ago.*
– *These results* ***appear to be*** *fairly robust across a variety of macroeconomic models.*
– *A first analysis* ***would seem to suggest that*** *the ancient cities survived well.*
– *The forecast values* ***appear to suggest that*** *the cyclical pattern will continue until 2017.*
– ***It seems reasonable to suggest that*** *the three families share a common ancestor.*
– ***It seems probable that*** *territorial birds had a survival advantage.*
– *These findings* ***may*** *reflect advances in technology.*
– ***We tentatively conclude that*** *wealth in Australia is more equally distributed than in other industrial societies.*
– *It is possible to draw only* ***tentative*** *conclusions.*

hedge /hedʒ/ *verb* **1** [T, usually passive] **~ sb/sth (about/around) (with sth)** to limit or reduce the force of sth with conditions or EXCEPTIONS (= things that are not included): *Advertising has been increasingly hedged about by laws and controls.* **2** [I, T] to avoid giving a direct answer or expressing a definite opinion: *Edelman is certainly hedging with all these 'mays' and 'mights'.* ◇ **~ sth** *The teacher used the word 'can' which is often used to hedge comments.* **3** [I, T] to protect yourself against the risk of losing money, for example by making deals or contracts that balance each other out: *Management will direct the firm to hedge if it can do so.* ◇ **~ sth** *They use the futures market to price their crops and hedge their price risks over time.*

IDM **ˌhedge your ˈbets** to reduce the risk of losing or making a mistake by refusing to completely support one idea or by keeping more than one option available: *Some species are able to hedge their bets, with some of their offspring adopting one strategy and the rest another.* ◇ *Locke hedges his bets and says only that it is 'probable'.*

PHR V **ˈhedge against sth** to do sth to protect yourself against problems, especially against losing money:

Portfolio entrepreneurship is another way for businesses to hedge against volatility of markets.

he·gem·ony /hɪˈdʒeməni; hɪˈgeməni; *BrE also* ˈhedʒɪməni; *NAmE also* ˈhedʒɪmoʊni/ *noun* (*pl.* **-ies**) [U, C] control by one country, organization or group over other countries, etc. within a particular group: *In the 18th century, several African writers posed a challenge to British political and cultural hegemony.* ◇ **~ over sb/sth** *In England, from time to time, the kings of the late Anglo-Saxon period claimed a hegemony over other rulers in Britain.* ■ **hege·mon·ic** /ˌhedʒɪˈmɒnɪk; ˌhegɪˈmɒnɪk; *NAmE* ˌhedʒɪˈmɑːnɪk; ˌhegɪˈmɑːnɪk/ *adj.*: *The author argues that the ultimate goal of all states is to achieve a hegemonic position in the international system.*

height /haɪt/ *noun* **1** [U, C] the measurement of how tall a person or thing is: *Average adult height is 164 cm in women and 177 cm in men.* ◇ *Limitations of the study include the fact that the parents' heights and weights were not measured, but were reported by the mother.* ◇ **~ of sth** *The height of the plant was measured as the distance between the stem base and the shoot top.* ◇ **in ~** *The palm has a thin trunk and averages 15 to 20 metres in height.* ◇ **with a ~ of...** *The sample used was cylindrical in shape, with a height of approximately 1 cm.* **2** [C, U] a particular distance above the ground: *In the test, a known weight is dropped on the specimen from a desired height.* ◇ *Each tree was measured for diameter at breast height.* ◇ **a ~ of...** *Ash from the volcano was injected into the air, reaching a height of 32 km.* **3** [sing.] the point when sth is at its best or strongest: *The railway boom reached its height in England in the 1840s.* ◇ **at the ~ of sth** *The play 'A Florentine Tragedy', begun when Oscar Wilde was at the height of his powers, remained unfinished.* **4 heights** [pl.] **~ (of sth)** a better or greater level of sth; a situation where sth is very good: *The arts and sciences in the Greek world reached new heights of excellence in the 7th and 6th centuries.* **5** [C, usually pl.] (often used in names) a high place or position: *Neo's powerlessness is emphasized through his fear of heights at the beginning of the film.* ◇ *The school is located in the neighbourhood of Washington Heights in New York City.*

height·en /ˈhaɪtn/ *verb* **~ sth** to make a feeling or an effect greater or stronger SYN INTENSIFY: *The awards were intended to heighten public awareness of the importance of international education.* ◇ *In some countries, widowhood has been associated with heightened risks of mortality.* ◇ *The use of the present tense helps to draw the reader in by heightening the sense of immediacy.*

heir /eə(r); *NAmE* er/ *noun* **1** a person who has the legal right to receive sb's property, money or title when that person dies: *When the last patriarch died without a male heir, the hereditary line died out.* ◇ **~ to sth** *Factions formed around the heir to the throne and other members of the royal family.* ◇ *She was the heir to vast estates in the north of England.* **2** a person who is thought to continue the work or a tradition started by sb else: **~ to sb/sth** *Heidegger's followers, or the heirs to his tradition, have gone in different ways.* ◇ **~ of sb/sth** *Antiochus maintained that the Stoics were the legitimate heirs of Plato's philosophy.* ◇ *The Ptolemies promoted themselves as the true heirs and champions of Classical Greek culture.* HELP Use **an**, not **a**, before **heir**.

held *past tense, past part. of* HOLD[1]

helix /ˈhiːlɪks/ *noun* (*pl.* **heli·ces** /ˈhiːlɪsiːz/) the shape formed by a line that curves around the length of a CYLINDER or CONE: *Crick and Watson demonstrated that DNA consisted of a double helix with interconnecting pairs of complementary bases.*

help[1] /help/ *verb* **1** [I, T] to make it easier or possible for sb to do sth by doing sth for them or by giving them sth that they need: **~ with sth** *By 2000 more and more husbands were coming home for dinner and helping with child rearing.* ◇ **~ sb** *Loans intended to help impoverished countries can have quite the opposite effect.* ◇ **~ sb with sth** *Desta and her older sister helped their mother with household chores.* ◇ **~ (sb) in doing sth** *A mnemonic commonly used in management is the SMART acronym, which helps managers in planning.* ◇ **~ sb (to) do sth** *Helping children to manage anger is not easy.* ◇ *Several million years ago, our ancestors lived in small, intimate groups with only the simplest tools to help them adapt for survival.* ◇ **~ (to) do sth** *Tom is the CEO of an online identity company which he helped to found in 2005.* HELP In verb patterns with a **to** infinitive, the 'to' is often left out, especially in informal or spoken English, but it is usually better to use it in written academic English. **2** [I, T] to improve a situation; to make it easier for sth to happen: *Her extensive knowledge of other languages also helped considerably.* ◇ **~ with sth** *Antipsychotic medications can help greatly with anxiety.* ◇ **~ in sth** *Technology can help significantly in the segmentation process.* ◇ **~ (to) do sth** *Strong winds help to disperse air pollution.* ◇ **~ that...** *It helped enormously that a new governor who identified with the Cajun group was elected.* ◇ **~ sth** *Steroids and antihistamines will reduce the rash and help symptoms.* **3** [T] **~ yourself/sb to sth** to give yourself/sb food, drinks, etc: *He no longer eats with the family and helps himself to food at night time.* **4** [T] **~ yourself to sth** (*informal, disapproving*) to take sth without permission SYN STEAL (1): *In what have been called the 'predatory' 1540s, the crown helped itself to a larger share of the national income than at any other time until the 1690s.*

IDM **sb can (not) help (doing) sth | sb cannot help but do sth** used to say that it is impossible to prevent or avoid sth: *Managers will probably not want to rush to lay employees off if they can help it.* ◇ *Earth scientists cannot help but suspect that earthquakes influenced ancient cultures more strongly than archaeologists have recognized.*

PHR V **ˌhelp ˈout | ˌhelp sb ˈout** to help sb, especially in a difficult situation: *During the First World War, she helped out in school kitchens.* ◇ *He helped out friends when they needed another hand in the fields.*

help[2] /help/ *noun* **1** [U] the act of helping sb to do sth: *He asked Medeia for her help.* ◇ **~ with sth** *All care homes should be able to give help with personal care.* ◇ **~ of sb/sth** *Anxious to restore England to papal obedience, she enlisted the help of her cousin, Cardinal Reginald Pole.* ◇ **with the ~ of sb/sth** *It is now possible to generate film-like scenes directly on a computer with the help of 3-D computer animation.* **2** [U] advice, money, etc. that is given to sb in order to solve their problems: *Some people feel ashamed of the disorder and embarrassed to ask for help.* ◇ *He was ill and in need of medical help.* ◇ *The USSR gave great economic, military and technical help to communist China.* ◇ **~ with sth** *She needed help with her rent after losing her job.* ◇ **~ in doing sth** *Successive governments have looked to the voluntary sector for help in tackling the most pressing social issues of the day.* ◇ **~ for sb/sth** *Despite the seriousness of much domestic violence, some agencies have been reluctant to provide help for the victims.* ◇ *Some men think it unmanly to seek help for minor ailments.* ⮌ *see also* SELF-HELP **3** [U] the fact of being useful: **be of ~ to sb/sth** *Specialist counselling services may be of help to some patients.* ◇ **with/without the ~ of sb/sth** *With the help of special algorithms, the straight edges of computer-generated objects are softened.* ◇ **with/without ~ from sb/sth** *It was discovered that a few RNA gene transcripts accurately self-spliced without any help from proteins.* **4** [sing.] a person or thing that helps sb: *Incentive programmes can be a big help when introducing a new product.* ◇ **a ~ to sb** *Western military supplies were a great help to the White Russians.* ◇ **a ~ that...** *Undoubtedly, in his job, it is a huge help that he speaks Arabic.*

help·ful /ˈhelpfl/ *adj.* **1** useful; able to improve a particular situation or provide help: *I would like to thank Dr Oliver Stuart for his helpful comments.* ◇ **it is ~ to do sth** *It is helpful to have a standard set of terms for describing trees.* ◇ **it is ~ for sb to do sth** *It is often helpful for a nurse to be present when the patient is given new information.* ◇ **~ in doing sth** *These two tests are particularly helpful in diagnosing infection.* OPP UNHELPFUL **2 ~ (to sb/sth)** willing to give help: *The research found that, overall, companies were more helpful and encouraging to white candidates.* OPP UNHELPFUL ■ **help·ful·ly** /ˈhelpfəli/ *adv.*: *The two theories are so closely related that they can more helpfully be considered as differing versions of the same general point of view.* **help·ful·ness** *noun* [U] **~ (of sb/sth)** *All participants were asked about the helpfulness of the standard callback service.*

H

hemi·sphere /ˈhemɪsfɪə(r); *NAmE* ˈhemɪsfɪr/ *noun* **1** one half of the earth, especially the half above or below the EQUATOR: *Anticyclones rotate clockwise in the northern hemisphere and anticlockwise in the southern.* **2** either half of the brain: *Generalized seizures involve both cerebral hemispheres at onset.* ◇ *Our perception of other people's emotions is processed in the right hemisphere.* **3** one half of a SPHERE (= a round solid object): *The simplest CRT screen would be a hemisphere, because any point on its surface is a constant distance from the focusing mechanism.*

hence AWL /hens/ *adv.* for this reason: *The major symptom is pain when the patient has not eaten for a while, hence waking at night.* ◇ *Both of these techniques essentially count photons and hence monitor the intensity of the light.* ➲ language bank *at* THEREFORE

IDM **... days, weeks, etc. ˈhence** (*formal*) a number of days, etc. from now: *Two hundred years hence, people may recognize in the Romantic period the beginning of environmental ways of understanding and acting.*

hence·forth /ˌhensˈfɔːθ; *NAmE* ˌhensˈfɔːrθ/ (*also* **hence·for·ward** /ˌhensˈfɔːwəd; *NAmE* ˌhensˈfɔːrwərd/) *adv.* (*formal*) starting from the present time or from a particular time and at all times following it: *Eurystheus forbade him henceforth to enter the city.* ◇ *This is the firm's unit labour cost, a concept I shall henceforth represent with the letters ulc.*

her¹ /hə(r); ɜː(r); ə(r); *strong form* hɜː(r)/ *pron.* **1** used as the object of a verb, after the verb *be* or after a preposition to refer to a woman or girl who has already been mentioned or is easily identified: *Naomi's final year project gave her the opportunity to research the subject in great depth.* ◇ *She was asked what success meant to her.* ◇ *Being a Christian is not, for her, a matter of seeking any reward.* **2** used as the object of a verb, after the verb *be* or after a preposition to refer to a person, male or female, whose sex is not stated or known, especially when referring to sb mentioned earlier HELP This use of **her** is often used by feminist writers instead of **him**, which is now considered sexist by many people when used in this way: *Empathy involves being able to recognize your child's anger and communicating to her that it is a natural reaction.* ➲ *compare* SHE

her² /hə(r); ɜː(r); ə(r); *strong form* hɜː(r)/ *det.* (the possessive form of *she*) **1** of or belonging to a woman or girl who has already been mentioned or is easily identified: *Pat begins to come to terms with the loss of her husband.* ◇ *In her book, she explores such topics as the human costs of emotional labour.* **2** of or belonging to sb, either male or female, who has already been mentioned or is easily identified HELP This use of **her** is often used by feminist writers instead of **him**, which is now considered sexist by many people when used in this way: *A person's wealth can be made to serve as an index of her well-being.* ➲ *see also* HERS

here /hɪə(r); *NAmE* hɪr/ *adv.* **1** used after a verb or preposition to mean 'in, at or to this position or place': *The data presented here clearly show the variability in results among these methods.* ◇ *Only the results for the behaviour of long chains will be discussed here.* **2** now; at this point: *Here the close-up moving image of McGoohan quickly fades into a black-and-white portrait shot.* HELP In this meaning, **here** is often used in spoken academic presentations; however, it may be considered too 'conversational' for formal academic writing: *Let me pause here to make it clear that I am not going to argue for the value of a feminine approach to adaptations.* **3** used when you are giving or showing sth to sb: *Here is an example of how trade expansion can hurt.* ◇ *Here are some of the adverse ways anger can impact someone.* **4 ~ to do sth** used to show your role in a situation: *This government is here to protect ordinary people, not just the rich.* **5** used after a noun, for emphasis: *The idea here is to measure changes in X, Y, Z over a period of time.*

IDM **be here to stay** used to say that sth will continue to happen or exist for a long time so people must accept or deal with it: *It looks as if the technology is here to stay.* **ˌhere and ˈthere** in various places: *The parkland is broken here and there by clumps of elm trees.* ◇ *There are a number of themes in his work that surface here and there throughout.*

here·after /ˌhɪərˈɑːftə(r); *NAmE* ˌhɪrˈæftər/ *adv.* **1** (*also* **here·in·after**) (*law*) in the rest of this document or later in this document: *Hereafter, we refer to these as nominal error levels.* ◇ *The importance of the working of this general law will be established hereafter.* ◇ *The Russian Corporate Governance Code (hereinafter the Code) has ten sections or chapters.* **2** (*formal*) after this time; in future: *This applies to any supplemental Agreements that may hereafter be made by the Employer and the Union.* ➲ *compare* THEREAFTER **3** (*formal*) after death: *They live in the hope of everlasting peace in the life hereafter.*

her·edi·tary /həˈredɪtri; *NAmE* həˈredɪteri/ *adj.* **1** (especially of illnesses) given to a child by its parents before it is born: *Hereditary cancers tend to occur at an earlier age.* ◇ *Counselling about the risk of hereditary disease is given to couples planning or expecting a child.* **2** that is legally given to sb's child, when that person dies: *Yet Tacitus knew well what hereditary monarchy would bring: mad rulers like Caligula and Nero.* ◇ *Japan had an emperor who inherited the throne in an unbroken line of hereditary succession.* **3** holding a rank or title that is hereditary: *In 1700 the majority of Europeans were subjects of hereditary rulers.* ◇ *Hereditary peers have, generally speaking, inherited the title that they hold from an ennobled ancestor.*

her·ed·ity /həˈredəti/ *noun* [U] the process by which mental and physical characteristics are passed GENETICALLY from one generation to the next: *The basic principle of heredity—that offspring tend to resemble their parents—has long been observed by human societies.*

here·in /ˌhɪərˈɪn; *NAmE* ˌhɪrˈɪn/ *adv.* (*formal*) in this place, document, statement or fact: *The Scripture quotations contained herein are from the New Revised Standard Version Bible.* ◇ *The uncertainties in predicting the time of a future earthquake can be large. Herein lies the basic problem in present earthquake prediction efforts.*

here·in·after /ˌhɪərɪnˈɑːftə(r); *NAmE* ˌhɪrɪnˈæftər/ *adv.* (*law*) = HEREAFTER (1)

her·it·able /ˈherɪtəbl/ *adj.* **1** (*biology*) (of a feature or medical condition) that can be passed from a parent to a child through the GENES: *To establish whether traits are heritable, it is important to know the identity of the true parents of individuals under study.* ◇ *Mutation is a permanent, heritable change to the information in the genome.* **2** (*law*) (of property or rights) that can be passed from one member of a family to another: *Heritable* *jurisdictions were courts and offices granted by the Crown and effectively owned as freeholds to be passed on.*

heri·tage /ˈherɪtɪdʒ/ *noun* [usually sing.] **1** the history, traditions and qualities that a country or society has had for many years and that are considered an important part of its character: *Sri Lanka has a rich and diverse cultural heritage.* ◇ *Panhellenic festivals reinforced a feeling that Greeks everywhere shared a common heritage.* **2** the country or part of the world where sb's family originally came from: *60% were European American, 19% were Asian American, 7% were of mixed heritage, 5% were Latino, and 1% were African American.* **3 + noun** used to describe things of special historical or natural value that are preserved for future generations of a country: *The city was declared a world cultural heritage site by UNESCO in 1988.* ◇ *A few examples of heritage tourism research include studies of historic preservation in Singapore (Chang, 1999) and Ireland (Johnson, 1996).*

hero /ˈhɪərəʊ; *NAmE* ˈhɪroʊ; ˈhiːroʊ/ *noun* (*pl.* **-oes**) **1** the main male character of a story, who usually has good qualities: *Hamlet's end contrasts with the more resolute deaths of Shakespeare's other tragic heroes.* ◇ *Packer's novels are totally devoid of either heroes or villains.* **2** a person, especially a man, who is admired by many people for doing sth brave or good: *When Taylor returned to Australia at the age of 70, he was treated as a national hero.* ◇ *The media depicted Howard Hughes as a war hero.*

hero·ic /həˈrəʊɪk; *NAmE* həˈroʊɪk/ *adj.* **1** showing extreme courage and admired by many people SYN COURAGEOUS: *She was awarded the cross of the Légion d'honneur and became a heroic figure in her own right.* ◇ *Gandhi achieved great things through his heroic passive resistance to British imperialism in India.* **2** that is about or involves a hero or heroes: *The Theban Wars and the Trojan War are the two great wars of the Greek heroic age.* ◇ *The Amazons make many appearances in heroic legend.* **3** showing great determination to succeed or to achieve sth, especially sth difficult: *He was deeply affected by the death of his third child, born prematurely and unable to survive despite heroic medical efforts.* ■ **hero·ic·al·ly** /həˈrəʊɪkli; *NAmE* həˈroʊɪkli/ *adv.*: *He died heroically in battle against Eumenes of Cardia.* ◇ *The injured were tended by doctors who worked heroically through the night.*

hero·ine /ˈherəʊɪn; *NAmE* ˈheroʊɪn/ *noun* **1** the main female character of a story, who usually has good qualities: *None of his novels has a central working-class hero or heroine.* ◇ *In this film, the heroine is represented as an ambitious, intelligent, pragmatic and successful career woman.* **2** a girl or woman who is admired by many people for doing sth brave or good: *the heroines of the revolution*

hero·ism /ˈherəʊɪzəm; *NAmE* ˈheroʊɪzəm/ *noun* [U] very great courage: *His shipmates praised his heroism and thanked him for risking his life to save theirs.* ◇ *Contemporary warfare does not usually lend itself to individual acts of heroism.*

hers /hɜːz; ɜːz; *NAmE* hɜːrz; ɜːrz/ *pron.* of or belonging to her: *The house and everything in it was hers.* ◇ *She found comfort in realizing that others had lived through experiences similar to hers.* ◇ *Hers was a remarkable case.*

her·self /hɜːˈself; *NAmE* hɜːrˈself *weak form* həˈself; *NAmE* hərˈself/ *pron.* **1** (the reflexive form of *she*) used when the woman or girl who performs an action is also affected by it: *This was the only way she could draw attention to herself.* ◇ *She had established herself as one of the leading authorities on Native American cultures.* **2** used to emphasize the female subject or object of a sentence: *She herself only moved to Britain after the death of her fiancé.* ◇ *As Thatcher herself would later acknowledge, it was 'one of the nation's worst-kept secrets'.*

IDM **by herˈself** **1** alone; without anyone else: *She lives by herself.* **2** without help: *She runs the business by herself.*

hesi·tate /ˈhezɪteɪt/ *verb* **1** [I] **~ to do sth** to be unwilling to do sth, especially because you are not sure that it is right or appropriate: *The outgoing president had already shown that he would not hesitate to use force to remain in power.* ◇ *They did not hesitate to criticize the prevailing employment model.* **2** [I] to be slow to speak or act because you feel uncertain or nervous: *At the first meeting, the participants hesitated before commenting on each others' lessons.* ■ **hesi·ta·tion** /ˌhezɪˈteɪʃn/ *noun* [U, C] **~ (to do sth)** *These women were strong leaders who showed no hesitation to use force in international conflicts.* ◇ *Natural speech is full of minor hesitations.*

het·ero·ge·neous /ˌhetərəˈdʒiːniəs/ *adj.* **1** (*formal*) consisting of many different kinds of people or things: *Most Africans entered the Americas as heterogeneous groups with varied ethnic origins.* ◇ *One problem is that proteins are very heterogeneous.* OPP HOMOGENEOUS (1) **2** (*chemistry*) used to describe a process involving substances in different PHASES (= solid, liquid or gas): *In heterogeneous hydrogenation reactions the gaseous reactants are temporarily attached to the solid surface of the metal catalyst.* OPP HOMOGENEOUS (2) ■ **het·ero·gen·eity** /ˌhetərədʒəˈniːəti/ *noun* [U] *Dendritic cells show considerable heterogeneity in both appearance and function.* ◇ *Results display significant heterogeneity across economies.*

het·ero·sex·ual /ˌhetərəˈsekʃuəl/ *adj.* sexually attracted to people of the opposite sex: *The objective now became to equalize partnership rights for gay and heterosexual couples.* ◇ *The studied respondents are living in heterosexual relationships (cohabiting or married).* ◇ *Participants were primarily white, heterosexual women in further or higher education.* ➲ *compare* HOMOSEXUAL ■ **het·ero·sex·ual** *noun*: *International resolutions from this period emphasized equality not only between women and men but also between heterosexuals and homosexuals.* **het·ero·sexu·al·ity** /ˌhetərəˌsekʃuˈæləti/ *noun* [U] *Traditionally, there are two recognized sexual identities: heterosexuality and homosexuality.*

hide /haɪd/ *verb* (**hid** /hɪd/, **hid·den** /ˈhɪdn/) **1** [T] **~ sth** to keep sth secret SYN CONCEAL: *For his safety, he hid his feelings and religious beliefs for about a decade.* ◇ *The answers to these questions may be hidden in the genome.* ◇ *For some people, the title 'Ms' carries the connotation that a woman is trying to hide the fact that she is single.* ◇ **~ sth from sb** *It turned out that millions of dollars of debt had been hidden from investors.* **2** [T] to put or keep sb/sth in a place where they/it cannot be seen or found SYN CONCEAL: **~ sb/sth** *Women were more often involved in low level political activities, for instance hiding people or passing messages.* ◇ **~ sb/sth +adv./prep.** *In the experiment, food was hidden within a large enclosed area.* ◇ **~ sb/sth from sb** *These small packs of tobacco can be easily hidden from teachers and parents.* **3** [I, T] to go somewhere where you hope you will not be seen or found: *If the moth hears the bat, it hides or flies away before the bat catches it.* ◇ **~ sb/sth (+ adv./prep.)** *He spent countless hours hidden away in his study.* ◇ **~ yourself (+ adv./prep.)** *Carriers are now liable if they transport passengers who hide themselves and gain entry to the country illegally.* **4** [T] **+ adv./prep** to cover sth so that it cannot be seen SYN CONCEAL: **~ sth** *She turned away and hid her face in her hands.* **~ sth**

PHR V **hide behind sth** to use sth to stop people from finding out the truth or information about you: *The gender of the author hiding behind the pseudonym had at first been kept a close secret.*

hier·arch·ic·al AWL /ˌhaɪəˈrɑːkɪkl; *NAmE* ˌhaɪəˈrɑːrkɪkl/ *adj.* arranged in a hierarchy: *Rome was a hierarchical society, but one also notable for its social mobility.* ◇ *Authority in the pre-colonial period was strictly hierarchical.* ◇ *Many networks have a hierarchical structure, in which the nodes* *that are close together are especially well connected.* ■ **hier·arch·ic·al·ly** /ˌhaɪəˈrɑːkɪkli; *NAmE* ˌhaɪəˈrɑːrkɪkli/ *adv.*: *Most people in a capitalist economy spend virtually their entire working lives in hierarchically organized jobs.*

hier·archy AWL /ˈhaɪərɑːki; *NAmE* ˈhaɪərɑːrki/ *noun* (*pl.* **-ies**) **1** [C, U] a system, especially in a society or an organization, in which people are organized into different levels of importance from highest to lowest: *Rural peasants were near the bottom of the Roman social hierarchy.* ◇ *He spent his career working his way up the managerial hierarchy until he reached board level.* **2** [C] a system that ideas or beliefs can be arranged into: *The increasing use of DNA sequence data to define taxonomic units has resulted in a great deal of rearrangement of taxonomic hierarchies.* ◇ **~ of sth** *In terms of people's hierarchy of priorities, the right to personal privacy remains extremely important.*

H

high[1] /haɪ/ *adj.* (**high·er**, **high·est**) **1** greater or better than normal in quantity or quality, size or level: *Open water has the highest evaporation rate.* ◇ *Use of the Internet is particularly high among university students.* ◇ *This scheme was designed to attract higher quality workers and to reduce labour turnover.* OPP LOW[1] (1) **2** measuring a long distance from the bottom to the top: *The canyon walls are steep and high.* ◇ *The Anasazi settlements were very advanced and contained America's largest and highest buildings until the skyscraper.* ◇ *The decrease in temperature with elevation allows permanent snow fields and glaciers to exist in high mountains.* OPP LOW[1] (4) **3** at a level which is a long way above the ground or above the level of the sea: *High clouds such as cirrus are composed entirely of ice crystals.* ◇ *Tea, coffee, and a wide variety of horticultural crops are grown at higher altitudes.* ◇ *The East Antarctic ice sheet is a high plateau that reaches a maximum elevation of over 4 000 m.* OPP LOW[1] (4) **4** used to talk about the distance that sth measures from the bottom to the top or how far above the ground or the level of the sea sth is: *They uncovered a large earthenware jar, about two feet high.* ◇ *Hydrologists decide how high to build flood defences by analysing meteorological statistics.* ◇ *Having defeated the insurgents at the barricade, he was carried shoulder-high in triumph by his fellow soldiers.* **5 ~ (in sth)** containing a lot of a particular substance or quality: *The wider availability of inexpensive foods that are high in fats is a primary cause of obesity.* ◇ *All shales in the Grand Canyon region are high in calcium.* ◇ *However, it is certainly the case that some anions are higher in energy than others.* ◇ *The trial concluded that a high-fibre diet could reduce the risk of colon cancer by up to 40%.* OPP LOW[1] (2) **6** near the top in importance or position: *Silver and gold ornament on weapons indicates persons of high status in the military hierarchy.* ◇ *The issue of international terrorism is high on the political agenda.* OPP LOW[1] (3) **7** [usually before noun] showing a lot of approval or respect for sb: *The principle of objectivity is held in high regard in science.* ◇ *It is possible for customers to have a relatively high opinion of a brand but not display repeat-buying behaviour.* OPP LOW[1] (6) **8** of great value or importance: *The stakes are high for managers when their decisions can precipitate industrial accidents.* ◇ *Jews, Christians and some pagans placed a high value on fasting.* **9** [usually before noun] morally good: *In order to stand for election by the Parliamentary Assembly, a candidate must be of high moral character.* ◇ *In emphasizing the economic origins of the Civil War, Egnal downplays the idea that the North was motivated by high ideals.* **10** at the upper end of the range of sounds that humans can hear; not deep or low: *Some people have naturally higher voices than others.* ◇ *The echoes from distant objects take longer to come back and therefore sound higher than the echoes from nearer objects.* OPP LOW[1] (7) **11** [only before noun] (of LATITUDES) near the North or South Pole: *At high latitudes, levels of the active hormone decline during winter.* OPP LOW[1] (9) IDM *see* MORAL[1]

▸ HIGH + NOUN **level • degree • rate • number • ratio • proportion • percentage • score • prevalence • concentration • frequency • risk • probability • incidence • standard • quality • priority** *During the last century, average temperatures have risen in response to increasingly high levels of greenhouse gas concentrations.* | **price • cost • value • income • wage • turnover • inflation • demand • profit • return • unemployment** *For many, diet is worsening because of high prices for meats, fruits and vegetables.* | **temperature • pressure • density • speed • energy • content • dose • mortality** *This fluid has a higher density and apparent viscosity than water.* | **status • rank • position • authority** *Under the notion of parliamentary sovereignty, there is no higher authority than Parliament.* | **esteem • regard • opinion** *Elders are held in high esteem and tribal communities want to care for their elders in ways that preserve and promote their dignity.*

▸ ADVERB + HIGH **relatively, comparatively • quite • moderately • sufficiently • very • extremely • particularly • unusually, exceptionally, abnormally • consistently • generally** *Low-income areas often suffer from relatively high unemployment.*

▸ ADVERB + HIGHER **significantly • considerably, substantially • somewhat • slightly • consistently • generally** *Men are at a statistically significantly higher risk than women.*

high[2] /haɪ/ *adv.* (**high·er**, **high·est**) **1** at or to a position or level that is a long way up from the ground or from the bottom: *Air Force strategy called for bombers to fly high and extremely fast, outrunning Soviet air defences.* ◇ *When a predator begins to chase them, gazelles may leap high into the air.* OPP LOW[2] (2) **2** at or to a large cost, value or amount: *Individuals who score high on this scale tend to be very uncomfortable around others and express a preference for being alone.* ◇ *Scientists are concerned about the outcome if ground temperatures rise high enough to melt the permafrost.* OPP LOW[2] (1) **3** at or to a position near the top in importance: *Africa ranks high as a source of US imports.* ◇ *Though only a tough and uneducated herdsman, he rose high in the army.*

high[3] /haɪ/ *noun* **1** the highest level or number: *Job dissatisfaction varied from 17% in Germany to a high of 60% in Japan.* ◇ *In July 2008, global oil prices hit record highs above US$147 a barrel.* ◇ *By 1994, public perception of crime as the most important problem in America reached an all-time high.* OPP LOW[3] (1) **2** an area of high air pressure: *These highs are slow-moving and produce long spells of fine weather.* OPP LOW[3] (2) **3** the feeling of extreme pleasure and excitement that sb gets after taking some types of drugs: *The nuts, when mixed with herbs and chewed, produce a mild high.*

high·er /ˈhaɪə(r)/ *adj.* [only before noun] at a more advanced level; greater in rank or importance than others: *Those with higher levels of education tend to be healthier than those of similar income who are less well educated.* ◇ *Reynolds belonged to a new kind of British engineering professor, well versed in higher mathematics.* ◇ *The interpretations and rulings of these higher courts take precedence over those of lower courts.* ➲ *see also* HIGHER EDUCATION

ˌhigher eduˈcation *noun* [U] (*abbr.* **HE**) education and training at college and university, especially to degree level: *The percentage of women in higher education has increased in all countries.* ◇ *Diabetes prevalence differed by 6.48% between women with higher education and those with no qualifications.* ◇ **+ noun** *Over a hundred higher education institutions around the world offer university degrees in project management.*

high·land[1] /ˈhaɪlənd/ *adj.* [only before noun] **1** connected with an area of land that has hills or mountains: *Wood,* *essential for fuel and construction, was originally abundant in the highland areas.* ➲ compare LOWLAND[1] **2 Highland** connected with the HIGHLANDS of Scotland: *Rebellious Highland clansmen made incursions into Lowland Scotland.*

high·land[2] /ˈhaɪlənd/ *noun* **1** [C, usually pl.] **~ (of sth)** an area of land with hills or mountains: *Axum was located in the northern highlands of Ethiopia.* ➲ compare LOWLAND[2] **2 the Highlands** [pl.] the high mountain region of Scotland: *Gaelic is the old Celtic language of the Highlands and Islands.*

ˌhigh-ˈlevel *adj.* [usually before noun] **1** senior or involving senior people: *The minister of education, chief medical officer and other high-level officials oversee the initiative.* ◇ *One recent development is the resumption of high-level talks between the two Koreas.* OPP LOW-LEVEL (2) **2** connected with the whole of an organization or process, as opposed to particular details or parts of it: *The strategic level, by definition, concerns long-term, high-level planning.* **3** in a high position or place: *An earthen dam backs up the river flow, forming a higher-level pool extending miles upstream.* OPP LOW-LEVEL (3) **4** (of nuclear waste) highly RADIOACTIVE: *The spent fuel and high-level waste create by far the most serious problems.* OPP LOW-LEVEL (1) **5** (*computing*) (of a computer language) similar to an existing language such as English, making it fairly simple to use: *Programmers writing in assembly language require a detailed knowledge of the architecture of their machines, unlike those operating in high-level languages.* OPP LOW-LEVEL (4)

high·light[1] AWL /ˈhaɪlaɪt/ *verb* **1** to emphasize sth, especially so that people give it more attention: **~ sth** *US research highlighted the role of street culture in the motivation to engage in robbery.* ◇ *Differences between breeds of dogs highlight differences in their genomes.* ◇ **~ that...** *The report highlighted that a number of departments were breaking the rules on appointments.* ◇ **~ how/what, etc...** *This case study highlights how depression may present in a person with severe learning disability.* **2 ~ sth (in sth)** to mark part of a text with a special coloured pen, or to mark an area on a computer screen, to emphasize it or make it easier to see: *These chemical bonds are shown highlighted in red.*

▸ HIGHLIGHT + NOUN **importance • significance • need • potential** *The study findings highlight the need for appropriate public health action.* | **fact • role • aspect • issue • trend • nature • extent • difference • disparity • contradiction • similarity • link** *These numbers highlight the fact that China's poor economic performance for much of the past 200 years has been atypical.* | **danger • problem • difficulty • tension • weakness • vulnerability • limitation • complexity • inadequacy • lack • challenge** *This study highlights the vulnerability of recently arrived older immigrants when it comes to having health insurance.*

high·light[2] AWL /ˈhaɪlaɪt/ *noun* **~ (of sth)** the best, most interesting or most exciting part of sth: *Unquestionably these two scenes are the highlights of the film.*

high·light·er /ˈhaɪlaɪtə(r)/ (*also* **ˈhighlighter pen**) *noun* a special pen used for marking words in a text in bright colours: *Use a highlighter to indicate any unfamiliar words.*

high·ly /ˈhaɪli/ *adv.* **1** very: *In recent years, spring precipitation has been highly variable.* ◇ *She is a highly skilled and knowledgeable teacher.* ◇ *It is highly unlikely that everyone will agree on all of the issues involved.* **2** at or to a high standard, level or amount: *He was a highly educated, upper-class man.* ◇ *Jakarta, Prague, Santiago and a number of other cities do not score highly on any world economic indicators.* **3** with admiration or praise: *Most prestige cars are bought as status symbols that gain value as more people think highly of them.* ◇ *They speak highly of traditional apprenticeship but opportunities for this kind of training are scarce in the modern world.*

ˌhigh ˈpressure *noun* **1** [U, C] the condition of air, gas or liquid that is kept in a small space by force: **at ~** *At high pressure, the CO_2 is dissolved in the water.* ◇ **under ~** *The hydrogen would be stored under high pressure in tanks.* ◇ *The central vessel is strong enough to withstand high pressures.* ➲ compare LOW PRESSURE (1) **2** [U] a condition of the air that affects the weather, when the PRESSURE is higher than normal: *There is fair weather in the ridge of high pressure which usually precedes a warm front.* ➲ compare LOW PRESSURE (2)

ˌhigh-ˈpressure *adj.* [only before noun] **1** using or containing a great force of a gas or a liquid: *The kaolinite is separated from the granite by washing it out with high-pressure water hoses.* ◇ *At the power station, coal, oil or gas is burnt to create high-pressure steam.* **2** connected with weather or with the earth's atmosphere when there is HIGH PRESSURE: *In the atmosphere, winds blow from high-pressure areas with relatively high temperatures to low-pressure areas.* ◇ *In September and October, massive high-pressure systems commonly develop over the western US.* **3** that involves a lot of worry and anxiety SYN STRESSFUL: *Under this high-pressure and competitive environment, it is difficult for people to achieve a balanced lifestyle.* ◇ *She has a high-pressure job as a chartered accountant.* **4** that involves aggressive ways of persuading sb to do sth or to buy sth: *Many companies have been criticized for using dubious, high-pressure sales techniques.*

H

ˌhigh-ˈprofile *adj.* [usually before noun] receiving or involving a lot of attention and discussion on television, in newspapers, etc: *Recent high-profile cases in the United Kingdom have shown up some of the failings of such an approach.*

ˌhigh-resoˈlution *adj.* [usually before noun] (of an image or a method of producing or displaying an image) showing a lot of clear sharp detail: *The goal of the international project was to produce a high-resolution 3D image.*

ˌhigh-ˈrisk *adj.* [usually before noun] **1** very likely to get a particular disease or suffer from a particular problem: *The study illustrates the importance of screening in this high-risk group.* ➲ compare LOW-RISK (1) **2** involving a high risk of loss, death, damage, etc: *Teenagers are vulnerable to getting involved with high-risk behaviours related to sex, drugs and violence.* ◇ *When there are lax controls in high-risk financial markets, the dangers are clear.* ➲ compare LOW-RISK (2)

ˈhigh school *noun* [C, U] (in the US and some other countries) a school for young people between the ages of 14 and 18: *About half of the participants (52.7 per cent) had ten years of education, 26.5 per cent had completed high school and 20.8 per cent had academic degrees.* ◇ *Students from 12 high schools in California took part on the project.* ◇ **+ noun** *I conducted focus groups with three groups of high school students and three groups of college students.* ◇ *a high school graduate/education*

ˌhigh-ˈspeed *adj.* [only before noun] that travels, works or happens very fast: *The wing motions were captured by two high-speed video cameras.*

ˌhigh-ˈtech *adj.* using the most modern methods and machines, especially electronic ones: *High-tech industries have more complex needs, including highly skilled workers and investment in research.* ◇ *More high-tech are supermarket chains that use loyalty cards to track individuals' purchases.*

high·way /ˈhaɪweɪ/ *noun* **1** (*especially NAmE*) a main road for travelling long distances, especially one connecting and going through cities and towns: *The trial subjects* *included women living in county towns located on a major highway.* **2** (*BrE, formal*) a public road: *The property is not situated on a public highway.* **3** (*computing*) a PATHWAY (or BUS) connecting parts of one computer system or between different systems: *An m-bit parallel data highway requires m wires to carry the data, and some additional wires to control the flow of information and, possibly, provide error correction.*

hill /hɪl/ *noun* an area of land that is higher than the land around it, but not as high as a mountain: *This small crab lives on steep wooded hills on the coast.* ◇ **+ noun** *Drainage is slower on middle and lower parts of hill slopes.*

him /hɪm; ɪm/ *pron.* **1** used as the object of a verb, after the verb *be* or after a preposition to refer to a male person or animal that has already been mentioned or is easily identified: *The Roman Senate gave him a new name, 'Augustus'.* ◇ *Nothing else is known about him.* **2** a person, male or female, whose sex is not stated or known, especially when referring to sb mentioned earlier or to a group in general: *A child may become quite upset when his parents refuse to buy a particular toy for him.* HELP This use is considered by many people to be sexist. To avoid this, use 'them' or 'him or her' instead. ➲ grammar note *at* THEY

him·self /hɪm'self/ *pron.* **1** (the reflexive form of *he*) used when the man or boy who performs an action is also affected by it: *He often had to defend himself against his critics.* ◇ *Morgan no longer preoccupied himself with experiments.* **2** used to emphasize the male subject or object of a sentence: *The buildings and estate at Monticello were designed by Jefferson himself.* ◇ *Stratton's model, as he himself admits, is oversimplified.*
IDM **by him'self** **1** alone; without anyone else: *He likes to sit by himself and look at the ocean.* **2** without help: *He does not have the money to complete the project by himself.*

hin·der /'hɪndə(r)/ *verb* to make it difficult for sb to do sth or for sth to happen SYN HAMPER, IMPEDE: **~ sb/sth** *Sometimes their personal problems hinder their ability to work effectively.* ◇ *Cultural diversity can hinder the development of social cohesion between employees (Cramton and Hinds, 2005).* ◇ **~ sb/sth from (doing) sth** *The chick spread its wings in order to hinder competing siblings from gaining access to the prey.*

hin·drance /'hɪndrəns/ *noun* **1** [C, usually sing.] a person or thing that makes it more difficult for sb to do sth or for sth to happen: *When making a speech, a prepared script can be a hindrance rather than a help.* ◇ **~ to sth/sb** *Small scale need not necessarily be a hindrance to export growth in sectors such as electronics.* **2** [U] (*formal*) the act of making it more difficult for sb to do sth or for sth to happen: *Between the walls of the container the molecule is free to move without hindrance.*

Hindu /'hɪnduː; ˌhɪn'duː/ *noun* a person whose religion is Hinduism: *Hindus in the West in general have achieved a very high educational level.* ■ **Hindu** *adj.*: *a Hindu temple*

Hin·du·ism /'hɪnduːɪzəm/ *noun* [U] the main religion of India and Nepal which includes the worship of one or more gods and belief in REINCARNATION: *Dharma is an important concept in Hinduism signifying order, law, duty and truth.*

hint¹ /hɪnt/ *noun* **1 ~ (of sth)** something that suggests what will happen in the future SYN SIGN¹ (1): *The first hint of the quantum revolution, unrecognized as such at the time, actually came in 1885.* ◇ *Few hints of fault structure were found by any of the studies.* **2** something that you say or do in an indirect way in order to show sb what you are thinking: **~ about/as to sth** *Hints as to why Soviet casualties were unnecessarily high are provided by several Russian war novels.* ◇ **~ that...** *Managers must learn to read between the lines or interpret subtle hints that a problem has developed.* **3** [usually sing.] **~ (of sth)** a small amount of sth SYN SUGGESTION (3), TRACE² (2): *There is just the hint of a smile on the faces of the two women on the extreme right.* **4 ~ (on sth)** a small piece of practical information or advice SYN TIP¹ (2): *The exercises are fairly simple, except in a few cases where a hint is given.*

hint² /hɪnt/ *verb* [I, T] to suggest sth in an indirect way: **~ at sth** *One study hints at local variation in growth.* ◇ **~ (that)...** *Very preliminary findings hint that this treatment may be effective in some cases.*

hip /hɪp/ *noun* **1** the joint at the top of the leg: **+ noun** *Hip fracture was the most frequent fall-related complication of hospitalized patients.* **2** the area at either side of the body between the top of the leg and the waist: **+ noun** *Weight, height, waist and hip circumference were measured.*

hire¹ /'haɪə(r)/ *verb* **1 ~ sb** (*especially NAmE*) to give sb a job: *Governments have come under pressure to make it easier to hire and fire workers.* **2 ~ sb/sth (to do sth)** to employ sb for a short time to do a particular job: *They spent heavily on advertising and hired prestigious consultants to evaluate their wines.* **3 ~ sth** (*especially BrE*) to pay money to borrow sth for a short time: *The company regularly hires limousines to collect important clients from their offices and airports.*
PHR V **ˌhire sb/sth 'out** (*especially BrE*) to let sb use sb/sth for a short time, in return for payment: *The richer peasants often owned machinery which they hired out at reasonable rates.*

hire² /'haɪə(r)/ *noun* **1** [U] (*especially BrE*) the act of paying to use sth for a short time: **for ~** *The UK has hundreds of village halls and church halls that are available for hire by research agencies.* ◇ **+ noun** *To succeed in attracting these customers, car hire companies need to operate internationally.* **2** [C] (*especially NAmE*) a person who has recently been given a job by a company: *The experienced salespeople mentor new hires.*

his¹ /hɪz; ɪz/ *det.* (the possessive form of *he*) **1** of or belonging to a man or boy who has already been mentioned or is easily identified: *Michell left Cambridge in 1767 and spent the rest of his life in Yorkshire.* ◇ *His wife had warned him not to seek work in that neighbourhood.* **2** of or belonging to sb, either male or female, who has already been mentioned or is easily identified: *A lazy student might try and get solutions from his classmates.* HELP This use is considered by many people to be sexist. To avoid this, use 'their' or 'his or her' instead. ➲ grammar note *at* THEY

his² /hɪz; ɪz/ *pron.* of or belonging to him: *Friends of his tried to help him escape.* ◇ *The choice was his.* ◇ *His was an especially important responsibility.*

histo·gram /'hɪstəgræm/ *noun* (*technical*) a diagram that uses RECTANGLES of different heights (and sometimes different widths) to show different amounts, so that they can be compared: *The histograms show the number of mussels of each size consumed by the crabs.* ➲ *compare* BAR CHART

his·tor·ian /hɪ'stɔːriən/ *noun* a person who studies or writes about history; an expert in history: *Historians disagree about the impact of the conflict on the nation's economy.*

his·tor·ic /hɪ'stɒrɪk; *NAmE* hɪ'stɔːrɪk; hɪ'stɑːrɪk/ *adj.* [usually before noun] **1** important in history; likely to be thought of as important at some time in the future: *The making of the Constitution of the Republic of Korea in 1948 was a historic event.* ◇ *It was clear even then, though, that historic changes were about to take place.* **2** (of a place or building) old and interesting, usually because important events happened there: *Historic buildings have often undergone successive phases of modification and repair.* ◇ *a historic town/city/monument/site* **3** from a period in history during which information was written down: *One of the* *world's biggest volcanic eruptions of historic times happened in 1815 on Sumbawa.* ➲ *compare* PREHISTORIC

WHICH WORD?

historic ◆ historical

- **Historic** describes an event or a situation that is likely to be remembered because it marks an important change that affects a lot of people: *Section 1.2 introduces the main historic events leading to the foundation of the European Union.* ◇ *Increasing global demand has pushed oil prices towards historic highs.*
- **Historical** describes sth that is connected with the past or with the study of history. It may also be used to emphasize that an event in the past really happened: *Historical records for Puerto Rico extend back roughly 500 years.* ◇ *Relating the sequence of historical events to the archaeological sequence is rarely straightforward.*

his·tor·ic·al /hɪˈstɒrɪkl; *NAmE* hɪˈstɔːrɪkl; hɪˈstɑːrɪkl/ *adj.* [usually before noun] **1** connected with the past: *Education can distort the meaning of historical events for political ends.* ◇ *This wider cultural and historical context is important to Walker's novel.* ➲ *usage note at* HISTORIC **2** connected with the study of history: *The historical record shows that once humans developed agriculture, intergroup hostility became even more common.* ➲ *usage note at* HISTORIC **3** (of a book or film) about people and events in the past: *Using the historical novel, women writers were able to challenge conventional accounts of the Victorian period.*

▸ HISTORICAL + ADJECTIVE **context, background, circumstances ◆ event ◆ moment ◆ perspective, overview ◆ reality ◆ precedent ◆ figure** *This extraordinary social and cultural institution emerged at a particular historical moment in Berlin.* | **record ◆ scholarship ◆ linguistics ◆ geography ◆ sociology** *In the 1960s, the Holocaust became a focus for historical scholarship.* | **fiction ◆ novel ◆ narrative, writing, account** *Most historical fiction, from the time of Scott onwards, had employed passive, fictional protagonists.*

his·tor·ic·al·ly /hɪˈstɒrɪkli; *NAmE* hɪˈstɔːrɪkli; hɪˈstɑːrɪkli/ *adv.* **1** in a way that is connected with people, places and events in history: *The novel does not give a historically accurate account of events.* ◇ *Life expectancy has risen to historically unprecedented levels on a global scale.* **2** in the past, often over a long period of time: *Historically, surgery was invariably risky and often fatal.*

his·tor·iog·raphy /hɪˌstɒriˈɒɡrəfi; *NAmE* hɪˌstɔːriˈɑːɡrəfi; hɪˌstɑːriˈɑːɡrəfi/ *noun* (*pl.* **-ies**) **1** [U] the study of writing about history: *This question is the most contentious issue in Macedonian historiography.* **2** [C] all the writing about a particular period or topic in history considered as a whole: *These subjects have accumulated a vast historiography.* ■ **his·tori·og·raph·ical** /hɪˌstɒriəˈɡræfɪkl; *NAmE* hɪˌstɔːriəˈɡræfɪkl; hɪˌstɑːriəˈɡræfɪkl/ *adj.*: *This essay examines current historiographical debates within feminist and social history.*

his·tory /ˈhɪstri/ *noun* (*pl.* **-ies**) **1** [U] all the events that happened in the past: *Throughout history, the progress of civilization has been inseparable from technological advances.* ◇ *Recent history shows that it is quite difficult for even a powerful government to prevent local conflict or civil war.* ◇ **in ~** *Global catastrophes have occurred many times in history.* **2** [U, sing.] **~ (of sth)** the past events concerned in the development of a particular place, subject, etc: *Analyses of shell fossils can be used to reconstruct the climatic history of the oceans.* ◇ *Popper viewed the history of science as a sequence of conjectures and refutations.* ◇ *For most of their evolutionary history, humans lived in small, sparsely settled communities.* ◇ *Polish nationalism has a long and complex history.* **3** [sing.] **~ (of sth)** a record of sth happening frequently in the past life of a person, family or place; the set of facts that are known about sb's past life: *There is a history of heart disease in the family.* ◇ *The patient's history shows dysfunctional parenting, a chaotic environment, and an absence of positive role models.* ➲ *see also* LIFE HISTORY **4** [C] **~ (of sth)** a written or spoken account of past events: *She has written a history of the labour movement.* **5** [U] the study of past events as a subject at school or university: *Subjects such as history and geography are made remarkably accessible to young people through the scheme.* ➲ *see also* NATURAL HISTORY, ORAL HISTORY

IDM **make ˈhistory** to do sth so important that it will be recorded in history: *Vodafone made history with the first UK mobile call on 1 January 1985.*

▸ ADJECTIVE + HISTORY **recent ◆ modern ◆ early ◆ ancient ◆ human** *Volcanic activity changed the nature of the crust of the Earth over long periods of early history.* | **long ◆ rich ◆ complex ◆ national ◆ cultural ◆ literary ◆ intellectual ◆ environmental ◆ political ◆ social ◆ economic ◆ colonial ◆ evolutionary** *These canals were part of the rich cultural history of the valley.* | **long ◆ past, previous ◆ family ◆ personal ◆ medical ◆ clinical ◆ psychiatric ◆ sexual** *There is no family history of breast cancer.* | **brief, short ◆ detailed ◆ full** *A brief history of the data is explained in this section.*

▸ VERB + HISTORY **study ◆ interpret ◆ rewrite** *Shelley uses myth to interpret history and to come to terms with the failure of the French Revolution.* | **study, research ◆ explore, examine ◆ read ◆ review ◆ trace, chart ◆ uncover ◆ record, document ◆ understand ◆ reconstruct ◆ tell** *The following sections trace the history of environmental thought.* | **have ◆ take ◆ review** *The patient has a history of cardiac failure.* | **narrate, recount, tell** *Film-maker Connie Field told the hidden history of women whose wartime jobs changed their lives.* | **study ◆ teach** *Parys taught US history in a high school classroom for thirteen years.*

hit[1] /hɪt/ *verb* (**hit·ting, hit, hit**) **1** to bring your hand, or an object you are holding, against sb/sth quickly and with force: **~ sb/sth** *An experienced tennis player will hit a ball without stopping to think how to do so.* ◇ **~ sb/sth with sth** *She assaulted him, hitting him with a metal bar.* **2 ~ sth/sb** to come against sth/sb with force, especially causing damage or injury: *Only objects more than a few metres across hit the ground fast enough to produce an impact crater.* **3 ~ sth (on/against sth)** to come against sth with force with a part of your body: *He fell and hit his head on the concrete floor.* **4** [often passive] **~ sb/sth** (of a bullet, bomb, etc. or a person using them) to reach and touch a person or thing suddenly and with force: *Government forces bombed rebel positions and inadvertently hit French military bases.* ◇ *One of the merchant ships in the convoy was hit and set on fire.* **5 ~ sb/sth** to have a bad effect on sb/sth: *Scotland was hit by a serious famine in 1697.* ◇ *Manufacturing areas have been very hard hit by the global economic recession.* ◇ *The collapse of the Soviet Union hit Finnish exports particularly hard.* ◇ *Thailand, Malaysia, Indonesia and South Korea were the countries worst hit by the crisis.* **6 ~ sth** to reach a particular level: *The government was on course for hitting its target of cutting child poverty by 25%.* ◇ *Once evolutionary growth hits its limits, companies are faced with more aggressive options such as mergers and acquisitions.* ◇ *In July 2008, global oil prices hit record highs above US$147 a barrel.* **7 ~ sth** (*rather informal*) to experience sth difficult or unpleasant: *In 2008, the global banking system hit major problems.*

IDM *see* NERVE

PHR V **ˈhit on/upon sth** [no passive] (*rather informal*) to think of a good idea suddenly or by chance: *The Aberbach brothers hit on a powerful yet simple formula.* ◇ *The two men who independently hit upon this idea lacked training in theoretical physics.*

hit² /hɪt/ *noun* **1** a person or thing that is very popular: *The film became an international hit after winning an award at the Sundance Film Festival.* ◇ **+ noun** *His image graced the covers of sheet music for popular hit songs.* **2** a visit by sb to a particular website; a result of a search on a computer, for example on the Internet: *Now the site receives 121 500 hits a minute.* ◇ *Search results were manually examined to eliminate irrelevant hits.* **3** an occasion when sth is damaged by sth, especially by sth that has been thrown or fired at it: *He had been shocked to discover that the centre could be destroyed by a direct hit from a Soviet missile.*

hith·er·to /ˌhɪðəˈtuː; *NAmE* ˌhɪðərˈtuː/ *adv.* (*formal*) until now; until the particular time you are talking about: *The new terrorism had two striking, hitherto unknown features.* ◇ *In the 'Communist Manifesto', it is argued that 'the history of all hitherto existing societies is the history of class struggle'.*

H

HIV /ˌeɪtʃ aɪ ˈviː/ *noun* [U] the abbreviation for 'human immunodeficiency virus' (the virus that can cause AIDS): *Each year, many thousands of individuals are diagnosed with HIV for the first time.* ◇ *An estimated 30% of people living with HIV are unaware of their infection, and may therefore transmit HIV to others, unknowingly.* ◇ **~ positive/negative** *Among youth ages 15–19 years, approximately 3% of males and 7% of females were HIV positive.* ◇ **+ noun** *Patients may present with symptoms or signs suggestive of HIV infection.*

hold¹ /həʊld; *NAmE* hoʊld/ *verb* (**held**, **held** /held/) **1** [T] **~ sth** to have a meeting, conversation, competition or other event: *Staff hold weekly team meetings to discuss progress.* ◇ *Prior to entry to the EU, Sweden held a national referendum.* **2** [T] **~ sth** to have a particular job or position: *Athenian women could not vote or hold office.* ◇ *He held a professorship at Heidelberg University.* **3** [T] **~ sth** to own or have sth: *The company holds a 70% global market share.* ◇ *They hold the land as joint tenants.* ◇ *Labour holds 41 seats.* **4** [T] **~ sth** to have a belief or an opinion about sb/sth: *He was a deeply religious man who held very strong views.* ◇ *Students who enjoy school hold positive attitudes towards academic activities.* ◇ *There is a widely held belief that consumers make purchases based on their socio-economic position.* **5** [T] to consider that sth is true or a fact: **~ that...** *Another important principle holds that all voters should count equally.* ◇ **~ sb/sth + adv./prep./adj.** *The trial judge held the defendants liable.* ◇ *Investors hold most companies in deep mistrust.* ◇ **~ sb/sth to be/have sth** *Hindus hold cows to be sacred.* **6** [T] to have sth possibly waiting to happen: **~ sth (for sb/sth)** *He does not know what the future holds for him.* ◇ **~ promise/potential** *Technology in the classroom holds much promise for new and exciting learning.* ◇ *The tensions of the Cold War held the potential for catastrophic nuclear conflict.* **7** [T] **~ sth (+ adv./prep.)** to keep sth so that it can be used later: *The money is held on trust.* ◇ *They have the right to find out what personal information is held on computer.* ◇ *Assets held abroad accounted for 46% of the company's total assets.* **8** [T] to keep sb/sth in a particular position: **~ sth (+ adv./prep.)** *The patient lies flat and the leg is held up.* ◇ *I used electrical tape to hold the switch in place.* ◇ **~ sth + adj.** *The pendulum is held still at an angle and then released.* **9** [T] **~ sb/sth (+ adv./prep.)** to carry sth; to have sb/sth in your hand, arms, etc: *The image depicts a girl holding a balloon.* **10** [T] **~ sth/sb** to have enough space for sth/sb; to contain sth/sb: *Clay deposits will hold more moisture than sandier layers.* **11** [I] to remain the same: *The same remarks hold for the transportation problem.* **12** [T] to keep sth at the same level, rate, speed, etc: **~ sth (at sth)** *The mixture was heated to 150°C and held at that temperature for 2 hours.* ◇ **~ sth + adj.** *Holding all else constant, imports of goods depress domestic output.* **13** [T] **~ sb/sth** to support the weight of sb/sth: *The base has to hold the total weight of the robot.* **14** [T] **~ sb** to keep sb and not allow them to leave: *He was arrested and held in custody.* **15** [T] **~ sth** to keep sb's attention or interest: *Adverts on the Internet must attract and hold attention.* **16** [T] **~ your breath** to take air into your lungs and not let it out for a period of time: *Hold your breath for 10 sec (or as long as comfortable).*

IDM Most idioms containing **hold** are at the entries for the nouns or adjectives in the idioms. For example, **hold your breath** is at **breath**. **hold ˈgood/ˈtrue** (of a statement, theory or idea) to remain true in different circumstances: *This principle still holds good.* ◇ *Their findings held true in a second study.*

PHR V **ˌhold sth aˈgainst sb** to allow sth that sb has done to make you have a lower opinion of them: *His earlier failings should not be held against him.*

ˌhold sb/sth ˈback to prevent the progress or development of sb/sth: *In the 1950s, heavy spending on the space programme held back other sectors of the economy.*

ˌhold sth ˈdown **1** to keep sth at a low level: *High rates of unemployment will hold down the income of all workers.* **2** [no passive] to keep a job for some time: *He could not hold down a job.*

ˌhold sb/sth ˈoff to stop sb/sth from defeating you: *The Cherokees and Iroquois held off the British long after the 'colonial' period supposedly ended.* ◇ *Having strong interpersonal connections can hold off despair.*

ˌhold ˈon to survive in a difficult or dangerous situation: *Labour just managed to hold on in many seats that they might have lost.* **ˌhold ˈon to sth | ˌhold ˈonto sth** **1** to keep sth that is an advantage for you; to not give or sell sth to sb else: *Prices will rise as employers attempt to hold on to their profit margins.* **2** to keep sth for a long time or for longer than usual: *They held on to many of the old religious ways.* ◇ *By holding on to her anger, she avoided mourning and acknowledging her sadness.*

ˌhold ˈout **1** to last or continue for a period of time, especially when this seems difficult or unlikely: *Galaxies will continue to make new stars as long as the gas supply holds out.* **2** to resist or survive in a dangerous or difficult situation: *The last survivors held out for two days in the temple.* **ˌhold ˈout sth** to offer a chance, hope or possibility of sth: *Some current researchers are holding out the possibility of finding a cure for this disorder.* ◇ *The agreement seemed to hold out the hope of peace.*

ˈhold sb to sth to make sb keep a promise: *The court decided that it would not be unjust to hold her to the terms of the agreement.*

ˌhold sth toˈgether to keep sth united or in one piece: *Coppice dunes are mounds of sand held together by shrubs.* ◇ *Primates live in groups that are held together by strong bonds between individuals.*

ˌhold ˈup to remain strong or working effectively: *This argument just does not hold up.* ◇ *In the early Depression, employment held up best in the South Atlantic region.* **ˌhold sb/sth ˈup** [often passive] **1** to delay or block the movement or progress of sb/sth: *Further progress on the treaty was held up by the Dutch.* **2** to use or present sb/sth as an example: *These two countries were frequently held up as models for other developing countries.*

hold² /həʊld; *NAmE* hoʊld/ *noun* **1** [sing.] **~ (of sb/sth) (on/over sb/sth)** influence, power or control over sb/sth: *The new government weakened the hold of the Church on education.* ◇ *The image of organizations as machines exerts a powerful hold over our thinking.* ◇ *The company was afraid it would lose its market hold.* **2** [C] **~ (of sth)** the part of a ship or plane where the goods being carried are stored: *The asbestos was transported in sacks in the holds of ships.*

IDM **get ˈhold of sth** (*rather informal*) **1** to find sth that you want or need: *When times were good, some lenders had made credit a little too easy for borrowers to get hold of.* **2** to learn or understand sth: *The idea of freedom of the will is a hard idea to get hold of.* **on ˈhold** delayed or remaining the same until a later time or date: *The debate has been put on hold until after the next election.* ◇ *The Bank of England has voted to keep interest rates on hold at 0.5%.* **take (a) ˈhold** to begin to have complete control over sb/sth; to become very strong: *Wherever capitalism took hold, people's incomes and consumption levels began to rise in a sustained way.* ◇ *Warming took hold in Antarctica about 12 500 years ago.*

hold·er /ˈhəʊldə(r); *NAmE* ˈhoʊldər/ *noun* (often in compounds) **1** a person who has or owns the thing mentioned: *If a patent is infringed, the patent holder will be entitled to damages.* ◇ *Border controls have now generally been reduced for EU passport holders.* **2** a thing that holds the object mentioned: *Whole blood samples are taken from the body and stored immediately in sample holders.*

hold·ing /ˈhəʊldɪŋ; *NAmE* ˈhoʊldɪŋ/ *noun* **1** [C] shares, property or items of value that a person, company or organization owns: *Investors reacted in alarm and began to sell their stock holdings.* ◇ *His global media holdings include major newspapers, a book publisher and a film company.* **2** [C] a piece of land that is rented by sb and used for farming: *Population growth in the region is resulting in soil degradation, dwindling land holdings and low agricultural productivity.* **3** [U] **~ of sth** the act of having, owning or holding sth: *A person's self-esteem is closely tied to the holding of a job.* ◇ *Catholics opposed the holding of a gay parade in Rome in 2000.*

ˈholding company *noun* a company that is formed to buy shares in other companies which it then controls: *The group is controlled by the pure holding company at the top of the entire organization.*

hole /həʊl; *NAmE* hoʊl/ *noun* **1** a hollow space in sth solid or in the surface of sth: *The women planted the seeds in clusters of six or seven kernels after digging small holes with sticks.* ◇ **~ in sth** *An urn containing the burned bones and ashes was placed into a hole in the ground accompanied by modest grave goods.* **2** a space or opening that goes all the way through sth: *Rivets were inserted in holes drilled through the pieces of steel to be joined.* **3 ~ (in sth)** a fault or weakness in sth such as a plan, law or story: *There are holes in Anderson's thesis that could bear further investigation.* **4** (*physics*) a position from which an ELECTRON is absent: *The first electron to depart leaves a hole in a low-lying orbital.* ➲ *see also* BLACK HOLE

holi·day /ˈhɒlədeɪ; ˈhɒlədi; *NAmE* ˈhɑːlədeɪ/ *noun* **1** [C] (*BrE*) (*NAmE* **vac·ation**) a period of time spent travelling or resting away from home: *He took a short holiday with his family before returning to Moscow.* ◇ **on ~** *They visited each other whenever possible and went on holiday together.* ◇ **+ noun** *The Balearic Islands are a popular holiday destination for young Europeans.* **2** [U] (*also* **holidays** [pl.]) (*both BrE*) (*NAmE* **vac·ation**) a period of time when you are not at work or school: *The study was conducted during Australian summer school holidays.* ◇ **+ noun** *The company will also have to pay any holiday pay due to employees.* **3** [C] a day when most people do not go to work or school, especially because of a religious or national celebration: *Lincoln declared the day a national holiday in 1863.* ◇ *This major religious holiday commemorates God's command to Abraham to sacrifice his son Ismail.*

hol·is·tic /həʊˈlɪstɪk; hɒˈlɪstɪk; *NAmE* hoʊˈlɪstɪk; hɑːˈlɪstɪk/ *adj.* **1** dealing with sth as a whole rather than just considering particular parts of it: *He suggested that a holistic approach should be taken, involving each department within the company at every level.* ◇ *What is lacking is a total and holistic view that draws on all of these areas of expertise.* **2** (*medical*) used to describe treatment that considers the whole person, including mental and social factors, rather than just the SYMPTOMS (= effects) of a disease: *Patients, particularly those from minority groups, are receiving less whole person and holistic care.*

■ **hol·is·tic·al·ly** /həʊˈlɪstɪkli; hɒˈlɪstɪkli; *NAmE* hoʊˈlɪstɪkli; hɑːˈlɪstɪkli/ *adv.*: *Many of these factors are likely to be interrelated and must therefore be assessed holistically.* ◇ *He firmly believes that doctors should treat patients holistically—body, mind and spirit.*

hol·low¹ /ˈhɒləʊ; *NAmE* ˈhɑːloʊ/ *adj.* **1** having a hole or empty space inside: *These ants dwell in fragile nests, such as hollow acorns, twigs or rock crevices.* ◇ *The anodes take the form of hollow graphite rods through which argon is passed.* **2** not sincere; without real meaning: *In the face of the worst recession since the 1930s, these claims look hollow.* **3** without real value: *He believed that life was wearisome and its enjoyments hollow.*

hol·low² /ˈhɒləʊ; *NAmE* ˈhɑːloʊ/ *noun* **1** an area that is lower than the surface around it, especially on the ground: *The collecting of cool air in hollows overnight produces quite sharp temperature contrasts.* **2** a hole in sth: *Water collects in hollows in living plants, such as tree holes.*

H

holy /ˈhəʊli; *NAmE* ˈhoʊli/ *adj.* (**holi·er**, **holi·est**) **1** [usually before noun] connected with God or a particular religion: *Pope Urban preached the radical doctrine of fighting a holy war.* ◇ *The Jews believed that the holiest place on earth was the Temple at Jerusalem.* **2** good in a moral and religious way: *He was in his thirties, and already enjoyed the reputation of a holy man.*

hom·age /ˈhɒmɪdʒ; *NAmE* ˈhɑːmɪdʒ/ *noun* [U, C, usually sing.] **~ (to sb/sth)** something that is said or done to show respect for sb: *At the traditional site of Troy, Alexander paid homage to his alleged ancestor Achilles.* ◇ *The book is a homage to Derrida.* HELP In history, kings and other rulers often required important people under their rule to **do/pay homage** to them: *Thus English kings paid homage, albeit usually reluctantly, to the kings of France.*

home¹ /həʊm; *NAmE* hoʊm/ *noun* **1** [C, U] the house, apartment, etc. that sb lives in, especially with their family: *Urbanization happened because individuals chose to leave their family homes in the countryside and move to cities.* ◇ *Adulthood milestones (e.g. leaving home, attending college and starting employment) were assessed at ages 18/19.* ◇ **at ~** *Conservative policies encouraged mothers to stay at home to look after their children.* ◇ **from ~** *Access to the Internet allows many people to work from home.* ◇ **away from ~** *We surveyed 200 first-year students living away from home for the first time.* **2** [C] a place where people who cannot care for themselves live and are cared for by others: *Long-term care in a home or hospital is needed for only a minority of the elderly.* ◇ *a care/residential home* ➲ *see also* NURSING HOME **3** [C] a house, apartment, etc, when you think of it as property that can be bought and sold: *The number of new homes sold fell by 26% between 2012 and 2013.* ◇ **+ noun** *Phoenix has the highest rate of home ownership among the large cities of America.* **4** [U, C] the town, district or country that you come from, or where you are living and that you feel you belong to: *Many of these immigrants had left their wives and families back home in India.* ◇ *Trotsky finally made his home in Mexico.* **5** [sing., U] the place where sb/sth can be found: **~ of sb/sth** *In the early 1990s, Geneva, the home of the Commission, became the site of intensive diplomatic struggle.* ◇ **~ to sb/sth** *A single oak tree may be home to 400 species of insect.*

home² /həʊm; *NAmE* hoʊm/ *adj.* [only before noun] **1** connected with the place where you live: *One-hour home visits are made biweekly throughout the year.* ◇ *Many companies will only deliver to the customer's home address.* ◇ *Most of these junior scientists return to their home countries to continue research.* **2** used at home: *The first telephone modem for home computer connection to a mainframe was developed in 1962.* **3** (*especially BrE*) connected with your own country rather than foreign countries SYN DOMESTIC (1): *Home governments can sometimes intervene in support of their own companies' self-interest.* ◇ *Each private secretary is responsible for a different area of policy: home affairs, foreign affairs, economic affairs and Parliament.* OPP FOREIGN (2), OVERSEAS[1]

home[3] /həʊm; *NAmE* hoʊm/ *adv.* to or at the place where you live: *Patients go home within 24 hours of the operation in most cases* ◇ *Although many students returned home as trained physicians, engineers and teachers, others chose to stay.* ◇ (*NAmE*) *Men tended to be the sole breadwinners, while their wives stayed home to take care of the children.*
IDM **bring sth ˈhome to sb** to make sb realize how important, difficult or serious sth is: *The Cuban missile crisis of 1962 brought home to many people the dangers of nuclear war.* ➲ *more at* DRIVE[1], PRESS[2]

home·land /ˈhəʊmlænd; *NAmE* ˈhoʊmlænd/ *noun* **1** the country where a person was born: *Southey's hero leaves his war-torn homeland and eventually lands in North America.* **2** an independent or partly independent state where a particular people live: *They have been fighting for an independent homeland for nearly 30 years.*

H

home·less /ˈhəʊmləs; *NAmE* ˈhoʊmləs/ *adj.* **1** having no home: *Studies report that homeless people have high levels of mental health problems.* **2 the homeless** *noun* [pl.] people who have no home: *The housing charity Shelter supports the homeless in a large percentage of Britain's towns and cities.* ■ **home·less·ness** *noun* [U] *High rates of poverty, homelessness, unemployment and crime place the community's youth at great risk.*

homi·cide /ˈhɒmɪsaɪd; *NAmE* ˈhɑːmɪsaɪd/ *noun* [U, C] (*especially NAmE, law*) the crime of killing sb deliberately SYN MURDER[1]: *The higher levels of homicide and suicide in the USA are claimed to be primarily due to the availability of guns.*

homo·ge·neous /ˌhɒməˈdʒiːniəs; *NAmE* ˌhoʊməˈdʒiːniəs/ *adj.* **1** (*formal*) consisting of things or people that are all the same or all of the same type: *The mentally disabled are not a homogeneous group.* OPP HETEROGENEOUS (1) **2** (*chemistry*) used to describe a process involving substances in the same PHASE (solid, liquid or gas): *Liquid acids and alcohols react together to produce a homogeneous mixture of esters and water.* OPP HETEROGENEOUS (2) ■ **homo·gen·eity** /ˌhɒmədʒəˈniːəti; *NAmE* ˌhɑːmədʒəˈniːəti/ *noun* [U] *In Africa, many states lack cultural and ethnic homogeneity.* ◇ *Low-value products tend to be highly price-elastic due to product homogeneity.*

homo·nym /ˈhɒmənɪm; *NAmE* ˈhɑːmənɪm; ˈhoʊmənɪm/ *noun* (*grammar*) a word that is spelt like another word (or pronounced like it) but which has a different meaning, for example *can* meaning 'be able' and *can* meaning 'put sth in a container': *Homonyms are reasonably rare, but the vast majority of words have multiple senses.*

homo·sex·ual /ˌhəʊməˈsekʃuəl; ˌhɒməˈsekʃuəl; *NAmE* ˌhoʊməˈsekʃuəl/ *adj.* sexually attracted to people of the same sex: *The rights of homosexual couples to shared parenting emerged on the political agenda with renewed strength.* ◇ *In many parts of the world, homosexual acts remain criminalized.* ➲ *compare* GAY[1], HETEROSEXUAL, LESBIAN ■ **homo·sex·ual** *noun*: *The government changed its policy to allow homosexuals to join the armed forces.* **homo·sexu·al·ity** /ˌhəʊməˌsekʃuˈæləti; ˌhɒməˌsekʃuˈæləti; *NAmE* ˌhoʊməˌsekʃuˈæləti/ *noun* [U] *Today, societal attitudes to homosexuality are changing, as are relevant legal issues.*

hon·est /ˈɒnɪst; *NAmE* ˈɑːnɪst/ *adj.* HELP Use **an**, not **a**, before **honest**. **1** always telling the truth, and never stealing or deceiving people: *They were treated not like honest men but like criminals.* OPP DISHONEST **2** not hiding the truth about sth: *An honest appraisal is needed of the probability that a child will fail the school year.* ◇ **~ about sth** *Speculation about climate change must be completely honest about the levels of uncertainty involved.* ◇ **~ with sb** *Physicians must be honest with their patients and empower them to make informed decisions.* ■ **hon·esty** /ˈɒnəsti; *NAmE* ˈɑːnəsti/ *noun* [U] *Non-profit organizations must be able to demonstrate trust, integrity and honesty.*

hon·est·ly /ˈɒnɪstli; *NAmE* ˈɑːnɪstli/ *adv.* **1** in an honest way: *You are protected in law from any repercussions provided you have acted honestly and in good faith.* OPP DISHONESTLY **2** used to emphasize that what you are saying is true, however surprising it may seem: *He honestly believed that he had a right in law to the property.*

honey /ˈhʌni/ *noun* [U] a sweet sticky yellow substance made by BEES that is spread on bread, etc: *The nomadic people, the Borans, seek out swarms of wild bees to collect their honey.*

honey·comb /ˈhʌnikəʊm; *NAmE* ˈhʌnikoʊm/ *noun* [U, C] a structure of cells with six sides, made by BEES for holding their honey and their eggs: *Hive bee honeycomb is always divided up into hexagons instead of some other polygons.*

honor, hon·or·able (*US*) = HONOUR[1], HONOUR[2], HONOURABLE

hon·or·ary /ˈɒnərəri; *NAmE* ˈɑːnəreri/ *adj.* HELP Use **an**, not **a**, before **honorary**. (*abbr.* **Hon**) **1** (of a university degree, a rank, etc.) given as an honour, without the person having to pass the usual exams, etc: *Professor Jackson was awarded an honorary doctorate from the University of Hamburg.* **2** (of a person) holding an honorary title or position: *Don Garden was made an honorary fellow at the University of Melbourne.* **3** (of a position in an organization) not paid: *The Geological Society has a salaried staff working under the direction of honorary officers and committees.* **4** treated like a member of a group without actually belonging to it: *Jantzen argues that women were denied authority as women; they had to become honorary men.*

hon·our[1] (*US* **honor**) /ˈɒnə(r); *NAmE* ˈɑːnər/ *noun* HELP Use **an**, not **a**, before **honour**. **1** [U] great respect and admiration for sb: *Individuals and groups pursued honour and glory, wealth or political power.* ◇ *It is the rich variety of the work that has given it a place of honour in the reception of Platonic ideas.* **2** [U] the quality of knowing and doing what is morally right: *His own personal sense of honour would not permit him to surrender.* ◇ *The code of honour was central to the Southern character: an obsession with personal bravery and a determination to live by one's word.* **3** [U] a good reputation; respect from other people: *The value of family honour emerges as an important issue in British Muslim life.* **4** [C] an award or official title given to sb as a reward for sth that they have done: *The Geological Society awarded him its highest honour, the Wollaston Medal, for his pioneering work in marine geology.* **5** [sing.] **~ (of doing sth)** something that you are very pleased or proud to do because people are showing you great respect SYN PRIVILEGE[1] (3): *Bebchuk had the honour of chairing the committee appointed to select the first recipient of the medal.* **6 honours, honors** [pl.] (*abbr.* **Hons**) (often used as an adjective) a university course that is of a higher level than a basic course: **+ noun** *She graduated with a first class honours degree in anatomy.* **7 honours, honors** [pl.] if you pass an exam or GRADUATE from a university or school **with honours**, you receive a special mark for having achieved a very high standard: *Alex received a scholarship to Miami University in Ohio, where he majored in physics, and graduated with honours.*
IDM **in ˈhonour of sb/sth | in sb's/sth's ˈhonour** in order to show respect and admiration for sb/sth: *Beethoven's third symphony, the 'Eroica', was originally composed in honour of his hero Napoleon.* ◇ *A statue was erected in Musa's honour.*

hon·our² (*US* honor) /ˈɒnə(r); *NAmE* ˈɑːnər/ *verb* **1 ~ sth** to do what you have agreed or promised to do: *The government had failed to honour its contractual obligations.* ◇ *There is a duty not to breach trust in any way, and this commitment must be scrupulously honoured.* **2 ~ sb/sth (with sth)** to do sth that shows great respect for sb/sth: *The Minoans honoured their gods with processions, music and dance.*

hon·our·able (*US* hon·or·able) /ˈɒnərəbl; *NAmE* ˈɑːnərəbl/ *adj.* HELP Use **an**, not **a**, before **honourable.** **1** deserving respect and admiration: *It is remarkable how little attention is given to questions of the governance of major companies, with some honourable exceptions.* **2** showing high moral standards: *Politics can be a decent activity pursued by honourable people to the benefit of the electorate.*

hope¹ /həʊp; *NAmE* hoʊp/ *verb* [I, T] to want sth to happen and think that it is possible: **~ for sth** *Over the next generation, the colonies attained self rule, and many hoped for democratic government for these new states.* ◇ **~ (that)...** *The government hoped that peace might follow from such an agreement.* ◇ **it is hoped (that)...** *Finally, it is hoped that treatment based on gene therapy will soon become an option for many single-gene disorders.* ◇ **~ to do sth** *Gorbachev had hoped to achieve a restructuring of Soviet society, and especially of the communist party.* HELP **Hope** can be used in the passive in the form **it is hoped that...** In other passive sentences, **hope** must always be followed by **for**: *The results were not as good as had been hoped for.* ◇ *The economy is more secure, but the hoped-for stability has not been achieved.*

hope² /həʊp; *NAmE* hoʊp/ *noun* **1** [U, C] a belief that sth you want will happen: **~ (of sth)** *It is very easy to give up trying if we believe there is no hope of success.* ◇ **~ (that...)** *She expressed the hope that her successors would continue the work.* ◇ *to offer/entertain/lose hope* ◇ **~ for sth** *Today, the best hope for a universal language rests with English.* ◇ **~ of doing sth** *The asylum seekers' hopes of gaining entry to Australian territory were short-lived.* ◇ **in the ~ that...** *When demand falls, firms hold on to workers in the hope that the recession will be short-lived.* ◇ **in the ~ of (doing) sth** *For eight years, he had been synthesizing molecules in the hope of finding a useful medicine.* **2** [C] something that you wish for: *The self is the source of our desires, opinions, hopes and fears.* ◇ **~ of/for sth** *Support is needed to help the patient accept the effects of the illness on his hopes for the future.* **3** [C, usually sing.] a person, a thing or a situation that will help you get what you want: **~ (of sth)** *Churchill recognized that his only hope of restoration was if colleagues came to require his support.* ◇ **~ for sth** *Grzimek saw himself and his fellow travellers as the last hope for Africa's wildlife.*
IDM **hold out (the) ˈhope (of sth/that...)** to hope and expect that sth will happen: *Some current investigators hold out hope of finding nervous system abnormalities with which to explain the disorder.*

hope·ful /ˈhəʊpfl; *NAmE* ˈhoʊpfl/ *adj.* **1** [not usually before noun] (of a person) believing that sth you want will happen SYN OPTIMISTIC: **~ (that...)** *Disability rights advocates are hopeful that this legislation will overturn some of these adverse rulings.* ◇ **~ about sth** *He was not hopeful about the future of capitalism.* **2** (of a thing) making you believe that sth you want will happen; bringing hope SYN PROMISING: *One hopeful sign in recent years is that most countries have moved away from negative policies such as forced eviction.*

hope·ful·ly /ˈhəʊpfəli; *NAmE* ˈhoʊpfəli/ *adv.* **1** used to express what you hope will happen: *Hopefully, future research will be able to provide more evidence.* HELP Although this is the most common use of **hopefully** in both general and academic English, it is a fairly new use and some people think it is not correct. **2** showing hope: *As Calder noted hopefully in 2006, 'Change is coming.'*

hope·less /ˈhəʊpləs; *NAmE* ˈhoʊpləs/ *adj.* **1** if sth is **hopeless**, there is no hope that it will get better or succeed: *Some pupils are seen as hopeless cases, and are not expected to attain the benchmark, even with extra support.* **2** feeling or showing no hope: *34.6% of students reported feeling sad or hopeless for more than two weeks in the last year.* ■ **hope·less·ly** *adv.*: *These explanations had proved hopelessly inadequate.* **hope·less·ness** *noun* [U] *In the extreme, pessimism can lead to a sense of helplessness and hopelessness.*

hori·zon /həˈraɪzn/ *noun* **1 the horizon** [sing.] the line at which the earth's surface and the sky appear to meet: **beyond the ~** *Curiosity as to what lay beyond the horizon motivated European overseas movement.* ◇ **below the ~** *The evening star appeared in the sky as the sun sank below the horizon.* **2** [C, usually pl.] the limit of your experience, knowledge or interests: *These young refugees are unable to leave the camps to broaden their intellectual horizons.* ◇ **~ of sth** *Information technology is expanding the horizons of data processing and storage techniques.* **3** (*earth science*) a layer of soil or rock with particular characteristics: *An individual soil horizon can form through several depositional layers.*
IDM **on the hoˈrizon** likely to happen soon: *Signs of America's economic decline were on the horizon.*

hori·zon·tal /ˌhɒrɪˈzɒntl; *NAmE* ˌhɔːrəˈzɑːntl; ˌhɑːrəˈzɑːntl/ *adj.* **1** flat and level; going from side to side rather than up and down: *Along the horizontal axis are levels of family income.* ◇ *In the diagram, the wires are shown as horizontal lines.* OPP VERTICAL (1) **2** (especially in business) at the same level; involving people or companies of the same level: *Horizontal relationships include those with organizations at the same point in the supply chain.* OPP VERTICAL (2) **3** [usually before noun] (*economics*) combining companies that do the same type of work or produce similar things: *Horizontal mergers and acquisitions constitute the largest component of cross-border mergers and acquisitions.*

hori·zon·tal·ly /ˌhɒrɪˈzɒntəli; *NAmE* ˌhɔːrəˈzɑːntəli; ˌhɑːrəˈzɑːntəli/ *adv.* **1** in a way that goes from side to side rather than up and down: *These plants have horizontally creeping stems.* OPP VERTICALLY (1) **2** (especially in business) in a way that involves people or companies of the same level: *Japan has without question a vertically organized society; however, it is also structured horizontally.* OPP VERTICALLY (2) **3** (*economics*) in a way that combines companies that do the same type of work or produce similar things: *This group of horizontally linked organizations produces about 3 000 quarter-ton bales of organic cotton a year.*

hor·mone /ˈhɔːməʊn; *NAmE* ˈhɔːrmoʊn/ *noun* [C, U] a chemical substance produced in the body or in a plant that encourages growth or influences how the cells and TISSUES function: *Epinephrine, or, as it used to be known, adrenaline, is the hormone that is released at times of panic.* ◇ *Dwarf mice are deficient in growth hormone.* ■ **hor·mo·nal** /hɔːˈməʊnl; *NAmE* hɔːrˈmoʊnl/ *adj.* [usually before noun] *Steroids and hormonal therapy can have an unwelcome impact on body image.*

hor·ror /ˈhɒrə(r); *NAmE* ˈhɔːrər; ˈhɑːrər/ *noun* **1** [U] a feeling of great shock or fear: **with ~** *Some commentators in the United States have observed British developments with horror.* ◇ **in ~** *There are those who recoil in horror at this idea.* **2** [sing.] **~ of (doing) sth** a great fear or dislike of sth: *There seems little doubt that Rasputin had a horror of war.* **3** [U] **the ~ of sth** the very unpleasant nature of sth, especially when it is shocking or frightening: *The horror of that fire led to the eventual passage of legislation to protect the* *safety of workers.* **4** [C, usually pl.] **the horrors of sth** a very unpleasant or frightening experience: *Their common experience of the horrors of war had made both decide to become international lawyers.* **5** [U] a type of book or film that is designed to frighten people: **+ noun** *Horror movies often have very complex, mixed representations of women.* ◇ *The film clearly references Price's previous screen appearances in the horror genre.*

hos·pital /ˈhɒspɪtl; *NAmE* ˈhɑːspɪtl/ *noun* a large building where people who are ill or injured are given medical treatment and care: **to ~** *A 62-year-old woman was admitted to hospital following an acute asthmatic attack.* ◇ **in ~** *Patients should expect to stay in hospital for at least 10 days after surgery.* HELP In British English, you say **to hospital** or **in hospital** when you talk about sb being there as a patient; in American English, it is usual to use **the**: (*NAmE*) *A 62-year-old woman was admitted to the hospital...* ◇ *Patients should expect to stay in the hospital...*

H

hos·pi·tal·ize (*BrE also* **-ise**) /ˈhɒspɪtəlaɪz; *NAmE* ˈhɑːspɪtəlaɪz/ *verb* [usually passive] to send sb to a hospital for treatment: *Further, patients were unnecessarily hospitalized 34% of the time.* ◇ **~ sb for/with sth** *He was hospitalized with severe pneumonia.* ■ **hos·pi·tal·iza·tion, -isa·tion** /ˌhɒspɪtəlaɪˈzeɪʃn; *NAmE* ˌhɑːspɪtələˈzeɪʃn/ *noun* [U] *A statistically significant association between smoking and duration of hospitalization was observed.*

host¹ /həʊst; *NAmE* hoʊst/ *noun* **1** (*biology*) an animal or a plant on which another animal or plant lives and feeds: *The host is infected by eating the eggs of the parasite.* ◇ **+ noun** *A phage attaches to the host cell wall and injects its genome into the cell.* **2** a country, a city or an organization that arranges and holds a special event: **play ~ to sth** *Washington, DC once again played host to the conference in 2012.* ◇ **+ noun** *Rio has been chosen as the host city of the 2016 Olympic Games.* **3** a country that provides homes and work for people who come from another country: **+ noun** *The aim of the legislation was the full integration of the migrant workers into the host state.* **4** a country where a company that is based in another country does business: **+ noun** *This management style sees each host country as unique, and sees real differences between these countries and the domestic one.* **5 ~ of sth** a large number of people or things: *People have developed a whole host of new ways to spend their leisure time.* ◇ *The scope of the assessment will depend on the relationship with the local community, and a host of other factors.* **6** the main computer in a network that controls or supplies information to other computers that are connected to it: **+ noun** *The ATM sends the card details to the host computer.*

host² /həʊst; *NAmE* hoʊst/ *verb* **1 ~ sth** to organize an event to which others are invited and make all the arrangements for them: *The conference will be hosted by the Department of Linguistics and Scandinavian Studies.* **2 ~ sth** to store a website on a computer connected to the Internet, usually in return for payment: *The .com domain, which hosts websites of commercial relevance, is the largest single Internet domain.*

hos·tile /ˈhɒstaɪl; *NAmE* ˈhɑːstl; ˈhɑːstaɪl/ *adj.* **1** very unfriendly or aggressive and ready to argue or fight: *Hostile media coverage has had a negative impact upon race relations.* ◇ **~ to/towards sb/sth** *The Tsar believed that anybody who was different was necessarily hostile to Russia.* **2 ~ (to sth)** strongly rejecting sth SYN OPPOSED (1): *Certain groups within society appear to be openly hostile to much arts-related activity.* **3** making it difficult for sth to happen or to be achieved: *She is particularly interested in how plants have adapted to survive in hostile environments.* **4** belonging to a military enemy: *The first action after a declaration of war was to send troops to ravage hostile territory.* **5** (*business*) (of an offer to buy a company, etc.) not wanted by the company that is to be bought: *Poor results would result quickly in the company being subject to hostile takeover bids.*

hos·til·ity /hɒˈstɪləti; *NAmE* hɑːˈstɪləti/ *noun* **1** [U] unfriendly or aggressive feelings or behaviour: *He aroused intense hostility among his opponents.* ◇ **~ to/towards sb/sth** *Hostility towards foreigners occurs in every society.* ◇ **~ between A and B** *At this period, the hostility between Yeltsin and Gorbachev became more open.* **2** [U] **~ (to/towards sth)** strong and angry opposition towards an idea, a plan or a situation: *Feedback showed a general pattern of caution or outright hostility towards genetically modified crops.* **3 hostilities** [pl.] (*formal*) acts of fighting in a war: *Internal factors within the Empire contributed to the outbreak of hostilities in 1618.*

hot /hɒt; *NAmE* hɑːt/ *adj.* (**hot·ter**, **hot·test**) **1** having a high temperature: *Most hot springs with temperatures above 60–70°C occur in volcanic belts.* ◇ *A hot summer boosts the demand for barbecues and lager.* ◇ *Galileo used the fact that hot air rises and so will escape from an open container when heated.* ◇ *Extracted energy will also be used for domestic hot water or space heating.* **2** (of a person) feeling heat in an unpleasant or uncomfortable way: *His breathing was constricted and he felt hot and uncomfortable.* **3** (of food) containing SPICES and producing a burning feeling in your mouth: *The patient complained of a sore tongue, particularly while eating hot or spicy foods.* ◇ *Capsaicin is the substance that makes chilli peppers taste hot.* **4** involving a lot of activity, argument or strong feelings: *Many of these questions are the subject of hot debate.* ◇ **~ issue/topic** *Poverty in Japan became a hot issue following the global financial crisis of 2008.*

hotel /həʊˈtel; *NAmE* hoʊˈtel/ *noun* a building where people stay, usually for a short time, paying for their rooms and meals: *Services include restaurants, recreation areas and a luxury hotel.* ◇ **+ noun** *a hotel room/chain* ◇ *More specific destination studies include analyses of Jamaica's hotel industry (Taylor, 1988, 1993).*

hotly /ˈhɒtli; *NAmE* ˈhɑːtli/ *adv.* **1** done in an angry or excited way or with a lot of strong feeling: *This remains a hotly debated issue amongst historians.* ◇ *The impact of these measures was hotly disputed at the time.* **2** done with a lot of energy and determination: *Voter participation jumped to nearly 60 per cent in the hotly contested election of 2004.* ⮌ *compare* CLOSELY (7)

hour /ˈaʊə(r)/ *noun* HELP Use **an**, not **a**, before **hour**. **1** [C] (*abbr.* **hr, hr.**) 60 minutes; one of the 24 parts that a day is divided into: *The interviews lasted approximately 1 hour.* ◇ *The flight from London to Istanbul takes less than 8 hours.* ◇ *No significant changes were observed in the number of hours that children spent watching television.* ◇ *The workers are paid $10 an hour.* ◇ *Women working more than 40 hours per week were found to have a significantly increased risk of depression.* **2 hours** [pl.] a fixed period of time during which people work, an office is open, etc: *In response, several supermarkets extended their opening hours.* ◇ *The government needs to introduce legislation to encourage flexible working hours.* ◇ *There are usually arrangements for contacting senior staff outside office hours.* **3 hours** [pl.] a long time: *Examinees were required to write for hours at a time.* ◇ *Writing your own software for the analysis of network data can take hours.* **4** [C] the time when sth important happens: *The period of the summer and autumn of 1940 was considered in popular memory to be Britain's finest hour.* ◇ *Phaedo tells the story of Socrates' last hours.* **5 hours** [pl.] used when giving the time according to the 24-hour clock, usually in military or other official language: *The majority of home visits were made at the weekend, between 08.00 hours and 18.00 hours* HELP These are pronounced '(o) eight hundred hours' and 'eighteen hundred hours'.

IDM **the ˈearly/ˈsmall hours** the period of time very early in the day before it is light: *She was brought in by ambulance in the early hours of the morning.*

hour·ly /ˈaʊəli; *NAmE* ˈaʊərli/ *adj.* HELP Use **an**, not **a**, before **hourly**. [only before noun] **1** done or happening every hour: *Accurate hourly data are required in very many applications.* ◇ *Constant weights of 222.45 g are recorded at three successive hourly intervals.* **2 ~ wage, fee, rate, etc.** the amount that you earn every hour or pay for a service every hour: *A French survey published in 1907 calculated the average hourly wage of a sample of skilled workers to be 0.87 francs in Paris.*

house¹ *noun* /haʊs/ (*pl.* **houses** /ˈhaʊzɪz/) **1** [C] a building for people to live in, usually for one family: *The family live in a two-storey house.* ◇ **at sb's ~** *Lewes recalled his first meeting with the young author at his house some 36 years before.* ◇ **move ~** (*BrE*) *These methods offer a means of estimating how many times people move house during their lives.* **2** [sing.] all the people living in a house SYN HOUSEHOLD: *The letters James and Amelia received from the children were read out to the whole house.* **3** [C] (in compounds) a building used for keeping animals or goods in: *Temperature and humidity levels in poultry houses are controlled automatically.* ◇ *In the mid-1790s, the Faradays moved to rooms over a coach house near Manchester Square.* **4** [C] (in compounds) a building used for a particular activity: *Wagner planned to build a new opera house at Bayreuth.* ◇ **~ of sth** *Their settlements are without houses of worship.* **5** [C] (in compounds) a company involved in a particular kind of business: *The big British and American publishing houses are more comfortable financially than their French counterparts.* ◇ *Currently, 25% of the top fashion houses in the world are located in Paris.* ➲ *see also* IN-HOUSE **6** [C] (in compounds) a restaurant: *In many other European cities by 1700 coffee houses began to appear.* **7** [C] (*often* **House**) a group of people who meet to discuss and make the laws of a country: *In Australia, elections for both houses are held concurrently.* **8 the House** [sing.] the House of Commons or the House of Lords in Britain; the House of Representatives in the US: *A motion requesting that the MP be suspended is voted on by the House.* **9** [C] a religious community that lives in a particular building: *Local bishops and the heads of religious houses were present.* **10** [C] an old and famous family: *Cynisca, a member of the Spartan royal house, won chariot races at Olympia.* ◇ **the House of sth** *The throne was to pass to the House of Hanover if Queen Anne died without heirs.* **11** [C] the part of a theatre where the audience sits; the audience at a particular performance: *The stage adaptation played to packed houses on Broadway.*
IDM **put/set/get your (own) ˈhouse in order** to take necessary action to deal with problems in your own business, life, etc, especially before you try to criticize sb else: *England ought to get its own house in order before finding fault elsewhere.*

house² /haʊz/ *verb* **1 ~ sb** to provide sb with a place to live or stay: *Ten temporary shelters housed 1 000 refugees.* **2 ~ sth** to be the place where sth is kept or where sth operates from: *The Indiana State Museum houses a large collection of historical objects.* ◇ *The offices also house a printing firm.*

house·hold /ˈhaʊshəʊld; *NAmE* ˈhaʊshoʊld/ *noun* all the people living together in a house or flat: *The risk of mortality is higher for children living in poorer households.* ◇ *low-income/wealthy households* ◇ *Male and female heads of households were interviewed in equal proportion.* ◇ **+ noun** *The respondents' monthly household income ranged from $455 to $12 000.* ◇ *The survey revealed that women spend almost twice as long on household chores as men.*

the ˌHouse of ˈCommons (*also* **the Com·mons**) *noun* [sing.+ sing./pl. v.] (in the UK and Canada) the part of Parliament whose members are elected by the people of the country: *He was elected to the House of Commons in 1906.* ➲ *compare* HOUSE OF LORDS

the ˌHouse of ˈLords (*also* **the Lords**) *noun* [sing.+ sing./pl. v.] (in the UK) the part of Parliament whose members are not elected by the people of the country: *The Liberals proposed to reform the House of Lords.* ➲ *compare* HOUSE OF COMMONS

the ˌHouse of Repreˈsentatives *noun* [sing.] the largest part of Congress in the US, or of the Parliament in Australia, whose members are elected by the people of the country: *The Democratic Party regained 22 seats in the House of Representatives.* ➲ *compare* SENATE (1)

house·wife /ˈhaʊswaɪf/ *noun* (*pl.* **house·wives** /ˈhaʊswaɪvz/) a woman who stays at home to cook, clean, take care of the children, etc. while her husband or partner goes out to work: *In the 1950s, once married with children, more women were full-time housewives.*

house·work /ˈhaʊswɜːk; *NAmE* ˈhaʊswɜːrk/ *noun* [U] the work involved in taking care of a home and family, for example cleaning and cooking: *Men with two children spent 0.7 fewer hours per week doing housework as compared with men without children.*

hous·ing /ˈhaʊzɪŋ/ *noun* **1** [U] houses, flats, etc. that people live in, especially when referring to their type, price or condition: *Disabled people are twice as likely to live in public housing as their non-disabled peers.* ◇ **+ noun** *The valley was being converted into new housing developments.* ◇ *As a mechanism for ensuring affordable housing for all social groups, one cannot say that the housing market works.* **2** [U] the job of providing houses, flats, etc. for people to live in: **+ noun** *From 1945 housing policy concentrated on reconstruction.* ◇ *Housing associations were expected to seek private finance to support new social housing provision.* **3** [C] a hard cover that protects part of a machine: *Figure 13.20 shows the configuration of the bearing housing bonded to the robot arm.*

how /haʊ/ *adv.* **1** in what way or manner: *How can tragedies like this be avoided?* ◇ *The mother alleged that she did not know how the injuries had been caused.* ◇ **~ to do sth** *The programme teaches people how to achieve their goals without violence.* **2** used before an adjective or adverb to ask or talk about the amount or degree of sth: *How often do you access the Internet? (Please tick one answer.)* ◇ *We do not even know how many languages are represented in the data.*

how·ever /haʊˈevə(r)/ *adv.* **1** used to introduce a statement that contrasts with sth that has just been said: *Down to the eighth century BC, there are no written records. After the seventh century BC, however, literary remains start to appear.* ◇ *Trust in business has been damaged. However, the authors see no viable alternative to free market capitalism.* **2** (with an adjective or adverb) to whatever degree: *Any deviation from religious tradition, however small, is perceived as dangerous.* ◇ *The end of the Cold War was a destabilizing event, however much one might welcome the collapse of communism.* ◇ *These supporters are likely to remain loyal, however badly the party is performing.* **3** in whatever way: *People should have an equal opportunity to live a good life, however they may conceive of this.* ◇ *However we may speculate about the future, certain historical realities ought to be clear.*

huge /hjuːdʒ/ *adj.* extremely large in size or amount; extremely great in degree SYN ENORMOUS, VAST: *Fires spread out of control, burning huge tracts of forest.* ◇ *The country has received huge amounts of foreign aid in recent decades.* ◇ *The recession has had a huge impact on the IT industry.*

LANGUAGE BANK

Ways of saying 'but'

The following words and expressions are useful when you want to contrast two statements or to introduce a point that contradicts or qualifies what has been stated.

however • although • yet • in fact • the fact remains that... • despite • in spite of • nevertheless

- *Some teachers claim that they treat all students the same. **However**, all students are not the same.*
- ***Although** humans may be biological organisms, they are social animals.*
- *We instinctively assume that everyone prefers socially desirable outcomes. **Yet**, people vary in the degree to which they value these outcomes.*
- ***In fact**, restrictions on budgets can often be even tighter here than in the private sector.*
- ***The fact remains that** research can be found to support either of these interpretations.*
- ***Despite** these political divisions, most Americans want to see the state help the deserving poor.*
- *These figures **nevertheless** conceal variations within regions.*

H

huge·ly /ˈhjuːdʒli/ *adv.* **1** extremely: *Henry Ford was a hugely successful entrepreneur.* ◇ *Economic factors are hugely important, and no serious study of history can ignore them.* **2** very much: *There are articles by a large number of authors, and the writing styles vary hugely.* ◇ *His books have hugely influenced biblical interpretation.*

human¹ /ˈhjuːmən/ *adj.* **1** [only before noun] of or connected with people rather than animals, machines or gods: *Human life may thus be seen as merely a struggle for survival and reproduction.* ◇ *The adult human body consists of more than 75 trillion cells.* ◇ *Most accidents with the reactors were due to equipment malfunctions or human error.* **2** showing the weaknesses that are typical of people, which means that other people should not criticize the person too much: *Saints, too, are only human, making mistakes on occasion.* **3** having the same feelings and emotions as most ordinary people: *Bryson makes scientists seem very human.* ➲ *compare* INHUMAN, NON-HUMAN
IDM **with a human ˈface** that considers the needs of ordinary people: *The Czechoslovak concept of 'socialism with a human face' was destroyed by the Soviet invasion of autumn 1968.*
▸ HUMAN + NOUN **life • condition • experience • development • activity, action • behaviour • population • body • mind • society • history • geography • health • disease • cell • genome** *Hobbes presents a pessimistic view of the human condition.* ◇ *AIDS is generally seen as the greatest threat to human health in the world.*
▸ ADVERB + HUMAN **fully • distinctively • uniquely • truly • essentially** *This group of Christians maintained that Jesus was both fully human and fully divine.*

human² /ˈhjuːmən/ *noun* (*also* ˌ**human ˈbeing**) a person rather than an animal, machine or god: *Particular compounds may be toxic in varying degrees to living organisms, including humans.* ◇ *Slaves were regarded as property, rather than as human beings.*

ˌ**human ˈcapital** *noun* [U] the skills, knowledge, and experience that an individual or population has, viewed in terms of their value or cost to an organization or country: *To measure the level of human capital in the economy, we include two measures of educational attainment in each region.*

hu·mane /hjuːˈmeɪn/ *adj.* showing kindness towards people and animals by making sure that they do not suffer more than is necessary: *The Qur'an commanded the just and humane treatment of slaves (16:71).* ◇ *Some meat eaters eat meat derived only from animals raised and slaughtered under the most humane conditions.*

hu·mani·tar·ian /hjuːˌmænɪˈteəriən; *NAmE* hjuːˌmænɪˈteriən/ *adj.* [usually before noun] **1** concerned with reducing suffering and improving the conditions that people live in: *The European Union has become the world's largest donor of humanitarian aid.* **2** used to describe a situation that involves a lot of human suffering, especially one in which food, etc. is needed by many people: *The report argued that the humanitarian crisis in the region required immediate action.* ■ **hu·mani·tar·ian** *noun*: *Humanitarians and Evangelicals sought to abolish pastimes such as cock-fighting and bear-baiting.*

hu·man·ity /hjuːˈmænəti/ *noun* **1** [U] people in general: *The most urgent issue facing humanity today is how the peoples of the world should share out its resources.* **2** [U] **~ (of sb)** the state of being a person rather than a god, an animal or a machine: *These early texts stress the humanity of Christ.* **3** [U] the quality of being kind to people and animals by making sure that they do not suffer more than is necessary; the quality of being humane: *Whatever the issues over border controls, it is still vital to treat asylum seekers with humanity.* **4 (the) humanities** [pl.] the subjects of study that are concerned with human culture, especially literature, history, art, music and philosophy: *It costs a lot more to run a course in physics or chemistry than in the humanities.* ◇ *The limited support given to arts and humanities is a direct result of the market-driven higher education system.* ➲ *compare* SCIENCE (3)

hu·man·kind /ˌhjuːmənˈkaɪnd/ *noun* [U] people in general: *Environmental crisis is the most urgent concern for humankind.* ➲ *see also* MANKIND

ˌ**human ˈnature** *noun* [U] the ways of behaving, thinking and feeling that are shared by most people and are considered to be normal: *Liberals generally take a positive view of human nature, whereas realists see human beings as capable of evil.*

the ˌ**human ˈrace** *noun* [sing.] all people, considered together as a group: *Trees are vital to the survival of the human race.*

ˌ**human reˈsources** *noun* **1** [pl.] people's skills and abilities, seen as sth a company or organization can make use of: *Financial and human resources were in short supply.* **2** (*abbr.* **HR**) [U+sing./pl. v.] the department in a company that deals with employing and training people: *The director of human resources cannot hire additional staff because of the shortage of space.*

ˌ**human ˈright** *noun* [usually pl.] one of the basic rights that everyone has to be treated fairly and not in a cruel way, especially by their government: *The international system for protecting human rights is not infallible.* ◇ **human rights + noun** *human rights abuses/violations*

hum·ble /ˈhʌmbl/ *adj.* (**hum·bler** /ˈhʌmblə(r)/, **hum·blest** /ˈhʌmblɪst/) **1** showing that you do not think that you are as important as other people SYN MODEST (4): *Christians believe that it is virtuous to be humble and meek.* **2** having a low rank or social position: *Born of humble origins in Normandy, Laplace became a professor of mathematics at the age of 20.* **3** (of a thing) not large or special in any way SYN MODEST (2): *Constructivism rose very quickly from rather humble beginnings to become one of the leading schools in International Relations.* ◇ *Households offered wheat cakes and other humble food to their family gods.* ■ **hum·bly** /ˈhʌmbli/ *adv.*: *Gandhi very humbly suggests that science itself is not infallible.*

humid /ˈhjuːmɪd/ *adj.* having a high level of water VAPOUR in the atmosphere: *The weather data recorded for Dubai is typical of the hot and humid climates under consideration in the study.*

hu·mid·ity /hjuːˈmɪdəti/ *noun* [U] the amount of water VAPOUR in the atmosphere: *Temperature and humidity were measured continuously.*

hu·mour (*US* **hu·mor**) /ˈhjuːmə(r)/ *noun* [U] **1** the quality in sth that makes it funny; the ability to laugh at things that are funny: *Jane tried to use humour to calm herself.* ◇ *It is not quite fair to suggest that he had no sense of humour.* **2** the state of your feelings or mind at a particular time: *The team approached challenges with good humour and creativity.*

hun·dred /ˈhʌndrəd/ *number* (*plural verb*) **1** 100: *Christianity grew from a few hundred followers to a few million.* ◇ *Europeans had little knowledge of the geography of Africa beyond fifty or a hundred miles from the coast.* ◇ *The total number of genes may be about a hundred for a large virus.* ◇ *The Club of Rome limited its membership to one hundred individuals.* HELP You say **a, one, two, several, etc. hundred** without a final 's' on 'hundred'. **Hundreds (of...)** can be used if there is no number or quantity before it. Always use a plural verb with **hundred** or **hundreds**, except when an amount of money is mentioned: *Four hundred (people) are expected to attend.* ◇ *Two hundred (pounds) was withdrawn from the account.* **2 hundreds (of...)** or **a hundred** a large number: *There are hundreds of factors that cause families stress.* ◇ (*rather informal*) *Has this been said a hundred times before?* ◇ *Most phylogeographic studies relate to events spread across thousands of years and hundreds of kilometres.* ◇ *The next step is to reduce the number of molecules being probed from many billions to a few tens or hundreds.* **3 the hundreds** [pl.] the numbers from 100 to 999: **in the hundreds** *Total casualties were probably in the hundreds.* ◇ *By the standards of ancient cities, Rome had a huge population, in the hundreds of thousands.* **4 the... hundreds** [pl.] the years of a particular century: *The late 1800s and early 1900s brought excitement over a wide array of inventions and developments.*

hung *past tense, past part. of* HANG

hun·ger /ˈhʌŋɡə(r)/ *noun* **1** [U] the state of not having enough food to eat, especially when this causes illness or death: *A prolonged drought meant hunger and poverty for entire villages and districts.* ◇ *The number of people suffering from chronic hunger in the region increased by 100 million.* **2** [U] the feeling caused by a need to eat: *Once the baby starts making these signs, it should be fed, since crying is regarded as a late sign of hunger.* **3** [sing.] **~ (for sth)** (*formal*) a strong desire for sth: *These writers set out to satisfy the new hunger for the printed word.*

hun·gry /ˈhʌŋɡri/ *adj.* (**hun·grier, hun·gri·est**) **1** not having enough food to eat: *There are still over 800 million hungry people in the world.* ◇ **go ~** *Ten per cent of children said they had gone hungry in the preceding month because of lack of money.* **2 the hungry** *noun* [pl.] people who do not have enough food to eat: *SGI has established humanitarian programmes to feed the hungry and meet the needs of the poor.* **3** feeling that you want to eat sth: *He often complains of feeling hungry and gets very thirsty.* **4** having or showing a strong desire for sth: **~ for sth** *Increasing prosperity has created markets hungry for Western luxury brands.* ◇ *The company's workforce sounds like an HR professional's dream: highly educated and hungry for success.* ◇ **- hungry** *Finally the republic was torn to pieces by rival power-hungry tribunes or dictators like Pompey and Julius Caesar.*

hunt¹ /hʌnt/ *verb* **1** [I, T] to go after wild animals or birds in order to catch or kill them for food, sport or to make money: *Baird and Dill (1996) tested the hypothesis that killer whales hunt in groups to maximize hunting success.* ◇ **~ sth** *Bats have to solve the problem of navigating and hunting insects at night.* **2** [I] **~ (for sth)** to look for sth that is difficult to find SYN SEARCH² (1): *Researchers have been hunting for genes associated with schizophrenia for decades.* **3** [T, I] to look for sb in order to catch them or harm them: **~ sb** *At one point he was hunted by the imperial secret police.* ◇ **~ for sb** *The local papers reported him as missing and the police hunted for him in vain.*
PHR V **ˌhunt sb ˈdown** to search for sb until you catch or find them, especially in order to punish or harm them: *Eumenes was condemned to death, and Antigonus was ordered to hunt him down.*

hunt² /hʌnt/ *noun* **1** (often in compounds) an act of going after wild animals to kill or capture them: *The bison hunt was a tradition undertaken twice a year in Kansa society.* **2** [usually sing.] **~ (for sb/sth)** (*rather informal*) an act of looking for sb/sth that is difficult to find: *The main focus of insulin research remains on diabetes, and the hunt for long-term treatments.* ◇ *The serious hunt for a theory of everything is on.*

hunt·er /ˈhʌntə(r)/ *noun* a person who hunts wild animals for food or sport; an animal that hunts its food: *50 000 years ago humans had certainly become resourceful and highly skilled hunters.* ◇ *African wild dogs are efficient hunters that rely on high hunting success rates at regular intervals.*

ˌhunter-ˈgather·er *noun* a member of a group of people who do not live in one place but move around and live by hunting, catching fish and gathering plants: *As human hunter-gatherers slowly accumulated more kinds of tools, clothes and skills, they were able to live in more kinds of places.* ◇ **+ noun** *Dunbar (1993) reviewed a number of documented hunter-gatherer societies.*

hunt·ing /ˈhʌntɪŋ/ *noun* [U] going after and killing wild animals and birds for food or sport: *Most of the hundred or so villagers support themselves through hunting and agriculture.* ◇ **+ noun** *Cats developing in different environments have different learning experiences and end up with different hunting behaviours.*

hur·dle /ˈhɜːdl; *NAmE* ˈhɜːrdl/ *noun* a problem or difficulty that must be solved or dealt with before you can achieve sth SYN OBSTACLE (1): *Various major technological hurdles must be overcome before fuel cells can compete effectively.*

hurt¹ /hɜːt; *NAmE* hɜːrt/ *verb* (**hurt, hurt**) **1** [T, I] **~ (sb/sth/yourself)** to cause physical pain to sb/yourself; to injure sb/yourself: *The intensity of the anger progresses from destroying things to physically hurting people.* ◇ *He felt nauseous and the light hurt his eyes.* ◇ *The procedure is simple and does not hurt.* **2** [I] to feel painful: *She complained that her back hurt.* ◇ **it hurts** *Ask the patient if it hurts anywhere in their chest when they swallow.* **3** [T, I] to make sb unhappy or upset: **~ sb/sth** *In his letters, he worries about having hurt the feelings of his mother.* ◇ **it hurts (sb) (to do sth)** *It hurts us to think of people we love dying.* ◇ *It hurts when the people we most want to love us are not available to provide that love.* **4** [T] **~ sb/sth** to have a bad effect on sb/sth: *Periods of high inflation hurt the poor most of all.* ◇ *This policy is likely to hurt the country's competitiveness in the long run.*

hurt² /hɜːt; *NAmE* hɜːrt/ *adj.* **1** injured physically: *She might have been seriously hurt or even killed.* **2** upset and offended by sth that sb has said or done: *Remarks like these soon found their way back to Hunt, who was deeply hurt.* ◇ *It is wrong to think that the harm of insult is entirely a matter of whether a person has hurt feelings.*

hurt³ /hɜːt; *NAmE* hɜːrt/ *noun* [U, sing.] a feeling of unhappiness because sb has not been fair or kind to you: *Hurt and disappointment are the foundation for pessimism.*

hus·band /ˈhʌzbənd/ *noun* the man that a woman is married to; a married man: *Husbands and wives commonly provide the day-to-day care when one partner is ill or disabled.*

hy·brid[1] /ˈhaɪbrɪd/ *adj.* **1** of mixed character; formed from two or more different things: *The European Commission is a hybrid organization, somewhere between an executive and a bureaucracy.* **2** (of an animal or a plant) having parents of different species or varieties: *The Kenyan Ministry of Agriculture recommends the use of hybrid seeds to increase maize yields.* **3** (of a vehicle, machine or system) using two different types of power, for example petrol and electricity: *Many observers believe that hybrid cars are destined to play a key role in the future.*

hy·brid[2] /ˈhaɪbrɪd/ *noun* **1** an animal or a plant that has parents of different species or varieties: *By 1959, 90% to 100% of all corn varieties planted were hybrids.* ◇ **~ of A and B** *The red wolf was found to be a hybrid of coyotes and grey wolves.* **2 ~ (between/of A and B)** something that is the product of combining two or more different things SYN MIXTURE (1): *Some agencies are more of a hybrid between state institutions and for-profit organizations.* ◇ *Most organizations will adopt an approach that is a hybrid of the two systems.* **3** a vehicle that uses two different types of power, for example petrol and electricity: *Pure electric cars, as opposed to hybrids, are cheap to run and produce almost no carbon emissions.*

hy·brid·ize (*BrE also* **-ise**) /ˈhaɪbrɪdaɪz/ *verb* [I, T] (of an animal or a plant) to be produced from parents of different species or varieties; to produce an animal or a plant from parents of different species or varieties: **~ with sth** *The invasive species may hybridize with the local species.* ◇ **~ sth** *Blows (1999) hybridized two species of Drosophila flies.* ■ **hy·brid·iza·tion, -isa·tion** /ˌhaɪbrɪdaɪˈzeɪʃn; *NAmE* ˌhaɪbrɪdəˈzeɪʃn/ *noun* [U] **~ (of sth)** *Mendel was chiefly concerned with the hybridization of species as an alternative to evolution.*

hydro·car·bon /ˌhaɪdrəˈkɑːbən; *NAmE* ˌhaɪdrəˈkɑːrbən/ *noun* (*chemistry*) a chemical COMPOUND of HYDROGEN and CARBON. There are many different hydrocarbons found in petrol, coal and natural gas: *Crude petroleum is essentially a mixture of hydrocarbons.* ◇ **+ noun** *Hydrocarbon emissions are often worse when an engine is first started.*

hydro·gen /ˈhaɪdrədʒən/ *noun* [U] (*symb.* **H**) the chemical element of ATOMIC NUMBER 1. Hydrogen is a gas that is the lightest of all the elements. It combines with OXYGEN to form water: **+ noun** *Two hydrogen atoms are joined to the oxygen atom by conventional chemical bonds, to form the water molecule.* ◇ *High energy is required to break the hydrogen bonds holding the polar molecules together.*

hy·droly·sis /haɪˈdrɒlɪsɪs; *NAmE* haɪˈdrɑːlɪsɪs/ *noun* [U] (*chemistry*) a reaction with water which causes a COMPOUND to separate into its parts: **+ noun** *Many hydrolysis reactions proceed with the liberation or uptake of a proton.*

hydro·philic /ˌhaɪdrəˈfɪlɪk/ *adj.* tending to mix with, dissolve in or be made wet by water: *Commonly used hydrophilic substances include soaps and detergents.* OPP HYDROPHOBIC

hydro·pho·bic /ˌhaɪdrəˈfəʊbɪk; *NAmE* ˌhaɪdrəˈfoʊbɪk/ *adj.* tending to REPEL or not mix with water: *Soap molecules possess a hydrophobic part which attracts grease and a hydrophilic part which helps to dissolve the grease in water.* OPP HYDROPHILIC

hy·droxyl /haɪˈdrɒksɪl; haɪˈdrɒksaɪl; *NAmE* haɪˈdrɑːksl/ *noun* (*symb.* **OH**) (in compounds) **+ noun** (*chemistry*) a chemical group with the formula OH, present in alcohols and many other ORGANIC COMPOUNDS: *When the alcohol was heated with concentrated acid, the hydroxyl group was removed and replaced with a bromine atom.*

hy·giene /ˈhaɪdʒiːn/ *noun* [U] the practice of keeping yourself and your living and working areas clean in order to prevent illness and disease: *At times, he neglects his personal hygiene.* ◇ *The level of sanitation and hygiene was extremely poor.* ◇ **+ noun** *Several different reports cite poor hygiene practices at the hospital.*

hy·phen /ˈhaɪfn/ *noun* the mark (-) used to join two words together to make a new one, as in *break-up*, or to show that a word has been divided between the end of one line and the beginning of the next: *Hyphens and dashes both function grammatically to join and separate.* ➲ *compare* DASH

hy·poth·esis AWL /haɪˈpɒθəsɪs; *NAmE* haɪˈpɑːθəsɪs/ *noun* (*pl.* **hy·poth·eses** /haɪˈpɒθəsiːz; *NAmE* haɪˈpɑːθəsiːz/) **1** [C] an idea or explanation of sth that is based on a few known facts but that has not yet been proved to be true or correct SYN THEORY (1): *Additional research is needed to test this hypothesis.* ◇ *The good genes hypothesis predicts that females will prefer to mate with the healthiest males.* ◇ **~ that...** *This supports the hypothesis that similarity to humans influences human attitudes towards animals.* ◇ **~ of sth** *De Vries was anxious to investigate ideas of inheritance in the light of Darwin's hypothesis of the origin of species.* ◇ **~ about sth** *Bacon used this to decide between two hypotheses about the ebb and flow of the tides.* ➲ *see also* NULL HYPOTHESIS **2** [U] guesses and ideas that are not based on certain knowledge SYN SPECULATION (1): *It is neccessary to use a fair degree of hypothesis when trying to reconstruct Viking aims and ambitions in north Britain.*

> **WORD FAMILY**
> hypothesis *noun*
> hypothesize *verb*
> hypothetical *adj.*
> hypothetically *adv.*

▸ ADJECTIVE + HYPOTHESIS **alternative • competing • main • working • simple • plausible • testable • a priori • scientific** *Diamond and Carey (1986) investigated an alternative hypothesis.*

▸ VERB + HYPOTHESIS **propose • test • support, corroborate • confirm, verify • accept • reject • refute • contradict • generate • formulate • develop • examine, investigate, explore • evaluate** *The authors proposed several hypotheses to explain this apparent discrepancy.* ◇ *These results confirm the hypothesis.*

THESAURUS

hypothesis • thesis • proposition • premise *noun*

These are all words for an idea that sb puts forward but that has not yet been proved, especially one used as the basis of an argument or a theory.

- the hypothesis/thesis/premise **of** sth
- a hypothesis/thesis/proposition **about** sth
- the hypothesis/thesis/proposition/premise **that...**
- the **central/main** thesis/premise
- a **general** thesis/proposition
- a **false** proposition/premise
- to **support/accept/reject** a hypothesis/thesis/proposition/premise
- to **develop** a hypothesis/thesis/proposition
- to **test** a hypothesis/proposition

- A **hypothesis** is an idea that you aim to prove to be either true or false through research; a **thesis** is a statement that you present, support and discuss in order to show that it is true: *Thus far, empirical results testing this hypothesis have been mixed...* ◇ *The central thesis of the article is that companies must monitor change in the external environment or they risk decline.*
- A **premise** and a **proposition** can both form the basis of a theory or an argument: **premise** is typically used to talk about a logical or reasonable idea; **proposition** can be used to talk about an opinion: *The underlying premise of Grameen is that, in order to emerge from poverty, landless peasants need access to credit.* ◇ *Consider the proposition that certain public health challenges, such as very high obesity levels, are a result of an accumulation of poor individual choices.*

hy·pothe·size (*BrE also* -ise) AWL /haɪˈpɒθəsaɪz; *NAmE* haɪˈpɑːθəsaɪz/ *verb* **1** [T] to suggest sth as a hypothesis: **~ sth** *The existence of a large asteroid with an orbit between Mercury and the Sun was hypothesized by Le Verrier in 1859.* ◇ **~ that...** *We hypothesized that the more educated parents are, the more demands they will place on schools.* ◇ **it is hypothesized that...** *It was hypothesized that people who are optimistic have better health.* **2** [I] to form a hypothesis: *Students are encouraged to hypothesize, be curious and take risks in answering questions.* ◇ **~ about sth** *He had hypothesized correctly about evolutionary links between birds and dinosaurs.*

hypo·thet·ic·al AWL /ˌhaɪpəˈθetɪkl/ *adj.* based on situations or ideas which are possible and imagined rather than real and true; based on or serving as a hypothesis: *This hypothetical example, however, is inconsistent with real-life observation.* ◇ *to take a hypothetical situation/case/scenario* ■ **hypo·thet·ic·al·ly** /ˌhaɪpəˈθetɪkli/ *adv.*: *Extreme outcomes cannot be eliminated altogether and are hypothetically possible.*

I i

I /aɪ/ *pron.* used as the subject of a verb when the speaker or writer is referring to himself/herself: *I know I am normal, but I am not so sure about anyone else.* ◇ *On this basic premise, she and I disagree.* ⊃ *see also* ME

ibid. /ˈɪbɪd/ (*also* **ib.**) *abbr.* in the same book or piece of writing as the one that has just been mentioned (from Latin 'ibidem'): *After the earthquake Gandhi said, 'This divine calamity has suddenly reminded us that all humanity is one' (ibid, p.40).*

ice /aɪs/ *noun* **1** [U] water that has frozen and become solid: *Sea ice covers a vast area of the world's surface.* ◇ **+ noun** *Frost, resulting in the formation of ice crystals in plant tissue, may lead to plant death.* **2** [sing.] (*usually* **the ice**) a layer of frozen water on the surface of water: *In the summer the bears can no longer hunt seals from the ice.* **3** [U] a piece of ice used to keep food and drinks cold: *It was noticed that consumers were adding ice to cider to cool it down.*

IDM **on ˈice** kept cold by being surrounded by ice: *The cells were kept on ice.*

ˈice age *noun* one of the long periods of time, thousands of years ago, when much of the earth's surface was covered in ice: *Shortly after the end of the last ice age, global temperatures soared by about 14°F in about a decade.*

ice·berg /ˈaɪsbɜːg; *NAmE* ˈaɪsbɜːrg/ *noun* an extremely large mass of ice floating in the sea: *As the West Greenland Current heads north, it collects icebergs from some of the most active glaciers in the world.* IDM *see* TIP[1]

ˈice cap *noun* a layer of ice permanently covering parts of the earth, especially around the North and South Poles: *Global warming is already causing the polar ice caps to melt.*

ˈice sheet *noun* a layer of ice that covers a large area of land for a long period of time: *As the ice sheets melted, world sea levels rose.*

icon /ˈaɪkɒn; *NAmE* ˈaɪkɑːn/ *noun* **1** a famous person or thing that people admire and see as a symbol of a particular idea, way of life, etc: *There are playful references to Shakespeare's status as a cultural icon.* **2** a small symbol on a computer screen that represents a program or a file: *The bottom row of icons is concerned with running the simulation.* **3** (in the Orthodox Church) a painting of a HOLY person, usually on a piece of wood, that is also thought of as a HOLY object: *Repin began his career painting icons.*

icon·ic /aɪˈkɒnɪk; *NAmE* aɪˈkɑːnɪk/ *adj.* acting as a sign or symbol of sth: *Nujoma is an iconic figure in Namibian history and politics.*

THESAURUS

idea ♦ **concept** ♦ **notion** *noun*

These are all words for a principle or an opinion about a topic.

- the idea/concept/notion **of** sth
- an idea/a notion **about** sth
- a/an **general/basic/important/fundamental/key/central** idea/notion/concept
- a/an **theoretical/traditional/abstract** idea/concept/notion
- to **have/develop/introduce** an idea/a concept/a notion
- to **discuss/explore/explain/understand** an idea/a concept/a notion
- to **support/reject/challenge** an idea/a concept/a notion

- **Idea** is the most general of these words; it can be used in both informal and formal academic contexts, about sth abstract, physical or creative; **concept** and **notion** are more formal words, used to talk mainly about abstract ideas: *Good science builds and refines good ideas—it does not reject them out of hand.* ◇ *Creative ideas become useful innovations when they are successfully applied.*
- A **concept** is typically an abstract principle that relates to a particular topic; **notion** is used more often to talk about a belief or an understanding of sth: *There are several key concepts that are fundamental to axiomatic design.* ◇ *Clans loom large in popular notions about the Scottish past, yet there is much about their historical reality which remains unclear.*

idea /aɪˈdɪə; *NAmE* aɪˈdiːə/ *noun* **1** [C] an opinion or a belief about sb/sth: *Marx used these ideas to sketch a history of economic change.* ◇ **~ about sth** *They discuss Leavis's ideas about the nature of literature and its place in social life.* ◇ **~ on sth** *Much of this thinking is not new or different from mainstream ideas on community development.* ◇ **~ of sth** *It is often claimed that the idea of race has a long history.* ◇ **~ that...** *Experimental evidence supports the idea that this enzyme is important in plant growth.* **2** [C] a plan, thought or suggestion as to a possible course of action: **~ to do sth** *It seemed like a bad idea to speak openly about such incidents.* ◇ **~ of sth** *Countries in the region are keen to embrace the idea of economic reform.* ◇ **~ of doing sth** *Most of them had accepted the idea of proclaiming martial law.* ◇ **~ for (doing) sth** *Each volunteer is asked to contribute his or her ideas for improvement and development.* **3** [U, sing.] a picture or impression in your mind: **~ of sth** *An idea of probable numbers can be gained by reference to contemporary anecdotes.* ◇ **~ (that)...** *One should not get the idea that this was a problem specific to that time or place.* **4 the idea** [sing.] the aim or purpose of sth: *The central idea was to learn from success stories outside the region.* ◇ **~ of (doing) sth** *The idea of a cipher system is to make confidential information unintelligible to an unauthorized person.*

IDM **have no iˈdea** to not know sth at all: *They had no idea how the war had started.* ◇ *The Internet user has no idea the data are being collected.*

▸ ADJECTIVE + IDEA **good** *For many children with behaviour problems, seeing a clinical child psychologist is a good idea.* ◇ *The company can get a good idea of potential consumer reactions using this kind of tool.* | **general** ♦ **basic, fundamental** ♦ **main** ♦ **key** ♦ **central** *Their basic ideas remained similar to Saint Augustine's.* | **new** ♦ **old** ♦ **traditional** ♦ **different** ♦ **clear** ♦ **simple** *This was a government in search of clear ideas for structural change.* | **theoretical** ♦ **liberal** ♦ **religious** ♦ **political** *This idea of testing theoretical ideas by the experimental method was radical.*

▸ VERB + IDEA **have** *The GP is likely to have some idea of the patient's priorities.* | **develop • generate • support • reinforce • promote • accept • reject • challenge • introduce • use • apply • present • discuss • explore • include • take • test • convey • illustrate** *The focus of the research is on how organizations develop new ideas for problem solving.* | **share • express** *He expressed his ideas in novels, plays and biographical studies.* | **get • give** *General product data give an idea of the standard of living in the country.*

ideal[1] /aɪˈdiːəl/ *adj.* **1** perfect; most suitable: *This was the ideal solution from the bishops' point of view.* ◇ **~ for sb/sth** *Much of the country is, however, ideal for livestock.* **2** [only before noun] the best that can be imagined, but not likely to become real: *Poor people in Aristotle's ideal state would be allowed to choose officials, but not to hold office.* IDM see WORLD

ideal[2] /aɪˈdiːəl/ *noun* **1 ~ (of sb/sth)** an idea or a standard that seems perfect and worth trying to achieve: *Kant was a supporter of the democratic ideals of the French Revolution.* ◇ *Legg attacked the National Trust for betraying the ideals of its Victorian founders.* **2** [usually sing.] **~ (of sth)** a person or thing considered as perfect: *His ideal of manhood was a strong, rugged, resourceful character.*

ideal·ism /aɪˈdiːəlɪzəm/ *noun* [U] **1** (*philosophy*) the belief that our ideas are the only things that are real or that we can know about: *Feuerbach was a stern critic of Hegel's idealism.* ➲ *compare* MATERIALISM (2), REALISM (3) **2 ~ (of sb/sth)** the belief that a perfect life, situation, etc. can be achieved, even when this is not realistic: *The idealism of the 1930s took some hard knocks in subsequent years.* ■ **ideal·ist** /aɪˈdiːəlɪst/ *noun*: *The thought of the minor German idealist Karl Krause was introduced to Spain by Julian Sanz del Rio.* ◇ *In the novel, Lydgate and Dorothea are portrayed as two young idealists committed to progress through social reform.*

ideal·is·tic /ˌaɪdiəˈlɪstɪk/ *adj.* having a strong belief in perfect standards and trying to achieve them, even when this is not realistic: *Many have a very idealistic view of marriage.*

ideal·ize (*BrE also* -ise) /aɪˈdiːəlaɪz/ *verb* **~ sb/sth** to consider or represent sb/sth as being perfect or better than they really are: *The book idealizes the past.* ◇ *The pastoral presents an idealized version of nature.* ■ **ideal·iza·tion, -isa·tion** /aɪˌdiːəlaɪˈzeɪʃn; *NAmE* aɪˌdiːələˈzeɪʃn/ *noun* [U, C] **~ (of sb/sth)** *Carter 'challenges the idealization of childhood as a natural state of innocence'.* ◇ *Kant defended the use of idealizations in scientific theories.*

ideal·ly /aɪˈdiːəli/ *adv.* **1** in an IDEAL situation: *Ideally, standards would be internationally agreed.* **2** perfectly: *Health visitors are ideally suited to undertake this work.*

iden·ti·cal AWL /aɪˈdentɪkl/ *adj.* **1** similar in every detail: *Even chickens kept in identical conditions and fed the same food will vary in weight.* ◇ *Consumers demand a large range of different varieties of similar, but not identical, products.* ◇ **~ to sb/sth** *The element has a crystal structure identical to that of carbon in diamonds.* ◇ **~ with sb/sth** *The wording is identical with the wording of Article 14 of the EU Directive on Electronic Commerce.* **2 the identical** [only before noun] the same: *The Court found that they were being taxed at a much higher rate than the identical products in Northern Ireland.*

iden·ti·cal·ly AWL /aɪˈdentɪkli/ *adv.* in exactly the same way: *The results indicate that the judges treat identically the requests of politicians from different parties.*

iden·ti·fi·able AWL /aɪˌdentɪˈfaɪəbl/ *adj.* that can be recognized: *Mass opposition was driven by clearly identifiable groups.* ◇ **~ by sth** *The plants are identifiable by their characteristic smell.*

iden·ti·fi·ca·tion AWL /aɪˌdentɪfɪˈkeɪʃn/ *noun* **1** [U] **~ (of sb/sth)** the process of finding or discovering sb/sth: *Screening has focused on the identification of persons with certain genetic disorders.* ◇ *The article provides an overview of approaches to the identification of the causes of environmental problems.* **2** [U, C] the process of recognizing sb/sth and being able to say who or what they are: *All birds were banded for individual identification.* ◇ **~ of sth** *The identification of the victim's body took place some eight hours after death.* ◇ *Developments of this kind offer the prospect of rapid and reliable identifications of many different species in future.* **3** (*abbr.* **ID**) [U] official papers or a document that can prove sb's identity: *The defendant was alleged to have shown identification stolen from Baker's wallet.* **4** [C, U] **~ (with sb/sth)** a strong feeling of sympathy, understanding or support for sb/sth: *The president proclaimed his identification with the average citizen.* ◇ *Members of a vulnerable group will feel a greater sense of identification with an institution devoted specifically to its interests.* **5** [U, C] **~ (of sb) (with sb/sth)** the process of making a close connection between one person or thing and another: *A common strategy was the identification of a Roman god or goddess with a native one.*

▸ ADJECTIVE + IDENTIFICATION **early • rapid • correct, accurate • visual** *Early identification of the condition is of paramount importance.* ◇ *Correct identification of nematode species is essential for treating infections.* | **strong • social • ethnic • personal** *Ethnic identification was measured with one item: 'Do you feel more Moroccan or more Dutch?'*

▸ NOUN + IDENTIFICATION **species** *A comprehensive evaluation of the reliability of species identification by fishing tourists was conducted throughout the study.* | **class • party** *My results show that individuals' attitudes towards class identification change a great deal over time.*

▸ VERB + IDENTIFICATION **allow, enable, permit • facilitate** *A systematic approach enabled the identification of local businesses that might sell these products.* | **make** *High levels of stress can reduce an eyewitness's ability to recall and make an accurate identification.*

iden·ti·fier /aɪˈdentɪfaɪə(r)/ *noun* **1** a thing that identifies sb/sth: *A barcode provides a unique identifier for each item in a retail store.* **2** (*computing*) a series of characters used to refer to a program or set of data within a program: *RDF fragment identifiers can contain any UNICODE characters.*

iden·tify AWL /aɪˈdentɪfaɪ/ *verb* (**iden·ti·fies, iden·ti·fy·ing, iden·ti·fied, iden·ti·fied**) **1** to find or discover sb/sth: **~ sb/sth** *The test was intended to identify patients with schizophrenia.* ◇ **~ sb/sth as sth** *Several social and economic factors have been identified as important in explaining this variation.* ◇ **~ what/which, etc...** *Employees learn to identify what the company recognizes as acceptable business practices.* ➲ thesaurus note *at* DETERMINE **2** to recognize sb/sth and be able to say who or what they are: **~ sb/sth/yourself** *Both men failed to identify him in court.* ◇ *There was an error in correctly identifying the sample.* ◇ **~ sb/sth/yourself as sb/sth** *One of the suspects identified himself as a security consultant.* **3** to make it possible to recognize who or what sb/sth is: **~ sb/sth** *Slaves were also obliged to wear a costume that identified them immediately.* ◇ **~ sb/sth as sb/sth** *These common traits identify individuals as members of a given culture.*

PHR V **iˈdentify with sb** to feel that you can understand and share the feelings of sb else: *They may identify with each other because of their similar social class or ethnic background.* **iˈdentify sb/sth with sb/sth** to consider sb/sth to be the same as sb/sth else SYN EQUATE (1): *The Romans identified the Greek god Zeus with their deity Jupiter.* ◇ *He believes that good people identify their own interests with those of society as a whole.* **be iˈdentified with sb/sth | iˈdentify yourself with sb/sth** to have a close association or connection with sb/sth: *The church became increasingly identified with opposition to the regime.* ◇ *Members of a film audience tend to identify themselves with the film's hero or heroine.*

▸ IDENTIFY + NOUN **factor • problem • issue • theme • area • number • group • individual • patient • type • need • source • study • cause • effect • difference • pattern • characteristic, feature • strategy • case • gene • protein** *The problems identified by Hobsbawm are complex.* ◇ *Soil samples were analysed, and the results were used to identify areas of human activity.*

▸ ADVERB + IDENTIFY **accurately • clearly • explicitly, specifically • easily, readily • quickly • initially • originally • commonly • uniquely** *The technique can be used to accurately identify the location of a tumour.* ◇ *The colour uniquely identified each chromosome.*

iden·tity AWL /aɪˈdentəti/ *noun* (*pl.* **-ies**) **1** [C, U] the characteristics that make a person or thing who or what they are and make them different from others: *He questions whether national identities and interests are gradually being replaced by European ones.* ◇ *Culture provides individuals within a society with a sense of identity.* **2** [C, U] (*abbr.* **ID**) **~ (of sb/sth)** the fact of being who or what a person or thing is: *The identity of the assailants was not known.* ◇ *Requests for access to medical records should include proof of identity.* **3** [U] the state of being the same as sb/sth; the feeling of having a close association or connection with sb/sth: **~ between A and B** *In an autobiography, there must be identity between the author, the narrator and the subject.* ◇ **~ with sb/sth** *The aim is to alter the attitudes of employees through the development of identity with the organization.* **4** [C] (*mathematics*) an EQUATION that is true for all possible values of the letters in the EQUATION, for example $(x + 1)^2 = x^2 + 2x + 1$: *In fact, this equation is an identity and there is no unique value of x.*

> **WORD FAMILY**
> identity *noun*
> identify *verb*
> identification *noun*
> identifiable *adj.*
> unidentified *adj.*

▸ ADJECTIVE + IDENTITY **new** *The couple have abandoned their past lives and assumed new identities.* | **different • distinct • personal, individual, own • collective • common • multiple • national • regional • cultural • ethnic, racial • religious • social • sexual • political • professional** *These refugees founded temples and cultural centres to maintain their cultural and religious identity.*

▸ NOUN + IDENTITY **gender • group** *Group identity also involves a belief that all members share a common fate.*

▸ VERB + IDENTITY **establish • determine** *Police have not yet established the identity of the wrongdoer.* | **create, develop, construct, build, form, forge • shape • define • maintain, preserve • reinforce • assert • retain • lose • share • express • acquire** *They failed to consider how identities are constructed in an increasingly multicultural world.* | **reveal** *Visitors to this site post questions anonymously, without revealing their identity.*

ideo·logic·al AWL /ˌaɪdiəˈlɒdʒɪkl; *NAmE* ˌaɪdiəˈlɑːdʒɪkl/ *adj.* (*sometimes disapproving*) connected with an ideology: *It is clear that whatever the ideological position of governments, they will always see economic success as crucial for their survival.* ◇ *Burns (1967: 198) notes that British academics in the 1920s had an 'ideological bias against business'.* ■ **ideo·logic·al·ly** AWL /ˌaɪdiəˈlɒdʒɪkli; *NAmE* ˌaɪdiəˈlɑːdʒɪkli/ *adv.*: *The claims have been dismissed as ideologically motivated, rather than empirically based.*

ideol·ogy AWL /ˌaɪdiˈɒlədʒi; *NAmE* ˌaɪdiˈɑːlədʒi/ *noun* (*pl.* **-ies**) [C, U] (*sometimes disapproving*) a set of ideas and beliefs that an economic or political system is based on, or that influences the way a person or group behaves: *The United States and the Soviet Union were both prepared to risk nuclear war for their political ideologies.* ◇ *Conservation became a key feature of Boy Scout ideology.* HELP The term **ideology** is sometimes used in a disapproving way to suggest a set of beliefs that are too fixed or not realistic or fair: *Their economic policy was based on ideology rather than sound economics.*

idiom /ˈɪdiəm/ *noun* **1** [C] a group of words whose meaning is different from the meanings of the individual words: *Comparisons have been made regarding the translators' handling of cultural concepts, idioms, metaphors, etc.* **2** [C] the kind of language and grammar used by particular people at a particular time or place: *Murray uses the Scottish idiom of his ancestors in his poetry.* **3** [C] the style of writing, music, art, etc. that is typical of a particular person, group, period or place: *In the show, the overall musical idiom is the pop song.* **4** [U] a form of expression natural to a language, person or group of people: *He has a keen ear for idiom.*

idiom·at·ic /ˌɪdiəˈmætɪk/ *adj.* **1** containing expressions that are natural to a NATIVE SPEAKER of a language: *The English translation is accurate and idiomatic.* **2** containing an idiom: *Idiomatic expressions often have a colourful literal meaning.*

i.e. /ˌaɪ ˈiː/ *abbr.* used to explain exactly what the previous thing that you have mentioned means (from Latin 'id est'): *Strict Jews eat kosher food, i.e. food that is fit to be eaten in accordance with Jewish law.*

> **LANGUAGE BANK**
>
> **Explaining what you mean**
>
> In academic writing, there are various ways of giving a more detailed explanation of what you mean.
>
> **i.e. • that is • In other words • or rather • or more precisely • specifically**
>
> – *Studies indicate that playing certain types of computer games (**i.e.** action games that involve rapid movement) improves visual intelligence skills.*
> – *The major purpose of the programme is to help students develop empathy; **that is**, the ability to understand the position of another person.*
> – *Most people in the industrialized world will have been hospitalized for some kind of operation. **In other words**, being ill is part of life.*
> – *The situation in England is radically different, **or rather** the textual evidence is.*
> – *We are interested in the voltage (**or more precisely**, the potential) which a cell produces when no current is flowing.*
> – *The plural morpheme can attach only to nouns—**specifically**, to singular countable nouns which do not have an irregular plural.*

if /ɪf/ *conj.* **1** used to say that one thing can, will or might happen or be true, depending on another thing happening or being true: *If this analysis is correct, several points follow.* ◇ *This will be the case if the government continues its current industrial and economic policies.* ◇ *The employer would be equally responsible if the act had been performed by an independent contractor.* ◇ **~ necessary** *It has powers to investigate breaches of EU law and, if necessary, to impose fines on governments.* **2** when; whenever; every time: *If a downward force is applied to the cylinder, more fluid flows into it.* ◇ *The pain becomes worse if he moves.* **3** used after *ask, know, find out, wonder*, etc. to introduce one of two or more possibilities SYN WHETHER: *There is no way of knowing if he is right.* ➲ grammar note *at* WHETHER **4** used before an adjective or adverb to introduce a contrast: *Hume offers a plausible, if rather depressing, explanation of this.* ◇ **~ at all** *The living conditions of the people improved little, if at all.*

IDM **ˌif and ˈwhen** used to say sth about an event that may or may not happen: *The information would only be revealed if and when the child required it as an adult.* **if ˈanything** used to suggest that sth may possibly be the case, especially the opposite of sth previously suggested: *The pace of change does not appear to have slowed, but if anything to have increased.* **if 'not 1** used to introduce a different suggestion, after a sentence with *if*: *If there is no improvement, a check should be made that the patient is taking the prescribed drugs. If not, the reason should be determined.* **2** used to suggest that sth may be even larger, more important, etc. than was first stated: *There is considerable evidence that most, if not all, of the Earth was covered with permanent ice.* **it is not as if** it is not the case that: *It is not as if we have only recently discovered that children raised in the same home still have distinct characters.* **'only if** used to state the only situation in which sth can happen: *A firm will reinvest profits only if it expects to earn more profits.*

ig·ne·ous /ˈɪgniəs/ *adj.* (*earth science*) (of rocks) formed when MAGMA (= melted or liquid material lying below the earth's surface) becomes solid, especially after it has poured out of a VOLCANO: *Igneous rocks are those that have formed from molten magma.* ◇ *Sedimentary rocks are generally much less dense than the deeper igneous material.* ⊃ *compare* METAMORPHIC, SEDIMENTARY

I

ig·nite /ɪgˈnaɪt/ *verb* **1** [I, T] to start to burn; to make sth start to burn: *The higher temperatures may have created greater opportunities for fires to ignite and spread.* ◇ **~ sth** *Just before the piston reaches the top dead centre (TDC), a spark ignites the fuel/air mixture.* **2** [T] **~ sth** to cause sth to start, especially sth dangerous or exciting: *A second crisis was ignited by the 1930 London naval conference.* ◇ *The incident ignited a heated public debate.*

ig·nor·ance AWL /ˈɪgnərəns/ *noun* [U] a lack of knowledge or information about sth: *The survey revealed a disturbing level of ignorance among Americans, especially in terms of geographical knowledge.* ◇ **~ of sth** *He theorized that the confusion resulted from contemporary ignorance of basic physical laws.* ◇ **~ about sth** *Through careful questioning, Socrates reveals the expert's ignorance about the very things he ought to know best.* ◇ **in ~ (of sth)** *Doctors left her in ignorance of her test results for over a month.*

ig·nor·ant AWL /ˈɪgnərənt/ *adj.* lacking knowledge or information about sth; not educated: *Newspapers characterized Russia's vast peasant population as ignorant, backward and passive.* ◇ **~ of sth** *Even scientists are largely ignorant of developments in fields outside their own specialism.* ◇ **~ about sth** *We are still relatively ignorant about the causes of ageing-related illnesses.*

ig·nore AWL /ɪgˈnɔː(r)/ *verb* **1 ~ sth** to deliberately pay no attention to sth SYN DISREGARD[1]: *During the 1930s, Britain and the US ignored Soviet warnings about the threat Hitler posed to world peace.* **2 ~ sth** to fail to consider an important aspect of sth: *He remarked that rational theories ignore the obvious fact that personal goals change over time.*

ill[1] /ɪl/ *adj.* **1** (*especially BrE*) (*NAmE usually* **sick**) [not usually before noun] suffering from an illness or disease; not feeling well: *These patients are often critically ill and require rapid assessment and intervention.* ◇ *Some individuals are at greater risk of becoming mentally ill than others.* ◇ *A further cause of increased levels of sickness absence was employees going to work despite feeling ill.* ◇ *Byron fell ill in Greece in 1823 with a fever and died the following spring.* ⊃ *see also* ILLNESS **2** [usually before noun] bad or harmful: *Compensation was paid to residents who suffered ill effects from the pollution.* ◇ *Smith was shocked at the poverty, overwork and ill treatment of many of the workers.*

IDM **ˌill at ˈease** feeling embarrassed and uncomfortable: *Respondents with a low score tend to be anxious and ill at ease in social situations.*

ill[2] /ɪl/ *adv.* **1** (especially in compounds) badly or in an unpleasant way: *It was claimed that they had been ill-treated in custody.* **2** badly; not in an acceptable way: *The courts have perhaps been ill served by the legislature, which has drafted laws that are rather imprecise.* **3** only with difficulty: *They could ill afford to lose existing financial backers.*

il·legal AWL /ɪˈliːgl/ *adj.* not allowed by the law: *Thousands of illegal immigrants entered the country on forged travel documents.* ◇ *Many illegal activities, such as the sale of illicit drugs, are part of the underground economy.* ◇ *Social, religious or national discrimination was declared illegal.* ◇ **it is ~ to do sth** *From 2003 it was illegal to advertise tobacco products.* OPP LEGAL (2) ■ **il·legal·ly** AWL /ɪˈliːgəli/ *adv.*: *In 2001, there were an estimated 3.5 million Mexicans living illegally in the United States.*

il·legal·ity AWL /ˌɪliˈgæləti/ *noun* [U] **~ (of sth)** the fact of not being allowed by law: *The 1936 Constitution, while restoring civil rights to priests, confirmed the illegality of religious propaganda.* ⊃ *compare* LEGALITY (1)

il·legit·im·ate /ˌɪləˈdʒɪtəmət/ *adj.* **1** not allowed by a particular set of rules or by law SYN UNAUTHORIZED: *The USA's decision to invade was viewed as illegitimate by many nations.* OPP LEGITIMATE (2) **2** born to parents who are not married to each other: *After 1733, fathers of illegitimate children were required by law to support them.* OPP LEGITIMATE (3) ■ **il·legit·im·acy** /ˌɪləˈdʒɪtəməsi/ *noun* [U] *One important factor is the degree of government repression or illegitimacy.* ◇ *Cook notes that the decline in illegitimacy, 1945–60, reflected the sexual restraint of the period.* **il·legit·im·ate·ly** *adv.*: *Marx argued that the working class was able to be exploited because they had been illegitimately deprived of access to the land.*

ˌill ˈhealth *noun* [U] the poor condition of a person's body or mind: *Older people are more susceptible to the disorder, especially when they already suffer from ill health.*

il·licit /ɪˈlɪsɪt/ *adj.* **1** not allowed by the law SYN ILLEGAL: *It is estimated that over 40% of 15- and 16-year-olds have used illicit drugs.* **2** not approved of by the normal rules of society: *Middle-class men satisfied their lusts in illicit relationships with women of a lower class.*

il·lit·er·ate /ɪˈlɪtərət/ *adj.* **1 ~ (in sth)** (of a person) not knowing how to read or write OPP LITERATE (1): *A large percentage of the rural population was illiterate.* **2** (usually after a noun or adverb) not knowing very much about a particular subject area: *They underestimated the extent to which the voters were politically illiterate.* OPP LITERATE (2) ■ **il·lit·er·acy** /ɪˈlɪtərəsi/ *noun* [U] *There were high rates of poverty and illiteracy.*

ill·ness /ˈɪlnəs/ *noun* **1** [U] the state of being physically or mentally ill: *An insurance scheme paid out compensation for an inability to work due to illness or injury.* ◇ *She argued that people who suffer from serious mental illness should be enabled to live within the community.* ◇ **with (...) ~** *New regulations governed the provision of care for those with chronic illness.* **2** [C] a type or period of illness: **(with a/an...) ~** *Stigma is a serious problem encountered by people with a mental illness.* ◇ *Serious and prolonged childhood illnesses had also affected the patient's emotional development.* ⊃ thesaurus note *at* DISEASE

▸ ADJECTIVE + ILLNESS **chronic, long-standing, long-term** • **acute** • **serious, severe** • **critical** • **life-threatening** • **terminal** • **minor** • **physical** • **mental, psychiatric, psychological** • **depressive** • **respiratory** *Some patients will need investigation to be convinced that they do not have a physical illness.*

▸ VERB + ILLNESS **cause** • **have** • **suffer (from), experience** • **develop** • **prevent** • **manage** • **treat** *Throughout history, people have used herbs and plant extracts to treat illnesses and to dress wounds.*

il·logic·al AWL /ɪˈlɒdʒɪkl; NAmE ɪˈlɑːdʒɪkl/ *adj.* not logical or sensible: *Depressed patients tend to think in illogical ways, such as drawing a general conclusion from a single event.* ◇ **~ to do sth** *Abadi shows that it would be illogical to argue for freedom and equality simultaneously.* OPP LOGICAL (2)

il·lu·min·ate /ɪˈluːmɪneɪt/ *verb* **1 ~ sth** to make sth clearer or easier to understand SYN CLARIFY: *Evolutionary thought illuminates medical issues from a fresh angle.* ◇ *Liu et al. (2002) provide evidence that illuminates the connections between these seemingly different trends.* ◇ **~ how/what, etc...** *Libet's results illuminate how free will operates.* **2 ~ sth** to shine light on sth: *The surface of the tympanum is illuminated by a laser beam.*

il·lu·min·at·ing /ɪˈluːmɪneɪtɪŋ/ *adj.* helping to make sth clear or easier to understand: *The answer was brief and not very illuminating.* ◇ *An illuminating example of the documentary approach in Civil War literature is Serafimovich's 'The Iron Flood'.*

il·lu·min·ation /ɪˌluːmɪˈneɪʃn/ *noun* **1** [U, C] light or a place that light comes from: *This method ensures that the maximum level of illumination reaches the specimen.* ◇ **~ of sth** *The illumination of her face by an unseen source of light is a common visual device in religious painting of this period.* **2** [U] understanding or explanation of sth: *The global epidemic of intergroup conflict—national, ethnic and religious—is badly in need of illumination.*

il·lu·sion /ɪˈluːʒn/ *noun* **1** [C, U] a false idea or belief: *Total security is, of course, an illusion.* ◇ **~ of sth** *Undoubtedly, humans have a need to establish and maintain the illusion of control over their environments.* ◇ **be under/have no illusions (that...)** *Campaigners were under no illusions that these goals would prove easy to achieve.* **2** [C] something that seems to exist but in fact does not, or seems to be sth that it is not: *Helmholtz was interested in visual illusions and the tricks that our senses can play on us.* ◇ **~ of sth** *Film has made it possible to create an illusion of reality in an unprecedented way.*

il·lus·trate AWL /ˈɪləstreɪt/ *verb* **1** to make the meaning of sth clearer by using examples, pictures, etc: **~ sth** *Two examples will serve to illustrate the point.* ◇ *The graph below illustrates the rising trend in obesity within Europe.* ◇ **~ how/what, etc...** *These models illustrate how social determinants of health influence individual health.* ◇ **be illustrated by sth** *The process is well illustrated by the case of competition regulation in the EU.* ◇ **~ sth with sth** *The argument is illustrated with field materials from research in Papua New Guinea.* ➲ grammar note *at* PRESENT[3] ➲ thesaurus note *at* SHOW[1] **2** to show that sth is true or that a situation exists SYN DEMONSTRATE (1): **~ sth** *This essay clearly illustrates the importance of social and cultural context.* ◇ **~ how/what, etc...** *Abbott's work illustrates how professional groups deploy their power to shape career paths.* ◇ **~ that...** *These results illustrate that changes in land temperature had a great effect on CO_2.* ➲ thesaurus note *at* SHOW[1] **3** [usually passive] to use pictures, photographs, diagrams, etc. in a book, etc: **(be) illustrated** *The library holds an illustrated manuscript containing Petrarch's 'Trionfi'.* ◇ **be illustrated with sth** *This book recounts the decades from the 1920s to the 1950s and is richly illustrated with photographs.*

▸ ILLUSTRATE + NOUN **way • fact • nature • difficulty • complexity • problem • difference, distinction** *This graph illustrates the difficulties in trying to assess the effectiveness of sales promotion activities.* | **point • principle • idea, concept • theme • effect • feature • relationship • application** *The analogy of the lock and key is often used to illustrate the concept of specificity.* | **importance • need** *The earthquake illustrated the need to make buildings not only earthquake-proof but also more fireproof.*

▸ NOUN + ILLUSTRATE **figure • diagram • example • case • story** *These concepts are conveniently illustrated by Venn diagrams.* | **fact** *The increase in world inequality is illustrated by the fact that average income in Western Europe is now about fifteen times higher than it is in Africa.*

▸ ADVERB + ILLUSTRATE **nicely, well, neatly • best • amply • perfectly • clearly • graphically, vividly • dramatically • further** *The power of consumer choice is most graphically illustrated by the widespread rejection of GM food by European consumers.*

il·lus·tra·tion AWL /ˌɪləˈstreɪʃn/ *noun* **1** [C, U] an example or a fact that clearly shows the meaning of sth or that sth is true: **as an ~** *Two useful examples can be given here as illustrations.* ◇ **~ of sth** *The case provides a clear illustration of a situation where the employer is not liable for costs.* ◇ **~ of how/what, etc...** *This case study is intended as an illustration of how a practice might start to provide additional support for carers.* ◇ **by way of ~** *By way of illustration, Kitagawa (1991) notes the following two examples:...* ◇ **for the purpose of ~** *For the purpose of illustration, only a two-cylinder engine will be considered here.* **2** [C] a picture or drawing in a book, etc. especially one that explains sth: *As shown in the illustration, buildings were remodelled and painted to resemble Alpine structures.* ◇ **~ to/for sth** *He was asked to draw the illustrations for a new edition of Shakespeare.*

il·lus·tra·tive AWL /ˈɪləstrətɪv; NAmE ɪˈlʌstrətɪv/ *adj.* helping to explain sth or show it more clearly SYN EXPLANATORY: *It should be stressed that this diagram is merely illustrative and is in no sense complete.* ◇ *In this illustrative example, there are two constraints on subsystem X.* ◇ *The city of San Francisco is illustrative: despite a general population increase 1990–2000, the number of black residents declined by 20 000.* ◇ **~ of sth** *The following example is illustrative of this point.*

image AWL /ˈɪmɪdʒ/ *noun* **1** [C, U] the impression that a person, an organization, a product, etc. gives to the public: *The campaign sought to help the company improve its public image.* ◇ *The company used advertising to project and promote brand image.* ◇ **~ of sb/sth** *Films such as 'Jurassic Park' seem to present positive images of strong, intelligent women.* **2** [C] a mental picture that you have of what sb/sth is like: *The visual images that came into my mind as she spoke were extremely vivid.* ◇ **~ of sth** *Respondents were asked to form a mental image of a farm animal.* ◇ **+ noun** *The patient was suffering from low self-esteem due to body image problems.* ➲ *see also* SELF-IMAGE **3** [C] a picture of sb/sth seen in a mirror, through a camera, or on a television or computer: *Earlier 3-D technology had failed to produce convincing images.* ◇ **~ of sth** *Citizens in the more affluent societies are often presented with televised images of human suffering.* ➲ *see also* MIRROR IMAGE **4** [C] **~ (of sth)** a copy of sb/sth in the form of a picture or statue: *They prayed to stone images of their gods.* **5** [C] a word or phrase used with a different meaning from its normal one, in order to describe sth in a way that produces a strong picture in the mind: *Beer (1993) discusses Romantic poetic images developed by Hardy, Forster, Woolf and Lawrence.* ◇ **~ of sth** *Plato uses the image of a mirror to describe the process via which artists produce their work.*

im·agery AWL /ˈɪmɪdʒəri/ *noun* [U] **1** pictures, photographs, etc: *The visual imagery employed in the advert was both unique and memorable.* ◇ *Using satellite imagery, it was possible to estimate how rapidly the forest is being cleared.* ◇ **~ of sth** *The advertising message is communicated through stunning imagery of the natural world.* **2** language that produces pictures in the minds of people reading or listening: *The poetry is sumptuous in imagery, form and mood.* ◇ **~ of sth** *All human relationships within the poems are conditioned by imagery of invasions and conquests.* ➲ *see also* METAPHOR

I

im·agin·ary /ɪˈmædʒɪnəri; *NAmE* ɪˈmædʒɪneri/ *adj.* existing only in the mind or imagination: *The rest of the novel describes Jack's imaginary adventures.* ◇ *A wavefront is an imaginary line that connects all the points representing a particular peak or trough in a wave.* OPP REAL (1)

iˌmaginary ˈnumber *noun* (*mathematics*) a number expressed as the SQUARE ROOT of a negative number, especially the square root of -1: *Imaginary numbers are all multiples of the number i which is defined to be the square root of minus one.* ➲ *compare* COMPLEX NUMBER, REAL NUMBER

im·agin·ation /ɪˌmædʒɪˈneɪʃn/ *noun* **1** [U, C] the part of your mind that can create a picture or idea, even if it is not real: **in ~** *The whole project as yet exists only in imagination.* ◇ **in sb's ~** *Such neighbourhoods never really existed except in people's imaginations.* ◇ **in the ... ~** *Crime levels were much exaggerated in the popular imagination.* HELP To **capture/catch sb's/the imagination** means to make sb/people very interested or excited: *The phenomenon of global warming has captured the public imagination in recent years.* **2** [U] something that you have imagined rather than sth real: *She discusses the difficulty of defining the difference between imagination and reality.* **3** [U] the ability to have new and exciting ideas: *The assessment measures an applicant's intelligence, imagination and verbal skills.* ◇ *Puckett and Johanek argue that this 'lack of imagination' on the part of politicians poses a major obstacle to education reform.*

im·agina·tive /ɪˈmædʒɪnətɪv/ *adj.* **1** connected with the imagination: *Colonial ideology had a significant influence on Victorian imaginative writing.* ◇ *These non-representational artists produce work that is purely imaginative.* **2** having or showing new and exciting ideas SYN INVENTIVE: *Channel Four's new, forthright, witty and imaginative approach revolutionized British television.* ■ **im·agina·tive·ly** *adv.*: *Used imaginatively, words and sounds can produce extremely effective advertising.*

im·agine /ɪˈmædʒɪn/ *verb* **1** to form a picture in your mind of what sth might be like: **~ sth** *Einstein made a series of 'thought experiments' in which he imagined situations according to the laws of physics.* ◇ *Products derived from organic polymers are so ubiquitous that it is difficult to imagine life without them.* ◇ **~ (that)...** *Participants in the role play were asked to imagine that they had recently become unemployed.* ◇ **~ how/what, etc...** *One can easily imagine how difficult it was for the city states to raise sufficient taxes.* ◇ **~ (sb/sth/yourself) doing sth** *The patient was then asked to imagine standing in the cathedral square of the city where he grew up.* **2** to think that sth is probably true SYN ASSUME (1), SUPPOSE (1): **~ sth** *In this scenario, it is easy to imagine 20 000 new cases of typhoid a year.* ◇ **~ (that)...** *We began working on the project by imagining that we had been commissioned by a board of directors.* ◇ **~ sb/sth to be/do sth** *They discuss a simplified universe consisting of a large number of masses, each imagined to represent a galaxy.*

im·aging /ˈɪmɪdʒɪŋ/ *noun* [U] the process of putting an image into a computer in a form it can use, storing it and showing it on a computer screen: *Brain imaging is now commonly used to aid diagnosis.* ◇ **+ noun** *Electron microscopy is an imaging technique that utilizes electrons rather than photons to probe a sample.*

im·bal·ance /ɪmˈbæləns/ *noun* [C, U] a situation in which two or more things are not the same size or are not treated the same, in a way that is unfair or causes problems: **~ in sth** *Keynes showed that it was output rather than prices that adjusted to global imbalances in trade.* ◇ *Affirmative action sought to redress racial imbalances in employment.* ◇ **~ between A and B** *The power imbalance between ruling and opposition parties has economic and cultural roots.* ◇ **~ (of sth)** *In recent years, courts have explicitly acknowledged that imbalance of power is a hallmark of employment relations.*

imbed = EMBED

imi·tate /ˈɪmɪteɪt/ *verb* **~ sb/sth** to copy sb/sth: *Girls learn the dances by watching and imitating their elders.* ◇ *The point of the test is to determine whether or not a computer can imitate a brain.*

imi·ta·tion /ˌɪmɪˈteɪʃn/ *noun* **1** [C] a copy of sth, especially sth expensive: *The product is threatened by inferior imitations.* ◇ **~ of sth** *Ginsberg's poem is a pale imitation of Whitman.* **2** [U] the act of copying sb/sth: **by ~** *Darwin assumed that dogs and cats learned by imitation.* ◇ **(in) ~ (of sb/sth)** *She wrote six comedies in imitation of Terence.*

im·ma·ter·ial /ˌɪməˈtɪəriəl; *NAmE* ˌɪməˈtɪriəl/ *adj.* **1** [not usually before noun] not important in a particular situation SYN IRRELEVANT: *The order of the elements is immaterial.* ◇ **~ to sb/sth** *This fact was immaterial to the Court of Justice.* ◇ **it is ~ whether...** *His Lordship added that it was immaterial whether the act occurred in public or in private.* **2** not having a physical form: *Plato and his followers taught that the soul was immaterial.* ➲ *compare* MATERIAL² (2)

im·ma·ture AWL /ˌɪməˈtjʊə(r); *NAmE* ˌɪməˈtʃʊr; ˌɪməˈtʊr/ *adj.* **1** not fully developed or grown: *The benefits from protecting immature fish are widely agreed to be significant.* ◇ *The newly hatched larva are sexually immature.* OPP MATURE¹ (1) **2** behaving in a way that is not sensible and is typical of people who are much younger: *The case concerned a mother with an immature and irresponsible daughter.* ◇ *His pattern of immature and unreliable behaviour contributed to his poor work record.* OPP MATURE¹ (2) ■ **im·ma·tur·ity** AWL /ˌɪməˈtjʊərəti; *NAmE* ˌɪməˈtʃʊrəti; ˌɪməˈtʊrəti/ *noun* [U] *Monkeys and apes have longer periods of immaturity and food dependence than other mammals.* ◇ *The protagonist of the novel is disappointed in her boyfriend because of his immaturity.*

im·me·di·ate /ɪˈmiːdiət/ *adj.* **1** happening or done without delay SYN INSTANT¹ (1): *The government's immediate response to the protests was to establish martial law.* ◇ *The nurse must have training in use of ventilators or immediate access to staff with adequate training.* **2** [usually before noun] existing now and needing urgent attention: *The residents in immediate danger were evacuated first.* ◇ *After the body's immediate needs are satisfied, surplus amino acids are converted to glycogen or fat.* **3** [only before noun] next to or very close to a particular place or time: *Housing prices are higher in the immediate vicinity of the park.* ◇ *In the immediate aftermath of the earthquake, fires broke out across the city.* **4** [only before noun] nearest in relationship or rank: *Her death had far-reaching implications for her immediate family and closest friends.* ◇ *Within the feudal army, loyalty was owed primarily to one's immediate superior.* **5** [only before noun] having a direct effect: *The obvious immediate causes of the famine were the drought and consequent crop failure.* IDM *see* EFFECT¹

im·me·di·ate·ly /ɪˈmiːdiətli/ *adv.* **1** without delay: *Barclay was appointed war minister and immediately began to strengthen the army.* ◇ *The murder was followed immediately by a campaign of terror.* ◇ *Immediately after breastfeeding, infants were weighed.* ◇ *Some of these issues may not be immediately obvious to the outside observer.* **2** (usually with prepositions) next to or very close to a particular place or time: *The family ruled the territory immediately south of the city of Dublin.* ◇ *The object appears either immediately before or immediately after the verb.* **3** (usually with past participles) closely and directly: *The charity's humanitarian work assists those immediately affected by conflict and natural disasters.* ◇ *It is arguably the developed nations that are immediately responsible for global warming.*

im·mense /ɪˈmens/ *adj.* extremely large or great SYN ENORMOUS: *An immense amount of work still lies ahead.* ◇ *Mass spectrometry was a development of immense importance.* ◇ *The financial burden of the war was immense.*

im·mense·ly /ɪˈmensli/ *adv.* extremely; very much SYN ENORMOUSLY: *Lansbury's reforms were immensely popular with the ordinary people of London.* ◇ *Rutherford calculated that the electric fields within the mica must be immensely powerful.* ➲ language bank *at* EXCEPTIONALLY

im·mi·grant AWL /ˈɪmɪɡrənt/ *noun* a person who has come to live permanently in a country that is not their own: *Each year, up to a million illegal immigrants also enter the country.* ◇ **+ noun** *Islam frequently forms an integral part of the ethnic identity of these immigrant communities.*

im·mi·grate AWL /ˈɪmɪɡreɪt/ *verb* [I] **~ (to...) (from...)** (*especially NAmE*) to come and live permanently in a country after leaving your own country: *The 'Latino' students are those whose parents immigrated to the United States from Central and Latin America.* ➲ *compare* EMIGRATE

im·mi·gra·tion AWL /ˌɪmɪˈɡreɪʃn/ *noun* [U] the process of coming to live permanently in a country that is not your own; the number of people who do this: *One of the best-known cases of illegal immigration is that of Mexicans moving into the US.* ◇ **~ from...** *There was a substantial rise in immigration from the Indian subcontinent in particular.* ➲ *compare* EMIGRATION

im·mi·nent /ˈɪmɪnənt/ *adj.* (especially of sth unpleasant) likely to happen very soon: *The Tibetan antelope is thought to be in imminent danger of extinction in the wild.* ◇ *Weight is a real and imminent threat to health in individuals who are morbidly obese.* ■ **im·mi·nence** /ˈɪmɪnəns/ *noun* [U] **~ (of sth)** *The imminence of the First World War led to the passing of much more restrictive immigration control legislation.*

im·mo·bile /ɪˈməʊbaɪl; *NAmE* ɪˈmoʊbl/ *adj.* **1** unable to move: *Gases like chloroform and nitrous oxide render the person who inhales them immobile.* OPP MOBILE (4) **2** not moving: *The camera then cuts to members of the public, who are immobile, watching the procession.* OPP MOBILE (2)

im·mo·bil·ity /ˌɪməˈbɪləti/ *noun* [U] **1** the lack of the ability to move: *In patients with long-standing immobility, corrective surgery may be necessary to restore limb function.* **2** a lack of movement: *Immobility and lack of exercise are widely accepted as risk factors for developing the condition.* OPP MOBILITY

im·mo·bil·ize (*BrE also* **-ise**) /ɪˈməʊbəlaɪz; *NAmE* ɪˈmoʊbəlaɪz/ *verb* **~ sb/sth** to prevent sb/sth from moving or from working normally: *The patient should be immobilized until a fracture is ruled out.* ◇ *Russia had been immobilized by war and revolution.* ■ **im·mo·bil·iza·tion, -isa·tion** /ɪˌməʊbəlaɪˈzeɪʃn; *NAmE* ɪˌmoʊbələˈzeɪʃn/ *noun* [U] **~ (of sb/sth)** *Local anaesthesia is required and immobilization of the fetus is essential.*

im·moral /ɪˈmɒrəl; *NAmE* ɪˈmɔːrəl; ɪˈmɑːrəl/ *adj.* **1** (of people and their behaviour) not considered to be good or honest by most people: *Can a resulting human good, such as material well-being, ever be used to justify an immoral act?* ◇ **it is ~ to do sth** *It is immoral to kill innocent civilians for their government's actions.* **2** not following accepted standards of sexual behaviour: *Poe was expelled from the University of Virginia for immoral behaviour.* ➲ *compare* MORAL[1] ■ **im·mor·al·ity** /ˌɪməˈræləti/ *noun* [U] **~ (of sb/sth)** *Activists gave public lectures on the immorality of the slave trade.* ◇ *For her immorality, Julia had been shut away by her father Augustus on the island of Pandateria.*

im·mor·tal /ɪˈmɔːtl; *NAmE* ɪˈmɔːrtl/ *adj.* **1** living or lasting for ever: *According to Christian teaching, only man has an immortal soul.* OPP MORTAL (1) **2** famous and likely to be remembered for ever: *The political unrest of the late 1790s prevented his 'homage to the immortal author of "Emile" and "The Social Contract"' from being completed.*

im·mune /ɪˈmjuːn/ *adj.* **1** [not usually before noun] **~ (to sth)** able to resist catching or being affected by a particular disease or illness: *Many were also naturally immune to yellow fever.* **2** [only before noun] (*biology*) connected with the IMMUNE SYSTEM: *Infants with low birthweight generally have an increased vulnerability to infectious diseases because of impaired immune function (e.g. Moore et al., 1999).* ➲ *see also* IMMUNE RESPONSE **3** [not usually before noun] **~ (to sth)** not affected or influenced by sth: *Three important geographical areas have, so far, proved relatively immune to the democratic trend.* **4** [not usually before noun] **~ (from sth)** protected from sth and therefore able to avoid it SYN EXEMPT[1]: *The Telecommunication Act of 1996 made Internet providers immune from legal prosecution for content.*

imˌmune resˈponse *noun* [C, U] the reaction of the body to an ANTIGEN (= a substance that can cause disease): *All immune responses originate in cells.* ◇ *Immune response may become impaired with age.*

imˈmune system *noun* **~ (of sb/sth)** the organs and processes in the body that produce substances to help it fight against infection and disease: *The immune system of an individual infected by HIV weakens over time.*

im·mun·ity /ɪˈmjuːnəti/ *noun* (*pl.* **-ies**) **1** [U] the body's ability to avoid or not be affected by infection and disease: **~ to sth** *They had developed immunity to the virus.* ◇ **~ against sth** *The vaccine would produce prolonged immunity against several diseases through a single dose.* **2** [U, C] **~ (from sth)** the state of being protected from sth: *Many states in North America grant health care professionals immunity from liability for negligent acts.* ◇ *The application of the theory acted effectively as an immunity from criminal prosecution for large corporate organizations.*

im·mun·ize (*BrE also* **-ise**) /ˈɪmjunaɪz/ *verb* **~ sb/sth (against sth)** to protect a person or an animal from a disease, especially by giving them an INJECTION of a VACCINE: *One million children have been immunized against the six major childhood diseases as a result of charitable donations.* ➲ *compare* VACCINATE ■ **im·mun·ization, -isa·tion** /ˌɪmjunaɪˈzeɪʃn; *NAmE* ˌɪmjunəˈzeɪʃn/ *noun* [U, C] **~ (of sb/sth) (against sth)** *Voluntary immunization of some American soldiers against typhoid fever began in 1909.* ◇ *The patient may also require a series of immunizations.*

im·muno·defi·ciency /ɪˌmjuːnəʊdɪˈfɪʃnsi; *NAmE* ɪˌmjuːnoʊdɪˈfɪʃnsi/ (*also* **imˈmune deficiency**) *noun* [U, C] a medical condition in which the body does not have the normal ability to resist infection: *These are opportunistic infections and cancers that occur as a result of immunodeficiency.* ◇ *As with many immunodeficiencies, recurrent infections can lead to irreversible long-term organ damage.* ➲ *see also* AIDS, HIV

im·mun·ology /ˌɪmjuˈnɒlədʒi; *NAmE* ˌɪmjuˈnɑːlədʒi/ *noun* [U] the scientific study of protection against disease: *Inoculation laid the groundwork for vaccination, immunology and medical statistics.* ■ **im·muno·logic·al** /ˌɪmjunəˈlɒdʒɪkl; *NAmE* ˌɪmjunəˈlɑːdʒɪkl/ *adj.*: *Immunological tests exploit the production of antibodies by many higher animals in response to foreign agents.*

im·pact[1] AWL /ˈɪmpækt/ *noun* [C, usually sing., U] **1** the powerful effect that sth has on sb/sth: **~ (on sb/sth)** *The injury may have a significant impact on the patient's daily life.* ◇ *Though it made little impact at first, this book acquired great importance in the years after World War*

I

II. ◇ ~ **of sth** *The economy took a considerable time to recover from the impact of the war.* ◇ ~ **of sth on sb/sth** *The series created nationwide public awareness of the profound impact of the civil rights movement on American history.* **2** the act of one object hitting another; the force with which this happens: *A large asteroid impact would eject massive amounts of soot into the atmosphere.* ◇ **on ~ (with sth)** *The fog of supercooled water droplets freezes on impact with any solid surface.* ◇ **+ noun** *Glass fibres have higher impact resistance properties and are much cheaper than carbon fibres.*

▸ ADJECTIVE + IMPACT **great, major, large, big, substantial, considerable • enormous, huge • significant • profound, strong • dramatic • limited • minimal • potential, likely • positive, beneficial • negative, adverse, detrimental • direct • indirect • immediate • long-term • overall • cumulative • environmental • ecological • economic • social • psychological • emotional • human** *Research shows that environmental policies can have long-term impacts on agricultural regions.* ◇ *Advanced technology permits humans to reduce their environmental impact.*

▸ VERB + IMPACT **have, exert • make • assess, evaluate • measure, quantify • determine • estimate • consider • analyse, examine, investigate, explore • understand • reduce, minimize, limit, moderate • mitigate** *The government introduced measures to minimize the impact of the crisis on the economy.*

im·pact² AWL /ɪmˈpækt/ *verb* [T, I] to have an effect on sth: ~ **sth** *Unreasonable levels of job stress can negatively impact individual salesperson performance.* ◇ ~ **on/upon sth** *The case highlights how the crisis has impacted on the local economy.*

im·pair /ɪmˈpeə(r); *NAmE* ɪmˈper/ *verb* ~ **sth** to damage sth or make sth worse: *His ability to carry out his duties was impaired by chronic illness.* ◇ *Sleepiness impairs driving performance and causes 20% of road accidents.*

im·paired /ɪmˈpeəd; *NAmE* ɪmˈperd/ *adj.* **1** damaged or not functioning normally: *Caution should be exercised in patients with impaired renal function.* **2 -im·paired** having the type of physical or mental problem mentioned: *Interestingly, the memory-impaired patients exhibit learning curves similar to the normal subjects.* ◇ *hearing-/speech-/learning-/brain-impaired* ➲ *usage note at* DISABILITY

im·pair·ment /ɪmˈpeəmənt; *NAmE* ɪmˈpermənt/ *noun* [U, C] (*technical*) the state of having a physical or mental condition which means that part of your body or brain does not work correctly; a particular condition of this sort: *The survey focused on the quality of nursing care for patients with visual impairment.* ◇ ~ **of sth** *The antidepressant drugs had caused an impairment of short-term memory.* ➲ *usage note at* DISABILITY

im·par·tial /ɪmˈpɑːʃl; *NAmE* ɪmˈpɑːrʃl/ *adj.* not supporting one person or group more than another SYN NEUTRAL (1), UNBIASED: *Everyone is entitled to a fair and public hearing by an independent and impartial tribunal.* OPP PARTIAL (2) ■ **im·par·ti·al·ity** /ˌɪmˌpɑːʃiˈæləti; *NAmE* ˌɪmˌpɑːrʃiˈæləti/ *noun* [U] ~ **(of sb/sth)** *At that time, there were substantial queries over the independence and impartiality of the judiciary.* **im·par·tial·ly** /ɪmˈpɑːʃəli; *NAmE* ɪmˈpɑːrʃəli/ *adv.*: *Even though a person may believe that he was acting impartially, his mind may unconsciously be affected by bias.*

im·pa·tient /ɪmˈpeɪʃnt/ *adj.* **1** quickly becoming slightly angry or upset, especially because you have to wait for a longer time than you want: ~ **with sb/sth** *Those with this personality type are impatient with people and can be abrasive.* ◇ ~ **at sth** *It is natural to be impatient at this kind of constraint.* **2** wanting to do sth soon; wanting sth to happen soon: ~ **to do sth** *The global community is impatient to enjoy the benefits of this technology now.* ◇ ~ **for sth** *Like many idealists, he was impatient for results.* **3** ~ **of sb/sth** unable or unwilling to accept sth unpleasant: *The government is impatient of interference and criticism.* ■ **im·pa·tience** /ɪmˈpeɪʃns/ *noun* [U] ~ **with sb/sth** *Some employees may exhibit impatience with clients.* ◇ ~ **at sth** *Impatience at the slow pace of reform voiced itself in two movements.*

im·pede /ɪmˈpiːd/ *verb* [often passive] ~ **sth** to delay or stop the progress of sth SYN HAMPER, HINDER: *Governments of rich countries often adopt policies that impede development in poor countries.* ◇ *The presence of inflammation impedes blood flow which results in limb pain.* ◇ *Economic progress in this area was significantly impeded by the Asian economic crash of 1997.*

im·pedi·ment /ɪmˈpedɪmənt/ *noun* something that delays or stops the progress of sth SYN OBSTACLE (1): ~ **to sth** *National borders are an impediment to international trade.* ◇ ~ **for sb/sth** *The size of the federal government is a major impediment for the president.*

im·pera·tive¹ /ɪmˈperətɪv/ *noun* a thing that is very important and needs immediate attention or action: *For some public health leaders, global health is a moral imperative.* ◇ ~ **of (doing) sth** *Welfare states are all driven in the same direction by the imperatives of international competition.*

im·pera·tive² /ɪmˈperətɪv/ *adj.* [not usually before noun] very important and needing immediate attention or action SYN VITAL (1): *Immediate action was imperative.* ◇ **it is ~ (for sb) to do sth** *It became imperative for the company to exploit opportunities in the leisure and luxury sectors.* ◇ **it is ~ that...** *It is imperative that the judiciary remain separate and independent from the executive.*

im·per·fect /ɪmˈpɜːfɪkt; *NAmE* ɪmˈpɜːrfɪkt/ *adj.* containing faults or mistakes; not complete or perfect SYN FLAWED: *With imperfect information, it is easy to make the wrong decisions.* ◇ *Knowledge of the causes of climatic changes is still highly imperfect.* ■ **im·per·fect·ly** *adv.*: *These processes are still imperfectly understood.* ◇ *Corporate reforms were introduced slowly and imperfectly.*

im·per·fec·tion /ˌɪmpəˈfekʃn; *NAmE* ˌɪmpərˈfekʃn/ *noun* [C, U] a fault or weakness in sb/sth: *Well-prepared polished sections always retain some scratches and other imperfections.* ◇ ~ **of sth** *Despite the imperfection of the mental process by which a belief is arrived at it, the belief itself may still be honest.*

im·per·ial /ɪmˈpɪəriəl; *NAmE* ɪmˈpɪriəl/ *adj.* [only before noun] **1** connected with an EMPIRE: *Britain went from being the world's leading imperial power at the turn of the twentieth century to a regional role within the EU.* ◇ *Sixty million conquered men and women around the Mediterranean were subject to Roman imperial rule.* **2** connected with a system of measurement that is used in some countries instead of the METRIC system of measurement: *Surveys are conducted in the USA using imperial systems of measurement, whilst the metric system is used in Europe.* ➲ *compare* METRIC

im·peri·al·ism /ɪmˈpɪəriəlɪzəm; *NAmE* ɪmˈpɪriəlɪzəm/ *noun* [U] **1** a system in which one country controls other countries, often after defeating them in a war: *During the era of Western imperialism, the rest of the world was dominated by Europeans.* **2** (*usually disapproving*) the fact of a powerful country or group increasing its influence through sth such as business, culture or language: *They tend to portray American products as agents of American cultural imperialism.* ◇ *Globalization has been perceived as a form of Western economic imperialism.* ■ **im·peri·al·ist** (*also* **im·peri·al·is·tic** /ɪmˌpɪəriəˈlɪstɪk; *NAmE* ɪmˌpɪriəˈlɪstɪk/) *adj.*: *He accused the Russians of showing towards China all the 'arrogance and conceit' of an imperialist power.*

im·peri·al·ist /ɪmˈpɪəriəlɪst; *NAmE* ɪmˈpɪriəlɪst/ *noun* (*usually disapproving*) a person, such as a politician, who supports or works in the interests of imperialism: *At this period, most British imperialists thought of themselves as conquerors and civilizers of the world.*

im·per·me·able /ɪmˈpɜːmiəbl; *NAmE* ɪmˈpɜːrmiəbl/ *adj.* (*technical*) not allowing a liquid or gas to pass through: *Overlying impermeable rocks prevent this water from moving upwards.* ◇ **~ to sth** *Lipid bilayers form a barrier that is relatively impermeable to most molecules.* OPP PERMEABLE

im·per·son·al /ɪmˈpɜːsənl; *NAmE* ɪmˈpɜːrsənl/ *adj.* **1** not referring to any particular person: *Old-age insurance became a national programme, administered in a completely impersonal way.* ◇ *The weather is a safe, impersonal topic that can be discussed between two strangers who want to be friendly.* **2** lacking friendly human feelings or atmosphere: *In vast impersonal cities individuals often feel isolated.* ◇ *Globalization is often seen in terms of impersonal forces wreaking havoc on the lives of ordinary people.* ■ **im·per·son·al·ity** /ɪmˌpɜːsəˈnæləti; *NAmE* ɪmˌpɜːrsəˈnæləti/ *noun* [U] **~ (of sth)** *Modern people periodically feel themselves frustrated by the impersonality and predictability of life.*

LANGUAGE BANK

Giving opinions using impersonal language

In academic writing, it is important to use impersonal language in order to sound more objective

- **It is important that...**
- **It is clear/obvious that...**
- **It is difficult (for sb) to do sth**
- **It would seem that...**
- **There is evidence that...**
- **There is no doubt that...**

– ***It is important that*** *these terms are used consistently.*
– ***It is clear that*** *the proposals now enjoyed much more support than had been the case previously.*
– ***It is difficult for us to*** *tell how Aristophanes really felt about the people he attacked in his plays.*
– ***It would seem that*** *cities should be fundamental to any definition of Roman culture.*
– ***There is evidence that*** *undernourishment in early childhood affects the development of cognitive faculties.*
– ***There is no doubt that*** *unconscious learning and perception occur.*

im·petus /ˈɪmpɪtəs/ *noun* [sing., U] something that encourages a process or activity to develop more quickly SYN STIMULUS (1): **~ to sth** *The pace of development was accelerated by two world wars which gave a huge impetus to aircraft and engine design innovation.* ◇ **~ for sth** *Additional impetus for reform came in the form of a Law Commission Report.* ◇ **~ (for/to sb) to do sth** *The new determination provided the political impetus to drive through more fundamental reforms.*

im·plaus·ible /ɪmˈplɔːzəbl/ *adj.* not seeming reasonable or likely to be true: *Marx's own argument for this claim is quite implausible.* ◇ **it is ~ to do sth** *It is implausible to expect that an authoritarian president would try to promote democracy in the regions.* ◇ **it is ~ that...** *It seems highly implausible that an expanding war on terrorism could stop such a powerful set of social processes as globalization.* OPP PLAUSIBLE ■ **im·plaus·ibly** *adv.*: *This rate is implausibly low in the context of other studies.*

im·ple·ment AWL /ˈɪmplɪment/ *verb* **~ sth** to start to use a new plan, system or law SYN CARRY STH OUT: *Such initiatives may be costly or otherwise difficult to implement.* ◇ *During its first term, Blair's government implemented an ambitious programme of constitutional reform.* ◇ *The plan was not fully implemented but many specific components were approved and put in place.*

▸ IMPLEMENT + NOUN **policy** • **strategy** • **programme** • **plan** • **initiative, measure** • **change** • **reform** • **system** • **law, legislation** • **directive** • **provision** • **decision** • **recommendation** • **guideline** • **intervention** • **algorithm** *The Australian federal government persuaded all states and territories to implement tough new gun control laws.*
▸ ADVERB + IMPLEMENT **fully** • **successfully, effectively** • **actually** • **properly** *The claimant argued that there was a failure to properly implement the relevant EU directive concerning pesticides.*

im·ple·men·ta·tion AWL /ˌɪmplɪmenˈteɪʃn/ *noun* [U, C] **~ (of sth)** the process or act of beginning to follow a particular plan, system or law: *Resources were made available to facilitate the implementation of these strategies.* ◇ *Community groups have been the key to the successful implementation of this programme.* ◇ *For these policy implementations, clear and mutual understanding is crucial.*

im·pli·cate AWL /ˈɪmplɪkeɪt/ *verb* **1** [usually passive] to show or suggest that sth is the cause of sth bad: **be implicated in sth** *Smoking is implicated in the development of several different cancers.* ◇ *He saw religious loyalties as deeply implicated in historic conflicts over particular places.* ◇ **be implicated as sth** *Two specific genes have been implicated as the probable cause of the syndrome.* **2 ~ sb (in sth)** to show or suggest that sb is involved in sth bad or criminal: *He details a rumour that implicated Tiberius in the poisoning of his own son Drusus.*

im·pli·ca·tion AWL /ˌɪmplɪˈkeɪʃn/ *noun* [C, usually pl.] **~ (of sth) (for sth)** a possible effect or result of an action or a decision: *The implications of these findings are far-reaching.* ◇ *This research has important implications for child-rearing and education.*

▸ ADJECTIVE + IMPLICATION **important, major** • **serious** • **significant** • **profound, far-reaching** • **wider, broader** • **full** • **obvious, clear** • **direct** • **possible, potential** • **long-term** • **negative** • **practical** • **theoretical** • **political** • **ethical** • **social** • **economic** • **legal** • **financial** *Meat-eating in excess can have serious adverse health implications.* ◇ *Potential implications for survey practice are presented in the discussion section.*
▸ VERB + IMPLICATION **have, carry** • **consider, explore, examine** • **assess** • **discuss** • **draw** • **understand** *Reich and Mankin (1986) discussed the implications of sharing technology across borders with potential competitors.*

im·pli·cit AWL /ɪmˈplɪsɪt/ *adj.* **1 ~ in sth** forming a necessary part of sth: *It is implicit in the right to a fair hearing that a person should be given sufficient notice to prepare their case.* ◇ *Work in the classroom may be supported by the values implicit in the organization and policies of the school.* **2** said or written in a way that suggests sth without expressing it directly: *There is an implicit assumption that decision-making is rational.* ◇ **~ in sth** *This same bias is implicit in other texts of the period.* OPP EXPLICIT (1)

im·pli·cit·ly AWL /ɪmˈplɪsɪtli/ *adv.* in a way that is not directly expressed: *This approach implicitly assumes that the entrepreneur starts the new business in the same labour market where he or she previously worked.* ◇ *Most human geography is explicitly or implicitly guided by one particular philosophical viewpoint.* OPP EXPLICITLY (1)

imply AWL /ɪmˈplaɪ/ *verb* (**im·plies, im·ply·ing, im·plied, im·plied**) **1** to make it seem likely that sth is true or exists SYN SUGGEST (2): **~ sth** *Paul's letters imply the existence of five or six house churches in the 50s and 60s of the first century AD.* ◇ **~ (that)...** *The rise of global law does not necessarily imply that a common law of humanity is in the making.* ⊃ thesaurus note *at* INDICATE **2** to suggest that sth is true or that you feel or think sth, without saying so directly: **~ (that)...** *Ancient arguments seem to imply that* *instrumental music was deemed inferior because it lacked words.* ◇ **be implied (by sb/sth)** *The consent to examination was assumed to be implied by the patient seeking assistance.* ◇ **(be) implied in sth** *The chronology implied in this second account differs.* **3** (of a fact or event) to suggest sth as a likely or necessary result: *The forecast traffic increase implied more roads and more air pollution.* ➲ thesaurus note *at* MEAN¹

im·port¹ /ˈɪmpɔːt; *NAmE* ˈɪmpɔːrt/ *noun* **1** [U, pl.] the act of bringing a product or service into one country from another: **~ of sth (from ...)** *The Clean Diamond Trade Act prohibited the import of 'blood diamonds' from conflict zones.* ◇ *Imports of goods depress domestic output because demand for home production goes down.* ◇ **(on) ~ into...** *On import into the country, products that do not comply should be identified and removed from the market.* ◇ **+ noun** *There are substantial import duties on tobacco products.* OPP EXPORT¹(1) **2** [C, usually pl.] a product or service that is brought into one country from another: **~ into...** *Trade restrictions on Chinese manufactures further increased the price of imports into Britain.* ◇ **~ from...** *Largely without natural resources, Japan is forced to rely on imports from around the world to run its industrial plants.* OPP EXPORT¹(2) **3** [U] (*formal*) importance: **of ~ to sb/sth** *These findings provide data of import to researchers and public health professionals.* **4 the ~ (of sth)** [sing.] (*formal*) the meaning of sth: *Had he asked for an increase in taxes, he could not have avoided alerting the country to the full import of his new policies.*

im·port² /ɪmˈpɔːt; *NAmE* ɪmˈpɔːrt/ *verb* **1** to bring a product or service into one country from another for sale: **~ sth** *They claimed that their right to import goods and sell them had been infringed.* ◇ **~ sth into...** *There are no domestic firearms manufacturers, so all firearms must be imported into the country.* ◇ **~ sth from...** *All manufactured products were imported from abroad.* OPP EXPORT²(1) **2 ~ sth (from...)** to introduce an idea or activity from another country or area: *New states established themselves using religious ideals imported from Europe.* OPP EXPORT²(2) **3** (*computing*) to get data from another program, changing its form so that the program you are using can read it: **~ sth** *When the documents have been imported, they can be read and edited.* ◇ **~ sth into sth** *Once all the data are collected, they are imported into specialized imaging analysis software.* OPP EXPORT²(3) ■ **im·port·ation** /ˌɪmpɔːˈteɪʃn; *NAmE* ˌɪmpɔːrˈteɪʃn/ *noun* [U] **~ (of sth)** *The European Union currently restricts the importation of many genetically modified products.*

im·port·ance /ɪmˈpɔːtns; *NAmE* ɪmˈpɔːrtns/ *noun* [U] the quality of being important: **~ of sth** *There is increasing recognition of the importance of health promotion.* ◇ **~ of sth for sb/sth** *Teachers often stress the importance of support at home for student success at school.* ◇ **~ of sth to sb/sth** *The report emphasizes the importance of corporate governance to the future growth of the economy.* ◇ **~ in sth** *A country's influence is determined broadly by its economic size and importance in international trade.* ◇ **~ as sth** *Researchers have increasingly recognized the Internet's importance as a promotional medium.* ◇ **be of... ~ (in sth/in doing sth)** *These traits are of central importance in determining the winner of contests against other males.* ◇ **a matter of ~ (to sb)** *The impact of industrialism on the behaviour of working people was a matter of special importance to these historians.* ◇ **in order of ~** *All risk assessments must identify the major risks and list them in order of importance.*

▸ ADJECTIVE + IMPORTANCE **great, major, enormous • considerable • growing, increasing • continuing • relative • particular, central, critical, crucial, paramount, fundamental, vital, primary, utmost, prime, special • equal • little • minor, secondary • economic • practical • strategic • historical** *It is of the utmost importance to be able to recognize those at risk of depression.*

▸ VERB + IMPORTANCE **recognize, acknowledge, realize • understand, appreciate • emphasize, highlight, stress, underscore, underline • attach ~ to, place ~ on • note • demonstrate, illustrate, show • indicate, suggest • reflect • underestimate • diminish • deny • discuss • reinforce, confirm • assume** *The British attach great importance to the continuation of an especially close relationship with the US.* ◇ *This technique has assumed enormous importance in DNA studies.*

▸ VERB + IN IMPORTANCE **grow, gain, increase • decline** *The worship of living emperors grew in importance as their position grew in power.*

THESAURUS

important • significant • notable *adj.*

These words all describe sth that has a great effect, is easy to notice or is of great value.

- to be important/significant/notable **for** sth
- to be important/signficant/notable **that...**
- an important/a significant/a notable **difference/contribution/change**
- an important/a significant **role/factor/part**
- a significant/notable **effect/increase**
- **particularly/especially/equally** important/significant/notable
- **extremely/highly/potentially/increasingly** important/significant
- **statistically** significant

- **Important** is the most general of these words; things are **significant** within a particular context or from a particular perspective: *Recycling of polymers has become an important environmental issue.* ◇ *Such small increases in risk can be highly significant in public health terms.*
- **Significant** is often used to describe sth that can be measured or proven by research: *In a significant proportion of cases...* ◇ *These trends are not statistically significant.*
- **Notable** is used to describe sth that deserves attention because it is unusual or interesting: *There is only one notable exception to these negative findings.*

im·port·ant /ɪmˈpɔːtnt; *NAmE* ɪmˈpɔːrtnt/ *adj.* **1** having a great effect on people or things; of great value: *The liver plays an important role in fat metabolism.* ◇ **~ in (doing) sth** *Mass media have become an important factor in influencing public opinion.* ◇ *By the 1980s, Robertson was arguing that class was no longer important in British politics (Heath et al., 1991).* ◇ **~ for sb/sth** *Visibility information is particularly important for shipping and aircraft.* ◇ **~ to sb/sth** *Understanding what drives trade is vitally important to managers.* ◇ **it is ~ (for sb/sth) to do sth** *It is important to note that soils can be irreversibly affected by excess salt concentration.* ◇ **it is ~ (that)...** *It is important that these samples resemble as closely as possible the samples to be analysed.* **2** (of a person) having great influence or authority: *The most important person in John Kennedy's early life was his father.* ◇ *When young Tacitus came to Rome, he met many of the important political figures.*

▸ IMPORTANT + NOUN **role • factor • part, element, component • feature, characteristic • aspect, respect • issue, question • topic • point • reason • difference, distinction • implications • consequence • influence • contribution • consideration • insight • source • determinant • predictor • step** *Product quality is an important element of competition in a wide range of markets.* ◇ *This research has important implications for child-rearing and education.*

▸ ADVERB + IMPORTANT **very, really, highly • extremely • particularly, especially • increasingly • potentially • critically, vitally, crucially • quite • clearly • functionally • strategically • economically • commercially • politically •**

historically *It will become increasingly important to prepare older workers for greater job mobility at the end of their careers.*

▸ IT IS IMPORTANT TO + VERB **note • recognize, realize, acknowledge • understand, appreciate • consider • remember, bear in mind • examine, study • emphasize, stress • identify • distinguish • ensure** *It is important to recognize that without proper nutrition, the body cannot develop properly.*

im·port·ant·ly /ɪmˈpɔːtntli; *NAmE* ɪmˈpɔːrtntli/ *adv.* in a way that has a great effect on people or things: *Finally, and most importantly, objectivity was maintained during all interviews.* ◇ *More importantly, however, Darwin was the first to fully address another question:...*

im·port·er /ɪmˈpɔːtə(r); *NAmE* ɪmˈpɔːrtər/ *noun* **~ (of sth)** a country, a company or a person that buys goods or services from another country in order to sell or use them in their own country: *China became a net importer of oil in 1993.* ◇ *Table 1.6 lists the top fifteen commercial services exporters and importers.* OPP EXPORTER

im·pose AWL /ɪmˈpəʊz; *NAmE* ɪmˈpoʊz/ *verb* **1** to introduce sth such as a new law, tax or system; to order that a law or punishment be used: **~ sth on/upon sth/sb** *Most states responded by imposing major restrictions on cross-border trade.* ◇ **~ sth** *The court imposed the relatively modest sentence of 4 years' imprisonment.* **2 ~ sth (on/upon sb/sth)** to make sb accept or follow the same opinions or beliefs as your own: *None of the major economic actors had the power to impose its will on the others.* **3 ~ sth (on/upon sb/sth)** to give sth that is difficult or unpleasant to sb/sth: *Crime imposes costs on victims, offenders, their families and society as a whole.* **4 ~ yourself (on/upon sb/sth)** to make sb/sth accept you or your ideas: *American hegemony has imposed itself upon the world.*

im·pos·ition AWL /ˌɪmpəˈzɪʃn/ *noun* **1** [U] **~ (of sth)** the act of introducing sth such as a new law, tax or system: *There was no possibility that Parliament would accept the imposition of extra taxation.* ◇ *Indonesia has a free-market economy but the government still plays a significant role through the imposition of price controls in selected industries.* **2** [C, usually sing.] an unfair or unreasonable thing that sb expects or asks you to do: *People sometimes perceive training as an imposition and not a process that allows them to develop their own learning goals.* ◇ **~ on sth** *Submission to religious authority came to be viewed as an imposition on the freedom of individual consciences.*

im·pos·si·bil·ity /ɪmˌpɒsəˈbɪləti; *NAmE* ɪmˌpɑːsəˈbɪləti/ *noun* (*pl.* **-ies**) **1** [U] **~ (of sth/of doing sth)** the fact of being impossible: *Totally accurate weather forecasting will never be practicable because of the impossibility of taking account of all the variables affecting the climate.* OPP POSSIBILITY (1) **2** [C, usually sing.] something that is impossible to do: *For both Herbert and Lacan, self-knowledge is in many ways an impossibility.* OPP POSSIBILITY (2)

im·pos·sible /ɪmˈpɒsəbl; *NAmE* ɪmˈpɑːsəbl/ *adj.* **1** that cannot exist or be done; not possible: **~ for sb/sth** *For all but a very few wealthy people, travel beyond a short distance from home was virtually impossible.* ◇ **~ to do** *In practice, the law proved almost impossible to enforce.* ◇ **it is ~ (for sb/sth) to do sth** *It is impossible for governments to raise the overall level of public expenditure without either increasing borrowing or taxes.* ◇ **make sth/it ~ (for sb/sth) (to do sth)** *The rigid outer skeleton makes it impossible for the animals to increase in size gradually.* OPP POSSIBLE (1) **2 the impossible** *noun* [sing.] a thing that is or seems impossible: *She considers that Western governments' attempts to control migration by controlling borders are an attempt to do the impossible.* **3** very difficult to deal with: *As soon as the interests of the two companies were in conflict, the directors were placed in an impossible position.* ■ **im·pos·sibly** /ɪmˈpɒsəbli; *NAmE* ɪmˈpɑːsəbli/ *adv.*: *Khrushchev introduced impossibly high growth rates for meat production.*

im·prac·ti·cal /ɪmˈpræktɪkl/ *adj.* not sensible or realistic: *'Romantic' love is often conceptualized as impractical or idealistic.* ◇ **it is ~ to do sth** *It would be impractical to evaluate the whole organization continuously.* ◇ **~ for sth** *Many of these techniques have limitations that make them impractical for large-scale field use.* OPP PRACTICAL (2) ■ **im·prac·ti·cal·ity** /ɪmˌpræktɪˈkæləti/ *noun* [U] **~ (of sth)** *Participation in a delegation to Rome impressed on Josephus the impracticality of resistance against Roman rule.*

im·pre·cise AWL /ˌɪmprɪˈsaɪs/ *adj.* not giving exact details or making sth clear: *Due to the small numbers of deaths involved, these estimates are imprecise and should be interpreted with care.* ◇ *Question comprehension is impeded by questions containing imprecise terms.* OPP PRECISE (1) ➲ *compare* INACCURATE ■ **im·pre·ci·sion** /ˌɪmprɪˈsɪʒn/ *noun* [U] **~ (of sth)** *The problem lies in the imprecision of the definitions.*

I

im·press /ɪmˈpres/ *verb* [T, I] if a person or thing **impresses** you, you feel admiration for them or it: **~ (sb)** *Young professionals rely on their cell phones to keep in touch, or simply to impress others.* ◇ *If the male fails to impress, he may never get to pass on his genes.* ◇ **be impressed by sth** *Even the board members were not impressed by the presentation.* ◇ **~ sb with sth/sb** *He impressed powerful people with his ability to get things done.*

PHR V **impress sth on/upon sb** to make sb understand how important sth is by emphasizing it: *The importance of what researchers have seen and heard has to be impressed on the audience.* **impress sth/itself on/upon sb** to have a great effect on sth, especially sb's mind or imagination: *Her efficiency was something that impressed itself upon her son's imagination.*

im·pressed /ɪmˈprest/ *adj.* feeling admiration for sb/sth because you think they are particularly good: **~ by sb/sth** *Durkheim was impressed by the work of the psychologist Wilhelm Wundt.* ◇ **~ with sb/sth** *The emperor was impressed with the young monk and his desire to create a new type of Buddhism.*

im·pres·sion /ɪmˈpreʃn/ *noun* **1** [C] an idea, a feeling or an opinion that you get about sb/sth, or that sb/sth gives you: **~ of sb/sth** *Participants were asked to describe their first impressions of the school.* ◇ **~ of being/having sth** *Brown gave the impression of being a reluctant European.* ◇ **~ that...** *During general election campaigns, political leaders try to give the impression that they are in control of events.* **2** [C, U] **~ (on sb/sth)** the effect that an experience, an action or a person has on sb/sth: *These people make favourable impressions on others and are described as being outgoing and self-confident.* ◇ *This argument made no impression on the Court.* ◇ *The paper made little impression at the time because it was published in an obscure Belgian journal.* **3** [C] an appearance that may be false: **~ (of sth)** *The architect arranged the fragments to convey the impression of a temple in ruins.* ◇ **~ that...** *Such policies create a false impression that regulators are making progress on environmental problems.* **4** [C] a mark that is left when an object is pressed hard into a surface: *The length of the foot was estimated from measurements of footprint impressions left on the soil.* ◇ **~ of sth** *Fossils are chemically altered remains or impressions of organisms left behind in rock.* **5** [C] **~ of sth** a drawing showing what a person looks like or what a place or a building will look like in the future: *Fig. 6.8 shows an impression of what the reactor will look like once completed.*

IDM **be under the imˈpression that...** to believe, usually wrongly, that sth is true or is happening: *Consumers may* be under the impression that animals on intensive farms experience high levels of welfare.

im·pres·sive /ɪmˈpresɪv/ *adj.* (of things or people) making you feel admiration, because they are very large, good, skilful, etc: *These arguments are supported by an impressive array of evidence.* ◇ *Cubans and Koreans have an impressive record of entrepreneurship in the US.* ◇ *With 37 per cent of the world's inventions, Japan's performance is particularly impressive.* ■ **im·pres·sive·ly** *adv.*: *The chapters on the Revolutionary period are impressively researched and original.*

im·prison /ɪmˈprɪzn/ *verb* [often passive] to put sb in a prison or another place from which they cannot escape: **~ sb** *He was imprisoned by the Nazis but escaped to England and returned to Norway in 1945.* ◇ **~ sb for sth** *He was imprisoned for four years without charge.* ◇ *Even under the best system of punishment, some people will inevitably be imprisoned for crimes they did not commit.* ■ **im·pris·on·ment** *noun* [U] *She was sentenced to life imprisonment.*

I

im·prob·able /ɪmˈprɒbəbl; *NAmE* ɪmˈprɑːbəbl/ *adj.* not likely to be true or to happen SYN UNLIKELY (1): *European patriotism on the American model seems rather improbable.* ◇ *Most seemingly improbable coincidences are produced by common causes.* ◇ **it is ~ that...** *It is highly improbable that particle accelerator experiments will cause an existential disaster.* OPP PROBABLE ■ **im·prob·abil·ity** /ɪmˌprɒbəˈbɪləti; *NAmE* ɪmˌprɑːbəˈbɪləti/ *noun* (*pl.* -ies) [U, C] **~ (of sth/doing sth)** *A low p-value is a measure of the improbability of obtaining a similar result if the variables are truly independent.*

im·proper /ɪmˈprɒpə(r); *NAmE* ɪmˈprɑːpər/ *adj.* **1** dishonest or morally wrong: *The press targeted other ministers with allegations of improper conduct.* OPP PROPER (3) **2** wrong; not correct: *Improper helmet use may affect helmet fixation in a crash.* ◇ *Improper vaccine storage was one of the principal factors in breakthrough infections.* ■ **im·prop·er·ly** *adv.*: *It was alleged that the Bank of England had acted improperly by granting a licence to the BCCI.*

im·prove /ɪmˈpruːv/ *verb* [I, T] to become better than before; to make sth/sb better than before: *Respondents were asked if their current work situation had improved.* ◇ **~ sth** *Innovation lowers costs and improves product quality in the industry.*

PHR V **imˈprove on/upon sth** to achieve or produce sth that is of a better quality than sth else: *The characteristics of disk drives vary, and are being improved on at an immense rate.* ◇ *It is very difficult to design a test that will improve upon the overall accuracy of predictions.*

▸ IMPROVE + NOUN **quality • performance • efficiency • effectiveness • outcome • accuracy • productivity • rate • chances • competitiveness • compliance • reliability • standards • capacity** *An approach had to be found to improve the performance of the loss-making part of the business.* | **understanding • capability • ability • communication • knowledge** *As computing power develops it will be possible to improve our understanding of climate change.* | **condition(s) • situation • position • status** *There were many strikes that led to government intervention to improve working conditions.* | **safety • health, well-being • access • skills • survival • symptoms • care** *These efforts are part of a general strategy to improve workplace safety.*

▸ ADVERB + IMPROVE | IMPROVE + ADVERB **greatly, considerably, substantially • significantly • steadily • gradually • dramatically • markedly** *Life expectancy and health have greatly improved over the last 50 years.* ◇ *Oral health has improved significantly over the past few decades.*

▸ ADVERB + IMPROVE **further • continually, continuously • potentially • actually • thereby, thus** *Information collection and storage technologies are continually improving.*

▸ VERB + TO IMPROVE **aim, seek, hope, intend • be designed • try, attempt • help • need • fail • continue** *The university aimed to improve its overall branding stategy.*

im·prove·ment /ɪmˈpruːvmənt/ *noun* **1** [U] the act of making sth better; the process of sth becoming better: **~ in sth** *The engine provides some improvement in efficiency at higher loads.* ◇ **~ over sth** *Levels of piracy ranged between 85 and 93 per cent, indicating little or no improvement over previous years.* ◇ **~ to sth** *Some reduction in noise has been achieved through improvement to the design of the wind turbines.* **2** [C] a change in sth that makes it better; sth that is better than it was before: *Most landlords refused to lend their tenants capital for farm improvements.* ◇ **~ in sth** *This study has shown a substantial improvement in immunization coverage in two urban slums.* ◇ **~ on sth** *The latest model is not always an improvement on its predecessors.* ◇ **~ over sth** *These figures are a considerable improvement over the 1970–1980 values.*

▸ ADJECTIVE + IMPROVEMENT **great, substantial • significant • continuous • further • incremental • dramatic • marked • modest • general • environmental • agricultural • clinical • technological** *There has been significant improvement in water quality.*

▸ NOUN + IMPROVEMENT **quality • health • performance • efficiency • productivity • safety** *Competition can generate substantial quality improvements.*

▸ VERB + IMPROVEMENT **achieve • show, demonstrate • report • suggest • see** *A central concern of public sector management has been to achieve continuous improvement in efficiency.* | **make** *It is clear that technical improvements must be made to fuel cells in order for them to become a realistic alternative technology for the future.*

▸ NOUN + FOR IMPROVEMENT **room, potential, scope • suggestion, recommendation** *There is room for improvement in the banking sector.* ◇ *The focus of this research was to explore experiences and identify suggestions for improvements.*

▸ IMPROVEMENT IN + NOUN **quality • performance • efficiency • productivity • outcome • standard • technology • health • survival** *The country has received huge amounts of aid without any improvement in the quality of life for the vast majority of the population.*

im·pulse /ˈɪmpʌls/ *noun* **1** [C, usually sing., U] a sudden strong wish or need to do sth, without stopping to think about the results: *The Titans were a warlike race of demons driven by violent impulses.* ◇ **~ to do sth** *There was a strong impulse among regional politicians to shield traditional farmers from global competition.* ◇ **on ~** *Sweets and desserts are usually bought on impulse rather than being planned purchases.* **2** [C, usually sing.] something that causes sb/sth to do sth or to develop and make progress: *Although not primarily motivated by a humanitarian impulse, they still had humanitarian intentions.* ◇ **~ to/towards sth** *The campaign created a powerful impulse towards social reform.* **3** [C] a brief electric current, for example one that travels from a NERVE to a muscle: *The key fact is that electricity travels along wires two or three million times faster than nerve impulses pass along nerves.* **4** [C] (*physics*) the change in MOMENTUM of an object due to a force: *Rocket motors on board the craft are fired and an impulse is imparted to the craft.*

im·pur·ity /ɪmˈpjʊərəti; *NAmE* ɪmˈpjʊrəti/ *noun* (*pl.* -ies) **1** [C] a substance that is present in small amounts in another substance, making it dirty or of poor quality: *Natural rainfall contains many impurities, including dissolved gases, dusts and salts.* ◇ *It is important to remove impurities before mixing the DNA with the purified protein sample.* **2** [U] the state of being dirty or not pure: *The people were required to repent and cleanse themselves of impurity.*

OPP PURITY **3** [C] (*engineering*) a TRACE ELEMENT that is added to a SEMICONDUCTOR: *The most common impurities used as dopants are boron, phosphorus and arsenic.*

in[1] /ɪn/ *prep.* HELP For the special uses of **in** in phrasal verbs, look at the entries for the verbs. For example **deal in sth** is in the phrasal verb section at **deal**. **1** at a point within an area, a space or an object: *The total number of illegal immigrants in the USA was estimated at around 11 million.* ◇ *His cousin lived in his house and paid a minimal rent.* ◇ *A fuller account of this process is given in Appendix D.* **2** surrounded by sth: *The samples were stored in liquid nitrogen.* **3** into sth: *The two birds were put in a holding box without food but with water.* **4** forming the whole or part of sth/sb; contained within sth/sb: *The total protein content in the samples was measured.* ◇ *The parent company holds a 51% stake in Central.* **5** used to show the form, shape, arrangement or quantity of sth: *The article was published in two parts.* ◇ *The storage cells are organized in a square matrix.* ◇ *The cores are typically 120 cm in length.* ◇ *The seats were arranged in rows, all facing the front.* ◇ *Customers in their millions allow Amazon to store their personal details.* **6** during a period of time: *Primary school fees were abolished in 2004.* ◇ *Data are collected in October each year.* ◇ *Departmental meetings were scheduled for early in the mornings.* ◇ *It has been shown that the risks of such side effects rise in old age.* ➲ language bank *at* TIME[1] **7** after a particular length of time: *The results will be ready in six weeks' time.* **8** (used after *first, last*, etc.) for a particular period of time: *In 1989 the coalition won the first presidential election in 19 years.* **9** used to show a state or condition: *Molotov was then in his twenties.* ◇ *A number of European dynasties were in a state of collapse.* ◇ *When we say we are in love, for example, we mean more than that we are in a particular bodily state.* **10** used to describe physical surroundings: *The soil surface hardens in the sun.* **11** used to show the language, material, etc. used: *Japan's constitution was written in English by American officials after 1945.* ◇ *It was important to obtain all patients' consent to the operation in writing.* ◇ *The images were reproduced in colour.* ◇ *Participants were paid in cash after the end of each experiment.* **12** wearing sth: *The emperor dressed in purple to emphasize his unique status.* **13** involved in sth; taking part in sth: *She was then cast in a film about the assasination of President Lincoln.* **14** used to show sb's job or profession: *Cajal served briefly as a medical lieutenant in the army.* **15** while doing sth; as a result of sth: *In attempting to address these questions, it is important to appreciate the role that coordination plays within organizations.* ◇ *IMF loans aided economic development, but in the process made the country into a debtor nation.* **16** used to show a rate or relative amount: *The accuracy was high, with an error rate of one in a million.* ◇ *One in ten Americans lives in California today.* IDM **in that** /ɪn ðət/ for the reason that: *The court declared that the company had acted unfairly in that it had not granted him an oral hearing.*

in[2] /ɪn/ *adv.* HELP For the special uses of **in** in phrasal verbs, look at the entries for the verbs. For example **write in (to sb/sth)** is in the phrasal verb section at **write**. **1** contained within an area, an object or a substance: *Prisoners were locked in for the night.* **2** into an area, an object or a substance: *She knocked on his door and went in.*

in·abil·ity /ˌɪnəˈbɪləti/ *noun* [U, sing.] **~ (of sb/sth) to do sth** the fact of not being able to do sth: *The inability of the UK to adapt to its changed international position meant a series of policy changes that depressed economic growth.* ◇ *Having a mental illness does not imply an inability to make decisions.* OPP ABILITY (1)

in·access·ible AWL /ˌɪnækˈsesəbl/ *adj.* difficult or impossible to reach or to get: *Many previously inaccessible markets, such as China and Russia, have now opened up.* ◇ **~ to sb/sth** *War had been declared in February 1793, rendering France virtually inaccessible to British citizens.* OPP ACCESSIBLE (1) ■ **in·access·ibil·ity** /ˌɪnækˌsesəˈbɪləti/ *noun* [U] **~ (of sth)** *In the short term, the inaccessibility of raw materials was a handicap.*

in·accur·ate AWL /ɪnˈækjərət/ *adj.* not exact or accurate; with mistakes: *Simulations based on incomplete or inaccurate information can be misleading.* ◇ *Concerns about the quality of data from the database remain, such as missing, incomplete or inaccurate data.* ◇ **it is ~ to do sth** *It would be inaccurate to draw general conclusions from this small amount of evidence.* OPP ACCURATE (1) ■ **in·accur·acy** AWL /ɪnˈækjərəsi/ *noun* (*pl.* **-ies**) [C, U] *The analysis of fresh samples reduces inaccuracies caused by sample deterioration.* ◇ **~ in (doing) sth** *Demographers cannot be held responsible for inaccuracy in forecasting population 20 years ahead.* **in·accur·ate·ly** *adv.*: *These terms of reference were often not translated at all, or were translated inaccurately.*

in·acti·vate /ɪnˈæktɪveɪt/ *verb* **~ sth** (*technical*) to make sth stop doing sth; to make sth no longer active: *When tumour suppressor genes are inactivated, the growth of altered cells is no longer prevented, and this permits the development of cancer.*

in·active /ɪnˈæktɪv/ *adj.* **1** not doing anything or showing much activity; not in use: *In 2007 only 22% of married women were economically inactive.* ◇ *Like many US cities in relatively inactive geological regions, New York City is not well prepared for the large earthquakes that might someday strike.* ◇ *Oil wells eventually become inactive because of diminished economic returns or mechanical problems.* HELP In medicine, an **inactive** disease is present, but is not showing any symptoms: *At the time of the examination, the patient's rheumatoid arthritis was inactive.* OPP ACTIVE[1] **2** not taking part in physical activity or exercise: *Diabetes prevalence has been shown to be highest among obese and physically inactive people.* OPP ACTIVE[1] (2) **3** having no chemical or biological effect: *Most of the key genes in development are initially in an inactive state and require activators to turn them on.* OPP ACTIVE[1] (5)

in·activ·ity /ˌɪnækˈtɪvəti/ *noun* [U] **1** the state of not being active: *Floodplain sedimentation is sporadic, with relatively long periods of inactivity.* ◇ **~ of sth** *Continued inactivity of a gene would require the continual presence of repressor proteins.* OPP ACTIVITY (3) **2** the fact of not taking part in physical activity or exercise: *Patients may have low levels of self-esteem due to their inactivity and poor fitness.* OPP ACTIVITY (3)

in·ad·equacy AWL /ɪnˈædɪkwəsi/ *noun* (*pl.* **-ies**) **1** [U] **~ (of sth)** the state of not being enough or good enough: *The disaster was largely due to the inadequacy of his military leadership.* OPP ADEQUACY **2** [C, usually pl.] a weakness; a lack of sth: **~ (of sth)** *Owing to the inadequacies of the geological record, the timing of events on the early Earth is open to considerable uncertainty.* ◇ **~ in sth** *Inadequacies in corporate governance have been brought to light since the financial crisis.* **3** [U] a state of not being able or confident to deal with a situation: *They typically exhibit low self-confidence and struggle with feelings of inadequacy, guilt and shame.*

in·ad·equate AWL /ɪnˈædɪkwət/ *adj.* **1** not enough; not good enough: *Malnutrition results from inadequate dietary intake.* ◇ **~ for sth** *Public transport provision is woefully inadequate for the needs of poor people.* ◇ **~ to do sth** *The educational institutions seem wholly inadequate to meet the challenges that the country now confronts.* OPP ADEQUATE **2** (of people) not able, or not confident enough, to deal with a situation: *Mothers often feel inadequate and guilty that they are not offering the best to their child.* ◇ **~ to sth** *Employees may suffer a loss of self-*

image because they feel inadequate to the job. ■ **in·ad·equate·ly** AWL *adv.*: *Managers need to evaluate the risk of launching an inadequately tested product.*

in·ad·mis·sible /ˌɪnəd'mɪsəbl/ *adj.* that cannot be allowed or accepted, especially in court: *The Court of Justice declared the application inadmissible.*

in·appro·pri·ate AWL /ˌɪnə'prəʊpriət; *NAmE* ˌɪnə'proʊpriət/ *adj.* not suitable or appropriate in a particular situation: *One person's perception of inappropriate behaviour may differ from another's.* ◇ **~ for sb/sth** *The health system may be culturally inappropriate for patients from minority ethnic groups.* ◇ **it is ~ (for sb/sth) to do sth** *It is usually inappropriate for a biomedical scientist to discuss the results of clinical tests with a patient.* ◇ **~ to sth** *A common source of measurement error is using variables that are inappropriate to the research problem.* OPP APPROPRIATE[1] ■ **in·appro·pri·ate·ly** AWL *adv.*: *People may say that they deserved the punishment because they behaved inappropriately.*

I

ˌin-ˈbuilt *adj.* = BUILT-IN

in·cap·able AWL /ɪn'keɪpəbl/ *adj.* not able to do sth: **~ of sth** *Paralysis may be so severe that it leaves the person incapable of speech.* ◇ **~ of doing sth** *Cities are experiencing intense pressure to provide housing but are incapable of responding adequately.* OPP CAPABLE (1)

in·cen·tive AWL /ɪn'sentɪv/ *noun* **1** [C, U] something that encourages you to do sth: **~ for/to sb/sth to do sth** *This programme has provided a great incentive for students to continue their studies.* ◇ **~ to do sth** *Governments have little incentive to introduce any reforms that might reduce their own powers.* ◇ **~ for sth** *It is necessary to look more closely at the incentives for innovation.* **2** [C] a payment or other encouragement that is given in order to increase investment or production: **~ for sb/sth (to do sth)** *This scheme offers a financial incentive for firms to create new drugs for neglected diseases.* ◇ **~ (to sb/sth) to do sth** *A firm may use output-based pay, which provides direct incentives to workers to produce more.*

inch /ɪntʃ/ *noun* (*abbr.* **in.**) a unit for measuring length, equal to 2.54 centimetres. There are 12 inches in a foot: *Sugar cane measures between six inches and a foot in diameter when fully grown.* ◇ *The resolution should be about 72 ppi (pixels per inch) for screen display.* ➲ grammar note *at* METRE

in·ci·dence AWL /'ɪnsɪdəns/ *noun* **1** [U, C, usually sing.] the number of times sth unpleasant, such as a disease or crime, happens in a particular group or particular situation: *A recent study of airline pilots showed no overall increase in cancer incidence.* ◇ **~ of sth** *The foundation is funding efforts to reduce the incidence of disease in the area.* ◇ *One of the root causes of conflict in these countries is the high incidence of poverty.* ➲ *compare* OCCURRENCE (1) **2** [U] (*physics*) the way in which a line, especially a line of light, meets a surface: *The angle of refraction is larger than the angle of incidence.* ◇ **+ noun** *The incoming ray may not actually strike the lens at the normal incidence angle.*

in·ci·dent[1] AWL /'ɪnsɪdənt/ *noun* **1** [C] **~ (of sth)** something that happens, especially sth unusual or unpleasant: *All incidents of abnormally high rainfall that occurred in the area were recorded.* ◇ *Following a serious pollution incident, the Assembly passed the Special Act to Punish Environmental Crime.* ◇ *A number of studies detail the effect of a patient safety incident on physicians.* **2** [C, U] a serious or violent event, such as a crime, an accident or an attack: *The policy was developed in the United States after a number of extremely violent incidents in public schools.* ◇ *He made his way to a police station to report the incident.* ◇ **without ~** *The demonstration passed off without incident.* **3** [C] a disagreement between two countries, often involving military forces: *What might have been a localized incident quickly sparked a general war.*

incident[2] /'ɪnsɪdənt/ *adj.* (*technical*) (especially of light or other RADIATION) falling on sth: *The units were then covered with black plastic to eliminate incident light.* ◇ **~ on sth** *The most efficient solar cells can convert nearly one quarter of the sunlight incident on them into electricity.*

in·ci·den·tal /ˌɪnsɪ'dentl/ *adj.* **1 ~ (to sth)** happening in connection with sth else, but not as important as it, or not intended: *The discovery was incidental to their main research.* **2 ~ to sth** (*technical*) happening as a natural result of sth: *Atrocities were not incidental to the conduct of war, but were routine and strategic.*

in·ci·den·tal·ly AWL /ˌɪnsɪ'dentli/ *adv.* **1** used to give some extra information, or to introduce a new topic: *All the contributors, incidentally, work in the United States.* **2** in a way that is not planned, or not of central importance, but that is connected with sth else: *Fifty per cent of all renal cancers are discovered incidentally.* ◇ *Details of weather forecasting are considered only incidentally in this book.*

in·clin·ation AWL /ˌɪnklɪ'neɪʃn/ *noun* **1** [C, U] a feeling that makes you want to do sth: **~ (to do sth)** *Many employees have a strong inclination to make the customer happy.* ◇ *The courts have shown little inclination to intervene in these matters.* ◇ **~ towards sth** *Education will not in itself be adequate to overcome inclinations towards violence.* **2** [C] a tendency to do sth or to behave in a particular way SYN TENDENCY (1): **~ (of sb)** *This study aims to examine the political inclinations of people in various social groups.* ◇ **~ (for sb) to do sth** *As vehicles are made safer, there is a natural inclination for drivers to take more risks.* **3** [C, usually sing., U] the fact or degree of sloping: **~ (of sth) (to sth)** *The vertical axis of the chart shows the inclination of the c axis to the microscope stage.* ◇ **~ towards sth** *The summer solstice is the time when the hemisphere reaches maximum inclination towards the sun.*

in·cline AWL /ɪn'klaɪn/ *verb* **1** [I, T] to tend to think or behave in a particular way; to make sb do this: **~ to/towards sth** *He was inclining more and more to the opinion that a Mathematical Department should be established.* ◇ **~ to do sth** *Generally, he inclined to agree with the conclusions they had reached.* ◇ **~ sb/sth to do sth** *Scholars should try to understand what inclines the practitioners of international relations to act the way they do.* **2** [I, T] to lean or slope in a particular direction; to make sth lean or slope: **~ (from...) (to...)** *The topography of the basin inclines from south-west to north-east.* ◇ **~ sth** *A double, conflicting flow is obtained by inclining the tube.*

in·clined AWL /ɪn'klaɪnd/ *adj.* **1 ~ to do sth** tending to do sth; likely to do sth: *Since the end of the Cold War, states have become less inclined to automatically condemn the actions of other states.* **2** [not before noun] **~ (to do sth)** wanting to do sth: *One might be inclined to dismiss such arguments as mere prejudice.* **3 ~ to agree, believe, think, etc.** used when you are expressing an opinion but do not want to express it very strongly: *I am inclined to think there is truth and nonsense on both sides.* ◇ *In such cases, I am inclined to say that priority must be given to needs over wants.* **4** (used with particular adverbs) having a natural ability for sth; preferring to do sth: *Scientifically inclined individuals took small but important steps towards a systematic exploration of earthquakes as a natural phenomenon.* **5** sloping; at an angle: *The ground surface is gently inclined and covered with fine sediment.*

in·clude /ɪn'kluːd/ *verb* **1** (not used in the progressive tenses) if one thing **includes** another, it has the second thing as one of its parts: **~ sth** *The questions addressed include the following:...* ◇ *There are many systems that are composed of individual parts linked together in some way.*

Examples include the Internet, and human societies. ◇ **~ doing sth** *The role includes reviewing the company's organizational structure.* **2** to make sb/sth part of sth, or part of a group of things: **~ sb/sth** *The content of the tests was expanded to include more spatial reasoning.* ◇ **be included** *The European Union is a major trading power, accounting for about 40 per cent of all global trade, if intra-EU trade is included.* ◇ **~ sb/sth in/within sth** *The steel sector was included within the scope of the Directive.* ◇ **~ sth with sth** *Return envelopes were included with the questionnaires to increase response rates.* ◇ **~ sb/sth as sth** *Frequency of attendance is included as a control variable in the test.* OPP EXCLUDE (1)

▸ INCLUDE + NOUN **the following • variable • measure • information • data • reference • material • item • factor • element • component • detail • aspect • feature • characteristics** *Key demographic variables were included in the final model.* ◇ *Descriptions of symptoms typically include references to poor concentration and anxiety.*

▸ ADVERB + INCLUDE **usually, generally • typically • therefore, thus • explicitly • necessarily** *Natural beech forests typically include trees both larger and older than trees in conventionally managed forests.*

▸ VERB + TO INCLUDE **expand (sth), broaden (sth) • extend sth** *This model has been extended to include exports and imports and international financial markets.*

▸ INCLUDE IN + NOUN **review • analysis • list • model • study • sample** *Studies included in this review were often limited by small samples.*

in·clud·ing /ɪnˈkluːdɪŋ/ *prep.* (*abbr.* **incl.**) having sth as part of a group or set: *Sometimes the problems are related to conditions at school, including bullying.* ◇ *Including this year, six of the seven warmest years on record have occurred since 2001.* ◇ **not ~** *By 1574 there were 100 000 copies in print, not including reprints.* OPP EXCLUDING

in·clu·sion /ɪnˈkluːʒn/ *noun* **1** [U] the fact of including sb/sth; the fact of being included: *The degree of social inclusion that children experience at school and at home is vital.* ◇ **~ in sth** *Some members of the population have little or no chance of being selected for inclusion in the sample.* ◇ **~ of sth** *The inclusion of an excessive amount of a selective agent, due to a dilution error, is also a potential source of error.* ◇ **for ~** *To be eligible for inclusion, reports had to be written between 2005 and 2011.* ◇ **+ noun** *Inclusion criteria for both studies were fluency in Dutch, and having children 4–18 years of age.* OPP EXCLUSION (1) **2** [C] a person or thing that is included: *A bibliography on this scale is an interesting inclusion.* HELP In geology, an **inclusion** is a very small piece of a different rock or other material inside a particular material: *Diamonds sometimes contain minute inclusions of the minerals garnet, olivine and pyroxene.* OPP EXCLUSION (2)

in·clu·sive /ɪnˈkluːsɪv/ *adj.* including a wide range of people, things or ideas: *The inclusive approach recognizes the interdependence between the employees, investors, customers and suppliers.* OPP EXCLUSIVE (3) ■ **in·clu·sive·ness** *noun* [U] **~ (of sth)** *The inclusiveness of these policies varies, but a constant across policies is the preference for consensus-building rather than conflict.*

in·co·her·ent AWL /ˌɪnkəʊˈhɪərənt; *NAmE* ˌɪnkoʊˈhɪrənt/ *adj.* **1** not logical or well organized: *The government's response to the situation was fragmented and incoherent, with various ministries and agencies pulling in different directions.* OPP COHERENT (1) **2** (of spoken or written language) not clear and hard to understand: *The same day, Kennedy received a rambling, incoherent message from Khrushchev.* ◇ *Other symptoms include disorganized thinking, incoherent speech, mood changes and sleep disturbances.* OPP COHERENT (2) **3** (*physics*) (of waves) not in PHASE with each other: *The individual light waves in light from the sun or from a lamp are incoherent.* OPP COHERENT (4) ■ **in·co·her·ence** /ˌɪnkəʊˈhɪərəns; *NAmE* ˌɪnkoʊˈhɪrəns/ *noun* [U] **~ (of sth)** *They criticized the apparent incoherence of US foreign policy during this period.*

in·come AWL /ˈɪnkʌm; ˈɪnkəm/ *noun* [C, U] the money that a person, region, country, etc. earns from work, from investing money or from business: *The nation's per capita income has risen to about $3 400 a year.* ◇ *Absolute poverty is the level of income below which it is impossible to lead a healthy life.* ◇ **~ of sb/sth** *Recent research relating the income of parents to the subsequent incomes of their grown children has shown that having rich parents pays off.* ◇ **~ of sth** *These adolescents come from households with an average income of $40 000.* ◇ **~ from sth** *The wife had income from her own investments and her farming activities.* ◇ **+ noun** *Income inequality rose dramatically between the early 1970s and the early 2000s.* ➲ *compare* EXPENDITURE (1) ➲ thesaurus note *at* MONEY

▸ ADJECTIVE + INCOME **disposable • personal • national • regional • annual • monthly • per capita • low • high • middle • average • median • mean • total • real • future • current • permanent • gross • net** *The total sample had a median family income level of $20 000–$29 000.* ◇ *The real wage, or real income, refers to wages or income corrected to take account of the effects of inflation.*

▸ NOUN + INCOME **household • family • farm** *In the countryside, household income increased by nearly 60 per cent across the decade.*

▸ VERB + INCOME **have • earn • receive • generate • redistribute • spend • raise • increase • reduce** *Most participants said that they could earn a much higher income in Shanghai than in their home towns.*

▸ INCOME + VERB **increase, rise • fall** *It is estimated that Chinese urban per capita incomes will increase by 200% over 20 years.*

▸ INCOME + NOUN **inequality • elasticity • distribution • gap • level • growth • poverty • tax** *The last dimension, income poverty, is defined as those whose household income is below 50% of the median income.*

▸ NOUN + OF INCOME **proportion, percentage, share • distribution • redistribution • source • level** *Coffee is an important source of income in the highland area of New Guinea.*

ˈincome tax *noun* [U, C] tax paid on personal income: *Taxation of companies' profits may be more beneficial than personal income tax.* ◇ *Higher income taxes may reduce the incentive to work.* ◇ **+ noun** *Income tax rates largely remained at the new higher levels.*

in·com·ing /ˈɪnkʌmɪŋ/ *adj.* [only before noun] **1** arriving somewhere; being received: *At the receiver end of the link, filters separate the incoming signal into four bands.* **2** recently elected or chosen: *The incoming government was pledged to nationalize the railways and the coal and steel industries.*

in·com·pat·ible AWL /ˌɪnkəmˈpætəbl/ *adj.* **1** (of ideas, policies or methods) not able to exist together or be used together because of basic differences: *The interests of the media and the president are very different and often incompatible.* ◇ **~ with sth** *These two different definitions of colonial modernity seem to be incompatible with each other.* OPP COMPATIBLE (1) **2** (of two or more things) of different types so that they cannot be used or mixed together: *Unfortunately, several mutually incompatible technologies were developed nearly simultaneously, forcing consumers to select a particular system.* OPP COMPATIBLE (2) ■ **in·com·pati·bil·ity** AWL /ˌɪnkəmˌpætəˈbɪləti/ *noun* (*pl.* **-ies**) [U, C] *The questions were sent in the body of the email, rather than as attachments, to solve problems of software incompatibility.* ◇ *The nature of education, citizenship and the nation-state presents a series of incompatibilities in the case of refugees.*

I

in·com·pe·tence /ɪnˈkɒmpɪtəns; *NAmE* ɪnˈkɑːmpɪtəns/ *noun* [U] the lack of skill or ability to do your job or a task as it should be done: *He was banned from practising medicine after the deaths of two of his patients as a result of his incompetence.* OPP COMPETENCE (1)

in·com·pe·tent /ɪnˈkɒmpɪtənt; *NAmE* ɪnˈkɑːmpɪtənt/ *adj.* not having the skill or ability to do your job or a task as it should be done: *The navy had a disproportionate number of incompetent officers.* OPP COMPETENT (2)

in·com·plete /ˌɪnkəmˈpliːt/ *adj.* **1** not having everything that it should have; lacking one or more of the necessary parts: *Surveys may underestimate coverage because of incomplete school records of immunization.* ◇ *The response rate was 89.9%. Four questionnaires were excluded due to incomplete data.* OPP COMPLETE[1] (1) **2** not finished or completely developed: *If there was insufficient air supply, incomplete combustion would be expected.* OPP COMPLETE[1] (3) ■ **in·com·plete·ly** *adv.*: *How chronic disorders contribute to lung cancer development is incompletely understood.* ◇ *Exhaust emissions of nitrogen oxides and incompletely burned fuel contribute to the formation of ground-level ozone in the atmosphere.* **in·com·plete·ness** *noun* [U] *Data were adjusted for incompleteness and misclassification.* ◇ **~ of sth** *Health care staff expressed frustration at the incompleteness of the Russian health reforms.*

I

in·com·pre·hen·sible /ɪnˌkɒmprɪˈhensəbl; *NAmE* ɪnˌkɑːmprɪˈhensəbl/ *adj.* **~ (to sb)** impossible to understand: *There are many passages in the book that are incomprehensible to the average reader.* OPP COMPREHENSIBLE

in·con·ceiv·able AWL /ˌɪnkənˈsiːvəbl/ *adj.* impossible to imagine or believe SYN UNTHINKABLE: *Up until now, such a project would have been almost inconceivable.* ◇ **it is ~ to do sth** *It is inconceivable to think of a city today that could develop and function without some planning activity.* ◇ **it is ~ that...** *In light of present sea ice trends, it is not inconceivable that Adelie penguins will continue to decline in the Palmer Station area.* OPP CONCEIVABLE

in·con·clu·sive AWL /ˌɪnkənˈkluːsɪv/ *adj.* not leading to a definite decision or result: *These studies have been criticized for producing inconclusive results.* ◇ *A CT scan is indicated for diagnostic purposes if the clinical findings are inconclusive.* OPP CONCLUSIVE

in·con·sis·tency AWL /ˌɪnkənˈsɪstənsi/ *noun* (*pl.* -ies) **1** [C, U] the fact of not matching sth else; something that does not match sth else: **~ in sth** *There may be missing information and inconsistencies in the report.* ◇ **~ between A and B** *Their analysis of the data revealed an inconsistency between some of the quantitative and qualitative data.* **2** [U] the fact of not always behaving in the same way, or of not always having the same opinions or standards: **~ in sth** *The apparent inconsistency in elements of US foreign policy can often be traced to power-sharing between the different branches of government.* ◇ **~ between A and B** *Inconsistency between beliefs and practices is to be expected because of the complexities of classroom life.*

in·con·sist·ent AWL /ˌɪnkənˈsɪstənt/ *adj.* **1** [not usually before noun] if two statements, etc. are **inconsistent**, or one is **inconsistent with** the other, they cannot both be true because they give the facts in a different way: *The researchers show evidence that what people say and do is inconsistent.* ◇ **~ with sth** *The present results are inconsistent with previous research.* OPP CONSISTENT (1) **2 ~ with sth** not matching a set of standards or ideas; different from sb's previous behaviour: *The present solution appears to be inconsistent with the best science.* ◇ *Children occasionally behave in ways that are inconsistent with their usual behaviour.* OPP CONSISTENT (3) **3** tending to change too often; not staying the same: *Given the inconsistent findings, there is clearly a need for further research.* ◇ **~ in sth** *Cialdini argued that people are often inconsistent in their choices.* OPP CONSISTENT (2) ■ **in·con·sist·ent·ly** *adv.* **~ (with sth)** *The government has a legal obligation not to act inconsistently with its own policy.* ◇ *Our research data suggest that in practice, the guidelines are differently interpreted and inconsistently applied.*

in·corp·or·ate AWL /ɪnˈkɔːpəreɪt; *NAmE* ɪnˈkɔːrpəreɪt/ *verb* **1** to include sth so that it forms a part of sth: **~ sth** *Customers tend to like buying new cars because they incorporate the latest design features.* ◇ **~ sth in/into/within sth** *Research results are incorporated in educational materials.* **2** [usually passive] (*business*) to create a legally recognized company: **be incorporated** *646 000 new businesses were incorporated in the US in 1990.*

in·corp·or·ation AWL /ɪnˌkɔːpəˈreɪʃn; *NAmE* ɪnˌkɔːrpəˈreɪʃn/ *noun* [U] **1** the act or process of including sth so that it forms part of sth: **~ in/into sth** *These compounds are commonly used as fire retardants by incorporation in many commercial and household products.* ◇ **~ of sth (into sth)** *The incorporation of vocabulary from one language into another is a normal aspect of language change.* HELP In law, the **incorporation** of an act is the process that legally includes it in the laws of a country for the first time: *The incorporation of the European Convention of Human Rights into English law provides questions for people working in public health.* **2** (*business*) the act or process of creating a legally recognized company: *The company had complied with the requirements of incorporation under Singaporean law.*

in·cor·rect /ˌɪnkəˈrekt/ *adj.* not accurate or true: *Positive feedback was given for correct answers and negative feedback for incorrect answers.* ◇ **it is ~ to do sth** *It would be incorrect to conclude from evidence of this kind that the Single Market Programme has failed.* OPP CORRECT[1] (1) ■ **in·cor·rect·ly** *adv.*: *20% of patients without the disease were incorrectly identified as test positive.*

in·crease[1] /ɪnˈkriːs/ *verb* [I, T] to become or make sth greater in size, amount or degree: **~ (from A) (to B)** *The percentage of the population living in poverty increased from 40 per cent to 60 per cent.* ◇ *By 1987 the market share had increased to 34%.* ◇ **~ in sth** *As Western cities increase in size, their overall population density falls.* ◇ **~ by sth** *The number of Americans lacking health insurance increased by at least 6 million during the 1980s.* ◇ **~ with sth** *Breast cancer increases with age and over 50 per cent of cases are diagnosed over the age of 60 years.* ◇ **~ sth** *Heavy advertising of strawberries may increase demand for strawberries.* ◇ **~ sth (from A) to B** *10 new states have joined the EU, increasing the number of language combinations from 110 to 380.* ◇ **~ sth by sth** *The government proposed to increase the number of police officers by 20 000.* OPP DECREASE[1] ➲ language bank *at* TREND ■ **in·creased** *adj.* [only before noun] *Those with fair skin, blue eyes and blond hair have at least a 60% increased risk of skin cancer.*

▸ INCREASE + NOUN **number • size • share • level • volume • quantity • rate • speed • frequency • pressure • temperature • density • concentration • likelihood, probability, odds • chance • risk** *Increasing the pressure results in a decrease in the volume.* ◇ *Human activities will increase the likelihood of natural disasters such as floods, wildfires and storms.* | **awareness • understanding • participation • activity • uptake • demand • supply • availability • coverage • incidence • competition • sensitivity • fitness** *Competitions can help increase awareness of a brand.* ◇ *A number of factors are likely to increase participation in training in the future.* | **spending, expenditure • price • cost • profit • revenue • sale • consumption • efficiency • productivity • capacity • output • production • effectiveness** *It was thought that a common currency would help increase economic efficiency in the EU.*

▸ NOUN + INCREASE **price • rate • number • demand • temperature** *As prices increase, this leads to an increase in the quantity supplied, because producers can afford to produce more.*
▸ ADVERB + INCREASE | INCREASE + ADVERB **greatly, substantially, considerably • significantly • rapidly • sharply • markedly • dramatically • exponentially • steadily • gradually • slightly** *The number of farms in the region increased dramatically.* ◇ *The share of jobs accounted for by small firms has steadily increased in most developed economies.*
▸ VERB + TO INCREASE **continue • tend • be expected • be found • be likely** *Other solids including carbon particles have also been found to increase the rate of oxidation by molecular oxygen.*
▸ INCREASE IN + NOUN **size • number • frequency • value • importance** *During the first 8 weeks after conception, the embryonic body does not increase greatly in size.*
▸ INCREASE WITH + NOUN **age • size • temperature • time • distance • length • increase** *The risk of infectious disease hospitalization increased 6% with each 1-year increase in vaccination age.*

in·crease² /ˈɪŋkriːs/ *noun* [C, U] a rise in the size, amount or degree of sth: *A strike could eventually produce substantial wage increases.* ◇ **~ of sth** *Imports and exports amounted to US$509.77 billion, an increase of 7.5%.* ◇ *The current rate of increase of atmospheric carbon dioxide concentration is unprecedented during at least the past 20 000 years.* ◇ **~ in sth** *Since 1995, there has been a 60 per cent increase in the number of people employed in the mills.* HELP Note that you use **increase in** to talk about the thing that is increasing, and **increase of** with a number to talk about how much sth increases. OPP DECREASE²
➲ language bank *at* TREND
IDM **be on the increase** to be increasing: *The use of knives by street gangs is on the increase.*
▸ ADJECTIVE + INCREASE **great, substantial, large • huge, massive • significant • rapid • sharp, steep • marked • dramatic • exponential • slight, modest, small • steady • gradual • average • overall • relative • corresponding • further • recent • annual • natural** *Routine testing resulted in a modest increase in the number of newly diagnosed infections.* ◇ *If demand falls, no further increases in employment can be expected.*
▸ NOUN + INCREASE **price • wage, pay • temperature • tax • output • percentage** *To prevent further price increases, the government wants to reduce demand.*
▸ VERB + INCREASE **experience • see • cause • result in, produce • show • indicate • observe, find • report • reflect • represent** *Most countries are experiencing an increase in the proportion of elderly people.*
▸ INCREASE IN + NOUN **number • amount • quantity • proportion, share, ratio • level • frequency • rate • prevalence • concentration • density • pressure • length • mass • temperature • risk • life expectancy • mortality** *There has been an increase in the prevalence of childhood asthma in developed countries.* | **demand • supply • efficiency • productivity • production • activity • cost • price • spending, expenditure • income • wages** *Sharp increases in the price of oil led some companies to reassess their global strategy.*

in·creas·ing·ly /ɪnˈkriːsɪŋli/ *adv.* more and more all the time: *Qualitative research has become an increasingly popular approach to social research.* ◇ *It is increasingly recognized that humans share 98% of their DNA with other higher primates.* ◇ *Increasingly, communication is recognized as the fundamental process by which organizations exist.*

in·cre·ment /ˈɪŋkrəmənt/ *noun* **1** an increase or addition, especially one of a series: *Both drugs are safe, if started at low doses with small increments.* **2** a regular increase in salary: *Tighter control of the pay bill was established by reducing annual increments.*

in·cre·men·tal /ˌɪŋkrəˈmentl/ *adj.* **1** happening in regular stages: *Incremental changes were made to the European Community's institutional structure.* **2** increasing by regular amounts: *This fund pays for the incremental costs of projects which provide additional benefits.* ■ **in·cre·men·tal·ly** /ˌɪŋkrəˈmentəli/ *adv.*: *Decentralization has proceeded incrementally since 1978.* ◇ *The Conservative Party has incrementally increased the ratio of female candidates to male.*

in·cu·bate /ˈɪŋkjubeɪt/ *verb* **1** [T] **~ sth** to keep cells, bacteria, etc. at a suitable temperature so that they develop: *Then cells were incubated in the dark for 15 minutes at room temperature.* **2** [T] **~ sth** (of a bird) to sit on eggs in order to keep them warm until they HATCH: *Each male has its own nest where it incubates the eggs.* **3** [I] (of a disease) to develop slowly without showing any signs that can be noticed: *The disease incubates for 4 to 12 days after exposure and before showing symptoms.*

in·cu·ba·tion /ˌɪŋkjuˈbeɪʃn/ *noun* **1** [U] the process of keeping cells, bacteria, etc. at a suitable temperature so that they develop: *The behaviour of bacteria may vary according to the temperature of incubation.* **2** [U] the process in which a bird sits on eggs in order to keep them warm until they HATCH: *Canada geese lay three to nine eggs on a 36-hour schedule and start incubation after the third egg is laid.* **3** [C] (*also* **incuˈbation period**) the time between sb getting a disease and the appearance of the first SYMPTOMS: *Most infectious diseases have a long incubation.* ◇ *The incubation period of hepatitis A is 4–6 weeks.*

in·cum·bent¹ /ɪnˈkʌmbənt/ *noun* a person who has an official position: *The parliamentary elections displaced a record number of incumbents.*

in·cum·bent² /ɪnˈkʌmbənt/ *adj.* **1** [only before noun] having an official position: *According to the Mexican constitution, an incumbent president could not stand for re-election.* **2** [not before noun] **~ on/upon sb (to do sth)** necessary as part of sb's duties: *The government realized that it was incumbent on them to act.*

incur /ɪnˈkɜː(r)/ *verb* (**-rr-**) **1 ~ sth** to have to pay costs as a result of your own behaviour or actions: *It is likely that the company will have incurred high costs in the development of such a product.* ◇ *to incur expenses/liabilities/debt/losses* **2 ~ sth** to have to deal with sth unpleasant as a result of your own behaviour or actions: *Raising taxes to maintain government revenues may incur the anger of the electorate.*

in·debt·ed /ɪnˈdetɪd/ *adj.* **1 ~ to sb (for sth)** grateful to sb for helping you: *I am indebted to Jane Roberts for reading and commenting on the first draft.* **2 ~ to sb/sth** influenced by or using information or ideas from sb/sth: *Marx was to remain deeply indebted to German idealist philosophy.* ◇ *Eliot's autobiographical masterpiece, 'Four Quartets', is indebted to Wordsworth's example in 'The Prelude'.* **3** owing money: *The government assisted heavily indebted business groups in contracting loans from nationalized banks.*

in·deed /ɪnˈdiːd/ *adv.* **1** (*especially BrE*) used to introduce a further and stronger or more surprising point: *Not all researchers perceive this as a disadvantage, and indeed feminist researchers often see it as an advantage.* ◇ *These public meetings frequently attracted large audiences; indeed, sometimes the hired accommodation could not hold all who wished to attend.* **2** (*especially BrE*) used after *very* and an adjective or adverb to emphasize a statement, description, etc: *The cases where this would be an appropriate course of action would be very rare indeed.* ◇ *Lunar rocks may have formed very recently indeed in the history of the universe.* **3** used to emphasize a statement that confirms sth that has already been suggested: *It was* *inevitable that he would be asked about these phenomena, and indeed he reported receiving 'numerous' requests for his opinion.*

in·def·in·ite AWL /ɪnˈdefɪnət/ *adj.* **1** lasting for a period of time that has no fixed end: *The father sought political asylum and was granted indefinite leave to remain in the UK.* **2** not clearly expressed or defined SYN IMPRECISE: *The action of folk tales takes place in generic settings and in an indefinite past.*

in͵definite ˈarticle *noun* (*grammar*) the word *a* or *an* in English, or a similar word in another language: *The use of the indefinite article with predicate nouns is a feature of English.* ➲ *compare* DEFINITE ARTICLE

in·def·in·ite·ly AWL /ɪnˈdefɪnətli/ *adv.* **1** for a period of time that has no fixed end or limit: *They argue that if the right policies are chosen, economic growth can continue indefinitely.* **2** to a degree or extent that is not known or stated: *Broadcasting today requires a transmission system that can carry an indefinitely large number of programmes.*

I

in·de·pend·ence /ˌɪndɪˈpendəns/ *noun* [U] **1** (of a country) freedom from political control by other countries: *Croatia had also declared independence.* ◇ **~ from sb/sth** *India gained independence from the British in 1947.* **2** the time when a country gains freedom from political control by another country: *Botswana has been one of the most politically stable countries in Africa since independence in 1966.* **3 ~ (of sb/sth)** freedom from outside control or influence: *The independence of the judiciary is of the greatest importance.* **4** the freedom to organize your own life and make your own decisions without needing help from other people: *Health and social care services need to help older people to maintain independence.* ◇ *Her financial independence allowed her to concentrate almost exclusively on research and writing.* ➲ *compare* DEPENDENCE (1)

in·de·pend·ent /ˌɪndɪˈpendənt/ *adj.* **1** (of a country) having its own government: *The former republics of the USSR are now 15 independent states.* ◇ **~ from/of sth** *Central America became independent from Spain in 1821.* **2** done or given by sb who is not involved in a situation and so is able to judge it fairly: *Prior to signing the agreement, the couple received independent legal advice.* **3** not connected with sth or with each other SYN SEPARATE[1] (2): *Three independent experiments were performed.* ◇ **~ of sb/sth** *The decision to undertake the project is independent of the question of how it should be financed.* ➲ *compare* DEPENDENT[1] (3) **4** not under the control or authority of sb/sth else: *Competition policy is entrusted to independent agencies and courts.* ◇ **~ of sb/sth** *The European Central Bank is completely independent of the national governments.* **5** supported by private money rather than government money SYN PRIVATE[1] (2): *In many continental European countries, health and education are services provided by the independent sector.* **6** confident and able to think or act for yourself without needing to be told what to do by other people: *In her novels, Gaskell creates very independent, strong women.* ◇ **~ of sb/sth** *These youths have reached a point in their lives where they are more independent of their parents.* ➲ *compare* DEPENDENT[1] (1) **7** having or earning enough money so that you do not have to rely on sb else for help: *Women are less likely to find jobs that allow them to be economically independent.* ◇ **~ of sb/sth** *They are self-sufficient and financially independent of their male partners.* ➲ *compare* DEPENDENT[1] (1) **8** not depending on other people for help or care: *Many patients can be helped to remain independent by attendance at a club or day centre.* ➲ *compare* DEPENDENT[1] (1) **9** not representing or belonging to a particular political party: *The remaining seat went to an independent candidate.*

in·de·pend·ent·ly /ˌɪndɪˈpendəntli/ *adv.* **1** without being controlled or influenced by sb/sth else: *The American College of Physicians independently reviewed the guidelines.* ◇ **~ of sb/sth** *These groups generally operate independently of direct government control.* **2** without help from other people: *Interviews were performed with people aged over 65 years, living independently or in sheltered accommodation.* **3** in a way that is not connected with sb/sth else SYN SEPARATELY: *It has been accepted that agriculture evolved independently in Asia, Africa, the Americas and Southern Europe.* ◇ **~ of sb/sth** *In his experiments, he found that different genes acted independently of each other.*

inde͵pendent ˈvariable *noun* (*mathematics*) a VARIABLE whose value does not depend on another variable: *Slight manipulations of the independent variable, price increases, are undertaken to determine their effect if any on sales, the dependent variable.* ➲ *compare* DEPENDENT VARIABLE

ˌin-ˈdepth *adj.* [usually before noun] very thorough and detailed: *The data for this paper were from in-depth interviews with 64 men from diverse socio-economic backgrounds.* ◇ *The report provides an in-depth analysis of the level of public support for adult education.* ➲ *see also* DEPTH (2)

in·de·ter·min·ate /ˌɪndɪˈtɜːmɪnət; *NAmE* ˌɪndɪˈtɜːrmɪnət/ *adj.* that cannot be identified easily or exactly: *The groupings are perhaps a little too vague and indeterminate.* ◇ *The material world is indeterminate; it needs to be interpreted.* ■ **in·de·ter·min·acy** /ˌɪndɪˈtɜːmɪnəsi; *NAmE* ˌɪndɪˈtɜːrmɪnəsi/ *noun* [U] **~ (of sth)** *Indeterminacy and ambiguity are recognized as effects of the modern way of life.*

index[1] AWL /ˈɪndeks/ *noun* **1** (*pl.* **in·dexes**) **~ (to sth)** (in a book or set of books) an alphabetical list of names, subjects, etc. with the numbers of the pages on which they are mentioned: *The topics covered are carefully detailed in the index to this book.* **2** (*pl.* **in·dexes** or **in·dices** /ˈɪndɪsiːz/) a number in a system or scale that represents the average value of particular prices, shares, etc. compared with a previous or standard value: *Whichever index is used, inflation is measured by how fast an average of prices is rising.* ◇ *Shares of large publicly listed companies are included in stock market indices.* **3** (*pl.* **in·dices** /ˈɪndɪsiːz/) **~ of sth** a sign or measure that sth else can be judged by: *One social historian points to this phenomenon as an index of social change.* **4** (in compounds) a number that gives the value of a physical quality in terms of a standard formula: *The decrease in PPV after fluid therapy correlates well with the resulting increase in cardiac index.* ➲ *see also* BODY MASS INDEX, REFRACTIVE INDEX **5** (*usually* **indices** [pl.]) (*mathematics*) a small number written above another number to show how many times the other number must be multiplied by itself. In the EQUATION $4^2 = 16$, the number 2 is an index: *The product is obtained by the base raised to the sum of the indices.* **6** (*pl.* **in·dexes**) (*computing*) a list of items, each of which identifies a particular record in a computer file or DATABASE and contains information about its address: *The computer compares input data with an index to find an address location.*

index[2] AWL /ˈɪndeks/ *verb* **1 ~ sth** to record names, subjects, etc. in an index: *Volunteers have been indexing the records of the Consistory Court of London.* **2 ~ sth** to provide an index to sth: *The Social Sciences Citation Index (SSCI) fully indexes over 1 700 major social science journals.* **3** [usually passive] **~ sth (to sth)** to link salaries, prices, etc. to the level of prices of food and other goods so that they both increase at the same rate: *The basic state pension continues to be indexed to inflation.*

THESAURUS

indicate • suggest • imply • point to *verb*

These words all mean to show that sth is likely to be true or exist, especially based on available evidence.

- to indicate/suggest/imply **that...**
- to point to **the fact that...**
- to indicate/suggest/imply/point to a **need/change/difference/relationship**
- to indicate/suggest/point to the **importance/effect** of sth
- **results/findings** indicate/suggest/imply/point to sth
- **evidence/studies/research/analysis** indicate/suggest/point to sth
- to **clearly** indicate/suggest/imply/point to sth
- to **strongly** indicate/suggest/imply sth
- **seem to** indicate/suggest/imply/point to sth

- **Indicate** and **suggest** are slightly more confident, often used where the evidence for sth is fairly clear; **imply** and **point to** are often more tentative, used where a conclusion is only a possible logical result of the evidence: *The results clearly indicated that these haemoglobins behaved differently.* ◇ *These instances point to the possibility of a more positive and promising approach.*
- **Suggest** and **imply** can often be used in the same way; however, **suggest** is often used to talk about how research or evidence shows a link or a relationship; **imply** is more usually used to talk about how evidence shows things like the need for sth or the existence of sth: *There is stronger data suggesting a possible relationship between multiple birth and postpartum depression.* ◇ *Decline rates imply a need for more upstream investment.*
- **Indicate** is often used to talk about evidence and conclusions that can be measured: *Items were rated using a five-point scale where higher total scores indicated higher levels of parental conflict.*

in·di·cate AWL /ˈɪndɪkeɪt/ *verb* **1** to show that sth is true or exists: **~ sth** *This experiment indicates the need to use higher concentrations of the solution.* ◇ **~ that...** *Bones excavated at the site indicate that its occupants ate a varied diet.* ◇ **~ how/what, etc...** *There is to date no research indicating how to do this.* **2** to be a sign of sth; to show that sth is possible or likely SYN SUGGEST (2): **~ sth** *Not being in the workforce, by itself, does not seem to indicate a higher risk of social exclusion.* ◇ **~ that...** *It is important to look out for signs that might indicate that the patient is becoming agitated.* **3 ~ sth** to represent information without using words: *Table 11.1 indicates the fixed currency conversion rates as agreed in December 1998.* **4** to give information in writing: **~ sth** *The main themes of the new novel would have been indicated on the cover of each monthly part.* ◇ **~ which/where, etc...** *A respondent indicates which items he/she agrees with.* **5** [usually passive] to suggest sth as a necessary or recommended course of action: **be indicated** *Blood transfusion is indicated when 30% of circulating volume is lost.* **6** to mention sth, especially in an indirect or brief way: **~ (to sb) that...** *At one stage the Bolsheviks were indicating that they might indeed accept help.* ◇ **~ sth (to sb)** *They indicated to him their great appreciation for what he had done.* ◇ **~ where/whether, etc...** *The account books do not indicate where the firm's start-up capital came from.* **7 ~ sth** (of an instrument for measuring things) to show a particular measurement: *An instrument may indicate a slightly different value every time a given input is fed into it.*

▸ INDICATE + NOUN **number** *The total fertility rate indicates the average number of children per woman.* | **effect • change • direction • relationship • importance • increase • value • position • rate • time • range** *Changes in these factors may indicate future changes in the economy as a whole.* | **level • degree, extent** *They had to indicate the degree to which they agreed or disagreed with six statements.* | **presence, existence • lack • difference • need • risk • role • nature • problem** *Abnormal patterns of activity might indicate an underlying problem.*

▸ ADVERB + INDICATE | INDICATE + ADVERB **clearly** *Protest demonstrations indicated clearly that a continuation of the authoritarian regime was unacceptable.*

▸ ADVERB + INDICATE **usually • strongly** *These results strongly indicate the value of taking a more flexible approach.* | **necessarily • generally • simply** *A low score might simply indicate that someone was feeling ill during the examination.* | **medically • clinically** *These operations are carried out on the NHS only if medically indicated.*

in·di·ca·tion AWL /ˌɪndɪˈkeɪʃn/ *noun* **1** [C, U] a sign or piece of information that shows that sth exists or is likely to happen: **~ that...** *The first significant indication that American policy might be changing occurred in the following year.* ◇ **~ (of sth)** *The chairman's statement gives some indication of the corporate strategy.* ◇ *Nonetheless, the data do provide a clear indication of the costs of different energy services over the centuries.* **2** [C] **~ (for sth)** a change in the body or mind that suggests that particular medical treatment is necessary: *If diarrhoea occurs in the elderly, then it is an indication for hospital admission.*

in·di·ca·tive AWL /ɪnˈdɪkətɪv/ *adj.* **1** [not usually before noun] **~ (of sth)** showing or suggesting sth: *These soils are also clearly indicative of local environmental conditions.* **2** [only before noun] (*grammar*) stating a fact: *Languages such as Italian and French possess a subjunctive mood which is clearly distinguishable from the indicative mood.*

in·di·ca·tor AWL /ˈɪndɪkeɪtə(r)/ *noun* a sign that shows you the state, existence or level of sth: *Table 17.4 shows the key economic indicators for each post-war decade.* ◇ **~ of sth** *An individual's gender has proved to be a good indicator of a tendency to buy a particular product or brand.*

in·dices *pl. of* INDEX[1]

in·dif·fer·ence /ɪnˈdɪfrəns/ *noun* [U] **~ (to sb/sth)** a lack of interest, feeling or reaction towards sb/sth: *The fundamental problem, Sen argued, was governmental indifference to the plight of the very poor.*

in·dif·fer·ent /ɪnˈdɪfrənt/ *adj.* [not usually before noun] **~ (to sb/sth)** having or showing no interest in sb/sth: *Foster (2001) suggests that many officials were indifferent to statistics and this produced poor legislation.*

in·di·gen·ous /ɪnˈdɪdʒənəs/ *adj.* belonging to a particular place rather than coming to it from somewhere else SYN NATIVE[1] (1): *In North and South America, entirely new populations came in, virtually eliminating the indigenous peoples.* ◇ **~ to...** *Both species are indigenous to Australia.*

in·dir·ect /ˌɪndəˈrekt; ˌɪndaɪˈrekt/ *adj.* [usually before noun] **1** not directly caused by or connected with sth: *There may, however, be a number of more indirect effects on environmental policymaking.* ◇ *Indirect health benefits from smoking bans are evaluated with smoking ban studies.* HELP **Indirect costs** are the costs not directly connected with making a product or providing a service, such as the cost of training, heating or rent: *Fixing the price is merely an issue of calculating all direct and indirect costs and adding a margin for profit.* HELP **Indirect taxes/taxation** are/is paid as an amount added to the price of goods and services rather than being paid on income or profits: *Changes to the rates of indirect taxation came into effect immediately.* OPP DIRECT[1] (1) **2** not done directly; done on sb's behalf by sb else: *Through Italy, the British government exercised an indirect control over the region.* OPP DIRECT[1] (1) **3** suggesting sth without clearly showing it: *There exists only indirect evidence on variations over time in the provision of care.* OPP DIRECT[1] (3) **4** avoiding saying sth in a clear and obvious way: *The speech was an* *indirect attack on the government's policy.* OPP DIRECT[1] (4) **5** (of a route) not going in a straight line; not following the shortest way: *Many got to England by indirect routes.* OPP DIRECT[1] (5)

in·dir·ect·ly /ˌɪndəˈrektli; ˌɪndaɪˈrektli/ *adv.* **1** in a way that is not directly caused by or connected with sth: *Human health may also be indirectly affected by the changes in land use.* ◇ *Energy from the sun drives a system that feeds, directly or indirectly, all the consumers on earth.* OPP DIRECTLY (1) **2** on sb's behalf by sb else: *At least a further 130 million people have jobs indirectly controlled by these corporations.* OPP DIRECTLY (1) **3** without saying sth directly: *The poem indirectly attacks the current political system.* OPP DIRECTLY (4)

in·dis·pens·able /ˌɪndɪˈspensəbl/ *adj.* too important to be without SYN ESSENTIAL[1] (1): *Mathematics plays an indispensable role in every technical discipline.* ◇ **~ to sb/sth** *The cultivation of a middle class is indispensable to economic development.* ◇ **~ for (doing) sth** *The high accuracy of the robot is indispensable for the correct assembly of parts.*

in·dis·tin·guish·able /ˌɪndɪˈstɪŋgwɪʃəbl/ *adj.* if two things are **indistinguishable**, or one is **indistinguishable from** the other, it is impossible to see any differences between them: *The nature of the interactions changes so that they become indistinguishable at sufficiently high energies.* ◇ **~ from sth** *If the oil and mineral are both colourless, the mineral grains may be almost indistinguishable from the oil.*

in·di·vid·ual[1] AWL /ˌɪndɪˈvɪdʒuəl/ *noun* **1** a person considered separately rather than as part of a group: *They would like to be able to identify individuals with personal characteristics best suited to job requirements.* ◇ *Bargaining among private individuals can often solve problems that governments or institutions cannot solve.* ◇ *Rousseau argued that each individual should be allowed to develop their own innate nature.* **2** a single member of a group or class: *They live in a group or as individuals, depending on the species.* ◇ **~ of sth** *Many patterns of animal behaviour appear spontaneously in all individuals of the species.* **3** a person who is very different from others and has lots of new and interesting ideas: *This type of accommodation is for true individuals who want a chance to design their own living space.*

> **WORD FAMILY**
> individual *noun, adj.*
> individually *adv.*
> individuality *noun*
> individualist *noun, adj.*
> individualistic *adj.*
> individualism *noun*

in·di·vid·ual[2] AWL /ˌɪndɪˈvɪdʒuəl/ *adj.* **1** [only before noun] considered separately rather than as part of a group: *Many interest groups, or even individual members of those groups, are able to exert influence over national governments.* ◇ **each ~** *The choice of treatment for each individual patient will depend on several factors.* **2** [only before noun] of or for a particular person: *From the age of 14, children could see the possibility of conflict between individual rights and public good.* **3** [only before noun] designed for use by one person: *Individual ready meals enjoy greater popularity in the UK.* **4** characteristic of a particular person or thing: *Behavioural responses to pain are very individual.* **5** (*usually approving*) having an unusual character SYN DISTINCTIVE, ORIGINAL[1] (2): *It is a highly individual crime novel.*

in·di·vidu·al·ism AWL /ˌɪndɪˈvɪdʒuəlɪzəm/ *noun* [U] **1** the belief that individual people in society should have the right to make their own decisions, rather than be controlled by the government: *Spencer strongly advocated individualism and laissez-faire economics as the foundations for social progress.* **2** the quality of being different from other people and doing things in your own way: *The whole film is a celebration of the hero's individualism.*

individualist AWL /ˌɪndɪˈvɪdʒuəlɪst/ *noun* **1** a person who believes that individual people in society should have the right to make their own decisions, rather than be controlled by the government: *The MP was condemned by the Labour leader as 'a nineteenth-century individualist'.* **2** a person who is different from other people and does things in their own way: *The major stars of the decade were James Dean and Marlon Brando, individualists through and through.*

in·di·vidu·al·is·tic AWL /ˌɪndɪˌvɪdʒuəˈlɪstɪk/ (*also* **in·di·vidu·al·ist** /ˌɪndɪˈvɪdʒuəlɪst/) *adj.* **1** believing that individual people in society should have the right to make their own decisions, rather than be controlled by the government: *Individualistic cultures are based on strong institutions that encourage people to strive and achieve success as individuals.* **2** different from other people and doing things in your own way: *These highly individualistic filmmakers did not have to struggle to find financing or distributors.*

in·di·vidu·al·ity AWL /ˌɪndɪˌvɪdʒuˈæləti/ *noun* [U] the quality of a particular person or thing that makes them different from others of the same kind: *Very often, adolescents need to demonstrate their individuality by their appearance.* ◇ *His music was characterized by great individuality.*

in·di·vidu·al·ize (*BrE also* **-ise**) /ˌɪndɪˈvɪdʒuəlaɪz/ *verb* **~ sth** to make sth different to suit the needs of a particular person, place, etc: *The answer is to individualize patient care.* ■ **in·di·vidu·al·iza·tion, -isa·tion** /ˌɪndɪvɪdʒuəlaɪˈzeɪʃn; *NAmE* ˌɪndɪvɪdʒuələˈzeɪʃn/ *noun* [U] **~ (of sth)** *Technology has made possible greater individualization of learning.*

in·di·vidu·al·ized (*BrE also* **-ised**) AWL /ˌɪndɪˈvɪdʒuəlaɪzd/ *adj.* designed for a particular person or thing; connected with a particular person or thing: *Each employee will have an individualized tax code.* ◇ **~ for sb/sth** *The treatment should be individualized for each patient.*

in·di·vidu·al·ly AWL /ˌɪndɪˈvɪdʒuəli/ *adv.* separately, rather than as a group: *Students are given opportunities to work individually, in small groups, and with the whole class.* ◇ *All birds were individually marked with numbered aluminium rings.*

in·di·vis·ible /ˌɪndɪˈvɪzəbl/ *adj.* that cannot be divided into separate parts: *The idea that matter was composed of indivisible basic particles first arose in the fifth century BC.* ◇ *The human rights of women are an inalienable, integral and indivisible part of universal human rights.* OPP DIVISIBLE ■ **in·di·vis·ibil·ity** /ˌɪndɪˌvɪzəˈbɪləti/ *noun* [U] **~ (of sth)** *The notion of interdependence and indivisibility of all human rights is central to human rights jurisprudence.*

in·door /ˈɪndɔː(r)/ *adj.* [only before noun] located, done or used inside a building: *Thus, indoor air pollution and its health implications are of particular concern in these settings.* OPP OUTDOOR

in·doors /ˌɪnˈdɔːz; *NAmE* ˌɪnˈdɔːrz/ *adv.* inside or into a building: *Given these negative images of the world outside, it seemed no wonder that more children were opting to stay indoors.* OPP OUTDOORS

in·duce AWL /ɪnˈdjuːs; *NAmE* ɪnˈduːs/ *verb* **1 ~ sth** to cause sth: *Certain drugs can induce depression.* ◇ *Major surgery induces profound physiological responses.* ◇ *Changes in daylength are known to induce changes in hormone secretion (Farner and Follett, 1979; Nicholls et al.,1988).* **2 ~ sb to do sth** to persuade or influence sb to do sth: *Big business is able to induce the government to do things that enhance profit-making.* ◇ *As a result of the campaign, the targeted firms were induced to sign codes of conduct pledging to improve working conditions.*

3 ~ sth (*physics*) to produce an electric charge or current, or a MAGNETIC state by induction: *The current in the primary winding is induced by the rotating magnet.* **4 ~ sth (from sth)** to use particular facts and examples to form a general rule or principle: *From the experimental evidence, one infers or induces the hypothesis.* ➲ *see also* INDUCTIVE

in·duc·tion AWL /ɪn'dʌkʃn/ *noun* **1** [U] (*technical*) a method of discovering general rules and principles from particular facts and examples: *Analytic induction is an extremely rigorous method of analysis.* ◇ **by ~** *Aristotle maintained that it is by induction that generalizations about forms are drawn from sense experience.* ➲ *compare* DEDUCTION (2) **2 ~ (of sth)** [U] the process or action of causing or starting sth: *Premedication refers to the administration of drugs 1-2 hours prior to the induction of anaesthesia.* HELP This meaning is used especially in medicine and biology and related areas of study. **3** [U] (*physics*) the process by which electricity or MAGNETISM passes from one object to another without them touching: *Faraday demonstrated electromagnetic induction in 1831.* ◇ **+ noun** *A copper induction coil surrounds the quartz tube to provide an alternating electromagnetic field within the flowing stream of argon gas.* **4** [U, C] **~ (into sth)** the process of introducing sb to a new job, skill, organization or group: *His prowess on the playing field led to his induction into the Baseball Hall of Fame in 1962.* **5** (*also* **mathe'matical induction**) [U] (*mathematics*) a method of proof to show that a given mathematical statement is true for all whole, positive numbers above zero, that begins by proving the statement for the smallest possible number, and then for the next term in the series: *Despite the name, proof by induction is a deductive form of reasoning.*

in·duct·ive /ɪn'dʌktɪv/ *adj.* (*technical*) using particular facts and examples to form general rules and principles: *Charmaz's (1997) research is an interesting illustration of an inductive approach.* ➲ *compare* DEDUCTIVE ■ **in·duct·ive·ly** *adv.*: *Categories for content were developed inductively from the data that were collected.*

in·dus·trial /ɪn'dʌstriəl/ *adj.* [usually before noun] **1** connected with industry: *Annual growth in the industrial sector fell dramatically.* ◇ *China has experienced the most rapid and remarkable industrial development in history.* ◇ *Water quality problems included groundwater contamination from agricultural and industrial chemicals.* **2** having many industries: *Poor working people crowded the industrial districts of the city.* ◇ *Advanced industrial societies have moved from being manufacturing economies to service sector economies.* ➲ *see also* PRE-INDUSTRIAL ■ **in·dus·tri·al·ly** /ɪn'dʌstriəli/ *adv.*: *Cities with industrially diversified economies are better able to sustain prosperity over the very long term.*

in·dus·tri·al·ist /ɪn'dʌstriəlɪst/ *noun* a person who owns or runs a large factory or industrial company: *Industrialists had the means to exert their influence on government choices.*

in·dus·tri·al·ize (*BrE also* **-ise**) /ɪn'dʌstriəlaɪz/ *verb* [I, T] to develop industries in a country or region on a large scale: *Most areas of eastern and east central Europe did not industrialize until after 1880.* ◇ **~ sth** *A small white minority used vast mineral wealth to industrialize the economy.* ■ **in·dus·tri·al·iza·tion, -isa·tion** /ɪn,dʌstriəlaɪ'zeɪʃn; *NAmE* ɪn,dʌstriələ'zeɪʃn/ *noun* [U] *Global industrialization currently depends on continual, increasing consumption of fossil fuels.* ◇ **~ of sth** *This readily available supply of iron ore contributed significantly to the rapid industrialization of North America*

in·dus·tri·al·ized (*BrE also* **-ised**) /ɪn'dʌstriəlaɪzd/ *adj.* (of a country, area or society) that has a lot of industry: *The Kyoto Protocol called for the major industrialized nations to cut their collective emissions by 5% from 1990 levels.* ◇ *By the late 1920s, Japan had become heavily industrialized.*

in,dustrial re'lations *noun* [pl.] relations between employers and employees in industry: *Unsurprisingly, industrial relations were often marked by conflict.*

the In,dustrial Revo'lution *noun* [sing.] the period in the 18th and 19th centuries in Europe and the US when machines began to be used to do work, and industry grew quickly: *Prior to the Industrial Revolution, industrial activity was domestic, small in scale, and dispersed.*

in·dus·try /'ɪndəstri/ *noun* (*pl.* **-ies**) **1** [C] the people and activities involved in producing a particular thing, or in providing a particular service: *The area's major industries are machinery, chemicals and food processing.* ◇ *General Motors entered the Korean automobile industry in 1972.* ◇ *The service industry grew along with manufacturing during the Industrial Revolution.* ◇ **in an ~** *In the pharmaceutical industry, regulations govern testing, approval, manufacturing, labelling, and the marketing of drugs.* **2** [U] the production of goods from raw materials, especially in factories: *The majority of air pollutants are caused by industry or transport.* ◇ *Japanese society is characterized by close relationships between government and industry.* ◇ **in ~** *Catalytic oxidation is widely used in industry.* **3** [U] (*formal*) the quality of working hard: *Prior to her marriage, she had been dependent upon her own industry for a living.* ◇ **~ of sb** *The industry of colonizers was said to grant legitimate ownership of the land they worked.*

▸ ADJECTIVE + INDUSTRY **heavy • light • manufacturing • domestic • local • private** *The economy is now much less dependent on heavy industry.* | **global • major • new • traditional • competitive • pharmaceutical • automotive • chemical** *Huge losses in recent years have tested the global insurance industry to the limit.*

▸ NOUN + INDUSTRY **service • film • food • gas • oil, petroleum • textile • airline • automobile, car • steel • construction • computer • music • electronics** *By the 1990s, film industries in Asia and Europe were increasingly integrated with the American studios.*

▸ VERB + INDUSTRY **enter • develop • protect • support • dominate • nationalize • regulate** *In 1971 Libya nationalized its oil industry.*

in·ef·fect·ive /,ɪnɪ'fektɪv/ *adj.* not achieving what you want to achieve; not having any effect: *Ineffective strategic management can bankrupt companies.* ◇ **~ in doing sth** *Merely giving advice seems to have been ineffective in addressing the problem.* ◇ **~ at doing sth** *The international regime has proved to be ineffective at implementing measures to prevent humanitarian catastrophes.* OPP EFFECTIVE (1) ■ **in·ef·fect·ive·ly** *adv.*: *Both Conservative and Labour governments of the early 1970s tried to intervene, but ineffectively and much too late.* **in·ef·fect·ive·ness** *noun* [U] **~ (of sth)** *The students urged voters to cast their ballots for McCarthy in protest against the ineffectiveness of Johnson's policies.*

in·ef·fi·cient /,ɪnɪ'fɪʃnt/ *adj.* not doing a job well and not making the best use of time, money, energy, etc: *In this situation, it is unlikely that inefficient firms will survive.* ◇ *Manual methods for this process are slow and relatively inefficient.* OPP EFFICIENT ■ **in·ef·fi·ciency** /,ɪnɪ'fɪʃənsi/ *noun* (*pl.* **-ies**) [U, C] *Revolutions may take place because the old regime simply collapses out of economic inefficiency.* ◇ *It is very hard for the central bankers to pinpoint market inefficiencies with certainty.* **in·ef·fi·cient·ly** *adv.*: *Cars and shipping burn fuel inefficiently.*

in·elas·tic /,ɪnɪ'læstɪk/ *adj.* **1** (*economics*) (of demand or supply) slow to be affected by changes in price or income: *The trade balance worsened as a result of the relatively inelastic demand for oil.* **2** (of a substance or material) unable to stretch and return to its original size and shape: *Inelastic skin is one of the signs of dehydration.*

I

in·eli·gible /ɪnˈelɪdʒəbl/ *adj.* not having the necessary qualifications to have or to do sth: *One participant was identified as ineligible.* ◇ **~ for sth** *Overall, 36 caregivers were ineligible for the study following the assessment.* ◇ **~ to do sth** *Individuals on probation are ineligible to vote in 30 states, while those on parole are ineligible in 35 states.* OPP ELIGIBLE ■ **in·eli·gi·bil·ity** /ɪnˌelɪdʒəˈbɪləti/ *noun* [U] *The legislative criteria for ineligibility are the same in both cases.*

in·equal·ity /ˌɪnɪˈkwɒləti; NAmE ˌɪnɪˈkwɑːləti/ *noun* (*pl.* **-ies**) [U, C] the unfair difference between groups of people in society, when some have more money, power or opportunities than others: *Greater growth may also lead to greater inequality as some people gain more than others.* ◇ *In recent decades, income and health inequalities have grown.* ◇ **~ in sth** *Dr Gordon summarized policies in the UK, the Netherlands and Sweden aimed at reducing inequalities in health.* ◇ **~ between sb/sth** *There is still widespread inequality between socio-economic classes.* ◇ **~ of sth** *Addressing the inequality of opportunities is fundamental to the pursuit of social justice.* OPP EQUALITY (1) ➲ *see also* UNEQUAL (1)

▸ ADJECTIVE + INEQUALITY **high • low • greater • increasing, growing, rising • global • social • economic • socio-economic • educational • ethnic • racial • structural** *In the developed world, rising social inequalities characterized the social landscape of the 1980s and 1990s.*

▸ NOUN + INEQUALITY **income • wage • health • gender • class** *Gender inequalities are considerably greater in the poor than in the rich world.*

▸ VERB + INEQUALITY **tackle, address • reduce • produce • increase • perpetuate • explain** *Tackling ethnic inequalities in health demands a comprehensive European strategy.*

in·equit·able /ɪnˈekwɪtəbl/ *adj.* not fair; not the same for everyone SYN UNFAIR: *Political philosophers have long argued that an inequitable distribution of economic resources is likely to distort politics.* OPP EQUITABLE (1)

in·equity /ɪnˈekwəti/ *noun* (*pl.* **-ies**) [U, C] something that is unfair; the state of being unfair SYN INJUSTICE: *The report painted a picture of increasing health inequity.* ◇ *Slower growth is unlikely to reduce inequity, and may increase it.* ◇ *In addition, he shows how big cities tend to perpetuate social inequities.*

inert /ɪˈnɜːt; NAmE ɪˈnɜːrt/ *adj.* **1** (*chemistry*) without active chemical or other properties: *The pressure within a reaction vessel can be increased by injecting an inert gas into it.* ◇ *Reduced gold is a stable and generally inert material highly suitable for medical applications.* **2** (*formal*) without power to move or act: *The peasants were not the inert conservative mass that had been supposed.*

in·er·tia /ɪˈnɜːʃə; NAmE ɪˈnɜːrʃə/ *noun* [U] **1** (*usually disapproving*) lack of energy; lack of desire or ability to move or change: *The powerful forces of organizational inertia mean that organizations respond only slowly and incrementally to change.* **2** (*physics*) a property of matter by which it stays still or, if moving, continues moving in a straight line unless it is acted on by a force outside itself: *Gravity and inertia are intimately connected with each other.*

in·er·tial /ɪˈnɜːʃl; NAmE ɪˈnɜːrʃl/ *adj.* (*technical*) connected with or caused by inertia: *Because of the equivalence of gravitational and inertial mass, the same acceleration is experienced by all bodies.*

in·escap·able /ˌɪnɪˈskeɪpəbl/ *adj.* (of a fact or a situation) impossible to avoid or deny SYN UNAVOIDABLE: *The inescapable conclusion is that these animals became extinct because of the influence of European settlers.* ■ **in·escap·ably** /ˌɪnɪˈskeɪpəbli/ *adv.* SYN UNAVOIDABLY: *Every economic policy question is inescapably political because it confers benefits upon some groups and losses upon others.*

in·ev·it·able AWL /ɪnˈevɪtəbl/ *adj.* **1** that you cannot avoid or prevent SYN UNAVOIDABLE: *Wilson and Kelling argue that crime is the inevitable result of disorder.* ◇ **it is ~ that...** *The complexity of the human genome is such that, during cell division, it is almost inevitable that errors will occur.* **2 the inevitable** *noun* [sing.] something that is certain to happen: *He took out further advances secured on the property; the inevitable happened, and he was unable to make the repayments.* ■ **in·ev·it·abil·ity** AWL /ɪnˌevɪtəˈbɪləti/ *noun* [U, sing.] *Most historians are now agreed that there was no inevitability about the political crisis of the 1640s.* ◇ **~ of sth** *The inevitability of ageing and death has been a major theme in philosophy and literature throughout the ages.*

in·ev·it·ably AWL /ɪnˈevɪtəbli/ *adv.* as is certain to happen: *Perhaps inevitably, there is a wide range of views on this issue.* ◇ *For Marx, the accumulation of capital by owners at the expense of workers inevitably leads to class conflict.*

in·ex·pen·sive /ˌɪnɪkˈspensɪv/ *adj.* not costing a lot of money: *This is a simple, quick and inexpensive technique.* ◇ **~ to do sth** *The tests are relatively inexpensive to perform.* OPP EXPENSIVE

in·ex·peri·enced /ˌɪnɪkˈspɪəriənst; NAmE ˌɪnɪkˈspɪriənst/ *adj.* having little knowledge or experience of sth: *Care of emergency admissions is still largely left to relatively inexperienced junior doctors.* OPP EXPERIENCED

in·ex·tric·ably /ˌɪnɪkˈstrɪkəbli; ɪnˈekstrɪkəbli/ *adv.* if two things are **inextricably linked**, etc, it is impossible to separate them: *Europe's foreign policy is inextricably linked with that of the US.* ◇ *Our future energy choices are now inextricably tied to the fate of our global climate.*

in·fancy /ˈɪnfənsi/ *noun* [U] **1** the time when a child is a baby or very young: *Sleep patterns and behaviour evolve significantly from infancy through childhood and adolescence.* ◇ **in ~** *Respiratory infection is a leading worldwide cause of death in infancy.* **2** the early development of sth: *Military geography in America has evolved from infancy during the course of the 20th century.* ◇ **in its/their ~** *Online surveys are clearly in their infancy but they have considerable potential.*

in·fant /ˈɪnfənt/ *noun* a baby or very young child: *Infants with a low birthweight are at a higher risk of expressing chronic diseases later in life.* ◇ *Turner syndrome affects approximately 1 in 5 000 newborn female infants.* ◇ **+ noun** *At the beginning of the twentieth century, infant mortality in Britain was about 140 per 1 000 live births.* HELP In American English, **infant** is only used for a baby, especially a very young one.

in·fect /ɪnˈfekt/ *verb* **1** to make a disease or an illness spread to a person, an animal or a plant: **~ sb/sth** *The virus leaves the host cell and can then infect other cells.* ◇ **~ sb/sth with sth** *Only about 5% of humans infected with tuberculosis develop the disease.* **2** to make a computer virus spread to another computer or program: **~ sth** *The computer virus replicates itself, infects your hard drive and destroys your files.* ◇ **~ sth with sth** *Once infected with the virus, the computer automatically sends copies of the document to people in the user's address book.*

in·fected /ɪnˈfektɪd/ *adj.* **1** having or containing a disease that was received from contact with sb/sth else: *Consumption of infected meat appears capable of infecting humans with a new variant of the disease.* **2** affected by or containing a computer virus: *In many cases, viruses are spread through users bringing infected disks into offices or educational establishments.*

in·fec·tion /ɪnˈfekʃn/ *noun* **1** [U] the act or process of giving or receiving a disease: *The main human protection against viral infection is the immune system.* ◇ **~ of sth** *The infection of a surgical wound is a relatively common event.* ◇ **~ with sth** *HIV antibodies generally appear within three months after infection with HIV.* **2** [C] a disease that is caused by sth such as bacteria or a virus: *Rabies is an acute viral infection that is usually transmitted through saliva via the bite of an infected animal.* ◇ **~ of sth** *Infections of the skin, nails and hair are caused by a group of fungi known as the dermatophytes.* ➲ thesaurus note *at* DISEASE

in·fec·tious /ɪnˈfekʃəs/ *adj.* **1** (of a disease) that can be passed easily from one person or animal to another, especially through the air they breathe: *Acute outbreaks of infectious diseases have dominated recent national security discussions of global health.* ◇ *Rubella is usually a mild, but highly infectious, viral condition.* **2** [not usually before noun] **~ to sb/sth** (of a person or an animal) having a disease that can be spread to others: *In the carrier state, an apparently cured patient can still be infectious to others.* ➲ *compare* CONTAGIOUS

infer AWL /ɪnˈfɜː(r)/ *verb* (**-rr-**) to reach an opinion or decide that sth is true on the basis of information that is available SYN DEDUCE: **~ sth** *Measurements of the radioactivity in rocks can be used to infer the age of the solar system.* ◇ **~ sth from sth** *Climate change in the dry valleys has been largely inferred from geomorphic evidence of past glacier positions.* ◇ **~ that...** *Some engineers at NASA had inferred that the Shuttle was becoming increasingly likely to have a catastrophic failure.*

in·fer·ence AWL /ˈɪnfərəns/ *noun* **1** [C] **~ (about sth) (from sth)** an opinion that you form based on what you already know SYN DEDUCTION (1): *He used geologic observations to draw inferences about prehistoric earthquakes.* ◇ *She refrains altogether from making biographical inferences from Shakespeare's works.* **2** [U] the act or process of forming an opinion, based on what you already know: **~ (about sth) (from sth)** *Statistical inference is the process of drawing conclusions from sample data about the characteristics of the population that has been sampled.* ◇ **by ~** *The owner of copyright in a work possesses the right to copy and, by inference, the right to prevent others from copying.*

in·fer·ior /ɪnˈfɪəriə(r); *NAmE* ɪnˈfɪriər/ *adj.* **1** low or lower in importance, position or quality: *In production, it is possible that some components will be of inferior quality to those tested.* ◇ **~ to sb/sth** *Learned opinion at that time held that women were morally, physically and intellectually inferior to men.* OPP SUPERIOR[1] (1) **2** (*anatomy*) low or lower in position: *In this patient the superior and inferior mesenteric arteries are blocked.* OPP SUPERIOR[1] (3)

in·fer·ior·ity /ɪnˌfɪəriˈɒrəti; *NAmE* ɪnˌfɪriˈɔːrəti; ɪnˌfɪriˈɑːrəti/ *noun* [U] the state of being lower in importance, position or quality than sb/sth else: *Low scorers are more prone to feelings of inferiority and inadequacy.* ◇ *Only 100 years ago, most people of European descent took the racial inferiority of others to be fact.* OPP SUPERIORITY (1)

in·fer·tile /ɪnˈfɜːtaɪl; *NAmE* ɪnˈfɜːrtl/ *adj.* **1** (of people, animals and plants) not able to have babies or produce young: *Some fertility specialists argue that a twin pregnancy is a desirable outcome for infertile couples.* OPP FERTILE (2) **2** (of land) not able to produce good crops: *The region has relatively infertile soils, particularly low in phosphate.* OPP FERTILE (1) ■ **in·fer·til·ity** /ˌɪnfɜːˈtɪləti; *NAmE* ˌɪnfɜːrˈtɪləti/ *noun* [U] *Both infertility itself and treatments for infertility can be sources of stress.*

in·fin·ite AWL /ˈɪnfɪnət/ *adj.* **1** very great; impossible to measure: *There is an almost infinite number of ways in which digital data may be organized or formatted on a disk.* ◇ *The number of theoretically possible different amino acid sequences is virtually infinite.* ◇ *Human beings can make and learn to recognize an almost infinite variety of speech sounds.* **2** without limits; without end: *It is impossible to complete an infinite series of tasks, since such a series has, by definition, no last member.* OPP FINITE (1)

in·fin·ite·ly AWL /ˈɪnfɪnətli/ *adv.* **1** with no limit or end: *The strings can be of finite length, infinitely long (without ends), or form closed loops.* ◇ *There is not just one such possible world, but infinitely many.* **2** (used especially in comparisons) very much: *The frequent disputes over EU policy are infinitely preferable to what went before.*

in·fini·tive /ɪnˈfɪnətɪv/ *noun* (*grammar*) the basic form of a verb such as *be* or *run*. In English, an infinitive is used by itself, for example *swim* in *She can swim* (this use is sometimes called the **bare infinitive**), or with *to* (the **to-infinitive**) as in *She likes to swim*: *The data show a slow but steady evolution towards the bare infinitive ('help him clean the room') from the 1920s to the 2000s.*

in·fin·ity /ɪnˈfɪnəti/ *noun* (*pl.* **-ies**) **1** (*symb.* ∞) [U, C] (*mathematics*) a number larger than any other: *As n approaches infinity, the energy goes to zero.* ◇ **~ of sth** *Suppose that there is an infinity of all possible universes having all possible sizes, ages, temperatures, shapes and contents.* **2** [U] a point far away that can never be reached: **at ~** *All four sets of planes intersect the z-axis at infinity.* ◇ **to/towards ~** *A uniform plane wave cannot exist physically because it stretches to infinity and would represent an infinite energy.* **3** [U] (*also* **in·fin·it·ies** [pl.]) **~ (of sth)** the state of having no end or limit: *Traherne's poems retain a sense of a free and urgent response to the wonder and infinity of God.* ◇ *Myth was full of images of terrifying abysses and infinities.*

in·flamed /ɪnˈfleɪmd/ *adj.* **1** (of a part of the body) red, sore and SWOLLEN because of infection or injury: *Local heat to the inflamed area may provide some relief.* **2** (of people, feelings or a situation) very angry or excited: *Long after the urban rebellion had been suppressed, the countryside was still inflamed.*

in·flam·ma·tion /ˌɪnfləˈmeɪʃn/ *noun* [U, C] a condition in which a part of the body becomes red, sore and SWOLLEN because of infection or injury: *Steroids are used to reduce the inflammation.* ◇ **~ of sth** *An acute inflammation of the lungs can occur within 1-2 weeks of starting treatment.*

in·flam·ma·tory /ɪnˈflæmətri; *NAmE* ɪnˈflæmətɔːri/ *adj.* **1** causing or involving inflammation: *Asthma is a chronic inflammatory condition of the lungs.* **2** intended to cause very strong feelings of anger: *It is important for both sides in the dispute to refrain from inflammatory statements or threats.*

in·flate /ɪnˈfleɪt/ *verb* **1** [T] **~ sth** to make sth appear to be more important or impressive than it really is: *They argue that the president inflated the security threat to the country.* **2** [T] **~ sth** to increase the amount of sth: *The average figure is inflated by two cases with very high amounts of compensation.* **3** [T, I] **~ (sth)** to fill sth with gas or air; to become filled with gas or air: *The pressure required to inflate a balloon is inversely proportional to the diameter of the balloon.* OPP DEFLATE (1)

in·flated /ɪnˈfleɪtɪd/ *adj.* **1** (especially of prices) higher than is acceptable or reasonable: *Food riots took place at markets where grain was for sale at inflated prices.* **2** (of ideas or claims) believing or claiming that sb/sth is more important or impressive than they really are: *Inflated claims have been made about what can be achieved.*

in·fla·tion /ɪnˈfleɪʃn/ *noun* [U] **1** a general rise in the prices of goods and services in a particular country, resulting in a fall in the value of money; the rate at which this happens: *The aim of the European Central Bank is to reduce inflation to less than 2%.* ◇ *Instead of a period of economic prosperity, the 1970s witnessed high inflation* *and economic stagnation.* ◇ *Escalating rates of inflation reduce the value of the domestic currency.* ◇ **+ noun** *Austria, Germany and Japan have had low inflation rates and low unemployment.* **2** the act or process of filling sth with air or gas: **by ~** *The coronary blood flow is stopped, by balloon inflation, for 2–4 minutes.* ◇ **~ of sth** *Inflation of a tourniquet is followed by the development of a dull, aching pain.* OPP DEFLATION

in·fla·tion·ary /ɪnˈfleɪʃənri; *NAmE* ɪnˈfleɪʃəneri/ *adj.* [usually before noun] causing or connected with a general rise in the prices of goods and services: *Oil price rises may intensify inflationary pressure and slow growth.*

in·flect /ɪnˈflekt/ *verb* **1** [I] (*grammar*) if a word **inflects**, its ending or the way it is spelled changes according to its GRAMMATICAL function in a sentence; if a language **inflects**, it has words that do this: *Modal verbs in English do not inflect for past tense.* **2** [T, usually passive] **~ sth** (*formal*) to influence sth: *His political position was to some extent mediated or inflected by contemporary theological disputes.* ■ **in·flect·ed** *adj.* [usually before noun] *The dictionary displays the inflected forms of each verb.*

in·flec·tion (*also* **in·flex·ion** *especially in BrE*) /ɪnˈflekʃn/ *noun* [C, U] **1** (*grammar*) a change in the form of a word, especially the ending, according to its GRAMMATICAL function in a sentence: *At more advanced levels, learners acquire a systematic knowledge of word inflections and derivations.* **2** a change in how high or low your voice is as you are speaking: *A lack of inflection in his voice made it harder to understand his questioning.*

in·flex·ible AWL /ɪnˈfleksəbl/ *adj.* **1** (*disapproving*) that cannot be changed or made more suitable for a particular situation SYN RIGID (2): *Policies that involve people should not be allowed to become rigid inflexible rules.* **2** (*disapproving*) (of people or organizations) unwilling to change their opinions, decisions or behaviour: *The company was inflexible when minor changes in customers' requirements occurred.* ■ **in·flex·ibil·ity** AWL /ɪnˌfleksəˈbɪləti/ *noun* [U] *One major disadvantage with a Criminal Code is its inflexibility.*

in·flict /ɪnˈflɪkt/ *verb* to make sb/sth suffer sth unpleasant: **~ sth on/upon sb/sth** *Alexander inflicted a severe defeat on the Illyrian king Cleitus.* ◇ **~ sth** *The damage to infrastructure inflicted by the flood was estimated to be around $260 million.* ■ **in·flic·tion** /ɪnˈflɪkʃn/ *noun* [U] **~ (of sth)** *Parental rights do not extend to the infliction of serious harm.*

in·flow /ˈɪnfləʊ; *NAmE* ˈɪnfloʊ/ *noun* **1** [C, U] the movement of a lot of money, people or things into a place from somewhere else SYN INFLUX: *At their peak, net private capital inflows accounted for as much as 17 per cent of Malaysia's GDP in 1993.* ◇ **~ of sb/sth (into/to...) (from...)** *There was an accelerated inflow of people to cities.* ◇ *Europe's brief prosperity in the 1920s depended on the continued inflow of capital from the US.* OPP OUTFLOW **2** [sing., U] **~ (of sth) (to/into...) (from...)** the movement of liquid or air into a place from somewhere else: *Global warming is hypothesized to cause an increased meltwater inflow from Arctic.* ◇ *Inflow into the heated Asian continent occurs as three main airstreams.* OPP OUTFLOW

in·flu·ence¹ /ˈɪnfluəns/ *noun* **1** [U, C] the ability to have an effect on the way that sth works or develops or the way that a person thinks or behaves; the effect itself: **~ (on/upon sb/sth)** *A number of recent studies have examined the influence of university research on industrial innovation.* ◇ *Victorian novelists had a great influence on public attitudes towards imprisonment.* ◇ **under the ~ of sb/sth** *Flow in rivers is unidirectional, proceeding downhill under the influence of gravity.* **2** [U] the power that sb/sth has to control what happens or what sb does: *Unions at the end of the 1970s wielded considerable political influence.* ◇ **~ over sb/sth** *Some drug companies use conferences to exert their influence over GPs.* ◇ **~ in/within sth** *Athens' inability to prevent the growth of Macedonian power and influence in Greece was clear.* ◇ **~ in doing sth** *Television and other media give heads of state enormous influence in shaping people's opinions.* **3** [C] a person or thing that affects the way a person thinks and behaves or the way that sth develops: *Their peers are powerful influences in young girls' lives.* ◇ **~ on sb/sth** *The chief influences on the price of copper in the 20th century were the two world wars, the Wall Street crash and the oil crisis in the 1970s.*

▸ ADJECTIVE + INFLUENCE **great, considerable • enormous • significant • powerful • political • economic** *Clay minerals exert a considerable influence on the properties of a soil.* | **strong • important • major • profound • positive • negative • formative** *The professor of French at Harvard was an important influence on T. S. Eliot.* | **direct • indirect • external • decisive** *The change in the price of one service has a direct influence on the demand for the other service.* | **pervasive • potential • growing • environmental • social • cultural • genetic • causal** *'Shared environment' includes all environmental influences that make children in a family similar to one another.* | **undue** *The Court held that the wife had suffered undue influence in agreeing to the mortgage.*

▸ VERB + INFLUENCE **have • exert, exercise • limit • minimize** *The Crystal Palace continued to exercise its influence on British design for the following 82 years—until it burnt down in 1936.* | **investigate, examine, explore • trace • reflect • acknowledge** *This article traces the influence of Wordsworth's 'Prelude' on several long, autobiographical poems.* | **wield • use • gain • extend • lose** *The balance of resources between government ministers and officials has changed and officials have lost influence.*

▸ NOUN + OF INFLUENCE **sphere** *Rome regarded Britain as lying within its sphere of influence and expected that British rulers should recognize its authority.*

in·flu·ence² /ˈɪnfluəns/ *verb* to have an effect on the way that sb/sth behaves or develops, or on the way that sb thinks: **~ sb/sth** *A number of writers have researched and identified the major needs that influence student behaviour.* ◇ *Public attitudes towards nuclear energy are strongly influenced by concerns about waste disposal.* ◇ **~ how/whether, etc...** *Many factors will influence how a patient behaves within an interview session.* ◇ **~ sb to do sth** *There is a range of theories to explain how people can be influenced to change their health attitudes, choices and behaviours.*

▸ INFLUENCE + NOUN **process • development • performance • outcome, result • behaviour • response • decision • choice • policy • pattern • attitude • perception • opinion • thinking** *The study aims to investigate how emigration and repatriation influence health outcomes.*

▸ NOUN + INFLUENCE **factor • consideration • experience • environment • culture • characteristic • gene** *At some level, similarity to humans is an important factor influencing human attitudes towards animals.*

▸ ADVERB + INFLUENCE **strongly, heavily, greatly • profoundly, deeply • highly • significantly • clearly • unduly** *In general, Vietnam has a humid tropical climate heavily influenced by the South East Asia monsoon.*

▸ ADVERB + INFLUENCE | INFLUENCE + ADVERB **directly • indirectly • positively • negatively** *Energy prices can be influenced directly by policy through energy and carbon taxes.*

in·flu·en·tial /ˌɪnfluˈenʃl/ *adj.* having a lot of influence on the way that sb/sth behaves or develops, or on the way that sb thinks: *Kant produced a number of highly influential books.* ◇ *The design of the main Wedgwood factory, founded in 1769, proved influential throughout Europe.* ◇ **~ in (doing) sth** *Changes in diet and physical activity may be influential in the development of type 2 diabetes.* ◇

~ among sb *A paper by Fraenkel was particularly influential among plant biologists.*

in·flux /ˈɪnflʌks/ *noun* [usually sing.] **~ (of sb/sth) (into...) (from...)** the fact of a lot of people, money or things arriving somewhere SYN INFLOW (1): *Archaeological evidence suggests that there was a large influx of refugees into southern Mesopotamia from the north.* ◇ *The anticipated influx of foreign investment into developing countries did not occur.*

in·form /ɪnˈfɔːm; *NAmE* ɪnˈfɔːrm/ *verb* **1** [T, I] to tell sb about sth, especially in an official way: **~ sb (of/about sth)** *The participants in the study were not informed of the purpose of the task in advance.* ◇ **~ sb that...** *Students were informed that their participation in the questionnaire was voluntary.* ◇ **~ sb how/when, etc...** *The Directive requires manufacturers to inform consumers how to recycle waste electrical goods.* ◇ **~ sb as to sth** *An employer has to inform the employee as to potential dangers when using equipment.* ◇ *All advertisements aim to inform and/or persuade.* **2** [T] **~ sth** to have an important influence on sth: *The chapter shows a range of ways that theories inform everyday teaching practices.* ◇ *The process of making health policy should be informed by scientific evidence.* PHR V **inˈform on sb** to give information to the police or sb in authority about the illegal activities of sb: *Many governments have now adopted a policy that encourages members of a cartel to inform on other members.* **inˈform on sth** to provide information about sth: *Signals such as alarm signals may also inform on environmental conditions.*

in·for·mal /ɪnˈfɔːml; *NAmE* ɪnˈfɔːrml/ *adj.* **1** not official; not following strict rules of how to do sth: *Informal caregivers often experience social isolation and financial strain.* ◇ *There is a danger that one party believes an informal agreement to be valid, where in fact it is not.* OPP FORMAL (1) **2** relaxed and friendly: *The data were gathered mainly from observation and informal conversations.* ◇ *The article highlights the ways that oral history may be used to engage adult learners in an informal community setting.* ➲ *compare* FORMAL (1) **3** (of business) done by people who do not work for an employer and often not official or legal: *In many cities, the informal sector is an important part of the urban economy.* **4** (of education or learning) not taking place in a school, college or other institution: *After the initial training, informal learning from supervisors and peers was a continuing feature that contributed to worker performance.* ➲ *compare* FORMAL (3) **5** (of language) suitable for normal conversation and writing rather than for serious speech and letters: *Only 2 of the 12 studies involving text-messaging reported using informal language.* ➲ *compare* FORMAL (2) ■ **in·for·mal·ity** /ˌɪnfɔːˈmæləti; *NAmE* ˌɪnfɔːrˈmæləti/ *noun* [U] **~ (of sth)** *The European Council has always attached the highest importance to the informality of its meetings.*

in·for·mal·ly /ɪnˈfɔːməli; *NAmE* ɪnˈfɔːrməli/ *adv.* **1** in a way that is not official; not following strict rules of how to do sth: *As long as they all agree, shareholders can alter their agreement either formally or informally (i.e. without a meeting).* OPP FORMALLY (1) **2** in a relaxed and friendly way: *Time was spent informally sitting with children while they went online, observing their decisions.*

in·form·ant /ɪnˈfɔːmənt; *NAmE* ɪnˈfɔːrmənt/ *noun* **1** a person who gives sb information about sth, for example to help them with their research: *The analysis is mainly based on semi-structured interviews with key informants.* **2** a person who gives secret information about sb/sth to the police or a newspaper: *With spies and informants heavily active in the area, they had to proceed with caution.*

in·for·ma·tion /ˌɪnfəˈmeɪʃn; *NAmE* ˌɪnfərˈmeɪʃn/ *noun* [U] **1** facts or details about sb/sth that are provided or learned: *Information was obtained from 9 715 pupils in 313 schools throughout England.* ◇ **~ about/on sb/sth** *Media reports are an important source of information about food safety issues for consumers.* ◇ *The basic Help documents provide detailed information about the purpose, function and features of a particular tool or service.* ◇ **~ from sb/sth** *Whenever possible, information from the patient is supplemented by information from another informant.* ◇ **piece of ~** *The media bombard us with thousands of new pieces of information every day.* ◇ **~ regarding/relating to/concerning sb/sth** *Further research is needed to collect more accurate information regarding personal exposures to pesticides.* ➲ *see also* FREEDOM OF INFORMATION **2** data that are stored, analysed or passed on by a computer: *Most computers have only one path along which information flows between the CPU and its memory.* ◇ **+ noun** *The percentage of private business investment going into information processing equipment and software grew steadily in the second half of the 20th century.* **3** what is shown by a particular arrangement of things: *Nucleic acids are responsible for storing and transmitting genetic information.*

▸ ADJECTIVE + INFORMATION **basic • new • additional, further • detailed • specific • accurate • reliable • relevant • useful • important, valuable • personal • public • confidential • sensitive • demographic • geographic • medical • environmental • political** *The census collects a variety of important demographic information, which is then used for planning welfare services and provision.*

▸ NOUN + INFORMATION **background • health • patient • market** *The gathering and exchange of market information has been facilitated by changes in technology.*

▸ VERB + INFORMATION **have • use • give, provide • present • yield • obtain, collect, gather • acquire • disclose • disseminate • exchange** *Human remains may yield useful information on the history of some diseases.* | **share • access • extract • retrieve • process** *Currently, users can access information from more than 62 distinct datasets covering some 400 million entries.* | **store • carry • transmit • transfer • encode** *The cost of storing information on disk is very low and this compensates for its relative slowness.*

▸ INFORMATION + NOUN **source • resource • service • provision • gathering • search • management • transfer • flow • exchange • processing** *The exchange begins with information flow from the manager to the salesperson.* | **leaflet, sheet, brochure • centre • overload** *People who were selected for the study were sent an information leaflet and reply slip with a prepaid envelope.* | **system • retrieval • society • age • revolution** *In the last few decades, the 'information revolution' has changed the way that businesses function.*

in·for·ma·tion·al /ˌɪnfəˈmeɪʃənl; *NAmE* ˌɪnfərˈmeɪʃənl/ *adj.* [usually before noun] providing or connected with information: *With informational advertising, black and white pictures can be quite effective.* ◇ *In the United States, personal informational privacy is safeguarded mainly by federal legislation.*

inforˈmation content *noun* [U] **~ (of sth)** the amount of useful information contained in sth, especially as contrasted with accompanying sounds, words, etc. that have no useful meaning: *The information content of animal signals varies widely among species.* ◇ (*disapproving*) *The information content of this article could have been set out in one sentence.* HELP In engineering, **information content** is the proportion of a received signal or measurement that is useful, as opposed to the **noise** that accompanies it.

inforˌmation techˈnology *noun* [U, pl.] (*abbr.* IT) the study or use of electronic equipment, especially computers, for storing, analysing and sending information: *Improvements in information technology should allow* *better information exchange between countries.* ◇ *The new information technologies should be viewed with an understanding of the diversity of their impacts.* ◇ **+ noun** *Firms may invest in a new factory or information technology system, for example.*

in·forma·tive /ɪnˈfɔːmətɪv; *NAmE* ɪnˈfɔːrmətɪv/ *adj.* giving useful information: *Cunningham's study provides a highly informative chronicle of Texas politics between 1963 and 1980.* ◇ **~ about sth** *B. A. Engel's 'Mothers and Daughters' is informative about the nineteenth-century Russian intelligentsia.*

in·formed /ɪnˈfɔːmd; *NAmE* ɪnˈfɔːrmd/ *adj.* **1** having or showing a lot of knowledge about a particular subject or situation: *The company sells luxury sports cars to a small but loyal, informed and wealthy customer base.* ◇ *She provides well-informed accounts of the developments and crises that shaped the period.* ◇ **~ about sth** *The proportion of women who are fully informed about and interested in politics is not far short of men.* **2** (of a decision or choice) based on an understanding of the facts: *Written informed consent was obtained from the participants.* ◇ *Making an informed decision is one of the basic principles of patient care.*

I

in·fra·red /ˌɪnfrəˈred/ *adj.* (*physics*) having or using ELECTROMAGNETIC waves that are just longer than those of red light in the visible SPECTRUM, but shorter than MICROWAVES: *The Earth's atmosphere absorbs a great deal of infrared radiation.* ◇ *infrared light/wavelengths* ◇ *an infrared lamp/laser* ➲ *compare* ULTRAVIOLET ■ **in·fra·red** *noun* [U] *A neodymium laser operates at a number of wavelengths in the infrared.*

in·fra·struc·ture AWL /ˈɪnfrəstrʌktʃə(r)/ *noun* [U, C] the basic systems and services that are necessary for a country or an organization to run smoothly, for example buildings, transport and water and power supplies: *He built the public infrastructure, such as highways and power plants, that the country needed.* ◇ *basic/physical/urban infrastructure* ◇ *Many communities in these countries lack well-developed health care and research infrastructures.* ■ **in·fra·struc·tural** /ˌɪnfrəˈstrʌktʃərəl/ *adj.* [usually before noun] *In South East Asia, the coastal zone continues to attract industries and infrastructural development.*

in·fre·quent /ɪnˈfriːkwənt/ *adj.* not happening often SYN RARE (1): *This is an arid region where storms, although infrequent, are often intense.* ◇ *In conclusion, it seems that relatively infrequent infectious diseases are receiving disproportionate attention.* ◇ *His visits were not infrequent.* HELP **Not infrequent** is used to mean 'fairly frequent'. OPP FREQUENT ■ **in·fre·quent·ly** *adv.*: *Not infrequently, the chairman would have made his decision before the meeting began.* ◇ *Unfortunately, he explains, such postive experiences occur infrequently.*

in·fringe /ɪnˈfrɪndʒ/ *verb* **1** [T] **~ sth** (of an action or a plan) to break a law or rule: *The production of a new computer program that infringes copyright in the original is not permitted.* **2** [T, I] to limit sb's legal rights or their freedom: **~ sth** *The tobacco industry claimed that government intervention infringed individual liberty.* ◇ **~ on/upon sth** *There were accusations that the strong growth of temporary help infringed on existing workers' rights.*

in·fringe·ment /ɪnˈfrɪndʒmənt/ *noun* [U, C] **1** the action of breaking a law or a rule: *The party had to stop using the song after the owner sued for copyright infringement.* ◇ **~ of sth** *It was a manifest infringement of the law.* **2** the action of limiting sb's legal rights or their freedom: **~ (of sth)** *The increasing number of unwanted calls received by many consumers is frequently seen as an infringement of domestic privacy.* ◇ **~ on sth** *There were concerns about infringement on civil liberties.*

in·gre·di·ent /ɪnˈɡriːdiənt/ *noun* **1** one of the substances from which sth is made: *The company produces drinks and food that are free of artificial ingredients.* ◇ **~ of/in sth** *The active ingredient in pepper spray is capsaicin, a chemical derived from plants in the genus Capsicum.* **2** one of the things or qualities that are necessary to make sth what it is: **~ for sth** *Systematic planning is a key ingredient for successful health promotion programming.* ◇ **~ of/in sth** *Social behaviour is an essential ingredient in successful business relationships.*

in·habit /ɪnˈhæbɪt/ *verb* **~ sth** to live in a particular place: *Almost all the ethnic groups that inhabit Europe today migrated originally from the lands to the north or east.* ◇ *Microbial communities inhabit melt holes in the glaciers (Wharton et al., 1985).* ◇ *In 1600, virtually all Europeans saw themselves as inhabiting a world where the natural and supernatural coexisted.*

in·hab·it·ant /ɪnˈhæbɪtənt/ *noun* a person or an animal that lives in a particular place: *Table 2 shows that the USA ranks third, with 291 million inhabitants.* ◇ *The policy of local autonomy required cooperation between local inhabitants and central bureaucrats.*

in·her·ent AWL /ɪnˈhɪərənt; ɪnˈherənt; *NAmE* ɪnˈhɪrənt/ *adj.* that is a permanent, basic or typical feature of sb/sth SYN INTRINSIC: *He believed there was no inherent contradiction between religion and science.* ◇ **~ in/within sb/sth** *The authors discuss the difficulties inherent in research involving more than one country.* ◇ **~ to sb/sth** *Crisp sees these five areas as inherent to the human experience.* ■ **in·her·ent·ly** AWL *adv.*: *In this view, power, like all social life, is inherently unstable.*

in·herit /ɪnˈherɪt/ *verb* **1** [T] (of a person or living thing) to have a medical condition, physical features or qualities that are the same as, or similar to, those of the parents, grandparents, etc: **~ sth** *On average, half of that parent's offspring will inherit the abnormal gene.* ◇ *The authors were able to show that early flowering of the plant was an inherited characteristic.* ◇ **~ sth from sb/sth** *His height and his blue eyes were inherited from his mother.* **2** [T, I] **~ (sth) (from sb)** to receive money or property from sb when they die: *At that time, women only inherited land from their parents if they had no brothers.* ◇ *Inherited wealth may also be a cause of bad relationships within families.* ◇ *Women were given the rights to own property and to inherit.* **3** [T] **~ sth (from sb)** to receive or be left with sth from a former owner or period of time: *The author suggests that 'education needs to leave behind the models inherited from the nineteenth century'.*

in·her·it·ance /ɪnˈherɪtəns/ *noun* **1** [U, C, usually sing.] the process of receiving sth such as a medical condition, physical characteristic or quality from parents, etc; the condition, characteristic, etc. that is received: *It cannot be claimed that there is no relationship at all between genetic inheritance and occupation.* ◇ **~ of sth** *Jennings described an interesting inheritance of shell pattern in a shelled amoeba.* **2** [C, U] the money or property that you receive from sb when they die; the fact of receiving sth when sb dies: *In 1176, another law was introduced to deal with disputed inheritances.* ◇ **by ~** *The family home has become a source of wealth that can be passed on, by inheritance, from parent to child.* **3** [C, usually sing.] a situation or tradition that you receive from a former owner or period of time: *For Romantic writers, the classical tradition was a rich cultural inheritance.*

in·hibit AWL /ɪnˈhɪbɪt/ *verb* **1** to prevent a process or an action from happening, or make it happen more slowly; to make sth less active: **~ sth** *The study shows that all three varieties of tomato were able to significantly inhibit the growth of cancer cells.* ◇ *Erosion of the rock is inhibited by dense vegetation cover.* ◇ **~ sb/sth from doing sth** *These retailers will be inhibited from importing goods that do not comply with the national law.* **2** to make sb nervous and unable to act in a relaxed and natural way: **~ sb** *Fieldworkers report that using a questionnaire designed to be read word by word inhibits them.* ◇ **~ sb from doing sth** *The interview situation may inhibit staff from expressing their views freely.*

in·hib·ition AWL /ˌɪnhɪˈbɪʃn; ˌɪnɪˈbɪʃn/ *noun* **1** [U, sing.] the act of preventing or slowing down a process or an action: *The study discusses the compounds likely to be responsible for the cell growth inhibition.* ◇ **~ of sth** *Data indicated that when fruit remained on the tree in November, a dramatic inhibition of flowering occurred the following spring.* **2** [C] **~ (against sth)** a control or limit on the way that sb expresses a natural feeling: *There were strong social and cultural inhibitions against the use of force by women.* **3** [C] a nervous feeling that stops sb from behaving in a relaxed and natural way: *The 14- and 15-year-olds in the study thought of drinking as a means of having fun and losing their inhibitions.*

in·hibi·tor /ɪnˈhɪbɪtə(r)/ *noun* **1** (*chemistry, biochemistry*) a substance that delays, slows or prevents a chemical or biochemical reaction: *Substances that reduce the action of a catalyst in a chemical reaction reversibly are known as inhibitors, whereas those that reduce it irreversibly are known as poisons.* ◇ *Sodium fluoride is a metabolic inhibitor which helps maintain the glucose level of the sample.* **2** (*biology*) a GENE or gene product that prevents another gene from being effective: *These inhibitors activate tumour suppressive genes.*

in·hibi·tory /ɪnˈhɪbɪtəri/ *adj.* [usually before noun] preventing an action or process: *Insulin has an inhibitory effect on appetite.*

ˌin-ˈhouse *adj.* [only before noun] existing or happening within a company or an organization: *Training costs might include external services and expenditure for in-house training.* ■ **ˌin-ˈhouse** *adv.*: *The main advantage of using agencies is that it is relatively cheap compared with undertaking the research in-house.*

in·human /ɪnˈhjuːmən/ *adj.* lacking the qualities of kindness and sympathy; very cruel: *He was found to be responsible for the deaths and inhuman treatment of 20 individuals.* ⮌ *compare* HUMAN[1], NON-HUMAN

ini·tial AWL /ɪˈnɪʃl/ *adj.* [only before noun] happening at the beginning; first: *Oral drugs are usually used in the initial stages of the disease.* ◇ *This planting system has higher initial costs, but reduces the wage bill for annual cultivation.* ◇ *The initial response of the government to the publication of the Scott Report was extremely disappointing.*

ini·tial·ly AWL /ɪˈnɪʃəli/ *adv.* at the beginning: *Data were assembled that initially appeared to provide support for the hypothesis.* ◇ *Initially developed for cancer treatment in the late 1970s, the drug was found to be highly effective in the treatment of sleeping sickness.* ◇ *An unfamiliar regional accent can sometimes cause difficulties for understanding, at least initially.*

ini·tials AWL /ɪˈnɪʃls/ *noun* [pl.] the first letters of all the names of a person or thing: *The initials 'TEU' are used to refer to articles in the Treaty on European Union.*

ini·ti·ate AWL /ɪˈnɪʃieɪt/ *verb* **1 ~ sth** to make sth such as a process or an action begin SYN SET STH IN MOTION: *A real estate boom in Southern California in the 1880s initiated a process of rapid growth.* ◇ *If the child does not return to school, legal proceedings may be initiated by the educational authorities.* **2 ~ sb (into sth)** to introduce sb to a particular skill or activity, especially a difficult one; to make sb a member of a particular group: *An assistant teacher had the task of 'initiating newcomers into the customs of the school'.*

ini·ti·ation AWL /ɪˌnɪʃiˈeɪʃn/ *noun* [U] **1** the act of starting sth: *The mean age for reported smoking initiation was 18.9 years.* ◇ **~ of sth** *GPs play a growing role in the initiation of antidepressant treatments.* **2 ~ (into sth)** the act of sb becoming a member of a group, often with a special ceremony; the act of introducing sb to an activity or a skill: *Initiation into a mystery religion was designed to be an emotionally moving, life-changing experience.*

ini·tia·tive AWL /ɪˈnɪʃətɪv/ *noun* **1** [C] a new plan for dealing with a particular problem or for achieving a particular purpose: *The supermarket chains are often the first with new customer initiatives such as loyalty cards.* ◇ *During the 3-month period 1 January to 30 March 2008, no major health initiatives were launched.* ◇ **~ to do sth** *Several national organizations have developed various initiatives to assess and improve patient safety in nursing homes.* **2** [U] the ability to decide and act on your own without waiting for sb to tell you what to do: *Individuality and personal initiative are encouraged and rewarded in the company.* ◇ **on your own ~** *Over 50 per cent of the participants read the passage again during the week on their own initiative.* **3 the initiative** [sing.] the power or opportunity to act before other people do: *The men in these stories find themselves lost in a world where women take the initiative and make important decisions.*

ini·ti·ator AWL /ɪˈnɪʃieɪtə(r)/ *noun* **~ (of sth)** the person or thing that starts a process or an activity: *The young elephant Tunga was the initiator of much play activity.* ◇ *Various forces work against government ministers being policy initiators.*

in·ject /ɪnˈdʒekt/ *verb* **1** [T, I] to put a drug or another substance into a person's or an animal's body using a SYRINGE: **~ sth into sb/sth/yourself** *The drug needs to be injected into a specific vein.* ◇ **~ (sth)** *A local anaesthetic was injected by a GP with the patient seated.* ◇ *The Court focused on the free and voluntary decision of the victim to inject.* ◇ **~ sb/sth/yourself (with sth)** *The patient now has to inject himself twice a day with insulin.* **2** [T] to put a liquid into sth using a SYRINGE or similar equipment: **~ A (into B)** *The plastic is injected into the mould by the pumping action of the screw.* ◇ *In diesel engines, the air pressure is fixed but the amount of fuel injected is varied.* ◇ **~ B with A** *Control experiments were carried out by injecting strawberry fruits with a tumour-causing bacterium.* **3** [T] **~ sth (into sth)** to add a particular quality to sth: *The new chief executive's strategy involved injecting glamour into the brand.* **4** [T] **~ sth (into sth)** to give money to an organization or a project so that it can function: *The major banks had a total of £37 000 million injected into them.*

in·jec·tion /ɪnˈdʒekʃn/ *noun* **1** [C, U] an act of injecting sb with a drug or another substance: *Patients were treated with one or two daily insulin injections.* ◇ **by ~** *The drugs are given by injection.* ◇ **~ (of sth) (into sth)** *The guidelines state 'do not offer injections of pain-killing substances into the back for low back pain'.* **2** [C] a large sum of money that is spent to help improve a situation, business, etc: *Investors provided the financial injection needed to save the firm.* ◇ **~ (of sth) (into sth)** *The President had promised to bring about economic recovery through large injections of government spending into the economy.* **3** [C, U] an act of forcing liquid or another substance into sth: **~ (of sth) (into sth)** *Prolonged droughts in the Sahel and Mexico during the past 14 000 years coincided with major injections of fresh water into the North Atlantic.* ◇ **+ noun** *The diagram illustrates a computerized fuel injection system that improves the performance of an engine.*

in·junc·tion /ɪnˈdʒʌŋkʃn/ *noun* **1** an official order given by a court which demands that sth must or must not be done: *The plaintiff sought an injunction to prevent any further harassment.* ◇ **~ against sb** *The court granted an injunction against the newspaper, prohibiting further publicity.* **2 ~ (to do sth)** (*formal*) a warning or an order from sb in authority: *This refers to the New Testament injunction to treat one's neighbour as one would wish to be treated oneself.*

in·jure AWL /ˈɪndʒə(r)/ *verb* **1 ~ sb/sth/yourself** to harm yourself or sb else physically, especially in an accident; to harm sb mentally: *The case dealt with a boy who was seriously injured in a motor accident at work.* ◇ *He stepped on the plug of an electric appliance, injuring his left foot.* ◇ *An elderly lady living alone who has a fall may not injure herself, but may lose her confidence.* **2 ~ sth** to damage sb's reputation, pride, etc: *A company has no feelings of dignity or pride that might be injured.*

in·jured AWL /ˈɪndʒəd; *NAmE* ˈɪndʒərd/ *adj.* **1** physically or mentally hurt; having an injury: *Arthritis was present in 63% of the injured knees and in 33% of the injured ankles.* ◇ *Families tried to cope with soldiers who survived the war, but came home physically or psychologically injured.* **2 the injured** *noun* [pl.] the people injured in an accident, a battle, etc: *After the earthquake, the injured were tended by doctors who worked throughout the night.*

I

the ˌinjured ˈparty *noun* [sing.] (*law*) the person who has been treated unfairly, or the person who claims in court to have been treated unfairly: *Where the goods are not of satisfactory quality, the injured party can reject them and refuse to pay the sum agreed.*

in·jury AWL /ˈɪndʒəri/ *noun* (*pl.* -ies) **1** [C, U] harm done to a person's or an animal's body, for example in an accident; harm done to a person's mind: *A substantial proportion of motorcycle riders who wear helmets still sustain head injuries in crashes.* ◇ *Employees of very small firms tend to work longer hours with a greater risk of major injury.* ◇ **~ to sb/sth** *Sixty per cent of injuries to children under 1 year occurred in the home environment.* ◇ *The plaintiff suffered an accidental injury to his hip in a fall.* **2** [U] **~ (to sth)** (*law*) damage to a person's feelings: *The judge awarded further sums for injury to feelings and loss of pride and dignity.* ➲ *usage note at* DAMAGE[1]

▸ ADJECTIVE + INJURY **serious, severe • significant • traumatic • fatal • life-threatening • major • minor • non-fatal • unintentional • accidental • non-accidental • intentional • personal • physical • bodily • psychiatric • psychological • occupational, work-related • sports-related** *Falls are common causes of occupational injuries.*

▸ NOUN + INJURY **head • brain • spine • ankle • knee • back • eye • road traffic • sports • burn** *Most knee injuries in children are due to twisting whilst playing sport.*

▸ VERB + INJURY **sustain, suffer, incur • cause • prevent • avoid • inflict • exacerbate, aggravate** *The Court of Appeal decided that the mother had inflicted the injuries on the baby.*

in·just·ice /ɪnˈdʒʌstɪs/ *noun* [U, C] **~ (of sth/doing sth)** the fact of a situation being unfair and of people not being treated equally; an unfair act or an example of unfair treatment: *The injustice of denying women the vote was increasingly recognized.* ◇ *Social action is needed to achieve concrete changes that redress social injustices.* OPP JUSTICE (1)

ink /ɪŋk/ *noun* [U, C] coloured liquid for writing, drawing and printing: **in ~** *The names are written in ink.* ◇ *The picture was drawn in coloured inks.*

inlet /ˈɪnlet/ *noun* **1** (*technical*) an opening through which liquid, air or gas can enter a machine, part of the body, etc: **+ noun** *Moving the open air inlet pipe within the container upwards increases the rainfall intensity.* OPP OUTLET (5) **2** a narrow area of water that stretches into the land from the sea or a lake: *Water enters the mouth of the estuary only through a tidal inlet.*

in·nate /ɪˈneɪt/ *adj.* (of a quality or feeling) that you have when you are born: *Higher animals possess both innate and adaptive immune systems.* ◇ *Such characteristics may be innate.* ■ **in·nate·ly** *adv.*: *This hypothesis suggests that humans are innately programmed to behave in a certain way.* ◇ *He believed that people were innately good.*

inner /ˈɪnə(r)/ *adj.* [only before noun] **1** inside sth; towards or near the centre of sth: *Most inner ear infections are viral.* ◇ *Embedded within the inner membrane are the photosynthetic reaction centres.* ◇ *Lehmann was able to show that there was a solid inner core at the very centre of the Earth.* OPP OUTER **2** involving your own thoughts and feelings; not involving or shown to other people: *The manager has to rely very much on his or her own inner resources.* ◇ *The author stresses external traits rather than exploring the inner life of his characters.*

ˌinner ˈcity *noun* the part near the centre of a large city, which often has social problems: *Dissatisfaction with government policy led to social unrest in several inner cities.* ◇ **+ noun** *an inner-city area/neighbourhood/school*

in·no·cence /ˈɪnəsns/ *noun* [U] **1** the fact of not being guilty of a crime, etc: *They struggled to prove their innocence since much of the evidence had been destroyed.* OPP GUILT (1) **2** lack of knowledge and experience of the world, especially of evil or unpleasant things: *Though apparently just a poor country girl, Mary Robinson quickly became a symbol for English purity and innocence.*

in·no·cent /ˈɪnəsnt/ *adj.* **1** not guilty of a crime, etc; not having done sth wrong: *It seems likely that many innocent defendants were convicted under these rules.* ◇ *The newspapers cast her as an innocent victim.* ◇ **~ of sth** *He had always maintained that he was innocent of all charges.* OPP GUILTY (1) **2** [only before noun] suffering harm or being killed because of a crime, war, etc. although not directly involved in it: *Those who suffered the most from the war were innocent civilians.* **3** having little experience of evil or unpleasant things, or of sexual matters: *These isolated societies have been seen by many as innocent and free from Western contamination.* **4** not intended to cause harm or upset sb SYN HARMLESS: *This may seem an innocent question, but it raises a number of difficult and complex issues.* ■ **in·no·cent·ly** *adv.*: *The court found that they had acted completely innocently.* ◇ *The stories illustrate the struggles of the islanders as they were innocently caught in the war.*

in·nov·ate AWL /ˈɪnəveɪt/ *verb* [I, T] to introduce new things, ideas or ways of doing sth: *The ability to innovate was a skill that he used to great advantage.* ◇ **~ sth** *Drawing on both photography and the stage, Melies innovated many cinematic techniques.* ■ **in·nov·ator** AWL /ˈɪnəveɪtə(r)/ *noun*: *The company is seen as a market innovator.*

in·nov·ation AWL /ˌɪnəˈveɪʃn/ *noun* **1** [U] the introduction of new things, ideas or ways of doing sth: *Technological innovation is considered essential for social progress.* ◇ **~ in sth** *The new TV channel was required to encourage innovation in programme-making.* **2** [C] a new thing, idea or way of doing sth that has been introduced: *Recent innovations include an online mentoring scheme.* ◇ **~ in sth** *His technical innovations in this area outpaced the insights of his contemporaries.*

▸ ADJECTIVE + INNOVATION **successful • radical • incremental • methodological • institutional • organizational • technological, technical • industrial** *The authors made claims to methodological innovation.* ◇ *He introduced radical organizational innovations.* | **major • recent** *The major innovations in economic analysis have originated in the US.*

▸ VERB + INNOVATION **promote, stimulate • foster, encourage • drive, spur • facilitate • implement • introduce • hinder • stifle** *Regulation may stifle innovation.* | **introduce • adopt • implement** *These are the people who implement organizational innovations.*

in·nova·tive AWL /ˈɪnəveɪtɪv; *BrE also* ˈɪnəvətɪv/ (*also less frequent* **in·nov·atory** /ˌɪnəˈveɪtəri; *NAmE also* ˈɪnəvətɔːri/) *adj.* (*approving*) introducing or using new things, ideas or ways of doing sth: *Highly innovative firms do not necessarily survive over long periods of time.* ◇ *There have been a variety of innovative approaches in recent years.*

in·or·gan·ic /ˌɪnɔːˈɡænɪk; *NAmE* ˌɪnɔːrˈɡænɪk/ *adj.* **1** not consisting of or coming from any living substances: *The surface of the inorganic material was altered so that its chemical properties were determined largely by the organic coating.* OPP ORGANIC (1) **2** (*chemistry*) involving substances that do not contain the element CARBON (except in the form of an OXIDE or CARBONATE): *In the process, the organic wastes are converted into simple organic and inorganic compounds.* OPP ORGANIC (2)

in·pa·tient /ˈɪnpeɪʃnt/ *noun* a person who stays in a hospital while receiving treatment: *Those with the more severe disorders were treated as inpatients.* ◇ **+ noun** *The study was conducted in 2007 as part of a programme to improve the quality of inpatient care.* ➲ *compare* OUTPATIENT

input¹ AWL /ˈɪnpʊt/ *noun* **1** [U, C] time, knowledge, ideas, money, etc. that you put into work or a project in order to make it succeed; the act of putting sth in: *She had provided no financial input for the purchase of the farmhouse.* ◇ **~ from sb** *He continues to receive input from his doctor.* ◇ **~ into/to sth** *There are many different inputs into the production process.* ◇ **~ on sth** *This section provides input on topic and language.* ➲ *compare* OUTPUT¹ (1) **2** [U, C] energy or information that enters a system or machine: *The nervous system depends on sensory input, such as that from the eye.* ◇ *The annual cycle of heat input and output in the subtropics is quite muted.* ◇ **~ from sth** *Inputs from externally provided data are in decimal.* ◇ **~ into sth** *Inputs into the system affect its outputs.* OPP OUTPUT¹ (2) **3** (*also* ˈ**input terminal**) [C] a place or means for electricity or data to enter a machine or system: *The voltage measured at the input is 2.5 mV.* OPP OUTPUT¹ (4) **4** [C] **~ (of sth)** something that is added to sth else: *These soils have received immense inputs of fertilizer.*

input² AWL /ˈɪnpʊt/ *verb* (**in·put·ting**, **input**, **input** or **in·put·ting**, **in·put·ted**, **in·put·ted**) to put data into a computer: **~ sth** *Information held on the system is only as accurate as the person who inputs the data.* ◇ **~ sth into sth** *Coded data is input into a computer manually or scanned.* ➲ *compare* OUTPUT²

in·quire (*BrE also* **en·quire**) /ɪnˈkwaɪə(r)/ *verb* [I, T] to ask for information about sth: *If a participant inquired, interviewers provided clarification about the services being addressed in the study.* ◇ **~ about sth** *It is important to inquire about family members who have suffered from the disease.* ◇ **~ as to sth/why, where, etc...** *I inquired as to why he came to see me.* ◇ **~ whether/what, etc...** *The Court only inquired whether the state had undertaken reasonable measures to fulfil its constitutional duty.*
PHR V **inˈquire into sth** to find out more information about sth SYN INVESTIGATE (1): *A long line of research has inquired into the relationship between democratic institutions and public policy.* HELP In general and academic British English, both **inquire** and **enquire** are used, but **inquire** is more frequent, especially when referring to an official or scientific investigation. In American English, **inquire** is usually used in all cases.

in·quir·ing (*BrE also* **en·quir·ing**) /ɪnˈkwaɪərɪŋ/ *adj.* [usually before noun] showing an interest in learning new things: *Having an inquiring mind, he was interested in a wide range of academic topics.*

in·quiry (*BrE also* **en·quiry**) /ɪnˈkwaɪəri; *NAmE* ˈɪnkwəri; ɪnˈkwaɪəri/ *noun* (*pl.* **-ies**) **1** [C] **~ (into sth)** an official process to find out the cause of sth or to find out information about sth: *The Committee was conducting an inquiry into immigration control.* ◇ *There were calls for a public inquiry into the deaths.* **2** [U, C] the process of asking questions or collecting information about sth: *Classical scientific inquiry begins with a question or problem.* ◇ *This issue merits further inquiry.* ◇ *This empirical inquiry seeks to contribute to public opinion literature in two ways.* ◇ **~ into sth** *Scholarly inquiry into the infrastructure of financial markets has tended to focus on price-setting phenomena.* ◇ **a line of ~** *The third line of inquiry is a variation of the second.* **3** [C] a question about sth; a request for information about sth : **~ about sth** *Inquiries about hallucinations should be made tactfully.* ◇ **~ as to sth/whether, how, etc...** *They have a duty to make inquiries as to how the monies are actually spent.* HELP In general and academic British English, both **inquiry** and **enquiry** are used, but **inquiry** is more frequent, especially when referring to an official or scientific investigation. In American English, **inquiry** is usually used in all cases.

in·scribe /ɪnˈskraɪb/ *verb* **1** [often passive] to write or cut words, your name, etc. onto sth: **~ A (on/in B)** *Ancient writings were inscribed on many different materials including clay, stone, metal and papyrus.* ◇ *The concept now constitutes a key policy objective of the Union, inscribed in the Lisbon Treaty.* ◇ **~ B (with A)** *The archaeologist Evans found three thousand clay tablets inscribed with a more elaborate version of the linear script.* **2** [often passive] **~ sth + adv./prep.** to make sth present in, on, etc. sth: *The book is a thorough analysis of the belief that God had inscribed his moral law on the heart of every person.*

in·scrip·tion /ɪnˈskrɪpʃn/ *noun* **~ (on sth)** words written in the front of a book or cut in stone or metal: *Some coins had Hebrew inscriptions on one side and Greek inscriptions on the other.*

in·sect /ˈɪnsekt/ *noun* any small creature with six legs and a body divided into three parts. Insects usually have wings. ANTS, BEES and flies are all insects: **+ noun** *Many insect pest species have evolved some resistance to insecticides.*

in·se·cure AWL /ˌɪnsɪˈkjʊə(r); *NAmE* ˌɪnsɪˈkjʊr/ *adj.* **1** not confident, especially about yourself or your abilities: *Profoundly insecure, he never overcame his resentment towards his predecessor.* ◇ **~ about sth** *They are likely to feel more insecure about their job prospects.* OPP SECURE² (3) **2** not safe or protected: *They feel financially insecure.* ◇ *This figure conceals a high turnover in part-time, casual and insecure low-paid work.* OPP SECURE² (1)

in·secur·ity AWL /ˌɪnsɪˈkjʊərəti; *NAmE* ˌɪnsɪˈkjʊrəti/ *noun* (*pl.* **-ies**) [U, C] **1** a feeling of lack of confidence: *They struggle with feelings of insecurity, self-doubt and inferiority.* ◇ *The aim is to address the anxieties and insecurities that people experience.* OPP SECURITY (5) **2** the fact that sb/sth is not safe or protected: *Many workers have experienced greater job insecurity.* ◇ **~ of sth** *The insecurities of the war had passed.* OPP SECURITY (2)

in·sensi·tive /ɪnˈsensətɪv/ *adj.* **1** not realizing or caring how other people feel, and therefore likely to hurt or offend them: *Raising the issue of organ donation just as patients were dying seems unfeeling and insensitive.* ◇ **~ to sth** *International NGOs were perceived as insensitive to local concerns.* OPP SENSITIVE (4) **2** not able to react to or feel sth: *Since customers rely entirely on these products, the market is relatively price insensitive.* ◇ **~ to sth** *Unfortunately, the instrument was relatively insensitive to the low wind speeds experienced.* ◇ *Nitrous oxide renders patients immobile, and insensitive to pain.* OPP SENSITIVE (2)
■ **in·sensi·tiv·ity** /ɪnˌsensəˈtɪvəti/ *noun* [U] **~ (to sth)** *The government was criticized for its insensitivity to the poor during the famine.* ◇ *Waist circumference over 100 cm in male adults increases the risk of insulin insensitivity.*

in·sep·ar·able /ɪnˈseprəbl/ *adj.* that cannot be separated or treated separately: *The reality seems to be that policing and corruption are inseparable in all cultures.* ◇ **~ from sth** *Of course, religion and morals are inseparable from* *their social framework.* ■ **in·sep·ar·ab·il·ity** /ɪnˌseprəˈbɪləti/ *noun* [U] **~ (of sth) (from sth)** *These approaches highlight the inseparability of civil society from the state.* **in·sep·ar·ably** /ɪnˈseprəbli/ *adv.*: *In this view, the physical and the spiritual are inseparably connected.*

in·sert AWL /ɪnˈsɜːt; *NAmE* ɪnˈsɜːrt/ *verb* **1** [often passive] to put sth into sth else or between two things: **~ sth** *The microscope should remain focused when another lens is inserted.* ◇ **~ sth into/in sth** *Electric connection is made when the rod is inserted into the tube.* ◇ **~ sth between A and B** *In the type of valve called a triode, a grid of fine wires is inserted between the cathode and the anode.* **2 ~ sth (into/in sth)** to add sth to a piece of writing: *The company will not insert this clause in any future contracts.* **3 ~ sth (into sth)** (*biology*) to include a piece of GENETIC material in a CHROMOSOME: *Genes can be inserted into animals and plants to give rise to different genotypes, and thus phenotypes.*

in·ser·tion AWL /ɪnˈsɜːʃn; *NAmE* ɪnˈsɜːrʃn/ *noun* [U, C] **1** the act of putting sth inside sth else; the thing that is put inside: **~ of sth** *Electrokinetic techniques require the insertion of electrodes.* ◇ **~ (of sth) into/in sth** *Acupuncture involves the insertion of needles into specific points of the body.* **2** the act of adding sth to a piece of writing; the thing that is added: **~ of sth** *In addition to brief insertions of new material, the last section has been reorganized.* ◇ **~ (of sth) into/in sth** *The insertion of illustrations in dictionaries seems to be justified.* **3** (*biology*) the inclusion of a piece of GENETIC material in a CHROMOSOME: *Thus, with respect to genes, insertion can be considered a random event.* ◇ *Targeted gene insertions have not been as important in Drosophila or C. elegans genetics as they have in yeast and mice.*

in·side¹ /ˌɪnˈsaɪd/ *noun* **1** [C, usually sing.] (*usually* **the inside**) the inner part, side or surface of sth: **on the ~ (of sth)** *Water vapour condensed on the inside of the bottle.* ◇ **from the ~ (of sth)** *The windows of the empty houses are boarded up from the inside.* OPP OUTSIDE¹ (1) **2 the inside** [sing.] the part of a curving river, road or movement nearest to the inner or shorter side of the curve: **on the ~ (of sth)** *The river was shallowest on the inside of the bend.* ◇ **~ of sth** *As the whale changes direction, its body rolls towards the inside of each turn.* OPP OUTSIDE¹ (4)

in·side² /ˌɪnˈsaɪd/ *adj.* [only before noun] **1** forming the inner part of sth; not on the outside: *These substances are found along the inside edge of the ring.* OPP OUTSIDE² (1) **2** known or done by sb in a group or an organization: *He was accused of selling inside information relating to the investment.* OPP OUTSIDE² (2)

in·side³ /ˌɪnˈsaɪd/ (*also* **in·side of** *especially in NAmE*) *prep.* on or to the inner part of sth; within sth: *The assistant teacher was sitting with the younger children inside the classroom.* ◇ *Both inside and outside Germany, commentators viewed these books with suspicion.* OPP OUTSIDE³ (1)

in·side⁴ /ˌɪnˈsaɪd/ *adv.* on or to the inside: *Each wheel was wired differently inside.* OPP OUTSIDE⁴ (1)

in·sider /ɪnˈsaɪdə(r)/ *noun* a person who knows a lot about a group or an organization, because they are part of it: *The legislation aimed to limit the ability of insiders to extract private benefits.* ◇ *As a Muslim writing about Muslims in the UK, Ikhlaq Din emphasizes the value of the insider's point of view.* ➲ *compare* OUTSIDER (1)

in·sight AWL /ˈɪnsaɪt/ *noun* **1** [C, U] an understanding of a particular situation or thing: *It is not yet clear if this approach will yield any valuable insights.* ◇ **~ into sth** *This discussion offers some insight into the issue.* **2** [U] the ability to see and understand the truth about people or situations: *If the patient lacks insight, it can be very difficult to take a history.* ◇ *Charkham (1994) summed this up with his usual intuitive insight.*

▸ ADJECTIVE + INSIGHT **important, key, crucial** • **valuable, useful** • **considerable** • **detailed** • **rich** • **interesting** • **fascinating** • **deep, profound** • **fundamental** • **penetrating** • **further, additional** • **new, fresh** • **unique** • **greater** • **theoretical** • **critical** *Understanding these uncertainties affords greater insight into the working of the economy.*

▸ VERB + INSIGHT **give, offer, provide, afford** • **generate, yield** • **reveal** • **lead to** • **gain, obtain, glean, derive** *Studies of these toxins have led to important insights into the role of this element in overall ribosome function.*

in·sight·ful AWL /ˈɪnsaɪtfʊl/ *adj.* [usually before noun] showing a clear understanding of sth SYN PERCEPTIVE (1): *This is a thorough and insightful analysis of the reform process.* ◇ *There are insightful comments about several films.*

in·sig·nifi·cant AWL /ˌɪnsɪɡˈnɪfɪkənt/ *adj.* not big or valuable enough to be considered important: *The calculation was based on a statistically insignificant coefficient.* ◇ *The differences are either insignificant or inconsistent.* OPP SIGNIFICANT (1) ■ **in·sig·nifi·cance** /ˌɪnsɪɡˈnɪfɪkəns/ *noun* [U] *Despite their seeming numerical insignificance, such variations in temperature can strongly affect agricultural production.* **in·sig·nifi·cant·ly** *adv.*: *Not insignificantly, this topic has now captured considerable political attention.*

in·sist /ɪnˈsɪst/ *verb* **1** [I, T] to say firmly that sth is true, especially when other people do not believe you: *English towns, as Taylor insisted, had less need to be surrounded by walls.* ◇ **~ on sth** *Far left groups continue to insist on the importance of state ownership of industry.* ◇ **~ (that)...** *Dobson insists that a sustainable society can be built only by ecologically motivated citizens.* ◇ **+ speech** *'This book is not a literary biography,' she insists.* **2** [I, T] to demand that sth happens or that sb agrees to do sth: **~ that...** *Of course, the law will always insist that authorities act legally.* ◇ **~ on sb/sth doing sth** *Shareholders have also insisted on more outside directors taking board positions.* PHR V **inˈsist on/upon sth** to demand sth and refuse to be persuaded to accept anything else: *The Assembly insisted on a programme of constitutional reforms.* ◇ **~ doing sth** *The UK insisted upon maintaining its traditional free-trade policy.*

in·sist·ence /ɪnˈsɪstəns/ *noun* [U, sing.] an act of demanding or saying sth firmly and refusing to accept any opposition or excuses: **on/upon doing sth** *Eisenhower's insistence on cutting spending weakened the economy.* ◇ **~ on/upon sth** *An insistence on a general right to social membership allows us to see citizenship in a more complex, multidimensional way.* ◇ **~ that...** *Most important is Rosenzweig's insistence that philosophy and theology must function together.* ◇ **at sb's ~** *Largely at French insistence, Germany was forced to give up the areas of Alsace-Lorraine and the Saar.*

in·sist·ent /ɪnˈsɪstənt/ *adj.* **1** demanding sth firmly and refusing to accept any opposition or excuses: *The immunization programme was the result of insistent pressure from the Department of Health.* ◇ **~ on (doing) sth** *Unlike many others writing in English at the time, Day is also insistent on using clear and simple prose.* ◇ **~ (that)...** *Talleyrand was insistent that the King of Saxony should not lose his throne.* **2** continuing for a long period of time in a way that cannot be ignored: *Rasta music is characterized by its use of drums to create an insistent, slow beat (Nagashima, 1984).* ■ **in·sist·ent·ly** *adv.*: *Both defendants insistently denied the charges against them.*

in situ /ˌɪn ˈsɪtjuː; ˌɪn ˈsaɪtjuː; *NAmE* ˌɪn ˈsaɪtuː/ *adv.* (*from Latin*) in the original or correct place: *Measurements are taken in situ, within the drill hole.* ■ **in situ** *adj.*: *The Committee visited a number of States for in situ information gathering.*

in·sol·uble /ɪnˈsɒljəbl; *NAmE* ɪnˈsɑːljəbl/ *adj.* **1 ~ (in sth)** (of a substance) that does not dissolve in a particular liquid: *These plants are relatively insoluble in water, but are soluble in fats.* OPP SOLUBLE (1) **2** (of a problem or mystery) that cannot be solved or explained: *She maintained that she would be able to solve some of these seemingly insoluble problems.* OPP SOLUBLE (2)

in·spect AWL /ɪnˈspekt/ *verb* [often passive] **1** to look closely at sth, especially to check that everything is as it should be SYN EXAMINE (2): **~ sth** *The specimen was visually inspected to assess these factors.* ◇ **~ sth for sth** *The plants are regularly inspected for disease.* **2 ~ sth** to officially visit a school, hospital, factory, etc. in order to check that rules are being obeyed and that standards are acceptable: *All schools are inspected regularly.* ◇ *Nursing facilities are inspected on a yearly basis to determine whether minimum standards are met.*

in·spec·tion AWL /ɪnˈspekʃn/ *noun* [U, C] **1** the act of looking closely at sth, especially to check that everything is as it should be SYN EXAMINATION (2): **on ~** *On closer inspection, not one of the cases offers firm support for this explanation.* ◇ **~ of sth** *A visual inspection of a dam, and its surrounding area, are an important part of a reservoir safety check.* **2** an official visit to a school, hospital, factory, etc. in order to check that rules are being obeyed and that standards are acceptable: *They found that regular inspections had been diligently carried out.* ◇ *There was a relatively weak regime of regulatory inspection and enforcement.*

in·spect·or AWL /ɪnˈspektə(r)/ *noun* **1 ~ (of sth)** a person whose job is to check that rules are being obeyed and that standards are high enough within an organization or system: *He was appointed an inspector of schools.* ◇ *Animal welfare inspectors have powers to investigate and prosecute instances of animal cruelty or neglect.* **2** (*abbr.* **Insp**) an officer of middle rank in the police: *A police officer of the rank of inspector may authorize these searches.*

in·spir·ation /ˌɪnspəˈreɪʃn/ *noun* **1** [U] the experience of being made to feel confident and excited about doing sth: *He could not fight, but his war songs brought inspiration to those who could.* ◇ **~ to do sth** *Formal education does not provide the skills or the inspiration to start a new business.* **2** [C, usually sing.] **~ (to sb)** a person or thing that makes you feel confident and excited about doing sth: *He remained an enduring inspiration to avant-garde artists.* **3** [U, C, usually sing.] the idea of doing sth or the reason for doing sth; the person or thing that provides this: *Shelley drew inspiration from his reading of Sir William Jones.* ◇ *These schools of thought all claim Marx as a direct inspiration.* ◇ **~ for sth** *The film provided the inspiration for her book.* ◇ **a source of ~** *Elizabethan England came to be seen as a Golden Age and vital source of inspiration for contemporary poets.*

in·spire /ɪnˈspaɪə(r)/ *verb* **1** to make sb feel confident and excited about doing sth: **~ sb** *As an exiled leader, he inspired a younger generation.* ◇ **~ sb to do sth** *The authors hope that readers will be inspired to enter and contribute to this fascinating area.* **2** [usually passive] to give sb the idea for sth; to be the reason why sb does sth: **be inspired by sb/sth** *He was inspired by the work of Karl von Frisch.* ◇ **~ sth** *Two major research questions initially inspired the creation of the database.* **3** to make sb have a particular feeling or emotion: **~ sth** *He was a charismatic figure who inspired fierce loyalty.* ◇ **~ sth in sb** *Public institutions must also inspire confidence in those they serve.*

in·spired /ɪnˈspaɪəd; *NAmE* ɪnˈspaɪərd/ *adj.* **1** having excellent qualities or abilities; produced with the help of inspiration: *She viewed Homer, not as a divinely inspired genius, but as a wandering poet.* **2** used with adverbs to form adjectives that show how sth has been influenced: *Public sector change has been largely politically inspired.*

in·stabil·ity AWL /ˌɪnstəˈbɪləti/ *noun* (*pl.* **-ies**) [U, C] **1** a situation in which things are likely to change or fail, or are already changing or failing: *Inequality is widening dramatically, which could cause instability and unrest.* ◇ *The country was displaying a growing macroeconomic instability.* OPP STABILITY ⊃ *see also* UNSTABLE (1) **2** a mental condition in which sb's emotions change suddenly, or are likely to do this: *There was evidence of emotional instability.* ◇ *They became more compassionate towards those suffering with mental instabilities.* ⊃ *see also* UNSTABLE (3) **3** the quality that sth has when it may change or fail suddenly: *The different types of genetic instabilities can be broadly divided into two categories.* ◇ *Postural instability causes patients to fall easily.* OPP STABILITY ⊃ *see also* UNSTABLE (4)

in·stall /ɪnˈstɔːl/ *verb* **1 ~ sth** to fix equipment into position so that it can be used: *The Queensland police have also installed video cameras in their vehicles.* ◇ *Cribb (1990) documents polluting companies that installed pollution control equipment in response to community complaints.* **2** to put a new program into a computer: **~ sth** *Many computer owners have installed anti-spam software to reduce junk email.* ◇ **~ sth on/onto sth** *As part of the study, participants were asked to install software onto their PCs.* **3** to put sb in a new position of authority, often with an official ceremony: **~ sb** *The purchasers of the company installed a new board of directors.* ◇ **~ sb as sth** *Once installed as leader, Hague began a process of radical reform of the party.*

I

in·stal·la·tion /ˌɪnstəˈleɪʃn/ *noun* **1** [U] the act of fixing equipment in position so that it can be used: **~ of sth (+ adv./prep.)** *The installation of electric power in a factory required a complete redesign of its layout.* ◇ **+ noun** *As installation costs come down, solar power will become an even more attractive option.* **2** [C] a piece of equipment or machinery that has been fixed in position so that it can be used: *For the operator of a renewable energy installation, the amount of additional financial support is crucial.* **3** [C] a place where specialist equipment is kept and used: *There were a number of terrorist attacks on US military installations.* **4** [U] **~ (of sb) (as sth)** the act of placing sb in a new position of authority, often with a ceremony: *The installation of his son as Tsar Alexander I allowed the modernization of the Russian army to recommence.* **5** [C] (*art*) a piece of modern art that is made using sound, light, etc. as well as objects: *Osorio employs unexpected spaces as stages for his installations.*

in·stance AWL /ˈɪnstəns/ *noun* a particular example or case of sth: *The instances cited highlight the need for the IT Department to be involved.* ◇ **~ of sth** *This is a particular instance of a more general problem.* ◇ **in... instance(s)** *In most instances, this is an adequate answer.*

IDM **for ˈinstance** for example: *There are frequently sets of regulations specific to certain industries. For instance, in the UK toy industry, regulation is covered by the Toys (Safety) Regulations 1995.* ⊃ language bank *at* EXAMPLE **in the ˈfirst instance** as the first part of a series of actions: *Oxygen and IV fluids are given in the first instance.*

in·stant¹ /ˈɪnstənt/ *adj.* [usually before noun] happening immediately SYN IMMEDIATE (1): *Information technology can provide almost instant access to medical information via the Internet.* ◇ *They examine how instant messaging allows friends to feel part of a larger peer group.* ■ **in·stant·ly** *adv.*: *The challenge was to design a logo that would be instantly recognizable.* ◇ *There was great pressure on emergency staff to react instantly.*

in·stant² /ˈɪnstənt/ *noun* [usually sing.] **1** a particular point in time SYN MOMENT (1): **at a... ~** *But animals do more than make decisions on the basis of the information they receive at any given instant; they learn and remember.*

2 a very short period of time SYN MOMENT (2): **in an ~** *Whole cultures cannot change in an instant.*

in·stant·an·eous /ˌɪnstənˈteɪniəs/ *adj.* **1** happening immediately: *The spark ignites the fuel and there is almost instantaneous combustion of the contents of the cylinder.* **2** (*physics*) existing or measured at a particular instant: *At each time step, the instantaneous velocity is calculated and applied to the model.* ■ **in·stant·an·eous·ly** *adv.*: *Huge sums of money can be transferred almost instantaneously.*

in·stead /ɪnˈsted/ *adv.* in the place of sth: *Some volunteers are not willing to travel. They prefer instead to seek opportunities nearer home.* ◇ *Historians might not be interested in personalities, instead focusing on wars or politics.* ◇ *None of these objectives was being achieved. Instead, American losses mounted.* ◇ *As far back as the 1850s, scientists tried to alert policymakers to the dangers of lead pipe, urging that safer materials be used instead.*

I

inˈstead of *prep.* in the place of sth: *Customers are now able to deal direct with a supplier instead of going through a middleman.* ◇ *Instead of financial rewards, these workers often find other reward strategies.*

in·sti·tute¹ AWL /ˈɪnstɪtjuːt; *NAmE* ˈɪnstɪtuːt/ *verb* **~ sth** to introduce a system or policy or start a process: *The government instituted a pension system which led to a dramatic increase in welfare provision.* ◇ *The Director can decide whether to institute legal proceedings.*

in·sti·tute² AWL /ˈɪnstɪtjuːt; *NAmE* ˈɪnstɪtuːt/ *noun* an organization that has a particular purpose, especially one that is connected with science, education or a particular profession: *Many universities and institutes are offering these courses.* ◇ *The interviewing was carried out by a leading independent social research institute.*

in·sti·tu·tion AWL /ˌɪnstɪˈtjuːʃn; *NAmE* ˌɪnstɪˈtuːʃn/ *noun* **1** [C] an important, often large, organization that has a particular purpose, for example, a university or bank: *Since the deregulation of financial institutions, all mortgage lenders have been able to diversify their operations.* ◇ *Schools and other public institutions should accommodate religious holidays.* **2** [C] a custom or system within society or among a particular group of people: *They believe that democratic institutions are the most secure protectors of human rights.* ◇ *The Civil Union Act created an institution that has identical legal consequences to those of marriage.* ◇ **~ of sth** *There is a passage in the 'Journal of Researches' in which Darwin attacks the institution of slavery.* **3** [U] **~ of sth** the act of starting or introducing sth such as a system or a law: *An outcry over corruption led to the institution of a commission of inquiry.* **4** [C] a building where people with special needs are taken care of, for example because they are old or mentally ill; the organization that takes care of them: *Some participants were excluded because they were living in an institution.* ◇ *Future studies should explore the response of managed care institutions.*

▸ ADJECTIVE + INSTITUTION **existing** • **central, key** • **powerful** • **new** • **informal** • **social** • **cultural** • **religious** • **traditional** • **political** • **financial, economic** • **formal** • **regulatory** • **democratic** *Informal social capital is often a more reliable source of financial assistance than finance from formal institutions.* | **international, supranational, global** • **national** • **governmental** • **public** • **private** • **multilateral** • **local, domestic** • **educational, academic** *All of the students in these educational institutions were given the opportunity to participate in the survey.*

▸ NOUN + INSTITUTION **banking, credit** *Banking institutions also began to internationalize in this period.*

▸ VERB + INSTITUTION **create** • **build** • **establish** • **shape** • **develop** • **reform** • **transform** • **strengthen** *The government did little to reform the political institutions.*

▸ INSTITUTION + VERB **emerge** • **operate** • **play a role (in)** • **shape** *EU institutions have shaped the EU's development as they vie for power with the member states.*

in·sti·tu·tion·al AWL /ˌɪnstɪˈtjuːʃənl; *NAmE* ˌɪnstɪˈtuːʃənl/ *adj.* [usually before noun] **1** connected with an institution or institutions: *Large pension funds and other institutional investors are active participants on the foreign exchange market.* ◇ *A relatively small percentage (4.1%) lived in institutional settings such as nursing homes.* ◇ *an institutional context/environment* ◇ *Changes over time, including institutional change, are in large measure a reflection of changes in technology.* ◇ *institutional structures/frameworks/arrangements* **2** involving customs or systems within society or among a group of people: *These codes and institutional practices then spread to other parts of the world.* ■ **in·sti·tu·tion·ally** AWL /ˌɪnstɪˈtjuːʃənəli; *NAmE* ˌɪnstɪˈtuːʃənəli/ *adv.*: *Institutionally, the treaty established a Commission, an Assembly, a Council and a Court of Justice.* ◇ *Some phenomena deserve to be described as institutionally racist.*

in·sti·tu·tion·al·ize (*BrE also* **-ise**) AWL /ˌɪnstɪˈtjuːʃənəlaɪz; *NAmE* ˌɪnstɪˈtuːʃənəlaɪz/ *verb* **1 ~ sth** to make sth become part of an organized system, society or culture, so that it is considered normal: *These were the earliest moves to institutionalize European cooperation.* **2 ~ sb** to send sb who is not capable of living independently to live in a special building, especially when it is for a long period of time: *She was interested in nineteenth-century reactions to people with mental handicaps who were not institutionalized.* ■ **in·sti·tu·tion·al·iza·tion, -isa·tion** /ˌɪnstɪˌtjuːʃənəlaɪˈzeɪʃn; *NAmE* ˌɪnstɪˌtuːʃənələˈzeɪʃn/ *noun* [U] **~ (of sth/sb)** *The adoption of the Universal Declaration of Human Rights was a milestone in the institutionalization of Enlightenment values.* ◇ *The aim is to identify effective home care projects that can delay institutionalization of frail older persons.*

in·sti·tu·tion·al·ized (*BrE also* **-ised**) AWL /ˌɪnstɪˈtjuːʃənəlaɪzd; *NAmE* ˌɪnstɪˈtuːʃənəlaɪzd/ *adj.* **1** (*usually disapproving*) that has become part of an organized system, society or culture, so that it is considered normal: *Segregation of non-whites was a form of institutionalized racism.* **2** (of people) living in an institution: *As many as 90 per cent of patients with dementia will be institutionalized before death.* HELP This meaning of **institutionalized** is often used to suggest a loss of the ability to live and think independently.

in·struct AWL /ɪnˈstrʌkt/ *verb* **1** to tell sb to do sth, especially in a formal or official way SYN DIRECT² (7): **~ sb to do sth** *Participants were instructed to press a key to indicate the location of the stimulus.* ◇ **~ sb how/where, etc...** *The owners instructed management how they wanted the assets diversified.* ◇ **~ sb** *A sedative was given, as instructed by the doctor.* ◇ **~ that...** *He instructed that strategic action be taken to control the problem.* **2** (*formal*) to teach sb a subject or skill: **~ sb in sth** *Bishop Remigius of Reims instructed Clovis privately in Christian beliefs.* ◇ **~ sb on sth** *Patients were instructed on what to do in case of emergency.* ◇ **~ sb** *Some educators believed that radio had potential for instructing both children and adults.* **3 ~ sb** (*law*) to employ a lawyer to act on your behalf: *Lack of economic resources and outside support make it extremely difficult to instruct a lawyer.*

in·struc·tion AWL /ɪnˈstrʌkʃn/ *noun* **1 instructions** [pl.] detailed information on how to do or use sth SYN DIRECTION (5): **~ on how to do sth** *The driving instructor initially gives the learner verbal instructions on how to change gears.* ◇ **~ about sth** *The hospital gave specific instructions about what clothes to bring.* ◇ **in accordance with... instructions** *The drug was given at a low dose in accordance with the manufacturer's instructions.* **2** [C, usually pl.] something that sb tells you to do SYN ORDER¹ (4): **~ to do sth** *The captain had instructions to establish a base on the island.* ◇ **~ that...** *Head office gave instructions that the* *agreement was to be cancelled.* ◇ **under ~ to do sth** *Crews were under strict instructions to destroy all code books before abandoning ship.* **3** [C] (*computing*) a code in a program that tells a computer to perform a particular operation: *The microprocessor executes instructions sequentially and will regard embedded data as instructions.* **4** [U] the act of teaching sth to sb: *The students with more hours of classroom instruction showed greater language skills.* ◇ **~ in sth** *All officers received instruction in risk management procedures.*

in·struct·ive AWL /ɪnˈstrʌktɪv/ *adj.* giving a lot of useful information: *Play in early life appears to be both enjoyable and instructive.* ◇ **~ to do sth** *It is instructive to compare Boswell with Lockhart, in terms of style.*

in·struct·or AWL /ɪnˈstrʌktə(r)/ *noun* **1** a person who teaches sth, especially a practical skill or sport: *There were few laws regulating the work of driving instructors.* **2** (*NAmE*) a teacher below the rank of assistant professor at a college or university: *She was an instructor in the Columbia zoology department.*

in·stru·ment /ˈɪnstrəmənt/ *noun* **1** a process or system that is used to discover or describe attitudes, experiences, skills, etc: *This is a screening instrument designed to identify psychosocial concerns among parents of children aged 4–16 years.* ◇ **~ to do sth** *There was no instrument to measure academic motivation across subject areas.* ◇ **~ for (doing) sth** *Valid and reliable instruments for measuring the quality of care are needed.* **2** something, for example a policy, situation or organization, that is used to achieve sth or that makes sth happen: **~ for (doing) sth** *Subsidies are a key fiscal policy instrument for the promotion of clean fuel.* ◇ **~ of sth** *Conflict is an inevitable instrument of change.* **3** a tool or device used for a particular task, especially for scientific work: *optical/surgical/scientific instruments* **4** a device that measures speed, distance, etc, or that shows information, in a vehicle or on a machine: **+ noun** *The first applications of this technology were in automobile instrument panels and mobile phones.* **5** (*law*) a formal legal document: *The Act was amended by the passing of a statutory instrument.* **6** = MUSICAL INSTRUMENT: *The instrument most commonly employed to represent the ancient qualities of Celtic music is the harp.*

in·stru·men·tal /ˌɪnstrəˈmentl/ *adj.* **1 ~ (in sth/in doing sth)** important in making sth happen; connected with sth's function as a way of making sth happen: *These reports have proved instrumental in changing air traffic regulations (Mewhinney, 2006).* ◇ *The main instrumental reason for choosing the course was simply to get a higher qualification.* **2** connected with a scientific instrument or measuring device: *Mass spectrometry is a widely used instrumental technique.* **3** made by or for musical instruments: *The play involved dances performed to the accompaniment of instrumental music.* ■ **in·stru·men·tal·ly** *adv.*: *Where parents seeem to use the telephone instrumentally, adolescents use it more expressively (Yttri, 2002).*

in·suf·fi·cient AWL /ˌɪnsəˈfɪʃnt/ *adj.* not enough for a particular purpose: *The available car parking was judged to be insufficient.* ◇ *The main cause of failure was that management provided insufficient time to prepare.* ◇ **~ for (doing) sth** *The evidence was insufficient for drawing firm conclusions.* OPP SUFFICIENT ➲ *compare* INADEQUATE (1) ■ **in·suf·fi·cient·ly** AWL *adv.*: *Alexander argues that Merton's approach is insufficiently ambitious.* **in·suf·fi·ciency** /ˌɪnsəˈfɪʃənsi/ *noun* [U, sing.] (*technical*)*He argued that vitamin D insufficiency might be partly responsible for Scottish ill health.*

in·su·late /ˈɪnsjuleɪt; *NAmE* ˈɪnsəleɪt/ *verb* **1** [T, I] to protect sth with a material that prevents heat, sound, electricity, etc. from passing through: **~ sth** *The bar is insulated so that there is no convection from the surface.* ◇ **~ sth from sth** *The gate electrode is electrically insulated from the device body.* ◇ **~ (sth) against sth** *The hairs on the leaves insulate against excessive cold or heat.* **2** [T] **~ sb/sth from/against sth** to protect sb/sth from unpleasant experiences or influences SYN SHIELD² (1): *Asian Americans are widely perceived to be insulated from racial discrimination by their success in education and the professions.*

in·su·la·tion /ˌɪnsjuˈleɪʃn; *NAmE* ˌɪnsəˈleɪʃn/ *noun* [U] **1** the act of protecting sth with a material that prevents heat, sound, electricity, etc. from passing through; the materials used for this: *Improving home insulation is one means of reducing energy consumption.* ◇ *Foam insulation was placed around the main fuel tank.* **2** the state of being separated or protected from sth: **~ from sth** *Independence refers to the judge's structural insulation from political pressure.* ◇ **~ of sth from sth** *The insulation of science from the rest of society has reduced significantly in the last half century.*

in·su·la·tor /ˈɪnsjuleɪtə(r); *NAmE* ˈɪnsəleɪtər/ *noun* a material or device used to prevent heat, sound, electricity, etc. from escaping from sth: *Aluminium nitride was chosen because it is a good electrical insulator.*

I

in·su·lin /ˈɪnsjəlɪn; *NAmE* ˈɪnsəlɪn/ *noun* [U] a chemical substance produced in the body that controls the amount of sugar in the blood by influencing the rate at which it is removed; a similar artificial substance given to people whose bodies do not produce enough naturally: *The drugs stimulate the cell to secrete insulin.*

in·sur·ance /ɪnˈʃʊərəns; ɪnˈʃɔːrəns; *NAmE* ɪnˈʃʊrəns/ *noun* **1** [U, C] an arrangement with a company in which you pay them regular amounts of money and they agree to pay the costs, for example, if you die or are ill, or if you lose or damage sth: *When the timber was destroyed in a fire, Macaura claimed on his insurance.* ◇ **~ against sth** *All car drivers must take out insurance against accidents.* ◇ **+ noun** *Such workers are not covered by any health insurance schemes.* ◇ *Smokers must pay higher life insurance premiums.* **2** [U] the business of providing people with insurance: **+ noun** *The government also regulates banks, insurance companies, and other financial institutions.* **3** [U] money paid by or to an insurance company: *Their travel insurance paid for new tickets.* **4** [U, C] **~ (against sth)** something you do to protect yourself against sth bad happening in the future: *The study showed that clutches of 50 eggs were no better insurance against early mortality.* ◇ *Investment in higher education was seen as an insurance against poverty.*

in·sure /ɪnˈʃʊə(r); ɪnˈʃɔː(r); *NAmE* ɪnˈʃʊr/ *verb* **1** [T, I] to buy insurance so that you will receive money if your property, car, etc. gets damaged or stolen, or if you get ill or die: **~ sth/yourself** *Taylor argues that global catastrophic risks can only be privately insured to a limited extent.* ◇ **~ sth/yourself for sth** *The community centre is insured for over $500 000.* ◇ **~ sth/yourself against sth** *Small farmers cannot afford to insure themselves against crop failure.* ◇ **~ against sth** *Losses from software defects are difficult to insure against.* **2** [T] **~ sb/sth** to sell insurance to sb for sth: *Japanese insurance companies insured the cargoes.* **3** (*especially NAmE*) = ENSURE

in·tact /ɪnˈtækt/ *adj.* [not usually before noun] complete and not damaged: *The disc florets in one plant were all removed while the other plant remained intact.* ◇ *When Khrushchev succeeded Stalin, he kept the structures of the country largely intact.*

in·take /ˈɪnteɪk/ *noun* **1** [U, C] the amount of food, drink, etc. that you take into your body: *All patients were advised to increase their fluid intake.* ◇ **~ of sth** *In fact, standard medical advice recommends that people should reduce their intake of meat.* **2** [C, U] **~ (of sb)** the number of people who enter a school, college, profession, etc. during a particular period: *All the schools studied had intakes of mainly socially disadvantaged pupils.* ◇ *The composition of the school intake was carefully analysed.* **3** [C, usually sing.] an act of taking sth in; a place or structure through which sth is taken in: *A leak from the air intake was discovered.* ◇ **+ noun** *Fuel and air are transferred into the cylinder through an intake valve.*

in·tan·gible /ɪnˈtændʒəbl/ *adj.* **1** that exists but that is difficult to describe, understand or measure: *There are intangible benefits to living in collective centres, such as a larger social support network and better access to services.* OPP TANGIBLE (1) **2** (*business*) that does not exist as a physical thing but is still valuable to a company: *The proportion of corporate value obtained from intangible assets like reputation rose over 50 per cent from 1981 to 1998.* ➲ *compare* TANGIBLE (2) ■ **in·tan·gible** *noun* [usually pl.] *An additional figure is often added to the selling price of a firm for intangibles, such as name worth or the value of the brands it owns.*

I

in·te·ger /ˈɪntɪdʒə(r)/ *noun* (*mathematics*) a whole number, such as 3 or 4 but not 3.5: *a positive/negative integer* ➲ *compare* FRACTION (2)

in·te·gral[1] AWL /ˈɪntɪgrəl; ɪnˈtegrəl/ *adj.* **1** being an essential part of sth: *Drums and drummers were an integral part of Akan culture on the Gold Coast.* ◇ **~ to sth** *Trading over long distances has been integral to the functioning of capitalism since its inception.* **2** [only before noun] (*mathematics*) connected with an integer; involving only integers: *The integers form an integral domain.* ■ **in·te·gral·ly** /ˈɪntɪgrəli; ɪnˈtegrəli; *NAmE* ɪnˈtegrəli/ *adv.*: *The rising trend in homelessness is integrally related to increased poverty levels.*

in·te·gral[2] /ˈɪntɪgrəl/ *noun* **~ (of sth)** (*mathematics*) an operation within CALCULUS used to determine the area under a GRAPH: *The integral can be thought of as the sum of rectangles with the smallest possible width.*

in·te·grate AWL /ˈɪntɪgreɪt/ *verb* **1** [T] to combine two or more things so that they work together: **~ A with B** *Descartes attempted to integrate philosophy with the 'new' sciences.* ◇ **~ A into B** *It is useful to consider how project work can be integrated into EFL training.* ◇ **~ A and B** *McNair seeks to integrate the Marxist concern with production and the realist concern with security.* **2** [I, T] to become or make sb become accepted as a member of a social group, especially when they come from a different culture: *Ethnic minority groups have faced many difficulties in their attempts to integrate.* ◇ **~ into/with sth** *Resident foreigners do not always find it easy to integrate into Japanese society.* ◇ **~ sb into/with sth** *Casper and Moore argue that the US military continues to have hostility to fully integrating women into its ranks.* ➲ *compare* SEGREGATE (1) **3** [T] **~ sth** (*mathematics*) to find the integral of sth: *The velocity profile can be obtained by integrating this equation.*

in·te·grated AWL /ˈɪntɪgreɪtɪd/ *adj.* [usually before noun] in which many different parts are closely connected and work successfully together: *Welsh schools promote an integrated approach that links school management with curriculum.* ◇ *The smart card would be valid on all parts of the integrated transport system.*

ˌintegrated ˈcircuit *noun* a small MICROCHIP that contains a large number of electrical connections and performs the same function as a larger CIRCUIT made from separate parts: *Without high-quality silicon, the integrated circuit would still be a mere concept.*

in·te·gra·tion AWL /ˌɪntɪˈgreɪʃn/ *noun* **1** [U, C] the act or process of combining two or more things so that they work together: *European economic integration has led to the creation of larger and more homogeneous markets in Europe.* ◇ *to facilitate/promote/achieve greater integration* ◇ **~ of A (into B)** *Integration of environmental considerations into industrial policy is clearly essential.* ◇ **~ of A and B** *It was decided that an integration of quantitative and qualitative methods would provide the best approach.* **2** [U] the act or process of mixing people who have previously been separated, usually because of colour, race or religion: *Osawa argues that social integration and participation, rather than redistribution, form new directions for 21st century welfare systems.* ◇ **~ (of sb) (into sth)** *Ethnic minority integration into society has been beset by misunderstandings and underfunding.* **3** [U, C] **~ (of sth)** (*mathematics*) the process of finding an INTEGRAL[2] or integrals: *The function p can be computed by numerical integration of the equation.*

in·teg·rity AWL /ɪnˈtegrəti/ *noun* [U] **1** the quality of being honest and having strong moral principles: *He suggests that one cannot be a good parent unless one exhibits moral integrity.* ◇ *The key need is for a new leader with high standards of personal and professional integrity.* ◇ **with ~** *During and after their term of office, Commissioners are required to behave with integrity.* **2 ~ of sth** the state of being whole and not divided SYN UNITY (1): *The new regime was predominantly concerned with strategies to defend the independence and territorial integrity of the new Polish state against foreign aggression.* ◇ *The DNA must be copied in its entirety, in order to maintain the integrity of the genome.* **3 ~ of sth** the state of not being spoilt, or of not having mistakes: *Using colleagues as informants may compromise the integrity of the data they provide, because they may just give the answers they think you want to hear.*

in·tel·lect /ˈɪntəlekt/ *noun* [U, C] the ability to think in a logical way and understand things, especially at an advanced level; your mind: *Aristotle suggests that the unique characteristic of the human intellect is our capacity for purely theoretical thought.* ◇ *Alexander III's intellect was far from outstanding.*

in·tel·lec·tual[1] /ˌɪntəˈlektʃuəl/ *adj.* [usually before noun] connected with or using a person's ability to think in a logical way and understand things SYN MENTAL: *Early treatment has allowed some affected children to survive with relatively normal intellectual development.* ◇ *intellectual abilities/disabilities/impairment* ◇ *Such private schools were a common feature of the intellectual life of the Graeco-Roman world.* ◇ *intellectual history/traditions* ➲ *see also* INTELLECTUAL PROPERTY ■ **in·tel·lec·tu·al·ly** *adv.*: *It seems that when students become involved in the community, they also became intellectually engaged.*

in·tel·lec·tual[2] /ˌɪntəˈlektʃuəl/ *noun* a person who is well educated and enjoys activities in which they have to think seriously about things: *Jean-Paul Sartre was a public intellectual in the sense that he expressed his philosophy in novels and plays.*

ˌintelˌlectual ˈproperty *noun* [U] (*law*) an idea, a design, etc. that sb has created and that the law prevents other people from copying: *The company claimed it had a right to withhold information from competitors in order to protect its intellectual property.* ◇ **+ noun** *This study will examine the impact of intellectual property rights on the global supply of medicines.*

in·tel·li·gence AWL /ɪnˈtelɪdʒəns/ *noun* [U] **1** the ability to learn, understand and think in a logical way about things; the ability to do this well: *Jane Austen makes Emma's intelligence and critical perception clear from the start of the novel.* ◇ **~ to do sth** *She had the intelligence to raise the alarm straight away.* ◇ **+ noun** *Intelligence tests measure performance on set tasks that require mental ability to solve correctly.* ➲ *see also* ARTIFICIAL INTELLIGENCE **2 ~ (on sth)** secret information that is collected, for example about a foreign country, especially one that is an enemy; the people that collect this information: *The agency* *gathered intelligence on enemy movements.* ◇ *He worked for British military intelligence between 1942 and 1945.*

in·tel·li·gent AWL /ɪnˈtelɪdʒənt/ *adj.* **1** good at learning, understanding and thinking in a logical way about things; showing this ability: *Miller was a leading playwright—intelligent, moral and respected.* ◇ *Laura Kalman's book is an intelligent, briskly written narrative.* **2** (of an animal) able to understand and learn things: *Weighing possible actions and comparing their likely outcomes is the sort of thing that intelligent animals are good at.* **3** (*computing*) (of a computer or program) able to use data it has stored in new situations and to react to changes: *Intelligent systems are computers whose responses to inputs mimic the responses that an informed human might make.* ■ **in·tel·li·gent·ly** AWL *adv.*: *Sales assistants were assessed on their ability to advise customers intelligently.*

in·tel·li·gible /ɪnˈtelɪdʒəbl/ *adj.* that can be easily understood SYN UNDERSTANDABLE: *There has been a vast amount of scholarship aimed at making Milton's poetry more intelligible and accessible.* ◇ **~ to sb** *Norwegian sociologists have tended to write in a way that was intelligible to ordinary Norwegians.* ■ **in·tel·li·gi·bil·ity** /ɪnˌtelɪdʒəˈbɪləti/ *noun* [U] *There is often a high degree of mutual intelligibility between neighbouring speech communities.*

in·tend /ɪnˈtend/ *verb* **1** to have a plan, result or purpose in your mind when you do sth: **~ to do sth** *The defendant claimed he had not intended to kill his brother.* ◇ **~ sb/sth to do sth** *The emperor never intended the regions to become truly independent.* ◇ **it is intended that...** *It is intended that the scheme would apply to couples who have had a child together.* ◇ **~ that...** *Parliament intended that the industry would agree a voluntary code of practice.* **2 ~ sth as sth| ~ sth to be sth** to plan that sth should have a particular meaning or use: *It is clear that she intended her contribution as a gift that did not need repaying.*

in·tend·ed /ɪnˈtendɪd/ *adj.* **1** meant or designed to be sth or to be used by sb: *Whewell was not certain that this was Newton's intended meaning.* ◇ **~ to be/do sth** *The following discussion is not intended to be an exhaustive review of the subject.* ◇ **~ as sth** *This effort is intended as a step towards developing the approach further.* ◇ **~ for sb/sth** *The material is intended for classroom use or self-study.* **2** [only before noun] that you are trying to achieve or reach: *The book's intended purpose and audience seem unclear.* ◇ *the intended target/recipients/beneficiaries of sth* ➲ *see also* UNINTENDED

in·tense AWL /ɪnˈtens/ *adj.* **1** very great; very strong SYN EXTREME[1]: *Monnet faced intense American pressure to devise a new policy towards Germany.* ◇ *Intense emotions such as terror, despair and anger were experienced by the victims of the bombing.* ◇ *Such productivity problems are predictably more intense in arid regions.* ◇ *As a result of intense competition for capable employees, the company lowered its recruitment standards.* **2** involving a lot of activity in a short period of time: *Boys tend to engage in more intense physical activity, with their activities typically based around competitive ball games.* ➲ *compare* INTENSIVE

in·tense·ly AWL /ɪnˈtensli/ *adv.* **1** extremely: *Although intensely competitive, the games also foster a profound cooperative spirit in each group.* **2** in a very serious or active way: *By focusing so intensely on student performance, teachers tended to neglect student creativity.* ◇ *Males will fight intensely to control mating territory.*

in·ten·sify AWL /ɪnˈtensɪfaɪ/ *verb* (**in·ten·si·fies, in·ten·si·fy·ing, in·ten·si·fied, in·ten·si·fied**) [I, T] to increase in degree or strength; to make sth increase in degree or strength SYN HEIGHTEN: *Friedman argues that globalization is intensifying.* ◇ **~ to sth** *The storm intensified to hurricane force.* ◇ **~ sth** *Cutting prices reduces margins and intensifies competition between sellers.* ◇ *Management intensified their demands for increased productivity.* ■ **in·tensi·fi·ca·tion** AWL /ɪnˌtensɪfɪˈkeɪʃn/ *noun* [U, sing.] **~ of sth** *Globalization involves the intensification and acceleration of social exchanges and activities.* HELP In agriculture, **intensification** means growing more crops or producing more animals in a smaller area: *This study investigates the relationship between population growth in high-density areas of Africa and agricultural intensification.*

in·ten·sity AWL /ɪnˈtensəti/ *noun* (*pl.* **-ies**) **1** [U, sing.] **~ (of sth)** the state or quality of being strong or intense: *The intensity of his anger was not justified by the situation.* ◇ *Cicero studied his adversary's case with even greater intensity than he studied his own.* **2** [U, C] the strength of sth, for example light, that can be measured: *Corals were affected by a reduction in light intensity.* ◇ *Observations showed that magnetic intensity increased as the climate became colder.* ◇ *There were green and yellow areas of varying intensities.* ◇ **~ of sth** *Intensity rating scales measure the intensity of pain, but other pain assessment tools are also available.*

in·ten·sive AWL /ɪnˈtensɪv/ *adj.* **1** involving a lot of work or activity in a short time: *British fears of French advances in India led to intensive diplomatic negotiations with the Persian emperor.* ◇ *All group leaders attended an intensive one-week leadership training workshop.* **2** done with a lot of attention, effort or care; extremely thorough: *More intensive treatment was provided for patients whose condition had not improved.* ◇ *An intensive search for similar fossils was eventually successful.* **3** (of methods of farming) aimed at producing as much food as possible using as little land or as little money as possible: *The intensive cultivation of watermelon involves the use of pesticides and artificial fertilizers.* **4** (in compounds) (especially in business and economics) using a lot of the thing mentioned: *Machinery began to replace simple labour-intensive production methods.* ◇ *These countries gave priority to development of capital-intensive heavy industries, even though capital in their economies was scarce.*

inˌtensive ˈcare *noun* [U] **1** continuous care and attention, often using special equipment, for people in hospital who are very seriously ill or injured: *Some patients may require intensive care for many days.* **2** (*also* **inˌtensive ˈcare unit** [C]) (*abbr.* **ICU**) the part of a hospital that provides intensive care: *He was still unconscious when transferred to intensive care.*

in·ten·sive·ly AWL /ɪnˈtensɪvli/ *adv.* **1** in a way that involves a lot of work or activity in a short time: *During this period, he lobbied Congress intensively for support of his civil rights legislation.* **2** with a lot of attention, effort or care: *Inorganic polymers are now being more intensively studied.* **3** using methods of farming that produce as much food as possible using as little land or as little money as possible: *The Corn Belt has been farmed intensively since the discovery of its rich soil base.*

in·tent /ɪnˈtent/ *noun* [U] (*formal* or *law*) what you intend to do SYN INTENTION: **~ to do sth** *The jury decided that there had been intent to cause serious injury.* ◇ **~ (of sth/sb)** *The intent of these questions is to identify patients at high risk of falls while in hospital.* ◇ *The creation of a new management committee was a clear signal of intent.*

IDM **to all intents and ˈpurposes** (*BrE*) (*NAmE* **for all intents and ˈpurposes**) in the effects that sth has, if not officially; almost completely: *To all intents and purposes, by the middle of 1997, the region's economy had more or less collapsed.*

in·ten·tion /ɪnˈtenʃn/ *noun* [C, U] what you intend or plan to do; your aim: *The President made her intentions clear in a television broadcast.* ◇ **~ of doing sth** *The council announced its intention of imposing a compulsory purchase order on a large area of land.* ◇ **with the ~ of doing sth** *After 1949, candidates for entry were classified with the* *intention of giving priority to those of peasant or worker origin.* ◇ **have no ~ of doing sth** *When questioned by concerned readers, Moran replied that he had no intention of changing his lifestyle.* ◇ **~ to do sth** *In this paper, it is my intention to outline the problem and propose a solution.* ◇ **~ that...** *Initially there was no intention that Reconstructionism should develop into a distinct movement.* ◇ **good intentions** *Such parents have good intentions but lack energy, time or skills to cope with their children.*

in·ten·tion·al /ɪnˈtenʃənl/ *adj.* done deliberately SYN DELIBERATE[1], INTENDED (2): *Parsons defines action as intentional behaviour oriented to the achievement of a goal.* ◇ *There is a risk of accidental or intentional overdose of prescribed drugs.* OPP UNINTENTIONAL ■ **in·ten·tion·al·ly** /ɪnˈtenʃənəli/ *adv.*: *The sampling rate was intentionally kept higher than the Nyquist sampling rate.* ◇ *Streets in 'New Urban' developments are intentionally narrow in an effort to reduce traffic speed.*

inter·act AWL /ˌɪntərˈækt/ *verb*

WORD FAMILY
interact *verb*
interaction *noun*
interactive *adj.*
interactively *adv.*
interactivity *noun*

1 [I] if one thing **interacts** with another, or if two things **interact**, one thing has an effect on the other, or the two things have an effect on each other: *These events involve numerous components and subsystems that interact in complicated ways.* ◇ **~ with sth** *The vast majority of drugs interact directly with molecules that are part of cells.* ◇ *There are competing views on how organizations interact with their environment.* ◇ **A and B ~ to do sth** *A patient's expectations and anxiety level interact to produce a person's unique level of therapeutic motivation.* **2** [I] **~ (with sb)** to communicate with sb, especially while you work or spend time with them: *The ability to interact with customers, and to be truly customer-focused is crucial.* ◇ *Teachers should spend time observing how individual children interact with each other at break time.*

inter·action AWL /ˌɪntərˈækʃn/ *noun* [U, C] **1** the effect that two things have on each other: **~ between A and B** *Our subsequent statistical analysis informed us that there was an interaction between all three factors.* ◇ **~ with sth** *Interactions with other drugs may increase the adverse effects of beta-blockers.* ◇ **~ of A with/and B** *All these factors seem to be crucial for the interaction of DNA with other molecules.* **2** the way that people communicate with each other, especially while they work or spend time with them: *Observations of parent-child interactions support the children's view of what is happening here.* ◇ **~ between A and B** *Trust that develops through social interaction between individuals can often be more important than legally binding contracts.* ◇ **~ (with sb)** *These results may be due to the fact that interactions with strangers are more likely to occur in cities.*

▸ ADJECTIVE + INTERACTION **significant • complex • favourable • dynamic • direct • weak • strong • reciprocal, mutual • competitive • strategic • repulsive • attractive • hydrophobic • intermolecular • molecular • electrostatic • electromagnetic** *As a significant interaction between species and colony size was found, we performed separate regression analyses for each species.* ◇ *The molecules are attracted to each other due to hydrophobic interactions.* | **social • face-to-face • interpersonal • human • everyday** *The respondents also provided advice on appropriate communication patterns, including the importance of face-to-face interactions.*

▸ NOUN + INTERACTION **protein-protein • cell-cell • drug** *ITC is now being increasingly applied to the study of protein-protein interactions.* | **parent-child • mother-child • student-student** *Observations of parent-child interactions support the children's view of what is happening here.*

▸ VERB + INTERACTION **involve • study, examine, analyse, explore • observe • describe • understand • shape • enhance** *However, this approach does not allow the researcher to study peer-group interaction.* | **mediate • govern • detect • facilitate • investigate • reveal • model** *Investigate the dipole-dipole interactions within the different compounds by comparing their boiling points.*

inter·active AWL /ˌɪntərˈæktɪv/ *adj.* **1** allowing information to be passed in both directions between a computer, etc. and a user; reacting to what a user does: *The nature of direct marketing has been transformed by the interactive media of telephone and Internet.* ◇ *Bottlenose dolphins were given interactive underwater keyboards with which they could ask and answer questions.* **2** (of two or more people or things) influencing each other: *The course involves interactive problem-solving for groups of up to ten participants.* ◇ *The project was designed to study the interactive effects of early life stress on urban childhood asthma risk.* ■ **inter·active·ly** AWL *adv.*: *Digitalization meant that television could now be used interactively.* **inter·activ·ity** /ˌɪntərækˈtɪvəti/ *noun* [U] *Websites are offering ever increasing degrees of interactivity.*

inter·change·able /ˌɪntəˈtʃeɪndʒəbl; *NAmE* ˌɪntərˈtʃeɪndʒəbl/ *adj.* that can be exchanged, especially without affecting the way in which sth works: *The parts produced by the company were not precise enough and were not fully interchangeable.* ◇ **~ with sth** *The use of human rights to identify persecution does not mean that refugee law is interchangeable with human rights protection.* ■ **inter·change·ably** *adv.*: *The words 'Web' and 'Internet' are often used interchangeably, but technically the two are quite distinct.*

inter·course /ˈɪntəkɔːs; *NAmE* ˈɪntərkɔːrs/ *noun* [U] (*formal*) **1** = SEXUAL INTERCOURSE **2** communication between people, countries, etc: *The three groups were deeply intertwined through intermarriage and social intercourse.*

inter·de·pend·ent /ˌɪntədɪˈpendənt; *NAmE* ˌɪntərdɪˈpendənt/ *adj.* that depend on each other; consisting of parts that depend on each other: *This paper will examine how China has been incorporated into the global, interdependent economy.* ◇ *Postmodern states are highly interdependent both economically and politically.* ■ **inter·de·pend·ence** /ˌɪntədɪˈpendəns; *NAmE* ˌɪntərdɪˈpendəns/ (*also less frequent* **inter·de·pend·ency** *pl.* **-ies**) *noun* [U, C] *In the modern world of global interdependence, a war can damage the well-being of a multitude of states.* ◇ **~ between A and B** *Continuous process technologies generate complex levels of interdependence between tasks.*

inter·dis·cip·lin·ary /ˌɪntəˈdɪsəplɪnəri; *NAmE* ˌɪntərˈdɪsəplɪneri/ *adj.* involving different areas of knowledge or study: *The laboratory established an interdisciplinary team comprising both chemists and physicists.* ◇ *We have adopted an interdisciplinary approach, combining historical methodologies with political philosophy.*

inter·est[1] /ˈɪntrəst; ˈɪntrest/ *noun* **1** [sing., U] the feeling that you have when you want to know or learn more about sb/sth: *This study has recently attracted considerable interest.* ◇ **with ~** *I read the article with great interest.* ◇ **~ in sb/sth** *Young people tend to have a relatively low level of interest in politics.* **2** [U] the quality that sth has when it attracts sb's attention or makes them want to know more about it: *The game of chess holds special interest for the study of the representation of human knowledge in machines.* ◇ **of ~** *During the last decade, nanotechnology has become a topic of intense interest.* ◇ **of ~ to sb** *This study is of interest to scholars and research students of the history of national identity.* ◇ **it is of ~ to do sth** *It is of interest to note here that...* **3** [C] an activity or a subject that you enjoy and that you spend time doing or studying: *He lived a decadent life centred on his artistic interests.* ◇ *Military history is my primary research interest.* **4** [U] the price of borrowing or lending money for a particular period of time (usually given as a PROPORTION of the original amount at an ANNUAL rate): **~ on sth** *They were* *paying 20% interest on their debt.* ◇ **with ~** *He was assured of the return of his money with interest.* ◇ **~ rate/rate of ~** *The interest rate now stands at 3%.* ◇ *The government does not control the rate of interest charged on borrowing.* **5** [C, usually pl., U] the advantage or benefit of a person or group: *The central task is to achieve a better balance between employer and employee interests at work.* ◇ *He wanted to compel the media to serve the national interest.* ◇ **~ of sb** *He argued that the interests of the producing and controlling classes are usually, but not always, in conflict.* ◇ **in the (best) ~ of sb/sth| in sb's/sth's (best) ~** *The death of the host animal is clearly not in the interest of the parasite.* ◇ *Developers saw that it was in their best interests to find a way in which both conservation and development could succeed.* ◇ **be in/against the public ~** *There are questions about whether it would be in the public interest for researchers to have access to patient data without consent.* ➲ *see also* SELF-INTEREST **6** [C, U] a connection with sth that affects your attitude to it, especially because you may benefit from it in some way: *MPs can be suspended from Parliament for failing to declare relevant financial interests.* ◇ **~ in sth** *All of the community had an interest in the outcome of the case.* ◇ **~ in doing sth** *They had a common interest in shortening food supply chains and empowering local communities.* ➲ *compare* VESTED INTEREST **7** [C] **~ (in sth)** a share in a business or company and its profits, or in a property: *The company has grown by acquisition to become a global mining house with interests in gold, platinum and coal.* ◇ *When the Crown acquired sovereignty over Australia, this destroyed all prior interests held by Aboriginal Australians.* **8** [C, usually pl.] a group of people or companies that are in the same business that they want to protect: *Business interests are careful not to be too closely associated with any one political party.*

IDM **in the interest(s) of (doing) sth** in order to help or achieve sth: *In the interests of French commerce, he arranged to have these trading rights awarded to French merchants.* ◇ *The Act was passed in the interest of protecting wild fauna and flora and conserving wild habitats.*

IDM *see* CONFLICT[1], GENERAL[1]

▸ ADJECTIVE + INTEREST **real • great, considerable • keen • general • widespread • growing • renewed • personal** *The data indicate a growing interest among Mexican nurses in migrating abroad for work.* | **special • particular • political • historical** *Of special interest is the reaction with calcium.* ◇ *The house was saved because of its historical interest.* | **best • common • mutual • national • public • material • political** *The war produced a spirit of solidarity and common interest that was built into the foundations of the Welfare State.* | **competing • private • foreign • domestic • economic • financial • commercial** *They were motivated by their own economic interests.*

▸ VERB + INTEREST **have • show • express • share • lose • attract, arouse • spark, stimulate, generate • revive • reflect** *A large number of families initially expressed interest in the project.* | **pay • earn • charge** *Basic forms of money holdings earn no interest but can be used immediately.* | **protect, safeguard • serve • defend • advance, promote, further • pursue • represent • balance** *The monopoly laws are designed to enhance competition and thus protect consumer interests.* | **have • acquire • secure** *In 1996 the company acquired a controlling interest in Prague Breweries when it increased its stake to 51%.*

▸ INTEREST + NOUN **rate • charge • payment** *A low interest rate will tend to stimulate investment.*

▸ NOUN + OF INTEREST **lack • level • focus** *Surveys show that levels of interest in public affairs have not declined but interest in parties and voting has.* | **area • topic • matter, question • point** *An important question of interest is whether these new registrations are the results of existing firms registering or of new firms starting up.*

inter·est² /ˈɪntrəst; ˈɪntrest/ *verb* to attract your attention and make you feel interested; to make sb/yourself give their/your attention to sth: **~ sb** *The mission was to find out where the target market (men and women aged 16–29) spent their spare time and what interested them.* ◇ **~ sb/yourself in sth** *In 1931 the French had attempted to interest the British in these documents.* ◇ *He interests himself in financial and international affairs.*

inter·est·ed /ˈɪntrəstɪd; ˈɪntrestɪd/ *adj.* **1** [not usually before noun] giving your attention to sth because you enjoy finding out about it or doing it; showing interest in sth and finding it exciting: **~ in sth/sb** *We were particularly interested in people's attitude to money.* ◇ **~ in doing sth** *She is interested in studying the influence of computers and the Internet on children's development.* ◇ **~ to see/hear/know, etc.** *I was interested to see what else might have been collected that was relevant to the topic.* ➲ *usage note at* INTERESTING **2** [usually before noun] in a position to gain from a situation or be affected by it: *There are many interested parties who may be affected by these research results.*

ˈinterest group *noun* a group of people who work together to achieve sth that they are particularly interested in, especially by putting pressure on the government, etc: *Those who represent interest groups are well situated to influence elected politicians.* ◇ *a public/special interest group* ➲ *compare* PRESSURE GROUP

inter·est·ing /ˈɪntrəstɪŋ; ˈɪntrestɪŋ/ *adj.* attracting your attention because it is special, exciting or unusual: *Some interesting research questions are raised by these data.* ◇ *These findings may prove quite interesting.* ◇ *I found her ideas interesting and wanted to read some of her work.* ◇ **it is ~ to note/see, etc...** *It is interesting to note that these two conditions very rarely occur together in the same baby.* ◇ **it is ~ that...** *It is interesting that strong political leaders so often fall spectacularly.* ■ **inter·est·ing·ly** *adv.*: *Interestingly, the distribution of population densities tends to be remarkably consistent for all urban areas.* ➲ language bank *at* SURPRISING

▸ INTERESTING + NOUN **question • example • illustration • insight • observation • finding, result • parallel • feature, aspect • case** *One of the interesting features of the periodic table is the division of the elements between metals and non-metals.*

▸ INTERESTING TO + VERB **note • see, observe • examine, investigate • compare • consider • speculate** *It is interesting to observe which aspects of the issue struck the court as being of importance.*

WHICH WORD?

interesting • interested

- A person or thing that is **interesting** attracts your attention because they are special, exciting or unusual: *An interesting discussion of idioms from a psycholinguistic point of view can be found in Gibbs (1990).* ◇ *an interesting question/example/case* ◇ ~~*an interested question/example/case*~~
- If you are **interested** in sb/sth, you are giving them your attention because you enjoy finding out about them: *Anyone interested in understanding the origins of Christianity should read the letters of Paul.* ◇ ~~*Anyone interesting in...*~~

inter·face /ˈɪntəfeɪs; *NAmE* ˈɪntərfeɪs/ *noun* **1** the way a computer program presents information to a user or receives information from a user, in particular the LAYOUT of the screen and the menus: *These user interfaces are designed for ease of use and have clear screen layouts.* **2 ~ (between A and B)** (*computing*) a a device or program for connecting two items of HARDWARE or software so that they can be used together or communicate with each other: *The architecture of a computer is the interface between its software and its hardware.* **3** the place where two surfaces meet or join: **~ between A and B** *Gas* *exchange in the lungs takes place at the interface between the alveoli and the pulmonary capillaries.* ◇ **~ of sth** *Friction at the sliding interface of metals is caused by the following mechanisms:...* **4 ~ between A and B** the point where two subjects, systems or organizations meet and affect each other: *There is a need for further research on the interface between the school community and the larger community.*

inter·fere /ˌɪntəˈfɪə(r); *NAmE* ˌɪntərˈfɪr/ *verb* **1** [I] **~ (in sth)** to get involved in and try to influence a situation that does not concern you, in a way that makes people angry or causes harm: *European governments frequently tried to interfere in the affairs of the Ottoman Empire.* **2** [I] (*physics*) (of light or other ELECTROMAGNETIC waves) to act on each other in a way that produces interference: *Diffracted light will interfere to produce bright and dark regions.* ◇ **~ with sth** *Background radiation will interfere with the signal and therefore represents a noise source.*
PHR V **interˈfere with sth** to prevent sth from succeeding or from being done or happening as planned: *Fortunately, his lack of competence in English did not really interfere with his academic work.*

I

inter·fer·ence /ˌɪntəˈfɪərəns; *NAmE* ˌɪntərˈfɪrəns/ *noun* [U, C] **1** the act of becoming involved in and trying to influence a situation that does not concern you, in a way that makes people angry or causes harm: *Until about 1850, many European cities grew without much political interference or control.* ◇ **~ in sth** *Entrepreneurs do not like government interference in their operations.* ◇ **~ with sth** *This was considered an unwarranted interference with personal liberty.* **2** the act of preventing sth from functioning correctly or normally: **~ with sth** *The major undesirable effect is interference with copper metabolism that could lead to copper deficiency.* ◇ **~ from sth** *This method of determining iron may suffer from interference from sulfate, cadmium or lead.* **3** the disturbing of received signals by signals from another source: *The amplifier suffered from interference that was assumed to have been introduced at the input of the amplifier.* **4** (*physics*) the combination of two or more waves to form a new wave of greater or lower AMPLITUDE: *If white light is shone on an oxidized wafer, constructive and destructive interference will cause certain colours to be reflected.*

inter·gov·ern·men·tal /ˌɪntəˌɡʌvənˈmentl; *NAmE* ˌɪntərˌɡʌvərnˈmentl/ *adj.* [only before noun] concerning the governments of two or more countries: *Other European intergovernmental organizations, such as the Council of Europe, have a wider membership than the EU.*

in·terim /ˈɪntərɪm/ *adj.* [only before noun] intended to last for only a short time until sb/sth more permanent is found: *An interim government took control of the situation.* ◇ *an interim agreement/measure*

in·ter·ior¹ /ɪnˈtɪəriə(r); *NAmE* ɪnˈtɪriər/ *noun* **1** [C, usually sing.] the inside part of sth: **(in the) ~ (of sth)** *The atoms in the interior of a protein fit together in a way that leaves very few gaps.* ◇ *Foreign automakers make slight modifications to vehicles' interiors to suit local tastes.* OPP EXTERIOR¹ **2 the interior** [sing.] **~ (of...)** the central part of a country or continent that is a long way from the coast: *The reasons why white men did not penetrate the interior of Africa are not hard to find.* **3 the Interior** [sing.] a country's own affairs rather than those that involve other countries: *The Minister of the Interior had perhaps the most influential office, for he controlled the police and censorship.*

in·ter·ior² /ɪnˈtɪəriə(r); *NAmE* ɪnˈtɪriər/ *adj.* [only before noun] **1** on the inside of sth; done or happening indoors: *Dublin's 18th-century architecture and interior decoration reflected Italian and German influences.* ◇ *In Euclidean geometry, the interior angles of triangles equal 180°.* OPP EXTERIOR² **2** connected with the part of a country or region that is a long way from the coast: *By the end of the colonial period, new settlements were spreading across the interior uplands.* **3** relating to a country's own affairs rather than those that involve other countries: *The interior minister was convinced that terrorists were lurking behind every corner.* **4** existing or happening in your mind: *They gave an impression of interior peace and serenity.*

inter·medi·ary /ˌɪntəˈmiːdiəri; *NAmE* ˌɪntərˈmiːdieri/ *noun* (*pl.* **-ies**) **~ (between A and B)** a person or an organization that helps other people or organizations by being a means of communication between them, especially in order to reach an agreement: *The interpreters acted as intermediaries between the different language groups.* ■ **inter·medi·ary** *adj.* [only before noun] *Distributors perform an important intermediary role in matching supply with demand.*

inter·medi·ate AWL /ˌɪntəˈmiːdiət; *NAmE* ˌɪntərˈmiːdiət/ *adj.* **1** [usually before noun] coming between two times, states, places or things: *A number of intermediate steps in the process had not beeen correctly followed.* ◇ **~ between A and B** *The region lay in an intermediate position between lower areas to the north-west and higher ones to the south-east.* HELP In business, **intermediate goods** are materials, such as cotton, or partly finished goods, such as car engines, which are used to produce **final goods** which are sold to the public: *Thailand raised import duties on intermediate goods to protect domestic manufacturers in certain industries like iron and steel.* **2** having more than a basic knowledge of sth but not yet advanced; suitable for sb who is at this level: *The book is targeted at intermediate and upper-intermediate learners.* ◇ *The class was following an intermediate-level course.*

inter·mit·tent /ˌɪntəˈmɪtənt; *NAmE* ˌɪntərˈmɪtənt/ *adj.* stopping and starting often over a period of time, but not regularly SYN SPORADIC: *Rainfall is sparse, intermittent and unreliable.* ◇ *The patient has had intermittent abdominal pain and has lost 5 kg.* ■ **inter·mit·tent·ly** *adv.*: *Renewable power is often available only intermittently: most obviously when the wind blows and the sun shines.*

inter·mo·lecu·lar /ˌɪntəməˈlekjələ(r); *NAmE* ˌɪntərməˈlekjələr/ *adj.* [only before noun] existing or taking place between MOLECULES: *The intermolecular forces are weaker in liquids and extremely small in gases*

in·tern·al AWL /ɪnˈtɜːnl; *NAmE* ɪnˈtɜːrnl/ *adj.* **1** [usually before noun] connected with the inside of sth: *Electron microscopy is very useful in studies of the internal structure of cells.* ◇ *The smallest tubing has an internal diameter of only 0.012 inches.* ◇ **~ to sth** *Climate variability also arises from atmospheric processes internal to the earth's system.* OPP EXTERNAL (2) **2** [only before noun] connected with the inside of a person's or animal's body: *Malignancies of the internal organs can reach an advanced stage before giving symptoms.* ◇ *A pelvic mass may be palpable on internal examination of patients.* OPP EXTERNAL (2) **3** involving or concerning only the people who are part of a particular organization rather than people from outside it: *In 2010 the company introduced an internal audit programme for all its manufacturing plants.* ◇ *The group's only internal tensions come when one member lets the others down.* ◇ **~ to sth** *They must consider every stakeholder, both external and internal to the organization.* OPP EXTERNAL (2) **4** [usually before noun] happening or existing within a country or region rather than involving other countries or regions SYN DOMESTIC (1): *Once internal conflicts cease, refugees are then able to return to their home states.* ◇ *On the other hand, trade liberalization also opens up the internal markets for foreign competition.* ◇ **~ to sth** *These factors are not just internal to the region.* OPP EXTERNAL (3) **5** [only before noun] coming from within a thing itself rather than from outside it: *To achieve internal consistency, several experiments were repeated.* ◇ *The wide range of ages for children in this study was a threat to internal validity.* ◇

Each body of law might have its own internal logic, rules and purposes that cannot easily be transplanted across to the other. OPP EXTERNAL (1) **6** happening or existing in a person's mind: *This limitation restricts the learning disabled child's ability to describe changes in internal feelings.*

in·tern·al·ize (*BrE also* -ise) AWL /ɪnˈtɜːnəlaɪz; *NAmE* ɪnˈtɜːrnəlaɪz/ *verb* **1 ~ sth** to make a feeling, an attitude or a belief part of the way you think and behave: *Early in life, children tend to internalize the accepted expectations of the culture.* ➲ *compare* EXTERNALIZE **2 ~ sth** (*economics*) to include the effects of an action, such as costs and benefits, in the price for performing that action: *The carbon tax was introduced so that producers would internalize the effect of their pollution on the environment.* ■ **in·tern·al·iza·tion, -isa·tion** /ɪnˌtɜːnəlaɪˈzeɪʃn; *NAmE* ɪnˌtɜːrnələˈzeɪʃn/ *noun* [U] **~ (of sth)** *The use of rewards to inhibit behaviour does not foster internalization of self-control.* ◇ *Internalization does not in itself raise wholesale electricity prices.*

in·tern·al·ly AWL /ɪnˈtɜːnəli; *NAmE* ɪnˈtɜːrnəli/ *adv.* **1** on or from the inside; within a thing itself: *When all the core has solidified, the internally generated magnetic field will cease to exist.* ◇ *Any good scientific theory should be internally consistent.* ➲ *compare* EXTERNALLY (1) **2** on the inside of the body: *Eggs are fertilized internally and so the very early stages of development occur within the mother hen.* ➲ *compare* EXTERNALLY (2) **3** in a way that involves or concerns only the people who are part of a particular organization rather than people from outside it: *It is sometimes more difficult for the EU to agree internally than for it to agree deals with its trading partners.* ◇ *The managers are all drawn internally from the sales force.* ➲ *compare* EXTERNALLY (1) **4** within a country or region rather than involving other countries or regions: *French Jews migrated internally, drawn to urban centres and especially to Paris.* ➲ *compare* EXTERNALLY (3) **5** in a person's mind: *Although the women in this study do not feel internally conflicted, some are concerned about potential external conflict.* ➲ *compare* EXTERNALLY (1)

inter·nation·al /ˌɪntəˈnæʃnəl; *NAmE* ˌɪntərˈnæʃnəl/ *adj.* [usually before noun] connected with or involving two or more countries: *The film was made by an international team.* ◇ *Certain authors of the era gained truly international reputations.* ◇ *Fortunately, the discovery of the 'ozone hole' triggered international efforts to stop the manufacture of CFCs.* ◇ *Globalization implies that product markets for goods and services are increasingly international.* IDM *see* COMMUNITY

▸ INTERNATIONAL + NOUN **relations • cooperation • agreement • treaty • rights • standard • instrument • obligation • affairs • order • peace • security • convention • migration • conflict • terrorism** *Technological innovation has profoundly shaped international relations.* | **law • politics • trade • business • market • investment • marketing • economy • competition** *These environmental regulations already exist under international law.* | **organization • institution • society • system • regime • tribunal • conference • agency** *Collaborations between international organizations can be the most challenging, particularly when they involve different national cultures.*

inter·nation·al·ize (*BrE also* -ise) /ˌɪntəˈnæʃnəlaɪz; *NAmE* ˌɪntərˈnæʃnəlaɪz/ *verb* [T, I] **~ (sth)** to bring sth under the control or protection of many nations; to make sth international: *Regulations on industrial pollution are increasingly internationalized.* ◇ *New technological infrastructure worldwide is providing opportunities for firms to internationalize.* ■ **inter·nation·al·iza·tion, -isa·tion** /ˌɪntəˌnæʃnəlaɪˈzeɪʃn; *NAmE* ˌɪntərˌnæʃnələˈzeɪʃn/ *noun* [U] **~ (of sth)** *Thus, the internationalization of firms through the establishment of multinational company networks has become a noticeable trend.*

inter·nation·al·ly /ˌɪntəˈnæʃnəli; *NAmE* ˌɪntərˈnæʃnəli/ *adv.* in, by or between two or more countries: *Companies are encouraged to comply with internationally recognized guidelines.* ◇ *The Middle East oil crisis of the early 1970s changed the way countries and organizations trade internationally.* ◇ *These results provide a backdrop for future research both nationally and internationally.*

the Interˌnational Phoˌnetic ˈAlphabet *noun* [sing.] (*abbr.* **IPA**) an alphabet that is used to show the pronunciation of words in any language: *Eighteen poems in dialect have been transliterated into the International Phonetic Alphabet.*

Inter·net (*also* **inter·net**) /ˈɪntənet; *NAmE* ˈɪntərnet/ *noun* (*usually* **the Internet**) [sing.] an international computer network which is used for finding and sharing information and for email: *In 2011, over 2.2 billion people had access to the Internet.* ◇ **on/over/via the ~** *There is a very wide variety of young adult literature available on the Internet.* ◇ **+ noun** *There is a growing tendency for Internet access to be considered a human right.*

inter·per·son·al /ˌɪntəˈpɜːsənl; *NAmE* ˌɪntərˈpɜːrsənl/ *adj.* [only before noun] connected with relationships between people: *Most of these patients are young, have unstable moods, and difficulties in interpersonal relationships.* ◇ *Recruiters who possess greater interpersonal skills seem to be an important reason why applicants decide to accept job offers.*

inter·play /ˈɪntəpleɪ; *NAmE* ˈɪntərpleɪ/ *noun* [U, sing.] the way in which two or more things or people affect each other SYN INTERACTION (1): **~ of sth** *The behaviour of children is affected by the complex interplay of personal, domestic and institutional factors.* ◇ **~ between A and B** *Some attention has been paid to the interplay between race and gender, and welfare provision.*

in·ter·pret AWL /ɪnˈtɜːprɪt; *NAmE* ɪnˈtɜːrprɪt/ *verb* **1** to explain the meaning of sth: **~ sth** *There may be several ways to interpret these findings.* ◇ **~ sth to do sth** *The dream was interpreted to mean that she would bear a son who would be a great emperor.* **2** to decide that sth such as an action or situation has a particular meaning and to understand it in this way: **~ sth as sth** *In Ancient Greece, earthquakes were interpreted as warning signs.* ◇ **~ sth + adv./prep.** *It is evident from these interviews that both husbands and wives interpret their roles in many different ways.* ➲ *compare* MISINTERPRET ■ **in·ter·pret·able** /ɪnˈtɜːprɪtəbl; *NAmE* ɪnˈtɜːrprɪtəbl/ *adj.*: *The survey is not computer scorable or interpretable.*

▸ INTERPRET + NOUN **findings • results • data • statistics • meaning • law, legislation • statute, clause • text • event** *These results should be interpreted cautiously.* ◇ *The task for the Tribunal was to interpret the law.*

▸ ADVERB + INTERPRET **correctly • properly • easily • broadly • widely, commonly • variously • best** *The actual rationale behind this decision has been variously interpreted.*

▸ INTERPRET + ADVERB **differently • correctly • cautiously, carefully • narrowly, restrictively • broadly** *Adherents of the same religion frequently interpret the scriptures differently.*

in·ter·pret·ation AWL /ɪnˌtɜːprɪˈteɪʃn; *NAmE* ɪnˌtɜːrprɪˈteɪʃn/ *noun* **1** [C] the particular way in which sth is understood or explained: *Later experiments supported this interpretation.* ◇ **~ of sth** *Kennedy and his aides worked strictly within a narrow interpretation of the law.* ◇ *a literal/strict/broad/radical interpretation of sth* **2** [U] **~ (of sth)** the action of explaining the meaning of sth: *The rationale for using this software was that it would make interpretation of the data easier.* HELP If sth is **open to interpretation**, its meaning is not clear and can be understood in different ways: *The facts of the case may be difficult to determine and open to interpretation.*

I

ine the ways in which racism intersects with other forms of discrimination.

in·ter·pret·ative AWL /ɪn'tɜːprɪtətɪv; *NAmE* ɪn'tɜːrprəteɪtɪv/ (*also* **in·ter·pret·ive** /ɪn'tɜːprɪtɪv; *NAmE* ɪn'tɜːrprɪtɪv/ *especially in NAmE*) *adj.* [usually before noun] connected with the particular way in which sth is understood or explained; providing an interpretation: *One of the inadequacies of this interpretative framework is its tendency to oversimplify.*

in·ter·pret·er /ɪn'tɜːprɪtə(r); *NAmE* ɪn'tɜːrprɪtər/ *noun* **1** a person whose job is to translate what sb is saying into another language: **through an ~** *Many of the characters speak different languages and can only communicate with each other through an interpreter.* ➲ *compare* TRANSLATOR **2** a person who explains or performs sth in a way that clearly shows their ideas about its meaning: *These problems seem not to have occurred to Hume or to any of his modern interpreters.* ◇ **~ of sth/sb** *Dai Jitao already had a reputation as a right-wing interpreter of Sun Yatsen's ideas.*

inter·relate /ˌɪntərɪ'leɪt/ *verb* [I, T, usually passive] if two or more things **interrelate**, or if they are **interrelated**, they are closely connected and they affect each other: *The participatory Internet, in combination with the hyperlink, allows sites to interrelate.* ◇ **be interrelated** *Mental and physical well-being are closely interrelated.* ◇ **be interrelated with sth** *Dust loadings in the atmosphere may be interrelated with changes in atmospheric carbon dioxide.* ■ **inter·related** *adj.*: *Repeated offending is associated with several interrelated factors.*

inter·rela·tion·ship /ˌɪntərɪ'leɪʃnʃɪp/ (*also* **inter·rela·tion** /ˌɪntərɪ'leɪʃn/) *noun* **~ (of/between A and B)** the way in which two or more things or people are connected and affect each other: *The interrelationships between explosive volcanic activity and climate are currently a priority area for research.* ◇ *The authors present evidence on the interrelations between parenting style and children's personality traits.*

inter·rupt /ˌɪntə'rʌpt/ *verb* **1** [I, T] to say or do sth that makes sb stop what they are saying or doing: *In mixed-sex conversations, men tend to interrupt more than women.* ◇ **~ sb/sth (with sth)** *Doctors were encouraged to let patients speak and not to interrupt them.* **2** [T] **~ sth** to stop sth from being continuous: *The quotations sometimes interrupt the flow of the argument.* ◇ *This humid period was, however, interrupted by a severe drought that lasted 200 years (Brooks, 2006).* **3** [T] **~ sth** to stop a line, surface or view from being even or continuous: *A narrow lagoon interrupts and modifies the course of the smaller streams.*

inter·rup·tion /ˌɪntə'rʌpʃn/ *noun* [C, U] **1** something that temporarily stops an activity or a situation; a time when an activity is stopped: *Care was taken to ensure that there were no visitors or other interruptions during interviews.* ◇ *The trade continued, with brief interruptions, through to 1739.* ◇ **without ~** *In the mid-1970s, President Ford threatened military action to keep the oil flowing without interruption.* ◇ **~ of sth** *Cigarettes were only made in this one factory, so the interruption of production had an enormous impact.* **2** the act of interrupting sb/sth and of stopping them from speaking: *It was noticeable that the Canadian negotiators used more interruptions than those from the United States.*

inter·sect /ˌɪntə'sekt; *NAmE* ˌɪntər'sekt/ *verb* **1** [I, T] (of lines, roads, etc.) to meet or cross each other: *The three types of plate margins commonly intersect.* ◇ **~ sth** *The straight line intersects the curve at three points.* **2** [T] **~ sth** to divide an area by crossing it: *Irregular cracks randomly intersect the rock surface.* **3** [I] to have some of the same features as sth else; to happen at the same time or in the same place as sth else: *This work lies at the boundary where myth and history intersect.* ◇ **~ with sth** *I will examine the ways in which racism intersects with other forms of discrimination.*

inter·sec·tion /ˌɪntə'sekʃn; *NAmE* ˌɪntər'sekʃn/ *noun* **1** [C, U] the place where two or more lines, surfaces, etc. meet or cross each other; the act of meeting or joining: *In the diagram, three intersections are shown.* ◇ **~ of sth** *The operating point will be at the intersection of the two curves.* ◇ *The line of intersection of these two planes marks the equinoxes.* ◇ **~ with sth** *We found that this is the shortest path from P to its intersection with the circle.* **2** [C, U] the place or moment at which two or more things affect each other or share similar features; the fact of two or more things affecting each other or sharing similar features: **~ of A and B** *Mike Savage has long explored the intersection of sociology and history.* ◇ **~ between A and B** *Environmental psychology examines the intersections between behaviour, mood, place and space.* ◇ **~ with sth** *These are issues about the role of the 'community' and its intersection with political and economic life.* **3** [C] (*especially NAmE*) = JUNCTION (2)

inter·spe·cif·ic /ˌɪntəspə'sɪfɪk; *NAmE* ˌɪntərspə'sɪfɪk/ *adj.* [only before noun] (*biology*) between different species: *Interspecific competition impacts the population dynamics of competing species (e.g, Zeineddine and Jansen, 2005; Kimura and Chiba, 2010).* ➲ *compare* INTRASPECIFIC

inter·twine /ˌɪntə'twaɪn; *NAmE* ˌɪntər'twaɪn/ *verb* **1** [I, T, usually passive] if two or more things **intertwine** or are **intertwined**, they are twisted together so that they are very difficult to separate: **~ with sth** *The coils intertwine with one another like strands of spaghetti.* ◇ **(be) intertwined (with sth)** *a net made of cotton intertwined with other natural fibres* **2** [T, usually passive, I] to be or become very closely connected with sth/sb else: **be intertwined (with sth)** *The impact of genetic factors is often closely intertwined with environmental factors.* ◇ **intertwined + noun** *The film follows a web of intertwined love stories that play out over the course of the February 14 holiday.* ◇ **~ with sth** *In some hunting narratives, the romantic intertwines with the tragic.*

inter·val AWL /'ɪntəvl; *NAmE* 'ɪntərvl/ *noun* **1** a period of time between two events: *These data cover many countries from 1950 to the present, in five-year intervals.* ◇ **~ of sth** *Hurricanes impact Puerto Rico with an average interval of 9.5 years.* ◇ **~ between A and B** *There is a long interval between sowing seed and receiving income for the crop.* HELP A **sampling interval** is the time between points at which data are measured and recorded in an experiment: *A soil core was collected from within a 30.5 cm radius of each flag at each sampling interval (day).* ➲ *see also* CONFIDENCE INTERVAL **2** [usually pl.] a period during which sth different happens from what is happening the rest of the time: *A cold climatic interval took place between 12 700 and 11 500 years ago.* ◇ **~ of sth** *The First Peloponnesian War consisted of a series of battles punctuated by considerable intervals of peace.* ◇ **time ~** *This mass extinction occurred over a relatively short time interval.*
IDM **at (...) intervals** **1** with time, or a particular length of time, between: *The interviews were conducted at regular intervals.* ◇ *The breath hydrogen is measured at 30-minute intervals over a three-hour period.* **2** with spaces between: *Auxiliary forts were evenly distributed on the wall at intervals of 8–10 miles.*

inter·vene AWL /ˌɪntə'viːn; *NAmE* ˌɪntər'viːn/ *verb* **1** [I] to become involved in a situation in order to improve it or stop it from getting worse: *Deciding when to intervene when students are arguing is often difficult for a teacher.* ◇ **~ in sth** *There are a number of reasons why governments intervene in business affairs.* ◇ **~ to do sth** *The courts could intervene to correct the erroneous decision.* **2** [I] to happen in the time between events: *In the intervening period, many changes have taken place in Jewish life.* ◇ *Some fifteen years were to intervene before a solution was discovered.* **3** [I] to exist or be found in the space between things: *The intervening galaxy acted as a kind of lens, bending the light.* ◇ **~ between A and B** *The number of words that intervene between parts of a sentence that are dependent on each other may be quite large.* **4** [I] to happen in a way that delays sth or prevents it from happening: *The intention had been to deploy these troops against Germany, but the Russian Revolution intervened.*

inter·ven·ing AWL /ˌɪntəˈviːnɪŋ; *NAmE* ˌɪntərˈviːnɪŋ/ *adj.* [only before noun] **1** happening between two periods or events: *In the intervening years, the price had gone up a lot.* **2** between two areas, objects or substances: *The logic of the greenbelt policy is to limit the outward expansion of urban areas in order to protect the intervening rural land.*

inter·ven·tion AWL /ˌɪntəˈvenʃn; *NAmE* ˌɪntərˈvenʃn/ *noun* [U, C] **1** the action of getting involved in a situation in order to improve it or stop it from getting worse: *Human intervention is needed to preserve threatened species.* ◇ **~ in sth** *In the second group of states, direct intervention in the economy was limited.* ◇ **~ to do sth** *They emphasize the importance of more immediate interventions to control crime.* **2** action by a country to become involved in the affairs of another country when they have not been asked to do so: *There had been interventions by the Warsaw Pact armies in 1956 and 1968.* ◇ **~ in sth** *Historical sources record military intervention in neighbouring states where it suited Rome's interests.* **3** action taken to improve a medical condition or illness: *Most patients make a recovery without further intervention.* ◇ *Effective non-surgical interventions are currently lacking.*

▸ ADJECTIVE + INTERVENTION **effective • early • specific • complex • future • preventive** *Early intervention may prevent worsening of the condition.* | **humanitarian • military** *The authors review the arguments in favour of humanitarian intervention.* | **medical • surgical • therapeutic • behavioural** *The physician then decides on the most appropriate medical interventions.*

▸ NOUN + INTERVENTION **government • state • policy** *The United States has seen much less government intervention.* | **health • nursing • lifestyle** *There has been some analysis of large-scale health interventions that have worked well.*

▸ VERB + INTERVENTION **require • justify • consider** *Maintaining and improving economic and social well-being requires intervention by governments.* | **deliver • implement • target • receive • plan • design • develop • evaluate • inform** *Typically, the intervention is delivered by one or more health professionals on a single occasion.*

inter·view¹ /ˈɪntəvjuː; *NAmE* ˈɪntərvjuː/ *noun* **1** a private meeting between people when questions are asked and answered: *The questionnaire-based survey was administered through face-to-face interviews.* ◇ **~ with sb** *One phase of the research entailed interviews with shoppers leaving the shopping centres.* **2** a conversation in which sb, especially a famous person, is asked questions by a JOURNALIST in order to find out about their work and opinions and that is printed in a newspaper, shown on television, etc: *In an interview on CNN, he outlined the problem as he saw it.* ◇ **~ with sb** *The journalist asks for an exclusive interview with the Prime Minister.* **3** a formal meeting at which sb is asked questions to see whether they are suitable for a particular job, or for a course of study at a college, university, etc: *In general, older candidates were less likely to receive offers of a job interview.* ◇ **~ for sth** *She was invited for an interview for a position as a primary school teacher.* **4 ~ (with sb)** a formal meeting at which sb is asked questions about a crime by the police: *In his first interview with the police, he claimed he had found the ransom by chance.*

▸ ADJECTIVE + INTERVIEW **structured • semi-structured • unstructured • in-depth • face-to-face • personal • individual • initial • follow-up • qualitative • clinical • judicial • diagnostic** *They had collected the data from in-depth interviews with women in two West African countries.*

▸ NOUN + INTERVIEW **telephone • group • research • exit** *Telephone interviews are quick, cheap, and usually have higher response rates.*

▸ VERB + INTERVIEW **conduct** *Researchers conducted interviews with residents in the Manchester area to explore changing attitudes to class.* | **give** *He gave interviews to local television stations when travelling outside Washington.* | **have • attend** *Of these patients, 88% had two interviews to assess their progress.* | **do, undertake • carry out, administer • obtain • arrange • hold • use, employ • complete • transcribe • record • analyse** *The data are based on an analysis of interviews carried out with 23 teachers.*

inter·view² /ˈɪntəvjuː; *NAmE* ˈɪntərvjuː/ *verb* **1** [T] to ask sb questions at a private meeting: **~ sb** *In each country, between 600 and 3 000 respondents were interviewed.* ◇ **~ sb about sth** *They interviewed a sample of people about their voting in the 1983 general election.* **2** [T] **~ sb (about sth)** to ask sb questions about their life, opinions, etc, especially on the radio or television or for a newspaper or magazine: *She is interviewed in a television studio about the publication of her latest novel.* **3** [T] **~ sb (for sth)** to talk to sb and ask them questions at a formal meeting in order to find out whether they are suitable for a job, course of study, etc: *She was interviewing applicants for a public health nursing degree programme.* **4** [I] **~ (for sth)** (*especially NAmE*) to talk to sb and answer questions at a formal meeting in order to get a job, a place on a course of study, etc: *They provide advice about how to interview for a job.* ◇ (*BrE, NAmE*) *Interviewers should aim to give the impression that they want every candidate to succeed and interview well.*

inter·view·ee /ˌɪntəvjuːˈiː; *NAmE* ˌɪntərvjuːˈiː/ *noun* the person who answers the questions in an interview: *The educational background of interviewees was relatively diverse.*

inter·view·er /ˈɪntəvjuːə(r); *NAmE* ˈɪntərvjuːər/ *noun* the person who asks the questions in an interview: *These people were contacted by telephone to answer questions put by experienced interviewers.*

inter·view·ing /ˈɪntəvjuːɪŋ; *NAmE* ˈɪntərvjuːɪŋ/ *noun* [U] the process of interviewing sb: *The interviewing was carried out by a leading independent social research institute.*

inter·war /ˌɪntəˈwɔː(r); *NAmE* ˌɪntərˈwɔːr/ *adj.* [only before noun] happening or existing between two wars, especially the First and the Second World Wars in Europe: *The interwar period saw a decline of the older established industries.* ◇ *interwar Britain/France/Europe*

in·tes·tine /ɪnˈtestɪn/ *noun* a long tube in the body that carries food away from the stomach. Food passes from the stomach to the **small intestine** and from there to the **large intestine** before it leaves the body: *This pathogen is closely related to the common and harmless E. coli strains that occur in the intestines of most animals.* ■ **in·tes·tinal** /ɪnˈtestɪnl; ˌɪnteˈstaɪnl/ *adj.* [usually before noun] *These symptoms are the hallmark of an intestinal obstruction.*

in·tim·ate /ˈɪntɪmət/ *adj.* **1** (of a link between things) very close: *Humans need to recognize their intimate relationship with nature.* ◇ *There is an intimate connection between the solid material and the air and water that surround it.* **2** (of people) having a close and friendly relationship: *Her father had been an intimate friend of Sir Walter Scott.* ◇ *He remained on intimate terms with them until his death.* **3** sexual: *Their relationship became intimate and lasted for at least two years.* ◇ *All the people in the study were either married or had an intimate partner.* **4** private and personal, often in a sexual way: *She did not want to disclose intimate details of her private life to strangers.* **5** (of a place or situation) encouraging close, friendly relationships: *There has been a move towards smaller and more intimate learning settings.* **6** (of knowledge) very detailed and thorough: *His intimate knowledge of Rome indicates that he spent many years there.* ■ **in·tim·acy** /ˈɪntɪməsi/ *noun* (*pl.* **-ies**) [U, C, usually pl.] *Real intimacy grows with an increased ability to share emotions.* ◇ **~ of sth** *Reality TV brings the intimacies of private life into public view.*

in·tim·ate·ly /ˈɪntɪmətli/ *adv.* **1** very closely (used especially when talking about things that are closely connected): *Gravity and inertia are intimately connected with each other.* ◇ *These are two intimately related problems.* **2** in a very detailed and thorough way: *He knew the city intimately.* ◇ *New managers must become intimately acquainted with the organizations they work for.*

into /ˈɪntə; *before vowels* ˈɪntu; *before vowels, strong form* ˈɪntuː; *strong form*/ *prep.* HELP For the special uses of **into** in phrasal verbs, look at the entries for the verbs. For example **look into sth** is in the phrasal verb section at **look**. **1** to a position in or inside sth: *The sample was placed directly into a sterile container.* ◇ *English captains and their crew stayed on shipboard in Africa; they did not venture into the interior.* **2** in the direction of sth: *She looked straight into the camera.* ◇ *You do work when cycling into the wind.* **3** to a point at which you hit sb/sth: *The asteroid crashed into the Earth at a location identified as the Yucatan Peninsula in Mexico.* **4** to a point during a period of time: *They would have debates long into the night.* ◇ *These differences continued well into the twentieth century.* **5** used to show a change in state: *It is easy to lapse into automatic behaviour.* ◇ *A water molecule could be split into hydrogen and oxygen atoms.* ◇ *The patient had gone into shock.* **6** used to show the result of an action: *He claims he did not coerce her into helping him.* **7** about or concerning sth: *She is conducting research into sleep.* ◇ *The book offers a number of new insights into the lives of ordinary soldiers.*

in·transi·tive /ɪnˈtrænsətɪv/ *adj.* (*grammar*) (of verbs) used without a DIRECT OBJECT: *The English verb 'grow' can be both transitive and intransitive.* OPP TRANSITIVE (1)

intra·spe·cif·ic /ˌɪntrəspˈsɪfɪk/ *adj.* [only before noun] (*biology*) within a species or between individuals of a single species: *With intraspecific competition, direct combat over a resource, be it a mate or food, is both costly and carries considerable risk.* ➲ *compare* INTERSPECIFIC

intra·ven·ous /ˌɪntrəˈviːnəs/ *adj.* (*abbr.* **IV**) (*medical*) (of drugs or food) going into a VEIN: *Intravenous drug users are at high risk of blood-borne infections.* ■ **intra·ven·ous·ly** *adv.*: *Most chemotherapy is given intravenously.*

in·tri·guing /ɪnˈtriːɡɪŋ/ *adj.* very interesting because of being unusual or not having an obvious answer: *Why and how organisms age are some of biology's most intriguing questions.* ◇ **it is ~ to do sth** *It will be intriguing to see how effective these measures will be.* ■ **in·tri·guing·ly** *adv.*: *Intriguingly, the rise in the incidence of obesity is not restricted to industrialized societies.*

in·trin·sic AWL /ɪnˈtrɪnsɪk; ɪnˈtrɪnzɪk/ *adj.* belonging to or part of the real nature of sth/sb; forming an essential part of sth: *Rather than possessing intrinsic value, souvenirs are valuable as holders of memories, experiences and ideas.* ◇ *Each molecule has intrinsic properties which affect the absorbance of light.* ◇ **~ to sth** *Clearly, the concept of value is intrinsic to the concept of a brand.* ➲ *compare* EXTRINSIC ■ **in·trin·sic·al·ly** AWL /ɪnˈtrɪnsɪkli; ɪnˈtrɪnzɪkli/ *adv.*: *These three features are intrinsically linked.* ◇ *The author cites many examples of cultural difference that demonstrate that no act is intrinsically good or bad.*

intro·duce /ˌɪntrəˈdjuːs; *NAmE* ˌɪntrəˈduːs/ *verb* **1** to bring sth, especially a product, system, law or idea, into use or operation for the first time SYN BRING STH IN: **~ sth** *Howard introduced the idea of the garden city, intended to be a blend of city and nature.* ◇ **~ sth into/to sth** *The company introduced new products into the highly competitive cosmetics market.* ◇ *Colonial powers have been introducing cultural changes to this part of the world since the mid 1800s.* **2 ~ sth** to formally present a new law so that it can be discussed in a parliament: *He introduced a bill to reduce military service from five years to three.* **3 ~ sth** (especially in a piece of writing) to bring sth into discussion: *This chapter introduces the topic of screening in public health and medical practice.* ◇ *The next section briefly introduces the analytical framework.* **4** to give sb the opportunity to learn about sth or do sth for the first time: **~ sb to sth** *From an early age, a child is introduced to Buddhist traditions by his or her parents.* ◇ **~ sth (to sb)** *Hunt was instrumental in introducing the work of both Shelley and Keats to a wider readership.* **5 ~ sth (into sth)** to put sth into sth: *Genetic manipulation makes it possible to introduce new genes into organisms.* **6 ~ sth (to/into sth)** to bring a plant, animal or disease to a place for the first time: *The British later introduced the crop to East Africa.* ◇ *Species introduced into one nation can often easily spread to neighbouring nations.* **7** to cause sth to contain mistakes: **~ sth** *Measurement error could have been introduced by respondents' recall errors.* ◇ **~ sth into sth** *The analyst's rankings rely on subjective information, which may introduce a bias into the rankings.* **8** to tell sb another person's name when they meet for the first time: **~ sb (as sth)| ~ A (to B) (as sth)** *Mr Meagles introduces him to Arthur Clennam as an engineer.* ◇ **~ yourself (to sb)** *Observers introduced themselves to the group and explained their purpose.* **9 ~ sb/sth** to provide a short description of sb/sth at the start of a television or radio show, book, speech, performance, etc: *He has also edited and introduced two volumes of screenplays by Preston Sturges.* ◇ *Her function was limited to introducing the panellists and asking the questions.* **10 ~ sth** to happen at the start of sth; to be the start of sth: *Wordsworth used this poem to introduce two sets of sonnets.*

▸ INTRODUCE + NOUN **concept, idea, notion • principle • distinction • technique • procedure • scheme, programme • innovation • technology • product • variation • change • regulation • legislation • reform • measure • ban • tax** *Grabher (2002) has introduced the concept of 'project ecology'.* ◇ *These companies failed to introduce commercial innovations that would have reduced trading costs.*

▸ ADVERB + INTRODUCE **first • originally • recently • newly** *The techniques were originally introduced by D.R. Hartree.* ◇ *These are key factors in identifying risks of invasiveness for species newly introduced.*

intro·duc·tion /ˌɪntrəˈdʌkʃn/ *noun* **1** [U] the act of bringing sth into use or operation for the first time: **~ (of sth)** *Problems have been made worse by the introduction of a new computing system.* ◇ **~ of sth into/to sth** *The authors discuss the introduction of a third language into Irish primary schools.* ◇ *The introduction of modern urban services to major Turkish cities was not generally carried out by local enterprises.* **2** [C] a thing that is brought into use or operation for the first time: *Successful new introductions provide increased sales, profits and competitive advantage.* **3** [U] **~ of sth (to/into sth)** the act of bringing a plant, animal or disease to a place for the first time: *The article traces the introduction of Chinese pig breeds to England around 1700.* **4** [C] a plant, animal or disease that is brought to a place for the first time: *Some deliberate introductions, such as the European rabbit in Australia, have had drastic ecological consequences.* **5** [U] **~ (of sth)** the act of formally presenting a new law so that it can be discussed in a parliament: *The Labour Party had pushed for the introduction of the bill.* **6** [C] the first part of a book, report or speech that gives a general idea of what is to follow: *These editions of the plays contain useful introductions and bibliographies.* ◇ **~ to sth** *In their* *introduction to the 1969 edition, the editors state that 'Intelligent Machinery' was 'written in September 1947'.* ➲ *compare* PREFACE **7** [C] **~ (to sth)** a book or course for people beginning to study a subject: *The book is recommended as the best general introduction to the study of Greek literature.* **8** [C, U] the act of making one person formally known to another, in which you tell each the other's name: *Introductions are made, and a certain number of handshakes take place.* ◇ **~ to sb** *Her first formal introduction to me occurred in my class during the first week.* **9** [sing.] **~ (to sth)** a person's first experience of a subject or thing: *This was his introduction to mountain scenery in the eastern tropics.* **10** [C] **~ (to sth)** a short section at the beginning of a piece of music: *The introduction to his Fifth Symphony features a solo trumpet.*

intro·duc·tory /ˌɪntrəˈdʌktəri/ *adj.* **1** written or said at the beginning of sth as an introduction to what follows SYN OPENING²: *The introductory chapter presents an overview of the developments to be reviewed.* **2** intended as an introduction to a subject or an activity for people who have never done it before: *A section on operating systems seems out of place in an introductory course on computer hardware.* **3** intended to persuade sb to buy sth for the first time: *The company tried enticing mobile phone users with introductory offers and free gifts.*

in·tu·ition /ˌɪntjuˈɪʃn; *NAmE* ˌɪntuˈɪʃn/ *noun* **1** [U] the ability to know sth by using your feelings rather than considering the facts: *To make a decision quickly, people have to rely on their intuition.* **2** [C] an idea or a strong feeling that sth is true although it is not proved: *Kennedy's initial intuition had been correct.* ◇ **~ that...** *The empirical studies mentioned earlier confirm the intuition that both numbers are significant.*

in·tui·tive /ɪnˈtjuːɪtɪv; *NAmE* ɪnˈtuːɪtɪv/ *adj.* **1** using or based on what is felt to be true, even without considering facts or evidence: *The fact is that we have an intuitive sense of right and wrong.* ◇ *Even teachers rarely move beyond an intuitive understanding of what constitutes fluency in speaking a foreign language.* **2** (of a system, computer software, etc.) easy to understand and to use, because it is clear what has to be done: *The program is intuitive to use.*

in·tui·tive·ly /ɪnˈtjuːɪtɪvli; *NAmE* ɪnˈtuːɪtɪvli/ *adv.* by using feelings rather than by considering facts: *Scholarly research has confirmed what most people know intuitively.* ◇ *This idea seems intuitively plausible.*

in·vade /ɪnˈveɪd/ *verb* **1** [I, T] to enter a country, town, etc. using military force in order to take control of it: *The Gauls of the Po valley had allied with Hannibal when he invaded.* ◇ **~ sth** *The French armies invaded Italy in 1859.* **2** [T] **~ sth** to spread into a living thing or body part: *Cancer cells have invaded nearby tissue.* **3** [T] **~ sth** (of an animal or plant) to move or spread into a place in large numbers: *In some places, pines have invaded areas formerly dominated by heather.* **4** [T] **~ sth** to disturb sth or have an unpleasant effect on it: *Technology has made it easy to invade the privacy of the individual.* **5** [T] **~ sth** to enter a place, situation or area of activity in large numbers, especially in a way that causes damage or confusion: *European manufacturers attempted to invade the US market again.* ➲ *see also* INVASION, INVASIVE

in·vader /ɪnˈveɪdə(r)/ *noun* **1** an army or a country that enters a country, town, etc. by force in order to take control of it; a soldier fighting in such an army: *King Alfred managed to strengthen his people's resistance to the invader.* ◇ *As these invaders moved south, they pillaged Buddhist monasteries.* **2** something that spreads into a living thing or body part: *However, these drugs can produce serious side effects because they prevent the body from mounting its usual defence against invaders.* **3** an animal or plant that moves or spreads into a place in large numbers: *By 1973 the plant had become a serious invader of riverbank vegetation and floodplains.*

in·valid /ɪnˈvælɪd/ *adj.* **1** not true because it is based on wrong information or bad reasoning: *Out-of-date diagnostic kits may deteriorate and produce invalid results.* ◇ *A comparison is invalid if we are not comparing like with like.* OPP VALID (1) **2** not legally or officially acceptable: *The Court declared the present arrangement invalid.* OPP VALID (2)

in·vali·date AWL /ɪnˈvælɪdeɪt/ *verb* **1 ~ sth** to cause or prove an idea, a story or an argument to be wrong: *This objection is correct, but it does not invalidate the foregoing argument.* OPP VALIDATE (1) **2 ~ sth** to make a document, contract, election, etc. no longer legally or officially valid or acceptable: *Only a fundamental mistake would invalidate a contract.* ■ **in·vali·da·tion** /ɪnˌvælɪˈdeɪʃn/ *noun* [U] **~ (of sth)** *In some fields of science, observation of a single exception to the theory results in invalidation of the theory.* ◇ *The arguments against the Act are unlikely to result in its invalidation.*

in·valu·able /ɪnˈvæljuəbl/ *adj.* extremely useful SYN VALUABLE (1): *Such insight can prove invaluable.* ◇ *These two accounts constitute an invaluable resource for researchers.* ◇ **~ to/for sb/sth** *The book is invaluable for anyone interested in the study of words.*

in·vari·able AWL /ɪnˈveəriəbl; *NAmE* ɪnˈveriəbl/ *adj.* always the same; never changing SYN UNCHANGING: *Linnaeus abandoned the idea that species were fixed and invariable.* ➲ *compare* VARIABLE² (1)

in·vari·ably AWL /ɪnˈveəriəbli; *NAmE* ɪnˈveriəbli/ *adv.* in every case; every time SYN ALWAYS (1): *If left untreated, the infection is invariably fatal.* ◇ *Almost invariably, parental consent will be given.*

in·vari·ant /ɪnˈveəriənt; *NAmE* ɪnˈveriənt/ *adj.* always the same; never changing SYN UNCHANGING: *The pattern of cell divisions was found to be invariant.* ■ **in·vari·ance** /ɪnˈveəriəns; *NAmE* ɪnˈveriəns/ *noun* [U] **~ (of sth)** *The invariance of the speed of light means that electromagnetic radiation is the best basis for standard measuring devices in space-time.*

in·va·sion /ɪnˈveɪʒn/ *noun* [C, U] **1** the act of an army entering another country by force in order to take control of it: **~ (of sth)** *Clinton decided to launch an invasion of the island nation in 1994.* ◇ **~ from sb/sth** *The Great Wall of China was constructed to prevent invasion from the north.* **2** the fact of a large number of people or things entering a place, situation or area of activity, especially people or things that are considered unpleasant: **~ by sb/sth** *South East Asian countries retain their own distinctive business practices despite an invasion by Western culture.* ◇ **~ from sb/sth** *Technological invasion from advanced industrial societies forces modernization on less technologically developed societies.* **3 ~ of sth** an act or process that disturbs sb/sth or has an unpleasant effect on it: *Without legal safeguards, the potential for unwarranted invasion of privacy is obvious.* ◇ *Requiring non-democratic states to be democratic seems to be an invasion of their sovereignty.* **4** the act of spreading into a living thing or body part: **~ of sth (into sth)** *The disease presents as a rash caused by invasion of cancer cells into the epidermis.* ◇ **~ of sth by sth** *It had recently been established that infectious diseases were caused by an invasion of the body by simple organisms such as bacteria.* **5** the fact of a large number of animals or plants moving or spreading into a place: **~ of sth** *The lowland grasslands of California were transformed by invasion of Mediterranean species brought by the Spanish.* ◇ **~ of sth by sth** *They discovered several invasions of shallow waters by deep-sea corals.* ➲ *see also* INVADE

in·va·sive /ɪnˈveɪsɪv/ *adj.* **1** (of animals or plants) moving or spreading into places in large numbers: *The impacts of invasive species range from negligible to extremely high.* **2** (especially of diseases within the body) spreading very quickly and in a harmful way: *One in two men will develop an invasive cancer in their lifetime.* **3** (of medical treatment) involving putting instruments or other objects into the body: *Minimally invasive surgery is generally associated with reduced pain and shorter hospital stay.* OPP NON-INVASIVE **4** disturbing sb/sth or having an unpleasant effect on it: *The legislation gives invasive new surveillance powers to law enforcement.* ➲ *see also* INVADE

in·vent /ɪnˈvent/ *verb* **1 ~ sth** to create or design sth that has not existed before: *Marx did not himself invent the concept of social classes.* ◇ *New technologies are invented almost on a daily basis.* **2 ~ sth** to say or describe sth that is not true, especially in order to deceive people: *In Homer's 'Odyssey', Odysseus is always quick to devise a strategy or invent a story about himself.*

in·ven·tion /ɪnˈvenʃn/ *noun* **1** [C] something that has been created or designed that has not existed before: *The automobile was then a relatively recent invention.* **2** [U] **~ of sth** the act of creating or designing sth that has not existed before: *Shockley's book describes the research leading to the invention of the transistor.* **3** [C, U] the act of saying or describing sth, and pretending that it is true, especially in order to deceive people; something that is said or described in this way: *The story may be an invention to discredit his reputation.* ◇ *Lawson himself admitted to an element of invention in his correspondence with Paterson.* **4** [U] the ability to have new and interesting ideas: *The story shows her exercising her powers of invention to the full.*

in·vent·ive /ɪnˈventɪv/ *adj.* **1** (especially of people) able to create or design new things or think of new ideas: *The inventive Daedalus constructed wings, so that he and his son might escape by flying away.* **2** (of ideas) new and interesting: *Investment bankers are seeking ever more inventive ways of financing companies' needs.* ■ **in·ven·tive·ness** *noun* [U] **~ (of sb/sth)** *European countries have long been renowned for the inventiveness of their entrepreneurs.*

in·vent·or /ɪnˈventə(r)/ *noun* **~ (of sth)** a person who has invented sth or whose job is inventing things: *Zvorykin is regarded as the inventor of modern television.*

in·ven·tory /ˈɪnvəntri; *NAmE* ˈɪnvəntɔːri/ *noun* (*pl.* **-ies**) **1** [C] **~ (of sth)** a written list of all the objects, animals, etc. in a particular place: *The study is based on a comprehensive inventory of all art galleries in Texas.* ◇ *The cattle inventory for this type of farm decreased significantly between 1980 and 2010.* **2** [U, C] (*especially NAmE*) all the goods in a shop or factory SYN STOCK[1] (3): *'Just-in-time' manufacturing reduces the cost of holding inventory.* ◇ *Of course, increased inventories tended to lead to higher prices.*

in·verse[1] /ˌɪnˈvɜːs; *NAmE* ˌɪnˈvɜːrs/ *adj.* [only before noun] opposite in amount, position, direction, order or effect to sth else: *The strong inverse relationship between air temperature and sea ice extent continues to be clearly evident.* HELP If sth changes **in inverse proportion to** sth else, it increases as the other decreases: *This potential varies in inverse proportion to the distance from the centre of mass of the Earth.* (That is, the potential is greater nearer to the centre of the Earth.)

in·verse[2] /ˌɪnˈvɜːs; *NAmE* ˌɪnˈvɜːrs/ *noun* **1** [C] **~ (of sth)** a quantity, an expression in mathematics, a GEOMETRIC figure, etc. that is the opposite of another: *The negative integers are the inverses of the positive ones.* **2 the ˈinverse** [sing.] the opposite of sth: *Poverty is the main cause of chronic hunger, and the inverse is also true: hunger traps people in poverty.*

in·verse·ly /ˌɪnˈvɜːsli; *NAmE* ˌɪnˈvɜːrsli/ *adv.* in a way that is opposite in amount, position, direction, order or effect to sth else: *The temperature of a black hole is inversely proportional to its mass.* ◇ *The availability of good medical care tends to vary inversely with the need for it in the population served.*

in·ver·sion /ɪnˈvɜːʃn; *NAmE* ɪnˈvɜːrʃn; ɪnˈvɜːrʒn/ *noun* [U, C] the act of changing the position or order of sth to its opposite, or of turning sth UPSIDE DOWN: *Tubes should be mixed gently by inversion.* ◇ **~ of sth** *These rules entail an inversion of logic.* HELP In climate science, an **inversion** (or **temperature inversion**) happens when the normal decrease of air temperature with increasing height is reversed: *During an inversion, cooler air remains close to the surface of the Earth.* An **inversion layer** is a layer of the atmosphere in which temperature increases with height.

in·vert /ɪnˈvɜːt; *NAmE* ɪnˈvɜːrt/ *verb* **~ sth** to change the normal position or order of sth, especially by turning it UPSIDE DOWN or by arranging it in the opposite order: *The image is inverted by the microscope.* ◇ *The word 'industry' has been put in inverted commas.*

in·ver·te·brate /ɪnˈvɜːtɪbrət; *NAmE* ɪnˈvɜːrtɪbrət/ *noun* any animal with no BACKBONE: *The fossil record for this part of the canyon has yielded more the 60 species of marine invertebrates.* ➲ *compare* VERTEBRATE ■ **in·ver·te·brate** *adj.* [usually before noun] *The invertebrate species varied between rivers (Table 2.3).*

inˌverted ˈcommas *noun* [pl.] (*BrE*) = QUOTATION MARKS

in·vest AWL /ɪnˈvest/ *verb* **1** [I, T] to put money into shares of a company, property or commercial project in the hope of making a profit: *Higher corporation taxes may reduce the incentive to invest.* ◇ **~ in sth** *The Korean government invested heavily in capital-intensive manufacturing businesses.* ◇ **~ sth** *Business owners invest money in order to make more money.* ◇ **~ sth in sth** *Excessively large amounts of speculative capital have been invested in the market.* **2** [I, T] (of an organization or government, etc.) to spend money on sth in order to make it better or more successful: **~ in sth** *The government should use the funds to invest in education.* ◇ **~ sth in sth** *China has invested a large amount of money in physical infrastructure.* **3** [T] to spend time, energy or effort on sth in the hope that it will be useful: **~ sth in sth** *The time invested in any given activity limits the time available for other activities.* ◇ **~ sth (in) doing sth** *Several other states have invested considerable effort in developing nuclear weapons.*

PHR V **inˈvest sb/sth with sth 1** to make sb/sth seem to have a particular quality: *Many of the stories invest him with divine qualities.* ◇ *Companies often go to great lengths to invest their brands with a distinctive visual identity.* **2** to formally give a person or organization a rank, position or authority: *Governments invest these regulatory bodies with the authority to decide on food safety.*

in·ves·ti·gate AWL /ɪnˈvestɪɡeɪt/ *verb* **1** [T, I] to find out information about a subject or problem by study or research: **~ sth** *This study investigates the effects of climate change on animal husbandry in Africa.* ◇ *These are issues that need to be investigated further.* ◇ **~ (how/what, etc...)** *This study investigated how Chinese students participate in classroom discourse.* ◇ *Once an opportunity has been identified, the decision to investigate further depends on the relevant information costs not being too high.* ➲ thesaurus note *at* EXPLORE **2** [T, I] **~ (sth)** to carefully examine the facts of a situation, an event, a crime, etc. to find out the truth about it or how it happened: *The Mission was established to investigate all violations of international human rights law.* ◇ *In the case of these two children, the local authority failed to investigate.* **3** [T] **~ sb (for sth)** to try to find out information about sb's character, activities, etc: *The Medical and Dental Council threatened to investigate him for misconduct.*

▸ INVESTIGATE + NOUN **association, relationship • interaction • effect, impact • influence • performance • mechanism • role • issue • phenomenon • hypothesis • possibility** *They investigated the relationship between culture and business performance in Japanese companies.* | **complaint • allegation • crime** *The Commissioner should be entitled to investigate complaints about hospitals.*

▸ NOUN + INVESTIGATE **study • research • analysis • article • author • researcher** *Educational researchers investigated the use of wireless technologies in the classroom.*

▸ ADVERB + INVESTIGATE **extensively • thoroughly, fully • systematically • experimentally** *To the best of our knowledge, this relationship has not been fully investigated in the literature.*

THESAURUS

investigation • study • research • experiment • observation • analysis *noun*

These words are all used to talk about research that is carried out in order to find out about sth.

- (a) **detailed** investigation/study/observation/analysis
- (a) **scientific** investigation/study/research/experiment/observation
- a **laboratory** investigation/experiment/study
- (a) **field** study/research/experiment/observation
- (an) **empirical/experimental** investigation/study/research/observation
- (a) **statistical** analysis
- to **carry out/conduct** (an) investigation/study/research/experiment/observations/analysis
- to **perform** (a/an) investigation/study/experiment/analysis
- to **do** (a/an) study/research/experiment

- **Research** is a general word for academic study of a subject, trying to discover new information about it. **Investigation** and **study** are both used to refer to a piece of research that is done to find out information: *The authors conducted social survey research using a structured interview approach.* ◇ *A laboratory investigation revealed the following results:...* ◇ *Our empirical study is partly based on survey data.*
- An **experiment** is a scientific test that is performed in a controlled way in a laboratory or in the field in order to answer a particular question and/or gain new knowledge: *A variety of field and laboratory experiments support the hypothesis.*
- **Observation** is the act of watching sb/sth to see what happens. It is often used to refer to the study of subjects in their natural environment, for example children in a classroom or a species of animal in the wild: *Observations were conducted on first nests attended by a male.*
- **Analysis** is the action or product of studying sth closely, for example the data collected as part of a study or an investigation, in order to understand it and/or to compare it with sth else: *A detailed statistical analysis of the literacy data is provided in Iversen and Stephens (2008).*

in·ves·ti·ga·tion AWL /ɪnˌvestɪˈɡeɪʃn/ *noun* [C, U] **1** a scientific or academic examination of the facts of a subject or problem: *The value of laboratory investigations in diagnosis and monitoring of treatment will be discussed.* ◇ **~ into sth** *Other research included investigation into the wind forces on roofs and structures.* ◇ **under ~** *Both the size and chemical composition of the molecule under investigation are important criteria to consider.* ◇ **~ of sth** *Despite strong growth in scientific investigation of the placebo effect, understanding of this phenomenon remains deeply confused.* **2** an official examination of the facts about a situation, crime, etc: *The EU Commission, having performed an initial investigation, rejected the claim.* ◇ *A 17-year-old kitchen porter confessed to the crime during police investigation.* ◇ **~ into sth** *These data are generally not used to aid investigations into crimes such as homicide.* ◇ **under ~** *The former interior minister was put under investigation.* ◇ **~ of sb/sth** *If the bank becomes bankrupt, there will be a close investigation of all its dealings*

▸ ADJECTIVE + INVESTIGATION **initial, preliminary • further • future • subsequent • ongoing • detailed, in-depth • thorough • appropriate • systematic** *There are several issues related to the spike in commodity prices that merit further investigation.* | **empirical • experimental • scientific** *Empirical investigations rely heavily on data and computer programs.* | **criminal • covert • forensic** *Various authorities conducted criminal investigations into his affairs.*

▸ VERB + INVESTIGATION **require • conduct, undertake, perform, carry out** *The court may direct the appropriate authority to undertake an investigation of the child's circumstances.* | **warrant, merit, deserve • need** *The themes outlined above appear to warrant further investigation.* | **order • launch** *Edward I ordered a wide-ranging investigation of government in the shires.*

in·ves·ti·ga·tive AWL /ɪnˈvestɪɡətɪv; *NAmE* ɪnˈvestɪɡeɪtɪv/ *adj.* [usually before noun] involving examining an event or a situation to find out the truth: *A member of the investigative team discussed the study with the patient.* ◇ *Criminal profiling is an investigative tool that has been the subject of considerable attention.* HELP **Investigative journalism** involves examining important public issues in order to tell people the truth about them in the media: *Investigative journalism may involve the use of tactics and techniques that would normally be considered unfair.*

in·ves·ti·ga·tor AWL /ɪnˈvestɪɡeɪtə(r)/ *noun* a person who carries out a formal investigation in order to find out information or the truth about sth: *The interviews were conducted by the principal investigator.* ◇ *In some cases, private investigators are sent to the applicant's neighbourhood to check on the truthfulness of the applicant's claims.*

in·vest·ment AWL /ɪnˈvestmənt/ *noun* **1** [U, C] the action or process of investing money for profit: *The government is trying to encourage foreign investment.* ◇ *They use other people's money to undertake investments designed to generate new sources of income for them.* ◇ **~ in sth** *The Act also had the effect of facilitating investment in large companies.* ◇ **+ noun** *Asia Pacific is a vibrant region with numerous investment opportunities.* **2** [C] an amount of money that you invest: *The company has given its shareholders a good return on their investment.* ◇ **~ of sth** *He promised a further investment of $1.1 billion.* **3** [C] something that you invest money in: *They had purchased the flat as an investment.* **4** [U, C] **~ in sth** the action or process of spending money on sth in order to make it better or more successful: *Employers want to see a return on their investment in training.* ◇ *Corporations have to recuperate the cost of investment in new technologies.* ◇ *The company is making significant investments in research and development.* **5** [U, C] the action of giving time, energy or effort to a task in order to achieve sth: **~ in sth** *Individuals' self-interest will be served by personal investment in the acquisition of qualifications and experience.* ◇ **~ of sth in sth** *Researchers make substantial investments of time, resources and effort in the collection of usable data.*

▸ ADJECTIVE + INVESTMENT **new • initial • long-term • foreign • international • direct • inward • financial** *The company lost over 70% of its initial investment of $1.88 billion.* | **large, substantial, significant • major • total** *Implementing such a system involves a significant investment of time and effort.* | **private • public** *Health, policing and transport are some of the areas that require public investment.*

I

▸ NOUN + INVESTMENT **capital** *The President stated that money would only be borrowed for capital investment.*
▸ VERB + INVESTMENT **require, need** *Only a relatively small investment is required and little risk is entailed.* | **reduce • limit • undertake** *Skills shortages are limiting investments in research and development.* | **attract • protect** *EU member states are using special tax schemes to compete with each other to attract investment.* | **make** *Many parents make a considerable investment in their children's education.* | **encourage • discourage • increase • promote, stimulate** *Central government agreed to increase investment in regional infrastructure.*
▸ INVESTMENT + NOUN **decision • fund • firm • product • opportunity • strategy • policy • activity • capital • behaviour • protection • criterion • law • treaty • agreement • flow** *Business owners have to make investment decisions based on estimates, guesses and hunches.*
▸ INVESTMENT IN + NOUN **education • infrastructure • system • research • development • human capital • technology • equipment • innovation • training** *Some countries have fallen behind despite quite substantial investments in higher education.*

I

in·vest·or AWL /ɪnˈvestə(r)/ *noun* a person or an organization that invests money in sth: *Russia and Ukraine were not nearly as successful in attracting foreign investors.* ◇ *private/corporate/institutional investors*

in·vis·ible AWL /ɪnˈvɪzəbl/ *adj.* **1** that cannot be seen: *The microscopic parasites that produce these effects are largely invisible.* ◇ *Advances in technology made it possible to view previously invisible planets and stars.* ◇ **~ to sb/sth** *The computer virus is invisible to the ordinary computer operator.* ◇ *Both these frequencies are invisible to the human eye.* OPP VISIBLE (1) **2** [not usually before noun] ignored or not considered: *International Relations has long been taught as if women were invisible.* ◇ **~ to sb/sth** *The majority of people with mental illness remain invisible to policymakers.* OPP VISIBLE (2) **3** [only before noun] (*economics*) connected with a service that a country provides, such as banks or TOURISM, rather than goods: *Earnings for technology and management services are one of the fastest growing components of world invisible trade.* ■ **in·visi·bil·ity** AWL /ɪnˌvɪzəˈbɪləti/ *noun* [U] **~ (of sth)** *The cystic fibrosis sufferers felt disadvantaged relative to other disabled groups because of the invisibility of their disorder.* ◇ *Despite their invisibility in much official data, the Irish in Britain experience considerable discrimination.*
IDM **the inˌvisible ˈhand** (*economics*) used to describe the way a market operates, with buyers and sellers each following only their own interest, but as a result (and without their intending it) creating a system for the exchange of goods and serivces that makes a society work. This idea was first suggested by the economist Adam Smith: *The invisible hand argument assumes that markets are competitive, with many actual or potential buyers and sellers in every market.*

in·vi·ta·tion /ˌɪnvɪˈteɪʃn/ *noun* **1** [C] a spoken or written request to sb to do sth or to go somewhere: *An email invitation was sent to university faculty, staff and students.* ◇ **~ to sth** *All three key opinion leaders accepted the invitation to the conference.* ◇ **~ to do sth** *Officials declined an invitation to be interviewed for the research.* **2** [U] the act of inviting sb or of being invited: **~ to do sth** *A letter of invitation to participate in the study accompanied the questionnaire.* ◇ **at the ~ of sb** *Anderson attended the performance at the official invitation of the Greek government.* ◇ **by ~** *Membership of these organizations is by invitation only.* **3** [C, usually sing.] something that encourages sb to do sth, usually sth bad: **~ (to sb) to do sth** *Some interpret the clause as an open invitation to expand federal power.* ◇ **~ to sth** *Policies that sound impressive can turn out to be invitations to disaster once the ministers discover their implications.*

in·vite /ɪnˈvaɪt/ *verb* **1** to ask sb formally to go somewhere, do sth or provide sth: **~ sb (to sth)** *When he was invited to a conference at Nankai University, he declined the invitation.* ◇ **~ sb for sth** *23 people were invited for an interview.* ◇ **~ sth (from sb)** *Comments were invited on the proposed changes.* ◇ **~ sb to do sth** *A representative from each school was invited to attend an information meeting.* ◇ **~ sb + adv./prep.** *The film's focus on the rhythms of daily life invites the viewer into the work and habits of the villagers.* **2 ~ sth** to make sth likely to happen, especially sth bad or unpleasant: *Many newer buildings omit these traditional beams, thereby inviting disaster in future earthquake events.* ◇ *Wilson's work will invite the criticism of some of its readers.*

in vitro /ɪn ˈviːtrəʊ; *NAmE* ɪn ˈviːtroʊ/ *adj.* (*from Latin, biology*) (of processes) taking place outside a living thing, in scientific APPARATUS: *The embryos are created through in vitro fertilization.* ◇ *The blocking process successfully inhibited fertilization in our in vitro experiment.* ■ **in vitro** *adv.*: *These features were all observed in vitro as well as in vivo.*

in vivo /ɪn ˈviːvəʊ; *NAmE* ɪn ˈviːvoʊ/ *adj.* (*from Latin, biology*) (of processes) taking place in a living thing: *A variety of in vivo and in vitro techniques were employed.* ■ **in vivo** *adv.*: *These proteins have a direct influence on DNA-associated processes occuring in vivo.*

in·vo·ca·tion /ˌɪnvəˈkeɪʃn/ *noun* [U, C] **~ (of sth)** (*formal*) **1** the act of mentioning or using a law or rule as a reason for doing sth: *The Court of Justice did not accept the invocation of Article 30 to justify the lack of action.* **2** the act of mentioning sb/sth as an example of sth, or as a way of supporting an argument or idea: *Despite its frequent invocation in the context of asylum seekers, the word 'terrorism' does not appear in the 1951 Convention.* **3** the act of making a request for help to sb, especially a god: *Mantras are powerful invocations addressed to the deities.* **4** (*computing*) the act of running a program, etc: *The invocation of a web service is performed by message passing.*

in·voke AWL /ɪnˈvəʊk; *NAmE* ɪnˈvoʊk/ *verb* **1 ~ sth** to mention or use a law or rule as a reason for doing sth: *The Court is invoking Article 21 of the Charter, which prohibits any discrimination based on age.* **2 ~ sb/sth (as sth)** to mention sb/sth as an example of sth, or as a way of supporting an argument or idea: *The Ural Mountains and the Caspian Sea are often invoked as the natural frontiers of Europe.* ◇ *Male primate behaviour is usually invoked as an explanation for men's propensity for warfare.* **3 ~ sb** to make a request (for help) to sb, especially a god: *Verse is used to invoke a deity or to gain protection.* **4 ~ sth** to make sb have a particular feeling or imagine a particular scene SYN EVOKE: *Humour is the ability to invoke laughter or see the funny side of a painful predicament.* **5 ~ sth** (*computing*) to begin to run a program, etc: *By clicking on the macro tag, the Template Editor window is invoked.*

in·vol·un·tary /ɪnˈvɒləntri; *NAmE* ɪnˈvɑːlənteri/ *adj.* **1** happening without the person concerned wanting it to: *Involuntary manslaughter arises where the defendant unlawfully causes the death of the victim, but has no intention of killing them.* ⊃ *compare* VOLUNTARY (1) **2** an **involuntary** movement, etc. is made suddenly, without you intending it or being able to control it: *Falling dreams often end with an involuntary muscle spasm.* OPP VOLUNTARY (3) ■ **in·vol·un·tar·ily** /ɪnˈvɒləntrəli; *NAmE* ɪnˌvɑːlənˈterəli/ *adv.*: *People found themselves being involuntarily transported from their places of birth in Africa to unfamiliar lands.*

in·volve AWL /ɪnˈvɒlv; *NAmE* ɪnˈvɑːlv/ *verb* **1** if a situation, an event or an activity **involves** sth, that thing is an important or necessary part or result of it SYN MEAN[1]:

~ sth *If a case involves matters of national security, a court may exercise its power to exclude the public.* ◇ *International business may involve exchange rate issues, which can make planning more difficult.* ◇ **~ doing sth** *Most formal education involved listening and reciting from memory.* ◇ **~ sb/sth doing sth** *Auctions involve many people bidding against each other for an item.* ➲ *compare* ENTAIL (1) **2** if a situation, an event or an activity **involves** sb/sth, they take part in it or are affected by it: **~ sb/sth** *He commanded the army and judged disputes involving non-citizens.* ◇ **be involved in sth** *The car had been involved in a serious accident.* **3** to make sb take part in sth: **~ sb (in sth)** *Difficulties might include failure to involve relevant people in the evaluation.* ◇ **~ sb in doing sth** *It is important to communicate with the patient and involve them in deciding what they eat.* ◇ **~ yourself (in sth)** *The UK was reluctant to involve itself in the negotiations.* **4 ~ sb (in sth)** to say or do sth to show that sb took part in sth, especially a crime SYN IMPLICATE (2): *If he played any part in encouragement, that would be sufficient to involve him in the murder.*

in·volved AWL /ɪn'vɒlvd; *NAmE* ɪn'vɑːlvd/ *adj.* **1** [not before noun] being part of sth; connected with or affected by sth HELP In this meaning, **involved** is often used directly after a noun: *It is clear that both environmental and genetic factors are involved.* ◇ *The reason why firms do not delay decisions is because there is a cost involved.* ◇ **~ in sth** *Examples of advances in this area include identification of the genes involved in ageing.* **2** [not usually before noun] taking part in sth; giving time or attention to sb/sth: *No other European country was as deeply involved as Britain.* ◇ *When people are not interested, they do not get involved.* ◇ **~ with sb/sth** *Parents and community members are involved with the school.* ◇ **~ in sth** *Telecom Italia is heavily involved in most aspects of the telecommunications industry.* **3** [not usually before noun] having a close personal relationship with sb/sth: **~ with sb** *We told him not to get involved with these kids.* ◇ **~ with sth** *He was too involved with past tradition and practices to develop the business successfully.* **4** complicated and difficult to understand SYN COMPLEX¹ (2): *The complete calculation is too involved to include here.* OPP SIMPLE (1)

▸ NOUN + INVOLVED **steps • stages • mechanism • process • issues • principles • factors, elements • skill • risk • challenge • difficulties, problems • cost • gene • protein • enzyme** *The producer concentrates on the skills and processes involved in producing the product.* | **actor • people, person • party • professional • individual • stakeholder • company • staff • organization** *The actors involved might be public officials, but they might equally well be non-governmental organizations.*

▸ ADVERB + INVOLVED **actively • directly • heavily, deeply • intimately, closely** *Citizens were not actively involved in the decision-making process.*

in·volve·ment AWL /ɪn'vɒlvmənt; *NAmE* ɪn'vɑːlvmənt/ *noun* [U, C] **1** the act of taking part in sth; the fact of being included in sth SYN PARTICIPATION: *The Nixon administration denied any involvement.* ◇ **~ of sb/sth** *The active involvement of the central bank is required to keep the inflationary process under control.* ◇ **~ with sth** *His involvement with the company goes back many years.* ◇ **~ in sth** *Patients complained about the lack of family involvement in the decision-making process.* ◇ *She studied diplomatic involvements in the oil industry in certain South American countries in the 1920s.* **2** the act of giving time and attention to sth you care about: *Parental involvement exerts a beneficial influence on children's school success.* ◇ **~ in sth** *He had a lifelong involvement in competitive sport.* ◇ **~ with sth/sb** *Employees are likely to exhibit a deep sense of involvement with the organization.* **3 ~ (with sb)** a romantic or personal relationship with sb: *Better co-parenting should affect parents' warmth and involvement with their child.*

in·ward¹ /'ɪnwəd; *NAmE* 'ɪnwərd/ *adj.* **1** towards the inside or centre of sth: *When these stars finally exhaust their reserves of nuclear fuel, they have no means of opposing the inward pull of gravity.* HELP In business, **inward investment** is money that is invested in a particular country from outside it: *During the 1990s, China was the largest developing country recipient of inward investment.* OPP OUTWARD (3) **2** [only before noun] inside your mind and not shown to other people: *Baptism is considered only an outward and visible sign of an inward and spiritual change.* OPP OUTWARD (1)

in·ward² /'ɪnwəd; *NAmE* 'ɪnwərd/ *adv.* (*also* **in·wards** *especially in BrE*) towards yourself and your interests: *Anger may be directed at others or turned inward at ourselves.* ◇ (*disapproving*) *Problems can arise when departments become self-contained, self-absorbed and inward-looking.* OPP OUTWARDS (2)

ion /'aɪən; 'aɪɒn; *NAmE* 'aɪɑːn/ *noun* (*physics, chemistry*) an atom or a MOLECULE with a positive or negative electric charge caused by its losing or gaining one or more ELECTRONS: *Sodium metal reacts vigorously with water to form hydrogen gas and a solution of sodium ions and hydroxide ions.* ◇ *Many enzymes require a metal ion for activity.* ➲ *see also* ANION, CATION

I

ionic /aɪ'ɒnɪk; *NAmE* aɪ'ɑːnɪk/ *adj.* **1** (*physics, chemistry*) connected with ions: *Positive ions have a smaller ionic radius than the atom from which they are derived, whereas the opposite is true for negative ions.* **2** (*chemistry*) (of a chemical BOND) using the electrical attraction between positive and negative ions: *The high melting point of sodium chloride is due to the strong ionic bond between the sodium and chloride ions.* ➲ *compare* COVALENT

ion·ize (*BrE also* **-ise**) /'aɪənaɪz/ *verb* [T, I] (*physics, chemistry*) (of an atom, a MOLECULE or a substance) to change or be changed into ions, typically when one or more ELECTRONS are removed: *Hydrogen chloride is fully ionized in aqueous solution to form hydrochloric acid.* ◇ *Radiotherapy is the therapeutic use of ionizing radiation to damage cancerous cells.* ◇ **~ sth** *At room temperature, only one in about 510 atoms is ionized.* ■ **ion·iza·tion, -isa·tion** /ˌaɪənaɪ'zeɪʃn; *NAmE* ˌaɪənə'zeɪʃn/ *noun* [U] **(+ noun)** *The ionization energy of helium is the highest of all the elements as its electrons are most strongly attracted to the nucleus.*

IPA /ˌaɪ piː 'eɪ/ *abbr.* **International Phonetic Alphabet** (an alphabet that is used to show the pronunciation of words in any language): **+ noun** *Material is cited in the text in IPA symbols.*

IQ /ˌaɪ 'kjuː/ *noun* the abbreviation for 'intelligence quotient' (a measurement of a person's intelligence that is calculated from the results of special tests): **~ (of sth)** *An IQ of 100 is, by an arbitrary definition, the population average.* ◇ *to have a high/low IQ* ◇ **+ noun** *an IQ test/score*

iron /'aɪən; *NAmE* 'aɪərn/ *noun* [U] (*symb.* **Fe**) the chemical element of ATOMIC NUMBER 26. Iron is a hard strong metal that is used to make steel and is also found in small quantities in blood and food: *Up to the early 1900s, Americans generally cooked on stoves made of cast iron.* ◇ **+ noun** *Iron ore is converted into sheets that can be used by car and aircraft manufacturers.* ◇ *Iron deficiency is associated with poverty, so it is particularly prevalent in the developing world.*

iron·ic /aɪ'rɒnɪk; *NAmE* aɪ'rɑːnɪk/ (*also less frequent* **iron·ic·al** /aɪ'rɒnɪkl; *NAmE* aɪ'rɑːnɪkl/) *adj.* **1** (of a situation) strange because it is very different from what you expect: *An ironic consequence of this colonialist war was that it brought about the end of colonialism in South East Asia.* ◇ **~ that...** *As Trewin points out, it is ironic that the wealthiest states favour 'free trade' but try to restrict international migration.* ➲ *see also* IRONY **2** showing that you really mean the opposite of what you are saying; expressing IRONY: *Personal film-makers often use an ironic approach to familiar objects, forcing a re-analysis of them.* ■ **iron·ic·al·ly** /aɪˈrɒnɪkli; *NAmE* aɪˈrɑːnɪkli/ *adv.*: *Ironically, the Roman Empire exerted its greatest influence on Ireland at the time of its own final decline.*

irony /ˈaɪrəni/ *noun* (*pl.* **-ies**) **1** [U, C] the strange aspect of a situation that is very different from what you expect; a situation like this: *The irony is that two of these anti-immigrant politicians were themselves the descendants of immigrants.* ◇ **~ of sth** *One of the ironies of modern times is that so many useful technologies also increase our risk of disease or catastrophe.* **2** [U] the use of words that say the opposite of what you really mean in order to emphasize sth or to be funny: *The main characters are portrayed with a mixture of irony and sympathy.* ◇ *Kuhn, without irony, claims a parallel between the training of scientists and monks.* **3** [U] a technique in literature, originally used in Greek TRAGEDY, where a character's words carry an extra meaning, especially because of what is going to happen that the character does not know about: **dramatic/tragic ~** *The dramatic irony in this scene revolves around Duncan's praise of Macbeth, even as Macbeth is plotting to kill him.*

I

ir·ration·al AWL /ɪˈræʃənl/ *adj.* not based on, or not using, clear logical thought SYN UNREASONABLE: *People are quite liable to have irrational beliefs, based on prejudice or personal bias.* ◇ **it is ~ (for sb) to do sth** *It would be irrational for one state to require its fishing industry to observe a fishing quota, if it is believed that the fishing industries in other states are intending to disregard the quota.* OPP RATIONAL ■ **ir·ration·al·ity** /ɪˌræʃəˈnæləti/ *noun* [U, C, usually sing.] *There is an element of irrationality in the way a crisis unfolds.* **ir·ration·al·ly** /ɪˈræʃnəli/ *adv.*: *The President had acted irrationally and had brought the country perilously close to disaster.*

ir·re·du·cible /ˌɪrɪˈdjuːsəbl; *NAmE* ˌɪrɪˈduːsəbl/ *adj.* (*formal*) that cannot be made smaller or simpler: *Concepts are our basic, irreducible mental dispositions.* ◇ **~ to sth** *Boas insisted that culture was irreducible to biology.* ■ **ir·re·du·cibly** /ˌɪrɪˈdjuːsəbli; *NAmE* ˌɪrɪˈduːsəbli/ *adv.*: *A significant trend has been towards the recognition of irreducibly universal human rights for individuals.*

ir·regu·lar /ɪˈregjələ(r)/ *adj.* **1** not happening at times that are at an equal distance from each other; not happening regularly: *These events seem to have occurred at irregular intervals.* ◇ *Supplies were irregular and a new source had to be found.* ◇ *There are many causes of an irregular pulse.* ➲ *compare* REGULAR (1) **2** not arranged in an even way; not having an even, smooth pattern or shape: *The coast of northern Brittany has an irregular pattern of bays and headlands.* OPP REGULAR (6) **3** not normal; not according to the usual rules: *What had happened was highly irregular.* ◇ *As with other forms of irregular warfare, terrorism is designed to achieve political change.* ➲ *compare* REGULAR (7) **4** (*grammar*) (especially of verbs or nouns) not changing their form in the same way as most other verbs and nouns: *an irregular verb/plural* OPP REGULAR (8)

ir·regu·lar·ity /ɪˌregjəˈlærəti/ *noun* (*pl.* **-ies**) [U, C] **~ (of sth) 1** an activity or a practice which is not according to the usual rules, or not normal: *The accountants had failed to identify irregularities in the accounts.* ◇ *procedural/financial irregularity* **2** something that does not happen regularly: *Workers manage the irregularity of earnings in different ways.* ➲ *compare* REGULARITY (3) **3** something that is not smooth or regular in shape or arrangement; the quality of being like this: *The sample is polished until all of the irregularities left by the grinding are removed.* ➲ *compare* REGULARITY (2)

ir·regu·lar·ly /ɪˈregjələli; *NAmE* ɪˈregjələrli/ *adv.* **1** at irregular times: *Traditionally, parliaments met only irregularly.* OPP REGULARLY (1) **2** not evenly or smoothly: *The surgeon removed an irregularly shaped mass of tissue.* OPP REGULARLY (3)

ir·rele·vant AWL /ɪˈreləvənt/ *adj.* not important to or connected with a situation: *The point is entirely correct, but it is irrelevant.* ◇ **~ to sb/sth** *Some of the discussion appears irrelevant to the topic in hand.* ◇ **~ for sb/sth** *The difference is so small as to be irrelevant for our purposes.* OPP RELEVANT (1) ■ **ir·rele·vance** AWL /ɪˈreləvəns/ *noun* [U, C, usually sing.] **~ (of sth) (to sth)** *the irrelevance of the curriculum to the children's daily lives* ◇ *This idea was rejected as an irrelevance.*

ir·re·spect·ive of /ɪrɪˈspektɪv əv/ *prep.* without considering sth or being influenced by it: **~ sth** *They will choose the best candidate irrespective of nationality.* ◇ **~ whether/how, etc...** *Irrespective of whether recreational drugs are legal or illegal, they are likely to have an impact on people's health.*

ir·re·spon·sible /ˌɪrɪˈspɒnsəbl; *NAmE* ˌɪrɪˈspɑːnsəbl/ *adj.* (*disapproving*) (of a person, attitude or action) not showing an appropriate sense of responsibility: *The company was accused of irresponsible marketing practices.* ◇ **it is ~ to do sth** *It would be professionally irresponsible to report information based on incomplete experiments.* OPP RESPONSIBLE (5) ■ **ir·re·spon·si·bil·ity** /ˌɪrɪˌspɒnsəˈbɪləti; *NAmE* ˌɪrɪˌspɑːnsəˈbɪləti/ *noun* [U] *The current economic crisis is the result of many years of irresponsibility in government and the private sector.* **ir·re·spon·sibly** /ˌɪrɪˈspɒnsəbli; *NAmE* ˌɪrɪˈspɑːnsəbli/ *adv.*: *Student militants had acted recklessly and irresponsibly.*

ir·re·vers·ible AWL /ˌɪrɪˈvɜːsəbl; *NAmE* ˌɪrɪˈvɜːrsəbl/ *adj.* that cannot be changed back to what it was before OPP REVERSIBLE (1): *Human activities inflict harsh and irreversible damage on the environment.* ◇ *For all practical purposes, the biochemical reaction is irreversible.* ■ **ir·re·ver·si·bil·ity** /ˌɪrɪvɜːsəˈbɪləti; *NAmE* ˌɪrɪvɜːrsəˈbɪləti/ *noun* [U] **~ (of sth)** *One aspect that has not been included is the possible irreversibility of salt reactions.* **ir·re·vers·ibly** /ˌɪrɪˈvɜːsəbli; *NAmE* ˌɪrɪˈvɜːrsəbli/ *adv.*: *Brainstem death occurs when the brainstem has been irreversibly damaged but the heart is still beating.*

ir·ri·gate /ˈɪrɪgeɪt/ *verb* **~ sth** to supply water to an area of land through pipes or channels so that crops will grow: *Rivers were diverted to irrigate fields.* ◇ *As much as 95 per cent of Indonesia's total annual production of rice is grown on irrigated land (Rose, 1982).*

ir·ri·ga·tion /ˌɪrɪˈgeɪʃn/ *noun* [U] the process of supplying water to an area of land through pipes or channels so that crops will grow: **~ (of sth)** *Water from the river is used for the irrigation of rice fields.* ◇ **+ noun** *irrigation ditches/canals* ◇ *Small-scale irrigation schemes are difficult to run.*

is /ɪz/ ➲ BE[1], BE[2]

Islam /ˈɪzlɑːm; ɪzˈlɑːm/ *noun* [U] **1** the Muslim religion, based on belief in one God and REVEALED through Muhammad as the Prophet of Allah: *Islam has grown and spread from the seventh-century Arabia of the Prophet Muhammad to a world religion with followers across the globe.* **2** all Muslims and Muslim countries in the world: *Paper was significant to the spread of religion and knowledge throughout Islam.* ■ **Is·lam·ic** /ɪzˈlæmɪk; ɪzˈlɑːmɪk/ *adj.*: *Islamic law*

is·land /ˈaɪlənd/ *noun* (*abbr.* **I, I., Is.**) a piece of land that is completely surrounded by water: *Iceland is the world's largest volcanic island.* ◇ **~ of sth** *For the islands of the eastern Caribbean, bananas have been the principal export crop since the early 1900s.* ◇ **on an ~** *Polynesian cultures developed independently, because when Polynesian people settled on an island, there were never any other* *people living there.* ◇ **+ noun** *The population of this small Indian Ocean island nation is about 1.2 million.*

isol·ate AWL /ˈaɪsəleɪt/ *verb* **1** to separate sb/sth physically or socially from other people or things: **~ sb/sth/yourself** *She isolates herself, reducing opportunities for social support and warmth.* ◇ **~ sb/sth/yourself from sb/sth** *Individuals with the disease must be isolated from the general population for a period.* ◇ *North Korea isolated itself economically from virtually all outside influences.* **2** to separate a single substance, cell, etc. from others so that you can study it: **~ sth** *Antibiotics inhibit the growth of bacteria and thus increase the likelihood of isolating target pathogens.* ◇ **~ sth from sth** *Once an organism has been isolated from a blood culture, it should be identified to species level.* **3** to separate a part of a situation, a problem or an idea so that you can see what it is and deal with it separately: **~ sth** *If all of the other factors change as well, it is not possible to isolate the relationship between price and the quantity demanded.* ◇ **~ sth from sth** *It has proved difficult to isolate the effect of a tsunami from the effects of the earthquake that generates it.*

isol·ated AWL /ˈaɪsəleɪtɪd/ *adj.* **1** far away from other places, buildings or people SYN REMOTE (1): *Isolated rural areas tend to lose their more entrepreneurial young people.* ◇ *There are practical problems with doing fieldwork among geographically isolated populations.* **2** without much contact with other people or other countries: *Divorce may leave family members feeling isolated.* ◇ *Class discussions took place on ways to reach out to socially isolated children.* ◇ **~ from sb/sth** *Workers became more isolated from one another.* **3** single; happening once: *This is not an isolated case.* ◇ *As in 1931, an isolated incident expanded into something bigger.*

isol·ation AWL /ˌaɪsəˈleɪʃn/ *noun* [U] **1** the act of separating sb/sth; the state of being separate: *The country escaped from plague because of its geographical isolation.* ◇ **~ of sb/sth** *The president's refusal to accept the election result led to the almost complete isolation of his regime.* ◇ **~ from sb/sth** *The Tokugawa brought peace and stability to Japan but isolation from the rest of the world.* ◇ **in ~** *Humans do not develop in isolation but in relation to their family, home, school and society.* ◇ **in ~ from sb/sth** *All these factors should not be considered in isolation from each other, as they are often interconnected.* HELP In medicine, **isolation** is often used before another noun when describing hospitals or other places for patients who have a disease that can easily be passed to other people: *Any clinical suspicion of tuberculosis should prompt transfer to an infectious diseases unit with isolation facilities.* In biology and chemistry, **isolation** is used to talk about the act of obtaining a substance or MICROORGANISM in a pure form: *Selection of the correct media is critical in the isolation of pathogens.* **2** the state of being alone or lonely: *Excessive alcohol intake can lead to social isolation and family conflict.* ◇ **~ from sb/sth** *These men were willing to endure isolation from home and family.*

iso·tope /ˈaɪsətəʊp; *NAmE* ˈaɪsətoʊp/ *noun* (*physics, chemistry*) one of two or more forms of a chemical element that have the same number of PROTONS but a different number of NEUTRONS in their atoms. They have different physical properties but the same chemical ones: **~ (of sth)** *The analysis of stable isotopes of carbon (C) and oxygen (O) is a rapidly expanding area of research (Bowen, 1991; Swart et al., 1993; Nordt et al., 1998).* ◇ **+ noun** *The oxygen isotope record plainly implies that sea level changed frequently and rapidly during the Pleistocene.*

issue[1] AWL /ˈɪʃuː; *BrE also* ˈɪsjuː/ *noun* **1** [C] an important topic that people are discussing or arguing about: *The creation of waste and its management have become major issues.* ◇ **~ of sth** *The research questions revolve around the issue of vegetarianism as a dietary choice.* ◇ **~ for sb/sth** *Locational questions and theories are central issues for geography.* ◇ **(not) be an ~** *Monarchy was not an issue in Belgium, whereas in France the republicans felt anxious about the survival of the republic.* **2** [C] (*often* **issues** [pl.]) a problem, concern or difficulty: *The management board should inform the supervisory board immediately of any issues.* ◇ **~ with sth** *Adolescents' issues with weight and eating are not necessarily going to become an illness unless eating patterns are unhealthy.* ◇ **~ about/around sth** *There are major issues about prenatal screening of this kind.* ◇ **(not) be an ~** *Geographic distance may not be an issue for the Internet, but it is when it comes to delivering products.* **3** [C] one of a regular series of magazines or newspapers: *Some of the articles in this issue consider America's political and cultural history.* ◇ *The December issue of the Journal will be a special issue devoted to equality law.* **4** [C, U] something that is supplied or made available for people to buy or use; the act of supplying or making available things for people to buy or use: *Share issues worth more than £2 000 billion had already been sold by three of the UK's largest property groups.* ◇ **~ of sth** *The system will involve the issue of permits for new waste-treatment facilities.* **5** [U] (*law*) children of your own: *The fund would pass to her issue or to her brother if she died without issue.*

IDM **be at ˈissue** to be the most important part of the subject that is being discussed: *What is at issue is the notion of critical inquiry.* ◇ *At issue in this case was a computer program designed for use by pharmacists.* **decide/settle the ˈissue** to answer a question or solve a problem that has been the subject of debate: *The delegates had to vote to decide the issue by majority.* **take ˈissue with sb/sth (about/on/over sth)** to disagree or argue with sb about sth: *This article takes issue with the first of these points—the idea of British honour.*

▸ ADJECTIVE + ISSUE **key, central, main, fundamental • important, major, big • critical, crucial • complex • difficult • sensitive • specific, particular • related • relevant • unresolved • technical** *The barely visible damage is a major design issue.* ◇ *The centre collaborates with researchers to clarify complex world issues that affect us all.* | **controversial, contentious • pressing • contemporary • broader • global • public • practical • theoretical • methodological • strategic • ethical, moral • legal • political • social • economic • environmental** *The party was able to capitalize on the strong focus on environmental issues throughout the election campaign.*

▸ NOUN + ISSUE **health • safety • gender** *Smoking has become a global health issue.* | **policy • security • human rights** *States have focused their attention on security issues to the detriment of human rights issues.*

▸ VERB + ISSUE **address, approach • tackle, handle • confront, face • raise • discuss, debate • consider • explore, examine, investigate, study • understand • cover • highlight • identify • frame • resolve • clarify • ignore, avoid** *No sustained efforts seem to have been made to tackle basic social issues such as inequality.*

▸ ISSUE + VERB **arise • affect • surrounding • involved • concerning • relating to • associated with • facing** *The complex ethical issues surrounding genetic testing and screening will be briefly reviewed.*

▸ NOUN + OF ISSUES **range • number • variety** *There are a number of issues that must be resolved before these benefits can be realized.* | **awareness • understanding • discussion, consideration • resolution** *Single discipline approaches can lead to an incomplete understanding of the issues involved.*

issue[2] AWL /ˈɪʃuː; *BrE also* ˈɪsjuː/ *verb* **1** to make sth known formally; to make sth available publicly: **~ sth** *The heads of government issued declarations on the economic situation regarding the euro.* ◇ *While thousands of firms issue environmental reports on their activities, these reports do not follow any common standard.* ◇ **~ sth to sb** *The National Hurricane Center issues a hurricane warning* to a community 24 hours before it expects the storm to hit land. **2** [often passive] to give sth to sb, especially officially: **~ sth** *The GPs in this study reported that they issued sickness certificates most frequently for mental health conditions.* ◇ **~ sb with sth** *Attendees on the course will be issued with a certificate of attendance.* ◇ **~ sth to sb** *An Application Registration Card is the identity document issued to asylum seekers.* **3 ~ sth** to start a legal process against sb, especially by means of an official document: *He failed to attend the court and a warrant was issued for his arrest.* **4 ~ sth** to produce new STAMPS, coins, shares, etc. for sale to the public: *The amount of gold coinage issued annually in Britain, France and the USA increased in the early 1850s.*

PHR V **ˈissue from sth** (*formal*) to come out of sth: *It is easy to overlook such examples of cultural influences entering the US, rather than issuing from it.* ■ **is·suer** *noun*: *As well as banks, today's credit card issuers include building societies, insurance companies and retailers.*

IT /ˌaɪ ˈtiː/ *noun* [U] the abbreviation for INFORMATION TECHNOLOGY: *IT is now part of every industry.* ◇ **+ noun** *He worked as an IT consultant.*

J

it /ɪt/ *pron.* (used as the subject or object of a verb or after a preposition) **1** used to refer to an animal or a thing that has already been mentioned or that is being talked about now: *If blood becomes too thin, it loses the ability to form clots.* ◇ *This approach is refreshing because it breaks down barriers.* ◇ *Seeing a cat and thinking of it being chased by a dog is a simple example of relational processing.* **2** used to refer to a baby, especially one whose sex is not known: *Other people can help a mother feed her baby by giving it a bottle.* **3** used to refer to a fact or situation that is already known or happening: *Banks were interested because it meant new clients.* ◇ *As Nietzsche sees it, human beings are naturally cruel.* **4** used to identify a person: *You can tell from a voice whether it is a man or a woman.* ◇ *At Troy, it was Odysseus who had the idea of the wooden horse.* **5** used in the position of the subject or object of a verb when the real subject or object is at the end of the sentence: *It can be difficult to sort out legend from fact.* ◇ *Many firms found it cheaper to pay outside companies for maintenance.* ◇ *It seems likely that most cities originated in one of four ways.* **6** used in the position of the subject of a verb when you are talking about time, the date, distance, the weather, etc: *It was two days before the Passover.* ◇ *Suppose it is 1 January 2050.* ◇ *When it is raining, there is nowhere to go.* **7** used when you are talking about a situation: *It was too complicated to explain.* ◇ *It is interesting that the same types of effects found in the early 1970s are still true today.* ◇ *If she does not like it here, she will not like it anywhere.* **8** used to emphasize any part of a sentence: *In India, it was the East India Company that provided the military power.* ◇ *It was during this period that the modern research laboratory became firmly established.* ➲ *see also* ITS

ital·ics /ɪˈtælɪks/ *noun* [pl.] (*also* **italic** [sing.]) printed letters that lean to the right: *Use italics for the names of books or plays.* ◇ **in ~** *Examples in this dictionary are in italics.* ■ **ital·ic** *adj.*: *The example sentences in this dictionary are printed in italic type.*

item AWL /ˈaɪtəm/ *noun* **1** a single object or thing, especially one that is part of a list, collection or set: *She bought the item online.* ◇ *The emphasis is on food items that are easy to prepare.* ◇ *It is the most urgent item on the agenda.* ◇ *Respondents rated items from (1) really disagree to (4) really agree.* ◇ *The universal core vocabulary includes items such as pronouns, numerals, body parts, geographical features, basic actions and basic states.* ◇ **~ of sth** *an item of clothing/equipment/furniture* ◇ *The habit of treating any item of information as a state secret meant that military units were not told what to expect.* **2** a single piece of news in a newspaper, on television, etc: *The story remained a major news item for three weeks.*

it·er·ation /ˌɪtəˈreɪʃn/ *noun* (*technical*) **1** [U, C] the process of repeating a MATHEMATICAL or COMPUTATIONAL process or set of instructions again and again, each time applying it to the result of the previous stage: *Direct iteration is used to solve the problem.* ◇ **~ of sth** *Over time, and multiple iterations of the analysis, recurrent themes and patterns were identified.* **2** [C] a version of sth: *The survey tools were all developed with the collaboration of front line staff and underwent several iterations.*

it·era·tive /ˈɪtərətɪv/ *adj.* (*technical*) involving ITERATION: *Data were analysed using a multi-step iterative process.*

its /ɪts/ *det.* belonging to or connected with a thing, an animal or a baby: *The theatre uses direct mail to keep in touch with its customers.* ◇ *He wrote about deforestation and its impact on climate change.* ◇ *The longer a baby lives, the greater its chances of continuing to survive.*

it·self /ɪtˈself/ *pron.* **1** (the reflexive form of *it*) used when the animal or thing that does an action is also affected by it: *The cycle then repeats itself.* ◇ *Watch how an animal grooms itself.* ◇ *Each group has different expectations of itself.* **2** used to emphasize an animal, a thing, etc: *The record itself is made from hard wax.* ◇ *Ratings were collected not only for the company itself, but for its main competitors.*

IDM **by itˈself 1** AUTOMATICALLY; without anyone doing anything: *Creative work sometimes seems to happen by itself.* **2** alone: *No theory can explain anything by itself.* **in itˈself** considered separately from other things; in its true nature: *Discipline is certainly not enough in itself to produce intelligence.* ◇ *They focused on meeting deadlines as a goal in itself.* ◇ *Definitions of health depend on a concept of what is normal, in itself a very complex field.*

Jj

jaw /dʒɔː/ *noun* **1** [C] either of the two bones at the bottom of the face that contain the teeth and move when you talk or eat: *He underwent surgery that removed half his upper jaw.* ◇ **+ noun** *Data on the daily use of jaw muscles are available for only a limited number of species.* **2** [sing.] the lower part of the face; the lower jaw: *One of the police officers hit him in the face with a baton, breaking his jaw.* **3 jaws** [pl.] the mouth and teeth of a person or an animal: *The fish are actively opening and closing their jaws well before hatching.*

jelly /ˈdʒeli/ *noun* (*pl.* **-ies**) [U, C] **1** (*BrE*) a cold sweet transparent food, that shakes when it is moved; any thick soft substance like this: *Encourage sips of cold clear fluid, then ice cream and jelly, then introduce normal diet as soon as possible.* **2** any thick soft substance like jelly: *Lubricate the end of the tube with jelly.*

jet /dʒet/ *noun* **1** a plane with engines that drive it forwards by pushing out streams of gases behind them: *In the late 1960s, Boeing invented the 747 jumbo jet.* ◇ **+ noun** *The Comet, the first commercial jet aircraft, had experienced widely reported crashes in 1952 and 1953.* ◇ *Mechanical engineers have been keen to build jet engines which run at higher temperatures.* **2 ~ (of sth)** a strong narrow stream of gas, liquid, steam or flame that comes very quickly out of a small opening. The opening is also called a jet: *Velvet worms hunt by shooting a jet of superglue at their prey to immobilize them.* ◇ *The design of the gas jets to produce a high velocity gas flow minimizes the risk of explosion.*

Jew /dʒuː/ *noun* a member of the people and cultural community whose traditional religion is Judaism and who come from the ancient Hebrew people of Israel; a person who believes in and practises Judaism: *Jews* *believe that a Jew is someone who is the child of a Jewish mother, and who has not adopted another faith.*

jew·el·lery (US **jew·el·ry**) /ˈdʒuːəlri/ *noun* [U] objects such as rings, etc. that people wear as personal decoration: *The lower classes often went barefoot and were not allowed to wear jewellery.*

Jew·ish /ˈdʒuːɪʃ/ *adj.* connected with Jews or Judaism; believing in and practising Judaism: *the local Jewish community*

job AWL /dʒɒb; NAmE dʒɑːb/ *noun* **1** work for which you receive regular payment: *If he loses his job, he will be in severe financial difficulties.* ◇ *The welfare state created new professional jobs in health, social security, housing and education.* ◇ **+ noun** *Thus, potential job losses lead to moderation in wage claims.* **2** a particular task or piece of work that sb/sth has to do: *Certain staff can be trained to do specific jobs or take on particular responsibilities.* ◇ *Most machinery developed for commercial purposes is intended to carry out some very specific job.* **3** [usually sing.] a responsibility or duty: **it is sb's ~ to do sth** *It is the adjudicator's job to make decisions on any objections that cannot be worked out between the parties.* ◇ **sb's ~ is to do sth** *The judge's job is to make rulings on the law, decide upon the admissibility of evidence, and summarize the case to the jury.* **4** an item of work that is done by a computer as a single unit: *There are various possibilities as to what happens next, depending on the way the job has been programmed.*
IDM **do the ˈjob (of doing sth)** to serve a particular purpose in a situation so that a task can be completed: *Local systems of social control and conflict resolution cannot do the job of keeping the peace.* **do a good ˈjob | do/make a good, poor, etc. job of (doing) sth** to do sth in a particular way, such as well or badly: *43% of respondents thought that Brown was doing a good job as Prime Minister.* ◇ *This book does an excellent job of linking inequality to a wide range of high-profile social and economic issues.* **on the ˈjob** while doing a particular job: *Learning on the job from peers and colleagues forms the basis for ongoing professional development.*
▸ ADJECTIVE + JOB **good, decent • demanding • new • part-time • full-time • permanent • temporary • skilled • unskilled • white-collar • blue-collar • well-paid • low-paid • manual • professional** *Part-time jobs now make up around one-quarter of all jobs, with three-quarters held by women.*
▸ VERB + JOB **do, perform • look for, seek • apply for • get, find, obtain, secure • offer sb • take, accept • have, hold • keep • lose • quit, leave • change • create • provide** *While doing his day job, he observed the way in which he and his colleagues actually worked.*
▸ JOB + NOUN **satisfaction • security • insecurity • strain, stress • description • title • creation • loss • applicant • seeker • offer • prospects • opportunities** *There is reason to believe that job security has been undermined for most employees.*

ˌjob satisˈfaction *noun* [U] the good feeling that you get when you have a job that you enjoy: *Evidence suggests that more committed employees experience greater job satisfaction.*

join /dʒɔɪn/ *verb* **1** [T, often passive] to fix or connect two or more things together: **be joined by sth** *Proteins are polymers composed of amino acids that are joined by covalent bonds.* ◇ **be joined to sth** *In diamond, each carbon atom is joined to four others.* ◇ **be joined together/up** *A polymer molecule consists of many identical chemical units joined together to make a long chain.* **2** [T] **~ sth** to become a member of an organization or a group: *The Czech Republic, Hungary and Poland all joined the EU in 2004.* ◇ *Women were banned from attending political meetings or joining political organizations.* ◇ *Galileo joined a small group of those who argued that the earth moved around the sun.* ◇ *The USA joined the ranks of the great powers, at first through industrial success, during the nineteenth century.* **3** [T, I] to take part in sth that sb else is doing or to go somewhere with them: **~ sth** *Global and regional institutions have joined the struggle over human rights.* ◇ *A growing number of established, respectable political figures had joined the outcry against the war.* ◇ **~ together** *It appears that at least some of these movements have been joining together under a common banner.* **4** [I, T] to come together to form one thing or group: **~ together** *Multiple fatty acid molecules join together to form the lipid membrane.* ◇ **~ to do sth** *More and more often, the unemployed, beggars and vagrants joined to form gangs that terrorized whole regions.* ◇ **be joined (to do sth)** *These DNA fragments will be eventually joined to form a continuous DNA strand.*
IDM **join ˈforces (with sb)** to work together in order to achieve a shared aim: *They may join forces so that they can combine their resources and energies.*
PHR V **ˌjoin ˈin (with sb/sth)** to take part in an activity with other people: *He finds it difficult to join in with other children in the playground due to his apparent lack of coordination.* ◇ *When it came to house-to-house fighting within the walls, even women joined in.* **ˌjoin ˈup (with sb)** to get together with sb else to do sth: *They marched north-west in the hope of joining up with He Long's forces in western Hunan.*

J

joint[1] /dʒɔɪnt/ *adj.* [only before noun] involving two or more people, groups or things together: *The study is a joint project of Maastricht University and the Corporation of Family Practices in Eindhoven.* ◇ *Ms Fowler and Mr Barron lived together for around 17 years, in a house registered in joint names.*

joint[2] /dʒɔɪnt/ *noun* **1** a place where two bones are joined together in the body in a way that enables them to bend and move: *He still suffers from pain in his joints and muscles.* ◇ *In Mary's case, surgical replacement of her right hip joint may lessen her disability.* **2** a place where two or more parts of an object are joined together, especially to form a corner: *Holes in the cement are especially dangerous if they occur at corner joints between floor and ceiling.* ◇ *Many large caverns developed along vertical joints or cracks in the limestone.*

joint·ly /dʒɔɪntli/ *adv.* in a way that involves two or more people, groups or things together: *Decisions about treatment should be made jointly with the patient.* ◇ *The throne was offered jointly to William and his wife Mary.*

ˌjoint ˈventure *noun* (*business*) a business project or activity that is begun by two or more companies, etc, which remain separate organizations: *Mergers and joint ventures have become increasingly common in the cultural industries.*

joule /dʒuːl/ *noun* (*abbr.* **J**) (*physics*) a unit of energy or work: *This drop in electrical energy will be measured in joules.*

jour·nal AWL /ˈdʒɜːnl; NAmE ˈdʒɜːrnl/ *noun* **1** a newspaper or magazine that deals with a particular subject or profession: *He has published in a range of academic journals.* ◇ *The review of the literature was conducted on 11 peer-reviewed journals.* ◇ *a leading/prestigious journal* ◇ *a scientific/scholarly/professional journal* **2** a written record of the things you do or see every day: *Ideally, researchers should always keep a journal from the beginning through to the end of the research.* ◇ *Many women wrote travel journals that were intended not for publication but for circulation amongst family and friends.* ➲ *compare* DIARY

jour·nal·ism /ˈdʒɜːnəlɪzəm; NAmE ˈdʒɜːrnəlɪzəm/ *noun* [U] the work of collecting and writing news stories for newspapers, magazines, radio or television: *He turned to journalism, first writing for a German newspaper.*

jour·nal·ist /ˈdʒɜːnəlɪst; *NAmE* ˈdʒɜːrnəlɪst/ *noun* a person whose job is to collect and write news stories for newspapers, magazines, radio or television: *Major human rights violations have been uncovered by investigative journalists.* ➲ *compare* REPORTER

jour·nal·is·tic /ˌdʒɜːnəˈlɪstɪk; *NAmE* ˌdʒɜːrnəˈlɪstɪk/ *adj.* [usually before noun] connected with the work of a journalist: *The newspaper has high journalistic standards.*

jour·ney /ˈdʒɜːni; *NAmE* ˈdʒɜːrni/ *noun* an act of travelling from one place to another, especially when they are far apart: *Many workers are forced to undertake long-distance weekly commuting journeys.* ◇ **~ (from...) (to...)** *Every year, migrating birds make long seasonal journeys from their breeding grounds to their wintering grounds and back.* ◇ (*figurative*) *This spiritual journey is intended to lead from the unenlightened life to an enlightened vision of the world.*

J

Ju·da·ism /ˈdʒuːdeɪɪzəm; *NAmE* ˈdʒuːdəɪzəm/ *noun* [U] the religion of the Jewish people, based mainly on the Bible and the Talmud (= a collection of ancient writings on Jewish law and traditions): *The Romans granted Judaism a special status on the grounds that it was an ancient national religion to which its members owed allegiance.*

judge[1] /dʒʌdʒ/ *noun* **1** a person in a court who has the authority to decide how criminals should be punished or to make legal decisions: *The more serious criminal offences are tried before a judge and jury.* ◇ *The Court of Appeal reversed the judge's decision.* ➲ *compare* MAGISTRATE **2** [usually sing.] **~ (of sth)** a person who has the necessary knowledge or skills to give their opinion about the value or quality of sb/sth: *Individuals are generally are the best judges of their own health and happiness.* **3** a person who decides who has won a competition: *The judges were stationed at strategic points around the race track.*

judge[2] /dʒʌdʒ/ *verb* **1** [I, T] to form an opinion about sb/sth, based on the information you have: **~ sb/sth** *An important responsibility of citizens is to monitor officials and judge their conduct.* ◇ **~ sb/sth on sth** *Each case has to be judged on its merits.* ◇ **~ sb/sth to be sth** *Twenty of the studies were judged to be of very good quality.* ◇ **~ sb/sth + noun** *The exhibition was judged a success, attracting 50 000 visitors during its eight days.* ◇ **~ sb/sth + adj.** *He saw trouble ahead on the slavery issue, which he judged incompatible with ideas of democracy and liberty.* ◇ **~ that...** *She judged that the relevant equations could not be solved in the near future.* ◇ **~ where/what, etc...** *It is sometimes quite hard to judge where each part of a network starts and ends.* **2** [T] to decide whether sb is guilty or not guilty in a court; to decide a case in a court: **~ sb (+ adj.)** *He was judged guilty and sentenced to be hanged.* ◇ **~ sth** *Other cases were judged by magistrates.* **3** [T] **~ sb** to give your opinion about sb, especially when you disapprove of them: *They have to be careful not to go too far or people will judge them negatively.*

judge·ment (*also* **judg·ment** *especially in NAmE*) /ˈdʒʌdʒmənt/ *noun* **1** [C, U] an opinion that you form about sth after thinking about it carefully; the act of making this opinion known to others: *Personal value judgements should not be mixed into classroom lectures.* ◇ **~ about sth** *The doctor has to make a judgement about the patient's mental state.* ◇ **~ (of sth)** *A pioneering study by Lichtenstein et al. (1978) examined absolute and relative probability judgements of risk.* ◇ *Ancient psychology sought not merely to understand an individual's actions but to pass moral judgement on them.* ◇ **in sb's ~** *In my judgement, the safest approach to these new technologies is freedom for individuals combined with heavy scrutiny for government.* ➲ *see also* VALUE JUDGEMENT **2** [U] the ability to make sensible decisions after carefully considering the best thing to do: *The GPs were asked to make a management decision based on their own judgement.* ◇ *In each of these cases, success was a combination of good luck, good judgement and good timing.* ◇ *Influential psychology texts have done little to dispel the impression that human judgement is inherently flawed and untrustworthy.* **3** (*usually* **judgment**) [C, U] the decision of a court or a judge: *All member states accept the principle of the rule of law and the moral authority of court judgments.* ◇ *Only about 5 per cent of cases reach final judgment.* ◇ **~ of sb/sth** *There is no appeal possible against the judgments of the Council of State.*

▸ ADJECTIVE + JUDGEMENT **initial • subjective, individual • own • intuitive • independent • sound • expert • moral, ethical • aesthetic • professional • clinical • political** *Absolute definitions of need and poverty are to a degree arbitrary, or a matter of subjective judgement.* ◇ *Haas believed that many, if not most, intuitive judgements are unreliable.* | **good • poor** *Poor judgement and an inability to manage stress are likely to interfere with effective parenting.* | **previous • final • summary • legal** *Trade unions suffered from a number of legal judgments in the 1980s.*

▸ VERB + JUDGEMENT **pass • base ~ on • reach** *People make judgements based on a range of quality related cues.* | **make • form** *He was anxious to form his own independent judgements.* | **use, exercise • require • suspend** *The great quantity of data meant that I had to use my own judgement as to what data were the most relevant to the aims of the research.* | **give, deliver, issue • comply with • enforce** *A Grand Chamber of the Court delivered its judgment on 1 June 2010.*

judge·men·tal (*BrE*) (*also* **judg·men·tal** *NAmE, BrE*) /dʒʌdʒˈmentl/ *adj.* **1** (*disapproving*) judging people and criticizing them too quickly: *It is important to avoid sounding judgemental.* **2** connected with the process of judging things: *The entrepreneur, having made a judgemental decision, must be able to implement the decision.*

ju·di·cial /dʒuˈdɪʃl/ *adj.* [usually before noun] connected with a court, judge or legal judgment: *Judicial decisions can be reversed when courts rule on non-constitutional matters.* ◇ *The Decembrists had placed reform of the judicial system high on their list of priorities.* ➲ *see also* JUDICIAL REVIEW ■ **ju·di·cial·ly** /dʒuˈdɪʃəli/ *adv.*: *The decisions may be judicially reviewed by the Federal Court and the Federal Court of Appeal.*

juˌdicial reˈview *noun* (*law*) **1** [C, U] (in the UK) a process in which a court examines an action or decision of a public body and decides whether it was right: **~ (of sth)** *They were granted a judicial review of the Ministry's order.* ◇ *The number of applications for judicial review has increased dramatically in recent years.* ◇ **+ noun** *The role of the court in judicial review proceedings is to determine the lawfulness of the decision-making process.* **2** [U] (in the US) the power of the Supreme Court to decide if sth is allowed by the Constitution: *The power of judicial review derives not from the Constitution, but from a series of cases dating back to the late 1700s.*

ju·di·ciary /dʒuˈdɪʃəri; *NAmE* dʒuˈdɪʃieri/ *noun* (*usually* **the judiciary**) (*pl.* **-ies**) [C+sing./pl. v.] the judges of a country or a state, when they are considered as a group: *The independence of the judiciary is of the greatest importance.* ➲ *compare* EXECUTIVE[1] (2), LEGISLATURE

juice /dʒuːs/ *noun* **1** [U, C] the liquid that comes from fruit or vegetables; a drink made from this: *Drink fruit juice and water to ensure adequate hydration.* ◇ *Fifty-nine commercial apple juices from concentrate were tested in the laboratory.* **2** [C, usually pl.] the liquid in the stomach that helps you to DIGEST food: *One of the most important ingredients of gastric juices is hydrochloric acid.*

jump¹ /dʒʌmp/ *verb* **1** [I] **+ adv./prep.** to move quickly off the ground or away from a surface by pushing yourself with your legs and feet: *The child who is hyperactive may jump around in a room.* ◇ *Eight of the interviewees believed that the barriers had been effective in preventing deaths by jumping from the bridge.* **2** [I] (*rather informal*) to rise suddenly by a large amount: **~ by...** *China's exports jumped by 46 per cent in February 2010 compared with the previous year.* ◇ **~ (from...) (to...)** *Average traffic speeds in this previously congested area jumped from 9.5 mph to 20 mph.* **3** [I] **~ (about) (from sth to sth)** (*rather informal*) to change suddenly from one subject to another: *He jumps from topic to topic within a single sentence.* IDM *see* CONCLUSION

PHR V ˈ**jump at sth** (*rather informal*) to accept an opportunity or offfer with enthusiasm: *He jumped at the chance to use the new accounting machine.*

jump² /dʒʌmp/ *noun* **1** an act of jumping: *Significant injury may also be caused by falls or jumps from a height.* **2 ~ (in sth)** (*rather informal*) a sudden increase in amount, price or value: *Following the broadcast there was a 19 per cent jump in the politician's credibility rating.* ◇ *In Sweden, there was a dramatic jump in unemployment to the European average in the early 1990s.*

junc·tion /ˈdʒʌŋkʃn/ *noun* **1** a place where two or more things meet or are joined: **~ with sth** *He discovered and crossed the Mississippi River just north of its junction with the Arkansas River.* ◇ **~ between A and B** *Special junctions between cells allow a neurological signal to spread throughout the muscle.* ◇ *Within the device, there is an electric field associated with the junction between the two layers of semiconductor.* ◇ **~ of A and B** *An X-ray demonstrated a 1.5 cm diameter stone at the junction of the left kidney and its ureter.* **2** (*especially BrE*) (*NAmE usually* **inter·sec·tion**) the place where two or more roads or railway lines meet: *A motorcyclist was injured in a collision at a junction where visibility was restricted by a bank of earth.* ◇ *a road/railway junction*

jun·ior /ˈdʒuːniə(r)/ *adj.* **1** [usually before noun] having a low rank in an organization or a profession: *junior doctors/officers/ministers/staff* ◇ *It is important to value the views of all team members, however junior.* OPP SENIOR¹ (1) **2** [only before noun] (*BrE*) (of a school or part of a school) for children under the age of 11 or 13: *Swain (2004) conducted a study of three junior schools in the UK in the late 1990s.* ➲ *compare* SENIOR¹ (3)

jur·is·dic·tion /ˌdʒʊərɪsˈdɪkʃn; *NAmE* ˌdʒʊrɪsˈdɪkʃn/ *noun* **1** [U, C] the authority that an official organization has to make legal decisions about sb/sth: *The court exercised its jurisdiction and authorized treatment.* ◇ **~ over sb/sth** *No single operating agency has jurisdiction over all systems.* ◇ **~ (of sb/sth) to do sth** *It was held that the minister had no jurisdiction to consider the scheme in the first instance.* ◇ **within/outside sb's/sth's ~** *The Commission had acted outside its jurisdiction.* **2** [C] an area or a country in which a particular system of laws has authority: *New South Wales was the first Australian jurisdiction to legally recognize same-sex relationships.* ■ **jur·is·dic·tion·al** *adj.*: *There have been jurisdictional disputes on just who is the responsible agency.*

jur·is·pru·dence /ˌdʒʊərɪsˈpruːdns; *NAmE* ˌdʒʊrɪsˈpruːdns/ *noun* [U] **1** the theory and philosophy of law: *He teaches International Law and Jurisprudence.* **2 ~ (of sth)** the legal system of a particular country or legal institution: *The domestic case law must be examined in the light of the jurisprudence of the Strasbourg court.*

jury /ˈdʒʊəri; *NAmE* ˈdʒʊri/ *noun* (*pl.* **-ies**) [C+sing./pl. v.] a group of members of the public who listen to the facts of a case in a court and decide whether or not sb is guilty of a crime: *The jury found him not guilty of murder but guilty of manslaughter.* ◇ *The trial judge in the Crown court directed the jury to acquit the defendant.* ◇ **trial by ~** *A defendant charged with a summary offence does not have a right to trial by jury.*

IDM **the jury is (still) ˈout on sth** (*rather informal*) used when you are saying that agreement has not yet been reached on a particular subject: *The jury is still out on genetically engineered crops.*

just¹ /dʒʌst/ *adv.* **1** exactly: **~ like...** *Tests found that at high dosages the drug cut through fatigue just like caffeine.* ◇ **~ as...** *Ambitious people from all over the empire moved to Rome, just as ambitious people today move to New York, Paris or Tokyo.* ◇ **~ what...** *The frog's eye tells the frog's brain just what it needs to know.* ◇ **~ how...** *Dreams show just how much more there is to the activity of the human mind than appears on the surface.* **2 ~ as important, easily, much, etc.** no less than; equally: *Numbers can be manipulated just as easily as words.* ◇ *CNN and the BBC refer to 'stories' just as much as they refer to 'news'.* ◇ *Such general statements are just as likely to mislead as to inform.* **3 ~ over, under, before, after, etc. sth** by a small amount: *The population of the city swelled from just over 4 000 in 1763 to about 19 000 in 1831.* ◇ *Just after World War II, he warned the American Economic Association of what he termed 'the march into socialism'.* **4** very recently: *His wife has just been discharged home from hospital following a stroke.* ◇ *Not all the Greek philosophers value knowledge in the ways just described.* ◇ *The topics just mentioned have all been widely discussed by listening specialists.* **5** at this/that moment; now: *His book was written in an earlier generation when Britain was just starting to industrialize.* ◇ **only ~** *Academic commentators are only just coming to terms with the complexity of the evaluative task.* **6** used to emphasize the simple reason for sth or the simple nature of sth SYN SIMPLY (1): *Special products or services that would just not be possible in a small society can thrive in a large society.* ◇ *Conservative ministers in the 1980s increasingly viewed local government as just another body delivering services to customers.* ◇ **~ because...** *No one should accept a particular approach to economics just because it is what some experts believe.* **7** only: *These are the results from just one study, conducted over 15 years ago.* ◇ **~ for sth** *This mechanism works not just for photons, but also for other types of particle.* ◇ **~ to do sth** *People use the technology to accomplish new goals, not just to achieve the old ones more efficiently.* **8 could/might/may ~** used to show a slight possibility that sth is true or will happen: *It could just be that the test companies are not testing appropriately representative groups of people.* **9** (*rather informal*) really; completely: *Those who had old computers and low-speed connections were annoyed by these limitations but insisted that the equipment was just fine for their purposes.*

IDM **could/might just as well...** used to say that one action or situation is as good or as possible as another: *This story is about fishing in a lake, but it might just as well be about dumping sewage in a river or polluting the air: the moral is the same.* **just about** (*rather informal*) **1** almost; very nearly: *The Union has become involved in just about every sphere of public policy.* ◇ *Vail manages to mention just about all of the demographic trends except for immigration.* **2** approximately: *The entire development cycle in Drosophila is very rapid, taking just about a week to develop from a fertilized egg into a mature fly.* **just ˈnow** at this moment; during this present period: *These types of approach are just now being explored.*

just² /dʒʌst/ *adj.* [usually before noun] **1** that most people consider to be morally fair and reasonable: *The women saw themselves as important contributors to a socially just society.* ◇ *It is wrong to fight in a war that lacks a just cause.* ◇ *Is there such a thing as a just war, and if so, what are the conditions of engagement?* OPP UNJUST **2** appropriate in a particular situation: *Criminals should get their just deserts—proportional punishment with fixed* *sentences.* ◇ *They believed that the workers were not receiving their just reward from the revolution they had made.* OPP UNJUST ■ **just·ly** *adv.*: *This may be the best chance for dealing justly and peacefully with the tensions of humanity.* ◇ *Kant's ethical theory is justly regarded as one of the best ever devised.*

just·ice /ˈdʒʌstɪs/ *noun* **1** [U] the fair treatment of people: *In a perfect society, truth and justice prevail.* ◇ *Social justice involves a high degree of economic equality.* HELP In English law, **natural justice** is a term that includes the right to a fair hearing and the right to be judged without BIAS: *The board's findings were null and void due to its failure to observe the principles of natural justice.* OPP INJUSTICE **2** [U] the quality of being fair or reasonable: *There is some justice in their complaint.* ◇ **~ of sth** *Elektra has no doubts about the justice of their cause.* OPP INJUSTICE **3** [U] the legal system used to punish people who have committed crimes: *There were also cases of miscarriage of justice.* ◇ **+ noun** *The criminal justice system focuses on punishment and blame.* **4** [U] a fair punishment for a crime, especially from the legal system: *to dispense/mete out/administer justice* ◇ **~ for sth** *They thought they were exacting justice for the murder of their parents.* **5** (*also* **Just·ice**) [C] a judge or MAGISTRATE in a court: *The justices in the magistrates' court acquitted the defendant.*

K

IDM **bring sb to ˈjustice** to arrest sb for a crime and put them on trial in court: *Human right violators would be brought to justice.* **do justice to ˈsb/ˈsth; do sb/sth ˈjustice** **1** to treat or represent sb/sth fairly, especially in a way that shows how serious, good, attractive, etc. they are: *No amount of data can do justice to the human suffering caused by AIDS.* **2** to deal with sb/sth correctly and completely: *The framework provides teachers with a way to do the main ideas justice, yet also keep them manageable.*

jus·ti·fi·able AWL /ˈdʒʌstɪfaɪəbl; ˌdʒʌstɪˈfaɪəbl/ *adj.* existing or done for a good reason, and therefore acceptable SYN LEGITIMATE (1): *They came to accept that military intervention was justifiable in cases of genocide and mass killing.* ◇ *Age differentiation is the treatment of people differently where there are justifiable reasons for this.* ■ **jus·ti·fi·ably** AWL /ˈdʒʌstɪfaɪəbli; dʒʌstɪˈfaɪəbli/ *adv.*: *Field justifiably claims that his account differs from its predecessors in that it examines a much wider range of material.*

jus·ti·fi·ca·tion AWL /ˌdʒʌstɪfɪˈkeɪʃn/ *noun* [C, U] a good reason why sth exists or is done: **~ for sth** *The classic justification for a social policy is that it will lead to greater social justice.* ◇ **~ for doing sth** *Neoclassical economics provides a justification for limiting the state's role in regulating both markets and the firms operating in them.* ◇ **in ~ of sth** *These results should be viewed as preliminary findings in justification of further study.*

jus·ti·fied AWL /ˈdʒʌstɪfaɪd/ *adj.* **1 ~ (in doing sth)** having a good reason for doing sth: *A doctor may be justified in performing an operation without consent on an unconscious patient in an emergency.* ◇ *Prussia felt justified in demanding all of Saxony as compensation for Prussian sacrifice and leadership in the War of Liberation.* OPP UNJUSTIFIED **2** existing or done for a good reason: *There are a surprising number of people who still believe that the arrests were fully justified.* ◇ *Terrorists deny the legitimacy of the state and claim that the use of violence against it is morally justified.* OPP UNJUSTIFIED

jus·tify AWL /ˈdʒʌstɪfaɪ/ *verb* (**jus·ti·fies, jus·ti·fy·ing, jus·ti·fied, jus·ti·fied**) to give an explanation or excuse for sth or for doing sth; to show that sb/sth is right or reasonable: **~ sth** *In a world ruled by market forces, archaeology needs to justify its existence.* ◇ *Napoleon's eastern threat was used to justify the extension of British dominance over India.* ◇ **~ (sb/sth) doing sth** *Government harassment involved using undercover agents to provoke violence to justify using police power.* ➲ *compare* DEFEND (1)
IDM *see* END[1]

WORD FAMILY
justify *verb*
justified *adj.*
justification *noun*
justifiable *adj.*
justifiably *adv.*
unjustified *adj.*

▸ JUSTIFY + NOUN **action • decision • choice • belief • refusal • intervention • measure • restriction • claim • assumption • conclusion • finding • use • existence** *The authors of the study fail to provide any robust evidence to justify their claims of success.*
▸ ADVERB + JUSTIFY **fully, entirely • morally • objectively** *Such measures can be objectively justified by imperative reasons of public interest.*
▸ VERB + TO JUSTIFY **seek • try, attempt • need • require • serve • use sth • be difficult** *It may be difficult to justify government financial support for the arts when other areas of need present themselves.*

ju·ven·ile¹ /ˈdʒuːvənaɪl; *NAmE* ˈdʒuːvənl/ *adj.* [only before noun] **1** (*formal* or *law*) connected with young people who are not yet adults: *There is evidence that juvenile crime increased during the 1950s and 1960s.* ◇ *Separate remand homes were set up for juvenile offenders.* **2** connected with young birds or animals: *Individual activities of three juvenile crabs were recorded on video over two nightly eight-hour periods.*

ju·ven·ile² /ˈdʒuːvənaɪl; *NAmE* ˈdʒuːvənl/ *noun* **1** (*formal* or *law*) a young person who is not yet an adult: *The US is the world leader in sentencing juveniles to life without parole.* **2** a young bird or animal: *It is to these areas that, in turn, juveniles and mature fish return to spawn (Rindorf and Lewy, 2006).*

Kk

keen /kiːn/ *adj.* (**keen·er, keen·est**) **1** (*especially BrE*) wanting to do sth or wanting sth to happen very much SYN EAGER: **~ to do sth** *Some people are not keen to divulge personal details such as their age or their income.* ◇ **~ that...** *William was keen that his new kingdom should enter the Nine Years War.* ◇ **~ on doing sth** *Germany and Japan are keen on keeping inflation rates low.* **2 ~ on sth** (*BrE*) enthusiastic about sth: *The European Parliament was not keen on the idea of a competing legislative body challenging its authority.* **3** [usually before noun] (*especially BrE*) very interested in an activity and doing it often: *He is a keen runner and usually exercises three times a week.* **4** [usually before noun] (of a feeling) strong or deep: *Both characters feel a keen sense of social responsibility.* ◇ **take a ~ interest in sth** *These are issues in which she began to take a very keen interest.* **5** [only before noun] (of the mind) quick to understand or see things SYN SHARP (7), ACUTE (5): *The historian describes the Emperor Tiberius's keen intelligence and sarcastic wit.* ◇ *It is Narayan's keen eye for detail that makes the novel so fascinating.* **6** involving people competing very hard with each other for sth: *There is keen competition between different companies.*

keen·ly /kiːnli/ *adv.* **1** very strongly or deeply: **~ aware/interested/felt** *The Emperor was keenly aware of the need for reform.* ◇ *Losses are more keenly felt than gains.* **2** by people with different opinions that they express strongly: **~ debated/contested** *This question is still keenly debated.*

keep /kiːp/ *verb* (**kept, kept** /kept/) **1** [I, T] to stay in a particular condition or position; to make sb/sth do this: **+ adj.** *Without access to wood, it was impossible to cook meals or keep warm.* ◇ **+ adv./prep.** *The director keeps close to the novel's plot structure.* ◇ **~ sb/sth + adj.** *Keeping customers happy leads to business profitability.* ◇ **~ sb/sth + adv./prep.** *Males and females were kept separately in visually isolated tanks.* ◇ **~ sb/sth doing sth** *A flying* *machine needs to supply energy to keep itself going forward.* **2** [I] to continue doing sth; to repeat an action many times: **~ doing sth** *Older employees who wish to keep working may demand flexible roles and schedules.* ◇ **~ on doing sth** *The number of casualties kept on increasing.* **3** [T] to continue to have sth and not give it back or throw it away: **~ sth** *Applicants should make sure to keep a copy of all job adverts they apply for.* ◇ **~ sth for sb/sth** *He sells the vans to the company for £12 000 but keeps one for his own company.* **4** [T] **~ sth + adv./prep.** to put or store sth in a particular place: *Doctors should keep a map in the car, and think about purchasing a satellite navigation device.* **5** [T] **~ sth** to own and care for animals: *On these garden patches they would grow vegetables and keep chickens.* **6** [I] to remain in good condition: *These foods would keep fresh longer in a refrigerator.* **7** [T] to know sth and not tell it to anyone: **~ a secret** *Keeping a secret involves increased awareness of those who are not allowed to know it.* ◇ **~ sth secret** *All banks instruct their customers to keep their PINs secret.* ◇ **~ sth (a) secret from sb** *Jack keeps his ancestry a secret from everyone.* **8** [T] **~ your promise/word**| **~ an appointment** to do what you have promised to do; to go where you have agreed to go: *The government could neither collect its taxes nor keep its promises.* ◇ *The applicant did not keep the appointment to be interviewed by the refugee advisory committee.* **9** [T] **~ a record, a diary, an account, etc.** to write down sth as a record: *Online merchants usually keep records of which customers bought which products.* ◇ *Some patients may benefit from keeping a reflective diary of their progress.* ◇ *In towns the police kept a list of all the inhabitants' addresses.*

IDM Most idioms containing **keep** are at the entries for the nouns and adjectives in the idioms, for example **keep track** is at **track**. ˌ**keep ˈgoing** to make an effort to live normally when you are in a difficult situation or when you have experienced great suffering: *The stories filled me with courage and the energy to keep going.*

PHR V ˌ**keep aˈway (from sb/sth)** to avoid going near sb/sth: *Some people think that this is a private matter which government needs to keep away from.* ˌ**keep sb/sth aˈway (from sb/sth)** to prevent sb/sth from going somewhere: *Children should be kept away from school until treatment is completed.*

ˌ**keep sth ˈback** to continue to have a part of sth: *Of this money, a proportion is kept back by the banks to meet requests for withdrawals.*

ˌ**keep sth ˈdown** to make sth stay at a low level; to avoid increasing sth: *A balanced healthy diet helps keep cholesterol levels down.*

ˈ**keep from sth** | ˈ**keep yourself from sth** to prevent yourself from doing sth: *Employees may do only as much as they need to do to keep from being fired.* ˈ**keep sb from sth** to prevent sb from doing sth: *The company relies on legal contracts to keep customers from leaving.* ˈ**keep sth from sb** to avoid telling sb sth: *One child said that her parents had kept secrets from each other.*

ˌ**keep sb ˈon** to continue to employ sb: *If the employer offers only the minimum wage, the employee may not care whether he or she is kept on or fired.*

ˌ**keep ˈout (of sth)** to not enter a place; to stay outside: *The visitor could have avoided the danger by obeying an instruction to keep out.* ˌ**keep sb/sth ˈout (of sth)** to prevent sb/sth from entering a place: *The single-storey dwellings keep out the rain and the sun.* ˌ**keep ˈout of sth** | ˌ**keep sb ˈout of sth** to avoid sth; to prevent sb from being involved in sth or affected by sth: *At the other end of the scale were those barely keeping out of debt.* ◇ *Women have been kept out of many kinds of work.*

ˈ**keep to sth** **1** to talk or write only about the subject that you are supposed to talk or write about: *Skills such as good timekeeping and keeping to an agenda are important.* **2** to do what you have promised or agreed to do: *It may be difficult to persuade the parents to keep to the new rules.*

ˌ**keep ˈup (with sb/sth)** to move, make progress or increase at the same rate as sb/sth: *Investment is essential to enable a business to keep up in the competitive race.* ◇ *The workers are not producing enough goods to keep up with incoming orders.* ˌ**keep ˈup with sth** **1** to learn about or be aware of the news, current events, etc: *They keep up with news from his hometown via the web.* **2** to continue to pay or do sth regularly: *The gangs threatened and tortured the debtors to make sure they kept up with their payments.* ˌ**keep sth ˈup** **1** to make sth stay at a high level: *Instead of seeking to restrict competition to keep prices up, he sought to maximize sales by minimizing costs.* **2** to continue sth at the same, usually high, level: *They need to borrow more money just to keep up the interest payments on their existing debt.* **3** to make sth remain at a high level: *Education is the only way we can keep up the standard.*

key[1] /kiː/ *adj.* [usually before noun] most important; essential SYN CRITICAL (1), VITAL (1): *As a member of NATO, Turkey has played a key role in European security.* ◇ **~ to sth** *Understanding global markets is often key to success here.*
➲ thesaurus note *at* MAIN[1]

▸ KEY + NOUN **issue, question • point • theme • concept, idea • principle • element, component, factor • feature, aspect, characteristic • role • term, word • variable • difference • area • determinant • driver • indicator • finding • assumption • event • account • figure, actor, player • informant • stakeholder** *National sovereignty is often seen as the key issue when European integration is discussed.* ◇ *Descartes was a key figure in the emergence of modern philosophical and scientific thinking.*

key[2] /kiː/ *noun* **1** a specially shaped piece of metal used for locking a door, starting a car, etc: *She inserts the front door key in the lock.* ◇ *He turned the key in the ignition.* **2** [usually sing.] a thing that provides a means of achieving or understanding sth SYN SECRET[2] (2): **~ to sth** *The key to success was education.* ◇ *Agriculture was the key to economic development.* ◇ *Value holds the key to both pricing and distribution.* ◇ **~ to doing sth** *Herder saw learning foreign languages as the key to understanding other cultures.* **3** any of the buttons that you press to operate a computer or telephone: *Each time the operator pressed a key, one or more wheels turned inside the machine.* ◇ *A better layout for the keys could be devised that would make it easier to type.* **4** a word or system for solving a code: *The message is encoded and decoded using the same key.* ◇ *The encryption key changes every time that authentication takes place.* **5** a set of answers to exercises or problems: *There is a number of exercises in each module, with a key at the back.* **6** a list explaining the symbols used in a map, plan, table, etc: *All Ordnance Survey maps come with detailed keys for easy identification of features.*

key·board /ˈkiːbɔːd; *NAmE* ˈkiːbɔːrd/ *noun* the set of keys for operating a computer: *Many people find it easier to use the arrow keys on their keyboard to move from cell to cell.*

key·word /ˈkiːwɜːd; *NAmE* ˈkiːwɜːrd/ *noun* **1** a word that tells you about the main idea or subject of sth: *'Representation' emerged as a keyword in urban geography in the 1990s.* **2** a word or phrase that you type on a computer keyboard to give an instruction or to search for information about sth: *Results are listed in order of the relevance of the match between the content of the web page and the keyword or phrase typed in.* ◇ **+ noun** *Advertising based on a keyword search could take place through a search engine such as google.com.*

kid·ney /ˈkɪdni/ *noun* either of the two organs in the body that remove waste products from the blood and produce URINE: *Waste products are excreted by the kidneys.* ◇ **+ noun** *kidney disease/failure*

K

kill /kɪl/ *verb* **1** [T, I] **~ (sb/sth/yourself)** to make sb/sth die: *Up to 100 000 civilians were killed.* ◇ *Antibiotics are small molecules that kill bacteria.* ◇ *He claimed that he had wanted to kill himself.* ◇ *The infection does not kill, but it could make you extremely ill.* **2** [T] **~ sth** to destroy or spoil sth or make it stop: *Background noise kills all hope of detecting a signal below about 10 Hz.*
PHR V **ˌkill sb/sth ˈoff** **1** to make a lot of plants, animals, etc. die: *They predicted a disaster large enough to kill off humanity.* **2** to stop or get rid of sth: *The long-term results of such policies will be effectively to kill off competition.*

kill·er /ˈkɪlə(r)/ *noun* a person, an animal or a thing that kills: *The case expands to be a hunt for a serial killer.* ◇ *Coronary heart disease, the country's biggest killer, is a preventable condition.*

kill·ing /ˈkɪlɪŋ/ *noun* [C, U] **~ (of sb/sth)** an act of killing sb/sth deliberately: *These groups regard the killing of foxes by hunting as an inhumane act.* ◇ *The worst mass killings of the twentieth century were committed by dictatorial states.* ◇ *The population had endured years of killing and destruction.* ➲ *compare* MURDER[1]

kilo·gram /ˈkɪləɡræm/ (*also* **kilo**) *noun* (*abbr.* **kg**) a unit for measuring weight; 1 000 grams: *The aircraft in question weighed approximately 60 000 kilograms.* ◇ **~ of sth** *Just a few kilograms of enriched uranium contains a vast destructive force.*

kilo·metre (*US* **kilo·meter**) /ˈkɪləmiːtə(r); kɪˈlɒmɪtə(r); *NAmE* ˈkɪləmiːtər; kɪˈlɑːmɪtər/ *noun* (*abbr.* **k, km**) a unit for measuring distance; 1 000 metres: *The town is approximately 100 kilometres from Cape Town city centre.* ◇ *The velocity is about one and a half kilometres per second.* ◇ *The floating ice island had an area of over 100 square kilometres before it began to break up.* ➲ grammar note *at* METRE

kin /kɪn/ *noun* [pl.] someone's family or relatives: *Networks of female kin helped and supported each other with domestic work.* ◇ **+ noun** *Irish secular society was organized around large kin groups.*

kind[1] /kaɪnd/ *noun* **1** [C] a group of people or things that have similar characteristics; a particular variety or type: **~ (of sb/sth)** *Nietzsche was concerned with what kind of person one should be.* ◇ *The kind of knowledge required to do well in tests is more abstract.* ◇ *Tinbergen distinguished four kinds of questions that can be asked.* ◇ **of all/various/different kinds** *And so the world became a place where microorganisms, plants and animals of all kinds could thrive.* ◇ **of this/that ~** *Each job, he argues, should be done only by those best suited to work of that kind.* ◇ **of its ~** *The new building would be the first of its kind in West Africa.* ◇ **of some ~** *About a quarter of patients in medical wards have a psychiatric disorder of some kind.* **2** [U] character or nature: *The difference was one of degree, not of kind.* ◇ **in ~** *Most of the problems they encounter are similar in kind to those of other patients.*
IDM **in ˈkind** **1** (of a payment) in goods or services, not money: *Serfs' rents were to be paid in kind, for example, two sheep and eight chickens.* **2** in the same way; with sth similar: *Individual states can increase their wealth by pursuing protectionist policies, providing other states do not respond in kind.* **your (own) kind** people who are like you because they have the same interests and ideas as you: *The desire to be amongst one's own kind is often the starting point for most volunteers in the movement.* **a kind of sb/sth** (*rather informal*) a person or thing that is similar to sb/sth else: *In effect, then, Plato is a kind of poet.* ◇ *The intervening galaxy acted as a kind of lens, bending the quasar's light.*

kind[2] /kaɪnd/ *adj.* (**kind·er, kind·est**) caring about others; friendly and generous: **~ (of sb) (to do sth)** *The community welcomed me and was kind enough to share some of its stories.* ◇ **~ to sb/sth** *Considerate behaviour includes sharing personal belongings with others and being kind to younger children.* ■ **kind·ly** *adv.*: *Financial support for the project was kindly provided by ICI.* **kind·ness** *noun* [U] *The correspondence constantly refers to the importance of acts of kindness in daily life.*

kin·et·ic /kɪˈnetɪk; *BrE also* kaɪˈnetɪk/ *adj.* [usually before noun] (*technical*) of or produced by movement: *Vehicle frames are designed to absorb the vehicle's kinetic energy in a crash while protecting the occupants from harm.* ◇ *He rejected the kinetic theory of gases developed by Maxwell and Boltzmann.*

king /kɪŋ/ *noun* **~ (of...)** the male ruler of an independent state that has a royal family: *Philip II became king of Macedon in 359 BC.* ◇ *The order was founded by King Edward III.*

king·dom /ˈkɪŋdəm/ *noun* **1** a country ruled by a king or queen: *By the eighth century, all the kingdoms of Anglo-Saxon England had accepted the discipline of Roman Christianity.* **2** one of the three traditional divisions of the natural world: *In the plant and animal kingdom, being male or female says much about an individual's ecology.* **3** (*biology*) one of the five main groups into which all living things are organized: *All modern animal phyla and a large part of the plant kingdom are represented.*

kin·ship /ˈkɪnʃɪp/ *noun* **1** [U] the fact of being related in a family: *People were linked by a strong support network with ties of kinship and lifelong familiarity.* ◇ **+ noun** *kinship groups/networks/ties* **2** [U, sing.] a feeling of being close to sb because you have similar backgrounds or attitudes SYN AFFINITY (1): *The farmers on both sides of the conflict may have felt more kinship with each other than with the aristocrats in their own city (Hanson, 1999).*

knee /niː/ *noun* the joint between the top and bottom parts of the leg where it bends in the middle: **+ noun** *About 80% of patients who had a knee replacement say that they are satisfied.*
IDM **bring sb/sth to their/its ˈknees** to defeat sb/sth; to badly affect an organization so that it can no longer function: *When large companies are brought to their knees it is often because of monumental leadership failure.*

knew *past tense of* KNOW

knife /naɪf/ *noun* (*pl.* **knives** /naɪvz/) a long, sharp piece of metal with a handle, used for cutting or as a weapon: *He stabbed the victim with a kitchen knife.*

knit /nɪt/ *verb* (**knit·ted, knit·ted**) HELP In sense 2 **knit** is usually used for the past tense and past participle. **1** [T, I] **~ (sth)** to make clothes, etc. from wool or cotton thread using two long thin KNITTING needles or a machine: *Emma Bovary signals her religious piety by knitting undershirts for orphans.* **2** [T] **~ sb/sth (together)** to join people or things closely together: *Globalization knits together the experiences of far-flung populations.* ◇ *These agricultural communities were tightly knit.*

know /nəʊ; *NAmE* noʊ/ *verb* (**knew** /njuː; *NAmE* nuː/, **known** /nəʊn; *NAmE* noʊn/) (not used in the progressive tenses) **1** [T, I] to have information in your mind as a result of experience or because you have learned or been told it: **~ sth** *We do not yet know the answer to this question.* ◇ **~ (that)...** *The West knew that the Soviet economy's growth rates had slowed in the 1960s.* ◇ **it is known that...** *It is now known that there are two main classes of these enzymes.* ◇ **~ where/what, etc...** *No one knew where in the brain the processing was taking place.* ◇ *Managers clearly need to know what is likely to happen in their key markets.* ◇ **~ of sth** *A person cannot always take steps to avoid a danger once he or she knows of its existence.* ◇ **~ (sth) about sth** *The Incas did not know about the arch but had perfected building techniques that were earthquake-proof.* ◇ *Little is known about the battle itself beyond two* *facts:...* ◇ **~ to do sth** *The patient knows to report any new symptoms or worsening of existing symptoms.* ◇ **~ sb/sth to be/do sth** *He had voluntarily joined an organization which he knew to be a terrorist organization.* ◇ *About 70 volcanoes in Indonesia are known to have erupted in the last 400 years.* **2** [T, I] to realize, understand or be aware of sth: **~ (that)...** *He knew that the situation would not soon be resolved.* ◇ *This was, as Quine must have known perfectly well, the position that Carnap had adopted.* ◇ **~ how/what, etc...** *Anyone who reads these poems would know how Larkin felt about marriage.* **3** [T] **~ (that)...** to feel certain about sth: *According to his account, he knew that he would be victorious in the upcoming battle.* **4** [T] to have developed a relationship with sb through meeting and spending time with them; to be familiar or friendly with sb: **~ sb** *Those who knew her say that she lived by the principles she taught.* ◇ **get to ~ sb** *Experienced teachers create a relaxed atmosphere in class and let the students get to know each other.* ◇ **be known to sb** *In general, the B2B customer is known to the supplier and is treated as an individual (Kotler, 2004).* **5** [T] to be familiar with sth through having read, seen or experienced it: **~ sth** *Plato must have known his work.* ◇ *Winston knew the place well.* ◇ **as we ~ it** *The first decades of the 20th century saw the beginnings of genetics as we know it.* **6** [T, usually passive] to think that sb/sth is a particular type of person or thing or has particular characteristics: **be known as sb/sth** *Thailand is known today as a Buddhist country.* ◇ **be known for sth** *Coulomb was known for his work on electricity, magnetism and mechanics.* ◇ **be known to be/do sth** *This is now known to be a gross oversimplification of the facts.* **7** [T] **(be) known as sth** [usually passive] to give sb/sth a particular name or title: *In later times he came to be known as 'the laughing philosopher'.* ◇ *The bell-shaped curve represents a distribution of data known as a 'normal distribution'.* **8** [T] **~ sb/sth** to recognize sb/sth: *The people who are asked to identify this man say they do not know him.* ◇ *They know a good personal opportunity when they see one.* **9** [T] **~ sb/sth from sb/sth** to be able to distinguish one person or thing from another SYN DIFFERENTIATE (1): *These characters lack the ability to know right from wrong.* **10** [T] to have learned a skill or language and be able to use it: **~ sth** *She is fluent in Mandarin and knows some Japanese.* ◇ **~ how/what, etc...** *Few people in ancient times knew how to read.* **11** [T] (only used in the perfect tenses) to have seen, heard or experienced sth: **~ sb/sth (to) do sth** *They had never known this to happen before.* ◇ **be known to do sth** *Applicants have been known to break down and cry.* **12** [T] **~ sth** to have personal experience of an emotion or situation: *She warns that he will never know peace if he kills his own mother.*

IDM **know 'best** to know what should be done, etc. better than other people: *There is a British political tradition that emphasizes the view that 'Government knows best'.* **know better (than to do sth)** to be sensible or polite enough to avoid doing sth: *As a pharmacist, she should have known better.* ◇ *He knows better than to be looking for a government subsidy.* **know full 'well** to be very aware of a fact and unable to deny or ignore it: *Tiberius knew full well that he was Augustus's fifth choice as his successor.* **let it be known/make it known that...** to make sure that people know about sth, especially by getting sb else to tell them: *The UK government made it known that it would not accept these terms.* **let sb 'know** to tell sb about sth: *President Johnson did not let the people know what was already taking place in Vietnam.* **make yourself 'known to sb** to introduce yourself to sb: *Odysseus made himself known to his son Telemachos.* IDM *see* FAR[1]

'know-how *noun* [U] (*rather informal*) knowledge of how to do sth and experience in doing it: *Labour skills and technological know-how are crucially important.*

know·ledge /ˈnɒlɪdʒ; *NAmE* ˈnɑːlɪdʒ/ *noun* **1** [U, sing.] the understanding of a subject that is gained through study, research or experience: *Scientific knowledge and technology were more advanced in China than in Europe.* ◇ **~ of sth** *Our knowledge of the biology of schizophrenia has developed significantly over the years.* ◇ *Clare's poetry conveys a detailed knowledge of the local flora and fauna.* ◇ **~ about sth** *Kant argued that we can obtain knowledge about the world, but it will always be subjective knowledge.* ◇ **+ noun** *The purpose of this article is to address these knowledge gaps and identify directions for future research.* ➲ *see also* GENERAL KNOWLEDGE **2** [U] the state of knowing about a particular fact or situation: **with/without sb's ~** *Spyware can enter the user's computer terminal without their knowledge.* ◇ **in the ~ that...** *Farmers raised yields, secure in the knowledge that any gains would go to them in profits.* ◇ **~ of sth** *The defendant denied any knowledge of how the injuries occurred.*

IDM **be common/public 'knowledge** to be sth that everyone knows, especially in a particular community or group: *These facts had been common knowledge among physicists for a long time.* **to (the best of) your 'knowledge** from the information you have, although you may not know everything: *To my knowledge, no one has yet attempted to answer these questions.* ◇ *The text is free of factual errors, to the best of my knowledge.*

▸ ADJECTIVE + KNOWLEDGE **basic • general • detailed • new • prior, existing, current • tacit • local • specialist, expert, specialized • professional • scientific • technical • medical • empirical • theoretical • a priori** *Without the acquisition of new knowledge, there could not have been an information revolution.* ◇ *Food is relatively 'culture bound' so local knowledge is vital to market success.*

▸ VERB + KNOWLEDGE **have, possess • lack • require • acquire, gain, accumulate • share, transfer, transmit, disseminate • generate, produce, create • develop, increase, improve, advance, deepen • use, exploit, apply • demonstrate** *South Korea acquired foreign knowledge through licences, overseas education, and capital goods imports.* ◇ *Long-term security encourages suppliers to innovate and to develop their knowledge.*

▸ KNOWLEDGE + NOUN **production, creation • acquisition • management • transfer • network • gap** *Knowledge creation and diffusion is at the heart of economic growth and development.*

▸ NOUN + OF KNOWLEDGE **body, stock • lack • source • acquisition** *A strong body of knowledge exists on the development of intergroup tensions.*

know·ledge·able /ˈnɒlɪdʒəbl; *NAmE* ˈnɑːlɪdʒəbl/ *adj.* **~ (about sth)** knowing a lot: *The nuns were an important force in the business: reliable, skilled and knowledgeable about market trends.*

'knowledge base *noun* all the information that is available to use or refer to in a particular organization, industry or area of research: *However, more research is needed to build on the current knowledge base.* ◇ *Any sector may be characterized by a specific knowledge base, technologies and inputs.*

'knowledge economy *noun* an economic system in which the main area of economic activity is producing and processing information: *Higher education is seen as the focal point for the knowledge economy.*

'knowledge worker *noun* a person whose job involves producing or processing information: *Advanced information technologies have increased the demand for highly skilled knowledge workers.*

known[1] /nəʊn; *NAmE* noʊn/ *adj.* [only before noun] known about, especially by a lot of people: *Huntington's disease is a genetic condition that has no known cure.* ◇ *Trilobites are the earliest known examples, occurring in rocks of Early Cambrian age.*

known[2] *past part. of* KNOW

Koran = QUR'AN

Ll

lab /læb/ *noun* (*informal*) = LABORATORY

label¹ AWL /ˈleɪbl/ *verb* (-ll-, *US* -l-) [often passive] **1 ~ sb/sth (as) sth** to describe sb/sth in a particular way, especially unfairly: *Starkie labels him a political and cultural conservative.* ◇ *These comments from dementia sufferers seemed to reflect a fear of being labelled as stupid.* **2** to attach a label to sth; to write information on sth in order to identify it: **~ sth** *Medicine bottles should be labelled clearly.* ◇ **~ sth with sth** *The container must be clearly labelled with the patient's name.* **3 ~ sth (with sth)** (*biology, chemistry*) to enable sth to be identified or TRACED by attaching a substance to it: *Many antigens can be labelled with fluorescent dyes.* **4 ~ sth** (*computing*) to refer to a particular instruction in a program using a series of characters: *We have labelled the beginning of the outer loop 'mainLoop'.*

label² AWL /ˈleɪbl/ *noun* **1** a piece of paper, plastic, etc. that is attached to an object and gives information about it: *Product labels do not distinguish added sugars from naturally occurring sugars.* ◇ *Products were automatically tagged with the 'made in New Zealand' label, which signalled environmental responsibility.* **2** a word or phrase that is used to describe sb/sth, sometimes in a way that seems too general, unfair or not correct: *Popular labels often attached to this decade include 'the swinging sixties'.* ◇ **under a/the ~ (of sth)** *Classic liberal ideas gained a new hearing, under the label of neo-liberalism.* ◇ **~ for sth** *'Chance' might only be a label for our current inability to identify the causes of these phenomena.* **3** (*biology, chemistry*) a substance that can be used to INDICATE the presence of sth: *An antibody that has an attached fluorescent label is added.* **4** (*computing*) a series of characters that are used to refer to an instruction in a program: *In Fig. 9.3 the label 'reset0' indicates the start of instructions to restore the program to its initial state.*

labor AWL (*US*) = LABOUR¹, LABOUR²

la·bora·tory /ləˈbɒrətri; *NAmE* ˈlæbrətɔːri/ *noun* (*pl.* -ies) (*also informal* **lab**) a room or building containing equipment for scientific experiments, research or teaching, or for making drugs or chemicals: **in a/the ~** *The study of soils often includes analysis of physical and chemical characteristics in the laboratory.* ◇ **+ noun** *Improved guidelines on the use and care of laboratory animals were established.* ◇ *A variety of field and laboratory experiments support the hypothesis that intergroup competition tends to strengthen social relations within each group.* ◇ *a laboratory test/investigation/study* ◇ **under ~ conditions** *It is a unicellular sexual microorganism that is easy to control under laboratory conditions.*

la·borer (*US*) = LABOURER

ˈlabor union *noun* (*NAmE*) = UNION (1)

la·bour¹ AWL (*US* **labor**) /ˈleɪbə(r)/ *noun* **1** [U] work, especially physical work: *A full-time job is 2 000 hours of labour in a year.* ◇ *More 40-year-olds have jobs that involve manual labour than 20-year-olds.* ➲ *see also* DIVISION OF LABOUR **2** [U] workers, considered as a group, especially people who use their hands or physical strength to do their work: *A notable characteristic of large farms in France was the efficiency with which they used labour.* ◇ **+ noun** *Labour costs constitute the largest proportion of operating costs.* **3** [U] workers considered as a social class or political force: *Representatives of labour, management and the government tried to address critical economic problems.* ◇ *Organized labour staged a series of general strikes.* ◇ **+noun** *The British Labour Party was committed to increasing public expenditure in 2010–2011.* **4** [C, usually pl.] a task or period of work: *These individuals all benefit directly from their labours.* **5** [U, C, usually sing.] the period of time or the process of giving birth to a baby: *The child was born at term by emergency caesarean following a difficult labour.* ◇ **in ~** *She was in labour for nearly 24 hours.*

▸ ADJECTIVE + LABOUR **skilled • unskilled • human • agricultural** *These men performed more skilled labour, often of a supervisory nature.* | **forced • domestic • manual • paid** *The Second Empire revived the practice of transporting convicts to do forced labour in French Guiana.* | **cheap • female • local** *Immigrants had at first been welcomed as cheap labour.*

▸ NOUN + LABOUR **child • slave** *President Grant's aim was to make slave labour unprofitable in the Caribbean.*

▸ VERB + LABOUR **require, need • provide** *A great deal of skill and labour had been required to develop the computer program.* | **supply • perform • sell** *She argues that a higher real wage leads workers to choose to supply more labour.* | **employ • use • hire** *It would not be profitable for them to employ any more labour.*

▸ LABOUR + NOUN **cost • productivity • supply • demand • shortage • flexibility • migration • mobility • law • standards • regulations • conditions** *Since the 1990s there has been renewed openness to labour migration.* | **movement • relations** *Addams defended the labour movement as a crucial institution for working-class Americans.*

la·bour² AWL (*US* **labor**) /ˈleɪbə(r)/ *verb* **1** [I] to try very hard to do sth difficult: **~ away** *They were still labouring away, trying to produce a draft law.* ◇ **~ to do sth** *However hard the department might labour to put things right, they were not going to succeed.* **2** [I] to do hard physical work: *Women and men laboured from before dawn to after dark.* ◇ *Less than half of the labouring class were literate by 1800.* **3** [I] **(+ adv./prep.)** to move with difficulty and effort: *On the night of April 9, 1825, the steamer Natchez laboured up the Mississippi River.*

IDM **labour the ˈpoint** to continue to repeat or explain sth that has already been said and understood: *It is not necessary to labour the point that international law already offers rules for ensuring environmental quality.*

PHR V **ˈlabour under sth** to believe sth that is not true: *Curll labours under the misapprehension that Swift's cousin Thomas was the author of the tale.*

la·bour·er (*US* **la·bor·er**) /ˈleɪbərə(r)/ *noun* a person whose job involves hard physical work that is not skilled, especially work that is done outdoors: *The migrants sustained themselves by working as agricultural labourers.*

ˈlabour force (*US* ˈ**labor force**) *noun* [C+sing./pl. v.] all the people in a country or organization who work or are looking for work SYN WORKFORCE: *As the number of children per woman declines, more women enter the labour force.* ◇ *A large labour force was needed to work on plantations.*

ˈlabour market (*US* ˈ**labor market**) *noun* the number of people who are available for work in relation to the number of jobs available: *The fortunes of working families rise and fall with conditions in the labour market.*

lack¹ /læk/ *noun* [sing., U] the state of not having sth or not having enough of sth SYN SHORTAGE: **~ of sth** *There is a lack of good evidence about the treatment and management of the disorder.* ◇ **through ~ of sth** *They failed, but not through lack of effort.* ◇ **for ~ of sth** *Legal proceedings were suspended for lack of evidence.* ◇ **no ~ of sb/sth** *There was no lack of people eager to assign blame for the country's problems.*

▸ ADJECTIVE + LACK **general • relative • apparent • perceived • alleged • current • complete, total • distinct, notable • serious, severe** *The report revealed a general lack of understanding of cultural differences among the population.*

▸ VERB + LACK **show, demonstrate, display, reveal, indicate, reflect • highlight • explain • suggest • find •**

note, report • overcome • imply • address *This indicates a substantial lack of knowledge amongst the consumers surveyed in this study.*

▸ LACK OF + NOUN **knowledge • skill • training • experience • understanding • awareness • interest • evidence • data, information • resources • support • clarity • transparency • time • control • access • confidence • trust • opportunity • attention • capacity • consensus • power** *He conceded that there was 'uncertainty and lack of clarity' in English law on the matter.*

lack[2] /læk/ *verb* [no passive] **~ sth** to have none or not enough of sth: *Children often lack the capacity to understand the consequences of expressing their anger.* ◇ *Poorer people usually lack the resources to move to better neighbourhoods.* ➲ *see also* LACKING

▸ LACK + NOUN **capacity • ability • competence • power • authority • legitimacy • information, data • evidence • knowledge • skill, expertise • experience • training • understanding • confidence • access • support • resources • means • incentive** *Respondents also indicated that they lacked the knowledge necessary to properly evaluate the materials.*

▸ ADVERB + LACK **completely, entirely • largely • generally, usually • typically • currently • simply • clearly • sadly • necessarily** *Most people simply lack the interest to become more politically active.*

lack·ing /ˈlækɪŋ/ *adj.* [not before noun] **1 ~ in sth** having none or not enough of sth: *Immature adolescents would be expected to be impulsive and lacking in self-awareness.* ◇ *The accounts are both limited and generally lacking in detail.* **2** not present; not available, or not available in a large enough quantity: *Attention from the father makes up for what is lacking in her relationship with her mother.* ◇ *Wherever tap water is lacking, it is the women who have to carry water in pots on their heads.* ➲ *compare* MISSING (1)

lady /ˈleɪdi/ (*pl.* **-ies**) *noun* **1** a word used to mean 'woman' that some people, especially older people, consider is more polite: *One 93-year-old lady with a history of falls was treated for around 8 weeks.* HELP Some women, however, prefer to be called **women**, as it suggests a more equal relationship with men: *These young women were highly motivated and determined to succeed.* ◇ ~~*These young ladies...*~~ ➲ *compare* GENTLEMAN (1) **2 Lady** (in the UK) a title used by a woman who is a member of the NOBILITY, or by sb who has been given the title 'lady' as an honour: *In June 1944, Lees-Milne visited Lord and Lady Braybrooke at Audley End.* ➲ *compare* LORD (1) **3** (in the past) a woman from a high social class: *Being a governess was the only employment option open to unmarried ladies of limited means.* ➲ *compare* GENTLEMAN (2)

lag[1] /læg/ *verb* (**-gg-**) [I] to move or develop slowly or more slowly than other people, organizations, etc: **~ behind sb/sth** *Profiling competitor strengths and weaknesses can allow an organization to see where its performance lags behind the competition.* ◇ **~ behind** *The result of this study indicates that support for homeless women may have lagged behind.*

lag[2] /læg/ (*also* ˈ**time lag**) *noun* the period of time between two connected events: *The effect of habitat destruction on animal populations is likely to show a lag, although it is not clear how long this might be.* ◇ **~ between A and B** *There is always a time lag between the environment changing and the organism's design responding.*

laid *past tense, past part. of* LAY[1]

lain *past part. of* LIE[1]

lake /leɪk/ *noun* (*abbr.* **L.**) a large area of water that is surrounded by land: *Gradually, the river deposited sediment in the lake behind the dam.* ◇ *In the vicinity of Lake Chad, land has been flooded by rising lake waters.* ◇ *saline/freshwater lakes*

lam·ent /ləˈment/ *verb* to feel or express disappointment about sth: **~ sth** *In this celebrated poem, Wordsworth lamented the loss of vision brought by age.* ◇ **~ (the fact) that...** *Miguel (2009) laments the fact that so few empirical findings forge links between the theory and data.*

lamp /læmp/ *noun* **1** a device that uses electricity, oil or gas to produce light: *In Great Britain, the Savoy Theatre was lit by electric lamps in 1881.* **2** an electrical device that produces RAYS of heat and that is used for medical or scientific purposes: *The transparent solutions were dried under a 120 V, 250 W infrared lamp for 24 hours.*

land[1] /lænd/ *noun* **1** [U] the part of the earth's surface that is not covered by water: *The tsunami caused much destruction when it reached land.* ◇ **on ~** *Such diverse life forms have been able to evolve on land and in the sea because of the unusual characteristics of water.* ◇ **by ~** *Many illegal immigrants travelled by air to Mexico, and then by land to the United States.* ◇ **over ~** *Over land during a cyclone, winds flatten crops, uproot trees and severely damage buildings.* ◇ **~ surface/area/mass** *Without human activity, forests would cover most of the earth's land surface.* ◇ **+ noun** *Early land plants were small, some only a few centimetres high.* **2** [U] (*also* **lands** [pl.]) the area of ground that sb owns, especially when you think of it as property that can be bought or sold: *A small number of houses and flats were built on the land in 1931.* ◇ *Many of the English lords acquired lands in Ireland.* ◇ **a piece of ~** *A group of travellers had occupied a piece of land owned by the council.* **3** [U] (*also* **lands** [pl.]) an area of ground, especially of a particular type or used for a particular purpose SYN TERRAIN: *When the lava reaches flat land, it spreads out to form a lava field.* ◇ *Dust storms are a common feature of arid lands.* ◇ *The proposed site is currently derelict industrial land.* ◇ *agricultural/arable land* ◇ **~ use** *Evidence points to both climate and human land use as having important impacts on this ecosystem.* **4** [C] a country or state: *The highest court in the land had condemned such practices as unacceptable.* ◇ *They had left their homes for foreign lands in pursuit of a better fate for their families.* ◇ **~ of sth** *One of the enduring cultural ideals for Americans is that the United States is a 'land of opportunity'.* **5 the land** [U] used to refer to country areas and the way of life in the countryside, or to ground or soil used for farming: *People left the land to move to the growing urban areas to work* ◇ *Capitalist farmers employed labourers to work the land.*

land[2] /lænd/ *verb* [I, T] to arrive on land or another surface; to put sb/sth on land or another surface: *Focusing on short-haul flights means that planes can land and return the same day.* ◇ **+ adv./prep.** *Astronauts Neil Armstrong and Buzz Aldrin landed on the moon in July 1969.* ◇ **~ sb/sth (+ adv./prep.)** *Before Japan declared war she landed troops at Chemulpo in Korea.*

land·ed /ˈlændɪd/ *adj.* [only before noun] owning a lot of land; connected with land that is owned: *Huge estates were owned by the landed gentry or an urban middle class copying its lifestyle.* ◇ *Well-to-do commoners used their money to acquire public office and landed property.*

land·ing /ˈlændɪŋ/ *noun* **1** [C, U] an act of bringing sth down to the ground: *Soon after the moon landing, public support for the space programme declined sharply.* ◇ *The pilot checks the length of the runway by radar, so that he can make a safe landing.* **2** [C] an act of bringing soldiers to land in an area that is controlled by the enemy: *The threat of a Normandy landing prevented Hitler from concentrating his troops against Russia.*

land·lord /ˈlændlɔːd; *NAmE* ˈlændlɔːrd/ *noun* a person or company who you rent a room, a house, an office, etc. from: *40 per cent of the population lives in properties owned by the local authority, private landlords or housing* *associations.* ◇ *Probably the worst-off peasants were those with an absentee landlord.* ➲ *compare* TENANT

land·mark /ˈlændmɑːk; *NAmE* ˈlændmɑːrk/ *noun* **1** something, such as a large building, that you can see clearly from a distance and that will help you to know where you are: *The screenplay is filled with references to familiar London landmarks—Battersea Power Station, Big Ben and Westminster Abbey.* ➲ *compare* MONUMENT (2) **2** an event, a discovery or an invention that marks an important stage in sth: **~ decision/case/study** *A consensus around racial integration led to the landmark decision to desegregate public schools in America.* ◇ **~ in sth** *Charlotte Brooke's 'Reliques of Irish Poetry' was a landmark in the history of Irish literature.* ➲ *compare* MILESTONE (1)

ˈland mass *noun* (*technical*) a large area of land, for example a continent: *The Arctic Ocean is a deep basin almost completely surrounded by continental land masses.*

land·owner /ˈlændəʊnə(r); *NAmE* ˈlændoʊnər/ *noun* a person who owns land, especially a large area of land: *There were destructive attacks on the property of local landowners and often on their families.* ■ **land·owner·ship** (*also* **land·owning**) *noun* [U] *Social reform spread landownership among the peasantry and middle classes.* **land·owning** /ˈlændəʊnɪŋ; *NAmE* ˈlændoʊnɪŋ/ *adj.* [only before noun] *Commerce, manufacture and technology had steadily shifted power away from the old landowning classes.*

L

land·scape /ˈlændskeɪp/ *noun* **1** [C] everything you can see when you look across a large area of land, especially in the countryside: *These physical landscapes were shaped by the pattern of human settlement.* ◇ **~ of sth** *The landscape of New England has undergone one of the most remarkable histories of transformation worldwide.* ◇ **in/on a/the ~** *New towns and cities were appearing on the Indian landscape.* ◇ **across a/the ~** *The distribution of soils across a landscape may be too complex to map accurately.* **2** [sing.] a situation or an activity of a particular type: *The war transformed the political landscape, with the creation of many new states.* ◇ **~ of sth** *It was a widely held view that Asia would dominate the global economic landscape of the twenty-first century.* **3** [C, U] a painting of a view of the countryside; this style of painting: *an artist famous for his landscapes* ◇ **+ noun** *The range of subject matter in Constable's major landscape paintings is surprisingly narrow.*

▸ ADJECTIVE + LANDSCAPE **changing** • **regional** • **natural** • **physical** • **rural** • **agricultural, agrarian** • **urban** • **industrial** *Many planned urban landscapes have been constructed to represent the power of an elite.* | **changing** • **contemporary** • **cultural** • **political** • **religious** • **social** • **economic** *The films reflected the changing social and cultural landscape of post-war Britain.*

▸ VERB + LANDSCAPE **create** • **dominate** • **characterize** • **shape** • **change, alter** • **transform** *This landscape is characterized by low limestone hills.*

lan·guage /ˈlæŋɡwɪdʒ/ *noun* **1** [C] the system of communication in speech and writing that is used by people of a particular country or area: *English has contributed a vast number of words to the Spanish language.* ◇ **in... ~** *The students are taught in their own language.* ◇ **the ~ of...** *Dutch is the official language of Suriname.* ◇ **+ noun** *The development of trusting relationships with customers generally required the language barrier to be overcome.* ➲ *see also* FIRST LANGUAGE, NATURAL LANGUAGE, SECOND LANGUAGE **2** [U] the use by humans of a system of sounds and words to communicate: *The acquisition of language occurs through interactions with others.* **3** [U] a particular style or form of speaking or writing: *At the end of the poem, the poetic language is not as elaborate.* ◇ *Lakoff (1987) has provided numerous examples of metaphors used in everyday language.* ◇ **the ~ of sth** *In the language of economics, peasant labour had no opportunity cost.* **4** [U, C] a way of expressing ideas and feelings using movements, symbols or sound: *Many species have complex forms of language.* ◇ *Sign language appears to be a more natural language of people who are deaf (Sacks, 1989).* ◇ *It is widely claimed that music is a universal language.* ➲ *see also* BODY LANGUAGE **5** [C, U] a system of symbols and rules that is used to operate a computer: *The use of high-level programming languages and tools has been extensively researched.* ◇ *Turing described different levels of programming language.*

▸ ADJECTIVE + LANGUAGE **native** • **indigenous** • **vernacular** • **official** • **first** • **second** • **foreign** • **modern** • **natural** • **original** • **common** *The book was translated into Latin and a number of modern languages, including German.* | **natural** • **human** *A major premise of this article is that human language can be and should be an object of scientific study.* | **spoken, verbal** • **written** • **everyday, ordinary** • **simple, plain** *Spoken language remains the primary medium for providing instruction in the classroom.*

▸ NOUN + LANGUAGE **target** • **minority** *Foreign-language learners typically have limited opportunities to speak the target language.*

▸ VERB + LANGUAGE **use, employ** • **learn** • **acquire** • **teach** • **study** • **understand** *Subjects with this syndrome suffer from severe mental retardation, but are reported to acquire language relatively normally.* | **speak** • **adopt** • **master** • **share** *Marketing language may be adopted and employed to disguise the negative effects of globalization.*

▸ NOUN + OF LANGUAGE **use** • **command** • **knowledge** • **understanding** • **variety** • **feature** • **aspect** *The older children's use of language reflects an increased capacity for higher order thinking.*

lapse¹ /læps/ *noun* **1 ~ (of sth)** a period of time between two things that happen SYN INTERVAL (1): *The lapse of time before the first written sources is considerable.* ◇ *It is apparent that students forget a significant amount of acquired words during a lapse of seven days.* **2 ~ (in sth)** a small mistake, especially one that is caused by forgetting sth or by being careless: *An intruder ended up in the Queen's bedroom due to lapses in security.* ◇ *EU nationals should not be deported as a sanction for administrative lapses or irregularities.* **3** an example or period of bad behaviour from sb who normally behaves well: *In a middle-aged or elderly person, any social lapse that is out of character should always suggest dementia.*

lapse² /læps/ *verb* **1** [I] (of a contract or an agreement) to be no longer valid because the period of time that it lasts has come to an end: *Construction has not begun as of 2013 and planning permission has lapsed.* ◇ *This jurisdiction lapsed in March 2005.* **2** [I] **~ (from sth)** to stop believing in or practising your religion: *Many who lapsed during persecution wanted to be readmitted to the churches.* ■ **lapsed** *adj.* [only before noun] *It is generally more profitable for companies to retain existing customers than to replace lapsed customers with new ones.*

PHR V **ˈlapse into sth** to gradually pass into a worse or less active state or condition: *By the time they arrived, he had lapsed into unconsciousness.*

large /lɑːdʒ; *NAmE* lɑːrdʒ/ *adj.* (**larger, larg·est**) **1** big in quantity or size: *The patient lost a large amount of blood.* ◇ *A large proportion of the US population already had Internet access.* ◇ *The second study made use of a much larger number of sources.* ◇ *It has been well documented that adolescents are the largest group of uninsured children.* ◇ *Fogel et al. (2005) showed that dominance by large firms hurt economy-wide growth.* ◇ **~ enough** *The sample was large enough to produce reliable estimates.* **2** wide in range and involving many things: *The capitalist producers were able to organize production on a larger scale.* ◇ *Private automobile use raises larger issues of social and environmental justice.*

IDM **at ˈlarge** (used after a noun) used to refer to the whole or most of a group, not just part of it; as a whole; in general: *The survey was criticized for being unrepresentative of the population at large.* ◇ *Benefits to society at large may be as significant as the benefits received by the individual.* **by and ˈlarge** used to say that sth is generally, but not completely, true: *The set of statistics corresponded by and large with the data evaluated in 2007.* **in large ˈmeasure | in ˈlarge part** to a great extent: *The decline in these unions has been due in large measure to globalization.* ◇ *The crisis appears to have resulted, in large part, from the failure to regulate the bank industry.* ➲ *more at* LOOM

large·ly /ˈlɑːdʒli; *NAmE* ˈlɑːrdʒli/ *adv.* to a great extent; mostly or mainly: *In the 1970s, its population was still largely rural.* ◇ *This project was largely a matter of routine laboratory work.* ◇ **~ because...** *Din does not address these issues, largely because his book is not about grand theories.*
▸ LARGELY + VERB **be based on • be determined by • be controlled by • be driven by • depend on • be composed of • be restricted to, be confined to • be superseded by • replace** *Areas of undisturbed forest are now largely confined to Borneo, Sumatra, Sulawesi and Papua.* | **disappear • eliminate • exclude • ignore • neglect • overlook • avoid • be forgotten** *These models of urban structure largely ignore social and cultural variables.* | **focus on • concern, be concerned with • explain • fail** *The psychological approach has largely failed to produce clear-cut results.*
▸ VERB + LARGELY **be based ~ on • derive ~ from • be driven ~ by • depend ~ on • consist ~ of • remain • focus ~ on** *These conclusions were based largely on an assessment of Web information.*
▸ LARGELY + ADJECTIVE **absent • invisible • unnoticed • unknown • unexplored • unchanged • unaffected • intact • independent • consistent • irrelevant • ineffective • due to • dependent on • responsible for** *Ferrel's work was largely unknown in Europe.*
▸ PHRASE **be largely a matter of** *The choice of anaesthetic drugs is largely a matter of personal and institutional preference.*

ˌlarge-ˈscale *adj.* [usually before noun] **1** involving many people or things, especially over a wide area: *A large-scale survey found that 20% of Europeans viewed television as their main source of health information.* ◇ *a large-scale study/project/enterprise* OPP SMALL-SCALE (1) **2** (of a map or model) drawn or made to a scale that shows a small area of land or a building in great detail: *Large-scale topographic maps became possible with the development of exact survey techniques in eighteenth-century France.* OPP SMALL-SCALE (2)

larva /ˈlɑːvə; *NAmE* ˈlɑːrvə/ *noun* (*pl.* **lar·vae** /ˈlɑːviː; *NAmE* ˈlɑːrviː/) an insect at the stage when it has just come out of an egg and has a short fat soft body with no legs: *The young feed on tiny insect larvae and other invertebrates.* ◇ *Females release larvae nightly over about a month.* ■ **lar·val** /ˈlɑːvl; *NAmE* ˈlɑːrvl/ *adj.* [only before noun] *In the life cycle of the nematode, there are four larval stages before the sexually mature adult develops.*

laser /ˈleɪzə(r)/ *noun* a device that gives out light in which all the waves OSCILLATE (= change direction and strength) together, typically producing a powerful beam of light that can be used for cutting metal, in medical operations, etc: **+ noun** *CD-ROM technology uses a laser beam to read tiny dots embedded on a layer within the disk.* ◇ *Laser therapy reduces the risk of visual loss by 50% and increases the chance of visual improvement.*

last¹ /lɑːst; *NAmE* læst/ *det., adj.* **1** happening or coming after all other similar things or people: *He was one of the last suspects to be guillotined during the Terror in May 1794.* ◇ *Parliament can propose amendments but the Council has the last say.* OPP FIRST¹ (1) **2** [only before noun] most recent: *Large ice sheets formed over Canada and Russia during the last ice age.* ◇ *In the last part of this paper, I look at six ways in which we can make children's rights count.* ◇ *This last point is critical.* OPP FIRST¹ (1) **3** [only before noun] only remaining: *Broadway Market was declared to be one of the last remaining sites in London with character.* ◇ *The army defeated the rebels and forced the last remnants of the German revolution to capitulate.* **4** used to emphasize that sb/sth is the least likely or suitable: *A peasant trade union was the last thing the party wanted, but despite their efforts the demand persisted.* IDM *see* ANALYSIS, WORD¹

last² /lɑːst; *NAmE* læst/ *adv.* **1** after anyone or anything else; at the end: *The word comprehension test came last.* OPP FIRST² (1) **2** most recently: *The president was last seen in public in August 2012.* OPP FIRST² (2)
IDM **ˌlast but not ˈleast** used when mentioning the last person or thing of a group, in order to say that they are not less important than the others: *Last but not least, I should like to thank all those who have made financial contributions to the conference.*

last³ /lɑːst; *NAmE* læst/ *pron.* **the last** (*pl.* **the last**) **1** the person or thing that comes or happens after all other similar people or things: *Farmers concentrated their production on vegetables, fruits, poultry and hay—the last too bulky for long-distance transport.* ◇ **~ (of sb/sth) to do sth** *Of these groups, the working classes were the last to gain political representation.* OPP FIRST³ **2 ~ of sth** the only remaining part or items of sth: *The Ching-t'u School is the last of the great Chinese schools of Buddhism.* OPP FIRST³
IDM **at (long) ˈlast** after much delay or effort; in the end SYN FINALLY (1): *Ritvo's book, at long last, gives this historic conflict the attention it deserves.*

last⁴ /lɑːst; *NAmE* læst/ *verb* **1** [I] (not used in the progressive tenses) to continue for a particular period of time: *it has been suggested that a drought that lasted at least 200 years occurred at this time.* ◇ *Suction should be performed in short bursts lasting only a few seconds.* ◇ **~ for...** *The inquiry was expected to last for three months.* **2** [I, T] to continue to exist or to function well; to survive sth or manage to stay in the same situation, despite difficulties: *Adolescents' friendships tend to last longer than do those of childhood.* ◇ *The government did not last long enough to fulfil its promises.* ◇ **~ for...** *Experiments in mice suggest that memory cells can survive in the complete absence of antigen (but mice do not last for 75 years as human memory does).* ◇ **~ sth** *Many legal relationships will not last the lifetime of the parties involved.* **3** [I] to be enough for what is needed, especially for a particular period of time: *The world's oil reserves were predicted to last only 50 years.* ◇ **~ for...** *New technology means these countries could have enough cheap gas to last for another 100 years.*

last·ing /ˈlɑːstɪŋ; *NAmE* ˈlæstɪŋ/ *adj.* [usually before noun] continuing to exist or to have an effect for a long time: *The government's agreed mission was to establish lasting peace in South Africa.* ◇ *Learning disability is a condition that tends to be present from birth and has a lasting effect on development.* ➲ *see also* LONG-LASTING

last·ly /ˈlɑːstli; *NAmE* ˈlæstli/ *adv.* **1** used to introduce the final point that you want to make SYN FINALLY (2): *Lastly, I will examine the impact of globalization on states and sovereignty.* ➲ language bank *at* ORGANIZE **2** at the end; after all the other things that you have mentioned: *This led in turn to the Maastricht Treaty, the Treaties of Amsterdam and Nice, and lastly the 2007 Lisbon Treaty.*

late¹ /leɪt/ *adj.* (**later, lat·est**) **1** [only before noun] near the end of a period of time, a person's life, etc: *By the late sixteenth century, the core of the capitalist world economy had become established.* ◇ *The medicine of the later Middle Ages was arguably also bad medicine.* ◇ *In later life, the Tsar surrounded himself with army officers.* ◇ *It appears*

L

that the introduction was added to the text at a much later date. ◇ It was only at this later stage of the experiment that the solution was discovered. ◇ Fairbanks's work anticipated many later developments in earthquake science. OPP EARLY[1] (1) **2** [not usually before noun] arriving, happening or doing sth after the expected, arranged or usual time: *Army pay was generally late.* ◇ **~ in doing sth** *Children with this condition are late in developing the skills of feeding, walking and dressing.* OPP EARLY[1] (2) **3** [only before noun] (*formal*) (of a person) no longer alive: *Other examples include the late Anita Roddick of the Body Shop, who promoted a number of environmental causes.* ■ **late·ness** /ˈleɪtnəs/ *noun* [U] *Lateness at work was always severely punished.* ➲ *see also* LATER[2], LATEST

IDM **be too ˈlate** happening after the time when it is possible to do sth: *The new management system should help the fishery to recover before it is too late.*

late[2] /leɪt/ *adv.* (*comparative* **later**, no *superlative*) **1 ~ (in sth)** near the end of a period of time, a person's life, etc: *Arriving late in the year of 1928, Eliade enrolled at the University of Calcutta.* ◇ *Later in the day, as the sun rises, pollution levels may drop.* ◇ *These genetic effects enhance fitness early in life but depress it late in life.* OPP EARLY[2] (1) **2** after the expected, arranged or usual time: *Pressure of work led to employees working late.* ◇ *The project started late due to funding difficulties.* OPP EARLY[2] (2) ➲ *see also* LATER[1]

IDM **of ˈlate** recently: *Of late, concerns about childhood obesity have dominated the news.* **too ˈlate (to do/be sth)** after the time when it is possible to do sth successfully: *The Spartan army arrived at Marathon too late to participate in the battle.* ◇ *In fact, the introduction of antibiotics came too late to explain the reduced mortality rate.* ➲ *more at* SOON

la·tent /ˈleɪtnt/ *adj.* [usually before noun] **1** existing, but not yet very obvious, active or well developed: *Bakunin wished to harness the latent anger of the slum-dwellers.* ◇ *This programme could not possibly be carried through without bringing to the surface the latent conflicts within the party.* **2** (*medical*) (of a disease or medical condition) not yet showing any SYMPTOMS: *In this case, the latent period from infection to the appearance of symptoms can be variable.* **3** (*biology*) (of a microorganism or other AGENT) present in the body without causing disease, but capable of doing so later: *The pool of virus on the surface of dendritic cells can remain latent for extended periods.* ■ **la·tency** /ˈleɪtənsi/ *noun* [U] *This was a period of latency for the religion, when it lay almost forgotten in the communal mind.* ◇ **+ noun** *The latency period from exposure onset to symptom onset is short.*

ˈlatent heat *noun* [U] (*physics*) the amount of energy that is absorbed or released by a substance as it changes from one state to another with no change in temperature, for example from solid to liquid or from gas to liquid: *As the water condenses, it releases latent heat.* ◇ **~ of sth** *As water evaporates, the latent heat of vaporization is absorbed from the surrounding air.*

ˌlatent ˈvariable *noun* (*statistics*) a VARIABLE whose value is calculated from the observation of other variables rather than by direct measurement: *Intelligence is a latent variable that IQ tests attempt to measure.*

later[1] /ˈleɪtə(r)/ *adv.* at a time in the future; after the time you are talking about: *In September 1778, Dominica was taken by the French, to be followed by St Lucia a few months later.* ◇ **~ in sth** *Short gestation may increase cardiovascular risk later in life.* OPP EARLIER

IDM **later ˈon** at a time in the future; after the time you are talking about: *Students were asked to agree or disagree with the statement: 'Achievement in school leads to job success later on.'* ◇ *Caregivers have to make difficult decisions later on in the progress of the disease.* **not/no later than...** by a particular time and not after it: *An earlier Greek version of the text was composed no later than the end of the second century.* ➲ *more at* SOON

later[2] /ˈleɪtə(r)/ *adj.* [only before noun] **1** near the end of a period of time, life, etc: *The temple walls date to the later eighth century.* ◇ *The questionnaire was designed to explore how gender relations shape unpaid labour in later life.* OPP EARLIER **2** coming after sth else or at a time in the future: *It is hoped that further research will be conducted at a later date.* ◇ *Later feminists, however, have argued that hysteria is a form of resistance to patriarchal control.* OPP EARLIER

lat·eral /ˈlætərəl/ *adj.* [usually before noun] connected with the side of sb/sth or with movement to the side: *The ends of the lateral branches bear female flowers.* ◇ *Lateral movement of the soil layer seems to have led to a landslide.* ◇ **~ to sth** *The injury was beneath and lateral to the kneecap.* ■ **lat·eral·ly** /ˈlætərəli/ *adv.*: *The cells proliferate and spread out laterally.* ◇ *At the rapids, the channel is constricted both laterally and vertically.*

lat·est /ˈleɪtɪst/ *adj.* [only before noun] the most recent or newest: *This review summarizes the latest developments in sleep research.* ◇ *Many businesses are investing in the latest technology to enable them to respond rapidly to changes in orders.*

lati·tude /ˈlætɪtjuːd; *NAmE* ˈlætɪtuːd/ *noun* **1** (*abbr.* **lat.**) [U] the distance of a place north or south of the EQUATOR, measured in degrees: *Because of its latitude, the days were shorter in winter.* ◇ *Throughout much of the last cold stage, the oceanic polar front was situated off northern Portugal around latitude 40°N.* ◇ **line of ~** *The seas around Scotland were divided into four zones by lines of latitude.* ➲ *compare* LONGITUDE **2 latitudes** [pl.] **~ (of...)** a region of the world that is a particular distance from the EQUATOR: *Similar rock formations are found in the cool northern latitudes of Finland and Sweden.* ◇ *The model projections of climate change indicate greater warming in the high latitudes.* **3** [U] freedom to choose what you do or the way that you do it SYN LIBERTY (1): *The region enjoyed considerable latitude when it came to issues of taxation.*

lat·ter[1] /ˈlætə(r)/ *adj.* **1** nearer to the end than the beginning of sth such as a book or a period of time: *The latter part of the article expores three possible solutions.* ◇ *The prices of most goods fell over the latter part of the 19th century.* **2 the latter...** used to refer to the second of two things or people mentioned, or the last in a list: *The London Society and the Victorian Society were both involved, and it was through the latter organization that John Betjeman arrived on the scene.* ➲ *compare* FORMER[1] (3)

lat·ter[2] /ˈlætə(r)/ *pron.* **the latter** (*pl.* **the latter**) the second of two things, people or groups that have just been mentioned, or the last in a list: *There were two separate questionnaires, one for employers and one for workers; the present study used the latter.* ➲ *compare* FORMER[2]

lat·tice /ˈlætɪs/ *noun* a structure that is made of long thin pieces that cross over each other with spaces shaped like a diamond between them: *Zeolites are a group of minerals with hollow crystal lattices that make them useful as industrial sieves.*

laugh /lɑːf; *NAmE* læf/ *verb* **1** [I] **~ (at sth)** to make the sounds and movements of your face that show you are happy or think sth is funny: *Laughing at a problem can distance it and reduce stress.* **2** [I] **~ (at sb/sth)** to show that you think sb/sth is ridiculous or not sensible: *David commonly worried about performing so badly in front of people that everyone would laugh at him.*

laugh·ter /ˈlɑːftə(r); *NAmE* ˈlæftər/ *noun* [U] the act or sound of laughing: *As you step into the school grounds you can hear the shouting, laughter and songs of children.*

L

launch[1] /lɔːntʃ/ *verb* **1 ~ sth** to start an activity, especially an organized one: *The Bolsheviks launched a propaganda campaign to discredit the Assembly.* ◇ *In 2003, the Ministry launched a new public health initiative.* ◇ *The airline launched an outspoken attack on environmental groups.* ◇ *South Vietnamese troops launched a major offensive.* **2 ~ sth** to make a product available to the public for the first time: *Isuzu has just launched a new product with an explicitly 'European flavour'.* ◇ *The Board of Education plans to launch three new courses in September.* **3 ~ sth** to send sth such as a SATELLITE, weapon, etc. into space, into the sky or through water: *The first meteorological satellites were launched in the early 1960s.* **4 ~ sth** to put a ship or boat into the water, especially one that has just been built: *The ship was launched in 1843 by Prince Albert.*

PHR V **ˈlaunch into sth** to begin sth in an enthusiastic way, especially sth that will take a long time: *The speaker then launched into a lengthy account of her research.*

launch[2] /lɔːntʃ/ *noun* the action of launching sth; an event at which sth is launched: *The company seeks tight control over all aspects of product launches (Grover et al., 2008).* ◇ **~ of sth** *She highlights the launch by UNESCO of the Living Human Treasures programme.*

lava /ˈlɑːvə/ *noun* [U, C] hot liquid rock that comes out of a VOLCANO; this type of rock when it has cooled and become hard: *As lava erupts, the pressure in the magma is reduced and the gas bubbles out.* ◇ **+ noun** *Wherever the side of a lava flow breaks, lava gushes out and starts to form a new flow.*

law /lɔː/ *noun* **1** (*also* **the law**) [U] the whole system of rules that everyone in a country or society must obey: *Contrary to popular belief, few psychiatric patients break the law.* ◇ *The government publishes guidance to help employers comply with the law.* ◇ *The Reform Act was passed by Parliament and became law in 1832.* ◇ **by ~** *Every apartment is required by law to have at least one working smoke alarm.* ◇ **against the ~** *Child recruitment is against the law in Nepal.* ◇ **under the ~** *The constitution specifies that all people are equal under the law.* ◇ **within the ~** *Transparency International gives the highest rating to regimes that always act within the law.* ◇ **in ~** *Shareholders' rights are enshrined in law.* ◇ **~ of sth** *All transactions are enforced by the law of contracts.* ◇ *Muhammad Iqbal believed that Islamic law should be the law of Pakistan.* **2** [U] a particular branch of the law: *Criminal law traditionally sought to balance the rights of defendants against the power of the state.* ➲ *see also* CASE LAW, CIVIL LAW, COMMON LAW, PRIVATE LAW **3** [C] a rule that deals with a particular crime, relationship or agreement: *A Virginian law of 1640 forbade slaves the right to bear weapons.* ◇ **~ against sth** *Laws against sex discrimination and increased support for child care helped open up the workplace to women.* ◇ **~ on sth** *The government introduced strict new laws on food hygiene.* ◇ **under a ~** *Persons convicted under these laws can receive up to two years' imprisonment.* **4** [U] the study of the law as a subject at university, etc; the profession of being a lawyer: *Jefferson studied law.* ◇ **+ noun** (*NAmE*) *She's in law school.* ◇ (*BrE*) *She's at law school.* ◇ *He practised law at a major Brussels law firm.* **5** [C] one of the rules that controls an organization or activity: *The Bible tells us that Moses inspired the people of Israel by giving them God's law.* ◇ **~ of sth** *The deliberate targeting of combatants is, in contrast, permitted by the laws of war.* **6** [C, U] a rule or system of rules for how people should behave: *Kant contended that all moral laws must be self-legislated.* ◇ *Blackstone regarded slavery as an affront to rationality and natural law.* ➲ *see also* NATURAL LAW **7** [C] the fact that sth always happens in the same way in an activity or in nature SYN PRINCIPLE (2): *Maxwell's equations describe underlying physical laws.* ◇ **~ of sth** *The fundamental laws of physics are constant and unchanging.* ◇ *Wages remained low because workers were subject to laws of supply and demand.* **8** [C] a scientific rule that sb has stated to explain a natural process: *The use of nodal voltages means that Kirchhof's first law is automatically satisfied.* ◇ **~ of sth** *The results were predictable in accordance with the second law of thermodynamics.* ➲ *see also* LEGAL, LEGISLATE

IDM **aˌbove the ˈlaw** not required to obey the law: *The judgment underlines the point that nobody, not even the executive, is above the law.* **ˌlaw and ˈorder** a situation in which people obey the law and behave in a peaceful way: *The civil war led to an almost total breakdown of law and order.* ◇ *The president considered using military force to maintain law and order.* ➲ *more at* RULE[1]

▸ ADJECTIVE + LAW **existing, current • international • national, domestic • federal • general** *In these cases, the UK Government is bound by international law.* | **common • customary • criminal • civil • public • private • administrative • constitutional • environmental** *Englishmen were proud of their free-born status, with legal rights in common law.*

▸ NOUN + LAW **human rights • immigration • refugee • family • company • competition • contract • employment • labour • copyright • patent** *This paper will concentrate on women's rights under international human rights law.*

▸ VERB + LAW **obey • follow • violate • be based on • formulate • apply** *Martin Luther King argued that immoral laws should not be obeyed.* | **break • breach, infringe • contravene • respect • comply with • codify • administer • implement • uphold • enforce • invoke • interpret • review • change, amend • reform** *Argentine Federal Police are responsible for enforcing federal law throughout Argentina.* | **pass, enact • make • introduce • adopt • repeal** *Gorbachev threatened to repeal the laws granting press freedom.* | **discover • deduce • satisfy** *Many philosophers have debated whether we discover laws of physics or invent them.*

▸ LAW + VERB **apply • govern** *Corporations remain governed by corporate law.* | **cover • allow, permit • authorize • prohibit • regulate • require • prescribe • protect** *These situations are not covered by EU law.* | **impose • confer • recognize** *Until 1994, South African law recognized only one form of marriage.*

▸ LAW + NOUN **enforcement • code • court • reform** *The investigation was conducted by the FBI and other law enforcement agencies.*

▸ NOUN + OF LAW **rule • principle • matter • body • area, field • source • court** *Arguably, a government's first priority is to enforce the rule of law.*

▸ NOUN + OF THE LAW **application** *The derivation of eqn. 4.2 involves application of the laws of thermodynamics.* | **interpretation • violation, breach • development** *Violations of the law can also have negative psychological consequences for the perpetrator.*

law·ful /ˈlɔːfl/ *adj.* (*formal*) allowed or recognized by law; legal: *The judge ruled that the police had a lawful excuse for entering M's house.* HELP **Lawful** is usually used when talking about whether a particular act is allowed according to the law, when this might not be immediately obvious. To talk more generally about acts that are allowed by law, use **legal**. OPP UNLAWFUL ■ **law·ful·ly** /ˈlɔːfəli/ *adv.*: *The court held that each of the defendants acted lawfully in the assessment of risk.* **law·ful·ness** *noun* [U] **~ (of sth)** *This article debates and defends the lawfulness of compulsory outpatient treatment.*

law·suit /ˈlɔːsuːt; *BrE also* ˈlɔːsjuːt/ (*also* **suit**) *noun* a claim or complaint against sb that a person or an organization can make in court: **file/bring a ~ (against sb)** *Three former employees filed a lawsuit against the company.*

law·yer /ˈlɔːjə(r)/ *noun* a person who is trained and qualified to advise people about the law, to represent them in court and to write legal documents: *Her lawyer argued that she had acted in self-defence.*

lay[1] AWL /leɪ/ *verb* (**laid**, **laid** /leɪd/) ➲ *see also* LIE[1] **1** to put sb/sth in a particular position, especially gently or carefully: **~ sb/sth (+ adv./prep.)** *President Barack Obama laid a wreath at the World Trade Center site.* ◇ **~ sb/sth + adj.** *The structure, when laid flat, can be seen to have three lobes.* HELP Some speakers confuse this meaning of **lay** with **lie**, especially in the present and progressive tenses. However, **lay** has an object and **lie** does not: *The victim was lying at the side of the road.* ◇ ~~*The victim was laying at the side of the road.*~~ **2 ~ sth** to put sth down, especially on or in the ground, ready to be used: *In three months, 2 000 mines were laid.* ◇ *The British now built railroads and laid telegraph cables.* **3 ~ the foundation/groundwork/basis (for sth)** to do the basic work on which further work or achievements can be based: *These pioneer studies laid the groundwork for all subsequent research in the Grand Canyon.* ◇ *Education lays the foundation for the acquisition of new behavioural norms, knowledge and experience.* **4 ~ sth + adv./prep.** to present a proposal or some information to sb for them to think about and decide on: *The proposed sale had not been laid before the creditors.* ◇ *Statutory instruments enacting EU law must be laid in draft and then approved by Parliament.* **5 ~ the obligation/responsibility/blame (for sth) on/upon sb** to make sb responsible for sth; to blame sb for sth: *Employers blatantly ignored the obligations laid upon them.* ◇ *It is inappropriate to lay the blame for this situation on one particular firm.* **6 ~ emphasis/stress on/upon sth** to emphasize a particular fact, idea, etc: *Emphasis should be laid on a physician-guided approach to treatment.* ◇ *Aristotle laid great stress upon the purpose of things as revealing their true meaning and significance.* **7 ~ eggs/an egg** (of a bird, an insect, a fish, etc.) to produce eggs/an egg from its body: *Adult mayflies emerge from the pond and fly only to mate and to lay eggs.*

IDM Idioms containing **lay** are at the entries for the nouns and adjectives in the idioms, for example **lay sth bare** is at **bare**.

PHRV **ˌlay sth aˈside** to not consider or not behave according to sth: *A mother's duty to her children is one that she cannot lay aside, no matter what the emergency.* **ˌlay sth ˈdown 1** to state officially that people must obey or follow a rule or principle: *The Maastricht Treaty of 1992 laid down five convergence criteria.* **2** to discover and express a rule or principle: *In 1687 Isaac Newton laid down the first universal laws of gravitation in his 'Principia'.* **3** [usually passive] to produce sth that is stored and gradually increases: *This eroded material is laid down by glacial deposition.* **ˌlay sb ˈoff** to stop employing sb because there is not enough work for them to do; to make sb REDUNDANT: *With fewer orders coming in, the managers of firms that produce the goods will have to lay off workers.* **lay sth ˈon** (*BrE*) to provide sth for sb, especially food or entertainment: *Lavish festivities were laid on for the betrothal of Louis XIV to Maria Theresa.* **ˌlay sth ˈout 1** to present a plan, an argument, etc. clearly and carefully: *Charles Darwin laid out his theory in a book published in 1859 entitled 'On the Origin of Species'.* ◇ **+ how/what, etc...** *The marketing plan lays out how marketing communication efforts will help meet profit objectives.* **2** [often passive] to plan how sth should look and arrange it in this way: *The chapters are clearly laid out.* ◇ *48 21.5 m plots were laid out, with 0.5-m spacing between adjacent plots.* ➲ *related noun* LAYOUT

lay[2] /leɪ/ *adj.* [only before noun] **1** not having expert knowledge or professional qualifications in a particular subject: *His book explains the theory for the lay public.* ◇ *The panel consists of medical practitioners, a lawyer chairperson and two lay members.* **2** not in an official position in the Church: *She is a Methodist lay preacher.* ◇ *Many Catholics, both priests and lay people, were imprisoned for opposing the regime.*

layer AWL /ˈleɪə(r); ˈleə(r); *NAmE* ˈler/ *noun* **1** a quantity of sth that lies over a surface or between surfaces: **~ of sth** *The soils are covered with a thick layer of partially rotted needles.* ◇ *As people age, the layer of fat under the skin thins.* ◇ **in a ~** *There are deposits of volcanic ash in a layer at least 2.5 cm thick.* ➲ *see also* OZONE LAYER **2 ~ (of sth)** a level or part within an organization, a society or a set of ideas: *These are the individuals who together constitute the various layers of the Council hierarchy.* ◇ *Mehta has added another layer of meaning to the narrative.*

▸ ADJECTIVE + LAYER **upper, top • middle • bottom • additional • multiple** *Thus, people in the top layer tend to have better chances in life than people in the bottom layer.* | **thin • thick • shallow • deep • outer • inner • lower • double • single • adjacent • active** *The wire is coated with a thin layer of silver chloride.*

▸ NOUN + LAYER **boundary • surface • soil** *Most of the ocean-atmosphere carbon exchange occurs within the surface layer of the ocean.*

▸ VERB + LAYER **form • deposit** *These cells form a layer called the retina at the back of the eye.*

▸ LAYER + VERB **surround • cover** *The stomach is a J-shaped, hollow structure surrounded by layers of muscle.*

▸ LAYER OF + NOUN **rock • sediment • soil • skin • fat • cells • material • air** *Roots and rhizomes were buried in a 4-cm bottom layer of sandy sediment.* | **hierarchy • management • meaning • complexity** *Model imperfections thus add another layer of complexity to the problem*

layered /ˈleɪəd; ˈleəd; *NAmE* ˈlerd/ *adj.* **1** arranged in a layer or in layers: *Graphite has a layered structure, and in each layer the carbon atoms form a hexagonal net.* **2** consisting of various levels or parts: *The authors attempt to explain 'Spain's layered and diverse identity'.*

lay·out /ˈleɪaʊt/ *noun* [usually sing.] **~ (of sth)** the way in which the parts of sth such as the page of a book, a garden or a building are arranged: *The new layout and design of the Indiana State Museum has substantially improved levels of visitor satisfaction.*

lead[1] /liːd/ *verb* (**led**, **led** /led/) **1** [T] to be the best at sth; to do sth first: **~ sth (in sth)** *Mumbai studios led the world in the volume of movie production through the 1990s.* ◇ **~ sth in doing sth** *Studies of breast cancer screening have led the way in clarifying these concerns.* **2** [T] **~ sth** to be in control of sth; to be the leader of sth: *He previously led the bioinformatics team at The Sainsbury Laboratory.* ◇ *The same year Napoleon led an expedition to Egypt.* **3** [I] **+ adv./prep.** to go in a particular direction or to a particular place: *There are two wires leading from the transducer terminals to the measuring instrument.* ◇ *Pontefract dominated the old Roman road leading north.* ◇ (*figurative*) *Your conclusion should lead out from the narrow topic of the dissertation to more general issues.* **4** [T] **~ sth** to have a particular type of life: *to lead a normal/double/quiet/happy life* ◇ *Despite leading a life of poverty, she shared whatever she had with others.* **5** [T] to be the reason why sb does or thinks sth: **~ sb to do sth** *In the experiment, participants are led to believe they are administering real electric shocks.* ◇ **~ sb to sth** *The differences between the two sets of results led me to the following conclusion...*

IDM **lead nowhere** to have no successful result for sb: *Five months of negotiations led nowhere.*

PHRV **lead on to sth** to develop into sth; to have sth as the next stage: *The chapter goes on to explore how customer data are collected and used by organizations. This leads on to a discussion of privacy.* **lead to sth** to have sth as a result SYN RESULT IN STH: *Lower interest rates will also lead to an increase in consumer spending.* ◇ *Analyses of the same data can lead to different conclusions.* ➲ language bank *at* CAUSE[1] **ˌlead ˈup to sth** to happen or come immediately before sth: *Bell examined the events leading up to the Constitution's development.* ◇ *The British military* *garrison in Jamaica had been reduced by 30% in the two years leading up to the rebellion.*

▸ LEAD + NOUN **army • team • party • expedition • rebellion • invasion • campaign** *Two philanthropic groups led the campaign to increase Londoners' access to green space.*

▸ LEAD + NOUN + TO DO STH **people • researchers, scholars • authors • critics • commentators, observers • scientists • firms, companies • the government** *The cost of materials has led researchers to search for lower-cost alternatives.*

▸ LEAD TO + NOUN **increase, rise • growth • reduction, decrease, fall, decline • formation, creation, establishment • production • emergence • loss • failure, breakdown • improvement • discovery • identification • understanding • conclusion • change, shift • outcome, result, consequence • problem, difficulty • confusion • conflict • death** *The enormous numbers of fatalities suffered by the army led to the formation of a new department, the Department for War Graves.* ◇ *Disguised or masked anger leads to confusion in the relationship.*

▸ ADVERB + LEAD TO | LEAD + ADVERB + TO **eventually, ultimately • inevitably • naturally** *Continued growth eventually led to a situation where growth was no longer possible.*

▸ ADVERB + LEAD TO **not necessarily • potentially, possibly • easily • usually, generally • always** *Satisfaction does not necessarily lead to loyalty (Varey, 2002).*

▸ LEAD + ADVERB + TO **directly** *It is difficult to conclude that the OECD work led directly to this result.*

lead² /li:d/ *noun* **1** [sing.] an example or action for people to copy: **the ~ of sb/sth** *Following the lead of France, the international community threw its support behind the new regime.* ◇ **take the/a ~** *The zealots took the lead in the violence that led up to the uprising of AD 66.* ◇ *European countries and the United States took a lead on data protection legislation.* **2 the lead** [sing.] **~ (in sth)** the position in front of everyone else: *The early lead in biotechnology research in Harvard University was lost to Stanford University.* **3** [sing.] the amount that sb/sth is in front of sb/sth else in an election or competition: **~ (over sb/sth)** *Just a few weeks earlier, Carter had enjoyed a comfortable lead over Ford in public opinion surveys.* ◇ **~ of sth (over sb/sth)** *Labour started out with a lead of 42 seats over the official Conservative opposition.* **4** [C] a piece of information that may help a company to get new business: *It was common practice among online marketers to use untargeted emails to generate leads.* ◇ *Sales leads should be chased quickly, before interest erodes.*

lead³ /led/ *noun* [U] (*symb.* **Pb**) the chemical element of ATOMIC NUMBER 82. Lead is a heavy soft grey metal, used especially in the past for water pipes or to cover roofs: *Researchers had to calculate the concentration of lead within the water sample.* ◇ **+ noun** *As far back as the 1850s, scientists tried to alert policymakers to the dangers of lead pipes.*

lead·er /ˈli:də(r)/ *noun* **1 ~ (of sth)** a person who leads a group of people, especially the head of a country or an organization: *A summit of world leaders was held at the UN.* ◇ *Party leaders are elected from a short list chosen by MPs.* ◇ **~ of sth** *The leaders of the French Revolution admired Tacitus's passion for freedom.* **2** an organization, a country or a person that is the most advanced or successful in a particular area: **~ (in sth)** *By the 1970s, Japanese companies had emerged as world leaders in factory automation.* ◇ **~ in doing sth** *Ford promised to be an industry leader in developing clean vehicles.* ➲ *see also* MARKET LEADER (1)

▸ ADJECTIVE + LEADER **prominent • effective • charismatic • former • national • local • religious, spiritual • political • military • nationalist • communist • tribal** *Charismatic leaders are distinguished by their ability to move people and organizations.*

▸ NOUN + LEADER **world • party • union • team • opposition • business • project • church • community • opinion** *The team leader's duties vary depending on the number and quality of workers in the team.* ◇ *Business leaders have tremendous indirect political power.* | **market • world • industry** *By the time he died in 1919, Henry J. Heinz's company was a market leader.*

lead·er·ship /ˈli:dəʃɪp; *NAmE* ˈli:dərʃɪp/ *noun* **1** [U] the ability to be a leader; the qualities a good leader should have: *Varying structures and styles of leadership can influence team process and performance.* ◇ *During periods of change and political turmoil, people feel the need for strong leadership.* **2** [U] the state or position of being a leader: **under sb's ~** *Under his political leadership, US fortunes began to soar.* **3** [C+sing./pl. v.] a group of leaders of a particular organization, etc: *The leadership became increasingly aware that it needed economic reforms.*

lead·ing /ˈli:dɪŋ/ *adj.* [only before noun] most important or most successful: *In men under 75, circulatory disease becomes the leading cause of death.* ◇ *Gorbachev was a leading figure in the Politburo.* ◇ *The US has taken a leading role in the creation of the World Trade Organization.* ◇ *a leading expert/scholar/thinker/theorist* ◇ *a leading exponent/advocate of sth*

leaf /li:f/ *noun* (*pl.* **leaves** /li:vz/) **1** [C] one of the thin flat green parts of a plant or tree: *Five mature leaves were collected from the plant and cut into cross-sections.* ◇ *Deciduous trees shed their leaves in winter because of the cost of respiration.* **2** [U] metal, especially gold or silver, in the form of very thin sheets: *Some of the sculptures were painted red and blue and were covered with gold leaf.*

leaf·let /ˈli:flət/ *noun* a printed sheet of paper or a few printed pages that are given free to advertise or give information about sth: *Women used their spare time to distribute leaflets, ask people to sign petitions, and publicize meetings.* ◇ *Patient information leaflets have been shown to reduce patient anxiety while improving knowledge.* ➲ *compare* PAMPHLET

leak¹ /li:k/ *verb* **1** [I, T] to allow liquid or gas to get in or out through a small hole: *In late July, the oil well stopped leaking.* ◇ **~ sth** *Oil and gas pipes may rupture and leak their contents.* ◇ **~ sth into sth** *The polyps often leak blood into the gut.* **2** [I] (of a liquid or gas) to get in or out through a small hole in sth: **~ into sth** *Toxic chemicals are leaking into the earth's groundwater.* ◇ **~ from sth (into sth)** *Haematoma consists of blood that has leaked from veins and capillaries into the tissues.* ◇ **~ out (to sth)** *Heat from the Earth's interior is leaking out to the surface at a rate of about 40 000 gigawatts.* **3** [T] **~ sth (to sb)** to deliberately give secret information to the public: *Louis XVI's ministers began to leak information to the press in the hope of obtaining favourable coverage.* ➲ *compare* DISCLOSE (1) **4** [I] (of secret information) to become known to the public: **~ to sb** *Word had leaked to the press about Westmoreland's request.* ◇ **~ out** *Valuable competitive knowledge may leak out.*

leak² /li:k/ *noun* **1** a small hole through which liquid or gas may accidentally pass: *Water companies have been heavily criticized for the amount of water lost through leaks.* **2** liquid or gas that escapes through a small hole in sth: *The oil rig exploded because of a methane gas leak.* ◇ *an air/oil leak* **3 ~ (to sb)** a deliberate act of giving secret information to the newspapers, etc: *Extensive leaks to the press ensure the meetings are not held entirely in secret.*

leak·age /ˈli:kɪdʒ/ *noun* **1** [C, U] an amount of liquid or gas escaping through a hole in sth; an occasion when there is a leak: **~ in sth** *Significant losses of methane occur from leakages in natural gas pipelines.* ◇ **~ of sth (from sth) (to sth)** *The moisture barrier layer minimizes leakage of water from the drainage layer to the landfilled waste.* **2** [U, C] a deliberate act of giving secret information to the newspapers, etc; an occasion when this happens: *Corruption does exist, mainly in the form of information leakage.* ◇ **~ of sth** *The King was extremely lax about state documents and there had been distressing leakages of information.*

lean¹ /liːn/ *verb* (**leaned, leaned**) (*BrE also* **leant, leant** /lent/) [I] **(+ adv./prep.)** to bend or move from a vertical position: *The headache is aggravated when the patient leans forward.* IDM *see* BACKWARDS

PHR V **ˈlean to/toward/towards sth** to prefer sth, especially a particular opinion or interest: *Coleridge leans towards the view that the language of poetry should differ from that of prose.*

lean² /liːn/ *adj.* (**lean·er, lean·est**) **1** (of people, animals or meat) thin in a healthy way; containing little fat: *He was tall and lean and appeared only about 25 years old.* ◇ *Eating a balanced diet of fresh fruit and lean meat is expensive and may be difficult for poorer families.* **2** (of an industry or a company) efficient and without any waste: **~ production/manufacturing** *Because the goal of lean production is to produce more with less, levels of exploitation can increase.* **3** [usually before noun] (of a period of time) difficult and not producing much money, food, etc: *A dry winter meant a lean year, and a prolonged drought meant hunger and poverty for entire villages.*

learn /lɜːn; *NAmE* lɜːrn/ *verb* (**learnt, learnt** /lɜːnt; *NAmE* lɜːrnt/) or (**learned, learned**) **1** [T, I] to gain knowledge or skill by studying, from experience or from being taught: **~ sth (by doing sth)** *He is learning English by attending language classes.* ◇ **~ sth from sb/sth** *Attitudes to taking medication are often learned from parents.* ◇ **~ sth from doing sth** *There is much to be learned from analysing such changes.* ◇ **~ to do sth** *More and more children learned to read and write.* ◇ **~ how/what, etc...** *There were few opportunities to learn how to use modern technologies.* ◇ **~ (about sth)** *Safely in contact with the mother, the infant begins to learn about the wider social world.* ◇ *Intelligence involves the ability to understand complex ideas and learn quickly.* **2** [I, T] to become aware of sth by hearing about it from sb else: **~ of sth** *Dutton did not learn of the earthquake until he reached Portland ten days later.* ◇ **~ about sth** *The radio was the way people learned about what was happening in the world.* ◇ **~ (that)...** *He was surprised to learn that the eclipse had been visible at Boston.* ◇ **~ what/who, etc...** *When she learned what had happened, she was furious.* ◇ **~ sth** *Xerxes quickly learned the wisdom of Artemisia's advice.* ➲ *compare* DISCOVER (1) **3** [T] **~ sth** to study and repeat sth in order to be able to remember it: *Learning new words involves working memory.* ➲ *compare* MEMORIZE **4** [I, T] to gradually change your attitudes about sth so that you behave in a different way: **~ from sth** *Managers must learn from past strategic mistakes.* ◇ **~ (that)...** *These children may have learned that tantrums will stop the parent from walking away.* ◇ **~ to do sth** *There is more to quitting smoking than learning to cope with cravings.*

IDM **learn a ˈlesson/learn lessons** to learn what to do or not to do in the future because of a bad experience in the past: *The case should be reviewed carefully to determine whether useful lessons can be learnt about future practice.*

learn·ed *adj.* [usually before noun] **1** /lɜːnd; *NAmE* lɜːrnd/ developed by training or experience; not existing at birth: *Culture is a set of learned behaviours that unite a group of people.* ◇ *Nausea and vomiting can be a learned response, e.g. following previous chemotherapy.* **2** /ˈlɜːnɪd; *NAmE* ˈlɜːrnɪd/ having a lot of knowledge because you have studied and read a lot: *His tutor was a grave and learned man.* ◇ *a learned judge/physician/scholar* **3** /ˈlɜːnɪd; *NAmE* ˈlɜːrnɪd/ connected with or for learned people; showing deep knowledge SYN SCHOLARLY (1): *It read more like a learned journal article than a court judgment.*

learn·er /ˈlɜːnə(r); *NAmE* ˈlɜːrnər/ *noun* a person who is learning a subject or skill, especially a foreign language: *Learners tend to prefer bilingual dictionaries.* ◇ *an advanced/intermediate learner* ◇ **~ of sth** *a learner of English/Spanish/Russian*

learn·ing /ˈlɜːnɪŋ; *NAmE* ˈlɜːrnɪŋ/ *noun* [U] **1** the process of learning sth: *Using games to facilitate learning is a growing field.* ◇ *The expansion of commerce and printing made the benefits of learning obvious.* ◇ **+ noun** *Males with Klinefelter syndrome may have mild learning difficulties.* **2** knowledge that you get from reading, study and experience: *He attended numerous church councils, where his learning and eloquence made him stand out.*

▸ ADJECTIVE + LEARNING **lifelong • cooperative, collaborative • experiential • adaptive • social • online** *The research on cooperative learning often highlights the positive benefits of increased student engagement.*

▸ NOUN + LEARNING **language • vocabulary • rote • classroom** *The new system of education encouraged understanding rather than conventional rote learning.*

▸ VERB + LEARNING **facilitate, foster, enhance, promote • impede, inhibit** *Frail older patients have physical and cognitive impairments that impede their learning.*

▸ LEARNING + NOUN **disability, difficulty • environment • style • objective • aid • opportunity • process • experience • outcome** *The learning environment was strictly regulated.*

least¹ /liːst/ *det., pron.* (*usually* **the least**) smallest in size, amount, degree, etc: *The aim is to choose the model that does the maximum amount of explanatory work with the least amount of fuss.* HELP **The least of sth** may be used to emphasize that sth is less important than other things: *If a firm can be assured of selling all that it produces, it may consider marketing to be the least of its worries.* **The least sb can say/do** may be used to suggest that sth could be stated more strongly/more action could be taken: *The least one can say is that the balance of the debate has shifted.*

IDM **at the (very) ˈleast** **1** at the minimum: *At the least there should be completely independent auditing of company accounts.* **2** (used with amounts) not less than: *He had, at the least, been twice to Greece and twice to Spain.* **3** considering sth in the worst way: *Good advertising should communicate quickly at the very least a good, positive brand attitude.* **ˌnot in the ˈleast** not at all: *The German government was not in the least embarrassed by the Petition.* ➲ *more at* SAY¹

least² /liːst/ *adv.* to the smallest degree: *These families are the least likely to be able to pay for childcare.* ◇ *Even the least disturbed sites have been dramatically changed by human disturbance.* ◇ **~ of all** *Not all environmentalists agree, least of all in Germany.*

IDM **at ˈleast** **1** not less than: *Humans have been in the Grand Canyon for at least four thousand years.* **2** used to limit what you have just said or make it less definite: *Such materials have useful properties, at least for limited periods of time.* **not ˈleast** especially: *Industrialization is difficult to achieve, not least because of the legacy of colonialism.* ➲ *more at* LAST²

leave¹ /liːv/ *verb* (**left, left** /left/) **1** [I, T] to go away from a place: *The defendant left without paying for the items.* ◇ **~ for...** *On January 17, 1871, the steamship 'Tennessee' left for Samana Bay.* ◇ **~ sth** *Parents were encouraged to leave the room during the interview as their presence might influence the responses given by their child.* **2** [I, T] to stop living at a place: *Individuals may decide to leave before having decided where to settle next.* ◇ **~ sth** *Rousseau was orphaned at age ten and left his native city at sixteen.* **3** [I, T] to stop going to a school or college, belonging to a group or working for an organization: *We wished to examine the extent to which job satisfaction scores predict staff members leaving.* ◇ **~ sth** *Both of his parents had left school at the age of 12.* ◇ *These issues need to be addressed*

in order to discourage more family doctors from permanently leaving the profession. **4** [T] **~ sb (for sb)** to leave your wife, husband or partner permanently: *The mother subsequently left her husband for another man.* **5** [T] **~ sth (until...)** to not do sth or not deal with sth immediately: *It was decided to leave these questions until towards the end of the interview.* **6** [T] to make or allow sb/sth to remain in a particular condition, place, etc: **~ sb/sth + adj.** *Respondents favoured leaving spending unchanged in a majority of policy areas.* ◇ **~ sb/sth doing sth** *No matter how long the mixture is left standing, only around 10% of it is found to have reacted.* **7** [T] to make or allow sb else to do or deal with sth: **~ sth to sb/sth** *If training is simply left to employers, the result is likely to be an undersupply of the skills needed in the economy.* ◇ **~ sb/sth to do sth** *In Africa, and elsewhere, regimes that had profited from Soviet support found that they were left to fend for themselves.* **8** [T] **~ sth** to cause sth to remain or happen as a result: *The process of soil formation is influenced by environmental factors that often leave traces in soils.* ◇ *Some accounts leave the impression that the countryside was stagnant during this period, but this was not the case.* **9** [T] **be left (of sth)** to remain: *Othello dies as a soldier intent on preserving what is left of his honour.* **10** [T] **~ sth (to sb)** to give sth to sb when you die: *She drew up a new will, leaving the vast majority of the estate to her son.* IDM *see* DESIRE², DOOR, FIELD
PHR V ˌ**leave sth aˈside** to not consider sth: *Again, leaving aside a few exceptions, HDI has been found to be low in poor countries, and high in rich countries.* ˌ**leave sb/sth beˈhind 1** [usually passive] to make much better progress than sb/sth else: *Those who cannot participate in this technology-based society will be left behind.* **2** to leave a place, state or person permanently: *Many immigrants continue to feel a strong attachment to the country they left behind.* ◇ *The glaciers left behind a terrain that slopes upward gradually from the lake-shore to a ridge about 50 km inland.* ˌ**leave ˈoff** to stop doing sth: *Morgan (2003) picks up where Schrecker's work leaves off.* ˌ**leave sb/sth ˈoff (sth)** to not include sb/sth on a list, etc: *The reason he gave for leaving her name off the title deeds was the fact that she was under the age of 21.* ˌ**leave sb/sth ˈout (of sth)** to not include or not mention sb/sth in sth: *The diagram simplifies the picture by leaving out Latin America, Africa and central Asia.* **be ˌleft ˈover (from sth)** to remain when all that is needed has been used: *Disposable income is the income that is left over after taxes and creditors are paid.*

leave² /liːv/ *noun* **1** [U, C] a period of time when you have permission to be away from work for a holiday or for a special reason: *Employees have the right to four weeks' paid annual leave.* ◇ *sick/maternity/paternity/parental/study leave* ◇ *Employees are allowed to take an unpaid leave of up to three months to care for a family member.* ◇ **on ~** *Although their leave is unpaid, employees retain their health benefits while they are on leave.* ➲ *see also* SICK LEAVE **2** [U] official permission to do sth: **~ of sth** *The company allows some employees to take six months' leave of absence for studying.* ◇ **without ~ (of sb/sth)** *No step can be taken about the child's future without leave of the court.* ◇ **~ to do sth** *In practice, indefinite leave to remain in the UK will be granted where certain conditions are met.*

leaves *pl. of* LEAF

lec·ture¹ AWL /ˈlektʃə(r)/ *noun* a talk that is given to a group of people to teach them about a particular subject, often as part of a university or college course: **~ (on/about sth) (to sb)** *She gave a series of lectures on psychology to students at Harvard.* ◇ *to prepare/deliver a lecture* ◇ **~ by sb** *In Paris he attended lectures by Henri Bergson.* ◇ **+ noun** *The question, then, is how to bring about successful learning in the lecture hall.*

lec·ture² AWL /ˈlektʃə(r)/ *verb* [I] **~ (in/on sth) (to sb)** to give a talk or a series of talks to a group of people on a particular subject, especially as a way of teaching in a university or college: *He lectured in physiology to bioscience graduates.* ◇ *Gilman began lecturing widely on feminism.*

lec·tur·er AWL /ˈlektʃərə(r)/ *noun* a person who gives lectures, especially as a teacher at a university or college in Britain: *As well as teaching students, university lecturers are involved in research projects.* ◇ **~ in sth** *For ten years, she was a senior lecturer in psychology.*

led /led/ **1** *past tense, past part. of* LEAD¹ **2 -led** (in adjectives) organized or influenced by: *Student-led demonstrations marched through the capital.* ◇ *Little effort was made to devise new product offerings that were customer-led rather than production-led.*

left¹ /left/ *adj.* [only before noun] on the side of your body which is towards the west when you are facing north: *After the accident, he continued to work with great fortitude, using his left hand to paint.* OPP RIGHT² (6) ■ **left** *adv.*: *The London Safety Unit wanted to highlight the dangers cyclists faced when lorries were turning left.*

left² /left/ *noun* **1** [sing.] the left part, side or direction: **on the ~** *Look at the drop-down menu on the lower left of the screen.* ◇ **to the ~** *In any given period, a particle spends half its time travelling to the left and half travelling to the right.* ◇ **from ~ to right** *The camera tracks slowly from left to right across the shabby, overcrowded dwellings of the workers.* OPP RIGHT¹ (4) **2** [sing.+ sing./pl. v.] a political group or party whose members are most in favour of social change: *The communists, or the radical left, have formed a group under various labels since 1973.* ◇ **on the ~** *Many on the far left believed it possible to move on immediately from collective ownership to full national ownership.* OPP RIGHT¹ (5)

left³ *past tense, past part. of* LEAVE¹

ˈ**left-hand** *adj.* [only before noun] on or towards the left side of sb/sth: *This quantity is the sum of the left-hand sides of the two equations.* ◇ *Match the items in the left-hand column with those on the right.* OPP RIGHT-HAND (1)

ˌ**left-ˈwing** *adj.* strongly supporting the ideas of SOCIALISM: *A younger generation of left-wing activists was determined to expand services and increase spending.*

leg /leg/ *noun* **1** each of the long body parts that connect the feet to the rest of the body: *She had a sharp pain in her right leg.* ◇ *The males shake their hind legs rhythmically.* ◇ **+ noun** *Patients may have leg pain, swelling or discoloration.* **2 ~ (of sth)** one of the long thin parts on the bottom of a table, chair, etc. that support it: *The vertical leg of a tower crane can carry a significant compression load.* **3 -legged** /ˈlegɪd; legd/ (in adjectives) having the number or type of legs mentioned: *These four-legged mammals took to the water not long after the oceans had been vacated by the great marine reptiles.* ◇ *Horses eventually evolved into taller, long-legged animals that fed on grass.* HELP When **-legged** is used with numbers, it is nearly always pronounced /ˈlegɪd/; in other adjectives it can be pronounced /ˈlegɪd/ or /legd/. **4 ~ (of sth)** one part of a journey or process: *Bauxite was loaded onto rail cars for the final leg of the journey to the upper Saguenay.*

leg·acy /ˈlegəsi/ *noun* (*pl.* -ies) **1** money or property that is given to you after sb dies SYN INHERITANCE (2): *William used a legacy from his parents to fund his purchase of the property.* **2** a situation that exists now because of events that took place in the past: *Each immigrant has their own cultural legacy and their own story of the struggle to assimilate.* ◇ **~ of sth** *This long history of conflict has left a legacy of mistrust and suspicion on all sides.*

prepare for sth: *Organizations cannot legislate for every contingency.*

legal AWL /ˈliːɡl/ *adj.* **1** [only before noun] connected with the law: *EU institutions put in place a robust legal framework for the single currency.* ◇ *The decision was political rather than legal.* ◇ *The manner in which companies buy and sell information about individuals raises a number of ethical and legal issues.* **2** allowed or required by law: *Almost every country in the world provides the legal right for women to participate in politics.* ◇ *There is no legal requirement currently to sell tobacco products behind the counter.* ◇ *Job advertisements that expressly require an applicant to be a certain gender or age are legal in some countries, unlike in the USA and UK.* OPP ILLEGAL

> **WORD FAMILY**
> legal *adj.*
> legally *adv.*
> legality *noun*
> illegal *adj.*
> illegally *adv.*
> illegality *noun*

▸ LEGAL + NOUN **system • order • regime • framework • basis • rule • norm • principle • regulation • status • authority • tradition • proceedings, action • aid • protection • representation • advice • adviser • scholar • profession • issue • position** *Access to justice is regarded by the judges as being a fundamental principle of the English legal system.* | **right • obligation, duty, requirement • owner** *In this case, the legal owner had left his farm to the claimant by will.*

▸ ADVERB + LEGAL **purely, strictly** *In the past, the territorial boundaries of states had a purely legal significance.*

ˌlegal ˈaid *noun* [U] money that is given by the government or another organization to sb who needs help to pay for legal advice: *To obtain legal aid in these cases, a person's income must be below the poverty line.*

le·gal·ity AWL /liːˈɡæləti/ *noun* (*pl.* -ies) **1** [U] **~ (of sth)** the fact of being allowed by law: *The Court of Justice reviews the legality of legislative acts.* ◇ *The most common route to challenge the legality of detention has been judicial review.* OPP ILLEGALITY (1) **2** [C, usually pl.] the legal aspect of an action or a situation: *The terms of business include legalities and details such as ownership of materials and intellectual property.*

le·gal·ly AWL /ˈliːɡəli/ *adv.* in a way that is allowed or required by law; in a way that is connected with the law: *They intend the agreement to be a legally binding contract.* ◇ *legally permissible/enforceable/valid* ◇ *legally responsible/liable/accountable* ◇ *A business group is defined here as a group of legally independent firms linked together in formal and informal ties (Khanna and Yafeh, 2007).* ◇ *Legally, Canada's claim to about one-third of the Arctic region appears well founded.*

le·gend /ˈledʒənd/ *noun* **1** [C, U] a story from ancient times about people and events, that may or may not be true; this type of story SYN MYTH (1): *Classical myths and heroic legends developed largely before the historical period.* ◇ **~ of sb/sth** *The legend of Cleopatra has proved even more powerful than her historical record.* ◇ **in ~** *Magna Carta became enshrined in English legend as the source of English liberties.* ◇ **according to ~** *According to legend, St Patrick banished all the snakes from Ireland.* **2** [C] (*technical*) the explanation of a map or a diagram in a book SYN KEY² (6): *See the figure legend for more information.*

le·gis·late AWL /ˈledʒɪsleɪt/ *verb* **1** [I, T] to make a law affecting sth: *The Carolingians legislated to try to safeguard the lands of the free peasantry.* ◇ **~ against sth** *Since the 1970s, the government has attempted to legislate against racial discrimination in Britain.* ◇ **~ for sth** *The government has now legislated for greater accountability in local government.* ◇ **~ on sth** *The question of where the power to legislate on same-sex marriage lies is very contentious in Australia.* ◇ **~ sth** *The coalition government succeeded in legislating a new law.* **2** [I] **~ (for/against sth)** to prepare for sth: *Organizations cannot legislate for every contingency.*

le·gis·la·tion AWL /ˌledʒɪsˈleɪʃn/ *noun* [U] **1** a law or set of laws passed by a parliament: *A directive is the most common form of EU legislation.* ◇ **~ on sth** *The EU introduced legislation on the labelling of GM food products.* ◇ **under ~** *Under the new legislation, all registration of religious organizations took place through the Ministry of Justice.* ◇ **~ to do sth** *The Conservatives promised to enact stronger legislation to prevent employers from discriminating against women.* **2** the process of making and passing laws: *The department recognized that the issue was suitable for legislation.*

▸ ADJECTIVE + LEGISLATION **national, domestic • federal • draft • relevant • primary • secondary • environmental** *Japan has some limited national legislation to promote family-friendly policies in the workplace.*

▸ NOUN + LEGISLATION **anti-discrimination • employment • immigration • data protection** *The USA was one of the earliest countries to pass comprehensive anti-discrimination legislation.*

▸ VERB + LEGISLATION **propose • draft, prepare • introduce, initiate • pass, approve, enact, adopt • implement • enforce • interpret, construe • review • amend • repeal** *Parliament had followed a standard formula in drafting the legislation.*

▸ LEGISLATION + VERB **govern, cover • prohibit • restrict • regulate • require** *Legislation governing the use of motorcycle helmets was implemented in Taiwan on 1 June 1997.*

▸ PHRASE **piece of legislation** *Congress passed several key pieces of legislation to improve existing parks and expand the national park system.*

le·gis·la·tive AWL /ˈledʒɪslətɪv; *NAmE* ˈledʒɪsleɪtɪv/ *adj.* [only before noun] connected with the act of making and passing laws: *Departmental Select Committees are likely to play a greater role in the legislative process in the future.* ◇ *The Scottish Parliament possesses legislative powers with responsibility for a variety of policy areas.* ◇ *legislative proposals/initiatives/procedures/acts/measures* ➲ *compare* EXECUTIVE² (2)

le·gis·la·tor AWL /ˈledʒɪsleɪtə(r)/ *noun* a member of a group of people that has the power to make laws: *In Argentina, female legislators are elected under a 1991 gender quota law.*

le·gis·la·ture AWL /ˈledʒɪsleɪtʃə(r)/ *noun* a group of people who have the power to make and change laws: *Republicans control majorities in both chambers in 25 state legislatures.* ◇ *The new family law was debated and passed by the legislature.* ➲ *compare* EXECUTIVE¹ (2), JUDICIARY

legitimacy /lɪˈdʒɪtɪməsi/ *noun* [U] **1 ~ (of sth)** the ability to be defended with a fair and acceptable reason: *Politicians try to apply scientific evidence in order to give legitimacy to their policies.* ◇ *The theory has increasingly gained legitimacy among social scientists.* ◇ *to question/challenge/undermine the legitimacy of sth* **2 ~ (of sth)** a way of behaving that obeys the law or rules: *People may see the police as legitimate, but may question the legitimacy of the laws they enforce.* **3 ~ (of sth)** the state of having the legal right to sth: *Conceptually, the rebels recognized the legitimacy of their rulers, as sanctioned by God.* **4 ~ (of sb)** the fact of a child being born when its parents are legally married to each other: *The question of the legitimacy of children is central to the Asian family.*

le·git·im·ate /lɪˈdʒɪtɪmət/ *adj.* **1** for which there is a fair and acceptable reason SYN VALID (1), JUSTIFIABLE: *The union had a perfectly legitimate expectation to be consulted.* ◇ *Companies should manage effectively relationships with anyone who has a legitimate interest in their activities.* **2** allowed and acceptable according to the law SYN LEGAL (2): *Where a global regulator does not enjoy* *legitimate authority it cannot legislate law norms.* OPP ILLEGITIMATE (1) **3** (of a child) born when its parents are legally married to each other: *Mothers, and the fathers of legitimate children, automatically have parental responsibility.* OPP ILLEGITIMATE (2) **4** having the legal right to have sb's title when that person dies: *He was Henry I's legitimate heir.*

legitimately /lɪˈdʒɪtɪmətli/ *adv.* **1** in a way that can be defended with a fair and acceptable reason: *Both sides in this debate can legitimately claim that they seek to protect the public interest.* **2** in a way that is allowed according to the law or rules: *There are also many migrants who are legitimately in the UK but who are in breach of their conditions of stay, for instance by working.*

le·git·im·ize (*BrE also* **-ise**) /lɪˈdʒɪtəmaɪz/ *verb* **1 ~ sth** to make sth that is wrong or unfair seem acceptable: *We should be suspicious about state leaders' motivation when they invoke human rights to legitimize military action.* **2 ~ sth** to make sth legal: *The fact that his wife worked in Ireland for six months could not legitimize his stay in the UK.* **3 ~ sb** to give a child whose parents are not married to each other the same rights as those whose parents are: *The Legitimacy Act, 1926, enabled a child born outside marriage to be legitimized by the subsequent marriage of the parents.*

leis·ure /ˈleʒə(r); *NAmE* ˈliːʒər/ *noun* [U] time that is spent doing what you enjoy when you are not working or studying; free time: *These days we have more money and more leisure to enjoy it.* ◇ **+ noun** *The river is used for rowing, waterskiing and other leisure activities.* ◇ *Parents of young children, especially mothers, enjoy very little leisure time.*

lend /lend/ *verb* (**lent**, **lent** /lent/) **1** [T, I] (of a bank or financial institution) to give money to sb on condition that they pay it back over a period of time and pay interest on it: **~ (sth) (to sb)** *The Federal Reserve System also lends money to private banks.* ◇ *Trying to get the financial system lending again was seen as a priority.* ◇ **~ sb sth** *In order to prevent a financial crisis, the IMF lent Argentina large sums of money in 2000.* OPP BORROW (1) **2** [T] to give sth to sb or allow them to use sth that belongs to you, which they have to return to you later: **~ sth (to sb)** *Achilles agreed to lend his armour to his companion Patroklos.* ◇ **~ sb sth** *The US effectively lent Britain equipment for the war.* OPP BORROW (3) **3** [T] **~ support/weight/credence/credibility/legitimacy (to sth)** to make sth seem more likely to be true or genuine: *The findings summarized here lend support to the conclusions.* ◇ *The results lend further credence to the hypothesis that climate change can force volcanism.* **4** [T] to give or provide help or support to sb/sth: **~ sth (to sb/sth)** *Governments routinely lend support to technological initiatives which they deem to be in the public interest.* ◇ **~ sb/sth sth** *The Ethiopians, led by Memnon, also lent the Trojans support.* **5** [T] to give a particular quality to a person or situation: **~ sth (to sb/sth)** *The large number of resident aliens who had market stalls must have lent a distinctly cosmopolitan air to commercial society.* ◇ **~ sb/sth sth** *The Japanese consumers have a marked preference for foreign-sounding brand names because they lend the product prestige.*

IDM **lend your name to sth** **1** to let it be known in public that you support or agree with sth: *Like other celebrities, the supermodel lends her name to an endless list of products.* **2** to have a place named after you: *Atlas lends his name to Atlantis, that is, '(Island) of Atlas'.*

PHR V **ˈlend itself to sth** to be suitable for sth: *Tourism, by its nature, is place-specific, and therefore lends itself to geographical analysis.*

lend·er /ˈlendə(r)/ *noun* an organization or a person that lends money: *Mortgage lenders risk losing their money if borrowers prove unable to maintain their repayments.* ➲ *compare* BORROWER

lend·ing /ˈlendɪŋ/ *noun* [U] the act of lending money: **+ noun** *Competition amongst banks and building societies will lead to changes in mortgage lending rates.*

length /leŋθ/ *noun* **1** [U, C] the size or measurement of sth from one end to the other: *The infant's weight and length were measured.* ◇ **~ of sth** *It was found that the pressure difference was proportional to the length of the pipe.* ◇ *The salmon reach a length of up to 90 cm.* ◇ **in ~** *The flame is directed through a gas jet slit approximately 10 cm in length.* ➲ *compare* BREADTH (2), WIDTH (1) **2** [U, C] the amount of time that sth lasts: **~ of sth** *The French government has passed a law limiting the length of the working week to 35 hours.* ◇ *The data were gathered over a considerable length of time.* ◇ **in ~** *Fourteen group interviews of around 1 hour in length were held.* **3** [U, C] the amount of writing in a book or document; the amount of time that a film lasts: *These sequences last for about a quarter of the film's length.* ◇ **in ~** *A complete listing of their entertainment and communications companies would run several pages in length.* **4** (in adjectives) having the length mentioned: *Quani (1982) provides a book-length treatment of the subject.* ➲ *see also* FULL-LENGTH **5** [C] **~ (of sth)** a long thin piece of sth: *The electrode consists of a length of silver wire, which is coated with a thin layer of silver chloride.* **6** [U] **~ of sth** the full distance that a thing goes on for: *The Green Mountain Uplands extend the length of New England.*

IDM **at... length** for a long time and in detail: *These concepts are discussed at great length.* **go to any, some, great, etc. ˈlengths (to do sth)** to put a lot of effort into doing sth, especially when this seems extreme: *Many multinationals have gone to great lengths to obscure their headquarters' location in order to present themselves as 'local'.* **the length and ˈbreadth of...** in or to all parts of a place: *Sometimes they would travel the entire length and breadth of the country.* ➲ *more at* ARM[1]

length·en /ˈleŋθən/ *verb* [I, T] to become longer; to make sth longer: *Growing seasons have lengthened as a result of the changing climate.* ◇ **~ sth** *The one big problem with consultation is that it lengthens the process.* OPP SHORTEN

lengthy /ˈleŋθi/ *adj.* (**length·ier**, **lengthi·est**) very long, and often too long, in time or size: *The effects of a recession can persist for a lengthy period.* ◇ *The drafting of the document was a lengthy process.*

lens /lenz/ *noun* **1** a curved piece of glass or plastic that makes things look larger, smaller or clearer when you look through it: **through a ~** *An SLR camera means a camera where the viewfinder looks directly through the camera lens.* ➲ *see also* CONTACT LENS, OBJECTIVE[1] (2) **2** (*anatomy*) the transparent part of the eye, behind the PUPIL, that FOCUSES light so that you can see clearly: *As a medical student, he had discovered how the lens of the eye changes shape as it focuses on objects at different distances.* **3** a way of understanding or thinking about sth: **through a ~** *Language ideology is the lens through which Philip Seargeant examines English in Japan.*

lent *past tense, past part. of* LEND

les·bian /ˈlezbiən/ *adj.* [only before noun] (of a woman) sexually attracted to other women: *Research finds that gay and lesbian couples tend to be relatively egalitarian (Heaphy, 2007).* ➲ *compare* GAY[1], HOMOSEXUAL ■ **les·bian** *noun*: *There are other equality issues of concern to gays and lesbians beyond discrimination in employment.* **les·bian·ism** *noun* [U] *She critically examines representations of lesbianism in film.*

le·sion /ˈliːʒn/ *noun* (*medical*) damage to the skin or part of the body caused by injury or illness: *The disease causes skin lesions.*

less¹ /les/ *det., pron.* used with uncountable nouns to mean 'a smaller amount of': *As less food gets into the patient, a large amount of weight is lost.* ◇ *Women with children generally spend less time working.* ◇ *Big firms tend to spend less on research (as a fraction of their total revenues).* ◇ **~ than sth** *Up to 38 cm of rain fell in less than 6 hours.* ◇ **~ of a... (than sth)** *Perhaps the curriculum offered in primary schools poses less of a challenge to children from advantaged backgrounds.* HELP In spoken English, people often use **less** with plural nouns. This is not considered correct in academic writing, and **fewer** should be used instead: *There has been a trend for women to have fewer children.* ◇ ~~*less children*~~ OPP MORE¹

IDM **ˌless and ˈless** smaller and smaller amounts: *The medication he was taking seemed to have less and less effect on his symptoms as time went on.* **no less than...** used to emphasize a large amount: *The results identified no less than 22 factors that might be involved.*

less² /les/ *adv.* to a smaller degree; not so much: *Workers in the US and Europe often lose their jobs because consumers are buying less expensive goods made elsewhere.* ◇ *On average, working-class families read less often to their children relative to professional middle-class families.* ◇ **no ~ a... (than...)** *No less a figure than Catherine II owed her crown to the overthrow and murder of her husband, Peter III.* OPP MORE²

IDM **ˌless and ˈless** continuing to become smaller in amount: *The immune system of an individual infected by HIV weakens over time, leaving the body less and less able to combat infection.* **less than** not at all: *The evidence on both sides is less than conclusive.*

less³ /les/ *prep.* used before a particular amount that must be taken away from the amount just mentioned SYN MINUS¹: *His share is 162 500 less 25 000, i.e., 137 500.*

less·en /ˈlesn/ *verb* [I, T] to become or make sth smaller, weaker or less important SYN DIMINISH (1): *The dose can be adjusted downwards as the symptoms lessen.* ◇ **~ sth** *The effect of a merger may be to substantially lessen competition.* ◇ *The website suggests techniques employers may adopt to lessen any adverse impact on employees with disabilities.* ■ **less·en·ing** *noun* [sing., U] **~ of sth** *Many people thought that the environmental crisis would be the key for the lessening of international tensions.*

less·er /ˈlesə(r)/ *adj.* [only before noun] **1** not as great in size, amount or importance as sth/sb else: *To a greater or lesser degree, this is a worldwide problem.* ◇ *Indonesia, Thailand, Japan, South Korea, and to a lesser extent Taiwan, restricted foreign direct investment.* ◇ *Diesel (CI) engines generally emit lesser amounts of CO and HC than SI engines.* OPP GREATER **2** used in the names of some types of animals, birds or plants that are smaller than similar kinds: *The herring gull (Larus argentatus) and the lesser black-backed gull (Larus fuscus) qualify as distinct species.* OPP GREAT (9) ■ **less·er** *adv.*: *The authors analyse works by lesser-known nineteenth-century novelists such as Reade and Frederick William Robinson.*

IDM **the ˌlesser of two ˈevils | the ˌlesser ˈevil** the less unpleasant of two unpleasant choices: *The newspaper called on Social Democratic voters to support the National Social candidate as the lesser evil, against the conservatives.*

les·son /ˈlesn/ *noun* **1** a period of time in which sb is taught sth: *The class has all its lessons in this room.* ◇ *A few quantitative studies have documented how Chinese university students participate in English lessons.* ◇ **~ in sth** *He was again forced to offer private lessons in mathematics to support himself.* ➲ *compare* CLASS¹ (4) **2** something that is learned or intended to be learned from experience or study: **~ from sth** *Keynes drew this lesson from the experience of the Great Depression.* ◇ *Harsh lessons were learned from the failure of this policy.* ◇ **~ about sth** *The long war taught Sparta a vital lesson about the centrality of naval power.* ◇ **~ of sth** *Section 6 applies the lessons of the chapter to the analysis of how a currency union operates.* **3** an experience, especially an unpleasant one, that sb can learn from so that it does not happen again in the future: *This lesson was not lost on the followers of Abd al-Wahhab.* ◇ **~ to sb** *Some unfortunates had their ears, nose or eyes cut away and were then released, as a lesson to others.* IDM *see* LEARN

let /let/ *verb* (**let·ting, let, let**) **1** [no passive] to allow sb to do sth or sth to happen without trying to stop it: **~ sb/sth do sth** *They maximized productivity by letting a robot transport the finished parts from machine to machine.* ◇ *Pores in the cell membrane let the potassium ions pass, but block the passage of sodium ions.* ◇ **~ sb/sth** *The justifications could probably go on forever, if we let them.* **2 ~ sb/sth do sth** to give sb permission to do sth: *They would not let him leave the country.* **3 ~ sb/sth + adv./prep.** to allow sb/sth to go somewhere: *The local neural network acts as a gate, deciding which signal to let through to the brain.* **4** [no passive] **~ me/us do sth** used to introduce what you are going to say or do: *Let me give some examples of how this works.* ◇ *Now let us consider the second row of the table.* HELP The phrase **Let me/us...** is a good way of moving your explanation forward when you are giving a spoken presentation. You will also find this phrase used a lot in textbooks written by experts for students, which often use the style and tone of a lecture. However, *Let me/us...* is not used in expert research articles and is best avoided in more formal academic writing. **5 ~ sb/sth do sth** (*technical*) used to say that you are supposing sth to be true when you calculate sth: *In the calculation below, let X be the partial pressure of nitrogen produced.*

IDM Most idioms containing **let** are at the entries for the nouns and adjectives in the idioms, for example **let alone** is at **alone**. **ˌlet ˈgo (of sth)** to give up an idea or an attitude; to give up control of sth: *The process involves letting go of preoccupation with past mistakes.* ◇ *Governments let go of power in favour of international corporations.* **let us ˈsay** used when making a suggestion or giving an example: *For now, let us say that the investment is simply a given amount, denoted by I.*

PHR V **ˌlet sb ˈdown** to fail to help or support sb as was hoped or expected: *Investors are being let down by their representatives.* **ˌlet sb/sth ˈdown** to make sb/sth less successful than they/it should be: *The interviews were let down by poor recording.*

le·thal /ˈliːθl/ *adj.* causing or able to cause death SYN DEADLY, FATAL (1): *This is approximately 75 times the lethal dose for human beings.* ◇ *Policy changes are urgently needed in light of the increasing use of lethal weapons amongst juveniles.*

let·ter /ˈletə(r)/ *noun* **1** [C] a message that is written down or printed on paper and usually put in an envelope and sent to sb: **~ (of sth) (to sb)** *He wrote a formal letter of complaint to the company.* ◇ **~ (from sb)** *Both defendants claimed that they had received no letter from the bank.* ◇ *Send a covering letter with your CV to show how you meet the essential criteria listed in the job specification.* **2** [C] a written or printed sign representing a sound used in speech: *Sets are usually denoted by capital letters such as S, A, B, X, etc.* ◇ *The title was written in large bold letters.* **3 the letter of sth** [sing.] the exact words of a rule or statement rather than its general meaning: *The court will apply the strict letter of the law.* ◇ *They risk going beyond the letter and the spirit of the treaty.*

IDM **to the ˈletter** doing exactly what sb/sth says, paying attention to every detail: *Once the manufacturer establishes the rules, they should be followed to the letter.*

level¹ /ˈlevl/ *noun* **1** [C] the amount of sth that exists in a particular situation at a particular time: *Disability increases with age, reaching very high levels after age 62.* ◇ **~ of sth** *Sweden achieved very low levels of unemployment that year.* ◇ *Shallow breathing increases the level of carbon dioxide in the bloodstream.* ◇ **at a... ~** *If government spending continues at the same level while tax revenues decline, the result will be a government deficit.* ➲ *see also* ENERGY LEVEL, HIGH-LEVEL (4), LOW-LEVEL (1) **2** [C, U] a particular standard or quality: *80% of European students achieve these levels in reading and maths.* ◇ *Candidates must be educated to degree level.* ◇ **~ of sth** *These national associations have reached a high level of training and experience.* ◇ **at a... ~** *The study emphasized that fundamental changes must occur in education at every level.* **3** [U, C] **at (the)... ~** a position or rank in a scale of size or importance: *Important decisions about the company's future are made at board level.* ◇ *These loci have revealed much about how natural selection acts at the molecular level.* ➲ *see also* HIGH-LEVEL (1), LOW-LEVEL (2) **4** [C] a particular way of looking at, reacting to or understanding sth: **on one/various, etc. level(s)** *Tantric teachings can be understood on various levels.* ◇ *On one level, the novel seems simply to tell the story of a Christian conversion.* ◇ **at a... ~** *Poetry communicates in unexpected ways and often at a deeper level than prose.* **5** [C, U] the height of sth in relation to the ground or to what it used to be: *Water levels were falling rapidly by evaporation alone.* ◇ **at... ~** *High pressure weather systems can result in the trapping of air pollution at ground level.* ◇ **above/below a... ~** *The terrain rises to a height of approximately 175 m above the lake level.* ➲ *see also* HIGH-LEVEL (3), LOW-LEVEL (3), SEA LEVEL

▸ ADJECTIVE + LEVEL **high • low • different • same • overall • average • minimum** *By controlling the overall level of emissions, governments hope to limit the impact on the environment.* | **elevated, increased • increasing • certain • current • general • optimal • appropriate • acceptable • normal** *Maximum acceptable nitrate levels in water are frequently set at 50 mg/l.* | **advanced • intermediate • basic • educational** *Improving the educational level of a potential workforce does not immediately create new jobs.* | **local • regional • state • national • international • global • individual • different • same • molecular** *Work at the local, state and national levels should be done collaboratively.* | **high • low • mean • global** *The ground surface is flat and lies 3 m above mean sea level .*

▸ NOUN + LEVEL **price • income • output • glucose • cholesterol • baseline** *This reduction was independent of the baseline level of cholesterol.* | **ground • water • sea • ocean • river • lake** *Over the last 20 000 years, melting glaciers have raised ocean levels by over one hundred metres.*

▸ VERB + LEVEL **achieve, reach, attain • raise** *Mothers who work full-time tend to have attained a higher level of education than other mothers.* | **raise, elevate • lower • indicate** *Such warming will melt polar ice caps and raise global sea levels.* | **have • report • increase • reduce • maintain, sustain • exceed • determine • measure • assess • monitor • compare • experience • exhibit, display, show • reflect • set • regulate, control** *Therapeutic drugs, known as statins, have been developed to reduce cholesterol levels.* ◇ *The surveys show a low level of oil pollution in the coastal waters.*

▸ LEVEL + VERB **rise • fall, drop, decline** *When water levels rise once more, aquatic species return.* | **increase • decrease • vary** *Income levels vary considerably across the country.*

▸ NOUN + IN LEVEL **increase, rise • fall, drop • change • fluctuation** *The rapids change with each change in water level of the river.* | **reduction, decrease • difference • variation** *Any variation in the level of oxygen might be expected to affect animal physiology.* | **increase • improvement** *There is a need for massive improvements in skill levels.*

level² /ˈlevl/ *adj.* **1** having a flat surface that does not slope: *Japanese houses are generally small on account of the severe shortage of level ground on which to build.* ◇ *Place the plate on a level surface for 30–40 minutes.* **2 ~ (with sth)** having the same height, position, value, etc. as sth: *The transducer needs to be kept horizontally level with the patient's heart.*

level³ /ˈlevl/ *verb* (**-ll-**, *US* **-l-**)

PHR V **ˈlevel sth against/at sb** to say in a public way that sb is to blame for sth, especially a crime or a mistake: *A criticism often levelled at teachers is that the parent was not given feedback.* ◇ *Many accusations were levelled against current or former members of the party.* **ˌlevel ˈoff/ˈout 1** to stop rising or falling and remain flat: *Additional hours of labour produce smaller and smaller increments of output, so the output curve on the graph levels off.* **2** to stay at a steady level of development or progress after a period of large rises or falls: *During the oil price increases of the 70s, industrial energy consumption levelled off.*

levy¹ AWL /ˈlevi/ *verb* (**lev·ies, levy·ing, lev·ied, lev·ied**) to use official authority to demand and collect a payment or tax: **~ sth** *A public authority may levy a charge for supply of information.* ◇ **~ sth on sb/sth** *Green taxes levied on goods are designed to encourage consumers to make purchases that are less environmentally damaging.*

levy² AWL /ˈlevi/ *noun* (*pl.* **-ies**) an extra amount of money that has to be paid, especially as a tax to the government: *Import duties and agricultural levies make up around 16 per cent of total revenue of the EU budget.* ◇ **~ on sth** *They imposed a climate change levy on fossil fuels burned by industry.*

lex·ic·al /ˈleksɪkl/ *adj.* [usually before noun] (*linguistics*) connected with the words of a language: *A lexical unit has three components: a meaning, a form and a set of combinatorial properties.* ◇ *New lexical items of this type also seem to be entering the English vocabulary in advertisements.* ■ **lex·ic·al·ly** /ˈleksɪkli/ *adv.*: *It is often stated that Quebec French is changing not only lexically but also syntactically in the direction of the dominant English language.*

lexi·cog·raphy /ˌleksɪˈkɒgrəfi; *NAmE* ˌleksɪˈkɑːgrəfi/ *noun* [U] the theory and practice of writing dictionaries: *Equivalence is likely to remain a concept central to bilingual lexicography.* ■ **lexi·cog·raph·er** /ˌleksɪˈkɒgrəfə(r); *NAmE* ˌleksɪˈkɑːgrəfər/ *noun* **lexi·co·graph·ic** /ˌleksɪkəˈgræfɪk/ (*also* **lexi·co·graph·ic·al** /ˌleksɪkəˈgræfɪkl/) *adj.*: *lexicographic traditions* ◇ *lexicographical theory/practice*

lexi·con /ˈleksɪkən; *NAmE also* ˈleksɪkɑːn/ *noun* **1** (*also* **the lexicon**) [sing.] all the words and phrases used in a particular language or subject; all the words and phrases used and known by a particular person or group of people: *These terms have become established words in the English lexicon.* ◇ **~ of sth** *These phrases do not belong to the lexicon of international law.* **2** [C] **~ (of sth)** a list of words on a particular subject or in a language in alphabetical order: *Excerpts translated here are from a lexicon of theological terms.*

li·abil·ity /ˌlaɪəˈbɪləti/ *noun* (*pl.* **-ies**) **1** [U, sing.] the state of being legally responsible for sth: *This Act imposes a strict liability on producers, importers and suppliers of goods that are faulty and cause loss or damage.* ◇ **~ for sth** *The investors of a corporation have only limited liability for its debts or other obligations.* ◇ **~ to do sth** *Potential defendants might incur liability to pay damages.* ➲ *see also* LIMITED LIABILITY **2** [C, usually pl.] the amount of money that a person or company owes: *The balance sheet provides a snapshot of the company's assets and liabilities at the end of the financial year.* ➲ *compare* ASSET (2) **3** [C, usually sing.] a person or thing that a company, person, etc. has that can

L

cause a lot of problems: *These allies might prove to be a liability rather than an asset.* ◇ *Having a large size can be a liability for leading, innovative firms.* ➲ compare ASSET (1)

li·able /ˈlaɪəbl/ *adj.* [not before noun] **1** legally responsible for paying the cost of sth: **~ for sth** *The shareholders are not personally liable for these debts.* ◇ *The component manufacturer is not liable for damage caused by the finished product if the component was not defective.* ◇ **hold sb/sth ~** *In this case, the physician is not held legally liable in the case of harm to the patient.* **2 ~ to do sth** likely to do sth: *Decision-makers are human and liable to make mistakes.* **3 ~ to sth** likely to be punished by law for sth: *Any individual found in possession of these products would be liable to prosecution.* ◇ *The company is liable to a fine for selling to an unlicensed buyer.* **4** having to do sth by law: **~ to do sth** *Managers of companies will be liable to pay compensation if they breach laws and regulations.* ◇ **~ for/to sth** *All classes of young men were liable to conscription into the Red Army.*

lib·eral¹ AWL /ˈlɪbərəl/ *adj.* **1** willing to understand and respect other people's behaviour and opinions, especially when they are different from your own; believing people should be able to choose how they behave: *Younger generations have more liberal views on divorce.* ◇ *Their ideas are fully consistent with liberal principles of freedom and equality.* **2** wanting or allowing a lot of political and economic freedom and supporting gradual social, political or religious change: *The basic ideals of liberal democracy include freedom of speech and freedom of cultural expression.* ◇ *In recent years, Japan has pursued more liberal trade policies.* ◇ *The liberal tradition in International Relations is closely connected with the emergence of the modern liberal state.* ➲ see also NEO-LIBERAL **3 Liberal** connected with the British Liberal Party in the past, or of a Liberal Party in another country: *These groups provided vital support for the social reforms embarked on by the governing Liberal Party.* **4** (of education) concerned with increasing sb's general knowledge and experience rather than particular skills: *The study of politics has always been at the centre of a liberal education.* **5** not completely accurate or exact: *Even in its most liberal interpretation, Orthodox law cannot be completely egalitarian.*

lib·eral² AWL /ˈlɪbərəl/ *noun* **1** a person who supports political, social and religious change: *Economic liberals argue in favour of world market integration in order to promote development.* ◇ *This concern with citizenship is found equally amongst liberals, radicals and feminists.* **2** a person who understands and respects other people's opinions and behaviour, especially when they are different from their own: *He is a liberal who cherishes individual autonomy.* **3 Liberal** a member of the British Liberal Party in the past, or of a Liberal Party in another country: *The 1918 general election witnessed Labour's replacement of the Liberals as the second largest party.*

lib·er·al·ism AWL /ˈlɪbərəlɪzəm/ *noun* [U] liberal opinions and beliefs, especially in politics: *Liberalism is fundamentally based around the liberty of the individual.* ◇ *Economic liberalism holds that the economic system works most efficiently free from political interference.* ➲ see also NEO-LIBERALISM

lib·er·al·ize (*BrE also* -ise) AWL /ˈlɪbrəlaɪz/ *verb* **~ sth** to make sth less strict, especially an economic or political system: *Markets were liberalized as state control over the structure of commodity chains was lifted.* ◇ *Freedom from exchange controls and a liberalized economy have brought a flood of foreign investment into Malaysia.* ■ **lib·er·al·ization, -isa·tion** AWL /ˌlɪbrəlaɪˈzeɪʃn; *NAmE* ˌlɪbrələˈzeɪʃn/ *noun* [U] *They argue that the best way to address global inequality is through trade liberalization.*

lib·eral·ly AWL /ˈlɪbərəli/ *adv.* **1** in large amounts SYN FREELY (4): *Christian traditions teach their members to give liberally.* ◇ *The different schools within Renaissance studies all borrow liberally from each other.* **2** in a way that is not completely accurate or exact: *The court has interpreted Article 8 liberally to include rights of access to personal data.*

lib·er·ate AWL /ˈlɪbəreɪt/ *verb* **1** to free a country or a person from the control of sb/sth else: **~ sb/sth** *Some landowners educated and even liberated favoured serfs.* ◇ **~ sb/sth from sb/sth** *He led the offensive in Greece, liberating Athens from the regime of Demetrius.* **2 ~ sb/sth (from sth)** to free sb/sth from sth that limits their ability to do things or enjoy life: ◇ *New communication technologies are liberating businesses from the need to be located near one another.* ◇ *Birth control was arguably the single most liberating influence for twentieth-century women.* **3** (*chemistry, physics*) to release gas, energy, etc. as a result of a chemical reaction or physical process: **~ sth into sth** *Magnesium reacts with acids to liberate both hydrogen and heat into the surroundings.* ◇ **~ sth from sth** *When atoms of sodium are excited, energy is liberated from them in the form of yellow light.* ■ **lib·er·ator** AWL *noun* **~ (of sb/sth)** *Direct testimonies of survivors and liberators of the concentration camps were collected.* ◇ *The Internet is advertised as a great liberator and equalizer.*

liberation AWL /ˌlɪbəˈreɪʃn/ *noun* **1** [U] the act of freeing a country or a person from the control of sb else: **~ from sb/sth** *The reform of Islam was inseparably connected with liberation from colonial rule.* ◇ **~ of sb/sth** *Presidents since Jimmy Carter have taken proactive roles in ensuring the liberation of captives.* ◇ **+ noun** *A few of these guerrilla groups have been accepted as national liberation movements.* **2** [U] the act of freeing sb from sth that limits their ability to do things or enjoy life; freedom from these limits: *She argues that feminism and gay liberation still have much to achieve.* ◇ *He campaigned in favour of sexual liberation through contraception.* ◇ **~ from sth** *The original teaching of the Buddha involves liberation from sufferings in the mundane world by individual effort.* **3** [U, sing.] **~ (of sth)** (*chemistry, physics*) the release of gas, energy, etc. as a result of a chemical reaction or physical process: *In a chemical reaction, there is a liberation of energy, but only part of this is available to do work.*

lib·er·tar·ian /ˌlɪbəˈteəriən; *NAmE* ˌlɪbərˈteriən/ *noun* a person who strongly believes that people should have the freedom to do and think as they like: *Left- and right-wing libertarians alike are sceptical of any laws that impede commercial free speech.*

lib·erty /ˈlɪbəti; *NAmE* ˈlɪbərti/ *noun* (*pl.* **-ies**) **1** [U] freedom to live as you choose without too much control by government or authority: *The government needs to find a balance between maintaining order and protecting individual liberty.* ◇ *The Union is founded on the principles of liberty, democracy and respect for human rights.* **2** [U] the state of not being a prisoner or a SLAVE: *Children may be deprived of their liberty on suspicion of committing a crime.* **3** [C] the legal right and freedom to do sth: *Each side accused the other of undermining democracy and basic liberties.* ◇ **~ to do sth** *The liberty to speak and think as one pleases is the test of a free country.* ➲ see also CIVIL LIBERTY

IDM **at liberty** (of a prisoner) no longer in prison SYN FREE¹ (3): *They were not detained, because there was no risk attached to their being at liberty.* **at liberty to do sth** having the right or freedom to do sth SYN FREE¹ (2): *A patient is at liberty to request treatment of a particular kind.* **take liberties with sth** to make important changes to sth, especially a book, in a way that is too free, and is not exactly correct: *Hawks's screenplay takes considerable liberties with the novel.*

li·brary /ˈlaɪbrəri; ˈlaɪbri; *NAmE* ˈlaɪbreri/ *noun* (*pl.* **-ies**) **1** a building or room in which collections of books, CDs,

DVDs, newspapers, etc. are kept for people to read, study or borrow: *The reports are usually stocked by university libraries or are easy to obtain on inter-library loan.* ◇ **+ noun** *Accessing texts, images and artefacts online is more convenient than visiting physical library collections.* **2 ~ (of sth)** a collection of books, CDs, DVDs, newspapers, etc. that is kept in a library or owned by sb: *The company hopes to capitalize upon its vast copyrighted library of films, music and TV programmes.* **3 ~ (of sth)** a collection of documents kept in electronic form, available on the Internet or on disks: *They are building a digital library of Internet sites and other cultural artefacts held in digital form.* **4 ~ (of sth)** (*biochemistry*) a collection of DNA FRAGMENTS (= pieces), representing some or all of the GENES of a particular ORGANISM (= living thing): *Regions of interest are hybridized with libraries of fragmented DNA.*

li·cence AWL (*US* **li·cense**) /ˈlaɪsns/ *noun* **1** [C] an official document that shows that permission has been given to do, own or use sth: *The police have the power to seize a vehicle where the driver cannot produce a valid driving licence.* ◇ *They had to decide whether to grant an export licence to the arms company.* ◇ **~ for sth** *The licence for supply and use of the software was costed at £116 000.* ◇ **~ to do sth** *In 1994, they obtained a licence to produce beer locally.* ◇ **+ noun** *Patients registered blind are entitled to a reduction of 50% on the television licence fee.* **2** [U, sing.] **~ to do sth** freedom to do or say whatever you want, often sth bad: *The nineteenth-century setting gives the novelist licence to select and adapt historical materials.* ◇ *Kingship was not a licence to act irresponsibly, since the king's power was circumscribed by law.*

IDM **artistic/poetic ˈlicence** the freedom of artists or writers to change facts in order to make a story, painting, etc. more interesting or beautiful: *Such statements of artistic licence are common in films based on true stories.* **under ˈlicence** (of a product) made with the permission of a company or an organization: *The firm is now planning production under licence in a number of countries.*

li·cense[1] AWL /ˈlaɪsns/ *verb* (*BrE also less frequent* **li·cence**) to give sb official permission to do, own or use sth: **~ sb/sth to do sth** *The government licensed around 1 000 shops to sell goods in foreign currency.* ◇ **~ sth for sth** *Some products are not licensed for use on infected wounds.*

li·cense[2] AWL /ˈlaɪsns/ *noun* (*US*) = LICENCE

li·censed AWL /ˈlaɪsnst/ *adj.* having official permission to do sth: *Research has shown for some years that the majority of drinking takes place outside of licensed premises.* ◇ *The number of licensed physicians in Russia was on average 4.21 per 1 000 population.*

lid /lɪd/ *noun* a cover over a container that can be removed or opened by turning it or lifting it: *The bottle lids should finally be securely sealed and the contents gently mixed.*

lie[1] /laɪ/ *verb* (**lies, lying, lay** /leɪ/, **lain** /leɪn/) **1** [I] (of a person or an animal) to be or put yourself in a flat or horizontal position so that you are not standing or sitting: **+ adv./prep.** *An illustration depicted a man lying on the ground.* ◇ **+ adj.** *The patient will be expected to lie flat for about 60 minutes.* **2** [I] (of a thing) to be or remain in a flat position on a surface: **+ adv./prep.** *Loose objects lying on a table would have rolled off.* ◇ **+ adj.** *A book lies open on a table next to their bed.* **3** [I] to be, remain or be kept in a particular state: **+ adj.** *These factories lay idle while at the same time a significant number of people were looking for work.* ◇ **+ adv./prep.** *Average depths of snow or hail lying on open ground are recorded at official sites.* **4** [I] (of ideas, qualities, problems, etc.) to exist or be found: *He makes clear where his sympathies lie.* ◇ **~ with sb/sth** *The main problem lay with the government rather than with the agency.* ◇ **~ in sth** *The answer lies in further empirical investigation.* **5** [I] **+ adv./prep.** (of a town, natural feature, etc.) to be located in a particular place: *The reef lies 60 km offshore.* ◇ *The city lay on the extreme western edge of the great empire.* ➲ *compare* LAY[1]

PHR V **lie aˈhead** to be going to happen to sb/sth in the future: *An immense amount of work still lies ahead.* **ˌlie beˈhind sth** to be the real reason for sth, often hidden: *Many analysts of social policy have suggested that the intentions that lie behind policies are less important than what they actually achieve.* **ˌlie ˈdown** to be or get into a flat position, especially in bed, in order to sleep or rest: *Patients should be warned to lie down if symptoms such as dizziness or fatigue develop.* **ˈlie with sb** to be sb's duty or responsibility: *The responsibility for change lies completely with the service user.*

lie[2] /laɪ/ *verb* (**lies, lying, lied, lied**) [I] to say or write sth that you know is not true: *The investigator could not tell when they were lying.* ◇ **~ (to sb) (about sth)** *Many people lied to the interviewer about the amount paid.*

lie[3] /laɪ/ *noun* a statement made by sb knowing that it is not true: *There is a strong moral distinction between telling the truth and telling lies.* ◇ *He said that the immigrants had refused assistance; that was an outright lie.*

life /laɪf/ *noun* (*pl.* **lives** /laɪvz/) **1** [U] living things that can grow and develop, for example animals and plants; the fact that they exist: *All life depends on the self-reproduction of cells.* ◇ *These complex ecosystems play an important role in sustaining life on earth.* ◇ *The Sonoran Desert offers the greatest diversity of plant life of any desert in the world.* ◇ *He offers a theory of the origin of life.* ◇ *There is overwhelming evidence that human beings have evolved from simpler forms of life.* ➲ *see also* LIFE FORM **2** [U] the existence of people: *The Constitution guarantees protection of life and liberty.* ◇ *The intention is to protect life rather than destroy it.* **3** [C, U] the existence of a particular person or of particular people: *Prompt treatment saves lives.* ◇ *The patient was displaying no signs of life.* ◇ *Breaches in product quality can lead to loss of life and grave injury.* **4** [U, C] the activities, events or situations that are experienced as part of being alive or as part of being in a particular situation: *Tensions remained part of everyday life.* ◇ *For many, life in urban areas is tough.* ◇ *The condition has considerable impact on the quality of life of affected children.* ◇ *They have all been married at some point in their lives.* ◇ *He began his political life as a revolutionary socialist.* ◇ **+ noun** *Numerous studies have indicated that there is a difference in life chances between social classes.* **5** [C, U] the period of time during which sb is alive: *He spent the rest of his life in a monastery.* ◇ *There is a fear that life must be prolonged at all costs, regardless of its quality.* ◇ *Midlife hypertension is associated with increased risk of dementia during later life.* ◇ **+ noun** *Murder carries a mandatory sentence of life imprisonment.* **6** [U, C, usually sing.] the period of time during which sth exists or functions: *The book started life as a doctoral dissertation.* ◇ **~ of sth** *Companies have sometimes extended the life of their product by licensing its production in a less developed country.* ➲ *see also* HALF-LIFE **7** [U] the fact that sth exists or functions: *The choice of a local partner can mean life or death for a foreign firm.* **8** [U] the quality of being active, exciting and full of energy SYN VITALITY: *She was full of life.* ◇ *These teachers breathed new life and energy into a somewhat tired and troubled school.* **9** [C] **~ (of sb)** a story of sb's life SYN BIOGRAPHY: *His 'Life of Euripides' was written in dialogue form.*

IDM **bring sb/sth to ˈlife** **1** to make sb/sth interesting or exciting: *These stories bring to life the personal histories of these individuals.* **2** to make sb/sth start to show signs of being alive: *The gods brought Pelops back to life again.* **claim/take sb's ˈlife** to kill sb: *The fire took the lives of 146 women and girls.* **come to ˈlife** **1** to become interesting or exciting: *He writes artfully, making his characters come to life.* **2** to start to show signs of being alive: *The*

L

clay birds come to life and fly off. ◇ *He wondered how a dead man can come back to life.* **for life** for the whole time until sb dies: *Judges were appointed for life.* **life after ˈdeath** the possibility or belief that people continue to exist in some form after they die: *Well over 50 per cent have some belief in life after death.* **a life of its ˈown** progress or development of an idea or a process that happens without sb intending to cause it: *Language can have a life of its own.* ◇ *The controversy, voiced through sports radio, newspapers and blogs, took on a life of its own.* **make life ˈdifficult (for sb/sth)** to cause problems for sb/sth: *Closely spaced trees make life difficult for ground-nesting birds.* **take your (own) ˈlife** to kill yourself: *His most famous heroine took her own life.* ➲ *more at* BREATHE, END², FACT, SPRING², WALK², WAY

▸ ADJECTIVE + LIFE **human • marine, aquatic** *Many countries have legislation to prohibit the release of aquatic life to waters where that species does not occur naturally.* | **real • everyday, daily, day-to-day • modern • contemporary • public • national • urban • rural • social • political • economic • cultural • religious** *The Internet plays an important role in many people's daily lives.* ◇ *He dominated Athenian political life.* | **normal, ordinary • healthy • stressful • personal • private • individual • inner • emotional • intellectual • spiritual • married • working • professional** *Community care plays a vital role in helping people live healthy lives.* ◇ *This type of journalism was redrawing the boundaries between public and private life.* ◇ *Employees often remained in the same organization throughout their working lives.* | **early • late, later • adult • entire, whole • long • short • eternal • previous, past** *Throughout her adult life, she suppressed these feelings.*

▸ NOUN + LIFE **plant • animal** *Vitamin D is a natural substance that plays a key role in all human and animal life.* | **family • home • community • village** *Social and family life has also been transformed in the capitalist era.*

▸ VERB + LIFE **threaten • destroy • sustain** *There are those who believe that new technology threatens family life.* | **value • protect • preserve • improve, enhance • endanger** *The State must take reasonable steps to preserve life.* | **risk • lose • sacrifice • give, dedicate, devote • save** *They feared they would lose their lives.* | **live, lead, have • experience • enjoy • rebuild • affect, shape • touch • transform, change • govern, regulate • dominate • disrupt • organize • enrich** *They had never experienced life in a Jewish community.* | **begin, start • extend, prolong** *If cure is not possible, treatment may extend life.*

▸ LIFE + NOUN **course • event • experiences • circumstances • situation • story, history • chances • goals • plan • choices • skills • satisfaction** *Sometimes a change in life circumstances is followed by an improvement in health.* ◇ *She recounts the life story of her grandfather.*

ˈlife course *noun* [usually sing.] the stages of human life that are defined by a person's culture rather than by exact periods of years or biological development: *The majority of citizens follow a standardized life course: marrying at a certain age, producing a family, gaining regular employment, and purchasing a home.*

ˈlife cycle *noun* **1 ~ (of sth)** the series of forms into which a living thing changes as it develops: *Four distinct root types can be observed during the life cycle of rice.* **2 ~ (of sth)** the period of time during which sth, for example a product, is developed and used: *This process should ideally happen across the whole project life cycle.*

ˈlife expectancy *noun* [U, C] the number of years that a person is likely to live: *Life expectancy was 82.4 years for women and 78.7 years for men.* ◇ **~ of sth** *While the national average is 79 years, the poorest men in this city have a life expectancy of 54 years.*

ˈlife form *noun* a living thing such as a plant or an animal: *Despite the diversity of life forms, at the molecular level all life is basically the same.*

ˌlife ˈhistory *noun* all the events that happen in the life of a person, an animal or a plant: *Climatic factors affect the fish at all stages of their life history.*

life·long /ˈlaɪflɒŋ; *NAmE* ˈlaɪflɔːŋ; ˈlaɪflɑːŋ/ *adj.* [only before noun] lasting or existing all through your life: *Technological advances underscore the importance of lifelong learning, as mastery of technology will never be finite.*

ˈlife sciences *noun* (*often* **the life sciences**) [pl.] the sciences concerned with studying humans, animals or plants: *The life sciences, by stimulating children's interest in understanding nature, can also lead to a deeper study of other scientific disciplines.* ◇ **+ noun** *Genetics plays a major role in life sciences research.* ➲ *compare* EARTH SCIENCE, NATURAL SCIENCE, PHYSICAL SCIENCE

life·span (*also* ˈ**life span**) /ˈlaɪfspæn/ *noun* the length of time that sth is likely to live, continue or function: *Recent developments provide some support for potential initiatives to extend human lifespan.* ◇ **across the ~** *Lifestyle, poverty, education, culture and the environment may influence health across the lifespan.*

ˈlife story *noun* the story of sb's whole life: *There is value in the individual life story as it connects to larger issues and contexts.* ◇ **the ~ of sb** *She recounts the life story of her grandfather.*

life·style /ˈlaɪfstaɪl/ *noun* [C, U] the way in which a person or a group of people lives and works: *These people tend to adopt healthier lifestyles.* ◇ **+ noun** *Positive lifestyle choices may affect the course of the disease.*

ˈlife table *noun* a table that, for each age group, gives the PROBABILITY of death or illness of a person before their next BIRTHDAY: *The life table is an essential foundation for estimates and projections in the life insurance industry and pension schemes.*

ˈlife-threaten·ing *adj.* that is likely to kill sb: *a life-threatening condition/illness/disease/complication* ◇ *They do not prescribe treatment unless the asthma is life-threatening.*

life·time /ˈlaɪftaɪm/ *noun* the length of time that sb lives or that sth lasts: *In Japan, business relationships are expected to last a lifetime.* ◇ **~ of sb/sth** *As a result of this agreement, we will save 1.8 billion barrels of oil over the lifetime of the vehicles sold in the next five years.* ◇ **+ noun** *Despite all the changes in work and family, women's lifetime earnings are about half men's, on average.*

lift¹ /lɪft/ *verb* **1 ~ sb/sth (+ adv./prep.)** to raise sb/sth or be raised to a higher position or level: *She has recovered well apart from being unable to lift her left arm.* ◇ *The ad shows a hand lifting the lid from a container of margarine.* **2 ~ sb/sth (+ adv./prep.)** to take hold of sb/sth and move them/it to a different position: *The operator could open the case of the machine, lift out two or more of the wheels, and replace them in a different order.* **3 ~ sth** to remove or end restrictions: *The French government refused to lift the ban on imported British beef.* ◇ *The government finally lifted martial law nationwide.* **4 ~ sth** to make the amount or level of sth greater: *The world economy's productivity levels would likely lift historic growth rates.* ◇ *Managers in these industries took steps to lift their share prices.* **5 ~ sth (from sth)** (*disapproving*) to use sb's ideas or words without asking permission or without saying where they come from: *Large chunks of the essay had been lifted from another source.* ➲ *compare* PLAGIARIZE

lift² /lɪft/ *noun* **1** [U] the upward pressure of air on an aircraft, a bird or an insect when flying: *A wing generates lift, but it also creates drag.* ◇ *In addition to finding the power needed to move forward, a flier needs to generate enough lift to stay in the air.* **2** (*BrE*) (*NAmE* **ele·va·tor**) [C] a machine that carries people or goods up and down to different levels in a building: *He had entered a lift alone on the ground floor.* ◇ *Tension exerted by the cable holding the lift prevents it from accelerating downwards.*

light[1] /laɪt/ *noun* **1** [U, C, usually sing.] energy from the sun, a lamp, etc. that makes it possible to see things, that shines or that is very bright: *Plants compete for light and nutrients.* ◇ *Below 1 000 m, no light penetrates.* ◇ *Plants can turn their leaves towards the light.* ◇ *This laser emits light for only 30 ns during each second of operation.* ◇ *Information is carried by pulses of laser light.* ◇ *This substance produces blue light at the edge of the UV region.* ◇ **+ noun** *The light source is from a laser.* ◇ *A light wave is a pattern of peaks and troughs in an electrical field which travels along at the speed of light.* **2** [C] a thing that produces light, especially an electric lamp: *The material change was enormous too: the rich now enjoyed modern water systems, ate under electric lights, and talked on telephones.* **3** [U] an area that seems brighter than other areas: *The distribution of light and shade in the photograph is evenly balanced.*

IDM **bring sth to ˈlight** to make information known to people: *The intense media publicity brought to light some previous eyewitness accounts of this kind of bridge wobble.* **cast/shed/throw ˈlight on sth** to help people to understand sth, especially in a new way, by providing new explanations or information: *Future field studies may shed light on this question.* ◇ *Since Darwin and Wallace, the evolutionary perspective has cast a new light on numerous unresolved questions.* **come to ˈlight** to become known to people: *Significantly, additional evidence has come to light since the publication of those studies.* **in (the) light of sth** when, or after, considering sth: *Reactions may change in the light of a more detailed description of the case.* ◇ *The results must be viewed in light of the study's limitations.* **in ˌa negative, positive, different, etc. ˈlight** in a negative, positive, etc. way: *These checks are generally seen in a positive light.* ◇ *All governments seek to present their policies in a favourable light.* **see the ˈlight (of ˈday)** to begin to exist; to become known to people: *A new model of car can take two years or more to see the light of day.*

▸ ADJECTIVE + LIGHT **bright • dim • visible • diffuse • ambient • artificial • fluorescent • ultraviolet, UV • infrared** *Each trial was staged under dim red light and recorded over a 24-hour period.*

▸ VERB + LIGHT **emit • transmit • produce • reflect • refract • polarize • scatter • absorb • detect • direct, shine** *Different molecules absorb light at different wavelengths.*

▸ LIGHT + VERB **travel • penetrate, pass through • illuminate** *Some molecules, if they are illuminated by light of one colour, re-emit the light with a different colour.*

▸ LIGHT + NOUN **level, intensity • source • emission • scattering • absorption • signal • ray, beam • pulse • wave • microscope • microscopy** *Light rays of shorter wavelengths are brought to different focal points.*

▸ VERB + IN (THE) LIGHT OF **be viewed • be read • be considered • be interpreted • be understood • be evaluated • be revised • be modified** *Even cautious conclusions may have to be revised in the light of further research.*

light[2] /laɪt/ *adj.* (**light·er**, **light·est**) **1** full of light; having the natural light of day: *The foyer of the building is light and spacious.* ◇ *Species living in dark habitats have white spots, whereas species living in light habitats do not.* ◇ *They left in the morning before it was light.* OPP DARK[1] (1) **2** [usually before noun] pale in colour: *Data paths are shown in light blue.* ◇ *New tissue was light green compared with dark green old tissue.* ◇ *The winter snow is lighter in colour.* OPP DARK[1] (2) **3** not weighing very much: *The boat was light enough to be carried when necessary.* ◇ *When water in a kettle boils, it becomes lighter as some of the molecules escape as a vapour.* OPP HEAVY (1) **4** [only before noun] used to describe machines, vehicles and weapons that are smaller and less powerful than others, or sth that uses these: *They manufacture light trucks and vans.* ◇ *Metro and light rail transit systems are expensive to expand.* ◇ *Examples include light industries that are not technologically advanced, such as food processing and textiles.* OPP HEAVY (3) **5** [usually before noun] less than usual in amount, size or degree: *The fast is broken by a light meal.* ◇ *Much of the rainfall occurs as light showers.* ◇ *These offences carry much lighter penalties.* HELP **Light** foods and drinks contain less than usual of a particular substance, for example fat, sugar or alcohol: *The aim was to replace unhealthy food with lighter options.* OPP HEAVY (2) **6** [only before noun] not serious, difficult or unpleasant: *She concludes the volume on a lighter note.* ◇ *When television first appeared in the United States, it was immediately clear that it affected other mass media that provided light entertainment.* **7** [not before noun] not containing enough important or serious information: *Theoretically the book is very light; and at times it can be repetitive.* ◇ **~ on sth** *Her novels are light on plot and context.* **8** [usually before noun] (of work) not requiring a lot of physical strength or effort: *Older workers were allocated lighter tasks.* OPP HEAVY (4) **9** (of a material or substance) not thick, solid or strong: *For patients wearing light clothes, this is a comfortable temperature.* **10** [only before noun] used to describe sb who does the thing mentioned, but not very much: *Lighter smokers were most likely to support banning smoking in cars with children.* ◇ *Customers may be classified according to whether they are heavy, medium or light users of the product.* OPP HEAVY (6) **11** (*physics*, *chemistry*) used to describe ISOTOPES that have a lower atomic mass than other isotopes of the same element: *When water evaporates, the lighter isotope, ^1H, is preferentially removed, leaving the residual water relatively enriched in the heavier isotope.* OPP HEAVY (7) ■ **light·ness** *noun* [U] *The bridge has an air of lightness and grace.* ◇ **~ of sth** *The book is written with a lightness of touch that makes it highly accessible.* ➲ *see also* LIGHTLY

IDM **(a) light touch** used for saying that sb deals with sb/sth in a gentle or relaxed way, rather than by using their authority: *They managed employees with a light touch.* **make ˈlight of sth** to treat sth as not being important or not serious: *Although Takahashi thought the role of the government for economic growth was important, he did not necessarily make light of the role of the market.*

light[3] /laɪt/ *verb* (**lit**, **lit** /lɪt/) HELP **Lighted** is also used for the past tense and past participle, especially before nouns. **1 ~ sth** to make sth start to burn: *At these ceremonies, small lamps are lit and presents are often given.* ◇ *She lit a cigarette and threw away the lighted match.* **2** [usually passive] to give light to a place: **be lit by sth** *In 1910 most homes were lit by coal gas.* ◇ **brightly/dimly lit** *Their leaves can photosynthesize even on the dimly lit forest floor.*

PHR V **ˌlight ˈup | ˌlight sth ˈup** to become bright with light or colour; to make sth bright with light or colour: *A star first lights up when it contracts from a 'protostar' and commences hydrogen burning.* ◇ *By 1900, a carbon filament lamp could light up a room at 3.7 lumens per watt.*

ˈlight bulb *noun* = BULB (1)

light·ing /ˈlaɪtɪŋ/ *noun* [U] **1** the arrangement or type of light in a place: *natural/artificial/electric/fluorescent lighting* ◇ **+ noun** *The second group, a control group, worked under normal lighting conditions.* **2** the use of electric lights in a place: *Employers have a duty to ensure that the correct heating, lighting and ventilation are available in the workplace.*

light·ly /ˈlaɪtli/ *adv.* **1** gently; with very little force or effort: *The probe is placed lightly on the skin, ensuring an air-free contact using gel or alcohol spray.* **2** to a small degree; not much: *The force was made up of lightly armed forces, using weapons only if attacked.* **3** without being seriously considered: *Changing the original deal was not something to be taken lightly.*

light·ning /ˈlaɪtnɪŋ/ *noun* [U] a flash, or several flashes, of very bright light in the sky caused by electricity: *Lightning strikes somewhere on the surface of the earth about 100 times every second.*

like¹ /laɪk/ *prep.* **1** similar to sb/sth; in the same way as sb/sth: *Profit is like health: you need it, and the more the better.* ◇ *Like her grandmother, she eventually settled in the Middle East.* ◇ *Workers are treated like commodities.* **2** used when giving an example SYN SUCH AS (1): *Writers like Walcott seem to contradict this view.* **3** used after *is, are*, etc. or after a word such as *seem, sound* or *look* to talk about how sth is or how it seems, sounds, etc: *They do not realize what war is like.* ◇ *This may seem like an unrealistic goal.* ◇ *Some of these conjectures sound more like science fiction than science.*
IDM **more like...** used to give a number or an amount that is more accurate than one previously mentioned: *In a macroscopic sample, there will not be twenty or 200 atoms in the chain, but more like 1 020 atoms.*

like² /laɪk/ *verb* (not usually used in the progressive tenses) **1 ~ sth** to find sth pleasant: *Children like the way the teachers treat them.* ◇ *Not everyone liked the idea.* ◇ *Many sufferers do not like the fact that their hair is thinning.* **2** [no passive] to enjoy sth or feel that you want to do sth: **~ to do sth** *Survey respondents do not like to display ignorance.* ◇ **~ doing sth** *They do not like accepting the authority of others.* ◇ **~ sb doing sth** *Young people do not like their parents monitoring their Internet use.* **3** used after *would* or *should* to say what sb wants: **~ sth** *He would like relationships, but feels unable to sustain them.* ◇ **~ to do sth** *People would like to deal with the issues more openly.* ◇ *I should like to make six brief points.* ◇ **~ sb to do sth** *Mrs B would like her grandchildren to know about their genetic heritage.*
IDM **if you ˈlike** (*rather informal*) used when you express sth in a new way: *It could have been a fact: it is, if you like, a possible fact.* HELP This phrase is suitable when you want to sound less formal, for example in speech or in an informal article. In more formal language, you can use **rather**: *Female labour was cheaper (or rather, was paid at half the wage).* **I/We, etc. (would) like to think (that)...** I/We etc. hope or believe that sth is true: *We like to think that our commitment to the school and to its students and families is long-term.*

like³ /laɪk/ *noun* **1 likes** [pl.] the things that sb likes: *Specific dietary advice is necessary, linked to the patient's likes and dislikes.* OPP DISLIKE² (2) **2** [U] sth/sb that is similar to sth/sb else: *Like is connected to like in a network.* ◇ **~ with ~** *The main difficulty is in comparing like with like.*
IDM **and the like | and such like** and similar things; etc: *Schools, hospitals, care homes and the like collectively spent some £60 million p.a. on food.* **the likes of** (*rather informal*) people such as: *The kind of work undertaken by the likes of Jaffe (and a few others) is still very much a minority enterprise.*

like⁴ /laɪk/ *adj.* [only before noun] having similar qualities to another person or thing: *The repulsion of like electric charges can be used to keep nanoscale particles and components apart.* ◇ *The court acts in conformity to the laws, and the government is in like manner governed by the constitution.*

like·li·hood /ˈlaɪklihʊd/ *noun* [U, sing.] the chance of sth happening; how likely sth is to happen SYN PROBABILITY (1): *Most of the risks classified as severe were considered of low likelihood (<1%).* ◇ **~ of sth** *This principle applies where there is a likelihood of environmental damage.* ◇ **~ of sb/sth doing sth** *The operation may reduce the likelihood of the ulcer returning.* ◇ **~ that...** *This difference is consistent with the likelihood that thermal gradients here are lower.* ◇ **the ~ is that...** *The likelihood is that some new products will fail after introduction.* ◇ **+ noun** *A likelihood ratio test compares the likelihood of observing a particular dataset under two (or more) alternative hypotheses.*
IDM **in all likelihood** used for saying that sth is very likely: *In all likelihood, the death toll of the Russians actually exceeded that of the Germans.*

like·ly¹ /ˈlaɪkli/ *adj.* (**like·lier, like·li·est**) (**more likely** and **most likely** are the usual forms.) **1** that can be expected SYN PROBABLE: *Research objectives will address each of the likely causes for the decline.* ◇ *36 possible outcomes exist, and all the outcomes are equally likely.* ◇ *Such an outcome now seems less likely.* ◇ **it is ~ that...** *It is likely that the explanations for health variation are complex.* ◇ **more than ~** *It is becoming more than likely that some of these low-cost airlines will soon cease to exist.* ◇ **how ~ it is that...** *The sales manager must determine how likely it is that the company will benefit from matching the price cut.* **2** if sb is **likely** to do sth, or sth is **likely** to happen, they will probably do it or it will probably happen: **~ to do sth** *Mass migration is likely to occur in response to climate change.* ◇ **more/less ~ (than sb) to do sth** *Older workers were more likely to report low job stress than younger workers.* ◇ **as ~ (as sb) to do sth** *Women are as likely as men to be employed in the informal labour market.* OPP UNLIKELY (1) **3** seeming suitable for a purpose: *Other cell types are more likely candidates for use in cardiac repair.*
▸ LIKELY + NOUN **explanation** • **diagnosis** • **cause** • **consequence** • **outcome** • **impact, effect** • **source** • **scenario** *A more likely explanation is that adults under-report symptoms.* ◇ *Good practice is to identify the most likely scenario.*
▸ LIKELY TO + VERB **occur, happen, arise** • **result in, lead to, cause** • **affect, influence** • **continue, persist, remain** • **increase** • **experience** • **suffer** • **die** • **survive** • **engage in, participate** • **encounter** • **report** • **respond** • **succeed** • **benefit** *These trees should be less likely to suffer from severe drought.*

like·ly² /ˈlaɪkli/ *adv.* probably: *This strong performance likely reflects the success of economic integration in the EU.* ◇ *This deterioration in living standards will likely exacerbate existing health inequalities.* ◇ **more/most ~** *Funding for such subsidies would most likely come from developed countries.*

liken /ˈlaɪkən/ *verb*
PHR V **ˈliken sth/sb to sth/sb** to compare one thing or person to another and say they are similar: *Richard Dawkins has famously likened the process of natural selection to the work of a blind watchmaker.*

like·wise AWL /ˈlaɪkwaɪz/ *adv.* **1** the same; in a similar way: *The researchers introduced themselves and asked participants to do likewise.* **2** also: *Managers agree that customer satisfaction is important, but likewise contend that this is hard to measure.*

limb /lɪm/ *noun* an arm or a leg; a similar part of an animal, such as a wing: *Intact animals moved a greater distance compared with animals that were missing a hind limb.* ◇ *the upper/lower limbs* ◇ *Some adult amphibians and insects can regenerate whole limbs after amputation.* ◇ **+ noun** *The ultimate cause of limb fractures is usually a fall.*

lime /laɪm/ *noun* [U] a white substance obtained by heating limestone, used in building materials and to help plants grow: *Previously drained soils can be treated with lime if the acidity is not too great.*

lime·stone /ˈlaɪmstəʊn; *NAmE* ˈlaɪmstoʊn/ *noun* [U] a type of SEDIMENTARY rock, mostly made up of, used for building and making CEMENT: *This limestone originates in part from shells and skeletons of past living creatures.* ◇ *Portland*

Limestone was loaded into boats on the Dorset coast for Wren's churches in London.

limit[1] /ˈlɪmɪt/ *verb* to keep sb/sth within or below a particular amount, level, size or area SYN RESTRICT (1): **~ sth** *There were several factors that limited the ability of women to work away from home.* ◇ *The existing statistical analyses all have one major problem which severely limits their usefulness.* ◇ **~ sth to sth** *Class sizes were limited to a maximum of 30.* ◇ **~ yourself to (doing) sth** *In this paper, I shall limit myself to describing the most widely used methods.*

PHR V **ˈlimit sth to sb/sth** [usually passive] to make sth exist or happen only in a particular area or within a particular group: *Breast examination should not just be limited to women.* ◇ *The use of this technique tends to be limited to the study of chromosome abnormalities in tumours.*

▸ LIMIT + NOUN **number • amount • extent • scope • range • capacity • use • application • ability • power • access • right • freedom • opportunity • potential • possibility • analysis • discussion • impact • effect • growth** *To limit the scope of the project, we chose to focus only on NGOs with an explicit social justice mission.* ◇ *A low educational level limits access to jobs and other social resources.*

THESAURUS

limit • restriction • control • restraint • constraint • limitation *noun*

These are all words for sth that limits what can happen or what sb/sth can do or achieve.

- limits/restrictions/controls/restraints/constraints/limitations **on** sth
- limits/restrictions/constraints/limitations **to** sth
- control **over** sth
- **within the** limits/constraints/limitations **of** sth
- **beyond the** limits/control/constraints/limitations **of** sth
- **in** control **of** sth
- to be **under/out of** control
- to be **subject to** limits/restrictions/control/constraints/limitations
- to **impose** limits/restrictions/controls/restraints/constraints/limitations
- to **place** limits/restrictions/constraints/limitations
- **tight** limits/restrictions/controls/constraints
- **severe** limits/restrictions/constraints/limitations

- A **limit** is a point or level beyond which sb/sth cannot go; it may be imposed by a law or rule, or it may be a natural limit imposed by the situation; a **restriction** is usually imposed by a rule or law: *The government may set limits on prices.* ◇ *The capitalist economy places certain limits on what the government can do.* ◇ *Foreign retailers operate under tight restrictions.*
- **Control** and **restraint** both refer to the act of limiting what sb/sth can do; **control** is usually imposed by authority; **restraint** may be imposed by authority, or it may be self-imposed, when sb deliberately stops him/herself from going too far: *The government has made visible progress in regaining full control over the country.* ◇ *New restraints were placed on the right of assembly.* ◇ *They were prepared to exercise restraint.*
- **Constraints** are often practical issues that limit what you can do; the **limitations** of a study are the factors that prevented it from achieving more: *Because of time and budget constraints, only the most critical features were thoroughly tested.* ◇ *Finally, the limitations of this study must be noted:...*

limit[2] /ˈlɪmɪt/ *noun* **1** the greatest or smallest amount or level of sth that is allowed SYN RESTRICTION (1): **~ (on sth)** *The treaty itself sets no mandatory limits on greenhouse gas emissions for individual countries.* ◇ *Parents who have difficulty setting limits with children often do not want their child to experience disappointment.* ◇ *to place/impose limits on sth* ◇ *a speed/an age limit* ◇ **~ for sth** *A sample of fish and shellfish from the bay exceeded the WHO limits for lead, mercury and cadmium.* ◇ **to the ~** *Each member state, it seemed, had its own agenda and was prepared to push it to the limit.* ➲ *see also* TIME LIMIT **2** a point at which sth stops being possible or existing: *Wherever the velocity of the fluid exceeds a certain upper limit, the pressure becomes negative.* ◇ **~ to sth** *Of course, there is a limit to the number of questions that can be asked in a survey.* ◇ **~ of sth** *The system has reached the limits of its capacity.* **3 ~ (of sth)** the furthest edge of an area or a place: *Soil analysis can be used to define the limits of an archaeological site.*

IDM **within ˈlimits** only up to a reasonable point or amount: *Provision is made for asylum seekers' access to health care, accommodation and education, albeit within limits.*

limi·ta·tion /ˌlɪmɪˈteɪʃn/ *noun* **1** [C, usually pl.] a limit on what sb/sth can do or how good they/it can be: *Several methods are available, but most have limitations.* ◇ *In order to overcome these limitations, more sensitive and quantitative techniques can be used.* ◇ *A major limitation was the relatively limited evidence base.* ◇ **~ of sth** *Finally, the limitations of this study must be noted.* ➲ thesaurus note *at* LIMIT[2] ➲ language bank *at* CRITICAL **2** [C] a rule, fact or condition that limits sth SYN RESTRAINT (1): *All rights are subject to limitations imposed by international law.* ◇ **~ on sth** *His later philosophy explores the social and economic limitations on human freedom.* ➲ thesaurus note *at* LIMIT[2] **3** [U] **~ (of sth)** the act or process of limiting or controlling sb/sth SYN RESTRICTION (2): *Management of chronic illness focuses on limitation of damage.* **4** (*also* **limitation period**) [C] (*law*) a legal limit on the period of time within which court PROCEEDINGS can be taken or for which a property right continues: *The 12-year limitation period was held by the judge to have ended in 1999.*

▸ ADJECTIVE + LIMITATION **major, severe, serious • important, significant • fundamental • main • inherent • potential • obvious • methodological • physical • practical • technical • functional • cognitive** *Some potential limitations of this study should be discussed.*

▸ VERB + LIMITATION **have • overcome • recognize, acknowledge, note • highlight • discuss • address** *To address these limitations, the present study utilized a relatively large sample of parents.*

limit·ed /ˈlɪmɪtɪd/ *adj.* **1** not very great in amount or extent: *There have been only a limited number of studies on this topic.* ◇ *There is only limited evidence to support this view.* ◇ *There is currently a limited understanding of these mechanisms.* ◇ *Given that resources are limited, cost is clearly a factor.* **2** kept within or below a particular limit of time, numbers, etc: *Tissues from very early embryos can be cultured for a limited time.* ◇ **~ to sth** *The age range was limited to 15–44.* HELP **Limited government** is government by a ruler or government whose power is kept within limits by a CONSTITUTION: *Spencer held that liberal democracy and limited government were the best adapted systems of resolving conflict in society.*

ˌlimited ˈcompany (*also* **ˌlimited liaˈbility company**) *noun* (*BrE*) a company whose owners only have to pay a limited amount of its debts: *There is the risk for those trading with the limited company that they may not be able to seek owed money from those who ran or owned the business.*

ˌlimited liaˈbility *noun* [U] (*law*) the legal position of having to pay only a limited amount of your or your company's debts: *In theory, limited liability makes raising capital easier, as individuals may feel more secure in their investment.*

limit·ing /ˈlɪmɪtɪŋ/ *adj.* putting limits on what is possible: *For many firms, the availability of resources is no longer a*

L

limiting factor in their location decisions. ◇ *The existing economic mechanism has become too limiting for a growing economy.*

line¹ /laɪn/ *noun* **1** a long thin mark on a surface: *Plot the three lines on the same graph.* ◇ *On Mercator's map, navigators could draw a straight line between two points and work out their direction of travel.* **2** an imaginary limit or border between one place or thing and another: *Because the earth is a sphere, the longest line of latitude lies midway between the poles: this is the equator.* ◇ *It is in fact impossible to draw a single line that marks the boundary between the two dialects.* ➲ *see also* DIVIDING LINE, POVERTY LINE **3 ~ between A and B** the division between one area of thought or behaviour and another: *He has blurred the line between fact and fiction.* ◇ *There may be a fine line between genius and insanity.* **4** the edge, outline or shape of sb/sth: *Clean lines emphasize the straightforward functionality of the design.* ➲ *see also* COASTLINE **5** a row of people or things behind each other or next to each other: **~ (of sth)** *At first there were long lines of cars at petrol pumps.* ◇ **in a ~** *The rules require that the dominos be placed in a line so that adjacent dominos have matching numbers.* ◇ (*NAmE*) *The company installed an easy pass system to minimize the hassle of waiting in lines.* **6** a system of making sth, in which the product moves from one worker to the next until it is finished: *an assembly/a production line* ◇ *Each assembly worker fits a part which enables the next person down the line to fit their part and so on until the finished car rolls off the line.* **7** [usually sing.] **~ of sb/sth** a series of people, things or events that follow one another in time: *Mitchell was one in a long line of naturalists and scholars who endeavoured to record basic data.* **8** [usually sing.] a series of people in order of importance: *The blame culture is passed down the line from senior management to middle management, who then blame staff for any inadequacy.* **9** [usually sing.] an attitude or a belief, especially one that sb states publicly: *The USA was unsuccessful in persuading her allies to take a strong line on trade.* ◇ *The official line is that there is no unauthorized migration between the two countries.* **10 ~ of sth** a method or way of thinking about sth: *The purpose of what follows is to suggest some of the possible lines of future thought and research.* ◇ *Critics of liberal culturalism have raised many objections to this entire line of argument.* **11** (*abbr.* l) a row of words on a page or the empty space where they can be written; the words of a song or poem: *The government policies are listed in lines 2 and 6 of the table.* ◇ *The first line of each verse is immediately repeated.* ◇ *In his review of the novel, Charles Baxter quotes the opening lines of the book.* **12** the words spoken by an actor in a play or film: *He delivers all his lines with little expressive variation and little emphasis on any specific words.* **13** a long piece of rope, etc, especially when it is used for a particular purpose: *The principle of the suspension bridge is that of a simple clothes line.* **14** a pipe or thick wire that carries water, gas or electricity from one place to another: *They are prepared for icy conditions because they do not require overhead power lines.* HELP In medicine, a **line** is a tube that carries liquid food, medicine or blood very slowly into a patient's body: *Patients should be started on oxygen and an arterial line should be inserted.* **15** a telephone or Internet connection; a particular telephone number: *It would be quite possible to arrange to control a distant computer by means of a telephone line.* ◇ **+ noun** *Broadband was given away for free, and the company made up for this with its pricing of line rental.* ➲ *see also* OFFLINE, ONLINE **16** a railway track; a section of a rail system: *New lines were almost always for the purpose of opening up new sources of raw materials, thereby adding to the railways' traffic.* ◇ **+ noun** *Some electrification of main line train services occurred in the early years of the twentieth century.* **17** [usually sing.] the direction that sb/sth is moving or located in: **in a ~** *When light passes through air, it travels in a straight line.* ◇ **~ of sth** *In an infinite and unchanging universe, every line of sight from an observer should hit a star.* **18** a route from one place to another, especially when it is used for a particular purpose: *Napoleon either had to abandon the enterprise or push on and extend his supply lines.* **19 ~ of sth** a type or area of business, activity or interest: *As they expanded, US industrial corporations tended to diversify into new lines of business.* ◇ *Our article builds on this line of work and provides evidence on the long-term impact of market potential on economic development.* **20** a type of product: *Micro-planning involves planning the production process for each product line.* ◇ **~ of sth** *The company initiated a $10 million campaign for a new line of basketball shoes.* **21** a company that provides transport for people or goods: *To trade with distant parts of the world, railways had to be built, shipping lines created and banks established.* ➲ *see also* AIRLINE **22** a row or series of military DEFENCES where the soldiers are fighting during a war: *He turned down a safe posting because he wanted to share the common dangers of the front line.* ◇ *They were trapped behind enemy lines.* ➲ *see also* FRONT LINE

IDM **along/on (the)... 'lines 1** in the way that is mentioned: *The Member States argued along the same lines as the District Court of Munich.* **2** similar to the way or thing that is mentioned: *Although this is a small initiative, a major curriculum along these lines would have much to contribute to the development of children.* **be, come, etc. on 'line** to be working or functioning: *New state-of-the-art production facilities were coming on line in each of these economies just as the crisis hit.* ➲ *see also* ONLINE **bring sb/sth, come, get, fall, etc. into 'line (with sb/sth)** to behave or make sb/sth behave in the same way as other people or how they should behave: *The government seemed to have found a way to bring the socialists into line.* ◇ *Members had to fall into line with German monetary policy.* **in 'line for sth** likely to get sth: *Many community members offered to volunteer as a way of getting themselves in line for a job with the organization.* **in 'line with sth** similar to sth; so that one thing is closely connected with another: *The economy failed to grow in line with expectations.* ◇ *The immediate adjustment of prices means that prices rise in line with the wage increase.* **(put sth) on the 'line** (*rather informal*) at risk: *Activists travel to conflict zones and quite literally put their lives on the line.* ◇ *The president refused to put his administration on the line over critical domestic issues.* **out of 'line (with sb/sth)** different from sb/sth: *This opinion now appears quite out of line with evidence on public attitudes.* ➲ *more at* DRAW, FRONT LINE, READ

line² /laɪn/ *verb* **1** [often passive] to cover the inside of sth with a layer of another material to keep it clean, make it stronger, etc: **~ sth** *The nausea was attributed to excessive levels of tin used to line the inside of the cans.* ◇ **~ sth with sth** *Seeds were germinated in a Petri dish lined with moist filter paper.* **2 ~ sth** to form a layer on the inner or outer surface of sth: *The pleura are membranes which line the outside of the lung and inside of the thoracic cavity.* **3** [often passive] to form lines or rows along sth: **~ sth** *Translations of manga comic books lined the shelves of bookstores around the globe.* ◇ **~ sth with sth** *The jaws were long and narrow and lined with small sharp teeth.*

PHR V **ˌline 'up** to stand in a line or row; to form a line: *A parent should walk the child to the place where children must line up to enter the building.* **ˌline sb/sth 'up** to arrange people or things in a straight line or row: *Children should be able to line up sticks in size order.*

lin·eage /ˈlɪniɪdʒ/ *noun* [U, C] **1** (*formal*) the series of families that sb comes from originally SYN ANCESTRY: *Many families in the region were proud of their lineage.* **2** (*biology*) a set of species, each member of which is considered to have EVOLVED from the one before: *This represents a group of related lineages united by descent from a common* *ancestral lineage.* HELP In biology, **lineage** is also used to talk about a set of cells which develop from a common cell: *The properties of such cells depend on their lineage or line of descent, and not environmental factors.*

lin·ear /ˈlɪniə(r)/ *adj.* **1** of or in lines: *In his art, he broke the laws of scientific linear perspective.* ◇ *The basic unit of collagen consists of three linear protein molecules wrapped round each other in a triple helix, like a rope.* **2** going from one thing to another in a single series of stages: *The film tells the story in a clear, linear narrative.* OPP NON-LINEAR (1) **3** (*mathematics*) involving one DIMENSION; that can be represented by a straight line on a GRAPH; of an EQUATION in which the highest power of its terms is one: *The linear momentum, p, of a particle of mass, m, is related to its velocity, v, by p = mv.* ◇ *We can compare this procedure with the technique for solving linear equations.* OPP NON-LINEAR (3) **4** (*mathematics*) involving or showing a relationship between quantities in which their rates of change are equal: *A linear relationship was shown to hold between time spent studying and final grades.* OPP NON-LINEAR (3) ■ **lin·ear·ity** /ˌlɪniˈærəti/ *noun* [U] *Lawrence abandons regular narrative linearity in the novel.* ◇ **~ of sth** *The method just described is another consequence of the linearity of the class of equations considered.* **lin·ear·ly** *adv.*: *The output noise amplitude in AM is constant with frequency, and does not increase linearly as in FM.*

lin·guist /ˈlɪŋɡwɪst/ *noun* **1** a person who studies languages or LINGUISTICS: *Historical corpus linguists are typically interested in analysing language change.* **2** a person who knows several foreign languages well: *He was a gifted linguist, speaking several oriental languages fluently.*

lin·guis·tic /lɪŋˈɡwɪstɪk/ *adj.* connected with language or the scientific study of language: *Modern linguistic theory is essentially a product of nineteenth-century European scholarship.* ◇ *The meanings of all linguistic expressions vary with the context in which they occur.* ■ **lin·guis·tic·al·ly** *adv.*: *The study was conducted in an ethnically and linguistically diverse urban school district.* ◇ *Psychological assessors should be culturally and linguistically sensitive in selecting their tests.*

lin·guis·tics /lɪŋˈɡwɪstɪks/ *noun* [U] the scientific study of language or of particular languages: *This issue does not get as much attention as it ought to in applied linguistics.* ◇ *corpus/historical/structural linguistics*

lin·ing /ˈlaɪnɪŋ/ *noun* **~ (of sth) 1** a layer of material used to cover the inside surface of sth: *Concrete segments which could be bolted together to form a circular lining were used to provide support.* **2** the covering of the inner or outer surface of a part of the body: *Gluten damages the lining of the small intestine in coeliac disease.* ◇ *It can cause mesothelioma, a cancer of the outer lining of the lung.*

link[1] AWL /lɪŋk/ *verb* [often passive] **1** to make a physical or electronic connection between one object, machine or place and another SYN CONNECT (1): **~ A to B** *Roads were quickly built linking new colonies to Rome.* ◇ **~ A with B** *The Baikal-Amur Railway links Siberia with the Pacific.* ◇ **~ A and B (together)** *The Internet links together millions of networks and individual users.* ◇ *The main chain is made from carbon atoms linked alternately by single and double bonds.* **2** to make or have a connection with sb/sth, especially where one thing affects the other: **~ A to/with B** *They motivate employees by linking rewards to high levels of performance.* ◇ *Vegetation is closely linked to climate.* ◇ *Tobacco is causally linked with 80–90 per cent of lung tumours.* ◇ **~ A and B** *This article holds that culture and politics are inextricably linked.* **3** to state that there is a connection or relationship between two things or people SYN ASSOCIATE[1] (1): **~ A to/with B** *There have been attempts to link these landforms to certain specific climatic environments.* ◇ *This study links coffee drinking with cigarette smoking.* ◇ **~ A and B** *There have been many studies attempting to link obesity and depression.*

PHR V ˌ**link ˈup (with sb/sth)** to join or become joined with sb/sth: *Organizations will often link up with their suppliers further down the supply chain to collaborate in the development of new products.*

▸ ADVERB + LINK **directly • clearly • explicitly • increasingly** *The analysis directly linked economic and racial issues.* | **closely • intimately • inextricably • intrinsically • tightly • strongly • loosely • necessarily • positively • causally • genetically** *Suppliers and customers are inextricably linked through a sequence of events that brings raw material to the ultimate customer (Lang, 2000).*

▸ LINK + ADVERB **together • directly • back** *The different parts of the city are linked together by transportation networks.* ◇ *Housing is linked directly to wealth.* | **closely** *Mark's gospel links closely the teaching and the healing activity of Jesus.*

link[2] AWL /lɪŋk/ *noun* **1** a connection between two or more people or things, especially where one affects the other: **~ between A and B** *The study demonstrated the causal link between smoking and lung cancer.* ◇ *This report did not explore any potential link between gender and achievement.* ◇ **~ to sth** *Entrepreneurship may provide what could be considered to be the missing link to economic growth.* **2** a relationship between two or more people, countries or organizations: **~ with sth** *The town maintained strong trading links with North Africa.* ◇ **~ between A and B** *Mass production broke the direct link between customer and producer.* **3** a means of travelling or communicating between two places: *New transport links — canals, railways and roads — were essential for moving raw materials to factories.* ◇ *Data can be transmitted across the world via satellite, terrestrial microwave links and fibre optic links at very high rates.* **4** (*computing*) a place in an electronic document that is connected to another electronic document or to another part of the same document: *The data can be accessed online directly by following the links provided on the website.* ◇ *Simply click on the link and the video will start playing.* ◇ **~ to sth** *The multimedia station includes a link to their online web page.*

IDM **a link in the ˈchain** one of the stages in a process or a line of argument: *In practice, the last two crucial links in the chain have seldom been discussed.* ➲ *more at* WEAK

▸ ADJECTIVE + LINK **close • direct • strong** *Work in the classroom may be supported and reinforced by closer links with parents and families.* | **clear • explicit • weak • important, significant • possible, potential • missing • causal • genetic** *There was no clear link between the meanings of the two words.*

▸ NOUN + LINK **transport • rail • video • radio • satellite** *Major investment projects include a high-speed rail link between Madrid and Barcelona.*

▸ VERB + LINK **provide • build • create** *Over 30 Russian and foreign airlines provide air links to 104 cities.* | **establish • strengthen • maintain, retain • break** *Nutritional studies have established a link between a diet high in saturated fats and an increased concentration of blood cholesterol.* | **demonstrate • suggest • make • highlight, emphasize • explore, investigate, trace, examine • form • acknowledge • mediate** *The Universal Declaration of Human Rights makes an explicit link between human rights and human dignity.* | **forge • sever** *It is desirable for many organizations to forge links with others in order to exert greater influence over their target market.*

link·age AWL /ˈlɪŋkɪdʒ/ *noun* **1** [U, C] the act of linking things; a link or system of links SYN CONNECTION (1): **~ between A and B** *The study involved record linkage between census and mortality data for the entire adult population.* ◇ **~ (of sth) (to sth)** *A focus on cascades leads us to concentrate more on the sequential linkage of one*

L

process to the next. ◇ *The region is dominated by industries with strong local linkages.* **2** [C] a device that links two or more things: *In a free piston engine, piston motion is not restricted by any mechanical linkages.* **3** [U] **~ (between A and B)** (*biology*) the tendency of groups of GENES on the same CHROMOSOME to be passed on together: *The physically closer two genes are on a chromosome, the greater the degree of genetic linkage between them.*

ˈlinking verb (*also* **cop·ula**) *noun* (*grammar*) a verb such as *be* or *become* that connects a subject with the adjective or noun (called the COMPLEMENT) that describes it: *The cue sentence is 'The novel would make a great film'. This is a linking verb usage of 'make'.*

lip /lɪp/ *noun* either of the two soft edges at the opening to the mouth: *This treatment has adverse effects including dry lips and skin.*

lipid /ˈlɪpɪd/ *noun* (*chemistry*) any of a group of biological substances including fats, oils and STEROIDS which do not dissolve in water but do dissolve in non-polar SOLVENTS: *High concentrations of blood lipids affect the accuracy of many clinical tests.*

li·quid¹ /ˈlɪkwɪd/ *noun* [C, U] a substance that flows freely and is not a solid or a gas, for example water or oil: *The oil is a viscous amber liquid.* ◇ *She has difficulty swallowing both solids and liquids.* ◇ *The samples were applied as drops of liquid.*

L

li·quid² /ˈlɪkwɪd/ *adj.* **1** in the form of a liquid, rather than a gas or a solid: *Smaller amounts of sulfur are present in liquid fuels.* ◇ *Water has one liquid phase but many different solid phases other than ordinary ice.* **2** used to describe a substance that is usually a gas but that has been changed into a liquid by cold or pressure: *The samples were frozen in liquid nitrogen.* **3** (*finance*) in cash; that can easily be changed into cash : *It is sensible to store some portion of income in liquid assets.* HELP A **liquid** market is one in which there are many active buyers and sellers, exchanging ASSETS for cash.

li·quid·ity /lɪˈkwɪdəti/ *noun* [U] (*finance*) the state of owning things of value that can easily be exchanged for CASH: *As a financial institution, the fundamental role of the stock market is to provide liquidity.* ◇ *A positive working capital serves as indicator for a firm's short-term liquidity.*

list¹ /lɪst/ *noun* a series of names, items, figures, etc, especially when they are written or printed: **~ (of sth)** *An initial search generated a list of 432 publications.* ◇ **on a ~** *159 manufacturing and mining firms appeared on the list.* ◇ **high on the ~** *Providing quotations for potential new transactions was not high on the list of most dealers' priorities.* ◇ **at the top of the ~** *The possible threat of inflation is at the top of their list of concerns.* ➲ *see also* WAITING LIST

▸ ADJECTIVE + LIST **long, lengthy, extensive • short, brief • detailed • exhaustive, comprehensive, complete, full • non-exhaustive • official • following** *These tables do not seek to provide an exhaustive list of all of the advantages and disadvantages of eLearning.*

▸ NOUN + LIST **reading • reference • mailing • word • price** *The address is included under 'Useful web links' in the reference list at the end of the chapter.*

▸ VERB + LIST **compile, draw up, make • generate, produce • publish • contain • provide • present • keep • review • top, head • join • narrow • search** *She compiled a list of more than 140 terms.*

list² /lɪst/ *verb* **1 ~ sth** to make a list of things in a particular order: *Consumers can simply be asked to list all the products they use for a particular task.* ◇ *Authors are listed alphabetically.* ◇ *Table 3.3 lists common plant names, with botanical equivalents.* **2 ~ sb/sth + adv./prep.** to mention or include sb/sth in a list: *The African wild dog is listed as endangered.* ◇ *The majority of US companies listed on the New York Stock Exchange are registered in Delaware.*

lis·ten /ˈlɪsn/ *verb* **1** [I] **~ (to sb/sth)** to pay attention to sb/sth that you can hear: *It is important for nurses to listen carefully to what the person has to say.* ◇ *In the focus groups, nearly all participants said that they listened to the radio regularly.* ◇ *Compared with adults, teenagers are much more likely to use the Internet for listening to music.* HELP You cannot 'listen sth' (without 'to'): ~~*to use the Internet for listening music*~~ **2** [I] **~ (to sb/sth)** to take notice of what sb says to you so that you follow their advice or believe them: *If apparently opposed groups listen to each other, such misperceptions may be overcome.*
PHR V **ˈlisten for sth** to be prepared to hear a particular sound: *Listen for breathing and any abnormal airway sounds.* **ˌlisten ˈin (on/to sth)** to listen to a conversation, especially one that you are not supposed to hear: *Call centre supervisors listen in to calls to monitor performance.*

lis·ten·er /ˈlɪsənə(r)/ *noun* **1** a person who listens: *A moderator should be a good listener, well organized and a quick learner.* **2** a person listening to a radio programme: *UK listeners tuned in to several stations that transmitted from continental Europe.*

list·ing /ˈlɪstɪŋ/ *noun* **1** a list, especially an official or published list of people or things, often arranged in alphabetical order: *A sampling of the 179 countries is included in Table 18.3, and the complete listing can be downloaded from their website.* ◇ **~ of sth** *This is a comprehensive and up-to-date listing of Romantic resources on the Internet.* **2** a position or an item on a list: *The position of the advertiser's listing on the screen will hugely influence the response it achieves.* HELP In business, a **listing** is a position for a company on the official SECURITIES list of the London Stock Exchange. To be on the list, particular requirements must be satisfied: *The process of gaining a listing on the London Stock Exchange is complex, costly and extremely time-consuming.*

lit *past tense, past part. of* LIGHT³

liter (*US*) = LITRE

lit·er·acy /ˈlɪtərəsi/ *noun* [U] **1** the ability to read and write: *There are guides for kindergarten teachers to improve literacy.* ◇ *Life expectancy in the country is just 42 years and adult literacy is 37 per cent.* **2** knowledge or skill in a particular area: *These students generally have higher computer literacy, which gives them a competitive edge in the programme.* ◇ *health/media/financial literacy*

lit·eral /ˈlɪtərəl/ *adj.* **1** [usually before noun] being the basic or usual meaning of a word or phrase: *The literal meaning of the Sanskrit word 'karma' is 'action'.* ◇ *The earthquake sent literal and figurative shock waves through local infrastructure.* ➲ *compare* FIGURATIVE (1), METAPHORICAL **2** [usually before noun] that follows the original words exactly: *The name sounds far more elegant in French than its literal English translation.* ➲ *compare* FREE¹ (9), LOOSE (4)

lit·er·al·ly /ˈlɪtərəli/ *adv.* **1** in a literal way SYN EXACTLY: *It is difficult to know whether the stories here were meant to be taken literally as things that happened.* ◇ *The term 'Beri-Beri' translates literally as 'man who walks like a sheep', the effect produced by the disease.* ➲ *compare* VIRTUALLY (1) **2** used to emphasize the truth of sth that may seem surprising: *Existing competitors within the market lost market share in the airline market as the low-cost carriers quite literally flew away with their business.* HELP In more informal contexts, you may see **literally** used to emphasize a word or phrase, even though it is not actually true: *I literally jumped out of my skin.* This use is common, but is not considered correct in more formal and academic contexts.

lit·er·ary /ˈlɪtərəri; *NAmE* lɪtəreri/ *adj.* **1** connected with literature: *a literary work/text/source* ◇ *Literary studies have incorporated and expanded this body of work.* ◇

Many Biblical scholars have used insights drawn from modern literary criticism. **2** (of a language or style of writing) suitable for or typical of a work of literature: *During the eighteenth century, common spoken Russian developed into a literary language.*

lit·er·ate /ˈlɪtərət/ *adj.* **1** able to read and write: *Rome was still an oral culture in which few were literate.* ◇ *Since the sample comprised both literate and illiterate respondents, the questionnaire was administered by a trained interviewer.* OPP ILLITERATE (1) **2** having education or knowledge, especially in a particular area: *Retail banks are operating in a highly competitive marketplace, characterized by increasingly financially literate customers.* OPP ILLITERATE (2)

lit·era·ture /ˈlɪtrətʃə(r); *NAmE also* ˈlɪtrətʃʊr/ *noun* **1** [U] pieces of writing that are considered to be works of art, especially novels, plays and poems (in contrast to technical books and newspapers, magazines, etc.): *The Romantic era was marked by a renewed interest in the art and literature of ancient Greece.* ◇ *Narrative poetry in English literature is often associated with the Middle Ages.* ◇ *Great works of literature can change the way people think.* **2** [U, C] pieces of writing or printed information on a particular subject: *The development of marketing strategy has been discussed extensively in the marketing literature.* ◇ **~ on sth** *An extensive literature exists on this topic.* ◇ **a body of ~** *There now exists a vast body of literature on all aspects of the canyon.* ◇ **+ noun** *The literature review discusses previous findings and hypotheses.*

▸ ADJECTIVE + LITERATURE **classical • ancient • modern • contemporary • nineteenth-century • Romantic • national • popular** *For the playhouse dramatists, classical literature provided a fund of historical and mythical figures and stories.* | **extensive • vast • rich • recent • current • existing, extant • growing, burgeoning • previous • relevant • published • secondary • academic, scholarly • peer-reviewed • empirical • theoretical • scientific • medical** *This book joins a growing literature on women in the black freedom struggle.*

▸ VERB + LITERATURE **read • write** *There is a body of contemporary immigrant American literature written by recent arrivals like Edwidge Danticat and Junot Diaz.* | **review • survey • search • summarize • read • consult • dominate • cite • publish** *Payne and colleagues review the available literature on older women's health in the workplace.*

liti·gant /ˈlɪtɪɡənt/ *noun* (*law*) a person who is making or defending a claim in court: *Small claims courts handle civil cases between private litigants.*

liti·ga·tion /ˌlɪtɪˈɡeɪʃn/ *noun* [U] (*law*) the process of making or defending a claim in court: **~ with sb/sth** *She was engaged in litigation with the company.* ◇ **~ for sth** *He had initiated litigation for occupational asthma.* ◇ **+ noun** *Settlement allows the firms to save on litigation costs.*

litre (*US* **liter**) /ˈliːtə(r)/ *noun* (*abbr.* l) a unit for measuring volume, equal to 1000 CUBIC centimetres: *3 litres of water* ◇ *a car with a 3.5-litre engine*

lit·ter /ˈlɪtə(r)/ *noun* **1** [U] (*ecology*) the dead leaves and other parts of plants that cover the ground, especially in a forest: *Nitrogen and phosphorus content in the leaf litter was about 30%.* ◇ *The three types of plant litter differed markedly in chemical properties.* **2** [C] a number of baby animals that one mother gives birth to at the same time: *In species that produce litters, competition within the litter will favour rapid development.* ◇ **~ of sth** *After a pregnancy of about three and a half months, the female gives birth to a litter of two to three cubs.* **3** [U] empty food and drink containers, pieces of paper, etc. that people have left in a public place: *Drying clothes hang from windows and litter covers the ground.*

lit·tle¹ /ˈlɪtl/ *det., pron.* **1** used with uncountable nouns to mean 'not much': *Very little research has yet been done.* ◇ *There is little evidence to support this theory.* ◇ *There can be little doubt that the Thatcher years had a major impact on the structure of the British economy.* ◇ *Many consumers know little about how their food is produced.* ◇ *The reforms had done little to remove the tensions between landowners and peasants.* ◇ **~ or no...** *In the control experiments, little or no change in concentration was seen.* **2 a little** used with uncountable nouns to mean 'a small amount' or 'some': *With a little practice this game could be played very successfully.* ◇ **~ of sth** *It is important here to know a little of the history of land law.*

IDM **ˌlittle by ˈlittle** slowly; gradually: *Little by little, the government attached more and more importance to gaining the Duma's approval for its measures.*

lit·tle² /ˈlɪtl/ *adv.* (**less, least**) **1** not much; only slightly: *Graunt's work is little known today.* ◇ *Cultivation techniques changed little until the green revolution of the 1960s.* **2 a little** to a small degree: *Each business cycle is a little different from the last.* ◇ *It is worth looking at this question a little more closely.*

lit·tle³ /ˈlɪtl/ *adj.* [usually before noun] HELP The forms **littler** /ˈlɪtlə(r)/ and **littlest** /ˈlɪtlɪst/ are rare. It is more common to use **smaller** and **smallest**. **1** not big; small; smaller than others: *The patient had some numbness in the little finger of his right hand.* **2** young: *The audience is invited to view the transformation of Emily from little girl to adolescent.* **3** (of distance or time) short: *Cells generated by stem cells continue to divide for a little time until they undergo differentiation.* ◇ *The influence of iron minerals extends a little way into the infrared.* ◇ *America caved in to the threats a little while later for two reasons.*

L

live¹ /lɪv/ *verb* **1** [I] **+ adv./prep.** to have your home in a particular place: *By 2040, 70% of the world's population will be living in urban areas.* ◇ *She lives in New York City.* ◇ *Curiously, these are terrestrial animals living in a marine habitat.* ◇ *Most sufferers of dementia live at home.* **2** [I, T] to spend your life in a particular way: *An early aim of the Labour government was to reduce the numbers of children living in poverty.* ◇ *Social, cultural and economic factors shape the experience of living with a disability.* ◇ *Man has a duty to live in harmony with nature and to respect and sustain the overall ecological balance (Eckersly, 1992; Goodin, 1992).* ◇ **~ sth** *Health care services play a central role in helping people live healthy lives.* **3** [I] to remain alive: *Women tend to live longer than men.* ◇ *By 2009, a newborn girl could expect to live to 82 years and a newborn boy to 78 years.* ◇ *Elderly Americans can now expect, on average, to live for three years longer than in 1965.* ➲ *see also* LONG-LIVED, SHORT-LIVED **4** [I] to be alive, especially at a particular time: *They lived in an age when riot, revolt and popular disturbances of one kind or another were commonplace.* ◇ *The fossilized feather was from a bird that lived during the Cretaceous, the last age of the dinosaurs.* ◇ *Robert May estimates that perhaps as many as 10% of all multicellular species that ever lived are alive now.*

PHR V **ˈlive by sth** to follow a particular belief or set of principles: *Those who knew her say that she lived by the principles she taught, with kindness and devotion to others.* **ˈlive by doing sth** to earn money or to get the things you need by doing a particular thing: *These early humans presumably lived by hunting and gathering.* **ˌlive sth ˈdown** to be able to make people forget about sth embarrassing you have done: *Jenner had to live down his association with radicalism to achieve acceptance in London.* **ˈlive off sb/sth** to receive money or the things that you need to live from sb/sth: *For a nobleman and his family to live entirely off servile labour, at least a hundred male serfs were needed.* **ˌlive ˈon** to continue to live or exist: *The ideas of Marx live on in many different interpretations and elaborations.* ◇ *Darby's memory lives on in his magnificent bridge which was opened on New Year's Day*

1781. ˈ**live on sth** to have enough money for the basic things you need to live: *Many elderly people live on limited resources.* ◇ *The one billion people who live on $1 per day not only lack vital medicines, but also lack food and school books.* ◇ *Families living on low incomes have a lower health status than those with higher incomes (Hirsch and Spencer, 2008).* ˌ**live ˈout sth** to spend the rest of your life in a particular way: *Most people lived out their lives within the framework of their local community.* ˌ**live ˈthrough sth** to experience a disaster or other unpleasant situation and survive it: *Soga lived through a period of enormous violence and deprivation.* ˈ**live together** (*also* ˈ**live with sb**) **1** to live in the same place with sb: *Professors and students lived together in the same building.* **2** to share a home and have a sexual relationship without being married SYN COHABIT: *They live together and have four children.* ˌ**live ˈup to sth** to do as well as or be as good as other people expect you to: *Unless the product or service sold is well known, there is always the risk that it will not live up to expectations.* ˈ**live with sb** = LIVE TOGETHER

live² /laɪv/ *adj.* [usually before noun] **1** living; not dead: *Elsewhere in the region, live animals are often sold in village markets.* ◇ *Spina bifida is a relatively common birth defect, affecting nearly 18 out of every 100 000 live births.* ◇ *This approach provides a powerful tool that enables researchers to follow chromosome movement in live cells.* **2** (of a performance) given or made when people are watching; not recorded: *Music videos were no longer just a stand-in for a recorded live performance of a song.* ◇ *live music/theatre* **3** (of a broadcast) sent out while the event is actually happening, not recorded first and broadcast later: *ITV's website featured a live video stream of the television coverage.* ◇ *The events were shown in a live television broadcast.* **4** of interest or importance at the present time: *The relationship between the EU and its member states is a live political issue.*

live·li·hood /ˈlaɪvlihʊd/ *noun* [C, U] a means of earning money in order to live SYN LIVING² (2): *The way people earn their livelihoods has changed.* ◇ *More people have gone into animal farming as a means of livelihood.*

live·ly /ˈlaɪvli/ *adj.* (**live·lier**, **live·li·est**) **1** (of a discussion or an argument) full of energy, excitement and strong feeling: *Each of these ideas has generated lively discussion amongst historians in recent years.* ◇ *There were lively debates between proponents of economic globalization and those who claimed that it was not helping to reduce world poverty.* **2** full of life and energy; active and enthusiastic: *The meeting is run in a lively, engaging manner.* ◇ *He developed a lively interest in observing the living world from an early age.*

liver /ˈlɪvə(r)/ *noun* a large organ in the body that cleans the blood and produces BILE: *Insulin also stops the breakdown of protein in the liver.* ◇ **+ noun** *Cirrhosis may lead to chronic liver failure and death.*

lives *pl. of* LIFE

live·stock /ˈlaɪvstɒk; *NAmE* ˈlaɪvstɑːk/ *noun* [U, pl.] the animals kept on a farm: *Contemporary mixed farming is intensive and commercial and integrates crops and livestock.* ◇ **+ noun** *livestock farming/production*

liv·ing¹ /ˈlɪvɪŋ/ *adj.* **1** having life; alive at the present time: *DNA is universal to all living things.* ◇ *living beings/creatures/organisms* ◇ *Fine electrodes are inserted into living cells to record their electrical activity.* **2** [only before noun] used or practised now: *Flexibility in word usage is an essential feature of living languages.* ◇ *It is an example of living history, an attempt to recreate the world that the first settlers experienced when they came to North America.*

IDM **within/in ˌliving ˈmemory** at a time, or during the time, that is remembered by people still alive: *The debate took place during one of the most closely fought general election campaigns in living memory.*

liv·ing² /ˈlɪvɪŋ/ *noun* **1** [U] a way or style of life: *The aim is to promote healthy living and reduce health inequalities.* ◇ *Older people suffer from functional disabilities related to the normal activities of daily living.* ◇ **~ conditions/standards** *Low socio-economic status and poor living conditions are the most important risk factors for infection.* ➲ *see also* STANDARD OF LIVING **2** [C, usually sing.] money to buy the things that you need in life: *Before the nineteenth century, most people in the world made their living by agriculture.* ◇ *Many of the town's men have left for the north, no longer able to earn a decent living in their own country.* ◇ *Darwin inherited enough money from his family to ensure that he never needed to work for a living.* **3 the living** [pl.] people who are alive: *Roman custom dictated that the dead be kept well away from the living.*

load¹ /ləʊd; *NAmE* loʊd/ *noun* **1** something that is being carried (usually in large amounts) by a person, vehicle, etc: *The birchbark canoe was able to carry heavy loads, and yet was light enough to be carried when necessary.* ◇ *During the night, the tankers dumped their loads in 18 areas around the city.* **2 ~ (of sth/sb)** (often in compounds) the total amount of sth/sb that sth can carry or contain: *A trainload of loyal troops was dispatched from east and west.* **3** [usually sing.] **~ (on sth)** the amount of weight that is pressing down on sth: *The total load on the bumper beam was 238 kN.* ◇ *Adhesive joints distribute the load over a larger area than mechanical joints.* ◇ *the load-bearing walls of the house* **4** an amount of work that a person, machine or system has to do: *Many faculty members expressed a wish to reduce their teaching load to allow more time for research.* ◇ **~ on sth** *Chronic heart disease and heart failure represent a significant load on the Western world's health care systems.* **5** the amount of electrical power that is being supplied at a particular time: *Energy efficiency improvements will help reduce the peak and overall electrical load at the poultry farm houses.* **6** a CIRCUIT connected to an electrical OUTPUT: *An electric heater is a large load and can cause lights in the house to dim.* **7** (*earth science*) the material carried along by a stream, an ocean current, a GLACIER, etc: *Here the river deposits its sediment load, typically as it approaches the sea and develops a delta or an estuary.*

load² /ləʊd; *NAmE* loʊd/ *verb* **1** to put a large quantity of things or people onto or into sth: **~ sth (up) (with sth)** *They hired students to load up delivery vans and deliver the product.* ◇ **~ sth/sb (into/onto sth)** *Portland Limestone was loaded into boats on the Dorset coasts.* OPP UNLOAD **2 ~ sb with sth** to give sb a lot of things, especially things they have to carry: *De Soto loaded them with presents.* ◇ (*figurative*) *He had been loaded with further honours for his part in defeating the rebels.* **3** to put sth into a weapon, camera or other piece of equipment so that it can be used: **~ sth (with sth)** *He mistakenly believed that he had loaded the gun with blank cartridges.* ◇ **~ sth (into sth)** *Swabs are loaded directly into a portable machine which measures the level of bacterial activity present.* **4 ~ sth** to put data or a program into the memory of a computer: *Focus group participants may not feel confident about loading the software.* ➲ *compare* DOWNLOAD¹

load·ing /ˈləʊdɪŋ; *NAmE* ˈloʊdɪŋ/ *noun* [U, C] the application of a weight or force to a structure: *The Millennium Bridge had a very high pedestrian loading at its opening.*

loan /ləʊn; *NAmE* loʊn/ *noun* **1** [C] money that an organization such as a bank lends and sb borrows: *Prospective purchasers often had to resort to taking out short-term loans at high rates of interest.* ◇ *Banks all over the world had been lending excessively and making high-risk loans.* ◇ **~ from sb** *With oil revenues increasing, Chad repaid its loan from the World Bank and withdrew from the* agreement. **2** [sing.] the act of lending sth; the state of being lent: **~ of sth** *The cases in which this rule has applied have almost all involved the loan of a motor vehicle.* ◇ **on ~ (from sb/sth)** *The Commission relies to a considerable extent on experts on loan from national ministries.* ■ **loan** *verb* **~ sth (out) (to sb)** *They loaned out money at high interest rates.* ◇ **~ sb sth** *The king forced merchants to loan him money.*

lobby[1] /ˈlɒbi; *NAmE* ˈlɑːbi/ *verb* (**lob·bies, lobby·ing, lob·bied, lob·bied**) [T, I] to try to influence a politician or the government and, for example, persuade them to support or oppose a change in the law: **~ sb/sth (for/against sth)** *The civil rights movement lobbied Congress for policies to rectify racial inequality and poverty.* ◇ **~ for/against sth** *Some mothers have set up pressure groups to lobby against the changes.* ■ **lobby·ist** /ˈlɒbiɪst; *NAmE* ˈlɑːbiɪst/ *noun*: *Within the EU, there are at least 70 professional car industry lobbyists.*

lobby[2] /ˈlɒbi; *NAmE* ˈlɑːbi/ *noun* (*pl.* **-ies**) [C+sing./pl. v.] a group of people who try to influence politicians on a particular issue: *What is perhaps surprising is how much the gun rights and gun control lobbies in the US have in common.* ◇ **+ noun** *Lobby groups representing the interests of business have incentives to affect election outcomes.*

local /ˈləʊkl; *NAmE* ˈloʊkl/ *adj.* [usually before noun] **1** belonging to or connected with the particular place or area that you are talking about or with the place where you live: *The Internet helps companies at both global and local levels.* ◇ *In the Baltic provinces, the Russian government again failed to win the support of the local population.* ◇ *The initiative is aimed at promoting access to sport and leisure facilities in the local community.* ⊃ *see also* LOCAL GOVERNMENT **2** affecting only one part of the body: *Local inflammation is one of the fundamental responses of the body to almost any kind of injury.* ◇ *Choice of local anaesthetic agent is usually determined by the duration and magnitude of surgery.* **3** (*computing*) used to describe devices available and connections over relatively short distances HELP A **local area network** is a collection of connected computers and other devices in a single building or on a single site: *The company's local network has no connection to the Internet.* A **local hard disk** is a disk connected to the user's computer directly, not over a network. **4** (*computing*) used to describe an ENTITY that is only available for use in one part of a program: *It looks for local keys, not over the Internet.*

ˌlocal ˈgovernment *noun* **1** [U] (*especially BrE*) the system of government of a town or an area by elected representatives of the people who live there: *The role of local government is also crucial.* ◇ *The relationship between central and local government has been especially significant in shaping these policy discourses.* ◇ **+ noun** *The future of local government finance is again under review.* **2** [C] (*NAmE*) the organization that is responsible for the government of a local area and for providing services, etc: *Federal, state and local governments are major players in America's market democracy.*

lo·cal·ity /ləʊˈkæləti; *NAmE* loʊˈkæləti/ *noun* (*pl.* **-ies**) **1** the place where sb/sth exists: *He described fossils said to have been discovered at various localities in the Himalayas.* ◇ *Commercial deposits of valuable minerals tend to be concentrated in a small number of localities.* ◇ *Juvenile fish are in freshwater from a few days to 4 years, depending on species and locality.* **2** the area that surrounds the place you are in or are talking about SYN VICINITY: **in the ~ (of sth)** *Analysis of surface dust samples in the locality also showed high lead concentrations.*

lo·cal·ize (*BrE also* **-ise**) /ˈləʊkəlaɪz; *NAmE* ˈloʊkəlaɪz/ *verb* **1 ~ sth** to find out or identify where sth is: *Barn owls are able to localize prey based solely on noise generated by the prey animal.* ◇ *Children will often find it hard to localize specific areas of pain.* **2 ~ sth** to limit sth or its effects to a particular area SYN CONFINE SB/STH TO STH: *Attempt to localize the fire using fire-fighting equipment but only if it is safe to do so.* **3 ~ sth** to organize an activity or a process so that it can all take place in a local area: *One way to avoid foreign companies taking advantage is to localize production: that is, to buy as many components as possible from local suppliers.* ■ **lo·cal·iza·tion, -isa·tion** /ˌləʊkəlaɪˈzeɪʃn; *NAmE* ˌloʊkələˈzeɪʃn/ *noun* [U] **~ (of sth)** *Bats make use of echoes of ultrasound for localization of prey animals during hunting.* ◇ *One explanation offered for this success is the localization of decision-making.*

lo·cal·ized (*BrE also* **-ised**) /ˈləʊkəlaɪzd; *NAmE* ˈloʊkəlaɪzd/ *adj.* happening within one small area: *The highly localized pain above his eyes suggests he may have developed an infection of his frontal sinuses.* ◇ *Area committees prepare contingency plans for response to oil spills in a localized area, such as a harbour.*

lo·cal·ly /ˈləʊkəli; *NAmE* ˈloʊkəli/ *adv.* within a particular area or place: *The majority of betel nuts consumed in Taiwan are grown and produced locally.* ◇ *Losing locally adapted breeding populations may not be reversible.* ◇ *British parties, locally and nationally, struggle to raise the money to run effective organizations.*

lo·cate AWL /ləʊˈkeɪt; *NAmE* ˈloʊkeɪt/ *verb* **1** [T] **~ sb/sth** to find the exact position of sb/sth: *Places referenced repeatedly in the text, such as Madeline Island, were difficult to locate on the map.* ◇ *Bright colours allow males to be located more easily by females.* **2** [T] **~ sth + adv./prep.** to put or build sth in a particular place: *It was essential to locate factories near a source of coal.* ⊃ *compare* RELOCATE **3** [I] **+ adv./prep.** (*especially NAmE*) to start a business in a particular place: *No businesses wish to locate there under the current economic and environmental conditions.*

lo·cated AWL /ləʊˈkeɪtɪd; *NAmE* ˈloʊkeɪtɪd/ *adj.* [not before noun] if sth is **located** in a particular place, it exists there or has been put there SYN SITUATED: *The site was located on a plateau 10–20 km from the sea.* ◇ *These volcanoes, located close to densely populated areas, are potentially extremely dangerous.* ◇ *More centrally located countries tend to be much richer than countries with few or small neighbours.*

lo·ca·tion AWL /ləʊˈkeɪʃn; *NAmE* loʊˈkeɪʃn/ *noun* **1** [C] a place where sth happens or exists; the position of sth: *Many small firms will tend to choose locations close to the major market leaders.* ◇ *Today, especially in the more developed world, producers and consumers are no longer in the same location.* ◇ **~ of sth** *Knowledge of the exact location of fishing grounds significantly increases the chance of a successful catch.* **2** [C, U] a place outside a film STUDIO where scenes of a film are made: *'Othello' exhibits evidence of having been filmed in different locations at different times, even within a single scene.* ◇ **on ~** *His films employ extensive exterior scenes shot on location.* **3** [U] **~ of sth** the act of finding the position of sb/sth: *The paper describes the acoustic location of prey by barn owls.* **4** [C] (*computing*) a position in computer memory: *The simulator uses an 8-bit memory with 256 locations.*

loci *pl. of* LOCUS

lock[1] /lɒk; *NAmE* lɑːk/ *verb* **1** [T, I] **~ (sth)** to fasten sth with a lock; to be fastened with a lock: *The factory owners routinely locked the doors of the plant during working hours.* **2** [T] **~ sth + adv./prep.** to put sth in a safe place and lock it: *The keys can be locked in a safe until they are required.* **3** [I, T] to become fixed in one position and unable to move; to make sth become fixed in this way: **+ adv./prep.** *The components are continually in motion rather than firmly locking into place.* ◇ **~ sth + adv./prep.** *The two wheels are locked together so that they will maintain their position.* **4** [T] **be locked in/into sth** to be

L

involved in a difficult situation, an argument, a disagreement, etc: *The Protestant allies and the Habsburgs were locked in a military stalemate.* ◇ *Wages are assumed to be fixed because employees are locked into contracts.*
PHR V **ˌlock sb/yourself ˈin (...)** to prevent sb from leaving a place by locking the door: *He has a recent history of locking himself in his room and shouting at family and visitors.* **ˌlock sb ˈup** (*rather informal*) to put sb in prison: *It is not helpful to troubled youth if courts lock up juveniles 'to protect the community'.* **ˌlock sth ˈup 1** to put money into an investment that you cannot easily turn into CASH: *As merchants, they were less interested in locking up capital in manufacturing.* **2 be locked up in sth** to be in a place where it cannot easily be obtained: *The American geologist Thomas Chamberlin speculated that there might be sources of energy locked up in atoms.*

lock² /lɒk; *NAmE* lɑːk/ *noun* **1** a device that keeps a door, window, lid, etc. closed, usually needing a key to open it: *The defendant had changed the locks on the doors of the house.* **2** a section of CANAL or river with a gate at either end, in which the water level can be changed so that boats can move from one level of the canal or river to another: *By creating dams, channels and locks, canal builders hoped to reconfigure the rivers to serve the needs of human commerce.*

L

locus /ˈləʊkəs; *NAmE* ˈloʊkəs/ *noun* (*pl.* **loci** /ˈləʊsaɪ; *NAmE* ˈloʊsaɪ/) **1 ~ (of sth)** (*formal*) the exact place or position where sth happens or which is thought to be the centre of sth: *The family is an important locus of the struggle for sexual equality.* ◇ *The real locus of power in society has shifted to institutions over which ordinary people have an almost complete lack of influence (Hertz, 2000).* **2** (*biology*) the position of a GENE or MUTATION on a CHROMOSOME: *The disease results from an alteration at a single genetic locus.* ◇ **~ for sth** *The majority of known risk loci for cancers are spread throughout the genome.* ◇ *If two loci are linked, this simply indicates that they are closely adjacent on the same chromosome.* **3 ~ (of sth)** the set of all points that share a particular property: *The locus of all points on a plane equidistant from a given point is a circle.* ◇ *A parabola is the locus of a point that moves so as to be equidistant from a fixed point and a straight line.*

lodge /lɒdʒ; *NAmE* lɑːdʒ/ *verb* **1 ~ sth (with sb) (against sb/sth)** to make a formal statement about sth to a public organization or authority SYN REGISTER¹ (1), SUBMIT (1): *The company subsequently lodged an appeal against the Commission's decision.* ◇ *Appeals could be lodged with the Aliens Appeals Board at any time.* **2** [usually passive] **be lodged in sth** to become fixed or stuck somewhere: *The bullet was still lodged in his spine.*

log¹ /lɒg; *NAmE* lɔːg; lɑːg/ *noun* **1** (*also* **log·book**) an official record of events during a particular period of time, especially a journey on a ship or plane: *For each aircraft journey, a log was kept of speed and altitude.* ◇ **~ of sth** *Diaries were written by social researchers as a log of their activities and reflections.* **2** (*rather informal*) = LOGARITHM **3** a thick piece of wood that is cut from or has fallen from a tree: *Slime moulds are typically found on rotting logs.*

log² /lɒg; *NAmE* lɔːg; lɑːg/ *verb* (**-gg-**) **1 ~ sth (into sth)** to put information in an official record or write a record of events SYN RECORD² (1): *Data for each transmitter were logged once every 20 minutes.* ◇ *After the fieldwork, all the input was logged into a database.* **2 ~ sth** to cut down trees in a forest for their wood: *Recently logged forests were far more likely to burn than those that had not been logged or had been logged long ago (Siegert et al., 2001).*
PHR V **ˌlog ˈin/ˈon** (*computing*) to perform the actions that allow you to begin using a computer system: *The percentage of children who logged on to the Internet for each time period is presented in Table 11.2.* **ˌlog ˈoff/ˈout** (*computing*) to perform the actions that allow you to finish using a computer system: *A common occurrence is to access a system when a user has logged in and not logged out.*

loga·rithm /ˈlɒgərɪðəm; *NAmE* ˈlɔːgərɪðəm; ˈlɑːgərɪðəm/ (*also rather informal* **log**) *noun* (*mathematics*) the power by which a number must be raised to produce a particular number: *The formulas may be expressed using common logarithms.* ◇ **~ of sth** *The natural logarithms of the numbers increase by a constant amount in each interval.* ◇ *The output voltage is proportional to the logarithm of the input voltage.* ■ **loga·rith·mic** /ˌlɒgəˈrɪðmɪk; *NAmE* ˌlɔːgəˈrɪðmɪk; ˌlɑːgəˈrɪðmɪk/ *adj.*: *Logarithmic units and logarithmic scales are very convenient when a variable has a large dynamic range.*

log·book /ˈlɒgbʊk; *NAmE* ˈlɔːgbʊk; ˈlɑːgbʊk/ *noun* = LOG¹ (1)

logic AWL /ˈlɒdʒɪk; *NAmE* ˈlɑːdʒɪk/ *noun* **1** [U, C] **~ (of sth)** a way of thinking or explaining sth, in which there is a connection between each idea and the next one: *The logic of this particular argument is not very compelling.* ◇ *It can be argued that the historical explanation follows not the logic of scientific causality but the logic of story.* ◇ *Actors try to resolve their disagreement by making a compromise between competing logics.* **2** [U, sing.] sensible reasons for doing sth: *Though this assumption might seem to have a certain logic, it is fatally mistaken.* ◇ **~ of sth** *Hollywood adaptations were almost exclusively subject to the economic logic of the Hollywood studios.* **3** [U] the science of thinking about or explaining the reason for sth using formal methods: *His approach rested on informal analysis of ordinary language rather than formal logic.* ◇ *Developments in mathematical logic have cast doubt on the ability of any theory to be completely self-contained.* **4** [U, C] (*computing*) a system or set of principles used in preparing a computer to perform a particular task: *Description Logics are used as a formal foundation in many practical knowledge-based systems.*

lo·gic·al AWL /ˈlɒdʒɪkl; *NAmE* ˈlɑːdʒɪkl/ *adj.* **1** following or able to follow the rules of logic in which ideas or facts are based on other true ideas or facts: *If this argument is followed to its logical conclusion, the world food crisis can only get worse.* ◇ *A number of economists started realizing on purely logical grounds that the formula was too simplistic.* **2** (of an action or event) seeming natural, reasonable or sensible: *At first glance, the decision appears perfectly logical.* ◇ **it is ~ to do sth** *It seems logical to assume that customers must be satisfied, or they will not stay with a business.* OPP ILLOGICAL (1) **3** (*computing*) connected to the system or set of principles used in preparing a computer to perform a particular task: *This first machine was relay-based, with some electronic circuits for performing simple logical operations.*

logic·al·ly AWL /ˈlɒdʒɪkli; *NAmE* ˈlɑːdʒɪkli/ *adv.* **1** in a way that follows the rules of logic: *These two sentences appear to be logically equivalent.* ◇ *The premises logically entail the conclusion.* **2** in a way that seems natural, reasonable or sensible: *It follows logically that change in the economic base ultimately leads to change in the legal and political superstructure.*

ˈlogic gate *noun* (*computing*) = GATE (2)

lo·gi·cian AWL /ləˈdʒɪʃn/ *noun* a person who studies or is skilled in logic: *To a mathematical logician, this argument is not valid.*

lo·gis·tics /ləˈdʒɪstɪks/ *noun* **1** [U+sing./pl. v.] **~ (of sth/doing sth)** the practical organization that is needed to make a complicated plan successful when a lot of people and equipment is involved: *The logistics of collecting and analysing the samples restricted the sample sizes.* **2** [U] (*business*) the business of transporting and delivering goods: *Outbound logistics are activities required to collect, store and distribute products or deliver services.* ◇ **+ noun**

All transport and logistics businesses today exist in a supply chain context. **3** [U] the activity of moving equipment, supplies and people for military operations: *The company developed very close relationships with the US government in planning wartime logistics.* ■ **lo·gis·tic** (*also* **lo·gis·tic·al** /lə'dʒɪstɪkl/) *adj.*: *The agency provides financial and logistic support directly to NGOs and community organizations.* ◇ *Logistical and cost constraints have served to limit the use of these techniques.* **lo·gis·tic·al·ly** /lə'dʒɪstɪkli/ *adv.*: *Admitting patients well before surgery is expensive and often logistically difficult.*

lone /ləʊn; *NAmE* loʊn/ *adj.* [only before noun] **1** without any other people or things SYN SOLITARY (3): *The clash between police and protesters claimed a lone victim.* ◇ *These early studies portrayed Faraday as a lone man of science working away in a basement.* **2** the only one of a kind: *The EU proved the lone champion of renewable energy against the US and developing countries who were pushing expanded fossil fuel use.* **3** (*especially BrE*) without a husband, wife or partner to share the care of children SYN SINGLE[1]: *The majority of lone parents are actually divorcees in their 20s or 30s.*

lone·ly /'ləʊnli; *NAmE* 'loʊnli/ *adj.* (**lone·lier**, **lone·li·est**) **1** unhappy because you have no friends or people to talk to: *Only 6% of participants reported that they felt lonelier as a result of using the Internet.* **2** (of a situation or period of time) sad and spent alone: *Meagre pensions and the fear of a lonely old age led some to share their homes and household expenses.* **3** [only before noun] (of places) where only a few people ever come or visit SYN ISOLATED (1): *The lonely landscapes of Keith Douglas's desert poems are indebted to the examples of Eliot and Auden.* ■ **lone·li·ness** *noun* [U] *Lack of significant relationships led to feelings of loneliness and isolation.*

long[1] /lɒŋ; *NAmE* lɔːŋ; lɑːŋ/ *adj.* (**long·er** /'lɒŋgə(r); *NAmE* 'lɔːŋgər; 'lɑːŋgər/**long·est** /'lɒŋgɪst; *NAmE* 'lɔːŋgɪst; 'lɑːŋgɪst/) **1** lasting or taking a great amount of time or more time than usual: *The rivers have been used for a very long time as an economic resource.* ◇ *For a new theory to survive, it must be tested over a long period of time by many different means.* ◇ *Humans have a long history of using plants.* ◇ *The Treaty of Lisbon entered into force on 1 December 2009 after a long process of negotiations and ratification.* OPP SHORT[1] (1) **2** used for asking or talking about particular periods of time: *The interviews were semi-structured and typically one to two hours long.* ◇ *How long have the symptoms been present?* **3** seeming to last or take more time than it really does because, for example, you are very busy or not happy: *The long years of fighting at the end of the fifth century had harmed the economy of many Greek states.* OPP SHORT[1] (2) **4** measuring or covering a great length or distance, or a greater length or distance than usual: *Proteins are large molecules made up of long chains of amino acids.* ◇ *Transporting the captured CO_2 over long distances by pipeline, rail or barges is expensive.* ◇ *This equation shows why X-rays with a shorter wavelength are absorbed less than those with a longer wavelength.* OPP SHORT[1] (3) **5** large in extent or larger than normal: *The IMF insisted on a long list of reforms.* ◇ *It is unusual for this guide to be longer than five pages; indeed, many are no longer than two sides.* OPP SHORT[1] (5) **6** used for asking or talking about particular lengths, distances or extents: *The small intestine is about five metres long and has three parts: the duodenum, jejunum, and ileum.* **7** (*phonetics*) a **long** vowel is pronounced for a longer time than other vowels: *A syllable is long if its vowel or diphthong is long.* OPP SHORT[1] (11) ➲ *see also* LENGTH

IDM **at long last** after a long time SYN FINALLY (1): *At long last, the old regime powers began to see that only a fundamental change of attitude could save them.* **have come a long 'way** to have made a lot of progress: *Since then, research in this field has come a long way.* **have a long way to 'go** to need to make a lot of progress before you can achieve sth: *Certain things, such as the status of women, have certainly improved but there is still a long way to go.* **in the 'long run** concerning a longer period in the future: *They argue that attempts by the government to reduce unemployment below the natural rate will, in the long run, simply lead to more inflation.* ◇ *In the long run, the sun will end up as a small block of hydrogen ice.* **'long on sth** (*rather informal*) having a lot of a particular quality: *Relationship marketing, to date, has been long on theoretical development but short on empiricism.* **take the 'long view (of sth)** to consider what is likely to happen or be important over a long period of time rather than only considering the present situation: *Given these many problems, the West had to be prepared to take the long view.* ➲ *more at* TERM[1], WAY

long[2] /lɒŋ; *NAmE* lɔːŋ; lɑːŋ/ *adv.* (**long·er** /'lɒŋgə(r); *NAmE* 'lɔːŋgər; 'lɑːŋgər/, **long·est** /'lɒŋgɪst; *NAmE* 'lɔːŋgɪst; 'lɑːŋgɪst/) **1** for a long time: *In most species of animals, females live longer than males.* ◇ *It did not take long for scientists in various parts of the world to appreciate the significance of the discovery.* ◇ *By late 1950, it became clear to Truman that the war would last longer than he had hoped.* **2** a long time before or after a particular time or event: **~ before/after...** *Climate variation was characteristic of the region long before agriculture was a significant factor in its ecology.* ◇ **before ~** *A new product may create a competitive advantage for a time, but before long a competitor will introduce something better.*

IDM **as/so 'long as** **1** only if: *The government is legitimate, according to Locke, as long as it protects the rights given to individuals by the law of nature.* **2** during the whole time that: *As long as war has existed, it has produced victims with physical and psychological injuries.* **for (so) 'long** for (such) a long time: *These children are restless and cannot sit still for long.* ◇ *Voters have tended to blame governments for having allowed banks to operate for so long in such a lightly regulated environment.* **no 'longer** used to say that sth that was possible or true before, is not now: *Increasingly, the most important ally of governments is no longer the police or the military; it is the media.* ◇ *Over half (56%) agreed that they had been away from work too long and no longer had the skills needed to return to work.*

ˌlong-'distance *adj.* [only before noun] operating or travelling between places that are far apart: *Long-distance trade in other goods was relatively insignificant.* ◇ *Wind-pollinated trees can increase their fitness through long-distance dispersal of pollen.*

lon·gev·ity /lɒn'dʒevəti; *NAmE* lɔːn'dʒevəti; lɑːn'dʒevəti/ *noun* [U] long life; the fact of lasting a long time: *Increasing longevity means that there are more older people needing treatment for chronic disease.* ◇ **~ of sb/sth** *Many factors will influence the quality and longevity of a customer relationship.*

lon·gi·tude /'lɒŋgɪtjuːd; 'lɒndʒɪtjuːd; *NAmE* 'lɑːndʒətuːd; 'lɔːndʒətuːd/ *noun* [U, C] (*abbr.* **long.**) the distance of a place east or west of the PRIME MERIDIAN, measured in degrees: *Lines of longitude converge at the poles.* ➲ *compare* LATITUDE (1)

lon·gi·tu·din·al /ˌlɒŋgɪ'tjuːdɪnl; ˌlɒndʒɪ'tjuːdɪnl; *NAmE* ˌlɑːndʒə'tuːdnl; ˌlɔːndʒə'tuːdnl/ *adj.* (*technical*) **1** concerning the development of sth over a period of time: *The study design comprised two cross-sectional surveys and one longitudinal analysis.* ◇ *longitudinal studies/research* ◇ *The longitudinal data show that heavier use of the Internet is associated with declines in television viewing.* ➲ *compare* CROSS-SECTIONAL **2** going downwards rather than across: *The electric cells are arranged in series along the longitudinal axis of the body.* ■ **lon·gi·tu·din·al·ly** /ˌlɒŋgɪ'tjuːdɪnəli; ˌlɒndʒɪ'tjuːdɪnəli; *NAmE* ˌlɑːndʒə'tuːdnəli; ˌlɔːndʒə'tuːdnəli/ *adv.*: *An ethnically diverse sample of 156*

L

youths was followed longitudinally for one year. ◇ *During development, this tube becomes divided longitudinally into two chambers: the atrial and ventricular chambers.*

ˌlong-ˈlasting *adj.* that can or does last for a long time: *Health shocks can have devastating and long-lasting consequences.* ◇ *Recent studies suggest that volcanic aerosols do not have a long-lasting effect on climate.*

ˌlong-ˈlived *adj.* having a long life; lasting for a long time: *This general model of consumer behaviour has proven to be remarkably long-lived.* ◇ *Governments will need to make financial arrangements to support a long-lived population.*

ˈlong-range *adj.* [only before noun] **1** travelling a long distance: *The crisis saw the deployment of American long-range bombers in Britain.* **2** made for a period of time that will last a long way into the future: *Government involvement in industry is often the product of political pressure rather than the outcome of long-range economic planning.*

ˌlong-ˈstanding *adj.* [usually before noun] that has existed or lasted for a long time: *As would be expected, older people were more likely to report a long-standing illness.* ◇ *There is a long-standing debate about how best to fight poverty.* ◇ *a long-standing tradition/practice/relationship*

ˌlong-ˈterm *adj.* [usually before noun] **1** that will last or have an effect over a long period of time into the future: *To truly investigate long-term effects, future research should include measurements at three consecutive time points.* ◇ *Long-term care for older adults has been a priority issue for the past two decades.* ◇ *This strategy involves extensive use of long-term contracts.* **2** that has lasted a long time and is not likely to change or be solved quickly: *Another important factor in keeping people out of the labour market is long-term sickness or disability.* ➲ *compare* SHORT-TERM

look¹ /lʊk/ *verb* **1** [I] **~ (at sb/sth)** to turn your eyes in a particular direction: *Subjects were asked to look at a blank screen and to imagine an object on it.* **2** [I] **~ (for sb/sth)** to try to find sb/sth: *Many conservatives began to look for a new leader.* ◇ *Nettle (2002) looked for evidence for natural selection on height in a cohort of several thousand British women.* ◇ *It is necessary to look elsewhere to find a really convincing answer to this question.* **3** *linking verb* to seem; to appear: **+ adj.** *The data for the post-1991 period look very different.* ◇ **+ noun** *The model does not look a viable option for the production of complex manufacturing goods.* ◇ **~ (to sb) like sb/sth** *This is starting to look like a far-fetched idea.* **4** [I] (not usually used in the progressive tenses) to have a similar appearance to sb/sth; to have an appearance that suggests that sth is true or will happen: **~ (to sb) like sb/sth** *A row of small dots very close together looks like a solid line.* ◇ **~ (to sb) as if.../as though...** *Many of these rural granite buildings look as if they have grown out of the ground.* HELP In spoken English people often use **like** instead of **as if** or **as though** in this meaning. This is not correct in academic English. **Like** can be used before a noun phrase (*a solid line*) but not before a clause (*they have grown out of the ground*). **5** [I] to seem likely: **~ (to sb) as if.../as though...** *It looks as if Aristotle could not bring himself completely to reject his Platonic heritage.* ◇ *It looked to many as though the alliance might well break apart.* **6** [I] **+ adv./prep.** to face a particular direction: *The towers look out over areas of nineteenth-century housing.*

IDM Most idioms containing **look** are at the entries for the nouns and adjectives in the idioms, for example **look the other way** is at **way**. **be looking to do sth** to hope or expect to do sth: *The legislation will have an impact on British firms looking to invest abroad.* **look ˈgood** to show success or that sth good might happen: *The business situation looks good at the moment.*

PHR V **ˌlook ˈafter sb/sth/yourself** (*especially BrE*) **1** to be responsible for or to take care of sb/sth/yourself: *Conservative policies encouraged mothers to stay at home to look after their children.* ◇ *It is the moral and humanitarian duty of the state to look after the welfare of refugees.* ◇ *Carers enable many who cannot look after themselves to maintain their independence.* **2** to make sure that things happen to sb's advantage: *States constantly look after their own best interests.*

ˌlook aˈhead (to sth) to think about what is going to happen in the future: *Looking ahead, he could see that the EU faced two key challenges.* ◇ *During periods of economic boom, firms should look ahead to the inevitable downturn that follows.*

ˌlook aˈround/ˈround to turn your head so that you can see sth: *None of the students seemed bothered by the music or was looking around.* **ˌlook aˈround/ˈround (sth)** to visit a place or building, walking around it to see what is there: *Potential buyers then come to look around the property.* ◇ *They give visitors plenty of time to look around on their own.* **ˌlook aˈround/ˈround for sth** to try to find or get sth: *In the summer of 1529, Henry began looking around for an alternative strategy to secure what he wanted.*

ˈlook at sth **1** to think about, consider or study sth: *The Inland Revenue will look at ways in which it can tax this income.* **2** to view or consider sth in a particular way: *They have the advantage of looking at things from a different perspective.* **3** to examine sth closely: *Of the 185 patients who had looked at their records online, 82 (44%) had experienced technical difficulties.*

ˌlook ˈback (on sth) to think about sth in your past: *Many Americans look back on the war years as the best years of their lives.* ◇ *Looking back, Robson regarded this as the major achievement of administrative law.* **ˌlook ˈback over sth** to consider again sth that you have read, written, done or experienced: *Organizations can also look back over the campaigns they have run in the past and refine their techniques.*

ˌlook ˈdown on sb/sth to think that you are better than sb/sth: *His fellow officers looked down on him.* ◇ *He was an aristocrat who looked down on manual work.*

ˈlook for sth to hope for sth; to expect sth: *When, for example, he attended a reception, the press were looking for signs of rebelliousness.*

ˌlook ˈforward to sth to be thinking with pleasure about sth that is going to happen (because you expect to enjoy it): *Many employees do not enjoy their work and spend their time looking forward to the weekend.* ◇ **~ forward to doing sth** *He was looking forward to going to college.*

ˌlook ˈinto sth to examine or investigate sth: *State governments rarely look into the affairs of corporations.*

ˌlook ˈon to watch sth without becoming involved in it yourself: *Archaeologists could only look on in helpless horror as the site was destroyed.* **ˈlook on sb/sth as sb/sth** to consider sb/sth to be sb/sth: *He came to be looked on as a heretic and extremist.* ◇ *Chandler looked on his youth as the golden period of his life.* **ˈlook on sb/sth with sth** to consider sb/sth in a particular way SYN REGARD¹: *People of this type are arrogant and tend to look on others with contempt.* ◇ *Their success is looked on with admiration.*

ˌlook ˈout for sb to take care of sb and make sure nothing bad happens to them: *When socializing, young women are advised to go out in groups and look out for their friends.* **ˌlook ˈout for sth** to try to notice or avoid sth bad happening SYN WATCH OUT FOR SB/STH (1): *Health care professionals should look out for signs of depression during pregnancy.*

ˌlook sth ˈover to examine sth to see how good, big, etc. it is: *The group spent one week looking over the data.*

ˈlook through sth [no passive] to examine or read sth quickly: *It may also be worth looking through the information provided to the public.*

ˈlook to sb for sth | **ˈlook to sb to do sth** to rely on or expect sb to provide sth or do sth: *They would be obliged* *to look to Austria and France for support.* ◇ *Japanese importers looked to Australian producers to fill the gap created by the absence of US products.* ˈ**look to sth** to consider sth and think about how to make it better: *Companies must look to the creation of meaningful relationships with those customers.*

ˌ**look sth ˈup** to search for information in a dictionary or other work of reference, or by using a computer: *Students are encouraged to look up any unfamiliar words in a dictionary.* ˌ**look ˈup to sb** to admire or respect sb: *Michels's analysis rested on the assumption that 'the masses' had a psychological need for leaders they could look up to.*

look² /lʊk/ *noun* **1** [C, usually sing.] **~ (at sth)** an act of examining or considering sth: *The present research takes a fresh look at the development of business groups.* ◇ *The chapter concludes with a brief look at social engineering.* ◇ *A close look at modern history reveals that large-scale violent confrontations could stop or even reverse this trend.* **2** [C, usually sing.] **~ (at sb/sth)** an act of looking at sb/sth: *Have a look at the plan in Figure 14.2.* **3** [C, usually sing.] the way sb/sth looks; the appearance of sb/sth: *To maintain their attractiveness, websites need constant updating, and sometimes a totally new look.* ◇ *Advertising and promotion must be unique, with its own consistent look and feel.* **4 looks** [pl.] a person's appearance, especially when the person is attractive: *Fashion is about looks, but it is also about money.* ◇ *She rejects Darcy's first proposal, despite his wealth, good looks and superior education.*

loom /luːm/ *verb* [I] to appear important or frightening and likely to happen soon: *Climate change looms as the twenty-first century's number one environmental challenge.*

IDM ˌ**loom ˈlarge** to be worrying or frightening and seem hard to avoid: *Fears of communism and nuclear war loomed large in the minds of many children.*

loop /luːp/ *noun* **1** a shape like a curve or circle made by a line curving right round and crossing itself; a piece of rope, wire, etc. in this shape: *These distant sites are able to control gene activity because DNA can form loops and bring them close to the promoter.* ◇ **~ of sth** *A loop of these polymer molecules is flexible, like a long piece of string.* **2** a structure, series or process, the end of which is connected to the beginning: *The goal is to close the information loop between the end users and the upstream operations of design and production.* ◇ **feedback ~** *The release of most hormones in the endocrine system is controlled by a series of feedback loops.* **3** (*computing*) a set of instructions that is repeated again and again until a particular condition is satisfied: *The right square bracket indicates the end of the loop.* **4 ~ (of sth)** a strip of film or tape on which the pictures and sound are repeated continuously: *The high-definition screen displayed a loop of nine three-minute videos.*

loose /luːs/ *adj.* (**loos·er**, **loos·est**) **1** not firmly fixed where it should be; that can become separated from sth: *Poor dental hygiene and loose teeth are commonplace in people with this condition.* **2** not tightly packed together; not solid or hard: *Loose soil material may be eroded by physical processes.* **3** not strictly organized or controlled: *Germany was, until 1871, only a loose confederation of 39 states.* **4** not exact; not very careful: *The word 'somatization' is often used in a looser sense as shorthand for unexplained medical symptoms.* ➲ *compare* FREE¹ (9), LITERAL (2) **5** (of clothes) not fitting closely: *Patients should be advised to wear loose cotton clothing.* OPP TIGHT (3) **6** not tied together; not held in position by anything or contained in anything: *Until marriage, women wore their hair long and loose.* **7** (*medical*) (of body waste) having too much liquid in it: *She has passed eight to ten loose stools over the last 12 hours.*

loose·ly /ˈluːsli/ *adv.* **1** in a way that is not exact: *Loosely speaking, capitalism can indeed mean any effort to gain wealth.* ◇ *Ethnic groups are often loosely defined.* **2** in a way that is not strictly organized or controlled: *Economic activities were only loosely regulated.* ◇ *With the disintegration of institutional order, government armies tend to degenerate into loosely organized armed groups.* **3** in a way that is not firm or tight: *In some minerals, water occurs in structural cavities and is only loosely bound to the crystal structure.*

lord /lɔːd; *NAmE* lɔːrd/ *noun* **1 Lord** (in the UK) a title used by a man of high rank in the NOBILITY, or sb who has been given the title 'lord' as an honour: *'The Daily Express' developed into a journal of substantial influence and circulation under the proprietorship of Lord Beaverbrook.* ➲ *compare* LADY (2) **2 Lord** a title used for some high official positions in Britain: *Philip Yorke, Lord Chancellor since 1737, was the prime mover behind the legislation.* **3** a powerful man in MEDIEVAL Europe, who owned a lot of land and property: *In the Middle Ages, all lands were owned by bishops of the church or by feudal lords.* **4 the Lords** [sing.+ sing./pl. v.] = HOUSE OF LORDS: *After both the Commons and the Lords agreed to an abolition of the slave trade, George III consented to the bill becoming law.*

lorry /ˈlɒri; *NAmE* ˈlɔːri; ˈlɑːri/ *noun* (*pl.* **-ies**) (*BrE*) = TRUCK (1)

lose /luːz/ *verb* (**lost**, **lost** /lɒst; *NAmE* lɔːst; lɑːst/) **1** [T] to stop having sth because it is taken away from you or destroyed: **~ sth** *Between 1983 and 1987, 4.6 million workers lost their jobs.* ◇ *If his dismissal were to be upheld, he would lose his pension rights.* ◇ **~ sth to sth** *This technical change could mean a new way of storing the animal feed so that less is lost to spoilage.* HELP If sth is **lost to sth**, it is lost because of that thing. **2** [T] to have less and less of sth, especially until there is none left: **~ sth** *He has lost his appetite and feels extremely tired.* ◇ *Between the birth of the young and their weaning, the older females lost more weight than the younger ones.* ◇ **~ sth to sth** *In the Greenland Sea, the ocean loses heat to the atmosphere, rapidly forming sea ice.* **3** [T] **~ sth** to no longer have part of your body or a physical ability because of an accident, illness or old age: *The injury caused him to lose the sight in his right eye.* ◇ *She lost control of her legs and could not walk for a little while.* ◇ *If blood becomes too thin, it loses the ability to form blood clots.* **4** [T] to have sth taken away by sb/sth: **~ sth** *It may be possible for a firm to raise its price without losing market share.* ◇ **~ sth to sb/sth** *The firm conducted research to explore why it was losing business to competitors.* **5** [T] **~ sth** to no longer have a particular quality or attitude: *They lost hope of finding formal employment.* ◇ *If the technology does not meet the advertised representations, credibility will be lost.* ◇ *Myths gain and lose credence over time.* **6** [T] to die; to have sb die: **~ sb/sth** *Hundreds of people lost their lives in the conflict.* ◇ *They were lost at sea when their ship foundered in a storm.* ◇ **~ sb to sth** *He lost his wife to cancer.* **7** [T, I] to be defeated; to fail to win a competition, a court case, an argument, etc: **~ (sth)** *The Tsar made peace with Napoleon after losing more battles than he could afford.* ◇ **~ sth to sb** *The party lost four seats, all to the Conservatives.* ◇ **~ to sb** *The sitting MP lost dramatically to a local farmer.* **8** [T, I] to fail to keep sth you want or need; to cause sb to fail to keep sth: **~ sth** *It was not long before he lost the confidence of his people.* ◇ **~ sth by doing sth** *Little would have been gained or lost by increasing or reducing the number of herring measured.* ◇ **~ sb sth** *This cooperation with the outsiders lost him the trust of the island community.* **9** [T] to make less money than you spend or use: **~ sth** *On a single day in 1998, the company lost more than $500 million.* ◇ *Many investors lost large amounts when the markets crashed.* ◇ **~ sth on sth/by doing sth** *Most manufacturers were losing money on computers.* **10** [T] **~ sth/sb** to be unable to find sth/sb: *She would request repeat prescriptions for her lithium well before they were* due, saying she had lost her tablets. **11** [T] **~ sth** to waste time or an opportunity: *In the aftermath of the insurrection, the Republic lost no time in rewarding those who had fought on the side of order.* ◇ *A person who loses the opportunity to receive education at a young age may not be able to compensate for that loss at a later age.*

IDM Idioms containing **lose** are at the entries for the nouns and adjectives in the idioms, for example **lose face** is at **face** *noun*.

PHR V **'lose yourself in sth** to become so interested in sth that it takes all your attention: *Marlowe's Faustus loses himself absolutely in Homer's imagined world.* **ˌlose 'out (on sth) (to sb/sth)** to not get sth, especially sth you wanted or feel you should have, because sb/sth else gets it instead: *If the competition for a resource between two species is very intense, one may lose out completely.* ◇ *In East Africa, many languages are losing out to Swahili.*

loss /lɒs; *NAmE* lɔːs; lɑːs/ *noun* **1** [U, C, usually sing.] the state of no longer having sth or as much of sth; the process that leads to this: *The long decline of the automobile industry has led to huge job losses.* ◇ *The patient was examined for signs of weight loss.* ◇ **~ of sth** *Rising ocean levels could cause the loss of immense amounts of arable land.* **2** [C, U] money that has been lost by a business or an organization: *They sustained substantial losses before selling out for a minimal sum.* ◇ **at a ~** *Expenditure calculations showed the business was operating at a substantial loss.* ◇ **~ to sb** *The activity was unlawful and involved significant financial loss to the defendants.* OPP PROFIT[1] (1) **3** [C, U] the death of a person: *The Soviet forces were soon in disarray, suffering enormous losses.* ◇ **~ of sb** *Over the next few months, Pat began to come to terms with the loss of her husband.* ◇ *In general, floods cause less loss of life than earthquakes, drought and famine.* **4** [C] a failure to win a contest: *After losses in several general elections, Labour steadily accepted a number of Conservative policies it had earlier opposed.* ◇ **~ to sb/sth** *After his loss to Johnson in 1964, Goldwater spent much of his free time raising money and lobbying.*

IDM **at a 'loss** not knowing what to say or do: *The community was at a loss to understand how a failing project could continue to be funded.* **cut your 'losses** to stop doing sth that is not successful before the situation becomes even worse: *They need to decide whether to persist in the hope of turning matters around or to quit and cut their losses.*

▸ ADJECTIVE + LOSS **great, heavy • potential** *Germanicus's army suffered heavy losses in the German campaign.* | **significant • substantial, massive, huge • total • net** *Revenues in 2007 were about $22 million, with a net loss of $30 million.* | **complete • severe • sudden • gradual • progressive • consequent • temporary • permanent, irreversible • excessive • sensory • visual** *The most dramatic political changes resulted from the emperors' gradual loss of influence.* | **financial • economic** *This type of infection accounts for many working days lost and consequently major economic losses.*

▸ NOUN + LOSS **job • heat • weight • hearing • memory • hair • blood • fluid • biodiversity** *Cloud cover reduces heat loss from the ground at night.*

▸ VERB + LOSS **suffer • experience • cause • inflict • bear • prevent** *Without question the earthquake caused devastating losses of both life and property.* | **incur, sustain • entail, imply, mean • represent • minimize, reduce • mitigate • offset • outweigh • compensate • recover • avoid** *By this time, the company had incurred losses of over $9 760 000.* | **mourn • lament** *She may still be mourning the loss of her natural parent.* | **make • recoup • absorb • cover** *The danger is that, if sales do not increase, the business will make a loss due to the low price.*

lost[1] /lɒst; *NAmE* lɔːst; lɑːst/ *adj.* **1** [usually before noun] that has been taken away, or cannot be brought back or created again: *It is estimated that depression costs the UK economy £9 billion/year in lost earnings.* ◇ *In her poems there is a pervasive theme of yearning for lost love.* **2** wasted; not used: *The limited investment in school-based crime prevention represents a lost opportunity for preventing crime.* ◇ *Obese workers have more lost workdays than do non-obese workers.* **3** that cannot be found: **(get) ~** *The probability of data getting lost or corrupted is very small.* ◇ *Exactly what Arab Spain was really like is not easy to see because its documents are almost wholly lost.* **4** killed or destroyed: *The hurricane drove the ship far out to sea where she was believed lost.* **5** unable to find your way; not knowing where you are: *As they are driving in the car, Kelly hesitates to say that she thinks they are lost.* ◇ **get ~** (*figurative*) *Short simple instructions ensured users of the web page did not get lost.* **6** [not before noun] unable to deal successfully with a particular situation: *Esther feels lost without her routine of eating, shopping and preparing food for her family.* ➲ *see also* LOSE

IDM **be 'lost in sth** to be giving all your attention to sth so that you do not notice what is happening around you: *I was lost in the music.* **be 'lost on sb** to not be understood or noticed by sb: *The implications of these trends were not lost on the food industry, particularly the suggestion that fast food may be 'addictive'.*

lost[2] *past tense, past part. of* LOSE

lot[1] /lɒt; *NAmE* lɑːt/ *pron.* **a lot, lots (to do)** (*informal*) a large number or amount: *I didn't know there were any young people in the Conservative Party, but apparently there are a lot.* ◇ *We still have lots to learn.* HELP **A lot/lots** is informal, especially in British English; in academic writing it is better to use **a large amount/number, many** or **much**: *There are a large number of young people in the Conservative party.* ◇ *There is still much to learn.*

lot[2] /lɒt; *NAmE* lɑːt/ *det.* **a lot of, lots of** (*informal*) a large number or amount of sb/sth: *A lot of research has been done on human personality.* ◇ *Without human intervention, forests experience lots of small fires.* HELP **A lot of/lots of** is informal, especially in British English; in academic writing it is better to use phrases such as **a large amount/number of, many** or **much**: *A large amount of research has been done on human personality.* ◇ *... forests experience many small fires.*

lot[3] /lɒt; *NAmE* lɑːt/ *noun* **1** [C+sing./pl. v.] (*especially BrE*) a group or set of people or things: *The middle class in this novel are a far from homogeneous lot.* ◇ **~ of sth** *They tested two different lots of the gel and noticed no difference between them.* **2** [C] (*especially NAmE*) an area of land used for a particular purpose: *Most of the homes are ranch-style detached houses on large lots.* ◇ *There were numerous unemployed men hanging out in the parking lots.* **3** [sing.] a person's luck or situation in life: *Dorothy's journal entries hint that she does not easily accept her lot as William's helpmate.* ◇ **~ of sb** *Malaysia introduced wealth-sharing programmes to improve the lot of ethnic Malays.* **4 the lot** [sing.+ sing./pl. v.] (*informal*) the whole number or amount of people or things: *They sorted the materials into eleven boxes, then transported the lot to the University Library.* ◇ *The new stage director turned out to be the worst of the lot.* HELP **The lot** is informal; in academic writing it is better to use phrases such as **all of them** or **them all**: *They transported all of them to the library.* ◇ *He turned out to be the worst of them all.*

IDM **by 'lot** using a method of choosing sb to do sth in which each person takes a piece of paper, etc. from a container and the one whose paper has a special mark is chosen: *Government positions were often filled by lot.* **throw in your 'lot with sb** to decide to join sb and share their successes and problems: *Romania was still waiting to make absolutely sure which side would win before throwing in her lot with the victor.*

loud /laʊd/ *adj.* **(loud·er, loud·est) 1** making a lot of noise: *Fear can be triggered by hearing a loud noise.* ◇

L

Loud voices are generally louder than the telephone or alarms. **2** (of a person or their behaviour) talking very loudly and too much: *He became loud and physically threatening while in the group.* ■ **loud·ly** *adv.*: *When people are angry, they often talk loudly and more quickly.* **loud·ness** *noun* [U] *Distress calls differ from alarm calls in terms of loudness, structure and function.*

love[1] /lʌv/ *noun* **1** [U] a strong feeling of affection for sb that you are sexually attracted to: *Novels reflected the evolving attitude towards romantic love.* ◇ **~ between A and B| ~ for sb** *Love between two men was certainly not a scandal in ancient Greece.* ◇ **fall/be in ~ with sb** *At the age of seventeen, he met and fell in love with his future wife.* ◇ **+ noun** *French was spoken to ladies at balls and written in love letters.* **2** [U] a strong feeling of deep affection for sb/sth, especially a member of your family or a friend: *They describe their families as lacking in love and support.* ◇ **~ of/for sb/sth** *His love of England was tempered by knowledge of the damage done by British imperialism to other parts of the world.* **3** [sing., U] the strong feeling of enjoyment that sth gives you: **~ of/for sth** *Bonaparte received a French education which deeply imbued him with a love for the classics.* ◇ **fall/be in ~ with sth** *In 1982 the marketing director fell in love with Italian coffee and introduced it at Starbucks.* **4** [C] a person, a thing or an activity that you like very much: **~ (of sth)** *She was the love of his life.* ◇ *Although lizards are his first love, his research has a broader significance.*

IDM **make ˈlove (to sb)** to have sex: *After they made love in his shepherd's hut, Aphrodite resumed her divine form and revealed her true identity to him.*

love[2] /lʌv/ *verb* **1 ~ sb** (not used in the progressive tenses) to have very strong feelings of affection for sb that you are sexually attracted to: *They did not love each other enough to be married.* **2 ~ sb/sth** (not used in the progressive tenses) to have very strong feelings of affection for sb/sth, especially a member of your family or a friend: *Keith, seven, loved his sister and often demonstrated his affection by hugging her.* ◇ *She felt very much loved by both parents.* **3** to like or enjoy sth very much: **~ sth** *As a boy he loved quiet places, science, stories and writing.* ◇ **~ doing sth** *He found he loved mixing and making things in the kitchen.* ◇ **~ to do sth** *In her spare time she loves to read.*

lover /ˈlʌvə(r)/ *noun* **1** a partner in a sexual or romantic relationship outside marriage: *The two families quarrel over a small piece of land and make marriage between the young lovers impossible.* **2** (often in compounds) a person who likes or enjoys a particular thing: *art/nature/music lovers* ◇ **~ of sth** *Hadrian was a lover of music and poetry.*

low[1] /ləʊ; *NAmE* loʊ/ *adj.* (**lower, low·est**) **1** less or worse than normal in quantity, quality, size or level: *Bigger firms will have lower average costs than smaller firms.* ◇ *Both of these metals have low densities.* ◇ *Voter turnout was very low at 37%.* ◇ *Mortality rates are much lower in middle-aged women than in men.* ◇ *Governments now acknowledge the difficulties arising from poverty, low educational standards and unemployment.* ◇ *The strongest effects were in low-income families.* OPP HIGH[1] (1) **2** having a reduced amount or not enough of sth: *The reservoirs were already low when the intense drought began.* ◇ *The supply of equipment and drugs is running low.* ◇ **~ in sth** *The average Soviet diet was low in protein.* OPP HIGH[1] (5) **3** below other people or things in importance or position: *Ordinary shareholders are low on the list of creditors when a company is wound up.* ◇ *Mental health remains a low priority in these countries.* OPP HIGH[1] (6) **4** not high or tall; not far above the ground: *The mountains and lower hills cut the land into many narrow coastal plains.* ◇ *These species are low bushes that retain their leaves over several years.* OPP HIGH[1] (2) **5** at or near the bottom of sth: *More than two-thirds of adults in Western countries will at some time suffer from low back pain.* ◇ *The lower slopes of volcanoes may be terraced to grow rice.* ➲ compare HIGH[1] (3) **6** [usually before noun] not showing much approval or respect for sb SYN POOR: *Many of the invaders held a low opinion of the people they had conquered.* OPP HIGH[1] (7) **7** (of sounds) not high; not loud: *The signal will be produced during a moment of low background noise.* ◇ *In the film, she dresses demurely and speaks in a low voice.* OPP HIGH[1] (10) **8** (of light) not bright SYN DIM (1): *Low light and low temperatures reduce growth.* **9** [only before noun] (of LATITUDES) near the EQUATOR: *The Nile provides a case study of how rivers in low latitudes have responded to environmental change.* OPP HIGH[1] (11)

▸ LOW + NOUN **level • rate • temperature • concentration • density • energy • frequency • weight • pressure • dose • score • quality • risk • probability • prevalence • incidence** *Sweden's relatively low level of unemployment has been accompanied by a rate of inflation somewhat higher than that in the US.* | **cost • price • value • income • wage • unemployment • inflation** *Its strong market share is a result of a marketing strategy designed to deliver quality products at low prices.* | **class • status • priority** *People in the lower social classes are more likely to smoke cigarettes.*

▸ ADVERB + LOW **relatively, comparatively • quite, rather, fairly • sufficiently • very • extremely • abnormally, exceptionally • consistently • generally** *Population grew at a relatively low 1.4% annual rate.*

▸ ADVERB + LOWER **significantly • considerably, substantially • somewhat • slightly • consistently • generally** *Enrolment rates are significantly lower for children with disabilities.*

low[2] /ləʊ; *NAmE* loʊ/ *adv.* (**lower, low·est**) **1** (often in compounds) at a level below what is usual or expected: *In general, service work is comparatively low-paid and less secure than most other kinds of work.* ◇ *Both these groups scored low on communication and problem-solving.* **2** in or into a low position, near the bottom of sth or not far above the ground: *They claimed that aircraft had flown low over villages to warn civilians of an imminent attack.*

low[3] /ləʊ; *NAmE* loʊ/ *noun* **1** a low level or point; a low figure: *The reputation of elected representatives sank to an all-time low.* ◇ **~ of sth** *Oil prices fell from a peak of $147 a barrel in July 2008 to a low of $40 in December 2008.* OPP HIGH[3] (1) **2** an area of low pressure in the atmosphere: *Forecasting of polar lows was almost impossible before the advent of regular polar-orbiting satellites.* OPP HIGH[3] (2)

lower[1] /ˈləʊə(r); *NAmE* ˈloʊər/ *adj.* [only before noun] **1** located below sth else, especially sth of the same type, or the other of a pair: *The fish's massive crushing teeth on the upper and lower jaws are used to feed on shellfish.* OPP UPPER (1) **2** at or near the bottom of sth: *Lower-back pain was the leading problem for which care was sought.* OPP UPPER (2) **3** (of a place) located towards the coast, on low ground or towards the south of an area: *During the dry season, seawater intrudes into the lower reaches of the river.* OPP UPPER (3)

lower[2] /ˈləʊə(r); *NAmE* ˈloʊər/ *verb* **1** to reduce sth in value, quality, etc: **~ sth** *By lowering prices, the firm may be able to increase its sales.* ◇ *Fibre can lower blood cholesterol levels in some cases.* ◇ *to lower the barrier/theshold for sth* ◇ *to lower the pressure/temperature/rate* ◇ **~ sth (from A) to B** *In 1943, the age for compulsory schooling was lowered from 8 to 7.* OPP RAISE[1] (3) **2** to let or make sth/sb go down: **~ sth** *Lowering the water table allows the soil to dry.* ◇ **~ sth/sb + adv./prep.** *The control rods can be lowered into the reactor core to slow down the reaction.* OPP RAISE[1] (7)

the ˌlower ˈclasses *noun* [pl.] (*also* **the ˌlower ˈclass** [sing.]) the groups of people who are considered to have the lowest social status and who have less money and/or power than other people in society: *For many of the families of soldiers from the lower classes, the absence of a male family member could result in severe financial difficulties.* ➲ *compare* MIDDLE CLASS, UPPER CLASS, WORKING CLASS ■ **ˌlower ˈclass** *adj.*: *Sport was seen as an occasion for lower-class spectators to experience a form of solidarity.*

ˌlow-ˈgrade *adj.* [usually before noun] **1** of low quality: *Reliance on low-grade coal as a source of energy generation affected the quality of the air, water and soil.* **2** (*medical*) of a less serious type: *Where it is possible, surgery alone may be enough to deal with some low-grade tumours.*

low·land¹ /ˈləʊlənd; *NAmE* ˈloʊlənd/ *adj.* [only before noun] connected with an area of land that is fairly flat and not very high above sea level: *In 1505, Portuguese colonists arrived in Sri Lanka and controlled the lowland coastal regions.* ◇ *These species are mainly distributed in tropical lowland habitats.* ➲ *compare* HIGHLAND¹ (1)

low·land² /ˈləʊlənd; *NAmE* ˈloʊlənd/ *noun* [U] (*usually* **lowlands** [pl.]) an area of land that is fairly flat and not very high above sea level: *It seems likely that diseases such as malaria in the coastal lowlands restricted population growth.* ➲ *compare* HIGHLAND² (1)

L

ˌlow-ˈlevel *adj.* [usually before noun] **1** on a small scale; not very important or serious: *The human response to low-level exposure to lead in the water supply is extremely varied.* ◇ *The police's power to take action against more everyday, low-level offences has also grown.* **2** of low rank; involving people of low rank: *These changes have resulted in increasing numbers of poorly paid low-level service jobs.* OPP HIGH-LEVEL (1) **3** close to the ground: *As the upper level clouds are becoming darker, low level clouds will become smaller or disappear altogether.* OPP HIGH-LEVEL (3) **4** (*computing*) (of a computer language) written in a form close to one that the computer can understand and act upon: *A key concept in computing in low-level languages is the addressing mode.* OPP HIGH-LEVEL (5)

ˌlow ˈpressure *noun* [U, C] **1** the condition of air, gas or liquid that is kept in a container with little force: *The quality of the water service has declined, and low pressure and intermittent supply are common.* ◇ **at ~** *Sulfur is relatively volatile at low pressure.* ◇ *A cell in the plasma display contains a gas at a low pressure.* OPP HIGH PRESSURE (1) **2** a condition of the air that affects the weather when the pressure is lower than average: *Temperatures were just over 25°C across the area of low pressure.* ◇ *Regions which undergo intense solar heating generally experience low pressures.* OPP HIGH PRESSURE (2)

ˌlow-ˈrisk *adj.* [usually before noun] **1** not very likely to get a particular disease or suffer from a particular problem: *It is recommended that patients who are in the low-risk group are treated with aspirin.* OPP HIGH-RISK (1) **2** involving only a small amount of danger and little risk of injury, death or damage: *Licensing is a low-risk and cheap method of accessing income from foreign markets.* OPP HIGH-RISK (2)

loyal /ˈlɔɪəl/ *adj.* **~ (to sb/sth)** not changing in your beliefs or support of sb/sth SYN TRUE (4): *The troops remained loyal to the Tsar.* ◇ *The banks are sending negative signals to their existing loyal customers when they offer preferential rates to new e-customers.* ■ **loy·al·ly** /ˈlɔɪəli/ *adv.*: *As a rule, German courts loyally apply EU law, but there are exceptions.*

loy·alty /ˈlɔɪəlti/ *noun* (*pl.* **-ies**) **1** [U] the quality of not changing in your beliefs or support of sb/sth: *Most attempts at building customer loyalty have focused on creating strong brands.* ◇ *brand/party loyalty* ◇ **~ to/towards sb/sth** *Loyalty to the nation is seen as basic to social solidarity.* ◇ **~ of sb** *As a general, he commanded the unflagging loyalty of his troops.* **2** [C, usually pl.] a strong feeling that you want to be loyal to sb/sth: *For many British Muslims, this raises complex issues of multiple identities and divided loyalties.*

luck /lʌk/ *noun* [U] **1** good things that happen to you by chance, not because of your own efforts or abilities: *More by luck than good management, this attempt was successful.* **2** chance; the force that causes good or bad things to happen to people SYN FORTUNE (1): **good/bad ~** *Bad luck or error do not appear to explain the data.*

lucky /ˈlʌki/ *adj.* (**luck·ier, lucki·est**) **1** having good luck SYN FORTUNATE: *He was also lucky in being the right man at the right place at the right time.* ◇ **~ to do sth** *They lost their possessions, and were lucky to escape with their lives.* ◇ **~ enough (to do sth)** *Workers who were lucky enough to keep their jobs at all were forced to take a pay cut.* **2** being the result of good luck: *Their success was a lucky accident.* ■ **luck·ily** /ˈlʌkɪli/ *adv.*: *Luckily, this worst-case scenario is not usually realized.*

lu·mi·nous /ˈluːmɪnəs/ *adj.* **1** shining in the dark; giving out light: *Only about 10% of this is accounted for by the luminous matter in stars and galaxies.* **2** (*physics*) connected with light as it is PERCEIVED by the eye, rather than in terms of its actual energy: *The candela is the unit of luminous intensity.* ■ **lu·mi·nos·ity** /ˌluːmɪˈnɒsəti; *NAmE* ˌluːmɪˈnɑːsəti/ *noun* [sing., U] **~ (of sth)** *the luminosity of a star*

lump¹ /lʌmp/ *noun* **1** a SWELLING under the skin, sometimes a sign of serious illness: *The patient reports that she noticed the lump in her right breast two days ago.* **2 ~ (of sth)** a piece of sth hard or solid, usually without a particular shape: *Hail consists of supercooled water droplets transformed into irregular lumps of ice.*

lump² /lʌmp/ *verb* to put or consider different things together in the same group: **~ A and B together** *The term 'hunter-gatherers' actually lumps together some very different ways of making a living.* ◇ **~ A (in) with B** *Wilmot did not like being lumped in with the radicals, as his own views and motivation were rather different.*

lung /lʌŋ/ *noun* either of the two organs in the chest that are used for breathing: *Few would now dispute that smoking causes lung cancer and many other diseases.* ◇ *If inhaled, the gas can cause damage to the lungs.*

lux·ury /ˈlʌkʃəri/ *noun* (*pl.* **-ies**) **1** [U] the enjoyment of special and expensive things, particularly food and drink, clothes and surroundings: *Their wives aspired to a life of luxury and social refinement.* ◇ **+ noun** *luxury goods/items/products* ◇ *a luxury car/cruise/hotel* **2** [C] a thing that is expensive and enjoyable but not essential: *The less well-off tend to spend more of their incomes on necessities and less on luxuries.* ◇ *Personal tuition is becoming a luxury in higher education.* **3** [U, sing.] **~ (of doing sth)** a pleasure or an advantage that you do not often have: *Few companies can have the luxury of producing just one product to satisfy a very large market.*

lying *pres. part. of* LIE¹

lyric¹ /ˈlɪrɪk/ *adj.* (of poetry or poets) expressing a person's personal feelings and thoughts: *Marvell's lyric poems are haunted by time and a sense of human failure.* ◇ *Schiller is best known as a dramatist and lyric poet.* ➲ *compare* EPIC² (1)

lyric² /ˈlɪrɪk/ *noun* **1** [C] a lyric poem: *Christopher Marlowe's 'The Passionate Shepherd to His Love' was probably the most popular of all Elizabethan lyrics.* ➲ *compare* EPIC¹ **2 lyrics** [pl.] **~ (of sth)** the words of a song: *The provocative lyrics of rap music highlight the social ills and inequality afflicting their communities.*

M m

ma·chine /məˈʃiːn/ *noun* **1** (often in compounds) a piece of equipment with moving parts that is designed to do a particular job. The power used to work a machine may be electricity, steam, gas, etc. or human power: *Workers could be trained to operate the new machines in one or two weeks.* ◇ *A washing machine may have its operation controlled by microprocessor chips.* ◇ **by ~** *This was the world's first attempt to sort mail by machine.* **2** a group of people who operate in an efficient way within an organization: *By July 1960, the Kennedy political machine was unstoppable.* ➲ *see also* MECHANICAL

ma·chin·ery /məˈʃiːnəri/ *noun* **1** [U] machines as a group, especially large ones: *The large-scale production of timber requires heavy machinery and substantial forest areas for economic returns.* **2** [U, sing.] the parts of a living thing that are involved in a particular process: *The goal of a virus is to enter a host cell and take advantage of the host's cellular machinery to promote its own replication and propagation.* **3** [U, sing.] the organization or structure of sth; the system for doing sth: **~ of sth** *One basic condition of sustainable democracy is that the machinery of government should be effectively honest and competent.* ◇ **~ for doing sth** *The government still had to put in place the machinery for enforcing compliance with the country's emissions standards.*

macro /ˈmækrəʊ; *NAmE* ˈmækroʊ/ *adj.* [only before noun] large; on a large scale: *Research will be needed at the macro level, for example tracking national trends in health inequalities.* OPP MICRO

macro·eco·nom·ics /ˌmækrəʊˌiːkəˈnɒmɪks; *NAmE* ˌmækroʊˌekəˈnɑːmɪks/ *noun* [U] the study of large economic systems, such as those of whole countries or areas of the world: *Macroeconomics involves the analysis of the economy as a whole, rather than one particular market.* ■ **macro·eco·nom·ic** *adj.*: *The basic idea of Keynesian macroeconomic policy is that unemployment is the result of insufficient spending by consumers and firms.* ◇ *macroeconomic stability/stabilization*

made *past tense, past part. of* MAKE

maga·zine /ˌmæɡəˈziːn; *NAmE* ˈmæɡəziːn/ *noun* **1** a type of large thin book with a paper cover published every week or month, containing articles, photographs, etc, often on a particular topic: *Weekly magazines such as 'Time' and 'Newsweek' are also sources of Americans' information.* ◇ **+ noun** *The database of newspaper, journal and magazine articles dates back to 1980.* **2** (*BrE also* **magaˈzine programme** *NAmE also* **magaˈzine program**) a regular radio or television programme consisting of a variety of topics: *Two common genres in primetime TV, news magazines and sport, include many promos within the programmes themselves.* ◇ *The evening magazine programme soon attracted a growing audience.*

magic¹ /ˈmædʒɪk/ *noun* [U] **1** the secret power of appearing to make impossible things happen by saying special words or doing special things: *The universe depicted in Shakespeare's plays of the late sixteenth and early seventeenth centuries was one of magic, mystery and wonder.* **2** a special quality or ability that sb/sth has, that seems too wonderful to be real: *By 1983, prosperity had returned, and with it the widespread belief that Reagan's economic policies had indeed finally worked their magic.*

magic² /ˈmædʒɪk/ *adj.* having or using special powers to make impossible things happen or seem to happen: *In this fantasy game, players wear armour, ride horses, fight battles and cast magic spells.* ◇ *There is no magic solution and there is no single, simple technological fix.*

magic·al /ˈmædʒɪkl/ *adj.* containing magic; used in magic: *The Arthurian romances differ from the sagas in their representation of healing and magical power.* ■ **ma·gic·al·ly** /ˈmædʒɪkli/ *adv.*: *The youth Teiresias is magically transformed into a girl.*

magis·trate /ˈmædʒɪstreɪt/ *noun* an official who acts as a judge in the lowest courts of law: *The defendants were convicted by magistrates of wilfully obstructing an officer in the execution of his duty.*

magma /ˈmæɡmə/ *noun* [U, C] very hot liquid rock found below the earth's surface: *Magma rises into the space and begins to solidify.* ◇ *The magmas produced were predominantly of alkaline type.* ◇ **+ noun** *The magma chamber is fed by a larger magma reservoir at the base of the crust or in the mantle.*

mag·ne·sium /mæɡˈniːziəm/ *noun* [U] (*symb.* **Mg**) the chemical element of ATOMIC NUMBER 12. Magnesium is a light, silver-white metal that burns with a bright white flame: *In some designs an alloy of magnesium is used.*

mag·net /ˈmæɡnət/ *noun* **1** a piece of iron or other material that attracts objects containing iron towards it, either naturally or because of an electric current that is passed through it: *Iron filings placed near a magnet will move to orient themselves along the lines of the magnetic field.* **2** [usually sing.] **~ (for sb/sth)** a person, place or thing that sb/sth is attracted to: *The city was a magnet for artists and intellectuals.* ◇ *A second magnet for funds was government bonds.*

M

mag·net·ic /mæɡˈnetɪk/ *adj.* [usually before noun] **1** behaving like a magnet: *The data are recorded on a thin band of flexible plastic coated with magnetic material.* **2** connected with or produced by magnetism: *Iron loses its magnetic properties as it is heated.* **3** attractive in a very powerful way: *They created an advertising campaign that linked the shoes to the basketball star's magnetic personality.*

magˌnetic ˈfield *noun* an area around a magnet or magnetic object, where there is a force that will attract some metals towards it: *When an electric current flows through the coil, it generates a magnetic field that causes the iron to act like a magnet.*

mag·net·ism /ˈmæɡnətɪzəm/ *noun* [U] a physical property of some metals such as iron, produced by electric currents, that causes forces between objects, either pulling them towards each other or pushing them apart: *For decades, theoretical physicists have struggled to combine theories of electricity, magnetism and gravity into one unified theory.*

mag·ni·fi·ca·tion /ˌmæɡnɪfɪˈkeɪʃn/ *noun* **1** [U] the act of making sth look larger: *Little can be seen of the individual cloud droplets without magnification.* **2** [C, U] the degree to which sth is made to look larger; the degree to which sth is able to make things look larger: *The tissue specimens were analysed at magnifications of 100, 200 and 400.* ◇ *The pieces were placed on a slide and examined under low magnification with a compound microscope.*

mag·nify /ˈmæɡnɪfaɪ/ *verb* (**mag·ni·fies**, **mag·ni·fy·ing**, **mag·ni·fied**, **mag·ni·fied**) **1 ~ sth** to make sth bigger, louder or stronger: *The negative impacts of rapid population growth are magnified and made more urgent in the context of climate change.* **2 ~ sth** to make sth seem more important or serious than it really is: *Political memories, myths and emotions can magnify fears of physical insecurity and cultural domination, driving groups further apart.* ➲ *compare* EXAGGERATE **3 ~ sth** to make sth look bigger than it really is, for example by using a LENS or MICROSCOPE: *The retinal image will be magnified.* ➲ *compare* ENLARGE

mag·ni·tude /ˈmæɡnɪtjuːd; *NAmE* ˈmæɡnɪtuːd/ *noun* **1** [U] **~ (of sth)** size: *Qualitative data are needed to determine the magnitude of impact that this might have.* ◇ *Advances of smaller magnitude have been identified in glaciers in the Alps.* ➲ *see also* ORDER OF MAGNITUDE **2** [U] **~ (of sth)** the great size or extent of sth: *The magnitude of the problem was not realized at first.* **3** [U] **~ (of sth)** great importance: *He made discoveries of such magnitude that he should have won several Nobel Prizes.* **4** [C, U] **~ (of sth)** the degree to which a star is bright: *Sixth and higher magnitudes were used to label stars visible only with telescopes.* ◇ *The scale runs from small values of magnitude for the brightest stars to large values for the faintest.* **5** [C, U] **~ (of sth)** the size of an EARTHQUAKE: *Using modern earthquake data, scientists have been able to estimate the magnitudes of the main shocks during that period.* ◇ *The two earthquakes were fairly close in magnitude.*

mail[1] /meɪl/ *noun* [U] **1** (*BrE also* **post**) the official system used for sending and delivering letters, packages, etc: **by ~** *The follow-up questionnaires were sent by mail.* **2** (*BrE also* **post**) letters, packages, etc. that are sent and delivered: *The company sent out 100 million pieces of mail each year.*

mail[2] /meɪl/ *verb* (*especially NAmE*) to send a letter, etc. to sb by mail: **~ sth (to sb/sth)** *The study involved mailing a survey to law enforcement agencies for cities with a population of 50 000 or more.* ◇ **~ sb sth** *Those who did not have Internet access were mailed paper surveys.*
PHRV ˌ**mail sth** ˈ**out** to send out a large number of letters, etc. at the same time: *Questionnaires were mailed out to nearly 8 000 people.*

M

mail·ing /ˈmeɪlɪŋ/ *noun* **1** [U] the act of sending items by mail: *The package contained a stamped addressed envelope for return mailing.* **2** (*NAmE also* **mailer**) [C] a letter or package that is sent by mail, especially one that is sent to a large number of people: *The study recruited people through mailings, general advertising and newsletters.*

main[1] /meɪn/ *adj.* [only before noun] being the largest or most important of its kind: *The oceans are the main source of water vapour in the atmosphere.* ◇ *There are four main reasons why US firms prefer to invest in rich countries rather than in poor ones.* ◇ *The two main parties together polled less than 70% of the total vote.*
▸ MAIN + NOUN **reason • cause • effect • point • factor • feature, characteristic • component • element • problem • concern • issue • theme • area • argument • focus • purpose, function • objective, aim, goal • task • challenge • advantage • source • findings • conclusion • difference • type • category • group • party • character • text • body of sth** *There are two main problems with this way of thinking.* ◇ *The main aim of the programme was to improve patient safety.* ◇ *The main body of the chapter is concerned with the European Convention on Human Rights.*

main[2] /meɪn/ *noun*
IDM **in the** ˈ**main** used to say that a statement is true in most cases: *The Law Commission's recommendations were, in the main, accepted.*

the main·land /ˈmeɪnlænd/ *noun* [sing.] the main area of land of a country, not including any islands near to it: *The island of Crete lies to the south, about midway between the Greek mainland and North Africa.* ■ **main·land** *adj.* [only before noun] *The company's entry into mainland China started in 1998 when it opened its first store in Shanghai.*

main·ly /ˈmeɪnli/ *adv.* **1** more than anything else SYN CHIEFLY, PRIMARILY: *Previous population-based studies focused mainly on specific diseases.* ◇ *Classical explanations are mainly concerned with trade between nations.* ◇ **~ because...** *Behaviours differ, mainly because cultures are very different from one country or group to another.* ◇ **~ due to...** *The sudden increase was mainly due to the fact that several large high street retailers launched their sales online on that day.* **2** in most cases; used to talk about the largest part of a group of people or things: *Part-time employees were mainly female.* ◇ *The countries taking part in the conference were mainly Eastern African countries.* ➲ language bank *at* BROADLY **3** concerning the greater part of sth: *The assessment of the development has been mainly positive.*

THESAURUS

main • major • key • central • principal • prime • primary *adj.*

These words all describe sth that is the largest or most important of its kind.

▸ to be key/central **to** sth
▸ a/the main/major/key/principal/prime/primary **factor/source**
▸ a/the main/major/key/central/principal/prime/primary **concern**
▸ a/the main/major/key/central/principal **component**
▸ a/the main/major/key/central/primary **issue/role**
▸ a/the main/major/principal/prime/primary **cause**
▸ to be **of** major/key/central/prime/primary **importance**

- **Main** tends to describe sth in fairly objective terms as the largest, most significant, etc; **major** can express a judgement about how important or serious sth is: *The main sources of water for the body are food and fluid ingestion.* ◇ *Illegal logging is a major problem in many parts of the region.*
- **Key** emphasizes that sth is the important thing in a particular context; **central** emphasizes that sth is important because other things depend on or are influenced by it: *Some commentators predict that resource shortages will play a key role in future conflicts.* ◇ *Ethical issues are nowadays more central to discussions about research than ever before.*
- **Principal** is mostly used for statements of fact about which there can be no argument; to state an opinion, it is more usual to use **key** or **central**: *Sulfuric acid is one of the principal acidifying components in precipitation.* ◇ *a key/central issue/question*
- **Prime** and **primary** can both describe sth that is the most important and so should be considered first; **prime** can emphasize one thing above all others; **primary** is often used where there are a number of things which can be ranked as ***primary***, ***secondary***, etc: *This phase is therefore of prime importance for the contractor.* ◇ *Obesity will soon overtake smoking as the primary preventable cause of death.*

the main·stream /ˈmeɪnstriːm/ *noun* [sing.] the ideas and opinions that are thought to be normal because they are shared by most people; the people whose ideas and opinions are most accepted: **in/into the ~ (of sth)** *The strategy was to bring formerly excluded groups into the mainstream.* ■ **main·stream** *adj.* [usually before noun] *The film draws attention to the exclusion of women's voices from the mainstream media.*

main·tain AWL /meɪnˈteɪn/ *verb* **1 ~ sth** to cause or enable a condition or situation to continue SYN PRESERVE[1] (1): *Walther argues that people can develop and maintain strong social relationships online.* ◇ *The authorities are determined to maintain control at any cost.* **2 ~ sth** to keep sth at the same level or rate: *The government meanwhile maintained a constant level of spending.* ◇ *In some countries, people maintain a high standard of living while working fewer hours than before.* **3** to state strongly that sth is true, even when some other people may not believe it: **~ (that)...** *Rowse maintains that Shakespeare's Sonnets were written between 1592 and 1595.* ➲ *compare* INSIST (1) ➲ thesaurus note *at* ARGUE **4 ~ sb/sth** to support sb/sth over a long period of time by providing money, paying for food, etc: *Failure to maintain a child as required by section 47 of the Children's Act 1998 is a criminal offence.* **5 ~ sth** to keep a building, machine, etc. in good condition by checking or repairing it regularly: *The company is responsible for establishing a reserve fund to maintain the property.* ◇ *If they are well maintained, even very old generators can give many additional years of service.* **6 ~ a record** to write sth down as a record and keep adding the most recent information SYN KEEP (9): *The employer is obliged to maintain records of the hours worked and payments made to workers.*

▸ MAINTAIN + NOUN **relationship, relations, ties, contact • control • balance • position • state • order • stability • peace • the status quo • continuity • independence • integrity • confidentiality • identity • distinction • system • structure • population** *What these elites want is to maintain their position in society.* | **level • rate • standard • value • temperature • pressure** *China has maintained rates of increase in output unparalleled by any of the world's capitalist economies.*

▸ ADVERB + MAINTAIN **still • always • consistently • usually, generally • often • long** *Economists such as Friedman have always maintained that this is the case.* ◇ *The kingdom had consistently maintained close cultural and political ties with France.* | **simply • largely • successfully • effectively** *The country largely maintained a liberal policy on film censorship.*

main·ten·ance AWL /ˈmeɪntənəns/ *noun* [U] **1** the act of keeping sth in good condition by checking or repairing it regularly: *The fuel tax is also used to generate revenue to finance road maintenance.* ◇ **~ of sth** *The safety aspects covered by the welfare regulations include the maintenance of equipment.* ◇ **+ noun** *Maintenance costs increase with the age of the equipment.* **2 ~ (of sth)** the act of making a condition or situation continue: *The principal objective of international law was the maintenance of peace and stability.* **3 ~ (of sth)** the act of keeping sth at the same level or rate: *The maintenance of strong levels of employment in wealthy countries depended on high levels of skill in the workforce.* **4** (*BrE*) money that sb must pay regularly to their former wife, husband or partner, especially when they have had children together: *The wife had applied for maintenance from her second husband.* ◇ *The Bill proposed to simplify how child maintenance was calculated.* ◇ **+ noun** *maintenance payments/obligations*

maize /meɪz/ (*BrE*) (*NAmE* **corn**) *noun* [U] a tall plant grown for its large yellow grains that are used for making flour or eaten as a vegetable; the grains of this plant: *At least half of the world's people rely on one of three cereal crops: wheat, maize and rice.*

major[1] AWL /ˈmeɪdʒə(r)/ *adj.* **1** [usually before noun] large, important or serious: *The period was dominated by a Tory Party that was opposed to major social changes.* ◇ *There is strong evidence that genetic factors play a major role in causing this disorder.* ◇ *Stroke is a major problem worldwide.* OPP MINOR[1] **2** [only before noun] greater or more important; main: *The major part of this huge territory became the new Russian province of Turkestan.* SYN MAIN[1]

▸ MAJOR + NOUN **role • part, component, element • feature • contribution • factor • determinant • reason • advantage • problem, issue • concern • theme • focus • challenge • change • shift • reform • difference • source • cause • effect • impact • influence • advance • city • area • centre • group • party • company • player • contributor • power • event • project • surgery** *Methane is the major component of most natural gases* ◇ *Four major ecological factors determine crop yield in agro-ecosystems:...*

major[2] AWL /ˈmeɪdʒə(r)/ *noun* (*NAmE*) **1** the main subject or course of a student at college or university: *According to the 2006 survey, 64 per cent of men choose a technical or industrial major.* ➲ *compare* MINOR[2] (2) **2** a student studying a particular subject as the main part of their course: *Geography majors at Texas A&M University rose from 70 in 1985 to 190 in 2001.*

ma·jor·ity AWL /məˈdʒɒrəti; *NAmE* məˈdʒɔːrəti; məˈdʒɑːrəti/ *noun* (*pl.* **-ies**) **1** [sing.+ sing./pl. v.] the greater number or part: **~ (of sb/sth)** *The majority of the time was spent collecting the data.* ◇ **the vast ~ (of sb/sth)** *The vast majority of such families save very little over the course of a lifetime.* ◇ **+ noun** *Their descendants are the majority population in Mauritius today.* OPP MINORITY (1) **2** [C] the number of votes by which one side in an election, a competition, a discussion, etc. wins: *It was unlikely that any one party would win an overall majority.* HELP A/an **overall/clear/absolute majority** is more votes than all the other people or parties together: **by/with a... ~** *This same government had been elected with a clear majority in 1945.* ◇ **by/with a ~ of sth** *The Bill was passed by a majority of 238 votes to 66.* ◇ **+ noun** *Today, Qualified Majority Voting (QMV) is applied to most EU decisions.* HELP In a vote, a **simple/bare majority** is over 50% of those voting; the term **qualified majority** is used when a proposal requires a majority set at a higher level (for example, two thirds) in order to pass. **3** [C] (*US*) the difference between the number of votes given to the candidate who wins the election and the total number of votes of all the other candidates: *Without this shift, Kerry would have had a popular majority of a million votes.* ➲ *see also* PLURALITY (2) **4** [U] the age at which a person is legally considered to be an adult: *The law recognizes that the young person is able to make decisions, despite the fact that he or she has not attained majority.*

IDM **be in the/a majority** to belong to or be the larger group or number: *In the over-50 age group, women are in the majority.*

▸ ADJECTIVE + MAJORITY **vast, great, overwhelming • large, substantial** *In the great majority of cases, a practical solution can be found.* | **• overall, clear, absolute • simple, bare • narrow • comfortable, large, substantial • qualified • two-thirds • parliamentary** *A director can be removed by a simple majority of votes.*

▸ VERB + MAJORITY **constitute, represent, comprise** *Women and children constitute the majority of the world's refugee population.* | **win, secure • command • form** *No one party could command a majority in the legislature.*

▸ MAJORITY + NOUN **population • group • view, opinion • decision • shareholder • ownership • stake** *There is no guarantee that the majority view is the correct one.* | **voting • vote • party • rule, government** *The chief argument in favour of majority rule is that it provides effective government by concentrating power in the hands of a single party.*

make /meɪk/ *verb* ➲ *see also* MADE (**made, made** /meɪd/) **1** to create or prepare sth by combining materials or putting parts together: **~ sth** *People in the US tend to buy more products made in other countries.* ◇ **~ sth (out) of sth** *The model is made of wood and plastic.* ◇ **~ sth from sth** *Historically, they made their artefacts and buildings from local, natural or renewable materials.* ◇ **~ sth into sth** *The seeds of the plants were boiled and made into porridge.* ◇ **~ sth for sb** *These giants made the thunderbolt for Zeus and the trident for Poseidon.* ◇ **~ sb sth** *She had made him some chicken soup.* ➲ *see also* MAN-MADE **2 ~ sth** to write, create or prepare sth: *It is also worth making a list of the patient's problems at this point.* ◇ *Parliament makes the laws and the judiciary interprets them.* ◇ *He made three more films in quick succession.* **3 ~ a decision, choice, contribution, claim, etc.** to decide, choose, etc. sth: *The decision must be made by the end of the month.* ◇ *Rich people make better use of health care systems.* HELP **Make** can be used in this way with a number of different nouns. These expressions are included at the entry for each noun. **4 ~ sth** to cause sth to exist, happen

M

or be done: *A mechanical device made a noise every 25 seconds.* ◇ *Teachers often make this mistake.* **5** to cause sb/sth to be or become sth: **~ sb/sth/yourself + adj.** *The aim is to make offenders aware of the harm they have caused.* ◇ *The political system in Germany makes reform difficult.* ◇ **~ sb/sth/yourself + noun** *Peter the Great's conquests made Russia a permanent part of Europe for the first time.* ◇ **~ it possible (for sb/sth) to do sth** *Modern communications technology has made it possible for people who do certain kinds of jobs to work from home.* ◇ **~ it clear (to sb) that...** *Commercial banks need to make it clear to firms that the old system of subsidies cannot continue.* ◇ **~ sth of sb/sth** *The innovator makes enemies of all who prospered under the old order.* **6 ~ sb/sth do sth** to cause sb/sth to do sth: *Nicotine is a highly addictive substance that makes people feel energized and alert.* **7** to force sb to do sth: **~ sb do sth** *Frederick III was able to make the nobility accept hereditary monarchy.* ◇ **be made to do sth** *They were made to work for the Spartans as serfs on what had been their own land.* **8 ~ sth** to earn or gain money: *Hospitals are making £78m a year from car park charges.* ◇ *The possibility of making a profit is what motivates business owners.* **9 ~ sb + noun** to elect or choose sb as sth: *She was made a director of the company.* **10** *linking verb* **+ noun** to become or develop into sth; to be suitable for sth: *Such a person would never make a good teacher.* ◇ *It also makes an excellent subject for multiple choice questions.* **11 ~ sth (+ adv./prep.)** to cause sth to appear as a result of breaking, tearing, hitting or removing material: *If a hole were made in the membrane, the protons would simply flood through it.* **12 ~ sth** to cause sth to be successful: *Konrad Lorenz made his reputation with his studies of animal behaviour.*

M

IDM Most idioms containing **make** are at the entries for the nouns and adjectives in the idioms, for example **make sense** is at **sense**. **make ˈdo (with sth)** to manage with sth that is not really good enough: *Women scrape together food and clothing for their children and make do.* ◇ *Their engineers had to make do with old equipment.* **make ˈgood** to become rich and successful: *Both are poor boys who have made good.* **make sth ˈgood 1** to pay for, replace or repair sth that has been lost or damaged: *The tenant must make good any damage done in removing the fixture.* **2** to do sth that you have promised, threatened, etc. to do: *He made good his threat.* **ˈmake it 1** to be successful in your career: *Many in the immigrant generation were struggling to make it in America.* **2** to succeed in reaching a place in time, especially when this is difficult: *About 40 per cent perished along the way, and of those who made it, 15 per cent died after their arrival.* **make it ˈthrough sth** to deal successfully with a difficult experience: *In New York City, thousands of children were failing to make it through the educational system.* **make the ˈmost of sth/sb/yourself** to gain as much advantage, enjoyment, etc. as you can from sth/sb: *The European Parliament has always made the most of its limited powers.* **make ˈmuch of sth/sb** to treat sth/sb as very important: *The Labour Party in Scotland was keen to make much of Gordon Brown's Scottish roots.* **ˌmake or ˈbreak sth** to be the factor that makes sth either a success or a failure: *Review criticism could make or break a reputation.*

PHR V **ˈmake for sth 1** to tend to result in sth: *Their report on conditions in the camps makes for grim reading.* **2** to move towards sth SYN HEAD[2] (2): *From Britain, he made for Spain, via southern Gaul.*

ˈmake sb/sth into sb/sth to change sb/sth into sb/sth SYN TURN SB/STH (FROM STH) INTO STH: *In his view, the early church sought to make the man Jesus into a divine figure.* ◇ *The novel by Robert James Waller was later made into a Hollywood film.*

ˈmake sth of sb/sth to understand the meaning or character of sb/sth: *The party's central committee never seemed quite sure of what to make of Kerensky.* ◇ *It is difficult to make anything of this collection of coincidences.*

ˌmake sb/sth ˈout 1 to say that sth is true about sb/sth when it may not be SYN CLAIM[2] (1): *Ethics is not as subjective as Hume makes out.* ◇ **~ to be sth** *British theatre is not as insular as it is sometimes made out to be.* **2** to manage to see sb/sth or read or hear sth SYN DISTINGUISH (5): *Herschel could barely make out the outlines of Uranus through his telescope.* **ˌmake sth ˈout** (used in negative sentences and questions) to understand sth; to see the reasons for sth: *It is difficult to make out the characteristics of the contemporary period.*

ˌmake sth ˈup 1 to form sth SYN CONSTITUTE (2): *Oxygen makes up roughly 20% of the atmosphere.* ➲ *related noun* MAKE-UP (1) ➲ language bank *at* PROPORTION **2** to put sth together from several different things: *The solution had been made up at the wrong concentration.* **3** to invent a story, lie, plan, etc: *It is common for people who see something strange to make up a story that explains it.* **4** to replace sth that has been lost; to COMPENSATE for sth: *Britain was able to make up the deficit on its commodity trade.*

ˌmake ˈup for sth to do sth that corrects a bad situation SYN COMPENSATE (2): *The proposed increase in funding could not make up for a half-century of neglect.*

maker /ˈmeɪkə(r)/ *noun* (often in compounds) a person, company or piece of equipment that makes or produces sth: *The company claims to have around half the global market for ice-cream makers.* ◇ **~ of sth** *Procter & Gamble, makers of Ariel detergent, wanted to test a new packaging design.* ➲ *see also* DECISION-MAKER, POLICYMAKER

ˈmake-up *noun* **1** [sing.] **~ (of sth)** the different things, people, etc. that combine to form sth; the way in which they combine: *Immigration has changed the social, ethnic and cultural make-up of Britain.* **2** [sing., U] **~ (of sb)** the different qualities that combine to form sb's character or being: *We can and do think of reason and appetite as part of our psychological make-up.* ◇ *Illness is essentially a failure of adaptation to an individual's environment, partly owing to genetic make-up.* **3** [U] substances used especially by women to make their faces look more attractive, or used by actors to change their appearance: *She refused to wear make-up or have her hair styled or generally conform to feminine stereotypes.*

mak·ing /ˈmeɪkɪŋ/ *noun* [U] (often in compounds) the act or process of making or producing sth: *Norway has made strenuous efforts to incorporate environmental values into policymaking.* ◇ **~ of sth** *Erwin Panofsky specifically compares the making of a film to the building of a cathedral.* ➲ *see also* DECISION-MAKING, NON-PROFIT

IDM **be the ˈmaking of sb** to make sb become a better or more successful person: *Syme remarks that 'exile may be the making of an historian'.* **in the ˈmaking** in the process of becoming sth or of being made: *The first edition of his dictionary, which was twelve years in the making, was published in Holland in 1690.* **of your own ˈmaking** (of a problem or difficulty) created by you rather than by sb/sth else: *The problems experienced by the urban poor are not of their own making.*

male[1] /meɪl/ *adj.* **1** (*abbr.* **m**) belonging to the sex that does not give birth to babies or lay eggs: *Male workers under 25 were paid 5 per cent more than their female counterparts.* ◇ *Participants in the study were predominantly male.* OPP FEMALE[1] (1) **2** connected with men or male animals: *The technique is a major advance in the treatment of male infertility.* ◇ *Lande (1981) showed that male traits and female preferences can co-evolve under some conditions.* OPP FEMALE[1] (2) ➲ *compare* MASCULINE **3** (*biology*) (of plants or flowers) producing POLLEN: *In maize, male and female flowers develop at particular sites on the shoot.* OPP FEMALE[1] (3)

male[2] /meɪl/ *noun* **1** a male animal or plant: *The evidence suggests that females prefer males with colourful beaks.* ◇ *Females benefit from being mated to dominant males by* *gaining a higher priority of access to food.* ◇ *Small pines are usually males and produce female flowers or cones only later.* OPP FEMALE[2] (1) **2** (*formal*) a man or boy: *Eczema is a skin condition that can affect both males and females of all ages.* ◇ *All free adult males had a theoretically equal right to participate in government.* HELP In this meaning, **male** is used mainly in formal and official language to talk about men or boys as a group. OPP FEMALE[2] (2)

ma·lig·nancy /məˈlɪɡnənsi/ *noun* (*pl.* -ies) **1** [C] a malignant mass of TISSUE in the body SYN TUMOUR: *Skin cancer is the most common malignancy in Western countries.* **2** [U] the state of being malignant: *An increased incidence of malignancy was seen in children exposed to radiation following the accident at Chernobyl.*

ma·lig·nant /məˈlɪɡnənt/ *adj.* (of a TUMOUR or disease) that cannot be controlled and is likely to cause death: *Surgery is commonly performed to diagnose and remove malignant tumours.* ➲ *compare* BENIGN (1)

mal·nu·tri·tion /ˌmælnjuːˈtrɪʃn; *NAmE* ˌmælnuːˈtrɪʃn/ *noun* [U] a poor condition of health caused by a lack of food or a lack of the right type of food: *In the world today, some 800 million people suffer from malnutrition.* ➲ *compare* NUTRITION

mam·mal /ˈmæml/ *noun* any animal, including humans, that gives birth to live babies, not eggs, and feeds its young on milk: *Marine mammals such as seals have fast reproductive rates for their size.* ◇ **+ noun** *Changes in farming practice have led to a decrease in many small mammal species.* ■ **mam·ma·lian** /mæˈmeɪliən/ *adj.*: *In many mammalian species, mates rather than material resources need defending.* ◇ *Mammalian cells lack a rigid cell wall.*

man /mæn/ *noun* (*pl.* **men** /men/) **1** [C] an adult male human: *Edwards was sent as a young man to Jamaica to live with his wealthy uncle.* ◇ *Men and women appear to be equally at risk from the disease.* **2** [U] humans as a group: *Not all pollution is caused by man.* HELP **Man** and **mankind** have traditionally been used to to mean 'all men and women'. Many people now prefer to use **humanity**, **the human race**, **human beings**, **people** or, especially in the field of life sciences, **humans**: *Studies of happiness around the world suggest that the human race is tremendously adaptable.* ◇ *Human beings tend to be social, existing in natural communities of about 150.* ◇ *Humans have a long history of using plants.* **3** [U] humans from a particular period of history: *Early man made use of stone for millennia, before discovering copper.* **4** [C] (*literary* or *old-fashioned*) a person, either male or female: *Later thinkers regarded it a self-evident truth that all men are born equal.* **5** [C] (in compounds) a male person connected with a particular place, activity or job: *In 1942 Newman received a letter from Frank Adcock, another Cambridge man.* ◇ *Boring formal speeches were made by party men and officials on all possible occasions.* ◇ *Medical men did not have the kinds of social power they do today.* **6** [C, usually pl.] a male worker in an organization who obeys the instructions of a person of higher rank: *Thirty thousand men worked on the tunnel for eleven years.* **7 men** [pl.] ordinary members of a military force as opposed to the officers: *The commander reported that he and his men were ready for battle.* **8** [C] a husband or sexual partner: *Although unmarried, they lived together as man and wife.* **9** [C] a person who is strong and brave or has other qualities that some people think are particularly male: *Real men were not supposed to show their feelings.*
IDM **the ˌman (and/or ˌwoman) in the ˈstreet** an average or ordinary person, either male or female: *It is one of the few archaeological finds that really interests the man in the street.* **a ˌman of the ˈpeople** a man, especially a politician, who understands and is sympathetic to ordinary people: *Abraham Lincoln was pre-eminently a man of the people.* **be your own ˈman/ˈwoman** to act or think independently and with confidence, not following others or being ordered: *In rejecting the precedent of his father, Billy becomes his own man and throws off the legacy of his father's failure.* **to a ˈman | to the last ˈman** used to emphasize that sth is true of all the people being described: *They were also communists, almost to a man.* ➲ *more at* ODD, THING

man·age /ˈmænɪdʒ/ *verb* **1** [T] to succeed in doing sth difficult: **~ sth** *Informed guesswork is all we can manage.* ◇ **~ to do sth** *Some researchers have managed to get access to government-owned survey data.* **2** [T] **~ sb/sth** to keep sb/sth under control; to deal with sb/sth: *Helping children to manage anger is not easy.* ◇ *Bridge engineers must manage risks carefully.* ◇ *The challenge lies in managing these patients in a sympathetic manner.* ◇ *To succeed, organizations must manage their relationships with government and regulatory bodies better than their competitors.* **3** [T, I] **~ (sth)** to be in charge of a business or an organization: *The directors manage the company on behalf of the shareholders.* ◇ *She could draw on their expertise and learn how to manage better than them.* **4** [T, I] **~ (sb)** to have the position of being in charge of staff at work: *The Harvard model was devised to inform managers of improved ways of managing people.* ◇ *When all is said and done, managers retain the power to manage and employees are still left with a basic obligation to obey.* **5** [T] **~ sth** to use money, time, information, etc. in a sensible way: *Ministers claim that some local authorities manage resources poorly.* ◇ *Students who manage their time effectively are more likely to do well at school.* ◇ *Financial and technical support enabled us to manage the data collected by hundreds of volunteers.* **6** [I] to be able to solve your problems or deal with a difficult situation SYN COPE: *The brothers and sisters of children with serious physical illness generally manage well.* ◇ **~ with/without sb/sth** *The Scottish economy, too, managed with little coinage before the 1140s.* ◇ *Human beings cannot manage without each other.* **7** [I] **~ (on sth)** to be able to live without having much money: *Social activities at school can be particularly difficult for families trying to manage on a low income.*

M

man·age·able /ˈmænɪdʒəbl/ *adj.* that can be dealt with or controlled without difficulty: *The debt has been reduced to a more manageable level.*

man·aged /ˈmænɪdʒd/ *adj.* [only before noun] carefully taken care of and controlled: *Beech is an important species in natural and managed forests in Europe.*

man·age·ment /ˈmænɪdʒmənt/ *noun* **1** [U] the act of running and controlling a business or similar organization: *He retired early from a job in management.* ◇ *Many of the tools of project management were developed in the early US missile programmes.* ◇ **~ of sth** *She had become a specialist in the management of voluntary organizations.* ◇ **+ noun** *Questioning the use of resources is a key management skill.* **2** [C+sing./pl. v., U] the people who run and control a business or similar organization: *If a corporation has too little debt, management has little incentive to work hard for greater efficiency.* ◇ **~ of sth** *Marketing research provides the management of a company with information to make better decisions on future activities.* ◇ **+ noun** *The senior management team had provided a clear statement of the problem.* **3** [U] the act or skill of dealing with people or situations in a successful way: *These teacher skills are essential in effective classroom management.* ◇ *waste/crisis/anger management* ◇ **~ of sb/sth** *Policies on the management of people should be consistent with the long-term business strategy of the organization.* ◇ *Such methods assist in the reduction or management of risk.* ◇ **+ noun** *Personality may affect risk management strategies.* **4** [U] (*medical*) the treatment or control of diseases or illnesses; the care of patients who suffer from them: *Burns require careful management to ensure optimal healing.* ◇ **~ of sb/sth** *The management of these patients can be complex.*

man·ager /ˈmænɪdʒə(r)/ *noun* a person who is in charge of running a business or similar organization or part of one: *Managers have to make strategic decisions about the future direction of their organization.* ◇ *senior/middle managers* ◇ *a marketing/sales/project manager* ◇ **~ of sth** *In-depth interviews were held with managers of hotels, bars and restaurants in the area.*

man·ager·ial /ˌmænəˈdʒɪəriəl; *NAmE* ˌmænəˈdʒɪriəl/ *adj.* [usually before noun] connected with the work of a manager: *This failure may be a sign of more widespread managerial problems.* ◇ *Employee resistance to managerial control can take a wide range of forms.* ◇ *Conflict is pervasive in managerial decision-making.*

ˌmanaging diˈrector *noun* (*abbr.* **MD**) **~ (of sth)** (*especially BrE*) the person who is in charge of a business: *The judge found that the managing director of the company had misinformed and deceived investors.*

man·date[1] /ˈmændeɪt/ *noun* **1** the authority to do sth, given to a government or other organization by the people who vote for it in an election: **~ for sth** *President Roosevelt had a clear mandate for change when he took office in March 1933.* ◇ **~ to do sth** *It was argued that the low turnout in the election meant that the government no longer possessed a legitimate mandate to govern.* **2 ~ (to do sth)** an official order given to sb to perform a particular task: *There is no specific international body with the mandate to focus on the rights of the elderly.*

M

man·date[2] /ˈmændeɪt; ˌmænˈdeɪt/ *verb* [often passive] **1 ~ sb/sth to do sth** to give sb, especially a government or committee, the authority to do sth: *The Government of Indonesia was mandated by the 1945 Constitution to control land, water and natural resources found in Indonesia.* **2** (*especially NAmE*) to order sb to behave, do sth or vote in a particular way: **~ sb (to do sth)** *Employers are not mandated to contribute to these pension plans.* ◇ **~ that...** *California's Proposition 227 mandated that all children in California public schools must be taught in English (Crawford, 1999).*

man·da·tory /ˈmændətəri; mænˈdeɪtəri; *NAmE* ˈmændətɔːri/ *adj.* required by law SYN COMPULSORY: *Pictorial warnings were not a mandatory requirement on cigarette packets until September 2009.* ◇ **~ for sb** *A few months later, immunization became mandatory for all soldiers.* ◇ **it is ~ (for sb) to do sth** *It is mandatory for people referred to specialist mental health services to have a health and social care assessment.*

man·eu·ver (*US*) = MANOEUVRE[1], MANOEUVRE[2]

mani·fest[1] /ˈmænɪfest/ *verb* **1** [T] **~ sth (in sth)** to show sth clearly, especially a feeling, attitude or quality SYN DEMONSTRATE (2): *The country's attitude towards immigration is manifested in a host of policies.* **2** [I, T] to appear or become easy to notice: *Symptoms usually manifest during childhood or adolescence.* ◇ **~ itself (in sth)** *Public opinion manifests itself in many forms.*

mani·fest[2] /ˈmænɪfest/ *adj.* (*formal*) easy to see or understand SYN CLEAR[1] (1): *The Court considered that the Commission had made a manifest error of assessment.* ◇ **~ in sth** *The contraction phase of the economy was manifest in a significant rise in unemployment.* ■ **mani·fest·ly** *adv.* SYN CLEARLY: *This theory is manifestly incorrect.* ◇ *Schools are manifestly failing to provide children with a sufficiently inclusive social environment for their needs.*

mani·fest·ation /ˌmænɪfeˈsteɪʃn/ *noun* [C, U] **~ (of sth)** (*formal*) an event, action or thing that is a sign that sth exists or is happening; the act of appearing as a sign that sth exists or is happening: *These were the first obvious manifestations of global warming.* ◇ *In some patients, this may be the sole manifestation of the disease.*

ma·nipu·late AWL /məˈnɪpjuleɪt/ *verb* **1 ~ sth** to change, correct or move text or data on a computer: *The task of organizing and manipulating the data to produce an image is considerable.* **2 ~ sth** to change or present data in a way that deceives sb: *They expressed concern that governments were deliberately manipulating the information that circulated the globe.* **3 ~ sth** to handle or control sth in a skilful way: *The ability to manipulate genes and genomes is central to molecular biology.* **4** (*disapproving*) to control or influence sb/sth, often in a dishonest way so that they do not realize it: **~ sb/sth** *Competing groups found innovative ways to manipulate the system.* ◇ **~ sb into (doing) sth** *Marketing was seen as manipulating people into purchasing goods they did not really want.* **5 ~ sth** to examine or treat a part of the body by feeling or moving it with the hand: *The hand is gently manipulated in a circular motion at the wrist.*

ma·nipu·la·tion AWL /məˌnɪpjuˈleɪʃn/ *noun* [U, C] **1** the action of changing, correcting or moving text or data on a computer: *This system really does simplify the calculations and manipulations.* ◇ **~ of sth** *A copy of the database was made available offline so that the necessary manipulation of data could take place.* **2** the action of changing or presenting data in a way that deceives sb: *Selective information, bad information and manipulation have always been with us.* ◇ **~ of sth** *Recognition of children's rights in this regard offers children protection against adult manipulations of truth.* **3** the action of handling or controlling sth in a skilful way: *There is concern about the development of genetic manipulation without proper ethical and legal controls.* ◇ **~ of sth** *We used experimental manipulations of the subtidal communities to test these hypotheses.* **4 ~ (of sb/sth)** (*disapproving*) the action of controlling or influencing sb/sth, often in a dishonest way so that they do not realize it: *The manipulation of the studio audience is a common device in television.* ◇ *This argument could also be applied to Chirac's manipulations of the 1997 election.* **5** the examination or treatment of a part of the body by feeling or moving it with the hand: *No other manipulations consistently affected the ligament.* ◇ **~ of sth** *He diagnoses the problem through manipulation of the joint.*

ma·nipu·la·tive AWL /məˈnɪpjələtɪv; *NAmE* məˈnɪpjəleɪtɪv/ *adj.* **1** (*disapproving*) skilful at controlling or influencing a person or situation, often in a dishonest way: *Some children come across as being overly demanding or manipulative.* **2** connected with the ability to handle an object or part of the body skilfully: *The devices require manipulative skill to set up.* ◇ *In certain cases, manipulative treatment or surgery can be beneficial.*

man·kind /mænˈkaɪnd/ *noun* [U] all humans, considered as one large group; the human race: *The largest building programme in the history of mankind is now under way.* ➲ *see also* HUMANKIND

ˌman-ˈmade *adj.* made or caused by people; not happening or made naturally SYN ARTIFICIAL (1): *Bridges, like all man-made objects, have a life cycle.*

man·ner /ˈmænə(r)/ *noun* **1** [sing.] the way that sth is done or happens: **~ of (doing) sth** *It is vital to find ways of improving the present manner of doing things.* ◇ *Much of our biographical information, especially the manner of his death, comes from contemporary poetry.* ◇ **in a... ~** *Silicon was first purified in a similar manner.* **2** [sing.] the way that sb behaves towards other people: *His manner was arrogant.* **3 manners** [pl.] behaviour that is considered to be polite in a particular society or culture: *They believed in the traditional values of hard work, the nuclear family, good manners and patriotism.* **4 manners (of sb/sth)** [pl.] the habits and customs of a particular group of people: *The poem criticizes the manners of aristocratic society.*

IDM **all ˈmanner of sb/sth** many different types of people or things: *The workers engaged in manufacturing* *produced all manner of goods.* **in the manner of sb/sth** in a style that is typical of sb/sth: *Byron's poem is digressive and comic in the manner of Sterne's novel 'Tristram Shandy'.*

man·oeuvre[1] (US man·eu·ver) /mə'nuːvə(r)/ *noun* **1** [C] a movement performed with care and skill: *In order to perform a complicated docking manoeuvre, it is essential that two spacecraft can be held at rest relative to each other.* **2** [C] a clever plan, action or movement that is used to give sb an advantage: *Many others lost their land as a result of a series of financial manoeuvres, some legal and others not.* **3 manoeuvres** [pl.] military exercises involving a large number of soldiers, ships, etc: *Russian officers attended German war colleges and German officers participated in Soviet military manoeuvres.*
IDM **freedom of/room for ma'noeuvre** the chance to change the way that sth happens and influence decisions that are made: *The party had little room for manoeuvre.*

man·oeuvre[2] (US man·eu·ver) /mə'nuːvə(r)/ *verb* **1** [I, T] to move or turn skilfully or carefully; to move or turn sth skilfully or carefully: *Many bats have sophisticated echolocation abilities that appear well designed for manoeuvring and hunting at night.* ◇ **~ sth (+ adv./prep.)** *It was difficult to manoeuvre these aircraft at high speeds.* **2** [I, T] to control or influence a situation or person in a skilful but sometimes dishonest way: *By the time of the Yalta conference, the Red Army occupied Poland, leaving Roosevelt little room to manoeuvre.* ◇ **~ sb/sth + adv./prep.** *The poem does not manoeuvre the reader into taking sides.*

man·slaugh·ter /'mænslɔːtə(r)/ *noun* [U] the crime of killing sb illegally but not deliberately: *Originally, he was charged with murder, but this was reduced to manslaughter.* ➲ *compare* HOMICIDE, MURDER[1]

man·tle /'mæntl/ *noun* **1** [sing.] **~ (of sth)** (*earth science*) the part of the earth below the CRUST and surrounding the CORE: *The aim was to drill through the ocean floor to reach the Earth's mantle.* **2** [sing.] **the ~ of sb/sth** the role and responsibilities of an important person or job, especially when they are passed on from one person to another: *There was uncertainty over who should claim the mantle of leadership.* ◇ *The third son, Richard, then assumed his father's mantle.* **3** [C] **~ (of sth)** a layer of sth that covers a surface: *Higher slopes are underlain by a thick mantle of weathered rock.*

man·ual[1] AWL /'mænjuəl/ *adj.* **1** [only before noun] **manual** work involves using mainly physical strength; a **manual** worker has a job that involves mainly physical work: *Tough manual labour characterized most stages of the production process.* ◇ *For all causes of death, mortality rates for unskilled manual workers in 1991–3 were 806 per 100 000.* **2** [usually before noun] done by sb with their hands rather than using a machine: *The computerized search was supplemented by a manual search of the bibliographies of all retrieved articles.* **3** [only before noun] connected with the hands: *The treatment is appropriate for patients with good manual dexterity.*

man·ual[2] AWL /'mænjuəl/ *noun* **1 ~ (of sth)** a book that tells you how to do sth: *Loyola's 'Spiritual Exercises' had been approved by the Pope as a manual of systematic devotion.* ➲ *compare* HANDBOOK **2** a book that describes the parts of a machine and explains how to operate it: *The engine manual specified that the pistons would run for 20 000 hours before replacement was necessary.* ➲ *compare* HANDBOOK

manu·al·ly AWL /'mænjuəli/ *adv.* using the hands rather than a machine or AUTOMATIC process: *Not only were the images created manually, they were also manually animated.* ◇ *The dispensing can be done either manually or using a robot.*

manu·fac·ture[1] /ˌmænju'fæktʃə(r)/ *noun* **1** [U] the process of producing goods in large quantities: *Cement manufacture results in significant amounts of dust, SO_2, NO_x, dioxin and CO_2.* ◇ **~ of sth** *Toyota use components from France, Spain and several other countries in the manufacture of their automobiles.* **2 manufactures** [pl.] goods that have been produced in large quantities: *The country became a major importer of cotton manufactures.*

manu·fac·ture[2] /ˌmænju'fæktʃə(r)/ *verb* **~ sth** to make goods in large quantities, using machinery: *'Just-in-time' production aims to manufacture goods rapidly to order.* ◇ *Europeans wanted to acquire raw materials and to sell their manufactured products.*

manu·fac·tur·er /ˌmænju'fæktʃərə(r)/ *noun* a person or company that produces goods in large quantities SYN MAKER: *a car/computer manufacturer* ◇ *The fibre was activated according to the manufacturer's instructions.* ◇ **~ of sth** *The company is a leading manufacturer of fast-moving consumer goods.*

manu·fac·tur·ing /ˌmænju'fæktʃərɪŋ/ *noun* [U] the business or industry of producing goods in large quantities using machinery: *The number of jobs in manufacturing declined sharply.* ◇ *car/chemical/textile manufacturing* ◇ **+ noun** *Wages in manufacturing industries are considerably lower in poor countries than they are in the US and Europe.*

manu·script /'mænjuskrɪpt/ *noun* (*abbr.* MS) **1** [C, U] a copy of a book, piece of music, etc. before it has been printed: *Approximately 400 manuscripts were submitted to the journal in 2010.* ◇ **~ of sth** *The dying Herbert entrusted the manuscript of his poems to his friend Nicholas Ferrar.* ◇ **in ~** *After circulating in manuscript for nearly 19 years, it was published in 1816.* **2** [C] a book, document or piece of music written by hand rather than typed or printed, especially a very old one: *The earliest surviving manuscript dates from the sixth century.*

many /'meni/ *det., pron.* **1** (used with plural nouns and verbs) a large number of: *In many cases, economic integration also involves some degree of political integration.* ◇ *Many studies compare the rate of disease in different geographical locations.* ◇ *Not many brands can survive without advertising for any extended period.* ◇ *Internet pharmacies have improved access and choice for many.* ◇ **~ of sb/sth** *Many of these questions have not yet been answered.* ◇ **so ~** *The existing members were worried that taking in so many new countries could impair the EU.* ◇ **too ~** *He had told Stalin that he was losing too many pilots because they were forced to fly in unsafe aircraft.* **2** used to ask about the number of people or things, or to refer to a known number: **how ~** *Given statistics of past earthquakes, how many people could be killed in a large future urban earthquake?* ◇ **as ~ ... as sb/sth** *China had six times as many university students as the UK in 2001.* **3 the many** used with a plural verb to mean 'most people': *Their policies blatantly favour the few at the expense of the many.* **4 many a** used with a singular noun and verb to mean 'a large number of': *Many a minority group has felt itself to be under threat from a dominant group.*
IDM **as many as...** used to show surprise that the number of people or things involved is so large: *As many as 250 000 were injured.*

map[1] /mæp/ *noun* **1 ~ (of sth)** a drawing or plan of the earth's surface or part of it, showing countries, towns, rivers, etc: *In 1815, Smith created the first geological map of England.* ◇ *Hardly anything remains of this topography today, but detailed maps reveal what once existed.* **2** a diagram or collection of data that shows how sth is arranged or organized: *The images show the electron density map as a mesh of thin, grey lines.* ◇ **~ of sth** *The markers are closely spaced enough to make a fine-scale map of*

M

chromosomes. **3** a description or diagram that shows how sb sees the world or thinks about a problem; a description of how sth has developed: *Cognitive maps visualize the elements and interactions within a complex problem.* ◇ **~ of sth** *'Reclaiming the Archive: Feminism and Film History' is a useful map of the field of feminist film history.* ➲ *see also* MIND MAP

map² /mæp/ *verb* **(-pp-)** **1** [T] **~ sth** to discover or give information about the way sth is arranged or organized: *Bowen (1998) mapped ethnic patterns in several large metropolitan areas.* ◇ *Mortimer isolated a large array of mutants that he and Hawthorne used to map the genome.* **2** [T, I] to link each element of a set with an element of another set; to be linked in this way: **~ sth to/onto/into sth** *A rotation of this graph diagram through 180° maps u onto w, w onto u, v onto x, and x onto v.* ◇ **~ to/onto/into sth** *Only one outcome maps into x = 0, whereas six outcomes map into x = 2.* **3** [T] **~ sth** to make a map of an area SYN CHART² (3): *Captain James Cook's second voyage of discovery in 1772-5 mapped the Antarctic region.*
PHR V ˈ**map sth on/onto/to sth** [usually passive] to link one thing to another in a way that shows sth about what it means or how it is organized: *Poorer sexual health outcomes can be closely mapped to deprivation and inequality.* ˌ**map sth ˈout** [usually passive] to plan, arrange or describe sth in a careful or detailed way: *A wide-ranging research agenda remains to be mapped out.*

map·ping /ˈmæpɪŋ/ *noun* [U] **1** the act or process of creating an account of the way sth is arranged or organized: *The gene for Huntington's disease was an early success story of genetic mapping.* ◇ **~ of sth** *The detailed case studies entailed a systematic mapping of social relationships.* **2 ~ (of sth)** the act or process of creating an image or plan of the earth's surface: *In the second section, new mapping of the distribution of coral reefs and mangrove forests in South East Asia is presented.*

M

mar·ble /ˈmɑːbl; *NAmE* ˈmɑːrbl/ *noun* [U] a type of hard, attractive stone that is usually white and often has coloured lines in it. It is used to make statues and parts of buildings: *Praxiteles, the Athenian sculptor, worked in both bronze and marble.*

march¹ /mɑːtʃ; *NAmE* mɑːrtʃ/ *verb* [I] (of soldiers, or of people who are protesting) to walk as part of an organized group: **(+ adv./prep.)** *As the army marched farther eastward, morale dropped steadily.* ◇ **~ on sth** *The students once again broke the ban on demonstrations and marched on the German embassy.* ➲ *compare* DEMONSTRATE (4)

march² /mɑːtʃ; *NAmE* mɑːrtʃ/ *noun* **1** [sing.] **the ~ of sth** the steady development or progress of sth: *The march of globalization has created losers as well as winners.* **2** [C] (of soldiers, or of people who are protesting) an act of walking as part of an organized group: *On 4 May 1919, 3 000 university students held a protest march.* ◇ **~ on sth** *Kornilov's march on Petrograd took place under the slogan 'In the Name of God and the Fatherland'.* ➲ *compare* DEMONSTRATION (2)

mar·gin AWL /ˈmɑːdʒɪn; *NAmE* ˈmɑːrdʒən/ *noun* **1** = PROFIT MARGIN: *Cutting prices reduces margins and intensifies competition across sellers.* ◇ *Higher margins in these markets give firms an incentive to offer greater availability.* HELP In economics and business, the phrase **at the margin** is used to refer to the point at which there is no further benefit to be obtained from a particular course of action: *Understanding costs and benefits at the margin is key.* **2** [usually sing.] the difference between two amounts, especially the amount by which sb wins sth: **~ between A and B** *There is a narrow margin between the therapeutic and toxic dose.* ◇ **by a... ~** *Environmentalists and planners proposed the initiative, but the public voted against it by a huge margin.* ◇ **by a ~ of sth** *Supporters of the existing regime outnumber its opponents by a margin of more than eight to one.* **3** [usually sing.] an amount of freedom or choice in a situation that allows sth to be successful: **~ of sth** *Employees frequently possess a considerable margin of discretion at work.* ◇ **~ for sth** *The procedures are based on strict rules, leaving little margin for political flexibility.* **4** [usually pl.] part of a group or situation that is not included in the main or most important part SYN FRINGE (2): **the ~ (of sth)** *The core and the margins of social policy have much to learn from one another.* ◇ **at/in/on/to the ~ (of sth)** *Accusations of moral crime usually were directed at women at the margins of the community.* **5 ~ (of sth)** the extreme edge or limit of a place or object: *In 1908, the majority of storms tracked eastward along the northern margin of the Great Lakes.* **6** the empty space at the side of a written or printed page: **in the margin(s)** *Added in small letters, in the margins, is a Latin translation of an early tenth century Arabic treatise on diet.*
IDM ˌ**margin of ˈerror** (when calculating sth) an amount that you allow for the possibility that a number is not completely accurate: *With quantitative data, there will always be a margin of error that must be accounted for.*

mar·gin·al AWL /ˈmɑːdʒɪnl; *NAmE* ˈmɑːrdʒɪnl/ *adj.* [usually before noun] **1** (of costs or benefits) connected with or caused by small changes: *If marginal costs are lower than average costs, an increase in production will reduce the cost per unit.* ◇ *There is a marginal benefit in screening for people with one affected first-degree relative aged under 45.* **2** small and not important SYN SLIGHT (1): *Many voters complained that there were only marginal differences between the main parties.* **3** not part of the main or central group, area or situation, and suffering difficulties as a result: *Migrants, marginal people and the poor were more likely to be prosecuted than their neighbours.* ◇ *A prolonged period of decreased temperatures would produce severe difficulty for the inhabitants of more marginal areas.* HELP **Marginal** land is land on which it is difficult to produce enough good crops to make a profit. **4** (*especially BrE*) (of a seat in parliament or on a council) won or lost by a very small number of votes and therefore at risk in an election: *In marginal seats, a popular candidate and good organization may be worth a few hundred votes.*

mar·gin·al·ize (*BrE also* **-ise**) /ˈmɑːdʒɪnəlaɪz; *NAmE* ˈmɑːrdʒɪnəlaɪz/ *verb* to cause sb to be or to feel not important and without any power: **~ sb** *In conservative regimes, public policy often marginalizes women and encourages them to stay at home with their children.* ◇ **marginalized + noun** *socially marginalized groups/sections of the population* ■ **mar·gin·al·iza·tion, -isa·tion** /ˌmɑːdʒɪnəlaɪˈzeɪʃn; *NAmE* ˌmɑːrdʒɪnələˈzeɪʃn/ *noun* [U] **~ (of sb)** *Critics of the system argued that marginalization of certain groups of refugees would increase rather than decline.*

mar·gin·al·ly AWL /ˈmɑːdʒɪnəli; *NAmE* ˈmɑːrdʒɪnəli/ *adv.* very slightly; not very much: *The Great Lakes Indians fared somewhat, if only marginally, better than most Native Americans.* ◇ *For the outcomes examined in this study, three outcomes were marginally significant.* HELP The phrase **marginally significant** is often used in the discussion of statistics, but it is not a technical term and has no technical definition. It means that the results of a study almost reached the level set as 'significant', but not quite.

mar·ine /məˈriːn/ *adj.* [only before noun] connected with or found in the sea: *Calcium carbonate is used by many marine organisms as a skeletal material.* ◇ *marine invertebrates/mammals/fauna* ◇ *Shales produced in a marine environment typically are high in sodium.*

mari·tal /ˈmærɪtl/ *adj.* [only before noun] connected with marriage or with the relationship between a husband and wife: *Nothing suggests that husbands could forcibly return their wives to the marital home.* ◇ *The renegotiation of traditional gender roles can be a source of marital conflict.*

ˌmarital ˈstatus *noun* [U] (used especially on official forms) (*formal*) the fact of whether sb is single, married, etc: *Demographic data collected included education level, marital status and employment.*

mark[1] /mɑːk; *NAmE* mɑːrk/ *verb* **1** [T] to be a sign that sth new is going to happen: **~ sth** *The 1960s marked a shift in the black freedom struggle from civil rights to black power.* ◇ *to mark a turning point/transition/watershed* ◇ **~ the beginning/end of sth** *It was hoped that Alexander's death would mark the beginning of a more liberal era.* ◇ *These events marked the end of the Cold War.* **2** [T, usually passive] to give sb/sth a particular quality or character SYN CHARACTERIZE (1): **be marked by sth** *American public life today is often marked by furious and unreasonable emotions.* ◇ **~ sb/sth as sth** *The quiver of arrows and the crescent moon headpiece mark this as a Diana figure.* **3** [T, usually passive] to write or draw a symbol, line, etc. on sth in order to give information about it: **be marked + noun** *The green line (marked ke) gives the kinetic energy of the electron.* ◇ **A is marked with B** *The location of each seed was marked with a painted nail so that we could track emergence of seedlings.* ◇ **~ B on A** *Wedgwood was the first in his industry to mark his name on his wares, denoting ownership of the design.* **4** [T] **~ sth** to show the position of sth: *The River Uruguay marks the boundary between Argentina and Uruguay.* **5** [T] **~ sth** to celebrate or officially remember an event that you consider to be important: *2011 marked the 60th anniversary of the 1951 Convention relating to the Status of Refugees.* **6** [T] **~ sth** (*especially BrE*) to give marks to students' work: *The teacher evaluates and marks the written work.* ➲ *compare* GRADE[2] (2)
PHR V **ˌmark sb/sth ˈoff (from sb/sth)** to make sb/sth seem different from other people or things: *The propertied class as a whole remained clearly marked off from the groups below them.* **ˌmark sb/sth ˈout (as/for sb/sth)** to make people recognize sb/sth as special in some way: *A special building, called a martyrium, was placed over the grave of a martyr to mark it out.* ◇ *The boys would occasionally hold hands, or act in ways that marked them out as different.* **ˌmark sth ˈout** to do sth that shows the edges or limits of sth: *Male bees collect the delicate lemon scent and use it to mark out their mating sites.* **ˌmark sth ˈup** to mark or correct a text, for example for printing: *The editor then marked up the manuscript for the typesetter.*

mark[2] /mɑːk; *NAmE* mɑːrk/ *noun* **1 ~ of sth** a sign that a quality or feeling exists: *There is a tradition of presenting gifts to caregivers as a mark of respect and appreciation.* ◇ *Unattainable luxuries were transformed into desirable marks of status or even into affordable necessities.* **2** an area on a surface that is different from the area around it: *Both of these tracks are relatively small, 1.5–3.0 cm in length, and show claw marks.* ◇ **~ on sth** *Not all injuries will leave a visible mark on the bone.* **3** a written or printed symbol that is used as a sign of sth: *Patients place a mark on the line to indicate the severity of their pain.* ➲ *see also* QUESTION MARK, TRADEMARK (1) **4** (*especially BrE*) a number or letter that is given to show the standard of sb's work or performance: *Even with the same pass mark, candidate 2 is seen to have performed better.* ➲ *see also* GRADE[1] (3)
IDM **ˌbear/carry the ˈmark(s) (of sth)** to show signs of what has happened to sb/sth or the way they have developed: *International financial institutions still bear the mark of the economic systems from which they have originated.* **ˌleave your/its/a ˈmark (on sth/sb)** to have an effect on sth/sb that lasts for a long time: *Catastrophes might leave a mark on cosmic evolution, in both the physical and biological senses.* **ˌmake your/a ˈmark (on sth)** to become famous or successful in a particular area: *Landor lived well into the Victorian era and continued to make a mark on Victorian letters.* ➲ *more at* WIDE

marked /mɑːkt; *NAmE* mɑːrkt/ *adj.* fairly large and easy to notice SYN DISTINCT (2), NOTICEABLE: *There is a marked tendency for these words to commence with a stressed syllable.* ◇ *The findings of this study are in marked contrast to qualitative studies in Scotland and Canada.* HELP **Marked** is used in academic writing especially when talking about how different things are, or how they change.
▸ MARKED + NOUN **contrast • difference, disparity • variation • shift, change • fluctuation • decrease, reduction, decline • deterioration • increase, rise • improvement** *A 2005 Scottish study found some marked differences in health between rural and urban dwellers (Iversen et al., 2005).*

mark·ed·ly /ˈmɑːkɪdli; *NAmE* ˈmɑːrkɪdli/ *adv.* to a large degree and in a way that is easy to notice ➲ *compare* SIGNIFICANTLY: *The two parasites differ markedly in the type of final host they must reach to complete their life cycle.* ◇ *The market for bottled water in the UK has increased markedly during the past couple of decades.* ◇ *The spectra of these molecules are markedly different.* HELP **Markedly** is used in academic writing especially when talking about how different things are, or how they change.

mark·er /ˈmɑːkə(r); *NAmE* ˈmɑːrkər/ *noun* **1** a feature or sign that shows that sth exists or what it is like: *Geographers today understand difference through socially produced markers, such as ethnicity.* ◇ **~ of sth** *Home ownership became a key marker of middle-class social identity.* ◇ **~ for sth** *The Film Festivals Yearbook has acted as a marker for current trends in film festival research.* **2** (*biochemistry*) one of two or more forms of a GENE that can be used to identify a CHROMOSOME or the location of other GENES: *The aim of the Icelandic genomic project is to identify genetic markers common to all human populations.* ◇ **~ of/for sth** *Various markers for infection have been used in epidemiological investigations.*

mar·ket[1] /ˈmɑːkɪt; *NAmE* ˈmɑːrkɪt/ *noun* **1** [C] a public open area or building where people meet to buy and sell goods: *The market complements the local shops and also the much larger street market in Ridley Road.* ◇ **+ noun** *The market stalls spread beyond the confines of the market building.* **2** [sing.] business or trade; the amount of trade in a particular type of goods: *The downturn in the housing market has affected all those firms involved in this sector.* ◇ *One of the major features of the oil market during the 1990s was the relative stability of the long-term oil price.* ◇ **~ in sth** *The global market in coffee, for example, is governed by a variety of treaties.* ◇ **share of the ~** *In 2005, the company sold 144 000 new cars in Britain, taking a 5.9% share of the market.* ◇ **+ noun** *For young people, labour market entry may have been delayed in response to low demand.* **3** [C] a particular area, country or section of the population that buys or might buy goods: *The company entered the Japanese market in December 2002.* ◇ *The ability to sustain a competitive advantage is vital to success in the global market.* ◇ **+ noun** *Companies analyse market segments to find niches that will give them a competitive edge.* **4** [C] **~ (for sth)** the number of people who want to buy sth SYN DEMAND[1] (1): *At this time the market for tobacco products was rapidly expanding.* ◇ *This is a fascinating study of how the market for avocados was created.* **5** (*often* **the market**) [sing.] the economic system in which goods are exchanged through trade, and prices, salaries, etc. are decided by competition between businesses, and by what and how much people buy and will pay: *There has been great discussion about what tasks government should assume and what should be left to the market and to individuals and families.* ➲ *see also* COMMON MARKET, FREE MARKET, LABOUR MARKET, OPEN MARKET, SINGLE MARKET **6** [C] a STOCK MARKET or financial market; a place where COMMODITIES or CURRENCIES can be bought and sold: *Many investors lost large amounts when the markets crashed.* ◇ *The high levels of unsecured debts made the world's financial markets uneasy.* ➲ *see also* MONEY MARKET
IDM **in the ˈmarket for sth** interested in buying sth: *Companies concentrate on attracting subscribers who*

M

make extensive use of their telephones and are in the market for other interactive services. **on the ˈmarket** available for people to buy: *The new product was different from anything else on the market.*

▸ ADJECTIVE + MARKET **competitive • internal • global** *In a perfectly competitive market, prices are determined solely by the market.* | **overseas, international, foreign • external • domestic • national • local • new • emerging • large • expanding • growing • active** *It is widely predicted that these emerging markets in Asia will fuel much of the world economic (GDP) growth in the immediate future.* | **existing • target • potential** *It is essential to ensure that there are mechanisms in place to gather adequate feedback from the target market.*

▸ NOUN + MARKET **retail • wholesale • B2B • labour • product • oil • housing • carbon • electricity • gas** *The company has the largest share of the retail grocery market.* ◇ *Countries differ widely in how their labour markets are organized.* | **home • world • export • consumer • niche** *The export tax was so high that the farmers could not sell their products on the world market.* | **capital • money • commodity • foreign exchange • futures** *The bank relied on money markets, from which it received the funds which it then loaned to borrowers.*

▸ VERB + MARKET **enter • penetrate • access • reach • dominate • supply • flood • serve • develop • exploit • segment • leave** *Honda entered the US motorcycle market in the late 1950s.* ◇ *De Beers dominates the global diamond market.* | **define • target** *It may make sense to define a target market in terms of particular demographic characteristics.* | **liberalize • open • regulate** *The EU now regulates a market of nearly 500 million consumers.*

▸ MARKET + NOUN **value • failure** *Market failures result when markets are controlled by a small number of buyers or sellers.* | **entry • competition • structure • segment • access • penetration • participant • conditions • price • performance • power • strategy • orientation • size • environment** *The company needs to adapt to local sensitivities in order to ensure successful market entry.* | **mechanism • reform • liberalization • regulation** *The outcome of Thatcher's labour market reforms was to decrease the power of the unions.*

mar·ket² /ˈmɑːkɪt; *NAmE* ˈmɑːrkɪt/ *verb* to advertise and offer a product or service for sale; to present sth in a particular way and make people want to buy it SYN PROMOTE (2): **~ sth** *The franchises aggressively market their products and offer discounts and sales to attract more customers.* ◇ **~ sth to sb** *The existing range of services continues to be marketed to the existing market segments.* ◇ **~ sth as sth** *VisitScotland exists to support the development of the tourism industry and to market Scotland as a quality destination.* ◇ **~ yourself (to sb) (as sth)** *Colleges must market themselves not only to prospective students, but also to their parents and local employers.* ➲ *see also* MARKETING

mar·ket·able /ˈmɑːkɪtəbl; *NAmE* ˈmɑːrkɪtəbl/ *adj.* **1** that can be sold or marketed: *Without these other scientists, Noyce's ideas would not have become marketable products.* **2** attractive to possible employers or customers: *The second type of immigrant is well educated, with marketable skills.*

mar·ket·er /ˈmɑːkɪtə(r); *NAmE* ˈmɑːrkɪtər/ *noun* (*business*) a person or company whose job is to advertise or present products or services for sale in a way that makes people want to buy them: *With the emergence of new media, marketers face choices about how to engage most effectively with customers.* HELP Note that an **advertiser** usually works for a separate company that produces advertisements for many different companies, while a **marketer** often works for the company that is selling a particular product.

ˌmarket ˈforces *noun* [pl.] a free system of trade in which prices and wages rise and fall without being controlled by the government: *In a free market economy, decisions about what to produce are determined by market forces of supply and demand.*

mar·ket·ing /ˈmɑːkɪtɪŋ; *NAmE* ˈmɑːrkɪtɪŋ/ *noun* [U] the activity of presenting, advertising and selling a company's products or services in the best possible way: **~ (of sth)** *Global marketing of tobacco has resulted in an increase in the number of people in the developing world who are now smoking.* ◇ **+ noun** *It was clear that the company would need a completely different marketing mix for each customer type.* ◇ *marketing communications/strategy* ◇ *a marketing department/manager/plan/campaign* ➲ *compare* ADVERTISING, PROMOTION (3) ➲ *see also* DIRECT MARKETING

ˌmarket ˈleader *noun* **1** the company that sells the largest quantity of a particular kind of product: *The company has a 51% share in the Indian market and has been market leader for a long time.* **2** a product that is the most successful of its kind: *It is the market leader in the flavoured soft drink segment in Asia.*

mar·ket·place /ˈmɑːkɪtpleɪs; *NAmE* ˈmɑːrkɪtpleɪs/ *noun* **1 the/a marketplace** [sing.] the activity of competing with other companies to buy and sell goods or services: *Being able to compete successfully in the global marketplace is now a critical factor in many industries.* ◇ *In a competitive marketplace, customer satisfaction can be an important reason for customers deciding to make a repeat purchase.* **2** [C] an open area in a town where a market is held: *Shopping centres and strip malls have partially replaced the old marketplaces.*

ˌmarket ˈprice *noun* the price that people are willing to pay for sth at a particular time: *Other potential producers will enter the market by selling at less than the current market price.*

ˌmarket reˈsearch (*also* ˌmarket ˈresearch) *noun* [U] the work of collecting information about what people buy and why: *Market research has shown that awareness of the need for sun protection does not necessarily lead to product purchase.* ◇ **+ noun** *a market research agency/survey*

ˌmarket ˈshare *noun* [U, C] (*business*) the amount that a company sells of its products or services compared with other companies selling the same things: *Corporations equate good branding with increased market share.* ◇ *The company had become China's most successful PC maker with a 17% market share.*

ˌmarket ˈvalue *noun* [U, sing.] **~ (of sth)** the amount for which sth can be sold on a particular market: *The market value of the firm is equal to the value of its shares plus its net debt.*

mark·up /ˈmɑːkʌp; *NAmE* ˈmɑːrkʌp/ *noun* **1** [C] an increase in the price of sth based on the difference between the cost of producing it and the price it is sold at: **~ (of sth)** *The computer giant will set the price at $3000, which means a markup of 50 per cent.* ◇ **~ on sth** *Markups on wine served in restaurants are typically between 200 and 300 per cent.* **2** [U] the symbols used in computer documents which give information about the structure of the document and tell the computer how it is to appear on the computer screen, or how it is to appear when printed: **+ noun** *In markup languages such as HTML, the formatting codes are embedded directly in the text.*

mar·riage /ˈmærɪdʒ/ *noun* **1** [C, U] the legal relationship between a husband and wife; the state of being married: *Many individuals were trapped in unhappy marriages.* ◇ *She had been brought up in England, and entered into an arranged marriage in Pakistan.* HELP A **mixed marriage** is one between partners of different races or religions. **outside ~** *There has been a dramatic increase in the number of births outside marriage.* ◇ **+ noun** *He needed to explain* *his feelings of anger resulting from the marriage breakdown.* ➲ *compare* CIVIL PARTNERSHIP **2** [C, U] (in some places) the legal relationship between partners of the same sex: *Iceland became the seventh member of the Council of Europe to recognize same-sex marriage.* **3** [C] the ceremony in which two people become husband and wife, or legal partners: *Marriages whilst skydiving or swimming underwater are not permissible under English law.* ◇ **+ noun** *The climax of the celebration was a grand marriage ceremony.* **4** [C] **~ of A and B** a combination of or close relationship between two things: *The negative consequences of this marriage of finance and culture are obvious.*

IDM **by ˈmarriage** when sb is related to you **by marriage**, they are married to sb in your family, or you are married to sb in their family: *The family was closely connected by marriage to the families of chiefs and royalty.*

mar·ried /ˈmærid/ *adj.* **1** (of a person) having a husband or wife: *She was a married woman with three children.* ◇ **~ to sb** *Today, more than in the past, high-income men tend to be married to highly educated women.* ◇ **get ~** *There is an idealized image of getting married to which one is exposed early in life.* ➲ *compare* UNMARRIED **2** (of two people) joined in marriage: *Married couples in the sample (84%) had been together for 17 years on average.* ◇ *They had been married for 35 years.* **3** [only before noun] connected with marriage: *The court held that it must take into full account the normal ups and downs of married life.*

mar·row /ˈmærəʊ; *NAmE* ˈmæroʊ/ *noun* [U] = BONE MARROW

marry /ˈmæri/ *verb* (**mar·ries**, **marry·ing**, **mar·ried**, **mar·ried**) **1** [T, I] to become the husband or wife, or legal partner, of sb; to get married to sb: **~ (sb)** *Oedipus knew he had killed a man and married a woman; he did not know they were his father and mother.* ◇ *None of the daughters married until they were in their thirties.* ◇ **+ adj.** *Bridget had married young and borne eight children.* **2** [T, often passive] to perform a ceremony in which two people become husband and wife or legal partners: **~ sb| be married** *Connolly and Douglas were married in an Anglican ceremony in 1838.* **3** [T] to find a husband or wife for sb, especially your daughter or son: **~ sb** *Extreme poverty has led some refugee families to marry their young daughters for dowry.* ◇ **~ sb to sb** *In 1500 Henry VII married his daughter Margaret to the king of Scotland.* **4** [T] to combine two different things or ideas successfully SYN UNITE (2): **~ sth** *Whether the partnership will enable them to marry the two cultures successfully is a difficult question.* ◇ **~ A and/to/with B** *The very idea of marrying general relativity to quantum theory is problematic.*

PHR V **ˌmarry ˈinto sth** to become part of a family or group because you have married sb who belongs to it: *French officials and soldiers often married into landed or business families.* **ˌmarry sb ˈoff (to sb)** (*disapproving*) to find a husband or wife for sb, especially your daughter or son: *Young women are married off against their will.*

mas·cu·line /ˈmæskjəlɪn/ *adj.* **1** having the qualities or appearance considered to be typical of men; connected with or like men: *Men often feel it is not very masculine to discuss health problems.* ◇ *He argues that masculine identity is established by risk-taking.* ➲ *compare* FEMININE (1), MALE[1] (1) **2** (in some languages) belonging to a class of nouns, pronouns or adjectives that have masculine GENDER, not FEMININE or NEUTER: *In both Greek and Latin, the noun 'sun' is grammatically masculine.*

mas·cu·lin·ity /ˌmæskjuˈlɪnəti/ *noun* [U] the fact of being a man; the qualities that are considered to be typical of men: *In such a system, masculinity is associated with income-earning.* ◇ *Subjects and information taught and presented to children help to reinforce conceptions of masculinity and femininity in our culture.*

mask[1] /mɑːsk; *NAmE* mæsk/ *noun* **1** a covering for part or all of the face, worn to protect it or hide it: *Masks must be worn to prevent inhalation of mining dust.* ◇ *People were running through the streets, wearing masks and smashing shop windows.* **2** an object that fits over sb's face and that is connected to a container of oxygen, used for helping them to breathe: *As soon as possible, give oxygen at a high flow rate using a mask with an oxygen reservoir.* **3** [usually sing.] a manner or an expression that hides sb's true character or feelings: *Security often comes from obscurity rather than identity; individuals hide behind many masks.*

mask[2] /mɑːsk; *NAmE* mæsk/ *verb* **~ sth** to hide a fact or feeling so that it cannot be easily seen or noticed: *These averages mask large differences between the countries and over time.* ◇ *Boys are raised to mask their real feelings and present an image of strength and self-confidence.*

mass[1] /mæs/ *noun* **1** [U, C] **~ (of sth)** (*technical*) the quantity of material that sth contains: *It is possible to calculate the mass of the sun from the velocity of the earth in its orbit.* ◇ *If 10 kg of hydrogen and 80 kg of oxygen burn to form water, it is predicted that the mass of water produced will be 90 kg.* HELP **Weight** is used in non-technical language for this meaning. ➲ *see also* BIOMASS, BODY MASS INDEX, CRITICAL MASS, RELATIVE MOLECULAR MASS **2** [C] a large amount of a substance that does not have a definite shape or form: *Monsoon precipitation originates from moist air masses over the Gulf of Mexico.* ◇ **~ of sth** *Most people believe that the earth is a mass of rock with an almost limitless supply of resources.* ➲ *see also* LAND MASS **3** [C, usually sing.] **~ of sth** a large amount or quantity of sth: *These works contain a mass of detail on economic and social history.* ◇ *A mass of evidence shows that all current life had a single origin.* **4** [C] **~ of sth** a large number of people or things grouped together, often in a confused way: *They were surrounded by a mass of faces.* ◇ *The most critical act is that of selecting what is most significant and relevant from the mass of information.* ◇ **masses of sb/sth** *The masses of refugees who might have survived were never given the assistance necessary.* **5 the masses** [pl.] the ordinary people in society who are not leaders or who are considered to be not very well educated: *Democracies have become effective only where the masses put the elites under pressure to respect their freedoms.* **6 the mass of sth** [sing.] the greater part of sth SYN MAJORITY (1): *For the great mass of the population, religious change continued throughout most of Europe.* **7** (*often* **Mass**) [U, C] (especially in the Roman Catholic Church) a ceremony held in memory of the last meal that Christ had with his DISCIPLES: *A priest received Christ's body and blood in communion each time he celebrated Mass.*

mass[2] /mæs/ *adj.* [only before noun] affecting or involving a large number of people or things: *The mass production of cars and telephones brought down the costs of technology to a level that most people could afford.* ◇ *Biological as well as nuclear technology can be used to build weapons of mass destruction.* ◇ *Our knowledge of the origin of major mass extinctions is still very limited.* ➲ *see also* MASS MEDIA

mas·sive /ˈmæsɪv/ *adj.* **1** extremely large in amount or degree: *The past thirty years have seen a massive increase in the amount of personal data recorded and processed.* ◇ *This massive eruption must have killed large numbers of people.* ◇ *In purely economic terms, losses are potentially massive.* **2** very large or heavy and solid: *In central Namibia, there is a group of massive boulders measuring well over 10 m across.* ◇ *The construction of massive defensive walls may mean that warfare was growing more frequent.* **3** (*physics*) containing a large quantity of material; having great MASS: *Black holes result from the death of the most massive stars.* **4** (*earth science*) (of rocks or minerals) without internal structure or layers: *Very massive granite*

M

releases relatively little debris and hence it may support a very steep slope.

mas·sive·ly /ˈmæsɪvli/ *adv.* to a very great degree: *These demands massively increased the cost of drug development.*

the ˌmass ˈmedia *noun* [pl.] sources of information and news such as newspapers, magazines, television and the Internet, that reach and influence large numbers of people: *The impact of the mass media upon race relations is not a new concern.* ◇ **in ~** *Policy experts appeared prominently in the mass media to offer their thoughts and advice.* ◇ **through ~** *Attitudes and beliefs are transmitted to children through their families and also through the mass media.*

ˌmass specˈtrometer *noun* (*technical*) a piece of equipment for measuring the masses of MOLECULES and MOLECULAR FRAGMENTS: *Samples are processed using a mass spectrometer.*

mas·ter¹ /ˈmɑːstə(r); *NAmE* ˈmæstər/ *noun* **1** (in the past) a man who had people working for him, often as SERVANTS in his home: *According to the code, there would no longer be a court of judgment for disputes between a master and a slave.* **2 ~ of sth** a person who is able to control sth: *He wished to be master of his own destiny.* **3** (in compounds) the most important plan or version of sth, on which elements in the plan, or other versions of the thing, are based: **+ noun** *A strategy is essentially a master plan setting out how the organization will achieve its mission and objectives.* ◇ *Some of these regions correspond to one of the 226 countries in the master list.* **4** (often in compounds) a person who is skilled at sth: *De Groot asked five grand masters to think aloud as they studied a chessboard.* ◇ **+ noun** *The master mason chosen for the task of rebuilding Canterbury Cathedral was a Frenchman, William of Sens.* **5 master's** (*also* ˈ**master's degree**) a second university degree, or, in Scotland, a first university degree, such as an MA: *Bloom holds a master's degree in clinical social work.* **6** (in some religions) a teacher or leader: *The Japanese Zen master Dogen (1200-1253) introduced this form of Ch'an into Japan.*

mas·ter² /ˈmɑːstə(r); *NAmE* ˈmæstər/ *verb* **1 ~ sth** to learn or understand sth completely: *By advanced level, the learners have mastered the necessary skills.* ◇ *Wilson had a great facility for mastering foreign languages.* **2 ~ sth** to manage to control an emotion: *Paris was considered weak because he was unable to master his desires.*

mas·tery /ˈmɑːstəri; *NAmE* ˈmæstəri/ *noun* [U, sing.] **1 ~ (of sth)** great knowledge about or understanding of a particular thing **SYN** COMMAND¹ (2): *Dickens praised Thackeray's refined knowledge of character and his mastery of the English language.* **2 ~ (of/over sb/sth)** control or power: *Margaret achieves an active mastery over her situation which is denied to Gaskell's other heroines.*

match¹ /mætʃ/ *verb* **1** [I, T] if two things **match** or if one thing **matches** another, they are the same or very similar, or they go well together: *Production and demand rarely match exactly.* ◇ *There was conflicting information: dates did not always match or names of locations differed.* ◇ **~ sth** *The sample closely matched the ethnic distribution of the US population at the time.* ◇ *The goal is to create cells that exactly match those of a patient.* **2** [T, often passive] to show the connection between two or more things; to find or provide sb/sth that goes together with or is connected with another person or thing: **A is matched with B** *Blood pressure recordings from the booklet were matched by date with the results from the monitor.* ◇ **A is matched to B** *This is a 'pull' system of manufacturing where production is matched to known demand.* ◇ **be matched for sth** *The two groups of clinicians were selected randomly and matched for age, gender and practice setting.* **3** [T] to be as good, interesting, successful, etc. as sb/sth else **SYN** EQUAL³ (2): **~ sb/sth** *The grain harvests of 1947 and 1948 failed to match pre-revolutionary levels.* ◇ *Korea, in particular, is close to Japan in most technology areas, even matching or exceeding it in some.* ◇ **be matched by sth** *The fall in revenue from sales of CDs has not been matched by a corresponding increase in revenue from online downloads.* **4** [T] to make sth the same as or better than sb/sth else: **~ sth/sb** *The Conservatives were promising to match Labour's spending totals.* ◇ **be well/evenly matched** *The two siblings were evenly matched as regards strength.* ➲ *compare* EQUAL³ (1) **5** [T] **~ sth** to provide sth that is suitable for or enough for a particular situation **SYN** MEET (1): *Producers worked towards a product that matched the expectations of consumers.* ◇ *Suppliers will need to provide components that match the requirements of Ford's manufacturing process.*
PHRV ˈ**match sth against sth** to compare sth with sth else in order to find things that are the same or similar: *The results are matched against electronic databases containing similar data for known samples.* ˌ**match ˈup to sb/sth** (usually used in negative sentences) to be as good, interesting, successful, etc. as sb/sth **SYN** MEASURE UP (TO STH/SB): *The majority of national currencies and sovereign central banks do not match up to these ideal economic conditions.* ˌ**match ˈup (with sth)** to be the same as or similar to sth; to happen in the same way as sth: *The information they provide often does not match up.* ◇ *It was believed that the wet conditions in lower latitudes matched up with the cold periods of high latitudes.* ˌ**match sth ˈup (to/with sth)** to find things that belong together: *The logistics supplier will then match up the PC system to the corresponding monitor.*

match² /mætʃ/ *noun* **1** [C] a thing that is exactly the same as or very similar to sth else, or that behaves in a similar way; the fact of sth being the same or very similar to sth else: *A fingerprint match revealed that she had claimed asylum in the Netherlands in 2003.* ◇ **good/close/exact ~ (to sth)** *The food provided to male beetles in the experiment was a very close match to their natural food supply.* ◇ **~ between A and B** *The probability of a chance match between an innocent person's DNA and that obtained at a crime scene is less than one in one billion.* **HELP** In computing, a **match** is a series of characters that meets the particular conditions of a computer search: *All that the computer did was to compare data with other data and display the results of any matches.* **2** [sing.] a person or thing that combines well with sb/sth else: *This merger is a perfect match, given Palm's marketing expertise and Treo's product competency.* **3** [sing.] a person who is equal to sb else in strength, skill, intelligence, etc: **a/no ~ for sb** *The lightly armed and untrained fighters were no match for an assertive professional army.* ➲ *compare* EQUAL² **4** [C] (*especially BrE*) a sports event in which people or teams compete against each other: *a tennis/football match* ◇ *Once he started fighting professionally, he won 27 consecutive matches.* ➲ *compare* GAME (2) **5** [C] a short thin piece of wood that is used for lighting a fire, cigarette, etc: *The fire was probably started by a discarded match.*

mate¹ /meɪt/ *noun* **1** either of a pair of birds or animals that are sexual partners: *In some species, males take over other nests in order to attract mates.* ◇ *Females choose mates for a variety of reasons.* ◇ **+ noun** *Male body coloration also plays an important role in female mate choice.* **2** a husband, wife or other sexual partner: *Humans are biologically programmed to make themselves attractive to potential mates.* **3** (in compounds) a person you share an activity with: *He had been chosen as Eisenhower's running mate in the election of 1952.* ◇ *The benefits of one person's education are enjoyed by neighbours and workmates.*

mate² /meɪt/ *verb* **1** [I] (of two animals or birds) to have sex in order to produce young: *Male-male competition is so intense that males frequently die before having the* *opportunity to mate.* ◇ **~ with sth** *One hypothesis is that females prefer to mate with males that have longer tails.* ➲ *see also* MATING **2** [T] to put animals or birds together so that they will have sex and produce young: **~ sth** *The two mice are mated to produce offspring with the gene.* ◇ **~ sth to/with sth** *In this study, males were mated with either 1 or 2 females.*

ma·ter·ial¹ /məˈtɪəriəl; *NAmE* məˈtɪriəl/ *noun* **1** [C, U] a substance from which a thing is or can be made; a substance with a particular quality: *Buying building materials is a major challenge for the poor.* ◇ *Organic material collected from the three units was dated using the radiocarbon method.* ◇ **materials science** *With advances in materials science, the process of developing new materials has become more sophisticated.* ➲ *see also* RAW MATERIAL **2** [U] information or ideas used in books or other work: *Darwin began to organize all the material collected over 17 years into a colossal book.* ◇ *A companion website contains much additional material that can be used to further understanding.* **3** [C, usually pl., U] things that are needed in order to do a particular activity SYN RESOURCE (2): *Several respondents complained about the lack of appropriate training materials.* ◇ *Instructors are encouraged to provide teaching material related to the book.* **4** [U, C] cloth used for making clothes, etc. SYN CLOTH (1), FABRIC (1): *The competitors wear badges made from pieces of coloured material.* ◇ *Patients with this skin condition should wear cotton clothing, and avoid wool and synthetic materials.*

▸ ADJECTIVE + MATERIAL **suitable • hazardous • solid • raw • starting • composite • organic • inorganic • synthetic • polymeric • genetic • biological • nuclear** *The genetic material of many viruses is a single molecule of double-stranded DNA.* | **supplementary, additional • archival • printed • online • visual** *The book is based on a large amount of archival material.* | **educational • teaching • promotional** *Companies have managed to get through to children by sponsoring educational materials used in schools.*

▸ NOUN + MATERIAL **bulk • plant • waste • building, construction** *The wasps construct their nests on flat surfaces using plant materials.* | **source • reference** *The findings provide useful reference material for those responsible for shaping policy.*

▸ VERB + MATERIAL **use • provide, supply** *China is now heavily involved in other countries that are able to supply needed raw materials.* | **collect • incorporate** *Many distribution channels already collect waste materials for recycling.* | **contain • deposit • remove • transport** *During spring and summer, when glacial meltwaters enter the lake, coarser material is deposited on the lake floor.* | **present • cover • include • publish • access** *The student might present material relating to each theme under a separate heading.*

▸ NOUN + OF MATERIAL **amount, quantity, volume • use • range • mass • source • type** *Mining often results in large amounts of waste material.* | **property, nature • layer** *The properties of composite materials in wet and hot conditions have been briefly introduced.*

ma·ter·ial² /məˈtɪəriəl; *NAmE* məˈtɪriəl/ *adj.* **1** [only before noun] connected with money and possessions rather than with the needs of the mind or spirit: *They belonged to a privileged class that enjoyed more material well-being than ordinary workers did.* ◇ *Refugees may have lost most of their material possessions, wealth and status.* ◇ *material culture/resources/goods/deprivation* OPP SPIRITUAL (1) **2** [only before noun] connected with the physical world rather than with the mind or spirit: *Shared beliefs in Africa include the belief that the spiritual influences the material world.* ◇ *The social and political world is not a physical entity or material object that is outside human consciousness.* ◇ *material culture/resources* ◇ *Friction between macroscale engineering surfaces is not an intrinsic material property like yield stress.* OPP SPIRITUAL (1) **3** important and needing to be considered: *Many material facts are dealt with in the book.* ◇ **~ to sth** *The husband's defence was rejected by the court as it was not considered material to the application.* HELP In law, **material** is used to describe evidence or facts that are important, especially when these facts might have an effect on the result of a case: *Information must be gathered from various sources, including interviewing eyewitnesses and gathering material evidence.* ➲ *see also* IMMATERIAL (1)

ma·teri·al·ism /məˈtɪəriəlɪzəm; *NAmE* məˈtɪriəlɪzəm/ *noun* [U] **1 ~ (of sb/sth)** (*usually disapproving*) the belief that money, possessions and physical comforts are more important than spiritual values: *They refuse to be engulfed in the consumerism and materialism of contemporary society.* **2** (*philosophy*) the belief that only material things exist and mental PHENOMENA like CONSCIOUSNESS are the result of physical INTERACTIONS: *Many philosophers today believe that materialism and naturalism are true.* ➲ *compare* IDEALISM (1)

ma·teri·al·ize (*BrE also* **-ise**) /məˈtɪəriəlaɪz; *NAmE* məˈtɪriəlaɪz/ *verb* [I] (usually used in negative sentences) to take place or start to exist as expected or planned: *The Liberal Democrat surge failed to materialize in the actual election.*

ma·teri·ally /məˈtɪəriəli; *NAmE* məˈtɪriəli/ *adv.* **1** in a way that is connnected with money and possessions rather than with the needs of the mind or spirit: *The projects seek to improve the health of people living in materially deprived districts.* **2** in a way that is connected with the physical world rather than with the mind or spirit: *These two themes are represented materially by objects that were placed in burial chambers alongside the dead person.* **3** in a way that is important and needs to be considered: *These new figures do not materially affect the results we obtained.*

ma·ter·nal /məˈtɜːnl; *NAmE* məˈtɜːrnl/ *adj.* **1** [usually before noun] connected with being a mother, especially during the time when a woman is pregnant or soon after the birth of a child: *In some less developed countries, maternal mortality is still one of the main causes of death for women of reproductive age.* ◇ *Maternal smoking in pregnancy is an important risk factor for several major birth defects.* ➲ *compare* PATERNAL (1) **2** having feelings that are typical of a caring mother towards a child: *Part of the argument is that women have a 'maternal instinct' and will put children before their careers.* ◇ *The poem reinforces the sentimental appeal of maternal love.* ➲ *compare* PATERNAL (2) **3** [only before noun] related through the mother's side of the family: *The girl was cared for from birth by her maternal grandmother.* ➲ *compare* PATERNAL (3) ■ **ma·ter·nal·ly** /məˈtɜːnəli; *NAmE* məˈtɜːrnəli/ *adv.*: *Mitochondrial DNA is usually maternally inherited.*

ma·ter·nity /məˈtɜːnəti; *NAmE* məˈtɜːrnəti/ *noun* [U] (usually in compounds) the state of being or becoming a mother: **+ noun** *She wished to return to work after her maternity leave.* ◇ *a maternity hospital/ward/service/unit*

math·em·at·ician /ˌmæθəməˈtɪʃn/ *noun* a person who is an expert in mathematics: *The Greeks were superb mathematicians and discovered much of the mathematics we still use today.*

math·emat·ics /ˌmæθəˈmætɪks/ (*also BrE informal* **maths** /mæθs/) (*also NAmE informal* **math** /mæθ/) *noun* **1** [U] the science of numbers and shapes. Branches of mathematics include ARITHMETIC, ALGEBRA, GEOMETRY and CALCULUS: *Friedlander had studied mathematics at the University of Berlin.* ◇ **pure/applied ~** *These results were originally proved as a piece of pure mathematics, without reference to DNA, by James White in 1969.* **2** [U+sing./pl. v.] the process of calculating using numbers: *While the mathematics may be difficult, the results are simple to understand.* ◇ *The precise detail of the mathematics is not important.*

➲ *compare* CALCULATION (1) ■ **math·emat·ic·al** /ˌmæθəˈmætɪkl/ *adj.*: *The computer has made it possible, with the help of mathematical models, to solve many practical problems of engineering.* **math·emat·ic·al·ly** /ˌmæθəˈmætɪkli/ *adv.*: *The difference between the observed and predicted number of shopping trips can be expressed mathematically.*

mat·ing /ˈmeɪtɪŋ/ *noun* [U, C] sex between animals: *This approaching behaviour is followed by courtship and mating.* ◇ *The optimal number of matings for a male is much higher than the optimal number for a female.*

mat·rix /ˈmeɪtrɪks/ *noun* (*pl.* **matri·ces** /ˈmeɪtrɪsiːz/) **1** [C] (*mathematics*) an arrangement of numbers, symbols, etc. in rows and columns, often used to represent LINEAR TRANSFORMATIONS: *In quantum mechanics, we may consider matrices with infinitely many rows and columns.* **2** [C] **~ (of sth)** an arrangement of data in rows and columns like a GRID, produced so that the data can be studied and compared: *The Boston Consulting Group's matrix of market growth against market share is particularly complex when applied to global markets.* **3** [C, U] (*earth science*) a mass of rock in which minerals are found in the ground: *Methane is held within the structure of the coal matrix.* ◇ *Such fossils will often be partly concealed by matrix.* **4** [C, U] (*biology*) the substance between cells, or in which structures are fixed: *This defect in the extracellular matrix results in osteoporosis that itself results in an increased tendency to fracture.* **5** [C] **~ (of sth)** the cultural, social or political situation from which sth/sb develops: *Brooks states that a software product is embedded in a cultural matrix of applications, users, laws and machine vehicles.*

M

mat·ter¹ /ˈmætə(r)/ *noun* **1** [U] a substance of a particular sort: *Carbon dating may be used for the dating of fossils containing organic matter derived from plants.* ◇ *There is always some mineral matter included in the coal.* **2** [U] physical substance in general that everything in the world consists of: *Chemistry is the study of the structure and properties of matter.* ◇ *A singularity occurs where matter is infinitely dense, such as at the centre of a black hole.* ➲ *see also* DARK MATTER **3** [C] a subject or situation that you must consider or deal with: *In this case, the board should discuss the matter with major shareholders.* ◇ *Domestic violence was considered as a private matter where legal intervention was not appropriate.* ◇ *The Human Rights Committee deals with matters relating to human rights in the UK.* **4 matters** [pl.] the present situation; the situation that you are talking about SYN THINGS: *To further complicate matters, these inexpensive tests may generate false positives.* ◇ *A number of media artists have sought to take matters into their own hands.* ◇ *To make matters worse, local people were spreading stories of disappointment and poor value for money.* **5** [sing.] **~ of sth** a situation that involves sth or depends on sth SYN QUESTION¹: *Whether an exposed subject does or does not develop the disease is largely a matter of luck.* ◇ *The historical period of 'Romanticism' is a matter of continuing debate.* **6** [U] written or printed material: *The middle classes demanded cheaper and more accessible reading matter.* ➲ *see also* SUBJECT MATTER

IDM **be another/a different ˈmatter** to be very different: *Local suffrage was seen as an extension of women's role in the local community, but national suffrage was a different matter altogether.* **for ˈthat matter** used to add a comment on sth that you have just said: *The refractive index of glass (and, for that matter, other solids) varies with the wavelength of the light involved.* **it's just/only a matter of ˈtime (before...)** used to say that sth will definitely happen, although you are not sure when: *It is only a matter of time before more data become publicly available.* **a matter of ˈhours, ˈminutes, etc.** | **a matter of ˈcentimetres, ˈmetres, etc.** only a few hours, minutes, etc: *A product designer developing a new design could see it produced directly from blueprints in a matter of hours.* **no matter who, what, where, etc...** used to say that sth is always true, whatever the situation is, or that sb should certainly do sth: *Interviews were heavily scripted, so that no matter who was giving the interview, the same questions would be asked.* ➲ *more at* FACT

▸ ADJECTIVE + MATTER **straightforward, simple • complicated • complex • serious • trivial • controversial • private • practical • technical • administrative • financial • religious • criminal** *Coping with risk is rarely a straightforward matter.*

▸ VERB + MATTER **settle, resolve • address • investigate • pursue • approach, handle • discuss • refer • clarify • concern, cover • decide** *In many cases the matter can be settled locally.*

▸ A MATTER OF + NOUN **luck, chance • faith • judgement • opinion • convenience • urgency • controversy, debate, dispute • speculation** *Whether a particular infant died shortly before or after birth was often largely a matter of chance.*

mat·ter² /ˈmætə(r)/ *verb* [I, T] (not used in the progressive tenses) to be important or have an important effect on sb/sth: *The aim is to invest in the parts of the company that matter most.* ◇ **~ to sb** *In the context of rail travel, what matters to most people is whether there is a direct train to their destination.* ◇ **~ (to sb) that...** *Does it matter that sales in the UK are declining, if the product is still doing well in the rest of the world?* ◇ **~ (to sb) how/whether, etc...** *If the customer does not have much choice, then managers may decide that it does not matter how they are treated.*

mat·ur·ation AWL /ˌmætʃuˈreɪʃn/ *noun* [U] **~ (of sth)** the process of becoming mature or adult: *This hormone stimulates growth and maturation of red blood cells from precursor cells in the bone marrow.* ◇ *This result might be an effect of sexual maturation, which usually happens earlier in females.*

ma·ture¹ AWL /məˈtʃʊə(r); məˈtjʊə(r); *NAmE* məˈtʃʊr; məˈtʊr/ *adj.* (**maturer** is occasionally used instead of **more mature**) **1** fully grown and developed physically: *The mouse has a life cycle of 9 weeks from fertilization to mature adult.* ◇ *27 sexually mature baboons were studied.* ◇ *The time of appearance of this tissue damage is determined by the lifespan of the mature cells within that tissue.* OPP IMMATURE (1) **2** behaving in a sensible way, as is expected of an adult: *These individuals remain emotionally less mature and independent than their peers.* OPP IMMATURE (2) **3** (of a system or organization) having reached an advanced stage: *Universal suffrage is one defining characteristic of a mature democracy.* HELP A **mature** economy, industry or market has developed to a point where it is unlikely that it will grow further: *The UK retail banking industry is a mature market, where the players are striving to create unique competitive advantage.* **4** created later in sb's life and showing greater understanding and skill: *Marx's mature works are marked by a shift away from the philosophical influences of his youth.*

ma·ture² AWL /məˈtʃʊə(r); məˈtjʊə(r); *NAmE* məˈtʃʊr; məˈtʊr/ *verb* **1** [I] to become fully grown or developed physically: *The African elephant does not mature until it is 15 years old.* ◇ **as sth/sb matures** *These processes occur as the dependent young grow and mature.* ◇ **~ into sth** *Not all of the daughter cells matured into effector cells.* **2** [I] to develop emotionally and behave like a sensible adult: *As we mature, we begin to recognize that we can have mixed or multiple emotions.* **3** [I] (of a system or organization) to reach an advanced stage: *Software testing is a relatively young profession that is gradually maturing.* ◇ **as sth/sb matures** *As these economies matured, their growth rates naturally slowed.*

ma·tur·ity AWL /məˈtʃʊərəti; məˈtjʊərəti; *NAmE* məˈtʃʊrəti; məˈtʊrəti/ *noun* [U] **1** the state of being fully grown or developed: *Chimpanzee females reach sexual maturity at younger ages than human females.* ◇ *This paper discusses marketing strategies suitable for markets that have reached maturity.* ➲ *compare* IMMATURITY **2** the quality of thinking and behaving in a sensible, adult manner: *Even the most intellectually bright child lacks emotional maturity.* ➲ *compare* IMMATURITY **3** (of an investment or insurance policy) the time when the money you have invested and any profit that has been made is ready to be paid: *They had invested in a series of Greek-law governed bonds with maturity dates ranging from 2011 to 2040.*

max·imal /ˈmæksɪml/ *adj.* [usually before noun] (*technical*) as great or as large as possible: *It takes several weeks for the treatment to have maximal effect.* ➲ *compare* MINIMAL

maxi·mize (*BrE also* **-ise**) AWL /ˈmæksɪmaɪz/ *verb* **1 ~ sth** to make sth as large or as great as possible: *The analysis is based on the assumption that firms want to maximize their profits.* ◇ *to maximize returns/gains/productivity/value* ◇ *Modifications were made in order to maximize fuel efficiency.* ◇ *The discussion was about how to maximize benefits from publicly funded health care.* OPP MINIMIZE (1) **2 ~ sth** to make the best use of sth: *They used the shared leadership process within the team to maximize the potential of the team as a whole.* ■ **maxi·miza·tion, -isa·tion** AWL /ˌmæksɪmaɪˈzeɪʃn; *NAmE* ˌmæksɪməˈzeɪʃn/ *noun* [U] *Profit maximization has no meaning for such subsistence farmers.*

max·imum[1] AWL /ˈmæksɪməm/ *adj.* [only before noun] (*abbr.* **max**) as large, fast, etc. as is possible; the most that is possible or allowed: *Maximum body length and width were measured for each specimen.* ◇ *There was no manager to check that resources were used to maximum effect.* ◇ *New regulations established a maximum working week of 49 hours.* ◇ **~ possible** *Respondents who had never smoked received the maximum possible score of 100 points.* OPP MINIMUM[1]

▸ MAXIMUM + NOUN **speed, velocity • flow • amplitude • temperature • density • amount • extent • depth • height • distance • load • capacity • efficiency • value • profit • yield • output • sentence • dose** *The maximum thermal efficiency can be increased by increasing the operating temperature.* ◇ *The maximum sentence is 14 years' imprisonment in the case of burglary of a dwelling.*

max·imum[2] AWL /ˈmæksɪməm/ *noun* (*pl.* **max·ima** /ˈmæksɪmə/) (*abbr.* **max**) the greatest amount, size, speed, etc. that is possible, recorded or allowed: *This index reached the maximum at day 2 and rapidly declined thereafter.* ◇ **~ of sth** *The percentage of drug dissolved reached a maximum of 26%.* ◇ *The time period for investigations can be extended up to a maximum of nine months.* OPP MINIMUM[2] (1)

may /meɪ/ *modal verb* (*negative* **may not**, *pt* **might** /maɪt/, *negative* **might not**) HELP Note that **might** is used as the past form for **may**, especially in indirect speech: *If he had requested consent to send her an email, she would have said that of course he might.* **may have** + past participle is also used to talk about past possibilities: *There may have been other factors that contributed to this result.* **1** used to say that sth is possible: *Free trade may lead to a deterioration of labour conditions in developed countries.* ◇ *The patient may have developed an ulcer.* ◇ **~ well** *However, after 10 or 20 minutes this action may well be too late and the patient may be unable to swallow.* ◇ **~ easily** *Children and teens who never express anger may easily go unnoticed.* ➲ grammar note *at* MIGHT **2** used when admitting that sth is true before introducing another point or argument: *She may have been old-fashioned in her approach, but she was an excellent teacher.* ◇ *The findings suggest that confidence in the health service has been undermined less than may at first appear.* **3** used to say that sth is allowed; used to ask for or give permission: *A representative of the European Commission may attend meetings but may not vote.* **4** used to express wishes and hopes: *May we wish you success and happiness in your nursing career.* ➲ grammar note *at* MODAL[1]

IDM **be that as it ˈmay** despite that SYN NEVERTHELESS: *There is no shortage of controversy concerning how the EU really works. Be that as it may, it is useful to resort to simplified models.* ➲ *more at* WELL[1]

maybe /ˈmeɪbi/ *adv.* (*rather informal*) HELP In more formal academic writing, it is better to use an alternative word such as **perhaps** or **possibly**. **1** used when you are not certain that sth will happen or that sth is true or is a correct number SYN PERHAPS: *Many people now accept that they will switch employers and maybe even change careers several times during their working lives.* **2** used when making a suggestion SYN PERHAPS: *Maybe teachers could spend time in one another's classrooms and get to know how their colleagues teach?*

me /mi; *strong form* miː/ *pron.* the form of *I* that is used when the speaker or writer is the object of a verb or preposition, or after the verb *be*: *My work has convinced me that there is a lot more to be done.* ◇ *Gandhi remains an inspirational figure for an outsider like me.* ◇ *You cannot know what it is like to be me.*

meal /miːl/ *noun* one of the regular occasions in a day when people sit down to eat food; the food that is eaten at a meal: *After a meal, blood glucose levels are high.* ◇ *Nearly 50% of adolescents eat at least five meals per week with their family.* ◇ *to prepare/cook/share a meal*

THESAURUS

mean • involve • entail • imply *verb*

These words all mean to have sth as a necessary part or result.

- to mean/imply **that...**
- to mean/involve/entail **doing sth**
- to mean/involve/entail/imply a **change**
- to mean/entail/imply a **loss**
- to involve/entail a **risk/cost/process**
- to **often/usually/always/necessarily** mean/involve/entail/imply sth

- **Mean** typically introduces a result; **involve** and **entail** are used to talk about a part of sth: *The enormous distance of stars from us means that the light we receive from them today left long ago.* ◇ *The cause of multiple sclerosis is unknown, but it is clear that both environmental and genetic factors are involved.*
- **Entail** and **imply** are used to talk about sth that is necessary and cannot be avoided; **involve** can be used to talk about sth that is not necessary but is an important part of sth: *Multivariate analysis entails the simultaneous analysis of two or more variables.* ◇ *Controlling a large territory implies substantial energy costs for males.* ◇ *This new breed of programmes tries to make entertainment out of real-life emergencies, often involving crime.*

mean[1] /miːn/ *verb* (**meant, meant** /ment/) **1** (not used in the progressive tenses) to have sth as a result or a likely result: **~ sth** *In ancient Greece, a prolonged drought meant hunger and poverty for entire districts.* ◇ **~ to be/do sth** *This essay will explore what it means to live in a multicultural society.* ◇ **~ (that)...** *Increased EU tariffs meant that the EU was criticized by countries outside Europe.* ◇ **~ doing sth** *For cohabitants, the absence of legal regulation meant living without legal rights.* ➲ *compare* ENTAIL (1) **2** (not used in the progressive tenses) to have sth as a meaning: **~ sth** *The generic name Hippophae means 'shiny horse'.* ◇ **what is meant by sth** *First, I shall discuss what is meant by 'theory of mind'.* ◇ **~ sth to sb** *The term 'consciousness' means different things to different people.* ◇ **~ (that)...** *The law means that both parties are permitted to submit assessments.* ◇ **what it means for sb/sth (to do sth)**

M

It is hard for us to understand what it meant for a Roman emperor to become a Christian. ➲ language bank *at* DEFINE **3** to have sth as a purpose or intention SYN INTEND (2): **~ what...** *The evidence that Gorbachev meant what he said slowly accumulated.* ◇ **be meant for sb/sth** *The ships carried huge cargoes meant for exchange at high profits.* ◇ *The Buddha offers a path of wisdom and truth meant for all.* ◇ **~ to do sth** *They did not mean to minimize the possible importance of such events.* ◇ **be meant to be/do sth** *The buses were always meant to be a temporary solution.* **4** (not used in the progressive tenses) to intend to say sth on a particular occasion: **~ sth** *What Mill means is that a happiness-producing act is good, regardless of motive.* ◇ **~ (that)...** *By describing business as crimogenic, he means that business people have to cheat to maintain their positions.*

mean[2] /miːn/ *noun* ➲ *see also* MEANS **1 ~ (between A and B)** a quality, condition or way of doing sth that is in the middle of two extremes and better than either of them: *Aristotle defined virtue as a mean between two extremes.* **2** (*also* **arith,metic 'mean**) (*technical*) the value found by adding together all the numbers in a group, and dividing the total by the number of numbers: *In rural China, the majority have incomes below 70% of the country mean.* ◇ *The arithmetic mean was $1.2 million, but the median was only $0.5 million.* ➲ *compare* MEDIAN[1] ➲ language bank *at* STATISTIC

mean[3] /miːn/ *adj.* [only before noun] (*technical*) calculated as a mean; average: *An increase in the mean global temperature of 3–5 degrees Celsius could have catastrophic consequences.* ◇ *Fifty audiotaped consultations were delivered by eight female and four male GPs with a mean age of 51 years.* ➲ *compare* MEDIAN[1]

M

mean·ing /ˈmiːnɪŋ/ *noun* **1** [C, U] the thing or idea that sth such as a word, a sign, an action or a fact represents: *In its common usage, the word 'evolution' has several different meanings.* ◇ **~ of sth** *French Jewish intellectuals redefined the meaning of Jewishness after the Holocaust.* ◇ *First, this paper will attempt to clarify the meaning of these physical properties.* **2** [U, C] the ideas that sb wishes to communicate through sth such as a book, film or painting: *Dr Barker's work uncovers the hidden layers of meaning in the texts of the Bible.* ◇ *The poem presents the reader with a series of conflicting meanings.* **3** [U] the quality or sense of purpose that makes you feel that sth, especially your life, is valuable: *Respondents noted how an increased focus on serving others brought new meaning to their lives.* **4** [U] the real importance and nature of an experience, a situation or an object: *These questions might be somewhat remote from the meaning of life.* ◇ *Narratives can give meaning to the everyday landscapes of home.*

▸ ADJECTIVE + MEANING **same • different • double • multiple • precise, exact • intended • original • usual • literal • symbolic • cultural • textual • technical** *The word 'snow' has different meanings to a northerner and a southerner.* | **true • deeper • special** *They argue that ceremonies disclose the true meaning of religion.*

▸ VERB + MEANING **express • convey • carry • understand, grasp • explore • interpret • explain, clarify • define • determine • construct, create • derive • reveal • assign, attribute, attach • change** *According to Derrida (1978), all texts carry at least a double meaning.* | **have • acquire, take on** *'User involvement' has taken on many meanings in today's health services.* | **find • lose • give** *Religion was enlisted to give meaning and purpose to warfare.*

mean·ing·ful /ˈmiːnɪŋfl/ *adj.* **1** serious, useful or important: *The training process encourages interviewers to build meaningful relationships with their interviewees.* ◇ *Perhaps the most meaningful way to help your child is to emphasize that you are there for her.* ◇ **~ to sb** *Direct involvement in the task makes the exercise much more meaningful to students.* **2** clearly showing the information that is required: *It remains difficult to make meaningful comparisons between diverse communities.* ◇ *In practice, we can only expect a statistically meaningful solution if we include many more equations.* ■ **mean·ing·ful·ly** /ˈmiːnɪŋfəli/ *adv.*: *Practitioners may lack the skills required to engage meaningfully with children and young people.* ◇ *If the same reference corpus is used, corpora of different sizes can be meaningfully compared with one another.*

mean·ing·less /ˈmiːnɪŋləs/ *adj.* **1** not having a meaning that is easy to understand: *This is such a broad statement that it is almost meaningless.* **2** without any purpose or reason and therefore not worth doing or having: *Today the practice survives, but as a meaningless custom whose original intent has been long forgotten.* **3 ~ (to sb/sth)** not considered important SYN IRRELEVANT: *The activities they teach are meaningless to students' lives, making school an ordeal.* ■ **mean·ing·less·ness** *noun* [U] *Industrialization gives humans power over natural resources, but it can also bring about a feeling of meaninglessness and moral emptiness.*

means /miːnz/ *noun* (*pl.* **means**) **1** [C] an action, an object or a system by which a result is achieved; a way of achieving or doing sth: **~ of sth** *Evidence suggests that patients would welcome the use of email as a means of communication with doctors.* ◇ *Many bus users have defected to other means of transport, particularly cars, over the last ten years.* ◇ **~ of doing sth** *Universities are tending to seek less labour-intensive means of delivering instruction.* ◇ **by... ~** *The conflict was resolved peacefully by political means.* ◇ **by ~ of sth** *This information was collected by means of a short questionnaire.* ◇ **~ to do sth** *The government has found other means, such as taxation, to modify behaviour.* ◇ **as a ~ to do sth** *Ghosh argues that child marriage serves as a means to perpetuate power imbalances between men and women.* ◇ **~ for (doing) sth** *Ragin and Becker (1989: 54) concluded that 'microcomputers provide important technical means for new kinds of dialogues'.* **2** [pl.] the money that sb/sth has: *The technology is within reach even of colleges of modest financial means.*

IDM **not by 'any means** not at all: *Darwin did not by any means ignore the importance of isolation in the process of speciation.* **a ,means to an 'end** a thing or an action that is not interesting or important in itself but is a way of achieving sth else: *Thirty-eight respondents viewed education simply as a means to an end.* ➲ *more at* END[1], WAY

▸ ADJECTIVE + MEANS **only • principal, primary • alternative • appropriate • best • peaceful • efficient • effective • powerful • illegal • technical • electronic** *They advocated a powerful government as the only means of controlling a large population.*

▸ VERB + MEANS **provide • offer • constitute • become • use, employ • choose • have • lack** *The original strategy was to use economic means to achieve political integration.*

▸ MEANS OF + NOUN **production • subsistence • exchange • communication • transport • identification** *It is clear that these means of production and of exchange originated in feudal society.*

meant *past tense, past part. of* MEAN[1]

mean·time /ˈmiːntaɪm/ *noun*

IDM **in the 'meantime** in the period of time between two times or two events; between now and a future event: *Rodham took weeks to collect his evidence; in the meantime, Nixon continued to fight back.*

mean·while /ˈmiːnwaɪl/ *adv.* **1** while sth else is happening: *Verdun was held with the aid of the Russian army. Meanwhile, the Russian south-western armies were successfully defending Poland.* **2** in the period of time between two times or two events: *It takes an average of 2.8 years to obtain a trademark registration. Meanwhile, the only protection available is under the Unfair*

Competition Law. **3** used to compare two aspects of a situation: *For the most part, people find a way to fix their damaged property. Public property, meanwhile, is repaired with public dollars.*

meas·ur·able /ˈmeʒərəbl/ *adj.* **1** that can be measured: *Eventually, measurable quantities of methane and some hydrogen are produced.* **2** [usually before noun] large enough to be noticed or to have a clear and obvious effect: *Women in the Scottish Parliament and Welsh Assembly have had a measurable effect on the political agenda in both countries.* ■ **meas·ur·ably** /ˈmeʒərəbli/ *adv.*: *The mutation rate is measurably higher in males than in females.*

meas·ure[1] /ˈmeʒə(r)/ *verb* **1** to find the size, quantity, etc. of sth in standard units: **~ sth** *Radar has been used to measure the distance to the moon with great accuracy.* ◇ **~ sth in sth** *Lines of latitude are measured in degrees.* ◇ **~ how much/how long, etc...** *The controller would measure how much the temperature differed from the set point.* ➲ language bank *at* RESEARCH[2] **2** to judge the importance, value or effect of sth SYN ASSESS (1): **~ sth** *One of the most important tools for measuring the performance of an organization is financial analysis.* ◇ **~ sth by sth** *Public opinion is typically measured by survey research.* ◇ **~ how/what, etc...** *We developed a survey that measured how well the social worker had satisfied the requirements.* **3** *linking verb* (not used in the progressive tenses) **+ noun** to be a particular size, length, amount, etc: *The cabins measured 18 by 27 feet.* ◇ *Some of these massive boulders split into two or more pieces, measuring well over 10 m across.*
PHR V **ˈmeasure sb/sth against sb/sth** to judge sb/sth by comparison with sb/sth: *But the risk has to be measured against the benefits.* ◇ *The defendant should be measured against an objective standard.* **ˌmeasure sth ˈout** to take an exact amount of sth from a larger amount: *Smaller quantities are then measured out.* **ˌmeasure ˈup (to sth/sb)** (usually used in negative sentences and questions) to be as good, successful, etc. as expected or needed SYN MATCH UP TO SB/STH: *There were concerns that the trial process failed to measure up to international standards.*

▸ MEASURE + NOUN **level • degree • extent • value • change • difference • activity • intensity** *Obviously, the price level is measured in euros in the EU and in dollars in the USA.* | **concentration • distance • length • rate • time • variable • pressure • temperature • number • amount** *Very robust landing probes have measured surface temperatures on Venus of about 730 K.* | **impact, effect • quality • performance • outcome • success** *Schneider, Klein and Murphy tried to measure the impacts of public policies on the demand for cigarettes.*

▸ ADVERB + MEASURE | MEASURE + ADVERB **directly • accurately, precisely • objectively • routinely** *Both voltage and current can be accurately measured and controlled.* ◇ *Survey questions are used that measure directly the extent of individual family ties.* | **experimentally • quantitatively** *Various methods may be used to quantitatively measure the intensity of radiation.*

▸ ADVERB + MEASURE **carefully • simply • easily • usually, generally, commonly • typically** *Serum antibody levels are easily measured.*

meas·ure[2] /ˈmeʒə(r)/ *noun* **1** [C] a plan or course of action taken in order to achieve a particular aim: *Countries may be reluctant to take precautionary measures.* ◇ **~ to do sth** *He suggests that measures to reduce the income gap would also reduce crime.* ◇ **~ against sb/sth** *Extremists within the party advocated violent measures against their opponents.* ◇ *Measures against oil pollution at sea resulted from oil tanker disasters.* **2** [C] **~ of sth** a way of judging or measuring sth: *There is much debate as to whether formal examinations provide an accurate measure of academic ability.* **3** [C] a standard unit used for stating the size, quantity or degree of sth; a system or scale of these units: *The question of the repeal of the Act arose in a dispute concerning the use of metric weights and measures.* ◇ **~ of sth** *These values can be converted into metres or another appropriate unit of measure.* ◇ *The pH scale is used as a measure of acidity.* **4** [sing., U] **~ of sth** a particular amount or degree of sth, especially a fairly large one SYN DEGREE (1): *A parliamentary committee enjoys a measure of independence.* ◇ *All human relationships involve some measure of give and take.* **5** [sing.] a sign of the degree, extent or quality of sth: *It is a measure of how far we have moved in our thinking that such questions are no longer even asked.* **6** [C] a written suggestion for a new law presented to a country's LEGISLATURE: *The Senate passed the measure by a 48–30 vote.*
IDM **beyond ˈmeasure** (*formal*) to a very great extent: *The living and working conditions of many working people had improved beyond measure.* **for good ˈmeasure** in addition to what has already been done or said: *The UK Government felt it necessary to add, for good measure, that 'the Guidelines are not binding on Member States'.* **the full ˈmeasure of sth** the whole of sth: *He has accepted a sum representing the full measure of his estimated loss.* **in full ˈmeasure** to the greatest possible degree: *Some settlers set up completely new societies which could reflect in full measure what they took to be right.* **in no small ˈmeasure | in some, equal, etc. ˈmeasure** (*formal*) to a large extent or degree; to some, etc. extent or degree: *Imperial ambitions and disappointments contributed in no small measure to France's domestic political instability.* ◇ *He argues that all progress is both good and bad simultaneously, though not necessarily in equal measure.* ➲ *more at* LARGE

▸ ADJECTIVE + MEASURE **appropriate • new • general • summary • specific • direct • simple • single • additional** *The most appropriate measures to protect their safety must be implemented.* | **effective • necessary • interim • preventive • protective • precautionary • legislative** *Vaccination is a widespread preventive measure in health systems.* | **good • valid • reliable • accurate • objective • subjective • quantitative** *The number of crimes reported by victims could act as a more objective measure of the public's cooperation with the police.* | **large • good** *The Irish parliament thus gained a large measure of autonomy from British control.*

▸ NOUN + MEASURE **control • public health • policy** *Rapid, effective control measures restricted the outbreak to fewer than 1 000 cases worldwide.* | **outcome • performance** *It is necessary to establish performance measures that hold organizations and officials accountable for their performance.*

▸ VERB + MEASURE **provide • introduce • require, need** *It was one of the most controversial measures introduced by the Labour government.* | **use, employ • include • develop • apply • design • consider** *Many economists have developed their own measures of economic welfare.* | **take • adopt • implement • impose • justify** *The US adopted protectionist measures to support her own economy.* | **construct** *Occupational information is used to construct the measures of class and status.*

▸ MEASURE OF + NOUN **success • support • control** *Profit provides a relatively easy measure of success.* ◇ *Direct payments give disabled people a degree of autonomy and some measure of control.* | **performance • quality • ability • status • uncertainty • size • degree, extent • similarity • concept** *In finance, the typical measure of performance is the return on a quoted security.*

meas·ure·ment /ˈmeʒəmənt; *NAmE* ˈmeʒərmənt/ *noun* **1** [U, C] the act or the process of measuring sth: *The United States has not adopted the metric system of measurement.* ◇ *Measurements made in different laboratories at different times will inevitably produce slightly different results.* ◇ **~ of sth** *Measurement of atmospheric pressure by barometer began in the early seventeenth century.* **2** [C, usually pl.] **~ (of sth)** the size, length or amount of sth, as established by measuring: *It is a criminal offence to*

M

give false or misleading statements about the measurements of a property.

▸ ADJECTIVE + MEASUREMENT **accurate, precise • detailed • quantitative • objective • physical** *Such accurate measurements make it possible to determine the molecular formulae of ions.* | **experimental • direct • repeated • serial** *The analysis involves direct measurement of emissions.*

▸ VERB + MEASUREMENT **include • require, need • report** *Finding the concentration of mercury in a body of water requires careful measurement.* | **make, perform, conduct, carry out • repeat • allow • enable • involve • describe • improve** *Repeating the measurement 100 times is likely to give 100 slightly different values.* | **take • obtain • use • provide • give • record • compare** *Geographers collecting data in the field need to specify the geographic locations at which they take measurements.*

▸ MEASUREMENT + NOUN **error • bias • variance • invariance • equivalence • validity • tool, instrument, device • technique • scale** *No account is taken of measurement errors and random fluctuations in the economy.*

meat /miːt/ *noun* [U, C] the parts of animals or birds that people eat: *Many Hindus do not eat meat at all.* ◇ *Low income groups are more likely to consume pizza, processed meats, whole milk and table sugar.* ◇ **+ noun** *World meat consumption tripled between 1961 and 2005.*

mech·an·ic·al /məˈkænɪkl/ *adj.* **1** connected with the physical laws of movement: *The rotor converts electrical energy into mechanical energy.* ◇ *We observed no change in the conductive properties of the membrane despite large changes in its mechanical properties.* **2** connected with machines and engines: *There exist uncertainties in flight departures because of unexpected events such as bad weather or mechanical problems.* ◇ *Beginning in 1991, a major effort was undertaken to redefine the discipline of mechanical engineering.* **3** operated by a machine or by a system of moving parts: *Huge mechanical devices for shovelling and loading were brought in and set to work.* ◇ *File storage on Babbage's 'Analytical Engine' was to be purely mechanical, using wheels and cards.*

M

mech·an·ic·al·ly /məˈkænɪkli/ *adv.* **1** in a way that is connected with the physical laws of movement: *Wave energy converters fall into several classes based on how they interact mechanically with waves.* **2** in a way that uses power from a machine or a system of moving parts: *Bed areas should be mechanically ventilated and cooled, with other areas naturally ventilated where possible.*

mech·an·ics /məˈkænɪks/ *noun* **1** [U] the science of movement and force: *Froude had an elementary knowledge of mathematics, but a very good understanding of the laws of mechanics.* ◇ *classical/fluid/molecular mechanics* ➲ *see also* QUANTUM MECHANICS **2** [pl.] **~ of sth** the way sth works or is done: *An approach to research was developed that focused not on the mechanics of the process, but on its human consequences.*

mech·an·ism AWL /ˈmekənɪzəm/ *noun* **1** a natural system or type of behaviour that performs a particular function: *A range of coping mechanisms have helped residents to manage the emotions caused by the conflict.* ◇ **~ by which...** *Similar experiments have investigated the molecular mechanism by which this regulation occurs.* ◇ **~ for (doing) sth** *A more general mechanism for shutting down genes involved in cell proliferation has also been found to operate in muscle cells.* ◇ **through/via a ~** *They kill bacteria through several mechanisms.* **2** a method or form of organization by which sth is achieved: **~ to do sth** *In the absence of democracy, people have created alternative mechanisms to influence policy outcomes.* ◇ **~ for (doing) sth** *Russian legislation created mechanisms for the support of environmentally friendly power generators.* ◇ **through/via a ~** *Both countries were unable to attract capital through market mechanisms.* ◇ **~ by which...** *There are thus three mechanisms by which human rights are protected within the OAS:...* **3** a set of moving parts in a machine that performs a task: *In printers, the filter must also remove the particles generated by the paper-feeding mechanism.*

▸ ADJECTIVE + MECHANISM **exact, precise • complex • main • basic • underlying • causal • proposed • possible • potential • alternative • effective** *The exact mechanisms involved in cellular function have been intensively studied.* | **biological • physiological • psychological • molecular • coping • protective** *There is no current consensus as to the exact physiological mechanism underlying acupuncture.* | **formal • institutional • regulatory** *Governments are expected to apply formal mechanisms such as legal codes and constitutions.*

▸ NOUN + MECHANISM **defence • control • feedback** *The family, religion and the police were all significant social control mechanisms.*

▸ VERB + MECHANISM **study, investigate, examine, explore • suggest, propose • provide • identify • reveal • outline • describe • discuss • clarify, elucidate • understand • use, employ • serve as, act as, function as • involve • lack** *The similarity between the histories of these two rivers suggests a common causal mechanism.* | **evolve** *Interestingly, some viruses have evolved mechanisms to suppress RNAi.* | **design • create • establish • provide** *The government established a legal mechanism to provide compensation to injured third parties.*

▸ MECHANISM + VERB **underlie • exist • operate** *The biological mechanisms underlying this phenomenon remain unknown.*

mech·an·is·tic /ˌmekəˈnɪstɪk/ *adj.* (*often disapproving*) connected with the belief that all things in the universe can be explained as if they were machines: *Mechanistic thinking sees emotion as irrational, and as undermining operational efficiency.*

media AWL /ˈmiːdiə/ *noun* **1 the media** [pl.] the main ways, such as television, newspapers and the Internet, that are used to communicate information and provide entertainment to large numbers of people HELP In general English, **media** is sometimes treated as singular: *the media reports that...* In academic English, however, it should be used with plural forms. The singular is **medium.** *Strobel (1996) argues that the media are more likely to follow politics than lead it.* ◇ *In many states, the national media remain largely under political control.* ◇ *the news/print/broadcast media* ◇ *the mainstream/popular/mass media* ◇ **in the ~** *Numerous studies have shown that violence in the media contributes to real-world violence.* ◇ **through the ~** *Patients are often anxious about hospital infections they have heard about through the media.* ◇ **+ noun** *A major study focused on the media coverage received by the two main political parties.* ➲ *see also* MASS MEDIA, MULTIMEDIA, NEW MEDIA, SOCIAL MEDIA **2** *pl. of* MEDIUM[1]

medi·aeval = MEDIEVAL

me·dian[1] /ˈmiːdiən/ *adj.* [only before noun] (*technical*) having a value in the middle of a series of values: *The workers had a median age of 57 years.* ◇ *median scores/values/income* ➲ *compare* MEAN[3]

me·dian[2] /ˈmiːdiən/ *noun* (*technical*) the middle value of a series of numbers arranged in order of size: *Hospitals were ranked by counting how many times they scored above the median.* ◇ *The miscarriage rate ranged from 21% to 40% (median 34%).* ➲ *compare* MEAN[2] (2) ➲ language bank *at* STATISTIC

me·di·ate AWL /ˈmiːdieɪt/ *verb* **1** [T, often passive] (*technical*) to influence sth and/or make it possible for it to happen: **be mediated by sth** *This model assumes that the effects are indirect and mediated by other factors.* ◇ **~ sth** *Spinath and O'Connor (2003) showed that genetic* *influences mediated the relationship between personality traits and parenting behaviours.* ◇ **be mediated through sth** *The design of the palace came directly from France, rather than being mediated through travellers or books.* **2** [I] **~ between A and B** to form a link between things: *World cities play a vital role mediating between the global economy and specific nation states.* ◇ *Simone de Beauvoir (1949) analysed the ways in which women mediate between nature and culture.* **3** [I, T] to try to end a disagreement between two or more people or groups by talking to them and trying to find things that everyone can agree on: **~ in sth** *Mediating in family disputes has an important role within these Muslim congregations.* ◇ **~ between A and B** *The UN mediated between the opposing sides in the civil war.* ◇ **~ sth** *The NLRB was established to mediate labour disputes.* **4** [T] **~ sth** to succeed in finding a solution to a disagreement between people or groups SYN NEGOTIATE (2): *An internationally mediated peace agreement led eventually to free elections.*

me·di·ation AWL /ˌmiːdiˈeɪʃn/ *noun* **1** [U] action that influences sth and/or makes it possible for it to happen: *The possibility that populations of L. littorea arrived in North America through human mediation was rejected.* **2** [U, C] an attempt to end a disagreement between two or more people or groups by talking to them and trying to find things that everyone can agree on: *Students perceive peer mediation as a way to think through and talk out problems.* ◇ *International mediations in these conflicts tend to focus heavily on ceasefire, power-sharing, elections and humanitarian issues.*

me·di·ator /ˈmiːdieɪtə(r)/ *noun* **1** a person or an organization that tries to get agreement between people or groups who disagree with each other: *In schools, the role of mediator can often be fulfilled by trained students.* ◇ **~ between A and B** *Financial analysts act as mediators between investors on the one hand and corporate management on the other hand.* **2** (*medical*) a substance such as an ENZYME or a HORMONE that acts in a chemical or biological process: *Chemical substances, called mediators, released from injured or activated cells, coordinate the development of the inflammatory response.*

med·ic·al AWL /ˈmedɪkl/ *adj.* [usually before noun] **1** connected with the science or practice of medicine: *She required urgent medical treatment.* ◇ *He had a number of other medical problems.* ◇ *The other principal treatment suggested by medical practitioners was physiotherapy.* **2** connected with medicine as opposed to SURGERY, PSYCHIATRY, etc: *The Commission's purpose is to assist in maintaining and improving standards of medical and surgical care in the UK.*

▸ MEDICAL + NOUN **care • treatment, therapy • intervention • history • condition • practice** *Chronic illness and medical conditions can obviously impact a child's school attendance.* | **records • information • problem • emergency • error • malpractice • school • education • student • practitioner • doctor • profession • professional • staff, personnel • research • science • ethics • attention • assistance, help • advice • consultation • examination • services • centre • equipment • device • costs, expenses • insurance • tourism** *Patients are increasingly accessing copies of their medical records.*

med·ic·al·ly AWL /ˈmedɪkli/ *adv.* **1** in a way that is connected with the science or practice of medicine: *Patients with medically unexplained symptoms are commonly referred to specialist clinics.* ◇ *Each laboratory has a lead consultant, who is medically qualified and acts as head of service.* **2** in a way that is connected with medicine as opposed to SURGERY, PSYCHIATRY, etc: *The vast majority of these conditions are treated medically and do not require surgery.*

medi·ca·tion /ˌmedɪˈkeɪʃn/ *noun* [C, U] a drug or another form of medicine that you take to prevent or to treat an illness: *The medications taken to treat angina should also be documented.* ◇ *Medication was prescribed for 17 children with ADHD, all by the child's primary care physician.*

me·di·cin·al /məˈdɪsɪnl/ *adj.* helpful in the process of curing illness or infection: *Review trials on medicinal products are now undertaken by the UK Ethics Committee Authority.* ◇ *medicinal plants/herbs* ◇ *The plant is valued for medicinal use.*

medi·cine /ˈmedsn; ˈmedɪsn/ *noun* **1** [U] the study and treatment of diseases and injuries: *A licensing system was introduced for anyone practising medicine in the UK.* ◇ *An estimated half of all drugs used in medicine are administered as salts.* ◇ *Modern medicine has been able to cure many of the scourges of earlier days.* ◇ *conventional/traditional/complementary/alternative medicine* ◇ *preventive/regenerative/evidence-based medicine* HELP In technical language, the term **medicine** is often considered not to include SURGERY (= treatment that usually involves cutting open a person's body). **2** [U, C] **~ (for sth)** a substance, especially a liquid that you drink or swallow in order to cure an illness: *The majority of children were taking medicine for their headaches.* ◇ *Two billion people, i.e. one third of the global population, lack access to essential medicines.*

medi·eval (*also* **medi·aeval**) /ˌmediˈiːvl; *NAmE also* ˌmiːdˈiːvl/ *adj.* [usually before noun] connected with the Middle Ages (about AD 1100 to AD 1450): *Parry (1975) suggests that in the early medieval period, crop failure was rare.* ◇ *Most states in medieval Europe were feudal in structure.*

medi·tate /ˈmedɪteɪt/ *verb* [I] to think deeply, usually in silence, especially for religious reasons or in order to make your mind calm: *Learning to meditate requires determination, commitment and daily practice.* ◇ **~ on/upon sth** *Dedicated to a life of prayer and fasting, they meditated on the words of the Qur'an.*

medi·ta·tion /ˌmedɪˈteɪʃn/ *noun* **1** [U] the practice of thinking deeply, usually in silence, especially for religious reasons or in order to make your mind calm: *Participants practised meditation together each day.* ◇ **in ~** *The image of the Buddha seated cross-legged in meditation is one of the most popular in Buddhist art.* **2** [C, usually pl.] **~ (on sth)** serious thoughts on a particular subject that sb writes down or speaks: *The poem offers a series of meditations on human suffering and endurance.*

me·dium[1] AWL /ˈmiːdiəm/ *noun* (*pl.* **media** /ˈmiːdiə/or **me·diums**) HELP In academic writing, the plural is usually **media**. **1** a way of communicating information to people: *The Internet is the latest medium to greatly increase promotional possibilities.* ◇ **through the ~ of sth** *Ayckbourn has reached a mass audience only through the medium of television.* ◇ **~ for (doing) sth** *This paper will evaluate choice of medium for product launches by three major manufacturers.* ➲ *see also* MASS MEDIA, MEDIA ➲ grammar note *at* DATA **2** something that is used for a particular purpose: **~ of sth** *Kennen (1995) suggests this is due to a single currency being used as the medium of exchange.* ◇ *Some parents will pay for their children to go to schools where English is the medium of instruction.* ◇ **through the ~ of sth** *The African Charter provided protection through the medium of procedural guarantees.* ◇ **~ for (doing) sth** *She discusses possible reasons why DNA has superseded RNA as the medium for storing genetic information.* **3** (*biology*) a substance that sth exists in or grows in or that it travels through: **culture ~** *Cells were removed from the culture medium by centrifugation.* ◇ **~ (of sth)** *Light was generated by a small device immersed in the medium of liquid nitrogen.*

me·dium[2] AWL /ˈmiːdiəm/ *adj.* [usually before noun] (*abbr.* **M**) in the middle between two sizes, amounts, times, temperatures, etc: *Daimler sold 467 000 heavy, medium and light trucks in 2007.* ◇ *Workers were classed*

M

as being at low, medium or high risk of occupational skin disease based on their job titles. ◇ *There are few data available for unlisted small and medium-sized enterprises.* IDM see RUN², TERM¹

meet /miːt/ *verb* (**met, met** /met/) **1** [T] **~ sth** to do what is needed or what sb asks for SYN FULFIL (1): *She believes that the welfare state has failed to meet the needs of modern parents and children.* ◇ *Some patients have symptoms that meet the criteria for more than one diagnosis.* **2** [T] **~ sth** to pay sth: *Parents will need to work more to meet the costs of child care.* ◇ *Her earnings are insufficient to meet her living expenses.* **3** [I, T, no passive] to come together formally in order to discuss sth: *The parliament met on 13 May and tried to change the constitution.* ◇ **~ sb** *Reagan refused to meet Soviet leaders during his first term.* **4** [I, T, no passive] to see and get to know sb for the first time: *The three soldiers had first met as boys at school.* ◇ **~ sb** *Key motives included the opportunity to meet people and make friends.* **5** [I, T, no passive] to be in the same place as sb by chance and talk to them: *After Lydia has married Wickham, Elizabeth and Darcy meet again.* ◇ **~ sb** *Junior staff still meet senior staff in the lift.* **6** [I, T, no passive] to come together socially after you have arranged it: **~ (for sth)** *Contacts may be maintained informally, for example, by meeting for lunch or talking on the telephone.* ◇ **~ sb (for sth)** *He arranges to meet her the following day at Rouen Cathedral.* **7** [T] **~ sb/sth** to go to a place and wait there for a person or means of transport to arrive: *Lenin was met at the Finland Station in Petrograd by a welcoming delegation.* ◇ *Lord Sheffield's supporters met his carriage and escorted him into the city.* **8** [I, T, no passive] to play, fight, etc. together as opponents in a competition: *The two armies finally met at Gaugamela in north-eastern Iraq.* ◇ **~ sb** *The Roman Emperor Valens met the Visigoths in battle at Adrianople.* **9** [T] **~ sth** to experience a particular situation or attitude, often an unpleasant one SYN COME ACROSS SB/STH, ENCOUNTER¹ (1): *The advancing French forces met no resistance.* **10** [I, T] to touch sth; to join: *Because of the curvature of spacetime, the statement that parallel straight lines never meet is untrue.* ◇ **~ sth** *This is the point where the Pennsylvania border meets the Ohio River.*

IDM **meet sb half'way** to reach an agreement with sb by giving them part of what they want: *President Eisenhower met the unions halfway by cooperating with Congress to raise defence expenditure.* **there is more to sth than meets the 'eye** a situation is more complicated or interesting than it might seem at first: *There is more to this apparently straightforward narrative than meets the eye.*

PHR V **ˌmeet 'up (with sb)** to meet sb, especially by arrangement: *After the show, the couple meet up with a friend.* **'meet with sb** to meet sb, especially for discussions: *He was called to the provincial capital to meet with British officials.* **'meet with sth** to experience a particular situation or attitude: *This strategy has so far met with limited success.* **'meet sth with sth** to react to sth in a particular way SYN RECEIVE (3): *The news was met with disbelief.*

▸ MEET + NOUN **need, requirement • demand • expectation • assumption • condition • criterion • specification • definition • standard • level • test • target • objective, goal • threshold • challenge • obligation • deadline** *The government's position is that Britain will only join monetary union when five conditions are met.* | **resistance • objection • death, end** *He met a violent end.*

▸ ADVERB + MEET **better • best • successfully • effectively • adequately • fully • easily • clearly** *Companies have had to look harder at how they can better meet the expectations of their customers.*

▸ MEET + ADVERB **regularly • face-to-face • annually • weekly • monthly** *Their finance ministers meet regularly to analyse the world's economic situation.*

▸ VERB + TO MEET **fail, be unable • struggle • be able • be designed** *Most participants were able to meet or exceed their goals.*

meet·ing /ˈmiːtɪŋ/ *noun* **1** [C] an occasion when people come together to discuss or decide sth: *The next meeting will be held on Tuesday, 19th December.* ◇ **~ of sb** *About 10 000 protesters attempted to disrupt the annual meeting of the IMF and the World Bank.* ◇ **~ with sb** *Newspaper editors had regular meetings with officials.* ◇ **~ on/about sth** *There has been a series of follow-up meetings on particular issues such as population and development.* ◇ **in a ~** *In a meeting last week, ministers discussed the measures the government should take.* ◇ **at a ~** *At a meeting on 17 May, it was agreed to change the club's name.* **2 the meeting** [sing.] the people at a meeting who discuss or decide sth: *The meeting passed the resolution.* **3** [C] a situation in which two or more people meet together, because they have arranged it or by chance SYN ENCOUNTER²: **~ with sb** *His first meeting with Ralph was at a dinner with Thomas Schelling.* ◇ **~ of/between A and B** *A seventeenth-century Persian chronicle tells of the meeting of a famous religious teacher and an unnamed wise woman.*

▸ ADJECTIVE + MEETING **initial • face-to-face** *The initial meeting of the inquiry took place in the autumn of 1954.* | **general • annual • monthly • weekly • regular • public • informal • formal • international • mass • political** *The minister stated at a public meeting that the project would go ahead.*

▸ NOUN + MEETING **council • group • team • board • committee • summit • town • planning • staff** *In these committee meetings, representatives submitted amendments.*

▸ VERB + MEETING **hold, have, conduct • attend • call, convene • organize, arrange • schedule • chair • host • address** *She called a meeting with supervisors to identify possible reasons for the rise in the number of complaints.*

▸ MEETING OF + NOUN **council • association • committee • company • board • society • group • assembly • shareholders • creditors • members** *The country holding the Presidency arranges and chairs all meetings of the Council.*

mei·osis /maɪˈəʊsɪs; *NAmE* maɪˈoʊsɪs/ *noun* [U] (*biology*) the division of a cell in two stages that results in four cells, each with half the number of CHROMOSOMES of the original cell: *Diploid germ cells undergo meiosis and differentiate into haploid eggs or sperm.* ◇ **during ~** *Recombination occurs during meiosis.* ⊃ *compare* MITOSIS

melt /melt/ *verb* [I, T] to become liquid as a result of heating; to make sth become liquid in this way: *Most substances melt at a higher temperature when subjected to pressure.* ◇ **~ sth** *If the amount of summer radiation is insufficient to melt the ice that accumulates over winter, the depth of ice thickens.*

PHR V **ˌmelt sth 'down** to heat a metal or glass object until it is liquid, especially so that the metal or glass can be used to make sth else: *Hideyoshi melted down the farmers' weapons to make temple bells and other implements.*

'melting point *noun* **~ (of sth)** the temperature at which a substance will melt: *Naphthalene is a solid at room temperature, and has a melting point of 80.5°C.*

mem·ber /ˈmembə(r)/ *noun* **1** a person, country or organization that has joined a particular group, club or team: *At the end of 2005, the World Trade Organization had 32 governments waiting to become members.* ◇ *Conservative policies seemed designed to please existing party members rather than attract new voters.* ◇ *group/board/union/team members* ◇ **~ of sth** *The decision of the Supreme Court of Canada involved a former member of the Irish National Liberation Army.* ◇ **+ noun** *Since 1945, the United Nations has striven to assist member states in limiting conflict.* **2** a person, an animal or a plant that belongs to a particular group: *Much of their work involves caring for family members, especially young children.* ◇

household/community/staff members ◇ **~ of sth** *All members of the community may attend these monthly meetings.* ◇ *Members of one species cannot interbreed with members of a different species.* **3 Member (for sth)** (in Britain) a Member of Parliament: *If the policy of the Member for Epping had been pursued, the result would have been war.*

ˌMember of ˈParliament *noun* = MP

mem·ber·ship /ˈmembəʃɪp; *NAmE* ˈmembərʃɪp/ *noun* **1** [U] the state of being a member of a group, club, organization, etc: **~ of sth** (*BrE*) *The UK's membership of the EU raises important constitutional questions.* ◇ **~ in sth** (*NAmE*) *In 1819, the citizens of the Missouri Territory applied for membership in the Union.* ◇ **+ noun** *Members pay a low annual membership fee.* **2** [C+sing./pl. v.] **~ (of sth)** the members of a group, a club, an organization, etc: *The membership of this committee has been almost exclusively female.* ◇ *The membership took the decision to go on strike.* **3** [sing., U] **~ (of sth)** the number of members of a group, a club, an organization, etc: *The IMF now has a membership of 185 countries.* ◇ *The decline in union membership was especially rapid during the 1980s and 1990s.*

mem·brane /ˈmembreɪn/ *noun* [C, U] **1** a thin layer of skin or TISSUE that connects or covers parts inside the body: *The lung is surrounded by two membranes.* ◇ **~ of sth** *The skin and mucous membranes of the body constitute efficient barriers against the entry of most pathogens.* **2 ~ (of sth)** (*biology*) a very thin layer found in the structure of cells: *These hormones are all water soluble and cannot cross the plasma membrane of the cell.* **3** a thin layer of material used to prevent air, liquid, etc. from entering a particular part of sth: *A thin plastic membrane is coated with a conducting material and spread over a printed circuit board.* ■ **mem·bran·ous** /ˈmembrənəs/ *adj.*: *It is a membranous structure in the form of a tube-shaped sac.*

mem·oir /ˈmemwɑː(r)/ *noun* **1 memoirs** [pl.] an account written by sb, especially sb famous, about their life and experiences: *Kissinger made no reference to the negotiations in his memoirs.* **2** [C] **~ (of sb/sth)** a written account of sb's life, a place or an event, written by sb who knows it well: *Ward wrote a memoir of his experiences in the California gold fields in 1851–52.*

me·mor·ial /məˈmɔːriəl/ *noun* **1** [C] a statue, stone, etc. that is built in order to remind people of an important past event or of a famous person who has died: *The Queen attended a wreath-laying ceremony at the war memorial.* ◇ **~ to sb/sth** *The building was constructed as a memorial to the nation's first president.* **2** [sing.] **~ to sb/sth** a thing that will continue to remind people of sb/sth: *The book functions as a sort of quiet-spoken memorial to its late author.* ■ **me·mor·ial** *adj.*: *a memorial plaque/mound/tomb/tablet*

mem·or·ize (*BrE also* **-ise**) /ˈmeməraɪz/ *verb* **~ sth** to learn sth carefully so that you can remember it exactly: *In the past, geography lessons focused on memorizing facts about the principal products of world regions.*

mem·ory /ˈmeməri/ (*pl.* **-ies**) *noun* **1** [C, U] your ability to remember things; the part of your mind in which you store things that you remember: *Everyone appreciates how useful it is to have a good memory.* ◇ **~ of sth** *It is possible their memory of events was inaccurate.* ◇ **~ for sth** *Memory for recent events is assessed by asking about news items from the last day or two.* ◇ **in sb's ~** *This scene had been deeply etched in her memory.* ◇ **+ noun** *Many mind-altering drugs reduce short-term memory span.* **2** [U] **in/within... ~** the period of time that sb is able to remember events: *The debate took place during one of the most closely fought general election campaigns in living memory.* ◇ *The most devastating earthquake in recent memory struck in December 2004.* **3** [C] a thought of sth that you remember from the past: *The interview brought up painful memories.* ◇ *to recall/revive/evoke memories* ◇ **~ of (doing) sth** *Hann had a vivid memory of staying up all night listening to radio reports of Charles Lindbergh's May 1927 solo flight from New York to Paris.* **4** [U, C] the part of a computer where data are stored; the amount of space in a computer for storing data: *The CPU needs to access the video memory in order to generate and modify the image being displayed.* ◇ **+ noun** *The processor may either read data from a memory location or write data to a memory location.* **5** [U] **~ (of sb)** what is remembered about sb after they have died: *These poems celebrate the memory of the poet's first wife, Emma.*

IDM **from memory** without reading or looking at notes: *Johnson was probably quoting from memory, hence the slight inaccuracy in the quotation.* **in memory of sb | to the memory of sb** intended to show respect and remind people of sb who has died: *The couple founded the charity in memory of their daughter.* ◇ *This book is dedicated to the memory of Dr Edwin Dinwoodie McKee (1906–1985).* ➲ *more at* LIVING[1]

men *pl. of* MAN

men·tal AWL /ˈmentl/ *adj.* **1** [usually before noun] connected with the state of health of the mind or with the treatment of illnesses of the mind SYN PSYCHOLOGICAL (1): *Health is a state of complete physical, mental and social well-being.* ◇ *Towards the end, Nixon's mental state became a source of concern to some.* ◇ *Some mental health problems may occur more often in families where there is a history of mental illness.* ➲ *compare* PSYCHIATRIC **2** [usually before noun] connected with or happening in the mind; involving the process of thinking: *Intelligence tests measure performance on set tasks that require mental ability to solve correctly.* ◇ *These tests are designed to examine the mental processes of the consumer.*

M

men·tal·ity AWL /menˈtæləti/ *noun* [usually sing.] (*pl.* **-ies**) **~ (of sb/sth)** the particular attitude or way of thinking of a person or group: *The teaching of Confucius still shapes the mentality of modern Koreans.* ◇ *This willingness to borrow superior weaponry or armour from their enemies is part of a wider Roman cultural mentality.*

men·tal·ly AWL /ˈmentəli/ *adv.* connected with or happening in the mind: *The aim is to keep patients functional both physically and mentally with an improved quality of life.* ◇ *People stay mentally competent with normal ageing.* ◇ *The majority of the public are likely to be unaware of how many mentally ill people they know and encounter every day.*

men·tion[1] /ˈmenʃn/ *verb* to write or speak about sth/sb, especially without giving much information: **~ sth/sb (as sth/sb)** *Many participants mentioned time and cost as reasons not to visit their health care provider.* ◇ **~ doing sth** *A few of these respondents mentioned going through financial struggles and difficult circumstances.* ◇ **~ how/where, etc...** *Several respondents mentioned how motherhood improved their status in their communities.* ◇ **~ that...** *It is important to mention that the number of observations for each of these groups was small, ranging from three to seven.* ◇ **the sth mentioned** *For the reasons mentioned in the previous section, continental climates are typically much more extreme than maritime climates.* ◇ **as mentioned + adv./prep.** *As mentioned above, indicators of sustainable development have been developed by many disciplines.* ➲ *see also* ABOVE-MENTIONED

IDM **not to mention** used to introduce extra information and emphasize what you are saying: *The issue of non-attendance at school has become a major topic of seminars and symposia, not to mention novels, comics and films.*

▸ MENTION + NOUN **reason • name • problem • study • example • case • work • factor** *One factor usually mentioned in studies of the correlation between poverty and disability is lack of access to schooling.*

▸ ADVERB + MENTION **already, previously • just • briefly • specifically, explicitly, expressly • frequently • rarely • never • barely, hardly, scarcely** *Examples specifically mentioned in the legislation include home modifications and assistive technology.*
▸ MENTION + ADVERB **above, earlier, previously, before, already • here • below • briefly** *As mentioned already, all relevant articles were analysed for additional citations.*
▸ VERB + TO MENTION **fail, neglect** *He fails to mention any case in which these conditions have been fulfilled.*

men·tion² /ˈmenʃn/ *noun* [U, C, usually sing.] an act of referring to sb/sth in speech or writing: *Several earlier cases are worthy of brief mention.* ◇ *specific/explicit/special mention* ◇ *Three other scientists of the same period deserve a mention.* ◇ **~ of sb/sth** *Less than a decade ago, the mere mention of an EU military capability was unthinkable.* ◇ **make no ~ of sb/sth** *The original Treaty of Rome made no mention of the environment.*

menu /ˈmenjuː/ *noun* **1** a list of possible choices that are shown on a computer screen: *Different options appear in the menus according to the item selected.* ◇ *The headings for each population are automatically displayed in drop-down menus.* ◇ **~ bar** *Detailed information about Excel is accessed by clicking Help on the menu bar.* **2** a list of the food that is available at a restaurant or to be served at a meal: *Rural schools offer a menu with many freshly prepared food items.* ◇ **on the ~** *As a response to a recent trend back to more traditional Japanese tastes, teriyaki burgers often appear on the menu.*

M

mer·chant /ˈmɜːtʃənt; *NAmE* ˈmɜːrtʃənt/ *noun* a person or company involved in buying and selling goods in large quantities, especially by importing and exporting goods or by supplying goods to a particular trade: *He was helped by one of the wealthiest merchants in New York.* ◇ *a coal/wine/sugar merchant* ◇ *Many of the products are sold in builders' merchants in the UK in the form of plywood.*

mere /mɪə(r); *NAmE* mɪr/ *adj.* [only before noun] (*superlative* **mer·est**, no *comparative*) **1** used to say that the fact that a particular thing is present in a situation is enough to have an influence on that situation: **~ fact** *The mere fact that people share similar beliefs about justice is not enough to sustain solidarity, social unity or political legitimacy.* ◇ **~ existence** *The mere existence of a hospital guideline does not guarantee its actual application.* ◇ **~ presence** *In the case of these viruses, the mere presence of antibodies is sufficient to make a definitive diagnosis.* **2** used when you want to emphasize how small or unimportant sb/sth is: *A mere 15 years ago, email, web shops and online banking were just dreams.*

mere·ly /ˈmɪəli; *NAmE* ˈmɪrli/ *adv.* used meaning 'only' or 'simply' to emphasize a fact or sth that you are saying: *These are not merely theoretical considerations.* ◇ *Economic reforms served merely to complicate the economic process in the USSR in the four years from 1985 to 1989.* ◇ *He argued that conflict within the state merely reflected the Roman concern for liberty and for the protection of civil rights.*

merge /mɜːdʒ; *NAmE* mɜːrdʒ/ *verb* **1** [I, T] to combine or make two or more things combine to form a single thing: *In the 1890s, thousands of small firms merged to form companies owned by shareholders.* ◇ **~ with sth** *The town of Haruna merged with the much larger city of Takasaki.* ◇ **~ into sth** *The process continues until the two galaxies merge into a single system.* ◇ **~ (A and B) (together)** *His work merges documentary style and avant-garde convention.* ◇ **~ A with B** *There are three forms of non-traditional news that merge entertainment with informational content.* ◇ **~ sth** *The government initiated a debate on whether to merge the existing institutions.* **2** [I] **~ (into sth)** if two things **merge**, or if one thing **merges into** another, the differences between them gradually disappear so that it is impossible to distinguish between them: *He taught his son, and for a time their artistic identities merged.* ◇ *Towards the south, the lowland merges into the large delta of the Irrawaddy river.*

mer·ger /ˈmɜːdʒə(r); *NAmE* ˈmɜːrdʒər/ *noun* the act of combining two or more things, especially organizations or businesses, into one: *The merger would have created a firm with a market share of 72 per cent.* ◇ **~ between/of A and B** *The European Commission prohibited the proposed merger between the two airlines.* ◇ **~ with sth** *Employee opposition to job losses prevented the restructuring of the company via a merger with a foreign partner.*

me·rid·ian /məˈrɪdiən/ *noun* an imaginary line on the surface of the earth that joins the North Pole to the South Pole and passes through a particular place: *The Royal Astronomer Nevil Maskelyne established Greenwich, England, as the location for the prime meridian, the place from which all clocks were set.*

merit¹ /ˈmerɪt/ *noun* **1** [C, usually pl.] a good feature that deserves praise, reward or admiration SYN STRENGTH (3): *Expert evidence should be assessed on its merits.* ◇ *When investigating any phenomenon, it is important to examine both merits and demerits.* ◇ **~ of sth** *The paper then considers the relative merits of these two theories.* **2** [U] the quality of being good and of deserving praise, reward or admiration SYN WORTH² (3): *Both points of view have merit.* ◇ *All of these novels have a high degree of artistic merit.* ◇ **on ~** *Promotion could only be achieved on merit.* ◇ **(not) without ~** *This is an interesting argument and not without merit.*

merit² /ˈmerɪt/ *verb* (not used in the progressive tenses) **~ sth** to do sth to deserve praise or attention SYN DESERVE: *There are some limitations of the study that merit attention in future research.* ◇ *Jenkins' project raises a number of interesting questions that merit further investigation.*

mesh /meʃ/ *noun* **1** [U, C] material made of pieces of plastic rope or wire that are twisted together like a net: *The top of each cup was covered with square of mesh.* ◇ *De Forest modified Fleming's diode by placing a wire mesh between the cathode and anode.* **2** [C, usually sing.] **~ of sth** a complicated system, pattern or situation, involving things that are closely connected to each other SYN WEB (1): *Decision-makers often have to work as a collective, within a mesh of dynamic and shifting power relationships.*

mes·sage /ˈmesɪdʒ/ *noun* **1** a piece of information sent in electronic form, for example by email or mobile phone: *The first email message was sent in 1971.* ◇ *Many parents reported using text messages for family communication.* ◇ *Even if a phone has been turned off, messages will be delivered when the phone is turned back on.* ➲ *see also* TEXT MESSAGE **2 ~ (of sth)** a written or spoken piece of information that you send to sb or leave for sb when you cannot speak to them yourself: *During their presidencies, both Reagan and Bush had sent messages of support.* **3** [usually sing.] an important idea that sth such as a book, speech or company is trying to communicate: *The number of articles containing an anti-smoking message dropped from 65% to 24%.* ◇ *Smaller or less well-funded bodies generally find it harder to put their message across.* ◇ *to convey/communicate/reinforce a message* ◇ *an advertising/a promotional/a marketing message* **4** [sing.] **~ (from sth)** something important that should be learned from an event: *The message from the Hoan Bridge disaster was clear: bridges susceptible to fatigue damage need to be carefully monitored.* **5** a piece of information or an instruction that is sent from one part of the body to another: *These calls transmit messages to the brain where specific smells and tastes are identified.*

mes·sen·ger /ˈmesɪndʒə(r)/ *noun* **1** a person who gives a message to sb or who delivers messages to people as a job: *Kings and emperors traditionally corresponded by messenger.* ◇ **~ of sb** *The second part of the confession of faith is the affirmation of Muhammad as the messenger of God.* **2** (*biochemistry*) a substance that carries information or instructions within the body: *Hormones produced by the endocrine system are but one of several types of chemical messengers.* ◇ **+ noun** *Messenger RNA (mRNA) is the RNA molecule that specifies the sequence of amino acids in a protein.*

met *past tense, past part. of* MEET

meta·bol·ic /ˌmetəˈbɒlɪk; *NAmE* ˌmetəˈbɑːlɪk/ *adj.* [usually before noun] connected with the chemical process of turning food or other substances in the body into energy: *The conclusion was that animals with a high metabolic rate would have a shorter lifespan than animals with lower rates.* ◇ *The blood samples are then analysed for evidence of a range of metabolic disorders.*

ˌmetabolic ˈpathway *noun* = PATHWAY (3)

me·tab·ol·ism /məˈtæbəlɪzəm/ *noun* [U, sing.] the chemical processes in living things that change food and other substances into energy and materials for growth: *The liver plays an important role in fat metabolism.* ◇ *The low temperatures result in a lower rate of metabolism for the fish.* ◇ **~ of sth** *Insulin is involved in the metabolism of carbohydrates, proteins and fats.*

me·tab·ol·ize (*BrE also* **-ise**) /məˈtæbəlaɪz/ *verb* **~ sth (to sth)** (*biology*) to turn food or other substances in the body into energy and waste products by means of chemical processes: *The liver rapidly metabolizes the glucose to water.*

metal /ˈmetl/ *noun* [C, U] a type of solid mineral substance that is usually hard and that heat and electricity can travel through, for example tin, iron and gold: *Gold, silver and copper were the first metals used by humans.* ◇ *They traded in luxuries such as spices and precious metals.* ◇ **+ noun** *Surgery realigns the spinal column and holds it together using metal plates and screws.* ◇ *a metal atom/ion/oxide* ➲ *see also* HEAVY METAL (1), TRANSITION METAL

me·tal·lic /məˈtælɪk/ *adj.* [usually before noun] **1** made of or containing metal: *Polymers may, in fact, never replace traditional metallic conductors like copper and aluminium.* **2** that looks, tastes or sounds like metal: *The condition has symptoms of fever, joint pain, fatigue, headache and a metallic taste in the mouth.*

meta·morph·ic /ˌmetəˈmɔːfɪk; *NAmE* ˌmetəˈmɔːrfɪk/ *adj.* (*earth science*) (of rocks) formed by the action of heat or pressure: *Biotite is a common mineral in a wide variety of igneous and metamorphic rocks.* ➲ *compare* IGNEOUS, SEDIMENTARY

meta·phor /ˈmetəfə(r); ˈmetəfɔː(r)/ *noun* [C, U] **1 ~ (for sth)** something that represents another situation or idea: *The concept of crime may act as a metaphor for wider troubles and social anxieties.* **2** a word or phrase used to describe sb/sth else, in a way that is different from its normal use, in order to show that the two things have the same qualities and to make the description more powerful; the use of such words and phrases: *Shakespeare frequently uses theatrical metaphors ('All the world's a stage...').* ◇ *The reader is directed to look for deeper levels of significance, through metaphor and imagery.* ➲ *compare* SIMILE

meta·phor·ical /ˌmetəˈfɒrɪkl; *NAmE* ˌmetəˈfɔːrɪkl/ *adj.* connected with or containing metaphors: *The author begins by exploring the literal and metaphorical journeys undertaken by the protagonists of three novels.* ➲ *compare* FIGURATIVE, LITERAL ■ **meta·phor·ic·al·ly** /ˌmetəˈfɒrɪkli; *NAmE* ˌmetəˈfɔːrɪkli/ *adv.*: *But now, speaking metaphorically, money came to be seen to have the power to direct economy and society.*

meta·phys·ics /ˌmetəˈfɪzɪks/ *noun* [U] the branch of philosophy that deals with the nature of existence, truth and knowledge: *The primary concern of metaphysics should be the investigation not of language but of reality.* ■ **meta·phys·ic·al** /ˌmetəˈfɪzɪkl/ *adj.*: *metaphysical claims/questions/principles*

meter /ˈmiːtə(r)/ *noun* **1** (especially in compounds) a device that measures and records the amount of electricity, gas, water, etc. that you have used or the time and distance you have travelled, etc: *The water companies were keen for customers to have water meters installed.* ◇ *In unlicensed cabs of this type, there is no meter.* **2 -meter** (in compounds) a device for measuring the thing mentioned: *Water temperature measurements were taken at the shoreline using a thermometer.* ◇ *The wavelengths are measured by a spectrometer.* **3** (*US*) = METRE

me·thane /ˈmiːθeɪn; *NAmE* ˈmeθeɪn/ *noun* [U] (*symb.* CH_4) a gas without colour or smell, that burns easily and is used as fuel. Natural gas consists mainly of methane: *Methane is principally produced through the anaerobic decay of organic matter.* ◇ **+ noun** *Wetlands are the source of over 40% of annual global methane emissions.*

method AWL /ˈmeθəd/ *noun* [C] a particular way of doing sth: *Managers are frequently not familiar with scientific methods.* ◇ **~ of sth** *Our results with these two methods of analysis are mutually supportive.* ◇ **~ (of sth) (that...)** *Firms will tend to introduce the methods of production that are most profitable.* ◇ **~ of doing sth** *There are several methods of delivering nursing care.* ◇ **~ for doing sth** *There are dozens of alternative technical methods for recording interviews.* ◇ **~ for sth** *Researchers have employed a variety of methods for the study of well-being in dementia.* ◇ **~ to do sth** *There are many methods to determine the water level, water velocity and discharge of a river.* ◇ **by a ~** *DNA from animal tissues can be obtained by several methods.* ◇ **according to a ~** *The reaction products were analysed according to the method of Tong et al.*

> **WORD FAMILY**
> method *noun*
> methodical *adj.*
> methodically *adv.*
> methodology *noun*
> methodological *adj.*
> methodologically *adv.*

▸ ADJECTIVE + METHOD **new • different, alternative • modern • traditional • conventional • standard • common • effective • efficient • reliable • direct • indirect • simple • sophisticated • appropriate • preferred** *The general consensus is to examine alternative methods of harnessing tidal energy.*

▸ **scientific • experimental • empirical • statistical • qualitative • quantitative • systematic • comparative • analytical • computational • numerical • mathematical • mixed** *Lockyer (2006) employed a mixed methods approach for her study of humour.*

▸ NOUN + METHOD **research • sampling • production • teaching • assessment** *A research method is simply a technique for collecting data.*

▸ VERB + METHOD **use, employ, apply, utilize • implement • develop • devise • propose • introduce • adopt, choose • adapt • follow • describe • outline • discuss** *Over the past decade, physical geographers have continued to develop new methods for data analysis.*

▸ METHOD + VERB **(be) based on • yield, produce • obtain • detect • measure • determine • work** *This method consistently yields lower figures.*

meth·od·ic·al AWL /məˈθɒdɪkl; *NAmE* məˈθɑːdɪkl/ *adj.* **1** done in a careful and logical way: *During the analysis, it was important to ensure a methodical approach.* **2** (of a person) doing things in a careful and logical way: *Crusoe is a methodical diarist, recording his experiences and* *achievements meticulously.* ■ **meth·od·ic·al·ly** /mə'θɒdɪkli; *NAmE* mə'θɑːdɪkli/ *adv.*: *The authors approach the topic methodically.*

meth·odo·logic·al AWL /ˌmeθədə'lɒdʒɪkl; *NAmE* ˌmeθədə'lɑːdʒɪkl/ *adj.* [usually before noun] connected with the methods and principles used to perform a particular activity: *methodological issues/principles/limitations* ◇ *The quality of the research is limited due to a number of methodological problems.* ◇ *Her methodological approach employs quantitative techniques to make sense of huge amounts of qualitative data.* ■ **meth·odo·logic·al·ly** /ˌmeθədə'lɒdʒɪkli; *NAmE* ˌmeθədə'lɑːdʒɪkli/ *adv.*: *Many of the studies are older and are methodologically limited.*

meth·od·ology AWL /ˌmeθə'dɒlədʒi; *NAmE* ˌmeθə'dɑːlədʒi/ *noun* (*pl.* **-ies**) [C, U] a set of methods and principles used to perform a particular activity: *The surveys are based on a standard methodology.* ◇ *The study makes use of recent advances in research methodology.* ◇ **~ for (doing) sth** *Marketers have developed methodologies for capturing information about the marketing environment.*

metre (*US* **meter**) /'miːtə(r)/ *noun* **1** [C] (*abbr.* **m**) a unit for measuring length; a hundred centimetres: *The city suffered major damage: an estimated 25 000 square metres of office space were destroyed.* ◇ *The resulting electric field will be up to a thousand volts per metre.* **2** [U] the arrangement of strong and weak stresses in lines of poetry that produces the rhythm: *He experimented with combining English metre and rhythm with Indian themes.*

M

GRAMMAR POINT

Using units of measurement

- Use the singular and plural forms: *Mud volcanoes range in diameter from less than* ***a metre*** *to* ***several hundred metres.*** ◇ *The velocity is about* ***one and a half kilometres*** *per second.* ◇ *Early land plants were small, some only* ***a few centimetres*** *high.*
- Note that *a* is often used instead of *one*: *The speed of the wave is about* ***a metre*** *per second.*
- When you are using the measurement as an adjective before a noun, use the singular form, with a hyphen: *Wilkinson devised a new boring machine that could make* ***a 72-inch cylinder***... ◇ *The film was shot in* ***eighty-millimetre film.***

met·ric /'metrɪk/ *adj.* based on the system of measurement that uses the metre and the kilogram as basic units: *It is estimated that between 3 and 4 million metric tons of oil are spilled annually into the world's rivers, lakes and oceans.* ➲ *compare* IMPERIAL (2)

met·ro·pol·itan /ˌmetrə'pɒlɪtən; *NAmE* ˌmetrə'pɑːlɪtən/ *adj.* [only before noun] **1** connected with a large or capital city: *The metropolitan area of Mexico City occupies an area of about 2 500 km²*. ◇ *In the United States, many cities and towns are clustered within larger metropolitan regions.* **2** connected with a particular country rather than with the other regions of the world that the country controls: *The unemployment rate for Guadeloupe is 26% compared with 9% in metropolitan France.* ◇ *The European powers tried to maintain a degree of metropolitan authority over their American colonies.*

micro /'maɪkrəʊ; *NAmE* 'maɪkroʊ/ *adj.* [only before noun] small; on a small scale: *At the micro level, we will need in-depth, qualitative studies to help us understand the impact of these policies on people living in poverty.* ➲ *compare* MACRO

mi·crobe /'maɪkrəʊb; *NAmE* 'maɪkroʊb/ *noun* an extremely small living thing that you can only see under a MICROSCOPE and that may cause disease: *Disinfectants kill microbes but may also damage human tissues.* ◇ *The most important biodegradation processes in aquatic and soil environments are carried out by microbes.*

mi·cro·bial /maɪ'krəʊbiəl; *NAmE* maɪ'kroʊbiəl/ *adj.* connected with microbes: *There is insufficient nitrogen for optimum microbial growth.* ◇ *Typically, highly fertile soils have a high organic content and an active microbial community.*

micro·chip /'maɪkrəʊtʃɪp; *NAmE* 'maɪkroʊtʃɪp/ *noun* (*also* **chip**) a very small piece of a material that is a SEMICONDUCTOR, used to carry a complicated electronic CIRCUIT: *The information is recorded in a microchip which is read by an electronic reader at immigration control.*

micro·organ·ism /ˌmaɪkrəʊ'ɔːgənɪzəm; *NAmE* ˌmaɪkroʊ'ɔːrgənɪzəm/ *noun* a very small living thing that you can only see under a MICROSCOPE: *Soil microorganisms play a key role in grassland ecosystems.* ◇ *Cleaning with soap and water removes most microorganisms from surfaces.*

micro·scope /'maɪkrəskəʊp; *NAmE* 'maɪkrəskoʊp/ *noun* an instrument used in scientific study for making very small things look larger so that you can examine them carefully: *The tissue section was visually analysed using a light microscope.* ◇ **+ noun** *The rock chip was then mounted on a clean microscope slide.* ➲ *see also* ELECTRON MICROSCOPE

micro·scop·ic /ˌmaɪkrə'skɒpɪk; *NAmE* ˌmaɪkrə'skɑːpɪk/ *adj.* **1** [only before noun] using a microscope: *Microscopic images of the stained sections were acquired and digitized.* ◇ *Microscopic examination of the surface revealed tiny abrasions and scratches.* **2** [usually before noun] extremely small and difficult or impossible to see without a microscope: *The microscopic features of the tubes were examined with a transmission electron microscope.* ◇ *Plankton refers to the microscopic organisms, including animals, plants and algae, that float in surface waters.* ■ **micro·scop·ic·al·ly** /ˌmaɪkrə'skɒpɪkli; *NAmE* ˌmaɪkrə'skɑːpɪkli/ *adv.*: *All the samples were examined microscopically.* ◇ *These sites are microscopically small.*

micro·scopy /maɪ'krɒskəpi; *NAmE* maɪ'krɑːskəpi/ *noun* [U] the use of a microscope to look at very small things: *Water droplet sizes ranging from 3 to 10 mm were determined by optical microscopy.* ◇ *Transmission electron microscopy showed the absence of intercellular spaces in the tissues.*

micro·wave /'maɪkrəweɪv/ *noun* **1** an ELECTROMAGNETIC wave that is shorter than a radio wave but longer than a light wave: **+ noun** *Because water vapour absorbs microwave radiation, the detectors have been flown on balloons at dry locations.* **2** (*also* ˌ**microwave** '**oven**) a type of OVEN that cooks or heats food very quickly using ELECTROMAGNETIC waves rather than heat: *The microwave oven essentially consists of a power supply, a waveguide feed and an oven cavity.*

mid·dle¹ /'mɪdl/ *adj.* [only before noun] **1** in a position in the middle of an object, a group of objects, a group of people, etc: *It was found that the iron concentration decreased in the following order: upper layer > middle layer > lower layer.* ◇ *Metabolism is the major area covered in the middle section of the book.* **2** at a point in the middle of a range: *The Eurozone and the US are at either end of the spectrum, while the UK occupies a middle position.* **3** between the beginning and the end of a period of time: *The Britannia Bridge was part of the rapid development of the railways in the middle part of the nineteenth century.* IDM **a middle** '**course** | **a/the middle** '**way** an acceptable course of action that avoids two extreme positions: *Steering a middle course between these two unacceptable positions involves a pragmatic approach.* ◇ *Keynes suggested that there may be a middle way between free market capitalism and full-blooded socialism.*

the mid·dle[2] /ˈmɪdl/ *noun* [sing.] **1 ~ of sth** a point or a period of time between the beginning and the end of sth: *In these conditions, the solar warming of the surface may become intense in the middle of the day.* ◇ *By the middle of the 20th century, most large private employers had to negotiate with a labour union in the hiring and management of labour.* **2** the part of sth that is at an equal distance from all its edges or sides: *These caldera lakes have islands in the middle, formed where magma has erupted in the lake.* ◇ **~ of sth** *Many synagogues oriented their seating towards the raised platform located in the middle of the synagogue floor.* **3** a point between two levels or ends of a range: *Rates are highest in Eastern Europe and lowest in Central and South America, with the United States falling in the middle.* ◇ **~ of sth** *Liberals are placed squarely in the middle of a spectrum of left-right political ideology.*
IDM in the middle of (doing) sth experiencing sth or busy with sth: *By 1982, the government was in the middle of an economic crisis.* ◇ *While he was in the middle of writing his memoir, Thomson went through a few weeks of despair.*

ˌmiddle ˈage *noun* [U] the period of your life when you are between the ages of about 40 and 60: *Most people reach their productivity and income peak in middle age.*

ˌmiddle-ˈaged *adj.* **1** (of a person) between the ages of about 40 and 60: *In Western countries, middle-aged adults often have to provide support to generations both above and below.* **2 the middle aged** *noun* [pl.] people who are middle-aged: *Such attitudes are more common in the middle-aged and elderly.*

the ˌMiddle ˈAges (*also* **the middle ages**) *noun* [pl.] in European history, the period from about AD 500 to AD 1450 **HELP** The earlier part of this period (around 500–1100) is sometimes considered a distinct period, known as the Dark Ages, while the later part (around 1100–1450) is thought of as the Middle Ages proper: *Throughout the Middle Ages, agriculture remained an important component of the economy of all towns.* ◇ **in ~** *The politics of Europe in the early middle ages have rarely been considered as a whole.*

ˌmiddle ˈclass *noun* [C+sing./pl. v.] the social class whose members are neither very rich nor very poor and that includes professional and business people: *Dickens was born into the lower middle class, a class of clerks, tradesmen and shopkeepers.* ◇ *Educational culture is based on the culture of the upper and middle classes (Delpit, 1995).* ➲ *compare* UPPER CLASS, WORKING CLASS

ˌmiddle-ˈclass *adj.* connected with the middle social class: *Data suggest that middle-class families are relatively successful in maintaining their social position.*

ˈmiddle ground *noun* [U] a set of opinions, decisions, etc. that two or more groups who oppose each other can agree on; a position that is not extreme: *Labour now aimed to occupy the middle ground, and govern from the political centre.*

might /maɪt/ *modal verb* (*negative* **might not**, *short form* **mightn't** /ˈmaɪtnt/) used when showing that sth is or was possible: *Much popular culture is part of what might be considered global culture.* ◇ *The next great earthquake to affect Asia might well be inland, perhaps along the Himalayas.* ◇ *Yet, although the writers might reject any influence of feminist writing, their texts seem to reveal the opposite.* ◇ *These names might have been in Shakepeare's mind as he was writing.* **IDM** *see* WELL[1] ➲ grammar note *at* MODAL[1]

mi·grant **AWL** /ˈmaɪɡrənt/ *noun* **1** a person who moves from one place to another, especially in order to find work: *Distinguishing between a refugee and an economic migrant may not be simple.* ◇ *Slaves and refugees are examples of forced migrants.* ◇ *Skilled migrants are unlikely to come to the UK if they do not have the option of settlement with their families.* **2** a bird or an animal that moves from one place to another according to the season: *Spring migrants are moving towards breeding grounds that may still have poor food supplies and inclement weather.* ■ **mi·grant** *adj.*: *In 2003, around 270 000 migrant workers entered the UK.* ◇ *These plantations were less suitable as habitat for resident and migrant birds.*

GRAMMAR POINT

might • could • may

- These modal verbs are each used to talk about present or future possibility: *A community **might** be defined on a geographical or neighbourhood basis.* ◇ *The authors suggest that long-term drought conditions **could** lead to changes in species composition.*
- To say that sth is *not* possible in the present or the future, use **may not** or **might not**: *In the absence of competition, existing institutions **might not** change at all.* ◇ *A business **may not** be able to increase its profits simply by raising its output price.* Note that **could not** has a different meaning: 'is/was not able to do sth'.
- To express what was possible in the past, use **might/may/could + have + past participle**: *Economic factors **may have played** some part in two of the rebellions.* ◇ *The number of Native Americans living in Virginia at this time **could have been** anything between 14 000 and 170 000.*
- To say that sth definitely would not have been possible in a given situation in the past, use **could not have + past participle**: *Recent examination by Wilch et al. (1993) argues that, based on their textural characteristics, the cinder cones **could not have erupted** under water.* **Could not have + past participle** is often used to say that sth would not have been possible without a particular action or event: *Without the acquisition of new knowledge, there **could not have been** an information revolution.* To say that it is possible that sth did not happen in a given situation in the past, use **might/may not have + past participle**: *Many salespeople **might not have mentioned** that the policy would not pay out for existing medical conditions.*

M

mi·grate **AWL** /maɪˈɡreɪt; *NAmE* ˈmaɪɡreɪt/ *verb* **1** [I] (of a lot of people) to move from one town, country or place to go and live and/or work in another: **~ (from sth) (to sth)** *It is estimated that about 18 million Chinese migrate from rural to urban areas each year.* ◇ **+ adv./prep.** *The Huns, a federation of nomadic tribes, migrated westward out of the central Asian grasslands.* ➲ *compare* EMIGRATE **2** [I] (of animals) to move from one part of the world to another according to the season: **~ (from sth) (to sth)** *Most terrestrial animals migrate to non-flooded areas during wet periods.* ◇ **+ adv./prep.** *Several species of sea turtle migrate over enormous distances.* ◇ **migrating + noun** *Turbines can kill migrating birds that attempt to fly through the turbine.* **3** [I] (*technical*) to move from one place to another: **~ to sth** *The infected cells then migrate to other areas of the body.* ◇ **~ (away) from sth** *Oil and gas may migrate away from the source rock to produce a petroleum accumulation.* ◇ **+ adv./prep.** *In certain diseases, cells migrate across the blood-brain barrier.*

mi·gra·tion **AWL** /maɪˈɡreɪʃn/ *noun* [U, C] **1** the movement of large numbers of people or animals from one place to another: *State control of population movement has decreased, resulting in massive internal rural-to-urban migration.* ◇ **+ adv./prep.** *Changes in the pattern of international migration into and out of the UK have contributed to population change.* ◇ **~ of sb/sth** *To obtain more complete figures, procedures are needed to estimate the net migration of children.* ◇ **+ noun** *Previous studies have shown that rivers are strong migration barriers for Bornean orang-utans.* **2** (*technical*) the slow or gradual movement of sth from one place to another: *There is virtually* *no cell migration in plants.* ◇ **~ of sth** *Mountain ranges and oceans both provide barriers for the migration of plants.* ◇ **~ (of sth) (from sth) (to sth)** *Permeability barriers may inhibit the migration of oil and gas from the source rock to the hydrocarbon reservoir.*

mi·gra·tory AWL /ˈmaɪɡrətri; maɪˈɡreɪtəri; *NAmE* ˈmaɪɡrətɔːri/ *adj.* (*technical*) connected with animals that migrate: *Pollution affected the river habitats used by migratory birds and other species.* ◇ *Migratory behaviour can have a strong genetic component.*

mild /maɪld/ *adj.* **(mild·er, mild·est) 1** not severe or strong: *Most patients have relatively mild symptoms which can be managed by diet.* ◇ *Mild learning disability generally represents the lower end of the normal distribution curve of intelligence.* **2** (of weather) not very cold, and therefore pleasant: *The central Transvaal Plateau is characterized by hot summers and mild dry winters.* ➲ *compare* HARD[1] (8) ■ **mild·ly** *adv.*: *The soil pH is mildly alkaline.* ◇ *In the interview, the patient admitted that he was mildly depressed.*

mile /maɪl/ *noun* **1** [C] a unit for measuring distance equal to 1 760 yards (approximately 1 609 metres): *She travelled 26 000 miles throughout the US.* ◇ *At this point, the river is about a half a mile wide.* ◇ *Japan has a small land area, covering just 145 000 square miles.* ◇ *Winds gusting to 150 miles per hour caused 19 deaths.* ◇ *Protests included a 144-mile march from Philadelphia to Washington, DC.* ◇ *They prepared for another invasion by building a twelve-mile-long defensive wall.* **2 miles** [pl.] a long distance or a large area: *The dam forms a pool extending miles upstream.* ◇ *The market was the only source of food for miles around.* ➲ grammar note *at* METRE

M

mile·stone /ˈmaɪlstəʊn; *NAmE* ˈmaɪlstoʊn/ *noun* a very important stage or event in the development of sth: *Young people with greater motivation are more likely to be successful in achieving various milestones.* ◇ **~ in sth** *The Bill has been described as a milestone in the history of human rights.* ➲ *compare* LANDMARK (2)

mili·tary[1] AWL /ˈmɪlətri; *NAmE* ˈmɪləteri/ *adj.* [usually before noun] connected with soldiers or the armed forces: *He was able to avoid military service on grounds of bad health.* ◇ *Throughout history, states have sought power by means of military force.* ◇ *American military power is currently greater than that of the next ten most powerful states combined.* ◇ *The first organized transport system in Britain was created by the Romans for political and military reasons.* ■ **mili·tar·ily** *adv.*: *The narrow Aegean tied the Greeks to the Near East and Egypt, commercially, culturally, politically and militarily.*

mili·tary[2] AWL /ˈmɪlətri; *NAmE* ˈmɪləteri/ *noun* **the military** [sing.+ sing./pl. v.] soldiers; the armed forces: *After 1985, the military was/were excluded from politics.*

milk /mɪlk/ *noun* [U] **1** the white liquid produced by cows and some other animals as food for their young and used as a drink by humans: *Animal products such as meat, milk and eggs are good sources of essential amino acids.* **2** the white liquid that is produced by women and female MAMMALS for feeding their babies: *The mother may feel worried that she is not producing enough milk.* ◇ **breast ~** *Infants who do not receive breast milk may experience poorer health outcomes.*

mil·len·nium /mɪˈleniəm/ *noun* (*pl.* **mil·len·nia** /mɪˈleniə/ or **mil·len·niums**) **1** a period of 1 000 years, especially as calculated before or after the birth of Christ: *The Persians were an Indo-European people who had settled in Iran by the early first millennium BC.* ◇ *For many millennia, human survival depended on belonging to a group.* **2 the millennium** the time when one period of 1 000 years ends and another begins: *By the turn of the millennium, China's economy was creating eight million jobs a year.*

milli·metre (*US* **milli·meter**) /ˈmɪlimiːtə(r)/ *noun* (*abbr.* **mm**) a unit for measuring length; a 1 000th of a metre: *Lengths range from about a quarter of a millimetre to several centimetres.*

mil·lion /ˈmɪljən/ *number* (*plural verb*) (*abbr.* **m**) 1 000 000: *By 1800, London's population was about a million.* ◇ *The error rate was one in a million.* ◇ *The influenza pandemic of 1918–1919 killed 20–50 million people (Kilbourne, 2006a).* ◇ *During the war, millions were sent to death camps.* ◇ **millions of...** *Companies spend millions of dollars to develop technologies to prevent illegal copying of discs.* HELP You say **a, one, two, several, etc. million** without a final 's' on 'million'. **Millions (of...)** can be used if there is no number or quantity before it. Always use a plural verb with **million** or **millions**, except when an amount of money is mentioned: *Four million (people) were affected.* ◇ *Two million (pounds) was withdrawn from the account.*

mimic /ˈmɪmɪk/ *verb* **(-ck-) ~ sth** (*technical*) to look or behave like sth else; to have the same effect as sth else SYN IMITATE (1): *Our model closely mimics and predicts the behaviour of Metapolybia wasps.* ◇ *Dieting may mimic the effects of nutritional stress in the short term.*

mind[1] /maɪnd/ *noun* **1** [C, U] the part of a person that makes them able to be aware of things, to think and to feel: *Meditation or prayer is used to calm and focus the mind.* ◇ *The plans he was making in his conscious mind reflected these deeper unconscious desires.* ◇ *In many people's minds, the King was responsible for the crisis.* ◇ *The eighteenth century brought new understandings of the human mind and body.* ◇ **state of ~** *The key issue was the defendant's state of mind at the time of the alleged offence.* ◇ **peace of ~** *To ensure peace of mind, the company offered its customers a three year warranty.* **2** [C] the ability to think and reason; sb's intelligence SYN INTELLECT: *The central character is a teenager with the mind of a 5-year-old.* ◇ *Locke tried to understand how the mind works.*

IDM **bear/keep sb/sth in ˈmind | bear/keep in ˈmind that...** to remember sb/sth; to remember or consider that...: *For Clifford, keeping in mind gender as a category for analysis is all-important.* ◇ *However, it should also be borne in mind that stated preferences may not reflect individuals' true preferences.* **bring/call sb/sth to ˈmind** to remind you of sb/sth SYN RECALL[1] (2): *In fact, the script brings to mind Sophocles' play 'Oedipus Tyrannus'.* **come/spring to ˈmind** if sth **comes/springs to mind**, you remember or think of it: *When we think of radical capitalists, the names that come to mind are Samuel Morse, Thomas Edison or Henry Ford.* **have/with sb/sth in ˈmind (for sth)** to be thinking of sb/sth, especially as a possible aim, target or solution: *The solutions we had in mind all involved equipment the laboratory did not possess.* ◇ *The books were written with a younger audience in mind.* **make up your ˈmind | make your ˈmind up** to decide sth: *Rather than provide a neat conclusion, she leaves readers to make their own minds up.* **on your ˈmind** if sb/sth is **on your mind**, you are thinking and worrying about them/it a lot: *The possibility of catastrophe was constantly on the minds of nuclear planners.* **to ˈmy mind** in my opinion: *This argument is, to my mind, quite a strong one.* ➲ *more at* BACK[2], CHANGE[2], FRAME[1], OPEN[1], OPEN[2], SPEAK

mind[2] /maɪnd/ *verb* **1** [T, no passive, I] (used especially in questions or with negatives) to be upset or worried by sth: **~ doing sth** *Some people do not mind taking risks; others prefer security.* **2 (not) mind doing sth** [T] to be (not) willing to do sth: *Shoppers were asked if they would mind paying 15% more for organic food.*

mind·ed /ˈmaɪndɪd/ *adj.* **1** (used with adjectives to form compound adjectives) having the way of thinking, the attitude or the type of character mentioned: *Romantic writers asserted their high-minded independence of both publishers and readers.* ◇ *They formed groups of committed, like-minded Muslims.* ◇ *She was described as a strong-minded and outgoing person with a large circle of friends.* **2** (used with adverbs to form compound adjectives) having the type of mind that is interested in or able to understand the areas mentioned: *For the religiously minded, the cause of this socio-economic breakdown was spiritual decay.* ◇ *Advice was sought from scientifically minded colleagues.*

ˈmind map *noun* **~ (of sth)** a diagram used to represent information VISUALLY: *Draw a mind map of your own ideas on the topic.*

mine¹ /maɪn/ *pron.* (the possessive form of *I*) of or belonging to the person writing or speaking: *A colleague is researching a project similar to mine.* ◇ *All italicization in the text is mine.* ◇ *Technology is not a strength of mine.*

mine² /maɪn/ *noun* **1** a deep hole or holes under the ground where minerals such as coal, gold, etc. are dug: *In Canada, Chinese Buddhists arrived on the West Coast in the 1850s to work in the mines.* ◇ *He seized control of the country's gold and silver mines.* ◇ *a coal/copper/diamond mine* ➲ *see also* MINING **2** a type of bomb that is hidden under the ground or in the sea and that explodes when sb/sth touches it: *The Russian ships went out at night to lay mines in enemy waters.*

mine³ /maɪn/ *verb* **1** [T, I] to obtain coal, gold, etc. by digging holes in the ground: **~ sth** *There is no clear evidence as to who mined gold in this region during pre-colonial times.* ◇ **~ sth (for sth)** *The plains have been mined for tin for at least 100 years.* ◇ **~ (for sth)** *The company was denied a gemstone licence and therefore could not start mining.* **2** [T] **~ sth** to analyse a DATABASE in order to produce new information: *By carefully mining the combined data, it may be possible to identify additional patterns.* **3** [T] **~ sth** to place mines below the surface of an area of land or water: *The area was heavily mined.* ◇ *HMS Ocean was mined in the Dardanelles in 1915.*

miner /ˈmaɪnə(r)/ *noun* a person who works in a mine taking out coal, gold, etc: *Coal miners in the US often work more than 40 hours a week.*

min·eral /ˈmɪnərəl/ *noun* [C, U] a substance that is naturally present in the earth and is not formed from animal or vegetable matter, for example gold and salt. Some minerals are also present in food and drink and in the human body and are essential for good health: *Quartz is one of the most common minerals in the earth's crust.* ◇ *Elderly patients may be malnourished or deficient in key vitamins and minerals.* ◇ **+ noun** *Mining firms have also begun to develop the islands' untapped mineral resources.* ◇ *Advances in the geological sciences have provided further valuable tools in the study of mineral deposits.* ➲ *compare* VEGETABLE (1)

min·imal AWL /ˈmɪnɪməl/ *adj.* **1** very small in size, amount or extent SYN NEGLIGIBLE: *The level of regulation is fairly minimal.* ◇ *Patients had effective analgesia with minimal side-effects.* **2** involving the smallest or lowest amount that is possible, required or recorded SYN MINIMUM¹: *Many countries fail to meet even minimal standards.* ◇ *The best approach is to err on the side of minimal intervention.* ➲ *compare* MAXIMAL ■ **min·im·al·ly** AWL *adv.*: *Participants were reimbursed minimally for time and travel costs.* ◇ *The tests are minimally invasive.*

mini·miza·tion (*BrE also* **-isa·tion**) /ˌmɪnɪmaɪˈzeɪʃn; *NAmE* ˌmɪnɪməˈzeɪʃn/ *noun* [U, C, usually sing.] the act of reducing sth, especially sth bad, to the lowest possible level: *Other elements, including cost minimization, may be relevant in determining choice of providers.* ◇ **~ of sth** *This allows for the minimization of missing data.*

min·im·ize (*BrE also* **-ise**) AWL /ˈmɪnɪmaɪz/ *verb* **1 ~ sth** to reduce sth, especially sth bad, to the lowest possible level: *This minimizes the risk of electric shock.* ◇ *This strategy was designed to minimize observer bias.* ◇ *Minimizing unit labour cost will have the effect of maximizing the profit rate.* ◇ *to minimize the effect/impact of sth* OPP MAXIMIZE (1) **2 ~ sth** to try to make sth seem less important than it really is SYN PLAY STH DOWN: *Neorealists minimize the importance of culture, traditions and identity.* **3 ~ sth** to make sth small, especially on a computer screen: *They minimize or switch between screens when parents are looking over their shoulder.*

min·imum¹ AWL /ˈmɪnɪməm/ *adj.* [usually before noun] (*abbr.* **min.**) the smallest or lowest that is possible, required or recorded: *These are the minimum standards expected.* ◇ *There are minimum legal requirements.* ◇ *Maximum and minimum air temperatures were also monitored daily.* ◇ *a minimum value/price/age* OPP MAXIMUM¹

min·imum² AWL /ˈmɪnɪməm/ *noun* (*pl.* **min·ima** /ˈmɪnɪmə/) (*abbr.* **min.**) the smallest or lowest amount that is possible, required or recorded: *Further suffering should be kept to a minimum.* ◇ *Some countries intended to do the bare minimum necessary to satisfy obligations under the Convention.* ◇ **a ~ of sth** *The trial judge recommended that he serve a minimum of 15 years in prison.* ◇ *This allows the evaluation to be conducted with a minimum of disruption.* HELP **The minimum of** is also used before a word referring to a state or activity. It is not usually used before a number: *The Court of Justice is required to act with the minimum of delay.* OPP MAXIMUM²
IDM **at (a/the) minimum | as a minimum** used for stating the smallest action or effort that is required: *At minimum, researchers need to focus on the drug's safety.* ◇ *As a bare minimum, the following records must be kept:...*

ˌminimum ˈwage *noun* [sing.] the lowest wage that an employer is allowed to pay by law: *On 1 April 1999, the UK government introduced a national minimum wage.* ◇ **+ noun** *minimum wage legislation/policy*

min·ing /ˈmaɪnɪŋ/ *noun* [U] **1** the process of getting coal and other minerals from under the ground; the industry involved in this: *Mining has been carried out in south-west England since the turn of the nineteenth century.* ◇ *Agriculture and much heavy industry, such as coal mining, have suffered a catastrophic decline.* ◇ **+ noun** *Mining companies had been benefiting from significant increases in commodity prices.* ➲ *see also* MINE² (1) **2 data/text ~** the process of looking at large quantities of data or documents that have been collected on a computer and using them to provide new information: *The data sets are large, so reanalysis and data mining are often possible.*

min·is·ter /ˈmɪnɪstə(r)/ *noun* **1** (*often* **Minister**) (in the UK and some other countries) a senior member of the government who is in charge of a government department or a branch of one: *Government ministers have refused to meet a coalition of ten environment groups to discuss their current policy.* ◇ *He suffered the resignation of two Cabinet ministers and a number of junior ministers.* ◇ *Fischer proved to be a popular foreign minister.* ◇ **~ of sth** *Tanaka became the new minister of education.* ➲ *see also* PRIME MINISTER **2** a trained religious leader, especially in some Protestant Christian churches: *They did not need churches or ministers for worship and they recognized no external authority.* ➲ *compare* PRIEST

min·is·ter·ial AWL /ˌmɪnɪˈstɪəriəl; *NAmE* ˌmɪnɪˈstɪriəl/ *adj.* connected with a government minister or ministers: *The Council consists of a representative of each member state at ministerial level.* ◇ *The doctrine of ministerial responsibility means that ministers receive both the praise and the blame for their departments' activities.*

min·is·try AWL /ˈmɪnɪstri/ *noun* (*pl.* **-ies**) **1** [C] (in the UK and some other countries) a government department that has a particular area of responsibility: *He was a former top official in the German foreign ministry.* ◇ **~ of sth** *the ministry of education/health/agriculture* **2** [C, usually sing.] the work and duties of a religious leader: *Jesus of Nazareth engaged in his public ministry, probably, in the late 20s of the first century CE.* ◇ **~ of sb** *In the next chapter, the twelve disciples are given authority to continue the ministry of Jesus.* **3 the Ministry** [sing.+ sing./pl. v.] ministers of religion when they are mentioned as a group: *Although women are now admitted to the Ministry in many Protestant churches, they remain largely excluded from the Catholic and Orthodox traditions.* **4** [C] (in some countries) a government; a period of government under one PRIME MINISTER: *In January 1870, Ollivier was invited to form a ministry.* HELP In this meaning, **ministry** is used especially to talk or write about governments in history.

minor[1] AWL /ˈmaɪnə(r)/ *adj.* [usually before noun] not very large, important or serious: *Health services may have only a minor role to play in reducing inequalities in health.* ◇ *Many of the accidents leading to minor injury are not reported.* ◇ *This relatively minor change could potentially have a substantial impact.* OPP MAJOR[1]

minor[2] AWL /ˈmaɪnə(r)/ *noun* **1** (*law*) a person who is under the age at which sb is legally an adult: *The findings will be of interest to professionals who encounter unaccompanied minors in their work.* **2** (*NAmE*) a subject that you study at university in addition to your MAJOR: *She majored in theoretical linguistics and took a minor in Finnish language.*

mi·nor·ity AWL /maɪˈnɒrəti; *NAmE* maɪˈnɔːrəti/ *noun* (*pl.* **-ies**) **1** [sing.+ sing./pl. v.] the smaller part of a group; less than half of the people or things in a large group: *A minority, 17.2%, were inclined to agree.* ◇ **~ of sb/sth** *'Effective democracies' still constitute a clear minority of the world's societies.* ◇ **+ noun** *These are, of course, minority views.* OPP MAJORITY (1) **2** [C] a group within a community or country that is different because of race, religion, culture or language: *Scotland has a sizeable South Asian minority.* ◇ *There are provisions designed to protect minorities.* ◇ *American Muslim issues, like those of other religious minorities, centre on their identity.* ◇ **+ noun** *Such programmes aim to increase the enrolment of minority students.* ➲ *see also* ETHNIC MINORITY **3** [sing.] (in a parliament, committee, etc.) the people who did not win enough votes to have a clear victory; the votes of these people: **~ (of sth)** *A blocking minority of 91 votes will prevent a proposal from being passed.* ◇ **+ noun** *There were also two periods of minority Labour government.* OPP MAJORITY (2) **4** [U] (*law*) the state of being under the age at which sb is legally an adult: *During the claimant's minority, the initial limitation period would not run.* ➲ *compare* MAJORITY (4)
IDM **be in a/the miˈnority** to form less than half of a large group: *By 1931 foreign firms were in a minority.* ◇ *Women entrepreneurs are in the minority in Europe.* OPP BE IN THE/A MAJORITY

▸ ADJECTIVE + MINORITY **visible, clear • distinct • small • tiny • growing • sizeable, substantial • significant • large** *There was always a substantial minority of claimants who reported not receiving paid care.* ◇ *They are culturally and politically significant minorities.* | **disadvantaged • oppressed, persecuted • privileged • ethnic • racial • national • cultural • religious • linguistic • sexual** *Racial minorities have been unfairly disadvantaged.* ◇ *Ethnic groups are often defined as belonging to a linguistic minority on the basis of their mother tongue.*

▸ VERB + MINORITY **constitute, form • represent • remain** *Although some participants were immediately comfortable sharing their ideas, they represented a minority.*

▸ MINORITY + NOUN **view, opinion • position • shareholder • shareholding, stake** *Those expressing these minority opinions remain less influential within the group.* | **group • community • population • representation • rights • status • background • culture • language • religion** *Political institutions remain weak, not least with regard to minority rights.*

minus[1] /ˈmaɪnəs/ *prep.* used when you SUBTRACT (= take away) one number or thing from another one: *Oil and minerals were valued at their market prices minus extraction costs.* OPP PLUS[1] IDM *see* PLUS[1]

minus[2] /ˈmaɪnəs/ *noun* **1** (*also* ˈ**minus sign**) the symbol (–), used in mathematics: *The pluses and minuses were added up.* ◇ *Minus signs indicate reduction of total magnetic intensity.* OPP PLUS[2] (1) **2 ~ (of sth)** (*rather informal*) a negative quality; a disadvantage: *All such labels have their pluses and minuses.* OPP PLUS[2] (2)

min·ute[1] /ˈmɪnɪt/ *noun* **1** [C] (*abbr.* **min.**) each of the 60 parts of an hour, that are equal to 60 seconds: *Each of the films lasts only five minutes.* ◇ *The whole test will take 45 minutes.* ◇ *Every few minutes a signal is transmitted.* ◇ *A heart rate of 70 beats per minute is assumed.* **2** [C] each of the 60 equal parts of a degree, used in measuring angles: *37 degrees 30 minutes (37° 30′)* **3 the minutes** [pl.] **~ (of sth)** a summary or record of what is said or decided at a formal meeting: *The minutes of the meetings of the Board of Directors are published online.*

mi·nute[2] /maɪˈnjuːt; *NAmE also* maɪˈnuːt/ *adj.* (*superlative* **minut·est**, no *comparative*) **1** extremely small SYN TINY: *Some molecules will be present in large amounts and some in minute amounts.* **2** very detailed, careful and thorough: *Their involvement was described in minute detail.*
■ **mi·nute·ly** *adv.*: *These proportions vary only minutely.* ◇ *The constituent parts are minutely described and analysed.*

mir·acle /ˈmɪrəkl/ *noun* **1** [C] an act or event that does not follow the laws of nature and is believed to be caused by God: *The gospels record that Jesus performed miracles and healed the sick.* **2** [sing.] an event or development that you did not expect or think was possible but has a very positive result: *A hugely successful export economy greatly contributed to the post-war economic miracle in West Germany.* ◇ **it is a ~ that...** *Under the circumstances, it is a miracle that the government achieved anything.* **3** [C] **~ of sth** a very good example or product of sth: *The second-generation optical mouse is a miracle of modern engineering.*

mir·ror[1] /ˈmɪrə(r)/ *noun* **1** a piece of special glass that reflects images and light: *When we look in a mirror, we recognize ourselves in the reflection.* ◇ *A reflecting mirror was utilized in order to concentrate sunlight on the panel surface.* **2** [usually sing.] **~ of sth** a thing that shows what sth else is like: *His transformation is a mirror of the broader social changes undergone by the nation.* HELP To **hold a mirror up to sth** is to examine it or show what it is like: *He is a ruthlessly realistic writer who has held a mirror up to himself and his culture.*

mir·ror[2] /ˈmɪrə(r)/ *verb* to have features that are similar to sth else, especially in a way that clearly shows what the other thing is like SYN REFLECT (1): **~ sth** *The results obtained closely mirror previous findings.* ◇ **be mirrored in/by sth** *These changes in legal processes were mirrored in institutional changes.*

ˌ**mirror** ˈ**image** *noun* **~ (of sth)** an image of sth that is like a REFLECTION of it, either because it is exactly the same or because the right side of the original object appears on the left and the left side appears on the right: *The two sides of the body are mirror images of each other.*

mis·car·riage /ˈmɪskærɪdʒ; *BrE also* ˌmɪsˈkærɪdʒ/ *noun* [C, U] the process of giving birth to a baby before it is fully developed and able to survive; an occasion when this happens: *She has previously had three miscarriages.* ◇ *In humans, from 10% to 25% of identified pregnancies end in miscarriage.* ➲ *compare* ABORTION

mis·con·cep·tion /ˌmɪskən'sepʃn/ *noun* [C, U] a belief or an idea that is not based on correct information, or that is not understood by people: *It is a common misconception that small earthquakes help prevent big earthquakes.* ◇ **~ about sth** *The book aims to dispel widespread misconceptions about Islam and politics in Muslim-majority states.* ➲ *compare* PRECONCEPTION

mis·con·duct /ˌmɪs'kɒndʌkt; *NAmE* ˌmɪs'kɑːndʌkt/ *noun* [U] (*formal*) unacceptable behaviour, especially by a professional person: *Two senior doctors were found guilty of serious professional misconduct.*

mis·in·ter·pret AWL /ˌmɪsɪn'tɜːprɪt; *NAmE* ˌmɪsɪn'tɜːrprɪt/ *verb* [often passive] to understand sth wrongly: **be misinterpreted** *There is a danger that anecdotal information can be misinterpreted.* ◇ **be misinterpreted as sth** *The signs of this condition may be misinterpreted as head injury.* ➲ *compare* INTERPRET (2) ■ **mis·in·ter·pret·ation** AWL /ˌmɪsɪntɜːprɪ'teɪʃn; *NAmE* ˌmɪsɪntɜːrprɪ'teɪʃn/ *noun* [U, C] *Discussions of human evolution are prone to misinterpretation.* ◇ **~ of sth** *Helmholtz apologized for having used phrases that could lead to misinterpretations of his true intention.*

mis·lead /ˌmɪs'liːd/ *verb* (**mis·led**, **mis·led** /ˌmɪs'led/) [T, I] to give sb the wrong idea and make them believe sth that is not true SYN DECEIVE (2): **~ (sb)** *The title might mislead potential readers.* ◇ *Such general statements are just as likely to mislead as to inform.* ◇ **~ sb about sth** *Companies may not make claims that might mislead consumers about eco-friendly practices.* ◇ **~ sb as to sth** *He had misled the Council as to his residential address.* ◇ **~ sb into doing sth** *The trustee had misled the widow into making the investment.*

mis·lead·ing /ˌmɪs'liːdɪŋ/ *adj.* giving the wrong idea and making people believe sth that is not true: *The book's title is somewhat misleading.* ◇ *The fossil record can give a misleading impression of the tempo and mode of evolution in some cases.* ■ **mis·lead·ing·ly** *adv.*: *The cracks look misleadingly like worm tracks.*

mis·match /'mɪsmætʃ/ *noun* **~ (between A and B)** a combination of things or people that do not go together well or are not suitable for each other: *The research focuses on the mismatch between growing global problems and the continuing lack of international solutions.*

mis·rep·re·sent /ˌmɪsˌreprɪ'zent/ *verb* [often passive] to give information about sb/sth that is not true or complete so that other people have the wrong impression about them/it: **~ sb/sth** *The media seemed to be deliberately misrepresenting the workers' demands.* ◇ **~ sb/sth as sth** *Government decisions were often misrepresented as scientifically based, with all risks concealed.* ■ **mis·rep·re·sen·ta·tion** /ˌmɪsˌreprɪzen'teɪʃn/ *noun* [U, C] **~ (of sb/sth)** *There has been continual misrepresentation of asylum seekers in the press.* ◇ *There were a number of inconsistencies and misrepresentations in the accounts of the revolt.*

miss /mɪs/ *verb* **1** [T] **~ sth** to fail to notice, understand or pay attention to sth; to not discover sth: *To pose this question is to miss a key point.* ◇ *Such fractures are easy to miss.* ◇ *This study focuses on a vulnerable group of pupils often missed by mainstream school surveys.* **2** [T] **~ sth** to not take the opportunity to do sth: *Here Reed misses an opportunity for careful theoretical analysis.* **3** [T] **~ sth** to be or arrive too late for sth: *Many people missed the deadline.* ◇ *Appointments are missed because of lack of transport.* **4** [T] **~ sth** to fail to do sth, have sth or attend sth: *He loathed military pomp and often found reasons to miss parades.* ◇ *Patients are offered a replacement meal if a meal is missed.* ◇ *Youths who miss school for longer periods require more complex interventions.* **5** [T] to feel sad because you can no longer see sb or do sth that you like: **~ sb/sth** *The child was missing his father.* ◇ **~ doing sth** *She misses having a partner.* **6** [T, I] to fail to hit, catch, reach, etc. sth: *Most of the torpedoes missed.* ◇ **~ sth/sb** *The artillery repeatedly missed its targets.*

PHR V ˌ**miss sb/sth** '**out** (*BrE*) to fail to include sb/sth in sth SYN OMIT (1): *She focuses on New York, thus missing out a significant part of the story.* ˌ**miss** '**out (on sth)** to fail to benefit from sth useful or enjoyable: *Many children missed out altogether.* ◇ *We miss out on some of Shakespeare's wordplay if we do not know how the words were pronounced.*

miss·ing /'mɪsɪŋ/ *adj.* **1** not available, for example because it has been removed, lost or destroyed; not included: *After correcting for the missing data, there is still substantial variation.* ◇ *Several lines are missing.* ◇ **~ from sth** *Data on turnout are missing from the analysis.* **2** used when it is not known where sb is, or whether sb is alive: *They demanded information about their missing children.* ➲ *compare* LOST[1] (5)

mis·sion /'mɪʃn/ *noun* **1** [C] **~ (to...)** an important official job that a person or group of people is given to do, especially when they are sent to another country; a group of people doing such a job: *Respected British socialists had by then returned from fact-finding missions to Soviet Russia.* ◇ *In the late 19th century, the Japanese government sent countless missions to Europe to learn about new techniques.* **2** [C] an important job that is done by a soldier, group of soldiers, etc: *The UN peacekeeping missions from 1992 to 1995 failed to restore peace to the country.* ◇ **~ to...** *Threats were made to cut off funds to US troops engaged in missions to Africa.* ◇ **on a ~** *On a dangerous mission over North Vietnam, his plane was shot down.* **3** [C] **~ (to...)** a flight into space: *Paine invited Soviet scientists to consider participating in the Viking mission to Mars.* **4** [C, U] the work of teaching people about Christianity, especially in a foreign country; a group of people doing such work: *It was his interest in mission that fostered these views.* ◇ **~ to...** *The Jesuit mission to Ulster in 1542 reported that there would be little support for this policy.* **5** [C] a building or group of buildings used by a Christian mission: *Two thirds of the 75 000 European Catholic priests, brothers and nuns working in missions overseas were French.* **6** [C] particular work that you feel it is your duty to do: *There is a need to evaluate how well these community schools are fulfilling their mission.* ◇ **~ to do sth** *Durkheim saw it as his mission to contribute to the development of a new French republican moral order.* ➲ *compare* VOCATION (1)

M

mis·take[1] /mɪ'steɪk/ *noun* **1** an action or opinion that is not correct, or that produces a result that is not wanted: *The industry has learned from its past mistakes.* ◇ *Try to avoid common mistakes during this process.* ◇ **make the ~ of doing sth** *William made the fatal mistake of sending royal troops to take control of Brussels.* ◇ **it is a ~ to do sth** *It would be a serious mistake to discontinue this work.* HELP **Make no mistake** is sometimes used in less formal writing to emphasize that what you are saying is correct: *Make no mistake: when we decided the case, we did not reach our position light-heartedly.* This use is best avoided in more formal writing. **2** a word, figure, fact, etc. that is not correct SYN ERROR: *Grammatical errors and small spelling mistakes are not corrected.* ◇ *Mistakes are often made in reading instruments or recording values.*

IDM **by mi'stake** by accident; without intending to: *Money paid by mistake should be returned.* ◇ *This may happen by mistake rather than by design.* HELP **By mistake** is very common in general English, and is also used in academic English. However, in academic English, the more formal **accidentally** and **unintentionally** are more common: *Varying the question order can result in* *questions being accidentally omitted.* ◇ *These policies either intentionally or unintentionally weaken the state.*

mis·take² /mɪˈsteɪk/ *verb* (**mis·took** /mɪˈstʊk/, **mis·taken** /mɪˈsteɪkən/)

PHR V **miˈstake sth/sb for sth/sb** [often passive] to think wrongly that sth/sb is sth/sb else: *These reactions are so unusual that they may be mistaken for a psychiatric disorder.* ➲ *compare* CONFUSE (2)

mis·taken /mɪˈsteɪkən/ *adj.* **1** based on a wrong opinion or bad judgement: *This is a common but mistaken belief.* ◇ *This assumption is mistaken.* ◇ **it is ~ to do sth** *It would be mistaken to ascribe change wholly to these factors.* **2** [not usually before noun] wrong in your opinion or judgement: *He admits that he may be mistaken.* ◇ **~ about sth** *Many people are mistaken about their own best interests.* ■ **mis·taken·ly** *adv.*: *Scholars have often mistakenly assumed that these methods are mutually exclusive.*

mis·un·der·stand /ˌmɪsʌndəˈstænd; *NAmE* ˌmɪsʌndərˈstænd/ *verb* (**mis·un·der·stood, mis·un·der·stood** /ˌmɪsʌndəˈstʊd; *NAmE* ˌmɪsʌndərˈstʊd/) [T, I] to fail to understand sb/sth correctly: **~ sb/sth** *About half the respondents misunderstood the first question on the questionnaire.* ◇ *Mental illness was often misunderstood by members of the general public.* ◇ **~ what/how, etc...** *Several witnesses admitted they might have misunderstood what they had seen.*

mis·un·der·stand·ing /ˌmɪsʌndəˈstændɪŋ; *NAmE* ˌmɪsʌndərˈstændɪŋ/ *noun* [U, C] a situation in which a comment, an instruction, etc. is not understood correctly: *Medical staff provided careful explanations to avoid any misunderstanding.* ◇ **~ of/about sth** *Darwin's reliance on Malthus led to much misunderstanding of the implications of Darwin's thought.* ◇ **~ between A and B** *Unfortunately, there were several misunderstandings between the agency and the two Japanese firms.*

mis·use¹ /ˌmɪsˈjuːs/ *noun* [U, C, usually sing.] the act of using sth in a dishonest way or for the wrong purpose SYN ABUSE¹ (1): *Many patients try to hide their drug or alcohol misuse.* ◇ **~ of sth** *Corruption is defined as, 'the misuse of public power for private benefits, e.g. bribery'.*

mis·use² /ˌmɪsˈjuːz/ *verb* **~ sth** to use sth in the wrong way or for the wrong purpose SYN ABUSE²: *Junior employees suspected their personal data were being misused by managers.* ◇ *Many different substances can be misused, from glue to cannabis, to 'hard' drugs such as heroin.*

miti·gate /ˈmɪtɪɡeɪt/ *verb* **~ sth** (*formal*) to make sth less serious or severe SYN ALLEVIATE: *In conclusion, it is clear that every effort must be made to mitigate the worst effects of global warming.* ◇ *Japanese buildings were traditionally designed to mitigate earthquake risk.*

miti·ga·tion /ˌmɪtɪˈɡeɪʃn/ *noun* [U] (*formal*) a reduction in how serious or severe sth is: **+ noun** *Appropriate prevention and mitigation measures were taken to protect local habitat from the effects of the road upgrade.*

IDM **in mitiˈgation** (*law*) with the aim of making a crime seem less serious or easier to excuse: *In mitigation, the defence lawyer said her client was seriously depressed at the time of the assault.*

mi·to·chon·drion /ˌmaɪtəʊˈkɒndriən; *NAmE* ˌmaɪtoʊˈkɑːndriən/ *noun* (*pl.* **mitochondria** /ˌmaɪtəʊˈkɒndriə; *NAmE* ˌmaɪtoʊˈkɑːndriə/) (*biology*) a small structure found in almost all EUKARYOTIC cells in which energy in food is released from complex MOLECULES: *The role of mitochondria as the seat of energy metabolism within eukaryotic cells had been established.* ■ **mito·chon·drial** /ˌmaɪtəʊˈkɒndriəl; *NAmE* ˌmaɪtoʊˈkɑːndriəl/ *adj.*: *Swedish scientists used mitochondrial DNA from 53 people to show that the evolutionary tree of human beings is firmly rooted in Africa.*

mi·tosis /maɪˈtəʊsɪs; *NAmE* maɪˈtoʊsɪs/ *noun* [U] (*biology*) a type of cell division that results in two cells, each with the same number and kinds of CHROMOSOMES as the original cell: *The megaspore divides repeatedly by mitosis to produce the female gametophyte.* ◇ **during ~** *During mitosis, the chromosomes are in a highly condensed phase and are inactive.* ➲ *compare* MEIOSIS

mix¹ /mɪks/ *verb* **1** [I, T] (of two or more substances) to combine, usually in a way that means they cannot easily be separated; to combine two or more substances in this way: *Alcohol is used to help the two liquids to mix.* ◇ **~ with sth** *As the solution mixes with seawater, precipitates of sulfides are often deposited.* ◇ **~ A and B** *The tubes were sealed and inverted several times to mix the contents.* ◇ **~ A and B together** *The two samples of DNA were mixed together.* ◇ **~ A with B** *The bitter taste of the medicine is masked by mixing it with fruit juices or syrups.* **2** [I] if substances **do not mix**, they cannot be combined to form one substance, but remain separate: *Oil and water do not mix.* **3** [T] **~ sth** to prepare sth by combining two or more different substances: *Parents may undertake practical tasks in the classroom like mixing paints or hearing children read.* **4** [T] to put together or use together different or separate things: **~ A and B** *Some criticized his attempt to mix different dramatic genres in one work.* ◇ **~ A with B** *Jews do not mix dairy products with meat.* ◇ *A trustee does not have the right to mix his own money with that of a beneficiary.* **5** [I] if two or more things, people or activities **do not mix**, they cannot successfully or easily be combined, so have to be kept separate: *In his view, the public and domestic spheres did not mix.* **6** [I] to spend time with different people or people from a different group: *There was a belief that different castes and classes should not mix.* ◇ **~ with sb** *These missionaries mixed with local people and spoke the local dialect.* **7** [T] **~ sth** to combine different recordings of voices and/or instruments to produce a single piece of music: *The music may be acoustic or electronically mixed.*

PHR V **ˌmix sth ˈin (with sth)** [usually passive] to combine one substance or thing with others: *The news footage is mixed in with dramatized scenes.* **ˈmix sth into sth** [often passive] **1** to combine one substance or thing with others: *This litter is mixed into the soil by macro organisms such as worms and beetles* **2** to produce sth by combining two or more substances or things: *The two goals, of creating brand loyalty and promoting sales, are mixed into a hybrid approach.* **ˌmix sth ˈup (with sth)** [often passive] **1** to put different things together so that it is difficult to separate them or to predict their order: *Different peoples, with different languages or religions, were often mixed up with each other.* **2** to think wrongly that sth is sth else SYN CONFUSE (2): *Many writers mix up ends and means in their writing.* ◇ *The samples were mixed up with other reagents.*

mix² /mɪks/ *noun* **1** [usually sing.] **~ (of sth/sb)** a combination of different things or people: *For the product launch, we used a mix of TV, radio and print.* ◇ *Demographic trends include an ageing population, smaller households and a greater ethnic mix.* **2 ~ (of sth)** a combination of substances used to make sth: *There may be a temptation to use less expensive steel or a thinner mix of cement to increase profits.* ◇ *Small amounts of an inhibitor were added to the liquid mix to prevent polymerization.*

mixed /mɪkst/ *adj.* **1** having a mixture of different qualities, especially some good and some bad: *States almost always have mixed motives for intervening militarily in other countries.* ◇ *Their track record on human rights advocacy has been very mixed.* ◇ *mixed findings/results/evidence* **2** consisting of different kinds of people, for example people from different races and cultures: *The policy was to establish new settlements with mixed populations.* ◇ *The types of students who enter medical school now are ethnically much more mixed.* ◇ *The study sample was racially diverse, with 33% of girls reporting that they* were white, 27% African-American, 11% Hispanic, 17% Asian and 12% of mixed race. **3** [usually before noun] consisting of different things or types of things: *Most businesses have a pragmatic, mixed approach where whatever method works best is used.* ◇ *There is wide support for a mixed economy, with both public and private ownership of companies and services.* **4** [usually before noun] of or for both males and females: *Some pupils, for religious or cultural reasons, are unable to participate in mixed swimming lessons.*

mix·ture /ˈmɪkstʃə(r)/ *noun* **1** [C, usually sing.] a combination of different things: *The organizations may be public, private or a mixture.* ◇ **~ of A and B** *The interview contained a mixture of different kinds of questions.* ◇ *Urban wastes comprise a complex mixture of materials.* **2** [C, U] a substance made by mixing other substances together: *100 ml of distilled water was added to the mixture.* ◇ *TFE is dangerous because it forms explosive mixtures with air.* ◇ **~ of A and B** *Food for fly larvae is a mixture of yeast, sugar and agar.* **3** [C] (*chemistry*) a combination of two or more substances that mix together without any chemical reaction taking place: *The constituent C is a true compound, not just an equimolar mixture.* ➲ *compare* COMPOUND[1] (1)

mo·bile /ˈməʊbaɪl; *NAmE* ˈmoʊbl/ *adj.* **1** [only before noun] involving mobile phones and small computers that can be carried around: *Mobile technology is changing the way businesses interface with customers.* ◇ *These flashcards can be downloaded to mobile devices.* ◇ *mobile operators/networks/services* **2** moving around rather than staying in one place; able to do this: *Climate change may have impacts for nomadic and other mobile communities.* ◇ *Some of the electrons are very mobile.* ➲ *compare* STATIONARY (1) **3** (of people) able or willing to move from one social class, job or area to another: *Married men with children are likely to be less mobile than single childless men.* ◇ *The population is urbanized and highly mobile.* HELP People who are **upwardly mobile** are moving towards a higher social position: *Upwardly mobile families had left the inner city for new jobs and better housing.* **4** [not usually before noun] (of a person) able to move or travel around easily: *Patients are mobile and active during dialysis and live a relatively normal life.* OPP IMMOBILE (1) **5** [usually before noun] in or using a vehicle so that a service can be provided or work can be done in different places: *They have a free medical clinic with mobile units to reach remote villages.*

ˌmobile ˈphone (*also* **mo·bile** /ˈməʊbaɪl; *NAmE* ˈmoʊbl/) (*both BrE*) (*also* **ˈcell phone**, **ˈcellular phone**, *informal* **cell** *NAmE, BrE*) *noun* a telephone that works by radio and that you can carry around with you: *One student was recording with her mobile phone.* HELP In non-academic English, **mobile** or **cell** is more frequent: *It was against school rules to use mobiles in class.*

mo·bil·ity /məʊˈbɪləti; *NAmE* moʊˈbɪləti/ *noun* (*pl.* **-ies**) **1** [U, C] the ability to move around; the fact that sb/sth moves around; the extent to which this happens: *Many of these patients have limited mobility.* ◇ *A country may deliberately implement a policy that aims to limit capital mobility.* ◇ *A similar ratio of electron mobilities might be expected.* **2** [U] the ability to move from one social class, job or area to another; the fact that this happens often: *Low occupational mobility was typical in this cohort.* ◇ *Being unmarried made upward mobility more difficult.* ◇ *There has been social and geographical mobility and rapid economic change.*

mo·bil·iza·tion (*BrE also* **-isa·tion**) /ˌməʊbɪlaɪˈzeɪʃn; *NAmE* ˌmoʊbələˈzeɪʃn/ *noun* [U] **1** the act of organizing a group of people to achieve a particular aim: *Unions have a long history of worker resistance and political mobilization.* **2** the act of finding and starting to use sth that is needed for a particular purpose: *There was a belief that involving the private sector would maximize resource mobilization for health projects.* **3 mobilization** of an army or a country is when it makes itself ready to fight in a war: *Mass mobilization for both world wars indirectly led to democratic reform (Kryder, 2000).*

mo·bil·ize (*BrE also* **-ise**) /ˈməʊbəlaɪz; *NAmE* ˈmoʊbəlaɪz/ *verb* **1** [T, I] to work together in order to achieve a particular aim; to organize a group of people to do this: *Students and workers mobilized around issues of world peace and the environment.* ◇ **~ sb/sth** *Clearly, the Internet has made it easier to mobilize support across national boundaries.* **2** [T] **~ sth** to find and start to use sth that is needed for a particular purpose: *The workshop aimed to teach local women how to mobilize community resources.* **3** [T, I] **~ (sb/sth)** if a country **mobilizes** its army, or if a country or army **mobilizes**, it makes itself ready to fight in a war: *Spain had no choice but to mobilize her armies to resist the French invasion.*

modal¹ /ˈməʊdl; *NAmE* ˈmoʊdl/ (*also* ˌ**modal** ˈ**verb**) *noun* (*grammar*) a verb such as *can*, *may* or *will* that is used with another verb (not a modal) to express possibility, permission, intention, etc: *Other modals indicate the degree of desirability of something becoming true.*

GRAMMAR POINT

Modal verbs

The modal verbs in English are **can**, **could**, **may**, **might**, **must**, **shall**, **should**, **will** and **would**.

- Modal verbs are followed by the infinitive of another verb without *to*: *Future work* ***could examine*** *these conditions further by...* ◇ *As markets are interdependent, we* ***should study*** *them together, not separately.*
- Modal verbs have only one form. They have no past and present participles and do not add -*s* to the third person singular form: *A behavioural reward programme* ***can*** *help a teen learn constructive ways to manage anger.* ◇ *Conservation today* ***must*** *work across a complex political landscape of public and private landownership.*
- In negatives, modal verbs are placed before *not*: *Extinction* ***may not be*** *complete due to strong dispersion.*

modal² /ˈməʊdl; *NAmE* ˈmoʊdl/ *adj.* [only before noun] **1** connected with the way in which sth is done: *Policy documents for London recommend a modal shift in travel, from cars to walking and cycling, to promote physical activity.* **2** connected with the value that occurs most frequently in a given set of data: *Most participants had completed a high school education (97%), and the modal income level was $73 000–$126 500 (35%).*

mo·dal·ity /məʊˈdæləti; *NAmE* moʊˈdæləti/ *noun* (*pl.* **-ies**) **1** (*formal*) the particular way in which sth exists, is experienced or is done: *We looked at the influence of different communication modalities, especially email as compared with phone.* ◇ *There are two treatment modalities available: home-based and hospital-based.* **2** (*biology*) any of the types of senses that the body uses to experience things: *The sensory modalities employed by migrating swallows were investigated in detail.*

mode AWL /məʊd; *NAmE* moʊd/ *noun* **1** [C] a particular way of doing sth or behaving: *Replacing car travel with more active modes could significantly improve physical activity rates.* ◇ *The narrative mode here is predominantly reported speech and thought.* ◇ **~ of sth** *Many teachers instinctively adopt this mode of instruction.* ◇ *Modern capitalism introduces a new mode of production: commercial manufacturing.* **2** [C, usually sing., U] a particular feeling, atmosphere or style: *They need to get in the right mode for listening.* ◇ **in... ~** *The piece opens in documentary mode.* **3** [C, U] the way in which a piece of equipment is set to perform a particular task: *To access these areas, the unit should be placed into a STOP or PAUSE mode.* ◇ **~ of**

M

sth *The autopilot has a second mode of operation that allows the pilot to assume responsibility.* ◇ **in... ~** *In automatic mode, the user needs only to specify a few parameters.* HELP In computing, a **mode** is a state of a program that enables particular tasks to be carried out: *The program has several modes of operation: managing images, editing images and printing images.* **4** [C] (*physics*) a distinct kind or pattern of VIBRATION: *The molecule would be expected to exhibit four normal modes of vibration.* **5** [sing.] (*statistics*) the value that appears most frequently in a set of data: *The mean price was 1.82, the mode 1.00 and the median 0.75.* ◇ *Descriptive statistics (median, mean, mode and standard deviations) were calculated from quantitative data.* ➲ language bank *at* STATISTIC

model¹ /ˈmɒdl; *NAmE* ˈmɑːdl/ *noun* **1** a simple description, especially a mathematical one, of a group of complex systems or processes, used for understanding or explaining how sth works: *This research uses fixed effects models for analysing longitudinal data.* ◇ *The Brown and Moore model, as modified by Popp (1976), is outlined in Figure 13.1.* ◇ **~ of sth** *Mathematical models of vaccine-driven evolution show the same thing.* ◇ **according to a... ~** *According to this model, planners underestimate costs to increase the likelihood that their projects gain funding.* ◇ **under/within/in a... ~** *Under this model, discrete groups can be categorically distinguished.* ◇ **+ noun** *Three indicators were used to assess model fit.* ➲ thesaurus note *at* THEORY **2** a way of doing sth that others can copy or refer to: **~ (for sth)** *This study may serve as a model for future text analyses.* ◇ *Field officers follow a formal model which ensures that they take into consideration a range of issues.* ◇ **~ of (doing) sth** *University staff worked with school staff in developing new models of student support.* ◇ **+ noun** *You can use the model texts to help you structure your own writing.* **3** an object that is a copy of sth, usually smaller than the original object: *The presentation includes scale models or architect's drawings.* ◇ **~ of sth** *Dalton introduced the practice of constructing models of compound atoms by joining together coloured wooden blocks.* **4 ~ of sth** a perfect example of sth: *His chapter is a model of tact.* ➲ *see also* ROLE MODEL **5** a particular design or type of product: *Both cars are the same model.* ◇ *The newer models are more reliable.* ◇ **~ of sth** *All these clinics had adopted the latest model of scanner.* **6** (in fashion and art) sb who sits, stands or moves around in order to display clothes or so that sb else can draw, paint or photograph them: *The fashion industry has finally decided not to use models younger than 16.*

▸ ADJECTIVE + MODEL **simple • basic • traditional • standard • alternative • original, initial • new • final • general • linear • multivariate • multilevel • hierarchical • mixed • full • dynamic • simplified • generalized • formal** *The data were analysed using standard models of species abundance.* ◇ *Results were similar to those of the original models.* | **mathematical • statistical • computational • theoretical • mental • conceptual • classical • neoclassical • structural • economic** *In the present study, a statistical model was applied to analyse the performance.*

▸ NOUN + MODEL **regression • prediction • growth • equilibrium • simulation** *The validity of the regression model is limited by the small sample size.*

▸ VERB + MODEL **estimate • propose, suggest • present, offer • provide • create • construct, build • develop • introduce • test • validate • use, adopt, employ, utilize • apply • implement • run • evaluate • outline • describe • consider, examine • discuss • compare • adjust, adapt, modify • specify • extend • select • reject • fit • support** *More research is required to validate these models in different populations.*

▸ MODEL + VERB **be based on • assume • posit, suggest, imply • predict • explain, account for • fit • capture • simulate, reproduce • represent • show • provide, yield, generate** *The model predicts that performance will differ across the groups.* ◇ *The goodness of fit indices show that the model fits the data well.*

▸ MODEL + NOUN **parameter • specification • prediction • fit • selection • simulation • validation • estimate • calibration • equation • assumption • system • organism • compound** *The estimated model parameters can be experimentally validated.*

model² /ˈmɒdl; *NAmE* ˈmɑːdl/ *verb* (-ll-, *US* -l-) **1** to create or use a description (especially a mathematical one), a computer program, a diagram or a copy of sth, in order to explain or calculate sth: **~ sth** *These processes can be modelled mathematically.* ◇ *His main interests are concerned with modelling evolution, biodiversity and climate change.* ◇ **be modelled as (doing) sth** *Water was modelled as a collection of several water molecules.* ➲ *compare* SIMULATE (1) **2 ~ sth** to show sb how to do sth, especially how to behave well SYN DEMONSTRATE (3): *Parents of these children tend to be nurturing and to consistently model prosocial behavior.* ◇ *Teachers model the values promoted in the classroom.*

PHR V **ˈmodel sth on/after sth** [usually passive] to make sth so that it is like sth else; to base sth on sth else: *National parks, modelled on US national parks, have arisen in many countries.* ◇ *Most authors recognize that the Italian health service was modelled after the British one.*

mod·el·ling (*US* **mod·el·ing**) /ˈmɒdəlɪŋ; *NAmE* ˈmɑːdəlɪŋ/ *noun* [U] the work of making a simple description of a system or a process that can be used to explain it, predict results, etc: **~ (of sth)** *The aim of this analysis was to improve modelling of the HIV epidemic.* ◇ *The results of mathematical modelling show that...* ◇ **+ noun** *We use a two-stage modelling technique to explore the relationship between diversity and disadvantage.*

mod·er·ate¹ /ˈmɒdərət; *NAmE* ˈmɑːdərət/ *adj.* **1** average rather than large or small in amount or level: *Even moderate exercise such as walking improves health and quality of life.* ◇ *Places with moderate temperatures, like coastal California, had significantly lower emissions than places with extreme temperatures like Texas.* ◇ *The patient's risk of developing a thrombosis is graded as low, moderate or high.* **2** having or showing opinions, especially about politics, that are not extreme: *It is important for the international community to encourage moderate leaders who favour peaceful coexistence.* ◇ *He was considered too moderate by many of his generals.* **3** staying within limits that are considered to be reasonable by most people: *The infringement of rights in this case can be considered relatively moderate.*

mod·er·ate² /ˈmɒdəreɪt; *NAmE* ˈmɑːdəreɪt/ *verb* **1** [T] **~ sth** to make sth become less extreme or severe: *Emotional support moderates the negative effects of physical assault on psychological health.* ◇ *The decree was never enforced, and a decade later the policy was moderated.* **2** [T, I] **~ (sth)** to be in charge of a discussion or debate, for example making sure that everyone has a chance to give their opinion: *A researcher was used to moderate the focus group.* ◇ *A manager must be able to manage conflict and willing to moderate for the team to continue effectively.*

mod·er·ate·ly /ˈmɒdərətli; *NAmE* ˈmɑːdərətli/ *adv.* **1** to an average extent; fairly but not very SYN REASONABLY: *Soil pH ranges from approximately neutral (6.9, Arizona) to moderately acidic (4.8, Florida).* ◇ *Brain-injured individuals commonly score moderately high on Scale 1.* ◇ *The test results correlated moderately with those of other measures of verbal intelligence.* ➲ language bank *at* EXCEPTIONALLY **2** within reasonable limits: *The patient is a 57-year-old man who has never smoked and drinks moderately.*

mod·er·ation /ˌmɒdəˈreɪʃn; *NAmE* ˌmɑːdəˈreɪʃn/ *noun* [U] the quality of being reasonable and not extreme: *Alcibiades praises Socrates for his virtues of wisdom,*

M

moderation and bravery. ◇ **in ~** *Patients are commonly advised to drink alcohol in moderation and to avoid overeating.*

mod·er·ator /ˈmɒdəreɪtə(r); *NAmE* ˈmɑːdəreɪtər/ *noun* **1** a person or organization whose job is to help the two sides in a disagreement to reach an agreement: *Egypt managed to assert its role as a regional moderator.* ➲ *see also* MEDIATOR (1) **2** (*especially NAmE*) a person whose job is to make sure that a discussion or debate is fair: *One student in each group acted as a moderator, starting and closing the debate.* **3** (*computing*) a person who is responsible for preventing offensive material from being published on a website: *In both chat rooms, offensive comments were quite quickly removed by the moderator.*

mod·ern /ˈmɒdn; *NAmE* ˈmɑːdərn/ *adj.* **1** [usually before noun] of the present time or recent times SYN CONTEMPORARY[1] (1): *In modern society, the social unit is the household.* ◇ *Lord Byron embraced Greek culture, both ancient and modern.* ◇ *The emergence of modern Europe as a major military, economic and political power ushered in the dawn of European colonialism.* ◇ *Anatomically modern humans migrated out of Africa some 50–100 000 years ago.* ➲ *compare* ANCIENT (1) **2** using the most recent technology, designs, materials, etc. SYN UP TO DATE: *With the use of more modern methods, the accuracy was recently reported to be 90 per cent.* ◇ *Cities like Shanghai and Beijing are very modern, and Shanghai in particular is a shopping and tourist paradise.* **3** [usually before noun] (of styles in art, music, fashion, etc.) new and intended to be different from traditional styles SYN CONTEMPORARY[1] (1): *The rejection of modern art is often supported by the argument that it is not true to nature.* **4** (of ways of behaving or thinking) new and not always accepted by most members of society: *Brand character includes things like: Is the brand fun or serious? Is it modern or traditional?* OPP TRADITIONAL (1) **5** (of a language) in the form that is used at the present time, as opposed to any earlier form: *She took a degree in modern languages from Queen's University, Belfast.* ◇ *modern English/Greek/German* ◇ *The modern Scandinavian languages are derived historically from a common Nordic ancestor.* OPP ANCIENT (1)

▸ MODERN + NOUN **society • culture • civilization • life • times, period, era, age • history • world • state, nation, nation state • city • economy • democracy • capitalism • thought • theory • scholarship • form • system • sense • human • scholar • historian • reader** *The use of mercenary armies was dominant in the Middle Ages and the early modern era.* ◇ *His ideas may seem uncomfortable to the modern reader.* | **method, technique • practice • science • medicine • physics • technology • computer** *Today, Italy remains at the forefront of modern earthquake science.* | **literature • art • music • architecture • dance** *These essays explore modern Irish literature (Heaney, Beckett, Yeats, Joyce) in relation to its political, post-colonial contexts.*

▸ ADVERB + MODERN **distinctly, distinctively • specifically, particularly • strikingly** *In some ways, 'The Secret Agent' looks back to Dickens, but it also conveys a distinctly modern sense of alienation.*

mod·ern·ism /ˈmɒdənɪzəm; *NAmE* ˈmɑːdərnɪzəm/ *noun* (*also* **Modernism**) [U] a style and movement in art, ARCHITECTURE and literature popular in the middle of the 20th century in which modern ideas, methods and materials were used rather than traditional ones: *French Romanticism can be seen as a bridge between neoclassicism and a more naturalistic modernism.* ➲ *compare* POSTMODERNISM

mod·ern·ist /ˈmɒdənɪst; *NAmE* ˈmɑːdərnɪst/ *adj.* [only before noun] **1** using modern ideas or methods: *It is important to acknowledge the development of modernist movements in Judaism.* **2** connected with a style and movement in art, ARCHITECTURE and literature popular in the middle of the 20th century in which modern ideas, methods and materials were used rather than traditional ones: *Leick questions the idea that modernist literature was 'an elite literature only understandable by literary specialists'.* ■ **mod·ern·ist** *noun*: *Many modernists undoubtedly viewed more traditional forms of mass culture in a negative light.*

mod·ern·ity /məˈdɜːnəti; *NAmE* məˈdɜːrnəti/ *noun* [U] the condition of being new and modern: *The adoption of a Western lifestyle was at first embraced as a symbol of progress and modernity.*

mod·ern·ize (*BrE also* **-ise**) /ˈmɒdənaɪz; *NAmE* ˈmɑːdərnaɪz/ *verb* **1** [T] **~ sth** to make a system, methods, etc. more modern and more suitable for use at the present time: *Wilson wanted to modernize the UK economy and to adapt to the technological revolution.* ◇ *The letters are reproduced here with modernized spelling and punctuation.* **2** [I] to start using modern equipment, ideas, etc: *While Japan, France and Germany had renewed their plant in the post-war period, Britain failed to modernize.* ■ **mod·ern·iza·tion, -isa·tion** /ˌmɒdənaɪˈzeɪʃn; *NAmE* ˌmɑːdərnəˈzeɪʃn/ *noun* [U] **~ (of sth)** *Most of a nation's individuals and businesses benefit from the modernization of the economy.*

mod·est /ˈmɒdɪst; *NAmE* ˈmɑːdɪst/ *adj.* **1** fairly limited or small in amount: *Profits generated by foreign sales are relatively modest.* ◇ *Reducing the phosphorus content of leaves resulted in modest increases in yield.* **2** not expensive, rich or impressive: *Students had to be given sufficient financial support, taking into account their modest backgrounds.* ◇ *The furnishing of their flats was modest, and they chose not to have televisions.* **3** (of people, especially women, or their clothes) not showing too much of the body; not intended to attract attention, especially in a sexual way: *The Qur'an and Islamic tradition enjoin modesty, and thus everyone is required to wear modest dress.* **4** (*approving*) not talking much about your own abilities or possessions: *Despite his achievements, Faraday remained a modest and humble person.* ■ **mod·est·ly** *adv.*: *The graph shows that average income grew only modestly for households in the lowest 25%.* ◇ *They themselves lived very modestly, in small mud-brick houses.* ◇ *They are expected to act modestly in public and in the company of men.* ◇ *He refers modestly to his 'homely language'.*

modi·fi·ca·tion AWL /ˌmɒdɪfɪˈkeɪʃn; *NAmE* ˌmɑːdɪfɪˈkeɪʃn/ *noun* [U, C] the act or process of changing sth in order to improve it or make it more suitable; a change that is made SYN ADAPTATION (1): *Some form of genetic modification has taken place.* ◇ *The tRNA adaptor molecule must undergo numerous chemical modifications in order to be able to carry out its function.* ◇ **~ of sth** *This aerial photograph predates later modification of the landscape.* ◇ **~ to/in sth** *It may be necessary to make some modifications to the method.*

modi·fier /ˈmɒdɪfaɪə(r); *NAmE* ˈmɑːdɪfaɪər/ *noun* (*grammar*) a word or group of words that describes a noun phrase or restricts its meaning in some way: *This type of structure is basically noun + modifier.*

mod·ify AWL /ˈmɒdɪfaɪ; *NAmE* ˈmɑːdɪfaɪ/ *verb* (**modi·fies, modi·fy·ing, modi·fied, modi·fied**) **1 ~ sth** to change sth slightly, especially in order to make it more suitable for a particular purpose or situation SYN ADAPT (1): *An individual increases its fitness in a given habitat by modifying its behaviour.* ◇ *These businesses have grown by being flexible enough to modify their structure.* ◇ *Users may decide to modify the programs to suit their objectives.* ◇ *In such circumstances, the parties are free to modify the contract.* ➲ *see also* GENETICALLY MODIFIED **2** [usually passive] to gradually change the structure of sth as a response to changes in the environment: **be modified** *The flow of the river has been modified by erosion.* ◇ **modified + noun** *Selection can act to favour a modified genotype.* **3 ~ sth** to make sth less

M

severe or more acceptable SYN ADJUST (2): *It may be difficult to change underlying character traits but it is possible to modify behaviour.* **4 ~ sth** (*grammar*) a word that **modifies** another word or group of words describes it or limits its meaning in some way: *In English, nouns can be modified by a preceding adjective, as in 'hot water'.*

modu·lar /ˈmɒdjələ(r); *NAmE* ˈmɑːdʒələr/ *adj.* **1** (of machines, buildings, etc.) consisting of separate parts or units that can be joined together: *Many car manufacturers have modular production systems.* **2** (of a course of study, especially at a British university or college) consisting of separate units from which students may choose several: *They offer short, modular courses aimed at professionals.*

modu·late /ˈmɒdjuleɪt; *NAmE* ˈmɑːdʒəleɪt/ *verb* **1 ~ sth** to influence sth by changing or controlling it: *The activity of some enzymes is modulated through the action of insulin.* **2 ~ sth** to change the rate at which a sound wave or radio signal VIBRATES so that it is clearer: *Each signal is modulated by a different carrier frequency.*

modu·la·tion /ˌmɒdjuˈleɪʃn; *NAmE* ˌmɑːdʒəˈleɪʃn/ *noun* [U, C] **1 ~ (of sth)** the action of influencing sth by changing or controlling it: *This effect indicates long-lasting modulation of neural activity.* **2 ~ (of sth)** the action of changing the rate at which a sound wave or radio signal VIBRATES so that it is clearer: *Radio transmission employs deliberate modulation of a complex audio signal.* ◇ *Traditional communication systems such as NTSC television signals are based on analogue modulations.*

M

mod·ule /ˈmɒdjuːl; *NAmE* ˈmɑːdʒuːl/ *noun* **1** a unit that can form part of a course of study or training, especially at a college or university in the UK: *The course consists of six modules covering the following topics:...* ◇ *I took a social policy module as part of my professional training as a social worker.* **2** one of a set of separate parts or units that can be joined together to make a more complex structure such as a machine, a piece of furniture or a building: *Car manufacturers need to encourage innovation in suppliers of modules or components, while ensuring their compatibility with overall design architectures.* ◇ *It has been estimated that over 2 million people in the developing world now rely on solar PV modules for their electricity.* **3** a unit of a computer system or program that has a particular function: *It includes a computer module to create population pyramids from any data.*

moist /mɔɪst/ *adj.* **1** slightly wet: *The substance is brittle when moist.* ◇ *moist air/soil/conditions* **2** having a lot of rain: *Mediterranean climates are characterized by long, hot, dry summers and warm, moist winters.* ◇ *Protection from fungi may be important in a moist subtropical environment.*

mois·ture /ˈmɔɪstʃə(r)/ *noun* [U] very small drops of water that are present in the air, on a surface or in a substance: *Vapour pressure affects the capacity of the air to absorb moisture from the surrounding environment.* ◇ *The depth of the thaw is affected by factors including air temperature and soil moisture.* ◇ **+ noun** *Electrostatics is used in agriculture to measure the moisture content of crops.*

mold (*US*) = MOULD[1], MOULD[2]

mole /məʊl; *NAmE* moʊl/ *noun* **1 ~ (of sth)** (*chemistry*) a unit for measuring the amount of substance HELP One **mole** of a substance is the quantity that contains as many ELEMENTARY units of that substance as the number of atoms in 12.0 grams of carbon-12: *The mass of a mole of these two different molecules would be vastly different.* **2** a small, dark brown mark on the skin, sometimes slightly higher than the skin around it: *Skin lesions, moles and warts may change as the skin ages.* **3** a small animal with dark grey fur that lives underground and is almost unable to see: *One Conservative MP had claimed regular sums for having moles removed from his land.*

mo·lecu·lar /məˈlekjələ(r)/ *adj.* [only before noun] connected with or consisting of molecules: *Dorothy Hodgkin carried out important research into molecular structure.* ◇ *Researchers hope to gain a more complete understanding of how life forms are ordered at the molecular level.* ➲ *see also* RELATIVE MOLECULAR MASS

moˌlecular biˈology *noun* [U] the branch of biology that studies the molecules, such as PROTEINS and NUCLEIC ACIDS, that are essential to life: *Taken together, classical genetics, molecular biology and genomics all help to provide a more complete answer than any of them would provide alone.*

mol·ecule /ˈmɒlɪkjuːl; *NAmE* ˈmɑːlɪkjuːl/ *noun* a group of atoms that forms the smallest unit that a substance can be divided into without a change in its chemical nature: *Heat is conducted through solids, liquids and gases as molecules collide with their neighbours.* ◇ *The process of forming large molecules from small ones is called polymerization.* ◇ *The condensation reaction releases a water molecule.* ◇ **~ of sth** *A molecule of water is made up of two hydrogen atoms and one oxygen atom.*

mol·ten /ˈməʊltən; *NAmE* ˈmoʊltən/ *adj.* (of metal, rock or glass) heated to a very high temperature so that it becomes liquid: *Magma is molten rock that has not yet reached the surface of the earth.*

mo·ment /ˈməʊmənt; *NAmE* ˈmoʊmənt/ *noun* **1** [sing.] a particular occasion or exact point in time: **~ in sth** *His stories dramatize key moments in history.* ◇ **~ of sth** *The development of an organism from the moment of conception through to maturity is an extremely complex process.* ◇ **at a... ~** *The static approach of conventional economics freezes time at a moment.* **2** [C] **~ (of sth)** a very short period of time: *Their analysis showed that the first few moments of a telephone call are of critical importance.*

IDM **at the/this ˈmoment** now; at the present time: *Although these ideas may seem fanciful at the moment, they are clearly not impossible.* **for the ˈmoment** for now: *Suppose for the moment that x = y.* HELP **For the moment** is used in writing to ask the reader to consider one particular aspect or possibility first, before going on to consider other aspects or possibilities.

mo·men·tum /məˈmentəm; *NAmE* moʊˈmentəm/ *noun* [U] **1** the ability of a process or course of events to keep increasing or developing: *The 1992 project gave European integration renewed political momentum.* ◇ **gain/gather ~** *The opposition movement against martial law gradually gained momentum.* ◇ **lose ~** *The villages kept growing in the 1700s, after the cities lost their momentum.* **2** (*physics*) the quantity of movement of a moving object, measured as its mass multiplied by its VELOCITY (= speed in a particular direction): *When no forces act on a body, its momentum is conserved.* ➲ *see also* ANGULAR MOMENTUM **3** a force that is gained by movement: *The rocks begin to move down the slope, gaining momentum and inflicting much damage on structures.*

mon·arch /ˈmɒnək; *NAmE* ˈmɑːnərk; ˈmɑːnɑːrk/ *noun* a person who rules a country, for example a king or queen: *Territorial states in early modern Europe were governed by absolute monarchs who regarded the state as their property.*

mon·archy /ˈmɒnəki; *NAmE* ˈmɑːnərki/ *noun* (*pl.* **-ies**) **1** [U, sing.] a system of government by a king or queen: *Under the prevailing French regime of absolute monarchy, Voltaire's thinking was highly subversive.* ◇ *The Provisional Government feared that officers would use the army to restore the monarchy.* **2** [C] a country that is ruled by a king or queen: *Britain is a constitutional monarchy, which means that the monarch plays a largely ceremonial role.* ➲ *compare* REPUBLIC **3 the monarchy** [sing.] the king or queen of a country and their family: *The monarchy in Thailand is central to Buddhist practice and culture.*

mon·as·tery /ˈmɒnəstri; *NAmE* ˈmɑːnəsteri/ *noun* (*pl.* **-ies**) a building in which a community of MONKS (= men leading a religious life) live: *Most medieval Christian monasteries housed monks who worked in a place of isolation.* ◇ *a Buddhist/Benedictine monastery*

mo·nas·tic /məˈnæstɪk/ *adj.* connected with MONKS or a monastery: *The essential framework of Benedict's monastic life was the worship of God.* ◇ *a monastic community/order*

mon·et·ary /ˈmʌnɪtri; *NAmE* ˈmʌnɪteri/ *adj.* [only before noun] connected with money, especially with the government's regulation of the MONEY SUPPLY of the country: *These changes in the government's monetary policies had unpredicted consequences for the economy.* ◇ *It was found that most shoplifting is of small items of relatively little monetary value.* ➲ thesaurus note *at* FINANCIAL

ˌmonetary ˈunion *noun* [U, C] (*economics*) a situation in which two or more states' currencies are fixed at an exchange rate of one for one: *Monetary union meant that East Germany abandoned its currency, the Ostmark, in favour of the Deutsche Mark.* HELP In the **European Monetary Union** (or **Economic and Monetary Union**) (**EMU**), monetary union is accompanied by a SINGLE MARKET and a **customs union** (= a free trade area with a common TARIFF on imports from outside the union). The SINGLE CURRENCY, the euro, was introduced in 2002 in 12 EU countries and is now the currency of 17 of the 28 member states.

THESAURUS

money • capital • funds • income • revenue • wealth
noun

These words can all be used to talk about money.

- to **earn** money/income/revenue
- to **raise** money/capital/funds/revenue
- to **invest** money/capital/funds
- to **spend** money/income/funds
- to **borrow** money/funds
- to **lend/save** money
- to **generate** income/revenue/wealth

- **Capital** and **funds** may each be used to refer to money that an organization uses to invest in a project or other business activity: *The average return on capital invested in land was only about 5 per cent.* ◇ *Funds were raised to build an impressive football stadium.*
- **Income** and **revenue** may each be used to refer to money that an organization receives, for example from the sales of its goods or services, but **income** may also be used to mean the money a person earns from their job: *The revenue generated by selling patents rose considerably in this period.* ◇ *Thus, each farmer earns an income from vegetable sales of around $1 000.*
- **Wealth** refers to the amount of money that a person, a group of people, a country, etc. has: *Market trading creates wealth through the exchange of scarce resources.*

money /ˈmʌni/ *noun* **1** [U] coins and paper notes used for buying and selling things HELP **Money** also refers to the *value* of coins and paper notes, or of ASSETS or promises that can be exchanged for coins and notes (such as the money in a bank account), even when no physical coins or notes are involved: *A lot of money is spent on training.* ◇ **~ to do sth** *Cathy gave him the money to pay off his debts.* ◇ **~ for sth** *Most of the money for the purchase came from Ms Dowden.* ◇ **~ from sth** *Money from donations goes to support their comfortable lifestyles.* ◇ **(in exchange) for ~** *He was likely to do anything for money.* **2 moneys** or **monies** [pl.] sums of money: *The trust required that the monies be used solely for the children's education.*

IDM **make ˈmoney** to earn a lot of money; to make a profit: *While the bourgeoisie made money, the aristocracy ran the government.* ◇ *Many major films made more money abroad than at home.* **pour/pump money into sth** to invest a lot of money in a business or a particular project, over a period of time: *The government had to pump money into the economy to prevent jobs, sales and markets from drying up.* **put (your) money into sth** to invest money in a business or a particular project: *Investors were encouraged to put their money into railways.* ➲ *more at* VALUE[1]

- ADJECTIVE + MONEY **extra, additional • cheap • public • federal** *Many women worked part-time to earn some extra money for the household.*
- NOUN + MONEY **purchase • loan • government • taxpayers'** *The new hospital has been financed through private banks rather than government money.*
- VERB + MONEY **spend • pay • cost • borrow • lend • earn • make • save • invest • recover • raise • owe • donate • waste • print • lose • withdraw • deposit • transfer • manage** *His mother took in laundry to earn money.* ◇ *Most manufacturers were losing money on computers.*

ˈmoney market *noun* the banks and other institutions that lend or borrow money, and buy and sell foreign money: *The money market plays a crucial role in the economy through its unique position relative to all other markets.*

ˈmoney supply *noun* [sing., U] (*economics*) the total amount of money that exists in the economy of a country at a particular time: *In the 1980s, UK governments tried to control the money supply in order to control inflation.*

M

moni·tor[1] AWL /ˈmɒnɪtə(r); *NAmE* ˈmɑːnɪtər/ *verb* **1** to watch and check sth over a period of time in order to see how it develops, so that you can make any necessary changes: **~ sth** *Students are tested regularly in literacy and numeracy to monitor progress.* ◇ *This device allows diabetics to monitor their blood glucose levels at home.* ◇ **~ whether/how, etc...** *The project engineer monitors whether everything is completed according to the plan specifications.* **2 ~ sb** to watch or check sb over a period of time, so that you can see if any problems develop and take action to stop or correct this: *If we can identify individuals at risk for recurrent depression, we may be able to monitor them more carefully.* **3 ~ sth** to listen to telephone calls, radio broadcasts, etc. in order to check them or find out useful information: *Telephone calls may be monitored or recorded for staff training purposes.*

moni·tor[2] AWL /ˈmɒnɪtə(r); *NAmE* ˈmɑːnɪtər/ *noun* **1** a piece of equipment used to check or record sth: *Some patients with hypertension purchase home blood pressure monitors.* ◇ *a cardiac/heart-rate/heart monitor* **2** a screen that shows information from a device such as a computer or camera, or a television screen: *The camera was connected to a monitor in the laboratory and the birds' behaviour was carefully noted.* ◇ *Air traffic information is available to the controllers on radar screens and computer monitors.* ◇ *a television/video/CCTV monitor* **3** a person whose job is to check that a process or activity happens in a fair, correct or legal way: *Election monitors expressed concerns about the conduct of the elections.*

monk /mʌŋk/ *noun* a member of a religious group of men who often live apart from other people in a MONASTERY and who do not marry or have personal possessions: *The medieval monks derived much of their power from their monopoly of handwriting skills.* ◇ *a Buddhist/Benedictine monk*

mono·graph /ˈmɒnəɡrɑːf; *NAmE* ˈmɑːnəɡræf/ *noun* **~ (on sth)** a detailed written study of a single subject, usually in the form of a short book: *He has published monographs on D.W. Griffith and Fritz Lang.*

mon·op·ol·ist /mə'nɒpəlɪst; *NAmE* mə'nɑ:pəlɪst/ *noun* (*technical*) a person or company that has a monopoly: *With barriers to the entry of new firms, a monopolist does not have to fear competition.*

mon·op·ol·is·tic /məˌnɒpə'lɪstɪk; *NAmE* məˌnɑ:pə'lɪstɪk/ *adj.* controlling or trying to get complete control over sth, especially an industry or a company: *Antitrust policy in the United States is about encouraging competition among firms and battling monopolistic practices.*

mon·op·ol·ize (*BrE also* **-ise**) /mə'nɒpəlaɪz; *NAmE* mə'nɑ:pəlaɪz/ *verb* **~ sth** to have or take control of all or most of sth so that others are prevented from sharing it: *Dominant groups are those that monopolize economic resources.* ◇ *Worker bees are responsible for tasks such as defence or feeding while reproduction is monopolized by the queen.* ■ **mon·op·ol·iza·tion, -isa·tion** /məˌnɒpəlaɪ'zeɪʃn; *NAmE* məˌnɑ:pələ'zeɪʃn/ *noun* [U] *Industries in Eastern Europe have shown a tendency towards monopolization.*

mon·op·oly /mə'nɒpəli; *NAmE* mə'nɑ:pəli/ *noun* (*pl.* **-ies**) **1** the complete control of trade in particular goods or the supply of a particular service: *At that time, London booksellers had a virtual monopoly, and were therefore able to keep prices high.* ◇ **~ on/of sth** *The East India Company had a strategy to break the Chinese monopoly on tea production.* **2** a type of goods or service that is completely controlled by one company or group: *Natural monopolies occur when the cost advantages of expanding are very high, for example with a gas or electricity network.* ◇ *The sale of spirits became a state monopoly.* **3** [usually sing.] **~ on/of sth** the complete control, possession or use of sth; a thing that belongs only to one person or group and that others cannot share: *These examples from the animal kingdom show that humans do not have a monopoly on innovation.*

M

mon·soon /ˌmɒn'su:n; *NAmE* ˌmɑ:n'su:n/ *noun* **1** a period of heavy rain in summer in S Asia; the rain that falls during this period: **+ noun** *During the monsoon season, however, floods often have catastrophic consequences.* **2** a wind in S Asia that blows from the south-west in summer, bringing rain, and the north-east in winter: **+ noun** *The western coastal areas receive more rainfall than the eastern, owing to the stronger south-west monsoon winds.*

month /mʌnθ/ *noun* **1** [C] any of the twelve periods of time into which the year is divided: *the month of August/December, etc.* ◇ *the summer/winter months* ◇ *There are at least two people whose birthdays fall in the same month.* **2** [C] a period of about 30 days: *Treatments may last several months.* ◇ **for a month/six months, etc.** *Fighting continued, however, for several months .* ◇ **in a month/six months, etc.** *She said she wanted to see me again in a month.* ◇ **per ~** *Six to twelve shops per month were changing hands in central Tokyo.* ➲ language bank *at* TIME[1] **3 months** [pl.] a long time, especially a period of several months: *He spent months living in a state of the most extreme poverty.*

month·ly[1] /'mʌnθli/ *adj.* **1** happening once a month or every month: *Monthly meetings are held in each precinct.* ◇ *Data are available on a monthly basis.* **2** paid, valid or calculated for one month: *Participants estimated total monthly household incomes.* ◇ *monthly expenditure/payments*

month·ly[2] /'mʌnθli/ *adv.* every month or once a month: *Municipal councils meet monthly.*

monu·ment /'mɒnjumənt; *NAmE* 'mɑ:njumənt/ *noun* **1 ~ (to sb/sth)** a building, column, statue, etc. built to remind people of a famous person or event: *There are numerous monuments to Queen Victoria in former British colonies.* ◇ *A monument was subsequently erected on the site of the battle.* **2** a building that has special historical importance: *Lansbury was responsible for preserving ancient monuments and managing the royal parks.* ➲ *compare* LANDMARK (1) **3 ~ to sth** a thing that remains as a good example of sth: *These recordings are a monument to his talent as a pianist.*

mood /mu:d/ *noun* **1** [C, U] the way you are feeling at a particular time: *32% of the patients reported using these drugs to improve their mood or to relax.* ◇ *Depressed mood is common after a stroke.* ◇ **in a... ~** *Individuals in a good mood tend to overestimate the likelihood of positive outcomes.* **2** [sing.] **~ (of sb/sth)** the way a group of people feel about sth; the atmosphere in a place or among a group of people: *The mood of the nation was changing.* ◇ *Until the Prime Minister calls the meeting to order, the mood is usually informal.*

moon /mu:n/ *noun* **1** *usually* **the moon,** *also* **the Moon** [sing.] the round object that moves around the earth once every 27½ days and shines at night by light reflected from the sun: **+ noun** *Soon after the moon landing, public and congressional support for the space programme declined sharply.* **2** [sing.] the moon as it appears in the sky at a particular time: *A full moon rose over the valley.* **3** [C] a natural SATELLITE that moves around a planet other than the earth: *It was Kuiper who first discovered that Titan, Saturn's largest moon, has an atmosphere.*

moral[1] /'mɒrəl; *NAmE* 'mɔ:rəl; 'mɑ:rəl/ *adj.* **1** [only before noun] concerned with principles of right and wrong behaviour: *Surgeons are required to make moral judgements on a daily basis.* ◇ *Locke believes there is a moral law that limits what governments may do.* ◇ *There are no hard-and-fast rules we can rely on for answers to our moral dilemmas.* **2** [only before noun] based on a sense of what is right and fair, not on legal rights or duties **SYN** ETHICAL (1): *Most individuals feel a moral obligation to obey the law.* **3** following the standards of behaviour considered acceptable and right by most people **SYN** GOOD[1] (8), HONOURABLE (2): *Flaxman was a deeply moral man.* ◇ *Officials were chosen for their moral worth rather than their expertise.* ➲ *compare* IMMORAL (1) **4** [only before noun] able to understand the difference between right and wrong: *All moral agents have an obligation not to harm others.*

IDM **claim/take the moral 'high ground** to claim that your side of an argument is morally better than your opponents' side; to argue in a way that makes your side seem morally better: *Some bars had bravely taken the moral high ground by introducing smoking bans.*

▸ MORAL + NOUN **judgement • authority • law • code • principle • reasoning • argument • justification • objection • issue • dilemma • panic • outrage • standards • values • sense • intuition • standing • virtue • order • philosophy • philosopher** *At the beginning of the 21st century, there is a moral panic about parenting, in particular working mothers and absent fathers.* ◇ *These young people were seen as a threat to the moral order of society.* | **responsibility • obligation • duty • imperative • right • claim** *Celebrities have a moral responsibility to ensure that the brands they endorse are not damaging the planet.*

moral[2] /'mɒrəl; *NAmE* 'mɔ:rəl; 'mɑ:rəl/ *noun* **1 morals** [pl.] standards or principles of good behaviour, especially in matters of sexual relationships: *This debate has associated mobile phones with bad manners and declining morals.* **2** [C] **~ of sth** a practical lesson that a story, an event or an experience teaches you: *The moral of the story is that the pursuit of individual self-interest can have very negative consequences.*

ˌmoral 'hazard *noun* [U, C] (*economics*) a situation in which sb's actions cannot be watched and checked by others: *The manager's frequent trips abroad created a moral hazard that the employees would not turn up for work.*

mor·al·ity /mə'ræləti/ *noun* (*pl.* -ies) **1** [U] principles concerning right and wrong or good and bad behaviour: *She argues strongly that morality does not come from religion.* ◇ *Internet censorship has been justified on the grounds of public morality.* ◇ *sexual/personal/political morality* ➲ *compare* ETHIC (1) **2** [U] the degree to which sth is right or wrong, or good or bad, according to moral principles: **~ of sth** *The morality of the action depends entirely upon the intention.* ◇ **~ of doing sth** *There are fundamental disagreements about the morality of altering the human genome.* **3** [U, C] a system of moral principles followed by a particular group of people: *In England, he says, people reject God but cling to Christian morality.* ◇ *Moralities diverge in terms of how they regard the good, the right and the virtuous.* ➲ *compare* ETHIC (2)

mor·al·ly /'mɒrəli; *NAmE* 'mɔːrəli/ *adv.* according to principles of good behaviour and what is considered to be right or wrong: *He felt that his actions were morally justified.* ◇ *It is the duty of good citizens to act in a morally responsible way.* ◇ *morally wrong/objectionable/repugnant* ◇ *morally right/permissible/acceptable*

mor·bid·ity /mɔː'bɪdəti; *NAmE* mɔːr'bɪdəti/ *noun* [U] (*medical*) **1** the number of people with a particular disease: *Areas with the highest mortality and morbidity tend to get those doctors who are least able to choose where they work.* **2** the state of having a particular disease: *A couple may be carriers of a genetic disease that may cause significant morbidity in the child.*

more[1] /mɔː(r)/ *det., pron.* (used as the comparative of *much, a lot of* and *many*) a larger number or amount of: *This topic is discussed in more detail in section 8.6.* ◇ **much ~** *This issue is far from resolved and much more experimentation is required.* ◇ **any ~** *The advent of democracy did not give women any more political power.* ◇ **even ~** *The early twentieth century saw the state taking even more responsibility for the provision of health care.* ◇ **~ (of sth) (than...)** *Excess demand exists when more of some good or service is demanded than is supplied.* ◇ **no ~ than...** *In the poorest nations, per capita annual incomes were no more than about $500.*
IDM **ˌmore and 'more** continuing to become larger in number or amount: *More and more companies are conducting business online.*

more[2] /mɔː(r)/ *adv.* **1** used to form the comparative of adjectives and adverbs with two or more syllables: *Future research is needed to provide more detailed tests of these predictions.* ◇ **~ ... than...** *He always seemed more interested in the past than in the politics of his own time.* ◇ **~ rather than less...** *Issues of equality of opportunity have become more rather than less important.* **2** to a greater degree than sth else; to a greater degree than usual: *For more advanced students, further conversational challenges arise once teacher and student reverse roles.* ◇ **~ ... than...** *Bridging the gap between student and staff nurse was more challenging than I had anticipated.* ◇ **~ than...** *By normal standards, Smith's evidence is more than adequate to support a claim to knowledge.* ◇ **little ~ than...** *Born to a poor family, he received little more than an elementary education.* ➲ *see also* ANY MORE
IDM **ˌmore and 'more** continuing to become larger in number or amount SYN INCREASINGLY: *As the banks' own security increases, customers more and more become the target for fraud.* **ˌmore or 'less 1** almost: *In the past 15 years, water rights in Australia have, more or less, been separated from land rights.* **2** approximately: *Baker divides the book into four parts, organized more or less chronologically.* **the more, less, etc..., the more, less, etc...** used to show that two things change to the same degree: *The more television children watch, the more likely they are to learn consumer skills.* ◇ *The more damaged stems became, the less they were likely to resprout.* **what is 'more** used to add a point that is even more important: *When this new monetary system was put to the test in 1929, it failed and, what is more, it deepened the crisis considerably.* ➲ language bank *at* ADDITION ➲ *more at* ONCE[1]

more·over /mɔːr'əʊvə(r); *NAmE* mɔːr'oʊvər/ *adv.* used to introduce some new information that adds to or supports what you have said previously: *The number of lone-parent families is increasing. Moreover, women head nine out of ten one-parent families.* ◇ *Closer analysis reveals deeper complexity. I shall argue, moreover, that...* ➲ language bank *at* ADDITION

morph·ology /mɔː'fɒlədʒi; *NAmE* mɔːr'fɑːlədʒi/ *noun* **1** [U, C] **~ (of sth)** the form and structure of animals, plants, rocks, soil, etc: *Exposure to competing demands shapes the morphology of species.* ◇ *The Isles of Scilly have a complex coastal morphology.* **2** [U] (*linguistics*) the forms of words, especially INFLECTED forms; the study of these forms: *Pidgins are simplified languages with little or no morphology and limited syntax.* ➲ *compare* GRAMMAR (1), SYNTAX (1) ■ **mor·pho·logic·al** /ˌmɔːfə'lɒdʒɪkl; *NAmE* ˌmɔːrfə'lɑːdʒɪkl/ *adj.*: *In carbon dioxide, the enzyme powders can undergo morphological changes.* ◇ *There are numerous lexical and morphological differences between the two varieties of the language.*

mor·tal /'mɔːtl; *NAmE* 'mɔːrtl/ *adj.* **1** that cannot live for ever and must die: *He was a mortal man and she was an immortal goddess.* OPP IMMORTAL (1) **2** causing death or likely to cause death; very serious: *Terror and shock in the face of mortal danger are completely natural.* ➲ *compare* FATAL **3** lasting until death: *These two mortal enemies could not meet without one destroying the other.*

mor·tal·ity /mɔː'tæləti; *NAmE* mɔːr'tæləti/ *noun* (*pl.* -ies) **1** [U] death, especially on a large scale: **~ from sth** *Cooks had unusually high mortality from viral hepatitis.* ◇ **~ among/amongst/in sb/sth** *Reduced mortality among newborns led to an increase in life expectancy.* ◇ **~ rate/rate of ~** *Today, infant mortality rates of more than 50/1 000 are regarded as high.* **2** [C] a death: *Electrofishing is a method for surveying fish communities but can cause fish mortalities.* **3** [U] the state of being unable to live for ever: *People did not wish to be reminded of their own mortality.*

mort·gage /'mɔːɡɪdʒ; *NAmE* 'mɔːrɡɪdʒ/ *noun* a legal agreement by which a bank or similar organization lends sb money to buy a house, etc, and they pay the money back over a particular number of years; the sum of money that they borrow: *It has become more difficult for people to obtain a mortgage.* ◇ *The couple had a £300 000 mortgage secured on their family home.*

most[1] /məʊst; *NAmE* moʊst/ *det., pron.* (used as the superlative of 'much', 'a lot of', 'many') **1 the most...** the largest in number or amount: *Africa has the most extensive savannah areas, which are rich in animal species.* ◇ *Pain is the most prominent symptom in the majority of patients.* ◇ *Residential schooling may be needed for the most severely affected children.* ◇ *Labour, as the major party in Scotland, had the most to lose fom the rise of the Scottish National Party.* **2** more than half of sb/sth; almost all of sb/sth: *Most people do not like change, because change can be disruptive.* ◇ *In most countries, there is great competition to get into good universities.* ◇ *In most cases, two researchers conducted semi-structured interviews in the homes of the participants.* ◇ **~ of sb/sth** *Conditions are very cold for most of the year.* HELP **The** is not used with **most** in this meaning.
IDM **at (the) 'most** not more than: *At most, only 7 years would be required for the water to fill the reservoir behind the highest dam completely.*

most[2] /məʊst; *NAmE* moʊst/ *adv.* **1** used to form the superlative of adjectives and adverbs of two or more syllables: **(the) ~** *Of all the countries in the region, the Philippines is the most affected by typhoons.* ◇ *The most*

M

pressing issue was how contracts would be awarded under the new system. ◇ *It is a rare disease that occurs most commonly in children and the elderly.* HELP When **most** is followed only by an adverb, **the** is not used: *This reason is mentioned most frequently*, but *This is the most frequently mentioned reason.* **2** to the greatest degree: *Different researchers have made different claims about what matters most.* ◇ **the ~** *Countries that benefit the most from price decreases will lose the most from price increases.* ◇ **~ of all** *What I enjoyed most of all about this project was the chance to apply my new knowledge and skills in a real working environment.* HELP In this meaning, **the** can be used but is is often left out. It is not used before **most of all.** **3** very; extremely; completely: *The cost would most certainly outweigh the benefits.* ◇ *In this case, net exports will most likely be positive.*

most·ly /ˈməʊstli; *NAmE* ˈmoʊstli/ *adv.* mainly; generally: *The discussion focuses mostly on China and India.* ◇ *Titan, a large satellite of Saturn, has a dense atmosphere consisting mostly of nitrogen.* ◇ *Many questions still remain unanswered, mostly due to a lack of empirical data.* ◇ *Their conclusions were mostly based on analyses of time trends.*

mother /ˈmʌðə(r)/ *noun* **1** a female parent: *In 1989, 27% of children born were born to unmarried mothers.* ◇ *a single/working/expectant mother* ◇ **~ of sb** *The mother of a starving child can be jailed for stealing a loaf of bread.* **2** (in compounds) **+ noun** a plant, cell, etc. from which another plant, cell, etc. develops: *When body cells divide, the daughter cells are identical to the mother cell.*

M

mother·hood /ˈmʌðəhʊd; *NAmE* ˈmʌðərhʊd/ *noun* [U] the state of being a mother: *Entering motherhood at such an early age is particularly problematic.* ◇ *Movies, television and marketing focus women's lives on marriage and motherhood.*

ˌmother ˈtongue *noun* the language that you first learn to speak when you are a child SYN FIRST LANGUAGE: *The online survey was answered by a majority of people whose mother tongue was not English.*

motif /məʊˈtiːf; *NAmE* moʊˈtiːf/ *noun* **1 ~ (of sb/sth)** a subject, idea or phrase that is repeated and developed in a work of literature or a piece of music SYN THEME: *This is not the first time Carter has employed the motif of a swan in her works.* **2** (*biochemistry*) a particular order in which a set of GENES or parts of MOLECULES are arranged on DNA or a PROTEIN: *A particular activity or role of a protein is often associated with a particular domain or motif.*

mo·tion /ˈməʊʃn; *NAmE* ˈmoʊʃn/ *noun* **1** [U, sing.] the act or process of moving; the way sth moves: *Newton predicted Kepler's three laws of planetary motion based on his own three laws.* ◇ **~ of sth** *Electric current is generally caused by the motion of electric charges.* ◇ **in ~** *According to Auerbach, what most fascinated early cinema audiences were bodies in motion.* **2** [C] a formal proposal that is discussed and voted on at a meeting: *The Council passed a motion cancelling further expenditure.*
IDM **go through the ˈmotions (of doing sth)** to do or say sth because you have to, not because you really want to: *While almost all regimes go through the motions of elections, the quality of electoral procedures is highly variable.* **set sth in ˈmotion** to start sth happening or moving: *Constantine set in motion a process that changed the course of Christian and imperial development.*

mo·tiv·ate AWL /ˈməʊtɪveɪt; *NAmE* ˈmoʊtɪveɪt/ *verb* **1** [often passive] to be the reason why sb does sth or behaves in a particular way: **be motivated by sth** *Gauthier assumes that people are ultimately motivated by self-interest.* ◇ *There is a widespread belief that shoppers are primarily motivated by convenience.* ◇ **a motivating factor/force** *Avoiding heat, rather than UV radiation, was reported as a motivating factor for using shade.* **2** to make sb want to do sth, especially sth that involves hard work and effort: **~ sb** *Bonuses are usually additional incentives designed to motivate salespeople.* ◇ **~ sb to do sth** *It is important to help motivate smokers to quit.* ■ **mo·tiv·ator** /ˈməʊtɪveɪtə(r); *NAmE* ˈmoʊtɪveɪtər/ *noun*: *Shame can be a very powerful motivator.* ◇ **~ to do sth** *Company cars are seen as a key motivator to perform well.*

mo·tiv·ated AWL /ˈməʊtɪveɪtɪd; *NAmE* ˈmoʊtɪveɪtɪd/ *adj.* **1 racially/politically/ideologicially, etc. motivated** done for racial, political, etc. reasons: *She alleges that the discrimination is racially motivated.* **2** wanting to do sth, especially sth that involves hard work and effort: *The teachers in the study appeared highly motivated.*

mo·tiv·ation AWL /ˌməʊtɪˈveɪʃn; *NAmE* ˌmoʊtɪˈveɪʃn/ *noun* **1** [C] a reason or reasons for doing a particular activity or behaving in a particular way: **~ for (doing) sth** *Booth maintained that profit was the motivation for business.* ◇ **~ behind sth** *Part of the motivation behind neural nets was to try to model the human brain more closely.* **2** [U, C] desire or willingness to do sth: **~ to do sth** *Older students reported lower levels of motivation to smoke for social reasons.* ◇ **~ for (doing) sth** *93.2% of parents believe that the motivation for learning can be raised.*

mo·tive AWL /ˈməʊtɪv; *NAmE* ˈmoʊtɪv/ *noun* a reason for doing sth: **~ for (doing) sth** *Her former husband had a motive for killing Monte.* ◇ *There are powerful profit motives pushing for timber exploitation and few incentives for sustainable forest management.* ◇ **~ behind sth** *Psychology seeks to understand the motives behind an individual's actions.*

motor¹ /ˈməʊtə(r); *NAmE* ˈmoʊtər/ *noun* **1** a device that uses a source of power, such as electricity or fuel, to make a vehicle or part of a machine move: *Because of electrical and mechanical losses in electric motors and generators, the output power is less than the input power.* ◇ *The up-down and forward-backward motions are driven by the two motors mounted on the back of the robot body.* ◇ **~ of sth** (*figurative*) *For Labour, the public sector had been a mechanism for social interventions and a motor of economic growth.* **2** (*biology*) a part of a living creature, such as BACTERIA, that is involved in moving it around: *Many simple bacteria have molecular motors that they use to propel themselves around.* ◇ *Bacteria like E. coli are equipped with rotary motors embedded in their cell walls.*

motor² /ˈməʊtə(r); *NAmE* ˈmoʊtər/ *adj.* [only before noun] **1** having an engine; using the power of an engine: *As the demand for motor vehicles rises with economic growth, pollution is likely to worsen.* **2** (*especially BrE*) connected with vehicles that have engines: *There was a growing demand for skilled workers in emergent sectors like the motor industry.* **3** (*technical*) connected with movement of the body that is produced by muscles; connected with the nerves that control movement: *Approximately half of the patients had limited motor functions.* ◇ *Play helps children learn how to relate to other children and adults, explore objects and increase their motor skills.*

ˌmotor ˈneuron (*also* **moto·neur·on** /ˌməʊtəˈnjʊərɒn; *NAmE* ˌmoʊtəˈnjuːrɑːn; ˌmoʊtəˈnuːrɑːn/) *noun* (*biology*) a nerve cell that sends signals to a muscle or GLAND: **+ noun** *A diagnosis of motor neuron disease was made.*

mould¹ (*US* **mold**) /məʊld; *NAmE* moʊld/ *noun* **1** [C, U] a fine soft green, grey or black substance like fur that grows on old food or on objects that are left in warm, wet air: *The cellular slime moulds have some properties similar to both animals and plants.* ◇ *Damp housing and mould on walls can cause serious health issues.* **2** [C] a container that you pour a liquid or soft substance into, which then becomes solid in the same shape as the container, for example when it is cooled or cooked: *The solution is then poured into a suitable mould and solidifies to form a gel as it cools.*

3 [C, usually sing.] a particular style showing the characteristics, attitudes or behaviour that are typical of sb/sth: *The case study introduced here is problematic since it does not fit the required mould.* ◇ **in the ~ of sb/sth** *He wanted to reinvent himself as a film mogul in the mould of Louis B. Mayer or Jack Warner.*
IDM **break the ˈmould (of sth)** to change what people expect from a situation, especially by acting in a new and original way: *Gorbachev gave little indication early on that he would break the mould of Soviet politics.*

mould² (*US* **mold**) /məʊld; *NAmE* moʊld/ *verb* **1 ~ sb/sth** to strongly influence the way sb/sth's character, opinions or behaviour develop: *They demonstrated that the state plays a key role in moulding civil society.* ◇ *When the Cold War ended, a new world view had emerged that was moulded by ideology rather than reality.* **2 ~ sth (into sth)** to shape a soft substance into a particular form or object by pressing it or by putting it into a mould: *Concrete could be more easily moulded into any required shape.*

mount /maʊnt/ *verb* **1** [T] **~ a campaign/challenge/attack/defence, etc.** to organize and begin sth: *Several national newspapers mounted a campaign against GM foods.* ◇ *Exploratory expeditions were mounted more and more frequently.* ◇ *The body mounts an immune response, producing antibodies to HIV.* **2** [I] to increase gradually: *Pressure was mounting for a military response.* ◇ *Concern began to mount that human activity might deplete the ozone layer.* **3** [T, often passive] to fix sth into position on sth else, so that you can use it, look at it or study it: **be mounted** *Once the sample is mounted, the procedure for polishing it is as follows...* ◇ **be mounted on/onto/in sth** *The spindle was mounted on a base plate.*

moun·tain /ˈmaʊntən; *NAmE* ˈmaʊntn/ *noun* **1** a large, steep, high hill, often with rocks near the top: *Radiotelescopes are often located at the tops of high mountains.* ◇ **in the mountains** *He left home for a period of solitary reading and meditation in the mountains.* ◇ **+ noun** *Proximity to an ocean or a mountain range can create local climates that support unique plant communities.* **2 ~ of sth** (*rather informal*) a very large amount or number of sth: *New studies have provided a mountain of data.*

mourn /mɔːn; *NAmE* mɔːrn/ *verb* [T, I] to feel and show sadness because sb has died; to feel sad because sth no longer exists or is no longer the same: **~ sth** *She may still be mourning the loss of her natural parent.* ◇ *Characters in the film mourn this lost past of prosperity and safety.* ◇ **~ for sb/sth** *The scene displays Niobe mourning for her children.*

mourn·ing /ˈmɔːnɪŋ; *NAmE* ˈmɔːrnɪŋ/ *noun* [U] sadness that you show and feel because sb has died or sth no longer exists SYN GRIEF (1): *This article examines female mourning in wartime Germany.* ◇ **~ for sb/sth** *There was little official mourning for the passing of the religious houses and the culture which had sustained them.*

mouse /maʊs/ *noun* (*pl.* **mice** /maɪs/) **1** a small animal that is covered in fur and has a long thin TAIL. Mice live in fields, in people's houses or where food is stored: *Subsequent laboratory mouse studies reported conflicting results.* **2** (*pl. also* **mouses**) (*computing*) a small device that is moved by hand across a surface to control the movement of the small mark on a computer screen that shows where writing, etc. will appear: *As an alternative to using the mouse, many people find it easier to use the arrow keys on their keyboard to move from cell to cell.*

mouth /maʊθ/ *noun* (*pl.* **mouths** /maʊðz/) **1** the opening in the face used for speaking and eating; the area inside the head behind this opening: *Occasionally, you would notice an acid taste in the mouth.* ◇ **by ~** *Drugs may be given by mouth or injection.* **2 ~ (of sth)** the entrance or opening of sth: *There was no grid at the mouth of the pipe to stop it from getting blocked.* ◇ *The expedition emerged from the mouth of the Grand Canyon three months later.* **3 ~ (of sth)** the place where a river joins the sea: *Doñana National Park lies on the Atlantic coast of Spain at the mouth of the Guadalquivir river.* IDM *see* WORD¹

move¹ /muːv/ *verb* **1** [I, T] to change position or make sb/sth change position in a way that can be seen, heard or felt: *He experiences prolonged periods when he is unable to move.* ◇ *Huge masses of earth and rock are still moving.* ◇ **+ adv./prep.** *The fluid keeps the ends of the bones apart, allowing the joint to move freely.* ◇ *Our neighbouring galaxy, M31, is actually moving towards the Milky Way.* ◇ **+ noun** *In solids, atoms cannot move significant distances.* ◇ **~ sb/sth** *Transport systems use specific modes (such as road, rail, water or air) to move people and materials.* ◇ **~ sb/sth + adv./prep.** *The frog moves its head downwards.* ◇ *It may be necessary to move the patient to a more private area.* **2** [I, T] to change or make sth change from one state, opinion or activity to another SYN SHIFT²: **(+ adv./prep.)** *They complained that the party has moved too far to the right.* ◇ **~ sth (+ adv./prep.)** *The current goal is to move the economy away from heavy industry and towards the service-based industries.* **3** [I] to make progress or develop in the way or direction mentioned SYN PROGRESS² (1): **+ adv./prep.** *Events moved fast in the first few years.* ◇ **~ on/ahead** *He rightly highlights that things have moved on since then.* ◇ *Plans for expansion were not moving ahead.* **4** [I] to take action; to do sth SYN ACT¹ (1): *There is a clear advantage to the government that is able to move first.* ◇ **~ to do sth** *Russia moved quickly to impose its grip on Eastern Europe.* ◇ **~ against sb/sth** *This may have been one of the reasons the authorities eventually moved against him.* **5** [I, T] to change the place where you live or have your work: *She decided to move because of the pollution from the factories in the town.* ◇ **~ (from...) (to...)** *Her family moved to the US from Russia when she was a child.* ◇ **~ away** *Children grow up and move away.* ◇ **~ house** (*BrE*) *The Dickenses moved house twice during the first two years of Charles's life.* **6** [T] **~ sb (from...) (to...)** to make sb change from one job, class, etc. to another SYN TRANSFER² (1): *Flexible contracts mean that staff can easily be moved from one job to another.* **7** [T] to suggest sth formally so that it can be discussed and decided: **~ sth** *A public company must move resolutions at a meeting of the members.* ◇ **~ that...** *In 27 BC he moved that Octavian be called Augustus.* **8** [T, often passive] to cause sb to have strong feelings, especially of sympathy or sadness: **be moved (by sth)** *The two women were deeply moved by the suffering of the poor.* ◇ **be moved to sth** *The entire audience was moved to tears.* **9** [T] **~ sb to do sth** to influence sb or cause them to do sth SYN PROMPT¹ (2): *It is his desire to concentrate on his work that moves him to do what he does.*
IDM **get sth ˈmoving** to cause sth to make progress: *He made great efforts to get things moving again.* ➲ *more at* FORWARD¹, TIME¹
PHR V **ˌmove ˈin | ˌmove ˈinto sth** to start to live in your new home: *The tenants had only moved in a few months before.* ◇ *Late in December 1824, they moved into a house in Johnson Street.* OPP MOVE OUT **ˈmove in sth** to live or spend your time in a particular social group: *He was living in Rome and moving in literary circles.* **ˌmove ˈin (on sb/sth)** to move towards sb/sth, especially in order to attack or take control: *They ordered the troops to move in.* ◇ *He met little resistance as he moved in on the city of Nanjing.* **ˌmove ˈin with sb** to start living with sb in the house, flat, etc. where they already live: *The woman in that case had moved in with a married man.* **ˌmove ˈon (to sth)** to start doing or discussing sth new: *It is vital to decide who should fill key roles in the business, should current staff move on, retire or die.* ◇ *The class then moves on to the next topic.* **ˌmove ˈout** to leave your old home: *The*

M

marriage broke down and he moved out. OPP MOVE IN, MOVE INTO STH

move² /muːv/ *noun* **1** an action that you do or need to do to achieve sth: *The CEO needs to be confident that big strategic moves will maintain profitable growth.* ◇ **~ to do sth** *In February 2011, the US made the first significant move to reduce the federal deficit.* ◇ **~ by sb** *In an earlier era, such a move by a Russian leader would have been inconceivable.* **2** a change in ideas, behaviour or policy SYN SHIFT¹ (1), TREND: **~ towards/to sth** *A number of obstacles held up the move to the next stage of political union.* ◇ **~ away from sth** *British politicians wished to see a move away from protectionism towards free trade.* **3 ~ (from...) (to...)** an act of changing the place where you live or work: *An early memory was of the family's move from sunny Sydney to cold, rainy Melbourne.* **4** [usually sing.] a change of place or position: *This happens each time the ion makes a move in a solution.* ➲ *see also* MOVEMENT

IDM **be on the ˈmove 1** to be travelling from place to place: *The nature of their job meant that medieval bishops were always on the move.* **2** to be making progress: *The economy was on the move at last.* **make the first ˈmove** to do sth before sb else, for example in order to end an argument or to begin sth: *The armies remained encamped opposite each other, each waiting for the other to make the first move.* **make a, your, etc. ˈmove** to do the action that you intend to do or need to do in order to achieve sth: *At this point Bismarck made a move.*

move·ment /ˈmuːvmənt/ *noun* **1** [C, U] an act of moving the body or part of the body: *There will be pain and restricted movement in the toes.* ◇ *Participants read sentences while having their eye movements tracked.* ◇ **~ of sb/sth** *The movement of the abdomen indicates the rate of breathing.* ◇ *A tiny on-board computer controls the movement of the robotic arm.* **2** [C, U] an act of moving from one place to another or of moving sth from one place to another: *Temporary population movements have a considerable effect on the distribution of population.* ◇ **~ of sb/sth** *An efficient transport system is vital for the free movement of goods and people.* ◇ **+ adv./prep.** *That sample of DNA could allow us to track whale movements across the globe.* ◇ *The Roman system focused specifically on facilitating rapid movement between London and the key Roman centres.* **3** [C] a group of people who share the same ideas or aims: *This was the era that witnessed the rise of the civil rights movement in America.* ◇ *New social movements emerged: women's rights, environmentalism, the anti-apartheid movement.* **4** [sing.] **~ (away from sth) (towards sth)** a gradual change in what people in society do or think SYN TREND: *There has been a movement away from a traditional, hierarchical structure in which employees have rigid, narrowly defined roles.* ◇ *The movement towards free trade can be interpreted as serving the interests of the major economic powers.* **5 movements (of sb)** [pl.] a person's activities over a period of time, especially as watched by sb else: *Networks of CCTV cameras can monitor the movements of specific individuals.* **6** [U] **~ (in sth)** progress, especially in a particular task: *There was finally some movement in this case when new evidence emerged.* **7** [U, C] **~ (in sth)** a change in amount: *Private financial institutions are able to force some movement in relative currency prices.* ◇ *A change in the money supply, however, results in an equal movement in the exchange rate.*

movie /ˈmuːvi/ *noun* (*especially NAmE*) **1** [C] = FILM¹ (1) **2 the movies** [pl.] = CINEMA (2) **3 the movies** [pl.] = CINEMA (3)

MP /ˌem ˈpiː/ *noun* the abbreviation for **'Member of Parliament'** (a person who has been elected to represent the people of a particular area in a parliament): *Tony Blair was elected an MP in 1983.* ◇ *Conservative/Labour MPs* ◇ **~ for...** *Jon Cruddas, the MP for Dagenham, expressed concerns about the impacts of immigration.*

MRI /ˌem ɑːr ˈaɪ/ *abbr.* (*medical*) **magnetic resonance imaging** (a method of using a strong MAGNETIC FIELD to produce an image of the inside of a person's body): **+ noun** *An MRI scan is the most useful test for confirming the diagnosis of multiple sclerosis.*

much¹ /mʌtʃ/ *det., pron.* used with uncountable nouns, especially in negative sentences to mean 'a large amount of sth': *The topic has not received much research attention.* ◇ *Profitability refers to how much profit is derived from a labour process.* ◇ **too ~** *It is desirable to split the roles of chair and CEO so that there is not too much power invested in one individual.* ◇ **so ~** *Teachers are often still unsure about using up so much class time on the project.* ◇ **as ~ (sth) as...** *The marketing audit is a systematic attempt to gather as much information as possible about the organization.* ◇ *Neglect is as much a form of abuse as a violent act.* ◇ **~ (of sth)** *Much of the time is spent on investigating complaints.* ◇ *The government did not do much to try and stop the practice.*

IDM **ˈnot much of a...** not a good...: *Wittgenstein was not much of a patriot.* **ˈthis much** used to introduce sth positive or definite: *This much of what Searle says is quite correct.*

much² /mʌtʃ/ *adv.* (**more, most**) to a great degree: *Currently, energy use is much higher in the more developed world than it is in the less developed world.* ◇ **so ~** *Developing oral skills is so much more than merely speaking and listening.* ◇ **very ~** *In many ways, the Korean and the US higher education systems are very much alike.* ◇ **~ too** *Much too little was known at the time to discard any of these hypotheses.* ◇ **~ the same (sth) as...** *Human geography can be studied in much the same way as any other science.*

IDM **ˈmuch as** although: *His thought begins to move in an Aristotelean direction, much as he might hate to admit it.*

mucus /ˈmjuːkəs/ *noun* [U] a thick liquid that is produced in parts of the body, such as the nose: *In this condition, the lungs produce too much mucus, clogging the airways and making it hard to breathe.* ■ **mu·cous** /ˈmjuːkəs/ *adj.*: *Poisons can enter the body by contact with skin or mucous membranes.*

mud /mʌd/ *noun* [U] wet earth that is soft and sticky: *Eventually, huge volumes of mud and water enter nearby rivers.*

multi·cel·lu·lar /ˌmʌltiˈseljələ(r)/ *adj.* [usually before noun] (*biology*) (of a living thing) having many cells: *Multicellular organisms contain many specialized cell types, which alone or in combination create multiple physiological systems.* ➲ *compare* UNICELLULAR

multi·cul·tural /ˌmʌltiˈkʌltʃərəl/ *adj.* for or including people of several different races, religions, languages and traditions: *The United States is a multicultural society composed of people from a variety of backgrounds.* ◇ *Britain has become increasingly multicultural.* ◇ *Just a few studies exist that show the effects of multicultural education.*

multi·cul·tural·ism /ˌmʌltiˈkʌltʃərəlɪzəm/ *noun* [U] the practice of giving importance to all cultures in a society: *Kobayashi (1993) and Hutcheon (1994) describe the official policy of multiculturalism in Canada.* ◇ *Miller distinguishes between multiculturalism as policy and multiculturalism as ideology.*

multi·di·men·sion·al AWL /ˌmʌltidaɪˈmenʃənl; ˌmʌltidɪˈmenʃənl/ *adj.* having several DIMENSIONS: *Research on age stereotypes suggests that views of older persons are complex and multidimensional.* ◇ *These results strongly indicate the value of taking a more multidimensional approach to the assessment of parenting behaviours.*

multi·dis·cip·lin·ary /ˌmʌltidɪsəˈplɪnəri; *NAmE* ˌmʌltiˈdɪsəpləneri/ *adj.* involving several different academic subjects or the work of several different professions: *Cancer care should be offered by a multidisciplinary team.* ◇ *The approach is multidisciplinary, making use of examples from history, anthropology and economics.*

multi·lat·eral /ˌmʌltiˈlætərəl/ *adj.* **1** in which three or more groups, nations, etc. take part: *The WTO launched a new round of multilateral trade negotiations.* **2** agreed on by three or more groups, nations, etc: *By the year 2000, there were over 130 multilateral environmental agreements.* **3** having members from several groups, especially several countries: *The WHO is the leading multilateral health institution.* ⊃ *compare* BILATERAL, UNILATERAL

multi·level /ˈmʌltɪlevl/ *adj.* [usually before noun] involving many levels: *Data are analysed using multilevel logistic models.*

multi·media /ˌmʌltiˈmiːdiə/ *adj.* [only before noun] **1** (in computing) using sound, pictures and film in addition to text on a screen: *The Internet allows also allows for the display of multimedia content.* **2** (in teaching and art) using several different ways of giving information or several different materials: *The project set out to generate a multimedia narrative involving stories, poetry, music, illustrations and textiles.* ■ **multi·media** *noun* [U] *The Internet and digital multimedia have driven the evolution of the PC.*

multi·nation·al[1] /ˌmʌltiˈnæʃnəl/ *adj.* **1** including or involving several countries, or people from several countries: *Protection could be assured only with the help of multinational troops.* ◇ *Grubert and Mutti studied US multinational activity in 33 countries.* **2** (of a business organization) operating in several countries: *The multinational corporations of advanced countries may locate new plants in poorer countries.* ◇ *a multinational company/enterprise/firm*

multi·nation·al[2] /ˌmʌltiˈnæʃnəl/ *noun* a company that operates in several different countries, especially a large and powerful company: *Lever Brothers Ltd. had become one of the largest multinationals in the world.* ⊃ thesaurus note *at* COMPANY

mul·tiple[1] /ˈmʌltɪpl/ *adj.* [only before noun] **1** many in number: *The size of glaciers is controlled by multiple factors, including temperature, precipitation and slope.* ◇ *An organism often has multiple copies of a particular gene with identical or related functions.* ◇ *The project was beneficial in helping the American students understand civil rights from multiple perspectives.* **2** involving several people, things or parts: *Women who had multiple births were more likely to suffer from depression.* ◇ *The veil has always had multiple significance for women.*

mul·tiple[2] /ˈmʌltɪpl/ *noun* a quantity that contains another quantity an exact number of times: *The Greeks and Romans made frequent use of three and its multiples.* ◇ **~ of sth** *75 is an exact multiple of 25.*

multi·pli·ca·tion /ˌmʌltɪplɪˈkeɪʃn/ *noun* [U] **1** the act or process of multiplying one number by another: *Some high-speed computers perform multiplication in a single operation.* ◇ **~ (of sth) by sth** *An arithmetic shift left is equivalent to multiplication by 2.* OPP DIVISION (2) **2** the process of increasing very much in number or amount: *Growth can occur by cell multiplication.* ◇ **~ of sth** *the further multiplication of the human species*

multi·pli·city /ˌmʌltɪˈplɪsəti/ *noun* (-ies) [usually sing.] **~ of sth** a great number and variety of sth: *Everyone's livelihood requires a multiplicity of goods and services supplied by others.*

multi·plier /ˈmʌltɪplaɪə(r)/ *noun* **1** a number by which another number is multiplied: *The quantities 1, 2 and k are adjustable constants, called undetermined multipliers.* **2** (*economics*) a factor that relates an INITIAL change in spending to the total change in activity that will result: *The output multiplier is the amount of additional output that results from a $1 change in aggregate demand.* ◇ **+ noun** *The multiplier effect explains how an initial increase in the planned injections into the economy increases national income by more than the initial amount of injection.*

multi·ply /ˈmʌltɪplaɪ/ *verb* (**multi·plies, multi·ply·ing, multi·plied, multi·plied**) **1** [T, I] to add a number to itself a particular number of times: **~ (A) by B** *Total sales is equal to the total number of units produced, multiplied by the price per unit.* ◇ *He divided the total expected deaths by the population, then multiplied by 1 000.* ◇ **~ A and B (together)** *A teacher may provide a child with verbal instructions for multiplying two numbers together.* **2** [I, T] to increase very much in number or amount; to make sth increase in this way: *The number of people wounded in industrial accidents multiplied like casualties on a battlefield.* ◇ **~ sth** *Ambrose paid for scribes who multiplied copies of his works.* **3** [I] (of an animal or other living thing) to increase in numbers by producing young animals or copies of itself: *The virus might then multiply and kill its host.*

multi·tude /ˈmʌltɪtjuːd; *NAmE* ˈmʌltɪtuːd/ *noun* (*formal*) **1** [C] **~ (of sth/sb)** an extremely large number of things or people: *The effectiveness of the training often depends on a multitude of factors.* ◇ *Singling out particular authors for attention, while excluding the work of a multitude of others, is clearly unfair.* **2 the multitude** [sing.+ sing./pl. v.] (*also* **the multi·tudes** [pl.]) (*sometimes disapproving*) the mass of ordinary people: *This fact raises important questions about the power of the multitude in India's democracy.*

multi·vari·ate /ˌmʌltɪˈveəriət; *NAmE* ˌmʌltɪˈveriət/ *adj.* [only before noun] (*statistics*) involving or depending on two or more VARIABLES: *In the final stage, multivariate analyses were conducted.* ⊃ *compare* BIVARIATE, UNIVARIATE

mu·ni·ci·pal /mjuːˈnɪsɪpl/ *adj.* [usually before noun] connected with or belonging to a town, city or district that has its own local government: *Local municipal governments play a major role in the form and functioning of cities today.* ◇ *Policies at a municipal level were not always coordinated with policies at the neighbourhood level.* ◇ *The site had been used as a chemical and municipal waste disposal site.*

mu·ni·ci·pal·ity /mjuːˌnɪsɪˈpæləti/ *noun* (*pl.* **-ies**) a town, city or district with its own local government; the group of officials who govern it: *Local municipalities are called cities, towns or townships.* ◇ *A recent report highlighted the deteriorating financial situation of municipalities across Canada.*

mur·der[1] /ˈmɜːdə(r); *NAmE* ˈmɜːrdər/ *noun* [U, C] the crime of killing sb deliberately: *Both defendants were convicted of attempted murder.* ◇ **~ of sb** *She witnesses Clytemnestra's brutal murder of Agamemnon.* ◇ *The rebels were responsible for the mass murder of 400 civilians.* ⊃ *compare* HOMICIDE, MANSLAUGHTER

mur·der[2] /ˈmɜːdə(r); *NAmE* ˈmɜːrdər/ *verb* **~ sb** to kill sb deliberately and illegally: *He was brutally murdered by his long-term companion.*

mur·der·er /ˈmɜːdərə(r); *NAmE* ˈmɜːrdərər/ *noun* a person who has killed sb deliberately and illegally SYN KILLER: *Polling data show that a substantial majority of Americans support capital punishment for convicted murderers.*

muscle /ˈmʌsl/ *noun* **1** [C, U] a piece of body TISSUE that you contract and relax in order to move a particular part

M

of the body; the TISSUE that forms the muscles of the body: *the jaw/abdominal/facial muscles* ◇ *Some of the cells make muscle or bone.* ◇ **+ noun** *Muscle relaxants were used to counter the spasms.* **2** [U] the power and influence to make others do what you want: *The unions wanted to use their industrial muscle through the general strike.*

mus·cu·lar /ˈmʌskjələ(r)/ *adj.* **1** connected with the muscles: *These muscular contractions cause severe pain.* ◇ *muscular strength/weakness* **2** having large strong muscles: *In Western contemporary cultures, the ideal male body is tall, muscular and agile.*

mu·seum /mjuˈziːəm/ *noun* a building in which objects of cultural, historical or scientific interest are kept and shown to the public: *Since opening in July 2002, the museum has attracted over 5 million visitors.* ◇ **~ of sth** *In 1998 the painting was lent to New York's Museum of Modern Art.* ◇ **+ noun** *a museum exhibit/collection*

mush·room /ˈmʌʃrʊm; ˈmʌʃruːm/ *noun* a FUNGUS with a round flat head and short STEM. Many mushrooms can be eaten: *The collection and cultivation of edible mushrooms has a long history.*

music /ˈmjuːzɪk/ *noun* [U] **1** sounds that are arranged in a way that is pleasant or exciting to listen to. People sing music or play it on instruments: *popular/folk/classical/world music* ◇ *Listening to or playing music gave the girls pleasure.* ◇ **a piece of ~** *He commissioned a special piece of music for the occasion.* ◇ **set sth to ~** *The poem was set to music by Henry Lawes.* **2** the art of writing or playing music: *He began to study music more formally.* ◇ **+ noun** *The music industry has experienced a rapid growth in downloading.* **3** the written or printed signs that represent the sounds to be played or sung in a piece of music: *He had to learn to read music before he could fulfil his dream of conducting a Mahler symphony.* **4** a book or piece of paper with musical notes printed on it: *There were display cases in which the music itself was gathered.*

mu·sic·al /ˈmjuːzɪkl/ *adj.* **1** [only before noun] connected with music; containing music: *By the end of the nineteenth century, German musical styles dominated much of Europe.* **2** (of a person) with a natural skill or interest in music: *She is very musical and loves sport.*

ˌmusical ˈinstrument (*also* **in·stru·ment**) *noun* an object used for producing musical sounds: *They played a wide range of musical instruments, from fiddles to horns and percussion.*

mu·si·cian /mjuˈzɪʃn/ *noun* a person who plays a musical instrument or writes music, especially as a job: *Employment and job security for professional musicians can be scarce.*

Mus·lim /ˈmʊzlɪm; ˈmʌzlɪm; ˈmʊzləm; ˈmʌzləm/ *noun* a person whose religion is Islam: *Muslims are proud that Islam is the fastest growing religion in the West.* ■ **Mus·lim** *adj.*: *Muslim communities*

must /məst; *strong form* mʌst/ *modal verb* (*negative* **must not**, *short form* **mustn't** /ˈmʌsnt/) HELP Unless you are quoting, the short form **mustn't** should not be used in academic writing. **1** used to say that sth is necessary or very important (sometimes involving a rule or law): *Each applicant must show a proficiency in speaking English.* ◇ *Pain relief must not be forgotten.* ◇ *Buyers must assume that sellers own the items they are offering.* ◇ *It must be emphasized that these studies are limited by a low number of subjects.* **2** used to say that sth is likely or logical: *The translations must have been made by scholars educated in both languages.* ◇ *If business owners spend their money on investment, it must be because they expect to benefit more from this activity than from other uses of their funds.* ➲ grammar note *at* MODAL[1]

GRAMMAR POINT

must ♦ have to

- These verbs may each be used to express obligation. They are both followed by the infinitive without *to*. **Must** is used especially when the obligation comes from a rule, law or other authority; **have to** is used especially when the obligation comes from circumstances that make sth necessary: *All contracts* ***must satisfy*** *certain legal requirements if they are to be valid.* ◇ *All states* ***have to collect*** *taxes.*
- **Must not** means 'is not permitted'. To say that sth is not obligatory, use **do not have to**: *Liberty* ***must not*** *be sacrificed for economy gain.* ◇ *There is an annual threshold below which capital gains tax* ***does not have to*** *be paid.*
- To express obligation in the past, use **had to**: *Companies* ***had to comply*** *with the requirements in the contract.* ◇ *Power plants built between 1970 and 1978* ***had to meet*** *a standard for particle emissions of...*

mu·tant[1] /ˈmjuːtənt/ *adj.* (of a living thing) different in some way from others of the same kind because of a change in its GENETIC structure: *The cultures would be expected to show similar numbers of mutant cells.* ◇ *The aberrant features of each mutant strain could be hereditarily transmitted over many generations.*

mu·tant[2] /ˈmjuːtənt/ *noun* a living thing with qualities that are different from its parents' qualities because of a change in its GENETIC structure: *Genetic analysis that begins by finding mutants is an extremely powerful first step for nearly any biological problem.*

mu·tate /mjuːˈteɪt; *NAmE* ˈmjuːteɪt/ *verb* **1** [I, T] to develop or make sth develop a new form or structure, because of a GENETIC change: *Parasites and viruses mutate regularly.* ◇ **~ into sth** *There is much concern about influenza mutating into a pandemic form.* ◇ **~ sth** *The next critical step is to identify which gene has been mutated.* **2** [I] **~ (into sth)** to change into a new form: *What started as a threat to one bank was allowed to mutate into a threat to the international financial system.* ➲ *see also* MUTATION

mu·ta·tion /mjuːˈteɪʃn/ *noun* [U, C] **1** a process in which the GENETIC material of a person, a plant or an animal changes in structure when it is passed on to children, etc, causing different physical characteristics to develop; a change of this kind: *The types of changes generated by mutation are not entirely random.* ◇ *Not all individuals carrying these mutations develop cancer during their lifetime.* ◇ *to detect/identify/find a mutation* ◇ **~ of sth** *Cancer is often attributed to mutation of cells that affect the cell cycle.* **2** a change in the form or structure of sth: *His book illustrates some of the mutations the twenty-first-century novel has undergone.* ◇ **~ of sth** *Glass's music is characterized by the mutation of repeated musical phrases by means of the addition of extra notes.*

mu·tual AWL /ˈmjuːtʃuəl/ *adj.* **1** used to describe feelings that two or more people have for each other equally, or actions that affect two or more people or things equally: *Mutual suspicion, rather than mutual trust, was too often the norm.* ◇ *The classroom climate is built on mutual respect and cooperation.* ◇ *mutual understanding/recognition/support/aid* ◇ *The principles could be altered by mutual agreement or unilateral notification.* **2** [only before noun] shared by two or more people: *They have mutual obligations in relation to the child.* ◇ *By working with Ministries of Education in other countries, joint programmes of mutual benefit can be created.* ■ **mu·tu·al·ity** /ˌmjuːtʃuˈæləti/ *noun* [U, sing.] (*formal*) *The term 'interdependence' implies a certain mutuality in terms of meeting the practical interests of different groups.*

M

mu·tu·al·ly AWL /ˈmjuːtʃuəli/ *adv.* done equally by two or more people or things: *Sharing of data would be on mutually agreed terms.* ◇ *Markets and hierarchies are mutually reinforcing elements in the capitalist profit-making process.* HELP If two ideas, states or things are **mutually exclusive** or **mutually incompatible**, they cannot both be true or exist at the same time or be used together: *The two perspectives are by no means mutually exclusive.* ◇ *Several mutually incompatible technologies were developed simultaneously, forcing consumers to select a particular system.*

my /maɪ/ *det.* (the possessive form of *I*) of or belonging to the speaker or writer: *I had never experienced anything like that in my life.* ◇ *My second example concerns the emission of greenhouse gases.*

my·self /maɪˈself/ *pron.* **1** (the reflexive form of *I*) used when the speaker or writer is also the person affected by an action: *I found myself becoming increasingly isolated.* ◇ *The statement, 'Most days I feel extremely good about myself,' reflects strongly positive well-being.* **2** used to emphasize the fact that the speaker is doing sth: *I would either test him in English myself or refer him to a Spanish psychologist.* ◇ *Sometimes such a machine is described as having free will (though I would not use this phrase myself).*
IDM **by myˈself** **1** alone; without anyone else: *I spend a lot of time reading by myself.* **2** without help: *'How am I meant to do everything by myself?' one wife complained.*

mys·teri·ous /mɪˈstɪəriəs; *NAmE* mɪˈstɪriəs/ *adj.* **1** difficult or impossible to understand or explain; strange: *The novel was evidently to be centred on the mysterious disappearance of its title character.* **2** (especially of people) strange and interesting because you do not know much about them: *It is a melodramatic tale of the doomed love of a mysterious woman and a runaway monk.* ■ **mys·teri·ous·ly** *adv.*: *Upon his release from prison, Dhakiyarr mysteriously disappeared.*

mys·tery /ˈmɪstri/ *noun* (*pl.* **-ies**) **1** [C] something that is difficult or impossible to understand or to explain: *The reasons for these omissions remain a mystery.* **2** [U] the quality of being difficult or impossible to understand or to explain, especially when this makes sb/sth seem interesting and exciting: *He is immediately fascinated by her air of mystery.* ◇ *The culture of early Japanese society has always been shrouded in mystery.* **3** [C] a story, film or play in which crimes and strange events are only explained at the end: *'The Golden Bough' begins like a good mystery.* ◇ **+ noun** *The mystery story 'The Strange Case of Dr Jekyll and Mr Hyde' stands apart from the rest of his fiction.* **4 mysteries** [pl.] **~ (of sth)** the skills or knowledge needed for a particular activity and regarded as too difficult to understand for those without such skills or knowledge: *Marx believed the working classes had the duty to master for themselves the mysteries of international politics.* **5** [C] **~ (of sb/sth)** a religious belief that cannot be explained or proved in a scientific way: *Isaiah describes the mysteries of Christ clearly in his prophecies.*

myth /mɪθ/ *noun* [C, U] **1** a story from ancient times, especially one that was told to explain natural events or to describe the early history of a people; this type of story SYN LEGEND (1): *The theme of transformation is a frequent feature of Greek myths.* ◇ *Jung applied psychoanalysis to the study of myth, folklore and fairy tales.* ◇ **~ of sb/sth** *He uses the myth of Iphigenia as a vehicle through which to discuss Argentine national identity.* **2** something that many people believe but that does not exist or is false: *Scientific research is finally dispelling three long-standing myths about human evolution.* ◇ *Contrary to popular myth, medieval people were not particularly superstitious.* ◇ **~ of sth** *Poetic forgeries, such as that of Thomas Chatterton, challenged the myth of original poetic genius.*

myth·ic·al /ˈmɪθɪkl/ (*also less frequent* **myth·ic** /ˈmɪθɪk/) *adj.* [usually before noun] **1** existing only in ancient myths: *Classical literature provided a fund of historical and mythical figures.* **2** not existing or not true; IDEALIZED, especially with reference to the past: *They look back to the mythical age of contentment and social order before the war.*

mytho·logic·al /ˌmɪθəˈlɒdʒɪkl; *NAmE* ˌmɪθəˈlɑːdʒɪkl/ *adj.* [usually before noun] connected with ancient myths: *The tree of life is one of the oldest of all mythological symbols.* ◇ *The Midas legends belong to a later period than that in which most mythological narratives are set.*

myth·ology /mɪˈθɒlədʒi; *NAmE* mɪˈθɑːlədʒi/ *noun* (*pl.* **-ies**) [U, C] **1** ancient myths in general; the ancient myths of a particular culture, society, etc: *Most works on classical mythology focus their attention on the stories.* ◇ **~ of sb/sth** *The legend of Atlantis occurs in the mythologies of many parts of Europe.* **2 ~ (of sth)** ideas that many people think are true but are in fact false: *The popular mythology of prohibition involves formerly law-abiding adults becoming flagrant lawbreakers.*

Nn

naive (*also* **naïve**) /naɪˈiːv/ *adj.* **1** (*disapproving*) lacking experience of life, knowledge or good judgement: *With my fellow students of the 1960s, I shared the naive view that we could revolutionize the world.* ◇ **~ to think/believe, etc. (that...)** *It would be naive to think that this could never happen again.* **2** (*approving*) (of people and their behaviour) simple and lacking experience of life: *In this version of the fairy tale, the heroine is naive, helpless and pretty.* ➲ *compare* SOPHISTICATED (3) ■ **naive·ly** (*also* **naïve·ly**) *adv.*: *It was naively assumed that free markets would take over where communism had left.* **naiv·ety** (*also* **naïv·ety**) /naɪˈiːvəti/ *noun* [U] *Many instances have been pointed out of the Tsar's political naivety.*

N

naked /ˈneɪkɪd/ *adj.* **1** not wearing any clothes: *Children usually ran about quite naked until they were ten years old.* ➲ *compare* BARE (2) **2** [usually before noun] without the usual covering SYN BARE (2): *The room is lit by a single naked bulb.* **3** (of emotions, attitudes, etc.) expressed strongly and not hidden: *The play is haunted by the notion that, beneath the surface, politics is a matter of naked self-interest.*
IDM **the naked ˈeye** the normal power of your eyes without the help of an instrument: *This microorganism is not usually visible to the naked eye.*

name[1] /neɪm/ *noun* **1** a word or words that a particular person, animal, place or thing is known by: *The young man's name was Max Planck.* ◇ **~ of sb/sth** *The names of firms violating environmental regulations were published.* ◇ **~ for sb/sth** *The Common Market was the popular name for the European Economic Community.* ◇ **~ and address** *It uses a database of customers' names and addresses built up through previous orders.* ◇ **change your ~** *These women married in their early twenties and changed their names.* ◇ **as the ~ implies/suggests** *White dwarfs, as the name implies, emit white light.* ➲ *see also* BRAND NAME, DOMAIN NAME **2** [usually sing.] a reputation that sb/sth has; the opinion that people have about sb/sth: *Shakespeare's father lost his business and his good name.* ◇ **make your ~ (as sth)** *He made his name in television by exporting British series to the United States.* ◇ **make a ~ for yourself (as sth)** *Huang Fu had made a name for himself as a diplomat at the Washington Conference.* ◇ **give sb/sth a bad ~** *These tactics have given the industry a bad name.* **3** a famous person: *Big names such as these draw big audiences.*

IDM **by ˈname** using the name of sb/sth: *In olden days, the village blacksmith would most probably know all of his customers by name.* **by the name of...** who is called: *One of the others was an obscure Russian physicist by the name of Alexander Friedmann.* **give your ˈname to sth** to invent, discover or be the source of sth that then becomes known by your name: *Thatcher gave her name to a political doctrine and a distinctive political style.* **go by the name of...** to be known or called by a particular name: *Those social processes go by the name of globalization.* **in ˌall but ˈname** used to describe a situation that exists in reality but is not officially recognized: *By 1930 Manchuria had become a colony in all but name.* **in the name of ˈsb/ˈsth | in sb's/sth's ˈname** **1** for sb; showing that sth officially belongs to sb: *The computer program creates a record of a reservation in the name of a particular passenger on a particular flight.* **2** using the authority of sb/sth; as a representative of sb/sth: *A priest speaks in the name of a god in whom he believes.* **3** used to give a reason or an excuse for doing sth, often when what you are doing is wrong: *His essay attacks the burning of books carried out in the name of religion.* **in ˈname only** officially recognized but not really existing: *By the thirteenth century, it was an empire in name only.* **under the name (of)...** using a particular name: *Mary Ann Evans published her novels under the name 'George Eliot' in order to conceal her true identity.* ➲ *more at* LEND

name² /neɪm/ *verb* **1** to give a name to sb/sth SYN CALL¹ (1): **~ sb/sth (after/for sb)** *The unit of electric charge, the coulomb, is named after him.* ◇ *Project 2061 was named for the year when Halley's comet will return.* ◇ **~ sb/sth + noun** *His father named his first son Eugene.* **2** to state the name of sb/sth SYN IDENTIFY (2): **~ sb/sth** *Participants were asked to name people in their social networks to whom they felt close.* ◇ *Such patients have difficulty in naming objects, despite being aware of what they are.* ◇ **~ sb/sth as sb/sth** *She was named in the will as a beneficiary.* **3 ~ sth** to state sth exactly SYN SPECIFY: *They hoped to avoid bargaining by forcing them to name a fair price at the outset.* **4 ~ sb (as) sth** to choose sb for a job or position SYN NOMINATE (2): *President Reagan named Stockman as head of the Office of Management and Budget.*

name·ly /ˈneɪmli/ *adv.* used to introduce more detailed information about sth that has just been mentioned: *The study looks at health expenditure in five countries of south-eastern Europe, namely Albania, Bosnia and Herzegovina, Montenegro, Serbia and Kosovo.*

nar·rate /nəˈreɪt; *NAmE also* ˈnæreɪt/ *verb* **1 ~ sth** to give a spoken or written report of sth; to tell a story SYN RELATE (2): *The story is narrated by an old Turkish fisherman.* **2 ~ sth** to provide a spoken description to accompany a film, programme, piece of music, etc: *Patrick Keiller's 1993 film, 'London', is narrated by Paul Scofield.*

nar·ra·tion /nəˈreɪʃn; næˈreɪʃn/ *noun* **1** [U, C] the act or process of telling a story, especially in a novel, film or play: *The novel constantly switches between first-person and third-person narration.* **2** [C] a description of events that is spoken during sth such as a television programme, film or play: *The film mixes documentary images and sound with a fictional narration.*

nar·ra·tive¹ /ˈnærətɪv/ *noun* **1** [C] a description of events, especially in a novel SYN STORY (1): *Her novel is a first-person narrative describing the worlds of a university-educated woman and her married sister.* ◇ **~ of sth** *The book provides a solid narrative of the events that led to the fall of the German Democratic Republic.* **2** [U] the act, process or skill of telling a story: *The use of narrative in history is a well-established way to describe and explain change over time.* **3** [U] the part of a work of literature that is narrated, as opposed to DIALOGUE: *The dialogue and narrative clearly owe a great deal to Hemingway.* **4** [C] a way of presenting a particular situation or process so that it makes clear or follows a set of aims or values: **~ about sth** *Owen and Fry have constructed a broader narrative about welfare and modernity.* ◇ **~ of sth** *This investigation reveals the range of competing narratives of national identity.*

nar·ra·tive² /ˈnærətɪv/ *adj.* [only before noun] connected with the act, process or skill of telling a story: *Boyd's film draws upon the narrative structure of Shakespeare's play.* ◇ *The romantic narrative poem is given a new dimension in Shelley's longest poem, 'The Revolt of Islam'.* ◇ *The female narrative voice and point of view give a strong sense of Elizabeth as subject, not as object.*

nar·ra·tor /nəˈreɪtə(r)/ *noun* **1** a person who tells a story, especially in a book, poem, etc: *Browning's poem has a first-person narrator.* ◇ **~ of sth** *Mary Shelley makes Walton, the narrator of 'Frankenstein', an Arctic explorer.* **2** a person who provides a spoken description to accompany a film, programme, piece of music, etc: *As the camera closes in, the narrator describes the scene.*

> **WHICH WORD?**
>
> **narrow • thin**
>
> - **Narrow** describes sth that is a short distance across from one side to the other: *a narrow band/strip/beam/gap/street/valley*
> - **Thin** describes sth that has a short distance through it from one side or surface to the other: *a thin layer/sheet/film/shell/slice/coating/crust/membrane*
> - **Narrow** and **thin** are both used with the meaning 'limited'. However, **narrow** suggests a deliberate choice or decision, while **thin** means 'so limited that it is not enough': *a narrow conception/definition/focus/interpretation/sense/view* ◇ *The account is very thin on details of what the move from one stage to the next actually entails.*

nar·row¹ /ˈnærəʊ; *NAmE* ˈnæroʊ/ *adj.* (**nar·row·er, nar·row·est**) **1** measuring a short distance from one side to the other, especially in relation to length: *A series of filters produces narrow bands of light.* ◇ *The area is characterized by steep mountains and narrow valleys.* OPP BROAD (1), WIDE (6) **2** limited in extent, amount or variety SYN RESTRICTED (1): *Consumers have only a narrow range of choices.* ◇ *The major drawback of these studies has been the narrow focus on a single disaster.* ◇ *The research presented here is narrower in scope.* OPP WIDE (1) **3** limited in range and unwilling or unable to accept opinions that are different from yours: *Some conservative researchers have narrow views about what constitutes 'real' educational research.* OPP BROAD (2) **4** strict in meaning: *Some people object to the narrow sense in which Chomsky uses the term 'language'.* OPP BROAD (3) **5** [usually before noun] only just achieved: *Muskie won by a surprisingly narrow margin in New Hampshire.* ◇ *The result was a narrow majority in favour of devolution.* ■ **nar·row·ness** /ˈnærəʊnəs; *NAmE* ˈnæroʊnəs/ *noun* [U] **~ (of sth)** *The very narrowness of the Channel meant that only short voyages were necessary.* ◇ *Those teaching in higher education have deplored for years the narrowness of these syllabuses.* OPP BREADTH

nar·row² /ˈnærəʊ; *NAmE* ˈnæroʊ/ *verb* [I, T] **1** to become or make sth more limited in extent, amount or variety: **~ (to sth)** *Although men are still more likely than women to smoke cigarettes, the gap has narrowed.* ◇ **~ sth** *Such a policy could still narrow the gap between rich and poor.* ◇ *to narrow the scope/range of sth* ◇ **~ sth to sth** *The initial review of published data led researchers to narrow their focus to a sample of 27 countries.* **2** to become or make sth less wide: **~ to sth** *Here the channel narrows to 30 feet in width.* ◇ **~ sth (to sth)** *As the vessels are narrowed, the bowel does not get sufficient blood.*

PHR V **ˌnarrow sth ˈdown (to sth)** to reduce the number of possibilities or choices: *The cause of the patient's asthma has been narrowed down to 20 possible compounds.*

nar·row·ly /ˈnærəʊli; *NAmE* ˈnæroʊli/ *adv.* **1** in a way that is limited: *It is a traditional structure in which employees have rigid, narrowly defined roles.* ◇ *Sociological liberalism rejects this view as too narrowly focused and one-sided.* **2** only by a small amount: *He narrowly escaped arrest and had to live in exile for the rest of his life.*

na·tion /ˈneɪʃn/ *noun* **1** [C] a country considered as a group of people with the same language, culture and history, who live in a particular area under one government: *For a long period, Ukraine was not an independent nation.* ◇ *Kennedy (1995) suggests that less developed nations are unable to compete fairly on the international scene.* ➲ *see also* NATION STATE ➲ thesaurus note *at* COUNTRY **2** [sing.] all the people in a country SYN POPULATION (1): *The entire nation was transfixed as it witnessed these events on TV.*

▸ ADJECTIVE + NATION **independent • sovereign • modern • developed • advanced • industrialized, industrial • wealthy, rich • major • powerful • developing • poor** *In advanced industrialized nations, regulation pervades the competitive environment (Shaffer, 1995).*

na·tion·al¹ /ˈnæʃnəl/ *adj.* [usually before noun] **1** connected with a particular nation; shared by a whole nation: *The national pension system was restructured.* ◇ *Once a state joins the European Union, national politics and policies tend to become 'Europeanized'.* **2** owned, controlled or paid for by the government: *The IMF demanded the privatization of the national airline.*

▸ NATIONAL + NOUN **government • authority • sovereignty • security • borders, boundaries • unity • interest • politics • policy • legislation, law • programme • system • economy • currency • bank • income • debt** *The absence of an effective national government has been a catastrophe for the country.* ◇ *The sale was declared to be 'not in the national interest'.* | **context • level • standard • guideline • average • survey • origin • identity • culture • curriculum • newspaper** *Human rights proponents in different national contexts have worked together on this issue.* ◇ *The president employed Islam as a source of national identity and legitimacy.*

na·tion·al² /ˈnæʃnəl/ *noun* a citizen of a particular country: *These figures included foreign nationals who made up just under 16 per cent of the population.*

na·tion·al·ism /ˈnæʃnəlɪzəm/ *noun* [U, C] **1** the desire by a group of people who share the same race, culture and language to form an independent country: *In the early nineteenth century, Europe saw the emergence of nationalism in Greece, Germany, Italy and Ireland.* ◇ *These were societies divided by competing nationalisms.* **2** (*sometimes disapproving*) a feeling of love for and pride in your country; a feeling that your country is better than any other: *There is a linkage between ethnocentric nationalism and hateful, violent behaviour.*

na·tion·al·ist¹ /ˈnæʃnəlɪst/ *adj.* [usually before noun] **1** connected with the desire by a group of people who share the same race, culture, language, etc. to form an independent country: *The Gold Coast was one of the first colonies to develop a mass nationalist movement.* ◇ *The nationalist parties favour greater autonomy for their nations, leading to independence in the case of Scotland.* **2** (*sometimes disapproving*) connected with a feeling of love for and pride in your country; connected with a feeling that your country is better than any other: *Nationalist sentiments soared in the mid-1890s when Japan and China fought over Korea.*

na·tion·al·ist² /ˈnæʃnəlɪst/ *noun* **1** a person who wants their country to become independent: *A popular front was formed between nationalists and those communists who supported independence.* ◇ *As a young man he had been an Indian nationalist.* **2** (*sometimes disapproving*) a person who has a great love for and pride in their country; a person who has a feeling that their country is better than any other: *The book showed that the new Prime Minister was an unabashed nationalist.*

na·tion·al·is·tic /ˌnæʃnəˈlɪstɪk/ *adj.* (*usually disapproving*) having very strong feelings of love for and pride in your country, so that you think that it is better than any other: *Nationalistic propaganda became a weapon in the fight for power.*

na·tion·al·ity /ˌnæʃəˈnæləti/ *noun* (*pl.* **-ies**) **1** [U, C] the legal right of belonging to a particular nation: *She holds dual French and British nationality.* ◇ *Commercial success depended on cooperation with other traders regardless of nationality, religion or ethnicity.* ◇ *At Vishwa Niketan, persons of all nationalities learn about Buddhism, inner peace and service to humankind.* **2** [C] a group of people with the same language, culture and history who form part of a political nation: *Our study provides an insight into the behaviours of different nationalities whilst on holiday.*

na·tion·al·ize (*BrE also* **-ise**) /ˈnæʃnəlaɪz/ *verb* **~ sth** to put an industry or a company under the control of the government, which becomes its owner: *In the past, the UK government nationalized many industries, such as coal, trains, airlines, water and gas.* OPP PRIVATIZE ■ **na·tion·al·iza·tion, -isa·tion** /ˌnæʃnəlaɪˈzeɪʃn; *NAmE* ˌnæʃnələˈzeɪʃn/ *noun* [U, C] **~ (of sth)** *A recent presidential decree will permit the nationalization of most loss-making industries.* ◇ *The growth in the welfare state was coupled with a series of nationalizations.*

na·tion·al·ly /ˈnæʃnəli/ *adv.* connected with a country as a whole; connected with a particular country: *Several large-scale, nationally representative studies have confirmed the link.* ◇ *Nationally, research has demonstrated that 79.4% of people agree that Australian police perform their job professionally.* ◇ *These trends in life expectancy have implications locally, nationally and internationally.*

na·tion·hood /ˈneɪʃnhʊd/ *noun* [U] the fact that a place is an independent nation: *The need was to create a shared sense of 'American nationhood' among all citizens and residents.*

ˌnation ˈstate *noun* an independent country in which most of the people share the same culture, language, etc: *Nepal emerged as a nation state in the eighteenth century.* ◇ *The modern nation state has to come to terms with considerable cultural diversity within its borders.*

na·tion·wide /ˌneɪʃnˈwaɪd/ *adj.* happening or existing in all parts of a particular country: *A nationwide survey of children and adolescents was carried out in the Czech Republic in 2001.* ◇ *a nationwide programme/campaign* ■ **na·tion·wide** *adv.*: *It was announced that the strategy would be applied nationwide.*

na·tive¹ /ˈneɪtɪv/ *adj.* **1** (of animals and plants) existing naturally in a place SYN INDIGENOUS: *Some studies suggest that fast-growing tree plantations use more water compared with native vegetation.* ◇ *native species/populations* ◇ **~ to...** *The Jacaranda bug is native to South America.* OPP NON-NATIVE (1) **2** [only before noun] connected with the place where sb was born and lived for the first years of their life: *The children came from families that had fled their native countries to avoid persecution.* ◇ *The campaign was run in the native language of each community.* ➲ *see also* NATIVE SPEAKER **3** [only before noun] (*sometimes offensive*) connected with the people who originally lived

N

in a country before other people, especially white people, came there: *There is suggestive evidence of forest management with fire by native peoples during the Woodland period.* **4** [only before noun] connected with the place where sb has always lived or has lived for a long time: *Victorian London seemed somewhat less daunting to native Londoners than to visitors.*

na·tive² /ˈneɪtɪv/ *noun* **1 ~ (of...)** a person who was born in a particular country or area: *The Roman general Gnaeus Julius Agricola was a native of southern Gaul.* **2** a person who lives in a particular place, especially sb who has lived there a long time: *The reality is that immigrants fill niches left vacant by natives (Abrahamson, 2004).* **3** (*old-fashioned, offensive*) a word used in the past by Europeans to describe a person who lived in a place originally, before white people arrived there: *Justifications for colonialism included the need to 'civilize' the natives, as they were called.* **4** an animal or a plant that lives or grows naturally in a particular area: *This depends on the species' ability to invade and withstand competition from natives.* ◇ **~ of...** *A native of South Africa, Asparagus asparagoides has now become one of the worst weeds in Australia.*

ˌnative ˈspeaker *noun* a person who speaks a language as their first language and has not learned it as a foreign language: *Yang said that his English was probably still not as good as that of a native speaker.* ◇ **~ of sth** *The students were all native speakers of Arabic.*

nat·ural /ˈnætʃrəl/ *adj.* **1** [only before noun] existing in nature; not made or caused by humans: *The migration of thousands of broad-wing hawks is one of the great spectacles of the natural world.* ◇ *Japan is a country with large resource needs but few endowments of natural resources.* ◇ *The twins provided a fascinating natural experiment in human variability.* ➲ *compare* SUPERNATURAL **2** normal; as you would expect: *Hayek claimed there is a natural order in society that governments should not try to change.* ◇ **perfectly ~** *These customs seeem perfectly natural to the islanders themselves.* ◇ **it is ~ (that)...** *It was only natural that the new constitution would represent a complete break with the past.* ◇ **it is ~ to do sth** *Without scientific knowledge, it was only natural to assume that the sun moved around the earth.* HELP If sb dies of **natural causes**, they die of old age or disease rather than violence: *His death occurred somewhat later, apparently due to natural causes.* ➲ *compare* UNNATURAL (1) **3** (of behaviour or an ability) part of the character that a person or an animal was born with: *The natural response of the owl is to turn its head to the source of the sound.* ◇ *They claimed that humans have a natural tendency towards laziness.* ◇ *Some learners believed that natural talent plays the key role in successful language learning.* ◇ **it is ~ (for sb/sth) (to be/do sth)** *It is natural for adolescents to seek acceptance, while also desiring independence.* **4** [only before noun] having an ability that you were born with: *He was a natural leader within his community.* **5** [only before noun] based on a sense of what is right and wrong: *The court held that the Board was in breach of the rules of natural justice.* **6** [only before noun] (of parents or their children) related by blood: *The Court of Appeal ruled that the boy be returned to his natural parents.*

▸ NATURAL + NOUN **world • environment • ecosystem • habitat • forest • vegetation • phenomenon • resource • hazard • disaster • enemy • population • setting • conditions • variation • process • experiment** *There were significantly more reports of flooding than any other natural hazard, except high winds.* ◇ *Several natural enemies of the comb jelly are known.*

ˌnatural diˈsaster *noun* a sudden and violent event in nature (such as an EARTHQUAKE or a flood) that kills a lot of people or causes a lot of damage: *Natural disasters affect agricultural output severely, and most farmers have limited means to cope with them.*

ˌnatural ˈgas *noun* [U] gas that is found under the ground or the sea and that is used as a fuel: *The natural gas extracted from the Sleipner gas fields contains on average 9.5% CO_2 by volume.* ◇ **+ noun** *natural gas markets/pipelines*

ˌnatural ˈhistory *noun* [U, C] **1** the study of plants and animals; a description of the plant and animal life of a particular place: *Darwin gained field experience in geology and natural history from his long voyage.* ◇ *From data gathered on the voyages came natural histories, reports, drawings and collections that celebrated the empirical world.* **2 ~ (of sth)** (*medical*) the usual way in which a disease develops, especially if it is not treated: *There is a need for an appropriate framework for understanding the diverse natural histories of cancers.*

nat·ur·al·ist /ˈnætʃrəlɪst/ *noun* a person who studies animals, plants, birds and other living things: *The early naturalists were not scientists and most simply catalogued and described animal species.*

nat·ur·al·is·tic /ˌnætʃrəˈlɪstɪk/ *adj.* **1** copying the way things are in the natural world: *Their responses were observed in both experimental and naturalistic settings.* ◇ *Not all writers accept the contention that focus groups are more naturalistic than individual interviews.* **2** (of artists, writers or their work) showing things as they appear in the natural world: *Gradually, sculptors moved towards a more naturalistic representation of the human body.*

nat·ur·al·ize (*BrE also* **-ise**) /ˈnætʃrəlaɪz/ *verb* [usually passive] **1** [T, I] **~ (sb)** to make sb who was not born in a particular country a citizen of that country; to become a citizen of another country: *He became a naturalized citizen of the United States in 1941.* ◇ *Policymakers urged immigrants to learn English and to naturalize.* **2** [I] (*biology*) (of a plant or an animal) to start growing or living naturally in a country where it is not NATIVE: *The species naturalized widely or expanded its range to suggest it could cover much of the continent (Humphries et al., 1991).* ◇ *The species has been reported to be a naturalized weed in China, Japan, northern Europe and South America.* ■ **nat·ur·al·iza·tion, -isa·tion** /ˌnætʃrəlaɪˈzeɪʃn; *NAmE* ˌnætʃrələˈzeɪʃn/ *noun* [U] **+ noun** *Language knowledge has been a formal requirement in naturalization law since 1914.* ◇ **~ of sth** *Several studies have shown the high degree of naturalization of introduced species along this coast.*

ˌnatural ˈlanguage *noun* [C, U] a language that has developed in a natural way and is not designed by humans: *The majority of words in a natural language are arbitrary.* ◇ **+ noun** *At the beginning of natural language processing, practical applications were preferred, such as fully automated translation.*

ˌnatural ˈlaw *noun* [U] a set of moral principles on which human behaviour is based: *Some theorists argue that human rights are derived from natural law; they are rights which people enjoy simply by virtue of being human.*

nat·ur·al·ly /ˈnætʃrəli/ *adv.* **1** existing or happening as a normal part of nature, without special help, treatment or action by sb: *Organic farming emphasizes the use of naturally occurring substances for pest management.* ◇ *Differences in languages and customs have arisen naturally as a result of the separation of human groups.* ◇ *Human beings, he observes, tend naturally to form groups.* **2** in a way that you would expect SYN OF COURSE: *There was naturally a range of opinion among those concerned.* ◇ *Being a research subject naturally exposes a person to risk.* **3** as a normal, logical result of sth: *The question naturally arises as to which source is genuine.* **4** in a way that shows or uses abilities or qualities that a person or an animal is born with: *Lenin had a naturally logical way of thinking*

and speaking. ◇ *One elitist argument is that those who get to the top of organizations are naturally gifted.*
IDM **come ˈnaturally (to sb/sth)** if sth **comes naturally** to you, you are able to do it very easily and very well: *She makes the point that childbirth comes naturally to female bodies.*

ˌnatural ˈnumber *noun* (*mathematics*) a positive whole number such as 1, 2 or 3, and sometimes also zero: *The set of natural numbers is denoted by N.*

ˌnatural ˈscience *noun* [C, U] a science concerned with studying the physical world. Chemistry, biology and physics are all natural sciences: *Ethics does not have the same kind of objective status as mathematics and the natural sciences.* ◇ *Natural science was introduced into Western Europe by the Arabs.* ➲ *compare* EARTH SCIENCE, LIFE SCIENCES, PHYSICAL SCIENCE, SOCIAL SCIENCE

ˌnatural seˈlection *noun* [U] the process by which plants, animals, etc. that can adapt to their environment survive and produce young, while the others disappear: *In some circumstances, natural selection favours competitors who stop at nothing in the fight to reproduce.* HELP The theory of **natural selection** was first fully explained by Charles Darwin and it is now thought to be the main process of EVOLUTION. ➲ *compare* SEXUAL SELECTION

na·ture /ˈneɪtʃə(r)/ *noun* **1** (*often* **Nature**) [U] all the plants, animals and things that exist in the universe that are not made by people: *The conventional wisdom is that Aboriginal peoples lived in harmony with nature.* ◇ *All such ethical theories insist that certain aspects of Nature have intrinsic value.* ◇ **in ~** *In nature, the search for a mate can expose females to greater predation risk.* ◇ **+ noun** *For many people, endangered animals such as the rhino embody the ethos of nature conservation.* HELP You cannot use 'the nature' when you are referring to the natural world: *an understanding of nature* ◇ ~~*an understanding of the nature*~~ **2** (*often* **Nature**) [U] the way that things happen in the physical world when it is not controlled by people: *It was decided to let nature take its course and allow the empty site to regenerate naturally.* ◇ **the laws of ~** *Superstring theory is the latest theory that is believed to unite all fundamental laws of nature.* ◇ **the forces of ~** *Humankind has gained an unprecedented degree of control over the forces of nature.* ◇ **in ~** *Descartes denied that a vacuum can exist in nature.* **3** [sing.] the basic character or qualities of sth: **the ~ of sth** *This paper will review research on the nature, extent and function of teenagers' online pretending.* ◇ *Due to the nature of the sample population used in this study, the results should be considered preliminary.* ◇ **in ~** *The statement was political in nature, calling for greater democracy.* ◇ **by ~** *As Schumpeter commented, 'Capitalism is by nature a form or method of economic change.'* **4** [sing.] a type or kind of sth: **of a... ~** *Differences between the standards are mainly of a technical nature.* ◇ *This imposes restrictions upon the ability to pursue research of a purely scientific nature.* **5** [U, C] the usual way that a person or an animal behaves that is part of their character: **by ~** *Just as we are naturally social beings, so too we are by nature rational.* ◇ **in sb's ~** *According to this stereotype, the virtuous wife would foster all that was best in her husband's nature.* ➲ *see also* HUMAN NATURE
IDM **against ˈnature** not natural; not moral: *Traditional natural law theorists argue that suicide is wrong because it is against nature.* **in the nature of ˈsth** similar to sth; a type of sth; in the style of sth: *The gift was in the nature of a trust.* **in the ˈnature of things** as a result of the way life or society normally functions: *It is an interesting historical conjecture, although in the nature of things difficult to prove.* ➲ *more at* FORCE[1]
▸ ADJECTIVE + NATURE **very** • **exact, precise** • **specific** • **true** • **fundamental, essential** • **inherent** • **distinctive** • **unique** *Conflict over the real price of imported inputs is obviously international by its very nature.* | **complex** • **limited** • **arbitrary** • **changing** • **cyclical** • **dynamic** • **diverse** • **dual** • **contingent** • **subjective** • **contested** • **contradictory** • **problematic** *The changing nature of technology is continuously re-shaping society.*
▸ VERB + NATURE **concern** • **explore, examine, consider, discuss** • **explain, clarify** • **illustrate, demonstrate** • **indicate** • **reveal** • **capture** • **reflect** *Various studies have explored the nature of parent-adolescent interactions.* | **understand** • **appreciate** • **acknowledge** • **recognize** • **emphasize, highlight, stress** *Care was taken to ensure that the patient understood the nature and purpose of the treatment.* | **change, alter, transform** • **shape, determine** *It is widely believed that the Internet has changed the nature of both work and leisure.*

naval /ˈneɪvl/ *adj.* connected with the navy of a country: *In the 1880s, Russia was the fifth largest naval power in terms of battleships.* ◇ *Naval officers came, in the main, from the upper-middle class.* ◇ *The United States established a naval base on the north-west coast of Trinidad.*

navy /ˈneɪvi/ *noun* (*pl.* **-ies**) [C+sing./pl. v.] the part of a country's armed forces that fights at sea; the ships that it uses: *The British navy had suppressed piracy on the South China coast, forcing the pirates upstream.* ◇ *The Russian fleet destroyed the Turkish navy at Sinope.* ➲ *see also* NAVAL

NB (*BrE*) (*also* **N.B.** *US, BrE*) /ˌen ˈbiː/ *abbr.* used in writing to make sb take notice of a particular piece of information that is important (from Latin 'nota bene'): *NB There is more than one possible answer to this question.*

near[1] /nɪə(r); *NAmE* nɪr/ *prep.* (*also* **near to**, **near·er (to)**, **near·est (to)**) HELP **Near to** is not usually used before the name of a place, person, festival, etc. **1** at a short distance away from sb/sth: *Major cities are often located near the sea, so they are vulnerable to sea level rises.* ◇ *Precipitation is greatest nearest the coast and decreases inland.* ◇ **~ to sth** *Typically, these items are located very near to the tills in supermarkets.* ◇ *The path of the radar beam moved nearer to the sun.* **2 ~ (to) sth** a short period of time from sth: *Near the end of the Cold War, churches in East Germany promoted freedom from dictatorial rule.* **3** used before a number to mean 'approximately', 'just below or above': *The respondents were near their full retirement age in 2012.* ◇ *For the last 20 years, unemployment was around 1% of the labour force; now it is nearer 8%.* ◇ **~ to sth** *In 1900, the average life expectancy at birth was around 30 years; in developed economies it was nearer to 50 years.* **4** close to a particular state: *He has returned to their farm, old and near death.* ◇ **~ to sth** *One language that is near to extinction is the Dyirbal language of Australia.* ◇ **~ to doing sth** *St. Thomas Becket's tomb in Canterbury was nearest to achieving the status of an international pilgrimage centre.* **5 ~ (to) sb/sth** similar to sb/sth in quality, size, etc: *Of the American States, New York is nearest to England in its laws of divorce.* IDM *see* HAND[1]

near[2] /nɪə(r); *NAmE* nɪr/ *adj.* (**near·er**, **near·est**) **1** a short distance away SYN CLOSE[3] (1): *The moon is a familiar object in our sky because it is our nearest neighbour.* HELP In this meaning, **near** and **nearer** do not usually go before a noun; **nearest** can go either before a noun or after a linking verb. **2** a short time away in the future: *Some Jews had a strong conviction that the end of this world was near.* ◇ **the ~ future** *The company was likely to close in the near future.* **3** (*usually* **nearest**) coming next after sb/sth: *The company has twice the market share of the nearest competitor.* ◇ *US companies invested just over twice as much as their nearest rivals.* **4** (*usually* **nearest**) similar; most similar: *The nearest equivalent to rice cultivation in British America was sugar production in the Caribbean.* ◇ *The state represented the nearest thing to omnipotence human beings could construct.* **5** [only before noun] (no comparative or superlative) close to being sb/sth: *The apparent economic boom was followed by a near* *collapse of the global financial system.* ◇ *This strategy gave the company a near monopoly in its local markets.* **6 ~ relative/relation** used to describe a close family connection: *The application must be made by a mental health professional or the patient's nearest relative.* HELP In biology, **near relative** is used to talk about two species that have a close biological connection: *Homo sapiens sapiens migrated northwards to join their near relatives, the Neanderthals.* ■ **near·ness** *noun* [U] **~ of sth** *Weather and climate are both influenced by the nearness or otherwise of oceanic waters.* ◇ **~ to sth** *Differences in skin colour result from our nearness to or distance from the sun.*

IDM **to the nearest...** followed by a number when counting or measuring approximately: *Height was measured without shoes to the nearest centimetre.* ◇ *The survey sizes in Table 3.3 have been rounded up or down to the nearest thousand.*

near³ /nɪə(r); *NAmE* nɪr/ *adv.* (**near·er, near·est**) **1** at a short distance away: *The observer happened to be standing near and saw every detail.* ◇ *Family members come from near and far to feast and exchange gifts in a celebration that lasts for three days.* **2** a short time away in the future: *Unpopular legislation can have a very damaging effect upon a government, particularly when a general election draws near.* **3** (especially in compounds) almost: *Japanese people had lived a peaceful life of farming and cultivation in near total isolation.*

IDM **as near as** as accurately as: *They fold the paper exactly in half, or as near as they can manage.* **not anywhere near/nowhere near** far from; not at all: *These questions have received a lot of attention in the past, yet are nowhere near being resolved.*

N

near·by¹ /ˌnɪəˈbaɪ; *NAmE* ˌnɪrˈbaɪ/ *adj.* [usually before noun] near in position; not far away: *The high price may also attract new suppliers from nearby cities where sellers are not able to get such a high price.* ◇ *Distances to relatively nearby stars can be gauged using the change in the star's position in the course of a year.*

near·by² /ˌnɪəˈbaɪ; *NAmE* ˌnɪrˈbaɪ/ *adv.* a short distance from sb/sth; not far away: *Mrs Bibi's area is very mixed, and there are many families from her cultural group living nearby.*

near·ly /ˈnɪəli; *NAmE* ˈnɪrli/ *adv.* almost; not quite; not completely: *The patients wore striped pyjamas nearly identical to the uniforms worn by prisoners.* ◇ *The economic crisis has sent car sales down by nearly one quarter in Europe this year.* ◇ *Sales of pickup trucks have nearly doubled since 1991.*

IDM **not ˈnearly** much less than; not at all: *The speciality coffee industry was growing, but still was not nearly as big as it became in the late 1990s.* ◇ *There were not nearly enough trained officers.* ➲ *usage note at* ALMOST

neat /niːt/ *adj.* (**neat·er, neat·est**) **1** in good order; carefully done or arranged: *She likes neat and tidy systems in which every detail finds its appropriate place.* ◇ *In practice, the distinction between the types of firms is not as neat as the above categorization suggests.* **2** simple but clever: *It was a neat solution to a difficult problem.* ◇ *His neat summaries of Piscator's ideas are illuminating.* **3** containing or made out of just one substance; not mixed with anything else: *The carboxylic acid is dissolved in neat thionyl chloride.* ■ **neat·ly** *adv.*: *Mistakes should be neatly crossed out, leaving the original material still visible.* ◇ *The introductory chapter neatly summarizes and clarifies the broader academic debate.* **neat·ness** *noun* [U] *He insisted on order, neatness and regularity, and was uneasy when these were disturbed.*

ne·ces·sar·ily /ˌnesəˈserəli; *BrE also* ˈnesəsərəli/ *adv.* used to say that sth cannot be avoided: *The list in Fig. 1.5 is necessarily incomplete.* ◇ *This novel of Bombay is necessarily also a novel of India.*

IDM **ˌnot necesˈsarily** used to say that sth is possibly true but not definitely or always true: *Working in small groups does not necessarily indicate learning.* ◇ *Cross argued that what was good for Australia was not necessarily good for Britain.*

ne·ces·sary /ˈnesəsəri; *NAmE* ˈnesəseri/ *adj.* **1** that is needed for a purpose or a reason SYN ESSENTIAL¹ (1): *The patient avoided leaving her flat unless strictly necessary.* ◇ *Few would deny that proficiency in English is a necessary condition for full participation in American society.* ◇ **if ~** *A data sheet, with telephone clarification if necessary, was used to validate the respondents' status.* ◇ **~ to do sth** *The nitrogen lacks the hydrogen necessary to form the hydrogen bond.* ◇ **it is ~ to do sth** *As a result of poor quality materials, it was necessary to replace several parts.* ◇ **~ for sb/sth** *Like most ancients, Tacitus believed that political experience was necessary for a historian.* ◇ *Good quality samples are necessary for diagnosis.* ◇ **(it is) ~ for sb/sth to do sth** *Some of the researchers doubted whether it was necessary for the questionnaires to ask such personal questions.* OPP UNNECESSARY (1) **2** [only before noun] that must exist or happen and cannot be avoided SYN INEVITABLE (1): *She argues that political centralization was a necessary consequence of urbanization.* ◇ *There is no necessary connection between the assets of the company and the value of the shares.*

IDM **a ˌnecessary ˈevil** something that is negative or not wanted but that must be accepted for a particular reason: *It is probably true that police repression was accepted by most Russians as a necessary evil (Westwood, 2002).*

▸ NECESSARY + NOUN **condition • precondition, prerequisite • ingredient • component • tool • skill • knowledge, information • resources • adjustment • step, measure** *The board of directors declared they would take any necessary steps to ensure the business remained solvent.*

▸ NECESSARY TO + VERB **achieve • build • enable • facilitate • ensure • maintain, keep, sustain • support • protect • specify • obtain • meet • address • prevent, avoid** *Further research is necessary to ensure that marine organisms will not be harmed (Fay and Golomb, 2011).* | **consider, examine, investigate, look at • distinguish • evaluate • understand • establish, determine, prove** *It is necessary to consider these two hypotheses separately.*

▸ ADVERB + NECESSARY **always • usually • often • absolutely • strictly • really • still • even** *For the US in 1941, a land line to Alaska seemed absolutely necessary.*

ne·ces·si·tate /nəˈsesɪteɪt/ *verb* (*formal*) to make sth necessary: **~ sth** *The lack of public funding necessitates the use of volunteer labour.* ◇ **~ doing sth** *The latter two situations necessitated combining the data in new ways.*

ne·ces·sity /nəˈsesəti/ *noun* **1** [U] the fact that sth must happen or be done; the need for sth: *During the war, women worked due to financial necessity.* ◇ **~ of (doing) sth** *The focus of diplomatic activity was the absolute necessity of avoiding a global nuclear conflict.* ◇ **~ for sth** *The necessity for iodine in the diet was recognized in the 1920s.* ◇ **~ (for sb) to be/do sth** *The minister stressed the necessity for members of the public to be financially responsible.* ◇ **of ~** *Women, of necessity, often choose part-time work to accommodate family responsibilities.* **2** [C] **~ (of sth)** a thing that you must have and cannot manage without: *Many inhabitants go short of the basic necessities of life: water, food, shelter.* **3** [C, usually sing.] a situation that must happen and that cannot be avoided: *The supposed need for an early revolution persuaded many to accept violence as a temporary necessity.*

neck /nek/ *noun* **1** the part of the body between the head and the shoulders: *This is a common condition that causes pain and stiffness in the neck.* ◇ *The male mallard duck has a dark green neck and head.* **2** a long narrow part of sth:

Small perfume flasks with very long narrow necks have been discovered in first-century tombs.

need[1] /niːd/ *verb* **1** to require sth/sb because they are essential or very important, not just because you would like to have them: **~ sth/sb** *The child may need professional help.* ◇ *The project needed more volunteers.* ◇ **sth is needed** *Research is needed to examine the role of cultural factors in technology use.* ◇ **~ to do sth** *The nursery needed to meet legal requirements concerning health and safety.* ◇ **~ doing sth** *The results need checking and evaluating.* **2 ~ to do sth** used to show what you should or have to do: *Roddick did not need to buy expensive advertising, since she was so newsworthy herself.*

need[2] /niːd/ *modal verb* (*negative* **need not**, *short form* **needn't** /ˈniːdnt/) (Unless you are quoting, the short form **needn't** should not be used in academic writing.) used to state that sth is/was not necessary or that only very little is/was necessary; used to ask if sth is/was necessary: **~ (not) do sth** *With electronic ticketing, the customer need only quote the booking number at the airport to receive a boarding pass.* ◇ **~ (not) have done sth** *Those ten thousand lives need not have been lost, if building regulations had been followed.*

need[3] /niːd/ *noun* **1** [sing., U] a situation when sth is necessary or must be done: **~ for sth** *The situation was resolved without the need for a formal meeting.* ◇ **~ (for sb/sth) to do sth** *The above observations suggest the need for farmers to adopt more sustainable systems.* ◇ **in ~ of sth (for sth)** *The Spanish king was in need of money for his wedding.* ◇ **according to ~** *Food aid was distributed according to need.* **2** [C, usually pl.] the things that sth/sb requires in order to function well or achieve sth: *The treatment was tailored to individual patient needs.* ◇ **the... needs of sth/sb** *Tax revenues were used to meet the financial needs of the army.* ◇ *Such a rigid curriculum cannot be responsive to the individual educational needs of a student.* **3** [U] the state of not having enough food, money or support SYN HARDSHIP: **in ~** *The government increased welfare provision for those in need.*

IDM **if need ˈbe** if necessary: *It was recommended that terrorist publications should be monitored and, if need be, censored.*

▸ ADJECTIVE + NEED **basic • universal • local • individual, personal • specific • unique • future • changing • perceived • unmet • complex • special • great • desperate • real • urgent, immediate, pressing • human** *The first priority was to identify the perceived needs of the target market.* | **social • material • educational • physiological • psychological, emotional • spiritual** *The charity was set up to satisfy local communities' basic material needs, such as food and housing.*

▸ NOUN + NEED **customer • patient • health • care, health care • housing** *The focus of the research was on adults with long-term health care needs.*

▸ VERB + NEED **meet, satisfy, serve, fulfil • address • accommodate • assess • identify • prioritize • recognize, acknowledge , accept • feel • understand • deny • balance • anticipate • suit, fit, match • reflect • create** *The Soviet Union purchased 400 million tons of American grain to satisfy a desperate need for more wheat.*

▸ VERB + THE/A NEED FOR STH/TO DO STH **highlight, emphasize, stress, underscore, underline, reinforce • suggest, indicate, imply • demonstrate, illustrate • avoid, remove, eliminate, obviate • reduce • be driven by** *These conflicting results highlight the need for additional regional studies.*

▸ NEED + VERB **arise** *All citizens should be able to access health care when the need arises.*

▸ A/THE NEED TO + VERB **consider • understand • distinguish • protect, preserve, keep, maintain • balance • engage • improve • develop • establish • ensure • avoid** *There is a powerful and growing need to develop courses in conflict resolution and peace with justice.*

nee·dle /ˈniːdl/ *noun* [C] **1** a very thin, pointed piece of steel used on the end of a SYRINGE: *Some agents can enter the body by injection with hypodermic needles.* **2** a thin piece of metal on a scientific instrument that moves to point to the correct measurement or direction: *It is not easy to explain why a compass needle points to magnetic north.* **3** a long thin piece of steel with a point at one end used for sewing: *She could no longer see well enough to thread a needle.* **4** [usually pl.] the thin, hard, pointed leaf of a PINE tree: *Nests are built using twigs, moss and pine needles.*

neg·ate AWL /nɪˈɡeɪt/ *verb* **1 ~ sth** to stop sth from having any effect: *It is not possible to negate the effect of inflation on rate of return.* **2 ~ sth** to state that sth does not exist: *This policy does not negate economic and ethical arguments in support of the free movement of people.*

neg·ation /nɪˈɡeɪʃn/ *noun* [C, usually sing., U] **~ (of sth)** the exact opposite of sth; the act of causing sth not to exist or to become its opposite: *Evil is not merely the negation of goodness.* ◇ *He stated: 'Monopoly of broadcasting is inevitably the negation of freedom.'*

nega·tive[1] AWL /ˈneɡətɪv/ *adj.* **1** bad or harmful: *When a strategy is viewed as costly in terms of time or money, it is frequently perceived as negative.* ◇ *The negative consequences of crime extend well beyond victims and offenders.* OPP POSITIVE[1] (1) **2** considering only the bad side of sth/sb; lacking enthusiasm or hope: *Questions were used to test the participant and provide positive or negative feedback.* ◇ *A general negative attitude towards language learning was noted.* ◇ *The students were well aware of the largely negative community perception of their school.* OPP POSITIVE[1] (2) **3** expressing the answer 'no': *The answers are loaded in favour of a positive rather than a negative reply.* OPP AFFIRMATIVE **4** containing a word such as 'no', 'not', 'never', etc: *In French, the form 'ne' marks the verb as being negative.* **5** (*abbr.* **neg.**) not showing any evidence of a particular substance or medical condition: *If she is tested, a negative result would reduce her concerns somewhat.* ◇ **~ for sth** *All the patients have tested negative for TB.* OPP POSITIVE[1] (6) **6** less than zero: *Keeping the project moving in the face of minimal or even negative economic growth became difficult.* ◇ *Weak demand leads inflation to fall and eventually become negative.* OPP POSITIVE[1] (7) **7** (of a relationship between two amounts or events) related in such a way that, when one increases, the other decreases: *There is a strong negative correlation between death rates and per capita GDP.* OPP POSITIVE[1] (8) **8** containing or producing the type of electricity that is carried by an ELECTRON: *The direction of current flow is opposite to that of the flow of negative charge.* ◇ *The positive atoms of sodium were attracted to the negative terminal.* OPP POSITIVE[1] (9)

▸ NEGATIVE + NOUN **effect, impact, consequence, outcome • relationship • aspect, side • influence** *The negative impact of these diseases is apparent very early in life.* | **attitude • emotion, feeling • feedback • stereotype • connotation, association • image, perception, view • reaction** *A recent survey of Asian women revealed that employers frequently held negative stereotypes.* | **result • outcome • finding** *As illustrated by the negative results of the first Irish referendum, public opinion remained highly sceptical of the EU.* | **relationship • correlation • association** *A number of studies have found a negative relationship between ethnic diversity and social capital.*

▸ ADVERB + NEGATIVE **strongly • significantly • potentially • slightly • largely, predominantly** *The term 'colonization' has strongly negative connotations.* ◇ *A significantly negative value indicates deceleration.*

nega·tive[2] AWL /ˈneɡətɪv/ *noun* **1** a word or statement that means 'no' or 'not': **in the ~** *When we asked if they felt their situation had improved, between 76% and 90%*

N

replied in the negative. **2** the result of a test or an experiment that shows that a substance or condition is not present: *There may be false negatives, i.e. the screening test failed to detect the cancer.* OPP POSITIVE[2] (1) **3** a disadvantage or problem: *Their bilingualism is seen as a negative, rather than a strength.* OPP POSITIVE[2] (2)

ˌnegative ˈfeedback *noun* **1** [U] (*engineering*) the return of part of an OUTPUT signal to the INPUT, tending to decrease the AMPLIFICATION, etc: *Negative feedback reduces the signal that appears at the input of the basic amplifier.* **2** [U, C] (*technical*) a situation in which the results of a process produce a reduction in the process itself or its effects: *The consequences include negative feedback, where the change in climate eventually results in lower emissions of methane.* ◇ *It has been suggested that the loss of ozone in the stratosphere could lead to a negative feedback that might allow more ozone to be produced.* ◇ **+ noun** *Growth hormone controls its own release by negative feedback signals to the hypothalamus.*

nega·tive·ly AWL /ˈnegətɪvli/ *adv.* **1** in a bad or harmful way: *The work of the police can involve exposure to events that impact negatively on health.* ◇ *The high oil price not only stimulated supply, but also negatively influenced demand for oil products.* OPP POSITIVELY (1) **2** in a way that considers only the bad side of sth/sb, or that lacks enthusiasm or hope: *She worries and thinks negatively about the future.* OPP POSITIVELY (2) **3** in a way that shows that you disapprove of or disagree with sth/sb: *Most Americans reacted negatively to the plan.* OPP POSITIVELY (3) **4** in such a way that, when one thing increases, another thing decreases: *Job satisfaction and job stress are negatively correlated.* OPP POSITIVELY (4) **5** in a way that contains or produces the type of electricity that is carried by an ELECTRON: *The stream of ions that is produced may consist of either positively or negatively charged ions.* OPP POSITIVELY (6)

N

neg·lect[1] /nɪˈglekt/ *verb* **1 ~ sb/sth** to fail to take care of sb/sth: *It is an offence for a person to wilfully neglect a child.* ◇ *Patients may neglect personal hygiene and their appearance.* **2 ~ sth** to not give enough attention to sth: *Marketers tend to neglect the fact that potential customers in foreign markets often need more information than customers in the home market.* ◇ *The development of a manufacturing sector was largely neglected by the communists after 1945.* **3 ~ sth** to ignore sth because it is not important, especially in a scientific experiment SYN DISREGARD[1]: *One may neglect the voltage drop altogether while calculating the current.* ◇ *Other factors influence the natural curves and twists and are neglected here.* **4 ~ to do sth** to fail or forget to do sth that you ought to do SYN OMIT (2): *The representative neglects to mention that the only jobs for local residents are in the low-wage service sector.* ➲ *see also* NEGLIGENCE

neg·lect[2] /nɪˈglekt/ *noun* [U] the fact of not giving enough care or attention to sb/sth; the state of not receiving enough care or attention: **~ (by sb/sth)** *A host of social problems result from years of neglect by political leaders.* ◇ **~ of sb/sth** *Chronic intoxication may lead to family problems including the neglect of children.* ◇ *Relative neglect of the oil industry and over-reliance on coal was a mistake.*

neg·lect·ed /nɪˈglektɪd/ *adj.* **1** not receiving enough attention: *This is an important study of a previously neglected area.* **2** not receiving enough care: *There is a need for engagement with abused and neglected children.*

neg·li·gence /ˈneglɪdʒəns/ *noun* [U] **~ (of sb/sth)** (*formal* or *law*) the failure to give sb/sth enough care or attention HELP In law, **negligence** is used to talk about a failure to give sb/sth enough care or attention, resulting in injury or damage: *His injury was due to the negligence of his employers.* ◇ *Claims for medical negligence most frequently fail due to an inability to establish causation.*

neg·li·gent /ˈneglɪdʒənt/ *adj.* (*formal* or *law*) failing to give sb/sth enough care or attention, especially when this has serious results: *The question for the jury is whether his behaviour was grossly negligent and consequently criminal.* ◇ *A single negligent act, damaging an electric cable for instance, would not be a nuisance.* ■ **neg·li·gent·ly** *adv.*: *The council accepted responsibility but negligently failed to carry out repairs promptly.*

neg·li·gible /ˈneglɪdʒəbl/ *adj.* of very little importance or size and not worth considering SYN INSIGNIFICANT: *It is arguable that this limitation has only negligible effects on the results of this study.* ◇ *Such an effect would be negligible over the size of the solar system.*

ne·go·ti·ate /nɪˈgəʊʃieɪt; *NAmE* nɪˈgoʊʃieɪt/ *verb* **1** [I] to try to reach an agreement by formal discussion: *Member states have to negotiate internally.* ◇ **~ with sb (for/about/on sth)** *The new party negotiated with opposition parties and the military about a new democratic constitution.* ◇ **~ with sb to do sth** *The company is negotiating with unions to cut another 3 400 jobs.* **2** [T] to arrange or agree sth by formal discussion: **~ sth** *He successfully negotiated a loan of £75 000 from the bank.* ◇ **~ sth with sb** *The US began to negotiate a free trade agreement with Canada.* **3** [T] **~ sth (+ adv./prep.)** to successfully get over or past a difficult part on a path or route: *The pedestrians were trying to negotiate their way through the underpasses.* **4** [T] **~ sth (+ adv./prep.)** to successfully solve a problem that is preventing you from achieving sth: *People have to negotiate a route through the bewildering range of services provided.*

ne·go·ti·ation /nɪˌgəʊʃiˈeɪʃn; *NAmE* nɪˌgoʊʃiˈeɪʃn/ *noun* [C, usually pl., U] formal discussion between people who are trying to reach an agreement: *Early in 2008 a new set of peace negotiations began in Cyprus.* ◇ **~ with sb** *In June the EU opened accession negotiations with Turkey.* ◇ **~ between A and B** *The process of negotiation between the parties took place over a considerable period of time.* ◇ **~ on/over sth** *The union represents doctors throughout the UK, for negotiation on pay and conditions.*

ne·go·ti·ator /nɪˈgəʊʃieɪtə(r); *NAmE* nɪˈgoʊʃieɪtər/ *noun* a person who is involved in formal political or financial discussions, especially because it is their job: *Congress created leverage for US trade negotiators through a number of changes in US trade laws.*

neigh·bour (*US* **neigh·bor**) /ˈneɪbə(r)/ *noun* **1** a person who lives next to you or near you: *Her neighbour says she lives alone.* **2** a country that is next to or near another country: *During this period, Ireland outpaced its European neighbours in job and wealth creation.* **3** a person or thing that is standing or located next to another person or thing: *Each person was asked to check their neighbour's scores.* ◇ *A negative charge on one atom will tend to repel electrons in its neighbour.* ◇ **nearest/immediate ~** *Each processor is connected only to its two nearest neighbours.* **4** any person in need of your help or kindness: *The biblical rule that you are to love your neighbour becomes, in law, you must not injure your neighbour.*

neigh·bour·hood (*US* **neigh·bor·hood**) /ˈneɪbəhʊd; *NAmE* ˈneɪbərhʊd/ *noun* **1** a district or an area of a town; the people who live there: *Fieldwork was conducted in socially and economically deprived neighbourhoods in Denmark.* ◇ **~ of...** *They came from the black working-class neighbourhoods of eastern Brooklyn.* ◇ **+ noun** *Neighbourhood groups were responsible for resolving some kinds of disputes.* **2** the area near a particular place or thing SYN VICINITY: *Many of the students' families worked and lived in or near the immediate school neighbourhood.* ◇ *Antibiotics are molecules produced by microorganisms and fungi, which they release to kill competing organisms in their neighbourhood.*

IDM in the neighbourhood of (of a number or an amount) approximately; not exactly: *Despite interest rates in the neighbourhood of 20%, money supply growth did not decrease in the early 1980s.*

neigh·bour·ing (*US* **neigh·bor·ing**) /ˈneɪbərɪŋ/ *adj.* [only before noun] located or living near or next to a place or person: *The overall impact will be increased food shortages in Russia and neighbouring countries.* ◇ *The strength of the bond between neighbouring carbon atoms in diamond is very strong.*

nei·ther[1] /ˈnaɪðə(r); ˈniːðə(r)/ *det., pron.* not one nor the other of two things or people; not either: *Neither side of the brain is dominant over the other.* ◇ *Full-scale war could have resulted in the annihilation of both powers, and so neither one made the first move.* ◇ *But which measure is correct? The answer is neither.* ◇ **~ of sth** *Neither of these conjectures has been proved.* ◇ *There are two distinct enterprises, neither of which can replace the other.*

nei·ther[2] /ˈnaɪðə(r); ˈniːðə(r)/ *adv.* **1** used to show that a negative statement is also true of sb/sth else: *Zimmern barely mentions Socrates, and neither does Brandeis.* ◇ *Neither could the agreement be interpreted as an acceptance of the situation by Argentina.* **2 neither... nor...** used to show that a negative statement is true of two things: *The most surprising fact about the EU is that neither Norway nor Switzerland opted to join.* ◇ *The children in the follow-up study were neither more aggressive nor more anxious.*

neo·clas·sic·al /ˌniːəʊˈklæsɪkl; *NAmE* ˌniːoʊˈklæsɪkl/ *adj.* [usually before noun] **1** used to describe art and ARCHITECTURE that is based on the style of ancient Greece or Rome, or music, literature, etc. that uses traditional ideas or styles: *Leo von Klenze was responsible for many neoclassical buildings in Munich.* ◇ *The eighteenth-century novel, written during the heyday of neoclassical theatre, enjoyed reminding its readers of the Greek myths they had seen dramatized.* **2** connected with the economic theory in which markets perfectly allow for all goods supplied to be bought at an EQUILIBRIUM price: *The 1980s saw a revival of neoclassical free market economics.* ◇ *The neoclassical view does not really consider the larger sociopolitical setting within which individual behaviour plays out.*

neo-liberal /ˌniːəʊˈlɪbərəl; *NAmE* ˌniːoʊˈlɪbərəl/ *adj.* [usually before noun] (*politics*) connected with a type of LIBERALISM that believes in an international free market, without government control, with businesses and industry controlled and run for profit by private owners: *A neo-liberal foreign policy promotes open markets and Western democratic values and institutions.* ■ **neo-liberal·ism** /ˌniːəʊˈlɪbərəlɪzəm; *NAmE* ˌniːoʊˈlɪbərəlɪzəm/ *noun* [U] *Neo-liberalism, as an ideology, has a long history, but has enjoyed a renaissance in the last 30 years.*

nerve /nɜːv; *NAmE* nɜːrv/ *noun* **1** [C] any of the long threads that carry messages between the brain and parts of the body, enabling you to move, feel pain, etc: *The optic nerve from each human eye is made up of over a million axons.* ◇ **+ noun** *As people age, the number of nerve endings in the skin decreases.* **2 nerves** [pl.] feelings of anxiety SYN ANXIETY (1): *The defendant took some valium tablets in order to calm his nerves.* **3** [U] the courage to do sth difficult or dangerous: *Without the army, the government lost its nerve and conceded the radicals' demands.*
IDM hit/touch a (raw/sensitive) ˈnerve to mention a subject that makes sb feel angry, upset or embarrassed: *The immigration issue has continued to touch a raw political nerve.*

ner·vous /ˈnɜːvəs; *NAmE* ˈnɜːrvəs/ *adj.* **1** anxious about sth; afraid of sth: *The Chancellor had to abandon his trip to Hong Kong because the markets were so nervous.* ◇ **~ about/of (doing) sth** *Students are often nervous about speaking in class.* OPP CONFIDENT (2) **2** easily made anxious or afraid: *He was a rather shy and nervous boy who found it difficult to make friends.* ◇ *During the breeding season, silver foxes are very nervous creatures.* **3** connected with the body's nerves and often affecting you mentally or emotionally: *It was a relatively new method of studying nervous tissue.* ◇ *He visited Paris to study nervous disorders.* ➲ *see also* CENTRAL NERVOUS SYSTEM, NERVOUS SYSTEM ■ **ner·vous·ness** *noun* [U] *She suffered acutely from anxiety and nervousness.*

ˈnervous system *noun* [usually sing.] the system of all the nerves in the body: *The connections made between neurons and muscles in the developing nervous system are highly specific.* ➲ *see also* CENTRAL NERVOUS SYSTEM

nest[1] /nest/ *noun* [C] a hollow place or structure that a bird or other creature makes in which to live and produce its young: *Moorhens often build their nests on the top of logs.* ◇ *Reptiles generally abandon their nests after the eggs have been laid.*

nest[2] /nest/ *verb* **1** [I] to make and use a nest: *This protected bird species had nested at the site for many years.* **2** [T] **~ sth (in/within sth)** (*technical*) to put types of information together, or inside each other, so that they form a single unit: *HTML tables can be nested within each other to produce a variety of different design layouts for websites.*

net[1] /net/ *adj.* **1** [usually before noun] (of an amount, value or price) that remains when nothing more is to be taken away to pay taxes, debts, etc: *The company's financial report showed a 31 per cent fall in net profit.* ◇ **~ of sth** *When there are regional tax differences, prices net of taxes will be different in different regions.* ➲ *compare* GROSS (1) **2** [only before noun] final, after all the important facts have been included SYN OVERALL[1]: *The total net migration for the decade is relatively low.* ◇ *The UK became a net importer of gas in 2004.* ◇ *The net effect of changes in the labour market has been to reduce the numbers of traditional 'men's jobs'.* ■ **net** *adv.*: *The plant generated 210kW gross electrical power and 40kW net.*

net[2] /net/ *noun* **1** [C] a piece of material that is made of string, thread or wire twisted or tied together, with small spaces in between: *Some of the fish entering the net subsequently escaped through the mesh.* ◇ *a fishing/mosquito net* ➲ *see also* SAFETY NET **2 the Net** (*also* **the net**) (*informal*) the Internet: *The longitudinal study found similar emailing patterns among early and late adopters of the net.*
IDM *see* CAST[1]

net·work[1] AWL /ˈnetwɜːk; *NAmE* ˈnetwɜːrk/ *noun* **1** a complicated system of roads, lines, tubes, etc. that cross each other and are connected to each other: *China's total road network is now the third longest in the world.* ◇ **~ of sth** *The hydra has no central nervous system but has a network of neurons distributed throughout the body.* **2 ~ (of sth)** a group or system of people or things that are connected to each other: *The company had an extensive network of factories throughout Asia.* ◇ *Exporters use a complex network of agents to get their produce to the market.* **3** a group of people who meet, exchange information, etc. for professional or social purposes: *An informal network developed in which practitioners met to exchange experiences and provide support.* ◇ *People with stronger social networks tend to be both healthier and happier (e.g. Diener, Lucas & Oishi, 2002).* **4** a number of computers and other devices that are connected together so that equipment and data can be shared: *She used her mobile phone to hack into the police computer network.* ◇ **+ noun** *The statistics show the number of network connections or number of people with access to a network.* ➲ *see also* NEURAL NETWORK **5** a group of radio or television stations in different places that are connected and that broadcast the same programmes at the same time: *Viacom owns US and global cable television networks.* ◇ **+ noun** *The* *company reduced its spend on network television ads in the USA by nearly 23%.*

net·work² AWL /ˈnetwɜːk; *NAmE* ˈnetwɜːrk/ *verb* **1** [T] **~ sth** to connect a number of computers and other devices together so that equipment and data can be shared: *Companies would network their computers together so that they could quickly exchange large amounts of data.* ◇ *Sharing data means setting up IT structures that are fully networked.* **2** [I] **~ (with sb)** to try to meet and talk to people who may be useful to you in your work: *Professional organizations contain subgroups dedicated to networking with their colleagues.* ➲ *see also* SOCIAL NETWORKING **3** [T, usually passive] to connect or operate as a network: **(be) networked** *Compared with the railways, the canals were less effectively networked.* ◇ *The main focus is on how firms survive in a complex networked business environment.*

neur·al /ˈnjʊərəl; *NAmE* ˈnʊrəl/ *adj.* (*biology*) connected with a NERVE or the NERVOUS SYSTEM: *The scan will detect major structural abnormalities such as severe neural tube defects.* ◇ *neural tissue/cells*

ˌneural ˈnetwork (*also* ˌneural ˈnet) *noun* (*computing*) a computer system with a structure that is similar to the human brain and nervous system: *In one experiment, an artificial neural network learned to form the past tenses of English verbs.*

neuro·logic·al /ˌnjʊərəˈlɒdʒɪkl; *NAmE* ˌnʊrəˈlɑːdʒɪkl/ *adj.* connected with NERVES or with the science of NEUROLOGY: *At least 6 per cent of the population have a neurological disorder in their lifetime.* ◇ *The symptoms are neurological in nature and result in severe abdominal pain.*

N

neurol·ogy /njʊəˈrɒlədʒi; *NAmE* nʊˈrɑːlədʒi/ *noun* [U] the scientific study of nerves and their diseases: *A panel of experts in neurology, psychiatry and psychology then reviewed all available data.*

neuron /ˈnjʊərɒn; *NAmE* ˈnʊrɑːn/ (*especially in BrE* **neur·one** /ˈnjʊərəʊn; *NAmE* ˈnʊroʊn/) *noun* a cell that carries information within the brain and between the brain and other parts of the body; a NERVE cell: *A typical sensory neuron in Aplysia, a sea slug, has about 1 200 synapses.* ➲ *see also* MOTOR NEURON

neuro·science /ˈnjʊərəʊsaɪəns; *NAmE* ˈnʊroʊsaɪəns/ *noun* [U] the science that deals with the structure and function of the brain and the NERVOUS SYSTEM: *The evidence suggests that out of body experiences must be explained in terms of psychology or neuroscience.* ■ **neuro·scientist** /ˈnjʊərəʊsaɪəntɪst; *NAmE* ˈnʊroʊsaɪəntɪst/ *noun*: *Cognitive neuroscientists are beginning to identify the neural pathways through which emotion modulates decision-making.*

neuro·trans·mit·ter /ˈnjʊərəʊtrænzmɪtə(r); *NAmE* ˈnʊroʊtrænzmɪtər/ (*also* **trans·mit·ter**) *noun* (*biology*) a chemical that carries messages from nerve cells to other nerve cells or muscles: *Calcium is also required for the release of neurotransmitters.*

neu·ter /ˈnjuːtə(r); *NAmE* ˈnuːtər/ *adj.* (*grammar*) (in some languages) belonging to a class of words whose GENDER is not MASCULINE or FEMININE: *Greek has three genders, each noun being masculine, feminine or neuter.*

neu·tral AWL /ˈnjuːtrəl; *NAmE* ˈnuːtrəl/ *adj.* **1** not supporting or helping either side in a disagreement, competition, etc. SYN IMPARTIAL: *Media owners are not politically neutral and often insert their own agendas into their media.* ◇ *My preference is to remain neutral on this matter.* **2** not belonging to or supporting any of the countries that are involved in a war: *Later that year, Stalin invaded the small, neutral state of Finland.* ◇ *Japan's economy had performed fairly well after World War I, during which Japan had remained neutral.* **3** neither acid nor ALKALINE: *A drug that is formulated for injection into the bloodstream needs to function at neutral pH.* ◇ *The solubility of soil material is larger when the water is neutral or mildly alkaline rather than acidic.* **4** (*abbr.* **N**) having neither a positive nor a negative electrical charge: *The number of electrons in a neutral atom will equal the number of protons within the nucleus.* ◇ *Since there are equal amounts of positive and negative charge, the whole molecule is electrically neutral.* **5** having no effect on other things; having neither positive nor negative characteristics: *Most mutations are neutral in effect.* ◇ *Cost-benefit assessment, moreover, is not morally neutral.* **6** deliberately not expressing any strong feeling: *Each word of each question should be read in a neutral voice.* ◇ *Stronger words can often change to become more neutral if used often enough.* **7** (of colours) not very bright or strong, such as grey or light brown: *Some garments are manufactured in neutral colours and then dyed to order.* ■ **neu·tral·ly** *adv.*: *The aim was to write clearly, neutrally and as simply as possible.*

neu·tral·ity AWL /njuːˈtræləti; *NAmE* nuːˈtræləti/ *noun* [U] **1** the state of not supporting either side in a disagreement, competition or war: *The president is obliged to maintain political neutrality.* ◇ *The foreign powers declared their neutrality in the revolutionary struggle.* **2** the condition of having neither a positive nor a negative electrical charge: *Electrical neutrality is maintained as more HCO_3^- is reabsorbed.* **3** (of chemicals) the condition of being neither acid nor ALKALINE: *Pepsin is unusual for an enzyme in that it works at acid pH, most enzymes requiring a pH near neutrality.*

neu·tral·ize (*BrE also* **-ise**) AWL /ˈnjuːtrəlaɪz; *NAmE* ˈnuːtrəlaɪz/ *verb* **1 ~ sth** to stop sth from having any effect: *Most of the samples were found to neutralize other viruses.* ◇ *The authorities must evaluate the resources necessary for neutralizing the threat of violent clashes.* ◇ *Price changes partially neutralize the effects of exchange rate movements.* **2 ~ sth** (*chemistry*) to make a substance chemically neutral: *Drugs that neutralize acid can be given depending on the severity of symptoms.* **3 ~ sth** to make a country or an area NEUTRAL: *Russia accepted that the Black Sea should be neutralized.* ■ **neu·tral·iza·tion**, **-isa·tion** AWL /ˌnjuːtrəlaɪˈzeɪʃn; *NAmE* ˌnuːtrələˈzeɪʃn/ *noun* [U] **~ (of sth)** *Neutralization of acids can occur within the soil.*

neu·tron /ˈnjuːtrɒn; *NAmE* ˈnuːtrɑːn/ *noun* (*physics*) a very small piece of matter that carries no electric charge and that forms part of the NUCLEUS (= central part) of an atom: *Neutrons are emitted as a consequence of nuclear fission.* HELP A **neutron** is a **subatomic particle.** ➲ *compare* ELECTRON, PROTON

never /ˈnevə(r)/ *adv.* not at any time; not on any occasion: *The Russian people never really accepted the Empress, especially after 1914.* ◇ *The car was never a commercial success.* ◇ *More than half of the respondents had never heard of this treatment.* ◇ *While some children have tantrums in early childhood, many children never do.*

never·the·less AWL /ˌnevəðəˈles; *NAmE* ˌnevərðəˈles/ *adv.* despite this fact SYN NONETHELESS: *Further research is needed in these areas. Nevertheless, some preliminary conclusions can be drawn:...* ◇ *The Cossack cavalry tended to be of the poorer families, but nevertheless were smart and full of pride.* ➲ language bank *at* HOWEVER

new /njuː; *NAmE* nuː/ *adj.* (**newer, new·est**) **1** not existing before; recently made, invented or introduced: *The President took credit for the creation of 10.5 million new jobs.* ◇ *Using electricity to relieve pain is not new.* ◇ *It is quite difficult to find any individual in a modern society that has not been touched by new communication technologies.* ◇ *The article examines the use of newer, interactive information technologies in young men's health promotion.* OPP OLD (4) **2 the new** *noun* [U] something that is new: *The library of the Institute of Psychiatry in London extends*

over two floors, roughly dividing the collection into the old and the new. **3** not used or owned by anyone before: *The question of value for money is important when customers are buying new cars, because new cars are so much more expensive than second-hand cars.* **4** recently bought; not owned by you before: *Zack had bought the new bike the month before.* **5** only recently produced or developed: *New leaves unfold in April when 2- or 3-year-old leaves are shed in about 1 month.* **6** different from a recent or the previous one: *Older workers may receive little help in finding new jobs.* OPP OLD (5) **7** in addition to sb/sth that already exists: *The director is on the management board and is responsible for securing new business.* ◇ *Hearing loss of this form is very common and impairs not just conversation, but the ability to make new friends.* **8** already existing but not seen or experienced before; not familiar: *Many minority students can develop communicative skills in a new language within two years.* ◇ **~ to sb/sth** *Open-ended questions can provide full answers and explore issues that are new to the researcher.* ◇ *Although these ideas became very influential from the 1950s, they were certainly not new to psychology.* **9** used to describe sb/sth that has only just arrived or started doing sth: *Ghana is set to become Africa's newest oil producer.* ◇ **~ to (doing) sth** *Many families in the inner city areas were new to British education and the British labour market.* **10** [usually before noun] just beginning or beginning again: *In 'David Copperfield', Mr Peggotty takes Emily to Australia to begin a new life.* ◇ *Many think that a global civil society marks the dawn of a new era of human cooperation.* **11** (usually with *the*) modern; of the most recent type: *The planned community of Seaside, Florida, is an early example of the movement known as the New Urbanism.* ◇ *It is not always clear, however, to what extent this 'new morality' is a departure from the traditional view.* **12** used in compounds to describe sth that has recently happened: *The majority of the participants expressed a new-found awareness of their own personal strengths from working together.*
■ **new·ness** *noun* [U] *In today's America, the idea of newness is linked to the idea of improvement.* ◇ **~ of sth** *The relative newness of the Internet means that this is an area that is fairly underused by social researchers.* ➲ *see also* NEWLY

IDM **ˌbreak new ˈground** to make a new discovery or do sth that has not been done before: *The book breaks new ground in showing how changes in ideas about childhood structured the toy industry as much as innovation in technology.* ➲ *more at* BRAVE, BREATHE

new·born /ˈnjuːbɔːn; *NAmE* ˈnuːbɔːrn/ *adj.* [only before noun] recently born: *Newborn babies show a preference for face-like visual patterns.*

newly /ˈnjuːli; *NAmE* ˈnuːli/ *adv.* (usually before a past participle) recently: *During the recession of 1920–1, many companies disbanded their newly formed personnel departments.* ◇ *Type 2 diabetes now accounts for about half of the newly diagnosed cases of diabetes in children and adolescents.* ◇ *In Central Asia, the newly independent republics began to go their own separate ways.*

▸ NEWLY + VERB+ED **formed, established • developed • discovered, found • arrived • acquired • introduced • diagnosed • elected • appointed • privatized • industrialized • constructed, built • opened • hatched** *The structure of 140 newly established companies employing more than 100 workers was analysed.*

▸ NEWLY + VERB+ING **emerging • arriving • developing • industrializing** *In newly industrializing economies in Asia, the state has played a prominent role in promoting investment in skills.*

▸ NEWLY + ADJECTIVE **independent • qualified • emergent • born • married • democratic** *Interviews were conducted with newly qualified nurses.*

ˌnew ˈmedia *noun* [pl.] new information and entertainment technologies, such as the Internet and DVDs: *Video games have become one of the most familiar ways for audiences to engage with new media.*

news /njuːz; *NAmE* nuːz/ *noun* [U] **1** new information about sth that has happened recently: *Robert Kennedy heard the news as he travelled by plane to Indianapolis.* ◇ **~ of sb/sth** *News of Columbus's discovery of America reached the Iberian peninsula.* ◇ **~ about sth** *News about interest rates has a big impact on foreign exchange markets.* ◇ **~ that...** *In this scene, Sergeant Dixon brings the news that Billy is missing in action.* **2** reports of recent events that appear in newspapers or on television or radio: *64 per cent of the sample followed international news.* ◇ **in the ~** *I shall begin with a discussion of two issues that are much in the news today.* ◇ **+ noun** *The issue of global warming is constantly addressed by the popular news media.* ◇ *news coverage/exposure* ◇ *a news item/story/event/report* **3 the news** a regular broadcast of the LATEST news: *People can watch the news overhead on commuter train monitors.* ◇ **on the ~** *Each night, on the television news, at least five minutes would be devoted to the latest outrages.* **4** a person, thing or event that is considered to be interesting enough to be reported as news: *Economic change often makes headline news because it has a direct effect on jobs.*

IDM **be bad ˈnews (for sb/sth)** to be likely to cause problems, or to be not helpful: *A natural source of a very important drug could be very bad news for threatened habitats.* **break the/bad ˈnews (to sb)** to be the first to tell sb some bad news: *Evidence shows that within their first year of qualifying, 79% of doctors break bad news to a patient at least once.* **be good news (for sb/sth)** to be likely to be helpful or give an advantage: *The finding is good news for many new democracies with diverse populations.*

news·paper /ˈnjuːzpeɪpə(r); *NAmE* ˈnuːzpeɪpər/ *noun* a set of large printed sheets of paper containing news, articles, advertisements, etc. and published every day or every week: *a local/national/regional/daily/tabloid newspaper* ◇ *Texts were sampled from 'The Guardian' newspaper online edition on three particular days.* ◇ *The trial was preceded by newspaper articles in which the accused were regarded as unquestionably guilty.* ➲ *see also* PAPER (3)

next¹ /nekst/ *adj.* [only before noun] (usually with *the*) coming straight after sb/sth in time, order or space: *Population ageing is likely to accelerate over the next 50 years.* ◇ *In the next section, the possibility of generating revenue from privately insured patients will be discussed.* ◇ *At various stages in the program, more than one choice as to the next step would be possible.* ◇ *After completion of training, the trainer is no longer present in the next room as a source of advice and guidance.*

next² /nekst/ *adv.* **1** after sth else; then; afterwards: *What happened next is not entirely clear.* ◇ *Next, two researchers reviewed the tables and identified thematic patterns.* ◇ *The number of landowners without noble titles was greatest in England. Next came France.* **2 ~ best, biggest, most important, etc... (after/to sb/sth)** following in the order mentioned: *After prostate cancer, lung cancer is the next commonest cancer in men.* ◇ *After mudstones and sandstones, limestones are the next most abundant type of sedimentary rock.*

next³ /nekst/ *noun* (*usually* **the next**) [sing.] a person or thing that is next: *Traditional stories were transmitted from one person to another and from one generation to the next.*

ˈnext to *prep.* **1** in or into a position right beside sb/sth: *The principal and the community school director have offices right next to each other.* ◇ *The bottle was placed next to the nest with the bottom edge touching the top of the nest.* ◇ *Most American states followed the practice of*

N

providing a ballot paper with boxes next to the names of the candidates. **2** following in order or importance after sb/sth: *Clearly, next to the family, schools provide the most highly significant experiences in children's lives.* ◇ *Next to carbon and oxygen, nitrogen is the third most abundant element in biological molecules.* **3** almost: *These five Greek texts were written by authors about whom we know next to nothing.* ◇ *Retaining donors for the party was next to impossible.*

NGO /ˌen dʒiː ˈəʊ; *NAmE* ˌen dʒiː ˈoʊ/ *abbr.* **non-governmental organization** (a charity, association, etc. that is independent of government and business): *Reporters Without Borders is an NGO that monitors press freedom.*

nice /naɪs/ *adj.* (**nicer, nicest**) **1** pleasing or good: *A nice example is given by the evolution of fruit flies.* ◇ *In summer the weather is nicer and therefore more people will visit the park.* ◇ **it is ~ to do sth** *It would be nice to see comparisons like these using more countries.* **2** (*formal*) involving a very small detail or difference SYN SUBTLE (3): *It is often necessary that nice distinctions be made.*

nice·ly /ˈnaɪsli/ *adv.* in a pleasing way; well: *This pattern fits nicely with the economic boom experienced in Asia in that period.* ◇ *Their debates nicely illustrate the difficulties of evaluating the impact of plague from surviving medieval sources.*

niche /niːʃ; nɪtʃ/ *noun* **1** (*business*) an opportunity to sell a particular product to a particular group of people: *The production of organic food represented a lucrative market niche.* ◇ **~ in sth** *After the age of sail had passed, a new niche was carved out for sail in recreational, sports and training applications.* ◇ **+ noun** *Ecotourism remains a small niche market.* **2** (*biology*) a position or role taken by a kind of living thing within its community. Different living things may fill the same niche in different places: *Although the wild worm lives in the soil, little is known about its ecological niche or natural history.* ◇ *After the extinction of the dinosaurs, many new life forms arose to fill the huge number of empty evolutionary niches.* **3** a comfortable or suitable role, job or way of life: *She found a niche as an arts administrator.* **4 ~ (in sth)** a small hollow place, for example in a rock or the side of a hill; a small hollow place in a wall to contain a statue, etc: *Higher sea levels may have produced the higher-level passages and horizontal niches visible in the landscape.*

N

night /naɪt/ *noun* [U, C] the time between one day and the next when it is dark, when people usually sleep: *Here, heavy traffic can be a serious problem at almost any time of the day or night.* ◇ *The jury had to spend the night in a hotel.* ◇ **at ~** *The pain usually occurs at night, due to the foot being elevated in bed.* ◇ **in/during the ~** *Some young children are repeatedly wakeful for long periods during the night.* ◇ **by ~** *Birds were kept in a temperature-controlled room maintained at 35°C by day and at 15°C by night.* ◇ **+ noun** *Another study focused on night shift health care workers.* OPP DAY (3)

nil /nɪl/ *noun* [U] nothing: *In these circumstances, the chances of controlling any infectious disease would be practically nil.*

nine /naɪn/ *number* 9 HELP There are examples of how to use numbers at the entry for **five**.

ni·trate /ˈnaɪtreɪt/ *noun* [U, C] (*chemistry*) a COMPOUND containing NITROGEN and OXYGEN. There are several different nitrates and they are used especially to make soil better for growing crops: **+ noun** *Nitrate pollution of rivers and lakes is a matter of serious environmental concern.*

ni·tro·gen /ˈnaɪtrədʒən/ *noun* [U] (*symb.* **N**) the chemical element of ATOMIC NUMBER 7. Nitrogen is a gas that is found in large quantities in the earth's atmosphere: *In the Middle East, peas and lentils were planted to replenish the soil's nitrogen content.* ■ **ni·tro·gen·ous** /naɪˈtrɒdʒənəs; *NAmE* naɪˈtrɑːdʒənəs/ *adj.*: *The 1960s saw the advent of large-scale chemical farming with nitrogenous fertilizers.*

no[1] /nəʊ; *NAmE* noʊ/ *det.* **1** not one; not any; not a: *There is no evidence that asylum seekers enter the country because they wish to benefit from free health care.* ◇ *No studies in non-English-speaking European shopping malls have been conducted so far.* ◇ *No individual is more important than the society itself.* ◇ *No two cases are exactly alike.* ⊃ *see also* NO ONE **2** used, for example on notices, to say that sth is not allowed: *Among responders, 90.1% saw 'no smoking' signs in their departments.* **3** used to express the opposite of what is mentioned: *Nietzsche was no German nationalist.* ◇ *The harvesting of the cane was no easy task.*

no[2] /nəʊ; *NAmE* noʊ/ *adv.* used before adjectives and adverbs to mean 'not': *After taxes, he might be left with no more than $30 000.* ◇ *The new rules require companies to publish accounts no later than six months after financial year end.*

the no·bil·ity /nəʊˈbɪləti; *NAmE* noʊˈbɪləti/ *noun* [sing.+ sing./pl. v.] people of high social position who have titles such as LORD SYN ARISTOCRACY (1): *They were tied to feudal landlords who could be members of the nobility or the clergy or both.* ◇ *In many European societies, the nobility sought to defend its privileged status.*

noble[1] /ˈnəʊbl; *NAmE* ˈnoʊbl/ *adj.* (**no·bler** /ˈnəʊblə(r); *NAmE* ˈnoʊblər/, **nob·lest** /ˈnəʊblɪst; *NAmE* ˈnoʊblɪst/) **1** belonging to a family of high social rank SYN ARISTOCRATIC: *One feature of the great noble families of Europe was their international flavour.* ◇ *Many of the earliest societies included a ruling group based on noble birth.* **2** having or showing fine personal qualities that people admire, such as courage, HONESTY and care for others: *Noble ambitions rarely motivate fictional politicians.* ◇ *Nero wanted to lead Rome from gladiatorial shows to nobler entertainments.*

noble[2] /ˈnəʊbl; *NAmE* ˈnoʊbl/ *noun* a person who comes from a family of high social rank; a member of the nobility SYN ARISTOCRAT: *The kings and nobles of ancient Greece built massive defensive walls and temples, as well as luxurious palaces and tombs.*

no·body /ˈnəʊbədi; *NAmE* ˈnoʊbədi/ *pron.* = NO ONE OPP SOMEBODY

noc·tur·nal /nɒkˈtɜːnl; *NAmE* nɑːkˈtɜːrnl/ *adj.* done, happening or active at night: *The activity and movement of nocturnal animals such as mice slows down in constant light.* ◇ *Most nocturnal coughs in children are not related to asthma.* OPP DIURNAL (2)

node /nəʊd; *NAmE* noʊd/ *noun* **1** a point in a network or diagram at which lines, paths or systems meet, cross or divide: *The hospital service has to be transformed from being a piece of real estate to becoming a node in a network delivering systems of care.* **2** a piece of equipment attached to a network: *As all messages pass through the central node, the loss of the central node brings down the network.* **3** a small hard mass of TISSUE, especially near a joint in the human body: **+ noun** *Lymph node disease was the second most common reported site of infection.* **4** (*biology*) a place on the STEM of a plant from which a branch or leaf grows: *Leaves can occur singly at each node, in pairs, or in groups of three or more.* **5** (*physics*) the points on a wave that have MINIMAL (= the smallest possible) AMPLITUDE: *A placed finger creates a node on a vibrating violin string.*

noise /nɔɪz/ *noun* **1** [U, C] a sound, especially when it is loud or unpleasant: *Noise is the most frequent occupational hazard.* ◇ *Some patients might find background noise and chatting reassuring.* ◇ *Fear can be triggered by hearing a loud noise.* ◇ **~ of sth** *Thunder is the noise of shock waves* *rippling out from the explosive expansion of air in the lightning flash.* **2** [U] (*technical*) extra electrical or electronic signals that are not part of the signal that is being broadcast or TRANSMITTED and that may damage it: **signal-to-noise ratio** *For each playback, we selected screeching calls of a particular group of mongooses with a good signal-to-noise ratio.* **3** [U] information that is not wanted and that can make it difficult for the important or useful information to be seen clearly: *The differences in the quality of the experts giving opinions will introduce a certain level of noise into the data.*

nom·in·al /ˈnɒmɪnl; *NAmE* ˈnɑːmɪnl/ *adj.* **1** (*economics*) (of a rate or value) expressed in terms of current prices or figures, without allowing for changes over time SYN UNADJUSTED: *The real and the nominal interest rates differ by the expected rate of inflation.* ◇ *While the average nominal wage increased by more than 23%, the rise in prices meant the average real wage increased by just 4%.* ➲ *compare* REAL (3) **2** (of a sum or amount) very small; much less than the usual or real value or amount SYN TOKEN² (1): *This software is provided free or at a nominal cost.* ◇ *A nominal amount (about 5 kg) of CO_2 gas is vented outside the plant.* **3** being sth in name only, and not in reality: *The king, although nominal commander, was totally dependent on the collaboration of the provincial assemblies.* **4** (*grammar*) connected with a noun or nouns: *Practically any verbal expressions, and most adjectival expressions, can be converted into a nominal expression.* ■ **nom·in·al·ly** /ˈnɒmɪnəli; *NAmE* ˈnɑːmɪnəli/ *adv.*: *His policies reduced public expenditure and nominally increased tax revenues.* ◇ *Volunteers were compensated only nominally with refreshments.* ◇ *He spent just twelve months in prison before being released from what was nominally a life sentence.*

nom·in·ate /ˈnɒmɪneɪt; *NAmE* ˈnɑːmɪneɪt/ *verb* **1** to formally suggest that sb/sth should be chosen for an important role, prize, position, etc. SYN PROPOSE (1): **~ sb/sth** *If a parent declines the invitation to attend, another family member may be nominated.* ◇ **~ sb/sth for sth** *A number of those making donations had subsequently been nominated for political honours.* ◇ **~ sb/sth as sth** *In Britain there is no opportunity for the public to decide who a party nominates as candidate.* ◇ **~ sb/sth to do sth** *In 2004, the film was nominated to represent Peru at the Academy Awards.* **2 ~ sb** to choose sb to do a particular job SYN APPOINT (1): *The bureaucracy was headed by the State Soviet, whose members were nominated by the tsar.* ◇ **~ sb to/as sth** *In the practice of papal provision, the pope actually nominated candidates to benefices.* ◇ **~ sb to do sth** *Galerius nominated an old military colleague, Licinius, to succeed the executed Severus.* **3 ~ sth** to officially choose a time, title, place, etc. for sth SYN SPECIFY: *A day was nominated for the exchange of contracts.*

nom·in·ation /ˌnɒmɪˈneɪʃn; *NAmE* ˌnɑːmɪˈneɪʃn/ *noun* [U, C] the act of suggesting or choosing sb/sth as a candidate in an election, or for a job or an award; the fact of being suggested for this: **~ (of sth)** *The committee is responsible for the nomination of directors and key executives.* ◇ **~ (for sth)** *He won the Republican Party nomination for President in 1860.* ◇ *The film had seven Oscar nominations.*

non- /nɒn; *NAmE* nɑːn/ *prefix* (in nouns, adjectives and adverbs) not: *By the following month, Nanjing and the Soviet Union had signed a non-aggression pact.* ◇ *non-alcoholic drinks* ◇ *Such behaviour causes fish to be non-uniformly distributed within the aquatic environment.* HELP Most compounds with **non** are written with a hyphen in British English but are written as one word with no hyphen in American English.

ˌnon-ˈcitizen *noun* (*NAmE*) = ALIEN²

ˌnon-comˈpli·ance *noun* [U] **~ (with sth)** the fact of failing or refusing to obey a rule: *European cities face high penalties for non-compliance with the limits on urban air pollution.* OPP COMPLIANCE

none /nʌn/ *pron.* not one of a group of people or things; not any: *Each factor influences the others; none is/are dominant.* ◇ *Electricity remained relatively expensive, and most rural homes had none at that time.* ◇ **~ of sb/sth** *None of the 2005 samples of avian influenza showed any resistance to the drug.* ◇ *Various attempts have been made to classify coastal landscapes, but none of them is ideal.*
IDM **none ˈother than** used to emphasize who or what sb/sth is, when this is surprising: *It was none other than Dickens who gave Griffith this idea.*

GRAMMAR POINT

none is/are

- **None** means *not one*, and, like **one**, it takes a singular verb: *Used alone, **none** of these methods **is** entirely satisfactory.* ◇ *Used alone, **not one** of these methods **is** entirely satisfactory.* ◇ ***None** of the correlations **is** significant at the 95% confidence level.*
- However, in more informal English, when **none** is used with a plural noun, the verb may be plural. In academic English, too, the plural verb is sometimes used, although less frequently than the singular verb: *In fact, **none** of these problems **are** actually rooted in human nature.* ◇ *There are an infinite number of complementary light colour sets, but **none that include** wavelengths in the green field.* This usage is sometimes considered incorrect, however, so it may be safer to use the singular verb, especially in British English.
- In general American English, when **none** is used with a plural noun, a plural verb is always used: ***None** of the trains **are** going to Boston.*

none·the·less AWL /ˌnʌnðəˈles/ *adv.* despite this fact SYN NEVERTHELESS: *Further research is needed in these areas. Nonetheless, some preliminary conclusions can be drawn:...* ◇ *By the end of 1922, he had lost the ability to write. He continued his work, nonetheless, dictating articles.*

ˌnon-eˈxistent *adj.* not existing; not real: *Flood protection measures in areas around the city were almost non-existent at that time.* ■ **ˌnon-eˈxistence** *noun* [U] **~ (of sb/sth)** *They refused to comment on the existence or non-existence of a waiting list.*

ˌnon-ˈhuman *adj.* not human: *There are some notable differences between humans and other mammals, including non-human primates.* ◇ *The key to understanding behaviour—human or non-human—lies in the complex interplay of genes and environment.* ➲ *compare* HUMAN¹, INHUMAN

ˌnon-interˈven·tion (*also* **ˌnon-interˈfer·ence**) *noun* [U] the policy or practice of not becoming involved in other people's disagreements, especially those of foreign countries: *Humanitarian principles often conflict with principles of sovereignty and non-intervention.*

ˌnon-inˈvasive *adj.* (of medical treatment) not involving cutting into the body: *Emerging non-invasive techniques have challenged conventional surgery for treating the condition.*

ˌnon-ˈlinear *adj.* **1** that does not develop from one thing to another in a single smooth series of stages: *These films tell their stories in a modernist non-linear fashion, moving between past and present.* ◇ *As warming continues, there is an ever-growing risk of 'tipping points' being crossed, leading to non-linear processes and abrupt changes.* OPP LINEAR (2) **2** (*mathematics*) involving two or more DIMENSIONS;

of an EQUATION with at least one term of power two or higher: *Projectile motion is non-linear as demonstrated by the curved line.* OPP LINEAR (3) **3** (*mathematics*) involving or showing a relationship between quantities in which the rates of change in those quantities are not equal: *The law of diminishing returns is based on a non-linear relationship between inputs and outputs.* OPP LINEAR (4)

ˌnon-ˈnative *adj.* **1** (of animals and plants) not existing naturally in a place but coming from somewhere else: *Non-native plants that have been brought to the UK can become invasive and damaging to other species.* OPP NATIVE¹ (1) **2** a **non-native** speaker of a language is one who has not spoken it from the time they first learnt to talk: *The participants comprised 23 non-native English speaking Indonesian students from a private university.* ➲ *compare* NATIVE SPEAKER

ˌnon-ˈpolar *adj.* (*physics, chemistry*) having no electrical or MAGNETIC POLARITY: *Water is a very poor solvent for non-polar molecules.* OPP POLAR (3)

ˌnon-ˈprofit (*BrE also* ˌnon-ˈprofit-making) *adj.* (of an organization) without the aim of making a profit: *Just Health Action (JHA) is a non-profit organization based in Seattle, Washington.* ◇ *In the non-profit sector, performance measurement is more challenging.*

ˌnon-speˈcif·ic *adj.* [usually before noun] **1** not definite or clearly defined; general: *The reference to 'group' is non-specific, with no indication of how group membership is determined.* **2** (*medical*) (of pain, a disease, etc.) with more than one possible cause: *Chest pain is a non-specific symptom that must be carefully assessed.*

N

ˌnon-ˈstandard *adj.* **1** not the usual size, type, etc: *Many customers wanted something out of the ordinary, such as frosted or coloured glass, or non-standard sizes of window.* ➲ *compare* STANDARD² (2) **2** (of language) not considered correct by most educated people: *The use of non-standard English often becomes stronger during adolescence.* ➲ *compare* STANDARD² (4)

ˌnon-ˈtrivial *adj.* **1** important: *Intensive study of diverse languages has made available a significant pool of non-controversial and non-trivial facts about languages.* **2** (*mathematics*) used to describe the solution given when at least one VARIABLE is not equal to zero or an IDENTITY: *No non-trivial solution had yet been found for the complete equation.*

ˌnon-ˈverbal *adj.* [usually before noun] not involving words or speech: *Non-verbal communication, such as whether to shake hands or not, varies according to culture.*

ˌnon-ˈwhite *adj.* belonging to a race of people who do not have white skin: *All but one of the non-white participants was African American.* ■ ˌnon-ˈwhite *noun*: *The initial reaction to immigrants and non-whites was mixed.*

ˈno one (*also* no·body) *pron.* not anyone; no person: *No one disputes that language is central to human affairs.* HELP **No one** is much more common than **nobody** in written English.

nor /nɔː(r)/ *conj., adv.* and not: **neither... nor...** *Miller is neither sentimental nor romantic.* ◇ *We can neither prove nor disprove these assertions.* ◇ **not... nor...** *The ice cover in the polar oceans is not continuous, nor is it complete.*

norm AWL /nɔːm; *NAmE* nɔːrm/ *noun* **1** [C, usually pl.] a standard or pattern of behaviour that is typical of or accepted within a particular group or society: *Mass media reflect as well as create social norms.* ◇ *The group controlled everything, and anyone who violated its norms risked forced exile.* ◇ *What is accepted as a cultural norm today may not exist or be demonstrated in the same way in the future.* ◇ **~ of sth** *In Ancient Greece, girls would absorb the norms of appropriate social behaviour in childhood, from their mothers and aunts.* **2** (*often* **the norm**) [sing.] a situation or a pattern of behaviour that is usual or typical SYN RULE¹ (2): *Over the past twenty years, it has become the accepted norm for women to be in employment.* ◇ *In many African cities, the informal sector is the norm, not the exception.* **3** [C] a required or agreed standard or amount: *The widely shared values concerning what it is fair to expect employees to do and employers to pay are termed work and pay norms.* ◇ *The government claims that background radioactivity is well below international norms.*

▸ ADJECTIVE + NORM **existing • accepted • dominant, prevailing • traditional • international • global • social • legal • cultural • behavioural • constitutional • democratic • moral • ethical** *Smith's lyric poetry marks a significant departure from the prevailing norms of late eighteenth-century verse.*

▸ NOUN + NORM **group • gender • human rights** *Zelda is unhappy with her adherence to traditional gender norms within marriage.* | **pay • work • industry** *These agreements were concluded on the basis of royalty rates that were close to industry norms.*

▸ VERB + NORM **accept • enforce • follow** *Individuals often act collectively by accepting the norms and values of a group of people.* | **create • adopt • internalize • promote • violate • challenge** *The alienated modern individual gains a sense of belonging by internalizing ethical norms that are celebrated as natural to his or her nation.* | **establish, set • develop • apply** *The company created a formula that set the norms for cat food advertising.*

▸ NORM + VERB **influence • govern • regulate • guide** *Some behaviours are powerfully influenced by peer norms.*

nor·mal¹ AWL /ˈnɔːml; *NAmE* ˈnɔːrml/ *adj.* **1** typical, usual or ordinary; what you would expect: *Observations show that, despite the patient's complaint, sleeping time is within the normal range.* ◇ *These clouds are so thin that under normal circumstances they cannot be seen.* ◇ *The novel ends with Jones losing his job, the girl he loves and his chance to lead a normal life.* ◇ **it is ~ to do sth** *Until recently, it was perfectly normal to see job adverts asking for a 'dynamic young individual' or stipulating a maximum age of 30 or 35.* **2** not suffering from any physical or mental DISORDER: *Patients with epilepsy may appear perfectly normal between seizures.* ◇ *The dividing line between normal and abnormal behaviour is sometimes difficult to draw.* OPP ABNORMAL **3 ~ to sth** (*technical*) (of a line, RAY or other feature) crossing a particular line or surface at an angle of 90 degrees: *The electric field E must be external to the conductor and normal to its surface.*

WORD FAMILY
normal *adj., noun*
normally *adv.*
normalize *verb*
normalization *noun*
normality *noun*
norm *noun*
abnormal *adj.*
abnormally *adv.*

nor·mal² AWL /ˈnɔːml; *NAmE* ˈnɔːrml/ *noun* **1** [U] the usual or average state, level or standard: *In 2001, rainfall for the study area was 40 cm below normal.* ◇ *Beneath features such as the Andes, the Alps or the Himalayas, the continental crust is much thicker than normal.* ◇ *After the boom time, the demand on the housing market returned to normal.* **2** (*technical*) a line at 90 degrees to a particular line or surface: *In general there are three normals to a parabola from any given point inside it.*

ˌnormal distriˈbution *noun* (*statistics*) the usual way in which a particular feature varies among a large number of things or people, represented on a GRAPH by a line that rises to a high SYMMETRICAL curve in the middle: *The distribution of the heights of a random sample of adult men follows a roughly normal distribution.*

nor·mal·ity AWL /nɔːˈmæləti; *NAmE* nɔːrˈmæləti/ (*also* nor·malcy /ˈnɔːmlsi; *NAmE* ˈnɔːrmlsi/ *especially in NAmE*) *noun* [U] **1** a situation where everything is normal or as you would expect it to be: *The article argues that women* *wanted to return to a sense of normality at the end of the war.* **2 ~ (of sb/sth)** a state of being free from physical or mental DISORDER: *The mother may have fears about the delivery, or doubts about the normality of the baby.*

nor·mal·ize (*BrE also* **-ise**) **AWL** /ˈnɔːməlaɪz; *NAmE* ˈnɔːr-məlaɪz/ *verb* **1** [T, I] **~ (sth)** to bring sth to, or to return to, a normal or standard pattern or condition: *When Coleridge revised the poem for publication, he normalized the spelling and removed archaic words.* ◇ *Once the infection has cleared, the heart rhythm often normalizes.* **2** [T] **~ sth** (*statistics*) to adjust a set of values, often in order to compare them with another set of values: *When we normalize the data, the area under the distribution curve is 1.* **HELP** If you want to compare two data sets representing scores marked on different scales, you can **normalize** the data by dividing each element of the data set by the value of its largest member. ■ **nor·mal·iza·tion, -isa·tion** **AWL** /ˌnɔːməlaɪˈzeɪʃn; *NAmE* ˌnɔːrmələˈzeɪʃn/ *noun* [U] **~ (of sth)** *A study of 58 patients showed that treatment with aspirin resulted in significant normalization of blood gases.* ◇ *Normalization of the extracted data removes experimental biases.*

nor·mal·ly **AWL** /ˈnɔːməli; *NAmE* ˈnɔːrməli/ *adv.* **1** usually; in normal circumstances: *The largest part of the parental leave is normally used during the child's first years.* ◇ *Stem cells are normally present in the blood in very small numbers.* ◇ *Most people who travel often seek out foods that they do not normally get at home.* **2** in the usual or ordinary way: *Girls with Rett's syndrome develop normally in the first year and then regress.* ◇ **~ distributed** (*statistics*) *When data are normally distributed, the mean and median are close together.*

nor·ma·tive /ˈnɔːmətɪv; *NAmE* ˈnɔːrmətɪv/ *adj.* describing, setting or connected with standards or rules; acting as a standard or saying what sth should be like: *Literature taught the proper use of words, and there is evidence for a normative approach to language in Plato.* ◇ *It is important to appreciate that the model is normative, aiming to describe an ideal situation, not to describe reality.* ➲ *compare* DESCRIPTIVE (1)

north¹ /nɔːθ; *NAmE* nɔːrθ/ *noun* [U, sing.] (*abbr.* **N**, **No.**) **1** (*usually* **the north**) the direction that is on your left when you watch the sun rise; one of the four main points of the COMPASS: *cold winds coming from the north* ◇ **to the ~ (of...)** *Mount Kenya is to the north of Nairobi.* ➲ *compare* EAST¹, SOUTH¹, WEST¹ **2 the north, the North** the northern part of a country, a region or the world: *birds migrating from the north* ◇ *Houses are less expensive in the North than in the South.* **3 the North** the richer and more developed countries of the world, especially in Europe and N America: *The summit was likely to be a failure due to the North's refusal to commit itself to safeguarding species diversity.*

north² /nɔːθ; *NAmE* nɔːrθ/ *adj.* [only before noun] (*abbr.* **N**, **No.**) in or towards the north: *North London* ◇ *the north bank of the river* ■ **north** *adv.*: *The house faces north.*

ˌnorth-ˈeast *noun* (*usually* **the north-east**) [sing.] (*abbr.* **NE**) the direction or region at an equal distance between north and east: *In winter, the monsoon blows from the north-east.* ■ **ˌnorth-ˈeast** *adv., adj.* **ˌnorth-ˈeastern** *adj.* [only before noun]

north·ern /ˈnɔːðən; *NAmE* ˈnɔːrðərn/ (*also* **Northern**) *adj.* [usually before noun] (*abbr.* **N**, **No.**) located in the north or facing north; connected with or typical of the north part of the world or a region: *the northern slopes of the mountain* ◇ *northern Scotland* ◇ *a northern accent*

ˌnorth-ˈwest *noun* (*usually* **the north-west**) [sing.] (*abbr.* **NW**) the direction or region at an equal distance between north and west: *The industrial heartland of Europe had moved from the north-west to the centre.* ■ **ˌnorth-ˈwest** *adv., adj.* **ˌnorth-ˈwestern** *adj.* [only before noun]

nose /nəʊz; *NAmE* noʊz/ *noun* the part of the face that sticks out above the mouth, used for breathing and smelling things: *During ascent in a plane, air in the ear, nose and throat cavities expands.*

not /nɒt; *NAmE* nɑːt/ *adv.* **1** used to form the negative of the verbs with *be*, *do* and *have* and modal verbs like *can* or *must*: *This pattern of migration is not a new phenomenon.* ◇ *This does not work when the commodity is non-renewable.* ◇ *Around two thirds reported that their business had not experienced any lost time.* ◇ *The food that the other rats are eating cannot be poisonous or they would not be alive.* **2** used to give the following word or phrase a negative meaning: *Not everybody uses this convention.* ◇ *Sometimes, but not often, pagan temples were taken over for Christian use.* ◇ *He decided not to go to hospital for further management of his pain.* ◇ *The survey begins with not one but two theorists whose writings are related.* **3 or ~** used to show a negative possibility: *Respondents reported whether or not they participate in team sports.* ◇ *This involves deploying scarce resources in projects that may or may not succeed.*

IDM **not a... | not one...** used for emphasis to mean 'no thing or person': *There is not a single Socialist Realist work of art set in the future.* **not only... (but) (also)...** used to emphasize that sth else is also true: *Photographs can be invaluable not only as records of historical landscapes but as evidence of cultural attitudes.* ➲ language bank *at* ADDITION **ˈnot that** used to state that you are not suggesting sth: *Not that there is anything necessarily wrong with this approach, but it does sidestep one major issue.*

not·able /ˈnəʊtəbl; *NAmE* ˈnoʊtəbl/ *adj.* deserving to be noticed or to receive attention; important: *The retirement age has declined substantially in nearly all cases, with the notable exceptions of Japan and Korea.* ◇ *a notable example/feature/difference/change* ◇ **it is ~ that...** *It is notable that over half of the TB cases in children in London were in children born in the UK.* ◇ **~ for sth** *These studies are notable for their focus on social as well as ecological processes.* ➲ thesaurus note *at* IMPORTANT

N

not·ably /ˈnəʊtəbli; *NAmE* ˈnoʊtəbli/ *adv.* **1** to a great degree; in a way that is interesting and that people notice: *Gender is notably absent from mainstream discussions of globalization.* ◇ *Recordings of blood pressure, BMI and smoking status were all notably high.* **2** used for giving a good or the most important example of sth **SYN** ESPECIALLY (1): *The British Caribbean, notably Jamaica, was the wealthiest area in the first British Empire.*

no·ta·tion /nəʊˈteɪʃn; *NAmE* noʊˈteɪʃn/ *noun* [U, C] **~ (for sth)** a system of signs or symbols used to represent information, especially in mathematics, science and music: *The mathematical notation for this is P(x), where P stands for predicate.* ◇ *In order to describe the complete algorithm, we use a standard notation.*

note¹ /nəʊt; *NAmE* noʊt/ *verb* **1** to mention sth because it is important or interesting: **~ sth** *Having noted the above strengths of the book, I now turn to some of its weaknesses.* ◇ **~ that...** *Carter notes that religion can be a powerful, unifying force in conflict situations.* ◇ **~ how/where, etc...** *Bauman notes how a new consumer society has emerged from processes of capitalist restructuring.* ◇ **it is noted that...** *In the article, it is noted that further theoretical as well as experimental researches are necessary.* ◇ **be worth noting (that...)** *Two important general results are worth noting at this point.* **2** to notice or pay careful attention to sth: **~ sth** *Note the difference between Figures 8.6 and 8.7.* ◇ **~ (that)...** *Note that there are no column headings at the start of the table.* ◇ **~ how/where, etc...** *Note how the faces are blanked out to protect the individuals in the photographs.* ◇ **be noted that...** *It should be noted that this research violates certain ethical principles.* ◇ **be worth**

noting (that/how, etc...) *It is worth noting in Figure 2.4 how the sales function has risen to a more dominant position.* **HELP** The abbreviation **NB** is used in writing to make sb take notice of a particular piece of information that is important (from Latin *nota bene*): *NB The drug should be used with caution in patients with hypertension and heart disease.*

PHR V **ˌnote sth ˈdown** to write down sth important so that you will not forget it: *The interviewer poses a range of questions, noting down the replies he/she receives for subsequent analysis.*

▸ NOTE + NOUN **importance • difference • similarity • change • point • problem • effect • fact** *Oliver and Wilkinson noted some similarities in practice between the USA and Japan towards unions.*

▸ NOTE + ADVERB **above, earlier, previously • here • below** *As noted above, the strength of linkage varies among different pairs of genes.*

▸ IT IS + ADJECTIVE + TO NOTE **important • useful • interesting** *It is important to note here that participants were not informed of the relative importance of these cues.*

note² /nəʊt; *NAmE* noʊt/ *noun* **1** [C] a short piece of writing to help you remember sth: **make a ~ (of sth)** *Make a note of any other medication taken by the patient.* ◇ **keep a ~ (of sth)** *The operator's assistant kept a note of which letters lit up on the lampboard.* **2 notes** [pl.] information that you write down while you are doing sth such as working on sth, reading sth or listening to sb speaking; information that is collected about a particular person: **take notes** *Detailed field notes were taken during the observations.* ◇ *Riebau suggested that he write directly to Davy and send his lecture notes and drawings.* ◇ *A patient has a right of access to their medical notes under the Data Protection Act.* **3** [C] a short comment on a word or passage in a book: *In some cases the translators have added explanatory notes.* ◇ *There is an extensive notes section and a short selected bibliography.* ➲ *see also* FOOTNOTE (1) **4** [sing.] a particular quality in sth, for example in sb's voice, or in what is said or happens: **~ of sth** *'Success', he added with a characteristic note of pessimism, 'is only a delayed failure.'* ◇ **on a... ~** *On a positive note, Dr Barrett documents the huge benefits to passengers of airline deregulation.* ◇ **sound a ~ (of sth)** *Lawler (1987) has sounded a note of caution about overgeneralizing about this particular climatic trend.* **5** [C] an official document with a particular purpose: *In a letter in the British Medical Journal, Hardy wrote that GPs write sick notes unthinkingly and irresponsibly.* ◇ *The delivery note corresponded to the purchase order.* **6** (*also* **bank·note**) (*both especially BrE*) (*NAmE usually* **bill**) [C] a piece of paper money: *The printing of additional notes must be authorized by the European Central Bank.* ◇ *The notes and coins that form a part of what goes by the name 'money' possess no intrinsic worth.* **7** [C] a short letter: *The next day Khrushchev sent a second note demanding that the United States withdraw its missiles in Turkey.* ◇ *It is extremely difficult to determine whether someone is the victim of suicide when there is no suicide note.* **8** [C] a single sound made by the voice or a musical instrument; the written or printed sign for a musical note: *Each segment of program thus had its own musical 'signature'—a series of squeaks and musical notes of rapidly changing pitches.*

IDM **of ˈnote** of importance or of great interest: *Hardly anybody of note foresaw the chain of events that unravelled.* ◇ *She has no past medical history of note and does not take any regular medications.* **of particular ˈnote** especially interesting: *The Malmö study is of particular note because it used sustained screening.* ◇ *Of particular note for the present discussion, the recent tenfold increase in human populations has occurred largely in cities.* **take ˈnote (of sth)** to pay attention to sth and understand its importance: *Watching a child and taking note of their body language can reveal much about how a child feels.* ➲ *more at* COMPARE

noted /ˈnəʊtɪd; *NAmE* ˈnoʊtɪd/ *adj.* well known because of a special skill or feature **SYN** FAMOUS: *The noted English economist John Hicks famously said that 'the best of all monopoly profits is a quiet life'.* ◇ **~ for sth** *This holiday is noted for popular street parades and large displays of 'lotus lanterns'.* ◇ **~ as sth** *South Africa's democratic transition in the early 1990s is noted as one of the success stories within the continent.*

note·worthy /ˈnəʊtwɜːði; *NAmE* ˈnoʊtwɜːrði/ *adj.* deserving to be noticed or to receive attention because it is unusual, important or interesting **SYN** SIGNIFICANT (1): *Many recent studies mention this problem, but three are especially noteworthy.* ◇ *Though he got a lot of screen work in Hollywood, none of it was particularly noteworthy.* ◇ **it is ~ that...** *It is noteworthy that in 1215 responses the students claimed to know the answers, but in over two thirds of the cases they were actually wrong.* ◇ **~ for (doing) sth** *Two other papers are noteworthy for considering more general processes and presenting empirical results.*

noth·ing /ˈnʌθɪŋ/ *pron.* not anything; no single thing: *Nothing can be done to restore memory in such cases.* ◇ *Very little labour could be expected from men who had nothing to eat.* ◇ *There may have been nothing wrong with the strategy, but the execution was flawed.* ◇ **~ else** *If nothing else changes, the result will be that aggregate demand is maintained at the same level.* ◇ **~ at all** *Over half of all people paid nothing at all for any service.*

IDM **be/have nothing to do with sb/sth** to have no connection with sb/sth: *There will be a number of other factors that affect their height that are nothing to do with gender.* ◇ *People routinely observe rituals that have nothing to do with spirits or deities.* **for ˈnothing** **1** without payment **SYN** FREE³ (1): *The video games industry gives away the software as a free download and users can therefore play for nothing.* **2** with no reward or result: *The thousands who had died in the war had given their lives for nothing.* **ˈnothing but** only; no more/less than: *The children of this generation have grown up speaking nothing but English.* ◇ *The admiral foresaw nothing but the total overthrow of his whole fleet.* **ˈnothing if not** extremely; very: *These matters are nothing if not controversial.* **ˈnothing less than** used to emphasize how great or extreme sth is: *Durkheim insisted that his subject required nothing less than a new scientific discipline to investigate it.* **nothing ˈlike** **1** not at all like: *A whale's flipper looks nothing like a sheep's hoof or a monkey's hand, and yet we can recognize the same underlying structure.* **2** not nearly; not at all: *In the rest of the world, there is nothing like this degree of globalization.* **ˌnothing ˈmuch** not a great amount of sth; nothing of great value or importance: *The implication of this theory for policy is that nothing much can be done to increase happiness.* ➲ *more at* COME

no·tice¹ /ˈnəʊtɪs; *NAmE* ˈnoʊtɪs/ *verb* **1** (not usually used in the progressive tenses) to see or hear sb/sth; to become aware of sb/sth: **~ sth/sb** *Individuals were asked whether they had noticed health warnings on cigarette packages during the past month.* ◇ **~ that...** *During the experiments, Heinsohn and Packer (1995) noticed that certain lionesses took on the role of leader.* ◇ **it is noticed that...** *It was noticed that a single serving of instant coffee contains 120 mg of polyphenols.* ◇ **~ what/how, etc...** *This presupposes that the public effectively notice what policymakers actually do.* ◇ **~ sb/sth do sth/doing sth** *The patient has noticed her heart beating fast.* **2** (not usually used in the progressive tenses) to pay attention to sb/sth: **~ sb/sth** *Respondents were asked to try and remember their dreams, noticing odd features or the way things behaved.* ◇ **be worth noticing (that...)** *It is worth noticing that age is insignificant in all models but one.* ◇ **it should be noticed that...** *It should be* *noticed that most often the choice of a breeding site and that of a mate happen at the same time.*

no·tice² /ˈnəʊtɪs; *NAmE* ˈnoʊtɪs/ *noun* **1** [U] the fact of sb paying attention to sb/sth or knowing about sth: *This change attracted little notice at the time.* ◇ *It is hard for any global brands to escape notice.* ◇ **take ~ of sth** *Several national newspapers took notice of this policy change, though federal health officials did little to publicize it.* **2** [U] information or a warning given in advance of sth that is going to happen: *One factory claimed it could make 100 000 car flags a week, given sufficient notice.* ◇ *At least six days' advance notice should normally be given by the organizer of a procession.* ◇ **without ~** *A sudden withdrawal of a product without notice may create bad publicity for a company.* **3** [U, C] a formal letter or statement saying that you will or must do sth, for example leave your job at the end of a particular period of time: *Employees who have worked between one month and two years continuously for the same employer are entitled to one week's notice.* ◇ *The council served a notice that required the removal of buildings belonging to the plaintiff.* **4** [C] a small advertisement or ANNOUNCEMENT in a newspaper or magazine, or on a website: *The sample was sought by posting a notice on an Internet forum inviting both males and females aged 50 years and older to participate in a research project.* **5** [C] a sheet of paper or an email giving written information about an event, etc: *There was positive feedback on receiving community-based information by email, such as notices from schools and community clubs.* **6** [C] a board or sign giving information, an instruction or a warning: *Warning notices for underage sale of tobacco were present in 53% of premises.*
IDM **at short ˈnotice** not long in advance; without warning or time for preparation: *Some customers may require service outside normal working hours and at very short notice.*

no·tice·able /ˈnəʊtɪsəbl; *NAmE* ˈnoʊtɪsəbl/ *adj.* easy to see or notice; clear or definite: *Many gene mutations do not have any noticeable effect.* ◇ *Their lack of confidence in speaking was particularly noticeable.* ◇ **it is ~ that...** *It is noticeable that most cities in these prefectures saw population decreases between 1999 and 2005.* ■ **no·tice·ably** /ˈnəʊtɪsəbli; *NAmE* ˈnoʊtɪsəbli/ *adv.*: *Although they are similar measures, they can in practice give noticeably different results.* ◇ *The proportion of female migrants increased noticeably between 1960 and 2000.*

no·ti·fi·ca·tion /ˌnəʊtɪfɪˈkeɪʃn; *NAmE* ˌnoʊtɪfɪˈkeɪʃn/ *noun* [U, C] the act of giving or receiving official information about sth: *The EC Treaty required prior notification before state aid payments could be made.* ◇ **~ of sth** *Parents must receive written notification of the health needs of their child and the type of treatment received.* ◇ *In the UK, notifications of cases of TB have not fallen since the 1980s.*

no·tify /ˈnəʊtɪfaɪ; *NAmE* ˈnoʊtɪfaɪ/ *verb* (**no·ti·fies, no·ti·fy·ing, no·ti·fied, no·ti·fied**) **1** [T] to tell sb about sth in a formal or official way **SYN** INFORM (1): **~ sb** *Parents should be notified immediately if a younger child has left the school grounds.* ◇ **~ sb about/of sth** *New vehicle purchasers are notified of the fuel economies for urban and highway travel.* ◇ **~ sb that...** *The company wrote to 161 000 customers, notifying them that their credit cards would be withdrawn within 35 days.* **2** [T, I] to report a particular disease, event or situation to an official authority: **~ sth (to sb)** *A clinically suspected case of Escherichia coli O157 infection must now be notified.* ◇ *Financial services merger cases have raised interesting issues regarding the failure to notify.* ■ **no·ti·fi·able** /ˈnəʊtɪfaɪəbl; *NAmE* ˈnoʊtɪfaɪəbl/ *adj.*: *TB is a notifiable disease and contact tracing is usually done through chest clinics.*

no·tion **AWL** /ˈnəʊʃn; *NAmE* ˈnoʊʃn/ *noun* an idea, a belief or an understanding of sth: *Communication is a fairly vague notion.* ◇ **~ of sth** *The notion of students as customers is now far from new.* ◇ *The very notion of what constituted being Greek changed over time.* ◇ *The new generation of writers wrote plays that challenged traditional notions of British theatre.* ◇ **~ that...** *The study supports the notion that the causes of obesity are complex.* ➲ thesaurus note *at* IDEA
▸ ADJECTIVE + NOTION **very • traditional • conventional • old • modern, contemporary • popular • general • basic • fundamental • broad • abstract • theoretical • preconceived • simplistic • vague • common-sense • romantic** *The study dispels some popular notions about bullying in schools.*
▸ VERB + NOTION **introduce • clarify • reinforce • support • accept • embrace • invoke • endorse • reject • challenge, question • undermine • dispel** *British observers reinforced the notion that America was indissolubly linked to Britain through ties of race and language.*
▸ NOTION(S) OF + NOUN **identity • self • citizenship • responsibility • justice • freedom • fairness • rationality • equality • autonomy • race** *Notions of justice permeate the 'Godfather' movies and Shakespeare's 'King Lear'.*

no·tori·ous /nəʊˈtɔːriəs; *NAmE* noʊˈtɔːriəs/ *adj.* well known for being bad: *There are thousands of harmful species and diseases that have invaded the United States from other continents. Notorious examples include the brown tree snake and the plague.* ◇ **~ for (doing) sth** *The processes of law are notorious for delay.* ■ **no·tori·ous·ly** *adv.*: *Young infants and children are notoriously difficult to assess when they become unwell.* ◇ *Notoriously, a plant or an animal introduced from another part of the world may flourish better than a related native species.*

not·with·stand·ing **AWL** /ˌnɒtwɪθˈstændɪŋ; *NAmE* ˌnɑːtwɪθˈstændɪŋ/ *prep.* (also used following the noun it refers to) without being affected by sth; despite sth: *Notwithstanding the accumulated evidence, many economists remain sceptical.* ◇ **~ the fact that...** *Notwithstanding the fact that there are not distinct human races, the idea of race remains important in the contemporary world.* ◇ **noun +** *Regulations notwithstanding, most villagers could conduct life as they pleased, as long as they avoided calling attention to themselves.* ■ **not·with·stand·ing** *adv.* **SYN** NEVERTHELESS: *Liberalization of imports had a severe impact on business. Notwithstanding, large Mexican business groups continued to grow and prosper.* **not·with·stand·ing that** *conj.*: *The court ruled that the boy should be returned to his biological parents, notwithstanding that he had expressed a wish to remain with his foster mother.*

nought /nɔːt/ *number* (*BrE*) = ZERO¹ (1)

noun /naʊn/ *noun* (*abbr.* **n.**) (*grammar*) a word that refers to a person, a place or a thing, a quality or an activity: *In many languages, plural nouns are longer than singular nouns.* ◇ *'Wisdom' is a feminine noun in both Greek and Hebrew.* ➲ *see also* PROPER NOUN

ˈnoun phrase *noun* (*grammar*) a word or group of words in a sentence that behaves in the same way as a noun, that is as a subject, an object, a COMPLEMENT, or as the object of a preposition: *In the phrase 'I spoke to the driver of the car', 'the driver of the car' is a noun phrase.*

novel¹ /ˈnɒvl; *NAmE* ˈnɑːvl/ *noun* a story long enough to fill a complete book, in which the characters and events are usually imaginary: *In all, Greene wrote 26 novels and nine volumes of short stories.*

novel² /ˈnɒvl; *NAmE* ˈnɑːvl/ *adj.* different from anything known before; new and interesting: *These strategies may provide a novel approach for treating drug-resistant disease.* ◇ *It is usually new firms that pioneer novel forms of organization.*

nov·el·ist /ˈnɒvəlɪst; *NAmE* ˈnɑːvəlɪst/ *noun* a person who writes novels: *This is a collection of feminist readings of Romantic women poets, novelists and dramatists.*

nov·elty /ˈnɒvlti; *NAmE* ˈnɑːvlti/ *noun* (*pl.* -ies) **1** [U] **~ (of sth)** the quality of being new, different and interesting: *The manufacturer is optimistic that customers will appreciate the novelty of their approach.* **2** [C] a thing, person or situation that is interesting because it is new, unusual or has not been known before: *There was a time when television was a novelty and when the TV star was a new and unfamiliar phenomenon.*

now /naʊ/ *adv.* **1** (at) the present time: *The organization is now known as Oxfam Great Britain.* ◇ *Most large companies now consider the entire world as the market for their products.* ◇ **for ~** *There are several important reasons for this, but for now I shall focus on just one:...* ◇ **until ~** *Until now, diet and lifestyle have been overlooked as risk factors in the condition.* ◇ **(for)... years, etc. ~** *For many years now, it has been illegal for an employer to discriminate between job applicants on the basis of gender or ethnicity.* **2** at or from this moment: *Having discussed the results in general terms, we are now ready to examine the survey data in detail.* **3** as a result of sth that has happened: *Having found out the patient's preferences, it should now be possible to establish a management plan.* ◇ **~ that...** *Now that both her children attend school, she does voluntary work in local education.*
IDM **(every) now and aˈgain/ˈthen** from time to time SYN OCCASIONALLY: *Every now and then, one of these new mutations might increase the chance of the mutant virus replicating.*

N

now·adays /ˈnaʊədeɪz/ *adv.* at the present time, in contrast with the past: *This is the technique most widely used nowadays.* ◇ *Nowadays, almost all new communication systems being installed are digital.*

no·where /ˈnəʊweə(r); *NAmE* ˈnoʊwer/ *adv.* not in or to any place: *After the war, the number of marriages doubled, and most of the new households had nowhere to go.* ◇ **~ (else)** *This ecosystem includes plants found nowhere else in the world.* ◇ *Nowhere are the issues of educating language minority students more complex than in California.*
IDM **get/go ˈnowhere** to make no progress or have no success: *Efforts to arrange such cooperation at the London World Economic Conference of 1933 went nowhere.* ➲ *more at* LEAD[1], NEAR[3]

nu·ance /ˈnjuːɑːns; *NAmE* ˈnuːɑːns/ *noun* [C, U] a very slight difference in meaning, sound, sb's feelings, etc. that is not usually very obvious: *Knights and McCabe (2000) reveal subtle nuances in employee experience of teamworking.* ■ **nu·anced** *adj.*: *Lindquist has offered a more nuanced understanding of this important figure in Indian history.*

nu·clear AWL /ˈnjuːkliə(r); *NAmE* ˈnuːkliər/ *adj.* [usually before noun] **1** of the NUCLEUS (= central part) of an atom: *This increase in nuclear charge means that the electron experiences a greater attraction to the nucleus.* ◇ *Heavier elements, like carbon, nitrogen and oxygen, are made in the stars, as a result of nuclear reactions that take billions of years to complete.* **2** using, producing or resulting from energy that is produced by splitting the NUCLEUS of atoms: *Nuclear power plants are much more complex and expensive to build and operate than fossil-fuelled plants.* ◇ *Public attitudes towards nuclear energy are strongly influenced by concerns about waste disposal.* **3** connected with weapons that use energy produced by splitting atoms: *Like a conventional weapon, a nuclear weapon produces a destructive blast, or shock wave.* ◇ *There are major uncertainties in estimating the consequences of nuclear war.* **4** (*biology*) of the NUCLEUS (= central part) of a cell: *Nuclear genes are those residing in the cell nucleus rather than in mitochondria or chloroplasts.*
▸ NUCLEAR + NOUN **charge • force • reaction • fission • fusion** *The protons and neutrons are held in a stable state in the nucleus by the binding energy of the strong nuclear force.* | **power, energy • plant • reactor • fuel • waste • programme • material** *The major sources of energy for modern nations are fossil fuels, nuclear fuels and hydropower.* ◇ *Their entire nuclear programme is continually being inspected and monitored.* | **weapon • war • proliferation • terrorism** *Further nuclear proliferation is likely to increase instability and the potential for conflict between states.* | **membrane • receptor • protein • gene • genome • DNA** *A sperm whale's nuclear DNA is carried on 44 chromosomes, located in the nucleus of each cell.*

ˌnuclear ˈfamily *noun* (*technical*) a family that consists of father, mother and children, when it is thought of as a unit in society: *The nuclear family may still be dominant, but it is nonetheless only one possible family form.* ➲ *compare* EXTENDED FAMILY

ˌnuclear ˈfission *noun* [U] = FISSION (1)

ˌnuclear ˈfusion *noun* [U] = FUSION (2)

ˌnuclear reˈactor *noun* = REACTOR

nu·cle·ic acid /njuːˌkliːɪk ˈæsɪd; njuːˌkleɪɪk ˈæsɪd; *NAmE* nuːˌkliːɪk ˈæsɪd; nuːˌkleɪɪk ˈæsɪd/ *noun* [C, U] (*biochemistry*) either of two acids, DNA and RNA, that are present in all living cells: *All viruses have a small amount of nucleic acid surrounded by a protein coat.*

nu·cleon /ˈnjuːkliɒn; *NAmE* ˈnuːkliɑːn/ *noun* a PROTON or NEUTRON: *The surviving number of nucleons in fact amounts to only about one billionth of the number of photons created.*

nu·cleo·tide /ˈnjuːkliətaɪd; *NAmE* ˈnuːkliətaɪd/ *noun* (*biochemistry*) MOLECULES that are the building blocks of NUCLEIC ACIDS: *Each nucleotide consists of a five-carbon sugar, a nitrogen-containing base and a phosphate group.* ◇ **+ noun** *Genes are nucleotide sequences (made of DNA) that code for specific proteins that affect the properties of cells.*

nu·cleus /ˈnjuːkliəs; *NAmE* ˈnuːkliəs/ *noun* (*pl.* **nu·clei** /ˈnjuːkliaɪ; *NAmE* ˈnuːkliaɪ/) **1** (*physics*) the central part of an atom that contains most of its mass and that carries a positive electric charge: *The atomic nucleus contains most of the mass of the atom.* ◇ **~ of sth** *Free neutrons are highly reactive with the nuclei of many atoms.* ◇ **in the ~** *All these isotopes contain six protons in the nucleus, but each has a different number of neutrons.* ➲ *see also* NEUTRON, PROTON **2** (*biology*) the central part of most EUKARYOTIC cells, containing the GENETIC material: *Most DNA in humans is located in the cell nucleus.* ◇ **~ of sth** *By combining the nuclei of two mouse eggs, a mouse had been created with two mothers.* ◇ **in the ~** *Human cells contain 46 chromosomes in the nucleus.* **3 ~ of sth** the central part of sth around which other parts are located or collected: *It was from scientists and academics that the nucleus of a new 'public opinion' seemed to be emerging.* ◇ *Each zone contained nuclei of older settlements around and between which the newer suburbs developed.*

nuis·ance /ˈnjuːsns; *NAmE* ˈnuːsns/ *noun* **1** [C, usually sing., U] a thing, person or situation that causes trouble or problems: *Anti-spam software reduces the extent of the nuisance caused by junk email.* ◇ **be a ~** *In coalfields, channel sandstones can be a great nuisance and hazard as they can contain explosive gas.* **2** [C, U] (*law*) behaviour by sb that harms or offends other people and that a court can order the person to stop: *The court held that night-time factory noise did not constitute an actionable nuisance to a family living close by.* ◇ *Anti-social behaviour orders were intoduced to combat 'neighbourhood nuisance'.*

null /nʌl/ *adj.* (*technical*) having the value zero: *Their reproductive success may become very low or even null at high altitudes.*

IDM ˌ**null and ˈvoid** (*law*) (of an election, agreement, etc.) having no legal force; not valid: *The terms of this contract are so particular that the slightest alteration would make them null and void.*

ˈ**null hypothesis** *noun* (*statistics*) the idea that is tested in an experiment, usually so that there are no SIGNIFICANT connections between two sets of OBSERVATIONS: *Experiments showed a relationship between smoking and lung cancer and so the null hypothesis was rejected.*

num·ber¹ /ˈnʌmbə(r)/ *noun* **1** [C, U] a quantity of people or things: *Large numbers were employed in menial jobs.* ◇ **~ of sb/sth** *The aim was to have an equal number of male and female delegates.* ◇ *Table 11.6 provides data on the number and size of mega-cities.* ◇ **in ~** *Immigrant communities grew in number and economic strength.* ◇ *Participants are few in number.* ◇ *This led to a decrease in the number of home visits.* ◇ *In absolute numbers, the trend is less obvious.* ◇ **in terms of ~** *Total television viewing—in terms of number of hours per week—continues to increase.* ◇ *In terms of numbers, the survey found that 70% had planned their purchases.* HELP A plural verb is often used with **number (of)**: *There are a large number of alternative approaches.* ◇ *By far the largest number—over 15 000—were employed in the postal service.* However, the use of a singular verb is more common in academic English than in general English: *There is a small number of potential claimants.* **2** [C, U] a word or symbol that represents a quantity SYN FIGURE¹ (1): *In 1999, this number was 1 614.* ◇ *x and y are numbers between 1 and 7.* ◇ *This number increased to 53% in March 2001.* ◇ *The program can generate random numbers.* ◇ *The groups are denoted with letters and numbers.* ◇ **by ~** *Each title is identified by number.* ➲ *see also* ATOMIC NUMBER, COMPLEX NUMBER, NATURAL NUMBER, REAL NUMBER **3** [C] (*abbr.* **No.**) (*symb.* **#**) used before a figure to identify sth, for example to show the position of sth in a series: *The cells on plate number 1 should remain uninfected.* **4** [C] (often in compounds) a set of figures that is used to identify sb/sth, for example on an official document: *Most suppliers ask customers to quote their account number in any correspondence.* ◇ *The study has been approved by the ethics committee (reference number 06-141).* **5** [pl.] **the numbers** data that consist of figures: *Overall, the numbers are not a reliable indicator of risk.* **6** [sing.] used to talk about the members of a group of people: **one/some, etc. of their ~** *Trustees may appoint one of their number to act as a custodian.* ◇ **among their ~** *The members select from among their number the person they regard as the most capable.* **7** [U] (*grammar*) the form of a word, showing whether one or more than one person or thing is being talked about: *The word 'men' is plural in number.* ◇ *The subject of a sentence and its verb must agree in number.*

IDM **a number of sb/sth** several people or things; some: *Joh (2004) identified a number of problems at the company.* **any number of sb/sth** several different people or things; a lot of different people or things: *Data may be incorrect in any number of ways and for any number of reasons.* HELP A plural verb is usually used with **a/any number of**: *A number of tests are required.* ◇ *There are any number of reasons for this.* However, in academic English it is also possible to use the singular: *There is a number of instrumental problems.*

▸ ADJECTIVE + NUMBER **large, great, substantial, high, considerable, significant • vast, huge, enormous • small, low** *Microorganisms are found in great numbers almost everywhere.* | **total • maximum • overall • (the) sheer • average, mean • minimum • expected • actual • equal • sufficient • limited, finite • fixed • certain • increased, increasing, growing • disproportionate • unprecedented • infinite** *The total number of cells is small.* ◇ *The data set includes data from only a limited number of species.* | **random • whole • decimal • binary • rational • natural • complex • absolute • fixed • real • even • odd • positive • negative** *A random number generator assigned a random number to each venue.*

▸ VERB + NUMBER **calculate • estimate • determine • compute • multiply, be multiplied by • divide, be divided by • add • represent • yield • indicate, show • record • compare** *This figure is then multiplied by the number of hours to give an energy consumption saving.* | **contain, include, have • comprise • involve • produce, generate • identify • show, present • list** *Snake venom contains a vast number of toxins.* ◇ *He lists a number of conditions.* | **count, measure • reduce, decrease • limit • minimize • increase, raise • double • maximize • exceed • equal • underestimate** *Strategies to reduce the number of people smoking require the efforts of doctors, politicians and health promotion staff.*

▸ NUMBER + VERB **rise, grow, increase • decline, fall** *By 2001 that number had risen to 57%.* ◇ *The number of these jobs fell sharply.*

▸ NOUN + IN NUMBER **increase, rise, growth, expansion • explosion • decrease, reduction, decline, drop, fall • variation, fluctuation, variability, difference, change** *The 1980s saw a huge increase in numbers of refugees.*

num·ber² /ˈnʌmbə(r)/ *verb* **1** [T, usually passive] to give a number to sth as part of a series or list: **(be) numbered (from)... to...** *Five distinct meanings, numbered from one to five, are listed.* ◇ **(be) numbered + noun** *They are numbered C1, C2 and C3.* ◇ **be numbered (+adv./prep.)** *The carbon atoms in cholesterol are numbered as shown in Figure 14.2.* **2** *linking verb* **+ noun** to make a particular quantity when added together: *Korean immigrants numbered nearly 300 000 by the end of the 1920s.* ◇ *State-owned enterprises, numbering well over 3 000, employed 45% of the workforce.* **3** [T, usually passive] **be numbered among sb** to be included in a particular group: *Syrians were numbered among the few industrialists in the city.*

nu·mer·ator /ˈnjuːməreɪtə(r); *NAmE* ˈnuːməreɪtər/ *noun* (*mathematics*) the number above the line in a FRACTION, for example 3 in the FRACTION ¾: *Multiply the numerator and the denominator on the right-hand side of the equation by 5.* ➲ *compare* DENOMINATOR

nu·mer·ic·al /njuːˈmerɪkl; *NAmE* nuːˈmerɪkl/ (*also less frequent* **nu·mer·ic** /njuːˈmerɪk; *NAmE* nuːˈmerɪk/) *adj.* [usually before noun] connected with numbers; expressed in numbers: *Numerical computations were performed for the environmental conditions.* ◇ *The numerical value of this ratio is very large.* ◇ *Numerical data are collected in Table 5.7.* ■ **nu·mer·ic·al·ly** /njuːˈmerɪkli; *NAmE* nuːˈmerɪkli/ *adv.*: *The model can be solved numerically.* ◇ *Mass number is numerically equal to the sum of the numbers of neutrons and protons.*

nu·mer·ous /ˈnjuːmərəs; *NAmE* ˈnuːmərəs/ *adj.* [usually before noun] existing in large numbers SYN MANY: *Numerous studies test this supposition.* ◇ *He had been left in her care on numerous occasions.* ◇ *These examples are too numerous to list.*

nun /nʌn/ *noun* a member of a religious community of women who promise to serve God all their lives: *Nuns live a lifestyle dedicated to study and spiritual discipline.* ➲ *compare* MONK

nurse¹ /nɜːs; *NAmE* nɜːrs/ *noun* a person whose job is to take care of sick or injured people, for example in a hospital: *The programme was delivered by trained nurses.* ◇ *They provide community-based health services such as school nurses and doctors.* ◇ *Mental health nurses work in a wide range of settings.*

nurse² /nɜːs; *NAmE* nɜːrs/ *verb* **1** [T] to care for sb who is sick or injured: **~ sb** *It is helpful if the nurse presenting the*

N

case has nursed the patient. ◇ **~ sb + adv./prep.** *She nursed him back to health.* **2** [T, I] **~ (sb)** to feed a baby with milk from the BREAST SYN BREASTFEED: *The mother was nursing the infant.* ◇ *Nursing mothers should not be detained.*

nurs·ing /ˈnɜːsɪŋ; *NAmE* ˈnɜːrsɪŋ/ *noun* [U] the job or skill of caring for people who are sick or injured: *The community health service provides home nursing.* ◇ **+ noun** *Specialist nursing care is required for these patients.*

ˈ**nursing home** *noun* a small private hospital, especially one where old people live and are cared for: *Older adults living in nursing homes sometimes become isolated and lose contact with the outside world.*

nur·ture /ˈnɜːtʃə(r); *NAmE* ˈnɜːrtʃər/ *verb* **1 ~ sb/sth** to care for and protect sb/sth while they are growing and developing: *Home is the place where children are nurtured and where their education begins.* **2 ~ sb/sth** to help sb/sth to develop and be successful: *They maintained their close ties to the United States but nurtured friendlier relationships with Arab countries to assure the flow of oil.* ◇ *The company seeks to nurture workers whose potential has been overlooked in the past.* **3 ~ sth** to have a feeling, an idea, a plan, etc. for a long time and encourage it to develop: *The public nurtured hopes that democracy would soon be restored.*

nut /nʌt/ *noun* a small hard fruit with a very hard shell that grows on some trees: *Humans are not unique in using tools; chimpanzees, for example, use stones to crack nuts.*

nu·tri·ent /ˈnjuːtriənt; *NAmE* ˈnuːtriənt/ *noun* a substance that is needed to keep people and other living things healthy and to help them to grow: *The patient has an inability to absorb nutrients.* ◇ *These foods are high in sugar and fat, but low in essential nutrients.*

O

nu·tri·tion /njuˈtrɪʃn; *NAmE* nuˈtrɪʃn/ *noun* [U] the process by which living things receive the food necessary for them to grow and be healthy; the food that is needed for this: *The website provides information on diet and nutrition.* ◇ *Patients with poor nutrition are at higher risk of developing complications.* ◇ *The nurse should ensure that the child receives adequate nutrition.* ➲ *compare* MALNUTRITION

nu·tri·tion·al /njuˈtrɪʃənl; *NAmE* nuˈtrɪʃənl/ *adj.* [only before noun] supplying or involving nutrition: *Nutritional supplements may be required if the patient is not eating.* ◇ *The baby's main nutritional intake will continue to be from milk.* ◇ *Poor maternal nutritional status has been related to adverse birth outcomes.* ■ **nu·tri·tion·al·ly** /njuˈtrɪʃənəli; *NAmE* nuˈtrɪʃənəli/ *adv.*: *The goal was to reduce caloric intake in a nutritionally sound manner.*

O o

obedi·ence /əˈbiːdiəns/ *noun* [U] the fact of doing what sb/sth tells you to do; the fact of obeying: *While a leader may demand obedience from his or her subordinates, that obedience is never guaranteed.* ◇ **~ to sb/sth** *The school instils critical thought and accountability to others rather than blind obedience to rules and authority.* ■ **obedi·ent** /əˈbiːdiənt/ *adj.* **~ (to sb/sth)** *A wife was expected to be obedient to her husband.*

obese /əʊˈbiːs; *NAmE* oʊˈbiːs/ *adj.* (of people) too fat, in a way that is bad for health: *This form of heart disease is more prevalent in obese patients.* ◇ *In the USA, two out of three adults are overweight or obese, compared with one in four in the 1960s (Manson and Bassuk, 2003).*

obes·ity /əʊˈbiːsəti; *NAmE* oʊˈbiːsəti/ *noun* [U] (of people) the fact of being too fat, in a way that is bad for health: *Concern has been expressed over the increasing problem of childhood obesity.* ◇ **+ noun** *The obesity epidemic is growing at an alarming rate with more than 20% of the UK population classed as obese.*

obey /əˈbeɪ/ *verb* **1** [T, I] **~ (sb/sth)** to do what you are told or expected to do: *It was considered the slave's Christian duty to obey his or her master.* ◇ *Even in democratic political systems, the people are compelled to obey the laws.* ◇ *The ambassador asked them to leave but they did not obey.* **2** [T] to behave in the way that is needed or expected according to an instruction, law or principle: *The transfers were effected by a stored program in which a list of instructions was obeyed sequentially.*

ob·ject[1] /ˈɒbdʒɪkt; *NAmE* ˈɑːbdʒekt; ˈɑːbdʒɪkt/ *noun* **1** a thing that can be seen and touched, but is not alive: *Palissy illustrated his lectures with fossils, rocks and other physical objects.* ◇ *Around the age of 40, many people start to notice that seeing objects closer than 1 m becomes difficult.* **2 ~ of analysis, interest, attention, criticism, etc.** a person or thing that sb studies or is interested in, or treats or thinks about in a particular way: *Keynes's basic views on economic policy have already been the object of extended analysis.* ◇ *This functionalist model became the object of intense criticism in the late 1960s and early 1970s.* **3** an aim or a purpose: **~ of sth** *The primary object of the survey is to study the effects of these administrative changes on the district.* ◇ **~ of doing sth** *The object of creating the Community was to engage in a close economic relationship with a number of European nations.* ◇ **the ~ is to...** *In an armed conflict, the object is to damage the military potential of the enemy in order to obtain a decisive advantage.* ◇ **with the ~ of doing sth** *In 1894 he supervised a series of experiments with the object of measuring the increase in gravity below the surface of the Earth.* ➲ thesaurus note *at* TARGET[1] **4** (*grammar*) a noun, noun phrase or pronoun that refers to a person or thing that is affected by the action of the verb (called the **direct object**), or that the action is done to or for (called the **indirect object**): *The object is the noun phrase that comes after the verb in English.* ◇ *Most languages have the order subject + verb + object (SVO): English is a language of this type.* ➲ *compare* SUBJECT[1] (6) **5** (*computing*) a package in which data and the operations on that data are bound together: *The interface treats most items, including cells, graphs and buttons, as objects.*

ob·ject[2] /əbˈdʒekt/ *verb* **1** [I] to say that you disagree with, disapprove of or oppose sth: *They have the right to object.* ◇ **~ to sth** *A number of people objected to the idea.* ◇ **~ to doing sth** *They object very strongly to killing innocent people.* **2** [T] **~ that...** to give sth as a reason for opposing sth SYN PROTEST[2] (2): *Some might object that Christianity and Islam are very different religions.*

ob·jec·tion /əbˈdʒekʃn/ *noun* [C, U] a reason why you do not like sth or are opposed to sth; the fact of not liking or supporting sth: *They continued to voice their objections.* ◇ *The vast majority of the population accept it without objection.* ◇ **~ to (doing) sth** *Sceptics have raised three main objections to this theory (Kentridge and Heywood, 1999; Weiskrantz, 1986).* ◇ **~ that...** *There is the principled objection that this simply solves one problem at the cost of creating another.*

ob·ject·ive[1] AWL /əbˈdʒektɪv/ *noun* **1** something that you are trying to achieve SYN GOAL, TARGET[1]: *Management have achieved their strategic objectives.* ◇ **the ~ of sth** *The specific objective of the study is to conduct an assessment of patient safety culture in hospitals.* ◇ **~ for sth** *Setting specific, realistic and measurable objectives for the sales training programme is critical.* ◇ **with the ~ of (doing) sth** *The project was launched with the objective of preventing new infections and raising awareness.* ➲ thesaurus note *at* TARGET[1] **2** (*also* **ob,jective ˈlens**) (*technical*) the LENS in a TELESCOPE or MICROSCOPE that is nearest to the object being looked at: *Most student-model microscopes* *are equipped with three objectives with magnifications of around 2.5, 10 and 40.*

▸ ADJECTIVE + OBJECTIVE **specific • main, primary, principal • key • overall • clear • strategic • political • social • economic • environmental • military • corporate** *The main objective of the article is to explain why and how such political struggles developed.*

▸ NOUN + OBJECTIVE **policy • research • business • learning • communication • marketing** *The state can more effectively attain its policy objectives by working together with other states.*

▸ VERB + OBJECTIVE **set • define, specify • pursue • achieve, meet, attain, accomplish, satisfy, fulfil, realize • further** *Unless clear objectives have been defined at the outset, it is very difficult to know whether the firm has achieved what it set out to achieve.*

ob·ject·ive² AWL /əbˈdʒektɪv/ *adj.* **1** not influenced by personal feelings or opinions; considering only facts SYN IMPARTIAL, UNBIASED: *It is difficult for managers at different levels to make objective assessments of employee performance.* ◇ *Future studies should include more objective measures to contribute to confidence in findings.* ◇ *an objective standard/criterion/test* ➲ *compare* SUBJECTIVE (1) **2** (*philosophy*) existing outside the mind; based on facts that can be proved: *Constructivists emphasize the absence of an objective social reality that exists beyond human activity or understanding.* ➲ *compare* SUBJECTIVE (2)

ob·ject·ive·ly AWL /əbˈdʒektɪvli/ *adv.* using facts and not influenced by personal feelings or beliefs: *There are aspects of well-being that can be measured objectively.* ◇ *Owing to costs and practicability, it was not possible to objectively assess patients' level of physical activity.*

ob·ject·iv·ity AWL /ˌɒbdʒekˈtɪvəti; *NAmE* ˌɑːbdʒekˈtɪvəti/ *noun* [U] the fact of sth being based only on facts or evidence, not on personal feelings; the fact of not being influenced by personal feelings: *There have been claims that this study was scientifically flawed and lacked objectivity.* ◇ **~ in sth** *It is important to ensure objectivity in board decisions.* ◇ **~ of sb/sth** *The objectivity of science is one cherished idea that may need to be re-examined.* ➲ *compare* SUBJECTIVITY (1)

ob·li·gated /ˈɒblɪɡeɪtɪd; *NAmE* ˈɑːblɪɡeɪtɪd/ *adj.* [not usually before noun] **~ (to do sth)** having a moral or legal duty to do sth: *The government would be obligated to pay.*

ob·li·ga·tion /ˌɒblɪˈɡeɪʃn; *NAmE* ˌɑːblɪˈɡeɪʃn/ *noun* [C, U] a duty to do sth because you have promised, or because of a law or rule: *The Belgian authorities had failed in their obligations under Articles 2 and 3 of the Convention.* ◇ **~ of sb** *The treaty specified the rights and obligations of the victorious and defeated powers.* ◇ **have an ~ to do sth** *An employer has an obligation to protect the safety of employees.* ◇ **be under an/no ~ to do sth** *He was under no legal obligation to answer the questions put to him.* ◇ **~ to sb/sth** *Employers with a strong sense of social obligation to workers are less likely to engage in these practices.*

▸ ADJECTIVE + OBLIGATION **general • international • mutual • legal • statutory • moral • ethical • social • contractual** *The parents have mutual obligations in relation to the child.* ◇ *In this case, the government failed to honour its contractual obligations.*

▸ NOUN + OBLIGATION **human rights • treaty • family** *Some states are inclined to hide information on their failure to fulfil their human rights obligations.*

▸ VERB + OBLIGATION **have • impose, place • create • accept • meet, fulfil, honour, discharge • breach, violate • evade** *The existence of a promise creates a special obligation between two people.*

▸ NOUN + OF OBLIGATION **performance, fulfilment • breach, violation • sense** *At trial, the judge found that the supplier was in breach of its obligations.*

ob·liga·tory /əˈblɪɡətri; *NAmE* əˈblɪɡətɔːri/ *adj.* **1** that you must do or obey, for example because of a law or moral rule SYN COMPULSORY: *A convention on the rights of older people would create obligatory and binding international law.* ◇ *Vaccination of children against common transmittable diseases is considered by many to be morally obligatory (Hasman and Holm, 2004).* ◇ **~ (for sb) (to do sth)** *In the Dutch health care system, it is obligatory for each citizen to be registered on the list of only one practice.* OPP OPTIONAL ➲ *compare* MANDATORY **2** that is expected, for example because other people in the same situation do it: *Many rich young men of the period made the obligatory European grand tour.*

ob·lige /əˈblaɪdʒ/ *verb* [T, usually passive] to make sb do sth, by law or because it is a rule or a duty: **be obliged to do sth** *Teachers are legally obliged to report child protection issues.* ◇ **feel obliged to do sth** *Examples include the captain who feels morally obliged to 'go down with his ship'.* ◇ **~ sb to do sth** *The greatest virtue of decision analysis is that it obliges decision-makers to make explicit all the bases of a decision.*

ob·scure¹ /əbˈskjʊə(r); *NAmE* əbˈskjʊr/ *verb* to cover sth; to make it difficult to see, hear or understand sth: **be obscured by sth** *Some days the sky is completely obscured by clouds.* ◇ **~ sth** *Headline figures tend to obscure genuine underlying problems of resource allocation.* ◇ **~ the fact that...** *These criticisms should not obscure the fact that there is much to admire in the book.*

ob·scure² /əbˈskjʊə(r); *NAmE* əbˈskjʊr/ *adj.* **1** not well known SYN UNKNOWN¹ (1): *Lemaitre's paper had made little impression because it was written in French and published in an obscure Belgian journal.* **2** difficult to understand: *The exact role or roles of protein kinase C within the cell remain surprisingly obscure.*

ob·scur·ity /əbˈskjʊərəti; *NAmE* əbˈskjʊrəti/ *noun* (*pl.* -ies) **1** [U] the state in which sb/sth is not well known or has been forgotten: *He died in relative obscurity in the 1730s.* **2** [U, C, usually pl.] **~ (of sth)** the quality of being difficult to understand; something that is difficult to understand: *The obscurity of the Court's language is unhelpful.* ◇ *His vocabulary is simple, although occasional obscurities may be found in his sentences.*

ob·serv·able /əbˈzɜːvəbl; *NAmE* əbˈzɜːrvəbl/ *adj.* that can be seen or noticed: *The scope of the survey is restricted to directly observable characteristics of organizations.* ◇ *Specialization is observable in the animal world, where the more highly developed the creature, the more highly differentiated its organs.*

ob·ser·vance /əbˈzɜːvəns; *NAmE* əbˈzɜːrvəns/ *noun* **1** [U] **~ (of sth)** the practice of obeying a law, celebrating a festival or behaving according to a particular custom: *Compliance officers enforce strict observance of corporate governance rules.* ◇ *There has been a decline in religious observance.* **2** [C, usually pl.] an act performed as part of a religious or traditional ceremony: *Ethnic or tribal allegiances could also be reflected in ritual observances.*

ob·ser·va·tion /ˌɒbzəˈveɪʃn; *NAmE* ˌɑːbzərˈveɪʃn/ *noun* **1** [U, C] the act of watching sb/sth carefully for a period of time, especially to learn sth: **~ (of sb/sth)** *Information was collected by direct observation of the animals' behaviour.* ◇ *Hubble's astronomical observations revealed that the universe contains galaxies which are moving apart from one another.* ◇ **under ~** *The decision was taken to keep her in hospital under observation.* ◇ **+ noun** *In-depth interviews are carried out with the participants at the end of the observation period.* ➲ thesaurus note *at* INVESTIGATION **2** [U] the ability to notice things, especially important details: **powers of ~** *Such activity promotes increased powers of observation.* **3** [C] **~ (about/on sth)** a comment, especially based on sth you have seen, heard or read SYN REMARK¹: *Latour's observations about the*

O

biosciences might equally apply to the social sciences. ◇ *Her book blends travel narrative with observations on the damaging effects of poverty.*

▸ ADJECTIVE + OBSERVATION **important • general • similar • simple • earlier • recent • interesting** *Mayer offers an interesting observation about this distinction.* | **direct • personal • careful • detailed • close • systematic • casual • behavioural • clinical • empirical • experimental • astronomical** *His ideas about the development of the cosmos were based more on personal observation.*

▸ VERB + OBSERVATION **make • include • provide • support • confirm** *Kinghorn makes a very astute observation.* ◇ *More recent evidence supports this observation in other species.* | **use • conduct, carry out • take • record • explain** *Gilbert was the first person to use geologic observations to draw inferences about prehistoric earthquakes.* | **submit, offer • report** *Each Member State has been given the opportunity to present its case and submit observations both orally and in writing.*

▸ OBSERVATION + NOUN **period • chart • schedule • task • error** *The aim of the observation schedule is to ensure that each participant's behaviour is systematically recorded.*

ob·ser·va·tion·al /ˌɒbzəˈveɪʃnl; *NAmE* ˌɑːbzərˈveɪʃnl/ *adj.* connected with or based on the observation of sb/sth in order to learn sth: *These data are largely from observational studies.* ◇ *observational evidence/data*

ob·serve /əbˈzɜːv; *NAmE* əbˈzɜːrv/ *verb* **1** [T] to see or notice sb/sth: **~ sb/sth** *No difference was observed between the two groups.* ◇ **~ sb/sth do sth** *Her parents observed her become increasingly tense and irritable.* ◇ **~ sb/sth doing sth** *Native speakers were asked what sorts of changes they were able to observe taking place in the language.* ◇ **~ that...** *In her frequent visits to schools, she has observed that trainee teachers have a strong interest in this topic.* ◇ **be observed to do sth** *Delays were observed to decrease by 40%.* HELP This pattern is only used in the passive. **2** [T, I] to watch sb/sth carefully, especially in order to learn more about them: **~ (sb/sth)** *Then the cells were observed under a microscope.* ◇ *The role of the researcher was simply to observe.* ◇ **~ what/how, etc...** *The research involves watching people as they go about their lives, observing what they do in a natural setting.* ➲ *compare* MONITOR[1] (1) **3** [T] **~ that...** to make a remark SYN COMMENT[2]: *Bateson observed that Wordsworth has been parodied more often than any other English poet.* **4** [T] **~ sth** to obey rules, laws, etc: *It is important to ensure that the rules are observed throughout the organization.* ◇ *Industry standards are generally observed.* ◇ *This distinction should be carefully observed.* **5** [T] **~ sth (as sth)** to celebrate festivals, special days, etc: *Muslims observe Friday as their holy day.*

▸ OBSERVE + NOUN **behaviour • interaction • process • phenomenon • activity** *These two phenomena are not observed within simple molecules.* | **difference • change • variation • increase • effect • result • pattern • trend • rate • level • association, correlation, relationship** *Few statistically significant changes could be observed.*

▸ ADVERB + OBSERVE **actually • easily** *Individual behaviour is more easily observed in bird species.* | **often, frequently • first • previously • already • recently** *The fungus was first observed in the north-eastern United States in 1977.* | **usually • generally • commonly, widely • rarely • readily • clearly • empirically • consistently** *Such market failures, however, are widely observed.* | **carefully • directly** *Only people 'on the spot' can directly observe an event.* | **rightly** *Constitutional lawyers have rightly observed that the South African approach is unique.*

▸ OBSERVE + ADVERB **directly • experimentally** *The decrease of the magnetic field was also observed experimentally.* | **elsewhere • earlier, previously • above** *As observed above, the party systems in England, Scotland and Wales differ significantly.*

ob·ser·ver /əbˈzɜːvə(r); *NAmE* əbˈzɜːrvər/ *noun* **1** a person who watches and studies particular events or situations and is therefore considered to be an expert on them: *These events have led some observers to talk of a 'crisis' of local government.* **2** a person who watches or notices sb/sth: *The speed of light in empty space is the same for all observers.* ◇ **to the casual ~** *To the casual observer, her paintings merely indicate a love of the sea.* **3** a person sent by a government or organization to an area to check political or military events: *International observers seemed to be happy with the way in which the election was conducted.* **4** a person who attends a meeting, lesson, etc. to listen and watch but not to take part: *They are employee-elected observers and may attend board meetings but have no voting rights.* ◇ **as an ~** *The trainee takes part purely as an observer.*

ob·so·lete /ˈɒbsəliːt; *NAmE* ˌɑːbsəˈliːt/ *adj.* no longer used because it has been replaced by a new invention, idea or way of doing sth: *New media technologies, as well as digital formats, can quickly become obsolete.*

obs·tacle /ˈɒbstəkl; *NAmE* ˈɑːbstəkl/ *noun* **1** a situation, event or fact that makes it difficult for you to do or achieve sth: *The second step will be discussing possible ways of overcoming these obstacles.* ◇ *to constitute/face/remove an obstacle* ◇ **~ to sth** *What Johanek calls 'a lack of imagination' poses a major obstacle to education reform.* ◇ **~ to doing sth** *The political obstacles to implementing these solutions are substantial.* ➲ *compare* HINDRANCE (1) **2** an object that is in your way and that makes it difficult for you to move forward: *The solar wind is deflected around obstacles in its path.*

ob·struct /əbˈstrʌkt/ *verb* **1 ~ sth** to block a road, an entrance, a passage, etc. so that sb/sth cannot get through, see past, etc: *The shopkeeper complained that a theatre queue obstructed access to his premises.* ◇ *A clot within a blood vessel often obstructs blood flow.* **2 ~ sb/sth** to prevent sb/sth from doing sth or making progress, especially when this is done deliberately SYN HINDER: *It is an offence to resist or wilfully obstruct a police officer.* ◇ *Combatants frequently attacked civilians and obstructed peace initiatives in the city.*

ob·struc·tion /əbˈstrʌkʃn/ *noun* **1** [U, C] **~ (of sth)** the fact of blocking a road, an entrance, a passage, etc; something that blocks a road, an entrance, etc: *Obstruction of the highway has been a criminal offence since the 11th century.* ◇ *The deposited sediment causes an obstruction in the river mouth in the form of a bar.* **2** [C, U] (*medical*) something that blocks a passage or tube in the body; a medical condition resulting from this SYN BLOCKAGE (1): *Airway obstruction may be due to an object, trauma or infection.* ◇ **~ of sth** *A simple obstruction of the small intestine causes swelling of the bowel.* **3** [U, C] **~ (of sth)** the fact of trying to prevent sth/sb from making progress: *In court, Mr Black was charged with obstruction of justice.*

ob·struct·ive /əbˈstrʌktɪv/ *adj.* **1** trying to prevent sb/sth from making progress: *Other artists complained about obstructive attitudes experienced during the visa application process.* ➲ *compare* CONSTRUCTIVE **2** [only before noun] (*medical*) connected with a passage, tube, etc. in your body that has become blocked: *chronic obstructive lung disease*

ob·tain AWL /əbˈteɪn/ *verb* **1** [T] **~ sth** to get sth, especially by making an effort: *A second study has obtained similar results.* ◇ *Written consent must be obtained before passing on personal information.* ◇ *More than one interview may be needed to obtain this information.* **2** [I] (*formal*) (not used in the progressive tenses) (of rules, systems or customs) to exist SYN APPLY (1): *It is possible that the same initial state of affairs obtains.* ◇ *Non-equilibrium conditions frequently obtain in water, soil and sediments.*

ob·tain·able AWL /əbˈteɪnəbl/ *adj.* [not usually before noun] that can be obtained SYN AVAILABLE (1): *Divorce is*

O

readily obtainable and its incidence in England and Wales is high.

ob·vi·ate /ˈɒbvieɪt; *NAmE* ˈɑːbvieɪt/ *verb* (*formal*) to remove a problem or the need for sth SYN PRECLUDE: **~ the need (for sth/to do sth)** *Air travel made cities closer, and obviated the need to spend days travelling across land.*

ob·vi·ous AWL /ˈɒbviəs; *NAmE* ˈɑːbviəs/ *adj.* **1** easy to see or understand SYN CLEAR[1] (1): *The household is the most obvious example of an institution based on affection.* ◇ *Where performance is below target, the reasons may not be immediately obvious.* ◇ **(it is) ~ (to sb) (that...)** *It was soon obvious to Colebrook that the ACE project was in a state of complete disarray.* ◇ **~ from sth** *This difference is obvious from even a very rapid comparison of the languages.* **2** that most people would think of or agree to: *Silicon is an obvious choice, but because of analytical difficulties it is rarely used.* ◇ **(it is) ~ (to sb) (that...)** *To many people, it will seem obvious that questions about ethics should be related to ones about religion.* ➲ thesaurus note *at* CLEAR[1]

▸ OBVIOUS + NOUN **example • way • sign • difference • similarity • point • connection • question • problem • limitation • advantage, benefit** *The most obvious point of comparison for UK financial oil markets is the US.* | **choice • candidate • solution, answer • explanation • reason • implication • objection** *Magnesium metal, a third lighter than aluminium, seemed an obvious candidate for more widespread use in a variety of industries, including aircraft.*

ob·vi·ous·ly AWL /ˈɒbviəsli; *NAmE* ˈɑːbviəsli/ *adv.* **1** used when giving information that you expect other people to know already or agree with SYN CLEARLY (1): *Obviously, a book of this nature cannot exhaust all possible aspects of poverty in the United States.* ◇ *Interest rates obviously have a big impact on the level of spending in the economy.* ◇ *This should ideally happen 14 days before surgery but it is obviously not possible in emergency cases.* **2** in a way that is easy to see or understand SYN CLEARLY (2): *Very often an emergency is not obviously an emergency.* ◇ *The appearance of the eggs (size, shape, colour) made them obviously different from those of the host.*

oc·ca·sion[1] /əˈkeɪʒn/ *noun* **1** [C] a particular time when sth happens: **on... ~** *The test was performed on two separate occasions.* ◇ *On rare occasions, a unilateral initiative may gain acceptance.* ◇ *On this occasion, however, he proposed a different subject:...* ◇ **on the ~ of sth** *Breaches of Article 9 had occurred on the occasion of both arrests.* ◇ **~ when...** *There are many occasions when it is preferable to...* **2** [C] a special event, ceremony or celebration: *Special occasions (for example, the birth of a sibling) are celebrated in school.* ◇ *Her best poetry tends to mark royal occasions.* ◇ *The ambassador will be present at ceremonial occasions.* **3** [C] a suitable time for sth SYN OPPORTUNITY: **~ for (doing) sth** *His retirement provides the perfect occasion for reflections on his career.* ◇ **~ (for sb) to do sth** *These differences can serve as an occasion to stimulate a constructive discussion.* **4** [C, U] (*formal*) a reason or cause: **~ for sth** *Ordinary citizens had many occasions for dissatisfaction.* ◇ *There was neither need nor occasion for precise constitutional definitions.* ◇ **~ to do sth** *He had occasion to complain.*

IDM **on ocˈcasion(s)** sometimes but not often: *On occasion, these statutes have been adopted in response to an instance of data misuse.* ◇ *Its decisions have on occasions provoked, rather than settled, conflict.* **when/if (the) occasion demands/arises** when/if necessary: *He was a man of abundant energy, bold and resolute when occasion demanded.* ◇ *Other data collection instruments can be implemented if the occasion arises.*

oc·ca·sion[2] /əˈkeɪʒn/ *verb* (*formal*) to cause sth: **~ sth** *Their account of the disaster occasioned universal dismay.* ◇ **~ sth to sb** *It is for the sentencing judge to consider the harm occasioned to the victim.*

oc·ca·sion·al /əˈkeɪʒənl/ *adj.* [only before noun] happening or done sometimes but not often: *Despite occasional lapses, adherence to this policy has improved.* ◇ *There are occasional references to non-Western traditions.*

oc·ca·sion·al·ly /əˈkeɪʒnəli/ *adv.* sometimes but not often: *The disease usually presents in adults, although it does occasionally occur in children.* ◇ *The changes occasionally caused tensions.* ◇ *Only occasionally were these considerations explicitly articulated.*

oc·cu·pancy AWL /ˈɒkjəpənsi; *NAmE* ˈɑːkjəpənsi/ *noun* [U] the act of living in or using a building, room, piece of land, etc: *The act also recognized a right of occupancy at 'fair and equitable' rates.* ◇ **+ noun** *The bed occupancy rate in the hospital was 83.2%.*

oc·cu·pant AWL /ˈɒkjəpənt; *NAmE* ˈɑːkəpənt/ *noun* **1** a person who lives or works in a particular house, room, building, etc: *The settlement included a dwelling for the human occupants and a barn for livestock.* ◇ **~ of sth** *The occupants of this building were affluent retired people.* **2** a person who is in a vehicle, seat, etc. at a particular time: *Of these fatalities, 50% are car occupants.*

oc·cu·pa·tion AWL /ˌɒkjuˈpeɪʃn; *NAmE* ˌɑːkjuˈpeɪʃn/ *noun* **1** [C] a job or profession: *Death rates amongst unskilled workers were three times higher than for those in professional occupations.* **2** [U] the act of moving into a country, town, etc. and taking control of it using military force; the period of time during which a country, town, etc. is controlled in this way: **~ (of sth)** *Russia continued its military occupation of the region.* ◇ **under ~** *Korea was under Japanese occupation for 36 years.* ◇ **during the ~** *The film was made during the German occupation of France.* **3** [U] the act of living in or using a building, room or piece of land: *The new house should be ready for occupation before Christmas.* ◇ **~ of sth** *The intention was that both couples would share occupation of the property.* ◇ **in ~ (of sth)** *This law may be used to allow family members a right to remain in occupation of the family home.* **4** [C] a way of spending time, especially when you are not working: *The organization was supposed to attract young adults to politically and socially useful leisure-time occupations.*

O

oc·cu·pa·tion·al AWL /ˌɒkjuˈpeɪʃənl; *NAmE* ˌɑːkjuˈpeɪʃənl/ *adj.* [only before noun] connected with a person's job or profession: *Service workers earn the least of all occupational groups.* ◇ *Only 1 in 25 GPs have any special training in occupational health.* ■ **oc·cu·pa·tion·al·ly** /ˌɒkjuˈpeɪʃənəli; *NAmE* ˌɑːkjuˈpeɪʃənəli/ *adv.*: *Some 3.6 million workers in the EU are estimated to be occupationally exposed to wood dust.*

oc·cu·pied AWL /ˈɒkjupaɪd; *NAmE* ˈɑːkjupaɪd/ *adj.* **1** [not before noun] busy: *Volunteering offered them the opportunity to keep themselves occupied.* ◇ **~ in sth** *They spend hours occupied in futile discussions.* ◇ **~ with sth** *The council is occupied with administrative issues.* **2** [not before noun] being used: *This central zone was to become densely occupied by industrial and commercial buildings.* OPP UNOCCUPIED **3** (of a country, etc.) controlled by people from another country, etc, using military force: *The Nazis kept close control over the media in occupied France.*

oc·cu·pier AWL /ˈɒkjupaɪə(r); *NAmE* ˈɑːkjupaɪər/ *noun* **1 ~ (of sth)** a person or company that lives in or uses a building, room or piece of land SYN OCCUPANT (1): *He said that the defendant's status as occupier of the premises was irrelevant.* **2** [usually pl.] a member of an army that takes control of a foreign country, etc. by force: *The United States still hoped to negotiate with the Soviet occupiers in the northern part of the Korean peninsula.*

oc·cupy AWL /ˈɒkjupaɪ; *NAmE* ˈɑːkjupaɪ/ *verb* (**oc·cu·pies, oc·cu·py·ing, oc·cu·pied, oc·cu·pied**) **1 ~ sth** to fill or use a space, area or amount of time SYN TAKE UP STH: *The city of Birmingham occupies an area of 268 km^2.* ◇ *A German text occupies about 30% more space than its English translation.* ◇ *The topic of computer crime has occupied much legislative time around the world.* **2 ~ sth** to live or work in a room, house or building: *A person occupying residential property with the permission of the owner will either be a tenant or a licensee.* **3 ~ sth** to enter a place in a large group and take control of it, especially by military force: *Catalonia had been partly occupied by French troops in the 1640s.* ◇ *Students occupied Harvard buildings to protest against the Vietnam war.* **4 ~ sth** to have an official job or position SYN HOLD¹ (2): *Once elected, the party leader usually occupies the post until the next election.* **5 ~ sth** to be in or at a particular position in a system SYN HOLD¹ (2): *Workers and employers occupy different positions in the production process.* **6** to fill your time or keep you busy doing sth: **~ sb/sth/yourself** *This task occupied him for some twenty years.* ◇ *Often they are playing games to occupy the time.* ◇ **~ sb/sth/yourself with sb/sth** *As a writer, she chiefly occupied herself with historical subjects.* ◇ **~ sb/sth/yourself (in) doing sth** *Participants were asked how long they occupied themselves watching TV each day.*

occur AWL /ə'kɜː(r)/ *verb* (-rr-) **1** [I] to happen: *A dramatic change occurred late in the eighteenth century.* ◇ *Destruction of ozone occurs rapidly.* **2** [I] **+ adv./prep.** to exist or be found somewhere: *The word occurs once in a collection of texts in 1990.* ◇ *Most new infections occur among young adults.*

PHR V **oc'cur to sb** (of an idea or thought) to come into your mind: *The idea occurred to Jack St Clair Kilby at Texas Instruments in 1958.* ◇ **it occurs to sb that...** *It never occurred to him that he might be endangering their lives.* ◇ **it occurs to sb to do sth** *It seemed not to have occurred to them to handle their discussions in any other way.*

▸ NOUN + OCCUR **event • process • reaction • change • variation • shift • growth • development • mutation • transition • transfer • death • damage • error • failure • earthquake • injury • accident • interaction • recombination** *Pilgrims thought they were standing in the actual places where the events had originally occurred.* ◇ *Death occurs usually within 5–8 years of the first signs of the disease.* | **effect • problem • behaviour • infection • disease • symptom • species • word** *Unhealthy behaviours often occur in combination.*

▸ ADVERB + OCCUR **often, frequently, commonly, generally, usually, normally, typically • rarely • actually • sometimes, occasionally • necessarily** *More intense thunderstorms generally occur in the mid to late afternoon.* | **naturally** *The analysis becomes more difficult if other naturally occurring sugars are present.*

▸ OCCUR + ADVERB **frequently, commonly, regularly • together • simultaneously • mainly, mostly • late • early • spontaneously • independently • primarily • predominantly • first** *Occasionally, however, a mutation will occur spontaneously in a gene.* | **naturally** *Silicon occurs naturally in the form of sand.*

oc·cur·rence AWL /ə'kʌrəns; *NAmE* ə'kɜːrəns/ *noun* **1** [C] something that happens: *Accidents at road junctions are not a frequent occurrence.* **2** [U, C] **~ (of sth)** the fact of sth happening: *The occurrence of earthquakes in such a region is not surprising.* ◇ *Action is required to prevent future occurrences of similar incidents.* **3** [C] a situation that exists: *Low blood pressure is a relatively common occurrence after surgery.* **4** [U, C] **~ (of sth)** the fact of sth existing or being found somewhere: *The increase in resistance among bacteria can partly be attributed to the occurrence of new species of soil microbes.* ◇ *The index will list important occurrences of those words in the documents.*

ocean /'əʊʃn; *NAmE* 'oʊʃn/ *noun* **1** (*often* **the ocean**) [sing., U] the salt water that covers most of the earth's surface: *The ice melts and flows back into the ocean.* ◇ *The sample is sediment from the deep ocean.* ◇ *Antarctica is surrounded by open ocean.* ◇ **+ noun** *Warm ocean water travels from Florida to north-west Europe.* ◇ *Marine geologists use a variety of tools to investigate the ocean floor.* ➲ *compare* SEA (1) **2** [C] one of the five large areas that the ocean is divided into: *the Antarctic/Arctic/Atlantic/Indian/Pacific Ocean* ◇ *It has become clear that most of the world's seas and oceans are over-fished.*

ocean·ic /ˌəʊʃi'ænɪk; *NAmE* ˌoʊʃi'ænɪk/ *adj.* [usually before noun] (*technical*) connected with the ocean or with an ocean: *These species are uncommon on most oceanic islands.*

odd AWL /ɒd; *NAmE* ɑːd/ *adj.* **(odder, oddest) 1** (no comparative or superlative) (of numbers) that cannot be divided exactly by the number two: *The molecule has an odd number of electrons.* OPP EVEN² (2) **2** strange or unusual: *A previously healthy 20-year-old male student had been behaving in an increasingly odd way.* ◇ *Given the arguments for free trade, the idea of protectionism may seem odd.* ◇ **it is ~ that...** *It is odd that she does not make this point more explicitly.* ◇ **it is ~ (for sb) to do sth** *They claim that in Spain it is odd for a man to be involved with the housework.* **3 the odd** [only before noun] (no comparative or superlative) happening or appearing occasionally; not very regular or frequent SYN OCCASIONAL: *The odd detail may be wrong.* **4** [only before noun] (no comparative or superlative) of no particular type or size; various: *The room contained some lamps and odd bits of candle.* **5** [only before noun] available; that sb can use SYN SPARE¹ (2): *This is something which any intelligent woman could do in any odd moments.* **6** (no comparative or superlative; usually placed immediately after a number) (*informal*) approximately or a little more than the number mentioned: *The EU deals with a much wider range of issues than its forerunners of fifty-odd years ago.*

IDM **the odd man/one 'out** a person or thing that is different from others or does not fit easily into a group or set: *Britain has so often appeared to be the odd man out in Europe.*

odds AWL /ɒdz; *NAmE* ɑːdz/ *noun* [pl.] **1** (*usually* **the odds**) the degree to which sth is likely to happen: **the ~ of (doing) sth** *The odds of success are very low.* ◇ **the ~ of sb/sth doing sth** *The odds of it becoming a viable commercial product have increased dramatically.* ◇ **the ~ against sth** *The odds against Shakespearean authorship seem to be strong.* ◇ **the ~ that...** *Conditions such as these greatly enhance the odds that a young person will pursue lifelong learning.* ◇ **the ~ are that...** *He thinks that the odds are that he will stay healthy.* **2** greater advantage; the state of being greater in strength, power or resources: **~ (against sb/sth)** *In the face of seemingly overwhelming odds against them, these teachers do not give up on their students.* ◇ **against all (the) ~** *Some cancer patients survive against all the odds.*

IDM **be at 'odds (with sth)** to be different from sth, when the two things should be the same SYN CONFLICT²: *Their world views are deeply at odds.* ◇ *Several ministers supported decisions that were at odds with government policy.* **be at 'odds (with sb) (over/on sth)** to disagree with sb about sth: *These two factions had been at odds since the late nineteenth century.*

of /əv; *strong form* ɒv; *NAmE* ʌv/ *prep.* **1** connected with sb; belonging to sb: *The role of women in society is changing.* ◇ *She was introduced to the works of Shakespeare as a young child.* HELP When you are talking about everything sb has written, painted, etc, use **of**; when you are referring to one or more examples of sb's work, use **by**: *a play by Shakespeare* **2** being part of sth; connected with sth; belonging to sth: *All the components of the test are considered.* ◇ *The effects of this are twofold:...* ◇ *Treated filter* *papers were placed inside the lids of 9-cm glass Petri dishes.* **3** living in a place; coming from a particular background: *The people of Virginia protested.* ◇ *No such studies have been performed in populations of African descent.* **4** concerning or showing sb/sth: *The allegations were presented as statements of fact.* ◇ *The researchers had taken a photograph of the participant.* **5** used to say what sb/sth is, consists of or contains: *The fire devasted much of the city of Rome.* ◇ *The issue of absence from school has gained much attention.* ◇ *She went to get a glass of water.* **6** used with measurements and expressions of quantity, time, age, etc: *The process uses large amounts of water.* ◇ *She has lost a lot of weight.* ◇ *The economy grew at a rate of 10% a year.* ◇ *The study presented 15 healthy children of 3–5 years of age.* **7** used to show that sb/sth belongs to a group, for example after *some, many* or *the most...*: *Some of these patients will require IV antibiotics.* ◇ *Many of the modern-day pollutants are less visible.* ◇ *The most famous of these was Karl Marx.* **8** used to show the position of sth in space or time: *They lie to the west and north of the Grand Canyon.* ◇ *Fathers married to the mother at the time of birth have parental responsibility.* **9** used after nouns formed from verbs: *Their ancestors were the first inhabitants of the area.* HELP The noun before **of** can be either the subject or object of the action: *There was resistance to the arrival of these ideas.* (= the ideas arrived); *Criticism of these ideas increased.* (= the ideas were criticized). **10** used after some verbs or after their object: *The story tells of a poor but happy couple who live on the land.* ◇ *They had failed to warn him of the risks involved in the treatment.* ◇ *The government accused him of being a spy.* ◇ *The women have not been deprived of their liberty.* ◇ *The defendant was acquitted of murder.* **11** used after some adjectives: *They were proud of their distinctive cultural heritage.* ◇ *The literature is largely devoid of well-controlled randomized trials.*

IDM **worst/biggest, etc. of ˈall | the worst/biggest, etc... of ˈall** used to say that sb/sth is worse, bigger, etc. than everyone/everything else: *Worst of all, the president seemed not to know.* ◇ *The biggest surprise of all was the discovery of two burial shafts.* ◇ *Diversification generally carries the greatest risk of all.*

off[1] /ɒf; *NAmE* ɔːf; ɑːf/ *adv.* HELP For the special uses of **off** in phrasal verbs, look at the entries for the verbs. For example **write sth off** is in the phrasal verb section at **write. 1** away from a place; at a distance in space or time: *The men went off to war.* ◇ *The defendant ran off without paying.* ◇ *A full understanding is some way off.* **2** away from an opinion or way of behaving: *They could not be frightened off by these threats.* **3** used to say that sth has been removed or separated: *The precipitate was filtered off and dried at 100°C under vacuum.* ◇ *The police cordoned off the street.* **4** not connected or functioning: *During an observation, a family might be asked to keep the television off.* ◇ *Genes are switched on and off during development.* OPP ON[2] (4) **5** used to say that sth is finished or will no longer happen: *These measures had the effect of killing off imports, especially luxury goods.* ➲ *see also* CUT-OFF **6** away from work or duty: *She was told to take time off and rest.* ◇ *They get a day off on their birthday.* ➲ *see also* WELL OFF

IDM **be better off (doing sth)** to be in a better situation (by doing sth): *Many will be better off doing a vocational course such as ICT.* **be well/better/badly, etc. ˈoff** used to say how much money sb has: *This does not mean that everyone is better off.* ◇ *The average household was 15 per cent worse off than in 2003.*

off[2] /ɒf; *NAmE* ɔːf; ɑːf/ *prep.* **1** down or away from a place; at a distance in space or time: *Children need to get off the sofa and onto the sports pitch.* ◇ *The island is situated 2 km off the coast of China.* ◇ *They are a long way off producing any really useful data.* **2** leading away from sth, for example a road or room: *He was in a room off the hall.* **3** used to say that sth has been removed: *The material is wiped off the swab.* ◇ *This approach took pressure off interviewees to reply quickly.* **4** away from work or duty: *Patients may take time off work.* ◇ *She has been off school.* **5** not wanting or liking sth that you usually eat or use: *He has been off his food for the last week.*

of·fence (*US* **of·fense**) /əˈfens/ *noun* **1** [C] an illegal act SYN CRIME (2): *a criminal/sexual/serious offence* ◇ **~ against sb/sth** *Theft is one of many offences against property.* ◇ **~ of sth** *The offence of fraud does not require the defendant to have actually obtained anything, such as goods or services.* ◇ **~ of doing sth** *Section 3 of the Act provides for the offence of driving without due care and attention.* ◇ **commit an ~** *The court held that no offence had been committed under the Computer Misuse Act 1990.* ◇ **it is an ~ to do sth** *It is an offence to resist or wilfully obstruct a police officer in the execution of his duty.* **2** [U] the act of upsetting sb by being rude to them, deliberately or by accident: **cause ~** *Doctors are often worried that they may cause offence by raising the issue of sexual health with older patients.* ◇ **give ~** *He has an ability to amuse and provoke without giving offence.* ◇ **take ~ (at sth)** *Hemphill and Hare took offence at Gendreau's criticisms.*

of·fend /əˈfend/ *verb* **1** [T, often passive, I] **~ (sb)** to make sb feel upset because of sth you say or do that is rude or embarrassing: *Many were offended by his insulting remarks.* ◇ *The photographs were designed to offend and scandalize.* **2** [T] **~ sb/sth** to seem unpleasant to sb: *The plays have been selected so as not to offend the sensibilities of audiences.* **3** [I] to commit an illegal act: *In deciding how to respond, the police need to consider whether this person is likely to offend again.* **4** [I, T] to be against what people believe is morally right: **~ against sb/sth** *States have a moral obligation to intervene in cases that offend against minimum standards of humanity.* ◇ **~ sth** *Stereotyping based on gender offends the principle of equality.*

of·fend·er /əˈfendə(r)/ *noun* **1** a person who commits a crime: *By punishing offenders, the criminal justice system seeks to encourage others to comply with the law.* ◇ *An example was the introduction of secure training orders for persistent young offenders.* **2** a person or thing that does sth bad: *When it comes to pollution, the chemical industry is a major offender.*

of·fen·sive[1] /əˈfensɪv/ *adj.* **1** rude in a way that causes you to feel upset: *This level of offensive language was extremely rare in any of the other blogs.* ◇ **~ to sb** *A small red triangle in the corner of the television screen indicated material that might be offensive to some.* **2** [only before noun] connected with the act of attacking sb/sth: *President Johnson authorized American ground troops to engage in offensive action.* ◇ **~ weapon** *He had been charged with carrying an offensive weapon.* ➲ *compare* DEFENSIVE (1) **3** extremely unpleasant: *Nausea without vomiting may be a reaction to offensive smells.*

of·fen·sive[2] /əˈfensɪv/ *noun* **1** a military operation in which large numbers of soldiers, etc. attack another country: *Spanish forces launched a successful offensive against the French in 1652.* **2** a series of actions aimed at achieving sth in a way that attracts a lot of attention: *The war was to be preceded by a well-conducted diplomatic offensive aimed at isolating the Dutch.*

offer[1] /ˈɒfə(r); *NAmE* ˈɔːfər; ˈɑːfər/ *verb* **1** [T] to give or provide sth: **~ sth** *She offered some wise advice.* ◇ *Cable television also offered some additional advantages.* ◇ *Roschelle et al. (2000) offered three explanations for these findings.* ◇ **~ sb sth** *Writing in a journal offers a child the opportunity to sort out their thoughts* ➲ thesaurus note *at* PROVIDE **2** [T] to say that you are willing to give sth to sb or to do sth for sb: **~ sth** *British ICT companies have been quick to offer their services.* ◇ **~ sth to sb** *Counselling should be offered to the family.* ◇ **~ sb sth** *His client was*

not even offered an interview. ◇ **~ to do sth** *Many mortgage lenders offer to pay the customer's switching costs.*
IDM **have sth to offer** to have sth available that sb wants: *The concluding chapter is a remarkable end to a book that has a huge amount to offer.* ◇ *The technologies currently in use are the best that modern science has to offer.*
▸ OFFER + NOUN **opportunity, chance, possiblity • prospect • potential • insight • perspective • glimpse • suggestion • explanation • interpretation, analysis • critique • information, evidence • advice • help, assistance, guidance • support • protection • advantage, benefit • solution • alternative • hope • overview • account • example • answer • definition • course • product • way** *Such discussions offer insights regarding a child's sense of security.* ◇ *Recent research has offered some empirical support for this assumption.*

offer[2] /ˈɒfə(r); *NAmE* ˈɔːfər; ˈɑːfər/ *noun* **1** an act of saying that you are willing to do sth for sb or give sth to sb: *The author accepted the job offer from the White House.* ◇ **~ of sth** *She received many offers of marriage and rejected them all.* ◇ **~ to do sth** *Kennedy refused an offer to debate with McCarthy.* **2 ~ (of sth)** an amount of money that sb is willing to pay for sth: *He made an offer of £4 500 which Arnold says he will consider.* **3** a reduction in the normal price of sth, usually for a short period of time: *Businesses try to attract new customers with special offers and price promotions.*
IDM **on ˈoffer** that can be bought, used, etc: *Marketers have to be able to persuade customers that they need the service on offer.*

of·fer·ing /ˈɒfərɪŋ; *NAmE* ˈɔːfərɪŋ; ˈɑːfərɪŋ/ *noun* **1** something that is produced for other people to use, watch, enjoy, etc: *Today's customers are seeking product offerings that match their individual requirements.* ◇ *Chekhov's plays became standard repertory offerings both inside Russia and abroad.* **2** something that is given to a god as part of religious worship: *Great numbers of Jews came to the Temple to pray and make offerings.*

of·fice /ˈɒfɪs; *NAmE* ˈɔːfɪs; ˈɑːfɪs/ *noun* **1** [C] a room, set of rooms or building where people work: *The principal shares her office with the coordinator, ensuring regular communication.* ◇ *These mobile workers are all out of the office a lot and use mobile phones, PDAs and laptops.* ◇ **+ noun** *office buildings/desks/space/workers* **2** [C] the local centre of a large business: *Over time, branch offices were opened in London, Chicago and Milan.* ◇ *The company will provide in-depth training at their Belgium head office.* **3** [U, C] an important position of authority, especially in government; the work and duties connected with this: **take/leave ~** *After leaving office, the President faced corruption charges.* ◇ **hold ~** *Catholics were excluded from becoming members of Parliament and holding other public offices.* ◇ **the ~ of sth** *He was elected to the office of chairman of the Defence Council.* ◇ **run for ~** *In almost every country in the world, women can vote and run for office.* ◇ **in ~** *After two years in office, he resigned as Secretary of State.* ◇ **out of ~** *A corrupt government can be voted out of office.* **4 Office** [C] used in the names of some British government departments: *In 2000, the Home Office and Foreign Office set up a joint unit to manage entry clearance.* ◇ *The Office of Fair Trading enforces competition policy in the UK.* **5** [C] (*NAmE*) = SURGERY (2): *The dispensing of drugs occurs through hospitals and doctors' offices.*

of·fi·cer /ˈɒfɪsə(r); *NAmE* ˈɔːfɪsər; ˈɑːfɪsər/ *noun* **1** a person who is in a position of authority in the armed forces: *army/military/naval officers* ◇ *The cavalry officers, especially the senior officers, were almost entirely to blame for the poor performance of their men in the Crimean War.* **2** (often in compounds) a person who is in a position of authority in the government or a large organization: *The defendant was accompanied by two prison officers.* ◇ *Defects in equipment or hazards should be reported to the health and safety officer.* ➲ *see also* POLICE OFFICER

of·fi·cial[1] /əˈfɪʃl/ *noun* (often in compounds) a person who is in a position of authority in a large organization: *Lobbying groups tried convince government officials of the need to impose trade restrictions.* ◇ *Senior public officials were accused of demanding or accepting bribes.* ◇ *Trade union officials tried to settle the case through negotiation.*

of·fi·cial[2] /əˈfɪʃl/ *adj.* **1** [only before noun] connected with the job of sb who is in a position of authority: *The Prime Minister spoke to the media outside his official residence in Downing Street.* ◇ *The Court of Justice requires proof of fault on the part of an employee acting in an official capacity.* ◇ *Beijing was quick to invite the new head of state for an official visit.* OPP UNOFFICIAL (2) **2** [usually before noun] agreed to, said or done by sb who is in a position of authority: *Official statistics from different nation states can be compared for a specific area of activity.* ◇ *Belgium recognizes both Flemish and French as official languages.* ◇ *official statements/documents/policy* OPP UNOFFICIAL (1) **3** [only before noun] that is told to the public but may not be true: *There has been no recognition of lived experiences that differ from the official version of events.*

of·fi·cial·ly /əˈfɪʃəli/ *adv.* **1** publicly and by sb who is in a position of authority: *In 1955, Cardiff was officially recognized as the capital of Wales.* **2** according to a particular set of rules or laws: *By definition, income from the black economy cannot be counted officially.* **3** according to information that has been told to the public but that may not be true: *Unemployment among nationals is officially 20 per cent and unofficially very much higher.*

off·line /ˌɒfˈlaɪn; *NAmE* ˌɔːfˈlaɪn; ˌɑːfˈlaɪn/ *adj.* [usually before noun] not directly controlled by or connected to a computer or to the Internet: *These questions never needed to be considered in the offline world.* OPP ONLINE ■ **off·line** *adv.*: *Data are available both online and offline.*

off·set[1] AWL /ˈɒfset; *NAmE* ˈɔːfset; ˈɑːfset/ *verb* (**off·set·ting, off·set, off·set**) to use one cost, payment or situation in order to cancel or reduce the effect of another: **~ sth** *Subsidies and assistance from central government were intended to offset the effects of mine closures.* ◇ **~ sth against sth** (*BrE*) *Losses incurred in one field could be offset against income from other work areas for tax purposes.*

off·set[2] AWL /ˈɒfset; *NAmE* ˈɔːfset; ˈɑːfset/ *noun* **1** a cost, payment or situation used in order to cancel or reduce the effect of another: *If a 500-year-old oak forest is destroyed by a development project, does a newly planted oak forest of equivalent size provide an acceptable offset?* **2** (*technical*) a constant value added to a varying quantity or signal: *The average output voltage differs from zero by a constant offset.*

off·shore /ˌɒfˈʃɔː(r); *NAmE* ˌɔːfˈʃɔːr; ˌɑːfˈʃɔːr/ *adj.* [usually before noun] **1** happening or existing in the sea, not far from the land: *Deepwater Horizon was the biggest oil well in the history of American offshore oil drilling.* ◇ *Offshore wind farms can interfere with other water uses, such as fishing and vessel navigation.* **2** (of winds) blowing from the land towards the sea: *Strong offshore wind drives air over the ocean surface, increasing the evaporation of seawater.* **3** (*business*) (of money, companies, etc.) kept or located in a country that has more generous tax laws than other places: *Proposals include the abolition of offshore financial centres that offer tax havens for the wealthy.* ■ **off·shore** *adv.*: *The fault zone to the west of Puerto Rico also lies offshore.* ◇ *The nature of the business has changed, as more research and development and manufacturing are located offshore.*

off·spring /ˈɒfsprɪŋ; *NAmE* ˈɔːfsprɪŋ; ˈɑːfsprɪŋ/ *noun* (*pl.* **off·spring**) the young of an animal or plant; someone's child/children: *Among these surviving offspring, 15 were females.* ◇ *36 clutches failed to produce an offspring.* ◇ *50%*

of male offspring will be affected. ◇ **~ of sb/sth** *They were usually the offspring of wealthy bankers.*

often /ˈɒfn; ˈɒftən; *NAmE* ˈɔːfn; ˈɑːfn; ˈɔːftən; ˈɑːftən/ *adv.* **1** in many cases or situations SYN COMMONLY: *Workers depend primarily on their jobs for income, but employers often have other means of support.* ◇ *It is often difficult to make accurate assessments of the eventual market value of new technology.* ◇ *All too often, the good suffer and evil-doers seem to flourish.* ◇ **as so ~ (happens)** *As so often happens, crisis forced change.* **2** many times SYN FREQUENTLY: *He would often say that the liberty to speak and think as one pleases is the test of a free country.* ◇ *Respondents indicated how often they had experienced each symptom in the previous week.*

IDM **as ˌoften as ˈnot** quite frequently: *In Germany, the bourgeoisie were as often as not university-educated.* **more ˌoften than ˈnot** usually: *The early naturalists more often than not simply catalogued and described animal species.*

oil /ɔɪl/ *noun* **1** [U] a thick liquid that is found in rock underground SYN PETROLEUM: *The price of oil soared.* ◇ **+ noun** *Oil companies are unlikely to stop extracting oil, even if they invest in renewable energy.* ◇ *Russia has huge oil reserves.* ◇ *The oil spill caused disruption along the US Gulf Coast.* ◇ *The oil and gas industry is highly competitive.* **2** [U] a form of PETROLEUM that is used as fuel and to make parts of machines move smoothly: **+ noun** *They had simple oil lamps.* **3** [U, C] a smooth thick liquid that is made from plants or animals and is used in food and medicines: *vegetable/olive oil* ◇ *They produce 85% of the world's palm oil.* ◇ *Fish oils have a beneficial effect on the symptoms.* **4** [C] (*chemistry*) any of a group of natural ESTERS, mainly found in plants, which are liquid at room temperature: *Vegetable oils can be hydrogenated to form saturated fats for use in margarine.* ➲ *compare* FAT² (3)

WHICH WORD?

older • oldest • elder • eldest

- **older** than
- the **older/oldest** rocks
- **older** children/adults/participants
- the **oldest** child/daughter/son
- the **elder** child/daughter/son
- the **eldest** (child/daughter/son)

- The comparative and superlative forms of **old** are **older** and **oldest**: *The eastern and highest cliff is far* ***older*** *than the western, younger scarp.* ◇ *The Palaeozoic rocks rest on successively* ***older*** *Precambrian rocks towards the south-west.* ◇ *Generally, the* ***oldest*** *outcropping rocks in Sinoburmalaya are of Cambrian age.*
- You can also use **older** and **oldest** when comparing people's ages: *We included all participants who were* ***older*** *than 50 years of age.* ◇ ***Older*** *children used the Internet more than did younger children.* ◇ *The* ***oldest*** *child in the family might experience home as a peaceful, supportive environment.* ◇
- However, when you are comparing members of the same family, it is considered correct to use **elder** and **eldest**. The comparative form **elder** is used only before a noun: *The throne was offered jointly to William and his wife Mary, the* ***elder*** *daughter of James II.* ◇ *As the* ***eldest*** *son, Lee inherited the family's mountain land.*

old /əʊld; *NAmE* oʊld/ *adj.* (**old·er**, **old·est**) **1** of a particular age: **be… years, months, etc. ~** *John is 33 years old and a primary school teacher.* ◇ *A 19-year-old woman presents with severe abdominal pain.* ◇ *Unemployment among 16–24-year-olds rose by 11 000 to 926 000.* ◇ **~ enough to do sth** *Herodotus was not old enough to remember the Persian wars.* **2** having lived for a long time; no longer young: *Children and old people are particularly vulnerable.* ◇ *When Tithonos grew old, he became too weak to move.* OPP YOUNG¹ (1) **3 the old** *noun* [pl.] old people: *Certain groups of people (women, the old, the very young) would be worse off.* **4** having existed or been used for a long time: *This theme is a very old one.* ◇ *The oldest known rocks on Earth are sedimentary deposits.* ◇ *Elements of what he proposed in his lecture were in fact very old.* OPP NEW (1) **5** [only before noun] belonging to past times or a past time in your life, and often having been replaced by sth else SYN FORMER¹ (1), PREVIOUS (1): *Her old job was abolished during the restructuring.* ◇ *This legislation was enacted to overcome the shortcomings of the old system.* ◇ *Comparing new and old ECGs is the easiest way to decide whether a cardiac event has occurred.* OPP NEW (6) **6** [only before noun] known for a long time: *He is one of her oldest friends.* ◇ *Kamenev and Zinoviev were already seeking an alliance with their old enemy Trotsky.* ➲ *compare* RECENT

ˌold ˈage *noun* [U] the time of your life when you are old: *Some elderly people see old age as the best time of their lives.* ◇ **in/during ~** *The effect will be to increase the uncertainties that people experience in old age.*

ˌold-ˈfashioned *adj.* (*sometimes disapproving*) **1** of a style or type that is no longer current or fashionable: *The 19th century translations are often written in very formal and old-fashioned English.* ◇ *Both the teaching and laboratory facilities are a little old-fashioned.* OPP MODERN (1) ➲ *compare* FASHIONABLE (1) **2** believing in old or traditional ways; having traditional ideas: *They are pretty old-fashioned, and believe the man should take charge of the household.* ◇ *His attitude is somewhat old-fashioned and backward-looking.*

omis·sion /əˈmɪʃn/ *noun* **1** [U] the act of not including sb/sth or not doing sth; the fact of not being included/done: *To ignore such determining considerations is a serious error of omission.* ◇ **~ (of sb/sth) (from sth)** *Klawans notes Cavell's omission of this film from his study of the genre.* **2** [C] **~ (from sth)** a thing that has not been included or done: *Notable omissions from Table 1 are Brazil, China, Estonia and the United States of America.* ◇ *There are some surprising omissions in Heller's bibliography.*

omit /əˈmɪt/ *verb* (**-tt-**) **1** to not include sth/sb, either deliberately or because you have forgotten it/them SYN LEAVE SB/STH OUT (OF STH): **~ sth/sb** *Birth statistics may omit many children who were born at home or who died in infancy.* ◇ **~ sth/sb from sth** *These data are omitted from the analysis.* **2 ~ to do sth** to not do or fail to do sth: *The police had omitted to provide the Board with a copy of the report.*

on¹ /ɒn; *NAmE* ɑːn; ɔːn/ *prep.* HELP For the special uses of **on** in phrasal verbs, look at the entries for the verbs. For example **depend on sth** is is covered at **depend**. **1** in or into a position covering, touching or forming part of a surface: *Hydrology concerns itself with water on and under the earth's surface.* ◇ *The solutions are given on page 285.* ◇ **~ to sth** *By moving the beam, characters can be written on to the surface of the paper.* HELP This could also be written ***onto*** *the surface of the paper* **2** used to show a date or day: *Approval was announced on 20 November 2001.* ◇ *At some schools, many classes run on Saturdays to increase accessibility and encourage participation.* ◇ *Lumière used the motif of smoke on several occasions.* **3** at the same time that sth happens or is done: *Symptoms include pain and burning on swallowing.* ◇ *On arrival, vessels discharged their cargoes and crew.* ◇ *He celebrated his grand triumph on his return to Rome.* **4** about sth/sb: *There are many books on gender.* ◇ *Further details on this project are provided in Ross et al. (2013).* ◇ *The children were tested on their knowledge of the alphabet.* ◇ *Most research on soils in archaeological contexts has taken place in North America and Europe.* **5** used to show that sb belongs to a group or an organization: *Everyone on the team has a part to play.* ◇ *He has been on the editorial boards of numerous* *academic journals.* **6** eating or drinking sth; using a drug or a medicine regularly: *They were fed on a diet of grain and vegetables.* ◇ *He is on a drug called eplerenone.* **7 ~ the left/right** used for saying what side sth is on: *The Plateau is visible in the distance on the right.* **8** at or near a place: *Many people had to live on the street.* ◇ *Most of his childhood was spent on the Greek island of Mykonos.* ◇ *They did manage to keep control of Rome and a few other places on the coast.* **9** used to show the basis or reason for sth: *Chalmers based his theory on the Latin American cases.* ◇ *They disagree with abortion on religious and moral grounds.* ◇ *The appointment of Cabinet ministers is made on the recommendation of the Prime Minister.* **10** earning or using a particular amount of money: *There is a need to cushion those on low incomes.* ◇ *They barely had enough money to live on.* **11** by means of sth; using sth: *It looks much better on television.* ◇ *Films are accessible on the Internet.* **12** used with some nouns or adjectives to say who or what is affected by sth: *Any increase in the money supply might have a relatively small impact on interest rates.* ◇ *There were height restrictions on buildings in the old town.* ◇ *This enormous catastrophe fell hardest on Belgium and France.* **13** compared with sb/sth: *Orders from some catering companies are down on previous years.*

on² /ɒn; *NAmE* ɑːn; ɔːn/ *adv.* HELP For the special uses of **on** in phrasal verbs, look at the entries for the verbs. For example **get on** is in the phrasal verb section at **get**. **1** used to show that sth continues: *The revolution was raging on.* ◇ *As the day wore on, most passengers had to endure a long wait to check in their bags.* ◇ *Darby's memory lives on in his magnificent bridge, which was opened in 1781.* **2** used to show that sth follows after another thing: *He then moves on to discuss the earthquake in its scientific context.* ◇ *Output rises until this point is reached and declines from then on.* **3** covering, touching or forming part of sth: *Make sure the lid is on.* OPP OFF¹ (3) **4** connected or operating; being used: *The test involves pressing a button as soon as a light comes on.* OPP OFF¹ (4) **5** happening: *The war had been on for several months.*

once¹ /wʌns/ *adv.* **1** on one occasion only; one time: *The word 'philosophy' appears only once in the New Testament.* ◇ *Some participants were interviewed more than once.* ◇ *91.1% reported having accessed the Internet at least once.* ◇ **~ a day, week, year, etc.** *The committee meets once a year.* **2** at some time in the past: *She confesses that she once wanted to go on the stage.* ◇ *Romantic literature was once seen as a new dawn.* ◇ *This once lively, bright and energetic child could no longer walk or talk.* **3** used in negative sentences to mean 'ever' or 'at all': *Green never once mentions his legal name, Henry Yorke.* ◇ *Not once does Kant characterize the genius as a breaker of rules.* IDM **once aˈgain | once ˈmore** one more time; another time: *Once again, he has been admitted to hospital.* ◇ *If passenger demand picks up once more, the airline may seek to increase its capacity by ordering more aircraft.*

once² /wʌns/ *conj.* as soon as; when: *Once such class differences develop, class conflict follows.* ◇ *Once present, deep infection is extremely difficult to eradicate.*

one¹ /wʌn/ *number, det.* **1** the number 1: *There were 750 adults reporting one or more illnesses or injuries per month.* ◇ *One more batch of six interviews was undertaken to test this assertion.* ◇ *There is only one active X chromosome per somatic cell.* **2** used in formal language or for emphasis before *hundred, thousand,* etc, or before a unit of measurement: *One thousand and forty-two patients were invited to participate in the survey.* ◇ *Rates of formation are estimated to be less than one tonne per hectare per year.* **3 ~ (of sb/sth)** a person or thing, especially when they are part of a group or pair: *Acute appendicitis is one of the most common surgical emergencies.* ◇ *Money and power often give one person or organization the ability to influence the actions of another.* ◇ *Some crystals are tapered, with a larger diameter at one end than at the other.* **4** used for emphasis to mean 'the only one': *Price is the one element of the marketing mix that directly affects the income that a company receives.* **5** used when you are talking about a time in the past or the future, without actually saying which one: *Retinal implants, or completely artificial eyes, may one day be possible.* **6** the same: *The authors of the 16 studies reviewed had one common focus.* IDM **as ˈone** (*formal*) in agreement; all together: *This is an external policy area where the member governments must act as one.* **(all) in ˈone** used to say that sb/sth has different roles, contains different things or is used for different purposes: *Marxism supplied its followers with politics, a religion and a moral identity all in one.* **ˌone after aˈnother/the ˈother** first one person or thing, and then another, and then another, up to any number or amount: *The holding company began to grow by buying up large companies one after another.* **ˌone and the ˈsame** used for emphasis to mean 'the same': *Capital and wage labour are two sides of one and the same relation.* **ˌone or ˈtwo** a few: *Before 1066 England had very few castles: just one or two on the Welsh border.*

one² /wʌn/ *pron.* **1** used to avoid repeating a noun, when you are referring to sb/sth that has already been mentioned, or that the person you are speaking to knows about: *The existence of these networks is critical for both small companies and larger ones.* ◇ *The question remains an important one today.* ◇ *This protein has several domains, including ones that can bind other proteins.* **2** used when you are identifying the person or thing you are talking about: *Each value is greater than or equal to the one above it on the graph.* ◇ *The author claims that, in British society, white, middle-class men are the ones who do best in terms of education and health care.* **3 ~ of sb/sth** a person or thing belonging to a particular group: *He was tutor to the young Nero and later one of his chief advisers.* ◇ *The patient complained of redness and tenderness over one of the calf veins.* **4** a person of the type mentioned: *Sudden death is a traumatic event for the family and loved ones of those involved.* ◇ **~ to do sth** *As a politician, he was not one to shy away from controversy.* **5** (*formal*) used to mean 'people in general': *Overtime is the difference between the total number of hours worked and the number of hours one is required to work according to one's employment contract.*

ˌone aˈnother *pron.* used to show that each member of a group does sth to or for the other members, or has the same relationship with them SYN EACH OTHER (1): *Oppositely charged ions attract one another.* ◇ *The rich countries are different from one another in many ways.* ◇ *The two ran against one another for office twice, in 2003 and 2006.*

one's /wʌnz/ *det.* (*formal*) the possessive form of *one*: *'Do one's best' is an idiom.*

one·self /wʌnˈself/ *pron.* (*formal*) **1** (the reflexive form of *one*) used as the object of a verb or preposition when 'one' is the subject of the verb or is understood as the subject: *One can train oneself not to have cigarettes.* ◇ *To insure oneself against a risk is to act in ways to reduce the risk.* ◇ *Self-reinforcement is the rewarding of oneself when a goal has been achieved.* **2** used to emphasize *one*: *Dieting is something that one can only do for oneself.*

ˌone-ˈsided *adj.* **1** (*disapproving*) (of an argument, opinion, etc.) showing only one side of the situation; not balanced SYN BIASED (2): *The problem with Parson's theory was that it was too one-sided.* ◇ *There is a need to move beyond the one-sided generalizations that prevail in the current literature.* **2** (of an activity or a relationship) with all the power, skill, etc. coming from one person or group: *Hitler's conversations became increasingly one-sided.* ◇ *For the democracies of the South, this one-sided economic dependence on the North looks set to continue.*

ˌ**one-to-ˈone** (*especially BrE*) (*NAmE usually* ˌ**one-on-ˈone**) *adj.* [usually before noun] **1** between two people only: *a one-to-one conversation/meeting/interview* ◇ *They want to cut class sizes and provide more one-to-one teaching.* **2** matching sth else in an exact way: *In Papua New Guinea, there is no one-to-one mapping between village names, groups and language names.* ◇ *There is a one-to-one correspondence between the set of men who are unmarried and the set of men who are bachelors.* ■ ˌ**one-to-ˈone** *adv.*: *A great deal of market research is undertaken one-to-one.*

ˌ**one-ˈway** *adj.* [usually before noun] **1** moving or allowing movement in only one direction: *Most road networks include one-way streets.* ◇ *The device forces air via a one-way valve into the patient's lungs.* **2** operating in only one direction: *Most traditional media provide one-way communications, where information passes from a source to a receiver but there is little opportunity for feedback.*

on·going AWL /ˈɒŋɡəʊɪŋ; *NAmE* ˈɑːnɡoʊɪŋ; ˈɔːnɡoʊɪŋ/ *adj.* [usually before noun] continuing to exist or develop: *It is clear that personal development is an ongoing process.* ◇ *There is an ongoing debate about whether management is an art or a science.* ◇ *Clinical trials are currently ongoing.*

on·line /ˌɒnˈlaɪn; *NAmE* ˌɑːnˈlaɪn; ˌɔːnˈlaɪn/ *adj.* connected to or available using a computer or the Internet: *There is growing evidence that online surveys typically generate lower response rates than postal surveys.* ◇ *online resources/materials/research/communication* ◇ *Finally, Hollensen suggests that organizations can create online communities where customers can share ideas and interact together.* OPP OFFLINE IDM *see* LINE[1] ■ **on·line** *adv.*: *Increasing numbers of customers now prefer to shop online.*

only[1] /ˈəʊnli; *NAmE* ˈoʊnli/ *adv.* **1** no one or nothing except: *There have been only a limited number of studies on this topic.* ◇ *Only three levels were used in the analysis presented.* ◇ *Capitalist production was only a small part of the economy.* ◇ *Thermodynamics applies only to bulk matter, not to individual molecules.* ◇ **sb ~ has to do sth** *One only has to note the growth of price comparison websites to see how these tools can be extremely important.* **2** in no other situation or place; for no other reason: *Thyroid eye disease only occurs in patients with Graves' disease.* ◇ **~ because** *He emerged victorious only because his opponents were more incompetent than he was.* ◇ **~ if** *A firm will reinvest profits only if it expects to earn more profits.* HELP In formal written English **only**, or **only if** and its clause, can be placed first in the sentence. In the second part of the sentence, **be**, **do**, **have**, etc. come before the subject and the main part of the verb: *Only in Burma and Thailand did Buddhism achieve the status of a state religion.* ◇ *Only if cost-cutting fails will enterprises make strategic changes within their existing operations.* **3** no more than; no longer than: *Some species grow to adult size and reproduce only once.* ◇ *Soil temperature increased only slightly.* ◇ *Climatic recovery takes only a decade or so.* **4** not until: *The census analysis has only recently been completed.* ◇ *Radiation damage may only become apparent many months or years after radiation exposure.* ◇ *Only then can the cell divide to form two daughter cells.* HELP When **only** begins a sentence **be**, **do**, **have**, etc. come before the subject and the main part of the verb. **5** used to say that sb can do no more than what is mentioned, although this is probably not enough: *Workers can only hope to shape or block technical change, not to initiate it.* ◇ *The President could only begin to come to grips with the enormity of what Hurricane Katrina revealed.* **6** used to say that sth has or will have a bad effect: *AIDS only serves to exacerbate poverty.* ◇ *He argues that pumping more money into the economy would only make things worse.* ◇ **~ to do sth** *Tall smokestacks are constructed on coal-burning power stations to reduce local pollution—only to cause acid rain elsewhere.*

IDM **only ˈjust 1** not long ago/before: *Progress in this direction is only just beginning.* **2** almost not: *Only just over 1% of the acid has dissociated.* ◇ *The very low cloud base is only just visible through the driving rain.* **only too...** very: *Governmental authorities are only too aware of their obligations under international law.* ◇ *They knew only too well how unpredictable and devastating earthquakes could be.* ➲ *more at* EVER, IF, NAME[1], NOT

only[2] /ˈəʊnli; *NAmE* ˈoʊnli/ *adj.* [only before noun] **1** used to say that no other or others of the same group exist or are there: *The only way a firm can stay in business is to make profits.* ◇ *He was the only person capable of bringing unity out of division.* ◇ *Scale is not the only difference between the two supermarkets.* **2** used to say that sb/sth is the best and you would not choose any other: *There was a developing belief that hospital was the only safe place to have children.*

onset /ˈɒnset; *NAmE* ˈɑːnset; ˈɔːnset/ *noun* [sing.] **~ (of sth)** the beginning of sth, especially sth unpleasant: *Treatment should be initiated within 60 minutes of the onset of symptoms.* ◇ *Only after the onset of the recession in 2008 did a clear policy divide on economic issues appear.* ◇ (*medical*) *the sudden/early/rapid/acute onset of sth*

onto /ˈɒntə; *NAmE* ˈɑːntə; ˈɔːntə; *before vowels* ˈɒntu; *NAmE* ˈɑːntu; ˈɔːntu/ (*also* **on to**) *prep.* **1** used with verbs to express movement on or to a particular place or position: *The sugar cane was loaded onto carts.* ◇ *Samples can be smeared directly onto a glass slide.* **2** used to show that sth faces in a particular direction: *Only a few small windows looked onto the street.*

ontol·ogy /ɒnˈtɒlədʒi; *NAmE* ɑːnˈtɑːlədʒi/ *noun* (*pl.* **-ies**) **1** [U] a branch of philosophy that deals with the nature of existence: *For such reasons as these, Heidegger believes that ontology and phenomenology coincide.* **2** [C, U] (*computing*) a list of ideas and categories in a subject area that shows the relationships between them: *An ontology is constructed so that the acquired knowledge can be classified.* ■ **onto·logic·al** /ˌɒntəˈlɒdʒɪkl; *NAmE* ˌɑːntəˈlɑːdʒɪkl/ *adj.*: *Any entity's ontological category is very plausibly one of its essential features.*

on·wards /ˈɒnwədz; *NAmE* ˈɑːnwərdz; ˈɔːnwərdz/ (*especially BrE*) (*NAmE usually* **on·ward** /ˈɒnwəd; *NAmE* ˈɑːnwərd; ˈɔːnwərd/) *adv.* **1 from... onwards** continuing from a particular time: *The Royal African Company's standing gradually declined from the 1710s onwards.* ◇ *From that point onwards, progress seemed unstoppable.* **2** forward: *The term 'cohort' is derived from the idea of a Roman troop of soldiers marching onwards together.* ◇ *The fear was that humankind might be regressing instead of striving onwards and upwards.*

opaque /əʊˈpeɪk; *NAmE* oʊˈpeɪk/ *adj.* **1** (of glass, liquid, etc.) not clear enough to see through or allow light through: *Most opaque minerals have colours in reflected light that range from nearly pure white to various shades of grey.* OPP TRANSPARENT (2) **2** (especially of language) difficult to understand; not clear: *There is a growing perception that decision-making in Brussels is remote, opaque and even undemocratic.* OPP TRANSPARENT (1)

open[1] /ˈəʊpən; *NAmE* ˈoʊpən/ *adj.* **1** allowing things or people to go through: *He supports the ideals of democratic peace, free trade and open borders.* ◇ *The family resource centre should be a welcoming space with an open door policy.* ◇ *The inlet and exhaust apertures remain open so that the exhaust products can be expelled.* OPP CLOSED (1) **2** (of sb's eyes or mouth) with the EYELIDS or LIPS apart: *The patient should breathe deeply with their mouth open.* OPP CLOSED (1) **3** spread out; with the edges apart: *Frost can damage open flowers, preventing seed set.* OPP CLOSED (1) **4** not blocked by anything: *Keep the*

O

airways open and look for chest movement. **5** not surrounded by anything: *Antarctica is surrounded by open ocean.* ◇ *Too often cities have inadequate provision of open space and green areas.* ◇ *Wind farms must be sited in open country.* **6** with no cover or roof on: *Any open wounds should be covered with sterile dressings.* HELP The **open air** is air that is outside, and not in a building: *In the open air, the concentration of radon is generally very low.* **7** [not usually before noun] (of a business) ready for business and to allow customers or visitors in: *The authority will not allow an insolvent company to remain open for business.* OPP CLOSED (2) **8** if a competition, etc. is **open**, anyone can enter it SYN PUBLIC[1]: *Recruitment to the civil service by open competition was established in 1870.* ◇ *Changes are not made to the constitution without full and open debate.* ◇ *The jury will deliver their verdict in open court.* ◇ *Open markets for skilled workers and free capital are essential to an entrepreneurial economy.* **9** [not before noun] **~ to sb** if a competition, building, etc. is **open** to particular people, those people can enter it: *Pharmacists carry out a major consulting role in pharmacies that are open to the public.* ◇ *Workshops and lectures were open to all in the community and in the university.* OPP CLOSED (4) **10** [not before noun] **~ (to sb)** to be available and ready to use: *Technological factors limit the range of options open to firms.* OPP CLOSED (4) **11 ~ (to sth)** that could be affected by argument, criticism or injury: *This concept is very much open to debate and interpretation.* ◇ *Chodorow's theory is open to criticism in some respects.* ◇ *He laid himself open to a charge of corruption.* ◇ *The protection afforded by limited liability is open to abuse.* ➲ *compare* VULNERABLE **12** known to everyone; not kept hidden: *The NHS provides open access to information about services, treatment and performance.* ◇ *Censorship of the media prevents free and open discussion of social and political issues.* **13** honest; not keeping thoughts and feelings hidden SYN FRANK: *There are demands for the government to be more open and transparent.* ◇ **~ (with sb) (about sth)** *Patients are more likely to forgive doctors who are open with them about errors.* **14 ~ to sth** (of a person) willing to listen to and think about new ideas: *Some volunteers described an increased ability to remain open to new ideas and experiences.* **15 ~ (to sth)** not yet finally decided or settled: *The evidence is open to different interpretations.* ◇ *This was not a matter open to negotiation.*

IDM **have/keep an ˌopen ˈmind (about/on sth)** to be willing to listen to or accept new ideas or suggestions: *Practitioners must keep an open mind and be prepared to review the diagnosis.* ➲ *more at* DOOR, FIELD, OPTION

open[2] /ˈəʊpən; *NAmE* ˈoʊpən/ *verb* **1** [I, T] to become no longer closed; to make sth no longer closed: *The valve opens and the piston moves downwards.* ◇ *With pea plants, self-fertilization occurs even before the flower opens.* ◇ **~ sth** *to open a door/window* ◇ *to open a bottle/box/can* ◇ *The patient could not open his eyes.* ◇ *Other Eastern Bloc nations opened their borders.* OPP CLOSE[1] (1) **2** [I, T] (of a business, hospital, school, etc.) to start business; to start to be available for people to use for the first time: *Before the two schools opened, several years were spent in preparation and planning.* ◇ **~ sth** *Up to March, the company had opened 267 new stores.* HELP If you say that a business **opens** at a particular time or on a particular day, you mean that it starts doing business at that time or that it does business on that day. OPP CLOSE[1] (3) **3** [T] **~ sth** to perform a ceremony showing that a building can start being used: *The New South Wales University of Technology was opened by the Governor of New South Wales on 11 September 1956.* **4** [I] (of a play, film, etc.) to start to be performed to the public: *They play opened in November and is still going strong.* **5** [T] **~ sth** to start an activity or event: *They had decided not to open an investigation.* ◇ *to open a dialogue/debate/meeting* ◇ *Some Athenians tried to open negotiations for peace with the Spartans.* **6** [I] **~ (with sth)** (of a story, film, etc.) to start in a particular way: *The narrative opens with him as a five-year-old, playing by a stream.* **7** [T] **~ a possibility/opportunity** to create the chance to do or discover sth new: *Technological advances have opened new opportunities.* ◇ *Surveying works in other languages opens the possibility of new revelations and discoveries.* **8** [T, I] **~ (sth)** to start a computer program or file so that you can use it on the screen: *Open a new file in your computer.* **9** [T] **~ your bowels** (*medical*) to pass solid waste out of the body: *He has not opened his bowels since the pain started.*

IDM **open ˈdoors for sb** to provide opportunities for sb to do sth and be successful: *Regime changes have opened doors for companies to start prestigious infrastructure projects.* **open sb's ˈeyes (to sth)** to make sb realize the truth about sth: *The sceptic is merely opening our eyes to how things are.* ◇ *Those horrors have opened the eyes of historians to other cruelties.* **open your/sb's mind to sth** to become or make sb aware of new ideas or experiences: *Diversity also matters because it opens people's minds to new ideas.* ◇ *They need to open their minds to new possibilities of technique and organization.* **open the way (for/to sth)** to make it possible for sb to do sth or for sth to happen: *New analytical technology is opening the way for more detailed investigations of sedimentary organic matter.*

PHR V **ˈopen into/onto sth** to lead to another area, place or room: *The narrow gorge opens into a wide valley of rolling hills.* **ˌopen ˈout** to become bigger or wider: *Most of these rivers open out in their lower courses to form wide estuaries.* **ˌopen ˈup (to sb)** to talk about what you feel and think; to become more willing to communicate: *A child will not automatically open up and share her inner thoughts and feelings.* **ˌopen sth ˈup** | **ˌopen ˈup 1** to become or make sth possible, available or able to be reached: *New technology is opening up possibilities for participation which have not existed in the past.* ◇ *The retail market has been opening up gradually to foreigners.* **2** to develop or start to happen or exist; to develop or start sth: *As some opportunities open up, others will close.* ◇ *This process opens up dialogue with the parties to the conflict.* **3** to appear and become wider; to make sth wider when it is narrow or closed: *They see a gap opening up between what they think they should receive and what they actually get.* **ˌopen sth ˈup** to make sth open that is closed, locked, etc: *When the statue is opened up, it reveals smaller images of the gods inside.*

ˌopen-ˈended *adj.* **1** without any limits, aims or dates fixed in advance: *She conducted open-ended interviews lasting three to five hours each with thirty flight attendants.* ◇ *Qualitative research is frequently very open-ended.* **2** (of a question) that can be answered in any way, rather than by 'yes' or 'no' or another particular answer: *They included many open-ended questions which gave the women the chance to talk freely.*

open·ing[1] /ˈəʊpnɪŋ; *NAmE* ˈoʊpnɪŋ/ *noun* **1** [C] a space or hole that sb/sth can pass through: *The trees near the canopy opening were unaffected.* ◇ **~ in sth** *Water exits through a lower opening in the dam.* **2** [C, usually sing.] **~ (of sth)** the beginning or first part of sth: *This is the decade which marks the opening of the age of print.* ◇ *At the opening of Act III, we learn that Banquo is suspicious.* OPP ENDING (1) **3** [C, usually sing.] a ceremony to celebrate the start of a public event or the first time a new building, road, etc. is used: *The Centre has had over 8 million visitors since its opening in 1984.* **4** [U, C] **~ (of sth)** the act or process of making sth open or of becoming open: *The main effect of pressure release is the opening of cracks in rocks.* ◇ *Kyrgyzstan underwent a dramatic opening following the demise of the USSR.* ➲ *compare* CLOSING[2] **5** [C] a job that is available SYN VACANCY (1): *Only the unemployed workers receive information about job openings.* **6** [C] a good opportunity for sb: *New employment opportunities*

O

and business openings were created. ◇ **~ for sth** *These ideas provide clear openings for the study of international law.*

open·ing² /ˈəʊpnɪŋ; *NAmE* ˈoʊpnɪŋ/ *adj.* [only before noun] first; beginning: *The opening scene unfolds at a police station.* ◇ *The opening chapter provides a good introduction to the subject.* OPP CLOSING¹

open·ly /ˈəʊpənli; *NAmE* ˈoʊpənli/ *adv.* without hiding any information, opinions or feelings: *The reform has been openly acknowledged by the government to have failed.* ◇ *She spoke openly about the shortcomings of past AIDS policies.* ◇ *There are now openly gay Congressmen and women.*

ˌopen ˈmarket *noun* [sing.] a situation in which companies can trade without restrictions, and prices depend on the amount of goods and the number of people buying them: **on the ~** *Workers are able to sell their labour on the open market.*

open·ness /ˈəʊpənnəs; *NAmE* ˈoʊpənnəs/ *noun* [U] **1** the quality of being honest and not hiding information or feelings: *Organizations may reduce stress by creating a climate which is conducive to trust and openness.* **2** the quality of being able to think about, accept or listen to different ideas or people: *Productive problem-solving involves openness and the freedom to be creative.* ◇ **~ to sth** *Developing these relationships takes time as well as openness to change.*

ˌopen ˈquestion *noun* **1** an issue that has not yet been decided: *It remains an open question whether the financial crisis will lead to a more prolonged downturn of the global economy.* **2** a question to which the answer is not just 'yes' or 'no': *The patient history should begin with open questions centred on the symptoms.* ➲ *compare* CLOSED QUESTION

op·er·ate /ˈɒpəreɪt; *NAmE* ˈɑːpəreɪt/ *verb* **1** [I] to work, happen or exist, especially in a particular way or place or at a particular time SYN FUNCTION² (1): *There are areas where non-governmental armed forces are operating.* ◇ *Once the issue is resolved, the group may cease to operate.* ◇ **+ adv./prep.** *Each of these services operates independently.* ◇ *These companies operate on a contractual basis.* **2** [T] **~ sth** to use or control a system, process or machine: *A number of hotel chains are now operating their own loyalty schemes.* ◇ *Patients should be given written advice not to drive or operate machinery for 24 hours.* **3** [I] **~ (on sb/sth)** to cut open sb's body in order to remove or repair a damaged part: *They have to make decisions about whether to operate on very sick patients.*

▸ NOUN + OPERATE **system • scheme • process • forces • organization • corporation • firm, company** *The scheme operated for about a year.* ◇ *They needed to augment the country's naval forces operating in the Caspian Sea.*

▸ OPERATE + NOUN **system • scheme • facility • plant • machinery • machine • device** *Two companies were granted licences to operate telecommunications systems.*

▸ OPERATE + ADVERB **successfully • smoothly • properly • efficiently, effectively • differently • independently • internationally, globally** *Agencies must have access to data if they are to operate efficiently.*

▸ OPERATE IN + NOUN **manner, fashion, way • mode • environment • sphere • sector • industry • market** *Firms operating in these industries undergo frequent reconfiguration and realignment.*

ˈoperating system *noun* software that controls the way a computer works and runs other programs: *At the time, Microsoft had about 90 per cent of the market for PC operating systems.*

op·er·ation /ˌɒpəˈreɪʃn; *NAmE* ˌɑːpəˈreɪʃn/ *noun* **1** [U] the action of working or of being used; the fact that sth exists or is happening: *The mine commenced operation in the 1920s.* ◇ **~ of sth** *The parties may agree to suspend the operation of the treaty.* ◇ **in ~** *The pumps are already in operation.* ◇ **come into ~** *Section 54 came into operation on 31 August 2006.* ◇ **be put into ~** *These strategic directions are put into operation through an array of activities.* **2** [C] an activity in which people are organized to work together: *The number of UN peacekeeping operations increased.* ◇ *Rescue operations become a frantic race against time.* ◇ *A military operation was launched.* **3** [C] a business or company; an activity in which a business or company is involved: *The firm began to establish its own manufacturing operations in Japan.* ◇ *Producers will scale back their operations, hoping to restore their previous level of profits.* **4** [C] one of the actions in a process, especially an action performed by a computer: *A circuit for the encoding operation is shown in Figure 10.6.* **5** [C] (*mathematics*) a process in which a number or quantity is changed by adding, MULTIPLYING, etc: *The most significant operation is the division by 2.* **6** [C] the process of cutting open a person's body in order to remove or repair a damaged part: **~ on sb/sth** *The centre has performed these operations on a small number of patients.* ◇ **~ to do sth** *She underwent an operation to remove the tumour.*

op·er·ation·al /ˌɒpəˈreɪʃənl; *NAmE* ˌɑːpəˈreɪʃənl/ *adj.* **1** [usually before noun] connected with the way in which a business, activity, process or machine works or happens: *Once established, a firm makes tactical and operational decisions.* ◇ *The military command followed their planned operational procedures.* ◇ *The reason for this poor operational efficiency was the lack of reliability of some machines.* **2** [not usually before noun] ready to be used; working: *After years of delay, the computerized database became fully operational.* ◇ *Cameras were operational 24 hours a day.* ■ **op·er·ation·al·ly** *adv.*: *Studies of this kind are operationally complex and expensive to implement.* ◇ *Intelligence might be said to be operationally defined by the tests used to measure it.*

op·era·tive /ˈɒpərətɪv; *NAmE* ˈɑːpərətɪv; ˈɑːpəreɪtɪv/ *adj.* **1** [not usually before noun] ready to be used; in use SYN FUNCTIONAL (1): *The system will be fully operative by the end of February.* **2** [only before noun] (*medical*) connected with a medical operation: *Operative treatment will vary depending upon the cause of the obstruction.* ➲ *see also* POST-OPERATIVE

op·er·ator /ˈɒpəreɪtə(r); *NAmE* ˈɑːpəreɪtər/ *noun* **1** (often in compounds) a person or company that runs a particular business: *Mobile phone operators are continually developing new services.* **2** (often in compounds) a person who operates equipment or a machine: *The virus is invisible to the ordinary computer operator.* ◇ *In the early 1930s, large numbers of women were employed as switchboard operators.* **3** (*mathematics*) a symbol or function which represents an operation in mathematics, e.g. ×, +: *In evaluating a formula, we perform multiplications and divisions before additions and subtractions: this rule is called precedence of operators.*

opin·ion /əˈpɪnjən/ *noun* **1** [C] someone's feelings or thoughts about sb/sth, rather than a fact SYN VIEW¹ (1): *This process resulted in a number of differing legal opinions.* ◇ **in sb's ~** *In Mearsheimer's opinion, the Cold War actually made the world a safer place after 1945.* ◇ **~ on/about/regarding sb/sth** *Individuals will have their own opinion on these matters.* ◇ **~ of sth** *Some argue that a favourable opinion of a product or service develops over a number of repeated purchases.* ◇ **~ that...** *A Commissioner has expressed the opinion that the Code has been breached.* ➲ language bank *at* ACCORDING TO **2** [U] the beliefs or views of a group of people: *The accuracy of this estimation has to remain a matter of opinion.* ◇ *There is a difference of opinion between experts as to the validity of the information.* ◇ *Archaeological opinion is divided on the dating of the theatre.* ◇ **+ noun** *One opinion survey in 1975 revealed that about 15 per cent of the population supported the Franco*

O

regime. ➲ *see also* PUBLIC OPINION **3** [C] advice from a professional person: *Even the most experienced GP can benefit from advice or a second opinion.* ◇ **~ on sth** *It seems valuable to consider expert opinions on effective management strategies.*

IDM **be of the opinion that...** (*formal*) to believe or think that...: *He was of the opinion that the current biological diversity had existed from the start.* ➲ language bank *at* ACCORDING TO **have/hold a good, bad, high, low, etc. opinion of sb/sth** to think that sb/sth is good, bad, etc: *The author compares the USA and the USSR and seems to have a high opinion of neither.*

▸ ADJECTIVE + OPINION **subjective • informed • political • professional • judicial, legal • medical • scientific** *They relied upon each doctor's professional opinion when making a diagnosis.* | **personal • favourable • dissenting, divergent, contradictory** *The interviewer will usually refrain from providing personal opinions during the interview.* | **public • popular • prevailing • expert • scholarly** *Conscious of prevailing opinion, he acknowledged that his views may not be popular.* | **second • expert, specialist** *A specialist opinion should be obtained before prescribing.*

▸ VERB + OPINION **form • influence • change** *Patients can and do form opinions about the quality of the health care product.* | **give, voice, express, state • have, hold • share** *Some economists hold the opinion that it is best for an economy to have small and weak trade unions.* | **mobilize • shape • polarize, divide** *He tried to mobilize public opinion to support his convictions.* | **seek • get • issue, deliver** *Board members may seek expert opinions as appropriate.*

▸ OPINION + VERB **differ** *Opinions wildly differ on this issue.*

▸ OPINION + NOUN **poll, survey • leader** *A short questionnaire was sent to key opinion leaders in 195 countries.*

▸ NOUN + OF OPINION **matter • body • climate • difference • consensus** *A growing body of opinion is suggesting that a more holistic approach should be taken.*

oˈpinion poll *noun* = POLL[1]

op·pon·ent /əˈpəʊnənt; *NAmE* əˈpoʊnənt/ *noun* **1** a person who disagrees with sth and tries to change or stop it: *Opponents argued that the new law would lead to discrimination.* ◇ *His political opponents blocked the discussion.* ◇ **~ of sth** *She was a fierce opponent of the reforms.* OPP ADHERENT, PROPONENT, SUPPORTER (1) **2** the person, organization or animal that sb/sth is fighting or competing against: *Animals faced with much larger opponents normally withdraw from the encounter.* ◇ *He remained on good terms with his main political opponent.* ➲ *compare* ADVERSARY, COMPETITOR (2)

op·por·tun·is·tic /ˌɒpətjuːˈnɪstɪk; *NAmE* ˌɑːpərtuːˈnɪstɪk/ (*also* **op·por·tun·ist** /ˌɒpəˈtjuːnɪst; *NAmE* ˌɑːpərˈtuːnɪst/) *adj.* **1** (*sometimes disapproving*) making use of an opportunity when it comes, rather than following a plan: *The cause of the problem is opportunistic behaviour.* ◇ *The more ambitious academics were described as pushy or opportunistic.* HELP In academic English, **opportunistic** and **opportunist** are also used without a negative meaning: *Attendance in pregnancy is a good chance for opportunistic health promotion.* **2** [only before noun] (*medical*) harmful to people who have been made weak by disease or drugs: *This is an opportunistic pathogen commonly infecting hospitalized patients.* ■ **op·por·tun·is·tic·al·ly** /ˌɒpətjuːˈnɪstɪkli; *NAmE* ˌɑːpərtuːˈnɪstɪkli/ *adv.*: *When the business partner has behaved opportunistically, there will be more problems.* ◇ *These bacteria opportunistically infect humans who have extensive burns.*

op·por·tun·ity /ˌɒpəˈtjuːnəti; *NAmE* ˌɑːpərˈtuːnəti/ *noun* (*pl.* **-ies**) [C, U] a situation or time that makes it possible to do or achieve sth SYN CHANCE (2): *Differences in educational opportunities correspond closely with income inequality.* ◇ *A commitment to equal opportunities will help to break the cycle of disadvantage.* ◇ **~ to do sth** *Professionals must seize the opportunity to work together.* ◇ **~ for sth** *They were refugees with few opportunities for economic advancement.* ◇ **~ for doing sth** *This study identified opportunities for disseminating research to physicians.* ◇ **~ of (doing) sth** *A large market provides the opportunity of increasing sales.* ◇ **~ for sb (to do sth)** *Opportunities for women in athletics have increased exponentially.* HELP As an uncountable noun, **opportunity** is used to talk about the existence or extent of opportunities: *The key to fairness is equality of opportunity.* ◇ *Staff are given ample opportunity to voice their concerns.* IDM *see* EARLY[1]

▸ ADJECTIVE + OPPORTUNITY **great, excellent, better, good • profitable • valuable • rare • exciting • ideal, golden • unique • new, unprecendented • future • reasonable • equal • limited • missed, lost • economic • commercial • corporate • entrepreneurial • technological • educational** *This affords a unique opportunity for 'policy learning', discerning lessons from best practices.*

▸ NOUN + OPPORTUNITY **employment, job • career • business • market • investment • training • learning • research** *It is difficult to detect whether these measures have been effective in improving employment opportunities for older people.*

▸ VERB + OPPORTUNITY **create • offer, provide, afford, present, bring • represent • open • maximize • expand • enhance, improve** *They felt unions offered the best opportunity for workers to exercise their voice.* | **seek • identify, spot • welcome • pursue • explore • enjoy, have, get • seize, take, grasp • benefit from • exploit, take advantage of, capitalize on** *As a surveyor, he took every opportunity to record the rocks he saw.* | **limit, restrict • lack • miss • lose** *The interviewers may miss opportunities to press for specific or deeper responses.*

▸ OPPORTUNITY + VERB **exist • arise • come • present itself** *Important research opportunities exist in the context of current agricultural restructuring.*

opporˈtunity cost *noun* (*economics*) the loss of the benefits of one possible course of action when a different course of action is chosen: *Choices will generally involve an opportunity cost.* ◇ **~ of sth** *A rise in the real interest rate increases the opportunity cost of investment in physical capital.*

op·pose /əˈpəʊz; *NAmE* əˈpoʊz/ *verb* **1** to disagree with sb's plan, policy, etc. and try to change it or prevent it from succeeding: **~ sth** *He opposed the death penalty.* ◇ **~ sb** *They have the ability to obstruct and oppose the president if they choose to do so.* ➲ *compare* PROPOSE (1) **2 ~ sb** to compete with sb in a contest: *Johnson would later oppose Harrison in the election of 1840.*

op·posed /əˈpəʊzd; *NAmE* əˈpoʊzd/ *adj.* **1** [not usually before noun] **~ to sth** (of a person) disagreeing with sth and trying to stop it: *They were strongly opposed to democratic reform.* **2** (of ideas or opinions) very different from sth: *They arrived at diametrically opposed conclusions.* ◇ **~ to sth** *This rigidity is not necessarily opposed to the requirements of art.*

IDM **as opposed to** used to make a contrast between two things or people: *The law changed to give authors—as opposed to publishers—rights over their works.* ◇ *Part 3 deals with grammatical, as opposed to lexical, meaning.*

op·pos·ing /əˈpəʊzɪŋ; *NAmE* əˈpoʊzɪŋ/ *adj.* [only before noun] **1** working, fighting or competing against each other: *Two opposing effects are involved.* ◇ *Few studies have noted that opposing forces might be at work.* ◇ *It is a policy on which little common ground can be found between the opposing sides.* **2** (of ideas or opinions) very different from each other: *Others may hold opposing viewpoints.* **3** opposite in direction or force: *We do work when we raise a weight against the opposing force of gravity.* ◇ *Balazs contemplates two opposing directions for the future of cinema.*

op·pos·ite¹ /ˈɒpəzɪt; ˈɒpəsɪt; *NAmE* ˈɑːpəzət/ *adj.* **1** [usually before noun] as different as possible from sth; involving two different extremes: *Their policies developed in opposite directions.* ◇ *Bad design will have the opposite effect and drive customers away.* ◇ *However, the findings do not support the opposite extreme either.* ◇ *The two strands have opposite chemical polarities.* ◇ **~ to sth** *This direction is opposite to the direction of the flow of electrons.* ➲ *compare* OPPOSING (2) **2** [usually before noun] on the other side of sth or facing sth: *The sites are on opposite sides of the river from one another.* ◇ *This picture (opposite page) was drawn from a photograph.* ■ **op·pos·ite** *adv.*: *The molecule's structure is shown opposite.*
IDM **the ˌopposite ˈsex** the other sex: *He struggled to develop relationships with members of the opposite sex.* ➲ *more at* PULL¹

op·pos·ite² /ˈɒpəzɪt; ˈɒpəsɪt; *NAmE* ˈɑːpəzət/ *noun* **1 the opposite** [sing.] the situation, idea or activity that is as different from another situation, etc. as it is possible to be SYN REVERSE³ (1): *The results of this study show the exact opposite.* ◇ *In the early 1990s, the opposite was true.* ◇ *Although the group claims to be active, a wealth of evidence suggests the opposite.* ◇ **~ of sth** *The patient reacts to guidance by doing the opposite of what is suggested.* **2 opposites** [pl.] people, ideas or situations that are as different as possible from each other: *The two men were opposites in every way.* ◇ *The schools were equally successful, yet their strategies were polar opposites.* IDM *see* EXACT

op·pos·ite³ /ˈɒpəzɪt; ˈɒpəsɪt; *NAmE* ˈɑːpəzət/ *prep.* on the other side of a particular area from sb/sth, and usually facing them: *At the end of the basilica, opposite the entrance doors, there was a raised platform.* ◇ *In preparation for combat, the ships deployed in a single line opposite the enemy.*

op·pos·ition /ˌɒpəˈzɪʃn; *NAmE* ˌɑːpəˈzɪʃn/ *noun* **1** [U] disagreement with a plan, policy, etc; attempts to change it or to prevent it from succeeding: *The measure encountered fierce opposition.* ◇ **~ to sth** *The early Christian church also voiced its strong opposition to the practice.* ◇ *Very often they face opposition to their research.* ◇ **in ~ (to sth)** *Her work has been rooted in opposition to a social system based on exploitation.* **2 the opposition** [sing.+ sing./pl. v.] the people you are competing against in business, politics, sport or war: *Pisistratus landed at Marathon and defeated the opposition in battle.* **3 the Opposition** [sing.+ sing./pl. v.] (*BrE*) the main political party that is opposed to the government; the political parties that are in a parliament but are not part of the government: *This decision was fiercely criticized by the Opposition.* **4** [U, C] the state of being as different as possible; two things that are as different as possible: **~ between A and B** *The modern mind tends to focus on the opposition between society and the individual.* ◇ **in ~ to sth** *This is in opposition to the findings of the present review.* ◇ *A number of binary oppositions and tensions were uncovered.*
IDM **in oppoˈsition** (of a political party) forming part of a parliament but not part of the government: *The party had been in opposition for 13 years.*

op·pos·ition·al /ˌɒpəˈzɪʃənl; *NAmE* ˌɑːpəˈzɪʃənl/ *adj.* [usually before noun] strongly disagreeing with sb/sth or very different from sb/sth: *Joyce was feted for his oppositional stance.* ◇ *He was becoming increasingly disobedient and oppositional at home.*

op·press /əˈpres/ *verb* **~ sb** to treat sb in a cruel and unfair way, especially by not giving them the same freedom, rights, etc. as other people: *Feminist writers have criticized the way in which these ideas have served to oppress women.* ■ **op·pres·sion** /əˈpreʃn/ *noun* [U] *Many immigrants came to America fleeing from religious intolerance and oppression.*

op·pressed /əˈprest/ *adj.* **1** treated in a cruel and unfair way and not given the same freedom, rights, etc. as other people: *They have become an impoverished and oppressed minority in their own country.* **2 the oppressed** *noun* [pl.] people who are oppressed: *She has always been an outspoken advocate for the oppressed.*

op·pres·sive /əˈpresɪv/ *adj.* treating people in a cruel and unfair way and not giving them the same freedom, rights, etc. as other people: *He remembers the everyday horrors of life under an oppressive regime.* ◇ *Medieval society was authoritarian and oppressive.*

opt /ɒpt; *NAmE* ɑːpt/ *verb* [I, T] to choose to take a particular course of action: **~ for sth** *Increasing numbers of men are opting for cosmetic surgery.* ◇ *They have always tended to opt for a low-risk strategy.* ◇ **~ to do sth** *After qualifying, these doctors can opt to go on a further two years of higher training.*
PHR V **ˌopt ˈin (to sth)** to choose to be part of a system or an agreement: *The UK is able to remain outside the new immigration and asylum provisions unless it opts in.* **ˌopt ˈout (of sth)** to choose not to take part in sth: *Denmark has opted out of the euro.* ➲ *related noun* OPT-OUT

optic /ˈɒptɪk; *NAmE* ˈɑːptɪk/ *adj.* [usually before noun] connected with the eye or the sense of sight: *Visual signals are transmitted from the eye to the brain via the optic nerve.*

op·tic·al /ˈɒptɪkl; *NAmE* ˈɑːptɪkl/ *adj.* [usually before noun] **1** connected with the sense of sight or the relationship between light and sight: *What we 'see' is a constructed image; hence the possibility of optical illusions.* **2** connected with the DETECTION (= act of finding/noticing) of light: *The presence of these microbes may be detected visually by a suitable optical device, such as a microscope.* ◇ *The optical disk was introduced as a key element in data storage for personal computers.* **3** (*physics*) using the visible part of the ELECTROMAGNETIC SPECTRUM: *Radio telescopes can have several advantages over optical telescopes.* ◇ *Due to their structural, mechanical, electrical and optical properties, nanotubes have been explored as biosensors (Chen et al., 2003).* ■ **op·tic·al·ly** /ˈɒptɪkli; *NAmE* ˈɑːptɪkli/ *adv.*: *Crystals are examined optically to check size and morphology.*

op·tics /ˈɒptɪks; *NAmE* ˈɑːptɪks/ *noun* [U] the scientific study of sight; the study of the TRANSMISSION and DEFLECTION of light and other forms of RADIATION: *As optics improved, microscopes required better and more reliable forms of illumination.*

op·ti·mal /ˈɒptɪməl; *NAmE* ˈɑːptɪməl/ *adj.* [usually before noun] (*also* **op·ti·mum**) the best possible; producing the best possible results SYN IDEAL¹ (1): *Producers maximize profits by choosing the optimal price level.* ◇ *The goal is to find optimal solutions to existing problems.* ◇ *In theory, the free market leads to the optimal allocation of resources.* ■ **op·ti·mal·ly** *adv.*: *Larger, optimally designed studies are needed to evaluate the public health impact.*

op·ti·mism /ˈɒptɪmɪzəm; *NAmE* ˈɑːptɪmɪzəm/ *noun* [U] a feeling that good things will happen and that sth will be successful; the tendency to have this feeling: **~ about sth** *The president's popularity ratings had fallen and there was less optimism about the future.* ◇ **~ that...** *There is cautious optimism that this discovery will lead to successful gene therapy.* OPP PESSIMISM ■ **op·ti·mist** /ˈɒptɪmɪst; *NAmE* ˈɑːptɪmɪst/ *noun*: *Optimists and pessimists give different answers to these questions.* OPP PESSIMIST

op·ti·mis·tic /ˌɒptɪˈmɪstɪk; *NAmE* ˌɑːptɪˈmɪstɪk/ *adj.* expecting good things to happen or sth to be successful; showing this feeling SYN POSITIVE¹ (2): *Their predictions were overly optimistic.* ◇ *The report expresses an optimistic view about reducing US dependence on foreign oil.* ◇ **~ about sth** *Businesses have become more optimistic about the state of the economy.* ◇ **~ that...** *They have remained cheerfully optimistic that the book will get finished.*

OPP PESSIMISTIC ■ **op·ti·mis·tic·al·ly** /ˌɒptɪˈmɪstɪkli; *NAmE* ˌɑːptɪˈmɪstɪkli/ *adv.*: *They were looking forward optimistically to the future.*

op·ti·mize (*BrE also* **-ise**) /ˈɒptɪmaɪz; *NAmE* ˈɑːptɪmaɪz/ *verb* **~ sth** to make sth as good as it can be; to use sth in the best possible way: *The aim is to optimize performance and minimize cost.* ◇ *They want to optimize the skills of each member of the team.* HELP In computing, data or software may be **optimized** in order to make searching or processing more efficient: *The structure of a database can be optimized for speed of searching.*

op·ti·mum¹ /ˈɒptɪməm; *NAmE* ˈɑːptɪməm/ *adj.* [usually before noun] = OPTIMAL: *The optimum pH was determined.*

op·ti·mum² /ˈɒptɪməm; *NAmE* ˈɑːptɪməm/ *noun* (*pl.* **op·tima** /ˈɒptɪmə/) the best possible result or set of conditions: *The plant grows within a range of 68 to 78°F, the optimum being 74°F.* ◇ **at the/an ~** *At the optimum, these marginal costs and benefits should be equal.* HELP The plural, **optima**, is used more commonly in academic English than in general English: *Mesophilic organisms have growth temperature optima in the range 20–37°C .*

op·tion AWL /ˈɒpʃn; *NAmE* ˈɑːpʃn/ *noun* **1** [C] something that sb can choose to do or have SYN CHOICE (2): *Online research is a viable option.* ◇ *an attractive/a cheap/a realistic/an alternative option* ◇ *the best/safest option* ◇ *Consumers who selected the healthy option often supplemented this with less healthy options.* ◇ **~ of sth** *There was the further option of overseas expansion.* ◇ **~ for (doing) sth** *Patients are informed about the options for treatment.* ◇ **~ for sb** *Surgery is the primary treatment option for these patients.* **2** [sing.] the right to do sth; the possibility of doing sth SYN CHOICE (3), OPPORTUNITY: **~ to do sth** *They were not given the option to refuse the test.* ◇ **~ of doing sth** *The company offered staff the option of working part-time.* **3** [C] **~ (to do sth)** the right to buy or sell sth at some time in the future: *Surviving children exercised an option to purchase the deceased child's share.* **4** [C] a subject that a student chooses to study as part of a course, in addition to the subjects that they must study: *She chose a social policy option.*

IDM **have no option but to do sth** to be in a situation in which you must do sth: *The directors had no option but to resign.* **keep/leave your ˈoptions open** to avoid making a decision now so that you still have a choice in the future: *Strategic choices that keep options open may be preferable.*

op·tion·al AWL /ˈɒpʃənl; *NAmE* ˈɑːpʃənl/ *adj.* that you can choose to do or have if you want to: *The referral system should be optional, not mandatory.* ◇ *These are mainstream issues rather than optional extras.* OPP COMPULSORY, MANDATORY, OBLIGATORY (1)

ˈopt-out *noun* **~ (from sth)** the ability to chose not to be involved in an agreement: *The UK, Ireland and Denmark have opt-outs from some EU border management issues.*

or /ɔː(r); *NAmE* ɔːr/ *conj.* **1** used to introduce another possibility: *The crystals may be nearly colourless, pink or pale brown.* ◇ *A referendum was called to vote 'yes' or 'no' on two questions.* ◇ **whether ~ not** *There is a substantial debate concerning whether or not the gap between rich and poor parts of the world is widening.* ➲ *compare* EITHER² (1) **2** used in negative sentences when mentioning two or more things: *Millions of people live without a clean or close water supply.* ◇ *She could not eat or sleep.* ➲ *compare* NEITHER² (2) **3** (*also* **or else**) used to warn or advise sb that sth bad could happen; otherwise: *He was told to go to the manager's office at once or he would be dismissed.* **4** used between two numbers to show approximately how many: *The sand was two or three feet deep.* **5** used to introduce a word or phrase that explains or means the same as what was just said or written: *Some restaurants may operate a 200–300% gross margin or 'mark-up', as it is known in the trade.*

IDM **or so** about; approximately: *During the first 100 000 years or so of human existence, most of our ancestors lived by hunting and gathering.*

oral /ˈɔːrəl/ *adj.* **1** [usually before noun] spoken rather than written: *Candidates take tests which cover written and oral exercises and interviews.* ◇ *They concluded that he had reasonably acted in reliance on the oral agreement.* OPP WRITTEN¹ (2) ➲ *compare* VERBAL **2** [only before noun] connected with the mouth: *The major risk factors for oral cancer are tobacco use and alcohol consumption.* ◇ *Intramuscular injections are often used instead of oral medication.* ■ **or·al·ly** *adv.*: *The express consent of the patient should be obtained either orally or in writing.* ◇ *The drug is administered orally.*

ˌoral ˈhistory *noun* [U] the collection and study of historical information using sound recordings of interviews with people who remember past events: *Oral history can tell us something about the history of a society, but it cannot take us very far back in time.*

orbit¹ /ˈɔːbɪt; *NAmE* ˈɔːrbɪt/ *noun* **1** [C, U] the curved path of sth that is moving around sth else, for example the path of the earth moving around the sun: **~ around sth** *The Earth has an elliptical orbit around the Sun.* ◇ **in ~** *The electromagnetic force holds electrons in orbit around atomic nuclei.* ◇ **into ~** *The first meteorological satellites took cameras into orbit in the 1960s.* HELP An **orbit** is also one of the movements all the way around sth: *The northern hemisphere is tilted towards the Sun and then away from it during the course of each complete orbit.* **2** [sing.] an area of activity, interest or influence: *Many of these states accepted a place within the Western, capitalist orbit.* ◇ **~ of sth** *Business was pulled into the political orbit of the EU institutions.*

orbit² /ˈɔːbɪt; *NAmE* ˈɔːrbɪt/ *verb* [T, I] to move in a curved path around sth, in the way that the earth moves aound the sun: **~ sth** *The International Space Station shown in Figure 5.1 is orbiting the Earth.* ◇ **~ around sth** *An internal magnetic field is produced by electrons orbiting around the nucleus.*

or·bit·al¹ /ˈɔːbɪtl; *NAmE* ˈɔːrbɪtl/ *adj.* [only before noun] connected with the movement in a regular pattern of one object around another: *As the ions are accelerated, the radius of their orbital motion will increase.*

or·bit·al² /ˈɔːbɪtl; *NAmE* ˈɔːrbɪtl/ *noun* (*chemistry, physics*) a region around an atom or MOLECULE in which an ELECTRON of a given energy and MOMENTUM can be found: *These electrons occupy atomic orbitals, with no more than two electrons in any one orbital.*

or·ches·tra /ˈɔːkɪstrə; *NAmE* ˈɔːrkɪstrə/ *noun* [C+sing./pl. v.] a large group of people who play various musical instruments together, usually playing CLASSICAL music: *Musicians in an orchestra only occasionally play unaccompanied solos.*

order¹ /ˈɔːdə(r); *NAmE* ˈɔːrdər/ *noun* **1** [U, C] the way in which people or things are placed or arranged in relation to each other: **~ of sth** *Marshall reversed the order of Sections 23 and 24.* ◇ **in ~** *References appear at the end of the dissertation in alphabetical order.* ◇ **in ~ (from A to B)** *The chromosomes are usually displayed by arranging them in order from the largest to the smallest.* ◇ *List the points you intend to cover and put them in order.* ◇ **in ~ of sth** *The risks should be arranged in order of severity.* ◇ **out of ~** *Film actors learn their parts in pieces, often out of chronological order.* **2** [U] the state in which everything is in the right place or sth is as it should be: **in ~** *The factory was in excellent order.* ◇ *Lucy ensured that all the bills were paid on time and that their accounts were all in order.* OPP DISORDER (3) **3** [U] the state that exists when people obey laws, rules or authority: *Government forces were called in* to restore order. ◇ *The imperial authorities saw the monks' defiance as a threat to public order.* ➲ *compare* DISORDER (2) **4** [C] something that sb is told to do by sb in authority: **~ (for sb/sth) to do sth** *Goude issued an order to 'drive out the rebels'.* ◇ **under orders** *Prison forces had acted under orders and were not punishable.* **5** [C] a written instruction by a court or judge: **~ to do sth** *She ignored a court order to return the children to England.* ◇ **~ for sth** *The court may make an order for the sale of the property.* ◇ **~ against sb** *Falsifying records is a criminal offence and may lead to an enforcement order against the employer.* **6** [C, U] a request to make or supply goods: *Customers can place orders online.* ◇ **~ for sth** *New orders for goods and services start to dry up.* ◇ **~ from sb** *Orders from other customers contributed to a more stable demand.* ◇ **on ~** *The company has 91 planes on order from Airbus.* ◇ **to ~** *Primers are usually made to order by commercial suppliers.* **7** [C, usually sing.] the way that a society, the world, etc. is arranged, with its system of rules and customs: *The social order is in a constant state of change.* ◇ *In a world order powered by multinational companies, colonialism is not a thing of the past.* **8** [sing.] a particular quality or degree: **of... ~** *Conrad's tales are of a different order to Kipling's.* ◇ *A land impact of this order could conceivably exterminate humanity.* ◇ **of a high/the highest ~** *Williams had powers of analysis and synthesis of a high order.* ➲ *see also* ORDER OF MAGNITUDE **9** [C] **~ (of sth)** (*biology*) a group into which animals, plants, etc. that are related are divided, smaller than a CLASS and larger than a FAMILY: *Beetles are the largest order of insects.* ➲ *compare* GENUS, KINGDOM (3), PHYLUM, SPECIES

IDM **in order for sb/sth to do sth** so that sb/sth can do sth: *Meeting targets is necessary in order for schools to avoid government pressure.* **in order that...** so that sth can happen: *In order that tones of voice may not help the interrogator, the answers should be written.* **in order to do sth** with the purpose or intention of doing or achieving sth: *An investigation must be performed in order to ensure patient safety.* ◇ *In order to develop as a team, the players needed to trust their leader.* ➲ language bank *at* PURPOSE **in working 'order** (especially of machines) working well, not broken: *Equipment used must be maintained and be in good working order.* **of/in the order of sth** (*BrE*) (*NAmE* **on the order of sth**) about sth; approximately sth: *Their length is typically of the order of 100 mm.* ➲ *more at* ASCEND, DESCEND, HOUSE[1], LAW, SHORT[1], TALL

▸ ADJECTIVE + NOUN **alphabetical • chronological • reverse • descending • ascending • random • linear • logical • fixed** *Subjects are asked to name the days of the week in reverse order.* | **international, global • old • new • natural • liberal • legal • social • political • economic • moral** *Many claim that Western bias still characterizes the international legal order.*

▸ NOUN + ORDER **rank • birth • word** *The notion that birth order is related to intelligence was put forward by Galton in the 19th century.* | **court • deportation • expulsion • residence • adoption • care** *He refused to regularize his immigration status and was served with a deportation order.*

▸ VERB + ORDER **determine • follow • change • reverse** *We used deduction to determine the order in which competing plans should be applied.* | **create, establish • impose** *Humans have an unconscious desire to establish order in their world.* | **restore • maintain, preserve, keep • enforce • threaten** *The continued unrest led to the military being called upon to maintain order.* | **give, issue • obey, follow • disobey** *He waited a few weeks, then gave the order to leave.* | **seek • obtain • grant • issue • impose • enforce • quash, revoke, set aside • obey • disobey • challenge** *There has been a reluctance to grant adoption orders to relatives.* | **create, establish • maintain • change • reverse • challenge • threaten** *Globalization is changing the established economic order.*

order[2] /ˈɔːdə(r); *NAmE* ˈɔːrdər/ *verb* **1** to use your position of authority to tell sb to do sth or say that sth must happen: **~ sb to do sth** *Troops were ordered to open fire.* ◇ **~ sb + adv./prep.** *Some senior diplomats were ordered home.* ◇ **~ sth** *The doctor ordered some blood tests and found that she was anaemic.* ◇ **~ that...** *The judge ordered that he be compulsorily detained for a period of seven days.* **2 ~ sth (from sb/sth)** to ask for goods to be made or supplied; to ask for a service to be provided: *They were able to order all of the drugs listed from the Internet.* **3 ~ sth** to organize or arrange sth: *The objects are put beside each other and ordered in sequence one after another.* ➲ *see also* ORDERED, DISORDERED (1)

or·dered /ˈɔːdəd; *NAmE* ˈɔːrdərd/ *adj.* [usually before noun] carefully arranged or organized: *Directories provide an ordered structure to the many websites in the world.* ◇ *Proteins often form highly ordered complexes that can have dozens of members.* ➲ *compare* ORDERLY (1) OPP DISORDERED (1)

order·ing /ˈɔːdərɪŋ; *NAmE* ˈɔːrdərɪŋ/ *noun* [C, U] the way in which sth is ordered or arranged; the act of putting sth into an order SYN ARRANGEMENT: *The tasks can be performed in a variety of different orderings.* ◇ **~ of sth** *The ordering of occupations in the status hierarchy is very similar in the two countries.*

or·der·ly /ˈɔːdəli; *NAmE* ˈɔːrdərli/ *adj.* **1** arranged or organized in a neat, careful and logical way: *Lung development takes place in an orderly sequence, with airways all in place by 16 weeks of gestational age.* ➲ *compare* ORDERED **2** behaving well; peaceful: *Customers were told to leave the building in an orderly manner.*

ˌorder of ˈmagnitude *noun* (*mathematics*) a level in a system of ordering things by size or amount, where each level is higher by a FACTOR of ten: *The productivity attained was an order of magnitude higher than with previous catalysts.*

or·din·al /ˈɔːdɪnl; *NAmE* ˈɔːrdənl/ *noun* connected with the order of sth in a series: *Ability was measured on a 4-point ordinal scale ranging from 'no difficulty' to 'unable to do so'.*

or·din·ar·ily /ˈɔːdnrəli; *NAmE* ˌɔːrdnˈerəli/ *adv.* used to say what normally happens in a particular situation, especially because sth different is happening this time SYN USUALLY: *Ordinarily, he works outside the UK.* ◇ *The word 'code' as it is ordinarily used is ambiguous.*

or·din·ary /ˈɔːdnri; *NAmE* ˈɔːrdneri/ *adj.* not unusual or different in any way: *Ordinary people typically identify happiness with pleasure, money or fame.* ◇ *Ordinary citizens had no channels of effective complaint.* ◇ *The details of the case are fairly ordinary.* ■ **or·din·ari·ness** *noun* [U] **~ (of sth)** *They try to see beneath the apparent ordinariness of everyday life.*

organ /ˈɔːgən; *NAmE* ˈɔːrgən/ *noun* **1** a part of the body that has a particular purpose, such as the heart or the brain: *This may result in damage to tissues and organs.* ◇ *The body tries to maintain blood flow to vital organs.* ◇ *sensory/reproductive/digestive organs* ◇ **+ noun** *Organ donation was a possibility.* HELP In scientific English, an **organ** is also a part of a plant that has a particular purpose: *Target plants were harvested and separated into organs (leaf, stem and root).* **2 ~ (of sth)** an official organization that is part of a larger organization and has a particular purpose: *Like all organs of the United Nations, the General Assembly must act within its powers.* ◇ *The council and the assembly would remain the essential organs of government.* **3 ~ of sth** a means of communicating the views of a particular group: *Reith was aware of the importance of radio as an organ of public opinion.*

or·gan·ic /ɔːˈgænɪk; *NAmE* ɔːrˈgænɪk/ *adj.* **1** [only before noun] produced by or from living things: *The soils are*

O

infertile, with relatively little organic matter. OPP INORGANIC (1) **2** [only before noun] (*chemistry*) involving substances containing the element CARBON together with HYDROGEN and sometimes other elements too: *Organic chemistry is an important branch of chemistry as carbon forms more known compounds than those formed by all the other elements put together.* ◇ *organic solvents/compounds/polymers/molecules* OPP INORGANIC (2) **3** [usually before noun] (of food or farming methods) produced or done without using artificial chemicals: *There has been a resurgence in small-scale organic farming.* ◇ *California is the premier state for both conventional and organic food production.* **4** happening or developing in a slow and natural way, rather than suddenly: *These are ad hoc systems that tend to be organic, in that they evolve according to perceived need.* **5** consisting of different parts that are all connected to each other: *These activities are significant in the development of the organic whole or collective identity.* **6** (*medical*) connected with the organs of the body: *Symptoms may not result from organic disease.* ◇ *The pain is likely to be organic.* ■ **or·gan·ic·al·ly** /ɔːˈɡænɪkli; *NAmE* ɔːrˈɡænɪkli/ *adv.*: *These are organically rich sediments.* ◇ *They deliver fresh, organically grown fruit and vegetables.* ◇ *Ideas for innovation grow organically.*

or·gan·ism /ˈɔːɡənɪzəm; *NAmE* ˈɔːrɡənɪzəm/ *noun* an individual plant, animal or other living thing, especially one that is so small that you can only see it under a MICROSCOPE. Some organisms consist of only one cell: *These toxins are carried by simple organisms like bacteria and fungi, as well as more complex ones like spiders and snakes.* ◇ *The causative organism was identified.* ◇ *This organism has evolved multi-drug resistance.* HELP **Organism** is sometimes used to refer to a system that is like a living thing: *Society could be understood as a social organism.* ➲ *see also* MICROORGANISM

O

▸ ADJECTIVE + ORGANISM **living • biological • simple • microscopic • single-celled, unicellular • multicellular • complex • higher • diploid • haploid • transgenic • genetically modified • mutant • causative • infectious, infecting • pathogenic • invasive • resistant • photosynthetic • aerobic • aquatic • freshwater • marine** *Many single-celled organisms can survive without interaction with any other living organism.*

▸ VERB + ORGANISM **identify • classify • isolate • kill** *These levels of radiation would be enough to kill any organism.*

▸ ORGANISM + VERB **live (in/within) • survive • reproduce • evolve • be adapted to sth • respond to sth** *Organisms adapted to the conditions become widely distributed.*

or·gan·iza·tion (*BrE also* **-isa·tion**) /ˌɔːɡənaɪˈzeɪʃn; *NAmE* ˌɔːrɡənəˈzeɪʃn/ *noun* **1** [C] an organized group of people with a particular purpose, such as a business or government department: **in an/the ~** *Everyone in the organization needs to know why change is necessary.* ◇ **~ for (doing) sth** *The Bank of International Settlements is an organization for central bank cooperation.* ◇ **~ for sb** *The Komsomol remained primarily an organization for young men.* ◇ **~ to do sth** *Software vendors have established an organization to monitor infringement of copyright.* ➲ thesaurus note *at* COMPANY **2** [U] the way in which the different parts of sth are arranged SYN STRUCTURE[1] (1): *These processors have, essentially, the same architecture but radically different internal organization.* ◇ **~ of sth** *The location and spatial organization of cities reflect economic, political, social and cultural circumstances.* **3** [U] the act of making arrangements or preparations for sth SYN PLANNING: *Such studies generally take a great deal of organization to set up.* ◇ **~ of sth** *They have a track record in the organization of conferences.* **4** [U] the quality of being arranged in a neat, careful and logical way; the ability to plan your work or life well and in an efficient way: *An increase in entropy represents a decrease of organization within a system.* ◇ *Students skipped lectures out of complacency, laziness or lack of organization.*

▸ ADJECTIVE + ORGANIZATION **international, multinational • national • regional, local • private • commercial, corporate • governmental • intergovernmental • non-governmental • non-profit, charitable, voluntary • professional • religious • humanitarian • community-based** *Transparency International is a non-governmental organization based in Berlin that promotes anti-corruption measures.* | **internal • formal • complex • hierarchical • bureaucratic • social • economic • industrial** *She acknowledged the power of a novel's formal organization to shape the reading of reality.*

▸ NOUN + ORGANIZATION **business • public sector • community • client • sales, selling • terrorist • health care • arts • human rights • umbrella** *He established a foundation as an umbrella organization for a number of charities he had set up during his life.*

▸ VERB + ORGANIZATION **join • leave • found, create, form, establish • run, manage • structure • restructure** *Not all problem drinkers are willing to join the organization because it requires total abstinence.*

or·gan·iza·tion·al (*BrE also* **-isa·tion·al**) /ˌɔːɡənaɪˈzeɪʃənl; *NAmE* ˌɔːrɡənəˈzeɪʃənl/ *adj.* **1** connected with an organization or with organizations in general: *Kolb and Shepherd studied the organizational culture of a technology company in New Zealand.* ◇ *Organizational restructuring does not always occur smoothly.* **2** connected with the ability to arrange or organize things well: *The project involved research on an individual and group scale, which required excellent organizational skills.* ■ **or·gan·iza·tion·al·ly, -isa·tion·al·ly** *adv.*: *Organizationally, the book is quite uneven.*

or·gan·ize (*BrE also* **-ise**) /ˈɔːɡənaɪz; *NAmE* ˈɔːrɡənaɪz/ *verb* **1** [T] **~ sth** to arrange for sth to happen or to be provided: *Bohr organized a conference on the application of physics to biology.* ◇ *Some of their supporters had attempted to organize street demonstrations.* **2** [T] to arrange sth or the parts of sth into a particular order or structure: **~ sth + adv./prep.** *Irish secular society was organized around large kin groups.* ◇ *Texts are made up of hierarchically organized groups of propositions.* ◇ **~ sth** *Before the fifth century, no one tried to organize the essential stuff of history.* **3** [T, I] to form a group of people with a shared aim, especially a union or political party: **~ sb (into sth)** *The anarchists were skilled workers who were organized into trade unions.* ◇ **~ (into sth)** *Workers organize and join unions to increase their strength in bargaining with employers.*

or·gan·ized (*BrE also* **-ised**) /ˈɔːɡənaɪzd; *NAmE* ˈɔːrɡənaɪzd/ *adj.* **1** [only before noun] involving large numbers of people who work together to do sth in a way that has been carefully planned: *Organized crime and terrorism often disregard borders.* ◇ *Organized consumer groups lobby for product safety legislation.* **2** arranged or planned in the way mentioned: *The kingdom of Pylos was large and highly organized.* ◇ *Polling was generally conducted in an organized and peaceful manner.* ➲ *compare* DISORGANIZED

or·gan·izer (*BrE also* **-is·er**) /ˈɔːɡənaɪzə(r); *NAmE* ˈɔːrɡənaɪzər/ *noun* a person or organization that organizes events, activities or services: *The festival organizers are not paid at all.* ◇ *Obama got his political training as a community organizer in Chicago.* ◇ **~ of sth** *The organizers of the rebellion were put on trial.*

ori·ent AWL /ˈɔːrient/ (*BrE also* **orien·tate** /ˈɔːriənteɪt/) *verb* **1** [usually passive] to make or adapt sb/sth for a particular purpose or group of people; to be suitable for this purpose or group: **be oriented to/towards sb/sth** *Some economic systems are oriented to commodity production.* ◇ **~ yourself (to/towards sth)** *Together, individuals orient themselves towards shared goals.* ◇ **religiously/socially/commercially oriented** *The first religiously oriented schools for Jewish girls from Orthodox families were established in 1918.* ◇ **goal-/market-/policy-oriented** *People*

LANGUAGE BANK

Organizing your writing

In academic writing, it is important to have a clear structure for your ideas and arguments, and to guide the reader through this structure by signposting your points and summarizing what will be discussed and in what order.

- **In this** essay/chapter/section, **I (shall)** argue/suggest...
- **I shall begin by** considering/describing/discussing...
- **To begin (with), I shall** consider/describe/discuss...
- **First/Firstly,... then/ followed by...**
- **First,... second,... third,...**
- **Firstly,... secondly,... thirdly,...**
- **This/The next/The following** chapter/section **deals with...**
- This **is/will be discussed/described/considered** in Chapter 3/in Part 2.
- This **is discussed/described below**.
- **I began by** considering/describing/discussing...
- **Next, I (shall)** consider/turn to/discuss...
- **I shall go on to** consider/describe/discuss...
- **Finally/Lastly,...**

– ***In this essay, I shall*** *argue that* ***the following*** *are two major differences between...*
– ***I shall begin by*** *analysing the arguments made by...*
– *I will* ***firstly*** *look at how spoken word recognition operates,* ***and then go on to*** *examine the visual modality.*
– *Rainforest removal has two principal ecological consequences.* ***First****, it is a major cause of species extinction.*
– *I should emphasize two points here.* ***Firstly****, this is only one way to...* ***Secondly****, I am not denying that...*
– ***The next*** *section* ***deals with*** *the end of communist regimes between 1989 and 1991.*
– *The study on which this builds* ***is described below.***
– ***I began by*** *describing how changes in commerce and technology changed the role of a number of cities.*
– ***Next****, I shall discuss how business groups have evolved in their approaches to product diversification.*
– ***Finally****, because many women asylum seekers begin as 'dependent' applicants, their claims may be treated as secondary.*

who are goal-oriented want to do things well and like challenges. **2** [usually passive] **be oriented +adv./prep.** to be placed in a particular position in relation to sth else: *Eurasia is oriented along an east-west axis.* **3 ~ yourself** to find your position in relation to your surroundings: *Most of us have used a magnetic compass to orient ourselves.* **4 ~ yourself** to make yourself familiar with a new situation: *The peer group can provide instruction in how to orient oneself in adult situations.*

orien·ta·tion AWL /ˌɔːriənˈteɪʃn/ *noun* **1** [U, C] the type of aims or interests that a person or an organization has; the act of directing your aims towards a particular thing: *It is common to find researchers adopting a problem-solving orientation.* ◇ *The company recognizes the strong price orientation of the UK market.* ◇ **~ to/towards sth** *Not all parents shared the school's orientation towards learning.* **2** [U, C] a person's basic beliefs or feelings about a particular subject: *political/religious/cultural orientations* ◇ **in ~** *Some religious organizations remain very conservative in orientation.* **3** [U, C] **sexual ~** whether a person is attracted to men, women or both: *Individuals should not be discriminated against because of sexual orientation.* **4** [C] the direction in which an object faces: **~ of sth** *The orientation of the strata reflects the nature of the surface on which they were deposited.* ◇ **in a/the ~** *The crystal and detector were positioned in the desired orientation.*

ori·gin /ˈɒrɪdʒɪn; *NAmE* ˈɔːrɪdʒɪn/ *noun* **1** [C, U] (*also* **origins** [pl.]) the point from which sth starts; the cause of sth: **~ of sth** *Various theories have sought to explain the origin of the universe.* ◇ *The letters of Paul are key to understanding the origins of Christianity.* ◇ **in ~** *Obesity is partly genetic in origin.* ◇ **of ~** *Goods can be tracked backwards to their point of origin.* ◇ *The term 'tor' is of ancient origin.* **2** [C, U] (*also* **origins** [pl.]) a person's social and family background: *In spite of his humble origins, his phenomenal career had won him great respect.* ◇ **of ~** *Families may move from their country of origin because of war or famine.* ◇ *68 per cent of the Muslim population was of South Asian origin.* **3** [C] (*mathematics*) a fixed point from which COORDINATES are measured: *Let S be a sphere with the centre at the origin.*

▸ ADJECTIVE + ORIGIN **foreign • national • geographical • social** *Genetic analysis can demonstrate the geographical origin of a population sample.* | **ancient • unknown • common • evolutionary • historical • divine** *All these languages share a common origin.* | **humble • ethnic • racial • paternal** *There are now approximately fifty million people of Chinese ethnic origin outside China.*

▸ VERB + ORIGIN **trace • betray** *As long as she pronounces her vowels and consonants correctly, Eliza Doolittle does not betray her working-class east London origins.* | **owe • understand • explain • identify, determine • examine** *The moon owes its origin to a giant impact between a moon-sized body and the primitive earth.*

▸ PHRASE **have its origin(s) in sth** *The Declaration of Independence clearly had its origins in the ideas of John Locke.*

ori·gin·al¹ /əˈrɪdʒənl/ *adj.* **1** [only before noun] present or existing from the beginning; first or earliest: *The original version was published in 1993.* ◇ *Many of the original settlers had already returned home.* **2** new and interesting in a way that is different from anything that has existed before; able to produce new and interesting ideas: *Von Thunen used a highly original method of analysis.* ◇ *Thomson is not a profound or original thinker.* **3** [usually before noun] painted, written, etc. by the artist rather than copied: *The illustration continues to be reproduced, so evocative is the original painting.*

▸ ORIGINAL + NOUN **version • work • research • paper • article • idea • form • design** *The preparation of the book required much original research.* ◇ *Push any material, and it will bend to some extent but then snap back to its original form.* | **intention, plan, purpose • position • value • owner • settler • inhabitant • text • data • meaning** *Napoleon still hoped to achieve his original intention of winning an early decisive victory.*

▸ ADVERB + ORIGINAL **highly • strikingly** *Plato had views about the sexes that were strikingly original in his time.*

ori·gin·al² /əˈrɪdʒənl/ *noun* **1** the earliest form of sth, from which copies are later made: *They produced their own new designs that were very close to the American originals.* **2** a book, text or play in the language in which it was first written: *The translator sought to retain the rich cultural texture of the Arabic original.*

IDM **in the oˈriginal** in the language in which a book, etc. was first written, before being translated: *He taught himself Latin and Greek in order to read the Classics in the original.*

ori·gin·al·ity /əˌrɪdʒəˈnæləti/ *noun* [U] the quality of being new and interesting in a way that is different from anything that has existed before: *The arguments are well rehearsed but lack originality.* ◇ **~ of sth** *Recent scholarship has restored credit to Palissy for the originality of his ideas.*

ori·gin·al·ly /əˈrɪdʒənəli/ *adv.* used to describe the situation that existed at the beginning of a particular period or activity, especially before sth was changed: *It was originally intended that the scheme would run for two years.* ◇ *Originally developed by European Marxist researchers, this approach has broad scope.*

ori·gin·ate /əˈrɪdʒɪneɪt/ *verb* **1** [I] **~ + adv./prep.** to happen or appear for the first time in a particular place or situation: *Mantle plumes originate deep within the Earth.* ◇ *When two rays of light originate from the same source, they are said to be coherent.* ◇ *The women in the study originated from nine countries.* **2** [T] **~ sth** to create sth new: *The general theory of intelligence was originated by Spearman (1927).*

ori·gin·ator /əˈrɪdʒɪneɪtə(r)/ *noun* **~ (of sth)** a person who creates or starts sth new: *Saussure is regarded as the originator of modern linguistics.*

ortho·dox /ˈɔːθədɒks; *NAmE* ˈɔːrθədɑːks/ *adj.* **1** (especially of beliefs or behaviour) generally accepted or approved of; following generally accepted beliefs SYN TRADITIONAL (1): *The orthodox view of citizenship is that it is a matter of treating people as individuals with equal rights under the law.* **2** following closely the traditional beliefs and practices of a religion: *In 1841, Feuerbach created a sensation with an attack on orthodox religion called 'The Essence of Christianity'.* **3 Orthodox** belonging to or connected with the Orthodox Church: *the schism between Roman and Orthodox Christianity in the eleventh century*

the ˌOrthodox ˈChurch *noun* [sing.] a branch of the Christian Church in eastern Europe and Greece: *the Greek/Russian Orthodox Church*

ortho·doxy /ˈɔːθədɒksi; *NAmE* ˈɔːrθədɑːksi/ *noun* (*pl.* **-ies**) [U, C, usually pl.] **1** an idea or view that is generally accepted: *Entrepeneurs challenge orthodoxy and make profits doing so.* ◇ *He questioned many of the established orthodoxies.* **2** the traditional beliefs or practices of a religion, etc: *He was a stern defender of religious orthodoxy.*

os·cil·late /ˈɒsɪleɪt; *NAmE* ˈɑːsɪleɪt/ *verb* **1** [I] **~ (between A and B)** to vary or change between two states or opinions SYN SWING[1] (1): *Trade with the Spanish colonies in Latin America oscillated between legality and illegality.* **2** [I] **(+ adv./prep.)** (*physics*) to vary in size, strength or position in a regular manner around a central point or value: *Energy is released as seismic waves that oscillate back and forth like sound waves in air.* ◇ *An oscillating charge in a radio transmitter generates an electromagnetic wave, which transports energy to the charges in the radio aerial.*

os·cil·la·tion /ˌɒsɪˈleɪʃn; *NAmE* ˌɑːsɪˈleɪʃn/ *noun* **1** [C, U] **~ (of sth)** a regular movement between one position and another: *Scientists investigated the effect of the ambient air on the oscillations of a pendulum.* **2** [C] **~ (between A and B)** a repeated change between different states, ideas, etc: *An oscillation between wet and dry conditions seems to be the norm for these arid and semi-arid ecosystems.* **3** [C] (*technical*) regular variation in size, strength or position around a central point or value, especially of an electrical current or electric field: *Maxwell found the speed of the waves to be 300 000 km each second, independent of the frequency of the oscillations.* ◇ **~ in sth** *Photosynthesis causes a yearly oscillation in atmospheric carbon dioxide of around 5 parts per million.*

other /ˈʌðə(r)/ *adj., pron.* **1** used to refer to people or things that are additional or different to people or things that have been mentioned or are known about: *The new economic system soon spread to other countries.* ◇ *After a full clinical examination, other forms of investigation should be used.* ◇ *Two buildings were destroyed and many others damaged in the explosion.* ◇ *This option is preferable to any other.* ◇ *Some designs are better than others.* ➲ *compare* ANOTHER ➲ language bank *at* ADDITION **2 the, its, their, etc. ~** used to refer to the second of two people or things: *On the other side of the board, we displayed the results.* ◇ **~ (one)** *If one sub-network fails, the other one will still connect.* ◇ *If one sub-network fails, the other will still connect.* **3 the, its, their, etc. ~** used to refer to the remaining people or things in a group: *Britain had maintained and strengthened its control of its other colonies in the Caribbean.* ◇ *2 tubs were 13.5 cm in depth, and the other 2 were 4.5 cm in depth.* ◇ *2 of the 4 tubs were 13.5 cm in depth; the others were 4.5 cm in depth.* **4 the other...** used to refer to the opposite place, direction, etc: *Dutton was on the other side of the country when the earthquake occurred.* ◇ *The argument works the other way too.* IDM *see* EVERY

ˈother than *prep.* **1** (usually used in negative sentences) except SYN APART FROM (1): *Historiographers often need to consider historical writing in languages other than English.* ◇ *Other than this observation, our findings were broadly consistent with previous studies.* **2** (usually used in negative sentences) different from; not: *Personal information cannot be used for any purposes other than those described.* ◇ *Rather than start price cutting, firms often compete in ways other than price.*

other·wise /ˈʌðəwaɪz; *NAmE* ˈʌðərwaɪz/ *adv.* **1** used to state what the result would be if sth did not happen or if the situation were different; or else: *Through these social policies, the state forces people to spend more on education than they otherwise would.* ◇ *Elizabeth cannot have been well off because otherwise she would not have taken a job at such a low salary.* **2** in a different way from the way mentioned; differently: *Many companies were effectively insolvent but pretended otherwise.* ◇ *Some of these isolated stones, otherwise known as menhirs, exceed 6 m in height.* ◇ *All the measures met basic criteria for reliability and validity, unless otherwise stated.* **3** apart from that: *She has felt a bit feverish for the past day or so but is otherwise well.* ◇ *They were allowed up on deck one or two hours a day, but were otherwise kept confined.*
IDM **or otherwise** used to refer to sth that is different from or the opposite of what has just been mentioned: *Miracles concerning individuals, human or otherwise, are not uncommon in Indic and Gujarati Hindu traditions today.*

ought to /ˈɔːt tə; *before vowels and finally* ˈɔːt tu/ *modal verb* (*negative* **ought not to**) **1** used to say what is the right thing to do: *He is not always as careful as he ought to be.* ◇ *Mothers are basically told that, unless they have HIV, they ought to breastfeed.* ◇ *Few people deny that we ought not to be cruel to animals.* **2** used to say what you expect or would like to happen: *The operation ought to be straightforward.* ◇ *As a doctor, she ought to be knowledgeable about common diseases.* **3** used to say what you advise or recommend: *She said that they ought to consider marriage guidance counselling.* HELP **Ought to** and **should** have the same meaning, although **should** is much more common. In questions, **should** is usually used instead of **ought to**. The negative form **oughtn't to** is not used in formal writing.

ounce /aʊns/ *noun* (*abbr.* **oz**) a unit for measuring weight, 1/16 of a pound, equal to 28.35 grams: *The device weighs just over 4 ounces.*

our /ɑː(r); ˈaʊə(r)/ *det.* (the possessive form of *we*) belonging to us; connected with us: *Our database included published and unpublished studies.* ◇ *We model behaviour for our children.* ◇ *Our work and leisure patterns are changing.*

ours /ɑːz; ˈaʊəz; *NAmE* ɑːrz; ˈaʊərz/ *pron.* the one or ones that belong to us or are connected with us: *This is not possible in a study like ours.* ◇ *Your answer might be quite different from ours.* ◇ *The environmental problems they faced were minor compared with ours.*

our·selves /ɑːˈselvz; ˌaʊəˈselvz; *NAmE* ɑːrˈselvz; ˌaʊərˈselvz/ *pron.* **1** (the reflexive form of *we*) used when you and another person or other people together cause and are affected by an action: *We try to learn from our mistakes and improve ourselves.* ◇ *We restricted ourselves to considering only inertial motion.* **2** used to emphasize *we*

or *us*; sometimes used instead of these words: *Always treat customers as we ourselves would like to be treated.* ◇ *Inside the cells of animals like ourselves are organelles known as mitochondria.*
IDM **by our'selves** without help: *We were told to sort it out by ourselves.* ◇ *We each have many needs that we cannot meet by ourselves.*

out /aʊt/ *adv.* HELP For the special uses of **out** in phrasal verbs, look at the entries for the verbs. For example **sell out** is in the phrasal verb section at **sell**. **1** away from the inside of a place or thing: *The damaged area of lung will not have any air getting in or out.* ◇ *The rod is pulled out another six inches.* **2** (of people) away from or not at home or their place of work: *The house was burgled while he was out.* ◇ *Prudent parents will not normally allow young children to go out unaccompanied.* ◇ **~ doing sth** *She collapsed while she was out shopping with her husband.* **3** away from a particular place: *Many small streams flow out to the sea in this area.* ◇ *The city was located on a peninsula that jutted out into the Bosporus.* **4** a long or a particular distance from a place or from land: *He had a farm out in the country.* ◇ *Each trial began approximately 12 nautical miles out.* **5** used to show that sth/sb is removed from a place, job, etc: *A flood the day before had washed out the road.* ◇ *Large corporate plantation owners have driven out smaller farmers.* **6** available to everyone; known to everyone: *The book's first edition came out in 1874.* ◇ *The secret is out now.* **7** in public; clearly and loudly so that people can hear: *Unfortunately, the victim is not willing to speak out.* ◇ *First, I asked him to count to ten out loud.* **8** (of fire, lights or burning materials) not or no longer burning or lit: *The child should be in bed with lights out 8–9 hours before having to rise again.* ◇ *He let the fire go out.* **9** at an end: *He was actually deposed before his term of office was out.* **10** to the end; completely: *The matter was fought out in the courts for months.* **11 ~ (by sth)** not correct or exact; wrong: *Some considered that the figures of the 1911 Census were out by some hundreds of thousands.*

out·break /ˈaʊtbreɪk/ *noun* **~ (of sth)** the sudden start of sth unpleasant, especially violence or a disease: *It was just three weeks before the outreak of war.* ◇ *Defending against likely disease outbreaks involves the stockpiling of vaccines.*

out·come AWL /ˈaʊtkʌm/ *noun* the result or effect of an action or event: *The programme may lead to positive outcomes such as a reduction in the number of school exclusions.* ◇ **~ of sth** *It is not clear whether the television debates actually influenced the outcome of the elections.*
➲ thesaurus note *at* RESULT[1]
▸ ADJECTIVE + OUTCOME **adverse, poor, negative, bad** • **positive, favourable, good, successful** • **primary, main** • **secondary** • **long-term** • **final, eventual, ultimate** • **possible** • **likely** • **clinical** • **educational** • **behavioural** *Some pollutants act immediately in producing adverse health outcomes.*
▸ NOUN + OUTCOME **health** • **learning** • **treatment** • **voting** • **pregnancy** • **birth** • **patient** *Technology is used in schools to enhance student learning outcomes.*
▸ VERB + OUTCOME **achieve, produce** • **influence, affect, shape** • **determine** • **lead to, result in** • **improve, enhance** • **predict** • **examine** • **evaluate, assess** • **measure** • **compare** • **report** *The equation can then be used to predict the outcome of an experiment under a new set of conditions.*

ˌoutcome ˈvariable *noun* (*statistics*) something that can be measured to judge the effects of a situation, a medical INTERVENTION, an experiment, etc: *Three respiratory symptoms, chest pain, dyspnoea and cough, were treated as outcome variables.*

out·dated /ˌaʊtˈdeɪtɪd/ *adj.* no longer useful because of being old-fashioned: *This model is based on a somewhat outdated view of women.* ◇ *The firm does not wish to invest in technology that will quickly become outdated.*

out·door /ˈaʊtdɔː(r)/ *adj.* [only before noun] used, happening or located outside rather than in a building: *Studies found that inner city and poor populations are less likely to participate in outdoor recreation activities.* OPP INDOOR

out·doors /ˌaʊtˈdɔːz; *NAmE* ˌaʊtˈdɔːrz/ *adv.* outside, rather than in a building: *Sunscreen was applied to children 15 minutes before they went outdoors.* OPP INDOORS

outer /ˈaʊtə(r)/ *adj.* [only before noun] on the outside of sth; furthest from the inside or centre of sth: *The crust is a rigid outer layer of the Earth.* ◇ *Hydrogen has just one electron in its outer shell.* ◇ *These outer membranes are relatively porous to small molecules.* ◇ *The outer fringe of the city comprised a series of residential areas.* ➲ compare EXTERNAL OPP INNER (1)

ˌouter ˈspace *noun* [U] = SPACE (8)

out·flow /ˈaʊtfləʊ; *NAmE* ˈaʊtfloʊ/ *noun* [usually sing.] **~ (of sth/sb) (from sth)** the movement of a large amount of money, liquid, people, etc. out of a place: *This loss of confidence led to a rapid outflow of capital from the affected countries.* OPP INFLOW

out·let /ˈaʊtlet/ *noun* **1 ~ (for sb/sth)** a way of expressing or making good use of strong feelings, ideas or energy: *Artistic expression can provide an outlet for survivors of trauma.* ◇ *During the Cold War, Hollywood artists and producers migrated to Europe to seek outlets for free expression.* **2** (*business*) a shop that sells goods of a particular type or made by a particular company: *Convenience goods are generally sold through many retail outlets so that buyers have easy access to the product.* ◇ **~ for sth** *Market traders remain significant outlets for many low-value products.* **3 ~ (for sth)** a market for goods or trade: *In the early eighteenth century, the Dutch sought foreign outlets for their abundant capital.* **4 ~ (for sth)** something that provides a way for research or information to be made available to people: *The journal has become a significant outlet for fundamental research in geography.* **5 ~ (for sth)** a pipe or hole through which liquid or gas can flow out: *The vents serve as outlets for ventilation and as smoke exhausts in the event of fire.* OPP INLET (1) **6** (*NAmE*) = SOCKET (2)

O

out·line[1] /ˈaʊtlaɪn/ *verb* **1** to give a description of the main facts or points involved in sth SYN SKETCH[1] (1): **~ sth** *The company report outlines its approach to sustainability.* ◇ *Some sites were excluded from further analysis for a number of reasons outlined below.* ◇ **~ how/what, etc...** *The first section outlines how international economic relations were shaped in the post-war economy.* ◇ **~ sth to sb** *If the patient is competent and continues to refuse consent, the consequences should be clearly outlined to him or her.* **2** [usually passive] **be outlined (+ adv./prep.)** to show or mark the outer edge of sth: *The affected areas were typically outlined in red on maps.*
▸ OUTLINE + NOUN **procedure** • **process** • **method** • **methodology** • **approach** • **strategy** • **step** • **proposal** • **framework** • **principle** • **reason** • **rationale** • **argument** • **vision** • **scenario** • **feature** *Many European political leaders have recently outlined their visions for the future organization and workings of the EU.*
▸ ADVERB + OUTLINE **briefly** • **clearly** *These effects are briefly outlined under five headings.*
▸ OUTLINE + ADVERB **above, earlier, previously** • **below** • **here** *In all the examples outlined above, officials were closely involved in the development of policy.*

out·line[2] /ˈaʊtlaɪn/ *noun* [C, U] **1** a description of the main facts or points involved in sth: **~ (of sth)** *Section 5.5 will present a brief outline of the methods employed in the study.* ◇ **in ~** *This topic has already been mentioned in outline.* ◇ *In outline, the principal events go as follows...* **2** the line that goes around the edge of sth, showing its main shape but not the details: *Clinically, the lesions become larger and gradually develop an irregular outline.* ◇ **in ~** *Viewed from the air, most beaches are curved in outline.*

out·look /ˈaʊtlʊk/ *noun* [usually sing.] **1** a person or group's attitude to life and the world: *Research has shown that children who have a positive outlook seem to adjust better.* ◇ **~ on sth** *The authors' outlook on obesity is clearly laid out in the introduction.* **2** what is likely to happen: *Recently, there has been a dramatic shift in the global economic outlook.* ◇ **~ for sth** *The outlook for premature babies is continually improving.* ➲ *compare* PROSPECT (3)

out·pa·tient /ˈaʊtpeɪʃnt/ *noun* a person who goes to a hospital for treatment but does not stay there: *A new outpatient was defined as a first-time visitor to the health facility for a specific condition.* ◇ **+ noun** *The woman asked about the possibility of an outpatient programme that would allow her to work during the day.* ➲ *compare* INPATIENT

out·put¹ AWL /ˈaʊtpʊt/ *noun* [U, C] **1** the amount of sth that a person, a machine or an organization produces: *The firm had to increase output in response to higher demand.* ◇ *to boost/expand/raise/reduce output* ◇ *output rises/falls* ◇ *Greater efficiency will lead to higher outputs.* ◇ *Labour productivity was so low that, to produce the same output, a Russian plant might be double the size of an equivalent American plant.* ➲ *compare* INPUT¹ (1) **2** the power, energy or data produced by a machine: *Noise is unwanted electrical output.* ◇ *Wind speed varies, causing the power output from a wind turbine to fluctuate.* ◇ *The digital output from the computer is applied to digital-to-analogue converters.* ➲ *compare* INPUT¹ (2) **3** (*biology*) the amount of sth that is produced by an organ in the body: *Cardiac output falls due to ineffective cardiac pumping.* **4** (*also* ˈ**output terminal**) a place or means for energy or data to leave a machine or system: *The amplifier has two input terminals that are distinct from the two output terminals.* OPP INPUT¹ (3)

O

out·put² AWL /ˈaʊtpʊt/ *verb* (**out·put·ting, out·put, out·put**) **~ sth** (of a computer or other device) to supply or produce data: *Each additional query boosts the probability of outputting the correct answer.* ➲ *compare* INPUT²

out·rage¹ /ˈaʊtreɪdʒ/ *noun* **1** [U] a strong feeling of shock and anger: *The massacre provoked genuine moral outrage.* ◇ *Many MPs expressed outrage at their colleagues' fraudulent behaviour.* **2** [C] an act or event that is violent, cruel or very wrong and that shocks people or makes them very angry: *This beating was the first of a long series of such outrages.*

out·rage² /ˈaʊtreɪdʒ/ *verb* [often passive] to make sb very shocked and angry: **be outraged (at sth)** *Many would be outraged at the suggestion that parental decisions about smoking in private homes should be regulated.*

out·set /ˈaʊtset/ *noun*
IDM **at/from the ˈoutset (of sth)** at/from the beginning of sth: *At the outset of the project, it was unclear how many people were likely to participate.* ◇ *It is important to develop a brand that is recognized from the outset.*

out·side¹ /ˌaʊtˈsaɪd/ *noun* **1** (*usually* **the outside**) [C, usually sing.] the outer side or surface of sth SYN EXTERIOR¹: **(on the) ~ (of sth)** *Parasites can live on the outside or inside of their host.* ◇ *There have been increasingly prominent messages on the outside of cigarette packaging.* OPP INSIDE¹ (1) **2** [sing.] the area that is near or around sth: **(on the) ~ (of sth)** *The air temperature inside the greenhouse was the same as that on the outside.* **3** (*usually* **the outside**) [sing.] the fact of not being part of or involved in a group or organization: **from the ~ (of sth)** *Friends of the Earth is a campaigning group that tries to influence government from the outside.* ◇ **on the ~ (of sth)** *This book will appeal to anyone who has ever felt on the outside of things.* **4 the outside** [sing.] the part of a curving river, road or track furthest from the inner or shorter side of the curve: **(on the) ~ (of sth)** *Banks are steep on the outside of the bend, where erosion generally takes place.* OPP INSIDE¹ (2)
IDM **on the outside** used to describe how sb appears or seems: *He is confused and may appear a little aggressive on the outside.*

out·side² /ˈaʊtsaɪd/ *adj.* [only before noun] **1** of, on or facing the outer side SYN EXTERNAL: *The mortality rate increases sharply when the outside air temperature falls below 0°C.* ◇ *Students created a colourful mural on the large outside wall of their local supermarket.* OPP INSIDE² (1) **2** not included in or connected with a particular group, organization, country, etc: *Most of the settlements were small and had little contact with the outside world.* ◇ *They appointed an outside expert to advise the school.* ◇ *outside investors/agencies/firms* ◇ *Despite various attempts to protect them from outside influences, their numbers are declining.* OPP INSIDE² (2)

out·side³ /ˌaʊtˈsaɪd/ (*also* **out·side of** *especially in NAmE*) *prep.* **1** away from or not in a particular place: *The pressures which cause migration often have their source outside the borders of a state.* ◇ *There are separate toilets in the corridor outside the cells.* ◇ *Disney opened its third theme park outside of the United States, in Hong Kong, in 2005.* OPP INSIDE³ **2** on or to a place beyond the edge of sth: *Many bird species show an egg-retrieval response when they see an egg outside their nest.* ◇ *For many people, the immediate environment outside their front door is of more importance than the state of the global environment.* OPP INSIDE³ **3** not part of sth: *The failure to meet its commitments arises from factors outside the company's control.* ◇ *The proportion of children born outside marriage quadrupled over this period.* OPP WITHIN¹ (1) **4 outside of** (*especially NAmE*) apart from: *Outside of arranging the interview, they had never spoken before.*

out·side⁴ /ˌaʊtˈsaɪd/ *adv.* **1** near but not in a room, building or container: *They were asked to wait outside.* ◇ *The bailiff remained outside in a car whilst the customs officers went inside the house.* OPP INSIDE⁴ **2** not inside a building; outdoors: *How many days of the week did you play outside or play a sport?*

out·sider /ˌaʊtˈsaɪdə(r)/ *noun* **1** a person who is not part of a particular organization or profession: *All trading blocs discriminate against outsiders.* ◇ *These terms are sometimes difficult to explain to outsiders.* **2** a person who is not accepted as a member of a society, group, etc: *For an outsider, trying to do business in these close-knit communities was very difficult.* ◇ *Resentment against outsiders had been building up.*

out·stand·ing /aʊtˈstændɪŋ/ *adj.* **1** extremely good; excellent: *He carried out some outstanding research in geochemistry.* ◇ *Few presidents these days are considered to be outstanding successes.* **2** [usually before noun] very obvious or important SYN PROMINENT (1): *The outstanding feature of the South East Asian region is the diversity of its environments.* ◇ *The outstanding events in personal and family life (births, marriages, deaths) were marked by religious services and feasting.* **3** (of payment, work, problems, etc.) not yet paid, done, solved, etc: *It was found that the property taken as security was worth much less than the outstanding debt.* ◇ *With French encouragement, some of the outstanding issues dividing Russia and Britain were settled.* ◇ *Finally, in 1906, the payments still outstanding were written off.*

out·strip /ˌaʊtˈstrɪp/ *verb* (**-pp-**) **1 ~ sth** to be greater than sth in number or amount SYN EXCEED (1): *Demand for transplants has continued to outstrip supply.* **2 ~ sb/sth** to be faster, better or more successful than sb/sth you are competing against SYN SURPASS: *Total sales of the product outstripped the rest of its sector, boosting brand share by nearly 10%.*

out·ward /ˈaʊtwəd; *NAmE* ˈaʊtwərd/ *adj.* [only before noun] **1** connected with the way people or things seem to be rather than with what is actually true: *The system may have altered in outward appearance, but in essence it has changed very little.* ◇ *Despite an outward show of support, Tiberius concealed a deep hatred for his adopted son.* OPP INWARD[1] (2) **2** going away from a particular place, especially one that you are going to return to: *It appears as though the pigeons store information during the course of their outward journey.* ◇ *During the 1920s, outward migration from Alabama alone topped 81 000.* **3** away from the centre or a particular point: *High-pressure gas in the cylinder exerts an outward force on the piston.* ◇ *The logic of the greenbelt policy is to limit the outward expansion of the urban areas.* OPP INWARD[1] (1)

out·wards /ˈaʊtwədz; *NAmE* ˈaʊtwərdz/ (*BrE*) (*also* **out·ward** *NAmE, BrE*) *adv.* **1** towards the outside; away from the centre or from a particular point: *Most cities are growing outwards along major roads.* ◇ *There is a force of several tonnes pushing outwards on the aircraft's doors.* ◇ **~ from sth** *There was a huge spread of Islam outwards from the Arabian peninsula towards the end of the 7th century.* **2** away from yourself or your interests: *Their limited natural resources forced them to look outwards.* OPP INWARD[2]

out·weigh /ˌaʊtˈweɪ/ *verb* **~ sth** to be greater or more important than sth: *The costs of such decisions are likely to far outweigh their benefits.*

ovary /ˈəʊvəri; *NAmE* ˈoʊvəri/ *noun* (*pl.* **-ies**) **1** either of the two organs in a woman's body that produce eggs; a similar organ in female animals, birds and fish: *Whether the right or left ovary provides the egg each month is relatively random.* **2** the part of a plant that produces seeds: *Frost may lead to plant death, or reduce the functioning of sensitive plant parts such as buds, ovaries and leaves.* ■ **ovar·ian** /əʊˈveəriən; *NAmE* oʊˈveriən/ *adj.* [only before noun] *The incidence of ovarian cancer increases with age.*

oven /ˈʌvn/ *noun* a piece of equipment for cooking or heating food, shaped like a box with a door at the front: *The plates are activated by heating in an oven at 100–120°C to remove free liquid.* ➲ *see also* MICROWAVE (2)

over[1] /ˈəʊvə(r); *NAmE* ˈoʊvər/ *adv.* HELP For the special uses of **over** in phrasal verbs, look at the entries for the verbs. For example **take sth over** is in the phrasal verb section at **take**. **1** downwards and away from a vertical position: *The pedestrian had been knocked over by a cyclist.* ◇ *The sliding material pushed against the foundations of the buildings, one of which eventually toppled over.* **2** from one side to another side: *SUVs are more likely than cars to roll over and kill their occupants.* ◇ *Make sure you turn over the page as the information may extend overleaf.* ◇ *It is difficult to determine exactly how far the canoe can be tipped before it will flip over.* **3** so as to cover sb/sth completely: *Most of the oceans must have been iced over.* ◇ *The whole building was demolished and covered over with a mound of earth and stones.* **4** above; more: *The study was confined to women aged 18 and over.* **5** remaining; not used or needed: *Small irregular galaxies are simply seen as bits and pieces left over from the early days of the universe.* **6** again: *Mr Crozier felt he was being required to pay twice over.* ◇ *This is an experimental result that has been proved many times over.* **7** ended: *When the interview is over, the transcription must be completed.* ◇ *Although the McCarthy era was over, anti-communism was still alive and well.* **8** used to talk about sb/sth changing position: *They then telephoned the FBI agent in Greenwood and asked him to come over.* ◇ *Roman officials demanded that they hand over the scriptures for burning.* IDM **(all) over aˈgain** a second time from the beginning: *The negotiation process would often start over again each time a new agreement was required.* ◇ *In effect, every sale is a new sale as the customer has to be persuaded all over again to buy that product instead of a rival one.* **over against sth** in contrast with sth: *Over against this orthodox view, Christian scholars of liberal inclinations pursued a more naturalistic understanding of things.* **ˌover and ˈover (aˈgain)** many times SYN REPEATEDLY: *People do not enjoy work when it involves performing the same task over and over again.*

over[2] /ˈəʊvə(r); *NAmE* ˈoʊvər/ *prep.* HELP For the special uses of **over** in phrasal verbs, look at the entries for the verbs. For example **get over sth** is in the phrasal verb section at **get**. **1** resting on the surface of sb/sth and partly or completely covering them/it: *The fabric is secured over the flat top of the cylinder with a ring.* ◇ *Women have to wear veils and something over their knees.* **2** in or to a position higher than but not touching sb/sth; above sb/sth: *The hummingbird hovered over the flower.* ◇ *The thunderstorms originate over the mountains and move over the lowlands.* **3** from one side of sth to the other; across sth: *In 1829 a design competition for a bridge over the Avon Gorge was held.* **4** on the far or opposite side of sth: *Refugees streamed in from over the border.* **5** so as to cross sth and be on the other side: *Several of the men, through fear, climbed over the walls of the courtyard.* ◇ *In March 1938, he dispatched German troops over the border.* **6** falling from or down from a place: *Upon hatching, the chick of the common European cuckoo (Cuculus canorus) pushes all host eggs over the edge of the nest.* **7 all ~** in or on all or most parts of sth: *Health care systems all over the world seem to be facing a funding crisis.* ◇ *Japanese Zen centres have grown up all over North America and Europe.* **8** more than a particular time, amount, cost, etc: *Aronson has over 40 years' experience as a social psychologist.* ◇ *Over 1 billion people do not have access to safe, clean drinking water.* ◇ *The company spends over $7 million a year on promoting its products.* **9** used to express a preference: *Holt et al. (2004) found that most people choose one global brand over another because of differences in the brands' global qualities.* ◇ *The benefits of absorption systems over vapour compression systems can be summarized as follows:...* **10** used to show that sb has control or authority: *The minister has a very wide scope of control over energy planning.* ◇ *The state wields a unique power and authority over its citizens.* ◇ *The Ruthenians of Galicia had no wish to be ruled over by Poles.* **11** during sth: *Earthquakes have exacted a heavy toll on India over the years.* ◇ *Rival families and factions continued to vie for power over the next few decades.* ◇ *They discussed the possibility of a National Mathematical Laboratory over lunch on 27 May 1943.* ➲ language bank *at* TIME[1] **12** past a particular difficult stage or situation: *He never got over his wife's death.* **13** because of or concerning sth; about sth: *There is disagreement over what precisely qualitative research is.* ◇ *These differences in their positions led to an argument over the economy.* **14** using sth; by means of sth: *Telemarketing or telesales is a form of non-store retailing when purchase occurs over the telephone.* ◇ *Listening to music online serves the same ends as listening to it over the radio with a small shift in mechanism.*
IDM **ˌover and aˈbove** in addition to sth: *There are also other factors over and above those discussed here.*

over·all[1] AWL /ˌəʊvərˈɔːl; *NAmE* ˌoʊvərˈɔːl/ *adj.* [only before noun] including all the things or people that are involved in a particular situation SYN GENERAL[1] (1): *It is useful to develop a single index that can be used to give an overall picture of air quality.* ◇ *Physicians were asked to rate their overall job satisfaction on a seven-point scale.*
▸ OVERALL + NOUN **picture • profile • shape • pattern • trend • rate • score • performance • efficiency • effectiveness • quality • accuracy • size • cost • satisfaction • prevalence • incidence • mortality • aim,**

O

objective, goal • strategy • effect, impact, impression • assessment • conclusion *The overall score is the mean of the responses to each of the 24 questions.* ◇ *The overall effectiveness of an organization's selling effort is thought to be determined by two factors.*

over·all² AWL /ˌəʊvərˈɔːl; *NAmE* ˌoʊvərˈɔːl/ *adv.* **1** including everything or everyone; in total: *Overall, 44% of children came from manual households.* ◇ *Rates for dementia overall appear to be comparable between countries.* **2** generally; when everything is considered: *Overall, this book does not fall short of its aim.* ◇ *The question is whether this policy will really achieve benefits for the European economy overall.* ➲ language bank *at* CONCLUSION

over·arch·ing /ˌəʊvərˈɑːtʃɪŋ; *NAmE* ˌoʊvərˈɑːrtʃɪŋ/ *adj.* [usually before noun] very important, because it includes or influences many things: *Their overarching aim was defined as 'preventing offending by children and young persons'.* ◇ *The overarching ethical principle is that patients should be treated in their best interests.*

over·come /ˌəʊvəˈkʌm; *NAmE* ˌoʊvərˈkʌm/ *verb* (**over·came** /ˌəʊvəˈkeɪm; *NAmE* ˌoʊvərˈkeɪm/, **over·come**) **1 ~ sth** to succeed in dealing with or controlling a problem that has been preventing you from achieving sth: *Any move abroad has to overcome barriers of unfamiliarity of location and culture.* ◇ *to overcome obstacles/difficulties/problems* ◇ *A visual aid can enable a person to overcome the limitations of their short-term memory.* ◇ *The parents need advice on how to help the child to gain confidence and overcome fear.* **2** [usually passive] **(be) overcome by sth** to be extremely strongly affected by sth SYN OVERWHELM (2): *They were overcome by fumes.* ◇ *Overcome by fear, the soldier began crying and shouting out loud.* **3 ~ sb/sth** to defeat sb: *The rebels were overcome in the siege of Alesia.*

over·dose /ˈəʊvədəʊs; *NAmE* ˈoʊvərdoʊs/ *noun* too much of a drug taken at one time: *Some people take overdoses repeatedly, often at times of stress.* ◇ **~ of sth** *An overdose of iron tablets can cause liver damage.*

over·esti·mate AWL /ˌəʊvərˈestɪmeɪt; *NAmE* ˌoʊvərˈestɪmeɪt/ *verb* **~ sth** to estimate sth to be larger, better, more important, etc. than it really is: *The importance of these ideas for novelists of Roth's generation cannot be overestimated.* ◇ *The percentage of the national budget devoted to foreign aid programmes is grossly overestimated.* OPP UNDERESTIMATE ■ **over·esti·mate** AWL /ˌəʊvərˈestɪmət; *NAmE* ˌoʊvərˈestɪmət/ *noun* [usually sing.] *Even this figure is most likely to be an overestimate.* ◇ **~ of sth** *Pregnancies were determined using chemical testing and could be an overestimate of real pregnancy rates.* **over·esti·mation** /ˌəʊvərestɪˈmeɪʃn; *NAmE* ˌoʊvərestɪˈmeɪʃn/ *noun* [U, C] *Questionnaires need to be designed carefully as there may be a tendency towards overestimation.* ◇ **~ of sth** *His empathy towards Weygand has led to an overestimation of his significance.*

over·lap¹ AWL /ˌəʊvəˈlæp; *NAmE* ˌoʊvərˈlæp/ *verb* (**-pp-**) **1** [T, I] if one thing **overlaps** another, or the two things **overlap**, part of one thing covers part of the other: **~ (with sth)** *Male home ranges overlap with several female territories.* ◇ *The butterflies' wings are covered with overlapping scales.* ◇ **~ sth** *Massive sulfide deposits commonly overlap areas where the vein gold deposits are found.* **2** [I, T] if two events **overlap** or **overlap** each other, the second one starts before the first one has finished: *Although these three stages follow each other roughly in developmental time, the later stages overlap considerably.* ◇ **~ sth** *His young life overlapped the later years of Chateaubriand.* **3** [I, T] to cover part of the same area of interest, knowledge, responsibility, etc: *The second and third meanings overlap considerably.* ◇ **~ with sth** *Climatology overlaps with meteorology in covering this area.* ◇ **~ sth** *Analytical chemistry overlaps the realms of biotechnology, materials science and many other subject areas.*

over·lap² AWL /ˈəʊvəlæp; *NAmE* ˈoʊvərlæp/ *noun* **1** [U, C] **~ (between sth and sth)** a shared area of interest, knowledge, responsibility, activity, etc: *There is a degree of overlap between the approaches.* ◇ *It is, however, the genuine overlap between family and business that makes family firms different.* **2** [U, sing.] a period of time in which two events or activities happen together: **~ with sth** *Most aquatic insects have short-lived adult stages with little temporal overlap with larval stages.* ◇ **~ (of sth)** *There is an overlap of several days in which both treatments are given.*

over·load¹ /ˈəʊvələʊd; *NAmE* ˈoʊvərloʊd/ *noun* [U, sing.] **~ (of sth)** too much of sth: *The overload of information made it difficult for central offices to separate the important from the unimportant.* ◇ *If there are signs of fluid overload, then diuretics may be considered.*

over·load² /ˌəʊvəˈləʊd; *NAmE* ˌoʊvərˈloʊd/ *verb* **1** to give sb too much of sth: **~ sb (with sth)** *Teachers complained that they were overloaded with paperwork.* ◇ **~ sth** *Complex syntactic structures quickly overload the processing capabilities of readers.* **2 ~ sth** to put too great a demand on a computer, an electrical system, etc. causing it to fail: *The demand for telephone service had become so heavy that the existing system was overloaded.*

over·look /ˌəʊvəˈlʊk; *NAmE* ˌoʊvərˈlʊk/ *verb* **1 ~ sth** to fail to see or notice sth SYN MISS (1): *It is important that this possibility is not overlooked.* ◇ *In particular, he overlooked the fact that sustained full employment had never been achieved either in Britain or the US.* **2 ~ sth** if a building, etc. **overlooks** a place, you can see that place from the building: *The incident took place in an area overlooked by flats.* ◇ *She lived in a splendid residence in Galata, overlooking the Bosporus.* **3 ~ sb (for sth)** to not consider sb for a job or position, even though they might be suitable: *Hearing Adrienne's story, I wondered how many of her peers were overlooked for similar opportunities.*

over·ly /ˈəʊvəli; *NAmE* ˈoʊvərli/ *adv.* (before an adjective) too; very SYN EXCESSIVELY: *This technique can give overly optimistic results unless used with great care.* ◇ *Many view the budget targets as overly restrictive and likely to inhibit recovery.*

over·ride /ˌəʊvəˈraɪd; *NAmE* ˌoʊvərˈraɪd/ *verb* (**over·rode** /ˌəʊvəˈrəʊd; *NAmE* ˌoʊvərˈroʊd/, **over·rid·den** /ˌəʊvəˈrɪdn; *NAmE* ˌoʊvərˈrɪdn/) **1 ~ sth** to use your authority to reject sb's decision, order, etc: *The veto was overridden by Congress.* ◇ *He overrode Dickens's express desire to be buried in Rochester.* **2 ~ sth** to be more important than sth: *Preserving life and health overrides lesser considerations.* ◇ *These concerns can override issues like price and delivery times.* ◇ *Minimizing delay sometimes overrides the efficient use of resources.* **3 ~ sth** (*technical*) to cover a particular area: *The island was overridden by an ice sheet moving from north-northwest.*

over·rid·ing /ˌəʊvəˈraɪdɪŋ; *NAmE* ˌoʊvərˈraɪdɪŋ/ *adj.* [only before noun] more important than anything else in a particular situation: *Water availability is the overriding concern in dry regions.* ◇ *Total population numbers are often the overriding consideration in planning.* ◇ *an overriding aim/goal/objective*

over·seas¹ AWL /ˌəʊvəˈsiːz; *NAmE* ˌoʊvərˈsiːz/ *adj.* connected with foreign countries, especially those separated from your country by the sea or ocean: *Overseas trade does, however, create the opportunity for more sales and growth.* ◇ *overseas markets/investments* ◇ *an overseas territory/empire/colony* ◇ *Overseas expansion has lessened the company's dependence on the increasingly saturated UK market.* ➲ *compare* HOME² (3)

over·seas² AWL /ˌəʊvəˈsiːz; NAmE ˌoʊvərˈsiːz/ *adv.* to or in a foreign country, especially those separated from your country by the sea or ocean SYN ABROAD (1): *In recent years, travelling overseas for work has become increasingly common.* ◇ *A substantial portion of manufacturing has been moved overseas.*

over·see /ˌəʊvəˈsiː; NAmE ˌoʊvərˈsiː/ *verb* (**over·saw** /ˌəʊvəˈsɔː; NAmE ˌoʊvərˈsɔː/, **over·seen** /ˌəʊvəˈsiːn; NAmE ˌoʊvərˈsiːn/) **~ sb/sth** to be in charge of sb/sth and make sure that a job or an activity is done correctly SYN SUPERVISE: *Today, the World Trade Organization oversees the implementation of more than 20 trade agreements.* ◇ *At the work camps, armed guards oversee the labourers who work long days and live in wretched conditions.*

over·sight /ˈəʊvəsaɪt; NAmE ˈoʊvərsaɪt/ *noun* **1** [U] the state of being in charge of sb/sth: **~ over sth** *The Ministry of Petroleum has regulatory oversight over the industry.* ◇ **~ (of sth)** *External oversight of antibiotic prescribing has been advocated by some authors.* ◇ *judicial/legislative oversight* **2** [C, U] the fact of making a mistake because you forget to do sth or you do not notice sth: *The failure to inspect was due to a careless oversight.* ◇ *You can never entirely eliminate human error and oversight.*

overt /əʊˈvɜːt; ˈəʊvɜːt; NAmE oʊˈvɜːrt; ˈoʊvɜːrt/ *adj.* [usually before noun] done in an open way and not secretly: *Visible, overt behaviour, like the clothes worn and eating habits, can be easily seen.* ◇ *Heaney has made overt reference to Wordsworth in the 'Glanmore Sonnets'.* ◇ *overt conflict/aggression/hostility* ➲ *compare* COVERT ■ **overt·ly** *adv.*: *Some scholars have replaced this overtly Christian way of expressing dates with a more neutral system.*

over·take /ˌəʊvəˈteɪk; NAmE ˌoʊvərˈteɪk/ *verb* (**over·took** /ˌəʊvəˈtʊk; NAmE ˌoʊvərˈtʊk/, **over·taken** /ˌəʊvəˈteɪkən; NAmE ˌoʊvərˈteɪkən/) **1** [T] **~ sb/sth** to become greater in number, amount or importance than sth else SYN OUTSTRIP: *Germany rapidly overtook Britain in industrial output.* ◇ *Nuclear energy may overtake oil as the main fuel.* ◇ *Quinine has been overtaken by newer drugs.* **2** [T, often passive] **~ sb/sth** if sth unpleasant **overtakes** a person, place, etc. it unexpectedly starts to happen and to affect them: *Disaster overtook the town in AD 296.* **3** [T, I] **~ (sb/sth)** (*especially BrE*) to go past a moving vehicle or person in front of you because you are going faster than they are: *The driver overtook a line of vehicles.*

over·throw¹ /ˌəʊvəˈθrəʊ; NAmE ˌoʊvərˈθroʊ/ *verb* (**over·threw** /ˌəʊvəˈθruː; NAmE ˌoʊvərˈθruː/, **over·thrown** /ˌəʊvəˈθrəʊn; NAmE ˌoʊvərˈθroʊn/) **~ sb/sth** to remove a leader or a government from a position of power by force: *The president was overthrown in a military coup.* ◇ *to overthrow a government/regime*

over·throw² /ˈəʊvəθrəʊ; NAmE ˈoʊvərθroʊ/ *noun* [usually sing.] **~ (of sb/sth)** the act of taking power by force from a leader or government: *The protests turned into riots, leading to the overthrow of the government.*

over·use /ˌəʊvəˈjuːz; NAmE ˌoʊvərˈjuːz/ *verb* **~ sth** to use sth too much or too often: *Some collocations are overused by learners, in comparison with native speakers.* ■ **over·use** /ˌəʊvəˈjuːs; NAmE ˌoʊvərˈjuːs/ *noun* [U, sing.] **~ (of sth)** *Widespread overuse of antibiotics has resulted in major problems with bacterial resistance.*

over·view /ˈəʊvəvjuː; NAmE ˈoʊvərvjuː/ *noun* **~ (of sth)** a general description or an outline of sth SYN SURVEY¹ (3): *The first section gives a comprehensive overview of three international organizations.* ◇ *Gold (1980: 7–15) and Martin (1991: 6–11) provide brief overviews of psychological approaches to the study of behaviour.* ◇ *a general/detailed/historical overview of sth* ➲ language bank *at* ABOUT²

over·weight /ˌəʊvəˈweɪt; NAmE ˌoʊvərˈweɪt/ *adj.* (of people) too heavy and fat: *Over half of the adult American population is overweight or obese (Ogden et al., 2006).* ◇ *Overweight patients tend to see their GP more frequently than others.* OPP UNDERWEIGHT

over·whelm /ˌəʊvəˈwelm; NAmE ˌoʊvərˈwelm/ *verb* [often passive] **1** to be so bad or so great that a person, organization or system cannot deal with it; to give too much of a thing to a person or thing: **~ sb/sth** *The huge quantity of data can easily overwhelm the capacity of the computers involved.* ◇ **be overwhelmed with sth** *Salespeople received so many demands from product managers that they became overwhelmed with information.* ◇ *Very soon after the attack, hospital facilities would be overwhelmed, especially with burn victims.* **2** to have such a strong emotional effect on sb that it is difficult for them to resist or know how to react SYN OVERCOME (2): **be overwhelmed by sth** *The bereaved person may be overwhelmed by the trauma.* ◇ **be overwhelmed with sth** *Some Christians were overwhelmed with terror and obeyed Pliny's order to sacrifice to the emperor.* **3 ~ sb** to defeat sb completely: *The Spartans captured 171 ships, and their infantry overwhelmed the Athenian camp.*

over·whelm·ing /ˌəʊvəˈwelmɪŋ; NAmE ˌoʊvərˈwelmɪŋ/ *adj.* very great or very strong; so powerful that you cannot resist it or decide how to react: *At this time, the overwhelming majority of the population lived in rural areas.* ◇ *Krueger found some, but not overwhelming, evidence to support this hypothesis.* ◇ *The scientific case for primary prevention of lung cancer by the elimination of tobacco smoking is overwhelming.* ■ **over·whelm·ing·ly** *adv.*: *The European economy in 1700 was still overwhelmingly agricultural.*

owe /əʊ; NAmE oʊ/ *verb* (not used in the progressive tenses) **1** to have to pay sb for sth that you have already received or return money that you have borrowed: *The total amount owed at any moment is called the 'national debt'.* ◇ *The amount of credit card debt owed by the average American cardholder is approximately $9 000.* ◇ **~ sb sth** *He owed the company a substantial sum of money.* ◇ **~ sth (to sb) (for sth)** *They owe $10 000 to various creditors.* ◇ *The company had owed some £16 500 for goods.* **2** to feel that you should do sth for sb or give them sth, especially because they have done sth for you: **~ sth to sb** *I owe a debt of gratitude to many people for their help.* ◇ **~ sb sth** *There is an unwillingness to receive unpaid material help from others, largely because they want to avoid owing others a favour.* ◇ **~ it to sb to do sth** *Rulers owe it to their subjects to provide leadership.* HELP The passive is not used in this meaning except with a person as the subject: *These people are owed an apology.* ◇ ~~*An apology is owed to these people.*~~ **3 ~ sth to sb/sth** to exist or be successful because of the help or influence of sb/sth: *The Internet owes its success to institutional as well as technological innovations (Mowery and Simcoe, 2002).* ◇ *Mountains such as the Appalachians owe their existence to plate tectonic forces that were active many millions of years ago.* **4 ~ allegiance/loyalty/obedience (to sb)** to have to obey or be loyal to sb who is in a position of authority or power: *Aliens were people who did not owe allegiance to the Crown.* ◇ *Members of the clan should act as members of a family, owing loyalty to the chief.*

ˈowing to *prep.* because of: *2009, owing to low gas prices, was a difficult time for gas producers.* ◇ *These differences may be owing to the fact that different methodologies were employed.* ◇ *Owing to its flat topography and close proximity to the sea, flooding threatens the city annually.* ➲ language bank *at* BECAUSE

own¹ /əʊn; NAmE oʊn/ *adj., pron.* **1** used to emphasize that sth belongs to or is connected with sb: *Publication was the playwright's own idea.* ◇ *The choice is her own.* ◇ *Her interest in this stems from her own experience of motherhood.* ◇ *The United States decided from the outset*

O

to fight the war on its own terms. ◇ **of sb's ~** *They were unable to have children of their own.* ◇ *Some people are worse off than others through no fault of their own.* HELP **Own** cannot be used after an article: *I need my own room.* ◇ ~~*I need an own room*~~ ◇ *It is good to have your own room.* ◇ ~~*It is good to have the own room.*~~ **2** done or produced by and for yourself: *Families laboured to grow their own food.*

IDM **come into your/its 'own** to have the opportunity to show how good or useful you are or sth is: *Here, the Internet really comes into its own with search engines able to scan masses of data in seconds.* **hold your 'own (against sb/sth) (in sth)** to remain in a strong position when sb is attacking you or competing with you: *At the Scotland-wide level, Labour was easily able to hold its own against the other parties.* **on your/its 'own 1** alone; without anyone/anything else: *She lives on her own.* **2** without help: *In 1948 Constanze conducted a survey of women managing on their own.* ◇ *This combination allows neurons to perform quite complex information processing tasks all on their own.* ➲ *more at* RIGHT¹

own² /əʊn; *NAmE* oʊn/ *verb* [T] (not used in the progressive tenses) **~ sth** to have sth that belongs to you, especially because you have bought it: *Land is often owned by more than one individual.* ◇ *CSV was a wholly owned subsidiary of two firms.* ◇ *Even today, there are numerous large British companies that are privately owned.* ◇ *Africa has also proved to be a difficult market for the American-owned corporations.* ◇ *King's in-house publishing company owned the copyright to the song.*

owner /'əʊnə(r); *NAmE* 'oʊnər/ *noun* a person who owns sth: *In this case, the legal owner had left his farm to the claimant by will.* ◇ *a factory/business/plantation owner* ◇ **~ of sth** *The owner of a patent is provided with a monopoly right to control the item.* ➲ *see also* LANDOWNER

own·er·ship /'əʊnəʃɪp; *NAmE* 'oʊnərʃɪp/ *noun* [U] the fact of owning sth: *home/car/business ownership* ◇ **~ of sth** *Private ownership of capital goods is one of the legal conditions that makes capitalist production possible.* ◇ **in/under... ~** *The only large companies left in public ownership were British Coal, British Railways and the Post Office.* ◇ *The company was already under foreign ownership.*

oxi·da·tion /ˌɒksɪ'deɪʃn; *NAmE* ˌɑːksɪ'deɪʃn/ *noun* [U] (*chemistry*) the process or result of oxidizing or being oxidized: *Incomplete oxidation of petrol produces carbon monoxide and carbon as well as carbon dioxide and water.* ➲ *compare* REDUCTION (4)

oxide /'ɒksaɪd; *NAmE* 'ɑːksaɪd/ *noun* [U, C] (*chemistry*) a COMPOUND of OXYGEN and another chemical element: *Emissions of nitrous oxide dropped by 12 per cent.* ◇ *Phosphorus forms a wide range of oxides.*

oxi·dize (*BrE also* **-ise**) /'ɒksɪdaɪz; *NAmE* 'ɑːksɪdaɪz/ *verb* [T, often passive] (*chemistry*) **1 ~ sth (to sth)** to combine or make sth combine with OXYGEN or to remove HYDROGEN: *When plants die, their carbon is ultimately oxidized back to carbon dioxide.* OPP REDUCE (3) **2 ~ sth (to sth)** to remove one or more ELECTRONS from a substance: *When sodium burns in chorine, it is oxidized to form sodium chloride.* ➲ *compare* REDUCE (4) ➲ *see also* OXIDATION

oxy·gen /'ɒksɪdʒən; *NAmE* 'ɑːksɪdʒən/ *noun* [U] (*symb.* **O**) the chemical element of ATOMIC NUMBER 8. Oxygen is a gas that is present in air and water and is necessary for people, animals and plants to live: *The need for oxygen is fundamental to life.* ◇ **+ noun** *The oxygen supply to the heart is inadequate.* ◇ *A water molecule consists of a central oxygen atom, bonded to two hydrogen atoms.*

ozone /'əʊzəʊn; *NAmE* 'oʊzoʊn/ *noun* [U] (*chemistry*) a poisonous gas with a strong smell that is a form of OXYGEN

HELP **Ozone** differs from normal oxygen (O_2) by having three atoms in its MOLECULE (O_3): *Ozone can be destroyed by reactions with nitrous oxide emissions from aircraft.* ◇ **+ noun** *Ozone depletion was first recognized as an issue in the 1970s.*

'ozone layer *noun* [sing.] a layer of OZONE high above the earth's surface that helps to protect the earth from harmful RADIATION from the sun: *In 1985 scientists discovered a hole the size of the USA in the ozone layer over the South Pole.*

Pp

pace /peɪs/ *noun* **1** [U, sing.] **~ (of sth)** the speed at which sth happens: *The pace of change in pop music increased as more artists became instant big sellers.* ◇ *The industrial boom gathered pace.* ◇ *Migration from south of the border continued at a rapid pace.* ◇ *The slow pace of ancient journeys facilitated intensive encounters with landscapes, sites and local people.* **2** [sing., U] the speed at which sb/sth walks, runs or moves: *These Spartan soldiers did not run at all, but advanced at a steady pace.* **3** [C] an act of stepping once when walking or running; the distance travelled when doing this: **within... paces of sb/sth** *The would-be assassin got to within three paces of Stolypin.* ➲ *compare* STEP¹ (3)

IDM **at your own 'pace** at a rate that is comfortable to you: *Students are encouraged to work at their own pace.* **keep 'pace (with sb/sth)** to move, increase, change, etc. at the same speed as sb/sth: *Public spending on social welfare has not kept pace with the increase in the portion of the population who are elderly or infirm.* ◇ *The review will assess whether market regulations have kept pace with changes in trading technology and practice.* **set the 'pace** to do sth at a particular speed or to a particular standard so that other people are then forced to copy it if they want to be successful: *Space movies set the pace for the development of special effects.* ➲ *more at* FORCE²

pack¹ /pæk/ *verb* **1** [T] **~ sth (up) (in/into sth)** to put sth into a container so that it can be stored, transported or sold: *Today, giant meat-packing plants can pack 400 or more animals an hour.* ◇ *Finally, women pasted labels on the cans and packed them in crates to be shipped to wholesalers.* **2** [T] to fill sth; to fill sth with a lot of people or things: **~ sth** *More than 17 000 people packed the courtyard of the temple.* ◇ **~ sth with sth** *The conservative veterans tried to pack the meeting with their own supporters.* ◇ **~ sb/sth into/on sth** *These newer chips, however, pack much more circuitry on the chip.* ➲ *see also* PACKED **3** [I, T, usually passive] to be close together; to position things close together: **+ adv./prep.** *If the silica spheres have a fairly uniform size, they can pack together in a regular manner.* ◇ **(be) packed (+ adv./prep.)** *While the maximum fraction of space that can be filled by packed cylinders is 91%, sheets can be packed together to fill up to 100% of space.* **4** [T] **~ sth (in sth)** to surround sth with a particular substance to protect or preserve it: *All fresh fish is packed in ice for transport.* **5** [T] **~ sth (down)** to press sth such as snow or soil to form a thick hard mass: *The floor was packed earth and the walls were of mud brick.*

PHR V **ˌpack sb/sth 'in** to put a lot of things or people into a limited space: *This book packs in a lot of information.* **ˌpack 'up | ˌpack sth 'up** to put your possessions into a bag, etc. before leaving a place: *With the return of drought in 1893 through 1897, many settlers finally packed up and left.*

pack² /pæk/ *noun* **1** [C] a container, usually made of paper, that holds items ready to be sold: *Tobacco warning labels on cigarette packs have been shown to reduce cigarette consumption.* ◇ *Bonus packs do create an immediate incentive to buy.* ➲ *compare* PACKAGE¹ (4), PACKET (1) **2** [C] a set of different things that are supplied together for a particular purpose: *This service pack included a firewall to prevent illegal access from the Internet.* **3** [C+sing./pl. v.] a group of wild animals that live and hunt together: **~ (of sth)** *Wolves in Europe live in packs of around 2–7 animals.* ◇ **in a ~** *In small packs, the loss of an individual can be detrimental for the entire pack.* **4** [C] a hot or cold piece of thick material, used for treating a wound: *Symptoms were temporarily relieved by an ice pack on his foot.*

pack·age[1] /ˈpækɪdʒ/ *noun* **1** a set of items or ideas that must be bought or accepted together: *The Marshall Plan (1947) was an aid package from the US of $13 billion to help rebuild West European economies after the war.* ◇ **~ of sth** *At the 2002 Seville summit, leaders approved a package of measures establishing minimum rules and standards on asylum.* ◇ **~ deal** *The EU's relations with its most important neighbours are usually conducted through package deals involving trade, aid and political dialogue.* **2** (*also* ˈ**software package**) (*computing*) a set of related programs for a particular type of task, sold and used as a single unit: *Many customers preferred all-inclusive software packages and did not want the hassle of having to download or buy everything separately.* **3** (*especially NAmE*) = PARCEL (1): *She received a package through the mail.* **4** (*NAmE*) a box, bag, etc. in which things are wrapped or packed; the contents of a box, etc: *Consumers are encouraged to check the list of ingredients on the side of the package.* ➲ *compare* PACK[2] (1)

pack·age[2] /ˈpækɪdʒ/ *verb* [often passive] **1 ~ sth (in sth)** to put sth into a box, bag, etc. to be sold or transported: *The product was packaged in heavy, chunky glass bottles.* ◇ *She noticed that what the parents put in the lunch boxes has changed to all packaged food and no fruit.* **2 ~ sb/sth (as sth)** to present sb/sth in a particular way: *In many cities, areas no longer used for their intended purposes, perhaps wharf areas or industrial sites, are packaged as tourist attractions.* **3 ~ sth (in sth)** to put several things of the same type together: *In a satellite radio system, 128 stations of stereo quality are to be packaged in one data stream.*

pack·aging /ˈpækɪdʒɪŋ/ *noun* [U] **1** materials used to wrap or protect goods that are sold in shops: *Lighter packaging can also lead to a reduction in shipping and transportation expenses.* ◇ **+ noun** *Polystyrene film is used extensively as a packaging material.* **2** the process of wrapping goods: *The company no longer had to use a separate contractor to manage its packaging.* ◇ **~ of sth** *The lead time needed for processing, packaging and distribution of these products is distinctly shorter than that for non-perishable goods.* ◇ **+ noun** *The injury had left him unable to work at the packaging company.*

packed /pækt/ *adj.* **1** extremely full of people SYN CROWDED (1): *The room was packed.* ◇ *A stage adaptation of the novel played to packed houses on Broadway.* **2** containing a lot of a particular thing: **~ with sth** *The text is densely packed with multiple perspectives on the wide variety of topics raised.* ◇ **~ -packed** *There is an action-packed rescue sequence at the novel's conclusion.* **3 tightly ~** pressed closely together: *Proteins are solid structures with tightly packed atoms.*

packet /ˈpækɪt/ *noun* **1** (*BrE*) a small box, bag, etc. in which goods are packed for selling: *For some years there has been a legal obligation for tobacco companies to print a health warning on cigarette packets.* ◇ **~ of sth** *a packet of biscuits/cigarettes/crisps* ➲ *compare* PACK[2] (1), PACKAGE[1] (4) **2** (*computing*) a block of data that forms part of a message sent through a computer network: *The Domain Name System (DNS) routes packets to a domain name rather than an IP address.* ◇ *The router calculates the route across the Internet that gets a data packet to its destination in the shortest time.* **3 ~ (of sth)** (*NAmE*) a set of documents that are supplied together for a particular purpose: *Families with children meeting this age criterion were mailed a packet of questionnaires.*

paedi·at·ric (*BrE*) (*NAmE* **pedi·at·ric**) /ˌpiːdiˈætrɪk/ *adj.* [usually before noun] connected with paediatrics: *Paediatric patients may be particularly vulnerable to certain toxins at specific stages of childhood.*

paedi·at·ri·cian (*BrE*) (*NAmE* **pedi·at·ri·cian**) /ˌpiːdiəˈtrɪʃn/ *noun* a doctor who studies and treats the diseases of children: *The child was discharged after examination by the paediatrician.*

paedi·at·rics (*BrE*) (*NAmE* **pedi·at·rics**) /ˌpiːdiˈætrɪks/ *noun* [U] the branch of medicine concerned with children and their diseases: *Improvements in paediatrics also contributed to this increased life expectancy.*

page /peɪdʒ/ *noun* **1** (*abbr.* **p**) one side or both sides of a sheet of paper in a book, magazine, etc: *The report appeared on the front page of the 'New York Times'.* ◇ *He devotes only twenty pages out of 268 to the events of the Haitian Revolution.* ◇ *The board was meeting over a weekend to discuss a 650-page document.* **2** a section of data that can be shown on a computer screen at any one time; a web page: *A total of 3 667 visitors accessed the introduction page of the digital questionnaire.* IDM *see* PRINT[1]

paid[1] /peɪd/ *adj.* [usually before noun] **1** (of work, etc.) for which people receive money: *Policies are needed to get more young people into paid work.* OPP UNPAID (1) **2** (of a person) receiving money for doing work: *It is estimated that there are, in the voluntary and community sectors, 470 000 paid workers.* OPP UNPAID (3)

IDM **put** ˈ**paid to sth** (*rather informal*) to stop or destroy sth, especially what sb plans or wants to do: *The reoccupation of Milan by the Austrians put paid to such schemes.*

paid[2] *past tense, past part. of* PAY[1]

pain /peɪn/ *noun* [U, C] **1** the feelings that sb has in their body when they have been hurt or when they are ill: *Warm baths may help relieve pain.* ◇ *Symptoms vary from mild breathlessness to severe chest pain.* ◇ *He has been getting aches and pains all over his body recently which he cannot explain.* ◇ **in ~** *Blood pressure may be high if the patient is in pain.* **2 ~ (of sth)** mental or emotional suffering: *He surely felt the pain of separation as he travelled on foot away from his home and loved ones.* ◇ *The country might need to go through the pain of social reform if it is to cope with a globalizing world.*

IDM **on pain of sth** with the threat of having sth done to you as a punishment if you do not obey: *Aphrodite instructed Anchises on pain of death never to reveal the child's true mother to anyone.*

- ADJECTIVE + PAIN **severe** • **acute** • **chronic** • **persistent** • **recurrent** • **post-operative** • **abdominal** *The treatment of severe chronic pain is difficult.*
- NOUN + PAIN **chest** • **back** • **shoulder** • **neck** • **joint** • **hip** • **leg** *It seems clear that back pain is more common in people in heavy manual occupations who undertake heavy lifting.*
- VERB + PAIN **experience, feel, suffer, endure** • **inflict, cause** *Do other species experience pain as we do?* ◇ *Our consciences inflict pain on ourselves in the form of guilt.* | **relieve, alleviate, ease, reduce** • **manage, treat, control** • **aggravate, exacerbate** *She took ibuprofen and paracetamol at night to alleviate the pain.*
- PAIN + NOUN **relief** • **management** *At that time, pain relief was seldom offered to women in normal labour.*

pain·ful /ˈpeɪnfl/ *adj.* **1** causing pain: *Since this morning, she has complained of painful leg swelling.* ◇ *The stings of venomous insects can be extremely painful.* **2** causing you to feel upset or embarrassed: *She tried to repress painful memories of the past.* ◇ *Some interviewees reported feeling relieved after relaying painful experiences.* **3** unpleasant or difficult to do: *The government confronted a painful* choice. ◇ ~ **(for sb) (to do sth)** *The Russo-Japanese War was painful for the army, but catastrophic for the navy.*

pain·less /ˈpeɪnləs/ *adj.* **1** causing no physical pain: *The condition is usually painless.* **2** not unpleasant or difficult to do: *Everything is designed to make the process of flying as painless and enjoyable as possible.*

paint¹ /peɪnt/ *verb* **1** [I, T] to make a picture or design using paints: *Many sculptors would also paint and draw.* ◇ ~ **sth/sb** *Rembrandt painted portraits of Dutch townsmen and their families.* ◇ *He was painted by Joshua Reynolds, one of the nation's foremost portrait artists.* **2** [T] to cover a surface or object with paint: ~ **sth (with sth)** *All sides of the square-shaped samples were painted with black paint.* ◇ ~ **sth + adj.** *The small shacks were painted green.* ◇ ~ **sth + noun** *The two types of building are painted different colours.* **3** [T] to give a particular impression of sb/sth SYN PORTRAY (2): ~ **sb/sth as sth** *Thirlwall paints Aristophanes as a politically and socially engaged poet.* ◇ ~ **sb/sth in...** *For such a complex issue, appeasement can be painted in remarkably black-and-white terms.*

paint² /peɪnt/ *noun* [U, C] a liquid that is put on surfaces to give them a particular colour; a layer of this liquid when it has dried on a surface: *Protesters were breaking windows, throwing bricks, spraying paint, turning over cars, etc.* ◇ *People with asthma should avoid working in places where paints, glues, foams or varnishes are used.* ◇ *Peeling paint can be seen on the walls and ceilings.*

paint·er /ˈpeɪntə(r)/ *noun* **1** an artist who paints pictures: *Painters like Turner and Constable were making daring experiments with effects of colour and light.* **2** a person whose job is painting buildings, walls, etc: *He works as a painter and decorator.*

paint·ing /ˈpeɪntɪŋ/ *noun* **1** [C] a picture that has been painted: ~ **(of sb/sth)** *This is one of the earliest paintings of a peasant scene.* ◇ ~ **by sb** *Paintings by the likes of Titian and Rubens were destroyed in the Lisbon earthquake.* **2** [U] the act or art of using paint to produce pictures: *He has written extensively about abstract painting, sculpture and photography.*

P

pair¹ /peə(r); *NAmE* per/ *noun* **1** [C] ~ **(of sth)** two things of the same type, especially when they are used or worn together: *The bond is formed by two atoms sharing a pair of electrons.* ◇ *No consumer reviews all the possible options when buying a shirt or pair of shoes.* **2** [C] ~ **(of sth)** an object consisting of two parts that are joined together: *The insect moves one front wing over the other in a motion resembling the closing of a pair of scissors.* ◇ *a pair of trousers/pants/glasses* HELP A plural verb is sometimes used with **pair** in the singular in senses 1 and 2. **3** [C +sing./pl. v.] two people who are doing sth together or who have a particular relationship: ~ **(of sb)** *The module is intended for use by small groups or pairs of students.* ◇ ~ **work** *The use of pair work promotes collaborative learning.* HELP In British English a plural verb is usually used: *A pair of elderly Chinese women beg on the busy Nanjing Road in Shanghai.* ◇ *The pair are depicted in the company of other gods.* **4** [C+sing./pl. v.] ~ **(of sth)** two animals or birds of the same type that are breeding together: *In an average year, a breeding pair of barn owls may consume as many as 5 000 small mammals.*
IDM **in ˈpairs** in groups of two objects or people: *Students worked in pairs.*

pair² /peə(r); *NAmE* per/ *verb* **1** [T, usually passive] to put people or things into groups of two: **be paired (with sb/sth)** *Each child was paired with another in play sessions.* **2** [I, T] to come together in order to breed: *It is generally evident that individuals do not pair randomly.* ◇ **(be) paired with sth** *Females paired with males that sing attractive songs also produce eggs with more testosterone (Gil et al., 2004).*
PHRV **ˌpair ˈup (with sth)** | **ˌpair sth ˈup (with sth)** to come together in groups of two; to cause two animals, birds or things to come together: *Larger males tend to pair up with larger females.*

pair·ing /ˈpeərɪŋ; *NAmE* ˈperɪŋ/ *noun* [C, U] two people or things that work together or are placed together; the act of placing them together: *These two writers, at first glance, seem a most unlikely pairing.* ◇ ~ **of sb/sth** *Customers must readily see the benefit in the pairing of services.*

pale /peɪl/ *adj.* **(paler, pal·est) 1** (of a person or their face) having skin that is almost white; having skin that is whiter than usual because of illness or a strong emotion: *On examination, she was pale and clammy with a firm, rapid pulse.* ◇ *Walker describes his friend's face turning 'pale as death' at the sight.* **2** light in colour; containing a lot of white: *The solution became pale yellow.* ◇ *Pumice is a very pale rock of low density.* OPP DARK¹ (2), DEEP¹ (11)

pal·lia·tive /ˈpæliətɪv/ *noun* **1** (*medical*) a medicine or medical treatment that reduces pain without curing its cause: *Cocaine was found to be a good palliative for toothache.* **2** (*formal, usually disapproving*) an action or a decision that is designed to make a difficult situation seem better without actually solving the cause of the problems: *The military intervention appears to have been little more than a short-term palliative which failed to address the long-term plight of the people.* ■ **pal·lia·tive** *adj.* [usually before noun] *Palliative care is intended neither to hasten nor postpone death.*

pamph·let /ˈpæmflət/ *noun* a very thin book with a paper cover, containing information or arguments about a particular subject: *Rosa Luxemburg published a pamphlet entitled 'Mass Strike, Party and Trade Unions' in 1906.* ➲ *compare* LEAFLET

pan·dem·ic /pænˈdemɪk/ *noun* a disease that spreads over a whole country or the whole world: *The influenza pandemic of 1918–19 resulted in 21 million deaths.* ■ **pan·dem·ic** *adj.*: *Pandemic influenza is a health threat which by definition does not respect national borders.* ➲ *compare* ENDEMIC, EPIDEMIC (1)

panel AWL /ˈpænl/ *noun* **1** [C+sing./pl. v.] a group of experts who give their advice or opinion about sth: *The expert panel was composed of 12 practising physicians.* ◇ ~ **of sb** *The case is presided over by a panel of judges.* **2** [C] a square or RECTANGULAR piece of wood, glass or metal that forms part of a larger surface such as a door or wall: *Windows of old historical buildings have glass panels set in sashes rather than a large single glass panel.* HELP A **solar panel** uses light and heat energy from the sun to produce electricity or heat water: *The cost of installing solar panels has dropped by 42 per cent in the past 2 years.* **3** [C] a flat board in a vehicle or on a piece of machinery where the controls and instruments are fixed: *First-generation plasma display panels used cells containing neon.* ◇ *The program turned on a row of 32 lights on the control panel.* **4** [C] a section of a page that shows a particular piece of information: *The top panel presents a standard measure of health in a population.* ◇ *This is shown graphically in the two panels on the right.*

panic /ˈpænɪk/ *noun* [U, C, usually sing.] **1** a sudden feeling of great fear that cannot be controlled and prevents clear thinking: *Her words sent him into a state of panic.* ◇ **in** ~ *Parents came running to the school in panic to get their children because of the terrorist attacks.* ◇ **in a** ~ *Everybody was getting in a panic.* ◇ ~ **attack** *Certain drugs reduce panic attacks.* **2** a situation in which people are made to feel very anxious, so that they act quickly and without thinking carefully: *The IMF directive to close down sixteen insolvent banks in the country caused panic.* ◇ ~ **about/over sth** *In the 1940s, there was something of a moral panic about the family in American society.*

paper /ˈpeɪpə(r)/ *noun* **1** [U] (often in compounds) material made in thin sheets, used for writing, drawing, covering things, etc: *a piece/sheet of paper* ◇ *The filter paper is covered with wax or a sheet of plastic to prevent evaporation.* ◇ **+ noun** *They have to submit a paper copy of their application form.* **2** [C] an academic article about a particular subject that is written by and for experts: *He published two papers in the field of animal behaviour.* ◇ *The results presented in this paper suggest obesity is a risk factor for both short- and long-term sickness absence.* ◇ **~ on sth** *Lamb himself was well known for his many detailed scientific papers on climate research.* **3** [C] a newspaper: *Some three quarters of British households take a daily paper.* ◇ *He was very fond of reading the papers.* HELP **The papers** is used to refer to newspapers in general. **4 papers** [pl.] pieces of paper with writing on them, such as letters, pieces of work or private documents: *His desk was overflowing with papers.* ◇ *This is a study based on a huge amount of research, mostly among company papers.* **5** [C] (*NAmE*) a piece of written work done by a student: *Students were asked to read aloud their papers about identity.* ◇ *In the late 1990s, citations to websites first began showing up in students' papers.* **6** [C] (*BrE*) a set of exam questions on a particular subject; the answers that people write to the questions: *Most contract law exam papers contain an orthodox problem question on offer and acceptance.* **7 papers** [pl.] official documents that prove your identity, give you permission to do sth, etc: *Those who had left their papers at home were taken to the police stations.*

IDM **on paper** **1** judged from written information only, but not proved in practice: *On paper these objections look strong.* ◇ *This scheme may be more difficult in practice than it appears on paper.* **2** when you put sth **on paper**, you write it down: *Monarchians left no writings; indeed, there is little sign at all that they put their ideas down on paper.*

▸ ADJECTIVE + PAPER **seminal • influential • classic • scientific • academic • published • unpublished** *In their seminal paper, they argued that it is the presence of both commitment and trust that leads to cooperative behaviour.*

▸ VERB + PAPER **publish • read • submit • draft • write • review • present • deliver** *In 1991, he delivered a conference paper at the Collège de France.*

▸ PAPER + VERB **cover, deal with • explore, examine • focus on • report • outline • propose • argue • demonstrate • reveal • conclude** *This paper demonstrates that there is no best way to manage supply chains.*

para·digm AWL /ˈpærədaɪm/ *noun* **1 ~ (of sth)** (*formal*) a typical example or pattern of sth: *Nigeria stands as the paradigm of a culturally complex African country.* ◇ *Kelsay's contribution serves as a paradigm for those who work in comparative ethics.* **2** (*technical*) a set of ideas that are used to explain how a particular subject should be understood or thought about: *Through much of the past century, the dominant paradigms were those offered by Freud and Marx.* ◇ *There are many instances where the prevailing scientific paradigm has dictated how data are interpreted.* ■ **para·dig·mat·ic** /ˌpærədɪɡˈmætɪk/ *adj.* (*formal* or *technical*) *An individual organism is a paradigmatic case of an autonomous system.*

ˈparadigm shift *noun* **~ (in sth)** a great and important change in the way sth is done or thought about: *This discovery led to a paradigm shift in atmospheric science.*

para·dox /ˈpærədɒks; *NAmE* ˈpærədɑːks/ *noun* **1** [C] a thing, situation or person that has two opposite features and therefore seems strange: **~ of sth** *The paradox of sovereignty is that nation states must be independent, yet must obey international law.* ◇ **~ that...** *There is a seeming paradox that people often feel advertising is untruthful, yet find it a useful source of information.* **2** [C, U] a statement containing two opposite ideas that make it seem impossible or not likely, although it is probably true; the use of this in writing: *It is a work full of paradox and ambiguity.* ■ **para·dox·ical** /ˌpærəˈdɒksɪkl; *NAmE* ˌpærəˈdɑːksɪkl/ *adj.*: *Weiser (2001) comes to the paradoxical conclusion that social uses of the Internet are associated with low social integration.* **para·dox·ic·al·ly** /ˌpærəˈdɒksɪkli; *NAmE* ˌpærəˈdɑːksɪkli/ *adv.*: *Paradoxically, many of the world's hungry people are farm workers or farmers.*

para·graph AWL /ˈpærəɡrɑːf; *NAmE* ˈpærəɡræf/ *noun* (*abbr.* **par.**, **para.**) a section of a piece of writing, usually consisting of several sentences dealing with a single subject. The first sentence of a paragraph starts on a new line: *The opening paragraph defines Islamic family law.* ◇ *The data cited in the previous paragraph suggest that the trend is downward.*

par·al·lel¹ AWL /ˈpærəlel/ *adj.* **1** two or more lines that are **parallel** to each other are the same distance apart at every point: *'Flat' space is space in which parallel lines never meet.* ◇ **~ to/with sth** *The vector is parallel to the x-axis.* **2** very similar; taking place at the same time: *The new policy direction in Britain echoed parallel developments in the United States.* ◇ **~ to sth** *This device plays a role parallel to that of the amplifier.* ■ **par·al·lel** AWL *adv.* **~ (to sth)** *The mountain range runs approximately parallel to the coast.* ◇ *Running parallel to economic transformations have been changes in people's perceptions and lifestyles.*

par·al·lel² AWL /ˈpærəlel/ *noun* **1** [C, U] a person, a situation or an event that is very similar to another, especially one in a different place or time SYN EQUIVALENT²: *The German approach has parallels in Austrian law.* ◇ **~ with sth** *There are strong parallels with the 1930s, when heavy industry and construction were also the hardest hit.* ◇ **without ~** *This is an achievement without parallel in modern times.* **2** [C, usually pl.] **~ between A and B** a comparison between two things: *Morgan and Moss drew parallels between biological and human communities.*

IDM **in ˈparallel (with sth)** with and at the same time as sth else: *All these things are happening in parallel with continuing natural climate change.* ◇ *We ran three experiments in parallel, randomly assigning each moth to only one of the different treatments.*

par·al·lel³ AWL /ˈpærəlel/ *verb* **1 ~ sth** to be similar to sth; to happen at the same time as sth: *The growth of geography in the nineteenth century paralleled that of other social sciences.* ◇ *This decreased equilibrium flexibility is generally paralleled by a decreased dynamic flexibility.* **2** to be the same distance apart from sth at every point: *These stranded ridges of sand and shells parallel the coastline.*

par·am·eter AWL /pəˈræmɪtə(r)/ *noun* [usually pl.] **1** something that decides or limits the way in which sth can be done: *It was employers who defined the parameters, objectives and evaluation criteria for the project.* ◇ **within the... parameters** *The local authority has made its final decision within the legal parameters.* **2** (*technical*) one of a set of factors that can be measured and that defines a system or sets the conditions of its operation: *The key climate parameters that influence this ecosystem are temperature, solar radiation and precipitation.* **3** (*statistics*) a characteristic of a whole population: *We use two different computational methods for estimating demographic parameters:...* HELP A **parameter** is different from a **statistic** of a population. One of the most common parameters measured is the **mean** of a population. **4 ~ (of sth)** (*mathematics*) a value in a function that is not one of the VARIABLES: *By changing the parameters of the quadratic equation, we produce a family of curves with the same form.*

para·mount /ˈpærəmaʊnt/ *adj.* more important than anything else: *Patients' needs are always paramount.* ◇ *The task was of paramount importance.* ◇ **~ in (doing)**

P

sth *The child's welfare was paramount in the decison.* ◇ **~ to sth** *Primary data have been paramount to Google's success.*

para·phrase[1] /ˈpærəfreɪz/ *verb* **~ sb/sth (as...)** to express what sb has said or written using different words, especially in order to make it easier to understand: *Almost half of the book either closely paraphrases or directly quotes de la Borde's treatise.*

para·phrase[2] /ˈpærəfreɪz/ *noun* **~ (of sth)** a statement that expresses sth that sb has written or said using different words, especially in order to make it easier to understand: *Her conclusion seems to be based on a somewhat misleading paraphrase of Wittgenstein's thought.*

para·site /ˈpærəsaɪt/ *noun* **1** a small animal or plant that lives on or inside another animal or plant and gets its food from it: *Infections caused by parasites are often associated with foreign travel.* ◇ *The movement of parasites from one host to another is a risky endeavour.* **2** (*disapproving*) a person who always relies on or benefits from other people and gives nothing back: *The nobility came to be seen as parasites living off the common people.*

para·sit·ic /ˌpærəˈsɪtɪk/ *adj.* **1** caused by a parasite: *Cats are the primary host of this parasitic infection.* **2** living on another animal or plant and getting its food from it: *As predicted, the host birds failed to discriminate the parasitic nestlings.* ◇ **~ on sth/sb** *Plasmodium is parasitic on both mammals and insects.* **3 ~ (on sth/sb)** (*disapproving*) (of a person) always relying on or benefiting from other people and giving nothing back: *The Conservative government elected in 1979 believed that state activity was parasitic on the private sector.*

par·cel /ˈpɑːsl; *NAmE* ˈpɑːrsl/ *noun* **1** (*especially BrE*) (*NAmE usually* **pack·age**) **~ (of sth)** something that is wrapped in paper or put into a thick envelope so that it can be sent by mail, carried easily, or given as a present: *Expatriate families would commonly send parcels of food and clothing to relatives in the home country.* **2** a piece of land: *The woodland was divided into parcels after being under communal ownership.* ◇ **~ of sth** *They have the power to allocate rights to particular parcels of land.* **3 ~ (of sth)** a quantity or amount of sth: *Small parcels of air rising because the atmosphere is unstable result in cumulus clouds.* IDM *see* PART

P

par·ent /ˈpeərənt; *NAmE* ˈperənt/ *noun* **1** [usually pl.] a person's father or mother: *The court ruled that the child should continue living with his adoptive parents.* ◇ *Dependency on tobacco is more than twice as likely in children of parents who smoke.* ➲ *see also* SINGLE PARENT **2** an animal or a plant that produces other animals or plants: *Mendel demonstrated that parents contributed equally to the progeny.* **3** (often used as an adjective) an organization that produces and owns or controls smaller organizations of the same type: **+ noun** *This research has shown that factories owned by larger parent companies were less affected by inspections.*

par·en·tal /pəˈrentl/ *adj.* [usually before noun] connected with a parent or parents: *There were no differences in parental age between the two groups.* ◇ *The court found that significant harm had occurred to the child due to the absence of proper parental care.*

par·en·thesis /pəˈrenθəsɪs/ *noun* (*pl.* **par·en·theses** /pəˈrenθəsiːz/) **1** (*formal* or *NAmE*) [usually pl.] = BRACKET[1] (1): **in parentheses** *The numbers in parentheses indicate percentage increases in previous years.* **2** a word, sentence, etc. that is added to a speech or piece of writing, especially in order to give extra information. In writing, it is separated from the rest of the text using brackets, COMMAS or DASHES: **in ~** *The manuscript also includes, in parenthesis, a recipe for cough syrup.*

par·ent·ing /ˈpeərəntɪŋ; *NAmE* ˈperəntɪŋ/ *noun* [U] the process of caring for your child or children: *Good parenting is associated with higher self-esteem in children.* ◇ **+ noun** *The court ordered an assessment of the mother's parenting skills.*

par·ity /ˈpærəti/ *noun* (*pl.* **-ies**) [U, C] **1** the state of being equal, especially the state of having equal value, pay or status: **~ with sb/sth** *By 1970 the USSR had achieved parity with the USA in numbers of intercontinental ballistic missiles.* ◇ *In the second half of 2008, the euro virtually attained parity with the pound.* ◇ *There must be mutual trust that the exchange rate parities agreed upon will be observed.* ◇ **~ between A and B** *The focus was primarily on parity between immigrants and native Norwegians in terms of social and economic rights.* **2** (*mathematics*) (of a number) the fact of being even or odd: *The identity has n cycles of length 1, so its parity is even.*

park /pɑːk; *NAmE* pɑːrk/ *noun* **1** an area of public land in a town or a city where people go to walk, play and relax: *Many areas in central, southern and eastern London contained no public parks.* **2** (in compounds) an area of land used for a particular purpose: *Rural land was converted into housing estates, shopping centres and industrial parks.* ◇ *The first international efforts to establish wildlife parks and reserves began as early as 1900.*

par·lia·ment /ˈpɑːləmənt; *NAmE* ˈpɑːrləmənt/ *noun* **1** [C, sing.+ sing./pl. v.] the group of people who are elected to make and change the laws of a country: *Compared with national parliaments, the European Parliament does appear weak.* **2 Parliament** [U+sing./pl. v.] the parliament of the United Kingdom, consisting of the House of Commons and the House of Lords: *In 2001, Parliament passed the Anti-terrorism, Crime and Security Act.* ◇ **in ~** *Questions were raised in Parliament.* ➲ *compare* CONGRESS (2) **3** (*also* **Parliament**) [C, U] a particular period during which a parliament is working; Parliament as it exists between one GENERAL ELECTION and the next: *Many politicians are planning to retire at the end of this parliament.* ◇ *In 1983, the Prime Minister dissolved Parliament and called an election.*

par·lia·men·tary /ˌpɑːləˈmentri; *NAmE* ˌpɑːrləˈmentri/ *adj.* [usually before noun] connected with a parliament; having a parliament: *The issue was the subject of extensive parliamentary debate.* ◇ *a parliamentary election/majority* ◇ *The war reinforced the British belief that parliamentary democracy was the best form of government in the world.*

part /pɑːt; *NAmE* pɑːrt/ *noun* **1** [C] a section, piece or feature of sth: *I will argue that there are two parts to this question.* ◇ **~ of sth** *In the first part of the article, I describe the relevant economic literature.* ◇ *This study will investigate whether such joints are the weakest parts of composite structures.* ◇ *Islam frequently forms an integral part of the ethnic identity of immigrant communities.* ◇ **into (...) parts** *This book is divided into three parts.* ◇ **in parts** *The sense that Shakespeare was good in parts, but needed tidying up, continued well into the eighteenth century.* ◇ **as ~ of sth** *The loan was made as part of an agreed structural adjustment programme.* **2** [U] **~ of sth** some but not all of a thing: *Part of the time the baby was with her mother, part of the time with her father.* ◇ *Part of the problem is that the word 'consciousness' is used in different ways.* ◇ *These negative images tell only part of the complex story of Africa's recent political evolution.* **3** [C] **~ (of sth)** an area or a region of the world, a country, a town, etc: *Of course, the concept of democracy is understood differently in different parts of the world.* ◇ *In 1945, the former Japanese parts of Sakhalin were absorbed into the USSR.* ◇ *These rocks are common in the western part of the Grand Canyon region.* **4** [C] a piece of a machine or structure: *Engine modifications resulted in much better dynamic performance for the moving parts.* **5** [C] **~ (of sth)** a separate piece or area of a human or animal body or of a plant: *The*

relaxation exercise involves tensing and relaxing the parts of the body. **6** [U] **~ of sth** a member of sth; a person or thing that, together with others, makes up a single unit: *These are critical issues for anyone working as part of a community mental health team.* ◇ *The project enabled residents to feel part of the community.* **7** [C, usually sing., U] **~ (in sth)** the way in which sb/sth is involved in an action or situation: *Kryuchkov was arrested for his part in the August coup.* **8** [C] a unit of measurement that allows you to compare the different amounts of substances in sth: *1 700 g of a simple syrup solution consisting of equal parts (1350 g) water and granulated sugar were then added to the extract.* ◇ *By 1950 the level of carbon dioxide in the atmosphere had increased to 300 parts per million.*
IDM **the best/better part of sth** most of sth, especially a period of time; more than half of sth: *The system put in place by the 1904 Act endured for the best part of a century.* **for ˈtheir, ˈhis, ˈmy, etc. part** as far as sb/you is/are concerned: *The government, for their part, aim to maximize revenues from the country's hydrocarbon resources.* **have a part to ˈplay (in sth)** to be able to help to achieve sth: *All countries have a part to play in protecting the environment.* **in ˈpart** partly; to some extent: *The project failure can in part be explained by inefficient resource allocation.* **on the part of sb/sth | on sb/sth's part** made or done by sb: *There was a reluctance on the part of consumers to deal with a foreign company.* **part and parcel of sth** an essential part of sth: *Tourism is now part and parcel of contemporary society.* **play/have a, their, etc. ˈpart (in sth)** to be involved in sth: *Governments are still expected to play a part in the financing of education.* **play/take/have no ˈpart in sth** to not be involved in sth: *The legality test plays no part in the assessment process.* ◇ *Piso took no part in the new regime until 23 BCE.* **take ˈpart (in sth)** to be involved in sth SYN PARTICIPATE: *After treatment, 75% of the children were able to take part in lessons.* ➲ *more at* GREAT, LARGE, SUM[1]

▸ ADJECTIVE + PART **large, substantial, significant, major • main, central • small** *In 64, a massive fire destroyed a large part of the city.* | **important • vital, crucial, essential, key • integral • constituent, component** *Working as a team, therefore, is an essential part of nursing.* | **early • final • latter** *Rural population numbers began to climb from the early part of the 20th century.* | **active** *Learning is a constructive process in which students take an active part.*

▸ VERB + PART **become • form • remain • occupy • cover • constitute, comprise • represent • spend • devote • explain** *All ancient texts remain part of a larger cultural context which is different from our own.* ◇ *Eventually, the Europeans occupied parts of Syria and Palestine.* | **have • contain • share • remove • replace** *The trend in all these industries is towards replacing heavier metal parts with lighter plastic parts.* | **reach • affect** *Infections can affect almost any part of the human body.*

▸ VERB + STH AS (A) PART OF STH **see, consider, view, regard • accept • treat • undertake • conduct • collect** *Humboldt insisted on seeing humans as a part of nature, not separate from it.*

par·tial /ˈpɑːʃl; *NAmE* ˈpɑːrʃl/ *adj.* **1** not complete or whole: *These measures are only a partial solution.* ◇ *These findings lend partial support to the social polarization thesis.* **2** [not usually before noun] showing or feeling too much support for one person, team, idea, etc, in a way that is unfair SYN BIASED (2): *De Mortillet founded several journals that were extremely partial, overpraising the work of his pupils and ignoring other scholars.* OPP IMPARTIAL

par·tial·ly /ˈpɑːʃəli; *NAmE* ˈpɑːrʃəli/ *adv.* partly; not completely: *The problem was partially addressed through the adoption of a more flexible strategy.* ◇ *Many of the drainage systems were partially blocked by dunes (Williams and Adamson, 1974).* ◇ *The attempt was only partially successful.*

par·tici·pant AWL /pɑːˈtɪsɪpənt; *NAmE* pɑːrˈtɪsɪpənt/ *noun* **~ (in sth)** a person who is taking part in an activity or event: *Patients need to be active participants in decisions about their care.* ◇ *The general agreement among research participants indicates that they all used similar strategies.*

▸ ADJECTIVE + PARTICIPANT **active • female • male • older • younger • adult • potential • eligible • prospective • full** *Five hospitals were contacted and asked to help in identifying potential participants.*

▸ NOUN + PARTICIPANT **research • study • project • trial • focus group** *Interviewees and focus group participants were given the same discussion topics.*

▸ VERB + PARTICIPANT **recruit • select • invite • ask, instruct, require • tell, inform • engage • involve • enable • allow • encourage • help** *Participants were asked to keep records of every instance of mobile phone use.*

▸ PARTICIPANT + VERB **receive • read • complete • tend • learn • experience • feel • view • rate • report, note, state, indicate, express • respond • speak • agree** *Experiences reported by Irish participants are broadly in accordance with previous research.*

par·tici·pate AWL /pɑːˈtɪsɪpeɪt; *NAmE* pɑːrˈtɪsɪpeɪt/ *verb* [I] **~ (in sth)** to take part in or become involved in an activity: *Internet users were invited to participate in an online study.* ◇ *Lack of resources prevents many states from participating fully in international agreements.* ◇ *Women actively participated in these groups.*

> **WORD FAMILY**
> participate *verb*
> participation *noun*
> participant *noun*
> participatory *adj.*

par·tici·pa·tion AWL /pɑːˌtɪsɪˈpeɪʃn; *NAmE* pɑːrˌtɪsɪˈpeɪʃn/ *noun* [U] the act of taking part in an activity or event: *Active political participation is limited across the region.* ◇ **~ in sth** *The company encouraged staff participation in decision-making.*

par·tici·pa·tory AWL /pɑːˌtɪsɪˈpeɪtəri; *NAmE* pɑːrˈtɪsəpətɔːri/ *adj.* [usually before noun] allowing everyone in a group or activity to give their opinions and to help make decisions: *76% of respondents cite the party's emphasis on participatory democracy as a reason for becoming a party member.*

par·ti·ciple /pɑːˈtɪsɪpl; *NAmE* ˈpɑːrtəsɪpl/ *noun* (*grammar*) (in English) a word formed from a verb, ending in *-ing* (= the **present participle**) or *-ed, -en*, etc. (= the **past participle**): *Participles can sometimes be used as attributive adjectives: the sleeping child, the leaning tower.*

par·ticle /ˈpɑːtɪkl; *NAmE* ˈpɑːrtɪkl/ *noun* **1** (*also* ˌ**elementary ˈparticle**, ˌ**subatomic ˈparticle**) (*physics*) a very small piece of matter, such as an ELECTRON or PROTON: *Electrical conduction is a phenomenon caused by a flow of charged particles.* **2** a very small piece of sth: *The vapour condenses on small particles such as dust.* ◇ **~ of sth** *Water running over the surface of the ground carries particles of clay, silt and fine sand.* **3** (*grammar*) an adverb or a preposition that can combine with a verb to make a phrasal verb: *In 'She tore up the letter', the word 'up' is a particle.*

par·ticu·lar[1] /pəˈtɪkjələ(r); *NAmE* pərˈtɪkjələr/ *adj.* [only before noun] **1** used to emphasize that you are referring to one individual person, thing or type of thing and not others SYN SPECIFIC (1): *Participants met to plan a course that would meet the needs of this particular community.* ◇ *this particular case/instance/situation/context* ◇ *Nationalism is created and experienced in particular historical circumstances.* ◇ *Some predators focus their energy on a particular type of prey, while others show much greater diversity.* **2** greater than usual; special: *The latest findings are of particular interest.* ◇ *to be of particular relevance/*

P

importance/concern ◇ *I will pay particular attention to gender and class as forces shaping these negotiations.*

IDM **in parˈticular** **1** especially or particularly: *Of the various models put forward, two in particular stand out.* ◇ *There are still a few gaps in the research. In particular, it is not yet clear how profitable the technique has been.* **2** special SYN SPECIFIC (1): *Ruth does not like school but cannot identify anything in particular that upsets her while she is there.* ➲ *more at* NOTE²

par·ticu·lar² /pəˈtɪkjələ(r); *NAmE* pərˈtɪkjələr/ *noun* **1** [C, usually pl.] a fact or detail, especially one that is officially written down: *He argues that God has knowledge of generalities but not particulars.* ◇ **particulars of sb/sth** *It was suggested that the different tests could be applied according to the particulars of the case.* ◇ **in every ~** *No case of a disease is exactly like every other case in every particular.* **2 particulars** [pl.] written information and details about a property, business, job, etc: *There was no ambiguity or misrepresentation in the sale particulars.* ◇ **particulars of sth** *All employees must have a written statement of the main particulars of employment within two months of their start date.*

par·ticu·lar·ity /pəˌtɪkjuˈlærəti; *NAmE* pərˌtɪkjuˈlærəti/ *noun* (*pl.* **-ies**) **1** [U] **~ (of sb/sth)** the quality of being individual or UNIQUE: *Geertz has a keen interest in the particularity of each culture he interprets.* **2** [U] attention to detail; the quality of being exact: *Parties must present their case with some degree of accuracy and particularity.* **3 particularities (of sth)** [pl.] the special features or details of sth: *Multinational firms are notably secretive about the particularities of these strategies.*

par·ticu·lar·ly /pəˈtɪkjələli; *NAmE* pərˈtɪkjələrli/ *adv.* especially; more than usual or more than others: *Proper product labelling is particularly important in the food, pharmaceutical and cosmetic industries.* ◇ *The fact that many societies have stories about talking animals is not particularly surprising.* ◇ *We were particularly interested in discovering the views of the local community.* ◇ *The patient reported pain, particularly at night.*

P

par·ticu·late /pɑːˈtɪkjələt; pɑːˈtɪkjuleɪt; *NAmE* pɑːrˈtɪkjələt; pɑːrˈtɪkjəleɪt/ *adj.* connected with, or in the form of, particles: *Air is normally drawn through filters to collect the particulate matter, which may then be analysed.*

par·ticu·lates / *NAmE* pɑːrˈtɪkjəleɪts/ *noun* [pl.] matter in the form of particles: *Diesel produces more particulates than petrol.*

par·ti·tion¹ /pɑːˈtɪʃn; *NAmE* pɑːrˈtɪʃn/ *noun* **1** [U] **~ (of sth)** the division of one country into two or more countries: *The partition of India in 1947 caused the movement of about 16 million people across the new borders.* **2** [C] a wall or screen that separates one part of a room or container from another: *Leong divided an aquarium into two parts using a glass partition.*

par·ti·tion² /pɑːˈtɪʃn; *NAmE* pɑːrˈtɪʃn/ *verb* [often passive] to divide sth into parts: **~ sth (between A and B)** *In 1939, it was agreed that Poland would be partitioned between Germany and Russia.* ◇ **~ sth into sth** *The data set was partitioned into separate training and test sets.*

part·ly /ˈpɑːtli; *NAmE* ˈpɑːrtli/ *adv.* to some extent; not completely: *Different data sources have produced different results, partly as a result of differences in recording practices and partly because of different definitions.* ◇ *These differences in mortality rates may be partly explained by socio-economic factors.* ◇ *Nuclear power is likely to increase, at least partly in response to concerns about global warming.*

part·ner¹ AWL /ˈpɑːtnə(r); *NAmE* ˈpɑːrtnər/ *noun* **1** the person that sb is married to or having a sexual relationship with: *Immigration rules on married partners have been amended to include civil partners.* ◇ *Kevin was able to find his ideal partner through online dating.* HELP Note that using the term **partner** allows you to avoid mentioning whether the person is married or not or whether they are male or female. **2** one of the people who owns a business and shares the profits, etc: *The assets of the firm are owned directly by the partners.* ◇ *She is the senior partner in an advertising firm.* **3** a country, a business or an organization that has an agreement with another country or organization: *The EU, the United States and Japan are China's three most important trading partners.* ◇ *Foreign firms were not authorized to own land, and needed to find a local partner in order to secure land rights.* ◇ **+ noun** *Services are often jointly marketed by the partner airlines.* **4** a person that you are doing an activity with, such as dancing or playing a game: *Astaire may dance by himself, with a partner, or with a company of dancers.* ◇ *Students thought individually on a given topic, then took turns to exchange ideas with their partners.* **5** (*biology*) either of a breeding pair of birds or animals: *Producing strong signals to attract sexual partners exposes the sender to exploitation by predators.*

part·ner² AWL /ˈpɑːtnə(r); *NAmE* ˈpɑːrtnər/ *verb* [T, I] to be the partner of sb/sth; to make two people, organizations, etc. become partners: **~ (with) sb/sth** *Small biotechnology firms may partner large pharmaceutical companies.* ◇ **~ A with B** *By partnering schools with community organizations, students will benefit through increased knowledge of world events and other subjects.*

part·ner·ship AWL /ˈpɑːtnəʃɪp; *NAmE* ˈpɑːrtnərʃɪp/ *noun* **1** [U] **(in/into) ~ (with sb/sth)** the state of being a partner in business: *Some UK universities have gone into partnership with Chinese colleges and universities.* ◇ *Companies offered to work in partnership with the government towards reducing greenhouse gas emissions.* **2** [C, U] a relationship between two people, organizations, etc; the state of having this relationship: *Immunization services in the city are provided through a public-private partnership.* ◇ **~ with sb/sth** *The EU has forged new partnerships with a variety of non-EU countries.* ◇ **~ between A and B** *Obama promised a new era of partnership between America and her allies.* ➲ *see also* CIVIL PARTNERSHIP **3** [C] a business owned by two or more people who share the profits HELP A **partnership** is usually a business that offers a professional service, such as a law firm or a medical practice: *Establishing a partnership is very simple and can amount to an agreement between people to form a business with a common goal.* ◇ **+ noun** *A new partnership agreement should be drawn up every time a new partner joins a practice.*

ˌpart of ˈspeech *noun* (*grammar*) one of the classes into which words are divided according to their grammar, such as noun, verb, adjective, etc: *Headwords in the dictionary are followed by an indication of part of speech.*

ˌpart-ˈtime *adj.* [usually before noun] for part of the day or week in which people work: *Women constituted 80% of all persons in part-time employment in 2000.* ◇ *part-time workers/jobs* ➲ *compare* FULL-TIME ■ **ˌpart-ˈtime** *adv.*: *Only a minority of the physicians worked part-time.*

party /ˈpɑːti; *NAmE* ˈpɑːrti/ *noun* (*pl.* **-ies**) **1** (*also* **Party**) [C+sing./pl. v.] a political organization that you can vote for in elections and whose members have the same aims and ideas: *This book analyses the development of political parties in four Central and Eastern European countries.* ◇ **~ of sb/sth** *The Labour Party was seen as the party of the working class.* ◇ **+ noun** *He was perceived to be a weak and ineffective party leader.* **2** [C] (especially in compounds) a social occasion, often in a person's home, at which people eat, drink, talk, dance, etc: *She refuses to attend play dates or birthday parties if one of her parents cannot be there.* **3** [C] one of the people or groups of people involved in a legal agreement or argument: *Both parties* *were seeking sole custody of their two children.* ◇ *Interested parties can submit information before the inquiry.* ➲ *see also* INJURED PARTY, THIRD PARTY **4** [C+sing./pl. v.] **~ (of sb)** a group of people who are doing sth together, such as travelling or visiting somewhere: *Each box could seat a small party of spectators.* ➲ *see also* WORKING GROUP

IDM **be (a) party to sth** to be involved in an agreement or action: *He was party to the discussions leading up to the creation of the new European currency.*

pass[1] /pɑːs; *NAmE* pæs/ *verb* **1** [T, I] **~ (sb/sth)** to move past or to the other side of sb/sth: *When a warm front passes a particular location, the air mass will change from cold to warm.* ◇ *A patient who has a cardiac arrest on a hospital corridor is owed a duty of care by any doctor who happens to be passing.* **2** [I] **+ adv./prep.** to go or move in the direction mentioned: *When light passes through the air, a certain amount of the light is scattered by the dust particles.* **3** [T] **~ sth + adv./prep.** to make sth move in the direction or into the position mentioned: *Cell cultures that are contaminated with bacteria should be passed through a bacterial filter.* **4** [T] to give sth to sb by putting it into their hands or in a place where they can easily reach it: **~ sth to sb** *The information will not be passed to a third party without the express permission of the respondent.* ◇ **~ sb sth** *I passed him the leaflet and asked him to take some time to digest the information I had given him.* **5** [I] **~ to sb** to be given to another person after first belonging to sb else, especially after the first person has died: *On his death, the throne passed to his son, Henry V.* ◇ *Power passed from generation to generation.* **6** [T] **~ sth** (of an amount) to become greater than a particular total SYN EXCEED (1): *The reported global inland fish catch passed 10 million tonnes in 2008.* ◇ *That was the decade in which the population passed 4 billion.* **7** [I] **~ from sth to/into sth** to change from one state or condition to another: *The business cycle generally runs its course, passing from expansion to recession and back to expansion in anything from 3 to 10 years.* **8** [I] (of time) to go by: *Almost exactly a decade had passed since the last major firestorm in southern California.* **9** [I] to come to an end; to be over: *They waited for the storm to pass.* **10** [T, I] **~ (sth)** to accept a proposal or law by voting; to be accepted: *Legislation was passed at the state and national levels to protect forests.* ◇ *to pass a law/an Act of Parliament/a resolution/a bill* ◇ *The ordinance passed without dissent.* **11** [I, T] to achieve the required standard in an exam or a test: *Most of the candidates passed.* ◇ **~ sth** *The proportion passing five English school-leaving exams (in different subjects) at age 16 ranged from 43% to 56%.* ◇ *The position of the UK government was that five tests must be passed before the UK would join the euro.* OPP FAIL (5) **12** [T] **~ sb** to test sb and decide that they are good enough, according to an agreed standard: *Academic institutions are there to pass students, rather than fail them, as a high pass rate reflects well on the teaching of the university.* OPP FAIL (5) **13** [I] to happen; to be said or done: *The whole nation wanted to know what passed weekly in Germany and Poland and all other parts of Europe.* ◇ **~ between A and B** *Sorting out what actually went on and what passed between the parties is particularly difficult.* ◇ **+ adj.** *Tsunamis generally pass unnoticed at sea.* **14** [T] **~ sth** to say or state sth, especially officially: *Having found the defendant guilty, the judge passed sentence.* ◇ *He aimed to discourage provincial corruption by preventing senators from passing judgement on their peers.* **15** [T] **~ sth** to send sth out from the body as or with waste matter: *He is concerned that he is often thirsty and passes urine more frequently.*

IDM **ˌcome to ˈpass** to happen: *Not all of the changes he had wished to see in England had come to pass.*

PHR V **ˌpass sth aˈround/ˈround** (*BrE*) to give sth to another person, who gives it to sb else, etc. until everyone has seen it: *One family member would write on behalf of others, and letters would be passed around or read aloud.* **ˈpass as sb/sth** = PASS FOR/AS SB/STH **ˌpass aˈway** to die. People say 'pass away' to avoid saying 'die': *He passed away in January 2010.* **ˌpass ˈby (sb/sth)** to go past: *For this thought experiment, he imagined a passenger on a train watching another train pass by.* **ˌpass sth ˈdown** [often passive] to give or teach sth to your children or people younger than you, who will then give or teach it to those who live after them, and so on SYN HAND STH DOWN (FROM SB) (TO SB) (1): *Traditional songs and ballads had been passed down through rural communities for many years.* **ˈpass for/as sb/sth** to be accepted as sb/sth: *One of our interviewees survived the war as a child, away from their family, by passing as a non-Jew.* ◇ (*disapproving*) *What passes for marketing may be little more than an attempt to bring best practice to their operations.* **ˈpass into sth** to become a part of sth: *Some of the concepts of European mechanics passed into the Chinese language.* **ˌpass sb/yourself/sth ˈoff as sb/sth** to pretend that sb/sth is sth they are not: *Younger employees who could pass themselves off as Bolshevik sympathizers found themselves promoted over the heads of others.* **ˌpass sth ˈon (to sb)** **1** to give sth to sb else, especially after receiving it or using it yourself: *There is little by way of inherited wealth to pass on.* ◇ *Classified documents had been passed on to him.* **2** (of a disease, a medical condition or a characteristic) to give sth to your children through your GENES: *Traits of parents tend to be passed on to their offspring.* **3** to make a customer pay for the cost of sth: *Companies would need to absorb the price increase or try to pass it on to customers.* **ˌpass ˈout** to become unconscious: *Mr Williams remembers feeling unwell and dizzy before passing out.* **ˌpass ˈover sth** to ignore or avoid sth SYN OVERLOOK (1): *This section fills in some of the details which were passed over in the earlier discussion.* **ˌpass ˈthrough (sth)** to go through a town, etc, stopping there for a short time but not staying: *On an ordinary day at the temple, 20 000 to 25 000 visitors may pass through.*

pass[2] /pɑːs; *NAmE* pæs/ *noun* **1** (*especially BrE*) a successful result in an exam: *The aim is to raise the number of pupils attaining five higher-grade passes.* ◇ **+ noun** *The answers are marked, with 17 correct answers constituting the minimum pass mark.* **2** an official document or ticket that shows that you have the right to enter or leave a place, to travel on a bus or train, etc: *Commuters purchase and print their own bus pass online.* ◇ *With the annual pass, lobbyists can enter the Parliament's buildings.* **3** a road or way over or through mountains: *Local supporters guided the rebels through the mountain passes.* **4** a stage in a process, especially one that involves separating things from a larger group: *The first pass in the statistical analysis was to determine whether there was a statistically significant change.* **5** an act of going or moving past or over sth: *On each pass, the satellite scans and measures large areas of the earth's surface.*

P

pas·sage /ˈpæsɪdʒ/ *noun* **1** [C] a short section from a book, other piece of writing or a piece of music SYN EXCERPT, EXTRACT[2] (1): *The passages quoted here are from articles that Gavin Stamp contributed to 'The Spectator'.* ◇ *The participants were instructed to read the three test passages.* **2** [C] a tube in the body through which air, gas or liquid passes: *In the lung, air passages lead to minute pockets, the alveoli.* ◇ *The tube is designed to be inserted into the nasal passage to secure an airway.* **3** (*also* **pas·sage·way** /ˈpæsɪdʒweɪ/) [C] a long narrow area with walls on either side that connects one room or place with another: *Most people in Rome were buried in underground passages cut into the soft stone that lay under the city.* ➲ *compare* CORRIDOR (1) **4** [sing.] **the ~ of time** the process of time passing: *Software will not deteriorate with the passage of time.* **5** [sing.] **~ (of sth) through sth** the process of discussing a BILL in a parliament so that it can become law: *The Scottish Bill had a fairly smooth passage through Parliament.* **6** [C, U] **(+ adv./prep.)** a journey from one place to another by ship; a ticket for such a journey: *These men would agree to work for a master for, say, four years to pay for their passage across the Atlantic.* **7** [U] **~ (of sth) (+ adv./prep.)** the action of going across, through or past sth: *The camera follows his elegant passage across the crowded dance floor.* ◇ *The channel allows the free movement of potassium ions through the pore but blocks the passage of sodium ions.* **8** [sing.] **~ across/through sth** a way through sth, especially when this is difficult: *To help Czechoslovakia, the Red Army would have needed to force a passage across Poland.* **9** [U, C, usually sing.] permission to travel across a particular area of land: *Often, disaster victims require shelter, food and water in addition to safe passage back to their communities.* **10** [sing.] **~ from A to/into B** a change from one state or condition to another: *The post-industrial phase involves a passage from industrial society to a society where the service sector dominates.* IDM *see* RITE

pas·sen·ger /ˈpæsɪndʒə(r)/ *noun* a person who is travelling in a car, bus, train, plane or ship and who is not driving it or working on it: *The airline carries approximately 30 000 passengers each year.* ◇ **+ noun** *Amtrak operates most of the nation's passenger trains.*

pass·ing /ˈpɑːsɪŋ; *NAmE* ˈpæsɪŋ/ *noun* [U] **1 the ~ of time/the years** the process of time going by: *Consumers' tastes change with the passing of time.* **2 ~ (of sb/sth)** the fact of sth ending or of sb dying: *The poem is more than a conventional lament for the passing of youth and beauty.* ◇ *Within a couple of centuries of his passing, partial accounts of his life began to appear.* **3 the ~ of sth** the act of making sth become a law: *There are restrictions on the ability of the House of Lords to prevent the passing of legislation.* IDM **in passing** done or said while you are giving your attention to sth else: *It is worth noting in passing that in 1917 Einstein himself for a time entertained a related idea.*

P

pas·sion /ˈpæʃn/ *noun* **1** [U, C] a very strong feeling of love, anger, enthusiasm, etc: *Research is always driven by passion: to know, to challenge, to prove, to disprove.* ◇ *Godwin's essay delves intensely into human passions and unveils the psyche's deepest truths.* **2** [U] a very strong feeling of sexual love: *It would not be long before questions of love and passion also became central to the novel in India.* ◇ **~ for sb** *This memoir tells the story of his passion for the daughter of his landlady.* **3** [C, usually sing.] **~ (for sth)** a very strong feeling of liking sth: *Frederick Lanchester was an automobile engineer and industrialist with a passion for aeronautics.*

pas·sion·ate /ˈpæʃənət/ *adj.* **1** having or showing strong feelings of sexual love or of anger, etc: *In widespread medieval understanding, passionate love was a disease of the soul.* **2** having or showing strong feelings of enthusiasm for sth or belief in sth: *She demonstrated a passionate commitment to justice.* ◇ **~ about sth** *The Italian Futurists were passionate about new technology, aeroplanes and fast cars.* ■ **pas·sion·ate·ly** *adv.*: *They argue passionately for a system based on trust and responsibility.*

pas·sive[1] AWL /ˈpæsɪv/ *adj.* **1** accepting what happens or what people do without trying to change anything or oppose them: *Rather than being a passive recipient of feedback from the teacher, each student plays an active part in the assessment process.* OPP ACTIVE[1] (1) **2** (*grammar*) connected with the form of a verb used when the subject is affected by the action of the verb, for example, 'The study was conducted by two researchers' is a passive sentence: *Researchers have found that passive sentences take longer to process correctly.* ➲ *compare* ACTIVE[1] (8)

pas·sive[2] AWL /ˈpæsɪv/ (*also* ˌ**passive** ˈ**voice**) *noun* (*often* **the passive (voice)**) [sing.] (*grammar*) the form of a verb used when the subject is affected by the action of the verb: *A search returns a list of sixty languages where the English translation contains a passive.* ◇ **in the ~** *All statements were written in the passive voice.* ➲ *compare* ACTIVE[2]

pas·sive·ly AWL /ˈpæsɪvli/ *adv.* by accepting what happens without reacting or trying to fight against it: *These people tend to behave passively in social relationships.* ◇ *The challenge was to make the consumer actively select milk, rather than just passively consume it out of habit.* OPP ACTIVELY (1)

pas·siv·ity AWL /pæˈsɪvəti/ *noun* [U] the state of accepting what happens without reacting or trying to fight against it: *Not all the women conformed to the cultural stereotype of passivity.*

past[1] /pɑːst; *NAmE* pæst/ *adj.* **1** gone by in time: *In past centuries, Buddhism made historic contributions to Chinese culture.* ◇ *In times past, cholera has been responsible for a number of major pandemics.* **2** [only before noun] gone by recently; just ended: *She has probably been losing weight for the past few months.* ◇ *38.7% of respondents reported eating at least five servings of fruits and vegetables in the past day.* ➲ language bank *at* TIME[1] **3** [only before noun] belonging to an earlier time: *Economic policy is often based on past experience.* ◇ *Past events in the family may help to explain the patient's concerns.* ◇ *Managers must learn from past mistakes and failure.* **4** [only before noun] (*grammar*) connected with the form of a verb used to express actions in the past: *Grammatical features included tenses (present continuous, past continuous and future simple) and modal verbs.*

past[2] /pɑːst; *NAmE* pæst/ *noun* **1** (*usually* **the past**) [sing.] the time that has gone by; things that happened in an earlier time: *In the past, treatment involved radical surgery.* ◇ *the recent/distant past* ◇ **a thing of the ~** *It appears that the small family farm is a thing of the past.* ◇ **a break with the ~** *During its first term, the government did not make a break with the past.* **2** [C] a person's past life or career, especially when this was difficult or included secrets: *He was unable to come to terms with the ghosts of his past.* **3 the past** [sing.] (*grammar*) = PAST TENSE

past[3] /pɑːst; *NAmE* pæst/ *prep.* **1** (*NAmE also* **after**) later than sth: *At about half past two in the afternoon, there was an earthquake which lasted about two minutes.* ◇ *Hawks went on working past the November date when the original schedule indicated completion.* **2** above or further than a particular point or stage: *Only approximately 1% of these salmon survive past the larval stage.* ◇ *Some 100 million European online shoppers spent an average of €1 000 each, driving online retailing past the €100 billion mark.* **3** on or to the other side of sb/sth: *The defendant was seen riding a motorcycle past the post office.*

past[4] /pɑːst; *NAmE* pæst/ *adv.* **1** used to describe time passing SYN BY[2] (1): *Several months had gone past.* **2** from one side of sth to the other: *The sample was selected by asking every fifth person who walked past to take part in the investigation.*

ˌ**past parˈticiple** (*BrE*) (*NAmE* ˌ**past** ˈ**participle**) *noun* (*grammar*) the form of a verb that in English ends in *-ed*, *-en*, etc. and is used with the verb *have* to form PERFECT tenses such as *I have eaten*, with the verb *be* to form passive sentences such as *It was destroyed*, or sometimes as an adjective as in *an upset stomach*: *With a small number of verbs, the past participle is the same as the base form (come/came/come).* ➲ *compare* PRESENT PARTICIPLE

the ˌ**past** ˈ**perfect** (*also* **the** ˌ**past** ˌ**perfect** ˈ**tense**) *noun* [sing.] (*grammar*) the form of a verb that expresses an action completed before a particular point in the past, formed in English with *had* and the past participle: *The past perfect tense ('had wrung') effects the time shift in the narrative.*

the ˌ**past** ˈ**tense** (*also* **the past**) *noun* [sing.] (*grammar*) the form of a verb used to describe actions in the past: *It is* *notable that fictional narratives—novels, stories, jokes—are usually told in the past tense.*

patch /pætʃ/ *noun* **1 ~ (of sth)** a small area of sth, especially one that is different from the area around it: *A small patch of woodland may consist of areas of closed canopy or open glades.* ◇ *The disease is characterized by thick patches of inflamed red skin covered with thick silvery scales.* ◇ *Food patches are attractive to females as the best place to lay their eggs.* **2** a piece of material that people can wear on their skin so that a drug or other substance can be absorbed gradually over a period of time: *Nicotine patches for smoking cessation were introduced in 1991.*

pa·tent[1] /ˈpætnt; *BrE also* ˈpeɪtnt/ *noun* [C, U] an official right to be the only person to make, use or sell a product or an invention; a document that proves this: *Patents are granted for technologies with commercial promise.* ◇ *The data contain patents from 84 patent offices, including patents filed in developing countries.* ◇ **+ noun** *A patent holder's bargaining power depends mostly on a patent's economic value.*

pa·tent[2] /ˈpætnt; *BrE also* ˈpeɪtnt/ *verb* **~ sth** to obtain a patent for an invention or a process: *Some US universities were patenting faculty inventions as early as the 1920s.* ◇ *The owner of a patented technology may have additional market power.*

pa·ter·nal /pəˈtɜːnl; *NAmE* pəˈtɜːrnl/ *adj.* **1** connected with being a father: *Greater paternal involvement has been associated with children having better health-related quality of life.* ◇ *The cells contain two copies of each chromosome, one maternal and one paternal.* ➲ *compare* MATERNAL (1) **2** behaving in a way that is typical of a kind father: *He is old enough to be her father and assumes a paternal role.* ➲ *compare* MATERNAL (2) **3** [only before noun] related through the father's side of the family: *He reminded her of her paternal grandfather.* ➲ *compare* MATERNAL (3) ■ **pa·ter·nal·ly** /pəˈtɜːnli; *NAmE* pəˈtɜːrnli/ *adv.*: *In most women, the paternally and maternally derived X chromosomes are each active in approximately 50% of cells.*

pa·ter·nity /pəˈtɜːnəti; *NAmE* pəˈtɜːrnəti/ *noun* [U] **~ (of sb)** the fact of being the father of a child: *The applicant sought blood and DNA tests to determine the paternity of the child.* ➲ *compare* MATERNITY

path /pɑːθ; *NAmE* pæθ/ *noun* (*pl.* **paths** /pɑːðz; *NAmE* pæðz/) **1** a way or track that is built or is made by the action of people walking: *The statue is in a small park with paths, trees and shrubs.* ◇ *All six men left the path and disappeared into the forest.* **2** [usually sing.] a line along which sb/sth moves; the space in front of sb/sth as they move: *The bird's flight path took it from one side of the lawn to the other.* ◇ *There is no defence against such a wall of water; everything in its path was completely destroyed.* ➲ *compare* WAY (2) **3** (*also* **path·way**) a way of achieving sth: *Kenya has a well-developed tourist industry, and other African countries are seeking to follow a similar path.* ◇ **~ to/towards sth** *School success is not necessarily a clear path to a better life.* ◇ *One common career path is from salesperson to district sales manager to top sales management.* **4 ~ (to sth)** (*computing*) the LOGICAL location of a file or DIRECTORY: *The path to the documents directory is C:\Users\username\Documents.*

patho·gen /ˈpæθədʒən/ *noun* (*medical*) a thing, such as a virus, that causes disease: *Candida is one of the ten most common pathogens isolated from blood cultures.* ◇ *There is a massive range of bacterial and fungal pathogens that infect humans.* ◇ **+ noun** *Naturally acquired immunity will often have little impact on pathogen evolution.* ■ **patho·gen·ic** /ˌpæθəˈdʒenɪk/ *adj.*: *37°C is higher than the optimal temperature for a number of pathogenic bacteria.*

patho·gen·esis /ˌpæθəˈdʒenɪsɪs/ *noun* **~ (of sth)** (*medical*) the way in which a disease develops: *The role of these antibodies in the pathogenesis of the disease remains uncertain.*

patho·logic·al /ˌpæθəˈlɒdʒɪkl; *NAmE* ˌpæθəˈlɑːdʒɪkl/ *adj.* **1** (*medical*) caused by, or connected with, disease or illness: *There are several pathological processes that can only be examined using electron microscopy.* ◇ *A number of pathological conditions result in low concentrations of albumin in the blood.* **2** (*medical*) connected with the scientific study of the causes and effects of diseases: *Pathological studies have shown an association between hypertension and Alzheimer's disease.* **3** not reasonable or sensible; impossible to control: *Pathological anxiety is a feeling of apprehension that is out of proportion to the actual situation.* ■ **patho·logic·al·ly** /ˌpæθəˈlɒdʒɪkli; *NAmE* ˌpæθəˈlɑːdʒɪkli/ *adv.*: *These disorders are pathologically distinct, but sometimes difficult to distinguish clinically.*

path·ology /pəˈθɒlədʒi; *NAmE* pəˈθɑːlədʒi/ *noun* **1** [U] (*medical*) the scientific study of the causes and effects of diseases: *Although knowledge of physiology and pathology is a necessary condition for competent medical practice, it is not sufficient.* ◇ **+ noun** *Every area of pathology laboratory testing is subject to regulation and inspection.* **2** [U] **~ (of sth)** (*medical*) the typical behaviour of a disease: *The first half of the book provides background into the pathology of Alzheimer's disease and risk factors.* **3** [U, C] (*medical*) a disease or medical condition: *Hip pathology may present as knee pain.* ◇ *The relationship between disabilities and underlying pathologies is complex.* **4** [C] an aspect of sb's behaviour that is extreme and unreasonable and that they cannot control: *Children who have endured such hardships are more prone to violence and other pathologies.* ◇ **~ of sth** *Klemperer's World War II diary offered acute observations about the pathology of Nazi Germany.*

path·way /ˈpɑːθweɪ; *NAmE* ˈpæθweɪ/ *noun* **1** = PATH (3): *It is important to uncover the pathways by which families came to inherit their current circumstances.* **2** (*biology*) a route, formed by a series of NERVE cells, along which signals of a particular kind usually travel: *The molecules activate signalling pathways.* ◇ *Some moral judgements involve the activation of different neural pathways.* **3** (*also* ˌ**metabolic** ˈ**pathway**) (*biochemistry*) a series of chemical reactions, usually controlled by ENZYMES, which follows a route of change from one COMPOUND to another within the cells or body of a living thing: *The metabolic pathway from pyruvate to glucose has to overcome three energy barriers.*

pa·tience /ˈpeɪʃns/ *noun* [U] **1** the ability to stay calm and accept delay, problems or suffering without complaining: **lose ~ with sb/sth** *The government may lose patience with the competition authorities.* ◇ **have little/no ~ for/with sth** *As a historian, he had little patience for general theories.* **2** the ability to spend a lot of time doing sth difficult that needs a lot of attention and effort: *Ruth demonstrated great patience and skill in seeing the project through.*

pa·tient[1] /ˈpeɪʃnt/ *noun* a person who is receiving medical treatment, especially in a hospital; a person who receives treatment from a particular doctor: *The patient is usually admitted on the day of operation.* ◇ *The general practitioner failed to inform his patient that there was a high risk that the patient was HIV positive.*

▸ ADJECTIVE + PATIENT **elderly, old** ◆ **adult** ◆ **young** ◆ **female** ◆ **male** ◆ **individual** ◆ **ill** ◆ **high-risk** ◆ **hospitalized** ◆ **diabetic** ◆ **obese** ◆ **depressed** ◆ **psychiatric** ◆ **paediatric** ◆ **surgical** *Diabetic patients are more prone to infection after surgery.*

▸ NOUN + PATIENT **cancer** ◆ **AIDS** *The programme was developed to improve care in hospital for cancer patients during the last 48 hours of life.*

▸ VERB + PATIENT **treat • diagnose • admit • examine • assess • monitor • refer • discharge • manage • protect • ask • inform, tell • advise • encourage • reassure • help • register • identify • recruit • exclude • classify** *These drugs are the best option for treating seriously ill patients whose cancer has spread.*
▸ PATIENT + VERB **undergo • experience • suffer • receive • present • complain • report • develop • die** *Patients presenting at A & E departments must be treated within 4 hours of arrival.*
▸ PATIENT + NOUN **safety • care • records • satisfaction • autonomy • choice • preferences • characteristics • outcomes • survey** *Chan et al. found a positive relationship between GPs' computer use and patient satisfaction.*
▸ PATIENT WITH + NOUN **disease • disorder • infection • failure • syndrome • pain • symptoms • injury, injuries • diagnosis • diabetes • cancer** *Anxiety disorders are widespread in patients with chronic diseases such as arthritis.*

pa·tient² /ˈpeɪʃnt/ *adj.* able to stay calm and accept delay, problems or suffering without complaining; showing this: *He was more sensitive and more patient than his father.* ◇ *She stressed the need for persistent, patient work to build up the party organization.* ◇ **~ with sb/sth** *Every kind of institution was made to listen to criticism and to be patient with opposition.* OPP IMPATIENT ■ **pa·tient·ly** *adv.*: *I would like to thank Dr Jane Graham who patiently answered my questions and corrected numerous errors.*

patri·arch /ˈpeɪtriɑːk; *NAmE* ˈpeɪtriɑːrk/ *noun* the male head of a family or community: *Gino Monetti's role within the narrative is that of domineering patriarch.*

patri·arch·al /ˌpeɪtriˈɑːkl; *NAmE* ˌpeɪtriˈɑːrkl/ *adj.* ruled or controlled by men; giving power and importance only to men: *The pressures of a strong patriarchal society often militated against women exercising their legal right to divorce.*

P

patri·archy /ˈpeɪtriɑːki; *NAmE* ˈpeɪtriɑːrki/ *noun* (*pl.* -ies) [U, C] a society, system or country that is ruled or controlled by men: *The communist government denounced patriarchy and the feudal family system.* ◇ *The film depicts a corrupt and decadent industrial patriarchy greedily pursuing wealth and fame.*

pat·tern¹ /ˈpætn; *NAmE* ˈpætərn/ *noun* **1** the regular way in which sth happens or is done: *The outcome has been disappointing because no clear pattern has emerged.* ◇ **~ of (doing) sth** *In the first year, the child develops a regular pattern of feeding and sleeping.* **2** a regular arrangement of lines, shapes, colours, etc. found in similar objects or as a design on material, etc: **in a ~** *At this stage, the epidermal cells are packed in a regular hexagonal pattern.* ◇ **+ noun** *Pattern recognition is common to all animals with sufficient neural machinery to store the information.* HELP In science, **pattern formation** is the scientific study of patterns in nature: *Pattern formation is a central process in the study of development.* **3** [usually sing.] **~ (for sth)** an example for others to copy: *The Act set the pattern for the legal structure of immigration control.*
▸ ADJECTIVE + PATTERN **similar • different • clear, distinct • characteristic, distinctive • complex • regular • consistent • changing • basic • typical, normal • common** *The hairs are arranged in characteristic swirling patterns.* | **overall • general, broad • observed • spatial • behavioural • temporal • seasonal • regional • traditional • global** *Data are from a single city, but overall patterns of health care use are similar to national averages.*
▸ NOUN + PATTERN **consumption • settlement • distribution • weather • migration • behaviour • sleep • voting** *It is difficult to generalize about consumer behaviour because consumption patterns vary.*
▸ VERB + PATTERN **exhibit, show, reveal, display • form • generate, produce • influence, affect • find • observe • describe • understand** *The ocean floors exhibit a regular striped pattern of variations in magnetic intensity.* | **follow • alter, change • fit • reflect • explain • examine, analyse • identify • determine, establish • compare** *A rise in sea level by about 0.5 m is sufficient to alter weather patterns and submerge coastal ecosystems.*
▸ PATTERN OF + NOUN **behaviour • activity • use • consumption • migration • movement • interaction • change, variation • evolution • inheritance** *Monkeys and apes develop patterns of behaviour that continue throughout adult life.*

pat·tern² /ˈpætn; *NAmE* ˈpætərn/ *verb* **~ sth** (*technical*) to give a clear or regular form to sth in nature or society: *The hormone plays a key role in patterning the growing root.* ◇ *Growing evidence suggests that obesity is socially patterned.*
PHR V **ˈpattern sth on sth** (*BrE*) (*NAmE* **ˈpattern sth after sth**) [usually passive] to use sth as a model for sth; to copy sth: *The novel patterns itself on Shakespeare's Hamlet.* ◇ *This model of education was patterned after undergraduate medical education.*

pat·terned /ˈpætənd; *NAmE* ˈpætərnd/ *adj.* having a regular arrangement or lines or shapes: *Male peacocks are brightly coloured with a splendid patterned train.*

pat·tern·ing /ˈpætənɪŋ; *NAmE* ˈpætərnɪŋ/ *noun* [U] **1 ~ (of sth)** the fact of a repeated pattern developing in behaviour or the way things happen: *The purpose of the present study is to investigate the social patterning of health among prison inmates.* **2** the arrangement of shapes or colours to make patterns: *The female moths' red/orange and black patterning functions as a warning signal to predators.*

pause¹ /pɔːz/ *verb* [I] to stop talking or doing sth for a short time before continuing: *Betty frequently paused and took more time than others to speak.* ◇ **~ to do sth** *Much earlier in the poem, Wordsworth pauses to consider William Wallace.*

pause² /pɔːz/ *noun* a period of time during which sb stops talking or doing sth, or sth stops happening: *After a pause, the questioner added: 'Where is England?'* ◇ *The relatively long pause between pulses allows for heat dissipation, principally through conduction and convection.*

pave /peɪv/ *verb* [often passive] to cover a surface with flat stones or bricks: **be paved (with sth)** *The streets intersect at perfect right angles and are paved with stone.*
IDM **ˌpave the ˈway (for sb/sth)** to create a situation in which sb will be able to do sth or sth can happen: *This decision paved the way for changes in employment rights for women.*

pay¹ /peɪ/ *verb* (**paid, paid** /peɪd/) **1** [I, T] to give sb money for work, goods, services, etc: *When the claimant had completed the works, the defendant refused to pay.* ◇ **~ for sth** *Buyers may become reluctant to pay for a product that they have seen being given away freely.* ◇ **~ for sb to do sth** *Parents will pay for their children to go to schools where English is the medium for learning.* ◇ **~ by sth** *Some utility companies have started applying a surcharge to customers who do not pay by direct debit.* ◇ **~ sth** *Paying higher wages would also reduce profits by adding directly to costs.* ◇ *to pay a fee/taxes/rent/a bill/your debts* ◇ **~ sth to sb** *An employer that fails to follow these procedures may have to pay compensation to the employee.* ◇ **~ sth for sth** *The amount of money paid by customers for flat-screen televisions actually fell 1 per cent.* ◇ **~ sb** *He left the family farm to earn money because his father could not afford to pay him.* ◇ **~ sb for sth** *Most support for older or disabled people comes from family, friends and neighbours, who are not paid for their work.* ◇ **~ sb sth** *Financial services computer professionals were consistently paid more than comparable staff in other sectors.* ◇ **~ sb/sth to do sth** *When* *paying someone to seek information, there is no guarantee that hours of work will provide any results.* **2** [I] (of a business, etc.) to produce a profit: *Companies have worked out how to make corporate social responsbility pay.* ◇ **it pays to do sth** *Shipping freight was so expensive that it did not pay to send anything but very valuable and lightweight goods such as spices and silks.* **3** [I, T] to result in some advantage for sb: *The 'job' of prisoners is to remind those on the outside that crime does not pay.* ◇ **it pays (sb) to do sth** *The common feeling is that 'when the future is highly uncertain, it pays to have a broad range of options open' (Coy, 1999: 118).* **4** [I, T] to suffer or accept a disadvantage because of your beliefs or actions: **~ (for sth) (with sth)** *Von Stulpnagel participated in the July 1944 bomb plot against Hitler and paid with his life.* ◇ **~ sth** *The selfish individual gets the benefit without paying the cost.* ◇ **~ sth for sth** *The main character pays a heavy price for a relentless pursuit of love in the modern world.* **5** [T] **~ attention/heed/regard/tribute/homage/respect (to sb/sth)** to give attention, etc. to sb/sth: *So long as they made an effort, paid attention and did the work, they classified themselves as good learners.* ◇ *Promotional techniques must pay due regard to the consumer's privacy.* ◇ *In much of his writing, Greene paid his respects to his literary precursors.* **6** [T] **~ a visit (to sb/sth)| ~ (sb/sth) a visit)** to visit sb/sth: *There may be no nearby aliens who have evolved enough to be capable of communicating with us, or paying us a visit.*

IDM **pay ˈdividends** to produce great advantages or profits: *At first, Kennedy's action appeared to pay dividends.* **ˌpay for itˈself** (of a new system, sth you have bought, etc.) to save as much money as it cost: *It is rare that any pollutant-reducing process pays for itself.* **pay your ˈway** to pay for everything you need or use yourself: *Gomez-Ibanez (1997) concludes that public transport users do not pay their way, largely because the fares they pay are not sufficient to cover the capital and operating costs.*

PHR V **ˌpay sb ˈback (sth) | ˌpay sth ˈback (to sb)** to return money that you borrowed SYN REPAY (1): *The banks cannot be sure that their loans will be paid back promptly.* ◇ *If they borrow from relatives or friends but fail to pay them back, they could lose their friendship and further support.* **ˌpay sth ˈdown** to reduce an amount of money that you owe by paying some of it: *In the stock market boom of the late 1920s, US corporations had sold stock at speculative prices to pay down debt.* **ˌpay sth ˈin | ˌpay sth ˈinto sth** to put money into a bank account or make payments towards sth such as a PENSION: *With conventional insurance, the benefits paid out will, more or less, equal the premiums paid in.* **ˌpay ˈoff** (of a plan or an action) to bring benefits or good results: *Most people think it is a good thing that hard work and education pay off.* **ˌpay sth ˈoff** to finish paying money owed for sth: *They can use the money from the sale to pay off their earlier debts.* **ˌpay sth ˈout** to pay money, usually a large sum of money, to one or more people: *A firm may pay out part of its profit in the form of dividends.* ◇ *A total of $1.94 billion was paid out in advertising by major studios in 1995.* **ˌpay ˈup** to pay all the money that you owe to sb: *Most consumers eventually paid up, under protest.*

pay² /peɪ/ *noun* [U] the money that sb gets for doing regular work: *The treaty established the principle that men and women should receive equal pay for equal work.* ◇ **+ noun** *a pay system/structure/scale/grade/increase* ◇ *In 2003, the gender pay gap meant that women employed full-time in Britain were paid 82% of average male full-time earnings (Olsen and Walby, 2004).*

pay·able /ˈpeɪəbl/ *adj.* [not before noun] that must be paid or can be paid: *The rent was payable in advance.* ◇ **~ to sb** *There are some rules which potentially constrain the amounts of compensation payable to directors who are removed from office.* ◇ **~ by sb** *Corporation tax is payable by companies on their profits.*

pay·ment /ˈpeɪmənt/ *noun* **1** [C] a sum of money paid or expected to be paid: *He makes monthly payments into a scheme that will cover college education for his children.* ◇ *The contract requires a down payment and states that it is not refundable.* ◇ **~ of sth** *The tribe received a payment of approximately 10 cents an acre for the land (Unrau, 1971).* ◇ **~ for sth** *The customer was late in making payments for the software.* ➲ *see also* BALANCE OF PAYMENTS **2** [U] the act of paying sb/sth or of being paid: *Under this form of pricing, organizations reward customers for early payment.* ◇ **(on) ~ of sth** *Her contract was cancelled on payment of $40 000 severance money.* ◇ **~ for sth** *Letters of credit and bills of exchange are the most commonly used form of payment for exports.* ◇ **in ~ (for sth)** *His friend asked him to supply £17 000 worth of electrical goods and to accept two stolen cheques in payment.*

PC /ˌpiː ˈsiː/ *abbr.* = PERSONAL COMPUTER

peace /piːs/ *noun* **1** [U, sing.] a situation or a period of time in which there is no war in a country or an area: *The West has an interest in maintaining peace in Europe.* ◇ *Napoleon's continuing colonial ambitions made a lasting peace impossible.* ◇ **~ between A and B** *The United Nations was set up to preserve peace between states after the Second World War.* ◇ **at ~** *The countries have been at peace for more than a century.* ◇ **+ noun** *In late 1995 a peace treaty was signed.* **2** [U] a situation in which there is no public violence or DISORDER: *Their drunken behaviour disturbs the peace and intimidates the public.* **3** [U] the state of being calm or quiet; mental or emotional calm: *The home is a place where a family is entitled to be left in peace.* ◇ *He chose the religious life in a quest for inner peace.* ◇ **~ of mind** *The death of friends has disturbed her peace of mind.* **4** [U] **~ (with sb)** the state of living in friendship with sb without arguing: *It was the duty of merchants to seek peace with each other.*

IDM **make (your) peace with sb** to end an argument with sb, usually by saying you are sorry: *Eisenstein returned to Russia and tried to make his peace with the government.* ➲ *more at* BREACH¹

P

peace·ful /ˈpiːsfl/ *adj.* **1** not involving a war, violence or argument: *Any periods of peaceful coexistence with neighbouring tribes are few and far between.* ◇ *The process of decolonization was relatively peaceful in many cases.* **2** quiet and calm; not anxious or disturbed in any way: *The more peaceful life away from the city might do her good.* ◇ *Dancing helps them relax and feel peaceful.* **3** trying to create peace or to live in peace; not liking violence or disagreement: *England was becoming more peaceful and prosperous.* ◇ *In Buddhism, a peaceful society is not understood as one that enjoys just the absence of war.* ■ **peace·ful·ly** /ˈpiːsfəli/ *adv.*: *The journey through Virginia and North Carolina proceeded peacefully.*

peace·keep·ing /ˈpiːskiːpɪŋ/ *adj.* [only before noun] intended to help prevent war or violence in a place where this is likely: *UN peacekeeping forces withdrew from the border zone in 2008.*

peace·time /ˈpiːstaɪm/ *noun* [U] a period of time when a country is not at war: *The men were psychologically weakened and poorly equipped to return to the routines of peacetime.* ◇ **in ~** *Feng's army worked in peacetime on the building of roads.* ➲ *compare* WARTIME

peak¹ /piːk/ *noun* **1** [usually sing.] the point when sb/sth is best or strongest SYN HEIGHT (3): *Cotton production reached a peak in 1978 and has declined steadily since.* ◇ **(at the) ~ of sth** *Towards the end of 1815, while at the peak of his popularity, Alexander presented the Poles with a constitution.* OPP TROUGH (1) **2** a point on a curve, wave or GRAPH, or a value of a physical quantity, that is higher than those around it: *If the peaks of the two waves are in correspondence, then the two waves will add up to make a* *single wave with a greater, combined intensity.* ◇ *The separated components of the mixture appear as discrete peaks on the chromatogram.* **3** the pointed top of a mountain; a mountain with a pointed top: *During the last full glacial period, alpine glaciers formed on high mountain peaks of New Mexico (Richmond, 1986).*

peak[2] /piːk/ *adj.* [only before noun] used to describe the highest level of sth, or the time when the highest number of people are using or doing sth: *The surface free energy reached a peak value of 66 mJ/m² at 2 minutes, then decreased slowly.* ◇ *He observed daily rhythms in the activity patterns of these mosquitoes and noted that the times of peak activity differed among species.* ◇ *They can flex capacity to have more staff on duty during peak times and less for slower times.* HELP **Peak oil** is the point in time when world oil production will reach its highest rate, after which production will gradually decrease: *In much of the peak oil literature, the scope for technical change in fossil fuel production is downplayed.*

peak[3] /piːk/ *verb* [I] to reach the highest point or value: *Hokkaido's population peaked in 1997 at 5 702 000 but had declined to 5 627 424 by the 2005 census.* ◇ **~ at sth** *Oil demand would peak at 88m barrels per day (mb/d) and then fall steadily to 81mb/d by 2035.*

peas·ant /ˈpeznt/ *noun* (especially in the past, or in poorer countries) a person who owns or rents a small piece of land for growing crops or keeping animals: *By the turn of the century, the richer peasants were acquiring land rapidly.* ◇ **+ noun** *Peasant farmers are usually conservative and reluctant to abandon traditional practices.* ◇ *Between 1875 and 1878, peasant revolts broke out in the Kiev region.*

pe·cu·liar /pɪˈkjuːliə(r)/ *adj.* belonging to or connected with one particular place, situation, person, etc, and not others: *This is by no means a peculiar feature of modern Europe, since it also pertains to other countries and other periods.* ◇ **~ to sb/sth** *Vocabulary peculiar to Australian English is labelled as such.*

P

pe·cu·li·ar·ity /pɪˌkjuːliˈærəti/ *noun* (*pl.* **-ies**) **1** [C] **~ (of sb/sth)** a feature that only belongs to one particular person, thing, place, etc: *The policies of the two states are also shaped by the peculiarities of history and politics of each country.* ➲ *compare* CHARACTERISTIC[1] **2** [C] **~ (of sb/sth)** a strange or unusual feature or habit: *He highlighted the peculiarities of usage of some words.* **3** [U] **~ (of sb/sth)** the quality of being strange or unusual: *The peculiarity of the phenomenon itself has been too little noted.*

peda·gogic /ˌpedəˈɡɒdʒɪk; *NAmE* ˌpedəˈɡɑːdʒɪk/ (*also* **peda·gogic·al** /ˌpedəˈɡɒdʒɪkl; *NAmE* ˌpedəˈɡɑːdʒɪkl/) *adj.* concerning methods of teaching: *The 'Headway' course has exerted a powerful influence on textbook design and pedagogic practice globally.* ◇ *The Internet is now regularly used for direct pedagogical purposes.* ■ **peda·gogic·al·ly** /ˌpedəˈɡɒdʒɪkli; *NAmE* ˌpedəˈɡɑːdʒɪkli/ *adv.*: *The second chapter explains how an interactive whiteboard works and presents a few ideas for exploiting this tool pedagogically.*

peda·gogy /ˈpedəɡɒdʒi; *NAmE* ˈpedəɡɑːdʒi/ *noun* (*pl.* **-ies**) [U, C] methods of teaching, especially as a subject of study or as a theory: *Kenway and Bullen (2001) discuss explicitly the lack of connection between consumer media culture and classroom pedagogy.* ◇ *Teachers started to read some current research on new pedagogies.*

pedi·at·ri·cian, pedi·at·ric, pedi·at·rics (*NAmE*) = PAEDIATRICIAN, PAEDIATRIC, PAEDIATRICS

peer /pɪə(r); *NAmE* pɪr/ *noun* **1** [usually pl.] a person who is the same age or who has the same social status as you: *These students had experienced social exclusion by their peers.* ◇ **~ pressure** *Hate crimes are commonly committed by males in groups as a result of peer pressure.* **2** (in Britain) a member of the NOBILITY: *In 1999, the House of Lords agreed to reduce the number of hereditary peers to 92.*

ˈpeer group *noun* a group of people of the same age or social position: *Mobile phones can be used to strengthen the ties within the adolescent peer group.*

ˌpeer reˈview *noun* [U] a judgement on a piece of scientific, academic or professional work by others working in the same area: *These publications have not undergone peer review.* ■ **ˌpeer-reˈviewed** *adj.*: *The search gathered peer-reviewed articles published from January 1960 to January 2009.*

pen /pen/ *noun* [C, U] an instrument made of plastic or metal used for writing with INK: *The data were recorded using a pen and notebook.* ◇ **in ~** *The final version of any work which is to be submitted for assessment should be done in pen.*

penal /ˈpiːnl/ *adj.* [usually before noun] **1** connected with or used for punishment, especially by law: *The idea that the penal system existed to rehabilitate offenders was central to this approach.* **2** that can be punished by law: *Everyone charged with a penal offence has the right to be presumed innocent until proven guilty.* **3** very severe: *After 1945, some regions became hostile to foreign firms or imposed penal rates of taxation.*

pen·al·ize (*BrE also* **-ise**) /ˈpiːnəlaɪz/ *verb* **1 ~ sb (for sth)** to put sb at a disadvantage by treating them unfairly: *The federal government was penalizing Newfoundland for its success by reducing subsidies.* **2 ~ sb (for sth)** to punish sb for breaking a rule or law by making them suffer a disadvantage: *It was argued that innocent service providers should not be penalized for the actions of their users.* **3 ~ sth** to make an act able to be punished by law: *The legislation creates new court orders and new measures to penalize breaches.*

pen·alty /ˈpenəlti/ *noun* (*pl.* **-ies**) a punishment for breaking a law, rule or contract: *The government has the power to impose penalties on anyone who breaks the rules.* ◇ *Individuals would be required to purchase health insurance or pay a financial penalty.* ◇ **~ for sth** *European cities and local governments face high penalties for non-compliance with these limits.* ◇ **+ noun** *Contracts often contain penalty clauses requiring payment if the contractor defaults.*

pen·cil /ˈpensl/ *noun* [C, U] an instrument for writing or drawing, usually made of wood and containing a thin stick of a black or coloured substance: *It would be extremely tedious to do these calculations using only pencil and paper.* ◇ **in ~** *The entries may be made in pencil or in ink.*

pene·trate /ˈpenətreɪt/ *verb* **1** [T, I] to go into or through sth: **~ sth** *These substances may cause minor health effects if they penetrate the skin.* ◇ **~ into/through sth** *Field observations show that roots can penetrate into rocks.* ◇ **~ to sth** *According to their energy, the charged particles penetrate to different levels in the atmosphere.* **2** [T, I] to succeed in entering an area, especially when this is difficult or has not been done before: **~ sth** *European explorers did not penetrate the interior of Africa until the nineteenth century.* ◇ **~ into sth** *As land developers penetrate into their traditional lands, these groups retreat even further into the forest.* **3** [T, I] to succeed in having an effect or influence in a particular area or with a particular group, especially when this has not been done before: **~ sth** *Revolving credit had not penetrated the economic world of the poor.* ◇ **~ into sth** *Awareness of environmental problems has penetrated deeply into contemporary thought and discussion.* **4** [T, I] to start to sell products in a particular market or area: **~ sth** *In telecommunications, the Japanese had failed to penetrate the major American market.* ◇ **~ into**

sth *Equipment conceived by Lord Kelvin back in 1852 has finally penetrated into the market.* **5** [T] **~ sth** to succeed in understanding sth: *He was mainly self-taught, which makes his writings sometimes difficult to penetrate.*

pene·trat·ing /ˈpenɪtreɪtɪŋ/ *adj.* **1** [usually before noun] involving sth entering an object or area, especially entering through sb's skin or body: *Open chest injuries develop as a result of penetrating trauma to the chest wall.* **2** showing clear and deep understanding: *In chapter 4, Gage provides some penetrating insights into the effects of this drought.*

pene·tra·tion /ˌpenɪˈtreɪʃn/ *noun* [U] **1** the act or process of going into or through an object or area: *According to this hypothesis, greater rainfall would lead to deeper water penetration.* ◇ **~ (of sth) (to sth)** *Herbivores remove the plant canopy, allowing increased penetration of light to the soil surface.* **2 ~ (of sth)** the process of starting to sell products in a particular market or area; the extent to which a product is bought or used by customers in a particular market or area: *These initiatives enhance US penetration of the local market.* ◇ *During that time frame, Internet penetration rose from 46% to 57% among respondents.*

pen·sion /ˈpenʃn/ *noun* an amount of money paid regularly by a government or company to sb who is considered to be too old or too ill to work: *People now have to work longer in order to qualify for less generous pensions.* ◇ *a state/public/private pension* ◇ *an occupational/disability/retirement/old-age pension* ◇ **on a ~** *A retired couple living on a pension will find the buying power of their income fall if inflation is high.* ◇ **+ noun** *In some countries, private pension funds predominate.*

people /ˈpiːpl/ *noun* **1** [pl.] persons; men, women and children: *10 000 people who worked in the factories lost their jobs.* ◇ *The disease affects people of all ages.* ◇ *A common way to protect people and buildings from lightning is to use lightning rods.* ◇ *Chernenko emphasized the need to discover what ordinary people really wanted.* **2** [pl.] persons in general; everyone: *These two views capture a fundamental split in the way people think about the nature of self.* ◇ *Gauthier believes that people are mostly self-interested.* **3** [C] all the persons who live in a particular place or belong to a particular country, race, etc: *On the evening of March 31, Johnson spoke to the American people:...* ◇ *Overseas empires brought non-European peoples under European control.* **4 the people** [pl.] the ordinary men and women of a country rather than those who govern or have a special position in society: *The phrase 'We the people' and the rest of the preamble are the most well-known part of the US Constitution.* ◇ *A small group of electors presented the caliph to the people for acceptance by public acclamation.* **5** [pl.] (in compounds) men and women who work in a particular type of job or are involved in a particular area of activity: *It is hardly surprising that there are close links between politicians and business people.* ◇ *The drink was marketed as an energy replacement for sportspeople.* **6** [pl.] the men, women and children that a person leads: *Moses adopted the Hebrew slaves as his people and led them out of captivity.* ◇ *Peter the Great drove his people hard to create a new empire and a new Russia.* IDM *see* MAN, THING

pep·tide /ˈpeptaɪd/ *noun* (*chemistry*) a chemical consisting of two or more AMINO ACIDS joined together: **+ noun** *The amino acids within proteins are linked by peptide bonds formed between an amino group of one amino acid and a carboxyl group of another.*

per /pə(r); *strong form* pɜː(r)/ *prep.* used to express the number, amount, cost, etc. of sth for each person, unit of time, unit of weight, distance travelled, etc: *The mortality rate per 100 000 population was calculated by age group for 16 countries.* ◇ *The patient smokes 20 cigarettes per day.* ◇ *Comparable workers in the United Kingdom earned $16.14 per hour.* ◇ *They will reduce smog by reducing vehicle emissions per mile of driving.*
IDM **as per sth** following a rule, plan, decision, etc. SYN ACCORDING TO (1): *This applies if they have revenues above US$100 million as per the current exchange rate.* ⊃ *more at* HEAD[1]

per annum /pər ˈænəm/ *adv.* (*abbr.* **p.a.**) (*from Latin*) for each year: *China's industrial production increased at 12 per cent per annum between 1980 and 1990.*

per cap·ita /pə ˈkæpɪtə; *NAmE* pər ˈkæpɪtə/ *adj.* for each person: *We control for the wealth available in an area by including per capita income, which is the total income from all sources divided by the number of people.* ■ **per cap·ita** *adv.*: *The country was ranked 5th in the world for prisoners per capita.*

per·ceive AWL /pəˈsiːv; *NAmE* pərˈsiːv/ *verb* **1** to notice or become aware of sth SYN NOTICE[1] (1): **~ sth** *This strategy only works if customers perceive the differences between the products.* ◇ **~ that...** *Girls perceive that boys get more personal and sexual freedom.* ◇ **be perceived to be/have sth** *When a student is perceived to have difficulties, the teacher reports this to his or her superior.* **2** to be aware of or experience sth using the senses: **~ sth** *Hallucinations, or perceiving things that do not exist, can be visual, auditory (i.e. hearing voices), tactile or olfactory.* ◇ **~ sth as sth** *When all of the visible spectrum is present, the eye perceives it as white.* **3** [often passive] to understand or think of sb/sth in a particular way; to believe that a particular thing is true SYN SEE (6): **~ sth + adv.** *Power affects how people perceive change.* ◇ *Risk and uncertainty may be perceived differently by individuals and organizations.* ◇ **~ sb/sth/yourself as sth** *The commercial world is frequently perceived as a ruthless one.* ◇ **~ sb/sth to be/have sth** *This depends on the degree to which an individual perceives the illness to be severe.* ◇ **~ that...** *43 per cent of those surveyed perceived that senior executives were only concerned with their own well-being.*

> **WORD FAMILY**
> perceive *verb*
> perceived *adj.*
> perception *noun*
> perceptive *adj.*
> perceptible *adj.*

perceived AWL /pəˈsiːvd; *NAmE* pərˈsiːvd/ *adj.* as understood or believed by a particular person or group: *The level of perceived risk varies from person to person and some people are less risk-averse than others.* ◇ *Whether real or perceived, lack of time is the main reason people say they do not exercise.*

per cent[1] AWL (*especially BrE*) (*NAmE usually* **per·cent**) /pə ˈsent; *NAmE* pər ˈsent/ *noun* [sing.+ sing./pl. v.] (*symb.* **%**) one part in every hundred: *The store announced it was reducing its workforce by 172 000 (around 7 per cent).* ◇ *When the wording was negative, a lower per cent agreed in both groups.* ◇ **~ of sb/sth** *Asia has 60 per cent of the world's population and 30 per cent of its land mass.*

> **GRAMMAR POINT**
>
> **Expressing percentages**
>
> - Percentages are written in words as *twenty-five per cent* and in figures as *25%*.
> - If a percentage is used with an uncountable or a singular noun, the verb is generally singular: *In 1955, only sixteen per cent of the revenue* ***was derived*** *from the progressive rate of taxation.*
> - If the noun is singular but represents a group of people, the verb may be singular or plural: *Twelve per cent of the population* ***works/work*** *in agriculture.*
> - If the noun is plural, the verb is plural: *Forty-five per cent of the respondents* ***were*** *female.*

P

per cent² AWL (*especially BrE*) (*NAmE usually* **per·cent**) /pə 'sent; *NAmE* pər 'sent/ *adj.* (*symb.* **%**) by, in or for every hundred: *The network had a 12 per cent share of prime-time viewers.* ■ **per cent** AWL *adv.*: *Federal revenues had declined 18 per cent over two years.*

per·cent·age AWL /pə'sentɪdʒ; *NAmE* pər'sentɪdʒ/ *noun* **1** [C+sing./pl. v.] the number, amount, rate of sth, expressed as if it is part of a total which is 100; a part or share of a whole: **~ (of sb/sth)** *Data on the status of women show a high percentage of women working at home for no pay.* ◇ *Their target was to increase the percentage of children doing at least two hours of sport at school each week from 25% to 75%.* ◇ **as a ~ of sb/sth** *Educational spending as a percentage of GDP was 3.32%.* ◇ **+ noun** *Table 5.10 shows the percentage change in average firm size.* ◇ *the percentage increase/reduction/share* ➲ grammar note *at* PER CENT¹ **2** [C, usually sing.] a share of the profits of sth: *The agent will usually take a percentage.* ◇ **on a ~** *Often, a new partner joining a practice will not start on a full percentage but will have to work towards parity.*

per'centage point *noun* a unit of one PER CENT: *Between 1995 and 2008, the participation rate for women aged 50–64 increased by around 11 percentage points, compared with just 4 points for men.*

per·cent·ile /pə'sentaɪl; *NAmE* pər'sentaɪl/ *noun* **~ (of sth)** (*statistics*) one of the 100 equal groups that a larger population can be divided into, according to their place on a scale measuring a particular value: *Households in the top 50th percentile of the living index were categorized as of high socio-economic status.*

per·cep·tible /pə'septəbl; *NAmE* pər'septəbl/ *adj.* **1** great enough to be able to be noticed SYN NOTICEABLE: *Emissions of carbon dioxide have brought about perceptible increases in average temperatures.* ◇ **barely ~** *Constitutional change may be gradual and barely perceptible.* **2** that can be noticed or felt with the senses: *According to Dalton, these particles were the building blocks of the perceptible world.*

P

per·cep·tion AWL /pə'sepʃn; *NAmE* pər'sepʃn/ *noun* **1** [U, C] an idea, a belief or an image you have as a result of how you see or understand sth: *Contrary to public perception, there is no shortage of water in the area.* ◇ **~ of sth** *Workers' perception of risk influences their behaviour in the workplace.* ◇ *Different people in different places will have different perceptions of any given situation.* ◇ **~ that...** *The attraction to cities is the perception that the city offers better schooling, medical services and employment prospects.* **2** [U] the way you notice things or the ability to notice things with the senses: *This is an attempt to understand the mental processes that contribute to sensation, perception and consciousness.* ◇ *Studies on brain injuries demonstrate the complexities involved in visual perception.* HELP In biology, **perception** refers to the processes in the nervous system by which a living thing becomes aware of events and things outside itself: *His thesis was on colour adaptation and light perception in minnows.* **3** [U] the ability to understand the true nature of sth SYN INSIGHT (2): *Engels with great perception remarked that 'every victory [over nature] brings its own vengeance'.*

per·cep·tive /pə'septɪv; *NAmE* pər'septɪv/ *adj.* (*approving*) having or showing the ability to see or understand things quickly, especially things that are not obvious: *In France, many people knew the perceptive analyses of society by Montesquieu, de Tocqueville and Comte.* ◇ *a perceptive observer/reader* ■ **per·cep·tive·ly** *adv.*: *Schumpeter wrote extensively and perceptively about Marx.* **per·cep·tive·ness** *noun* [U] *Ammianus Marcellinus, who continued Tacitus' history down to his own time, shows some of his predecessor's psychological perceptiveness.*

per·cep·tual /pə'septʃuəl; *NAmE* pər'septʃuəl/ *adj.* [only before noun] connected with the ability to PERCEIVE (= notice) things or the process of perceiving: *They found that doctors' perceptual skills can be improved with training.* ◇ *Given a different perceptual system, we might see the world in black and white.*

per·fect¹ /'pɜːfɪkt; *NAmE* 'pɜːrfɪkt/ *adj.* **1** having everything that is necessary; complete and without faults or weaknesses: *There is no perfect solution to this problem.* ◇ *The intricate and delicate apparatus had to be kept in perfect condition.* ◇ *The cellular machinery responsible for the copying is highly reliable, but not perfect.* **2** completely exact or accurate SYN EXACT: *The correlation between the two scores is almost perfect.* ◇ *A bank of 100 000 specimens could potentially supply 99% of the US population with a perfect genetic match for transplantation.* ◇ *The Earth does not have perfect spherical symmetry.* ◇ *a perfect circle/square/sphere* **3** as good as it is possible to be: *In a perfect world, there would be no need for displays of moral virtue.* ◇ *A lot of misery can be traced to the one mistaken notion that we need to be perfect for people to love us.* **4** very good of its kind: *The story of the company is a perfect example of how a private enterprise is subject to a country's changing political fortunes.* **5 ~ for sb/sth** exactly right for sb/sth SYN IDEAL¹ (1): *These unused areas would be perfect for crop processing.* **6** (*grammar*) connected with the form of a verb that in English consists of part of the verb *have* with the past participle of the main verb, used to express actions completed by the present or a particular point in the past or future: *Some languages display a variation in the choice of auxiliary used to form a past or perfect tense.* ➲ *compare* PROGRESSIVE¹ (5), SIMPLE (5) IDM *see* WORLD

per·fect² /pə'fekt; *NAmE* pər'fekt/ *verb* **~ sth** to develop sth so that it becomes perfect or as good as possible: *Drew perfected the method of preserving blood plasma.* ◇ *The best way for doctors to perfect their skills is within practice.*

per·fect³ /'pɜːfɪkt; *NAmE* 'pɜːrfɪkt/ **the perfect** (*also* **the ˌperfect 'tense**) *noun* [sing.] (*grammar*) the form of a verb that expresses actions completed by the present or a particular point in the past or future, formed in English with part of the verb *have* and the past participle of the main verb: *The non-progressive perfect refers to an event in the past with current relevance.* ➲ *see also* PAST PERFECT, PRESENT PERFECT

per·fec·tion /pə'fekʃn; *NAmE* pər'fekʃn/ *noun* **1** [U, sing.] the state of being perfect: *We can never achieve moral perfection.* ◇ **~ of sth** *Paley drew a parallel between the technical perfection of the eye and that of the telescope.* **2** [U] **~ (of sth)** the development of sth so that it becomes perfect or as good as possible: *These extraordinary advances have arisen from the rapid perfection of a single manufacturing technique.*

per·fect·ly /'pɜːfɪktli; *NAmE* 'pɜːrfɪktli/ *adv.* **1** in a way that could not be better: *This example perfectly illustrates the problem.* ◇ *Such measures do not fit perfectly within the traditional models of armed conflict.* **2** (used to emphasize an adjective or an adverb) completely : *In these terms, splitting the infinitive is a perfectly acceptable and grammatical form of language.* ◇ *Like other people with similar brain damage, he manages perfectly well for most purposes.* ◇ *In a perfectly competitive market, firms are unable to use marketing strategies to affect the price at which they sell.*

per·form /pə'fɔːm; *NAmE* pər'fɔːrm/ *verb* **1** [T] **~ sth** to do sth, such as a piece of work, task or duty SYN CARRY STH OUT: *People do not enjoy work when it involves performing the same task over and over again.* ◇ *Firstly, analyses were performed on data gathered in the taxonomy project.* ➲ thesaurus note *at* CARRY **2** [I] **+ adv./prep.** to work or function well or badly: *The country's two largest software companies have performed well this year.* ◇ *The younger* *participants performed at a higher level than the older participants.* **HELP** In this meaning, where there is no adverb or preposition, **perform** means 'perform well': *There is continuous pressure to perform in the sales forces of most organizations.* **3** [T, I] **~ (sth)** to entertain an audience by playing a piece of music, acting in a play, etc: *The play was first performed at the Blackfriars theatre.* ◇ *She performs on stage for about 90 minutes.* **IDM** *see* MIRACLE

▸ PERFORM + NOUN **task • work • analysis • examination • test • experiment • study • assessment • search • act, action • activity • behaviour • function • role • duty • service • operation • surgery • procedure • calculation • measurement** *Galileo was the first to propose testing this idea by performing experiments.*

▸ PERFORM + ADVERB **well • effectively • correctly • satisfactorily, adequately • badly, poorly** *Their region's economy was performing poorly.*

per·form·ance /pəˈfɔːməns; *NAmE* pərˈfɔːrməns/ *noun* **1** [U, C] how well or badly you do sth; how well or badly sth works: *The company should offer employees a series of incentives to improve performance.* ◇ **~ of sb/sth** *What governments do greatly affects the performance of economic systems.* ◇ **~ by/from sb/sth** *Future economic historians will be intrigued by the different performances by various countries today.* **2** [U, sing.] **~ of sth** the action or process of performing a task or function: *The emperor was conscientious in the performance of his duties.* ◇ *It was no more than an adequate performance of a difficult task.* **3** [C] **~ (of sth)** an act of presenting a play, concert or some other form of entertainment: *1991 saw the first performance of the play.* **4** [C] an act of performing a song, a piece of music, or a role in a play or film: *Olivier gave a great performance in the role of Othello.* ◇ **sb's ~ (as sb)** *Cagney's performance as the gangster in 'Public Enemy' was even more memorable.* ◇ **~ by/from sb** *The evening's entertainment included a performance from a Leeds-based West African drumming group.*

▸ ADJECTIVE + PERFORMANCE **good • improved • superior • poor • overall • actual • individual • economic • environmental • financial • organizational • academic • cognitive** *The poor academic performance of many children in care has been of particular concern.*

▸ NOUN + PERFORMANCE **firm • business • market • job • school • system** *A change in firm structure may make firm performance better.*

▸ VERB + PERFORMANCE **improve, enhance • affect, influence • analyse • examine • investigate • assess, evaluate • measure • monitor • compare • predict • achieve • show • maintain** *The Conservatives achieved their best performance since 1992.*

▸ PERFORMANCE + NOUN **indicator, measure • standard • management • evaluation, assessment • appraisal • measurement • monitoring • test • criterion • target, goal • outcome • improvement • characteristics** *All employees are subject to performance evaluation and monitoring.*

per·form·er /pəˈfɔːmə(r); *NAmE* pərˈfɔːrmər/ *noun* **1** a person or thing that behaves or works in the way mentioned: *Sales reps who are poor performers either resign or are sacked.* ◇ *'Moneyweek' was the best performer in this sector of the magazine market.* **2** a person who performs for an audience in a show or concert: *Performers who had made their names on the small screen were turned into film stars.*

per·haps /pəˈhæps; præps; *NAmE* pərˈhæps/ *adv.* **1** used when saying that sth may be true **SYN** POSSIBLY (1): *More experienced pilots perceived situations as less risky than more junior pilots, perhaps because they understood the dynamics of a situation more thoroughly.* ◇ *Her work may perhaps be criticized for its lack of innovation.* **2** used when you want to make a statement or opinion less definite **SYN** MAYBE (1): *Two of the most important earthquakes in the United States were, perhaps surprisingly, nowhere near California.* ◇ *Perhaps the best example of a shock appeal used in advertising is that used by governments to reduce tobacco smoking.* **3** used when giving a number or estimate that is not exact **SYN** APPROXIMATELY, ROUGHLY (1): *42 500 troops were levied for service in Ireland, representing perhaps 19 per cent of available manpower in England and Wales.*

period **AWL** /ˈpɪəriəd; *NAmE* ˈpɪriəd/ *noun* **1** a particular length of time: **~ (of sth)** *Japan's economy has enjoyed a period of decent growth.* ◇ **over a ~ (of sth)** *The writings were composed over a long period.* ◇ **for a ~ (of sth)** *Replanted forest cannot be utilized for a period of 30 years.* ◇ **(for) a ~ of time** *Some drugs should be discontinued for a period of time prior to surgery.* ◇ **a two-hour/four-day, etc. ~** *Bach studied dune development in the area over a three-year period.* ➲ language bank *at* TIME¹ **2** a length of time in the life of a particular person, the history of a particular country, etc: *For much of the post-war period, the economy has been under tight government control.* ◇ **~ of sth** *There have been few periods of history that compare with the present for the rapidity and scale of change.* ◇ *The poem is typical of his middle period.* ➲ language bank *at* TIME¹ **3** (*earth science*) a length of time that is a division of an ERA. A period is divided into EPOCHS: *A further mass extinction occurred at the end of the Cretaceous period.* ➲ language bank *at* TIME¹ **4** **~ (of sth)** (*physics*) the length of time it takes to reach the same point in a cycle each time: *As energy is lost, the size of the orbit decreases and the period of rotation becomes shorter.* **5** **~ (of sth)** any of the parts that a day is divided into at a school or college for a lesson or other activity: *This school dedicates one period of classroom practice every day to a programme entitled 'Let's Improve Our Scores'.* **6** (*chemistry*) a set of elements that OCCUPY a horizontal row in the periodic table: *First, let us take an overview of how the properties of the elements vary across the periods and down the groups.* **7** the flow of blood each month from the body of a woman who is not pregnant: *The 33-year-old woman has not had a period for the last 3 months.* **8** (*NAmE*) = FULL STOP

▸ ADJECTIVE + PERIOD **long, lengthy • short, brief • extended • prolonged • given • entire** *They can go without food or water for extended periods.* | **early • late • entire • historical • modern • current • post-war • interwar • medieval** *Human rights have a much higher profile than in earlier historical periods.*

▸ NOUN + PERIOD **time • study • follow-up • incubation** *In contrast, over the same time period, wealth grew in the twenty wealthiest nations.*

▸ VERB + PERIOD **cover • study, examine • enter** *The data cover the period between 19 March and 17 May 1982.* | **spend • experience, undergo • represent • span • specify • identify • compare** *These young men spend a period of three months in monasteries practising Buddhism.* | **characterize • mark** *Political, social, and cultural entanglements characterized the colonial period.*

▸ PERIOD OF + NOUN **time • years • months • weeks • days • hours • growth, development, expansion • decline • change, transition • stability • activity • study • observation • unemployment • detention • leave • service** *Since the mid-1970s, the Western world has seen the end of this period of stability.* | **history • life • rule** *Adolescence is a relatively short period of life.*

peri·od·ic **AWL** /ˌpɪəriˈɒdɪk; *NAmE* ˌpɪriˈɑːdɪk/ *adj.* **1** [usually before noun] happening fairly often and regularly: *States are required to send periodic reports to the Committee on Economic, Social and Cultural Rights.* ◇ **on a ~ basis** *All such hospital policies are reviewed on a periodic basis.* **2** with a repeated pattern: *The blocks were laid out in a periodic structure.* ◇ *The shape of the signal was periodic.*

peri·od·ical **AWL** /ˌpɪəriˈɒdɪkl; *NAmE* ˌpɪriˈɑːdɪkl/ *noun* a magazine that is published every week, month, etc,

P

especially one that is concerned with an academic subject: *In September 1952, Schaefer submitted his manuscript to a major geographical periodical.*

peri·od·ic·al·ly AWL /ˌpɪəriˈɒdɪkli; *NAmE* ˌpɪriˈɑːdɪkli/ *adv.* fairly often and regularly: *Cyclins are proteins that periodically rise and fall in concentration during the cell cycle.* ◇ *These decisions re patient care should be reviewed periodically.*

peri·od·icity /ˌpɪəriəˈdɪsəti; *NAmE* ˌpɪriəˈdɪsəti/ *noun* [U] **1 ~ (of sth)** the quality of being periodic; the tendency to happen at regular intervals: *The periodicity of these fluctuations seems to be largely comparable with the periodicity of the ice advances and retreats of the Pleistocene.* **2** (*chemistry*) relating to the regularly repeating properties shown by sets of elements in the periodic table: *A graph of the melting points of the elements in the second and third periods in the periodic table plotted against atomic number shows periodicity as the pattern repeats.*

the ˌ**periodic** ˈ**table** *noun* [sing.] (*chemistry*) a way of arranging all the chemical elements in groups and PERIODS in increasing order of their ATOMIC NUMBER: *Thallium is the heaviest element in group 13 of the periodic table.*

per·iph·eral[1] /pəˈrɪfərəl/ *adj.* **1** [usually before noun] connected with the outer edge of an area: *These lands were retained for agricultural use, but the peripheral areas and the poorest were left to lie fallow.* ◇ *Testing showed some loss of peripheral vision in both eyes.* **2** not as important as the main aim or part of sth: *Ageing is often regarded as a peripheral issue on the legislative agenda.* ◇ **~ to sth** *The time available for activities defined as peripheral to the core academic curriculum has been severely curtailed.* **3** [only before noun] (*medical*) connected with parts of the body that are near its surface or edge rather than in the centre or in one of the body's central systems: *Components of the neurological system include the brain, spinal cord and peripheral nervous system.* **4** [only before noun] (of equipment) connected to a computer: *Canon successfully diversified from cameras into photocopying and computer peripheral products.*

per·iph·eral[2] /pəˈrɪfərəl/ *noun* a piece of equipment that is connected to a computer: *Networking computers has many advantages, not least of which is the ability to share peripherals such as printers and scanners.*

per·iph·ery /pəˈrɪfəri/ *noun* (*pl.* **-ies**) [usually sing.] **1** the outer edge of an area or object: **on the ~ (of sth)** *Eventually, those communities on the periphery of the empire began to revolt.* ◇ **at the ~ (of sth)** *Starch granules are usually located at the periphery of the cells.* **2 ~ (of sth)** the less important part of sth, for example of a particular activity or of a social or political group: *These people have been marginalized, oppressed and pushed to the periphery of society.*

per·man·ence /ˈpɜːmənəns; *NAmE* ˈpɜːrmənəns/ *noun* [U] the state of lasting for a long time or for all time in the future: *The presence of many carefully maintained old buildings suggests permanence and stability.*

per·man·ent /ˈpɜːmənənt; *NAmE* ˈpɜːrmənənt/ *adj.* lasting for a long time or for all time in the future; existing all the time: *Mutation is defined as a permanent change to the genome that will be included in any copies made of that genome.* ◇ *These are the five permanent members of the UN Security Council.* ◇ **on a ~ basis** *The victims were allowed to remain in the host country on a temporary or permananent basis.* OPP TEMPORARY ■ **per·man·ent·ly** *adv.*: *By then, nearly 1.8 million Canadians were estimated to have settled permanently in the United States.* ◇ *Permanently frozen ground poses a broad array of problems for engineering.* OPP TEMPORARILY

per·me·able /ˈpɜːmiəbl; *NAmE* ˈpɜːrmiəbl/ *adj.* allowing a liquid or gas to pass through: *Where the regional bedrock is highly permeable, salts may not be retained in the lake.* ◇ **~ to sth** *The cell membrane is freely permeable to water but only selectively permeable to different ions.* OPP IMPERMEABLE ■ **per·mea·bil·ity** /ˌpɜːmiəˈbɪləti; *NAmE* ˌpɜːrmiəˈbɪləti/ *noun* [U] *Soils with low permeability can become waterlogged.* ◇ **~ (of sth) (to sth)** *Aspirin may alter the permeability of the cell membrane.* ◇ *These polymers have much higher permeability to gases.*

per·me·ate /ˈpɜːmieɪt; *NAmE* ˈpɜːrmieɪt/ *verb* **1** [T] **~ sth** (of an idea, an influence, a feeling, etc.) to affect every part of sth: *A feeling of unease permeates the novel.* ◇ *Technology has permeated the field of global health interventions over the past decade or more.* **2** [I, T] **~ (sth)** (of a liquid, gas, etc.) to spread to every part of an object or a place: *Membranes are porous materials allowing gaseous molecules to permeate through the pores.*

per·mis·sible /pəˈmɪsəbl; *NAmE* pərˈmɪsəbl/ *adj.* **~ (for sb) (to do sth)** acceptable according to the law or a particular set of rules: *It is no longer permissible for businesses to refuse to hire black employees.*

per·mis·sion /pəˈmɪʃn; *NAmE* pərˈmɪʃn/ *noun* **1** [U] the action of allowing sb to do sth, especially officially: **~ for sth** *Essentially, the licence would grant permission for the use of software in specified circumstances.* ◇ **~ to do sth** *In 816, the emperor gave Kukai permission to build a monastery on Mt Koya.* ◇ **~ for sb/sth to do sth** *The Ministry of Defence refused permission for them to attend the inquiry.* ◇ **with (the) ~ of/from sb/sth** *This article is reprinted with the permission of the London Mathematical Society.* ◇ **without (sb's) ~** *There are legal rules specifying that no one should enter another's land without permission.* ➲ *usage note at* CONSENT[1] **2** [C, usually pl.] **~ to do sth** an official document allowing sb to do sth: *This figure includes the costs of obtaining the necessary permissions to use patented ideas.*

per·mis·sive /pəˈmɪsɪv; *NAmE* pərˈmɪsɪv/ *adj* **1** allowing or showing a freedom of behaviour that many people do not approve of, especially in sexual matters: *Children of divorced mothers held more permissive attitudes towards premarital sex.* **2** (*biology*) allowing a biological process to occur: *The mutants grow well at the permissive temperature.* ■ **per·mis·sive·ness** *noun* [U] *He was highly critical of the materialism and sexual permissiveness that he perceived in modern society.*

per·mit[1] /pəˈmɪt; *NAmE* pərˈmɪt/ *verb* (**-tt-**) **1** [T] to allow sb to do sth or to allow sth to happen, especially officially: **~ sth** *The law permits and recognizes various types of marriages.* ◇ **~ sb/yourself sth** *Estes and Grant permit themselves a measure of literary licence when they describe these events.* ◇ **~ sb/yourself to do sth** *In the 1960s, the British government permitted the USA to construct a large military base on an island in British Indian Ocean Territory.* **2** [T, I] to make sth possible: **~ (sth)** *New communications technology has permitted the creation and rapid growth of television shopping networks.* ◇ *Mistakes will be avoided if the assessment is as complete as the circumstances permit.* ◇ **~ sb/sth to do sth** *It was unlikely that time would permit the committee to have anything other than a decision-making role.*

per·mit[2] /ˈpɜːmɪt; *NAmE* ˈpɜːrmɪt/ *noun* an official document that gives sb the right to do sth, especially for a limited period of time: *Thousands of work permits were issued for specific groups and purposes, e.g. to Italian men for coal mining.* ◇ **~ to do sth** *Power plants can sell their permits to emit carbon dioxide to others.*

per·mu·ta·tion /ˌpɜːmjuˈteɪʃn; *NAmE* ˌpɜːrmjuˈteɪʃn/ *noun* any of the different ways in which a set or number of things can be ordered or arranged: *Ten lists of five words were made up of random permutations within each* pool. ◇ ~ **of sth** *Let G be a group of permutations of a set X, and let x be any chosen element of X.*

per·pen·dicu·lar /ˌpɜːpənˈdɪkjələ(r); *NAmE* ˌpɜːrpənˈdɪkjələr/ *adj.* ~ **(to sth)** forming an angle of 90° with another line or surface; going straight up: *The Earth's equatorial plane is perpendicular to its axis of spin.* ◇ *The explorer suddenly finds himself facing a high perpendicular wall of rock.*

per·pet·rate /ˈpɜːpətreɪt; *NAmE* ˈpɜːrpətreɪt/ *verb* to commit a crime or do sth wrong or evil: ~ **sth** *It was novels like Solzhenitsyn's which made Russians realize the enormity of the abuses perpetrated by Stalin.* ◇ ~ **sth against/upon/on sb** *For Hausner, the Holocaust was the last and worst in a long line of atrocities perpetrated against the Jews.* ■ **per·pet·ra·tion** /ˌpɜːpəˈtreɪʃn; *NAmE* ˌpɜːrpəˈtreɪʃn/ *noun* [U] ~ **(of sth)** *They would never condone the perpetration of voilence against any group or individual.*

per·pet·ra·tor /ˈpɜːpətreɪtə(r); *NAmE* ˈpɜːrpətreɪtər/ *noun* ~ **(of sth)** a person who commits a crime or does sth that is wrong or evil: *Most victims and perpetrators of Nazism are now dead.* ◇ *Many witnesses express uncertainty when asked to identify the perpetrator of a crime from a line-up (Pike et al., 2001).*

per·pet·ual /pəˈpetʃuəl; *NAmE* pərˈpetʃuəl/ *adj.* [usually before noun] **1** continuing for a long period of time without interruption SYN CONTINUOUS (1): *Technical progress, the growth of knowledge, and conflict among classes all foster perpetual change.* **2** frequently repeated SYN CONTINUAL (1): *Characters with weaknesses were a perpetual source of fascination for audiences.* ■ **per·petu·al·ly** /pəˈpetʃuəli; *NAmE* pərˈpetʃuəli/ *adv.*: *The Spartans were perpetually at war and therefore needed to be prepared to fight year round.*

per·petu·ate /pəˈpetʃueɪt; *NAmE* pərˈpetʃueɪt/ *verb* ~ **sth** to make sth continue for a long time, especially sth bad: *It is important to challenge those economic and political structures that perpetuate inequalities.* ◇ *In film studies, there are many examples of arguments perpetuating this myth.* ■ **per·petu·ation** /pəˌpetʃuˈeɪʃn; *NAmE* pərˌpetʃuˈeɪʃn/ *noun* [U] ~ **(of sth)** *The result was perpetuation of misery and the development of an ever-widening gap between rich and poor.*

per se /ˌpɜː ˈseɪ; *NAmE* ˌpɜːr ˈseɪ/ *adv.* (*from Latin*) used meaning 'by itself' to show that you are referring to sth on its own, rather than in connection with other things: *Nuclear power per se does not pollute, but the residue from nuclear power plants is extremely polluting and long-lasting.*

per·se·cute /ˈpɜːsɪkjuːt; *NAmE* ˈpɜːrsɪkjuːt/ *verb* [often passive] **1** to treat sb in a cruel and unfair way, especially because of their race, religion or political beliefs: ~ **sb** *All nation states, whatever their political ideology, have persecuted minorities in the past.* ◇ ~ **sb for sth** *Many of the early American colonists had been persecuted for religious deviation in the European states they had left.* **2** ~ **sb** to deliberately say and do unpleasant things to sb all the time, in order to make tham anxious or unhappy: *Neighbours had shouted abuse from outside her house and continually persecuted her.*

per·se·cu·tion /ˌpɜːsɪˈkjuːʃn; *NAmE* ˌpɜːrsɪˈkjuːʃn/ *noun* [U, C] cruel and unfair treatment of sb, especially because of their race, religion or political beliefs: *He was judged to have a well-founded fear of persecution in his home state because of his political opinions.* ◇ ~ **of sb** *The Nazi persecutions of Jews began in 1933.*

per·sist AWL /pəˈsɪst; *NAmE* pərˈsɪst/ *verb* **1** [I] to continue to do sth despite difficulties or opposition, in a way that can seem unreasonable: ~ **in doing sth** *Many people persist in holding these beliefs.* ◇ ~ **in sth** *Mao persisted in his criticisms of current literature.* ◇ ~ **with sth** *They have no alternative but to persist with the policy.* **2** [I] to continue to exist: *If symptoms persist, surgery may be required.* ◇ ~ **into sth** *In a minority of people, acne may persist well into adulthood.*

per·sist·ence AWL /pəˈsɪstəns; *NAmE* pərˈsɪstəns/ *noun* [U] **1** ~ **(of sth)** the state of continuing to exist for a long period of time: *Bourdieu uses this theory to explain the persistence of class inequalities in education.* **2** the fact of continuing to do sth despite difficulties or opposition: ~ **with sth** *In general, patience and persistence with standard therapies are as effective.* ◇ ~ **in (doing) sth** *The party continued to show innovative persistence in trying to meet the needs of its membership.*

per·sist·ent AWL /pəˈsɪstənt; *NAmE* pərˈsɪstənt/ *adj.* **1** continuing for a long period of time, especially in a way that causes problems and cannot be stopped: *Bullying is a persistent problem in UK schools.* ◇ *He suffers persistent back pain following a sprain 12 months ago.* **2** determined to do sth despite difficulties or opposition, in a way that can seem unreasonable: *Burglary rates would be cut by 50% by targeting 100 000 persistent offenders.* ■ **per·sist·ent·ly** AWL *adv.*: *A persistently elevated and irregular pulse is unlikely to be related to anxiety.* ◇ *The US government had persistently refused to sign any international deals to limit its carbon emissions.*

per·son /ˈpɜːsn; *NAmE* ˈpɜːrsn/ *noun* (*pl.* **people** /ˈpiːpl/ or, especially in formal use, **per·sons**) **1** a human, especially one who is not identified: *The person concerned shall be informed of the outcome of the claim.* ◇ *In 2007, the USA spent approximately $7 400 per person on health care.* ◇ *Each cell had an official capacity of five persons.* ◇ *It was determined that a criminal offence had been committed by a person or persons unknown.* ➲ *see also* PEOPLE **2** a human considered as an individual: *Socrates was a real person but here is more of a fictional character speaking on Plato's behalf.* ◇ *Flaherty established a strong bond with the people he lived and worked with.* ◇ ~ **of sth** *Chih-i was regarded as a person of great wisdom.* HELP Use **everyone** or **everybody** instead of 'all people'. **3 -person** (in compounds) a person working in the area of business mentioned; a person concerned with the thing mentioned: *A good salesperson listens and gains an understanding of a buyer's needs.* ◇ *A spokesperson for the World Food Programme in the city reported that hundreds of houses had been destroyed.* **4** (*grammar*) any of the three classes of personal pronouns. The **first person** (*I/we*) refers to the person(s) speaking; the **second person** (*you*) refers to the person(s) spoken to; the **third person** (*he/she/it/they*) refers to the person(s) or thing(s) spoken about: *Some languages have different forms for each person and number of the subject.*

IDM **in ˈperson** with the personal presence or action of the individual mentioned: *About 24% of non-Internet users said they contacted the government last year, by phone, by writing a letter, or in person.* **in the person of sb** in the form or shape of sb: *The Bourbon dynasty was restored to the thrones of France and Spain in the person of Ferdinand VII.*

per·sona /pəˈsəʊnə; *NAmE* pərˈsoʊnə/ *noun* (*pl.* **per·son·ae** /pəˈsəʊniː; pəˈsəʊnaɪ; *NAmE* pərˈsoʊniː; pərˈsoʊnaɪ/ or **per·so·nas**) the aspects of a person's character that they show to other people, especially when their real character is different: *His public persona is quite different from the family man described in the book.*

per·son·al /ˈpɜːsənl; *NAmE* ˈpɜːrsənl/ *adj.* **1** [only before noun] your own; not belonging to or connected with anyone else: *The rise in online fraud has left many customers feeling worried about their personal data.* ◇ *Members of these societies have a weak sense of personal identity, but a correspondingly strong sense of community.* **2** [only before

P

noun] connected with individual people, especially their feelings, characters and relationships: *People maintain only a limited number of personal relationships.* ◇ *In premodern societies, dress was never a matter of purely personal choice.* **3** not connected with a person's job or official position: *New technologies make it difficult for salespeople to separate work from personal life.* ◇ *Men tend to spend more than women on personal interests and leisure pursuits.* **4** [only before noun] done by a particular person rather than by sb who is acting for them: *Medical staff may have no personal contact with those patients being assessed.* ◇ *Children should be taught to take personal responsibility for their actions.* **5** [only before noun] made or done for a particular person rather than for a large group of people or people in general: *Most personal care for older people is provided by their families.* ◇ *I am indebted to Suzanne Webb for her account of this matter (personal communication, 9 January 2012).* **6** [only before noun] connected with a person's body: *Staff often have to deal with clients with poor personal hygiene.* ◇ *She received £950 as damages for personal injury.* **7** connected with a particular person's character, appearance or private life in a way that is offensive: *He made offensively personal remarks to a woman colleague about her physical appearance.* ◇ *The discussion got too heated and personal.*

▸ PERSONAL + NOUN **data, information, details • identity • circumstances • history • experience • conduct • development • gain • income • property, asset, wealth • assistant** *Larger items of personal property tend to be funded by the highest earner in the family.* | **relationship • autonomy, freedom, liberty • characteristics, traits, attributes • feelings • beliefs • preference • choice** *Two other personal characteristics influenced children's Internet use.* | **life • matter • interest** *It was argued that religion was a personal matter and not one for official inquiry by the state .* | **contact • selling • responsibility • liability • interview • observation** *I also conducted personal one-to-one interviews with the former directors of the national AIDS programme.* | **care • service • communication** *In the 1980s there was a greater demand by the wealthy for personal services.*

▸ ADVERB + PERSONAL **highly • deeply • purely** *For these activists, political issues were deeply personal.* | **intensely • essentially** *The nature of these relationships was intensely personal.*

ˌpersonal comˈputer *noun* (*abbr.* **PC**) a small computer that is designed for one person to use at work or at home: *With a personal computer and Internet access, the organization can reach a community of millions.*

per·son·al·ity /ˌpɜːsəˈnæləti; *NAmE* ˌpɜːrsəˈnæləti/ *noun* (*pl.* **-ies**) **1** [C, U] the various aspects of a person's character that combine to make them different from other people: *Physically attractive people are generally believed to have appealing personalities.* ◇ *Vice-President Gerald Ford believed that Nixon had undergone a significant change of personality in the White House.* ◇ **+ noun** *Austin et al. identified personality traits associated with a higher concern for animal welfare in farmers.* **2** [U] the qualities of a person's character that make them interesting and attractive: *As a film-maker, Bergman does not lack personality.* **3** [C] a famous person, especially one who works in entertainment or sport SYN CELEBRITY (1): *Gilbert Harding was to be Britain's first major television personality.* **4** [C] a person whose strong character makes them easy to notice: *Sir Richard Greenbury was a very dominant personality.* **5** [U] the qualities of a place or thing that make it interesting and different SYN CHARACTER (1): *The majority of brands do not have this depth of personality.*

persoˈnality disorder *noun* (*medical*) a serious mental condition in which sb's behaviour makes it difficult for them to have normal relationships with other people or a normal role in society: *There is ongoing debate over the helpfulness of the diagnosis of personality disorder.*

per·son·al·ize (*BrE also* **-ise**) /ˈpɜːsənəlaɪz; *NAmE* ˈpɜːrsənəlaɪz/ *verb* **1 ~ sth** to cause an issue, argument, etc. to become concerned with particular people or feelings rather than with general matters: *What can be measured is the media's tendency to personalize politics.* **2 ~ sth** to design or change sth so that it is suitable for the needs of a particular person: *They offer a bewildering array of extra features which allow customers to personalize their new car.* ◇ *Personalized medicine targets treatments to the characteristics of individual patients.* **3 ~ sth** to mark sth in some way to show that it belongs to a particular person: *One strategy is to personalize covering letters, by including the respondent's name and address.*

per·son·al·ly /ˈpɜːsənəli; *NAmE* ˈpɜːrsənəli/ *adv.* **1** by a particular person rather than by sb acting for them: *Wilson had known several of these writers personally.* **2** in a way that is connected with one particular person rather than a group of people SYN INDIVIDUALLY: *The Chief Executive of the agency is personally responsible for the agency's performance.* **3** in a way that is connected with sb's personal life rather than with their job or official position: *Sexual relationships with colleagues could complicate a politician's life both personally and professionally.* **4** with the personal presence or action of the individual mentioned: *He debated personally or in writing with contemporary religious opponents.* **5** used to show that you are giving your own opinion about sth: *Personally, I find these answers to Fermi's question to be the most plausible.* **6** in a way that is intended to be offensive: *It was hard not to feel personally attacked.*

IDM **take sth ˈpersonally** to believe that a remark or action is directed against you and be upset or offended by it: *It is best not to take criticism personally as this can adversely affect the response that should be made.*

per·son·nel /ˌpɜːsəˈnel; *NAmE* ˌpɜːrsəˈnel/ *noun* [pl.] the people who work for a business, an organization or one of the armed forces: *Formal and informal interviews were carried out with a total of seven key personnel from the Queensland Police Headquarters.* ◇ *military/medical/sales personnel* ◇ *armed/skilled/trained personnel* ➲ *see also* HUMAN RESOURCES

per·spec·tive AWL /pəˈspektɪv; *NAmE* pərˈspektɪv/ *noun* **1** [C] a particular attitude towards sth; a way of thinking about sth SYN VIEWPOINT (1): *They believed women bring a different perspective to politics.* ◇ **~ on sb/sth** *Mitchell (1998) provides various perspectives on the problems of poverty.* ◇ **from a... ~** *This is the first work to approach the subject from a historical perspective.* ◇ **from the ~ of sb/sth** *The book discusses risk from the perspective of an investor.* **2** [U] the ability to think about problems and decisions in a reasonable way without making them seem more serious or more important than they really are: *Setting objectives helps the children to maintain a sense of perspective.* ◇ *A broader view allows us to gain perspective.* ◇ **in/into ~** *To put these numbers in perspective, Germany's entire electricity system in 2005 was 124 GW (Eurostat, 2008).* **3** [U] the art of creating an effect of depth and distance in a picture by representing people and things that are far away as being smaller than those that are nearer the front: *Sizes and shapes do not appear on the screen in their true proportions but distorted in perspective.* ◇ *Camera lenses organize their visual field according to the laws of perspective.*

▸ ADJECTIVE + PERSPECTIVE **own • different, alternative • new, fresh • unique • broad • multiple ~s • diverse ~s • global, international • long-term • critical • comparative • theoretical • historical • ethical • cultural • sociological • societal • social • political • economic • evolutionary • ecological • disciplinary • feminist • Marxist • postmodern** *These data inform politicians and members of the public alike of how their own perspective compares*

P

with others. ◇ *From a broader comparative perspective, a common American pattern of appointing business people has emerged.*

▸ VERB + PERSPECTIVE **adopt, take** ◆ **offer, provide** ◆ **introduce, bring** ◆ **present** ◆ **broaden** ◆ **gain** ◆ **embrace** ◆ **share** ◆ **integrate** *Japanese companies adopt a long-term product perspective as opposed to the short-term approach of the USA.* ◇ *Travel broadens our perspectives and challenges our assumptions.*

WHICH WORD?

persuade ◆ **convince**

- The main meaning of **persuade** is to get sb to agree to do sth by giving them good reasons for doing it: *Her father persuaded her to return to the family home.* The main meaning of **convince** is to make sb believe that sth is true: *His experience convinced him that schools can become the hub of the community.*
- It is quite common, however, for each of these words to be used with either meaning: *The firm must convince non-users to buy this type of product.* ◇ *This was the mutation that persuaded scientists that genes were part of chromosomes.*
- Both **persuade** and **convince** are often preceded by verbs like *attempt, try* and *seek*: *70 per cent of consumers feel advertising seeks to persuade people to buy things they do not want.* ◇ *They tried to convince him of the correctness of their view.*
- Both verbs are used with noun objects such as *audience, reader* and *public*: *Political and business leaders have struggled to persuade the American public of the virtues of globalization.* ◇ *A great deal of information is needed to convince the reader to make a decision 'right now'.*
- If you are **convinced/persuaded** of sth, you believe it to be true. **Persuaded** in this meaning is rather formal: *By this time, Stalin was persuaded that fertilizers were overrated.*

per·suade /pəˈsweɪd; *NAmE* pərˈsweɪd/ *verb* **1** to make sb do sth by giving them good reasons for doing it: **~ sb to do sth** *Franklin's skill lay in persuading his colleagues to solve their own practical problems.* ◇ **~ sb** *Manifestos are designed to persuade the voters.* ◇ **~ sb into (doing) sth** *Europeans struggled to persuade Indians into alliance.* **2** to make sb believe that sth is true SYN CONVINCE (1): **~ sb/yourself that...** *People are choosing private medicine instead of trying to persuade the government that health policy is wrong.* ◇ *They persuaded themselves that they were a superior people entrusted with the care of the natives.* ◇ **be persuaded of sth** *Younger men may not be persuaded of the need for preventive health care.*

per·sua·sion /pəˈsweɪʒn; *NAmE* pərˈsweɪʒn/ *noun* **1** [U] the act of persuading sb to do sth or to believe sth: *They tried to improve sales through persuasion.* ◇ *Lenin needed all his powers of persuasion to convince his party of this.* **2** [C, U] a particular set of beliefs, especially about religion or politics: *People of all political persuasions began to object that many programmes were biased.*

per·sua·sive /pəˈsweɪsɪv; *NAmE* pərˈsweɪsɪv/ *adj.* able to persuade sb to do or believe sth: *He offers a persuasive argument that scholars who neglect the influence of faith miss an important part of the story.* ◇ *The messages were persuasive enough to encourage hundreds of thousands of people to join.* ➲ thesaurus note *at* CONVINCING ■ **per·sua·sive·ly** *adv.*: *Satia argues persuasively that local political officers were crucial in the formation of this brutal regime.* **per·sua·sive·ness** *noun* [U] **~ (of sth)** *It is a valuable text because of the breadth of his knowledge and the persuasiveness of his arguments.*

per·tain /pəˈteɪn; *NAmE* pərˈteɪn/ *verb* [I] (*formal*) to exist or to apply in a particular situation or at a particular time: *The Japanese culture of company loyalty was probably stronger by far than that pertaining in any other part of the globe.*

PHR V **perˈtain to sth/sb** to be connected with sth/sb: *Two key issues pertaining to this debate still remain unexplored.*

per·tin·ent /ˈpɜːtɪnənt; *NAmE* ˈpɜːrtnənt/ *adj.* appropriate to a particular situation SYN RELEVANT (1): *In the introduction, Zamindar raises a number of pertinent questions.* ◇ **~ to sth** *National policy documents pertinent to the subject were retrieved from official government web pages and key informants.* ■ **per·tin·ent·ly** *adv.*: *Wright's authority was overruled on two occasions, most pertinently in the selection of essays.* **per·tin·ence** /ˈpɜːtɪnəns; *NAmE* ˈpɜːrtnəns/ *noun* [U] **~ (to sth)** *In the present study, this technique was used to investigate themes of particular pertinence to child and family ill health.*

per·vade /pəˈveɪd; *NAmE* pərˈveɪd/ *verb* **~ sth** to spread through and be easy to notice in every part of sth SYN PERMEATE (1): *Religion pervaded all aspects of life in ancient Greece.* ◇ *The country continues to be pervaded by racial divisions.*

per·va·sive /pəˈveɪsɪv; *NAmE* pərˈveɪsɪv/ *adj.* (especially of sth bad) spreading through all parts of a place or thing: *The distrust was fuelled by the pervasive influence of racism.* ◇ *Extravagant consumption had become so pervasive that the state no longer felt able to check it.* ■ **per·va·sive·ly** *adv.*: *The country remains a pervasively patriarchal society.* **per·va·sive·ness** *noun* [U] **~ (of sth)** *The percentages of occurrence reported in the studies indicate the pervasiveness of the problem.*

pes·sim·ism /ˈpesɪmɪzəm/ *noun* [U] **~ (about sth)** a feeling that bad things will happen or that sth will not be successful: *The swing towards pessimism about global prospects was extreme, especially after the collapse of Lehman Brothers in September 2008.* OPP OPTIMISM ■ **pes·sim·ist** /ˈpesɪmɪst/ *noun*: *Pessimists and optimists base their forecasts on very different kinds of assumptions.* OPP OPTIMIST

P

pes·sim·is·tic /ˌpesɪˈmɪstɪk/ *adj.* **~ (about sth)** expecting bad things to happen or sth not to be successful: *The women I interviewed resolutely avoid being pessimistic about love and marriage.* OPP OPTIMISTIC

pest /pest/ *noun* an insect or animal that destroys plants, food, etc: *Often the fastest way to control a pest is to use chemical methods.* ◇ *They attempted to introduce predators for the control of insect pests.*

pesti·cide /ˈpestɪsaɪd/ *noun* [C, U] a chemical used for killing pests, especially insects: *Larger farmers may use more pesticides and fertilizers.* ◇ **+ noun** *From a food policy perspective, pesticide residues on fresh foods are a major concern.*

pe·ti·tion¹ /pəˈtɪʃn/ *noun* **1** a written document signed by a large number of people that asks sb in a position of authority to do or change sth: *Probably more than one fifth of all British males aged over 15 signed the anti-slavery petitions of 1833.* **2 ~ (for sth)** (*law*) an official document asking a court to take a particular course of action: *Her husband has already filed a petition for divorce.* ◇ *In Hateley v Morris (2004), the petition was presented some two years after the events complained of.* **3** (*formal*) a formal request to God or to sb in authority: *The second petition of the Lord's Prayer asks, 'Your kingdom come' (Matt. 6:10; Luke 11:2).*

pe·ti·tion² /pəˈtɪʃn/ *verb* **1** [I, T] to make a formal request to sb in authority, especially by sending them a petition: **~ for/against sth** *In 1649 Morfa went to Seville to petition for more troops.* ◇ **~ sb/sth (for sth)** *Millions of people petitioned Parliament, demanding an end to the slave trade.* ◇

~ sb/sth to do sth *A Romanian National Party petitioned the Emperor in 1892 to restore autonomy to Transylvania.* **2** [I, T] (*law*) to formally ask for sth in court: **~ (sb) (for sth)** *The parties would then have to wait two years before petitioning for divorce.* ◇ **~ sb/sth to do sth** *An unpaid creditor petitioned the court to wind up the company.*

pe·ti·tion·er /pəˈtɪʃənə(r)/ *noun* **1** (*law*) a person who asks a court to take a particular course of action: *The petitioner, O, was employed by the company in 1983 as a manual worker.* **2** (*formal*) a person who makes a formal request to sb in authority: *Don Corleone holds court as petitioners line up to request favours from him on the day of his daughter's wedding.*

pet·rol /ˈpetrəl/ (*BrE*) (*NAmE* **gas, gas·oline**) *noun* [U] a liquid obtained from petroleum, used as fuel in car engines, etc: *Supermarkets moved into the retailing of petrol in the early 1990s, undercutting the prices of petrol companies.*

pet·rol·eum /pəˈtrəʊliəm; *NAmE* pəˈtroʊliəm/ *noun* [U] mineral oil that is found under the ground or the sea and is used to produce petrol, oil, etc: *This activity has been driven by the discovery of petroleum and gas in these marine regions.* ◇ **+ noun** *The petroleum industry is very familiar with the changing fortunes of oil and gas prices.* ◇ *petroleum products/reserves/companies*

pH /ˌpiː ˈeɪtʃ/ *noun* [U, sing.] (*chemistry*) a measurement of the level of acid or ALKALI in a SOLUTION or substance. In the pH range of 0 to 14, a reading of below 7 shows an acid and of above 7 shows an alkali: *Very high soil pH can indicate salt accumulation.* ◇ *a high/low/alkaline/acidic/neutral pH* ◇ **+ noun** *The output of the pH electrode is displayed directly as a pH value.* ◇ *Methyl orange is a commonly used indicator, changing from red to yellow over the pH range 3.0–4.4.*

P

pharma·ceut·ical[1] /ˌfɑːməˈsuːtɪkl; ˌfɑːməˈsjuːtɪkl; *NAmE* ˌfɑːrməˈsuːtɪkl/ *adj.* [only before noun] connected with making and selling drugs and medicines: *In the pharmaceutical industry, regulations govern testing, approval, manufacturing, labelling and the marketing of drugs.* ◇ *pharmaceutical companies/firms/products*

pharma·ceut·ical[2] /ˌfɑːməˈsuːtɪkl; ˌfɑːməˈsjuːtɪkl; *NAmE* ˌfɑːrməˈsuːtɪkl/ *noun* [usually pl.] a drug or medicine: *Developing new pharmaceuticals is a time-consuming process.*

pharma·cist /ˈfɑːməsɪst; *NAmE* ˈfɑːrməsɪst/ *noun* a person whose job is to prepare medicines and sell or give them to the public in a shop or hospital: *Forty-four per cent of respondents reported asking pharmacists about the effects of non-prescription medications.* ➲ *compare* CHEMIST

pharma·col·ogy /ˌfɑːməˈkɒlədʒi; *NAmE* ˌfɑːrməˈkɑːlədʒədʒi/ *noun* [U] the scientific study of drugs and their use in medicine: *The target in this area of clinical pharmacology is clear and simple: the elimination of seizures.* ■ **pharma·co·logic·al** /ˌfɑːməkəˈlɒdʒɪkl; *NAmE* ˌfɑːrməkəˈlɑːdʒɪkl/ *adj.*: *Both psychological and pharmacological treatments are important in managing depression in chronic disease.*

phar·macy /ˈfɑːməsi; *NAmE* ˈfɑːrməsi/ *noun* (*pl.* **-ies**) **1** [C] a shop or a place in a hospital where medicines are prepared or sold: **+ noun** *The primary reason for the pharmacy visit was to obtain a prescription medication (71.0%).* ➲ *compare* CHEMIST **2** [U] the study of how to prepare medicines and drugs: **+ noun** *Data were collected by trained pharmacy students and supervised by the survey manager.*

phase[1] **AWL** /feɪz/ *noun* **1** a stage in a process of change or development: **~ (of sth)** *By the end of that conflict, Europe was entering a new phase of historical development.* ◇ **in the... ~** *Diversified business groups played a critical role in the early phase of modern economic growth.* ◇ **during the... ~** *The protein polyhedrin is produced in large amounts during the very late phase of the viral life cycle.* **2** (*chemistry*) a form of a substance, such as a particular solid, liquid or gas, that is separated by its surface from other forms: **+ noun** *Oil and water form a two phase mixture as there is a physical boundary between the two liquids.* **3** (*physics*) the relationship in time between the states or cycles of a repeating system (such as an alternating electric current or a light or sound wave) and either a fixed point or the states or cycles of another system: **+ noun** *When the amplifier is inverting, there is a 180° phase shift between the input and the output.*

IDM **in/out of phase (with sth)** in/not in the same phase or stage of variation in a cycle: *The two reflected rays are not in phase with each other.* ◇ *The driving cycle is a quarter of a period out of phase with the swing's cycle.*

phase[2] **AWL** /feɪz/ *verb* [usually passive] to arrange to do sth gradually in stages over a period of time: **phased + noun** *The expected costs are used as the main argument for a phased approach.*

PHRV **ˌphase sth ˈin** to introduce or start using sth gradually in stages over a period of time: *The new age limit will be phased in from 2002 to 2027.* **ˌphase sth ˈout** to stop using sth gradually in stages over a period of time: *Switzerland gradually phased out its restrictions on parts exports.*

phe·nom·enal **AWL** /fəˈnɒmɪnl; *NAmE* fəˈnɑːmɪnl/ *adj.* **1** very great or impressive **SYN** EXTRAORDINARY (2): *The inward flows of financial capital made significant contributions to the phenomenal economic growth in Latin America.* **2** that can be felt through the senses or through immediate experience: *The mind automatically attends to an array of phenomenal experiences, including motivation, memory and emotion.*

phe·nom·enon **AWL** /fəˈnɒmɪnən; *NAmE* fəˈnɑːmɪnən/ *noun* (*pl.* **phe·nom·ena** /fəˈnɒmɪnə; *NAmE* fəˈnɑːmɪnə/) a fact or an event in nature or society, especially one that is not fully understood: *Globalization is a complex phenomenon that affects many aspects of our lives.* ◇ *Deserts are natural phenomena, but desertification is the expansion of desert areas.* ◇ **the ~ of sth** *These theories do not adequately explain the phenomenon of religion.* ➲ grammar note *at* DATA

▸ ADJECTIVE + PHENOMENON **recent, new • widespread • global • complex • interesting • observable • empirical • natural • physical • biological • mental • social • cultural • linguistic • electromagnetic** *This population explosion is a new social phenomenon seen only in the capitalist epoch.*

▸ VERB + PHENOMENON **observe • experience • exhibit • describe • investigate, study, explore, examine, analyse • explain • understand • know • discover • illustrate • model** *Companies must understand the social networking phenomenon, and be aware of the possibilities afforded by advertising and sponsorship.*

▸ PHENOMENON + VERB **arise** *Religious healing was a phenomenon arising in the late fourth century.*

phe·no·type /ˈfiːnətaɪp/ *noun* (*biology*) the set of characteristics of a living thing, resulting from its combination of GENES and the effect of its environment: *It is always the phenotype that produces the greatest number of descendants that increases within the population.* ➲ *compare* GENOTYPE ■ **phe·no·typic** /ˌfiːnəˈtɪpɪk/ *adj.*: *Phenotypic variation can result from differences in the genetic information contained in the fertilized eggs.* ◇ *phenotypic traits/characteristics* ◇ *phenotypic changes/differences/development* **phe·no·typ·ic·al·ly** /ˌfiːnəˈtɪpɪkli/ *adv.*: *North American barn swallows differ phenotypically from the European race.*

phil·oso·pher **AWL** /fəˈlɒsəfə(r); *NAmE* fəˈlɑːsəfər/ *noun* a person who studies or writes about philosophy: *The Greek philosopher Democritus said that everything in the universe is the fruit of chance and necessity.* ◇ *Political* *philosophers have long argued that high levels of inequality are problematic for democracy.*

philo·soph·ical AWL /ˌfɪləˈsɒfɪkl; *NAmE* ˌfɪləˈsɑːfɪkl/ (*also* **philo·soph·ic** /ˌfɪləˈsɒfɪk; *NAmE* ˌfɪləˈsɑːfɪk/) *adj.* connected with philosophy: *The first question is a matter of philosophical debate.* ◇ *Coleridge's later philosophical writing is preoccupied with religious issues.* ◇ *The more philosophical question of whether advertising helps create unnecessary wants is much more difficult to answer.* ◇ *a philosophical problem/issue/argument/discussion/position/theory/approach* ■ **philo·soph·ic·al·ly** /ˌfɪləˈsɒfɪkli; *NAmE* ˌfɪləˈsɑːfɪkli/ *adv.*: *Questions of intervention and human rights can be studied philosophically, historically and legally.*

phil·oso·phy AWL /fəˈlɒsəfi; *NAmE* fəˈlɑːsəfi/ *noun* (-ies) **1** [U] the study of the nature and meaning of the universe and of human life: *Western/contemporary/political/moral philosophy* ◇ *For a year Marx studied philosophy and law at the University of Bonn.* ◇ **~ of sth** *They anticipated some of the advances in the philosophy of science that came later.* HELP **Natural philosophy** is an old term for the study of the physical world, which developed into the natural sciences. The term may still be used in the study of the history of science: *He took up the chair in natural philosophy at Glasgow in 1846.* **2** [C] a particular set or system of beliefs resulting from the search for knowledge about life and the universe: *Aristotle's political philosophy differed from Plato's in two key respects.* ◇ *This chapter is devoted primarily to the Buddhist philosophies of India.* **3** [C] a set of beliefs or an attitude to life that guides sb's behaviour: *The Sales and Marketing departments have developed very different philosophies and strategies to fulfil their roles within the organization.* ◇ **~ of sth** *Spiritual awareness is at the core of the general Japanese philosophy of life.*

phone /fəʊn; *NAmE* foʊn/ *noun* [C, U] an electronic device that people use for talking to other people over long distances; the system that makes this possible SYN TELEPHONE: *Almost all schools officially ban phones from the classrooms.* ◇ **over the/by ~** *Increasingly, marketing research is being conducted by phone.* ◇ **+ noun** *Cheaper international phone calls and air transport have facilitated moving production and services to low-cost countries.* ➲ *see also* MOBILE PHONE

phon·et·ic /fəˈnetɪk/ *adj.* **1** using special symbols to represent each different speech sound: *A number of glossaries helpfully provide phonetic transcriptions alongside definitions.* **2** connected with the sounds of human speech: *When phonetic change takes place, it is often in the direction of a strong sound to a weak sound.* ■ **phon·et·ic·al·ly** /fəˈnetɪkli/ *adv.*: *These last three forms are all quite similar phonetically.*

phon·et·ics /fəˈnetɪks/ *noun* [U] the study of speech sounds and how they are produced: *There are many scholars in phonetics who would not accept the conclusions in this chapter.*

phos·phate /ˈfɒsfeɪt; *NAmE* ˈfɑːsfeɪt/ *noun* [U, C] (*chemistry*) an ION made from one phosphorus atom and four OXYGEN atoms, or a COMPOUND containing this ion, used in industry or needed by plants to grow: *The use of synthetic detergents has increased the amount of phosphate in rivers and lakes.*

phos·phorus /ˈfɒsfərəs; *NAmE* ˈfɑːsfərəs/ *noun* [U] (*symb.* **P**) the chemical element of ATOMIC NUMBER 15. Phosphorus is found in several different forms, including as a poisonous, pale yellow substance that shines in the dark and starts to burn as soon as it is placed in air: *Phosphorus is an essential component of proteins, cell membranes, teeth and bones.* ◇ **+ noun** *Plant growth and productivity are frequently limited by low phosphorus availability.*

photo /ˈfəʊtəʊ; *NAmE* ˈfoʊtoʊ/ *noun* (*pl.* **-os**) (*rather informal*) = PHOTOGRAPH[1]

photo·chem·ical /ˌfəʊtəʊˈkemɪkl; *NAmE* ˌfoʊtoʊˈkemɪkl/ *adj.* (*chemistry*) caused by or connected with the chemical action of light: *The vertical distribution of ozone can be principally explained by photochemical reactions.*

photo·graph[1] /ˈfəʊtəgrɑːf; *NAmE* ˈfoʊtəgræf/ (*also rather informal* **photo**) *noun* **~ (of sb/sth)** a picture that is made by using a camera: *The earliest aerial photographs of the Jornada region were taken in 1936.* ◇ *Figure 4.27 shows a photograph of a small portable rainfall simulator.*

photo·graph[2] /ˈfəʊtəgrɑːf; *NAmE* ˈfoʊtəgræf/ *verb* **~ sb/sth** to take a photograph of sb/sth: *In the 1850s successful attempts were made to photograph subjects in motion.*

pho·tog·raph·er /fəˈtɒgrəfə(r); *NAmE* fəˈtɑːgrəfər/ *noun* a person who takes photographs, especially as a job: *Many professional photographers still prefer to use traditional 35 mm cameras rather than the newer digital cameras.*

photo·graph·ic /ˌfəʊtəˈgræfɪk; *NAmE* ˌfoʊtəˈgræfɪk/ *adj.* connected with photographs or photography: *The photographic image is a mechanical reproduction of reality and we therefore accept as real the object reproduced.*

pho·tog·raphy /fəˈtɒgrəfi; *NAmE* fəˈtɑːgrəfi/ *noun* [U] the art, process or job of taking photographs or filming sth: *The colour inkjet printer created the mass market in desktop digital photography.* ◇ *The use of aerial photography for map-making was in its infancy at this time.*

pho·ton /ˈfəʊtɒn; *NAmE* ˈfoʊtɑːn/ *noun* (*physics*) a unit of ELECTROMAGNETIC energy: *An atom in its excited state may spontaneously emit a photon into the field.* ◇ **+ noun** *A high-power UV lamp with short wavelength or high photon energy may reduce treatment time.*

photo·syn·thesis /ˌfəʊtəʊˈsɪnθəsɪs; *NAmE* ˌfoʊtoʊˈsɪnθəsɪs/ *noun* [U] (*biology*) the process by which green plants turn CARBON DIOXIDE and water into food using energy obtained from light from the sun: *Cacti survive in hot deserts using their swollen stems for water storage and photosynthesis.* ■ **photo·syn·thet·ic** /ˌfəʊtəʊsɪnˈθetɪk; *NAmE* ˌfoʊtoʊsɪnˈθetɪk/ *adj.*: *Growth of the plants and photosynthetic rate of G. robertianum were found to be primarily dependent on light availability.*

phrasal /ˈfreɪzl/ *adj.* (*grammar*) of or connected with a phrase: *The dictionary offers two sorts of examples: phrasal examples and sentence examples.*

ˌphrasal ˈverb *noun* (*grammar*) a verb combined with an adverb or a preposition, or sometimes both, to give a new meaning, for example *come across, put up with* and *see to*: *One Latinate verb may match several phrasal verbs, with 'demolish' matching 'knock down', 'tear down' and 'blow up'.*

phrase[1] /freɪz/ *noun* **1** (*grammar*) a group of words without a FINITE verb, especially one that forms part of a sentence. 'the economic situation' and 'in this study' are phrases: *Even more frequently used than 'likely' and 'probably' are the verb phrases 'may have' and 'may mean'.* ◇ *The text is peppered with foreign words and phrases.* ➲ *see also* NOUN PHRASE **2** a group of words that have a particular meaning when used together: *The EU continues to disappoint those who wish to see it become, in Tony Blair's memorable phrase, 'a superpower, not a super-state'.* IDM *see* TURN[2]

phrase[2] /freɪz/ *verb* [often passive] to say or write sth in a particular way: **be phrased (+ adv./prep.)** *Each question is phrased differently.* ◇ **be phrased as sth** *The questions were phrased as attitude questions, with the wording: 'To what extent do you agree with...?'*

P

phylum /ˈfaɪləm/ *noun* (*pl.* **phyla** /ˈfaɪlə/) (*biology*) a group into which animals, plants or other living things are divided, smaller than a KINGDOM and larger than a CLASS: *Most of the individual organisms are arthropods, but representatives of almost all of the animal phyla are present.* ➲ *compare* FAMILY[1] (5), GENUS, ORDER[1] (9), SPECIES

phys·ic·al AWL /ˈfɪzɪkl/ *adj.* **1** [usually before noun] connected with a person's body rather than their mind: *The survey collected information about lifestyle such as smoking and drinking habits, physical activity and diet.* ◇ *The disease spreads easily from person to person via physical contact or shared objects.* **2** [only before noun] connected with things that actually exist or are present and can be seen, felt, etc. rather than things that only exist in a person's mind: *Tribal peoples use deceptively simple technologies to live in close harmony with their physical environment.* **3** [only before noun] according to the laws of nature or what is likely: *They are faced with either high marginal costs or the physical impossibility of additional short-term supply.* **4** [only before noun] connected with physics: *Every physical event is determined by purely physical causes in accordance with physical laws.* ◇ *Many advances have been made in developing surface treatments to alter chemical and physical properties of polymer surfaces.*

▸ PHYSICAL + NOUN **activity • exercise • inactivity • examination • health • fitness • condition • illness • disability, impairment • injury • damage, harm • symptom • functioning • appearance • characteristic • contact • abuse • violence • aggression • restraint • barrier • education** *These behaviours may be detrimental to physical health in the long term.* | **environment • landscape • world • space • reality • object • entity • phenomenon • infrastructure • proximity • presence • location • dimension • distance • quantity • parameter • property • cause • damage • disturbance • science** *The idea that one can learn about the physical world using logic and reason marked the beginning of the scientific era.*

P

ˌphysical geˈography *noun* [U] **1 ~ (of sth)** the way in which the natural features of a place are arranged: *Humboldt's explorations recast long-standing assumptions about the physical geography of the New World.* **2** the scientific study of the natural features on the surface of the earth: *Traditionally, students of the earth sciences, physical geography, environmental sciences and civil engineering learn about the principles of hydrology during their studies.*

phys·ic·al·ly AWL /ˈfɪzɪkli/ *adv.* **1** in a way that is connected with a person's body rather than their mind: *The individual changes both physically and mentally throughout life.* ◇ *The patient used to be physically active and involved in several different sports.* **2** in a way that is connected with things that actually exist or are present and can be seen, felt, etc. rather than things that only exist in a person's mind: *New species are generated where populations are physically separated from one another.* **3** according to the laws of nature or what is likely: *Getting to the scene of the crime would have been physically impossible for him.*

ˌphysical ˈscience *noun* [U] (*also* **the physical sciences** [pl.]) the areas of science concerned with studying natural forces and things that are not alive, for example physics and chemistry: *The greatest achievement of physical science in modern times has been the development and use of quantum theory.* ➲ *compare* LIFE SCIENCES

phys·ician /fɪˈzɪʃn/ *noun* a doctor, especially one who is a specialist in general medicine and not SURGERY: *17% of respondents had consulted their primary care physician in the last month.* HELP In British English, **physician** is used mainly in academic and formal English. In general English, **doctor** or **GP** is used instead. In American English, however, **physician** is used in both academic and general English. ➲ *compare* SURGEON

physi·cist /ˈfɪzɪsɪst/ *noun* a scientist who studies physics: *In quantum mechanics, many physicists would argue that a subatomic particle is never at rest.* ◇ *a mathematical/theoretical/nuclear physicist*

phys·ics /ˈfɪzɪks/ *noun* [U] the scientific study of matter and energy and the relationships between them, including the study of forces, heat, light, sound, electricity and the structure of atoms: *The fundamental laws of physics are constant and unchanging.* ◇ *Two apparently quite different concepts dominate modern physics: the idea of the particle and the idea of the field.*

physio·logic·al /ˌfɪziəˈlɒdʒɪkl; *NAmE* ˌfɪziəˈlɑːdʒɪkl/ *adj.* connected with the way in which a living thing functions: *Inflammation is a characteristic physiological response of tissues to injury.* ◇ *physiological functions/changes/effects/processes*

physi·ology /ˌfɪziˈɒlədʒi; *NAmE* ˌfɪziˈɑːlədʒi/ *noun* **1** [U] the scientific study of the normal functions of living things: *In 1873, he began research in anatomy and physiology at the University of Vienna.* **2** [U, sing.] the way in which a particular living thing functions: *Acoustic signals have been shown to influence female reproductive physiology in birds.* ◇ **~ of sth** *Substantial differences exist between the physiology of plants growing in high- and low-phosphorus conditions.*

pick /pɪk/ *verb* **1 ~ sb/sth** (*rather informal*) to choose sb/sth from a group of people or things: *The assumption that people pick their friends at random is seriously flawed.* HELP In this meaning, **pick** is a slightly informal word and can suggest choosing sb/sth without much thought. In most cases, **choose** is a better word to use in academic writing. **2 ~ sth** to take flowers or fruit from the plant or the tree where they are growing: *Berry consumption was surprisingly low, considering the continued tradition of picking berries from forests.* **3 ~ sth + adv./prep.** to pull or remove sth or small pieces of sth from sth else: *Most monkeys and apes will pick parasites off each other.*

IDM **ˌpick and ˈchoose (sth)** to choose only those things that you like or want very much: *Consumers want to pick and choose which products they buy.* **pick a ˈwinner** (*rather informal*) to choose sth that will be successful or perform well: *Policymakers have a dismal track record in picking winners.*

PHR V **ˌpick sb/sth ˈoff 1** to choose a person, an animal or an aircraft, especially one of a group, and then shoot or kill them: *Prey rarely sits around waiting to be picked off by a predator.* **2** (*business*) to take away business or particular customers from a another company: *The company found a number of its activities were being picked off by smaller specialist organizations.*

ˌpick sb/sth ˈout 1 to choose sb/sth carefully from a group of people or things SYN SELECT[1] (1): *Screening is used to pick out individual cells with the desired cloned insert.* **2** to recognize sb/sth from among other people or things: *The human eye is enormously gifted at picking out patterns.* **ˌpick sth ˈout 1** to discover or recognize sth after careful study: *It is easy to pick out some potentially important differences between these studies.* **2** to make sth easy to see or hear: *The sphere picked out in red is in contact with the six spheres picked out in a darker shade of green.*

ˌpick sth ˈover to examine a group of things carefully, especially to choose the ones you want: *Officials will pick over the details of these proposals line by line.*

ˌpick ˈup to get better, stronger, faster or higher: *It was not until the onset of the Industrial Revolution that the pace of urbanization really picked up.* **ˌpick sb/sth ˈup 1** to take hold of sb/sth and lift them/it up: *At the age of 32, he began to notice a feeling of weakness when picking up his children, aged 3 and 5.* ◇ *The sand-sized particles are easily* *picked up by the wind.* **2** to collect sb/sth from a place SYN COLLECT (5): *Contrary to expectations, when the fines were imposed, the number of parents picking up their kids late more than doubled.* **ˌpick sth ˈup 1** to notice, identify or recognize sth: *Could it be that unhappy people tend to be unemployed rather than the other way around, and that is what the surveys are picking up?* **2** to receive an electronic signal, sound or picture: *A radio receiver can pick up any station by tuning to the band of the desired station.* **3** to learn information or a skill without much effort: *Children in every culture pick up the language around them with extraordinary speed.* **4** to continue a discussion or an activity that has stopped for while or that was started earlier by sb else SYN TAKE STH UP (1): *Ong and Yeung pick up this theme.* **ˌpick ˈup on sth 1** to notice sth and perhaps react to it: *He initially does not seem to pick up on her fear.* **2** to return to a point that has already been mentioned or discussed: *This strand of liberalism picks up on earlier liberal thought about the beneficial effects of international institutions.*

pic·tor·ial /pɪkˈtɔːriəl/ *adj.* [usually before noun] using, containing or connected with pictures: *Fig. 15.1 is a pictorial representation of the graph given in the example above.* ◇ *Christian Metz noted some of the fundamental distinctions between linguistic and pictorial modes of communication.*

pic·ture¹ /ˈpɪktʃə(r)/ *noun* **1** a painting or drawing, etc. that shows a scene, person or thing: *Engaging the children in drawing pictures helped them to talk around a difficult subject.* ◇ **~ of sb/sth** *In one experiment, patients were shown two pictures of a house.* **2** a photograph: *Satellite pictures (Fig.12.6) show a large area of middle- and high-level cloud.* ◇ **~ of sb/sth** *This technique involves using a gamma camera to take pictures of the heart.* **3 ~ (of sb/sth)** an image on a television screen: *Television pictures of buildings after an earthquake are stark reminders of the harrowing events.* **4 ~ (of sb/sth)** a description that gives you an idea in your mind of what sb/sth is like: *The Clinton campaign painted a picture of economic well-being and future glory.* ◇ *Results of such analysis give a picture of the vegetation at a given point in time.* ◇ *The company placed buyers and marketing teams in the regions in order to gain a clearer picture of local markets.* **5** (*usually* **the picture**) [sing.] the general situation concerning sb/sth: *Material facts enter the picture but they are secondary to ideas.* ◇ *We need to take the radiation into account to get the full picture.* ◇ **in/out of the ~** *The industry is becoming more market-driven, but one cannot reasonably leave technology out of the picture.* IDM *see* BIG

▸ ADJECTIVE + PICTURE **accurate, realistic • complete, comprehensive, full • detailed • overall, general • clear • coherent • vivid • bleak • mixed • complex • mental** *Such data cannot provide a complete picture of symptoms, illness or disease occurring in society.* | **overall, broad • full, whole** *The overall picture in 2006 was of trade expanding in real terms faster than output.*

▸ VERB + PICTURE **paint, draw • present, give, offer, provide • yield, reveal • get, gain, obtain • build • complete • complicate, confuse, distort • fit (into)** *The United States in the early 1920s presents a very different picture.*

▸ PICTURE + VERB **emerge** *If we compare the energy consumption per GDP, a different picture emerges.*

pic·ture² /ˈpɪktʃə(r)/ *verb* **1** to imagine sb/sth; to create an image of sb/sth in your mind: **~ sb/sth (as sth)** *A gas can be pictured as a collection of molecules (or atoms) in continuous random motion.* ◇ **~ what/how, etc...** *Picture what happens from the point of view of an observer at rest who is watching the train from the track.* **2** [usually passive] to describe or present sb/sth in a particular way SYN PORTRAY (2): **be pictured as sth** *The state was pictured as a cause of excessive taxation and over-regulation.* **3** [usually passive] to show sb/sth in a photograph or picture: **be pictured (+ adv./prep/adj.)** *Both front and back of the manuscript are pictured here.* ◇ *The key elements of the network are pictured in Figure 5.8.*

piece /piːs/ *noun* **1 ~ (of sth)** an amount of sth that has been cut or separated from the rest of it; a standard amount of sth: *A complete new plant can develop from a small piece of stem or root.* ◇ *a piece of paper/meat/wood/string* ◇ *Over time, every small piece of land was filled up with houses.* **2** [usually pl.] one of the parts that sth breaks into or is divided into; one of the parts that sth is made of: **into pieces** *As the rocks fell, they crashed into other rocks, breaking into pieces.* ◇ **in pieces** *A stage actor memorizes an entire role in proper order, while film actors learn their parts in pieces, often out of chronological order.* ◇ **to pieces** *If a watch is taken to pieces for cleaning, it goes on existing in a disassembled state.* ◇ *Finally, the republic was torn to pieces by rival power-hungry tribunes.* **3 ~ of sth** a single item of a particular type: *a piece of equipment/machinery/furniture* ◇ *Every piece of software will contain errors that may not show up until a particular set of circumstances occurs.* **4 ~ of sth** a single example or an amount of sth: *Both pieces of legislation reflected the outlook of the new Energy Secretary.* ◇ *A second piece of evidence pointing to the existence of supermassive black holes is provided by active galaxies.* ◇ *The media bombard us with thousands of new pieces of information every day.* **5 ~ (of sth)** a single item of writing, art, music, etc. that sb has produced or created: *Any piece of writing is a product of its time.* ◇ *A piece of music recorded by a pianist is also an analogue signal.* ◇ *This is a collection of 23 pieces whose original publication dates stretch from 1976 to 2008.* **6** an article in a newspaper or magazine or a broadcast on television or radio: *He wrote a short piece on the subject that was published in the 'Edinburgh Review'.*
IDM **(all) of a ˈpiece** the same or similar: *The first three objections to this theory are all of a piece.* ◇ *For the most part, the country is geologically of a piece.*

P

ˈpie chart *noun* a diagram consisting of a circle that is divided into sections to show the size of particular amounts in relation to the whole: *The pie chart below indicates the share of the vote won by each candidate.* ➲ language bank *at* TABLE

pig·ment /ˈpɪɡmənt/ *noun* [U, C] **1** a substance that exists naturally in people, animals and plants and gives their skin, leaves, etc. a particular colour: *When we expose our skin to sunlight, we produce more pigment and our skin becomes darker.* ◇ *The typical red/orange/yellow pigments in many fruits can also signal the 'ripeness' of the fruit.* **2** a substance that is mixed with another substance, such as oil or water, to produce paint, etc: *Titanium dioxide is a cheap and abundant material that is widely used as a pigment in white paint.*

pig·men·ta·tion /ˌpɪɡmenˈteɪʃn/ *noun* [U] the presence of pigment in skin, hair, leaves, etc. that causes them to be a particular colour: *Increasing skin pigmentation is very common, affecting some 70% of pregnant women.*

pile /paɪl/ *noun* **1 ~ (of sth)** a number of things that have been placed on top of each other: *A pile of bricks is no stronger than the mortar that glues them together.* **2 ~ (of sth)** a mass of sth that is high in the middle and wider at the bottom than at the top: *The city was reduced to a pile of rubble.* ◇ *a pile of sand/sediment*

pilot¹ /ˈpaɪlət/ *noun* a person who operates the controls of an aircraft, especially as a job: *Studies were conducted on commercial airline pilots in 23 countries.*

pilot² /ˈpaɪlət/ *adj.* [only before noun] done on a small scale in order to see if sth is successful enough to do on a large scale: *Based on the pilot testing, we shortened and simplified the instructions.* ◇ *a pilot project/study/scheme*

pilot³ /ˈpaɪlət/ *verb* **~ sth** to test a new product, idea, etc. with a few people or in a small area before it is introduced everywhere: *In 2002 the community school model was piloted in seven locations.*

pin¹ /pɪn/ *noun* **1** a short thin piece of stiff wire with a sharp point at one end and a round head at the other, used to hold or attach things: *His nerves have been damaged as a result of diabetes and he cannot feel it when the doctor pricks his feet with a pin.* **2** a short piece of metal or other material, used to hold things together: *External fixation involves inserting pins into the bone on either side of the fracture.* **3** a piece of metal with a sharp point, worn for decoration: *Personal ornaments found at the burial site included a pin and six silver brooches.* **4** one of the metal parts that stick out of an electric PLUG and fit into a SOCKET: *a three-pin plug*

pin² /pɪn/ *verb* (-nn-) **~ sth (+ adv./prep.)** to attach sth onto another thing or join things together with a pin, etc: *Snapshots of his former life were pinned to his hospital wall.* ◇ *Connections are pinned, bolted or clamped with no welding.*

PHR V **ˌpin sth ˈdown** to explain or understand sth exactly: *The concept of ethnicity, like so many other social science concepts, is difficult to pin down.*

pine /paɪn/ *noun* [C, U] (*also* **ˈpine tree** [C]) a forest tree with leaves like needles: *Open late glacial environments were replaced by forests of birch and pine.*

pin·point /ˈpɪnpɔɪnt/ *verb* **1 ~ sth** to find and show the exact position of sb/sth or the exact time that sth happened: *In 20 minutes, police pinpointed and confirmed the exact location of the bomb.* **2 ~ sth** to be able to give the exact reason for sth or to describe sth exactly: *Larry Polivka pinpoints two major reasons for our lack of understanding of assisted living.*

P

pi·on·eer¹ /ˌpaɪəˈnɪə(r); *NAmE* ˌpaɪəˈnɪr/ *noun* **1** a person who is the first to study and develop a particular area of knowledge, culture, etc. that other people then continue to develop: **~ in sth** *He was a pioneer in the field of special education.* ◇ **~ of sth** *Alfred Lotka, one of the pioneers of stable population theory, proved this principle mathematically in 1907.* **2** one of the first people to go to a particular area in order to live and work there: *Like the generations of pioneers before them, early settlers arrived in California well aware of the hazards of life in the Wild West.*

pi·on·eer² /ˌpaɪəˈnɪə(r); *NAmE* ˌpaɪəˈnɪr/ *verb* **~ sth** to be one of the first people to do, discover or use sth new: *Marx pioneered the use of official statistics in social science writing.* ◇ *to pioneer a technique/method*

pi·on·eer·ing /ˌpaɪəˈnɪərɪŋ; *NAmE* ˌpaɪəˈnɪrɪŋ/ *adj.* [usually before noun] introducing ideas and methods that have never been used before: *The pioneering work in this area was done by Gould and White (1986).* ◇ *In a pioneering study, Pavitt (1984) distinguished between four basic firm types.*

pipe¹ /paɪp/ *noun* **1** a tube through which liquids and gases can flow: *Breeding grounds in urban areas can include pools of fresh water from leaking water pipes or taps.* ➲ *see also* EXHAUST¹ (2) **2** a narrow tube with a bowl at one end, used for smoking TOBACCO: *In the UK, 25% of adults smoke cigarettes, 1% smoke a pipe regularly and 4% of men smoke at least one cigar a month.*

pipe² /paɪp/ *verb* **~ sth (+ adv./prep.)** to send water, gas, oil, etc. through a pipe from one place to another: *59 per cent of households had public water piped into their dwelling.* ◇ *192 towns had piped water systems, and 38 some kind of piped sewage.*

pipe·line /ˈpaɪplaɪn/ *noun* a series of pipes that are usually underground and are used for carrying oil, gas, etc. over long distances: *Carbon steel material is used to build the pipelines.* ◇ *the construction of a gas/an oil pipeline*

IDM **in the ˈpipeline** something that is **in the pipeline** is being discussed, planned or prepared and will happen or exist soon: *Denmark has only two official projects, although a handful of projects are in the pipeline.*

pis·ton /ˈpɪstən/ *noun* a part of an engine that consists of a short CYLINDER that fits inside a tube and moves up and down or backwards and forwards to make other parts of the engine move: *The combusting air and fuel mixture drives the piston downwards.*

pit·fall /ˈpɪtfɔːl/ *noun* **~ (of sth)** a danger or difficulty, especially one that is hidden or not obvious at first: *Generally speaking, researchers must always understand the limitations and potential pitfalls of their study.* ◇ *The authors suggest ways in which common pitfalls can be avoided.* ➲ *compare* TRAP¹ (3)

piv·otal /ˈpɪvətl/ *adj.* of great importance because other things depend on it: *The film's cultish features have played a pivotal role in attracting its core audiences.* ◇ *This pivotal moment structurally divides the play into two halves.* ◇ **~ to sth** *Hydrogen is widely considered to be pivotal to our world's energy requirements for the twenty-first century.*

place¹ /pleɪs/ *noun* **1** [C] a particular position, point or area: *Schools are one of the safest places for children.* ◇ *Parts of East Antarctica are probably the windiest places on Earth.* ◇ **~ of sth** *They travel in the autumn from the place of their birth to wintering grounds in warmer regions.* **2** [C, U] a particular city, town, building, etc: *In the course of his life, he visited such places as Rome, Athens, Palestine, Asia Minor and Arabia.* ◇ *The Caribbean was a risky place to live during the eighteenth century.* ◇ **+ noun** *Many place names in England have spellings that do not reflect their actual pronunciations.* ◇ **a sense of ~** *In all three plays, Wesker conveys an acute sense of place by capturing distinctive ways of speaking.* **3** [C] (especially in compounds or phrases) a building or an area of land used for a particular purpose: *Eventually, all underground burial places were called 'catacombs'.* ◇ *In a nation full of swamps and forests, hiding places were easy to find.* ◇ **~ of sth** *Mosques in America serve not only as places of worship but also as community centres.* **4** [C] a particular area on a surface: *The lava spilled over the rim of the inner gorge at several places.* ◇ *The image has been marked in three places.* ◇ **in places** *The ice may have been over 1500 m thick in places.* **5** [sing.] the role or importance of sb/sth in a particular situation, usually in relation to others: *They promoted the idea that women's proper place was in the home.* ◇ **~ as sth** *After her death, her place as editor was taken by William Miles.* ◇ **~ in sth** *Finding their place in the world can create insecurity in young people.* ◇ **have no ~ in sth** *Some critics argued that theories had no place in geography because all locations, indeed all geographic facts, are unique.* ◇ **no ~ for sth** *Stalin's command economy offered no place for popular participation and popular initiative.* ◇ **in... place** *Technology remains the dominant engine of growth, with human capital investment in second place.* **6** [C] the position that sb/sth is in; the natural or correct position that sb/sth should be in: *The less dense air below changes places with the more dense air above.* ◇ *She put the book back in its place on the shelf.* **7** [C] a point in a book, speech, piece of music, etc: *The equations for rods are given in several places in this article.* ◇ *There are places in this account which are still dependent on the research of a single author.* **8** [C] an opportunity to take part in sth, especially to study at a school or university or on a course: *Places in medical schools are scarce.* **9** [C, usually sing.] a position among the winners of a race or competition: *The Liberal Democrat vote fell by 3.7% and dropped behind the SNP to third place.* ◇ *Three people tied for first place.*

IDM all ˈover the place (*informal*) everywhere: *Political poems on these subjects sprouted up all over the place.* **fall into ˈplace** if sth complicated or difficult to understand **falls into place**, it starts to happen as planned, or becomes clear in your mind: *Kennedy won a string of impressive primary victories, and the ingredients for victory fell into place.* **in the ˈfirst place** used at the end of a sentence to talk about why sth was done or whether it should have been done or not: *The desire for technology is one of the reasons China opened its markets in the first place.* **in the ˈfirst, ˈsecond, etc. place** used at the beginning of a sentence to introduce the different points you are making in an argument: *In the first place, any given instance of behaviour is determined by a range of influences.* **in ˈplace** (*also* **into ˈplace**) **1** in the correct position; ready for sth: *Lung development happens in an orderly sequence, with airways all in place by 16 weeks of gestational age.* ◇ *Cranes lifted each steel piece into position and the bridge builders riveted them into place.* **2** working or ready to work: *There are agreements in place with all of these schools to provide health and dental services to their students.* **in place of sb/sth | in sb's/sth's ˈplace** instead of sb/sth: *He repeated Toricelli's experiment but, in place of mercury, he used water and wine.* ◇ *A director cannot appoint a delegate to act in his place should he be prevented from attending board meetings.* **out of ˈplace** not in the correct place; not suitable for a particular situation: *Such practices convey a message that women are out of place in these 'masculine' environments.* **put sth in ˈplace** to start or provide sth: *The Department of Conservation in New Zealand has now put in place a rat extermination programme on several islands.* **take ˈplace** to happen: *Crust formation took place in several steps.* ◇ *Millions of online transactions take place each day.* **take sb's/sth's ˈplace | take the place of sb/sth** to replace sb/sth: *With robots and computers increasingly taking the place of skilled workers, structural unemployment soared.* **take your ˈplace** to take or accept the position in society that is correct or that you deserve: *He seemed destined to take his place in history alongside other great transformers.* ➲ *more at* PRIDE

place² /pleɪs/ *verb* **1 ~ sth + adv./prep.** to put sth in a particular place, especially when you do it carefully or deliberately: *Seeds were placed in a Petri dish and moistened with distilled water for 1 day.* **2 ~ sb/sth/yourself + adv./prep.** to put sb/sth/yourself in a particular situation; to make sb/sth/yourself experience sth: *An ageing population can place an enormous financial burden on the working population.* ◇ *The capitalist economy places certain limits on what the government can do.* ◇ *to place obligations/demands/restrictions on sb* ◇ *They had no choice but to place themselves at the mercy of the emperor.* **3 ~ sth on (doing) sth** used to express the attitude sb has towards sb/sth: *Governments now place more emphasis on interactive approaches.* ◇ *Freudian theory places great importance on childhood.* ◇ *to place reliance/weight/a priority on sth* ◇ *Conversely, those who place a high value on social cohesion will be willing to sacrifice some freedom of choice.* **4 ~ sb/sth + adv./prep.** to decide that sb/sth has a particular position or rank compared with other people or things: *Both Germany and Poland have placed this issue high on the political agenda.* ◇ *The debate was seen by 9.68 million viewers, placing it second only to the channel's top rated show.* ◇ *Typically, Mandela is placed alongside great peacemakers like Mahatma Gandhi and Martin Luther King.* **5** to arrange for sb to live, be treated, etc. somewhere: **~ sb with sb/sth** *In 2010, the child was made a ward of court and placed with foster parents.* ◇ **~ sb in sth** *Patients may be placed in an intermediate care facility for up to 4 weeks.* **6 ~ sth** to give instructions about sth or make a request for sth to happen: *The current trend of manufacturing offshore means that an order must be placed some six to nine months in advance.* ◇ *Advertisements were placed in the media.* **7 ~ sb/sth + adj.** used to describe a person or team finishing in a particular position in a race or competition: *In an opinion poll immediately after the third debate, the Conservatives were placed first.*

IDM be well, ideally, uniquely, better, etc. placed for sth/to do sth 1 to be in a good, very good, etc. position; to have a good, etc. opportunity to do sth: *The competition is intense, and companies with particular skills or experience are better placed for success.* ◇ *GPs are ideally placed to identify and offer advice to drug misusers.* **2** to be located in a good or convenient place: *Bristol was well placed geographically to trade with Africa and the Atlantic world.* ➲ *more at* PREMIUM, RECORD¹

pla·cebo /pləˈsiːbəʊ; *NAmE* pləˈsiːboʊ/ *noun* (*pl.* **-os**) [C, U] a substance that has no physical effects, given to patients who do not need medicine but think that they do, or used when testing new drugs; the use of such a substance: *However, the response of patients who receive a placebo may represent a genuine therapeutic effect.* ◇ **~ effect** *The placebo effect could be operating here, because similar improvements were observed in both groups.*

place·ment /ˈpleɪsmənt/ *noun* **1** [U] **~ (of sth)** the act of putting sth somewhere: *The placement of outdoor advertising is strictly controlled by local authorities.* **2** [U, C] **~ (of sb)** the act of finding sb a suitable job or place to live; the place that is found: *The study highlighted issues surrounding the recruitment and placement of nurses.* ◇ *The five siblings went into two separate foster placements.* **3** [C, U] (*BrE*) a job, often as part of a course of study, where you get some experience of a particular kind of work: *Students were set a project to complete during their work placement.* ◇ **on ~** *While on placement, I interviewed, under supervision, a client who experiences continuous voices in her head.* ➲ *compare* WORK EXPERIENCE

pla·giar·ism /ˈpleɪdʒərɪzəm/ *noun* [U, C] (*disapproving*) an act of copying another person's ideas, words or work and pretending that they are your own: *The fact that the copying or plagiarism was unintentional will not serve as a defence.* ◇ *Numerous minor plagiarisms were noted in the article.*

pla·giar·ize (*BrE also* **-ise**) /ˈpleɪdʒəraɪz/ *verb* [I, T] (*disapproving*) to copy another person's ideas, words or work and pretend that they are your own: *The ease with which students can now plagiarize has been much discussed and debated.* ◇ **~ sth** *Generations of authors plagiarized this text without acknowledging their source.* ➲ *compare* COPY² (2)

plain¹ /pleɪn/ *adj.* (**plain·er**, **plain·est**) **1** easy to see or understand SYN CLEAR¹ (1): **it is ~ that...** *It is quite plain that the marriage has broken down.* ◇ **make it ~ that...** *He made it plain that he was seeking considered advice and intended to act on that advice.* **2** [only before noun] expressed in a clear and simple way, without using technical language: *The documents in which these criticisms were made were in plain straightforward language.* ◇ *The organization increased access to quality information by posting user-friendly reports, written in plain English, on its website.* **3** not trying to deceive anyone; honest and direct: *These are routines which we all use to avoid plain speaking or uncomfortable issues.* ◇ *It is a plain fact that different people have different needs for information.* **4** not decorated or complicated; simple: *Textile technology is one of the oldest technologies, perhaps going back to 5000 BC, when Egyptians produced plain linen textiles.* HELP In computing, **plain text** is data representing text that is not written in code or using special FORMATTING and can be read, displayed or printed without much processing: *Mathematical formulae are an example of content that cannot be represented satisfactorily via plain text.* **5** without marks or a pattern on it: *The introduction of plain packaging for cigarettes will not restrict a smoker*

P

from buying or using tobacco. **6** [only before noun] (used for emphasis) simple; nothing but SYN SHEER (1): *Neighbouring groups may be seen as possessing certain negative characteristics, such as inferiority, greed or plain nastiness.*

plain² /pleɪn/ *noun* (*also* **plains** [pl.]) a large area of flat land: *These are mountainous islands with a narrow coastal plain from which volcanic slopes rise steeply.* ◇ *The narrator of 'Shane' is brought up on the Wyoming high plains.*

plain·ly /ˈpleɪnli/ *adv.* **1** in a way that is easy to see, hear, understand or believe SYN CLEARLY (2), OBVIOUSLY (2): *Eisenstein plainly sees no theoretical bar to adapting novels successfully for the screen.* ◇ *The judge's decision cannot be challenged unless plainly wrong.* **2** using simple words to say sth in a direct and honest way: *She has the ability to cut through the rhetoric and speak plainly and perceptively.* ◇ *This statement must be plainly written and explain any scientific terminology and acronyms.* **3** in a simple way, without decoration: *She was plainly dressed and wore no make-up.*

plain·tiff /ˈpleɪntɪf/ (*BrE less frequent* **com·plain·ant**) *noun* (*law*) a person who makes a formal complaint against sb in a court of law: *Agreeing that the board had violated their constitutional rights, the judge found for the plaintiffs.* HELP In England and Wales, the term **plaintiff** was officially replaced by **claimant** in 1999. ➲ *compare* DEFENDANT

plan¹ /plæn/ *noun* **1** a set of things to do in order to achieve sth, especially one that has been considered in detail in advance: *A comprehensive long-term plan was prepared but never fully implemented.* ◇ *The government developed strategic plans that set out common goals.* ◇ *a care/management/marketing plan* ◇ **~ for (doing) sth** *He proposed a plan for profit-sharing among his workers.* ◇ **~ to do sth** *Plans are underway to introduce a national colorectal cancer screening programme in the UK.* ◇ **according to ~** *So far, data collection has progressed according to plan.* **2** [usually pl.] something that you intend to do or achieve: *The plan is to roll out the reforms across the whole country by 2017.* ◇ **~ to do sth** *Napoleon had no plans to create an Italian nation state.* ◇ **~ for sth** *When he left school he had no plans for the future.* **3 ~ (of sth)** a detailed map of a building, town, etc: *Figure 1.3b. Plan of the Mycenaean palace at Pylos.* ◇ *Anaximander is credited with drawing the first plan of the stars.* HELP In architecture, a **plan** is a detailed drawing or diagram showing the LAYOUT of a building or one floor of a building. ➲ *compare* ELEVATION (6)

plan² /plæn/ *verb* (-nn-) **1** [T, I] to make detailed arrangements for sth you want to do in the future: **~ sth** *Minor reforms were planned and implemented in the course of the 1980s.* ◇ *The experiments were all carefully planned in advance.* ◇ **~ for sth** *The high inflation rate made it harder for businesses to plan for the future.* ◇ **~ sth for sth** *No new employment legislation was planned for the 2010-2011 Parliamentary Session.* ◇ **~ how/what, etc...** *Patients became involved in planning how the new clinic would operate.* **2** [I, T] to intend or expect to do sth: **~ to do sth** *The Board of Education was planning to build a number of new schools in Washington Heights.* ◇ **~ on (doing) sth** *The logging companies were planning on liquidating all old growth areas within thirty years.* ◇ **~ that...** *The authors had not planned that the report would be made public.* ◇ **~ sth** *Gustavus Adolphus planned a series of campaigns which would bring him to the gates of Vienna.* **3** [T] **~ sth** to make a design or an outline for sth: *The Ancient Greeks planned these colonial cities as a grid pattern with a central space.*

pla·nar /ˈpleɪnə(r)/ *adj.* (*mathematics*) of or relating to a flat surface: *The three bonds around the nitrogen are found to be arranged in a planar geometry.*

plane /pleɪn/ *noun* **1** (*BrE also* **aero·plane**) (*NAmE also* **air·plane**) a flying vehicle with wings and one or more engines: **by ~** *The most contentious food miles are clocked up by fresh fruit and vegetables flown in by plane from overseas.* ◇ **+ noun** *Similar sources were employed by Weick (1990) in his study of the Tenerife plane crash in 1977.* **2** any flat or level surface; an imaginary flat surface through or joining material objects: **~ of sth** *A water molecule has two vertical planes of symmetry.* ◇ **in a/the... ~** *If two waves vibrate in the same plane and travel along the same path, they can interfere with each other.* **3 ~ (of sth)** a level of thought, existence or development: *In tragedy, the characters and acting style were on a much higher plane than the normal life of the audience.*

planet /ˈplænɪt/ *noun* **1** [C] a large round object in space that moves around a star (such as the sun) and receives light from it: *Newton's laws accounted for the motions of the planets.* ◇ *The planet Venus has an atmosphere about 100 times the mass of Earth's atmosphere.* **2 the planet** [sing.] used to mean 'the world', especially when talking about the environment: *The film's message is that only human action can save the planet.*

plan·et·ary /ˈplænətri; *NAmE* ˈplænəteri/ *adj.* [only before noun] connected with a planet or planets: *Kepler's first law of planetary motion stated that planets move in elliptical orbits.*

plan·ner /ˈplænə(r)/ *noun* **1** a person whose job is to plan the growth and development of a town: *Urban planners redesigned the city centre.* **2** a person who makes plans for a particular area of activity: *British military planners developed these tactics before the war.*

plan·ning /ˈplænɪŋ/ *noun* [U] **1** the act or process of making plans for sth: *Profiles of customers were developed by the bank for use in strategic planning.* ◇ *careful/long-term/central planning* ◇ **+ noun** *Local residents were involved in the planning process.* ➲ *see also* FAMILY PLANNING **2** the job of planning the growth and development of a town: *Urban planning in many countries has focused on the physical design of new suburbs.*

plant¹ /plɑːnt; *NAmE* plænt/ *noun* **1** [C] a living thing that grows in the earth and usually has a STEM, leaves and roots. Plants typically take in water and other substances through their roots, and make food in their leaves by PHOTOSYNTHESIS: *Iron toxicity has occasionally been observed in rice plants grown in lowlands.* ◇ *The majority of the flowering plants rely on animals for pollination and seed dispersal.* ◇ **+ noun** *Most of the plant species of the Mediterranean Basin came from the temperate north.* ◇ *plant growth/material/communities* **2** [C] a factory or place where power is produced or an industrial process takes place: *Many US workers attribute job losses to the fact that US firms are building new manufacturing plants outside the US.* ◇ *The dam's hydropower turbines will generate as much electricity as 18 nuclear power plants.* ➲ *see also* POWER PLANT **3** [U] the large machinery that is used in industrial processes: *The decision to purchase new plant and machinery requires consideration of the future cash flows generated by the capital item.*

plant² /plɑːnt; *NAmE* plænt/ *verb* **1 ~ sth** to put plants or seeds in the ground to grow: *Planting trees can have a cooling effect on surrounding areas by providing additional moisture.* ◇ **~ sth in sth** *Ten seedlings from the nine study species were planted in each subplot.* **2** to cover or supply an area of land with plants: **~ sth** *The settlers cleared the forests and planted fields.* ◇ **~ sth with sth** *The global area planted with GM crops has increased annually by more than 10% since they were introduced in 1996.* **3 ~ sth (in sth)** to make an idea become established in a person's mind or people's minds: *These new ideas are becoming more firmly planted in the public*

P

mind. **4 ~ sth (+ adv./prep.)** to hide sth such as a bomb in a place where it will not be found: *Historically, rebels and revolutionaries have planted bombs in civilian areas.*

plan·ta·tion /plɑːnˈteɪʃn; *NAmE* plænˈteɪʃn/ *noun* **1** a large area of land, especially in a hot country, where crops such as coffee, sugar, rubber, etc. are grown: *Slaves worked long hours on sugar plantations.* ◇ **+ noun** *The family originated in a French creole community of small plantation owners.* **2** a large area of land that is planted with trees to produce wood: **+ noun** *Areas of deforestation are permitted only in plantation forests.*

plant·ing /ˈplɑːntɪŋ; *NAmE* ˈplæntɪŋ/ *noun* [U, C] **~ (of sth)** an act of planting sth; something that has just been planted: *Opposition has substantially restricted the commercial planting of GM crops in Northern Europe.* ◇ *An initial planting of 1500 trees has helped to stabilize the coastline.*

plasma /ˈplæzmə/ (*also* **plasm** /ˈplæzəm/) *noun* [U] **1** (*biology* or *medical*) the clear liquid part of blood, in which the blood cells, etc. float: **+ noun** *Plasma levels were elevated in women with endometriosis.* **2** (*physics*) a gas that contains approximately equal numbers of positive and negative electric charges and is present in the sun and most stars: *If we pass a current through a column of plasma, it will generate a magnetic field around it.*

plas·tic[1] /ˈplæstɪk/ *noun* **1** [U, C, usually pl.] a light strong material that is produced by chemical processes and can be formed into shapes when heated. There are many different types of plastic, used to make different objects and FABRICS: *The wheel is made of plastic or metal and is very lightweight.* ◇ *Plastics are very good insulators.* **2 plastics** [U] the science of making plastics: *The Sun Belt became a haven for the new high-tech industries of aerospace, plastics, chemicals and electronics.*

plas·tic[2] /ˈplæstɪk/ *adj.* **1** made of plastic: *Take loose samples of the soil and put these into well-sealed plastic bags.* ◇ *No air should enter the plastic tube once the experiment starts.* **2** (of a material or substance) easily formed into different shapes: *Concrete was a much more plastic material than masonry.* **3** (*biology*) (of a living thing) able to adapt to change or variety in the environment: *Other plastic reproductive tactics in fish include sex change and reproductive suppression.*

plas·ti·city /plæˈstɪsəti/ *noun* [U] **1** (*technical*) the quality of being easily made into different shapes: *Fireclays are generally less pure and lack plasticity and strength.* **2** (*biology*) the ability of a living thing to adapt to changes in its environment or differences between its various HABITATS: *The major organ responsible for phenotypic plasticity in humans is the brain.*

plate /pleɪt/ *noun* **1** one of the very large pieces of rock, sometimes as large as a continent, that form the earth's surface: **+ noun** *Tectonic plate movements opened up and destroyed land bridges between islands.* ◇ *The earthquake occurred several hundred kilometres from India's active plate boundaries.* ➲ *see also* PLATE TECTONICS **2** a thin flat piece of metal, used especially to join or make sth stronger, or to pass an electric current: *A sheet of abrasive paper was bonded on a flat steel plate of a width of 10 cm.* ◇ *Several charging wires are suspended between two parallel metal plates.* **3** a shallow glass dish in which cells may be grown: *The sample is then placed onto a fresh plate.* **4** (*biology*) one of the thin flat structures that cover and protect other parts of an animal: *The head and front of the body of these animals were covered by bony plates.* **5** a thin sheet of glass, metal, etc. that is covered with chemicals so that it reacts to light and can form an image: *A photographic plate is used as a detector.* **6** a photograph that is used as a picture in a book, especially one that is printed on a separate page on high quality paper: *As we can see on Plate 1, the interference colours go through a repeating sequence.*

plat·eau /ˈplætəʊ; *NAmE* plæˈtoʊ/ *noun* (*pl.* **plat·eaux** or **plat·eaus** /ˈplætəʊz; *NAmE* plæˈtoʊz/) **1** an area of flat land that is higher than the land around it: *The mountain glaciers on the Tibetan plateau are receding rapidly.* **2** a time of little or no change after a period of growth or progress: *The town's population reached a plateau before rising again in the second half of the 1930s.*

ˌplate tecˈtonics *noun* [U] (*earth science*) the movements of the large sheets of rock (called PLATES) that form the earth's CRUST; the scientific study of these movements: *The theory of plate tectonics drastically changed our understanding of the dynamics of the Earth's interior.* ➲ *see also* CONTINENTAL DRIFT

plat·form /ˈplætfɔːm; *NAmE* ˈplætfɔːrm/ *noun* **1** a raised level surface on which people or things can stand: *There are viewing platforms where visitors may gape at the canyon.* ◇ *The company was forced to abandon its plans to sink the disused oil platform in the North Sea.* HELP A **platform** may be used by public speakers or performers; to *share a platform* is to speak or perform at the same event: *Welsh and Scottish nationalists shared a platform in speaking against the expected expenditure cuts.* **2** [usually sing.] the aims of a political party and the things that they say they will do if they are elected to power: *Plaid Cymru had perhaps the most distinctive platform for campaigning in the election.* ◇ **on a ~ (of/that...)** *The party won the 2009 general election on a platform that stressed a strong commitment to decentralization.* **3** an opportunity or a place for sb to express their opinions publicly or make progress in a particular area: *The Internet has become a global trading platform.* ◇ **~ for sth** *The forum will provide a platform for discussion of communication issues.* ◇ **~ for sb to do sth** *The tribunal offered an instructive platform for the government to devise ways of reducing ethnic tensions* **4** the type of computer system which determines what kind of software it can use: *Gambling and gaming services specially developed for mobile platforms are increasing rapidly.*

THESAURUS

plausible • credible • reasonable *adj.*

These words all describe sth that seems possible, sensible or likely to be true.

- it is plausible/credible/reasonable **that...**
- a plausible/reasonable **explanation/assumption/response**
- a plausible **hypothesis/scenario**
- credible **evidence**
- a reasonable **estimate**
- to **seem** plausible/credible/reasonable
- **highly/equally** plausible/credible

- **Plausible** describes an idea that seems possible or likely; **credible** emphasizes that sth seems likely because it comes from a source that can be believed or trusted: *There are two plausible explanations for these findings.* ◇ *Trade magazines are often perceived as credible sources of information.*
- **Reasonable** describes sth that seems likely because it is sensible or logical: *The most reasonable explanation is that the lake alkalinity is an indicator of changes in soil chemistry.*

plaus·ible /ˈplɔːzəbl/ *adj.* (of an excuse or explanation) reasonable and likely to be true: *Helmholtz did not regard internal friction as a plausible explanation for this phenomenon.* ◇ *These claims seem to be quite plausible.* ◇ **~ that...** *Similar work is under way in many countries and it is plausible that this approach will be useful on a world-wide basis.* ◇ **~ to do sth** *It was plausible to argue that city and state governments were prisoners of the market.*

OPP IMPLAUSIBLE ■ **plausi·bil·ity** /ˌplɔːzəˈbɪləti/ *noun* [U] *The subgroup effects lack biological plausibility and are likely to have arisen by chance.* ◇ **~ of sth** *This essay will examine the plausibility, or otherwise, of these various theories.* **plaus·ibly** /ˈplɔːzəbli/ *adv.*: *It has been plausibly argued that Bertram was of partially Roman descent.*

play[1] /pleɪ/ *verb* **1** [T] **~ a role/part (in sth)** to be involved in sth and have an effect on it: *John Maynard Keynes played a major role at the 1944 Bretton Woods conference.* ◇ *Nutritional deficiency also played a part in these high mortality rates.* **2** [I, T] to do things for pleasure, as children do; to enjoy yourself, rather than work: *The children were asked how many days a week they played outside.* ◇ **~ with sb** *Most of the boys loved to play with friends.* ◇ **~ with sth** *The older girls refused to play with clay.* ◇ **~ sth** *Numbers of children playing traditional games declined sharply.* **3** [T, I] to be involved in a game or sport; to compete against sb in a game or sport: **~ sth** *Increasing numbers of children began to play video games.* ◇ **~ (against) sb** *In 1997, the computer Deep Blue played against the world chess champion and beat him.* **4** [T, I] **~ (sth) (to sb) (on sth)** to perform on a musical instrument; to perform music: *to play the piano/violin/flute, etc.* ◇ *The god Pan played a song on his reed pipes.* ◇ *The orchestra played throughout the programme.* **5** [T, I] **~ (sth)** to make a radio, CD, etc. produce music or other sounds; to produce music or other sounds: *It is a device for storing and playing digital music files.* ◇ *Music playing in the background can increase customer satisfaction levels.* **6** [T] to act in a play, film, etc; to act the role of sb: **~ sth** *The part is played by a little-known Australian actor.* ◇ **~ sb** *Ben Kingsley played Gandhi.* **7** [T] **~ sth + adv./prep.** to deal with or present a situation in the way mentioned: *He played the situation carefully for maximum advantage.* IDM *see* HAND[1], PART

PHR V **ˌplay sth ˈback (to sb)** to play music, film, etc. that has been recorded on a CD, video, etc: *The teacher filmed the scene and then played it back on the big screen.* **ˌplay sth ˈdown** to try to make sth seem less important than it is: *Subsequent historians have tried to play down the Paris Commune's revolutionary and working-class nature.* OPP PLAY STH UP **ˌplay A ˈoff against B** (*BrE*) (*NAmE* **ˈplay A off B**) to put two people or groups in competition with each other, especially in order to get an advantage for yourself: *The Soviet government appeared to be playing one church off against the other.* **ˈplay on/upon sth 1** to make use of sth in order to create an effect: *The film plays on the tension between the illusion and reality.* **2** to take advantage of sb's feelings, etc. SYN EXPLOIT (3): *She played on the Emperor's fears until he had Asiaticus arrested.* **ˌplay ˈout** to develop in a particular way: *The research aimed to reveal how racial, ethnic and class issues play out in the classroom.* **ˌplay sth ˈup** to try to make sth seem more important than it is: *Applicants are often advised to play up their work experience.* OPP PLAY STH DOWN **ˈplay with sth** to use things in different ways to produce an interesting effect, or to see what effect they have: *In this poem Fitch plays with words which sound alike.*

play[2] /pleɪ/ *noun* **1** [U] the state of being active or in operation; the influence of one thing on another: **be in ~** *There are several external elements in play that make a democratic outcome more probable.* ◇ **come into ~** *Although effective fundraising was the key to their success, many other factors did come into play.* ◇ **bring/put sth into ~** *Clearly, new regulations need to be brought into play to restrain the behaviour of financial institutions.* ◇ **be at ~** *There were several motives at play here.* ◇ **~ of sth** *In conclusion, the free play of information and ideas across the world will be a vital factor in future innovation.* **2** [C] a piece of writing performed by actors in a theatre or on television or radio: *The play was first performed at the Blackfriars Theatre.* **3** [U] things that people, especially children, do for pleasure rather than as work: *It was one of the first academic studies of children's play.* ◇ **+ noun** *A safe play space is vital for every school.*

IDM **a play on ˈwords/sth** the use of a word or phrase that can have two different meanings, to create a particular effect: *The novel is set in a fictionalized city called 'Nakhlau', a play on 'Lucknow'.*

play·er /ˈpleɪə(r)/ *noun* **1** a company, country or person involved in a particular activity or area, especially in business or politics: *The market has no clear market leader but five major players.* ◇ **~ in (doing) sth** *The UK and India are global players in science and technology.* ◇ *Supermarkets have become the key players in shaping food consumption patterns in the UK.* **2** (in compounds) a machine for playing or showing sound or pictures that have been recorded on CDs, etc: *Freezing the frame on VCRs and DVD players opened up non-linear ways of viewing to audiences.* **3** a person who takes part in a game or sport: *Football players were sustaining significant levels of injuries.* **4** (usually in compounds) a person who plays a musical instrument: *This case involved an American saxophone player who came to England to play at a jazz club in London.*

play·wright /ˈpleɪraɪt/ *noun* a person who writes plays for the theatre, television or radio SYN DRAMATIST: *He is one of the greatest playwrights of the twentieth century.*

plea /pliː/ *noun* **1** an urgent emotional request: *Lincoln's pleas, of course, fell on deaf ears.* ◇ **~ for sth** *The Soviets rejected all pleas for help.* ◇ **~ to sb** *He then made his personal plea to the emperor.* ◇ **~ to do sth** *Bonine's plea to generate a larger group of scholars to study this region has not been met.* **2** (*law*) a statement made by or for sb who is accused of a crime: *The defendant changed his plea to guilty.* ◇ **~ to sth** *The prosecution accepted a guilty plea to the lesser offence of manslaughter.* **3 ~ of sth** (*law*) a reason given to a court for doing or not doing sth: *A successful plea of insanity results in a special verdict of 'not guilty by reason of insanity'.*

plead /pliːd/ *verb* (**pleaded, pleaded**) (*NAmE also* **pled, pled** /pled/) **1** [I, T, no passive] to state in court that you are guilty or not guilty of a crime: *A person can suffer from severe mental disorder and still be fit to plead.* ◇ **~ guilty/not guilty (to sth)** *They pleaded not guilty to the charges.* ◇ **~ sth** *The defendant was charged with murder and pleaded provocation.* **2** [I] to ask sb for sth in a very strong and serious way SYN BEG (1): **~ (with sb) (to do sth)** *At the end of Act II, Katherine pleads with Thomas to focus on what is best for his children.* ◇ **~ for sth** *States and localities pleaded for help from Washington.* **3** [T, no passive] to give sth as an explanation or excuse for sth: **~ sth** *The Wall Street analysts and large banks who lent Enron billions pleaded ignorance.* ◇ **~ that...** *They can legitimately plead that the decision is out of their hands.* **4** [I, T] to argue in support of sb/sth: **~ for sth** *In Chapter 11, Braj Kachru pleads for the acceptance of Asian writings in the canon of English literature.* ◇ **~ sth** *She appeared on television to plead the cause of political prisoners everywhere.*

pleas·ant /ˈpleznt/ *adj.* (**pleas·ant·er, pleas·ant·est**) (**more pleasant** and **most pleasant** are more common) enjoyable, pleasing or attractive: *Patients were asked to categorize each sensation as pleasant, unpleasant or neutral.* ◇ *It seems that visitors to the theme park only keep photographs of pleasant experiences (Sutton, 1992: 283).* OPP UNPLEASANT (1) ■ **pleas·ant·ly** *adv.*: *We were pleasantly surprised by the positive reaction from the local community.*

please /pliːz/ *verb* **1** [T, I] **~ (sb)** to make sb satisfied and happy: *A protective tariff which pleased both industrialists and agrarians was passed in January 1879.* ◇ *He was always eager to please.* **2** [I] often used after *as* or *what, where*, etc. to mean 'to want', 'to choose' or 'to like' to do

P

sth: *Most villagers were allowed to conduct life as they pleased, as long as they paid their taxes.*

pleased /pli:zd/ *adj.* feeling satisfied and happy about sth: *To their surprise, managers were not pleased, but horrified.* ◇ **~ with sb/sth** *It was expected that Ghanaian economists would be pleased with the news.* ◇ **~ (that)...** *Participants were pleased that someone was taking an interest in their condition.* ◇ **~ to have, learn, see, think, etc. sth** *Many Canadians are pleased to think of their country as being open to religious and cultural diversity.*

pleas·ing /ˈpli:zɪŋ/ *adj.* **~ (to sb/sth)** that gives you pleasure SYN APPEALING: *These refinements add strength to the building and are aesthetically pleasing to the viewer.*

pleas·ure /ˈpleʒə(r)/ *noun* **1** [U] a state of feeling or being happy or satisfied; the activity of enjoying yourself SYN ENJOYMENT (2): **~ in (doing) sth** *It is clear that a virtuous person will take pleasure in doing good.* ◇ **~ of (doing) sth** *Singer argues that, in practice, the suffering of animals inevitably exceeds the pleasure of meat-eating.* ◇ **for ~** *Academic reading is a different activity from reading for pleasure.* **2** [C] a thing that makes you happy or satisfied: *Many early Christians believed in avoiding such worldly pleasures as the public games and the theatre.*

pled (*NAmE*) *past tense, past part. of* PLEAD

pledge¹ /pledʒ/ *noun* a serious promise SYN COMMITMENT (2): *If a party is likely to win an election, it has little reason to make many specific pledges.* ◇ **~ of sth** *The EU and other developed countries made pledges of future emissions reductions.* ◇ **~ to do sth** *The countries made a series of pledges to cut emissions by 2020.* ◇ **~ that...** *The students were required to sign a pledge that they would teach in the state system for six years after graduation.*

pledge² /pledʒ/ *verb* to formally promise to give or do sth: **~ sth** *The donors' conference was held in Brussels, at which a total sum of $213 million was pledged.* ◇ **~ sth to sb/sth** *Foreign allies pledged their support to him and his family.* ◇ **~ to do sth** *He came into office pledging to restore decency, pride and integrity to the American political process.* ◇ **~ (that)...** *He pledged that there would no increase in income tax rates for the first two years.*

plen·ti·ful /ˈplentɪfl/ *adj.* available or existing in large amounts or numbers SYN ABUNDANT (1): *China in particular has a strongly expanding industry and relatively cheap and plentiful supplies of coal.*

plenty /ˈplenti/ *pron.* a large amount; as much or as many as you need: **~ (of sth)** *There is plenty of evidence that unemployment has many far-reaching effects other than loss of income.* ◇ **~ to do/say/offer, etc.** *So far, the practice side of project management has given the theorists plenty to think about.*

plot¹ /plɒt; *NAmE* plɑ:t/ *noun* **1** [C] **~ (of sth)** a GRAPH showing the relationship between two sets of numbers, quantities or factors: *Figure 1.10 shows a plot of the cross-section as a function of energy.* **2** [C, U] the series of events that form the story of a novel, play, film, etc: *The novel has three interconnected plots.* ◇ *Austen shifted the focus from plot to character.* **3** [C] a small piece of land that is used or intended for a particular purpose: *Three seedlings were planted per plot.* ◇ **~ of land** *They rented small plots of land on which to grow vegetables.* **4** [C] a secret plan made by a group of people to do sth wrong or illegal: *Most plots and revolts in the Caribbean were easily dealt with by the authorities.* ◇ **~ to do sth** *In 1820 a plot to assassinate the Cabinet was uncovered.*

plot² /plɒt; *NAmE* plɑ:t/ *verb* (**-tt-**) **1** [T] to mark points on a GRAPH and draw a line or curve connecting them; to show information on a graph: **~ sth** *We then plot a graph of the heat input against temperature.* ◇ *Figure 3.1 plots the ozone distribution in two ways.* ◇ **~ sth on sth** *Rates of inflation are plotted on the vertical axis and rates of unemployment on the horizontal axis.* ◇ **~ sth against sth** *The total monthly use was plotted against time to investigate trends in the utilization data.* **2** [T] **~ sth (on sth)** to mark sth on a map, for example the position or course of sth: *We plotted our original data on enlarged vertical aerial photographs.* **3** [I, T] to make a secret plan to harm sb, especially a government or its leader: **~ (with sb) (against sb)** *The king refused to hand over the fleece and plotted against Jason and his companions.* ◇ **~ to do sth** *He was charged with plotting to murder Lenin.* ◇ **~ sth** *The same men had plotted the assassination of the king.* **4** [T] **~ sth** to write the plot of a novel, play, etc: *At their most brilliant, his plays are carefully plotted, logical mystery tours.*

plug /plʌg/ *noun* **1** a small plastic object with two or three metal PINS, that connects a piece of electrical equipment to the main supply of electricity: *The cable is fitted with a two-pin plug.* **2** a thick round piece of plastic, rubber or metal that you put in the hole in a bath or sink to stop the water from flowing out: *She pulled out the plug and let the water drain away.*

plural¹ /ˈplʊərəl; *NAmE* ˈplʊrəl/ *noun* (*grammar*) (*abbr.* **pl.**) a form of a noun or verb that refers to more than one person or thing: **~ (of sth)** *In old English, the plural of 'child' was 'childer'.* ◇ **in the ~** *There exists a smaller group of nouns which occur only in the plural, including clothes, oats and groceries.* ⊃ *compare* SINGULAR¹

plural² /ˈplʊərəl; *NAmE* ˈplʊrəl/ *adj.* **1** (*abbr.* **pl.**) (*grammar*) connected with or having the plural form: *In many languages, plural nouns are longer than the corresponding singulars.* **2** more than one in number: *Representatives will reflect the plural and varied viewpoints of constituents.* **3** containing several different groups or elements: *A diversity of religions is an inevitable part of modern plural societies.*

plur·al·ism /ˈplʊərəlɪzəm; *NAmE* ˈplʊrəlɪzəm/ *noun* [U] **1** the existence of many different groups of people in one society, for example people of different races or of different political or religious beliefs: *Modern societies are said to be characterized by deep diversity and cultural pluralism.* **2** the belief that it is possible and good for different groups of people to live together in peace in one society: *A robust religious pluralism is a prerequisite in our modern globalized world.* **3** (*philosophy*) a theory or system that recognizes more than one set of principles or beliefs: *Moral pluralism has been both recognized and denied since the ancient world.*

plur·al·ist /ˈplʊərəlɪst; *NAmE* ˈplʊrəlɪst/ *adj.* (*also* **plur·al·is·tic** /ˌplʊərəˈlɪstɪk; *NAmE* ˌplʊrəˈlɪstɪk/) **1** (of a society) having many different groups of people and different political parties in it: *It is an important principle of broadcasting in a free, pluralist society that all sectors of society should be fairly represented on the screen.* **2** (*philosophy*) not based on a single set of principles or beliefs: *For Judge Power, neutrality required a pluralist approach on the part of the state, not a secularist one.*

plur·al·ity /plʊəˈræləti; *NAmE* plʊˈræləti/ *noun* (*pl.* **-ies**) [usually sing.] **1 ~ (of sth)** a large number: *Organizations reflect a plurality of interests.* **2 ~ (of sth) (over sb/sth)** (*US, politics*) the number of votes given to one person, political party, etc. when this number is less than 50% but more than any other single person, etc. receives: *This substantial swing gave them a large plurality of votes over the next largest party.* ⊃ *compare* MAJORITY (3)

plus¹ AWL /plʌs/ *prep.* **1** used when the two numbers or amounts mentioned are being added together: *The claimant demanded the return of $2 million plus interest.* OPP MINUS¹ (1) **2** as well as sth/sb; and also: *Intensified competition plus changes in technology have had dramatic results.*

P

IDM **plus or ˈminus** used when the number mentioned may actually be more or less by a particular amount: *The aim was to establish the value for the Hubble Constant to an accuracy of plus or minus 10 per cent.*

plus² AWL /plʌs/ *noun* **1** (*also* **ˈplus sign**) the symbol (+), used in mathematics: *The individual participant was scored with either a plus or a minus.* ◇ *The purpose of the bracket around the plus sign is to remind us that a full positive charge is not present.* OPP MINUS² (1) **2** **~ (of sth)** (*rather informal*) an advantage; a good thing: *The introduction highlighted some pluses and minuses of globalization.* OPP MINUS² (2)

poem /ˈpəʊɪm; *NAmE* ˈpoʊəm/ *noun* a piece of writing arranged in short lines. Poems try to express thoughts and feelings with the help of sound and rhythm: *The 'Voyage of the Argonauts' is an epic poem written in the third century BC.* ◇ *lyric/narrative poems*

poet /ˈpəʊɪt; *NAmE* ˈpoʊət/ *noun* a person who writes poems: *British Romantic poets influenced both the poetry and fiction of the century that followed their own.*

poet·ic /pəʊˈetɪk; *NAmE* poʊˈetɪk/ (*also less frequent* **poet·ical** /pəʊˈetɪkl; *NAmE* poʊˈetɪkl/) *adj.* **1** [only before noun] connected with poetry: *The article led to a critical re-evaluation of the British poetic tradition.* ◇ *At the end of the poem, the poetic language is not as elaborate.* **2** (*approving*) like or suggesting poetry, especially because it shows imagination and deep feeling: *The process of birth is described in poetic and idealized prose.* IDM *see* LICENCE ■ **poet·ic·al·ly** /pəʊˈetɪkli; *NAmE* poʊˈetɪkli/ *adv.*: *The 1937 film, 'The River', poetically argued the need for government intervention in water management.*

poet·ry /ˈpəʊətri; *NAmE* ˈpoʊətri/ *noun* [U] a collection of poems; poems in general SYN VERSE: *Symons (1907) emphasizes the intensity and suggestive power of Blake's poetry.* ◇ *Many of the students in this study love to write poetry but have little interest in the poets of the past.* ◇ *lyric/epic/narrative/Romantic poetry* ➲ *compare* PROSE

P

point¹ /pɔɪnt/ *noun* **1** [C] a thing that sb says or writes giving their opinion or stating a fact: *The article makes three key points.* ◇ *Korsgaard uses a variety of analogies to make her point.* ◇ *Finally, it is necessary to highlight one further point.* ◇ *There is an important point raised here:...* ◇ **~ that...** *In a way, this proves his point that police corruption is widespread.* **2** [C] (*usually* **the point**) the main or most important idea in sth that is said or done: *This argument is partly correct but misses the key point.* ◇ *He talked round the subject, but never really got to the point.* ◇ **~ that...** *Kent and Taylor (2002) emphasize the point that communication is a means of managing relationships.* **3** [U, sing.] the purpose or aim of sth: *Yet this argument simply misses the point.* ◇ **~ (of sth) (is to do sth)** *The point of the argument is to demonstrate that the working class is being dissolved.* ◇ **(no) ~ in doing sth** *There is no point in reasoning about how we should live if everything we do is in fact quite pointless.* **4** [C] a particular detail or fact: *Case studies are presented to illustrate particular points and principles.* **5** [C] **~ (that...)** a particular quality or feature that sb/sth has: *It is a major selling point that users can access their accounts from anywhere in the world.* ◇ *One of the book's strong points is that a number of contributors write from the perspective of non-Anglophone countries.* **6** [C] a particular time or stage of development: *The number of horses on farms continued to decline, reaching a low point in the late 1950s.* ◇ **at some ~ (in sth)** *A method for dealing with change is to construct possible scenarios that might emerge at some point in the future.* ◇ **on the ~ of sth** *He believed Germany was on the point of revolution.* ➲ *see also* STARTING POINT, TURNING POINT, VANTAGE POINT **7** [C] a particular place or area: *Coarse sand and gravel were deposited as sediments at the point where the Colorado River entered the lake.* ➲ *see also* FOCAL POINT **8** [C] a mark or unit on a scale of measurement: *The proportion of 19-year-olds who achieved this standard rose by 3 percentage points between 2002 and 2004.* ◇ *Perceived discrimination increased by .03 points on the 0-1 scale.* ➲ *see also* BOILING POINT (1), DATA POINT, MELTING POINT, PERCENTAGE POINT, REFERENCE POINT **9** [C] a unit of credit towards a score, award or benefit: *One point was awarded for each correct answer and scores were converted to percentages.* ◇ *There are no points available for professional qualifications, even when these involve several years' postgraduate study.* **10** [C] the sharp thin end of sth: *He then used a sharp point to incise details into the clay surface.* **11** [C] a small dot used in writing, especially the dot that separates a whole number from the part that comes after it: *The larger figures have been rounded off to eliminate decimal points.* ◇ *Twenty-one point four per cent of the children had a consultation with a physician.* ➲ *see also* FIXED POINT, FULL STOP **12** [C] **~ (of sth)** a very small dot of light or colour: *As this little point of light is scanned across the sample, the detector signal is recorded to build up an image.*

IDM **in point of ˈfact** used to say what is true in a situation: *In point of fact, their participants were by no means exclusively members of minority ethnic groups.* **make a ˈpoint of doing sth** to make sure you do sth because it is important or necessary: *The resolution made a point of stressing that corrupt officials should be dealt with 'no matter who they might be'.* **ˌmore to the ˈpoint** used to say that sth is more important than sth else: *We need to figure out not just what a 'minority' is but, more to the point, what is important about being a 'minority'.* **ˌpoint of ˈcontact** a place where you go or a person that you speak to when you are dealing with an organization: *Staff should be briefed about how to handle media inquiries and usually a central point of contact for the media is assigned.* **a ˌpoint of deˈparture** **1** an idea, a theory or an event that is used to start a discussion, an activity, etc: *Brunn's point of departure is man's innate artistic drive.* **2** a place where a journey starts: *More than 1 000 migrants were diverted back to their points of departure at ports on the West African coast.* **to the ˈpoint** expressed in a simple, clear way without any extra information or feelings SYN PERTINENT: *I have tried to keep general descriptions brief and to the point.* **to the ˈpoint of (doing) sth** to a degree that can be described as sth: *Some teenagers engage in physical exertion to the point of exhaustion as an indirect way of coping with anger.* **up to a (certain) ˈpoint** to some extent; to some degree but not completely: *Each component within this definition can be challenged, up to a point.* ➲ *more at* BESIDE, CASE, LABOUR²

point² /pɔɪnt/ *verb* **1** [I, T] to lead to or suggest a particular development or logical argument: **+ adv./prep.** *These arguments all point in the same direction.* ◇ **~ the way + adv./prep.** *Recent data and policy development point the way towards a better future.* ➲ thesaurus note *at* INDICATE **2** [I] **+ adv./prep.** to face in or be directed towards a particular direction: *A compass needle naturally points north.* ◇ *These three axes must pass through the centre of mass of the molecule, but can otherwise point in any direction.* **3** [T] **~ sth (at sb/sth)** to aim sth at sb/sth: *He pointed a gun at his victim.* **4** [I] **~ (at/to/towards sb/sth)** to stretch out your finger towards sb/sth in order to show sb where that sb/sth is: *The patient pointed towards her left foot.*

IDM **point a/the ˈfinger (at sb/sth)** to accuse sb of doing sth; to claim that sb/sth is responsible for sth negative: *In the face of growing child obesity, many are pointing the figure at television advertising by food manufacturers.*

PHRV **ˌpoint ˈout (to sb)** | **ˌpoint sth ˈout (to sb)** to mention sth in order to provide information or an opinion about it; to mention sth in order to make sb notice it: *As Hardie (1987) points out, we do not understand this* *process very well.* ◇ *Someone needs to point out to them the risks they are running.* ◇ **~ that...** *However, the authors point out that there are unsolved problems associated with their approach.* ˈ**point to sth** **1** to mention sth that you think is important and/or the reason why a particular situation exists: *Critics point to a number of continuing problems within the Civil Service.* **2** to suggest that sth is true or likely: *The results pointed strongly to folic acid being the effective preventive agent.* ˌ**point sth ˈup** to emphasize sth so that it becomes easier to notice SYN HIGHLIGHT[1] (1): *The article points up the remarkable differences between the male Romantic writers and their female peers.*

point·ed /ˈpɔɪntɪd/ *adj.* **1** having a sharp end: *Many of the smaller forms had small pointed teeth but the large species were often toothless.* **2** aimed in a clear and often critical way against a particular person or their behaviour: *The novel is a pointed satire on the popular newspaper industry.*

point·er /ˈpɔɪntə(r)/ *noun* **1** a sign that sth exists; a sign that shows how sth may develop in the future: *Although further analysis is required, these initial comparisons have offered some promising pointers.* ◇ **~ to sth** *Artistic style can be a useful pointer to the intrinsic cultural values of a society.* **2** (*rather informal*) a piece of advice: *The translations provide helpful pointers for the interpretation of tricky French passages.* **3** (*computing*) a small symbol that marks a point on a computer screen: *Put the mouse pointer on the rectangle again and double-click.*

point·less /ˈpɔɪntləs/ *adj.* having no purpose; not worth doing: *New misunderstandings will lead to pointless conflict.* ◇ **it is ~ doing sth** *It is pointless training the workforce if managers do not have the same level of knowledge.*

ˌ**point of ˈreference** *noun* (*pl.* **points of reference**) = REFERENCE POINT

ˌ**point of ˈview** *noun* (*pl.* **points of view**) **1** the particular attitude or opinion that sb has about sth SYN OPINION (1): *They often respected points of view that were at odds with their own.* ◇ *His point of view has been influenced by that of Mikhail Bakhtin.* **2** a particular way of considering or judging a situation SYN ANGLE (4), PERSPECTIVE (1): **from a... ~** *From a historical point of view, this idea is of considerable significance.* ◇ **from sb/sth's ~** *From the country's point of view, timber exports are underpriced.*

poi·son¹ /ˈpɔɪzn/ *noun* [U, C] **1** a substance that causes death or harm if it is swallowed or absorbed by a living thing: *He killed himself by taking poison.* ◇ *Patients suspected of being exposed to a poison or drug should be monitored closely.* **2 ~ (of sth)** an idea, a feeling, etc. that is extremely harmful: *In Buddhism these impulses are represented by the three poisons of greed, anger and stupidity.*

poi·son² /ˈpɔɪzn/ *verb* **1 ~ sb/yourself (with sth)** to harm or kill a person or an animal by giving them poison either deliberately or by accident: *He apparently poisoned himself in jail in 1759.* **2 ~ sth** to put poison in or on sth: *The rebel troops moved in, poisoning wells and systematically destroying crops.* **3 ~ sth** to have an extremely harmful effect on sth: *Continuing assassinations of senior government and military figures further poisoned the political atmosphere.*

poi·son·ing /ˈpɔɪzənɪŋ/ *noun* [U, C] **1** the fact or state of having swallowed or absorbed poison: *Most accidental poisoning in young children results from them exploring their environment and placing things in their mouths.* ◇ *An increase in acute alcohol poisonings was found.* **2** the act of killing or harming sb/sth by giving them poison: *The judge found that death had been caused by salt poisoning administered by the mother.*

poi·son·ous /ˈpɔɪzənəs/ *adj.* **1** (of a plant or substance) causing death or illness if swallowed or absorbed by a living thing SYN TOXIC (1): *The cloud of poisonous gas killed thousands of people.* ◇ **~ to sb/sth** *The plant is poisonous to livestock.* **2** (of an animal or insect) producing a poison that can cause death or illness if the animal or insect bites you: *Tourists were advised to wear boots to protect against poisonous snakes.* **3** extremely unpleasant; showing a desire to harm or upset sb: *He refers frequently to the country's poisonous political culture.*

polar /ˈpəʊlə(r); *NAmE* ˈpoʊlər/ *adj.* [only before noun] **1** connected with, or near the North or South Pole: *The last time the polar regions were significantly warmer than today was about 125 000 years ago.* ◇ *Global warming is already causing the polar ice caps to melt.* **2** directly opposite in character: *Their strategies were polar opposites.* **3** (*physics, chemistry*) having electrical or MAGNETIC polarity: *Water is a polar molecule, as oxygen has a greater electronegativity than hydrogen.* OPP NON-POLAR

po·lar·ity /pəˈlærəti/ *noun* (*pl.* **-ies**) **1** [U, C] (*physics*) the condition of having two poles with opposite qualities; the direction of a MAGNETIC or electric field: *It exhibits polarity when presented to a magnetic needle.* ◇ *The magnetic field peaks in strength immediately after switching polarity.* ◇ *Sunspots can be classified according to their magnetic field polarities.* **2** [U] **~ (between A and B)** a situation where two tendencies, opinions, etc. oppose each other: *The revival of the polarity between agriculture and trade goes back to the early twentieth century.* **3** [U, C] (*biology*) the tendency of living organisms or parts to develop with clearly different top and bottom or front and back ends, or to grow or lie in different directions: *As well as anteroposterior and dorso-ventral polarity, vertebrates also have bilateral symmetry.*

po·lar·iza·tion (*BrE also* **-isa·tion**) /ˌpəʊləraɪˈzeɪʃn; *NAmE* ˌpoʊlərəˈzeɪʃn/ *noun* [U, C] **1 ~ (of sth)** the act of making people separate into two groups with completely opposite opinions: *The summit was a contributory factor in the polarization of South African politics.* ◇ *This religious divide can be seen as another version of the polarizations in Enlightenment thinking.* **2 ~ (of sth)** the action of making waves of light, etc. VIBRATE in a single direction: *The polarization of the light is modified somewhat by reflection.* ◇ *The two polarizations of these waves travel at different velocities.* **3 ~ (of sth)** the action of giving polarity to sth: *If the tip is heated in the presence of a sufficiently strong electric field, polarization forces will draw migrating atoms towards the highest-field regions (Dyke and Dolan, 1956).*

po·lar·ize (*BrE also* **-ise**) /ˈpəʊləraɪz; *NAmE* ˈpoʊləraɪz/ *verb* **1** [I, T] to separate or make people separate into two groups with completely opposite opinions: *In the end, opinion polarized on a range of issues.* ◇ **~ sb/sth** *Increases in inequality polarize societies.* **2** [T] **~ sth** to make waves of light, etc. VIBRATE in a single direction: *If the vibrations are all along the same axis, the light is polarized.* **3** [T] **~ sth** to give polarity to sth: *It is possible to polarize a material with a suitably strong magnet.*

pole /pəʊl; *NAmE* poʊl/ *noun* **1** either of the two points at the opposite ends of the line on which the earth or any other planet turns: *No sunlight is present during the dark winter months at the poles.* ◇ **the North/South Pole** *The bears on these islands close to the North Pole are relatively isolated.* **2 ~ (of sth)** either of the two ends of a MAGNET, or the positive or negative points of an electric battery: *When a wire is moved between the poles of a magnet, a current will flow in the wire.* **3 ~ (of sth)** either of two opposite extremes: *These positions fall at opposite poles of the debate.* **4** a long thin straight piece of wood or metal, especially one with the end placed in the ground, used as a support: *Trees and wooden poles were worshipped in early antiquity.*

po·lice[1] /pəˈliːs/ *noun* (*often* **the police**) [pl.] an official organization whose job is to make people obey the law and to prevent and solve crime; the people who work for this organization: *He was arrested by the police for armed robbery.* ◇ **+ noun** *A 17-year-old kitchen porter confessed to the crime during the police investigation.*

po·lice[2] /pəˈliːs/ *verb* **1 ~ sth** (of the police, army, etc.) to go around a particular area to make sure that no one is breaking the law there: *The new industrial districts were harder to police.* **2 ~ sth** (of an official or a committee) to make sure that a particular set of rules is obeyed: *The regulations will be policed by factory inspectors.*

poˈlice force *noun* the police organization of a country, district or town: *The local police force has more calls on its time than it can meet.*

poˈlice officer (*also* **officer**) *noun* a member of the police: *A number of high-ranking police officers were interviewed.*

pol·icy AWL /ˈpɒləsi; *NAmE* ˈpɑːləsi/ *noun* (*pl.* **-ies**) **1** [C, U] a plan of action agreed or chosen by a political party, a business, etc: **~ of sth** *The government adopted a policy of gradual change.* ◇ **~ of doing sth** *Labour followed Conservative policy of allowing business to operate freely within the market.* ◇ **~ (on sth)** *Academic authorities had begun a campaign to reverse established policies on education.* ◇ *A matter will be referred to Cabinet if there is a major change in policy.* ➲ *see also* PUBLIC POLICY **2** [C, U] a principle that you believe in that influences how you behave; a way in which you usually behave: **~ of sth** *Losses will occur either way, but a policy of honesty will minimize those losses.* ◇ **~ of doing sth** *The policy of ignoring change until it is inevitable is not to be recommended.* **3** [C] a written statement of a contract of insurance: *She took out a policy to cover funeral expenses for her mother.* ◇ **insurance ~** *He attempted to claim on the insurance policy.*

▸ ADJECTIVE + POLICY **common** ◆ **foreign** ◆ **national** ◆ **domestic** ◆ **local** ◆ **public** ◆ **social** ◆ **monetary** ◆ **economic** ◆ **fiscal** ◆ **environmental** ◆ **industrial** *The EU could not come even remotely close to a common policy on the issue*

▸ NOUN + POLICY **government** ◆ **state** ◆ **health** ◆ **trade** ◆ **competition** ◆ **immigration** *Government policies are always subject to change.*

▸ VERB + POLICY **implement** ◆ **adopt** ◆ **introduce** ◆ **pursue**, **follow** ◆ **develop** ◆ **influence**, **affect**, **inform** ◆ **shape** ◆ **determine** ◆ **make**, **formulate** ◆ **set** ◆ **design** ◆ **aim** ◆ **change** ◆ **support** ◆ **promote** ◆ **evaluate** *The policies were implemented over the next three years.* ◇ *The United States has been heavily involved in shaping policy.*

▸ POLICY + NOUN **development** ◆ **process** ◆ **area** ◆ **issue** ◆ **agenda** ◆ **objective**, **goal** ◆ **debate** ◆ **change** ◆ **decision** ◆ **option** ◆ **recommendation** ◆ **implication** ◆ **initiative** ◆ **intervention** ◆ **implementation** ◆ **document** ◆ **instrument** ◆ **integration** *The Prime Minister also has the ability to intervene in any policy area.*

pol·icy·maker /ˈpɒləsimeɪkə(r); *NAmE* ˈpɑːləsimeɪkər/ *noun* a person responsible for or involved in forming policies, especially in politics: *Many economists and policymakers believe high employment will cause inflation.* ■ **pol·icy·mak·ing** /ˈpɒləsimeɪkɪŋ; *NAmE* ˈpɑːləsimeɪkɪŋ/ *noun* [U] *Democratization opened up more avenues for business participation in policymaking.*

po·lite /pəˈlaɪt/ *adj.* (**po·liter**, **po·litest**) HELP **more polite** and **most polite** are also common **1** having or showing good manners and respect for the feelings of others: *He was a relatively young man, very polite and with a quiet self-confidence.* **2** socially correct but not always sincere: *She endeavoured to maintain polite conversation at dinner.* **3** [only before noun] from a class of society that believes it is better than others: *In St Petersburg, the language of polite society was French.*

pol·it·ical /pəˈlɪtɪkl/ *adj.* **1** connected with the state, government or public affairs: *The political system in Germany makes reform difficult.* ◇ *Violence sometimes becomes widespread as ethnic groups compete for political power.* **2** connected with the different groups working in politics, especially their policies and the competition between them: *A question on the agenda is whether Britain should provide state funding for political parties.* **3** (of people) interested in or active in politics: *Dietrich was also very political.* **4** concerned with the competition for power within an organization, rather than with matters of principle: *Some employees feel they have to attend meetings for some internal political reason.*

▸ POLITICAL + NOUN **system** ◆ **power** ◆ **institution** ◆ **community** ◆ **process** ◆ **life** ◆ **culture** ◆ **participation** ◆ **activity** ◆ **action** ◆ **change** ◆ **theory** ◆ **philosophy** ◆ **ideology** ◆ **rights** ◆ **context** *Keohane suggests that political institutions have simply not kept pace with the changes in the international economy.* | **party** ◆ **leader** ◆ **elite** ◆ **issue** ◆ **agenda** ◆ **debate** ◆ **influence** *Political leaders are being pressed for action.*

▸ ADVERB + POLITICAL **highly** ◆ **intensely** ◆ **deeply** ◆ **explicitly**, **overtly** ◆ **inherently** ◆ **purely** ◆ **primarily** *Public ownership was a highly political issue.*

poˌlitical aˈsylum *noun* [U] = ASYLUM

pol·it·ic·al·ly /pəˈlɪtɪkli/ *adv.* in a way that is connected with politics: *As in many other countries, immigration is a politically sensitive issue.* ◇ *Politically motivated assassinations and further economic crises combined to weaken the government.* ◇ *They organized politically to win citizenship rights from the state.*

poˌlitical ˈscience (*also* **pol·it·ics**) *noun* [U] the study of government and politics: *The question of why some politicians run for higher office while others do not continues to be an important one in political science.*

poˌlitical ˈscientist *noun* an expert in political science: *Political disaffection in present-day democracies has received extensive attention from political scientists in recent years.*

pol·it·ician /ˌpɒləˈtɪʃn; *NAmE* ˌpɑːləˈtɪʃn/ *noun* a person whose job is concerned with politics, especially as an elected member of parliament, etc: *Labour politicians regularly argued for the need to address these problems.* ◇ *These people tend to mistrust elected politicians and parties.*

pol·iti·cize (*BrE also* **-ise**) /pəˈlɪtɪsaɪz/ *verb* [often passive] **1** to make a situation, activity or event more political: **~ sth** *Presidents have been more successful with their efforts to politicize the civil service and make career bureaucrats more responsive to political leadership.* ◇ **highly politicized** *The issue of GM foods has become highly politicized.* **2 ~ sb/sth** to make sb become more involved in politics; to make sth become more influenced by politics: *Often led by newly politicized women, the citizens' movements energized Japan's political scene in the early 1970s.* HELP It is often seen as a positive thing when people become **politicized**; however, when **politicize** is used to talk about issues or institutions, this may be seen as a negative thing. ■ **pol·iti·ciza·tion, -isa·tion** /pəˌlɪtɪsaɪˈzeɪʃn/ *noun* [U] **~ (of sb/sth)** *A number of commentators have complained about increased politicization of civil servants.* ◇ *The return of many Algerian migrants to Algeria was marked by a process of politicization.*

pol·it·ics /ˈpɒlətɪks; *NAmE* ˈpɑːlətɪks/ *noun* **1** [U+sing./pl. v.] the activities involved in getting and using power in public life, and being able to influence decisions that affect a country or society: *These men were to dominate*

Chinese politics from the late thirties until the seventies. ◇ *domestic/national/local politics* ◇ **go into ~** *Disillusioned with university life, he went into politics instead.* **2** [U +sing./pl. v.] the activities of governments concerning the political relations between states: *Britain's role in world politics during the 19th and 20th centuries was defined to a significant degree by Empire and by the retreat from Empire.* ◇ *global/international politics* **3** [U+sing./pl. v.] matters concerned with getting or using power within a particular group or organization: *Poorer-performing companies may be focused on internal politics rather than on the customer.* **4** [pl.] a person's political views or beliefs: *Debates over her politics, publications and lifestyle have fascinated generations.* **5** [U] = POLITICAL SCIENCE: *He questions whether there has been a distinctively British approach to teaching and studying politics in its universities.* **6** [sing.] **~ (of sth)** a system of political beliefs; a state of political affairs: *America had no need for a politics of the left committed to altering the basic economic structure.* **7** [sing., U+sing./pl. v.] **~ (of sth)** the principles connected with a particular area of activity or interest, especially when concerned with power and status: *Feminism is viewed as a politics of gender equality.* ◇ *identity/gender/feminist/sexual/racial/green politics*

pol·ity /ˈpɒləti; *NAmE* ˈpɑːləti/ *noun* (*pl.* **-ies**) (*formal*) **1** [U, C] a form or process of government: *The rules of the free market require a mutual separation of economy and polity.* ◇ *Western imperial expansion made possible for the first time the formation and operation of a global economy (Parry, 1966) and a global polity (Bull and Watson, 1984).* **2** [C] a society as a political unit: *As far as Hay is concerned, 'democratic polities get the level of participation they deserve'.*

poll¹ /pəʊl; *NAmE* poʊl/ *noun* **1** (*also* **oˈpinion poll**) [C] an act of questioning people who are representative of a larger group in order to get information about the general opinion SYN SURVEY¹ (1): *Public opinion polls show that there is a widespread support for environmental and green views.* ◇ *A poll conducted in August 1993 found that 38 per cent of the public trusted government scientists.* ◇ **+ noun** *Some poll questions directly asked respondents to evaluate one of the four claims.* **2** [C] (*also* **the polls** [pl.]) the process of voting at an election; the process of counting the votes: *The Liberals were again defeated at the polls in July 1886.* ◇ **go to the polls** *90 per cent of the potential electorate had gone to the polls.* **3** [sing.] the number of votes given in an election: *In the 2009 European elections, the Conservatives had actually topped the poll.* ◇ *He was returned with just 50.9 per cent of the poll.*

poll² /pəʊl; *NAmE* poʊl/ *verb* **1** [T, I] to receive a particular number of votes in an election: **~ sth** *The Conservatives polled 31% of the vote and won 14 seats.* ◇ **+ adv./prep.** *The party polled well in East Anglia.* **2** [T, usually passive] **~ sb** to ask a large number of members of the public what they think about sth SYN SURVEY² (1): *Only 14 per cent of those polled disapproved of the plan.*

pol·len /ˈpɒlən; *NAmE* ˈpɑːlən/ *noun* [U] fine powder, usually yellow, that is formed in flowers and carried to other flowers of the same kind by the wind or by insects, to make those flowers produce seeds: *The field bee forages primarily upon flowers that produce pollen and secrete nectar.* ◇ **+ noun** *Two types of pollen grains were detected:...*

pol·lin·ate /ˈpɒləneɪt; *NAmE* ˈpɑːləneɪt/ *verb* **~ sth** to put POLLEN into a flower or plant so that it produces seeds: *These bees were equally effective at pollinating both types of plants.* ■ **pol·lin·ation** /ˌpɒləˈneɪʃn; *NAmE* ˌpɑːləˈneɪʃn/ *noun* [U] *Many plants rely on insects for pollination.*

poll·ing /ˈpəʊlɪŋ; *NAmE* ˈpoʊlɪŋ/ *noun* [U] **1** the activity of voting: *Polling was generally conducted in an organized and peaceful manner.* ◇ **+ noun** *Many people went back to Labour in the final days of the campaign and even on polling day.* **2** the act of asking questions as part of an opinion poll: *Quota sampling is used intensively in commercial research, such as market research and political opinion polling.* ◇ **+ noun** *The study asks whether polls really represent public opinion, given that the questions are developed by polling organizations.*

pol·lu·tant /pəˈluːtənt/ *noun* a substance that pollutes sth, especially air and water: *By 1993, the Ministry of the Evironment had identified 25 808 major facilities emitting pollutants into the air.* ◇ *air/atmospheric/environmental pollutants*

pol·lute /pəˈluːt/ *verb* **1** [T, I] to add harmful or poisonous substances to land, air, water, etc. so that it is no longer pleasant or safe to use: **~ (sth)** *They want heavy taxes on the profits of firms that pollute the environment.* ◇ *Nuclear power itself does not pollute.* ◇ **~ sth with sth** *These weapons would pollute the atmosphere with very dangerous chemicals.* **2** [T] **~ sb/sth** to have a bad effect on people, society, etc: *Flaherty believed Inuit culture was polluted by contact with the outside world.*

pol·lu·tion /pəˈluːʃn/ *noun* [U] **1** harmful or poisonous substances that make land, air, water, etc. no longer pleasant or safe to use; the process of adding these substances to the environment: **air/water ~** *Strong winds help to disperse air pollution.* ◇ **~ (of sth)** *A government may reduce pollution of the environment by allowing emissions permits to be traded.* ◇ **+ noun** *Expenditure on pollution control is still low.* **2 noise/light ~** harmful or unpleasant levels of noise, or of artificial light at night: *Noise pollution can permanently impair hearing over time.*

poly·mer /ˈpɒlɪmə(r); *NAmE* ˈpɑːlɪmər/ *noun* (*chemistry*) a natural or artificial substance consisting of large MOLECULES that are made from combinations of small simple molecules: *At the environmental level, few organic polymers degrade at an acceptable rate in the biosphere.* ◇ **+ noun** *The polymer chain can be represented by the formula shown in 1.1.* ■ **poly·mer·ic** /ˈpɒlɪmerɪk; *NAmE* ˈpɑːlɪmerɪk/ *adj.*: *Many properties of a polymeric material are improved when the polymer chains are sufficiently long.*

P

poly·mer·ize (*BrE also* **-ise**) /ˈpɒlɪməraɪz; *NAmE* ˈpɑːlɪməraɪz; pəˈlɪməraɪz/ *verb* [I] (*chemistry*) to combine, or to make units of a chemical combine, to make a polymer: *The substances begin to polymerize, and are forced into a mould to create the desired shape.* ■ **poly·mer·iza·tion** /ˌpɒlɪməraɪˈzeɪʃn; *NAmE* ˌpɑːlɪmərəˈzeɪʃn; pəˌlɪmərəˈzeɪʃn/ *noun* [U] *Small amounts of an inhibitor are added to the liquid mix to prevent premature polymerization during storage.*

poly·no·mial /ˌpɒliˈnəʊmiəl; *NAmE* ˌpɑːliˈnoʊmiəl/ *noun* (*mathematics*) an expression that consists of two or more VARIABLES raised to whole-number POWERS: *The air properties were correlated by quadratic polynomials, as a function of temperature.*

poly·pep·tide /ˌpɒliˈpeptaɪd; *NAmE* ˌpɑːliˈpeptaɪd/ *noun* (*biochemistry*) a MOLECULE consisting of many AMINO ACIDS joined together. They form part of (or the whole of) PROTEIN molecules: **+ noun** *The hormone glucagon is composed of a single polypeptide chain of 29 amino acids.*

pool¹ /puːl/ *noun* **1** a small area of still water, especially one that has formed naturally: *Rain at any time of year may reduce salinity in pools almost to fresh water in a few hours.* HELP A **swimming pool** is an area of water that has been created for people to swim in. **2 ~ (of sth)** an amount of sth that is available and can be used when needed: *From the remaining pool of 72 rural counties, 40 were randomly selected.* ◇ *Underlying the skin, there is a pool of stem cells that can give rise to all the various types of skin cells.* HELP In biology, a **gene pool** is all of the GENES that are available within breeding populations of a particular species of animal or plant: *The genetic variation of some plants from their parents results in expansion of the gene pool for a particular species.* **3 ~ (of sb/sth)** a group of people, especially of people who are available for work when needed: *At the bottom, there is a pool of cheap labour providing services for the advanced sector.*

pool² /puːl/ *verb* **1** to put together information from different sources so that it can be considered together: **~ sth** *To our knowledge, no research pooling data from different years is available for the Swiss general population.* ◇ **pooled + noun** *Pooled estimates were substantially more reliable than individual assessments.* **2 ~ sth** to put together money, resources etc. from different people so that all of them can use it: *The skills of teachers can be pooled and shared.*

poor /pɔː(r); pʊə(r); *NAmE* pɔːr; pʊr/ *adj.* (**poor·er, poor·est**) **1** having very little money; not having enough money for basic needs: *More than 70% of people in poor countries live in villages.* ◇ *In general, rich people have better chances in life than poor people.* ◇ *poor households/neighbourhoods* OPP RICH (1) **2 the poor** *noun* [pl.] people who have very little money: *The right direction for the redistribution of wealth is from the rich to the poor, not vice versa.* OPP RICH (2) **3** not good; of a standard or quality that is low or lower than expected: *There is a strong association between low income and poor health.* ◇ *poor diet/nutrition/housing/hygiene* ◇ *The Sale of Goods Act 1979 does not give the consumer any rights where the product is of poor quality.* ◇ *However, the relatively poor performance of the country's economy has meant that educational success has not been translated into economic success.* **4 ~ in sth** lacking in sth: *They have a diet that is poor in fresh fruit and vegetables.* ◇ *These sediments are remarkably poor in iron.* OPP RICH (3) **5** (of a person) not good or skilled at sth: *Grant had no political experience and was a poor judge of character.* ◇ **~ at (doing) sth** *Collectives are notoriously poor at decision-making.*

P

poor·ly /ˈpɔːli; ˈpʊəli; *NAmE* ˈpɔːrli; ˈpʊrli/ *adv.* in a way that is not good enough: *The pathways in the brain responsible for the processing of pain signals are poorly understood.* ◇ *The companies had been performing poorly for many years.*

pope /pəʊp; *NAmE* poʊp/ *noun* (*often* **the Pope**) the leader of the Roman Catholic Church, who is also the Bishop of Rome: *the election of a new pope* ◇ *Pope Francis*

popu·lar /ˈpɒpjələ(r); *NAmE* ˈpɑːpjələr/ *adj.* **1** liked or admired by many people or by a particular person or group: *Email is a popular method of communication.* ◇ *Organic farming is becoming increasingly popular in many Western countries.* ◇ **~ with sb** *If changes take place, these may be popular with some employees, but not others.* OPP UNPOPULAR **2** [only before noun] (*sometimes disapproving*) made for the tastes and knowledge of ordinary people: *No other environmental issue receives quite as much attention in the popular press.* **3** [only before noun] (of an idea, belief or opinion) shared by most or many people: *Some scholars argue that this popular view is deeply flawed.* ◇ *Frankenstein in the popular imagination has virtually nothing to do with Shelley's novel.* **4** [only before noun] (of political activity) done by the ordinary people of a country rather than limited to politicians or political parties: *A party can win an absolute majority of seats with less than half the popular vote.* ◇ *There has been little popular support for Welsh independence.* IDM *see* CONTRARY¹

▸ POPULAR + NOUN **culture • music • song • media • press • fiction • literature • magazine • entertainment** *Naremore's scholarly work began with an interest in both modernist literature and popular culture.* | **belief • view • opinion • imagination • perception** *According to popular belief, pilgrimages to these sites bring luck and prosperity to the pilgrims.* | **support • sovereignty • vote • participation • movement** *Dynastic sovereignty gave way to popular sovereignty and states have accepted increasing limitations on their freedom to do as they choose.*

popu·lar·ity /ˌpɒpjuˈlærəti; *NAmE* ˌpɑːpjuˈlærəti/ *noun* [U] the state of being liked, enjoyed or supported by a large number of people: *Walter Scott enjoyed enormous popularity because his novels appealed to men as well as women.* ◇ **~ (of sth) (among/with sb)** *These ideas are gaining popularity among scholars in the field.* ◇ *Despite the immense popularity of films like 'Crocodile Dundee', cinema audiences were falling.*

popu·lar·ize (*BrE also* **-ise**) /ˈpɒpjələraɪz; *NAmE* ˈpɑːpjələraɪz/ *verb* **1 ~ sth** to make a lot of people know about sth and enjoy it: *His books have done much to popularize the sport.* **2 ~ sth** to make a difficult subject easier to understand for ordinary people: *The theories of Bowlby and others were popularized through women's magazines.* ■ **popu·lar·iza·tion, -isa·tion** /ˌpɒpjələraɪˈzeɪʃn; *NAmE* ˌpɑːpjələrəˈzeɪʃn/ *noun* [U] **~ (of sth)** *The popularization of home ownership in post-war Japan can hardly be seen as a natural outcome of economic growth.* ◇ *Newton's work started the popularization of science for the general public in the English language.*

popu·lar·ly /ˈpɒpjələli; *NAmE* ˈpɑːpjələrli/ *adv.* **1** by many or most people SYN COMMONLY: *Zhukov was popularly regarded as the outstanding Soviet war leader.* **2** by ordinary people, not by experts SYN COMMONLY: *They were members of the Church of Jesus Christ of Latter-day Saints, popularly known as Mormons.* **3** by the ordinary people of a country voting in an election: *The government was accountable to the monarch and not to a popularly elected parliament.*

popu·late /ˈpɒpjuleɪt; *NAmE* ˈpɑːpjuleɪt/ *verb* **1** [often passive] to live in an area and form its population SYN INHABIT: **be (densely/sparsely) populated** *Rural areas are typically much less densely populated than urban areas.* ◇ **(be) populated by sb** *It was possible to find villages entirely populated by widows and children.* **2 ~ sth (with sb/sth)** to move people or animals to an area to live there: *He hoped to populate the Midwest with settlers.* **3** to fill or be present in sth: **~ sth** *The galaxies, stars and planets that populate the universe today will some day disappear.* ◇ **~ sth with sb/sth** *The aim is to populate commercials with characters that viewers can identify with.* **4 ~ sth (with sth)** to add data to a document: *It is important that the database is populated with data which can be accessed and used effectively.*

popu·la·tion /ˌpɒpjuˈleɪʃn; *NAmE* ˌpɑːpjuˈleɪʃn/ *noun* **1** [C+sing./pl. v., U] (*abbr.* **pop.**) the total number of people who live in a particular area, city or country; all the people who live there: *Kuwait has a small population.* ◇ *The period from 1870 to 1880 saw a threefold increase in population in the region.* ◇ **~ of sth** *The vast majority of the population of the country are poverty-stricken.* **2** [C+sing./pl. v.] a particular group of people or animals living in a particular area: *There were massive casualties on both sides, with the civilian population suffering most.* ◇ **~ of sb/sth** *Their colleagues have studied populations of both species in the UK.* HELP In statistics, a **population** is the collection of items being STATISTICALLY analysed: *When populations are small, random events can lead them to behave atypically.*

▸ ADJECTIVE + POPULATION **total, entire, whole • large • small • local • old, elderly • diverse • indigenous, native** *The 1930 census reports a total population of 98 723 047 US citizens.* ◇ *A large population of rats was found present on the island.* | **general • ageing • national** *Scores for students were consistently higher than those for the general population.* | **human • adult • rural • urban •**

natural • **civilian** • **working** • **wild** • **vulnerable** *In Africa, 13% of the adult population now owns a mobile phone.*

▸ NOUN + POPULATION **world** *The world population increased to 1.6 billion by 1900.* | **study** • **target** • **patient** • **minority** • **immigrant** *In practice, however, collection of data from all members of the study population was impossible.*

▸ VERB + POPULATION **represent** • **reflect** • **estimate** • **study** • **target** • **sample** • **divide** • **cover** • **compare** • **protect** • **maintain** • **support** • **serve** *The members of the jury are intended to represent the population as a whole.* ◇ *The vast majority of studies sampled US populations.*

▸ POPULATION + VERB **grow, increase, rise** • **double** • **decline, fall, decrease** • **consist of** • **live** • **experience** • **(be) exposed to** *Most of India's vast, diverse population lives in peace and growing prosperity.*

▸ POPULATION + NOUN **growth, increase** • **decline** • **size** • **numbers** • **density** • **health** • **level** • **group** • **structure** • **change** • **dynamics** • **data** • **statistics** • **study** • **distribution** • **sample** • **estimate** • **movement** • **characteristics** • **pressure** *The Asiatic regions include some areas with very high rural population densities.* | **ageing** • **projections** *Population ageing is one of the major global challenges of the 21st century.* | **genetics** • **mean** *Work on the population genetics of the organism began in the 1970s.*

pore /pɔː(r)/ *noun* **1** ~ **(of/in/on sth)** one of the very small holes in the skin that sweat can pass through: *Some chemicals can enter the body this way through pores on the surface of the skin.* **2** ~ **(of/in/on sth)** one of the very small holes in the surface of a living thing or rock: *Pores develop in the cell membrane of infected cells.*

por·os·ity /pɔːˈrɒsəti; *NAmE* pɔːˈrɑːsəti/ *noun* [U] the quality or state of being porous: *Because of their porosity and permeability, sandstones act as hosts for water.*

por·ous /ˈpɔːrəs/ *adj.* **1** having many small holes that allow water or air to pass through slowly: *The deep basins themselves consist of permeable, porous rock.* ◇ *Activated charcoal is porous and has a very large surface area.* **2** (of a border or line) easy to cross because it is not fixed or protected enough: *The boundaries of the firm are often porous and alter through time.*

port /pɔːt; *NAmE* pɔːrt/ *noun* **1** [C] a town or city where ships load and UNLOAD goods: *Athens developed into a major naval and commercial port.* ◇ **+ noun** *Tokyo was already a bustling urban centre and port city.* **2** [C, U] (*abbr.* **Pt.**) a place where ships can load and UNLOAD goods or be protected from storms: *On July 8, 1853, US Commodore Matthew Perry sailed into Edo Bay and demanded that Japan open its ports to American vessels.* ◇ **in** ~ *The tonnage charge is based on ship size and berth hire for the time the vessel is in port.* ➲ *see also* AIRPORT **3** [C] (*computing*) a place on a computer where another piece of equipment can be attached: *The output port is the device that is responsible for moving the data between the processor and the peripheral.* **4** [C] an opening in an engine or machine for steam, liquid or air to enter or leave: *The mixing cylinder in the middle has two intake ports and two exhaust ports.*

IDM ˌ**port of ˈcall** one of a series of places that you visit on a journey or steps that you take in a process: *Growing numbers of people regard the Internet as their first port of call for both general and specific information about companies.* ˌ**port of ˈentry** a place where people and goods can enter or leave a country: *Asylum applications may be made at the port of entry.*

port·able /ˈpɔːtəbl; *NAmE* ˈpɔːrtəbl/ *adj.* easy to carry or move: *The recorder and the unit for storage of data were placed in a portable device.* ■ **port·abil·ity** /ˌpɔːtəˈbɪləti; *NAmE* ˌpɔːrtəˈbɪləti/ *noun* [U] *Respondents cited portability, speed and convenience as factors in their choice of device.*

port·folio /pɔːtˈfəʊliəʊ; *NAmE* pɔːrtˈfoʊlioʊ/ *noun* (*pl.* **-os**) **1** ~ **(of sth)** the range of products or services offered by a company or organization; the range of customers it has: *The aim is to achieve a balanced portfolio of products and services.* ◇ *There will be a mix of new and retained customers, but the proportions of each in the overall customer portfolio may vary.* **2** a set of shares or other ASSETS owned by a particular person or organization: *Large banks are better able to diversify their loan and investment portfolios.* ◇ **+ noun** *Portfolio management is based on an analysis of business by relative market share and market growth rate.* **3** a collection of examples of sb's work or documents relating to their work, especially for showing to a possible employer: *For the pieces of work that made up my portfolio, I tried to pull in as many aspects of biomedical science as I could.* ◇ ~ **of sth** *The NMC recommends that all nurses keep a portfolio of evidence of their ongoing professional development and learning.* **4 + noun** used to describe sth that combines a range or series of different activities, options, jobs, etc. into a whole: *Portfolio careers combining a number of different roles that a GP can perform have become more common.* **5** the particular area of responsibility of a government minister: *At the Office of Science and Technology Policy, her portfolio included climate change policy, carbon science research and energy issues.*

por·tion AWL /ˈpɔːʃn; *NAmE* ˈpɔːrʃn/ *noun* **1** ~ **(of sth)** one part of sth larger: *These figures represent a relatively small portion of total retail transactions.* ◇ *Simply copying large portions of text and changing a few words will also be regarded as plagiarism.* **2** ~ **(of sth)** an amount of food that is large enough for one person: *Eating five portions of fruit or vegetables a day will contribute to half of the daily recommended fibre intake.* **3** [usually sing.] ~ **(of sth)** a part of sth that is shared with other people SYN SHARE[2] (2): *Secular nobles spent their portion of the surplus product on things that demonstrated and enhanced their power and prestige.*

P

por·trait /ˈpɔːtreɪt; ˈpɔːtrət; *NAmE* ˈpɔːrtrət/ *noun* **1** ~ **(of sb/sth)** a painting, drawing or photograph of a person, especially of the head and shoulders: *Leading British artists such as Sir Joshua Reynolds painted portraits of West Indian absentee families.* **2** ~ **(of sb/sth)** a detailed description of sb/sth SYN DEPICTION (1): *He painted a gloomy portrait of the harsh existence of workers in Russia.*

por·tray /pɔːˈtreɪ; *NAmE* pɔːrˈtreɪ/ *verb* **1** to show sb/sth in a picture or film; to describe sb/sth in a piece of writing SYN DEPICT: ~ **sb/sth** *The show portrays real events as they happened.* ◇ ~ **sb/sth as sth** *In these paintings, he is portrayed as a young man without a beard.* **2** to describe or show sb/sth in a particular way, especially when this does not give a complete or accurate impression of what they are like SYN REPRESENT (4): ~ **sb/sth + adv./prep.** *These writers had various agendas and incentives to portray Michigan in a positive light.* ◇ *Political processes are shaped by the way in which the media portray political events.* ◇ ~ **sb/sth as sth** *She argues that women are traditionally portrayed as 'wives, mothers and victims' rather than 'policy experts, authorities and leaders'.* **3** ~ **sb/sth** to act a particular role in a film or play SYN PLAY[1] (6): *He chose Trevor Howard to portray Captain Bligh.*

por·tray·al /pɔːˈtreɪəl; *NAmE* pɔːrˈtreɪəl/ *noun* [C, U] ~ **(of sb/sth) (as sth)** a picture or description of sb/sth in a work of art or literature, a film, etc; a particular way in which this is done: *The portrayal of elderly people in advertising, soap operas, books, plays and cinema is often as figures of fun.* ◇ *an accurate/a sympathetic/a positive/a negative portrayal of sb/sth*

pose AWL /pəʊz; *NAmE* poʊz/ *verb* **1** [T] **~ sth** to create a problem that has to be dealt with: *They argue forcefully that GM crops pose a serious threat to biodiversity and human health.* ◇ *Parents are often unaware of the risks the Internet poses for their children.* **2** [T] **~ sth** to ask a question, especially one that needs serious thought SYN RAISE[1] (1): *Bodmer and Witten (1984) posed an interesting question:...* **3** [I] **~ as sb/sth** to pretend to be sb/sth that you are not: *A mystery shopper will pose as a real customer in order to evaluate how good the service is.* **4** [I] **~ (for sb/sth)** to sit or stand in a particular position in order to be painted, drawn or photographed: *The figures on Greek vases are portrayed in action, not contemplation: they almost never appear to be posing for the artist.*

▸ POSE + NOUN **problem • challenge • difficulty • dilemma • threat • risk, danger, hazard • obstacle, barrier** *Mapping the surface of ice sheets poses a challenge to scientists.*

posit /ˈpɒzɪt; *NAmE* ˈpɑːzɪt/ *verb* (*formal*) to suggest or accept that sth is true so that it can be used as the basis for an argument or a discussion SYN POSTULATE[1]: **~ sth** *Texts from early Hinduism posit the existence of an absolute ultimate reality (Brahman) and its identity with the soul (Atman).* ◇ **~ that...** *Raymond Williams posited that capitalism could function only with the help of advertising.*

pos·ition[1] /pəˈzɪʃn/ *noun* **1** [C] the place where sb/sth is located: **~ (of sb/sth)** *By determining the position of at least three satellites, the receiver can compute its own position.* ◇ **in a ~** *If two lights in different positions are flashed quickly one after the other, the observer seems to see one light that moves.* ◇ **at a ~** *If you enter a character, it will appear at the position indicated by the cursor.* **2** [U] the place where sb/sth is meant to be; the correct place: **into/out of ~** *Washington moved his troops into position to meet the British assault.* ◇ **in ~** *To ensure animals were not responding to the researcher, taping did not begin until 2–3 minutes after the researcher was in position.* **3** [C, U] **(in/into a) ~** the way in which sb is sitting or standing; the way in which sth is arranged: *The image represents a child a few feet tall in a standing position.* ◇ *Place the arm in the correct position, usually with the shoulder and elbow at 90 degrees.* ◇ *There may be pain on laughing, coughing, movement, or changing position when in bed.* **4** [C, usually sing.] the situation that sb is in, especially when it affects what they can and cannot do SYN SITUATION (1): *The legal position is clear enough: officers are employees and servants of the council.* ◇ **~ of sth** *The case example illustrates how people in positions of power can interpret the rules to their advantage.* ◇ **in a ~** *As soon as the interests of the two companies were in conflict, the directors were placed in an impossible position.* ◇ **~ to do sth** *Some immigrants are not in a position to bargain aggressively with their employers.* ➲ thesaurus note *at* SITUATION **5** [C] an opinion on or attitude towards a particular subject: **~ on sth** *At no point does she state her own position on these issues.* ◇ **~ that...** *He took the position that social science, like other sciences, must be a value-free endeavour.* **6** [C, U] **~ (of sb/sth)** the level of importance of a person, organization or thing when compared with others SYN STATUS (2): *Feminism seeks equal rights for women and men, and commitment to improve the position of women in society.* ◇ *The novel shows how Tom and Daisy can use their wealth and position to escape the consequences of their actions.* **7** [C] a job SYN POST[1] (1): *In 1937 he took a position at Stanford University as a professor.* ◇ **in a ~** *She has been in her current position for three to four years.* **8** [C] a place in a race, competition or test, when compared with others: *Schools that select their students are more able to control their league table position.* ◇ *The Liberal Democrats retained a prominent position in the polls for the rest of the campaign.*

▸ ADJECTIVE + POSITION **good • strong • current • unique • bargaining • legal • financial • political** *Community nurses are in a good position to offer support to young carers.* ◇ *Russia's bargaining position had been improved by military successes against Turkey.* | **current • original, starting, initial • common • strong • philosophical • political** *They are writing from very different philosophical positions.* | **dominant • strong • high • privileged • central • current • competitive • social • socio-economic** *Better-off people and countries will attempt to preserve and defend their privileged position.* | **key, senior, top • current** *Khrushchev as party secretary began to place his own nominees in key positions.*

▸ VERB + POSITION **hold • have • assume • adopt • change • maintain** *In the 1920s, America came to assume a pivotal position in the global economy.* ◇ *Pain may be relieved by adopting different positions.* | **occupy • reach • determine, find, establish • specify, describe, give • indicate, represent, show** *The butte occupies a position between the east and west forks of Carbon Canyon in the eastern Grand Canyon.* | **change • maintain • strengthen • improve** *They knew that violent protest only strengthened the position of the reactionaries.* | **take • define • support • defend** *Morgan appears to take the position that a manager's place is to resolve conflict.* | **establish, secure • strengthen, improve • occupy • reach • defend • use • abuse • lose** *The company was seeking to secure a dominant market position in the Far East.* | **hold, have • take, take up, assume • fill** *She has held positions at Yale, the National Research Council and Carnegie Mellon University.*

pos·ition[2] /pəˈzɪʃn/ *verb* **1** to put sb/sth in a particular position: **~ sb/sth** *Use the arrow keys to position the cursor.* ◇ **~ sb/sth + adv./prep.** *The camera is often positioned closer to the actors than in his previous films.* **2** [often passive] to put sb/sth in a particular situation, especially when it affects what they can and cannot do: **~ sb/sth +adv./prep.** *He sees the fundamental role of strategy as positioning the enterprise for the future.* ◇ **~ sb/sth/yourself to do sth** *Some large corporations are already positioning themselves to take advantage of these opportunities.* ◇ **be well positioned to do sth** *The UN is well positioned to put to use new information and communication technologies for pedagogical purposes.* **3** to advertise a product, service or business as satisfying the needs of a particular group of customers: **~ sth** *A firm's pricing objectives could be to position the brand so that it is perceived to be of a certain quality.* ◇ **~ sth as sth** *Red Bull is positioned as an energy drink for young adults.* ◇ **~ sth + adv./prep.** *There are various possibilities open to B2B marketing managers when choosing how to position their organization in the marketplace.*

pos·ition·al /pəˈzɪʃənəl/ *adj.* [only before noun] connected with the position of sb/sth: *This technology gives an absolute positional accuracy of 10 m, which is insufficient for survey purposes.*

pos·ition·ing /pəˈzɪʃənɪŋ/ *noun* [U] **1** the act of putting sb/sth in a particular position; the fact that sb/sth is in a particular position: *The quality of the barcode and its correct positioning on the specimen tube are critical for efficient processing.* **2** the act of advertising a product, service or business as satisfying the needs of a particular group of customers: *Market positioning is the adoption of a specific market stance in relation to the competition.* ◇ **~ of sth** *Packaging has also been found to be strongly associated with the positioning of a brand.*

posi·tive[1] AWL /ˈpɒzətɪv; *NAmE* ˈpɑːzətɪv/ *adj.* **1** good or useful: *Globalization processes can be understood as having both negative and positive impacts.* ◇ *84 per cent of teachers reported positive changes in classroom behaviour.* ◇ *Some positive signs are emerging in the battle against AIDS.* OPP NEGATIVE[1] (1) **2** noticing or emphasizing what is good in sb/sth; showing confidence or hope:

These students had more positive attitudes towards school than the comparison students. ◇ *The historian Ikei Masaru wrote: 'Americans... have many positive images of Japan and the Japanese.'* ◇ **~ about (doing) sth** *He feels very positive about enjoying the time he has got left with his family.* OPP NEGATIVE[1] (2) **3** expressing agreement, support or permission: *Electric commuter trains have now been introduced and have received a positive response from the public.* OPP NEGATIVE[1] (3) **4** aimed at dealing with sth; taking action to produce a particular result SYN ACTIVE[1] (1): *The occupier has a duty to take positive steps to keep the premises in good repair.* ◇ *The publication of these books is a positive move towards reducing the gap in the literature.* **5** giving clear or definite proof or information SYN CONCLUSIVE: *Positive evidence for the toxicity of nanotubes remains to be found.* ◇ **proof ~** *A publication like this is proof positive that the world has grown a lot smaller.* **6** (of a scientific test) showing that a substance or medical condition is present, or that a particular event has happened: *In latent TB infection, symptoms are absent but skin or blood tests are positive.* ◇ *Hyman argued that the positive results could all be explained by methodological errors and multiple analyses.* ◇ **~ for sth** *When a patient tests positive for HIV, he or she will be questioned about recent sexual contacts.* OPP NEGATIVE[1] (5) **7** (of a number or value) greater than zero: *In Equation 11.6, the amount invested, I, is always a positive number.* ◇ *All the countries experienced a collapse in GDP, with positive growth rates only appearing in the mid-1990s.* OPP NEGATIVE[1] (6) **8** (of a relationship between two amounts or events) related in such a way that, when one increases, the other also increases: *There is a positive relationship between good teaching practices and student achievement.* ◇ *These chemicals are found in salted, smoked or pickled meat and have a positive correlation with the development of certain cancers.* OPP NEGATIVE[1] (7) **9** containing or producing the type of electricity that is carried by a PROTON: *The resultant atom is electrically neutral, the positive protons and negative electrons balancing one another precisely.* ◇ *Current flows due to the movement of positive charge towards the negative electrode and negative charge towards the positive electrode.* OPP NEGATIVE[1] (8)

▸ POSITIVE + NOUN **impact, effect, influence • result, outcome • change • sign • value • role • contribution • aspect, side • experience • relationship** *Psychological research has demonstrated that these techniques are related to positive outcomes in mental health.* | **attitude, view, outlook • emotion, feeling • association, connotation • image** *Literature on resiliency has shown that children who have a positive outlook seem to adjust better.* | **feedback • response • answer** *The majority of feedback was very positive.* | **action • step, move • obligation** *This case suggests that local authorities have a positive obligation to protect the lives of children known to them.* | **number, integer • value • rate • growth** *This relation holds for any positive integer p.* | **relationship • correlation • association** *The available evidence does on balance suggest a positive association between green spaces and better health.*

▸ ADVERB + POSITIVE **generally, largely • consistently • highly** *The people I interviewed had generally positive memories of the period.* | **significantly • strongly • strictly** *Such results indicated that the level of physical activity had a significantly positive relationship to a child's self-concept.*

posi·tive² AWL /ˈpɒzətɪv; *NAmE* ˈpɑːzətɪv/ *noun* **1** the result of a test or an experiment that shows that a substance or condition is present: *Laboratory reports were often unreliable, with, for instance, contaminated swabs producing false positives.* OPP NEGATIVE[2] (2) **2** a good or useful quality or aspect; the aspects of a situation that are good or useful: *The positives clearly outweigh the negatives.* ◇ **the ~** *In focusing on the positive, this approach helps teachers view behaviour from a different perspective.* OPP NEGATIVE[2] (3)

ˌpositive ˈfeedback *noun* **1** [U] (*engineering*) the return of part of an OUTPUT signal to the INPUT, tending to increase the AMPLIFICATION, etc: *Too much positive feedback results in higher output distortion.* **2** [U, C] a situation in which the results of a process produce an increase in the process itself or its effects: *Glaciers would have provided positive feedback, reflecting incoming solar radiation and leading to further cooling.* ◇ *There are indications of a positive feedback in which increases in global temperature lower the ability of present soils and other parts of the biosphere to absorb CO_2.* ◇ **+ noun** *Capital accumulation is both a result and a cause of the firm's growth in economic strength—a positive feedback loop operating over time.*

posi·tive·ly AWL /ˈpɒzətɪvli; *NAmE* ˈpɑːzətɪvli/ *adv.* **1** in a way that is good or useful: *Research shows that peers influence the behaviour of children both positively and negatively.* OPP NEGATIVELY (1) **2** in a way that shows you are considering what is good in sb/sth, or are feeling confidence or hope: *The novelist and philosopher Iris Murdoch has argued that we can work to make ourselves feel more positively about other people.* OPP NEGATIVELY (2) **3** in a way that shows you approve or agree, or that involves giving the answer 'yes': *In the spring of 1894, China responded positively to Korea's request for military aid.* ◇ *For the question 'I try to follow what I'm taught about health', about 78% of the participants answered positively.* OPP NEGATIVELY (3) **4** in such a way that, when one thing increases, another thing also increases: *Academic achievement positively correlated with the number of days students attended extended-day programmes.* OPP NEGATIVELY (4) **5** in a way that leaves no possibility of doubt: *The claimant must positively prove that she was subjected to undue influence to enter into the transaction.* **6** in a way that contains or produces the type of electricity that is carried by an PROTON: *Each atom consists of a positively charged nucleus surrounded by a number of negatively charged electrons.* OPP NEGATIVELY (5)

pos·sess /pəˈzes/ *verb* (not used in the progressive tenses) **1 ~ sth** to have or own sth: *These women writers demanded improved education for women and the right of women to possess property.* ◇ *Britain was a founder member of NATO and possessed nuclear weapons.* **2** to have a particular quality or feature: **~ sth** *The new substance could possess properties that are new and enhance the functioning of the cell.* ◇ *Many non-profit service providers are highly trained professionals who possess expert knowledge in their field.* ◇ *to possess skills/capabilities/characteristics* ◇ **be possessed of sth** (*formal*) *Coleridge regards the nightingale as an embodiment of nature, possessed of mysterious powers.*

pos·ses·sion /pəˈzeʃn/ *noun* **1** [U] the state of having or owning sth: **~ of sth** *In the nineteenth-century novel, as in broader society, social status was based on the possession of property.* ◇ **in ~ of sth** *Oligarchy is rule by a few, usually those in possession of wealth.* ◇ **take ~ of sth** *The mortgagee was legally entitled to take possession of the property.* ◇ **in/into sb's/... ~** *Jamaica was easily the largest West Indian island to come into British possession.* **2** [C, usually pl.] something that you own or have with you at a particular time: *They lost their possessions and were lucky to escape with their lives.* ◇ *Entrants to his community had to give up all personal possessions.* **3** [C] a country that is controlled or governed by another country: *The French had Caribbean possessions mainly in Guadeloupe, Martinique and Saint-Domingue.* **4** [U] the state of having illegal drugs or weapons with you at a particular time: *He had been convicted in the UK on a number of occasions*

P

for drugs possession. **5** [U] the situation when sb's mind is believed to be controlled by an evil spirit: *They believed in the reality of evil spirits and demonic possession.*

pos·ses·sive /pəˈzesɪv/ *adj.* [usually before noun] (*grammar*) showing that sth belongs to sb/sth: *We use the possessive pronouns 'my' and 'mine' in a number of different ways.* ■ **pos·ses·sive** *noun* **~ (of sth)** *The form 'its' as a possessive of 'it' is only a few hundred years old*

pos·si·bil·ity /ˌpɒsəˈbɪləti; *NAmE* ˌpɑːsəˈbɪləti/ *noun* (*pl.* **-ies**) **1** [U, C] the fact that sth might exist, happen, or be true, but is not certain: *The expansion of the programme remains a distinct possibility.* ◇ **~ that...** *This raises the possibility that the two phenomena might be linked.* ◇ **~ of sth** *A rapid increase in size suggests the possibility of malignancy.* ◇ **~ of doing sth** *Scientists have explored the possibility of using DNA sequence data to trace the source of the outbreaks.* **2** [C, usually pl.] one of the different things that you can do in a particular situation: *Respondents are asked to give simple answers from a limited range of possibilities such as 'Strongly agree/Agree/Neutral/Disagree/Strongly disagree'.* ◇ **~ of sth** *Through this sequence of plays, Yeats began to explore the possibilities of an innovatory stage technique.* ◇ **~ for (doing) sth** *We applied this strategy to existing medicines to identify new possibilities for drug development.*

▸ ADJECTIVE + POSSIBILITY **interesting, intriguing, exciting • realistic • future** *A third possibility is biologically the most intriguing.* ◇ *Shelley's political thought explores future possibilities and not past defeats.* | **very • real, distinct, strong • remote • alternative • theoretical, logical** *This kind of anarchism denies the very possibility of legitimate authority.* ◇ *There was a real possibility that the child would suffer significant harm.*

▸ VERB + POSSIBILITY **explore, investigate, examine • consider • discuss • open (up), create • reduce, limit** *Residents considered the possibility that it might be an earthquake.* | **raise, suggest • exclude, eliminate, rule out, preclude • deny, ignore, reject • recognize, acknowledge, accept** *The evidence does not preclude the possibility of a common parentage.* | **offer, provide • see • exhaust** *Imaginative ideas emerge from individuals with the capacity to think differently and see possibilities.*

pos·sible /ˈpɒsəbl; *NAmE* ˈpɑːsəbl/ *adj.* **1** [not usually before noun] that can be done or achieved: *The models show that, under some conditions, such an evolution is theoretically possible.* ◇ **it is ~ to do sth** *Unfortunately, it is not yet possible to accurately identify those individuals who will develop the disease.* ◇ **it is ~ for sb to do sth** *It is now possible for anyone who owns a personal computer and a digital video camera to make movies and distribute them over the Internet.* ◇ **if ~** *We need to be able to detect and, if possible, correct errors.* OPP IMPOSSIBLE (1) **2** that might exist, happen or be true but is not certain: *The data could be invaluable for studying the possible effects of climate change.* ◇ *possible causes/reasons/solutions/outcomes* ◇ *The Middle East oil crisis of the early 1970s stimulated considerable research into possible alternative energy sources.* ◇ **it is ~ that...** *It is possible, and indeed likely, that the Dutch or the English were the first to trade some kind of brandy with Amerindians.* ➲ *compare* POTENTIAL[1] **3** reasonable or acceptable in a particular situation: *There are many possible explanations for this phenomenon.* ◇ *It is important to look into possible ways that recent conflicts could have been prevented.* **4** used after adjectives to emphasize that sth is the best, worst, etc. of its type: *With this system, its proponents argue, profit and loss calculations will bring about pollution reduction in the most efficient possible way.*

IDM **as quickly, much, soon, etc. as ˈpossible** as quickly, much, soon, etc. as you can: *This strategy aims at keeping wages as low as possible while forcing employees to give high levels of effort.*

pos·sibly /ˈpɒsəbli; *NAmE* ˈpɑːsəbli/ *adv.* **1** used to say that sth might exist, happen or be true, but it is not certain SYN PERHAPS (1): *Findings were not significant for the type 1 diabetes group, possibly due to the smaller sample size.* ◇ *This was possibly the largest volcanic eruption in history.* ◇ *Radiation absorbed by tissues leads to cell damage and mutations in DNA and may possibly lead to cancer.* **2** used to say that sb will do or has done as much as they can in order to make sth happen: *Advertisers need to find out everything they possibly can about the exact segment of the population they are targeting.*

post[1] /pəʊst; *NAmE* poʊst/ *noun* **1** [C] a job, especially an important one in a large organization SYN POSITION[1] (7): *Candidates for senior posts need to demonstrate solid management experience.* ◇ *From 1907, Michels held an academic post at the University of Turin.* ◇ *He picked personal supporters to fill key administrative posts.* **2** (*especially NAmE*) = POSTING (2) **3** (*BrE*) (*also* **mail** *NAmE, BrE*) [U] the official system used for sending and delivering letters and packages; letters and packages that are sent and delivered: **by ~** *A particular problem with questionnaires sent by post is that they frequently produce a low response rate.* **4** (*also* **post·ing**) [C] a piece of writing that forms part of a BLOG; a message sent to a discussion group on the Internet: *The full set of 62 blogs generated thousands of posts and many more comments.*

post[2] /pəʊst; *NAmE* poʊst/ *verb* **1** [T, I] to put information or pictures on a website: **~ sth (on/to sth)** *A message posted on an Internet discussion group can be accessed by anyone who has an Internet connection.* ◇ **~ on/to sth** *On Facebook, visitors can comment and post on the wall providing a potential forum for users.* **2** (*BrE*) (*NAmE* **mail**) [T] **~ sth (to sb)** to send a letter, etc. to sb by post: *Only a small percentage of letters posted were written by women.* ➲ *compare* MAIL[2] **3** [T] **~ sth + adv./prep.** to put a notice, etc. in a public place so that people can see it SYN DISPLAY[1] (1): *I recruited interviewees by posting fliers around a medium-size midwestern city.* **4** [T, usually passive] to send sb to a place for a period of time as part of their job: **be posted + adv./prep.** *He was posted to Washington as military attaché.* **5** [T] **~ sb + adv./prep.** to put sb, especially a soldier, in a particular place so that they can guard a building or area: *Guards were posted along the border.*

post[3] /pəʊst; *NAmE* poʊst/ *prep.* after: *American poetry post the 1950s has not had the same impact.*

pos·tal /ˈpəʊstl; *NAmE* ˈpoʊstl/ *adj.* [only before noun] **1** (*especially BrE*) involving things that are sent by post: *Many studies have used postal surveys sent to single responders such as a senior HR manager.* **2** connected with the official system for sending and delivering letters, etc: *Unlike postal services, telephone systems were not always placed under the direct control of the state.*

pos·ter /ˈpəʊstə(r); *NAmE* ˈpoʊstər/ *noun* **1** a large notice, often with a picture on it, that is put in a public place to advertise sth: **+ noun** *As with radio, poster campaigns can be very effective at reinforcing messages conveyed by other media.* **2** a large piece of paper that sb puts up at a conference to present the results of their research: **+ noun** *The team coordinated the poster presentation and stand at a recent conference.* **3** a person who posts sth on a BLOG or an Internet discussion group: *This issue seemed to be the only concern for posters.*

pos·ter·ior /pɒˈstɪəriə(r); *NAmE* pɑːˈstɪriər/ *adj.* [only before noun] located behind sth or at the back of sth: *The cerebellum is located in the posterior region of the head and is made up of two hemispheres.* ◇ *If the posterior end of the egg is irradiated with ultraviolet light, no germ cells develop.* OPP ANTERIOR

P

post·gradu·ate /ˌpəʊstˈɡrædʒuət; *NAmE* ˌpoʊstˈɡrædʒuət/ *noun* (*especially BrE*) a person who already holds a first degree and who is doing advanced study or research; a GRADUATE student: **+ noun** *They aimed to advertise the archive as a research resource and so attract postgraduate students to the university.* ◇ *postgraduate courses/education/training/study*

post hoc /ˌpəʊst ˈhɒk; *NAmE* ˌpoʊst ˈhɑːk/ *adj.* (*from Latin*) happening after the event: *These findings are post hoc analyses and do not constitute proof of effectiveness.* HELP In science, **post hoc** is often used to describe the analysis of data produced by an experiment or test, looking for sth that was not part of the original reason for the experiment or test. ■ **post hoc** *adv.*: *Field notes were written up more fully post hoc.*

post·hu·mous /ˈpɒstjʊməs; *NAmE* ˈpɑːstʃəməs/ *adj.* [usually before noun] happening, done, published, etc. after a person has died: *She approved the posthumous publication of Philip Sidney's works.* ◇ *His family began a campaign for a posthumous pardon.* ■ **post·hu·mous·ly** *adv.*: *Saussure presented this thesis in a series of lectures published posthumously by his students in 1916.*

ˌpost-inˈdustrial *adj.* [only before noun] (of a place or society) no longer relying on heavy industry (= the production of steel, large machinery, etc.): *Some geographers contend that the emerging post-industrial society is increasingly service-oriented.*

post·ing /ˈpəʊstɪŋ; *NAmE* ˈpoʊstɪŋ/ *noun* **1** = POST[1] (4) **2** (*especially BrE*) (*NAmE usually* **post**) **~ (to...)** a job that sb is sent to a particular place to do, especially for a limited period of time; the act of sending them there: *Before the 1880s, most European diplomats regarded a posting to the US as a form of social and political exile.*

post·mod·ern /ˌpəʊstˈmɒdn; *NAmE* ˌpoʊstˈmɑːdərn/ *adj.* connected with or influenced by postmodernism: *Postmodern theory has suggested new directions for research.* ◇ *In the postmodern world of new technologies, the concept of childhood is under challenge.*

post·mod·ern·ism /ˌpəʊstˈmɒdənɪzəm; *NAmE* ˌpoʊstˈmɑːdərnɪzəm/ *noun* [U] an attitude or approach to sth, such as a particular subject, that is a reaction against the accepted modern way of thinking about it HELP **Postmodernism** has influenced many fields including art, ARCHITECTURE, literature and cultural and social studies. A **postmodernist** AESTHETIC deliberately mixes features from traditional and modern styles and different artistic media; it tends to show a distrust of general theories and encourage critical engagement with a particular subject: *Since the late 1980s, the influence of postmodernism can be clearly documented in feminist research.* ◇ *It is helpful to see postmodernism as a critique of certain tendencies within modern thought, but not as the proclamation of an entirely new kind of society.* ➲ *compare* MODERNISM ■ **post·mod·ern·ist** /ˌpəʊstˈmɒdənɪst; *NAmE* ˌpoʊstˈmɑːdərnɪst/ *noun, adj.* [usually before noun] *Postmodernists question the legitimacy of all modern urban theories.* ◇ *Much postmodernist writing has opened social theory to new dimensions.*

post-natal /ˌpəʊstˈneɪtl; *NAmE* ˌpoʊstˈneɪtl/ (*BrE*) (*NAmE* **post-partum** /ˌpəʊst ˈpɑːtəm; *NAmE* ˌpoʊst ˈpɑːrtəm/) *adj.* [only before noun] connected with the period after the birth of a child: *Post-natal depression can have a huge immediate impact on the mother.* ➲ *compare* ANTENATAL

ˌpost-ˈoperative *adj.* [only before noun] connected with the period after a medical operation: *Post-operative intensive care will be required.*

post·pone /pəˈspəʊn; *NAmE* poʊˈspoʊn/ *verb* to arrange for an event, etc. to take place at a later time or date SYN PUT STH OFF: **~ sth** *The election was postponed because of the death of one of the candidates.* ◇ **~ sth to/until sth** *The patient may have their surgery postponed until the results of the tests are available.* ◇ **~ doing sth** *The success of the feminist movement enabled more women to pursue career paths and to postpone having children.* ➲ *compare* CANCEL (1) ■ **post·pone·ment** *noun* [U, C] *Roosevelt accepted a policy of postponement on any discussion of post-war economic arrangements.* ◇ **~ of sth** *Reproductive rates have risen among older women, suggesting a postponement of childbearing to the thirties or forties.*

pos·tu·late[1] /ˈpɒstjuleɪt; *NAmE* ˈpɑːstʃəleɪt/ *verb* (*formal*) to suggest or accept that sth is true so that it can be used as the basis for a theory SYN POSIT: **~ sth** *Mendel's theory postulated distinct causal factors that are passed on from parents to offspring.* ◇ **~ that...** *He postulated that the canyons had initially been cut by rivers during a lower stand of the sea in the Pleistocene epoch.*

pos·tu·late[2] /ˈpɒstjʊlət; *NAmE* ˈpɑːstʃələt/ *noun* (*formal*) a statement that is accepted as true, that forms the basis of a theory: *Like any theory, quantum mechanics starts out by making a number of postulates on which the theory is based.*

ˌpost-ˈwar *adj.* [only before noun] existing, happening or made in the period after a war, especially the Second World War: *Life in post-war Britain was hard.* ◇ *the post-war era/period/years* ◇ *European governments wanted American dollars for post-war reconstruction.*

pot /pɒt; *NAmE* pɑːt/ *noun* **1** a deep round container used for cooking things in: *Fragments of iron cooking pots were found at the site.* **2** (*especially BrE*) a container made of glass, CLAY or plastic, in which food or drink is stored: *The oldest physical evidence for the production of beer is in the remains of 5 000-year-old pots from Iran.* **3** a container of various kinds, made for a particular purpose: *After germination, plants were raised in a glasshouse in individual pots.*

po·tas·sium /pəˈtæsiəm/ *noun* [U] (*symb.* **K**) the chemical element of ATOMIC NUMBER 19. Potassium is a soft silver-white metal that exists mainly in COMPOUNDS which are used in industry and farming: *Some metals such as potassium and calcium are important nutrients required by plants and animals.*

P

po·tato /pəˈteɪtəʊ; *NAmE* pəˈteɪtoʊ/ *noun* (*pl.* **-oes**) [C, U] a round white vegetable with a brown or red skin that grows underground as part of the root of a plant also called a potato: *By the early nineteenth century, potatoes were the dominant staple in the diet of the Irish peasant class.* ◇ *Potato is one of the very few foods that is high in calories, protein, minerals and vitamins.*

po·tency /ˈpəʊtnsi; *NAmE* ˈpoʊtnsi/ *noun* [U] the power that sb/sth has to affect your body or mind: *Their accusations have lost potency due to the successful campaign to discredit them.* ◇ *The two drugs have the same potency.*

po·tent /ˈpəʊtnt; *NAmE* ˈpoʊtnt/ *adj.* having great power or influence; having a strong effect on your body or mind SYN POWERFUL (2): *It is apparent that financial markets have an extremely potent effect on corporate strategy.* ◇ *Symbolic rewards and punishments can be highly potent.* ◇ *Patients receiving potent topical steroids should be kept under regular review.*

po·ten·tial[1] AWL /pəˈtenʃl/ *adj.* [only before noun] that can develop into sth or be developed in the future SYN POSSIBLE (2): *The potential benefits of the treatment are great.* ◇ *Soils are a potential source of much information in archaeological studies.*

▸ POTENTIAL + NOUN **benefit, advantage, gain • problem, complication, pitfall • danger, threat, risk, hazard • harm • impact, effect, consequence • conflict • solution • source • target • bias • customer, buyer • competitor • donor • investor • partner, mate • participant** *There are* *potential problems associated with herbicide use, however.* ◇ *Businesses are well aware of the potential impact of the media for their activities and sales.*

po·ten·tial² AWL /pəˈtenʃl/ *noun* **1** [U] the possibility of sth happening or being developed or used: **~ for sth** *There was always the potential for misunderstanding.* ◇ **~ for doing sth** *Corporations have already recognized the potential for advertising products to schoolchildren.* ◇ **~ to do sth** *Genetic testing has the potential to improve public health outcomes.* **2** [U] qualities that exist and can be developed SYN PROMISE¹ (2): **with ~** *She was considered a young broadcaster with great potential.* ◇ **~ of sb/sth** *Shared leadership maximizes the potential of the team as a whole.* ◇ **~ as sth** *Africa had potential as both a supplier of raw materials for industrial Europe and a market for finished goods.* **3** [U, C] (*physics*) the difference in VOLTAGE between two points in an electric field or CIRCUIT: *The EEG measures changes in electrical potential using electrodes on the scalp.*

▸ ADJECTIVE + POTENTIAL **full • great, enormous • considerable, significant • future • economic** *After very promising starts with the company, they had never reached their full potential.*

▸ VERB + POTENTIAL **have, hold, possess • demonstrate, show • offer • maximize • exploit • explore • limit • highlight • recognize** *Integrative frameworks offer the potential to improve our understanding of organizations.* ◇ *Staff were unable to exploit the potential of computer software.* | **realize, fulfil, reach • evaluate, assess, measure** *Many things can prevent children from realizing their full potential.*

poˌtential ˈdifference *noun* **~ (between A and B)** (*physics*) the difference of electrical potential between two points: *Initially, both recording electrodes are left outside the cell; thus, no potential difference between the two electrodes is measured.* ◇ *A flow of an electrical current only occurs when there is a potential difference between two points within a circuit.*

poˌtential ˈenergy *noun* [U] (*physics*) the form of energy that an object gains due to its position or ALIGNMENT: *A rock perched up on the cliff has gravitational potential energy, which converts to kinetic energy when it falls.* ◇ **~ of sth** *Figure 23.24 shows how the potential energy of a molecule varies with its distance from the substrate surface.*

po·ten·tial·ly AWL /pəˈtenʃəli/ *adv.* possibly going to develop or be developed into sth, especially sth bad: *Only a very small minority of patients are potentially dangerous.* ◇ *potentially harmful/damaging/life-threatening/fatal/lethal* ◇ *Such negative publicity could potentially undermine the entire project.*

pound /paʊnd/ *noun* **1** [C] (*also technical* **ˌpound ˈsterling**) (*symb.* **£**) the unit of money in the UK, worth 100 pence: *Every pound spent on the website will generate a 10p donation to Oxfam.* ◇ *The US dollar is the most traded currency on the foreign exchange market, followed by the euro, the Japanese yen and the pound sterling.* ◇ **+ noun** *Dickens was replaced on the ten pound note by Charles Darwin in 2000.* ◇ *A spreadsheet program may be used in the course of preparing a multimillion pound construction contract.* HELP The **pound** is also the name of the unit of currency in several other countries, including Egypt, Syria and Lebanon. **2 the pound** [sing.] (*finance*) the value of the British pound compared with the value of the money of other countries: *The strong pound means that customers can buy products from overseas competitors more cheaply.* ◇ *The pound recovered strongly and both inflation and unemployment figures fell sharply.* **3** [C] (*abbr.* **lb**) a unit for measuring weight, equal to 0.454 of a kilogram: *Mark is six feet, five inches tall and weighs over three hundred pounds.* ◇ *Wheat flour sold wholesale for about $10 per 100 pounds.* HELP The **pound** is the standard unit of weight in the US. The UK now uses kilograms, but many older people still understand and use pounds as well.

pour /pɔː(r)/ *verb* **1** [I] **+ adv./prep.** (of liquid, smoke, light, etc.) to flow quickly in a continuous stream: *Eventually, molten lava pours out.* **2** [T] **~ sth (+ adv./prep.)** to make a liquid or other substance flow from a container in a continuous stream: *The reaction mixture was poured into 50 ml of water.* **3** [I] **+ adv./prep.** to come or go somewhere continuously in large numbers SYN FLOOD² (3): *Complaints poured in.* ◇ *The Taiping rebels of the south were pouring down the Yangtze towards Nanjing.* IDM *see* MONEY

PHR V **ˌpour sth ˈinto sth** to give a lot of money, attention or effort to sth over a period of time: *They began to pour government money into the industry.* ◇ *The King poured all his energy into restoring direction and unity to the movement.* **ˌpour sth ˈout** to express your feelings, especially after keeping them secret or hidden: *Many writers poured out their feelings onto the page as an emotional compensation for the toughness of war.*

pov·erty /ˈpɒvəti; *NAmE* ˈpɑːvərti/ *noun* **1** [U] the state of being poor: *The programme has assisted in alleviating poverty and improving food security in the most vulnerable populations.* ◇ **in ~** *The proportion of people living in extreme poverty fell from 29% to 23%.* ◇ **+ noun** *The problem of poverty reduction has moved to the forefront of government attention.* **2** [U, sing.] a lack of sth; poor quality: *One of the best predictors of Internet poverty is being a lone parent.* ◇ **~ of sth** *Policymakers have revealed a poverty of imagination when addressing this issue.*

the ˈpoverty line (*also* **the ˈpoverty level** *especially in US*) *noun* [sing.] the official level of income that is necessary to be able to buy the basic things you need, such as food and clothes, and to pay for somewhere to live: *Sixty per cent of the population live below the poverty line.*

pow·der /ˈpaʊdə(r)/ *noun* [U, C] a dry mass of very small fine pieces or grains: *If the family was poor and used insufficient milk powder, the baby was undernourished.* ◇ *Each dried plant sample was ground to a fine powder using a ball mill.*

power¹ /ˈpaʊə(r)/ *noun* **1** [U] the ability to control people or things: **~ (over sb/sth)** *Employers are able to exercise power over their employees because good jobs are scarce.* ◇ **~ to do sth** *Technology has the power to shape society.* ◇ **+ noun** *Aboriginal voices have been largely unheard because of unequal power relations.* **2** [U] political control of a country or an area: *The military again seized power in 1984.* ◇ *The election in May 1997 brought a change of government when Tony Blair's Labour Party came to power.* ◇ **in ~** *After decades in power, the leadership turned corrupt.* ◇ **+ noun** *The king died and a power struggle ensued.* ➲ *see also* BALANCE OF POWER **3** [U] (*also* **powers** [pl.]) (in people) the ability or opportunity to do sth or to act in a particular way: **~ to do sth** *Empowerment means acquiring the power to think and act freely.* ◇ **in/within sb's ~** *Anorexics often do not accept that it is within their power to change.* ◇ **~ of sth** *Lenin needed all his powers of persuasion to convince his party.* **4** [U, C, usually pl.] the right or authority of a person or group to do sth: **~ to do sth** *Only the Security Council has the power to enforce international law.* ◇ **~ (of sth)** *The 2006 Act gave increased powers of arrest to immigration officers.* **5** [C] a country with a lot of influence in world affairs: *At the turn of the 20th century, Britain was the world's leading imperial power.* ➲ *see also* SUPERPOWER **6** [U] (in compounds) strength or influence in a particular area of activity: *Their efforts to exercise collective bargaining power against multinational companies have failed.* ◇ **~ of sth** *The market exchange rates do not necessarily reflect the relative purchasing power of currencies.* ➲ *see also* BARGAINING

P

POWER, PURCHASING POWER **7** [U] the influence of a particular thing or group within society: *Democracy is about people power.* ◇ **~ of sb/sth** *The power of the supermarkets means that traditional brands are struggling.* **8** [U] **~ (of sth/sb)** the physical strength of sth/sb: *Sandy coasts tend to enhance the power of waves.* **9** [U] **~ (of sth)** the quality of being effective or of having a strong effect on people's feelings or thoughts: *The power of his argument lay in the many historic examples he listed.* **10** [U] energy that can be collected and used to operate a machine, to make electricity, etc: *Electric power is clean and convenient.* ◇ *nuclear/wind power* ◇ *Generating mechanical power from the combustion of fossil fuel is not a straightforward matter.* ◇ **+ noun** *The current drawn from the power supply remains constant.* ➲ *see also* POWER PLANT **11** [C, U] **~ (of sth)** (*mathematics*) the number of times that an amount is to be multiplied by itself: *4 to the power of 3 is 64 (= 4 × 4 × 4 = 64).*

▸ ADJECTIVE + NOUN **considerable • absolute • relative • real • symbolic • political** *They had always defended and respected the king's absolute power.* | **legislative • regulatory • decision-making • executive • sovereign • formal** *Local authorities have few legislative powers of their own.* | **great • global • economic • military** *Moreover, men with greater economic power than their partners tended to share less than those without such power.* | **major • dominant • foreign • imperial, colonial • sovereign** *China emerged as a major military power.* | **considerable • great • explanatory • predictive • statistical** *The ability to explain this complex behaviour illustrates the great explanatory power of evolutionary reasoning.*

▸ VERB + POWER **possess, have • use • lack** *He possessed great intellectual powers, originality and drive.* | **enjoy • exercise, exert • abuse • give • limit • lose** *The rules were designed to prevent directors from abusing their considerable powers.* | **hold • wield • retain • consolidate • share** *Pro-business administrations have held power for most of the period since 1970.* | **gain, acquire • confer • delegate** *The board may delegate power to the chairman.* | **seize • come to** *Darius I seized power and reorganized the empire.*

▸ POWER + NOUN **relations, relationship • dynamics • structure • imbalance • struggle • politics** *Processes constitute a vital part of the power structure within an organization.*

power² /ˈpaʊə(r)/ *verb* [usually passive] to supply a machine or vehicle with the energy that makes it work: **be powered (by sth)** *Almost all highway vehicles are powered by four-stroke cycle engines.*

power·ful /ˈpaʊəfl; *NAmE* ˈpaʊərfl/ *adj.* **1** (of people, organizations or groups) able to control and influence people and events SYN INFLUENTIAL: *Shaftesbury was a powerful ally of Charles II.* ◇ *Global corporate structures have become more powerful than many nations.* **2** having great power or force; very effective: *More powerful engines employ more cylinders.* ◇ *Zeus wields the most powerful weapon in the universe, the thunderbolt.* ◇ *With the aid of powerful computers, we can predict, with quite good accuracy, the shapes of small- to medium-sized molecules.* **3** having a strong effect on people's feelings or thoughts: *Religious belief systems can be immensely powerful.* ◇ *Language has a powerful influence in shaping our attitudes towards disability.* ◇ *The framework provides a powerful analytical tool for understanding the dynamics of an industry.*

power·ful·ly /ˈpaʊəfəli; *NAmE* ˈpaʊərfəli/ *adv.* in a way that has a strong effect or people's feelings or thoughts: *The book powerfully evokes the miseries of life in the slums.* ◇ *He argues powerfully in favour of promoting diversity.*

power·less /ˈpaʊələs; *NAmE* ˈpaʊərləs/ *adj.* **1** without power to control or influence sb/sth: *States are by no means powerless in the face of economic globalization.* **2 ~ to do sth** completely unable to do sth: *They felt powerless and incompetent to do anything about the situation.* ■ **power·less·ness** *noun* [U] *Volunteering can lessen feelings of powerlessness that may accompany the transition to retirement.*

ˈpower plant (*BrE also* **ˈpower station**) *noun* a building or group of buildings where electricity is produced

PR /ˌpiː ˈɑː(r)/ *noun* [U] the abbreviation for PUBLIC RELATIONS: *a PR department/agency/campaign* ◇ *The article is very good PR for the theatre.*

prac·tic·able /ˈpræktɪkəbl/ *adj.* that can be done or used successfully SYN FEASIBLE, WORKABLE (1): *The Act requires employers to ensure employees' safety, health and welfare as far as is reasonably practicable.* ◇ **it is ~ (for sb) to do sth** *It is not always practicable to use a tape recorder in interviews, for example in a noisy environment.* ■ **prac·tic·abil·ity** /ˌpræktɪkəˈbɪləti/ *noun* [U] *Due to costs and practicability, it was not possible to objectively assess patients' level of physical activity.*

prac·tical /ˈpræktɪkl/ *adj.* **1** connected with real situations rather than with ideas or theories: *I gained practical experience working with animals as a volunteer at rescue centres in South America.* ◇ *There is a world of difference between theoretical and practical machines.* ◇ *In purely practical terms, driving a motor vehicle is one of the most risky activities that the vast majority of the population ever undertakes.* ➲ *compare* THEORETICAL (1) **2** (of an idea, a method or a course of action) right or sensible; possible and likely to be successful SYN FEASIBLE, WORKABLE (1): *In the 1920s, the central generation of electricity made electrification of lighthouses a practical proposition.* ◇ **it is ~ (for sb) to do sth** *It is not always practical for patients to modify their footwear to the extent necessary to avoid pain.* OPP IMPRACTICAL (1) **3** (of things) useful or suitable for a particular purpose: *It has long been recognized that legal codes were more than just a practical tool of government and order.* OPP IMPRACTICAL **4** (of a person) sensible and realistic in the way they approach a problem or situation: *Results-based leadership is exemplified by eminently practical people who are very effective in getting things done.*

IDM **for (all) ˈpractical purposes** used to say that sth is so nearly true that it can be considered to be so: *In classical Athens, there was for all practical purposes no law enforcement agency.*

▸ PRACTICAL + NOUN **experience • skill • work • help • advice • example • use, application • implementation • approach • consequence • implication • value • problem, difficulty • limitation • issue, matter • consideration • significance, importance • relevance • reason** *A free online support service provides anonymous and practical advice about money matters and debt.* | **approach • solution • suggestion** *The group made a number of very practical suggestions for improving their class discussions.*

prac·ti·cal·ity /ˌpræktɪˈkæləti/ *noun* **1 practicalities** [pl.] the real facts and circumstances rather than ideas or theories: *Concentrate upon identifying as many ideas as possible without worrying about the practicalities.* ◇ **~ of (doing) sth** *For most, the details and practicalities of achieving a good diet are not always clear.* **2** [U] **~ (of sth)** the quality of being suitable, or likely to be successful SYN FEASIBILITY: *Even Nesselhauf is sceptical about the practicality of her own suggestion.*

prac·tic·al·ly /ˈpræktɪkli/ *adv.* **1** almost; very nearly SYN VIRTUALLY: *These two translations are practically identical, with minor, insignificant differences in word order and word choice.* ◇ *It is becoming practically impossible for law students to do without at least a basic knowledge of European law.* **2** in a realistic or sensible way; in real situations: *The experiences of China, Malaysia and Singapore demonstrate that policy integration is practically possible and that it works.* ◇ *Several practically important themes were touched on in this meeting.* ◇ *Practically speaking, there could be large-scale ranching of cattle and horses only in times of low population density.* ➲ *compare* THEORETICALLY

prac·tice¹ /ˈpræktɪs/ *noun* **1** [U] action rather than ideas or theories: *Systems have developed to make sure that new research findings are implemented in clinical practice.* ◇ **~ of sth** *The earliest book on the theory and practice of Chinese medicine was written during the period 770 BC to 221 BC.* ◇ **put sth into ~** *The modern secret ballot was initially put into practice in Australia, but the idea first emerged in France.* **2** [U, C] a way of doing sth that is the usual or expected way; a custom or habit: *It is good practice to ask clients what they think will happen in counselling and what they expect to get out of it.* ◇ *Investigations suggested that poor working practices had led to contamination within the factory.* ◇ *The chewing of coffee beans was a practice adopted by those seeking an aid for keeping alert on long journeys.* ➲ *see also* BEST PRACTICE, CODE OF PRACTICE **3** [U, C] **~ (of sth)** the work or business of some professional people such as doctors, dentists and lawyers; the place where they work: *Many men had devoted their lives to study in the hopes of making a living from the practice of law.* ◇ *Two doctors bought a property together, from which they ran a medical practice.* ➲ *see also* GENERAL PRACTICE **4** [U] doing an activity or training regularly so that you can improve your skill; the time you spend doing this: *Performance improves with practice, regardless of what is being learned.* ◇ **~ in sth** *Students do a lot of practice in comprehension by reading books that they can understand on their own.*

IDM **in ˈpractice** used to talk about what actually happens as opposed to what is meant or believed to happen: *At the time of its design in the 1970s, it was expected that the Thames Barrier would be used once every few years. In practice, however, it has been used 6 times a year, on average, over the past 6 years.*

▸ ADJECTIVE + PRACTICE **good • common • everyday • current • new • standard • traditional • professional • social • cultural • religious • medical** *It is common practice to speak of cat, house and car as 'countable nouns'.*

▸ NOUN + PRACTICE **management • work • business • health** *There is a need to understand the relationship between management practices, worker experiences and consumer outcomes.*

▸ VERB + PRACTICE **adopt • follow • share • implement • support • promote • inform • influence • shape • identify • change • adapt • develop • improve** *Film-makers whose work shapes current practice include Britain's Kim Longinotto and China's Wang Bing.* ◇ *Nations and businesses realize that they are beginning to need to adapt their practices to a changing climate.*

▸ PRACTICE + NOUN **guideline • standard • guidance** *75% of therapists used practice guidelines in clinical practice.* | **nurse • staff • manager • team • setting • meeting** *Sixteen GPs took part in the four focus groups, along with two practice nurses, a practice manager and a medical student.*

prac·tice² /ˈpræktɪs/ *verb* (*US*) = PRACTISE

prac·tise (*US* **prac·tice**) /ˈpræktɪs/ *verb* **1** [T] **~ sth** to do sth regularly as part of your normal behaviour: *Shintoism is not so widely practised in Japan today.* ◇ *Hand washing between clients was practised by 94 of 105 hairdressers (89.5%).* **2** [I, T] to work as a doctor, lawyer, etc: *All trainee doctors practising in the UK at the time of the survey were eligible to take part.* ◇ **~ sth** *Many private health care providers were not licensed to practise medicine.* ◇ **~ as sth** *He moved to Melbourne in 1854 to practise as a lawyer.* **3** [I, T] to do an activity or train regularly so that you can improve your skill: *One respondent said: 'Even though I practised for about an hour every few days, after three months I still couldn't play very well.'* ◇ **~ (doing) sth** *In extensive reading, learners are practising reading.*

prac·ti·tion·er AWL /prækˈtɪʃənə(r)/ *noun* **1** a person who works in a profession, especially medicine or law: *The other principal treatment suggested by medical practitioners for low back pain was physiotherapy.* ◇ *'United Nations, Divided World' is an important collection of readings by practitioners and academics.* ➲ *see also* GENERAL PRACTITIONER **2 ~ (of sth)** a person who regularly does a particular activity, especially one that requires skill: *Practitioners and fans of Celtic music would object to the suggestion that it was no longer folk music, but world music.*

prag·mat·ic /prægˈmætɪk/ *adj.* **1** solving problems in a practical and sensible way rather than by having fixed ideas or theories SYN REALISTIC: *The International Court of Justice has taken a pragmatic approach in resolving this dilemma.* ◇ *English language-only papers were included for pragmatic reasons.* **2** (*philosophy*) connected with philosophical or political PRAGMATISM: *The pragmatic nature of Confucianism has been criticized by other Chinese philosophers.* **3** (*linguistics*) connected with the way that language is used in a particular situation: *Exemplification and identification are basic pragmatic functions in both academic speech and writing.* ◇ *The entries in this kind of dictionary contain morphological, semantic and pragmatic information.* ➲ *see also* PRAGMATICS ■ **prag·mat·ic·al·ly** /prægˈmætɪkli/ *adv.*: *Marx has something relevant to say, both pragmatically and intellectually.*

prag·mat·ics /prægˈmætɪks/ *noun* [U] (*linguistics*) the study of language in use and the way in which CONTEXT contributes to meaning: *Semantics deals with the question of meaning, while pragmatics deals with questions of use.*

prag·ma·tism /ˈprægmətɪzəm/ *noun* [U] **1** the practice of thinking about solving problems in a practical and sensible way rather than by having fixed ideas and theories: *Their support for a Supreme Court was based on principle rather than pragmatism.* **2** (*philosophy*) an approach that considers and judges theories or beliefs in terms of the success of their practical application: *An instrumental conception of truth is closely associated with pragmatism.* ■ **prag·ma·tist** /ˈprægmətɪst/ *noun*: *Pentagon insiders saw Clifford as a tough-minded pragmatist.*

praise¹ /preɪz/ *verb* **1** to express your approval or admiration for sb/sth: **~ sb/sth (for sth)** *Critics praised the play for its examination of the current state of politics.* ◇ **~ sb/sth as sth** *Kennedy has been widely praised as a moderating voice throughout the crisis.* **2 ~ God** to express your thanks to or your respect for God: *Angels exist to praise God, carry his messages, bear witness and act as ministering spirits.*

praise² /preɪz/ *noun* [U] **1** (*also less frequent* **praises** [pl.]) words that show approval of or admiration for sb/sth: **~ for (doing) sth** *They expect no praise for doing their job well.* ◇ **~ from sb/sth** *The Beveridge Report drew praise from both sides of the political spectrum.* ◇ **in ~ of sb/sth** *He was put to work editing newsreels in praise of Stalin.* **2** the expression of worship to God: **of ~** *a hymn/song of praise* ◇ **~ to God** *It is the act of giving praise to God that binds religious communities together.* IDM *see* SING

pray /preɪ/ *verb* [I, T] to speak to God, especially to give thanks or ask for help: **~ (to sb) (for sb/sth)** *Alexander prayed to Poseidon for a safe voyage to Babylonia.* ◇ **~ (to sb) that...** *'I hope and pray that commercialization of television will be decisively defeated,' wrote the Bishop of Manchester.*

pray·er /preə(r); *NAmE* prer/ *noun* **1** [C] words that you say to God giving thanks or asking for help: *They held a* *firm belief that God would listen and that he would answer their prayers.* ◇ **~ for sb/sth** *Church services offered prayers for the royal family.* **2** [U] the act or habit of praying: *The young people talked about seeking God's support through prayer.* ◇ *He sat in prayer, his head bowed.*

pre·car·ious /prɪˈkeəriəs; *NAmE* prɪˈkeriəs/ *adj.* not safe or certain; dangerous: *Such long-term dependence on imported gas is a precarious situation for any nation.* ◇ *But every now and then, that precarious balance will break down and war is likely to follow.* ■ **pre·car·ious·ly** *adv.*: *The good news is that the great majority of the region's native species still survive, however precariously.* ◇ *On coasts exposed to waves, granite boulders are often precariously balanced, resulting in rockfalls.* **pre·car·ious·ness** *noun* [U] **~ (of sth)** *The precariousness of a life in trade ensured that family members would have to pool their resources.*

pre·cau·tion /prɪˈkɔːʃn/ *noun* [usually pl.] something that is done in advance in order to prevent problems or to avoid danger: *The employer failed to take proper safety precautions.* ◇ *Every practical possibility must be considered and every reasonable precaution must be taken.* ◇ **~ against sth** *It is important to anticipate dangers and take the necessary precautions against them.* ■ **pre·cau·tion·ary** /prɪˈkɔːʃənəri; *NAmE* prɪˈkɔːʃəneri/ *adj.*: *The government had adopted several precautionary measures against financial instability before the crisis.*

pre·cede AWL /prɪˈsiːd/ *verb* **~ sb/sth** to happen before sth or come before sth/sb in order: *Anxiety may precede the onset of depression.* ◇ *The study reported here was preceded by a pilot in the same school carried out by one of the authors (E.H.).* ■ **pre·ceding** *adj.*: *the preceding paragraph/page/section*

pre·ce·dence AWL /ˈpresɪdəns/ *noun* [U] the condition of being considered more important than sb/sth else and therefore coming or being dealt with first SYN PRIORITY (2): *Giving precedence to safety will entail costs.* ◇ **~ over sb/sth** *US economic interests took precedence over environmental considerations.*

pre·ce·dent AWL /ˈpresɪdənt/ *noun* [C, U] an earlier action, event or way of doing sth that is seen as an example or a rule to be followed in a similar situation later: **~ (for sth)** *The design of this factory set a precedent for virtually all mass production factories that followed.* ◇ *Historical precedent would suggest that prices would continue to rise.* ◇ **without ~** *Global warming will confront us with challenges utterly without precedent.* HELP In law, a **precedent** is a previous case or legal decision that must be followed in similar cases: *The fact that a settlement was reached prior to trial means that the case is of no value as a legal precedent.* ➲ *see also* UNPRECEDENTED

pre·cipi·tate[1] /prɪˈsɪpɪteɪt/ *verb* **1** [T] **~ sth** to make sth, especially sth bad, happen suddenly or sooner than it should SYN SPARK[1]: *The end of the Cold War precipitated a crisis in national political culture.* ◇ *Angina pain is precipitated by exertion.* **2** [I, T] (*chemistry*) to separate a solid substance from a liquid in a chemical process: *The material with higher molecular mass is less soluble and precipitates first.* ◇ **~ (sth) from sth** *Calcium carbonate can be precipitated from solution.* ◇ **~ (sth) out** *Much of the material brought into the ocean by rivers is precipitated out as sediment.*

pre·cipi·tate[2] /prɪˈsɪpɪteɪt/ *noun* (*chemistry*) a solid substance that has been separated from a liquid in a chemical process: *An insoluble black precipitate is formed with hydrogen sulfide.*

pre·cipi·ta·tion /prɪˌsɪpɪˈteɪʃn/ *noun* **1** [U] (*technical*) rain, snow, etc. that falls; the amount of this that falls: *These clouds produce heavy precipitation and sometimes hail.* ◇ *The annual average precipitation at this site is 3 400 mm.* **2** [U, C] **~ (of sth)** (*chemistry*) a chemical process in which solid material is separated from a liquid: *Stalactites and stalagmites develop by the precipitation of calcium carbonate.*

pre·cipit·ous /prɪˈsɪpɪtəs/ *adj.* (of a decrease) very large and unexpected: *In the early 1980s, American farmers experienced a precipitous decline in grain exports.* ■ **pre·cipit·ous·ly** *adv.*: *In these areas, large mammal populations declined precipitously when faced with the new human predators.*

pre·cise AWL /prɪˈsaɪs/ *adj.* **1** clear and accurate SYN EXACT (1): *Terms such as 'upper social class' have a precise academic definition.* ◇ *New equipment led to more precise estimates of the magnitude of earthquakes.* ◇ **~ about sth** *It is difficult to be precise about the size of many Chinese cities.* **2** [only before noun] used to emphasize that sth happens at a particular time or in a particular way: *At that precise moment, a bomb went off.* ◇ *The Court did not express a view on the precise manner in which the principle was to be implemented.*

IDM **to be (more) preˈcise** used to show that you are giving more detailed and accurate information about sth you have just mentioned: *The British constitution is unwritten or, to be more precise, 'uncodified'.*

pre·cise·ly AWL /prɪˈsaɪsli/ *adv.* **1** exactly: *Pakistan spends almost precisely the same amount per person on health care as Uganda.* ◇ *The quantity of the product supplied is precisely equal to the quantity demanded.* **2** accurately; carefully: *The term is rarely defined precisely.* ◇ *To measure rainfall precisely, you need a recording rain gauge.* **3** used to emphasize that sth is very true or obvious: *This is, of course, precisely the point.* ◇ *It is precisely because the book explores human suffering with such poignancy and insight that it has had such a profound impact on Western culture.*

IDM **more preˈcisely** used to show that you are giving more detailed and accurate information about sth you have just mentioned: *People who work for wages make their living by renting themselves out, or more precisely, by selling their time.* ➲ language bank *at* I.E.

P

pre·ci·sion AWL /prɪˈsɪʒn/ *noun* [U] the quality of being exact and accurate SYN ACCURACY (1): *To improve the precision of the instrument, they added new items to the scale.* ◇ **with ~** *This term is difficult to define with precision.*

pre·clude /prɪˈkluːd/ *verb* (*formal*) to prevent sth from happening or sb from doing sth; to make sth impossible: **~ sth** *Determinism precludes free action and moral responsibility.* ◇ *The complexity of making comparisons does not preclude the possibility of rational decision-making.* ◇ **~ sb from doing sth** *The Commissioner is precluded from questioning policy.* ◇ **~ (sb) doing sth** *The shallow and rocky soils precluded ploughing by early European American settlers and their successors.*

pre·con·ceived /ˌpriːkənˈsiːvd/ *adj.* [only before noun] (of ideas or opinions) formed before you have enough information or experience of sth: *Patients enter treatment with preconceived notions regarding therapy.*

pre·con·cep·tion /ˌpriːkənˈsepʃn/ *noun* [usually pl.] an idea or opinion that is formed before you have enough information or experience SYN ASSUMPTION (1): *One of the great strengths of this book is that it challenges such preconceptions.* ◇ **~ about sth** *When a person acts in a certain way, they do so based on their preconceptions about the situation.* ➲ *compare* MISCONCEPTION

pre·con·di·tion /ˌpriːkənˈdɪʃn/ *noun* something that must happen or exist before sth else can exist or be done SYN PREREQUISITE: **~ for sth** *Protection of minorities was stipulated as a precondition for membership of the League.* ◇ *Drought and wildfire destroy the surface soil structure,* *creating the preconditions for severe erosion.* ◇ **~ of sth** *They argued that consolidating the institutional structure was a necessary precondition of enlargement.*

pre·cur·sor /priːˈkɜːsə(r); *NAmE* priːˈkɜːrsər/ *noun* a person or thing that comes before sb/sth similar and that leads to or influences their development: **~ (of sth)** *At an early stage, the precursors of white blood cells are indistinguishable from those of red blood cells.* ◇ **~ to sth** *Obtaining access may well be used as the precursor to some fraudulent scheme.* HELP In biology, a **precursor** can also be a substance from which another substance is made, especially as part of a METABOLIC reaction: *Plasminogen is the inactive precursor of plasmin, an enzyme important in the control of clot formation.*

pre·date /ˌpriːˈdeɪt/ (*also* **ante·date**) *verb* to be built or formed, or to happen, at an earlier date than sth else in the past: **~ sth** *Few of the town's buildings predate the earthquake of 1755.* ◇ **~ sth by sth** *Telecommunications predate the electronic digital computer by over a century.*

pre·da·tion /prɪˈdeɪʃn/ *noun* [U] (*ecology*) the act of an animal killing and eating other animals: *Mice may only live for a few months in the wild; they generally die early from predation or cold.* ◇ **+ noun** *Sparrows suffer predation risks when feeding.*

preda·tor /ˈpredətə(r)/ *noun* an animal that kills and eats other animals: *Pheasant chicks cannot fly to escape predators.* ◇ *Large changes in abundance of predators and prey have been reported in recent years.*

preda·tory /ˈpredətri; *NAmE* ˈpredətɔːri/ *adj.* **1** (*technical*) (of animals) living by killing and eating other animals: *Predatory fish are often key components of lake ecosystems.* ◇ *Behavioural mechanisms that allow prey to escape from predatory attacks can represent important adaptations.* **2** (of people or behaviour) treating sb badly in order to gain control of sth: *Large British firms often had a predatory attitude to small firms.* ◇ *Competition authorities have only rarely investigated allegations of predatory pricing in the airline industry.*

pre·de·ces·sor /ˈpriːdɪsesə(r); *NAmE* ˈpredəsesər/ *noun* **1** a person who did a job, or filled a role, before sb else: *The new President's foreign policy was very similar to that of his predecessor.* ◇ *Unlike their earlier twentieth-century predecessors, the new immigrants were primarily Asian and Hispanic.* ➲ *compare* SUCCESSOR **2** a thing, such as a machine, that has been followed or replaced by sth else: *Modern automobiles emit much smaller amounts of pollutants than their predecessors.* ➲ *compare* SUCCESSOR

pre·de·ter·mine /ˌpriːdɪˈtɜːmɪn; *NAmE* ˌpriːdɪˈtɜːrmɪn/ *verb* **~ sth** to decide sth in advance so that it does not happen by chance: *These strategy documents often predetermine future EU action.* ◇ *He lets his desire for a particular result override his commitment to truth, and predetermine his conclusion.* ■ **pre·de·ter·mined** *adj.*: *All trials were assessed following predetermined criteria.*

predi·cate¹ /ˈpredɪkət/ *noun* (*grammar*) a part of a sentence containing a verb that makes a statement about the subject of the verb, such as *went home* in *John went home*: *Traditional grammar tells us that the simplest whole sentences are composed of a subject and a predicate.* ➲ *compare* OBJECT¹ (4)

predi·cate² /ˈpredɪkeɪt/ *verb* (*formal*) **1** [usually passive] **~ sth on/upon sth** to base sth on a particular belief, idea or principle: *The idea is predicated upon a redistribution of resources from one citizen to another.* **2** to state that sth is true SYN ASSERT (1): **~ that...** *The article predicates that the market collapse was caused by weakness of the dollar.* ◇ **~ sth** *a word which predicates something about its subject*

LANGUAGE BANK

Discussing predictions

In academic language, you often need to write about what is expected or predicted to happen.

- to be **expected/likely** to happen
- to **be set to** continue/increase/reach sth
- to **predict/forecast/anticipate/envisage** sth
- **By** July/next year/2030, etc, sth **will** happen
- to be lower/higher/better, etc. **than expected/predicted**
- **in line with expectations/predictions**
- a **probable** outcome/result
- **In all probability...**

– *The demand for tea would be* ***expected*** *to increase if the price of coffee were to increase.*
– *Infection is much more* ***likely*** *to occur in elderly patients.*
– *This figure* ***is set to*** *reach 200 million by 2016.*
– *We do not have enough information to* ***predict*** *the outcome with certainty.*
– *Recent scientific studies have* ***forecast*** *adverse global climate changes.*
– *We* ***anticipated*** *that we would get a response rate of 55% to 60%.*
– *He* ***envisaged*** *continued progress in human culture.*
– ***By*** *2017, roughly half of all minorities in Canada* ***will*** *be South Asian or Chinese.*
– *Temperatures could be as much as 4°C warmer* ***than predicted.***
– *The economy failed to grow* ***in line with expectations.***
– *What could be the* ***probable*** *results of these policies over the next few years?*
– *Nationalism, in all its forms, will,* ***in all probability****, remain part of the life of each country and of the international system.*

pre·dict AWL /prɪˈdɪkt/ *verb* to say, expect or suggest that a particular thing will happen in the future or will be the result of sth SYN FORECAST²: **~ sth** *The factors that predict outcome in acute illness in the very old require further exploration.* ◇ **as predicted** *As predicted, children's early success in solving computer problems was related to greater Internet use.* ◇ **~ how/what, etc...** *The authors predict how readers would normally divide a written text into pronounceable phrases.* ◇ **~ that...** *The good genes hypothesis predicts that females will prefer to mate with the healthiest males.* ◇ **it is predicted that...** *In the UK alone, it is predicted that by 2024 over 40% of the population will be over 50.* ◇ **be predicted to do sth** *An impact on the earth of energy 1 000 megatons or more was predicted to occur every 60 000 years (Morbidelli et al., 2002).*

▸ PREDICT + NOUN **outcome • future • response • consequence • occurrence • risk • likelihood • behaviour • performance • intention • increase • decline • mortality • score** *Models have been developed to predict consumer behaviour.*

▸ NOUN + PREDICT **model • theory • hypothesis** *The observed pattern is as predicted by the theory.*

▸ PREDICTED + NOUN **value • probability • rate • number • grade • score • change • pattern • outcome • duration • incidence** *The observed and predicted values are seen to agree precisely within the errors of less than one part in 10 million.* ◇ *The data did not follow the predicted pattern.*

▸ ADVERB + PREDICT **accurately • correctly • independently • significantly • reliably • strongly • well • successfully • confidently** *Animal and experimental models do not reliably predict the value of experimental vaccines.*

▸ PREDICT + ADVERB **accurately • correctly • exactly, precisely • well** *The effects of financial innovations have not always been easy to predict exactly.*

▸ ADJECTIVE + TO PREDICT **difficult, hard • impossible • possible • easy** *It is not difficult to predict a malaria outbreak because the disease is so closely related to local weather circumstances.*

▸ VERB + TO PREDICT **be able** ♦ **fail** ♦ **attempt** *Grzimek failed to predict how the tourist industry would transform the Serengeti into a marketable 'sight'.*

pre·dict·able AWL /prɪˈdɪktəbl/ *adj.* if sth is **predictable**, you know in advance that it will happen or what it will be like: *In a bureaucratic firm, the employer pays wages that increase in a predictable way with an employee's seniority.* ◇ *The outcomes of such contests are highly predictable.* ■ **pre·dict·abil·ity** AWL /prɪˌdɪktəˈbɪləti/ *noun* [U] **~ (of sth)** *Very little is known about the predictability of natural environments.* **pre·dict·ably** AWL /prɪˈdɪktəbli/ *adv.*: *Predictably, children who possess more empathy show less aggressive behaviour.*

pre·dic·tion AWL /prɪˈdɪkʃn/ *noun* [C, U] a statement that says what you think will happen; the act of making such a statement: *Kahneman and Lovallo (1993) pointed out the difficulties that managers have in making accurate predictions.* ◇ *The experimental results are then compared with theoretical predictions.* ◇ *to test/support/verify a prediction* ◇ **~ of sth** *Prediction of future farming incomes is complex.* ◇ **~ about sth** *Our results confirmed the predictions about the function of the jumping behaviour in tadpoles.* ◇ **~ that...** *The evidence is consistent with Jovanovic's prediction that company growth rates decline with size.* ➲ language bank *at* PREDICT

pre·dict·ive /prɪˈdɪktɪv/ *adj.* connected with the ability to show what will happen in the future: *A hypothesis is only as good as its explanatory and predictive power.* ◇ **~ of sth** *Childhood mental distress is strongly predictive of poor mental health in adult life.*

pre·dic·tor /prɪˈdɪktə(r)/ *noun* something that can help to show accurately what will happen: *The study shows lower reading times among IT users, even after education and other predictors are taken into account.* ◇ **~ of sth** *Age was a significant predictor of memory performance.* ◇ *a strong/good/independent predictor of sth* ◇ **~ for sth** *Small body size at birth appears to be an important predictor for long-term health.*

preˌdictor ˈvariable *noun* a VARIABLE that can be measured and used to predict the value of another VARIABLE: *Variables associated with prior injury are commonly used as predictor variables in injury risk factor investigations.*

pre·dis·pose /ˌpriːdɪˈspəʊz; *NAmE* ˌpriːdɪˈspoʊz/ *verb* **1** [T, I] to make it likely that sb will suffer from a particular illness or condition: **~ sb to (doing) sth** *Several physical factors have been shown to predispose individuals to developing fatigue.* ◇ **~ to sth** *Chronic lung inflammation predisposes to lung cancer.* **2** [T] to influence sb so that they are likely to think or behave in a particular way: **~ sb to sth** *The lack of constructive options has predisposed many young people to hostility.* ◇ **~ sb to do sth** *Failure at school and low parental supervision may predispose young people to become involved in crime.*

pre·dis·pos·ition /ˌpriːdɪspəˈzɪʃn/ *noun* [C, U] a condition that makes sb/sth likely to behave in a particular way or to suffer from a particular disease: **~ to sth** *The strong genetic predisposition to schizophrenia makes attempts at primary prevention difficult.* ◇ **~ to do sth** *Individuals bring to the purchase decision a predisposition to act in a particular way.*

pre·dom·in·ance AWL /prɪˈdɒmɪnəns; *NAmE* prɪˈdɑːmɪnəns/ *noun* **1** [sing.] **~ (of sth) (in sth)** the situation of being greater in number or amount than other things or people SYN DOMINANCE (2): *There is a predominance of evergreen trees in regions with nutrient-poor soils.* ◇ *We analysed a total of 1 607 cases of the disease, with a slight predominance in women (54%).* **2** [U] **~ (of sb/sth) (over sb/sth)** the state of having more power or influence than others SYN DOMINANCE (1): *Liberal democracy upholds the belief in the predominance of individual rights over collective rights.*

pre·dom·in·ant AWL /prɪˈdɒmɪnənt; *NAmE* prɪˈdɑːmɪnənt/ *adj.* **1** largest or most frequent; most obvious or important SYN DOMINANT (2): *Family-owned firms in most Latin American economies are the predominant form of corporation.* ◇ *Varieties of wheat, barley and millet were the predominant crops.* **2** having more power or influence than others SYN DOMINANT (1): *The predominant economic goal at the time was to keep a tight control on inflation.*

pre·dom·in·ant·ly AWL /prɪˈdɒmɪnəntli; *NAmE* prɪˈdɑːmɪnəntli/ (*also less frequent* **pre·dom·in·ate·ly** /prɪˈdɒmɪnətli; *NAmE* prɪˈdɑːmɪnətli/) *adv.* mostly; mainly: *The balance of the population has shifted from predominantly rural to overwhelmingly urban.* ◇ *In the UK, which is predominantly a service economy, labour costs are a very significant part of the total costs of a business.* ➲ language bank *at* BROADLY

pre·dom·in·ate AWL /prɪˈdɒmɪneɪt; *NAmE* prɪˈdɑːmɪneɪt/ *verb* **1** [I] to be greater in amount or number than sth/sb else in a place or group: *Cool and wet conditions predominated in Sydney from January 1788 to winter 1790.* **2** [I] **~ (over sb/sth)** to have the most power, influence or importance: *It is difficult to determine where the authority of ministers and central government will predominate over local government.*

pref·ace /ˈprefəs/ *noun* an introduction to a book, especially one that explains the author's aims: *Coleridge wrote this preface for the poem's first publication.* ◇ **in the ~** *The new material is helpfully summarized in the preface.* ◇ **the ~ to sth** *The prefaces to his many books provided an ideal forum for expounding on his ideas.*

pre·fer /prɪˈfɜː(r)/ *verb* (-rr-) (not used in the progressive tenses) to like sb/sth more than sb/sth else; to choose one person or thing rather than another because they/it are more suitable: **~ sth** *Both men and women tend to prefer female friends for sharing and emotional support.* ◇ *Soil depth is important for vine growth; moderately deep soils are, in general, to be preferred.* ◇ **~ sth to/over sth** *Recent studies have shown that both sexes of the fish are choosy about mates: close kin are preferred over non-kin.* ◇ **~ to do sth** *Local banknotes were hardly used and people preferred to use overseas currencies if they had them.* ◇ *Bolivar's vision was not anti-American, but he preferred not to include the USA.* ◇ **~ doing sth** *Most developers prefer building the projects but not maintaining them over the long term.* ◇ **~ that...** *Many Health Trusts prefer that a formal request to see medical records is made in writing.* ◇ **~ sb/sth to do sth** *Some people would prefer local government to address purely localized problems.*

P

pref·er·able /ˈprefrəbl/ *adj.* more attractive or more suitable; to be preferred to sth: **~ to sth** *The argument for democracy is not that it is perfect but that it is preferable to the alternatives.* ◇ **it is ~ to do sth** *It is preferable to use no more than five or six categories.* ◇ **~ to doing sth** *Work may be preferable to doing nothing, but in many cases it does not make an individual feel creative or fulfilled.* ■ **pref·er·ably** /ˈprefrəbli/ *adv.*: *Preferably, at least part of the observations should be conducted in the field.* ◇ *The ceremony is conducted normally by an older male, preferably the head of a family.*

pref·er·ence /ˈprefrəns/ *noun* **1** [C, usually sing., U] a greater interest in or desire for sb/sth than sb/sth else: **~ for doing sth** *While some teachers expressed a preference for creating their own tasks, others preferred to use ready-made material.* ◇ **~ for sb/sth** *It is possible that adolescents have a stronger preference for technology than adults.*

◇ **in order of ~** *Voters are required to rank the candidates in order of preference.* **2** [C] a thing that is liked better or best: *Food preferences were consistently identified as a major influence on the food choices of young people.*
IDM **give (a) preference to sb/sth** to treat sb/sth in a way that gives them/it an advantage over other people or things: *We gave preference to studies with the largest sample size.* **in preference to sb/sth** rather than sb/sth: *In lower-income households, bananas were selected in preference to more expensive berries and other fresh fruit.*

pref·er·en·tial /ˌprefəˈrenʃl/ *adj.* [only before noun] **1** giving an advantage to a particular person or group: *The shares are offered for sale at preferential rates to existing workers and managers.* ◇ *The state's opposition to minority religions reflected the preferential treatment granted to more mainstream religions.* **2** preferring one thing or action to another: *A large part of the water generally flows through vertical preferential pathways such as cracks, root holes or wormholes.* ■ **pref·er·en·tial·ly** /ˌprefəˈrenʃəli/ *adv.*: *The researchers created situations in which one group of children would be treated preferentially.* ◇ *Predators preferentially attack prey on the periphery of a group.*

pre·fix /ˈpriːfɪks/ *noun* **1** (*grammar*) a letter or group of letters added to the beginning of a word to change its meaning, such as *un-* in *unhappy* and *re-* in *rethink*: *The mark, in the case of opposites, is invariably a negative prefix: possible:impossible, kind:unkind.* ➲ *compare* SUFFIX **2** a word, letter or number that is put before another: *For the definition of the various prefixes used in electronics, see Appendix H.*

preg·nancy /ˈpregnənsi/ *noun* (*pl.* **-ies**) [U, C] the state of being pregnant: *There has been an alarming rise in teenage pregnancies.* ◇ **during/in ~** *Excessive alcohol consumption during pregnancy can damage the developing fetus.*

P

preg·nant /ˈpregnənt/ *adj.* (of a woman or female animal) having a baby or young animal developing inside her/its body: *The girls in the study showed a lack of concern about becoming pregnant.* ◇ **~ with sth** *His wife is pregnant with their third child.*

pre·his·toric /ˌpriːhɪˈstɒrɪk; *NAmE* ˌpriːhɪˈstɔːrɪk/ *adj.* connected with the time in history before information was written down: *Most of today's human diseases go back to prehistoric times.* ◇ *In Ireland, archaeologists have shown much greater interest in prehistoric sites than in medieval ones.*

ˌpre-inˈdustrial *adj.* [only before noun] connected with a time before there was large-scale industry in a country or an area: *Agricultural production is fundamental to any pre-industrial society.*

preju·dice /ˈpredʒudɪs/ *noun* [U, C] an unreasonable dislike of a person, group, etc, especially when it is based on their race, religion, sex, etc: *Racial prejudice was deeply entrenched in European culture.* ◇ *Dickens shared some of the cultural prejudices of his time.* ◇ **~ against sb/sth** *An agenda for future research might include greater understanding of how prejudice against women harms societies.*
IDM **without ˈprejudice (to sth)** (*law*) without affecting any other legal matter: *The Code is to be applied without prejudice to the rights of refugees.*

pre·lim·in·ary AWL /prɪˈlɪmɪnəri; *NAmE* prɪˈlɪmɪneri/ *adj.* happening or done before a more important event or action SYN INITIAL: *Preliminary analysis of the data suggests that educated women have educated spouses.* ◇ *Prior to the main experiment, a preliminary study was carried out.* ■ **pre·lim·in·ary** *noun* (*pl.* **-ies**) **~ (to sth)** *An engagement is viewed as a preliminary to the formal relationship of marriage or civil partnership.*

pre·ma·ture /ˈpremətʃə(r); *NAmE* ˌpriːməˈtʃʊr; ˌpriːməˈtʊr/ *adj.* **1** happening before the normal or expected time: *The premature deaths of two elephants raised concerns about the unhealthy zoo environment.* ◇ *His 1984 visit to England and Scotland came to a premature end, when he learned that Ustinov had died.* **2** (of a birth or a baby) happening or being born before the normal length of PREGNANCY has been completed: *Antenatal steroids have improved the survival rates of premature babies.* ◇ *Amanda's baby was premature and initially fed by bottle.* **3** happening or made too soon: *We should be careful not to jump to a premature conclusion.* ◇ **it is ~ to do sth** *It would be premature to draw any firm conclusions at this stage.* ■ **pre·ma·ture·ly** *adv.*: *Half of all smokers die prematurely, but stopping significantly extends life expectancy.*

prem·ise (*BrE also less frequent* **prem·iss**) /ˈpremɪs/ *noun* a statement or an idea that forms the basis for a reasonable line of argument: *Her argument is founded on four basic premises.* ◇ *Business marketing in the 1970s was based on the premise that marketing and purchasing were separate activities.* ◇ *However, this criticism rests on a false premise.* ➲ thesaurus note *at* HYPOTHESIS

prem·ised /ˈpremɪst/ *adj.* **~ on/upon sth** based on a particular idea or belief that is considered to be true: *This idea is premised on two assumptions.* ◇ *This article is premised on the idea that health promotion research is inherently political.*

prem·ises /ˈpremɪsɪz/ *noun* [pl.] the building and land near to it that a business owns or uses: *The landlord did not have the right to enter the premises.* ◇ *A piece of land may be used for a family house, flats, offices or business premises.*

pre·mium /ˈpriːmiəm/ *noun* **1** an amount of money that you pay once or regularly for an insurance policy: *A business that does not implement widely accepted standards for workplace safety may face higher insurance premiums.* ◇ *Specific premiums paid depend on the applicant's age, risk status, and coverage levels chosen.* **2** a sum added to an ordinary price or charge: *Many consumers are willing to pay a premium for products that are socially responsible.* ◇ *Sellers of highly differentiated products are able to charge a premium in their prices.* **3** an extra payment added to the basic rate SYN BONUS (1): *Registered growers receive a Fairtrade premium of US$0.15 per pound.* ◇ *Vocational graduates earn a wage premium in Egypt, Israel and Thailand.* ■ **pre·mium** *adj.* [only before noun] *The premium prices reflected the investment, the product attributes, and the benefits brought to users.* ◇ *These are services developed specially for mobile phones and provided at a premium rate.*
IDM **at a ˈpremium** **1** if sth is **at a premium**, there is little of it available and it is difficult to get: *In Japan space is at a premium, and this has given rise to all sorts of miniaturized hotel formats.* **2** at a price that is higher than normal: *The US dollar was selling at a premium.* **put/place/set a premium on sb/sth** to think that sb/sth is particularly important or valuable: *Where you shop depends primarily on where you live and whether you put a premium on high quality or low price.*

pre·natal /ˌpriːˈneɪtl/ *adj.* [only before noun] (*especially NAmE*) = ANTENATAL

pre·occu·pa·tion /priˌɒkjuˈpeɪʃn; *NAmE* priˌɑːkjuˈpeɪʃn/ *noun* [U, C] a state of thinking about sth continuously; sth that you think about frequently or for a long time: *People followed the election campaign with intense preoccupation.* ◇ *Economic growth has been a major preoccupation of economists, dating back at least to Adam Smith.* ◇ **~ with sth** *These girls were more likely to have low self-esteem and a preoccupation with their appearance.*

pre·occu·pied /priˈɒkjupaɪd; *NAmE* priˈɑːkjupaɪd/ *adj.* thinking and/or worrying continuously about sth so that you do not pay attention to other things: *Some patients appear awkward in their social behaviour, preoccupied and withdrawn.* ◇ **~ with sth** *The government was preoccupied with the question of who 'belonged' to the UK, largely seen in terms of birth and parentage.*

pre·occupy /priˈɒkjupaɪ; *NAmE* priˈɑːkjupaɪ/ *verb* (**pre·occu·pies, pre·occu·py·ing, pre·occu·pied, pre·occu·pied**) **~ sb** if sth is **preoccupying** you, you think or worry about it very often or all the time: *The failure of the bank Northern Rock preoccupied the government during the autumn of 2007.*

prep·ar·ation /ˌprepəˈreɪʃn/ *noun* **1** [U] the act or process of making sth/sb ready or of getting ready for sth: *Patients selected for this treatment require thorough preparation.* ◇ *The women performed the domestic tasks of spinning and weaving, food preparation and childcare.* ◇ **~ of sth** *Accused individuals are entitled to legal assistance in the preparation of their defence.* ◇ **~ for sth** *In preparation for washing, the coal is crushed at the mine mouth to less than centimetre size.* **2** [C, usually pl.] things that you do to get ready for sth or to make sth ready: *Wedding preparations are often handled by women friends of the bride.* ◇ **~ for sth** *Parents were asked how long it should take their child to make final preparations for school in the morning.* ◇ **~ to do sth** *The generals had not made adequate preparations to meet an attack.* **3** [C] a substance that has been specially prepared for use as a medicine, COSMETIC, etc: *A small area of skin can be treated by short-term antibiotic preparations.*

pre·para·tory /prɪˈpærətri; *NAmE* prɪˈpærətɔːri/ *adj.* done in order to prepare for sth: *Much of the preparatory work has already been done.* ◇ *This study provides a preparatory step in developing a model for risk assessment.*

pre·pare /prɪˈpeə(r); *NAmE* prɪˈper/ *verb* **1** [T] to make sth/sb ready to be used or to do sth: **~ sth/sb** *The Health Facility Committee prepared quarterly work plans and budgets.* ◇ **~ sth/sb for sb/sth** *One MP prepared a report on the flu pandemic for the Council of Europe.* ◇ *Students offered suggestions about how their school experiences could have better prepared them for college or the world of work.* **2** [I, T] to make yourself ready to do sth or for sth that you expect to happen: **~ for sth** *The programme was established in 1997 to help UK organizations prepare for the impacts of climate change.* ◇ **~ yourself (for sth/to do sth)** *Male youths were thought to need a period in which to prepare themselves for adult life.* ◇ **~ to do sth** *Merely preparing to commit a criminal offence is not in itself a crime.* **3** [T] **~ sth** to make food ready to be eaten: *During harvest season, farm women also prepared meals for large crews while still tending to animals and gardens.* **4** [T] **~ sth (from sth)** to make a medicine or chemical substance, for example by mixing other substances together: *Rayleigh prepared some samples of nitrogen by removing oxygen, carbon dioxide and water vapour from air.*

IDM **prepare the ˈground (for sth)** to make it possible or easier for sth to happen or to be achieved: *The Prime Minister holds small meetings with trusted or senior ministers to prepare the ground for sessions of the full Cabinet.*

pre·pared /prɪˈpeəd; *NAmE* prɪˈperd/ *adj.* **1** [not before noun] ready and able to deal with sth: *In the second test, participants were generally better prepared and less anxious about the test.* ◇ **~ for sth** *The stories in the film focus on accidents that one is unlikely to be prepared for.* ◇ **~ to do sth** *The question asked was: How well prepared do you think you are to take care of your family member's physical needs?* **2** **~ to do sth** willing to do sth: *A takeover cannot succeed unless a sufficient proportion of the shareholders are prepared to accept the offer.* OPP UNWILLING **3** done, made or written in advance: *Many cafes and high-street chains offer freshly prepared salads and sandwiches.*

prep·os·ition /ˌprepəˈzɪʃn/ *noun* (*grammar*) a word or group of words, such as *in, from, to, out of* and *on behalf of*, used before a noun or pronoun to show place, position, time or method: *In English (and many other languages), prepositions precede the noun phrases they govern.* HELP The preposition is sometimes placed at the end of the clause. In written academic language, this is sometimes considered incorrect, even though it may sound more natural. If in doubt, put the preposition before the noun or pronoun to which it relates. Compare the following examples: *For the task, learners chose the person they wanted to write about.* ◇ *For the task, learners chose the person about whom they wanted to write.* ■ **prep·os·ition·al** /ˌprepəˈzɪʃənl/ *adj.*: *We looked at occurrences of three- and four-word prepositional phrases, e.g. 'in this situation'.*

pre·requis·ite /ˌpriːˈrekwəzɪt/ *noun* [usually sing.] something that must exist or happen before sth else can happen or be done SYN PRECONDITION: **~ for (doing) sth** *A college degree became an essential prerequisite for a decent job.* ◇ **~ of sth** *In academic and health policy, living conditions are referred to as 'prerequisites of health'.* ◇ **~ to (doing) sth** *The prerequisite to walking across a busy city street is the ability to make quick judgements.* ◇ **~ to do sth** *All the respondents agreed that cooperation between managers and doctors is an absolute prerequisite to attain higher quality.*

pre·roga·tive /prɪˈrɒgətɪv; *NAmE* prɪˈrɑːgətɪv/ *noun* [C, U] **1** a right or an advantage belonging to a particular person or social group: *It's a parent's prerogative to give a car to a child as a gift.* ◇ *Government reforms were designed to restrict union power and restore managerial prerogative.* ◇ **~ of sb/sth** *Permanent stone monuments became the prerogative of the emperors.* **2** **~ (of sb/sth)** (*law*) the special rights of a king or queen: *The Prime Minister advises the monarch on the exercise of the Royal Prerogative to dissolve Parliament.*

pre·scribe /prɪˈskraɪb/ *verb* **1** (of a doctor) to tell sb to take a particular medicine or have a particular treatment; to write a PRESCRIPTION for a particular medicine, etc: **~ sth** *Most people pay directly for drugs prescribed outside hospital.* ◇ **~ sb sth** *Her GP had prescribed her antibiotics and painkillers.* ◇ **~ sth for sb/sth** *17% of participants were taking medications prescribed for mood problems.* **2** (of a person or an organization with authority) to say what should be done or how sth should be done SYN STIPULATE: **~ sth** *Inspections of products are prescribed by EU law in the general interest of the Union.* ◇ **~ that...** *The rules prescribe that individuals have a right to information about data collection and use.* ◇ **~ how/what, etc...** *The Constitution does not prescribe how Congress should be organized internally.*

P

pre·scrip·tion /prɪˈskrɪpʃn/ *noun* **1** [C] an official piece of paper on which a doctor writes the type of medicine a patient should have, and which enables them to get it from a PHARMACY: **~ for sth** *Many doctors said that the patient expects them to write a prescription for antibiotics when they have spent money on consulting a doctor.* ◇ **on ~** (*BrE*) *Both these drugs are only legally available on prescription.* ◇ **by ~** (*NAmE*) *Both these drugs are only legally available by prescription.* ◇ **+ noun** *People over the age of 65 years are the greatest consumers of prescription drugs.* **2** [C] medicine that a doctor has ordered for a patient: *We could not assess whether the prescription is actually dispensed or taken.* **3** [U] **~ (of sth)** the act of prescribing medicine: *We did not have any information about the prescription of antidepressants by other specialists.* **4** [C] **~ (for sth/for doing sth)** a plan or suggestion by sb in authority for making sth happen or for improving it: *Over time, a set of prescriptions for increasing the motivational qualities of jobs has been developed.* **5** [C] **~ (that...)** the way that sth has been done for a long time and which is accepted as right: *The study demonstrated that men simply accept the cultural prescription that the mother should take primary responsibility for the baby.*

pre·scrip·tive /prɪˈskrɪptɪv/ *adj.* **1** telling people what should be done or how sth should be done: *It seems that public food safety regulation is becoming less detailed and less prescriptive.* ◇ *The book tries not to present prescriptive solutions to marketing problems, but encourages discussion about causes and effects.* **2** (*linguistics*) telling people how a language should be used, rather than describing how it is used: *Dictionaries for translators (but also business people, scientists, etc.) might be both prescriptive and descriptive.* ◇ *Many speakers of English do not follow the rules of prescriptive grammars.* OPP DESCRIPTIVE (1)

pres·ence /ˈprezns/ *noun* **1** [C, U] the state or fact of existing or being present in a particular place: **~ of sth** *Yellow-brown to red colours generally indicate the presence of iron oxides.* ◇ *to detect/confirm/reveal the presence of sth* ◇ **~ (of sth) (in sth)** *The presence in the soil of quartz may be another factor.* ◇ **~ at sth** *The applicant had failed to explain his presence at a property in the city where a suspected terrorist was also found.* ◇ **~ or absence (of sth)** *Quantitatively, there was a relationship between humidity and the presence or absence of ticks.* OPP ABSENCE (1) **2** [C, usually sing.] the fact of sb/sth being in a place and having an influence: *The party has a strong electoral presence in the region.* ◇ *In central and northern Wales, the Romans maintained a military presence into the fourth century.* ◇ *Outside of Europe, the company has in recent years established a significant presence in Japan, China and India.* **3** [C] a person or thing that is not seen, but is believed to exist: *He believed that his scientific work affirmed a divine presence in the universe.*

IDM **in the presence of sb/sth** where sb/sth is in a particular place; where sth exists: *Interviewees may respond differently in the presence of another person.* HELP In scientific language, the phrase **in presence of sb/sth** is also used: *The reaction between hydrogen and nitrogen to form ammonia goes much faster in presence of an iron catalyst.* **make your presence ˈfelt** to have a strong influence; to make sb aware that you are there: *New technology has certainly made its presence felt.*

pres·ent¹ /ˈpreznt/ *adj.* **1** [only before noun] existing or happening now SYN CURRENT¹ (1): *In its present form, the theory has two serious weaknesses.* ◇ **(at) the ~ time** *At the present time, natural gas vehicles are restricted to fleet vehicles with a limited daily range.* ◇ **past and ~** *Figure 3.4 shows the past and present distribution of tropical rainforests.* ◇ *A number of authors, past and present, have made significant contributions to our understanding of student behaviour.* ➲ *see also* PRESENT DAY ➲ *usage note at* ACTUAL **2** [only before noun] (of a piece of work, etc.) being considered now: *The aim of the present study was to explore these associations.* HELP **The present author** refers to the author of the work that you are reading: *Studies by the present author have also examined these implications.* ➲ *usage note at* ACTUAL **3** [not before noun] (of a thing or substance) existing in a particular place, group or situation: *Assessing how many species are present is not simple.* ◇ **~ in/within/throughout sth** *These differences were present within every socio-economic and ethnic group.* ◇ **~ on sth** *Large feathers are only present on the dorsal surface.* **~ in/at sth** (used for talking about amounts) *Ammonia is present in trace quantities.* ◇ *The two parent isotopes are present at low concentrations in many geological materials.* OPP ABSENCE (1) **4** [not before noun] (of a person) being in a particular place: *The decisions are to be taken by a two-thirds majority of those present.* ◇ **~ at sth** *Shareholders do not have to be physically present at the meeting to vote.* ◇ **~ throughout/during sth** *Government officials had been present during the exercise.* OPP ABSENT (2)

▸ PRESENT + NOUN **context** • **situation** • **circumstances** • **arrangement** • **position** • **climate** • **state** • **form** • **case** • **purposes** *The concern in the present context is with the social theory.* ◇ *What is important for present purposes is a recognition of these opportunities.* | **time** • **moment** • **century** • **era** • **age** *At the present moment, there are conflicting ideas.* | **study** • **work** • **investigation** • **experiment** • **results** • **findings** • **discussion** • **review** • **analysis** *The present investigation is aimed at establishing the nature of this phenomenon.* | **paper** • **article** • **volume** • **edition** • **book** • **chapter** • **section** *The aim of the present paper was to test this hypothesis.*

pres·ent² /ˈpreznt/ *noun* **1** (*usually* **the present**) [sing.] the time now: **at ~** *At present, China and India are home to almost 38 per cent of the world's population.* ◇ *The processes that could cause a rapid breakdown of ice sheets are not fully understood at present.* ◇ **in the ~** *Things only exist momentarily in the present, not in the future.* ◇ **(up) to the ~** *Figure 1.4 charts the advance of lighting technology from 1700 to the present.* ➲ *usage note at* ACTUAL **2** a thing that you give to sb as a gift: *He gave her many expensive presents.* ◇ *She hoped for a jump in sales in December as customers bought last-minute Christmas presents from her bookshop.* **3 the present** [sing.] (*grammar*) = PRESENT TENSE

pres·ent³ /prɪˈzent/ *verb* **1** [T] to show or offer information or ideas for other people to consider: **~ sth** *Table 2 presents the results of our analysis evaluating Hypotheses III-V.* ◇ *The author presents an insightful and convincing argument.* ◇ **~ sth + adv./prep.** *These data are presented in Figure 17.9.* ◇ **~ sth to sb** *Groups present their findings to the entire class.* SYN PROVIDE **2** [T] to show or describe sb/sth in a particular way: **~ sb/sth as (doing) sth** *Globalization tends to be presented as an external force.* ◇ *Leading figures have attempted to present the movement as non-denominational.* ◇ **~ sth** *The organization needs to present a robust financial image.* **3** [T] to be the cause of a problem, difficulty or opportunity: **~ sth** *Specific illnesses may present additional difficulties.* ◇ *This constitutional constraint presents a huge challenge for the country.* ◇ **~ sb with sth** *Globalization presents organizations with unlimited opportunities.* **4** [T] **~ itself (to sb)** (of an opportunity, an idea or a solution) to happen or become available: *When an opportunity presents itself, it is often seized without proper evaluation.* ➲ *compare* ARISE (1) **5** [T] to give sth to sb in a formal situation: **~ sth** *Parents were asked to present the child's vaccination card.* ◇ **~ sb with sth** *The company has been presented with awards for its good corporate governance.* ◇ **~ sth to sb** *They signed antislavery petitions presented to Parliament in 1833.* **6** [T] **~ sth** to produce a show, TV programme, etc: *That year, the National Theatre Company presented its inaugural production of 'Hamlet'.* HELP In British English, to **present** a show, etc. also means to introduce the items in it: *The ceremony was broadcast on BBC1 and presented by television personality Graham Norton.* **7** [I] (*medical*) (of a condition or patient) to be seen: *Typically, the disease presents in early childhood.* ◇ **~ with sth** *Patients may present with back pain.*

▸ PRESENT + NOUN **information** • **material** • **topic** • **facts** • **data** • **statistics** • **findings** • **results** • **evidence** • **analysis** • **review** • **summary** • **list** • **example** • **paper** *Evidence presented here came from women across a spectrum of ages.* | **overview** • **view** • **concept** • **idea** • **argument** • **discussion** • **approach** • **hypothesis** • **framework** • **proposal** • **theory** • **model** • **methodology** • **study** • **estimate** • **solution** *Table 12.3 presents an overview of the content areas included.* ◇ *The ideas presented are very speculative.* | **picture** • **image** • **perspective** • **scenario** • **story** • **account** • **version** *Other newspapers presented a very different story.* | **challenge** • **problem** • **difficulty** • **dilemma** • **obstacle** • **barrier** • **threat** • **risk** • **opportunity** • **option** *Schools in disadvantaged areas present a problem for policymakers in England.*

▸ NOUN + PRESENT **table ◆ figure ◆ chapter ◆ section ◆ article ◆ paper ◆ book** *The next section presents the relevant theoretical concepts.*

▸ (BE) PRESENTED + ADVERB **here ◆ herein ◆ below ◆ above ◆ elsewhere ◆ separately** *Much of the information presented here is an update and refinement of earlier works.*

GRAMMAR POINT

present ◆ describe ◆ examine

- These verbs are followed by a noun phrase; they may not be followed by a *that-* clause:

– *The next section **presents** the theoretical framework.*
– *The following sections **describe** methods that are the most feasible, portable and time efficient.*
– *The next two chapters **examine** locations, activities and lifestyles within global cities.*

- The passive is also used:

– *This model **is presented** in Figure 3.1.*

illustrate ◆ reveal ◆ show

- These verbs may be followed by a *that-* clause:

– *The example **illustrates that** price is not the only factor in persuading more customers to buy the product.*
– *Evidence from the Levant trade **shows that** a 10 per cent return on capital was acceptable.*

- They may also be followed by a dependent clause (= a clause that is not a full sentence) without *that*:

– *Figure 2 **shows** the various payment rates measured in the study.*

- The passive is also used. A full sentence is followed by *as* + passive form:

– *The nature of these structures **is shown** in Figure 17.3.*
– *The model predicted..., **as illustrated** in the figure.*

pre·sen·ta·tion /ˌpreznˈteɪʃn; *NAmE* ˌpriːzenˈteɪʃn/ *noun* **1** [C, U] the act of showing or offering information or ideas for other people to consider; an occasion when this happens: *Dedicated staff will tour local schools, giving presentations and offering advice.* ◇ **~ (of sth) (to sb/sth)** *We then made oral presentations of findings to the Health and Medical Board.* ◇ *The questions were 'field tested' in conference presentation and in print (Greenland, 1999).* **2** [C, U] **~ of sth** the way that sb/sth is shown or described: *The selection and presentation of all data must reflect these priorities.* ◇ *The audience sees a refined cinematic presentation of the subject.* ◇ *Choice of language is part of a speaker's presentation of self.* **3** [U] the act of giving or showing sth to sb in a formal situation: **~ (of sth) (to sb)** *The company might commission a copy for presentation to a patron or benefactor.* ◇ **on ~ (of sth)** *EU citizens are normally waved through on presentation of proof of the right to travel.* **4** [C, U] (*medical*) the way that a condition or patient is or appears; the occasion when a condition or patient is seen or examined: *Hers is an atypical presentation, but the disease can present in a variety of ways.* ◇ *Laboratory testing is guided by clinical presentation.* ◇ **~ of sth** *This is the most serious presentation of gallstone disease and carries a mortality of about 15%.* ◇ **at ~** *The majority of our patients had total paralysis at presentation.*

the ˌ**present** ˈ**day** *noun* [sing.] the situation that exists in the world now, rather than in the past or the future: **to the ~** *From the 1870s up to the present day, the canyon has been scientifically explored and studied.* ◇ **at/in the ~** *In the period 1066–1280, most of the inhabitants of the British Isles lived, not in towns as they do at the present day, but in the countryside.* ■ ˌ**present-**ˈ**day** *adj.* [only before noun] *It has been noted that women use more personal pronouns than men in present-day British English.* ◇ *It was traditionally thought that agriculture first emerged in a few Asian centres, most notably south-west Asia (present-day Iraq).*

pre·sent·er /prɪˈzentə(r)/ *noun* **1** a person who makes a speech or talks to an audience about a particular subject: *Presenters at the workshops included paediatricians, an asthma educator and GPs.* **2** (*BrE*) a person who introduces the different sections of a radio or television programme: *a radio/television presenter* ◇ *Listening to a BBC presenter even up to the 1960s and 1970s, it is apparent how class distinctions in accents have softened.*

pres·ent·ly /ˈprezntli/ *adv.* **1** (usually used before the word or sentence that it refers to) at the time you are speaking or writing; now SYN CURRENTLY: *As the law presently stands, it is possible to claim compensation.* ◇ *Only very limited information is presently available.* ◇ *Presently, more older adults are alive than at any other time in our society's history.* ➲ *usage note at* ACTUAL **2** (usually used at the end of a sentence or CLAUSE) at a later time, for example at a later point in the text that you are writing: *A number of these differences will be reviewed presently.* ◇ *As will be discussed presently, it is this author's contention that...*

ˌ**present parˈticiple** (*BrE*) (*NAmE* ˌpresent ˈparticiple) *noun* (*grammar*) the form of the verb that in English ends in *-ing* and is used with the verb *to be* to form progressive tenses such as *I was running* or sometimes as an adjective as in *running water*: *It is not surprising that present participles can sometimes function as prepositions.* ➲ *compare* PAST PARTICIPLE

the ˌ**present** ˈ**perfect** *noun* [sing.] (*grammar*) the form of a verb that expresses an action done in a time period up to the present, formed in English with the present tense of *have* and the past participle of the verb, as in *I have eaten*: *You can use the present perfect to talk about your life experiences.*

ˌ**present** ˈ**tense** (*also* **the present**) *noun* [usually sing.] (*grammar*) the form of a verb that expresses an action that is happening now or at the time of speaking: *Sometimes participants expressed themselves using the past tense and at other times in the present tense.*

pre·ser·va·tion /ˌprezəˈveɪʃn; *NAmE* ˌprezərˈveɪʃn/ *noun* [U] **1 ~ of sth** the fact or process of making sure that a particular quality or feature is kept: *It is clear that one such duty is the preservation of the peace.* ◇ *She is interested in conservation biology and the preservation of biodiversity.* **2** the fact or process of keeping sth safe from harm, in good condition or in its original state: *Wilderness preservation is a key goal of the US network of national parks.* ◇ **~ of sth** *His works stressed the importance of the preservation of forests.* ◇ **+ noun** *Some preservation techniques destroy the DNA of the sample.* **3 ~ (of sth)** the degree to which sth has not been changed or damaged by age, weather, etc: *The excellent preservation of these echinoderms suggests relatively quiet water environments.*

pre·serve[1] /prɪˈzɜːv; *NAmE* prɪˈzɜːrv/ *verb* **1 ~ sth** to keep a particular quality or feature: *The convention recognizes the need to preserve biodiversity.* ◇ *Exposure times are reduced to preserve sample integrity.* ◇ *They were unable to preserve the peace indefinitely.* **2** to keep sth safe from harm, in good condition or in its original state: **~ sth** *Local farmers have acted to preserve a remnant of the primordial ecosystem.* ◇ **well/poorly preserved** *Most of the fossil specimens are poorly preserved.* ◇ **~ sth + adj.** *Their main aim was to preserve the company's assets intact.* **3** to prevent sth from decaying, by treating it in a particular way: **~ sth** *Salt is used in preserving meat and fish.* ◇ **be preserved in sth** *Nematodes were preserved in 4% formaldehyde.* ➲ *compare* CONSERVE

pre·serve[2] /prɪˈzɜːv; *NAmE* prɪˈzɜːrv/ *noun* [sing.] an activity, job or interest that is thought to be suitable for one particular person or group of people: *Foreign policy and military policy is largely a male preserve.* ◇ **~ of sb/sth** *In*

P

truth, the enforcement of laws is not the exclusive preserve of the courts.

pre·side /prɪˈzaɪd/ *verb* [I] **~ (at/over sth)** to lead or be in charge of a meeting, ceremony, etc: *Central courts presided over most criminal trials for major offences.* ◇ *The presiding judge could not be removed.* ◇ (*figurative*) *The government presided over a very rapid increase in public spending.*

presi·dency /ˈprezɪdənsi/ *noun* (*pl.* **-ies**) [usually sing.] the job of being president of a country or an organization; the period of time sb holds this job: *In 1800 Jefferson won the presidency from John Adams.* ◇ *This was one of the most controversial bills of the Bush presidency.* HELP The **presidency** of an organization is sometimes held by a country rather than a single person: *The meetings are ordinarily hosted by the country holding the presidency.*

presi·dent /ˈprezɪdənt/ *noun* **1** (*also* **President**) the elected leader of a REPUBLIC: *He later became Greece's first elected president.* ◇ *The president appoints the District's judges.* ◇ **~ of...** *the President of the United States* ◇ *President Obama* **2** (*also* **President**) **~ (of sth)** the person in charge of some organizations, clubs, colleges, etc: *She became the first woman to be elected president of the American Anthropological Association.* ◇ *The committee was composed of educators, ranging from university presidents through elementary school principals.* **3 ~ (of sth)** (*especially NAmE*) the person in charge of a bank or commercial organization: *The last of these reorganizations was carried out under James Wolfensohn, president of the Bank between 1995 and 2005.*

presi·den·tial /ˌprezɪˈdenʃl/ *adj.* connected with a president: *International observers declared the presidential elections generally free and fair.* ◇ *The expansion of presidential power has been aided by the willingness of some presidents to interpret their role liberally.*

P

press¹ /pres/ *noun* **1** (*usually* **the press, the Press**) [sing.+ sing./pl. v.] the people or companies that produce articles and programmes for newspapers, magazines, websites, etc; the newspapers, etc. that they produce: *They claimed that the press was undermining respect for the political process.* ◇ **in the (...) press** *The incident was widely reported in the national press.* ◇ **the popular ~** *Scientific literature describes research articles published in 'scholarly' (professional science) journals, rather than in the popular press.* ◇ **+ noun** *The issue has received widespread press coverage.* ◇ *Official Chinese press reports indicated that further changes were likely.* **2** [sing., U] the things that are written or said about sb/sth in newspapers, etc: *Banks generally do not get a very good press.* ◇ *These varieties faced none of the bad press associated with genetically modified crops.* **3** [C] a business that prints or publishes books: *The article was published in 'Law and Geography' (Oxford University Press, Oxford 2002).* **4** [C] a machine for printing books, newspapers, etc: *This was well before Gutenberg's invention of the printing press in the fifteenth century.* **5** [C] a piece of equipment that uses force or weight to produce sth, to make sth flat or to get liquid from sth: *This mixture is then put into a press and compressed to form a disc.* **6** [C, usually sing.] **~ (of sth)** an act of pushing sth with your hand or with a tool that you are holding: *The information is available at the press of a few computer keys.* **7** [sing.] **~ of sth** the large number of people or things competing for space or attention; the difficulties caused by this: *There was no environmental regulation to mitigate the press of so many people living in close proximity.*

IDM **go to ˈpress** to be printed or published: *There were changes in the law after the book went to press in 2010.* **in ˈpress** used after a reference to say that a book, etc. is about to be published: *A simple model was used to reconstruct the impacts of each storm (Boose et al, in press).*

press² /pres/ *verb* **1** [T, I] to push sb/sth firmly against or into sth; to be pushed in this way: **~ sb/sth + adv/prep.** *When a finger is pressed against the material, the drop in its electrical resistance is detected.* ◇ **+ adv./prep.** *The higher you go, the less weight of air there is above you, pressing down on you.* **2** [T, I] to push a switch, button, etc. in order to make it work: **~ sth** *A rat can be trained to press a lever for food.* ◇ **+ adv./prep.** *Participants were instructed to press down on the corresponding key as quickly as possible.* **3** [T, often passive] to use force or weight to create an object or to get liquid from sth: **(be) pressed** *Olive oil pressed in Italy from Greek olives can be labelled 'made in Italy'.* **4** [I] **+ adv./prep.** to continue to move in a determined way in a particular direction: *The settlers' life was not easy, yet they pressed westward.* **5** [T, often passive, I] to make a determined effort to persuade or force sb to do sth SYN PUSH¹: **~ sb (to do sth)** *If pressed to defend this approach, few pure mathematicians would do so.* ◇ **~ sb into (doing) sth** *People are routinely pressed into pleading guilty to crimes that nobody thinks they committed.* ◇ **~ sb for sth** *When pressed for specific points, the participants found it difficult to come up with answers.* ➲ *compare* URGE¹ (1) **6** [T] **~ sth** to express or repeat an opinion or demand strongly: *Both men press the case for poetry as the foremost of the human arts.* ◇ *Minority ethnic communities are starting to press their claim for full citizenship.*

IDM **ˌpress sth ˈhome** to succeed in communicating sth clearly, by arguing or attacking in a powerful way: *A number of slogans were developed to press home the message that erosion control was necessary.* ◇ *Henry V was intent on pressing home his claim to the throne of France.* **ˌpress sb/sth into ˈservice** to use sb/sth for a particular purpose, sometimes when this is not suitable: *Local labourers, both skilled and unskilled, were pressed into service in the rebuilding effort.* ➲ *more at* CHARGE¹, HARD²

PHR V **ˌpress aˈhead/ˈon (with sth)** to continue doing sth in a determined way: *The Commission pressed ahead with the drafting process.* ◇ *He made serious mistakes, but pressed on regardless.* **ˈpress for sth** to keep asking for sth: *The first directly elected parliament rapidly started pressing for bolder reforms.*

press·ing /ˈpresɪŋ/ *adj.* [usually before noun] needing to be dealt with immediately SYN URGENT (1): *There is a pressing need to discover errors in strategy sooner rather than later.* ◇ *The most pressing issues in Scotland during the election focused on the economy and public finances.* ◇ *Reducing health inequalities is a pressing concern.*

pres·sure¹ /ˈpreʃə(r)/ *noun* [C, U] **1** the force with which sb/sth presses against sth: **~ (of sth)** *When the river froze, the bridge collapsed under the pressure of the ice.* ◇ *The needle is then withdrawn and pressure applied through a piece of gauze.* ◇ **+ noun** *Pressure sores and leg ulcers are the most common serious skin problems in old age.* **2** (*technical*) the force produced by a solid, liquid or gas on a particular area, for example when pressing against a surface or when in or leaving a closed space: *A pin exerts more pressure than a finger pushed with the same force.* ◇ **~ on sth** *The gas exerts a pressure on the walls of its container.* ◇ **at... ~** *The heating occurs at constant pressure.* ◇ **at a ~ of sth** *Experiments were performed at a pressure of 01 GPa.* ◇ **under ~** *The powder was heated under pressure to form a film.* ◇ **under a ~ of sth** *The bottle was filled under a pressure of more than one atmosphere.* ➲ *see also* HIGH PRESSURE (1), LOW PRESSURE (1) **3** the force of the atmosphere on the earth's surface: *Pressure has been falling in the last 36 hours.* ◇ *The cold phase occurs when cool currents and increased atmospheric pressures predominate.* ◇ **high/low ~** *Air flows from a region of high pressure to one of low pressure.* ➲ *see also* HIGH PRESSURE (2), LOW PRESSURE (2) **4** (*medical*) the force with which blood travels around the body SYN BLOOD PRESSURE: *In this condition, the pulmonary artery pressure is elevated.* **5** the feeling that it is necessary to do sth; the action of making sb feel this; the problems caused by this: **under ~ to do sth** *Schools are under increasing pressure to lift standards.* ◇ *Governments have come under pressure to increase labour flexibility.* ◇ **under (...) ~** *Diagnoses were less accurate under time pressure.* ◇ **~ for sth** *From the 1960s, there were considerable pressures for change.* ◇ **~ on sb** *This increased the pressure on the government.* ◇ **(put) ~ (on sb) to do sth** *This situation puts pressure on the company to improve its performance.* ◇ **~ on sth** *The result is greater pressure on prices.* ◇ **~ from sb** *Despite strong pressures from the unions, the state has been reluctant to regulate employer-sponsored education.* ◇ **~ of sth** *The pressures of competition mean that speed is becoming increasingly important.*

▸ ADJECTIVE + PRESSURE **high • internal • external • constant** *A new combination of internal and external pressures after 2000 made reform more likely than ever before.* | **standard • normal • partial • low • negative** *Both electrodes are encapsulated within a glass envelope that is filled with neon at low pressure.* | **strong • intense • considerable, great • enormous • increasing, growing, mounting • increased • upward • downward** *This development will put upward pressure on prices.* | **international • popular • competitive • selective • evolutionary • environmental • social • political • regulatory • institutional • economic • financial • commercial • inflationary** *Oil price rises may intensify inflationary pressure and slow growth.*

▸ NOUN + PRESSURE **gas • vapour • air • water • surface** *This sensor measures the air pressure.*

▸ VERB + PRESSURE **generate, create • maintain • apply • exert, put ~ on, place ~ on • increase • reduce • relieve • be subject to • withstand, resist** *In knee joints, cartilage has to withstand enormous pressures.* ◇ *These populations are subject to intense pressure from predators.* | **raise • lower • measure • monitor** *The gas will expand by a very small amount, lowering the internal pressure infinitesimally.* | **bring, bring to bear, impose • put sb under • intensify • ease • face, be/come under • feel • experience • be driven by • respond to • cope with** *Attempts to impose direct pressure on government usually fail.*

▸ PRESSURE + VERB **decrease, fall, drop • rise, increase • exceed** *As the solution was vented, the pressure dropped.*

▸ PRESSURE + NOUN **change • drop • gradient • difference • ratio • overload • gauge • sensor** *As the dissolved carbon dioxide in the spray solution leaves the nozzle, it undergoes a rapid decompression due to the sudden pressure drop.*

pres·sure² /ˈpreʃə(r)/ *verb* [often passive] (*disapproving*) to try to persuade sb to do sth, especially by making them feel that they must or should do it: **be pressured to do sth** *Regulations are needed to ensure that owners are not pressured to sell their homes.* ◇ **be pressured into (doing) sth** *Many firms are pressured into pursuing cost-based competitive strategies.*

ˈpressure group *noun* a group of people who try to influence the government and ordinary people's opinions in order to achieve the action they want, for example a change in a law: *Individuals have come to regard pressure groups as an effective channel for political expression.* ➲ *see also* INTEREST GROUP

pres·tige /preˈstiːʒ/ *noun* [U] respect and admiration that sb/sth receives, because people consider them/it to have great importance, quality or value: *It is interesting to see how different languages begin to acquire prestige and others are devalued.* ◇ *Education plays an important part in political influence, economic advantage and social prestige.* ➲ *compare* STATUS (4)

pres·ti·gious /preˈstɪdʒəs/ *adj.* [usually before noun] (not usually used about people) respected and admired; considered to have great importance, quality or value: *She was the recipient of the prestigious Franz Liszt Prize for musical excellence.* ◇ *a prestigious university/journal*

pre·sum·ably AWL /prɪˈzjuːməbli; *NAmE* prɪˈzuːməbli/ *adv.* used to say that you think that sth is likely or probably true, based on what you already know: *This is learned behaviour and presumably can be unlearned.* ◇ *Presumably, even the control mice will experience some stress from being handled and kept in the lab.*

pre·sume AWL /prɪˈzjuːm; *NAmE* prɪˈzuːm/ *verb* **1** [I, T] to suppose that sth is true or exists, although it is not definitely proved or known SYN ASSUME (1): **~ (that)...** *Researchers sometimes presume that meaning is a constant.* ◇ **it is presumed that...** *It is presumed that an owner of goods knows their condition.* ◇ **~ sb/sth to be/have sth** *Adults are presumed to be competent.* ◇ **~ sth** *The court will never presume shared ownership just because people share a home.* ◇ **~ sb/sth + adj.** *He was missing at sea, presumed dead.* HELP In legal contexts, **presume** often means that sth is being accepted as true until it is shown not to be true: *Everyone has the right to be presumed innocent until proven guilty.* **2** [T] to accept that sth is true or that it exists, and to act on that basis: **~ sth** *The work presumes a standard of education corresponding to that of a university entrance examination.* ◇ **~ (that)...** *This acquisition model presumes that knowledge is owned and held by a sole person (the teacher) and transmitted to others (the learners).* **3** [T] **~ to do sth** to do sth without having the right or ability to do it: *Practitioners must not presume to know the patient's thoughts.*

pre·sump·tion AWL /prɪˈzʌmpʃn/ *noun* [C, U] the act of supposing or accepting that sth is true or exists, although it has not been proved; a belief that sth is true or exists SYN ASSUMPTION (1): **~ that...** *The presumption is that an action is permissible unless an argument can be found that shows otherwise.* ◇ **~ of sth** *The concept of human rights rests on the presumption of the intrinsic moral worth of the individual.* HELP In legal contexts, **presumption** often means that sth is being accepted as true until it is shown not to be true: *The Human Rights Act 1998 has as its main principle the presumption of innocence.*

pre·sup·pose /ˌpriːsəˈpəʊz; *NAmE* ˌpriːsəˈpoʊz/ *verb* **1** to accept that sth is true and argue a case or take action on that basis, before it has been proved to be true SYN ASSUME (1), PRESUME (2): **~ that...** *This type of thinking presupposes that clear rules and appropriate control mechanisms can prevent risk and danger.* ◇ **~ sth** *However, this theory presupposes a society made up entirely of people who can be relied on to act rationally in their own interests.* **2 ~ sth** to require sth or accept sth as needing to exist: *The book presupposes relatively little prior knowledge on the part of the student.* ◇ *Scientific validation presupposes the existence of a model.*

pre·sup·pos·ition /ˌpriːsʌpəˈzɪʃn/ *noun* [C, U] something that you accept as being true and that you use when you argue sth, even though it has not been proved; the act of accepting that sth is true or exists SYN ASSUMPTION (1): **~ about sth** *The practice of science rests upon a number of presuppositions about the nature of reality.* ◇ **~ of sth** *The presupposition of continuous progress in the effectiveness of language teaching is open to serious doubt.*

pre·tend /prɪˈtend/ *verb* **1** to behave in a particular way, in order to make other people believe sth that is not true: **~ that...** *He pretended that he was buying a property in Trinidad on the account of his funders.* ◇ **~ to do sth** *Sixty per cent of participants reported that they had never pretended to be someone else.* **2** (usually used in negative sentences and questions) to claim to be, do or have sth, especially when this is not true: **~ (that)...** *There is no*

P

point in pretending there is no prejudice. ◇ **~ to be/do/have sth** *The result does not pretend to be comprehensive.*

pretty /ˈprɪti/ *adv.* (with adjectives and adverbs) (*rather informal*) **1** to some extent; fairly: *People in advertising get pretty good at defensively arguing that it does little, if any, harm.* **2** very: *The answer was pretty clear: yes.* ◇ *He seems pretty sure that the donations will never reach those in need.*
IDM **pretty ˈmuch/ˈwell** (*rather informal*) almost; almost completely: *GDP per capita in sub-Saharan Africa remained pretty much constant.*

pre·vail /prɪˈveɪl/ *verb* **1** [I] to exist or be very common at a particular time, in a particular place or among particular people: *Different geographical, political and cultural concepts of Europe have prevailed at different times.* ◇ **~ in sth** *The economic conditions prevailing in a particular country may have a bearing on competitiveness.* ◇ **~ among sb** *For the first few months, a similar mood prevailed among state educational leaders.* **2** [I] (of ideas or opinions) to be accepted as being stronger or more important in a particular situation: *For the moment, these arguments have not prevailed.* ◇ **~ over sth** *Reason, he argued, must prevail over fear.* **3** [I] to defeat an opponent, or opposing system, especially after a long struggle: *The pro- and anti-reformists appeared closely matched, each facing a tough fight to prevail.* ◇ **~ over sb/sth** *In stories such as this, we desire the forces of good to prevail over the forces of evil.*
PHR V **preˈvail on/upon sb to do sth** to persuade sb to do sth: *Bismarck had prevailed on Hesse-Darmstadt and Baden to accept military reforms.*

pre·vail·ing /prɪˈveɪlɪŋ/ *adj.* [only before noun] **1** existing, most common or having most influence at a particular time SYN CURRENT[1] (2): *The government's approach was strongly influenced by the prevailing economic conditions.* ◇ *Under the prevailing view, talented people are entitled to expect greater income.* **2** the **prevailing wind** in an area is the one that blows over it most frequently: *In general, the coastal currents in South East Asia are driven by prevailing monsoon winds.*

preva·lent /ˈprevələnt/ *adj.* that exists or is very common at a particular time or in a particular place SYN COMMON[1] (1), WIDESPREAD: **~ in sb/sth** *This condition is more prevalent in patients with diabetes.* ◇ *Family ownership of firms is the prevalent form of ownership in many countries around the globe.* ◇ **~ among sb** *Some inherited illnesses are disproportionately prevalent among minority ethnic communities.* ■ **preva·lence** /ˈprevələns/ *noun* [U] **~ (of sth)** *This high prevalence of smoking in pregnancy has important consequences for child health.*

pre·vent /prɪˈvent/ *verb* to stop sth from existing or happening; to stop sb/sth from doing sth: **~ sth** *GPs have a crucial role to play in promoting health and preventing disease.* ◇ **in order to ~ sth** *The product had to be accompanied by a certificate of origin, in order to prevent fraud.* ◇ **~ sb/sth (from) doing sth** *The Arafura Shelf prevented cooler water from the Pacific from crossing to the Banda Sea during the southern winter.*
▸ PREVENT + NOUN **damage • harm • loss • disease • infection • injury • complications • death • formation • development • spread • transmission • recurrence • conflict** *The presence of contaminants can often prevent the formation of crystals suitable for X-ray analysis.*

pre·vent·able /prɪˈventəbl/ *adj.* that can be prevented: *Cigarette smoking is the leading preventable cause of disease and death in the United States.* ◇ *preventable diseases/deaths*

pre·ven·tion /prɪˈvenʃn/ *noun* [U] the act of stopping sth bad from happening: *There are restrictions on access to data that are held for the purpose of crime prevention.* ◇ *The idiom 'prevention is better than cure' is a central message in many public health interventions.* ◇ **~ of sth** *The prevention of crime was presented as a community responsibility.* ◇ **+ noun** *Research has shown that these diseases can be delayed or prevented through use of disease prevention strategies.*

pre·vent·ive /prɪˈventɪv/ (*also* **pre·venta·tive** /prɪˈventətɪv/) *adj.* [only before noun] intended to try to stop sth that causes problems or difficulties from happening: *Vaccination is a widespread preventive measure in health systems.* ◇ *Early preventive intervention tends to be exceptionally cost-effective.* ◇ *Resources spent on preventive medicine are far from adequate.* ➲ *compare* CURATIVE

pre·view /ˈpriːvjuː/ *verb* **~ sth** to give a short account of sth that is going to happen, be studied, etc: *This chapter previews a topic that is further expanded upon in Chapters 6 and 7.*

pre·vi·ous AWL /ˈpriːviəs/ *adj.* [only before noun] **1** happening or existing before the event or object that you are talking about SYN PRIOR (1): *The next section focuses on previous studies on business groups in Argentina.* ◇ *Previous research has shown that around one quarter of children have been bullied in school (Whitney and Smith, 1993).* ◇ *This result is consistent with previous findings.* ◇ *The experimenter had roughly 125 hours of previous observer experience.* **2** immediately before the time or section you are talking about SYN PRECEDING: *She had felt increasingly breathless over the previous three months.* ◇ *the previous year/decade/century* ◇ *As discussed in the previous section,...* ◇ *the previous chapter/paragraph/page* ■ **pre·vi·ous to** *prep.*: *Previous to the introduction of the law, anyone could call themselves a nurse and care for the sick.*

pre·vi·ous·ly AWL /ˈpriːviəsli/ *adv.* before now; before a particular time: *As previously noted, Tokyo is the most significant exception to this pattern.* ◇ *Cells were maintained using the culture conditions described previously by Campbell et al.* ◇ *An important eleventh-century Arabic atlas, previously unknown to modern geographers, was discovered in a private collection in 2002.* ◇ *Previously, applicants entering the country for work or study had to show that they could maintain themselves without needing public funds.* ◇ **...years, months, etc. ~** *He had smoked heavily for 25 years, but had given up 5 years previously.*

ˌpre-ˈwar *adj.* [usually before noun] happening or existing before a war, especially before the Second World War: *Silverman focuses on contemporary France and does not discuss the pre-war period.* ◇ *Business groups in pre-war Japan had both positive and negative traits.*

prey[1] /preɪ/ *noun* [U, sing.] an animal that is hunted, killed and eaten by another: *Group hunting is required to capture larger prey, such as zebra or buffalo.* ◇ **a bird of ~** *The Cape Verde kite is considered to be one of the rarest birds of prey.*
IDM **be/fall ˈprey to sth** to be harmed or affected by sth bad: *Rome never fell prey to raiding groups from the mountains.* ◇ *The language of natural rights has always been prey to this kind of criticism.*

prey[2] /preɪ/ *verb*
PHR V **ˈprey on/upon sb/sth** **1** (of an animal or a bird) to hunt and kill another animal for food: *A food web is a network that represents which species prey on which others in a given ecosystem.* **2** to harm or take advantage of sb who is weaker than you: *They fear the Internet as a tool of potentially violent people who prey on children.*

price[1] /praɪs/ *noun* **1** [C, U] the amount of money that you have to pay for sth: *In the first six months of the year, average house prices rose by 10.9%.* ◇ **~ of sth** *Taxation can be used to increase the price of goods and services.* ◇ **~ for sth** *They will be able to charge lower prices for their*

P

product. ◇ **in ~** *Such a strategy can work well if shares are rising in price.* ➲ *see also* MARKET PRICE **2** [sing.] the unpleasant things that you must do or experience in order to achieve sth or as a result of achieving sth: **~ of sth** *Chernyshevsky was well aware of the price of revolution but many of those whom he inspired were not.* ◇ **~ for (doing) sth** *The bishops of Rome paid a price for their freedom from imperial control.* ◇ **~ to pay (for sth)** *The extra work involved is a small price to pay for the rich data that are provided.*

IDM **at ˈany price** whatever the cost or the difficulties may be: *Two thirds of those surveyed would not knowingly purchase a shirt made under bad sweatshop conditions at any price.* ◇ *Retention of power at any price meant that, when Lenin died, he bequeathed overwhelming problems to his successors.* **at a ˈprice 1** involving sth unpleasant: *But economic progress comes at a price: vast factory developments scar the landscape and add to already high levels of pollution.* **2** costing a lot of money: *The luxury and freedom of car ownership comes at a price.*

▸ ADJECTIVE + PRICE **high • low • rising • falling • full • fair • average • wholesale • minimum • domestic • current** *Relatively high oil prices increase the revenues and profits of oil companies and benefit oil-exporting countries.*

▸ NOUN + PRICE **oil • energy • food • commodity • house • share • stock • purchase • market • retail** *The company's share price has fallen 40 per cent in the last three months.*

▸ VERB + PRICE **charge • pay • set • lower, cut, reduce • raise, increase • fix • determine** *In most markets the sellers, not the buyers, set prices.* ◇ *The companies had used their dominance in the market to fix prices.*

▸ PRICE + VERB **rise, increase • fall • change • remain** *During this period, US natural gas prices remained stable.*

▸ NOUN + IN (THE) PRICE (OF STH) **rise, increase • decrease, fall, drop, reduction, decline • change • difference • variation • fluctuation** *Temporary increases in the price of energy have occasionally depressed investment and growth.* ◇ *A fall in price may lead to an increase in revenue.*

price² /praɪs/ *verb* [usually passive] to set the price of sth at a particular level: *How a company prices its products depends on what its pricing objectives are.* ◇ **~ sth + adv./prep.** *An adequate, secure, clean and competitively priced supply of energy is vital for sustainable development.* ◇ **~ sth at sth** *The company was buying components from the USA priced at US$400 each.*

pri·cing /ˈpraɪsɪŋ/ *noun* [U] the act of deciding how much to charge for sth: **~ of sth** *There has already been a significant effect on the pricing of natural gas in Europe.* ◇ **+ noun** *Setting a pricing strategy is not easy because of the huge number of factors to be taken into account.*

pride /praɪd/ *noun* **1** [U, sing.] a feeling of pleasure that you get when you or people who are connected with you have done sth well or have sth that other people admire: *Despite the pain of defeat and humiliation after World War II, a renewed sense of national pride was emerging in West Germany.* ◇ **~ in (doing) sth** *All but two of the students expressed a strong pride in their racial and ethnic heritages.* ◇ **take ~ in (doing) sth** *Most people are capable of enjoying work and take pride in doing good work.* ◇ **with ~** *They declare and display their identity within the Melawi society with pride.* **2** [U] the feeling of respect for yourself; the feeling that you are better than other people: *The terms of the Paris peace treaty dealt a series of heavy blows to Russian power and Russian pride.*

IDM **pride of ˈplace** a central position that is given to sb/sth that is considered important: *The peasant family farm was given pride of place in West Germany's agricultural policy.*

priest /priːst/ *noun* a person who is qualified to perform religious duties and ceremonies in some religions: *He was ordained as a priest and was soon pressed into service as a bishop.* ◇ *The kings functioned as the chief priests and conducted all the public sacrifices.* ➲ *compare* MINISTER (2)

pri·macy AWL /ˈpraɪməsi/ *noun* (*pl.* **-ies**) [U] the fact of being the most important person or thing: *Primacy must be given to the welfare of the child.* ◇ **~ (of sth) (over sth)** *The new doctrine sought to defend the primacy of international law over domestic law.*

pri·mar·ily AWL /praɪˈmerəli; *BrE also* ˈpraɪmərəli/ *adv.* mainly SYN CHIEFLY: *Their argument focuses primarily on two basic issues.* ◇ *The questionnaire was primarily concerned with attitudes towards household recycling.* ◇ *This labour shortage was regarded as primarily due to poor wages and conditions.*

pri·mary AWL /ˈpraɪməri; *NAmE* ˈpraɪmeri/ *adj.* **1** [usually before noun] main; most important; basic SYN PRIME¹ (1): *A primary cause of land pollution is waste disposal.* ◇ *The primary focus of the article is on species protection law.* ◇ *The primary objective of the Word Bank is to fight poverty and assist developing countries.* ◇ *sb's primary aim/goal/concern* ◇ *The primary data source for this study is the Indonesia Family Life Survey (IFLS).* ➲ *compare* SECONDARY (1) ➲ *see also* PRIMARY SOURCE ➲ thesaurus note *at* MAIN¹ **2** [usually before noun] developing or happening first; earliest: *The model suggests five primary stages in the development and implementation of a strategy.* HELP **Primary** is used especially in biology and medicine to refer to the first stage of development or growth of sth: *Clinical examination reveals an extensive primary tumour.* ➲ *see also* PRIMARY CARE **3** [only before noun] (*especially BrE*) connected with the education of children aged around 5–11: *Local education authorities provide state primary and secondary education.* ◇ *Primary school teachers from a minority ethnic group accounted for only 0.5 per cent of all primary teachers.* ➲ *compare* ELEMENTARY (1), SECONDARY (4), TERTIARY **4** (*chemistry*) (of an ORGANIC COMPOUND) having its FUNCTIONAL GROUP located on a CARBON atom which is BONDED to no more than one other carbon atom; containing a NITROGEN atom bonded to one carbon atom: *Unlike tertiary alcohols, secondary and primary alcohols are readily oxidized to carbonyl compounds.* ➲ *compare* SECONDARY (5), TERTIARY (4)

ˌprimary ˈcare (*also* **ˌprimary ˈhealth care**) *noun* [U] the medical treatment that you receive first when you are ill, for example from your family doctor: *Primary care was provided by 8 000 GPs, 60% of whom worked part-time.* ◇ *Village clinics act as primary health care in rural areas of China.* ◇ **+ noun** *a primary care physician/team/setting*

ˈprimary source *noun* a document, etc. that contains information obtained by research or observation, not taken from other books, etc: *Primary sources cited in Ludlum (1963) were consulted wherever possible.* ➲ *compare* SECONDARY SOURCE

prime¹ AWL /praɪm/ *adj.* [only before noun] **1** main; most important; basic: *Many economists regard the production of new ideas as the prime factor behind economic progress.* ◇ *In a developing knowledge society, dictionaries are cultural tools of prime importance.* ➲ thesaurus note *at* MAIN¹ **2** a **prime example** of sth is one that is typical of it: *Denmark is often hailed as the prime example of the successful development of wind energy.* **3** most likely to be chosen for sth; most suitable: *A prime target of political organization is control over the media.* ◇ *The power to dissolve Parliament has long been considered a prime candidate for reform.*

prime² AWL /praɪm/ *noun* **1** (*also* **ˌprime ˈnumber**) (*mathematics*) a number that can be divided exactly only by itself and 1, for example 7, 17 and 41: *The primes less than 100 are shown in Fig. 7.1.* ◇ *N is the product of two primes.* **2** [sing.] **~ (of sth)** the time in your life when you

P

are strongest or most successful: *Shakespeare was 48, in the prime of life and at the zenith of his career.* ◇ *He ruled for only ten years and died while still in his prime.*

prime[3] AWL /praɪm/ *verb* **1 ~ sth (for sth)** to make sth ready for use or action SYN PREPARE (1): *Sex hormones evidently primed these cells for mating.* ◇ *Keynesian economics (the use of deficit spending to prime the economy during periods of economic downturn) were put into practice.* **2 ~ sb (to do sth)** to prepare sb to react to a situation in a particular way, especially by giving them particular information SYN BRIEF[3]: *If respondents are repeatedly asked about terrorism in a survey, for example, they may be primed to respond that terrorism is the most important issue.*

ˌprime ˈminister (*also* ˌ**Prime ˈMinister**) *noun* (*abbr.* **PM**) the main minister and leader of the government in some countries: *Both the US president and British prime minister telephoned Yeltsin to convey their best wishes.* ◇ *The decision to dissolve Parliament is formally exercised by the monarch, who acts on the Prime Minister's advice.*

primer /ˈpraɪmə(r)/ *noun* (*biology*) a MOLECULE that serves as a starting material for a POLYMERIZATION process: *The primer is a short RNA molecule to which deoxynucleotides are added.*

primi·tive /ˈprɪmətɪv/ *adj.* **1** [usually before noun] belonging to a very simple society with no industry, etc: *Primitive tribes lived by fishing, hunting and gathering.* ◇ *He argued that ritual, rather than myth, was the defining feature of primitive religions.* **2** [usually before noun] belonging to an early stage in the development of humans or animals: *At first, primitive man could learn only the hard way, by the consequences of experience.* ◇ *Very primitive forms of life are known to have developed as early as 4 billion years ago.* **3** very simple and old-fashioned, especially when it is also not convenient and comfortable SYN CRUDE (1): *105 English settlers established a small and rather primitive village at Jamestown.* ◇ *Computers were still in a very primitive state of development during the 1950s.* **4** [usually before noun] (of a feeling or desire) very strong and not based on reason, as if from the earliest period of human life: *Rhoda protects herself with the primitive instinct for avoiding danger.* **5** [usually before noun] (*biology*) (of a part or structure) in the first or early stage of development; not developed from anything else: *The remaining primitive endoderm cells form the visceral endoderm.*

P

prin·ci·pal[1] AWL /ˈprɪnsəpl/ *adj.* [only before noun] main; most important: *Methane is the principal component of natural gas.* ◇ *In many countries, fuel taxes are among the principal sources of government revenue.* ◇ *Measles was one of the principal causes of death among the troops.* ◇ *Gellner (1983) argued that industrialization was a principal reason for the emergence of national languages and cultures.* ➲ thesaurus note *at* MAIN[1]

WHICH WORD?

principal • principle

- **principal** *adj.* main; most important: *the principal aim/cause/concern/reason* ◇ ~~*the principle aim/cause, etc.*~~
- **principle** *noun* a law, rule, theory or belief: *the general principles of political science* ◇ ~~*the general principals of sth*~~

Principal is also a noun with a range of meanings including: a head teacher in the US; a person who is being represented by sb else; and an amount of money invested.

prin·ci·pal[2] AWL /ˈprɪnsəpl/ *noun* **1** (*NAmE*) = HEAD TEACHER: *Elementary school principals are mostly male in the United States and Canada but female in Mexico and Israel.* ◇ *There are three assistant principals, each of whom is responsible for about six classes.* **2** (*technical*) a person that you are representing, especially in business or law: *The agent's role is to act on the principal's behalf.* **3** [usually sing.] (*finance*) an amount of money that you lend to sb or invest to earn interest: *Money may be spent in ways that prevent the lender from getting back their principal.*

prin·ci·pal·ly AWL /ˈprɪnsəpli/ *adv.* mainly SYN CHIEFLY: *In Stage 1, the focus is principally, but not exclusively, on data gathering.* ◇ *In its natural state, uranium consists principally of nuclei of two isotopes: ^{235}U and ^{238}U.* ◇ *The novel is principally concerned with examining the commercial and material ethos of American culture.*

prin·ciple AWL /ˈprɪnsəpl/ *noun* **1** [C] a law, rule or theory that sth is based on: *Accounting principles and practices vary from country to country.* ◇ **~ of sth** *A number of general principles of administrative law have been established in immigration cases.* ◇ **on the ~ that...** *The classification technique operates on the principle that people living in similar areas have the same needs and lifestyles.* ➲ *see also* FIRST PRINCIPLES **2** [sing.] a general or scientific law that explains how sth works or why sth happens: **~ behind sth** *This is a fundamental principle behind any scientific process.* ◇ **~ that...** *A large number of medieval writers defended the principle that nature always chooses the simplest path.* ◇ **on the ~ that...** *This technique is based on the principle that solubility of noble gases in the atmosphere is a function of temperature.* **3** [C] a belief that is accepted as a reason for acting or thinking in a particular way: *This dilemma can be examined using ethical principles.* ◇ **~ of sth** *The principles of democracy are very different from the principles that govern a capitalist economy.* ◇ **the ~ that...** *In Islam, respect for the natural world is founded on the principle that Allah created all things.* **4** [C, usually pl., U] a moral rule or a strong belief that influences your actions: **against your principles** *He decided that it would be against his principles to marry anyone whom he was unable to support.* ◇ **on ~** *Most Populists were against violence on principle.* ◇ **as a matter of ~** *Many were reluctant, as a matter of principle, to accept the reassertion of Party control.* ➲ *usage note at* PRINCIPAL[1]

IDM **in ˈprinciple 1** if sth can be done **in principle**, there is no good reason why it should not be done although it has not yet been done and there may be some difficulties: *Although in principle this issue can be resolved technically, in practice it is still likely to pose problems.* **2** in general but not in detail: *In principle, the computer is a remarkably simple device.*

▸ ADJECTIVE + PRINCIPLE **general • universal • basic, fundamental • key, core • underlying • scientific** *Weismann defined two key principles of heredity.* | **guiding • overarching • abstract • ethical, moral • legal • constitutional • democratic • liberal** *The segment explores the impact this arrest has on the fundamental constitutional principle that a citizen is innocent until proven guilty.*

▸ VERB + PRINCIPLE **formulate • establish • outline • illustrate • accept • apply, use • follow • invoke • satisfy • violate** *States always apply principles of humanitarian intervention selectively, resulting in an inconsistency in policy.* | **embody • lay down • enshrine • respect, uphold • endorse • adopt • embrace • undermine • defend** *These Articles embody three basic principles.*

▸ PRINCIPLE + VERB **govern • apply • underlie** *Universal principles govern the process of development.* ◇ *In the case of environmental legislation, the same principles apply.* | **guide** *He concluded that rulers must allow themselves to be guided by the principles of peace, justice and charity.*

prin·cipled AWL /ˈprɪnsəpld/ *adj.* **1** based on rules or truths: *These two options seem equally valid and there is no principled way to choose between them.* **2** based on strong beliefs about what is right and wrong: *There are* *both pragmatic and principled reasons for supporting reform.*

print[1] /prɪnt/ *verb* **1** [T, I] **~ sth** to use a machine to produce letters, pictures or patterns on paper: *It has been possible to print colour images for a long time, but inexpensive colour printing is relatively recent.* **2** [T] **~ sth** to produce sth such as books or newspapers by printing them: *The government can increase its spending without raising taxes simply by printing money and spending it.* ◇ *The catalogue is printed in 52 editions in 25 languages.* **3** [T] **~ sth** to publish sth in printed form: *The letter was printed in 'The Spectator', 30 May 1987.*

IDM **the ˌprinted ˈword/ˈpage** what is published in books, newspapers or magazines: *From the early 1790s, radicals and reformists saw the printed word as an agent of change.*

PHR V **ˌprint sth ˈoff/ˈout** to produce a document or information from a computer in printed form: *Information sheets can be printed off for the client.*

print[2] /prɪnt/ *noun* **1** [U] letters, words, numbers, etc. that have been printed onto paper: **in... ~** *The opt-out box appears in small print at the bottom of the order form.* ◇ **+ noun** *At the moment, the journal publishes online and print editions at the same time.* **2** [U] used to refer to the business of producing newspapers, magazines and books: *Films, television, print, radio and the Internet have immense power to reach people with powerful messages.* ◇ **+ noun** *The US Supreme Court ruled that the Internet more resembles print media than broadcast media.* **3** [C] a picture that was made by printing: *The prints depict scenes of rural life.* **4** [C] a photograph produced from film: *The grain of the image that ensures the uniqueness of every photograph or film print gets lost in the digital image.* ➲ *see also* FINGERPRINT, FOOTPRINT (1)

IDM **in print** **1** (of a book) still available from the company that publishes it: *The 'Origin' went through six editions in Darwin's lifetime and has remained in print ever since.* **2** (of a person's work) printed in sth such as a book or newspaper: *Relatively few of Wyatt's poems appeared in print in his lifetime.*

print·er /ˈprɪntə(r)/ *noun* **1** a machine for printing text on paper, especially one connected to a computer: *By the late 1990s, high-quality, low-cost colour printers were widely available.* **2** a person or company whose job is printing sth such as books: *The new publication attracted the interest of other printers and booksellers and unauthorized copies appeared.*

print·ing /ˈprɪntɪŋ/ *noun* [U] the act of using a machine to produce letters, pictures or patterns on paper: *The invention of printing on paper provided a technology with which information could be stored over the long term.* ◇ **+ noun** *Johannes Gutenberg established the first printing press in Mainz around 1450.*

prior AWL /ˈpraɪə(r)/ *adj.* [only before noun] happening or existing before sth else or before a particular time: *Audience expectations are also built on prior experience.* ◇ *This research confirms the results of prior studies (Kendler et al., 1993b, 2006c).* ◇ *The legislation was introduced before Parliament without the prior knowledge of the king.*

pri·ori ➲ A PRIORI

pri·ori·tize (*BrE also* **-ise**) AWL /praɪˈɒrətaɪz; *NAmE* praɪˈɔːrətaɪz/ *verb* **1** [T] to treat sth as being more important than other things: **~ sth** *In the Chilean education system, the subjects prioritized are mathematics and language.* ◇ **~ A over B** *When Germany declared war on the USA, President Roosevelt decided to prioritize the European war over the war against Japan.* **2** [T, I] **~ (sth)** to put tasks or problems in order of importance, so that you can deal with the most important first: *Next, we prioritized the remaining tasks.* ■ **pri·ori·tiza·tion, -isa·tion** AWL /praɪˌɒrətaɪˈzeɪʃn; *NAmE* praɪˌɔːrətəˈzeɪʃn/ *noun* [U] **~ (of sth) (over sth)** *The vice-provost defended the prioritization of research over teaching.* ◇ *Policymakers need more guidance in the prioritization of competing policy goals.*

pri·or·ity AWL /praɪˈɒrəti; *NAmE* praɪˈɔːrəti/ *noun* (*pl.* **-ies**) **1** [C] something that you think is more important than other things and should be dealt with first: *Dealing effectively with bullying is currently a very high priority within schools.* ◇ *Mental health remains a low priority in many countries.* ◇ *the top/main/key priority* ◇ *Setting priorities in health involves making decisions about how to allocate resources between competing health issues.* **2** [U] the condition of being considered or treated as more important than other things or people SYN PRECEDENCE: *A debate took place as to whether industrial investment should give priority to electronics or to steel.* ◇ **A takes/has ~ over B** *Under the new management, quality service took priority over productivity.*

ˈprior to *prep.* before sth: *Prior to 2000, water use was even higher.* ◇ *Samples of solid polystyrene were saturated with gas at high pressure prior to measurement.* ◇ **~ doing sth** *High temperature has been used to reduce exotic weeds prior to planting native species (Bainbridge, 1990, 2007).*

prison /ˈprɪzn/ *noun* [C, U] a building where people are kept as a punishment for a crime they have committed, or while they are waiting for trial: *Unlike other countries, Italy does not have maximum-security prisons reserved for very dangerous criminals.* ◇ **in ~** *He was arrested during a visit to Europe and served four years in prison.* ◇ **to ~** *She was sent to prison for contempt of court.* ◇ **+ noun** *With only 5 per cent of the world's population, America holds approximately 25 per cent of the global prison population.* ◇ *the prison service/system/authorities*

pris·on·er /ˈprɪznə(r)/ *noun* **1** a person who has been captured, for example by an enemy, and is being kept somewhere: *They took prisoners to sell back for ransom.* ◇ **~ of war** *Many detainees see themselves as prisoners of war.* **2** a person who is kept in prison as a punishment, or while they are waiting for trial: *Between July 1846 and July 1847, he released about 2 000 political prisoners.*

priv·acy /ˈprɪvəsi; *NAmE* ˈpraɪvəsi/ *noun* [U] **1 ~ (of sb)** the state of being free from the attention of the public: *To protect the privacy of respondents in the survey, we did not have access to their medical records.* **2** the state of being alone and not watched or disturbed by other people: *A separate room provided privacy for those wishing to pray.*

pri·vate[1] /ˈpraɪvət/ *adj.* **1** [usually before noun] belonging to or for the use of a particular person or group; not for public use: *He envisaged a society in which private property would be abolished.* ◇ *Between 2002 and 2007, the number of private cars in Beijing increased from 1.5 to 3 million.* OPP PUBLIC[1] (2) **2** [usually before noun] owned or managed by an individual person or an independent company rather than by the state: *A survey of patient satisfaction at private hospitals was undertaken.* ◇ *In contrast, private enterprises played a much greater role in the United States from the beginning.* OPP PUBLIC[1] (3) ➲ *see also* PRIVATE COMPANY, PRIVATE SCHOOL, PRIVATE SECTOR **3** [only before noun] working or acting for yourself, rather than for the state or for a group or company: *Nationalized industries were sold off to private investors.* ◇ *The Commission received complaints from a number of corporations and private individuals.* **4** [usually before noun] not connected with your work or official position: *Such groups monitor interference by the state in an individual's private life.* OPP PUBLIC[1] (4) **5** intended for or involving a particular person or group of people; not for others or for people in general to know about: *Senior officials held private discussions.* OPP PUBLIC[1] (5) **6** that you do not want other people to know about SYN SECRET[1] (2): *Macy destroyed*

P

her diary so her private thoughts went unrecorded. **7** where you are not likely to be disturbed; quiet: *It was hard to find a private place for the interview.* OPP PUBLIC[1] (5)

pri·vate² /ˈpraɪvət/ *noun*
IDM **in ˈprivate** with no one else present: *Research assistants conducted post-test interviews with participants in private.* ➲ *compare* IN PUBLIC

ˌprivate ˈcompany (*also* **ˌprivate ˌlimited ˈcompany**) *noun* (*business*) a business that may not offer its shares for sale to the public: *The energy sector comprises a mix of public and private companies.* ➲ *compare* PUBLIC COMPANY

ˌprivate ˈlaw *noun* [U] (*law*) the part of the law that concerns individual people and their property: *The plaintiffs commenced an action in private law for recovery of the money due.*

pri·vate·ly /ˈpraɪvətli/ *adv.* **1** in which sth is owned, managed or provided by an individual person or an independent company rather than by the state: *It is the largest privately owned decorating and property services company in the UK.* OPP PUBLICLY (2) **2** in a way that is not known to people in general: *The Prime Minister privately sympathized with the reform campaign.* OPP PUBLICLY (1)

ˌprivate ˈschool *noun* a school that receives no money from the government and where the education of the students is paid for by their parents: *Many of the children cannot be enrolled at state-run schools and their parents are often too poor to send them to private schools.* ➲ *compare* PUBLIC SCHOOL

the ˌprivate ˈsector *noun* [sing.] the part of the economy of a country that is not under the direct control of the government: *The Conservatives aimed to reduce the role of the state and expand the private sector.* ➲ *compare* PUBLIC SECTOR

P

pri·vat·ize (*BrE also* **-ise**) /ˈpraɪvətaɪz/ *verb* **~ sth** to sell a business or an industry so that it is no longer owned by the government: *The newly privatized British Telecom was concerned to be profitable.* OPP NATIONALIZE ■ **pri·vat·iza·tion, -isa·tion** /ˌpraɪvətaɪˈzeɪʃn; *NAmE* ˌpraɪvətəˈzeɪʃn/ *noun* [U] **~ (of sth)** *As Freedland (2001) has shown, privatization of service delivery alters the relationship between citizens and public authority.*

priv·il·ege¹ /ˈprɪvəlɪdʒ/ *noun* **1** [C] a special right or advantage that a particular person or group of people has: *They enjoyed special privileges because of their links to the government.* ◇ *Citizenship in the classical period was a jealously guarded privilege.* ◇ **the ~ of sb** *The ability to experience higher education is no longer the privilege of a select few.* **2** [U] (*disapproving*) the rights and advantages that rich and powerful people in a society have: *Her formative years reflected the wealth and privilege that she experienced as a child of New York 'society'.* **3** [sing.] something that you are proud and pleased to have the opportunity to do SYN HONOUR[1] (5): **~ of doing sth** *I had the privilege of working with many extremely capable people.* ◇ **it is a ~ to do sth** *It is a rare privilege to carry out research with such distinguished colleagues.* **4** [U, C] (*technical*) a special right to do or say things without being punished: *MPs, even though protected by parliamentary privilege, generally withhold comment on judges and on legal matters which are pending.*

priv·il·ege² /ˈprɪvəlɪdʒ/ *verb* (*formal*) to give sb/sth special rights or advantages that others do not have SYN FAVOUR[2] (2): **~ sb/sth** *English inheritance law privileged the eldest son.* ◇ **~ A over B** *Such institutions privilege some groups over others.*

priv·il·eged /ˈprɪvəlɪdʒd/ *adj.* **1** (*sometimes disapproving*) having special rights or advantages that most people do not have: *National governments retain a privileged position in the EU.* ◇ *Shelley came from a privileged background and attended Eton and Oxford University.* ◇ *The privileged classes would rely on state repression to prevent working class parties from gaining power.* **2** (*law*) (of information) known only to a few people and legally protected so that it does not have to be made public SYN CONFIDENTIAL: *He was dismissed when he published privileged information regarding treaty negotiations with France.* **3** [not before noun] **~ (to do sth)** having an opportunity to do sth that makes you feel proud: *I have been privileged to work with some extremely talented teachers.*

prize¹ /praɪz/ *noun* **1** an award that is given to a person who wins sth such as a competition or race, or who does very good work: *The Wellcome Trust awards an annual prize for books with a medical theme.* ◇ **~ for sth** *For this discovery, Shirakawa, MacDiarmid and Heeger won the Nobel prize for chemistry in 2000.* **2 ~ (of sth/doing sth)** something very important or valuable that is difficult to achieve or obtain: *The prize of raising the long-term growth potential of the British economy was not achieved.*

prize² /praɪz/ *verb* [often passive] **~ sth (above sth)** to value sth highly: *Archery was a skill highly prized by the Persians.* ◇ *He prized rationality above all other human qualities.*

pro·active /ˌprəʊˈæktɪv; *NAmE* ˌproʊˈæktɪv/ *adj.* (of a person, an organization or a policy) controlling a situation by making things happen rather than waiting for things to happen and then reacting to them: *Encourage patients to take a proactive role in the management of their symptoms.* ◇ *Public relations strategy may be thought of as being either proactive or reactive.* ➲ *compare* REACTIVE (2) ■ **pro·active·ly** *adv.*: *'Helping hand' governments proactively manage their economies to advance social and economic development.*

prob·abil·ist·ic /ˌprɒbəbɪˈlɪstɪk; *NAmE* ˌprɑːbəbɪˈlɪstɪk/ *adj.* [usually before noun] (*technical*) (of methods or arguments) based on the idea that, as we cannot be certain about things, we can base our beliefs or actions on what is likely: *Both of these problems can be tackled by taking a probabilistic approach.*

prob·abil·ity /ˌprɒbəˈbɪləti; *NAmE* ˌprɑːbəˈbɪləti/ *noun* (*pl.* **-ies**) **1** [U, C] how likely sth is to happen SYN LIKELIHOOD: *The probability is that prices will rise rapidly.* ◇ *These are risks with seemingly low probability, but with colossal consequences.* ◇ **~ of (doing) sth** *The system must be designed to maximize the probability of success.* ◇ **~ that...** *Invertebrates adopt strategies that reduce the probability that they will be caught by fish.* **2** [C, U] (*mathematics*) a RATIO, PERCENTAGE or FRACTION showing the chances that a particular thing will happen: *List all the outcomes and assign probabilities to each of them.* ◇ **~ of (doing) sth** *That individual has a 50% probability of being female.* ◇ **~ that...** *If the bearer has only one offspring, there is a 50% probability that the mutation will be lost.* **3** [C] a thing that is likely to happen: *A fall in interest rates is a strong probability in the present economic climate.* ◇ *This now seems a probability rather than just a possibility.*
IDM **in ˌall probaˈbility...** very likely; it is very likely that: *In all probability, many will gain nothing from taking drug treatment.* ➲ *more at* BALANCE[1]

▸ ADJECTIVE + PROBABILITY **high** • **increased, greater** • **low** • **equal** *If both parents have the disease, then there is an increased probability of offspring being affected.* | **total, overall, cumulative** • **average** • **predicted** • **estimated** *What is the overall probability that a lottery ticket wins at least one prize?*

▸ NOUN + PROBABILITY **error** • **survival** *The error probability can be reduced even further.*

▸ VERB + PROBABILITY **have • increase, raise • reduce, decrease, lower • maximize • minimize • affect** *Pavlov studied the way that repetition increased the probability of various behaviours.* | **estimate • predict • assign • calculate, compute • determine, find • give** *Dividing the average number alive in each five-year age group by 5 000 gives the probability of surviving to each age.*

prob·able /ˈprɒbəbl; *NAmE* ˈprɑːbəbl/ *adj.* likely to happen, exist or be true: *Massive volcanic eruptions were the probable cause of these extinctions.* ◇ **it is ~ that...** *It is highly probable that this situation will be repeated in the future.* OPP IMPROBABLE

prob·ably /ˈprɒbəbli; *NAmE* ˈprɑːbəbli/ *adv.* used to say that sth is likely to be true or to happen: *The church at Tours probably had an archive, but it does not survive.* ◇ *This variation in the results is probably due to sampling errors.* ◇ *We will probably never know just how many cities of the ancient world were razed by earthquakes.*

probe[1] /prəʊb; *NAmE* proʊb/ *noun* **1** (*technical*) a small device put inside sth and used by scientists to test sth or record information: *This test entails driving a conical probe into the soil at 20 mm.* **2** (*medical*) a long thin metal tool used by doctors for examining inside the body: *Access may be limited by the size of the probe.* **3 ~ (into sth)** a thorough and careful investigation of sth: *In August 2010, the European Commission opened a formal probe into marine insurance arrangements.*

probe[2] /prəʊb; *NAmE* proʊb/ *verb* **1** [I, T] to ask questions in order to find out secret or hidden information about sb/sth SYN INVESTIGATE (2): *It becomes necessary to probe beneath the surface in order to ask deeper questions about what is happening.* ◇ **~ sth** *It is necessary to probe the relationship between national security and international security.* **2** [T] **~ sth (for sth)** to touch, examine or look for sth, especially with a long thin instrument: *The doctor probed the wound for signs of infection.*

prob·lem /ˈprɒbləm; *NAmE* ˈprɑːbləm/ *noun* **1** a thing that is difficult to deal with or to understand: *Leakage of gasoline from underground storage tanks is a common problem worldwide.* ◇ **~ of sth** *The end of the Cold War did not solve the problem of nuclear weapons.* ◇ **~ for sb/sth** *Lack of funding posed a serious problem for the second phase of the project.* ◇ **~ with sth/sb** *12% of patients had problems with choking and/or swallowing.* ◇ **+ noun** *We looked at some of the causes of problem behaviour that can lead students to become disengaged with learning.* **2** a question that can be answered by using logical thought or mathematics: *He proved that not all mathematical problems can be solved by computing machines.*

▸ ADJECTIVE + PROBLEM **common • complex • difficult** *This seems a workable solution to a complex problem.* | **serious, major, big • main • fundamental, basic • real • significant • potential • obvious • global • chronic** *One potential problem is that yeast cells can acidify the culture medium.* | **practical • technical • methodological • environmental • social • behavioural • medical • physical • sexual • mental, psychological • emotional** *It seems clear that environmental problems often cannot be addressed without cooperation among nations.*

▸ NOUN + PROBLEM **health** *Mental health problems in children are a major deterrent to learning.*

▸ VERB + PROBLEM **solve • address, tackle, approach, attack • study, investigate • analyse • consider • discuss • understand** *The authoritarian strategy created more problems than it solved.* ◇ *It is advisable to attack the problem in stages.* | **have, experience, encounter • present • pose • raise • cause, create • exacerbate, compound • identify • report • highlight • illustrate • deal with, face, confront, handle • overcome • resolve • eliminate • correct • avoid, circumvent • reduce, alleviate, mitigate, minimize • remain** *The assessment is designed to identify any possible psychological problems.* ◇ *To overcome the problem of confused brand values, firms often develop different brand names to serve different market segments.*

▸ PROBLEM + VERB **arise • occur • exist • stem from, emerge • lie with/in • relate to, concern • be associated with • affect • face • persist** *Major problems arose when the predatory snails attacked snails native to the islands (Civeyrel and Simberloff, 1996).*

prob·lem·at·ic /ˌprɒbləˈmætɪk; *NAmE* ˌprɑːbləˈmætɪk/ (*also less frequent* **prob·lem·at·ical** /ˌprɒbləˈmætɪkl; *NAmE* ˌprɑːbləˈmætɪkl/) *adj.* difficult to deal with or understand; full of problems; not certain to be successful: *The theory remains deeply problematic.* ◇ *This remains the most problematic aspect of the subject.* OPP UNPROBLEMATIC

ˈproblem-solving *noun* [U] the act of dealing with or understanding problems, especially by using logical or sensible thinking: *The changes led to greater emphasis on problem-solving, teamwork and self-management.* ◇ **+ noun** *Some adolescents may get angry easily because they lack problem-solving skills.*

pro·ced·ural AWL /prəˈsiːdʒərəl/ *adj.* connected with a procedure: *The Court of Justice stated that each EU state should follow its own procedural rules.* ◇ *procedural fairness/justice/safeguards*

pro·ced·ure AWL /prəˈsiːdʒə(r)/ *noun* **1** [C, U] a series of actions done in a particular order and way, especially the usual or correct way: *The precise procedures used in making the calculations are presented below.* ◇ *Welsh legal procedure was reformed.* ◇ **~ for sth** *Once the sample is mounted, the procedure for polishing the surface is as follows:...* ◇ **under a/the ~** *National parliaments could raise objections under the procedures introduced by the Treaty of Lisbon* **2** [C] (*medical*) a medical operation: *These surgical procedures were all performed in hospital rather than in the clinic.* ◇ *More than 10% of patients undergoing the procedure required a blood transfusion.*

▸ ADJECTIVE + PROCEDURE **formal • standard, standardized • correct • systematic • routine • ordinary • special • urgent • preliminary** *The Secretary General ensures that all committees act in accordance with formal procedures.* | **legislative • democratic • administrative • judicial • statistical • experimental • analytical** *There were many defects in administrative procedure affecting the way the Foreign Office reached its decision.* | **surgical • medical • invasive • routine** *For minor and routine procedures, oral or implied consent is usually sufficient.*

▸ NOUN + PROCEDURE **operating • decision-making • selection • screening • sampling • grievance, complaints** *Evidence indicates that refugee decision-making procedures may be failing to identify those most in need of protection.*

▸ VERB + PROCEDURE **use, follow, employ, apply • adopt, implement • repeat • develop, design, devise • establish, introduce, lay down • describe** *Society has developed very robust procedures for testing the safety and efficacy of vaccines.* | **perform, carry out • undergo** *Invasive medical procedures were carried out in units with poor hygiene.*

pro·ceed AWL /prəˈsiːd; *NAmE* proʊˈsiːd/ *verb* **1** [I] to continue doing sth that has already been started; to continue being done: *The doctor contacted the hospital to check how best to proceed.* ◇ *As the reaction proceeded, the catalyst was produced.* ◇ *During the war, railway construction proceeded at a rapid pace.* ◇ **~ with sth** *It was decided to proceed with laboratory work despite the lack of funding.* **2** [I] **~ to do sth** to do sth next, after having done sth else first SYN GO ON TO DO STH, GO ON TO STH: *King Richard accepted the surrender of Acre and then proceeded to massacre all its inhabitants.* **3** [I] **+ adv./prep.** to move or travel in a particular direction: *The pilgrims enter the city of Mecca and proceed to the Grand Mosque.*

P

PHR V **pro'ceed against sb** (*law*) to start a court case against sb: *US antitrust agencies proceeded against the companies concerned.* **pro'ceed from sth** to be caused by sth; to be the result of sth: *The 2003 constitution proceeded from the same logic.*

pro·ceed·ings AWL /prə'si:dɪŋz/ *noun* [pl.] (*formal*) **1 ~ (against sb) (for sth)** the process of using a court to settle a disagreement or to deal with a complaint: *The plaintiff brought proceedings against the defendant in respect of the damage to his reputation.* **2 ~ (against sb) (for sth)** an event or a series of actions that takes place in a particular, official way: *The General Medical Council initiated disciplinary proceedings against the doctor for negligence.* **3 ~ (of sth)** the official written report of a meeting: *He has given more than 100 invited talks, published in the proceedings of international conferences.*

pro·ceeds AWL /'prəʊsi:dz; *NAmE* 'proʊsi:dz/ *noun* [pl.] the money that you receive when you sell sth: *A company can dispose of assets and use the proceeds to pay creditors.* ◇ **~ of sth** *The claimant may have an entitlement to a share in the proceeds of sale.* ◇ **~ from sth** *Successive governments overspent the proceeds from the oilfields.*

pro·cess[1] AWL /'prəʊses; *NAmE* 'prɑ:ses; 'proʊses/ *noun* **1** a series of actions that are taken in order to achieve a particular result: *Data from the market research informed the decision-making process.* ◇ **~ of (doing) sth** *The term 'remote sensing' describes the process of obtaining data using both photographic and non-photographic sensor systems.* **2** a series of things that happen, especially ones that result in natural changes: *These behaviours have survived through the long evolutionary process.* ◇ *The enzymes increased the rate at which the process occurred.* ◇ **~ of sth** *The communications revolution has been central to the process of globalization.* **3** a method of doing or making sth, especially one that is used in industry: *Metal ions can originate from industrial processes such as metal purification.*

P

IDM **in process** being done; continuing: *The reforms are still in process at the time of writing.* **in the process** while doing sth else, especially as a result that is not intended: *Suburbs became magnets for commercial and industrial growth, weakening downtown areas in the process.* **in the process of (doing) sth** in the middle of doing sth that takes some time to do: *This is a problem of considerable complexity which is still in the process of being unravelled.*

▸ ADJECTIVE + PROCESS **whole, entire • complex** *The whole labour process was divided into many small tasks.* | **ongoing • continuous • iterative • dynamic • random • natural • developmental** *Personal development is an ongoing process that arises naturally during the course of a professional person simply doing his or her job at work.* | **political • democratic • legislative** *Since the 1950s, Japanese firms have spent an enormous amount of resources in mastering the American political process (Hansen and Mitchell, 2000).* | **social • historical • evolutionary • physical • biological • chemical • cellular • cognitive** *These biological processes naturally produce hydrogen.*

▸ NOUN + PROCESS **research • policy • planning • decision • decision-making • policymaking • assessment • selection • learning • thought** *The research process generated powerfully significant correlations between practices, commitment and performance (Wright, Gardner and Moynihan, 2003).* | **production • manufacturing** *Customers were also involved in the design and production process (cf Harris and Cohen, 2003).*

▸ VERB + PROCESS **study • consider • examine, analyse • describe, characterize, outline • explain • model • illustrate • discuss • understand** *This theory is insufficient to explain the ageing process.* | **involve • influence, affect • control, regulate, govern • begin, initiate, start • drive • facilitate • guide • inform • accompany • accelerate • disrupt • reverse • undergo • reflect** *Everyday behaviour involves multiple cognitive processes.* ◇ *Modern technology greatly facilitates this process.* | **manage • improve • simplify, streamline • complete • repeat** *Due to the lack of precision in parts manufacturing, streamlining the assembly process proved impossible.*

▸ PROCESS + VERB **continue • work • involve • take • affect • lead to, produce, generate, result in • cause • contribute to** *Many industrial and commercial processes involve chemical reactions.* | **begin • operate • act • govern • underlie** *Further studies are needed to provide a deeper understanding of the social processes underlying such criminal behaviour.*

LANGUAGE BANK

Describing a process

The following words and expressions are useful in academic writing when explaining the process by which sth happens, or describing the process by which something is done. See also the Language Banks at **cause** *noun* and **conclusion**.

- the author/diagram/chapter **illustrates/describes the process** of...
- the author/diagram/chapter **shows/describes how**...
- **first/first of all**,...
- **next/second**,...
- **following/after this**,...
- **once/after** X has been done/has happened,...
- **at the same time/simultaneously**
- **as/while** X happens,...
- **finally/lastly**,...
- **the first/next/final stage/step is...**
- **at this point/stage**,...
- this **allows/enables/leads to/causes...**

– *This chapter **describes the** asylum **process** from application through to cessation of refugee status.*
– *Figure 14.4 **shows how** a message may be routed through an unconstrained topology.*
– ***First**, the empty weighing container is placed centrally on the pan.*
– ***Next**, we match the complaint data sources to each other.*
– ***Following this**, 300 µl of sodium carbonate solution (250 g/ml) was added and the reactants were mixed.*
– ***Once** the partners have been identified, the stakeholders must come to agreement about their respective roles and responsibilities.*
– *Dispense the gel solution under the oil **simultaneously** with all the other components to form one drop.*
– ***As** this happens, some of the catalyst C is converted back to B again.*
– ***Finally**, work out the concentration of OH, and enter this into the final column.*
– ***The final stage is** monitoring, which involves tracking effectiveness in the market over time.*
– *Having identified a potential problem, **the next step is to** quantify the problem.*
– ***At this point**, the conductivity rises dramatically.*
– *The Internet facilitates the processing of information, which in turn **enables** the rapid diffusion of ideas and technologies.*

pro·cess[2] AWL /'prəʊses; *NAmE* 'prɑ:ses; 'proʊses/ *verb* **1** to treat raw material, food, etc. in order to change it, preserve it, etc: **~ sth (into sth)** *The raw milk produced by UK dairy farmers is processed into a number of different products.* ◇ **processed + noun** *These highly processed foods are high in fat, sugar and salt.* **2 ~ sth** to deal officially with sth such as a document, application or request: *Previously, the department took six weeks to process each passport application.* **3 ~ sth** to deal with information by performing a series of operations on it, especially using a computer: *Project feedback will be processed by the university statistics department.* ◇ *The use of surveillance* *cameras relies on computers to digitize and process the information received.* ■ **pro·cess·ing** AWL *noun* [U] *Speed of information processing is a crucial factor.* ◇ **+ noun** *Hendrickson and Heffernan (2002: 2) analyse the restructuring taking place in the milk processing sector.* ➲ *see also* DATA PROCESSING

pro·ces·sion /prəˈseʃn/ *noun* **1** [C, U] a line of people or vehicles that move along slowly, especially as part of a ceremony; the act of moving in this way: *They took part in a grand procession to the Capitol on 15 July every year.* ◇ **in ~** *Effigies of the leaders were carried in procession down the boulevard.* **2** [C] **~ of sb/sth** a number of people or things that come one after the other: *During that time, a procession of foreigners visited the USSR and later published their revelations.*

pro·ces·sor /ˈprəʊsesə(r); *NAmE* ˈprɑːsesər; ˈproʊsesər/ *noun* **1** a machine or person that processes things: *The early years of computing were dominated by the mainframe, which was largely used as a data processor.* ◇ *Consumers have put pressure on producers and processors to ensure that their foods are safe and nutritious.* **2** (*computing*) a part of a computer that controls all the other parts of the system: *CMOS technology dominates in the design and manufacture of integrated circuits for computer memories and central processors.*

pro·claim /prəˈkleɪm/ *verb* to publicly and officially tell people about sth important SYN DECLARE (1): **~ sth** *Rhodesia proclaimed independence from Great Britain in 1965.* ◇ **~ that...** *The conference proclaimed that illiteracy was a barrier to the promotion of education.* ◇ **~ sb/sth/yourself + noun** *Schumpeter often proclaimed himself an admirer of Karl Marx.* ◇ **~ sb/sth/yourself to be/have sth** *He not only disputed the election results but even proclaimed himself to be President.*

proc·lama·tion /ˌprɒkləˈmeɪʃn; *NAmE* ˌprɑːkləˈmeɪʃn/ *noun* [C, U] an official statement about sth important that is made to the public; the act of making an official statement: *Abraham Lincoln issued his emancipation proclamation to free slaves in the United States during the American Civil War.* ◇ *In 1970, Malaysia's Rukunegara ('National Principles') was adopted by royal proclamation.*

pro·duce¹ /prəˈdjuːs; *NAmE* prəˈduːs/ *verb* **1 ~ sth** to make or grow things to be sold, especially in large quantities: *The firm chiefly produced goods for export.* ◇ *These smallholder coffee farmers produce some of the world's best coffee.* ➲ *compare* MANUFACTURE² **2** (of an area) to grow or supply sth; to be the source of sth: *Bolivia therefore produces more food than it consumes.* ◇ *Many supermarkets proudly promote locally produced ranges of food.* ◇ *Mali, Senegal and Togo are part of a wider cotton-producing region.* **3 ~ sth** to grow or make sth as part of a natural process; to have a baby or young animal: *Some trees produce resin in large quantities.* ◇ *Bile is a complex chemical mixture produced in the liver.* ◇ *Offspring are normally produced one at a time, spaced several years apart.* **4 ~ sth** to create or make sth as part of a physical process: *The hydraulic motor drives a generator to produce electricity.* ◇ *The sound is produced by blowing air through a slit.* ◇ *Irregular weathering produces a wide variety of plant habitats.* ◇ **~ sth from sth** *Synthetic gas (syngas) is produced from coal.* **5** to create or make sth using imagination and skill: *In Australia, aboriginal groups produced work describing their struggles.* ◇ *Jerome spent the rest of his life there producing his huge literary output.* **6 ~ sth** to cause sth to happen SYN BRING STH ABOUT: *Every attempt at expansion quickly produced an increase in imports and higher inflation.* ◇ *These reforms may produce unintended outcomes.* ◇ *This response produces changes in the body.* ➲ language bank *at* CAUSE¹ **7 ~ sth** to show or provide sth for sb to see, consider or use: *The two commissions have produced several important reports.* ◇ *Studies of children's Internet use in the United States are sparse and have produced mixed results.* **8 ~ sb** if a place, situation, period of time or group of people **produces** sb with a particular skill or quality, the person comes from that place, time or group of people: *The era produced fewer prominent female writers.* **9 ~ sth** to be in charge of preparing a film or play for the public to see: *The film was produced by an Indian-Tamil company.*

▸ PRODUCE + NOUN **goods • commodity • product • food • unit • output** *Historically, international prices for most commodities produced in Chile have been high.* | **antibody • hormone • protein • toxin • eggs • offspring • seed • embryo • molecule • chemical • acid • product** *The amount of antibody produced in response to foreign antigens decreases with age.* ◇ *Cod produce several million eggs a year.* | **signal • electricity • sound • pattern • image • product • output** *The machine produces a significant output of heat.* | **effect • result • outcome • change • increase • benefit • response** *By the 1990s, failing economies and widespread public unrest produced an unexpected result.* | **report • estimate • image • document • work • list • text • evidence • result** *These findings also explained why so many previous studies had failed to produce positive results.*

pro·duce² /ˈprɒdjuːs; *NAmE* ˈprɑːduːs; ˈproʊduːs/ *noun* [U] things that have been grown or made, especially things connected with farming: *The amount of fresh produce in US supermarkets has expanded dramatically.* ◇ *Not only does local produce support the local economy, it is also seen as environmentally friendly.*

pro·du·cer /prəˈdjuːsə(r); *NAmE* prəˈduːsər/ *noun* **1** a person, company or country that grows or makes food, goods or materials: *There are many producers supplying to the market.* ◇ *In some cases, differing standards were clearly introduced in order to protect domestic producers.* ◇ **~ of sth** *As in every industry, the producers of computer animation stay competitive by differentiating their products.* HELP In economics, a **primary producer** is a company, industry, etc. that provides raw materials to be made into goods, for example by farming or MINING: *The balance of power between supermarkets and primary producers is heavily weighted in favour of the former.* ➲ *compare* CONSUMER (1) **2 ~ (of sth)** a person or living thing that makes or causes sth: *The mould is the producer of the toxin aflatoxin.* HELP In ecology, a **primary producer** is a living thing, such as a plant, that produces ORGANIC material from INORGANIC substances: *Primary producers convert sunlight into chemical energy through the process of photosynthesis.* **3 ~ (of sth)** a person who is in charge of the practical and financial aspects of making a film or play: *The Toronto Film Festival is an important market in which producers and directors sell the rights to their films to international distributors.* ➲ *compare* DIRECTOR (3) **4 ~ (of sth)** a person or company that arranges for sb to make a programme for radio or television, or a CD, etc: *The corporation also owns 20th Century Fox Television, a major producer of network television shows.*

prod·uct /ˈprɒdʌkt; *NAmE* ˈprɑːdʌkt/ *noun* **1** a thing that is grown or produced, usually for sale: *The export tax is so high that the farmers cannot sell their products on the world market.* ◇ *Wealth is created when new jobs and new products spur economic activities.* ◇ *Meat, milk and dairy products, and leafy green vegetables are rich sources of vitamin A.* ➲ *see also* END PRODUCT, GDP, GNP **2** a thing produced during a natural, chemical or industrial process: *Compounds isolated from natural products have been important sources of new drugs.* ◇ *The dumping of waste products into the sea, air and land means that pollution problems are widespread.* ◇ **~ of sth** *Formaldehyde is a minor product of combustion of all types of fuel.* ➲ *see also* BY-PRODUCT (1) **3** (*chemistry*) a substance that is formed

P

as a result of a chemical reaction: *The reaction has proceeded as far as is favourable and the relative amounts of reactant and product will change no further.* ➲ *compare* REACTANT **4 ~ of sth** a person or thing that is the result of sth: *She was the product of a mixed marriage.* ◇ *As products of popular culture, shopping malls encourage the further acceptance of popular culture.* **5** (*mathematics*) a quantity obtained by multiplying one number by another: *The product of two negative numbers is positive.*

▸ ADJECTIVE + PRODUCT **new • final • finished • innovative • existing • agricultural • dairy • commercial • industrial • imported • branded** *The finished product is transported to the US for sale.*

▸ NOUN + PRODUCT **food • tobacco • consumer • software** *For business or high-end consumer products, local adaptation is less important.*

▸ VERB + PRODUCT **sell • buy, purchase • market, advertise, offer, promote • launch • export • import • supply, deliver, distribute • produce, manufacture • differentiate • consume • price • develop • design** *The franchises aggressively market their products and offer discounts and sales to attract more customers.*

pro·duc·tion /prəˈdʌkʃn/ *noun* **1** [U] the process of growing or making food, goods or materials, especially in large quantities: *A 3–4°C average local temperature drop would halt all Canadian grain production.* ◇ **~ of sth** *The production of electricity from renewable energy sources is increasingly considered as a priority.* ◇ **in ~** *Some oil deposits have been found and are in production.* ◇ **out of ~** *In the United States alone, 105 acres of agricultural land go out of production every hour.* ◇ **+ noun** *Many manufacturing jobs have been moved to China, where production costs are lower.* **2** [U] the total quantity of goods or materials that is produced: *From 1960 to 2000, global food production more than kept up with global population increase.* ◇ **+ noun** *Oil production levels have been flattening in recent years.* **3** [U] the act or process of making sth naturally: *Foods and drinks that stimulate saliva production may increase pain and should therefore be avoided.* ◇ **~ of sth** *As well as insulin, these cells are responsible for the production of another important hormone, glucagon.* **4** [C, U] **~ (of sth)** a film, play or broadcast that is prepared for the public; the act of preparing a film, play, etc: *The production of his play 'Dangerous Liaisons' was forced to move to a much smaller venue.* ◇ *The high cost of film production led the company to co-produce films with other studios.* **5** [U] **~ of sth** the act of making or supplying sth for sb to see, use or consider: *If a party refuses to disclose documents, the judge may order the production of the documents.* **6** [U] (*linguistics*) the ability to produce language or information that you have learned in speech or writing; the process of doing this: *The language production and reasoning of these children is surprising.* ➲ *compare* RECEPTION (5)

▸ ADJECTIVE + PRODUCTION **large-scale • commercial • intensive • agricultural • industrial** *The soil beneath the grasslands was found to be extremely fertile for agricultural production.* | **annual • domestic • global** *Domestic production of food staples in developing countries has declined.*

▸ NOUN + PRODUCTION **food • oil • electricity • commodity • grain • crop • biofuel • ethanol • hydrogen • gas • steel • milk • sugar • energy** *Oil accounted for 35% of global energy production in 2001.*

▸ VERB + PRODUCTION **encourage • regulate • control** *He imported foreign specialists and encouraged the domestic production of textile machinery.* | **relocate • organize • rationalize • concentrate • subsidize** *There may be redundancies as firms try to rationalize their production and make it more efficient.* | **maximize • intensify • limit, restrict • reduce** *To maximize production from grains and other crops, heavy applications of nitrogen fertilizers are widely used.* | **boost • expand** *Many of these countries are well poised to expand oil production.* | **stimulate • induce • inhibit • suppress • enhance** *A range of drugs are used to inhibit the production of male sex hormones.*

▸ VERB + PRODUCTION **cease, halt, stop** *The idea was to halt the production of additional nuclear weapons.* | **increase • decrease** *Argentina, Brazil, India and China are all increasing GM crop production.*

▸ PRODUCTION + VERB **cease, halt, stop** *Opening the market to subsidized American grain meant that local production virtually ceased.* | **drop, fall, decline, decrease • rise, increase • exceed** *Biomass and phytoplankton production generally increase throughout the summer.*

▸ PRODUCTION + NOUN **process • cost • capacity • technology • capability • line • run • schedule • technique, method • worker • system • engineer • plant** *In 1950, production workers in manufacturing constituted about 40% of the total workforce.*

pro·duct·ive /prəˈdʌktɪv/ *adj.* **1** making goods or growing crops, especially in large quantities: *Relatively small farms can be highly productive.* ◇ *The greater productive capacity of tractors was a boon to those farmers who could afford them.* OPP UNPRODUCTIVE **2** doing or achieving a lot SYN FRUITFUL: *This line of research was very productive.* ◇ *Older adults who engage in multiple productive activities, such as caregiving and volunteering, report better health.* ➲ *compare* COUNTERPRODUCTIVE **3 ~ of sth** resulting in sth or causing sth: *There was strong evidence that peer-led debate was more productive of higher level discussion than tutor-led debate.* **4** (*linguistics*) connected with producing language or information that you have learned, in speech or writing: *This paper introduces a new approach to developing productive language and thinking skills in students.* ➲ *compare* RECEPTIVE (4) **5** (*medical*) (of a cough) that produces MUCUS: *This patient has a productive cough and is not breathless at rest.* ◇ **~ of sth** *Mr Crick has a history of recurrent cough productive of green sputum.* ■ **pro·duct·ive·ly** *adv.*: *Tobacco could not be grown productively on the same land for more than three years in a row.* ◇ *They worked together productively for more than a decade.*

prod·uct·iv·ity /ˌprɒdʌkˈtɪvəti; *NAmE* ˌprɑːdʌkˈtɪvəti; ˌproʊdʌkˈtɪvəti/ *noun* [U] the rate at which a worker, a company or country produces goods; the amount produced, compared with how much time, work and money is needed to produce them: *The system is designed to maximize productivity.* ◇ *The volcanic winter that would follow such an eruption would cause a drop in agricultural productivity.* ◇ **~ of sb/sth** *Managers are always eager to find ways of increasing the productivity of their workforce.*

pro·fes·sion /prəˈfeʃn/ *noun* **1** [C] a type of job that needs special training or skill, especially one that needs a high level of education: *the medical/legal/teaching profession* ◇ *As members of a profession, bioscientists have a responsibility to preserve its professional standards.* **2 the profession** [sing.+ sing./pl. v.] all the people who work in a particular profession: *Society is changing and the teaching profession is changing with it.* **3 the professions** [pl.] the traditional jobs that need a high level of education and training, such as being a doctor or lawyer: *Increasing numbers of women entered the professions.* **4** [C] **~ of sth** a statement about what you believe, feel or think about sth, that is sometimes made publicly SYN DECLARATION (3): *The first of the Five Pillars of Islam is making a profession of faith in God.*

pro·fes·sion·al[1] AWL /prəˈfeʃənl/ *adj.* **1** [only before noun] connected with a job that needs special training or skill, especially one that needs a high level of education: *63% of the teachers surveyed said they needed more time for professional development.* ◇ *professional qualifications/expertise* ◇ *The stress of professional practice was considerable.* **2** (of people) having a job that needs special training and a high level of education: *These sensible,*

P

quality designs were traditionally aimed at professional people such as lawyers and doctors. **3** showing that sb is well trained and extremely skilled SYN COMPETENT (2): *Larger retailers have become highly professional in handling their purchasing from suppliers.* **4** suitable or appropriate for sb working in a particular profession: *The Code of Professional Conduct contains these guidelines.* **5** doing sth as a paid job rather than just for pleasure: *a professional team/player/singer*

pro·fes·sion·al² AWL /prəˈfeʃənl/ *noun* a person who does a job that needs special training and a high level of education: *Questionnaires were sent to a selection of 400 professionals and managers (i.e. doctors, architects, solicitors, corporate executives).* ◇ *A range of different doctors and other health care professionals were interviewed.*

pro·fes·sion·al·ism AWL /prəˈfeʃənəlɪzəm/ *noun* [U] **~ (of sb/sth)** the high standard that you expect from a person who is well trained in a particular job: *Smart, well-trained staff should reassure potential customers of the professionalism of the organization.*

pro·fes·sion·al·ly AWL /prəˈfeʃənəli/ *adv.* **1** in a way that is connected with a person's job or training: *Staff were left in a difficult position, ethically, legally and professionally.* **2** in a way that shows skill and experience: *The selling process does not seem to have been managed professionally.* **3** by a person who has the right skills and qualifications: *The tapes were transcribed professionally.*

pro·fes·sor /prəˈfesə(r)/ *noun* (*abbr.* **Prof.**) **1** (*especially BrE*) (*NAmE* ˈ**full professor**) a university teacher of the highest rank: *By 1948, he had reached the rank of full professor.* ◇ **~ of sth** *She is Professor of History at Monash University.* HELP **Full professor** is used to describe a rank, but is not used as a title. **2** (*NAmE*) a teacher at a university or college: *These documents illustrate the attitudes of Harvard professors towards Jewish students at this time.*

pro·fi·cient /prəˈfɪʃnt/ *adj.* able to do sth well because of training and practice: *Less proficient students attributed success to easy tests.* ◇ **~ in sth** *Participants were all proficient in English.* ■ **pro·fi·ciency** /prəˈfɪʃnsi/ *noun* [U] **~ (in sth)** *The German participants tended to have higher levels of proficiency in English.*

pro·file¹ /ˈprəʊfaɪl; *NAmE* ˈproʊfaɪl/ *noun* **1 ~ (of sb/sth)** a description of sb/sth that gives useful information: *It is assumed that wages will rise in line with the academic profile of the workforce.* **2** the general impression that sb/sth gives to the public and the amount of attention they receive: **~ (of sb/sth)** *The impact of the campaign was to raise the profile of the brand as a whole.* ◇ **a high/low ~** *The plight of minority groups has attracted a higher profile.* ◇ *Outside New York and Chicago, the Catholic Church kept a low profile.* ➲ *see also* HIGH-PROFILE **3** the outline of sb/sth as seen from the side, not the front; a CROSS SECTION of a structure or geographical feature: **(in) ~** *She stands in profile to the left of the screen.* ◇ *Canyons cut in hard, resistant rocks have steep walls and narrow, V-shaped or vertical profiles.*

pro·file² /ˈprəʊfaɪl; *NAmE* ˈproʊfaɪl/ *verb* **~ sb/sth** to give or write a description of sb/sth that gives the most important information: *Profiling competitor strengths and weaknesses can allow an organization to see where its performance lags behind the competition.*

pro·fil·ing /ˈprəʊfaɪlɪŋ; *NAmE* ˈproʊfaɪlɪŋ/ *noun* [U] the act of collecting information about sb/sth so that you can identify them or describe what they are likely to be like: *DNA profiling is an extremely decisive method for excluding suspects in a case.*

profit¹ /ˈprɒfɪt; *NAmE* ˈprɑːfɪt/ *noun* **1** [C, U] the money that you make in business or by selling things, after paying the costs involved: *If a firm is not making a profit, it cannot grow.* ◇ *The company's annual financial report showed a 31% fall in net profit.* ◇ **~ on sth** *By the 1820s, the profits on his Jamaican estates were declining.* ◇ **~ from sth** *The company continued to reap great profits from its ongoing service contracts.* ◇ **at a ~** *Japanese swords marketed in China at a 500% profit.* ◇ **for ~** *Unfortunately, much donated food goes to governments, which then sell it for profit.* ◇ **in ~** *In 2007–8, the company made in excess of £2.8 billion in profit.* ◇ **+ noun** *They decided to introduce new products in order to raise their profit rates.* OPP LOSS (2) **2** [U] the advantage that you get from doing sth: *He was a tyrant, who ruled his realm for his own profit and not for the good of the community.*

▸ ADJECTIVE + PROFIT **high • low • great, large • net • gross • total • future • expected • short-term • long-term • marginal • economic • corporate** *Firms that achieve high profits in one period will have more to reinvest in the next period.*

▸ VERB + PROFIT **make • earn, realize, accrue • reap • boost • maximize • generate, yield • reinvest, invest • pursue • lose • increase • calculate** *Their goal is to maximize short-term profits and stimulate a positive cash flow.*

▸ PROFIT + VERB **increase, rise • fall** *The company's gross profits had increased under his management.*

▸ PROFIT + NOUN **rate • margin • maximization • share • motive • potential** *Partners in a practice still draw their profit share if they are unable to work.*

profit² /ˈprɒfɪt; *NAmE* ˈprɑːfɪt/ *verb* [I, T] to get sth useful from a situation; to be useful to sb or give them an advantage: **~ from sth** *He was amongst the first English novelists to have profited from free elementary education for the poor.* ◇ **~ by (doing) sth** *Some firms may profit by not following the rules.* ◇ **~ sb** *The new legislation did not profit them directly.*

prof·it·abil·ity /ˌprɒfɪtəˈbɪləti; *NAmE* ˌprɑːfɪtəˈbɪləti/ *noun* [U] the fact that sth makes money or is likely to make money: *Profitability occurs when a firm's sales revenues exceed its costs.* ◇ *Increased technical efficiency may lead to greater profitability.* ◇ **~ of sth** *Because of the low profitability of vaccines, many pharmaceutical companies are cautious of embarking on vaccine development.*

prof·it·able /ˈprɒfɪtəbl; *NAmE* ˈprɑːfɪtəbl/ *adj.* **1** that makes or is likely to make money: *Guano mining quickly proved a highly profitable business.* ◇ **it is ~ (for sb) to do sth** *It is often more profitable to sell direct to the public.* **2** that gives sb an advantage or a useful result: **it is ~ (for sb) to do sth** *It can be profitable for a very hungry individual to delay flight from a predator, so that it can eat for a longer period of time.* ■ **prof·it·ably** /ˌprɒfɪtəbli; *NAmE* ˌprɑːfɪtəbli/ *adv.*: *He was not able to run the farm profitably.* ◇ *It is felt that US teachers could profitably emulate these teaching methods.*

ˈ**profit margin** (*also* **margin**) *noun* (*business*) the difference between the cost of buying or producing sth and the price that it is sold for: *Often, the aftermarket in servicing can generate better profit margins than the original car sale.* ◇ *a high/low profit margin*

pro·found /prəˈfaʊnd/ *adj.* **1** very great; felt or experienced very strongly: *Hurricanes have a profound effect on many coastal ecosystems.* ◇ *The implications of this discovery are profound.* **2** showing great knowledge or understanding: *These methods have yielded profound insights into the inner workings of the cell.* **3** needing a lot of study or thought: *Most religions attempt to answer profound questions about the universe and the human individual.* **4** (*medical*) very serious; complete: *Clinical examination has revealed profound brain damage.*

pro·found·ly /prəˈfaʊndli/ *adv.* **1** in a way that has a very great effect on sb/sth: *Augustine's writings profoundly influenced later Christian thought.* ◇ *They differed*

P

profoundly on many matters. **2** extremely: *The nineteenth century remained a profoundly religious age.* **3** (*medical*) very seriously; completely: *Studies in the 1980s of infants born before 29 weeks found approximately one third to be profoundly disabled.*

prog·no·sis /prɒgˈnəʊsɪs; *NAmE* prɑːgˈnoʊsɪs/ *noun* (*pl.* **prog·no·ses** /prɒgˈnəʊsiːz; *NAmE* prɑːgˈnoʊsiːz/) **1** (*medical*) an opinion, based on medical experience, of the likely development of a disease or an illness: *Larger tumours are more likely to have spread and have a poor prognosis.* ◇ *If the long-term prognosis is poor, heart transplantation should be considered.* ◇ **~ for sth** *For most cancers, early detection greatly improves the prognosis for treatment.* **2 ~ (for sth)** a judgement about how sth is likely to develop in the future SYN FORECAST[1]: *Russ Britt offered a pessimistic prognosis for the future of print journalism in the USA.* ■ **prog·nos·tic** /prɒgˈnɒstɪk; *NAmE* prɑːgˈnɑːstɪk/ *adj.*: *Studies suggest that never smokers have improved survival compared with smokers, independent of other prognostic factors.*

pro·gram¹ /ˈprəʊgræm; *NAmE* ˈproʊgræm/ *noun* **1** (*computing*) a set of instructions in code that control the operations or functions of a computer: *The mathematical analysis is undertaken using a computer program.* **2** (*NAmE*) = PROGRAMME[1]

pro·gram² /ˈprəʊgræm; *NAmE* ˈproʊgræm/ *verb* (**-mm-**, *NAmE also* **-m-**) **1** to give a computer, etc. a set of instructions to make it perform a particular task: **~ sth (to do sth)** *A robotic arm is programmed to add oil at various time intervals.* ◇ **~ sth (into sth)** *The equation is not easily remembered but can be programmed into laboratory computer systems.* **2** (*NAmE*) = PROGRAMME[2]

pro·gramme¹ (*BrE*) (*NAmE* **pro·gram**) /ˈprəʊgræm; *NAmE* ˈproʊgræm/ *noun* **1** a plan of things that will be done or included in the development of sth: *The breast screening programme aims to detect small cancers which can be cured surgically.* ◇ *There are fears that the country is pursuing an undeclared nuclear programme.* ◇ **~ of sth** *Under China's programme of economic reform, the country has grown rapidly and progressively entered the world economy.* **2** something that people watch on television or listen to on the radio: *Several studies have analysed the content of advertising broadcast during children's TV programmes.* **3 ~ (of sth)** an organized order of performances or events: *The city has planned a spectacular programme of events for next year.* **4** (*NAmE*) a course of study: *Geoscience training is not a common component of most archaeology degree programs.*

▸ NOUN + PROGRAMME **screening • training • education • research • health • immunization, vaccination • marketing • reform • surveillance • nuclear** *Immunization programmes have even eradicated some diseases.*

▸ VERB + PROGRAMME **implement • launch, initiate, institute, introduce • fund, finance • design • develop • deliver • undertake • run • pursue • complete** *Following their election, the new government implemented a programme of non-fee primary education as promised.*

pro·gramme² (*BrE*) (*NAmE* **pro·gram**) /ˈprəʊgræm; *NAmE* ˈproʊgræm/ *verb* [usually passive] to make a person, an animal, etc. behave in a particular way, so that it happens AUTOMATICALLY: **be programmed to do sth** *He argues that humans are innately programmed to behave in a certain way.* ⊃ *compare* PROGRAM² (1)

pro·gram·mer /ˈprəʊgræmə(r); *NAmE* ˈproʊgræmər/ *noun* **1** a person whose job is writing programs for computers: *These jobs are predominantly in highly skilled, knowledge-intensive services involving accountants, lawyers, computer programmers and so on.* **2** (*computing*) a device that AUTOMATICALLY controls the operation of sth according to a particular program: *The central heating boiler is controlled by a programmer which has different programs for weekdays and weekends.*

pro·gram·ming /ˈprəʊgræmɪŋ; *NAmE* ˈproʊgræmɪŋ/ *noun* [U] **1** the process of writing and testing programs for computers: *Turing and his group pioneered the science of computer programming.* **2 ~ (of sth)** the activity of planning which television or radio programmes to broadcast; the programmes that are broadcast: *Cable channels relied heavily on the programming of feature films.* ◇ *Television programming has a clear impact on the behaviour of both younger and older children.* **3** factors, ranging from GENETIC to social, that instruct a person or animal to behave in a certain way: *This work led to the concept of fetal programming which suggests that maternal poverty can affect the development of the foetus (Earle and O'Donnell, 2007).* ◇ **~ of sth** *As a result of the differing mental programming of societies, there are significant variations in behaviour and social norms which impact on all forms of business.*

pro·gress¹ /ˈprəʊgres; *NAmE* ˈprɑːgres; ˈprɑːgrəs/ *noun* [U] **1** the process of improving or developing, or of getting nearer to achieving or completing sth: **~ (of sb/sth)** *Teachers carefully monitor the progress of each student.* ◇ **~ in (doing) sth** *Finland has made substantial progress in reducing pollution levels.* ◇ **~ on sth** *However, as Stacey notes, progress on the Bill was slow.* ◇ **~ towards sth** *Progress towards this goal will be limited until existing problems are solved.* ◇ **~ with sth** *They saw this as the way to achieve further progress with European integration.* **2 ~ (of sb/sth) (+ adv./prep.)** movement forwards or towards a place: *The army's progress through the province was marked by massacres and destruction.*

IDM **in progress** happening at this time: *Negotiations are still in progress.*

▸ ADJECTIVE + PROGRESS **significant • considerable, substantial • remarkable • great • real • steady • rapid • slow • recent • further • continued** *There has been significant progress in understanding the basic causes of ageing.* | **technological • technical • scientific • academic • economic • social • moral • human • historical** *In Khrushchev's early years, there was new confidence in Soviet technological progress.*

▸ VERB + PROGRESS **make, achieve • monitor, follow, track • measure • review, examine • assess, evaluate • see • impede, hinder • promote • show • bring • represent • report • accelerate** *The twentieth century saw great progress in physics.*

▸ NOUN + OF PROGRESS **rate, pace • lack • idea, notion • possibility • review** *The size and quality of a country's natural resources determine its rate of economic progress.*

pro·gress² /prəˈgres/ *verb* **1** [I] to develop over a period of time to a better or more advanced state; to make progress SYN ADVANCE² (2): *The disease progresses at a variable rate.* ◇ *Science progresses through the construction of theories and the derivation of laws.* **2** [I] to go forward in time SYN GO ON (1): *As the twentieth century progressed, car ownership increased.* **3** [I] **+ adv./prep.** to move forward: *Weakness begins in the facial muscles and progresses down the body.* **4** [T] **~ sth** to cause a task, project, etc. to make progress: *Account managers handle and progress the day-to-day work the agency carries out for its clients.*

PHRV **proˈgress to sth** to move on from doing one thing to doing sth else: *As students, they may get involved in this kind of extremist politics and then progress to armed violence.*

pro·gres·sion /prəˈgreʃn/ *noun* **1** [U, C] the process of developing gradually from one stage or state to another: *Career progression was based primarily on length of service.* ◇ **~ of sth** *The aim is to treat early to slow the progression of the disease.* ◇ **~ (from sth) (to sth)** *Aristotle viewed scientific inquiry as a progression from* *observations to general principles.* **2** [C] **~ (of sth)** a number of things that come in a series: *A progression of scandals has left the public disenchanted with the profession.*

pro·gres·sive[1] /prəˈgresɪv/ *adj.* **1** in favour of new ideas, modern methods and change: *The twentieth century was marked by progressive movements in art and architecture.* **2** happening or developing gradually or in stages: *The decades from 1950 to 1970 were a period of progressive economic growth.* **3** (of a medical condition) becoming more and more severe: *It is a slow, progressive disease with no real effective treatment.* **4** (of a tax) increasing as the amount to be taxed increases: *The budget deficit grew despite the introduction of a progressive income tax.* **5** (*also* **con·tinu·ous**) (*grammar*) connected with the form of a verb (for example *I am waiting* or *It is raining*) that is made from a part of *be* and the present participle. Progressive forms are used to express an action that continues for a period of time: *The basic meaning of the progressive form is to indicate that a process, activity or action is in progress.* ➲ *compare* PERFECT[1] (6), SIMPLE (5)

pro·gres·sive[2] /prəˈgresɪv/ *noun* [usually pl.] a person who is in favour of new ideas, modern methods and change: *Traditionalists and progressives differ strongly on the benefits of gun ownership and gun control.*

pro·gres·sive·ly /prəˈgresɪvli/ *adv.* (often with a comparative) in a steady and continuous way: *The average size of the fish is becoming progressively smaller.* ◇ *Tariffs are being progressively reduced as they form a barrier to trade.*

pro·hibit AWL /prəˈhɪbɪt; *NAmE also* proʊˈhɪbɪt/ *verb* **1** [often passive] to stop sth from being done or used, especially by law SYN FORBID (1): **~ sth** *New Zealand is among the countries that prohibit discrimination against people on the basis of sexual preference.* ◇ *This conduct is expressly prohibited by Article 102 (c).* ◇ **~ sb from doing sth** *Should parents be prohibited from smoking in the vicinity of their children?* ◇ **~ (sb) doing sth** *The European Union passed legislation in 2004 that prohibits keeping electronic addresses without the owners' consent.* **2 ~ sth/sb from doing sth** (of a fact or situation) to make sth impossible to do SYN PREVENT: *Patients were excluded from the study if their physical condition prohibited them from completing the questionnaire.*

pro·hib·ition AWL /ˌprəʊɪˈbɪʃn; *NAmE* ˌproʊəˈbɪʃn/ *noun* **1** [U] **~ (of sth)** the act of stopping sth from being done or used, especially by law: *The prohibition of smoking in public places may have the unintended consequence of increasing children's exposure to smoke at home.* **2** [C] a law or rule that stops sth from being done or used: **~ against (doing) sth** *The city had a prohibition against building any high-rise edifice that would block the public's views of historic landmarks.* ◇ **~ on (doing) sth** *The prohibition on torture is regarded as fundamental by the international community.*

pro·hibi·tive AWL /prəˈhɪbətɪv; *NAmE also* proʊˈhɪbətɪv/ *adj.* **1** (of a price or cost) so high that it prevents people from buying sth or doing sth: *Because of the prohibitive costs of the clinical trials, the project was abandoned.* **2** preventing people from doing sth by law: *He called on Congress to pass prohibitive legislation against the spread of slavery.* ■ **pro·hibi·tive·ly** *adv.*: *Radiotherapy is indicated for 55% of new cancer cases in the region, but is often unavailable or prohibitively expensive.*

pro·ject[1] AWL /ˈprɒdʒekt; *NAmE* ˈprɑːdʒekt/ *noun* **1** a planned piece of work that is designed to find information about sth, to produce sth new or to improve sth: *Other major projects include a dam being constructed in Laos.* ◇ **~ to do sth** *They have undertaken a large-scale project to develop fuel-efficient cars that can meet US emissions standards.* ◇ **~ for sth** *There have been several pilot projects for population management of termites.* ◇ **+ noun** *Many large firms now provide formal training in project management.* **2** a piece of research work done by a school or college student: **do a ~** *When doing projects, students clearly need to do their research with very limited resources.* ◇ **~ on sth** *Her project on dolphins was due the following week.* **3 ~ (of sth/of doing sth)** a set of aims, ideas or activities that sb is interested in or wants to bring to people's attention: *It was thought that a common currency would help keep a unified Germany tied to the project of European integration.*

▸ ADJECTIVE + PROJECT **large • major • ambitious • new** *Demand for water led to the construction of the Arizona Canal, the state's most ambitious project to date.* | **large-scale • pilot • individual • public • collaborative** *The aim is to facilitate collaborative projects between psychologists and epilepsy health care providers.* | **political** *Numerous voices have emerged to champion the leftist political project.*

▸ NOUN + PROJECT **research** *The small Texas town was involved in the local high school students' research project.* | **development • investment • infrastructure • construction** *The World Bank also invested in Korean development projects.*

▸ VERB + PROJECT **complete** *No one company can provide all the products and services necessary to complete the project.* | **support • develop • pursue** *Blair and Brown together developed the New Labour project.* | **undertake, conduct, carry out • design • approve • fund, finance • initiate, launch • implement • manage • lead • describe • evaluate** *Managers were seemingly hesitant to initiate risky investment projects.*

▸ PROJECT + NOUN **work** *This aspect of the project work was relatively similar across the different police districts.* | **management • organization • governance • execution • implementation • design • development • performance • success • activity • network • plan • goal** *Processes and steps required to meet the project goals were well understood.* | **manager • leader • coordinator • member, participant • team** *From the 1990s, there was an unprecedented rise in demand for project managers, particularly in construction and IT.*

pro·ject[2] AWL /prəˈdʒekt/ *verb* **1** [T, usually passive] to estimate what the size, cost or amount of sth will be in the future, based on what is happening now SYN FORECAST[2]: **be projected (for sth)** *Steady growth is also projected for perfumes, shampoos and powders.* ◇ **be projected to do sth** *The world's population is projected to rise by 2 billion in the next 25 years.* ◇ **it is projected that...** *It is projected that the health care of the elderly will account for an increasing proportion of future health budgets.* **2** [T, usually passive] **be projected (for sth)** to plan an activity, a project, etc. for a time in the future: *The other colonies were told that a new government would be imposed upon them, like that projected for Quebec.* **3** [T] to present sb/sth/yourself to other people in a particular way, especially one that gives a good impression: **~ sth** *The Conservatives have generally tried to project an image of being the more patriotic party.* ◇ **~ sb/sth/yourself (as sb/sth)** *The reporter chose to project Keeler as a naive young woman.* **4** [I] **+ adv./prep.** to stick out beyond an edge or surface: *Another group of dinosaurs had large crests projecting from their heads.* **5** [T] **~ sth/sb (+ adv./prep.)** to throw sth or make sth move forward or away: *A particle is projected from ground level in such a way that it passes through two points.* **6** [T] **~ sth (on/onto sth)** to make light, an image, etc. fall onto a flat surface or screen: *Images are projected onto the retina of the eye.*

PHR V **proˈject sth onto sb** to imagine that other people have the same feelings, problems, etc. as you, especially when this is not true: *Anxious parents may project their own anxieties onto their child.*

P

pro·jec·tion AWL /prəˈdʒekʃn/ *noun* **1** [C] an estimate or forecast of a future situation based on what is happening now SYN FORECAST[1]: *It is difficult to make detailed projections beyond 2020.* ◇ **~ of sth** *Figure 3.3 summarizes the World Bank's projections of the global population.* **2** [U, C] **~ (of sth) (on/onto sth)** the act of putting an image of sth onto a surface; an image that is shown in this way: *The projection of images on a screen takes place at 24 frames per second.* ◇ *The films were initially presented as frozen unmoving images, projections of still photographs.* **3** [C] a method for representing a solid shape or object on a flat surface: *Other researchers have also developed new map projections.* **4** [C] **~ (+ adv./prep.)** something that sticks out from a surface: *A nose leaf is a small upward projection from the nose of some bats.* **5** [U, C] **~ (of sth)** the act of giving a form and structure to thoughts and feelings; the form and structure given to thoughts and feelings: *Cyberspace provides opportunities for the projection of desires, frustrations and anxieties.* ◇ *Native Americans appeared in American literature as symbolic projections of fear and savagery.* **6** [U] the act of imagining that sb else has the same feelings, thoughts and reactions as you: *People with this personality type are more prone to utilize projection.*

pro·lif·er·ate /prəˈlɪfəreɪt/ *verb* **1** [I] to increase quickly in number or amount SYN MULTIPLY (2): *Women's journals proliferated, running instructions on household management alongside fashion advice.* **2** [I] (*biology*) (of a cell, structure or ORGANISM) to REPRODUCE quickly SYN MULTIPLY (3): *Several types of leukaemia are caused by cells continuing to proliferate instead of differentiating.*

pro·lif·er·ation /prəˌlɪfəˈreɪʃn/ *noun* **1** [U, sing.] **~ (of sth)** a RAPID increase in the number or amount of sth; a large number of a particular thing: *The proliferation of weapons of mass destruction may result in a new era of inter-state rivalries.* ◇ *There has been a proliferation of regional economic groupings or trade blocs around the world in recent years.* **2** [U] (*biology*) the RAPID REPRODUCTION of a cell, part or ORGANISM: *Mammals have renewable tissues that need to be replenished by cell proliferation.* ◇ *to stimulate/inhibit cell proliferation*

pro·lif·ic /prəˈlɪfɪk/ *adj.* **1** (of an artist, a writer, a period of time, etc.) producing many works of art, literature, etc. SYN PRODUCTIVE (2): *He was a prolific writer, author of 240 works.* **2** (of plants or animals) producing a lot of fruit, flowers or young: *Some farmers kept pumpkins in production because they were so prolific and easy to propagate.* **3** able to produce a large amount of sth such as food or a natural resource: *They are prolific source rocks for natural gas since they are rich in organic matter and rarely expel any generated oil.* **4** existing in large numbers SYN NUMEROUS: *Although lakes originate in many ways, they may be as prolific today as at any time in the geological past.*

pro·long /prəˈlɒŋ; *NAmE* prəˈlɔːŋ; prəˈlɑːŋ/ *verb* **~ sth** to make sth continue longer SYN EXTEND (4): *Renal dialysis treatment has prolonged the life of countless patients.*

pro·longed /prəˈlɒŋd; *NAmE* prəˈlɔːŋd; prəˈlɑːŋd/ *adj.* continuing for a long time: *Prolonged exposure to stress can lead to exhaustion.* ◇ *Cities throughout the developed world typically experienced a prolonged period of substantial growth.*

prom·in·ence /ˈprɒmɪnəns; *NAmE* ˈprɑːmɪnəns/ *noun* **1** [U, sing.] the state of being important, well known or easy to notice: *Michel Foucault first came to prominence in Parisian intellectual life in the early 1960s.* ◇ *to gain/achieve prominence* ◇ *Her controversial views on Australian history have been given a prominence they scarcely deserve.* **2** [C, U] (*medical* or *formal*) a thing that sticks out from sth; the fact or state of sticking out from sth: *Small skin lumps form on bony prominences like elbows.* ◇ **~ of sth** *This leads to prominence of abdominal wall veins.*

prom·in·ent /ˈprɒmɪnənt; *NAmE* ˈprɑːmɪnənt/ *adj.* **1** important or well known: *Women appear to have played a more prominent role in the early Christian church than in society at large.* ◇ *Parental care is probably the most prominent example of this type of 'altruism'.* **2** easily seen SYN NOTICEABLE: *Shore platforms are prominent features of rock costs.* **3** sticking out from sth: *The head is now much more developed with prominent eyes, and the limbs are beginning to develop.*

prom·in·ent·ly /ˈprɒmɪnəntli; *NAmE* ˈprɑːmɪnəntli/ *adv.* **1** in a position of importance: *Earthquakes and volcanoes have figured prominently in human history since the dawn of recorded time.* **2** so as to be easily seen: *Charles Dickens had portraits of his friends, Carlyle and Tennyson, prominently displayed in his library.*

prom·ise[1] /ˈprɒmɪs; *NAmE* ˈprɑːmɪs/ *noun* **1** [C] a statement in which you say that you will definitely do sth, or that sth will definitely happen: **make/keep/break a ~** *To compete for funds against other regions, they were inclined to make promises they could not keep.* ◇ *Politicians who break promises are likely to get into trouble with their own supporters.* ◇ **~ to do sth** *The army appears to be delivering on its promise to return the country to democratic rule.* ◇ **~ of sth** *These countries have received a promise of EU membership.* ◇ **~ that...** *Khrushchev procured from Washington a promise that America would not invade Cuba.* **2** [U] the quality of being likely to be excellent or successful SYN POTENTIAL[2] (2): *He never fulfilled his early promise and had to earn a living painting children's portraits.* ◇ *He asked Harris whether his work showed any promise.* **3** [U, sing.] a sign or a reason for hope that sth may happen, especially sth good: **~ for (doing) sth** *In the environmental field, nanomaterials hold promise for providing elegant solutions to numerous problems.* ◇ **~ of sth** *The recent rapid economic growth in China and India brings the promise of a better life to much of the world's population.*

prom·ise[2] /ˈprɒmɪs; *NAmE* ˈprɑːmɪs/ *verb* **1** [I, T] to tell sb that you will definitely do sth, or that sth will definitely happen: **~ to do sth** *The government promised to increase spending on defence, law and order, and health.* ◇ **~ sth** *Loans totalling $3 billion were promised by Denmark.* ◇ **~ (that)...** *He had to promise that the decision would be reviewed every five years.* ◇ **~ sb (that)...** *Hitler promised Chamberlain that their two countries would never go to war with each other again.* ◇ **~ sth to sb** *They had promised anonymity to participants in the study.* ◇ **~ sb sth** *Britain's biggest bank had promised employees a job for life.* **2** [T] to make sth seem likely to happen; to show signs of sth: **it promises to be sth** *It promises to be a discovery of immense medical importance.* ◇ **~ sth** *The future really did seem to promise great things.*

prom·is·ing /ˈprɒmɪsɪŋ; *NAmE* ˈprɑːmɪsɪŋ/ *adj.* showing signs of future success: *Two new drugs have shown promising results in clinical trials.* ◇ *One promising new approach came from an EU funded research project.*

pro·mote AWL /prəˈməʊt; *NAmE* prəˈmoʊt/ *verb* **1 ~ sth** to help sth to happen or develop SYN ENCOURAGE (1): *The importance of diet in promoting health is hardly a new discovery.* ◇ *The USA claimed to be promoting democracy in the region.* **2** to help sell a product or service or make it more popular by advertising it or offering it at a special price: **~ sth** *They use celebrities to promote their products.* ◇ **~ sth as sth** *By 2007, the supermarket chain claimed to have 7 000 regional lines from throughout the UK that were promoted as local produce.* **3** [often passive] to move sb to a higher rank or more senior job: **~ sb** *Unless she increases her scholarly output in respected journals, she is in danger of not being promoted.* ◇ **~ sb (from sth) (to sth)** *He was*

P

promoted from president and chief executive officer to chairman of the board.

▸ PROMOTE + NOUN **health • well-being • welfare • development • growth • interests • rights • values • use • behaviour • activity • equality • change • cooperation • understanding • learning • idea • view • policy • formation • competition • integration • democracy** *They stressed the role of the state in promoting economic development.* ◇ *Organizations lobby for legislation and regulations which promote their own interests.*

▸ ADVERB + PROMOTE **actively • vigorously • strongly • successfully • widely** *Governments around the world have actively promoted collaboration as a source of innovation.*

pro·moter AWL /prəˈməʊtə(r); *NAmE* prəˈmoʊtər/ *noun* **1** **~ of sth** a supporter of a cause, project or aim SYN CHAMPION¹ (2): *King Charles II was a great promoter of science.* **2** a person or company that organizes or provides money for a sports event, concert or theatre production: *The concert is held because someone, the promoter, is hoping to make a profit.* **3** (*biochemistry*) a region of a DNA MOLECULE which forms the site at which TRANSCRIPTION of a gene starts: *Gene promoters called estrogen response elements (EREs) control the differential gene transcription in the sexes (Sanchez et al., 2002).*

pro·mo·tion AWL /prəˈməʊʃn; *NAmE* prəˈmoʊʃn/ *noun* **1** [U] activity that supports or encourages a cause, project or aim: **~ (of sth)** *A primary role of the Commission is the promotion of human rights.* ◇ **+ noun** *There is a tendency for health promotion campaigns to be targeted at young and middle-aged adults.* **2** [U, C] a move to a more important job or rank in a company or organization: *There now exists in organizations less opportunity for promotion than there was in the past.* ◇ **~ to sth** *Promotions to positions with more responsibility provide recognition for good performance.* **3** [U, C] **~ (of sth)** activities done in order to increase the sales of a product or service: *French cooperatives have only recently become concerned with the marketing and promotion of their products.* ◇ *Firms pass the cost of the promotions and advertisements on to consumers in the price of the product.*

pro·mo·tion·al /prəˈməʊʃənl; *NAmE* prəˈmoʊʃənl/ *adj.* connected with activities done in order to increase the sales of a product or service, or in order to gain support for a cause, project or aim: *They may have to update their promotional material to reflect the higher prices.* ◇ *It is very important to monitor and evaluate the effectiveness of an organization's promotional activities.*

prompt¹ /prɒmpt; *NAmE* prɑːmpt/ *verb* **1** **~ sth** (of an event or fact) to cause an action or feeling SYN PROVOKE (1): *Both issues prompted discussion about the proper limits of federal power.* ◇ *The results of the study prompt the question of why managers did not follow recommendations.* **2** **~ sb to do sth** to make sb decide to do sth: *The discovery prompted a number of scientists to expand the search for microbes in the soil.* **3** to encourage sb to speak by asking them questions or suggesting words that they could say: **~ sb** *She prompted him on the answers he should give to reporters.* ◇ **~ sb to do sth** *The child would then see two of these toys and be prompted to say what they were.* **4** **~ sb (to do sth)** (of a computer) to request a user to take action: *A hand-held computer prompts the respondent to enter data at random or preset times.*

prompt² /prɒmpt; *NAmE* prɑːmpt/ *adj.* **1** done without delay SYN IMMEDIATE (1): *Early detection and prompt treatment are critical to the survival of the patient.* **2** [not before noun] **~ (in doing sth)** (of a person) acting without delay: *Sparta complained that her allies had not been prompt in supporting her campaigns.*

prompt³ /prɒmpt; *NAmE* prɑːmpt/ *noun* **1** a word or suggestion that encourages sb to speak or reminds them what to say or write: *A series of scripted prompts was used by the interviewer.* **2** (*computing*) a sign on a computer screen that shows that the computer is ready for instructions: *At the command prompt, type the following:...*

prompt·ly /ˈprɒmptli; *NAmE* ˈprɑːmptli/ *adv.* **1** without delay: *The deteriorating situation forced politicians to act promptly.* **2** exactly at the correct time or at the time mentioned: *The client arrived at the office promptly.* **3** (always used before the verb) immediately: *Dahlmann and his colleagues protested, and were promptly dismissed.*

prone /prəʊn; *NAmE* proʊn/ *adj.* **1** likely to suffer from sth or to do sth bad SYN LIABLE (2): **~ to sth** *Some official statistics are particularly prone to error, such as those relating to crime.* ◇ **~ to do sth** *Studies suggest that boys are more prone to be aggressive than girls.* **2** **-prone** (in adjectives) likely to suffer or do the thing mentioned: *This is a time-consuming and error-prone process.* ◇ *The machine is relatively trouble free and not very accident-prone.* **3** lying flat with the front of your body touching the ground: *The patient was arranged in a prone position with a pillow under the abdomen.*

pro·noun /ˈprəʊnaʊn; *NAmE* ˈproʊnaʊn/ *noun* a word that is used instead of a noun or noun phrase, for example *he, it, hers, me, them,* etc: *Men tend to use the pronoun 'I' in order to claim the credit for success, whereas women are more likely to say 'we'.*

pro·nounce /prəˈnaʊns/ *verb* **1** **~ sth** to make the sound of a word or letter in a particular way: *Brand names that are difficult to pronounce are unlikely to be accepted by customers.* ➲ *see also* PRONUNCIATION **2** to say or give sth formally, officially or publicly: **~ sth** *The art film attempts to pronounce judgements on 'modern life' as a whole.* ◇ **~ sb/sth + adj./noun** *She was pronounced dead on arrival at the hospital.* ◇ **~ sb/sth to be/have sth** *He pronounced the country to be in a state of war.* ◇ **~ that...** *The poet John Donne (1572–1631) pronounced that 'no man is an island'.* PHR V **pro'nounce on/upon sth** (*formal*) to state your opinion on sth; to give a decision about sth: *In January 1973, the Supreme Court pronounced on the issue.*

pro·nounced /prəˈnaʊnst/ *adj.* very obvious or easy to notice SYN DEFINITE (3): *This process can result in a pronounced change in the course of the river.* ◇ *The under-representation of women is even more pronounced for advanced degrees.*

pro·nounce·ment /prəˈnaʊnsmənt/ *noun* a formal public statement: *A series of judicial pronouncements have lent support to this position.* ◇ **~ on sth** *It is difficult to make clear-cut pronouncements on the correctness or otherwise of grammar forms in spoken language.*

pro·nun·ci·ation /prəˌnʌnsiˈeɪʃn/ *noun* **1** [U, C] the way in which a language or a particular word or sound is pronounced: *Chapter 6 discusses several aspects of English pronunciation, including phonetics and prosody.* ◇ **~ of sth** *The correct pronunciation of a word often depends on the context.* **2** [sing.] the way in which a particular person pronounces the words of a language: *He needed to improve his pronunciation and vocabulary to communicate more effectively with his colleagues.*

proof /pruːf/ *noun* **1** [U, C] information, documents, etc. that show that sth is true SYN EVIDENCE¹ (1): *Proof may be needed to establish ownership.* ◇ **~ of sth** *Proof of negligence is not required.* ◇ *to have conclusive/definitive proof of sth* ◇ **~ that...** *This is a clear proof that globalization is not an irreversible process.* ➲ *see also* BURDEN OF PROOF ➲ thesaurus note *at* EVIDENCE¹ **2** [U] the process of testing whether sth is true or a fact: *The idea is attractive but incapable of proof on current evidence.* ➲ *see also* BURDEN OF PROOF **3** [C] **~ (of sth)** a series of stages by which you show that a statement in mathematics or philosophy is true, or that a calculation is correct: *The proof of this* *theorem is quite simple.* ◇ *To give a formal proof, it is necessary to have a careful definition of the integers.* **4** [C, usually pl.] a copy of printed material that is produced so that mistakes can be corrected: *He made very few corrections to the proofs.*

proof·read /ˈpruːfriːd/ *verb* (**proof·read**, **proof·read** /ˈpruːfred/) [T, I] **~ (sth)** to read and correct a piece of written or printed work: *Check your spelling and, if possible, have someone else proofread your work.* ■ **proof·read·ing** *noun* [U] *Proofreading is an important stage of the process.*

propa·ganda /ˌprɒpəˈɡændə; *NAmE* ˌprɑːpəˈɡændə/ *noun* [U] (*usually disapproving*) ideas or statements that may be false or give a false impression and that are used in order to gain support for a political leader, party, etc: *The war, the war economy and wartime propaganda had prepared the way for social change.* ◇ *government/political propaganda* ◇ **+ noun** *The exhibition formed a crucial part of the large imperial propaganda campaign staged in Britain during the inter-war years.*

propa·gate /ˈprɒpəɡeɪt; *NAmE* ˈprɑːpəɡeɪt/ *verb* **1** [T] **~ sth** (*formal*) to spread an idea, a belief or a piece of information among many people: *They founded the newspaper in 1847 to propagate their ideas.* **2** [I, T] (*biology*) to produce new plants or animals from parent plants or animals: *For cells and organisms to survive and propagate, they must accurately pass on their genetic information to the next generation.* ◇ **~ sth** *Highly endangered species can sometimes be propagated in this way.* **3** [I, T] (*physics*) (of a wave or signal) to travel in a particular direction or through a particular MEDIUM; to send a wave or signal in a particular direction or through a particular medium: **+ adv./prep.** *In all three cases, a shock wave propagates into the driver gas.* ◇ **~ sth + adv./prep.** *In seismic reflection surveying, seismic waves are propagated through the subsurface.*

P

propa·ga·tion /ˌprɒpəˈɡeɪʃn; *NAmE* ˌprɑːpəˈɡeɪʃn/ *noun* [U] **1 ~ (of sth)** (*formal*) the action of spreading an idea, a belief or a piece of information among many people: *Both Protestant and Catholic reformers were conscious of the need for improved literacy to facilitate the propagation of the faith.* **2 ~ (of sth)** (*biology*) the process of producing new plants or animals from parent plants or animals: *These are the cells that produce the sperm and eggs for the propagation of the species.* **3 ~ (of sth)** (*physics*) the action of sending a wave or signal in a particular direction or through a particular MEDIUM: *The electric and magnetic fields on the line are perpendicular to each other and transverse to the direction of wave propagation.*

pro·pel /prəˈpel/ *verb* (-ll-) [often passive] **1 ~ sth (+ adv./prep.)** to move, drive or push sth forward or in a particular direction: *The ancient Greek warship was propelled by three banks of oars.* ◇ *These explosions propel clouds of dust out of the crater of the volcano.* **2 ~ sb + adv./prep.** to force sb to move in a particular direction or to get into a particular situation: *NATO was propelled into action by a mixture of humanitarian concern and self-interest.*

pro·pen·sity /prəˈpensəti/ *noun* (*pl.* -ies) a tendency to a particular kind of behaviour SYN TENDENCY (1): **~ for (doing) sth** *This group has the greatest propensity for Internet shopping.* ◇ **~ towards sth** *The Turkish population in Germany shows a high propensity towards self-employment (Constant et al., 2003).* ◇ **~ to do sth** *Non-European minority students have a generally higher propensity to choose an academic education.* HELP In economics, the **marginal propensity to consume (MPC)** is a measure of how spending changes in relation to changes in income; the **marginal propensity to save (MPS)** is a measure of how saving changes in relation to changes in income.

proper /ˈprɒpə(r); *NAmE* ˈprɑːpər/ *adj.* **1** [only before noun] (*especially BrE*) right, appropriate or correct; according to the rules: *Everything had to be kept in its proper place.* ◇ *Steps must also be taken to ensure that proper procedures are followed.* OPP IMPROPER (2) **2** [only before noun] (*BrE*) considered to be real and of a good enough standard: *They may find it difficult to find time for exercise or a proper meal.* **3** socially and morally acceptable: **~ for sb** *They believe such things are not proper for girls.* ◇ **it is ~ (for sb) to do sth** *It would not be proper to make too much of this finding.* ◇ **right and ~** *According to the early nineteenth-century view, it was right and proper for humans to use environments as they saw fit.* OPP IMPROPER (1) **4** [after noun] according to the most exact meaning of the word: *Urban authorities are making efforts to integrate squatter settlements into the city proper.* **5 ~ to sb/sth** belonging to a particular type of person or thing; natural in a particular situation or place: *Some mythical beasts possess a trait that is proper to another animal, such as wings.*

prop·er·ly /ˈprɒpəli; *NAmE* ˈprɑːpərli/ *adv.* **1** (*especially BrE*) in a way that is correct and/or appropriate: *A smoothly operating money market allows an economy to function properly.* ◇ *The history of British race relations after the Second World War cannot be properly understood without appreciation of the preceding era.* **2** in a way that is socially or morally acceptable: *The values of one's faith should be guides for how to behave properly.* OPP IMPROPERLY **3** in the strict sense: *He argues that it is only possible to steal from someone that which properly belongs to him.* ◇ **~ speaking** *Directors of companies are not, properly speaking, trustees.*

ˌproper ˈnoun (*also* ˌproper ˈname) *noun* (*grammar*) a word that is the name of a person, a place, an institution, etc. and is written with a capital letter, for example *Tom, Rome, Texas, the Rhine, the White House*: *The dictionary contains a lot of foreign words and loan words, including common nouns as well as proper nouns.*

prop·erty /ˈprɒpəti; *NAmE* ˈprɑːpərti/ *noun* (*pl.* -ies) **1** [C, usually pl.] **~ (of sth)** a quality or characteristic that sth has: *They investigated the physical and chemical properties of soils.* ◇ *Essential properties are those without which an object would not be what it is.* ➲ thesaurus note at FEATURE[1] **2** [U] a thing or things that are owned by sb; a possession or possessions: *The court held that the furniture was the husband's property.* ◇ **~ of sb** *The capital goods used in production are the private property of capitalists.* ➲ *see also* INTELLECTUAL PROPERTY **3** [U, C] land and buildings; a particular piece of land or a particular building and its surrounding land: *He could not own property, so he rented buildings outside the city.* ◇ *The bank commenced proceedings to sell the property.*

▸ ADJECTIVE + PROPERTY **intrinsic, inherent • essential, fundamental, basic • unique • special • unusual • desirable • important • common • physical • chemical • material • biological • biochemical • mechanical • electrical • thermal • thermodynamic • magnetic • optical • structural** *Each molecule has intrinsic properties which affect the absorbance of light.* | **private • personal • cultural** *People in the working class typically do own cars, homes and other personal property.*

▸ VERB + PROPERTY **possess, have • acquire** *Things belong to categories because they possess certain properties in common.* | **exhibit, show, display • share • attribute • describe • define • investigate, study, examine • affect • determine • alter, change** *CO_2 exhibits excellent heat transfer properties.* | **own, hold • sell • transfer • purchase, buy • inherit • damage • destroy • seize, appropriate • protect** *In the fifth century, probably three quarters of the citizens owned some rural property.*

▸ PROPERTY + NOUN **rights • law • developer • owner • ownership • tax** *Property developers are able to charge buyers a premium for a flat on the eighth floor.*

proph·ecy /ˈprɒfəsi; *NAmE* ˈprɑːfəsi/ *noun* (*pl.* -ies) **1** [C] a statement that sth will happen in the future, especially one made by sb who claims religious or magic powers: *While he was at Gordium, Alexander fulfilled the prophecy by slashing through the knot with his sword.* HELP A **self-fulfilling prophecy** is a statement or theory about sth that will happen in the future that itself causes the thing to happen: *Subsequently, in what might be described as a self-fulfilling prophecy, numerous Nazi supporters lost hope as the regime collapsed.* **2** [U] the power of being able to say what will happen in the future: *Cassandra's gift of prophecy came with a curse: she would see the future, but no one would ever believe her.*

prophet /ˈprɒfɪt; *NAmE* ˈprɑːfɪt/ *noun* **1** [C] (in the Christian, Jewish and Muslim religions) a person sent by God to teach the people and give them messages from God: *Christians relied heavily on the argument that the Hebrew prophets foretold events in Jesus's life.* **2 the Prophet** [sing.] Muhammad, who established the religion of Islam: *As was the case with the Prophet, God's chosen are sometimes orphaned young.* **3** [C] **~ (of sth)** a person who teaches or supports a new idea, theory, etc: *In the eyes of the founders of the Royal Society, Francis Bacon was the prophet of a new scientific methodology.*

proph·et·ic /prəˈfetɪk/ *adj.* **1** correctly stating or showing what will happen in the future: *Wollstonecraft's ideas were shocking to her contemporaries but have proved remarkably prophetic.* **2** [only before noun] like or connected with a prophet or prophecy: *Morna Hooker (1997, pp. 38–54) has drawn attention to several further prophetic actions of Jesus.*

pro·pon·ent /prəˈpəʊnənt; *NAmE* prəˈpoʊnənt/ *noun* a person who supports an idea or course of action SYN ADVOCATE[2] (1): *Proponents argue that GM crops increase yields without decreasing biodiversity.* ◇ **~ of sth** *Edward Young was one of the most influential proponents of originality in literature.*

pro·por·tion AWL /prəˈpɔːʃn; *NAmE* prəˈpɔːrʃn/ *noun* **1** [C+sing./pl. v.] a part or share of a whole: *53% of the sample reported driving to work; a smaller proportion used public transport.* ◇ **~ of sth** *Minority groups constitute a significant proportion of the population.* ◇ *a large/high/substantial/low/tiny proportion of sb/sth* ◇ *We then calculated the proportion of offspring born to females in each category.* **2** [U] the relationship of one thing to another in size, amount or number SYN RATIO: **~ of sth to sth** *The proportion of air to fuel must be correct.* ◇ **in ~ to sth** *The states collect fees from companies in proportion to the size of their workforces.* **3 proportions** [pl.] the size and shape of one part of sth in relation to the other parts: *The female is not just a miniature copy of the male. Her proportions differ.* **4** [U] the correct relationship in size between one thing and another or between the parts of a whole: *The architecture of the time was based on principles of order and proportion.* ◇ **in ~ (with sth)** *The two feet of a human being are roughly the same size, and their bodies are in proportion.* IDM **of huge/epic, etc. proportions** extremely large or serious: *Such an epidemic would represent a humanitarian crisis of catastrophic proportions.* **out of (all) proˈportion (to sth)** larger or more serious in relation to sth than is necessary or appropriate: *Pathological anxiety is a feeling of apprehension that is out of proportion to the actual situation.*

WORD FAMILY
proportion *noun*
proportional *adj.*
proportionally *adv.*
proportionate *adj.*
proportionately *adv.*
disproportionate *adj.*
disproportionately *adv.*

pro·por·tion·al AWL /prəˈpɔːʃənl; *NAmE* prəˈpɔːrʃənl/ *adj.* of an appropriate size, amount or degree in comparison with sth SYN PROPORTIONATE: *The response to violence and aggression must be proportional.* ◇ **~ to sth** *Transport costs are not always directly proportional to distance.* ◇ *The amplitude of the oscillations is inversely proportional to the wavelength.* ■ **pro·por·tion·al·ly** AWL /prəˈpɔːʃənəli; *NAmE* prəˈpɔːrʃənəli/ *adv.*: *The thickness of the sample must decrease proportionally as the length increases.*

LANGUAGE BANK

Describing proportions and relative quantities

In academic writing, it is often necessary to describe a quantity or group as a proportion of a larger quantity or group, or to compare two quantities. This is often done using fractions, percentages or ratios.

- **a/one third/quarter** of X
- **almost/approximately half** of X
- **less/fewer than/over/more than half** of X
- **one in three/four/five** is...
- **twice/three times as much** time/money, etc.
- **twice/three times as many** people/species, etc.
- X **is three/four times** higher/greater/larger than...
- **the ratio of** X **to** Y is...
- **a high/large proportion** of X
- **the largest/greatest proportion of** X is...
- X **accounts for/makes up/comprises/represents...**

– ***A quarter of*** *adults in the US own at least one gun.*
– *Supermarket groups now account for* ***almost half of*** *all food retail sales in Europe.*
– ***Fewer than one third of*** *the males manage to mate during a mating season.*
– ***Over a fifth (21%) of*** *those aged 85 and over could not do this personal care task for themselves.*
– *The outlook is extremely poor for these patients and only* ***one in four*** *will survive.*
– *Households headed by men have, on average,* ***five times as much*** *wealth as those headed by women.*
– *Table 22.1 shows that China had* ***six times as many*** *university students as the UK in 2001.*
– *It produces a magnetic field* ***many thousand times*** *stronger than the earth's.*
– ***The ratio of*** *females* ***to*** *males in sub-Saharan Africa is 102 to 100.*
– *We may expect* ***a higher proportion of*** *errors in the elementary student group.*
– ***The largest proportion (27%) of*** *questions posted concerned sexual health.*
– *These elements* ***comprise*** *about 34% of the human genome.*

pro·por·tion·al·ity /prəˌpɔːʃəˈnæləti; *NAmE* prəˌpɔːrʃəˈnæləti/ *noun* [U] (*formal*) the principle that sth should be appropriate in size, amount or degree to sth else: *The principle of proportionality embodies the concept that the punishment should fit the crime.*

pro·por·tion·ate AWL /prəˈpɔːʃənət; *NAmE* prəˈpɔːrʃənət/ *adj.* increasing or decreasing in size, amount or degree according to changes in sth else SYN PROPORTIONAL: *The expansion of higher education places was achieved without a proportionate increase in university funding.* ◇ **~ to sth** *Pay is reduced for part-time teachers in a manner proportionate to their working hours.* ➲ *compare* DISPROPORTIONATE ■ **pro·por·tion·ate·ly** AWL *adv.*: *Rising labour productivity ensured that extra output could be produced with proportionately fewer workers.*

pro·posal /prəˈpəʊzl; *NAmE* prəˈpoʊzl/ *noun* **1** a formal suggestion or plan: *The interested parties were invited to submit proposals before October 30.* ◇ **~ to do sth** *Proposals to introduce identity cards were rejected.* ◇ **~ for sth** *He welcomed proposals for legislative reform.* ◇ **~ that...** *The proposal that enterprises should be charged for the capital they used was not accepted.* **2 ~ (that...)** an explanation suggested for people to consider: *The*

P

findings support the proposal that human attitudes to animals are affected by species' similarity to humans.

pro·pose /prəˈpəʊz; *NAmE* prəˈpoʊz/ *verb* **1** to suggest a plan or an idea for people to consider and decide on: **~ sth** *Three solutions have been proposed.* ◇ **~ sth as sth** *Remote Internet voting has been proposed as a solution to the problem of low voter turnout.* ◇ **~ to do sth** *The government proposed to abolish the office of Lord Chancellor.* ◇ **~ that...** *No one dared propose that they should be freed.* ◇ **~ doing sth** *The Bretton Woods Conference proposed setting up three international organizations.* ➲ language bank *at* ARGUMENT **2** to suggest an explanation of sth for people to consider: **~ sth** *They proposed the following hypothesis:...* ◇ **~ sth as sth** *Operational sex ratio has been proposed as one of the key factors in inter-sexual selection (Emlen and Oring, 1977).* ◇ **~ that...** *Chomsky proposed that language is rule-based.* ➲ thesaurus note *at* SUGGEST ➲ language bank *at* ACCORDING TO

▸ PROPOSE + NOUN **solution • framework, model • scheme • plan • strategy • method, approach • classification • definition • mechanism • amendment • legislation • reform** *Sawa proposed a plan for profit-sharing among his workers.* | **hypothesis, theory • model • explanation** *Ackley and Sullivan (1994) have proposed a conceptual model of the seasonal cycle of sea ice with the following characteristics:...*

▸ ADVERB + PROPOSE **originally, first • recently** *None of the schemes originally proposed came to fruition.*

prop·os·ition /ˌprɒpəˈzɪʃn; *NAmE* ˌprɑːpəˈzɪʃn/ *noun* **1 ~ (that...)** a statement that expresses an opinion or a possible fact: *This study tests the proposition that increased economic interdependence between states reduces conflict.* ◇ *The proposition that Mars has an ocean is not true.* HELP A **proposition** can express an opinion that can be tested or studied in order to see if it is accurate; in logic, a **proposition** states a fact that is either true or false. ➲ thesaurus note *at* HYPOTHESIS **2** a project, task or idea considered in terms of how successful or difficult it is likely to be: *Targeting a small but expanding middle class may be a very attractive proposition for a new entrant to the market.* **3** (*also* **Proposition**) (in the US) a suggested change to the law that people can vote on: *They voted overwhelmingly for the proposition.*

P

prop·os·ition·al /ˌprɒpəˈzɪʃnəl; *NAmE* ˌprɑːpəˈzɪʃnəl/ *adj.* containing or connected with a proposition, especially in philosophy or LINGUISTICS: *The propositional content of 'kick the bucket' is the same as that of 'die'.*

pro·pri·etary /prəˈpraɪətri; *NAmE* prəˈpraɪəteri/ *adj.* [usually before noun] **1** (of goods) made and sold by a particular company and protected by a TRADEMARK: *Several proprietary database software packages are available to marketers.* **2** connected with an owner or the fact of owning sth: *Both parties have proprietary rights in the family home.*

pro·pri·etor /prəˈpraɪətə(r)/ *noun* (*formal*) the owner of land, a business or property: *The registered proprietor has the power to transfer the land.* ◇ *Commentators were disturbed by the political influence of newspaper proprietors.*

prose /prəʊz; *NAmE* proʊz/ *noun* [U] writing that is not poetry: *They are the editors of a new multi-volume edition of Milton's poetry and prose.* ◇ **+ noun** *Lipsius admired Tacitus's pithy prose style.* ◇ *prose fiction/writing/narrative*

pros·ecute /ˈprɒsɪkjuːt; *NAmE* ˈprɑːsɪkjuːt/ *verb* **1** [T, I] to officially charge sb with a crime in court: **~ sb/sth for (doing) sth** *He was successfully prosecuted for manslaughter.* ◇ **~ (sb/sth)** *National courts may be unwilling to investigate or prosecute such crimes.* ◇ *Roman officials varied in their willingness to prosecute.* HELP In a court case, the **prosecuting** lawyer acts for the person or organization that is charging sb with a crime. **2** [T] **~ sth** (*formal*) to continue taking part in or doing sth: *They had overwhelming public support to prosecute the war.*

pros·ecu·tion /ˌprɒsɪˈkjuːʃn; *NAmE* ˌprɑːsɪˈkjuːʃn/ *noun* **1** [U, C] the process of trying to prove in court that sb is guilty of a crime; the process of being officially charged with a crime in court: *It was unlikely that he would escape prosecution.* ◇ *The vast majority of criminal prosecutions are brought by the State.* **2 the prosecution** [sing.+ sing./pl. v.] a person or an organization that prosecutes sb in court, together with their lawyers, etc: *The prosecution must prove that the defendant committed a criminal offence.* ◇ **+ noun** *Ten prosecution witnesses refused to appear in court.* **3** [U] **~ (of sth)** (*formal*) the act of continuing a course of action: *He insisted that such measures were essential to successful prosecution of the war.*

pros·ecu·tor /ˈprɒsɪkjuːtə(r); *NAmE* ˈprɑːsɪkjuːtər/ *noun* **1** a public official who charges sb officially with a crime and prosecutes them in court: *The prosecutor offers each of the prisoners the choice of confessing to or denying involvement in the crime.* **2** a lawyer who leads the case against a DEFENDANT in court: *The jury is aware that the prosecutor might be silent about evidence favourable for the defendant.*

pro·social /ˌprəʊˈsəʊʃl; *NAmE* ˌproʊˈsoʊʃl/ *adj.* [usually before noun] used to describe positive, helpful behaviour that is intended to benefit others or society as a whole: *Teachers sought to encourage prosocial behaviours of cooperation, helping and generosity.*

pro·spect AWL /ˈprɒspekt; *NAmE* ˈprɑːspekt/ *noun* **1** [U, sing.] the possibility that sth will happen: **~ of (doing) sth** *There was no realistic prospect of a successful prosecution.* ◇ *At no time, however, did Britain face the immediate prospect of war.* ◇ **~ that...** *This raises the prospect that GM disease-resistant strains might soon be developed.* ◇ **in ~** *No treatment seems to be in prospect.* **2** [sing.] an idea of what might or will happen in the future: *Giving feedback to a colleague can often be a daunting prospect.* ◇ **~ of (doing) sth** *The child may be nervous about the prospect of having to return to school.* **3 prospects** [pl.] the chances of being successful: *career/employment/job prospects* ◇ **~ for sth** *High levels of inequality will inhibit future prospects for poverty reduction.* ◇ **~ of sth** *This turn of events put an end to German prospects of a quick victory.*

pro·spect·ive AWL /prəˈspektɪv/ *adj.* [usually before noun] **1** expected to do sth or to become sth SYN POTENTIAL[1]: *Prospective employers typically base their offers upon a candidate's existing salary.* ◇ *Peacocks display their coloured tails to prospective mates.* ◇ *prospective buyers/purchasers/customers* **2** expected to happen soon: *The authorities were facing a prospective deficit of $47.3m.* **3** following the development of a disease or situation, in a selection of the population, as it happens, rather than after it has happened: *Prospective studies followed hundreds of patients with functional dyspepsia.* ➲ *compare* RETROSPECTIVE (3)

pros·per /ˈprɒspə(r); *NAmE* ˈprɑːspər/ *verb* [I] to develop in a successful way; to be successful, especially in making money SYN THRIVE: *Whereas Greek culture prospered under Roman rule, the same was not true of the non-Greek cultures of Egypt and the Near East.* ◇ *New companies are created, while others change as they try to survive and prosper.*

pros·per·ity /prɒˈsperəti; *NAmE* prɑːˈsperəti/ *noun* [U] the state of being successful, especially in making money SYN AFFLUENCE: *The country now enjoyed a long period of peace and prosperity.* ◇ *They see the government's task as delivering economic prosperity and social justice.*

pros·per·ous /ˈprɒspərəs; *NAmE* ˈprɑːspərəs/ *adj.* rich and successful SYN AFFLUENT: *John was only six years old when his father, a prosperous farmer, died.*

prot·ag·on·ist /prəˈtæɡənɪst/ *noun* **1 ~ (of sth)** the main character in a play, film or book: *The novel's main protagonist lives a lower middle-class life as a bank clerk.* ◇ *The female protagonist is disappointed in the men in her life.* ➲ *compare* HERO (1), HEROINE (1) **2** one of the main people in a real event, especially a competition, battle or struggle: *The Soviet Union was a principal protagonist in the Cold War.* **3 ~ (of sth)** an active supporter of a policy or movement, especially one that is trying to change sth SYN ADVOCATE[2] (1), CHAMPION[1] (2): *The German economist Friedrich List came to be known as the chief protagonist of this approach.* ◇ *The world is not nearly as homogeneous as the protagonists of globalization like to claim.*

pro·tect /prəˈtekt/ *verb* **1** [T, I] to keep sb/sth safe from harm or injury: **~ sb/sth** *Parents worry about how to protect their children.* ◇ *to protect civilians/citizens/the public* ◇ *Responsibility for protecting the environment rests with us all.* ◇ *The international system for protecting human rights is not perfect.* ◇ *The government acted quickly to protect its economic interests.* ◇ **~ sb/sth/yourself against/from sth** *The Refugee Convention is aimed at protecting individuals from persecution.* ◇ **~ against/from sth** *Diets that are high in fruit and vegetables may protect against certain cancers.* **2** [T, usually passive] to introduce laws that make it illegal to kill, harm or damage a particular animal, area of land, building, etc: **be protected** *Certain types of forests will be protected under the Habitats Directive.* ◇ **protected + noun** *The Eurasian lynx is listed as a protected species.* **3** [T] to help an industry in your own country by taxing goods from other countries so that there is less competition: **~ sth** *To protect their domestic car industries, the governments of the EU countries pushed for protective tariffs.* ◇ **~ sth from sth** *The state singled out strategic industries and protected them from outside competition.* **4** [T, I] to provide sb/sth with insurance against fire, injury, damage, etc: **~ sb/sth** *Depositors knew that their deposits were protected by federal deposit insurance.* ◇ **~ (sb/sth) against sth** *Protection and indemnity insurance protects against environmental damage.*

pro·tec·tion /prəˈtekʃn/ *noun* **1** [U] the act of protecting sb/sth; the state of being protected: **~ for/of sb/sth** *The ozone in the atmosphere provides vital protection for life on Earth.* ◇ **~ against/from sth** *There was no statutory right to protection against unfair dismissal.* ◇ **for ~** *They began building shelters for protection.* ◇ **under ~** *A section of the Kazakh people put themselves under Russian protection.* ➲ *see also* DATA PROTECTION **2** [C] **~ (against sth)** a thing that protects sb/sth against sth: *Tumour-suppressor genes are a protection against the development of cancer.* **3** [U] the system of helping an industry in your own country by taxing foreign goods: *An industry struggling to become established may benefit from import protection.*

▸ ADJECTIVE + PROTECTION **adequate, sufficient • effective • strict • special • equal • temporary • environmental • humanitarian • social • financial • diplomatic • legal, judicial** *Appropriate security and technical processes need to be in place for adequate protection of the individual's data.*

▸ NOUN + PROTECTION **consumer • child • investor • refugee • minority • patent • data • copyright • privacy • employment • human rights • health • sun • flood** *There is a need to start thinking more deliberately about coastal defences and flood protection.*

▸ VERB + PROTECTION **afford, offer, provide, confer, grant, give • extend • ensure, guarantee • receive, enjoy • seek • need, require** *The filtration process offers only very limited protection against water-borne pathogens.*

pro·tec·tion·ism /prəˈtekʃənɪzəm/ *noun* [U] (*economics*) the principle or practice of protecting a country's own industry by taxing foreign goods: *Trade protectionism disadvantages low-income countries seeking economic growth through exports.* ■ **pro·tec·tion·ist** /prəˈtekʃənɪst/ *adj.*: *protectionist policies/measures* ◇ *There were clear differences between the more protectionist 'old' EU states and the more market liberal newcomers.*

pro·tect·ive /prəˈtektɪv/ *adj.* **1** [only before noun] providing or intended to provide protection: *The protective effect of fruit and vegetable consumption has been consistently demonstrated.* ◇ *protective clothing/equipment* **2 ~ (of sb/sth)** having or showing a wish to protect sb/sth: *The Japanese are proud and protective of their national language and culture.* **3** intended to give an advantage to your own country's industry: *Protective tariffs were imposed by Austria in 1887, in order to ensure that railway-building benefited its own iron and steel industry.*

pro·tect·or /prəˈtektə(r)/ *noun* **~ (of sth)** a person, an organization or a thing that protects sb/sth: *A politically free and critical press is one of the strongest protectors of individual liberty.*

pro·tein /ˈprəʊtiːn; *NAmE* ˈproʊtiːn/ *noun* **1** [C] a natural substance that is an essential part of all living things, especially for forming the structure of muscle, hair, ENZYMES, blood, etc: *The sequence of amino acids within a protein is known as its primary structure.* ◇ *On binding of substrates to enzymes, the protein often changes shape.* ◇ *to synthesize/produce/secrete proteins* **2** [U] proteins found in meat, eggs, fish and some vegetables that are an essential part of what humans and animals eat to help them grow and stay healthy: *Songbirds' diets are insect-based and relatively high in protein.*

pro·test[1] /ˈprəʊtest; *NAmE* ˈproʊtest/ *noun* [U, C] the expression of strong disagreement with or opposition to sth; a statement or an action that shows this: *The use of animals in experiments has for long been the focus of much political protest.* ◇ **~ against sth** *Activists organized protests against the regime in the 1980s.* ◇ **in ~** *A number of editorial staff resigned in protest.* ◇ **+ noun** *Global protest movements have been largely responsible for the heightened global sensitivity to environmental degradation.* HELP A **protest** can take the form of a **demonstration**, a march involving a number of people. A **protest** is always to show disagreement or oppostion, whereas a **demonstration** can be to show support.

P

pro·test[2] /prəˈtest; *NAmE also* ˈproʊtest/ *verb* **1** [I, T] to say or do sth to show that you disagree with or disapprove of sth, especially publicly: *Women's rights groups continued to protest.* ◇ **~ about/against/at sth** *It is the right of citizens to protest against unjust legislation.* ◇ **~ sth** (*NAmE*) *Architects worldwide protested the planned demolition.* **2** [T] to say firmly that sth is true, especially when you have been accused of sth or when other people do not believe you: **~ sth** *Despite protesting his innocence, he was convicted and imprisoned.* ◇ **~ that...** *Pro-migrant organizations protested that immigration rules were too strict.*

Prot·est·ant /ˈprɒtɪstənt; *NAmE* ˈprɑːtɪstənt/ *noun* a member of a part of the Western Christian Church that separated from the Roman Catholic Church in the 16th century: *He was brought up a Protestant.* ■ **Prot·est·ant** *adj.*: *The majority of the population is Protestant.* ◇ *a Protestant church/country* **Prot·est·ant·ism** /ˈprɒtɪstəntɪzəm; *NAmE* ˈprɑːtɪstəntɪzəm/ *noun* [U] *the advance of Protestantism in the 16th century*

pro·test·er /prəˈtestə(r); *NAmE also* ˈproʊtestər/ *noun* a person who makes a public protest SYN DEMONSTRATOR: *The vice-president condemned anti-war protesters.*

proto·col AWL /ˈprəʊtəkɒl; *NAmE* ˈproʊtəkɔːl; ˈproʊtəkɑːl/ *noun* **1** [C, U] the accepted way of doing sth or behaving in a particular organization or situation: *Most*

NHS Trusts have protocols defining how such requests should be made. ◇ *Protocol requires that the mortgagor must allow the mortgagee to communicate with professionals involved in the sale.* **2** [C, U] a system of fixed rules and formal behaviour used at official meetings, usually between governments: *The meeting appeared to be orderly and to follow procedures and protocols.* **3** [C] a plan for performing a scientific experiment or medical treatment: *The study protocol was approved by the Independent Scientific Advisory Committee of the UK.* ◇ *Nurses are required to follow strict protocols during courses of chemotherapy.* ◇ **according to a/the ~** *After cooling to room temperature, the remaining reagents were added according to the experimental protocol.* **4** [C] the first or original version of an agreement, especially a TREATY between countries, etc; an extra part added to an agreement or TREATY: *The Kyoto protocol of 1997 followed on from the UN Framework Convention on Climate Change.* **5** [C] a set of rules that control the way data are sent between computers: *The IP (Internet protocol) address is a logical address identifying nodes across the entire Internet.*

pro·ton /ˈprəʊtɒn; *NAmE* ˈproʊtɑːn/ *noun* a very small piece of matter with a positive electric charge that forms part of the NUCLEUS (= central part) of an atom: *Deuterium has a nucleus consisting of one proton and one neutron.* ◇ *Water has the ability to both accept and donate protons from other substances.* HELP A **proton** is a **subatomic particle**. ➲ *compare* ELECTRON, NEUTRON

proto·type /ˈprəʊtətaɪp; *NAmE* ˈproʊtətaɪp/ *noun* **1** the first design of sth from which other forms are copied or developed: *Industry was to decide which designs to build as prototypes.* ◇ **~ for sth** *The prototype for lean production was a system developed by Toyota in the 1950s.* ◇ **~ of sth** *Three movies dating from the 1930s are regarded as the prototype of the gangster genre.* **2 ~ (of sth)** the first, original or typical form of sth: *He was in many ways the prototype of the 'angry young man'.* ◇ *These objects are the prototypes of a category of rapidly spinning neutron stars.* ■ **proto·typ·ical** /ˌprəʊtəˈtɪpɪkl; *NAmE* ˌproʊtəˈtɪpɪkl/ *adj.*: *Prototypical examples of large-scale, centralized energy projects in the US include the Hoover Dam and the Shippingport Nuclear Reactor.*

proud /praʊd/ *adj.* (**proud·er**, **proud·est**) **1** feeling pleased and satisfied about sth that you own or have done, or are connected with: **~ (of sb/sth/yourself)** *These immigrants remain proud of their heritage.* ◇ **~ to be/have/do sth** *They are proud to work for an organization with a good name.* **2** [only before noun] causing sb to feel pride: *The NHS has a proud tradition of providing health services to all according to their needs.* **3** (*disapproving*) feeling that you are better and more important than other people: *As these freedmen acquired great wealth, they also adopted the proud arrogance of their masters.* **4** having respect for yourself and not wanting to lose the respect of others: *They were too proud to ask for help.*

proud·ly /ˈpraʊdli/ *adv.* in a way that shows that sb is proud of sth: *The Saudis proudly proclaim their Islamic heritage and traditions.*

prov·able /ˈpruːvəbl/ *adj.* that can be shown to be true SYN VERIFIABLE: *Some knowledge is analytic, i.e. it is provable by pure reasoning.*

prove /pruːv/ *verb* (**proved**, **proved** or **proved**, **proven** /ˈpruːvn/) HELP In British English, **proved** is the more common form. Look also at **proven**. **1** [T, I] to use evidence or argument to show that sth is true: **~ sth (to sb)** *God's existence can be neither proved nor disproved by science or logic.* ◇ **~ (to sb) (that)...** *Christians had to prove to the Romans that their movement was politically harmless.* ◇ **~ otherwise** *In these cases, a dismissal is automatically considered to be unfair until the employer proves otherwise.* ◇ **~ sb/sth + adj./noun** *Testing should consist of attempts to prove a theory wrong.* ◇ **~ sb/sth to be/have sth** *This makes this assumption reasonable, but does not prove it to be correct.* ◇ **be proved/proven to do sth** *The treatment has not been proved to have lasting benefits.* ◇ **~ where/what, etc...** *The government cannot prove where the pollution is coming from.* HELP In mathematics or logic, proving a statement involves showing that it is always true by means of mathematical statements: *From these axioms, we can prove the following theorem:...* OPP DISPROVE ➲ *compare* CONFIRM (1), VERIFY (1) ➲ *see also* PROOF (1) ➲ thesaurus note *at* SHOW[1] ➲ language bank *at* EVIDENCE[1] **2** *linking verb* if sth **proves** dangerous, expensive, etc. or if it **proves to be** dangerous, etc, you discover that it is dangerous, etc. over a period of time: **+ adj.** *Achieving these aims has proved very difficult.* ◇ **+ noun** *Jackson's election in 1828 proved a turning point in American history.* ◇ **~ to be sth** *As Bishop of Alexandria, he proved to be a man of energy and bravery.* **3** [T] **~ yourself (to sb)** to show other people how good you are at doing sth or that you are capable of doing sth: *Proving themselves to each other is fundamentally important to these men.* **4** [T] to show other people that you are a particular type of person or that you have a particular quality SYN SHOW[1] (4): **~ yourself + adj/noun** *They have proved themselves able to adapt to many new challenges.* ◇ **~ yourself to be sth** *She had proved herself to be a shrewd politician.*

proven /ˈpruːvn; *BrE also* ˈprəʊvn/ *adj.* [only before noun] tested and shown to be true: *Some drug combinations are of proven value for specific purposes.*

pro·vide /prəˈvaɪd/ *verb* **1** to give sth to sb or make it available for them to use SYN SUPPLY[2]: **~ sth** *The state must enforce the rule of law and provide essential public services.* ◇ *Their results provide insight into the geographic effects of climate variability.* ◇ *Arid lands tend to be more sparsely populated, providing opportunities for comparing cultivated and uncultivated soils.* ◇ **~ sth for sb** *Special day centres have been developed to provide care for older people.* ◇ **~ sb with sth** *The International Monetary Fund and the World Bank provided Brazil with about $50 billion in loans during the 1990s.* ➲ thesaurus note *at* SUPPLY[2] **2 ~ that...** (*formal*) (of a law or rule) to state that sth will or must happen SYN STIPULATE: *If there is evidence of mental disorder, mental health laws provide that the patient can be held in hospital for a brief period.* ➲ *see also* PROVISION

PHR V **proˈvide for sb** to give sb the things that they need to live, such as food, money and clothes: *Under Islam, a woman's husband was obliged to provide for her and her children.* **proˈvide for sth** **1** to make preparations to deal with a possible future event or to make sure that sth happens or exists: *A school has a duty to provide for health, safety and security.* **2** to supply the money or other things that are needed to live or to do a particular thing: *The monks worked at the tasks needed to manage a farm and provide for the needs of the community.* **3** (of a law or rule) to state that sth will or must happen or be done: *The draft constitution provided for a bicameral legislature and assured equal rights for women.* ◇ **~ for sb/sth to do sth** *The scheme provided for all children to receive at least a basic education.*

▸ PROVIDE + NOUN **information • data • evidence • insight • overview • example • detail • answer • account, description • estimate • explanation • analysis** *A wealth of behavioural data has provided compelling evidence for the existence of a magnetic sense in a variety of animals.* | **service • care • support • guidance • advice • protection • assistance • benefit • resources • source** *Personal journals and peer discussion groups provide strong educational support for students.* | **opportunity • means, way • basis • framework • context • access • mechanism • solution • measure • incentive** *Having less or more* *income and wealth provides individuals with less or more access to goods and services.*

THESAURUS

provide • give • offer • present *verb*

These words all mean to make sth, especially information, available for people to consider or use.

- to provide/give/offer/present sth **for/to** sb
- to provide/give/offer/present sth **in** sth
- to provide/give/offer/present **information/evidence**
- to provide/give/offer/present an **example**
- to provide/give/offer (an) **account/insight/support**
- to provide/offer (an) **opportunity/guidance**

- **Provide** is more formal than **give**; **provide** is more impersonal and often used when sth is made available to people in general; **give** can be more personal, when sth is made available by or to a particular person: *Further investigations may provide useful information in this case.* ◇ *Clear explanations of what is happening must be given to patients and their families.*
- **Offer** emphasizes that sth is made available for people to use/accept or not: *Consumers often want the specialist advice offered by knowledgeable, expert retailers.* ◇ *Genetic engineering offers new opportunities but also presents new challenges in environmental protection.*
- **Present** is often used to talk about showing ideas or information in writing or in a presentation: *Summary statistics for the nine scales are presented in Table 4.3.*

See also the Thesaurus note at **supply** *verb*.

pro·vided /prəˈvaɪdɪd/ (*also* **pro·vid·ing** /prəˈvaɪdɪŋ/) *conj.* **~ (that)...** used to say what must happen or be done to make it possible for sth else to happen SYN IF: *Provided that conditions are sufficiently wet, plant matter will accumulate more quickly than it is decomposed, forming peat.* ◇ *Geothermal heat pumps are saving over four million tons of carbon dioxide a year (provided they displace gas as the heating fuel).*

pro·vider /prəˈvaɪdə(r)/ *noun* a person or an organization that supplies sb with sth they need or want: *Health system records include records maintained by hospitals, doctors and other health care providers.* ◇ **~ of sth** *CLT-UFA is a major provider of films, sports and other entertainment to European and American networks.* ➲ *see also* SERVICE PROVIDER

prov·ince /ˈprɒvɪns; *NAmE* ˈprɑːvɪns/ *noun* **1** [C] one of the areas that some countries are divided into with its own local government: *Ontario is the largest Canadian province.* ◇ **~ of sth** *Cantonese is widely spoken in the southern provinces of China.* **2 the provinces** [pl.] (*BrE*) all the parts of a country except the capital city: *He played in London and in the provinces to ecstatic audiences.* **3** [sing.] **~ (of sb)** a particular area of knowledge, interest or responsibility: *Empirically testing hypotheses is often presumed to be wholly the province of scientists.*

pro·vin·cial /prəˈvɪnʃl/ *adj.* **1** [only before noun] connected with one of the large areas that some countries are divided into, with its own local government: *Educational services were decentralized from the federal to the provincial governments.* ◇ *In Indonesia, the equator runs through Pontianak, the provincial capital of West Kalimantan.* **2** [usually before noun] connected with the parts of a country that do not include the capital city: *Sleepy provincial towns had become bustling commercial cities.* **3** (*disapproving*) unwilling to consider new or different ideas or things: *Contemporary artists offer an antidote to provincial and conventional habits of thought.*

pro·vi·sion /prəˈvɪʒn/ *noun* **1** [U] the act of supplying sb with sth that they need or want; sth that is supplied: *Titmuss argued that state welfare provision should be universal.* ◇ **~ of sth** *The principle of public provision of services, funded by governments, is widely accepted but not universally applied.* ◇ *Applications of the solar battery have included the provision of power for spacecraft and for pocket calculators and watches.* **2** [U, C] **~ for sb/sth** preparations that you make to deal with sth that may or will happen or be needed: *Governments and communities have responsibilities in terms of provision for people with special needs.* ◇ *Provisions must be made for appropriate back-up when regular staff are not available.* **3** [C] a condition or an arrangement in a legal document: *The Act contains a further provision allowing different levels of fees to be charged.* ◇ **~ for sth** *The Montreal Protocol included provisions for a phase-out of methyl bromide by 2005.* ➲ *see also* PROVIDE

pro·vi·sion·al /prəˈvɪʒənl/ *adj.* made for the present time, possibly to be changed when more information is available or when a more permanent arrangement can be made: *It is often possible to make a provisional diagnosis on these results.* ◇ *A committee of peers and privy councillors formed themselves into a provisional government in the absence of the king.* ■ **pro·vi·sion·al·ly** /prəˈvɪʒənəli/ *adv.*: *He began to tell the story which he provisionally entitled 'Alice's Adventures Underground'.*

provo·ca·tion /ˌprɒvəˈkeɪʃn; *NAmE* ˌprɑːvəˈkeɪʃn/ *noun* [U, C] **1** the act of doing or saying sth deliberately in order to make sb react strongly, especially with anger: *They made sure that their demonstrations remained peaceful in the face of provocation.* ◇ *The defence of provocation is not suitable in cases where the defendant kills out of revenge.* **2** (*medical*) the process of performing a test on sb in order to get a particular response: **+ noun** *The reaction was confirmed with a provocation test.*

pro·voca·tive /prəˈvɒkətɪv; *NAmE* prəˈvɑːkətɪv/ *adj.* intended to produce arguments or discussion, or to cause strong reactions: *The book raises some provocative questions about American psychoanalysis and its understanding of race.* ◇ *In the eyes of the 'establishment', these views were provocative and outrageous.* ■ **pro·voca·tive·ly** *adv.*: *Derrida declared famously and provocatively that 'there is nothing outside the text'.*

P

pro·voke /prəˈvəʊk; *NAmE* prəˈvoʊk/ *verb* **1 ~ sth** to cause a particular reaction or have a particular effect: *The book provoked a heated debate over Korean historiography.* ◇ *Entering online environments and recording the conversation for research purposes can provoke hostile responses from users.* ➲ *see also* THOUGHT-PROVOKING **2** to say or do sth in order to produce a strong reaction from sb, usually anger: **~ sb** *Bishops advised their followers not to seek martyrdom or to provoke the authorities.* ◇ **~ sb into (doing) sth** *Nothing could have been more calculated to provoke them into action.* ◇ **~ sb to do sth** *The other person reacted in a way which then provoked the defendant to lose his self-control.*

prox·imal /ˈprɒksɪməl; *NAmE* ˈprɑːksɪməl/ *adj.* (*anatomy*) located towards the centre of the body; furthest from the end part: *The proximal small intestine appears dilated.* ◇ **~ to sth** *Swelling developed just proximal to the knee joint.* OPP DISTAL (1)

prox·im·ate /ˈprɒksɪmət; *NAmE* ˈprɑːksɪmət/ *adj.* [usually before noun] (*technical*) nearest in time, space or order to sth; most immediate: *Although the proximate causes of pandemics are microbial or viral, there are ancillary causes of almost equal importance.* ◇ *He defines a cluster as 'a geographically proximate group of companies and associated institutions in a particular field'.*

prox·im·ity /prɒkˈsɪməti; *NAmE* prɑːkˈsɪməti/ *noun* [U] the state of being near sb/sth in distance or time: *Marine organisms often occur as genetically distinct populations* *despite geographical proximity.* ◇ **in ~** *All three schools were in close proximity.* ◇ **~ to sb/sth** *Patterns of soil moisture depend on proximity to water sources.* ◇ **~ of sb/sth** *The number of early retirement predictors was clearly dependent on the proximity of old-age retirement.*

proxy /ˈprɒksi; *NAmE* ˈprɑːksi/ *noun* (*pl.* **-ies**) **1** [U] the authority that you give to sb to do sth for you, when you cannot do it yourself: **by ~** *The ability of shareholders to vote at meetings is limited, with widespread difficulty reported in voting by proxy.* ◇ **+ noun** *The proxy voting process is a key mechanism by which shareholders monitor corporate managers.* **2** [C, U] a person who has been given the authority to represent sb else: *A member is entitled to vote through a proxy and the company may not deny this right.* ◇ **~ for sb** *In the past, health professionals may have been useful proxies for their patients.* **3** [C] (*technical*) something that you use to represent sth else that you are trying to measure or calculate: **~ for sth** *Using free lunch status as a proxy for socio-economic status, we found that 44% of Latino students received free or reduced-price lunch.* ◇ **+ noun** *Two Nordic studies used proxy measures to assess trends.*

pru·dent /ˈpruːdnt/ *adj.* making judgements and decisions in a sensible and careful way, especially in order to avoid unnecessary risks: *The most pressing concern for every prudent emperor was the identification and grooming of a successor.* ◇ **it is ~ to do sth** *It is prudent to advise pregnant women to abstain from alcohol throughout pregnancy.* HELP In law, the terms **prudent** and **prudence** are used to refer to a person or behaviour that most reasonable people would regard as careful and sensible: *The standard of behaviour expected of a minor is not that of an adult, but rather that of a prudent and reasonable child.* ■ **pru·dence** /ˈpruːdns/ *noun* [U] *There is a need to exercise prudence in such important matters.* **pru·dent·ly** *adv.*: *It became apparent that the banking system had not been supervised prudently and effectively enough.*

P

psy·chi·at·ric /ˌsaɪkiˈætrɪk/ *adj.* connected with psychiatry or with mental illness: *Obsessional symptoms occur also in other psychiatric disorders, especially anxiety and depression.* ◇ *They studied a sample of 176 psychiatric patients with schizophrenia, bipolar disorder or major depression.* ◇ *psychiatric hospitals/treatment/care*

psych·iatrist /saɪˈkaɪətrɪst/ *noun* a doctor who studies and treats mental illnesses: *Most patients with anorexia nervosa are very reluctant to see a psychiatrist.*

psych·iatry /saɪˈkaɪətri/ *noun* [U] the study and treatment of mental illness: *In psychiatry, the term 'disorder' is preferred because few conditions have the established physical pathology that is implied by the term 'disease'.*

psy·chic /ˈsaɪkɪk/ (*also less frequent* **psych·ical** /ˈsaɪkɪkl/) *adj.* **1** connected with strange powers of the mind and not able to be explained by natural laws: *Schizophrenics may be convinced that people with psychic powers are forcing them to act the way they do.* **2** connected with the mind rather than the body: *The novel can be read as depicting 'the physical and psychic landscapes of the East'.*

psy·cho·analy·sis /ˌsaɪkəʊəˈnæləsɪs; *NAmE* ˌsaɪkoʊəˈnæləsɪs/ (*also* **an·aly·sis**) *noun* [U] a method of treating mental illness by investigating the influence of the unconscious mind, by getting sb to talk about their fears, past experiences, dreams, etc: *Freudian psychoanalysis understands childhood as the source of repression and anxiety.* ■ **psy·cho·ana·lyt·ic** /ˌsaɪkəʊˌænəˈlɪtɪk; *NAmE* ˌsaɪkoʊˌænəˈlɪtɪk/ *adj.* [only before noun] *Psychoanalytic theories interpret denial as a coping strategy based on childhood experiences.*

psy·cho·logic·al AWL /ˌsaɪkəˈlɒdʒɪkl; *NAmE* ˌsaɪkəˈlɑːdʒɪkl/ *adj.* **1** [usually before noun] connected with a person's mind and the way it works: *There may be a tendency to channel psychological distress into physical symptoms.* ◇ *psychological well-being/health* ◇ *psychological factors/problems/symptoms* ◇ *The awareness of wind turbine noise varies greatly and appears to be partly psychological.* **2** [only before noun] connected with the study of psychology: *A large body of psychological research shows that women place greater value on group relationships than men do.* ◇ *Psychological tests are more frequently admitted as evidence in court today.* ■ **psy·cho·logic·al·ly** AWL /ˌsaɪkəˈlɒdʒɪkli; *NAmE* ˌsaɪkəˈlɑːdʒɪkli/ *adv.*: *Benedict's community was cut off physically and psychologically from the surrounding world.*

psych·olo·gist AWL /saɪˈkɒlədʒɪst; *NAmE* saɪˈkɑːlədʒɪst/ *noun* a scientist who studies psychology: *Attitudes are what psychologists call affective, in that they are linked to our emotional states.* ◇ *a cognitive/clinical/paediatric psychologist*

psych·ology AWL /saɪˈkɒlədʒi; *NAmE* saɪˈkɑːlədʒi/ *noun* **1** [U] the scientific study of the mind and how it influences behaviour: *The field of psychology has contributed greatly to our understanding of customers' perceptions of prices.* ◇ *cognitive/social/evolutionary psychology* **2** [U, sing.] the way that people think and therefore behave in a particular situation: *Understanding buyer psychology is of fundamental importance to marketing.* ◇ **~ of sth** *The article brings into focus the importance of understanding the psychology of dispute resolution.*

psych·osis /saɪˈkəʊsɪs; *NAmE* saɪˈkoʊsɪs/ *noun* (*pl.* **psych·oses** /saɪˈkəʊsiːz; *NAmE* saɪˈkoʊsiːz/) [U, C] a serious mental illness that makes a person lose contact with reality: *Symptoms of psychosis include hallucinations, delusions and disorganized thought.*

psy·cho·ther·apy /ˌsaɪkəʊˈθerəpi; *NAmE* ˌsaɪkoʊˈθerəpi/ (*also* **ther·apy**) *noun* [U] the treatment of mental illness by discussing sb's problems with them rather than by giving them drugs: *Options for those who fail to respond to standard treatments include changing to a different form of psychotherapy.* ■ **psy·cho·ther·ap·ist** /ˌsaɪkəʊˈθerəpɪst; *NAmE* ˌsaɪkoʊˈθerəpɪst/ (*also* **ther·ap·ist**) *noun*: *The sessions were led by trained psychotherapists and all sessions were supervised.*

psych·ot·ic /saɪˈkɒtɪk; *NAmE* saɪˈkɑːtɪk/ *adj.* suffering from or connected with psychosis: *Once she is alone in the flat, Carol becomes increasingly psychotic and delusional.* ◇ *In schizophrenia, the patient suffers from psychotic symptoms and functional impairment.*

pu·berty /ˈpjuːbəti; *NAmE* ˈpjuːbərti/ *noun* [U] the period of a person's life during which their sexual organs develop and they become capable of having children: *About one third of children died before reaching puberty.* ⊃ *compare* ADOLESCENCE

pub·lic[1] /ˈpʌblɪk/ *adj.* **1** [only before noun] connected with ordinary people in society in general: *The fairness of these rules is a matter of public interest.* ◇ *Pressure groups can have an impact by winning a high level of public support.* ◇ *public concern/confidence/awareness/participation* ⊃ *see also* PUBLIC OPINION, PUBLIC RELATIONS **2** [only before noun] provided or available for the use of people in general: *Several countries have now introduced a ban on smoking in public places.* ◇ *Many communities have been eliminating virtually all public spaces, like parks, playgrounds and beaches.* OPP PRIVATE[1] (1) ⊃ *see also* PUBLIC SERVICE, PUBLIC TRANSPORT **3** [only before noun] paid for or connected with the government as opposed to a private company or individual: *There were relatively high levels of public expenditure and taxation.* ◇ *Public authorities include central and local government, schools and universities, the National Health Service, the police, and publicly* *owned companies.* ◇ *public spending/education/institutions* OPP PRIVATE¹ (2) ➲ *see also* PUBLIC SCHOOL (2), PUBLIC SECTOR, PUBLIC WORKS **4** involving activities and people not connected to sb's home, family or private life: *They established secular states and limited the role of religion in public life.* ◇ *After the transition to democracy, women gained more presence in the public sphere.* OPP PRIVATE¹ (4) ➲ *see also* PUBLIC AFFAIRS, PUBLIC DOMAIN **5** able or intended to be seen, heard or known by people in general: *These monuments were highly public advertisements of a family's or an individual's status in the community.* ◇ *The agreement was made public only in the form of a press release.* OPP PRIVATE¹ (5)

IDM **go ˈpublic 1** to tell people in general about sth that has only been known to a few people: *The head of the inquiry went public to say that 'the state had lost the momentum for reform'.* **2** (of a company) to start selling shares on the STOCK EXCHANGE: *After ten years, the company went public and the share price doubled to US$50 in the first month.* **in the public ˈeye** well known to many people, for example through newspapers and television: *Organizations with famous brand names are more likely to engage the attention of campaigners because they are in the public eye.* ➲ *more at* KNOWLEDGE

pub·lic² /ˈpʌblɪk/ *noun* **1 the public** [sing.+ sing./pl. v.] ordinary people in society in general: *News media have the potential to educate the public on a variety of health issues.* ◇ *The jury consisted of 15 members of the public.* ◇ *Since the 1960s, the American public has demanded increasingly more goods and services from their government.* ➲ *see also* GENERAL PUBLIC **2** [C+sing./pl. v.] a group of people who share a particular interest or who are involved in the same activity: *Between 1780 and 1820, the reading public grew in numbers, income and sophistication.* ◇ *The Romantic poet communicated directly with his public, rejecting politeness and form.* ◇ *These novelists brought the issue of factory conditions to the attention of a much wider public.*

IDM **in ˈpublic** in a place when other people, especially people you do not know, are present: *Women were ridiculed and arrested for speaking in public and marching in the streets.* ➲ *compare* IN PRIVATE

ˌpublic afˈfairs *noun* [pl.] issues, activities and questions connected with society, the economy and politics, and that affect ordinary people in general: *Women have a right to seek employment and to participate in public affairs.*

pub·li·ca·tion AWL /ˌpʌblɪˈkeɪʃn/ *noun* **1** [U] the act of printing a book, a report, an article, etc. and making it available to the public: *The novel sold over two million copies in the year following its publication.* ◇ *The article was accepted for publication in May 1953.* ◇ **~ of sth** *Since the publication of the Acheson report into health inequalities in 1988, the need for a radical approach has been recognized.* **2** [C] a book, an article, etc. that has been published: *His recent publications include 'Rififi: a French Film Guide' (2009) and, with Julian Stringer, 'Japanese Cinema: Texts and Contexts' (2007).* ◇ *Scepticism is built into the refereeing process for scientific publications submitted to academic journals.* **3** [U] **~ (of sth)** the act of making sth generally known, for example by printing it in a newspaper: *A period of months might elapse between students taking an examination and publication of the results.*

ˌpublic ˈcompany (*also* **ˌpublic ˌlimited ˈcompany**) (*both BrE*) (*NAmE* **ˌpublic corpoˈration**) *noun* (*abbr.* **plc, PLC**) a company that sells shares in itself to the public: *Public companies are subject to a stricter regulatory regime than private companies because of their dealings with the general public.*

ˌpublic doˈmain *noun* [sing.] something that is in the **public domain** is available for everyone to use or to discuss and is not secret: **in the ~** *Commercially sensitive information will have no competitive advantage if it is placed in the public domain.*

ˌpublic ˈgood *noun* **1** [C] (*economics*) something that is provided to all members of a society without profit, either by the government or by a private individual or organization: *Local governments are more capable than national governments of tailoring the provision of public goods and services to the needs of local citizens (Tiebout, 1956; Klugman, 1994).* **2 the public good** [sing.] the benefit or general health and happiness of the public: *The organization needs to give broader and more concrete meaning to its claims to serve the public good.*

ˌpublic ˈhealth *noun* [U] services to protect the health of the public, such as providing SANITATION and preventing disease: *The additive does not constitute a real danger to public health.* ◇ **+ noun** *Many public health measures aim specifically at protecting and promoting the health of children.*

pub·li·city /pʌbˈlɪsəti/ *noun* [U] **1** the attention that is given to sb/sth by newspapers, television, etc: *The case received much publicity in Britain.* ◇ *The decision led to considerable negative publicity when the story was leaked.* **2** the business of attracting the attention of the public to sth/sb; the things that are done to attract attention: **~ (for sth/sb)** *Sponsorship can be used very effectively to generate favourable publicity for the sponsor.* ◇ **+ noun** *The company signed up 340 000 customers in the first eight weeks following a big publicity campaign.*

pub·li·cize (*BrE also* **-ise**) /ˈpʌblɪsaɪz/ *verb* **~ sth** to make sth known to the public: *He publicized his ideas on computer design in a series of lectures.* ◇ *Since 1995 in Chile, average school test scores have been widely publicized in newspapers.* ◇ *There have been a number of highly publicized pollution incidents.*

ˌpublic ˌlimited ˈcompany *noun* (*BrE*) (*abbr.* **plc, PLC**) = PUBLIC COMPANY

pub·lic·ly /ˈpʌblɪkli/ *adv.* **1** in a way that can be seen, heard or known by people in general: *He did not speak publicly about his personal suffering until well into the 1970s.* ◇ *Many of these drugs are publicly available over the Internet.* ◇ *Obama publicly supported this action.* OPP PRIVATELY (2) **2** by the state or government, rather than by a private company or individual: *Supports for working families, such as publicly funded childcare, are only minimally available.* ◇ *Much of the infrastructure of a city—including streets, sewers, lighting and the water supply system—is publicly owned.* OPP PRIVATELY (1) **3** in a way that affects or concerns ordinary people in society in general: *Parliament is publicly accountable through direct elections.* **4** on a STOCK EXCHANGE: *For diversified business groups, shares of operating companies are often listed and publicly traded.*

ˌpublic oˈpinion *noun* [U] the opinions that people in society have about an issue: *The mass media have become more influential in shaping public opinion.*

ˌpublic ˈpolicy *noun* [U, C] the principles, especially those which have not been officially written down, on which social laws are based: *Many who seek to influence public policy do so by telling legislators what they want.* ◇ **+ noun** *There are a few public policy issues, such as abortion, gun control and school prayer, about which Americans have strong opinions.* ◇ *The public policy aspects of wind energy are wide-ranging and very complicated.*

ˌpublic reˈlations *noun* **1** [U] (*abbr.* **PR**) the business of giving the public information about a particular organization or person in order to create a good impression: *Many party leaders in the past were not particularly skilful at public relations and presentation.* ◇ **+ noun** *Corporations*

P

hire public relations firms and spend billions on advertising. **2** [pl.] the state of the relationship between an organization and the public: *Offering community services can be a useful way of building good public relations in the local area.*

ˌpublic ˈschool *noun* [C, U] **1** (in the UK, especially England) a private school for young people between the ages of 13 and 18, whose parents pay for their education. The students often live at the school while they are studying: *Conservative MPs usually come from established middle-class families and many have been to public schools.* ➲ *compare* PRIVATE SCHOOL **2** **ˈpublic school** (in the US, Australia, Scotland and other countries) a free local school paid for by the government: *The vast majority of American children go to public schools that are financed not by tuition payments but by tax dollars.*

the ˌpublic ˈsector *noun* [sing.] the part of the economy of a country that is owned or controlled by the government: *The expected decrease in the number of jobs in the public sector is likely to have a disproportionate impact on women.* ◇ **+ noun** *It was claimed that public sector enterprises achieve inferior performance in terms of the efficient use of resources.* ➲ *compare* PRIVATE SECTOR

ˌpublic ˈservice *noun* **1** [C] a service such as transport or health care that a government or an official organization provides for people in general in a particular society: *All of the villages studied are poor and lack public services.* **2** [C, U] something that is done to help people rather than to make a profit: *This is a definition of broadcasting as a public service rather than a business.* ◇ *He was rewarded for his years of outstanding public service.* **3** [U] the government and government departments: *He spent forty years in public service as a legislator, governor, congressman and diplomat.*

ˌpublic ˈtransport (*BrE*) (*NAmE* ˌpublic transporˈtation) *noun* [U] the system of buses, trains, etc. provided by the government or by companies, which people use to travel from one place to another: *In cities there is better provision of public transport, which is more energy-efficient than private vehicle use.* ◇ **+ noun** *More investment is required to renew the public transport system.*

ˌpublic ˈworks *noun* [pl.] building work, such as that of hospitals, schools and roads, that is paid for by the government: *They undertook extensive public works, including major repairs and extensions to the sewage system.* ◇ **+ noun** *The public authority can use the revenue to finance additional roads or other public works projects.*

pub·lish AWL /ˈpʌblɪʃ/ *verb* **1** [T] **~ sth** to produce a book, magazine, etc. and sell it to the public: *The Foundation publishes books, magazines and newspapers.* ◇ *The novel's first edition was published by W. H. Allen in 1958.* **2** [T] to print a letter, an article, etc. in a newspaper or magazine: **~ sth** *The diversity of approaches is evident in the range of journals that publish articles on student behaviour.* ◇ **~ sth in sth** *Only articles published in peer reviewed journals were included in this review.* **3** [T, I] (of an author) to have your work printed in a newspaper, magazine, etc, or printed and sold to the public: **~ (sth)** *He has published numerous books on film aesthetics and history.* ◇ *James decided to publish under the pseudonym Danny Santiago.* ◇ **~ on sth** *Professor Henri Bejoint has published extensively on lexicography.* **4** [T] to make information available to the public SYN RELEASE[1] (5): **~ sth** *The Commission's final report was published in June 2009.* ◇ **~ sth on/in sth** *The project is a good example of reporting using the Internet: results are published on a purpose-built website.*

▸ PUBLISH + NOUN **newspaper • magazine • journal • volume • edition** *There, during the First World War, a small group of anarchists published a journal called 'New Society'.* | **book • work • novel • memoir • biography • monograph** *He published his major philosophical work, 'Meditations on First Philosophy', in 1641.* | **article • paper • study • essay • poem • pamphlet • document • review • material** *Only four of Wilfred Owen's poems were published in his lifetime.* | **report • study • research • work • letter** *Wright et al. (2003) published a very interesting study of raven roosts.* | **findings, results • data, information • guidelines, guidance • statement** *Their findings were published in January 2011.*

▸ ADVERB + PUBLISH **recently • previously • first, originally** *In a recently published study conducted in 13 European countries, Borrell et al. showed that...*

▸ PUBLISH + ADVERB **posthumously • anonymously • separately • together** *While pregnant, Wollstonecraft wrote 'Maria: or, The Wrongs of Women', published posthumously in 1798.* | **extensively, widely • jointly** *The author has published widely on animal consciousness.* | **annually • regularly • elsewhere** *The results are published annually on the NCQA website.*

pub·lish·er AWL /ˈpʌblɪʃə(r)/ *noun* a person or company that prepares and prints books, magazines, newspapers or electronic products and makes them available to the public: *It was very difficult for Popper to find a publisher for what became one of the century's most influential philosophical works.*

pub·lish·ing AWL /ˈpʌblɪʃɪŋ/ *noun* [U] the profession, business or activity of preparing books, articles, etc. and selling them or making them available to the public: *Access to scientific publications will be addressed by electronic publishing.* ◇ **+ noun** *Calder and Boyars was a small independent publishing house specializing in avant-garde writing.*

pull[1] /pʊl/ *verb* **1** [T, I] **~ (sth)** to hold sth firmly and use force in order to move it or try to move it towards yourself: *Concrete is strong when squashed but weak when pulled.* ◇ *The chain is connected to a pulling mechanism.* **2** [T] **~ sth + adv./prep.** to remove sth from a place by pulling: *Pull out the plug when the machine is not in use.* **3** [T] to move sb/sth in a particular direction by pulling: **~ sb/sth + adv./prep.** *As there is an attractive force here, the electron is pulled towards the nucleus.* ◇ **~ sth** *Wagons were pulled either by people or by animals.* **4** [T] **~ sth/yourself + adv./prep.** to move your body or a part of your body in a particular direction, especially using force: *The spinning figure skater increases her rate of spin by pulling in her extended arms.* ◇ (*figurative*) *Education will enable them to pull themselves out of poverty.* **5** [T] **~ sth** to move a switch, etc. towards yourself or down in order to operate a machine or piece of equipment: *When the handle is pulled in one of the carriages, the driver knows that a problem has arisen.* **6** [T] **~ sb/sth (in)** to attract the interest or support of sb/sth: *The ability of a brand name to pull customers in is therefore crucial.*

IDM **pull in different/opposite diˈrections** to have different aims that cannot be achieved together without causing problems: *These different demands may seem to pull in different directions, since some promote integration while others seem to reinforce segregation.* **pull your ˈweight** to work as hard as everyone else in a job or activity: *Ackroyd and Crowdy (1990) report that workers perceived as not pulling their weight were continually harassed by their colleagues.*

PHR V **ˌpull sth aˈpart** to separate sth into pieces by pulling different parts of it in different directions: *Today, earth scientists generally reserve the word 'rift' for places where the earth's crust is being pulled apart.* **ˌpull ˈback** **1** (of an army) to move back from a place SYN WITHDRAW (1): *Troops were visibly weakening and starting to pull back from their positions.* **2** to decide not to do sth that you were intending to do, because of possible problems SYN WITHDRAW (5): *Since the early 1980s, there has been a* *tendency for government to pull back from direct intervention in economic affairs.* **ˌpull sth ˈdown 1** to destroy a building or other structure completely: *Cortes had ordered that all houses should be pulled down and burnt.* **2** to cause prices or the level of sth to decrease: *A decline in aggregate demand pulls down employment.* **ˌpull ˈout (of sth)** to move away from sth or stop being involved in it SYN WITHDRAW (5): *Norway was to have joined them but pulled out after a referendum.* **ˌpull toˈgether** to act or work together with other people in an organized way and without fighting: *In our focus groups, participants talked about everyone pulling together at a time of crisis.* **ˌpull sth toˈgether** to gather different ideas or facts into one account or argument: *This book pulls together a wide range of evidence supporting the theory.* **ˌpull sth ˈup** to cause prices or the level of sth to increase: *High demand pulls up prices.*

pull² /pʊl/ *noun* **1** [sing.] a strong physical force that makes sth move in a particular direction: **~ (of sth)** *Waves are caused by wind; tides result from the gravitational pull of the moon.* ◇ **~ on sth** *These filaments exert a pull on the cell membrane.* **2** [C, usually sing.] the fact of sth attracting you or having a strong effect on you: **~ (of sth)** *Although the family did not spend much time in Palestine during his early life, they continued to feel the pull of their ancestral homeland.* ◇ **+ noun** *Push factors are those that drive a person away from his place of residence, while pull factors are those which draw him to a new destination.* ➲ *compare* PUSH² (2)

pul·mon·ary /ˈpʌlmənəri; *NAmE* ˈpʌlməneri/ *adj.* [only before noun] (*medical*) connected with the lungs: *A history of cardiac or pulmonary disease may indicate right heart failure.*

pulse¹ /pʌls/ *noun* **1** [usually sing.] the regular beat of blood as it is sent around the body, that can be felt in different places, especially on the inside part of the wrist; the number of times the blood beats in a minute: *There are many causes of an irregular pulse.* ◇ *Patients should be taught how to take their own pulse.* ◇ **+ noun** *The patient looks flushed and has a pulse rate of 120/min.* **2** a single short increase in the amount of light, sound, electricity or other wave produced by sth: *The two sources each emit a pulse at the exact same instant (see Figure 6a).* ◇ *A short laser pulse is composed of a wide range of frequencies.*

pulse² /pʌls/ *verb* [usually passive] to make a wave or BEAM become a series of pulses: **be pulsed** *The frequency at which the lamp is pulsed is normally 50 Hz.* ◇ **pulsed + noun** *The CO_2 lasers can produce high average power and generate both continuous and pulsed beams.*

pump¹ /pʌmp/ *noun* a machine that is used to force liquid, gas or air into or out of sth: *A ground source heat pump is an energy-efficient method of supplying heat to a building.*

pump² /pʌmp/ *verb* **~ sth (+ adv./prep.)** to make water, air, gas, etc. flow in a particular direction by using a pump or sth that works like a pump: *The left side of the heart pumps blood to the rest of the body.*
PHR V **ˌpump sth ˈinto sth** to put a lot of a particular thing into sth: *This would have the effect of pumping more money into the economy.*

punc·tu·ate /ˈpʌŋktʃueɪt/ *verb* **1** [T, often passive] to happen occasionally during a period of time; to be located in various places all through an area: **~ sth** *The European conflicts which punctuated the king's long reign also gave rise to several peace conferences.* ◇ **~ sth with sth** *The text is nicely punctuated with photos and maps.* **2** [I, T] **~ (sth)** to divide writing into sentences and phrases by using special marks, for example COMMAS, question marks, etc: *The guide will help editors of texts to decide how to punctuate.*

punc·tu·ation /ˌpʌŋktʃuˈeɪʃn/ *noun* [U] the marks used in writing that divide sentences and phrases; the system of using these marks: *Students audit the oral history interviews, correcting spelling and adding punctuation as necessary.* ◇ **+ noun** *a punctuation mark/symbol*

pun·ish /ˈpʌnɪʃ/ *verb* **1** to make sb suffer because they have broken the law or done sth wrong: **~ sb** *Restorative justice focused on repairing the harm caused by crime rather than punishing offenders.* ◇ **~ sb for (doing) sth** *Relatives of servicemen who deserted could no longer be punished for the desertion.* **2 ~ sth (by/with sth)** to set the punishment for a particular crime: *Failure to follow the requirements constitutes a criminal offence that may be punished with a fine.*

pun·ish·ment /ˈpʌnɪʃmənt/ *noun* [U, C] an act or a way of punishing sb: *Ottoman sultans were allowed to inflict punishment, including execution, without even proof of crime, to preserve public order.* ◇ **~ for sth** *Punishments for quite minor crimes could also be severe.* ➲ *see also* CAPITAL PUNISHMENT

pupil /ˈpjuːpl/ *noun* **1** (*especially BrE*) a person who is being taught, especially a child in a school: *The first of these studies focuses on primary school pupils.* **2** a person who is taught particular skills by an expert: *It was Plato's star pupil Aristotle who founded the great institution of scientific learning at Athens, the Lyceum.* **3** the small round black area at the centre of the eye: *Causes of an abnormally dilated pupil include drugs, nerve damage and glaucoma.*

pur·chase¹ AWL /ˈpɜːtʃəs; *NAmE* ˈpɜːrtʃəs/ *noun* **1** [C, U] the act or process of buying sth: *Men are more likely than women to make purchases on the web.* ◇ **~ of sth** *As more people have jobs, there is more wage income to pay for the purchase of consumer goods.* **2** [C] something that sb has bought: *Customers buying from a shop usually take possession of their purchases straight away.* **3** [U, sing.] **~ (on sth)** (*formal*) a way of understanding or controlling sth: *He starts with an examination of whether Freud, Klein or Winnicott might offer some purchase on the phenomenon.*

P

pur·chase² AWL /ˈpɜːtʃəs; *NAmE* ˈpɜːrtʃəs/ *verb* to buy sth: **~ sth** *Consumers typically purchase products on the basis of price, convenience and quality.* ◇ **~ sth from sb** *The treaties ensured that a certain quantity of beans would be purchased from particular suppliers each year.*

pur·chaser AWL /ˈpɜːtʃəsə(r); *NAmE* ˈpɜːrtʃəsər/ *noun* **~ (for/of sth)** a person who buys sth SYN BUYER (1): *The absence of a public market may make it more difficult for a shareholder to find a purchaser for his or her shares.*

pur·chas·ing AWL /ˈpɜːtʃəsɪŋ; *NAmE* ˈpɜːrtʃəsɪŋ/ *noun* [U] the activity of buying things: **~ (of sth)** *These characteristics make the purchasing of business services a relatively high-risk decision for potential customers.* ◇ **+ noun** *A large amount of information about consumer purchasing behaviour is available.*

ˈpurchasing power *noun* [U] **1 ~ (of sb/sth)** money that people have available to buy goods and services with: *The purchasing power of the younger age group has also increased.* HELP In economics, the term **purchasing power** is only used in the second meaning (below). **2 ~ (of sth)** (*economics*) the amount that a unit of money can buy: *GDP is measured at market exchange rates that do not necessarily reflect the relative purchasing power of currencies.*

pure /pjʊə(r); *NAmE* pjʊr/ *adj.* (**purer** /ˈpjʊərə(r); *NAmE* ˈpjʊrər/, **purest** /ˈpjʊərɪst; *NAmE* ˈpjʊrɪst/) **1** not mixed with anything else; with nothing added: *Copper generally is fairly pure, but may contain some other metallic or semimetallic elements.* ◇ *The resulting rock is often pure white, and is a favoured material for ornamental building stone or sculpture.* **2** not containing anything that is not important or not necessary: *They cherished a romantic* *notion of pure art, devoid of social responsibility.* ◇ *In no respect, according to Spencer, does industrial society exist in a pure state.* **3** not containing any harmful substances, or substances that are not wanted: *The marketing campaign for the bottled water implied that tap water was not pure.* **4** [only before noun] complete and total SYN SHEER (1): *These similarities must be due to more than pure chance.* **5** [only before noun] concerned with the knowledge of a particular subject, rather than with using this knowledge in practical ways: *It is also highly instructive to examine the relationship between pure and applied science in the development of practical ideas.* ➲ *compare* APPLIED **6** morally good, especially with regard to sexual matters: *Young people often sit uncomfortably somewhere in between being a child, innocent, pure, and in need of adult protection, and being an independent adult.* **7** (of a sound) clear and perfect: *The note produced by an instrument is not a pure tone.* ➲ *see also* PURIFY, PURITY

IDM ˌ**pure and** ˈ**simple** [after noun] involving only the thing mentioned: *As a writer he was regarded as apolitical, 'a man of letters, pure and simple'.*

pure·ly /ˈpjʊəli; *NAmE* ˈpjʊrli/ *adv.* only; completely: *In purely economic terms, losses are potentially massive.* ◇ *These partnerships are based purely on self-interest.* ◇ **~ as sth | ~ for sth** *These cases have been lumped together into one category purely for convenience.* ◇ **~ in terms of sth** *Few firms can afford to think of marketing purely in terms of their domestic market.*

puri·fi·ca·tion /ˌpjʊərɪfɪˈkeɪʃn; *NAmE* ˌpjʊrɪfɪˈkeɪʃn/ *noun* [U, C] **1** the act or process of making sth pure by removing anything that is bad, unpleasant or not wanted: **~ (of sth)** *Purification of the sample requires several changes of solvent.* ◇ **+ noun** *This is a relatively new water purification technique.* **2 ~ (of sth) (from sth)** (*technical*) the act or process of separating a pure form of a substance from a mixture that contains it, or of removing IMPURITIES from a substance: *The experiment outlined in Fig. 7.14 describes the efficient purification of ADH from the bakers' yeast.* **3** the act or process of making sb pure by removing evil, especially in a ceremony: *The pilgrimage requires ritual purification.*

P

pur·ify /ˈpjʊərɪfaɪ; *NAmE* ˈpjʊrɪfaɪ/ *verb* (**puri·fies**, **puri·fy·ing**, **puri·fied**, **puri·fied**) **1 ~ sth** to make sth pure by removing anything that is bad, unpleasant or not wanted: *The survey showed that 40 per cent of households were purifying their water.* **2** [often passive] (*technical*) to separate a pure form of a substance from a mixture that contains it; to remove the IMPURITIES from a substance: **be purified (from sth)** *The aspirin was purified from the pain relieving tablets by recrystallization.* **3 ~ sb/yourself** to make sb/yourself pure by removing evil, especially in a ceremony: *The people were encouraged to pray, repent and purify themselves.*

pur·ity /ˈpjʊərəti; *NAmE* ˈpjʊrəti/ *noun* **1** [U, sing.] the state or quality of not being mixed with anything else or of not having anything added: *The degree of purity can be improved by this method.* ◇ **~ of sth** *The pharmaceutical form of heroin, diamorphine, has a purity of 99.5%, whereas the purity of street heroin is typically about 40%.* ➲ *compare* IMPURITY (2) **2** [U] the fact of being morally good, especially in sexual matters; the fact of not containing or being affected by anything bad or unpleasant: *Her beauty became a symbol of spiritual purity and innocence.*

pur·port /pəˈpɔːt; *NAmE* pərˈpɔːrt/ *verb* **~ to be/have/do sth** (*formal*) to claim to be, have or do sth, when this may not be true: *Some critics have taken issue with the ways in which aid agencies purport to speak on behalf of refugees.*

pur·ported /pəˈpɔːtɪd; *NAmE* pərˈpɔːrtɪd/ *adj.* [only before noun] (*formal*) that has been stated to have happened or to be true, when this may not be correct: *Many migrants abandoned their 'transit' through the United States long before reaching their purported destination in Canada.* ■ **pur·port·ed·ly** *adv.*: *In Kansas, squatters quickly moved in to establish residence on land purportedly reserved for Native American tribes.* ➲ *compare* SUPPOSEDLY

LANGUAGE BANK

Stating purpose

It is often important to state the purpose of a piece of academic writing or of a particular study, experiment or action.

- **the purpose of** this study/test/book **is...**
- **with the purpose/aim of** comparing/determining/establishing
- **for the purpose of** comparison/illustration/finding out
- **for** practical/research/political/diagnostic **purposes**
- **the** main/primary/ultimate **aim is to...**
- the study/article/model **aims to...**
- **in order to** assess/compare/determine
- **so that** we/they/it can...
- I/we **will attempt to** explain/address/describe
- this **is/represents an attempt to...**

– ***The purpose of*** *the study* ***was to*** *document shifts in the boundary between the two habitats.*
– *I developed a simulator for each of the three machines* ***with the aim of*** *systematically comparing their performance.*
– *The diagram is merely given* ***for the purpose of*** *visualization.*
– ***For*** *descriptive* ***purposes****, we have divided the genetic analysis into sections.*
– ***The main aim*** *of this paper* ***is to*** *examine comparative evidence on wealth-related health inequalities.*
– *This study* ***aimed to*** *reveal the antioxidant capacity of nutmeg oil.*
– *The study was carried out for different heat fluxes* ***in order to*** *demonstrate the effect of input heat.*
– *Political parties now collect data* ***so that*** *they can rapidly rebut charges from opponents.*
– *I have* ***attempted to*** *explain the basic principles involved.*
– *The theory* ***represents an attempt to*** *offer a better explanation for the behaviour of states.*

pur·pose /ˈpɜːpəs; *NAmE* ˈpɜːrpəs/ *noun* **1** [C, U] the aim, intention or function of sth; the thing that sth is supposed to achieve: *Such an analysis can serve several purposes.* ◇ *The oxygenation reaction, so far as is known at present, serves no useful purpose.* ◇ **~ of sth** *The sole purpose of strategic planning is to enable a firm to gain a sustainable edge over its competitors.* ◇ **for/with the ~ of (doing) sth** *A standardized form was developed specifically for the purpose of extracting data.* ◇ **~ for (doing) sth** *The primary purpose for collecting, analysing and disseminating this information is to support policymaking.* **2 purposes** [pl.] what is needed or being considered in a particular situation: **for (the) ~ of sth** *For the purposes of this article, 'self-employment' refers to those who are not employees but who do not employ others.* ◇ **for... purposes** *For present purposes ,these distinctions are not very important.* **3** [U, C] the feeling that what you are doing is valuable; sth important that you want to achieve: *Participants gain a sense of common purpose and a commitment to action.* ◇ *This belief is what gives meaning, purpose and hope to their lives.* ◇ *Work also provides a purpose in life.*

IDM **on** ˈ**purpose** not by accident SYN DELIBERATELY, INTENTIONALLY: *Many of the temples were burned—whether on purpose or accidentally, they cannot say.* HELP This expression is much more common in general English than in academic writing, where more formal words such as INTENTIONALLY are likely to be used instead: *Sometimes invaders intentionally destroy the culture they conquer.* **to little/no** ˈ**purpose** with little/no useful effect or result:

The costs incurred and the time spent in litigation had been to little or no purpose. ➲ *more at* FIT³, INTENT, PRACTICAL

▸ ADJECTIVE + PURPOSE **sole • main, primary, principal, central • specific, particular • stated • special • express • intended • sb's own • original • ultimate • underlying • present • dual • useful • legitimate • moral • peaceful** *The ideal respondent will vary, depending on the specific purpose of the investigation.*

▸ ADJECTIVE + PURPOSES **illustrative • descriptive • comparative • administrative • educational • commercial • charitable • political • military • civic • diagnostic • therapeutic** *This example is for illustrative purposes only.*

▸ NOUN + PURPOSES **research • management • identification • insurance • tax** *The models have been widely used for management purposes.*

▸ VERB + PURPOSE **serve • fulfil, achieve, realize • suit • pursue • defeat • state** *The policy achieved its central purpose to a reasonable degree.*

pur·sue AWL /pəˈsjuː; *NAmE* pərˈsuː/ *verb* **1 ~ sth** to do sth or try to achieve sth over a period of time: *More women were pursuing careers outside the home.* ◇ *In other countries, governments have pursued different strategies.* ◇ *They see the state as designed to guarantee individuals the freedom to pursue their private goals.* ◇ *to pursue an objective/aim/agenda* ◇ *The governments of Reagan in the US and Thatcher in Britain pursued neo-liberal economic policies.* ◇ *EU member states are under pressure at home to continue to pursue national interests.* **2 ~ sth** to continue to discuss, find out about or be involved in sth: *Evans-Pritchard does not really pursue this question.* ◇ *The fundamental logic behind this approach has been further pursued by Meinig.* **3 ~ sb/sth** to follow sb/sth, especially in order to catch them: *An offender who is being pursued by the police can be liable for injury to an officer if he acts carelessly or recklessly.*

pur·suit AWL /pəˈsjuːt; *NAmE* pərˈsuːt/ *noun* **1** [U] the act of trying to find, obtain or achieve sth: **~ of sth** *Traditionally, the pursuit of profit has been the key driver in business.* ◇ **in ~ of sth** *In other cases, lobby groups will join together in pursuit of a common policy goal.* **2** [C] an activity, especially one that you do because you enjoy it: *Reducing working hours allows more time for leisure pursuits.* ◇ *The 1800s was an era when interest in Buddhism in Europe was primarily an intellectual pursuit.* **3** [U] the act of following or trying to catch sb: **~ of sb/sth** *The police are unable to make any significant headway in the pursuit of such criminals.* ◇ **in ~ (of sb/sth)** *The vehicle sped off with police in pursuit.*

push¹ /pʊʃ/ *verb* **1** [T, I] to make sth move with force in a particular direction; to move in this way: **~ sth** *It is similar to the effect you get when you push a child's swing.* ◇ **~ sth + adv./prep.** *The force with which the gas is pushed out diminishes quickly away from the vent.* ◇ **+ adv./prep.** *The sliding material pushed against the foundations of the buildings.* **2** [T] **~ sth** to make a switch, button, etc. move in or down, in order to operate a machine SYN PRESS² (2): *The reader controlled the pace at which the words were presented by pushing a button.* **3** [I] **~ adv./prep.** to move in a particular direction: *As farmers pushed into upland regions, they discovered that the soils made excellent pasture.* **4** [T] **~ sb/sth + adv./prep.** to make sb/sth react in a particular way or be in a particular situation: *Overselling to the same customers could end up pushing them away.* ◇ *Falling demand pushed many workers into extended spells of unemployment.* **5** [T, I] to change sth or make sth develop so a new level or limit is reached: **~ sth + adv./prep.** *Prices were pushed upwards.* ◇ *One should not push the comparison too far.* ◇ **~ (at) sth** *The great bridge builders of the nineteenth century were pushing at the very boundaries of what was possible.* **6** [T] to force or try to persuade sb to work hard or do sth: **~ sb/yourself (+ adv./prep.)** *They pushed themselves to their physical and mental limits.* ◇ **~ sb to do sth** *The legislative can use its authority to push the government to take further action.* **7** [T] **~ sth** to try hard to persuade people to accept or agree with a new idea, etc: *It became a geopolitical game, with various regional players pushing their own specific agendas.* **8** [T] **~ sth (on/onto/to sth)** (*computing*) to transfer data to the top of a STACK: *The parameters and return address are pushed to the stack to form a stack frame.*

PHR V **ˌpush aˈhead/ˈforward (with sth) | push sth aˈhead/ˈforward** to continue with a plan or activity in a determined way: *The group pushed ahead with the mining project.* ◇ *Successful innovation can push the existing technological frontier forward.* **ˌpush sth ˈaside** to not accept or not consider sth: *Kindt and Muller push aside this understanding of the concept from the outset.* **ˈpush for sth** to keep asking for sth or try to make sth happen because you think it is very important: *It is part of their job to push for change.* **ˌpush sb/sth ˈout** [often passive] to make sb/sth go or become less important, and replace them/it with sb/sth else: *She argues that women are not opting out of the workplace; they are being pushed out.* **ˌpush sth ˈthrough (sth)** to make a plan happen: *The government pushed through reforms.* ◇ *It is vital to have sufficient resources to push projects through.* ◇ *The Act was pushed through Congress by the Bush administration.*

push² /pʊʃ/ *noun* **1** [C, usually sing.] **~ (of sth)** an act of making sb/sth move in a particular direction, especially using your hands: *It required only the push of a button.* **2** [sing.] encouragement or a strong effort to do sth: *Bilingual education had been given a strong push in the 1970s.* ◇ **~ to do sth** *The company began a major push to establish bottling operations outside the USA.* ◇ **~ for (doing) sth** *A significant push for democratization has not occurred.* ◇ **~ towards (doing) sth** *The push towards achieving greater equality remains high on the political agenda.* ◇ **+ noun** *This movement into the cities was characterized by the classic features of migrations—the combination of push and pull factors.* HELP A **push** factor is sth that drives sb/sth away; a **pull** factor attracts them/it. For example, in the Industrial Revolution, poor farm workers experienced lack of work and food as a push factor, and new factories in the cities offering employment as a pull factor. ➲ *compare* PULL² (2)

put /pʊt/ *verb* (**put·ting, put, put**) **1** to bring sb/sth into the state or condition mentioned: **~ sb/sth + adv./prep.** *Higher pay levels can put employers in a stronger position against labour market competitors.* ◇ *Field Marshal Paskevich was put in charge of an army of 190 000 Russian troops.* ◇ *Landslides and fires constantly put local residents at risk.* ◇ **~ sth into action/practice** *A new advertising strategy was agreed and put into action.* **2 ~ pressure/strain/a burden on sb/sth** to make sb/sth be affected by sth: *In the eighth century, population growth put pressure on the land.* ◇ *Gentzkow and Shapiro (2008b) detail how the US government puts pressure on the media not to publish certain stories.* **3 ~ an end/a stop to sth** to make sth end: *The advent of World War II put an end to many experiments in film-making.* ◇ *The Great Depression of the 1930s put an abrupt stop to this growth.* **4 ~ sth + adv./prep.** to express or state sth in a particular way: *This argument was originally put by Pettigrew (1985) in his study of ICI.* ◇ *Put another way, the EU has evolved into a political system in its own right that is more than the sum of its member states.* ◇ *To put the question in a more contemporary form, is growth in real GDP compatible with sustainable economic development?* **5** to give or attach a particular level of importance, force or value to sth: **~ emphasis, weight, a premium, limits, etc. on sth** *The literature puts a strong emphasis on the socialization processes.* ◇ *All these factors put limits on the way individuals could readily use their land.* ◇ **~ faith, trust, etc. in sth**

Dostoevsky put his faith in Christian humility and the 'Russian soul'. **6 ~ sth + adv./prep.** to move sth into a particular place or position: *The study focused on student strategies for getting attention, such as putting a hand up or calling out.* ◇ *Herodotus reports that the Libyans put some gold on the ground to pay for the goods.* **7 ~ sb/sth + adv./prep.** to cause sb/sth to go to a particular place: *He was put in prison after publicly criticizing the government.* ◇ *The money was put into a savings account.* **8 ~ sth (+ adv./prep.)** to write sth or make a mark on sth: *He was reluctant to put his name in the register.*

IDM Idioms containing **put** are at the entries for the nouns and adjectives in the idioms, for example **put (your) money into sth** is at **money**. **put to'gether** used when comparing or contrasting sb/sth with a group of other people or things to mean 'combined' or 'in total': *The total mass of microorganisms on the planet is far greater than that of all the larger animals put together.*

PHR V **,put sth a'cross (to sb)** to communicate your ideas or feelings successfully to sb: *Electronic means of communication help interest groups to put their message across swiftly and efficiently.*

,put sth a'side 1 to ignore or forget sth, usually a feeling or difference of opinion SYN DISREGARD[1]: *The parents attempted to put aside their own feelings in the interests of all the children.* **2** to save sth or keep it available to use: *As the economy grew, individuals were able to put aside more of their income.*

'put sb/sth at sth to calculate sb/sth to be a particular age, weight, amount, etc: *Estimates by the World Wildlife Fund put the total amount of burnt forest at 2.5 million hectares.*

,put sth/sb 'back to return sth/sb to its/their previous state or position: *The female birds were then put back in the home cage.* ◇ *The penetration of the UK economy by foreign firms did not put British businesses back in competition.*

'put sth before sth to treat sth as more important than sth else: *After the Revolution, Bolshevik trade unionists tended to put workers before party.*

,put sth be'hind sth/sb 1 to give support to sth/sb: *The President put his power and energy behind the project.* **2** to try to forget about an upleasant experience and think about the future: *For the most part, Reagan put these problems behind him, achieving instead a reputation for strength and leadership.*

,put sth 'down 1 to stop sth such as a protest by force SYN CRUSH (2): *Eighty people were killed when the military put down demonstrations in Milan in May 1898.* **2** to write sth; to make a note of sth: *The editor encouraged him to put his views down on paper.* **'put sth down to sth** to consider that sth is caused by sth SYN ATTRIBUTE[1] (1): *Many changes in fish numbers can be put down to overfishing and climate change (Russell et al., 1971).*

,put sth 'forward (*also formal* **'put forth**) to suggest sth for discussion: *The 'Energy Review' (2006) put forward proposals for tackling the UK's energy and climate change challenges.* ◇ *Hoch (2000) put forward several explanations for the increase in woody species.* ➲ thesaurus note *at* SUGGEST

'put sth into sth 1 to spend a lot of time or make a lot of effort doing sth: *The assumption is that if wages go up, employees will put more effort into their work.* ◇ **~ sth into doing sth** *We are delighted at this recognition of the work we have put into making the modules interactive.* ➲ *related noun* INPUT[2] **2** to spend money on sth: *Voters did not see the need to put scarce public resources into ecotourism.* ◇ **~ sth into doing sth** *Some countries have put significant amounts of money into developing biological control of insects.*

,put sb 'off (sth/sb) to make sb lose interest in or enthusiasm for sth/sb: *Many potential customers were put off by the price.* ◇ **~ off doing sth** *An early negative experience of language learning may put children off learning a language later.* **,put sth 'off** to change sth to a later time or date SYN POSTPONE, DELAY[2] (1): *By the 1990s, many Japanese women were putting off marriage or rejecting it altogether.*

,put sth 'on 1 to dress yourself in sth: *They put on a white garment to symbolize their new state of purity.* OPP TAKE STH OFF (2) **2** to become heavier, especially by the amount mentioned SYN GAIN[1] (3): *Question 7 asked, 'Over what period of time have you put on this weight?'*

,put sth 'out 1 to stop sth from burning or shining: *However, the wind strengthened and the authorities did not succeed in putting out the fire.* **2** to publish or broadcast sth: *Decisions were based on annual reports put out by the city council.* **3** to give a job or task to a worker who is not your employee or to a company that is not part of your own group or organization: *The contract was put out to tender.*

'put sth to sb to express sth such an opinion, a suggestion or a question to sb: *People whose conduct is being investigated hardly ever have the opportunity to put their case to the Commissioner.*

,put sth to'gether to make or prepare sth, especially by collecting parts together: *Three companies were asked to put together a fully costed design.*

,put 'up sth to show a particular level of skill or determination in a fight or contest: *The Ligurians put up a fierce, century-long resistance to Roman expansion.* **,put sb 'up (for sth)** to suggest or present sb as a candidate for a job or position: *All the directors were put up for re-election.* **,put sth 'up 1** to place sth somewhere so that it will be seen, such as on a wall or on a website SYN DISPLAY[1] (1): *Posters were put up around the hospital reminding staff and patients to wash their hands.* ◇ *The images and accompanying text were put up on the company website.* **2** to build sth or place sth somewhere: *The council planned to put a multi-storey car park up along the town's ancient walls.* **3** to raise or increase sth: *After six months, the publishers put the price up.* **,put 'up with sb/sth** to accept sb/sth that is unpleasant without complaining SYN TOLERATE (2): *Customers are increasingly unwilling to put up with low quality food and poor service.*

pu·ta·tive /ˈpjuːtətɪv/ *adj.* [only before noun] (*formal* or *law*) believed to be the person or thing mentioned SYN PRESUMED, SUPPOSED: *the putative father of her children*

puz·zle[1] /ˈpʌzl/ *noun* **1** a game, etc. that you have to think about carefully in order to answer it or do it: *Most people, when they are trying to solve a jigsaw puzzle, like to look at the picture on the box.* ◇ *Her hobbies include crossword puzzles and gardening.* **2** [usually sing.] something that is difficult to understand or explain SYN MYSTERY (1): *The interesting puzzle is that the data do not fit the theoretical expectations.* ◇ *A major puzzle addressed is the shift from a militaristic foreign policy before 1945 to a pacifist foreign policy after the war.*

puz·zle[2] /ˈpʌzl/ *verb* **~ sb** to make sb feel confused because they do not understand sth: *The question of how Chinese lexis has developed across centuries has puzzled historical linguists for decades.* ■ **puz·zling** /ˈpʌzlɪŋ/ *adj.*: *The lack of clinical assessment research on this population is somewhat puzzling.*

Qq

quad·rat·ic /kwɒˈdrætɪk; *NAmE* kwɑːˈdrætɪk/ *adj.* (*mathematics*) involving an unknown quantity that is multiplied by itself once only: *a quadratic form/term/equation/element*

quake /kweɪk/ *noun* = EARTHQUAKE

quali·fi·ca·tion /ˌkwɒlɪfɪˈkeɪʃn; *NAmE* ˌkwɑːlɪfɪˈkeɪʃn/ *noun* **1** [C] (*BrE*) an exam that you have passed or a course of study that you have successfully completed: *Many care workers possess entry-level qualifications.* ◇ *They were likely to hold vocational qualifications.* ◇ *Those without formal qualifications were least likely to have Internet access.* **2** [U] the fact of reaching the necessary standard for sth, for example by passing an exam: *A survey done one month after qualification showed that 46% failed to find permanent positions.* **3** [C] a skill, type of experience, or quality that is needed for a particular job or activity, or to be a particular thing: **~ to do sth** *The vast majority lack the qualifications necessary to engage fully with complex economic information.* ◇ **~ for sth** *Geographers generally agree that great size is not the only qualification for world city status.* **4** [C, U] information that you add to a statement to limit the effect that it has or the way it is applied: *This statement captures an important truth, but it needs certain qualifications.* ◇ **without ~** *She states without qualification that the system needs to change.*

quali·fied /ˈkwɒlɪfaɪd; *NAmE* ˈkwɑːlɪfaɪd/ *adj.* **1** having passed the exams or completed the training necessary in order to do a particular job: *Keeping control in the classroom can be a challenge for newly qualified teachers.* ◇ **~ for sth** *The individual must be qualified for the job for which she or he applied.* **2** [not before noun] having the knowledge, experience or skills to do sth: **~ to do sth** *The concerns triggered questions regarding who was best qualified to address the problems.* ◇ **~ for sth** *Board members should be qualified for their positions.* **3** [usually before noun] (of support, approval, etc.) limited in some way: *The data provide only qualified support for the hypothesis.* ◇ *He gave qualified approval to these guidelines.*

quali·fy /ˈkwɒlɪfaɪ; *NAmE* ˈkwɑːlɪfaɪ/ *verb* (**quali·fies, quali·fy·ing, quali·fied, quali·fied**) **1** [I] to reach the standard of ability or knowledge needed to do a particular job, for example by completing a course of study or passing exams: *The doctor was a German national, who had qualified in Germany.* ◇ **~ as sth** *She qualified as a doctor at a time when this was unusual for women.* **2** [T] to give sb the skills and knowledge they need to do sth: **~ sb to do sth** *Having experience in local government qualifies you to be a parliamentary candidate.* ◇ **~ sb for sth** *Women traditionally invested in non-market skills (qualifying them for homemaking and caregiving).* **3** [I, T] to do or have what is needed in order to do sth, have sth or be included in sth: *The guidelines did not clearly define the circumstances in which an applicant could qualify.* ◇ **~ for sth** *2 669 subjects qualified for the study.* ◇ **~ sb for sth** *Fleeing the instability of civil war does not qualify an individual for asylum.* **4** [I, T] to have the right qualities to be described as a particular thing: **~ as sth** *Those who qualify as refugees are eligible for a temporary residence status.* ◇ **~ as + adj.** *A number of regions qualify as relatively underdeveloped.* ◇ **~ sth as sth** *These boroughs were physically very small, their economies barely qualifying them as small towns.* **5** [T] **~ sth** to add sth to a previous statement to make the meaning slightly different, usually less strong or less general: *He carefully qualified his views and did not insist that they were true in all cases.* **6** [T] **~ sth (with sth)** (of a word) to describe another word in a particular way: *In Britain, the term 'minority' is usually qualified with the word 'ethnic'.*

quali·ta·tive AWL /ˈkwɒlɪtətɪv; *NAmE* ˈkwɑːləteɪtɪv/ *adj.* [usually before noun] connected with or measuring the quality of sth, rather than with how much of it there is: *The findings from both qualitative and quantitative research show a positive outcome.* ◇ *The assessor gathered qualitative data on parent-child interactions.* ◇ *The discussion in this paper is largely based on a qualitative analysis of organizational documents.* ➲ *compare* QUANTITATIVE ■ **quali·ta·tive·ly** AWL *adv.*: *Data were analysed qualitatively using thematic analysis.*

qual·ity /ˈkwɒləti; *NAmE* ˈkwɑːləti/ *noun* (*pl.* **-ies**) **1** [U, C] the standard of sth when it is compared with other things like it; how good or bad sth is: *A diet may be deficient in quantity, quality or both.* ◇ **of... ~** *If the input data are of poor quality, the results cannot be trusted.* ◇ **~ of sth** *Studies found no clear-cut relationship between population size and the quality of service provided by the local government.* ◇ **~ of life** *Prospective parents have a right to receive complete information about persons with disabilities, including their potential for a good quality of life.* ◇ **+ noun** *An essential component of good quality prenatal care is education.* ◇ *A quality improvement programme was undertaken.* **2** [U] a high standard: *These indicators are considered important for assuring quality.* ◇ **~ of sth** *Staff were obviously keen to ensure the quality of their product.* ◇ **+ noun** *Sample material is stored for checking or quality assurance purposes.* **3** [C] a feature of sb's character or of a thing or substance: *He lacked the necessary qualities required to be a leader.* ◇ *While Turkish cinema possesses its unique qualities, it is nonetheless part of a wider movement in cinema.* ➲ thesaurus note *at* FEATURE[1]

▸ ADJECTIVE + QUALITY **poor, low, inferior • variable • acceptable • good, high • better, superior • excellent • overall • methodological • nutritional • environmental** *There are sectors of very low quality housing.* ◇ *The methodological quality of studies was assessed independently.* | **desirable • necessary • intrinsic • aesthetic • personal • moral** *People would be expected to value these landscapes because of their aesthetic qualities.*

▸ NOUN + QUALITY **air • water • soil • habitat • diet • product • service • data** *These measures have brought about a marked improvement in water quality.*

▸ VERB + QUALITY **monitor, check • measure • assess, judge, evaluate, appraise, rate • determine • reflect • indicate • perceive • predict** *It was not possible to assess the quality of the interventions reported.* | **affect, impact, influence • compromise, impair, degrade • reduce, diminish • improve, enhance, upgrade • maximize, optimize** *They may need to compromise product quality in order to reduce costs.* | **ensure • assure • guarantee • maintain • promote** *The most prevalent method of maintaining quality is storage at low temperatures.* | **possess, have • exhibit, demonstrate • lack • attribute** *He did not possess the warlike qualities of his predecessor.*

▸ QUALITY + NOUN **control • assessment, evaluation • rating, score • indicator, measure • criteria • objective • standard • programme, initiative • improvement** *Quality assessment of included studies was performed independently by two authors.*

ˈquality control *noun* [U, C] the practice of checking that the goods or services that an organization produces or provides are of a high standard: *Japanese quality control moved towards broader organizational strategies for improving product quality.*

quanta *pl. of* QUANTUM[1]

quan·ti·fier /ˈkwɒntɪfaɪə(r); *NAmE* ˈkwɑːntɪfaɪər/ *noun* (*grammar*) a determiner or pronoun that expresses quantity, for example 'all' or 'both': *The distinction between determiners and quantifiers is not an absolute one.*

quan·tify /ˈkwɒntɪfaɪ; *NAmE* ˈkwɑːntɪfaɪ/ *verb* (**quan·ti·fies, quan·ti·fy·ing, quan·ti·fied, quan·ti·fied**) **~ sth** to describe or express sth as an amount or a number: *These effects can be difficult to quantify.* ◇ *We did not attempt to quantify the magnitude of the sex difference in coloration.* ■ **quan·ti·fi·able** *adj.*: *If the objectives are specific and quantifiable, measurement would seem to be easy.* **quan·ti·fi·ca·tion** /ˌkwɒntɪfɪˈkeɪʃn; *NAmE* ˌkwɑːntɪfɪˈkeɪʃn/ *noun* [U, sing.] *Two internal standards were used for more accurate quantification.* ◇ **~ of sth** *Scoring systems allow a quantification of the severity of illness.*

Q

quan·ti·ta·tive /ˈkwɒntɪtətɪv; *NAmE* ˈkwɑːntəteɪtɪv/ *adj.* [usually before noun] connected with or measuring the amount or number of sth rather than its quality: *An important tool in quantitative research is the structured questionnaire.* ◇ *Using both qualitative and quantitative analyses, Hill et al. (1998) showed that...* ➲ compare QUALITATIVE ■ **quan·ti·ta·tive·ly** *adv.*: *This shift has been demonstrated quantitatively by Wilkinson and Walker (1989).*

ˌquantitative aˈnalysis *noun* [U, C] **~ (of sth)** (*chemistry*) measurement of the quantities of particular substances within a particular sample: *Quantitative analysis of a particular hydrocarbon showed that it contained 14.3% hydrogen and 85.7% carbon by mass.*

quan·tity /ˈkwɒntəti; *NAmE* ˈkwɑːntəti/ *noun* (*pl.* **-ies**) **1** [C, U] the amount of sth; a particular amount or number of sth: *We cannot assume that the total quantity produced equals the total quantity consumed.* ◇ *The data are limited in terms of both quality and quantity.* ◇ **~ of sth** *Governments collect and analyse vast quantities of information.* ◇ *Small quantities of imported goods found their way into the shops.* ◇ **in ... ~** *Water was not available in unlimited quantities.* **2** [C] (*mathematics*) a value that can be expressed in numbers; the symbol that represents it: *This quantity is generally denoted by the symbol v.* ◇ *We suppose that a quantity z, called the dependent variable, depends on two independent variables x and y.*
IDM **in quantity** in large amounts or numbers: *Air conditioning had existed for some time, but it was only after World War II that residential-size units were produced in quantity.*

quan·tum¹ /ˈkwɒntəm; *NAmE* ˈkwɑːntəm/ *noun* (*pl.* **quanta** /ˈkwɒntə; *NAmE* ˈkwɑːntə/) (*physics*) a very small quantity of energy: *He specified that the energy content of one of these quanta would be proportional to the frequency of the radiation.*

quan·tum² /ˈkwɒntəm; *NAmE* ˈkwɑːntəm/ *adj.* [only before noun] (*physics*) suggesting behaviour that is due to the rules of quantum theory: *Nuclear radiation is a quantum process.*

Q

ˌquantum meˈchanics *noun* [U] (*physics*) the branch of MECHANICS that deals with movement and force in MICROSCOPIC (= very, very small) objects which obey the rules of quantum theory: *Quantum mechanics deals predominantly with the behaviour of matter on the very small scale.*

ˈquantum theory *noun* [U] (*physics*) a theory based on the idea that energy exists in units that cannot be divided: *Quantum theory deals in probabilities rather than certainties.* ◇ *Gravity has a perplexing nature that seems to resist attempts to put it together with quantum theory.*

quar·ter /ˈkwɔːtə(r); *NAmE* ˈkwɔːrtər/ *noun* **1** (*also* **fourth** *especially in NAmE*) [C] one of four equal parts of sth: *About half the soldiers could read, and about a quarter could read and write.* ◇ **~ of sth** *The Black Death killed at least a quarter of the population of Europe.* ◇ *Over a quarter of a million Melanesians in Vanuatu and the Solomon Islands speak related varieties of Tok Pisin.* ◇ **+ noun** *Their partnership went back a quarter century to when both attended the same high school.* ➲ language bank *at* PROPORTION **2** [C] a period of three months, used especially as a period for which bills are paid or a company's income is calculated: *This led to a reported fall of 2.6% in construction growth in the first quarter.* ◇ **~ of sth** *By the fourth quarter of 2000, the real wage had risen from $7.79 to $8.33.* **3** [C] a person or group of people, especially as a source of help, information or a reaction: *There is growing public pressure from some quarters to ban these products.* ◇ **in... quarters** *The announcement was received with surprise in many quarters.* **4** [C, usually sing.] a district or part of a town: *It offers an excellent description of the life of women in the Jewish quarter.* ◇ **~ of sth** *Many working-class quarters of London had been 'invaded by the middle classes'.* **5 quarters** [pl.] rooms that are provided for soldiers, SERVANTS, etc. to live in: *Servants' quarters typically offered little space or privacy.* ◇ *Tuberculosis is essentially a disease of poverty, crowded living quarters and malnutrition.* IDM see CLOSE³

quar·ter·ly /ˈkwɔːtəli; *NAmE* ˈkwɔːrtərli/ *adj.* produced or happening every three months: *All health facilities have to complete financial reports on a quarterly basis.* ◇ *One of the most reliable sources is a quarterly survey of American consumers conducted by the University of Michigan.* ■ **quar·ter·ly** *adv.*: *The full database is updated quarterly and made available to subscribers.*

quar·tile /ˈkwɔːtaɪl; *NAmE* ˈkwɔːrtaɪl; ˈkwɔːrtl/ *noun* (*statistics*) one of four equal groups into which a set of things can be divided according to the DISTRIBUTION of a particular VARIABLE: *The ratio is the same when one compares the top wealth quartile with the bottom wealth quartile.* ➲ compare QUINTILE ➲ language bank *at* STATISTIC

quartz /kwɔːts; *NAmE* kwɔːrts/ *noun* [U] a hard, very common mineral, often found in CRYSTAL form. It is used to make scientific equipment and accurate clocks and watches: **+ noun** *Manufactured quartz crystals are used as oscillators in all types of radios, telephones and satellites.*

quash /kwɒʃ; *NAmE* kwɔːʃ; kwɑːʃ/ *verb* **~ sth** (*BrE, law*) to officially say that a decision made by a court is no longer valid or correct: *The defendant's conviction was quashed on appeal.*

queen /kwiːn/ *noun* **1** the female ruler of an independent state that has a royal family: *The kings and queens who ruled these states justified their power by appealing to the doctrine of divine right.* ◇ **~ of sth** *The first Queen Elizabeth had been queen of England, not of Scotland.* **2 ~ (of sth)** the wife of a king: *Eleanor of Aquitaine became queen of France when she married King Louis VII.* **3** a large female insect that lays eggs for the whole group: *In ants with multiple queens per colony, young queens often stay in their mother's nest.*

query¹ /ˈkwɪəri; *NAmE* ˈkwɪri/ *noun* (*pl.* **-ies**) **1** a question, especially one asking for information or expressing a doubt about sth: *Respondents answered each query by selecting one of the following five responses:...* **2** a search for information that is entered into an Internet search engine: **+ noun** *Ginsberg et al. (2009) presented a novel approach for detecting influenza outbreaks using search engine query data.*

query² /ˈkwɪəri; *NAmE* ˈkwɪri/ *verb* (**quer·ies, query·ing, quer·ied, quer·ied**) to express doubt about whether sth is correct or not: **~ sth** *Several researchers have queried the emphasis that has been placed on national culture.* ◇ **~ why/whether, etc...** *There is a basis for querying why this is even necessary.*

quest /kwest/ *noun* a long or difficult search for sth, especially for a quality such as knowledge or truth: **~ for sth** *The quest for truth in the court room is different from the quest for truth in the laboratory.* ◇ **~ to do sth** *The quest to investigate these problems has absorbed considerable amounts of scholarly energy.* ◇ **in the/sb's ~ (to do sth)** *Historians based in Tasmania have embraced these methodologies in their quest to reconstruct the early colonial period on the island.* ◇ **in ~ of sth** *The novel tells the story of a hero in quest of special knowledge.*

ques·tion¹ /ˈkwestʃən/ *noun* **1** [C] a sentence, phrase or word that asks for information: **~ about sb/sth** *The doctor asks her detailed questions about herself.* ◇ **~ on sth** *Questions on family-friendly management were included in the survey for the first time in 1998.* ◇ **an answer to a ~** *There are a number of possible answers to this question.* **2** [C] a matter or topic that needs to be discussed or dealt with: *There are still many unresolved research questions in climate research.* ◇ **~ of sth** *Such issues raise wide-ranging matters of concern, including questions of authority and accountability.* **3** [U, C] doubt or confusion about sth: **beyond ~** *The value of such an approach seems beyond question.* ◇ **open to ~** *How many are distinct species is open to question.* ◇ **there is no ~ (that...)** *There is no question that the commercial was clever and funny.* ◇ **~ about/as to sth** *Questions remain, however, about the validity of the results.* **4** [C] a task or request for information that is intended to test your knowledge or understanding, for example in an exam or a competition: *The following broad topics are frequently set as exam questions:...* ◇ **~ on/about sth** *Students may read the paper and find a really difficult question on a topic that they thought was straightforward.*

IDM **be a question of (doing) sth** to be a matter depending on or involving a particular condition or thing: *It is also often just a question of personal preference.* ◇ *It is no longer a question of competing for market share.* **bring/throw sth into 'question** to cause sth to become a matter for doubt and discussion: *The proposed changes have been brought into question by market analysts.* **come into 'question** to become a matter for doubt and discussion: *President Bush's standing at home suffered as his leadership abroad came into question.* **in 'question 1** being considered or discussed: *The places in question are sub-Saharan Africa, Bangladesh, India, Nepal and Pakistan.* **2** in doubt; uncertain: *The validity and reliability of the results may be in question.* **out of the 'question** impossible or not allowed and therefore not worth discussing: *In such a context, the use of military force to solve conflicts is out of the question.* **there is no question of (sth/sb doing) sth** there is no possibility of sth: *There could be no question of the abolition of taxes.* ◇ *There is no question of the company being liable.* **without 'question 1** used for saying that there can be no doubt about sth: *Without question, the earthquake caused devastating loss of life and property.* **2** without asking any questions or expressing any feelings of doubt: *In antiquity, miracles were not accepted without question.* ⊃ more at BEG, CALL[1]

▸ ADJECTIVE + QUESTION **important • key • fundamental, basic • central • crucial, critical • open • interesting • specific • difficult • further • general • broad • ethical • philosophical** *On important questions, all or most member states still want to present their positions.* | **following • closed • open-ended • unanswered • follow-up** *Closed and open-ended questions were both present in the first version of questionnaire but a large number of answers given to open-ended questions were missing or illegible.*

▸ NOUN + QUESTION **survey • interview • discussion • research** *On the basis of these findings, a clear answer to the first research question emerges.* | **policy • research** *The Joint Cabinet Committee discussed constitutional matters and other policy questions.*

▸ VERB + QUESTION **raise • pose • consider • identify • address, tackle • respond to • ignore • avoid** *The article raised the question of Michels's theoretical understanding of Marxism.* ◇ *Investigators do their best to pose questions and record answers in a uniform fashion.* | **ask, put • prompt • formulate, frame • answer, reply to • use** *Patients with dementia are usually willing to reply to questions but make mistakes.* | **explore, examine, investigate • discuss • approach • settle, resolve • concern** *Many contemporary women writers explore questions of gender, sexuality and identity.*

▸ QUESTION + VERB **arise • remain** *Thus, the question arises: why did the Prime Minister continue with this policy?*

ques·tion[2] /ˈkwestʃən/ *verb* **1** to have or express doubts about sth: **~ sth** *Recent studies have questioned the assumption that Japan remained closed to outsiders in the Enlightenment period.* ◇ **~ whether/how, etc...** *Some observers are questioning whether organic foods really are better for consumers.* SYN CHALLENGE[2] ⊃ thesaurus note at CHALLENGE[2] **2** to ask sb questions about sth, especially officially: **~ sb** *Only 2% of those questioned understood the meaning of the term.* ◇ **~ sb about/on sth** *Smokers are questioned about their reasons for smoking.*

ques·tion·able /ˈkwestʃənəbl/ *adj.* **1** that you have doubts about because you think it is not accurate or correct SYN DEBATABLE: *These assumptions, however, are highly questionable.* ◇ **it is ~ whether...** *It is questionable whether the current practice is justifiable in terms of the suffering inflicted on the animals.* **2** likely to be dishonest or morally wrong SYN SUSPECT[3]: *Many growing businesses adopted some very questionable practices to grab a larger slice of the market.*

ques·tion·ing /ˈkwestʃənɪŋ/ *noun* [U] the activity of asking sb questions: *Inevitably, recording of police questioning influences the conduct of officers.* ◇ **~ of sb** *Direct questioning of experimental subjects is probably the most common method of determining the structure of social networks.*

'question mark *noun* **1** the mark (?) used in writing after a question: *The question mark indicated that the participant was undecided or did not know the answer.* **2** used to say that sth is not certain: *A question mark exists as to whether adequate value has been placed upon environmental resources.* ◇ **~ over sth** *The models remain useful as reference points, even if there is a question mark over their relevance today.*

ques·tion·naire /ˌkwestʃəˈneə(r); *NAmE* ˌkwestʃəˈner/ *noun* a written list of questions that are answered by a number of people so that information can be collected from the answers: *Ten per cent of eligible students completed the questionnaire.* ◇ *to develop/administer/use a questionnaire* ◇ **~ on/about sth** *All participants received a postal questionnaire about their health, employment situation and work-related problems.*

quick /kwɪk/ *adj.* (**quick·er**, **quick·est**) **1** done with speed; taking or lasting a short time: *Mobile phones are often the cheapest and quickest way to communicate.* ◇ **in ~ succession** *He made three more films in quick succession.* **2** doing sth fast: *He was not a quick thinker by nature.* ◇ **~ to do sth** *Critics were quick to point out some of the weaknesses in the company's approach.* **3** [only before noun] happening very soon or without delay: *Such private colleges generally appeal to students requiring quick results.*

quick·ly /ˈkwɪkli/ *adv.* **1** fast: *This region is characterized by weather systems which move quickly.* **2** soon; after a short time: *Multinational companies need to respond quickly to changing circumstances.* ◇ *It quickly became apparent that the venture was not a success.*

quiet /ˈkwaɪət/ *adj.* (**quiet·er**, **quiet·est**) **1** making little or no noise: *Aircraft became quieter, flew higher and offered passengers more comfort.* **2** (of a place, period of time or situation) without many people or much noise, activity or excitement: *Initial assessment of the patient should take place in a quiet room with adequate lighting.* ◇ *Travel companies can generate some income in quiet periods through cutting prices.* ◇ *He was a wealthy landowner who wanted so far as possible to lead a quiet life.* **3** (of a person) tending not to talk very much: *They are quiet, shy, polite and not at all spoilt by their success.* **4** (of a feeling or attitude) definite but not expressed in an obvious way: *With a quiet determination, they set about reducing inequalities within their own communities.*

IDM **keep quiet about sth** | **keep sth quiet** to say nothing about sth; to keep sth secret: *Politicians also kept quiet*

Q

about this fact. ◇ *The Jewish leaders begged Pilate to keep the story quiet.*

quiet·ly /ˈkwaɪətli/ *adv.* **1** in a quiet manner; without noise: *The gas may escape relatively quietly.* **2** with little activity or excitement; without attracting attention: *In the face of mounting opposition, the proposal was quietly dropped.* ◇ *He was quietly confident that local politicians would do what he wanted.*

quin·tile /ˈkwɪntaɪl/ *noun* (*statistics*) one of five equal groups into which a set of things can be divided according to the DISTRIBUTION of a particular VARIABLE: *In the United States, greater income inequality was due both to a decreased share for the lowest quintile and to an increased share for the highest quintile.* ◇ **in a ~** *Households in the highest quintile (or the top 20 per cent) had an average income of £60 310.* ➲ *compare* QUARTILE ➲ language bank *at* STATISTIC

quit /kwɪt/ *verb* (**quit·ting, quit, quit**) (*BrE also* **quit·ting, quit·ted, quit·ted**) **1** [I, T] to leave your job, school, etc: *At such a wage level, the employee might well decide to quit.* ◇ **~ as sth** *Ford quit as chief executive in 2006.* ◇ **~ sth** *She had quit her job as an administrative assistant in an accounting firm.* **2** [T, I] (*especially NAmE*) to stop doing sth: *In the present study, 80% of smokers said they wanted to quit.* ◇ **~ doing sth** *These are the key reasons volunteers quit working for non-profit organizations.* ◇ **~ sth** *If no one around them is smoking, they may find it easier to quit the habit themselves.* **3** [T] **~ sth** to leave a place, especially permanently: *The difficulty in properly housing his troops forced Napoleon to quit Moscow.*

quite /kwaɪt/ *adv.* **1** (*BrE*) (not used with a negative) to some degree SYN FAIRLY (1), PRETTY: *In their views of humanity, however, the two men were quite similar.* ◇ *The case of Morocco illustrates this trend quite well.* ◇ *The Bill stands quite a good chance of becoming law.* HELP When **quite** is used with an adjective before a noun, it comes before *a* or *an*. You can say: *This is quite a difficult concept to explain* or *This concept is quite difficult to explain* but not ~~*This is a quite difficult concept to explain.*~~ **2** (*BrE*) to the greatest possible degree SYN ABSOLUTELY, COMPLETELY, ENTIRELY: *Progress in this area of technology over the last decade has been quite remarkable.* ◇ *The next parliament would be elected under quite a different system.* ◇ **not ~** *Terrorism is not quite so easy to define as might be expected.* ◇ *Today things are not quite the same.* ◇ **~ the opposite/contrary/reverse** *Freud's approach to religion is quite the opposite of that taken by people who are themselves religious.* ◇ **~ apart from sth** *Quite apart from these theoretical issues, there were practical reasons for limiting the sample.* **3** to a great degree; very; really: *Figure 10.20 shows this happening quite clearly at the 300 m level.*

IDM **quite a ˈlot (of sth)** (*also BrE* **quite a ˈbit**) (*informal*) a large number or amount of sth: *A national survey showed that seven out of ten Australians had 'quite a lot of confidence' in the police.* **ˈquite some sth** a large amount of sth: *This market has been growing very rapidly for quite some time now.* ➲ *more at* CONTRARY[2]

quota /ˈkwəʊtə; *NAmE* ˈkwoʊtə/ *noun* the limited number or amount of people or things that is officially allowed: **~ on sth** *Spanish rules imposed a quota on the amount of wine available for export in bulk to other Member States.* ◇ **~ (of sth)** *The country may be exceeding its OPEC quota of 1 100 000 barrels of oil per day.* ◇ *Import quotas restrict the value or volume of a particular good which may be imported from specified countries.*

quota·tion AWL /kwəʊˈteɪʃn; *NAmE* kwoʊˈteɪʃn/ *noun* **1** [C, U] words from another speaker or writer that sb uses in his/her own writing or speech, showing clearly that the words are from this source; the act of quoting the words of another speaker or writer: *Each of these challenges is discussed and quotations are used to illustrate them.* ◇ *His heavy use of direct quotation clearly emphasizes the primacy of the interviews.* ◇ **~ from sb/sth** *Quotations from the interviews are presented in Table 8.1.* ◇ **above/following ~** *Willmott (1993) cites as evidence the following quotation from the literature on excellence:...* ➲ thesaurus note *at* REFERENCE[1] **2** [C] an estimate of how much sth will cost; a statement of the value of sth, especially shares in a company: *All potential suppliers will be asked for submission of a price quotation for supplying goods and services.* ◇ *They may wish to check the accuracy of the market quotations.*

quoˈtation marks (*also* **ˈspeech marks**) (*BrE also* **inˌverted ˈcommas**) *noun* [pl.] a pair of marks (' ') or (" ") placed around a word, sentence, etc. to show that it is what sb said or wrote, that it is a title or that you are using it in an unusual way: *When you ask the patient questions, write down their exact words and enclose them in quotation marks.*

quote[1] AWL /kwəʊt; *NAmE* kwoʊt/ *verb* **1** [T, I] to use words from another speaker or writer in your writing or speech, showing clearly that the words are from this source: **~ sth** *The passage just quoted is an excellent summary of the situation.* ◇ **~ sth above/below** *In essence, this criticism is the same as the Hayek criticism quoted above.* ◇ **~ sb as saying sth** *Edison is quoted as saying: 'Inspiration can be found in a pile of junk.'* ◇ **~ sb** *To quote Al Gore, 'We must not leap from denial to despair.'* ◇ **~ from sth** *The Committee quoted extensively from her pamphlet.* **2** [T, often passive] to mention sb/sth in a particular way; to give sth as an example: **~ sth + adv./prep.** *The data for Argentina and Brazil quoted here were from the 1985–7 period.* ◇ **~ sth as sth** *Most patients were quoting chest pain as a reason for the consultation.* ◇ **~ sth** *In this context, Mahmud and Vargas (2008) quote the examples of Botswana and Norway.* **3** [T, often passive] to give a price for sth: **be quoted (+ adv./prep.)** *The prices of many currencies are quoted in dollars.* HELP If shares or companies **are quoted** on a STOCK EXCHANGE, the prices of the shares are listed there: *Several football clubs are now quoted on the Stock Exchange.*

quote[2] AWL /kwəʊt; *NAmE* kwoʊt/ *noun* (*rather informal*) a quotation: *It is interesting to consider a quote from Jules Verne's novel 'L'Ile Mysterieuse':...*

quo·tient /ˈkwəʊʃnt; *NAmE* ˈkwoʊʃnt/ *noun* **1** (in compounds) a degree or amount of a particular quality or characteristic: *The location quotient LQ describes the employment share of any sector in any region, relative to the national share of employment in the sector.* ➲ *see also* IQ **2** (*mathematics*) a number which is the result when one number is divided by another: *The way of finding the quotient and remainder is very similar to the division algorithm for integers.* ➲ *compare* REMAINDER (2)

Qur'an (*also* **Koran, Quran**) /kəˈrɑːn/ *noun* **the Qur'an** [sing.] the HOLY book of the Islamic religion, written in Arabic, containing the word of Allah as REVEALED to the Prophet Muhammad

Rr

race /reɪs/ *noun* **1** [C, U] one of the main groups that humans can be divided into according to their physical differences, for example the colour of their skin: *This is a medical condition that is equally common in both sexes and all races.* ◇ *Laws and policies which discriminated against people on the basis of race or gender have gradually been changed.* ➲ *see also* RACE RELATIONS **2** [C] a group of people who share the same language, history, culture, etc: *The Scots were, to the twelfth-century William of*

R

Newburgh, 'an uncivilized race'. ➲ *see also* HUMAN RACE **3** [sing.] a situation in which a number of people, groups, organizations, etc. are competing, especially for political power or to achieve sth first: **~ for sth** *The author shows how religious forces, themes and imagery affected the race for the White House.* ◇ **~ to do sth** *Germany lost the race to build a viable nuclear weapon during World War II.* **4** [C] **~ (between A and B)| ~ (against sb)** a competition between people, animals, vehicles, etc. to see which one is the faster or fastest: *Malthus compared the economic and social history of Britain to a race between a hare and a tortoise.* **5** [C] **~ (of sth)** (*biology*) a particular breed or type of animal or plant within a species: *For the different species and races of rhinoceros, the details of their decline differ.*

IDM **ˌrace to the ˈbottom** a situation in which countries or organizations compete with each other by cutting taxes, wages, standards, etc. in order to try to gain an advantage, with the result that overall tax or wage levels or standards are reduced, but no real advantage is gained by one country or organization over another: *This situation results in a 'race to the bottom' whereby nations try to underbid each other by offering ever-lower wages, ever-lower rates of taxation, and ever-more residual forms of state welfare.*

ˌrace reˈlations *noun* [pl.] the relationships between people of different races who live in the same community: *The Commission for Racial Equality was set up to investigate complaints of unlawful racial discrimination and to promote harmonious race relations.*

ra·cial /ˈreɪʃl/ *adj.* **1** [only before noun] happening or existing between people of different races: *President Kennedy promised he would abolish racial discrimination in federally aided housing.* **2** [usually before noun] connected with a person's race: *Her fiction explores notions of gender and racial identity.* ◇ *The data suggest that friendships are still made mainly within rather than across racial groups.*

ra·cial·ly /ˈreɪʃəli/ *adv.* **1** in a way that is caused by difference in race: *For the year 1999 to 2000, there were over 21 000 racially motivated attacks reported.* **2** in a way that is connected with race: *Britain has become a more racially mixed society than at any time in its history.*

ra·cism /ˈreɪsɪzəm/ *noun* [U] (*disapproving*) **1** the unfair treatment of people who belong to a different race; violent behaviour towards them: *He demanded action on institutional racism in the police force.* ◇ *Despite the racism and sexism they encountered at school, these young women have high levels of achievement.* ➲ *compare* DISCRIMINATION (1) **2** the belief that some races of people are better than others: *Racism is the belief that human progress is inevitably linked to the existence of distinct races.* ➲ *compare* PREJUDICE (1) ■ **ra·cist** /ˈreɪsɪst/ *noun*: *The march was attended by the extreme right, racists and fascists.* **ra·cist** *adj.*: *They were routinely subjected to racist attitudes and behaviours.* ◇ *It would be exaggerated to describe such a policy as intentionally racist.*

ra·dial /ˈreɪdiəl/ *adj.* having a pattern of lines that go out from a central point towards the edge of a circle: *The basic radial pattern is common to all flowers.* ■ **ra·di·al·ly** /ˈreɪdiəli/ *adv.*: *The effect can be observed for light moving radially out from the earth.*

ra·di·ant /ˈreɪdiənt/ *adj.* [only before noun] (*technical*) sent out in RAYS from a central point: *Radiant energy from the sun is absorbed in the top centimetres of land surfaces.*

ra·di·ate /ˈreɪdieɪt/ *verb* **1** [T] **~ sth** to send out energy, especially light or heat in all directions SYN GIVE OFF STH: *Electrons do not radiate energy continuously.* **2** [I] **+ adv./prep.** (of energy, especially light or heat) to be sent out in all directions: *Without appropriate insulation, heat radiates downwards from the building into the ground.* **3** [I] **+ adv./prep.** (of lines, etc.) to spread out in all directions from a central point: *Russian railways mainly radiated from Moscow and Petrograd.* ◇ *Pain may radiate to the shoulder or abdomen.* **4** [T] **~ sth** (of a person) to show clearly that you have a strong feeling or quality through your expression, attitude or behaviour: *As a leader, John F. Kennedy radiated vigour and charisma.*

ra·di·ation /ˌreɪdiˈeɪʃn/ *noun* **1** [U, C] powerful and very dangerous RAYS that are sent out from RADIOACTIVE substances: *The individual contracted cancer as a result of exposure to radiation.* ◇ *The nature and severity of the threat posed by different kinds of particles and radiations vary greatly.* ◇ **+ noun** *For other tissues, radiation damage may only become apparent many months or years after radiation exposure.* **2** [U] energy that is sent out in the form of RAYS: *Lightning is a major natural source of electromagnetic radiation.* ◇ *to emit/absorb radiation* ◇ *Absorption of solar radiation by the surfaces and faces of the glaciers generates meltwater.* **3** (*also* **ˌradiˈation therapy**) [U] the treatment of cancer and other diseases using radiation: *Late reactions occur more than 90 days after commencing a course of radiation.* ➲ *compare* RADIOTHERAPY

rad·ical[1] AWL /ˈrædɪkl/ *adj.* [usually before noun] **1** concerning the most basic and important parts of sth; thorough and complete SYN FAR-REACHING: *This period was one of radical change in the universities.* ◇ *The rapid population growth of the past 250 years is a radical departure from the previous trend.* **2** new, different and likely to have a great effect: *The need for a radical approach to improving the health of the population has been recognized.* **3** in favour of thorough and complete political or social change: *In this highly charged political climate, radical groups were viewed with great suspicion.* **4** (of medical treatment) thorough and intended to cure sth completely: *Radical surgery for this condition is of uncertain value, with high mortality and few long-term survivors reported.*

rad·ical[2] AWL /ˈrædɪkl/ *noun* **1** a person with radical opinions: *Before 1919, anarchism was more popular than socialism among young radicals.* **2** (*chemistry*) a group of atoms that behave as a single unit in a number of COMPOUNDS: *An acid radical is the anion formed when a hydrogen ion is removed from an acid.* ➲ *see also* FREE RADICAL

rad·ic·al·ism /ˈrædɪkəlɪzəm/ *noun* [U] belief in radical ideas and principles: *Much of the civil rights energy in the 1940s grew out of economic and political radicalism.*

rad·ic·al·ly AWL /ˈrædɪkli/ *adv.* completely; to a very great extent: *British politics is radically different now from how it was 30 or 40 years ago.* ◇ *New technologies may radically reduce the carbon emissions associated with certain types of energy production.*

radii *pl. of* RADIUS

radio /ˈreɪdiəʊ; *NAmE* ˈreɪdioʊ/ *noun* **1** (*often* **the radio**) [U, sing.] the activity of broadcasting programmes for people to listen to; the programmes that are broadcast: *They watch a lot of television, listen to the radio, and read magazines.* ◇ **on ~** *British political parties are provided with free broadcasting time on radio and television.* ◇ **on the ~** *They are asked about adverts they see on TV and hear on the radio.* **2** [C] a piece of equipment used for listening to radio programmes: *Sony started by making transistor radios in the 1950s.* **3** [U] the process of sending and receiving messages through the air using ELECTROMAGNETIC waves: *Guglielmo Marconi is credited with being the first to use radio to span the Atlantic in 1901.* ◇ **by ~** *The message was then sent to its recipient by radio in Morse code.* ◇ **+ noun** *Such galaxies emit radio waves from their central cores.* **4** [C] a piece of equipment for sending and receiving radio signals: *When they have finished speaking,* *they say 'over' and switch the radio from transmit mode to receive mode.*

radio·active /ˌreɪdiəʊˈæktɪv; *NAmE* ˌreɪdioʊˈæktɪv/ *adj.* sending out harmful RADIATION caused when the NUCLEI (= central parts) of atoms are broken up: *Radioactive decay involves the disintegration of atomic nuclei.* ◇ *No country has yet devised a safe and permanent method of radioactive waste disposal.* ◇ *a radioactive element/isotope/substance* ◇ *Almost all fission products of these isotopes are highly radioactive.* ■ **radio·activ·ity** /ˌreɪdiəʊækˈtɪvəti; *NAmE* ˌreɪdioʊækˈtɪvəti/ *noun* [U] *Radioactivity affects humans and animals, causing somatic and genetic effects.* ◇ **~ of sth** *The radioactivity of a sample is measured by electrical or photographic methods.*

radi·ology /ˌreɪdiˈɒlədʒi; *NAmE* ˌreɪdiˈɑːlədʒi/ *noun* [U] the study and use of different types of RADIATION in medicine, for example to treat diseases: *Radiology may be useful in less acute cases.* ■ **radio·logic·al** /ˌreɪdiəˈlɒdʒɪkl; *NAmE* ˌreɪdiəˈlɑːdʒɪkl/ *adj.*: *Further radiological investigations may be required to establish the cause of the condition.*

radio·ther·apy /ˌreɪdiəʊˈθerəpi; *NAmE* ˌreɪdioʊˈθerəpi/ *noun* [U] the treatment of disease, especially cancer, by RADIATION: *Patients who undergo radiotherapy should be advised about skin care.*

ra·dius /ˈreɪdiəs/ *noun* (*pl.* **radii** /ˈreɪdiaɪ/) **1 ~ (of sth)** a straight line between the centre of a circle or SPHERE and any point on its outer edge; the length of this line: *The two circles will have radii of 5 mm and 10 mm.* ➲ *compare* DIAMETER **2** a round area that covers the distance mentioned from a central point: **within a ~ (of sth)** *Nearly all residents had access to fruits and vegetables within a 1-mile radius of their homes.* ◇ **at a ~ of sth** *At a radius of 90 miles, death would occur within two weeks of exposure to radiation from the bomb.*

rage¹ /reɪdʒ/ *noun* [U, C] a feeling of violent anger that is difficult to control: *Children and adolescents with bipolar disorder may demonstrate intense rage.*

R

rage² /reɪdʒ/ *verb* **1** [I] (of a storm, a battle, an argument, etc.) to continue in a violent way: *As this war has been raging for many years, it has consumed many lives on both sides.* ◇ *Debates rage in the archaeological literature over the degree of its effect on ancient societies (e.g. Ackerley, 1988; Artzy and Hillel, 1988).* **2** [I] **~ (at/against/about sb/sth)** to show that you are very angry about sth or with sb, especially by shouting: *In Act III, the King madly rages against human ingratitude.*

rail /reɪl/ *noun* **1** [U] (often before another noun) railways as a means of transport: **by ~** *Coal is delivered to a power plant by rail.* ◇ **+ noun** *The building of extensive road and rail systems is a major undertaking.* ◇ *a rail service/line/operator/network* ◇ *The air pollution cost per passenger of rail transport depends on the occupancy rate.* **2** [C, usually pl.] each of the two metal bars that form the track that trains run on: *The freight train left the rails.* **3** [C] a wooden or metal bar placed around sth as a barrier or to provide support: *An occupational therapist may be able to arrange for adaptations to the patient's home, such as ramps and grab rails.*

rail·way /ˈreɪlweɪ/ (*BrE*) (*NAmE* **rail·road** /ˈreɪlrəʊd; *NAmE* ˈreɪlroʊd/) *noun* **1** (*BrE also* **ˈrailway line**) a track with rails on which trains run: *The military was keen to build a railway across Bulgaria to Constantinople.* **2** a system of tracks, together with the trains that run on them, and the organization and people needed to operate them: *Plans to privatize the railways came to nothing in Switzerland and Germany.* ◇ **+ noun** *Car travel times to the nearest railway station were also computed.*

rain¹ /reɪn/ *noun* **1** [U, sing.] water that falls from the sky in separate drops: *Areas are defined as arid if they receive less than 255 mm of rain per annum.* ◇ *Acid rain (with a pH less than 5.65) is another example of aerial pollution.* ◇ *A cold rain had fallen for several days prior to the disaster.* ◇ **in the ~** *Thousands of drivers fail to take even the most basic precautions, such as slowing down in the rain.* ➲ *see also* RAINY **2 rains** [pl.] falls of rain: *During the winter months, there are usually heavy rains.* **3 the rains** [pl.] the season of heavy continuous rain in tropical countries: *The rains do not reach India until late May or early June.* **4** [sing.] **~ of sth** a large number of things falling from the sky at the same time: *A rain of perhaps 10 million boulders would be expected from such an explosion.*

rain² /reɪn/ *verb* **1** [I] when **it rains**, water falls from the sky in drops: *It was raining heavily when they set off.* **2** [I, T] to fall or to make sth fall on sb/sth in large quantities: **~ (sth) (down) (on sb/sth)** *The bombs that rained down on Germany killed many civilians.* ◇ **it rains sth** *When they looked out, they saw that it was raining ash.*

rain·bow /ˈreɪnbəʊ; *NAmE* ˈreɪnboʊ/ *noun* a curved band of different colours that appears in the sky when the sun shines through rain: **+ noun** *Light from any hot object, including the sun and stars, can be spread out using a prism to make a rainbow pattern, or spectrum.*

rain·fall /ˈreɪnfɔːl/ *noun* [U, sing.] the total amount of rain that falls in a particular area in a particular amount of time; an occasion when rain falls: *The river basin receives an average annual rainfall of 2 000 mm.* ◇ *the daily/seasonal rainfall* ◇ *high/extreme/intense rainfall* ◇ *A bridge over a river collapsed after a heavy rainfall.* ◇ **+ noun** *This suggests significant changes in tropical rainfall patterns.*

rain·for·est /ˈreɪnfɒrɪst; *NAmE* ˈreɪnfɔːrɪst; ˈreɪnfɑːrɪst/ *noun* [C, U] a thick forest in tropical parts of the world that have a lot of rain: *The most threatened, and most diverse, natural ecosystems on earth are the tropical rainforests.* ◇ *The refuges were mainly areas of lowland rainforest.*

rainy /ˈreɪni/ *adj.* (**rain·ier**, **rain·iest**) having or bringing a lot of rain: *The river widens to about 15 km during the rainy season.*

raise¹ /reɪz/ *verb* **1 ~ sth** to mention sth for people to discuss or sb to deal with: *Buzan's work raises some interesting questions (Buzan, 1983: 214–42).* ◇ *One of the key issues raised in 'The Da Vinci Code' involves the role of the feminine in Christianity.* ◇ *Ethical objections are raised by vegetarians to the killing of farm animals for human consumption.* **2 ~ sth** to cause or produce a feeling or reaction; to make a problem appear: *Increasing costs raised serious doubts among investors as to the viability of the project.* ◇ *Many complex ethical issues are raised by modern medicine.* **3** to increase the amount or level of sth: **~ sth** *The aim of the project was to raise students' awareness of the dangers of drug use.* ◇ *Patients were advised to avoid talking for long periods or raising their voice.* ◇ **~ sth to sth** *Demand remained unchanged when the price was raised to $44.* OPP LOWER² (1) **4 ~ sth** to collect or bring money or people together: *The revenue raised from the production tax was US$10 million.* ◇ *The film 'Throw Me a Dime' showed how young children raised money by begging to feed their families.* ◇ *The estates of Brabant raised an army to oppose the policies and troops of Joseph II.* **5** to care for a child or young animal until it is able to take care of itself: **~ sb/sth** *In many species, up to 80% of the chicks in a nest are not fathered by the male that raises them.* ◇ **~ sb/sth as sth** *None of the four men were raised as Jews.* ➲ *compare* BRING SB UP **6 ~ sth** to breed particular animals; to grow particular crops: *Insects raised on a high protein diet showed stronger mating preferences.* **7 ~ sth** to lift or move sth to a higher level: *Students raise their hand when they want to speak.* ◇ *Development in Bangkok commonly involves raising land to protect it against local flooding.* OPP LOWER² (2) **8 ~ sb (from sth)** to make sb who has died come to life again: *In myth, Asklepios was a famous surgeon who could raise people from the dead.*

IDM **raise your 'voice (about/against sth)** to clearly express your opinon about sth: *In 1637, the synod of the Reformed Church of France raised its voice against the slave trade.*

▸ RAISE + NOUN **question • issue • possibility, prospect • problem, difficulty • challenge • concern • doubts • objection • suspicion** *Kwon (2002) raised some methodological concerns.* ◇ *Plans to drill oil wells off Greenland have raised concerns about oil pollution.* | **rate • level • standards • expectations • temperature • price • taxes • wages • productivity • profile • awareness • probability • stakes** *A higher proportion of short-wavelength light was generated as the temperature was raised.* | **money, funds, capital, finance • revenue • taxes** *Funds were raised to build a football stadium.*

WHICH WORD?

raise • rise

- **Raise** is a verb that must have an object; **rise** is used without an object: when you **raise** sth, you increase its number or quantity; when sth **rises**, it increases in number or quantity: *Firms may absorb losses rather than raise prices.* ◇ *Prices will be raised by 8%.* ◇ *Prices have risen steadily.*
- When you **raise** sth, you lift it to a higher position; when people or things **rise**, they move from a lower to a higher position: *More than two thirds of the audience raised their hands.* ◇ *The hot humid air rises in a vertical column.*
- **Raise** is used in academic writing meaning 'to mention sth for people to discuss or sb to deal with': *This study raises two important questions...*

raise² /reɪz/ *noun* (*NAmE*) = RISE¹ (3)

rais·ing /ˈreɪzɪŋ/ *noun* **1** [U] the activity of breeding particular animals or growing particular crops: *Until the mid-twentieth century, most farms combined livestock raising and grain growing.* **2** [U, sing.] **~ (of sth)** the act of increasing the amount or level of sth: *With the raising of the retirement age, the topic of age discrimination is at the forefront of public scrutiny.* **3** [U] **awareness/consciousness ~** the activity of making people more aware of an issue that you think is important: **+ noun** *Educational and awareness-raising activities can empower individuals and communities to understand and protect their human rights.*

ran *past tense of* RUN¹

ran·dom¹ AWL /ˈrændəm/ *adj.* **1** [usually before noun] done, chosen, etc. so that all possible choices have an equal chance of being considered: *We used a random sample of 1 250 Montgomery county residential addresses.* ◇ *Participants are recruited through random selection.* **2** without any regular pattern: *The length of time a molecule spends in each phase is random and highly unpredictable.* ◇ *Heat increases the random motion of molecules.* ◇ *Random variation makes it difficult to draw general conclusions from single observations.* ■ **ran·dom·ness** AWL *noun* [U] *Two processes introduce randomness into evolution: mutations and meiosis.*

ran·dom² AWL /ˈrændəm/ *noun*

IDM **at 'random** without deciding in advance what is going to happen; without any regular pattern: *Individuals are assigned to treatment groups completely at random.* ◇ *to be drawn/allocated/chosen/selected at random*

ˌrandom eˈffect *noun* (*statistics*) the treatment of VARIABLES within a study as a random selection from a larger population, intended to be representative of that population: *We designated the test population and their interaction as random effects and the base population as a fixed effect.* ◇ **+ noun** *Because the sample is a subset of Asian countries, a random effects model appears more appropriate.* ➲ *compare* FIXED EFFECT

ran·dom·ize (*BrE also* **-ise**) /ˈrændəmaɪz/ *verb* [usually passive] (*technical*) to use a method in an experiment or a piece of research that gives all choices an equal chance of being considered; to put things in a random order: **(be) randomized** *Randomized controlled trials of the new designs took place in Ethiopia.*

ran·dom·ly AWL /ˈrændəmli/ *adv.* **1** in a way that gives every possible choice an equal chance of being considered: *One member from each family was randomly selected.* **2** without any regular pattern: *Imprinted genes are not randomly distributed in the genome, but tend to occur predominantly in clusters.*

ˌrandom ˈvariable *noun* (*statistics*) a function that gives a UNIQUE number to the possible OUTCOMES of an experiment: *X is a discrete random variable that represents the number of 'tails' we get when we toss a fair coin ten times.*

rang *past tense of* RING³

range¹ AWL /reɪndʒ/ *noun* **1** [C, usually sing.] a variety of things of a particular type: **~ (of sth)** *This technique has a wide range of applications.* ◇ **across/over a ~** *The results stimulated discussion across a broad range of issues.* **2** [C, usually sing.] the limits between which sth varies: *The plant community has adapted to the large temperature range created by high altitude.* ◇ **~ of sth** *The actual price range of hair products was enormous.* ◇ **in/within a ~ of sth** *The average value for each species falls within a range of about 12–16%.* ◇ **outside a ~ of sth** *The result fell outside the predicted range of values.* ◇ **over a ~ (of sth)** *This result is generally consistent with the recent study over a wider pressure range.* ➲ language bank *at* STATISTIC **3** [C] **~ (of sth)** a set of products of a particular type: *Amway produced a new range of beauty products called 'Satinique'.* **4** [C] **~ (of sth)** a line or group of mountains or hills: *Glaciers were present in the Pyrenees and other mountain ranges in Spain.* **5** [C, U] the distance that a vehicle will travel before it needs more fuel; the distance over which a weapon can hit things: *Vehicles using natural gas have a limited range.* ◇ *Rifles had a much greater range and accuracy than muskets.* ➲ *see also* LONG-RANGE (1)

IDM **within 'range (of sth)** near enough to be reached, seen or heard: *The planes could not get within range of their targets.*

▸ ADJECTIVE + RANGE **wide, large • broad, extensive • great, vast, huge, enormous • diverse • narrow, limited, small, restricted • whole, entire, full** *Consumers had a narrow range of choices.* | **normal • acceptable • potential • dynamic • continuous • geographical** *The results were within the recommended acceptable range.*

▸ NOUN + RANGE **age • temperature • frequency** *The age range of these young authors was 15 to 20 years.*

▸ VERB + RANGE **have • show, exhibit, illustrate, demonstrate, display • represent • indicate • cover, span • extend, expand, broaden • limit, restrict, narrow • consider, examine • produce** *Members of the icefish family exhibit a range of activity levels.* ◇ *Collins (1998) considers a wide range of environmental conditions.* | **include, encompass, incorporate, comprise • identify • capture • highlight • explore • address • provide, offer • draw on, utilize** *Standard surveys of the general population fail to capture the full range of health care concerns of women.* | **fall within, lie within** *This difference falls within the range of values predicted for future global warming (IPCC, 2001).*

range² AWL /reɪndʒ/ *verb* **1** [I] to vary between two particular amounts, sizes or levels, including others between them: **~ (in sth) (from A to B)** *Settlements ranged in size*

R

from individual farmsteads to small villages. ◇ *Participants ranged widely in age.* ◇ **~ between A and B** *The operating temperature ranged between 40 and 90K.* **2** [I] to include a variety of different things in addition to those mentioned: **~ from A to B** *In the post-war period, a vast array of services was provided by central government, ranging from education to telecommunications.* ◇ **+ adv./prep.** *Subjects for cartoons ranged widely in this period, but particular favourites involved political corruption and military incompetence.* ➲ *see also* WIDE-RANGING **3** [I] **+ adv./prep.** to move around an area: *Some predators range over large distances.*

PHR V **ˌrange yourself/sb aˈgainst/ˈwith sb/sth** [usually passive] to join with other people to oppose or support sb/sth: *His army could match in size the combined forces of all the Greek city states ranged against him.* **ˈrange over sth** to include a variety of different subjects: *Save for the omission of politics, Plotinus's essays range over the whole field of ancient philosophy.*

rank¹ /ræŋk/ *noun* **1** [C, usually pl., U] the position that sb has in a particular organization or society: *The campaign was aimed at party officials in the middle and lower ranks.* ◇ *The aim was to include writers of both genders and all social ranks from 1415–1681.* ◇ *Reproductive success tends to be higher for individuals of high rank.* ◇ **~ of sth** *Lenin's father had been a schoolteacher but had risen to the rank of schools inspector.* ➲ *see also* RANKING **2 the ranks** [pl.] the members of a particular group or organization: *The movement gained strength as more and more people joined their ranks.* ◇ **~ of sth** *Some freedmen became very wealthy and joined the ranks of the upper classes.* **3** [C] **~ (of sth)** the position that sb has in the army, navy, police, etc: *Braithwaite served in the army as a private and rose to the rank of major.* **4** [sing.] the degree to which sb/sth is higher or lower on a scale of quality, importance, success, etc: *Weber was widely recognized throughout his life as an academic scholar of the first rank.* ◇ **~ order** *The countries are listed below in rank order, from highest to lowest.*

rank² /ræŋk/ *verb* [T, I] (not used in the progressive tenses) to give sb/sth a particular position on a scale according to quality, importance, success, etc; to have a position of this kind: **~ sb/sth** *Based on the interviews, the school ranked all 800 students and selected the best 150.* ◇ **~ sb/sth + adv./prep.** *Question 4 asks customers to rank these factors in order of importance.* ◇ *Surveys reveal that voters did not rank these issues highly.* ◇ **~ (sb/sth) as sth** *All groups ranked gang and gun violence as the most serious forms of violence.* ◇ **~ (sb/sth) + adj.** *In 2005, the UK ranked 17th out of 24 industrialized nations in terms of child poverty.* ◇ **+ adv./prep.** *Table 7.3 shows the 10 countries that rank highest in terms of human development.*

rank·ing /ˈræŋkɪŋ/ *noun* the position of sb/sth on a scale that shows how good or important they are in relation to other similar people or things: *These rankings are based on opinion surveys.* ◇ **~ in sth** *Getting a high ranking in search engines has become a critical skill.* ◇ **~ of sth** *Table 4.1 presents a ranking of cities averaged by total market size.*

rape¹ /reɪp/ *noun* [U, C] the crime, typically committed by a man, of forcing sb to have sex with him, especially using violence: *The defendant was convicted of rape.* ◇ *There was an increase in the number of reported rapes.* ◇ **+ noun** *rape victims*

rape² /reɪp/ *verb* **~ sb** (usually of a man) to force sb to have sex with him when they do not want to by threatening them or using violence: *In some states, abortion is legal when a woman has been raped, or her life or health are in danger.*

rapid /ˈræpɪd/ *adj.* [usually before noun] happening in a short period of time or at a fast rate: *Rapid evolutionary change at the level of the gene was taking place.* ◇ *India has experienced rapid increases in economic growth since 1980.* ◇ *Alexander captured Babylon, Susa and Persepolis in rapid succession.* ◇ *At 2 weeks, she was admitted to hospital with rapid breathing that required oxygen.* ■ **rap·id·ity** /rəˈpɪdəti/ *noun* [U] **~ (of sth)** *The rapidity of global warming was not fully appreciated until the 1990s.* ◇ *Figure 1.1 illustrates the rapidity with which farm output has increased during the capitalist era.*

▸ RAPID + NOUN **growth, increase, expansion, rise, proliferation • development • advance • progress • spread, diffusion • response • recovery • decline, decrease • deterioration • pace • rate • change • turnover • succession • urbanization • industrialization • evolution • assessment • identification** *These cities all experienced rapid population growth during the Industrial Revolution.* ◇ *The rapid pace of economic development in today's world is striking.*

rap·id·ly /ˈræpɪdli/ *adv.* in a short period of time or at a fast rate: *Internet adoption in homes has grown rapidly since the early 1990s.* ◇ *The situation is rapidly worsening.* ◇ *Women readers were a rapidly expanding market at this time.* ◇ *The polymer is cooled rapidly from -23°C to -28°C.*

▸ VERB + RAPIDLY **increase, rise • grow • expand • spread • change • develop • evolve • progress • decline • decrease • deteriorate • decay** *Wind turbine technology has evolved rapidly over the last twenty years.* ◇ *Overfishing during the years 2002–2009 decreased rapidly.*

▸ RAPIDLY + VERB-ING **changing • growing, increasing, rising • expanding • developing • evolving • industrializing • declining** *This applies espeically to the rapidly industrializing economies of East Asia.*

rap·port /ræˈpɔː(r)/ *noun* [sing., U] a friendly relationship in which people understand each other very well: **~ with sb** *Interviewers worked hard to establish a rapport with the young interviewees.* ◇ **~ (between A and B)** *Building a good rapport between patient and professional was considered vital.* ◇ *Rapport-building techniques included active listening and open body language.*

rare /reə(r); *NAmE* rer/ *adj.* (**rarer, rar·est**) **1** not done, seen, happening, etc. very often: *In rare cases, death may ensue.* ◇ *On rare occasions, hurricanes reach category 5, with devastating impacts on both human and natural systems.* ◇ *Thus, with rare exceptions, all the cells contain identical genetic information.* ◇ *Patients with rare diseases need targeted effective therapies.* ◇ **it is ~ (for sb/sth) to do sth** *It is rare for individual fish to reach ages beyond 7 or 8.5 years for males and females, respectively.* **2** existing only in small numbers and therefore valuable or interesting: *Though commonly found in the Harz Mountains during the 1990s, it is a rare species today.* ➲ *see also* RARITY

rare·ly /ˈreəli; *NAmE* ˈrerli/ *adv.* not often: *It is rarely used as an anaesthetic for humans.* ◇ *Only rarely did textbooks refer to the African soldiers in the French army.* ◇ *Half of all Americans aged 12 to 30 'rarely, if ever, read a newspaper'.*

rar·ity /ˈreərəti; *NAmE* ˈrerəti/ *noun* (*pl.* **-ies**) **1** [C] a person or thing that is unusual and is therefore often interesting or valuable: *Single mothers are still a rarity in Japan.* **2** [U] **~ (of sb/sth)** the quality of being rare: *However, there are some limitations, not least of which is the relative rarity of twins in the general population.*

rate¹ /reɪt/ *noun* **1** a measurement of the speed at which sth happens: *A number of European countries experienced steeply rising inflation rates.* ◇ **~ of sth** *The Soviet Union achieved very high rates of economic growth between the 1920s and the 1980s.* ◇ *The addition of enzymes increased the rate of chemical reaction by a factor of 1 000.* ◇ **at a ~ (of sth)** *Per capita GDP has grown at an average annual rate of 2.4% in rich countries.* **2** a measurement of the number of times sth happens or exists during a particular period: *Generally, the native mammals have excellent survival rates.* ◇ *Mortality rates from cholera were 9 times higher in households supplied by the Southwark company.* ◇ **~ of sth** *The patient looked tired and had a heart rate of 60 beats per minute.* ➲ *see also* BIRTH RATE **3** a fixed amount of money that is charged or paid for sth: *These studies compared the impacts of fixed and flexible foreign exchange rates.* ◇ **~ of sth** *There was a sharp rise in the rate of interest.* ◇ **at a ~ (of sth)** *These businessmen were given loans at very low interest rates.* ➲ *see also* DISCOUNT RATE

IDM **at ˈany rate 1** used to show that you are being more accurate about sth that you have just said: *Management has often been perceived as hostile, or at any rate unsupportive.* **2** used to say that a particular fact is true despite what has happened in the past or what may happen in the future: *Further studies are needed but, at any rate, our results show indications of significant progress so far.*

▸ ADJECTIVE + RATE **high • low • average • constant • increased • increasing • overall • annual • real** *The overall rate of violent crime in US schools decreased over the period.*

▸ NOUN + RATE **growth • inflation • reaction** *When the temperature was lowered, the reaction rate slowed.* | **response • participation • success • mortality, death • birth • fertility • pregnancy • survival • heart • unemployment** *Teenage pregnancy rates were very high.* | **exchange • interest • tax • wage** *Higher tax rates were associated with lower levels of private investment.*

▸ VERB + RATE **have • show, exhibit • experience • yield • achieve • exceed • equal** *The rate of erosion exceeded the rate of oxidation.* | **calculate, determine, estimate, measure • underestimate • observe • report • assume • predict • compare** *Using colonoscopy, some experts have reported tumour detection rates of 90–100%.* | **increase, raise • accelerate • maximize • enhance • improve • reduce, lower, decrease, cut • set, fix • maintain • adjust, alter • control • affect, influence** *The aim was to reduce adult smoking rates to 21% or less by 2010.* | **charge • pay** *Borrowers were being charged an interest rate of 5%.*

▸ RATE + VERB **rise, increase • fall, decline, decrease, drop • exceed • reach • vary • differ • range from... to... • depend on • remain • tend to** *In 1995, the unemployment rate rose to 5.7 per cent.* ◇ *The rate of technological advance remained slow.*

rate² /reɪt/ *verb* (not used in the progressive tenses) **1** to consider that sb/sth has a particular level of quality, value, etc: **~ sb/sth + adv./prep.** *The department is highly rated.* ◇ *Only 45% of customers rated the company favourably.* ◇ **~ sb/sth (as) sth** *There was one debate between Kennedy and McCarthy, which most observers rated as a draw.* ◇ **~ sb/sth + adj.** *Most children were also rated high in inhibitory control.* **2** to place sth/sb in a particular position on a scale in relation to similar things or people SYN RANK²: **~ sb/sth (+ adv./prep.)** *GPs were asked to rate how important these barriers were, using a five-point Likert scale.* ◇ **~ sth/sb (as) + sth** *The patient rated the pain as 8 out of 10.* ◇ **~ sb/sth + noun** *The university is currently rated the top Korean university.* **3 ~ sth** to be good, important, etc. enough to be treated in a particular way SYN MERIT²: *The problem does not even rate a mention in the literature.*

ra·ther /ˈrɑːðə(r); *NAmE* ˈræðər/ *adv.* **1** used to mean 'fairly' or 'to some degree', often when expressing slight criticism or surprise: *The definition of molecular biology given above is rather limited.* ◇ *At first sight, the results are rather surprising.* ◇ *Islam arrived later in Indonesia than in Morocco and took a rather different form.* ◇ *This is rather a difficult question that requires a complex answer.* **2** used to correct sth you have said, or to give more accurate information: **or ~** *For Crosland, education, or rather comprehensive education, was a central issue.* ➲ language bank *at* I.E. **3** used to introduce an idea that is different or opposite to the idea that you have stated previously: *Race is not a biological fact. It is, rather, a historical outcome of how people of different ancestries have lived with one another.* ◇ **but ~** *Oil has not been a solution to the country's economic weakness, but rather a prime cause of deeper problems.*

IDM **would rather... (than...)** would prefer to: *Anna would rather sit and chat with her friends than do schoolwork.*

ˈrather than *prep.* instead of sb/sth: *The tissue sample was processed into resin, rather than wax.* ◇ **~ doing sth** *New members have generally joined existing groups rather than forming completely new ones.*

rat·ify /ˈrætɪfaɪ/ *verb* (**rati·fies, rati·fy·ing, rati·fied, rati·fied**) **~ sth** to make an agreement officially valid by voting for or signing it: *150 countries have ratified the treaty.* ◇ *Workers finally ratified a contract that provided higher wage increases.* ■ **rati·fi·ca·tion** /ˌrætɪfɪˈkeɪʃn/ *noun* [U] **~ (by sb/sth)** *The Convention required ratification by five states in order to enter into force.*

rat·ing /ˈreɪtɪŋ/ *noun* a measurement of how good, popular, important, etc. sb/sth is, especially in relation to other people or things: *A follow-up study found that better trained teams had significantly higher customer satisfaction ratings.* ◇ **~ of sth** *Poor self-reported health was defined as a rating of 4 or 5 on a five-point scale.* ◇ *Parents were asked to provide their own ratings of their child's social skills.*

ratio AWL /ˈreɪʃiəʊ; *NAmE* ˈreɪʃioʊ/ *noun* (*pl.* **-os**) the relationship between two groups of people or things that is represented by two numbers showing how much larger one group is than the other: *An unbalanced sex ratio added to the problems for white settlers in the Caribbean.* ◇ **~ of A to B** *The ratio of male migrants to female migrants is 2:1.* ◇ *The X-ray observations allow us to estimate the ratio of the mass of hot gas to dark matter.* ◇ *to calculate/find/determine/measure the ratio of A to B* ◇ **A-to-B ~** *The new type of antenna provides a better signal-to-noise ratio.* ➲ language bank *at* PROPORTION

ra·tion·al AWL /ˈræʃnəl/ *adj.* **1** (of behaviour or ideas) based on reason rather than emotions: *Delusions are not affected by rational argument.* ◇ *Economic theories of rational decision-making focus narrowly on prices and quantities.* ◇ **it is ~ (for sb/sth) to do sth** *In such circumstances, it is rational for companies to raise prices.* OPP IRRATIONAL **2** (of a person) able to think clearly and make decisions based on reason rather than emotions SYN REASONABLE: *As Kant points out, no rational person wants to be a slave.* OPP IRRATIONAL ■ **ra·tion·al·ly** AWL /ˈræʃnəli/ *adv.*: *It is assumed that managers will act rationally in the pursuit of profit optimization.*

ra·tion·ale /ˌræʃəˈnɑːl; *NAmE* ˌræʃəˈnæl/ *noun* the principles or reasons that explain a particular decision, course of action or belief: *The underlying rationale is that competition removes monopolies.* ◇ **~ for sth** *This explanation provides a compelling economic rationale for the formation of alliances.* ◇ **~ behind sth** *The rationale behind this approach was to shift power away from service providers towards consumers.*

ra·tion·al·ism AWL /ˈræʃnəlɪzəm/ *noun* [U] the belief that all behaviour and opinions should be based on reason rather than on emotions or religious beliefs: *The Catholic Church was challenged by the growth in rationalism.*

ra·tion·al·ist /ˈræʃnəlɪst/ *noun* a person who believes in rationalism: *Economic rationalists see no real difficulties in applying the same logic here.* ■ **ra·tion·al·ist** (*also* **ra·tion·al·is·tic** /ˌræʃnəˈlɪstɪk/) *adj.* [usually before noun] *rationalist* *theories of international relations ◇ a rationalist approach/perspective/position*

ra·tion·al·ity AWL /ˌræʃəˈnæləti/ *noun* [U] ideas based on reason rather than emotion; the ability to have such ideas: *Practical rationality enables humans to navigate their environments successfully and achieve their purposes.*

ra·tion·al·ize (*BrE also* **-ise**) AWL /ˈræʃnəlaɪz/ *verb* **1** [T, I] **~ (sth)** to find or try to find a logical reason to explain why sb thinks or behaves in a particular way: *an attempt to rationalize his violent behaviour ◇ However we rationalize our actions in terms of conscious beliefs and desires, a great deal is going at the subconscious level.* **2** [T] **~ sth** to make changes to a business, system, etc. in order to make it more efficient, especially by spending less money: *Pharmaceutical companies have attempted to rationalize research processes in order to reduce costs.* ■ **ra·tion·al·iza·tion, -isa·tion** AWL /ˌræʃnəlaɪˈzeɪʃn; *NAmE* ˌræʃnələˈzeɪʃn/ *noun* [U, C] *Rationalizations often involve self-deception.* ◇ **~ of sth** *Continuous rationalization of production is the key to generating cost reductions in manufacturing.*

ˈrational number *noun* (*mathematics*) a number that can be expressed as the RATIO of two whole numbers: *Real numbers themselves are divided into rational and irrational numbers.*

raw /rɔː/ *adj.* **1** [usually before noun] (of a material) in its natural state; not yet changed, used or made into sth else: *Raw wool was exported for processing abroad.* ➲ *see also* RAW MATERIAL **2** (of food) not cooked: *Eating raw meat is a major route of T. gondii infection in humans. ◇ Whale blubber is eaten raw in Japan.* **3** [usually before noun] (of data) not yet organized into a form in which they can be easily used or understood: *Approximately 20% of the raw data were considered unreliable and unfit for processing.* **4** [usually before noun] (of qualities and emotions) powerful and natural; not limited or trained: *They are songs full of raw emotion. ◇ The first issue is the question of power—the raw power exercised by masters over enslaved people.*

ˌraw maˈterial *noun* [C, U] a basic material that is used to make a product: *Taiwan imports most of the raw materials needed to maintain industrial production.* ◇ **~ for sth** (*figurative*) *After the fall of the Berlin wall in 1989, government archives became raw material for documentary films re-examining history.*

R

ray /reɪ/ *noun* a narrow line of light, heat or other energy: *When parallel light rays pass through a lens, they are refracted by the lens and brought to a common focus. ◇ gamma/ultraviolet rays* ◇ **~ of sth** *The two rays of light are absorbed differently as they pass through the coloured mineral and therefore have different colours.* ➲ *see also* X-RAY

reach¹ /riːtʃ/ *verb* **1** [T] **~ sth** to achieve a particular aim SYN ARRIVE AT STH: *They were all close to reaching the same conclusion. ◇ Only if they fail to reach an agreement can the matter be referred to arbitration. ◇ Reaching consensus on what constitutes terrorism is difficult. ◇ to reach a decision/verdict/compromise ◇ to reach a goal/target* ➲ *see also* FAR-REACHING **2** [T] **~ sth** to increase or decrease to a particular level, over a period of time: *Current begins to flow through the valve once the grid voltage reaches a certain level. ◇ Growth in Africa has maintained a strong pace, reaching almost 5.6% in 2006. ◇ The ice cube melts as heat flows from oven to ice, warming it up until it reaches melting point. ◇ to reach a peak/a maximum/its climax ◇ to reach a threshold/minimum* **3** [T] **~ sth** to arrive at a particular point or stage of sth after a period of time: *The vaccine delivery system has reached the stage of human clinical trials. ◇ Evolution had reached a critical point: the emergence of anatomically modern humans. ◇ She was dismissed approximately four weeks after reaching the age of 62. ◇ to reach maturity/adulthood* **4** [T] **~ sth** to arrive at the place that sb/sth has been travelling to: *The goods typically pass through several countries before reaching their final destination. ◇ Much of the aid never reached the front line, being sold for private profit en route. ◇ The ash from Krakatoa was injected into the stratosphere, reaching a height of 32 km.* **5** [I, T] to be big or long enough to go to a particular point or place: *This is a tall grass species that can reach up to 2 m in height.* ◇ **~ sth** *Sea mounts are undersea mountains that rise steeply from the floor of the ocean but do not reach the surface.* ◇ **+ adv./prep.** *Much more violent eruptions may occur where major faults reach down to the roof of a magma chamber.* **6** [T] **~ sb** to be seen or heard by sb: *By this time, literature was reaching a wider audience among the middle classes. ◇ Trade and professional journals are ideal for reaching particular target markets.* **7** [T] **~ sb** to communicate with sb, especially by telephone: *Of the 190 families meeting initial eligibility criteria, 52 could not be reached by phone.* **8** [T] **~ sb** to come to sb's attention: *News of the crisis reached him on Anglesey.*

PHR V **ˌreach ˈback to sth** to go back from the present to a particular earlier time: *The rising significance of the English language has a long history, reaching back to the birth of British colonialism in the late 16th century.* **ˌreach ˈout to sb** to show sb that you are interested in them and/or want to have contact with them or help them: *The programme's staff and volunteers make a sustained effort to reach out to youth organizations and schools.*

reach² /riːtʃ/ *noun* **1** [U, sing.] the limit to which sb/sth has the power or influence to do sth: **~ (of sb/sth)** *The reach of the federal government grew steadily after the New Deal. ◇ China has extended its reach into Africa in search of the raw materials needed to sustain its expansion.* ◇ **beyond (the) ~ (of sb/sth)** *A complete, encyclopedic description of the world was now beyond the reach of a single scholar.* **2** [U] the distance over which you can stretch your arms to touch sth; the distance over which a particular object can be used to touch sth else: **out of (sb's) ~** *Small objects such as buttons and batteries should be kept out of a child's reach.* ◇ **within (sb's) ~** *An urgent impulse or threat would drive them to seize any weapon within reach.* **3** [C, usually pl.] a straight section of water between two bends on a river: *Navigation and drainage play a key role in the commercial life of the lower reaches of the river.* **4 reaches** [pl.] **the outer, further, etc. ~ of sth** the parts of an area or a place that are a long way from the centre: *Manuscripts were obtained from the far reaches of the empire and translated into Arabic.*

IDM **within (easy) ˈreach (of sth)** close to sth: *These areas were within easy reach of maritime trade.*

react AWL /riˈækt/ *verb* **1** [I] to change or behave in a particular way as a result of or in response to sth SYN RESPOND (1): *Each person reacts in their own individual way.* ◇ **~ (to sth) (by doing sth)** *The industry has reacted to changes in business conditions by restructuring. ◇ Male stickleback fish react aggressively to the distinctive coloration of another male on their territory.* **2** [I] **~ (with sth) (to do sth)** (*chemistry*) (of substances) to experience a chemical change when coming into contact with another substance: *The acid and base will react to form a salt and water. ◇ It burns spontaneously in air and reacts violently with water. ◇ The moment that nitric oxide (NO) is exposed to air, it reacts with the oxygen to give nitrogen dioxide (NO_2).* **3** [I] **(+ adv./prep.)** to become ill after eating, breathing or coming into contact with a particular substance: *They often reported reacting badly to smoke because of asthma.*

PHR V **reˌact aˈgainst sb/sth** to show dislike or opposition in response to sth, especially by deliberately doing the opposite of what sb wants you to do: *Like his contemporary Karl Marx, Kierkegaard reacted against Hegel's philosophy, but in a very different direction.*

react·ant /riˈæktənt/ *noun* (*chemistry*) a substance that takes part in and is changed by a chemical reaction: *Encounters between reactants in solution occur in a very different manner from encounters in gases.* ➲ *compare* PRODUCT (3)

re·ac·tion AWL /riˈækʃn/ *noun* **1** [C, U] what you do, say or think as a result of sth that has happened: *The initial UN reaction was to dismiss the problem.* ◇ **~ to sb/sth** *People can have very different emotional reactions to events.* ◇ **in ~ to sth** *The City Beautiful movement was proposed in reaction to the pollution and crowding of industrial cities.* ➲ *see also* CHAIN REACTION (2) **2** [C] (*chemistry*) a chemical change produced by two or more substances acting on each other: *Enzymes increase the rate of chemical reactions.* ◇ *In an electrochemical cell, the reduction reaction occurs at one electrode, and the oxidation reaction at the other electrode.* ◇ **+ noun** *For high salt concentrations, a dramatic increase in reaction rate was observed.* ➲ *see also* CHAIN REACTION (1) **3** [C, U] (*medical*) a response by the body, usually a bad one, to sth such as a drug or a chemical substance: *A profound allergic reaction can follow exposure to a foreign protein or drug.* ◇ **~ to sth** *Drugs are tested in patient volunteers to monitor adverse reactions to long-term use.* ◇ **in ~ to sth** *Headaches and gastrointestinal upset are just two symptoms that children may experience in reaction to such stress.* **4** [U, C] (*physics*) a force shown by sth in response to another force, which is of equal strength and acts in the opposite direction: *Newton's third law of motion says that action and reaction are equal and opposite.* ◇ **+ noun** *Where any part of the bridge is prevented from moving, a reaction force is created.* **5** [C, usually sing.] **~ (against sth)** a change in people's attitudes or behaviour caused by strong disapproval of other very different attitudes: *Nationalism can be seen as a reaction against globalization.* **6** [U] opposition to social or political progress or change: *As globalized modernity challenged all societies, the forces of reaction gathered.* **7 reactions** [pl.] the ability to move quickly in response to sth, especially if in danger: *Wasps show quick reactions to a variety of perturbations.*

▸ ADJECTIVE + REACTION **chemical • biochemical • enzymatic • catalytic • electrochemical • photochemical • reverse • overall** *There are thousands of biochemical reactions, each catalysed by a separate enzyme.* | **adverse • acute, severe • allergic • inflammatory** *No inflammatory reaction was observed.*

▸ VERB + REACTION **provoke, elicit, trigger** *The fall in inflation triggers a reaction from the central bank: it cuts the interest rate.* | **undergo • initiate • produce, cause • drive • catalyse • accelerate • facilitate • inhibit • stop • reverse** *The heat from the molten rock, combined with high ambient temperatures at depth, caused chemical reactions.* | **suffer • have • cause, induce** *He suffered a serious allergic reaction to an anti-tetanus injection given to him by a doctor.*

▸ REACTION + VERB **occur, take place • proceed** *If the reaction takes place in a sealed container, the total pressure will change as the reaction proceeds.*

re·ac·tion·ary AWL /riˈækʃənri; *NAmE* riˈækʃəneri/ *adj.* opposed to political or social change: *The throne was claimed by Ferdinand's reactionary brother, Don Carlos.* ■ **re·ac·tion·ary** AWL *noun* (*pl.* -ies)*They knew that violent protest only strengthened the position of the reactionaries.*

re·act·ive AWL /riˈæktɪv/ *adj.* **1** (*chemistry*) tending to show chemical change when mixed with another substance: *Free radicals are highly reactive and can damage both DNA and proteins.* **2** showing a reaction or response: *Senior management began to recognize the importance of a proactive rather than a purely reactive approach.* ◇ **~ to sth** *Her pupils are equal and reactive to light.* ➲ *compare* PROACTIVE

re·activ·ity /ˌriːækˈtɪvəti/ *noun* [U] (*chemistry*) the degree to which sth reacts, or is likely to react: *Because of the high reactivity, dry iron nanoparticles tend to explode in contact with air.*

re·act·or AWL /riˈæktə(r)/ (*also* ˌnuclear reˈactor) *noun* a large structure used for the controlled production of nuclear energy: *The first controlled nuclear reactor was built and demonstrated by Enrico Fermi in 1942.* ◇ **in a ~** *As the reaction occurs, temperature rises or falls in the reactor.*

read /riːd/ *verb* (**read**, **read** /red/) **1** [I, T] to go through written or printed words in silence or speaking them to other people: **~ to sb/yourself** *Parents reported how often they read to their child.* ◇ **~ sth** *Reading a book on logic or philosophy is not like reading a novel.* ◇ *'The Iliad' was the most widely read book in the Greek world.* ◇ **~ (sth) aloud** *She always read her work aloud while writing, to see if it sounded right.* **2** [I, T] (not used in the progressive tenses) to look at and understand the meaning of written or printed words or symbols: *More than 90% of the population is able to read and write.* ◇ **~ sth** *He could read English but not Arabic.* **3** [I, T] (not used in the progressive tenses) to discover or find out about sb/sth by reading: **~ about/of sth** *The treatment may be actively sought by patients who have read about its benefits in the media.* ◇ **~ that...** *People are more likely to take a new drug if they read that medical studies support the claim that it is effective.* **4** [T] to understand sth in a particular way: **~ sth** *The institutional history of the European Union can be read in several ways.* ◇ **~ sth as sth** *Though it may not seem so at first, this turn to religion can be read as a sign of progress.* **5** [T] (of a computer or the person using it) to take data from a place where the data are stored, such as a disk: **~ sth** *The punched card was read by machine and the computer held a record of the readings.* ◇ **~ sth from sth** *The computer reads the instruction from memory and decodes it.* **6** [T] **+ speech** (of a piece of writing) to be written in a particular way: *The fourth paragraph now reads as follows:...* **7** [I] **+ adv./prep.** (of a piece of writing) to give a particular impression when read: *This ground-breaking article continues to read well today.* ◇ *The conclusion reads like notes collected in a hurry without the author developing a precise thesis.* **8** [T] **~ sth (from sth)** to get information from a measuring instrument: *The pressures of generator and absorber can be read from the pressure gauges.* **9** [T] **~ sth** (of measuring instruments) to show a particular value such as weight, speed or pressure: *When both the input terminals are grounded, the probe at the output reads the dc voltage 0.574 V.* **10** [T, I] (*BrE*) to study a subject, especially at a university: **~ sth** *She read pharmacology for her undergraduate degree at Leeds University.* ◇ **~ for sth** *Currently, Iskander is reading for a PhD at Queen Mary University.*

IDM **ˌread between the ˈlines** to look for or discover a meaning in sth that is not clearly stated: *Managers must learn to read between the lines or interpret subtle hints that a problem has developed.* **ˌtake it/sth as ˈread** to accept sth without discussing it: *Most realists, unsurprisingly, took it as read that other great powers would in time emerge to balance the USA.*

PHR V **ˌread sth ˈback** to read a message to the person who gave it to you in order to check that it is correct: *The aircraft acknowledges receipt of the message and reads back any crucial data.* **ˌread sth ˈinto sth** to think that sth means more than it really does: *It would be unwise to read too much into this particular finding.* **ˌread ˈon** to continue reading: *Before reading on, please pause a moment.* **ˌread sth ˈout** to read sth using your voice, especially to other people: *The interviewers' role was to read out the questionnaire on the computer screen and record the responses of each participant.* **ˌread sth ˈover/ˈthrough** to read sth from beginning to end in order to get a general impression of it or look for mistakes: *The participants read* *through the set of problems and then grouped together those problems they considered to be mathematically similar.* **ˌread sth ˈup | ˌread ˈup on sb/sth** to read a lot about a subject in order to research it: *Parents may well have read up on various treatments or alternative therapies that they would like to try.*

read·able /ˈriːdəbl/ *adj.* **1** (of a book, an article, etc.) that is easy, interesting and enjoyable to read: *It is an extremely readable book, written in a very engaging style.* ◇ *This survey of the research field is highly readable.* **2** (of written or printed words) clear and easy to read: *Sans-serif fonts are the most appropriate online, as their simple form makes them more readable at low resolutions.* HELP **Machine readable** documents contain text or code that can be read by a machine: *a machine readable passport* ■ **read·abil·ity** /ˌriːdəˈbɪləti/ *noun* [U] **~ (of sth)** *The following actions can increase the size of the display and enhance the readability of information.*

read·er /ˈriːdə(r)/ *noun* **1** a person who is reading sth: *St Paul keeps reminding his readers that the time is short.* ◇ **~ of sth** *There are many different readers of research reports and these audiences all have very different expectations.* **2** a person who reads a particular newspaper, magazine, etc: *As with the network television news shows, the average newspaper reader is nearing retirement age.* ◇ **~ of sth** *The pro-Conservative swing occurred across readers of most papers, including those of the Labour-supporting 'Mirror'.* **3** (*computing*) an electronic device that reads data stored in one form and changes them into another form so that a computer can perform operations on them: *The information is recorded in a microchip which is read by an electronic reader at immigration control.* **4** (*usually* **Reader**) **~ (in sth)** a senior teacher at a British university just below the rank of a professor: *Nicholas Kinnie is Reader in Human Resource Management at the University of Bath.*

read·er·ship /ˈriːdəʃɪp; *NAmE* ˈriːdərʃɪp/ *noun* [usually sing.] the number or type of people who read a particular newspaper, book, etc: *The issues and arguments presented here should attract a wide readership.* ◇ *a broad/mass/general readership* ◇ **~ of sth** *The populist papers have a combined readership of 4.3 million.*

R

read·ily /ˈredɪli/ *adv.* **1** quickly and without difficulty SYN FREELY (2): *Carbohydrates are used up first, as they are the most readily available store of energy.* ◇ *Two main issues are readily apparent from these developments.* **2** in a way that shows that you do not object to sth SYN WILLINGLY: *The plan was readily accepted by Germany.* ◇ *Both physicians and patients readily acknowledge that current treatments for LBP are ineffective.*

readi·ness /ˈredinəs/ *noun* **1** [U] **~ (for sth)** the state of being ready or prepared for sth: *A professional standing army was maintained in constant readiness for action.* ◇ *Adrenaline molecules make their way to all parts of the body, putting it into a state of readiness for sudden physical activity.* **2** [U, sing.] **~ (of sb) to do sth** the state of being willing to do sth: *In January 1971, Chou indicated his readiness to receive a presidential representative.* ◇ *Regulatory changes have affected the readiness of investors to implement renewable energy projects.*

read·ing /ˈriːdɪŋ/ *noun* **1** [U] books or articles that are intended to be read: *Directions for further reading are given at the end of each chapter.* ◇ *Dictionaries and definitions seldom make compelling reading.* **2** [sing., U] an act of reading sth: **~ (of sth)** *A careful reading of this narrative is very revealing.* ◇ *On close reading, the book reveals much about the motivations of the people involved.* ◇ **~ of sth from sth** (*technical*) *This example concerns the reading of binary data from the input device.* **3** [U] the activity of sb who reads: *With the advent of the web, the challenges to teachers of reading and writing have shifted.* ◇ **+ noun** *In each reading group, participants discussed a novel they had all read.* **4** [C] **~ (of sth)** the particular way in which you understand sth, such as a book or a situation SYN INTERPRETATION (1): *Deconstruction questions the established readings of a text and highlights alternative readings.* ◇ *The book encourages a critical reading of the political economy of the media in Kenya.* **5** [C] one of the stages during which a BILL must be discussed and accepted by a parliament before it can become law: *A bill in support of the plan had two readings in parliament in April 1626, but then was set aside.* ◇ *On the second reading, the bill's contents are subject to a fuller debate.* **6** [C] the amount or number shown on an instrument used for measuring sth: *The blood pressure reading taken this morning was 170/100.* **7** [C] **~ (of sth)** an event at which sth is read to an audience for entertainment; a piece of literature that is read at such an event: *In late December 1853, Dickens gave two public readings of 'A Christmas Carol' in Birmingham Town Hall.*

ready /ˈredi/ *adj.* (**read·ier, readi·est**) **1** [not before noun] fully prepared for what you are going to do: **~ for sth** *His mother had been unable to get him ready for school in the mornings.* ◇ **~ to do sth** *At the end of the second act, Hamlet is finally ready to take action.* **2** [not before noun] **~ to do sth** willing and quick to do or give sth: *Authorities in general seem more ready to act after a disaster than before its occurrence.* **3** [not before noun] completed and available to be used: **~ for sth** *The questionnaire should now be ready for use in the field.* ◇ **~ to do sth** *Many of the centres were not ready to accept refugees until the early eighties.* **4** available to be used easily and immediately: *Ensure all equipment necessary to assess the patient is ready and in working order.* ◇ *These individuals should have ready access to appropriate treatment.* ◇ *Nitrogen is commonly used due to its low cost and ready availability in a highly pure form.* **5** **~ for sth** needing sth as soon as possible: *An educated audience, impatient with inherited conventions, was ready for change.* ➲ *see also* READILY, READINESS

re·affirm /ˌriːəˈfɜːm; *NAmE* ˌriːəˈfɜːrm/ *verb* **~ sth** to state sth again in order to emphasize that it is still true: *Labour governments have reaffirmed their commitment to the use of private-sector capital for funding major projects.* ■ **re·affirm·ation** /ˌriːˌæfəˈmeɪʃn; *NAmE* ˌriːˌæfərˈmeɪʃn/ *noun* [C, U] **~ (of sth)** *The Bicentennial celebrations of the Constitutional Convention in 1987 provided the opportunity for a public reaffirmation of its virtues.*

re·agent /riˈeɪdʒənt/ *noun* (*chemistry*) a substance or mixture for use in chemical analysis or other reactions: *Certain reagents can be used in organic chemistry to make a wide range of different compounds.*

real /rɪəl; ˈriːəl; *NAmE* ˈriːəl/ *adj.* **1** actually existing or happening and not imagined: *But, in the real world, keeping variables constant is often difficult.* ◇ *People who break the rules but succeed are often praised, whether in real life or in television dramas.* ➲ *see also* REAL-LIFE, REAL-WORLD **2** [only before noun] used to emphasize how important or serious a situation is: *These pathogens constitute a real problem for the immune system.* ◇ *There was no real risk of violence or any other harm to the child.* ◇ *There was also a very real concern about the geographical distribution of grants.* **3** [only before noun] (*economics*) when the effect of price rises on the power of money to buy things is included in the sums: *This figure shows the average real wage of skilled construction workers.* ◇ *A fall in the real interest rate will boost output further.* ◇ *In the UK, the minimum wage is lower in real terms than it was two decades ago.* ➲ *compare* NOMINAL (1) **4** [only before noun] actual or true, rather than what appears to be true: *Boys are raised to mask their real feelings and present an image of strength and self-confidence.* **5** [only before noun] having all the important qualities that it should have to deserve to be called what it is called: *Opposition leaders were in doubt on how to continue their peaceful struggle for real democracy in the country.* ◇ *Searle argues that, whereas computers and robots behave as if they understand language, only human beings have the real thing.*

ˈ**real estate** *noun* [U] (*especially NAmE*) **1** property in the form of land or buildings: *In Japan, the price of real estate dropped dramatically in the late 1980s.* **2** the business of selling houses or land for building: *The company enlarged its range of activities in the 1970s, entering the businesses of real estate, mining, textiles and finance.*

real·ism /ˈriːəlɪzəm; *BrE also* ˈrɪəlɪzəm/ *noun* [U] **1** (*politics*) the view that the subject matter of politics is political power, not matters of principle: *It was the political realism of Machiavelli's work that led to its instant condemnation by the religious and political leaders of the day.* HELP In non-academic language, **realism** often refers to a way of seeing, accepting and dealing with situations as they really are without being influenced by your emotions or false hopes: *There was a new mood of realism among the leaders at the peace talks.* However, although this use is frequent in journalism, in academic writing **realism** is mostly used more precisely in its political, artistic or philosophical meaning. **2** (in literature, art and film) the quality of being very like real life: *Reviews of the first edition emphasized the novel's working-class realism.* **3** (*philosophy*) the view that the kinds of things that exist and the nature of those things are independent of human beings and the way in which they PERCEIVE things: *According to scientific realism, snow is made from water molecules, but is not necessarily cold and white.* ➲ *compare* IDEALISM (1)

real·ist /ˈriːəlɪst; *BrE also* ˈrɪəlɪst/ *noun* **1** (*politics*) a person who believes that the subject matter of politics is political power, not matters of principle: *Realists argue that globalization does not have radical consequences.* HELP In non-academic language, a **realist** is a person who accepts and deals with a situation as it really is and does not try to pretend that it is different. However, in academic writing, **realist** is mostly used more precisely in its political, artistic or philosophical meaning. **2** a writer, artist, etc. whose work represents things as they are in real life: *Dickens was a convinced realist who occasionally indulged in fantasy and grotesquerie.* **3** (*philosophy*) a person who believes that reality exists independently of how people view it: *The realist supports Galileo's position against the Catholic Church that the Earth revolves around the Sun.* ■ **real·ist** *adj.*: *The second major element in the realist view concerns the nature of international relations.* ◇ *A realist novel, such as 'Middlemarch', advances precepts of how the social world operates.*

real·is·tic /ˌriːəˈlɪstɪk; *BrE also* ˌrɪəˈlɪstɪk/ *adj.* **1** sensible and appropriate; possible to achieve SYN FEASIBLE, VIABLE (1): *Participants gained knowledge and skills on setting realistic goals.* ◇ *Tropical reforestation can be a realistic prospect only where the needs of local people are taken into account.* ◇ *By developing more realistic expectations, a child or teen becomes less prone to experience frustration or anger.* ◇ *a realistic option/alternative* OPP UNREALISTIC **2** accepting in a sensible way what it is actually possible to do or achieve in a particular situation: *a realistic view/assessment* ◇ **~ about sth** *Every project leader stressed the importance of being realistic about the time and resources required.* ◇ **it is ~ to do sth** *It might be more realistic to focus preliminary efforts on those top priority species.* OPP UNREALISTIC **3** representing things as they are in real life: *These films are characterized by their realistic portrayal of daily life.* OPP UNREALISTIC

real·is·tic·al·ly /ˌriːəˈlɪstɪkli; *BrE also* ˌrɪəˈlɪstɪkli/ *adv.* **1** used to say what you think can actually be achieved in a particular situation: *It is important to clarify what may realistically be expected from industry participation.* ◇ *In short, government should promise only what it can realistically deliver.* ◇ *Realistically, the small amount of material on healthy eating within the curriculum is not enough to dramatically alter established behaviours and habits.* **2** in a way that shows that sb accepts in a sensible way what it is actually possible to do or achieve: *They speak more realistically than romantically about the institution of marriage.*

real·ity /riˈæləti/ *noun* (*pl.* **-ies**) **1** [U] the true situation and the problems that actually exist in the world, especially in contrast to how people would like it to be: *However, it is unlikely that such models reflect reality.* ◇ *Political reality places many constraints on this legal doctrine.* ◇ **~ of sth** *The reality of most markets is fierce competition between suppliers.* **2** [C] a thing that is actually experienced or seen, in contrast to what people might imagine: *A universal system of health care and social security became a reality.* ◇ **~ of sth** *The harsh realities of problematic peer relationships are bullying and exclusion.* **3** [U] **~ television/TV/shows/series/contestants** television/shows, etc. that use real people (not actors) in real situations, presented as entertainment: *More young people vote in reality TV shows than in general elections.*
IDM **in reˈality** used to say that a situation is different from what has just been said or from what people believe: *This approach sounds simple but, in reality, a large number of different assumptions must be made in order to decide between different possible solutions.*

▸ ADJECTIVE + REALITY **harsh, grim, stark • practical • everyday • underlying • complex • material, concrete • empirical • social • historical • political • economic** *The approach is analytical because it encourages participants to question the everyday realities of their lives.* | **objective • external • ultimate • physical** *According to this theory, there is no objective reality: everything involving human beings is subjective.*

▸ VERB + REALITY **reflect • depict, represent • capture • grasp • acknowledge • ignore • obscure • confront • construct** *Education cannot ignore the realities of the global market.* | **deny • distort • mask** *It is useless to deny the reality of current economic changes.*

real·iza·tion (*BrE also* **-isa·tion**) /ˌriːəlaɪˈzeɪʃn; ˌrɪəlaɪˈzeɪʃn; *NAmE* ˌriːələˈzeɪʃn/ *noun* **1** [U, sing.] **~ (that)...** the process of becoming aware of sth SYN AWARENESS (1): *This has led to the realization that many receptors have a common structure.* ◇ *There is a growing realization that the ownership of English is shared by all its speakers.* **2** [U] **~ (of sth)** the process of achieving a particular aim, etc. SYN ACHIEVEMENT (2): *To ensure the realization of such goals, a number of provisions have been made.* **3** [U, C] **~ (of sth)** (*formal*) the act of producing sth in an actual or physical form; the thing that is produced: *The immediate physical realization of the information in the genetic code is not the cell but a collection of protein molecules.* ◇ *I shall present different realizations of this principle in different examples.*

real·ize (*BrE also* **-ise**) /ˈriːəlaɪz; *BrE also* ˈrɪəlaɪz/ *verb* **1** [T, I] (not used in the progressive tenses) to understand or become aware of a particular fact or situation: **~ (that)...** *You do not need to be a nurse long to realize that the demands are high.* ◇ **~ how/what, etc...** *It requires a historical perspective to realize how much daily life has changed.* ◇ **~ (sth)** *Governments realized the importance of building a business-friendly environment.* ◇ *Science and ethics are also much more closely interrelated than many people realize.* ◇ **it is realized that...** *However, it was soon realized that there were even better options with this new material.* **2** [T] **~ sth** to achieve sth important: *The company provides coaching programmes to help managers to realize their full potential.* ◇ *There are a number of challenges that must be solved before this goal can be fully* *realized.* **3** [T, usually passive] **be realized** to happen or become real: *These fears were realized in December 1941.* **4** [T] **~ sth** to make a profit or an amount of money SYN MAKE (8): *It usually takes about two to three years to realize profit.* **5** [T] **~ your assets** to sell things that you own, for example property, in order to get the money that you need for sth: *Having realized these assets, the proceeds are then distributed to the creditors.* **6** [T] **~ sth** to give actual or physical form to sth: *So-called 'zero emission buildings' can be realized with existing planning approaches and technologies.*

ˌreal-ˈlife *adj.* [only before noun] actually happening or existing in life: *Poor decisions in real-life situations can have devastating consequences.*

real·ly /ˈriːəli; *BrE also* ˈrɪəli/ *adv.* **1** used to say what is actually the fact or the truth about sth: *Even these accounts are not problem-free for historians interested in knowing what really happened.* **2** used, often in negative sentences, to reduce the force of sth you are saying: *A problem with the technique is that the temperature never really stabilizes.* ◇ *Therefore, individual companies can only really grow by taking market share from their competitors.* **3** used to emphasize sth you are saying or an opinion you are giving: *What we really want to find out is what organisms were in the sample at that point.* ◇ *The question is how much social relations really mattered politically.* **4** used to emphasize an adjective or adverb: *The defendants argued that they had not intended to kill or cause really serious injury.*

realm /relm/ *noun* **1** an area of activity, interest or knowledge: **in/within/into/outside the ~ (of sth)** *Ageing is a random process that falls outside the realm of natural selection.* ◇ *Often, refusals to answer will be based on a feeling that certain questions delve into private realms.* ◇ *Based on their experiences in the public realm of paid work, men tend to approach care work as tasks to master and problems to solve.* **2** (*formal*) a country ruled by a king or queen SYN KINGDOM (1): *In the medieval realm, the king was the leader of his vassals, who in turn were responsible for those beneath them.*

R

ˌreal ˈnumber *noun* (*mathematics*) any number that is not an IMAGINARY NUMBER: *The square of any real number is positive.* ➲ *compare* COMPLEX NUMBER

ˌreal ˈtime *noun* [U] (*computing*) **1** the fact that there is only a very short time between a computer system receiving data and dealing with them: **in ~** *The interactive parts of some computer games are animated in real time.* **2** the actual time during which a process or event happens: **in ~** *Speech is constructed in real time and this imposes greater working memory demands than writing.*

ˈreal-world *adj.* existing in the real world and not specially invented for a particular purpose: *It will then be necessary to show that microbicides are effective outside of trial conditions and in the real-world setting.*

reap /riːp/ *verb* **~ sth** to obtain sth, especially sth good, as a direct result of sth that you have done: *The company continued to reap great profits from its ongoing service contracts with the Pentagon.* ◇ *An innovative firm is able to secure markets to enable it to reap the rewards of investment in R&D in the future.* ◇ *We cannot reap the benefits of science without accepting some risks—that has always been the case.*

re·appear /ˌriːəˈpɪə(r); *NAmE* ˌriːəˈpɪr/ *verb* [I] to appear again after not being heard of or seen for a period of time: *Democracy was important for a period in classical Greece, but only in the nineteenth century did it reappear as a major idea.* ■ **re·appear·ance** /ˌriːəˈpɪərəns; *NAmE* ˌriːəˈpɪrəns/ *noun* [U, sing.] **~ (of sb/sth)** *The first reappearance of Tacitus in Italy was in an eleventh-century manuscript from Germany.*

rear¹ /rɪə(r); *NAmE* rɪr/ *verb* **1 ~ sb/sth** [often passive] to care for young children or animals until they are fully grown SYN RAISE¹ (5): *Lions usually manage to rear about half the number of cubs born to them.* ◇ *Identical twins reared apart are very similar in intelligence.* **2 ~ sth** to breed or keep animals or birds, for example on a farm: *Visits to farms where animals were reared increased both awareness of, and concern for, the welfare of animals on farms.*

IDM **sth rears its ˈhead** (of sth unpleasant) to appear or happen: *As fervent nationalism reared its head, the international organization was powerless to prevent state action.*

rear² /rɪə(r); *NAmE* rɪr/ *noun* (*usually* **the rear**) [sing.] the back part of sth: *A remodelling in the ninth century added another room at the rear and a bigger courtyard in front.* ◇ **~ of sth** *As Officer A was heading around to the rear of the house, he heard voices and returned to the front door.*

rear³ /rɪə(r); *NAmE* rɪr/ *adj.* [only before noun] at or near the back of sth: *All new cars are now supplied with rear seat belts.* ◇ *The rear ranks evidently did not join combat, but stood ready to take their place.*

re·arrange /ˌriːəˈreɪndʒ/ *verb* **~ sth** to change the position or order of things: *In many cases, it is necessary to rearrange an equation to put it into a form appropriate for plotting and subsequent analysis.* ■ **re·arrange·ment** *noun* [C, U] *Chromosomal rearrangements can move large chunks of DNA around the genome.* ◇ **~ of sth** *There is no rearrangement of atoms at the transition temperature.*

rea·son¹ /ˈriːzn/ *noun* **1** [C] a cause or an explanation for sth that has happened or that sb has done: **~ why...** *Population movement is the main reason why it is difficult to produce accurate estimates.* ◇ **~ for sth** *There are numerous reasons for these differences.* ◇ **~ for doing sth** *There are many reasons for rejecting this view.* ◇ **~ that...** *The greater scattering of light of lower wavelengths by dust particles in the atmosphere is the reason that the sky appears blue, rather than red.* ◇ **for... ~** *Natural gas is a desirable fuel for several reasons.* ◇ **by ~ of sth** (*formal*) *Some patients, by reason of their illness, are not capable of informed consent.* ➲ language bank *at* THEREFORE **2** [U] a fact that makes it right or fair to do sth: **~ to do sth** *He had good reason to distrust the political system.* ◇ **~ why...** *There is no reason why such advances should cease.* ◇ **~ for (doing) sth** *There was no good reason for extending the policy.* **3** [U] the power of the mind to think in a logical way, to understand and form opinions: *Philosophy is the attempt to use reason to solve problems that cannot be solved in other ways.* ◇ *The Enlightenment was characterized by a belief in the power of human reason to change society.* **4** [U] what is possible, practical or right: **within ~** *This means trusting employees and giving them, within reason, the right to do what they want.*

▸ ADJECTIVE + REASON **good • sufficient • compelling** *There is no compelling reason to doubt this account.* | **main, major, primary, principal, key • important • valid, legitimate, sound • strong • possible • different • various • common • the following • obvious • real • underlying • political • economic • historical • practical • technical • pragmatic • moral** *There are two main reasons for unemployment.* ◇ *Location is important for the following reasons:...*

▸ VERB + REASON **have • see** *We see no reason why the same arguments should not apply to managers.* | **give, provide, offer • outline • state, cite, advance • mention • explain • discuss • explore • understand • suggest • identify • constitute** *Morgan gives some practical reasons why conflict can be an advantage.*

▸ REASON TO + VERB **believe, think • suppose, assume • expect • doubt, question • suspect • fear** *There is no particular reason to think this figure should vary greatly.*
▸ PHRASE **for this/that very reason • for the simple reason that...** *They have turned away from external reality but, for that very reason, they know more about internal, psychical reality.*

rea·son² /ˈriːzn/ *verb* **1** [T] **~ (that...)** to form a judgement about a situation by considering the facts in a logical way: *Noticing this unsatisfied demand, banks will reason that they can charge a higher rate.* ◇ *Consumption, supporters reasoned, had the potential to improve the economy as a whole.* **2** [I] to use your power to think and understand: *The task seems to reveal the conditions under which people can reason logically.*
PHR V ˈ**reason with sb** to talk to sb in order to persuade them to be more sensible: *Parents who reason with their children are more likely to have altruistic children.*

rea·son·able /ˈriːznəbl/ *adj.* **1** fair, practical and sensible: *The information provides reasonable grounds for suspicion.* ◇ *a reasonable assumption/suspicion* ◇ *The instruction is so obviously wrong that no reasonable person would follow it.* ◇ **it is ~ to do sth** *It would be reasonable to expect stronger bonds to be harder to stretch.* OPP UNREASONABLE ➲ thesaurus note *at* PLAUSIBLE **2** appropriate in a particular situation: *There was no breach as the surgeon had exercised reasonable care and skill.* ◇ *The employee has to claim within a reasonable time.* ◇ *This method provides reasonable estimates of ancient CO_2 levels.* **3** (of prices) not too expensive SYN FAIR¹ (1): *The objective was to make food available at reasonable prices.* ◇ *Great accuracy can be achieved at a reasonable cost.* **4** [usually before noun] fairly good, but not very good: *A reasonable level of English was required to complete the survey.*

rea·son·able·ness /ˈriːznəblnəs/ *noun* [U] **1 ~ (of sth)** the quality of being fair, practical and sensible: *The tribunal will assess the reasonableness of an employer's decision to dismiss someone.* **2 ~ (of sth)** the quality of being appropriate in a particular situation: *They must assess the reasonableness of the time taken to act.*

rea·son·ably /ˈriːznəbli/ *adv.* **1** to a degree that is fairly good but not very good SYN FAIRLY (1): *The analysis is reasonably accurate.* ◇ *The premises have to be reasonably safe.* ◇ *For most pupils, a reasonably clear pattern of friendships did emerge.* **2** in a logical, sensible or fair way: *One might reasonably expect that a more expensive product will be of better quality.* ◇ *Provided he acted reasonably, he will not be guilty of negligence.* ◇ *The item must be returned as soon as reasonably practicable.*

rea·soned /ˈriːzənd/ *adj.* [only before noun] (of an argument or opinion) presented in a logical way that shows careful thought: *There are some reasoned arguments in favour of psychometric tests.* ◇ *a reasoned opinion/judgment*

rea·son·ing /ˈriːzənɪŋ/ *noun* [U] the process of thinking in a logical way; opinions and ideas that are based on logical thinking: *He suggested that scientific reasoning should be applied to the study of language.* ◇ *If it were valid, this line of reasoning would have many other implications.* ◇ *They explained their reasoning as follows:...*

re·assur·ance /ˌriːəˈʃʊərəns; ˌriːəˈʃɔːrəns; *NAmE* ˌriːəˈʃʊrəns/ *noun* **1** [U] the fact of giving advice or help that takes away a person's fears or doubts: *It is important to provide reassurance and support as the patient may be very anxious and stressed.* ◇ **~ that...** *This group requires reassurance that the product works and has been proven in the market.* **2** [C] something that is said or done to take away a person's fears or doubts: *Overly detailed reassurances can also create false perceptions of safety.*

re·assure /ˌriːəˈʃʊə(r); ˌriːəˈʃɔː(r); *NAmE* ˌriːəˈʃʊr/ *verb* to say or do sth that takes away a person's fears or doubts: **~ sb (about sth)** *It is important that everything is done to inform and reassure witnesses about the legal process.* ◇ **~ sb that...** *Reassure the patient that seizures do not necessarily mean a diagnosis of epilepsy.*

re·assur·ing /ˌriːəˈʃʊərɪŋ; ˌriːəˈʃɔːrɪŋ; *NAmE* ˌriːəˈʃʊrɪŋ/ *adj.* making you feel less worried or uncertain about sth: *These results are reassuring.* ◇ **it is ~ to do sth** *It may be reassuring to know that this is a very normal reaction.* ◇ **it is ~ that...** *It is reassuring that both data sets give very similar results.* ■ **re·assur·ing·ly** *adv.*: *Reassuringly, the more experienced and skilled the clinicians were, the more accurate their diagnoses.*

rebel¹ /ˈrebl/ *noun* **1** a person who fights against the government of their country: *As popular support waned, the rebels were defeated by government forces.* ◇ **+ noun** *Rebel groups went on the offensive against the government.* **2** a person who opposes sb in authority over them within an organization such as a political party: *88 Labour MPs rebelled, with former ministers and cabinet ministers among the rebels.* **3** a person who does not like to obey rules or who does not accept normal standards of behaviour or appearance: *She is a rebel who refuses to be intimidated by rank or wealth.*

rebel² /rɪˈbel/ *verb* (-ll-) [I] to fight against or refuse to obey an authority, for example a government, a system or your parents: *Accused of inciting the slaves to rebel, Smith was thrown into jail and sent for trial.* ◇ **~ against sb/sth** *Despite further reforms, by the late 1820s, ratepayers were dissatisfied and the poor began to rebel against the system.*

re·bel·lion /rɪˈbeljən/ *noun* **1** [C, U] **~ (against sb/sth)** an attempt by some of the people in a country to change their government, using violence SYN UPRISING: *Boudicca was a British queen who led a rebellion against Rome.* ◇ *The whole region rose in rebellion, with thousands of deaths and atrocities.* **2** [U, C] **~ (against sb/sth)** opposition to authority within an organization such as a company or a political party: *If rebellion breaks out, even on a small scale, it may prove difficult to stop it from spreading.* ◇ *Major's government, hit by rebellions, struggled to find a parliamentary majority.* **3** [U] opposition to authority; being unwilling to obey rules or accept normal standards of behaviour or appearance: *Crusoe's decision to go to sea is an act of rebellion.* ◇ **~ against sb/sth** *Many teenagers start smoking as a form of rebellion against parental authority.*

re·bel·li·ous /rɪˈbeljəs/ *adj.* **1** unwilling to obey rules or accept normal standards of behaviour or appearance: *Among older adolescents, rebellious behaviour is common.* ◇ *Linda's parents sought treatment because she was increasingly angry and rebellious.* **2** opposed to the government of a country; opposed to those in authority within an organization: *Britain sought to subdue its rebellious American colonists in 1775–6.* ◇ *MPs in the two main parties have become more rebellious, even to the point of voting against their own party.* ■ **re·bel·li·ous·ness** *noun* [U] *Hip-hop culture has a reputation for rebelliousness.*

re·build /ˌriːˈbɪld/ *verb* (**re·built, re·built** /ˌriːˈbɪlt/) **1 ~ sth** to build or put sth together again: *In the aftermath of the Persian destruction, the Athenians completely rebuilt their city.* **2 ~ sth** to make sth/sb complete and strong again: *They needed to rebuild the war-torn economies of Europe.*

re·call¹ /rɪˈkɔːl/ *verb* **1** (not used in the progressive tenses) to remember sth: **~ sth** *Participants were recalling events that had happened several weeks earlier.* ◇ **~ (sb/sth) doing sth** *The respondent could not recall reading or hearing about the event described.* ◇ **~ that...** *It is important to recall that these are all growth measures.* ◇ **~ how/when,**

R

etc... *Mateus recalls how the way he and his wife share domestic chores puzzles his neighbours.* ◇ **+ speech** *'All of us were afraid,' another demonstrator recalled. 'But we went and did it anyway.'* **2 ~ sth** (not used in the progressive tenses) to make sb think of sth SYN EVOKE: *Much of the poetry in the early volumes recalls images, scenes or incidents from a personal past.* **3 ~ sb (to sth)** to order sb to return: *The patient should be recalled to hospital for treatment.* **4 ~ sth** to ask for sth to be returned, often because there is sth wrong with it: *Where there is considered to be a risk of injury, a product should be recalled.*

re·call[2] /rɪˈkɔːl; ˈriːkɔːl/ *noun* **1** [U] **~ (of sth)** the ability to remember sth that you have learned or sth that has happened in the past; the action of remembering sth: *They tested the children's understanding and subsequent recall of the stories.* **2** [sing.] **~ (of sth)** an official order or request for sb/sth to return, or for sth to be given back: *This was the largest recall of consumer products in US history.*

re·cede /rɪˈsiːd/ *verb* **1** [I] to move gradually away from a previous position: *When the floodwaters receded, settlers returned to the mess left behind.* ◇ **~ from sth** *In this model, each galaxy recedes equally from every other galaxy.* **2** [I] (especially of a problem, feeling or quality) to become gradually weaker or smaller: *The immediate threat to the state receded, but the result was chronic social violence.* ◇ **~ into sth** *The study of what makes life worth living has receded into the background.*

re·ceipt /rɪˈsiːt/ *noun* **1** [U] (*formal*) the act of receiving sth: **in ~ of sth** *The applicant was unemployed and in receipt of income support.* ◇ **on/upon ~ of sth** *On receipt of the consent form, the researcher contacted the participants by telephone.* **2 receipts** [pl.] (*business*) money that a business, bank or government receives: *Slowing economic growth meant that tax receipts would be less than expected.* **3** [C] **~ (for sth)** a piece of paper that shows that goods or services have been paid for: *Without submitting any receipts, he also claimed reimbursement for travel.*

re·ceive /rɪˈsiːv/ *verb* **1** to get or accept sth that is sent or given to you: **~ sth** *Adolescents and parents received written information about the study.* ◇ *Giving and receiving feedback among colleagues is a key part of medical education.* ◇ *to receive a message/complaint/letter* ◇ **~ sth from sb/sth** *Academic scientists often receive funding from commercial companies.* **2** to experience, suffer or be given a particular type of attention or treatment: **~ sth** *Such issues received widespread attention.* ◇ *This is a concept that has recently received criticism in the literature.* ◇ *Patients may also receive care in the home.* ◇ *They receive ongoing training and supervision.* ◇ *to receive treatment/therapy/assistance* ◇ **~ sth from sb** *The initiative has received positive support from human rights organizations.* **3** [usually passive] to react to sth new, in a particular way: **be received + adv./prep.** *His work was not well received at the time.* ◇ *The decision has been received rather critically.* ◇ **be received with sth** *The announcement was received with surprise in many quarters.* **4** to change broadcast signals into sounds or pictures on a television or other equipment: **~ sth** *The MRI signals received by a probe can be analysed.* ◇ **~ sth from sth** *Signals received from satellites and deep space vehicles are often very weak.* **5 ~ sb** to welcome or entertain a visitor: *Tourism is booming and in 2007 the city received more than a million visitors.* **6 ~ sb (into sth)** (*formal*) to officially recognize and accept sb as a member of a group: *In October 1845, he was received into the Roman Catholic Church.*

re·ceived /rɪˈsiːvd/ *adj.* [only before noun] accepted by most people as being correct: *The author challenges the received view of Pope's poem.* ◇ *At that time, the received wisdom was that the universe was static.*

R

re·ceiver /rɪˈsiːvə(r)/ *noun* **1** a piece of electrical equipment that picks up broadcast signals, such as television or radio: *A radio receiver can pick up any station by tuning to the band of the desired station.* ◇ *A GPS receiver operates by measuring its distance from a group of satellites in space.* ➲ *compare* TRANSMITTER (1) **2** (*law*) a person who is chosen by a court to be in charge of a company that is BANKRUPT: *The lender could sell the property or appoint a receiver.* **3 ~ (of sth)** a person who receives sth: *He contrasts this with the largely passive role students assume as receivers of knowledge.*

re·cent /ˈriːsnt/ *adj.* [usually before noun] that happened or began only a short time ago: *In recent years, the trend towards working outside the home has reversed for some.* ◇ *Two other recent studies found only weak associations.* ➲ language bank *at* TIME[1]

▸ RECENT + NOUN **years, decades, times • history, past • study, research, work, scholarship • literature, publication • book • article, paper • review • report • survey • advance, development • trend • change • example • case • evidence • data • discovery, findings • analysis • debate • event • crisis • immigrant** *Advances for minority groups in recent decades are dramatic.* ◇ *Some recent examples demonstrate the range of such activity.*

▸ ADVERB + RECENT **relatively, comparatively • fairly • very** *This is a relatively recent development.*

re·cent·ly /ˈriːsntli/ *adv.* not long ago: *The WHO have recently published new guidelines on managing the disease.* ◇ *This hypothesis is supported by a recently conducted survey by Wordsworth et al.* ◇ *More recently, radar satellites have measured sea surface elevations with precisions of the order of a few centimetres.*

re·cep·tion /rɪˈsepʃn/ *noun* **1** [U] the act of receiving sth or welcoming sb: **~ (of sb/sth)** *They lay down minimum standards for the reception of asylum seekers.* ◇ **+ noun** *There are only reception centre spaces for 770 refugees.* **2** [sing.] the type of welcome or reaction that is given to sb/sth: *In Australia the book received a mixed critical reception.* ◇ *In general, this compulsory programme received a positive reception.* **3** [U] (*especially BrE*) the area inside the entrance of a hotel, an office building, etc. where guests or visitors go first when they arrive: *People register by handing in their medical card to the practice reception.* ◇ **+ noun** *Reception staff make a note of who requests repeat prescriptions.* **4** [U] the quality of reception of ELECTROMAGNETIC signals, such as radio and television signals, that are broadcast: *Tenants complained of poor television reception.* ◇ *Mobile phone reception is completely lost when entering a tunnel.* ➲ *compare* TRANSMISSION (2) **5** [U] (*linguistics*) the ability to understand language or information that you hear or read; the process of doing this: *The dictionary was originally designed for both language reception and production.* ➲ *compare* PRODUCTION (6) **6** [C] a formal social occasion to welcome sb or celebrate sth: *Hotels regularly host wedding or business receptions.*

re·cep·tive /rɪˈseptɪv/ *adj.* **1 ~ (to sth)** willing to listen to or to accept new ideas or suggestions: *Some developed countries seemed receptive to such ideas.* ◇ *The young are particularly receptive to advertising.* ◇ *His ideas found a receptive audience in literate circles from Lisbon to Moscow.* ➲ *compare* RESPONSIVE (2) **2** able to receive signals or STIMULI: *It is used as a coating material to provide a receptive surface for printing ink.* ◇ **~ to sth** *The goldfish's vision is receptive to a wider band of light than a human's.* **3** (of a female animal) ready to MATE: *Calling songs are generated to attract sexually receptive females.* **4** (*linguistics*) connected with understanding language or information that you hear or read: *Receptive knowledge was measured by asking participants to provide a translation for each target word.* ➲ *compare* PRODUCTIVE (4) ■ **re·cep·tive·ness** *noun* [U] **~ (of sb/sth) (to sth)** *Future research is* *needed to gauge the receptiveness of stakeholders to the restrictions.* ◇ *Dominant males may vary their response depending on female receptiveness.* **re·cep·tiv·ity** /ˌriːsepˈtɪvəti/ *noun* [U] **~ (of sb/sth) (to sth)** *A number of factors will influence a person's receptivity to health education messages.*

re·cep·tor /rɪˈseptə(r)/ *noun* (*biology*) an organ or nerve ending in the body that responds to heat, light, taste, pain, etc. and causes a nerve to send a signal: *T2R receptors allow the detection of bitter tastes.* ◇ **+ noun** *The retina contains receptor cells which are sensitive to light.*

re·ces·sion /rɪˈseʃn/ *noun* **1** [C, U] a difficult time for the economy of a country, lasting months or years, during which trade and industrial activity are reduced, and more people are unemployed HELP The actual definition of a **recession** is a fall in GDP for two quarters of the year (i.e. over a period of six months): *If the economy moves into a recession, it would be easier for managers to recruit staff.* ◇ *The onset of the global economic recession in the second half of 2008 saw a pronounced fall in the US natural gas price.* ◇ *a deep/severe/sharp/prolonged recession* ◇ *These were measures intended to pull the economy out of recession.* **2** [U] **~ (of sth) (+ adv./prep.)** (*formal*) the movement backwards of sth from a previous position: *Redshifting is caused by the recession of distant galaxies away from us.*

re·ces·sive /rɪˈsesɪv/ *adj.* (*biology*) connected with a characteristic that only appears in an individual if it has two GENES for this characteristic, one from each parent. This characteristic does not appear if a DOMINANT gene is also present: *A recessive disorder is one in which an otherwise healthy parent has a defective allele in their genome.*

re·cipi·ent /rɪˈsɪpiənt/ *noun* (*formal*) a person who receives sth: *Most cardiac transplant recipients are discharged within 7–14 days.* ◇ *The familial relationship of the caregiver to the care recipient was not included in the data.* ◇ **~ of sth** *Consumers are no longer passive recipients of marketing messages; they have become more sophisticated.* ◇ **+ noun** *There are three steps in the delivery of aid to recipient countries:...*

re·cip·ro·cal /rɪˈsɪprəkl/ *adj.* involving two people or groups who agree to help each other or behave in the same way to each other; involving two ideas that balance each other and must exist together: *Many countries have reciprocal arrangements with the UK, enabling citizens of each country to receive medical care while abroad.* ◇ *Political philosophers would argue that there is a reciprocal relationship between rights and duties.* ■ **re·cip·ro·cal·ly** /rɪˈsɪprəkli/ *adv.*: *The possession of rights means that migrants can legitimately make claims on the institutions of British society, and, reciprocally, these institutions can make demands on them.*

re·cip·ro·cate /rɪˈsɪprəkeɪt/ *verb* **1** [I, T] **~ (sth) (with sth)** to behave or feel towards sb in the same way as they behave or feel towards you: *Germany reciprocated with its own declaration of war against the United States two days later.* ◇ *The support that is offered must be reciprocated, should the need arise.* **2** [I] (*technical*) to move backwards and forwards in a straight line: **reciprocating + noun** *The early water wall boilers were used in conjunction with reciprocating piston steam engines.* ■ **re·cip·ro·ca·tion** /rɪˌsɪprəˈkeɪʃn/ *noun* [U] *Blau (1964) suggests that when one employee performs a task that is beneficial to another, there is an expectation of reciprocation.*

reci·procity /ˌresɪˈprɒsəti; *NAmE* ˌresɪˈprɑːsəti/ *noun* [U] a situation in which two people, countries, etc. provide the same help or advantages to each other: *Ethical principles of reciprocity and solidarity help support the practice of data sharing.*

rec·og·ni·tion /ˌrekəgˈnɪʃn/ *noun* **1** [U] the act of remembering who sb is when you see them, or of identifying what sth is: *Brand recognition is built by creating an aura around a product.* ◇ *A definitive answer as to just how different face recognition is from general object recognition has yet to be provided.* **2** [U, sing.] the act of accepting that sth exists, is true or is official SYN ACKNOWLEDGEMENT (2): *The United States granted diplomatic recognition to the Soviet Union in 1933.* ◇ **~ that...** *Despite widespread recognition that smoking was harmful, allowing it in bars satisfied the needs of many bar owners and customers.* ◇ **~ of sth** *There is a growing recognition of the global threat posed by weapons of mass destruction.* **3** [U] public praise and reward for sb's work, achievements or actions: *Her work did not gain wide recognition until after her death.* ◇ **~ for sth** *Dr Noble has received broad recognition for this important work.* ◇ **in ~ of sth** *He received the Nobel Prize for physics in recognition of his work on radioactivity.*

IDM **to change, alter, etc. beyond/out of (all) recogˈnition** to change so much that it is almost impossible to recognize: *Over the past 30 years, the pattern of higher education in the UK has changed almost beyond all recognition.*

rec·og·niz·able (*BrE also* **-is·able**) /ˈrekəgnaɪzəbl; ˌrekəgˈnaɪzəbl/ *adj.* easy to know or identify: **~ as sth/sb** *In the earth's atmosphere, the water vapour condenses to form very small water droplets, recognizable as cloud.* ◇ **~ by sb** *The brand will have a unique name and packaging, which will be easily and instantly recognizable by its target market.* ■ **rec·og·niz·ably, -is·ably** /ˈrekəgnaɪzəbli; ˌrekəgˈnaɪzəbli/ *adv.*: *Historical social thought in the West began to take a recognizably modern form during the eighteenth century.*

rec·og·nize (*BrE also* **-ise**) /ˈrekəgnaɪz/ *verb* (not used in the progressive tenses) **1 ~ sb/sth** to know who sb is or what sth is when you see or hear them, because you have seen or heard them before: *The immune system has evolved to recognize many foreign antigens.* ◇ *A 3D object-centred description would allow the object to be recognized from virtually any angle.* **2** to admit or to be aware that sth exists or is true SYN ACKNOWLEDGE (1): **~ sth** *Reid recognized the limitations of his theory.* ◇ **~ sth as sth** *Asbestos has been recognized as a cause of lung cancer through inhalation.* ◇ **~ how/what, etc...** *Fast-food companies immediately recognized how diets in India are impacted on by religion.* ◇ **~ that...** *The government recognizes that wealth is primarily created by the action of businesses operating in free markets.* ◇ **it is recognized that...** *It is recognized that different communities globally may view disabilities in different ways.* ◇ **be recognized to be/have sth** *Some categories of drugs are recognized to be effective against both depression and anxiety.* **3** to accept and approve of sb/sth officially: **~ sb/sth** *The United States was the first country to recognize the new state of Israel.* ◇ *The qualification is recognized in hundreds of countries across the planet.* ◇ **~ sb/sth as sth** *The person whom tradition recognizes as founder of Zen Buddhism in Japan is Eisai (1141–1215).* **4** to be thought of as very good or important by people in general: **be recognized as sth** *Margaret Fuller was swiftly recognized as a significant figure in American letters.* ◇ **recognized + noun** *He is the recognized authority on the geology of South East Asia.* **5 ~ sb/sth** to give sb official thanks for sth that they have done or achieved: *His scientific contributions and leadership have been recognized by awards and honours in seven countries.*

▸ RECOGNIZE + NOUN **face • emotion • sign** *We can recognize a face that is familiar to us even when quite large changes have been introduced.* | **importance, significance • existence • validity • fact • nature • need, necessity • right • limitation, limit • danger • difficulty • complication • distinction • potential • contribution •**

R

role • complexity • extent • possibility • reality • diversity *Schools are increasingly recognizing the need for emotional education for all children.*
‣ ADVERB + RECOGNIZE **widely, universally, generally, commonly • increasingly • long • well • fully • clearly • easily • readily • immediately • first** *It is widely recognized that supermarkets increasingly dictate the way agriculture is practised.* | **internationally • officially, formally • legally • increasingly • explicitly** *Further evidence of ownership may be supplemented through the use of the internationally recognized copyright symbol.*

re·com·bin·ation /ˌriːkɒmbɪˈneɪʃn; *NAmE* ˌriːkɑːmbɪˈneɪʃn/ *noun* [U] **1 ~ (of sth)** the process of combining or causing sth to combine again or differently: *Dierickx and Cool (1989) noted that knowledge flows are vital for the creation of new knowledge, as well as recombination of existing knowledge.* **2 ~ (between A and B)** (*biology*) the process of forming new combinations of characteristics not found in the parents HELP **Recombination** can refer to two processes: the RANDOM separation of CHROMOSOME pairs and the exchange of chromosome pieces; both happen in the first division of MEIOSIS. When the GAMETES formed from meiosis FUSE, the new combinations of GENES can appear. **Recombination** is frequently reserved for the exchange of chromosome pieces: *There is considerable evidence to support the phenomenon of recombination between different animal mitochondrial DNA (mtDNA) molecules.*

rec·om·mend /ˌrekəˈmend/ *verb* **1 ~ sb/sth (to sb) (for/as sth)** to tell sb that sth is good or useful, or that sb would be suitable for a particular job, etc: *Kitamura's book can be highly recommended to all scholars and students of the US occupation of Japan.* ◇ *10 patients were recommended for exercise ECG testing.* **2** to advise a particular course of action: **~ sth** *The guidelines do not recommend the use of chest physiotherapy in these cases.* ◇ *The recommended dose is 20 mg every 8 hours.* ◇ **~ (that) ...** *In its report, the Commission recommended that a separate agency be created.* ◇ **it is recommended that...** *It is recommended that all immunization programmes use MMR or measles-rubella vaccine.* ◇ **~ (sb) doing sth** *The author strongly recommends running a test case.* ◇ **~ how/what, etc...** *Reichheld (2006) recommends how survey results be used to classify individual customers.* ➲ language bank *at* REPORT[1] **3 ~ sb/sth (to sb)** to make sb/sth seem attractive or good: *Hardman's approach has much to recommend it.*

rec·om·men·da·tion /ˌrekəmenˈdeɪʃn/ *noun* an official suggestion about the best thing to do: *Professional planners collect and analyse data, prepare reports and make policy recommendations.* ◇ **~ (to sb) (for/on/about sth)** *The health report details specific recommendations for evaluation and management of the condition.* ◇ *In June 2002, the CVM issued recommendations on corporate governance.* ◇ *Central government makes recommendations to local authorities about how they should work with refugees in the integration process.* ◇ **(on) the ~ of sb/sth** *to accept/follow/implement the recommendations of sb/sth* ◇ *Appointment of Cabinet ministers is made on the recommendation of the Prime Minister.*

rec·on·cile /ˈrekənsaɪl/ *verb* **1** to find a way of dealing with two or more ideas, needs, etc. that seem to be opposed to each other: **~ sth** *The challenge for contemporary democracies is to understand and reconcile these two contrasting patterns.* ◇ **~ sth with sth** *It was difficult to reconcile the theory with the evidence.* **2** [often passive] to make people become friends again after an argument or a disagreement: **~ sb** *The peace conference is seeking to reconcile all sides of the conflict on the basis of their common values.* ◇ **~ sb to sb** *The two writers were reconciled to one another shortly before Thackeray's death in 1863.* **3 ~ sb/yourself (to sth)** to make sb/yourself accept an unpleasant situation because it is not possible to change it SYN RESIGN YOURSELF TO STH: *Among the émigré writers who reconciled themselves to the new regime and returned were Aleksei Tolstoy and Gorki.*

rec·on·cili·ation /ˌrekənsɪliˈeɪʃn/ *noun* **1** [U, sing.] an end to a disagreement and the start of a good relationship again: *This should be viewed as an opportunity to bring about lasting peace and reconciliation.* ◇ **~ between A and B** *In general, French and German churches welcomed the Schuman Plan as it promoted reconciliation between their countries.* ◇ **~ with sb** *Moscow made a diplomatic retreat and sought a reconciliation with the US.* **2** [U] **~ (between A and B)** the process of making it possible for two different ideas, facts, etc. to exist together without being opposed to each other: *The author questions if there can be any possibility of reconciliation between such clearly opposed positions.*

re·con·sider /ˌriːkənˈsɪdə(r)/ *verb* [T, I] to think about sth again, especially because you might want to change a previous decision or opinion: **~ (sth)** *The court has at times to reconsider earlier decisions in the light of changed social conditions.* ◇ *The senators' response was to urge him to reconsider.* ◇ **~ how/what, etc...** *Teachers must reconsider how they observe and document student learning.* ■ **re·con·sid·er·ation** /ˌriːkənˌsɪdəˈreɪʃn/ *noun* [U, sing.] *Any policy must be subject to reconsideration in the light of changed circumstances.* ◇ **~ of sth** *A reconsideration of policies could be helpful.*

re·con·struct AWL /ˌriːkənˈstrʌkt/ *verb* **1** to build or make sth again that has been damaged or that no longer exists: **~ sth** *Government forces worked to reconstruct villages destroyed in battles.* ◇ **~ sth from sth** *A number of his sermons were reconstructed from shorthand notes.* **2 ~ sth** to be able to describe or show exactly how a past event happened, using the information you have gathered: *Lewis carried out extended taped interviews with the family members to reconstruct their life histories.*

re·con·struc·tion AWL /ˌriːkənˈstrʌkʃn/ *noun* **1** [sing., U] **~ (of sth)** the process of changing or improving the condition of sth or the way it works; the process of putting sth back into the state it was in before: *A huge reconstruction of the welfare state was undertaken in Britain in the 1980s.* ◇ *Directly related to each of these issues was the problem of postwar economic reconstruction* **2** [U] **~ (of sth)** the activity of building again sth that has been damaged or destroyed: *Archaeological reconstruction of the slave quarters at Monticello has been aided by a precise plan made by Jefferson in 1796.* **3** [C] **~ (of sth)** an impression, model or short film showing events that are known to have happened in order to try and get more information or better understanding: *Historical reconstructions of the early Greek world tend to rely most heavily on written sources.*

re·cord[1] /ˈrekɔːd; *NAmE* ˈrekərd/ *noun* **1** [C] something that gives you information about the past, especially an account kept in writing or some other permanent form so that it can be looked at and used in the future: *Historical records tell us little about Muhammad's early years.* ◇ **~ of sth** *Participants were asked to keep records of every instance of mobile phone use.* ◇ **on ~** *The ten warmest years on record have all been since 1990.* **2** [C] the best result or the highest or lowest level that has ever been reached: *In 2006, the company set a new annual sales record in the UK.* ◇ *Bauer broke three world records in the backstroke.* ◇ **~ for sth** *'Fahrenheit 9/11' (2004) broke all box office records for a documentary.* ◇ **+ noun** *2008 saw a record number of foreigners living in the UK.* **3** [sing.] the facts that are known about sb/sth's past behaviour, character, achievements, etc: *The company has a proven, impressive safety record over its 50 years of*

R

operation. ◇ **~ on sth** *It is now not uncommon for suppliers to be asked about their lrecord on environmental issues.* **4** (*also* **ˌcriminal ˈrecord**) [C] the fact of having committed crimes in the past: *A person with no criminal record might, upon conviction, be sentenced to a term of imprisonment of five years or more.* **5** [C] a piece or collection of music released on CD, the Internet, etc: **+ noun** *The availability of downloadable music on the web deprives record companies of millions in lost revenues.*

IDM **put/place sth on (the) ˈrecord | be/go on (the) ˈrecord (as saying...)** to say sth publicly or officially so that it may be written down and repeated: *Officials at the World Bank have gone on record in support of capital controls.* **put/set the ˈrecord straight** to give people the correct information about sth in order to make it clear that what they previously believed was in fact wrong: *The novel is in fact a public attempt to set the record straight.*

▸ ADJECTIVE + RECORD **detailed • accurate • complete • incomplete • official • written • documentary • manual • electronic, computerized • daily • past • historical, historic • medical • archaeological • geological • diplomatic • administrative • archival** *No medical records could be obtained to confirm this diagnosis.* | **poor • impressive • past** *The company's reputation suffered when it applied its brand name to train services with a very poor reliability record.*

▸ NOUN + RECORD **patient • hospital • court • safety • voting • fossil • pollen** *The use of electronic patient records allows doctors to see much more of a person's medical history than do paper files.*

▸ VERB + RECORD **keep, maintain • access • review • compile, complete • update • check • leave • preserve • hold** *Employers may maintain records of Internet use associated with particular computers.* | **set • hold • break** *The Universal Declaration of Human Rights holds the world record as the most widely translated document.*

THESAURUS

record • document • register • chart • enter *verb*

These words all mean to make a list or an account of information or events by writing them down, storing them on a computer, etc.

- to record/document/register sth **as/in** sth
- to record/document **that...**
- to record/enter **data**
- to document/chart **changes/history**
- to record/register **names**
- to **carefully/systematically** record/document sth
- to **officially** record/register sth

- **Record** can be used to talk about putting information into written form, into a computer, on film, etc; **document** is usually used to talk about recording details in writing, either on paper or in electronic form; **enter** is used especially about putting information into a computer: *Responses should be recorded verbatim.* ◇ *These correlates of poverty are well documented in the literature.* ◇ *The nursing team may enter data direct onto the GP patient record.*
- **Document** and **chart** are used to talk about information recorded over a period of time, especially to show trends or progress: *These pairs systematically document their home-buying process.* ◇ *Saxenian (2002) has charted the development of this industry.*
- **Register** is used to talk about putting sb's name on an official list or document: *The father's name is registered on the certificate of birth.*

re·cord² /rɪˈkɔːd; *NAmE* rɪˈkɔːrd/ *verb* **1** [T] to keep a permanent account of facts or events by writing them down, filming them, storing them in a computer, etc: **~ sth** *There are well-tried methods of both generating and recording*

the data. ◇ *All the interviews were recorded and transcribed subject to written consent by the interviewees.* ◇ **~ what/how, etc...** *Patients are asked to record what is eaten and when it is eaten.* ◇ **~ that...** *Inscriptions record that Greeks were among the workforce who built the royal buildings.* ◇ **it is recorded that...** *It is recorded that, in the eighteenth century, only 20 or 30% of the farmers grew rice.* **2** [T, I] **~ (sth)** to make a copy of music, a film, etc. by storing it on tape or a disc so that you can listen to or watch it again: *A third of all recorded music is bought in the USA.* ◇ *You will need to inform the audience that you are recording.* **3** [T] to show a particular measurement or amount: **~ sth** *Wedgwood invented a pyrometer, or thermometer, that recorded the high temperatures in kilns.* ◇ **~ how/what, etc...** *Computer software records how much time it takes employees to deal with incoming calls.* **4** [T] **~ sth** to make an official or legal statement about sth: *Jury members recorded their vote by secret ballot.*

re·cord·ing /rɪˈkɔːdɪŋ; *NAmE* rɪˈkɔːrdɪŋ/ *noun* **1** [C] **~ (of sth)** sound or pictures that have been recorded on CD, DVD, video, etc: *The group viewed and discussed video recordings of their class discussions.* ◇ *Following the focus group meetings, the recordings were transcribed verbatim.* **2** [U] the process of making a record, film, radio or television show, etc: *Digital audio recording allows exceptional closeness to the data, easy access and storage.* ◇ **+ noun** *The availability of cheap sound and image recording equipment has helped to make online sessions with remote audiences possible.* **3** [U] **~ (of sth)** the process or act of writing down and storing information for official purposes: *Recording of children's height and weight is routine in many preschools.*

re·count /rɪˈkaʊnt/ *verb* to tell sb about sth, especially sth that you have experienced: **~ sth (to sb)** *'The Lay of the Last Minstrel' recounts the story of a family feud in the sixteenth century.* ◇ **~ how/what, etc...** *Refugees recount how their experiences have affected their progress in learning about a country and its language.*

re·coup /rɪˈkuːp/ *verb* **~ sth** to get back an amount of money that you have spent or lost SYN RECOVER (4): *The museum needed to attract 1.5 million visitors paying an average admission fee of 1 000 yen just to recoup construction costs.*

R

re·course /rɪˈkɔːs; *NAmE* ˈriːkɔːrs/ *noun* [U] something that sb has to do or can do to help themselves in a difficult situation: *Surgery may be the only recourse.* HELP If sth is done **without recourse to** sth, it is done without having to use that thing: *Diagnosis can be done without recourse to surgery.* If sb **has recourse to** a particular course of action, they can use it if they need to: *Researchers have recourse to all sorts of resources.*

re·cover AWL /rɪˈkʌvə(r)/ *verb* **1** [I] **~ (from sth)** to get well again after being ill or hurt: *He was still in hospital, recovering from back surgery.* **2 be recovered (from sth)** [T] to be well again after being ill or hurt: *The patient should be at work after 2 weeks and should be fully recovered by 6 weeks.* **3** [I] to return to a normal state after an unpleasant or unusual experience or a period of difficulty: *The cleared areas were soon grown over and the forest recovered quickly.* ◇ **~ from sth** *When an economy recovers from a recession, productivity typically rises relative to its long-run trend.* **4** [T] to get back the same amount of money that you have spent or that is owed to you SYN RECOUP: **~ sth** *The firm must charge enough to recover its costs.* ◇ **~ sth from sb/sth** *The company set up by the council went into liquidation and the bank sought to recover its money from the council.* **5** [T] to get back or find sth that was lost, stolen or missing: **~ sth** *It was impossible to recover the bodies of all those killed.* ◇ **~ sth from sb/sth** *The picture shows stone artefacts that were* *recovered from the site.* **6** [T] **~ sth** to win back a position or level that has been lost SYN REGAIN (1): *Between 1989 and 1993, the country recovered its status as Africa's most open political regime.* **7** [T] **~ sth** to get back the use of your senses or control of your emotions SYN REGAIN (1): *She died the next day without recovering consciousness.*

re·cov·er·able AWL /rɪˈkʌvərəbl/ *adj.* **1** that you can get back after it has been spent or lost: *These financial losses are recoverable.* **2** that can be obtained from the ground: *Recoverable shale oil from the marine black shales of the eastern United States is said to exceed 400 billion barrels.*

re·cov·ery AWL /rɪˈkʌvəri/ *noun* (*pl.* **-ies**) **1** [C, usually sing., U] the process of becoming well again after an illness or injury: *90% of patients make a full recovery in 4–6 weeks.* ◇ **~ from sth** *There are a number of things that patients can do themselves to promote recovery from depression.* **2** [U, C, usually sing.] the process of improving or becoming stronger again: *European otter populations are showing signs of recovery throughout the UK.* ◇ *An economic recovery has begun.* ◇ **~ in sth** *The Roosevelt administration contributed to a recovery in world trade by relaxing these tariff barriers.* **3** [U] **~ (of sth)** the action or process of getting sth back that has been lost or stolen: *States must admit actions for recovery of lost or stolen cultural property brought by or on behalf of rightful owners.* **4** [U] (*also* **reˈcovery room** [C]) the room in a hospital where patients are kept immediately after an operation: *The patient developed breathing difficulties in the recovery room after spinal anaesthesia.*

re·create AWL /ˌriːkriˈeɪt/ *verb* **~ sth** to make sth that existed in the past exist or seem to exist again: *The author discusses the attempt by Martin Scorsese's 'Gangs of New York' (2002) to recreate the look of nineteenth-century New York.* ■ **re·cre·ation** /ˌriːkriˈeɪʃn/ *noun* [C, U] **~ (of sth)** *Much of the quality of this analysis derived from an imaginative recreation of dramatic events.*

rec·re·ation /ˌrekriˈeɪʃn/ *noun* **1** [U] the fact of people doing things for enjoyment, when they are not working: *Retailing sites increasingly offer opportunities for leisure, recreation and other activities.* **2** [C] (*BrE*) a particular activity that sb does when they are not working: *The chief executive lists his recreations in 'Who's Who' (2002) as 'pigs, theatre, gardening'.*

rec·re·ation·al /ˌrekriˈeɪʃənl/ *adj.* **1** connected with activities that people do for enjoyment when they are not working: *The mountains, hills, rivers and lakes provide numerous recreational activities, including mountain climbing, hiking, canoeing and sailing.* **2** (of drugs) taken for enjoyment, but only taken occasionally: *Estimates of illegal drug use suggest that cannabis is the most widely used recreational drug in Britain.*

re·cruit¹ /rɪˈkruːt/ *verb* **1** [T, I] to find new people to join a company, an organization, the armed forces, etc: **~ (sb) (to sth)** *Over the next decade, the company recruited 3 000 employees.* ◇ *The company is having difficulties recruiting staff to its UK headquarters.* ◇ **~ (sb) from sth** *Some firms try to recruit senior executives from their competitors in order to get real insight into their strategic intentions.* ◇ **~ sb to do sth** *The company was looking to recruit an engineer to analyse, test and improve the layout of its website.* **2** [T] to get people to help with or be involved in sth: **~ sb to do sth** *All health facilities recruited a minimum of 50 patients to participate in each survey.* ◇ **~ sb from sth** *The participants were recruited from 10 teaching hospitals.* ◇ **~ sb to sth** *All those recruited to the study completed the questionnaire.* **3** [T] **~ sth (from sth)** to form a new army, team, etc. by persuading new people to join it: *Much of the early CIA leadership was recruited from Wall Street.* ■ **re·cruit·er** *noun*: *Students prevented recruiters from companies with war contracts from appearing on university campuses.*

re·cruit² /rɪˈkruːt/ *noun* **1** a person who has recently joined the armed forces or the police: *Intelligence tests were used in 1917 to assign US Army recruits to different roles.* **2** a person who joins an organization, a company, etc: *The new recruits are put through rigorous training programmes.*

re·cruit·ment /rɪˈkruːtmənt/ *noun* [U] **1** the action of finding new people to join a company, an organization, the armed forces, etc: **~ (of sb) (to sth)** *For many schools, the recruitment of appropriately qualified staff is a significant issue.* ◇ **+ noun** *Ethical issues are becoming crucial in the recruitment process as companies with poor reputations are unable to attract top talent.* **2** the action of getting people to help with or be involved in sth: **~ (of sb) (to sth)** *Recruitment of patients to the study was initially very slow.* ◇ **+ noun** *Suggestions for reporting the success of recruitment strategies, as well as ideas for future research in this area, are presented.* **3** (*ecology*) the increase in a natural population as the number of young animals or plants grow and new members arrive: *Our findings are in line with other studies concerning seed germination and seedling recruitment in subarctic species.*

rect·angle /ˈrektæŋgl/ *noun* a flat shape with four straight sides, two of which are longer than the other two, and four angles of 90°: *She shows the children how to combine rectangles and triangles to create houses.* ■ **rect·angu·lar** /rekˈtæŋgjələ(r)/ *adj.*: *The streets are laid out in a rectangular grid pattern.*

rect·ify /ˈrektɪfaɪ/ *verb* (**rec·ti·fies**, **rec·ti·fy·ing**, **rec·ti·fied**, **rec·ti·fied**) **~ sth** (*formal*) to put right sth that is wrong SYN CORRECT²: *The court requested that the school board rectify the situation of inequality of educational opportunity.* ■ **rec·ti·fi·ca·tion** /ˌrektɪfɪˈkeɪʃn/ *noun* [U] **~ (of sth)** *Individuals enjoy the right to reply or obtain rectification of false information after publication.*

recur /rɪˈkɜː(r)/ *verb* (**-rr-**) [I] to happen again or a number of times: *Symptoms recur in 50% of women within 2 years of withdrawal of therapy.* ◇ **recurring + noun** *One recurring theme of the research is that our society is increasingly globalized.*

re·cur·rence /rɪˈkʌrəns; *NAmE* rɪˈkɜːrəns/ *noun* [U, C, usually sing.] if there is **a recurrence of** sth, it happens again: **~ (of sth)** *The huge expansion of UN peacekeeping operations has arguably helped prevent recurrence of conflict.* ◇ *Among the lessons that need to be learned are how the outbreak of the disease occurred and how to prevent a recurrence.* ◇ **+ noun** *Follow-up is required as there is a 5% recurrence rate.*

re·cur·rent /rɪˈkʌrənt; *NAmE* rɪˈkɜːrənt/ *adj.* that happens again and again: *Recurrent infections can have an effect on a patient's general well-being.* ◇ *Youth culture is a recurrent theme in the novel.*

re·cur·sive /rɪˈkɜːsɪv; *NAmE* rɪˈkɜːrsɪv/ *adj.* involving a process that is repeated many times in order to obtain a result: *Academic writing is a recursive process in which you draft, review and revise your work several times.*

re·cycle /ˌriːˈsaɪkl/ *verb* **~ sth** to treat things that have already been used so that they can be used again: *435 million tonnes of steel is recycled every year worldwide.* ◇ *The pencils are made from recycled plastic cups.* ■ **re·cyc·ling** *noun* [U] **~ (of sth)** *The recycling of glass and aluminium saves energy.* ◇ **+ noun** *a recycling centre/facility/plant*

red¹ /red/ *adj.* (**red·der**, **red·dest**) having the colour of blood or fire: *A red coloration indicates a positive result, that is that nitrate has been reduced.* ■ **red·ness** *noun* [U]

R

Early symptoms may be redness, swelling and pain in the affected part of the body.

red[2] /red/ *noun* [C, U] the colour of blood or fire: *Bright reds and yellows are often used to signify speed and white is often associated with purity.* ◇ **in ~** *The recommended group numbers are shown in red at the top of each group.*

re·define AWL /ˌriːdɪˈfaɪn/ *verb* to change the nature or limits of sth; to make people consider sth in a new way: **~ sth** *Policymakers were concerned to redefine the relationship between the state and its citizens.* ◇ **~ how/what, etc...** *This report has sought to redefine how health care should be planned in a more collaborative way at a global level.* ■ **re·def·in·ition** /ˌriːdefɪˈnɪʃn/ *noun* [U, C] **~ (of sth)** *Bell (1999) outlines the redefinition of national identity in Uzbekistan.*

re·dis·trib·ute AWL /ˌriːdɪˈstrɪbjuːt; ˌriːˈdɪstrɪbjuːt/ *verb* **~ sth (from sb/sth) (to sb/sth)** to share sth out among people in a different way: *The welfare state has had a major role in redistributing income and resources from men to women.* ■ **re·dis·tribu·tive** /ˌriːdɪˈstrɪbjətɪv/ *adj.*: *Social movements work for redistributive policies in favour of the disadvantaged.*

re·dis·tri·bu·tion AWL /ˌriːdɪstrɪˈbjuːʃn/ *noun* [U, sing.] the act of sharing sth out among people in a different way: *All the major political factions included land redistribution in their campaign pledges for the general election.* ◇ **~ (of sth) (from sb/sth) (to sb/sth)** *Maximizing social welfare calls for a redistribution of wealth from the rich to the poor.*

re·draw /ˌriːˈdrɔː/ *verb* (**re·drew** /ˌriːˈdruː/, **re·drawn** /ˌriːˈdrɔːn/) **~ sth** to make changes to sth such as the borders of a country or region, a plan or an arrangement: *Mass movements of the population occurred because boundaries had been redrawn.*

re·dress[1] /rɪˈdres/ *verb* **~ sth** to correct sth that is unfair or wrong: *Affirmative action programs seek to redress racial imbalances in employment.*

IDM **redress the ˈbalance** to make a situation equal or fair again: *Minority groups may experience health deprivation, and health workers can redress the balance by positive discrimination in favour of deprived groups.*

re·dress[2] /rɪˈdres; ˈriːdres/ *noun* [U] payment, etc. that you should get for sth wrong that has happened to you or harm that you have suffered: **~ against sth** *Enslaved Africans effectively had no legal redress against maltreatment by whites.* ◇ **~ for sth** *It is difficult for rural residents to seek redress for pesticide spray drift or odours from animal operations.* ➲ *compare* COMPENSATION (1)

re·duce /rɪˈdjuːs; *NAmE* rɪˈduːs/ *verb* **1** [T, often passive] to make sth less or smaller in size, amount or degree: **~ sth** *Many companies were cutting hours to reduce costs.* ◇ **~ sth by sth** *The naval budget had been reduced by 71.4% since the end of the war.* ◇ **~ sth by (doing) sth** *Inflation can be reduced by macroeconomic policies that raise the rate of unemployment.* ◇ **~ sth (from sth) (to sth)** *The temperature was reduced from 60 to 40°C to avoid damage to the pump.* ◇ **reduced + noun** *Cultural diversity may lead to reduced communication and to reinforcement of existing stereotypes.* **2** [I] **~ (from sth) (to sth)** to become less or smaller in size, amount or degree: *The main rate of corporation tax will reduce from 28% to 27%.* **3** [T, often passive] **~ sth (to sth)** (*chemistry*) to remove OXYGEN from a substance or add HYDROGEN to a substance: *In the human body, nitrate is reduced to nitrite by the digestive system.* ◇ *Trying to dissolve a powerful reducing agent in water may simply result in the water itself being reduced to hydrogen gas.* ➲ *compare* OXIDIZE (1) **4** [T, often passive] **~ sth (to sth)** (*chemistry*) to add one or more ELECTRONS to a substance; to have one or more ELECTRONS added: *In the second equation, the copper ions gain electrons, and so are reduced.* ➲ *compare* OXIDIZE (2)

PHR V **reˈduce sb/sth to sth** [usually passive] to force sb/sth into a worse state or condition: *Education is reduced to employability; self-worth to market worth; citizens to consumers.* ◇ **~ to doing sth** *The king was reduced to raising money as his immediate forebears had done, by ad hoc means.* **reˈduce sth to sth | reˈduce to sth** to change sth to a more general or more simple form; to be changed in this way: *Not all information can or should be reduced to a number.* ◇

▸ REDUCE + NOUN **risk, harm • cost, price • demand • need • amount, rate, size, level, load, number • likelihood, chance, probability • incidence • burden • impact, effect • pressure • complexity • uncertainty • error, bias • intake, consumption, absorption • exposure • transmission • disparity, gap, deficit, loss** *The common method adopted in the financial world to reduce risk is to spread the risk over many people.* | **emission • pollution • inequality • stress, anxiety • poverty • unemployment • mortality • morbidity** *Reducing inequalities in health is now a priority for most European countries.*

▸ ADVERB + REDUCE | REDUCE + ADVERB **considerably, significantly, substantially • drastically • dramatically** *Costs can be significantly reduced by using the supply chain in two key ways.* ◇ *Fossil carbon emissions to the atmosphere will need to be reduced drastically.*

▸ ADVERB + REDUCE **greatly • markedly • severely, sharply • gradually, progressively • effectively • potentially • actually** *Mortality progressively reduces numbers in each older age group.*

re·du·cible /rɪˈdjuːsəbl; *NAmE* rɪˈduːsəbl/ *adj.* **~ (to sth)** that can be described or considered in a simpler way: *Even the most complex statement is reducible to discrete elements.*

re·duc·tion /rɪˈdʌkʃn/ *noun* **1** [C, U] the action or fact of making sth smaller or less in amount, size or degree: **~ in sth** *The Climate Change Act sets a target of a 26% reduction in emissions by 2020.* ◇ **~ of sth** *The biggest impact of the Immigration and Nationality Act was the reduction of discrimination against Asians.* **2** [U] **~ of sth to sth** an explanation of a subject or problem in terms of another simpler or more basic one: *Sociobiology argues for a reduction of human behaviour to biological concepts.* **3** [C] an amount of money by which sth is made cheaper: *Although the wage increases benefited mainly the lowest-paid, there were also price reductions which benefited all.* **4** [U, C] **~ (of sth)** (*chemistry*) the fact of removing OXYGEN from a substance or adding HYDROGEN to a substance: *The reduction of iron ore in a blast furnace occurs at high temperatures.* OPP OXIDATION **5** [U, C] (*chemistry*) the fact of adding one or more ELECTRONS to a substance: **+ noun** *When electricity is passed through molten sodium chloride, the reduction process occurs at the negative electrode.* ➲ *compare* OXIDATION

▸ ADJECTIVE + REDUCTION **significant, substantial, great • dramatic • drastic • gradual, progressive • rapid • sharp • modest, slight • relative • overall • considerable • absolute • consequent • corresponding** *Improvements in medicine and living conditions resulted in a dramatic reduction in mortality rates.*

▸ NOUN + REDUCTION **cost • price • tax • deficit • weight • poverty • mortality • carbon, CO_2 • emission, pollution** *The problem of poverty reduction has moved to the forefront of government attention.*

▸ VERB + REDUCTION **achieve • cause, produce, lead to, result in, bring about • show, demonstrate, indicate • imply • suggest • report • represent • observe • experience • involve** *The results show a reduction in the risk of death from all causes per kilogram increase in birthweight.*

re·duc·tive /rɪˈdʌktɪv/ *adj.* (*sometimes disapproving*) that tries to explain sth complicated by considering it as a

R

combination of simple parts: *It is important to avoid the potential risk of adopting a rather one-dimensional, reductive approach to patient assessment.*

re·dun·dancy /rɪˈdʌndənsi/ *noun* (*pl.* -ies) **1** [U, C, usually pl.] (*BrE*) the situation when sb has to leave their job because there is no more work available for them: *voluntary/compulsory redundancy* ◇ *The firm is looking for 3 000 redundancies among crew and administrative staff.* ◇ **+ noun** *To qualify for redundancy payments, the claimant must have been continuously employed by the employer for at least two years.* **2** [U, sing.] **~ (of sth)** (*formal* or *technical*) the state of not being necessary or useful: *If all the redundancy of English were removed, it would take about half the time to transmit a telephone conversation.* HELP In ecology or genetics, **redundancy** or **functional redundancy** is used to refer to a situation in which more than one species or GENE is available to perform the same role within an ECOSYSTEM or a GENOME: *With a large measure of functional redundancy, species could be lost with little loss of performance or stability in the system.* ◇ *Having multiple codons specifying the same amino acid is known as the redundancy of the genetic code.* ➲ *see also* FUNCTIONAL GROUP (2)

re·dun·dant /rɪˈdʌndənt/ *adj.* **1** (*BrE*) (of a person) without a job because there is no more work available for you in a company: **make sb ~** *The introduction of a new IT system would allow 46 employees to be made redundant.* **2 ~ (to sb)** not needed or useful: *This undermines the notion that women's wartime experience had rendered men redundant to them.*

reef /riːf/ *noun* a long line of rocks, CORAL or sand near the surface of the sea: *Disturbance is part of the ecology of all coral reefs and probably contributes to their diversity.* ◇ **+ noun** *The abundance of 134 reef fish species was recorded in each sampled area.*

refer /rɪˈfɜː(r)/ *verb* (-rr-) **~ sb/sth (to sb/sth) (for sth)** to send sb/sth to a person, place or organization with more knowledge or authority: *The patients were referred to the specialist clinics for allergy treatment.* ◇ *Under the rules, the court was free to refer the matter even if the case was clear.*

PHR V **reˈfer to sb/sth (as sth)** to mention sb/sth, usually in a way that gives particular information about them: *Firms at the frontier are described as 'leaders', while less successful firms are referred to as 'backward' firms.* ◇ **~ back to sth** *Arthur Koestler, referring back to an article he had written some years earlier, pressed for the idea of a supranational federation.* **reˈfer to sth 1** if a word, phrase or symbol **refers to sth**, that is what it means: *'Praxis' for the Greeks referred to human beings' way of acting and conducting their lives.* **2** to read or use a source of information in order to find out sth SYN CONSULT (3): *For a short definition of the terms used, please refer to Table 12.*

ref·er·ee /ˌrefəˈriː/ *noun* a person who reads and checks the quality of a technical article before it is published: *Revised versions of articles are usually sent back to the referees for further comment.*

ref·er·ence[1] /ˈrefrəns/ *noun* **1** [C, U] a thing you say or write that mentions sb/sth else; the act of mentioning sb/sth: **~ to sb/sth** *Most references to Dryden in translation studies relate to his preface to his translation of Ovid's 'Epistles' (1680).* ◇ *Article 51 makes express reference to the right of self-defence 'if an armed attack occurs'.* ◇ **by ~ to sb/sth** *The commonest explanation of the tragedy of Hamlet is by reference to the fatal flaw of indecisiveness.* **2** [C] a mention of a source of information in a book, an article, etc; a source of information that is mentioned in this way: *In the references section, the full details are given for each cited reference in the numerical order.* ◇ **~ on sth** *Solow (1957) is often quoted as the standard reference on growth accounting.* ➲ *see also* CROSS REFERENCE **3** [U] the act of looking at sth for information: **~ to sth** *A bookmarking feature allows for quick reference to any page.* ◇ **for ~** *Having a complete genome sequence available for reference is an enormous benefit for researchers.* **4 + noun** a measure, substance, set of values, etc. that is regarded as normal or typical and used when making comparisons: *Female (56.7 per cent of the sample) is the reference category for gender.* ◇ *The total protein was 66 g/L (reference range 63–79 g/L).* ➲ *see also* FRAME OF REFERENCE **5** [C] (*abbr.* ref.) a number, word or symbol that shows where you can find a piece of information: *Recently, a second population has colonized an area known as Red Bridge (grid reference is given below).* ◇ **+ noun** *The study has been approved by the ethics committee of the University at Lübeck (reference number 06-141).* ➲ *see also* CROSS REFERENCE

IDM **with/in reference to sth** used to say what sth refers to or is about: *The word 'cult' is often used with reference to ancient religions.* ◇ *Chakravorty shows, particularly in reference to Calcutta, how big cities tend to perpetuate social inequities.* HELP The expression *with special reference to sth* is used in academic writing to show that it is a particular area of a subject that is mainly being discussed: *Lamb H. 'Climate in the 1960s with special reference to East African lakes'. Geographical Journal, 1966,132: 183–212.* **without reference to sth** used to say that a particular aspect or factor has not been considered or included: *The idea is to boost the general activity of the immune system without reference to any particular antigen.* ➲ *more at* TERMS

▸ ADJECTIVE + REFERENCE **explicit** • **implicit** • **direct** • **frequent** • **occasional** • **specific, particular** • **brief** *The question 'what should be' cannot even be addressed without explicit reference to values.*

▸ VERB + REFERENCE **make** • **include, contain** • **omit** • **exclude** • **avoid** • **add** • **remove** *The UN Charter contains references to both the rights of states and the rights of people* | **provide** • **cite** • **give** • **include** • **consult** *Each chapter provides specific references to relevant web links.*

THESAURUS

reference • **citation** • **quotation** *noun*

These are all words for sth you say or write that repeats the words or ideas of sb else.

- a reference/citation **to** sb/sth
- a quotation/citation **from** sb/sth
- to **include/contain/provide** a reference/citation/quotation

- A **quotation** is where you state the ***exact words*** that sb said or wrote, in order to support your own ideas or argument; a **citation** is where you use the ***ideas*** of another author: *Direct quotations from interview transcripts are identified by interview number.* ◇ *Before this, few of the works included citations to previous research.*
- A **reference** is always used in academic writing with a **quotation** or a **citation** to give details about the source; an ***in-text reference*** appears in the text and full reference details are given in a ***reference list*** or ***bibliography*** at the end: *Table 5.5 provides references to selected erosion studies carried out in granite areas.*
- **Citation** is also used as a general term to refer to any information from a source: a **citation**, a **quotation** or a **reference**: *A full list of citations is included at the end.*

NOTE Use a quotation only when the exact wording is important. Remember that quotations and citations may be used to support, but not to replace, your own ideas. It is essential to make it clear to the reader whose idea you are stating; if you do not do this, the reader will assume the idea is yours, which is plagiarism. For information on avoiding plagiarism, see pages AWT6–7.

R

▸ REFERENCE + NOUN **range** ◆ **point** ◆ **group** ◆ **category** ◆ **class** ◆ **sequence** ◆ **value** ◆ **price** *The reference values used for the model calculations are described in Table 5.*

ref·er·ence² /ˈrefrəns/ *verb* **1** **~ sth** (*formal*) to refer to sth: *60% of all responses from white students specifically referenced the need to speak English.* **2** [usually passive] to provide a book, an article, etc. with references: **be referenced** *When comparing analytical results, all terms and techniques must be clearly defined and referenced.*

ˈreference frame *noun* = FRAME OF REFERENCE

ˈreference point (*also* ˌ**point of ˈreference**) *noun* **~ (for sth)** a standard by which sth can be judged or compared: *The organism becomes a reference point for investigations of other organisms with which it shares features of interest.*

ref·er·en·dum /ˌrefəˈrendəm/ *noun* (*pl.* **ref·er·en·dums** or **ref·er·enda**) [C, U] an occasion when all the people of a country can vote on an important issue: **~ on sth** *The government held a referendum on whether people wanted regional government in the north-east.* ◇ **by ~** *The treaty was rejected by referendum.*

re·fer·ral /rɪˈfɜːrəl/ *noun* [U, C] the act of sending sb/sth to a person, place or organization with more knowledge or authority: *The only time referral is not necessary is if a patient has previously been fully investigated.* ◇ **~ (to sb/sth) (for sth)** *Providing support for parents includes parenting classes, support groups and referrals to specialists for children with learning difficulties.*

re·fine AWL /rɪˈfaɪn/ *verb* **1** **~ sth** to make sth such as a theory or method better or clearer by making small changes to it: *Nine focus groups were conducted to review and refine the wording of the questions.* ◇ *Clearly, more investigation is needed to refine our understanding of the mechanisms by which climate and ecosystems interact.* **2** **~ sth** to make a substance pure by taking other substances out of it: *The discovery of oil and the techniques to refine it led to the possibility of the internal combustion engine.*

re·fined AWL /rɪˈfaɪnd/ *adj.* **1** [usually before noun] (of a theory or method) improved by having had small changes made to it: *The least refined demographic measures may not be immediately applicable in comparative studies of populations.* **2** [usually before noun] (of a substance) made pure by having other substances taken out of it: *The high intake of refined sugar and starch may increase the risk of inflammatory bowel disease.* **3** (of a person) able to make judgements about the quality or value of things; showing such an ability SYN CULTURED (2): *The speaker represents himself as a member of an exclusive group with more refined tastes than at least some of his contemporaries.*

re·fine·ment AWL /rɪˈfaɪnmənt/ *noun* **1** [C, U] **~ (of sth)** a small change to sth such as a theory or method that improves it; the process of improving sth in this way: *In addition to refinements of North and Weingast's argument, there have been significant direct challenges.* ◇ *Arguably, these system approaches are in need of substantial elaboration and refinement.* **2** [C] **~ of sth** a thing that is an improvement on an earlier, similar thing: *This concept is illustrated in Fig. 3.2 which is a refinement of Fig. 3.1.* **3** [U, sing.] **~ (of sth)** the ability to judge the quality and value of things; the fact of having high quality or value: *Proust's greatness lay in, among other things, an unmatched refinement of artistic taste.* ◇ *Mass-produced cars offer acceptable levels of comfort, refinement and reliability.*

re·flect /rɪˈflekt/ *verb* **1** [T] to show or be a sign of what sth is like or how sb thinks or feels: **~ sth** *The novel reflects the social realities of frontier life.* ◇ *The aim was to collect a sample that could reflect the views of both genders and differing age bands.* ◇ **~ how/what, etc...** *A company's share price is important because it reflects how much investors value the business.* **2** [T] to throw back light, heat, sound, etc. from a surface: **~ sth (back)** *Green light is not absorbed and is reflected back, giving plants their characteristic green colour.* ◇ **reflected + noun** *In addition to the regular reflected wave, a pulse-like wave is found.* **3** [I, T] to think carefully and deeply about sth: **~ on/upon sth** *It is worth reflecting critically on how Darwin's work has been presented to the general public.* ◇ **~ that...** *Emily reflected that her eating disorder was allowing her to hurt her parents, at whom she was quite angry.* ◇ **~ how/what, etc...** *Our project participants were invited to record and reflect how they live within their communities.*
IDM **reflect well, badly, etc. on sb/sth** to make sb/sth appear to be good, bad, etc. to other people: *These failures reflect badly on the company as a whole.*

▸ REFLECT + NOUN **fact** ◆ **reality** ◆ **nature** ◆ **concern** ◆ **interest** ◆ **difference, diversity, variation** ◆ **change, shift** ◆ **view** ◆ **belief** ◆ **attitude** ◆ **preference** ◆ **bias** ◆ **trend, tendency** ◆ **pattern** ◆ **importance** ◆ **influence** ◆ **complexity** ◆ **difficulty** ◆ **degree** ◆ **lack** ◆ **need** ◆ **process** *The dramatic increases in population since about 1650 reflect the fact that the death rate began to fall before the birth rate did.*

▸ ADVERB + REFLECT **accurately, truly** ◆ **adequately** ◆ **best** ◆ **closely** *Dicey believed that the Commons accurately reflected the will of the people and controlled the executive.* | **probably, likely, presumably** ◆ **perhaps, possibly** ◆ **clearly, undoubtedly** ◆ **simply, merely** ◆ **partly, partially** ◆ **largely, primarily, generally** ◆ **(not) necessarily** ◆ **inevitably** *The vocabulary of any language necessarily reflects the environment in which its speakers live.*

re·flect·ance /rɪˈflektəns/ *noun* [U, C] (*physics*) a measure of how much light is reflected off a surface, considered as a part of the total light that shines onto it: *Cool materials have high solar reflectance and stay cool in the sun.* ◇ *Reflectances are correlated with surface colour perceptions.*

re·flec·tion /rɪˈflekʃn/ *noun* **1** [C] **~ of sth** an account or description of what sb/sth is like; a thing that is a result of sth else: *How do researchers ever know that the version they have recorded is an accurate reflection of the refugee experience?* ◇ *Cervantes' sympathy for the prisoners is almost certainly a reflection of his own years in a North African prison.* **2** [U] careful thought about sth, especially your work or studies: *Freire proposes that this model of education encourages passivity and does not encourage critical reflection.* ◇ **on ~** *On reflection, it might have been better to have gathered more data at this early stage.* **3** [C, usually pl.] **reflections (on sth)** written or spoken thoughts about a particular subject: *In his memoir 'In Search of Mind' (1983), Bruner shared his reflections on the origins of the cognitive revolution.* **4** [U] **~ (of sth)** the action or process of sending back light, heat, sound, etc. from a surface: *In terms of reflection of solar radiation, plants are unique.* ◇ *The reflected ray follows the principle that the angle of reflection equals the angle of incidence.* **5** (*also* **reflexion**) [C, U] **~ (of sth)** (*mathematics*) an operation on a shape to produce its MIRROR IMAGE: *The wings of a butterfly are related by reflection in the xy-axis.*

R

re·flect·ive /rɪˈflektɪv/ *adj.* **1** thinking carefully about things, especially about your work or studies: *Although some doctors develop skills through reflective practice, most do not.* ➲ language bank *on* page 676 **2** **~ of sth** typical of a particular situation or thing; showing the state or nature of sth: *Even verbally expressed anger can be reflective of more serious difficulties when it is intense.* **3** **reflective** surfaces send back light or heat: *Silicon dioxide is a transparent film, and the silicon surface is highly reflective.*
■ **re·flect·ive·ly** *adv.*: *She writes reflectively about her experiences in the country.*

re·flex /ˈriːfleks/ *noun* **1** [C, U] an action or a movement of your body that happens naturally in response to sth

LANGUAGE BANK

Reflective writing

In your studies, you may be asked to reflect on and write about a particular aspect of your course. The main purpose is to show that you can think critically about your course and about yourself as a learner. These words and phrases can help you to get started.

- Expressing your beliefs and feelings:
  - ▸ I believe/I feel…
  - ▸ I am sure that…
  - ▸ For me,…
  - – *I believe I can communicate effectively…*
- Expressing what you have learnt:
  - ▸ …has taught me (that)…
  - ▸ I have been made aware…
  - ▸ I noticed/realized that…
  - ▸ As a result of…
  - ▸ On reflection/In thinking back/Looking back on it,…
  - ▸ On balance, I would say…
  - – *This course has taught me the importance of listening to others attentively.*
- Expressing a change in your thinking:
  - ▸ I am now more…
  - ▸ I am becoming more aware…
  - ▸ Much better is to…
  - ▸ I now feel…
  - ▸ I now undertand/see that…
  - – *However, I now understand that other people may have been brought up with a different belief system.*
- Admitting weaknesses:
  - ▸ I would find it difficult to…
  - ▸ I need to try to…
  - ▸ … challenges me personally.
  - ▸ It was very difficult to…
  - – *I would find it difficult to deal with prejudiced people.*
- Expressing positive changes:
  - ▸ … is/has been extremely/most beneficial for…
  - ▸ … has provided me with the opportunity to…
  - ▸ … has taught me the importance of…
  - ▸ … is a valuable skill.
  - – *This course has provided me with the opportunity to reflect on my belief system.*

R

and that you cannot control; sth that you do without thinking: *A newborn baby is equipped with basic reflexes.* ◇ **by ~** *If your hand comes into contact with a hot surface, then you will pull it away by reflex.* **2** [C] (*linguistics*) a word or sound formed by development from an earlier stage of a language: *It is often possible to reconstruct some of the aspects of the original language from the reflexes in the daughter languages.*

re·flex·ive /rɪˈfleksɪv/ *adj.* **1** a **reflexive** word or form of a word shows that the action of the verb affects the person who performs the action HELP A **reflexive** pronoun is a pronoun such as *herself* or *themselves*. A **reflexive** verb is a verb such as *wash yourself*: *In non-standard English, theirselves is a reflexive pronoun.* **2** (of a reaction) happening as a reflex, without you thinking about it: *Anger is the reflexive response to a number of difficult experiences.* **3** (of a method or theory) taking account of itself or of the effect of the personality or presence of the researcher on what is being investigated: *They urge a reflexive approach to social work practice, involving a constant revaluation of the workers' own power and perspectives.*

re·form¹ /rɪˈfɔːm; *NAmE* rɪˈfɔːrm/ *noun* [U, C] change that is made to a social system, an organization, etc. in order to improve or correct it: *Only gradual economic reform will create the conditions for states to mature.* ◇ *Major reforms during the Great Depression permanently changed the country's big-business sector.* ◇ **~ of sth** *Portugal is going through a massive organizational reform of primary health care.*

▸ ADJECTIVE + REFORM **major • significant • radical • far-reaching • recent • structural • economic • social • institutional • electoral • constitutional • political • parliamentary • legal, legislative • educational • regulatory • administrative** *The Panel concluded that radical reforms were needed, including the dismissal of many judges.*

▸ NOUN + REFORM **land • policy • law • market • welfare • education • health** *After the liberation of Italy in 1945, a political struggle for land reform broke out.*

▸ VERB + REFORM **institute • introduce, initiate • implement • undertake • advocate, call for • recommend • support • promote • pursue • urge • drive • need, require • oppose • achieve** *According to Nakamura, the Nippon Railway Co. implemented two major organizational reforms before the 1900s.*

▸ REFORM + NOUN **programme • agenda • package • proposal • plan • strategy • process • effort • initiative** *Alongside the military reform programme, police reform has been equally comprehensive.*

re·form² /rɪˈfɔːm; *NAmE* rɪˈfɔːrm/ *verb* **~ sth** to make changes to a system, an organization, a law, etc. in order to improve it: *Both India and Pakistan are now reforming their educational systems.* ◇ *The Treaty of Nice (2001) marked an attempt to reform the EU's institutions to prepare the Union for enlargement.*

re·form·er /rɪˈfɔːmə(r); *NAmE* rɪˈfɔːrmər/ *noun* a person who works to achieve political or social change: *The Commission's eighteen members included leading social reformers and campaigners.*

re·form·ist /rɪˈfɔːmɪst; *NAmE* rɪˈfɔːrmɪst/ *adj.* wanting or trying to change political or social situations: *Various reformist organizations took on issues such as child marriage and female education.* ■ **re·form·ist** *noun*: *From the early 1790s, radicals and reformists saw the printed word as an agent of change.*

re·fract /rɪˈfrækt/ *verb* **1 ~ sth** (*physics*) (of a material or substance) to make waves, such as those of light, sound or energy, change direction when they go through at an angle: *The rays of light are refracted by the material of the lens.* **2 ~ sth (through sth)** used to describe how sth changes when considered from a particular point of view: *Films such as this reproduce things not as they really are but as they appear when refracted through ideology.* ■ **re·frac·tion** /rɪˈfrækʃn/ *noun* [U] **~ (of sth)** *Atmospheric refraction of light is a significant source of error.*

re·fract·ive /rɪˈfræktɪv/ *adj.* (*physics*) causing, caused by or connected with refraction: *Sunlight comprises rays of differing colours and refractive properties.*

re,fractive ˈindex *noun* (*physics*) a measurement of how much an object or a substance refracts light: *A beam of light changes direction when it passes from a region of one refractive index to a region with a different refractive index.*

re·frain /rɪˈfreɪn/ *verb* [I] **~ from (doing) sth** to stop yourself from doing sth, especially sth that you want to do: *The patient was advised to refrain from heavy arm activities for the next 2 weeks.*

ref·uge /ˈrefjuːdʒ/ *noun* **1** [U] protection from danger or trouble: **~ from sb/sth** *Asylum seekers are exercising a legal right to seek refuge from persecution.* ◇ **take ~ in sth** (*figurative*) *He condemns those on the Left who take refuge in the past in order to avoid political action in the present.* **2** [C] a place, person or thing that provides protection or safety for sb/sth: **~ from sb/sth** *A burrowing lifestyle offers* *a refuge from predation.* ◇ **~ for sb/sth** *The walled citadels served as a refuge for the inhabitants of the unfortified towns below.*

refu·gee /ˌrefju'dʒiː/ *noun* a person who has been forced to leave their country or home, in order to escape war, natural disaster or political or religious PERSECUTION: *Since 2000, Canada has resettled approximately 11 000 refugees per year.* ◇ **+ noun** *The paper characterized the percentage of asylum seekers who were granted refugee status as 'disturbingly low'.*

re·fusal /rɪ'fjuːzl/ *noun* [U, C] an act of saying or showing that you will not do, give or accept sth: *Although we did not measure reasons for refusal, emails indicated that a lack of time was a likely factor.* ◇ **~ to do sth** *The high refusal to participate may have produced a skewed sample.* ◇ **~ of sth** *In the case of refusal of a visa, the question is whether the entry clearance officer's decision was unreasonable.*

re·fuse /rɪ'fjuːz/ *verb* **1** [I] to say that you will not do sth that sb has asked you to do: *The applicants had requested the Commission to take action but the Commission refused.* ◇ **~ to do sth** *Of the 4 971 selected subjects, 13% refused to participate.* **2** [T] **~ sth** to say that you do not want sth that has been offered to you SYN TURN SB/STH DOWN: *Cromwell refused the offer of the Crown but was proclaimed Lord Protector in December 1653.* **3** [T] to say that you will not give or allow sb sth that they want or need SYN DENY (3): **~ sth** *If the application is refused, the applicant can present it directly to the Court.* ◇ *to refuse permission for/consent to sth* ◇ **~ sb sth** *One of the researchers was refused a visa to attend a conference in the UK.*

re·fute /rɪ'fjuːt/ *verb* **~ sth** to prove that a statement or theory is wrong SYN DISPROVE (1): *These claims have not been convincingly refuted.* ◇ *to refute an argument/a hypothesis/a theory* HELP In general English, **refute** is often used to mean simply 'deny', without any proof being involved: *I absolutely refute the charges made against me.* Some people consider this use incorrect and it is best avoided in academic writing; use **deny** or **reject** instead. ⊃ thesaurus note *at* REJECT ■ **refu·ta·tion** /ˌrefju'teɪʃn/ *noun* [C, U] **~ (of sth)** *He anticipates other possible refutations of his argument.* ◇ *Scientists tried to protect their theories from refutation.*

re·gain /rɪ'geɪn/ *verb* **~ sth** to get back sth you no longer have, especially an ability or a quality: *After a seizure, the patient gradually regains consciousness.* ◇ *They need to regain control over their lives.* ◇ *In 357, the Phocians made a desperate effort to regain their independence.*

re·gard¹ /rɪ'gɑːd; *NAmE* rɪ'gɑːrd/ *verb* [often passive] to think about sb/sth in a particular way: **be + adv. + regarded** *The film is now highly regarded, even if it had a mixed reception on its first appearance.* ◇ **be regarded (by sb) as sth** *Plagiarism is commonly regarded as a form of academic cheating.* ◇ *Research that is likely to harm participants is regarded by most people as unacceptable.* ◇ **~ sb/sth/yourself as sth** *The younger Pitt did not regard himself as a party man.*

IDM **as regards sb/sth** concerning or in connection with sb/sth: *As regards using cable as an advertising medium, the company increased its advertising spending on cable networks by 64 per cent.*

re·gard² /rɪ'gɑːd; *NAmE* rɪ'gɑːrd/ *noun* **1** [U] attention to or thought and care for sb/sth: *Due regard must be given to national security interests.* ◇ **~ for sb/sth** *Today's decisions often are taken with little regard for tomorrow's consequences.* ◇ **~ to sb/sth** *There is a profession-dominated service ethic that pays scant regard to patient-centred care.* **2** [U] **~ (for sb/sth)** respect or admiration for sb/sth: *Faraday never lost his regard for Davy's science.* HELP If you **hold sb in high regard**, you have a good opinion of them: *Even Handel held Purcell in high regard.* **3 regards** [pl.] used to send good wishes to sb at the end of a letter or email: *With kind regards, Yours...*

IDM **have re'gard to sth** (*law*) to remember and think carefully about sth: *The court must have regard to all the circumstances of the case.* **in this/that re'gard** concerning what has just been mentioned: *The landmark case in this regard is City of Richmond v. Croson (1989).* **in/with regard to sb/sth** concerning sb/sth: *These studies have provided valuable information with regard to diagnosis of the disease.*

re·gard·ing /rɪ'gɑːdɪŋ; *NAmE* rɪ'gɑːrdɪŋ/ *prep.* concerning sb/sth; about sb/sth: *The terminology regarding ethnicity, culture, race and diversity is complex.* ◇ *The Commission issued specific recommendations regarding the simplification of criminal justice proceedings.*

re·gen·er·ate /rɪ'dʒenəreɪt/ *verb* **1** [I, T] (*biology*) to grow again; to make sth grow again: *Once destroyed, brain cells do not regenerate.* ◇ *Renewable resources naturally regenerate to provide a new supply.* ◇ **~ sth** *Some insects can regenerate whole limbs after amputation.* ◇ **~ itself** *If the woodland is left alone, it will regenerate itself in a few years.* **2** [T] **~ sth** to make an area, institution, etc. develop and grow strong again: *The site is a regenerated industrial area.* ◇ *Schools are increasingly seen as providing a focal point for regenerating community.* ■ **re·gen·er·ation** /rɪˌdʒenə'reɪʃn/ *noun* [U] **~ (of sth)** *The rapid regeneration of the weed slowed down.* ◇ *Partnerships are seen as a mechanism for delivering urban regeneration.* **re·gen·era·tive** /rɪ'dʒenərətɪv/ *adj.*: ◇ *The focus of regenerative medicine is currently on stem cells.* ◇ *Governments should focus on regenerative programmes such as poverty eradication.*

re·gime AWL /reɪ'ʒiːm/ *noun* **1** a government, especially one that has not been elected in a fair way: *The communist regime collapsed in November 1989.* ◇ **under a ~** *Under authoritarian regimes, freedom of expression is usually limited.* **2** a method or system of organizing or managing sth: *There are difficulties of a political nature in imposing a visa regime on friendly states.* ◇ **under a ~** *A key finding was that there was a significantly better response from staff under the new regime.* **3** the conditions under which a natural, scientific or industrial process occurs: *Ice cores reveal large and rapid changes in the North Atlantic climate regime during the Late Glacial Stage (Taylor et al., 1993).* ◇ **under a ~** *We maintained birds under three thermal regimes: constant cold, constant thermoneutrality and natural seasonal variation.* **4** = REGIMEN

regi·men /'redʒɪmən/ (*also* **re·gime**) *noun* a course of medical treatment and sometimes changes to diet and behaviour that sb has to follow in order to recover from or control an illness: *Diabetes treatment regimens are complicated, encompassing lifestyle changes and medication intake.*

re·gion AWL /'riːdʒən/ *noun* **1** [C] a large area of land, usually without exact limits or borders: *Most coastal regions have at least moderate rainfall.* ◇ *The Dakota people inhabited the region.* **2** [C] one of the areas that a country is divided into, that has its own customs and/or its own government: *Terrorist bombings and street demonstrations in the Basque region threatened state unity.* **3 the regions** [pl.] (*BrE*) all of a country except the capital city: *He travelled around the regions, promising more state funds for them after his re-election.* **4** [C] **~ (of sth)** an area of sth, especially one that has a particular character: *The radiance curves span the far infrared region of the electromagnetic spectrum.* ◇ *The strongly connected components of the network in Fig. 6.13 are highlighted by the shaded regions.* **5** [C] a part of the body, usually one that has a particular character or problem: *It is most likely that many* genes are involved in specifying the different heart regions. ◇ ~ **of sth** *Blastomere removal identifies regions of the embryo that are essential for further development.* **6** [C, usually sing.] an area of activity or thought: *Adaptation studies has traditionally occupied a nebulous region between film and literature.*

IDM **in the region of sth** used when you are giving a number, price, etc. to show that it is not exact SYN APPROXIMATELY: *The unemployment rate in the US has been in the region of 6% for a number of years.*

re·gion·al AWL /ˈriːdʒənl/ *adj.* [usually before noun] connected with a region: *A new regional development policy was introduced in 1980.* ◇ *Regional differences between urban and rural areas have widened.* ◇ *regional variation/disparities* ◇ *Sustainability is an issue at regional and local levels too.* ◇ *A third component of Oklahoma's regional identity is the tragic image of the 'Dust Bowl' of the 1930s.* ◇ *regional geography/climate* ■ **re·gion·al·ly** AWL /ˈriːdʒənəli/ *adv.*: *Typhoon is a regionally specific term for a tropical cyclone.*

regis·ter[1] AWL /ˈredʒɪstə(r)/ *verb* **1** [T, I] to record the name of sb/sth on an official list: ~ **sth** *The clinic registered 465 new patients.* ◇ ~ **sth on/in sth** *The father's name is registered on the certificate of birth.* ◇ ~ **(sb/sth) as sth** *Boric acid was first registered as an insecticide in 1948 by the US Environmental Protection Agency.* ◇ ~ **(sb/sth) with sb/sth** *Companies have to register with Companies House in order to obtain a trading certificate.* ◇ ~ **(sb/sth) (for sth)** *The list was used to track down those who had failed to register for military service.* ➲ thesaurus note *at* RECORD[2] **2** [T] ~ **sth** to make your opinion known officially or publicly: *The French President, Charles de Gaulle, registered his opposition to the creation of the European Economic Community.* **3** [I] + **noun** (of a measuring instrument) to show or record an amount: *The thermometer registered 74 degrees below zero.* **4** [T] ~ **sth** to achieve a particular score or result: *The Conservative performance in Wales was impressive, registering the biggest increase in vote share for the party of any region of Britain.* **5** [T] ~ **sth** to notice sth and remember it: *One final general point to register is that there is growing interest in the use of online focus groups.*

R

regis·ter[2] AWL /ˈredʒɪstə(r)/ *noun* **1** [C] ~ **(of sth)** an official list or record of names or items; a book that contains such a list: *Every company is required to maintain a register of its directors.* ◇ *The parish register records the burial of the poet's only son.* **2** [C, U] (*linguistics*) the level and style of a piece of writing or speech, that is usually appropriate to the situation that it is used in: *Some features occur more often in formal written registers rather than in spoken registers.* ◇ *The concept of register is typically concerned with variation in language conditioned by the situation or context of use.* **3** [C] (*computing*) (in electronic devices) a location in a store of data, used for a particular purpose and with quick access time: *Microprocessors use registers to hold temporary data.*

regis·trar /ˌredʒɪˈstrɑː(r); ˈredʒɪstrɑː(r)/ *noun* **1** a doctor working in a British hospital who is training to become a specialist in a particular area of medicine: *There are plenty of topics to which registrars have little or no exposure during training.* ➲ *compare* CONSULTANT (2), RESIDENT[1] (4) **2** ~ **(of sth)** a person whose job is to keep a REGISTER or official records, especially of births, marriages and deaths: *The memorandum and articles of a company are public documents, filed with the registrar of companies.*

regis·tra·tion AWL /ˌredʒɪˈstreɪʃn/ *noun* [U, C] the act of making an official record of sth/sb: *Voter registration was conducted from 9 January to 21 February 2010.* ◇ ~ **of sth** *In 2004, there were 36 939 new registrations of breast cancer in women in the UK.* ◇ + **noun** *All subscribers pay an annual registration fee.*

regis·try /ˈredʒɪstri/ *noun* (*pl.* **-ies**) a place where REGISTERS or records are kept: *Patients must give informed consent for their data to be included in the registry.* ◇ ~ **of sb/sth** *A random sample of older adults was drawn from the population registries of 11 municipalities in the Netherlands.*

re·gress /rɪˈgres/ *verb* **1** [I] to return to an earlier or less developed state or way of behaving: *50% of tumours completely regressed.* ◇ ~ **to sth** *In Shakespeare's world, when the solidity and truth of women are undermined, the world regresses to savagery.* **2** [T] ~ **sth (on sth)** (*statistics*) to perform a regression analysis: *Overtime hours worked were regressed on the four predictor variables.*

re·gres·sion /rɪˈgreʃn/ *noun* [U, C] **1** the process of going back to an earlier or less developed state or way of behaving: ~ **(to sth)** *Regression back to military rule in South Korea has become inconceivable.* ◇ *Regression occurs commonly among physically ill people.* ◇ ~ **of sth** *Excessive erosion of soil may lead to a regression of soil development* **2** (*also* **reˈgression analysis**) (*statistics*) a method of establishing the relationship between a VARIABLE and a DEPENDENT VARIABLE such that the value of the dependent variable can be predicted from the value of the other (the INDEPENDENT VARIABLE): *Using regression analysis, we can predict the height of a child from his or her age.*

re·gres·sive /rɪˈgresɪv/ *adj.* **1** becoming or making sth less advanced: *There are several regressive aspects of the recent reforms.* **2** (of a tax) having less effect on the rich than on the poor: *These programmes will help to lower social inequities and diminish the effects of regressive taxation.*

regu·lar /ˈregjələ(r)/ *adj.* **1** following a pattern, especially with the same time and space in between each thing and the next: *These interviews were conducted at regular intervals.* ◇ *The patient must undergo regular blood monitoring.* OPP IRREGULAR (1) **2** done or happening often: *Newspaper editors had regular meetings with officials.* ◇ *Eighty-seven per cent of the town's residents use the Internet on a regular basis.* OPP IRREGULAR (1) **3** [only before noun] (of people) doing the same thing or going to the same place often: *Half of all regular cigarette smokers will eventually be killed by their habit.* ◇ *Younger and better-educated people tend to be more regular users of the Internet.* **4** lasting or happening over a long period: *Service contracts provide the firm with a regular income.* ◇ *In the 1950s, most of these people had to live in poverty and without regular employment.* ➲ *compare* CASUAL (4) **5** [only before noun] usual or standard: *These high school students spend more than twelve hours a day in their regular school and then in private cram schools.* ◇ *For many children, regular classrooms have already been superseded by a new kind of classroom that is the postmodern technological world.* **6** having an even shape: *Mormon towns were laid out according to a regular grid pattern.* OPP IRREGULAR (2) **7** [only before noun] belonging to or connected with the permanent armed forces or police force of a country: *The British government recruited over 200 000 volunteers to supplement the regular army.* **8** (*grammar*) (especially of verbs or nouns) changing their form in the same way as most other verbs and nouns: *For example, regular verbs in the language take subject agreement forms, whereas these verbs do not agree with anything.* OPP IRREGULAR (4)

re·gu·lar·ity /ˌregjuˈlærəti/ *noun* **1** [U] the fact that the same thing happens again and again, and usually with the same length of time between each time it happens: *The new generation of entrepreneurs apply scientific approaches to achieve regularity and safety in production processes.* **2** [U] ~ **(of sth)** the fact that sth is arranged in an even way or in an organized pattern: *The regular external form of crystals implied an internal regularity of their* *constituents.* ➲ *compare* IRREGULARITY (3) **3** [C] a thing that has a pattern to it: *The history of the capitalist world economy shows clear regularities and its future development is subject to prediction.* ◇ **~ in sth** *Others (e.g. Barabasi, 2002) provide additional analyses of the regularities in the structure and growth of the Web.* ➲ *compare* IRREGULARITY (2)

regu·lar·ly /ˈreɡjələli; *NAmE* ˈreɡjələrli/ *adv.* **1** at regular times: *Shareholders elect a board of directors that meets regularly.* ◇ *These students participated in this study as part of their regularly scheduled German language course.* **2** often: *People who exercise regularly are significantly less likely to develop this form of cancer.* ◇ *Regularly updated, this website provides 1 487 links to nearly every source of economic information on the Internet.* **3** in an even or balanced way: *Many structures, such as the feathers on a bird's skin, are found to be more or less regularly spaced with respect to one another.*

regu·late AWL /ˈreɡjuleɪt/ *verb* **1** to control the rate of a machine or process so that it works in the correct way; to control how sb/sth behaves: **~ sth** *The control devices can regulate circulating water temperatures, flow rates and pressures.* ◇ *This is a clear example of how genes can regulate behaviour.* ◇ **be regulated by sth** *Production of thyroid hormones is regulated by another hormone (thyrotropin).* ◇ **highly/tightly regulated** *Fibre development is a highly regulated process which consists of four distinctive but overlapping stages:...* **2** to control sth by means of rules: **~ sth** *Many professions have adopted a code of practice to regulate their activities.* ◇ **be regulated by sth** *In Slovenia, drug markets are regulated by EU and state legislation.* ◇ **highly/tightly regulated** *Public companies are more tightly regulated than private companies.*

regu·la·tion AWL /ˌreɡjuˈleɪʃn/ *noun* **1** [C, usually pl.] an official rule made by a government or some other authority: *Firms must comply with environmental regulations.* ◇ *Strict health and safety regulations must be adhered to.* ◇ *legal/federal/government regulations* ◇ *These regulations were rarely enforced.* ◇ *to adopt/implement/enact regulations* ◇ **~ on sth** *The EU introduced regulations on the labelling of GM foods.* ◇ **under ~** *Under existing regulations, a simple share buyout could occur.* ◇ **rules and regulations** *Governments have a key role to play in passing rules and regulations to enhance sustainable development in society.* **2** [U] the act of controlling sth by means of rules: *Strict regulation has protected some coastlines as wildlife refuges and recreational areas.* ◇ *legal/statutory/federal/government regulation* ◇ **~ of sth** *The decline of government regulation of television resulted in a decline in public affairs documentaries.* ◇ **under ~** *Increasingly, industrial effluents are under stringent regulation.* **3** [U] the act of controlling how a machine or system operates or how sth behaves: *The circulation of ocean currents has an important effect upon world temperature regulation* ◇ **~ of sth** *The regulation of gene expression takes place at many levels.*

regu·la·tor AWL /ˈreɡjuleɪtə(r)/ *noun* **1** a person or an organization that officially controls an area of business or industry and makes sure that it is operating fairly: *In 1997, both the water and electricity regulators imposed price reductions.* ◇ *In 2001, Enron, a huge US company that went bankrupt, was investigated by the US financial regulator.* **2** a device that AUTOMATICALLY controls sth such as speed, temperature or pressure: *Voltage regulators provide a constant DC voltage that varies little with variations in power supply voltage.* **3** (*biology*) a substance or process that controls the function of another substance or process: *Plant growth regulators play an important role in seed germination.*

regu·la·tory AWL /ˈreɡjələtəri; *NAmE* ˈreɡjələtɔːri/ *adj.* [usually before noun] **1** having the power to control an area of business or industry and make sure that it is operating fairly: *The British Independent Television Commission, a regulatory body, fined the television channel that aired the film.* ◇ *a regulatory agency/authority* ◇ *Governments established a regulatory framework to prevent fraud and provide security to savers.* **2** (*biology*) (of a substance or process) controlling another substance or process: *Calcium ions and regulatory proteins play key roles in muscle contraction and relaxation.*

re·habili·tate /ˌriːəˈbɪlɪteɪt/ *verb* **1 ~ sb** to help sb to have a normal, useful life again after they have been very ill or in prison for a long time: *At present, it is not possible to rehabilitate Alzheimer's patients.* **2 ~ sb/sth (as sth)** to begin to consider that sb/sth is good or acceptable after a long period during which they were considered bad or unacceptable: *In recent years, the genre of melodrama has been critically rehabilitated in Western film studies.* ◇ *He played a major role in rehabilitating Magritte as an artist.* **3 ~ sth** to return a building or an area to its previous good condition: *The top priority was to rehabilitate the park and develop it into a place for youth activities.*
■ **re·habili·ta·tion** /ˌriːəˌbɪlɪˈteɪʃn/ *noun* [U] **~ (of sb/sth)** *The paper emphasized the importance of psychological factors in the rehabilitation of the back-injured worker.* ◇ *Tannock's 'Nostalgia critique' is perhaps the landmark essay in the recent theoretical rehabilitation of nostalgia.* ◇ **+ noun** *The facility was used as a rehabilitation centre for juvenile offenders.*

reign[1] /reɪn/ *noun* **1 ~ (of sb)** the period during which a king, queen, EMPEROR, etc. rules: *The humanist tradition of the Tudors came to full flower during the reign of Elizabeth.* **2 ~ of sth** the period during which an idea, a system, etc. has a lot of influence or control: *To Kipling, the British Empire meant the world-wide reign of justice.*

reign[2] /reɪn/ *verb* [I] **1** to rule as king, queen, EMPEROR, etc: *Queen Victoria reigned from 1837 to 1901.* **2** to be the best or most important in a particular situation or area of skill: **~ supreme** *By the late nineteenth century, industrial capitalism reigned supreme in the United States.*

rein /reɪn/ *noun* **the reins** [pl.] **~ (of sth)** the state of being in control or the leader of sth: *It is still national governments that hold the reins of power: they can choose when and whether to accept international rules.*
IDM **give/allow sb/sth (a) free/full ˈrein | give/allow (a) free/full ˈrein to sb/sth** to give sb complete freedom of action; to allow sth to be expressed freely: *The moderator generally tries to allow a relatively free rein to the discussion.* ◇ *Individuals, he suggests, need to give full rein to their individuality if they are to be noticed.*

re·incar·na·tion /ˌriːɪnkɑːˈneɪʃn; *NAmE* ˌriːɪnkɑːrˈneɪʃn/ *noun* [U] the belief that after sb's death their soul lives again in a new body: *Belief in reincarnation is widespread in many cultures.*

re·inforce AWL /ˌriːɪnˈfɔːs; *NAmE* ˌriːɪnˈfɔːrs/ *verb* **1 ~ sth** to make a feeling, idea, habit or tendency stronger: *Some argue that the media serve to reinforce rather than change political views* ◇ *to reinforce an idea/a message* ◇ *The slump in European trade was reinforced by a contraction in the world economy.* **2 ~ sth** to make a structure or material stronger, especially by adding another material to it: *Because concrete is strong when squashed but weak when pulled, steel bars are used to reinforce it.* **3 ~ sth** to send more people or equipment in order to make an army, etc. stronger: *The US forces needed to be reinforced by 200 000 troops.*

re·inforce·ment AWL /ˌriːɪnˈfɔːsmənt; *NAmE* ˌriːɪnˈfɔːrsmənt/ *noun* **1 reinforcements** [pl.] extra soldiers or police officers who are sent to a place because more are needed: *Macedonian reinforcements from Asia enabled Antipater to defeat the Greek army.* **2** [U, sing.] the act of making a feeling, idea, habit or tendency stronger: **~ (of sth)** *The stories are often set in the late 1950s, a time of reinforcement of 'old' values, following World War II.* ◇ **positive/negative ~** *Undesirable behaviour would be linked to a stimulus such as a very mild electric shock that acted as a negative reinforcement.* **3** [U] the act of making a structure or material stronger, especially by adding another material to it: *The walls of mud houses had straw in them as reinforcement so as to prevent their fracture.*

re·inter·pret AWL /ˌriːɪnˈtɜːprɪt; *NAmE* ˌriːɪnˈtɜːrprɪt/ *verb* **~ sth** to INTERPRET sth in a new or different way: *Parejo and Aviles (2007) reinterpret previous results in view of their new idea.* ■ **re·inter·pret·ation** AWL /ˌriːɪnˌtɜːprɪˈteɪʃn; *NAmE* ˌriːɪnˌtɜːrprɪˈteɪʃn/ *noun* [C, U] **~ (of sth)** *Sulak proposes a modern reinterpretation of the principles of Buddhism.* ◇ *International law is subject to interpretation and reinterpretation over time.*

re·invest AWL /ˌriːɪnˈvest/ *verb* [T, I] to put profits that have been made on an investment back into the same investment or into a new one: **~ (sth)** *A firm must reinvest its profits from one year if it wants to remain competitive in the next year.* ◇ **~ (sth) in sth** *The money accumulated was shifted into other forms of investment rather than reinvested in industry.* ■ **re·invest·ment** AWL *noun* [U, C] **~ (in sth)** *Reinvestment can be either in business or social projects, or in environmental schemes.*

re·iter·ate /riˈɪtəreɪt/ *verb* to repeat sth that you have already said, especially to emphasize it: **~ sth** *To reiterate the key point: the majority of people do not consistently act selfishly.* ◇ **~ that...** *In December 2009, the Tuvaluan Prime Minister reiterated that his government rejected resettlement.* ■ **re·iter·ation** /riˌɪtəˈreɪʃn/ *noun* [U, C] **~ (of sth)** *The approach to human rights has been characterized by constant reiteration of the premise that all people are created equal.*

THESAURUS

reject • deny • contradict • refute *verb*

These words all mean to say or believe that sth is not true.

- to reject/deny/contradict/refute a **claim**
- to reject/contradict/refute a/an **hypothesis/view/idea/notion/theory**
- to reject/deny/refute a **possibility**
- to **completely/explicitly** reject/deny sth

- **Reject** means to disagree with an idea, a claim or a theory put forward by sb else; **refute** means to show that sth is wrong or false by using evidence: *Most people strongly reject the idea of reproductive cloning.* ◇ *It is extremely difficult to provide evidence that would confirm or refute this hypothesis.*
- **Deny** means to say that sth is not true; it is also commonly used with a negative to say that a fact must be accepted: *Extreme realists deny the existence of an international society.* ◇ *The impact of these costs cannot be denied.*
- **Contradict** means to claim that sth is not true by putting forward an opposite idea or evidence: *However, this general rule has now been contradicted by recent findings.*

re·ject AWL /rɪˈdʒekt/ *verb* **1 ~ sth** to refuse to accept or consider sth: *This hypothesis can be rejected on a number of grounds.* ◇ *to reject an idea/a view/an argument/a claim* ◇ *This kind of scientific approach to ethics is rejected by Kant.* ◇ *The US Supreme Court rejected Dred Scott's appeal for freedom.* **2 ~ sb** to refuse to accept sb for a job or position: *Workers who are fortunate to be hired are better off than those who are rejected.* **3 ~ sth** to decide not to use, sell, publish, etc. sth because its quality is not good enough: *The novel was rejected six times by publishers.* **4 ~ sth** (of the body) to not accept a new organ after a TRANSPLANT operation, by producing substances that attack the organ: *The patient's body rejected the new liver within two weeks.* **5 ~ sb/sth** to fail to give a person or an animal enough care or affection: *The lioness rejected the smallest cub, which died.* ◇ *She feels she was rejected by her mother, who chose her stepfather over her.*

re·jec·tion AWL /rɪˈdʒekʃn/ [U, C] **1** the act of refusing to accept or consider sth: *The plan collapsed following its rejection by the French National Assembly in 1954.* ◇ **~ of sth** *Turner proposes a thoroughgoing revision rather than a wholesale rejection of the concept of national identity.* **2** the act of refusing to accept sb for a job or position: *Such optimism is similarly evidenced by the sixteen-year-old who tries out for the school swim team in spite of a rejection the previous year.* **3** the decision not to use, sell, publish, etc. sth because its quality is not good enough: *Any flaws in products or deliveries lead to product rejections.* **4 ~ (of sth)** an occasion when sb's body does not accept a new organ after a TRANSPLANT operation, by producing substances that attack the organ: *These drugs are frequently used to prevent graft rejection of organ transplants.* **5** the act of failing to give a person or an animal enough care or affection: *Attitudes to older people are sometimes negative, which may reinforce a sense of social rejection or exclusion.*

re·lapse[1] /rɪˈlæps; ˈriːlæps/ *noun* [C, U] the fact of becoming ill again after making an improvement: *She appears to have suffered a relapse in her illness.* ◇ *To prevent relapse, medication should be continued for about 6 months.*

re·lapse[2] /rɪˈlæps/ *verb* [I] to go back into a previous condition or into a worse state after making an improvement: *Some patients relapse after radiotherapy.* ◇ **~ into sth** *He had relapsed into his old ways.*

re·late /rɪˈleɪt/ *verb* **1** to show or make a connection between two or more things SYN CONNECT (2): **~ sth** *A bilingual dictionary relates the vocabularies of two languages by means of translation equivalents.* ◇ **~ A to B** *This theory relates climate changes to periodic variations in the orbit of the Earth around the Sun.* **2** to give a spoken or written report of sth; to tell a story: **~ sth** *A church member related the story of the man's conversion.* ◇ **~ how/what, etc...** *The famous inscription relates how Darius I ascended the Persian throne.* ◇ **~ that...** *Goethe relates that he left Leipzig to study law in Strasbourg.*

PHR V **reˈlate to sth/sb 1** to be connected with sth/sb; to refer to sth/sb: *The figures presented in the Annual Report relate to various matters.* ◇ *Article 29 provides extensive guidance when data relate to an individual.* **2** to be able to understand and have sympathy with sb/sth: *Play helps children learn how to relate to other children and adults.*

re·lated /rɪˈleɪtɪd/ *adj.* **1** connected with sth/sb in some way: *Attention and memory are closely related.* ◇ *A separate but related issue is the potential for terrorists to use nuclear explosives.* ◇ **~ to sth/sb** *These movements of humans were, of course, related to continuing climatic changes.* OPP UNRELATED (1) **2** belonging to the same group: *A genus is a group of related species.* ◇ **~ to sth** *In practice, an investigator will probably use several of these methods to find genes related to the gene of interest.* OPP UNRELATED (2) **3 ~ (to sth/sb)** connected by a family relationship or by marriage: *The young and rich Prince Yusupov was related to the Tsar by marriage.* ◇ *Closely related family members inherit large blocks of the genome from a common ancestor.* OPP UNRELATED (2)

▸ RELATED + NOUN **issue, problem, question, topic • factor • field, area • concept, idea • word, term • activity • industry** *Researchers in diverse but related fields of study were brought together to examine the current situation.* | **species • organism • gene • protein** *Community refers to a group of related organisms in a particular area.*

▸ ADVERB + RELATED **closely** *The two proteins are closely related, both in structure and ancestry.* | **directly** *The amount of improvement these patients showed was directly related to the length of their therapy.* | **significantly** • **strongly** • **highly** • **intimately** • **clearly**, **obviously** • **specifically** • **positively** • **negatively**, **inversely** • **causally** • **functionally** • **structurally** • **semantically** • **linearly** *Population densities are clearly related to land productivity.*

re·lated·ness /rɪˈleɪtɪdnəs/ *noun* [U] **~ (between A and B)** the fact of belonging to the same group: *This method can be used to measure the degree of relatedness between two species.*

re·la·tion /rɪˈleɪʃn/ *noun* **1 relations** [pl.] the way in which two people, groups or countries behave towards each other or deal with each other: *War has always been a central focus of the study of international relations.* ◇ **~ with sb/sth** *European integration has altered British relations with other European countries.* ◇ **~ between A and B** *By the mid-1980s, relations between the two groups had deteriorated.* ➲ *see also* INDUSTRIAL RELATIONS, PUBLIC RELATIONS, RACE RELATIONS **2** [U, C] the way in which two or more people or things are connected SYN RELATIONSHIP (2): **~ between A and B** *Price is determined by the relation between supply and demand.* ◇ **~ (of sb/sth) to sth** *The book has as its central theme the relation of fact to fiction.* ◇ **bear no ~ to sth** *According to Marx, the payment of wages in the nineteenth century bore no relation to profits.* **3** [C] a person who is in the same family as sb else SYN RELATIVE² (1): **~ (of sb)** *She was a relation of Sir Walter Scott's.* ◇ **be no ~ (to sb)** *Prime Minister Indira Gandhi was no relation to Mahatma Gandhi.* **4 relations** [pl.] (*formal*) sex with sb: **~ with sb** *She had relations with a gardener employed at the mental hospital.* ◇ **sexual ~** *The church teaches that marriage should precede sexual relations.*

IDM **in relation to sth 1** in connection with sth: *In recent times, matters of consent in relation to medical treatment have achieved a high profile with the public.* **2** in comparison with sth: *Companies' influence in the political process has become greater in relation to that of individuals.*

▸ ADJECTIVE + RELATIONS **good** • **close** • **positive** • **personal** • **interpersonal** • **international** • **external** • **social** • **economic** *The newly independent Ukrainian state quickly established good relations with the state of Israel.*

▸ ADJECTIVE + RELATION **positive** • **complex** • **causal** • **spatial** *There is also weak evidence supporting a causal relation between meat consumption and breast cancer.*

▸ NOUN + RELATIONS **power** • **gender** • **labour** • **family** *There has been a change in the nature of the power relations between ministers and civil servants.*

▸ VERB + RELATIONS **have** • **create** • **develop** • **establish** • **maintain** • **improve** • **regulate** • **examine**, **analyse** • **understand** • **explain** • **define** • **describe** • **characterize** • **affect** • **transform** *They all tend to maintain reasonably friendly relations with each other*

▸ VERB + RELATION **have** • **bear** • **examine** • **analyse** • **establish** • **find** • **understand** • **show** • **define** • **describe** • **explain** • **express** *Fig. 1 shows the relation between technical efficiency and overall performance.*

re·la·tion·al /rɪˈleɪʃənl/ *adj.* concerning the way in which two or more people or things are connected: *These differences between transactional and relational approaches to fund-raising are summarized in Table 9.1.*

re·la·tion·ship /rɪˈleɪʃnʃɪp/ *noun* **1** [C] the way in which two people, groups or countries behave towards each other or deal with each other: *Over fifteen years, the company and its advertising agency have established a good working relationship.* ◇ **~ between A and B** *The 1962 Act marked an historic shift in the relationship between the UK and its Commonwealth citizens.* ◇ **~ with sb** *The GP is likely to have already built up a relationship with the patient.* **2** [C, U] the way in which two or more people or things are connected SYN RELATION (2): **~ between A and B** *The second stage, data analysis, involves calculating relationships between variables.* ◇ **~ (of sb/sth) to sb/sth** *The relationship of religion to politics remains an important issue in the West today.* ◇ **bear little/no ~ to sth** *The curriculum seems to bear little relationship to their life experiences and opportunities.* ◇ **in ~ to sb/sth** *A social class can exist only in relationship to some other social class.* **3** [C] a loving and/or sexual friendship between two people: **~ between A and B** *Several myths consider the implications of a committed relationship between a mortal and an immortal.* ◇ **~ with sb** *He engaged in sexual relationships with Hollywood starlets.* ◇ **be in a ~ (with sb)** *At that time, she was not in a relationship.* **4** [C, U] the way in which a person is related to sb else in a family: *In these societies, mother-daughter relationships are more culturally important than father-son relationships.* ◇ *Marriage within certain prohibited degrees of relationship risks the birth of children with genetic defects.* ◇ **~ between A and B** *There was no familial relationship between them.*

▸ ADJECTIVE + RELATIONSHIP **close** • **strong** • **intimate** • **new** *Her once close relationship with her mother had deteriorated during the past year.* | **positive** • **negative** • **significant** • **special** • **complex** *Analyses also revealed a significant relationship between marital status and income.* | **good** • **long-term** *In 1955, 27% of people aged between 25 and 64 were not married or in a long-term relationship.* | **social** • **personal** • **interpersonal** • **working** *Some argue that Internet use cuts people off from genuine social relationships.* | **causal** • **direct** • **linear** • **inverse** *The findings have identified a causal relationship between education and health.*

▸ NOUN + RELATIONSHIP **customer** • **employment** • **family** • **power** *Managing customer relationships via the Internet can be equally challenging.*

▸ VERB + RELATIONSHIP **have** • **examine** • **explore** • **analyse** • **establish** • **understand** • **consider** • **discuss** • **define** • **use** • **mediate** *There are a number of factors involved in establishing relationships with stepchildren.* | **form** • **develop** • **maintain** • **build** • **create** *Children and teens need to be helped to develop relationships with others around their own age.* | **find** • **show** • **suggest** • **determine** • **explain** *Another table shows the relationship between social class and educational attainment.*

rela·tive¹ /ˈrelətɪv/ *adj.* **1** considered and judged by being compared with sth else: *It is possible to discover the relative importance of the various factors responsible for economic growth.* ◇ *The article addresses the relative merits of each theory.* **2** [only before noun] existing or having a particular quality only when compared with sth else SYN COMPARATIVE¹ (2): *Bush was able to win his party's nomination to the presidency with relative ease.* ◇ *The evidence of the country's relative economic decline discredited the party elites.* ➲ *compare* ABSOLUTE¹ (2) **3** (*grammar*) referring to an earlier noun, sentence or part of a sentence: *Indian English uses fewer relative clauses.*

IDM **relative to sb/sth 1** in comparison with sb/sth: *One of the most striking features of humans is the large size of their brains relative to those of chimpanzees.* **2** in relation to sb/sth: *Friction arises whenever bodies in contact move or try to move relative to each other.* **3** about or concerning sb/sth: *The focus was on gaining participants' perspectives relative to the issues outlined above.*

rela·tive² /ˈrelətɪv/ *noun* **1** a person who is in the same family as sb else SYN RELATION (3): *They promised new support for families where one parent was not in paid work because of caring for children or a dependent relative.* ◇ *a close/distant relative* **2** a type of animal or plant that belongs to the same group as sth else: *Like our close* *relatives the chimpanzees, we humans live in highly complex social groups.*

rela·tive·ly /ˈrelətɪvli/ *adv.* to a fairly large degree, especially in comparison with sth else: *Their army was relatively small.* ◇ *The side effects are serious in relatively few cases.* ◇ *relatively low/high levels of sth* ➲ language bank *at* EXCEPTIONALLY

IDM **ˈrelatively speaking** used when you are comparing sth with all similar things: *Temperatures in the summer of 2003 could be regarded, relatively speaking, as being on the cool side.*

rela·tiv·ism /ˈrelətɪvɪzəm/ *noun* [U] the belief that truth is not always and generally valid, but can be judged only in relation to other things, such as your personal situation: *The beginning of the twenty-first century saw something of a comeback for relativism within analytical philosophy.* ■ **rela·tiv·ist** /ˈrelətɪvɪst/ *adj.*: *A totally relativist position rejects any objective view of knowledge.* **rela·tiv·ist** *noun*: *Relativists are suspicious of objective truth.*

rela·tiv·ity /ˌreləˈtɪvəti/ *noun* [U] **1 ~ (of sth)** the state of being relative and only able to be judged when compared with sth else: *His teaching emphasizes the historical relativity of human knowledge and experience.* **2** (*physics*) the principle that the laws of physics are the same in all FRAMES OF REFERENCE: *These ideas, which are the basis of Einstein's theory of relativity, formed a completely new world view.* HELP Einstein's **special theory of relativity** is based on the principle that the speed of light has the same value (= is a CONSTANT) in all INERTIAL (= non-accelerating) frames of reference. This theory is necessary to make the EQUATIONS of MECHANICS obey the same transformation rules as the equations of ELECTROMAGNETISM in changing from one inertial frame of reference to another. His **general theory of relativity** extends this to accelerating frames of reference and includes the effects of GRAVITY.

relax AWL /rɪˈlæks/ *verb* **1** [I] to rest while you are doing sth enjoyable, especially after work or effort: *Manage stress by, for example, talking things through and making time to relax.* **2** [I, T] to become calmer and less anxious; to make sb calmer and less anxious: *By learning how to relax, she will ultimately be able to calm herself when she experiences anger or anxiety.* ◇ **~ sb** *The aim of sedation is to relax the anxious patient.* **3** [I, T] to become less tight or stiff; to make sth less tight or stiff: *Direct the patient to allow her lower jaw to relax.* ◇ **~ sth** *The drug is effective in relaxing smooth muscle.* **4** [T] **~ sth** to allow rules, laws, etc. to become less strict: *In an effort to improve Soviet-American relations, the regime relaxed emigration restrictions.* ◇ *We have relaxed two assumptions inherent in previous research.*

re·lax·ation AWL /ˌriːlækˈseɪʃn/ *noun* **1** [U] ways of resting and enjoying yourself; time spent resting and enjoying yourself: *Women are somewhat more likely than men to go to the gym for relaxation.* **2** [U] ways of becoming calmer and less worried: **+ noun** *Relaxation techniques will help patients to keep as calm as possible.* **3** [U] **~ (of sth)** the loss of tension in a part of the body, especially in a muscle: *The relaxation of muscles is a sign of calm.* **4** [U, C, usually sing.] **~ (of sth)** the act of making a rule, law, etc. less strict: *The relaxation of foreign currency regulations has made it much easier for the company to be paid directly.*

re·laxed AWL /rɪˈlækst/ *adj.* **1** (of a person) calm and not anxious or worried: *It is important to ensure that the patient feels relaxed.* **2 ~ (about sth)** not caring too much about making people follow rules: *British society became more relaxed about premarital sex in the 1960s.* **3** (of a place or situation) calm and informal: *A relaxed, friendly atmosphere was created.*

re·lease¹ AWL /rɪˈliːs/ *verb* **1** to let sb/sth come out of a place where they have been kept or trapped: **~ sb/sth** *Soldiers and workers invaded the prisons and released political prisoners.* ◇ **~ sb/sth from sth** *When a whole city collapses, there is insufficient time for rescuers to release victims from the collapsed debris.* **2 ~ sth** to allow sth to move, fly or fall freely: *A nuclear explosion releases thermal energy (heat) at very high temperatures.* **3 ~ sth** to express feelings such as anger or anxiety in order to get rid of them: *Like alcohol, these drugs can release aggression by reducing inhibitions in people* **4 ~ sb from sth** to free sb from a duty, responsibility or contract: *In Britain, a 1994 Act released local authorities from the obligation to provide sites for mobile populations.* **5 ~ sth** to make sth available to the public: *The 'Broadband Difference' report, released in June 2002, focused on home broadband users.* **6 ~ sth** to make sth available that had previously been held back: *The Research Council will not release funds until there is a written confirmation that the ethical approval has been completed.*

re·lease² AWL /rɪˈliːs/ *noun* **1** [U, sing.] **~ (of sb) (from sth)** the act of setting a person or an animal free; the state of being set free: *The release of the two men from prison defused the crisis.* **2** [C] a thing that is made available to the public, especially a new CD or film; the act of making sth available to the public: *Any compilation of top-grossing films tends to be dominated by recent releases made in the United States.* ◇ **~ of sth** *The release of too much information can have an adverse impact on public expectations.* **3** [U, C] the act of letting a gas, chemical, etc. come out of the place where it has been contained: *High blood glucose levels stimulate insulin release.* ◇ **~ (of sth) (from sth)** *The release of the drug from an implanted device needs to be controlled.* **4** [U, sing.] **~ (of sth)** the feeling that you are free from pain, anxiety or some other unpleasant feeling: *The release of tension produces tears.*

rele·vance AWL /ˈreləvəns/ *noun* [U] **1** the fact of being valuable and useful to people in their lives and work: *Plato's pioneering thought is still of great contemporary relevance.* ◇ **~ (of sth) (to sth/sb)** *He attempts to make clear to his students the relevance of this play to their lives.* ◇ *These methods for the analysis of population composition have particular relevance in planning and decision-making.* **2 ~ (of sth) (to sth/sb)** the fact of being closely connected with the subject you are discussing or the situation you are thinking about: *The relevance of these findings to currently proposed medical applications is uncertain.*

rele·vant AWL /ˈreləvənt/ *adj.* **1** closely connected with the subject you are discussing or the situation you are thinking about: *They have all the relevant information needed to make the decision.* ◇ **~ to sth/sb** *A number of measures adopted by the EU are relevant to any discussion of e-commerce.* OPP IRRELEVANT **2** [not usually before noun] valuable and useful to people in their lives and work: *Malthusian theory was first presented in 1798 and remains relevant today.* ◇ **~ to sth/sb** *People in societies undergoing significant changes would have to decide which rituals and beliefs were still relevant to their lives.* ■ **rele·vant·ly** *adv.*: *Most relevantly perhaps, economic opportunities for immigrants have changed since the 1960s.*

▸ RELEVANT + NOUN **information, data • fact • evidence • research • knowledge • literature • article • study • factor • consideration • issue, question • market • provision • law • legislation • variable • part, section • aspect • authority • stakeholder • sense** *It will be necessary to undertake a thorough economic analysis, drawing upon all relevant supporting facts and data.*

▸ ADVERB + RELEVANT **extremely, highly • particularly, especially • increasingly • immediately • socially • culturally** *Concerns about the cost of cancer treatment are highly relevant to the debate over the funding of this drug.* | **directly • potentially • clearly, obviously • equally** *A more* *directly relevant decision is that made by the Court of Appeal last year.*

re·li·abil·ity AWL /rɪˌlaɪəˈbɪləti/ *noun* [U] **1 ~ (of sth)** the fact of being likely to be correct or true: *Unfortunately, the quality and reliability of this information will vary wildly.* ◇ *An analysis was performed to assess the statistical reliability of the tree topology.* OPP UNRELIABILITY **2 ~ (of sb/sth)** the quality of being able to be trusted to do sth well; the quality of being able to be relied on: *Some retailers raised questions about the reliability of the new products.* ◇ *Ways of improving the reliability of the technique have been suggested.* OPP UNRELIABILITY

re·li·able AWL /rɪˈlaɪəbl/ *adj.* **1** likely to be correct or true: *Reliable data are difficult to obtain as much criminal activity goes unreported.* ◇ *The most reliable source of information on refugee numbers today is the UNHCR.* ◇ *There is a lack of reliable evidence on which to base general conclusions.* ◇ *Tree rings are a reliable indicator of the state of a tree's health or vigour.* ◇ *Astronomers began to develop an understanding of how stars work, and to derive reliable estimates of their ages.* OPP UNRELIABLE **2** that can be trusted to do sth well; that can be relied on: *He stationed some of the more reliable troops at strategic points.* OPP UNRELIABLE ■ **re·li·ably** AWL /rɪˈlaɪəbli/ *adv.*: *At present, there is no single test that will reliably predict liver failure.* ◇ *The volunteers were judged to have performed reliably with no reported breaches of confidentiality.*

re·li·ance AWL /rɪˈlaɪəns/ *noun* **1** [U, sing.] **~ (on/upon sb/sth)** the state of needing sb/sth in order to survive or be successful SYN DEPENDENCE (1): *One of the company's objectives was reducing its reliance on developing markets.* ◇ *He suggested that friendship with the United States was preferable to a reliance on the Soviet Union.* **2** [U, sing.] **~ (on/upon sb/sth)** the fact of being able to trust or rely on sb/sth: *There are several problems with reliance on intuition.* ◇ *A continued reliance has been placed on performance targets as a means of increasing productivity.*

re·li·ant AWL /rɪˈlaɪənt/ *adj.* needing sb/sth in order to survive or be successful SYN DEPENDENT[1] (1): **~ on/upon sb/sth** *Women are especially reliant on social security benefits for retirement income.* ◇ **~ on/upon sb/sth for sth** *Today, most countries are heavily reliant on these sources for their energy.*

re·lief /rɪˈliːf/ *noun* **1** [U, sing.] the feeling of happiness that you have when sth unpleasant stops or does not happen: *Their feelings of relief after the election were based on the recognition that losses could have been worse.* ◇ **to sb's ~** *The contract was renewed, much to her relief.* ◇ **a sigh of ~** *Union leaders breathed a sigh of relief at the news.* **2** [U] the act of removing or reducing pain, anxiety, etc: *It may be necessary to give increasing doses to achieve the same amount of pain relief.* ◇ **~ from sth** *Exercise is a good way to obtain relief from tension.* ◇ **~ of sth** *ECT is also an option for rapid relief of symptoms of depression.* **3** [U] food, money, medicine, etc. that is given to help people in places where there has been a war or natural disaster SYN AID[1] (1): *Paragraph 38 imposes obligations on states to provide relief to victims of disasters.* ◇ **+ noun** *Relief organizations supplied the affected areas with 22 tonnes of aid.* **4** [U] financial help given by the government to people who need it: *Mill called for limited state action in some areas, including education and relief for the poor.* **5** [U, sing.] something that is interesting or enjoyable that replaces sth boring, difficult or unpleasant for a short period of time: **comic/light ~** *When these people do appear in literature, it is nearly always as comic relief.* ◇ **~ from sth** *His highly theatrical performance provides an unexpected relief from the impassive expressions of the film's other actors.* **6** [U] the quality of a particular situation, problem, etc. that makes it easier to notice than before: **bring/throw sth into (sharp) ~** *The crisis brought into sharp relief the differences between the two parties.* **7** [U] (*geography*) difference in height from the surrounding land: *This landscape is characterized by low relief.* **8** [U, C] a way of decorating wood, stone, etc. by cutting designs into the surface of it so that some parts stick out more than others; a design that is made in this way: *The column is decorated in high relief with scenes from Greek mythology.* ◇ *The bronze doors are covered with sculpted reliefs.* **9** [C+sing./pl. v.] a person or group of people that replaces others who have been on duty: **+ noun** *In 1858 he defeated a relief force from the southern camp.* **10** [sing.] **~ of...** the act of freeing a town, etc. from an enemy army that has surrounded it: *British troops were involved in the relief of Peking.*

re·lieve /rɪˈliːv/ *verb* **1 ~ sth** to remove or reduce an unpleasant feeling or pain: *Warm baths may help relieve the pain.* ◇ *Open and honest explanation can help to relieve anxiety.* **2 ~ sb** to prevent sb from experiencing an unpleasant feeling or pain: *Patients will have more positive expectations if it is explained to them how this intervention will relieve them.* **3 ~ sth** to make a problem less serious SYN ALLEVIATE: *Radicals pressed for more government intervention to relieve poverty and unemployment.* ◇ *More and better roads do not relieve congestion but instead increase demand.* **4 ~ sth** to free a town, etc. from an enemy army that has surrounded it: *Demetrius defeated the fleet Ptolemy sent to relieve the city.*
PHR V **reˈlieve sb of sth** **1** to free sb from a responsibility or duty: *Privatization relieved the state of the responsibility for providing the investment for modernizing the system.* **2** (*ironic*) to take or steal sth from sb: *The intention was to relieve speculators of their ill-gotten gains.*

re·li·gion /rɪˈlɪdʒən/ *noun* **1** [U] the belief in the existence of a god or gods, and the activities that are connected with the worship of them: *Some scientists believe science and religion to be mutually exclusive.* **2** [C] one of the systems of belief that are based on the belief in the existence of a particular god or gods: *Buddhism differs from other religions in many ways.* ◇ *Most of the great world religions have struggled historically with issues of religious pluralism and tolerance.* ◇ *Those practising no religion, according to the census in 1991, numbered just under 250 000.*

re·ligi·os·ity /rɪˌlɪdʒiˈɒsəti/; *NAmE* rɪˌlɪdʒiˈɑːsəti/ *noun* [U] (*sometimes disapproving*) the state of being religious or too religious: *Anti-intellectualism was combined with a rising tide of religiosity which emerged as early as the 1730s.*

re·li·gious /rɪˈlɪdʒəs/ *adj.* **1** [only before noun] connected with religion or with a particular religion: *They were put to death for their religious beliefs.* ◇ *The Ottoman Empire was composed of many ethnic and religious groups.* **2** (of a person) believing strongly in the existence of a god or gods: *He was a deeply religious man.*
▸ RELIGIOUS + NOUN **belief • faith • group • organization • institution • community • order • minority • leader • authority • tradition • identity • affiliation • life • experience • practice • observance • service, ceremony • ritual • symbol • freedom • toleration • diversity • pluralism • education** *This is a challenging time for those whose lives are shaped by religious faith.*

re·li·gious·ly /rɪˈlɪdʒəsli/ *adv.* **1** in a way that is connected with religion: *China, India and Russia are among the world's most religiously diverse countries.* **2** very carefully or regularly: *The World Trade Organization follows this principle religiously.*

re·lin·quish /rɪˈlɪŋkwɪʃ/ *verb* (*formal*) to stop having sth such as power or control, especially when sb is unwilling to do this SYN GIVE SB/STH UP: **~ sth** *It is difficult to imagine governments being prepared to relinquish control of fiscal policy.* ◇ **~ sth to sb** *When it was time for Eteokles*

R

to relinquish the throne to his brother, he refused to give it up.

re·locate AWL /ˌriːləʊˈkeɪt; *NAmE* ˌriːˈloʊkeɪt/ *verb* [I, T] (especially of a company or workers) to move to a new place to work or operate; to move a company or workers to a new place: **~ (from...) (to...)** *Docks and warehouses closed when the shipping industry relocated to deeper ports elsewhere.* ◇ **~ sb/sth (from...) (to...)** *The government aimed to relocate 37 000 staff from the south-east of England to areas of lower employment.* ■ **re·loca·tion** AWL /ˌriːləʊˈkeɪʃn; *NAmE* ˌriːloʊˈkeɪʃn/ *noun* [U] **~ (of sb/sth) (from...) (to...)** *The airline's relocation of its headquarters from the Pacific Northwest to Chicago is unimaginable without the communication abilities provided by the Internet.*

re·luc·tant AWL /rɪˈlʌktənt/ *adj.* hesitating before doing sth because you do not want to do it or because you are not sure that it is the right thing to do: *Human rights have indeed often been forced on reluctant governments.* ◇ **~ to do sth** *It is natural that employees will be reluctant to accept a reduction in their wages.* ■ **re·luc·tance** AWL /rɪˈlʌktəns/ *noun* [U, sing.] **~ (of sb/sth) (to do sth)** *These examples also show the reluctance of the private sector to become involved.* **re·luc·tant·ly** AWL *adv.*: *The mother reluctantly agreed to give the information.*

rely AWL /rɪˈlaɪ/ *verb* (**re·lies, rely·ing, re·lied, re·lied**)

> **WORD FAMILY**
> rely *verb*
> reliable *adj.*
> reliably *adv.*
> reliability *noun*
> reliance *noun*
> reliant *adj.*
> unreliable *adj.*
> unreliability *noun*

PHR V **reˈly on/upon sb/sth 1** to need or depend on sb/sth: *This study relies on data generated from a national survey.* ◇ **~ on/upon sb/sth to do sth** *These industries rely on an immigrant workforce to do almost all of the most unpleasant jobs.* ◇ **~ on/upon sb/sth doing sth** *The plotters relied on the army obeying their* **~ on/upon sb/sth for sth** *This is an example of an invasive aquatic plant that relies solely on seed production for its spread.* **2** to trust or have confidence in sb/sth: *He relies heavily on the judgement of his experienced advisers.* ◇ **~ on/upon sb/sth to do sth** *Injections are given to patients who cannot be relied on to take their medications regularly by mouth.*

R

re·main /rɪˈmeɪn/ *verb* (not usually used in the progressive tenses) **1** *linking verb* to continue to be sth; to be still in the same state or condition: **+ adj.** *Many questions remain unanswered.* ◇ *Levels of output and employment remain unchanged.* ◇ **+ noun** *This task remains a challenge for many firms.* ◇ *In the end, the secret remained a mystery.* ◇ **it remains + adj./noun** *It remains possible that new evidence could challenge this theory.* ◇ *It remains a possibility that...* **2** [I] **~ (of sth)** to still be present after the other parts have been removed or used; to continue to exist: *Piles of rubble were all that remained of the historic city centre.* ◇ *Doubts remained over the loyalties of the young men.* ◇ *questions/uncertainties/challenges/problems remain* ◇ *With only two days remaining, ten states drafted a proposal.* **3** [I] to still need to be done, said or dealt with: **there remains/remain sth** *There remain significant unanswered questions.* ◇ **the fact remains that...** *The fact remains that only the artist can tell you what the art represents and what its purpose was.* ◇ **~ to be done** *Much analysis still remains to be done.* ◇ **it remains to do sth/to be done** *It remains to be established whether these findings have a wider application.* **4** [I] **+ adv./prep.** to stay in the same place; to not leave: *He was deported but his family remained in the UK.* ◇ *The women were so determined that the soldiers could not persuade them to remain behind.*

IDM **it remains to be ˈseen (whether/what, etc.) | sth remains to be ˈseen** used to say that you cannot yet know sth: *It remains to be seen whether the models will reveal general patterns.* ◇ *What this change will mean in the present context remains to be seen.*

re·main·der /rɪˈmeɪndə(r)/ *noun* **1** (*usually* **the remainder**) [sing.+ sing./pl. v.] the remaining people, things or time SYN REST[1] (2): *Over half the world's tropical forests are located in Latin America, with the remainder split between Africa and Asia.* ◇ **~ of sth** *The remainder of this chapter will focus on the development of a marketing communications campaign.* ◇ *He was jailed in 1926 and spent the remainder of his life in prison.* HELP When **the remainder** refers to a plural noun, the verb is plural: *The remainder of his notes seem to have been lost.* **2** [C, usually sing.] (*mathematics*) the numbers left after one number has been divided into another: *Divide 2 into 7, and the answer is 3, remainder 1.* ➲ *compare* QUOTIENT

re·main·ing /rɪˈmeɪnɪŋ/ *adj.* [only before noun] **1** not yet used, dealt with or RESOLVED: *The remaining chapters of the book are devoted to strategy implementation.* **2** still existing, present or in use: *Most of the remaining parts of the British Empire achieved independence over the next few years.*

re·mains /rɪˈmeɪnz/ *noun* [pl.] **1** the parts of sth that are left after the other parts have been used, eaten, removed, etc: *The cloud begins a process of dissolution which is completed in a few minutes, leaving no visible remains.* ◇ **~ of sth** *The carbonized remains of trees and plants can be used to date recent lava flows.* **2** the parts of ancient objects and buildings that have survived and are discovered in the present day: *The evidence from archaeological remains and early texts does not provide a clear picture.* ◇ **~ of sth** *British and Indian archaeologists uncovered the remains of several early cities in what is now Pakistan.* **3** the body of a dead person or animal: *During the 1830s, several experts condemned the practice of burying human remains in densely populated areas.*

re·mark[1] /rɪˈmɑːk; *NAmE* rɪˈmɑːrk/ *noun* something that you say or write that expresses an opinion or a thought about sb/sth SYN COMMENT[1]: *The article ends with a few concluding remarks.* ◇ **~ about sth** *First, I would like to make some introductory remarks about the research project itself.* ◇ **~ that...** *Warren (2002: 99) makes the interesting remark that...*

re·mark[2] /rɪˈmɑːk; *NAmE* rɪˈmɑːrk/ *verb* [I, T] to say or write a comment about sth/sb SYN COMMENT[2]: **~ on/upon sth/sb** *Student teachers often remarked on how little time was allotted for the study of history in schools.* ◇ **~ how...** *He remarked how standards of beauty differed between societies.* ◇ **+ speech** *As Byron famously remarked, 'I awoke one morning and found myself famous.'* ◇ **~ that...** *The judge remarked that there are many cases in which it becomes impossible for two people to work together, without obvious fault on either side.* ◇ **be remarked on/upon** *The selection of authors is not remarked on by the editors.*

re·mark·able /rɪˈmɑːkəbl; *NAmE* rɪˈmɑːrkəbl/ *adj.* unusual or surprising in a way that causes people to take notice: *He claims that it was a remarkable achievement, and it is hard to disagree.* ◇ **it is ~ how...** *It is remarkable how little dissent was expressed.* ◇ **it is ~ that...** *It is remarkable that no specific UN Convention exists to regulate the rights of elderly people.* ◇ **~ for sth** *Those looking for their first job were remarkable for their low educational levels.* ◇ **~ about sb/sth** *What was truly remarkable about the invention of the transistor was its short timescale.* OPP UNREMARKABLE

re·mark·ably /rɪˈmɑːkəbli; *NAmE* rɪˈmɑːrkəbli/ *adv.* **1** in a way that is surprising or worth taking notice of: *Results for Norway are remarkably similar to those reported for the*

United Kingdom. ➲ language bank *at* EXCEPTIONALLY **2** used for emphasizing that sth is surprising: *Remarkably, fossils of alligators have been found as far north as Ellesmere Island to the west of Greenland.* ◇ *The destruction, remarkably, is not even mentioned in these accounts.*

re·med·ial /rɪˈmiːdiəl/ *adj.* [only before noun] **1** aimed at solving a problem, correcting sth or making sth better: *The results enabled the company to identify poorly performing staff and to take remedial action where necessary.* **2** connected with school students who are slower at learning than others: *Researchers argue that these boys need remedial teaching in order to help them achieve.*

rem·edy¹ /ˈremədi/ *noun* (*pl.* -ies) **1** a way of dealing with or improving an unpleasant or difficult situation SYN SOLUTION (1): **~ for sth** *The lack of resources meant there could not be an instant remedy for six decades of underfunding.* ◇ **~ (to sth)** *Some favoured wage cuts as the remedy to the huge level of unemployment.* ◇ *The appropriate remedy involved imposing a tax on the emissions from a polluting activity.* **2** a treatment or medicine to cure a disease or to reduce pain that is not very serious: *Patient surveys have reported 4.8% of patients in the UK use herbal remedies.* ◇ **~ for sth** *Quinine has long been used as a remedy for malaria.* ➲ *compare* CURE¹ (1) **3** (*law*) a way of dealing with a problem, using the processes of the law SYN REDRESS²: **~ against sth** *A person who is injured through using a product that he knows to be defective has no remedy against the manufacturer.* ◇ **~ for sth** *The client had an adequate remedy for breach of contract.*

rem·edy² /ˈremədi/ *verb* (**rem·ed·ies, rem·edy·ing, rem·ed·ied, rem·ed·ied**) **~ sth** to correct or improve sth: *The government's proposals to remedy the situation were regarded as acceptable.*

re·mem·ber /rɪˈmembə(r)/ *verb* (not usually used in the progressive tenses) **1** [T, I] to have or keep an image in your memory of an event, a person, a place, etc. from the past: **~ (sb/sth)** *He can remember events from long ago easily, but struggles to recall what he ate for breakfast.* ◇ *The two communities had lived side by side for as long as anyone could remember.* ◇ **~ (sb/sth) doing sth** *People are called the day after a commercial has run on television and asked if they remember seeing it.* ◇ **~ (that)...** *He remembered that he had lost his sister.* **2** [T, I] to bring back to your mind a fact, piece of information, etc. that you knew: **~ sth** *There is evidence to suggest that we can remember the names of schoolfriends over long periods of time.* ◇ **~ what/how, etc...** *Patients do not always remember what has been said completely or correctly.* **3** [T] to keep an important fact in your mind: **~ (that)...** *It is important to remember that not every salesperson needs the same training.* ◇ *Remember, consumers do not distinguish one type of marketing communication from another.* ◇ **be remembered that...** *It must be remembered that the glass prevents the air in a greenhouse from mixing with the colder air outside.* **4** [T] to not forget to do sth; to actually do what you have to do: **~ sth** *When patients have limited English, doctors need to remember their key communication skills.* ◇ **~ to do sth** *The patient needs to remember to take the medication.* HELP Notice the difference between **remember doing sth** and **remember to do sth**: *I remember sitting in the clinic.* means 'I have an image in my memory of doing it'; *Remember to give the exact location.* means 'Do not forget to do it.'

IDM **be reˈmembered for sth | be reˈmembered as sth** to be famous or known for a particular thing that you have done in the past: *She is best remembered for her 26 novels.* ◇ *He will be remembered as one of the more important geologists of the twentieth century.*

re·mind /rɪˈmaɪnd/ *verb* to help sb remember sth, especially sth important that they must do: **~ sb (about/of sth)** *Everyone needs to be reminded about brands they like, but which slip from their minds.* ◇ **~ sb to do sth** *Follow-up calls were used to remind respondents to submit their survey.* ◇ **~ sb that...** *Shareholders are reminded that they have responsibilities as well as rights.* ◇ **~ sb how/what, etc...** *Incidents like these reminded them how vulnerable they were.*

PHR V **reˈmind sb of sb/sth** to make sb remember or think about another person, place or thing by being similar to them in some way: *He tries to keep very busy and avoids everything he can that reminds him of the war.*

re·mind·er /rɪˈmaɪndə(r)/ *noun* **1** something that makes you think about or remember sb/sth that you have forgotten or would like to forget: **~ of sb/sth** *These cases serve as a reminder of the risks investors face in the region.* ◇ *Slums are a constant reminder of the state's incapacity or unwillingness to tackle poverty.* ◇ **~ that...** *Globalization provides a reminder that the privileged isolation of Australia is under increasing threat.* **2** a letter or note telling sb that they have not done sth: *A month after the first mailing, a reminder was sent.*

remit /ˈriːmɪt; rɪˈmɪt/ *noun* [usually sing.] (*BrE*) the area of activity over which a particular person or group has authority, control or influence: **within the ~ of sb/sth** *The court decided that the scheme was within the general management remit of the council.* ◇ **~ to do sth** *Interviewees highlighted the absence of any one agency with a clear remit to promote health within higher education.*

re·mote /rɪˈməʊt; *NAmE* rɪˈmoʊt/ *adj.* (**re·moter, re·mot·est**) **1** far away from places where other people live SYN ISOLATED (1): *The Pacific still seemed remote to Americans of that time.* ◇ *Her father was a retired general living in a remote village.* ◇ **~ from sth** *Bearn was a small province remote from Paris.* **2** [only before noun] far away in time or space SYN DISTANT (1): *Depressed patients often express guilt about experiences in their recent or remote past.* ◇ *Darwin claimed that organisms all derived from some remote common ancestor.* ◇ *Light beams appear to be coming from remote galaxies.* ◇ **~ from sth** *During earlier geological history, many continents that are now remote from polar regions were in the reach of ice sheets.* **3** that you can operate from far away, using an electronic link: *Remote sensors are becoming more widely used to provide information throughout a distribution network.* ◇ *The computer's capacity to store and process large amounts of personal information and to allow remote access to databases are factors causing legitimate public concern.* HELP In computer science, a **remote** device is one that can only be accessed by means of a network: *ssh gives you more secure access to remote machines than telnet.* ➲ *see also* REMOTE SENSING **4 ~ from sth** very different from sth: *The arguments can seem rather remote from the reality of general practice.* ➲ *compare* IRRELEVANT **5** not very great SYN SLIGHT: *The prospects for a vaccine seem rather remote.* ◇ *Proper precautions should be taken to prevent even remote possibilities of injury or death.* **6** (of people or their behaviour) not very friendly or interested in other people SYN DISTANT (4): *'Aloof', 'remote' and 'passive' were all words used repeatedly by memoirists to describe the president.*

re·mote·ly /rɪˈməʊtli; *NAmE* rɪˈmoʊtli/ *adv.* **1** from a distance: *A patient's condition can be monitored remotely.* **2** (usually in negative sentences) to a very slight degree SYN SLIGHTLY: *The two situations are not even remotely comparable.*

re·mote·ness /rɪˈməʊtnəs; *NAmE* rɪˈmoʊtnəs/ *noun* [U] **1** the state of being distant in space or time: **~ (of sth)** *The process of change began in the remoteness of geological time.* ◇ **~ from sth** *All three locations share an apparent remoteness from any settlement.* ➲ *compare* ISOLATION (1) **2 ~ (of sth)** (*disapproving*) the state of not being involved with ordinary people: *The increased remoteness of the*

R

political world means that ordinary people feel excluded from the forces that shape their lives.

re,mote 'sensing *noun* [U] the use of SATELLITES to search for and collect information about the earth: *Remote sensing is especially valuable in aiding understanding of human use of the earth.*

re·moval AWL /rɪˈmuːvl/ *noun* **1** [U, C] the act of taking sb/sth away from a particular place, or of getting rid of sth: *Following weed removal, grassland areas can be reseeded with native species.* ◇ **~ (of sb/sth) (from sth)** *Airlines may be unwilling to undertake enforced removals of failed asylum seekers.* ◇ *The disease is treated by complete removal of milk from the diet.* **2** [U] **~ (of sb) (from sth)** the act of making sb leave their job SYN DISMISSAL (1): *He is charged with crimes that could result in his removal from office.*

re·move AWL /rɪˈmuːv/ *verb* **1** to take sth/sb away from a place: **~ sth/sb** *If the natural vegetation is removed, the soil is soon impoverished.* ◇ **~ sth/sb from sth/sb** *In 2008, 67 980 people were removed from the UK.* **2** to get rid of sth; to make sth disappear: **~ sth** *A single market does not occur simply by removing barriers to trade.* ◇ *to remove obstacles/restrictions* ◇ *It is important to remove impurities before mixing the DNA with the protein sample.* ◇ **~ sth from sb/sth** *Fish called 'cleaner fish' remove parasites from the skin and mouths of larger fish.* **3 ~ sth** to take off clothing, etc. from the body: *Simple cooling techniques (e.g. removing clothing, cooling ambient temperature) are usually sufficient.* **4 ~ sb (from sth)** to make sb leave their job: *Once installed in the White House, presidents can only be removed from office by the impeachment process.*
IDM **be (far/further/furthest) removed from sth** **1** to be at a distance from sb/sth: *The settlers were allowed a claim of 320 acres of dryland in areas removed from known sources of irrigation.* **2** to be very different from sth; to not be connected with sth: *An experimental situation in the laboratory is often far removed from reality.*

re·mu·ner·ation /rɪˌmjuːnəˈreɪʃn/ *noun* [U] (*formal*) an amount of money that is paid to sb for the work they have done: *The area of executive remuneration is an issue that attracts a lot of attention from investors.* ◇ **+ noun** *The company's 2008 remuneration package included a 16 per cent rise in basic salary and bonus for the chief executive.* HELP **Remuneration** is used especially when talking about the salaries and other benefits given to business people who are very highly paid.

R

re·nais·sance /rɪˈneɪsns; *NAmE* ˈrenəsɑːns/ *noun* [sing.] **1 the Renaissance** the period in Europe during the 14th–16th centuries when people became interested in the ideas and culture of ancient Greece and Rome and used these influences in their own art, literature, etc: *The number of people who adequately learned Greek remained small throughout the entire Renaissance.* **2** a situation when there is new interest in a particular subject, area or idea after a period when it was not very popular SYN REVIVAL (2): *The notion that attitudes, values and preferences shape politics has undergone something of a renaissance.*

renal /ˈriːnl/ *adj.* [usually before noun] (*medical*) connected with the KIDNEYS: *Acute renal failure normally responds to treatment.*

ren·der /ˈrendə(r)/ *verb* **1 ~ sb/sth + adj.** to cause sb/sth to be in a particular state or condition SYN MAKE (5): *This mistake should not render the contract void.* ◇ *Factory-based mass production rendered many workers' skills obsolete.* **2 ~ sth (to sb/sth)** to give sb sth, especially in return for sth or because it is expected: *The duty to render assistance to persons in distress at sea constitutes 'one of the most ancient and fundamental features of the law of the sea'.* **3 ~ sth** (*formal*) to announce sth, especially when it is done officially: *In some cases, a scientific body is called on formally to render a verdict.* ◇ *It is hoped that a decision will be rendered soon.*

ren·der·ing /ˈrendərɪŋ/ *noun* **1 ~ (of sth)** a piece of writing that has been translated into a different language; the particular way in which it has been translated: *There were by this time numerous other renderings of Aristotle's 'Politics' in both European and non-European languages.* ◇ *The statement in the English introduction is a misleading rendering of the Arabic.* **2 ~ (of sth)** a performance of a piece of music, a role in a play, etc; the particular way in which sth is performed: *Olivier's rendering of Henry V stands out in what is a great film version of Shakespeare's original play.*

ren·di·tion /renˈdɪʃn/ *noun* **1** [C] **~ (of sth)** a translation of a word, phrase or piece of writing from another language; the particular way in which it has been translated: *It is a faithful rendition of the original Latin text.* **2** [C] **~ (of sth)** the performance of sth, especially a song or piece of music; the particular way in which it is performed: *The 1999 film features renditions of beat poetry and prose by actors portraying the group's core writers.* **3** (*also* **ex,traordinary ren'dition**) [U] **~ (of sb)** (especially in the US) the practice of sending foreigners who are thought to be guilty of a crime to be questioned in another country where the laws about the treatment of prisoners are less strict: *The move was an attempt to legalize extraordinary rendition.*

renew /rɪˈnjuː; *NAmE* rɪˈnuː/ *verb* **1 ~ sth** to begin sth again after a pause or an interruption, often with more energy or effort than before: *Committees should renew their efforts to inform and improve the work of Parliament generally.* ◇ *Researchers spent a week in the village, renewing their acquaintance with the participants.* ➲ compare RESUME (1) **2 ~ sth** to make sth valid for a further period of time: *The police force did not renew the contracts of a number of female police officers.* **3 ~ sth** to emphasize sth by saying or stating it again SYN REITERATE, REPEAT[1] (2): *The established TV channels were required to renew their commitment to core public service values.* **4** to change sth that is old or damaged and replace it with sth new of the same kind: **~ sth** *Certain groups of cells are constantly renewed throughout the life of an organism.* ◇ **~ itself** *Survival is dependent upon the organization's ability to adapt and to renew itself.*

re·new·able /rɪˈnjuːəbl; *NAmE* rɪˈnuːəbl/ *adj.* **1** [usually before noun] (of energy and natural resources) replaced naturally or controlled carefully and therefore able to be used without the risk of none being left: *Renewable energy is the most attractive energy source in environmental terms.* ◇ *A renewable resource, wood crops replace themselves every 50 to 100 years.* **2** that can be made valid for a further period of time after it has finished: *The members elect a president for a three-year renewable term.*

re·new·ables /rɪˈnjuːəblz; *NAmE* rɪˈnuːəblz/ *noun* [pl.] types of energy that can be replaced naturally, such as energy produced from wind or water: *The government wants 20% of the UK's electricity to come from renewables by 2020.* HELP **Renewables** are more commonly referred to as **renewable energy (sources).**

re·newal /rɪˈnjuːəl; *NAmE* rɪˈnuːəl/ *noun* [U, C] **1** the act of making a contract, etc. valid for a further period of time after it has finished: *Insurance companies will remind customers that their policies are due for renewal.* ◇ **~ of sth** *She is offered a renewal of the contract with the employer.* **2 ~ (of sth)** a situation in which sth is replaced, improved or made more successful: *Major world events such as the Olympics provide opportunities for urban renewal.* ◇ *The relative prosperity of Britain in this period may have been based on illusions of an economic renewal.* **3 ~ (of sth)** a situation in which sth begins again after a pause or an interruption: *His policy was, in short, to seek a renewal of* *the war.* ◇ *In Gray's sonnet, the joyous springtime renewal of life is set against the poet's lonely grief.*

re·newed /rɪˈnjuːd; *NAmE* rɪˈnuːd/ *adj.* [usually before noun] happening again with increased interest or strength: *There has been renewed interest in technologies to treat water in the home.*

rent[1] /rent/ *noun* [U, C] an amount of money that you regularly pay so that you can use a house, etc: *Tenants are generally required to pay their rent in advance.* ◇ **~ (on sth)** *The peasants were now forced to pay high rents on land that they had formerly owned.* ⊃ *compare* HIRE[2] (1)

rent[2] /rent/ *verb* **1** [T, I] to regularly pay money to sb so that you can use sth that they own, such as a house, some land, a machine, etc: **~ sth** *The costs of renting an apartment in an urban area are prohibitively high.* ◇ *People living in Scotland were more likely to live in rented accommodation.* ◇ **~ (sth) from sb** *The migrants were likely to resort to renting from private landlords.* **2** [T] **~ sth (out) (to sb)** to allow sb to use sth that you own such as a house or some land in exchange for regular payments: *They tried to make a living out of renting out rooms to students.* **3** [T] **~ sth** (*especially NAmE*) to pay money to sb so that you can use sth for a short period of time: *He had been involved in an accident while driving a rented car.* ⊃ *compare* HIRE[1] (3)

re·organ·ize (*BrE also* **-ise**) /riˈɔːɡənaɪz; *NAmE* riːˈɔːrɡənaɪz/ *verb* [T, I] **~ (sth)** to change the way in which sth is organized or done: *One of the most effective things they can do is to reorganize the formal structure of the business.* ◇ *In 1996 it reorganized, putting all its global television activities into a single division.* ■ **re·organ·iza·tion, -isa·tion** /riˌɔːɡənaɪˈzeɪʃn; *NAmE* riːˌɔːrɡənəˈzeɪʃn/ *noun* [U, C] *Some have tried structural reorganization, for example by abolishing or merging departments.* ◇ **~ of sth** *General Albrecht von Roon planned a reorganization of the army in 1860.*

re·pair[1] /rɪˈpeə(r); *NAmE* rɪˈper/ *verb* **1 ~ sth** to put sth that is old, broken or damaged back into good condition: *Healthy cells are more successful at repairing DNA damage than tumour cells.* ◇ *Safety defects have not been repaired sufficiently quickly.* ◇ **~ itself** *Damaged hearts do not repair themselves as other muscles do.* ⊃ *compare* RESTORE (3) **2 ~ sth** to say or do sth in order to improve a bad or unpleasant situation: *Restorative justice focused on repairing the harm caused by crime to people and relationships.* ■ **re·pair·er** *noun*: *Many service industries, such as plumbers and car repairers, never advertise, as they rely on their existing customers to bring them business.*

re·pair[2] /rɪˈpeə(r); *NAmE* rɪˈper/ *noun* [C, U] an act of repairing sth: *He has kept the pump maintained since he bought it by undertaking repairs himself.* ◇ *The injury requires surgical repair.* ◇ **~ of sth** *Stem cells from outside sources can contribute to the repair of the injured lung.* ◇ **+ noun** *Specialized repair mechanisms for UV damage have been found in nearly all cells from bacteria to mammals.*

IDM **in good, poor, etc. reˈpair | in a good, poor, etc. state of reˈpair** in good, etc. condition: *All work equipment must be maintained in an efficient state, and kept in good repair.*

repay /rɪˈpeɪ/ *verb* (**re·paid, re·paid** /rɪˈpeɪd/) **1** to pay back the money that you have borrowed from sb: **~ sth** *The country is looking to repay its international debts.* ◇ **~ sth to sb** *Once the money was repaid to governments, it would be spent on public infrastructure.* ◇ **~ sb** *He undertook to repay his employer from any compensation he received.* **2** to give sth to sb or do sth for them in return for sth that they have done for you: **~ sb (for sth)** *During my last placement, I took the opportunity to repay my primary school teacher for all she had done for me.* ◇ **~ sth** *The widespread perception was that you could never trust people to repay a favour.* ◇ **~ sth with sth** *The company's investment in managing relationships has been repaid with near-perfect customer service.* **3 ~ sth** if sth **repays** your attention, interest, study, etc, it is worth spending time to look at it, etc: *It is a complex article but one that repays close attention.*

re·pay·ment /rɪˈpeɪmənt/ *noun* **1** [U] the act of paying back money that you have borrowed from a bank, etc: *When debt repayment is higher than a country's economic growth, the debt is considered unsustainable.* ◇ **~ of sth** *The businesses had to tackle the difficult task of rescheduling repayment of these debts.* **2** [C, usually pl.] a sum of money that you pay regularly to a bank, etc. until you have returned all the money that you owe: *She has been unable to keep up her mortgage repayments.* ◇ **~ of sth** *The household undertakes to make monthly repayments of the loan to the lender.*

re·peal /rɪˈpiːl/ *verb* **~ sth** if a government or other group or person with authority **repeals** a law or part of a law, that law, or that part of it, is no longer valid: *Parliament has the power to make or repeal any legislation.* ◇ *The Irish Republic undertook to repeal Articles 2 and 3 of the 1937 constitution.* ■ **re·peal** *noun* [U] **~ (of sth)** *Following the repeal of the state monopoly, the market became highly fragmented.*

re·peat[1] /rɪˈpiːt/ *verb* **1** [T] **~ sth** to do or produce sth again or more than once: *Researchers later repeated the same experiment with both children and adults as participants.* ◇ *to repeat a process/procedure* ◇ *to repeat a calculation/measurement* ◇ *The initial dose for adults is usually 0.8 mg, repeated at 2–3 minute intervals if necessary.* **2** [T] to say or write sth again or more than once: **~ sth** *These details are well documented in the literature and will not be repeated here.* ◇ **~ yourself** *At the risk of repeating myself, I should like to draw attention to these points again.* ◇ **~ that...** *It is worth repeating that this book has an ambitious goal.* **3** [T, I] **~ (sth/itself)** to happen more than once in the same way: *So little appears to have been learnt and history seems to be repeating itself.* ◇ *The rhymes repeated at line-beginnings as well as line-endings.* **4** [T] **~ sth (to sb)** to tell sb sth that you have heard or been told by sb else: *These accusations were repeated to her husband.* **5** [T] to say sth that sb else has said, especially in order to learn it: **~ sth** *She was required to learn history by committing long passages to memory, before repeating it word for word.* ◇ **~ what...** *His colleagues were simply repeating what he himself had argued in his speech.*

re·peat[2] /rɪˈpiːt/ *noun* **1** an event that is very similar to sth that happened before: **~ of sth** *The policy response prevented a repeat of the trauma of the Great Depression.* ◇ **+ noun** *Loyalty programmes are clearly designed to encourage repeat purchase of and loyalty to a brand.* **2** a pattern that is repeated on a surface or in a series HELP This meaning is used in GENETICS to refer to repeated SEQUENCES of DNA: *Simple sequence repeats have mutation rates in excess of 1 in 1 000 per locus per generation.*

re·peated /rɪˈpiːtɪd/ *adj.* [only before noun] happening, said or done several or many times: *Cognitive therapy is sometimes tried for patients who have repeated episodes of depression.* ◇ *Recent examples of press excesses have led to repeated calls in the UK for greater state intervention in the press.*

re·peat·ed·ly /rɪˈpiːtɪdli/ *adv.* many times; again and again: *The government has repeatedly emphasized the importance of involving the private sector.* ◇ *Children often communicate distress by complaining repeatedly of physical symptoms for which no physical cause can be found.*

repel /rɪˈpel/ *verb* (**-ll-**) **1** [T] **~ sb/sth** to successfully fight sb who is attacking you, your country, etc. and drive them away: *Although the government was able to repel the*

R

attack, the fighting led to 250 civilian deaths. ◇ *Male crabs have been seen to leave their own territory to help familiar neighbours repel intruders.* **2** [T] **~ sth** to drive, push or keep sth away: *When a material repels water to a large extent, it is called hydrophobic.* ◇ *These compounds may be useful for repelling cockroaches.* **3** [T] **~ sb** (not used in the progressive tenses) to give sb a strong feeling of dislike, disapproval or horror: *The soldiers were repelled by the cruelties of their enemies.* ➲ *see also* REPULSION (2), REPULSIVE (2) **4** [T, I] **~ (sth)** (*physics*) if one thing **repels** another, or if two things **repel** each other, an electrical or MAGNETIC force pushes them apart: *The small charged particles repel each other.* ◇ *The well-known rule about electric charges is that opposites attract and like charges repel.* OPP ATTRACT (4) ➲ *see also* REPULSION (1), REPULSIVE (1)

rep·er·toire /ˈrepətwɑː(r); *NAmE* ˈrepərtwɑːr/ *noun* all the skills or types of behaviour that sb is able to use: *The learners had a limited lexical repertoire.* ◇ **~ of sth** *A child may need to develop a repertoire of anger management strategies.*

repe·ti·tion /ˌrepəˈtɪʃn/ *noun* **1** [U, C] the act of repeating sth that has already been done, said or written: **~ (of sth)** *Speech is often rapid and disorganized with frequent repetition of words and phrases.* ◇ *There are unnecessary repetitions and omissions in the text.* ◇ **without ~** *In many situations, we have to make an ordered selection without repetition.* **2** [C] **~ of sth** the fact of an action or event happening again in the same way as before: *Blair wished to avoid a repetition of the situation under John Major when MPs openly criticized their own party leadership.* ➲ *compare* RECURRENCE

re·peti·tive /rɪˈpetətɪv/ *adj.* **1** saying or doing the same thing many times, so that it becomes boring: *Computers are very good at solving problems involving tedious, repetitive tasks.* **2** repeated many times: *Some forms of work, especially those that involve repetitive movement, are likely to affect women differently.* ◇ *About half the DNA of the genome is made up of repetitive sequences of different types.*

R

re·place /rɪˈpleɪs/ *verb* **1** to be used instead of sth/sb else; to do sth instead of sb/sth else: **~ sth/sb** *New products often simply replace old ones, with limited economic effects.* ◇ **~ sth/sb as sth** *John Major replaced Thatcher as Prime Minister in 1990.* **2** to remove sb/sth and put another person or thing in their place: **~ sb/sth** *Because there are fewer skilled workers than unskilled workers, it is usually more difficult to replace skilled workers.* ◇ **be replaced by sth** *In 2002 twelve national currencies were replaced by the euro.* ◇ **~ sb/sth with sb/sth** *It is generally more profitable for companies to retain existing customers than to replace lapsed customers with new ones.* **3 ~ sth** to change sth that is old, damaged, etc. for a similar thing that is newer or better: *He is buying equipment to replace old machines that have stopped working.*

re·place·ment /rɪˈpleɪsmənt/ *noun* **1** [U] the act of replacing one thing with another, especially sth that is newer or better: **~ of sth** *Correction of the problem may require replacement of the component in question.* ◇ **~ of sth with sth** *At its most basic level, farming is the replacement of some natural vegetation community with some sort of artificial vegetation.* ◇ **+ noun** *Before replacement therapy was discovered, this disease was invariably fatal.* **2** [C] a thing that replaces sth, especially because the first thing is old or damaged: *Care should be taken with patients who have hip replacements.* ◇ **~ for sth** *In its early days, the transistor was essentially seen as a possible replacement for the valve.* **3** [C] **~ (for sb)** a person who replaces another person in an organization, especially in their job: *The managers sacked Payne; there was no mention of finding a replacement for him.*

rep·li·cate¹ /ˈreplɪkeɪt/ *verb* **1** [T] **~ sth** to produce the same thing again SYN REPRODUCE (1): *Another study did not replicate these findings.* ◇ *This effect is also hard to replicate.* **2** [I, T] (of a cell or virus) to produce exact copies of itself: *No plasmids that can replicate autonomously could be found.* ◇ **~ sth** *If a cell cannot replicate its DNA, then it cannot divide.* ◇ **~ itself** *Like a biological virus, a computer virus replicates itself.*

rep·li·cate² /ˈreplɪkət/ *noun* **1** something that is done or produced in the same way as sth else: *In this study, three biological replicates were carried out.* ◇ **+ noun** *Replicate samples were very similar in the amount of product.* **2** a close or exact copy of a cell or virus: *Five viral replicates were analysed from each collection date.*

rep·li·ca·tion /ˌreplɪˈkeɪʃn/ *noun* [U, C] **1** the act or process of producing the same thing again: *Attempts at replication produced varying results.* ◇ **~ of sth** *There has not yet been an exact replication of this research.* **2** the process by which GENETIC material, a cell or a virus makes a copy of itself: *Acyclovir has the effect of inhibiting viral replication in infected cells.* ◇ **~ of sth** *In their experiment, Meselson and Stahl found that after one generation (one replication of DNA), all the DNA of the cells was intermediate in density.*

reply¹ /rɪˈplaɪ/ *verb* (**re·plies**, **re·ply·ing**, **re·plied**, **re·plied**) **1** [I, T] to say or write sth as an answer to sb/sth: **~ (to sb/sth) (with sth)** *Three studies could not be included as the authors did not reply to the email request.* ◇ *Some philosophers may want to reply to this question with a firm 'No'.* ◇ **~ that...** *Tinbergen politely replied that Keynes had totally misunderstood his methods.* ◇ **+ speech** *Her mother replied, 'Finish school and college first.'* **2** [I] **~ (to sth) (with sth)** to do sth as a reaction to sth that sb has said or done: *They replied to the shelling with a heavy mortar attack.*

reply² /rɪˈplaɪ/ *noun* (*pl.* **replies**) [C, U] an act of replying to sth/sb in speech or writing: *We received replies from 1 767 people.* ◇ **~ to sth/sb** *It would be nice to have an accurate reply to this question.* ◇ **in ~ to sth/sb** *Stokes, in reply to Thomson, agreed with almost all of this.*

re·port¹ /rɪˈpɔːt; *NAmE* rɪˈpɔːrt/ *verb* **1** [T, often passive, I] to tell people that sth has happened or exists, or to provide other information about sth: **~ sth** *Surveys of UK workers report similar findings.* ◇ *There has been a reported decline in the fish population.* ◇ **~ doing sth** *More than half of the respondents reported feeling tired.* ◇ **~ that...** *Of the participants questioned, 44.4% reported that they had a family history of cancer.* ◇ **~ whether/how, etc...** *The children were asked to report whether they had experienced pain.* ◇ **~ on sth** *Subjects were asked to report on their food consumption.* ◇ **(be) reported by sb** *These results are similar to those reported by Dozier (2005).* ◇ **be reported + adv./prep.** *This is a phenomenon that has been widely reported in the literature.* ◇ **be reported as (doing) sth** *The scale was reported as being valid for primary care patients.* ◇ **be reported to do sth** *Several hundred agents have been reported to cause occupational asthma.* ◇ **it is reported that...** *It has been reported that viral replication is inhibited by nitric oxide.* **2** [T, often passive, I] to present information in a newspaper, on television, etc. about sth that has happened: **be reported in sth** *This was widely reported in the press.* ◇ **~ that...** *The 'Daily Mail' and other newspapers reported that the Human Rights Act was the reason for the ruling.* ◇ **~ on sth** *Journalists reporting on the government crackdown were harassed and intimidated.* **3** [T] to tell a person in authority about a crime or about sth else that is wrong: **~ sth** *She was reluctant to report the crime.* ◇ **~ sth to sb** *The number of racial incidents reported to the police has risen steadily.* ◇ **~ sb (to sb) (for sth/for doing sth)** *He had reported her for making a false benefit claim.* **4** [I] to go somewhere and tell sb in authority that you have arrived: **~ to sb/sth** *They may be required to report* *regularly to a police station.* ◇ **~ for sth** *The next day, he reported for duty in the army.*

PHR V **re͵port ˈback (to sb/sth) (on sth)** to provide information for others, after doing sth or after returning somewhere: *The psychologist informs the parents before reporting back to the team meeting.* **reˈport to sb** (not used in the progressive tenses) (*business*) if you **report to** sb, they are in charge of you or are responsible for your work: *District managers report to regional directors.*

▸ REPORT + NOUN **findings, results • data • statistics • level • score • increase • decrease • rate • frequency • incidence • prevalence • correlation • coefficients • association • estimates** *Older adults tend to report higher levels of happiness.* | **case • event • instance • outcome • difference • improvement • effect • experience • problems • difficulties • symptoms • pain • feelings • thoughts** *One study reported outcomes for two motivational categories.*

▸ NOUN + REPORT **investigators • author • study • survey • table • respondent • participant** *In accordance with Gorski's data, the authors reported a 50% risk of miscarriage.*

▸ (BE) REPORTED + ADVERB **elsewhere • separately • here • below • above • earlier • previously** *Results are reported in more detail elsewhere.*

▸ ADVERB + REPORT **previously • initially, originally • subsequently • recently • frequently • consistently • rarely • regularly • commonly • routinely • typically • generally** *Members of this group generally report higher levels of job satisfaction.*

LANGUAGE BANK

Reporting verbs

These verbs are each used to refer to what a source said. The subject of the verb may be the researcher(s), the research or the text that reports on the research.

demonstrate • describe • document • illustrate • indicate • provide • report • reveal • show • state • suggest

- *Hereford's 1977 study* ***documented*** *a continuum of tidal flat deposits.*
- *Valenzuela (1999)* ***reported*** *that the recent immigrants in her study had high levels of social capital.*
- *This result* ***reveals that*** *incubation temperature influences adult behaviour.*
- *The researchers* ***showed*** *that teachers' expectations of students were influential in students' performance.*
- *Sharir and Lerner's analysis (Sharir and Lerner, 2006)* ***suggests*** *that successful entrepreneurs are dedicated to the social goals they want to achieve.*

Reporting verbs that focus on an author's thought processes are also referred to as **thinking verbs**.

argue • assert • challenge • claim • conclude • contend • maintain • predict • question • recommend • refute • reject

- *Harris (1997)* ***argued*** *that river restoration should be part of the management strategy for common carp in Australia.*
- *Recent studies* ***challenge*** *the assumption that wellbeing could be represented by material prosperity.*
- *Berger (1996) and Slonczewski (1996) independently* ***predicted*** *that a spin-polarized current...*
- *Some studies have* ***questioned*** *the efficacy of governmental regulation.*
- *He* ***refuted*** *the widespread view that famines occur only when there is a sharp decline in food available.*

See also the Language Bank on research verbs at **research** *verb*.

re·port² /rɪˈpɔːt; *NAmE* rɪˈpɔːrt/ *noun* **1** a written document in which a particular situation or subject is examined or discussed: *According to the WHO report, these hazards are more prevalent in lower-grade occupations.* ◇ **~ on sth** *The Commissioner is required to submit an annual report on his work to Parliament.* ◇ **~ of sth** *The Board then rejected the report of the inquiry.* ◇ **~ from/by sb/sth** *A recent report from the American Heart Association provides a review of cohort studies.* ◇ **~ to sb/sth** *In her report of 24 July 2002 to the UN Security Council, she denounced the lack of cooperation.* **2** a statement that sth has happened or exists; a piece of information about sth: **~ that...** *The study confirms anecdotal reports that such behaviour is common.* ◇ **~ of sth** *These trends are consistent with reports of dramatic increases in obesity worldwide.* ◇ **~ of (sb) doing sth** *There have been numerous reports of artists experiencing difficulties.* **3** information that is presented in a newspaper, on television, etc. about sth that has happened: *The newspaper reports were exaggerated.* ◇ **~ of/about sth** *Media reports about food safety concerns are relatively common.* **4** (*BrE*) (*NAmE* **reˈport card**) a written document about a student's progress at school: *Her mother proudly exhibited her daughter's report cards.*

▸ ADJECTIVE + NOUN **early • previous • subsequent • recent • numerous** *The study confirms earlier reports that homeless people have poorer mental health than the general population.* | **original • initial, preliminary • interim • periodic • final • annual • quarterly • weekly • daily • special • official • formal • joint • detailed, full, comprehensive • brief • written • narrative • technical • medical • published • influential • confidential • computer-based, computerized** *The final report of the review panel, published in 2006, recommended that...* | **verbal • anecdotal • retrospective** *Retrospective verbal reports are often collected to establish what actually took place.*

▸ NOUN + REPORT **draft • summary • research • incident • inspection • audit • credit • laboratory • police • progress** *Next, the auditor sent a draft audit report to the contact person.*

▸ VERB + REPORT **commission • produce, prepare • draft • write, compile • submit, file, send • publish, issue, release • present • read • review** *The group was asked to draft a report on institutional reform.*

▸ REPORT + VERB **state • note • indicate • highlight • conclude • recommend, suggest** *A 1979 report, 'The Effects of Nuclear War', noted that the results of a war would go far beyond the immediate casualties.*

re·port·ed·ly /rɪˈpɔːtɪdli; *NAmE* rɪˈpɔːrtɪdli/ *adv.* according to what some people say (used to express the belief that the information given may not actually be true): *He attracted huge numbers of followers, reportedly preaching to as many as 10 000 at a time.*

re·port·er /rɪˈpɔːtə(r); *NAmE* rɪˈpɔːrtər/ *noun* a person who presents information in a newspaper, on television, etc. about sth that has happened: *Reporters were banned from the courtroom.* ◇ *In his early years, he was a newspaper reporter.* ➲ *compare* JOURNALIST

re·port·ing /rɪˈpɔːtɪŋ; *NAmE* rɪˈpɔːrtɪŋ/ *noun* [U] **1** the act or process of giving information or official reports about sth: *An effective system of error and incident reporting is necessary.* ◇ *26.5% would support mandatory reporting for severe cases.* ◇ **+ noun** *They could also impose global corporate reporting requirements.* **2** the activity of presenting and writing about news on television, in newspapers, etc: *There was a growing awareness of bias in news reporting.*

rep·re·sent /͵reprɪˈzent/ *verb* **1 + noun** *linking verb* (not used in the progressive tenses) to be sth; to be equal to sth SYN CONSTITUTE, AMOUNT TO STH (2): *This approach represented a shift of emphasis.* ◇ *This represents a departure* *from standard practice.* ◇ *Chinese business represents 73% of the Indonesian corporate sector.* ➲ language bank *at* PROPORTION **2** (not used in the progressive tenses) **~ sth** to be a symbol or sign of sth SYN SYMBOLIZE: *The triangles and circles represent boys and girls respectively.* ◇ *Here, n represents a positive integer.* ◇ *The polymer chain can be represented by this formula.* **3** [no passive] **~ sth** to be typical of sth: *The study's findings might not represent migrant populations in smaller cities.* ◇ *The comment represents his honest opinion.* **4** to show or describe sb/sth in a particular way SYN PRESENT[3] (2): **~ sb/sth + adv./prep.** *Data were represented graphically by a scatterplot.* ◇ *The diagram accurately represented their opinions.* ◇ *The six countries represented in Figure 17.1 are similar in many ways.* ◇ **~ sb/sth as sth** *Martin is represented as a dedicated family man.* ◇ *A variety of systems can be represented as networks.* **5** (not used in the progressive tenses) **~ sb/sth** to include a particular type or number of people or things: *The studies represented a variety of clinical settings.* ◇ *A total of 114 countries were represented, reflecting our international nature.* **6 be represented + adv./prep.** to be present to a particular degree: *Italian traders were well represented in Egypt.* ◇ *Households headed by women are disproportionately represented among the poorest sections of society.* **7** to act or speak for sb/sth; to attend or take part in an event on behalf of sb: **~ sb/sth** *There have been protests from activists representing various indigenous populations.* ◇ *The non-executive directors have a duty to represent the interests of the shareholders.* ◇ **~ sb/sth in sth** *All UN member states are represented in the General Assembly.* **8 ~ sb/sth** to show sb/sth, especially in a picture or diagram SYN DEPICT (1): *The image represents a child a few feet tall, pointing to heaven.* **9 ~ sth** to say or suggest sth that you want sb to believe or pay attention to: *She makes sense of the myriad of ways in which the issues have been represented by different authors.*

rep·re·sen·ta·tion /ˌreprɪzenˈteɪʃn/ *noun* **1** [U, C] the act of presenting sb/sth in a particular way; something that shows or describes sth SYN PORTRAYAL: *The offence of fraud by false representation has been committed.* ◇ **~ of sth** *This flow chart is only a representation of the ideal situation.* ◇ *a graphical/pictorial/visual/schematic representation of sth* **2** [U] the fact of having sb who will speak or vote for you: *The importance of legal representation was clear.* ◇ **~ from sb** *The composition of the Task Force ensured representation from all the community stakeholders.* HELP **Proportional representation** is a system that gives each party in an election a number of seats in relation to the number of votes its candidates receive. **3 representations** [pl.] formal statements made to sb in authority, especially in order to make your opinions known or to protest: *The magistrate declined to hear their representations.* ◇ **~ to sb** *He was not afforded an opportunity to make representations to the committee.*

rep·re·sen·ta·tion·al /ˌreprɪzenˈteɪʃnl/ *adj.* **1** involving the act of presenting or showing sth in a particular way: *Cities now often sell themselves on the basis of particular representational strategies.* HELP A **representational** style in art, cinema, etc. is one in which things are shown as they are really are: *Every representational film adapts a prior conception.* ➲ *compare* ABSTRACT[1] (4) **2** involving sb who will speak or vote for other people: *Account managers have a key representational role in the client/agency relationship.*

rep·re·sen·ta·tive[1] /ˌreprɪˈzentətɪv/ *noun* **1** a person who has been chosen to act, speak or vote for sb/sth; a person who has been chosen to attend or take part in an event on behalf of sb: *He was the king's official representative.* ◇ *Citizens of the Member States can elect representatives to the European Parliament.* ◇ **~ of sb/sth** *The ambassador is the direct representative of a sovereign monarch.* ◇ **~ from sth** *Its members included representatives from each of the major political parties.* HELP In the US, the House of Representatives is the lower house of Congress, whose members are called **Representatives**: *Among the southerners were Senator Lister Hill and Representative Carl Elliot, both Democrats from Alabama.* ➲ *see also* HOUSE OF REPRESENTATIVES **2 ~ (of sth)** a person, animal or thing that is a typical example of a particular group: *A biological species is a population of similar individuals, each of which is a representative of that species.* **3** a person who works for a company and travels around selling its products: *Many sales representatives operate out of offices in their homes.* HELP In general and Business English, the less formal **rep** is used: *Sales reps can quote prices to customers immediately.*

rep·re·sen·ta·tive[2] /ˌreprɪˈzentətɪv/ *adj.* **1 ~ (of sb/sth)** typical of a particular group; that can be used as an example: *Findings may not be truly representative of the general population.* ◇ *The examples reproduced below are representative of their work.* **2** (*technical*) (of a sample or piece of work) containing or including examples of all the different types of people or things in a large group: *They used a representative sample of items.* ◇ *This is comparable with rates seen in other nationally representative surveys.* ◇ **~ of sth** *The study is based on a sample of 1 000 workers broadly representative of the UK working population with respect to age, gender and occupational status.* ◇ **~ for sth** *The study is not representative for the whole of Italy and Spain.* **3** (of a system of government, etc.) consisting of people who have been chosen to speak or vote for other people: *They favour representative democracy.* ◇ *Constitutional and representative government had never existed.* ■ **rep·re·sen·ta·tive·ness** *noun* [U] **~ (of sb/sth)** *It is important to ensure the representativeness of the sample.*

re·press /rɪˈpres/ *verb* **1 ~ sth** to try not to have or show an emotion, a thought, etc: *If we repress or suppress our anger and the other emotions related to it, we feel less connected to others.* HELP In Freudian psychology, **repress** has a particular meaning, which is to stop yourself having particular thoughts or feelings so completely that they become or remain unconscious: *Interviewees may have forgotten or even repressed some memories.* ➲ *compare* CONTROL[2] (4) **2** [often passive] **~ sb/sth** to use political and/or military force to control a group of people and restrict theirfreedom SYN PUT STH DOWN, SUPPRESS (1): *Autocracies, according to this view, do not need legitimacy, since they can repress even widespread opposition.* **3 ~ sth** (*biology*) to prevent a GENE from being expressed: *The protein products of the two genes bind to each other to repress their own transcription.*

re·pressed /rɪˈprest/ *adj.* **1** (of emotions) not expressed: *The main character is driven by barely repressed rage.* **2** (of a person) having emotions or desires that are not allowed to be expressed: *He grew up in a very repressed Victorian household.*

re·pres·sion /rɪˈpreʃn/ *noun* [U] **1** the act of using force to control a group of people and restrict their freedom: *The students sparked off events that ended in brutal repression.* **2 ~ (of sth)** the act of controlling strong emotions and desires and not allowing them to be expressed so that they no longer seem to exist: *The repression of anger can be positively harmful.* **3** (*biology*) the act or process of preventing a GENE from being expressed: *The signalling leads to the repression of genes by switching transcription off.*

re·pres·sive /rɪˈpresɪv/ *adj.* (of a system of government) controlling people by force and restricting their freedom: *Marxist intellectuals, fleeing repressive regimes, tended to congregate in Switzerland.*

re·pro·duce /ˌriːprəˈdjuːs; *NAmE* ˌriːprəˈduːs/ *verb* **1** [T] **~ sth** to produce sth again; to make sth happen again in the same way: *These findings have not been reproduced.* ◇ *Perucci and Wysong (Ch. 61) focus on the way that*

R

universities reproduce social inequalities. **2** [T] **~ sth** to make a copy of a picture, piece of text, etc; to include a copy of a picture, etc: *These children can draw, but only to reproduce images that they have previously seen.* ◇ *The image is reproduced here with the kind permission of the publisher.* **3** [I, T] (of people, animals, plants, etc.) to produce young: *Animals compete with each other to survive and reproduce.* ◇ *Most animals and plants are sexually reproducing organisms.* ◇ **~ itself** *The population failed to reproduce itself during the period.*

re·pro·du·cible /ˌriːprəˈdjuːsəbl; *NAmE* ˌriːprəˈduːsəbl/ *adj.* **1** that can be produced again: *This method leads to highly reproducible results with relatively little technical variation.* **2** that can be copied: *Graphic art became mechanically reproducible for the first time.*

re·pro·duc·tion /ˌriːprəˈdʌkʃn/ *noun* **1** [U] the act or process of producing babies, young animals or plants: *Dominant birds monopolized reproduction, accounting for 95.2% of all chicks.* ◇ *sexual/asexual reproduction* **2** [U] the act or process of producing sth again or of making sth happen again in the same way: *Schools are key sites of socialization and cultural reproduction.* ◇ **~ of sth** *He was primarily concerned with class-based reproduction of social inequality.* **3** [U] the act or process of producing copies of sth, especially of a document, book, picture, etc: *He applied the latest advances in typography and photographic reproduction.* **4** [C] a thing that has been reproduced; a copy, especially of a document, book, picture, etc: *The reproductions that accompany the text are of very high quality.* ◇ **~ of sth** *Verbatim reproductions of previous published papers are not accepted.*

re·pro·duct·ive /ˌriːprəˈdʌktɪv/ *adj.* [only before noun] connected with producing babies, young animals or plants: *Female reproductive success was lower in larger groups.* ◇ *Testosterone stimulates the development of male reproductive organs.* ◇ *Flowers contain the reproductive cells of higher plants.*

rep·tile /ˈreptaɪl; *NAmE also* ˈreptl/ *noun* an animal that has cold blood and skin covered in SCALES, and that lays eggs: *In many reptiles, the sex that an egg develops into depends on the temperature of incubation.* ■ **rep·til·ian** /repˈtɪliən/ *adj.*: *In proportion to body size, mammals have brains about ten times the size of reptilian brains.*

re·pub·lic /rɪˈpʌblɪk/ *noun* a country that is governed by a president and politicians elected by the people and where there is no king or queen: *Nigeria became a republic in 1963.* ◇ *As an export market, Japan is less important for Germany than the Czech Republic is.* ◇ **~ of sth** *China (officially the People's Republic of China) has one fifth of the world's population.* ➲ *compare* MONARCHY

re·pub·lic·an[1] /rɪˈpʌblɪkən/ *noun* **1** a person who supports a form of government with a president and politicians elected by the people with no king or queen: *In France, a republic had been established and the republicans felt anxious about its survival.* **2 Republican** (*abbr.* **R**, **Rep.**) a member or supporter of the Republican Party of the US: *The Republicans in Congress slashed the budget for environmental protection.* ◇ *For most of the past half century, high-income people have tended to be Republicans and lower-income people Democrats.* ➲ *compare* DEMOCRAT

re·pub·lic·an[2] /rɪˈpʌblɪkən/ *adj.* **1** connected with or like a republic; supporting the principles of a republic: *The new republican government in France faced a difficult situation.* ◇ *He was involved in the republican movement of the early 1830s.* **2** (*also* **Republican**) (*abbr.* **R**, **Rep.**) connected with the Republican Party in the US: *The next Republican president, Ronald Reagan, left a profoundly different mark on environmental policy.*

re·pul·sion /rɪˈpʌlʃn/ *noun* **1** [U, C] (*physics*) the force by which things push each other away: *The rearrangement of the electrons results in a change in the electron-electron repulsion.* ◇ *This conformation should minimize the internal repulsions and generate the lowest energy.* OPP ATTRACTION (5) ➲ *see also* REPEL (4) **2** [U] a strong feeling of dislike towards sb/sth that you find extremely unpleasant: *People talked about the case with a mixture of fascination and repulsion.* OPP ATTRACTION (1)

re·pul·sive /rɪˈpʌlsɪv/ *adj.* **1** [usually before noun] (*physics*) involving or causing the force by which things push each other away: *This is the point at which the attractive and repulsive forces are in balance.* OPP ATTRACTIVE (4) **2** causing a strong feeling of dislike; very unpleasant: *It was a repulsive thought.* ◇ *She claims to find him physically repulsive.* OPP ATTRACTIVE (1)

repu·ta·tion /ˌrepjuˈteɪʃn/ *noun* the opinion that people have about what sb/sth is like, based on what has happened in the past: *The brand had an excellent reputation.* ◇ **~ of sth** *The resultant publicity could disproportionately damage the reputation of the organization.* ◇ **~ as sth** *The firm earned a reputation as a leader in its field.* ◇ **~ for (doing) sth** *The Roman church enjoyed a reputation for generosity.*

re·quest[1] /rɪˈkwest/ *noun* **1** [C, U] the action of asking for sth formally and politely; the thing that you ask for: *His request was refused.* ◇ **~ for sth** *The court rejected her request for a retrial.* ◇ **~ to do sth** *He made a request to have a fresh claim considered.* ◇ **~ that...** *She concludes with the request that her name not be used.* ◇ **~ from sb** *Sending money to a charitable organization is usually a response to a request from someone working for that organization.* ◇ **on/upon ~** *Results for all variables are available upon request.* ◇ **at the ~ of sb| at sb's ~** *The scheme was originally introduced at the request of the federal government.* **2** [C] **~ (to sth) (to do sth)** a message to a computer asking for data or the performance of some action: *A web browser sends requests to a server which responds by sending data to be displayed.*

re·quest[2] /rɪˈkwest/ *verb* to ask for sth; to ask sb to do sth in a polite and formal way: **~ sth** *He requested $38 bn for homeland security programmes.* ◇ **~ sth from sb** *The Ministry of Health requested technical assistance from the World Health Organization.* ◇ **~ sb to do sth** *The applicant may request the court to reconsider its decision.* ◇ **~ that...** *The court may request that this procedure be utilized.*

R

re·quire AWL /rɪˈkwaɪə(r)/ *verb* (not usually used in the progressive tenses) **1** to need sth; to depend on sb/sth: **~ sth** *Some patients may never require treatment.* ◇ *The skills required did not change much from generation to generation.* ◇ *Recruits may not be able to meet the required standard in training.* ◇ **~ sth for sth** *General anaesthesia is required for this type of procedure.* ◇ **~ sth (in order) to do sth** *Soils require time to form.* ◇ **~ sb/sth to do sth** *This approach requires the analyst to produce detailed transcripts of natural conversation.* ◇ **~ that...** *These jobs require that these young men embrace 'soft' skills in addition to academic training.* **2** [often passive] to make sb do or have sth, especially because it is necessary according to a particular law or set of rules: **(be) required (of sb)** *The company should clarify the standards of ethical behaviour required of company directors.* ◇ **be required by sth** *Cancer registration is required by law in many countries.* ◇ **be required under sth** *After the judgment, the state is required under Article 228 to take the necessary measures to comply.* ◇ **~ sb to do sth** *The law requires the father to assist in the financial support of the child.* ◇ **~ that...** *The Data Protection Directive already requires that personal data be protected.*

re·quire·ment AWL /rɪˈkwaɪəmənt; *NAmE* rɪˈkwaɪərmənt/ *noun* **1** (*often* **requirements**) [pl.] something that sb needs or wants: *This technique can be used to deliver* all of a patient's nutritional requirements. ◇ A normal energy requirement is 25–35 kcal/kg per day. ◇ It is not likely that the existing products will satisfy customer requirements. ◇ **~ of sb/sth** *They are developing new membranes that can meet the requirements of the automobile industry.* ◇ **~ for sth** *Growth is a requirement for social stability.* **2** something that is necessary according to a particular law or set of rules: *All manufacturers must meet the essential requirements listed in Annex 1 of the directive.* ◇ **~ of sth** *The Commission's decision complied with the requirements of Article 20.* ◇ **~ for sth** *The legal requirements for registration have been completed.* ◇ **~ under sth** *This is a statutory requirement under the Control of Pesticides Regulations 1986.* ◇ **~ to do sth** *There may be a requirement to notify the supervisory authority.*

▸ ADJECTIVE + REQUIREMENT **basic, fundamental • essential • minimum, minimal • strict, stringent • specific • additional** *Beyond these minimum requirements, contributors are encouraged to annotate their data as thoroughly as possible.* | **mandatory • formal • substantive • legal • statutory • legislative • constitutional • regulatory • procedural** *There is a legal requirement to carry out specific risk assessments for certain types of work.*

▸ NOUN + REQUIREMENT **eligibility • residence • disclosure, reporting, notification** *Eligibility requirements were relaxed.*

▸ VERB + REQUIREMENTS **meet, satisfy, fulfil, suit • match • exceed** *Commissioners can be removed if they do not fulfil the requirements of their post.* | **impose, lay down, specify, implement, introduce, set • outline • relax, reduce • waive • remove • comply with, conform to • be subject to • violate, contravene** *Both sets of rules impose reporting requirements.*

res·cue[1] /ˈreskjuː/ *verb* to save sb/sth from a dangerous or difficult situation: **~ sb/sth** *Ships' captains have a duty to rescue people in distress at sea.* ◇ **~ sb/sth from sth/sb** *He studied people who rescued Jews from the Nazis during World War II.* ◇ *The state had to rescue ailing industries from the threat of bankruptcy.* ■ **res·cuer** *noun*: *Their analyses showed several reasons why the rescuer was motivated to act.*

R

res·cue[2] /ˈreskjuː/ *noun* [U, C] the act of saving sb/sth from a dangerous or difficult situation; the fact of being saved: **~ (of sb/sth)** *the dramatic rescue of 33 trapped copper miners* ◇ *Ten fishermen were saved in a daring sea rescue.* ◇ **come to the ~** *They were found by soldiers who had come to the rescue.* ◇ **+ noun** *Rescue workers continued their search for survivors.* ◇ *Greece was given a financial rescue package from the EU.* ◇ *a rescue mission/operation/attempt*

re·search[1] AWL /rɪˈsɜːtʃ; ˈriːsɜːtʃ; *NAmE* rɪˈsɜːrtʃ; ˈriːsɜːrtʃ/ *noun* [U] careful study of a subject, especially in order to discover new facts or information about it: *There is a need for further qualitative research in this area.* ◇ *Linguists need to do more research to find out what motivates the spread of linguistic changes in these societies.* ◇ **~ on sth/sb** *Research on the effect of a Mediterranean-style diet on dementia is explored.* ◇ **~ into sth/sb** *This paper brings together 25 years of research into organizational buying behaviour.* ◇ **+ noun** *Some interesting research questions are raised by these data.* HELP The plural form **researches** is also sometimes used in British English, but is much less frequent: *The distinction between science and technology is often claimed by scientists who wish to pursue their researches without worrying about how their discoveries might be used in the future.* ➲ *see also* MARKET RESEARCH ➲ thesaurus note *at* INVESTIGATION

▸ ADJECTIVE + RESEARCH **future, further • previous, prior • recent • current • basic • extensive • qualitative • quantitative • comparative • empirical • scientific • academic • participatory • social • ethnographic • medical, clinical • geographic, geographical • historical** *Early academic research suggested that the media more often reinforced than changed political views.*

▸ VERB + RESEARCH **conduct, undertake, carry out, do • need, require • focus on • draw on • review • describe • report • present • publish • be based on** *Many large companies employ market research agencies to conduct their research for them.*

▸ RESEARCH + VERB **be based on • focus on • examine, explore • show, demonstrate • suggest, indicate • provide • reveal • identify** *Gond's research focuses on the topic of corporate social responsibility.*

▸ RESEARCH + NOUN **question • interest • project • programme • study • process • strategy • method • design • group • team • assistant • participant** *His major research interest is the ecology of human impact on species-rich tropical ecosystems in South East Asia.*

▸ NOUN + OF RESEARCH **area, field • type, form • nature • subject • focus • aim, goal, purpose • line • piece • body** *There is a large body of research examining the governance of independent firms.*

LANGUAGE BANK

RESEARCH STUDY

Claiming that your research is important or relevant

If you are writing up a research study, for instance as part of your dissertation, you will need to describe why your general study area is relevant or important in your field or in the world. This is usually done in the Introduction.

- Mention the large amount of previous research:

– ***Numerous*** *empirical studies have examined...*
– ***Much*** *research has been devoted to...*
– *In recent years, there has been* ***increasing*** *interest in...*

- State the importance of your topic using adjectives:

– *A* ***major*** *issue of concern is...*
– *A* ***key*** *factor in... is...*
– *It is* ***important*** *to consider...*

LANGUAGE BANK

RESEARCH STUDY

Indicating a gap, problem or need in current research

In your research study, you will also need to show that there is a need for your particular study. This is done in the Introduction and/or the Literature Review, by establishing that there is a gap or problem in previous research.

- Use a **contrast marker** (*however, but, yet*) to introduce these steps:

– ***However****, little attention has been paid to...*
– *...* ***but*** *only a small number of studies have focused on...*
– *...* ***yet*** *there is no systematic survey of...*

- Use **negatives** and **restrictive expressions** (*no, not, lack, little, few, limited, only*):

– *To date, there has* ***not*** *been much research on...*
– *However, we still* ***lack...***
– *So far,* ***few*** *studies have addressed...*
– *Most studies have been* ***limited*** *to...*

re·search[2] AWL /rɪˈsɜːtʃ; *NAmE* rɪˈsɜːrtʃ/ *verb* **1** [T, I] to study sth carefully and try to discover new facts about it: **~ sth** *She is currently researching the history of public health in nineteenth-century Scotland.* ◇ **~ in sth** *He has worked, taught and researched in this field for several years.* ◇ **~ how/what, etc...** *Environmental economists research how environmental goods and services may be provided more efficiently by putting a price on them.* **2** [T] to collect information for an article, a book, etc: *The work is well researched and thoroughly referenced.*

LANGUAGE BANK

Research verbs

These verbs are each used to describe the research process, including its **aims**, **processes** and **results**. Note the use of the passive form (*were conducted* / *were examined*):

analyse ◆ **assess** ◆ **categorize** ◆ **conduct** ◆ **examine** ◆ **find** ◆ **investigate** ◆ **measure** ◆ **select** ◆ **use**

– *In this study, we* ***analyse*** *the mechanism of...*
– *Statistical tests* ***were conducted*** *to assess group differences.*
– *Data* ***were examined*** *both within and across practices.*
– *In an Australian study, Barrett (1980)* ***found*** *that...*
– *In this study, we* ***use*** *Norwegian register data covering all children born in 2004–2009.*

For reporting verbs, see the Language Bank at **report** *verb*.

re,search and de'velopment *noun* [U] (*abbr.* **,R & 'D**) (in industry) work that is done to develop new products and processes or to improve existing ones: *The company was accused of having invested too little in research and development.* ◇ **~ of sth** *The money was intended for the research and development of medical treatment* ◇ **+ noun** *Their production, marketing and R & D activities are concentrated in a few favourable locations.*

re·search·er AWL /rɪˈsɜːtʃə(r); *NAmE* rɪˈsɜːrtʃər/ *noun* a person who does research: *In the 1980s, cheap computer power allowed researchers to use information technology to good effect.* ◇ *The interviews were conducted by a researcher who had been appointed for this specific role.* ◇ **~ in sth** *There is now a considerable amount of evidence on education markets, from researchers in political science, law, education, sociology and economics.* ◇ **~ from sth** *Researchers from several disciplines were involved in writing this book.*

▸ ADJECTIVE + RESEARCHER **leading** ◆ **international** ◆ **academic** ◆ **critical** ◆ **qualitative** ◆ **quantitative** ◆ **empirical** ◆ **medical** ◆ **social** *For academic researchers, professional recognition and advancement depend crucially on being first to disclose and publish their result.*

▸ NOUN + RESEARCHER **university** ◆ **(public) health** ◆ **market** ◆ **management** *The article explored the attitudes of policymakers towards health researchers.*

▸ VERB + RESEARCHER **allow, enable** ◆ **encourage** ◆ **interest** ◆ **lead ~ to** *These concerns have led some researchers to suggest that there is a need for an ethics code for Internet research.*

▸ RESEARCHER + VERB **use, employ** ◆ **seek (to)** ◆ **attempt to, try to** ◆ **conduct** ◆ **study** ◆ **examine** ◆ **consider** ◆ **find** ◆ **identify** ◆ **suggest** ◆ **argue** *Currently, researchers are using a variety of approaches to study the biology of smallpox.*

re·sem·blance /rɪˈzembləns/ *noun* [C, U] the fact of being or looking similar to sb/sth: **~ to sb/sth** *These rites bear a striking resemblance to the midsummer fire rituals found in Scandinavia.* ◇ *The broad categories naturally bear some resemblance to each other.* ◇ **~ between A and B** *The resemblance between family members comes mostly from shared genetics.*

re·sem·ble /rɪˈzembl/ *verb* [no passive] (not used in the progressive tenses) **~ sb/sth** to look like or be similar to another person or thing: *Offspring tend to resemble their parents.* ◇ *Their demographic characteristics closely resembled the general population.*

re·sent /rɪˈzent/ *verb* to feel angry about sth, especially because you feel it is unfair: **~ sth/sb** *She bitterly resented the fact that she had not attended college.* ◇ *Flora is forced to marry a man who resents her because she is pregnant.* ◇ **~ doing sth** *The wealthy may resent having to pay higher taxes to ensure social equality for others.*

re·sent·ment /rɪˈzentmənt/ *noun* [U, C] a feeling of anger or unhappiness about sth that you think is unfair: *Breaking promises can cause resentment.* ◇ *Resentment was aroused by immigrants taking jobs.* ◇ *Some people harbour resentments going back many years.* ◇ **~ at sth** *Voters' resentment at tax increases led to the party's defeat at the polls.*

re·ser·va·tion /ˌrezəˈveɪʃn; *NAmE* ˌrezərˈveɪʃn/ *noun* **1** [C, U] a feeling of doubt about a plan or an idea: **~ about sb/sth** *Britain had reservations about the agreement.* ◇ **without ~** *St Paul seems here to approve this concept without reservation.* **2** (*also* **re·serve**) [C] an area of land in the US that is kept separate for Native Americans to live in: *The Hualapai were at that time living on a tiny reservation inside the canyon.* **3** [C] an arrangement for a seat on a plane or train, a room in a hotel, etc. to be kept for you: *The new system also had a link to several hotels at which reservations could be made.*

re·serve[1] /rɪˈzɜːv; *NAmE* rɪˈzɜːrv/ *noun* **1** [C, usually pl.] a supply of sth that is available to be used in the future or when it is needed: *Russia has huge oil reserves.* ◇ *Leptin is produced when the body's fat reserves are depleted.* ◇ **~ of sth** *In the 1990s, developing countries built up large reserves of US foreign currency.* ◇ *In this situation, the central bank will be obliged to sell foreign exchange reserves in order to maintain the exchange rate.* **2** (*NAmE also* **pre·serve**) [C] a piece of land that is a protected area for animals, plants, etc: *Singapore aimed to set aside 5 per cent of her total land area as nature reserves.* ◇ *Animals are moved between reserves in East Africa to improve the genetic constitution of each population.* **3 the reserve** [sing.] (*also* **(the) reserves** [pl.]) an extra military force, etc. that is not part of a country's regular forces, but is available to be used when needed: *These men became second lieutenants in the reserve and did not serve in the active forces.* ◇ *The army began calling up reserves for combat training.* **4** [U] a feeling that you do not want to accept or agree to sth until you are quite sure that it is all right to do so: *Chesterton managed, with some reserve, to admire the novels of Virginia Woolf.* ◇ **without ~** *The new leadership accepted Deng's recommendations without reserve.* **5** [U] the quality that sb has when they do not talk easily to other people about their ideas or feelings: *Kwang is also like Henry in his reserve, formal restraint or self-discipline.* **6** (*also* **re'serve price**) [C] (*BrE*) the lowest price that sb will accept for sth: *In a standard auction model, reserve prices increase the auctioneer's expected revenues.* **7** [C] = RESERVATION (2)

IDM **in re'serve** available to be used in the future or when needed: *The government might instruct banks to keep more funds in reserve.* ◇ *The drug is mainly held in reserve for those patients who have not responded to other treatments.*

re·serve[2] /rɪˈzɜːv; *NAmE* rɪˈzɜːrv/ *verb* **1 ~ sth** to have or keep a particular power: *Ministers reserve the power to order a referendum if they are not satisfied with the intentions of the council.* ◇ **~ the right to do sth** *The government has reserved the right to opt out of aspects of the European directives on human rights.* **2** to keep sth for sb/sth, so that it cannot be used by any other person or for any other reason: **~ sth for sb/sth** *The medical school reserved sixteen places for members of educationally or economically disadvantaged minorities.* ◇ **~ sth** *DVDs reserve a control area at the inside edge of the track that contains the disk's identification.*

res·er·voir /ˈrezəvwɑː(r); *NAmE* ˈrezərvwɑːr/ *noun* **1** a natural or artificial lake where water is stored before it is taken by pipes to houses, etc: *Water would fill the reservoir behind these dams in a matter of months.* **2** a place where a liquid or gas is available or is kept: *Oil and gas reservoirs are usually covered by an impenetrable layer of rock.* ◇ *Liquid mercury from a reservoir is passed through a*

R

fine capillary tube at a fixed rate. **3 ~ (of sth)** a supply or source of sth: *Long-serving managers may have vast reservoirs of knowledge about market potential.* ◇ *The other large terrestrial reservoir of carbon is organic material in various stages of chemical modification.* HELP In medicine, **reservoir** is used to refer to sth that can be a source of infection: *The main reservoirs for the disease are livestock.*

res·ide AWL /rɪˈzaɪd/ *verb* [I] **+ adv./prep.** (*formal*) to live or be found in a particular place or situation: *Most children continue to reside with their mothers after marital breakdown.* ◇ *Respondents residing in urban areas were compared with their rural counterparts.* ◇ *This technique can reveal exactly where particular types of cells reside within a soil or sediment community.*
PHR V **reˈside in sth** to be caused by sth: *The uniqueness of human beings resides in our biological attributes and in our ability to adapt culturally.* **reˈside in/with sb/sth** (of power or a right) to belong to sb/sth: *Ultimately, the power to take action resides with senior managers and particularly the chief executive.*

resi·dence AWL /ˈrezɪdəns/ *noun* **1** (*also* **resi·dency** /ˈrezɪdənsi/) [U] the legal right to live in a country that is not your own: *She claimed a right of residence in the United Kingdom on the basis that her daughter was in education there.* ◇ *After having been entitled to only temporary residency for more than ten years, they finally received permanent residency in 2002.* **2** [U] the fact of living in a particular place: *The city was the principal place of residence of the governing elite.* ◇ *The new bride took up residence in the house of her husband.* **3** [C] a house, especially a large or impressive one: *The creation of palatial private residences was very much a characteristic of the towns of the Mediterranean in the late Roman period.*

resi·dent[1] AWL /ˈrezɪdənt/ *noun* **1** a person who lives in a particular place: *The police have asked local residents to keep a record of any problems.* ◇ *The patient population includes a mix of urban, suburban and rural residents.* ◇ **~ of sth** *Although he had been a resident of the UK for many years, he had his application for British citizenship turned down.* **2** a bird or MAMMAL that lives in a particular area, especially one that does not MIGRATE: *In some cases, residents help their neighbours defend their territory against intruders.* **3** a person who is staying in a place where they are looked after by other people, such as a care home or a hotel: *More than half of residents in care homes have fees paid by local authorities.* **4** a doctor working in a hospital in the US who is receiving special advanced training: *Formal training is offered to hospital residents and other physicians.* ⊃ *compare* REGISTRAR (1)

resi·dent[2] AWL /ˈrezɪdənt/ *adj.* **1** living or found in a particular place: *Project leaders found it challenging to address the various needs of the resident population.* ◇ *Within each plot of ground, all resident species were identified and recorded.* ◇ **~ in sth** *The appellant was a Lebanese citizen who had been resident in the UK for 15 years.* **2** used to describe a species of bird or MAMMAL that does not MIGRATE: *When passing through the estuary, the migrant birds do not compete with the resident birds, because they feed in different areas.*

resi·den·tial AWL /ˌreziˈdenʃl/ *adj.* [usually before noun] **1** (of an area of a town) suitable for living in; consisting of houses rather than factories or offices: *The outer fringe of the city comprised a series of residential areas.* **2** connected with the place where sb lives, or the places where people live: *Directors were not required to disclose their residential address on these documents.* ◇ *There was a question about whether the water would be suitable for residential use.* **3** requiring a person to live at a particular place; offering living accommodation: *A decision was made in Mr Jones's best interests to move him into residential care.* ◇ *She was placed in a residential home for adolescents.*

re·sid·ual /rɪˈzɪdjuəl; *NAmE* rɪˈzɪdʒuəl/ *adj.* [only before noun] (*formal*) **1** remaining after most of sth has gone: *The ritual is clearly some residual form of tree worship.* **2** (of a physical state or property) remaining when the thing that causes it is removed or not present: *Aftershocks are generally the result of the release of residual stress in areas not ruptured in the main shock.*

resi·due /ˈrezɪdjuː; *NAmE* ˈrezɪduː/ *noun* **1** a small amount of sth that remains at the end of a physical or chemical process: *Hard water leaves an insoluble residue after it has been boiled.* ◇ *From a food policy perspective, pesticide residues on fresh foods are a major concern.* **2 ~ (of sth)** (*figurative*) what is left behind after sth has happened: *Legislation in the UK is usually detailed and tightly drafted, leaving only a residue of power to the executive.* **3 ~ (of sth)** (*law*) the part of the money, property, etc. of a person who has died that remains after all the debts, gifts, etc. have been paid: *The residue of the estate was divided equally among his children.*

re·sign /rɪˈzaɪn/ *verb* [I, T] to officially tell sb that you are leaving your job, an organization, etc: *He lost a vote of confidence in the Bavarian parliament and was forced to resign.* ◇ **~ from sth** *The defendant resigned from his position, but continued to work as an independent contractor.* ◇ **~ as sth** *Amid rising international pressure, Taylor resigned as president.* ◇ **~ sth** *In 1763 Smith resigned his post at Glasgow to become tutor to a young duke.*
PHR V **reˈsign yourself to sth** to accept sth unpleasant that cannot be changed or avoided: *No longer did girls from poor families have to resign themselves to textile mills, dressmaking and domestic service.* ◇ **~ yourself to doing sth** *After secondary school, obeying his father's wishes, he resigned himself to going through medical school.*

res·ig·na·tion /ˌrezɪɡˈneɪʃn/ *noun* **1** [U, C] **~ (as sth)** the act of giving up your job or position; the occasion when you do this: *The crisis forced his resignation as prime minister.* ◇ *Further resignations are expected.* **2** [C] a letter, for example to your employers, to say that you are giving up your job or position: *He left in disgust for Shanghai and from there submitted his resignation.* **3** [U] patient willingness to accept a difficult or unpleasant situation that you cannot change: *They accepted their defeat with resignation.*

re·sili·ence /rɪˈzɪliəns/ (*also less frequent* **re·sili·ency** /rɪˈzɪliənsi/) *noun* [U] **1** the ability of people or things to recover quickly after sth unpleasant, such as shock or an injury: *With confidence comes the resilience to cope with situations that arouse frustration and anger.* ◇ *This article highlights strategies and skills that promote resilience.* **2** the ability of a substance to return to its original shape after it has been bent, stretched or pressed: *Wooden structures have built-in resilience.*

re·sili·ent /rɪˈzɪliənt/ *adj.* **1** able to recover quickly after sth unpleasant such as shock or an injury: *Most children are resilient.* ◇ **~ to sth** *If a community has a strong foundation, it can be very resilient to economic shocks.* **2** (of a substance) returning to its original shape after being bent, stretched or pressed: *Rubber is a highly resilient material.*

re·sist /rɪˈzɪst/ *verb* **1** [T, I] to refuse to accept sth and try to stop it from happening SYN OPPOSE (1): **~ (sth)** *Governments will have to resist pressure, in all forms, from powerful industries and other vested interests.* ◇ *The energy market has been particularly difficult to liberalize because France has resisted so strongly.* ◇ **~ doing sth** *She has resisted going to the doctors for 18 months now.* **2** [T] **~ sth** to not be harmed, damaged or changed by sth: *A deeper beam has more capacity to resist bending than a shallower one.* ◇ *Buffers are special solutions that resist*

R

changes in pH upon the addition of an acid or base. **3** [T, I] (often in negative sentences) to stop yourself from having sth you like or doing sth you very much want to do: **~ (sth)** *They discuss how resisting the temptation to give a diagnostic label might benefit the patient.* ◇ *Most people would not take active steps to receive a bribe, but, if offered one, many would be unable to resist.* ◇ **~ doing sth** *TV journalists could not resist starting to analyse the MPs' performances before the debate had actually ended.* **4** [I, T] to fight back when attacked; to use force to stop sth from happening: *Local officials were taking land from the peasants and persecuting those who resisted.* ◇ **~ sth** *The citizens united and prepared to resist the invasion.*

re·sist·ance /rɪˈzɪstəns/ *noun* **1** [U, sing.] the power not to be affected by sth; the fact of not being affected by sth: *Ceramic materials are very hard and brittle, but have high temperature resistance.* ◇ *Antibiotic resistance makes the treatment of some bacterial infections difficult.* ◇ **~ to sth** *There are a number of alleles of the human beta globin gene that confer some resistance to malaria.* ◇ *Some people have a lower resistance to cold than others.* **2** [U, sing.] dislike of or opposition to a plan or an idea; refusing to accept sth or to obey: **~ to sb/sth** *Resistance to change is minimized if transformation is conducted appropriately.* ◇ **~ from sb/sth** *The UN encountered resistance from the US on the subject of global warming.* **3** [U, sing.] the act of using force to oppose sb/sth: **~ to sb/sth** *The Sadducees did not favour armed resistance to Roman rule.* ◇ **~ from sb/sth** *They met with little resistance from the forces still loyal to James II en route to London.* ◇ **~ against sb/sth** *There were still a few instances of violent resistance against the occupiers.* **4** (*often* **the Resistance**) [sing.+ sing./pl. v.] an organization that resists the authorities, especially in a country that an enemy has control of: *The local communist parties made no attempt to seize power, even though they had a fine record in the Resistance and a stock of arms.* ◇ **+ noun** *The various resistance movements called for overt opposition to the Romans.* **5** [U, C] (*symb.* **R**) (*physics*) the opposition of a substance or device to the flow of an electrical current **HELP** By Ohm's law, **resistance** is equal to the VOLTAGE divided by the CURRENT: **~ (of sth)** *The electrical resistance of several materials varies with temperature.* ◇ **high/low output/input ~** *To avoid the loss of signal strength, voltage amplifiers are required to have a high input resistance.* **6** [U, sing.] a force that stops sth from moving or makes it move more slowly: *Objects with different masses fall at the same rate when air resistance is negligible.* ◇ **~ to sth** *This leads to an increase in resistance to blood flow, resulting in an increased blood pressure.*

▸ NOUN + RESISTANCE **drug • antibiotic • insulin** *There has been increasing concern about the emergence of drug resistance among a broad range of pathogenic microorganisms.*

▸ VERB + RESISTANCE **increase • reduce** *Sales leadership can reduce the resistance of the sales force to expansion.* | **have • confer • lead to • overcome** *We assumed that a mutation conferring resistance to one drug does not confer resistance to any of the other drugs in use.* | **face • encounter • overcome** *The Flavian army attacked the city and overcame Vitellian resistance in fierce street fighting.*

▸ RESISTANCE TO + NOUN **drug • antibiotics • infection • disease • stress • parasites** *These potato plants, after infection by potato blight, seemed to have some acquired resistance to further infection.* | **treatment • change • the idea • policy** *There is a lot of resistance to the idea that language can at all be the object of scientific inquiry.*

re·sist·ant /rɪˈzɪstənt/ *adj.* **1** not affected by sth; able to resist sth: *Overuse of antibiotics makes it easier for resistant strains to colonize a patient.* ◇ **~ to sth** *The vertical walls of the canyon are highly resistant to erosion.* **2 ~ to sth** opposing sth; trying to stop sth from happening: *There is evidence that both women and men are resistant to major change in domestic divisions of labour.* ◇ *Understanding why some people are resistant to pressures to become smokers offers many opportunities for prevention.* **3 -resistant** (in adjectives) not damaged by the thing mentioned: *Kevlar is heat-resistant, five times stronger than steel, and about half as light as fibreglass.* ◇ *The intensive and extensive use of antibiotic agents has resulted in the emergence of highly drug-resistant bacterial pathogens.*

re·sis·tor /rɪˈzɪstə(r)/ *noun* (*physics*) a device that has resistance to an electric current in a CIRCUIT: *A resistor is connected between the positive input terminal and ground.* ◇ *The voltage across a resistor is directly proportional to the current flowing through it.*

reso·lution **AWL** /ˌrezəˈluːʃn/ *noun* **1** [U, sing.] the act of solving or settling a problem or disagreement: *The fight raged without resolution for ten years.* ◇ *Public interest in education for conflict resolution has increased in response to the violence of recent years.* ◇ **~ of sth** *The EU opted for a policy that did not result in a peaceful resolution of the conflict.* ◇ **~ to sth** *Knowing these mechanisms may enable a more speedy resolution to business problems.* **2** [U, C] the ability of a scientific instrument to separate or distinguish small images or images that are very close to each other: *When viewed at high resolution, the spots are found to be clusters of smaller particles.* ◇ *Modern electron microscopes have resolutions that are less than 0.2 nm when used with biological specimens.* **3** [U, sing.] **~ (of sth)** the ability of sth such as a computer screen or PRINTER to give a clear image; the amount of detail that can be seen in an image: *In the 1980s, inkjet printers had maximum resolution of 300 dpi (dots per inch).* ⊃ *see also* HIGH-RESOLUTION **4** [C] **~ (on sth)** a formal statement of an opinion agreed on by an organization, especially by means of a vote: *Since 1999, the Security Council has adopted seven resolutions on children and armed conflict.* ◇ *Public and private companies may reduce the share capital through passing a special resolution that is confirmed by a court.* **5** (*chemistry*) the process of reducing or separating a substance into the parts or substances it is made of: **~ (of sth)** *Gas chromatography allows the resolution of carbohydrates of very similar structure.* ◇ **+ noun** *The high resolution nuclear magnetic spectrum of the compound was used to obtain its exact structure.* **6** [U] the quality of being determined **SYN** RESOLVE[2]: *He handled the last British actions of the war with resolution.*

re·solve[1] **AWL** /rɪˈzɒlv; *NAmE* rɪˈzɑːlv; rɪˈzɔːlv/ *verb* **1** [T] **~ sth** to find an acceptable solution to a disagreement or problem **SYN** SETTLE (1): *They have provided a legal system to resolve disputes and regulate trade.* ◇ *Disagreements between reviewers were resolved by consensus.* ◇ *Students learn ways to resolve conflict constructively.* ◇ *More detailed functional analysis of completely sequenced genomes may offer the key to resolving this issue.* ◇ *The end of the Cold War produced a new mood of optimism that diplomacy could resolve all major international problems.* ◇ *to resolve a dilemma/difficulty* ◇ *How can this apparent contradiction be resolved?* ◇ *to resolve the ambiguities/tensions in sth* ◇ *Differences in interpretation were resolved through discussion.* **2** [T] to make a firm decision to do sth: **~ to do sth** *The Athenians resolved to keep fighting rather than to make peace.* ◇ **~ that...** *Othello resolves that Desdemona must die.* **3** [T] (of an organization) to reach a decision, usually by means of a formal vote: **~ that...** *In 1978, the European Parliament resolved that the three communities should be referred to collectively as 'the European Community'.* ◇ **it is resolved that...** *At a board meeting attended by the defendant, it was resolved that his service contract should be terminated.* ◇ **~ to do sth** *The meeting resolved to invite all London County Council members to join them.* **4** [I, T] (*medical*) if a medical condition resolves or is resolved, it improves or disappears: *These symptoms may resolve spontaneously but recur*

R

without treatment. ◇ *We have lost much of our ability to resolve bacterial infection using antibiotics.*

PHR V **re'solve into sth | re'solve sth into sth** **1** to separate or to be separated into its parts: *The broad peak in the spectrum was resolved into separate lines at specific wavelengths by using a more powerful spectrometer.* **2** (of sth seen or heard at a distance) to gradually be seen in a different form when it is seen or heard more clearly: *At high magnification, some of this material could be resolved into regularly sized, quasi-spherical molecules.*

re·solve[2] AWL /rɪ'zɒlv; *NAmE* rɪ'zɑːlv; rɪ'zɔːlv/ *noun* [U] strong determination to achieve sth SYN RESOLUTION: *The difficulties in their way merely strengthened their resolve.* ◇ **~ to do sth** *The government reiterated its resolve to uncover the truth.*

res·on·ance /'rezənəns/ *noun* **1** [U] (of sound) the quality of being deep and clear and continuing for a long time: *The condition can cause decreased vocal resonance.* **2** [U, C] (*physics*) the VIBRATION of an object caused by an external vibration at the same FREQUENCY as its own natural frequency: *If wind applies a force to the bridge at the same frequency as the natural frequency, then resonance occurs and the vibrations can become very large indeed.* ➲ *see also* MRI **3** [U, C] the power to bring images, feelings or memories into the mind of the person reading or listening: *This line of argument had special resonance in Germany.* ◇ *Lack of power has a particular resonance in children's lives.*

res·on·ant /'rezənənt/ *adj.* **1** having the power to bring images, feelings or memories into your mind: *Clearly, these stories struck a resonant note with many readers.* **2** (*physics*) connected with or causing resonance in a CIRCUIT, atom or other object: *The separate electron clouds about each atom vibrate with different resonant frequencies.*

res·on·ate /'rezəneɪt/ *verb* **1** [I] to remind sb of sth; to be similar to what sb thinks or believes: *Many of the problems the women discuss continue to resonate, including patriarchy, motherhood and childcare.* ◇ **~ with sb/sth** *These word choices were intended to resonate with readers.* ◇ *Their platform resonated strongly with the aims of regional and local governments elsewhere.* **2** [I] (of a voice, an instrument, etc.) to make a deep, clear sound that continues for a long time: *The strings of a guitar resonate when you pluck them.* **3** [I] (*physics*) to come to resonance: *The crystal resonates at 16 MHz.*

R

re·sort[1] /rɪ'zɔːt; *NAmE* rɪ'zɔːrt/ *noun* **1** [C] a place where a lot of people go on holiday: *Acapulco is a seaside resort which has grown rapidly in the last 40 years.* ◇ *a tourist/holiday resort* **2** [U] **~ to sth** the act of using sth, especially sth bad or unpleasant, because nothing else is possible SYN RECOURSE: *There is no cause that justifies resort to violence.* ◇ *Companies can export their surplus without resort to sophisticated pricing policy.*

IDM **a/the last re'sort** the last course of action that you should or can take in a particular situation: *Intervention should only be considered as a last resort.*

re·sort[2] /rɪ'zɔːt; *NAmE* rɪ'zɔːrt/ *verb*

PHR V **re'sort to sth** to make use of sth, especially sth bad, as a means of achieving sth, often because there is no other possible solution: *As abolitionists escalated their campaign, anti-abolitionists increasingly resorted to violence.* ◇ **~ to doing sth** *She held that courts should take into account all the circumstances before resorting to imprisoning offenders.*

re·source AWL /rɪ'sɔːs; rɪ'zɔːs; *NAmE* 'riːsɔːrs; rɪ'sɔːrs/ *noun* **1** [C, usually pl.] a supply of sth that a country, an organization or a person has and can use: *Japan has few natural resources and depends on massive imports of raw materials.* ◇ *Investment in renewable energy resources is crucial in countering climate change.* ◇ **+ noun** *Decisions regarding resource allocation are ultimately taken by headquarters.* ➲ *see also* HUMAN RESOURCES (1) **2** [C] something that can be used to help achieve an aim, especially as a part of work or study: *In addition to printed material, there is an extensive range of online resources covering issues of globalization and social policy.* ◇ **~ for (doing) sth** *These movies can serve as an excellent resource for generating school-based discussions of anger management.* ◇ **~ to do sth** *This article aims to provide a resource to help GPs manage patients with chronic neurological disease.* ◇ **+ noun** *The family resource centre helps to make the school a friendly and welcoming place for parents and the community.* **3 resources** [pl.] personal qualities that help you deal with a situation: *Speakers of languages make use of their own linguistic resources in creating new words.*

▸ ADJECTIVE + RESOURCE **available • scarce, limited • additional • valuable • renewable • natural • financial • material • economic** *Despite their limited financial resources, they demonstrate a remarkable capacity to control their budget.*

▸ VERB + RESOURCE **use • require, need • allocate, devote • mobilize • invest • provide • lack • invest • manage** *Growth requires resources (both raw materials and energy).*

▸ RESOURCE + NOUN **allocation • management • use • availability • depletion • scarcity • base** *Climate change and resource depletion present challenges to the modern ideal of unlimited economic growth.*

re·spect[1] /rɪ'spekt/ *noun* **1** [C] a particular aspect or detail of sth: **in... respect(s)** *Chodorow's theory is open to criticism in some respects.* ◇ *Notwithstanding its strengths, the present study is limited in several important respects.* ◇ **in this ~** *He had failed to accurately inform Parliament of government policy on the issue. In this respect, the minister's failings were serious.* **2** [U, sing.] polite behaviour towards or reasonable treatment of sb/sth: *Patients should be treated with respect whatever their life choices and beliefs.* ◇ **~ for sb/sth** *The new rulers showed little respect for human rights.* ◇ *Fundamental principles include a respect for civil liberties.* ◇ **due ~** *Several countries have undertaken measures to manage and develop fishery resources with due respect for the ecosystem and biodiversity.* **3** [U, sing.] a feeling of admiration for sb/sth because of their good qualities or achievements: *Forming a strong partnership based on mutual respect and trust was essential.* ◇ *Kennedy was the only national leader who commanded respect and enthusiasm.* ◇ **~ for sb/sth** *She had failed as a manager and her team had little respect for her.* ➲ *see also* SELF-RESPECT

IDM **in respect of sth** (*formal*) **1** concerning: *The local authority commenced proceedings in respect of the three surviving children.* **2** in payment for sth: *The producer will incur no liability in respect of damage to the product itself.* **with re'spect** used when you are going to disagree, usually quite strongly, with sb: *Paragraph 151 of the decision is not, with respect, entirely clear.* ◇ *With respect, this seems to be incorrect.* **with respect to sth** concerning: *Several observations can be made with respect to Figure 9.3.* ◇ *The moisture content of the soil is low and varies with respect to the distance from the coast.*

▸ ADJECTIVE + RESPECT **great • deep • equal • mutual** *He enjoyed great respect for his judgement and trustworthiness.*

▸ VERB + RESPECT **have • show • deserve** *Professionals need to show respect for others' opinions, listening and providing feedback when asked.* | **require • demand • pay** *It is interesting that in this paper some respect is paid to the principle of 'one man, one vote, one value'.* | **earn • win, gain • command • lose** *To succeed in Korea, you must cultivate close personal relationships with business associates and earn their respect and trust.*

re·spect² /rɪˈspekt/ *verb* **1 ~ sth** to agree not to break a law or principle: *The decision must respect the principles laid down in Article 14.* ◇ *The Community should respect international law in the exercise of its powers.* **2** to be careful not to do sth that people would consider to be wrong; to treat sb in a way that shows that you think they are important: **~ sth** *Children's privacy, dignity and confidentiality should be respected.* ◇ **~ sb (as sth)** *Each patient must be respected as an individual with unique needs.* **3** [often passive] (not usually used in the progressive tenses) to have a good opinion of sb/sth; to admire sb/sth: **~ sb/sth** *Mondale was bright, he worked hard, and his colleagues respected him.* ◇ **~ sb/sth as sth** *Buddhism is widely respected as one of the world's most ethical religions.* ◇ **~ sb/sth for sth** *Greek heroes were respected for the specific passions they displayed.*

re·spect·abil·ity /rɪˌspektəˈbɪləti/ *noun* [U] **1** the state or quality of being considered socially acceptable: *The Victorian drawing room is the very image of middle-class comfort and respectability.* **2** the state or quality of being accepted as valid or important in a particular area of activity: *Ecological economics is gradually acquiring academic respectability.*

re·spect·able /rɪˈspektəbl/ *adj.* **1** considered by society to be acceptable, good or correct: *Many former members of terrorist groups came from respectable families.* **2** acceptable in number, size or amount: *Allister polled a respectable 17% of the vote.*

re·spect·ful /rɪˈspektfl/ *adj.* showing or feeling respect: *Research shows that these groups respond positively to fair and respectful treatment by police.* ◇ **~ of sb/sth** *Citizens today are more respectful of others' rights.* ◇ **~ towards sb/sth** *The Emperor Tiberius was respectful towards Livia and avoided any public confrontation.* ■ **re·spect·ful·ly** /rɪˈspektfəli/ *adv.*: *Listening respectfully to the other person's point of view is the mark of a civilized debate.*

re·spect·ing /rɪˈspektɪŋ/ *prep.* (*formal*) concerning SYN WITH RESPECT TO STH: *The Court noted the existence of a generally accepted international law respecting the treatment of aliens.*

re·spect·ive /rɪˈspektɪv/ *adj.* [only before noun] belonging or relating separately to each of the people or things mentioned: *Members of the European Parliament are directly elected by voters in their respective countries.*

re·spect·ive·ly /rɪˈspektɪvli/ *adv.* in the same order as the people or things mentioned: *The height, width and thickness of the beam are 70 mm, 120 mm and 5 mm respectively.* ◇ *The book is divided into two parts dealing respectively with old and new media.*

res·pir·ation /ˌrespəˈreɪʃn/ *noun* **1** [U] the act of breathing: *Changes in respiration can be an early indicator of changes in the patient's condition.* HELP In medicine, **respiration** can also be a countable noun: *Vital signs must be recorded, especially pulse, blood pressure, respirations per minute and temperature.* **2** [U] (*biology*) a process in living things that involves the release of energy, typically by taking in OXYGEN and releasing CARBON DIOXIDE: *Carbon recycling occurs through photosynthesis, respiration and decomposition.* ◇ *Like animals, some bacteria can conduct aerobic respiration.* ◇ *All multicellular animal life is dependent on the uptake of oxygen during respiration.* HELP Energy release that does not use OXYGEN is called ANAEROBIC **respiration**: *During fermentation, the absence of oxygen forces yeast to carry out anaerobic respiration.*

re·spira·tory /rəˈspɪrətri; ˈrespərətri; *NAmE* ˈrespərətɔːri/ *adj.* connected with breathing: *Lower respiratory tract infections may be caused by viruses, bacteria, fungi or parasites.*

re·spond AWL /rɪˈspɒnd; *NAmE* rɪˈspɑːnd/ *verb* **1** [I] to do sth as a reaction to sth that sb has said or done SYN REACT (1): **~ (to sth) (with sth)** *Politicians may respond to popular concerns with legislation that poses problems for business.* ◇ *Some polluters respond positively to complaints and protests.* ◇ *China was slow to respond to new economic opportunities.* ◇ **~ (to sth) (by doing sth)** *Farmers responded to greater demand for grain by increasing the amount of land used for grain production.* **2** [I] **~ (to sth)** to improve as a result of a particular kind of treatment: *His depression responded to treatment.* ◇ *Something like half of patients will fail to respond to these drugs.* **3** [I, T] to give a spoken or written answer to sb/sth SYN REPLY¹ (1): *The disadvantage of mobile email is that there are few legitimate excuses for not responding.* ◇ **~ (to sb/sth) (with sth)** *Consumers are promised attractive rewards if they respond to a questionnaire.* ◇ **~ that...** *The president responded that existing legislation was sufficient.*

▸ RESPOND TO + NOUN **change • challenge • problem • issue • call • demand • request • event • environment • conditions** *She wanted the UK to lead the world effort in responding to the challenge of climate change.* | **situation • concerns • need • pressure • threat • crisis • cue • signal • stimulus** *One child may become upset, while another child responds calmly to the same situation.* | **treatment • therapy** *Currently it is not possible to predict who will respond to therapy.* | **question • survey • questionnaire • call • request** *A total of 984 people responded to the survey.*

▸ RESPOND + ADVERB **differently • quickly, rapidly • well • adequately • favourably, positively • negatively** *These infections respond well to antibiotics.* ◇ *Investors are likely to respond favourably to these incentives.* | **similarly • strongly • directly • immediately • effectively • appropriately • accordingly • flexibly • aggressively • correctly** *The government did not respond effectively to the disaster.* ◇ *They demonstrated a strong desire to respond aggressively to the financial crisis.* | **directly • affirmatively, positively • negatively • appropriately** *They responded affirmatively to the question.*

re·spond·ent AWL /rɪˈspɒndənt; *NAmE* rɪˈspɑːndənt/ *noun* **1 ~ (to sth)** a person who answers questions, especially in a survey: *Over 60% of respondents to the online questionnaire regarded digital resources as 'essential' to their research.* **2** (*law*) a person who is accused of sth: *The respondent denied that there was a valid marriage.*

re·sponse AWL /rɪˈspɒns; *NAmE* rɪˈspɑːns/ *noun* **1** [C, U] a reaction to sth that has happened or been said: *Thus far, the response has been insufficient to slow the rise in domestic greenhouse emissions.* ◇ **~ to sb/sth** *Outcomes will depend on the policy responses of governments to expected increases in pollution.* ◇ **in ~ to sb/sth** *High-profile arrests for these offences were increasing, largely in response to sensationalist news reports.* **2** [C, U] a physical reaction to a particular situation or STIMULUS: **~ to sth** *This may help explain individual variation in the brain's response to psychological stress.* ◇ **in ~ to sth** *The increase in heart rate seen in young people in response to exercise may not be evident in older people.* ⊃ *see also* IMMUNE RESPONSE **3** [C, U] a spoken or written answer: *There were 1 568 usable survey responses.* ◇ **~ to sb/sth** *He offers the following cautious response to a query about women's issues in Tunisian cinema:...* ◇ **in ~ to sb/sth** *She received 42 letters in response to this advertisement.* ◇ **+ noun** *The response rate to the questionnaires dropped over time.*

▸ ADJECTIVE + RESPONSE **good • positive • negative • possible • initial** *If there is a good response, the medication may be withdrawn temporarily.* | **rapid • strong • direct • emotional** *Ensuring a rapid response to customer demands is critical.* | **appropriate** *The teacher poses a question and gives students a few minutes to think about an appropriate response.* | **behavioural • physiological • inflammatory • adaptive • cellular** *This*

R

triggers additional physiological and behavioural responses that are not seen at lower hormonal levels (Wingfield and Ramenofsky, 1999).

▸ VERB + RESPONSE **produce, generate • elicit, evoke • obtain • influence, affect, shape • determine • predict • compare • record** *The same signal can be used to elicit different responses in different cells.* | **show, exhibit • trigger • induce • provoke** *Entering online environments and recording the conversation for research purposes can provoke hostile responses from users.* | **give, provide • receive** *More than 150 workers gave incomplete responses or refused to participate in the study.* | **stimulate • inhibit • monitor** *These vaccines stimulate an immune response.*

▸ RESPONSE TO + NOUN **change • event • situation • conditions • environment • pressure** *The molecules can change their shape in response to a change in their environment.* | **problem • crisis • challenge • threat • issue • concern • need • demand • request** *Decisions were made in response to the requests of church leaders.* | **treatment • stimulus • stimulation • stress • infection • signal • cue** *Just 1.2% had no response to treatment.* | **question • request** *These data are based on parents' responses to questions about their children.*

re·spon·si·bil·ity /rɪˌspɒnsəˈbɪləti; *NAmE* rɪˌspɑːnsəˈbɪləti/ *noun* (*pl.* **-ies**) **1** [U, C] a duty to deal with or take care of sb/sth, so that you may be blamed if sth goes wrong: **~ for sth** *The questionnaire was sent to managers with responsibility for health and safety.* ◇ **~ for doing sth** *Responsibility for protecting the environment rests with us all.* ◇ **~ to do sth** *It is the nurse's responsibility to ensure that patients have reading glasses and hearing aids, if used.* **2** [U] **~ (for sth)** blame for sth bad that has happened: *Austria has to bear some responsibility for the outbreak of the war.* **3** [C, U] a moral duty to behave well with regard to sb/sth: **~ to/towards sb** *Britain has finally come to recognize its responsibilities towards developing countries.* ◇ **~ to do sth** *When people realize that something is morally wrong with their society, they have some responsibility to do something about it.*

IDM **on your own responsibility** without official permission and being willing to take the blame if sth goes wrong: *He argued that the police should decide on their own responsibility what action to take in a particular situation.*

▸ ADJECTIVE + RESPONSIBILITY **personal • individual • collective • shared • corporate** *Board members are to take collective responsibility for the annual report and accounts.* | **great • primary • sole** *William Henry Ireland claimed sole responsibility for the forgeries.* | **main • overall • new • parental • ministerial • professional • financial** *The main responsibility for maintaining international peace and security lies with the UN Security Council.* | **moral • ethical • social • legal • professional** *All these religions place a strong emphasis on moral responsibility and accountability.*

▸ VERB + RESPONSIBILITY **take • assume • accept • bear • retain • share • assign • attribute • place • avoid** *It was held that he did not share responsibility for the bank's heavy losses.* | **have • fulfil • meet • discharge** *The company aims to fulfil its responsibilities to the societies and communities in which it operates.* | **take on, take over • acquire • give • shift • transfer • exercise • carry out • hold • carry • delegate • abdicate** *The new system was intended to give greater responsibility and greater independence to managers.*

re·spon·sible /rɪˈspɒnsəbl; *NAmE* rɪˈspɑːnsəbl/ *adj.* **1** [not before noun] having the job or duty of doing sth or taking care of sb/sth, so that you may be blamed if sth goes wrong: **~ for sb/sth** *The local authority in which the child resides is responsible for the child.* ◇ *The directors are responsible for the management of the company's business.* ◇ **~ for doing sth** *The coastguard were responsible for coordinating the rescue.* **2** [not before noun] that can be blamed for sth: **~ for sth** *Normally, all the persons responsible for the damage will be sued.* ◇ **find/hold sb ~ (for sth)** *Each commander was found responsible for the crimes committed by members of his unit.* **3** [not before noun] **~ (for sth)** being the cause of sth: *Freud was mainly responsible for the development of this theory.* ◇ *Tobacco is currently responsible for the death of one adult in ten worldwide.* **4 ~ to sb/sth** having to report to sb/sth with authority or in a higher position and explain to them what you have done: *A revised constitution made ministers responsible to the King, not to Parliament.* **5** (of people, actions or behaviour) that can be trusted and relied on: *Teenagers are encouraged to involve parents or another responsible adult in these decisions.* ◇ *It is the duty of good citizens to act in a morally responsible way.* ◇ *Socially responsible companies pay heed to the environmental consequences of their activities.* OPP IRRESPONSIBLE ➲ *compare* CONSCIENTIOUS (1) **6** [usually before noun] (of a job or position) needing sb who can be trusted and relied on; involving important duties: *Both men and women held responsible positions in the early church.*

re·spon·sibly /rɪˈspɒnsəbli; *NAmE* rɪˈspɑːnsəbli/ *adv.* in a sensible way that shows you can be trusted: *Many companies are trying to show that they are acting responsibly by minimizing their impact on the environment.* OPP IRRESPONSIBLY

re·spon·sive AWL /rɪˈspɒnsɪv; *NAmE* rɪˈspɑːnsɪv/ *adj.* **1** [not usually before noun] **~ (to sb/sth)** reacting quickly and in a positive way: *These companies are less adaptable and responsive to the customer.* ◇ *They have sought to make health services more responsive to the needs of the population.* OPP UNRESPONSIVE **2** reacting with interest or enthusiasm SYN RECEPTIVE (1): *The patient apparently remains alert and responsive.* ◇ **~ to sth** *Guinea pigs injected with the drug became lethargic and less responsive to external stimuli.* OPP UNRESPONSIVE ■ **re·spon·sive·ness** AWL *noun* [U] **~ (to sb/sth)** *Educational leaders must demonstrate responsiveness to the needs of society.* ◇ *Students demonstrated a lack of responsiveness to the topics proposed for discussion.*

rest¹ /rest/ *noun* **1** [sing.] **the ~ (of sth)** the remaining part of sth: *He spent the rest of his life in a town on the Black Sea.* ◇ *Most of the rest of the world lagged behind economically.* ◇ *Part of the money placed in a bank is kept to meet requests for withdrawals and the rest is lent out.* **2** [pl.] **the ~ (of sth)** the remaining people or things; the others: *A third of those machines were driven by steam and the rest were horse-powered.* ◇ *He was met there by an aunt, and the rest of his family joined him a few months later.* **3** [U, C] a period of relaxing, sleeping or doing nothing after a period of activity: *Treatment is likely to involve bed rest.* ◇ **~ from sth** *There is no rest from the continual noise of the crowded streets.* ◇ **have/take a ~ (from sth)** *He encouraged her to have a rest.* ◇ **+ noun** *Many industries worked non-stop and individual workers had different rest days.* **4** [C] (often in compounds) an object that is used to support or hold sth: *The subject's head posture was maintained with a chin rest.*

IDM **at ˈrest** not moving: *According to Newton, bodies acted upon by no forces remain at rest.* **come to ˈrest** to stop moving: *Most of the lava flows come to rest at the bottom of the slope.* **for the ˈrest** (*BrE*) apart from that; as far as other matters are concerned: *He had no principles beyond a hatred of all things foreign, and for the rest was willing to encourage the queen in her personal extravagance.* **lay/put sth to ˈrest** to stop sth by showing it is not true: *Dickens laid these rumours to rest in a letter of May 1870.*

rest² /rest/ *verb* **1** [I] to relax, sleep or do nothing after a period of activity or illness: *The Buddha sat under a tree to rest.* **2** [T] **~ sth** to not use a part of your body for some time: *It is advisable to rest the ankle if the sprain is serious.*

R

3 [I, T] **~ (sth) + adv./prep.** to support sth by putting it on or against sth; to be supported in this way: *One hand rests on a globe that is turned to display the continent of Africa.* **4** [I] (of a problem or subject) to be left without further investigation or discussion: *The matter could no longer rest.*

PHR V **ˈrest on/upon sb/sth** to depend or rely on sb/sth: *The party's electoral success rested on its ability to extend its support to a large minority of the working class.* **ˈrest on sth** to be based on sth: *They maintained that traditional forms of theology rested on irrational and unscientific assumptions.* **ˈrest with sb** to be the responsibility of sb: *The burden of proof in a criminal trial rests with the prosecution.* ◇ **it rests with sb to do sth** *It will ultimately rest with Parliament to address the central flaws of the Act.*

re·state /ˌriːˈsteɪt/ *verb* **~ sth** to state sth again or in a different way, especially so that it is more clearly or strongly expressed: *The Companies Act 2006 essentially restates the law in this respect.* ■ **re·state·ment** *noun* [C, U] **~ (of sth)** *An evaluation of Gayer's case may be aided by a brief restatement of his argument.* ◇ *Certain points may be in need of restatement.*

res·taur·ant /ˈrestrɒnt; *NAmE* ˈrestrɑːnt; ˈrestərɑːnt/ *noun* a place where you can buy and eat a meal: *Fast-food restaurants have been associated with the development of many strong international brands.*

res·tor·ation AWL /ˌrestəˈreɪʃn/ *noun* **1** [U, C] **~ of sth** the act of bringing back a system, a law, etc. that existed previously: *James Rothschild arrived in Paris in 1811 and helped finance the restoration of the monarchy.* ◇ *Devout Anglicans prayed for a restoration of the old order in Church and State.* HELP In British history, **the Restoration** was the time after 1660 when, following a period with no king or queen, Charles II became king: *Most of the verse written by Marvell after the Restoration was of a political or satirical character.* **2** [U] **~ (of sth) (to sb/sth)** the act of returning sth to its correct place, condition or owner: *They founded a Central National Committee which planned for the restoration of land to the peasants.* **3** [U, C] the work of repairing and cleaning an old building, a painting, etc. so that its condition is as good as it originally was: *Sources of building stone are seldom recorded, but they are important to those concerned with restoration.* ◇ **~ of sth** *In addition to his restorations of ancient sculptures, Pierantoni also made several new works.*

re·stora·tive /rɪˈstɔːrətɪv/ *adj.* **1** making you feel strong and healthy again: *The restorative effects of physical environments have been studied by various researchers.* **2** connected with treatment that repairs the body or a part of it: *Dental care includes preventive and restorative treatment as necessary.* **3** used to describe a system of justice or discipline in which criminals or OFFENDERS are expected to do things to COMPENSATE for the harm they have done, rather than simply being punished: *Referral orders reflect the principles of restorative justice, whereby the young offender is encouraged to understand the impact of their crime and make restoration to the victim, through apology or community service.*

re·store AWL /rɪˈstɔː(r)/ *verb* **1** to bring back a situation or feeling that existed before: **~ sth** *He ordered fresh troops to go to the capital to restore order.* ◇ *The recommendations set out to restore public confidence in the profession.* ◇ **~ sth to sb/sth** *Surgery may be necessary for restoring function to the limb.* **2 ~ sb/sth to sth** to bring sb/sth back to a former condition, place or position: *The young Greek hero Hippolytus was restored to life by the goddess Diana.* ◇ *International support enabled the exiled government to be restored to power.* **3 ~ sth** to repair a building, work of art, piece of furniture, etc. so that it looks as good as it did originally: *In 1927, it was decided to restore the building at a cost of more than a million pounds.* **4 ~ sth** to bring a law, tradition, way of working, etc. back into use: *Kerensky had agreed to restore the death penalty for soldiers at the front.* **5 ~ sth (to sb/sth)** to give sth that was lost or stolen back to sb: *These treasures needed to be recovered and restored to their legitimate owners.*

re·strain AWL /rɪˈstreɪn/ *verb* **1 ~ sth** to stop sth that is growing or increasing from becoming too large SYN BRING/GET/KEEP STH UNDER CONTROL: *The Japanese government had cooperated with industry to restrain foreign competition.* **2** to stop sb/sth from doing sth, especially by using physical force: **~ sb/sth** *The police officer had taken hold of his arm in order to restrain him.* ◇ **~ sb/sth from (doing) sth** *They agreed that if Turkey won the war, it should be restrained from taking vengeful action.* **3** to stop yourself from feeling an emotion or doing sth that you would like to do: **~ sth** *Brewster could hardly restrain his enthusiasm.* ◇ **~ yourself (from doing sth)** *They were unable to restrain themselves from expressing loud disapproval.*

re·straint AWL /rɪˈstreɪnt/ *noun* **1** [C, usually pl.] **~ (on sb/sth)** a rule, fact, idea, etc. that limits or controls what people can do: *The following year, new restraints were placed on workers.* ◇ *They failed in their attempts to put effective legal restraints on royal powers.* ➲ thesaurus note *at* LIMIT² **2** [U] the act of controlling or limiting sth, especially because it is necessary or sensible to do so: *The government may introduce wage restraint in the public sector.* ◇ **~ of sth** *The Supreme Court found the company guilty of illegal restraint of trade.* ➲ thesaurus note *at* LIMIT² **3** [U] the quality of behaving calmly and with control SYN SELF-CONTROL: *The Swedish unions were willing to exercise restraint up to a point.* ◇ **with ~** *He acted with characteristic restraint.* **4** [U] **~ (of sb)** the use of physical force to control sb who is behaving in a violent way: *Restraint of violent or aggressive prisoners was permitted.* **5** [C] a device that limits or prevents sb's freedom of movement: *The study found that few children were using car safety restraints appropriate for their age group.*

re·strict AWL /rɪˈstrɪkt/ *verb* **1** to limit or control the size, amount or range of sth: **~ sth** *Severe climate restricted crop yields.* ◇ *It is not difficult to restrict access to sections of the website for particular users.* ◇ **~ sb/sth to (doing) sth** *Before the 1970s, the activities of multinational organizations tended to be restricted to such things as car production.* **2** to limit sth to a particular time, place or group: **~ sth** *Attendance at the meetings was tightly restricted.* ◇ **~ sth to sb/sth** *Membership of the craft union was restricted to workers in the same craft or occupation.* **3 ~ sb (from sth/from doing sth)** to not allow sb to do sth or to go somewhere: *Other cheese companies were restricted from using the name 'Cheddar'.* **4 ~ yourself/sb/sth (to sth/to doing sth)** to allow yourself or sb to have, do or consider only a limited amount of sth or to do only a particular kind of activity: *In this short paper, I will restrict myself to an outline evaluation of the system as a whole.* ◇ *By restricting the analysis to currently employed older adults, our sample does not include information on workers who have already left the labour force.* **5 ~ sth/sb** to stop sth/sb from moving freely SYN IMPEDE: *Pain and disability can severely restrict movement and the ability to perform activities of daily living.*

▸ RESTRICT + NOUN **use • scope • entry • membership** *In the 1850s, thirteen states adopted laws restricting the use and local sale of alcohol.* | **movement • flow • growth • development** *The water flow was so restricted by the arches that dangerous 'rapids' formed under the bridge.* | **number • access • activity • competition • choice • right • freedom • ability • imports • immigration** *Both countries controlled wage rates and severely restricted workers' rights to unionize and strike.* | **analysis • attention • sample • discussion** *The discussion will be restricted to*

R

four aspects of the patterns that emerged from the experiment.

re·stricted AWL /rɪˈstrɪktɪd/ *adj.* [usually before noun] **1** limited or controlled in size, amount or range: *Many minerals are made from the same restricted range of compositions but under different conditions.* ◇ *Birds with restricted access to drinking water renewed body tissue very slowly.* ◇ **~ to sb/sth** *Some infections are still mainly restricted to animals.* OPP UNRESTRICTED **2** controlled by rules or laws: *Freedom of expression and religion were severely restricted.* ◇ *Mini-radar systems were used by the police for monitoring vehicle speeds in restricted areas of the road system.* OPP UNRESTRICTED **3** only open or available to a small number of people or those with special permission: *A number of states became increasingly unhappy about the restricted membership of the Security Council.* OPP UNRESTRICTED **4** physically prevented from moving freely: *The development of basins with restricted water circulation extended over vast areas.* OPP UNRESTRICTED

re·stric·tion AWL /rɪˈstrɪkʃn/ *noun* **1** [C] a rule or law that limits what you can do or what can happen: *Producers may try to convince government officials of the need to impose trade restrictions.* ◇ **~ on sth** *Communist regimes typically placed heavy restrictions on migration.* ◇ *By the late 1990s, the government had relaxed restrictions on foreign ownership.* ◇ *to lift/remove restrictions on sth* ➲ thesaurus note *at* LIMIT² **2** [U] the act of limiting or controlling sb/sth: *Severe calorie restriction in certain stages of pregnancy was associated with reduced birth weight.*

re·strict·ive AWL /rɪˈstrɪktɪv/ *adj.* limiting sth; preventing people from doing what they want: *Most developed countries have implemented restrictive immigration policies.* ◇ *The patient was advised to avoid restrictive clothing.*

re·struc·ture AWL /ˌriːˈstrʌktʃə(r)/ *verb* **1** [T, I] **~ (sth)** to organize sth such as a system or company in a new and different way: *Spain had achieved some success in restructuring its economy.* ◇ *Their competitors were restructuring more rapidly.* **2** [T] **~ sth** (*finance*) to change the debt of a business in difficulty into another kind of debt: *Greece faced the immediate prospect of having to restructure its debt.* ■ **re·struc·tur·ing** AWL *noun* [U, C, usually sing.] **~ (of sth)** *These reforms triggered a massive restructuring of US industry.* ◇ *The findings have implications for the likely restructuring of the country's debt.*

R

re·sult¹ /rɪˈzʌlt/ *noun* **1** [C] a thing that is caused or produced because of sth else: *The new techniques produced similar results when compared with the traditional ones.* ◇ **~ of sth** *Cities were formed as a direct result of the need to trade and procure other resources.* ◇ **as a ~ (of sth)** *Trade was greatly disrupted as a result of Napoleon's Continental Blockade.* ◇ **with the ~ that...** *During the Industrial Revolution, there was a decline in infant mortality, with the result that populations became more youthful.* ➲ *see also* END RESULT ➲ language bank *at* BECAUSE, CAUSE¹ **2** [C] **~ (of sth)** the information that you get from a piece of research or from a scientific or medical test: *The experimental results are then compared with theoretical predictions.* ◇ *These results suggest that migration was a primary driver of rural growth in the 1990s.* ◇ *The results presented in this article are also fully reproducible.* **3 results** [pl.] (*business*) the financial profit or loss that a business has made during a particular period: *The company achieved good financial results in 2005 despite a challenging market environment.* **4 results** [pl.] things that are achieved successfully: *Griffin (1991) reports on a job enrichment exercise in a bank which took two to four years to show results.* **5** [C, usually pl.] (*BrE*) the grade you get in an exam or in a number of exams: *The table shows the national education targets set and the results achieved on a year by year basis since 1997.* **6** [C] **~ (of sth)** the winner in an election; the final score in a sports event, competition, etc: *The consequences of election results for business appear to be much greater in recent decades.*

▸ ADJECTIVE + RESULT **overall** • **significant** • **important** • **positive** • **mixed** *The study did not yield any statistically significant results.* | **direct** • **net** *The net result of these changes was a sharp decrease in oil production.* | **experimental** • **empirical** • **negative** *A pregnancy test may give a false negative result if performed too early in the pregnancy.*

▸ NOUN + RESULT **test** • **research** • **survey** *This paper discusses research results from anthropological fieldwork carried out in Malta.*

▸ RESULT + BE + ADJECTIVE **consistent** • **inconsistent** • **conflicting** • **generalizable** • **reproducible** • **representative** • **true** • **valid** • **robust** • **surprising** • **disappointing** • **encouraging** *The sample was exclusively male and so the results may not be generalizable to women.*

▸ VERB + RESULT **obtain** • **find** • **produce, give, yield** • **provide** • **achieve** • **present** • **report** • **summarize** • **interpret** • **publish** • **confirm** • **affect** • **influence** *The results obtained here provide relevant information for future actions.*

▸ RESULT + VERB **show** • **suggest, indicate** • **demonstrate** • **illustrate** • **reflect** • **highlight** • **reveal** • **confirm** • **support** • **imply** • **generalize to** *The present results may not generalize to more severely injured children.*

THESAURUS

result • **outcome** • **finding** • **consequence** *noun*

These words can all refer to things that happen because of sth else.

- the result/outcome/consequence **of** sth
- the results/outcomes/findings/consequences **for** sb/sth
- findings **from** sth
- **as a** result/consequence
- **with the** result/consequence that...
- **with...** consequences
- **experimental/empirical** results/findings
- **test** results
- to **be consistent with/in line with** the results/findings
- to **report/present** the results/outcomes/findings
- to **publish/interpret** the results/findings
- the results/findings **confirm/indicate/show/suggest** that...

- **Results**, **outcomes** and **consequences** are things that happen because of sth else; **outcomes** can be things that happen at the end of a series of events: *In the Andalucian region of Spain, an estimated 80 million tonnes of topsoil are lost annually as a result of intensive olive production.* ◇ *The ambition was to improve the outcomes for all children.*
- **Consequences** is used most frequently to talk about possible negative results of an action: *Global warming could have serious consequences for public health, agriculture and the area of habitable land.* ◇ *to have negative/adverse/disastrous/severe/dire/unfortunate consequences*
- You can use the words **results**, **outcomes** and **findings** to refer to things that are observed in an experiment or a study; **results** or **findings** are most likely to be used when the data involve quantities: *These results are presented in Table 8.8.* ◇ *The outcomes presented here highlight the contextual role of social and political factors.* ◇ *This is in line with the findings from the A.C. Nielsen/NetRatings (1999) study.*

re·sult² /rɪˈzʌlt/ *verb* [I] to happen because of sth else that happened first: *Agriculture and logging expanded rapidly in the area and great environmental damage resulted.* ◇

Trained researchers conducted interviews and analysed some of the resulting data. ◇ **~ from sth** *A high total workload is likely to result from the combination of full-time work and long housework hours.*
PHR V **re'sult in sth** to make sth happen SYN LEAD TO STH: *Weather problems resulted in the closure of the airport.* ◇ *The government was convinced that the creation of the new pipeline would ultimately result in huge economic savings.* ◇ **~ in (sb/sth) doing sth** *These policies resulted in many elderly people suffering hardship.* ➲ language bank *at* CAUSE¹

re·sult·ant /rɪ'zʌltənt/ *adj.* [only before noun] caused by the thing that has just been mentioned: *The board is reporting on the implementation of current policies and the resultant changes and benefits.* ◇ *The computer system was effectively unusable for several days, with resultant losses to the firm estimated at some $36 000.*

re·sume /rɪ'zjuːm; *NAmE* rɪ'zuːm/ *verb* (*formal*) [I, T] (of an activity) to begin again after an interruption; to begin an activity again after an interruption: *Although vaccination resumed in 2004, the halt in the programme caused a polio outbreak that spread to at least five other countries.* ◇ **~ sth** *Following surgery, patients should expect that it will take at least 6 weeks until they are able to resume normal activities, such as driving.* ◇ **~ doing sth** *Drugs to aid smoking cessation should not be prescribed again within 6 months if the patient resumes smoking.*

re·tail /'riːteɪl/ *noun* [U] the selling of goods to the public, usually through shops: *Women are concentrated in service sector jobs or in jobs in retail, personal services and tourism.* ◇ **+ noun** *There has been considerable consolidation within the retail market for electrical goods.* ➲ *compare* WHOLESALE (1)

re·tail·er /'riːteɪlə(r)/ *noun* a person or business that sells goods to the public: *Faced with tough conditions, many retailers slashed their prices before Christmas.* ◇ **~ of sth** *The Swedish-based company is the world's largest retailer of home furnishing products.*

re·tail·ing /'riːteɪlɪŋ/ *noun* [U] the business of selling goods to the public, usually through shops: *The increase in employment in retailing and leisure is small.*

re·tain AWL /rɪ'teɪn/ *verb* **1 ~ sb/sth** to keep sb/sth; to continue to have sth and not lose it or get rid of it: *Smaller or weaker countries often try to retain control over their domestic industry.* ◇ *Loyalty programmes have also helped the company to retain its customers.* ◇ *Both copies of the gene will be retained in the genome as they both fulfil useful functions.* ➲ *see also* RETENTION (1) **2 ~ sth** to take in a substance and keep holding it: *Trees in a rainforest moderate the local water cycle by retaining water in the soil.* ➲ *see also* RETENTION (2) **3 ~ sth** to remember or continue to hold sth: *Studies of implicit memory show that people retain more information than they are aware of remembering.* ◇ *This information is no longer retained within the computer's main memory.* ➲ *see also* RETENTION (3) **4 ~ sb/sth** (*law*) to employ a professional person such as a lawyer or doctor; to make regular payments to such a person in order to keep their services: *For asylum seekers, the short time to present an asylum appeal may prevent them from finding and retaining a lawyer before the filing deadline.* ◇ *Many of these patients retained the services of an attorney in order to ensure the maintenance of insurance benefits.*

re·ten·tion AWL /rɪ'tenʃn/ *noun* [U] **1** the act of keeping sb/sth rather than losing or getting rid of them/it: **~ (of sb/sth)** *The proposal advocated the retention of the present system.* ◇ **+ noun** *Companies with poor customer retention rates will end up spending more on customer acquisition.* ➲ *see also* RETAIN (1) **2** the act of keeping sth, such as liquid or heat, inside sth rather than letting it escape: *Fluid retention in the lungs causes difficulty in breathing and shortness of breath.* ➲ *see also* RETAIN (2) **3** the ability to remember information: *Vocabulary retention is conditional upon the amount of involvement while processing these words.* ◇ **~ of sth** *It is helpful to break down the information into smaller parts to maximize retention of information.* ➲ *see also* RETAIN (3)

re·think /ˌriː'θɪŋk/ *verb* (**re·thought, re·thought** /ˌriː'θɔːt/) [T, I] **~ (sth)** to think again about an idea, a course of action, etc, especially in order to change it: *The teacher observed the students exchanging, defending and rethinking ideas.* ■ **re·think·ing** /'riːθɪŋkɪŋ/ (*also* **re·think** /'riːθɪŋk/) *noun* [sing.] **~ (of/about sth)** *Globalization has caused a serious rethinking of both political and economic geographies.*

ret·ina /'retɪnə; *NAmE* 'retənə/ *noun* (*pl.* **ret·inas** or **ret·inae** /'retɪniː; *NAmE* 'retəniː/) a layer of TISSUE at the back of the eye that is sensitive to light and sends signals to the brain about what is seen: *The protein prevents the formation of tumours in the retina in humans.* ■ **ret·inal** /'retɪnl; *NAmE* 'retənl/ *adj.*: *All patients with a suspected retinal detachment need to be referred immediately to an ophthalmologist.*

re·tire /rɪ'taɪə(r)/ *verb* [I] to stop doing your job, especially because you have reached a particular age: *Those who have retired early are more likely to be financially secure.* ◇ **~ from sth** *He had recently retired from government service.*

re·tired /rɪ'taɪəd; *NAmE* rɪ'taɪərd/ *adj.* having retired from work: *72% of those interviewed were retired.* ◇ *a recently retired high-school teacher*

re·tire·ment /rɪ'taɪəmənt; *NAmE* rɪ'taɪərmənt/ *noun* **1** [U, C] the fact of stopping work because you have reached a particular age; the time when you do this: *She was forced to take early retirement.* ◇ *Those men approaching retirement were more open to self-management.* ◇ **~ of sb** *The company announced the retirements of several senior personnel.* ◇ **+ noun** *There are plans to increase the retirement age.* **2** [U] the period of your life after you have stopped work at a particular age: *People save for their retirement by paying into a pension fund.* ◇ **in ~** *He continued his writing and research in retirement.* **3** [U] **~ from sth** the act of stopping a particular type of work, especially in sport or politics, etc: *Both times Jordan announced his retirement from professional basketball, Nike's stock price fell.*

re·treat¹ /rɪ'triːt/ *verb* **1** [I] to move away from a place or an enemy because you are in danger or because you have been defeated: *The Roman army could not contain the revolts and began to retreat.* ◇ **+ adv./prep.** *They then retreated north-west with their forces intact.* OPP ADVANCE² (1) **2** [I] to move away or back: *In the Himalayas, most glaciers are retreating.* ◇ **+ adv./prep.** *Colder temperatures may cause red squirrels to retreat downhill into marginally warmer altitudes.* OPP ADVANCE² (1) ➲ *compare* RECEDE (1) **3** [I] **+ adv./prep.** to change your mind or plans because of criticism or because a situation has become too difficult SYN BACK OFF (FROM STH): *Kennedy accused the Eisenhower administration of retreating from the principles of independence and anti-colonialism.* **4** [I] **(+ adv./prep.)** to escape to a place that is quieter or safer: *He retreated to the monastery he founded on his south Italian estate.*

re·treat² /rɪ'triːt/ *noun* **1** [C, usually sing., U] a movement away from a place or an enemy because of danger or defeat: **~ (from...) (to...)** *The Russian winter devastated Napoleon's army on the retreat from Moscow.* ◇ **in ~** *The Russian armies were in retreat on both the northern and south-western fronts.* **2** [C, usually sing., U] a movement away or back: **~ (of sth) (from/to sth)** *The retreat of the ocean from the shore revealed a reef off the northern point of the island.* ◇ *Global warming is causing a general retreat*

R

of the jet stream to a more northerly location. ◇ **in ~** *The Scandinavian ice sheet had been in retreat until about 12 000 years ago.* **3** [C, usually sing.] **~ (from sth)** an act of changing a decision because of criticism or because a situation has become too difficult: *This ruling by the European Court is a clear retreat from its earlier decision.* **4** [U, C, usually sing.] **~ (from sth) (into sth)** an act of trying to escape from a particular situation to one that you think is safer or more pleasant: *The hero is depicted as seeking small consolations in retreat from existential despair.* ◇ *Pennybacker also offers evidence to explain the retreat into racially reactionary politics in the immediate post-war period.* ➲ *compare* ESCAPE² (2) **5** [U, C] a period of time when sb stops their usual activities and goes to a quiet place for prayer and thought; an organized event when people can do this: *After a few months of meditation in retreat, he re-emerged from the monastery.* **6** [C] a quiet, private place that you go to in order to get away from your usual life: *Macaulay's English holidays were spent in cathedral towns or rural retreats.*

re·trieval /rɪˈtriːvl/ *noun* [U] **1** (*computing*) the process of finding information that is stored on a computer; the process of finding information in your memory: *The Internet has brought changes which have revolutionized information storage and retrieval.* ◇ **~ (of sth) (from sth)** *The test assesses recall and retrieval from long-term memory.* ➲ *compare* RECALL² (1) **2 ~ (of sth)** the process of getting sth back, especially sth that is lost or difficult to find SYN RECOVERY (3): *One aspect of women's history is dedicated to the retrieval of the lost or untold stories of women in specific social and cultural contexts.*

re·trieve /rɪˈtriːv/ *verb* **1 ~ sth (from sth)** (*computing*) to find information that is stored on a computer; to find information in your memory: *First, all the references retrieved from the databases were examined and titles were read.* ◇ *The more times words are retrieved from memory, the more likely they are to be learned.* **2 ~ sth (from sb/sth)** to bring or get sth back, especially sth that is lost or difficult to find SYN RECOVER (5): *It has now proved possible to retrieve carbon dioxide from bubbles in layers of ice of known age.* **3 ~ sth** to make a bad situation better: *A defeat in 190 BC was retrieved by a victory in the following year.* ■ **re·triev·able** /rɪˈtriːvəbl/ *adj.*: *Information about the child and its family was retrievable from the original school health records.*

R

retro·spect /ˈretrəspekt/ *noun*

IDM **in retrospect** thinking about a past event or situation, often with a different opinion of it from the one you had at the time: *In retrospect, this was a mistake.* ◇ *We may see this film differently in retrospect.*

retro·spect·ive /ˌretrəˈspektɪv/ *adj.* **1** thinking about or connected with sth that happened in the past: *The story is really a retrospective account.* ◇ *Individuals often provide themselves with retrospective justification for violent acts.* **2** (of a new law or decision) intended to take effect from a particular date in the past rather than from the present date: *There were complaints because of the retrospective way in which the tax was applied.* ◇ *Despite the fact that retrospective legislation is said to be contrary to the rule of law, arguably it is quite commonplace.* **3** examining the development of a disease or situation after it has happened, rather than as it happens: *In the retrospective study, patients who had been diagnosed 1–5 years previously were approached to participate.* OPP PROSPECTIVE (3) ■ **retro·spect·ive·ly** *adv.*: *His education, he realized retrospectively, added up to an extensive knowledge of geography and the environment.* ◇ *Legislation should not be introduced retrospectively.*

re·turn¹ /rɪˈtɜːn; *NAmE* rɪˈtɜːrn/ *verb* **1** [I] **~ (to...) (from...)** to come or go back from one place to another: *In 1586, Drake returned from his first voyage as a naval commander.* ◇ *Orwell served in Burma and returned to England after five years.* ◇ *9 per cent of skilled migrants report planning to return home.* **2** [T] to bring, give, put or send sth/sb back to a particular person or place: **~ sth** *In total, 78% of the questionnaires were returned.* ◇ **~ sb/sth to sb/sth** *Doctors try to return patients back to work as soon as possible.* **3** [I] to come back again SYN REAPPEAR: *Symptoms return soon after the drug is withdrawn.* **4** [I] **~ (to sth)** to start discussing a subject you were discussing earlier, or doing an activity you were doing earlier: *To return to the key question identified in the introduction...* ◇ *These issues will be returned to in the next three chapters.* **5** [I, T] to go back, or to make sth go back, to a previous state: **~ to sth** *Oil prices then rose again, returning to a $70 to $80 range by autumn 2009.* ◇ *The law states that women should be entitled to return to work after paid maternity leave.* ◇ **~ sth to sth** *There was a clear need to return the Colorado River to its free-flowing state.* **6** [T] **~ sth** to do sth or give sth to sb because they have done or given the same to you first: *About 10% of people contacted did not return calls.* ◇ *Children have to learn the social norm in which an individual returns the favour of help from another.* **7** [T] **~ sth** to give or produce sth such as a response, a result, a particular amount of money, etc: *A web search for articles with 2 medical subject headings returned over 5 000 results.* ◇ *A start-up business requires time, energy and investment to grow before returning profits.* **8** [T, often passive] **~ sb (to sth)**| **~ sb (as sth)** (*BrE*) to elect sb to a political position: *The Athenians returned Pericles to office at the next elections.* **9** [T] **~ a verdict** to give a decision about sth in court: *The jury returned a verdict of accidental death.*

re·turn² /rɪˈtɜːn; *NAmE* rɪˈtɜːrn/ *noun* **1** [sing.] the action of arriving in or coming back to a place that you were in before: **~ (to...) (from...)** *Huang had been forced to flee to Japan. On his return, he devoted himself to education.* ◇ *After his return from his epic voyage, Darwin settled down to marriage, a large Victorian family and a life of science.* ◇ **+ noun** *The visitor and any dependants must be able to meet the cost of the return journey.* **2** [sing., U] the action of giving, putting or sending sth/sb back: *A total of 16 questionnaires were returned, a 64% return.* ◇ **~ (of sb/sth) (to sb/sth)** *The court granted the fathers' applications for return of the children.* ◇ **+ noun** *The postmark, return address and signature were all illegible.* **3** [sing.] **~ (of sth)** the situation when a feeling or state that has not been experienced for some time starts again SYN REAPPEARANCE: *The poem welcomes the return of spring.* **4** [sing.] **~ to sth** the action of going back to an activity that you used to do, or to a situation that you used to be in: *A high proportion of this group of patients achieved a return to work.* **5** [U, C, usually pl.] **~ (on sth)** the amount of profit that you get from sth SYN EARNINGS (2), YIELD²: *The rate of return on saving is currently 5% a year.* ◇ *Riskier stocks were expected to produce higher returns.* ◇ *to generate/provide/earn/yield high financial returns* ◇ *There is an emphasis on maximizing return on investment.* **6** [C] an official report or statement that gives particular information to the government or another body: *The data in this table are based on tax returns.* ◇ *Anyone receiving a bequest or gift is required to file a return.*

IDM **in reˈturn (for sth)** as an exchange or a reward for sth; as a response to sth: *In return for his hospitality, the gods gave Oineus a grapevine, naming 'wine' (Greek 'oinos') after him.* ◇ *When someone becomes angry with a person, it is normal for them to become angry in return.*

reˌturns to ˈscale *noun* [pl.] (*economics*) changes in production OUTPUT that result from a PROPORTIONAL change in all production INPUTS HELP If output changes in the same proportion as inputs, there are **constant returns to scale (CRS)**. **Decreasing returns to scale (DRS)** and **increasing returns to scale (IRS)** occur when output changes in a lesser/greater proportion than inputs: *It is possible for a* *production function to exhibit increasing returns to scale when it is small, constant returns to scale when it has achieved a medium size, and decreasing returns to scale when it is very large.*

re·veal AWL /rɪˈviːl/ *verb* **1** to make sth known to sb SYN DISCLOSE: **~ sth** *Further analysis revealed a difference between newer and more experienced drivers.* ◇ **~ sth to sb** *Teens are often reluctant to reveal personal problems to others.* ◇ **~ (that)...** *The survey revealed that a significant number of employees felt that technology was being used to control their activities.* ◇ **it is revealed that...** *He resigned after it was revealed that one of his closest aides was an East German spy.* ◇ **~ how/what, etc...** *Opinion polls revealed how unsuccessful they had been in winning over the public.* ◇ **~ sb/sth/yourself to be/have sth** *He was subsequently revealed to have had no involvement in the matter.* ➲ *see also* REVELATION (1) ➲ grammar note *at* PRESENT[3] ➲ language bank *at* REPORT[1] **2** to show sth that previously could not be seen: **~ sth** *An MRI scan revealed a tumour.* ◇ *Excavation has revealed the impressive remains of a major Roman villa.* ◇ **~ yourself (to sb) (as sth)** *The Green Knight then reveals himself to Gawain as the lord of the castle.*

▸ REVEAL + NOUN **pattern • structure • presence • feature** *Genetics can be used to reveal the underlying logical structure of a biological process.* | **difference • effect • information • details • evidence • truth • relationship • association • extent • number • level • importance • aspect • nature • problem • change • variation • trend • existence • identity • complexity** *Long-term exposure to the chemical may only reveal adverse effects after several years.*

▸ NOUN + REVEAL **analysis • study • examination • investigation • inspection • observation • test • experiment • research • results • findings • data • evidence • history • story • account • survey • interview • work • comparison • approach** *Additional studies have revealed other unanticipated ecological risks.*

▸ ADVERB + REVEAL **clearly • recently • subsequently** *The outline of the temple was recently revealed by new excavations.* | **usually • divinely** *The texts are said to have been divinely revealed.*

re·veal·ing AWL /rɪˈviːlɪŋ/ *adj.* providing interesting or important important information, especially of a personal nature, that was not known before: *Gorbachev, Shevardnadze and Yeltsin have all published their memoirs, but they are not very revealing.*

reve·la·tion AWL /ˌrevəˈleɪʃn/ *noun* **1** [C] a fact that people are made aware of, especially one that has been secret and is surprising SYN DISCLOSURE (2): *Although the new research has not produced any spectacular revelations, it has answered some long-standing questions.* ◇ **~ about/concerning sth** *The former MP stood down following revelations about his private life.* ◇ **~ that...** *The biomedical community was shocked by the revelation that Smith had fabricated scientific data.* ➲ *see also* REVEAL (1) **2** [U] **~ (of sth)** the act of making people aware of sth that has been secret SYN DISCLOSURE (1): *The revelation of the horrors of the Holocaust caused a wave of international revulsion.* ➲ *see also* REVEAL (1) **3** [C, U] something that is considered to be a sign or message from God: *They question the authority of a religious tradition based on a claimed divine revelation.*

rev·enue AWL /ˈrevənjuː; *NAmE* ˈrevənuː/ *noun* [U] (*also* **revenues** [pl.]) money that a government receives from taxes or that an organization receives from its business SYN RECEIPTS: *The government can raise revenue via taxes placed on products, households and firms.* ◇ *Shares may be issued to generate revenue for the company.* ◇ *In Nigeria, oil accounts for more than 85% of government revenues.* ◇ *tax/sales/advertising revenue* ◇ **+ noun** *Intellectual property may provide a significant revenue stream for businesses.* ➲ thesaurus note *at* MONEY

re·ver·sal AWL /rɪˈvɜːsl; *NAmE* rɪˈvɜːrsl/ *noun* **1** [C, U] a change of sth so that it is the opposite of what it was: **~ (of sth)** *The last decade has seen a reversal of the trend towards early retirement among men.* ◇ *The paper examines the impact of policy reversal on economic performance in East Africa.* ◇ **~ in sth** *It is considered necessary to reduce emissions considerably by 2050 so as to bring about a reversal in global warming.* **2** [C] **~ (in sth)** a change from being successful to having problems or being defeated: *Following independence in 1991, the country experienced a major reversal in both economic and social development.* **3** [C, U] **~ (of/in sth)** an exchange of positions or functions between two or more people: *This reversal of gender roles has profound implications.* ◇ *These figures show that role reversal is relatively uncommon.*

re·verse[1] AWL /rɪˈvɜːs; *NAmE* rɪˈvɜːrs/ *verb* **1** [T, I] to change sth completely so that it is the opposite of what it was before; to change in this way: **~ sth** *This attempt to revive the language appears to have reversed the enormous decline over the previous hundred years.* ◇ *As the piston reverses its direction and moves up, the fuel/air mixture is compressed.* ◇ *to reverse a trend/pattern/process* ◇ **~ (itself)** *US policy reversed itself in the 1930s.* ◇ *Although a decline in research productivity occurred from 1970 to 1980, this trend reversed in the early 1980s.* **2** [T] **~ sth** to change a previous decision, law, etc. to the opposite one SYN REVOKE: *The Court of Appeal reversed the decision of the High Court.* **3** [T] **~ sth** to exchange the positions or functions of two things: *There was a long tradition of masters and slaves pretending to reverse social roles at the Saturnalia.*

re·verse[2] AWL /rɪˈvɜːs; *NAmE* rɪˈvɜːrs/ *adj.* [only before noun] opposite to what has been mentioned: *The birds travel in summer from the place of their birth to wintering grounds in the Congo. In the spring, they make the journey in the reverse direction.* ◇ *The items were read in one order for half the respondents and in reverse order for the other half.* ◇ *the reverse reaction/process/effect*

re·verse[3] AWL /rɪˈvɜːs; *NAmE* rɪˈvɜːrs/ *noun* **1 the reverse** [sing.] the opposite of what has just been mentioned: *Heat will flow from a hotter object to a colder object and will never, by itself, do the reverse.* ◇ *This study found that, in developing countries, the majority of firms with less than 10 employees are female-owned, while the reverse is true for larger firms.* ◇ **~ of sth** *There were more mothers with asthma than fathers, which is the reverse of the male/female difference in childhood asthma.* **2** a loss or defeat; a change from success to failure SYN SETBACK: *Military reverses led to increasing dissatisfaction with the government.* **3 the reverse** [sing.] **~ (of sth)** the back of a coin, piece of material, piece of paper, etc: *The conditions were printed on the reverse of the document with no notice of them on the front.*

IDM **in reˈverse** in the opposite order or way SYN BACKWARDS (1): *A heat pump is a refrigerator operating in reverse.*

R

re·vers·ible AWL /rɪˈvɜːsəbl; *NAmE* rɪˈvɜːrsəbl/ *adj.* **1** (of a process, an action or a disease) that can be changed so that sth returns to its original state or situation: *At this stage of the disease, the damage is seen to be reversible.* OPP IRREVERSIBLE **2** (*chemistry*) (of a reaction) happening at the same time as the opposite reaction, producing an EQUILIBRIUM mixture of REACTANTS and products: *The cycle is readily explained in terms of the reversible chemical reactions corresponding to these two processes.* **3** (*physics*) (of a process) that can be reversed by the smallest change in the conditions in the surroundings: *A reversible process is not something that can be achieved in practice—rather, it is an idealization or limit of a real process.* ■ **re·vers·ibil·ity** /rɪˌvɜːsəˈbɪləti; *NAmE* rɪˌvɜːrsəˈbɪləti/ *noun* [U] **~ (of**

sth) *With some patients, there may be some reversibility of the condition.*

re·ver·sion /rɪˈvɜːʃn; *NAmE* rɪˈvɜːrʒn/ *noun* **1** [U, sing.] **~ (to sth)** the act or process of returning to a former state or practice: *For these liberal democracies, reversion to authoritarianism is almost unthinkable.* ◇ *Socialist countries were expected to intervene in any country of the Soviet bloc to prevent a reversion to capitalism.* **2** [U, C] **~ (to sb/sth)** (*law*) the return of land or property to sb: *For fifty years after reversion to China, Hong Kong would retain its political, economic and judicial systems.*

re·vert /rɪˈvɜːt; *NAmE* rɪˈvɜːrt/ *verb*
PHR V **reˈvert to sb/sth** (*law*) (of property or rights) to return to the original owner: *Ownership of the adjacent railway reverted to him once the line was abandoned.* **reˈvert to sth** **1** to return to a former state or practice: *Two of these new democracies have reverted to authoritarian rule.* ◇ *When challenged, people will often revert to coping strategies that have proved successful over time.* **2** to return to an earlier topic or subject: *He here reverts to a topic he first tackled in an earlier book in 1962.*

re·view¹ /rɪˈvjuː/ *noun* **1** [C, U] an examination and discussion of a range of information relevant to a particular subject: *We conducted a targeted literature review, concentrating on US-based studies in the past 15 years.* ◇ **~ of sth** *A comprehensive review of the subject is available in Thomas (2011).* ◇ **+ noun** *Readers are referred to many outstanding review articles on this subject (Behr, 1988b).* ➲ *see also* PEER REVIEW **2** [U, C] an examination of sth, with the intention of changing it if necessary: *The claimant made an application for judicial review to challenge the decision.* ◇ **~ of sth** *The government asked Kate Barker to conduct a review of the planning system and come up with precise recommendations.* ◇ **under ~** *The issue of local government finance is under review, with a major report expected in 2015.* ◇ **subject to ~** *Decisions by the trustees are subject to review by the courts.* ◇ **+ noun** *The policy review process includes consulting with patients as well as medical staff.* ➲ *see also* JUDICIAL REVIEW **3** [C] a report in a newspaper or magazine, or on the Internet, television or radio, in which sb gives their opinion of a book, play, film, etc: *Balasz wrote film reviews for the newspaper 'Der Tag'.*

▸ ADJECTIVE + REVIEW **recent • present, current • regular • periodic • annual • systematic, comprehensive, thorough, extensive, detailed • brief, short • excellent • critical • independent** *Sir Andrew Leggatt conducted a comprehensive review of the tribunal system on behalf of the government.* | **narrative • retrospective** *In their retrospective review of 425 patient records, Bell and colleagues found 25 (5.9%) having had a diagnosis of epilepsy.* | **urgent • judicial • ethical • medical** *The ward sister, who took the urgent phone call, has asked for an urgent medical review.*

▸ NOUN + REVIEW **peer • literature** *Only articles that have gone through a process of peer review are accepted for publication.*

▸ VERB + REVIEW **conduct, undertake, perform • provide, present • write • publish** *Cheung (2004) provides an excellent review of this cross-cultural research.*

re·view² /rɪˈvjuː/ *verb* **1 ~ sth** to examine, consider and discuss a range of information relevant to a particular subject: *First, I shall briefly review the evidence for these claims.* ◇ *Hayden (1998) reviewed the existing literature on these climatic interactions.* **2 ~ sth** to carefully examine and consider sth again, especially so that you can decide if it is necessary to make changes: *Every treatment plan is reviewed at six weeks.* ◇ *Risk assessments must be regularly reviewed.* ◇ *The management team reviewed progress after six months and made a number of recommendations.* ◇ *Patients have the right to ask a judge to review this decision if they do not agree.* **3 ~ sth** to write a report of a book, play, film, etc. in which you give your opinion of it: *He worked as a civil servant but also reviewed books for magazines such as 'The New Statesman'.* **4 ~ sth** (*especially NAmE*) to check a piece of work to see if there are any mistakes: *Drafts of the questionnaire were reviewed for content, clarity and utility.*

▸ REVIEW + NOUN **literature • study • research • work • article, paper • report • findings • evidence • records** *Goss (2004) reviews studies of geographies of consumption.*

▸ ADVERB + REVIEW **briefly • systematically • extensively • critically** *In the next section, we will systematically review research on effective reading programmes for English language learners.*

re·view·er /rɪˈvjuːə(r)/ *noun* **1** a person who examines or considers sth carefully, for example to see if any changes need to be made: *Anonymous reviewers offered instructive feedback during the development of this chapter.* **2** a person who writes reviews of books, films, plays, etc: *A 'New York Times' reviewer referred to 'The Big Lebowski' as the Coen brothers' 'finest film'.*

re·vise AWL /rɪˈvaɪz/ *verb* **1** [T] **~ sth** to change sth, such as a book, process or rule, in order to improve it or make it more suitable: *The essay was first published in 1798 and substantially revised in 1803.* ◇ *The department revised its procedures to make sure that the problem did not occur again.* **2** [T] **~ sth** to change an opinion or a plan, usually because of new information: *The new model revises the familiar thesis that global capitalism originated since the fifteenth century (Frank and Gills, 1993).* ◇ *To cope with this sudden change, the banking world was obliged to revise its ideas drastically.* **3** [T] **~ sth (+ adv./prep.)** to change sth, such as an estimate or price, in order to correct or improve it: *The National Bureau of Statistics has recently revised China's GDP growth up by half a percentage point.* ◇ *The revised budget was submitted to the House committee.* **4** [I] **~ (for sth)** (*BrE*) to prepare for an exam by looking again at work that you have done: *She started to revise for her exams.*

re·vi·sion AWL /rɪˈvɪʒn/ *noun* **1** [C] a change or set of changes to sth, especially a text: *The editor made substantial revisions to the introduction.* ◇ **subject to ~** *Her paper was accepted, subject to some minor revisions, for publication in 'Bioscience Horizons'.* **2** [C] **~ (of sth)** a changed and improved version of sth, especially a text: *This paper uses the third revision of the guidelines, published in 2010.* **3** [U, C] **~ (of sth)** the act of changing sth, especially a text, or of examining it with the intention of changing it: *The report noted the need for further revision of the treaty provisions.* ◇ *Constitutional revisions took place in 1992 and 1994.* **4** [U] (*BrE*) the process of learning work for an exam: *Exam revision can take a number of different forms.*

re·visit /ˌriːˈvɪzɪt/ *verb* **1 ~ sth** to visit a place again: *He revisited the city several times.* ◇ *No further efforts were made to revisit the deepest sea floor areas for over three decades.* **2 ~ sth** to return to an idea or a subject and discuss it again: *The concluding chapter revisits three key themes.* ◇ *Several of the authors revisit old debates from new perspectives.*

re·vival /rɪˈvaɪvl/ *noun* **1** [U, C] an improvement in the condition or strength of sth: *Neither fiscal nor monetary policy was used as a tool for economic revival.* ◇ **~ of sth** *King George III enjoyed a revival of popularity.* **2** [C] the process of sth becoming or being made popular or fashionable again: *Taiwan has experienced a Buddhist revival.* **3** [C] **~ (of sth)** a new production of a play that has not been performed for some time: *He wrote additional speeches for a revival of Kyd's play.*

re·vive /rɪˈvaɪv/ *verb* **1** [I, T] to become, or to make sb/sth become, CONSCIOUS or healthy and strong again: *During the first half of 1931, the economy revived.* ◇ **~ sb/sth** *He*

R

then collapsed, and attempts to revive him failed. **2** [T] **~ sth** to make sth start to be used or done again: *Graf is responsible for reviving interest in ancient magic.*

re·voke /rɪˈvəʊk; *NAmE* rɪˈvoʊk/ *verb* **~ sth** to officially cancel sth so that it is no longer valid: *The company's export licence was revoked.*

re·volt /rɪˈvəʊlt; *NAmE* rɪˈvoʊlt/ *noun* [C, U] a protest against authority, especially that of a government, often involving violence; the action of protesting against authority SYN UPRISING: **~ (against sb/sth)** *Mackenzie led an armed revolt against British rule in Canada.* ◇ *to suppress/crush a revolt* ◇ **in ~ (against sb/sth)** *The peasants rose in revolt against their landlords.*

revo·lu·tion AWL /ˌrevəˈluːʃn/ *noun* **1** [C, U] a great change in conditions, ways of working, beliefs, etc. that affects large numbers of people: *Popular culture has absorbed the information revolution easily, as sales of digital musical downloads show.* ◇ *The seventeenth century witnessed a scientific revolution.* ◇ *an agricultural/a technological/a cultural revolution* ◇ *The 1790s was a decade of political and social revolution.* ◇ **~ in sth** *The 2001 film is a carefully constructed history of a revolution in the sport of skateboarding.* ➲ *see also* INDUSTRIAL REVOLUTION **2** [C, U] an attempt, by a large number of people, to change the government of a country, especially by violent action: *The King of Prussia had taken the leading role in suppressing the 1848 revolution in Germany.* ◇ *Fear of revolution brought growing internal repression.* ➲ *compare* REVOLT **3** [C, U] a complete CIRCULAR movement around a point: *A high-performance disk drive of the late 1990s had a rotational speed of 90 revolutions per second.* ◇ **~ around sth** *In Copernicus's view, the moon's motion involves both a monthly revolution around the earth and a monthly period of rotation on its axis.* ➲ *see also* REVOLVE (1)

revo·lu·tion·ary[1] AWL /ˌrevəˈluːʃənəri; *NAmE* ˌrevəˈluːʃəneri/ *adj.* **1** [usually before noun] connected with political revolution: *The revolutionary movement of Garibaldi had exploited the masses rather than benefited them.* ◇ *The revolutionary period of 1776–1787 receives only cursory treatment in this account.* **2** involving a great or complete change: *In the 17th century, Nicolaus Steno stated his revolutionary new idea about fossils in his famous book.* ◇ *Revolutionary social change was the goal.*

revo·lu·tion·ary[2] AWL /ˌrevəˈluːʃənəri; *NAmE* ˌrevəˈluːʃəneri/ *noun* (*pl.* **-ies**) a person who starts or supports a revolution, especially a political one: *For the French revolutionaries, the power of the popular uprising had unexpected disadvantages.*

revo·lu·tion·ize (*BrE also* **-ise**) AWL /ˌrevəˈluːʃənaɪz/ *verb* to completely change the way that sth is done: **~ sth** *These discoveries have revolutionized our understanding of early Chinese society.* ◇ *Technology revolutionized the industry.* ◇ **~ how/what, etc.** *The Internet has revolutionized how consumers purchase goods.*

re·volve /rɪˈvɒlv; *NAmE* rɪˈvɑːlv; rɪˈvɔːlv/ *verb* [I] **~ (around sth)** to go in a circle around a central point: *Galileo sought to demonstrate the truth of the theory that the earth revolved around the sun.*

PHR V **reˈvolve around/round sb/sth** to have sb/sth as the main interest or subject: **~ around doing sth** *Dietary recommendations specifically revolved around encouraging a high-fibre diet.* ◇ **~ around whether/what, etc...** *One major problem revolves around whether surveys can validly obtain information on racial prejudice.*

re·ward[1] /rɪˈwɔːd; *NAmE* rɪˈwɔːrd/ *noun* **1** [C, U] a thing that you are given, or sth good that happens, because you have done sth good, worked hard, etc: ◇ **~ for (doing) sth** *Both participants and counsellors received rewards for each session completed.* ◇ **~ (of sth)** *Aristotle assumed that happiness is the reward of a virtuous life.* ◇ *Film festivals demand huge personal commitment and hard work, but offer very little financial reward.* **2** [C] an amount of money that is offered to encourage people to do sth, such as help the police find a criminal, find sth that is lost, etc: *The New South Wales government offered a $100 000 reward for information leading to the conviction of offenders.*

re·ward[2] /rɪˈwɔːd; *NAmE* rɪˈwɔːrd/ *verb* [often passive] to give sth to sb because they have done sth good, worked hard, etc: **~ sb for (doing) sth (with sth)** *Kroto and Smalley were rewarded for their discovery with a Nobel prize.* ◇ **~ sb with sth** *Each time the owls turn their head in response to a sound, they are rewarded with a small piece of meat.* ◇ **~ sb/sth** *Parents were encouraged to reward success and not to focus attention on failure.*

re·ward·ing /rɪˈwɔːdɪŋ; *NAmE* rɪˈwɔːrdɪŋ/ *adj.* **1** (of an activity) worth doing; that makes you happy because you think it is useful or important: *Learning a language and enjoying ways of socializing with a host are some of the most rewarding experiences for an international manager.* ◇ **it is ~ to do sth** *It is immensely rewarding to work collaboratively with communities and students.* **2** producing a lot of money SYN PROFITABLE (1): *Minority women fill low-wage jobs, while white women disproportionately pursue more financially rewarding careers.*

re·write /ˌriːˈraɪt/ *verb* (**re·wrote** /ˌriːˈrəʊt; *NAmE* ˌriːˈroʊt/, **re·writ·ten** /ˌriːˈrɪtn/) to write sth again in a different way, for example in order to improve it or because there is some new information: **~ sth** *Gandhi reportedly gave Anand feedback and he rewrote the novel.* ◇ **~ sth as sth/in terms of sth** *The equation can be rewritten as...*

rhet·oric /ˈretərɪk/ *noun* [U] **1** (*often disapproving*) speech or writing that is intended to influence people, but that is not completely honest or sincere: *The labels 'citizenship' and 'community development' may be nothing more than political rhetoric.* ◇ **~ of sth** *The education reforms use the rhetoric of professionalism, but in reality they limit rather than empower teachers.* **2** the skill of using language in speech or writing in a special way that influences or entertains people: *Many listeners were moved by his rhetoric and agreed with him.*

rhet·oric·al /rɪˈtɒrɪkl; *NAmE* rɪˈtɔːrɪkl/ *adj.* **1** connected with the art of rhetoric: *The poem uses rhetorical devices, such as metaphor and exaggeration, to produce its effect.* **2** (*often disapproving*) (of a speech or piece of writing) intended to influence people, but not completely honest or sincere: *Media references to the Nazi death camps are often little more than rhetorical gestures that hide widespread public ignorance.* **3** (of a question) asked only to make a statement or to produce an effect rather than to get an answer: *Frequently, Downes asks rhetorical questions such as 'Who wouldn't want X?'* ■ **rhet·oric·al·ly** /rɪˈtɒrɪkli; *NAmE* rɪˈtɔːrɪkli/ *adv.*: *The book is rhetorically strong but it is weak on theory.* ◇ *Abram Courtney asked rhetorically: 'If you prick a blind man, does he not bleed?'*

rhyme[1] /raɪm/ *noun* **1** [U] the use of words in a poem or song that have the same sound, especially at the ends of lines: *Coleridge employed a quick-moving ballad stanza, often with internal rhyme in the first and third lines.* **2** [C] a word that has the same sound or ends with the same sound as another word: *Shakespeare has two hundred rhymes not found in the other sonnet sequences, while Sidney has only sixty.* ◇ **~ for sth** *Can you think of a rhyme for 'beauty'?* **3** [C] a short poem in which the last word in the line has the same sound as the last word in another line, especially the next one: *Street criers and peddlers promoted their wares with combinations of chants, rhymes and humour.*

rhyme[2] /raɪm/ *verb* [I, T] (of two words or syllables) to have or end with the same sound; to put words that sound

R

the same together, for example when writing poetry: *Only two of six lines fully rhyme in the first stanza.* ◇ **~ (sth) (with sth)** *The couplet rhymes 'leave' with 'believe'.*

rhythm /ˈrɪðəm/ *noun* **1** [C] **~ (of sth)** a regular pattern of changes or events: *The majority of ancient people lived in the countryside and observed the seasonal rhythms of agricultural life.* ◇ *Disturbed biological rhythms appear to underlie many of the health problems of shift workers.* **2** [C, U] a strong regular repeated pattern of sounds or movements: *The drums often imitated speech rhythms and tones.* ◇ *In this German translation of 'Paradise Lost', the unique sound and rhythm of Milton are lost.*

rhyth·mic /ˈrɪðmɪk/ (*also less frequent* **rhyth·mic·al** /ˈrɪðmɪkl/) *adj.* having a regular pattern of sounds, movements or events: *The heart's rhythmic beating is caused by the contraction of its myocardial cells.* ■ **rhyth·mic·al·ly** /ˈrɪðmɪkli/ *adv.*: *Teach the patient to slow their respiratory rate and to breathe slowly and rhythmically.*

rice /raɪs/ *noun* [U] short, narrow white or brown grain grown on wet land in hot countries as food; the plant that produces this grain: **+ noun** *The plains are seasonally flooded and are used for rice cultivation.*

rich /rɪtʃ/ *adj.* (**rich·er, rich·est**) **1** having a lot of money or property; producing a lot of wealth: *The investors became very rich.* ◇ *By the turn of the century, the richer peasants were acquiring land rapidly.* ◇ *Less than 10% of the population in rich countries lives in rural areas.* OPP POOR (1) **2 the rich** *noun* [pl.] people who have a lot of money or property: *The gap between the rich and the poor was widening.* OPP POOR (2) **3** (often in compounds) containing or providing a large supply of sth: *Sewage is a rich source of organic carbon.* ◇ *The 1990s produced a rich literature on the urban geography of Japan and Korea.* ◇ *It is known that antioxidant-rich foods offer protection against many diseases.* ◇ **~ in sth** *The equatorial climate resulted in the waters becoming very rich in algae.* OPP POOR (4) **4** very interesting and full of variety: *The study focuses on three localities in Brazil with a rich history of Japanese immigration.* ◇ *The aim was to construct a much richer, more broad-based model of democracy.* **5** (of soil) containing the substances that make it good for growing plants in SYN FERTILE (1): *The rich soils of the plains enabled the development of highly productive agricultural societies.* OPP POOR (3) **6** (of colours, sounds, smells and tastes) strong or deep; very beautiful or pleasing: *The walls were painted in rich colours.*

rich·ly /ˈrɪtʃli/ *adv.* **1** used to express the fact that the quality or thing mentioned is present in large amounts: *Naylor provides a richly detailed examination of the city over this period.* ◇ *Germany is richly endowed with coal and iron ore.* **2** in a generous way: *Tacitus describes Seneca as a courtier who is usually richly rewarded for his loyal services.* **3** in a beautiful and expensive manner: *The temple was richly adorned with sculpture.* **4** used to express the fact that sth has a pleasant strong colour, taste or smell: *The interiors of the houses are often richly coloured.*

rich·ness /ˈrɪtʃnəs/ *noun* [U] the state of being rich in sth, such as a variety of types or interesting qualities: *It was found that the pathways were different from the rough grassland in terms of species richness.* ◇ **~ of sth** *This article will attempt to convey the richness and diversity of Buddhism across Asia.* ➲ *compare* WEALTH

rid /rɪd/ *verb* (**rid·ding, rid, rid**)

IDM **get ˈrid of sth/sb** to make yourself free of sth/sb that is a problem or that you do not want; to throw sth away: *The first step was to get rid of a number of false assumptions.* ◇ *In order to get rid of his rival, Alvaro informs Clara's father about the secret love affair between them.* **be ˈrid of sth/sb** (*formal*) to be free of sth/sb that is a problem or that is not wanted: *A common currency means that firms and consumers will be rid of foreign exchange transaction costs.*

PHR V **ˈrid sth/sb of sth/sb** to remove sth/sb that is causing a problem from a place, group, etc: *Their goal was to rid the world of nuclear weapons.* **ˈrid yourself of sth/sb** to make yourself free from sth/sb that is a problem: *Happiness can only be attained after we rid ourselves of false fears and expectations.*

ridge /rɪdʒ/ *noun* **1** a long narrow area of high land along the top of a line of hills or under the sea: *A series of deep, steep-sided valleys are separated by narrow ridges.* ◇ *New crust is being formed at ocean ridges.* **2** a raised line on the surface of sth; the point where two sloping surfaces join: *The roofs are unusual due to the relative heights of the eaves and the ridge.*

ri·dicu·lous /rɪˈdɪkjələs/ *adj.* not at all sensible or reasonable: *The idea that a plastic could conduct electricity for a long time seemed quite ridiculous.* ■ **ri·dicu·lous·ly** *adv.*: *The chances of a successful guess are ridiculously small.*

rift /rɪft/ *noun* **1** a serious disagreement between people that stops their relationship from continuing SYN BREACH[1] (2), DIVISION (3): **~ (over sth)** *There were management rifts over the company's direction.* ◇ **~ between A and B** *During the second century, the rift between Jewish Christians and other Jews widened.* **2** (*earth science*) a break in the earth's CRUST, where TECTONIC plates are separated or are moving apart: *The Rhine rift is another well-known example of a continental rift.* ◇ **+ noun** *In East Africa, the rift valleys are occupied by numerous lakes.*

right[1] /raɪt/ *noun* **1** [C, U] a legal or moral claim to have or get sth or to behave in a particular way: *Workers still had very few employment rights.* ◇ **~ to do sth** *The Data Protection Act 1998 states that individuals have a right to know who holds data on them.* ◇ **~ to sth** *Surely every child has an equal right to education?* ◇ **~ of sb/sth** *The group campaigns for the rights of the disabled.* ◇ **by ~ (of sth)** *The Anglo-Welsh lords claimed to hold their lands by right of conquest, independently of the king.* ➲ *see also* CIVIL RIGHTS, HUMAN RIGHT **2 rights** [pl.] the authority to make, publish, perform, etc. a particular product, text, etc: *Copyright ©1961 Massachusetts Medical Society, all rights reserved.* ◇ **~ to do sth** *The company earns millions by selling the rights to use its technology.* ◇ *The two theatres were granted exclusive rights to stage comedies and tragedies by the 1737 Licensing Act.* **3** [U, C] what is morally good or correct: *Sociopaths have no sense of right and wrong.* ◇ *A gulf has opened up between many scientists and many of the public about the rights and wrongs of genetic modification.* OPP WRONG[3] (1) **4 the/sb's right** [sing.] the right side or direction: *Shivwits Plateau is visible in the distance on the right.* OPP LEFT[2] (1) **5 the right, the Right** [sing.+ sing./pl. v.] political groups that most strongly support the CAPITALIST system: *The Right tends to assume that choice can only be provided by the market.* OPP LEFT[2] (2)

IDM **in its/their, etc. own ˈright** because of the qualities that sth/sb has, not because of a connection with sth/sb else: *The Metis are descendants of Cree First Nations and French settlers, but are now an independent group in their own right.*

▸ ADJECTIVE + RIGHT **human • fundamental, basic • universal • individual • equal • moral • natural • exclusive • social • cultural • civil • legal, statutory • political • international • indigenous • gay** *To be democratic, a constitution must uphold fundamental rights.*

▸ NOUN + RIGHT **property, land • intellectual property • employment • voting • citizenship • disability • minority** *It is claimed that to ensure justice between ethnic groups, minority rights must supplement individual human rights.*

R

▸ VERB + RIGHT **have, possess • grant • acquire • retain • reserve • protect, enforce • infringe • lose** *A government is legitimate, according to Locke, as long as it protects the rights of its citizens.* | **confer • recognize • establish • extend • guarantee, defend, uphold, safeguard • respect • enshrine • promote • claim, assert, demand • secure • enjoy • exercise • fulfil • balance • affect • deny • violate • restrict, limit • waive** *Emancipation conferred on Jews the same rights and responsibilities as other French citizens.*

▸ HUMAN/CIVIL, ETC. RIGHTS + NOUN **issue • organization, institution • framework • regime • standards, norms • record • protection • activist, defender • movement • activism • violation, abuse** *Activists were drawing attention to human rights issues under the country's military dictatorship.*

▸ RIGHT TO + NOUN **freedom, liberty • life • health • education • respect • privacy • self-determination** *Marketing is seen by some as invading an individual's right to privacy.*

▸ RIGHT TO + VERB **vote • marry • live • work • strike • participate • choose • refuse** *In the United States, many citizens who have the right to vote have not been exercising this right.*

right[2] /raɪt/ *adj.* **1** correct for a particular situation or thing, or for a particular person: *In agricultural societies, the right amount of rain at the right time is crucial.* ◇ *The Americans waited until the moment was right before invading.* ◇ *Evans-Pritchard saw his own work as a necessary step in the right direction.* OPP WRONG[1] (3) **2** [not before noun] correct in your opinion or judgement: **~ about sth** *Turing was absolutely right about the way our perceptions of computers would change.* ◇ **~ to do sth** *It seems right to say that Fresnel completely misidentified the nature of light.* ◇ **~ in doing sth** *It is clear that Lewes was right in concluding that Dickens was well-read, but not a scholar.* OPP WRONG[1] (1) **3** [not usually before noun] morally good or acceptable; correct according to law or a person's duty: *Confucius proposed doing what is right simply because it is morally right.* ◇ **do the ~ thing** *Polly is faced with a decision between doing the right thing or simply indulging a selfish desire.* ◇ **~ to do sth** *Consequentialists believe that it can be right to commit murder, in certain extraordinary circumstances.* OPP WRONG[1] (5) **4** [not before noun] in a normal or good enough condition: *The misbehaving students were highlighting that something important in their lives was not quite right.* ◇ *The regulations specify the steps required to put matters right after a data protection breach.* OPP WRONG[1] (4) **5** true or correct as a fact: *Since we did not know which answer was right, we checked all our calculations.* OPP WRONG[1] (2) **6** [only before noun] of, on or towards the side of the body that is towards the east when a person faces north: *Higher temperatures are shown on the right side of the diagram.* ◇ *She has an ulcer on her right leg.* OPP LEFT[1] (1) ➲ *see also* RIGHT-WING ■ **right·ness** /ˈraɪtnəs/ *noun* [U] **~ (of sth)** *Green firmly believed in the rightness of the decisions made by the public.* ◇ **~ of doing sth** *The paper did not discuss the rightness or wrongness of not treating these patients.* IDM *see* TRACK[1]

right[3] /raɪt/ *adv.* **1** all the way; completely: *These spectacular ridges extend right across ocean basins.* **2** exactly; directly: *The same problems began to occur right in the heart of the city.* **3** in the way that things should happen or are supposed to happen: *When it is done right, risk taking can be seen as a type of social engineering.* ◇ *After the funding was cut, nothing went right.* OPP WRONG[2]
IDM **right aˈway** immediately; without delay: *Staff needed information right away.* **right ˈnow** at this moment; in this period: *The development of a new model is the challenge facing the field right now.*

ˈright angle *noun* an angle of 90°, as in the corner of a square: **at a ~** *The horizontal and vertical lines are joined at a right angle.*

ˈright-hand *adj.* [only before noun] on or towards the right side of sth: *The right-hand column lists the top 15 countries in terms of import value.* ◇ *It can be shown that the right-hand side of the equation is equivalent to marginal revenue.* OPP LEFT-HAND

right·ly /ˈraɪtli/ *adv.* **1** for a good reason SYN JUSTIFIABLY: *The judge quite rightly rejected this argument.* ◇ *Tsiolkovsky is rightly regarded as one of the fathers of space flight.* ◇ *For years, scholars have been concerned (and perhaps rightly so) that women do more than their share of housework.* **2** in a correct or accurate way SYN CORRECTLY: *Goldstein rightly points out that 'a lot of classroom images are... treated simply as decoration'.*

ˌright-ˈwing *adj.* strongly supporting the CAPITALIST system: *It is a right-wing party promoting social conservatism.* ◇ *extreme right-wing groups/organizations* OPP LEFT-WING

rigid AWL /ˈrɪdʒɪd/ *adj.* **1** (of an object or substance) stiff and difficult to move or bend: *The bacterial cell has a rigid cell wall around it.* ◇ *Arthropods have a rigid outer skeleton, the cuticle.* **2** (of rules, methods, etc.) very strict and difficult to change or adapt SYN INFLEXIBLE (1): *Despite their rigid class structure, Romans had a respect for ability rather than birth or descent.* ◇ *The government approach can, through the very nature of legislation, be too rigid.* **3 ~ (about sth/doing sth)** (of a person or organization) not willing to change or adapt ideas or behaviour SYN INFLEXIBLE (2): *It is important not to be too rigid about applying these rules.* ■ **ri·gid·ity** AWL /rɪˈdʒɪdəti/ *noun* [U] *Glucose binds to proteins, increasing rigidity.* ◇ **~ of sth** *One cause of graduate unemployment is the rigidity of the curriculum.* **ri·gid·ly** AWL *adv.*: *Some idioms, for example 'How do you do?', are rigidly fixed.* ◇ *The Chancellor, Gordon Brown, stuck rigidly to the plans for public spending inherited from the Conservatives.*

rig·or·ous /ˈrɪɡərəs/ *adj.* **1** done carefully and with a lot of attention to detail SYN THOROUGH (1): *This study exemplifies the importance of rigorous statistical analysis to distinguish competing hypotheses.* **2** demanding that particular rules or processes are strictly followed SYN STRICT (1): *She attempted to follow a particularly rigorous diet and exercise programme.* ■ **rig·or·ous·ly** *adv.*: *A distinguished jury rigorously evaluated the hundreds of eligible applications.*

rig·our (*US* **rigor**) /ˈrɪɡə(r)/ *noun* **1** [U] the fact of being careful and paying great attention to detail: *Skinner recognized the need for scientific rigour and objective, verifiable measurement.* ◇ *Some scholars saw this early work as lacking rigour and being overly descriptive.* **2 the rigours of sth** [pl.] the difficulties and unpleasant conditions of sth: *Life was wretched for boys who were unable to cope with the rigours of military life in Sparta.*

ring[1] /rɪŋ/ *noun* **1** an object, area, group of objects, etc. in the shape of a circle with a large hole in the middle: *Agricultural activities are located in a series of concentric rings around the central market.* HELP In chemistry, a **ring** is a number of atoms joined to form a circle in a MOLECULE: *All steroids contain four hydrocarbon rings joined together in a distinct shape.* ◇ *The protons on a benzene ring are in a region where the magnetic field is slightly strengthened.* In astronomy, a **ring** is a thin disc around a planet consisting of very small pieces of rock and ice. **2** a piece of jewellery that you wear on your finger: *The custom of giving an engagement ring began in 1477 when Maximilian, the Archduke of Austria, presented his fiancée, Mary of Burgundy, with a diamond ring.*

R

ring² /rɪŋ/ *verb* **(ringed, ringed) 1** [usually passive] **be ringed by/with sth** to be surrounded by sth: *As shown in Fig. 14.1, the plateau is ringed by zones of intense deformation.* **2 ~ sth** to put a metal ring around a bird's leg so that it can be easily identified in the future: *For identification purposes, birds were ringed with standard coloured plastic rings.*

ring³ /rɪŋ/ *verb* (**rang** /ræŋ/, **rung** /rʌŋ/) **1** [I, T] (of a bell or telephone) to produce a sound; to make a bell produce a sound: *Her parents cannot get her to enter the school building when the bell rings at 8:50 a.m.* ◇ **~ sth** *He realized that if he rang the bell before serving food, the dogs would associate the sound with the presentation of food and begin salivating.* **2** [T, I] (*BrE*) to telephone sb/sth SYN CALL¹ (6): **~ (up)** *They often ring up to ask how he's getting on.* ◇ **~ sb/sth (up)** *After taking his blood pressure and temperature, the GP rang the hospital for his blood results.* IDM *see* ALARM¹

rise¹ /raɪz/ *noun* **1** [C] an increase in an amount, a number or a level: *It was realized that freeing prices would inevitably result in sudden and enormous price rises.* ◇ *There was a dip from 2000 to 2003, then a gradual rise.* ◇ **~ in sth** *In post-glacial times, there has been a rapid rise in sea level.* ◇ *Developed and developing countries alike are experiencing rises in life expectancy.* ◇ **~ of sth** *This is equivalent to a rise of 40 million in a million years.* HELP Note that you use a **rise in sth** to talk about the thing that rises, and a **rise of sth** to talk about how large or small the rise is. OPP FALL² (2) ➲ language bank *at* TREND **2** [sing.] **~ (of sb/sth)** the process of becoming more important, successful or powerful: *The changes encouraged the rise of small-scale capitalism.* ◇ *The rise and fall of human societies has been driven by a complex set of factors.* **3** [C] (*BrE*) (*NAmE* **raise**) an increase in the money you are paid for the work you do: *Pay rises and promotion were assessed on the basis of the previous six months' work.* **4** [sing.] an upward movement: *This technique will provide oxygenation but will not ventilate; there will be no chest rise and fall.*

IDM **give ˈrise to sth** to cause sth to happen or exist: *Relatively small temperature changes give rise to glacier melt, ice shelf collapse, and sea ice reduction.*

▸ ADJECTIVE + RISE **rapid • sharp, steep • sudden • dramatic • exponential • significant, substantial • large • steady • small • slow • gradual • inexorable • recent** *Even a tiny transfer of heat to the system results in a significant rise in temperature.*

▸ NOUN + RISE **temperature • sea level • price • wage** *We measure the temperature rise of the sample as a known amount of energy is supplied.*

▸ VERB + RISE **cause, produce, trigger • see, witness • experience • show • follow, accompany • be accompanied by, be followed by • be caused by • predict, expect • examine • reflect • limit • prevent** *Physical damage to plant cells was often accompanied by a rapid rise in the production of the gas ethylene.* | **see, witness • chart, trace, document, describe • encourage** *The later eighteenth century saw the rise of Protestant movements that emphasized the individual's personal experience of faith.*

▸ RISE IN + NOUN **price, cost, value • rate, ratio • level • number • incidence • temperature • pressure • concentration • inflation • wages, income • demand • output • unemployment • inequality • population** *US data show a rise in the incidence of the disease since the early 1980s.*

rise² /raɪz/ *verb* (**rose** /rəʊz; *NAmE* roʊz/, **risen** /ˈrɪzn/) **1** [I] to increase in amount or number: *Net exports will be reduced when the foreign exchange rate rises.* ◇ *There are several reasons for rising oil prices.* ◇ **~ (from...) (to...)** *In 1920, only 10% of property in the UK was owner-occupied; in 2007, this figure had risen to 70%.* ◇ **~ by sth** *Money wages have risen by 4% and so unit labour costs have risen by 4%.* ◇ **~ above sth** *If the concentration rises above the toxic threshold, adverse effects may be apparent.* ◇ **~ 2°C, 5%, etc.** *Average global temperature is predicted to rise 2°C before the year 2100.* ➲ *usage note at* RAISE¹ ➲ language bank *at* TREND **2** [I] to come or go upwards; to reach a higher level or position: *Because warm air is less dense, the air rises.* ◇ **~ 10 m, etc.** *Sea level rose 100 m in 10 000 years, flooding low-lying areas.* ◇ **+ adv./prep.** *In calm weather, smoke rises vertically.* ➲ *usage note at* RAISE¹ **3** [I] to become more successful, important or powerful: *A gifted speaker, Malcolm X rose quickly through the ranks of the Nation of Islam.* ◇ **~ to sth** *Environmental issues rose to prominence on the political agenda.* ◇ **~ to do sth** *Christianity would one day rise to become a great world religion.* **4** [I] to begin to fight against a ruler, government or army that controls you: **~ (up)** *According to Marx, the proletariat must one day rise up to destroy bourgeois capitalism.* ◇ **~ (up) in sth** *Agricultural labourers rose in revolt across the southern counties in 1830.* ◇ **~ (up) against sb/sth** *Revolutionary France appealed to other nations to rise up against their governments.* ➲ *compare* REBEL² ➲ *related noun* UPRISING **5** [I] (of the sun or moon) to appear above the HORIZON: *A belief is the acceptance of the truth of something (e.g. that the sun will rise tomorrow).* OPP SET¹ (8) ➲ *usage note at* RAISE¹ **6** [I] **+ adv./prep.** (of land or mountains) to slope upwards from or be visible above the surroundings: *The gorges are separated by rugged, high mountain ranges rising to 6 000 m.* IDM *see* CHALLENGE¹

PHR V **ˈrise to sth** to show that you are able to deal with an unexpected situation or problem: *Researchers must rise to the current challenges and provide evidence-based approaches that clinicians can effectively apply.*

▸ NOUN + RISE **price • rate, ratio • level • figure, number • incidence • concentration • population • temperature • pressure • wage, income • cost • value • unemployment • output • demand • profit • inflation** *The incidence of the disease rises significantly with increasing age.*

▸ RISE + ADVERB | ADVERB + RISE **rapidly, quickly • sharply, steeply • steadily • slowly • gradually** *The increase in GDP approaches 5 per cent and gradually rises thereafter.*

▸ RISE + ADVERB **fast • dramatically • significantly, considerably, substantially, markedly • exponentially • slightly • progressively • high** *Worldwide use of the Internet rose dramatically from approximately 3 million people in 1994 to 377 million by 2000.*

ris·ing /ˈraɪzɪŋ/ *noun* a situation in which a group of people join together in order to fight against the people who are in power SYN REVOLT, UPRISING: *After six months of war, the rising was suppressed and the kingdom was placed under military rule.*

risk¹ /rɪsk/ *noun* **1** [C, U] the possibility of sth bad happening at some time in the future; a situation that could be dangerous or have a bad result: *Most were aware of the health risks associated with smoking.* ◇ *The common method adopted in the financial world to reduce risk is to spread the risk over many people.* ◇ **~ of (doing) sth** *The overall risk of contracting the disease is very much higher with hepatitis.* ◇ **~ that...** *Care has to be taken to design questions that minimize the risk that people do not respond truthfully.* ◇ **~ to sb/sth** *The government issued statements assuring the population that there were no risks to health.* ◇ **+ noun** *Smoking is a major risk factor for cancer.* ➲ *see also* AT-RISK, LOW-RISK, RISK ASSESSMENT **2** [C] **~ (to sth/sb)** a person or thing that is likely to cause problems or danger at some time in the future: *The law gave powers to detain a foreign national if their presence was believed to be a risk to national security.* **3** [C] **a good/bad/poor ~** a person or business that a bank or company is willing/unwilling to lend money to, sell insurance to, or do business with because the bank or company is unlikely/likely to lose money: *Previous customers were chosen because they were thought to be good risks.*

R

IDM **at ˈrisk (from/of sth)** in danger of sth unpleasant or harmful happening: *A poor capital equipment purchase may put the entire organization at risk.* ◇ *Patients undergoing surgery are at risk of developing a deep vein thrombosis (DVT).* **at the ˈrisk of (doing) sth** although there may be a particular bad result: *At the risk of oversimplifying, I shall divide responses into four categories.* **run a/the ˈrisk (of sth/of doing sth) | run ˈrisks** to be or put yourself in a situation in which sth bad could happen to you: *Entrepreneurship involves the motivation to overcome obstacles and the willingness to run risks.* **take a ˈrisk | take ˈrisks** to do sth even though you know that sth bad could happen as a result: *Making any investment necessarily involves taking a risk.*

▸ ADJECTIVE + RISK **high, great • increased, elevated • signficant • low • relative • potential • perceived • real • political • environmental • financial** *There is only a very low risk that a person will ever die in an earthquake.*

▸ VERB + RISK **have • involve, carry, include • present, pose • create • face • reduce, mitigate, decrease • minimize • manage • avoid, eliminate • increase • affect, influence • assess, identify • accept** *Existing regional nuclear tensions already pose serious risks.*

▸ RISK + VERB **be associated with • increase • vary, differ** *At 30–34 years, the average risk increases to 1.5 per 1 000 births.*

▸ RISK + NOUN **factor • assessment, analysis, estimate, prediction • reduction, management • model, profile • aversion • category • perception** *Risk management entails making decisions about whether to ban or regulate a substance or process.*

risk² /rɪsk/ *verb* **1 ~ sth** to put sth valuable or important in a dangerous situation, in which it could be lost or damaged: *His shipmates praised his heroism and thanked him for risking his life to save theirs.* ◇ *Trying a new candy bar would be a low-involvement decision, because you would not really be risking much money.* **2** to be in a situation where something dangerous or bad may happen to you: **~ sth** *In a cyclone, exposed livestock and people risk death and injury from flying debris.* ◇ **~ (sb/sth) doing sth** *Employees may risk losing their jobs in exposing the unethical practices of their employers.* **3** to do sth that you realize may not succeed or may have bad results: **~ sth** *The more people have to lose through aggressive behaviour, the less likely they are to risk it (Gottfredson, 1987).* ◇ **~ doing sth** *The US naval commanding group believed that the Japanese would never risk attacking the US.*

ˈrisk assessment *noun* [C, U] the act of identifying possible risks, calculating how likely they are to happen and estimating what effects they might have: *The global marketer is advised to carry out a risk assessment at all levels.*

ˈrisk-taking *noun* [U] the practice of doing things that involve risks in order to achieve sth: *The Bank of England feared that big bonuses linked to short-term performance measures encouraged excessive risk-taking by traders.*

risky /ˈrɪski/ *adj.* (**risk·ier, riski·est**) (You can also use **more risky** and **most risky**.) involving the possibility of sth bad happening **SYN** DANGEROUS: *Individuals engage in risky behaviour in the form of dares and challenges to establish status in the group.* ◇ *Any energy or climate change policy that rests on a bet on the future price of oil is inherently risky.* ■ **riski·ness** /ˈrɪskinəs/ *noun* [U] **~ (of sth)** *Risk perception is an individual's assessment of the riskiness of a situation.*

rite /raɪt/ *noun* **~ (of sth)** a ceremony performed by a particular group of people, often for religious purposes: *Whatever the mood of society, the rites of religion will invariably reflect and reinforce it.* ◇ *burial/initiation/religious rites*

IDM **ˌrite of ˈpassage** a ceremony or an event that marks an important stage in sb's life: *In some cases, gaining full membership of a community is marked by a rite of passage.*

rit·ual /ˈrɪtʃuəl/ *noun* [C, U] a series of actions that are always performed in the same way, especially as part of a religious ceremony: *People kept worshipping their gods and performing religious rituals.* ◇ *Funerals were observed with a high degree of ritual.*

rival¹ /ˈraɪvl/ *noun* a person, organization or thing that competes with another in business, politics, sport, etc: *Although growing in size, the company is still smaller than its two main rivals.* ◇ **~ to sb/sth** *From the 1990s, there was no longer any serious rival to American power.* ◇ **~ for sth** *His chief rival for the Democratic presidential nomination was Hillary Clinton.*

rival² /ˈraɪvl/ *adj.* [only before noun] competing with another person, organization, thing or idea: *A financial services team may break away from the 'parent' organization and establish a rival firm.* ◇ *Agriculture, in this conception, is just another part of the consumer goods industry. In recent years, however, a rival interpretation has emerged.*

rival³ /ˈraɪvl/ *verb* (**-ll-**, *NAmE also* **-l-**) **~ sb/sth** to be as good or impressive as sb/sth else: *Some championed the euro as a way to develop a strong, stable counterpart to rival the dollar internationally.* ➲ *compare* COMPARE (4)

ri·val·ry /ˈraɪvlri/ *noun* (*pl.* **-ries**) [U, C] a state in which two people, companies, etc. are competing for the same thing: **~ (with sb/sth) (for sth)** *A child who experiences sibling rivalry for parental attention may demonstrate aggression.* ◇ *The writer examines McQueen's competitive rivalries with fellow stars such as Paul Newman and Dustin Hoffman.* ◇ **~ (between A and B) (for sth)** *In the market for commercial aircraft, there was fierce rivalry between dominant manufacturers Boeing and Airbus.*

river /ˈrɪvə(r)/ *noun* **1** (*abbr.* **R.**) a natural flow of water that continues in a long line across land to the sea: *China has extensive water storage capabilities along all of its major rivers.* ◇ *the Colorado/Mississippi/Amazon River* ◇ *the River Thames/Congo/Danube* ◇ **+ noun** *a river basin/channel/corridor/valley* **2 ~ (of sth)** a large amount of liquid that is flowing in a particular direction: *The disastrously wet winter buried homes in rivers of mud as massive debris flows occurred on hillsides throughout greater Los Angeles.*

RNA /ˌɑːr en ˈeɪ/ *noun* [U] a chemical present in all living cells, which carries instructions from DNA and is a type of NUCLEIC ACID **HELP** **RNA** is short for 'ribonucleic acid': *Work with animal materials led to the demonstration of the importance of RNA in protein synthesis.*

road /rəʊd; *NAmE* roʊd/ *noun* **1** a hard surface built for vehicles to travel on: *Most cities are growing outward along major roads.* ◇ *The problem of traffic congestion has been addressed by building new roads.* ◇ **by ~** *Logs are exported across the Mekong to Thailand and by road to the port of Vinh in central Vietnam.* ◇ **+ noun** *road traffic/safety* ◇ *road accidents/users* **2 (on the) ~ to sth** the way to achieving sth: *Labour's central claim was that Britain was on the road to recovery.*

IDM **(further) along/down the ˈroad** to or at a later point in a process; to or in the future: *The Asia-Pacific Economic Cooperation forum (APEC) is attempting to move even further along the road of trade liberalization.* **on the ˈroad** **1** travelling in vehicles using roads: *Every year there are more cars on the road in the UK.* **2** moving from place to place, and not staying in one place for very long: *He collected information from fellow journalists who spent much time on the road.*

robot /ˈrəʊbɒt; *NAmE* ˈroʊbɑːt/ *noun* a machine that can perform a complicated series of tasks AUTOMATICALLY, especially one that is programmed by a computer: *Many*

R

of these techniques have been automated and are performed by robots. ■ **ro·bot·ic** /rəʊˈbɒtɪk; *NAmE* roʊˈbɑːtɪk/ *adj.*: *Computer-controlled robotic systems were used to analyse samples.*

ro·bust /rəʊˈbʌst; *NAmE* roʊˈbʌst/ *adj.* **1** (of a system, an organization, a method or evidence) likely to remain successful, strong or valid, even in changing or difficult circumstances: *The findings highlighted a lack of robust evidence to support the proposals.* ◇ *Maximum likelihood is a robust method that has been shown to perform well under many circumstances.* ◇ *Britain also had a robust banking system; the series of banking panics that began to hit the US from October 1930 had no parallel in the UK.* HELP In statistics, a test or result is **robust** if it is not affected very much by changes in the INITIAL conditions used in the test or to arrive at the result: *Results are robust to expanding this cut-off to 5 years.* **2** physically strong and unlikely to break or be damaged or destroyed: *The structure is robust enough to be preserved in many sediments.* **3** strong and determined; showing that you are sure about what you are doing or saying: *Countries which have taken a more robust approach to reform have seen major progress being made in increasing economic growth.* ◇ *While allegiance to institutional religion has declined, religious beliefs are still fairly robust.* ■ **ro·bust·ly** /rəʊˈbʌstli; *NAmE* roʊˈbʌstli/ *adv.*: *The conclusion is that exclusion along ethnic lines is strongly and robustly associated with civil war.* ◇ *They should be robustly made, out of metal rather than fibreglass.* ◇ *Member governments defend their own economic interests robustly at all stages.* **ro·bust·ness** /rəʊˈbʌstnəs; *NAmE* roʊˈbʌstnəs/ *noun* [U] **~ (of sth)** *There are a number of difficulties involved in assessing the robustness of the evidence.* ◇ *The physical robustness of distilled alcohol was a vital factor in this growth in production because it withstood long sea voyages much better than beer or wine.*

rock /rɒk; *NAmE* rɑːk/ *noun* **1** [U, C] the hard solid material that forms part of the surface of the earth and some other planets: *Granite tors are essentially outcrops of solid rock rising above the surface.* ◇ *Igneous petrogenesis is the process or set of processes by which igneous rocks are formed.* ◇ *sedimentary/volcanic/metamorphic rock* **2** [C] a large single piece of rock: *The female baboon was behind a rock where she began grooming a young male.* **3** [C] (*NAmE*) a small piece of rock SYN STONE (2): *Women on the picket lines also jumped on cars and threw rocks at strike-breakers.* **4** (*also* ˈ**rock music**) [U] a type of loud popular music, developed in the 1960s, with a strong beat, played on electric instruments: *Several unlicensed 'pirate' radio stations began broadcasting alternative pop and rock music in 1964.* ◇ **+ noun** *a rock concert/band*

rocky /ˈrɒki; *NAmE* ˈrɑːki/ *adj.* (**rock·ier, rocki·est**) made of rock; full of rocks: *Rocky shores occur on the coasts of many islands in South East Asia.*

rod /rɒd; *NAmE* rɑːd/ *noun* **1** (often in compounds) a long straight piece of wood, metal or glass: *We want to find out whether copper rods expand when heated.* ◇ *The basic ingredients of a nuclear reactor are fuel rods, a moderator, control rods and a coolant.* **2** a type of light-sensitive cell that is found in the part of the eye called the RETINA, responsible mainly for seeing black and white in poor light: *The control of light perception in the rods and cones of the eyes is a complex interplay of many signalling components.* ➲ *compare* CONE (4)

role AWL /rəʊl; *NAmE* roʊl/ *noun* **1** the function that sb/sth has or the part sb/sth plays in a particular situation: **~ of sb/sth** *Students alternate between the roles of teacher and student.* ◇ *The role of surgery is to treat any underlying disease process.* ◇ **~ as sth** *Her role as a wife involved cooking, cleaning and childrearing.* ◇ **~ in sth** *Culture has an important role in the development of humans.* ◇ *Governments played a minor role in most people's daily lives.* ◇ **in sb/sth's ~** *He became unable to function in his role as a professor.* ◇ **+ noun** *In this story, we witness a role reversal as the mother rather than the child is 'taught a lesson'.* ➲ *see also* ROLE MODEL **2** an actor's part in a play, film, etc: *The comedian Harry Secombe took the title role.* ◇ **~ of sb/sth** *She played the role of Jo in 'Little Women'.* ◇ **in a ~** *The films all starrred Niki Karimi in the leading role.*
▸ ADJECTIVE + ROLE **leading • minor** *Governments often take a leading role in technology transfer.* | **important, major • key, crucial, critical, vital, essential • significant • prominent • fundamental • central, pivotal • specific, precise • unique • dominant • dual • primary • active • traditional • causal • potential • decisive • positive • strategic • functional • physiological • regulatory • social • political** *The EGF receptor plays a key role in both normal development and cancer.*
▸ NOUN + ROLE **gender, sex • leadership** *Gender roles enforced by society influence students' personal identities.*
▸ VERB + ROLE **play • perform** *In perfoming a role, the actor creates a kind of life.* | **have • take, assume • fulfil, serve, occupy • emphasize, highlight, stress • examine, explore, investigate • consider, discuss, assess • clarify • define • describe • understand • recognize • acknowledge • assign • strengthen • ignore** *Sen explores the role of ethical norms in our individual behaviour.*
▸ ROLE + NOUN **reversal • play • model • conflict, ambiguity • expectations** *Role ambiguity occurs when salespeople are not certain about actions they should take.*

ˈ**role model** *noun* a person that other people admire and try to copy: *Extended family members can serve as positive role models.* ◇ **~ for sb** *She became a role model for other girls.*

roll[1] /rəʊl; *NAmE* roʊl/ *verb* **1** [I, T] to turn over and over and move in a particular direction; to make an object do this: **+ adv./prep.** *The rock rolled away.* ◇ **~ sth + adv./prep.** *Smears are made by rolling the swab across wax on a slide.* **2** [I, T] to turn over to face a different direction; to make sb/sth do this: **~ (over) (onto sth)** *SUVs are more likely than cars to roll over and kill their occupants.* ◇ **~ sb/sth onto sth** *They rolled the patient onto her side.* **3** [I, T] **~ (sth) + adv./prep.** to move smoothly (on wheels or as if on wheels); to make sth do this: *In 1929, 4.5 m passenger vehicles rolled off assembly lines.* **4** [T] to make sth into the shape of a ball or tube: **~ sth into sth** *The plates are very thin and are rolled into a cylinder to save space.* ◇ **~ sth up** *He rolled up the scroll and gave it back to his attendant.*
PHR V ˌ**roll sth** ˈ**back** to return sth to how it was in the past after progress had been made; to reduce the power or importance of sth: *The reforms weakened the unions and rolled back some of the gains of the early 1970s.* ˌ**roll sth** ˈ**out** (*rather informal*) to officially make a new product available or start a new political CAMPAIGN SYN LAUNCH[1] (1): *In 2006, the company rolled out its brand of cider across the UK.*

roll[2] /rəʊl; *NAmE* roʊl/ *noun* **1** [C] **~ (of sth)** a long piece of paper, cloth, film, etc. that has been wrapped around itself or a tube several times so that it forms the shape of a tube: *a roll of paper/canvas/film* **2** [U] **~ (of sth)** the movement of a ship from side to side in the water or of an aircraft in the air so that one side is higher than the other: *This movement has been likened to the roll of a ship.* **3** [C] an official list of names: *Electoral rolls have been used to estimate small area populations.* ◇ **on a ~** *She and her children ended up on the welfare rolls.*

Roman Catholic /ˌrəʊmən ˈkæθlɪk; *NAmE* ˌroʊmən ˈkæθlɪk/ (*also* **Cath·olic**) *noun* (*abbr.* **RC**) a member of the part of the Christian Church that has the POPE as its leader: *She was brought up a Roman Catholic.* ■ ˌ**Roman** ˈ**Catholic** (*also* **Cath·olic**) *adj.*: *the Roman Catholic Church*

R

ˌ**Roman Caˈtholicism** (*also* **Cath·oli·cism**) *noun* [U] *his conversion to Roman Catholicism*

ro·mance /rəʊˈmæns; ˈrəʊmæns; *NAmE* ˈroʊmæns/ *noun* **1** [C] **~ (with sb)** an exciting, usually short, relationship between two people who are in love with each other: *Titus had a well-known romance with the Jewish princess Berenice.* **2** [U] love or the feeling of being in love: *While women have realistic perspectives on marriage, they also believe romance is important.* **3** [U] **~ (of sth)** a feeling of excitement and adventure, especially connected with a particular place or activity: *Pyle wrote, not about the romance of war, but about the details of death and dying.* **4** [C, U] a story about a love affair; these stories as a type of literature: *As in a conventional romance, the final scenes involve marriage.* **5** [C, U] a story of excitement and adventure, often set in the past; these stories as a type of literature: *In the Middle Ages, romances were considered to be stories of adventure told in rhyme.*

ro·man·tic /rəʊˈmæntɪk; *NAmE* roʊˈmæntɪk/ *adj.* **1** involving love between two people who are sexually attracted to each other: *We typically assume that marriages are built on romantic love.* ◇ *Desiderio has romantic liaisons with various women.* **2** connected with love, especially in a way that is too obvious or perfect: *The Hollywood romantic comedy reached its peak in the 1930s.* ◇ *Childs sees the final shots of the film as a clichéd romantic ending.* **3** having an attitude to life in which imagination and the emotions are especially important; not looking at situations in a realistic way: *Many people had romantic visions of agrarian life.* **4 Romantic** [usually before noun] used to describe literature, music or art, especially of the 19th century, that is concerned with strong feelings, imagination and a return to nature, rather than reason and order: *The nature of religious feeling and the significance of the imagination figure prominently in Romantic literature.* ■ **ro·man·tic·al·ly** /rəʊˈmæntɪkli; *NAmE* roʊˈmæntɪkli/ *adv.*: *About one fifth of the couples were unmarried but were romantically involved with one another at the time of their child's birth.* ◇ *There are constant references to the romantically dangerous draw of the sea.*

ro·man·ti·cism /rəʊˈmæntɪsɪzəm; *NAmE* roʊˈmæntɪsɪzəm/ *noun* [U] **1** (*also* **Romanticism**) a style and movement in art, music and literature in the late 18th and early 19th century, in which strong feelings, imagination and a return to nature were more important than reason and order: *Eighteenth-century Romanticism asserts the value of aesthetic and emotional experience.* **2** the quality of seeing people, events and situations as more exciting and interesting than they really are: *A commercial hit, the film was criticized for its romanticism.* ➲ *compare* REALISM (2)

roof /ruːf/ *noun* (*pl.* **roofs**) **1** the structure that covers or forms the top of a building or vehicle: *Roofs of houses and buildings collapsed under the weight of accumulating volcanic ash.* **2** the top of an underground space such as a tunnel or CAVE: *Much more violent eruptions may occur where major faults reach down to the roof of a magma chamber.*
IDM **under sb's/the same ˈroof** in a particular building or house: *In this historical definition, the 'family' included all those living under the same roof, including servants.*

room /ruːm; rʊm/ *noun* **1** [U] empty space that can be used for a particular purpose: **~ for sb/sth** *Most of the canals have been backfilled to make room for road construction.* ◇ **~ to do sth** *Small farmers had neither room to expand nor access to grazing land (Wibking, 1963).* **2** [U] the possibility of sth existing or happening; the opportunity to do sth: **~ for sth** *This explanation still leaves room for ambiguity.* ◇ *There is room for improvement in the way the programme is managed.* ◇ **~ to do sth** *This policy left the government with very little room to manoeuvre.* **3** [C] a part of a building that has its own walls, floor and ceiling and is usually used for a particular purpose: *On three occasions, the teacher asked students to leave the room when they got into personal arguments with each other.* ◇ *a waiting/dining/operating room* **IDM** *see* MANOEUVRE[1]

ˈ**room temperature** *noun* [U] the normal temperature inside a building: **at ~** *Plant samples were air-dried at room temperature.*

root[1] /ruːt/ *noun* **1** [C] the part of a plant that grows under the ground and absorbs water and minerals that it sends to the rest of the plant: *Large trees have deep roots, giving access to a large volume of soil.* ◇ **~ of sth** *The roots of each plant were washed to remove any remnants of soil.* **2** [C, usually sing.] **~ of sth** the main cause of sth, such as a problem or difficult situation: *These considerations, while important, fail to get to the root of the problem.* **3** [C usually pl.] the basis of sth: *Some of the major multinational chocolate manufacturers can trace their roots to this period.* ◇ **have roots in sth** *Ethics has its roots in the study of philosophy.* **4 roots** [pl.] the feelings or connections that you have with a place because you have lived there or your family came from there: *The powerful can come from vastly different backgrounds: many politicians have working-class roots.* ◇ *Many people feel that their spiritual roots lie in the land where their ancestors lived and farmed.* **5** [C] (*linguistics*) the part of a word that has the main meaning and that its other forms are based on; a word that other words are formed from: *Grammatical words like 'the', 'and' and 'of' have no lexical roots at all.* ◇ *The word 'haram' (sacred or forbidden) shares the same root with 'harim'—the part of the household reserved for women.* **6** [C] **~ (of sth)** (*mathematics*) a quantity which, when multiplied by itself a particular number of times, produces another quantity: *My calculator tells me that the square root of 75 is 8.66.* ➲ *see also* SQUARE ROOT
IDM ˌ**root and ˈbranch** thorough and complete: *Farmers welcomed a root and branch reform of agricultural policy.* **take ˈroot 1** (of a plant) to develop roots: *Some shrubs and small trees take root in the crevices of the limestone.* **2** (of an idea) to become widely accepted: *Mill argued that human rights cannot take root if they are imposed by outsiders.*

root[2] /ruːt/ *verb* [I] (of a plant) to grow roots: *Crops will not root, grow and flourish without water to nourish them.*
PHR V ˌ**root sth/sb ˈout** to find a person or thing that is causing a problem and remove or get rid of them: *The government was determined to root out corruption linked with expenses.*

root·ed /ˈruːtɪd/ *adj.* **1 ~ in sth** developing from or being strongly influenced by sth: *The characters are firmly rooted in a comic tradition, with important roles for slaves, soldiers and cooks.* **2 ~ in sth** fixed in one place; not moving or changing: *Chinese management is deeply rooted in cultural traditions that will take a long time to change.*

rope /rəʊp; *NAmE* roʊp/ *noun* [C, U] very strong thick string made of thinner strings or wires twisted together: *For this, a cable rope made of strands of thin steel wires is used.* ◇ *a piece/length of rope*

rose *past tense of* RISE[2]

ro·tate /rəʊˈteɪt; *NAmE* ˈroʊteɪt/ *verb* **1** [I, T] to move or turn around a central fixed point; to make sth do this: *Some disks rotate at 15 000 rpm.* ◇ **~ about/around sth** *Every spherical body rotates around an axis.* ◇ **~ sth** *The object had only been rotated a few degrees.* **2** [I, T] to regularly change who does a particular job or activity: **+ adv./prep.** *A roster is drawn up and students rotate through the jobs during the year.* ◇ **~ sth** *The new computers made it easier for workers to rotate jobs.* ■ **ro·tat·ing** *adj.* [only before noun] *The fibre band is fed onto a rotating mandrel.* ◇ *A board exhibits a rotating selection of children's work.*

ro·ta·tion /rəʊˈteɪʃn; *NAmE* roʊˈteɪʃn/ *noun* **1** [U, C] the action of sth moving in a circle around a central fixed point; one complete movement in a circle around a fixed point: **~ (of sth)** *Clockwise rotation of wind direction is known as veering.* ◇ **~ around/about sth** *The fall of the card from a horizontal position usually implies a rotation around its axis of symmetry.* **2** [U, C] the act of regularly changing the thing that is being used in a particular situation, or of changing the person who does a particular job: *Firms can achieve greater flexibility through job rotation.* ◇ *Crop rotation is standard, because it has both environmental and economic advantages.* ◇ **in ~ (with sth)** *Irrigated rice is grown in rotation with dry crops.*

ro·ta·tion·al /rəʊˈteɪʃənl; *NAmE* roʊˈteɪʃənl/ *adj.* connected with the movement of objects in a circle around a central fixed point: *A pin-joint allows rotational motion about its axis.* ◇ *The maximum rotational speed of the shaft is 6 500 rpm.*

rote /rəʊt; *NAmE* roʊt/ *noun* [U] (often used as an adjective) the process of learning sth by repeating it until you remember it rather than by understanding the meaning of it: **by ~** *At the grammar schools, students learned the classics by rote.* ◇ **+ noun** *The new system of education encouraged understanding rather than conventional rote learning.*

rough /rʌf/ *adj.* (**rough·er, rough·est**) **1** having a surface that is not even, regular or smooth: *The rough surface is then coated with a thin layer of resin.* ◇ *rough grassland/pasture/terrain* OPP SMOOTH[1] (1) **2** not exact; not including all details SYN APPROXIMATE[1]: *These potential increases are only rough approximations.* ◇ *He gave a rough sketch of his plan.* ◇ *It is possible to make a rough estimate of the number of genes that remain to be identified.* OPP EXACT (1), PRECISE (1) ➲ *see also* ROUGHLY **3** not gentle or careful; violent: *Most complaints received concern rough handling by police.* ◇ *Boys were expected to be rough.*

rough·ly /ˈrʌfli/ *adv.* approximately but not exactly: *The gender split was roughly equal, with 11 males and 13 females.* ◇ *'Advertere' may be roughly translated as 'to turn towards'.*

IDM **roughly speaking** used to introduce sth that is true in a very general way and is not precise or exact: *Roughly speaking, 'resources' are 'goods'.* ◇ *The set N is, roughly speaking, the simplest infinite set.*

rough·ness /ˈrʌfnəs/ *noun* [U] the quality of having a surface that is not even, regular or smooth: *The boulders appear fresh with little surface roughness.*

round[1] /raʊnd/ *adj.* (**round·er, round·est**) **1** shaped like a circle or a ball: *They were armed with short swords and small round shields.* ◇ *It is a fact that the earth is round.* HELP You can also use **circular** for sth that is shaped like a circle and **spherical** for sth that is shaped like a ball. **2** having a curved shape: *The script is characterized by large round letters.* ◇ *Impressive round towers made of stone became characteristic features of major ecclesiastical sites.*

round[2] /raʊnd/ *adv.* (*especially BrE*) (*NAmE usually* **around**) For the special uses of **round** in phrasal verbs, look at the entries for the verbs. For example, **come round** is in the phrasal verb section at **come**. **1** in a circle or in a curve to face another way: *Each time the planet goes round, it rotates a little.* **2** marking the edge or outside of sth: *Large temples had columns all round.* **3** on all sides of sb/sth: *Everyone huddled round to look at the computer screen.* **4** from one place, person, etc. to another: *He travelled round collecting folk songs and stories.* ◇ *There is barely enough food to go round.*

IDM ˌ**round aˈbout** approximately: *Round about 50 million years ago, Antarctica separated from Australia.* ➲ *see also* THE OTHER WAY ROUND

round[3] /raʊnd/ *prep.* (*especially BrE*) (*NAmE usually* **around**) **1** in a circle: *The children formed a circle round the teacher.* ◇ *The experiment used two aircraft going round the earth in opposite directions.* **2** on, to or from the other side of sth: *Ships began regularly sailing round the Cape of Good Hope en route to the East Indies.* **3** on all sides of sb/sth; surrounding sb/sth: *The ring is like a tyre mounted round the core of each wheel.* **4** in or to many parts of sth: *Email means you can communicate with people all round the world.* ◇ *The baby was crawling round the floor in a filthy nappy.* **5** to fit in with particular people, ideas, etc: *A number of Ford films are built round the theme of the quest for the Promised Land.*

round[4] /raʊnd/ *noun* **1 ~ (of sth)** a set of events that form part of a longer process: *A new round of negotiations towards further reductions in barriers to trade began in March 2000.* ◇ *For its part, the Commission launched successive rounds of reform.* **2 ~ (of sth)** a regular series of activities: *They desperately wish to escape the daily round of labour and struggle.*

round[5] /raʊnd/ *verb* **1 ~ sth (up/down) (to sth)** to increase or decrease a number to the next highest or lowest whole number: *Percentages are often rounded up or down in frequency tables.* **2 ~ sth** to go around sth in order to move in another direction: *As sea transport improved, ships were able to round the Cape of Good Hope en route to the East Indies.* **3 ~ sth** to make sth into a round shape: *We should use a fillet to round the sharp inside corners.*

round·ed /ˈraʊndɪd/ *adj.* [usually before noun] **1** having a round shape: *The landscape is dominated by outcrops of massive granite and scattered rounded boulders.* **2** having a wide variety of qualities that combine to produce sth that is complete and balanced: *A good business biography has a rounded and balanced treatment of the subject's career and personal qualities.*

route[1] AWL /ruːt; *NAmE also* raʊt/ *noun* **1** a way that sb/sth follows to get from one place to another: *In the spring, the birds take the same route back.* ◇ *to follow a different/alternative route* ◇ **~ between A and B** *They recommend varying the route between office and home.* ◇ **~ (from A) to B** *The map helps us find the correct route to our destination.* ◇ **by/via ~** *A virtual circuit first establishes a route through the network and then sends all the packets, in order, via this route.* **2** a fixed way along which a bus, train, etc. regularly travels or goods are regularly sent: *Low-cost operators knew the cost of flying each route.* ◇ *Before about 1450, Europe, Asia and Africa were linked only by a few overland trade routes.* **3** a particular way of achieving sth: *Most countries chose a middle route somewhere between the two strategies.* ◇ **~ to sth** *Education was one of the preferred routes to social mobility.* ◇ **by/via ~** *The production of ceramics by this novel route has generated a great deal of interest.*

route[2] AWL /ruːt; *NAmE also* raʊt/ *verb* (**rout·ing** or **route·ing, rout·ed, rout·ed**) **~ sb/sth (+ adv./prep.)** to send sb/sth by a particular route: *To minimize fuel wastage, flights are individually routed to avoid flying against strong winds.*

rou·tine[1] /ruːˈtiːn/ *adj.* [usually before noun] **1** done or happening as a normal part of a particular job, situation or process: *All children have a routine check-up at the child health clinic.* ◇ *Routine use of the vaccine has almost eliminated the disease.* **2** not unusual or different in any way: *By 1800, sailing across the Atlantic had become almost routine.* **3** ordinary and boring, especially because of being repeated many times in the same way:

Even the lowliest, most routine jobs in organizations can be made meaningful.

rou·tine² /ruːˈtiːn/ *noun* **1** [C, U] the normal order and way in which things are regularly done: *Some autistic children are distressed by changes in their daily routine.* ◇ *They consulted monolingual English learners' dictionaries as a matter of routine.* **2** [C] a series of movements, funny stories, etc. that are part of a performance: *The dance routine was carefully choreographed.* ◇ *John Cleese did a 15-minute comedy routine.* **3** [C] (*computing*) a list of instructions that enable a computer to perform a particular task: *Most statistical computer packages contain routines to select a subset of the explanatory variables.*

rou·tine·ly /ruːˈtiːnli/ *adv.* as a normal part of a job, situation or process: *By the 1930s, the EEG was routinely used in neurology.* ◇ *Increased numbers of homeless people were seen searching routinely through garbage containers.*

row /rəʊ; *NAmE* roʊ/ *noun* **1** one of the horizontal sections into which a table is divided: *The top row of Table 1 shows the recommended target values.* ➲ *compare* COLUMN (1) **2** ~ **(of sb/sth)** a line of numbers, things or people: *This is shown by a row of zeros.* ◇ *The plan shows a row of beech trees along the boundary of the car park.*
IDM **in a ˈrow** **1** if sth happens several times **in a row**, it happens in the same way each time, and nothing different happens in the time between: *Tony Blair is the only Labour leader to have won three elections in a row.* **2** if sth happens for several days, etc. **in a row**, it happens on each of those days: *The city then suffered drought for three years in a row.*

royal /ˈrɔɪəl/ *adj.* [only before noun] connected with or belonging to the king or queen of a country: *The royal family lived in splendour in the Topkapi palace.* ◇ *In Denmark, the slave trade was ended by royal decree in 1803.*

roy·alty /ˈrɔɪəlti/ *noun* (*pl.* **-ies**) **1** [U] one or more members of a royal family: *Major new collections were visited by royalty and aristocracy.* **2** [C, usually pl.] a sum of money that is paid by an oil or MINING company to the owner of the land that they are working on: *Landowners may receive royalties of 12–20% of well revenues.* ◇ **+ noun** *Firms in extractive industries were pressured to reveal their royalty payments to host country governments.* **3** [C, usually pl.] a sum of money that is paid to sb who has written a book, piece of music, etc. each time that it is sold or performed: *The costs of paying royalties to artists must be taken into account.*

rub·ber /ˈrʌbə(r)/ *noun* [U] a strong substance that can be stretched and does not allow liquids to pass through it, made from the liquid inside a tropical plant or produced using chemicals: *Malaysia remains the world's largest supplier of natural rubber.* ◇ *Synthetic rubber is also available.* ◇ **+ noun** *a rubber band/tube/tyre/bullet*

rub·bish /ˈrʌbɪʃ/ *noun* [U] (*especially BrE*) things that you throw away because you no longer want or need them SYN GARBAGE: **+ noun** *Visual pollution includes billboards, rubbish dumps and other man-made structures that destroy the beauty of a landscape.*

rude /ruːd/ *adj.* (**ruder, rud·est**) having or showing a lack of respect for other people and their feelings: *He was known as a rather rude, aggressive and occasionally violent man.* ◇ *Most of the students considered her remarks rude and inappropriate.* ◇ **~ to sb (about sb/sth)** *A secretary had complained that Brown had been rude to her.* ◇ **it is ~ to do sth** *In many countries, it is rude to openly disagree with someone.* ■ **rude·ly** *adv.*: *When she was asked to get more involved, she responded rudely.*

ruin¹ /ˈruːɪn/ *noun* **1** [U] **~ (of sth)** the state or process of being destroyed or badly damaged: *The second shock completed the ruin of those buildings which had already been severely damaged.* ◇ *It was a policy that led to the ruin of Catholicism and the triumph of the Protestant party.* **2** [U] the fact of having lost all your money or your social position: *Divorce often spelled financial ruin for women.* ◇ *A steep fall in sugar prices brought colonial plantations to the brink of ruin.* **3** [C] (*also* **ruins** [pl.]) the parts of a building that remain after it has been destroyed or severely damaged: *A path runs through the ancient ruins.* ◇ **~ of sth** *In 1870, Heinrich Schliemann excavated the ruins of Troy in north-west Anatolia.*
IDM **in ˈruins** destroyed or badly damaged: *Much of the city lay in ruins.* ◇ *Their dreams of empire were in ruins.*

ruin² /ˈruːɪn/ *verb* **1 ~ sth** to damage sth so badly that it loses all its value or pleasure: *The damage done to his face ruined his chances as an actor.* ◇ *a ruined building/city/temple* **2 ~ sb/sth** to make sb/sth lose all their money or their social position: *The Great Fire of London destroyed his house and ruined him economically (Boorstin, 1984).*

rule¹ /ruːl/ *noun* **1** [C] a statement of what may, must or must not be done in a particular situation: *The same rules apply to all applicants.* ◇ **~ for sth/sb** *The UK was one of the first nations to establish rules for the operation of companies.* ◇ **according to ~** *Crimes are categorized according to Home Office rules.* ◇ **rules and regulations** *The changes in the rules and regulations governing higher education were substantial.* **2** [C, usually sing.] the normal state of things; what is true in most cases: *It was not until the growth of capitalism that rapid population growth became the rule rather than the exception.* ◇ **an exception to the ~** *Corporate bias in the media has undoubtedly increased, with independent journalists becoming exceptions to the rule.* ◇ **as a (general) ~** *As a rule, local leaders in British cities do not gain significant national media attention.* **3** [U] the government of a country or control of a group of people by a particular person, group or system: *In Northern Ireland, the British government imposed direct rule from London in 1972.* ◇ *Military rule in Argentina eventually collapsed for internal reasons.* ◇ *Arguably, majority rule provides more effective government.* ◇ **under... ~** *Sudan was under joint British and Egyptian rule between 1899 and 1955.* ◇ **against... ~** *The last revolt against Soviet-communist rule happened in Poland in 1980.* **4** [C] **~ (of sth)** a statement of what is possible according to a particular system, for example the grammar of a language: *By the age of five, children have mastered very complex rules of language, although they cannot consciously understand them.*
IDM **play by the ˈrules** (*rather informal*) to follow the rules of a particular system and act fairly and honestly: *China, as a rising capitalist power playing by the rules of the market, may turn out to be the most formidable threat ever faced by the USA.* **the rules of the ˈgame** (*rather informal*) the standards of behaviour that most people accept or that actually operate in a particular area of life or business: *As in sports, it is the rules of the game that distinguish one economic system from another.* **the rule of ˈlaw** the condition in which all members of society, including its rulers, accept the authority of the law: *Their priority was to establish the rule of law and orderly administration.* **a rule of ˈthumb** a practical method of doing or measuring sth, usually based on past experience rather than on exact measurement: *The common rule of thumb is to delay any potential surgery until skeletal maturity is reached.* ➲ *more at* BEND¹, DIVIDE¹, GENERAL¹

▸ ADJECTIVE + RULE **strict • simple • basic • common • new • formal • informal • legal • voting • international** *Strict health and safety rules were followed.* | **democratic • authoritarian • military • colonial • imperial** *In 1992, the country re-established democratic rule after massive protests ousted the military-backed government.*

▸ VERB + RULE **create, formulate, set • introduce, implement • adopt • observe, abide by • break • bend**

R

Many organizations have created voluntary rules or codes of conduct for transacting business internationally. | **establish** • **enforce, impose** • **accept** *The Government of India Act (1858) established British colonial rule over India.* | **use** • **violate** • **follow, obey, adhere to, conform to** • **satisfy** , **learn** • **change, modify, alter** • **apply** *Using the same rule, we then determined the final answer.* ◇ *Both generals were accused of committing war crimes by violating the rules of war.*

▸ RULE + VERB **govern** • **relate to, concern, regarding** • **apply** *There are simple rules governing the way these molecular structures are formed.*

▸ NOUN + OF RULES/A RULE **set, system, body, framework** • **application** • **enforcement** • **breach, violation** *Attempting to follow a set of rules inevitably brings problems of interpretation.* ◇ *Breaches of this rule were to be punished most severely.*

rule² /ruːl/ *verb* **1** [T, I] to control and have authority over a country or group of people: **~ sth** *In fact, the Conservative Party had ruled Britain for around three quarters of the twentieth century.* ◇ (*figurative*) *Eighty million years ago, dinosaurs ruled the earth.* ◇ **~ (over sb/sth)** *This was the period in which Spain ruled over Portugal.* ◇ *Ptolemy VII ruled briefly together with his father in 145 BC.* ◇ (*figurative*) *After the revolution, anarchy ruled.* **2** [T, often passive] **~ sth** (*often disapproving*) to be the main thing that influences and controls sb/sth: *The pursuit of money ruled his life.* ◇ *We live in a society where we are ruled by the clock.* **3** [I, T] to give an official decision about sth SYN PRONOUNCE (2): **~ on sth** *The Crown Court felt that it was unable to rule on this question.* ◇ **~ against/in favour of sb/sth** *The House of Lords ruled in her favour.* ◇ **~ sb/sth + adj.** *The deal may be ruled illegal.* ◇ **~ sb/sth to be/have sth** *The deal was ruled to be illegal.* ◇ **~ that...** *The court ruled that the women had been unfairly dismissed.* ◇ **it is ruled that...** *It was ruled that the women had been unfairly dismissed.* IDM see DIVIDE¹

PHR V ˌ**rule sb/sth ˈout (as sth) 1** to state that sth is not possible or that sb/sth is not suitable SYN EXCLUDE (3): *Therefore, we cannot rule out the possibility of selection or publication bias in the review.* ◇ *However, some studies have ruled out fruit and vegetable intake as an explanation for these differences.* **2** to prevent sb from doing sth; to prevent sth from happening: *His age effectively ruled him out as a possible candidate.*

ruler /ˈruːlə(r)/ *noun* a person who rules or governs: *Egypt very early on became a united kingdom under a single ruler, the pharaoh.*

rul·ing¹ /ˈruːlɪŋ/ *noun* an official decision made by sb in a position of authority, especially a judge: **~ (on sth)** *The Court must give a preliminary ruling on such cases within three months.* ◇ *The ruling was reversed in the appeal court.* ◇ **~ that...** *Discrimination continued even after the 1954 Supreme Court ruling that black and white US children had an equal right to education.*

rul·ing² /ˈruːlɪŋ/ *adj.* [only before noun] having control over a particular group or country: *In Taiwan, the leaders of the ruling party played greater leadership roles.* ◇ *Willis argues that working-class resistance to the authority of the ruling class is generally futile.*

run¹ /rʌn/ *verb* (**running, ran** /ræn/, **run**) **1** [T] to be in charge of a business or organization SYN MANAGE (3): **~ sth** *The iTunes Store is an online business run by Apple Inc.* ◇ **~ sth + adv./prep.** *Some of the leading colleges are now run as companies (Thrift, 2005: 35).* ➲ *see also* RUNNING (1) **2** [T] **~ sth** to make a service, course of study, etc. available to people SYN ORGANIZE (1): *Many training institutions run specialist courses for post-registration students.* ◇ *In 2003, the Ontario government ran a campaign to encourage voter turnout at the next election.* **3** [I, T] to operate or function; to make sth operate or function: **+ adv./prep.** *The earlier machines were incapable of running at the required speed.* ◇ *All the software ran on IBM computers.* ◇ **~ sth** *The hydrogen was burnt and the heat produced was used to run a steam engine.* ◇ *The computer was running a spreadsheet program.* **4** [T] **~ a test, an experiment, an analysis, etc.** to do a test, an experiment, etc: *Accidental errors were identified by running the tests after each major modification.* ◇ *Variants of Swinney's experiment have been run many times.* **5** [T] **~ a deficit/surplus** (*economics*) to manage a country's economy so that the country is in debt/not in debt: *Germany ran a small deficit throughout the 1980–2001 period.* **6** [I] to be a candidate in an election for a political position, especially in the US: *In the 1992 elections, Ross Perot ran as a third-party candidate.* ◇ **~ for sb/sth** *In most Muslim countries, women can vote and run for political office.* ◇ **~ in sth** *After being sentenced to twelve months in prison, he was no longer able to run in the 2011 election.* ➲ *compare* STAND¹ (12) **7** [I] (usually used in the progressive tenses) **+ adv./prep.** to happen at the time or in the way mentioned: *Technological innovation is now running at an unprecedented rate.* ◇ *The meeting did not run as smoothly as anticipated.* **8** [I] to continue for a particular period of time without stopping: **~ for sth** *'The Fate of Frankenstein' ran for 37 performances at the English Opera House in 1823.* ◇ **~ from A to B** (*especially BrE*) *The current holder of the post is Richard Toms, whose term of office runs from June 2013 to June 2015.* ◇ **~ from A through B** (*NAmE*) *The fiscal year of the federal government runs from October 1 through September 30.* **9** [I] **+ adv./prep.** to be at or near a particular level: *Estimates for the number of visitors to the site run as high as 3 million.* **10** [I] **+ adj.** to become different in a particular way, especially a bad way: *Within days of the strike starting, petrol stations began to run short of petrol and diesel.* ◇ *The river currently runs dry during the peak irrigation season (Zhongmin et al.).* **11** [I, T] to lead or stretch from one place to another; to make sth do this: **+ adv./prep.** *The village lies within the fertile strip that runs along the river bank.* ◇ **~ sth** *This trench runs the length of the Andes, about 75 km offshore.* ◇ **~ sth + adv./prep.** *Easements include the right to run cables and pipes over (or under) land belonging to others.* **12** [I] **~ from A to B** to range from one thing or person to another: *As a consequence of its vast size, China's climate runs from one extreme to the other.* **13** [I] to move using your legs, going faster than when you walk: *Factory-farmed chickens may suffer from weaknesses that can impair their ability to run.* ◇ **+ adv./prep.** *Most of the children were frightened and ran off.* **14** [I] (**+ adv./prep.**) (of liquid) to flow: *The rainwater runs down the rock faces.* ◇ *Many of these rural homes have no electricity or running water.* **15** [I, T] (of a story or an argument) to have particular words or contents: *Australian literature, so the argument runs, is both producer and product of continuing racial tensions.* **16** [T] **~ sth** to print and publish an item or a story: *In 2000, the 'Daily Mail' ran 200 stories about asylum seekers.*

IDM Most idioms containing **run** are at the entries for the nouns and adjectives in the idioms, for example **run a risk** is at **risk** *noun*. ˌ**up and ˈrunning** (*rather informal*) working fully and correctly: *It took two months to get the website up and running.*

PHR V ˌ**run aˈway (from sb/...)** to leave sb/a place suddenly; to escape from sb/a place: *Slaves ran away from their owners for many different reasons.*

ˌ**run sth ˈdown** to make sth gradually stop functioning or become smaller in size or number: *Monetary authorities had completely run down their foreign exchange reserves.*

ˈ**run into sth 1** to experience problems: *The company's plan soon ran into difficulty.* **2** to reach a particular level or amount: *The cost of such software management systems can run into many millions of pounds.*

ˌ**run ˈout** (of a supply of sth) to be used up or finished: *Even in the 1860s, economists were predicting that coal* *would soon run out.* ◇ *He said he felt under pressure and that time was running out.*

ˌ**run sb/sth ˈover** (of a vehicle or its driver) to hit a person or an animal and drive over their body or a part of it: *The defendant was accused of running over the victim in his car.*

ˌ**run ˈthrough sth 1** [no passive] to be present in every part of sth: *A key thread running through all these documents is the idea of cooperation.* **2** to discuss, repeat or read sth quickly: *In his speech, the prime minister ran through a long list of the problems the country was facing.*

ˈ**run to sth** to be of a particular size or amount: *Justinian's summary of all Roman law ran to over a million words.* ◇ *The total investment runs to around a billion dollars.*

ˌ**run sth ˈup** to allow a debt or bill to reach a large total SYN ACCUMULATE (1): *Clearly, poor banking regulation allowed banks to run up too much debt.* ˌ**run ˈup against sth** to experience a difficulty: *It seemed that almost every topic would run up against the restrictions of school censorship.*

run² /rʌn/ *noun* **1** [C] an act of running; a period of time spent running; the distance that sb runs: *They gradually picked up speed and then broke into a run.* ◇ *She sometimes goes for a run with her mother.* **2** [C] an occasion when a system or test is carried out from start to finish: *This pH gradient was used after a trial run with pH 3-10.* ◇ **~ of sth** *Each sequence represents one run of the experiment.* **3** [C] the amount of a product that a company decides to make at one time: *Such huge print runs soon dropped.* ◇ **~ of sth** *Managers tend to prefer long production runs of standardized products.* **4** [C] a series of performances of a play or film: *'Fargo' grossed three times its $7 million budget in its initial run.* **5** [C] **~ of sth** a period of sth good or bad happening; a series of successes or failures SYN SPELL² (1): *However, his run of good luck was not to last.* ◇ *Frequent runs of bad harvests had set firm limits to population growth.* **6** [C, usually sing.] **~ on the dollar, pound, etc.** a situation when many people sell dollars, etc. and the value of the money falls: *The run on the schilling intensified.* **7** [C, usually sing.] **~ on sth** a situation when many people suddenly want to buy sth: *A run on gold in 1797 forced the government to suspend cash payments.* **8** [C, usually sing.] **~ on a bank** a situation when many people suddenly want to take their money out of a bank: *Reports of liquidity problems at Northern Rock prompted a run on the bank.*

IDM **in the ˈlong/ˈshort/ˈmedium run** used to describe what will happen a long, short, etc. time in the future: *Better relationships with staff may cost more in the short run, but can lead to greater performance in the long run.* **on the ˈrun** trying to avoid being captured: *Younger runaway slaves were better able to cope with the difficulties of life on the run.*

run·away /ˈrʌnəweɪ/ *adj.* [only before noun] **1** happening very easily or quickly, and not able to be controlled: *She has little hope that runaway climate change can be prevented.* **2** (of a person) having left without telling anyone: *The law undermined the ability of slaveholders to recover runaway slaves.*

rung *past part. of* RING³

run·ning /ˈrʌnɪŋ/ *noun* [U] **1** the activity of managing or operating sth: **~ (of sth)** *Founders may become somewhat detached from the running of the business.* ◇ *It is these norms that ensure the smooth running of society.* ◇ **+ noun** *Once an electrode and meter have been purchased, the running cost is low.* **2** the action or sport of running: *She enjoyed the running for its own sake as well as for the competition.* ◇ *long-distance/cross-country running*

ˈ**run-off** *noun* **1** [U, C] rain, water or other liquid that runs off land into streams and rivers: *First, the total volume of annual river run-off into East Juyan Lake was calculated.* ◇ *The water has been polluted by run-offs from farmland.* **2** [C] a second vote or competition that is held to find a winner: **+ noun** *In Marburg, the result was a run-off election between von Gerlach and the conservative von Pappenheim.*

rup·ture¹ /ˈrʌptʃə(r)/ *noun* [C, U] **1 ~ (of sth)** an injury in which sth inside the body breaks apart or bursts: *This type of haemorrhage is caused by the sudden rupture of a blood vessel over the surface of the brain.* **2 ~ (of sth)** a situation when sth breaks or bursts: *After an earthquake, buildings may suffer explosions after the rupture of underground pipes.* **3 ~ in/with/between sb/sth** the ending of agreement or of good relations between people, countries, etc: *These acts of violence created deep ruptures in the fabric of society.*

rup·ture² /ˈrʌptʃə(r)/ *verb* **1** [T, I] **~ (sth)** to burst or break apart sth inside the body; to be broken or burst apart: *The internal bleeding was due to a ruptured spleen.* ◇ *Blisters can rupture, leaving large painful areas on the skin.* **2** [T, I] **~ (sth)** to make sth break or burst; to be broken or burst: *A large earthquake ruptures a fault area of about 1 000 km.* ◇ *Segments of the San Andreas fault ruptured in very large earthquakes.* **3** [T] **~ sth** to make an agreement or good relations between people or countries end: *Crises rupture our social communities and expose conditions beyond our control.*

rural /ˈrʊərəl; *NAmE* ˈrʊrəl/ *adj.* [usually before noun] connected with or like the countryside: *Much of the industry is small-scale and scattered in villages in rural areas of the country.* ◇ *Subsistence farming is the major source of livelihood for the country's rural poor.* ◇ *Since 1950, the balance of the population has shifted from predominantly rural to overwhelmingly urban.* ➲ *compare* URBAN

▸ RURAL + ADJECTIVE **area • district • county • settlement • village • setting • landscape • life • community • society • population • resident, dweller • household • economy • development • poverty • poor** *Rural communities began to meet many of their material needs through imports.*

S s

sa·cred /ˈseɪkrɪd/ *adj.* **1** connected with God or a god and thought to deserve special respect SYN HOLY: *Hindus regard cows as sacred and not to be consumed.* ◇ *Formally opened in 1995, the temple today is a sacred space for Buddhists.* ◇ *The study of the sacred text is considered the most central act of devotion to God.* **2** very important and treated with great respect: *In some organizations, the group meeting is sacred and the search for consensus critical.* ◇ **~ to sb** *Marx's writings are as sacred to some communists as is the Bible to the most sincere and devout of Christians.* ■ **sa·cred·ness** *noun* [U] **~ of sb/sth** *One main aspect of Hinduism is the belief in the sacredness of all living creatures.*

sac·ri·fice¹ /ˈsækrɪfaɪs/ *noun* **1** [C, U] the fact of giving up sth important or valuable to you in order to get or do something that seems more important; sth that you give up in this way: *Each of these communities depends on the willingness to make some personal sacrifices for a more general good.* ◇ **~ of sth** *Setting the same net price in both markets will involve some sacrifice of profit.* **2** [C, U] the act of offering sth to a god, especially an animal that has been killed in a special way; an animal, etc. that is offered in this way: *The gods were honoured with animal sacrifices and other offerings.* ◇ **~ to sb** *Alexander offered sacrifice to Babylon's chief god Marduk.*

sac·ri·fice² /ˈsækrɪfaɪs/ *verb* **1** [T] to give up sth that is important or valuable to you in order to get or do sth that seems more important for yourself or for another person:

~ sth *They were accused of sacrificing their professional integrity to serve the interests of power.* ◇ **~ sth for (the sake of) sb/sth** *Sometimes it may be necessary to sacrifice a lesser good for a greater good* ◇ **~ yourself** *He was the first Tamil soldier to willingly sacrifice himself in battle.* **2** [T, I] to kill an animal or a person and offer it/them to a god, in order to please the god: **~ sb/sth** *Agamemnon decided to sacrifice his own daughter to save his community.* ◇ **~ to sb/sth** *Rural communities often sacrificed to their gods and goddesses on simple open-air altars.*

sad /sæd/ *adj.* (**sad·der, sad·dest**) **1** unhappy; showing that you are unhappy: *Girls are more likely than boys to report feeling sad or losing sleep over worries.* **2** that makes you feel unhappy: *King Minos of Crete was on the island of Paros when he received the sad news of his son's death.* **3** (of a fact or situation) very bad; deserving blame or criticism: *It is a sad fact that many of those killed were children.*

sadly /ˈsædli/ *adv.* used to say that a particular situation or fact makes you sad or disappointed SYN UNFORTUNATELY: *Research in some areas of non-profit marketing is often sadly lacking.*

sad·ness /ˈsædnəs/ *noun* [U] the feeling of being sad: *Students who were bullied frequently reported feelings of sadness, loneliness and insomnia.*

safe /seɪf/ *adj.* (**safer, saf·est**) **1** [not before noun] protected from any danger or harm: *Students thrive in caring learning environments where they feel safe and supported.* ◇ *A government may protect certain selected industries to keep jobs safe within them.* ◇ **~ from sb/sth** *Virtually no place on earth can be deemed safe from all natural disasters.* OPP UNSAFE (2) **2** not likely to lead to any physical harm or danger: *Building safer cars can induce faster and less careful driving.* ◇ *During the period of exile, refugees watch social and political developments in their country of origin, evaluating the potential for a safe return.* ◇ **~ (for sb) (to do sth)** *The equipment must be safe to use and be routinely checked.* OPP UNSAFE (1) **3** where sb/sth is not likely to be in danger or to be lost: *It is the duty of the employer to maintain a safe working environment.* ◇ *Schools are still among the safest places in the community.* OPP UNSAFE (1) **4** not involving much or any risk; not likely to be wrong or to upset sb: *Because the trustee chooses the safest investments, the income produced will often be relatively less.* ◇ **~ to do sth** *It is safe to say that this technique has revolutionized immunology.*

IDM **on the ˈsafe side** being especially careful; taking no risks: *To be on the safe side, factory managers inflated their requirements for raw materials.* **play (it) ˈsafe** to be careful; to avoid risks: *The government played safe and delivered a programme which was thought to be more acceptable to the general public.*

safe·guard¹ /ˈseɪfɡɑːd; *NAmE* ˈseɪfɡɑːrd/ *verb* [T, I] to protect sth/sb from loss, harm or damage; to keep sth/sb safe: **~ sb/sth (against/from sth)** *Protection rights require that children are safeguarded against all forms of abuse, neglect and exploitation.* ◇ **~ against sth** *19th century workingmen's associations were intended to safeguard against socialism.*

safe·guard² /ˈseɪfɡɑːd; *NAmE* ˈseɪfɡɑːrd/ *noun* something that is designed to protect people from harm, risk or danger: *The data will be publicly available, after suitable safeguards have been put in place.* ◇ **~ against sth** *The 1844 Act provided safeguards against fraud by insisting on full publicity and a Registrar of Companies.*

safe·ly /ˈseɪfli/ *adv.* **1** without being harmed, damaged or lost: *Passengers are entitled to expect that they will arrive safely at their intended destination.* **2** in a way that does not cause harm or that protects sb/sth from harm: *Influenza vaccine can be safely and effectively administered during any trimester of pregnancy.* **3** without much possibility of being wrong: *It cannot be safely assumed that colour-deficient individuals will be able to recognize green LED signals.* **4** without any possibility of the situation changing: *Only when the crisis was safely over did Khrushchev affirm that an attack on China would be regarded as an attack on the Soviet Union.* **5** without any problems being caused; with no risk: *Can major food processing companies safely ignore the success of Fairtrade products?*

safety /ˈseɪfti/ *noun* [U] **1** the state of being safe and protected from danger or harm: *Appropriate assessment must be performed in order to ensure patient safety.* ◇ *public/personal safety* ◇ *It is everyone's birthright to live in safety without fear of discrimination.* ➲ *see also* HEALTH AND SAFETY **2** the state of not being dangerous: *Concerns about food safety have increased in recent years.* ◇ **+ noun** *These road safety measures led to fewer deaths on the roads.* ◇ *Regulations enforcing health and safety standards impose costs on firms.* **3** a place where you are safe: *School buses brought the flood victims to safety.*

ˈsafety net *noun* an arrangement that helps to prevent disaster if sth goes wrong: *Today, in western Europe, many people expect governments to provide a social safety net, especially during periods of economic decline.*

said *past tense, past part. of* SAY¹

sail¹ /seɪl/ *verb* **1** [I] **(+ adv./prep.)** (of a boat or ship or the people on it) to travel on water using sails or an engine: *A large Japanese fleet had sailed for Korea.* **2** [I, T] to control or travel on a boat with a sail, especially as a sport: **go sailing** *She likes to go sailing at weekends.* ◇ **~ sth (+ adv./prep.)** *He managed to sail the boat between the rocks.*

sail² /seɪl/ *noun* [C, U] a sheet of strong cloth which the wind blows against to make a boat or ship travel through the water: *As the boat moved down the river, the wind began to fill the sails.* ◇ **under ~** *a ship under sail*

IDM **set ˈsail (from/for...)** to begin a trip by sea: *He set sail for England in June 1923.*

sake /seɪk/ *noun*

IDM **for sth's sake** because of the interest or value sth has, not because of the advantages it may bring: *Data are not generated for their own sake, but rather to facilitate further research.* ◇ *In organizational contexts, most people do not welcome conflict for the sake of it.* **for the sake of sb/sth | for sb's/sth's sake** in order to help sb/sth or because you like sb/sth: *Parents usually cooperate on the same nest for the sake of their offspring.* **for the sake of (doing) sth** in order to get or keep sth: *The assumption was made for the sake of simplicity, but it was not realistic.* **for the sake of ˈargument** for the purpose of having a discussion: *Suppose, for the sake of argument, that the price of manufactures rises as a result of international trade.*

sal·ary /ˈsæləri/ *noun* (*pl.* **-ies**) money that employees receive for doing their job, especially professional employees or people working in an office, usually paid every month: *In the UK, the average annual salary of a sales manager is around £40 000.* ◇ *Besides paying high salaries, the company also provided travelling expenses.* ➲ *compare* WAGE¹

sale /seɪl/ *noun* **1** [U, C] **~ (of sth)** an act or the process of selling sth: *The industry spends over $1 billion a year on advertising in order to promote the sale of its products.* ◇ *Mass marketing concentrates on making a sale by offering the best product at the best price.* **2 sales** [pl.] the number of items sold: *While total retail sales on the Internet are still small in comparison with sales on the high street, the number of Internet shoppers is increasing.* ◇ *Basically, sales forces are generating more sales with fewer salespeople.* ◇ *Shares in the company lost 28 per cent of their value and*

S

sales fell by 50 per cent. ◇ **~ of sth** *In cold weather, there is an increase in sales of comfort foods, such as root vegetables and soups.* **3 sales** [U] the part of a company that deals with selling its products: *Sales and marketing have a special part to play in gaining customer insight.* ◇ **+ noun** *The sales manager and the sales force together are key to an organization's selling effort.* **4** [C] an occasion when a shop sells its goods at a lower price than usual: *Shoppers were waiting for bargains in the January sales.*

IDM **for ˈsale** available to be bought, especially from the owner: *The art dealer claimed he had a Renoir for sale.* ◇ *The railway company was offered for sale in 1992 and sold to a consortium.* **on ˈsale** available to be bought, especially in a shop: *The first GM food to be on sale in the UK was tomato purée.*

sales·per·son /ˈseɪlzpɜːsn; *NAmE* ˈseɪlzpɜːrsn/ *noun* (*pl.* **-people**) a person whose job is to sell goods: *A good salesperson will know which customers can be dealt with online and which prefer a personal visit.*

sa·li·ent /ˈseɪliənt/ *adj.* most important or obvious: *Salient features of the machine are summarized in Table 13.1.* ◇ *Kolk and Pinkse (2008) suggest that, for many firms, environmental issues may not be particularly salient.* ■ **sa·li·ence** *noun* [U, sing.] *The most likely effect from using product placements is raising brand awareness and salience.* ◇ *Religion has assumed a growing salience in the politics of countries in Europe.*

sa·line¹ /ˈseɪlaɪn; *NAmE* ˈseɪliːn/ *adj.* [usually before noun] (*technical*) containing salt: *Farmers have adopted the practice of allowing saline water onto the rice fields for the rearing of prawns.* ◇ *Rinse the wound with saline solution.* ■ **sal·in·ity** /səˈlɪnəti/ *noun* [U] **~ (of sth)** *Atmospheric pressure and oxygen content mean that the surface temperature and the salinity of the oceans are closely regulated.*

sa·line² /ˈseɪlaɪn; *NAmE* ˈseɪliːn/ *noun* [U] a solution of salt in water: *The patient received 750 ml of saline intravenously and no longer feels thirsty.*

salt /sɔːlt; *BrE also* sɒlt/ *noun* **1** [U] a white substance that is added to food to give it a better flavour or to preserve it. Salt is obtained from mines and is also found in sea water. HELP **Salt** is sometimes called **common salt** to distinguish it from other chemical salts. Its chemical name is **sodium chloride**, formula NaCl: *Sea salt in the atmosphere affects the chemistry of surface waters.* ◇ *The consumption of foods high in fat, sugar and salt is associated with high levels of obesity.* ◇ **+ noun** *Fresh water is less dense than salt water.* **2** [C] (*chemistry*) any chemical COMPOUND formed from the reaction of an acid with a BASE: *The solution is then washed with water to remove salts.* ◇ *Some inorganic salts are used as drugs.* ◇ **+ noun** *Many of these peptides are inhibited at high salt concentrations.*

same¹ /seɪm/ *adj.* **1** exactly the one or ones mentioned; not different: *Keynes was born in the same year in which Karl Marx died.* ◇ **the ~... as sth** *Rosalind Franklin was working on the structure of DNA at the same time as Watson and Crick.* ◇ **exactly the ~** *The two scientists came to exactly the same conclusion.* ◇ **much the ~** *Human geography can be studied in much the same way as any other science.* ◇ **the very ~** *Shakespeare uses the very same phrase in 'Troilus and Cressida'.* **2** exactly like the one or ones mentioned: *Different shops charge different prices for the same things.* ◇ **the ~... as sth** *Switzerland has about the same levels of income per capita as the US.*

same² /seɪm/ *pron.* **1 the ~ (as...)** the same thing or things: *The physical reactions to anger are the same as those aroused by stress in general.* ◇ *Tito in Yugoslavia had already created his own national road to socialism. Mao Zedong was now free to do the same.* **2 the ~ (as...)** having the same number, colour, size, quality, etc: *Teachers should not treat all children the same, because they are not all the same.* ◇ *The number of people employed in US call centres is roughly the same as the number of people working as truck drivers.*

IDM **ˌall/ˌjust the ˈsame** despite this SYN NEVERTHELESS: *The autocracy was in no danger. All the same, Russia could no longer be regarded as the dominant power of Europe.* **ˌone and the ˈsame** the same person or thing: *Marketing investment and advertising investment are one and the same for brand valuation purposes.*

same³ /seɪm/ *adv.* (*usually* **the same**) in the same way: *Under an ethic of justice, everyone is treated the same, regardless of differing needs and abilities.*

ˈsame-sex *adj.* [only before noun] **1** of the same sex: *Same-sex parents are considered as more important role models than opposite-sex parents during adolescence.* **2** involving people of the same sex: *Australian same-sex couples have in most areas achieved largely equal rights to opposite-sex couples.*

sam·ple¹ /ˈsɑːmpl; *NAmE* ˈsæmpl/ *noun* **1** a number of people or things taken from a larger group and used in tests to provide information about the group: *70 products were included in the final sample.* ◇ **~ of sb/sth** *Data are collected from a random sample of the population.* ◇ *The survey covers a nationally representative sample of babies born in the United Kingdom over a 12-month period.* **2** a small amount of a substance taken from a larger amount and tested in order to obtain information about the substance: *Soil samples from five different valleys exhibited significant differences.* ◇ *A blood sample is analysed for its alcohol level.* **3 ~ (of sth)** a small amount or example of sth that can be looked at or tried to see what it is like: *One of the tasks is concerned with getting free samples of a product into the hands of potential customers.*

▸ ADJECTIVE + SAMPLE **representative • random • systematic • small • large • total, entire, full, whole • final • original • current • independent • national • diverse • select • unknown • stratified • normative • clinical** *The response rate for this national sample for all ages was 71.1%.* | **small • entire, whole • original • clinical • biological • solid** *The entire sample of cells is then printed onto a fresh plate.*

▸ NOUN + SAMPLE **patient • convenience • probability • quota • validation** *The convenience sample uses respondents who are easily or conveniently available.* | **blood • urine • serum • tissue • DNA • soil • water** *DNA sequence changes are difficult to detect in cells or tissue samples from humans or animals.*

▸ VERB + SAMPLE **take • select • use • analyse** *The social introversion scale was designed by L.E. Drake (1946) using a sample of female college students.* | **draw • recruit • comprise, compose • divide, split • restrict • generate • bias** *The British Crime Survey is a regular survey of a national sample drawn from the populations of England and Wales.* | **collect, obtain • test • dilute • process, prepare • store • send • transport • screen • incubate • centrifuge** *The samples were obtained by the method of Judd and Weldon.*

▸ SAMPLE + VERB **consist of • comprise • contain** *Some samples contained only benign tissue.*

▸ SAMPLE + NOUN **size • selection • survey • member • characteristic • design • stratum • bias • mean** *Due to the rarity of the disorders, a large sample size is needed.* | **preparation • collection** *Any distinguishing textural features could have been destroyed during sample preparation.*

sam·ple² /ˈsɑːmpl; *NAmE* ˈsæmpl/ *verb* **1 ~ sb/sth** to test, question, etc. part of sth or of a group of people in order to find out what the rest is like: *They randomly sampled 25 000 women aged 45–64 years who were registered with one of the practices.* ◇ *133 sites were sampled by dredging* the sea floor. ◇ **~ sb/sth from sth** *Three medical professionals were sampled from each department.* **2 ~ sth** to try a small amount of a particular food to see what it is like; to experience sth for a short time to see what it is like: *Customers are invited to sample and test new products.* **3** (*technical*) to take repeated samples of a continuous ANALOGUE signal in order to represent it in a DIGITAL form: *Typically, a signal may be sampled at up to five times the rate of its maximum frequency component.*

sam·pling /ˈsɑːmplɪŋ; *NAmE* ˈsæmplɪŋ/ *noun* [U] the process of taking a sample: *The most common technique used for selecting respondents is random sampling.* ◇ **+ noun** *In three of the studies, sampling methods were not clearly specified.*

ˈsampling error *noun* [U, C] (*statistics*) a situation in which a set of results or figures does not show a true situation, because the group of people or things it was based on was not typical of a wider group: *The findings suggest that the differences found in previous individual studies can be explained by sampling error.* ◇ *Obtaining the data continuously will make the analysis more reliable, since the effect of sampling errors is eliminated.*

ˈsampling frame *noun* (*statistics*) a list of the items or people forming a population from which a sample is taken: *We used the National Population Register as the sampling frame.*

sanc·tion¹ /ˈsæŋkʃn/ *noun* **1** [C, usually pl.] **~ (against/on sb)** an official order that limits trade or contact with a particular country, in order to make it do sth, such as obey international law: *The United States imposed sanctions against the Soviet Union in the early 1980s.* **2** [U] **~ (of sb/sth)** official permission or approval for an action or a change SYN AUTHORIZATION (1): *He had repeatedly issued orders without the sanction of the party.* **3** [C] a course of action that can be used, if necessary, to make people obey a law or behave in a particular way SYN PENALTY: *Industrial action was commonplace and legal sanctions were very rarely invoked.* ◇ **~ against/on sb/sth** *Immigration policy did little to stop the use of illegal workers, since sanctions against employers were rarely imposed.*

sanc·tion² /ˈsæŋkʃn/ *verb* **1 ~ sth** to give permission for sth to take place: *The UN did not expressly sanction NATO's use of force.* ◇ *Domestic violence was legally sanctioned until the late nineteenth century.* **2 ~ sb/sth** to punish sb/sth; to put a sanction on a country: *The law typically sanctions citizens who refuse to perform their legal duties.* ◇ *US trade sanctions restrict trade, investment and financial transactions with sanctioned countries.*

S

sand /sænd/ *noun* [U, C, usually pl.] a substance that consists of very small fine grains of rock. Sand is found on beaches, in DESERTS, etc: *Coastal deposits of sand or shingle were transported by waves.* ◇ *When sands have been deposited very quickly, the particles do not adopt their most stable packing.*

sandy /ˈsændi/ *adj.* (**sand·ier, sand·iest**) covered with or containing sand: *The shallow, sandy soils are low in fertility and have poor moisture retention.*

sang *past tense of* SING

sani·ta·tion /ˌsænɪˈteɪʃn/ *noun* [U] the equipment and systems that keep places clean, especially by removing human waste: *disease resulting from poor sanitation* ◇ *A lack of clean water and sanitation were the main problems.*

sank *past tense of* SINK¹

sat *past tense, past part. of* SIT

sat·el·lite /ˈsætəlaɪt/ *noun* **1** [C, U] an electronic device that is sent into space and moves around the earth or another planet. It is used for communicating by radio, television, etc. and for providing information: *The first meteorological satellites were launched in the early 1960s.* ◇ **by/via ~** *Data can be transmitted across the world via satellite at very high rates.* ◇ **+ noun** *satellite television/channels/communications/images* **2** [C] a natural object that moves around a larger natural object in space: *The moon is the Earth's only natural satellite.* **3** [C] a town, a country or an organization that is controlled by and depends on another larger or more powerful one: **+ noun** *The Soviet satellite states in Eastern Europe collapsed in 1989.*

sat·ire /ˈsætaɪə(r); *NAmE* ˈsætaɪər/ *noun* [U, C] the use of HUMOUR to criticize a person, an idea or an institution and to show their faults or weaknesses; a piece of writing that uses this type of criticism: *The plays of Aristophanes are characterized by their biting social and political satire.* ◇ **~ on sth** *'Hard Times' is a succinct and often bitter satire on the effects of the Industrial Revolution in northern England.* ■ **sa·tir·ic·al** /səˈtɪrɪkl/ (*also less frequent* **sa·tir·ic** /səˈtɪrɪk/) *adj.*: *a satirical novel/poem*

sat·is·fac·tion /ˌsætɪsˈfækʃn/ *noun* **1** [U, C] the good feeling that you have when you have achieved sth or when sth that you wanted to happen does happen; something that gives you this feeling: *Many carers derive high levels of personal satisfaction from their role.* ◇ **~ of (doing) sth** *The pressures and satisfactions of living in the public gaze appeal to only a minority of people.* ◇ **+ noun** *The programme has been highly popular with the hospital achieving 90% 'exceptional' ratings on its patient satisfaction surveys.* OPP DISSATISFACTION ⊃ *see also* JOB SATISFACTION **2** [U, sing.] **~ (of sth)** the act of satisfying a need or desire: *Children often lack the capacity to postpone the satisfaction of their needs.* **3** [U] **~ (of sth)** (*formal*) an acceptable way of dealing with a complaint, a debt, an injury, etc: *The company's creditors were pressing for satisfaction of their debts.*

IDM **to sb's satisˈfaction** **1** if you do sth **to sb's satisfaction**, they are pleased with it: *The question is unlikely ever to be settled to everyone's satisfaction.* **2** if you prove sth **to sb's satisfaction**, they believe or accept it: *None of his critics has so far proved that point to general satisfaction.*

sat·is·fac·tory /ˌsætɪsˈfæktəri/ *adj.* good enough for a particular purpose: *None of these methods is entirely satisfactory.* ◇ *The inquiry procedure has not produced a satisfactory solution.* ◇ *a satisfactory explanation/answer/result* ◇ *The patient's health and general condition were satisfactory.* OPP UNSATISFACTORY ■ **sat·is·fac·tor·ily** /ˌsætɪsˈfæktərəli/ *adv.*: *The issue of whom the money belonged to was not satisfactorily resolved.*

sat·is·fied /ˈsætɪsfaɪd/ *adj.* **1** pleased because you have achieved sth or because sth that you wanted to happen has happened: *Many companies regard satisfied customers as their best form of promotion.* ◇ **~ with sb/sth** *The local council wants to know how satisfied residents are with its refuse collection service and recycling facilities.* OPP DISSATISFIED **2 ~ (that...)** believing or accepting that sth is true SYN CONVINCED (1): *The court was satisfied that the child had understood the relevant information and had arrived at a clear choice.*

sat·isfy /ˈsætɪsfaɪ/ *verb* (**sat·is·fies, sat·is·fy·ing, sat·is·fied, sat·is·fied**) **1 ~ sth** to provide what is wanted, needed or asked for: *The company must produce goods that satisfy customers' requirements efficiently and effectively.* ◇ *When produce is plentiful, we no longer seek to satisfy our needs but our desires.* ◇ *The cell replicates DNA when all the conditions are satisfied.* ◇ *To qualify for a patent, a product must satisfy certain criteria:...* **2** (not used in the progressive tenses) to make sb certain that sth is true or has been done: **~ sb** *Darwin's gradualist explanation did not satisfy* *some scientists.* ◇ **~ sb/yourself (that)...** *The evidence must satisfy the judge that internal relocation is a safe and reasonable option.* ◇ **~ sb/yourself of sth** *People need to be satisfied of the need for a new system.* **3 ~ sb** (not used in the progressive tenses) to make sb pleased by doing or giving them what they want: *In ethical dilemmas, there is no easy way to get answers that satisfy everyone.* **4 ~ an equation** (*mathematics*) (of a quantity) to make an EQUATION true: *There are only two ways this equation can be satisfied.*

sat·is·fy·ing /ˈsætɪsfaɪɪŋ/ *adj.* giving pleasure because it provides sth that you need or want: *Developing mutually satisfying relationships between suppliers and their customers is fundamental.* ◇ **it is ~ (to sb) to do sth** *It is always satisfying to investigators to identify the molecular basis for a genetic disease.*

sat·ur·ate /ˈsætʃəreɪt/ *verb* **1 ~ sth (with sth)** to make sth completely wet: *Evaporation may cause overlying air to become saturated with water vapour.* **2** [often passive] **~ sth (with sth)** to fill sth completely with sth so that it is impossible to add any more: *Samples of solid polystyrene were saturated with gas at high pressure prior to measurement.* ◇ (*figurative*) *The European car market was already saturated with a large number of competitors.*

sat·ur·ated /ˈsætʃəreɪtɪd/ *adj.* **1** completely wet: *The zone below this water table is the saturated zone and the water stored there is groundwater.* **2** [usually before noun] (*chemistry*) (of a chemical solution) containing the greatest possible amount of the substance that has been dissolved in it: *Bacteria can grow under a wide range of conditions, including in a saturated salt solution.* **3** (*chemistry*) (of a MOLECULE) containing the largest possible number of HYDROGEN atoms without double or triple CARBON-to-carbon bonds: *Unsaturated hydrocarbons burn in air with a more smoky yellow flame than saturated hydrocarbons.*

sat·ur·ation /ˌsætʃəˈreɪʃn/ *noun* [U] **1** (*often figurative*) the state or process that happens when no more of sth can be accepted or added because there is already too much of it/too many of them: *Where domestic market saturation has been reached, companies may turn to exporting as a solution.* ◇ **+ noun** *British military planners had developed the tactic of saturation bombing before the war began.* **2** (*chemistry*) the degree to which sth is absorbed in sth else, expressed as a PERCENTAGE of the greatest possible amount: *If oxygen saturation is lower than 95%, oxygen therapy should be prescribed.*

save /seɪv/ *verb* **1** [T] to keep sb/sth safe from death, harm, loss, etc: **~ sb/sth** *Aeneas escaped death at the hands of Achilles after Poseidon saved him.* ◇ *More lives have been saved by public health measures than by all of the biomedical discoveries.* ◇ **~ sb/sth from sth** *The new product line may have saved the company from failure.* ◇ **~ sb/sth from doing sth** *In every 1 000 women who undergo screening, one will be saved from dying of breast cancer.* **2** [I, T] to keep money instead of spending it, especially in order to buy a particular thing: **~ (up) (for sth)** *The stock market enables investors to spread their risks even while saving for the future.* ◇ **~ sth (up) (for sth)** *If you want to save money for a trip, you have to reduce costs.* **3** [T, I] to avoid wasting sth or using more than necessary: **~ sth** *Increasingly, business meetings are conducted through teleconferences, saving the time and energy formerly expended on travel.* ◇ **~ (sth) (on sth)** *With the railcard, customers will save one third on most rail fares.* ◇ **~ sb sth (on sth)** *Use of alternative fuels has saved the company 7.2% on its thermal equivalent fossil fuel costs.* **4** [T] to avoid doing sth difficult or unpleasant; to make sb able to avoid doing sth difficult or unpleasant: **~ sth** *With Internet shopping, customers might save a trip to the store but invariably they have to wait for their purchases.* ◇ **~ sb/yourself sth** *With hindsight, the parties could have saved themselves a great deal of trouble and expense.* ◇ **~ (sb from) doing sth** *Such schemes have the obvious advantage of saving the government from finding large capital sums.* **5** [T, I] **~ (sth)** to make a computer keep work, for example by putting it on a disk: *Frustration and extra work are easily prevented by saving the data on a secondary data storage system.*

IDM **save (sb's) ˈface** to avoid or help sb avoid EMBARRASSMENT: *Compromise is a means of allowing all parties in a situation to save face.*

sav·ing /ˈseɪvɪŋ/ *noun* **1** [C] an amount of sth such as time or money that you do not need to use or spend: *The commercial sector could also realize large energy savings.* ◇ *Some innovations result in significant time savings.* ◇ **~ of sth** *In the year ending March 2004, the company achieved a cost saving of $869 million.* ◇ **~ in sth** *The savings in labour cost exceed the additional transportation costs.* ◇ **~ on sth** *Consumers will make considerable savings on their electricity bills.* **2 savings** [pl.] money that has been saved, especially in a bank, etc: *People will use their savings to buy treasury bonds if the rate of interest on them is high enough.* ◇ **+ noun** *Many banks try to encourage current account customers to move their savings accounts to the same bank too.* **3 -saving** (in adjectives) that prevents the waste of the thing mentioned or stops it from being necessary: *Energy-saving light bulbs are increasingly being used in hotels and public buildings.* ◇ *Many technical changes are both capital-saving and labour-saving.* ◇ *Antibiotics can be life-saving in cases of meningitis.*

saw *past tense of* SEE

say[1] /seɪ/ *verb* (**says** /sez/, **said**, **said** /sed/) **1** [T, I] to use words to express an opinion or idea, or state a fact: **~ sth** *In the focus group, we were interested not just in what people said but in how they said it.* ◇ *The central analytical problem, he says, is how we analyse change generated within the economic system.* ◇ **+ speech** *She said quite directly, 'That's an elitist view.'* ◇ **~ sth about sth** *In 'Notebooks', Sartre says some interesting things about pure reflection.* ◇ **~ (that)...** *Some economists say that society will increasingly be stratified into two classes, depending on wealth and education.* ◇ **~ how/whether, etc...** *More research is needed before we can say with certainty how retirement affects health.* ◇ **as sb says...** *As Lewis says: Pain is a feeling. To have pain and to feel pain are one and the same.* ◇ **~ so** *Even if he does not explicitly say so, Pomey was obviously in favour of modern orthography.* ◇ **have to ~ (about sth)** *It is important to consider what anthropologists have to say about rites of passage.* ◇ **~ sth on a subject, topic, etc.** *I shall have more to say on this issue later in the paper.* **2** [T] (of a text, picture, etc.) to communicate information: **~ sth** *It is important to look at what the data actually say.* ◇ **~ sth (to sb) (about sth)** *These films all have things to say to us about the human condition.* **3** [T, no passive] to suggest sth as an example or a possibility: *Attaining, say, an upper-middle-class position is very important for those who have their background in this class.* ◇ **~ (that)...** *Say a local community organizes a protest against a dirty plant, and the plant subsequently cuts its emissions...* ◇ **let us say...** *The term 'world music' is itself relatively new, let us say two decades old.*

IDM **sb/sth is said to be/have/do sth** used to describe what sb/sth is like: *In a democratic society, everyone is said to be 'equal under the law'.* ◇ *A drug that binds very strongly to its receptor is said to have a high affinity.* **it ˌgoes without ˈsaying (that)...** it is very obvious; it does not need to be said: *It goes without saying that no single cultural heritage exists for Australian literature.* **it is said (that)...** used to report what sb has said, or what people in general have said: *About 5 000 antibiotics are known, and it is said that about 300 are discovered each year.* **ˈnot to say** used to introduce a stronger way of describing sth: *This is an elegant, not to say ingenious, explanation.* **that**

S

ˈ**said** used to introduce an opinion that makes what you have just said seem less strong: *The idea that genes 'seal your fate' might be popular, but it is not science. That said, it is also true that individuals really differ as a result of the genes they inherit from their parents.* **there's something, not much, etc. to be said for (doing) sth** there are/are not good reasons for doing sth, believing sth or agreeing with sth: *There is much to be said for seeing the period 1286 to 1547 as a unit.* **this/that is ˈnot to say (that)** used to give added information that corrects or changes slightly sth you have just said: *Nature needed to be conquered for human society to thrive. This is not to say there were not some critics of the industrialization movement.* **to ˌsay the ˈleast** used to suggest that a situation is worse, better, more serious, etc. than you are saying: *The announcement of the passing of the nation state is, to say the least, premature.* ◇ *Their take-home pay is modest, to say the least.* **to say ˈnothing of sth** used to introduce a further fact or thing in addition to those already mentioned SYN NOT TO MENTION: *The amounts of waste produced by agriculture and industry are staggering, to say nothing of waste generated by ordinary citizens.* ➲ *more at* LET, SUFFICE

say² /seɪ/ *noun* [sing., U] the right to speak, or the right to influence sth by giving your opinion before a decision is made: **have your ~** *The chair of the meeting must make sure that everyone is allowed to have their say.* ◇ **have a ~ (in/on/over sth)** *Referendums mean voters can have a say over a particular issue.* ◇ **have the final ~ (in/on/over sth)** *Ultimately, the physician has the final say on treatment options and will act in the patient's best interest.*

say·ing /ˈseɪɪŋ/ *noun* **1** [C] a well-known phrase or statement that expresses sth about life that most people believe is sensible and true; something that sb has said: **~ that...** *There is an old saying in business that no matter how good your prices are, someone somewhere will be charging less.* **2 sayings (of sb)** [pl.] things said by a religious or political leader, or by a PHILOSOPHER, that have been collected and written down: *The Analects consists of scattered sayings of Confucius that were compiled by his disciples after his death.*

sca·lar /ˈskeɪlə(r)/ *adj.* (*mathematics*) (of a quantity) having size but no direction: *These are scalar functions: the values they take up are ordinary numbers.* ■ **sca·lar** *noun*: *Another class of physical quantities is called tensors, of which scalars and vectors are special cases.* ➲ *compare* VECTOR

S

scale¹ /skeɪl/ *noun* **1** [sing., U] the size or extent of sth, especially when compared with sth else: *Imperial building projects impressed by their sheer scale and grandeur.* ◇ **the ~ of sth** *The small scale of the community was a strength because they all knew each other so well.* ◇ **on a... ~** *Technology has made it possible to share risks on an international scale.* ◇ **at a... ~** *The cost of fishing is still poorly documented and studied in most regions, particularly at a global scale.* ➲ *see also* FULL-SCALE, LARGE-SCALE, RETURNS TO SCALE, SMALL-SCALE **2** [C] a range of levels or numbers used for measuring sth: **on a ~ of/from... to...** *Values represent how respondents valued each place on a scale of 1 to 7.* ◇ *For each country, we assessed the quantity of data available on a scale ranging from + (few) to + + + + (many).* ◇ **on the ~** *There was a middle point on the scale that allowed for a neutral response.* ◇ **four-point/five-point, etc. ~** *Multiple health complaints were assessed using a symptom checklist with a five-point scale.* ➲ *see also* TIME-SCALE **3** [C, usually sing.] the set of all the different levels of sth, from the lowest to the highest: *At the other end of the biological scale are multicellular organisms that are composed of vast numbers of cells.* ◇ **up/down a ~** *As with agriculture, slave ownership in the city extended well down the social scale.* **4** [C] a series of marks on an instrument that is used for measuring: *The water level in the cylinder is determined by reading the scale C attached to the floating disc D.* **5** [C] (*also* **scales** [pl.]) an instrument for weighing people or things: *Participants' weight was determined using a calibrated weighing scale.* **6** [C, U] the relation between the actual size of sth and its size on a map, diagram or model that represents it: **~ of sth** *They worked with maps at a scale of 1:250 000.* ◇ **to ~** *The diagram is not drawn to scale.* ◇ **~ model** *The scale models built for the measurements differ in scale and material.* **7** [C] any of the thin plates of hard material that cover the skin of many fish and REPTILES: *Digital images of fish and scales from adult cod from two farms were analysed.* IDM *see* TIP²

▸ ADJECTIVE + SCALE **grand • massive, vast • large, broad, wide • unprecedented • small • modest • sheer • global, worldwide • regional • national** *Conceived on a grand scale, New Madrid enjoyed urban planning well ahead of its time.* | **multiple • sliding • binary • logarithmic • atomic • molecular • microscopic • vertical • spatial • temporal • clinical • geographic, geographical** *Payment is based on a sliding scale so that low-income patients pay according to their resources.* ◇ *When examined on an atomic scale, the classical concepts of particle and wave melt together.*

▸ VERB + SCALE **construct, devise, design, create • develop • use** *Rosen (1962) attempted to develop better diagnostic scales.*

scale² /skeɪl/ *verb* **1** [T, usually passive] to calculate or measure sth according to a scale: **be scaled from A to B** *Answers to each survey question were scaled from 1 to 4, with 4 being the most affirmative and 1 being the most negative.* ◇ **be scaled by sth** *Each of the 30 items is scaled by frequency.* **2** [T, usually passive] to show or represent sth relative to its size or another feature: **(be) scaled (according to sth)** *A diagram scaled according to how much people are paid produces a pyramid.* **3** [I] **~ (with sth)** to vary according to a scale: *The difficulty in finding new prime numbers scales rapidly with the size of the number.* PHR V **ˌscale sth ˈback** (*also* **ˌscale sth ˈdown**) to reduce the size, number or extent of sth: *When the Japanese economy was hit by the oil crises in the 1970s, plans for the railways had to be scaled back.* **ˌscale sth ˈup** to increase the size, number or extent of sth: *A spider scaled up to the size of a horse sounds frightening, but would probably be completely incapable of standing up.*

scan¹ /skæn/ *verb* (**-nn-**) **1** [T, I] to look at every part of sth carefully, especially because you are looking for a particular thing or person: **~ sth** *The company should be scanning the environment to keep on top of technological developments.* ◇ **~ for sth** *It is hard for the animals to feed and scan for danger at the same time.* ◇ **~ sth for sth** *Using a qualitative data analysis software package, all journals were scanned for the words 'antenatal', 'prenatal' or 'natal'.* ◇ **~ sth + adv./prep.** (*technical*) *Light was scanned over the surface to measure the height.* **2** [T] **~ sth (for sth)** to look quickly at sth in order to find relevant information: *The on-screen report will be scanned for the main points.* **3** [T, usually passive] to use a machine to get an image of the inside of sb's body and show it on a computer screen: **be scanned| have sth scanned** *In these 11 studies, 432 people had their brains scanned to measure the size.* **4** [T, usually passive] to use a machine that uses light or another means to read data or to produce an image of an object or document in digital form: **be scanned** *These response forms were then electronically scanned, verified and entered into a separate database for statistical analysis.*

scan² /skæn/ *noun* **1** a medical test in which a machine produces an image of the inside of a person's body and shows it on a computer screen: *This was a twin pregnancy in which an ultrasound scan at 20 weeks gestation showed that the twins were of the same sex.* ◇ **~ of sth** *A CT scan of the abdomen and pelvis showed no abnormalities.* **2 ~ (of sth)** the use of a machine to read data or produce an image of sth: *The solar radiation data have been produced from satellite-based scans of terrestrial cloud cover.* **3 ~ (of sth)** the act of looking quickly through sth written or printed, usually in order to find sth or to get a general idea about what is in it: *A quick scan of these studies shows that a large number of volatile compounds have been identified in berries.*

scan·dal /ˈskændl/ *noun* [C, U] behaviour or an event that people think is morally or legally wrong and causes public feelings of shock or anger: *New regulations were brought in as a result of financial scandals involving gross inflation of revenues by companies.* ◇ *Investigative reporters uncovered the Watergate scandal.* ◇ *There is scandal as the corruption becomes too gross to ignore.*

scan·ner /ˈskænə(r)/ *noun* **1** a machine used in medical examinations to produce an image of the inside of a person's body on a computer screen: *For brain scanning, the head has to be placed inside the scanner and kept very still.* **2** a machine that uses light or another means to read data, or to produce an image of an object or document in digital form: *The root systems were gently washed and then scanned with a desktop optical scanner.*

scarce /skeəs; *NAmE* skers/ *adj.* (**scar·cer, scar·cest**) if sth is **scarce**, there is not enough of it and it is only available in small quantities: *The country had to juggle scarce resources, such as medicine and equipment, to provide services for a wide range of health issues.* ◇ *In years when food is scarce, birds of various species lay a smaller number of eggs.*

scarce·ly /ˈskeəsli; *NAmE* ˈskersli/ *adv.* only just; almost not SYN HARDLY: *The ethical debate has scarcely moved on since the 1960s.* ◇ *After the earthquake, there was scarcely a house left standing.* ◇ *It is scarcely surprising that this arbitrary rule engendered a great deal of resentment.*

scar·city /ˈskeəsəti; *NAmE* ˈskersəti/ *noun* (*pl.* **-ies**) [C, U] **~ (of sth)** if there is a **scarcity of** sth, there is not enough of it and it is difficult to obtain it SYN SHORTAGE: *There is a growing scarcity of resources throughout the world, such as energy and water.* ◇ *Population growth, in turn, contributes to resource scarcity and environmental stress, often resulting in conflict.*

scat·ter[1] /ˈskætə(r)/ *verb* **1** [I, T] (*physics*) to change direction or spread in many directions; to make sth change direction or spread in many directions: *X-ray waves bounce off the molecule and combine with one another as they scatter in different directions.* ◇ **~ sth** *Gases and aerosols in the earth's atmosphere absorb or scatter radiation.* **2** [T, often passive] **~ sth (on/over/around sth)** to throw or drop things in different directions so that they cover an area: *Members of the family of the deceased will collect the ashes to be scattered on the sea or land.* **3** [T, often passive] to be found spread over an area rather than all together: **be scattered (across/along/throughout sth)** *Thailand has several religious monuments and pilgrimage sites scattered across the country.* **4** [I, T] (of people or animals) to move very quickly in different directions; to make people or animals do this SYN DISPERSE (1): **(+ adv./prep.)** *The men scattered in all directions in their haste to follow their sergeant's orders.* ◇ **~ sb/sth (+ adv./prep.)** *Massacres and deportations destroyed over 1.5 million people and scattered the survivors to the far corners of the globe.*

scat·ter[2] /ˈskætə(r)/ (*also* **scat·ter·ing** /ˈskætərɪŋ/) *noun* [sing.] **~ (of sth)** a small amount of sth or a small number of people or things spread over an area: *Upland farming could not support more than a thin scatter of people.*

scat·tered /ˈskætəd; *NAmE* ˈskætərd/ *adj.* **~ (throughout/across/around sth)** spread far apart over a wide area SYN DISPERSED: *The men earned decent wages in factories and automobile plants scattered throughout the Midwest.*

scen·ario AWL /səˈnɑːriəʊ; *NAmE* səˈnærioʊ/ *noun* (*pl.* **-os**) **1** a description of a possible series of events or situations: *The source of climate data for these scenarios is the University of East Anglia.* ◇ **in/under this/the following, etc. ~** *Under both scenarios, average carbon gain differed significantly across species.* ◇ **~ of sth** *The main method of examination is to test design ideas against scenarios of use that describe typical activities.* **2** a description of what takes place in a film, play, novel, etc: *A cinematograph film, and consequently also a scenario, is always divided into a great number of separate pieces.*

▸ ADJECTIVE + SCENARIO **worst-case • hypothetical • future • plausible • possible • unlikely • extreme • optimistic • realistic • alternative • typical • the following** *The worst-case scenarios indicate that 50% of people more than 85 years of age will become demented.*

▸ VERB + SCENARIO **imagine • construct, generate • propose, present • outline • describe • consider • analyse** *The government's Strategy Unit performed a cost-benefit analysis of the issues, in which it outlined five possible scenarios.*

scene /siːn/ *noun* **1** [C, usually sing.] the place where sth happens, especially sth unpleasant or dangerous: *The area was declared a crime scene and secured.* ◇ **~ of sth** *The suspect claims to have been miles from the scene of the crime.* ◇ **on/at the ~** *The emergency team were among the first on the scene.* **2** [C] **~ (of sth)** an event or a situation that you see, especially one of a particular type: *Making his way through choking clouds of dust, Davy encountered a scene of utter chaos.* **3 the... scene** [sing.] a particular area of activity or way of life and the people or organizations that are part of it: *These groups energized Japan's political scene in the early 1970s.* **4** [C] a part of a film, play or book in which the action happens in one place or is of one particular type: *The opening scene unfolds at a police station.* **5** [C] one of the short sections that a play is divided into: *In the closing scene of the play, all but Tiresias and the dead Antigone are assembled together.* **6** [C] a view that you see; a painting, photograph, etc. that shows a place and the things that are happening there: *The cartoon depicts a street scene in contemporary Manhattan.*

IDM **arrive, appear, etc. on the scene** to start to exist or be part of a situation or activity: *Earthquake rates around the globe have remained the same since Homo sapiens first arrived on the scene.* ◇ *In 1995, Daewoo came on the scene with a major investment proposal.* **behind the ˈscenes** in a way that people in general do not know about: *Even before the first meeting, trouble was brewing behind the scenes.* **set the ˈscene (for sth) 1** to create a situation in which sth can easily happen or develop: *Faraday's work set the scene for a gradual accumulation of experimental data.* **2** to give sb the information they need in order to understand what comes next: *The paper begins by setting the scene with a profile of older men in the labour market.*

scep·tic (*BrE*) (*NAmE* **skep·tic**) /ˈskeptɪk/ *noun* **1** a person who usually doubts that claims or statements are true, especially those that other people believe in: *Gradually, the potential of penicillin became clearer to sceptics.* ◇ *Sceptics argued that high-tech solutions would never come to pass.* **2** (*philosophy*) a person who doubts the possibility of real knowledge of any kind: *The sceptic's claim that knowledge is impossible could mean that no belief is ever completely justified.*

scep·tical (*BrE*) (*NAmE* **skep·tical**) /ˈskeptɪkl/ *adj.* **~ (about/of sth)** not easily convinced; having doubts that a claim or statement is true or that sth will happen: *Presently, the global public remains deeply sceptical about nuclear waste disposal.* ◇ *Many scientists are highly sceptical of the chances of success.* ■ **scep·tic·al·ly** (*BrE*) (*NAmE*

S

skep·tic·al·ly) /ˈskeptɪkli/ *adv.*: *Headlines about national educational performance should be treated sceptically.*

scep·ti·cism (*BrE*) (*NAmE* **skep·ti·cism**) /ˈskeptɪsɪzəm/ *noun* **1** [U, sing.] an attitude of doubting that claims or statements are true or that sth will happen; an attitude of not being easily convinced: *The report was met with a degree of scepticism.* ◇ **~ about sth** *There is increasing public scepticism about health claims in the media.* **2** [U] (*philosophy*) the theory that certain knowledge is impossible: *Radical scepticism is the thesis that our beliefs are completely unjustified.*

sched·ule¹ AWL /ˈʃedjuːl; *NAmE* ˈskedʒuːl/ *noun* **1** [C, U] a plan for doing sth, giving times when events should happen: *Chicago's weather affects the flight schedules at all the airports.* ◇ **~ of sth** *Each woman will have a planned schedule of care, with 10 routine antenatal care visits.* ◇ **~ for sth** *The firm did not commit to making any payments during the three-year schedule for development and production.* ◇ **on ~** *Out of 135 departures, 117 (87%) were on schedule.* ◇ **ahead of/behind ~** *The customs union came into existence in 1968, eighteen months ahead of schedule.* **2** [C] a plan for the things that a particular person has to do, and the times when they have to do them SYN TIMETABLE (1): *I am very grateful to Laura Gaines, who took much time out of her very busy schedule to guide me through the final stages of revision.* ◇ *Meetings were held at lunchtimes to minimize the inconvenience to individual schedules.* **3** [C] a written list of things, for example prices or questions: *Managers from 79 manufacturing plants were interviewed using a semi-structured interview schedule.* ◇ **~ of sth** *Article 5 (3) requires public authorities to publish and make available a schedule of charges.* **4** (*NAmE*) = TIMETABLE (2) **5** [C] (*law*) an addition to a formal document, especially one that is in the form of a list: *The details of the covenants are set out in a schedule at the end of the register.* **6** [C] a list of the television and radio programmes that are on a particular channel and the times that they start: *It is a common complaint that the British television schedules are dominated by crime drama.*

sched·ule² AWL /ˈʃedjuːl; *NAmE* ˈskedʒuːl/ *verb* [often passive] to arrange for sth to happen at a particular time: **~ sth** *One employer agreed to undertake a risk assessment and schedule regular meetings with managers.* ◇ **~ sb/sth for sth** *All participants were scheduled for a follow-up visit after one year.* ◇ **~ sb/sth to do sth** *The conference was scheduled to take place in London during the summer of 1923.*

S

sched·uled /ˈʃedjuːld; *NAmE* ˈskedʒuːld/ *adj.* [only before noun] included in or planned according to a schedule: *The company began operating scheduled air services in 2003.*

schema /ˈskiːmə/ *noun* (*pl.* **sche·mas** or **sche·mata** /ˈskiːmətə; skiːˈmɑːtə/) **~ (of sth)** (*technical*) an outline of a plan or theory: *Regulation 139/2004 retains the general schema of the original Regulation.*

sche·mat·ic AWL /skiːˈmætɪk/ *adj.* showing or describing the main features or relationships of sth but not the details; showing sth as a diagram: *A schematic diagram of a ligand binding to its receptor is shown in Figure 10.6.* ■ **sche·mat·ic·al·ly** AWL /skiːˈmætɪkli/ *adv.*: *Figure 4.4 schematically depicts the major DNA-repair pathways in mammalian cells.* ◇ *A typical calibration curve is shown schematically in Figure 2.9.*

scheme AWL /skiːm/ *noun* **1** (*BrE*) a plan or system for doing or organizing sth: *Recently, the Indian government launched health insurance schemes for the poor.* ◇ **~ of sth** *The Liberal government of 1870 introduced a scheme of universal primary education.* ◇ **~ for (doing) sth** *The grandiose schemes for diverting northern rivers into the arid south were abandoned.* ◇ **~ to do sth** *Companies such as Ford have developed schemes to encourage employees to return to learning.* ◇ **under a ~** *Under the current free-market scheme, consumers pay high prices for essential drugs.* **2** a system for organizing information: *Barbarin (1999) noted that about 20 different classification schemes exist in the literature.* ◇ **~ of sth** *Lamarck established several taxonomic classes that still form part of today's scheme of zoological classification.* ◇ **~ for (doing) sth** *Goldthorpe devised a seven-category scheme for classifying social class.* IDM **the (...) ˈscheme of things** the way things seem to be organized in the world, in which everything has a place that relates to the general system: *Bookchin reserved a special place for humanity in the natural scheme of things.* ◇ *The danger of dying in a natural catastrophe is really very small in the larger scheme of things.*

▸ ADJECTIVE + SCHEME **pilot** • **voluntary** • **mandatory** • **regulatory** *In the United States, the US Department of Agriculture administers several voluntary environmental schemes.* | **conceptual** *The basic structure of our conceptual schemes lies deep in our thought and practice.*

▸ NOUN + SCHEME **incentive** • **training** • **pension** • **insurance** • **compensation** • **support** • **irrigation** *Share incentive schemes should be available to employees and executive directors but not to non-executive directors.* | **classification** • **coding** • **weighting** • **sampling** *In principle, any weighting scheme is open to testing.*

▸ VERB + SCHEME **devise, design, develop** • **propose** *Elaborate classification schemes were proposed by Kay and others in the USA.* | **introduce, launch** • **adopt** • **implement, operate, run** *By the end of the century, 160 such bodies had been founded in England to implement schemes of street paving, widening, cleansing and lighting.*

scholar /ˈskɒlə(r); *NAmE* ˈskɑːlər/ *noun* **1** a person who knows a lot about a particular subject because they have studied it in detail: *Some scholars argue that the capacity of states to regulate and control their societies has increased over time.* ◇ **~ of sth** *She is an eminent scholar of French literature.* HELP **Scholar** is usually used in connection with the humanities or social sciences, or in historical contexts: *At this time, in the late 16th century, continental scholars were busy collecting and classifying all manner of geological and biological objects.* In modern contexts, to talk about natural sciences, use **scientist**. **2** a person who has a scholarship to study at a university or other institution: *She is currently a visiting scholar at the Max Planck Institute for the Study of Societies in Cologne, Germany.*

▸ ADJECTIVE + SCHOLAR **eminent, distinguished** • **prominent, well-known** • **leading** • **influential** • **modern, contemporary** • **young** • **international** • **feminist** • **literary** • **legal** • **classical** • **religious** *Feminist scholars have proposed a variety of explanations for why women might be less likely to support war.*

▸ SCHOLAR + VERB **debate** • **argue (about)** • **agree** • **accept** • **recognize** • **disagree** • **argue (that)** • **claim** • **suggest** • **believe, think** • **point out** • **emphasize** • **focus on** • **note** • **study** • **work** • **write** *Scholars debate the extent to which public support for democracy is intrinsic or instrumental.*

schol·ar·ly /ˈskɒləli; *NAmE* ˈskɑːlərli/ *adj.* **1** involving or connected with serious academic study SYN ACADEMIC¹ (2): *China's contemporary engagement with the African continent is the subject of a growing body of scholarly literature.* ◇ *Little scholarly work has been done on the relationship between law and retail market activity.* ◇ *to attract scholarly attention/interest* **2** having or showing a lot of knowledge as a result of serious academic study: *Weber gave a new and controversial answer to this question, which he demonstrated in an extremely scholarly and rigorous manner.*

schol·ar·ship /ˈskɒləʃɪp; *NAmE* ˈskɑːlərʃɪp/ *noun* **1** [U] the serious study of an academic subject; the work that is produced as a result: *Recent scholarship has demonstrated that the issue is far more complex than was* *previously acknowledged.* ◇ *classical/historical/legal/feminist scholarship* ◇ **~ on sth** *Scholarship on the role of universities in the innovation process has grown rapidly since 1970.* ◇ **~ in sth** *Recent scholarship in the field provides key pointers for detailed consideration of these issues.* **2** [C] an amount of money given to sb by an organization to help pay for their education or study at a particular institution: *Florida also sponsors the McKay Scholarships for students with disabilities.*

school /skuːl/ *noun* **1** [C] a place where children go to be educated: *Although a younger brother attends the local school, neither Gloria nor her sister has ever been enrolled there.* ◇ *Population composition is a necessary consideration in decisions about where to build schools.* ➲ *see also* HIGH SCHOOL, PRIVATE SCHOOL, PUBLIC SCHOOL **2** [U] (used without *the* or *a*) the time children spend at school; the things they do there: **go to ~** *Many of these children will never have the opportunity to go to school.* ◇ **leave ~** *Many students graduate or leave school without much work experience.* ◇ **at ~** *Training focuses on critical life skills such as communication both at school and in the home.* ◇ **in ~** *These educators not only had an impact on their students while they were in school, but also years later.* ◇ **+ noun** *A combination of school curriculum and family-based strategies were used to promote children's physical activity.* **3** [U] (used without *the* or *a*) the time during the day when children are working in a school: *School starts with an assembly, which all are required to attend.* ◇ **after/before/during ~** *Young adolescents may not be independent enough to move around and meet with peers after school.* **4 the school** [sing.] all the students, teachers and other staff in a school: *Anti-bullying schemes involving the whole school have been shown to be effective.* **5** [C] **~ (of sth)** a group of writers, artists, etc. whose style of work or opinions have been influenced by the same person or ideas: *Along with Adam Smith, he was a founder of the classical school of political economy.* **6** [C] **~ (of sth)** a department of a college or university that teaches a particular subject: *He questioned whether every national university required a medical school, school of architecture, law school or engineering school.* **7** [C, U] (*NAmE, rather informal*) a college or university: *Elite schools in the United States that confer great advantages on their graduates probably number about thirty.* **8** [C] **~ (of sth)** a large number of fish or other sea animals swimming together: *The size of fish in any given school tends to be similar.*
IDM **school(s) of ˈthought** a way of thinking about a particular subject that is shared by number of people: *There are two principal schools of thought on minority treatment: assimilation and recognition.*

school·ing /ˈskuːlɪŋ/ *noun* [U] the education you receive at school: *Although he had little formal schooling, Clare was an avid reader of English poetry.* ◇ **primary/secondary ~** *In 1960, 75 per cent of Kingston's population had only primary schooling.* ◇ **home ~** *Parents increasingly see home schooling as a viable method of educating their children.*

sci·ence /ˈsaɪəns/ *noun* **1** [U] knowledge about the structure and behaviour of the natural and physical world, based on facts that you can prove, for example by experiments: *He describes how science progresses despite the many obstacles in its path.* ◇ *Modern science has tended to explain events much more in terms of causes than reasons.* **2** [U] the study of science: **+ noun** *Science teachers in elementary schools lacked training.* **3** [C, U] a particular branch of science, especially biology, chemistry or physics: *The quantity of data produced in the sciences has increased significantly in the last decade.* ◇ *Biomedical science requires multidisciplinary approaches to the study of human diseases.* ◇ *Demography is a science concerned with the analysis of the size, characteristics and processes of a population.* ➲ *compare* ART (5), HUMANITY (4) ➲ *see also* COMPUTER SCIENCE, EARTH SCIENCE, LIFE SCIENCES, NATURAL SCIENCE, PHYSICAL SCIENCE, POLITICAL SCIENCE, SOCIAL SCIENCE **4** [sing.] **~ of sth** a system for organizing the knowledge about a particular subject: *At that time, scientists and engineers began to probe deeper into the science of earthquakes.* IDM *see* EXACT

sci·en·tif·ic /ˌsaɪənˈtɪfɪk/ *adj.* [usually before noun] **1** involving science; connected with science: *Observation and experience are keys to constructing and judging scientific theories.* ◇ *These decisions required political, rather than purely scientific, judgements.* **2** done in a careful and organized way SYN METHODICAL (1): *Creativity combined with a scientific approach can be essential for innovation.*
▸ SCIENTIFIC + NOUN **knowledge • understanding • research • method, approach • evidence • study • inquiry, investigation • analysis • discovery • explanation • theory, hypothesis • principle • progress • revolution • discipline • community • literature • paper • journal** *Scientific knowledge and technology were more advanced in the Islamic world and China than they were in Europe.*

sci·en·tif·ic·al·ly /ˌsaɪənˈtɪfɪkli/ *adv.* **1** in a way that is connected with science: *There is still a lack of scientifically valid data to explain these differences.* ◇ *The idea that language can be studied scientifically is rejected by many people.* **2** in a careful and organized way: *The Classical School of Management argued that all organizations should be designed scientifically.*

sci·en·tist /ˈsaɪəntɪst/ *noun* a person who studies one or more of the NATURAL SCIENCES: *Scientists have discovered how to block the effects of a gene in the brain.* ◇ *Even as recently as the 1970s, some earth scientists did not accept the concept of continental drift.* ➲ *see also* COMPUTER SCIENTIST, POLITICAL SCIENTIST, SOCIAL SCIENTIST

scope AWL /skəʊp; *NAmE* skoʊp/ *noun* **1** [U] the opportunity or ability to do or achieve sth SYN POTENTIAL[2] (1): **~ for sth** *There is significant scope for improvement in the way mental health complaints are managed.* ◇ **~ to do sth** *There is clearly considerable scope to improve the quality of data.* **2** [U] the range of things that a subject, an organization, an activity, etc. deals with: *Studies with more limited geographic scope are consistent with the national studies.* ◇ **~ of sth** *The scope of intellectual property rights was restricted by a right to life-saving medicines for the poor in developing countries.* ◇ **in ~** *This study was limited in scope, involving a small sample of young people in one part of Greece.* ◇ **beyond/outside/within the ~ of sth** *These issues lie beyond the scope of this article.* ➲ *compare* RANGE[1] (2) **3** [C] a MICROSCOPE or TELESCOPE: *Sorting was done under a dissecting scope, and individuals were counted and identified to the lowest possible taxon, usually species.*
▸ ADJECTIVE + SCOPE **limited • narrow • considerable • wide • broad** *There is limited scope for a public authority to legitimately withhold information.*
▸ VERB + SCOPE **broaden, widen • expand, extend • limit, restrict • define** *One consequence of society's increasing globalization is that researchers are encouraged to broaden the scope of their research.*
▸ ADJECTIVE + IN SCOPE **broad • limited • narrow • global • national • international** *Six categories address specific adverse event types, whereas the remaining two categories were broader in scope.*

score[1] /skɔː(r)/ *noun* the number of points sb gets for correct or positive answers in a test: *People with better intelligence test scores are, on average, faster in their reactions.* ◇ *The total scores ranged from 3 to 12 with a higher score indicating greater support from supervisors.* ◇ *to calculate/compute/obtain/produce/yield a score*◇ **~ of sth**

S

A score of 16 or greater indicates that the individual may have clinically significant depressive symptoms.

score² /skɔ:(r)/ *verb* **1** [T, I] to gain marks or points in a test: **~ sth** *If you are consistently scoring 9 out of 10 or above, you are progressing well.* ◇ **+ adv./prep.** *European firms generally score well in these areas.* ◇ *Participants were defined as having 'high job strain' if they scored high on job demands and low on job control.* **2** [T] **~ sth/sb (+ adv./prep.)** to give sth/sb a particular number of points: *Items are scored on a four-point scale.* ◇ *Computerized scoring systems have been developed to help with case finding.* **3** [T] **~ sth** to succeed; to have an advantage: *They scored an impressive victory in a huge naval battle off the Arginusae Islands.* ◇ *Clinton had scored a major legislative success in getting the NAFTA treaty ratified.*

screen¹ /skri:n/ *noun* **1** [C] the flat surface at the front of a television, computer or other electronic device, on which you see pictures or data: *A potential criticism of e-relationships is impersonality, because all business is done on a computer screen.* ◇ **on ~** *Questions may be shown on screen or on a printed questionnaire.* ◇ **+ noun** *Parents play a central role in a child's screen viewing.* **2** [C] the data or images shown on a computer screen: *Users need to scroll down through multiple screens when searching, since each screen can only display a limited amount of information.* **3** [C] the large flat surface that films or pictures are shown on: *The images we receive of the physical world differ from those on the movie screen.* ◇ **on ~** *She first appeared on screen in 1922.* **4** [sing., U] (*often* **the screen**) films or television in general: *The stories and characters were adapted for the screen.* ◇ **+ noun** *He established himself as a mature and accomplished screen actor.* **5** [C] a piece of furniture or equipment that is used to divide a room, or to keep one area of sth hidden or separate: *The participants can be hidden from each other, either in another room or behind a screen.* **6** [C] a system of checking sb/sth for the presence of sth, often a disease: *Conventional genetic screens would not have detected the presence of these genes.* ◇ **~ for sth** *Several relatively inexpensive methods have been developed to carry out an initial screen for the presence of a mutation.* ➲ *see also* SCREENING (1)

S

screen² /skri:n/ *verb* **1** [often passive] to examine people in order to find out if they have a particular disease or illness: **~ sb** *Selected high-risk women are routinely screened in North America.* ◇ **~ sb for sth** *Patients with recurring fungal infections should be screened for diabetes.* **2 ~ sth for sth** to examine sth in order to see if sth is present in it: *By 1995, 18 000 extracts had been screened for anti-cancer activity.* **3 ~ sth** to check sth to see if it is suitable or if you want it: *All papers are screened by the editor and many are rejected before review.* **4 ~ sb** (of a company or an organization) to find out information about people who work or who want to work for you in order to make sure that they can be trusted: *Candidates are screened and sorted by other criteria.* **5 ~ sth/sb from sth/sb** to hide or protect sth/sb by placing sth in front of or around it/them: *The electrode was screened from the light source using masking tape.* **6** [usually passive] to show a film, etc. to the public: **be screened** *In 2007, three new adaptations of Jane Austen novels were screened.*

PHR V **ˌscreen sb ˈout** to decide not to allow sb to join an organization, enter a country, etc. because you think they may cause problems: *Individuals can be screened out if they seem to have unrealistic expectations of the job.* **ˌscreen sth ˈout** to prevent sth harmful from entering or going through sth: *Sunscreens are ineffective in screening out UVA radiation.*

screen·ing /ˈskri:nɪŋ/ *noun* **1** [U, C] the act of testing or examining a person or a group of people to see if they have a disease or condition: *The majority of women felt it was important that women of their age should undergo cancer screening.* ◇ *Health screenings can decrease the negative effects of health problems by identifying them early.* ◇ **~ for sth** *Population-based trials of screening for prostate cancer are currently ongoing.* ◇ **~ of sb** *With a compliance rate of 60%, screening of 50–69-year-olds would be expected to prevent 1 200 deaths per year in the UK.* ◇ **+ noun** *The benefit from the screening programme should outweigh the possible harm caused by the test.* **2** [U] **~ of sth** the act of testing or examining sth, for example to see if a particular substance is present, or if it is suitable for sth: *This process involves the random screening of large numbers of compounds to find one that may act as a useful drug.* **3** [U] the act of checking whether sb is suitable for a particular job or role, or whether they have the right to receive sth: *The department is mainly responsible for screening, hiring and assigning all new college graduates employed by the company.* **4** [C, U] the act of showing a film or television programme: *Male-oriented comedies have built audiences through screenings on channels like Comedy Central.* ◇ **~ of sth** *The screening of this programme caused a lot of controversy at the time.*

script /skrɪpt/ *noun* **1** [C] a written text of a play, film, broadcast, talk, etc: *In Paris, he wrote radio scripts and essays on art, culture, literature and film for a number of journals.* ◇ *The interviewer follows a set script and simply poses a range of questions, noting down the replies for subsequent analysis.* **2** [U, C] a set of letters in which a language is written SYN ALPHABET (1): *Croats write their language in Roman script, while Serbs write theirs in Cyrillic.* ◇ *One of the main problems of Greek scripts lies in the regional varieties.* **3** [C] (*computing*) a series of instructions for a computer, carried out in a particular order, for example when a link in a website is used: *The tool generates a downloadable Perl script that can be executed locally to retrieve data.*

scru·tin·ize (*BrE also* **-ise**) /ˈskru:tənaɪz/ *verb* **~ sth** to look at or examine sth carefully: *Foreign policy is closely scrutinized by the media, public opinion and opposition parties.*

scru·tiny /ˈskru:təni/ *noun* [U] careful and thorough examination SYN INSPECTION (1): *Neither of these arguments withstands close scrutiny.* ◇ **~ of sth** *Despite the careful scrutiny of scientific papers before publication, there are occasional examples where the work described in a paper cannot be replicated.* ◇ **be/come under ~** *Some organizations have come under increasing scrutiny from environmentalists.* ◇ **subject sth to ~** *This allegation was soon subjected to intense scientific scrutiny and criticism.*

sculp·ture /ˈskʌlptʃə(r)/ *noun* [C, U] **~ (of sb/sth)** a work of art that is a solid figure or object, made by cutting or shaping wood, stone, metal, etc; these works of art taken together; the skill of making them: *a marble sculpture of Venus* ◇ *Greek painting and sculpture achieved what they did within the constraints posed by a variety of conventions.* ■ **sculp·tural** /ˈskʌlptʃərəl/ *adj.*: *The dramatic growth in sculptural production reflects an extension of patronage from monasteries.*

sea /si:/ *noun* **1** [U] (*often* **the sea**) (*especially BrE*) the salt water that covers most of the earth's surface: *The deep sea is a very stable environment.* ◇ **by ~** *The agreement did not include the right to transport oil and its products by sea.* ◇ **in/into the ~** *Fish for food is either caught in the open sea or raised in fish farms close to the shore.* ◇ **out to ~** *Eggs deposited on the surface of a mudflat risk being carried out to sea by a receding tide.* ◇ **go to ~** *Crusoe's decision to go to sea is an act of rebellion against his parents.* ◇ **+ noun** *Glaciers and sea ice have tended to retreat in recent decades.* ◇ *The majority of the sea floor consists of soft sediments.* HELP In literary language, in historical contexts and in some phrases, the plural form **seas** is sometimes used: *Some of the money Athens received to police the seas was diverted to the celebration of religious festivals.* ➲ *compare* OCEAN (1) **2** [C] (often **Sea**, especially as part of a name) a large area of salt water that is part of an ocean or surrounded by land: *Temperatures of water in shallow seas increased or decreased as continents moved across latitudes.* ◇ *He died while holidaying in the resort town of Sochi on the Black Sea coast.* **3** [C] (*usually* **seas** [pl.]) the movement of the waves of the sea: *Access to offshore wind turbines is restricted by poor weather conditions, in particular strong winds or high seas.* **4** [sing.] **~ of sth** a large amount of sth: *The church would be an island of stability in a sea of chaos.* **HELP** Note that **sea** is often used in this meaning to talk about negative feelings and situations: *The clinic gradually drowned in a sea of bureaucracy.*

IDM **at ˈsea** **1** on the sea, especially in a ship; in the sea: *He often worked an 18-hour day at sea.* ◇ *Huge quantities of waste have been dumped at sea.* **2** confused and not knowing what to do: *He confessed to still being at sea in some critical parts of the discussion.*

seal[1] /siːl/ *noun* **1** [sing.] a thing that makes sth definite: **~ of approval** *This policy option was given the seal of approval by the Congressional Budget Office.* **2** [C] a device or substance used to join two things together or fill a crack so that air or liquid cannot get in or out: *Desert pavement acts as an efficient seal, preventing ready entry of rainwater into the material below.* **3** [C] a sea animal that eats fish and lives around coasts. There are many types of seal, some of which are hunted for their fur: *Elephant seals and fur seals prey on a wide variety of species.*

IDM **set the ˈseal on sth** (*formal*) to make sth definite or complete: *The move set the seal on Dickens's new status.*

seal[2] /siːl/ *verb* **1** [often passive] **~ sth (with sth)** to close a container tightly or fill a crack, especially so that air or liquid cannot get in or out: *Glass pressure tubes were sealed with Teflon screw caps.* ◇ *If the reaction takes place in a sealed container, the total pressure will change as the reaction proceeds.* **2** **~ sth** to close an envelope, etc. by sticking the edges of the opening together: *Questionnaires were returned to the teacher in a sealed envelope.* **3** **~ sth** to make sth definite, so that it cannot be changed or argued about: *Victory was sealed when the enemy asked permission to recover their own dead, thereby formally admitting defeat.* ◇ *The landing of Columbus sealed the fate of many millions in America because the native peoples had no immunity to the diseases carried by the conquistadors.* **4** **~ sth** (of the police, army, etc.) to prevent people from passing through a place: *In response to the perceived threat of globalized terrorism, governments sought to seal their borders.*

PHR V **ˈseal sth in sth** to put sth in a container and seal it: *The spirit drips through ten feet of charcoal for 11 days before being sealed in barrels of American oak.* **ˌseal sth ˈoff (from sth)** to prevent people or animals from entering or leaving a particular area: *Nature reserves were sealed off to halt the spread of avian influenza.* ◇ *Few cultures are hermetically sealed off from cultural interaction.*

ˈsea level *noun* [U, C, usually pl.] the average height of the sea, used as the basis for measuring the height of all places on land: *The sea level during the peak of the last ice age was 120 metres lower than today.* ◇ *Millions of people now living in coastal areas may need to leave their homes if sea levels rise as predicted.* ◇ **above/at/below ~** *High-grown teas, produced 1 200 m above sea level, are the best that Sri Lanka produces.*

search[1] /sɜːtʃ; *NAmE* sɜːrtʃ/ *noun* **1** an attempt to find sb/sth, especially by looking carefully for them/it: **~ of sth** *An officer carried out a search of the yard looking for Irwin but he was unable to locate him.* ◇ **in ~ of sth** *Historically, people have moved to cities in search of employment.* ◇ **~ for sb/sth** *The search for solutions to new marketing problems must begin by asking the right question.* **2** an act of looking for information in a computer DATABASE, on the Internet, etc; an act of looking for information in official documents: *We performed a large literature search in order to summarize the current knowledge in this field.* ◇ *I attempted to narrow the search by including additional keywords.* ◇ **~ of sth** *Users can conduct complex searches of the data, and download data files.*

search[2] /sɜːtʃ; *NAmE* sɜːrtʃ/ *verb* **1** [I, T] to look carefully for sth/sb; to examine a particular place when looking for sth/sb: *At some point, the animal stops searching and returns to its burrow.* ◇ **~ for sth/sb** *Only 10% of consumers actively search for animal welfare information when making their food purchases.* ◇ **+ adv./prep.** *Increased numbers of homeless people were seen searching routinely through garbage containers for food.* ◇ **~ sth** *The police may obtain a warrant to enter and search premises.* ◇ **~ sth for sth/sb** *He was afraid that his house would be searched for clues.* **2** [T] **~ sb (for sth)** (especially of the police) to examine sb's clothes, etc. in order to find sth that they may be hiding: *A police officer may stop and search a driver or passenger for articles that could be used in connection with terrorism.* **3** [I, T] to look in a computer DATABASE, on the Internet, etc. in order to find information; to look at official documents in order to find information: **~ sth** *The authors searched seven online databases using keywords that included 'mental health'.* ◇ **~ for sth** *The program allowed me to search systematically for patterns and collate responses.* ◇ **~ sth for sth** *Patients will often search the Internet for new and experimental treatments.* **4** [I] **~ for sth** to think carefully, especially in order to find the answer to a problem: *There is a need to search for practical answers to these questions.*

PHR V **ˌsearch sth/sb ˈout** to look for sth/sb until you find them: *More flexibility allows firms to search out the lowest-cost alternatives.*

ˈsearch engine *noun* a computer program that searches the Internet for information, especially by looking for documents containing a particular word or group of words: *Most Internet search engines search for the exact sequence of letters that you type in the search box.*

sea·son /ˈsiːzn/ *noun* **1** any of the four main periods of the year: spring, summer, autumn and winter: *Species in some communities have been seen to shift with changing seasons.* ◇ **during the... ~** *During the summer season from April to October, warm air is drawn into the bay from the south.* **2** [usually sing.] **dry/rainy/wet/monsoon ~** a period of the year in some countries when it is either very dry or it rains a lot: *Where a regular dry season occurs, forests are extremely vulnerable to fire.* ◇ **during the... ~** *During the monsoon season, floods often have catastrophic consequences.* **3** [usually sing.] a period of time during a year when a particular activity happens or is done: *The hurricane season in North America lasts from 1 June to 30 November.* ◇ **during the... ~** *Each year during the breeding season, all nest boxes are checked weekly.* ➲ *see also* GROWING SEASON **4** a period of time in which a play is shown in one place; a series of plays, films or television programmes: *Three of the directors featured in the season visited Manchester to discuss their work.* ◇ *The series finished at the end of its fifteenth season in April 2009.*

IDM **in ˈseason** (of fruit or vegetables) easily available and ready to eat because it is the right time of year for them: *People should buy fresh fruit in season when it tastes best and costs less.*

sea·son·al /ˈsiːzənl/ *adj.* **1** happening or needed during a particular season; changing with the seasons: *Seasonal variations always exist for agricultural products.* ◇ *Irish migrants filled the need for seasonal labour in the agricultural sector.* ◇ *Malaria is highly seasonal, with the highest transmission occurring during and immediately after the rainy season.* **2** typical of or suitable for a particular time of year: *All the meals are cooked on site and are seasonal.* ■ **sea·son·al·ly** /ˈsiːzənəli/ *adv.*: *The data are not strictly comparable since health expenditure may vary seasonally.* ◇ *Safety stock levels are usually based on historical sales data, often seasonally adjusted.*

seat¹ /siːt/ *noun* **1** a place where you can sit, for example a chair: *It is a fairly small theatre with 1 300 seats.* **2** a place where you pay to sit in a plane, train, etc: *The airline has online booking and no reserved seats to make the booking process cheaper and quicker.* **3** an official position as a member of a parliament, council, committee, etc: *Republicans won over 675 seats in the 46 states with legislative elections in 2010.* ◇ *to gain/hold/lose a seat* ◇ *96 per cent of corporate investors take a seat on the board.* ◇ *They won the by-election in a previously safe Conservative seat.* **4 ~ of sth** (*formal*) a place where people are involved in a particular activity, especially a city that has a university or the offices of a government: *Men occupied the seats of power in the town and would not willingly share their privilege.* ◇ *The great palace of Versailles became the seat of government after 1680.* ◇ *Cordoba was a seat of learning and great literary and artistic achievement.*
IDM **be in the ˈdriving seat** (*BrE*) (*NAmE* **be in the ˈdriver's seat**) (*rather informal*) to be the person in control of a situation: *This challenge must be faced if rural people are to be in the driving seat of development activities that affect their own lives.*

seat² /siːt/ *verb* **1 ~ sb/yourself** to give sb a place to sit; to sit down in a place: *We see Zeus seated on a throne holding a lightning bolt.* **2 ~ sb** to have enough seats for a particular number of people: *The parliamentary chambers are equipped to seat 750 members.*

sec·ond¹ /ˈsekənd/ *det., ordinal number* **1** happening or coming next after the first in a series of similar things or people; 2nd: *This was the second time within a week that he had been called to see this patient.* ◇ *The second step a firm must take is to determine the cost of an investment.* ◇ *Most scholars now agree that his works were written towards the end of the 2nd century CE.* ◇ *The Archbishop of Canterbury was assassinated by supporters of King Henry II in 1170.* HELP In this example, **Henry II** is pronounced 'Henry the second'. **2** next in order of importance, size, quality, etc. to one other person or thing: *The EU is the world's leading importer and second-largest exporter of food.* ◇ **~ only to sb/sth** *At the time, Canada ranked second only to the United States in total aluminium output.* ◇ **~ to none** *The company's influence as a grocer is second to none.* **3** [only before noun] another; in addition to one that you already own or use: *In India, perhaps 70 million people speak English as a second language.* ◇ *Many of them have a high income to spend on holidays, second homes and eating out.* IDM *see* THOUGHT¹

sec·ond² /ˈsekənd/ *adv.* **1** after one other person or thing in order or importance: **come ~** *He came second with 17 per cent of the votes.* ◇ *The policies cast women as mothers first and workers second.* **2** used to introduce the second of a list of points you want to make in a speech or piece of writing SYN SECONDLY: *The lawyer is wary of representing Manion, first because he does not like him, and second because he thinks he is likely to be guilty.* ➲ language bank *at* ORGANIZE

sec·ond³ /ˈsekənd/ *noun* [C] **1** (*symb.* ") (*abbr.* **sec.**) a unit for measuring time. There are 60 seconds in one minute: *The speed at which sound waves travel in sea water ranges between about 1 400 and 1 500 metres per second.* ◇ *The prices of shares of public limited companies are changing every few seconds due to constant changes in demand.* **2** (*also* **arc second, second of arc**) (*symb.* ") a unit for measuring angles. There are 60 seconds in one minute: *The gravitational deflection of such a light ray can be calculated to be 1.75 seconds of arc.*

sec·ond·ary /ˈsekəndri; *NAmE* ˈsekənderi/ *adj.* **1** less important than sth else: *The emphasis was on rapid expansion in output; costs and quality were of secondary importance.* ◇ **~ to sth** *In Britain, the European Parliament has been regarded as secondary to the House of Commons.* ➲ *compare* PRIMARY (1) **2** happening as a result of sth else: *Sick animals become weak and quickly pick up secondary infections.* ◇ *The hazards from earthquakes can be classified into two categories, based on whether they are primary or secondary effects.* ◇ **~ to sth** *Personal injuries secondary to the explosion were reported by 10% of both men and women.* ➲ *compare* PRIMARY (2) **3** [only before noun] (of writing) based on other books, etc, not on direct research or observation: *These films have received little attention in the secondary literature on Weimar cinema.* ➲ *see also* SECONDARY SOURCE **4** [only before noun] connected with the education of children aged around 11–18: *He began teaching at secondary schools in the vicinity of Paris.* ◇ *They received four years of secondary education followed by two years of professional training.* ➲ *compare* ELEMENTARY (1), PRIMARY (3), TERTIARY (2) **5** (*chemistry*) (of an ORGANIC COMPOUND) having its FUNCTIONAL GROUP located on a CARBON atom which is BONDED to two other carbon atoms; containing a NITROGEN atom bonded to two carbon atoms: *Unlike tertiary alcohols, secondary and primary alcohols are readily oxidized to carbonyl compounds.* ◇ *Reaction with nitrous acid is used to distinguish between primary, secondary and tertiary amines.* ➲ *compare* PRIMARY (4), TERTIARY (4) ■ **sec·ond·ar·ily** /ˈsekəndrəli; *NAmE* ˌsekənˈderəli/ *adv.*: *This essay primarily discusses technology ads on TV and only secondarily examines the technology itself.*

ˈsecondary source *noun* a book or other source of information where the writer has taken the information from some other source and not collected it himself or herself: *Most of the information was taken from secondary sources.* ➲ *compare* PRIMARY SOURCE

ˌsecond-geneˈration *adj.* **1** used to describe people who were born in the country they live in but whose parents came to live there from another country: *She was a second-generation American.* ◇ *Previous studies show that, in most countries, second-generation immigrants are disadvantaged when it comes to educational attainment.* **2** (of a product or technology) at a more advanced stage of development than an earlier form: *Second-generation biofuels are produced from cellulose, hemicellulose or lignin.*

ˌsecond ˈlanguage *noun* a language that sb learns to speak well and that they use for work or at school, but that is not the language they learned first: *Classes typically include adult basic education and English as a Second Language (ESL).* ◇ **+ noun** *Her research explores second language acquisition processes within the context of computer-mediated communication.*

sec·ond·ly /ˈsekəndli/ *adv.* used to introduce the second of a list of points you want to make in a speech or piece of writing: *Firstly, the new technology is expensive; secondly, it would mean considerable additional staff training.* ◇ *Secondly, and importantly, cultural influences and their effects on buyer behaviour are discussed.* ➲ language bank *at* ORGANIZE

the ˌsecond ˈperson *noun* [sing.] (*grammar*) the form of a pronoun or verb used when addressing sb: *In the phrase 'you are', the verb 'are' is in the second person and the word 'you' is a second-person pronoun.* ➲ *compare* FIRST PERSON, THIRD PERSON

se·crecy /ˈsiːkrəsi/ *noun* [U] the fact of making sure that nothing is known about sth; the state of being secret: *The report states that selection processes are 'shrouded in secrecy'.*

S

se·cret¹ /ˈsiːkrət/ *adj.* **1** known about by only a few people and kept hidden from others; not done in the presence of other people: *The leaders signed a secret agreement that they would not support any attacks on the rebel regime.* ◇ *The file remained secret until 1946.* ◇ *Voting was by secret ballot.* ◇ **keep sth ~ (from sb)** *She kept her background secret from everyone all her life.* **2** [only before noun] used to describe actions and behaviour that you do not want other people to know about: *Eleanor Roosevelt was told that Johnson was a secret liberal.* **3** [only before noun] working secretly against a government's political opponents: *Beria was chief of the secret police and considered Stalin's most likely successor.* ■ **se·cret·ly** *adv.*: *Comecon (the Council for Mutual Economic Assistance) began meeting secretly in 1949.*

se·cret² /ˈsiːkrət/ *noun* **1** [C] something that is known about by only a few people and not told to others: *Typical examples of trade secrets include company databases and suppliers' agreements.* ◇ **keep sth a ~** *The discovery was for some time kept a closely guarded secret.* ◇ **make no ~ of sth** *The government made no secret of its wish to change the direction of policy in the public sector.* **2** [C, usually sing.] (*usually* **the secret**) the best or only way to achieve sth; the way a particular person achieves sth: *At a time of self-doubt, the secret was to stick to certainties.* ◇ **the ~ of sth** *The secret of the company's success is a host of innovative features that deliver better service for clients.* **3** [C, usually pl.] **~ (of sth)** a thing that is not yet fully understood or that is difficult to understand: *Descartes called for a universal mathematics to unlock the secrets of the universe.*
IDM **in ˈsecret** without other people knowing about it: *Members who had previously met only in secret could now gather openly to celebrate their faith.*

sec·re·tary /ˈsekrətri; *NAmE* ˈsekrəteri/ *noun* (*pl.* **-ies**) **1** a person who works in an office, working for another person, dealing with letters and telephone calls, keeping records, arranging meetings, etc: *One study showed that 93 per cent of secretaries and personal assistants were women compared with 61 per cent of teaching professionals (Grimshaw and Rubery, 2001).* **2** (*also* **Secretary**) **~ (of sth)** the head of a government department: *The president's instructions to his secretary of defense highlighted the degree to which he had already made up his mind.*
HELP In the UK the title **Secretary** or **Secretary of State** is used for particular, important government departments: *the Home/Foreign/Education Secretary* ◇ *the Secretary of State for Education.* In the US, **secretary** is the usual term for the head of a government department, chosen by the president; the **Secretary of State** is specifically the head of the government department that deals with foreign affairs: *US Secretary of State, John Kerry* **3** an assistant of a UK government minister or AMBASSADOR: *The private office of a minister consists of a private secretary and up to three assistant private secretaries.*

se·crete /sɪˈkriːt/ *verb* **1** (of part of the body or a plant) to produce a substance, usually a liquid: **~ sth** *Thyroxine is the major hormone secreted by the thyroid gland.* ◇ *These cells can secrete molecules capable of killing cells infected with a virus.* ◇ **~ sth from sth (into sth)** *The digestive enzyme ribonuclease is secreted from the pancreas into the intestine.* **2 ~ sth/sb + adv./prep.** to hide sb/sth: *Dynamite was secreted under the dining room of the Winter Palace.*

se·cre·tion /sɪˈkriːʃn/ *noun* **1** [U] the process by which substances, usually liquids, are produced by parts of the body or plants, either as waste or for a particular function: *As blood sugar levels rise, insulin secretion will increase.* ◇ **~ of sth** *The drugs inhibit the secretion of gastric acid.* **2** [C, usually pl.] a substance, usually a liquid, produced by parts of the body or plants: *The principal endocrine secretions of the testis and ovary differ.*

sec·tion AWL /ˈsekʃn/ *noun* **1** [C] a separate part of a book, document, website, etc: *The book is divided into three sections.* ◇ *This section discusses the demographic models of widest interest in the analysis of populations.* ◇ *Section 28 (3) of the Act deals with unmarried couples.* ◇ **~ on sb/sth** *The RNIB site includes a particularly useful section on how to guide people with sight problems.* ◇ **~ of sth** *The next sections of this chapter trace the main developments in interpretive thinking after 1920.* **2** [C] any of the parts into which sth is divided: *The African wild dog reserve consists of 2.2 acres of grassland divided into two sections by a tarmac road.* ◇ **~ of sth** *Even a very short section of DNA can have a very large number of different configurations or sequences.* **3** [C] (*medical, biology, earth science*) a very thin and flat slice cut from sth in order to be examined, especially under a MICROSCOPE: *Sections are stained and examined under a microscope.* ◇ *Visual analysis of the tissue section was done using a light microscope.* ◇ **~ of sth** *For root structure analysis, longitudinal sections of the 10 mm root tip region were prepared.* ➲ *see also* CROSS SECTION (2) **4** [C, U] a view or image of sth when it has been cut from top to bottom or from one side to the other: **~ of sth** *Figure 9a shows a side view section of six layers.* ◇ **~ through sth** *Sections through crystals are usually six-sided or rectangular.* ◇ **in ~** *When looked at in section, hailstones show a series of alternately opaque and clear ice rings.* ➲ *see also* CROSS SECTION (1) **5** [C] **~ of sth** a separate group within a larger group of people: *In some countries, large sections of society have tolerated the police employing harsh tactics against crime.* ◇ *The health complex saw increased demand for services, especially by the poorer sections of the community.* ➲ *see also* CROSS SECTION (3) **6** [C] **~ (of sth)** (*NAmE*) a district of a town, city or county: *His family lived in the poorest section of the city.*

▸ ADJECTIVE + SECTION **opening, introductory • present • main • previous, preceding • next, following • later, subsequent • final, concluding, closing** *This issue will be explored further in the concluding section of the chapter.* | **longitudinal • vertical • transverse • horizontal** *Figure 13.12 represents a vertical section through a severe tropical cyclone.*

▸ VERB + SECTION **conclude • see • include, contain** *The report included a special section describing the heightened vulnerability of teachers.*

▸ SECTION + VERB **discuss, consider • examine, explore • deal with, focus on, be devoted to • address • apply to • present • provide** *The following section is devoted to discussing the sources of family-related motivation.*

sec·tor AWL /ˈsektə(r)/ *noun* **1** a part of an area of activity, especially of a country's economy: **~ (of sth)** *The shrinkage of the manufacturing sector of the economy has led to the loss of many skilled jobs.* ◇ **in/within a/the ~** *Within the financial sector, the accumulation of debt was even greater.* ◇ **across ~** *Technological innovation takes place unevenly across sectors.* ➲ *see also* PRIVATE SECTOR, PUBLIC SECTOR **2** (*geometry*) a part of a circle lying between two straight lines drawn from the centre to the edge: *If percentages are plotted, 1 per cent is represented by a sector with an angle of 3.6 degrees.* **3** an area of land or sea that is part of a larger area: *The pact divided Poland into Russian and German sectors.* ◇ **~ of sth** *This sector of the Rocky Mountains was apparently relatively dry throughout the Late Pleistocene.*

▸ ADJECTIVE + SECTOR **private • public • voluntary • informal • formal • agricultural • industrial • financial • commercial • corporate • economic • social** *The support of corporate donors remains an important source of income for the voluntary sector.*

▸ NOUN + SECTOR **service • manufacturing • energy • business • banking • education • retail • transport • health • food** *Employment rates in the service sector are*

S

increasing at the expense of those in the manufacturing sector.

▸ VERB + SECTOR **regulate • dominate • enter • represent** *The agency has extensive powers to regulate the transportation sector by setting rules for new vehicles.*

secu·lar /ˈsekjələ(r)/ *adj.* **1** not connected with spiritual or religious matters: *This article examines the place of religion in modern European secular societies.* ◇ *He had an excellent secular education in Greek literature and philosophy.* **2** (of a change or a trend) occurring or continuing over a long period: *Secular trends in childhood obesity in Greece were assessed by Krassas et al. (2001).* ◇ *There is evidence that the slump is not cyclical but secular.*

se·cure¹ AWL /sɪˈkjʊə(r); *NAmE* səˈkjʊr/ *verb* **1** to obtain or achieve sth, especially when this means using a lot of effort: **~ sth** *Ultimately, the key to securing universal human rights is education.* ◇ **~ sth for sb/sth/yourself** *It is very difficult to secure a parliamentary majority for such proposals.* ◇ **~ sb/sth/yourself sth** *Despite fierce opposition, he secured himself a potentially lucrative command in Gaul.* **2 ~ sth on/against sth** to legally agree to give sb property or goods that are worth the same amount as the money that you have borrowed from them, if you are unable to pay the money back: *The couple had a £300 000 mortgage secured on their family home.* **3 ~ sth (against sth)** to protect sth so that it is safe and difficult to attack or damage: *Henry VII was concerned to secure the new dynasty against internal and external enemies.* **4 ~ sth (to sth)** to attach or fix sth firmly: *Secure the elbow in the sling with tape or a safety pin.*

se·cure² AWL /sɪˈkjʊə(r); *NAmE* səˈkjʊr/ *adj.* **1** safe from being attacked, harmed or damaged; protected and/or made stronger so that it is difficult for people to enter or leave, or to take sth: *Money and valuables should be kept in a secure place, e.g. a safe.* ◇ *Children need a stable and secure family environment.* ◇ *The findings are entered as de-identified data into a secure, password-protected database maintained on-site.* ◇ **~ from sth** *Without a home in which to live and the knowledge that they are secure from eviction, no family can thrive satisfactorily.* OPP INSECURE (2) **2** likely to continue or be successful for a long time SYN SAFE (1): *Many faculty members do not need to excel because their jobs are secure and stable.* ◇ *She has a secure home within the family where everything is provided.* OPP INSECURE (2) **3** feeling happy and confident about yourself or a particular situation, so that you do not need to worry: *Training supported by a mentoring programme and a help desk can help staff feel more secure.* OPP INSECURE (1) **4** fixed or attached firmly: *Check to ensure that all equipment is secure.* ■ **se·cure·ly** AWL *adv.*: *Credit card companies have sought to develop structures that will enable bank card transactions to be conducted securely across the Internet.* ◇ *The bottle lids should finally be securely sealed and the contents gently mixed.*

se·cur·ity AWL /sɪˈkjʊərəti; *NAmE* səˈkjʊrəti/ *noun* (*pl.* **-ies**) **1** [U] the activities involved in protecting a country, building or person against attack or danger: *Some states see all other states as potential enemies and threats to their national security.* ◇ *Overall, the UN's record on the maintenance of international peace and security has been mixed.* ◇ **+ noun** *The end of the Cold War also had major implications for defence, foreign and security policy.* **2** [U] protection against sth bad that might happen in the future; the degree to which sth is safe and protected: *As the cost of higher education for students has increased, job security for academics has fallen.* ◇ *The effects of global climate change can exacerbate poverty in poor developing countries and threaten food security.* ➲ *see also* SOCIAL SECURITY **3 securities** [pl.] (*finance*) documents that can be bought and sold giving sb the rights to money earned from a particular business or VENTURE: **+ noun** *Much like global banking, transborder securities trading is mainly conducted through computerized clearing systems.* **4** [U] the fact of agreeing that a valuable item, such as a house, will be given to sb if you are unable to pay back the money that you have borrowed from them: **as ~** *The assets that they have used as security or collateral for the debt are shrinking in value.* **5** [U] the state of feeling happy and safe from danger or worry: *Children look to adults for safety and security.* ◇ **a sense of ~** *Unhappily, staff were lulled into a false sense of security by a lack of previous fatal fires.*

▸ ADJECTIVE + SECURITY **national, internal, state • international, global, collective • physical • personal** *Host states are often unable or unwilling to provide adequate physical security for refugee camps.* | **social • economic • financial** *To run for Parliament an individual must have financial security.*

▸ VERB + SECURITY **provide • ensure • enhance • threaten • achieve** *States seek nuclear weapons both to enhance their own security and to deter potential adversaries.*

▸ NOUN + SECURITY **job • food • health • energy** *Concerns about energy security and high oil prices led to policies that promoted the use of biofuels.*

▸ SECURITY + NOUN **policy • issue • force • service • system • measures • interests • threat** *Supercomputers are used by the security services to crack codes and to monitor telecommunications traffic for certain words and phrases.*

sed·en·tary /ˈsedntri; *NAmE* ˈsednteri/ *adj.* **1** (of work or a way of life) in which you spend a lot of time sitting down: *Health professionals seek to promote physical activity and reduce sedentary behaviour in children.* ◇ *The food industry argues that sedentary lifestyles are the root cause of the problem.* **2** (of people) spending a lot of time sitting down and not moving: *Prescribing walking for sedentary individuals has proved to be effective at low cost.* **3** (*technical*) (of people or animals) that stay and live in the same place or area: *Most African tribes in the region are sedentary crop farmers.*

sedi·ment /ˈsedɪmənt/ *noun* **1** [U, C] (*earth science*) mud, sand and stones carried by water or wind and left, for example, on the surface of the land or the bottom of a lake or the sea: *The major types of sediment deposited were mud and silt.* ◇ *His study suggested that extensive chemical weathering of Precambrian rocks occurred prior to deposition of Cambrian sediments.* **2** [U] the solid material that settles at the bottom of a liquid: *The sample is centrifuged to remove any sediment.*

sedi·ment·ary /ˌsedɪˈmentri/ *adj.* (*earth science*) connected with or formed from the mud, sand and stones that settle on the surface of the land or the bottom of lakes or the sea: *Feldspars are an important constituent in many sedimentary rocks.* ◇ *The best-known sedimentary kaolin deposits are from Georgia in the USA.* ➲ *compare* IGNEOUS, METAMORPHIC

sedi·men·ta·tion /ˌsedɪmenˈteɪʃn/ *noun* [U] **1 ~ (of sth)** (*earth science*) the process of leaving sediment at the bottom of a river, etc: *The rapid sedimentation of this reservoir is being intensively studied.* **2 ~ (of sth)** (*biology*) the process of solid material settling at the bottom of a liquid, or of causing it to do this: *the sedimentation of dead yeast cells during the process of fermentation* HELP In chemistry, the usual term for this process is **precipitation**. ➲ *see also* PRECIPITATION (2)

see /siː/ *verb* (**saw** /sɔː/, **seen** /siːn/) **1** [T] (used in orders) to look at sth in order to find information: **~ sth** *One way of describing society is using socio-economic classes (see Chapter 7).* ◇ *Once DNA and chromatin replication is complete, nuclear division follows (see below).* ◇ *These findings have been replicated at other venues and indeed in other countries (see, for example, Sargeant, 1997).* ◇ **~ sth for sth**

S

See Fig.12.4 for a list of symbols. **2** [T] (not used in the progressive tenses) to become aware of sb/sth by using your eyes: **~ sb/sth** *Many zooplankton are too small to be seen individually with the naked eye.* ◇ **~ (that)...** *Check to see that the substage assembly is properly installed.* ◇ **~ what/how, etc...** *Consumers could not peer into the can to see what the food looked like.* ◇ **~ sb/sth doing sth** *On numerous occasions, he was seen chatting with reporters and others on the news set.* ◇ **~ sb/sth do sth** *As parents arrive to see their children perform, they are encouraged to stop and look at the work that covers the walls and tables.* **3** [I] (not usually used in the progressive tenses) to have or use the power of sight: *On waking next morning, he could not see clearly out of either eye.* **4** [T] (not usually used in the progressive tenses) to have an opinion of sth: **~ sth + adv./prep.** *Each of these groups has different clients and may well see things differently.* ◇ *Seen from a historical perspective, terrorism has almost never emerged in a political vacuum.* ◇ **~ sth as sth** *Most people see housework as an undesirable task which they attempt to avoid.* ◇ *Community care should not be seen as opposite to hospital care.* **5** [T] (not usually used in the progressive tenses) **~ sth** to watch sth such as a game, television programme or performance: *People feel pressured to see a particular movie while everyone is talking about it.* ◇ *The average number of food advertisements seen every day on kids' programmes in the USA is 17.* **6** [T] (not usually used in the progressive tenses) to understand sth: **~ sth** *Some students may not see the point of working hard and therefore make less effort.* ◇ **~ (that)...** *It is important to see that the issues here are different.* ◇ **~ how/what, etc...** *It is easy to see how an error of this type can occur.* ◇ *No one else saw what was about to happen.* **7** [T] (not used in the progressive tenses) **~ sth** to be the time when an event happens SYN WITNESS[2] (2): *The past decade has seen tremendous advances in this field.* ◇ *The twentieth century, especially the period after 1950, saw the rise of a large number of highly industrialized countries.* **8** [T] (not used in the progressive tenses) to experience or suffer sth: **~ sth** *Most farmers saw times grow worse with the adoption of the land tax.* ◇ **~ what/how, etc...** *It is quite common for young children to steal items from a store just to see what it feels like.* **9** [T] (not used in the progressive tenses) **~ sth** to be the place where an event happens SYN WITNESS[2] (2): *Spain has seen a fall in exports and in domestic consumption due to a change in consumer habits.* **10** [T] **~ sb (about sth)** to have a meeting with sb: *Patients are seen three or more times a week, for at least a year.* **11** [T] **~ sb** to visit sb: *She says that they are all 'busy people' and see each other occasionally when work permits.* **12** [T] (not used in the progressive tenses) to consider sth as a future possibility; to imagine sb/sth as sth: ◇ **~ sb/sth doing sth** *Some observers see either Beijing or Shanghai emerging as the dominant world city.* ◇ **~ sb/sth as sth** *Early on, Rosenberg saw Ukrainians as an important future ally.* **13** [T, I] (not usually used in the progressive tenses) to find out sth by looking, asking or waiting: **~ what/which, etc...** *We must see what impact this reform has.* ◇ *We will need to see which of the two approaches works best.* ◇ **it is seen that...** *It is seen that each atom is in direct contact with only six others.* ◇ **~ (that)...** *Turning from households to families, we can see that changes have also taken place in the demography of the family.* ◇ **wait and ~** *Rather than having to wait and see, it would be helpful to be able to predict which pathogens are most likely to emerge.*

IDM Most idioms containing **see** are at the entries for the nouns and adjectives in the idioms, for example **see the light** is at **light**. **for all (the world) to 'see** clearly visible; in a way that is clearly visible: *Blogs and message boards have been added to the site and customer reviews of products are posted for all to see, whether good or bad.* **ˌsee for your'self** to find out or look at sth yourself in order to be sure that what sb is saying is true: *The entire transcript is shown in Appendix B, so readers can see for themselves what has been excluded.* **see sb/sth for what they 'are/it 'is** to realize that sb/sth is not what they/it at first seem to be: *The human 'individual' must be seen for what he or she is: a large organism carrying and inhabited by a host of smaller ones.* **seeing that...** because of the fact that...: *Seeing that both accounts were published almost simultaneously, possible influencing effects are unlikely.*

PHR V **ˌsee sb 'off** **1** to go to a station, etc. with sb who is starting a journey: *Appiah saw Nkrumah off at Euston Station when he headed back to Ghana in 1947.* **2** (*BrE*) to defeat sb in a game, fight or contest: *Grant easily saw off Greely's challenge for the Republican nomination.* **ˌsee 'through sb/sth** (not used in the progressive tenses) to realize the truth about sb/sth: *The public could see through the policy and was not impressed.* **ˌsee sth 'through** (not usually used in the progressive tenses) to not give up doing a task or project until it is finished: *Some find that life gets in the way and they are unable to see the project through.* **'see to sth** to deal with sth: *In the bourgeois family, it was the women who saw to the business of consumption.* **'see to it that...** to make sure that...: *The state saw to it that they had everything they needed.*

seed /siːd/ *noun* **1** [C, U] the small hard part produced by a plant, from which a new plant can grow: *For the cultivation of crop plants, seeds are usually sown a few centimetres or less beneath the soil surface.* ◇ *A tree has to exist for years or decades in the same place before it produces seed.* ◇ **+ noun** *Carbon monoxide was shown to be beneficial for seed germination under salt stress conditions.* **2** [C, usually pl.] **~ (of sth)** the beginning of a feeling or a development which continues to grow: *It was the absence of answers to such questions that planted the first seeds of doubt among the voters.*

seed·ling /ˈsiːdlɪŋ/ *noun* a young plant that has grown from a seed: *Seeds were germinated and seedlings grown under aerobic conditions for 2 days.* ◇

seek AWL /siːk/ *verb* (**sought, sought** /sɔːt/) **1** [T] to ask for sth from sb, such as help or support: **~ sth** *He arrived in the UK seeking political asylum.* ◇ *True obsessive-compulsive disorders are difficult to treat and specialist help should be sought.* ◇ **~ sth from sb** *The on-duty nurse advised him to go home and seek advice from his own doctor the following morning.* **2** [T, I] to try to obtain or achieve sth: **~ sth** *More and more American workers were forced to seek employment in low-wage service industries.* ◇ *Under an extreme right-wing regime, Germany sought a solution to its problems through outward expansion.* ◇ **~ to do sth** *Sometimes institutions such as the Parliament or the Commission have actively sought to expand their influence.* **3** [I] **~ to do sth** to try to do sth SYN ATTEMPT[2]: *Levy-Bruhl sought to explain the influence of these social factors on how people think.* ◇ *These strategies seek to maximize the effectiveness of scarce resources.* ◇ *Kantor constantly sought to challenge the boundaries between art and life.* **4 -seeking** (in adjectives and nouns) looking for or trying to get the thing mentioned; the activity of doing this: *The child may display attention-seeking behaviours such as truancy and running away.* ◇ *Marketing can be adopted by both profit-seeking and not-for-profit organizations.* ◇ *Neo-Marxist theories argue against the idea that individuals are always rational and self-seeking.*

IDM **seek your 'fortune** (*literary*) to try to find a way to become rich, especially by going to another place: *The majority of residents in Bulyanhulu were immigrants who had come to seek their fortune from mining.*

PHR V **ˌseek sb/sth 'out** to look for and find sb/sth, especially when this means using a lot of effort: *In these cases, buyers will seek out information about the alternative ways in which they can satisfy their needs.*

▸ SEEK + NOUN **advice** • **help, assistance** • **information** • **care, treatment** • **consent** • **support** • **asylum** *Linda's parents sought treatment because she was increasingly angry and rebellious.* | **ways** • **solution** • **work,**

employment ◆ **damages** *From the mid-1980s, many states sought ways of reducing the overall cost of services (Whitfield, 2001).*

▸ SEEK TO + VERB **understand** ◆ **explain** ◆ **address** ◆ **identify** ◆ **establish** ◆ **achieve** ◆ **maximize** ◆ **challenge** ◆ **ensure** ◆ **protect** ◆ **promote** ◆ **avoid** *Her account highlights the complexities involved in seeking to address issues of poverty for girls through education.*

seek·er /ˈsiːkə(r)/ *noun* (often in compounds) a person who is trying to find or get the thing mentioned: *An additional 2.7 million new jobseekers were entering the labour market at a time of no job creation.* ➲ *see also* ASYLUM SEEKER

seem /siːm/ *linking verb* **1** (not used in the progressive tenses) to give the impression of being or doing sth SYN APPEAR (1): **+ adj.** *Although the reality of economic globalization seems clear, the details of its impact are contested.* ◇ **+ noun** *Improved technology seemed the best way of improving the growth rate.* ◇ **~ like sth** *This may seem like an attractive option, but there are severe problems.* ◇ **~ as though...** *It seems as though they will need more time.* ◇ **it seems that...** *It seems that in almost all societies, the attitudes that people have to language change are basically the same.* ◇ **~ to do/be/have sth** *In major media centres, there seemed to be a lot of support for Putnam's ideas.* ◇ **~ to sb** *This view, it seems to me, has little to recommend it.* **2 ~ to do/be/have sth** used to make what you say about your thoughts, feelings or actions less strong: *The history of the early twentieth century seemed to suggest that there was a flaw in classic Marxist analysis.* ◇ *The authors' findings seem to indicate that some changes in immigration policy can have a dramatic impact on immigration.* **3 it seems| it would seem** used to suggest that sth is true when you are not certain or when you want to be polite: **~ (that) ...** *It seems that each side in the debate has failed to learn the lesson taught by the other side.* ◇ **+ adj.** *It would seem reasonable to expect photosynthesis to increase as atmospheric carbon dioxide levels rise.*

seem·ing /ˈsiːmɪŋ/ *adj.* [only before noun] appearing to be sth that may not be true SYN APPARENT (2): *Most studies focus on a seeming contradiction between 'international approaches' and 'local approaches'.*

seem·ing·ly /ˈsiːmɪŋli/ *adv.* in a way that appears to be true but may in fact not be SYN APPARENTLY: *Because light behaves in two seemingly contradictory ways, two different theories have been developed to explain it.* ◇ *The seemingly endless cycle of war and conflict confirmed in their minds the essentially aggressive impulses in human nature.*

seen *past part. of* SEE

seg·ment¹ /ˈsegmənt/ *noun* **1** a part of sth that is separate from the other parts or can be considered separately: *Companies analyse market segments to find niches that will give them a competitive edge.* ◇ *As replication proceeds, newly synthesized DNA segments are joined together to finally generate two identical daughter DNA molecules.* ◇ **~ of sth** *Large segments of the population experienced no significant improvement in their standard of living.* **2** (*geometry*) part of a shape separated from the rest by at least one line or PLANE; the line between two points: *A circle divided in half by a single line is a semi-circle; dividing a circle by a single line anywhere else makes a segment of the smaller part.*

seg·ment² /segˈment/ *verb* [often passive] **~ sth** (*technical*) to divide sth into different parts: *A company may segment a market on the basis of how often a customer uses its products or services.* ◇ *The Andes are segmented into five zones, only three of which have active volcanoes.*

seg·men·tal /segˈmentl/ *adj.* [only before noun] consisting of or divided into segments: *The segmental structure is also evident in the embryonic brain, which is composed of three segments (neuromeres).*

seg·men·ta·tion /ˌsegmenˈteɪʃn/ *noun* [U, C] (*technical*) the act of dividing sth into different parts; one of these parts: *Market segmentation is used to identify groups that may be willing to pay higher prices.* ◇ *The first visible signs of segmentation in the embryo are transient grooves that appear on the surface of the embryo.* ◇ **~ of sth** *The advent of digital television is producing a growing demographic segmentation of audiences.*

seg·re·gate /ˈsegrɪgeɪt/ *verb* [usually passive] to separate people of different races, religions, sexes or classes and treat them in a different way: **be segregated (from sb)** *In the feudal era, elites were not only physically segregated from peasants, but also spoke a different language.* ◇ **segregated + noun** *The plaintiffs accused the board of education of maintaining racially segregated schools.* OPP INTEGRATE (2)

seg·re·ga·tion /ˌsegrɪˈgeɪʃn/ *noun* [U] **1** the act or policy of separating people of different races, religions, sexes or classes and treating them in a different way: *For African Americans, segregation increased throughout much of the 20th century.* ◇ *Inequalities resulting from racial segregation are still evident in the socio-economic status of the population.* **2 ~ (of A and B) (into sth)** the act of separating people or things from a larger group: *the segregation of pupils with learning difficulties* ◇ *This may justify the segregation of the study of religion and the study of race into separate fields of academic inquiry.*

seis·mic /ˈsaɪzmɪk/ *adj.* [only before noun] **1** connected with or caused by EARTHQUAKES: *Ground shaking is the result of seismic waves reaching the Earth's surface.* ◇ *By recording large amounts of seismic data, good estimates of the Earth's radial and lateral seismic velocities can be obtained.* **2** having a very great effect; of very great size: *There is a requirement for a seismic shift in cancer research philosophy.*

seize /siːz/ *verb* **1 ~ sth** to be quick to take advantage of sth such as a chance or an opportunity: *The new government seized the opportunity to pursue new tactics.* ◇ *He showed that, in competitive electoral politics, it is essential to seize the initiative.* **2** to take control of a place or situation, often suddenly and violently: **~ sth** *Hitler seized power in 1933.* ◇ *On 11 December, Communist forces seized the city.* ◇ **~ sth from sb** *Italian troops seized control of the country from Haile Selassie.* **3 ~ sth** (of the police, etc.) to take possession of sth by legal right: *Documents belonging to the plaintiff had been seized by the police.* **4 ~ sb** to arrest or capture sb: *French and British officials sent to open negotiations were seized and imprisoned.* **5 ~ sb/sth (from sb)** to take hold of sb/sth suddenly and using force: *She tried to seize the gun from him.*

PHR V **ˈseize on/upon sth** to suddenly show a lot of interest in sth, especially because you can use it to your advantage: *The press were quick to seize on claims of procedural failings by the police.*

seiz·ure /ˈsiːʒə(r)/ *noun* **1** [C] a sudden attack of an illness, especially one that affects the brain: *She had two further seizures while in the ambulance.* ◇ *He has suffered epileptic seizures three to four times a month.* **2** [U] **~ (of sth)** the act of using force to take control of a country, town, etc: *He criticized the Bolsheviks' seizure of power in 1917.* ◇ *The attack on Egypt was precipitated by Colonel Nasser's seizure of the Suez Canal.* **3** [U] **~ (of sth)** the use of legal authority to take sth from sb: *Sections 60 and 66 of the Act are concerned with searching premises and the seizure of property.*

sel·dom /ˈseldəm/ *adv.* not often SYN RARELY: *These drugs are seldom used today because they interact with certain foodstuffs.* ◇ *Markets are seldom static.* ◇ **~, if ever** *This is seldom, if ever, possible.*

S

se·lect¹ AWL /sɪˈlekt/ *verb* **1** to choose sb/sth from a group of people or things, usually according to a system: **~ sb/sth** *Each GP selected a random sample of his/her patients.* ◇ *A total of 2 125 people were randomly selected to participate in this experiment.* ◇ **~ sb/sth for sth** *Two periods, 1999–2003 and 2004–06, were selected for analysis.* ◇ **~ sb/sth from sth** *The panel of judges is selected from a list of names which have been put forward.* ◇ **~ sb/sth as sth** *Truman was selected as a candidate for the US Senate in 1934.* ◇ **~ sb/sth to do sth** *The families were selected to represent a range of social classes.* ◇ **~ which/what, etc...** *There are three fundamental factors involved in selecting which media sector to use for an advertising campaign.* ➲ language bank *at* RESEARCH² **2 ~ sth (from sth)** to mark sth on a computer screen for a particular purpose; to choose sth on a computer screen, especially from a menu: *The student selects a block of HTML text from the page to use as a potential quotation.*

PHR V **select for/against sth** (*biology*) (in terms of EVOLUTION) to be the deciding factor in whether a particular living thing or characteristic of a living thing survives: *The heavy egg loss may have selected for larger females, able to lay more eggs at shorter intervals.*

▸ SELECT + NOUN **item • option** *Participants are asked to select items repeatedly at random from a restricted pool.* | **sample • value • variable • individual • patient • respondent • participant • candidate • group • audience • model • site • study • strategy • case • school • material • product** *Management decides which skills the team requires and selects individuals with these competencies.*

▸ ADVERB + SELECT **randomly • arbitrarily • carefully • positively • purposively, deliberately • specially • initially • sexually** *Females of these crabs carefully select the sites at which they release their larvae.*

▸ SELECT + ADVERB **randomly • at random** *Customers were selected at random as they entered the store and followed by two observers until they left.*

se·lect² AWL /sɪˈlekt/ *adj.* [only before noun] carefully chosen as the best out of a larger group of people or things: *The survey is based on interviews with a select group of expert mediators in the New York area.* ◇ *A select bibliography of major works on British slavery and abolitionism is appended.*

se·lec·tion AWL /sɪˈlekʃn/ *noun* **1** [U, C] the process of choosing sb/sth from a group of people or things, usually according to a system: **~ (of sb/sth)** *The selection of the countries was based on two criteria.* ◇ *The company evaluates potential markets before making a final selection.* ◇ *Today, mate selection clearly appears as one of the major mechanisms in evolution.* ◇ **+ noun** *The use of a random selection process does not guarantee a representative sample.* **2** [C] a number of people or things that have been chosen from a larger group: **~ of sb/sth** *The study concentrates on a selection of authors.* ◇ **~ from sb/sth** *These are only brief selections from the longer interview conversations.* **3** [C] **~ (of sth)** a collection of things from which sth can be chosen SYN RANGE¹ (1): *There is a wide selection of techniques to support this analysis.* **4** [U] (*biology*) (in EVOLUTION) a process in which environmental or GENETIC factors influence which types of living thing are more successful than others: *There has been more than enough time for selection to generate specific DNA sequences of the required length.* ➲ *see also* NATURAL SELECTION, SEXUAL SELECTION

se·lect·ive AWL /sɪˈlektɪv/ *adj.* **1** [usually before noun] affecting or choosing only a small number of people or things from a larger group; causing particular people or things from a group to be chosen: *The species were modified genetically through selective breeding.* ◇ *Females have an important selective advantage if they can distinguish and choose to mate with males of higher quality.* **2** tending to be careful about what or who you choose: **~ about sth** *He believed that biographers had a duty to be selective about what they revealed.* ◇ **~ in sth** *Mortgage lenders are becoming increasingly selective in their lending policy.* ■ **se·lect·ive·ly** AWL *adv.*: *The regime was selectively targeting federal funds for social spending and construction projects.* **se·lect·iv·ity** /səˌlekˈtɪvəti/ *noun* [U] *This type of fishing net has long been considered ecologically harmful because of its inherent lack of selectivity.*

self /self/ *noun* (*pl.* **selves** /selvz/) **1** [C] the type of person you are, especially the way you normally behave, look or feel: *Some people felt better able to express their true selves over the Internet.* ◇ *People display different selves in purchasing and consumption.* ◇ *The Russia whose armies had crossed Europe to Paris in 1814 was now a pale shadow of its former self.* **2** [U] (*also* **the self** [sing.]) a person's personality or character that makes them different from other people: *For many teens, developing a sense of self is a relatively smooth process.* ◇ *Social competence is frequently associated with positive beliefs about the self.* **3** [U] used to refer to sb as the one affected by their own actions: *The initial assessment of the patient is of vital importance in determining the risk of harm to self or others.*

ˌself-asˈsess·ment *noun* [U] the process of judging your own progress or achievements: *To facilitate student self-assessment, the students were asked to analyse their language production.* ◇ **~ of sth** *There should be self-assessment of the board's work on an annual basis.*

ˌself-aˈwareness *noun* [U] knowledge and understanding of your own character: *Through such open discussion, children and teens develop increased self-awareness.* ■ **ˌself-aˈware** *adj.*: *If we are aware of our own values and beliefs, the task of becoming self-aware is much easier.*

ˌself-ˈconscious *adj.* **1** nervous or embarrassed about your appearance or what other people think of you: *Detailed note-taking in front of participants may make them extremely self-conscious.* ◇ **~ about sth** *The patient presents to her GP because she is becoming increasingly self-conscious about a lump in the front of her neck.* **2** (*often disapproving*) done in a way that shows you are aware of the effect that is being produced: *The self-conscious artifice of the film contributes to a distancing effect.* **3** (*philosophy, psychology*) having knowledge of your own existence: *If there is no self-concept without language, then other animals are not self-conscious.* ■ **ˌself-ˈconscious·ly** *adv.*: *Ziegler's book inspired a range of theories—some more popular, others self-consciously scholarly.* **ˌself-ˈconscious·ness** *noun* [U, sing.] **~ about sth** *Prufrock reveals an acute self-consciousness about the opinions of others.* ◇ **~ (of sth)** *the stylistic self-consciousness of musicals* ◇ *If you are not only aware of the world around you but of yourself as an observer, then you have self-consciousness.*

ˌself-conˈtained *adj.* able to operate or exist without outside help or influence SYN INDEPENDENT (3): *The four essays are self-contained and can be read independently of each other.* ◇ *Within ecological theory, ecosystems are usually treated as self-contained units with no outside interactions.*

ˌself-conˈtrol *noun* [U] the ability to control your emotions and desires, especially in difficult situations: *The jury may decide that the defendant was provoked to lose his self-control.*

ˌself-deˈfence (*BrE*) (*NAmE* **ˌself-deˈfense**) *noun* [U] **1** the act of protecting yourself when you are being attacked or criticized: *A state's right of self-defence is explicitly recognized in international law.* ◇ **act in ~** *The burden of proving that the defendant did not act in self-defence rests with the prosecution.* **2** the skill of being able to protect yourself from physical attack, especially without using

S

weapons: **+ noun** *Medical staff were advised to consider enrolling in a self-defence class.*

ˌself-deˌtermiˈnˑation *noun* [U] **1** the right of a country or a region and its people to be independent and to choose their own government and political system SYN INDEPENDENCE (1): *Reconciling principles of national self-determination with national security was a formidable task.* **2** the right or ability of a person to control their own FATE: *The right to self-determination is a closely guarded value in Britain, and raises many ethical and legal issues.*

ˌself-emˈployed *adj.* **1** working for yourself and not employed by a company, etc: *The greater independence of self-employed persons is believed to be largely responsible for their job satisfaction.* **2 the self-employed** *noun* [pl.] people who work for themselves and are not employed by a company, etc: *The self-employed are granted rights under the Treaty to move to another member state to work.* ■ **ˌself-emˈploy·ment** *noun* [U] *They found that when unemployment is low, people are more likely to enter self-employment.*

self-esteem *noun* [U] a feeling of being happy with your own character and abilities: *Children and teens with low self-esteem may be highly sensitive to criticism and exclusion.*

ˌself-ˈevident *adj.* obvious and needing no further proof or explanation: *Euclid's geometry begins with axioms, which he regarded as 'self-evident truths'.* ◇ **it is ~ that...** *It is self-evident that foreign policy should serve to defend and advance national interests.* ■ **ˌself-ˈevident·ly** *adv.*: *This claim should not be regarded as self-evidently true.*

ˌself-ˈgovern·ment *noun* [U] the government or control of a country, region or organization by its own people or members, not by others: *From 1972, local self-government in Northern Ireland had been suspended and direct rule imposed from London until 1999.* ■ **ˌself-ˈgovern·ing** *adj.*: *Citizenship denotes full membership of a self-governing community.*

ˌself-ˈharm *noun* [U] the practice of deliberately injuring yourself, for example by cutting yourself, as a result of having serious emotional or mental problems: *Every act of deliberate self-harm should be assessed thoroughly.* ■ **ˌself-ˈharm** *verb* [I] *If the patient is self-harming, their mental health needs should be considered.*

S

ˌself-ˈhelp *noun* [U] the act of relying on your own efforts and abilities in order to solve your problems, rather than depending on other people for help: *Self-help can take many forms, including learning to identify symptoms and take actions to counteract them.* ◇ **+ noun** *Self-help groups can also be a valuable source of support.*

ˌself-ˈimage *noun* the opinion or idea you have of yourself, especially of your appearance or abilities: *Clark showed that black children educated in segregated schools developed a negative self-image.*

ˌself-ˈinterest *noun* [U] (*often disapproving*) the fact of sb only considering their own interests and of not caring about things that would help other people: *The pursuit of self-interest does not always benefit society as a whole.* ◇ **in sb's ~** *Williamson (1985) argues that some decision-makers tend to act in their own self-interest whenever this is profitable.* ■ **ˌself-ˈinterest·ed** *adj.*: *States are rarely prepared to sacrifice their own soldiers overseas unless they have self-interested reasons for doing so.*

self·ish /ˈselfɪʃ/ *adj.* caring only about yourself rather than about other people: *In early childhood, one first becomes aware of the need to balance selfish desires and consideration for others.* ◇ *Critical Theorists are likely to argue that capitalism is inherently selfish.* ■ **self·ish·ly** *adv.*: *Thomas Hobbes expected that people would selfishly pursue their own interests rather than the common good.* **self·ish·ness** /ˈselfɪʃnəs/ *noun* [U] *Selfishness can have benefits when it comes to reproductive fitness.*

ˌself-reˈspect *noun* [U] a feeling of pride in yourself that what you do, say, etc. is right and good: *For many people, having a job is essential to their self-respect.*

ˌself-sufˈficient *adj.* **~ (in sth)** able to do or produce everything that you need without the help of other people: *Dongtan is being designed to be self-sufficient in energy, food and water.* ◇ *Huge numbers of women work in jobs that fail to make them economically self-sufficient.* ■ **ˌself-sufˈficiency** *noun* [U] *Fairtrade assists these producers in achieving economic self-sufficiency.*

sell /sel/ *verb* (**sold, sold** /səuld; *NAmE* sould/) **1** [T, I] to give sth to sb in exchange for money: **~ sth (to sb) (for sth)** *He sold the company to the American retail giant for $6.7bn in 1999.* ◇ **~ sb sth (for sth)** *Mortimer offered to sell him the watch for £50 000.* ◇ **~ (sth) (at sth)** *Bondholders therefore willingly sell bonds at the existing price.* ◇ *Farmers refused to sell until prices rose.* ◇ **~ (sth) at a profit/loss** *The goods were transported from the colonies back to the mother countries where they could be sold at a profit.* **2** [T] **~ sth** to offer sth for people to buy: *The shops also sell products from developing countries.* **3** [T, I] to be bought by people in the way or in the numbers mentioned; to be offered at the price mentioned: **~ (sth)** *By 1902, the 'Daily Mail' was selling 1.2 million copies a day.* ◇ *Their products were of a high quality and sold well.* ◇ *The firm discovers that its dolls are not selling.* ◇ **~ for sth** *The painting sold for $106 million.* ◇ **~ at sth** *The jeans sell at considerably higher prices in the UK than in the USA.* **4** [I, T] to make people want to buy sth: *In such a competitive media environment, celebrity sells.* ◇ **~ sth** *Journalists have long known that scare stories sell newspapers.* **5** [T] **~ sth/ yourself (to sb)** to persuade sb that sth is a good idea, service, product, etc; to persuade sb that you are the right person for a job, position, etc: *It is easier to sell the idea to primary teachers.* ◇ *People attending interviews do not always sell themselves well.* **6** [T] **~ yourself (to sb)** (*disapproving*) to accept money or a reward from sb for doing sth that is against your principles: *The worker sells himself to the capitalist in return for wages.* ➲ *see also* SALE

IDM **sell sb/yourself ˈshort** to not value sb/yourself highly enough and show this by the way you treat or present them/yourself: *When he talks about his lack of success, it is hard not to feel that he is selling himself short.*

PHRV **ˌsell sth ˈoff 1** to sell things cheaply because you want to get rid of them or because you need the money: *The country's poor are becoming poorer as they sell off their few possessions.* **2** to sell all or part of an industry, a company or land: *By 1992, the Conservatives had sold off nearly all the major utilities.* **ˌsell sth ˈon** to sell to sb else sth that you have bought not long before: *The contract involved property which had been sold on before the complainant brought his claim.* **ˌsell ˈout | be ˌsold ˈout** to be all sold: *The first edition sold out on the day of publication.* **ˌsell ˈout (of sth) | be ˌsold ˈout (of sth)** to sell all of your stock of sth: *Suppliers were often sold out before demand was satisfied.* **ˌsell ˈout (to sb/sth) 1** (*disapproving*) to change or give up your beliefs or principles in order to gain an advantage: *His fellow Russians thought that he was selling out to the West.* **2** to sell your business or a part of your business: *These decades saw many shareholders sell out.* **ˌsell ˈup** (*especially BrE*) to sell your home, possessions, business, etc, usually because you are leaving the country or retiring: *If things do not improve, she will have to think about selling up.*

sell·er /ˈselə(r)/ *noun* a person or company that sells sth: *A market occurs when buyers and sellers come together to trade.*

selves *pl. of* SELF

se·man·tic /sɪˈmæntɪk/ *adj.* [usually before noun] (*linguistics*) connected with the meaning of words and sentences: *The most obvious effect of context is to add semantic content, that is, to enrich a meaning or make it more specific.* ◇ *Compare for example, the semantic units [dog] and [animal].* ■ **se·man·tic·al·ly** /sɪˈmæntɪkli/ *adv.*: *The words in the thesaurus are grouped semantically.*

se·man·tics /sɪˈmæntɪks/ *noun* [U] (*linguistics*) **1** the study of the meanings of words and phrases: *The study of extensions of meaning is an important task for semantics.* **2 ~ (of sth)** the meaning of words, phrases or systems: *The effect of combining the progressive form with a verb in English depends on the semantics of the verb.*

se·mes·ter /sɪˈmestə(r)/ *noun* one of the two periods that the school or college year is divided into in some countries, for example the US: *Beginning in the second semester of seventh grade, students are required to take six semesters of Global Studies.* ➲ *compare* TERM[1] (5)

semi·colon /ˌsemiˈkəʊlən; *NAmE* ˈsemikoʊlən/ *noun* the mark (;) used to separate the parts of a complicated sentence or items in a detailed list, showing a pause that is longer than a comma but shorter than a full stop: *Instructions are separated by semicolons.* ➲ *compare* COLON (1)

semi·con·duct·or /ˌsemikənˈdʌktə(r)/ *noun* (*engineering, computing*) **1** a solid substance that CONDUCTS electricity in particular conditions, better than an INSULATOR but not as well as a CONDUCTOR: *Semiconductors conduct electricity poorly but the conductivity increases with temperature.* ◇ **+ noun** *Semiconductor materials have low reactivity and high surface hardness.* **2** a device containing a semiconductor used in ELECTRONICS: *In both semiconductors and computers, new firms grew to positions of considerable size and market share.* ◇ **+ noun** *It represents one of the simplest and cheapest semiconductor devices ever developed.*

sem·inal /ˈsemɪnl/ *adj.* very important and having a strong influence on later developments: *Maslow's (1943) seminal work on human needs is also particularly relevant.* ◇ *This was proved by Claude Shannon in two seminal papers in 1948 and 1949.*

ˌsemi-ˈstructured *adj.* (of interviews) allowing the INTERVIEWER to ask questions based on what the INTERVIEWEE says in addition to asking pre-prepared questions: *Semi-structured interviews were chosen as the research method to avoid limiting the responses of the people being interviewed.*

sen·ate /ˈsenət/ *noun* (*usually* **the Senate**) [sing.] **1** one of the two groups of elected politicians who make laws in some countries, for example in the US, Australia, Canada and France. The Senate is smaller than the other group but higher in rank. Many state parliaments in the US also have a Senate: *The Senate must ratify any treaty with a two-thirds majority.* ➲ *compare* CONGRESS (2), HOUSE OF REPRESENTATIVES **2** (in ancient Rome) the most important council of the government; the building where the council met: *His father, Cassius Apronianus, entered the Senate, attaining a consulship and several governorships.*

sen·ator /ˈsenətə(r)/ *noun* (*often* **Senator**) (*abbr.* **Sen.**) a member of a senate: *The idea was endorsed by the first African American US Senator, Hiram Revels.* ◇ *The prime source is the Latin writings of Cornelius Tacitus, a Roman senator probably from Gallia Narbonensis.* ■ **sen·at·or·ial** /ˌsenəˈtɔːriəl/ *adj.* [only before noun] *The PDP won 75 of the 109 senatorial seats.*

send /send/ *verb* (**sent, sent** /sent/) **1** to make sth go or be taken to a place, especially by mail, email, radio, etc: **~ sth** *The first email was sent in 1971.* ◇ **~ sth by mail/post** *The follow-up questionnaires were sent by mail.* ◇ **~ sth to sb/sth** *The capsule cannot send any signals to the spaceship.* ◇ **~ sth back (to sb/sth)** *Darwin sent many boxes of flora and fauna back to London for study.* ◇ **~ sb sth** *The bank has sent her a letter asking her to nominate a solicitor.* **2** to tell sb to go somewhere or do sth; to arrange for sb to go somewhere: **~ sb (+ adv./prep.)** *Wealthier parents could send their children to a private school.* ◇ *Patients with minor head injuries are usually sent home after treatment.* ◇ **~ sb to do sth** *German troops were sent to help Austria.* **3** to tell sb sth by sending them a message: **~ sth (to sb)** *Eyewitnesses sent the news to London.* ◇ **~ sb sth** *Disagreements between parents might also send the child confusing messages.* ◇ **~ sth (that)...** *The emperor sent word that the old philosopher would have to die.* **4** to make sth/sb move quickly or suddenly: **~ sth/sb doing sth** *A severe storm sent the Mongols fleeing.* ◇ **~ sth/sb + adv./prep.** *The eruption sends a column of hot gases up into the atmosphere over the volcano.* **5** to cause sb/sth to be in a particular state: **~ sb/sth into sth** *A restrictive monetary policy sent the economy into a recession.* ◇ **~ sb/sth to sth** *Between 1936 and 1938, Stalin sent up to 6 million Soviet citizens to their deaths.*

PHR V **ˈsend for sb** to ask or tell sb to come to you, especially in order to help you: *He promised to send for his future wife as soon as he was settled in America.* **ˈsend for sth** to ask sb to bring or deliver sth to you: *Students were encouraged to send for adult education booklets and college prospectuses.* **ˌsend sb ˈin** to order sb to go to a place to deal with a difficult situation: *Metternich sent in Austrian troops to crush the rebellions in Naples and Piedmont.* **ˌsend sth ˈin** to send sth by mail to a place where it will be dealt with: *Of the 155 respondents who sent in completed questionnaires, 16 agreed to be interviewed* **ˌsend sb ˈoff (to...)** to tell sb to go somewhere; to arrange for sb to go somewhere: *In 1492, Queen Isabella sent Christopher Columbus off to the New World.* **ˌsend sth ˈoff** to send sth to a place, especially by mail: **~ (to sb/sth) (for sth)** *Dickens used to send copy off to his printers only days before an issue appeared on the streets.* **ˌsend sth ˈon** to send sth from one place or person to another: **~ (from sb/sth) (to sb/sth)** *The information is sent on from these sites to other brain areas.* **ˌsend sth ˈout 1** to send sth to a number of different people or places: *A thousand questionnaires can be sent out through the post in one batch.* **2** to produce sth such as light, a signal, sound, etc. SYN EMIT: *The transmitter sends out a signal at a frequency of 2 kHz.*

send·er /ˈsendə(r)/ *noun* a person who sends sth: *Completed questionnaires are to be returned to the sender electronically.*

se·nior¹ /ˈsiːniə(r)/ *adj.* **1** having a high rank in an organization or a profession: *A senior manager authorizes expenditure over a certain limit.* ◇ *She had served in senior positions in the US government.* OPP JUNIOR (1) **2** [only before noun] older, especially having now retired from work: *Many smaller businesses offer discounts for students and senior citizens.* **3** [only before noun] (*BrE*) (of a school or part of a school) for children over the age of 11 or 13: *She wanted to show how senior school curriculum choices were shaped by the subjects that led to university entrance.* ➲ *compare* JUNIOR (2)

se·nior² /ˈsiːniə(r)/ *noun* **1** (*especially NAmE*) an older person, especially sb who has now retired from work: *This measure boosts income for seniors aged 85 years and older.* **2** a person who has a higher rank in an organization or a profession: *No individual HR professional is able to challenge his or her more powerful seniors on sensitive firm issues.* **3** (in the US and some other countries) a student in the last year at a HIGH SCHOOL or college: *They used a sample of 500 high school seniors for the survey.*

se·ni·or·ity /ˌsiːniˈɒrəti; *NAmE* ˌsiːniˈɔːrəti; ˌsiːniˈɑːrəti/ *noun* [U] **1** the fact of being older or of a higher rank than others: *Senators spoke in order of seniority, so there was minimal opportunity for young men to influence the deliberations.* **2** the rank that you have in a company because of the length of time you have worked there: *There is a rigid career structure based on merit and seniority.*

sen·sa·tion /sen'seɪʃn/ *noun* **1** [C] a feeling that you get when sth affects your body: *The patient reported a burning sensation in his legs.* ◇ **~ of sth** *Feelings of exhaustion accompanied a sensation of dizziness.* **2** [U] the ability to feel through your sense of touch SYN FEELING (8): *She has not noticed any loss of sensation or power in her lower limbs.* **3** [C, usually sing.] **~ (of sth)** a general feeling or impression that is difficult to explain; an experience or a memory: *Many viewers reported a sensation of liberation and new possibilities as a result of watching the film.* **4** [C, usually sing.] very great surprise, excitement or interest among a lot of people: *Feuerbach created a sensation with an attack on orthodox religion called 'The Essence of Christianity'.*

sense[1] /sens/ *noun* **1** [C] the meaning that a word or phrase has; a way of understanding sth: *The word 'former' has at least two senses.* ◇ **in... sense** *The machine could, in a sense, be described as intelligent.* ◇ *The agreement in no sense represented a surrender of China's sovereign rights.* ◇ *Health and fitness are not synonyms when fitness is understood in its genetic sense.* ◇ **in the ~ of sth** *Words do not directly refer to their objects in the sense of 'copying' or 'resembling' them.* ◇ **in the ~ that...** *Economic growth is important in the sense that lower growth rates have a big opportunity cost over time.* **2** [C] **~ of sth** a feeling about sth important: *The festivals contributed towards a growing sense of Greek national identity.* ◇ *The five-year strategic plan succeeded in giving a sense of purpose to all staff.* ◇ *Unfortunately, staff were lulled into a false sense of security by a lack of previous fatal fires.* **3** [sing.] an understanding about sth; an ability to judge sth: *Saadia claims that our innate moral sense is itself a form of rationality.* ◇ **~ of sth** *The passage of time helps the development of a sense of proportion and greater objectivity.* ◇ *The first two essays give you a good sense of the gulf between the two theoretical approaches.* ➲ *see also* COMMON SENSE **4** [C] one of the five powers (sight, hearing, smell, taste and touch) that your body uses to get information about the world around you: *'The senses', Shelley writes, 'are the sources of all knowledge to the mind.'* ◇ **~ of sth** *Following the operation, the patient's sense of smell was impaired.* ◇ **+ noun** *These problems do not affect all the sense organs equally.*

IDM **make 'sense 1** to have a meaning that can be understood: *The data seemed to make no sense.* **2** to be a sensible thing to do: *In the ambassador's opinion, the plan made perfectly good sense.* ◇ **~ to do sth** *It made sense to use proven methods to analyse the results.* ◇ **~ for sb/sth** *Full independence would have made no sense for the region.* **make 'sense of sth** to understand sth that is difficult or has no clear meaning: *The aim was to help the children use poetry to make sense of traumatic events in their lives.*

▸ ADJECTIVE + SENSE **broad, wide • general • loose • strict, narrow • literal • absolute • ordinary • usual • traditional, conventional • modern • real • meaningful • technical** *In its broadest sense, 'replication' means simply the building of a copy.* | **strong, keen • clear • heightened • growing • deep, profound • real • false** *Inspectors noted a strong sense of community among both students and staff.*

▸ VERB + SENSE **create, generate • instil • develop • foster, promote • reinforce • give • maintain • get, gain • have • retain • lose • lack** *The meetings helped foster a sense of solidarity among staff.* | **feel, experience • express, convey** *Low-income students may experience a sense of alienation from school culture (Kaplan, 2007).*

▸ SENSE OF + NOUN **self • identity • belonging • community • solidarity • ownership • pride • well-being • security • purpose • urgency • continuity • superiority • guilt • alienation** *The new figures created a sense of urgency among policymakers.* | **responsibility, duty • justice** *Putnam (1983) defined 'social capital' as citizens' ability to trust, willingness to participate and sense of justice.*

sense[2] /sens/ *verb* (not used in the progressive tenses) **1** to become aware of sth even though you cannot clearly see it, hear it, etc: **~ sth** *Traditionalists opposed the change, sensing a threat to established community authority.* ◇ **~ (from sth) (that)...** *The reader senses from this passage that something profound has taken place.* ◇ **~ how/what, etc...** *Politicians at Kyoto had difficulties sensing how far they could take the process without losing support.* **2 ~ sth** to become aware of sth by seeing it, hearing it, etc: *Nietzsche believes that there is no other world more real than the one we sense.* **3 ~ sth** (of a device) to discover and record or react to sth: *The circuit sensed the temperature of the chip and turned on the transistor.* ◇ *Remotely sensed data was used to estimate energy use across the region.* ➲ *see also* REMOTE SENSING

sens·ibil·ity /ˌsensə'bɪləti/ *noun* (*pl.* **-ies**) **1** [U, C] the ability to experience and understand deep feelings, especially in art and literature: *Pasternak was a man of great literary sensibility.* ◇ *Flowers, fields and forests appeal to our aesthetic sensibilities.* **2 sensibilities** [pl.] a person's feelings, especially when the person is easily offended or influenced by sth: *Historic accounts are sometimes shocking to modern sensibilities.*

sens·ible /'sensəbl/ *adj.* **1** (of actions, plans, decisions, etc.) done or chosen with good judgement based on reason and experience rather than emotion; practical: *Given the difficult situation, their approach seems sensible and appropriate.* ◇ *All long-haul travellers were advised to take sensible precautions.* ◇ **it is ~ to do sth** *For the robot design process, it seemed sensible to start with a series of simplified actions.* **2** (of people) able to make good judgements based on reason and experience rather than emotion: *He is a sensible and capable boy.* ■ **sens·ibly** /'sensəbli/ *adv.*: *These were risks that could not sensibly be ignored.*

sen·si·tive /'sensətɪv/ *adj.* **1** that you have to treat with great care because it may offend people or make them angry or embarrassed: *The choice of official language for the event is a politically sensitive issue.* ◇ *Information regarding a patient's mental health is considered sensitive data.* **2** reacting quickly or more than usual to sth: *Those with sensitive skin should avoid over-exposure to the sun.* ◇ **~ to sth** *The coral reefs are sensitive to oil pollution impacts.* OPP INSENSITIVE (2) **3** able to measure very small or particular changes: *The very low levels of contamination demand highly sensitive detection systems.* ◇ **~ to sth** *A photographic system sensitive to ultraviolet light was employed.* OPP INSENSITIVE (2) **4** aware of and able to understand other people and their feelings: *Parents trusted the school to carry out the sex education project in a sensitive manner.* ◇ **~ to sth** *Policymakers failed to be sensitive to local concerns.* OPP INSENSITIVE (1) **5** easily offended or upset: *Adolescents are often particularly sensitive on the subject of sexual health.* ◇ **~ about sth** *China and Russia remained very sensitive about any action that might weaken the rules of sovereignty.* ■ **sen·si·tive·ly** /'sensətɪvli/ *adv.*: *With only a limited budget, we decided to analyse a limited range of chemicals very sensitively.* ◇ *The wind energy industry will need to respond sensitively to these concerns.*

sen·si·tiv·ity /ˌsensə'tɪvəti/ *noun* (*pl.* **-ies**) **1** [U, C, usually pl.] the quality of reacting to sth, especially quickly or more than usual, and often with harmful results: *Skin sensitivity was measured.* ◇ **~ to sth** *This is a list of common sensitivities to antibiotics and analgesics.* ◇ **~ of sth to sth** *First, the sensitivity of demand to the changes in*

S

income was calculated. OPP INSENSITIVITY **2** [U, sing.] the ability to measure very small changes: *The technique is simple and rapid but has the disadvantages of lacking sensitivity and precision.* ◇ **~ of sth** *The newer tests have a sensitivity of 70–90% and a specificity of 90–95%.* **3** [U] the fact of needing to be treated very carefully because it may offend or upset people: *The decision was made by the Prime Minister herself because of its political sensitivity.* ◇ **~ of sth** *The bank is very aware of the sensitivity of personal finance information.* **4** [U] the ability to understand other people's feelings: *Kevin et al. (2006) reported that firms' performance can be improved by cultural sensitivity in external relationships.* ◇ **~ to sth** *The adolescents displayed a lack of sensitivity to the pain of others.* OPP INSENSITIVITY **5** [C, usually pl.] a tendency to be easily offended or upset by sth: *The company modified the marketing campaign to respect local sensitivities.* **6** [U] the ability to understand art, music and literature and to express yourself through them: *She sang with great emotional sensitivity.*

sen·si·tize (*BrE also* **-ise**) /ˈsensətaɪz/ *verb* [usually passive] **1 ~ sb/sth (to sth)** to make sb/sth more aware of sth, especially a problem or sth bad: *Customers and shareholders are becoming increasingly sensitized to environmental issues.* **2 ~ sb/sth (to sth)** (*technical*) to make sb/sth sensitive to physical or chemical changes, or to a particular substance: *As a result of being pre-tested, subjects in an experiment may become sensitized to the experimental treatment.* ■ **sen·si·tiza·tion, -isa·tion** /ˌsensətaɪˈzeɪʃn; *NAmE* ˌsensətəˈzeɪʃn/ *noun* [U] **+ noun** *Sensitization programmes highlight the individual and social harm caused by the marginalization of women.* ◇ **~ to sth** *This study confirmed an anticipated relationship between sensitization to workplace allergens and flour exposure.*

sen·sor /ˈsensə(r)/ *noun* a device that can react to levels of light, heat, etc. and can record these or cause a machine to react to them: *The fire detection system uses four sensors, one in each room.* ◇ *a/an temperature/pressure/oxygen/earthquake sensor*

sens·ory /ˈsensəri/ *adj.* [usually before noun] connected with the physical senses: *Patients had a range of sensory impairments, including visual and hearing difficulties.* ◇ *In the case of the external world, all the evidence we will ever have comes from our sensory experience.*

sent *past tense, past part. of* SEND

sen·tence¹ /ˈsentəns/ *noun* **1** [C] (*grammar*) a set of words expressing a statement, a question or an order, usually containing a subject and a verb. In written English, sentences begin with a capital letter and end with a full stop (.) or a question mark (?): *'The Social Contract' opens with the famous sentence, 'Man is born free, and is everywhere in chains.'* **2** [C, U] the punishment given by a court: *He served a long prison sentence for supplying illegal drugs.* ◇ **~ (of sth)** *Murder carries a mandatory sentence of life imprisonment.* ◇ *If the jury finds the defendant guilty, the judge passes sentence.*

sen·tence² /ˈsentəns/ *verb* [often passive] to say officially in court that sb is to receive a particular punishment: **be sentenced (to sth)** *He was convicted and sentenced to one year in prison.* ◇ **be sentenced to do sth** *The former chairman was sentenced to pay a $7.5 million fine.*

sen·ti·ment /ˈsentɪmənt/ *noun* **1** [C, U] a feeling or an opinion: *Nationalist sentiments soared in the mid-1890s when Japan and China fought over Korea.* ◇ *patriotic/religious/moral sentiments* ◇ *Film directors have the ability to affect public sentiment.* ◇ **~ that...** *An HR executive expressed the sentiment that 'there is no best way to recruit new employees'.* **2** [U] (*sometimes disapproving*) feelings of romantic love, sadness, etc. which may be too strong or not appropriate: *Sentiment and love—traditional female concerns—were now prevailing in mainstream literary culture.*

sen·ti·men·tal /ˌsentɪˈmentl/ *adj.* **1** connected with emotions, rather than reason: *He denied any sentimental desire to resurrect the past.* ◇ *The poem reinforces the sentimental appeal of maternal love.* **2** (*often disapproving*) producing emotions such as romantic love or sadness, which may be too strong or not appropriate; feeling these emotions too much: *Reviewers regarded the poems as childish and sentimental.*

sep·ar·able /ˈsepərəbl/ *adj.* that can be separated from sth, or considered separately: *The sections are not easily separable.* ◇ **~ from sth** *The writer ceases to be separable from his material.* OPP INSEPARABLE ■ **sep·ar·abil·ity** /ˌseprəˈbɪləti/ *noun* [U] **~ (of sth)** *This process depends on the degree of separability of tasks.*

sep·ar·ate¹ /ˈseprət/ *adj.* **1** forming a unit by itself; not joined to, touching or close to sth/sb else: *Caregivers and children were interviewed in separate rooms.* ◇ *He concluded that the mind or soul must be a separate entity from the body.* ◇ *Separate analyses for both age groups revealed age differential explanation patterns.* ◇ **~ from sth/sb** *The Committee wanted educational radio to be entirely separate from commercial radio.* ◇ **keep sth/sb ~ from sth/sb** *The trustee must keep the trust property separate from his or her own.* **2** [usually before noun] different; not connected: *The pair met on two separate occasions.* ◇ *That is a separate issue and one that will be returned to later.* ■ **sep·ar·ate·ness** *noun* [U] **~ (of sth/sb) (from sth/sb)** *Northern Ireland's physical separateness from the British mainland emphasizes its distinctiveness.*

IDM **go your (own) separate ˈways** to end a relationship with sb: *In Central Asia, the newly independent republics began to go their own separate ways.*

sep·ar·ate² /ˈsepəreɪt/ *verb* **1** [I, T] to divide into different parts or groups; to divide things into different parts or groups: *The individual components of the mixture do not separate.* ◇ **~ sth** *This process separates the proteins in the sample.* ◇ **~ A from B** *Energy is released when the carbon and hydrogen atoms are separated from each other.* ◇ **~ A and B** *Einstein's theory does not give an unambiguous way of separating space and time.* ◇ **~ sth into sth** *The equation can be separated into two parts.* **2** [I, T] to move apart; to make people or things move apart: *These huge land masses separated and drifted apart.* ◇ **~ from sth** *Molecules separate from each other according to differences in their sizes.* ◇ **~ into sth** *They separated into smaller hunting groups in the winter.* ◇ **~ sb/sth** *Burt claimed to have studied 53 pairs of identical twins separated at birth.* ◇ **~ A from B** *Deportation would separate him from his wife and child.* ◇ **~ A and B** *Boys and girls are then separated by gender.* **3** [T] to be between two people, areas, countries, etc. so that they are not touching or connected: **~ sb/sth** *In Canada, large geographical distances separate the population.* ◇ **~ A from B** *Seven hundred years separate the Greek poet Homer from the Roman poet Ovid.* ◇ **~ A and B** *They want to break down the barriers that have traditionally separated the arts and sciences.* **4** [I] to stop living together as a couple with your husband, wife or partner: *His parents separated when he was two years old.* ◇ **~ from sb** *She appears to have separated from her partner.* **5** [T] to make sb/sth different in some way from sb/sth else SYN DIVIDE¹(3): **~ sb/sth** *Two cultures, two languages and two religions separated them.* ◇ **~ A from B** *There was little to separate any of the main political parties from one another any longer.*

PHR V **ˌseparate ˈout | ˌseparate sth ˈout** to divide into different parts; to divide sth into different parts: *A mixture of water and ethanol does not separate out.* ◇ *Scientists*

S

now understand enough about biology to be able to separate out the cell's components.

sep·ar·ated /ˈsepəreɪtɪd/ *adj.* **1** not joined to, close to or touching sth else SYN SEPARATE[1] (1): *The dark matter appeared in two distinctly separated regions.* ◇ **~ from sth** *Communities that are separated from each other, but are otherwise identical, could behave very differently.* **2** divided into different parts or groups: *In America's separated system, the president shares power with Congress.* ◇ **~ from sth** *Legislative and operational tasks should be clearly separated from one another.* **3** no longer living with your husband, wife or partner: *African Americans were more likely to be divorced or separated than the non-African American sample.* ◇ **~ from sb** *Mr Constance, who was separated from his wife, began to cohabit with Mrs Paul.*

sep·ar·ate·ly /ˈseprətli/ *adv.* as a separate person or thing; not together: *I will consider the three cases separately.* ◇ *These data were analysed separately for the two ethnic groups.* ◇ **~ from sb/sth** *He seems to say that the soul can exist separately from the body.*

sep·ar·ation /ˌsepəˈreɪʃn/ *noun* **1** [U, sing.] the act of separating people or things; the state of being separate: **~ (of sb/sth) (from sb/sth)** *The Civil Code prohibits the separation of a child under 16 from his/her guardian without the guardian's consent.* ◇ **~ of A and B** *As a result of this, France initiated the separation of Church and State.* ◇ **~ between A and B** *In modern democracies, there is a separation between the executive and the legislature.* **2** [U, C] the state in which a husband and wife live apart while they are still legally married: *Many marriages end in separation or divorce.* ◇ *Following a separation, the husband obtained a mortgage on the family home without the wife's knowledge.* **3** [C] a period of time that people spend apart from each other: *They needed to become reacquainted with each other after a long separation.*

sep·tic /ˈseptɪk/ *adj.* infected with harmful bacteria: *This was done to prevent the sores turning septic.* ➲ *see also* SHOCK[1] (3)

se·quence[1] AWL /ˈsiːkwəns/ *noun* **1** [C] **~ (of sth)** a set of connected events, actions, numbers, etc. that have a particular order: *This action sets in motion a sequence of events that can bring about profound changes.* ◇ *These techniques use a sequence of pulses separated by different time intervals.* **2** [C, U] the order that connected events, actions, etc. happen in or should happen in: *A questionnaire should follow a sequence that is logical from the respondent's point of view.* ◇ **in a... ~** *In most standard psychological tests, everyone is administered the same items in a fixed sequence.* ◇ **in ~** *The model defines clear steps to be performed in sequence.* **3** [C] (*biology*) the order in which a set of GENES or parts of MOLECULES are arranged: *An allele is one of two or more alternative forms of a DNA sequence.* ◇ **~ of sth** *A great advance has been the complete determination of the base sequence of the human genome.* **4** [C] a part of a film that deals with one subject or topic or consists of one scene: *The opening sequence shows Johnny Case returning from holiday.* ◇ **~ of sth** *The villain remains out of frame until the last sequences of the film.* ◇ **~ from sth** *Carroll describes a sequence from 'The Birds' where Hitchcock seems to violate this principle.* **5** [C] (*mathematics*) an ordered list of numbers: *A Fibonacci sequence is defined as a sequence in which any term is the sum of the two preceding terms.* ➲ *compare* SERIES (4)

se·quence[2] AWL /ˈsiːkwəns/ *verb* **1 ~ sth** (*biology*) to identify the order in which a set of GENES or parts of MOLECULES are arranged: *As the databases grew, so did ambitions to sequence entire genomes.* **2 ~ sth** to arrange things in a sequence: *The latter approach shows how processes of information collection should be sequenced.*

se·quen·cing AWL /ˈsiːkwənsɪŋ/ *noun* [U] **1** (*biology*) the process of identifying the order in which a set of GENES or parts of MOLECULES are arranged: *DNA sequencing requires a very large number of copies of the same DNA sequence.* ◇ **~ of sth** *The recent sequencing of the human genome has led to the identification of a large number of genes on chromosome 21.* **2 ~ (of sth)** the action of arranging things in a sequence: *The recording may be replayed repeatedly for analysis of the timing and sequencing of events.*

se·quen·tial AWL /sɪˈkwenʃl/ *adj.* forming or following in a logical order: *Marketing planning is a sequential process.* ■ **se·quen·tial·ly** AWL /sɪˈkwenʃəli/ *adv.*: *These processes always occur sequentially and are never simultaneous.*

sera *pl. of* SERUM

ser·ial /ˈsɪəriəl; *NAmE* ˈsɪriəl/ *adj.* **1** [usually before noun] (*technical*) arranged in a series, one after another: *Many normally serial activities were scheduled concurrently in order to save time.* **2** [only before noun] doing the same thing in the same way several times: *Police said they had no proof that a serial killer was responsible for the four murders.* **3** [only before noun] (of a story, etc.) broadcast or published in several separate parts: *Dickens wrote his novels for serial publication.* ■ **seri·al·ly** /ˈsɪəriəli; *NAmE* ˈsɪriəli/ *adv.*: *The tasks are executed serially.* ◇ *A version of the novel was published serially in 'Cosmopolitan' magazine.*

ser·ies AWL /ˈsɪəriːz; *NAmE* ˈsɪriːz/ *noun* (*pl.* **ser·ies**) **1** [C, usually sing.] **~ of sth** several events or things of a similar kind that come or happen one after the other: *We do not know the exact series of events that led to this outcome.* ◇ *I asked each group a series of questions designed to get their response to the report.* ◇ *A series of recent studies examines the direct impact of media on social behaviour and public attitudes.* ◇ *a series of experiments/steps* ◇ *a series of articles/papers/lectures* **2** [C] a set of radio or television programmes that deal with the same subject or that have the same characters: *Paramount Studios produce the series 'Entertainment Tonight'.* ◇ *a television/TV/radio/drama series* **3** [U, C] (*technical*) an electrical CIRCUIT in which the current passes through all the parts in the correct order: **in ~** *The switches were used in series rather than in parallel.* ◇ **+ noun** *The circuit consists of the series connection of a diode D and a resistor R.* **4** [C] (*mathematics*) the sum of the terms in a SEQUENCE: *This is an infinite geometric series with a common ratio of 3.*

ser·ious /ˈsɪəriəs; *NAmE* ˈsɪriəs/ *adj.* **1** important and worrying because of possible danger or risk: *AIDS remains a very serious worldwide health problem.* ◇ *There are potentially serious consequences from false positive errors.* ◇ *Conflicts pose serious threats to economic recovery and sustainability.* ◇ *a serious illness/disease/condition/injury* ◇ *The banking crisis was serious enough to threaten the national currency.* **2** that must be treated as important and thought about carefully: *There are now serious doubts about the validity of the model.* ◇ *The interactive and uncontrollable nature of the Internet raises serious issues for media strategy.* **3** thinking about things in a careful and sensible way: *Alternative anti-smoking strategies deserve serious consideration.* ◇ *The inspector commented that all staff she had met had been serious, responsible and cooperative.* **4 ~ about (doing) sth** sincere about sth: *The government of South Africa seems to be serious about tackling these domestic issues.*

ser·ious·ly /ˈsɪəriəsli; *NAmE* ˈsɪriəsli/ *adv.* **1** to a degree that is important and worrying: *The parliament building was seriously damaged by the explosion.* ◇ *The argument*

S

put forward by Figueira (1998) has been seriously undermined by new evidence. **2** carefully and sincerely: *The government seriously considered introducing a new education system.*

IDM **take sb/sth 'seriously** to think that sb/sth is important and deserves attention and respect: *Of course, the company takes all breaches of security extremely seriously.* ◇ *Eventually, classical mythology stopped being taken seriously as actual history.*

ser·ious·ness /ˈsɪəriəsnəs; *NAmE* ˈsɪriəsnəs/ *noun* [U, sing.] **~ (of sth)** the state of being serious: *The seriousness of the drought took the authorities by surprise.* ◇ *Fines to plaintiffs reflect the seriousness of the offence.*

serum /ˈsɪərəm; *NAmE* ˈsɪrəm/ *noun* (*pl.* **sera** /ˈsɪərə; *NAmE* ˈsɪrə/ or **ser·ums**) **1** [U] (*biology, medical*) the thin yellow liquid that remains from the blood when the CLOTTING elements have been removed: *The majority of biological analyses are performed within whole blood, blood serum, blood plasma or urine.* ➲ *compare* PLASMA (1) **2** [U, C] (*medical*) serum taken from the blood of an animal and given to people to protect them from disease or poison: *At that time, tetanus infection was treated by injection of horse serum.*

ser·vant /ˈsɜːvənt; *NAmE* ˈsɜːrvənt/ *noun* **1** a person who works in another person's house, and cooks, cleans, etc. for them: *During the 1930s, over 70 per cent of employed black women worked as domestic servants in private homes.* **2** a person who works for a government or ruler: *An efficient tax-collecting system requires many public servants to gather and process the information.* ➲ *see also* CIVIL SERVANT **3** **~ of sth** a person or thing that is controlled by sth: *Education is increasingly seen as a servant of the economy.*

serve /sɜːv; *NAmE* sɜːrv/ *verb* **1** [I, T] to have a particular effect, use or result: **~ as sth** *Although Shakespeare served as a model to later writers of tragedy, he was less influential in the field of comedy.* ◇ **~ to do sth** *Two examples will serve to illustrate the point.* ◇ **~ only to do sth** *It is important to recognize that these communications often serve only to confirm decisions that have already been made.* **2** [T] to be useful to sb in achieving sth: **~ sth** *Perhaps the only medieval maps that served a practical purpose were the ones known as Portolano (meaning 'handy') charts.* ◇ **~ sb + adv./prep.** *At times of crisis, his man-of-action character usually served him well.* ◇ **be well, etc. served (by sth)** *The Court of Appeal clearly considered that the child's interests would be best served by living with the mother.* **3** [T] to provide an area or a group of people with a product or service: **~ sb/sth** *In the Philippines, 100 per cent foreign ownership in businesses serving the domestic market is allowed.* ◇ **~ sb/sth with sth** *Almost 85 per cent of Malaysia's rural population is served with a piped water supply.* ◇ **be well, etc. served by sth** *Eastern North America was by then well served by rail.* **4** [I, T] to work or perform duties for a person, an organization, a country, etc: **~ as sth** *The author served as chair of the Department of Anthropology for a period of nine years.* ◇ **~ in/on/with sth** *Each Cossack male was required to serve in the army, providing his own horse.* ◇ **~ under/with sb** *Teacher instructors, without teacher qualifications, serve under fully qualified teachers in the classroom.* ◇ **~ sth** *A seamstress had to serve a two-year apprenticeship.* ◇ **~ sb/sth (as sth)** *Haydn had for many years served the Esterházy family as court composer.* **5** [T] **~ sth** to spend a period of time in prison: *The scheme allows prisoners serving sentences of between three months and four years to be considered for early release.* **6** [T] to give sb food or drink, for example at a restaurant or during a meal: **~ sth (at/with sth)** *Most parents reported that they 'usually' or 'always' served fruits and vegetables at meals.* ◇ **~ sb** *The 'New York Times' noted that the restaurant was serving 1 500 customers a day.* ◇ **~ sth to sb| ~ sb sth** *He spent some time cooking and serving food to hungry pilgrims.* **7** [T] (*law*) to give or send sb an official document, especially one that orders them to appear in court: **~ sth (on sb)** *The Commissioner may serve notice on data controllers where he or she is satisfied that there has been a breach of data protection principles.* ◇ **~ sb with sth** *D was served with a notice to quit the property.*

PHR V **ˌserve sth ˈup** to give, offer or provide sth: *For many pupils in the group, the curriculum was something served up by teachers and government that they themselves had little control over.*

ser·ver /ˈsɜːvə(r); *NAmE* ˈsɜːrvər/ *noun* (*computing*) a computer program that controls or supplies data to several computers connected in a network; the main computer on which this program is run: *An item of data is transmitted by a web server to a client computer.*

ser·vice¹ /ˈsɜːvɪs; *NAmE* ˈsɜːrvɪs/ *noun* **1** [C] a system that provides sth that the public needs, organized by the government or a private company: *All of the villages studied are poor and lack public services.* ◇ *Local governments also made steep cuts in spending on various essential services they provided.* ◇ **+ noun** *Service users may fear that negative responses will lead to cuts in services.* ➲ *see also* PUBLIC SERVICE (1), SERVICE PROVIDER (1) **2** (*also* **Service**) [C] an organization or a company that provides sth for the public or does sth for the government: *A unified national health service was created in Brazil in the early 1990s.* ◇ *The principal federal agency involved in soil survey is the National Resource Conservation Service.* ➲ *see also* CIVIL SERVICE, HEALTH SERVICE, PUBLIC SERVICE (3), SOCIAL SERVICES **3** [C, U] a business whose work involves doing sth for customers but not producing goods; the work that they do: *Other cities with significant clusters of financial services have also been hit by job losses.* ◇ **+ noun** *From 2003 to 2007, service sector employment grew at roughly four per cent per year.* ◇ *Other service industries, especially banking and information services, are also expanding in major urban centres.* **4** [U, C] help, information or advice given to customers by a business during and after the sale of goods: *Doing business electronically can increase revenues, cut costs and improve customer service.* ◇ *The table shows that, overall, good quality of service was the number one reason for seeking health care from different providers.* ◇ *It is possible that if a few firms dominate a market, they will charge high prices and provide a poor service to customers.* **5** [C, usually pl.] the particular skills or help that a person is able to offer; an act of helping sb: *Ejected from Sparta, Alcibiades offered his services to Persia.* ◇ **~ of sb** *Trials may enlist the services of GPs to recruit patients during the consultation process.* ◇ **~ as sth** *Hecht was paid up to $5 000 a week for his services as a screenwriter.* ➲ *see also* PUBLIC SERVICE (2) **6** [U] the work that sb does for an organization, etc, especially when it continues for a long time or is admired very much: *The average length of service of police officers in the study was 5 years.* ◇ **~ to sth** *The company's philosophy is to put service to society before profits.* HELP **Domestic service** is work that sb does cooking, cleaning, etc. in sb else's home. **7** [U] the use that you can get from a vehicle, machine or tool; the state of being used: *The Concorde entered service with Air France and British Airways in 1976.* ◇ **in ~** *There are about 8 000 container ships currently in service around the world.* **8** [C, U] an examination of a vehicle, machine or piece of equipment followed by any work that is necessary to keep it operating well: *A garage might use such a database to advise its customers that their cars are due for a service.* ◇ **+ noun** *The firm holds service contracts for most of China's large chemical plants.* **9** [C, usually pl., U] the army, the navy or the AIR FORCE; the work done by people in them: **the (armed) services** *Of the patients with hearing problems, most were in the armed services or were call centre operators.* ◇ *Ammianus saw service in northern Italy, Gaul* *and Germany.* **10** [C, usually sing.] a bus, train, etc. that goes regularly to a particular place at a particular time: *The bus service is slow, crowded and uncomfortable.* **11** [C] a religious ceremony: *Attending religious services at least once a month increases social trust by 16 points on the trust scale.* ◇ *These services are held during specific years at a temple and are conducted by priests.* **12** [U] **~ (of sth)** (*law*) the act of formally giving an official document, etc. to sb: *He claimed he was not in the UK at the time of the service of the notice.*

IDM **at the 'service of sb/sth | at sb's 'service** completely available for sb to use or to help sb: *The Huguenots placed themselves at one time at the service of the king.* **be of 'service (to sb)** (*formal*) to be useful or helpful: *This work is of service to specialist and non-specialist alike.* **(not) do sb a 'service | (not) do a service (to/for sb/sth)** to do sth that is helpful/not helpful to sb: *He believed that television has done a service to democracy by allowing people to participate in public events.* ➲ *more at* PRESS[2]

▸ ADJECTIVE + SERVICE **public • social • local • essential • basic • specialist • medical • personal • educational • postal** *In rural areas, prior to the arrival of medical services, twins died within the first month of life at roughly double the rate of single babies.* | **financial • professional • personal** *Competition has led to a greater focus on business development and the marketing of professional services.* | **good • poor • after-sales • personal** *In China, India and Russia, good service and product quality were listed as crucial.*

▸ NOUN + SERVICE **health, health care • hospital • support • emergency • welfare • energy • police • transport • telephone • telecommunication** *By 2004, 60% of calls to the UK emergency services were made from mobiles.* | **police • prison • probation • fire** *In Europe, civic duties can include compulsory fire service work (or payment in lieu).* | **Internet • information • banking • catering • cleaning • business** *In analysing the market for banking services, Chen (1999) suggests that there are four critical success factors.*

▸ VERB + SERVICE **provide, offer, supply • access** *This study highlights the vulnerability of recently arrived older immigrants when it comes to accessing health services.* | **deliver • run • improve • develop • maintain • use, utilize • receive • evaluate** *The new hospitals will have even more control over how they use funds and deliver services.* | **advertise • purchase, buy** *No practices advertised travel vaccination services in South Asian languages.*

▸ SERVICE + NOUN **user • provider • utilization, use • delivery • provision** *Levels of maternal health service utilization are very low in this region.* | **organization, firm, company • industry • sector • worker • personnel, staff** *Service workers typically receive lower fringe benefits than workers in other major occupational categories.*

ser·vice[2] /ˈsɜːvɪs; *NAmE* ˈsɜːrvɪs/ *verb* **1 ~ sb/sth** to provide people with sth they need, such as products to buy or a transport system SYN SERVE (3): *The Internet has become a powerful medium for reaching and servicing customers around the world.* ◇ *The three main ports are all serviced by rail and roads.* **2 ~ sth** (*technical*) to pay interest on money that has been borrowed: *The ability of the country to service short-term debt had deteriorated during the first half of the 1990s.* **3** [usually passive] to examine a vehicle, machine or piece of equipment and repair it if necessary so that it continues to work correctly: **have sth serviced** *A landlord who failed to have a gas fire serviced for eight years was found to be in breach of the law.*

ˈservice provider *noun* **1** a company that provides a service to customers: *I worked alongside mental health service providers and service users.* **2** a company that connects customers to the Internet: *Many people use more than one Internet service provider.*

ses·sion /ˈseʃn/ *noun* **1** [C] a period of time that is spent doing a particular activity: *Most club members attended regular football training sessions.* ◇ *Patients received ten group counselling sessions.* **2** [C, U] a formal meeting or series of meetings of a court, a parliament, etc; a period of time when such meetings are held: *In the 2007–08 parliamentary session, the government published nine draft bills.* ◇ **in ~** *Under the Public Order Act 1936, no march may be held within a mile of Parliament when it is in session.*

set[1] /set/ *verb* (**set·ting, set, set**) **1** [T] to establish a standard or limit that people must follow: **~ sth** *Societies set their own rules, and continuously opt to constrain some freedoms while defending others.* ◇ **~ sth for sth** *The Nursing and Midwifery Council sets the standards for education, training, conduct and performance.* ◇ **~ sth for sb/yourself** *Some patients set daily calorie limits for themselves.* **2** [T] to give sb a target or task to achieve: **~ sth** *Access to the data will enable us to set priorities more systematically.* ◇ *The goals are set in terms of reducing poverty and improving health and education.* ◇ **~ sth for sth** *Writing a proposal is useful in encouraging you to set realistic objectives for your research project.* ◇ **~ sth for sb/yourself** *The directive has set targets for each member state to improve waste recovery.* ◇ **~ sb/yourself sth** *The researchers have set themselves a difficult task.* **3** [T] **~ sth** to fix sth so that others copy it or try to achieve it: *There is an implicit onus on health care workers to set a good example by living healthy lifestyles.* ◇ *They argued that carving out chunks of a national park for private interests set a very dangerous precedent.* **4** [T] **~ sth** to arrange or fix sth; to decide what will happen or what sth will be like: *The Prime Minister advises the monarch to dissolve Parliament, and sets a date for a general election.* ◇ *The paper was largely theoretical, an attempt to set the agenda for future research.* ◇ *This early work set the tone and direction of strategic management in several important ways.* **5** [T] **~ sth (at sth)** to decide on the price or value of sth: *Beijing set the price of the Jetta at $16 750.* ◇ *In 1938, the Fair Labor Standards Act set a minimum wage of 25 cents per hour.* ◇ *The central bank can set the interest rate as soon as it observes current data.* **6** [T] to cause sb/sth to be in a particular state; to start sth happening: **~ sb/sth + adv./prep.** *The Roman Emperor Constantine set in motion a process that changed the course of Christian development.* ◇ **~ sb/sth + adj.** *Setting the hostages free was the only option that accorded with Ward's conscience.* ◇ **~ sb/sth doing sth** *This idea set Einstein thinking about the definition of velocity, and the concepts of absolute and relative.* **7** [T, usually passive] **~ sth + adv./prep.** to place the action of a play, novel or film in a particular place or time: *'King Lear' is set in pre-Christian Britain.* **8** [I] (of the sun or moon) to go down below the HORIZON: *As the sun was setting, Mara and his armies fled.* OPP RISE[2] (5)

IDM Idioms containing **set** are at the entries for the nouns and adjectives in the idioms, for example **set the scene** is at **scene**.

PHR V **ˌset about ˈdoing sth | ˈset about sth** [no passive] to start doing sth: *Once elected, the new government set about drawing up legislative proposals.* ◇ *The new Cable Authority set about its task with great enthusiasm.*

set sth (off) against sth to judge sth by comparing good or positive qualities with bad or negative ones: *There is the potential for continuing or new emissions from one activity to be set off against reductions in emissions elsewhere.*

ˌset sb/sth aˈpart (from sb/sth) to make sb/sth different from or better than others: *Humans can be set apart from nature by virtue of their reasoning capacities.* **ˌset sth aˈpart (for sth)** [usually passive] to keep sth for a special use or purpose: *A special building was always set apart for sacred functions.*

ˌset sth aˈside 1 to not consider sth, because other things are more important SYN DISREGARD[1]: *The lessons of two world wars prompted Europeans to set aside issues of*

S

sovereignty and nationalism, and build an economic community. **2** to stop discussing or thinking about sth for a period of time in order to consider sth else: *Setting aside these concerns, however, I shall return now to the question of...* **3** to save or keep money for a particular purpose in the future: *'Retained earnings' refers to the total profit that is set aside by corporations for future investment.* **4** to decide that sth can be used for a particular purpose: *Substantial tracts of land, including some along the river, were set aside for parks.* **5** (*law*) to state that a decision made by a court is not legally valid: *The court allowed the appeal and set aside the original order.*

ˌset sth/sb ˈback to delay the progress of sth/sb by a particular time: *The cataclysm of 1787–89 set back the Parisian economy in spectacular manner.* ➲ *related noun* SETBACK

ˌset sth ˈdown 1 to give sth as a rule or principle: *The 1999 EC Directive on air quality set down specific requirements relating to air pollutants.* **2** to write sth down on paper in order to record it: *Gildas was one of the earliest of a group of western writers to set down a regional view of history.*

ˌset sth ˈforth (*formal*) to present sth or make it known: *The Atlantic Charter set forth the common goals that would guide America over the next few years.*

ˌset ˈoff to begin a journey: *In 1492, Columbus set off to find the western route, with the source of spices being his main goal.* **ˌset sth ˈoff 1** to start a process or series of events: *A poor harvest combined with existing hunger set off a series of peasant attacks on landowners' estates.* **2** to cause sth to start operating: *Most car airbags are set off by MEMS acceleration sensors.*

ˈset on/upon sb/sth [usually passive] to attack sb/sth suddenly: *Sweden was set upon by her neighbours, losing most of her overseas territories.*

ˌset ˈout 1 to begin a job or task with a particular aim or goal: *This study deliberately sets out to provide different perspectives on the environment and sustainability.* **2** to leave a place and begin a journey: *With a group of companions, Jason set out from Lolkos in Greece.* **ˌset sth ˈout** to present ideas, facts, etc. in an organized way, in speech or writing: *Miliband used the speech to set out a post-Blair foreign policy.*

ˌset sb/yourself ˈup (as sb) to claim that sb is/you are a particular type of person: *Demosthenes sets himself up as the champion of Greek freedom against a 'barbarian'.* **ˌset (yourself) ˈup (as sb)** to start running a business: *Attracted by the opportunities available to work on the new railroads, migrants set themselves up in the growing towns and cities.* ➲ *related noun* SET-UP (2) **ˌset sth ˈup 1** to create sth or start it: *The Securities and Exchange Commission (SEC) was set up in 1934 to regulate financial markets.* ➲ *related noun* SET-UP (2) **2** to arrange for sth to happen: *The clinician should offer to set up a meeting with the medical team.* **3** to start a process or a series of events: *Free radicals set up chain reactions of chemical destruction in the body.* **4** to build sth or put sth somewhere: *The device gives drivers a warning when a police radar trap has been set up nearby.* **5** to make a machine ready for use: *The recipient would set up his own machine in the same way as the sender's, in order to decode the message.* ➲ *see also* SET-UP (3)

set² /set/ *noun* **1 ~ (of sth)** a group of similar things that belong together in some way: *The owner of the house gave her a set of keys.* ◇ *Of course, each individual has two sets of grandparents.* ◇ *The law distinguishes between international and non-international armed conflict, with a distinct set of rules for each.* ➲ *see also* DATA SET **2** (*mathematics*) a group of things that have a shared quality: **~ (of sth)** *Y is the set of all natural numbers n such that n is a multiple of 11.* ◇ **+ noun** *Boole attempted to turn set theory (and logic) into algebra.* **3** a piece of equipment for receiving television or radio signals: *With the spread of television, audiences abandoned their radio sets and movie theatres closed.* **4** (*BrE*) a group of school students with a similar ability in a particular subject: *The school organized its pupils into ability sets for each subject.*

▸ ADJECTIVE + SET **complete, full • whole, entire • large • broad, wide • comprehensive • small • limited, restricted • minimum • distinct • unique • single • standard • common • consistent • coherent • diverse • rich • complex • final** *McKendall argues that organizational change efforts focus on a limited set of values.* | **finite • unique • large • small • complete** *The set given by (35.1) defines a finite set A.*

▸ NOUN + SET **data • skill** *The Human Resource Manager provided details of the skill sets needed for the post.*

▸ VERB + SET **develop, generate, produce, create, establish • obtain • introduce, present • offer, provide, yield • use, adopt • have • constitute • comprise • identify • describe • analyse • consider** *In the first stage, students develop a set of arguments in favour of a position.* | **denote • define • represent • form** *Let X denote the set of corners of a cube.*

▸ SET + VERB **contain • consist of** *The set contains an infinite number of elements.*

▸ SET OF + NOUN **rules • guidelines • instructions • standards • principles • norms • beliefs, ideas • assumptions • criteria • circumstances • genes • institutions** *In another study, a set of 80 genes was selected for investigation.* | **data • values • variables • indicators • parameters • conditions • propositions • questions • equations** *A comprehensive set of variables was considered.* | **numbers • elements** *The number of binary operations on a set of n elements is nn.*

set³ /set/ *adj.* **1** [usually before noun] planned or fixed: *There is a set budget of £20 000.* ◇ *Intelligence tests measure performance on set tasks that require mental ability to solve correctly.* ◇ *Students are required to study three set texts for the examination.* **2** likely to do sth; ready for sth or to do sth: **~ to do sth** *The arguments look set to continue.* ◇ **~ for sth** *Wall Street and European stocks look set for a third consecutive month of gains.*

set·back /ˈsetbæk/ *noun* a difficulty or problem that delays or prevents sth, or makes a situation worse: *This approach suffered a major setback in the early 1980s.* ◇ **~ to sth** *Thus, the loss of effective antibiotics would be an enormous setback to medical practice.*

set·ting /ˈsetɪŋ/ *noun* **1** the place at which sth happens; a set of surroundings: *Most recent migrants to the city have come from rural settings.* ◇ *The study focuses on pain relief in emergency care settings.* ◇ *Some actions take on radically different meanings in different social settings.* ◇ **~ for sth** *Her conclusion was that a diversified urban economy provides the best setting for innovation.* **2** the place and time at which the action of a play, novel, etc. takes place: *A fascination with Arabian settings is characteristic of much Romantic fiction.* ◇ **~ for sth** *The interior of a silk-weaving shop provides the setting for one of William Hogarth's morality tales.* **3** a position at which the controls on a machine can be set, to set the speed, height, temperature, etc: *The motor has two settings available.* ◇ *Customers are free to change the default settings on their PCs.*

set·tle /ˈsetl/ *verb* **1** [T] **~ sth** to put an end to an argument or a disagreement: *Christians had often asked their bishops to settle disputes among them.* ◇ *The case was eventually settled out of court.* ◇ *Young's observations appeared to have settled the matter.* ◇ *to settle a question/an issue/a claim* **2** [T, I] **~ (sth)** to cure a medical problem or to make it less serious; to be cured or to become less serious: *Antibiotics will settle the problem in most cases.* ◇ *When the pus is discharged, the pain settles.* **3** [T, often passive] to decide or arrange sth finally: **~ sth** *The queen persisted in refusing either to marry or to settle the succession by legislation.* ◇ **it is settled that...** *It has long been settled that a promoter is not the agent of the*

S

company he is promoting. **4** [I] **+ adv./prep.** to make a place your permanent home: *He eventually settled in Atlanta where he remarried.* **5** [I, T, usually passive] (of a group of people) to make your permanent home in a country or an area as COLONISTS: **+ adv./prep.** *Most settled in the colonies and forged new lives and communities there.* ◇ **be settled by sb** *This region was settled by the Dutch in the nineteenth century.* **6** [I] to fall from above and come to rest on sth; to stay for some time on sth: **~ on sth** *Sediment carried into a lake by streams settles on top of older sediment on the lake bottom.* ◇ **~ to sth** *The particles will eventually settle to the bottom of their container.* **7** [T] **~ sth** to pay the money that you owe: *Most families were still unable to settle their debts.* ◇ *After settling accounts, customers could then stock up on new supplies for the following month.* IDM see ISSUE[1]

PHR V ˌ**settle ˈdown 1** to become less severe; to no longer change as much: *Poverty rates increase in the wake of recession and then slowly settle down.* **2** to start to have a quieter way of life, living in one place: *Peta is not ready to settle down.* **3** to become less excited: *The class soon settled down.* **settle down to sth** to begin to give your attention to sth: *After the holiday, he settled down to a typical corporate career.* ˈ**settle for sth** to accept sth that is not exactly what you want but is the best that is available: *They were not prepared to settle for less than their full legal rights.* ˈ**settle on sth** to choose or make a decision about sth after thinking about it: *She has settled on a style of teaching that enables the students to be quiet and get on with their work.* ˈ**settle sth on sb** (*law*) to formally arrange to give money or property to sb, especially in a WILL: *He settled part of his estate on his son.*

settle·ment /ˈsetlmənt/ *noun* **1** [C] an official agreement that ends an argument between two people or groups: *The parties reached an out-of-court settlement.* ◇ *Yeltsin negotiated a settlement that did not include Gorbachev's resignation.* **2** [U] the action of reaching an agreement: **~ (of sth)** *It is a solution that facilitates the settlement of claims.* ◇ **+ noun** *GATT was replaced by the WTO, which has a more effective dispute settlement mechanism.* **3** [U, sing.] the action of paying back money that you owe: **~ (of sth)** *Often a partial settlement of a debt is a commercially sensible arrangement.* ◇ **in ~ of sth** *Constance received £950 in settlement of an action for personal injuries.* **4** [C] a place where people have come to live and make their homes, especially where few or no people lived before: *Ponce de Leon entered Florida and attempted to establish a permanent settlement.* ◇ *It is one of the oldest Viking settlements in western Europe.* **5** [U] **~ (of sth)** the process of people making their homes in a place: *Slavery in the British Empire resulted from the English settlement of colonies in the Americas.* **6** [C] (*law*) the conditions on which money or property is given to sb; a document stating these conditions: *She has been well provided for by her divorce settlement.* ◇ *a marriage/property settlement*

set·tler /ˈsetlə(r)/ *noun* a person who goes to live in a new country or region: *White settlers regarded themselves as culturally superior to the Native Americans.*

ˈ**set-up** *noun* **1** [C, usually sing.] a way of organizing sth; a system: *The EU's institutional set-up means that the committee makes recommendations rather than decisions.* **2** [U] the act of organizing an activity or process, especially for the first time: **+ noun** *Set-up costs are very high for firms trying to enter such high-tech markets.* **3** [C, usually sing.] a set of equipment used for a particular purpose: *The whole experimental set-up was put in a temperature-controlled box.*

seven /ˈsevn/ *number* 7 HELP There are examples of how to use numbers at the entry for **five**.

sever /ˈsevə(r)/ *verb* **1 ~ sth** to completely end a relationship or all communication with sb: *The new president's objective was to sever the connection between state and religion.* **2 ~ sth** to cut sth into two pieces; to cut sth off sth: *The bullet entered the skull and severed the optic nerve.*

sev·eral /ˈsevrəl/ *det., pron.* more than two but not very many: *Several factors seem to be involved in the rapid spread of the disease.* ◇ *Researchers looking for alternatives have found several in the past year.* ◇ **~ of sth** *Several of these studies come from the south-central United States.*

se·vere /sɪˈvɪə(r); *NAmE* sɪˈvɪr/ *adj.* (**se·verer, se·ver·est**) (**more severe** and **most severe** are more frequent.) **1** extremely bad or serious: *On examination, the patient is clearly in severe pain.* ◇ *In severe cases, multiple organ failure may occur.* ◇ *severe disability/illness/disease/disorders/symptoms* ◇ *severe problems/damage* ◇ *The soil studies in the region illustrate the severe limitations on agriculture.* ◇ *Major El Niño events have occurred in 1925–26, 1982–83 and 1997–98, the last being particularly severe.* ◇ **~ enough** *Anxiety disorder is diagnosed when the anxiety is severe enough to cause significant problems in social functioning.* **2** punishing sb in an extreme way when they break a particular set of rules SYN HARSH: *When Draco introduced his new laws in 621 BC, the penalties were very severe.* ◇ **~ on/with sb** *The Court was more severe with Spain for not complying with its judgment in an earlier case.* **3** extremely difficult and requiring a lot of skill or ability: *The 2007 report called the crisis 'the most severe challenge to the UK financial system for several decades'.* **4** not kind or sympathetic and showing disapproval of sb/sth: *Parents who are severe and exacting in educating their children usually had strict parents themselves.*

se·vere·ly /sɪˈvɪəli; *NAmE* sɪˈvɪrli/ *adv.* **1** very badly or seriously: *The results of the present study may not generalize to more severely injured children.* ◇ *The small sample size in each study may have severely limited the studies' ability to detect cultural differences among the students.* **2** in a very strict way: *Members were reminded that infringement of the rules would be severely punished.*

se·ver·ity /sɪˈverəti/ *noun* (*pl.* **-ies**) **1** [U, C] the fact or condition of sth being very bad or serious: *Vaccines reduce disease severity and spread.* ◇ **~ of sth** *One weakness in the study is that there is little information on severity of symptoms.* ◇ *By late in 1931, the frequency and severity of regional banking crises in the US were increasing rapidly.* ◇ *All severities of pain require practical and psychological interventions.* **2** [U] the fact of sth being very strict or extreme; the fact of sb being strict or not kind and sympathetic: *There were six consequences listed for breaking school rules, increasing in severity from minor actions up to suspension.* ◇ *He was, in his conservative way, a reformer, but his severity made him bitter enemies.* ◇ **~ of sth** *42% of drivers cited the 'severity of the punishment if I was caught' as a factor that helps them to adhere to road laws.*

sew /səʊ; *NAmE* soʊ/ *verb* (**sewed, sewn** /səʊn; *NAmE* soʊn/) or (**sewed, sewed**) [I, T] to use a needle and thread to make things with cloth; to attach sth using a needle and thread: *Even in the most prosperous Hakka houses, the women still spun and sewed.* ◇ **~ sth (on/in/into sth)** *Employees were paid $0.50 for each piece of work completed (sewing a collar on a shirt, for example).*

sex AWL /seks/ *noun* **1** (*also formal* **intercourse, sexual intercourse**) [U] the physical act in which the sexual organs of two people touch and which can result in a woman having a baby: *The legal age for young people to have sex is still sixteen.* ◇ **+ noun** *By the early 1970s, sex education was improving in schools in Britain.* **2** [U, C] the state of being either male or female SYN GENDER: *Sex is determined by environmental factors in many reptiles and some fish.* ◇ **~ of sb/sth** *It is no longer the case that a*

S

pregnant woman has to wait until birth to find out the sex of her child. ◇ + **noun** *Laws against sex discrimination have helped open up the workplace to women in many countries.* ➲ *see also* SAME-SEX **3** [C] either of the two groups that people, animals and plants are divided into according to their function of producing young: *Within breeding pairs, each sex will benefit from the parental care efforts of the opposite sex.*

sex·ism AWL /ˈseksɪzəm/ *noun* [U] the unfair treatment of people, especially women, because of their sex; the attitude that causes this: *Unlike racism and sexism, it is likely that all people may suffer from ageism.* ■ **sexist** *adj.*: *There is much evidence that sexist attitudes are learned from peers.*

sex·ual AWL /ˈsekʃuəl/ *adj.* **1** [usually before noun] connected with the physical activity of sex: *The study looks at sexual behaviour and attitudes in the UK.* ◇ *A broad definition of sexual health is adopted to include relationships, emotions and well-being.* **2** [only before noun] connected with the process of producing young: *The data show sexual reproduction in the plants in five areas of the eastern Alps.* **3** [usually before noun] connected with the state of being male or female: *Male and female flies are easily distinguished by secondary sexual characteristics.*

ˌsexual ˈintercourse *noun* [U] (*formal*) = SEX (1)

sexu·al·ity AWL /ˌsekʃuˈæləti/ *noun* [U] the feelings, attitudes and activities connected with a person's sexual desires: *Many teachers in the study see female sexuality as incompatible with intelligence and achievement at school.*

sex·ual·ly AWL /ˈsekʃəli/ *adv.* **1** in a way that is connected with the physical activity of sex: *The analysis was restricted to sexually active people.* **2** in a way that is connected with the process of producing young: *These species of lizards are thought to be hybrids of two sexually reproducing ancestral species.*

ˌsexual seˈlection *noun* [U] (*biology*) SELECTION that happens when a member of one sex, usually female, chooses to MATE with a member of the opposite sex with particular characteristics: *Examples in the animal kingdom have shown that sexual selection may lead to the evolution of male ornaments.*

shade /ʃeɪd/ *noun* **1** [U] an area that is dark and cool under or behind sth, for example a tree or building, because the sun's light does not get to it: **in the ~** *In hot weather, most children ate lunch inside or in the shade.* ◇ **in the ~ of sth** *A large group of people would sit in the shade of the mango trees, waiting to see the doctor.* **2** [C] **~ (of sth)** a particular form of a colour, that is, how dark or light it is: *Although many sedimentary rocks are coloured various shades of grey, truly black examples are rare.* **3** [U] the dark areas in a picture, especially the use of these to produce variety: *Every good film shot is satisfying when the distribution of light and shade in the image is evenly balanced.* **4** [C, usually pl.] **~ of sth** a different kind or level of opinion or feeling: *The doctrine created interest amongst philosophers and theologians of all shades of opinion.*

shadow /ˈʃædəʊ; *NAmE* ˈʃædoʊ/ *noun* **1** [C] the dark area or shape produced by sb/sth coming between light and a surface: *The close-up shows her shadow on the wall.* ◇ *Diffuse light casts no shadows and penetrates deeper into canopies than direct sunlight.* **2** [U] (*also* **shadows** [pl.]) DARKNESS, especially that produced by sb/sth coming between light and a surface: *Patches of light and shadow moved across the screen.* ◇ **in ~** *A considerable area will be left in shadow.* ◇ **in the shadows** *Strangers may be lurking in the shadows.* **3** [sing.] the strong (usually bad) influence of sb/sth: **the ~ of sb/sth** *By 1700 the British company was coming out of the shadow of its Dutch rival.* ◇ **in/under the ~ of sb/sth** *Conrad grew up under the shadow of Russian imperialism.* IDM *see* CAST[1]

shaft /ʃɑːft; *NAmE* ʃæft/ *noun* **1** (often in compounds) a long, narrow passage in which sth can go up and down in a building or underground: *A sensor was positioned at the base of the shaft.* ◇ + **noun** *New safety legislation pushed up the costs of deep shaft mining.* **2** (often in compounds) a metal bar that joins parts of a machine so that power can pass between them: *The propeller shaft was made of steel.*

shake /ʃeɪk/ *verb* (**shook** /ʃʊk/, **shaken** /ˈʃeɪkən/) **1** [I, T] to move with short quick movements from side to side or up and down; to make sb/sth move in this way: *Buildings shook in Sacramento and tremors were felt in Reno.* ◇ **~ sb/sth** *Earthquakes shake the ground because there is a sudden movement in the Earth's crust.* ◇ **~ hands (with sb)**| **~ sb's hand** *John Foster Dulles refused to shake hands with Chou En Lai at the conference.* **2** [T] (not used in the progressive tenses) **~ sb** to shock or upset sb very much: *Plato became a disciple of Socrates and was profoundly shaken by his death.* **3** [T] **~ sth** to make a belief or an idea less certain: *The Great Depression shook the faith of many in the future of capitalism.* ◇ *A series of medical scandals have shaken public confidence in the medical profession.* **4** [T] to get rid of sth: **~ sth off** *The GDR was never able to shake off its negative image in the British media.* ◇ **~ sth** *It is hard to shake the feeling that an opportunity has been missed.*

IDM **shake the ˈfoundations of sth | shake sth to its ˈfoundations** to cause people to question their basic beliefs about sth: *Two major occasions in the 20th century shook the foundations of world politics: the First World War and the Second World War.* ◇ *The launch of Sputnik shook Congress and the nation to its foundations.*

PHR V **ˌshake sth ˈup** (*rather informal*) to make important changes in an organization, a profession, etc. in order to make it more efficient: *They have helped to shake things up by forcing new issues onto the table.*

shall /ʃəl; *strong form* ʃæl/ *modal verb* (*negative* **shall not** *short form* **shan't** /ʃɑːnt; *NAmE* ʃænt/, *pt* **should** /ʃʊd/ *negative* **should not** *short form* **shouldn't** /ˈʃʊdnt/) HELP Unless you are quoting, the short form **shan't** should not be used in academic writing. The form **shouldn't** should also be avoided, unless you are quoting or deliberately using a less formal style. **1** (*especially BrE*) used with *I* and *we* for saying what you intend to do HELP Academic writers often use 'I shall' or 'we shall' when describing or explaining what they are going to talk about, or not talk about: *In the next section, I shall consider two contrasting approaches to this problem.* ◇ *We shall see later how Plato attempts to cope with this difficulty.* ◇ *I shall not attempt to explain this idea of 'intuition' any more explicitly.* **2** (*formal*) used in legal and official language to say what must happen: *Personal data shall be processed fairly and lawfully.* ➲ grammar note *at* MODAL[1]

S

shal·low /ˈʃæləʊ; *NAmE* ˈʃæloʊ/ *adj.* (**shal·low·er**, **shal·low·est**) **1** not having much distance between the top or surface and the bottom: *Results demonstrated that young plaice prefer shallow warmer water.* ◇ *The beech tree dominates on drier shallow soils.* OPP DEEP[1] (1) **2** (*disapproving*) (of a person, an idea, a comment, etc.) not showing serious thought or feelings about sth: *The psychological insight of the novels is shallow.* OPP DEEP[1] (4) **3** (of breathing) taking in only a small amount of air each time: *Anger can produce, for example, increased heart rate, shallow breathing and sleep or eating disturbances.* OPP DEEP[1] (9)

shame /ʃeɪm/ *noun* **1** [U] the feelings of sadness, EMBARRASSMENT and GUILT that you have when you know that sth you have done is wrong or stupid: *A person with HIV may also feel a sense of shame or guilt for having contracted the disease.* **2** [U] the loss of respect that is caused when you do sth wrong or stupid: *Her parents told her that her refusal to marry would bring shame on the family.* **3 a shame** [sing.] used to say that sth is a cause for feeling sad or disappointed: *It is a great shame that Runia's works are not yet translated into English.*

shape¹ /ʃeɪp/ *noun* **1** [C, U] the form of the outer edges or surfaces of sth; an example of sth that has a particular form: *Normally, the lens changes its shape to help the eye focus.* ◇ *In the ancient world, clay vessels had to be made in all shapes and sizes because they served so many purposes.* ◇ **in ~** *The field is irregular in shape and is surrounded on all sides by mature woodland.* ◇ **in the ~ of sth** *The texts mention luxury items including racehorses, purple textiles and gold jewellery in the shape of serpents.* ◇ (*figurative*) *There have been limited moves to more openness by the government in the shape of the Freedom of Information Act 2000.* **2** [U] the physical condition of sb/sth; the state of sth: **in ~** *Being permitted to work out with the team helped him to keep in shape.* ◇ *The Botswana economy is generally in good shape.* **3** [U] **~ (of sth)** the particular qualities or characteristics of sth: *Fast innovation can enable management to change the shape of its business.*

IDM **give 'shape to sth** to express or explain a particular idea, plan, etc: *Tagore painted pastoral scenes of a peaceful Bengal, to give shape to his patriotic feelings for the region.* **take 'shape** to develop and become more complete or organized: *Distinctive industries took shape in Britain in the second century.*

shape² /ʃeɪp/ *verb* **1** to have an important influence on the way that sth is done or the way that sb/sth develops: **~ sb/sth** *It is likely that new technologies will influence medical treatment and shape health policy.* ◇ *These findings suggest that parents continue to shape the behaviours and attitudes of their adolescents.* ◇ **~ how/what, etc...** *The experience of living through the war shaped how people thought about politics and the state.* ◇ **~ A into B** *It was British merchants who shaped the small port of Bombay into a great city tailored to the needs of British commerce.* **2 ~ sth** to make sth into a particular shape: *Water shapes its course according to the nature of the ground over which it flows.*

S

shaped /ʃeɪpt/ *adj.* having the type of shape mentioned: *The asteroids are irregularly shaped rocky or iron-rich bodies.* ◇ **~ like sth** *More than 5 000 of the tombs in the region were shaped like keyholes.* ◇ **-shaped** *These windows have small diamond-shaped or rectangular panes of glass.*

share¹ /ʃeə(r); *NAmE* ʃer/ *verb* **1** [T, I] to have the same feelings, ideas, etc. as sb else; to have the same qualities as sb/sth else: **~ sth** *Social relationships tend to arise among people who share common experiences.* ◇ *All three animals share a great many features of cell structure and organization.* ◇ **shared + noun** *Historically, trade guilds were formed to protect shared interests.* ◇ **~ sth with sb/sth** *Gayer shared with Hayek the view that US monetary policy in the 1920s was responsible for the Great Depression.* ◇ **~ in sth** *Greeks, no matter where they lived in the wide Mediterranean world, shared in a common culture.* **2** [T] **~ sth (with sb)** to tell other people about sth, for example your ideas or experiences, or some information that you have: *The group were now ready to share their ideas with each other.* **3** [T, I] to be equally involved in sth or responsible for sth: **~ sth (with sb)** *European nation states also share power with the institutions of the EU.* ◇ *Responsibility for town and country planning is shared with district councils.* ◇ **be shared between sb (and sb)** *Care is usually shared between the general practitioner and a specialist doctor.* ◇ **~ in sth** *Congress has a constitutional responsibility to share in the task of governing the country.* **4** [T, I] **~ (sth) (with sb)** to have or use sth at the same time as sb else: *A majority of the families in the area share overcrowded apartments with other families or extended family.* **5** [T, I] **~ (sth) (with sb)** to give some of what you have to sb else; to let sb use sth that is yours: *My new friends insisted on sharing their food with me.* **6** [T] **~ sth (out) (among/between sb)** to divide sth between two or more people: *Food is shared equally among all group members.* ◇ *In the two smaller doctors' practices, staff shared out tasks flexibly.*

share² /ʃeə(r); *NAmE* ʃer/ *noun* **1** [C] any of the units of equal value into which a company is divided and sold to raise money. People who own shares receive part of the company's profits: **~ (in sth)** *The country's major banks hold shares in each other.* ◇ **+ noun** *Lack of confidence in the company caused a sharp fall in share price.* ➲ *compare* STOCK¹ (1) **2** [C, usually sing.] one part of sth that is divided between two or more people: **~ (of sth)** *In 2005, the French car manufacturer Peugeot sold 144 000 new cars in Britain, taking a 5.9% share of the market.* ◇ *In this study, a larger share of men had employers in the private sector than in the public sector.* ◇ **~ in sth** *Her husband had offered to give her a share in the proceeds of sale of the family home.* ➲ *see also* MARKET SHARE **3** [sing.] **~ (of sth)** the part that sb has in a particular activity that involves several people: *Children were expected to do their share of the work on the farm.* **4** [sing.] **~ (of sth)** an amount of sth that is thought to be normal or acceptable for one person or group: *World music has already produced its fair share of popular music stars.* IDM *see* FAIR¹

share·hold·er /ˈʃeəhəʊldə(r); *NAmE* ˈʃerhoʊldər/ *noun* an owner of shares in a company or business: *Minority shareholders should have the same rights as larger shareholders, but often this is not the case.*

share·hold·ing /ˈʃeəhəʊldɪŋ; *NAmE* ˈʃerhoʊldɪŋ/ *noun* the amount of a company or business that sb owns in the form of shares: *a minority/majority shareholding* ◇ **~ in sth** *She had a 50% shareholding in the company.*

sharp /ʃɑːp; *NAmE* ʃɑːrp/ *adj.* (**sharp·er, sharp·est**) **1** [usually before noun] (especially of a change in sth) sudden and fast: *There was a sharp decline in life expectancy in the early 1990s.* ◇ *Exporters of these goods have seen some of the sharpest falls in exports.* ◇ *a sharp increase/rise/drop/reduction* **2** [usually before noun] (especially of a difference in sth) clear and definite: *Political theory makes a sharp distinction between public and private responsibility.* ◇ **in ~ contrast** *These findings were in sharp contrast to most organizational research conducted up to then.* ◇ **into ~ focus/relief** *The scandal threw the whole issue of party funding into sharp focus.* **3** (especially of sth that can cut or make a hole in sth) having a fine edge or point: *Constant collision of grains smooths the sharp edges of the crystals.* ◇ *Some of the fish had small sharp teeth and fed on small invertebrates.* OPP BLUNT¹ (1) **4** (of a person or what they say) critical or severe: *Even NASA was subjected to sharp criticism.* ◇ *The mixture of fact and fiction has come under sharp attack from critics.* **5** (of a physical feeling or an emotion) very strong and sudden, often like being cut or wounded SYN INTENSE (1): *The pain can at times be very sharp.* **6** changing direction suddenly: *The river runs in 10–20 km long straight reaches separated from each other by sharp bends.* **7** (of people or their minds or eyes) quick to notice or understand things or to react: *They revealed a sharp awareness of the subtler nuances of clothing codes.* ◇ *Wedgwood demonstrated his sharp commercial eye.*

sharp·en /ˈʃɑːpən; *NAmE* ˈʃɑːrpən/ *verb* **1** [I, T] **~ (sth)** to become stronger and/or clearer; to make sth stronger and/or clearer: *The smaller shoots die off as the competition for resources sharpens.* ◇ **~ sth** *The differences between those standpoints sharpen the issues that need to be addressed.* ◇ *Competition demands that one constantly prepare, practise and sharpen skill sets.* ◇ *The regional divide is sharpened by economic disparities between the* *relatively successful south and the impoverished north.* **2** [T] **~ sth** to make an edge or point sharper: *Tools were simple, handheld tools with a sharpened edge.*

sharp·ly /ˈʃɑːpli; *NAmE* ˈʃɑːrpli/ *adv.* **1** suddenly and by a large amount: *Investment levels declined sharply after the stock crash of 1987.* ◇ *The risk of hypothermia rises sharply in the winter months.* ◇ *The number of part-time students has increased sharply.* ◇ *to fall/drop/decrease sharply* **2** in a way that clearly shows the differences between two things; in a way that clearly emphasizes sth: *This perspective contrasted sharply with standard economic theory.* ◇ *Parenting behaviour differs sharply among the high and low educated.* ◇ *Scholars are sharply divided on how to read the texts.* ◇ *Most galaxies do not have sharply defined outer edges.* ◇ *These changes have brought the poverty of older single women more sharply into focus.* **3** in a critical way: *These plans were sharply criticized by the European Parliament.* ◇ *This idea is expressed in sharply critical terms.* **4** used to emphasize that sth has a sharp point or edge: *Samples of sodic pyroxene have sharply pointed crystals.*

she /ʃi; *strong form* ʃiː/ *pron.* (used as the subject of a verb) **1** a female person or animal that has already been mentioned or is easily identified: *The wife maintained that she could not marry again.* ◇ *She became the first woman ever to lecture at Oxford University.* ➲ *compare* HER[1] (1) **2** a person of either sex who has already been mentioned or is easily identified: *Tell your child she should not be angry with a new step-parent.* HELP This use of **she** is often used by feminist writers instead of **he**, which is also sometimes used to refer to a male or female but is considered sexist by many people. ➲ *compare* HER[1] (2) ➲ grammar note *at* THEY

shear /ʃɪə(r); *NAmE* ʃɪr/ *noun* [U] the application of forces which SLIDE layers of solid (or liquid) over each other: *Bicycle brake blocks are designed to withstand shear in the rubber.* ◇ **+ noun** *As the car corners, there is a shear strain across the tyres.*

sheath /ʃiːθ/ *noun* (*pl.* **sheaths** /ʃiːðz/) **1** a structure in living TISSUE that fits closely over another: *The tumour tends to spread along nerve sheaths.* **2** any covering that fits closely over sth for protection: *The optical fibre in the cables is tiny and lightweight. It needs a suitable sheath to protect it from mechanical damage or corrosion.*

shed /ʃed/ *verb* (**shed·ding, shed, shed**) **1 ~ sth** if an animal sheds its skin, or a plant sheds leaves, it loses them naturally: *Some species live in soil where they live on skin and feathers shed by animals and birds.* ◇ *Deciduous trees shed their leaves in winter because of the cost of respiration.* **2 ~ sth** to let sth fall; to drop sth: *The ice shelf shed a floating ice island which had an area of over 100 square kilometres before it began to break up.* **3 ~ sth** to get rid of sth that is no longer wanted: *Britain has shed a number of overseas responsibilities and its armed forces have been withdrawn from various countries.* **4 ~ blood** to kill or injure people, especially in a war: *Under this view, political leaders do not have the moral right to shed the blood of their own citizens on behalf of suffering foreigners.*
IDM *see* LIGHT[1]

sheep /ʃiːp/ *noun* (*pl.* **sheep**) an animal with a thick coat, kept on farms for its meat or its wool: **+ noun** *He worked on the family sheep farm.*

sheer /ʃɪə(r); *NAmE* ʃɪr/ *adj.* **1** [only before noun] used to emphasize the size, degree or amount of sth; nothing but: *The sheer number of very large cities in the country is remarkable, with about 100 cities greater than one million people.* ◇ *Imperial building projects, at Rome and elsewhere, impressed by their sheer scale and grandeur.* ◇ *Modern development economists have shown that famine is seldom caused by sheer lack of food.* ➲ *compare* UTTER[1] **2** very steep: *The height of the sheer cliffs on Mt Desert Island approaches 250 m.*

sheet /ʃiːt/ *noun* **1** a piece of paper for writing or printing on, etc. usually in a standard size: **~ (of sth)** *Children sat around a table covered with large sheets of paper and pens.* ◇ *The answer sheets show that subjects frequently changed their minds, on occasion up to five times per test.* ◇ **+ noun** *The website enables access to over 2 700 pieces of sheet music published in California between 1852 and 1900.* **2** a flat thin piece of any material, normally square or RECTANGULAR: **~ (of sth)** *All 13 000 kg of the material had to be dried by spreading it thinly on sheets of black plastic in full sun.* ◇ **+ noun** *The connecting pipes are protected by a sheet metal cover.* **3 ~ (of sth)** a wide flat area of sth, covering the surface of sth else: *The new type of shield was round and made of wood covered with a thin sheet of bronze.* ◇ *Horizontal sheets of shallow cloud at all levels produce virtually no precipitation to the surface.* ➲ *see also* ICE SHEET **4** a large piece of thin cloth used on a bed to lie on or lie under: *The hospital was under-staffed, water shortage was acute and there was no supply of sheets and pillows.*

shelf /ʃelf/ *noun* (*pl.* **shelves** /ʃelvz/) **1** a flat piece of wood, plastic, metal, etc. for things to be placed on and often forming part of a set: *The product was taken off supermarket shelves.* ◇ **~ space** *The more shelf space you give an item, the more likely you are to sell it.* **2** (*earth science*) a piece of rock sticking out from a larger area of rock or from the edge of a mass of land under the sea: *The reef traps seawater on the shallow coastal shelf.* ➲ *see also* CONTINENTAL SHELF
IDM **off the ˈshelf** that can be bought immediately and does not have to be specially designed or ordered: *A computer customized directly to a customer's requirements provides more value than one off the shelf from a retailer.*

shell /ʃel/ *noun* **1** [C, U] (often in compounds) the hard outer part of eggs, nuts, some seeds and some animals: *There are likely to be many factors that affect the thickness of an eggshell.* ◇ *The lower layer was a mixture of sand and fragments of human debris (e.g. charcoal, shell, bone, plaster and brick).* **2** [C] **~ (of sth)** any structure that forms a hard outer frame: *Liquid rock is scarce in the earth; it is found only in the outer shell of the earth's core.* ◇ *The cylindrical shell of the water tank is acting as the single support for all loads, including the weight of water to be stored.* **3** [C] the walls or outer structure of sth, for example an empty building after a fire, or a vehicle when the inside has not yet been made: *In 1934, both the large country houses owned by the Trust were empty shells.* **4** [C] a metal container that explodes when it is fired from a large gun: *The first shells that fell destroyed the fuel stock and all food supplies.*

shel·ter[1] /ˈʃeltə(r)/ *noun* **1** [U] the fact of having a place to live or stay, considered as a basic human need: *One of the functions of a city is to provide shelter for those who live there.* ◇ *In the immediate aftermath of the quake, a million people were without food or shelter.* **2** [U] protection from rain, danger or attack: *Refugees were forced to take shelter in makeshift camps.* ◇ **~ from sth** *They need places where they can nest and feed and find shelter from predators.* **3** [C] (often in compounds) a structure built to give protection, especially from the weather or from attack: *They constructed temporary shelters of organic materials such as wood, bone or hides.* ◇ *Kennedy urged American citizens to build nuclear fallout shelters.* **4** [C] a building, usually owned by a charity, that provides a place to stay for people without a home, or protection for people or animals who have been badly treated: *She moves between the homes of friends, squats and homeless shelters.*

shel·ter[2] /ˈʃeltə(r)/ *verb* **1** [T] to give sb/sth a place where they are protected from the weather or from danger: **~ sb/sth** *The camp was established in 1997 and*

S

currently shelters over 19 000 refugees. ◇ **~ sb/sth from sb/sth** *Fringing reefs are associated with sites sheltered from the south-west monsoon.* **2** [T] **~ sb/sth from sth** to protect sb/sth, especially from competition or taxes: *The government sheltered the company from competitors by imposing duties on imported cars.* **3** [I] **~ (from sth)** to stay in a place that protects you from the weather or from danger: *This situation is determined principally by the necessity to shelter from predators.*

shelves *pl. of* SHELF

shield¹ /ʃiːld/ *noun* **1** a person or thing used to protect sb/sth, especially by forming a barrier: *Charring acts as a protective shield to protect plants against further burning.* ◇ *There is still no shield that can deflect a nuclear explosion.* **2** a plate or screen that protects a machine or the person using it from damage or injury: *Lead shields may be required for more penetrating types of radiation.* **3** a large piece of metal or wood carried by soldiers in the past to protect the body when fighting: *Each soldier carried a small shield and a short sword.* **4** (*earth science*) an area of the earth's surface with generally flat LANDSCAPE made of rock from the earliest period of the earth's history, that has not been changed by TECTONIC forces: **+ noun** *Extensive flat relief is present in shield areas formed in the Precambrian and Palaeozoic.*

shield² /ʃiːld/ *verb* **1 ~ sb/sth (from sb/sth)** to protect sb/sth from danger, harm or sth unpleasant: *They believed that children needed to be shielded from the adult world.* ◇ *Persian rule brought Macedon great advantages by shielding the kingdom from attack by its neighbours.* **2 ~ sth** to put sth around a piece of machinery, etc. in order to protect the person using it: *Microwave ovens can pose a hazard if not properly shielded.*

shift¹ AWL /ʃɪft/ *noun* **1** [C] a change in position or direction: **~ (in sth)** *In recent years, there has been a shift in consumer attitudes.* ◇ *This policy change represented a profound shift.* ◇ **~ of sth (in sth)** *One result was a gradual shift of emphasis in educational policy.* ◇ **~ from A (to B)** *The disease may have spread because of demographic shifts from rural to urban living.* ◇ **~ to/towards sth** *He found a shift towards the blue end of the spectrum.* ➲ *see also* PARADIGM SHIFT **2** [C] a period of time worked by a group of workers who start work as another group finishes: *Most drivers work eight-hour shifts.* ◇ *The plant operates 24 hours a day, with workers alternating night and day shifts.* ◇ **+ noun** *Research has also suggested that shift work might result in stress.* **3** [U] the system on a keyboard that allows capital letters or a different set of characters to be typed; the key that operates this system: *Important keys like enter, shift and space are often made larger than other keys to make it easy to hit them.*

▸ ADJECTIVE + SHIFT **major, significant, important • large • fundamental, profound • dramatic, radical, seismic • abrupt, sudden • rapid • decisive • small, slight, subtle • gradual • upward • downward • cultural • demographic • climatic** *In times of heightened family change, even ten years can bring major shifts in household formation.* ◇ *A slight upward shift of temperatures was observed.*

▸ NOUN + SHIFT **policy • power** *Radical policy shifts are more easily made in a crisis atmosphere.*

▸ VERB + SHIFT **represent • mark, indicate, show, signal • suggest • see, witness • reflect • cause, lead to, contribute to • undergo** *Recent years have seen a shift in the delivery of health care.*

▸ SHIFT + VERB **occur, take place** *It is clear that a shift has occurred in the nation's approach to energy security.*

▸ SHIFT IN + NOUN **emphasis • focus • perspective • attitudes • direction • the balance of • demand • supply** *These changes represented a seismic shift in the balance of control from the state to the private sector.*

shift² AWL /ʃɪft/ *verb* **1** [T] **~ sth (away from/from A) (to/towards B)** to change the attention, direction or focus of sth: *Low unemployment shifts the balance of power towards workers.* ◇ *During the 1980s, philosophers of science sought to shift attention to laboratory practice.* ◇ *Many Japanese firms have now shifted their focus to core businesses and away from diversification.* **2** [I] (of the emphasis or direction of sth) to change from one state or position to another: **~ (away from/from A) (to/towards B)** *The research focus gradually shifted from basic to applied research.* ◇ *In recent years, attention has shifted away from these issues.* ◇ **+ adv./prep.** *The balance of power between parties shifted back and forth.* **3** [I, T] to move from one position or place to another; to move sth in this way: *Friction prevents the stonework from shifting in an earthquake.* ◇ *The EU's external borders are constantly shifting.* ◇ **~ sth (to sth)** *Companies can shift production to developing countries.* ◇ **~ from A to B** *There has been a tendency for population to shift from large cities to smaller towns.*

IDM **shift your ˈground** (*usually disapproving*) to change your opinion about a subject, especially during a discussion: *Dryden tactfully shifted his poetic ground away from tributes to Cromwell to celebrations of the returning Charles II.*

shine /ʃaɪn/ *verb* (**shone, shone** /ʃɒn; *NAmE* ʃoʊn/) HELP In sense 2 in *NAmE* **shined** can also be used for the past tense and past participle. **1** [I] to produce or reflect light; to be bright: *The smallest stars will shine for trillions of years.* **2** (*NAmE also* **shined, shined**) [T] **~ sth + adv./prep.** to aim or point a light in a particular direction: *The effect of shining a light on an electron is to shake it back and forth.* ◇ *The thickness of the base can be monitored by shining an infrared beam through it.*

PHR V **ˌshine ˈthrough (sth)** (of a quality) to be easy to see or notice: *His integrity and honesty shine through.*

ship¹ /ʃɪp/ *noun* a large boat that carries people or goods by sea: *Products can be moved around the world cheaply on huge container ships.* ◇ **by ~** *For decades Alaska could only be reached by ship.*

ship² /ʃɪp/ *verb* (**-pp-**) **1** [T] **~ sb/sth + adv./prep.** to send or transport sb/sth by ship or by another means of transport: *Japanese electronics goods are shipped to markets all over the world.* ◇ *The product is then shipped directly to the customer by courier.* ◇ *The government shipped workers from the mainland to work on the island.* **2** [I, T] to be available to be bought; to make sth available to be bought: *The software is due to ship next month.* ◇ **~ sth** *Profits are generated from producing and shipping large quantities of a limited number of products.*

ship·ping /ˈʃɪpɪŋ/ *noun* [U] **1** the activity of carrying people or goods from one place to another by ship: **~ (of sth)** *Commercial shipping of propane requires special handling due to the associated hazards.* ◇ **+ noun** *a shipping company* ◇ *the shipping industry* **2** ships in general or considered as a group: *Cars, lorries, aviation and shipping have been almost exclusively reliant on oil.* ◇ **+ noun** *Major shipping lanes run through the Malacca Strait.*

shock¹ /ʃɒk; *NAmE* ʃɑːk/ *noun* **1** [C, usually sing., U] a strong feeling of surprise as a result of sth happening, especially sth unpleasant; the event that causes this feeling: **~ to sb** *This election result was a shock to the parliamentary party.* ◇ **+ noun** *Many modern artists use shock tactics to focus on issues.* **2** [C] (*economics*) a sudden event or change that disturbs an economy: *The oil shocks of the 1970s left a scar on the global economy.* ◇ **~ to sth** *Recessions tend to be caused by adverse shocks to the economic system.* **3** [U] (*medical*) a serious medical condition, usually the result of injury in which a person has lost a lot of blood and they are extremely weak: *Internal bleeding should be suspected if a patient develops signs of shock*

S

without obvious blood loss. **4** [C, U] a violent shaking movement that is caused by an explosion, EARTHQUAKE, etc: *The damage was caused not by the first earthquake, but by one of the large shocks later in the morning.* ➲ *see also* SHOCK WAVE (1) **5** [C] = ELECTRIC SHOCK: *The shock delivered is 'synchronized' with the patient's pulse.*

shock[2] /ʃɒk; *NAmE* ʃɑːk/ *verb* **1** [I, T] (of bad language, behaviour, etc.) to offend sb's feelings of what is morally right and wrong: *These movies deliberately set out to shock.* ◇ **~ sb** *The play certainly shocked its first audiences.* ◇ *Some observers were shocked by the violence.* **2** [T] to surprise and upset sb: **~ sb** *He posed a question that shocked many economists.* ◇ **be shocked to do sth** *Some of the refugees were shocked to find that their story was public knowledge.*

shock·ing /ˈʃɒkɪŋ; *NAmE* ˈʃɑːkɪŋ/ *adj.* **1** that offends or upsets people; that is morally wrong: *Shocking images of brutal atrocity and death helped to make that message vivid.* **2** (*BrE, rather informal*) very bad: *Many of the school buildings are in a shocking state of repair.* ■ **shock·ing·ly** *adv.*: *There was a shockingly high mortality rate.*

ˈshock wave *noun* **1** a movement of very high air pressure that is caused by an explosion, EARTHQUAKE, etc: *When the asteroid hit the ocean, the atmospheric shock wave moved at several times the speed of sound across North America.* **2 shock waves** [pl.] feelings of shock that people experience when sth bad happens suddenly: *William's victory at Hastings sent shock waves through the British Isles.*

shoe /ʃuː/ *noun* one of a pair of outer coverings for your feet: *Athletic footwear sales increased because wearing these shoes enabled people to convey a desirable picture of themselves.*

shone *past tense, past part. of* SHINE

shook *past tense, past part. of* SHAKE

shoot[1] /ʃuːt/ *verb* (**shot**, **shot** /ʃɒt; *NAmE* ʃɑːt/) **1** [I, T] to fire a gun or other weapon; to fire sth from a weapon: *The troops were ordered to shoot to kill.* ◇ **~ sth** *Many deaths were caused by shooting poisoned arrows.* ◇ **~ (sth) at sb/sth** *The passenger in the car had been shot at two weeks previously and feared another attack.* ◇ **~ sth down** *On a dangerous mission over North Vietnam, his plane was shot down.* **2** [T] to kill or wound a person or an animal with a bullet, etc: **~ sb/sth/yourself** *Troops shot his grandfather in the head and killed him.* ◇ **~ sb/sth dead** *One protester was shot dead by police.* **3** [T] to make a film or photograph of sth: **~ sth** *Mixing takes place after the film has been shot.* ◇ **~ sth adv./prep.** *The Hollywood production was shot on location in and around Melbourne.*

IDM **be shot through with sth** to contain a lot of a particular quality or feature: *The poem is shot through with intelligence and deep ironies.*

PHR V **ˌshoot ˈup** to rise suddenly by a large amount: *As a consequence, unemployment shot up.* ◇ **~ (from sth) to sth** *Three months later, the company's shares had shot up to $110.*

shoot[2] /ʃuːt/ *noun* **1** the part that grows up from the ground when a plant starts to grow; a new part that grows on plants or trees: *Seedlings given an 8 week period at 5°C produced green shoots.* **2** an occasion when sb takes professional photographs for a particular purpose or makes a film: *The production itself involved an 8-hour film shoot and final editing took 2 weeks.*

shoot·ing /ˈʃuːtɪŋ/ *noun* **1** [C] a situation in which a person is shot with a gun: *There have been at least 25 high school shootings involving multiple victims in the United States.* **2** [U] the process of filming a film: *Every day before shooting they added material to the screenplay.*

shop[1] /ʃɒp; *NAmE* ʃɑːp/ *noun* **1** [C] (*especially BrE*) a building or part of a building where you can buy goods or services SYN STORE[1] (1): *The market is run to complement rather than rival the local shops.* ◇ *The company sells franchises to run retail health food shops.* ◇ *The retailer has grown to a successful chain of 12 shops.* ◇ **in a ~** *The prices of most goods in the shops do not change every day.* **2** (*also* **work·shop**) [C] (especially in compounds) a place where things are made or repaired, especially part of a factory where a particular type of work is done: *A car repair shop might use benchmarks such as the average time taken to book a car in.*

IDM **ˌset up ˈshop** to start a business: *The company first set up shop in Asia Pacific in 1996.*

shop[2] /ʃɒp; *NAmE* ʃɑːp/ *verb* (**-pp-**) **1** [I] to buy things in shops or using the Internet: *Many people shop at the same supermarket each week.* ◇ *As more people shop online, there are more opportunities for businesses to collect personal data.* ◇ **~ for sth** *Difficulties in performing activities such as shopping for groceries reduce older adults' sense of independence.* **2 go shopping** [I] to spend time going to shops and looking for things to buy: *When we go shopping we are tempted by many different things on the shelves.*

PHR V **ˌshop aˈround (for sth)** to compare the quality or prices of goods or services that are offered by different shops or companies so that you can choose the best: *Most people would not bother to shop around for the best deal.*

shop·ping /ˈʃɒpɪŋ; *NAmE* ˈʃɑːpɪŋ/ *noun* [U] the activity of buying things from shops or the Internet: *Parents were encouraged to involve their children in grocery shopping and meal preparation.* ◇ *Online shopping is set to account for nearly 40% of all UK retail sales by 2020.* ◇ **+ noun** *We asked respondents about their shopping trips in the past month.*

shore /ʃɔː(r)/ *noun* **1** [C, U] the land along the edge of the sea or ocean, a lake or another large area of water: *Rocky shores occur on the coasts of many islands in South East Asia.* ◇ **~ of sth** *Dairying was increasingly concentrated in north-western Vermont, along the eastern shore of Lake Champlain.* ◇ **on ~** *Fishermen were permitted to spread, dry and mend their nets on shore.* **2 shores** [pl.] (*especially literary*) a country, especially one with a coast: *The Greeks were irresistibly drawn to distant shores.*

S

short[1] /ʃɔːt; *NAmE* ʃɔːrt/ *adj.* (**short·er**, **short·est**) **1** lasting or taking a small amount of time or less time than usual: *The plan was approved in a relatively short time.* ◇ *Volcanic activity ceased for a short period of time.* ◇ *This insect has a relatively short life cycle.* OPP LONG[1] (1) **2** [only before noun] (of a period of time) seeming to have passed very quickly: *Within a few short years, the industry has gone from analogue, clunky TVs to digital hang-on-the-wall displays.* OPP LONG[1] (3) **3** measuring or covering a small length or distance, or a smaller length or distance than usual: *The majority of migrants travel only a short distance.* ◇ *A geodesic is defined to be the shortest path between any pair of its points.* ◇ *Short wavelengths have higher indices of refraction.* OPP LONG[1] (4) **4** (of a person) small in height: *Children with the condition are at higher risk of short stature.* OPP TALL (1) **5** small in extent; smaller than normal: *Unsurprisingly, shorter questionnaires tend to achieve better response rates than longer ones.* ◇ *After a short introduction, the topics were addressed one by one.* ◇ *The short answer to this question is that no consensus has emerged.* OPP LONG[1] (5) **6** [not before noun] **~ (of sth)** not having enough of sth; lacking sth: *40% of the world's population are short of basic resources such as water and food.* ◇ *The Navy was under great strain, short of adequate ships and of air cover.* **7** [not before noun] not easily available; not supplying as much as you need: *Food was short, and products like meat, eggs and butter could* *fetch a good price.* ◇ *When time is short, background can be covered only in outline.* **8** [not before noun] **~ (of sth)** less than the number, amount or distance needed or mentioned: *They recruited 109 patients—11 short of the target.* ◇ *Republicans picked up 40 seats, leaving them only 13 seats short of a majority.* **9 ~ of breath** having difficulty breathing, for example because of illness: *The patient becomes short of breath when walking uphill.* **10 ~ for sth** being a shorter form of a name or word: *QR codes, short for Quick Response, were invented in 1994.* **11** (*phonetics*) a **short** vowel is pronounced for a shorter time than other vowels: *The Cree vocabulary has a set of seven long and short vowels.* OPP LONG[1] (7) ➲ *see also* SHORTLY, SHORTNESS

IDM **give sb/sth short 'shrift | get/receive short 'shrift** to give sb/sth or get/receive little attention or sympathy: *The important role of the manufacturing and design process receives short shrift in this account.* **in ˌshort 'order** quickly and without trouble: *Unemployment, poor housing and slum formation could not be put right in short order.* **in the 'short run** concerning the immediate future: *Better relationships with staff may cost more in the short run, but can lead to greater productivity in the long run.* **in ˌshort sup'ply** not existing in large enough quantities to meet demand: *Fat, sugar and salt were in short supply through nearly all of our evolutionary history.* **little/nothing short of 'sth** used when you are saying that sth is almost true, or is equal to sth: *The company's success has been nothing short of a global phenomenon.* **'short on sth** (*rather informal*) not having much of a particular quality: *Relationship marketing, to date, has been long on theoretical development but short on empiricism.* ➲ *more at* NOTICE[2], TERM[1]

short² /ʃɔːt; *NAmE* ʃɔːrt/ *adv.* **(short·er, short·est)**

IDM **cut sth 'short** to end sth before the time expected or arranged or before the natural time: *Tragically, his life was cut short by smallpox.* ◇ *Feng, being the fourth son, had to cut his education short.* **fall 'short of sth 1** to be less than sth: *Total demand may exceed or fall short of supply.* **2** to fail to reach the standard that you expected or need: *An initially promising example fell short of their expectations.* **run 'short of sth** to not have enough of sth: *Petrol stations were rapidly running short of petrol and diesel.* **short of (doing) sth** without sth; without doing sth; unless sth happens: *It is unlikely that another massive wave of immigrants will arrive in Israel, short of an unforeseen event.* ◇ *Short of using computer software, the simplest method of solving equations involves systematic elimination.* ➲ *more at* STOP[1]

short³ /ʃɔːt; *NAmE* ʃɔːrt/ *noun*

IDM **in 'short** in a few words: *His novels belong to a great but vanished age. They are, in short, old-fashioned.*

short·age /ˈʃɔːtɪdʒ; *NAmE* ˈʃɔːrtɪdʒ/ *noun* [C, U] a situation where there is not enough of the people or things that are needed: *Chronic food shortages are not the only problem confronting the country.* ◇ *These demographic shifts will create a severe labour shortage in developed countries.* ◇ **~ of sth** *The biggest problem we face is the shortage of financial resources.* ◇ *There is a critical shortage of health professionals outside the urban areas.*

short·com·ing /ˈʃɔːtkʌmɪŋ; *NAmE* ˈʃɔːrtkʌmɪŋ/ *noun* [usually pl.] a fault in a piece of research, a plan, a system, etc: **~ (of sth)** *This legislation was enacted to overcome the shortcomings of the old system.* ◇ **~ in sth** *The BSE crisis exposed serious shortcomings in the overall coordination of European policies on agriculture.* ➲ *compare* DEFECT[1]

short·en /ˈʃɔːtn; *NAmE* ˈʃɔːrtn/ *verb* [T, I] to make sth shorter; to become shorter: **~ (sth)** *The treatment should shorten recovery times by two days on average.* ◇ *During this period of observations, the sea ice season has shortened.* ◇ *The third phase of the research involved using a shortened version of the questionnaire.* ◇ **~ sth to sth** *The activity was shortened to around 30 minutes.* OPP LENGTHEN

ˌshort-ˈlived *adj.* lasting only for a short time: *The effects of the drug are relatively short-lived; repeated administration is required.* ◇ *Most of the record relates to major but short-lived events, such as volcanic eruptions.* ◇ *The anchovy (Engraulis encrasicolus) is a short-lived species.*

short·ly /ˈʃɔːtli; *NAmE* ˈʃɔːrtli/ *adv.* **1 + adv./prep.** a short time; not long: *The condition may be diagnosed at or shortly after birth.* ◇ *At some point shortly afterwards, they moved to London.* ◇ *Many of the studies measured the impact shortly following completion of the programme.* **2** soon: *This topic will be discussed shortly.* ◇ *As we will see shortly, in many cases the distinction is not so straightforward.*

short·ness /ˈʃɔːtnəs; *NAmE* ˈʃɔːrtnəs/ *noun* [U] **1** the fact of being short in length or height: *His shortness is caused by a deficiency in growth hormone.* ◇ **~ of sth** *The shortness of the list is not surprising.* **2 ~ of breath** difficulty breathing, for example because of illness: *Shortness of breath can be a sign of many disease conditions.*

ˌshort-ˈterm *adj.* [usually before noun] lasting a short time; designed only for a short period of time in the future: *The central bank can affect the short-term interest rate.* ◇ *The majority of the studies found evidence of a short-term effect.* ◇ *Individuals are encouraged to set both short-term goals and long-term goals.* HELP **Short-term memory** is the ability to remember things that happened a short time ago: *Symptoms include short-term memory loss, confusion and excessive daytime sleepiness.* ➲ *compare* LONG-TERM

shot¹ /ʃɒt; *NAmE* ʃɑːt/ *noun* **1 ~ (at sb/sth)** the act of firing a gun; the sound this makes: *The soldier fired four shots at a car which had broken through a checkpoint.* **2 ~ (of sb/sth)** a scene in a film that is filmed continuously by one camera: *The movie's opening shot is of a character walking across a featureless landscape.*

shot² *past tense, past part. of* SHOOT[1]

should /ʃəd; *strong form* ʃʊd/ *modal verb* (*negative* **should not**, *short form* **shouldn't** /ˈʃʊdnt/) HELP The form **shouldn't** should not be used in academic writing, unless you are quoting or deliberately using a less formal style. **1** used to show what is right or appropriate, especially when criticizing sb's actions: *The national government should play a greater role in dealing with social problems.* ◇ *Future research should include more diverse groups and better measures of social effects.* **2** used to say that you expect sth is true or will happen: *As work in this area is in its early stages, results should improve significantly in the future.* ◇ *By now, pupils should be able to read with a large degree of independence.* **3** used to say that sth that was expected has not happened: *The court held that any decision should have taken into account implications for all the individuals affected.* **4** used to refer to a possible event or situation: *The first group would include the five large countries (Germany, France, Spain, Italy and the UK, if it should adopt the euro).* ◇ *If it should turn out that no evidence could justify this belief, then we had better stop holding the belief.* **5** (*BrE*) used after *that* when sth is suggested: *As a safeguard, it was recommended that all personal genetic information should be anonymized.* HELP In both American and British English, this idea can be expressed without 'should': *As a safeguard, it was recommended that all personal genetic information be anonymized.* **6** used after *that* after many adjectives that describe feelings: *It is interesting that Harris should draw such a conclusion.* ◇ *It is not surprising that the European Patent Office should modify its approach in this manner.* ➲ grammar note *at* MODAL[1]

shoul·der /ˈʃəʊldə(r); *NAmE* ˈʃoʊldər/ *noun* either of the two parts of the body between the top of each arm and the

S

neck: **on sb's shoulders** *In classical mythology, Atlas was condemned to support the sky on his shoulders.* ◇ **+ noun** *Sixty per cent of patients complained of neck and shoulder pain.*

shout¹ /ʃaʊt/ *verb* [I, T] to speak or cry out in a very loud voice: **~ for sth** *He shouted for help.* ◇ **~ at sb** *They were shouting at each other* ◇ **~ sth (at/to sb)** *Protesters shouted slogans and abuse at police.* ◇ **~ (sth) out** *She shouted out in pain when she tried to move her leg.* ◇ **+ speech** *'Go back!' she shouted.*

shout² /ʃaʊt/ *noun* a loud cry of anger, fear, excitement, etc: *There were angry shouts as the board announced its decision.*

show¹ /ʃəʊ; *NAmE* ʃoʊ/ *verb* (**showed, shown** /ʃəʊn; *NAmE* ʃoʊn/ or, rarely, **showed, showed**) **1** to make sth clear; to prove sth SYN DEMONSTRATE (1): **~ (that)...** *Evidence shows that children learn best in their own language.* ◇ **~ sth** *Investigations have shown important differences in the use of media by children of different ages.* ◇ **~ sb/sth to be/have sth** *No single process can be shown to be solely responsible for the sudden drastic reduction of animal and plant numbers.* ◇ **~ how/what, etc...** *Sociologists have shown how different cultures and civilizations can be modern in different ways.* ➲ grammar note *at* PRESENT³ **2** (not usually used in the progressive tenses) to give particular information, or a time or measurement SYN ILLUSTRATE (1): **~ sth** *Figure 2.1 shows this hierarchical relationship.* ◇ **be shown in sth** *A diagram of a flower is shown in Figure 2.35.* ◇ **be shown on sth** *The total labour force is shown on the horizontal axis.* ◇ **be shown by sth** *The total energy is shown by the black line.* ◇ **as shown in/on/by sth** *The percentage marks are as shown in Table 41.6.* ➲ grammar note *at* PRESENT³ **3** to let sb see sth: **~ sth** *Subjects are shown four such pictures or videos.* ◇ **~ sth to sb** *The ECG should be shown to a clinician able to interpret it.* ◇ **~ sb how to do sth** *By showing consumers how to serve the product, it helped to create a clear point of difference for the brand.* **4** to make it clear that you have a particular quality or feeling: **~ sth** *He showed considerable diplomacy and was talented in building the right team.* ◇ *Historians have recently shown great interest in these notions.* ◇ *Some children may not show anger at home but instead express it in the classroom.* ◇ **~ yourself + adj.** *Parliament showed itself unsympathetic to workers' calls for the regulation of industry.* ◇ **~ yourself to be/have sth** *She showed herself to be a pragmatic politician.* **5 ~ sth** to clearly have a particular quality or feature: *Most patients will show signs of dehydration.* ◇ *This fuel cell has shown promise for combined heat and power systems.* ◇ *Many plants and animals show characteristics which sit between the two extremes.* **6 ~ sth (for/to sb)** to behave in a particular way towards sb: *Courts must function in a manner which shows due respect for children's rights.* **7** (of a picture or photograph) to be of sb/sth; to represent sb/sth: **~ sth** *The first drawing shows a very traditional classroom, with desks in rows.* ◇ **~ sb/sth doing sth** *This photograph shows women protesters being removed by police.* **8 ~ sth** to make sth available for the public to see: *Over 90 per cent of the films shown in Eastern European cinemas were American films.* ◇ *He has continued to work as a new media artist, showing his work in several international exhibitions.*

PHR V **ˌshow sb/sth ˈoff** to show people sb/sth that you are proud of: *The contestants showed off their speed, strength and endurance.* **ˌshow ˈup** to arrive where you have arranged to meet sb or to do sth: *Some families did not show up for the study visit or did not return calls.* **ˌshow ˈup | ˌshow sth ˈup** to become visible; to make sth become visible: *Unreported crime does not show up in the official statistics.* ◇ *The effects may show up only in the medium or long term.*

▸ SHOW + NOUN **effect • result • evidence • example • difference, variation • level, rate • pattern • relationship, association, correlation • structure • distribution • increase • decrease, reduction, decline • improvement • change • trend** *However, other studies have failed to show such effects.* ◇ *Table 6.5 shows the results of one such analysis.* | **promise • characteristic • similarity • difference • tendency • behaviour • (no) signs of • little/no sign of** *An ancient skeleton found in Portugal shows characteristics of both subspecies.* ◇ *The cloned mice showed no signs of premature ageing.*

▸ NOUN + SHOW **study, research • experiment • survey • results, findings • analysis • data • evidence • statistics • example, case • calculation** *Experiments have shown that loss of soil leads to lower crop yields.* | **figure • table • diagram • map • curve, line • arrow** *This leads to a reduction in energy, as shown by the blue curve.*

▸ ADVERB + SHOW **clearly • consistently • convincingly • usually, generally, typically • previously • recently** *These data clearly show the desired decrease in water content.*

▸ SHOW + ADVERB **clearly • convincingly, conclusively • explicitly • experimentally • empirically** *It has been shown conclusively that fluoride in drinking water substantially reduces dental decay.* | **here • below • above • diagrammatically, graphically • schematically** *Some typical shapes are shown below [Fig. 2].* ◇ *This approach is shown diagrammatically in Fig. 3.10.*

▸ BE SHOWN TO + VERB **have • reduce, decrease • improve, increase • affect, influence** *These programmes have been shown to reduce overall school dropout rates.*

THESAURUS

show • demonstrate • illustrate • prove *verb*

These words all mean to make sth clear or show that sth is true.

- to show/demonstrate/illustrate/prove **that/what/how...**
- **results/research/evidence/findings** show/demonstrate/prove sth
- **studies/experiments/data** show/demonstrate/illustrate sth
- a **diagram/example** shows/illustrates sth
- to show/demonstrate/illustrate the **effect/difference/relationship**
- to **clearly/convincingly/consistently** show/demonstrate sth
- to show/demonstrate/prove sth **conclusively**
- to show/illustrate sth **schematically/graphically**

- **Prove** is the strongest of these words, used to mean there is very clear evidence that sth is true, so that any doubts are removed: *It is difficult to prove conclusively, but all the data point in this direction.*
- **Show, demonstrate** and **illustrate** can all be used to talk about presenting facts and evidence for sth; **show** and **illustrate** can also be used to talk about presenting information visually; **demonstrate** often refers to showing the truth of sth in a practical way: *Studies have shown that a child's concern and caring behaviours deepen as time goes on.* ◇ *The domain structure is illustrated schematically in Figure 11.3.* ◇ *This experiment clearly demonstrates the movement of ions across a membrane.*

show² /ʃəʊ; *NAmE* ʃoʊ/ *noun* **1** a programme on television or the radio SYN PROGRAMME¹ (2): *Many of the earliest television shows were essentially former radio programmes.* ◇ *More than 60 million people watched network news shows every evening.* **2** a theatre performance, especially one that includes singing and dancing: *It became a stage show and subsequently a film.* **3** an occasion when a collection of things are brought together for people to look at: *Trade shows offer a good opportunity for marketers and consumers to meet.* ◇ **on ~** *He put his paintings on show in the capital.* ➲ *compare* EXHIBITION (1) **4 ~ of sth** an action or a way of behaving that shows how you feel SYN DISPLAY[2] (2): *In a show of force, tanks and security police advanced against citizens surrounding public buildings.* ◇ *The fact that elections are held requires the government to organize a show of support.*

IDM **(a) show of 'hands** a group of people each raising a hand to vote for or against sth: *Elections to office were by show of hands.*

show·ing /'ʃəʊɪŋ; *NAmE* 'ʃoʊɪŋ/ *noun* **1** [usually sing.] evidence of how well or how badly sb/sth is performing: *The administration made a fairly good showing in the recovery up to 1937.* ◇ *The main reason for the poor showing in the war against Finland was the lack of winter training.* **2 ~ (of sth)** an act of showing a film or television programme: *Plans for a sequel were being made while showings of the first series were still in progress.*

shown *past part. of* SHOW[1]

shrank *past tense of* SHRINK

shrift /ʃrɪft/ *noun* IDM *see* SHORT[1]

shrink /ʃrɪŋk/ *verb* (**shrank** /ʃræŋk/, **shrunk** /ʃrʌŋk/) or (**shrunk, shrunk**) **1** [I, T] to become smaller in size or amount; to make sth smaller in size or amount: *In 2008, the UK economy was shrinking.* ◇ **~ sth** *Chemotherapy is used to shrink the tumour prior to surgery.* **2** [I] **+ adv./prep.** to move back or away from sb/sth because you are frightened or shocked: *They shrink away in fear from the soldiers.*

PHR V **'shrink from sth** to be unwilling to do sth that is difficult or unpleasant: *France shrank from a war against Germany.* ◇ **~ from doing sth** *This is a church that too easily shrinks from speaking out about injustice.*

shut /ʃʌt/ *verb* (**shut·ting, shut, shut**) [T, I] **~ (sth)** to make sth close; to become closed: *to shut the door/window*

PHR V **ˌshut 'down** (of a factory, shop, etc. or a machine) to stop opening for business; to stop working: *If a firm's gross profit is not sufficient to cover its fixed cost, then in the long run it must shut down.* **ˌshut sth 'down** to stop a factory, shop, etc. from opening for business; to stop a machine from working: *In the highest wind speeds, the wind turbine is shut down.* ◇ *The company said that it would shut down unprofitable businesses.* **ˌshut sb/sth 'out (of sth)** to prevent sb/sth from entering a place or from being involved in sth: *Laboratory conditions shut out, as far as possible, all potentially disruptive exterior factors.*

sib·ling /'sɪblɪŋ/ *noun* a brother or sister: *It has been shown that children are more likely to smoke if their parents or older siblings do (Royal College of Physicians, 1992).* ◇ **+ noun** *Often, parents are quick to assess a child's anger as just typical sibling rivalry.*

sic /sɪk; siːk/ *adv.* (*from Latin*) written after a word that you have copied from somewhere, to show that you know that the word is wrongly spelled or wrong in some other way: *A new and more beautiful, more finished city had sprang [sic] up in the ruins of the old.*

sick /sɪk/ *adj.* **1** physically or mentally ill: *The drink was first marketed for sick children and then rebranded to target athletes.* ◇ *The infection usually develops in hospitalized patients who are elderly or very sick.* ◇ **be off ~** *Several employees have been off sick for more than six months.* ◇ **get ~** (*NAmE*) *Some began to get sick and die as a result of contamination of the water supply.* **2 the sick** *noun* [pl.] people who are ill: *Social security systems to provide incomes for the unemployed, the sick and the retired were then set up.* **3** [not usually before noun] (*especially BrE*) feeling that you want to VOMIT: **feel ~** *He has been feeling sick, although he has not actually vomited.* **4** (*rather informal*) bored with or angry about sth that has been happening for a long time, and wanting it to stop: **~ of sb/sth** *The country had been at war for twenty years and the people were sick of it.* ◇ **~ of doing sth** *English schools have become so sick of testing their students that most did not take part in these surveys.*

IDM **be 'sick** (*BrE*) to bring food from the stomach back out through the mouth SYN VOMIT: *He has been sick twice since he arrived at the hospital half an hour ago.* **fall 'sick** to become ill: *In its earliest years, the NHS struggled to provide basic care when people fell sick.* IDM *see* FEEL[1]

'sick leave *noun* [U] permission to be away from work because of illness; the period of time spent away from work: *Those driving for 20 hours a week or more were more likely to take sick leave due to low back symptoms.* ◇ **on ~** *The study evaluated a rehabilitation programme for patients on long-term sick leave (three months or more).*

sick·ness /'sɪknəs/ *noun* **1** [U] illness; bad health: *The National Insurance Act provided insurance for workers in time of sickness.* ◇ **+ noun** *The condition is a leading cause of sickness absence and retirement due to ill health.* **2** [U, C, usually sing.] a particular type of illness or disease: *The drug tends to be used mainly for motion sickness.* ◇ *The conditions in which they were kept brought on a sickness among the slaves.* **3** [U] (*especially BrE*) the feeling that you are likely to VOMIT; the fact of VOMITING: *The patient experienced a 24-hour episode of sickness and diarrhoea.*

side[1] /saɪd/ *noun* **1** a particular aspect of sth: *Consumerism also had a darker side.* ◇ **~ to sth** *All the same, these apparent limitations do have a positive side to them.* ◇ *Critics of this view highlight that there is also a negative side to globalization.* **2 ~ (of sth)** one of the opinions, attitudes or positions held by sb in an argument, a business arrangement, etc: *It is this ability to see both sides of an issue that makes Emily Brontë one of the great Romantics.* ◇ *On the opposite side of the argument, a further question arises:...* ⊃ *see also* ONE-SIDED (1) **3** one of the two or more people or groups taking part in an argument, a war, etc: *After some fluctuations, England had chosen the Protestant side in the conflict.* ◇ *He later changed sides and supported the Roman cause.* **4** [usually sing.] **~ (of sth)** either of the two halves of a surface, an object or an area: *Now even the poor of Japan or Germany will own goods made on the other side of the world.* ◇ *Carcinoid heart disease classically affects the right side of the heart.* **5 ~ (of sth)** a part or an area of sth near the edge and away from the middle: *Additional sampling on the north side of the road showed a further increase in traffic pollutants.* ◇ *If a town is built on two sides of a river, the data may mistakenly identify it as two communities instead of one.* **6** [usually sing.] either the right or left part of a person's body, especially from under the arm to the top of the leg: *The patient should lie on her right side for at least two hours following the procedure.* **7 ~ (of sth)** the part of an EQUATION that is either to the left or the right of the equals sign: *We have multiplied both sides of the original equation by 2.* **8 ~ (of sth)** the vertical or sloping surface around sth, but not the top or bottom of it: *Rainforests are formed on the southern side of the mountains, with arid areas to the north in central Asia.* **9 ~ (of sth)** any of the flat surfaces of a solid object: *The box has six sides of 1 m by 1 m.* **10 ~ (of sth)** any of the lines that form a flat shape such as a square or triangle: *A trapezium has two parallel sides, which are the top and the bottom flanges.* **11 -sided** used in adjectives to state the number or type of sides: *Sections through crystals are usually six-sided or rectangular.*

IDM **from ˌside to 'side** moving to the left and then to the right and then back again: *The electromagnetic field oscillates in space from side to side, but does not move forwards.* **on/from all 'sides** in or from all directions; everywhere: *The Roman Empire had lost the west in the fifth century and was now under attack on all sides.* **to one 'side** to be dealt with later: *Leaving this issue to one side,*

S

there is the question of what rules should be in place during the phase-in period. **the other side of the ˈcoin** the aspect of a situation that is the opposite of or contrasts with the one you have been talking about: *Severe climate events have presented us with challenges; however, the other side of the coin is that we humans have been affecting environmental change.* **ˌside by ˈside 1** close together and facing in the same direction: *The steel panels can be stacked either side by side or on top of each other.* **2** together, without any difficulties: *Western and indigenous care systems could exist side by side, supplementing and complementing one another.* **take ˈsides** to express support for sb in a disagreement: *Social researchers are sometimes put in a position where they take sides.* ➲ *more at* ERR, SAFE

side² /saɪd/ *verb*
PHR V **ˈside with sb (against sb/sth)** to support one person or group in an argument against sb else: *The report suggested that when air pollution cases reached the courts, judges often sided with industry.* ◇ *Workers may side with managers, or they may instead side with shareholders against management.*

ˈside effect *noun* [usually pl.] **1 ~ (of sth)** an extra and usually bad effect that a drug has on sb, as well as curing illness, RELIEVING pain, etc: *Common side effects of radiotherapy include nausea, hair loss and risk of infection.* ◇ *Most of the treatments available are relatively non-toxic and do not cause significant side effects.* **2** an unexpected result of a situation or course of action that happens as well as the result you were aiming for: *Attempting to suppress markets through prohibition can have unintended side effects.*

sight /saɪt/ *noun* **1** [U] the ability to see: *These statistics include people who have restricted sight, hearing or speech.* ◇ *The accident caused the child to lose his sight in one eye.* **2** [U] **~ of sb/sth** the act of seeing sb/sth: *This scale measures the extent of highly specific fears, such as the sight of blood or snakes.* ◇ *We are made sad by the sight of someone crying, and happy by the sight of someone smiling.* **3** [U] the area or distance within which sb can see or sth can be seen: **out of ~ (of sb)** *Keep medicines in a cool, dark place and out of sight and reach of children.* ◇ **within ~ (of sth)** *People living within sight of a danger such as a volcano tend to develop a sort of acceptance.* **4** [C] a thing that you see or can see: *A wind farm is becoming an increasingly familiar sight in the countryside today.* ◇ *Cormorants are a very common sight on Shapwick Heath.* **5 sights** [pl.] **~ (of...)** the interesting places, especially in a town or city, that are often visited by tourists: *The opening scene shows a young couple taking in the sights of Paris.*
IDM **at first ˈsight** when you first begin to consider sth: *What may, at first sight, be considered a disadvantage turns out to be the major strength of the Golgi method.* **in sight** about to happen soon: *An end to this controversy seems to be in sight because of the latest developments in technology.* **lose ˈsight of sth** to stop considering sth; to forget sth: *We should not lose sight of the fact that there still remain several areas of debate.* ◇ *Caught up in our busy lives, we can easily lose sight of our original goals.*

sight·ed /ˈsaɪtɪd/ *adj.* **1** able to see; not blind: *the blind parents of sighted children* **2 sighted** (in compounds) able to see in the way mentioned: *When you are guiding someone who is blind or partially sighted, ask them what kind of help they want from you.* ➲ *usage note at* DISABILITY

sign¹ /saɪn/ *noun* **1** an event, action or fact that shows that sth exists, is happening or may happen in the future SYN INDICATION (1): **~ of sth/sb** *Death occurs usually within 5–8 years of the first signs of the disease.* ◇ **~ of doing sth** *The economic slump has only now begun to show signs of ending.* ◇ **~ that...** *There are signs that this situation is changing.* HELP In medicine, the **signs** of disease may be noticed by a doctor but not by the patient; they contrast with **symptoms** which the patient can feel or see: *A continuous watch should be kept for suggestive clinical signs, particularly lethargy and substantial weight gain.* ➲ *compare* SYMPTOM (1) **2** a piece of paper, wood or metal that has writing or a picture on it that gives you information, instructions or a warning: *In Quebec, all signs and posters must be in the official language, French.* **3 ~ (to sb) (to do sth)** a movement or sound that you make to tell sb sth: *He made a sign to him to enter.* **4** a symbol or word used to represent sth, especially in mathematics: *Thus everything under the square root sign must be multiplied.* ◇ *The minus signs on each side of the equation cancel out.* **5** (*mathematics*) the fact of a quantity being positive or negative: *The negative sign shows that the direction of E is opposite to the direction in which V increases.* ◇ **~ of sth** *The sign of the slope tells us whether the curve is increasing or decreasing.*
IDM **a ˌsign of the ˈtimes** something that you feel shows what things are like now, especially how bad they are: *The increase in the number of towns surrounding themselves with defensive walls was considered to be a sign of the times.*

sign² /saɪn/ *verb* [I, T] to write your name on a document, letter, etc. to show that you have written it, that you agree with what it says, or that it is genuine: *The President of the Czech Republic refused to sign until concessions were made for his country.* ◇ **~ sth** *In May 2010, the government of Greece signed an agreement for a three-year loan package.* ◇ *They did not sign their names on any document.* ◇ *to sign a form/contract/treaty/petition* ◇ **~ yourself + noun** *1883 was the year in which he stopped signing himself 'Henry James Junior'.*
PHR V **ˌsign sth aˈway** to lose your rights or property by signing a document: *They did not want to sign away ownership rights to the inventions.* **ˌsign sth ˈoff** to give your formal approval to sth, by signing your name: *For several years in a row, the Court has refused to sign off the EU accounts.* **ˌsign ˈon/ˈup | ˌsign sb ˈon/ˈup** to sign a form or contract which says that you agree to do a job or become a soldier; to persuade sb to sign a form or contract like this: *The recruits, who were peasants of good character, then signed on formally.* ◇ *The publisher signed him up on the spot.* ➲ *compare* ENLIST (2) **ˌsign ˈup (for sth)** to arrange to do a course of study by adding your name to the list of people doing it: *Those unable to perform such work ought not to sign up for such courses.* **ˌsign ˈup to sth** (*BrE*) to commit yourself to a project or course of action, especially one that you have agreed with a group of other people, countries or organizations: *The Schengen Agreement applies to the Member States which have signed up to it.* **ˌsign ˈup to do sth** (*BrE*) to agree to take part in sth: *This draft envisages industry members signing up to comply with a range of standards.*

sig·nal¹ /ˈsɪɡnəl/ *noun* **1** a series of electrical waves that carry sounds, pictures or messages, for example to a radio, television or mobile phone: *Each connector can transmit many electrical signals at the same time.* ◇ *Signals received from satellites are often extremely weak.* ◇ **+ noun** *The power drawn from the signal source is usually small.* **2** an event, action or fact that shows that sth exists or is likely to happen SYN INDICATION (1): *No political leader likes to send a signal which will upset his supporters in the party.* ◇ **~ of sth** *Appointments to these prestigious positions are signals of achievement.* ◇ **~ that...** *The declaration was understood as a clear signal that the Russians were escalating the struggle for global dominance.* **3** a movement or sound that you make to give sb information, instructions or a warning SYN SIGN¹ (3): *Many animals employ visual signals for communication.* ◇ *No light signals could reach the Earth from beyond this horizon at the present time.* ◇ **at a ~** *All rose at the signal that indicated the emperor's entrance.* **4** a piece of equipment that uses different coloured lights to tell drivers to go slower, stop, etc, used especially on railways and roads: *Computerized traffic signals also improve the traffic flow.*

▸ ADJECTIVE + SIGNAL **strong • large • small • original • received • modulated • modulating • desired • digital • analogue • electrical • periodic • differential** *A strong signal on one pair of wires may be picked up by an adjacent pair of wires.*

▸ NOUN + SIGNAL **input • output • message • voltage • control** *The frequency of the input signal is then lowered.*

▸ VERB + SIGNAL **send • provide • give** *By doing this, those firms will be giving a positive signal to the market.* | **produce** *Numerous species produce acoustic signals that summon other individuals to surround a predator.* | **transmit • emit • deliver • generate • receive • detect • obtain • observe • apply • amplify • convert • sample • process • pass** *Background radiation frequently plays an essential role in generating the signal.*

▸ SIGNAL + NOUN **source • pathway • power • strength • intensity • amplitude • voltage • current • processing • sequence • level • spectrum • energy • transmission • detection • bandwidth** *No more than 10% of the signal strength is lost in the connection to the amplifier input.*

sig·nal[2] /ˈsɪɡnəl/ *verb* (-ll-, *US* -l-) **1** [T] to be a sign that sth exists or is likely to happen SYN INDICATE (2): **~ sth** *The proposal for a new, looser union of sovereign states signalled the end of the old USSR.* ◇ **~ that...** *The crisis signalled that some important changes were taking place in English political culture.* **2** [T] to show sth such as a feeling or opinion through your actions or attitude: **~ sth** *His government signalled a willingness to abandon the UK's national veto.* ◇ **~ that...** *The company raised its prices significantly, signalling that it did not want a prolonged costly price war.* **3** [I, T] to make a movement or sound to give sb a message, an instruction or a warning: *The other ship signalled back.* ◇ **~ to sb** *He was waving his arm, signalling to his wife.* ◇ **~ (to) sb to do sth** *The emperor signalled his chamberlain to show in another delegation.* ◇ **~ sth** *The charge was signalled by trumpets.* ◇ **~ that...** *As the driver could not see the road behind him, it was the duty of the conductor to signal that the road was clear.*

sig·na·ture /ˈsɪɡnətʃə(r)/ *noun* **1** [C] your name as you usually write it, for example at the end of a letter: *Two weeks later, the newspaper delivered a petition to the Prime Minister containing 1.5 million signatures.* ◇ **sb's ~** *The artist's signature appears on the picture.* **2** [U] the act of signing sth: *Under the terms of the Treaty, this agreement should have been concluded within 18 months of signature.* ◇ **for ~ (by sb/sth)** *The Convention is open for signature by countries which are not members of the Council of Europe.* ◇ **~ of sth** *Stalin achieved the signature of the Japanese-Soviet Neutrality Pact in April 1941.* **3** [C] a particular quality that makes sth different from other similar things and makes it easy to recognize: **sb's ~** *Over a group of films, a director must exhibit certain recurrent characteristics of style, which serve as his signature.* ◇ **~ (of sth)** *The vast assemblages of different molecules making up a living organism can give a form of molecular signature of that life for the fossil record.* ◇ **+ noun** *Vollin also recalls Lugosi's signature role, Count Dracula.*

sig·nifi·cance AWL /sɪɡˈnɪfɪkəns/ *noun* [U, C] **1** the importance of sth, especially when this has an effect on what happens in the future: **~ (of sth) (for sb/sth)** *The significance of these findings has yet to be fully determined.* ◇ *This legislation has particular significance for older workers.* ◇ *In the Berlin of the early 20th century, this form of architecture had acquired a special significance.* ◇ **of... ~** *Two developments in the 1990s were of major significance.* OPP INSIGNIFICANCE **2 ~ (of sth)** the meaning of sth: *There are several scenes in the novel in which Nick ponders the significance of a word.* ◇ *Like so many scientific terms, it has taken on a more precise significance.* **3** (*also* sta,tistical sigˈnificance) (*statistics*) the extent to which a result is different from what would be expected from RANDOM variation or errors: *However, no tests were made for statistical significance, and no comparison with other schools was included.* ◇ **reach ~** *Among 18–64 year-old respondents, however, this discrepancy did not reach significance.*

▸ ADJECTIVE + SIGNIFICANCE **great • major • considerable • particular • special • real • relative • full • increasing • increased** *The important contributions to astronomy by Kuiper were also of great significance for the geological sciences.* | **practical • functional • symbolic • political • social • historical • cultural • economic • moral • religious • legal • biological • clinical** *This finding has practical significance, in that empathy can be learned and applied in real-life situations.*

▸ VERB + SIGNIFICANCE **have • understand • explain • discuss** *It must be established that the car owner understood the significance of a notice warning that parked cars would be clamped.* | **assume • acquire • attach • recognize, see, acknowledge • appreciate • consider, examine • assess, evaluate • determine • emphasize, highlight • test • demonstrate, show, indicate • lose • give** *It is a disease that will assume increasing significance as the population ages.*

sig·nifi·cant AWL /sɪɡˈnɪfɪkənt/ *adj.* **1** large or important enough to have an effect or to be noticed: *These voters could have a significant effect on the outcome of the election.* ◇ *Although population ageing is a global phenomenon, there are significant regional differences.* ◇ **~ for sb/sth** *The contributions of Islamic civilization proved to be as significant for the West.* ◇ **it is ~ that...** *It was significant that its nearest rival only had a 5.5 per cent share of the market.* OPP INSIGNIFICANT ➲ thesaurus note *at* IMPORTANT **2** having a particular meaning: *The lighting of a candle may be symbolically significant if it denotes the bringing of light, that is, enlightenment.* ◇ **it is ~ that...** *It is particularly significant that Branagh selected Belfast for the play's United Kingdom debut.* **3** (*statistics*) having statistical significance ➲ *see also* SIGNIFICANCE (3): *After 3 years, results for breast cancer were no longer statistically significant.* ◇ *Munafo et al. (2003) found significant associations between personality and polymorphisms in three genes.* OPP INSIGNIFICANT

WORD FAMILY
significant *adj.*
significantly *adv.*
signify *verb*
significance *noun*
signification *noun*
insignificant *adj.*
insignificantly *adv.*
insignificance *noun*

▸ SIGNIFICANT + NOUN **number • amount • part • proportion • way • effect, impact, influence • difference • change • variation • increase • decrease, reduction • improvement • role • factor • contribution • risk • problem** *Shopping centres bring significant increases in traffic.* ◇ *This graph highlights the significant improvements in human development throughout much of the world.* | **association, relationship, correlation • interaction • predictor** *The percentage of managers and professionals in a neighbourhood is a significant predictor of educational outcomes for children (Crane, 2008).*

▸ ADVERB + SIGNIFICANT **highly, extremely • particularly • potentially** *Their choice of the word 'degrade' is highly significant.* | **especially • increasingly • equally • politically • socially • historically • culturally • economically • morally** *Three technological changes are especially significant.* | **strongly • consistently • statistically** *It turns out, however, that this relationship is strongly significant (Figure 3.2).*

sig·nifi·cant·ly AWL /sɪɡˈnɪfɪkəntli/ *adv.* **1** in a way that is large or important enough to have an effect on sth or to be noticed: *At that time, the sea level was significantly higher than it is today.* ◇ *The party systems in England, Scotland and Wales differ significantly.* ◇ *A small change that lowers the temperature below the melting* *point significantly reduces water production.* **2** in a way that has a particular meaning: *Significantly, however, the Law Commission recommended that the offence should be regarded as a relatively minor one.* **3** (*statistics*) in a way that has statistical significance ➲ *see also* SIGNIFICANCE (3): *The sum of the two coefficients is positive, but it is not statistically significantly different from zero.* ◇ *The breeding pair density was significantly correlated with the number of fledglings.*

sig·ni·fi·ca·tion /ˌsɪɡnɪfɪˈkeɪʃn/ *noun* [U, C] **1 ~ (of sth)** (*formal*) the ideas that sth represents: *The novel's central character works for a waste management company, and is very much aware of garbage and all its cultural significations.* **2 ~ (of sth)** (*formal* or *linguistics*) the exact meaning of a word or phrase: *Here, 'liberty' is understood according to the proper signification of the word: the absence of external impediments.*

sig·nify AWL /ˈsɪɡnɪfaɪ/ *verb* (**sig·ni·fies, sig·ni·fy·ing, sig·ni·fied**) (*formal*) **1** [T] to be a sign of sth SYN MEAN[1] (1): **~ sth** *Some saw Obama's election as signifying the end of racism in America.* ◇ **~ that...** *Consultation signifies that the other person or group is important.* **2** [T] to show or state sth such as a feeling or intention: **~ sth** *The most widespread of gestures signifying an agreement is the handshake.* ◇ **~ that...** *The court will look for some conduct by the defendant signifying that he assumes responsibility.* **3** [I] (usually used in questions or negative sentences) to be important or to matter: *The fact that the current increases slightly as it passes through the network does not signify.*

sign·ing /ˈsaɪnɪŋ/ *noun* [U] **~ (of sth)** the act of writing your name at the end of an official document to show that you accept it: *A significant advance was the signing of the US-EC cooperation agreement in 1991.*

si·lence[1] /ˈsaɪləns/ *noun* **1** [C, U] a situation when no one is speaking: *After telling the dramatic story of her family's flight, she took a slow, deep breath, followed by a long silence.* ◇ **in ~** *For much of the meeting time, participants sat in silence absorbing the input.* **2** [U, sing.] a situation in which sb refuses to talk about sth or to answer questions: *A day later the government finally broke its silence, confirming that it had struck a military target.* ◇ **~ about/on sth** *There was an official silence about the violence committed on either side during the war.* **3** [U] a complete lack of noise or sound: *People who lived through the bombing talk of the silence that came between the raids.*

si·lence[2] /ˈsaɪləns/ *verb* **~ sb/sth** to make sb stop expressing opinions that are opposed to yours: *By the mid-1990s, the government appeared to have effectively silenced its opposition.*

si·lent /ˈsaɪlənt/ *adj.* **1** (of a person) not speaking: *In 2001 and 2002, with interest rates low and falling, critics of the government fell silent.* ◇ *The sceptical could only remain silent.* **2** not giving information about sth; refusing to speak about sth: *He remained silent and refused to discuss his inability to act and resolve his financial difficulties.* ◇ **~ about/on sth** *Much of the related literature is largely silent on this question.* **3** where there is little or no sound; making little or no sound SYN QUIET (1): *The war is not yet over, although the guns fell silent over three years ago.* **4** [only before noun] not expressed with words or sound: *Delgado continued his silent protest.* **5** [only before noun] (of films) with pictures but no sound: *The heightened style of silent film acting could be considered an extension of stage acting.* ■ **si·lent·ly** *adv.*: *More than 43 000 demonstrators paraded silently around the White House.* ◇ *Not everyone stood by silently or participated in the killing.*

sil·icon /ˈsɪlɪkən/ *noun* [U] (*symb.* **Si**) the chemical element of ATOMIC NUMBER 14. Silicon exists as a grey solid or as a brown powder and is found in rocks and sand. It is used in making glass and TRANSISTORS: *As microprocessor technology improved, it became possible to put more and more transistors on larger and larger chips of silicon.* ◇ **+ noun** *The experiments were made possible by the availability of high quality silicon crystals.*

sil·ver[1] /ˈsɪlvə(r)/ *noun* [U] (*symb.* **Ag**) the chemical element of ATOMIC NUMBER 47. Silver is a grey-white valuable metal used for making coins, jewellery, DECORATIVE objects, etc: *In the sixteenth century, the value of silver in Europe decreased as a result of the discovery of new silver mines in America.* ◇ **+ noun** *In the coffin was a silver drinking cup.*

sil·ver[2] /ˈsɪlvə(r)/ *adj.* shiny grey-white in colour: *Lithium is a soft, very light, silver-white metal.*

simi·lar AWL /ˈsɪmələ(r)/ *adj.* like sb/sth but not exactly the same: *Similar results were found in a study of adolescents.* ◇ **~ to sb/sth** *In Italy the situation was very similar to that of Germany.* ◇ **~ in sth** *The trees were all similar in size.* ◇ **in a ~ way/manner/fashion** *Proteins from these organisms respond to temperature changes in a similar way.* ◇ **in a ~ vein** *In a similar vein, Chang and Shin argued that the financial crisis gave rise to a greater emphasis on efficiency.* OPP DIFFERENT (1), DISSIMILAR ➲ language bank *at* COMPARE

▸ SIMILAR + NOUN **result • finding • pattern • trend • level • rate • size • structure • effect • approach • problem • issue • situation • case • argument • study • analysis • process • conclusion • product** *Studies in the USA show a similar pattern.* ◇ *All three drugs had similar effects.*

▸ ADVERB + SIMILAR **quite, somewhat, rather • relatively • fairly • sufficiently • broadly, generally, essentially, roughly, largely, substantially • superficially • highly • remarkably, strikingly • apparently • exactly • closely • structurally • functionally • chemically** *Hospitals throughout the world are broadly similar in the way that they deliver medical care.*

simi·lar·ity AWL /ˌsɪməˈlærəti/ *noun* (*pl.* **-ies**) **1** [U, sing.] the state of being like sb/sth but not exactly the same SYN RESEMBLANCE: **~ (of A and B)** *Products can be grouped according to the similarity of their marketing requirements.* ◇ **~ between A and B** *Moore et al. reported a striking similarity between the two groups.* ◇ **~ to sb/sth** *Ives's work is said to bear a certain similarity to that of writers such as Borges.* ◇ **~ in sth** *These so-called 'global consumers' often share a degree of similarity in tastes and interests.* OPP DIFFERENCE (1), DISSIMILARITY **2** [C] a feature that things or people have that makes them like each other: **~ between A and B** *Some kinds of similarities between languages are in fact due to chance.* ◇ **~ in/of sth** *There are similarities in the strategies used.* ◇ **~ to/with sb/sth** *The school has many similarities to New York City schools.* OPP DIFFERENCE (1), DISSIMILARITY

simi·lar·ly AWL /ˈsɪmələli; *NAmE* ˈsɪmələrli/ *adv.* **1** in almost the same way: *Competitors may enter the market with similarly low prices, but offering higher levels of service.* ◇ *The longer the history of aggression, the more likely an individual will behave similarly in the future.* ◇ *Behind this category is a similarly sized grouping of third-tier cities.* **2** used to say that two facts, actions or statements are like each other: *These winds form the Amazon rainforest by bringing moisture-laden air from the Atlantic Ocean. Similarly, the Congo rainforest forms where air from the Indian Ocean brings moisture.*

sim·ile /ˈsɪməli/ *noun* [C, U] a word or phrase that compares sth to sth else, using the words *like* or *as*, for example *a face like a mask* or *as white as snow*; the use of such words and phrases: *Parables, metaphors and similes formed an important part of the Buddha's teaching repertoire.* ◇ *The following discussion of simile is based mainly on Croft and Cruse (2004).* ➲ *compare* METAPHOR

S

sim·ple /ˈsɪmpl/ *adj.* (**sim·pler**, **sim·plest**) (You can also use **more simple** and **most simple**.) **1** not complicated; easy to understand or do: *A simple example demonstrates the relevance of this approach.* ◇ *This concept is not easy to explain in simple terms.* ◇ *Molecular techniques offer relatively simple ways to detect this mutation.* ◇ **it is ~ to do sth** *It is simplest to think of a rise in the real interest rate as reducing productivity.* **2** [usually before noun] consisting of only a few parts; not complicated in structure: *Harmful toxins may be carried by simple organisms like bacteria and fungi, as well more complex ones like spiders and snakes.* ◇ *Other scientists experimented with the use of steam to operate simple machines.* HELP In grammar, a **simple** sentence is one that has only one verb. **3** basic or plain without anything extra or unnecessary: *She lived in seclusion, wore coarse clothing and ate simple food.* ◇ *He presents a people whose material life may be very simple but whose theology is abstract and sophisticated.* **4** used before a noun to emphasize that it is exactly that and nothing else: *The simple fact that there are similarities does not necessarily mean that two languages belong in the same subgroup.* ◇ *It is difficult for historians to reconstruct what actually happened in the past for the simple reason that the events of history can never be proven.* **5** (*grammar*) used to describe the present or past tense of a verb that is formed without using an auxiliary verb, as in *She loves him* (= the simple present tense) or *He arrived late* (= the simple past tense): *To speakers of South Asian English, 'wanting' may sound more natural than the simple present.* ➲ *compare* PERFECT¹ (6), PROGRESSIVE¹ (5) ➲ *see also* SIMPLY IDM *see* PURE

▸ SIMPLE + NOUN **example, case • way, method, approach • process, procedure • system • rule • measure, test • matter • idea • question • solution, answer • explanation • terms** *Kepler had derived elegantly simple rules to predict the motions of the planets.* | **model • form • structure** *In the earliest, simplest form of society, both the boat and the net are commonly owned by everyone in the village.*

▸ ADVERB + SIMPLE **relatively, comparatively • quite, rather, fairly, reasonably, somewhat • apparently, seemingly • very, extremely, particularly • remarkably** *The solution is remarkably simple, although deriving it is not.*

sim·pli·city /sɪmˈplɪsəti/ *noun* [U] **1** the quality of being easy to understand or use: *For the sake of simplicity, I will concentrate mainly on two-dimensional examples.* ◇ **~ of sth** *Despite the great simplicity of this approach, it has proven to be extremely successful.* **2** (*approving*) the quality of being natural and plain or not complicated in design: *The urban designs of Frank Lloyd Wright reflected the modernist taste for purity and simplicity in design.* ◇ **~ of sth** *Missing the peace and simplicity of his hometown, Buddhadasa returned to the south.*

sim·pli·fi·ca·tion /ˌsɪmplɪfɪˈkeɪʃn/ *noun* **1** [U] **~ (of sth)** the process of making sth less complicated, or easier to do or understand: *Lulu and Berhane call for further simplification of the questionnaire.* **2** [C] a change that makes a problem, statement, system, etc. less complicated or easier to understand or do: *The theory presented here includes some major simplifications.*

sim·plify /ˈsɪmplɪfaɪ/ *verb* (**sim·pli·fies**, **sim·pli·fy·ing**, **sim·pli·fied**, **sim·pli·fied**) **1 ~ sth** to make sth less complicated, or easier to do or understand: *Engineers sought to simplify work processes to improve product quality and reduce cycle times.* ◇ *To simplify matters, we shall assume there are no limits on the number of fish in the pond.* ◇ *The determination of blood glucose levels has been greatly simplified due to the development of glucose biosensors.* **2 ~ sth (to sth)** (*mathematics*) to rewrite an EQUATION in its simplest form by, for example, gathering common terms together and cancelling repeated terms where appropriate: *We can simplify the expression by dividing both sides by y and we are left with dx = dt.*

sim·plis·tic /sɪmˈplɪstɪk/ *adj.* (*disapproving*) treating complicated issues and problems as if they were much simpler than they really are: *Much of the existing literature on relationships has taken a rather simplistic view of conflict.* ◇ **it is ~ to do sth** *It is too simplistic to suggest that all environmental degradation can be traced back to the explosion of the human population.* ■ **sim·plis·tic·al·ly** /sɪmˈplɪstɪkli/ *adv.*: *Since rivers flow into the sea, an observer might simplistically conclude that the global sea level must be rising continuously.*

simp·ly /ˈsɪmpli/ *adv.* **1** used to emphasize how basic sth is SYN JUST¹ (6): *In literary theory, this term may simply mean the 'theory of criticism'.* ◇ *Some of Orwell's modern critics argue that he was simply wrong about the effect of technology (Huber, 1994).* ◇ **(not) ~ a matter of sth** *Living standards are not simply a matter of material goods.* **2** in a way that is easy to understand: **~ put** *Simply put, sociology was to be the science of society.* ◇ **put ~** *Put simply, different human experiences in different regions of the world result in differences in regional consciousness and culture.* ◇ **to put it ~** *To put it simply, democracy implies a process of participation in which all are considered equal.* **3** used to introduce a summary or an explanation of sth that you have just said or done: *Quite simply, maps are an efficient means of portraying and communicating spatial data.* **4** in a way that is natural and plain: *He was committed to living simply and helping the poor.*

simu·late AWL /ˈsɪmjuleɪt/ *verb* **1 ~ sth** to create particular conditions that exist in real life using a computer model, usually for study or training purposes: *An engineer can design a circuit and simulate its behaviour using a software package.* ◇ *A random weather model can be used to simulate given climatic conditions.* **2 ~ sth** to copy the appearance or character of sth: *Rain is simulated by water dripping through small holes from a water container.*

simu·la·tion AWL /ˌsɪmjuˈleɪʃn/ *noun* [C, U] **~ (of sth)** a situation in which a particular set of conditions is created artificially in order to study or experience sth that could really exist: *Computer simulations show how galaxies could grow in a variety of different model universes.* ◇ *The cost of running large simulations may be very high.* ◇ *Other studies focused on the modelling and simulation of potential climate change.*

sim·ul·tan·eous /ˌsɪmlˈteɪniəs; *NAmE* ˌsaɪmlˈteɪniəs/ *adj.* happening or done at the same time as sth else: *Current technology permits the simultaneous analysis of tens of thousands of genes.* ◇ **~ with sth** *Causes precede (or are at least simultaneous with) their effects.* ■ **sim·ul·tan·eity** /ˌsɪmltəˈneɪəti; *NAmE* ˌsaɪmltəˈniːəti/ *noun* [U] **~ (of sth)** *For Wagenfuhr, the simultaneity of event, transmission and reception was the characteristic feature of television.*

ˌsimulˌtaneous eˈquations *noun* [pl.] (*mathematics*) EQUATIONS involving two or more unknown quantities that have the same values in each equation: *Linear simultaneous equations can be solved by using algebraic manipulation to eliminate one of the variables.*

sim·ul·tan·eous·ly /ˌsɪmlˈteɪniəsli; *NAmE* ˌsaɪmlˈteɪniəsli/ *adv.* at the same time as sth else: *Elections for both chambers of the parliament occur simultaneously.* ◇ **~ with sth** *Major scientific discoveries and technological innovations emerged simultaneously with capitalism.*

sin¹ /sɪn/ *noun* **1** [C] a crime against God or against a religious or moral law: *The woman apparently stated, 'I am innocent and have committed no sin.'* **2** [U] the act of breaking a religious or moral law: *With the confession of sin comes the recognition that God forgives sin.*

sin² *abbr.* (*mathematics*) (in writing) SINE

since[1] /sɪns/ *prep.* (usually used with the present perfect or past perfect tense) from a time in the past until a later past time; until now: *The UK has been a Member State since 1973.* ◇ *Estimates indicate that 2 million people have emigrated from the country since independence.* ◇ **~ doing sth** *This was the first conference organized by the association since changing its name.* ◇ **~ then** *Little progress has been made since then.* ◇ **ever ~** *Ever since the Industrial Revolution, many approaches have been tried to maximize industrial productivity.* HELP Use **for**, not **since**, with a period of time: *The company has been active in this market for ten years.* ◇ ~~*since ten years*~~ ➲ language bank *at* TIME[1]

since[2] /sɪns/ *conj.* **1** (used with the present perfect, past perfect or simple present tense in the main clause) from an event in the past until a later past event; until now: *It is now sixty years since the last book focusing exclusively on his life and career.* ◇ **ever ~** *Pathogens have surely been evolving in humans ever since humans first appeared as a separate species.* **2** because; as: *Since capitalism is an economic system, understanding capitalism requires some knowledge of economics.* ➲ language bank *at* BECAUSE

since[3] /sɪns/ *adv.* (used with the present perfect or past perfect tense) **1** from a time in the past until a later past time; until now: *Strachey was not, ultimately, a great biographer, but the art of biography has never been quite the same since.* ◇ **ever ~** *This policy was condemned at the time, and has been ever since, as completely irrational.* **2** at a time after a particular time in the past: *The strategy was put in place by the marketing director, who has since left the company.*

sin·cere /sɪn'sɪə(r); *NAmE* sɪn'sɪr/ *adj.* (*superlative* **sincerest**, no *comparative*) **1** (of feelings, beliefs or behaviour) showing what a person really thinks, believes or feels SYN GENUINE (2): *These initiatives reflected a sincere attempt to improve living conditions for the poor.* **2 ~ (in sth)** (of a person) saying only what you really think, believe or feel SYN HONEST (2): *Some colonialists were undoubtedly sincere in their belief that they were bringing civilization to the places they colonized.* ■ **sin·cer·ity** /sɪn'serəti/ *noun* [U] **~ (of sth)** *This was an attempt to demonstrate the sincerity of the policy of 'peaceful coexistence' with the west.*

sin·cere·ly /sɪn'sɪəli; *NAmE* sɪn'sɪrli/ *adv.* in a way that shows what you really feel or think about sb/sth: *He sincerely believed that it would be wrong to participate.*

sine /saɪn/ *noun* (*abbr.* **sin**) (*mathematics*) the RATIO of the length of the side opposite one of the angles in a RIGHT-ANGLED triangle that are less than 90° to the length of the longest side: *The mathematics of navigation uses trigonometry, which requires an accurate knowledge of the sine, cosine and tangent of an angle.* ➲ *compare* COSINE, TANGENT

sing /sɪŋ/ *verb* (**sang** /sæŋ/, **sung** /sʌŋ/) [I, T] to make musical sounds with your voice in the form of a song: *A well-educated Athenian man did not just exercise in the gymnasium, but was also able to sing and dance well.* ◇ **~ sth** *There were reports that officers joined with students in singing revolutionary songs on the streets.*
IDM **sing the praises of sb/sth** to express your approval or admiration for sb/sth: *The president sang the praises of New York City's firefighters.* ◇ *Ex-radicals of the thirties were now singing the praises of big business and capitalism.*

sing·er /'sɪŋə(r)/ *noun* a person who sings, or whose job is singing, especially in public: *Yam began her career as an opera singer in the 1920s.*

sing·ing /'sɪŋɪŋ/ *noun* [U] the activity of making musical sounds with your voice: *Patients reported that playing music or singing gave them pleasure, but also a feeling of peace and quiet.*

sin·gle[1] /'sɪŋgl/ *adj.* **1** [only before noun] only one: *In medieval Wales, there was a single word for 'language' and 'nation'.* ◇ *By 2008, 15 countries and over 300 million consumers used this single currency.* ◇ *Fungi grow as single cells (yeasts) or as hyphae (filamentous fungi).* **2** [only before noun] used to emphasize that you are referring to one particular person or thing on its own: *Despite some myths or beliefs, no single factor has been pinpointed as the cause of aggression.* ◇ **~ most...** *Language is probably the single most important human achievement.* ◇ **every ~** *It may not always be necessary to vaccinate every single member of the population.* **3** (of a person) not married or having a romantic relationship with sb: *During the late nineteenth and early twentieth centuries, single women were the traditional carers, particularly for parents.* ◇ *More people were choosing to remain single and fewer were having children (McRae, 1999).* **4** [only before noun] intended to be used by only one person: *Nurse the patient in a single room with en suite facilities if possible.* ➲ *compare* DOUBLE[1] (4)

sin·gle[2] /'sɪŋgl/ *verb*
PHR V ˌ**single sb/sth** ˈ**out** to choose sb/sth from a group for special attention: *In his book, Weber singles out three main types of social authority: traditional, legal and charismatic.* ◇ **~ for sth** *Singling out an individual for attention can be embarrassing to the person concerned.* ◇ **~ as sb/sth** *The in-house training of a new health care assistant was often singled out by respondents as a major challenge.*

ˌ**single** ˈ**currency** *noun* a type of monetary union in which all the member countries use the same currency HELP The **single currency** or **single European currency** can be used to refer to the system of money called the EURO that was introduced between 1999 and 2002 and is now used in many European countries: *The introduction of the single currency had a number of practical implications for companies operating across European borders.*

ˌ**single** ˈ**market** *noun* [usually sing.] (*economics*) a group of countries that have few or no controls on the movement of goods, money and people between the members of the group: *It could be argued that a single market requires a single currency; otherwise, currency fluctuations will form internal barriers.* HELP **The single market** (or **the Single Market**) is often used to refer to the European single market, which came into effect on 1 January 1993: *The proposal is a logical step in support of the single market and European financial integration.*

ˌ**single** ˈ**parent** *noun* a person who takes care of their child or children without a husband, wife or partner: *A quarter of families with dependent children in the UK are headed by a single parent.* ◇ **+ noun** *Low-income and single-parent families are more likely to have a smoker in the home.*

sin·gly /'sɪŋgli/ *adv.* separately; one at a time SYN INDIVIDUALLY: *Leaves can occur singly at each node, in pairs, or in groups of three or more.* ◇ *Socio-economic deprivation and endemic infections can singly or together make the persistence of a disease more likely.*

sin·gu·lar[1] /'sɪŋgjələ(r)/ *noun* [sing.] (*grammar*) a form of a noun or verb that refers to one person or thing: *The singular of 'bacteria' is 'bacterium'.* ◇ **in the ~** *Countable nouns cannot occur in the singular without a determiner.* ➲ *compare* PLURAL[1]

sin·gu·lar[2] /'sɪŋgjələ(r)/ *adj.* **1** (*grammar*) connected with or having the form of a noun or verb that refers to one person or thing: *a singular noun/pronoun* ◇ *The same pattern holds for the second person singular forms.* ➲ *compare* PLURAL[2] (1) **2** especially great or obvious SYN OUTSTANDING (1): *His singular contribution to Tory thinking was a genuine concern about social deprivation.*

S

3 (*mathematics*, *physics*) connected with a singularity: *The term 'Big Bang' suggests that a sudden explosion occurred at a singular point in space-time.*

sin·gu·lar·ity /ˌsɪŋɡjuˈlærəti/ *noun* (*pl.* -ies) **1** [U] (*formal*) the quality of sth/sb that makes them unusual, strange or UNIQUE: *For all his efforts to join in, inside he cannot shake off the sense of his singularity.* **2** [C] (*mathematics*, *physics*) a point at which a mathematical function or physical quantity takes an INFINITE value: *Either side of the singularity, the function has opposite signs.* HELP A **singularity** occurs especially in SPACE-TIME when matter is infinitely dense, such as at the centre of a BLACK HOLE.

sink[1] /sɪŋk/ *verb* (**sank** /sæŋk/, **sunk** /sʌŋk/) or (*less frequent* **sunk, sunk**) **1** [I] to go down below the surface or towards the bottom of a liquid or soft substance: *1 517 people died when the British liner Titanic sank on April 14, 1912.* ◇ **~ to sth** *Cooled surface water sinks to the bottom, forcing bottom water upwards.* **2** [T] **~ sth** to damage a boat or ship so that it goes below the surface of the sea, etc: *In one month alone, November 1942, 134 merchant ships were sunk by the enemy.* **3** [I] (of an object) to move slowly downwards: *The foundations of the building were starting to sink.* **4** [I] **~ (to sth)** to decrease in amount, volume, strength, etc: *Foreign trade sank to a very low level.*
PHR V **ˌsink ˈin** | **ˌsink ˈinto sth** to go down into another substance through the surface: *Most of this new oceanic crust eventually sinks back into the mantle.* **ˈsink into sth** to go gradually into a less active, happy or pleasant state: *Mazarin had allowed the navy to sink into decay.* **ˌsink sth ˈinto sth** to spend a lot of money on a business or an activity, for example in order to make money from it in the future: *Many investors sank their life savings into the company.*

sink[2] /sɪŋk/ *noun* **1** a large open container that has TAPS to supply water and that you use for washing dishes in: *The water that drains from a kitchen sink or bathtub rotates every few seconds and flows fast.* **2** (*technical*) a body or process which acts to absorb or remove energy or a particular COMPONENT from a system: *Carbon dioxide serves as a good heat sink for thermally unstable compounds.* ◇ *Added to the natural sources and sinks, human activities have a significant impact on the global carbon cycle.* OPP SOURCE[1] (1)

S

sis·ter /ˈsɪstə(r)/ *noun* a girl or woman who has the same mother and father as another person: *He settled in Dove Cottage with his sister Dorothy in December 1799.* ◇ *She does not want to follow her older sister who got married at the age of 14.* ◇ *Loretta was working part-time to help her mother support her younger brother and sister.* ➲ *see also* SIBLING

sit /sɪt/ *verb* (**sit·ting, sat, sat** /sæt/) **1** [I] to rest your weight on your bottom, for example on/in a chair: *People with back pain should adopt good posture when sitting, standing and walking.* ◇ **+ adv./prep.** *Sitting on a low bench is more comfortable for those not used to sitting on the floor.* ◇ **+ adj.** *The traditional posture for meditation is to sit cross-legged.* ◇ **~ doing sth** *Students have been passive recipients of knowledge as they sit listening to teachers.* **2** [T] **~ sb + adv./prep.** to put sb in a sitting position: *Sit the patient upright in order to allow the blood cells to settle.* **3** [I] to be in a particular place: **+ adv./prep.** *In the Atlantic, this rise sits in the middle of the ocean between continents.* ◇ **+ adj.** *The plane can land and return the same day, meaning that it does not need to sit idle.* **4** [I] to have an official position as sth or as a member of sth: **~ on/in sth** *He sits on the editorial boards of several academic journals.* ◇ **~ as sth** *Sir Christopher Slade sat as a judge of the Chancery Division between 1975 and 1982.* **5** [I] (of a parliament, committee, court of law, etc.) to meet in order to do official business: *When Parliament is sitting, the monarch receives daily reports on parliamentary proceedings.* **6** [T, I] to do an exam: **~ sth** (*BrE*) *An individual may be asked to provide evidence of study such as submitting coursework or sitting a written examination.* ◇ **~ for sth** (*especially NAmE*) *Dobbs sat for a research scholarship in science at Cambridge.*
IDM **sit comfortably, easily, well, etc. (with sth)** to seem right, natural, suitable, etc. in a particular situation: *Neither alternative sits altogether comfortably with traditional theological doctrines.*
PHR V **ˌsit ˈdown** to move from a standing position to a sitting position: *Fast food makes it unnecessary for members of a family to sit down to a meal together.* **ˌsit ˈdown and do sth** to give sth time and attention in order to try to solve a problem or achieve sth: *There must be some forum where policymakers can sit down and discuss studies or research results.* **ˌsit ˈin (on sth)** to attend a meeting, class, etc. in order to listen to or learn from it rather than to take an active part: *The child's mother did not sit in on the interview.* **ˌsit ˈup** to be in or move yourself into a sitting position, rather than lying down or leaning back: *Patients with airway and breathing problems may prefer to sit up as this will make breathing easier.*

site AWL /saɪt/ *noun* **1** a place where sth has happened or that is used for sth: *Tourists flock to such archaeological sites as the Parthenon.* ◇ **~ of sth** *The rabies virus takes weeks to get from the site of infection (usually a dog bite) to the brain.* ◇ **+ noun** *Site visits were timed for low tide and consequently temperature measurements were not taken at the same time each day.* **2** a place where a building, town, etc. was, is or will be located: **~ (of sth)** *In 324, Constantine began to build a new city on the site of a small Greek city called 'Byzantion'.* ◇ **~ for sth** *The Catholic bishops asked for another site for the church.* ◇ **on ~** *Engineers on site unfortunately made some basic errors.* **3** a place on the Internet where a company, an organization, a university, etc. puts information SYN WEBSITE: *Most participants (85.9%) reported visiting these sites several times per week.*

situ ➲ IN SITU

situ·ate /ˈsɪtʃueɪt/ *verb* **1 ~ sth + adv./prep.** to build or place sth in a particular position: *The narrator of this tale does not situate the events in a particular locality.* ◇ *There is a tendency to situate toxic waste sites and poor and minority communities adjacent to one another.* **2 ~ sth + adv./prep.** to consider how an idea, event, etc. is related to other things that influence your view of it: *To develop this proposition, it is important to situate it in the context of critical race theory.* ◇ *Chu situates her work in relation to early twentieth-century discourses about governance, law, nationalism and statehood.*

situ·ated /ˈsɪtʃueɪtɪd/ *adj.* [not before noun] **1 + adv./prep.** in a particular place or position: *The bulk of Russia's industrial workers were employed in factories, which were often situated far from towns.* ◇ *Situated in the Indian Ocean, Christmas Island is closer to Asia than to Australia.* **2 + adv./prep. (to do sth)** (of a person, an organization, etc.) in a particular situation or in particular circumstances: *Some citizens, especially those who represent important corporations and interest groups, are well situated to influence elected politicians.*

situ·ation /ˌsɪtʃuˈeɪʃn/ *noun* **1** all the circumstances and things that are happening at a particular time and in a particular place: *There were changes of policy as the political situation changed.* ◇ *These problem-solving skills can be applied to real-life situations.* ◇ **in a... ~** *They felt that what had been asked of them placed them in a difficult situation.* ◇ **the ~ where/in which...** *This is intended to deal with the situation in which the previous owner has abandoned the land.* **2** the area or place where sth is located: *Corals flourish where water movement is moderate and in situations close to the open sea.* ◇ *Canterbury* *also attracted royalty, in part because of its convenient situation en route from the Channel ports to London.*

▸ ADJECTIVE + SITUATION **current, present • particular, specific, certain • similar • different • difficult • complex • dangerous, precarious • stressful • real, actual • real-life • ideal • economic • financial • political** *Box 8.6 presents an overview of the current situation in Canada.*

▸ VERB + SITUATION **describe • apply to, refer to • consider • assess, analyse • imagine • create, lead to • change • remedy, rectify • improve • face • deal with, respond to, address, handle • avoid** *The population increase, by flooding the labour market, created a situation where employers could afford to pay less.*

▸ SITUATION + VERB **arise, exist • change • improve • deteriorate, worsen** *In the event, such a situation rarely arose.*

THESAURUS

situation • circumstances • position • conditions • the case *noun*

These words are all used to talk about the way that things are.

- a situation **where/in which** ...
- a situation/circumstances/a position/conditions **of** sth
- **in a...** situation/position/condition
- **in...** circumstances/conditions
- **it is the case that...**
- **This is** the situation/position/case.
- the **current/present** situation/circumstances/conditions
- sb's/the **economic/financial/social** situation/circumstances/position/conditions
- to **lead to** a situation/condition...
- a situation/circumstances/conditions **lead(s) to sth/arise(s)**
- the situation/the position/conditions **deteriorate(s)/worsen(s)**

- **Situation** is the most general of these words, used to talk about all the things that are happening at a particular time and in a particular place; **position** often refers to the situation of a particular person, especially when it affects what they can and cannot do; **the case** is the true situation: *This has led to a situation of lawlessness.* ◇ *Situations arise in which it is important to have this information.* ◇ *This put him and his colleagues in a difficult position.* ◇ *It appears to be the case that scores are distorted.*
- The **circumstances** that affect an event are the facts surrounding it; the **conditions** that affect it are often physical ones, such as the weather. A person's **circumstances** are their financial situation; the **conditions** they live in refer to things such as the quality and amount of food or shelter they have: *Some organizations are less focused on such strategies in the face of current economic circumstances.* ◇ *Living in poor social conditions in childhood is associated with poorer health in later life.*

situational /ˌsɪtʃuˈeɪʃənl/ *adj.* [usually before noun] connected with or changing according to the particular situation that exists: *There may be a number of situational factors determining purchase behaviour, such as brand availability (Dick and Basu, 1994).* ◇ *All the learners get are sentence fragments deprived of their situational context.*

six /sɪks/ *number* 6 HELP There are examples of how to use numbers at the entry for **five**.

size[1] /saɪz/ *noun* **1** [C, U] how large or small sth is: **~ (of sth)** *The particles have an average size of 20 nm (20 billionths of a metre).* ◇ *The flexibility of a material is determined by the shape and size of the cross-section.* ◇ **in ~** *Species that are similar in size may differ in feeding behaviour.* ◇ **of... ~** *In 1850 there were only three cities with populations over 1 million people, but by 2000 there were cities of this size in all parts of the world.* ◇ **of all sizes** *Populations of all sizes may suffer in variable environments.* ◇ **the same ~** *In one industry there are 100 firms, all about the same size, whereas in the other industry there are only four firms.* ➲ *see also* EFFECT SIZE **2** [U] the large amount or extent of sth: *Visitors to the ruins of Knossos are dazzled by its size and complexity.* ◇ **~ of sth** *There was public concern at the size of some compensation payments given to directors.* **3** [C] one of a number of standard measurements in which clothes, shoes and other goods are made and sold: *The merchants' primary concern was speed of delivery as they did not want to stock a huge range of different sizes themselves.* **4 -size, -sized** (in adjectives) having the size mentioned: *They are an entrepreneurial nation, with many small and medium-size businesses as well as large multinationals.* ◇ *The sample is divided into four, approximately equal-sized groups.*

IDM **one size fits 'all** (*rather informal*) used to refer to the idea that the same solution or method can be applied in every case, usually when this idea is wrong: *As organizations and consumers become more diverse, the search for a 'one size fits all' marketing solution will prove self-defeating.*

▸ ADJECTIVE + SIZE **small • large • average • different • similar • relative** *When the population size is small, natural selection becomes less efficient at weeding out such characteristics.*

▸ NOUN + SIZE **sample, set • population • family, household • group • class • market • body • particle** *Once body size is taken into account, whales have the smallest relative brain size among all mammals.*

▸ VERB + SIZE **have • reach, achieve • increase • reduce, decrease • estimate • measure, calculate, assess • be affected by, be limited by, be determined by** *The size of the adult is determined by the size the larva reaches before pupation.*

▸ SIZE + VERB **increase • decrease • vary, change • range** *'Villa' was used to designate territories whose size might range from one hundred to several thousand hectares.*

▸ VERB + IN SIZE **vary, range, differ • increase, grow • double • be reduced, decrease, shrink** *Eggs vary enormously in size among different animals.*

size[2] /saɪz/ *verb* [usually passive] **(be) sized + adv./prep.** to have or be given a particular size: *High sales force turnover can be a signal that a sales force is not sized correctly.*

size·able (*also* **siz·able**) /ˈsaɪzəbl/ *adj.* fairly large SYN CONSIDERABLE: *In the USA, the Hispanic population and the black population together represent a sizeable proportion of the total population.* ◇ *There are now some 3.5 million Turks in Germany, making them a very sizeable minority.*

skel·etal /ˈskelətl/ *adj.* **1** [usually before noun] connected with the skeleton of a person or an animal: *Tendons transfer contraction forces from skeletal muscle to bone.* **2** that exists only in a basic form, as an outline: *The author offers only a skeletal account of this social phenomenon.*

skel·eton /ˈskelɪtn/ *noun* **1** a structure made of bone or other hard material supporting or containing the body of an animal or plant: *Archaeologists found a mass grave near Athens containing seventeen skeletons with iron collars around the necks.* ◇ **~ of sb/sth** *A large proportion of global carbon is locked away as calcium carbonate in the shells and skeletons of marine organisms.* **2** [usually sing.] **~ (of sth)** the main structure that supports a building, etc: *The two-by-four skeleton of timber is typically clothed with plywood.* **3** [usually sing.] **~ (of sth)** the basic outline of a plan or piece of writing to which more details can be added later: *The skeleton of the original literary work can become the skeleton of a film.*

skep·tic, skep·tical, skep·ti·cism (*NAmE*) = SCEPTIC, SCEPTICAL, SCEPTICISM

sketch[1] /sketʃ/ *verb* **1** [T] **~ sth (out)** to give a general description of sth, giving only the basic facts SYN OUTLINE[1] (1): *The approach to genre sketched out in this article of course raises some questions of its own.* **2** [T, I] **~ (sth)** to make a quick drawing of sth: *Sketching the diagram makes the problem easier to solve.*

sketch[2] /sketʃ/ *noun* **1 ~ (of sth)** a short report or description that gives only basic details about sth: *This article first provides a brief sketch of the theoretical background.* ◇ *It would take another book to explain it in detail; what follows is only a rough sketch.* **2** a simple picture that is drawn quickly and does not have many details: *These paintings were intended as sketches for more finished pictures to be done later.* ◇ **~ of sth** *a rough sketch of a human face* **3** a short funny scene on television, in the theatre, etc: *He loved dancing, acting, writing sketches and performing in them.*

skies *pl. of* SKY

skil·ful (*US* **skill·ful**) /ˈskɪlfl/ *adj.* having or showing the ability to do sth well, especially sth that needs a particular ability or special training: *Once the driver has become more skilful, the difficulty of combining actions disappears.* ◇ *Skilful questioning is important so that relevant information is obtained on the patient's condition.* ■ **skil·ful·ly** (*US* **skill·ful·ly**) /ˈskɪlfəli/ *adv.*: *Taillon has skillfully used a variety of primary sources.*

skill /skɪl/ *noun* **1** [C] a particular ability or type of ability: *Workers need incentives to acquire new skills.* ◇ *New media require digital skills that not all people master to the same degree.* ◇ **~ of (doing) sth** *Children with this disorder are late in developing the skills of feeding, walking and dressing.* ◇ **~ to do sth** *Some individuals lack the necessary skills to set up and manage a business.* **2** [U] the ability to do sth well, especially sth that is difficult for most people: *Special training enables some people to see things others miss: it takes skill to use a microscope.* ◇ **~ in/at (doing) sth** *He was a courtier known for his great learning, his skill in the arts and his love affairs.* ◇ *The maiden Arachne, who boasts of her skill at weaving, is changed by Athena into a spider.*

▸ ADJECTIVE + SKILL **good • basic, general • special, specialized, specialist • necessary, requisite • transferable • social, interpersonal • cognitive • motor • practical • analytical • managerial • clinical** *Others suffer from a poor diet because they have never been taught basic cooking skills.* | **great • technical • professional** *Kersh's ethnographic method was more successful but requires great skill to implement effectively.*

▸ NOUN + SKILL **communication • language • critical thinking • management • leadership • coping • problem-solving • parenting • life** *Being able to interpret and evaluate data is a key life skill.*

▸ VERB + SKILL **have, possess • demonstrate • use, apply, exercise, utilize • develop, learn, acquire, gain • improve, enhance • practise • master • teach • provide • require, need, involve • lack** *Learning these skills is a process that takes time.*

▸ SKILL + NOUN **acquisition, development • set, mix • base • shortage** *To accomplish these new objectives, a different skill set is required of the sales manager.*

▸ SKILLS+ NOUN **level • training, development** *Investment in human skills development is a primary determinant of industrial competitiveness.*

skilled /skɪld/ *adj.* **1** having enough ability, experience and knowledge to be able to do sth well SYN EXPERT[2] (2): *They were skilled horsemen and fierce warriors who terrified their enemies.* ◇ *Haider and Frensch have shown that, as we become more skilled, we learn to ignore redundant information.* ◇ **~ in/at (doing) sth** *Craftsmen in south-eastern Europe and western Asia were already skilled at smelting and casting copper.* **2** having special experience or training in doing a particular job: *The contract system is sometimes used to hire electricians, plumbers and other highly skilled workers.* ◇ *The industry has capitalized on the availability of skilled labour at low cost.* OPP UNSKILLED **3** (of a job) needing special abilities or training: *Assembly remained a highly skilled job requiring experienced watchmakers.* OPP UNSKILLED

skill·ful (*NAmE*) = SKILFUL

skim /skɪm/ *verb* **(-mm-) 1** [I, T] to read sth quickly in order to find a particular point or the main points: **~ through/over sth** *Certain behaviour can be performed with little if any focused attention (for example, skimming through a magazine).* ◇ **~ sth** *The students were shown the verb they needed was related to 'order', and were asked to skim the entry for this word.* **2** [T] **~ sth** to remove a substance such as fat from the surface of a liquid: *The surface is skimmed to remove any scum which may float at the top.* **3** [I, T, no passive] to move quickly and lightly over a surface, not touching it or only touching it occasionally: **~ along/over, etc. sth** *Just before impact, one car was lifted up on curved rails and skimmed over the top of the other.* ◇ **~ sth** (*figurative*) *Necessarily, this introduction only skims the surface of what could be said.*

skin /skɪn/ *noun* **1** [U, C] the layer of TISSUE that covers the body: *People apply sunscreen to protect their skin from UV radiation.* ◇ *Many sufferers develop dry skin and brittle nails.* ◇ **+ noun** *skin cancer/disease/conditions* ◇ *Height, like skin colour, has an important genetic component and is highly visible.* **2 -skinned** (in adjectives) having the type of skin mentioned: *'Ethiopian' was the ordinary Greek word for a dark-skinned person.* **3** [C, U] (often in compounds) the skin of a dead animal, with or without its fur, used for making things: *Textiles replaced animal skins as the material for clothing.* **4** [C, U] the outer layer of some fruits and vegetables: *Foods that should be consumed include brown rice, wholemeal breads, and fruit and vegetables that have edible skins.*

skip /skɪp/ *verb* **(-pp-) 1** [T] **~ sth** to not do sth that you usually do or should do: *A recent study shows that skipping breakfast can adversely affect cardiovascular health.* ◇ (*especially NAmE*) *Some youths periodically skip classes or miss school altogether for a day here and a day there.* **2** [T, I] to leave out sth that would normally be the next thing that you would do or read: **~ sth** *If time does not permit, some of the later sections in Chapter 4 can be skipped.* ◇ **~ over sth** *Because the results of their work are well known, it is tempting to skip over the details of how they reached their conclusions.* ◇ **~ to sth** *If you have answered 'No', please skip to question 11.*

sky /skaɪ/ *noun* (*pl.* **skies**) [C, U] the space above the earth that you can see when you look up, where clouds and the sun, moon and stars appear: *The Milky Way forms a band of light across the night sky.* ◇ *This accounts for the blue appearance of a cloudless sky well away from the sun's disc.* ◇ *Descending air is associated with clear skies.* ◇ **in the ~** *The weather was sunny, with no trace of clouds in the sky.* ◇ **+ noun** *Measurements were taken under stable sky conditions.*

slang /slæŋ/ *noun* [U] very informal words and expressions that are more common in spoken language, especially used by a particular group of people, for example, children, criminals, soldiers, etc: *Her fiction incorporates words from Arabic alongside English and Scottish street slang.* ◇ **+ noun** *The expression 'in country' was a slang term for the battle areas of Vietnam.*

slave /sleɪv/ *noun* **1** a person who is owned by another person and is forced to work for them: *Slaves were freed in*

S

the Danish and French colonies in 1848–9. ◇ **+ noun** *Slavery and the slave trade were thus widespread phenomena on several continents for centuries.* **2** a person who is so strongly influenced by sth that they cannot live without it, or cannot make their own decisions: **~ of sth** *Devotees of the movement were hopeless slaves of fashion.* ◇ **~ to sth** *While IT may have freed people from certain repetitive and tedious tasks, it has also made them slaves to their workstations.*

slav·ery /ˈsleɪvəri/ *noun* [U] **1** the state of being a slave: *He destroyed the city and sold the inhabitants into slavery.* OPP FREEDOM (3) **2** the practice of having slaves: *Between 1842 and 1854, slavery was abolished in Uruguay, Ecuador, Peru and Venezuela.*

sleep[1] /sliːp/ *verb* (**slept, slept** /slept/) [I] to rest with your eyes closed and your mind and body not active: *During her depressive episodes, she would sometimes spend the entire day watching television, eating and sleeping.* ◇ **+ adv./prep.** *Anthony has stated that he is not sleeping well.*

PHR V ˈ**sleep together** | ˈ**sleep with sb** to have sex with sb, especially sb you are not married to: *After Aphrodite slept with Anchises, she forbade him ever to boast of it.*

sleep[2] /sliːp/ *noun* **1** [U] the natural state of rest in which your eyes are closed and your mind and body are not active: *People vary in the amount of sleep they need.* ◇ *Irritability may be due to hunger, lack of sleep and other factors.* ◇ **go/get to ~** *When she wakes up in the night, it takes around 15 mins for her to go back to sleep.* ◇ **+ noun** *Use of technology allows clinicians to more easily track changes in sleep patterns over time.* **2** [sing.] a period of sleep: *Coleridge claimed to have fallen into an opium-induced sleep and awoken three hours later.*

slide[1] /slaɪd/ *verb* (**slid, slid** /slɪd/) **1** [I, T] to move easily over a surface while keeping contact with it; to make sth move in this way: **+ adv./prep.** *The water content must be sufficient for the particles to slide freely past each other.* ◇ *The slopes became unstable and slid down the mountainside.* ◇ **~ sth + adv./prep.** *First, slide the sling under the injured arm.* **2** [I] **+ adv./prep.** to change gradually to a worse condition or lower value: *Why do some new democracies slide backwards while others flourish?* ◇ *They hoped to rescue the company before it slid into insolvency.* ◇ *When the government abolished the managed exchange rate, the rupiah slid immediately to 2 755.*

slide[2] /slaɪd/ *noun* **1** [usually sing.] a change to a lower or worse condition: **~ into sth** *Governments are working together to prevent a slide into a global depression.* ◇ **~ in sth** *Nothing has arrested the slide in sales.* **2** a sudden fall of a large amount of rock or earth down a slope: *Where sediments are unstable, a relatively small disturbance can trigger a slide.* **3** a small piece of glass that sth is placed on so that it can be looked at under a MICROSCOPE: *The rock chip is then glued to a clean microscope slide.* ◇ *The tissue or cultured cell substrate is fixed to a glass slide.* **4** one page of an electronic PRESENTATION, that may contain text and images: *The patients could press a button to see the next slide.*

slight /slaɪt/ *adj.* (**slight·er, slight·est**) very small in degree: *The activity of the enzyme can be shut down by slight increases in temperature.* ◇ *Slight differences in procedures among laboratory technicians may also produce differences in results.* ◇ *With slight modifications, all 40 proposals submitted were approved.*

slight·ly /ˈslaɪtli/ *adv.* a little: *Every teacher of applied ethics approaches the task in a slightly different way.* ◇ *This suggests that murder rates were slightly higher at the beginning of the 20th century than the beginning of the 21st.* ◇ *The methodology varied slightly from that used in previous studies.* ◇ *After 60 days, the mass loss slightly increased to 10.2%.* ◇ *All participants were asked to fill in a slightly modified version of the questionnaire.*

slope[1] /sləʊp; *NAmE* sloʊp/ *noun* **1** [C, usually pl.] an area of land that is part of a mountain or hill: *Geological factors have great control on the form and development of rock slopes.* ◇ *Common sense suggests that steep slopes are more prone to landsliding than gentle slopes.* ◇ **on the slopes of sth** *Field investigations were conducted at a study site located on the slopes of Mt Fuji about 2 000 m above sea level.* **2** [C] a surface or piece of land that slopes: *Sampling was carried out at a site with a gentle slope.* ◇ **on a ~** *On a slope, water will move laterally under the influence of gravity.* **3** [sing., U] **~ (of sth)** the amount by which sth slopes: *The slope of a supply curve will depend on how sensitive it is to changes in price.* ◇ *If no weight loss is observed, the thermogram will have a slope of zero (i.e. a horizontal line).*

slope[2] /sləʊp; *NAmE* sloʊp/ *verb* [I] **(+ adv./prep.)** (of a surface or line) to be higher at one end than the other: *The field sloped down towards the south-east.* ◇ *Most price-volume relationships slope downwards, indicating that, as price rises, demand falls.*

slow[1] /sləʊ; *NAmE* sloʊ/ *adj.* (**slow·er, slow·est**) **1** not moving, acting or done quickly; taking a long time: *Their accounts indicate the slow pace of change in this field.* ◇ *Changing an organization's core beliefs is likely to be a slow process.* ◇ *Europe has had a considerably slower population growth rate than the world as a whole.* OPP FAST[1] (1) **2** hesitating to do sth; not doing sth immediately: **~ to do sth** *The BBC was slow to develop a robust independence from the state.* ◇ **~ in doing sth** *New transfers of finance to developing countries have been slow in coming.* OPP QUICK (2) ■ **slow·ness** *noun* [U] *The cost of storing information on disk is very low indeed and this compensates for its relative slowness.*

slow[2] /sləʊ; *NAmE* sloʊ/ *verb* [I, T] to go or to make sth/sb go at a slower speed or be less active: **~ (down/up)** *It now appears that rapid growth is slowing down.* ◇ **~ sth/sb down/up** *Different designs use one or other of these materials in the heart of the reactor core to slow the neutrons down.* ◇ **~ sth** *The pattern of China's growth has slowed the pace of poverty reduction.* OPP SPEED[2] ➲ *see also* SLOWDOWN (1)

slow[3] /sləʊ; *NAmE* sloʊ/ *adv.* (**slow·er, slow·est**) (used especially in the comparative and superlative forms, or in compounds) at a slow speed SYN SLOWLY: *They found that drivers who owned their own trucks drove slower.* ◇ *Caterpillars are slow-moving eating machines.*

slow·down /ˈsləʊdaʊn; *NAmE* ˈsloʊdaʊn/ *noun* a reduction in speed or activity: *The worldwide economic slowdown reduced demand for Russia's chief exports: oil and gas.* ◇ **~ in sth** *The new government in Slovakia orchestrated a slowdown in the speed of privatization there.*

slow·ly /ˈsləʊli; *NAmE* ˈsloʊli/ *adv.* at a slow speed; not quickly: *The importance of gas as an energy source has grown slowly.* ◇ *Child poverty started slowly increasing in the 1970s.* ◇ *Lizards were located by moving slowly through the habitat and scanning the ground and trees.*

IDM ˌ**slowly but** ˈ**surely**/ˈ**steadily** making slow but definite progress: *China's massive investment in infrastructure is moving this enormous nation forward slowly but steadily.*

small /smɔːl/ *adj.* (**small·er, small·est**) **1** not large in size, number, degree or amount: *The modern international business environment is dominated by a relatively small number of nations.* ◇ *To complete the project, the class is divided into small groups of five students.* ◇ *Small amounts of vitamins can have a huge effect on the body.* ◇ *Viruses*

S

are much smaller than cells. ◇ *GPS receivers have become small enough to be carried by just about everyone in cars and boats.* **2** [usually before noun] not doing business on a very large scale: *The figures for failure rates of small firms contrast dramatically with those for large firms.* ◇ *Attention focused upon identifying and helping small businesses with growth potential.* ◇ *Roughly five million small farmers grew cashews in this former British colony.* **3** not as big as sth else of the same kind: *Absorption of most nutrients occurs in the small intestine.* **4** young: *Anyone with small children knows how quickly and easily they can get into danger.* **5** [usually before noun] not written or printed as capitals: *Formulae representing undetermined positive integers will be represented by small letters in heavy type.* ■ **small·ness** *noun* [U] **~ (of sth)** *Measurement of the potential difference is complicated by the smallness of the current.* ◇ *Smallness is argued to provide flexibility in a firm's relations with other firms (Saxenian, 1994).* IDM see HOUR, GREAT, WAY, WONDER[2]

ˌsmall-ˈscale *adj.* **1** (of an organization or activity) not large in size or extent; limited in what it does: *a small-scale farmer/fishery* ◇ *Translating the achievements of previous small-scale studies into national-level policies is likely to prove challenging.* OPP LARGE-SCALE (1) **2** (of a map or model) drawn to a small scale so that not many details are shown: *The existing maps were too small-scale to outline the hazard zones with accuracy.* OPP LARGE-SCALE (2)

smell[1] /smel/ *noun* **1** [C, U] the quality of sth that people and animals sense through their noses: *Nausea without vomiting may result from fear and anxiety or may be a reaction to offensive smells.* ◇ **~ of sth** *This ester is largely responsible for the characteristic smell of a banana.* **2** [U] the ability to sense things with the nose: *Monkeys have a more sensitive sense of smell than humans.*

smell[2] /smel/ *verb* (**smelled, smelled**) (*BrE also* **smelt, smelt** /smelt/) **1** [I] to have a particular smell: *Chemicals that smell the same may have very differing structures.* ◇ **+ adj.** *The hospital environment should smell fresh and have no unpleasant odours.* ◇ **~ of sth** *The scented leaf geraniums can smell of apple, peppermint, cedar, rose and lemon.* **2** [T, no passive] (not used in the progressive tenses; often with *can* or *could*) **~ sth** to notice or recognize a particular smell: *At the time he could smell petrol and thought the car might ignite.*

S

smoke[1] /sməʊk; *NAmE* smoʊk/ *noun* [U] the grey, white or black cloud that is produced by sth burning: *Cigarette smoke contains several thousand components with diverse effects.* ◇ **~ from sth** *Research indicates that smoke from cooking fires can pose a major health hazard.*

smoke[2] /sməʊk; *NAmE* smoʊk/ *verb* **1** [T, I] **~ (sth)** to SUCK smoke from a cigarette, etc. into your mouth and let it out again: *He smokes 40 cigarettes per day.* ◇ *It was socially unacceptable for women to smoke pipes or cigars.* ◇ *Despite the risks, many women still smoke during pregnancy.* **2** [I] to use cigarettes, etc. in this way as a habit: *Have you ever smoked?* ◇ *He has smoked heavily for many years.*

smoker /ˈsməʊkə(r); *NAmE* ˈsmoʊkər/ *noun* a person who smokes TOBACCO regularly: *Heavy users of alcohol also tend to be heavy smokers and may have a poor diet.*

smok·ing /ˈsməʊkɪŋ; *NAmE* ˈsmoʊkɪŋ/ *noun* [U] the activity or habit of smoking cigarettes, etc: *More impulsive individuals often lack the ability to quit smoking.* ◇ *Smoking is the main risk factor for the development of many cancers.*

smooth[1] /smuːð/ *adj.* (**smooth·er, smooth·est**) **1** completely flat and even, without any holes or rough areas: *Platelets are normally discoid in shape with a smooth surface.* ◇ *Erosion reduced the underlying metamorphic rocks to a nearly smooth, flat plain.* OPP ROUGH (1) **2** happening or continuing without any problems: *The smooth functioning of a free market depends on political power.* ◇ *Most of the former British colonies experienced a relatively smooth transition to independence.* **3** (of a series of numbers or data) progressing in an even way or at a steady rate: *The rates move up and down in long, smooth curves that are visible only when traced over 100 years or more.* ◇ *Migration rates have shown a relatively smooth downward trend over the last two decades.* **4** (of movement) even and regular, without sudden stops and starts: *Road networks could be modified to create a smoother flow of traffic.* ■ **smooth·ness** *noun* [U] **~ (of sth)** *The plains ecosystem is unlike most similar grasslands in the world in the relative smoothness of its environmental gradients.*

smooth[2] /smuːð/ *verb* to make sth even and regular, without sudden stops, starts or changes: *The very large heat capacities of the ocean surface layers smooth seasonal temperature variations.*

PHR V **ˌsmooth sth ˈout** to remove differences between different examples of sth; to make problems or difficulties disappear: *One of the objectives of macroeconomic policy is to smooth out business cycle fluctuations.* ◇ *They help smooth out the difficulties their clients would otherwise face in dealing with foreign companies.* **ˌsmooth sth ˈover** to make problems or difficulties seem less important or serious: *Wilson appears willing to smooth over detail in order to make his points.*

smooth·ly /ˈsmuːðli/ *adv.* **1** without problems or difficulties: *Human societies rely on rules and conventions to ensure that they run smoothly.* **2** in an even way, without suddenly stopping and starting again: *Ideally, traffic should flow smoothly at the speed limit.*

snow /snəʊ; *NAmE* snoʊ/ *noun* [U] small soft white pieces of frozen water that fall from the sky in cold weather; this substance when it is lying on the ground: *Six inches of snow fell within two hours.* ◇ *Widespread melting of snow and ice and rising sea levels were reported.* ◇ **+ noun** *The key is the association between snow cover and glacier growth and decay.*

so[1] /səʊ; *NAmE* soʊ/ *adv.* **1** to such a great degree: *The story may not be quite so simple.* ◇ *The best way to appreciate why Mendel is so important is to review his experiments.* ◇ **~ ... (that)...** *The pace of economic transformation is so great that it has created a new world politics.* ◇ **~ ... as to do sth** *The gravity associated with black holes is so powerful as to be able to bring time to a complete standstill.* **2** very; extremely: *As so often happens, crisis forced change.* ◇ *The example of Greek democracy seemed so much better in theory than in practice.* ◇ *Like so many emperors before him, he had to defend the eastern border, which was threatened by the Persian Empire.* **3** used to refer back to sth that has already been mentioned: *If they cannot make an identification, they should say so.* ◇ **to do ~** *Many rich residents of Athens did not own land, as it was illegal for them to do so without special dispensation.* ◇ **in ~ doing** *The defendant returned to the flat and in so doing woke the victim.* **4 not ~ ... (as...)** (used in comparisons) not to the same degree: *The effect is not so strong as in reaction R2.* ◇ *Each firm is not so concerned about the economy-wide profit rate as it is about its own profit rate.* ◇ *Organizations use customer satisfaction questionnaires not so much to improve product or service quality but to monitor employees.* **5** also: *As incomes fall during a recession, so do taxes.* ◇ *As the campaign intensified, so, too, did Kennedy's rhetoric.* **6** used to show the size, amount or number of sth: *There are only so many jobs that can be created through research, development and design work.* **7** used when you are explaining how sth happened: *So it was that all those writers of the Romantic era felt, with Keats, that they 'must tell a tale of chivalry'.*

IDM ... or so used after sth such as a number or an amount to show that it is not exact: *The extent of changes in climate over the last 100 years or so is greater than was formerly believed.* **so as to do sth** with the intention of doing sth: *LEDs can be designed so as to produce coherent light with a very narrow bandwidth.* **so 'be it** (*formal*) used to show that you accept sth and will not try to change it or cannot change it: *Improvements are thus needed urgently, and if subsidies are necessary, so be it.* **ˌso much for 'sth** used to show that you have finished talking about sth: *So much for the similarities—now for a profound difference:...* **IDM** *see* FAR[1]

GRAMMAR POINT

so that • in order to • *to*-infinitive

- These phrases each express purpose. The ***to*-infinitive** and **in order to** are often used to explain the methods used in a study. In this context, passive forms are common: *Blood tests are used **to measure** the concentration of hormones.* ◇ *Additionally, **in order to reduce** heterogeneity, analyses were also performed in these subgroups...*
- **So that** is similar in meaning but is followed by a main clause (= with a subject and verb): *In this study, the interview questions were explicit **so that** there was little room for misinterpretation.* ◇ ***So that** the knowledge that is produced with public funds is available to all, employment contracts include the condition that...*

so[2] /səʊ; *NAmE* soʊ/ *conj.* **1** used to introduce the result of sth that has just been mentioned: *Major cities are often located near the sea, so they are vulnerable to sea level rises caused by global warming.* **2 ~ (that)...** with the result that: *Latin changed gradually so that it came to look like a different language.* **3 ~ (that)...** used to show the reason for or purpose of sth: *Digital circuits are designed so that each transistor operates as a switch.* ➲ language bank *at* PURPOSE **4** used to introduce the next step in a process: *So after the planning, there was a great deal of hard work to be done.* **5** used when stating that two events or situations are similar: *Just as states enact legislation, so too do non-state armed groups.*

ˌso-ˈcalled **AWL** *adj.* **1** [usually before noun] used to introduce the word that people usually use to describe sth: *In Sweden, the so-called 'Golden Age' of Gustav I ended in the mid-sixteenth century.* **2** [only before noun] used to show that you do not think that the word or phrase that is being used to describe sb/sth is appropriate: *So-called higher education is often just training people to become bureaucrats.*

so·cial /ˈsəʊʃl; *NAmE* ˈsoʊʃl/ *adj.* **1** [only before noun] connected with society and the way it is organized: *In recent decades, China has witnessed a host of economic, social and cultural changes.* ◇ *The social policies of the present are rooted in their historical origins.* ◇ *Social movements may play important roles in the expansion of democracy.* ➲ *see also* SOCIAL SCIENCE, SOCIAL SECURITY, SOCIAL SERVICES, SOCIAL WORK **2** [only before noun] connected with activities in which people meet each other for pleasure: *Human development is dependent on social interaction.* ◇ *People in their 50s are at a higher risk of lacking activities and social relations.* ◇ *It is recognized that personal and social networks can play a big part in terms of trust and belonging.* **3** [only before noun] connected with a person's position in society: *Women from all social classes consult the doctor more often than men do.* ◇ *Social inequalities in health in the UK persist despite attempts to reduce them.* **4** [only before noun] (*ecology*) (of animals) living naturally in groups, rather than alone: *Elephants are very social individuals.* ◇ *Human beings are social animals.*
▸ SOCIAL + NOUN **policy • context • order • world • theory • research • structure • cohesion • reality • norm • change • movement • justice • responsibility • institution** *Much social research is funded by organizations such as firms and government departments.* | **network • interaction • relation • life • world • relationship • environment** *The family provides the first social environment for the child.* | **class • status • group • mobility, movement • welfare • support • care • inequality • exclusion** *In a feudal society, people were defined by their social class and social mobility was extremely limited.*

ˌsocial ˈcapital *noun* [U] the networks of relationships among people who live and work in a particular society, enabling that society to function effectively: *One of Putnan's (1993) key indicators of social capital was membership in voluntary associations.* ◇ *Crucially, social capital can be built or eroded, depending on how people interact in their communities.*

ˌsocial ˈcontract *noun* [sing.] an agreement among citizens to behave in a way that benefits everyone: *The country's leaders are committing to a new social contract with the people.*

so·cial·ism /ˈsəʊʃəlɪzəm; *NAmE* ˈsoʊʃəlɪzəm/ *noun* [U] a set of political and economic theories based on the belief that everyone has an equal right to a share of a country's wealth and that the government should own and control the main industries: *At this period, Marx was exposed to many influences which pulled him towards socialism.* ➲ *compare* CAPITALISM, COMMUNISM (1)

so·cial·ist /ˈsəʊʃəlɪst; *NAmE* ˈsoʊʃəlɪst/ *adj.* [usually before noun] supporting socialism: *Marx called for a socialist revolution in the form of a class struggle.* ◇ *He gave advice and assistance to socialist parties in France and Germany.* ◇ *a socialist society/economy* ■ **so·cial·ist** *noun*: *The main disagreements between Marxists and other socialists is over means rather than ends.*

so·cial·iza·tion (*BrE also* **-isa·tion**) /ˌsəʊʃəlaɪˈzeɪʃn; *NAmE* ˌsoʊʃələˈzeɪʃn/ *noun* [U] the process by which sb, especially a child, learns to behave in a way that is acceptable in their society: *Culture may be understood as a shared system of meanings, values and beliefs learned through socialization.* ◇ **+ noun** *Schools have come to play an essential role in the socialization process.*

so·cial·ize (*BrE also* **-ise**) /ˈsəʊʃəlaɪz; *NAmE* ˈsoʊʃəlaɪz/ *verb* **1** [T, often passive] to teach people to behave in ways that are acceptable to their society: **~ sb** *Parents nurture and socialize their children by setting an example.* ◇ **~ sb into sth** *Journalists are being socialized into the culture of self-censorship that now dominates news organizations (Phillips, 1998).* **2** [I] to meet and spend time with people in a friendly way, in order to enjoy yourself **SYN** MIX[1] (6): *Some nursing home residents viewed recreational activities as a welcome opportunity to socialize.* ◇ **~ with sb** *She socialized primarily with friends of her own gender.* **3** [T] **~ sth** to organize sth according to the principles of socialism: *It may be impossible to equalize productive resources in modern economies except through socializing ownership.*

so·cial·ly /ˈsəʊʃəli; *NAmE* ˈsoʊʃəli/ *adv.* **1** in a way that is connected with society or social class: *Growing numbers of investors are keen to invest in socially responsible companies.* ◇ *The countries of the region are economically, socially and culturally diverse.* ◇ *While health care for all may be socially desirable, it is not necessarily economically efficient.* **2** in a way that is connected with rules about polite behaviour in a society: *Participants in the study understood women's drinking to have become more socially acceptable than it was in the past.*

ˌsocial ˈmedia *noun* [pl.] websites and applications that enable users to create and share content or to take part in social networking: **+ noun** *The past few years have seen a*

S

rapid increase in the use of social media sites, such as Twitter, YouTube or Facebook.

ˌsocial ˈnetworking *noun* [U] communication with people who share your interests using a website or other service on the Internet: *The growth of public interest in online social networking was mirrored by politicians in the lead-up to the election.* ◇ **+ noun** *Blogging and social networking websites are powerful ways in which consumers can influence the choices of other consumers.*

ˌsocial ˈscience *noun* **1** [U] (*also* **ˌsocial ˈstudies**) the study of people in society: *Culture is one of the most difficult concepts to interpret in all of social science.* ◇ **+ noun** *Social science research has sometimes ignored the interactions of race, ethnicity, gender and class.* ➲ *compare* NATURAL SCIENCE **2** [C] a particular subject connected with the study of people in society, for example geography, ECONOMICS or SOCIOLOGY: *Gender issues have received increasing attention in many areas of the social sciences in recent decades.* ◇ *The chapter concludes with a look at the current status of human geography as a social science.*

ˌsocial ˈscientist *noun* a person who studies social science: *'Complexity' has been an intriguing topic to engineers, natural scientists and social scientists.*

ˌsocial seˈcurity (*BrE*) (*also* **wel·fare** *NAmE, BrE*) *noun* [U] money that the government pays regularly to people who are poor, unemployed, sick, etc: *More was spent on health and social security and less on housing and education.* ◇ **+ noun** *Social security benefits have declined relatively in recent years.*

ˌsocial ˈservices *noun* [pl.] a system that is organized by the local government or another organization to help people who have financial or family problems; the department or the people who provide this help: *Worldwide Islamic organizations provide social services in many nations.* ◇ *He referred Iris to social services for a needs assessment.*

ˈsocial work *noun* [U] work that involves giving help and advice to people living in the community who have financial or family problems: *Many of the nuns are active in social work.* ◇ *Since the 1970s, professional social work has demonstrated commitment to ideas such as multiculturalism.* ◇ **+ noun** *The primary aim was to make social work practice more accountable.*

S

ˈsocial worker *noun* a person whose job is social work: *Doctors and social workers, for example, may have day-to-day contact with the public.*

so·ci·etal /səˈsaɪətl/ *adj.* [only before noun] connected with society and the way it is organized: *To achieve these societal goals, regulators employ a multitude of policy tools.*

so·ci·ety /səˈsaɪəti/ *noun* (*pl.* **-ies**) **1** [U, C] people in general, living together in communities; a particular community of people who share the same customs, laws, etc: *The pursuit of self-interest does not always benefit society as a whole.* ◇ *Social institutions must treat all members of society as equals.* ◇ *The dominant world trend is towards an ageing society.* ◇ *These social reform movements would transform American society.* ◇ **within/in ~** *Within any society, there will always be some people dissatisfied with the status quo.* ◇ **throughout/across ~** *The government would ensure that prosperity was shared across society.* **2** [C] a group of people who join together for a particular purpose: *There are a number of guidelines put forth by professional societies.* ◇ *Radical elements formed secret societies and prepared for active resistance.* HELP The written abbreviation **Soc.** is used in the names of particular societies: *Reproduced by courtesy: Chem. Soc. Rev. 26 (1997) 169. Copyright, Royal Society of Chemistry.* **3** [U] **~ (of sb)** the state of being with other people SYN COMPANY (3): *Family life includes the society of close relatives.*

▸ ADJECTIVE + SOCIETY **human • international, global • civil • wider, broader • mainstream • secular • multicultural** *This was the culture which confronted them in school and in wider society.* | **ancient • primitive • traditional • agrarian • rural • pre-industrial • industrial, industrialized • post-industrial • post-war • modern • contemporary • urban • advanced** *Rainfall is crucial to an agrarian society.* ◇ *In modern industrial society, capitalist owners need a huge pool of movable workers.* | **hierarchical • tribal • patriarchal • feudal • civilized • capitalist • bourgeois • democratic • socialist • communist • pluralistic, pluralist, plural • divided** *In a feudal society, people were defined by their social class and social mobility was extremely limited.* | **liberal • open • free • egalitarian • just • affluent** *They should unite to work for a just society.*

▸ NOUN + SOCIETY **host • settler • hunter-gatherer • peasant • consumer** *A very small proportion of immigrants speak the language of the host society upon arrival.*

▸ VERB + SOCIETY **build • create • organize • structure • shape • underpin • transform • benefit • divide • govern • dominate** *Older people are frequently not valued by the society they helped to create.*

so·cio·cul·tural /ˌsəʊsiəʊˈkʌltʃərəl; *NAmE* ˌsoʊsioʊˈkʌltʃərəl/ *adj.* connected with society and culture: *Companies that fail to recognize changes in the sociocultural environment, and adapt accordingly, typically fail.*

ˌsocio-ˌecoˈnomic *adj.* connected with society and economics: *A consistent relation was shown between socio-economic status and lifestyle.* ◇ *Health inequalities between socio-economic groups in Scotland have increased over recent decades.* ◇ *Most participants were women and came from a wide range of socio-economic backgrounds.* ◇ *socio-economic position/class* ◇ *Childhood socio-economic disadvantage may be an important factor.* ◇ *socio-economic disparities/inequalities/factors*

socio·lin·guis·tics /ˌsəʊsiəʊlɪŋˈɡwɪstɪks; *NAmE* ˌsoʊsioʊlɪŋˈɡwɪstɪks/ *noun* [U] the study of the way language is affected by differences in social class, region, sex, etc: *She provides a critical review of sociolinguistics in relationship to interview analysis.* ■ **socio·lin·guis·tic** *adj.*: *There is significant variation in these sociolinguistic patterns that reflects access to education.*

soci·olo·gist /ˌsəʊsiˈɒlədʒɪst; *NAmE* ˌsoʊsiˈɑːlədʒɪst/ *noun* a person who studies sociology: *The way sociologists study domestic divisions of labour has also changed.*

soci·ology /ˌsəʊsiˈɒlədʒi; *NAmE* ˌsoʊsiˈɑːlədʒi/ *noun* [U] the scientific study of the nature and development of society and social behaviour: *Anthropology and sociology evolved as separate disciplines in the nineteenth century.* ◇ **~ of sth** *Sociology of education has had little to say about theories of learning.* ■ **socio·logic·al** /ˌsəʊsiəˈlɒdʒɪkl; *NAmE* ˌsoʊsiəˈlɑːdʒɪkl/ *adj.*: *The sociological study of food and eating is a growing area of research.* **socio·logic·al·ly** /ˌsəʊsiəˈlɒdʒɪkli; *NAmE* ˌsoʊsiəˈlɑːdʒɪkli/ *adv.*: *MPs are sociologically unrepresentative of the population, being disproportionately male, middle-aged and middle class.*

socket /ˈsɒkɪt; *NAmE* ˈsɑːkɪt/ *noun* **1** a device on a piece of electrical equipment that you can fix a PLUG, a light BULB, etc. into: *The operator of the machine was able to pull electrical leads out of sockets and plug them back into different sockets.* **2** (*BrE*) (*NAmE* **out·let**) a device in a wall that you put a PLUG into in order to connect electrical equipment to the power supply of a building: *All sockets in domestic and commercial premises accept standard plugs.* **3** a curved hollow space in the surface of sth that another part fits into or moves around in: *The eye sockets offer physical protection to the eyes.*

so·dium /ˈsəʊdiəm; *NAmE* ˈsoʊdiəm/ *noun* [U] (*symb.* **Na**) the chemical element of ATOMIC NUMBER 11. Sodium is a soft silver-white metal that is found naturally only in COMPOUNDS, such as salt: *High levels of sodium in the diet have been linked to hypertension.* ◇ **+ noun** *Examples of ionic compounds include acids, bases and salts, such as sodium chloride.*

soft /sɒft; *NAmE* sɔːft/ *adj.* (**soft·er, soft·est**) **1** changing shape easily when pressed; not stiff or firm: *There is a thick, soft clay layer at the subsurface.* OPP HARD[1] (3) **2** less firm or hard than other things of the same type: *The underlying soft rock is exposed.* ◇ *Optical glass is softer than common glass and scratches easily.* OPP HARD[1] (3) ➲ *see also* SOFT TISSUE **3** not feeling hard or rough when touched: *A clean, soft cloth should be used.* **4** not clear or bright; not loud or strong: *The first heart sound is soft.* ◇ *Soft pink lights adorned the tree.* **5** (*usually disapproving*) sympathetic rather than strict (usually used to suggest weakness): *Some of these governments had been inclined to take a soft line.* ◇ *One essential motive was to avoid being considered too soft.* ◇ **~ on sb/sth** *He believed his predecessors had been soft on crime.* OPP HARD[1] (6), TOUGH (3) **6** that cannot be measured or described easily, but still has a value or quality that can be recognized: *Employers look for 'soft' or non-cognitive skills such as a certain type of communicative style.* ◇ *These models did not use soft qualitative data and this limited their ability to mimic reality.* ➲ *compare* HARD[1] (4), TANGIBLE (1) ■ **soft·ness** *noun* [U, sing.] **~ (of sth)** *The apparent softness of graphite is deceptive.*

ˌ**soft** ˈ**drink** *noun* a cold drink that does not contain alcohol: *Reducing consumption of soft drinks was described as one of the simpler ways to reduce obesity in the United States.*

soft·en /ˈsɒfn; *NAmE* ˈsɔːfn/ *verb* **1** [I, T] to become softer or less solid; to make sth softer or less solid: *These substances soften or melt on heating.* ◇ **~ sth** *Use ear drops to soften the wax.* **2** [I, T] to become less severe; to make sb/sth less severe: *By the end of the project, their antagonistic attitudes towards one another had softened.* ◇ **~ sb/sth** *Nothing softens her or inspires her compassion.* ◇ *These measures were intended to soften the impact on the poor and low-income families.*

ˌ**soft** ˈ**tissue** *noun* [U, C] (*anatomy*) the parts of the body that are not bone, for example the skin and muscles: *MRI is excellent for assessing the bone and soft tissues.* ◇ **+ noun** *soft tissue injury/infection*

soft·ware /ˈsɒftweə(r); *NAmE* ˈsɔːftwer/ *noun* [U] the programs used by a computer for doing particular jobs: *An operating system is the most important piece of software in a computer system.* ◇ *Many computer owners have installed anti-spam software to try and reduce the extent of the nuisance caused by junk email.* ◇ **+ noun** *a software developer/engineer* ➲ *compare* HARDWARE (1) ➲ *see also* PACKAGE[1] (2)

ˈ**software package** *noun* (*computing*) = PACKAGE[1] (2)

soil /sɔɪl/ *noun* [U, C] the top layer of the earth in which plants grow: *Sandy soils are more vulnerable to wind erosion than rocky or clayey soils.* ◇ **in the ~** *The dormant seeds can survive for decades in the soil.* ◇ **+ noun** *The protection that trees provide against soil erosion depends on the existing grass cover.*

solar /ˈsəʊlə(r); *NAmE* ˈsoʊlər/ *adj.* [only before noun] **1** of or connected with the sun: *Measures of solar radiation are also required.* **2** using the sun's energy: *Solar heating could be more widely utilized.* ◇ *Demand for solar energy technologies increased.*

ˈ**solar system** *noun* **1 the solar system** [sing.] the sun and all the planets that move around it: *Of the planets in the solar system, Mercury has almost no atmosphere.* **2** [C] any group of planets that all move around the same star: *Some began to posit the revolutionary idea that the stars were suns at the centre of distant solar systems.*

sold *past tense, past part. of* SELL

sol·dier /ˈsəʊldʒə(r); *NAmE* ˈsoʊldʒər/ *noun* a member of an army: *He served as a Russian soldier and saw active duty.*

sole AWL /səʊl; *NAmE* soʊl/ *adj.* [only before noun] **1** only; single: *Its sole purpose was to increase profits.* ◇ *Unemployment levels largely remained below 20 per cent, the sole exception being the early 1980s.* **2** involving only one person or group: *He took sole responsibility for the events.* ◇ *Independent retail stores are typically run by a sole trader or as a family business.*

sole·ly AWL /ˈsəʊlli; *NAmE* ˈsoʊlli/ *adv.* only; not involving sb/sth else: *Explanations which rely solely on culture are problematic.* ◇ *The problem was not solely or even mainly one of shrinking markets.* ◇ *Individuals were no longer solely responsible for their own welfare.*

solid[1] /ˈsɒlɪd; *NAmE* ˈsɑːlɪd/ *adj.* [usually before noun] **1** not in the form of a liquid or gas: *There is a tax on solid waste destined for landfills.* ◇ *The patient had discomfort swallowing solid food.* ◇ *In this earliest period of the Earth's life, the solid materials present in its core consisted of iron and alloys of iron.* **2** hard or firm, with a surface that does not move when pressed: *The flow around a solid obstacle was unstable when the velocity exceeded a certain value.* **3** having no holes or empty spaces inside: *Outcrops of solid rock rise from grasslands.* ◇ *The deposit is buried to a great enough depth for pressure to force the grains together into a solid mass.* **4** having a strong basis; reliable: *The firm had a solid position as the market leader.* ◇ *Their insights provide a solid foundation for future research.* ◇ *There is currently no solid evidence to suggest this was the case.* **5** (*technical*) having a shape with length, width and height: *A solid three-dimensional object cannot be reflected in this way.* **6** [only before noun] made completely of the material mentioned: *She believed the necklace to be solid gold.* **7** (of a line or colour) without spaces: *The different sectors are represented by solid and broken lines.*

solid[2] /ˈsɒlɪd; *NAmE* ˈsɑːlɪd/ *noun* **1** [C] a substance that is not a liquid or a gas: *Sodium chloride (salt) is a crystalline solid.* **2** [C] (*geometry*) a shape that has length, width and height: *There are only five of these regular polyhedra, the so-called Platonic solids.* **3 solids** [pl.] food that is not liquid: *She had difficulty in swallowing liquids and solids.*

soli·dar·ity /ˌsɒlɪˈdærəti; *NAmE* ˌsɑːlɪˈdærəti/ *noun* [U] support by one person or group of people for another because they share feelings, opinions, aims, etc: **~ between/among sb** *The study focused on the presence (or absence) of social solidarity among mine workers.* ◇ **~ with sb/sth** *The words people choose may be used to show solidarity with ideas held by other group members.*

so·lid·ify /səˈlɪdɪfaɪ/ *verb* (**so·lidi·fies, so·lidi·fy·ing, so·lidi·fied, so·lidi·fied**) **1** [I, T] to become a solid rather than a liquid or a gas; to make sth do this: *Some of the rising magma solidifies without erupting.* ◇ **~ sth** *Shrinkage occurs when the molten plastic is solidified in the mould.* **2** [I, T] to become more definite and less likely to change; to make this happen: *Significant trends have either emerged or solidified.* ◇ **~ sth** *He imposed martial law to solidify his power.* ■ **so·lidi·fi·ca·tion** /səˌlɪdɪfɪˈkeɪʃn/ *noun* [U] **~ (of sth)** *These deposits can be ascribed to the cooling and solidification of magmas.* ◇ *The liaisons enabled the creation or solidification of particular business groups.*

soli·tary /ˈsɒlətri; *NAmE* ˈsɑːləteri/ *adj.* **1** [usually before noun] done alone; without other people: *Research is not*

S

a solitary activity. ◇ *Subjects show a lack of interest in social involvement and a preference for solitary pursuits.* ◇ *He was placed in solitary confinement for 29 days.* **2** (of a person or an animal) usually or frequently spending time alone: *Tigers are solitary animals.* **3** (of a person, thing or place) alone, with no other people or things around SYN SINGLE[1] (1): *Standing under a solitary tree in a thunderstorm is no protection.*

solu·bil·ity /ˌsɒlju'bɪləti; *NAmE* ˌsɑːlju'bɪləti/ *noun* [U] the fact that a substance can be dissolved in a liquid; the degree to which this is possible: *The polymer has low water solubility, even at pH above 7.* ◇ **~ (of sth) (in sth)** *The solubility of oxygen in water is temperature dependent.*

sol·uble /'sɒljəbl; *NAmE* 'sɑːljəbl/ *adj.* **1** that can be dissolved in a liquid: *The soluble salts in saline soils are mostly neutral.* ◇ *The nitric acid and hydrogen peroxide are water soluble and are removed from the atmosphere by precipitation.* ◇ **~ in sth** *The drug is highly soluble in water, making it ideal for injection.* OPP INSOLUBLE (1) **2** (of a problem) that can be solved: *Often the technical problems are soluble, but what seem insuperable are the political, social and cultural problems.* OPP INSOLUBLE (2)

solute /'sɒljuːt; sɒ'ljuːt; *NAmE* 'souljuːt; sou'ljuːt/ *noun* a substance that is dissolved in a SOLVENT forming a solution: *Ten grams of the solute is dissolved in 50 cm^3 of water.*

so·lu·tion /sə'luːʃn/ *noun* **1** [C] a way of solving a problem or dealing with a difficult situation SYN ANSWER[1] (4): *Most ethical dilemmas encountered by nurses do not have simple solutions.* ◇ **~ to sth** *The goal is to find optimal solutions to existing problems.* ◇ **~ for sth** *One approach is to look for a technical solution for each issue.* **2** [C] **~ (to/for/of sth)** an answer to a problem in mathematics: *With modern, high-speed computers, numerical solutions to the Schrödinger equation can be found.* **3** [C, U] a liquid in which a substance has been dissolved, so that the substance has become part of the liquid; the state of being dissolved in a liquid: *The solution contains a relatively high concentration of sulfuric acid.* ◇ *The viscosity of the solution was controlled by adjusting the polymer level.* ◇ *The filtered solutions were diluted at least 10 times with 1/1 ethanol/water.* ◇ **~ of sth** *Traditional leather-tanning processes involve treating the hides with an aqueous solution of chromium.* ◇ **in/out of ~** *These molecules rotate freely in solution.*

▸ ADJECTIVE + SOLUTION **simple • obvious • possible, potential • optimal, ideal • complete • satisfactory, acceptable • practical • technical, technological • innovative** *What appears to be an optimal solution from a local point of view may be less than optimal when the situation is viewed globally.* | **exact • approximate • complete • unique • general • numerical • analytical • non-trivial • closed-form** *No non-trivial solution had yet been found for the complete equation.* | **concentrated • dilute • aqueous • saturated • saline • alkaline • acidic, acid** *Most metals are soluble in acidic solutions.*

▸ NOUN + SOLUTION **buffer** *Similar results were obtained when a buffer solution with a pH of 9 was used instead of pure water.*

▸ VERB + SOLUTION **seek, search for • demand • find • offer • propose, present • provide, deliver • impose • implement • adopt** *Fisher (1930,1938) proposed a solution to this problem.* | **obtain, find • construct • devise • plot • derive • compute • yield** *The solution obtained in this way is plotted in Fig.14.16.*

▸ PHRASE **part of the solution** *The debate about British economic decline centres on the issue of whether social and political institutions were part of the solution or whether they were part of the problem.*

solve /sɒlv; *NAmE* sɑːlv; sɔːlv/ *verb* **1** [T] **~ sth** to find a way of dealing with a problem or difficult situation: *International agreement is the best way to solve environmental problems.* ◇ *Social skills give students the tools they need to solve complex conflicts.* ➲ *see also* PROBLEM-SOLVING **2** [T, I] to find the correct answer or explanation for sth: **~ sth** *Site-specific soil surveys have proved helpful in solving particular archaeological research questions.* ◇ *The distribution of these elements is obtained by solving this equation:...* ◇ **~ for sth** *We can solve for x and y separately and then substitute our solutions into the equation.*

solv·ent /'sɒlvənt; *NAmE* 'sɑːlvənt/ *noun* [C, U] a liquid that can dissolve another substance: *The product was soluble in organic solvents.* ◇ *Evaporation of the solvent leaves a thin film of protein molecules on the plate for analysis.*

soma /'səumə; *NAmE* 'soumə/ *noun* [usually sing.] (*biology*) the parts of an ORGANISM other than the REPRODUCTIVE cells: *The distinction between germ line and soma exists only in animals.*

som·at·ic /sə'mætɪk/ *adj.* [usually before noun] **1** (*medical*) connected with the body, especially as opposed to the mind: *Somatic symptoms of anxiety include abdominal discomfort, indigestion and poor appetite.* **2** (*biology*) connected with the soma: *Cancer emerges when a cell lineage accumulates specific somatic mutations.* HELP In biology, a **somatic cell** is any cell of a living ORGANISM other than the REPRODUCTIVE cells: *In sexually reproducing organisms, a fundamental distinction is between germ cells and somatic cells.*

some[1] /səm; *strong form* sʌm/ *det.* **1** used with uncountable nouns or plural countable nouns to mean 'an amount of' or 'a number of', when the exact amount or number is not important or is not stated: *32% of low-skilled migrants send some money home, compared with 27% of university-educated migrants.* ◇ *Patients with a history of cardiovascular disease will require some simple investigations.* HELP In negative sentences and in questions, **any** is usually used instead of **some**: *She has not noticed any change.* **2** /sʌm/ used to refer to certain members of a group or certain types of a thing, but not all of them: *This feeling was shared by some parents, particularly parents from the Traveller community.* ◇ *The same process is likely to work better in some contexts than others.* **3** /sʌm/ a limited amount of sth: *This approach had some success (e.g. Wong et al., 1987) but was fairly soon abandoned.* ◇ *There is some evidence to support this view.* **4** /sʌm/ a large or fairly large amount or number of sth: *This process has been underway for quite some time.* ◇ *For some years he shared the work with his brother.* **5** used with a singular noun to refer to sb/sth that is not known or not identified: *They attributed these feats to some great figure from the past.* ◇ **~ kind of sth** *She felt that people deserved some kind of explanation.* ◇ **~ ... or other** *All the contributors have at some time or other been involved in fieldwork.* **6** used before a number that is not exact: *This industrial region is home to some four million people.* ◇ *In the 1980s, the South Korean working week was some ten hours longer than Japan's.*

some[2] /sʌm/ *pron.* **1** used to refer to an amount of sth or a number of people or things when the amount or number is not given: *Some disapprove of this idea.* ◇ *Her forthrightness offended some in high places.* ◇ *She has spots all over her face and some on her back.* HELP In negative sentences and questions **any** is usually used instead of 'some': *I don't want any.* ◇ *Do you have any of the following conditions?* **2** a part of the whole number or amount being considered: *A sizeable percentage of immigrants hope eventually to return, and some do.* ◇ **~ of sb/sth** *I found it difficult to understand some of his arguments.* ◇ *Changes in climate may destroy some of the world's prime food-growing areas.*

some[3] /sʌm/ *adv.* used before numbers to mean 'approximately': *This sandstone bed is some 16 feet in thickness.* ◇

At Toolik Lake, some 40% of the total annual precipitation falls as snow. ◇ *The foundation now has some 16 000 members in the United States.*

some·body /ˈsʌmbədi/ *pron.* = SOMEONE **OPP** NOBODY

some·how /ˈsʌmhaʊ/ *adv.* **1** in a way that is not known or certain: *He has somehow managed to keep his visits to the clinic secret.* ◇ *Most common was the desire to help somehow.* ◇ *These natural products are considered by many to be somehow different—safer, healthier—than synthetic products such as plastics.* **2** (*rather informal*) for a reason that you do not know or understand: *Somehow, I didn't like the place.* ◇ *The fireworks look much better on TV. They look more real somehow.*

some·one /ˈsʌmwʌn/ (*also less frequent* **some·body**) *pron.* used when referring to or describing a person whose name is not known, not stated or not important: *The firm was looking for someone with his qualifications.* ◇ *When you smile at someone, it is almost impossible for them not to smile back.* ◇ **~ else** *60% per cent of participants reported that they had never pretended to be someone else; 40% had.* ◇ **+ adj.** *Although we might not know all of these people personally, we know that we can trust them, because they are already known and trusted by someone close to us.* ◇ **~ who...** *He was someone who could be relied upon.* **HELP** In negative sentences and questions, **anyone** is usually used instead of **someone**: *Neither he nor anyone else had the right to use the company's money in that way.*

some·thing /ˈsʌmθɪŋ/ *pron.* **1** a thing that is not known or mentioned by name: *When someone said something that was difficult to interpret, we first asked the group to respond, rather than giving our own opinion.* ◇ **~ about sth** *It is helpful to know something about the accuracy of the scale and what it will and will not give information about.* ◇ **~ else** *Often interviewees reveal aspects of their attitudes while answering a questionnaire about something else entirely.* ◇ **+ adj.** *Many people feel that there is something wrong with this approach.* **HELP** In negative sentences and questions, **anything** is usually used instead of **something**: *These parasites are specific to flies and do not attack anything else.* **2** used when describing an important or particular thing: *They have a responsibility to make something of their lives.* ◇ *If those were the only things that mattered, there might be something in this argument.* **3** used when describing a thing in a way that is not exact: *There are something in the order of 14 000 appeals a year.* ◇ **~ like sth** *Her argument goes something like this:...* ◇ **be/have ~ to do with sth** *This may have something to do with the tendency to view children as passive learners.* **HELP** The informal expression **or something**, meaning 'or something like that', is very common in spoken English, but should be avoided in academic English. Instead, you can use a more formal expression such as **something similar**: *Experiment with a rubber block, or something similar.*

IDM **something of a/an...** (*also* **somewhat of a/an...**) used to say that sb/sth is the thing mentioned, but only to a certain degree: *Luther was also something of a German nationalist, in reaction against the power of Rome.* ➲ *more at* SAY[1]

some·times /ˈsʌmtaɪmz/ *adv.* occasionally but not all of the time or in every case: *These fractures are sometimes slow to heal.* ◇ *Sometimes, a manufacturer's most significant competitor is the 'own label' product of the supermarket itself.* ◇ *Computer-assisted cartography, sometimes called digital mapping, is discussed separately from traditional cartography.*

some·what **AWL** /ˈsʌmwɒt; *NAmE* ˈsʌmwʌt/ *adv.* to some degree **SYN** RATHER (1): *While this result appears to be somewhat surprising, in fact it is quite consistent with the AWGN analysis.* ◇ *The sample sizes for each analysis described below vary somewhat due to missing data for some measures used.* ◇ **~ of a/an...** *He became somewhat of an expert on US antitrust policy.*

some·where /ˈsʌmweə(r); *NAmE* ˈsʌmwer/ *adv.* in, at or to a place or position that you do not know or do not mention by name: *No matter how good the prices are, someone somewhere will be charging less.* ◇ **~ between sth** *Most cases lie somewhere between these extremes.* ◇ **~ in between (sth)** *This is somewhat less true in elementary schools and more the case in high schools, with middle schools somewhere in between.* ◇ **~ in/on sth** *More than half of those polled said that their standard of living was somewhere in the middle.* ◇ **~ else** *If business people see an area as having a bad investment climate, they will not invest in that area but will choose instead to invest somewhere else.* **HELP** In negative sentences and questions, **anywhere** is usually used instead of **somewhere**: *Immigrants who came to America found a freedom that they could not find anywhere else in the world.* ■ **some·where** *pron.*: *The refugees had somewhere to sleep, but no food.*

son /sʌn/ *noun* a person's male child: *They have a son, Christopher, aged two.* ◇ *Hannibal was born in 247 BC, the eldest son of Hamilcar Barca.* ◇ *Only the sons and daughters of the most privileged classes attended college.* **IDM** *see* FATHER

song /sɒŋ; *NAmE* sɔːŋ/ *noun* **1** [C] a short piece of music with words that you sing: *He collected Hungarian folk songs.* **2** [U] songs in general; music for singing: *They represented their social history in song.* **3** [C, U] the musical sounds that birds and some other creatures make: *The calling songs of different species may differ considerably.* ◇ *Song in both songbirds and whales is socially learned.*

soon /suːn/ *adv.* (**soon·er**, **soon·est**) **1** in a short time from now; a short time after sth else has happened: *The firm will soon be outpaced by others.* ◇ *It soon became clear that adult norms were misleading when applied to college students.* ◇ **~ afterwards** *Soon afterwards, following a final battle, probably in Kent, Caesar decided to return to Gaul.* **2** quickly: *These conservatives did not realize how soon their ideas would become dominant in national politics.* ◇ *Recent archaeological findings indicate that some regions within Greece recovered much sooner than others.* ◇ **as ~ as...** *As soon as an inventor firm introduces a new innovation in the market, other companies will copy the innovation.* ◇ **as ~ as possible** *Patients who are in need of transplant as soon as possible due to acute liver failure are given priority over everyone else on the list in the UK.* ◇ **the sooner...** *The earlier severe disease is identified, the sooner aggressive treatment can begin.*

IDM **no sooner... than...** used to say that sth happens immediately after sth else: *No sooner had the meeting closed than the police arrived.* **ˌsooner or ˈlater** at some time in the future, although the exact time may not be known: *Sooner or later the loans will have to be paid back.*

so·phis·ti·cated /səˈfɪstɪkeɪtɪd/ *adj.* **1** (of things, systems, methods or ideas) clever and complicated: *There are more sophisticated techniques that can be applied.* ◇ *Sophisticated software is used to reconstruct an image.* ◇ *As cars become increasingly sophisticated, most customers cannot identify problems themselves.* **2** [usually before noun] able to deal with complicated ideas: *The demand for these services is from increasingly sophisticated clients.* ◇ *Such studies generated a more sophisticated understanding of technical change.* **3** knowing a lot about the modern world and about things that people consider to be socially important: *She was not the elegant, sophisticated woman he remembered.* ◇ *The result was the emergence of a sophisticated urban population.*

so·phis·ti·ca·tion /səˌfɪstɪˈkeɪʃn/ *noun* [U] **1** the fact of being clever or complicated: *Increasing technological*

S

sophistication in communications has brought about a more integrated trading system. ◇ **~ of sth** *The sophistication of the analysis is unrivalled.* **2** the ability to understand or use sth that is clever or complicated: *Consumers often show a high degree of sophistication in making complex purchasing choices.* **3** the fact of knowing a lot about the modern world and about things that people consider to be socially important: *Together with increased prosperity and sophistication, a culture of wasteful energy usage has become established.*

sore /sɔː(r)/ *adj.* (of a part of the body) painful, especially because of infection or because a muscle has been used too much: *Sore throat is a common complaint and is mostly viral in origin.* ◇ *I am unable to undertake any exercise while my knee is sore.* ■ **sore·ness** *noun* [U] *Unaccustomed exercises can cause muscle soreness.*

sorry /ˈsɒri; *NAmE* ˈsɑːri; ˈsɔːri/ *adj.* (**sor·rier, sor·ri·est**) HELP **Sorry** is much more frequent in all its meanings in spoken English than in written English, especially formal or academic writing. **1** [not before noun] feeling sad or sympathetic about sb else's bad luck or problems: **~ (that)...** *I'm really sorry this has happened to you.* ◇ **~ to see, hear, etc.** *I'm so sorry to hear about your son's illness.* **2** [not before noun] feeling sad or ashamed about sth that you have done: **~ about sth** *I hope my decision to step down will show people how sorry I am about my actions.* ◇ **~ for (doing) sth** *Lesley is sorry for all the trouble she has caused.* **3** [not before noun] realizing that you made the wrong decision and wishing that you had done sth different: **~ (that)...** *I am sorry we did not go to Sweden or Germany.* ◇ **~ to do sth** *We should give protection to any unique groups of animals that we would be sorry to lose.* **4** [only before noun] very sad or bad, especially making you feel sympathy or disapproval: *This outcome was a sorry result for the House of Lords.* ◇ *Some were just roaring with laughter at the whole sorry performance.*

IDM **be/feel sorry for sb** to feel sympathy for sb: *I am sorry for him but he has brought it on himself.* **I'm sorry 1** used when you are apologizing for sth: *I'm sorry. Are you all right?* **2** used for disagreeing with sb or politely saying 'no': *I'm sorry, I don't feel like talking right now.* **3** used for introducing bad news: *I'm sorry to say that the results were not as good as we had hoped.*

S

sort¹ /sɔːt; *NAmE* sɔːrt/ *noun* a group or type of people or things that have similar characteristics; a particular variety or type SYN KIND¹ (1): **~ of sth** *The current crisis has provoked precisely the same sort of reaction.* ◇ *This sort of analysis provides quantitative evidence.* ◇ *Some sort of intercellular signalling is involved.* ◇ **what sort(s) of sth** *It is valid to ask what sorts of goals are involved.* ◇ **~ of thing** *This sort of thing was a nuisance to us, but never became sufficiently widespread to cause serious difficulty.* ◇ **of some ~** *At that time, the great majority of South East Asia (around 80 per cent; Flint, 1994) was still under forest of some sort.* ◇ **all sorts of sth** *Globalization has produced all sorts of implications for the multicultural configurations of local communities in the United States.* ◇ **of this/that ~** *Something of this sort took place in the Middle Ages.* ◇ **of a... ~** *Lessons of a different sort are revealed by the British experience.* ◇ **of... sorts** *To build a Roman villa required specialist craftsmen of various sorts.* ◇ **of one ~ or another** *Keating's account is drawn mainly from official sources of one sort or another.*

IDM **of ˈsorts | of a ˈsort | a sort of sth** used when you are saying that sth is the thing mentioned, but only to a certain degree, or that sth is not a good example of sth: *This, however, created a paradox of sorts.* ◇ *For a brief space, there was a sort of democracy.*

sort² /sɔːt; *NAmE* sɔːrt/ *verb* [often passive] to arrange things in groups or in a particular order according to their type or to what they contain: **~ sth** *There are a number of programs for sorting and coding qualitative data.* ◇ **be sorted into sth** *These predictors can generally be sorted into three categories.* ◇ **be sorted by/according to sth** *There seem to be four groups of economies sorted by their ability to generate and absorb new ideas.*

PHR V **ˌsort sth ˈout** (*rather informal*) to deal with sth successfully; to stop sth from being a problem: *The record of international agencies in sorting out problems is generally poor.* HELP **Sort sth out** is much more common in general English; in academic English, a more formal word or expression such as **resolve** or **deal with** is more common: *It is unclear how this conflict could be resolved.* ◇ *This potential problem was dealt with by ensuring regular observations.* **ˌsort sth ˈout (from sth)** to separate sth from sth else; to recognize sth as different from sth else: *We went through all the results, sorting out those that were potentially abnormal.* ◇ *In this context, it is difficult to sort out legend from fact.* **ˈsort through sth** to look at or consider different things in order to find the most useful or important ones: *The project provides document summaries to enable the researcher to sort through search results.*

sought AWL *past tense, past part. of* SEEK

soul /səʊl; *NAmE* soʊl/ *noun* **1** [C] the spiritual part of a person, believed to exist after death: *The book deals with the immortality of the human soul.* ◇ **~ of sth** *The service for the dead is a plea to God to save the souls of the dead from Hell.* **2** [C] a person or group's inner character, containing their particular beliefs, desires and characteristics: *Nothing has been able to quiet the longings of her soul.* ◇ **the ~ of sth/sb** *For Rushdie, the conflict between racists and anti-racists is an epic struggle for the soul of Britain.* **3** [sing.] the spiritual and moral qualities of humans in general: *Since Plato, philosophers have tended to value the rational mind or the soul above the earthly and 'corrupt' body.*

sound¹ /saʊnd/ *noun* **1** [C] something that can be heard: *Popping and cracking sounds were audible.* ◇ *Robots have been built that can make sounds, detect each other's sounds and imitate them.* ◇ **~ of sth/sb (doing sth)** *This sequence of the movie is accompanied by the sound of wind in the palm trees.* ➲ *compare* NOISE (1) **2** [U] continuous movements (called VIBRATIONS) that travel through air or water and can be heard when they reach a person's or an animal's ear: *We infer the presence of objects in our environment from patterns of light or sound.* ◇ **the speed of ~** *The information passes along the tube at the speed of sound.* ◇ **~ wave** *The sound waves generated by a human can be converted into electrical signals by using a microphone.* **3** [U] what you can hear coming from a television, radio, etc, or as part of a film: **+ noun** *During the early adoption of cell phones, the sound quality was often inferior to that of landlines.* ◇ *This point was illustrated by comparing sound recordings of interviews with completed questionnaires.*

sound² /saʊnd/ *verb* (not usually used in the progressive tenses) **1** *linking verb* to give a particular impression when heard or read about: **+ adj.** *None of these options sounds very plausible.* ◇ **~ (to sb) like sb/sth** *The noise of the flood waters sounded to the drivers like an approaching vehicle.* ◇ **~ as if/as though...** *In his speeches, he sounded as if he was entirely unaware of the likely results of such extreme measures.* HELP In spoken English, people often use **like** instead of **as if** or **as though** in this meaning. This is not correct in academic English. **Like** can be used before a noun phrase (*an approaching vehicle*) but not before a clause (*he was entirely unaware of the likely results...*). **2 -sounding** (in adjectives) giving the impression of being sth: *There is a range of similar-sounding conditions that are invariably treated by some form of steroid.* **3** [I, T] to give a signal such as a warning by making a sound: *The alarm failed to sound when the fire started.* ◇ **~ sth** *to sound an alarm/a siren* **4** [T] to express a particular opinion about a situation or idea : **~ the alarm** *In a speech, the president sounded the alarm about 'a different kind of enemy'.* ◇ **~ a note of sth** *Lawler (1987) sounded a note of caution about overgeneralizing about this particular climatic trend.*

sound[3] /saʊnd/ *adj.* (**sound·er**, **sound·est**) **1** sensible; that can be relied on and that will probably give good results: *Around 1900, several scientists realized that Mendel's principles provided a sound basis for explaining heredity.* ◇ *Although regulated competition is a theoretically sound model, it is a technically complicated one* **2** in good condition; not damaged or hurt: *Some would insist that the American economy was always fundamentally sound.* **3** [only before noun] good and thorough: *Companies need a sound knowledge of the markets in which they operate.* ◇ *Nurses need a sound understanding of the healing process.* ■ **sound·ness** *noun* [U] **~ (of sth)** *Reiss has expressed serious doubts about the soundness of these assumptions.*

source[1] AWL /sɔːs; *NAmE* sɔːrs/ *noun* **1** a place, thing or person that you get sth from: *An additional heat source was used to provide a constant internal temperature.* ◇ **~ of sth** *The Internet provides a rich source of information on psychological tests.* ◇ **~ for sth** *The best food sources for zinc are red meats, shellfish, nuts, whole grains and legumes.* ◇ **from a... ~** *Exposure to radiation in the UK is mainly from natural sources, such as radon gas in bedrock.* ◇ **+ noun** *After crushing the source materials, we sorted the particles into four size classes.* **2** [usually pl.] a text or person that provides information, especially for study, a piece of written work or news: *See also the many sources cited in Cain (2000).* ◇ *In the 1960s, geographers began to use many more government data sources in their ethnic studies.* ◇ **~ for sth** *The historical sources for the first forty years of the Jewish-Christian sect are few.* ⇨ *see also* PRIMARY SOURCE **3 ~ (of sth)** a thing, situation or person that causes sth, especially a problem: *GM food is widely acknowledged to be the source of both potential economic benefits and serious concerns.* ◇ *It may prove impossible to eliminate all sources of error.* ◇ *Living in neighbourhoods with high levels of violent crime could also be a source of chronic stress.* **4 ~ (of sth)** the place where a river or stream starts: *Great public interest was aroused by the search for the source of the Nile.*

IDM **at ˈsource** at the place or the point that sth comes from or begins: *For full-time employees, national insurance payments are deducted by employers at source.*

▸ ADJECTIVE + SOURCE **main, primary, principal • major • important • various • different • multiple • additional • common** *Next, the principal sources of stress in the patient's life were identified.* | **rich • good • valuable • useful • reliable • key • independent • original • single** *The most reliable source of information on refugee numbers today is the UNHCR.* | **potential • possible • significant • constant** *The threat of disappearance is a constant source of anxiety in the stories.* | **renewable • alternative • new • natural • large • external** *Renewable energy sources have fewer environmental effects than conventional energy sources.* | **primary • secondary • literary • written • textual • documentary • historical • official • authoritative • early** *I have not found earlier sources for this statement (though they may exist).*

▸ NOUN + SOURCE **heat • energy • carbon • light • food • funding • data • information** *By 1800, a light source, the tallow candle, had been developed that was more than 32 times as efficient as a campfire.*

▸ VERB + SOURCE **identify • find, locate** *By the nineteenth century, the demand for cereals was increasing so rapidly that concerted efforts were made to find new sources of nitrogen.* | **have • use (as), utilize • rely on, depend on** *Using various sources, we estimated the changes in the total fraction of tax-exempt assets in aggregate private wealth.* | **become • constitute, represent • remain • remove** *The best way to make cities healthier, he argued, was to remove the sources of disease, such as sewage and garbage.* | **require • provide • offer • serve as • derive from, come from, originate from • seek** *These volcanic rocks were derived from a large variety of sources (Polat and Kerrich, 2001).* | **examine • analyse • consult • cite • list • draw on • be based on** *In preparing this article, a wide range of documentary sources were consulted.*

▸ SOURCE + NOUN **material • area, region • text • document** *The source text for Mamet's second film adaptation was a popular legal thriller entitled 'The Verdict' (1980).*

▸ SOURCE OF + NOUN **information, data • knowledge • inspiration • power, authority • strength • advantage • supply • energy • support • income, revenue, finance • funding** *Oil continues to be the chief source of industrial energy.* | **error • bias • variation • uncertainty • confusion • conflict • infection** *In practice, many sources of bias remain, particularly those associated with participant subjectivity.*

source[2] AWL /sɔːs; *NAmE* sɔːrs/ *verb* [often passive] **~ sth** to get sth from a particular place: *There has been debate about whether sourcing fruit and vegetables locally actually reduces greenhouse gas emissions.* ◇ **~ sth from sth** *Equally important at the early stages of development was the use of free software sourced from the Internet.*

south[1] /saʊθ/ *noun* [U, sing.] (*abbr.* **S**, **So.**) **1** (*usually* **the south**) the direction that is on your right when you watch the sun rise; one of the four main points of the COMPASS: *warmer weather coming from the south* ◇ **to the ~ (of...)** *They trade with countries to the south.* ⇨ *compare* EAST[1], NORTH[1], WEST[1] **2 the south, the South** the southern part of a country, a region or the world: *Seven of the Democrats who voted in favour were from the South.* **3 the South** the poorer countries in the southern half of the world: *These policies may pose challenges for producers in the Global South.*

south[2] /saʊθ/ *adj.* (*abbr.* **S**, **So.**) [only before noun] in or towards the south: *South Wales* ◇ *the south coast* ■ **south** *adv.*: *The house faces south.*

ˌsouth-ˈeast *noun* (*usually* **the south-east**) [sing.] (*abbr.* **SE**) the direction or region at an equal distance between south and east: *These cultural changes began in London and the south-east.* ■ **ˌsouth-ˈeast** *adv., adj.* **ˌsouth-ˈeastern** *adj.* [only before noun]

south·ern /ˈsʌðən; *NAmE* ˈsʌðərn/ (*also* **Southern**) *adj.* (*abbr.* **S**) [usually before noun] located in the south or facing south; connected with or typical of the south part of the world or a region: *the southern slopes of the mountain* ◇ *southern Spain* ◇ *a southern accent*

ˌsouth-ˈwest *noun* (*usually* **the south-west**) [sing.] (*abbr.* **SW**) the direction or region at an equal distance between south and west: *In summer, the monsoon blows from the south-west.* ■ **ˌsouth-ˈwest** *adv., adj.* **ˌsouth-ˈwestern** *adj.* [only before noun]

sov·er·eign[1] /ˈsɒvrɪn; *NAmE* ˈsɑːvrən/ *adj.* **1** [only before noun] (of a country or state) free to govern itself; completely independent SYN AUTONOMOUS (1): *According to realists, war is always a possibility in a system of sovereign states.* **2** having complete power, or the greatest power in a country, etc: *The state's control over these resources relied on its sovereign power.* ◇ *The Westminster model assumes that Parliament is sovereign and ministers are accountable to Parliament.*

sov·er·eign[2] /ˈsɒvrɪn; *NAmE* ˈsɑːvrən/ *noun* (*formal*) a king or queen: *His execution illustrates the high price to be paid for open opposition to the sovereign.*

sov·er·eign·ty /ˈsɒvrənti; *NAmE* ˈsɑːvrənti/ *noun* [U] **1** complete power to govern a country, etc: *Dynastic sovereignty gave way to popular sovereignty, with government by consent of the people.* ◇ **~ of sth** *In the past, the*

S

sovereignty of Parliament was without any formal limits. ◇ **~ over sth** *Canada claimed sovereignty over the entire Arctic Archipelago of North America in 1895.* **2** the state of being a country with freedom to govern itself: *He asserted that states claiming sovereignty would inevitably develop offensive military capabilities.* ◇ *national/state sovereignty*

space /speɪs/ *noun* **1** [U] the whole area in which all things exist and move: *The speed of light in empty space is the same for all observers.* ◇ *With the Global Positioning System, an observer can determine his or her position in space with extreme accuracy.* **2** [U, C] a real or imagined area where activities take place or are possible: *Both main political parties increasingly came to occupy the same political space.* ◇ *The study looked at people—women, children, the elderly—who most often experience fear in public spaces.* ◇ **~ between A and B** *Fantasy fiction inhabits the space between reality and dreams.* ◇ **~ for sth** *One of Agamben's aims is to open up a space for an alternative, non-metaphysical politics.* **3** [U] an amount of an area or of a place that is empty or that is available for use: *At the time, there was a severe shortage of office space in central London.* ◇ *The aim was to fund the website through the sale of online advertising space.* ◇ **~ for (doing) sth** *There was extremely limited space available in the building for conducting confidential interviews.* ◇ **~ (for sb) to do sth** *There is not enough space here to discuss the different proposals in detail.* ◇ **+ noun** *We calculated carbon dioxide emissions from space heating, water heating, cooking, lightsandappliances.* ➲ *compare* ROOM (1) **4** [C] **~ (between A and B)** an area between things that is empty: *The spaces between the plates are filled with polystyrene.* ◇ *More severe injuries usually occur when a blast occurs in confined spaces.* **5** [C] an area that is used for a particular purpose: *The council's policies stipulate maximum building heights and minimum requirements for parking spaces.* ◇ **~ for (doing) sth** *Planners neglected to create spaces for strolling, looking, comparing and choosing.* ◇ **~ (for sb/sth) to do sth** *The Internet provides a space for adolescents to explore their identities and address their concerns.* **6** [C, U] a large area of land that has no buildings on it: *Davis lists the public spaces, especially parks, that have been built over since 1945.* ◇ *There is a consumer preference for low-density housing near open space.* **7** [C, U] the part of a line, page or document that is empty or that is available for use: *Participants were asked to record their thoughts in the spaces provided on the questionnaire.* **8** (*also* ˌ**outer** ˈ**space**) [U] the area outside the earth's atmosphere where all the other planets and stars are: *In 1961, Gagarin became the first human to fly in space.* ◇ *One recent proposal is for the commercialization of outer space by placing commercial messages in orbit.* **9** [C, usually sing.] a period of time: *For a brief space in January 1967, there was a sort of democracy.* ◇ **~ of sth** *A million years is a short space of geological time for such an incredible volume of lava to be deposited.* ◇ **in the ~ of sth** *The book examines how communist economies can be transformed into their opposite in the space of a few years.* **10** [U] the freedom and the time to think or do what you want to: **~ to do sth** *The school introduced a new discipline procedure that gave children space to understand their emotions and their disruptive behaviour.* ◇ **~ for sth** *This imagery of certainty leaves little space for search and experimentation.*

spaced /speɪst/ *adj.* **+ adv./prep.** (of a number of things) arranged or located with a distance or time between them: *100 wooden nest boxes were spaced at 30-metre intervals for hole-nesting passerines.* ◇ *At location F, the contours are widely spaced so the slopes are comparatively gentle.* ◇ *Haig mentions that closely spaced birth intervals tend to increase infant mortality.*

ˈ**space-time** (*also* **space·time**) *noun* [U] (*physics*) the universe considered as a CONTINUUM with four measurements —length, width, depth and time—inside which any event or physical object is located: *The curvature of space-time can also become infinite in certain situations.*

spa·cing /ˈspeɪsɪŋ/ *noun* **1** [U, C] the amount of space that there is between things: **~ (of sth)** *There is regular spacing of trees in a forest caused by competition for sunlight and nutrients.* ◇ **~ between A and B** *The spacing between adjacent turbines is 10 rotor diameters.* **2** [U] the amount of time that is left between things happening: *Effective contraception offers choice in determining family size and spacing.* ◇ **~ between A and B** *On average, educated women have fewer, but healthier, children, partly due to longer spacing between births.*

span¹ /spæn/ *noun* **1** the length of time that sth lasts or is able to continue: *The teachers make special arrangements that take account of these children's short attention span.* ◇ **~ of sth** *Over the span of human history, people have organized their economic activities in many different ways.* ◇ *Daewoo is a good example of how a Korean company could globalize its operations in a short span of time.* ➲ *see also* LIFESPAN, TIME SPAN **2 ~ (of sth)** a range or variety of sth: *Due to the broad span of the study, it has not been possible to describe each measure in detail.* **3 ~ (of sth)** the part of a bridge or an ARCH between one vertical support and another: *Larger spans could be achieved but the bridge builder had to ensure that their designs made the bridges safe.* **4 ~ (of sth)** the width of sth from one side to the other: *The Sarawak Chamber in Sarawak, Malaysia, has a roof span of 300 m.*

span² /spæn/ *verb* (-nn-) **1** [T, I] to last all through a period of time or to cover the whole of it: **~ sth** *Yam Kim-fai's career and fame spanned more than four decades.* ◇ *The author's investigation spans two generations and explores internal and transnational migration.* ◇ **~ from A to B** *We acquired monthly incidence data for accidental deaths for 204 months spanning from 1990 to 2006.* **2** [T] **~ sth** to include many things or a large area: *These articles span a wide range of topics.* ◇ *Research for this review spanned more than 1 000 articles.* ◇ *The influence of Martin Luther spans religion, language and culture.* ◇ *A cross-sectional study was undertaken, spanning eight European cities.* **3** [T] **~ sth** to stretch right across sth, from one side to the other: *This wave formed a formidable barrier across the river: it was more than 20 feet in height and spanned nearly the entire navigable channel.*

spare¹ /speə(r); *NAmE* sper/ *adj.* **1** [usually before noun] that is not being used or is not needed at the present time: *The market in spare parts, e.g. for cars and electrical goods, is traditionally an area where good profits can be made.* ◇ *The lack of spare capacity in schools meant that parents had little choice as to where to send their children.* **2** (of time) available to do what you want with rather than work: *We work on average fewer hours per week than our grandparents and we have more spare time.*

spare² /speə(r); *NAmE* sper/ *verb* **1** [often passive] to allow sb/sth to escape harm, damage or death, especially when others do not escape it: **~ sb/sth** *Some lost their livelihoods while others were spared.* ◇ *His life was spared after his wife intervened with the emperor.* ◇ **~ sb/sth from sth** *Fortunately, the spinal cord was spared from injury.* ◇ **~ sb/sth sth** *He offered to spare them the death penalty if they conformed.* **2** to make sb/sth available to sb else, especially when it requires an effort for you to do this: **~ sb/sth for sth** *Now that many women are employed outside the home, it is more difficult for them to spare the time for volunteer activities.* ◇ **~ sb/sth** *The general was so important that the country could not spare him.*

IDM **to** ˈ**spare** if you have time, money, etc. **to spare**, you have more than you need: *Retired people with more time* *to spare are more likely to volunteer.* ◇ *The government has no funds to spare for such research.*

spark[1] /spɑːk; *NAmE* spɑːrk/ *verb* to cause sth to start or develop, especially suddenly: **~ sth** *Speculation about a likely depreciation of the exchange rate sparked a currency crisis.* ◇ *Publication of the study sparked a renewed interest in the subject.* ◇ **~ sth off** *Napoleon's deposition of the Spanish king sparked off a revolt in Madrid.* ◇ **(be) sparked by sth** *In the 1860s, they staged more than 800 uprisings, mostly to protest against financial difficulties sparked by crop failures.*

spark[2] /spɑːk; *NAmE* spɑːrk/ *noun* **1** a small flash of light produced by an electric current: *The cable was cut and sparks from the resulting short-circuit ignited leaking petrol.* **2** a very small burning piece of material that is produced by sth that is burning or by hitting two hard substances together: *A piece of flint was used for striking a spark.* **3** an action or event that causes sth important to develop, especially trouble or violence: *Aeneas's son kills a pet stag while hunting, and from that small spark a full-blown war develops.* **4** [usually sing.] **~ of sth** a small amount of a particular quality or feeling: *She claims that all humans have a spark of the divine within them.*

sparse /spɑːs; *NAmE* spɑːrs/ *adj.* (*comparative* **sparser**, no *superlative*) only present in small amounts or numbers and often spread over a large area: *The sparse vegetation does little to prevent erosion.* ◇ *Currently, only sparse data are available.* ◇ *Rainfall is sparse, intermittent and unreliable.* ■ **sparse·ly** *adv.*: *Arid lands also tend to be more sparsely populated.*

spa·tial /ˈspeɪʃl/ *adj.* connected with space and the position, size, shape, etc. of things in it: *More research is needed into the inequitable spatial distribution of public services across the city.* ◇ *Hupp and Bazemore (1993) described both spatial and temporal patterns of sedimentation in western Tennessee.* ◇ *Temporal and spatial variations in water availability have prompted studies into water conservation practices among Prairie farmers.* ◇ *Quantitative spatial analysis tends to focus on large areas and populations.* ■ **spa·tial·ly** /ˈspeɪʃəli/ *adv.*: *The environmental impacts of hunter-gatherers are limited, both spatially and temporally.* ◇ *Jobs in the United States became more spatially concentrated between 1972 and 1992.*

spawn /spɔːn/ *verb* **1** [I, T] (of fish and some other creatures) to lay eggs: *The fish spawn among fine-leaved plants.* ◇ **~ sth** *Eggs are spawned and in the water embryos quickly develop into larvae.* **2** [T] to cause sth to develop or be produced in large numbers: *The question of whether globalization is a good or a bad thing has spawned heated debates in classrooms, boardrooms and on the streets.* ◇ *The Internet has spawned a new generation of researchers who seem to have boundless amounts of web-generated data.*

speak /spiːk/ *verb* (**spoke** /spəʊk; *NAmE* spoʊk/, **spoken** /ˈspəʊkən; *NAmE* ˈspoʊkən/) **1** [I] to talk to sb about sth; to have a conversation with sb: **~ to/with sb** *There were strict rules on who could speak to the emperor.* ◇ **~ (to/with sb) (about sth/sb)** *Many students are reluctant to speak to their teachers about their problems.* **2** [I] to use your voice to say sth: *A strategy was devised for dealing with participants who were reluctant to speak.* ◇ *For some patients, speaking on the telephone can be a cause of significant stress.* **3** [I] to mention, describe or present sth/sb: **~ of sth/sb** *The Scottish government spoke of the need to modernize the law.* ◇ **~ of sth/sb as sth** *To speak of Roman commanders as 'generals' is somewhat misleading.* ◇ **~ about sth/sb** *The manifesto spoke about 'reducing international conflict'.* ◇ **~ in favour of/against sth** *I shall examine the reasons that speak in favour of increased openness and sharing of data.* ◇ **~ in terms of sth** *So far, I have spoken in terms of marketing being essentially about providing what the customer wants.* **4** [T] (not used in the progressive tenses) **~ sth** to be able to use a particular language: *He could speak English, French, Dutch, Danish and Portuguese.* ◇ *The language spoken in aristocratic European circles was French.* **5** [T, I] to use a particular language to express yourself: **~ sth** *Approximately 32% of Los Angeles County households report speaking Spanish in the home.* ◇ **~ in sth** *Most language teachers ask students to speak in the target language as much as possible in class.* **6 -speaking** (in adjectives) speaking the language mentioned: *In the 1960s, US television programmes became important parts of the television schedule in many English-speaking nations.* **7** [I] to make a speech to an audience: **(+ adv./prep.)** *Nanbara Shigeru spoke at the extraordinary session of the national legislature in 1946.* ◇ **~ in favour of/against sth** *The Liberal MP spoke in favour of the amendment.* **8** [T] to say or state sth: **~ sth** *The poet Theocritus spoke the truth when he described Egypt as a land of opportunity for immigrants.* ◇ **the spoken word** *It seems that the Roman elite were more concerned by the power of the spoken word than the written word.*

IDM **ˈgenerally, ˈbroadly, ˈroughly, ˈrelatively, etc. speaking** used to show that what you are saying is true in a general, etc. way: *Types of therapy differ widely, but broadly speaking, they all aim to make people happier and less anxious.* ◇ *Globally speaking, less was known about the origin of the HIV epidemic than other emerging infectious diseases.* **ˌso to ˈspeak** used to emphasize that you are expressing sth in an unusual way: *Types of relationships and norms of conduct are passed down the generations: we are, so to speak, locked in from birth.* **speak for itˈself/themˈselves** to be so easy to see and understand that you do not need to say anything else about it/them: *Murrow and Friendly determined to use a compilation of existing footage, letting the evidence speak for itself.* **speak for myˈself/herˈself/himˈself, etc.** to express what you think or want yourself, rather than sb else doing it for you: *Care was taken to allow respondents to speak for themselves.* **speaking as sth** used to say that you are the type of person mentioned and are expressing your opinion from that point of view: *Michel Camdessus, speaking as Managing Director of the IMF, has referred to poverty as the ultimate systemic threat (Camdessus, 2000).* **speak your ˈmind** to say exactly what you think, in a very direct way: *Students who visit the mental health clinic can speak their minds, knowing that confidentiality will be respected.* **speak ˈvolumes (about/for sth/sb)** to tell you a lot about sth/sb, without the need for words: *Different scents communicate different things to those around you and speak volumes about yourself* ➲ *more at* STRICTLY, TRUTH

PHR V **ˈspeak for sb** to state the views or wishes of a person or a group; to act as a representative for sb: *Loach was apparently 'speaking for the British film community', when he made these comments.* **ˌspeak ˈout (against sth)** to state your opinions publicly, especially in opposition to sth and in a way that takes courage: *Local leaders who spoke out against the violence were imprisoned and tortured.* **ˈspeak to sth/sb** to be relevant to or deal with sth/sb: *Their new political strategy spoke specifically to the interests and sensibilities of the urban poor.* **ˌspeak ˈup (for sb/sth)** to say what you think clearly and freely, especially in order to support or defend sb/sth: *Some people are, because of their condition, less able to speak up for their needs.*

speak·er /ˈspiːkə(r)/ *noun* **1** a person who speaks a particular language: *Current circumstances are producing increasing numbers of English speakers around the world.* ◇ **~ of sth** *Competent speakers of the language should be able to identify these grammar rules.* ➲ *see also* NATIVE SPEAKER **2** a person who is or was speaking: *It seems that for men, the point of conversation is to be the speaker, whereas women value listening much more.* **3** a person who gives a talk or makes a speech: *Dr Lee is a regular*

S

speaker on these issues at international conferences. **4 (the) Speaker (of sth)** the title of the person whose job is to control the discussions in a parliament: *The Speaker presides over the most important debates in the House of Commons.* **5** the part of a piece of equipment that the sound comes out of: *Sound imitating the noise made by a prey animal comes from a speaker.*

spe·cial /ˈspeʃl/ *adj.* **1** [usually before noun] not ordinary or usual; different from what is normal SYN EXCEPTIONAL (1): *In special cases, additional funding may be given.* ◇ *The experience unites him with his family in a special way that brings them together.* **2** designed or organized for a particular person, purpose or occasion: *There has been a growing number of special issues of journals on this topic.* **3** belonging to one particular person, group of people, or place: *Britain continued to value its special relationship with the United States.* **4** [only before noun] better or greater than usual: *These are particularly serious problems that require special attention.* **5** more important than others; deserving or getting more attention than usual: *The Sun God had a special place in the lives of these people.*

▸ SPECIAL + NOUN **case • circumstances • kind, type • feature • treatment • purpose • way • place** *The period might, in special circumstances, be extended by a further 14 days.* | **issue • procedure • resolution • law** *No special procedure is required for constitutional change.* | **relationship • status • role • place • way • property** *The Romans granted Judaism special status.* | **interest • attention • consideration** *This issue is of special interest to economists.*

spe·cial·ist¹ /ˈspeʃəlɪst/ *noun* **1** a doctor who has SPECIALIZED in a particular area of medicine: *It is generally not possible for the patient to see a specialist without first consulting a general practitioner.* ◇ **~ in sth** *Breuer was a leading Viennese specialist in internal medicine.* **2 ~ (in sth)** a person who is an expert in a particular area of work or study: *Their arguments can only be understood by specialists in economics.* ➲ *compare* GENERALIST

spe·cial·ist² /ˈspeʃəlɪst/ *adj.* [only before noun] **1** connected with a doctor who has SPECIALIZED in a particular area of medicine: *Patients from more deprived areas are less likely to be referred for specialist care.* **2** having or involving detailed knowledge of a particular topic or area of study: *Such products typically require specialist knowledge on the part of the salesperson.*

S

spe·ci·al·ity /ˌspeʃiˈæləti/ (*BrE*) (*also* **spe·cial·ty** *NAmE, BrE*) *noun* (*pl.* **-ies**) **1** a particular area of medicine that sb studies and becomes an expert in: *Most specialities have a minimum of five years' training.* **2** a type of food or product that a restaurant or place is famous for because it is so good: *There was a flourishing trade in luxury goods and local specialities.* ◇ **~ of sth** *Often, there is an opportunity to taste the culinary specialities of the area.* **3** (in compounds) **+ noun** satisfying particular tastes or needs: *Speciality goods are sold in relatively few outlets.* **4** an area of work or study that sb gives most of their attention to and knows a lot about; something that sb is good at: *Textbooks of New Testament theology have long been a German speciality.* ◇ **sb's ~** *Robinson's speciality is military history.*

spe·cial·iza·tion (*BrE also* **-isa·tion**) /ˌspeʃəlaɪˈzeɪʃn; *NAmE* ˌspeʃələˈzeɪʃn/ *noun* **1** [U] **~ (in sth)** the practice of limiting yourself to providing a particular product or service: *There was a move away from cereal farming towards specialization in other commodities.* **2** [U] **~ (in sth)** the process of becoming an expert in a particular area of work or study: *The company's organizational structure encouraged a high degree of specialization in finance, accounting, etc.* **3** [C] **~ (in sth)** a particular area of work or study that sb becomes an expert in: *Candidates need a specialization in the exact scientific area.*

spe·cial·ize (*BrE also* **-ise**) /ˈspeʃəlaɪz/ *verb* **1** [I] **~ (in sth)** to limit yourself to providing a particular product or service: *The company specializes in the production of small vehicles suited to urban traffic.* **2** [I] **~ (in sth)** to become an expert in a particular area of work or study: *He specializes in property law.*

spe·cial·ized (*BrE also* **-ised**) /ˈspeʃəlaɪzd/ *adj.* **1** connected with a particular area of work or study: *Each profession requires particular aptitudes and specialized knowledge.* **2** requiring or involving detailed and particular knowledge or training: *People with severe learning disability often find themselves needing specialized care.* **3** designed or developed for a particular purpose or area of knowledge: *Makers of specialized dictionaries have traditionally focused on the selection and translation of terms.*

spe·cial·ly /ˈspeʃəli/ *adv.* for a particular purpose, person, etc: *They offer a variety of services specially designed for mobile phones.* ➲ *usage note at* ESPECIALLY

spe·cialty /ˈspeʃəlti/ *noun* (*pl.* **-ies**) (*especially NAmE* or *medical*) = SPECIALITY

spe·cies /ˈspiːʃiːz/ *noun* (*pl.* **spe·cies**) **1** a group into which animals, plants, etc. that are able to breed with each other and produce healthy young are divided, smaller than a GENUS and identified by a Latin name: **~ (of sth)** *The forest is home to more than 300 species of birds.* ◇ *Most plant species cannot survive in these habitats.* ◇ *Up to 80% of endangered species worldwide could be adversely affected by competition or predation by invasive species.* ◇ **+ noun** *Major droughts have affected species diversity and killed some trees.* ➲ *compare* CLASS¹ (6), FAMILY¹ (5), KINGDOM (3), ORDER¹ (9), PHYLUM **2** (*chemistry, physics*) a particular kind of atom, MOLECULE, ION or PARTICLE: *Most, but not all, of the various different chemical species present in sea water can be removed by distillation.*

▸ ADJECTIVE + SPECIES **different • various • particular • individual • single • new • related • native • alien • invasive • dominant • endangered • human • marine** *Conservationists have taken action to protect the diversity of native species in the region.*

▸ VERB + SPECIES **find • detect • identify • define • study • record • compare • introduce • protect • preserve** *There are many advantages to using DNA sequences to identify species.*

▸ SPECIES + VERB **live • occur • survive • occupy • dominate • invade • colonize • differ • show, exhibit • evolve** *One species may simply dominate a resource such as a water supply.*

▸ SPECIES + NOUN **richness, abundance • diversity • distribution • composition • identification • trait • interaction • conservation • protection • management • extinction • pool • assemblage** *Species richness recovered quickly thereafter.* ◇ *Rainforest removal is a major cause of species extinction.*

spe·cif·ic AWL /spəˈsɪfɪk/ *adj.* **1** [usually before noun] connected with one particular person, thing or group only SYN PARTICULAR¹ (1): *Companies can develop the products and services that specific types of customers want.* ◇ *Regardless of the specific context, the following recommendations apply:...* ◇ *These unplanned cities often grew haphazardly in response to specific local circumstances.* ◇ **noun + specifc** *Kloeppel et al. report that drought effects in the Appalachian forests are species specific.* **2 ~ to sb/sth** existing only in one place; limited to one person, thing or group SYN PECULIAR (1): *Some illnesses are specific to minority ethnic groups.* **3** detailed and exact SYN PRECISE (1): *This rather general question can be supplemented by some more specific questions.* ◇ **~ about sth** *Article 32 of the draft treaty was more specific about these powers than the Single European Act.*

spe·cif·ic·al·ly AWL /spəˈsɪfɪkli/ *adv.* **1** in a way that is connected with or intended for one particular person, thing or group only: *A booklet containing health recommendations specifically designed for the elderly was distributed to patients.* ◇ *The Roman system focused specifically on facilitating rapid movement between London and the key Roman centres.* **2** in a detailed, exact and clear way: *The rules specifically mention the possibility of holding extraordinary meetings of the European Council.* **3** used when you want to add more detailed and exact information: *The post-1815 period, or more specifically the time of Victoria's reign (1837–1901), represented the great age of British colonization.* ➲ language bank *at* I.E.

speci·fi·ca·tion AWL /ˌspesɪfɪˈkeɪʃn/ *noun* **1** [C] a detailed description of how sth is, or should be, designed or made: *To meet specifications in these cases, producers must adhere to tight guidelines.* ◇ **~ of sth** *Sophisticated users will read the detailed specifications of any computer they are thinking of buying.* ◇ **to sb's specifications** *A chip produced to his specifications would have an appearance distinct from any other piece of circuitry.* ◇ **to a... ~** *The development is built to a very high specification.* **2** [C, U] **~ (of sth)** a clear and exact statement of a fact or of sth that is required: *The first stage involves a clear specification of the marketing problem.* ◇ *Greater specification of how goals are to be achieved may increase the individual's efficiency.* **3** [C, U] **~ (of sth)** an act of identifying sb/sth clearly and definitely: *An allocation of goods and services means a complete specification of who produces what and who consumes what.*

speci·fi·city AWL /ˌspesɪˈfɪsəti/ *noun* [U] the quality of being specific: *The legislation lacked the specificity needed for making various operational decisions.*

spe·cif·ics AWL /spəˈsɪfɪks/ *noun* [pl.] **~ (of sth)** the details of a subject that you need to think about or discuss: *It is beyond the scope of this paper to go into the specifics of each approach.*

spe·cify AWL /ˈspesɪfaɪ/ *verb* (**speci·fies**, **speci·fy·ing**, **speci·fied**, **speci·fied**) to identify sb/sth clearly and definitely; to state a fact or sth that is required clearly and exactly: **~ sth** *Three coordinates are needed to specify the location of the centre of mass of the molecule.* ◇ **~ who/what, etc...** *This part of the plan should specify who is responsible for the various activities and actions.* ◇ **~ that...** *The Canadian constitution specifies that provinces have ownership of natural resources.*

speci·men /ˈspesɪmən/ *noun* **1** a single example of sth, especially an animal or a plant: *A total of 147 specimens from 56 species were examined.* ◇ **~ of sth** *Two well-preserved specimens of* Eocrinus *have been reported from the Bright Angel Shale.* **2** a small amount of sth that shows what the rest of it is like: *Sampling programmes brought up rock specimens from the oceanic plains.* ◇ **~ of sth** *Specimens of his writing were analysed for particular stylistic features.* **3** a small quantity of blood, URINE, etc. that is taken from sb and tested: *If a driver is stopped by the police and refuses to provide a breath specimen, they are guilty of an offence.* ◇ **~ of sth** *Timed specimens of urine were collected from all the patients.*

spec·tacle /ˈspektəkl/ *noun* **1** [C, U] **~ (of sth)** a performance or an event that is very impressive and exciting to look at: *Athletic events, after all, are the great public spectacles of our time.* ◇ *The spectacle of public execution provided a warning to the audience.* ◇ *Speech, song and visual spectacle remained the principal means of communicating folk culture.* **2** [sing.] **~ (of sth)** an unusual, embarrassing or sad sight or situation that attracts a lot of attention: *The spectacle of human misery is harder to ignore than it used to be.* **3 spectacles** [pl.] (*formal*) = GLASS (3)

spec·tacu·lar /spekˈtækjələ(r)/ *adj.* very impressive: *In the 1950s, the party had a number of spectacular electoral successes.* ◇ *The most spectacular recorded example of coastline changes was caused by the eruption of Krakatau in 1883 (Simkin and Fiske, 1983).* ■ **spec·tacu·lar·ly** *adv.*: *Ayler (2009) argues that the World Trade Organization has been spectacularly successful in increasing the volume of world trade.*

spec·ta·tor /spekˈteɪtə(r)/ *noun* a person who is watching a performance or an event: *Female spectators naturally identified with the protagonist at the film's climax.*

spec·tra *pl. of* SPECTRUM

spec·tral /ˈspektrəl/ *adj.* (*technical*) connected with a spectrum: *The spectral lines enabled the molecular composition of the gas sample to be identified.*

spec·trom·eter /spekˈtrɒmɪtə(r); *NAmE* spekˈtrɑːmɪtər/ *noun* (*technical*) a piece of equipment for measuring the WAVELENGTHS of spectra: *Dynamic light scattering (DLS) measurements were conducted at 25°C using a light-scattering spectrometer.* ➲ *see also* MASS SPECTROMETER

spec·tros·copy /spekˈtrɒskəpi; *NAmE* spekˈtrɑːskəpi/ *noun* [U] (*chemistry*, *physics*) the study of forming and looking at spectra using a spectrometer, etc: *One method used to determine the amount of alcohol in a car driver's breath involves infrared spectroscopy.*

spec·trum /ˈspektrəm/ *noun* (*pl.* **spec·tra** /ˈspektrə/) **1** a pattern of coloured bands formed when light is split into its CONSTITUENT WAVELENGTHS, as seen, for example, in a RAINBOW: *The light from stars or galaxies is analysed by spreading it out into a spectrum.* ◇ *Sunrises and sunsets take on colours in the red end of the spectrum.* **2** (*physics*) any signal ordered by one of its properties, such as its energy or mass: *The composition of a material can be found by studying its mass spectrum.* ➲ *see also* MASS SPECTROMETER **3** [usually sing.] a complete or wide range of people or things: **~ (of sb/sth)** *His writing appealed to an exceptionally broad spectrum of Victorian readers.* ◇ **across the... ~** *The movement gathered widespread support across the political spectrum.*

specu·late /ˈspekjuleɪt/ *verb* **1** [I, T] to form an opinion about sth without knowing all the details or facts: **~ about sth** *Ancient and modern historians have speculated about Alexander's ultimate goals.* ◇ **~ on sth** *She considers the future political role of global cities and speculates on the possibility that they will evolve into city states.* ◇ **~ as to sth** *One can only speculate as to whether such criticisms may influence future decisions.* ◇ **~ that...** *The fossil evidence led Resser (1946) to speculate that these molluscs occupied shallow-water habitats.* ◇ **~ why/how, etc...** *It is interesting to speculate why this phenomenon has not received more attention.* **2** [I] to buy goods, property, shares, etc, hoping to make a profit when you sell them, but with the risk of losing money: *George Soros, for example, is believed to have made over US$1000 million by speculating.* ◇ **~ in sth** *Grundy speculated in land, often preferring urban real estate.*

specu·la·tion /ˌspekjuˈleɪʃn/ *noun* [U, C] **1** the act of forming opinions about what has happened or what might happen without knowing all the facts: *The explanation for this remarkable coincidence is still a matter of intense speculation and debate.* ◇ **~ that...** *There is speculation that Canadian cities will become more like American cities if cuts to the Canadian welfare state continue (Dear and Wolch, 1993; Lemon, 1996b).* ◇ **~ about/over sth** *Relying on mere speculations about potential consequences is not enough in this context.* **2 ~ (in sth)** the activity of buying and selling goods or shares in a company in the hope of making a profit, but with the risk of losing money: *In 1926 the company faced financial difficulties because of failed speculation in a trading business.* ◇

S

Keynes's speculations in financial markets increased the assets of King's College tenfold.

specu·la·tive /ˈspekjələtɪv; *NAmE also* ˈspekjəleɪtɪv/ *adj.* **1** based on guessing or on opinions that have been formed without knowing all the facts: *The causes of the revolt remain speculative.* ◇ *The suggestion that these surfaces are of the same age is highly speculative in the absence of any radiometric rock dating.* **2** (of business activity) done in the hope of making a profit but involving the risk of losing money: *Eventually, the speculative bubble collapses and the boom-bust cycle starts again.* ■ **specu·la·tive·ly** *adv.*: *He also suggests, more speculatively, that this change could have been the origin of human language.*

speech /spiːtʃ/ *noun* **1** [C] a formal talk that sb gives to an audience: *The Governor of the Bank of Thailand made a speech supporting capital controls.* ◇ *to give/deliver a speech* ◇ **in a ~** *In a 1982 speech, President Ronald Reagan blamed the recession on the increase in women in the workforce.* ◇ **~ on/about sth** *Sir William Jones delivered a famous speech about Sanskrit, pointing out its similarities to Greek and Latin.* **2** [U] the ability or right to speak: *She argues that human speech is not always as distinct from communication between other animals as it might seem.* ◇ **free ~** *The right to free speech is the cornerstone of any democratic society.* ◇ **freedom of ~** *The constitutional rights to freedom of speech guarantee that people can say and write whatever they please.* **3** [U] the way in which a particular person speaks: *Jumbled speech and hearing voices are two symptoms traditionally associated with insanity.* **4** [U] the language used when speaking: *We compared the vocabulary used in academic speech with that employed in academic writing.* ◇ **+ noun** *Speech recognition systems are used to handle some routine customer inquiries at call centres.* **5** [C] a group of lines that an actor speaks in a play in the theatre: *Hamlet then makes his famous speech, declaring, 'What a piece of work is a man...'*

ˈspeech marks *noun* [pl.] = QUOTATION MARKS

speed¹ /spiːd/ *noun* **1** [C, U] the rate at which sb/sth moves or travels: *By 8 o'clock, wind speeds had reached nearly 100 mph.* ◇ **~ of sth** *Raising the temperature of a gas increases the average speed of its molecules.* ◇ **at (a)... ~** *The cylinder rotates at a constant speed.* ◇ *The turbine units can become unstable at high speed.* ◇ **+ noun** *Highway speed limits are effective at reducing fatalities only when drivers observe them.* ➲ *see also* HIGH-SPEED **2** [U, C] the rate at which sth happens or is done: **~ of sth** *The merchants' primary concern was speed of delivery.* ◇ *The quickening speed of technological change is leading to shorter product life cycles.* ◇ **at a... ~** *The two ant species foraged at different speeds.* **3** [U] the quality of being quick or fast: *Smaller organizations can have the advantage of speed and flexibility over larger ones.*

speed² /spiːd/ *verb* (**speed·ed, speed·ed**) **~ sth** to make sth happen more quickly: *The aim is to speed detection of possible outbreaks and epidemics.* ◇ *Border security measures have been relaxed to speed deliveries.*

PHR V ˌ**speed ˈup** | ˌ**speed sth ˈup** to move or happen faster; to make sth move or happen faster: *More steam is fed to the engine to cause it to speed up.* ◇ *The diagnosis of breast cancer has been speeded up in recent years.*

spell¹ /spel/ *verb* (**spelt, spelt** /spelt/ or **spelled, spelled**) **1** [T, I] **~ (sth)** to write or say the letters of a word in the correct order; to form words correctly from individual letters: *The word was spelled correctly.* ◇ *Many others have not even learned to spell.* **2** [T] **~ sth** (of letters) to form a word when they are put together in a particular order: *The task requires participants to indicate whether or not a string of letters spells a real word.* **3** [T] **~ sth (for sb/sth)** to have sth, usually sth bad, as a result; to mean sth, usually sth bad: *In an earlier era, divorce often spelled financial ruin for women.*

PHR V ˌ**spell sth ˈout** to explain sth in a simple, clear way: *The Prime Minister spelt out his foreign policy approach in April 1999 in a speech in Chicago.* ◇ **~ out what/why, etc...** *The author's primary concern is to spell out what he takes to be the full significance of these events.*

spell² /spel/ *noun* **1** [C] a short period of time during which sth lasts or sb does sth: *Prolonged dry spells are not uncommon in this area.* ◇ *He said he had often experienced headaches and dizzy spells.* ◇ **~ of sth** *University graduates are likely to experience spells of unemployment as they search for the best job.* **2** [sing.] a quality that sb/sth has that gives them control or influence over people as if in a magical way: **under the ~ of sb/sth** *He fell under the spell of the sea at an early age.* IDM *see* CAST¹

spell·ing /ˈspelɪŋ/ *noun* **1** [U] the process or activity of forming words correctly from individual letters: *Many parents believe that accuracy in spelling is of major educational importance.* ◇ **+ noun** *Some spelling mistakes in the original report have been corrected.* **2** [C] **~ (of sth)** the way that a particular word is written: *Variant spellings of these words are numerous.*

spelt *past tense, past part. of* SPELL¹

spend /spend/ *verb* (**spent, spent** /spent/) **1** [T] to use time for a particular purpose; to pass time: **~ sth + adv./prep.** *Over 70% of fathers surveyed reported a wish to spend more time with their children.* ◇ **~ sth on sth** *On average, individuals spent 2.9 hours per week on activities related to sports.* ◇ **~ sth doing sth** *He spent 20 years working in sales and marketing.* ◇ **~ sth in doing sth** *The Roman army in Britain spent long periods in establishing and maintaining frontiers.* **2** [I, T] to give money to pay for goods or services: **~ (sth)** *No business likes to spend money unless it has to.* ◇ *The need for governments to spend heavily was regarded as a priority.* ◇ **~ sth on (doing) sth** *The amount spent on foreign goods and services will increase.* ◇ **~ sth doing sth** *They spend enormous sums of money obtaining celebrity endorsements.* **3** [T, often passive] to use energy or effort, especially until it has all been used: **~ sth on (doing) sth** *This energy would be better spent on other activities.* ◇ **~ sth doing sth** *We spent too much effort generating the data and not enough on analysing it.*

spend·ing /ˈspendɪŋ/ *noun* [U] the amount of money that is spent by a government, an organization or a particular group of people: *Lower interest rates will also lead to an increase in consumer spending.* ◇ *In the US, public spending accounts for less than half of total health spending.* ◇ *government/federal spending* ◇ *social/welfare/military/defence spending* ◇ **~ on sth** *These are policies aimed at reducing the spending on imports specifically.* ◇ **+ noun** *The Japanese public does not want to see spending cuts in any social policy areas.*

sperm /spɜːm; *NAmE* spɜːrm/ *noun* (*pl.* **sperm** or **sperms**) [C, U] a cell produced by the sex organs of a male that can combine with a female egg to produce young; the liquid that contains these cells: *All the sperm produced by a male bee are identical.*

sphere AWL /sfɪə(r); *NAmE* sfɪr/ *noun* **1** a solid figure that is completely round, with every point on its surface at an equal distance from the centre: *Those theorems determine the surface area and volume of a sphere.* **2** any object that is completely round, for example a ball: *The newly formed planet was a solid sphere with a core made up of iron alloys.* **3** an area of activity, influence or interest; a particular section of society SYN DOMAIN (1): **in a... ~** *Increasingly, women were wielding equal power in the public sphere.* ◇ *the private/domestic sphere* ◇ **~ of**

influence *Bishops struggled to protect or enlarge their spheres of influence.*

spher·ic·al AWL /ˈsferɪkl; *NAmE also* ˈsfɪrɪkl/ *adj.* shaped like a sphere SYN ROUND¹ (1): *Both the earth and the moon are nearly spherical.* ■ **spher·ic·al·ly** AWL /ˈsferɪkli; *NAmE also* ˈsfɪrɪkli/ *adv.*: *The particles are more regularly sized and spherically shaped.*

spice /spaɪs/ *noun* [C, U] one of the various types of powder or seed that come from plants and are used in cooking. Spices have a strong taste and smell: *Demand for salt and spices played a major role in the development of transport routes and cultural contact.*

spill¹ /spɪl/ *verb* (**spilled**, **spilled**) (*BrE also* **spilt**, **spilt** /spɪlt/) [I, T] (usually of liquid) to flow over the edge of a container by accident; to make liquid do this: **(+ adv./prep.)** *If a river overtops its banks, water spills out over the floodplain.* ◇ **~ sth (+ adv./prep.)** *A woman successfully sued a restaurant after spilling hot coffee on herself.*
PHR V ˌ**spill ˈover (into sth) 1** to fill a container and go over the edge: *A levee reduces the number of times a river will spill over onto its floodplain.* ➲ *related noun* SPILLOVER (2) **2** to start in one area and then affect other areas: *Violent conflict and insecurity can spill over into neighbouring countries.* ➲ *related noun* SPILLOVER (1)

spill² /spɪl/ (*also* **spill·age** /ˈspɪlɪdʒ/) *noun* an act of letting a liquid come or fall out of a container; the amount of liquid that comes or falls out: *About 700 000 tons of oil spilled into the Gulf, the largest oil spill in the world's oceans ever.*

spill·over /ˈspɪləʊvə(r); *NAmE* ˈspɪloʊvər/ *noun* [C, U] **1 ~ (of sth) (from sth) (into sth)** the results or the effects of sth that have spread to other situations or places: *Developing economies could benefit from technology spillovers from more developed economies.* ◇ *There was concern about spillover of French revolutionary sentiment into English proletarian radicalism.* **2 ~ (of sth) (from sth) (into sth)** something that is too large or too much for the place where it starts, and spreads to other places: *The village was a spillover from a neighbouring, larger village.*

spin¹ /spɪn/ *noun* **1** [U, C] a very fast turning movement: *The graph shows the geometry of the earth's orbit and spin.* ◇ *The two electrons can have either parallel spins or opposite spins.* **2** [sing., U] (*rather informal*) a particular way of presenting information or a situation, especially one that makes you or your ideas seem good: *It was the media advisers whose role it was to put a positive spin on news items.*

spin² /spɪn/ *verb* (**spin·ning**, **spun**, **spun** /spʌn/) **1** [I, T] to turn round and round quickly; to make sth do this: **~ round/around sth** *Electrons spinning around an atom also satisfy certain functions.* ◇ **~ sth (round/around)** *For each candidate, the wheel was spun to produce a random question.* ◇ *One millilitre of the liquid Agrobacterium culture was spun for 5 minutes at the standard speed.* **2** [I, T] to make thread from wool, cotton, etc. by twisting it: *The 'Spinhuis' was a women's prison, whose inmates were employed spinning and sewing for the textile industry.* ◇ **~ A (into B)** *The factory spun cotton into yarn.* **3** [T] **~ sth** (*rather informal*) to present information or a situation in a particular way, especially one that makes you or your ideas seem good: *From this perspective, Virgil and Horace could be seen as spinning high-class propaganda for the state.*
PHR V ˌ**spin sth ˈoff (as sth)** (*especially NAmE, business*) to form a new company from parts of an existing one: *In-house communications services were spun off as separate IT service companies.*

spinal /ˈspaɪnl/ *adj.* [usually before noun] connected with the spine: *The boards were originally designed to transport patients with possible spinal injuries.*

ˌ**spinal ˈcord** *noun* the mass of nerves inside the spine that connects all parts of the body to the brain: **+ noun** *The majority of spinal cord injuries, involving previously healthy young adults, result from trauma.*

spine /spaɪn/ *noun* **1** the row of small bones that are connected together down the middle of the back SYN BACKBONE (1): *This condition is seen in young people and affects the spine.* **2** any of the sharp pointed parts like needles on some plants and animals: *These generally small fish had long spines in front of their fins.* **3 ~ (of sth)** the narrow part of the cover of a book that the pages are joined to: *On the spine of the book, only the first part of the title appears.*

spiral /ˈspaɪrəl/ *noun* **1** a shape or design, consisting of a continuous curved line that winds around a central point, with each curve further away from the centre: *Data are recorded along a continuous spiral on a CD-ROM.* **2** a continuous harmful increase or decrease in sth, that gradually gets faster and faster: *The economy went into a downward spiral and, by 1933, one quarter of the workforce was unemployed.* ◇ **~ of sth** *Thus, once the elite lost contact with Rome, they entered a spiral of cultural and economic decline.* ■ **spiral** *adj.*: *A spiral staircase winds up into the tower.* ◇ *In large spiral galaxies like the Milky Way, new stars are being made from hydrogen gas.*

spirit /ˈspɪrɪt/ *noun* **1** [U, C] the part of a person that includes their mind, feelings and character rather than their body: *His achievement is presented as a liberation of both body and spirit.* ◇ *It is a story that reveals the breadth and depth of the human spirit in the face of failure and defeat.* **2** [sing., U] an attitude or way of thinking: **(in a) ~ of sth** *Human beings should act towards one another in a spirit of brotherhood.* ◇ **in ~** *Golding's work is often closer in spirit to that of Eliot than to that of Conrad.* **3** [U, sing.] loyal feelings towards a group, team or society: *Individuals of outstanding public spirit would be chosen from among the community.* ◇ *Religious doctrines give worshippers a moral core, a community spirit and a guide to social stability.* **4** [sing.] **~ (of sth)** the typical or most important quality or mood of sth: *The book seemed to capture the spirit of the age.* ◇ *The progressive spirit of the 1960s left its mark on debates concerning law and order.* **5** [U] **~ (of sth)** the real or intended meaning or purpose of sth: *The Soviets had broken the spirit, if not the letter, of the Yalta accords.* **6** [U] courage, determination or energy: *The young hero was portrayed as a British lad of spirit.* **7** [C] **~ (of sb)** the part of a person that many people believe still exists after their body is dead: *They claimed to be communicating with the spirit of a man buried beneath their wooden house.* ➲ *compare* SOUL (1) **8** [C] an imaginary creature with magic powers: *Illness was explained in terms of sorcery and evil spirits.* **9** [C, usually pl.] (*especially BrE*) a strong alcoholic drink: *This was equivalent to a 25% decrease in the price of the cheaper brands of spirits.*

spir·it·ual /ˈspɪrɪtʃuəl/ *adj.* [usually before noun] **1** connected with the human spirit, rather than the body or physical things: *It is possible to have spiritual experiences without being religious or following a particular faith.* OPP MATERIAL² (1) **2** connected with religion: *The media portrayed him not as a monk from Vietnam but as a world spiritual leader.* ➲ *compare* TEMPORAL (2) ■ **spir·itu·al·ly** /ˈspɪrɪtʃuəli/ *adv.*: *It was an illness that was both physically and spiritually debilitating.*

spir·itu·al·ity /ˌspɪrɪtʃuˈæləti/ *noun* [U] the quality of being concerned with religion or the human spirit: *People borrow from eastern and western traditions to create unique forms of spirituality and religion.*

S

spite /spaɪt/ *noun* [U] a feeling of wanting to hurt or upset sb: **out of ~** *Largely out of spite, they withheld their approval.*
IDM **in ˈspite of sth** if you say that sb did sth **in spite of** a fact, you mean it is surprising that that fact did not prevent them from doing it SYN DESPITE: *In spite of the difficulties, they have a drive to succeed.* ◇ *English became the official language for business in spite of the fact that the population was largely Chinese.* ➲ grammar note *at* DESPITE ➲ language bank *at* HOWEVER

split¹ /splɪt/ *verb* (**split·ting**, **split**, **split**) **1** [I, T] to divide into two or more parts; to make sth divide into two or more parts: **~ into sth** *The molecule can thus split into its component atoms.* ◇ **~ sth (into sth)** *In 2007, it was announced that the Home Office would be split into two.* **2** [I, T] to divide into smaller groups that have very different opinions; to make a group of people do this: *The Liberals split over Irish Home Rule in 1886.* ◇ **~ sth** *Allende's radical policies had split Chilean society.* **3** [T] to divide sth into two or more parts and share it between different people, activities, etc: **~ sth** *Three residents share each flat, splitting the costs of rent and utilities.* ◇ **~ sth with sb** *The company agreed to split the profits with her so that both would get 50%.* ◇ **~ sth between A and B** *France had to split its resources between the army and the navy.*
PHR V **ˌsplit aˈway/ˈoff (from sth)** | **ˌsplit sth aˈway/ˈoff (from sth)** to separate from a larger object or group; to separate sth from a larger object or group: *The left wing split away from the rest of the party.* **ˌsplit ˈup (with sb)** to stop having a relationship with sb: *She has recently split up with her husband and is finding it difficult to cope.* **ˌsplit sb ˈup (into sth)** | **ˌsplit ˈup (into sth)** to divide a group of people into smaller parts; to become divided up in this way: *During slave sales, families were often split up.* ◇ *It is possible to split up the high-income group into two quite distinct categories.* **ˌsplit sth ˈup (into sth)** to divide sth into smaller parts: *By splitting up this industry into smaller firms, the unit costs of smaller firms will be higher.*

split² /splɪt/ *noun* **1** [C] a disagreement that divides a group of people or makes sb separate from sb else: **~ within sth** *There was a genuine split within the Conservative party about the strategy it should adopt.* ◇ **~ with sb/sth** *In 256-7, his theology led to a split with Rome.* ◇ **~ between A and B** *Albania aligned itself with China in the growing split between the Soviet Union and China.* **2** [sing.] a division between two or more things: *They would collect the revenues in exchange for a fixed salary or a profit split.* ◇ **~ between A and B** *The apprenticeship system reinforced the split between education and training.*

S

spoil /spɔɪl/ *verb* (**spoiled**, **spoiled** /spɔɪld/) (*BrE also* **spoilt**, **spoilt** /spɔɪlt/) **1** [T] **~ sth** to change sth good into sth bad, unpleasant, etc. SYN RUIN² (1): *The dispute very effectively spoiled their relationship.* **2** [I] (of food) to become bad so that it can no longer be eaten: *Much of the seed had spoiled during the voyage.* **3** [T] **~ sb** to give a child everything they ask for in a way that has a bad effect on their character and behaviour: *Like a spoiled child, MacArthur repeatedly insisted that he alone knew what was best.*

spoke *past tense of* SPEAK

spoken¹ *past part. of* SPEAK

spoken² /ˈspəʊkən; *NAmE* ˈspoʊkən/ *adj.* [only before noun] involving speaking rather than writing; expressed in speech rather than in writing: *While Hebrew was the language of the Scriptures, Aramaic was the everyday spoken language of the time.* ◇ *This was primarily a culture of the spoken word and gesture, not of print.*

spokes·man /ˈspəʊksmən; *NAmE* ˈspoʊksmən/, **spokes·woman** /ˈspəʊkswʊmən; *NAmE* ˈspoʊkswʊmən/, **spokes·per·son** /ˈspəʊkspɜːsn; *NAmE* ˈspoʊkspɜːrsn/ *noun* (*pl.* **-men** /-mən/, **-women** /-wɪmɪn/, **-persons** or **-people** /-piːpl/) a person who speaks on behalf of a group or an organization: *Party spokesmen were shouted down when they refused to concede the workers' demands.* ◇ **~ for sb/sth** *She is the government spokeswoman for Women and Equality.*

spon·sor¹ /ˈspɒnsə(r); *NAmE* ˈspɑːnsər/ *noun* **~ (of sth)** **1** a company or government that supports research or training: *The role of the federal government as a sponsor of health-related research had grown significantly since the late 1950s.* **2** a person or company that pays for a radio or television programme, or for a concert or sports event, usually in return for advertising: *The majority of sports clubs reported that they received less than a quarter of their income from sponsors.* **3** a person who agrees to be officially responsible for another person: *Immigration authorities require sponsors to sign an undertaking that they will be responsible for their relative's maintenance.* **4** a person who introduces and supports a proposal for a new law, etc: *The Bill was eventually dropped by its sponsor.*

spon·sor² /ˈspɒnsə(r); *NAmE* ˈspɑːnsər/ *verb* **1 ~ sth** (of a government or other organization) to arrange for sth official to take place: *In 1975, the United Nations sponsored the first World Conference on Women in Mexico City.* ◇ *She has argued forcefully that a UN-sponsored treaty is the only realistic solution to the crisis.* **2 ~ sth/sb** (of a company, government, etc.) to support research or training by paying for it: *Daewoo Foundation sponsors various academic projects.* ◇ *The Committee sponsored a series of educational seminars.* **3 ~ sth** (of a company) to pay the costs of a particular event, programme, etc. as a way of advertising: *From 2002, Hewlett-Packard sponsored the BMW Williams racing team.* **4 ~ sth** to introduce a proposal for a new law, etc: *Congressman Justin Smith Morrill sponsored the Morrill Act (1862), which established land-grant colleges.*

spon·sor·ship /ˈspɒnsəʃɪp; *NAmE* ˈspɑːnsərʃɪp/ *noun* [U] financial support from a person or an organization, especially from a company in return for advertising; the act of providing this support: *Many oral history programmes in the US relied heavily on corporate sponsorship for their funding.* ◇ *Sport sponsorship can be a significant marketing tool.* ◇ **~ of sth (by sb/sth)** *Doubts have been expressed about sponsorship of children's sport by companies that sell unhealthy food.*

spon·tan·eous /spɒnˈteɪniəs; *NAmE* spɑːnˈteɪniəs/ *adj.* **1** happening naturally, without being made to happen: *Recovery is usually spontaneous, prompt and complete.* ◇ *Spontaneous abortion or miscarriage is a common outcome of pregnancy.* ◇ *Approximately 65% of cases are caused by spontaneous mutation.* **2** not planned but done because you suddenly want to do it: *Lynx avoid people whenever possible and no spontaneous attacks have been recorded.* ◇ *The leaders claimed that the riot was spontaneous, not prearranged.* ■ **spon·tan·eous·ly** *adv.*: *Bleeding may cease spontaneously.* ◇ *Extroverts tend to act spontaneously.*

spor·ad·ic /spəˈrædɪk/ *adj.* happening only occasionally or at intervals that are not regular; happening in only a few places: *These subjects had difficulty maintaining employment and had sporadic and unstable work histories.* SYN INTERMITTENT ■ **spor·ad·ic·al·ly** /spəˈrædɪkli/ *adv.*: *Even before Constantine, Christianity began to spread sporadically beyond the imperial borders.*

sport /spɔːt; *NAmE* spɔːrt/ *noun* **1** [U] (*BrE*) (*NAmE* **sports** [pl.]) activity that you do for pleasure and that needs physical effort or skill, usually done in a special area and according to fixed rules: *The aim is to increase young people's participation in sport.* **2** [C] a particular form of sport: *Many may find their role models in football or other sports.* **3** [C] (*biology*) a plant or an animal that is different from its usual type in a way that can be clearly noticed:

Sports such as this shell from the common garden snail demonstrate the variation that can exist within a population.

sport·ing /ˈspɔːtɪŋ; *NAmE* ˈspɔːrtɪŋ/ *adj.* [only before noun] connected with sports: *The venue is designed primarily for sporting events.* ◇ *Participation in sporting activities was highest among this age group.*

spot[1] /spɒt; *NAmE* spɑːt/ *noun* **1** a small round area that has a different colour or feels different from the surface it is on: *The adult herring gull has a red spot near the end of the lower mandible.* ◇ **~ of sth** *In the dark shales were spots of the mineral cordierite.* **2** [usually pl.] a small mark or lump on a person's skin: *Petechiae are small red spots on the skin.* **3** a particular area or place: *Commuters often pass the same spots at the same time every day.* ◇ *It was only by continually monitoring trouble spots that conflicts could be avoided.*

IDM **on the ˈspot** (*rather informal*) **1** immediately: *He apologized on the spot and then left.* **2** at the actual place where sth is happening: *Only people on the spot can directly observe an event.*

spot[2] /spɒt; *NAmE* spɑːt/ *verb* (-tt-) (not used in the progressive tenses) (*rather informal*) to see or notice a person or thing, especially suddenly or when it is not easy to do so: **~ sb/sth** *These seabirds spot fish schools from high in the air.* ◇ *Direct discrimination is usually fairly easy to spot.* ◇ *The disease was first spotted in 1952.* ◇ **~ sb/sth doing sth** *She was spotted walking at night on the beach.* ◇ **~ that...** *Einstein spotted that there was something strange going on.*

spouse /spaʊs; spaʊz/ *noun* (*formal* or *law*) a husband or wife: *At some points in most marriages, one spouse concentrates on earning the family's income, while the other concentrates on child-rearing.* ■ **spou·sal** /ˈspaʊzl; ˈspaʊsl/ *adj.* [only before noun] *The spousal relationship remains a key social tie in the late adulthood years.*

sprang *past tense of* SPRING[2]

spread[1] /spred/ *verb* (**spread**, **spread**) **1** [I, T] to affect or be known or used by more and more people; to make sth do this: *Rumours spread about his having an illegitimate child.* ◇ **+ adv./prep.** *In recent years, the problem has spread to parts of Asia.* ◇ *Christianity spread rapidly through the Roman Empire.* ◇ **~ sth (+ adv./prep.)** *Viral marketing is a quick and inexpensive means of spreading a message.* **2** [I, T] to be in a number of different places; to cause sth to be in a number of different places: **+ adv./prep.** *Mystery shopping can be traced to the early 1970s in the USA, but it has spread worldwide.* ◇ **~ sth + adv./prep.** *Marine fish may be spread to new regions by the construction of canals.* **3** [I, T] to cover a larger and larger area; to make sth cover a larger and larger area: *They took immediate action to stop the blaze spreading.* ◇ **~ out** *Drop a stone into water and a wave spreads out.* ◇ **~ (sth) + adv./prep.** *Volcanic eruptions spread dust high into the stratosphere.* **4** [T] to separate sth into parts and divide them between different times or different people: **~ sth** *To spread risk, some entrepreneurs may choose to own multiple businesses.* ◇ **~ sth over/across sth** *The aim was to spread the costs of training more equally across industry.* **5** [T] to DISTRIBUTE sth in a particular way: **~ sth between/among sb/sth** *Family-friendly policies are not spread evenly among companies.* ◇ **~ sth over sth** *The negotiating process may be spread over several days in some cultures.* **6** [T] **~ sth (out)** to open sth that has been folded so that it covers a larger area than before: *They spread nets to capture the birds.* **7** [T] to put a layer of a substance onto the surface of sth: **~ A on/over B** *Salts are commonly spread on highways during winter to prevent build-up of ice.* ◇ **~ B with A** *In the laboratory, C. elegans lives on agar plates spread with E. coli bacteria.*

spread[2] /spred/ *noun* **1** [U] **~ (of sth)** an increase in the amount or number of sth that there is, or in the area that is affected by sth: *Measures were taken to limit the spread of the disease.* ◇ *The persecutions of the mid-third century failed to prevent the spread of Christianity.* ◇ *Bacterial enzymes cause rapid spread of the infection.* ◇ *Non-residential space demands are the major contributors to urban spread.* ➲ *compare* PROLIFERATION (1) **2** [C, usually sing.] a range or variety of people or things: *This group tended not to have such a wide spread in scores.* ◇ **~ of sth** *149 people returned completed questionnaires, representing a good spread of researchers.* **3** [U] **~ (of sth)** the area that sth exists in or happens in: *Increasing geographical spread allows firms to become more efficient.* **4** [C] **~ (between A and B)** (*finance*) the difference between two rates or prices: *The spread between the bid price and the ask price is very small.*

spread·sheet /ˈspredʃiːt/ *noun* a computer program in which figures and other data are entered in rows and columns in order to calculate costs, etc. Spreadsheets are often used in financial and project planning: *Data were entered into an Excel spreadsheet.*

spring[1] /sprɪŋ/ *noun* **1** [U, C] the season between winter and summer when plants begin to grow: *Intense thunderstorms during the spring and early summer can bring heavy rain, strong winds and tornadoes.* ◇ **in (the) ~** *This process starts again when sunlight returns in spring.* ◇ **in the ~ of...** *The army was severely weakened by disease in the spring of 1776.* **2** [C] a place where water comes naturally to the surface from under the ground: *The well is fed by mountain springs.* ◇ **+ noun** *Spring water tends to be less contaminated than groundwater.* **3** [C] a twisted piece of metal that can be pushed, pressed or pulled but which always returns to its original shape or position afterwards: *The springs inside the joint expand to extend the leg.*

spring[2] /sprɪŋ/ *verb* (**sprang** /spræŋ/ **sprung** /sprʌŋ/) (*NAmE also* **sprung**, **sprung**) **1** [I] to move suddenly and with one quick movement in a particular direction: **+ adj.** *When the pressure is removed, the membrane springs open.* ◇ **+ adv./prep.** (*figurative*) *His supporters in the party sprang to his defence.* **2** [I] to appear or come somewhere quickly or suddenly: **~ up** *New groups dedicated to public health sprang up after the First World War.* ◇ **+ adv./prep.** *Ideas do not just spring out of nowhere.*

IDM **spring into/to life** to suddenly start working or doing sth: *Elsewhere in the city, businesses sprang back to life wherever and however they could.* ➲ *more at* MIND[1]

PHR V **ˈspring from sth** to be caused by sth; to start from sth: *The Alternative Technology movement sprang from the environmental concerns and the counterculture of the 1960s and 1970s.*

sprung *past part. of* SPRING[2]

spun *past part. of* SPIN[2]

spur[1] /spɜː(r)/ *verb* (-rr-) **1** to encourage sb to do sth or to encourage them to try harder to achieve sth: **~ sb/sth to/into sth** *The prospect of profits spurs them to action but competition channels their activity.* ◇ **~ sb/sth (on) (to do sth)** *Other countries then began to support one side or the other, spurred on by their political sympathies or economic interests.* ◇ *Poor parents are more likely to spur their children to abandon school in favour of a job.* **2 ~ sth** to make sth happen faster or sooner: *Many of these initiatives seek to spur local economic development.*

spur[2] /spɜː(r)/ *noun* **1** [usually sing.] a fact or an event that makes you want to do sth better or more quickly SYN INCENTIVE (1), MOTIVATION (1): *The integration process was given an additional spur at the beginning of the 1990s.* ◇ **~ to sth** *A large competitive market of this kind should act as a spur to efficiency and innovation.* **2 ~ (of sth)** an area of high ground that sticks out from a

S

mountain or hill: *The Great Wall of China follows the narrow crests and spurs of a granite mountain range.*

square[1] /skweə(r); *NAmE* skwer/ *noun* **1** a shape with four straight sides of equal length and four angles of 90°; a piece of sth that has this shape: *The patterns are made up of red and white squares and triangles.* **2** an open area in a town, usually with four sides, surrounded by buildings: *People protested in the city's streets and squares.* **3 ~ of sth** the number obtained when you multiply a number by itself: *The output is the square of the input.* ➲ *see also* SQUARE ROOT

square[2] /skweə(r); *NAmE* skwer/ *adj.* **1** having the shape or approximate shape of a square: *The points are arranged on a square grid.* **2** having angles of 90° exactly or approximately: *Translations are given in square brackets.* **3 ~ kilometre/mile/metre, etc.** used to refer to a unit of measurement equal to the area of a square whose side is of the unit mentioned: *Table 5.3 shows the number of people per square kilometre in each country.* **4** (*abbr.* sq) **3 metres/6 feet/25 miles, etc. square** used to give the size of a square object or space, by giving the length of each of its sides: *The painting was nearly two metres square.*

square[3] /skweə(r); *NAmE* skwer/ *verb* **1** [T, usually passive] **~ sth** to multiply a number by itself: *The body mass index is equal to body weight divided by height squared.* **2** [T, I] to make two ideas, facts or situations agree or combine well with each other; to agree or be CONSISTENT with another idea, fact or situation **SYN** RECONCILE (1): **~ A and B** *It is difficult to square these two arguments.* ◇ **~ A with B** *His values seem hard to square with those of Christians in general.* ◇ **~ with sth** *The book did not quite square with the expectations of his admirers.* **3** [T] **~ sth (off)** to make sth have straight edges and corners: *A very sharp axe is used to square off the tree trunks.*

ˌsquare ˈbracket (*BrE*) (*NAmE* **bracket**) *noun* [usually pl.] either of a pair of marks, [ ], placed at the beginning and end of extra information in a text, especially comments made by sb who is checking the text: **(in/inside/within) ~s** *Editor's comments have been placed in square brackets.*

ˌsquare ˈroot *noun* **~ (of sth)** (*mathematics*) a number which, when multiplied by itself, produces a particular number: *The square root of 64 (√64) is 8 (8 × 8 = 64).*

S

sta·bil·ity **AWL** /stəˈbɪləti/ *noun* **1** [U, sing.] the quality or state of not changing or being disturbed in any way: *Switzerland is known for its political stability.* ◇ *Exchange rate stability may be threatened.* ◇ *These materials are reported to have a very high thermal stability, a property needed for use as high temperature coatings.* ◇ **~ of sth** *Clearing forests reduces the diversity and stability of local ecosystems.* **OPP** INSTABILITY (1) **2** [U] **~ (of sth)** the quality of being unlikely to move or fall over: *The operation had given him significantly greater stability of the knee.* **OPP** INSTABILITY (3)

sta·bil·ize (*BrE also* **-ise**) **AWL** /ˈsteɪbəlaɪz/ *verb* **1** [I, T] to become firmly established and not likely to change; to make sth do this: *Prices have stabilized to some degree.* ◇ **~ sth** *Central banks engage in monetary policy to stablize the economy.* ➲ *compare* DESTABILIZE (1) **2** [T] **~ sth** to make sth firm or steady so that it is not likely to move or fall over: *The upper body is thrown forward while the pelvis is stabilized by the seat belt.* **3** [I, T] (of a patient or their medical condition) to stop getting any worse after an injury or operation; to make a patient or their condition do this: *Her condition had stabilized on medication.* ◇ **~ sb/sth** *The patient must be stabilized before being sent to the CT scanner.* ■ **sta·bil·iza·tion, -isa·tion** **AWL** /ˌsteɪbəlaɪˈzeɪʃn; *NAmE* ˌsteɪbələˈzeɪʃn/ *noun* [U] **~ (of sth)** *The stabilization of the currency was his economic priority.* ◇ *Surgical shoulder stabilization may be recommended.*

stable **AWL** /ˈsteɪbl/ *adj.* **1** not likely to change or fail; firmly established: *The population has remained relatively stable.* ◇ *India has enjoyed stable democracy for over half a century.* ◇ *The economy had high but stable inflation.* ➲ *compare* CONSTANT[1] (2), STEADY (2) **OPP** UNSTABLE (1) **2** (of a substance) staying in the same chemical or ATOMIC state: *A sugar such as glucose is stable at body temperature.* ◇ *The elements of which water is composed, hydrogen and oxygen, both have stable isotopes.* **3** firmly fixed; not likely to move or fall over: *Wire mesh can be used to cover the debris and provide a stable surface for plants.* ➲ *compare* STEADY (3) **OPP** UNSTABLE (4) **4** (of a patient or their medical condition) not becoming worse after an injury or operation: *The test may be performed once the patient is stable.* ◇ *Mr Monkton is in a stable condition.*

> **WORD FAMILY**
> stable *adj.*
> stability *noun*
> stabilize *verb*
> unstable *adj.*
> instability *noun*
> destabilize *verb*

stack[1] /stæk/ *noun* **1** a PILE of sth, usually neatly arranged: *The American space shuttle has 96 individual fuel cells arranged in three stacks.* ◇ **~ of sth** *The mirrors are formed by a stack of alternating layers of two different semiconductors.* **2** (*computing*) a way of storing data in a computer in which only the most recently stored item can be RETRIEVED (= found or got back): *The addition of a new item to the top of the stack causes all other items on the stack to be pushed down and become inaccessible.* **HELP** **Stacks** are often called 'last in, first out' data structures.

stack[2] /stæk/ *verb* [T, often passive] **~ sth (+ adv./prep.)** to arrange objects neatly, especially in a PILE: *The bases are stacked directly on top of each other.* ◇ *An additional transistor is now stacked between the power-supply rails.*

staff[1] /stɑːf; *NAmE* stæf/ *noun* **1** [pl.] (*BrE*) all the workers employed in an organization considered as a group: *Staff were not trained in passenger safety procedures.* ◇ *The advice line is manned by specially trained nursing staff.* ◇ **+ noun** *Staff turnover was extremely high.* **HELP** In this meaning, **staff** is plural and takes a plural verb; it is the most common meaning in British English but is not used in American English. You can sometimes use **staff members** instead: *Staff members were not trained in passenger safety procedures.* ➲ *compare* WORKFORCE (1) **2** [C] **~ (of sb)** a group of workers employed by an organization or a particular person: *Airlines employ large staffs of researchers whose sole task is to find new ways to optimize aspects of their business.* **HELP** In this meaning, **staff** is singular and the plural is **staffs**; it is used in both British and American English. **3** [pl.] (*BrE*) the teachers in a school or college: *He was sometimes aggressive towards other pupils and staff.* ◇ *A senior member of staff patrols the school at all times.* **HELP** In American English, **the staff** is the people who work at a school or college, but who do not teach students: *students, faculty and staff* **4** [C+sing./pl. v.] a group of senior army officers who help the officer who is in charge of a military unit: *Dreyfus was the only Jew on the army's general staff.*

staff[2] /stɑːf; *NAmE* stæf/ *verb* [T, often passive] to work in an organization; to provide people to work in an organization: **be staffed by/with sth** *The centre is staffed by a lawyer, paralegals and volunteers.* ◇ **~ sth** *Resources were stretched to staff very large projects.* ■ **staf·fing** *noun* [U] *The project depends on extra staffing.* ◇ **+ noun** *Staffing problems exacerbated the situation.*

stage[1] /steɪdʒ/ *noun* **1** [C] a point, period or step in a process or in the development of sth: **~ of sth** *Females reach several stages of social development more quickly than males.* ◇ **at a/the... ~ (of sth)** *If tumours are detected at an early stage, treatment is usually easier.* ◇ **in a/the... ~ (of sth)** *The bridge had to be dismantled in the final stage of its construction.* ◇ **in stages** *The idea is to solve the problem in stages.* ➲ *compare* PHASE[1] (1) **2** [C] a raised area where actors, dancers, speakers, etc. perform: **on a/the ~** *The play was performed on the Royal Shakespeare Company's main stage in Stratford-upon-Avon.* ◇ **on ~** *They listened to the speakers on stage.* **3** (*often* **the stage**) [sing.] the theatre and the world of acting as a form of entertainment: **on (the) ~** *He had long craved to perform on the stage.* **4** [sing.] an area of activity where important things happen, especially in politics: *Mikail Gorbachev entered the political stage in 1985.* ◇ **on the... ~** *The city would never regain its former power and prestige on the world stage.* ➲ *see also* CENTRE STAGE **5** [C] the part of a MICROSCOPE on which you put the object you are looking at: *He placed the sample on the microscope stage and examined it.*

IDM **set the 'stage for sth** to make it possible for sth to happen; to make sth likely to happen: *Scientific advances have set the stage for unprecedented technological innovations in computers.*

▸ ADJECTIVE + STAGE **early, initial, preliminary • late, final, latter • advanced • intermediate • formative • various, different • distinct • successive • main • key, crucial • developmental • larval • embryonic** *In the advanced stages of the disease, a significant number of patients require hospitalization.*

▸ NOUN + STAGE **planning • design • committee • decision • life • growth • adult** *The hypothesis had been carefully formulated at the planning stage.*

▸ VERB + STAGE **reach • enter • go through, pass through • mark, represent • outline • identify, determine • involve • complete** *Not every patient and family will reach a stage of acceptance.* ◇ *The consumer goes through six key stages in the product acquisition process.*

stage² /steɪdʒ/ *verb* **1 ~ sth** to organize and present a play or an event for people to see: *There is intense competition to stage major world events such as the Olympics.* **2 ~ sth** to organize and take part in action that needs careful planning, especially as a public protest: *The military staged a coup against Chavez.* ◇ *In 1902–3, many industrial workers staged strikes.* **3 ~ sb/sth** (*medical*) to say how far a disease, especially cancer, has progressed in a patient: *It is important that patients are staged correctly.* ◇ *MRI scan is used to stage rectal cancers.*

stain¹ /steɪn/ *verb* **1** [T, I] to leave a mark that is difficult to remove on sth: *Vitamin D has the advantage that it does not smell or stain.* ◇ **~ sth (with sth)** *His clothes were stained with blood.* ◇ **~ sth + adj.** *Dithranol stains skin and clothing yellow.* **2** [T] to change the colour of sth using a coloured liquid: **~ sth (with sth)** *Chromosomes can be stained with a dye and examined directly under the microscope.* ◇ **~ sth + adj.** *The photograph shows a section through a rat spinal cord with the axons stained green.*

stain² /steɪn/ *noun* **1** [C, U] a liquid used for changing the colour of sth: *By using a protein-selective stain, the molecules of interest can be visualized.* ◇ *The stained sections were rinsed with distilled water so that excess stain was removed.* **2** [C] a dirty mark on sth, that is difficult to remove: *There was a greenish stain on the shirt.* ◇ *coffee/blood/ink stains*

stake¹ /steɪk/ *noun* **1** [C] a share of a business that sb owns because they have invested money in it SYN HOLDING (1): *Foreign shareholders acquired major stakes.* ◇ **~ in sth** *Tesco now owns an 84% stake in the firm.* ➲ *compare* SHARE² (1) **2** [sing.] **~ in sth** a part in sth that is important to you and that you want to be successful: *The monarch had a strong personal stake in the maintenance of peace in northern Europe.* ◇ *Decision-making tends to exclude many with a legitimate stake in the outcomes.* ➲ *compare* INTEREST¹ (6) **3 stakes** [pl.] something that you risk losing when you are involved in an activity that can succeed or fail: *The stakes are much higher because the entire human population is put at risk.* ◇ *He raised the stakes by committing American 'honor' and manpower to avert defeat.* **4** [C] a wooden or metal post that is pointed at one end and pushed into the ground in order to support sth, mark a particular place, etc: *Tall plants can be secured by tying them to stakes.* **5 the stake** [sing.] (in the past) a wooden post that sb could be tied to before being burnt to death as a punishment: **at the ~** *Heretics and unbelievers were persecuted and even burned at the stake.*

IDM **at 'stake** that can be won or lost, depending on the success of a particular action: *There was a lot at stake.* ◇ *The issues at stake were of public importance.* ◇ *What is at stake is not just America's freedom.* **in the... stakes** used to say how much of a particular quality sb/sth has, as if they were in a competition in which some people are more successful than others: *The acknowledged leaders in the environmental stakes include countries such as Germany and Japan.*

stake² /steɪk/ *verb* **1 ~ sth on (doing) sth** to risk money or sth important on the result of sth: *Mayor Ken Livingstone staked his political future on the charge.* ◇ *The Persians had staked everything on killing Alexander.* **2** to state your opinion or position on sth very clearly: **~ sth** *It was important that he stake his position and stand behind it.* ◇ **~ sth out** *Swyngedouw (1997) stakes out a political-economic analysis of urban water crises in Ecuador.*

IDM **stake your 'claim (to/for/on sth)** to say or show publicly that you think sth should be yours or that you should be considered in a particular way: *Settlers of European descent had begun to stake their claims in the frontier region.* ◇ *Russia staked its claim to be regarded as a major European power.*

stake·hold·er /'steɪkhəʊldə(r); *NAmE* 'steɪkhoʊldər/ *noun* a person or company that is involved in a particular organization, project or system, especially because they have invested money in it: *Stakeholders should be involved in critical decisions.* ◇ *It is important to identify who the key stakeholders might be and the demands they might place on the organization.*

stamp¹ /stæmp/ *noun* **1** [sing.] the mark or sign of a particular quality or person: *When westerners did accept monasticism, they put their own cultural stamp on it.* ◇ **the ~ of sb/sth** *Those parts of the country that had been rebuilt bore the distinctive stamp of social engineering.* **2** [C] a small piece of paper stuck to sth to show that an amount of money has been paid, in particular a **postage stamp**: *Each envelope bore the name of the addressee, a box number address and a stamp.* HELP In the US, a **food stamp** is a piece of paper that is given by the government to poor people, for them to buy food with.

IDM **stamp of approval** a formal or official expression of agreement or permission: *Recently this type of approach has been given the stamp of approval by authorities both in the US and in the UK.*

stamp² /stæmp/ *verb* **1** [T, usually passive] **~ sth** to stick a stamp on a letter or package: *The students received a paper questionnaire with a stamped return envelope.* **2** [T, often passive] to print letters, words, a design, etc. onto sth using a special tool: **~ A (with B)** *The coins were stamped with a symbol that indicated their weight.* ◇ **~ B on A** *A symbol was stamped on the coins to indicate their weight.*

PHR V **'stamp sth on sth** to make sth have an important effect or influence on sth: *The European Union is trying to stamp its authority on the international scene.* **,stamp sth 'out** to get rid of sth that is bad, unpleasant or dangerous, especially by using force or a lot of effort SYN ELIMINATE (1): *Persecution and torture were employed in attempts to stamp out heresy.* ◇ *Insurrection had quickly been stamped out in Poland.*

S

stance /stæns; *BrE also* stɑːns/ *noun* the opinions that sb has about sth and expresses publicly SYN POSITION[1] (5): **~ on sth** *Companies, therefore, have to take a stance on such issues.* ◇ **~ towards sb/sth** *Some authors have adopted a more critical stance towards the reforms.* ◇ **~ against sth** *Some countries have taken a strong public stance against age discrimination.* ◇ **~ that...** *They have maintained their stance that prices must stay high.*

stand[1] /stænd/ *verb* (**stood**, **stood** /stʊd/) **1** [I] to be on your feet; to be in a vertical position: *The pain is so bad that the child cannot stand or walk.* ◇ **+ adj.** *Standing still next to the track, an observer will hear the train as it approaches.* **2** [I] **~ (up)** to get up onto your feet from another position: *Paul stood up and began to speak.* **3** [I] **+ adv./prep.** to be in a particular place: *He built the Church of Hagia Sophia, which still stands in Istanbul.* **4** [I] to be in a particular condition or situation: *As things stand, children can be obliged to act as donors, whereas adults cannot.* ◇ *You need to be clear where you stand before you engage in managing change.* ◇ **+ adj.** *The refugee system is meant to stand separate from and parallel to the system of immigration control.* **5** [I] **~ at sth** to be at a particular level, amount, height, etc: *The Philippine population now stands at around 90 million.* ◇ *In the third year after the war, production stood at 37% of pre-war levels.* **6** [I] **+ noun** to be a particular height: *The statue stood 9 metres high.* **7** [I] (of a liquid or mixture) to remain still, without moving or being moved: *No matter how long the mixture is left standing, only around 10% of A is found to have reacted.* **8** [I] if an offer, a decision, etc. made earlier **stands**, it is still valid: *The points made in this discussion still stand.* **9** [I] **~ to do sth** to be in a situation where you are likely to do sth: *The larger a firm is, the less profit it stands to gain by cutting price and stealing customers from smaller rivals.* **10** [I] to have a particular attitude or opinion about sth or towards sb: *It was a time when Britain was confident of its values and people knew where they stood.* ◇ **~ on sth** *Writers do not always tell their readers how they stand on this issue.* **11** [T] **~ sth** used especially with *can/could* to say that sb/sth can survive sth or can TOLERATE sth without being hurt or damaged: *These materials can stand compressive stress, but cannot stand tensile stress.* ◇ *British television stands comparison with that of any other country.* **12** (*especially BrE*) (*NAmE usually* **run**) [I] to be a candidate in an election: **~ as sth** *He was not selected to stand as a Labour candidate for the Scottish parliamentary elections.* ◇ **~ for sth** *Constitutionally, the president could not stand for re-election.*

IDM Idioms containing **stand** are at the entries for the nouns and adjectives in the idioms, for example **stand a chance** is at **chance**.

PHR V ˌ**stand ˈback (from sth) 1** to move back from a place: *Citizens could do little more than stand back and watch the city burn nearly to the ground.* **2** to think about a situation as if you are not involved in it: *There are cases where people stand back and do nothing even where people need help.*

ˌ**stand beˈtween sb/sth and sth** to prevent sb/sth from getting or achieving sth: *By the 1970s, he claimed, government was the chief obstacle standing between the American people and honest opportunity.*

ˌ**stand ˈby** to be present while sth bad is happening but not do anything to stop it: *They claimed the police stood by and did nothing while their homes burned.* ˈ**stand by sth** to still believe or agree with sth you said, decided or agreed earlier: *The parties will stand by their policy promises.*

ˌ**stand ˈdown (as sth)** to leave a job or position: *The general election provided an opportunity for a fresh start, with a record number of MPs standing down.* ◇ *The organization appointed him as its envoy only hours after he stood down as Prime Minister.*

ˈ**stand for sth** [no passive] (not used in the progressive tenses) to be an abbreviation or symbol of sth: *Few people these days know what the acronym AIDS stands for.* ◇ *The ultimate goal is to get their brands to stand for the same thing in all parts of the world.*

ˌ**stand ˈout (as sth)** to be much better or more important than sb/sth: *Two particular strengths of the book really stand out.* ◇ *Several issues stand out clearly as central themes in the discussion.* ➲ *see also* OUTSTANDING (1) ˌ**stand ˈout (from/against sth)** to be easily seen: *The in-focus parts of the image stand out from the background.* ◇ *Labels are a primary way in which manufacturers try to make their brands stand out among the competition.*

ˌ**stand ˈup** to be on your feet: *Headaches that are worse when standing up are common after a lumbar puncture.*

ˌ**stand ˈup for sb/sth** to support or defend sb/sth: *He knew that it was important for the party to be seen as 'standing up for Britain'.* ˌ**stand ˈup (to sth)** to remain valid even when tested or examined closely: *The approach does not stand up to rigorous scrutiny.* ˌ**stand ˈup to sb** to resist sb; to not accept bad treatment from sb without complaining: *The boy believed that he should always stand up to bullies.* ˌ**stand ˈup to sth** (of materials, products, etc.) to remain in good condition despite rough treatment SYN WITHSTAND: *They did not know how well existing machines would stand up to this test.*

stand[2] /stænd/ *noun* **1** [usually sing.] an attitude towards sth or an opinion that you make clear to people: *The courts must, for the sake of law and order, take a firm stand.* ◇ **~ on sth** *The Senator must take a stand on policy issues affecting state and regional interests.* **2** [usually sing.] a strong effort to defend yourself or your opinion about sth: *At his headquarters, he unwisely made a stand, and after a two-week battle was forced to retreat.* ◇ *He backed Muhammad Ali in his stand against the Vietnam War.* **3** a table or structure that goods are sold from, especially in the street or at a market: *The programme had developed 19 farmers' markets by 1999 as well as four roadside stands.* **4** (*especially BrE*) a table or a structure where things are displayed or advertised, for example at an EXHIBITION: *Each product group had its own stand, and they all had different marketing brochures and sales literature.* **5** (*ecology*) **~ (of sth)** a group of plants or trees of one kind: *These old-growth eucalyptus forests were replaced, following fire, by dense stands of younger trees.*

ˈ**stand-alone** *adj.* [usually before noun] (especially of a computer) that can be operated on its own without being connected to a larger system: *The evolution from stand-alone computers to the telecommunications network environment of today has been rapid.*

stand·ard[1] /ˈstændəd; *NAmE* ˈstændərd/ *noun* **1** [C] a level of quality, especially one that people think is acceptable: *Since parents want their children to succeed, they will prefer schools that meet high standards.* ◇ **~ of sth** *The family complained of an inadquate standard of care.* ◇ **~ for sth** *Managers set clear standards for employee performance.* ◇ **below a/the ~** *Their conduct fell below the standards expected of Members of Parliament.* ◇ **according to/against a/the ~** *He tested his hypotheses according to standards of the field.* ➲ *see also* GOLD STANDARD (2), STANDARD OF LIVING **2** [C, usually pl.] a level of quality that is normal or acceptable for a particular person, place or situation and that you compare sb/sth else with: *Shame involves our awareness of not living up to our own standards.* ◇ **by... standards** *Cities were very small by modern standards.* ◇ *Neither couple was rich by American standards.* **3 standards** [pl.] a level of behaviour that sb considers to be morally acceptable: *She holds the view that we should not impose our moral standards on others.* HELP A **double standard** is a moral rule that is unfair because it is used in one situation or for one group of people but not another: *There was a double standard for sexual conduct and many husbands kept mistresses.* **4** [C] a system or method that is the usual way of measuring, producing or doing a particular thing in a particular field of activity: *The models had to be revised several times before they became accepted as the industry standard.* ◇ **~ for sth** *Beaufort's scale became the international standard for wind observations until 1946.*

▸ ADJECTIVE + STANDARD **international, global** ◆ **national** *The country has a low level of economic development by global standards.* | **high** ◆ **low** ◆ **acceptable, adequate, appropriate** ◆ **minimal, minimum** ◆ **strict, stringent** ◆ **objective** ◆ **uniform** ◆ **common** ◆ **internal** ◆ **environmental** ◆ **ethical** ◆ **professional** ◆ **technical** ◆ **legal** ◆ **educational** *Adopting higher environmental standards can raise a firm's costs.*

▸ NOUN + STANDARD **living** ◆ **safety** ◆ **quality** ◆ **performance** ◆ **human rights** ◆ **emissions** *Organizations need to find ways of utilizing scarce human resources to meet quality standards.*

▸ VERB + STANDARD **meet** ◆ **set, establish** ◆ **develop** ◆ **impose** ◆ **apply, implement** ◆ **enforce** ◆ **maintain** ◆ **adopt** ◆ **raise, improve** ◆ **lower** ◆ **exceed** ◆ **achieve, reach** ◆ **require** *It is part of a radical strategy to promote social inclusion and raise educational standards.*

stand·ard² /ˈstændəd; *NAmE* ˈstændərd/ *adj.* **1** average or normal rather than having special or unusual features: *There is no standard interview procedure.* ◇ *It is standard practice to use cells from mice of two different colours.* ◇ *In a standard contract, each party enjoys a degree of freedom.* ◇ **as ~** *Many new features were fitted as standard.* **2** [usually before noun] (of a size, measurement or design) regularly used or produced and not special in any way: *For adults, the standard sizes are 35, 37, 39 and 41.* ◇ *The bricks all conform to a standard format.* ➲ *compare* NON-STANDARD (1) **3** [only before noun] read by most people who are studying a particular subject: *Such questions are largely ignored in the standard textbooks.* **4** [usually before noun] (of spelling, pronunciation, grammar, etc.) believed to be correct and used by most people: *They might speak standard English at school and a non-standard dialect at home.* ➲ *compare* NON-STANDARD (2)

ˌstandard deviˈation *noun* **~ (of sth)** (*statistics*) the amount by which measurements in a set vary from the MEAN value for the set: *Across industries, the mean tariff reduction is 4.0 percentage points with a standard deviation of 2.9 percentage points.* ➲ *see also* MEAN² (2) ➲ language bank *at* STATISTIC

ˌstandard ˈerror *noun* (*statistics*) a measure of how accurate an estimate is: *The mean relative consumption and the estimated standard error are calculated for five predator groups.*

stand·ard·ize (*BrE also* **-ise**) /ˈstændədaɪz; *NAmE* ˈstændərdaɪz/ *verb* **~ sth** to make things of the same type have the same features or qualities; to make sth standard: *It is notoriously difficult to standardize definitions of disorders.* ◇ *The product is standardized to make its production less expensive.* ■ **stand·ard·iz·ed, -is·ed** *adj.*: *Information was obtained using standardized questionnaires.* **stand·ard·iza·tion, -isa·tion** /ˌstændədaɪˈzeɪʃn; *NAmE* ˌstændərdəˈzeɪʃn/ *noun* [U] **~ (of sth)** *Standardization of tests is critical.*

ˌstandard of ˈliving *noun* (*pl.* **ˌstandards of ˈliving**) the amount of money and level of comfort that a particular person or group has: *The positive consequences of the economic reforms for the Chinese standard of living were enormous.*

stand·ing¹ /ˈstændɪŋ/ *adj.* [only before noun] **1** existing or arranged permanently, not formed or made for a particular situation SYN PERMANENT: *Shielded by the Alps from war with neighbours, Switzerland never needed a standing army.* ◇ *He serves on the standing committee of China's association of teacher education and development.* **2** (of water) not moving; still: *The disease developed as humans lived together in closer association and near standing water.*

stand·ing² /ˈstændɪŋ/ *noun* [U] **1** the position or reputation of sb/sth within a group of people or in an organization SYN STATUS (2): *These individuals may behave in ways that allow them to keep or increase their social standing.* ◇ **of... ~** *The Committee consists of ten experts of high moral standing.* **2 of... ~** the period of time that sth has existed: *In 1737, he married his mistress of long standing.* ◇ *The senior reviewers are all consultants of many years' standing.* ➲ *compare* DURATION ➲ *see also* LONG-STANDING

stand·point /ˈstændpɔɪnt/ *noun* [usually sing.] an opinion or a way of thinking about ideas or situations SYN PERSPECTIVE (1): *He voiced his disapproval of the standpoint adopted by Montesquieu.* ◇ **from a... ~** *From an ethical standpoint, we have a responsibility to welcome asylum seekers.* ◇ **from the ~ of sb/sth** *Justice was not considered here from the standpoint of the person ultimately affected by the decision.*

star¹ /stɑː(r)/ *noun* **1** a large ball of burning gas in space that is seen as a point of light in the sky at night: *The path of light from a distant star changes direction as it passes the sun.* ◇ *Black holes result from the death of the most massive stars.* **2** an object, a decoration, a mark, etc, usually with five or six points, whose shape represents a star: *Jews were forced to wear yellow stars.* **3** a star-shaped symbol that tells you how good sth is: *Reviewers were asked to grade the book out of four stars.* ◇ **+ noun** *Star ratings for overall quality are given.* **4 ~ (of sth)** a famous and excellent singer, actor, sports player, etc: *Fewers became a star of the London music hall.* ◇ *a pop/film/movie/Hollywood star* **5 ~ of sth** a person who has the main part, or one of the main parts, in a film, play, etc: *The real star of the film is Hay Petrie.* **6** a person or thing that is the best of a group: **+ noun** *Plato's star pupil Aristotle founded the Lyceum.* ◇ *Japan's domestic motor and electronic goods manufacturers were once its star performers.*

star² /stɑː(r)/ *verb* (-rr-) **1** [I] to have one of the main parts in a film, play, etc: **~ in sth** *Olivier also starred in an adaptation of 'Pride and Prejudice'.* ◇ **~ with/opposite sb** *Lamarr starred with famous colleagues such as Clark Gable and Spencer Tracy.* **2** [T, no passive] **~ sb (as sb/sth)** if a film, play, etc. **stars** sb, that person has one of the main parts: *The film starred Bing Crosby as Father Chuck O'Malley.*

starch /stɑːtʃ; *NAmE* stɑːrtʃ/ *noun* [U, C] a white food substance found in potatoes, rice, etc. It functions as a CARBOHYDRATE store and is an important part of the human diet: *Carbohydrates stored in the root systems as starch are converted into simple sugars.* ◇ *Ethanol can be produced from the fermentation of sugars or starches.*

stark /stɑːk; *NAmE* stɑːrk/ *adj.* (**stark·er, stark·est**) **1** unpleasant; real, and impossible to avoid: *The study looks at the stark realities of dying in a hospital* ◇ *Politicians are faced with stark choices about how to allocate scarce resources.* **2** very different from sth in a way that is easy to see SYN MARKED: *In stark contrast to the United States, Japan spends more on earthquake research than on national defence.* **3** looking severe and without any colour or decoration: *The room is stark and bare.* ■ **stark·ly** /stɑːkli; *NAmE* stɑːrkli/ *adv.*: *The ruling starkly illustrated the subordination of British to European law.* ◇ *These theories offer starkly contrasting images of the world.*

start¹ /stɑːt; *NAmE* stɑːrt/ *verb* **1** [T, I] to begin doing or using sth: **~ sth** *Treatment should be started as soon as possible following exposure to the virus.* ◇ **~ to do sth** *The Japanese national population has started to decline.* ◇ **~ doing sth** *Individuals who start smoking in adolescence frequently continue to smoke as adults.* ◇ **~ (sb) on sth**

S

She was started on a new treatment programme. ◇ **~ (sth) by doing sth** *I shall start by considering a very simple example:...* **2** [I, T] to start happening; to make sth start happening: *The control of fire risks requires knowledge of how a fire starts.* ◇ *Sessions started at 9:00 a.m. and subjects were asked not to eat or smoke for at least 1 hour before.* ◇ **~ sth** *Only some of these collisions are energetic enough to start a reaction.* ◇ *He started his academic career at Cornell University.* **3** [I, T] (of a machine or vehicle) to begin to operate; to make a machine or vehicle begin to operate: *The car will not start if the petrol tank is empty.* ◇ **~ sth** *Note the position at which the stop occurred and then start the motor again.* **4** [I, T] to make sth, especially a business, begin to exist; to begin to exist: **~ sth** *Most workers cannot raise enough money to start their own businesses.* ◇ **~ sth up** *The government is offering loans to graduates to start up their own businesses.* ◇ **~ up** *An established firm may be able to borrow money at lower rates of interest than a new firm starting up.* ➲ *see also* START-UP² **5** [I, T] to begin, or to begin sth such as a career, in a particular way that changed later: **~ as sth** *He started as a medical student in Italy.* ◇ **~ out/off as sth** *The company started out as an online bookseller but has broadened its offering.* ◇ **~ sth as sth** *Stetson started life as the son of a small town banker and ended it as a leading American financier.* **6** [I] **+ adv./prep.** to begin from a particular place, amount or situation: *The drug is usually started at 400 mg daily but may be increased up to 800–1 000 mg.* ◇ *Doses vary, but start low and are increased gradually.* ◇ *In my view the problem started here.*

IDM get ˈstarted (on sth) to begin doing sth: *Patients may be anxious to get started on treatment as soon as possible.* **to ˈstart with 1** used when you are giving the first and most important reason for sth: *The firms make an important contribution on several dimensions. To start with, they generate economic output in a relatively stable manner.* **2** at the beginning: *To start with, everything sounded wonderful.* ◇ *Most patients receive injections to start with and then take high-dose vitamin B_{12}.*

PHR V ˌstart ˈoff 1 to begin happening; to begin doing sth: *A number of famous pop stars have complained that their managers took advantage of them when they were starting off.* **2** to begin by doing or being sth: *What started off as a sales tool evolved to become sales and marketing software.* ◇ **~ off by doing sth** *Section 2 starts off by reviewing the recent transformations taking place in economics.* ◇ **~ off + adj.** *The scales started off fine but something went wrong during the study.* **ˌstart ˈout (on sth)** to begin to do sth, especially in business or work: *He asked her what advice she would give to women starting out on their careers.* **ˌstart ˈover** (*especially NAmE*) to begin again: *A few students decided to start over during the exercise in order to repeat the individual steps.*

start² /stɑːt; *NAmE* stɑːrt/ *noun* **1** [C, usually sing.] the point at which sth begins **SYN** BEGINNING (1): **~ (of sth)** *Spain only began to build a stable democracy in the early 1980s, marking the start of a period of rapid transformation.* ◇ **from the ~** *He warmly supported the project from the very start.* ◇ **from ~ to finish** *The project took just four months from start to finish.* ◇ **+ noun** *The tenancy is fixed, in that it has a certain start date and a certain end date.* **2** [sing.] the act or process of beginning sth: *Japanese trade unionism made a fresh start during the period following the war.* ◇ *In August 1951, an official start was made on rebuilding the old town.* **3** [C, usually sing.] the opportunity that you are given to begin sth in a successful way: *In the UK, mothers are told that 'breastfeeding gives babies the best start in life'.*

IDM for a ˈstart used to emphasize the first of a list of reasons, opinions, etc: *These theories face several problems. For a start, the empirical evidence does not support their claims.*

ˈstarting point *noun* a thing, an idea or a set of facts that can be used to begin a discussion or process: **~ for sth** *This model is a useful starting point for discussion.* ◇ **~ for doing sth** *These preliminary findings should be considered a starting point for planning future research.*

ˈstart-up¹ *adj.* [only before noun] connected with starting a new business or project: *The Internet giant spent $500 million in advertising and start-up costs before it reached its position of dominance.*

ˈstart-up² *noun* a company that is just beginning to operate, especially an Internet company: *There is evidence that the jobs created by new start-ups are of lower average quality than those created by larger established firms.*

state¹ /steɪt/ *noun* **1** [C] the mental, emotional or physical condition that a person or thing is in: **~ (of sb/sth)** *Diagnosis depends on thorough examination of the physical and mental state of the patient.* ◇ *It is vital to examine the current state of relations between the groups in question.* ◇ *His state of mind varies from hysterical to coolly determined.* ◇ **in a/the ~** *An important feature of manganese is its ability to exist in several different oxidation states.* **HELP** In physics and chemistry, the **state** of a substance is whether it is a solid, liquid or gas: *At its triple point, water exists in all of its three states, solid, liquid and gas.* ➲ *compare* CONDITION¹ (6) ➲ *see also* GROUND STATE, STEADY STATE **2** (*also* **State**) [C] a country considered as an organized political community controlled by one government: *Core questions used in the survey are also used in equivalent surveys conducted by EU member states.* ◇ *After the collapse of the Soviet Union, the IMF helped the Baltic states set up treasury systems for their central banks.* ◇ **~ of sth** *In 1971 the eastern section seceded, creating the independent state of Bangladesh.* ➲ *see also* HEAD OF STATE, NATION STATE, WELFARE STATE ➲ thesaurus note *at* COUNTRY **3** (*also* **State**) [C] (*abbr.* **St.**) **~ (of sth)** an organized political community forming part of a country: *The states of the Midwest, especially Wisconsin, are traditionally regarded as the 'dairy states'.* ◇ *The evolution began in the 1990s, mostly in the states of New South Wales and Victoria.* ◇ *In New York State, the advent of managed care created a shift in Medicaid policy.* **4** (*also* **the State**) [sing., U] the government of a country: *Certainly, the role of the state is changing.* ◇ *The state maintains the rule of law and protects citizens from foreign aggression.* ◇ *The table shows the main companies that are still state-owned.* ◇ **affairs of ~** *The Church was frequently dominant in affairs of state.* ➲ thesaurus note *at* COUNTRY **5** [U] the formal ceremonies connected with high levels of government or with kings and queens: **in ~** *At their meeting, she sat in state under a canopy, with a crown upon her head.*

IDM a state of afˈfairs a situation: *She suggests a number of options to improve the current state of affairs.* **state of the ˈart** the most modern or advanced techniques or methods in a particular field: *Therefore, we present a detailed overview of the current state of the art, with a particular emphasis on practical solutions.* ◇ *state-of-the-art techniques/systems*

▸ ADJECTIVE + STATE **current, present • initial, original • new • final • excited • stable • conscious • emotional • mental, psychological • electronic** *In an excited state, the energy of an atom or molecule has increased by a fixed amount or quantum.* | **individual • small • weak • powerful • independent • democratic • liberal • secular** *Previously, the left in most Western liberal states was receptive to arguments about inequality.*

▸ NOUN + STATE **member • sovereign • nation** *If a country is a sovereign state, it will be generally recognized as such.*

▸ VERB + STATE **reach, enter • return to • change • maintain • determine • describe, define • represent** *When this state has been reached, the molecule is in its state of maximum entropy.* | **create • establish** *They called for a revolution to establish a socialist state.*

▸ STATE + VERB **agree • fail • adopt • seek • play a role** *Ten New England and Mid-Atlantic states agreed to adopt legislation establishing a regional market for carbon allowance.*

▸ STATE OF + NOUN **mind • consciousness • flux • motion • emergency • nature • knowledge • the economy • the world** *English culture was in a state of conspicuous flux in the early sixteenth century.* ◇ *In the state of nature, Rousseau argued, man is innocent.*

state² /steɪt/ *adj.* (*also* **State**) [only before noun] **1** provided by, controlled by or belonging to the government of a country: *The cost of state pensions represents one of the biggest calls on public spending.* ◇ *The successful state education system equips the majority of workers with a high level of skills that employers respect.* ◇ *state aid/support/subsidies* ◇ *state control/regulation/ownership/protection* ◇ *Starting in the 1980s, state policy shifted its emphasis to liberalization.* ◇ *In the Cold War period, the principle of state sovereignty blocked intervention in other states.* **2** connected with the leader of a country attending an official ceremony: *The president of Mexico visited the White House on a state visit.* **3** connected with a particular state of a country, especially in the US: *New Jersey's state legislature authorized the state to finance $6 billion of school facilities improvements.*

state³ /steɪt/ *verb* **1** to formally write or say sth, especially in a careful and clear way: *As stated above, there are no formal rules regarding the steps to be taken in these cases.* ◇ **~ sth** *Of those asked to take part in the study, 154 declined without stating any reason.* ◇ **~ how/what, etc...** *The plan should state how and when changes are to be implemented.* ◇ **~ that...** *The regulations typically state that people can be excluded if they create a nuisance.* ◇ **it is stated that...** *It is stated that governments will have to resist pressure from powerful industries.* ◇ **sth is stated to be/have sth** *This arrangement was explicitly stated to be a replacement for the abolished system.* ➲ language bank *at* REPORT¹ **2** [usually passive] to fix or announce the details of sth, especially on a written document: **(be) stated** *Only use the inhaler for the number of doses stated on the label.* ➲ *see also* STATED IDM *see* DIFFERENTLY

▸ ADVERB + STATE | STATE + ADVERB **clearly • explicitly • otherwise • simply • already, previously** *The email clearly stated the aims of the project.*

▸ ADVERB + STATE **expressly, specifically** *The article expressly states that persons are born free and equal in dignity and rights, not in talents.*

▸ STATE + ADVERB **above, earlier** *As stated earlier, the effects of insulin are fairly numerous.*

stated /ˈsteɪtɪd/ *adj.* [only before noun] clearly or formally expressed: *Their stated aim is to get the best person for the job.* ◇ *The subjects are asked if they are comfortable with the data being used for the stated purpose.*

state·hood /ˈsteɪthʊd/ *noun* [U] **1** the fact of being an independent country with the rights and powers of such a country: *Since 1947, more than thirty other colonies have obtained statehood.* **2** the fact of being one of the states within a country such as the US or Australia: *Utah achieved statehood in 1896.*

state·ment /ˈsteɪtmənt/ *noun* **1** [C] something that you say or write that gives information or an opinion: *It is not possible to make precise statements about the historical impacts of the project.* ◇ *The statements quoted in this article are the most representative ones supporting the explanations.* **2** [C] a formal or official account of facts, opinions or plans, especially one that appears in the newspapers, on television, etc. SYN DECLARATION, ANNOUNCEMENT (1): *Some MPs addressed the matter by issuing a press statement.* ◇ *The publicity that the strike generated forced the company into making a public statement.* ◇ **~ on/about sth** *The government publishes an annual statement on progress towards sustainable development.* **3** [C] a formal account of facts or events that is given by a WITNESS or other person to the police or in a court: *None of the statements made by him in the investigation proceedings were used at his trial.* **4** [C] a printed record of money paid, received, etc: *Quarterly financial statements should be published, along with details of the factors that have affected business performance.* ◇ *He produced bank statements proving that there had been no financial wrongdoing.* ➲ *compare* ACCOUNT¹ (5) **5** [U] (*formal*) the act of stating or expressing sth in words SYN EXPRESSION (1): *Interviews were recorded and notes were taken to enable precision of statement.* ◇ *The theory's basic propositions are capable of statement in a clear and concise fashion.*

IDM ˌ**make a ˈstatement** to express or show an opinion or characteristic in a very clear way, although often without words: *It is a film that makes a statement about the current state of the nation.*

states·man /ˈsteɪtsmən/ *noun* (*pl.* **-men** /-mən/) a man who is a skilled, experienced and respected political leader: *Elton considered Thomas Cromwell to have been one of the greatest statesmen in the whole of English history.*

states·per·son /ˈsteɪtspɜːsn; *NAmE* ˈsteɪtspɜːrsn/ *noun* (*pl.* **-people**) a skilled, experienced and respected political leader: *Many statespeople feared that military intervention would actually make the problem worse.*

static /ˈstætɪk/ *adj.* not moving, changing or developing: *Sales to the USA were relatively static.* ◇ *The population of France remained almost static.* OPP DYNAMIC² (1)

sta·tion¹ /ˈsteɪʃn/ *noun* **1** a place where trains stop so that passengers can get on and off; the buildings connected with this: *Being near a main train station may be crucial for attracting a target market of urban professionals.* ◇ (*BrE*) *a railway station* **2** (usually in compounds) a place where buses stop; the buildings connected with this: *A new library building is promised, together with a bus station.* HELP In British English, the word **station** on its own usually means a train station: *Many cities have suffered due to not having a station on the line.* In American English, it is usual to say which type of station you mean. **3** (usually in compounds) a place or building where a service is organized and provided or a special type of work is done: *The temperature for each month between 1981 and 2005 was obtained from the nearest weather station.* ◇ (*BrE*) *Petrol stations were rapidly running short of petrol.* ◇ (*NAmE*) *Gas stations were rapidly running short of gas.* **4** (often in compounds) a radio or television company and the programmes it broadcasts: *Commercial television and radio stations are now dominant in the market.*

sta·tion² /ˈsteɪʃn/ *verb* **1** [often passive] **~ sb + adv./prep.** to send sb, especially from one of the armed forces, to work in a place for a period of time: *Nearly 90 000 American troops were stationed in Vietnam.* **2 ~ sb/yourself + adv./prep.** to go somewhere and stand or sit there, especially to wait for sth; to send sb somewhere to do this: *The company could also arrange for security guards to be stationed outside the sealed office.*

sta·tion·ary /ˈsteɪʃənri; *NAmE* ˈsteɪʃəneri/ *adj.* **1** not moving; not intended to be moved: *In this design, the X-ray camera is stationary while the sample is rotated.* OPP MOBILE (2) **2** not changing in condition or quantity SYN STATIC (1): *In a stationary population, the number of births is equal to the number of deaths.* HELP In mathematics, a **stationary point** is a point on a curve where the GRADIENT is zero: *This approach successfully found all the stationary points on the path.*

stat·is·tic AWL /stəˈtɪstɪk/ *noun* **1 statistics** [pl.] a collection of information shown in numbers: *The statistics show that the number of complaints has declined in recent years.* ◇ *The use of official statistics for purposes of social research*

S

has been a very controversial area for many years. ◇ *These population statistics can be interpreted in a number of different ways.* HELP **Vital statistics** are figures that show the number of births, marriages and deaths in a country: *We employed vital statistics data from the state of Missouri covering the period 1989–2005.* **2 statistics** [U] the science of collecting and analysing statistics: *He obtained his PhD in Statistics from the University of Wisconsin in 2004.* ◇ *Survey data were analysed using descriptive statistics and significance tests.* **3** [C] a piece of information shown in numbers: *This statistic was presented as an interesting finding rather than as a major social problem.*

LANGUAGE BANK

Describing statistics

In academic writing, it is often necessary to cite statistical evidence or describe statistical data that show, for example, how frequent an event is, how two events are linked, or how an outcome changes in relation to a particular variable.

- The data/results show **a correlation between** X and Y.
- **a positive/negative/significant/strong correlation**
- to show/describe/examine **the distribution of** X
- to follow/assume/tend towards a **normal distribution**
- **deviation from** the mean/norm
- to show/calculate/estimate the **standard deviation**
- to find/determine/calculate **the mode/mean/median**
- **the range of** values/temperatures/sizes, etc.
- the **frequency/incidence** increases/decreases/varies with...
- to study/compare a **population/sample**
- to measure/identify/include **variables**
- the **lowest/highest/top/bottom quartile/quintile**

– *The data displayed show **a correlation** of -0.85 **between** total years of schooling and fertility rates.*
– *Irrespective of the level of analysis considered, there was **a significant and positive correlation**.*
– *Figure 4.1 shows **the age distribution of** PC ownership.*
– *The results will tend ever closer to a **normal distribution** with a mean at 10.*
– *These **deviations from** the mean were expressed in terms of z-scores.*
– *Figure 9.3c shows the **standard deviations of** the monthly mean surface air temperatures.*
– *A technique for **calculating the median** from grouped data is required.*
– *This difference falls within the **range of values** predicted by the model.*
– *The normalized **frequency** increases in each five-year period since the early 1990s.*
– *A report from a group in Oslo (Boberg et al., 1998) gives a mean annual incidence as 1.9/100000 of the **population** studied.*
– *Column E's results include all **variables** whose coefficient is positive and highly significant.*
– *Vitamin D levels **in the lowest quartile** were associated with a significant increase in mortality.*

S

stat·is·tic·al AWL /stəˈtɪstɪkl/ *adj.* connected with statistics: *The researchers used different statistical methods to help them decide on their conclusions.* ◇ *statistical techniques/models* ◇ *Effective government hinges on careful statistical analysis of data describing the economy and society.* ◇ *This observational conclusion needs to be confirmed by more rigorous statistical tests.* ➲ *see also* SIGNIFICANCE (3)

stat·is·tic·al·ly AWL /stəˈtɪstɪkli/ *adv.* in a way that is connected with statistics: *The results were not statistically significant.* ◇ *Images were taken and statistically analysed by the software.* ➲ *see also* SIGNIFICANT (3)

statistical sigˈnificance *noun* = SIGNIFICANCE (3)

stat·is·ti·cian AWL /ˌstætɪˈstɪʃn/ *noun* a person who studies or works with statistics: *The eminent statistician George Box asserted that 'all models are wrong, some models are useful'.*

statue /ˈstætʃuː/ *noun* a figure of a person or an animal in stone, metal, etc, usually the same size as in real life or larger: *In the 2nd century AD, a statue was erected in his honour.* ◇ *A number of monumental stone and bronze statues have survived.*

sta·tus AWL /ˈsteɪtəs; *NAmE also* ˈstætəs/ *noun* **1** [U, C] the legal position of a person, group or country: *A growing population of immigrant workers are often in the country without legal status or citizenship.* ◇ *Private schools face losing charitable status over lack of free places.* ◇ *This opens the door for the inclusion of gender (and other minority statuses) into theory on democracy.* ➲ *see also* MARITAL STATUS **2** [U, C, usually sing.] the social or professional position of sb/sth in relation to others: *Silver and gold ornament on weapons indicates persons of high status in the military hierarchy.* ◇ *Dickens insisted on his own professional status as a self-made man of letters.* ◇ **~ of sb/sth** *Factors such as changes in the role and status of women in society contribute to shifts in marriage patterns.* ◇ **+ noun** *The ordering of occupations in the status hierarchy is very similar in the two countries.* **3** [U] high rank or social position: *The author states that the pursuit of power, status and wealth is rarely absent from international deliberations.* ◇ **+ noun** *As the most prestigious animals for sacrifices and feasts, cattle were a status symbol for the rich.* **4** [U, C, usually sing.] the level of importance that is given to sth: *Not all areas of the empire were of equal status in the eyes of the Roman government.* ◇ *The success of these schools can be attributed to the prestigious status accorded to Spanish.* **5** [U] **~ (of sth)** the situation at a particular time during a process: *The introduction of non-native waterbird species would prejudice the conservation status of wild fauna and flora.*

▸ ADJECTIVE + STATUS **current • equal • special** *Many religions ascribe a special status to certain features of the physical environment.* | **marital • legal • official • constitutional • charitable • moral • parental • consultative** *In many societies, women are disadvantaged with respect to access to household income, regardless of their age and marital status.* | **high • low • privileged • socio-economic • social • economic • professional • educational • occupational • financial** *Where people live is closely associated with a number of indicators of their socio-economic status and lifestyle.* | **poor • nutritional • mental • functional • cognitive** *Poor maternal nutritional status has been related to adverse birth outcomes.*

▸ NOUN + STATUS **refugee • immigration, immigrant • migration • minority • insurance** *An asylum seeker may find it much easier to obtain refugee status in Sweden as compared with Greece.* | **health • employment • smoking • weight • HIV • vaccination • conservation** *Nurses should be aware of the extent to which social problems influence the health status of older people.*

▸ VERB + STATUS **have • give** *In Won Buddhism, men and women priests have equal status.* | **achieve, attain, acquire, gain, secure • accord, confer • claim • enjoy • retain, maintain • associate** *Their concern is to gain status in the eyes of their particular peer groups.* ◇ *The family that lived in the house clearly enjoyed very high status in Nichoria.* | **elevate • assume** *In the contemporary world, cinema has assumed the status of a dominant medium of communication.* | **grant, award • lose • determine • examine • deny • recognize • reach** *If such people acquire any other citizenship, they lose their British subject status.* | **reflect • enhance, improve** *The government will implement policies to improve the economic status of regions that are less developed.* | **assess, evaluate • monitor • disclose • confirm • check • record** *He was* *asked to go to Korea and assess the status of the industrial development projects.*

status quo /ˌsteɪtəs ˈkwəʊ; *NAmE* ˌsteɪtəs ˈkwoʊ/ *noun* (*usually* **the status quo**) [sing.] (*from Latin*) the situation as it is now, or as it was before a recent change: *New challenges to the status quo include terrorism and the spread of nuclear weapons.* ◇ *Frederick the Great would have been happy to maintain the status quo.* ◇ *to preserve/challenge the status quo*

stat·ute /ˈstætʃuːt/ *noun* **1** a law that is passed by a parliament, council, etc. and formally written down: *The first data protection statute was enacted in the German state of Hesse in 1970.* ◇ **by ~** *There are numerous organizations set up by statute which are not part of any government department.* ◇ **+ noun** *Once a bill becomes law, it is entered in the statute book.* **2** a formal rule of an organization or institution: *A new university statute was introduced and student numbers were cut.* ◇ **~ of sth** *In the past, the statutes of most European central banks were rather vague in terms of final objectives.*

statu·tory /ˈstætʃətri; *NAmE* ˈstætʃətɔːri/ *adj.* [usually before noun] fixed by law; that must be done by law: *The council was under a statutory duty to increase the average rents by a specified amount.* ◇ *In most countries, recording of death is a statutory requirement for all age groups.* ◇ *Citizenship by descent has always been statutory in English law.* ⊃ *compare* OBLIGATORY (1)

staunch /stɔːntʃ/ *adj.* (*superlative* **staunch·est**, *no comparative*) strong and loyal in your opinions and attitude SYN FAITHFUL: *Hazlitt was a staunch supporter of Napoleon against the monarchies of Europe.* ◇ *a staunch defender/ally/advocate* ■ **staunch·ly** *adv.*: *This idea was staunchly defended by the government as central to its restructuring of the welfare state.*

stay[1] /steɪ/ *verb* **1** [I] **+ adv./prep.** to continue to be in a particular place for a period of time without moving away: *2 000 forced migrants decided to stay in Slovenia permanently.* ◇ *In a traditional nuclear family structure, the woman stays at home and works in the domestic sphere.* ◇ *Data comparison shows that snow stayed longer in the northern sites than in the southern sites.* **2** *linking verb* to continue to be in a particular state or situation SYN REMAIN (1): **+ adj.** *In an FM signal, the amplitude stays constant and the frequency varies with time.* ◇ *Poorer women have less access to information about how to stay healthy in pregnancy.* ◇ **+ adv./prep.** *The stars within a galaxy are gravitationally bound and stay together.* ◇ *External costs must stay below an acceptable level.* **3** [I] **+ adv./prep.** to live in a place temporarily as a guest or visitor: *Survivors of the earthquake moved to the outskirts or stayed with relatives in distant towns.* **4** [T] (*law*) to stop, delay or prevent sth, especially a legal process: *The court is empowered to stay proceedings in order to allow the parties time to settle the dispute.*

IDM **be here to ˈstay | have come to ˈstay** to be accepted or used by most people and therefore become a permanent part of our lives: *Regionalism as a global phenomenon may be here to stay.* **stay ˈput** (*rather informal*) if sb/sth **stays put**, they continue to be in the place where they are or where they have been put: *By perhaps 5 000 BCE, many communities were staying put, living in a single location throughout the year.*

PHR V ˌ**stay aˈway (from sb/sth)** to not go near a particular person or place: *Some studies show that children from poor family backgrounds are more likely to stay away from school than children without economic problems.* ˌ**stay ˈon** to continue studying, working, etc. somewhere for longer than expected or after other people have left: *The chart shows the rate at which girls stay on to the final year of secondary education.*

stay[2] /steɪ/ *noun* a period of staying; a visit: *Complications of major surgery can lead to prolonged hospital stays.* ◇ *It is important to understand what foreign tourists expect during their stay in Japan.*

IDM **a** ˌ**stay of exeˈcution** (*law*) a delay in following the order of a court: *An application for a stay of execution must be lodged prior to the appeal against the order.*

stead·ily /ˈstedɪli/ *adv.* **1** gradually and in an even and regular way: *Agricultural production has been steadily increasing in Brazil.* ◇ *The company's sales have been falling steadily for a number of years now.* **2** without any change or interruption: *Press the canister down and continue to inhale steadily and deeply.* IDM *see* SLOWLY

steady /ˈstedi/ *adj.* (**stead·ier**, **steadi·est**) **1** developing, growing, etc. gradually and in an even and regular way SYN CONSTANT[1] (1): *Many families have left the area due to a steady decline in real estate value.* ◇ *St Andrew's attracts a steady stream of visitors.* ◇ *During this period, there were steady increases every year in world trade in music.* **2** not changing and not interrupted SYN REGULAR (4): *The hot air balloon ascended at a steady speed of 10 m/s.* ◇ *Most of these energy devices can be modelled as a steady flow of matter into and out of a control volume.* ◇ *He initiated an ambitious building project in order to provide steady employment to the restless urban poor.* **3** firmly fixed, supported or balanced; not shaking or likely to fall down: *The trembling makes it impossible to hold a cup steady.* ◇ *Such fine work requires a good eye and a steady hand.*

ˌ**steady ˈstate** *noun* [C, U] the state of a system or process that allows the VARIABLES being described not to change over time: *The economy is initially in a steady state in which there is no growth of output per capita.* ◇ **in ~** *The heat and mass transfer is in steady state.* ◇ **+ noun** *The continuous creation of matter proposed in the steady state theory of the universe was a radical idea.*

steal /stiːl/ *verb* (**stole** /stəʊl; *NAmE* stoʊl/, **stolen** /ˈstəʊlən; *NAmE* ˈstoʊlən/) [I, T] to take sth from a person, shop, etc. without permission and without intending to return it or pay for it: *The defendant broke into a house intending to steal.* ◇ **~ sth** *Trade in stolen goods generally is limited to high-value, easily transported goods.* ◇ **~ (sth) from sb/sth** *The missing painting was stolen from the museum in the 1960s.*

steam /stiːm/ *noun* [U] **1** the hot gas that water changes into when it boils: *This hot stream of gas may be used to generate steam in a boiler.* **2** the power that is produced from steam under pressure, used to operate engines, machines, etc: *A third of those farm machines were driven by steam and the rest were horse-powered.* ◇ **+ noun** *These steam turbines generated rotary motion directly.* ◇ *steam power/engines*

steel /stiːl/ *noun* [U] a strong hard metal that is made of a mixture of iron and CARBON: *Demand for steel and stainless steel has been on the increase in recent years.* ◇ **+ noun** *Conventional steel side-door impact beams are mounted on the car body.* ◇ *Layoffs have been widespread in the US steel industry.*

steep /stiːp/ *adj.* (**steep·er**, **steep·est**) **1** (of a slope, hill, etc.) rising or falling quickly, not gradually: *Given the steep slopes, glacial movement in mountainous regions is fast.* **2** [usually before noun] (of a rise or fall in an amount) sudden and very big SYN SHARP (1): *Sales for most US newspapers are in steep decline.* ■ **steep·ly** *adv.*: *The mountainous islands have a narrow coastal plain from which volcanic slopes rise steeply.* ◇ *The numbers of manual industrial jobs fell steeply through much of the 1980s.* **steep·ness** *noun* [U] **~ (of sth)** *Slope steepness is one of the most important factors affecting soil moisture.*

stem[1] /stem/ *noun* **1** the main long thin part of a plant above the ground from which the leaves or flowers grow; a

S

smaller part that grows from this and supports flowers or leaves: *These species have taller stems and broader leaves than wetland plants.* **2** (*grammar*) the main part of a word that stays the same when endings are added to it: *The plural morpheme combines with a slightly distorted form of the noun stem.*

stem² /stem/ *verb* (**-mm-**) **~ sth** to stop sth that is flowing from spreading or increasing: *The clotting agent serves to stem blood loss in case of wounds.* ◇ *Politicians seemed powerless to stem the tide of violence.*

PHR V **ˈstem from sth** (not used in the progressive tenses) to be the result of sth: *The view that Europe is internationally uncompetitive stems from the fact that Western European labour and other production costs are high.*

ˈstem cell *noun* a basic type of cell which can divide and develop into cells with particular functions. All the different kinds of cells in the human body develop from stem cells: *Since 1998 it has been possible to isolate embryonic stem cells (ESC) from human embryos.* ◇ **+ noun** *Stem cell therapy offers a new and potentially very powerful form of treatment for inherited disorders.*

step¹ /step/ *noun* **1** one of a series of things that you do in order to achieve sth: **+ adv./prep.** *Nuclear power is the first step along the road to the production of nuclear weapons.* ◇ *The next theorem is the crucial step towards defining subtraction.* ◇ *Strong liberals go one step further.* ◇ **take steps to do sth** *The government began taking steps to bring the economy wholly under its supervision.* **2** one of a series of things that sb does or that happen, which forms part of a process: *There are three key steps in the process of genetic divergence.* ◇ *The initial step is to decide whether the itching is due to skin disease.* ◇ **step by step** *Such a matrix is formed step by step as follows:...* ◇ *The notes below provide a step-by-step approach for beginners.* ➲ *compare* STAGE¹ (1) **3** the act of lifting your foot and putting it down in order to walk or move somewhere: *By about 14 months, most children can take a few steps unaided.* **4** a surface that you put your foot on in order to walk to a higher or lower level, especially one of a series: *The tenant fell down an external flight of steps which had no handrail and was unlit.*

IDM **in/out of ˈstep (with sb/sth)** having ideas that are the same as/different from other people's: *Some of Brunswik's positions were out of step with the mainstream psychology of his day.*

▸ ADJECTIVE + STEP **crucial, essential, key • initial, first, preliminary, preparatory • final • further, additional • subsequent • following • basic • logical • analytical • single** *Yeltsin sanctioned further steps towards a market economy.* | **important, major, significant • main • critical, vital • necessary • decisive • reasonable • unprecedented • unusual • positive • concrete • short • small • practical • appropriate** *The most significant steps in this direction were taken by Islamic and East Asian specialists.* | **early • intermediate • extra • sequential • discrete • individual** *Some proteins unfold by more complex mechanisms, which may involve one or more intermediate steps.*

▸ VERB + HEADWORD **take • represent, mark, constitute** *These studies represent an important step forward in working with culturally diverse populations.* | **require • follow, take • outline, summarize • involve • complete, perform • repeat • skip** *Briefly, this approach involves three steps.*

▸ NOUN + OF STEPS **series, sequence** *Progress is usually by a series of small steps, punctuated by failures.*

step² /step/ *verb* (**-pp-**) [I] **+ adv./prep.** to lift your foot and move it in a particular direction or put it on or in sth: *We may cringe when we accidentally step on an insect, whether or not we believe they feel pain.*

PHR V **ˌstep aˈside/ˈdown** to leave an important job or position and let sb else take your place: *In 2008 ill-health prompted Fidel Castro to step down in favour of his brother, Raul.* **ˌstep ˈback (from sth)** to move away from a situation in order to think about it calmly, as if you are not involved in it yourself: *I found it useful to step back and consider the project in distinct stages.* **ˌstep ˈforward** to offer to help sb or give information: *It is important for GPs to know when to step forward and take the lead.* **ˌstep ˈin** to help sb in a disagreement or difficult situation: *It was assumed that the government would step in and save a project if it got into financial difficulties.* **ˌstep ˈup** to come forward: *It requires a strong movement of people to step up and force the necessary changes.* **ˌstep sth ˈup** to increase the amount, speed, etc. of sth: *Fast-food companies have stepped up their efforts to develop new foreign markets.*

stereo·type /ˈsteriətaɪp/ *noun* **~ (of sb/sth)** a fixed idea or image that many people have of a particular type of person or thing, but which is often not really true: *The campaign was designed to challenge negative stereotypes of people with mental illness.* ◇ *The evidence revealed how the policy reinforced existing racial stereotypes.* ◇ *cultural/sexual/gender/age stereotypes* ■ **stereo·typ·ical** /ˌsteriəˈtɪpɪkl/ *adj.*: *Politicians regularly employ crude and stereotypical images of the homeless.* **stereo·typ·ical·ly** /ˌsteriəˈtɪpɪkli/ *adv.*: *Female respondents with high scores on the scale are seen as having stereotypically masculine interests.*

ster·ile /ˈsteraɪl; *NAmE* ˈsterəl/ *adj.* **1** (of humans or animals) not able to produce children or young animals SYN INFERTILE (1): *Very occasionally, the normally sterile mule may parent its own offspring, but other hybrids are consistently sterile.* ➲ *compare* FERTILE (2) **2** completely clean and free from bacteria: *The fluid is placed in a sterile container and transported to the laboratory.* ◇ *a sterile dressing/glove/swab* **3** (of a discussion, an argument, etc.) not producing any useful result: *This situation led to a long and ultimately sterile debate over whether prime ministerial government had replaced Cabinet government.* ■ **ster·il·ity** /stəˈrɪləti/ *noun* [U] *Sexually transmitted diseases such as these can cause sterility.*

ster·oid /ˈsterɔɪd; ˈstɪərɔɪd; *NAmE* ˈstɪrɔɪd/ *noun* (*biochemistry*) any of a large class of ORGANIC COMPOUNDS with a characteristic structure containing four rings of CARBON atoms. They include many HORMONES and some VITAMINS: *Steroids are the mainstay of the treatment and work by reducing inflammation.* ◇ **+ noun** *Steroid hormones are derived from cholesterol.*

stick /stɪk/ *verb* (**stuck, stuck** /stʌk/) **1** [T, I] to fix sth to sth else, usually with a sticky substance; to become fixed to sth in this way: **~ sth + adv./prep.** *The most convenient way would be to stick a numbered label on each of the boxes.* ◇ *The ends should be stuck together with glue or tape.* ◇ **+ adv./prep.** *The particles are located inside the cells and do not stick on the cell surface.* ◇ *Some pairs of amino acids will tend to stick to each other; others will be repelled by each other.* **2** [I] (*rather informal*) to become accepted: *Data to support such excessive fear of crime are usually lacking, but the perception sticks.*

PHR V **ˌstick ˈout** | **ˌstick sth ˈout** to be further out than sth else or come through a hole; to push sth further out than sth else or through a hole: *At the bottom of the diagram, several lines stick out.* ◇ *The lump does not move when the patient is asked to swallow or stick out his tongue.* **ˈstick to sth** **1** to act according to an agreement or decision that you have made: *Kravchuk stuck to this agreement.* **2** to continue doing or using sth and not change it: *The Chancellor stuck rigidly to the plans for public spending inherited from the Conservatives.* **ˈstick with sth** [no passive] to continue with sth or continue doing sth: *Buyers tend to stick with brand names with which they are familiar.*

S

sticky /ˈstɪki/ *adj.* (**stick·ier, sticki·est**) **1** made of or covered in a substance that sticks to things that touch it: *Tiny hairs and sticky mucus in the nose trap particles, preventing their entry into the lung.* **2** (*economics*) (of prices, wages, etc.) slow to change or react to change: *The level of output is determined by aggregate demand in the short run with sticky wages and prices.* OPP FLEXIBLE (1) ■ **sticki·ness** *noun* [U] **~ (of sth)** *Stickiness of the eyes often only occurs in the morning when the watery discharge has dried.* ◇ *A common argument in support of price stickiness is that there are costs associated with changing prices.*

stiff /stɪf/ *adj.* (**stiff·er, stiff·est**) **1** firm and difficult to bend or move: *The aim was to find a breakthrough fibre to be used to make tyres lighter and stiffer.* **2** when a person or part of their body is **stiff**, their muscles hurt when they move them: *Ligaments become less elastic as people age, making joints feel tight or stiff.* **3** more difficult or severe than usual: *Stiffer competition and falling prices gave employers an incentive to mechanize.* ◇ *Cities and communities face stiff financial penalties if they are not in compliance with the directive's requirements.* **4** (of a person or their behaviour) not friendly or relaxed: *The reviewer describes the translator's language as stiff and awkward.* ■ **stiff·ness** *noun* [U] **~ (of sth)** *The strength and stiffness of polymers are low compared with metals and ceramics.* ◇ *The patient presented with a history of back pain and morning stiffness.*

stifle /ˈstaɪfl/ *verb* **~ sth** to prevent sth from happening; to prevent a feeling from being expressed: *Supervisory intrusion into product design could stifle innovation.* ◇ *Corporate monopolies are formed to stifle competition, not to encourage it.*

stigma /ˈstɪɡmə/ *noun* **1** [U, C, usually sing.] feelings of disapproval that people have about particular illnesses or ways of behaving: *The Catholic Church has had to accept that any stigma attached to divorce has eroded.* ◇ *Their work aims to reduce the stigma associated with HIV.* **2** [C] (*biology*) the part in the middle of a flower where POLLEN is received: *In male plants, the large stigmas in disc florets were not found to serve as an important pollinator attractant.*

stig·ma·tize (*BrE also* **-ise**) /ˈstɪɡmətaɪz/ *verb* **~ sb/sth (as sth)** to describe or consider sb/sth as having qualities that deserve strong criticism or disapproval: *Such moves could be seen to stigmatize asylum seekers.* ◇ *Workhouses were stigmatized as a last resort for the destitute.* ■ **stig·ma·tiza·tion, -isa·tion** /ˌstɪɡmətaɪˈzeɪʃn; *NAmE* ˌstɪɡmətəˈzeɪʃn/ *noun* [U] **~ (of sb/sth)** *The strategy aims to fight prejudice against, and stigmatization of, people living in low-income situations.*

still[1] /stɪl/ *adv.* **1** continuing until a particular point in time and not finishing: *The importance of these organisms is still unclear.* ◇ *Many questions still remain.* ◇ *Taxpayers are still waiting for refunds.* ◇ *Descendants of these people still exist in small numbers in North Africa.* **2** despite what has just been said: *The rate of divorce has declined slightly in recent years, but it still remains high.* ◇ *Despite the fact that no one was ever convicted, many people still believe they know the identities of the killers.* **3** used for making a comparison stronger: *Still more important was the fact that many children of poorer families were taught to read in Sunday schools.* ◇ *The challenge to global marketers is to monitor, match or, better still, anticipate changes in technology.* **4 ~ more/another** even more: *The world has moved since the 1940s to still more complex levels of organization and technology.* ◇ *The merger was not fully implemented before still another merger occurred.*

still[2] /stɪl/ *adj.* not moving; calm and quiet: *The sun stays still whilst the earth rotates, thus giving the illusion that the sun is rising and then descending.* ◇ *The eggs are laid in still water, from which larvae hatch and sink to the bottom and seek a host.*

stimu·lant /ˈstɪmjələnt/ *noun* a drug or substance that makes you feel more awake and gives you more energy: *Patients should avoid stimulants such as caffeine, heavy meals and too much alcohol.*

stimu·late /ˈstɪmjuleɪt/ *verb* **1 ~ sth** to make sth develop or become more active, especially in a positive way: *Broader access to land stimulated economic growth.* ◇ *The authors hope that these suggestions stimulate further discussion about proposed screening programmes.* ◇ *The curriculum proved to stimulate the interest of adolescents in science.* ➲ *compare* ENCOURAGE (1) **2** to make sb interested and excited about sth: **~ sb** *The book provided much to inform, stimulate and entertain readers.* ◇ **~ sb to do sth** *Working in groups often stimulates poorly motivated students to become active participants.* **3 ~ sth** (*biology*) to make a part of the body function: *In the male, the hormone stimulates testosterone secretion.* ◇ *The pituitary gland plays a crucial role in stimulating other endocrine glands.*

stimu·lat·ing /ˈstɪmjuleɪtɪŋ/ *adj.* **1** full of interesting or exciting ideas; making people feel enthusiastic: *The editors' introductions are clear, informative and intellectually stimulating.* ◇ *A balanced diet and a stimulating environment provide a sound basis for improving mental function.* **2** making you feel more active and healthy: *It is advisable to take this drug in the morning to avoid this stimulating effect at night.*

stimulation /ˌstɪmjuˈleɪʃn/ *noun* [U] **1** the act or process of making a part of the body function: *In the 1930s, the pioneer of electrical brain stimulation was American neurosurgeon Wilder Penfield.* ◇ **~ of sth** *Chronic pain can arise from stimulation of pain receptors or from damage to the nerves themselves.* **2** the act of making sb interested and excited about sth: *One participant stressed the value of intellectual stimulation for people living with mental illnesses.*

stimu·lus /ˈstɪmjələs/ *noun* (*pl.* **stim·uli** /ˈstɪmjəlaɪ/) **1** [usually sing.] something that helps sb/sth to develop better or more quickly: **~ to sth** *The formation of Romania acted as a powerful stimulus to Balkan nationalism.* ◇ **~ for sth** *Demands that racial discrimination should be tackled provided the stimulus for legislation.* ◇ **~ to do sth** *There is a time lag between the stimulus to establish new schools and the ability to plan, construct and staff them.* **2** something that produces a reaction in a human, an animal or a plant: *Response of the fetus to painful stimuli occurs from 22 weeks' gestation.* ◇ *Fast and accurate responses to changing visual stimuli are essential for catching prey.* ◇ **~ to do sth** *Giving too much oxygen in these cases can actually remove the stimulus to breathe.*

stipu·late /ˈstɪpjuleɪt/ *verb* to state clearly and firmly that sth must be done, or how it must be done SYN SPECIFY: **~ sth** *The ban was introduced because the club had ignored a number of requirements stipulated by the council.* ◇ **~ that...** *The Data Protection Act stipulates that individuals have the right to know who holds data on them.* ◇ **~ how/what, etc...** *Every country has rules and regulations that stipulate how the bridge builders should decide on loads and strengths.* ■ **stipu·la·tion** /ˌstɪpjuˈleɪʃn/ *noun* [C, U] **~ (that...)** *The six students in each class were selected randomly but with the stipulation that three boys and three girls would be sampled.*

stir /stɜː(r)/ *verb* (**-rr-**) **1** [T] to use an object to move a liquid or substance round and round in order to mix it thoroughly: **~ sth** *Stir the solution well and thoroughly mix the salt and water.* ◇ **~ sth into sth** *He observed a spiral structure, like the pattern of cream stirred into a cup of black coffee.* **2** [I, T] to move; to make sb/sth move: (*figurative*) *By 1816 the revolutionary spirit was stirring again*

S

in England. ◇ ~ **sth/sb** *Marine shelves are vigorously stirred by tidal currents capable of moving sediment of almost all sizes.* **3** [T] to make sb excited or make them feel sth strongly: ~ **sth** *India held a fascination for Dickens and stirred his imagination.* ◇ ~ **sb to do sth** *One of the chapters Wells wrote stirred Anna to write to the author.*
PHR V ˌ**stir sth ˈup** to cause problems or make people feel strong emotions: *It is an offence to stir up hatred on the grounds of sexual orientation.*

sto·chas·tic /stəˈkæstɪk/ *adj.* (*technical*) having a RANDOM pattern that can be analysed STATISTICALLY but cannot be predicted exactly: *Genetic drift is a stochastic process: it emphasizes the random nature of transmitting alleles from one generation to the next.* ◇ *Many commodity price series have been shown to possess stochastic trends.*

stock[1] /stɒk; *NAmE* stɑːk/ *noun* **1** [U, C, usually pl.] the value of the shares in a company that have been sold; a share that sb has bought in a company or business: *There are millions of Americans who buy or sell stock through their stockbrokers.* ◇ *Wall Street and London saw the value of stocks and shares hit their lowest in 2002–03.* ◇ **+ noun** *Falling stock prices are an indication of poor management and the beginning of exposure to takeover.* ➲ *compare* SHARE[2] (1) **2** [C, U] a supply of sth that is available for use: *New housing currently represents only 1% of the total housing stock.* ◇ *Over-fishing is causing a reduction in fish stocks and is harming the marine environment.* ◇ ~ **of sth** *The stock of fresh water accessible to humans on earth is limited.* **3** [U, C] a supply of goods that is available to be sold in a shop: *Ideally, a company should carry enough stock to meet customers' orders immediately.* ◇ **in ~** *The more products a store carries, the more difficulty it will have keeping everything in stock.* ◇ **out of ~** *A store with a reputation for frequently running out of stock may irritate customers.*
IDM **take ˈstock (of sth)** to stop and think carefully about the way in which a particular situation is developing in order to decide what to do next: *The article takes stock of the recent procedural and institutional reforms.*

stock[2] /stɒk; *NAmE* stɑːk/ *verb* **1 ~ sth** (of a shop) to keep a supply of a particular type of product to sell: *Retailers who choose not to stock certain major brands run the risk of losing customers.* **2** [often passive] **~ sth (with sth)** to fill sth with food, books, etc: *They have warehouse-sized stores stocked with basic household goods.*
PHR V ˌ**stock ˈup (on sth)** to buy a lot of sth so that you can use it later: *In the build-up to an event such as the Olympics, retail sales are high as people stock up.* ◇ *Customers could then stock up on new supplies for the following month.*

ˈ**stock exchange** *noun* [usually sing.] a place where shares in companies are bought and sold; all of the business activity involved in doing this: *India has a range of business forms, including public limited companies, which are listed on the stock exchange.* ◇ *The Budapest stock exchange also fell by almost 3%.*

ˈ**stock market** (*also* **market**) *noun* the business of buying and selling shares in companies; the place where this happens; a stock exchange: *In 1998 the company was floated on the stock market.* ◇ *The Japanese government wished to restore confidence in the stock market.*

stole *past tense of* STEAL

stolen *past part. of* STEAL

stom·ach /ˈstʌmək/ *noun* the organ inside the body where food goes when you swallow it; the front part of the body below the chest: *These penicillins should be taken on an empty stomach.* ◇ **in/into the ~** *For many years, it was thought that ulcers were caused only by increased acid in the stomach.* ◇ **+ noun** *Most knowledge of cephalopods still originates largely from analysis of stomach contents collected from their predators.*

stone /stəʊn; *NAmE* stoʊn/ *noun* **1** [U] the hard solid mineral substance of which rock is made, often used for building: *Impressive round towers made of stone became characteristic features of important churches.* ◇ **+ noun** *The city was defended with a stone wall.* ➲ *see also* LIMESTONE **2** [C] (*especially BrE*) a small piece of rock of any shape found on the ground: *Ripples form when a stone is thrown into a pond.* **3** [C] (usually in compounds) a piece of stone shaped for a particular purpose: *Standing stones and pillars mark a place of worship.* ◇ *These words are carved on the stone beside his grave.* ➲ *see also* CORNERSTONE **4** [C] (often in compounds) a small piece of hard material that can form in the body, for example in the KIDNEY, and cause pain: *About 20% of the population have small stones in their gallbladder.* ◇ *Kidney stones can be extremely painful.* **5** (*pl.* **stone**) [C] (*abbr.* **st**) (in the UK) a unit for measuring weight, equal to 6.35 kg or 14 POUNDS: *He has lost 3 stone in the last 2 months.*
IDM **set in ˈstone** that cannot be changed: *The works of Jewish scripture were at that time not yet set in stone.*

stood *past tense, past part. of* STAND[1]

stop[1] /stɒp; *NAmE* stɑːp/ *verb* (**-pp-**) **1** [I, T] to no longer continue to do sth; to make sb/sth no longer do sth: *Patients who smoke should be advised to stop.* ◇ ~ **doing sth** *Volunteers are entitled to stop participating at any point and withdraw from the study.* ◇ ~ **sb/sth** *It may be expected that over time symptoms will recur when treatment is stopped.* **2** [I, T] to end or finish; to make sth end or finish: *When the rain stops, the clouds usually clear rapidly.* ◇ ~ **sth** *The reaction was stopped by the addition of 100 μl of dimethyl sulfoxide to the cell culture.* ◇ *All herbal medication should be stopped for between 2 and 3 weeks before surgery.* **3** [T] **~ sb/sth (from) doing sth** to prevent sb from doing sth; to prevent sth from happening: *Numerous European countries have brought in legislation to stop supermarkets from wielding excessive power.* ◇ *It was school policy for students to stay on campus during school time and measures were in place to stop students from leaving.* HELP In British English, it is possible to leave out the word **from**: *to stop supermarkets wielding excessive power* ◇ *to stop students leaving* In American English, **from** should not be left out. **4** [I, T] to no longer work or function; to make sth no longer work or function: *Earthquake shaking of a certain amplitude will often cause pendulum clocks to stop.* ◇ ~ **doing sth** *Unless the timelock function was removed by the supplier, the software would stop working.* ◇ ~ **sth** *To stop the clock, press the Esc key and click End on the menu.* **5** [I, T] to no longer move; to make sb/sth no longer move: *I braked and waited for a moment as the car to my left stopped.* ◇ ~ **sb/sth** *He was stopped by the police on his way home.* **6** [I] **~ to do sth** to end an activity for a short time in order to do sth: *She becomes short of breath when walking uphill, but feels much better if she stops to catch her breath for a minute.* **7** [T] **~ sth** to prevent money from being paid: *By the time the plaintiffs had discovered the fraud, it was too late to stop the payment.* IDM *see* TRACK[1]
IDM **stop short of (doing) sth** to nearly do sth, but not actually do it, especially because it may involve a risk: *The protest stopped short of a violent confrontation.* ◇ *Berthin stops short of proposing any of these explanations as a definitive key to the novel.*

stop[2] /stɒp; *NAmE* stɑːp/ *noun* **1** [usually sing.] an act of stopping or stopping sth; the state of being stopped: **~ to sth** *A legal stop to immigration was implemented in 1973.* ◇ **put a ~ to sth** *It took a strenuous campaign to put a stop to these discriminatory practices.* ◇ **come to a ~** *The reaction has appeared to have come to a stop before all the reactants have been converted into products.* **2** a place where a bus or train stops regularly for passengers to get

S

on or off: *The bus stop is 10 minutes' walk away and buses are infrequent.* ➲ *see also* FULL STOP

stor·age /ˈstɔːrɪdʒ/ *noun* [U] **1** the process of keeping sth in a particular place or form until it is needed; the place or form that sth can be kept in: **~ (of sth)** *Another function of bone is storage of minerals, particularly calcium and phosphate.* ◇ **for ~** *This is the system of water reaches and lakes where water is pumped for temporary storage.* ◇ **+ noun** *Typical energy storage devices are compared in Figure 6.* **2** (*computing*) the process of keeping data on a computer; the way it is kept: *The optical disk was introduced as a key element in data storage for personal computers.* ◇ **+ noun** *In the last few years, storage capacities have increased at up to 100% a year.*

store[1] /stɔː(r)/ *noun* **1** a large shop that sells many different types of goods: *Up to March, the company had opened 267 new stores, to bring its total to over 2 400 in Europe.* ◇ *She pulled her products out of department stores in 2001 to sell direct to the public via an Internet site.* **2** (*especially NAmE*) a shop, large or small: *Compared with supermarkets, small grocery stores and convenience stores may be more expensive.* **3** a quantity or supply of sth that sb has and uses: *Fatty acids are an important source of energy, particularly when the body's glycogen stores are depleted.* ◇ **~ of sth** *The subject matter of the research was 'capable of adding usefully to the store of human knowledge'.* ◇ *The electrodes provide the store of chemical energy that is converted to electrical work as the battery is discharged.*

IDM **in store (for sb/sth)** waiting to happen to sb: *A similar fate lies in store for the sun, the galaxy and the universe.*

store[2] /stɔː(r)/ *verb* **1 ~ sth** to keep information or facts in sth, for example in a computer or a brain: *The cost of storing data on disk is very low indeed and this compensates for its relative slowness.* **2** to put sth somewhere and keep it there to use later: **~ sth** *The pots were used for a variety of functions: boiling seaweed, steaming vegetables, serving and storing food.* ◇ **~ sth in sth** *To calculate the volume of water stored in sea ice, we must know its thickness.* ◇ **~ sth up (in sth)** *When a spring is stretched, potential energy is stored up in the spring.*

PHR V ˌ**store sth ˈup** to not express strong feelings or deal with problems when you have them, especially when this causes problems later: *Not to take the appropriate policy actions now may store up further trouble later.*

storm /stɔːm; *NAmE* stɔːrm/ *noun* **1** very bad weather with strong winds and rain, and often THUNDER and LIGHTNING: *Mangrove forests are often subject to damage from severe tropical storms.* **2** (in compounds) very bad weather or conditions of the type mentioned: *When electric charges build up in clouds and exceed a critical limit, they are discharged to the earth during a thunderstorm.* ◇ *Heavy snowstorms in central China contributed to severe electricity shortages in 31 provinces.* **3 ~ of protest/criticism/controversy/publicity** a situation in which a lot of people suddenly express very strong feelings about sth: *Holmes's research caused a storm of protest, and heated debates ensued.* ◇ *Lomborg met a storm of criticism from environmentalists and scientists.*

story /ˈstɔːri/ *noun* (*pl.* **-ies**) **1 ~ (about/of sth/sb)** a description, often spoken, of what happened to sb or of how sth happened: *A documentary film tells a story about real life, with claims to truthfulness.* ◇ *Asking victims to recount their story in the context of an armed conflict is a complex and sensitive process.* ➲ *see also* LIFE STORY **2** a situation considered in terms of the information that is known about it: *The longitudinal results tell a different story.* ◇ *These facts are noteworthy, to be sure, but they do not represent the whole story.* **3** a description of events and people that the writer or speaker has invented in order to entertain people: *In all, he wrote 26 novels and nine volumes of short stories.* ◇ *Reading a detective story, we look for clues in a way we do not when reading a tragedy.* ◇ **~ about/of sth/sb** *Elizabeth Barrett Browning's 'Aurora Leigh' (1857) tells the story of an aspiring young woman poet.* **4** a report in a newspaper, magazine or news broadcast: *An airliner crash is a sensational news story.* ◇ *They carried out an extensive analysis of health-related stories in major Canadian newspapers over an 8-year period.* **5** (*also* **story·line** /ˈstɔːrilaɪn/) the series of events in sth such as a book, film or play SYN PLOT[1] (2): *A romantic narrative is a story in which the protagonist confronts obstacles and emerges victorious (Jacobs, 1996).*

straight[1] /streɪt/ *adj.* (**straight·er**, **straight·est**) without a bend or curve; going in one direction only: *When light passes through air, it travels in a straight line.* ◇ *The river runs in 10–20 km long straight reaches separated from each other by sharp bends.* ➲ *compare* CURVED IDM *see* RECORD[1]

straight[2] /streɪt/ *adv.* (**straight·er**, **straight·est**) **1** not in a curve or at an angle; in a straight line: *If she looks straight ahead and an object is placed on her blind side, she cannot see it.* **2** by a direct route; immediately: *The GP had sent him straight to hospital as soon as he found out the results.* ◇ *This argument leads straight back to the problem.* ◇ *Most direct entrants are still recruited straight from university.* **3** in or into a level or vertical position; in or into the correct position: *Sitting up straight may make breathing easier.*

IDM ˌ**straight aˈway** immediately; without delay: *Fagen agreed to go to Geneva straight away.*

straight·for·ward AWL /ˌstreɪtˈfɔːwəd; *NAmE* ˌstreɪtˈfɔːrwərd/ *adj.* easy to do or to understand; not complicated SYN EASY (1): *There are a variety of straightforward ways in which empirical research could be extended.* ◇ *With many traditional works, ascertaining the date of publication is a relatively straightforward matter.* ◇ *This process is straightforward in theory but complicated in practice.* ■ **straight·for·ward·ly** *adv.*: *The book is straightforwardly organized into three main parts.*

strain[1] /streɪn/ *noun* **1** [U, C] pressure on sb/sth because they have too much to do or manage, or sth very difficult to deal with; the problems or anxiety that this produces: *The association between high job strain and depression was present for both men and women.* ◇ **~ of sth** *She finds it hard to cope with the stresses and strains of everyday life.* ◇ **~ on sb/sth** *An ageing population placed additional strain on the health care system.* ◇ **under ~** *Relations between central and local government came under growing strain in the 1980s.* ◇ **under the ~ of sth** *The bank's website collapsed under the strain of Internet customers trying to access their accounts.* **2** [U, C] the pressure that is put on sth when a physical force stretches, pushes or pulls it: *The local strain in the fibres is insufficient to cause significant numbers of fibres to fail.* ◇ **~ on sth** *The usual type of chair puts an enormous strain on the spine.* ◇ **+ noun** *Without an understanding of strain energy, no modern bridge could be built.* **3** [C] a particular type of plant or animal, or of a disease caused by bacteria or viruses: *Many inbred strains were developed by selectively breeding rats.* ◇ *New mutant strains develop even during a single infection.* **4** [C, U] an injury to a part of the body, such as a muscle, that is caused by putting too much pressure on it: *The most frequent injury types were sprains and strains.* ◇ *Musculoskeletal trauma can range from simple muscle strain to multiple fractures and soft tissue damage.*

strain[2] /streɪn/ *verb* **1** [T] **~ sth** to try to make sth do more than it is able to do: *Inflationary pressures and growing populations strained municipal resources.* ◇ *The US security strategy focused on a 'war on terrorism' has strained relations across the Atlantic (Ikenberry, 2002).*

2 [I] **~ (to do sth)** to make an effort to do sth, using all your mental or physical strength: *His voice was so quiet that I had to strain to hear it.*

strained /streɪnd/ *adj.* **1** (of a situation) not relaxed or friendly SYN TENSE² (1): *Relations with Korea became strained in the ninth century.* **2** showing the effects of worry or pressure SYN TENSE² (2): *The face looks strained, the posture is tense and the patient is restless.*

strand /strænd/ *noun* **1** a single thin piece of thread, wire, hair, etc: *The DNA strands are separated by heat.* ◇ **~ of sth** *A cable rope made of strands of thin steel wires was employed.* **2** one of the different parts of an idea, a plan, a story, etc: **~ in sth** *The first strand in Crosby's argument was cultural.* ◇ **~ of sth** *This section aims to analyse and compare the four main strands of liberal political thought.*

strange /streɪndʒ/ *adj.* (**stran·ger, stran·gest**) **1** unusual or surprising, especially in a way that is difficult to understand or explain: *A man with no training in religious matters, he was a strange choice for the position.* ◇ **it is/seems ~ that...** *It seems strange that two potentially competing species would operate together.* ◇ **it is ~ how...** *It is strange how community identities evolve.* **2** not familiar because you have not visited, seen or experienced it before: *They found themselves crossing a large and diverse Roman empire, often strangers in a strange land.* ◇ **~ to sb** *The book opens up a world that is at once both familiar and strange to the North American reader.* ■ **strange·ness** *noun* [U] **~ (of sb/sth)** *Several other critics have commented on the strangeness of the film's ending.* ◇ *The ability of the text and photographs to convey the strangeness of the New World for Europeans is particularly impressive.*

strange·ly /ˈstreɪndʒli/ *adv.* in an unusual or surprising way: *Plato and Aristotle are strangely silent on the matter.* ◇ **~ enough** *Strangely enough, parents of children who learn better in Chinese than English want them to continue to be taught in English.*

strang·er /ˈstreɪndʒə(r)/ *noun* a person that you do not know: *Younger children with this disorder are abnormally anxious in the presence of strangers.* ◇ *They are offended when complete strangers address them by their first names.* ◇ **~ to sb** *The offender was likely to be a stranger to the victim.*

IDM **be no/a ˈstranger to sth** to be familiar/not familiar with sth because you have/have not experienced it many times before: *The Romans were no strangers to Greek culture.*

strata *pl. of* STRATUM

stra·tegic AWL /strəˈtiːdʒɪk/ *adj.* [usually before noun] **1** done as part of a plan that is meant to achieve a particular purpose or to gain an advantage: *The strategic planning process commences at corporate level.* ◇ *Effective strategic management can transform the performance of an organization.* ◇ *Firms establishing strategic alliances with large partners grew at a higher rate than firms without access to such partners.* ➲ *usage note at* STRATEGY **2** connected with gaining an advantage in a war or other military situation: *Historically, the region has always been of strategic importance.* ◇ *Khrushchev had hoped to improve Russia's strategic situation by installing nuclear missiles in Cuba.* ➲ *compare* TACTICAL (3) **3** (of weapons, especially nuclear weapons) intended to be fired at an enemy's country rather than used in a battle: *While the threat of strategic nuclear war has receded, the global problem of nuclear weapons remains an urgent concern for humanity.* ➲ *compare* TACTICAL (4)

stra·tegic·al·ly AWL /strəˈtiːdʒɪkli/ *adv.* **1** in a way that is connected with achieving a particular purpose or gaining an advantage: *Relationships can be developed with strategically important customers.* ◇ *The company has more than 1 700 offices strategically located in popular airports and holiday destinations.* **2** in a way that is connected with gaining an advantage in a war or other military situation: *Colonies formed vital strongholds for Rome and all were strategically placed.*

strat·egist AWL /ˈstrætədʒɪst/ *noun* a person who is skilled at planning things, especially military activities: *Between the wars, military strategists in France and Germany developed plans for protecting civilians in the event of an air war.* ◇ *Political strategists learned from advertising experts how to market a product on television.*

WHICH WORD?

strategy *noun* ◆ **tactics** *noun* ◆ **strategic** *adj.* ◆ **tactical** *adj.*

- These words are each used to refer to a set of actions that is planned and carried out in order to achieve a specific aim or objective. **Strategy** is used to mean a plan of action to achieve a long-term or overall aim; **tactics** is used to mean actions that are planned in the short-term to achieve a discrete aim: *The Lisbon strategy aims to increase the employment rate of older workers.* ◇ *A market leader may have to adopt defensive tactics to protect its position.*
- **Tactics** sometimes has a negative connotation: *Middle-class people were sometimes oppressed by the strong-arm tactics of the Roman army.*
- The adjectives **strategic** and **tactical** are also used: *The remuneration scheme should support the long-term strategic interests of the company.* ◇ *The company had to make short-term tactical decisions but with long-term horizons; to maximize current year profits but maintain long-term viability.*

strat·egy AWL /ˈstrætədʒi/ *noun* (*pl.* **-ies**) **1** [C] a plan that is intended to achieve a particular purpose: *The three most recent Prime Ministers have had very different strategies and tactics.* ◇ *A firm's business strategy can be defined as the action managers take to attain the goals of the firm.* ◇ **~ for sth** *A strategy for the management of this disease needs to be developed.* ◇ **~ for doing sth** *Peace education gives a long-term strategy for dealing with problems of violence.* ◇ **~ to do sth** *Emotional maturity involves using 'coping strategies' to solve gradually more complex social problems.* ◇ **~ of sth** *South Korea and Taiwan are classic examples of countries pursuing a strategy of export-led development.* HELP In ecology, **strategies** are ways that have EVOLVED (= developed) in plants and animals that enable them to survive and be successful in their environment: *Some plants have evolved alternative strategies for capturing the nitrogen they need.* **2** [U] the process of planning sth or putting a plan into operation in a skilful way: *Followers of Marx have disagreed about political strategy.* ◇ *This paper provides an assessment of the role of the Internet within marketing strategy.* ◇ **+ noun** *The design of the strategy process must cause strategic thinking to happen.* **3** [U, C] the skill of planning the movements of armies in a battle or war; an example of doing this: *Atomic weapons transformed foreign policy and military strategy.* ◇ *Part of the Anglo-French grand strategy was to reduce Russian naval power.* ➲ *compare* TACTIC (2)

WORD FAMILY
strategy *noun*
strategic *adj.*
strategically *adv.*
strategist *noun*

▸ ADJECTIVE + STRATEGY **effective, successful** ◆ **optimal** ◆ **alternative** ◆ **new** ◆ **appropriate** ◆ **overall** ◆ **global** ◆ **long-term** ◆ **corporate** ◆ **competitive** ◆ **creative** ◆ **reproductive** ◆ **adaptive** ◆ **preventive** *Tutin (1979) studied mating patterns and reproductive strategies in a community of wild chimpanzees.*

S

▸ NOUN + STRATEGY **business** ◆ **marketing** ◆ **communication** ◆ **media** ◆ **advertising** ◆ **research** ◆ **search** ◆ **sampling** ◆ **coping** ◆ **management** ◆ **development** ◆ **prevention** ◆ **intervention** ◆ **recruitment** ◆ **pricing** ◆ **teaching** *The goal of this project was to develop a theoretically grounded research strategy to improve health communication campaign reach.*

▸ VERB + STRATEGY **adopt, implement, employ, use, pursue, follow, deploy** ◆ **develop, devise, formulate** ◆ **identify** ◆ **discuss** ◆ **propose, suggest, recommend** ◆ **choose, select** ◆ **adapt** ◆ **outline** ◆ **describe** ◆ **evaluate** *Strategic global considerations have led companies to adopt different pricing strategies.*

strati·fi·ca·tion /ˌstrætɪfɪˈkeɪʃn/ *noun* **1** [U, C] the division of people or things into different levels or groups: *Social stratification was accentuated.* ◇ *Risk stratification can be further improved with specialized testing.* ◇ **~ of sb/sth** *There is clearly a stratification of living conditions.* **2** [U] (*earth science*) the arrangement of rocks or earth in layers: *Burrowing organisms can affect stratification.* ◇ **~ of sth** *The strongly developed stratification of many of the rocks is clearly shown.*

strat·ify /ˈstrætɪfaɪ/ *verb* (**strati·fies, strati·fy·ing, strati·fied, strati·fied**) **1** [often passive] to divide people or things into levels or groups: **be stratified by/for/according to sth** *The patients were stratified by age.* ◇ **~ sth** *This would help stratify the risk.* **2** [usually passive] **(be) stratified** (*earth science*) used for saying that different types of rock, earth, etc. are arranged in layers: *The subsurface consists of horizontally stratified rock sequences.*

stra·tum /ˈstrɑːtəm; *NAmE* ˈstreɪtəm/ *noun* (*pl.* **strata** /ˈstrɑːtə; *NAmE* ˈstreɪtə/) **1** a level or group, for example within society: *The decline in smoking is not occurring uniformly across social strata.* ◇ **~ of sth** *The developers originally identified three strata of risk.* ◇ **in a ~** *Workers in this stratum were considered to be the most vulnerable.* ➲ grammar note *at* DATA **2** (*earth science*) a layer or set of layers of rock or earth: *This can cause folds to develop in the overlying strata.*

stream¹ /striːm/ *noun* **1** a small narrow river: *Russian villages were typically situated near the bank of a lake, river or stream.* **2 ~ (of sth)** a continuous flow of liquid, air or gas: *Samples were washed with a gentle stream of water on a 0.5-mm mesh screen.* ◇ *This hot stream of gas may be used to generate steam in a boiler.* ➲ *see also* BLOODSTREAM **3 ~ (of sb/sth)** a continuous flow of people or things: *A small town with an ancient university, St Andrew's attracts a steady stream of visitors.* ◇ *The ions are formed by collision with the stream of electrons.* **4 ~ (of sth)** (*computing*) a continuous flow of computer data or instructions: *Some interfaces cannot deal with a continuous stream of data at high speeds.* **5 ~ of sth** a large number of things that happen one after the other: *Discerning eras or stages in a historical stream of events always involved some arbitrariness.*

IDM **be/come on ˈstream** to be/start to be in operation or available: *Less than 10 per cent of these reactors have come on stream since 2000.* ◇ *There remains concern that oil demand will exceed supply before alternative supplies of energy are on stream.*

stream² /striːm/ *verb* **1** [I] **+ adv./prep.** (of liquid, air, gas, etc.) to move or pour out in a continuous flow: *Light streams through a small window.* ◇ *Moderate drizzle causes windows and road surfaces to stream with moisture.* ◇ *Blood was streaming from his mouth.* **2** [I] **+ adv./prep.** (of people or things) to move somewhere in large numbers, one after the other: *Refugees streamed in from over the border.* ◇ *The photons will then stream away.* **3** [T] **~ sth** (*computing*) to play video or sound on a computer by receiving it as a continuous flow, from the Internet for example, rather than needing to wait until the whole of the material has been DOWNLOADED: *The public hearings held in Minneapolis were streamed live.*

stream·line /ˈstriːmlaɪn/ *verb* **1 ~ sth** to make a system or organization work better, especially in a way that saves money, by using faster or simpler methods of working: *The measures attempted to streamline the immigration process for skilled workers.* **2** [usually passive] to give sth a smooth even shape so that it can move quickly and easily through air or water: **streamlined + noun** *These mammals adapted to aquatic life by evolving streamlined bodies and flippers rather than legs.*

street /striːt/ *noun* (*abbr.* **St**) a public road in a city or town that has houses and buildings on one or both sides: **~ (of...)** *In 1705, Tory candidates were chased by an angry crowd through the streets of Chester.* ◇ *At that time, security measures around 10 Downing Street were limited.* ◇ *Police are using surveillance to help remove 'dangerous' persons from city streets (Davis, 1990; Herbert, 1996).* ◇ **+ noun** *Fruit was sold by women on most street corners.* ◇ *Politicians began to worry that rising levels of street crime might deter foreign investment.*

IDM **on the ˈstreets/ˈstreet** without a home; outside, not in a house or other building: *A 1997 survey estimated that there were 4 500 homeless children living on the streets of the city.* ➲ *more at* MAN, WALK¹

strength /streŋθ/ *noun* **1** [U, sing.] the quality that a person or animal has of being physically strong: *Physical strength and endurance abilities are very specific to the individual.* ◇ *Exercises to increase muscle strength are of benefit in preserving joint function.* ◇ *The female lions combine their strength to overpower a wildebeest.* OPP WEAKNESS (1) **2** [U] the quality that an object or substance has of being strong and not easily broken or damaged: *Carbon fibre has very high stiffness and strength.* ◇ *A box-type beam has better bending strength than a circular one.* ◇ *They form polymers that have great mechanical strength.* ◇ **~ of sth** *Historically, engineers have always been concerned with strength of materials.* OPP WEAKNESS (1) **3** [C] a quality or ability that a person or thing has that gives them an advantage: *Each of these approaches has strengths and weaknesses.* ◇ **~ of sth** *One of the great strengths of this book is that it challenges such preconceptions.* ◇ *The main strength of the present study is its design.* ◇ *The relative strengths of traditional advertising versus promotion are summarized in Fig. 15.1.* OPP WEAKNESS (2), LIMITATION (1) ➲ language bank *at* CRITICAL **4** [U] the power and influence that sb/sth has: *Economic strength is an important basis for political power.* ◇ *But now Russia was recovering its military strength.* ◇ **~ of sth** *The decline in the strength of trade unions has reduced the bargaining power of workers.* **5** [U] how strong a natural force is: *These winds may be almost constant in their strength and direction.* ◇ *Electric field strength is defined as voltage per unit length.* ◇ *These signals have varied in strength over time.* ◇ **~ of sth** *The strength of the tide varies over the tidal cycle.* **6** [U, C] how strong a drug, chemical or drink is SYN CONCENTRATION (1): *The final result depends on solution strength.* ◇ *Administrative staff were authorized to change drug dosage and strength.* ◇ **~ of sth** *The pKa value indicates the relative strength of an acid.* ➲ *see also* STRONG (13), STRONG (14) **7** [U] **~ (of sth)** how clear and reliable an argument, evidence or a connection is: *It is important to review the strength of evidence before new techniques are added.* ◇ *Further research is needed to quantify the strength of association between green spaces and urban health.* ◇ *Correlation is a measure of the strength of the relationship between two variables.* **8** [U, sing.] the quality of being brave and determined in a difficult situation: **~ (of sth)** *His courage to express often controversial views may have derived from his personal strength of character.* ◇ **~ to do sth** *It takes a lot of strength*

S

to keep working when you see little point. **9** [U] **~ (of sth)** how strong or deeply felt an opinion or a feeling is: *Neither man had anticipated the strength of public opposition to their strategy.* ◇ *Strength of feeling on an issue in the House of Commons can influence a minister.* **10** [U] the number of people in a group, a team or an organization: **~ of sth** *The peacetime strength of the army was 415 000.* ◇ **in ~** *The King again invaded the empire in strength.* ◇ **below ~** *Documents suggest that army units might be up to 25 per cent below strength.*

IDM **on the strength of sth** because sb has been influenced or persuaded by sth: *He was chosen largely on the strength of his experience in wielding real power.*

strength·en /ˈstreŋθn/ *verb* **1** [T, I] **~ (sb/sth)** to make sb/sth physically stronger; to become physically stronger: *These muscles strengthen the shoulder and prevent dislocation.* ◇ *Masonry structures can be strengthened by steel reinforcement.* ◇ *Differences in heart rate may only be detected when the heartbeat strengthens.* OPP WEAKEN (2) **2** [T] **~ sth** to make an organization, a position or an argument stronger or more powerful: *He immediately began to strengthen the army.* ◇ *Cooperation enables partners to strengthen their market positions.* ◇ *These arguments are strengthened by the fact that there are scientific studies in respected journals that cast doubt on the claims.* OPP WEAKEN (1) **3** [I, T] to become or make sb become more determined or certain about sth: *His determination to remain in power strengthened.* ◇ **~ sth** *The purpose of this convention was to strengthen the resolve of the international community to take action on the issue.* OPP WEAKEN (3)

strenu·ous /ˈstrenjuəs/ *adj.* **1** showing great energy and determination: *Norway has made strenuous efforts to incorporate environmental values into policymaking.* **2** needing great effort and energy: *There is mixed evidence about the effect of strenuous exercise on symptoms.* ■ **strenu·ous·ly** *adv.*: *The software giant strenuously denied these allegations.*

stress[1] AWL /stres/ *noun* **1** [U, C] pressure or anxiety caused by the problems in sb's life: *Achieving a good life balance is known to reduce work-related stress.* ◇ *The questionnaire assesses the level of stress experienced by a parent of an adolescent.* ◇ *These changes are evidenced by the considerable increase in scholarly research regarding issues such as job stresses and strains (Bhuian, Menguc and Borsboom, 2005).* ◇ **~ of (doing) sth** *The stress of adapting to a new environment can be greater for the partner.* ◇ **~ on sb** *Increased stress on families could have a serious negative effect on the well-being of children.* ◇ **under ~** *The person may panic under stress and make inappropriate decisions.* ◇ **+ noun** *Care plans that teach stress management techniques may prove to be effective.* **2** [U, C] pressure put on sth that can damage it or make it lose its shape SYN PRESSURE[1] (1): **~ on sth** *The effect of pressure or stress on a material is to deform it.* ◇ **~ in sth** *Shear stresses in a beam tend to make an element deform into a lozenge or diamond shape.* ◇ **under ~** *Any one of these flaws, when the material is put under stress, may be where the material starts to fail.* **3** [U, C] pressure put on resources, the environment, the economy or a system that can cause problems or failure of the system: **~ on sth** *The huge elderly non-working population is expected to place great stress on the national economy.* ◇ **under... ~** *The study sites were under water stress during most of the growing season.* ◇ *Serious stresses involving population, resources and environment are clearly visible ahead.* **4** [U] illness or damage caused by difficult physical conditions: *Plants can avoid drought stress by maximizing water uptake or minimizing water loss.* ◇ **+ noun** *MRI or bone scans are useful to detect stress fractures.* **5** [U] **~ on sth** special importance given to sth SYN EMPHASIS (1): *The Act laid stress on the principle of parental responsibility.* ◇ *This approach places great stress on human overpopulation as the cause of the problem.* **6** [U, C] (*phonetics*) an extra force used when pronouncing a particular word or syllable: *Key information is marked in speech through word stress.* ◇ **~ on sth** *There is no stress on the first vowel.*

stress[2] AWL /stres/ *verb* to give particular emphasis or importance to a fact, an idea or a statement SYN EMPHASIZE (1): **~ sth** *Teachers often stress the importance of support at home for student success at school.* ◇ *The European Parliament stressed the need for a common approach across member states.* ◇ *Some analysts stress the role played by culture and identity factors.* ◇ **~ that...** *Taylor stressed that training should be undertaken systematically.* ◇ **it is stressed that...** *It should be stressed that vaccine development is problematic.* ◇ **~ how/what, etc...** *Some studies stress how some companies primarily use global strategies.*

stressed AWL /strest/ *adj.* **1** [not before noun] too anxious and tired to be able to relax: *Both groups of GPs reported feeling highly stressed.* ◇ *The more stressed the carer becomes, the more this can impact upon their relative.* **2** (*technical*) that has had a lot of physical pressure put on it: *These washers cushioned the highly stressed points of contact between blocks.* **3** (*phonetics*) pronounced with emphasis: *A stressed syllable is such only in contrast to an unstressed syllable.*

stress·ful AWL /ˈstresfl/ *adj.* causing a lot of anxiety: *Emotional responses to stressful events are of two kinds.* ◇ *The child can use this method in different stressful situations.* ◇ **~ for sb** *Interviewing can be stressful for interviewers.*

stretch[1] /stretʃ/ *verb* **1** [T, I] to make sth longer, wider or looser, for example by pulling it; to become longer, etc. in this way: **~ (sth)** *If you stretch a rubber band, then you feel a force.* ◇ *The fully stretched spring has a greater energy than the slightly stretched spring.* ◇ *In fact, all materials stretch when pulled, and some stretch more than others.* ◇ **~ out sth** *If you stretch out a single molecule of human DNA, it would extend for over 2 m.* OPP COMPRESS (1) **2** [T] **~ sth + adv./prep.** to pull sth so that it is smooth and tight: *They carried large shields made of ox hide stretched over a wooden frame.* **3** [I] **+ adv./prep.** to spread over an area of land or space SYN EXTEND (6): *The river basin stretches from the Northern Highland to the Central Plain.* ◇ *Sandy beaches stretch along the coastline.* ◇ (*figurative*) *These relationships and networks stretch across the organization.* **4** [I] **+ adv./prep.** to continue over a period of time: *The roots of capitalism stretch back many centuries.* ◇ *The origins of these policies stretch back to the 1930s.* ◇ *This region experiences a dry season stretching from November to April.* **5** [I, T] to put out an arm, a leg, etc. in order to reach sth; to put your arms or legs out straight and contract your muscles: *In his classic example, giraffes acquired long necks by stretching to reach leaves higher on the tree.* ◇ **~ sth (out)** *He stretches his leg out in an athletic pose.* **6** [T, often passive] to make use of a lot of your money, time or other resources: **be stretched** *Resources were stretched to open new offices and to staff very large projects.* ◇ **be stretched to capacity/the limit/the maximum** *A service provider is stretched to its full capacity during periods of high demand.* **7** [T, I] **~ (sb/sth)** to make use of all sb's skill or intelligence: *Such tasks may potentially stretch learners' language.* ◇ *The performance targets were not viewed as being particularly stretching.* **8** [T] **~ sth** to apply sth in a way that would not normally be considered reasonable: *The inclusion of Israel slightly stretches the traditional definition of 'European'.*

stretch[2] /stretʃ/ *noun* **1** [C] an area of land or water, especially a long one: *Three further landslides occurred within a 7-kilometre stretch.* ◇ **~ of sth** *Most large wetlands incorporate stretches of open water.* HELP In biochemistry,

stretch is also used to describe a length or SEQUENCE of DNA or PROTEIN: *The same polymerase adds a short stretch of DNA, about 30 nucleotides long.* **2** [C] a continuous period of time SYN PERIOD (1): *Women sat at sewing machines for long stretches in a poorly lit building.* ◇ **~ of sth** *This study examined only a shorter stretch of time.* ◇ **at a ~** *Coach drivers are allowed to drive for up to 15 hours at a stretch.* **3** [U] the ability to be made longer or wider without breaking or tearing: *The amount of stretch in a material is crucially important in bridge building.*

strict /strɪkt/ *adj.* (**strict·er**, **strict·est**) **1** that must be obeyed exactly: *They recommended that there should be strict controls on genetic testing.* ◇ *There are strict rules on the deductions that an employer may make to an employee's pay.* ◇ *California has adopted its own stricter emissions standards.* ◇ *strict laws/regulations/limits/requirements/criteria* ◇ *Legislation against environmental pollution has become very strict.* **2** [usually before noun] very exact and clearly defined: *He was not regarded as a priest in the strict sense of that word.* ◇ *Unfortunately, the term has no strict definition in law and has been subject to multiple legal rulings.* ◇ *The Court of Appeal adopted a strict interpretation of the requirement.* **3** obeying the rules of a particular religion or belief exactly: *Some strict Christians criticized the use of any personal jewellery.* ■ **strict·ness** *noun* [U] **~ (of sth)** *Most striking here is the strictness of the regime.* ◇ *There is a wide variety of interpretation and degree of strictness in observance of cultural traditions.*

strict·ly /ˈstrɪktli/ *adv.* **1** with a lot of control and rules that must be obeyed: *Regulations strictly limited the amount of phosphorus allowed in detergents.* ◇ *It is of importance that the water balance is set for a strictly defined area.* **2** used to emphasize that sth happens or must happen in all circumstances SYN ABSOLUTELY: *Building a settlement inside a so-called Reserved Forest is strictly forbidden.* **3** in all details; exactly: *Patient-identifiable information that is not strictly necessary should be excluded.* ◇ *This is strictly true only in a small region of space.* **4** used to emphasize that sth only applies to one particular person, thing or situation SYN PURELY: *This does not appear to be a strictly economic issue.*
IDM **ˈstrictly speaking** if you are using words or rules in their exact or correct sense: *Strictly speaking, all chemical reactions are reversible.* ◇ *The following groups are, strictly speaking, subject to immigration control but do not need leave to enter.*

strife /straɪf/ *noun* [U] (*formal* or *literary*) angry or violent disagreement between people or groups of people SYN CONFLICT[1] (2): *Some of these countries have been torn apart by civil strife.*

strike[1] /straɪk/ *verb* (**struck**, **struck** /strʌk/) **1** [T] **~ sb/sth** to hit sb/sth hard or with force: *The molecules of gas are in ceaseless, random motion and exert a force when they strike the walls of the container.* **2** [T] **~ sb/sth** to hit sb/sth with your hand or a weapon: *In this case, the defendant struck his wife, knocking her unconscious.* ◇ *A man about to be attacked does not have to wait for his assailant to strike the first blow.* **3** [I, T] to attack sb/sth, especially suddenly: *When Nero removed the detachment of guards, enemies took it as a signal to strike.* ◇ **~ sb/sth** *The missile was designed to strike targets in the United States.* **4** [I, T] to happen suddenly and have a harmful or damaging effect on sb/sth: *When conflict or natural disaster strikes, women survivors usually bear the heaviest burden of relief and reconstruction.* ◇ **~ sb/sth** *Ikeda reported that a 7.2-magnitude earthquake struck the Kobe-Nara region of central Honshu on 17 January 1995.* **5** [I, T] (of LIGHTNING) to hit and hurt or damage sb/sth on the ground: *Lightning strikes somewhere on the surface of the earth about 100 times every second.* ◇ **(be) struck by lightning** *For the Greeks, a person or place struck by lightning became sacred.* **6** [T] **~ sth** (of light) to fall on a surface: *At any given time, solar radiation strikes half of the globe, but not directly.* **7** [T, often passive] to cause sb to notice or be interested; to make a particular impression on sb: **~ sb** *The moral and intellectual shortcomings of the clergy struck certain English observers with particular force.* ◇ **~ sb as (doing) sth** *People in this category strike others as being conventional, moralistic and narrow-minded.* ◇ **it strikes sb that...** *On the other hand, it strikes me that Carlson's terminology undermines his line of defence.* **8** [I] to refuse to work, because of a disagreement over pay or conditions: *The right to strike is not seen as the exclusive prerogative of trade unions.*
IDM **strike a ˈbalance (between A and B)** to manage to find a way of being fair to two opposing things; to find an acceptable position which is between two things: *In our work, it was necessary to strike a balance between the analytical approach and a numerical one.* **strike a ˈbargain/ˈdeal** to make an agreement with sb in which both sides have an advantage: *Individual companies are able to strike bargains with organized labour.* ◇ *March's agent, Ivan von Auw, sent the book to Rinehart and soon struck a deal.* ➲ more at HARD[1]
PHR V **ˈstrike at sb/sth** to cause damage to sth; to have a serious effect on sb/sth: *This observation strikes at the heart of the standard description of cosmology embodied in the Friedmann equations.* **ˌstrike ˈback (at/against sb)** to try to harm or defeat sb in return for an attempt to harm or defeat you: *Kennedy struck back, mobilizing his own liberal supporters.* **ˌstrike sth ˈdown** (*especially NAmE*) to decide that a law is illegal and should not apply: *In France, courts have the power to strike down actions of government as unlawful.* **ˌstrike sb/sth ˈoff (sth)** (*also* **ˌstrike sb/sth ˈfrom sth**) [often passive] to remove sb/sth's name from sth, such as the list of members of a professional group: *A biomedical scientist was struck off the register following allegations that the registrant had failed to maintain adequate records.* **ˌstrike sth ˈout** to remove sth from a list or document or refuse to consider it: *The courts have the ability to strike out unreasonable clauses.*

strike[2] /straɪk/ *noun* **1** [C, U] a period of time when an organized group of employees of a company stops working because of a disagreement over pay or conditions: *The new Independent Federation of Trade Unions called a one-hour strike involving millions of workers.* ◇ *a miners'/coal/railway strike* ◇ **on ~** *They went on strike in July 2000, when negotiations over the new contract broke down.* ◇ **+ noun** *Public sector bargaining is regulated by detailed legal arrangements that aim to minimize the risk of strike action.* **2** [C] a military attack, especially by aircraft dropping bombs: *The air strikes left an estimated 1 200 people dead, most of them civilians.* **3** [C] an act of hitting sth/sb: *Lightning rods can be used to conduct the enormous electrical currents when lightning strikes occur.*

strik·ing /ˈstraɪkɪŋ/ *adj.* interesting and unusual enough to attract attention: *Another striking feature of humans is their use of language.* ◇ *Experiments in birds provide a particularly striking example of the importance of circadian rhythms for behaviour.* ◇ *Striking differences in cultural norms and attitudes produced a threatening situation.* ◇ *a striking resemblance/similarity* ◇ **it is ~ that...** *It is striking that no research into the problem is being carried out.* ■ **strik·ing·ly** *adv.*: *Although both aim to transform the individual, their methods are strikingly different.* ◇ *Strikingly, 57% of these academic keywords are among the 2 000 most frequent words in English.* ➲ language bank *at* SURPRISING

string /strɪŋ/ *noun* **1** [C] a series of characters (= letters, numbers, etc.): *A simple search string is easily constructed.* ◇ **~ of sth** *Each natural number is represented by a string of symbols.* ◇ *In this way, a picture becomes a very long string of zeros and ones.* **2** [C] **~ of sth** a set or series of things that are joined together: *Proteins are made of long*

S

strings of 20 different species of amino acids. ◇ *A string of three diodes is used to provide a constant voltage.* **3** [C] **~ of sth** a series of things or people that come closely one after another: *This controversy was the latest in a string of disputes.* ◇ *Understanding a simple spoken sentence involves a whole string of abilities.* **4** [U, C] long, strong material like very thin rope, used for tying things: *Imagine a weight tied to a piece of string.* **5 strings** [pl.] (*rather informal*) special conditions or restrictions: *Money was not loaned without strings.* ◇ *European governments wanted American dollars for post-war reconstruction, but without any strings attached.*

strin·gent /ˈstrɪndʒənt/ *adj.* (of a law, rule, regulation, etc.) very strict and that must be obeyed exactly: *To satisfy more stringent emissions standards, a new engine must be designed.* ◇ *The US President George Bush decided not to ratify the treaty, considering it too stringent.* ■ **strin·gency** /ˈstrɪndʒənsi/ *noun* [U] **~ (of sth)** *Policymakers can loosen the stringency of the target to keep costs down.*

strip[1] /strɪp/ *noun* **1** a long narrow piece of paper, metal, cloth, etc: *The cylinder is magnetized so that the iron strips are attracted.* ◇ **~ of sth** *The strips of material were sorted and labelled.* **2** a long narrow area of land, sea, etc: *The area was dry and well drained except for a narrow strip along the lowest part of the valley.* ◇ **~ of sth** *Gambia is a narrow strip of land bordering the Gambia River.*

strip[2] /strɪp/ *verb* **(-pp-)** **1** [T] to remove all of a particular type of thing, person or quality from a structure, place, organization, etc: **~ A from B** *Even though the electrons have been stripped from the atoms, the positively charged nuclei remain.* ◇ **~ B of A** *Gildas claimed that the Emperor Maximus stripped Britain of its troops, who never returned.* ◇ *These policies, stripped of their racist aspects, were allowed to continue after the war.* ◇ **~ sth out** *'Downsizing' meant that large numbers of middle management were stripped out in the belief that this furthered 'lean production'.* ◇ **~ sth + adj.** *Grotowski stripped the theatre bare of all props and scenery.* **2** [T] **~ sb of sth** to take away property, honours or rights from sb, as a punishment: *On 24 February 303, Christians were stripped of legal rights.* **3** [T] **~ A (off/from B)** to remove a layer from sth, especially so that it is completely exposed: *The sedimentary layers were stripped off the rock by glacial action.* **4** [I, T] to take off all or most of your clothes or another person's clothes: *They were ordered to strip and lie down on the grass.* ◇ **~ sb + adj.** *The prisoners had been stripped naked, sprayed with cold water and beaten with sticks.*

PHR V **ˌstrip sth aˈway** **1** to remove a layer from sth: *Here, weathering has stripped away the layers of periglacial deposits to reveal the bedrock underneath.* **2** to remove anything that is not true or necessary: *The article strips away any notion of rational strategy to reveal fear and superstition as the real drivers of presidential policy.*

strive /straɪv/ *verb* (**strove** /strəʊv; *NAmE* stroʊv/, **striven** /ˈstrɪvn/) or (*less frequent* **strived**, **strived**) [I] to try very hard to achieve sth: **~ to do sth** *At first, the EU strove to adopt common standards for each of the regulated professions.* ◇ *Those who strive to succeed in life do not always have the skills required to be effective leaders.* ◇ **~ for sth** *In her work, she strives for a higher degree of objectivity than did earlier biographers.* ■ **striv·ing** *noun* [U, sing.] *Freud claimed that all human striving is ultimately motivated by hunger and sexual desire.* ◇ **~ for sth** *Veblen writes that capitalism has encouraged 'a ceaseless striving for prestige'.*

stroke /strəʊk; *NAmE* stroʊk/ *noun* **1** [C, U] a sudden serious illness when a blood VESSEL in the brain bursts or is blocked, which can cause death or the loss of the ability to move or to speak clearly: *The husband suffered a major stroke and could no longer speak or write.* ◇ *A public health campaign in 2006 informed the Dutch public about the risk of stroke.* **2** [C] a single successful action or event: **~ of sth** *Sejanus had an amazing stroke of good fortune which is graphically recounted by Tacitus.* ◇ **by a ~ of sth** *He went after them and, by a stroke of poetic justice, was captured by pirates and himself sold as a slave.*

IDM **at a ˈstroke** with a single immediate action: *The arrests and executions wiped out the Jewish leadership at a stroke.*

strong /strɒŋ; *NAmE* strɔːŋ/ *adj.* (**strong·er** /strɒŋɡə(r); *NAmE* strɔːŋɡər/, **strong·est** /strɒŋɡɪst; *NAmE* strɔːŋɡɪst/) **1** (of evidence, an argument, etc.) difficult to attack or criticize: *Our results are strong evidence for a common evolutionary origin.* ◇ *This hypothesis has not yet received strong empirical support.* ◇ *There remains a strong argument for the development of a performance management framework.* ◇ *A strong case can be made for including a detailed family history as a core component of every medical case history.* ◇ *Many of these studies were not methodologically strong.* OPP WEAK (8) ➲ thesaurus note *at* CONVINCING **2** (of a connection) firmly established; clearly shown to exist: *During this period, the department established strong links to industry.* ◇ *There is a strong relationship between maternal education and child health.* ◇ *The duration of smoking is important because of its strong association with lung cancer.* ◇ *The study found a strong correlation between the two data sets.* OPP WEAK (5) **3** having a powerful effect on sth; having a lot of power or influence: *An individual's level of education has by far the strongest effect on earnings.* ◇ *The pH value has a strong influence on the solubility.* ◇ *The climatic impact is particularly strong during the monsoons.* ◇ *Governments can put strong pressure on newspapers not to publish stories.* ◇ *The role of strong political leadership has been crucial.* ◇ *International human rights law is becoming stronger.* OPP WEAK (3) **4** powerful and difficult for people to fight against or defeat: *There was strong competition in many markets from cheap imports.* OPP WEAK (3) **5** of a high standard; performing or performed well: *Russia has maintained a strong economic growth rate in recent years.* ◇ **~ in sth** *According to the school policy, students who were weak in English were not allowed to have lessons with their peers who were stronger in English.* OPP WEAK (7) **6** (of an opinion, a belief or a feeling) very powerful: *These governments received strong popular support for the reform programme.* ◇ *There was strong opposition from the US and the UK.* ◇ *Japanese workers have a strong sense of pride in their work.* ◇ *Indigenous identity also remains strong in other parts of Latin America.* ◇ *Guilt and grief are strong emotions that are sometimes expressed as anger.* **7** [only before noun] (of a person) holding an opinion or a belief very firmly and seriously: *These arguments have found their strongest supporters in the US.* ◇ *They are strong advocates of increasing investment in new technologies.* **8** likely to succeed or happen: *In this case, the worker is in a strong bargaining position.* ◇ *In our analysis, we took into consideration the strong possibility of reporting bias.* ◇ *These antibodies are also the strong candidates to be investigated further as potential diagnostic tools.* **9** (of people or animals) having a lot of physical power so that you can lift heavy weights, do hard physical work, etc: *Knowledge economies shift from a physically strong workforce in manufacturing to an intellectually skilled workforce in services.* OPP WEAK (1) **10** (of objects or materials) not easily broken or damaged; made well: *These synthetic fibres are very strong and light, and have a high chemical and heat resistance.* OPP WEAK (2) **11** (of a natural or physical force) having great power: *Such strong winds are more common in tropical coastlands.* ◇ *Being the nearest to the sun, it feels the strongest gravitational force.* OPP WEAK (6) **12** easy to see, hear, feel or smell; great or INTENSE: *These pigments appear golden under strong light.* ◇ *Workers are often exposed to irritants and strong odours.* OPP WEAK (6) **13** having a powerful effect on the body or mind: *Some*

S

GPs may be reluctant to prescribe strong opioids for osteoarthritis. **14** (*chemistry*) completely separated into its IONS when dissolved in water: *Strong electrolytes are good conductors of electricity as the solution contains many ions.* OPP WEAK (10) HELP In non-scientific language, a **strong** liquid is one that contains a lot of a substance: *a strong cup of tea* In scientific terms, the word for this is **concentrated**: *a concentrated solution of sulfuric acid* and its opposite is **dilute**. **15** (of prices, an economy, etc.) having a value that is high or increasing: *GDP growth in the Asian countries was strong.* ◇ *Demand is particularly strong for agricultural products.* OPP WEAK (9) **16** great in number; used after numbers to show the size of a group: *There was a strong British military presence in the Caribbean.* ◇ *The community is some 7 000 or 8 000 strong.* **17 the strong** [pl.] people who are rich or powerful: *The law and its representatives did very little to protect the weak against the strong.* OPP WEAK (4) **18** not easily upset or frightened; not easily influenced by other people: *Their films typically feature strong female characters.*

strongly /strɒŋli; *NAmE* strɔːŋli/ *adv.* **1** in a clear or important way: *These conclusions are strongly supported by a recent study.* ◇ *The exchange current density depends strongly on the nature of the electrode surface.* ◇ *The amount of free time is strongly related to social and demographic characteristics.* OPP WEAKLY **2** with a lot of feeling or belief: *Many Labour MPs were strongly opposed to this legislation.* ◇ *Nearly all of them strongly agree that education is the key to success.* ◇ *Whitley (1999) argues strongly for the persistence of distinctive company forms in many parts of the world.* **3** to a great degree or extent: *The term colonization has strongly negative connotations.* ◇ *The soils are strongly acidic, with surface pH values of 4.5.* ◇ *Such a perspective contrasts strongly with traditional notions of education.* **4** with a lot of power or force: *The earthquake was felt more strongly in the upper floors of tall buildings than at ground levels.*

strove *past tense of* STRIVE

struck *past tense, past part. of* STRIKE[1]

struc·tural AWL /ˈstrʌktʃərəl/ *adj.* [usually before noun] connected with the way in which sth is built or organized: *The two cities have undergone similar structural changes.* ◇ *These structural features have the effect of increasing the dynamic flexibility of the chain.* HELP In economics, **structural unemployment** occurs when the structure of an economy changes and companies need fewer workers, especially because of changes in technology and organization; it is distinct from unemployment caused by regular changes in supply or demand: *Over-capacity led to high and persistent structural unemployment in the regions where these industries were dominant.* ■ **struc·tur·al·ly** AWL /ˈstrʌktʃərəli/ *adv.*: *Molecules that are structurally very similar can have very different effects.*

struc·tur·al·ism /ˈstrʌktʃərəlɪzəm/ *noun* [U] (in literature, language and social science) a theory that considers any text as a structure whose various parts only have meaning when they are considered in relation to each other: *The Swiss linguist Ferdinand de Saussure was the inventor of structuralism.* ➲ *compare* DECONSTRUCTION ■ **struc·tur·al·ist** /ˈstrʌktʃərəlɪst/ *adj., noun*: *A well-known structuralist approach to word meaning is that developed by Lyons.* ◇ *French structuralists, however, were not much concerned with questions of gender at this time.*

struc·ture[1] AWL /ˈstrʌktʃə(r)/ *noun* **1** [U, C] the way in which the parts of sth are connected together, arranged or organized; a particular arrangement of parts: *Proteins are, in basic chemical structure, more complex molecules than DNA.* ◇ *A human hair strand has a complex structure, made of bundles of intertwined fibres.* ◇ **~ of sth** *I begin by describing the structure of a simple generic CPU.* ◇ *Marx aimed to facilitate a change in the economic and political structure of society.* **2** [C] a thing that is made of several parts arranged in a particular way, for example a building: *Termites build extraordinary structures that look as though they must be built to a plan.* ◇ *Wood frame structures are tough; they bend and creak, but they rarely fail catastrophically during an earthquake.* ◇ *The fertilized egg divides to give rise to many millions of cells, which form structures as complex and varied as eyes, arms, heart and brain.* **3** [U, C] the state of being well organized or planned with all the parts linked together; a careful plan: *Essays are not simply collections of written facts; they need structure.* ◇ *He gives the performances a dramatic structure and a moral force.*

> **WORD FAMILY**
> structure *noun, verb*
> structural *adj.*
> structurally *adv.*
> unstructured *adj.*
> restructure *verb*
> restructuring *noun*

▸ ADJECTIVE + STRUCTURE **complex • basic • internal • underlying • overall • hierarchical • social • economic • political • organizational, institutional • corporate • industrial • chemical • molecular • atomic • narrative • semantic • syntactic** *The basic structure of Aristotle's theory remained, but the list of virtues changed.* ◇ *In the 1960s, researchers in the spatial analysis school used simple models to focus on the internal structure of cities.*

▸ NOUN + STRUCTURE **market • family • power • crystal • protein** *Silver iodide has a crystal structure very similar to ice.*

▸ VERB + STRUCTURE **have, possess • form, produce • make, create, develop, build • adopt • affect • shape • alter, change, modify • determine • reveal • describe • examine, analyse • understand** *These communities develop social structures appropriate to their needs.*

▸ STRUCTURE + VERB **consist of, contain • determine, influence • emerge, appear • evolve • change** *New structures emerged that transformed how resources were used.*

▸ STRUCTURE OF + NOUN **system, organization • network • society, community • economy • market • industry • state • government • protein • DNA • gene • molecule** *A flow diagram defines the structure of a system at a conceptual level.*

struc·ture[2] AWL /ˈstrʌktʃə(r)/ *verb* [often passive] to arrange or organize sth into a system or pattern: **be structured** *The way societies are structured can play an important role in shaping population health.* ◇ **~ sth (around sth)** *I will structure my discussion around the following statements:...*

struc·tured AWL /ˈstrʌktʃəd; *NAmE* ˈstrʌktʃərd/ *adj.* having a clearly defined pattern or organization: *The research was based on structured interviews with a national, random sample of individuals.* ➲ *see also* SEMI-STRUCTURED

strug·gle[1] /ˈstrʌɡl/ *noun* **1** [C] a hard fight in which people try to obtain or achieve sth, especially sth that sb else does not want them to have SYN BATTLE[1] (2): *Power struggles were frequently handled by violence.* ◇ **~ for sth** *International politics is driven by an endless struggle for power.* ◇ **~ against sth** *The film-maker worked with demonstrators to document their struggle against government corruption.* ◇ **~ (with sb/sth) (over sth)** *The union was involved in a struggle with employers over the introduction of machine tools.* ◇ **~ between A and B** *There is usually a struggle between competing groups.* ➲ *see also* CLASS STRUGGLE **2** [sing.] **~ to do sth** something that is difficult for you to do or achieve SYN EFFORT (2): *Many poor farmers were losing the struggle to survive.* ◇ *It has been a struggle to maintain the unique wilderness of the Antarctic.* **3** [C] a physical fight between two people or groups, especially when one of them is trying to escape, or to get sth from the other SYN FIGHT[2] (2): *One of the officers took him by the*

S

arm and led him away, whereupon a violent struggle ensued.

strug·gle² /ˈstrʌgl/ *verb* **1** [I] to try very hard to do sth when it is difficult or when there are a lot of problems: *The online business had previously been struggling.* ◇ *Women who had to support a family on their own often struggled financially.* ◇ **~ for sth** *They overcame tremendous adversity, successfully struggling for recognition.* ◇ **~ to do sth** *The poor therefore have to struggle hard to make their voices heard.* **2** [I] to fight against sb/sth in order to prevent a bad situation or result: **~ with sth** *They may struggle with feelings of insecurity and self-doubt.* ◇ **~ against sth** *In many respects, it was the foreign-owned firms which had to struggle against disadvantages.* **3** [I] to compete or argue with sb, especially in order to get sth: **~ for sth** *Local families were still struggling for dominance, as they had done for centuries.* ◇ **~ against sb** *Rival chiefs struggled against each other.*

stuck *past tense, past part. of* STICK

stu·dent /ˈstjuːdnt; *NAmE* ˈstuːdnt/ *noun* **1** a person who is studying at a university or college: *Between 1990 and 2002, the number of international students enrolled in Australian universities increased from 24 998 to 185 058.* ◇ *college/university/graduate/undergraduate students* ◇ *medical/law students* ◇ **+ noun** *a student nurse/teacher* **2** a person who is studying at a school, especially a SECONDARY school: *Students created an online classroom to teach other high school students about the problem via the World Wide Web.* ➲ *compare* PUPIL (1) **3** **~ of sth** (*formal*) a person who is very interested in a particular subject: *Ginzberg was also a student of folklore and was partially inspired by Frazer.*

study¹ /ˈstʌdi/ *noun* (*pl.* **-ies**) **1** [C] a piece of research that examines a subject or question in detail: *A recent study calculated the effect of globalization on union bargaining power.* ◇ *One study found that having a home computer was associated with higher test scores in reading.* ◇ **~ of sth** *In the 1980s, the political scientist James Flynn conducted a study of IQ test results from 14 nations.* ◇ **~ on sth** *Their studies on spontaneous mutation appeared in 1943.* ◇ **~ into sth** *In a major study into the US retail banking sector, Schneider (1980) noted...* ◇ **+ noun** *Several factors governed the choice of study design.* ➲ *see also* CASE STUDY (1) ➲ thesaurus note *at* INVESTIGATION **2** [U, sing.] the act of considering or examining sth in detail: *However, this finding still needs further study.* ◇ *The authors stated that there were few blood samples available for study.* ◇ **~ of sth** *Writer Richard de Mille made a thorough study of Castaneda's works.* ➲ thesaurus note *at* INVESTIGATION **3** [U] the activity of learning or gaining knowledge, either from books or by examining things in the world: *In 2008, 30% of all those who entered the UK came for study.* ◇ *Foreign language study is worthy of attention at all levels of education.* ◇ **~ of sth** *Soil science is the study of soils as a natural resource on the earth's surface.* **4 studies** [pl.] a particular person's learning activities, for example at a college or university: *The German social scientist Max Weber began his studies at the University of Berlin.* **5 studies** [U+sing./pl. v.] used in the names of some academic subjects: *Mary Ann Doane has written about film theory, feminist theory, cultural studies and semiotics.* ◇ *Traditionally, the Bronze Age has been considered part of Classical Studies.* **6** [C] a room, especially in sb's home, used for reading and writing: *Soil science students never saw a farm but sat in their studies reading textbooks.* **7** [C] **~ (of sth)** a drawing or painting of sth, especially one done for practice or before doing a larger picture: *a study of Chartres Cathedral*

▸ ADJECTIVE + STUDY **large • detailed • recent • previous • early • pilot • classic • present, current • scientific • empirical • comparative • qualitative • experimental • observational • longitudinal, cross-sectional • prospective, retrospective** *In a large study of 2 231 cancer patients, 87% wanted as much information as possible—good or bad.*

▸ NOUN + STUDY **cohort • research • field** *Future field studies, especially in tree physiology, may shed light on this question.*

▸ VERB + STUDY **conduct, undertake, carry out, perform, do • publish • design • present • describe, report • review • discuss • cite • identify • select • exclude • approve • fund • replicate** *Hearing is one of the last senses to disappear according to studies carried out in intensive care units.*

▸ STUDY + VERB **show, demonstrate, indicate, reveal • find • suggest • report • support, confirm • conclude • identify • highlight • document** *Studies have shown that a large percentage of students are not fully engaged in their classroom studies.* | **focus on • address • aim • investigate, explore, examine, look at • analyse • assess, evaluate • include, involve • compare** *Relatively few studies have focused on the role of social cues in animal behaviour.*

▸ STUDY + NOUN **design • participant • population • sample • period • site • area • protocol • findings** *During the study period of nearly four decades, the relative abundance of the species present at this site has changed little.*

study² /ˈstʌdi/ *verb* (**stud·ies, study·ing, stud·ied, stud·ied**) **1** [I, T] to spend time learning about a subject by reading, going to college, etc: *When in high school, Takashi studied abroad in Ireland for one month.* ◇ **~ for sth** *Aboulela studied for a master's degree in statistics at the London School of Economics.* ◇ **~ sth** *The Committee contended 'that the accumulation of facts is not the sole, or perhaps not the leading, purpose of studying history'.* ◇ **~ (sth) at...** *David Hume was born in Edinburgh and studied law at Edinburgh University.* ◇ **~ (sth) under...** *He studied under Naropa, who had once been the head scholar of Nalanda University.* **2** [T] to examine a problem, situation, group, etc. in detail in order to analyse or understand it: **~ sth** *Cimbura (2000) studied the effects of stress on police officers.* ◇ *The prevalence of personality disorder varies depending upon the population group studied.* ◇ **~ how/what, etc...** *These models can be used to study how various internal and external factors affect the ultimate outcome of biological systems.* **3** [T] **~ sth** to watch or look at sb/sth carefully in order to find out sth: *She visited important sites, studied documents and conducted interviews.* ◇ *A microfossil is any fossil that is best studied by means of a microscope.*

stuff /stʌf/ *noun* [U] **1** something that sth else is based on or is made from; the most important feature of sth : *The physical components of the brain are composed of exactly the same stuff as the rest of the physical universe.* ◇ **~ of sth** *Tsunami warning systems are not the stuff of science fiction.* ◇ *Formerly, montage was the very stuff of cinema.* **2** (*informal*) used to refer to a substance, a material, a group of objects, some information, etc. when you do not know the name, when the name is not important or when it is obvious what you are talking about: *We're sending and communicating stuff that we should not be communicating by email.* ➲ *see also* FOODSTUFF

stu·pid /ˈstjuːpɪd; *NAmE* ˈstuːpɪd/ *adj.* (**stu·pider, stu·pidest**) (**more stupid** and **most stupid** are also common.) **1** showing a lack of thought or good judgement: *Most people hate being made to look stupid.* ◇ *a stupid question/mistake* **2** (*offensive, disapproving*) (of a person) slow to learn or understand things; not clever or intelligent: *Giants were represented as cruel and stupid.*

style AWL /staɪl/ *noun* **1** [C, U] the particular way in which sth is done: *Different cultures have different communication styles.* ◇ *a leadership/parenting/learning/teaching style* ◇ *Party members were encouraged to adopt* *a military style in language and dress.* ◇ **~ of sth** *The style of questioning used was very informal.* ➲ *see also* LIFESTYLE **2** [C, U] the features of a book, painting, building, etc. that make it typical of a particular author, artist, historical period, etc: *His style is succinct and very readable; the jargon of social science and development studies is largely absent.* ◇ **in (a) ~** *Harshly realist in style, 'The Bad Seed' created controversies from the beginning.* ◇ *In the 1970s and 1980s, Hindu communities across the nation constructed temples in traditional architectural styles.* **3** [C] a particular design of sth, for example clothes: *Cars are supplied with different styles, engines, seats, colours.* ◇ *Our social groups effectively socialize us to see particular dress and hair styles as being more attractive than others.* **4** [U] the quality of being elegant or fashionable and made to a high standard: *Advertising becomes less about telling us why we should buy a product and more about associating the product with style and image.* **5** [U] the correct use of language: *While this is not considered good style today, it does make a text easier to read.* **6** (in adjectives) having the type of style mentioned: *It offers an arcade-style interactive game.* ◇ *This is American-style capitalism.* **7** [C] (*biology*) the long thin part of a flower that carries the STIGMA: *It is also possible that flowers with protruding styles might deter some prospective flower pollinators.*

styl·is·tic /staɪˈlɪstɪk/ *adj.* [only before noun] connected with the style that a writer, artist or musician uses: *Detailed studies confirmed that the same stylistic features are found in all parts of the text.* ■ **styl·is·tic·al·ly** /staɪˈlɪstɪkli/ *adv.*: *The previous 'Star Trek' films were stylistically conservative.*

styl·ized (*BrE also* -ised) **AWL** /ˈstaɪlaɪzd/ *adj.* drawn, written, etc. in a way that is not natural or realistic: *the stylized gestures of silent cinema*

sub- /sʌb/ *prefix* **1** (in nouns and adjectives) below; less than: *There are very large seasonal swings of temperature from searing summer heat to sustained sub-zero temperatures in winter.* ◇ *There is growing evidence that the quality of informed consent in clinical research is often sub-optimal.* **2** (in nouns and adjectives) under: *Some countries in sub-Saharan Africa have the highest mortality in the range 20–25 per thousand.* ◇ *In Ruttmann's film 'Berlin' there is a scene of two subway trains passing each other in opposite directions.* **3** (in verbs and nouns) a smaller part of sth: *C-fibres are subdivided into two types.* ◇ *As a group, we each wrote a literature review for one of the subtopics.*

sub·atom·ic /ˌsʌbəˈtɒmɪk; *NAmE* ˌsʌbəˈtɑːmɪk/ *adj.* [usually before noun] (*physics*) smaller than, or found in, an atom: *Subatomic entities manifest particle-like properties in certain contexts and wave-like properties in other contexts.*

ˌsubatomic ˈparticle *noun* = PARTICLE (1)

sub·cul·ture /ˈsʌbkʌltʃə(r)/ *noun* the behaviour and beliefs of a particular group of people in society that are different from those of most people; a particular group of people in society with such behaviour and beliefs: *In the late 1950s and 1960s, a steady stream of youth subcultures emerged.*

sub·div·ide /ˈsʌbdɪvaɪd; ˌsʌbdɪˈvaɪd/ *verb* [T, often passive, I] **~ (sth) (into sth)** to divide sth into smaller parts; to be divided into smaller parts: *This potentially dangerous UV radiation is subdivided into three categories.* ◇ *Larger social groups, such as an army division, tend to subdivide into many duplicate parts.*

sub·div·ision *noun* **1** /ˌsʌbdɪˈvɪʒn/ [U] **~ (of sth)** the act of dividing a part of sth into smaller parts: *Further subdivision of these subtypes can be made.* **2** /ˈsʌbdɪvɪʒn/ [C] **~ (of sth)** one of the smaller parts into which a part of sth has been divided: *The US Bureau of Economic Analysis is a subdivision of the US Department of Commerce.* **3** /ˈsʌbdɪvɪʒn/ [C] (*NAmE*) an area of land that has been divided up for building houses on: *The San Fernando Valley unfolds in a mass of freeways, office towers and residential subdivisions.*

sub·group /ˈsʌbgruːp/ *noun* a smaller group made up of members of a larger group: *Additional surveys were conducted with population subgroups (adolescents, women of reproductive age and older adults) during 2003.* ◇ **~ of sb/sth** *Market segmentation involves the analysis of mass markets to identify subgroups of consumers with similar wants and buying requirements.*

sub·head·ing /ˌsʌbˈhedɪŋ/ *noun* a title given to any of the sections into which a longer piece of writing has been divided: **under a ~** *This chapter is organized under two main subheadings.*

sub·ject¹ /ˈsʌbdʒɪkt; ˈsʌbdʒekt/ *noun* **1** a thing or person that is being discussed, described or dealt with: *Atkins treats this subject in considerable detail.* ◇ **~ of sth** *Much attention has been paid to the subject of silicate mineral weathering.* ◇ *The reason for this dramatic increase has been the subject of much debate.* ◇ **on a ~** *Many books and articles have been written on this subject.* ◇ **+ noun** *Classical vases frequently took their subject matter from mythology.* **2** a person being used to study sth, especially in an experiment: *When subjects were asked to write a description of what they had seen, only 33% mentioned the change in actor.* ◇ *The median age of participating study subjects was 54 years.* **3** an area of knowledge studied in a school, college, etc: *In a public primary school, class teachers teach almost all subjects, but only one class.* ◇ *These students were all native speakers of Arabic who started learning English as a school subject at the age of 12.* ◇ **+ noun** *International content will be integrated into all the core subject areas.* **4** a person or thing that is the main feature of a picture or photograph, or that a work of art is based on: *Robert Walter Weir was an American painter of historical subjects.* ◇ **~ of sth** *While the main subject of the photograph is Alva, he is framed off-centre, at the top of the picture.* **5** a member of a state who is not its ruler, especially when that ruler is a king or queen: *Where their countries gained independence, they would be citizens of those countries and British subjects as well.* **6** (*grammar*) a noun, noun phrase or pronoun representing the person or thing that performs the action of the verb (*I* in *I sat down.*), about which sth is stated (*the house* in *the house is very old*) or, in a passive sentence, that is affected by the action of the verb (*the tree* in *the tree was blown down in the storm*): *The second sentence has a plural subject and a plural verb form.* ◇ **~ of sth** *In languages like Italian, the subject of a finite clause can be dropped.* ➲ *compare* OBJECT¹ (4), PREDICATE¹

S

sub·ject² /ˈsʌbdʒekt; ˈsʌbdʒɪkt/ *adj.* **1 ~ to sth** affected or likely to be affected by an event, action or process: *In general, folk cultures are more traditional and less subject to change than popular culture.* ◇ *Budgets and labour processes became subject to greater management scrutiny and control.* **2 ~ to sth** depending on sth in order to be completed or agreed: *All the interviews were recorded and transcribed subject to written consent by the interviewees.* ◇ *This requirement is subject to the limitation of 'reasonable practicability'.* **3 ~ to sth/sb** under the authority of sth/sb: *In all jurisdictions, financial agreements are subject to the law of contract.* ◇ *The liquidator is an officer of the court and is subject to its control.* **4** [only before noun] under the control of another ruler, country or government: *The European colonial powers refused to allow the subject peoples of Asia and Africa to attain independence.*

sub·ject³ /səbˈdʒekt/ *verb* (*formal*) to bring a country or group of people under your control or rule, especially by using force: *Imperialism is the desire to create empires that subject other peoples.* ◇ **~ sb/sth to sth** *Vitoria had asked: 'By what right were the barbarians subjected to Spanish* rule?' ■ **sub·jec·tion** /səbˈdʒekʃn/ *noun* [U] **~ (of sb/sth) (to sb/sth)** *Serfdom was an essential social relationship in feudalism that involved the legal subjection of peasants to a lord.*

PHR V **subˈject sb/sth to sth** [often passive] to make sb/sth experience or suffer sth, usually sth unpleasant: *Patients must not be subjected to any treatment they consider inhumane or degrading.* **subˈject sth to sth** [usually passive] to make sth go through or be affected by a particular process, often as part of an experiment: *These data were subjected to statistical analyses, which yielded five major factors.* ◇ *It was observed that in cells subjected to temperatures higher than normal, certain proteins increased in amounts.*

sub·ject·ive /səbˈdʒektɪv/ *adj.* **1** based on a particular person's beliefs or opinions, rather than on facts or evidence that everyone can recognize: *It could be argued that Strachey's observations are highly subjective and therefore scientifically unsound.* ◇ *Using the model requires a subjective judgement of the contribution of each activity to the achievement of the mission.* OPP OBJECTIVE² (1) **2** [usually before noun] (of ideas, feelings or experiences) existing in sb's mind rather than in the real world: *Pain is an inherently subjective experience, though it is typically expressed in behaviour detectable by others.* OPP OBJECTIVE² (2) ■ **sub·ject·ive·ly** *adv.*: *The initial identification must be done empirically, not subjectively.* ◇ *These factors influence how the child subjectively experiences the traumatic event.* OPP OBJECTIVELY

sub·ject·iv·ity /ˌsʌbdʒekˈtɪvəti/ *noun* (*pl.* -ies) **1** [U] the fact of being based on or influenced by personal beliefs and opinions rather than only on facts or evidence: *Use of computer-based test results avoids or minimizes subjectivity in selecting interpretive material.* ◇ **~ of sth** *He had the idea of a 'middle ground' between the objectivity and the subjectivity of judgements of beauty.* OPP OBJECTIVITY **2** [C] the particular, subjective way in which one person views and experiences the world: *In these novels, the question of rival subjectivities is brought into focus.*

ˈsubject matter *noun* [U] **~ (of sth)** the ideas or information contained in a book, speech, painting, etc: *The subject matter of his last play was more serious.*

S

sub·mis·sion AWL /səbˈmɪʃn/ *noun* **1** [U] **~ (of sb/sth) (to sb/sth)** the act of accepting that sb has defeated or is greater than you and that you must obey them SYN SURRENDER² (1): *The Greek communities of the Aegean coast were forced into submission to the Persian empire.* ◇ *Since Islam means submission to the will of God, Muslims emphasize the need to obey Islamic law.* **2** [U, C] **~ (of sth)** the act of giving a proposal, application or other document to sb in authority so that they can consider or judge it; a proposal, etc. that is given in this way: *The membership process requires the submission of an application form.* ◇ *The deadline for submissions is 5 August 2014.* **3** [C] (*law*) a statement that is made to a judge in court or to a committee: *According to the Equality Authority, the requirement for written submissions can be a factor in claimants not proceeding.*

sub·mis·sive /səbˈmɪsɪv/ *adj.* willing to accept sb else's authority and to obey them without question: *White males are depicted in positions of power and females in more submissive and accepting roles.*

sub·mit AWL /səbˈmɪt/ *verb* (-tt-) **1** [T] to give a proposal, application or other document to sb in authority so that they can consider or judge it: *The completed manuscript was submitted in 1903 but not published until 1917.* ◇ **~ sth to sb/sth** *Inspectors visited the factory in summer 2001 and submitted a highly critical report to the Health and Safety Executive.* ◇ **~ sth for sth** *Ten proposals were submitted by minority stockholders for consideration at the annual general meeing.* **2** [I, T] to accept the authority, control or greater strength of sb/sth; to agree to sth because of this SYN GIVE IN TO STH/SB, YIELD¹: *Independent women like Clytemnestra who defy male hegemony and refuse to submit are condemned and excluded.* ◇ **~ to sb/sth** *Czechoslovakia was forced to submit to Nazi Germany in 1939.* ◇ **~ yourself (to sb/sth)** *He submitted himself to a search by the guards.* **3** [T] **~ that...** (*law* or *formal*) to say or suggest sth: *The government submitted that such measures were justified.*

sub·or·din·ate¹ AWL /səˈbɔːdɪnət; *NAmE* səˈbɔːrdɪnət/ *adj.* **1** having less power or authority than sb else in a group or an organization: *Most newly independent countries were far from satisfied with their subordinate position in the international economic system.* ◇ *Subordinate males have chronically elevated levels of corticosterone compared with dominant individuals (Abbott et al., 2003).* ◇ **~ to sb/sth** *Despite devolution, the Scottish Parliament is still subordinate to the Westminster Parliament.* **2** less important than sth else SYN SECONDARY (1): *The initial high-level categories were further subdivided into a number of subordinate categories.* ◇ **~ to sth** *It was widely accepted that trade was subordinate to politics.*

sub·or·din·ate² AWL /səˈbɔːdɪnət; *NAmE* səˈbɔːrdɪnət/ *noun* a person who has a position with less authority and power than sb else in an organization: *Occupational status was divided into three categories: managers, middle managers or subordinates.* OPP SUPERIOR²

sub·or·din·ate³ AWL /səˈbɔːdɪneɪt; *NAmE* səˈbɔːrdɪneɪt/ *verb* **~ sb/sth (to sb/sth)** to treat sb/sth as less important than sb/sth else: *In his narratives, Tacitus subordinates military details to dramatic and psychological elements.* ■ **sub·or·din·ation** AWL /səˌbɔːdɪˈneɪʃn; *NAmE* səˌbɔːrdɪˈneɪʃn/ *noun* [U] **~ (of sb/sth) (to sb/sth)** *The subordination of tenants to their landlords was an accepted part of social arrangements.*

sub·scribe /səbˈskraɪb/ *verb* **1** [I] **~ (to sth)** to pay money regularly to receive or use a service or to support an organization or cause: *Two thirds of the world's population does not subscribe to a mobile phone.* ◇ *Teachers could be dismissed for subscribing to journals of 'advanced' views.* ◇ *More than half the adult population are subscribing members of at least one organization (such as a trade union).* **2** [I] **~ (for sth)** (*finance*) to apply to buy shares in a company: *Other investors in the company subscribed for a total of 5 000 shares.*

PHR V **subˈscribe to sth** to agree with or support an opinion or a theory SYN BELIEVE IN STH: *Most professionals subscribe to the view that contact with the mother is almost always in the child's best interests.*

sub·scriber /səbˈskraɪbə(r)/ *noun* a person who pays money regularly to receive or use a service or to support an organization or cause : *The mobile phone network offered new subscribers a digital camera.* ◇ *Amnesty International has more than one million members, subscribers and regular donors in over 140 countries and territories.* ◇ **~ to sth** *Subscribers to the journal have access to online articles, features and reviews from 1996 to the present.*

sub·script *adj.* (*technical*) (of a letter, figure or symbol) written or printed below the normal line of writing or printing: *subscript numerals* ➲ *compare* SUPERSCRIPT

sub·scrip·tion /səbˈskrɪpʃn/ *noun* [C, U] **1** an amount of money that you pay, usually once a year or once a month, to receive a service or be a member of an organization; the act of paying this money: *The UN obtains its funding from annual subscriptions from member countries.* ◇ **~ to sth** *Most academic libraries will have subscriptions to a wide range of journals.* ◇ **+ noun** *The company offers a subscription service whereby customers pay a monthly fee in return for the right to download music tracks onto their*

PC. **2** the act of people paying money for sth to be done: **by ~** *Novik was one of 23 warships built by public subscription.*

sub·sec·tion /ˈsʌbsekʃn/ *noun* a part of a section, especially of a legal document: *The following subsections describe the key assumptions of the methodology.* ◇ *The case is described in subsection (6) below.*

sub·se·quent AWL /ˈsʌbsɪkwənt/ *adj.* happening or coming after sth else: *The findings of the initial investigation were confirmed by subsequent radiocarbon analysis.* ◇ *Subsequent events did not prove Taylor wrong.* ◇ *This work had a tremendous influence on subsequent generations of economists.* OPP PREVIOUS (1)

WHICH WORD?

subsequent • consequent • successive • consecutive

- **Subsequent** means happening or coming after sth else; **consequent** means happening as a result of sth else: *Subsequent studies have broadly confirmed these findings.* ◇ *Any delay would have resulted in a loss of business and the consequent loss of profits.*
- **Successive** and **consecutive** both describe series that occur without interruption; **consecutive** is used especially with nouns relating to time: *successive administrations/generations/governments* ◇ *The leaders attended successive rounds of talks.* ◇ *After 17 consecutive days of demonstrations, the government agreed to popular demands for democratic reforms.*

sub·se·quent·ly AWL /ˈsʌbsɪkwəntli/ *adv.* afterwards; after sth else has happened: *Subsequently, further analysis was performed.* ◇ *Schaefer became a political refugee in England and subsequently moved to Iowa City.*

ˈsubsequent to *prep.* (*formal*) after; following: *The theory was developed subsequent to the earthquake of 1906.* ◇ *Subsequent to discussions with users, it became apparent that the resource pack was unsuitable.*

sub·set /ˈsʌbset/ *noun* (*technical*) a smaller group of things or people formed from the members of a larger group: *The data set was split into five subsets.* ◇ **~ of sth/sb** *A small subset of these forests had escaped direct human influence (Cogbill et al., 2002).*

sub·sidi·ar·ity /səbˌsɪdiˈærəti; ˌsʌbsɪdiˈærəti; NAmE səbˌsɪdiˈerəti; ˌsʌbsɪdiˈerəti/ *noun* [U] the principle that a central authority should not be very powerful, and should only control things which cannot be controlled by local organizations: *According to the principle of subsidiarity, actions should be taken at the lowest appropriate administrative level.*

sub·sid·iary¹ AWL /səbˈsɪdiəri; NAmE səbˈsɪdieri/ *noun* (*pl.* -ies) a business or company that is owned or controlled by another larger company: *The Act defines 'operator' to include the parent company, its subsidiaries and any joint venture partners.*

sub·sid·iary² AWL /səbˈsɪdiəri; NAmE səbˈsɪdieri/ *adj.* **1 ~ (to sth)** connected with sth but less important than it: *Smith argued that culture was the main social divisor in Jamaica, with colour and class playing subsidiary roles.* ◇ **~ to sb/sth** *Women's lives and activities, previously seen as subsidiary to men's, are documented (Mattley, 2006: 143).* **2** (of a business or company) owned or controlled by another company: *In order to facilitate its expansion into the UK, Domino's established a subsidiary company, Domino's Pizza Group Ltd.*

sub·sid·ize (*BrE also* -ise) AWL /ˈsʌbsɪdaɪz/ *verb* [often passive] **~ sb/sth** to give money to sb or an organization to help pay for sth; to give a subsidy: *In the UK, health care is heavily subsidized by the government.* ◇ *Legislation exists in South Africa to support the use of free and subsidized medicines.* ➲ *compare* FUND² ➲ thesaurus note *at* FUND²
■ **sub·sid·iza·tion, -isa·tion** /ˌsʌbsɪdaɪˈzeɪʃn; NAmE ˌsʌbsɪdəˈzeɪʃn/ *noun* [U] **~ (of sth)** *By 1995, there was a trend towards the state subsidization of private and personal care for the elderly.*

sub·sidy AWL /ˈsʌbsədi/ *noun* (*pl.* -ies) [C, U] money that is paid by a government or an organization to reduce the costs of services or of producing goods, especially so that their prices can be kept low: *In the Environmentally Sensitive Areas scheme, farmers are paid subsidies to preserve the environment.* ◇ *The rail service now operates without subsidy.* ◇ **~ for sth** *State subsidies for universal childcare, such as Denmark's, are expensive.*

sub·sist /səbˈsɪst/ *verb* **1** [I] (*formal* or *law*) to exist; to be valid: *Copyright will subsist during the lifetime of the author and for a period of 70 years after the author's death.* **2** [I] **~ (on sth)** to manage to stay alive, especially with limited food or money: *Often they subsisted on a diet of bread and potatoes.*

sub·sist·ence /səbˈsɪstəns/ *noun* [U] **1** the state of having just enough money or food to stay alive: *In 1899, a third of the working-class households in York lacked the minimum income necessary for subsistence.* ◇ **+ noun** *Her earnings were below the subsistence level.* **2** (in compounds) **+ noun** connected with production at a level that provides just enough for your own use, without any extra to sell: *The local population gain their livelihoods mainly from fishing and subsistence agriculture.*

sub·spe·cies /ˈsʌbspiːʃiːz/ *noun* (*pl.* sub·spe·cies) a group into which animals, plants, etc. that are related are divided, smaller than a species : *Chimpanzees are classified into four subspecies (Gonder et al., 1997; Groves, 2001).*

sub·stance /ˈsʌbstəns/ *noun* **1** [C] a type of solid, liquid or gas that has particular qualities: *Over 4 000 chemical substances, both gases and particulates, have been identified in tobacco smoke.* ◇ *Dialysis removes toxic substances from the blood.* ◇ *a hazardous/harmful/radioactive substance* **2** [C] a drug or chemical, especially an illegal one, that has a particular effect on the mind or body: *He was suspended from the sport for using a banned substance.* ◇ **+ noun** *A significant proportion of adolescents admitted substance abuse or alcohol abuse.* **3** [U] the most important or main part of sth: **the ~ of sth** *The notes contained the substance of the discussion.* ◇ **in ~** *The new government proposals were very different in substance from those of the year before.* **4** [U] (*formal*) importance: *A series of decisions in the early 1960s gave real substance to the European legal system.* ◇ **sb/sth of ~** *Yeats was by that time widely recognized as a writer of substance.* **5** [U] the quality of being based on facts or the truth: *A close examination of the evidence shows that the charges were not completely without substance.*

sub·stan·tial /səbˈstænʃl/ *adj.* large in amount, value or importance SYN CONSIDERABLE: *Very substantial sums of money have been provided by governments to bail out the banking sector.* ◇ *A substantial part of the forest is already in a degraded state.* ◇ *The severity of the drought prompted substantial changes in public policy on urban water use.* ◇ *Results indicate that the health risks are substantial, with few employees having no risk factors.*
▸ SUBSTANTIAL + NOUN **amount, quantity • degree • body • number • part • proportion, portion • majority • minority • fraction** *Substantial amounts of polystyrene (but not all) have been extracted from the blend samples.* | **impact • influence • difference • change • variation • reduction • increase • gain • benefit • improvement • progress • contribution • damage • loss • burden • evidence • investment • sum • savings** *The 2008-9 financial crisis had a substantial impact on these groups.*

S

sub·stan·tial·ly /səbˈstænʃəli/ *adv.* **1** very much SYN CONSIDERABLY: *This programme has been successful in substantially reducing the carp population in both lakes.* ◇ *It was found that these choices were not substantially affected by gender.* ◇ *The net value of the dry-season crop is substantially higher (Tawatchai and Singh, 1996).* **2** (*formal*) mainly; in most details, even if not completely: *The procedures for Experiment 2 were substantially similar to those of Experiment 1.*

sub·stan·ti·ate /səbˈstænʃieɪt/ *verb* **~ sth** to provide information or evidence to prove that sth is true: *There is no shortage of evidence to substantiate this claim.* ■ **sub·stan·ti·ation** /səbˌstænʃiˈeɪʃn/ *noun* [U] **~ (of sth)** *They have to show that the evidence is relevant to the substantiation of their claim.*

sub·stan·tive /səbˈstæntɪv; ˈsʌbstəntɪv/ *adj.* **1** dealing with real, important or serious matters: *Several substantive issues have been identified.* **2** (of law) defining rights and duties, as opposed to giving the rules by which those rights and duties are put into effect: *The present case concerned a matter of substantive law.*

sub·sti·tute[1] AWL /ˈsʌbstɪtjuːt; *NAmE* ˈsʌbstɪtuːt/ *verb* [I, T] to take the place of sb/sth else; to use sb/sth instead of sb/sth else: **~ for sb/sth** *Outside professionals can support community projects, but cannot substitute for indigenous leaders.* ◇ **~ A for B** *The aim was to reduce carbon dioxide emissions by substituting biofuels for petroleum.* ◇ **~ B with/by A** *The aim was to substitute petroleum with biofuels.*

sub·sti·tute[2] AWL /ˈsʌbstɪtjuːt; *NAmE* ˈsʌbstɪtuːt/ *noun* a person or thing that you use or have instead of the usual one: *For the purposes of the experiment, it was decided to use natural rubber rather than an artificial substitute.* ◇ **~ for sb/sth** *Although virtual training has advantages, there are no substitutes for authentic experience.*

sub·sti·tu·tion AWL /ˌsʌbstɪˈtjuːʃn; *NAmE* ˈsʌbstɪˈtuːʃn/ *noun* [U, C] **~ (of A for B)** the act of using sb/sth instead of another person or thing; the fact of sb/sth appearing in place of sb/sth else: *The substitution of TBI for chemotherapy in treating cancer proved to be controversial.* ◇ *Modification or substitution of a particular amino acid results in loss of enzyme activity.* ◇ *Most modern ciphers do not involve letter substitutions.*

S

sub·strate /ˈsʌbstreɪt/ *noun* (*technical*) **1** an underlying substance or layer: *Where volcanic material has been extruded on to a soft substrate, the rate of erosion of the substrate can exceed that of the lava flow.* **2** the surface or material on which a living thing grows and feeds: *Initially, 35 forms of life that live on or within ocean substrates were considered.* **3** the substance on which an ENZYME acts to produce a chemical reaction: *The enzyme is then provided with a substrate that it converts into a coloured product.* **4** a material that provides the surface on which sth is put or marked, for example in making INTEGRATED CIRCUITS: *Manufacturing integrated circuits usually starts with a silicon substrate onto which various layers can be deposited and patterned.*

sub·stra·tum /ˈsʌbstrɑːtəm; *NAmE* ˈsʌbstreɪtəm/ *noun* (*pl.* **sub·strata** /ˈsʌbstrɑːtə; *NAmE* ˈsʌbstreɪtə/) (*technical*) a layer of sth, especially rock or earth, that is below another layer: *The salt disperses before reaching the substratum.* ◇ *The range of different seabed substrata was evenly sampled.*

sub·title /ˈsʌbtaɪtl/ *noun* **1** a second title of a book, article, etc. that appears after the main title and gives more information: *Both the title and subtitle are misleading.* ◇ **~ of sth** *As the subtitle of her work suggests, they were 'writers in a common cause'.* **2** [usually pl.] **~ (of sth)** words that appear on a TV or cinema screen so that you can understand what is being said: *The English subtitles of the Hindi in 'Slumdog Millionaire' appear during key action scenes.*

sub·tle /ˈsʌtl/ *adj.* (**sub·tler**, **sub·tlest**) (**more subtle** is also common.) **1** (*often approving*) (especially of a change or difference) not very obvious; not easy to notice: *There seems to be a subtle difference between 'pure' episodic memory and autobiographical memory.* ◇ *Changes in local water levels were very subtle but were nonetheless signficant over the ten-year period.* **2** (of a person or their behaviour) behaving in a clever way and using indirect methods in order to achieve sth: *The restrictions forced companies to advertise to children in more subtle ways, such as educational sponsorship.* **3** showing a good understanding of things that are not obvious to other people: *The book contains a wealth of subtle ideas.* ◇ *Aristotle gives a subtle philosophical analysis of self-control and the lack of it in Book VII.*

subtle·ty /ˈsʌtlti/ *noun* (*pl.* **-ies**) **1** [U] the quality of being not very obvious: *It seems that class differences grew in subtlety as society as a whole became more affluent.* **2** [U] the ability to notice and understand things that are not obvious to other people: *Lydgate's work tends to lack Chaucer's subtlety and delicacy of touch.* ◇ **~ of sth** *Weber's achievement lies in the precision of his concepts and the subtlety of his analyses.* **3** [C, usually pl.] **~ (of sth)** a small but important detail or aspect of sth: *Companies need to understand and respect the subtleties of local cultures.*

subtly /ˈsʌtli/ *adv.* **1** in a way that is not obvious: *These temperature changes subtly affected growth rates.* **2** in a way that is clever and uses indirect methods to achieve sth: *The decor in 'fast food' restaurants is designed to subtly control customer behaviour.* **3** in a way that shows the ability to notice and understand things that are not obvious to other people: *The novel subtly avoids any simple opposition between the rural and the urban.* ◇ *More subtly, it has been argued that some full-time care workers should be considered 'partial volunteers'.*

sub·tract /səbˈtrækt/ *verb* [T, I] **~ (sth) (from sth)** to take a number or an amount away from another number or amount: *All negative scores were then subtracted from all positive scores for every participant.* ◇ *Older mathematics curricula are typified with the learning of algorithms for adding, subtracting, multiplying and dividing.* OPP ADD (3) ■ **sub·trac·tion** /səbˈtrækʃn/ *noun* [U, C] *Mechanical computing devices were developed that could perform addition, subtraction, multiplication and division.* ◇ *Many additions and subtractions were involved in the full calculation.* OPP ADDITION (3)

sub·trop·ic·al /ˌsʌbˈtrɒpɪkl; *NAmE* ˌsʌbˈtrɑːpɪkl/ *adj.* in or connected with regions that are near the tropical parts of the world: *This species is found in tropical and subtropical regions of Africa, Asia and Australia.*

sub·urb /ˈsʌbɜːb; *NAmE* ˈsʌbɜːrb/ *noun* an area where people live that is outside the centre of a city: *They may live in the suburbs or the city.* ◇ *The growth of the suburbs swelled London's population.* ◇ **~ of...** *They studied a random sample of a thousand households in Gurgaon, a suburb of Delhi.*

sub·ur·ban /səˈbɜːbən; *NAmE* səˈbɜːrbən/ *adj.* in or connected with a suburb: *I use the term 'city' here to mean both the municipality and the extended suburban area.* ◇ *One of the largest malls in the United States is the Mall of America, in suburban Minneapolis.*

sub·ver·sive /səbˈvɜːsɪv; *NAmE* səbˈvɜːrsɪv/ *adj.* trying or likely to destroy or damage a system or institution by attacking it secretly or indirectly: *He was accused of engaging in subversive activity.*

sub·vert /səbˈvɜːt; *NAmE* səbˈvɜːrt/ *verb* (*formal*) **1** **~ sth** to try to destroy the authority of a political, religious, etc.

system by attacking it secretly or indirectly SYN UNDERMINE (1): *In 'The Enemy Within', Kennedy describes the hidden forces in America that attempted to subvert the country's freedoms.* **2 ~ sth** to try to destroy a person's belief in sth/sb SYN UNDERMINE (1): *I do not intend to subvert the clear themes of loss that emerge in studies of children's responses to divorce.* ■ **sub·ver·sion** /səbˈvɜːʃn; *NAmE* səbˈvɜːrʒn/ *noun* [U] *Subversion may include a variety of techniques, including propaganda, intelligence activities and assisting rebel groups.*

suc·ceed /səkˈsiːd/ *verb* **1** [I] to achieve sth that you have been trying to do or get; to have the result or effect that was intended: *Most African governments viewed the operation as dangerous and unlikely to succeed.* ◇ **~ in doing sth** *After lengthy experiments, Joseph Aspdin eventually succeeded in making the first artificial cement, which he patented in 1824.* HELP When sb/sth **only succeeds in doing sth**, the opposite of what was intended is achieved: *The publicity generated by their managers was meant to connect the two celebrities, but it only succeeded in driving them apart.* ⊃ *see also* SUCCESS **2** [T] **~ sb/sth** to come next after sb/sth and take their/its place or position SYN FOLLOW (1): *These traditions continued through the later Roman Empire and the societies that succeeded it.* ◇ **~ sb/sth as sth** *Theseus succeeded his father as ruler of Athens.* ◇ **succeeding + noun** *The village was founded in 1845 by Swiss immigrants, and succeeding generations have retained their Swiss-German traditions.* ⊃ *see also* SUCCESSION (1) **3** [I] **~ (to sth)** to gain the right to a title, property, etc. when sb dies: *After Herod's death in 4 BCE, his sons succeeded to his subdivided kingdom.* ⊃ *see also* SUCCESSION (3)

suc·cess /səkˈses/ *noun* **1** [U] the fact that sth/sb achieves a good result: *The questionnaire shows that many students attribute both success and failure in education to luck.* ◇ **~ in doing sth** *Mexico has had remarkable success in using the soap opera format to encourage family planning and literacy.* ◇ **~ in sth** *The presence of educational resources in the home, including computers, is a strong predictor of academic success in maths and science.* ◇ **~ of sth** *Further funding is essential to ensure the continued success of the immunization project.* ◇ **+ noun** *This approach has a success rate of 70%.* ◇ **the key to ~** *Nearly all respondents strongly agreed that education is the key to success.* OPP FAILURE (3) **2** [U] **~ (as sth)** the fact that sb achieves a high position in a particular activity; the fact of becoming rich or famous: *Pryor achieved great popular success as a comic.* **3** [C] a thing or person that has achieved a good result and been successful: *Initially, the IBM Personal Computer was a huge success, capturing 40% of the market.* ◇ *Sales management scholars have emphasized the importance of learning from successes and failures in the field (Chonko et al., 2003).* ◇ **make a ~ (of sth)** *To make a success of the new policies required leaders who could show flexibility and practicality.* OPP FAILURE (4)

▸ ADJECTIVE + SUCCESS **great, remarkable, notable, huge, spectacular, enormous, phenomenal • considerable • relative • limited, partial • mixed • apparent • past • initial, early • long-term • future • ultimate • overall** *The travelling exhibitions enjoyed great success.* ◇ *Despite initial successes in controlling avian influenza, a high number of human cases were recorded from January to June 2005 (WHO).* | **economic • commercial • academic, educational • military • electoral • reproductive** *Russia's position had been improved by military successes against Turkey in the Caucasus.*

▸ VERB + SUCCESS **achieve • meet with • have, enjoy, experience • evaluate, assess • explain • attribute • predict** *The ADEPT model may be useful to explain successes and failures of health promotion policy.* | **affect, influence • determine • ensure, guarantee • promote, enhance • maximize • limit • measure** *Attempts to restore water quality of contaminated aquifers by pumping met with limited success.*

▸ SUCCESS + NOUN **story • rate • factor** *The belief that the British political system is a success story has become less fashionable recently.*

suc·cess·ful /səkˈsesfl/ *adj.* **1** achieving your aims or what was intended: *Successful completion of the construction project depended on multi-agency cooperation.* ◇ *After a successful career in direct sales, Mary Kay Ash retired and started Mary Kay Inc.* ◇ **~ in (doing) sth** *The introduction of the flea beetle has been highly successful in controlling this weed (Buckingham, 2002).* ◇ **~ at (doing) sth** *In the initial years of her administration, Thatcher was successful at building alliances in order to achieve her goals.* OPP UNSUCCESSFUL **2** having become popular and/or made a lot of money: *Boeing's new jet, the 707, was tremendously successful.*

suc·cess·ful·ly /səkˈsesfəli/ *adv.* in a way that achieves your aims or intentions: *Four US cities successfully implemented this training programme for school administrators.* ◇ *Being able to compete successfully in the global marketplace is now a critical factor for survival in many industries.* ◇ *Both these ambitions were realized quite successfully.*

suc·ces·sion AWL /səkˈseʃn/ *noun* **1** [C, usually sing.] a number of things or people that follow each other in time or order SYN SERIES (1): **~ of sth** *Since 1991, a succession of books has appeared covering the break-up of the USSR.* ◇ **in ~** *The 1992 election was the sixth in succession in which the party gained less than 40% of the votes.* ◇ **in quick/rapid ~** *Alexander conquered Lydia, Caria and Lycia in quick succession.* ⊃ *see also* SUCCEED (2) **2** [U] the act of taking over an official position or title: **~ to sth** *Agrippina was responsible for a series of dynastic murders to secure Nero's succession to the imperial throne.* ◇ **in ~ to sb** *Masefield was appointed Poet Laureate in succession to Robert Bridges.* ⊃ *see also* SUCCEED (3) **3** [U] the right to take over an official position or title, especially to become the king or queen of a country: *In ancient Sparta, the succession was hereditary.* ◇ **~ to sth** *The main contenders for the succession to the leadership were all veteran revolutionaries.* ⊃ *see also* SUCCEED (3)

suc·ces·sive AWL /səkˈsesɪv/ *adj.* [only before noun] following immediately one after the other SYN CONSECUTIVE: *Each successive generation was found to be larger.* ◇ *Throughout the 1920s, successive British governments were under pressure to extend the provision of birth control.* ⊃ *usage note at* SUBSEQUENT ■ **suc·ces·sively** AWL *adv.*: *As part of the rehabilitation process, the gibbons are successively moved further and further from human contact.* ◇ *Christopher Codrington was successively councillor (1666) and deputy governor of Barbados (1669–72).*

suc·ces·sor AWL /səkˈsesə(r)/ *noun* a person or thing that comes after sb/sth else and takes their/its place: *Ptolemy I and his immediate successors encouraged prominent Greek scholars and scientists to come to Egypt.* ◇ **~ to sb/sth** *The 704 was the successor to the 700 series of IBM mainframe computers.* ◇ **~ as sth** *Beadle became Morgan's successor as chairman of the Biology Division.* ⊃ *compare* PREDECESSOR

such /sʌtʃ/ *det., pron.* **1** of the type already mentioned: *Some studies have focused on populations of single species inhabiting separate environments. In such cases, species comparisons are problematic.* ◇ *Free trade did not significantly influence British policies until half a century after Adam Smith first advocated such a system.* ◇ **many/some ~** *The early Christians were a secretive group and, like many such groups, they developed a set of secret symbols.* ◇ **as ~** *These judgements are individual interpretations, and, as such, cannot claim any finality.* **2** of the type that you are just going to mention: **in ~ a way (that/as to...)**

The principle is that winners should compensate losers in such a way that eventually everyone is better off. ◇ **no ~ thing (as...)** *Jackson argued that there is no such thing as a static or finished landscape.* ◇ **~ that...** *The distances of the asteroids were such that many astronomers believed the answer had been found.* **3** used to emphasize the great degree of sth: **~ (a) sth that...** *Water is such a common substance that it is easy to forget the fact that it has very special characteristics.* ◇ *This issue assumed such importance that the PIU set up a special taskforce to look at it.* ◇ **sth is/was, etc. ~ that...** *Wartime shortages were such that smuggling became commonplace.* ◇ **~ is/was, etc. sth that...** *Such was the power of vested interests in the USSR that it took thirty years or more to change the system.*

IDM **as 'such** as the word is usually understood; in the exact sense of the word: *Although the novel is not magical-realist as such, it does contain elements of myth and magic.* **such as 1** for example: *Most South East Asian governments have plans for large prestige projects, such as new airports and new industrial zones.* ◇ *A number of these countries, such as the UK, have relatively high rates of multiple sclerosis.* ◇ **~ ... as** *Inflation makes it difficult for families to plan for such things as retirement income and college expenses.* ➲ language bank *at* EXAMPLE **2** of a kind that; like: *Events such as those shown in Fig. 3.6 have been observed through measurement since 1984.* **ˌsuch as it 'is/ they 'are** used to say that there is not much of sth or that it is of poor quality: *Glen Hodgson noted that the case law (such as it was) was not particularly clear.*

suck /sʌk/ *verb* **1 ~ sth (+ adv./prep.)** to take liquid, air, etc. into your mouth by using the muscles of your lips: *He sucked the blood from a cut on his finger.* **2** to take liquid, air, etc. out of sth: **~ sth + adv./prep.** *The pump sucks air out through the valve.* ◇ **~ sth + adj.** *Greenfly can literally suck a plant dry.*

sud·den /'sʌdn/ *adj.* happening or done quickly and unexpectedly: *His sudden death in 319 BC set off a new round of conflict.* ◇ *Tree ring data point to a sudden climatic change at this time.* OPP GRADUAL ■ **sud·den·ness** *noun* [U] **~ (of sth)** *The suddenness of the collapse of communism in the USSR defied the predictions of experts.*

sud·den·ly /'sʌdənli/ *adv.* quickly and unexpectedly: *Alexander died suddenly and mysteriously at the age of 32.* ◇ *Antarctica suddenly became largely ice-covered around 34 million years ago.* OPP GRADUALLY

S

sue /suː; *BrE also* sjuː/ *verb* **1** [T, I] **~ (sb) (for sth)** to make a claim against a person, company, etc. in court about sth that they have said or done to harm you: *Former miners are currently suing the government for hundreds of millions of pounds in compensation.* ◇ *The widow of one of the victims wanted to sue.* ◇ *She is entitled to sue for breach of contract.* **2** [I] **~ for sth** (*formal*) to formally ask for sth: *Napoleon thought that Alexander would sue for peace.*

suf·fer /'sʌfə(r)/ *verb* **1** [I] to be badly affected by a disease, pain, sadness, a lack of sth, etc: *The policy must change or else people will suffer unacceptably.* ◇ **~ from sth** *Over 2 million older people in the UK suffer from depression.* ◇ *Many of these cities suffer from problems of overcrowding.* **2** [T] **~ sth** to experience sth unpleasant, such as injury, defeat or loss: *The buildings had suffered severe earthquake damage.* ◇ *OECD countries might suffer an annual loss of $25 billion.* **3** [I] to become worse: *She knew that her health would suffer in prison.*

▸ SUFFER + NOUN **loss • damage • injury • harm • defeat • decline • fate • consequences • effects • problems • disadvantage • setback • abuse • violence • hardship • injustice • discrimination • illness • pain • attack • stroke** *55 fishermen had suffered injuries in the past 12 months while at sea.* ◇ *Labour suffered its heaviest defeat in modern times.*

▸ SUFFER + ADVERB **disproportionately • badly, severely, greatly** *The other group that suffered disproportionately was women.*

▸ SUFFER FROM + NOUN **illness • disease • disorder • condition • symptoms • pain • depression • stress • problem • difficulties • lack • limitations • effects • bias • loss • defect • weakness • drawback** *It was known that he was suffering from a terminal disease.*

suf·fer·er /'sʌfərə(r)/ *noun* a person who suffers, esecially sb who is suffering from a disease: *A history of depression can be found in at least 80% of sufferers.* ◇ *Some migraine sufferers point to certain foods as triggers.*

suf·fer·ing /'sʌfərɪŋ/ *noun* **1** [U] physical or mental pain: *There is a moral duty not to cause unnecessary suffering.* ◇ *It is questionable whether this practice is justifiable in terms of the suffering inflicted on the animals.* ◇ **~ of sb** *There are other ways to alleviate the suffering of the patient.* ◇ **pain and ~** *They had endured unimaginable pain and suffering.* **2 sufferings** [pl.] **~ (of sb)** feelings of pain and unhappiness: *Dickens's boyhood experience at Warren's factory made him sympathetic to the sufferings of the poor.*

suf·fice /sə'faɪs/ *verb* [I] (not used in the progressive tenses) to be enough for sb/sth: **~ to do sth** *A few examples will suffice to illustrate the point.* ◇ **~ for sth** *No definition is perfect, but this one will suffice for present purposes.*

IDM **suffice (it) to say (that)...** used to suggest that, although you could say more, what you do say will be enough: *Suffice it to say that such cases present a serious problem.*

suf·fi·cient AWL /sə'fɪʃnt/ *adj.* enough for a particular purpose; as much as you need: *The city lacks sufficient water resources.* ◇ *There is sufficient evidence to show that good mental health can be supported by social factors.* ◇ **~ to do sth** *The threat of sanctions is often sufficient to make the Member State comply.* ◇ **~ for sth/sb** *An informal approach is sufficient for our purposes.* HELP In logic, a **sufficient condition** of a statement is a condition that, if true, makes the statement true. It is often combined with a **necessary condition**, which must be true in order for the statement to be true: *A receptive corporate culture is a necessary, though not a sufficient, condition for the success of this strategy.* OPP INSUFFICIENT ➲ *see also* SELF-SUFFICIENT

> **WORD FAMILY**
> sufficient *adj.*
> sufficiently *adv.*
> suffice *verb*
> insufficient *adj.*
> insufficiently *adv.*
> insufficiency *noun*

suf·fi·cient·ly AWL /sə'fɪʃntli/ *adv.* to the necessary degree: *The challenge for government will be in convincing sufficiently large numbers of businesses to participate.* ◇ *This problem is sufficiently serious to make simple cascading an impractical proposition.* ➲ language bank *at* EXCEPTIONALLY

suf·fix /'sʌfɪks/ *noun* (*grammar*) a letter or group of letters added to the end of a word to make another word, such as *-ly* in *quickly* or *-ness* in *sadness*: *Tok Pisin does not have a suffix like English -s to mark plurals.* ➲ *compare* PREFIX

sugar /'ʃʊgə(r)/ *noun* **1** [U] a substance obtained from various plants that is used to make food and drink sweeter. Sugar is usually dry and white, like salt, or brown: *Brazil exported sugar, tobacco and cotton.* ◇ *Consumption of cane and beet sugar declined.* ◇ **+ noun** *Slaves worked long hours on sugar plantations.* **2** [C, usually pl., U] a substance that is a source of energy found in plants and fruit; dissolved in the blood, it can supply energy to the cells of the body: *Solar energy is converted into chemical energy in the form of sugars by photosynthetic plants.* ◇ *The high intake of refined sugar and starch may increase the risk of this disease.* ◇ **+ noun** *He had a low blood sugar level.*

3 [C] (*biochemistry*) the general name given to simpler CARBOHYDRATES: *The basic unit is a monosaccharide (sugar) such as glucose, fructose or galactose.*

THESAURUS

suggest • propose • put sth forward • advance *verb*
These words all mean to tell people about a new idea or theory for them to discuss or consider.

- to suggest/propose/put forward/advance sth **as/for** sth
- to suggest/propose/put forward a/an **strategy/approach/model/idea**
- to propose/put forward/advance a **theory/hypothesis**
- to put forward/advance a/an **view/argument**
- to suggest/propose/put forward/advance sth **to explain** sth

- **Suggest** is often slightly less confident than **propose**, **put forward** and **advance**; **suggest** can be used to make possible suggestions; **propose**, **put forward** and **advance** are used in a confident way when you want your idea to be accepted: *He suggests three approaches that may keep large firms innovative.* ◇ *He proposed an alternative definition of social distance.*
- **Suggest** is often used to make practical suggestions; **advance** is used in more theoretical contexts to talk about an idea, a theory or an argument: *The report suggests ways of mobilizing communities to support children.* ◇ *The Court dismissed the two arguments advanced as lacking any credence.*

sug·gest /sə'dʒest; *NAmE also* səg'dʒest/ *verb* **1** to put forward an idea or a plan for other people to consider SYN PROPOSE (1): **~ sth** *Inkpen and Ross suggest several reasons why this might be.* ◇ **~ sth to sb** *Lazar rejects a response to the problem suggested to him by Fabre and Frowe.* ◇ **~ (that)...** *He suggested that they try again.* ◇ **~ doing sth** *The Conservative Party suggested going further in its manifesto.* ◇ **it is suggested that...** *It is suggested that checkpoints be deployed in strategic areas.* ➲ language bank *at* ACCORDING TO, ARGUMENT **2** to put an idea into sb's mind; to make sb think that sth is true SYN INDICATE (2): **~ (that)...** *Research suggests that consumers may be getting more adventurous.* ◇ **~ sth** *Estimates suggest turnover rates for employees ranging from 30–60 per cent.* ◇ **~ to sb that...** *These results suggested to Fitzpatrick that the toxic factor in the two strains is identical.* ➲ thesaurus note *at* INDICATE **3** to recommend sb/sth for a particular job or purpose SYN RECOMMEND (1): **~ sb/sth for sth** *Rosenberg had suggested McDonald for the post in August 1933.* ◇ **~ sb/sth as sth** *The method was being suggested as a tool for monitoring and improving work in other fields.* ◇ **~ sb/sth** *He was able to suggest only a few useful books on the subject.* HELP You cannot 'suggest somebody something': ~~*He was able to suggest me only a few books.*~~ **~ how/what, etc...** *The Court did not suggest how much weight the lower court should give to this new evidence.* **4** to state or express sth in an indirect way SYN IMPLY (2): **~ (that)...** *In effect, he is suggesting that most people think of ethics as a kind of social contract.* ◇ **~ sth** *The sceptic is suggesting something more radical: that we have no reason to think that anything we believe about such things has a shred of justification.* ◇ *Shading was used to suggest a forest in the mists.* **5 ~ itself (to sb)** (of an idea) to come into sb's mind: *The same answer suggested itself to two British naturalists within a few years of each other.*

▸ SUGGEST + NOUN **way • approach • strategy • mechanism • need • possibility • effect • role • relationship • link • association • change • reason • model • use** *The European Commission is suggesting a novel way of determining retirement age.* | **presence • existence • importance • cause** *The data suggest the presence of additional genetic variants.*

▸ NOUN + SUGGEST **author • researcher** *The author suggests four specific measures for dealing with the problem.* | **evidence • data • result • finding • research • study • literature • report • survey • analysis • observation • experiment • experience • history • theory • argument • model • estimate • work • name • example** *The most recent studies suggest that obesity rates are continuing to rise in men.*

▸ ADVERB + SUGGEST | SUGGEST + ADVERB **strongly • further • therefore • here • previously • again • perhaps** *Ethnographic studies strongly suggest that this assumption is false.*

▸ ADVERB + SUGGEST **clearly • immediately • certainly • thus • often, frequently • sometimes • already • even • first • initially • then • now** *The following steps are frequently suggested.* | **recently • originally** *Grant has recently suggested that the last battle of the Hundred Years War was in fact Bosworth Field.*

▸ SUGGEST + ADVERB **otherwise** *Here, again, the evidence suggests otherwise.* | **above • earlier** *However, as suggested above, the usefulness of each tool may depend on the type of user.*

sug·ges·tion /sə'dʒestʃən; *NAmE also* səg'dʒestʃən/ *noun* **1** [C] an idea or a plan that you put forward for sb else to consider: *The suggestion was rejected.* ◇ **make a ~** *Employees must feel free to make suggestions and complaints.* ◇ **~ for sth** *She offers suggestions for future lines of research.* ◇ **~ about sth** *Holmes provides some helpful suggestions about how to protect participants' confidentiality.* ◇ **~ on sth** *They were asked to give suggestions on treatment options for patients.* ◇ **~ that...** *The suggestion that different decisions might easily have been taken does seem reasonable.* **2** [U, C, usually sing.] a reason to think that sth is true SYN HINT[1] (1): **~ of sth** *There is a suggestion of an IQ difference within pairs of twins.* ◇ **~ that...** *There is no suggestion that the current rules will be amended.* **3** [C, usually sing.] **~ (of sth)** a slight amount or sign of sth SYN HINT[1] (3), TRACE[2]: *The novel gives not the slightest suggestion of anything but a personal impression of India.* **4** [U] the action of putting an idea into people's minds by connecting it with other ideas: *He was capable of hypnotizing unsuspecting audiences through the power of suggestion.*

IDM **at/on sb's sug'gestion** because sb suggested it: *At Turing's suggestion, Newman had approached Thomas H. Flowers for help.*

LANGUAGE BANK

RESEARCH STUDY

Giving suggestions for future research

- Use **markers of uncertainty** or **modal verbs** (especially *could, may* and *would*) to show that these are suggestions:
  - *There are number of* ***possible*** *extensions to this research...*
  - *These findings* ***suggest the possibility*** *for further research on...*
  - *Further work* ***could*** *extend the range of phenomena studied...*
  - *These results* ***may*** *be important for future studies on...*
  - *Examining a wider context* ***would*** *lead to...*
- Use **markers of necessity/obligation or value** to show what research is needed:
  - *There is still a* ***need*** *for further research to determine...*
  - *Further studies* ***should*** *be undertaken to discover...*
  - *It would be* ***worthwhile*** *to investigate...*
  - *...* ***merits*** *further investigation*

sug·gest·ive /sə'dʒestɪv; *NAmE also* səg'dʒestɪv/ *adj.* reminding you of sth or making you think about sth: *China's recent history gives some suggestive evidence in*

S

favour of this view. ◇ **~ of sth** *Patients may present with symptoms suggestive of HIV infection.*

sui·cidal /ˌsuːɪˈsaɪdl; *BrE also* ˌsjuːɪˈsaɪdl/ *adj.* (of people) very unhappy or DEPRESSED and feeling that they want to kill themselves; (of behaviour) showing this: *This study will focus on the use of health care services by suicidal adults in the decade 2000–2010.* ◇ *The authors reviewed government data on the links between depression and suicidal behaviour.*

sui·cide /ˈsuːɪsaɪd; *BrE also* ˈsjuːɪsaɪd/ *noun* [U, C] the act of killing yourself deliberately: *It was found that patients who expressed a sense of hopelessness were eleven times more likely to commit suicide.* ◇ *Suicides from the bridge halved after the barriers were erected.* ◇ **+ noun** *The highest male suicide rate was in 15–34-year-olds.*

suit[1] /suːt; *BrE also* sjuːt/ *verb* [no passive] (not used in the progressive tenses) to be convenient or useful for sb: **~ sb/sth** *A product may need to be adapted to suit the needs of a local market.* ◇ **it suits sb to do sth** *The powerful only intervene when it suits them to do so.* **IDM** *see* FOLLOW
PHR V ˈ**suit sth to sth/sb** to make sth appropriate for sth/sb: *An adaptation is a feature of an organism that suits it to a particular way of life.*

suit[2] /suːt; *BrE also* sjuːt/ *noun* **1** = LAWSUIT: *His father filed a suit challenging his detention.* **2** a set of clothes made of the same cloth and designed to be worn together: *The men wore suits and hats.* **IDM** *see* FOLLOW

suit·able /ˈsuːtəbl; *BrE also* ˈsjuːtəbl/ *adj.* right or appropriate for a particular person, purpose or occasion: *Suitable climatic conditions do not automatically mean that a plant will establish itself in an area.* ◇ **~ for sth/sb** *The data of 6 999 respondents were found suitable for statistical analysis.* ◇ **~ to do sth** *He judged the moment suitable to resume his attack on his rival.* **OPP** UNSUITABLE ■ **suit·abil·ity** /ˌsuːtəˈbɪləti; *BrE also* ˌsjuːtəˈbɪləti/ *noun* [U] **~ (of sth/sb) (for sth/sb)** *The information is to be used for assessing an employee's suitability for promotion.* ◇ **~ (of sth/sb) (to do sth)** *He questioned her suitability to be Prime Minister.*

suit·ably /ˈsuːtəbli; *BrE also* ˈsjuːtəbli/ *adv.* **1** in a way that is right or appropriate for a particular person, purpose or occasion: *There is a shortage of suitably qualified translators and interpreters.* **2** in a way that shows the feelings, etc. that you would expect in a particular situation: *His presidential address was suitably earnest in tone.*

suite /swiːt/ *noun* **1 ~ (of sth)** a number of things that form a set or collection: *The growing suite of health promotion journals reflects the expanding business of addressing health inequities and promoting health.* **2 ~ (of sth)** a set of rooms, especially in a hotel, hospital or medical centre: *The full suite of rooms includes two examining rooms, a meeting room, three private offices and a waiting room.* **3 ~ (of sth)** (*earth science*) a group of minerals, rocks or FOSSILS that occur together and are characteristic of a location or period: *The principal minerals of both suites of rocks are also similar.* **4 ~ (of sth)** (*computing*) a set of computer programs with the ability to share data: *a suite of software development tools*

suit·ed /ˈsuːtɪd; *BrE also* ˈsjuːtɪd/ *adj.* [not before noun] right or appropriate for sb/sth: **~ to (doing) sth** *She is uniquely suited to this task.* ◇ **~ for sth** *A senior clinician may be ideally suited for this role.* ◇ **~ to do sth** *Geographers are particularly well suited to lend their expertise in this arena.* ◇ **~ to sb** *This curriculum is especially suited to middle-grade students.*

sul·fate (*BrE also* **sul·phate**) /ˈsʌlfeɪt/ *noun* [C, U] a COMPOUND of SULFURIC ACID and a chemical element: *ammonium sulfate*

sul·fide (*BrE also* **sul·phide**) /ˈsʌlfaɪd/ *noun* [C, U] a COMPOUND of sulfur and another chemical element: *hydrogen sulfide*

sul·fur (*BrE also* **sul·phur**) /ˈsʌlfə(r)/ *noun* [U] (*symb.* **S**) the chemical element of ATOMIC NUMBER 16. Sulfur is a pale yellow substance that produces a strong unpleasant smell when it burns and is used in medicine and industry: *All fossil fuels contain some sulfur.* **HELP** The spelling **sulfur** has been adopted by the International Union of Pure and Applied Chemistry and by the Royal Society of Chemistry in the UK. However, in non-scientific British English, **sulphur** still remains the usual spelling.

sul·fur·ic acid (*BrE also* **sul·phur·ic acid**) /sʌlˌfjʊərɪk ˈæsɪd; *NAmE* sʌlˌfjʊrɪk ˈæsɪd/ *noun* [U] (*symb.* H_2SO_4) a strong clear acid: *In nature, sulfuric acid is released into the air by volcanoes.*

sul·phate, sul·phide, sul·phur, sul·phur·ic acid (*BrE*) = SULFATE, SULFIDE, SULFUR, SULFURIC ACID

sum[1] **AWL** /sʌm/ *noun* **1** [C] **~ (of sth)** an amount of money: *Large sums of money were owed to the company.* ◇ *The sum of £100 000 is borrowed over a 25 year term at an annual interest rate of 6.5%.* **2** [C, usually sing.] **~ (of sth)** the total amount resulting from the addition of two or more numbers, amounts or items: *Her share is half of the sum of £300 000 and £25 000, i.e., £162 500.* **3** (*also* ˌ**sum ˈtotal**) [sing.] **the ~ of sth** the total amount of sth that exists: *Hawks would be a lesser director if his adventure dramas were the sum of his work.* **4** [C] a simple problem that involves calculating numbers: *We can do a simple sum to illustrate this point.*
IDM **be greater/more than the ˌsum of its ˈparts** to be better or more effective as a group than you would think just by looking at the individual members of the group: *As a whole, the corporation is greater than the sum of its parts.* **in ˈsum** used to introduce a short summary of the main points of a discussion, speech, etc: *In sum, the book provides a valuable analysis of Spanish federalism.*

sum[2] **AWL** /sʌm/ *verb* (**-mm-**)
PHR V ˌ**sum ˈup** | ˌ**sum sth ˈup** **1** to state the main points of sth in a short and clear form **SYN** SUMMARIZE: **to ~** *To sum up, the impact of the Internet on marketing strategy has been as follows:...* ◇ **~ up what...** *Summing up what has been said thus far,...* ➲ language bank *at* CONCLUSION **2** (of a judge) to give a summary of the main facts and arguments in a legal case, near the end of a trial: *On the following day the judge summed up the case.* ˌ**sum sth ˈup** **1** to describe or show the most typical characteristics of sth, especially in a few words: *The words of Burton in the last-named case probably sum up the courts' and tribunals' approach.* **2** to form or express an opinion of sth: *He had summed up the situation there before anyone else had even begun to analyse it.*

sum·mar·ily /ˈsʌmərəli; *NAmE* səˈmerəli/ *adv.* immediately, without paying attention to the normal process that should be followed: *He was summarily dismissed on the ground of gross misconduct.*

sum·mar·ize (*BrE also* **-ise**) **AWL** /ˈsʌməraɪz/ *verb* [T, I] **~ (sth)** to give a summary of sth: *Meyer et al. (2007) summarized the results from these studies.* ◇ *Table 2 summarizes some of the key findings.* ◇ *So, to summarize, the UK can choose from various internationally available, standardized systems that are being built elsewhere.*

sum·mary[1] **AWL** /ˈsʌməri/ *noun* (*pl.* **-ies**) a short statement that gives only the main points of sth, not the details: **~ (of sth)** *Wymer and Starnes (2001) provide a useful summary of the available research.* ◇ *The article concludes with a brief summary of the findings.* ◇ **in ~** *So, in summary, knots can be found or created in both single-stranded and double-stranded DNA molecules.*

sum·mary² AWL /ˈsʌməri/ *adj.* [only before noun] **1** giving only the main points of sth, not the details: *The summary report of the parliamentary debate of 31 May 1787 reveals a sharp division of opinion.* **2** done immediately, without paying attention to the normal process that should be followed: *The court is thus allowed to enter summary judgment without the delay and expense of a trial.*

sum·ma·tion AWL /sʌˈmeɪʃn/ *noun* **1** [C, usually sing.] **~ (of sth)** a summary of what has been done or said: *The book provides an intelligent summation of a thriving historical field.* **2** [C] **~ (of sth)** a collection of different parts that forms a complete account or impression of sb/sth: *Pliny's great work represented a real summation of universal knowledge.* **3** [U, C] **~ (of sth)** the process of adding things together; a total amount resulting from adding things together: *An aggregate score was constructed through summation of the individual totals.*

sum·mer /ˈsʌmə(r)/ *noun* [U, C] the warmest season of the year, coming between spring and autumn: *Bradley's observations show low temperatures during the summer and early autumn.* ◇ **in (the) ~** *In summer, growth is much faster.* ◇ *The young fish grew best in warm and relatively dry summers.* ◇ **in the ~ of...** *He resigned his appointment in the summer of 1836.* ◇ **+ noun** *Over the summer months, several competitors withdrew from the presidential race.* ◇ *Summer temperatures at Toolik Lake are significantly warmer than on the coast.*

sum·mit /ˈsʌmɪt/ *noun* **1** the highest point of sth, especially the top of a mountain: **~ (of sth)** *Almost all climbers use oxygen-enriched air to reach the summit of Mount Everest.* ◇ **at the ~ of sth** (*figurative*) *When he succeeded to the consulship in 102 BC, Lutatius Catulus was at the summit of his popularity.* **2** an official meeting or series of meetings between the leaders of two or more governments at which they discuss important matters: *The First International Earth Summit was held in Rio de Janeiro in 1992.* ◇ **+ noun** *There are annual summit meetings, but the more regular work is done in meetings of ministers and officials.*

sum·mon /ˈsʌmən/ *verb* **1** to order sb to appear in court: **~ sb** *The inquiry has powers equivalent to those of the High Court to summon witnesses.* ◇ **~ sb to do sth** *She was summoned to testify as a prosecution witness.* **2 ~ sb (to sth) (to do sth)** to order sb to come to you: *Aristotle was summoned to the Macedonian court to tutor young Alexander.* **3 ~ sth** to arrange an official meeting SYN CONVENE (1): *He then decided to summon a meeting of the company's creditors.* **4 ~ sth** to call for or try to obtain sth: *The patient triggers an alarm to summon help in the event of a fall in their home.* **5 ~ sth (up)** to make an effort to produce a particular quality in yourself, especially when you find it difficult: *These warrior nobles and knights must summon the courage to face death.*

PHR V **ˌsummon sth ˈup** to make a feeling, an idea, a memory, etc. come into your mind SYN EVOKE: *These images are designed to summon up a feeling of nostalgia in the viewer.*

sun /sʌn/ *noun* **1 the sun, the Sun** [sing.] the star that shines in the sky during the day and gives the earth heat and light: *The earth's atmosphere lets through most of the sun's radiation.* **2** (*usually* **the sun**) [sing., U] the light and heat from the sun: *Technologies that rely on sun and wind are not reliable as the power supply is intermittent.* ◇ **in the ~** *Australian adolescents demonstrate the highest-risk behaviours by spending long periods of time in the sun.* **3** [C] any star around which planets move: *They put forward the revolutionary idea that the stars were suns at the centre of distant solar systems.*

IDM **under the ˈsun** (*rather informal*) used to emphasize that you are talking about a very large number of things: *Newsgroups allow anyone to express views on almost any topic under the sun.*

sung *past part. of* SING

sun·light /ˈsʌnlaɪt/ *noun* [U] the light from the sun: *The plant should not be exposed to direct sunlight.* ◇ *A solar thermal power plant absorbs sunlight to heat steam in a power cycle.*

super·fi·cial /ˌsuːpəˈfɪʃl; ˌsjuːpəˈfɪʃl; *NAmE* ˌsuːpərˈfɪʃl/ *adj.* **1** connected with or existing on the surface of sth: *The technique involves taking samples of soils and other superficial deposits for analysis.* **2** located or existing on the skin or just below it: *Reduced blood flow in superficial veins increases the risk of developing such blood clots.* **3** (of a wound or damage) only affecting the surface and therefore not serious: *Many of the superficial injuries can be treated easily with simple first aid.* **4** appearing to be true, real or important until you look at it more carefully: *Despite all their superficial similarities, the European and American systems are essentially quite different.* **5** (*often disapproving*) not thorough, deep or complete; concerned only with what is obvious: *A superficial reading of the sources may lead one to believe that they all tell the same story.*

super·fi·cial·ly /ˌsuːpəˈfɪʃəli; ˌsjuːpəˈfɪʃəli; *NAmE* ˌsuːpərˈfɪʃəli/ *adv.* **1** in a way that appears to be true, real or important until you look at it more carefully: *The expression has been used to describe several superficially similar but slightly different kinds of information.* ◇ *Superficially, at least, much in the 1280s was still as it had been 120 years earlier.* **2** in a way that is not thorough, deep or complete; in a way that is concerned only with what is obvious: *Much of the language's grammar has only been studied superficially so far.* **3** on the surface of sth: *The plant can fix the topsoil superficially with its long horizontally spreading roots.* **4** on the skin or immediately below it: *The blood tracks more superficially along the nerve fibre layer.*

su·per·ior¹ /suːˈpɪəriə(r); sjuːˈpɪəriə(r); *NAmE* suːˈpɪriər/ *adj.* **1** better in quality than sb/sth else: *They are sold at a higher price to reflect their superior quality and flavour.* ◇ **~ to sb/sth** *Their cavalry units were far superior to any they encountered.* OPP INFERIOR (1) **2** greater than sb/sth else: *Because of their far superior military force, they were able to issue an ultimatum to the enemy.* ◇ **~ (in sth) (to sb/sth)** *They were vastly superior in numbers to the rebels.* **3** higher in rank, importance or position: *Robinson was accused of refusing to obey the lawful orders of a superior officer.* ◇ **~ to sb** *He was superior to his two partners in social rank.* OPP INFERIOR (1) **4** (*anatomy*) further above or out; higher in position: *The inferior vena cava is longer than the superior vena cava.* OPP INFERIOR (2)

su·per·ior² /suːˈpɪəriə(r); sjuːˈpɪəriə(r); *NAmE* suːˈpɪriər/ *noun* **(sb's) ~** a person of higher rank or position: *They sought to share in the advantages enjoyed by their social superiors.*

su·per·ior·ity /suːˌpɪəriˈɒrəti; sjuːˌpɪəriˈɒrəti; *NAmE* suːˌpɪriˈɔːrəti; suːˌpɪriˈɑːrəti/ *noun* [U] **1** the state or quality of being better, more skilful, more powerful, greater, etc. than others: **~ (of sth/sb) (in sth)** *The advantages of technological superiority in warfare were realized long ago.* ◇ **~ (of sth/sb) (to/over sth/sb)** *They believe in the superiority of the market to the state in generating economic growth.* ◇ *The initial military successes demonstrated the French army's clear superiority over the Dutch forces.* OPP INFERIORITY **2** behaviour that shows that you think you are better than other people: *His air of intellectual superiority seemed threatening to some.*

S

su·per·la·tive¹ /su'pɜːlətɪv; sjuː'pɜːlətɪv; *NAmE* suː'pɜːrlətɪv/ *adj.* **1** of the highest quality or degree; excellent: *These shortcomings diminish an otherwise superlative work.* **2** (*grammar*) connected with adjectives or adverbs that express the highest or a very high degree of a quality, for example *best, worst, slowest* and *most difficult*: *Such adjectives occur normally in the comparative and superlative degrees.* ➲ *compare* COMPARATIVE¹ (3)

su·per·la·tive² /su'pɜːlətɪv; sjuː'pɜːlətɪv; *NAmE* suː'pɜːrlətɪv/ *noun* (*grammar*) the form of an adjective or adverb that expresses the highest degree of sth, for example *best, worst, slowest* and *most difficult*: *Only superlatives seem appropriate to describe the mobile phone 'revolution' in Africa.* ➲ *compare* COMPARATIVE²

super·nat·ural /ˌsuːpə'nætʃrəl; ˌsjuːpə'nætʃrəl; *NAmE* ˌsuːpər'nætʃrəl/ *adj.* **1** that cannot be explained by the laws of science and that seems to involve gods or magic: *Durkheim thinks it misleading to define religion as belief in gods or supernatural beings.* ➲ *compare* NATURAL (1) **2 the supernatural** *noun* [sing.] events, forces or powers that cannot be explained by the laws of science and that seem to involve gods or magic: *Around this time, interest in the supernatural was at its height among the Victorians.*

super·power /'suːpəpaʊə(r); 'sjuːpəpaʊə(r); *NAmE* 'suːpərpaʊər/ *noun* one of the countries in the world that has very great military or economic power and a lot of influence, for example the US: *After the Second World War, the world was dominated by the two superpowers, the USA and the USSR.* ◇ *China is a rising economic superpower.*

super·script /'suːpəskrɪpt; 'sjuːpəskrɪpt; *NAmE* 'suːpərskrɪpt/ *adj.* (*technical*) (of a letter, figure or symbol) written or printed above the normal line of writing or printing: *superscript numbers* ➲ *compare* SUBSCRIPT

super·sede /ˌsuːpə'siːd; ˌsjuːpə'siːd; *NAmE* ˌsuːpər'siːd/ *verb* **~ sth** to take the place of sth that is considered old-fashioned, no longer appropriate or no longer the best: *The 1996 monograph supersedes several earlier versions.* ◇ *The 1994 Act has now been largely superseded by the Regulatory Reform Act 2001.* HELP Note that the correct spelling of this word is **supersede**, although it is quite frequently spelled wrongly as 'supercede'.

S

super·sti·tion /ˌsuːpə'stɪʃn; ˌsjuːpə'stɪʃn; *NAmE* ˌsuːpər'stɪʃn/ *noun* [U, C] the belief that particular events happen in a way that cannot be explained by reason or science; the belief that particular events bring good or bad luck: *Our understanding of earthquakes and volcanic eruptions has progressed from the realm of religion and superstition to that of modern science.* ◇ *The first reformers considered certain aspects of contemporary culture as pagan superstitions.*

super·sti·tious /ˌsuːpə'stɪʃəs; ˌsjuːpə'stɪʃəs; *NAmE* ˌsuːpər'stɪʃəs/ *adj.* believing in superstitions: *Much of the hostility to the missionaries was based on superstitious fears.* ◇ *Some cultures are much more openly superstitious.*

super·vise /'suːpəvaɪz; 'sjuːpəvaɪz; *NAmE* 'suːpərvaɪz/ *verb* [T, I] to be in charge of sb/sth and make sure that everything is done in a correct or safe way: **~ sb/sth** *The role of these bodies is to supervise the implementation of the various human rights documents by member states.* ◇ **~ sb doing sth** *Her two young children have to spend most summer days indoors because she cannot be outside to supervise them playing.*

supervision /ˌsuːpə'vɪʒn; ˌsjuːpə'vɪʒn; *NAmE* ˌsuːpər'vɪʒn/ *noun* [U] the act of supervising sb/sth: *Lack of parental supervision is found to be related to early adolescent problem behaviour.* ◇ **under ~** *Patients should practise slow, controlled breathing, at first under supervision and then at home.* ◇ **under the ~ of sb/sth** *They work under the close supervision of a trainer.*

super·visor /'suːpəvaɪzə(r); 'sjuːpəvaɪzə(r); *NAmE* 'suːpərvaɪzər/ *noun* a person who supervises sb/sth: *Clinical supervisors are responsible for overseeing day-to-day clinical practice.* ◇ *The company decided to hire more supervisors to control the pace of work.* ■ **super·vis·ory** /ˌsuːpə'vaɪzəri; ˌsjuːpə'vaɪzəri; *NAmE* ˌsuːpər'vaɪzəri/ *adj.*: *A single supervisory body was established to plan and monitor the project.*

sup·ple·ment¹ AWL /'sʌplɪment/ *verb* to add sth to sth in order to improve it or make it more complete: **~ sth** *In order to supplement their household income, she brews a local drink made from maize.* ◇ **~ sth with sth** *One week after giving birth, 27% of the women had supplemented breastfeeding with one bottle or more of formula.* ■ **sup·ple·men·ta·tion** /ˌsʌplɪmen'teɪʃn/ *noun* [U] *Multivitamin, iron and calcium supplementation are recommended lifelong for all patients after weight loss surgery.*

sup·ple·ment² AWL /'sʌplɪmənt/ *noun* **1** a thing that is added to sth else to improve or complete it: *Parents may ask advice about special diets and dietary supplements.* ◇ **~ to sth** *A useful supplement to this kind of data is behavioural information.* **2 ~ (to sth)** a book or a section at the end of a book or online that gives extra information or deals with a special subject: *Almost all of these findings were recently published in a special supplement to the Journal.* ◇ *More information can be found in an online supplement.*

sup·ple·men·tary AWL /ˌsʌplɪ'mentri/ (*NAmE also* **sup·ple·men·tal** /ˌsʌplɪ'mentl/) *adj.* [usually before noun] provided in addition to sth else in order to improve or complete it SYN ADDITIONAL: *The treaty was accompanied by supplementary agreements on labour and the environment.* ◇ *Supplementary data were obtained by telephone and email communications.*

sup·plier /sə'plaɪə(r)/ *noun* a person or company that supplies goods: *Initial preference was given to local suppliers.* ◇ **~ (of sth) (to/for sb/sth)** *Most of the major suppliers of equipment to cement firms were based in OECD countries.* ◇ *Suppliers to the airline industry suffered a downturn as global demand for new aircraft declined.*

sup·ply¹ /sə'plaɪ/ *noun* **1** [C] an amount of sth that is provided or available to be used: *The demand for skilled foreign workers first outstripped the supply in 1997.* ◇ *Communities are concerned that hazardous material will contaminate drinking water supplies.* ◇ **~ of sth** *Unless the brain has adequate supplies of glucose, it will cease to function normally.* ➲ *see also* MONEY SUPPLY, SUPPLY AND DEMAND, WATER SUPPLY **2** [U, sing.] **~ (of sth) (to sb/sth) (for sth)** the act of supplying sth: *In healthy people, the supply of oxygen to the heart increases when demand increases.* ◇ *Irrigation schemes need to ensure a reliable supply of water for rice cultivation.* ➲ *see also* SUPPLY CHAIN **3 supplies** [pl.] the things such as food, medicines, fuel, etc. that are needed by a group of people, for example an army or EXPEDITION: *Disaster victims require shelter, food, water and other emergency supplies.* ◇ *The absence of medical supplies meant that millions of soldiers died from disease.* ◇ *They waited for fresh supplies to arrive.* IDM *see* SHORT¹

▸ ADJECTIVE + SUPPLY **unlimited • plentiful, abundant • adequate • limited • inadequate • available • total** *At low altitudes, there is a plentiful supply of molecular oxygen.* | **constant • reliable • steady** *The constant supply of energy from the sun is either absorbed, stored by chemical reactions, or reflected back into space by the earth.*

▸ NOUN + SUPPLY **money • water • food • labour • electricity • blood • oil • oxygen • gas • power • energy • fuel** *With abundant food supplies, appetite triggers eating rather than hunger.*

▸ VERB + SUPPLY **secure** ◆ **restrict** ◆ **control** *A computer controls the electrical power supply.* | **increase, boost** ◆ **reduce** ◆ **outstrip, exceed** *Less union power may increase the supply of labour.* | **interrupt, disrupt** ◆ **ensure** *The war may affect international commodities' prices, for example by interrupting the supply of oil.*

sup·ply² /sə'plaɪ/ *verb* (**sup·plies, sup·ply·ing, sup·plied, sup·plied**) to provide sb/sth with sth that they need or want, especially in large quantities: **~ sb/sth** *Coal was initially used to supply domestic heat and fuel.* ◇ **~ sb/sth with sth** *They focus on supplying customers with the services they actually need.* ◇ *Each adrenal gland is supplied with blood through three arteries.* ◇ **~ sth to sb/sth** *He supplied confidential information to the police relating to a serious crime.*

THESAURUS

supply ◆ **provide** ◆ **yield** ◆ **generate** *verb*

These words all mean to make sth, such as product or service, available for people to use.

▸ to supply/provide sth **to/for** sb
▸ to supply/provide sb **with** sth
▸ to supply/provide/yield/generate **information/data**
▸ to supply/provide (a) **service/product/goods**
▸ to supply/generate **heat/power/energy/electricity**
▸ to yield/generate **results/profit/returns**

- **Provide** and **supply** are both used to talk about making goods and services available to people; **supply** is used especially about providing sth in large quantities: *Local councils may fail to provide adequate services for all city residents.* ◇ *The Dutch plantations in Java supplied 80% of the world market.*
- **Yield** and **generate** are used to talk about producing sth such as a benefit or a profit: *Does this ability to retain employees yield economic benefits?* ◇ *There is also evidence that such movies generate more revenue.*
- **Generate** is used to talk about producing power, energy, etc; **supply** is used to talk about making power, energy, etc. available to sth/sb: *'Biogas' is a methane/carbon dioxide mixture that can be burned to generate power or heat.* ◇ *The cooling system could be operated with thermal energy supplied by solar collectors.*

See also the Thesaurus note at **provide**.

sup,ply and de'mand *noun* [U] (*economics*) the relationship between the amount of goods or services that are available and the amount that people want to buy, especially when this controls prices: *The fluctuations of supply and demand continually bring the price of a commodity back to the cost of production.*

sup'ply chain *noun* (*business*) the series of processes involved in the production and supply of goods: *The global supply chain is changing the way organizations are responding to customers.* ◇ **+ noun** *The firm has a good level of support from its supply chain partners.*

sup·port¹ /sə'pɔːt; *NAmE* sə'pɔːrt/ *verb* **1 ~ sth** to help to show that sth is true or correct SYN CORROBORATE (1): *The evidence generally supports this view.* ◇ *Despite the politicians' complaints about television bias, survey evidence consistently fails to support the claims.* ➲ thesaurus note *at* CONFIRM **2** to agree with and encourage an idea, plan, person, group, etc. SYN BACK⁴ (1): **~ sb/sth** *The tabloid newspapers strongly supported her 'tough stand' on law and order.* ◇ **~ sb/sth in sth** *It is important that GPs support mothers in their wish to breastfeed.* **3** to help or encourage sb to do sth: **~ sb** *Groups can be used to support patients or their relatives.* ◇ **~ sb to do sth** *Children should be encouraged and supported to voice their anger openly.* ◇ **~ sb in (doing) sth** *In 402, Sparta had agreed to support Cyrus in his bid to usurp the Persian throne from his brother.* **4 ~ sb/sth/yourself** to provide money so that sb can buy what they need: *She got a part-time job to help her mother support her younger brother and sister.* ◇ *His wife had supported him financially.* ➲ thesaurus note *at* CONTRIBUTE **5 ~ sth** to help or encourage sth to be successful by giving it money SYN SPONSOR² (2): *The projects were supported by Home Office funding.* ◇ *The grant supports work in six community schools.* ➲ thesaurus note *at* FUND² **6 ~ sth** to produce enough food and water for sb/sth; to provide a good environment for sb/sth to live in: *The droughts meant that the remaining prairies to the west could no longer support large numbers of cattle.* ◇ *In only 1 or 2 billion years, the earth will probably become too hot to support life.* **7 ~ sb/sth** to hold sb/sth in position; to prevent sb/sth from falling: *In all structures, the materials have to support their own weight.* ◇ *Once four walls have been erected, they have sufficient mass and strength to support a domed roof.*

▸ SUPPORT + NOUN **view** ◆ **idea** ◆ **use** ◆ **proposal** *Not all of Skinner's followers could support his views.* | **hypothesis, theory** ◆ **notion** ◆ **thesis** ◆ **conclusion** ◆ **finding** ◆ **argument** ◆ **claim, assertion** ◆ **contention** ◆ **interpretation** ◆ **diagnosis** ◆ **prediction** ◆ **assumption** ◆ **suggestion** ◆ **proposition** ◆ **belief** ◆ **research** *However, more recent studies have not supported this hypothesis.* | **work** ◆ **project** ◆ **effort** ◆ **development** *Even many conservatives supported the development of European welfare states.* ◇ *Funding to support microbicide development and testing comes primarily from public and philanthropic sources.* | **decision** ◆ **ban** *Smokers who believed that cigarette smoke was dangerous to non-smokers were more likely to support bans.*

▸ NOUN + SUPPORT **evidence** ◆ **data** ◆ **facts** ◆ **finding** ◆ **results** ◆ **study** ◆ **observation** ◆ **experiment** ◆ **argument** | **grant** ◆ **funding** ◆ **donor** *The research was supported by grants from the National Science Foundation*

sup·port² /sə'pɔːt; *NAmE* sə'pɔːrt/ *noun* **1** [U, C] approval, encouragement, help or comfort that is given to sb/sth; a person or thing that provides this: *Her faith seemed to give her comfort and emotional support during a very stressful time.* ◇ **~ of sb/sth** *It was her failure to gain the support of MPs, rather than of the electorate, that proved decisive.* ◇ **~ (for sth)** *Declining support for the two main parties meant that one could form a government backed by less than 40% of the votes.* ◇ *They are firm in the belief that any child can excel with the proper supports.* **2** [U] money or items that are provided to a person or organization that needs them: **~ (for sth)** *Financial support for much of this work was provided by grants.* ◇ *The EU has emphasized the need to reduce state support for agriculture.* ◇ **in ~ of sb/sth** *She attended a gala event in support of her local hospital.* **3** [U] evidence that helps to show that sth is true or correct: *A series of observations lend support to the proposed hypothesis.* ◇ **~ for sth** *Most notably, such research is providing support for the idea that many plant and animal species were domesticated more than once.* ➲ thesaurus note *at* EVIDENCE¹ **4** [U] the act of holding sth firmly in position or preventing it from falling: *By about 7 months, most children can sit without support.* ◇ *Use plenty of pillows or cushions for support.* **5** [C] a thing that holds sth in position or prevents it from falling: *In this test, the specimen is placed on rigid supports and a known weight is dropped onto it from a desired height.*

▸ ADJECTIVE + SUPPORT **great, considerable** ◆ **strong** ◆ **widespread, broad** ◆ **popular, public** ◆ **mutual** ◆ **parental** ◆ **emotional** ◆ **social** ◆ **political** ◆ **electoral** ◆ **technical** ◆ **organizational** ◆ **logistical** ◆ **nutritional** ◆ **psychological** ◆ **military** ◆ **online** ◆ **administrative** *Popular support for democracy is high among ordinary citizens of the region.* ◇ *The company offers phone and online technical support.* | **financial** ◆ **material** *They mostly focused on providing material support, such as food and clothing.* | **empirical** ◆

S

evidential *There is interesting empirical support for the existence of both these effects.*

▸ NOUN + SUPPORT **peer** ◆ **family** ◆ **carer** *Along with education, peer support is an important part of the fight against AIDS.*

▸ VERB + SUPPORT **lend, provide, give** ◆ **offer** ◆ **receive, obtain, get** ◆ **find** ◆ **have** ◆ **lack** *Failing initially to obtain commercial support, the project eventually won financial backing from the Rockefeller Foundation.* | **gain, garner** ◆ **attract** ◆ **enlist** ◆ **secure** ◆ **ensure** ◆ **need, require** ◆ **seek** ◆ **pledge** ◆ **acknowledge** ◆ **lose** ◆ **withdraw** ◆ **withhold** *The petition attracted widespread support.* ◇ *He pledged British military support for the war.* | **win** ◆ **enjoy** ◆ **mobilize** ◆ **command** ◆ **draw** ◆ **rally** ◆ **muster** ◆ **voice, express** *Truman's tactics were designed to win some support from all sides.*

▸ SUPPORT + NOUN **package** ◆ **measure** *Wide-ranging structural reforms were adopted as part of the IMF-led US $17.2 billion support package.* | **staff** ◆ **scheme** ◆ **network** ◆ **service** ◆ **mechanism** ◆ **group** ◆ **system** ◆ **programme** ◆ **worker** *Social support systems facilitate the development of coping strategies.*

sup·port·er /sə'pɔːtə(r); *NAmE* sə'pɔːrtər/ *noun* **~ (of sb/sth)** a person who supports a political party, an idea, etc: *They were fervent admirers of Britain and staunch supporters of a Franco-British alliance.* ◇ *Understandably, one of the main goals of a party's election campaign is to mobilize traditional supporters.*

sup'port group *noun* a group of people who meet or communicate with each other in order to help each other with a particular problem: *People who used Internet support groups reported feeling that they received more support, in general, than those who relied only on offline social networks.*

sup·port·ing /sə'pɔːtɪŋ; *NAmE* sə'pɔːrtɪŋ/ *adj.* [only before noun] **1** helping to achieve or prove sth: *Staff in the service firm act in a supporting role to assist the service personnel as necessary.* ◇ *Learners can access the supporting materials instantly.* ◇ *Much supporting evidence for this result has been reported in the literature.* **2** carrying the weight of sth: *a supporting beam/structure*

S

sup·port·ive /sə'pɔːtɪv; *NAmE* sə'pɔːrtɪv/ *adj.* giving help, encouragement or sympathy to sb: *A young person who grows up in a supportive environment will attach to positive and caring adults.* ◇ **~ of sb/sth** *These six countries have been very supportive of international initiatives for environmental protection.*

sup·pose /sə'pəʊz; *NAmE* sə'poʊz/ *verb* **1** [I, T] to think or believe that sth is true or possible but without proof or certain knowledge: *Few, I suppose, would dispute this claim.* ◇ **~ (that)...** *It seems reasonable to suppose that these known cases may constitute a representative sample.* ◇ *Many of the surviving examples date from the fifteenth century, but there is no reason to suppose that they did not exist earlier.* ◇ **~ sb/sth to be/do sth** *One would suppose prosperous farmers to be more likely than poor ones to try to conceal their assets.* ◇ **~ sb/sth + noun/adj.** (*formal*) *They were wrong in supposing him a radical.* **2** [T] **~ (that)...** to think of sth as being true so that you can imagine what would happen as a result: *Suppose the price of X is P.* ◇ *Now suppose there are two antennas separated by distance r in free space.* ◇ *The dominant models and theories suppose that action follows decision.*

IDM **be supposed to do/be sth** **1** to be expected, required or intended to do/be sth according to a rule, a custom, an arrangement, etc: *The soldiers did not seem to have a clear idea of what they were supposed to do.* ◇ *Reporting is supposed to be annual, but many countries fail to make timely reports.* **2** to be generally believed to be/do sth: *This is a non-verbal mental ability test and is supposed to be quite good at testing general intelligence.* ◇ *Despite her comparatively advanced age of 40, she is supposed to have borne him seven children.* **not be supposed to do sth** to not be allowed to do sth: *Women in the US military are not supposed to serve in combat.* HELP The use of **not supposed to...** in this meaning often suggests that the thing that is not allowed may still happen.

sup·posed·ly /sə'pəʊzɪdli; *NAmE* sə'poʊzɪdli/ *adv.* according to what is generally thought or believed but not known for certain SYN ALLEGEDLY: *Supposedly feminine ways of thinking are actually employed by many men.* ◇ *During the Cold War, America supposedly protected the 'free world' against the communist bloc.*

sup·pos·ing /sə'pəʊzɪŋ; *NAmE* sə'poʊzɪŋ/ *conj.* **~ (that)** used to ask sb to think of sth as being true or to imagine that sth will happen: *Supposing that this argument is broadly correct, the implications are serious.*

sup·pos·ition /ˌsʌpə'zɪʃn/ *noun* (*formal*) **1** [C] an idea that you think is true although you may not be able to prove it SYN ASSUMPTION (1): *Unfortunately, scant data are available to assess this supposition.* ◇ **~ about sth** *Their research is full of suppositions about how people think and behave.* ◇ **~ that...** *Does the evidence support the supposition that the tamarins are teaching their young where to search for prey?* **2** [U] the act of believing or claiming that sth is true even though it cannot be proved: *Unpleasant debates arose based on supposition and anecdote.* ◇ **~ of sth** *These beliefs definitely rest on the supposition of the existence of causal circumstances.*

sup·press /sə'pres/ *verb* **1 ~ sth** (of a government or ruler) to stop sth by force, especially an activity or group that is believed to threaten authority: *Russia had supported Austria in suppressing the Hungarian revolt in 1849.* **2 ~ sth** to prevent sth from growing, developing or continuing: *Plant growth was suppressed because of low temperatures and scarce rainfall.* **3 ~ sth** (*usually disapproving*) to prevent sth from being published or made known: *The corporate willingness to suppress information is particularly disturbing.* **4 ~ sth** to prevent yourself from having or expressing a feeling or an emotion: *While boys are supported in accepting anger and encouraged to express it, girls are taught to ignore and suppress their anger.*

sup·pres·sion /sə'preʃn/ *noun* [U] **1 ~ (of sth)** the act of a government or ruler stopping sth by force: *The suppression of the Polish revolt in 1831 snapped the link between the Russian autocracy and the Polish gentry.* **2 ~ (of sth)** the act of preventing sth from growing, developing or continuing: *A common side effect of all these drugs is immune suppression leading to increased risk of infection.* **3 ~ (of sth)** the act of preventing sth from being published or made known: *A fair trial could not be guaranteed because of the suppression of evidence.* **4 ~ (of sth)** the act of preventing yourself from having or expressing a feeling or an emotion: *In Indonesia, the suppression of strong emotions is a virtue instilled from childhood.*

sup·pres·sor /sə'presə(r)/ *noun* a thing that prevents sth from growing, developing or continuing: *Appetite suppressors are associated with pulmonary hypertension.* ◇ **~ of sth** *The inference is that gene B is a suppressor of gene A.*

supra·nation·al /ˌsuːprə'næʃnəl; *BrE also* ˌsjuːprə'næʃnəl/ *adj.* [only before noun] involving more than one country: *The EU is a unique form of supranational governance.* ◇ *Supranational regulation is especially important in the context of Internet sales.*

su·prem·acy /suː'preməsi; *BrE also* sjuː'preməsi/ *noun* [U] a position in which sb/sth has more power, authority or status than anyone or anything else: *Their research explored how African Americans eventually defeated white supremacy in Mississippi.* ◇ *A battle for supremacy took place between the older gods and the younger gods.* ◇ **~ of sth/sb** *The legislative supremacy of the UK Parliament* is underlined in the Scotland Act 1998.* ◇ **~ of A over B** *In 1964 (Costa v. ENEL), the Court established the supremacy of EU law over national law.*

su·preme /suːˈpriːm; *BrE also* sjuːˈpriːm/ *adj.* [usually before noun] **1** highest in rank or position: *The European Council is the supreme political authority in the European Union.* ◇ *The constitution of the UK is very clear that Parliament is supreme and the judiciary are subservient.* ◇ **reign ~** *By the late nineteenth century, industrial capitalism reigned supreme in the United States.* **2** very great or the greatest in degree: *As Hans Kohn observed, 'Nationalism is a state of mind in which the supreme loyalty of the individual is felt to be due the nationstate.'*

sure /ʃʊə(r); ʃɔː(r); *NAmE* ʃʊr/ *adj.* (**surer**, **sur·est**) (You can also use **more sure** and **most sure**, especially in sense 1.) **1** [not before noun] confident that you know sth or that you are right SYN CERTAIN[1] (2): **~ (that)...** *Darwin was sure that the Cambrian explosion represented the start of the record of animal evolution.* ◇ **~ of sth** *States can never be sure of the intentions of their neighbours and, therefore, must always be on their guard.* ◇ **~ about sth** *If a junior doctor is not sure about the diagnosis, he or she must ask the patient to wait for a senior doctor review.* ◇ **~ how/whether, etc...** *Nobody can be quite sure where the supermassive black holes at the hearts of galaxies today came from.* OPP UNSURE **2** [not before noun] **~ of (doing) sth** certain that you will receive sth or that sth will happen: *The firm wishes to avoid full launches of new product lines until it is sure of adequate market demand.* **3** certain to do sth or to happen: *The shift in national energy policy from coal to oil in 1959 condemned Japan's coal industry to a slow but sure death.* ◇ **~ to do sth** *Rebellion against the empire was sure to get any emperor's attention.* **4** [usually before noun] that can be trusted or relied on: *The Conservatives changed their leader four times between 1997 and 2005, a sure sign that they could not find an adequate response to New Labour.* ◇ *The surest way to stay ahead is to produce better goods or services at lower cost.* **5** [usually before noun] steady and confident: *Clinton was a superb politician in public with a sure grasp of issues and a winning campaign style.*

IDM **be sure to do sth** used to tell sb to do sth: *Be sure to cover all cases in your argument.* **make ˈsure (that...)** **1** to do sth in order to be certain that sth else happens: *It is the nurse's responsibility to make sure that each patient receives all of the appropriate nursing care they require.* **2** to check that sth is true or has been done: *She checked to make sure that their medications were correct.*

sure·ly /ˈʃʊəli; ˈʃɔːli; *NAmE* ˈʃʊrli/ *adv.* **1** used when you are expressing an opinion and want other people to agree with you: *It is surely reasonable for states to take into account the pattern of past terrorist attacks to assess the risk of future attack.* ◇ *Atwood's portrayal of Oryx is surely meant as a critique of these racist and patriarchal structures.* **2** used with a negative to show that sth surprises you and you do not want to believe it: *Are we to suppose that his actions were not discussed and debated? Surely not.* **3** (*formal*) without doubt; certainly: *The household's share of total per capita carbon emissions will surely grow.*
IDM *see* SLOWLY

sur·face[1] /ˈsɜːfɪs; *NAmE* ˈsɜːrfɪs/ *noun* **1** [C] the outside part or top layer of sth: *When unpolarized light strikes a smooth surface, such as a piece of glass, the reflected light is polarized.* ◇ *If the air in the very low troposphere is cold enough, precipitation will reach the earth's surface as snow.* ◇ **on a/the ~** *Mercator tackled the crucial problem of projection: how to represent a sphere on a flat surface.* ◇ **+ noun** *Fine litter dries quickly because of its high ratio of surface area to volume.* **2** [C, usually sing.] the top layer or upper limit of an area of water or an amount of liquid: *Eventually, the deep water rises to the surface.* ◇ **on/beneath/below/near the ~** *The damselfly lays its eggs millimetres beneath the water surface.* ◇ **+ noun** *Glacial

meltwater freshens and warms coastal surface waters.* **3** [sing.] the outer appearance of a person, thing or situation; the qualities that you see or notice, that are not hidden: **on/beneath/below the ~** *Even within the Roman province, the Celtic world continued below the surface.* ◇ **~ of sth** *Beneath a surface of friendly relations lay a deep antagonism.* **4** [C] the flat upper part of a piece of furniture, that is used for working on: *The work surface needs to be at a comfortable height.* **5** [C] (*geometry*) an object with one fewer DIMENSIONS than the space it OCCUPIES: *A surface can be highly complex, as in the case of fractals, or quite simple, as in the case of planes.*
IDM **on the ˈsurface** when not thought about deeply or thoroughly; when not looked at carefully SYN SUPERFICIALLY: *There was little, on the surface at least, to suggest that he would become a protest leader.*

sur·face[2] /ˈsɜːfɪs; *NAmE* ˈsɜːrfɪs/ *verb* [I] **+ adv./prep.** to appear or become obvious after having been hidden or not known SYN EMERGE (1): *Conflict surfaced in many of their relationships.* ◇ *Two themes surfaced from the surveys.*

surge /sɜːdʒ; *NAmE* sɜːrdʒ/ *noun* **1** a sudden increase in the amount or number of sth; a large amount of sth: *Public reporting on the environment experienced a similar surge.* ◇ **~ in sth** *The smoking ban in the UK led to a surge in the demand for patio heaters as customers were forced to smoke outside.* ◇ **~ of sth** *There has been a powerful surge of interest in the politics of national identity.* **2** a sudden, strong forward or upward movement: *The city is vulnerable to flooding during high tides and storm surges.* ◇ **~ of sth** *Cold surges of air occur during winter from the vast pool of air north and east of the Himalayas.* **3** a sudden increase in the flow of electrical power through a system: *The repeater usually includes circuitry to protect the electronics from power surges.*

sur·geon /ˈsɜːdʒən; *NAmE* ˈsɜːrdʒən/ *noun* a doctor who is trained to perform surgery: *The surgeon had decided to operate.*

sur·gery /ˈsɜːdʒəri; *NAmE* ˈsɜːrdʒəri/ *noun* (*pl.* **-ies**) **1** [U, C] medical treatment of injuries or diseases that involves cutting open a person's body, sewing up wounds, etc: *Most studies report a recurrence rate of about 10% after surgery.* ◇ *An estimated 140 000 gastric bypass surgeries were performed.* ◇ **~ for sth** *He underwent surgery for a colonic carcinoma.* ◇ **~ to do sth** *He had surgery to correct a mitral valve defect.* **2** [C] (*BrE*) a place where a doctor sees patients: *The patient is probably well enough to visit the surgery.* **3** [C] (*BrE*) a time during which a doctor, an MP or another professional person is available to see people: *MPs hold regular surgeries for constituents.*

sur·gi·cal /ˈsɜːdʒɪkl; *NAmE* ˈsɜːrdʒɪkl/ *adj.* [only before noun] used in or connected with surgery: *These patients required a surgical procedure.* ◇ *surgical treatment/intervention/techniques* ■ **sur·gi·cal·ly** /ˈsɜːdʒɪkli; *NAmE* ˈsɜːrdʒɪkli/ *adv.*: *The tumour can be surgically removed.*

sur·pass /səˈpɑːs; *NAmE* sərˈpæs/ *verb* **~ sb/sth** to be better or greater than sb/sth SYN EXCEED: *The project has surpassed all expectations.* ◇ *Sales for the year look as if they will surpass one million.*

sur·plus[1] /ˈsɜːpləs; *NAmE* ˈsɜːrpləs/ *noun* [C, U] **1** an amount that is extra or more than you need: *Some areas produced food surpluses.* ◇ *If the state quotas were met, peasants could sell the surplus on the free market.* ⇨ *see also* CONSUMER SURPLUS **2** (*economics*) the amount by which the amount of money received is greater than the amount of money spent; the amount by which the amount of sth available is greater than the amount being used or sold: *A business will focus on those activities that are likely to generate a surplus.* ◇ *The effect of a labour surplus is likely

S

to be a fall in wages due to excess supply. ◇ **in ~** *The government budget was in surplus.* HELP A **trade surplus** is a situation in which the value of a country's exports is greater than the value of its imports: *By 1987, Japan's annual trade surplus exceeded $60 billion.* ➲ *compare* DEFICIT (1) ➲ *see also* CONSUMER SURPLUS

sur·plus² /ˈsɜːpləs; *NAmE* ˈsɜːrpləs/ *adj.* [usually before noun] more than is needed or used SYN EXCESS²: *Peasants now had shorter distances to travel in order to sell their surplus produce.* ◇ *Banks invested surplus funds abroad.* HELP A person or thing that is **surplus to requirements** is not needed: *The employee may be surplus to the requirements of the business.*

sur·prise¹ /səˈpraɪz; *NAmE* sərˈpraɪz/ *noun* **1** [U] a feeling caused by sth happening suddenly or unexpectedly: *The announcement was received with surprise in many quarters.* ◇ **to sb's ~ | to the ~ of sb** *To the great surprise of the investigators, some particles were substantially deflected.* ◇ **in ~** *The two orang-utans gazed at their own images in surprise, often moving and changing their point of view.* ◇ **~ at sth** *None of the authors expresses much surprise at his treatment by the authorities.* ◇ **~ that...** *In light of these issues, it is of little surprise that lower-income countries are often less able to adapt.* **2** [C] an event, a piece of news, etc. that is unexpected or that happens suddenly: *The data contain few surprises in respect of the major parties.* ◇ **come as a ~ (to sb)** *The Nazi-Soviet Pact came as a surprise to the Russian people too.* ◇ **+ noun** *The Japanese made a surprise attack on the US fleet at Pearl Harbor.* **3** [U] the use of methods that cause feelings of surprise: *The element of surprise was essential to the success of the operation.*

IDM **catch/take sb/sth by surˈprise** to attack or capture sb/sth unexpectedly or without warning: *For many predators, hunting success depends on their ability to catch prey by surprise.* **catch/take sb by surˈprise** to happen unexpectedly so that sb is slightly shocked; to surprise sb: *The results of their research, published in 1990, took many by surprise.*

sur·prise² /səˈpraɪz; *NAmE* sərˈpraɪz/ *verb* to make sb feel surprised: **~ sb** *In many ways, this narrative will not surprise experts in the field.* ◇ **it surprises sb that...** *It might surprise some readers that a scientist should be writing about 'belief'.*

sur·prised /səˈpraɪzd; *NAmE* sərˈpraɪzd/ *adj.* feeling or showing surprise: **~ by sth** *The economists who designed the experiment were quite surprised by the results.* ◇ **~ at sth** *They were surprised at the volume of sales.* ◇ **~ to hear, discover, learn, etc.** *Many people are surprised to learn that there is a difference between these two.* ◇ **~ that...** *She seemed pleasantly surprised that he acknowledged his shortcomings.*

sur·pris·ing /səˈpraɪzɪŋ; *NAmE* sərˈpraɪzɪŋ/ *adj.* causing surprise: *This result is not surprising.* ◇ *A somewhat surprising finding is that nitrate levels are also declining in the lakes.* ◇ **it is ~ that...** *It is hardly surprising that food scares often have dramatic economic effects.* ◇ **it is ~ how/what, etc...** *In many respects, it is surprising how little these cultures have changed over time.*

surprisingly /səˈpraɪzɪŋli; *NAmE* sərˈpraɪzɪŋli/ *adv.* in a way that causes surprise: *Surprisingly little attention has been paid to this question.* ◇ *Surprisingly, having a science-based degree did not significantly increase scores in the knowledge test.* ◇ **not ~** *Perhaps not surprisingly, the Court of Appeal reversed the judge's decision.*

sur·ren·der¹ /səˈrendə(r)/ *verb* **1** [I, T] to admit than you have been defeated and want to stop fighting; to allow yourself to be caught, taken prisoner, etc: *The queen was eventually forced to surrender.* ◇ **~ to sb** *The guerrillas refused to surrender to the government.* ◇ **~ yourself (to sb)** *The gunman later surrendered himself to police.* **2** [T] to give up sth/sb when you are forced to SYN RELINQUISH: **~ sth/sb** *Member states have been very cautious about surrendering control over policy areas such as immigration and defence.* ◇ **~ sth/sb to sb** *The people, in making their pact with the ruler, had surrendered all their rights to him.*
PHR V **surˈrender to sth | surˈrender yourself to sth** to give in to sth, such as a strong feeling or an influence: *He surrendered himself to the charm of Italy and the beauty of the Tuscan landscape.*

LANGUAGE BANK

Highlighting interesting data

In academic writing, there are various ways of saying that you think information or results are interesting or surprising

- **It is surprising that...**
- **It is interesting to note that...**
- **Surprisingly/Interestingly/Strikingly,...**
- **One of the most interesting** findings/developments/features, etc.
- **The most striking** feature/example/difference, etc.

– *It is* ***surprising*** *that so few studies have directly addressed the question.*
– ***It is interesting to note that*** *both boys and girls demonstrated similar strategies for managing conflict.*
– ***Interestingly****, Sauer's ideas failed to attract much interest in British geography.*
– ***One of the most interesting*** *examples of environmental change in the 20th century has been the fluctuating level of lakes in the tropics.*
– ***The most striking*** *aspect of the change has been the decline in baby adoptions.*

sur·ren·der² /səˈrendə(r)/ *noun* [U, sing.] **1 ~ (to sb/sth)** an act of admitting that you have been defeated and want to stop fighting: *This chapter examines how Nazi Germany's surrender was received in Japan in the final stages of the Pacific War.* **2 ~ of sth (to sb)** an act of giving sth to sb else even though you do not want to, especially after a battle, etc: *The provisions entailed a total surrender of royal power to the council.*

sur·round /səˈraʊnd/ *verb* **1 ~ sth/sb** to be all around sth/sb: *A barbed wire fence surrounded the camp.* ◇ *Eggs are usually surrounded by several protective layers.* **2** to move into position all around sb/sth, especially so as to prevent them from escaping; to move sb/sth into position in this way: **~ sb/sth** *The police surrounded the lakeside hut where he was holding the boy hostage.* ◇ **~ sb/sth with sb/sth** *On his return to Rome, he surrounded the city with walls to protect it against further barbarian attacks.* **3 ~ sth/sb** to be closely connected with sth/sb: *Controversy surrounds the achievements of a whole series of EU programmes.* ◇ *An inquiry was ordered into the circumstances surrounding the death of an eight-year-old child.* **4 ~ yourself with sb/sth** to choose to have particular people or things near you all the time: *He liked to surround himself with people he could trust.*

sur·round·ing /səˈraʊndɪŋ/ *adj.* [only before noun] **1** that is near or around sth: *The tower soars 200 m above the surrounding countryside.* ◇ *Being so much warmer, the storm core is significantly less dense than the surrounding air.* **2** that is closely connected with sth/sb: *The question entirely depends on the surrounding circumstances.*

sur·round·ings /səˈraʊndɪŋz/ *noun* [pl.] everything that is around or near sb/sth: *A sunspot is a region of the sun's surface that is marked by a lower temperature than its surroundings.* ◇ *Points at which rainwater is funnelled into the ground from the immediate surroundings will experience greater erosion.*

S

sur·veil·lance /sɜːˈveɪləns; *NAmE* sɜːrˈveɪləns/ *noun* [U] **1** the act of carefully watching sb/sth, especially in order to prevent crime SYN OBSERVATION (1): *The authors evaluate the trend towards electronic surveillance in the workplace.* ◇ **under ~** *He was under constant police surveillance.* ◇ **~ of sb/sth** *In the United States, technological surveillance of city streets has increased markedly.* ◇ **+ noun** *Surveillance programmes aim to collect baseline information on the identity and numbers of species within areas.* **2 ~ (of sb/sth)** the act of carefully watching another country's military activities to see what they are planning to do: *The agreement would have permitted each nation to conduct surveillance of the other's military potential.* **3** the act of carefully watching the development of a disease in a group of people: **health/disease/HIV, etc. ~** *Global health surveillance is an important mechanism for detecting changes in the epidemiologic patterns of diseases.* ◇ **~ of sth** *Surveillance of cerebral palsy cannot be based on a simple case count as the condition varies by type and severity.*

sur·vey[1] AWL /ˈsɜːveɪ; *NAmE* ˈsɜːrveɪ/ *noun* **1 ~ (of sb/sth)** an investigation of the opinions, behaviour, etc. of a particular group of people, which is usually done by asking them questions: *In 1995, Katz and Aspden conducted the first national survey of the public's use of the Internet.* ◇ *The survey revealed important trends in consumer spending.* ◇ **+ noun** *The Internet has emerged as an alternative to the telephone for conducting survey research.* **2** an act of examining and recording the measurements, features, etc. of an area of land in order to make a map or plan of it: *Published soil surveys contain a wealth of data on landscapes as well as soils.* ◇ *Early archaeological field surveys appeared to bear out this view.* **3 ~ (of sth)** a general study, view or description of sth: *He provides a comprehensive survey of the major developments in world politics from 1945 to 1990.* ◇ *The literature survey revealed that, generally, employers are more reluctant to adopt telecommuting than workers are.*

▸ ADJECTIVE + SURVEY **previous • subsequent • detailed • comprehensive, extensive • general** *Chapter 2 offers an extensive survey of the large empirical literature on this subject.* | **large-scale • national, nationwide • initial** *Large-scale field surveys using aerial photography show that there is an ongoing colonization of new areas by deciduous shrubs.* | **recent • annual • original • follow-up • conventional • retrospective • representative • population-based • cross-sectional • longitudinal • quantitative • online • postal • face-to-face • social • epidemiological** *In a recent survey, 69% of UK companies cited security as a major inhibitor to purchasing across the Internet.* | **aerial • geological • archaeological** *In the twentieth century, geological surveys over land and sea areas have covered most of the western half of the Arctic basin.* | **brief • annual • historical** *The journal commissioned a brief survey of modern letters from G.K. Chesterton.*

▸ NOUN + SURVEY **telephone • email • mail • questionnaire • Internet, Web • household • patient • panel • opinion • satisfaction • baseline** *The project is based on a household survey of 1 750 homes in each of six countries.*

▸ VERB + SURVEY **conduct, undertake • carry out • plan • design • commission • administer • distribute • answer • complete** *60% of respondents completed the survey online, and all others completed a mail survey.*

▸ SURVEY + VERB **show, reveal • cover** *Field surveys revealed high variability in the number of newborns per pool.* | **indicate, suggest • ask** *For decades, numerous surveys have asked Americans: 'What do you think is the most important problem facing this country today?'*

▸ SURVEY + NOUN **data • evidence • respondent • design • methodology • question, item • questionnaire • instrument • interview • response • result • error • research • researcher • estimate** *In China, survey data were collected in three provinces.*

sur·vey[2] AWL /səˈveɪ; *NAmE* sərˈveɪ/ *verb* **1 ~ sb/sth** to investigate the opinions or behaviour of a group of people by asking them a series of questions: *Of those surveyed, 71.1% were single.* ◇ *The study surveyed 51 junior doctors in a variety of specialties.* ◇ *65% of surveyed companies based at least some part of their wages on individual performance.* ➲ *compare* INTERVIEW[2] (1) **2 ~ sth** to study and give a general description of sth: *Chapple surveys a range of traditions in modern yoga.* ◇ *This chapter surveys the literature on the political economy of trade policy.* **3 ~ sth** to measure and record the features of an area of land, for example in order to make a map or in preparation for building: *Sixteen sites were surveyed on the south-west coast of British Columbia.* **4 ~ sth** to look carefully at the whole of sth, especially in order to get a general impression of it SYN INSPECT (1): *Upon arriving in town after the flood, they set out to survey the damage.*

sur·vey·or /səˈveɪə(r); *NAmE* sərˈveɪər/ *noun* a person whose job is to examine sth in order to get information about it or to check its quality: *The surveyors included in their notes observations about vegetation, soils and topography.* ◇ *The valuation was undertaken by an independent surveyor.*

sur·vival AWL /səˈvaɪvl; *NAmE* sərˈvaɪvl/ *noun* **1** [U] the state of continuing to live or exist, often despite difficulty or danger: *Chemotherapy may shrink the cancer and improve long-term survival.* ◇ *Organizations realize that they need to adopt a new approach to ensure survival and compete successfully.* ◇ *the battle/struggle for survival* ◇ *Early detection is crucial to improve patients' chances of survival.* ◇ **+ noun** *A typical brood of a crab will contain 60–120 eggs; information on survival rates is not available.* **2** [C] **~ (of sth)** something that has continued to exist from an earlier time: *Women's exclusion from the military is a survival of stereotypes of their proper sphere.*
IDM **the surˌvival of the ˈfittest** the idea that only the people or things that are best adapted to their surroundings will continue to exist: *Survival strategies are based on the survival of the fittest in the marketplace.*

sur·vive AWL /səˈvaɪv; *NAmE* sərˈvaɪv/ *verb* **1** [I] to continue to live or exist: *Few animals in the wild survive long enough to experience old age.* ◇ *They were the only surviving direct heirs of Augustus.* ◇ **~ from sth** *Thousands of vases survive from the Classical period.* ◇ **~ on sth** *A third of the nation survives on $1 per day or less.* ◇ *Herbivorous mammals were able to survive on seeds, nuts and vegetation.* ◇ **~ as sth** *A number of scenarios could test our ability to survive as a species.* **2** [T] to continue to live or exist despite a dangerous event or time: **~ sth** *The Picto-Scottish kingdom grew into a strong political unit which survived the Viking onslaught.* ◇ **~ sth + adj./adv.** *Singapore survived the Asian currency crisis in remarkably good shape.* **3** [T] **~ sb/sth** to live or exist longer than sb/sth: *He was survived by his wife and six children.* ◇ *The surviving spouse will receive the property of the deceased.*

sur·vivor AWL /səˈvaɪvə(r); *NAmE* sərˈvaɪvər/ *noun* a person who continues to live, especially despite being nearly killed or experiencing great danger or difficulty: *Those women who are treated for cancer and survive five years are considered as cancer survivors.* ◇ **~ of sb/sth** *After the massacre, emperor Julian and his elder brother Gallus were left as sole survivors of this side of the family.* ◇ **~ from sth** (*figurative*) *The two companies were the two really substantial survivors from the nineteenth century to enter the twenty-first century in Asia Pacific.*

sus·cep·ti·bil·ity /səˌseptəˈbɪləti/ *noun* (*pl.* **-ies**) **1** [U, C] the level to which sth is likely to be influenced, harmed or affected by sth: *Measures of magnetic susceptibility indicate how easily a material can be magnetized.* ◇ **~ to sth** *Clinical symptoms manifest in early childhood, with an*

S

increased susceptibility to viral infections. **2 susceptibilities** [pl.] a person's feelings which are likely to be easily hurt SYN SENSIBILITIES: *Humans are animals with bodily instincts but also with strong social susceptibilities and rational capacities.*

sus·cep·tible /sə'septəbl/ *adj.* **1** [not usually before noun] **~ (to sb/sth)** very likely to be influenced, harmed or affected by sb/sth: *These features make the lung particularly susceptible to injury and disease.* ◇ *A susceptible individual is exposed to an allergen and forms antibodies specific to that antigen.* **2 ~ (of sth)** (*formal*) allowing sth; capable of sth: *The question of whether data are accurate will not always be susceptible of a straightforward answer.*

sus·pect¹ /sə'spekt/ *verb* (not used in the progressive tenses) **1** [T, I] to have an idea that sth is probably true or likely to happen, although you do not have proof: **~ (that)...** *There is no reason to suspect that these findings are invalid.* ◇ *It may be, as I suspect, that these three factors are the most important.* ◇ **it is suspected that...** *It is suspected that other actions may contribute to this response.* ◇ **be suspected of doing sth** *In the past, many patients suspected of having cancer required surgery to confirm the diagnosis.* ◇ **be suspected to be/have sth** *The death is suspected to have been the result of unnatural or unknown causes.* ◇ **(be) suspected** *Silver coinage was more common than previously suspected.* ◇ **~ sth** *The doctor suspects a viral infection.* **2** [T] to have an idea that sb is guilty of sth, without having proof: **~ sb/sth of doing sth** *Local people strongly suspect the company of having bribed councillors.* ◇ **~ sb/sth of sth** *He and others were suspected of various criminal offences.* ■ **sus·pected** *adj.*: *The procedure can confirm the presence of a clinically suspected heart condition.* ◇ *The authorities were allowed to imprison suspected terrorists.*

sus·pect² /'sʌspekt/ *noun* **1** a person who is thought to be guilty of a crime or of having done sth wrong: *The suspects had been arrested.* **2** (*rather informal*) a person or thing that is thought to be a possible reason for sth or cause of sth: *Obesity is one of the prime suspects.* HELP **The usual suspects** is a slightly informal expression for the people or things that are often mentioned or involved in sth: *The article covers all the usual suspects.*

S

sus·pect³ /'sʌspekt/ *adj.* that may be false or dangerous and that cannot be relied on SYN QUESTIONABLE (2): *It may be wise to take further readings before rejecting the suspect data.* ◇ *The motives for the ban were highly suspect.*

sus·pend AWL /sə'spend/ *verb* **1 ~ sth** to officially stop sth for a time; to prevent sth from being active, used, etc. for a time: *In Zimbabwe, the company had to suspend its operations at the request of the government.* ◇ *Yeltsin temporarily suspended the activities of the communist party in the Russian Republic.* ➲ *see also* SUSPENSION (1) **2 ~ sth** to officially delay sth; to prevent sth from happening as early as planned: *The regulation suspends the introduction into the European Union of certain species of wild flora and fauna.* ◇ *On the other issues, we should suspend judgement until more data are available.* ➲ *see also* SUSPENSION (1) **3** [usually passive] **~ sb (from sth)** to officially prevent sb from doing their job, going to school, etc. for a time: *Labour MPs were suspended from the Commons for failing to declare relevant financial interests.* ➲ *see also* SUSPENSION (2) **4 ~ sth (from sth) (by/on sth)** to hang sth from sth else: *Three identical small spheres of mass m are suspended from a common point by threads of equal length.* **5 (be) suspended (in sth)** (*technical*) to float in liquid or air without moving: *Aerosols are solid and liquid particles suspended in atmosphere.* ◇ *The floodplains receive mainly suspended sediment during overbank flooding.* ➲ *see also* SUSPENSION (3)

sus·pen·sion AWL /sə'spenʃn/ *noun* **1** [U, sing.] **~ (of sth)** the act of delaying sth for a period of time, especially until a decision has been taken: *The temporary suspension of diamond exports was a move to address these concerns.* ◇ *Dramatists rely on their audiences' active and willing suspension of disbelief.* ➲ *see also* SUSPEND (1) **2** [U, C] **~ (from sth)** the act of officially removing sb from their job, school, etc. for a period of time, usually as a punishment: *Serious breaches of the Charter result in suspension from the organization.* ◇ *There are five or six consequences listed, from minor actions increasing in severity up to suspensions or exclusions.* ➲ *see also* SUSPEND (3) **3** [C, U] (*technical*) a liquid or gas with very small pieces of solid material floating in it; the state of such a liquid or gas: **~ (of sth) (in sth)** *Dust can be loosely defined as a suspension of solid particles in air.* ◇ **in ~** *The finest particle sizes are carried in suspension great distances from shore by wind or water.* ➲ *see also* SUSPEND (5) **4** [U, C] the system by which a vehicle is supported on its wheels and which makes it more comfortable to travel in when the road surface is not even: **+ noun** *The suspension system for automobiles must provide two different functional requirements: precise steering and ride comfort.*

sus·pi·cion /sə'spɪʃn/ *noun* **1** [U, C] a feeling that sb has done sth bad or cannot be trusted, even though you have no proof: *The police must have reasonable grounds for suspicion before they can act.* ◇ **~ that...** *The evidence confirms the suspicion that the vessel is engaged in smuggling.* ◇ **~ of sth** *Moreover, in much of America there exists a deep suspicion of government.* ◇ **~ of sb** *The boy aroused the suspicion of the police officers.* **2** [C, U] a feeling or belief that sth is true, even though you have no proof: **~ that...** *Once Hamlet has raised the suspicion that Claudius is a murderer, he is in deadly danger.* ◇ **~ of sth** *There is clinical suspicion of a fracture, but no fracture on the X-ray.*

IDM **under su'spicion (of sth)** thought to be guilty of doing sth wrong, illegal or dishonest: *They were all people who, for one reason or another, were under suspicion.*

sus·pi·cious /sə'spɪʃəs/ *adj.* **1** [not usually before noun] feeling that sb cannot be trusted or has done sth bad, even though you have no proof: **~ (of sb/sth)** *He remained deeply suspicious of his nephew.* ◇ **~ about sth** *Respondents may feel suspicious about the research.* ◇ **~ that...** *This made them suspicious that there was some truth in the allegations.* ➲ *compare* SCEPTICAL **2** making you feel that sth is wrong, illegal or dishonest: *A number of cases involved deaths in suspicious circumstances.* ◇ *Police did not treat the fire as suspicious.*

sus·tain AWL /sə'steɪn/ *verb* **1 ~ sb/sth** to provide enough of what sb/sth needs in order to live or exist: *There is little appreciation of the role played by complex ecosystems in sustaining life on earth.* ◇ *During Ramadan, families rise before sunrise to take their first meal of the day, which must sustain them until sunset.* ◇ *A certain level of income is required to sustain a middle-class lifestyle.* **2** to make sth continue for some time without becoming less SYN MAINTAIN (1): **~ sth** *Financial development is essential to sustaining economic growth.* ◇ *She argues that television uses emotion to sustain the interest of potentially distracted viewers.* ◇ **sustained + noun** *This view has come under sustained attack.* **3 ~ sth** (*formal*) to experience sth bad SYN SUFFER (2): *The patient had sustained injuries to the chest wall.* ◇ *The structure of the hotel did sustain some damage.* ◇ *The injured party will be compensated for any losses sustained under the breach of the contract.* **4 ~ sth** to provide evidence to support an opinion, a theory, etc. SYN UPHOLD (1): *It will be useful to consider what sort of argument might sustain the claim that globalization can cause fundamental change.* **5 ~ sth** (*law*) to decide that a claim, etc. is valid SYN UPHOLD (2): *The Commission will bring the case to the European Court, and if its claim is* *sustained, the member state in violation of the rules can be fined.*

sus·tain·abil·ity AWL /səˌsteɪnəˈbɪləti/ *noun* [U] **1** the use of natural products and energy in a way that does not harm the environment: *Industrialized countries must reduce resource use and emissions to ensure global environmental sustainability.* **2 ~ (of sth)** the ability to continue or be continued for a long time: *The agency is committed to the long-term financial sustainability of the initiative.*

sus·tain·able AWL /səˈsteɪnəbl/ *adj.* **1** involving the use of natural products and energy in a way that does not harm the environment: *Environmental protection and sustainable development continue to occupy a prominent place in the objectives of the European Union.* ◇ *sustainable energy/agriculture* OPP UNSUSTAINABLE (2) **2** that can continue or be continued for a long time: *The company's concentration in the steel industry was not good for sustainable long-term growth.* ◇ *The overriding aim of marketing is to develop a sustainable competitive advantage.* OPP UNSUSTAINABLE (1) ■ **sus·tain·ably** /səˈsteɪnəbli/ *adv.*: *Each country's population has to live sustainably within the earth's resources.*

swal·low /ˈswɒləʊ; *NAmE* ˈswɑːloʊ/ *verb* **1** [I, T] to make food, drink, etc. go down your throat into your stomach: *The patient has difficulty breathing and swallowing.* ◇ **~ sth** *He feels pain on trying to swallow solid foods.* **2** [T] **~ sth (up)** (*rather informal*) to make sth disappear by using it, taking it in or covering it: *Ongoing projects already swallowed up their time and budget allocation.* ◇ *This led to the conclusion that a supermassive black hole has swallowed up many stars.*

swam *past tense of* SWIM

sweat[1] /swet/ *noun* **1** [U] drops of liquid that appear on the surface of your skin when you are hot, ill or afraid: *Sodium is also lost through the skin in sweat.* ◇ **~ gland** *The sweat glands can be divided into two groups.* **2** [C] the state of being covered with sweat: *She also reports fever, night sweats and weight loss.*

sweat[2] /swet/ *verb* [I] when you **sweat**, drops of liquid appear on the surface of your skin, for example when you are hot, ill or afraid: *She was anxious and sweating profusely.*

sweep[1] /swiːp/ *verb* (**swept**, **swept** /swept/) **1** [T] **~ sth/sb + adv./prep.** to move or push sth/sb suddenly and with a lot of force: *A strong current sweeps the water along the coast.* **2** [I, T] to spread suddenly and/or with a powerful effect over an area: **+ adv./prep.** *The south-west monsoon sweeps northwards across the Indian subcontinent.* ◇ *Cholera swept across Europe in 1832.* ◇ *A wave of democratic change swept through Latin America in the 1980s.* ◇ **~ sth** *In 2009 an even larger wave of protest swept South Africa.*

PHR V ˌ**sweep sth aˈside** to ignore sth completely: *Arguably, values such as freedom, choice and community have been swept aside in pursuit of supposed 'school effectiveness'.* ˌ**sweep sth aˈway** to get rid of sth completely: *Mass opposition protests have swept away authoritarian regimes in many countries over the last three decades.*

sweep[2] /swiːp/ *noun* [U] **~ (of sth)** the range of a law, an idea, a piece of writing, etc. that includes many different things: *Hegel reinterpreted the whole sweep of human history as a process of increasing self-awareness.* ◇ *The broad sweep of the Pure Food and Drugs Act of 1906 was certainly encouraged by the Progressive Movement.*

sweet /swiːt/ *adj.* (**sweet·er**, **sweet·est**) tasting or smelling of sugar: *Sweet tastes were associated with honey and ripe fruit.* ➲ *compare* BITTER (3)

swell /swel/ *verb* (**swelled** /sweld/, **swol·len** /ˈswəʊlən; *NAmE* ˈswoʊlən/) or (**swelled**, **swelled**) **1** [I] to become bigger or rounder: *These soils have a tendency to shrink and swell.* ◇ *The material swelled in organic solvents such as benzene.* ◇ *Her ankle started to swell.* **2** [T, I] to make sth increase; to increase: **~ sth** *The war on drugs led drug offenders to swell the ranks of prisoners.* ◇ *The homeward flow of diplomats was swollen by the expulsions.* ◇ **~ to sth** *Union membership swelled to 10 million by 1940.* OPP SHRINK (1) ➲ *see also* SWOLLEN[1]

swell·ing /ˈswelɪŋ/ *noun* **1** [U] the condition of being larger or rounder than normal: *The classical symptoms are severe pain, swelling and fever.* ◇ **~ of sth** *The doctor noted mild swelling of the ankles.* ◇ *Moisture absorption by polymeric matrices can induce swelling of the structure.* **2** [C] a part of the body that has become larger or rounder than normal, because of illness or injury: *Painless swellings may appear in the lower abdomen.*

swept *past tense, past part. of* SWEEP[1]

swim /swɪm/ *verb* (**swim·ming**, **swam** /swæm/, **swum** /swʌm/) **1** [I, T] (of a person) to move through water in a horizontal position using the arms and legs: *Some sailors never learned to swim.* ◇ **~ sth** *'Beer' (1988) is an account of two men who swam the whole length of the river.* **2** [I] (of a fish, etc.) to move through or across water: *As fish swim they generate turbulence.* ◇ **+ adv./prep.** *Some species of angler fish, when threatened, emit a flash before swimming away.*

swim·ming /ˈswɪmɪŋ/ *noun* [U] the sport or activity of swimming: *Swimming is a good form of exercise.*

swing[1] /swɪŋ/ *verb* (**swung**, **swung** /swʌŋ/) **1** [I, T] to change or make sb/sth change from one opinion or mood to another: *Although liberals and radicals welcomed the outbreak of the French Revolution, opinion soon swung the other way.* ◇ **~ (from A) (to B)** *The patient's mood swings from mania to severe depression.* ◇ **~ between A and B** *Debate about the explanation of this change swings between medical discoveries and environmental causes.* ◇ **~ sb/sth (to sth)** *Voters who decided after the conventions swung the election to the eventual winner.* **2** [I, T] to turn or change direction suddenly; to make sth do this: **+ adv./prep.** *One part of the molecule swings round into its new position.* ◇ *This is one reason why economies swing from booms to slumps.* ◇ **~ sth + adv./prep.** *Gravitational force swings the pendulum downwards.* **3** [I, T] to move backwards or forwards or from side to side while hanging from a fixed point; to make sth do this: *The lever arm swings to cause the power stroke.* ◇ **~ sth** *The sugar planters believed that men swung the heavy cane knives more effectively than did women.* **4** [I, T] to move or make sth move with a wide curved movement: **+ adv./prep.** *A crane that swings over the claimant's land is a trespass.* ◇ **~ sth + adv./prep.** (*figurative*) *How can we swing the pendulum back to a healthier BMI level?*

swing[2] /swɪŋ/ *noun* a change from one opinion or situation to another; the amount by which sth changes: **~ in sth** *There have been major swings in public opinion on the existence of climate change.* ◇ **~ of sth** *In the positive direction, a swing of +0.2 V would not cause the transistor to cut off.* ◇ **~ (from sb/sth) (to/towards sb/sth)** *The biggest surprise among Liberal Democrat performances was the 20% swing to the party from Labour in Redcar.*

IDM **in full ˈswing** having reached a high level of activity: *By the end of 2000, the technology boom was in full swing.*

switch[1] /swɪtʃ/ *verb* **1** [I, T] to change from one thing to another; to make sth do this: **~ (over/back/away) (from sth) (to/into sth)** *The acceleration will switch over into a deceleration at some point.* ◇ *Some Liberal Democrat voters switched back to the Conservatives.* ◇ *High fuel prices caused Americans to switch away from big cars.* ◇ **~ between A and B** *Gaps are required between data*

S

structures to switch between read and write operations. ◇ **~ sth (over) (from sth) (to sth)** *In December, the Bolsheviks switched their attention to Moscow.* **2** [T] to exchange one thing for another: **~ sth over/around/round** *Customers have been able to switch their debts around, moving from one interest-free deal to another.* ◇ **~ sth with sb/sth** *In this scene, the countess has switched positions with her maid.*

PHR V **ˌswitch ˈoff/ˈon | ˌswitch sth ˈoff/ˈon** to turn a light, machine, etc. off/on by pressing a button or switch: *Parts of the interview took place after the tape had been switched off.*

switch² /swɪtʃ/ *noun* **1** a small device that you press or move up and down in order to turn a piece of electrical equipment on and off: *Current only flows if both switches are closed.* **2 ~ (in/of sth) (from A to B)** a change from one thing to another, especially when this is sudden and complete: *A further recent trend is the switch in land use from food production to crops for the biofuel industry.*

swol·len¹ /ˈswəʊlən; *NAmE* ˈswoʊlən/ *adj.* larger or rounder than normal (used mainly about a body part that is like this because of illness or injury): *The joint is swollen and deformed.* ◇ *She has a painful and swollen right ankle.*

swol·len² *past part. of* SWELL

swum *past part. of* SWIM

swung *past tense, past part. of* SWING¹

syl·lable /ˈsɪləbl/ *noun* any of the units into which a word is divided, containing a vowel sound and usually one or more consonants: *'Potato' is stressed on the second syllable.*

syl·la·bus /ˈsɪləbəs/ *noun* (*pl.* **syl·la·buses** or *less frequent* **syl·labi** /ˈsɪləbaɪ/) a list of the topics, books, etc. that students should study in a particular subject at school or college: **on a/the ~** *It is only since the 1970s that marketing has featured significantly on university syllabuses.* ➲ *compare* CURRICULUM

sym·bol AWL /ˈsɪmbl/ *noun* **1** a person, an object, an event, etc. that represents a more general quality or situation: *Students had the right to wear discreet religious symbols to school.* ◇ **~ of sth** *Rokossovsky became to the Poles a symbol of Russian domination.* **2** a sign, number, letter, etc. that has a fixed meaning, especially in science, mathematics and music: *The speed of light is traditionally denoted by the symbol c.* ◇ *A potent brand symbol can act as a strong consumer force.* ◇ **~ for sth** *The logical symbol for an OR operation is an addition sign.*

sym·bol·ic AWL /sɪmˈbɒlɪk; *NAmE* sɪmˈbɑːlɪk/ *adj.* containing symbols; being used as a symbol: *This combined device has its own symbolic representation shown in Fig. 36.4b.* ◇ *The Church of England today seems to possess largely symbolic rather than real political power.* ◇ **~ of sth** *Significantly, the flowers are calla lilies, symbolic of death.* ■ **sym·bol·ic·al·ly** AWL /sɪmˈbɒlɪkli; *NAmE* sɪmˈbɑːlɪkli/ *adv.*: *Wars are often fought over targets which are strategically worthless but symbolically significant.*

sym·bol·ism AWL /ˈsɪmbəlɪzəm/ *noun* [U] **1** the use of symbols to represent ideas or qualities: *As a result of the Islamic revival, religious symbolism and social values were re-emphasized.* **2 ~ (of sth)** the symbolic meaning attached to objects or facts: *She examines the symbolism of food in Gisele Pineau's novels.*

sym·bol·ize (*BrE also* **-ise**) AWL /ˈsɪmbəlaɪz/ *verb* **~ sth** to be a symbol of sth SYN REPRESENT (2): *In China the colour white symbolizes death and mourning.*

sym·met·rical /sɪˈmetrɪkl/ (*also* **sym·met·ric** /sɪˈmetrɪk/) *adj.* (of a body, a design, an object, etc.) made up of exactly similar parts facing each other or around an AXIS: *The blades of the turbine are symmetrical.* ◇ *He replaced late medieval irregularity with a comprehensively symmetrical design.* OPP ASYMMETRIC (1) ■ **sym·met·ric·al·ly** /sɪˈmetrɪkli/ *adv.*: *In a normal distribution, the values of a continuous variable are distributed symmetrically around the mean value.*

sym·metry /ˈsɪmətri/ *noun* (*pl.* **-ies**) **1** [U, C] the quality of being made up of exactly similar parts facing each other or around an AXIS: *An organism is said to have bilateral symmetry if it is identical with its own reflection in some plane.* ◇ *They were working with two-dimensional shapes to see if it was possible to put a line of symmetry through them.* **2** [C] (*physics, mathematics*) the property of an object or physical law of not being changed after certain TRANSFORMATIONS, such as REVERSING time, a ROTATION or a REFLECTION: *The interactions of elementary particles appear to be dictated by mathematical symmetries.* **3** [U] **~ (between A and B)** the quality of being very similar or equal: *The term 'equivalence' presents an illusion of symmetry between languages which hardly exists in reality.*

sym·pa·thet·ic /ˌsɪmpəˈθetɪk/ *adj.* **1** showing that you approve of sb/sth or that you share their views and are willing to support them: *The film 'The Madness of King George' gives a more sympathetic portrayal.* ◇ **~ to/towards sb/sth** *The Catholic Church at the time was not in any way sympathetic to abolitionism.* **2 ~ (to/towards sb)** kind to sb who is hurt or sad; showing that you understand and care about their problems: *GPs' practices should ensure that they are sympathetic towards the needs of disabled employees.* ■ **sym·pa·thet·ic·al·ly** /ˌsɪmpəˈθetɪkli/ *adv.*: *As a character, Prospero is not entirely sympathetically presented.*

sym·pa·thize (*BrE also* **-ise**) /ˈsɪmpəθaɪz/ *verb* **1** [I] **~ (with sb/sth)** to feel sorry for sb; to show that you understand and feel sorry about sb's problems: *He sympathized with the plight of the women.* **2** [I] **~ with sb/sth** to support or approve of sb/sth: *The court clearly sympathized with her point of view.*

sym·pathy /ˈsɪmpəθi/ *noun* (*pl.* **-ies**) **1** [U, C, usually pl.] **~ (for sb)** the feeling of being sorry for sb; showing that you understand and care about sb's problems: *Humans tend to feel less sympathy for those who seem strange and alien.* ◇ *Film music has an emotional dimension: it can regulate our sympathies.* **2** [C, usually pl., U] the act of showing support for or approval of an idea, a cause, an organization, etc: *Dubois makes clear where his sympathies lie.* ◇ *political/communist sympathies* ◇ **~ for sth** *She had no sympathy for democracy.*

IDM **in ˈsympathy with sth** happening because sth else has happened: *The amplitude of the oscillation increases in sympathy with the rise in temperature.* **in/out of ˈsympathy with sb/sth** agreeing/not agreeing with sb/sth; wanting/not wanting to support sb/sth: *Forms of Marxism that are more in sympathy with religion have come into existence.*

sym·phony /ˈsɪmfəni/ *noun* (*pl.* **-ies**) a long complicated piece of music for a full ORCHESTRA, usually divided into three or four sections: *Beethoven's Eroica Symphony, completed in 1804, recast the symphony as a psychological journey of struggle and triumph.*

symp·tom /ˈsɪmptəm/ *noun* **1** a change in your body or mind that shows that you are not healthy: *Symptoms include sore throat, fever, headache, and occasionally nausea and vomiting.* ◇ *Up to a third of patients experience withdrawal symptoms when the drug is stopped.* ◇ **~ of sth** *Early symptoms of respiratory disease may often be ignored by the public.* HELP **Symptoms** can be felt or seen by the patient; they contrast with **signs** of disease which may only be noticed by a doctor. ➲ *compare* SIGN¹ (1) **2 ~ of sth** a sign that sth has been caused by sth else SYN INDICATION (1): *The April coup was a symptom rather than a*

S

cause of the collapse of revolutionary unionism. ◇ *One early symptom of rapid urban growth is the transformation and, in many cases, the deterioration of the natural environment.*

▸ ADJECTIVE + SYMPTOM **common • severe • mild • persistent • unexplained • physical, somatic • psychological, mental • clinical • depressive • psychotic • neurological • respiratory • work-related** *Patients with medically unexplained symptoms are commonly referred to specialist clinics.*

▸ VERB + SYMPTOM **have, experience • report • present • cause • develop • relieve, alleviate, reduce • treat** *57 per cent reported low back symptoms in the last 12 months.*

▸ SYMPTOM + VERB **occur • develop, appear • persist** *Further treatments should be considered if symptoms persist.*

▸ NOUN + OF SYMPTOMS **onset • level • severity • presence • prevalence** *The onset of symptoms can be surprisingly abrupt.*

symp·tom·at·ic /ˌsɪmptəˈmætɪk/ *adj.* **1** **~ of sth** being a sign of a problem or an unpleasant situation: *The emergence of a diffuse protest movement against globalization is symptomatic of a new wave of resistance to it.* **2** (*medical*) showing or connected with symptoms of illness: *Symptomatic patients were significantly younger than asymptomatic.* ◇ *Correction of the underlying condition is the first priority, followed by symptomatic relief.* OPP ASYMPTOMATIC

syn·apse /ˈsaɪnæps; ˈsɪnæps/ *noun* (*biology*) a connection between two nerve cells: **at a ~** *Communication between neurons occurs at synapses.* ◇ **+ noun** *A variety of molecules coordinate synapse formation.* ■ **syn·ap·tic** /saɪˈnæptɪk; sɪˈnæptɪk/ *adj.*: *Synaptic transmission begins shortly after a contact is made.*

syn·drome /ˈsɪndrəʊm; *NAmE* ˈsɪndroʊm/ *noun* **1** a set of physical conditions that show that sb has a particular disease or medical problem: *Heart failure is a complex clinical syndrome caused by impaired ventricular performance.* **2** **~ (of sth)** a set of opinions or a way of behaving that is typical of a particular type of person, attitude or social problem: *The region suffers from a syndrome of political dependency: solutions are expected to come from outside.*

syno·nym /ˈsɪnənɪm/ *noun* a word or expression that has the same or nearly the same meaning as another in the same language: *In the American vernacular, 'federal' and 'national' are synonyms.* ◇ **~ for sth** *The term 'competitive strategy' is sometimes used as a synonym for 'business strategy'.*

syn·onym·ous /sɪˈnɒnɪməs; *NAmE* sɪˈnɑːnɪməs/ *adj.* **1** **~ (with sth)** so closely connected with sth that the two things appear to be the same: *The ruling party regards itself as synonymous with the state, ignoring completely any political opposition.* **2** (of words or expressions) having the same, or nearly the same, meaning: *To many people, direct marketing has become synonymous with 'junk mail'.* ■ **syn·onym·ous·ly** *adv.*: *In the Christian tradition, the name Lucifer is used synonymously with that of Satan.*

syn·tac·tic /sɪnˈtæktɪk/ *adj.* (*linguistics*) connected with SYNTAX: *Question comprehension is impeded by questions containing imprecise terms or complex syntactic structures.* ■ **syn·tac·tic·al·ly** /sɪnˈtæktɪkli/ *adv.*: *Syntactically, this expression is a perfectly regular and unexceptional Adj-N combination.*

syn·tax /ˈsɪntæks/ *noun* [U] **1** (*linguistics*) the way that words and phrases are put together to form sentences in a language; the rules of grammar for this: *These passages are nearly identical in both vocabulary and syntax.* ➲ *compare* MORPHOLOGY (2) **2** (*computing*) the rules that state how words and phrases must be used in a computer language: *Figure 2.10 illustrates the syntax that is used to express these features.*

syn·the·sis /ˈsɪnθəsɪs/ *noun* (*pl.* **syn·the·ses** /ˈsɪnθəsiːz/) **1** [U] the natural chemical production of a substance in animals and plants: *Protein synthesis is carried out by cellular bodies called ribosomes.* ◇ *Errors in DNA synthesis cause changes in the genetic code that will be passed to all subsequent cells.* ◇ **~ of sth** *Synthesis of a protein molecule can be divided into three phases.* **2** [U] the artificial chemical production of a substance from two or more simpler substances: *During the 1990s, the chemical industry focused on ways to reduce pollution caused by chemical synthesis and manufacturing.* ◇ **~ of sth** *The synthesis of these polymers required a special approach.* **3** [C, U] **~ (of sth)** the act of combining two or more separate ideas, beliefs, styles, etc; a mixture or combination of ideas, beliefs, styles, etc: *Giddens has always sought to produce new insights through syntheses of existing ideas.* ◇ *The power of the work lies in its synthesis of intellect and emotion.*

syn·the·size (*BrE also* **-ise**) /ˈsɪnθəsaɪz/ *verb* **1** **~ sth** to produce a substance by means of chemical or biological processes: *Vitamin D is synthesized in skin exposed to sunlight.* ◇ *Citrulline is not one of the 20 amino acids used for synthesizing proteins.* **2** **~ sth** to combine separate types of sth such as ideas, beliefs or information: *A strength of this review is that it synthesizes evidence from controlled trials and experimental studies.*

syn·thet·ic /sɪnˈθetɪk/ *adj.* **1** made by combining chemical substances rather than being produced naturally by plants or animals SYN ARTIFICIAL (2), MAN-MADE: *There are many types of synthetic and natural fibres.* ◇ *Chemicals made by organisms are not inherently 'safer' than synthetic chemicals.* **2** (*linguistics*) (of languages) using changes to the ends of words rather than word order to show the functions of words in a sentence: *The modern Romance languages, like Latin, have a synthetic form of the future tense.* ➲ *compare* ANALYTIC (2) **3** (*philosophy*) (of a statement) that may be either true or false, depending on experience: *Synthetic sentences are those which express true propositions in some (conceivable) contexts and false ones in others.* ➲ *compare* ANALYTIC (3) ■ **syn·thet·ic·al·ly** /sɪnˈθetɪkli/ *adv.*: *The chemical structure of penicillin was studied to ascertain whether it would be possible to make the chemical synthetically.*

syr·inge /sɪˈrɪndʒ/ *noun* **1** a plastic or glass tube with a long hollow needle that is used for putting drugs, etc. into a person's body or for taking a small amount of blood from a person: *When taking blood cultures, blood is usually collected from a patient's vein using a syringe.* **2** a plastic or glass tube with a rubber part at the end, used for SUCKING up liquid and then pushing it out: *High-purity water was introduced through a plastic tube attached to a glass syringe.*

sys·tem /ˈsɪstəm/ *noun* **1** [C] an organized way of doing sth; an organized set of ideas or theories : *Health care systems all over the world seem to be facing a funding crisis.* ◇ *The administration persisted in reforms which liberalized the legal system to a significant extent.* ◇ **~ of sth** *Establishing effective systems of financial management is a challenge.* ◇ **~ for sth** *A system for the management of knowledge must be capable of adapting to local requirements.* ◇ **~ for doing sth** *The international system for protecting human rights is not infallible.* ➲ *see also* VALUE SYSTEM **2** [C] a group of things that work together in a particular way or for a particular purpose: *Kirlik (1993) studied pilots' use of an automated flight control system in a simulated flight environment.* ◇ **+ noun** *The section concludes with a discussion of the various styles of digital system design.* ➲ *see also* ECOSYSTEM, OPERATING SYSTEM, SOLAR

S

SYSTEM **3** [C] a human or animal body, or a part of it, when it is being thought of as the organs and processes that make it function: *The nervous system is the most complex of all the organ systems in the animal embryo.* ◇ *Virtually every reaction that occurs in biological systems is catalysed by an enzyme.* ◇ *In some cases, air pollution may affect the cardiovascular system.* ➲ *see also* CENTRAL NERVOUS SYSTEM, IMMUNE SYSTEM, NERVOUS SYSTEM **4 the system** [sing.] (*rather informal, usually disapproving*) the rules or people that control a country or an organization, especially when they seem to be unfair because you cannot change them: *Despite further reforms, by the late 1820s ratepayers were dissatisfied and the poor began to rebel against the system.*

▸ ADJECTIVE + SYSTEM **new • complex** *The Council is a complex system with multiple levels*. | **international, global • national • state • legal • political • economic • social • financial • educational** *Nothing has been left untouched by the expansion of the capitalist economic system.*

▸ NOUN + SYSTEM **health (care) • education • management • production • justice • banking** *Some animal production systems, such as organic farming, place a high priority on animal welfare.*

▸ VERB + SYSTEM **have • use • develop • create • design • implement • operate • describe** *The Ministry of Education commissioned the university to design and implement an information system for the education sector.* | **establish • introduce • provide • adopt** *The advent of the World Trade Organization has resulted in many more countries introducing systems of patent protection.*

WHICH WORD?

systematic • systemic

- **systematic** means done according to a system or plan; caused by the system or plan that is used: *The notion is intriguing but rarely studied in a systematic fashion.* ◇ *Systematic errors cause all of the data to be shifted in one direction.*
- **systemic** means affecting a whole system, and in particular the whole of the body: *These quotes also hint at systemic discrimination within the organization.* ◇ *These infections cause a severe systemic disease, with fever, sore throat, headache, and progressive multi-organ dysfunction.*

T

sys·tem·at·ic /ˌsɪstəˈmætɪk/ *adj.* **1** done according to a system or plan, in a thorough, efficient or determined way: *A systematic review of the literature was conducted in November 2009.* ◇ *Recent technical advances are leading to more systematic approaches to gene identification.* ◇ *Meaning is a difficult topic to address in a systematic way.* ◇ *a systematic method/procedure/study/analysis/investigation* **2** (of an error) happening in the same way all through a process or set of results; caused by the system that is used: *Systematic error produces measurements differing from the true value by a constant amount in the same direction.* ◇ *Randomized controlled trials have important elements which aim to reduce systematic bias.*

sys·tem·at·ic·al·ly /ˌsɪstəˈmætɪkli/ *adv.* **1** in a way that follows a system: *All these studies were systematically reviewed.* ◇ *The survival probabilities vary systematically with the age of the firm.* **2** in the same way all through a process or set of results because of the system that is used: *If some respondents perceive 5 to be the midpoint of a 1-to-10 scale, then responses should be systematically biased in favour of 5 relative to 6.*

sys·tem·ic /sɪˈstemɪk; sɪˈstiːmɪk/ *adj.* **1** affecting or connected with a whole system, not just parts of it: *The Council is tasked to identify and manage systemic risk in the financial system.* ◇ *Regardless of method, systemic change in a school never comes easily.* ➲ *usage note at* SYSTEMATIC **2** (*medical*) affecting or connected with the whole body: *Allergy is a systemic disease and not an organ-specific disease.* ➲ *usage note at* SYSTEMATIC **3** (of chemicals or drugs used to treat diseases) entering the plant or body and spreading to all parts of it: *In very severe cases, systemic drugs such as ciclosporin may be prescribed.* ■ **sys·tem·ic·al·ly** /sɪˈstemɪkli; sɪˈstiːmɪkli/ *adv.*: *If these measures do not resolve symptoms or she becomes systemically unwell, then antibiotics are required.*

Tt

LANGUAGE BANK

Referring to visuals

Visuals include **tables, bar charts, line graphs** and **pie charts**, and are a useful way to present your data effectively. Charts and graphs are usually referred to as **figures**.

SUMMARIZE WHAT THE VISUAL IS ABOUT

Note the use of both active and passive forms, and the use of the personal pronouns *I* and *We*.

▸ Figure 1 **illustrates/shows...**
▸ Table 1 **displays/gives/illustrates/presents/provides/shows/summarizes...**
▸ **... are/is displayed/given/illustrated/presented/provided/shown/ summarized** in Figure/Table 2.
▸ I/We **illustrate/show** in Figure 3
▸ I/We **give/illustrate/present/provide/show/summarize** in Table 3...

– *Figure 1 **illustrates** the variation in average prices.*
– *Table 2 **gives** a summary of three major cardiovascular risk factors.*
– *Frequencies of Internet use **are presented** in Table 2.*
– *In Fig. 3, **we show** the circuit excited by two separate but equal voltage sources.*

EXPLAIN OR STATE THE IMPLICATIONS OF THE DATA

Note the use of *that* after the verb. You can also use an *as* phrase.

▸ Figure/Table 1 **illustrates/indicates/shows that...**
▸ **As** Figure/Table 2 **illustrates/indicates/shows,...**
▸ **As illustrated/shown in** Figure/Table 3,...

– *Figure 1 **shows that** income and longevity are both rising.*
– ***As** the figure **shows**, the algal growth cycle increases aqueous oxygen concentrations in daytime.*
– ***As shown in** Table 5.2, a similar proportion of respondents had used the Internet as had not.*
– *The model predicted large emissions reductions, **as illustrated** in Figure 3.*

table /ˈteɪbl/ *noun* **1** a list of facts or numbers arranged in a special order, usually in rows and columns: *The total population of the Empire when Napoleon invaded was 41 million (see table, p. 606).* ◇ *As is clear from Table 2.6, the EU is more efficient in the production of these goods.* ◇ **the ~ above/below** *The table below shows ozone concentrations measured every hour on a high pollution day in Los Angeles.* ◇ **in the ~** *All drug doses listed in this table are adult doses and not children's doses.* ◇ **~ of contents** *Readers may need to consult the table of contents and the index to locate topics.* ➲ *see also* LIFE TABLE, PERIODIC TABLE **2** a list that shows how well an organization such as a school or a hospital is performing compared with others: **~ (of sth)** *The government planned to compile a league table of universities, based on 'student satisfaction' surveys.* ◇ **in/on the ~** *Ranking on the table is based on exam score averages.* **3** a piece of furniture that consists of a flat top supported by legs: **on a ~** *They argued that, if computers were placed on kitchen tables rather than in studies,* technophobia could be transformed into technofamiliarity. ◇ **at a ~** *The technical assistant was seated at a table next to the respondent.* **4** (*computing*) a collection of data stored in memory as a series of records: *The members table in the database contained name and address data for each member.* ➲ *see also* WATER TABLE

IDM **on the ˈtable** (of a plan, a suggestion or an idea) offered to people so that they can consider or discuss it: *All the options had to be put on the table and explored.* **turn the ˈtables (on sb)** to change a situation so that you are now in a stronger position than the person who used to be in a stronger position than you: *By the mid-eighteenth century, the British were to turn the tables completely on the Dutch and win an unchallenged supremacy among Europeans in Asia.*

tab·let /ˈtæblət/ *noun* **1** (*especially BrE*) a small round solid piece of medicine that you swallow: *The side effects are best managed by taking the tablets with food.* **2** a flat piece of stone, etc. with words or symbols on it: *This early map was engraved on a clay tablet c. 2200 BCE.* **3** (*also* ˌ**tablet comˈputer**) (*trademark* in the UK) a small, light, flat computer that can be used without a keyboard or mouse, by touching the screen: *In March 2012, 31% of US Internet users were reported to have a tablet.*

tabu·late /ˈtæbjuleɪt/ *verb* [often passive] **~ sth (+ adv./prep.)** to arrange facts or figures in columns or lists so that they can be read easily: *The results are tabulated below.* ◇ *Their frequency and distribution are tabulated in Appendices 1 and 2.* ■ **tabu·la·tion** /ˌtæbjuˈleɪʃn/ *noun* [U, C] *Simple tabulation was used to produce results on broad trends.* ◇ **~ of sth** *Appendix B contains tabulations of optical properties.*

tacit /ˈtæsɪt/ *adj.* [usually before noun] that is suggested indirectly or understood, rather than expressed in words or made known: *Business functions on the tacit understanding that favours are returned.* ◇ *Interest in tacit knowledge stems from Polanyi's (1956) argument that we frequently know a good deal more than we can express verbally.* ➲ *compare* EXPLICIT ■ **tacit·ly** *adv.*: *There are many cases where the use of forced labour has been tacitly accepted by companies using these workers.*

tackle /ˈtækl/ *verb* **~ sth** to make a determined effort to deal with a difficult problem or situation: *Several innovative strategies have been used to tackle this problem.* ◇ *Social marketing has been used to good effect in order to tackle many social issues worldwide (Andreasen, 2003).*

tac·tic /ˈtæktɪk/ *noun* **1** [C, usually pl.] the particular method you use to achieve sth: *Tactics employed in these campaigns include petitions, student referendums, forums and lobbying meetings.* ◇ *A market leader has to adopt defensive tactics to protect its position.* ◇ **~ for (doing) sth** *Tactics for improving a child's diet should not be solely food-based.* ➲ *usage note at* STRATEGY **2 tactics** [pl.] the art of moving soldiers and military equipment around during a battle or war in order to use them in the most effective way: *Philip II's reign coincided with a revolution in military tactics and weaponry.* ➲ *compare* STRATEGY (3)

tac·tic·al /ˈtæktɪkl/ *adj.* **1** [usually before noun] connected with the particular method that is used to achieve sth: *The tools can be used to develop both long-term strategies and short-term tactical plans.* ➲ *usage note at* STRATEGY **2** [usually before noun] carefully planned in order to achieve a particular aim: *Concessions made to the working class were merely tactical decisions made to ensure that the ruling elite remained in power.* ➲ *usage note at* STRATEGY **3** [only before noun] connected with military tactics: *They launched the first tactical and strategic air raids on civilian populations.* ➲ *compare* STRATEGIC (2) **4** [only before noun] (especially of weapons) used or having an effect over short distances or for a short time: *Of particular concern are tactical nuclear weapons (TNW), of which thousands exist, none of them covered by formal arms control accords.* ➲ *compare* STRATEGIC (3) ■ **tac·tic·al·ly** /ˈtæktɪkli/ *adv.*: *Traditionally, sales promotion has been used tactically to encourage brand switching.*

tag¹ /tæg/ *noun* **1** (often in compounds) a label, object or substance that is attached to sth to identify it or give information about it or its movements: *Items in a shop with a price tag attached did not constitute an offer to sell.* ◇ *The habitat utilization of top predators has been studied using electronic tags to follow their movements.* ◇ *The nucleic acid is labelled either radioactively or with a fluorescent chemical tag.* **2** (*computing*) a set of letters or symbols that are put into or around a piece of data, an image, etc. in order to identify it or show that it is to be treated in a particular way: *You are invited to help describe the photographs on Flickr, either by adding tags or leaving comments.* ◇ *Paragraphs are divided by the p tag, just as in HTML.* **3** [usually sing.] a name or phrase that is used to describe a person or thing in some way: *Television was thought of as a 'window on the world', to use the tag adopted by the BBC's current affairs programme 'Panorama'.*

tag² /tæg/ *verb* (**-gg-**) **1 ~ sth/sb** to attach a tag to identify sth/sb or give information: *13 000 cod were tagged, yielding valuable information on cod migration patterns.* ◇ *The relative level of gene expression in two cell types can be determined by fluorescently tagging mRNA molecules.* **2** (*computing*) to add a set of letters or symbols to a piece of text or data in order to identify it or show that it is to be treated in a particular way: **~ sth** *A learner is trained to tag a document with these five tags.* ◇ **~ sth as sth** *We extracted every instance of words tagged as proper nouns.*

tail /teɪl/ *noun* **1** [C] the part that sticks out and can be moved at the back of the body of a bird, an animal or a fish: *One hypothesis is that females prefer to mate with males that have longer tails.* **2 -tailed** (in adjectives) having the type of tail mentioned: *Carr was able to unravel the complex mating system of white-tailed deer.* **3** [C] the back part of a plane, etc: *Transmitting coils may be mounted in the nose and at the tail of the survey aircraft.* **4** [C] a long part at the back or end of sth: *The pancreas is divided into head, body and tail.* ◇ *The popular conception that a comet's tail streams away behind it is wrong.* HELP In statistics, a **tail** is a long line at the end of a curve on a GRAPH that gradually slopes down towards the horizontal AXIS, or a series of small changes that can be represented by a line like this: *Climatic events are marked by a large change in the ecosystem at the time of the occurrence, followed by a long tail of less obvious adjustments.* **5 tails** [U] the side of a coin that does not have a picture of the head of a person on it: *I cannot say whether a coin will come up heads or tails on a particular toss.* ➲ *compare* HEAD¹ (4)

T

take /teɪk/ *verb* (**took** /tʊk/, **taken** /ˈteɪkən/) **1** [T] **~ sth (to sb/sth)** to carry or move sth from one place to another: *They loaded the fish on carts and took them to the market.* **2** [T] to remove sth/sb from a place or a person: **~ sth/sb + adv./prep.** *Children were able to control the rate of the experiment by taking their hands out of the liquid.* ◇ *The new tax legislation took money away from the poorest households.* ◇ **~ sb's life** *In Europe, a deadly bubonic plague took the lives of up to a quarter of the population.* **3** [T] **~ sth (from sth/sb)** to get sth from a particular source: *Water samples were taken from the river.* ◇ *The data are taken from the 2011 report.* **4** [T] to capture a place or person; to get control of sth: **~ sth (from sb)** *With his more experienced army, Vitellius managed to defeat Otho and take Rome.* ◇ *In 1995, the Republicans took control of the House of Representatives.* ◇ **~ sb prisoner/captive** *In 1944, Lorenz was taken prisoner by the Russian army.* **5** [T] **~ sb (to sth)** to go with sb from one place to another, especially to lead or guide them:

When the police arrived, they took her straight to jail. **6** [T] **~ sb/sth + adv./prep.** to make sb/sth go from one level, situation, etc. to another: *A modest rate of economic growth took living standards in China to a significantly higher level.* **7** [T] **~ sth** to use a particular course of action in order to deal with or achieve sth: *In 1991, the army took action against the independence movement.* ◇ *Specific steps were taken to increase employees' sense of participation in decision-making.* ◇ *Care was taken to minimize any risks.* ◇ *The unions took the lead in the campaign for workplace safety legislation.* ➲ *see also* RISK-TAKING **8** [T] **~ sth** used with nouns to say that sb is doing sth, performing an action, etc: *Patients were advised to take a 30-minute walk every day.* ◇ *He took several deep breaths and tried to keep calm.* ◇ *Employees demanded the right to take regular rest breaks.* **9** [T] (not usually used in the progressive tenses) **~ sth** to have a particular feeling, opinion or attitude: *Constantine also took an active interest in the church's internal life.* ◇ *Hemphill and Hare (2004) took offence at Gendreau et al.'s (2002) criticisms.* ◇ *The judge took a different view.* ◇ *Moreover, Adam Smith often took the side of the poor against the rich.* ◇ *She takes a psychoanalytical approach to the subject.* **10** [T] (not used in the progressive tenses) to consider or understand sth in a particular way: **~ sth** *Taking the average scores, it was found that the results had not changed.* ◇ **~ sth + adv./prep.** *Taken together, the wealth of the 400 richest Americans was equal to the combined assets of the 83 million poorest households in the US.* ◇ **~ sth as sth** *The dismissal of the EU Commission in 1999 can be taken as a sign of this changing balance of power.* ◇ **~ sth to do sth** *Government policy led to allegations of 'privatizing' the welfare state, which is usually taken to mean that commercialism is destroying the welfare ethos.* **11** [T] **~ sb/sth** used to introduce sb/sth as an example: *Taking China as an example, its annual biomass resource amounts to 650 million tons of standard coal.* **12** [T] **~ sth/sb + adv./prep.** to react to sth/sb in a particular way: *Unfortunately, the school did not take these threats of violence seriously.* **13** [T] **~ sth** to have a particular form, position or state: *Payment sometimes took the form of crops or cash.* ◇ *Jose Manuel Barroso took office as European Commission President in late 2004.* ◇ *The welfare of the child took greater priority.* **14** [T] (not usually used in the progressive tenses or in the passive) **~ sth** to accept or receive sth: *In 1937 Beadle took a position at Stanford University as a professor.* ◇ *In the 2008 survey, 61% of respondents said they believed that MPs do not generally take bribes.* ◇ *She took his advice and made significant changes to the novel's structure.* ◇ *Governments increasingly took responsibility for providing assistance to the unemployed.* ◇ *As a young, inexperienced teacher, he found it hard to take criticism.* **15** [T, no passive, I] to need or require a particular amount of time: **~ sth (to do sth)** *The processs took two years to complete.* ◇ *Congress took more time than expected to respond to the rapidly developing crisis.* ◇ **~ sth for sb/sth to do sth** *It took nearly a thousand years for Europe to emerge from the so-called Dark Ages.* ◇ **+ adv.** *It did not take long for scientists around the world to appreciate the significance of the discovery.* **16** [T] **~ sth** to test or measure sth: *A proportion of patients preferred to take their blood pressure in the comfort of their own home.* ◇ *Measurements were taken at the beginning, middle and end of the year.* **17** [T] **~ sth** to find out and record sth; to write sth down: *The secretary took notes of everything that was said during each meeting.* **18** [T] **~ sth** to photograph sb/sth: *These photographs of the town were taken in 1952.* **19** [T] **~ sth** to eat, drink, etc. sth: *Patients were informed of the need to take the medication with food.* **20** [T] **~ sth** to use a particular method to find out people's opinions: *Due to the unprecedented level of disagreement, it was decided to take a vote.* ◇ *A poll of working women taken during the war found that 80 per cent wanted to keep their jobs after the war was over.* **21** [T] **~ sth** to study a subject at school, college, etc: *In Canadian schools, children take classes in how to watch and analyse the media.* **22** [T] **~ sth** to do an exam or a test: *Students had the option of taking the test in English or in Spanish.* **23** [T] **~ sth** to use a form of transport, a road, a path, etc. to go to a place: *When the CEO heard of the success story, he immediately took a plane and flew directly to the factory.* **24** [T] (not used in the progressive tenses) **~ sth** (of verbs, nouns, etc.) to have or require sth when used in a sentence or other structure: *In Italian, a singular masculine noun takes the definite article 'il'.*

IDM Idioms containing **take** are at the entries for the nouns and adjectives in the idioms, for example **take root** is at **root**.

PHR V **ˌtake sb ˈback (to...)** to cause sb to start thinking about or discussing sth, especially sth previously mentioned or sth in the past: *This comment takes us back to a seminal paper published in 1967 by Andrei Sakharov.* **ˌtake sth ˈback** to return a product to the store where you bought it, for example because it is the wrong size or does not work: *This study will focus on customers who reverse a purchase decision by taking a product back.*

ˌtake sth ˈdown 1 to write sth down: *No attempt was made by the police to take down the witness's exact words.* **2** to remove a structure, especially by separating it into pieces: *Part of the scaffolding was then taken down.*

ˌtake sth ˈforward to develop sth such as a plan or an idea, especially by discussing or researching it and planning future actions: *Issues around further European integration were taken forward at the next meeting of European foreign ministers.*

ˌtake sb ˈin [often passive] to make sb believe sth that is not true SYN DECEIVE (1): *The public was not taken in by these false claims.* **ˌtake sth ˈin 1** [no passive] to include or cover sth: *Subsequent research took in a broader range of factors than previous studies.* **2** to understand or remember sth that you hear or read: *A diagnosis generally had to be explained several times before patients could take in all the implications.* **3** to take notice of sth with your eyes: *The study seemed to show that participants could take in the key elements of the scene at a glance.* **4** to absorb sth into the body, for example by breathing or swallowing: *The first assumption was that people need to take in a certain number of calories per day.* ➲ *related noun* INTAKE (1)

ˌtake ˈoff 1 to become successful or popular very quickly or suddenly: *These moves enabled the Social Democrats to take off as a real political force.* **2** (of an aircraft, etc.) to leave the ground and begin to fly: *Planes could not land or take off due to the storm.* OPP LAND[2] **ˌtake sth ˈoff 1** to have a period of time as a break from work: *The pay gap is partly due to the time women take off from paid work in order to raise children.* **2** to remove sth, especially a piece of clothing, from your/sb's body: *The patient was asked to take off his shirt.* OPP PUT STH ON (1)

ˌtake on sth [no passive] to begin to have a particular quality or appearance: *After the attacks, attempts to tighten security took on a new urgency.* **ˌtake sth/sb ˈon 1** to agree to do sth or be responsible for sth/sb: *After her promotion, she took on more of a leadership role within the company.* **2** to oppose or fight sb/sth, especially sb/sth powerful: *The television series 'Decade of Destruction' successfully took on the World Bank.*

ˌtake sth ˈout to obtain a service such as insurance, a loan or an advertisement: *The company took out several large loans but this only led to further financial difficulties.*

ˌtake ˈover (from sth) to become bigger or more important than sth else; to replace sth: *In Norway, timber was the most common bridge-building material until the late nineteenth century when steel and concrete took over.* **ˌtake ˈover (from sb)** | **ˌtake sth ˈover (from sb) 1** to begin to do a job or take responsibility for sth after sb else has stopped doing this: *London employees worked until midnight, when their colleagues in Tokyo took over.* ◇ *During the Second World War, the state took over the management*

T

of the economy. **2** to gain control of a country, etc, usually by force: *The French ruled the Tyrol, which had been taken over from the Austrians in 1805.* ➲ *related noun* TAKEOVER (2)
ˌ**take sth ˈover** to gain control of a business, a company, etc, especially by buying shares: *These newer powerful families took over a variety of businesses in the 1990s (Djankov et al., 2003).* ➲ *related noun* TAKEOVER (1)
ˌ**take sb ˈthrough sth** to help sb learn or become familiar with sth, for example by talking about each part in turn: *The course takes students through all the various processes of scientific inquiry.*
ˈ**take to sth** [no passive] to go to a place, especially to escape or to protest: *Protesters took to the streets in the capital, Budapest.*
ˌ**take ˈup sth** to use or fill an amount of time or space: *The entertaining subplot takes up nearly half the play.* ◇ *It became clear that a vertical format would take up too much space.* ˌ**take sth ˈup 1** to continue sth that has been started or mentioned before: *The ideas of Fisher were then taken up and developed by George Williams (1966).* **2** to start or begin to do sth such as a job: *Williams then took up the position of Professor of ElectroTechnics at the University of Manchester.* ◇ *She also took up the cause of oppressed workers abroad.* **3** to accept sth that is offered or available: *Many researchers took up the challenge to design applications for the new technology.*

take·over /ˈteɪkəʊvə(r); *NAmE* ˈteɪkoʊvər/ *noun* **1** [U, C] an act of taking control of a company by buying most of its shares: *Fending off the threat of hostile takeover becomes a preoccupation in many firms.* ◇ **~ of sth** *This was part of an attempted takeover of the whole group.* ◇ **~ bid** *They made a successful takeover bid for the company.* **2** [C] an act of taking control of a country, an area or a political organization by force: *This led to growing corruption, and ended in a military takeover.*

ˈ**take-up** *noun* [U, sing.] (*especially BrE*) the rate at which people accept sth that is offered or made available to them: *Unfamiliarity is sometimes given as a reason for low take-up.* ◇ **~ of sth** *The take-up of loans is only 10 per cent.*

tale /teɪl/ *noun* **1** a story created using the imagination, especially one that is full of action and adventure: *The fairy tales we read to children include many stories of cruel step-parents, often stepmothers.* ◇ **~ of sth** *Byron's tales of exotic love and adventure quickly won him fame.* **2** an exciting spoken description of an event, which may not be completely true: *Herodotus tells the following tale:...* ◇ **~ of sth** *The first European explorers were met with tales of earthquakes from Native Americans.*

tal·ent /ˈtælənt/ *noun* **1** [C, U] a natural ability to do sth well: *His parents encouraged him to develop his talents as a naturalist.* ◇ *Film-makers had to prove not just that they had talent but that they could work profitably.* ◇ *Some learners seemed to believe that natural talent plays the key role in successful language learning.* ◇ **~ for (doing) sth** *He was a scientist with an obvious talent for popularization.* **2** [U, C] people or a person with a natural ability to do sth well: *The function of this new industry was to recruit the best creative talent.* ◇ *The 'B' film could operate as a training ground for new talents.*

tal·ent·ed /ˈtæləntɪd/ *adj.* having a natural ability to do sth well: *Sakharov was a respected and highly talented physicist.*

talk¹ /tɔːk/ *verb* **1** [I] to say things or have a conversation with sb; to use words in order to give information or to express feelings or ideas: *People often multitask while talking on their cell phones.* ◇ **~ (to/with sb) (about sb/sth)** *This case provides a good example of what I am talking about.* ◇ *During the task, participants were not allowed to talk to each other.* ◇ *Under pressure from his European Allies, President Reagan agreed to meet and talk with Gorbachev.* ◇ **~ of sth** *It is common to talk of trust between organizations, yet it could be argued that organizations are not really things that can trust each other.* **2** [I, T] to use words; to say words in a language: *Although she is a year and a half old, she cannot sit, stand, walk or talk.* ◇ **~ sth** *Sometimes people are uncomfortable around other people because they do not talk the same language, or do the same things.*
PHR V ˌ**talk sth ˈdown** (*rather informal*) to make sth seem less important or successful than it really is: *The media talked down the success of the project.* ˌ**talk ˈdown to sb** to speak to sb as if they were less important or intelligent than you: *Staff are talked down to at meetings and occasionally humiliated if they express criticism.* ˌ**talk sth ˈover (with sb)** to discuss sth thoroughly, especially in order to reach an agreement or make a decision: *These problems should be talked over, and resolved as far as possible.* ◇ *They may sit down and try to think the problem through or talk it over with a friend.* ˌ**talk sb ˈthrough sth** to explain to sb how sth works or should be done so that they can do it or understand it: *Doctors need to be talked through the process of how to break bad news.* ˌ**talk sth ˈthrough** to discuss sth thoroughly until you are sure you understand it: *Spend time listening to patients and talking through anxieties.* ˌ**talk sb/sth ˈup** (*rather informal*) to describe sb/sth in a way that makes them/it sound better, larger or more important than they really are/it really is: *The sense of a Britain in crisis had been talked up intermittently since the OPEC oil crisis of 1972–3.*

talk² /tɔːk/ *noun* **1** [C] an informal speech or lecture on a particular subject: **in a ~** *In this talk I shall try to explain the ideas behind the various possible points of view.* ◇ **~ (on sth)** *Betjeman began giving short talks for the BBC on a range of subjects in the early 1930s.* **2 talks** [pl.] formal discussions between governments or organizations: *The Commission was granted the power to act as sole negotiator for the Community in world trade talks.* ◇ **~ between A and B** *Talks between the two parties failed to produce any movement towards reunification.* ◇ **~ on sth** *Soviet and American negotiators proved unable to make progress in talks on long-range and intermediate-range weapons.* ➲ thesaurus note *at* DISCUSSION **3** [U] (often in compounds) conversation or a way of speaking: *He recorded his classes and analysed how his own classroom talk shaped student interaction and participation.* ◇ **~ about sth** *There seemed to be a common structure beneath talk about a variety of topics.* **4** [U] stories and statements that suggest a particular thing might happen in the future: **~ of sth** *Throughout autumn 2007 and early 2008, there was much talk of future possible price increases.* ◇ **~ of doing sth** *Despite all the talk of maintaining peace, war became a fixture of life.* **5** [C] **~ (with sb)** a conversation or discussion: *These facts were discovered by the author through informal talks with students during class breaks.* ➲ thesaurus note *at* DISCUSSION **6** [U] words that are spoken, but without the necessary facts or actions to support them: *The hatred of Roman rule was not just talk.*

tall /tɔːl/ *adj.* (**tall·er**, **tall·est**) **1** having a greater than average height: *Contemporary descriptions and photographs indicate that Lincoln was a very tall man of around 193 cm.* ◇ *Virtually all the tall buildings in Kuala Lumpur have had to pay particular attention to foundation problems.* ◇ *Rebels would lie in wait in the tall grass.* ➲ *compare* SHORT¹ (4) **2** used to describe or ask about the height of sb/sth: *Men on average are taller than women.* **3 a metre/six feet, etc. ~** used after a measurement to give the height of sb/sth: *Early land plants did not grow more than a metre tall.*
IDM **be a tall ˈorder** (*rather informal*) to be very difficult to do: *Consolidating democracy in the country through elections remains a tall order, though not impossible to deliver.*

tan·dem /ˈtændəm/ *noun*
IDM **in ˈtandem (with sb/sth)** a thing that works or happens **in tandem** with sth else works together with it or happens at the same time as it: *Rapid population growth acts in tandem with climate change to deplete key natural resources, such as water, fuel and soil fertility.*

tan·gent /ˈtændʒənt/ *noun* **1** (*geometry*) a straight line that touches the outside of a curve but does not cross it: *This slope can be found by drawing a tangent to the curve and then measuring the slope of the tangent.* **2** (*abbr.* **tan**) (*mathematics*) the RATIO of the length of the side opposite an angle in a RIGHT-ANGLED triangle to the length of the side next to it: *The mathematics of navigation uses trigonometry, which requires an accurate knowledge of the sine, cosine and tangent of an angle.* ➲ *compare* COSINE, SINE

tan·gen·tial /tænˈdʒenʃl/ *adj.* **1** (*geometry*) of or along a tangent: *Flowing liquids may generate tangential viscous stress.* ◇ **~ to sth** *The reduced friction between the ice and the tyres would cause the car to drive off the road tangential to the curve.* **2 ~ (to sth)** (*formal*) having only a slight or indirect connection with sth: *These are important questions, but only tangential to my interest here.* ■ **tan·gen·tial·ly** /tænˈdʒenʃli/ *adj.*: *The heavier material is thrown tangentially outwards by the system's rotational winds.*

tan·gible /ˈtændʒəbl/ *adj.* **1** [usually before noun] that can be clearly seen to exist: *Some of these policies have produced tangible benefits for children in the developing world.* OPP INTANGIBLE (1) **2** that you can touch and feel: *Software might be downloaded over the Internet so that no tangible objects change hands.* ◇ *Capital, in the form of tangible assets (such as machinery) or intangible assets (such as money), can be a key locational consideration.* OPP INTANGIBLE (2)

tank /tæŋk/ *noun* **1** a large container for holding liquid or gas; the liquid or gas contained in a tank: *Leakage of gasoline from underground storage tanks is a common problem worldwide.* ◇ *a fuel/water tank* ◇ **~ of sth** *The empty bottle has its tube closed and is immersed in a tank of water.* ◇ *The 184-foot yacht is capable of circumnavigating the globe on a single tank of fuel.* **2** a military vehicle covered with strong metal and armed with guns. It can travel over very rough ground using special wheels: *He knew that military bridges had to carry heavy tanks.*

tap¹ /tæp/ *verb* (**-pp-**) **1** [T, I] to make use of a source of energy, knowledge, money, etc. that already exists: **~ sth** *If consumption of fossil fuels decreased, the demand to tap the Alaskan reserve would be unnecessary.* ◇ *Merchants formed trading companies in the hope of tapping wealth from overseas.* ◇ *Many of the wells tap shallow subsurface water.* ◇ **~ into sth** *Memory works by tapping into the neural network necessary to find the information you are trying to remember.* ◇ *The company has been very successful in tapping into this new market.* **2** [T, I] to hit sb/sth quickly and lightly; to hit your fingers, feet, etc. quickly and lightly on a surface: **~ sb/sth** *Some people pace around, tap their feet or fidget when they are anxious.* ◇ **+ adv./prep.** *He was busy tapping away at his computer.*

tap² /tæp/ (*especially BrE*) (*NAmE usually* **faucet**) *noun* a device for controlling the flow of water from a pipe: *They now have access to a community water tap and washing area as part of the programme.* ◇ *The patient says he is finding it difficult to open bottles or turn on taps.*

tape¹ AWL /teɪp/ *noun* **1** [U] a long narrow strip of MAGNETIC material that is used for recording sounds, pictures or information: **on ~** *Data are recorded on magnetic tape at 9600 bpi along each track of nine-track tape.* ◇ *Computer programs were then supplied on some storage device such as a disk or tape.* **2** [C] a plastic case that contains a length of tape; the sounds, or sounds and pictures, that have been recorded on a tape: *This feature allowed a user to copy the contents of one cassette tape onto another.* ◇ *She had her parents and a close friend listen to the tapes.* ◇ **+ noun** *For years, the cassette tape recorder was the accepted medium for recording interviews and focus group sessions.* **3** [U] a long narrow strip of material with a sticky substance on one side that is used for sticking things together: *The electrode was screened from the light source using masking tape.*

tape² AWL /teɪp/ *verb* **~ sb/sth** to record sb/sth on MAGNETIC tape using a special machine: *All sessions were taped with permission and transcribed verbatim for analysis.*

THESAURUS

target • aim • objective • goal • object • end *noun*
These are all words for sth that you are trying to achieve.

- the target/aim/objective/goal/object **of** sth
- **with** the aim/objective/object **of** doing sth
- **for…** ends
- the **major/specific/key/main/primary** targets/aims/objectives/goals
- **short-term** targets/objectives/goals
- **long-term** aims/objectives/goals
- **political/social** aims/objectives/goals/ends
- the/sb's target/aim/objective/goal/object **is to** …
- to **agree (on)/set/meet/reach** a/an target/objective/goal
- to **achieve** a/an target/aim/objective/goal/end
- to **attain** a/an target/objective/goal/end

- A **target** is usually a fairly short-term result that you are trying to achieve; it is usually officially recorded in some way, for example by an employer or a government committee; it is likely to involve specific numbers or amounts: *Managers had strong incentives to attain targets.*
- People often set their own **aims** or **objectives**; these are things that they wish to achieve, often as part of a project or piece of writing. A **goal** may be more long-term and relate to a person's life, study or career plans or to the long-term plans of a company or an organization: *The aim of this chapter is to describe the methods used in the collection of the data.* ◇ *In cooperative learning, the objective is to engage groups of learners in accomplishing mutual learning goals.*
- The **object** of an activity is its purpose; **ends** are a particular kind of purpose. The term **ends** is sometimes (but not always) used to suggest disapproval of sb's aims or their reasons for doing sth: *The object of the exercise is to understand the factors driving the business cycle.* ◇ *The author suggests that Constantine simply used Christianity for his own political ends.* ◇ *They are all working to achieve the same ends.*

tar·get¹ AWL /ˈtɑːɡɪt; *NAmE* ˈtɑːrɡɪt/ *noun* **1** a result that you try to achieve: *Asset purchases were intended to boost spending and so help to meet the inflation target.* ◇ **against a ~** *The government itself publicly sets targets against which to monitor its own performance.* ◇ **~ for sth** *The participating states could not agree to a legally binding set of targets for the reduction of gas emissions.* ◇ **~ of sth** *Within weeks of the product being launched, the first-year target of 30 000 sales had been exceeded.* ◇ **above/below (the, its, etc.) ~** *The organization's total UK membership of 322 845 in 1954 was well below its target of 470 000.* ◇ **on ~** *The inflation rate was on target at 2%.* **2** an object, a person or a place that people direct sth towards, such as an attack, advertising, etc: *In 1941 work began on a radar system to help bombers find their targets.* ◇ **~ for sb/sth** *Their unoccupied homes make tempting daytime targets for burglars.* ◇ **~ of sb/sth** *The nuclear industry has long been a target of environmental campaigners.* ◇ *Women are the primary targets of the cosmetic surgery industry.* ◇

T

+ noun *Twenty-nine randomly selected students from the target audience completed the pre-resource assessment.* HELP **Target** is frequently used before another noun. In linguistics, the **target language** is a language you are learning or translating into: *Teachers were asked to speak the target language as much as possible.* In genetics, a **target gene/protein/sequence** is the gene, etc. being studied: *First, the target gene is cloned using an E. coli host which does not contain the T7 polymerase gene.* In biology, a **target cell** is a cell in the body which responds to a particular HORMONE or chemical MESSENGER: *The action of the hormone on a target cell implies the existence of a specific hormone receptor.*

▸ ADJECTIVE + TARGET **specific • main, primary • important** *Even though a specific target for blood pressure will be set, the message to the patient must always be 'lower, lower, lower'.* | **potential • easy • prime • intended • legitimate** *These enzymes are potential targets for cytotoxic drugs.*

▸ NOUN + TARGET **inflation • performance • sales** *Senior managers often spoke of a persistent failure to achieve performance targets.*

▸ VERB + TARGET **reach • hit** *The sales department is desperate to hit its sales targets.* | **set • meet, achieve** *There is pressure on hospitals to achieve set waiting-time targets.* | **become • identify • provide** *Since the late 1990s, a number of transnational companies have become the targets of anti-globalization protesters.*

▸ TARGET + NOUN **audience • market • group • population** *The target population of the survey is children 19–35 months of age living in US households.*

tar·get[2] AWL /ˈtɑːɡɪt; *NAmE* ˈtɑːrɡɪt/ *verb* (**tar·get·ing, tar·get·ed, tar·get·ed**) [often passive] **1** to try to have an effect on a particular group of people: **~ sb** *The claim is that tobacco companies use marketing strategies that specifically target low-income groups.* ◇ **be targeted at sb** *Many parts of the book are targeted at a more advanced readership.* ◇ **be targeted to sb** *Public relations activities can be targeted to a small specialized audience if the right media vehicle is used.* ◇ **be targeted for sth** *People with a diagnosis of mental illness are rarely targeted for health promotion initiatives.* **2 ~ sb/sth** to aim an attack or a criticism at sb/sth: *Children with disabilities are often targeted by bullies.* ◇ *Putnam's critique has targeted classical theories of international relations.* **3** to direct money or resources towards a particular thing or group of people: **be targeted at sb/sth** *Scarce resources can be targeted at only those aspects of the service that are perceived as being of the greatest importance.* **4** (*biology*) to try to have an effect on a particular thing; to direct sth to a particular location: **~ sth (for sth)** *Proteins targeted for destruction are fed into a multiprotein complex where they are degraded by enzymes.* ◇ **~ sth to sth** *Modification of the lipid parts generally target these proteins to the cell membrane.*

tar·iff /ˈtærɪf/ *noun* **1** a tax that is paid on goods coming into or going out of a country: *Export-oriented industries had been damaged by protective tariffs.* ◇ **~ on sth** *The government imposed high tariffs on all imported goods.* ◇ **+ noun** *Rules were drawn up to facilitate the trade of health-related goods, notably through tariff reductions.* **2** a payment or level of payment: *The government intended to reduce the feed-in tariffs paid to renewable energy installations.*

task AWL /tɑːsk; *NAmE* tæsk/ *noun* a piece of work that has to be done: **~ (to do sth)** *It would be a relatively simple task to identify the documents.* ◇ *In the comprehension task, subjects were asked whether the words were in a meaningful order.* ◇ **~ of sb/sth** *It is a task of future research to analyse whether these differences can be confirmed.* ◇ **~ of (doing) sth** *Practitioners have the crucial task of working out the programme elements.* ◇ **+ noun** *Body size is correlated with task performance in insects such as ants.*

IDM **take sb to ˈtask (for sth/for doing sth)** to criticize sb for sth: *Thompson (2004) takes Fournier and Grey to task for ignoring the politics of the workplace.*

▸ ADJECTIVE + TASK **difficult • ambitious • demanding, challenging, arduous • daunting, formidable • impossible • complex, complicated • time-consuming • urgent** *The calculation is a fairly arduous task.* ◇ *It was a challenging task the company was facing, as it meant that it had to develop the system in twelve months.* | **easy, simple, straightforward • trivial • repetitive • routine • everyday • daily • ongoing** *It was not an easy task to embark on a new path.* | **main, principal • major • important • essential • crucial • primary • central, core • basic • specific, particular • specialized** *One of the main tasks of personality theory is to make accurate predictions of an individual's behaviour.* | **cognitive • functional • interactive • productive • administrative • managerial • regulatory • academic • experimental • developmental • manual • domestic** *One experimental task required subjects to estimate various quantities.*

▸ NOUN + TASK **comprehension • decision, decision-making • classification, categorization • selection • problem-solving • memory • learning • communication • research • management • production • household** *Household tasks were predominantly women's responsibilities.*

▸ VERB + TASK **set, assign • design • complicate • simplify • automate • delegate • manage • facilitate** *Tasks were assigned according to age and sex.* | **face, be faced with • handle • approach • undertake, take on • engage in • accomplish, perform, execute, carry out, do • complete, finish • fulfil • solve** *They are incapable of accomplishing daily tasks on their own.*

▸ NOUN + OF TASK(S) **variety, range • number • series • nature • complexity • performance • completion** *They changed the nature of the task from a complex decision-making task to a simple reporting task.*

ˈtask force *noun* a group of people who are brought together to deal with a particular problem: *A task force was set up to tackle health inequalities.*

taste[1] /teɪst/ *noun* **1** [C, U] the flavour that is experienced and recognized by people or animals when a particular food or drink touches their mouth or tongue: *Limoncello is a liqueur with a sweet lemony taste that is not sour.* ◇ *The defence systems of plants have various components, for example thorns, hard structures, hairy leaves, bitter taste, etc.* ◇ **~ of sth** *Two genes appear to be involved in how one perceives the taste of ethanol.* **2** [U] the sense that allows people or animals to recognize different foods and drinks when they touch their mouth or tongue: *In many animals, the key senses of taste and smell have evolved in this way.* **3** [C, U] what sb likes or prefers: *Consumer tastes change quickly.* ◇ **a matter of (...) ~** *Whether Constable is a better painter than Picasso is largely a matter of taste.* ◇ *Which method you choose is a matter of personal taste.* ◇ **~ of sb** *Bourdieu carried out extensive research into the habits and tastes of social classes in France in the 1970s.* ◇ **~ in sth** *His taste in music was linked to his political convictions.* ◇ **~ for sth** *By this time, Europeans had developed a taste for American goods and wanted to import more of them.* ◇ **to the ~ of sb| to sb's ~** *The new styles of painting were not to the taste of traditionalists.* **4** [U] the ability to recognize what is right or appropriate: *These rights need to be balanced with considerations of taste and decency.* ◇ **(in) good/bad ~** *Glorifying the war in a video game demonstrates very poor judgement and bad taste.* **5** [sing.] **~ of sth** a short experience of sth: *These early publications gave the country its first taste of journalism.*

taste[2] /teɪst/ *verb* (not used in the progressive tenses) **1** *linking verb* **+ adj.** to have a particular flavour: *These compounds frequently taste bitter.* ◇ *The wines taste quite different from one another.* **2** [T] **~ sth** to recognize

T

flavours in food and drink: *Studies suggest that chickens cannot taste sugar.* **3** [T] **~ sth** to eat or drink a small amount of sth and experience its flavour: *Each panellist was asked to taste the samples in the order presented.* **4** [T] **~ sth** to experience sth: *Following a period of difficulty at the end of 1949, the group finally tasted success.*

taught *past tense, past part. of* TEACH

tax¹ /tæks/ *noun* [C, U] money that people have to pay to the government so that it can pay for public services: HELP People pay tax according to their income and businesses pay tax according to their profits. Tax is also often paid on goods and services: *A law was proposed to abolish highway tolls and introduce a fuel tax.* ◇ **pay tax/taxes** *All families that paid income tax and had a child under 16 were eligible to receive this benefit.* ◇ **levy/impose taxes/a tax** *The system was designed to benefit small producers by imposing lower taxes on lower volumes of production.* ◇ **high/low taxes** *Another unpopular measure needed to reduce carbon emissions would be much higher taxes on air travel.* ◇ **~ on sth** *They pay tax on their taxable income.* ◇ **before/after ~** *Accounting profits before tax were 2 800 million pounds.* ◇ **in ~** *The amount paid in tax will increase.* ◇ **through/via taxes** *Research institutes were largely funded from the public purse via taxes.* ◇ **~ rate** *The income tax rate for Singapore resident individuals is tiered, subject to a maximum of 20 per cent.* ◇ **~ cut/increase** *Voters are often won over by promises of tax cuts and tax rebates.* ◇ **~ revenue** *As people's incomes fall, the state's tax revenues will also fall.* ⮌ *see also* INCOME TAX

tax² /tæks/ *verb* **~ sb/sth** to put a tax on sth; to make sb pay tax: *They tax some individuals at higher rates than others.* ◇ *Governments normally tax the net income of firms in their jurisdictions.*

tax·ation /tæk'seɪʃn/ *noun* [U] **1** money that has to be paid as taxes: *The government had been able to reduce direct taxation.* **2** the system of collecting money by taxes: *This system of taxation was regarded as efficient and equitable.*

tax·onomy /tæk'sɒnəmi; *NAmE* tæk'sɑːnəmi/ *noun* (*pl.* **-ies**) **1** [C] **~ (of sth)** a particular system of CLASSIFYING things (= arranging them into groups): *Research on taxonomies of technical occupations is just beginning to emerge.* **2** [U] the scientific process of CLASSIFYING things: *Since the genome is contained in almost every cell, DNA taxonomy can be applied to partial specimens.* ■ **taxo·nom·ic** /ˌtæksə'nɒmɪk; *NAmE* ˌtæksə'nɑːmɪk/ *adj.*: *Tasmanian tigers are actually marsupials, belonging in the same taxonomic group as kangaroos and koalas.*

T

tax·pay·er /'tækspeɪə(r)/ *noun* a person who pays tax to the government, especially on the money that they earn: *It has recently been announced in the budget that taxpayers submitting income tax returns electronically will qualify for a (small) discount.* ◇ **the ~** *The cost to the taxpayer of this policy is $465 million.*

teach /tiːtʃ/ *verb* (**taught**, **taught** /tɔːt/) **1** [T] to help sb learn sth or learn how to do sth, by providing information or opportunites to experience things: **~ sth** *Films have the potential to teach important lessons about the prevention of conflict.* ◇ **~ sb sth** *The women had an influential role in teaching the children the value of rural life.* ◇ **~ sth to sb** *These programmes teach thinking skills to high-risk youths.* ◇ **~ sb to do sth** *One response is to teach learners to distinguish between 'generalized' and 'specialized' technical vocabulary.* ◇ **~ sb how/what, etc...** *The training session teaches people how to achieve their personal goals.* ◇ **~ sb that...** *Further observation taught them that this was not, in fact, the case.* ◇ **~ sb about sth** *The process teaches students about conflict resolution.* **2** [I, T] to give lessons to students, for example in a school, college or university: *One of the teachers interviewed was teaching in a middle school.* ◇ **~ sb** *He preferred teaching adults to teaching children.* ◇ *The two groups are taught separately.* ◇ **~ sth** *Dutch is the official language and is taught in schools.* ◇ **~ sth to sb** *The teacher was teaching history to a Year 10 group of largely unmotivated students.* **3** [T] to state that sth is true; to present sth as real or necessary: **~ that...** *Plato and his followers taught that the soul was immaterial.* ◇ **~ sth** *The Church teaches deference to authority.* ◇ **~ sb to do sth** *The party and the population had been taught to regard Stalin almost as a god.*

teach·er /'tiːtʃə(r)/ *noun* a person who teaches, especially a person whose job is to teach in a school: *The programme encouraged qualified people to become teachers and to remain in the educational system.* ◇ *an English/a history, etc. teacher* ◇ **~ of sth** *This is an indispensable resource for students and teachers of Renaissance literature.* ◇ **primary/secondary (school) ~** *The data were gathered from trainee secondary school teachers in Germany.* ◇ **~ education/training** *The development officers are supported by the university's department of teacher training.*

teach·ing /'tiːtʃɪŋ/ *noun* **1** [U] the work of a teacher: *She opted for a career in teaching.* ◇ *Questions were raised about how resources for language teaching should best be allocated.* ◇ **+ noun** *The next decade saw the range of teaching materials expand, particularly with increased use of the Internet.* **2** [C, usually pl., U] the ideas of a particular person or group, especially about politics, religion or society, that are taught to other people: *Buddhist/Christian/Jewish teachings* ◇ *Islamic finance is about how to conduct business in accordance with religious teaching.* ◇ **~ of sb/sth** *Mass socialist parties were formed, which subscribed to the teaching of Karl Marx.* ◇ **~ on sth** *A clear and consistent set of teachings on modern issues has emerged.*

team AWL /tiːm/ *noun* [C+sing./pl. v.] **1** a group of people who work together at a particular job: *The research team was able to advise on how the training should be organized.* ◇ *He was supported by a small multidisciplinary team.* ◇ **~ of sb** *A team of researchers carried out structured interviews with employers and employees.* ◇ **in a ~** *Students worked in teams to complete the background research.* ◇ **a member of a/the ~** *After she and other members of the team had piloted the interview schedule, they decided that it was not sufficiently structured.* ◇ **~ member** *Support from team members for each other is important.* ◇ **+ noun** *Team working is an essential aspect of primary health care.* **2** a group of people who play a particular game or sport against another group of people: *College and high school sports teams in the United States often receive huge support from local people.*

team·work /'tiːmwɜːk; *NAmE* 'tiːmwɜːrk/ *noun* [U] the activity of working well together as a team: *Teamwork should be encouraged.* ◇ **+ noun** *The cooperative learning groups are taught teamwork skills.*

tear¹ /teə(r); *NAmE* ter/ *verb* (**tore** /tɔː(r)/, **torn** /tɔːn; *NAmE* tɔːrn/) **1** [T, I] to damage sth by pulling it apart or into pieces or by cutting it on sth sharp; to become damaged in this way: *The paper tapes tended to stretch and tear.* ◇ **~ sth** *Fig. 5.3 shows irreversible stretching induced by tearing a polyethylene sheet.* ◇ **~ (sth) + adv./prep.** *Muscle injuries rarely tear a muscle in two.* **2** [T] **~ sth + adv./prep.** to remove sth from sth else by pulling it violently: *He then tore off his disguise and revealed his true identity.* **3 -torn** (in adjectives) very badly affected or damaged by sth: *Foreign aid has brought relief to millions who live in war-torn and impoverished regions.*

IDM **tear sb/sth aˈpart, to ˈpieces, etc.** to destroy or defeat sb/sth completely: *New democracies are easily torn apart by political controversies.* ◇ *Finally, the republic was torn to pieces by rival power-hungry tribunes.* **be torn (between A and B)** to be unable to decide or choose between two people, things or feelings: *She was torn between her desire to compete and her desire to please her parents.*

PHR V ˌ**tear sth aˈpart** **1** to destroy sth violently, especially by pulling it to pieces: *The earthquake tore apart the region's transportation systems.* **2** to make people in a country, an organization or other place fight or argue with each other: *It is a society that is torn apart by ethnic and religious rivalries.* ˌ**tear sth ˈdown** to destroy a building, wall, etc: *Many residents wanted to remain but their homes were torn down.* ˌ**tear sth ˈup** **1** to destroy a document, etc. by tearing it into pieces: *She tore up papers on his desk and did other damage.* ◇ (*figurative*) *Officials were reluctant to take the matter any further because of the threat to tear up the agreement.* **2** to remove or destroy a tree, building, etc, usually violently: *Long lengths of railway track had been torn up.*

tear[2] /teə(r); *NAmE* ter/ *noun* **~ (in sth)** damage or a hole in sth made by tearing: *Such fractures can cause tears in the membranes surrounding the brain.* IDM *see* WEAR[2]

tear[3] /tɪə(r); *NAmE* tɪr/ *noun* [usually pl.] a drop of liquid that comes out of your eye when you cry: *The penitents were expected to shed tears, to wear sackcloth and to ask publicly for forgiveness.* ◇ *Those who witnessed this touching scene had tears in their eyes.*

tech·nical AWL /ˈteknɪkl/ *adj.* **1** [usually before noun] connected with the use of science or technology; involving the use of machines: *Capital investment and technical innovations produced new infrastructures.* ◇ *At that time, technical change was revolutionizing production.* **2** [usually before noun] connected with a particular type of activity, or the skills and processes needed for it: *Some issues require technical knowledge that few people have.* ◇ **highly ~** *Self-regulation plays a significant role in highly technical areas such as industrial standardization.* **3** [usually before noun] (of language, writing or ideas) requiring knowledge and understanding of a particular subject: *No attempt is made to explain the technical terms used.* ◇ *Section 4 introduces subject matter of a somewhat more technical nature.* **4** connected with the details of a law or set of rules: *The more technical aspects of the law relating to appeals are outside the scope of this study.*

▸ TECHNICAL + NOUN **matter** ♦ **aspect** ♦ **detail** ♦ **reason** ♦ **complexity** ♦ **support, assistance, help** ♦ **advice** ♦ **information** ♦ **cooperation** ♦ **difficulty, problem** ♦ **issue** ♦ **challenge** ♦ **solution** ♦ **feasibility** ♦ **efficiency** ♦ **sophistication** *The technical assistance from the World Bank ended in 2009.* ◇ *We encountered various technical difficulties with recording interviews.* | **change** ♦ **development** ♦ **progress, advance** ♦ **innovation** ♦ **information** ♦ **means** ♦ **specifications** ♦ **standards** ♦ **procedure** *A full array of technical specifications for the wind energy sector will be developed.* | **expert** ♦ **staff, team** ♦ **adviser** ♦ **worker** ♦ **work** ♦ **education, training** ♦ **school, college, institute** ♦ **subject** *In the curricula, practical and technical subjects were emphasized.* | **knowledge** ♦ **expertise** ♦ **skill** ♦ **competence** ♦ **capability, ability** ♦ **know-how** *The pressure of acquiring technical skill sometimes prevents dancers from exploring the aesthetic concepts of their art.* | **nature** ♦ **sense** ♦ **meaning** ♦ **language** ♦ **vocabulary** ♦ **jargon** ♦ **term** ♦ **definition** ♦ **report** *The term 'perspective' is used here in a technical sense.*

tech·nic·al·ly AWL /ˈteknɪkli/ *adv.* **1** in a way that is connected with the use of science or technology; in a way that involves the use of machines: *This was probably not technically feasible at the time.* ◇ *An ordinary citizen in any of the technically advanced countries has opportunities not available to kings in earlier centuries.* **2** in a way that involves the skills and processes needed for a particular activity: *Handling such small volumes of liquid is technically challenging.* **3** according to the exact meaning or facts SYN STRICTLY, STRICTLY SPEAKING: *The child is not technically a witness and should not be cross-examined.* ◇ *Technically, a species can have only one scientific name, although it may be known by any number of 'common names'.* ◇ **~ speaking** *A dolphin is technically speaking a mammal, but superficially appears more similar to a fish.*

tech·ni·cian /tekˈnɪʃn/ *noun* a person whose job is looking after technical equipment or doing practical technical work, for example in a laboratory: *The quality and amount of the reagents, as well as the skill of the laboratory technicians, can significantly affect results.* ◇ *She had worked in hospitals as a medical technician and researcher.*

tech·nique AWL /tekˈniːk/ *noun* **1** [C] a particular way of doing sth that involves using a special skill or process: *The company implemented new selling techniques.* ◇ *The design can be made robust using the techniques discussed in section 2.5.* ◇ **~ for (doing) sth** *The same mathematical techniques for constructing the images are used in newer forms of scanning.* ◇ **~ of sth** *These disciplines are continually developing new techniques of analysis.* ◇ **~ in sth** *This section discusses the principal approaches and techniques in the analysis of population growth.* **2** [U, sing.] a person's skill or ability in a particular activity: *The actors welcomed these opportunities to work on their technique.* ◇ *Good experimental technique can reduce variation, but it will rarely completely remove it.*

▸ ADJECTIVE + TECHNIQUE **basic, simple** ♦ **common** ♦ **traditional** ♦ **conventional, standard** ♦ **formal** ♦ **different** ♦ **alternative** ♦ **new** ♦ **innovative, novel** ♦ **modern** ♦ **advanced** ♦ **sophisticated** ♦ **special** ♦ **specialized** ♦ **appropriate** ♦ **useful** ♦ **effective** ♦ **powerful** *This is a sophisticated technique for dealing with change at a personal or group level.* | **experimental** ♦ **analytical** ♦ **diagnostic** ♦ **qualitative** ♦ **quantitative** ♦ **numerical** ♦ **statistical** ♦ **mathematical** ♦ **computational** ♦ **participatory** ♦ **surgical** *A range of analytical techniques has made it possible to date land surfaces.*

▸ NOUN + TECHNIQUE **relaxation** ♦ **imaging** ♦ **dating** ♦ **modelling** ♦ **sampling** ♦ **measurement** ♦ **management** ♦ **production** ♦ **marketing** ♦ **interviewing** *New dating techniques have enabled some generalizations to be put forward.*

▸ VERB + TECHNIQUE **devise, design** ♦ **develop** ♦ **refine, improve** ♦ **pioneer** ♦ **introduce** ♦ **teach** ♦ **apply** ♦ **adopt, implement** ♦ **employ, use, utilize** ♦ **practise** ♦ **learn, master** ♦ **combine** *The group claimed to have pioneered a new technique.*

▸ TECHNIQUE + PAST PARTICIPLE **described** ♦ **discussed** ♦ **outlined** ♦ **based on** *Some of the techniques outlined here are fairly straightforward.*

▸ NOUN + OF + TECHNIQUE(S) **variety** ♦ **range** ♦ **number** ♦ **use** ♦ **application** ♦ **development** ♦ **limitation** ♦ **effectiveness** *With the development of techniques to manipulate genetic material and reintroduce it into cells, it has become possible to study biochemical pathways as never before.*

tech·no·logic·al AWL /ˌteknəˈlɒdʒɪkl; *NAmE* ˌteknəˈlɑːdʒɪkl/ *adj.* [usually before noun] connected with or using technology: *Technological progress has undoubtedly reduced the unit cost of products.* ◇ *Individuals are finding their skills becoming obsolete because of the pace of technological change.* ◇ *It was a remarkable period of scientific and technological innovation.* ■ **tech·no·logic·al·ly** AWL /ˌteknəˈlɒdʒɪkli; *NAmE* ˌteknəˈlɑːdʒɪkli/ *adv.*: *During the past half-century, biological sciences have been changing the world, scientifically, technologically and socially.* ◇ *Even the largest, most technologically advanced countries cannot provide strong innovation systems to all their industries.*

tech·nol·ogy AWL /tekˈnɒlədʒi; *NAmE* tekˈnɑːlədʒi/ *noun* (*pl.* -ies) [U, C, usually pl.] equipment, machines and

T

processes that are developed using knowledge of engineering and science; the knowledge used in developing them: *Technology is changing the way children learn.* ◇ *The key is to use technology to enhance the customer experience.* ◇ *The Internet and digital technologies have enabled new interactive forms of communication.* ◇ *The revolution in communication technology may further accelerate these processes.* ◇ **~ for (doing) sth** *The technology for accomplishing regeneration is complex.* ◇ **use, etc. of ~** *The civilian use of this military technology turned out to be one of the most important and unexpected growth areas in the late 1990s.* ◇ **~ of sth** *There were massive production increases in much of the less-developed world through new technologies of production.* ➲ *see also* HIGH-TECH, INFORMATION TECHNOLOGY

▸ ADJECTIVE + TECHNOLOGY **existing, current • available • new, novel • modern • innovative • the latest, state-of-the-art • emerging • advanced, sophisticated • next-generation • foreign, imported • expensive • efficient • clean • low-carbon • renewable** *The first approach basically develops the existing technologies.* ◇ *Advanced technology permits humans to reduce their environmental impact.* | **digital • electronic • wireless • nuclear • military • agricultural • medical • reproductive • alternative** *Alternative technologies may offer a more cost-effective manufacturing process.*

▸ NOUN + TECHNOLOGY **communication(s) • mobile • Internet • computer • production** *At the end of the 1970s, new computer technology was introduced into printing.*

▸ VERB + TECHNOLOGY **invent • develop • adapt • be based on • embrace • acquire • adopt • introduce • import • use, employ, utilize, deploy • integrate, incorporate • exploit • license • transfer** *In the 1970s, the USA planned a military navigation system that was based on satellite technology.* ◇ *Private firms transfer technology to developing countries in three ways:...*

▸ TECHNOLOGY + VERB **enable, facilitate, permit, allow • enhance • change, evolve • advance** *In the twentieth century, new technologies facilitated worldwide communication.*

▸ TECHNOLOGY + NOUN **policy • infrastructure • adoption • upgrading • transfer • diffusion • frontier • gap** *The issue of international technology transfer is high on the political agenda.*

▸ NOUN + OF TECHNOLOGY **advent • emergence • availability • adoption • introduction • implementation • use, deployment • application • development • diffusion • transfer • impact** *The advent of wireless technology meant that remotely located laptops could also tap into the database.*

▸ NOUN + IN TECHNOLOGY **advances • innovation • developments • improvements • revolution • investment** *Advances in technology now made it possible to view previously invisible planets and stars.*

tec·ton·ic /tek'tɒnɪk; *NAmE* tek'tɑːnɪk/ *adj.* [only before noun] (*earth science*) connected with the structure of the earth's surface and the processes that take place within it: *Most earthquakes occur at the margins of tectonic plates.* ◇ *The Middle Cambrian was a time with almost no tectonic activity.* ➲ *see also* PLATE TECTONICS

teen·age /'tiːneɪdʒ/ (*also rather informal* **teen** /tiːn/ *especially in NAmE*) *adj.* [usually before noun] between 13 and 19 years old; connected with people of this age: *Another study found that teenage girls used the Internet less than did teenage boys.* ◇ *The UK has the highest rate of teenage pregnancies in Europe.*

teen·ager /'tiːneɪdʒə(r)/ (*also rather informal* **teen** /tiːn/ *especially in NAmE*) *noun* a person who is between 13 and 19 years old: *Traditional systems of educating children and teenagers changed.*

teens /tiːnz/ *noun* [pl.] the years of a person's life when they are between 13 and 19 years old: *The group comprised young people in their teens and early twenties.* ◇ *These people ranged in age from the late teens to the 80s.*

teeth *pl. of* TOOTH

tele·com·mu·ni·ca·tions /ˌtelikəˌmjuːnɪ'keɪʃnz/ (*also informal* **tele·coms** /'telikɒmz; *NAmE* ˌtelikɑːmz/) *noun* [pl.] the technology of sending signals, images and messages over long distances by radio, telephone, television, SATELLITE, etc: *In the US in the 1970s, monopolies in telecommunications and transportation were broken up.* ◇ **+ noun** *There has been a growth in importance of the information and telecommunications industries.* ■ **tele·com·mu·ni·ca·tion** (*also informal* **tele·com** /'telikɒm; *NAmE* 'telikɑːm/) *adj.* [only before noun] *Markets characterized by inertia include energy supply, telecommunication services and banks.*

tele·phone /'telɪfəʊn; *NAmE* 'telɪfoʊn/ *noun* [C, U] an electronic device that people use for talking to other people over long distances; the system that makes this possible SYN PHONE: *mobile/cellular/wireless/landline telephones* ◇ *The patient struggles to lift anything and is too weak even to use the telephone.* ◇ **by/via ~** *Interviews were conducted via telephone.* ◇ **on/over the ~** *They were unavailable to talk on the telephone.* ◇ **+ noun** *Marketing messages were delivered by direct mail, telephone calls, emails and text messages.*

tele·scope /'telɪskəʊp; *NAmE* 'telɪskoʊp/ *noun* a piece of equipment shaped like a tube, containing LENSES, that you look through to make objects that are far away appear larger and nearer: *Stars, in general, cannot be resolved even by the most powerful telescopes.* ◇ *He looked for comets and asteroids through a telescope and calculated their orbits.*

tele·vi·sion /'telɪvɪʒn/ *noun* (*abbr.* **TV**) **1** [U] the system and business of broadcasting pictures and sounds using electronic signals and creating programmes for people to watch: *digital/satellite/cable television* ◇ **on ~** *They maintain that watching violence on television leads to aggressive behaviour among children.* ◇ **+ noun** *a television channel/station* ◇ *A ban on advertising during children's television programmes is being considered.* ◇ *He was the winner of the Channel 4 'Big Brother' reality television series.* **2** [U] the programmes that are broadcast on television: *Evidence suggests that people are watching more television than ever before.* ◇ **+ noun** *Families were asked about their television viewing habits.* **3** (*also* **television set**) [C] a piece of electrical equipment with a screen on which people watch programmes that are broadcast: *flat-screen/high-definition televisions* ◇ *The average American household had its television set on for six hours a day.*

tell /tel/ *verb* (**told, told** /təʊld; *NAmE* toʊld/) **1** [T] to give information to sb by speaking or writing; to express sth in words: **~ sb** *Delighted customers told friends and customer numbers grew.* ◇ **~ sb about sth** *The applicants were told in detail about the work that they would be doing.* ◇ **~ sb of sth** *Patients should always be told of the potential risks involved.* ◇ **~ sb sth** *If the clinician never tells the patient anything, it is no wonder if the patient fails to return.* ◇ **~ sb + speech** *Truman reportedly told one colleague: 'You know I'm against this.'* ◇ **~ sb (that)...** *Doctors told his parents that he might never walk again.* ◇ *Everyone, Freud tells us, has at least some grasp of everyday conscious thought.* ◇ **~ sb how/where, etc...** *Good management depends on telling the patient how to obtain help quickly if needed.* ◇ **~ the truth** *Some of these novels not only told the truth about the past, but also tried to explain it.* ◇ **~ a story** *Students will want to tell their story to trusted adults.* **2** [T] to order or advise sb to do sth: **~ sb to do sth** *She was told to take time off and rest.* ◇ **~ sb that...** *No one told them that they should inform the authorities.* **3** [T] to show sth; to give information about sb/sth: **~ sb sth** *This equation tells us something interesting.* ◇ **~ sb (that)...**

T

Experience told him that the sessions would not be well attended. ◇ *Anger is a signal that tells us something is wrong.* ◇ **~ sb how/where, etc...** *The laws of thermodynamics tell us how much work can be generated.* **4** [T, I] (not used in the progressive tenses) to know, see or judge sth correctly; to see the difference between one thing or person and another: **~ sth** *Light travels in lines that are so nearly straight that we cannot tell the difference.* ◇ **(it is easy, hard, etc. to) ~ what/whether, etc...** *It is still too early to tell what all of these changes in staff will mean for company policy.* ◇ **~ A from B** *The inability to tell green from red is not uncommon.* ◇ **~ A and B apart** *It is only possible to them apart by examining them under a microscope.* IDM *see* TIME[1], TRUTH

PHR V **'tell of (doing) sth** to make sth known; to report sth: *The story tells of the adventures of a cheeky young boy in a small village.*

tem·per·ate /'tempərət/ *adj.* [usually before noun] (*technical*) **1** (of a region or climate) not having extreme temperatures; never very hot or very cold: *The plants flourished in temperate latitudes.* ◇ *In temperate zones, such adaptations are rare.* **2** growing or living in an area that is never very hot or very cold: *Temperate deciduous forests are the dominant vegetation of southern Appalachia.* ◇ *Studies on temperate bat species have found that many species have very specific roosting preferences.*

tem·pera·ture /'temprətʃə(r); *NAmE also* 'temprətʃʊr/ *noun* (*abbr.* **temp**) **1** [C, U] the measurement in degrees of how hot or cold a thing or place is: *Low temperatures result in slow plant growth.* ◇ *There was no change in temperature.* ◇ **~ of sth** *From its core to its surface, the temperature of the earth varies by several thousand degrees.* ◇ **+ noun** *Nearly all structures are exposed to temperature change during their lifetimes.* ➲ *see also* ROOM TEMPERATURE **2** [C, U] the measurement of how hot sb's body is: *He developed abdominal pain and a high temperature.* ◇ **~ of sb/sth** *On examination, she has a temperature of 39.2°C.* ◇ **body ~** *Body temperature should be monitored throughout.* ◇ **take your/sb's ~** *He has felt generally unwell but has not taken his temperature.*

▸ ADJECTIVE + TEMPERATURE **high • low • average, mean • constant • maximum • ambient • global • potential • annual** *Towards the poles, average temperatures decline further.*

▸ NOUN + TEMPERATURE **air • water • fluid • sea • room • surface • melting • operating** *These winds can raise air temperatures by 10 degrees within 15–20 minutes.*

▸ VERB + TEMPERATURE **increase, raise • reduce, lower, decrease • reach • maintain • measure • record • estimate • calculate • control • experience • indicate • predict • withstand** *Reducing the temperature rapidly will slow the reaction significantly.*

▸ TEMPERATURE + VERB **rise, increase • fall, decrease, drop • vary • range • reach • exceed • remain • affect, influence** *Temperatures will rise fastest in the northern hemisphere.* ◇ *Water temperatures here rarely exceed 2°C.*

▸ TEMPERATURE + NOUN **difference • change, variation, fluctuation • gradient • range • increase, rise • lapse • dependence • profile • coefficient • ratio • scale • inversion • measurement • record** *There is a smaller seasonal temperature range in the North American continent.*

▸ NOUN + IN TEMPERATURE **change, variation, fluctuation • difference • increase, rise • decrease, reduction, drop, fall** *The largest differences in temperature are between the equatorial regions and the poles.*

tem·plate /'templeɪt/ *noun* **1** something that is used as a model for producing other similar examples of sth: *What is revealed is a range of strategies, rather than a standard template.* ◇ **~ for sth** *The procedures might serve as a template for future risk research.* ◇ **~ of sth** *The aim is to provide a template of care to guide health care professionals with limited experience.* **2** (*biochemistry*) a MOLECULE of DNA or RNA that acts as a pattern for building a PROTEIN or other large molecule: **~ for sth** *DNA serves as a template for mRNA synthesis; mRNA serves as a template for polypeptide synthesis.* ◇ **+ noun** *Behind the enzyme, the template strand pairs again with the coding strand to reform the DNA duplex.* **3** (*computing*) a set FORMAT for a document: *In some web document templates, double braces {{...}} indicate items that should be replaced by specific values.*

tem·ple /'templ/ *noun* **1** a building used for the worship of a god or gods, especially in religions other than Christianity: *Uisang founded many of the most famous Buddhist temples in Korea.* ◇ **~ of sb** *One key example is the temple of Zeus at Olympia.* ◇ **~ to sb** *A temple to Venus stood on this spot.* **2** each of the flat parts at the sides of the head, at the same level as the eyes and higher: *He had black hair, greying at the temples.*

tem·poral /'tempərəl/ *adj.* **1** connected with or limited by time: *The focus tends to be on spatial and temporal variations in voting patterns.* **2** connected with the real physical world, not spiritual matters: *They were afraid that Buddhism was gaining too much temporal power.* **3** (*anatomy*) near the temples at the side of the head: *The temporal lobe is divided into discrete regions with clearly different functions.*

tem·por·ary AWL /'temprəri; *NAmE* 'tempəreri/ *adj.* lasting or intended to last or be used for a limited period of time: *The article discusses the temporary nature of many areas of water.* ◇ *Most of these firms have cut back on their part-time and temporary workers.* ◇ *The improvement seen in the condition with the use of steroids is temporary, lasting 6–8 weeks.* ◇ *The family may be permitted to remain in the country on a temporary or permanent basis.* OPP PERMANENT ■ **tem·por·ar·ily** AWL /'temprərəli; *NAmE* ˌtempə'rerəli/ *adv.*: *The company announced that it would be temporarily closing the factory because of the global downturn.* ◇ *They estimate that 5.3 million Americans have temporarily or permanently lost their voting rights as a result of a felony conviction.* OPP PERMANENTLY

tempt /tempt/ *verb* **1** [usually passive] to make sb feel that they might want to do or believe sth: **be tempted by sth** *Like many philosophers, McTaggart was tempted by the view that time is an illusion.* ◇ **be tempted to do sth** *In considering these various possibilities, one might be tempted to think that the correct one is obvious.* **2 ~ sb into (doing) sth** to persuade sb to do sth that you want them to do, for example by offering them sth: *The schemes failed to tempt ex-servicewomen into domestic work.* ◇ *The block grant is intended to tempt individual states into cutting their benefit bills.* **3** [often passive] to attract sb or make sb want to do or have sth, even if they know it is wrong: **~ sb** *He is not tempted by the things of this world.* ◇ **~ sb into (doing) sth** *Television appearances doubtless tempted many into inventing or exaggerating their stories.* ◇ **~ sb to do sth** *She argues that prison makes many who are tempted to commit a crime think twice.*

temp·ta·tion /temp'teɪʃn/ *noun* **1** [C, U] the desire to do or have sth that you know is bad or wrong: **~ to do sth** *There is a temptation to seize on the similarities while ignoring the differences.* ◇ **resist the ~ (to do sth)** *They want the EU to resist the temptation to regulate all matters from Brussels.* ◇ **give in to ~** *Eve is represented as giving in to temptation and then persuading Adam to follow her.* ◇ **~ of sth** *The decision should be made by someone who is not exposed to the temptation of self-interest.* **2** [C] a thing that makes sb want to do or have sth that they know is bad or wrong: **~ of sth** *After-school programmes protect children from the temptations of the streets.* ◇ **~ to sb** *The high*

T

price fetched by the rhino horn is a major temptation to local peoples with meagre incomes.

tempt·ing /ˈtemptɪŋ/ *adj.* something that is **tempting** is attractive, and makes people want to have it, do it, etc, even though it may be wrong: *Homes of people out at work make tempting daytime targets for burglars.* ◇ **it is ~ to do sth** *In our fast-changing societies, it is tempting to conclude that history has few lessons to teach us.*

ten /ten/ *number* 10 HELP There are examples of how to use numbers at the entry for **five**.

ten·ant /ˈtenənt/ *noun* a person who pays rent for the use of a room, building, land, etc. to the person who owns it: *In the nineteenth century, the vast mass of urban households were private tenants.* ◇ **~ farmer** *In some cases, improvements have led to the displacement of poor tenant farmers.*

tend /tend/ *verb* **1** [I] **~ to do sth** to regularly or frequently behave in a particular way or have a particular characteristic: *Rich people tend to have better chances in life than poor people.* ◇ *Too much research has tended to focus on the academic failure of African American students, rather than their successes.* ➲ language bank *at* BROADLY **2** [I] **~ (to/towards sth)** (*mathematics*) to come close to a particular quantity as a limit: *This supports the argument that the value will approach zero as n tends to infinity.* **3** [I] **~ (to/towards sth)** to be likely to have or show a particular characteristic: *This type of religious authority tends towards conservatism.* **4** [I] **+ adv./prep.** to go or move in a particular direction: *The European consensus tends in a completely different direction.* **5** [T, I] to care for sb/sth: **~ sb/sth** *He withdrew to Mapperton where he tended his formal gardens.* ◇ **~ to sb/sth** *For many women, staying home and tending to children is not enough.*

ten·dency /ˈtendənsi/ *noun* (*pl.* **-ies**) **1** [C] if sb/sth has a particular **tendency**, they are likely to behave or act in a particular way: *Governments everywhere exhibit certain bureaucratic tendencies.* ◇ **~ (for sb/sth) to do sth** *There was a general tendency for firms to begin with simple tasks and accumulate capabilities gradually.* ◇ **~ to/towards sth** *It may be more appropriate to think of learners as having a tendency towards a particular mindset.* ◇ **~ for sth** *Japanese firms show strong tendencies for collective action (Zhao, 1993).* **2** [C] a new custom that is starting to develop SYN TREND: **~ (for sb/sth) (to do sth)** *There is an increasing tendency for small firms to be more competitive.* ◇ **~ to/towards sth** *There was a growing tendency towards nationalism.* **3** [C+sing./pl. v.] (*BrE*) a group within a larger political group, whose views are more extreme than those of the rest of the group: *Their findings identify three major tendencies within the party.*

ten·der¹ /ˈtendə(r)/ *adj.* (**ten·derer**, **ten·derest**) (**more tender** and **most tender** are also common.) **1** (of a part of the body) painful when touched SYN SORE: *On examination, his abdomen was tender.* **2** kind, gentle and loving: *Such people may be superficially charming but they lack tender feelings.* ■ **ten·der·ness** *noun* [U] *The patient will complain of pain and tenderness directly over the joint.* ◇ *She always treated him with tenderness and compassion.*

ten·der² /ˈtendə(r)/ *verb* **1** [I] **~ (for sth)** to make a formal written offer to supply goods, do work, etc. at a stated price: *The two companies had been preparing to tender for the same contract.* **2** [T] **~ sth (to sb)** to offer or give sth to sb formally: *He tendered his resignation immediately.*

ten·der³ /ˈtendə(r)/ *noun* [C, U] a formal offer to supply goods or do work at a stated price: *Eight foreign companies submitted their tenders to work on the development of the gas field.* ◇ *In 1922 the design and construction of the Sydney Harbour Bridge was put out to tender.* ◇ *Bidding for the work is by sealed competitive tender.*

tenet /ˈtenɪt/ *noun* **~ (of sth)** one of the principles or beliefs that a theory or larger set of beliefs is based on: *That meaning is essentially conceptual in nature is one of the central tenets of cognitive linguistics.* ◇ *the basic/fundamental tenets of sth*

tense¹ AWL /tens/ *noun* any of the forms of a verb that may be used to show the time of the action or state expressed by the verb: **~ (of sth)** *The past tense of 'lead' is 'led'.* ◇ **in the... ~** *The story is narrated in the present tense.* ➲ *compare* ASPECT (3)

tense² AWL /tens/ *adj.* **1** (of a situation, an event, a period of time, etc.) making people have strong feelings such as anger or anxiety that often cannot be expressed: *The security situation is still tense.* ◇ *Relations between Downing Street and senior civil servants were sometimes tense.* **2** (of a person) nervous or anxious and unable to relax: *They may be so tense that it is necessary to reduce their anxiety levels before starting treatment.* **3** (of a muscle or other part of the body) stretched tight rather than relaxed: *His breathing is rapid and shallow and his muscles are tense.*

ten·sion AWL /ˈtenʃn/ *noun* **1** [U, C, usually pl.] a situation in which people do not trust each other, or feel unfriendly towards each other, and which may cause them to attack each other: *Evidence of racial tension in some parts of the country is growing.* ◇ *The Great Depression exacerbated class tensions in Britain.* ◇ *The early modern state was ill equipped to regulate or resolve tensions in rural society.* ◇ **~ between A and B** *Both cities have recently experienced tensions between members of the two groups.* **2** [C, U] **~ (between A and B)** a situation in which the fact that there are different needs or interests causes difficulties: *Tensions between the priorities of British governments and those of other EU member states have always existed.* ◇ *There is a degree of tension between the common and civil law legal traditions.* **3** [U] a feeling of anxiety and stress that makes it impossible to relax: *Emotional exhaustion may be accompanied by feelings of frustration or tension.* **4** [U] the feeling of fear and excitement that is created by a writer or a film director: *Many admired his technique, his control of tone and his ability to create tension.* **5** [U] the state of being stretched tight; the extent to which sth is stretched tight: *Yoga or relaxation techniques may be used to reduce tension in the back, neck and jaw.* ◇ **~ of sth** *The tension of the steel belt was increased by turning the lock nut.*

ten·sor /ˈtensə(r); ˈtensɔː(r)/ *noun* (*mathematics*) a quantity that has different values in different directions. A VECTOR is a special simple case of a tensor: *Next above a vector are tensors of order 2, which are often referred to as matrices.*

ten·ta·tive /ˈtentətɪv/ *adj.* **1** (of an arrangement, agreement, etc.) not definite or certain because you may want to change it later: *Despite these limitations, it is possible to draw some tentative conclusions.* ➲ language bank *at* HEDGE **2** not behaving or done with confidence: *The first tentative steps towards reform were taken the following year.* ■ **ten·ta·tive·ly** *adv.*: *The ruined structure has been tentatively identified as a Roman temple.* ◇ *Initially, adolescents explore these new possibilities tentatively.* ➲ language bank *at* HEDGE

ten·ure /ˈtenjə(r)/ *noun* **1** [C] **~ (as sth)** the period of time when sb holds a job: *During his tenure as Home Secretary, he introduced a range of such measures.* ◇ *Shorter employment tenures tend to be associated with low levels of training.* **2** [U] the right to stay permanently in your job, especially as a teacher at a university or in a public position: *Once in office, a judge enjoys security of tenure.* **3** [U] **~ (over sth)** the legal right to live in a house or use a

T

piece of land: *The peasants owned or had tenure over their land.*

term[1] /tɜːm; *NAmE* tɜːrm/ *noun* ➲ *see also* TERMS **1** [C] a word or phrase used to describe a thing or to express an idea, especially in a particular kind of language or area of study: *Warren Weaver coined the term 'molecular biology' in 1938.* ◇ **~ for sb/sth** *'Community' is today more frequently used as an alternative term for 'ethnic group'.* ◇ **~ of sth** *The 1990s generation turned the word 'sad' into a term of abuse.* ➲ language bank *at* DEFINE **2** [C] **~ (of sth)** (*mathematics*) each of the various parts in a series, an EQUATION, etc: *Navier treated each term of this equation separately.* **3** [C] a fixed or limited period of time for which sth lasts: **~ (of sth)** *A Commissioner's term of office lasts for a period of five years.* ◇ **serve a ~** *Trumbo had only recently been released after serving a ten-month prison term.* **4** [sing., U] the end of a particular period of time, especially one for which an agreement, etc. lasts: **~ (of sth)** *In some cases, a fixed-term contract may continue beyond the term of the agreement.* ◇ **at/to full ~** *The pregnancy was allowed to go to full term.* ➲ *see also* LONG-TERM, SHORT-TERM **5** (*NAmE also* **tri·mes·ter**) [C, U] (especially in the UK) one of the three periods in the year during which classes are held in schools, universities, etc: *Rules, routines and expectations in the classroom will need to be reviewed throughout the term.* ◇ **the end of ~** (*BrE*) *Towards the end of term, she had a breakthrough in her research.* ◇ **the end of the ~** (*NAmE*) *Near the end of the term, the teachers were asked to complete a questionnaire.* ➲ *compare* SEMESTER

IDM **in the ˈlong/ˈshort/ˈmedium term** used to describe what will happen a long, short, etc. time in the future: *These behaviours may be detrimental to physical health in the long term.* ➲ *more at* CONTRADICTION, EQUAL[1], TERMS

▸ ADJECTIVE + TERM **general** • **standard** • **generic** • **specific** • **key** • **relative** • **similar** • **positive** • **negative** • **technical** • **economic** • **theoretical** • **legal** • **political** *Psychology, sociology and anthropology all suffer from poorly defined key terms.*

▸ NOUN + TERM **search** • **umbrella** *'Homicide' is an umbrella term which encompasses both lawful and unlawful killings.*

▸ VERB + TERM **include** • **contain** • **introduce** • **add** • **consider** *In any case, the equation should include this term.* ◇ *The term is now considered obsolete.* | **use, employ** • **define** • **interpret** • **coin** • **apply, give** • **associate** *'Lagoon' is a term given to a shallow water body that is connected with the sea or a large lake through a narrow entrance.*

▸ TERM + VERB **represent** • **describe** • **appear** *The term describes the surface that separates two distinct layers of sedimentary rocks.* | **mean, denote, signify** • **refer to** • **cover** • **capture** • **imply** *The two terms mean the same thing.* | **dominate** • **vanish** • **correspond to** • **cancel** *All the terms cancel except for two.*

▸ NOUN + OF + TERM **use, usage** • **sense, meaning** • **understanding** • **definition** • **interpretation** • **explanation** • **list** • **glossary** • **set** • **variety** • **number** *The 'Oxford English Dictionary' attributes the first use of the term 'international' to Bentham in 1780.* | **number** • **sum** • **magnitude** • **coefficient** *These sequences all have only a finite number of terms.*

term[2] /tɜːm; *NAmE* tɜːrm/ *verb* [often passive] **~ sb/sth + noun/adj.** to use a particular name or word to describe sb/sth: *One would normally term these leading legal and political figures 'conservative'.* ◇ *By contrast, West Germany had what is termed a capitalist economy.*

ter·min·al[1] AWL /ˈtɜːmɪnl; *NAmE* ˈtɜːrmɪnl/ *adj.* **1** (of an illness or a disease) that cannot be cured and will lead to death, often slowly: *In February 1922, Rosenzweig was diagnosed with a terminal illness.* **2** (of a person) suffering from a terminal illness: *The drug is able to offer only a small life extension to terminal patients.* **3** certain to get worse and come to an end: *The company appeared to be in terminal decline.* **4** [only before noun] (*technical*) forming or located at the end of sth: *The amino-acid chain constituting a protein has two terminal points.* ◇ *At the wrist, the radial nerve is separated into numerous terminal branches.*

ter·min·al[2] AWL /ˈtɜːmɪnl; *NAmE* ˈtɜːrmɪnl/ *noun* **1 ~ (of sth)** a point at which connections can be made in an electric CIRCUIT: *An electric field is applied across the sample by connecting the terminals of a battery across it.* ◇ *an input/output terminal* **2** a piece of equipment, usually consisting of a keyboard and a screen that links the user to a central computer system: *Details of sales transactions were entered into a computer terminal.* **3** a place, building or set of buildings where journeys by train, bus or boat begin or end: *The initiative obliges foreign ports to establish terminals dedicated to US-bound shipping.* **4** a building or set of buildings at an airport where air passengers arrive and leave: *Enormous public controversy was generated by proposals for a fifth terminal at Heathrow Airport.*

ter·min·al·ly /ˈtɜːmɪnəli; *NAmE* ˈtɜːrmɪnəli/ *adv.* in a way that cannot be cured and is predicted to lead to death: *Opiates are commonly used in terminally ill patients suffering with chronic pain.*

ter·min·ate AWL /ˈtɜːmɪneɪt; *NAmE* ˈtɜːrmeɪt/ *verb* **1** [I, T] to end; to make sth end: *When they reach the age of sixteen, the child allowance and other benefits paid to their parents terminate.* ◇ **~ sth** *It was claimed that the defendant had acted wrongfully in terminating the contract.* **2** [T] **~ sth** to end a PREGNANCY at an early stage by a medical operation: *The Abortion Act 1967 states that a pregnancy may only be terminated by a registered medical practitioner.* **3** [I] **~ in sth** (of a thing) to end at a particular place or in a particular form: *The larger glaciers terminate in vertical ice cliffs about 20 m high.*

ter·min·ation AWL /ˌtɜːmɪˈneɪʃn; *NAmE* ˌtɜːrmɪˈneɪʃn/ *noun* **1** [U, C] **~ (of sth)** the act of ending sth; the end of sth: *Legislation in the past made the costs of termination of employment prohibitive.* ◇ *The offence may be sufficiently serious to justify a termination of the contract.* **2** [C, U] a medical operation to end a PREGNANCY at an early stage SYN ABORTION (2): *If the test shows that the baby is affected, she may choose to have a termination.* ◇ **~ of sth** *During this period, the mother has the option of termination of pregnancy.*

ter·min·ology /ˌtɜːmɪˈnɒlədʒi; *NAmE* ˌtɜːrməˈnɑːlədʒi/ *noun* (*pl.* **-ies**) **1** [U, C] the set of technical words or expressions used in a particular subject: *The website provides information to help patients understand medical terminology.* ◇ *The lack of a standardized terminology is a serious handicap for an emerging field of study.* **2** [U] words used with particular meanings: *The court called for clearer use of terminology in such cases.* ■ **ter·mino·logic·al** /ˌtɜːmɪnəˈlɒdʒɪkl; *NAmE* ˌtɜːrmənəˈlɑːdʒɪkl/ *adj.*: *The design of a terminological database for a specialized domain is extremely complex.*

terms /tɜːmz; *NAmE* tɜːrmz/ *noun* [pl.] ➲ *see also* TERM[1] **1** the conditions that people offer, demand or accept when they make an agreement, an arrangement or a contract: **~ (of sth)** *The dispute related to the terms of the contract between the two parties.* ◇ **under the ~ of sth** *All EU members offer asylum under the terms of the Geneva Convention of 1951.* ◇ **~ and conditions (of sth)** *Often there is no choice but to accept poor terms and conditions of employment.* **2** conditions that you agree to when you buy, sell or pay for sth; a price or cost: *The bank is able to offer its clients good borrowing terms.* ◇ **on easy/favourable, etc. ~** *Unused land was released for sale on easy*

T

terms to peasants. **3** a way of expressing yourself or of saying sth: **in ... ~** *Hegel's system of thought is not easy to explain in simple terms.*

IDM **be on good/friendly/bad, etc. 'terms (with sb)** to have a good, friendly, etc. relationship with sb: *Clovis was on good terms with the bishops in his kingdom.* **come to 'terms (with sb)** to reach an agreement with sb; to find a way of living or working together: *The peoples of these areas also quickly came to terms with Alexander the Great.* **come to 'terms with sth** to accept sth unpleasant by learning to deal with it: *The bereaved person gradually comes to terms with the loss.* **in terms of 'sth | in...terms** used to show what aspect of a subject you are talking about or how you are thinking about it: *The USA compares surprisingly poorly with other countries in terms of overall health outcomes.* ◇ *In practical terms, this means that police have to be more adaptable.* **on your own 'terms | on sb's 'terms** according to the conditions that you or sb else decides: *Many scientists want to be in the media spotlight, but only on their own terms.* ◇ *If firms want to do business in Asia, they must do so on Asia's terms.* **ˌterms of 'reference** the limits that are set on what an official committee or report has been asked to do: *The matter, they decided, lay outside the commission's terms of reference.* ➲ *more at* CONTRADICTION, EQUAL[1], UNCERTAIN

ˌterms of 'trade *noun* [pl.] (*economics*) the relationship between a country's export and import prices, indicating the quantity of imports that can be bought when a fixed quantity of exports is sold: *Unequal terms of trade create differential living standards across countries.*

ter·rain /təˈreɪn/ *noun* [U, C] **1** used to refer to an area of land when you are mentioning its natural features, for example, if it is rough, flat, etc: *The aeroplane crashed into mountainous terrain several miles short of the airport.* ◇ *Landslides are rare in many granite terrains.* **2** an area of activity or study, especially one where there is disagreement: *Douglas Kellner in 'Cinema Wars' explores how Hollywood film has been a dynamic and politically contested terrain.*

ter·res·trial /təˈrestriəl/ *adj.* **1** (of animals and plants) living or growing on land, rather than in water, in/on trees or in the air: *These early peoples would have relied on a diet of terrestrial mammals, birds and fish.* **2** connected with or on the land, rather than the sea or the air: *Bacteria are probably the most abundant type of microorganism found in both aqueous and terrestrial environments.* **3** connected with the planet Earth: *Terrestrial radiation is also emitted to space at the Earth's surface.* **4** (of television and broadcasting systems) operating on Earth rather than from a SATELLITE: *Signals in this frequency range are used for terrestrial broadcasting.*

T

ter·ri·tor·ial /ˌterəˈtɔːriəl/ *adj.* **1** connected with the land or sea that is owned by a particular country: *Territorial expansion brought millions of Germans into the Reich.* ◇ *Traditionally, security meant protection of the sovereignty and territorial integrity of states from external military threats.* **2** (of an animal or species) defending an area of land that it believes to be its own: *Males of this species are highly territorial.* ■ **ter·ri·tori·al·ity** /ˌterəˌtɔːriˈæləti/ *noun* [U] *The US government accepts the principle of territoriality.* ◇ *With domesticated animals, their instinct of territoriality is greatly diminished.* **ter·ri·tori·al·ly** /ˌterəˈtɔːriəli/ *adv.*: *By 1939 Japan had expanded territorially and developed into an industrial power.*

ter·ri·tory /ˈterətri; *NAmE* ˈterətɔːri/ *noun* (*pl.* -ies) **1** [U, C] land that is under the control of a particular country or ruler: *The USSR apologized for the incursion of Soviet troops into Chinese territory.* ◇ *Alexander put into action a policy of land development in the conquered territories.* **2** [C, U] an area that an animal or group of animals considers as its own and defends against others who try to enter it: *Some species are solitary and defend a territory, while others nest in colonies.* ◇ *One third of birds changed territory between consecutive breeding seasons.* **3** [U, C] an area of knowledge, activity or experience: *The formation of the coalition plunged Westminster politics into uncharted territory.* ◇ *The term 'narrative' tends to cover a wider and wider territory.* **4** [C] an area of a town, country, etc. that sb has particular rights in or responsibility for in their work or another activity: *Sales territories might be based on counties or individual nations within the UK.* **5** [U] a particular type of land: *The objective is to provide a better separation of urban and rural territory.* **6** (*also* **Territory**) [C] a country or an area that is part of the US, Australia or Canada but is not a state or PROVINCE: *The island is an Australian external territory of outstanding conservation significance.*

IDM **ˌcome/ˌgo with the 'territory** (*rather informal*) to be a normal and accepted part of a particular job or situation: *For a teacher, dealing with difficult children is a challenge that comes with the territory.*

ter·ror /ˈterə(r)/ *noun* **1** [U] a feeling of extreme fear: *The other sailors leaped into the sea in terror.* ◇ *The shield features the Gorgon's head and other images intended to inspire terror.* **2** [U] violent action or the threat of violent action that is intended to cause fear, usually for political purposes SYN TERRORISM: *The attacks of 9/11 led to the so-called global war on terror.* ◇ **+ noun** *The House of Lords ruled that the detention of 12 foreign terror suspects without trial breached human rights.* **3** [C] a person, situation or thing that makes you very afraid: *Even tragic art is positive: it shows fearlessness in the face of terrors.*

ter·ror·ism /ˈterərɪzəm/ *noun* [U] the use of violent action in order to achieve political aims or to force a government to act: *Al-Qaeda was linked to a series of acts of terrorism.* ◇ *Security is not confined to combating terrorism.*

ter·ror·ist /ˈterərɪst/ *noun* a person who uses terrorism to achieve political aims or to force a government to act: *Police were allowed to detain suspected terrorists for seven days without charge.* ◇ **+ noun** *The 9/11 terrorist attacks on the US shifted global priorities.* ◇ *a terrorist group/organization/network*

ter·tiary /ˈtɜːʃəri; *NAmE* ˈtɜːrʃieri; ˈtɜːrʃəri/ *adj.* **1** third in order, rank or importance: *The growth of the secondary sector (industry) entailed the expansion of the tertiary sector, including the retail trade and services.* ◇ *Race, the third topic in the title, plays an important but tertiary role.* ➲ *compare* PRIMARY (1), SECONDARY (1) **2** [only before noun] (*especially BrE*) connected with education after the age of 18: *Unemployment rates are much higher for those who have not completed secondary school, as compared with those with tertiary education.* ◇ *The research involved visiting six lecturers in tertiary institutions in England.* ➲ *compare* PRIMARY (3), SECONDARY (4) **3** (*biology, chemistry*) used to refer to the THREE-DIMENSIONAL structure of some MOLECULES: *Polypeptides may become mature proteins simply by folding into their natural tertiary structure.* **4** (*chemistry*) (of an ORGANIC COMPOUND) having its FUNCTIONAL GROUP located on a CARBON atom which is BONDED to three other carbon atoms; containing a NITROGEN atom bonded to three carbon atoms: *Unlike tertiary alcohols, secondary and primary alcohols are readily oxidized to carbonyl compounds.* ◇ *Reaction with nitrous acid is used to distinguish between primary, secondary and tertiary amines.* ➲ *compare* PRIMARY (4), SECONDARY (5)

test[1] /test/ *noun* **1** a procedure to discover how good or reliable sth is, or to find out more information about it: *The test determines the resistance of a material to a shock loading.* ◇ **~ of sth** *Many tests of these hypotheses have been conducted.* ◇ **~ on sb/sth** *Tests on animals have serious limitations.* ◇ **in ~** *Girls typically show more* *emotional concern in these tests than boys.* HELP In chemistry, a **test** may be used to identify a substance or to find out if a particular chemical is present in a substance: *All the sugars gave a positive test with Fehling's solution which confirmed that they were all reducing sugars.* ➲ *see also* CHI-SQUARE TEST **2** a medical examination to discover if sb has a particular illness or condition HELP Medical **tests** are usually done by taking samples of body tissues or fluids, rather than by physically examining a patient's body. When a doctor examines a person's body, it is called an **examination**: *He went for an HIV test.* ◇ *Hypothyroidism is easily confirmed by a blood test.* ◇ **~ for sth** *It is useful as a screening test for urinary tract infection.* ➲ *compare* EXAM (2), EXAMINATION (2) ➲ *see also* BLOOD TEST **3** an examination of sb's knowledge or ability, consisting of questions for them to answer or activities for them to perform: *Some children are simply better at taking tests.* ◇ **~ on sth** *Tests on English language are being introduced.* ◇ **in a ~** (*BrE*) *In the numeracy test, 11 questions on risk are presented.* ◇ **on a ~** (*NAmE*) *She did well on her science test.* ➲ *compare* EXAM (1), EXAMINATION (3) **4 ~ of sth** a situation, event or activity that shows how good, strong, etc. sb/sth is: *Stressful events work as tests of a relationship.* ◇ *Some young people see smoking as a test of their sophistication and 'cool'.* **5** a way of proving or deciding whether an action or situation is an example of a particular quality: *The Court of Justice applied two tests to determine whether the goods were similar or not.* ◇ **~ of sth** *Each clause of the contract must satisfy the test of reasonableness.* HELP In law, a **test case** is a legal case whose result will be used as an example when decisions are being made on similar cases in the future. However, the term is also used in other disciplines to mean a situation whose result may help you predict the results of similar situations: *Introductions of alien species to islands in the Pacific have provided a test case of the effects of sexual selection on the probability of extinction.*

IDM **put sb/sth to the 'test** to put sb/sth in a situation which will show what their/its true qualities are: *Problem questions enable students to put their knowledge to the test.* **stand the test of 'time** to prove to be good, popular, etc. over a long period of time: *Darwin's theory for evolutionary change has stood the test of time.*

▸ ADJECTIVE + TEST **standard • simple • diagnostic** *Sickle-cell disease can be detected by a simple blood test.* | **statistical • empirical • experimental • clinical • biochemical • psychological • cognitive • objective • subjective** *Statistical tests can be applied to examine particular hypotheses.* | **routine • positive • negative • abnormal • genetic** *Patients with any of the risk factors should be offered a routine HIV test.*

▸ NOUN + TEST **laboratory** *The thermal properties of the ground were investigated by means of laboratory tests.* | **screening • blood • skin • liver • thyroid • HIV • pregnancy** *Screening tests can be performed on those with a family history of breast cancer.* | **intelligence, IQ • memory • vocabulary** *A youngster who seems bright may score poorly on intelligence tests.*

▸ VERB + TEST **do, perform, undertake, carry out, administer, conduct, run • complete • develop, design • use • undergo** *A liver function test should be done.* ◇ *A sample from a person may give a false negative result if the test is performed too soon.* | **take • pass • fail** *Passing your driving test is more than just luck.*

▸ TEST + VERB **show, indicate, reveal • identify • confirm • measure** *Tests have shown that the temperature on the outside of the pile was significantly higher than that on the inside.*

▸ TEST + NOUN **result • procedure • site** *Those who have the disorder will have a positive test result.* | **statistics, data • item** *The test data were taken from the earlier study.* | **score** *IQ test scores can vary widely in the same person over time.*

test² /test/ *verb* **1** [T, I] to do sth to check how good or reliable sth is or to find out more information about it: **~ sth** *More research is needed to test the hypothesis.* ◇ *The model was developed and rigorously tested by Muneer et al. (2010).* ◇ **~ sth out** *It is important to test out adverts before running them.* ◇ **~ (sth) for sth** *They then tested for the robustness of the results.* ◇ **~ sth on sth** *First the product is tested on animals.* HELP In chemistry, to **test** a substance is to examine a substance using a REAGENT, especially in order to find out if another chemical is present: *The solutions were tested with universal indicator paper to determine their pH.* ◇ *She tested the air to see whether any of the pollutants were above their recommended safety levels.* **2** [T] to examine the blood, a part of the body, etc. to find out what is wrong with a person, or to check the condition of their health: **~ sb/sth** *A urine sample should have been tested by the GP.* ◇ **~ sb/sth for sth** *Some people do not want to be tested for HIV.* ◇ **~ for sth** *To test for allergy, a small amount of the suspected allergen is injected into the skin.* **3** [I] **~ positive/negative (for sth)** to produce a particular result in a medical test, especially a drugs test or HIV test: *Of the 14 patients, eight had tested HIV-positive.* **4** [T] to find out how much sb knows or what they can do by asking them questions or giving them activities to perform: **~ sb (on sth)** *The children were tested on their knowledge of the alphabet.* ◇ **~ sth** *The first chapter tests students' ability to identify different topics contained within one question.* **5** [T] **~ sb/sth** to be difficult and therefore need all your strength, ability, etc: *Some of the games are designed to test or stress participants.* ◇ *The patient may be severely tested physically and emotionally.* ➲ *compare* CHALLENGE² (4) IDM *see* TRIED¹

▸ TEST + NOUN **hypothesis, theory • idea • proposition • prediction • assumption • model • method • effect, impact • validity • robustness • efficacy, effectiveness • significance • ability** *To test the effect of ionic strength on the reaction, different concentrations of NaCl were added to the reaction mixture.*

▸ ADVERB + TEST **empirically, experimentally • directly, explicitly • formally • rigorously** *Previous cross-linguistic studies have empirically tested this prediction.*

▸ TEST + ADVERB **empirically, experimentally • statistically • separately, individually • simultaneously** *The aim of the study was to test experimentally whether survival of birds depends on age.*

test·able /ˈtestəbl/ *adj.* that can be tested: *To make this a testable hypothesis, we need something to examine.* ◇ *As more data become available, these propositions become empirically testable.*

tes·ta·ment /ˈtestəmənt/ *noun* (*formal*) **1** [C, usually sing., U] **~ (to sth)** a thing that shows that sth else exists or is true SYN TESTIMONY (2): *These examples bear testament to the truth of his claims.* **2 Testament** [C] a division of the Christian Bible HELP The **Old Testament** tells the history of the Jews, their beliefs and their relationship with God before the birth of Christ. The **New Testament** describes the life and teachings of Jesus Christ.

test·ify /ˈtestɪfaɪ/ *verb* (**testi·fies, testi·fy·ing, testi·fied, testi·fied**) **1** [I, T] to make a statement that sth happened or that sth is true, especially as a WITNESS in court: *Slaves were denied the right to testify in court.* ◇ **~ against/for sb** *Grüber was the only German to testify against Eichmann at his trial.* ◇ **~ to (doing) sth** *They must produce expert witnesses who will testify to the fact that the danger was not foreseeable.* ◇ **~ (that)...** *The witness testified that no one was home when he arrived.* **2** [I, T] to show or be evidence that sth is true: **~ to sth** *His own work testifies to the fact that these global interests persisted.* ◇ **~ (that)...** *Geological records testify that life on Earth has developed and adapted itself to slowly changing conditions.* **3** [T] **~ (that)...** to say

T

that you believe sth is true because you have evidence of it: *Anybody with practical experience of commentary writing will testify that this is a difficult task.*

tes·ti·mony /ˈtestɪməni; *NAmE* ˈtestɪmoʊni/ *noun* (*pl.* -ies) **1** [U, C] a formal written or spoken statement saying what you know to be true, usually in court: *Their rights to make a will, to inherit or to give testimony in court were curtailed.* ◇ *Expert testimony disclosed that the tapes had been deliberately tampered with.* ◇ **~ (of sb)** *We then hear the testimonies of two witnesses.* **2** [U, sing.] **~ (to sth)** a thing that shows that sth else exists or is true: *He successfully predicted the eclipse of the sun of 28 May 585 BC, which bears testimony to his ability.* ◇ *The temple architecture is a testimony to the way in which Hindus sought to praise their gods.* IDM *see* BEAR

test·ing /ˈtestɪŋ/ *noun* [U] **1** the activity of examining blood, a part of the body, etc. to find out what is wrong with a person, or to check the condition of their health: *Older pregnant women often undergo genetic testing of the fetus.* ◇ **~ for sth** *He is calling for routine testing for HIV.* **2** the activity of testing how good or reliable sth is, or in order to find out more information about it: *The hypotheses are then subject to rigorous testing.* ◇ **~ of sth** *They announced that they would resume the testing of nuclear weapons.* **3** the activity of testing people's knowledge by asking them questions or giving them activities to perform: *She believes we have enough testing in schools.*

text AWL /tekst/ *noun* **1** [C] a book, or other written or printed work HELP When a book is referred to as a **text**, it is the content that is being considered rather than its physical form: *Morgan's book has now become a classic text.* ◇ *He then turned to the investigation of ancient Latin texts.* ◇ *The relation between a source text and its translation is interesting.* HELP In British English, a **set text** is a book, play, etc. that students have to study for an exam. **2** [U] the written or printed words that go together to form a piece of writing: *We cannot read text if it is too small.* ◇ *In narrative text, there have to be temporal links that order the events in the story.* HELP In computing, **text** is data in the form or words or letters. **3** [sing.] the main printed part of a book or magazine, not the notes, illustrations, etc: *The boxes in the text present additional facts about the economy.* ◇ *By glancing at the text and images of the magazine, you can see that it caters for a white readership.* HELP To refer to the main text from an illustration, table, etc, insert a note **(see text)**: *This figure shows that high unemployment still exists (see text).* **4** [C] the written form of a speech, a play, an article, etc: *All the corrections he made on the drafts passed directly into the report's final text.* ◇ **~ of sth** *The full text of the articles is freely available online.* ➲ *compare* SCRIPT (1) **5** [C] (*NAmE*) = TEXTBOOK: *The book is an introductory text.* **6** [C] = TEXT MESSAGE

▸ ADJECTIVE + TEXT **key, important, standard • original • early • ancient • classical • classic, canonical • literary • medical • legal • religious, sacred** *She argued that literary texts such as plays and epic should not be considered accurate representations of everyday life.*

▸ VERB + TEXT **read • write, produce • translate • study • edit • interpret • analyse • publish • understand** *Attention must be paid to the historical context in which the text was produced.* ◇ *Subjects were asked to read text on a computer screen.*

text·book /ˈtekstbʊk/ (*NAmE also* **text**) *noun* a book that teaches a particular subject and that is used especially in schools and colleges: *a history/an economics/a medical textbook* ◇ **~ on sth** *These are the definitions that are given in almost all standard textbooks on the subject.*

tex·tile /ˈtekstaɪl/ *noun* **1** [C] any type of cloth made by WEAVING or KNITTING: *The new machines and factories produced cotton textiles.* ◇ **+ noun** *The textile industry continued to develop.* ◇ *a textile mill/worker* **2 textiles** [pl.] the industry that makes cloth: *Most low-tech industries today are not structured like textiles and clothing.*

ˈtext message (*also* **text**) *noun* a written message that you send using a mobile phone: *Sending text messages on a mobile phone became much cheaper.*

text·ual AWL /ˈtekstʃuəl/ *adj.* [usually before noun] connected with or contained in a text: *She performed a textual analysis of different newspapers' coverage of the story.* ◇ *There is no textual evidence to support this interpretation.* ■ **text·ually** *adj.*: *Other studies are more textually focused.*

tex·ture /ˈtekstʃə(r)/ *noun* [C, U] **1** the way a surface or substance feels when you touch it, for example how rough, smooth, hard or soft it is: *This material has a finer texture.* ◇ *Subjects had to picture various objects, including their colours and textures.* ◇ *Soils that are coarse in texture (sandy) generally have high infiltration rates.* **2 ~ of sth** the way that different parts of a piece of music or literature are combined to create a final impression: *He is particularly alert to the acoustic texture of verse.*

than /ðən; *rare strong form* ðæn/ *prep.* **1** used to introduce the second part of a comparison: *She knew more than they thought.* ◇ *He is sixteen years younger than his wife.* ◇ *Everyday resistance was more common than open revolt.* **2 more/less/fewer, etc. ~** used for comparing amounts, numbers, distances, etc: *Mortality rates are low (less than 1 in 1 000).* ◇ *This estimate was lower than their original figure.* ➲ *see also* OTHER THAN, RATHER THAN IDM *see* SOON

thank /θæŋk/ *verb* **~ sb (for sth/for doing sth)** to tell sb that you are grateful for sth: *She thanked the students for their contributions to the discussion.*

thanks /θæŋks/ *noun* [pl.] words or actions that show that you are grateful to sb for sth SYN GRATITUDE: *It is not considered necessary in these cultures to express thanks in words.* ◇ **~ for sth** *Haris Kountouris deserves special thanks for the chapter on EU law.* ◇ **~ to sb (for sth)** *They gave thanks to God for the safe return of their friends.*
IDM **thanks to sb/sth** used to say that sth has happened because of sb/sth: *Thanks to the Internet, anyone can access this information.*

that¹ /ðæt/ *det.* (*pl.* **those** /ðəʊz; *NAmE* ðoʊz/) **1** used to refer to sb/sth that has already been mentioned or is already known about: *Keats does not just describe the idea he has, but also tells us how that idea arose and grew.* ◇ *The physical environment which supported those people is the Mongolian steppe.* **2** used to refer to a person or thing that is not near the speaker or as near to the speaker as another, or for contrasting with 'this': *Every film makes a selection of elements based on a set of possibilities (e.g. this actor and performance style rather than that one).*

that² /ðæt/ *pron.* (*pl.* **those** /ðəʊz; *NAmE* ðoʊz/) **1** used to refer to sth that has already been mentioned, or is already known about: *There was nothing they could do about that.* ◇ *The movie is about real life, and that is precisely the problem.* **2** [usually pl.] used to refer to people of a particular type: *Those who most need medical services tend to use them least.* ◇ *This will not surprise those familiar with his writing.* **3** /ðət; *rare strong form* ðæt/ (*pl.* **that**) used as a relative pronoun to introduce a part of a sentence which refers to the person, thing or time you have been talking about: *The results that he obtained were very surprising.* ◇ *Himes was one of the people that he met.* ◇ *1953 was the year that the structure of DNA was announced.*
IDM **that is** used to say what sth means or to give more information: *A firm grows by investing, that is, by using its profits to increase the quantity of its capital goods.* ◇ *They concentrated on the core engineering subjects, that is design and manufacturing.* ➲ language bank *at* I.E.

T

that³ /ðət; *rare strong form* ðæt/ *conj.* **1** used after some verbs, adjectives and nouns to introduce a new part of the sentence: *Muslims believe that each of us has a soul created by God.* ◇ *It is essential that this patient's vital signs are assessed quickly.* ◇ *It leads to the conclusion that war is inevitable.* **2 so... that...** used to express a result: *The format of the show is so successful that it has been exported around the world.* ◇ *The membranes are so weak that molecules of oxygen and carbon dioxide can diffuse across them.*

that⁴ /ðæt/ *adv.* **1** used when referring to an amount, distance, etc. that has already been mentioned or is already known about: *He must have felt a lot of pain to have had that much anger.* ◇ *The rate at which you travel might be estimated as the number of kilometres you cover divided by the time took you to travel that far.* **2 not (all) ~** (*rather informal*) not very; not as much as has been said: *This poem is, by Hughes's best standards, not all that good.*

the /ðə; ði; *strong form* ðiː/ *definite article* **1** used to refer to sb/sth that has already been mentioned or is easily understood: *This raises two questions. The first is relatively easy to answer but the second is not.* ◇ *The temperature was well over 100 degrees.* ◇ *The winters are extremely wet in this mountainous region.* **2** used to refer to sb/sth that is the only, normal or obvious one of their kind: *Her duties included answering the telephone.* ◇ *He designed three bridges over the Thames.* ◇ *He was asked by Vincenzo Perugia to steal the Mona Lisa.* **3** used when explaining which person or thing you mean: *A convenient summary can be found in the book by Smith.* ◇ *Every important historic earthquake represents a unique challenge for the scientists who endeavour to understand it.* ◇ *Racine was the greatest exponent of French classical tragedy.* ◇ *It was only the second Australian Royal Commission to be composed entirely of medical practitioners.* ◇ *Alexander the Great conquered much of the world in the fourth century BC.* **4** used to refer to a thing in general rather than a particular example: *A total of 52 students can play the piano.* ◇ *A warning was broadcast on the radio.* ◇ *During this epoch, the horse appeared in North America.* ◇ *One fifth of children between 1 and 2 years of age are repeatedly wakeful for long periods during the night.* **5** used with adjectives to refer to a thing or a group of people described by the adjective: *Heath resisted mounting pressure for a general election, but was only delaying the inevitable.* ◇ *In 1930, only 2.6 per cent of the unemployed had been without work for more than a year.* ◇ *For the British in particular, Spain is a popular holiday destination.* **6** used before the plural of sb's last name to refer to a whole family or a married couple: *Garibaldi's forces began to lose ground against the Bourbons.* ◇ *In 1903 the Curies shared the Nobel Prize for physics with Henri Becquerel for the discovery of radioactivity.* **7** enough of sth for a particular purpose: *Not all companies are able to develop strong brands, because they simply do not have the resources.* **8** used with a unit of measurement to mean 'every': *The scale was 5 miles to the inch.* ◇ *Senior workers were paid by the piece.* **9** used with a unit of time to mean 'the present': *The petitioning campaign was a highly successful way of exerting popular pressure on the government of the day.* **10** /ðiː/ used, stressing *the*, to show that the person or thing referred to is famous or important: *This is very definitely the next thing to read on human intelligence.*

IDM the more, less, etc..., the more, less, etc... used to show that two things change to the same degree: *The more the term is used, the more credibility it gains.* ◇ *The less skill a task involves, the lower the pay and the greater the monotony.*

the·atre (*US* **theater**) /ˈθɪətə(r); *NAmE* ˈθiːətər/ *noun* **1** [C] a building or an outdoor area where plays and similar types of entertainment are performed: *A trip to the theatre is still an infrequent event for many people.* ◇ **+ noun** *Up to that time, Brecht's work was little known to British theatre audiences.* **2** (*also* ˈ**movie theater**) (*both NAmE*) [C] = CINEMA (1): *A good movie is one that makes you leave the theatre thinking.* **3** [U] plays considered as entertainment: *Kathakali is a highly formal style of theatre.* ◇ *For Billington, the best theatre is resolutely social in form.* **4** [U] (*also* **the theatre** [sing.]) the work of writing, producing and acting in plays: *Cinema is profoundly different from the theatre.* ◇ *Maxwell Anderson dominated American theatre in the 1930s.* ◇ **in ~** *The director began his career in theatre.* **5** [C, U] (*BrE*) (*also* **operating theatre** *BrE* **operating room** *US*) a room in a hospital used for medical operations: *The patient was being prepared for theatre.* ◇ **in ~** *She arrived in theatre for a routine operation.* **HELP** **Operating theatre** and **operating room** cannot be used as uncountable nouns. Only **theatre** can be used in this way. **6** [C, usually sing.] **~ of war** the place in which a war or fighting takes place: *Russia opened up a new theatre of war in the Balkans.*

the·at·ri·cal /θiˈætrɪkl/ *adj.* [only before noun] connected with the theatre: *There is nothing better than a live theatrical performance.*

theft /θeft/ *noun* [U, C] **~ (of sth)** the crime of stealing sth from a person or place: *The defendant was charged with the theft of various products from a supermarket.* ➲ *see also* THIEF

their /ðeə(r); *NAmE* ðer/ *det.* (the possessive form of *they*) **1** of or belonging to them: *They lived in London with their baby daughter.* ◇ *Tom and Jane were having problems in their relationship.* ◇ *Their aim is to ensure that they receive the largest possible budget.* **2** used instead of *his* or *her* to refer to a person whose sex is not mentioned or not known: *Ask the patient to describe the characteristics of their pain.* ◇ *It is not easy to make a person change their behaviour.* ➲ grammar note *at* THEY

theirs /ðeəz; *NAmE* ðerz/ *pron.* (the possessive form of *they*) of or belonging to them: *Our feelings on this issue are the same as theirs.* ◇ *Theirs is hot, dangerous work.*

them /ðəm; *strong form* ðem/ *pron.* (the object form of *they*) **1** used when referring to people, animals or things as the object of a verb or preposition: *Staff received letters encouraging them to take early retirement.* ◇ *There are not enough goods to meet the demand for them.* ◇ *Drugs are essential, but a doctor must know how to use them correctly.* **2** used instead of *him* or *her* to refer to a person whose sex is not mentioned or not known: *You cannot just stop someone in the street and ask them inappropriate questions.* ➲ grammar note *at* THEY

T

the·mat·ic **AWL** /θɪˈmætɪk; θiːˈmætɪk/ *adj.* [usually before noun] connected with the theme or themes of sth: *Durgnat divides film noir into eleven thematic categories.* ◇ *We conducted eight focus groups and then performed a qualitative thematic analysis of the interviews.* ■ **the·mat·ic·al·ly** **AWL** /θɪˈmætɪkli; θiːˈmætɪkli/ *adv.*: *The chapters are organized thematically.*

theme **AWL** /θiːm/ *noun* the subject of a talk, piece of writing, EXHIBITION, etc; an idea that keeps returning in a piece of research or a work of art or literature: *The fear of female infidelity is a common theme in Shakespeare's plays.* ◇ **~ of sth** *The theme of the book is how ecosystems respond to climate variability.* ➲ *compare* SUBJECT¹ (1), TOPIC (1)

▸ ADJECTIVE + THEME **key, central, main, major, dominant • important • broad, general • familiar • common • recurring, recurrent • underlying, basic** *A key theme of this chapter is the need for companies to integrate their communications.*

▸ VERB + THEME **explore, address, discuss • develop • focus on • identify • illustrate • return to • echo** *'The Pirate'*

explores the theme of identity. ◇ *I shall return to and develop this theme in the next chapter.*
▸ THEME + VERB **emerge** *Similar themes emerge in each of the chapters.*

them·selves /ðəm'selvz/ *pron.* **1** (the reflexive form of *they*) used when people or animals performing an action are also affected by it: *The accused were allowed to defend themselves.* ◇ *Although individuals may claim to value privacy, they frequently appear to do little to protect themselves.* ◇ *Because of disagreements among themselves, the Communists had not offered military assistance.* **2** used to emphasize *they* or a plural subject: *Most families consumed only what they themselves produced.* ◇ *The children of obese mothers are themselves prone to obesity.* **3** used instead of *himself* or *herself* to refer to a person whose sex is not mentioned or not known: *Previous to this, anyone could call themselves a nurse and care for the sick.* ◇ *Around one person in every 14 described themselves as being a member of a minority ethnic group.* ➲ grammar note *at* THEY
IDM **by them'selves 1** alone; without anyone or anything else: *Women live longer and are more likely to live by themselves later in life.* ◇ *Cultural differences by themselves cannot explain differences in national economic performance.* **2** without help: *Many older people are unable to carry out self-care tasks by themselves.*

then¹ /ðen/ *adv.* **1** used to refer to a particular time in the past or future: *Albert was then 17.* ◇ *The river was not as low then as it is now.* ◇ **since ~** *The book was published in 1985, and since then over 30 000 copies have been sold.* ◇ **up to ~** *Up to then, he had planned on deserting the army.* ◇ **until ~** *It may well prove to be correct, but until then it should be remembered that it is just a model and not a proven scientific fact.* ◇ **back ~** *There was a lot of racism back then.* ◇ **from ~ on** *Output per dollar of wage rises until this point is reached and declines from then on.* **2** used to introduce the next item in a series of actions, events, instructions, etc. SYN AFTERWARDS (1), NEXT² (1): *Goods are bought and then sold for a profit.* ◇ *The numbers are then added together.* **3** used to show the logical result of a particular statement or situation: *If you have a Y chromosome, then you almost certainly got that from your father.* **4** used to introduce a summary of sth that has just been said: *Overall, then, the results of this study should be a cause for some optimism.* IDM *see* THERE

T

then² /ðen/ *adj.* [only before noun] used to describe sb/sth that had a particular title, job, etc. at the time in the past that is being discussed: *The then president, Charles De Gaulle, thought Britain was too close to the US.* ◇ *The Moon was the main focus of the 1960s–1970s 'space race' between the USA and the then Soviet Union.*

theo·lo·gian /ˌθiːə'ləʊdʒən; *NAmE* ˌθiːə'loʊdʒən/ *noun* a person who studies theology: *Calvin was a brilliant theologian, the main architect of the Protestant doctrinal system.*

the·ology /θi'ɒlədʒi; *NAmE* θi'ɑːlədʒi/ *noun* (*pl.* **-ies**) **1** [U] the study of religion and beliefs: *Thomas Aquinas adapted Aristotle's philosophy to Christian theology.* ◇ *Communist governments either abolished faculties of theology or separated them from universities.* **2** [C] a set of religious beliefs: *Female gurus have propagated alternative Hindu theologies.* ■ **theo·logic·al** /ˌθiːə'lɒdʒɪkl; *NAmE* ˌθiːə'lɑːdʒɪkl/ *adj.*: *Vigorous theological debates marked the later Roman Empire.* **theo·logic·al·ly** /ˌθiːə'lɒdʒɪkli; *NAmE* ˌθiːə'lɑːdʒɪkli/ *adv.*: *Such a notion is historically inaccurate and, from a Muslim perspective, theologically false.*

the·orem /'θɪərəm; *NAmE* 'θiːərəm; 'θɪrəm/ *noun* (*mathematics, physics*) a rule or principle that can be proved to be true: *Once we have proved a theorem by using the basic axioms, we can apply it to equations.* ◇ *Menger's theorem states:...*

the·or·etic·al AWL /ˌθɪə'retɪkl; *NAmE* ˌθiːə'retɪkl/ *adj.* [usually before noun] **1** concerned with the ideas on which a particular subject is based, rather than with practice and experiment: *The book combines theoretical perspectives with policy and practice issues.* ◇ *Complexity theory provides a broad theoretical framework for understanding and designing complicated systems.* ◇ *Gauge theories are central to modern theoretical physics.* ◇ *He conducts theoretical and empirical research on information technology usage.* OPP EMPIRICAL (1), EXPERIMENTAL (1), PRACTICAL (1) **2** that could possibly exist, happen or be true, although this is unlikely: *Any possibility that the French government would not impose the quota was purely theoretical.*
▸ THEORETICAL + NOUN **framework • perspective, standpoint • foundation, basis, grounding, underpinning • approach • prediction • construct, entity • model • justification, rationale • explanation • assumption • argument • reflection • background • concept, idea • proposition • orientation • understanding • reasoning • debate, discussion • implication • tradition • paradigm • consideration • insight • stance, position • work • knowledge • literature • physics • physicist** *Several authors have suggested theoretical approaches to guide data collection efforts.*

the·or·etic·al·ly AWL /ˌθɪə'retɪkli; *NAmE* ˌθiːə'retɪkli/ *adv.* **1** in a way that is concerned with the ideas on which a particular subject is based, rather than with practice and experiment: *These views were challenged both theoretically and empirically.* ◇ *The journal focuses on applied research that is theoretically sound.* **2** in a way that is possible in theory but unlikely in practice: *Such a situation is, although theoretically possible, also unlikely to be sustainable in the long-run.* ◇ *Theoretically, all of these activities can be performed by one organization.*

the·or·ist AWL /'θɪərɪst; *NAmE* 'θiːərɪst; 'θɪrɪst/ (*also less frequent* **the·or·et·ician** /ˌθɪərə'tɪʃn; *NAmE* ˌθiːərə'tɪʃn; ˌθɪrə'tɪʃn/) *noun* a person who develops ideas about a particular subject in order to explain why things happen or exist: *Feminist theorists emphasize that the differential treatment of boys and girls is a nearly universal, cross-cultural circumstance.* ◇ *Since antiquity, many political theorists have admired Sparta's government.*

the·or·ize (*BrE also* **-ise**) /'θɪəraɪz; *NAmE* 'θiːəraɪz/ *verb* [I, T] to suggest facts and ideas to explain sth; to form a theory or theories about sth: **~ about/on sth** *Long ago, Montesquieu theorized about the impact of climates on human behaviour.* ◇ **~ that...** *He theorized that the atolls marked the sites of vanished volcanoes.* ◇ **it is theorized that...** *It has been theorized that this rate of cognitive decline can be slowed by changes to the social environment.* ◇ **~ sth** *Cox theorizes a complex interplay between politics and economics.* ■ **the·or·iz·ing, -is·ing** *noun* [U] *In his early theorizing, he talked of 'self-preservative' instincts.*

the·ory AWL /'θɪəri; *NAmE* 'θɪri; 'θiːəri/ *noun* (*pl.* **-ies**) **1** [C, U] a formal set of ideas that is intended to explain why sth happens or exists: *There are various theories concerning the origin of this expression.* ◇ *Coleridge coined the term 'psycho-analytical' in 1805, long before Freud developed a theory and practice under that name.* ◇ *Evolutionary theory can inform the study of antibiotic resistance.* ◇ **~ of sth** *Conley intends his work to offer a grand theory of cinema.* ➲ *see also* CRITICAL THEORY, GAME THEORY, QUANTUM THEORY **2** [U] the system of ideas on which a particular subject is based: *Political theory has a long-standing position in the history of Western thought.* ◇ *Carby (1982) criticizes received concepts of the family,*

WORD FAMILY
theory *noun*
theoretical *adj.*
theoretically *adv.*
theorist *noun*
theorize *verb*

patriarchy and reproduction in feminist theory. **3** [C] **~ (that...)** an opinion or idea that sb believes is true but that is not proved: *Dickens is attempting to demonstrate his theory that history is a pattern of causes and effects.*
IDM **in ˈtheory** used to say that a particular statement is supposed to be true but may in fact be wrong: *This process is in theory rather simple, but the proposed methods may be more difficult to apply in practice.* ◇ *In theory, a new Parliament could repeal the Human Rights Act 1998, although in reality this would be very unlikely.*
▸ ADJECTIVE + THEORY **modern, contemporary** • **international** • **traditional** • **conventional** • **standard** • **basic** • **general** • **liberal** • **critical** • **scientific** • **evolutionary** • **political** • **economic** • **legal** • **moral, ethical** • **philosophical** • **mathematical** • **physical** • **psychological** • **normative** *Publicly verifiable evidence is the ultimate test of scientific theories.* | **current, existing** • **recent** • **early** • **competing** • **alternative** • **underlying** • **successful** • **adequate** • **explanatory** • **grand** *Current theories seek to link these ideas to recent advances in molecular genetics.* | **social** • **feminist** • **democratic** • **literary** • **classical** • **neoclassical** • **multicultural** • **cognitive** • **psychoanalytic** • **ecological** • **behavioural** • **linguistic** • **sociological** *Social theory is closely related to the discipline of sociology.*
▸ VERB + THEORY **develop, formulate, construct, build** • **test** • **propose, advance, present, outline** • **apply** • **criticize** • **challenge** • **reject** • **abandon** • **accept** • **defend** • **support** • **discuss** • **summarize** • **review** *I will look briefly at how this theory can be applied, its successes and its limitations.*
▸ THEORY + VERB **suggest, postulate** • **inform** • **explain** • **guide** • **imply** • **emphasize** • **predict** • **assume** • **account for** • **be based on** • **be grounded in** *Globalization theory predicts the end of the national economy.*

THESAURUS

theory • **model** • **approach** • **framework** *noun*

These are all words for an idea or a set of ideas that help to explain, understand or do sth.

- the theory/model/approach/framework **of** sth
- a model/framework **for** sth
- an approach **to** sth
- a **general/new** theory/model/approach/framework
- a **theoretical** model/approach/framework
- a/an **simple/traditional/alternative** model/approach
- to **develop/have/use/apply** a/an theory/model/approach/framework
- to **present/propose/discuss** a/an theory/model/approach/framework
- to **base** a/an theory/model/approach/framework **on** sth
- a/an theory/model/approach/framework **has/provides** sth

- A **theory** only helps sb explain or understand sth; a **model**, an **approach** or a **framework** can also have a more practical application: *the Frankfurt school of Marxist critical theory* ◇ *a strong legal framework for environmental regulation* ◇ *Few archaeologists have used this approach.*
- A **model** or a **framework** typically describes the structure of sth; a **model** is often used to predict a possible pattern or structure; a **framework** is often used as a basis for doing sth; an **approach** is a way of thinking about or doing sth: *In the low-density environment, the crabs behaved as predicted by the model.* ◇ *Establish a framework for analysing the results.* ◇ *They have pioneered innovative approaches to environmental management.*

thera·peut·ic /ˌθerəˈpjuːtɪk/ *adj.* **1** [usually before noun] designed to help treat an illness: *The procedure is used for diagnostic and therapeutic purposes.* ◇ *Cannabis is being investigated as a therapeutic agent for multiple sclerosis.* **2** helping you to relax: *She found it therapeutic to have so much time to think and speak.* ■ **thera·peut·ic·al·ly** /ˌθerəˈpjuːtɪkli/ *adv.*: *The 'statin' drugs are widely used therapeutically to reduce cholesterol levels in blood.*

ther·ap·ist /ˈθerəpɪst/ *noun* **1** (especially in compounds) a specialist who treats a particular type of illness or problem, or who uses a particular type of treatment: *A speech and language therapist can help with communication problems.* **2** = PSYCHOTHERAPIST

ther·apy /ˈθerəpi/ *noun* (*pl.* **-ies**) **1** [U, C] treatment for a physical problem or an illness: *She has been receiving antibiotic therapy for the last 5 days.* ◇ *Complementary therapies such as massage and aromatherapy may help.* ◇ **~ for sth** *Therapy for diabetes is monitored using measures of blood glucose.* ➲ *see also* RADIOTHERAPY **2** [U] = PSYCHOTHERAPY: **~ for sth** *He is receiving therapy for depression.* ◇ **in ~** *Women in therapy report significantly more problems than men.*

there /ðeə(r); *NAmE* ðer/ *adv.* **1 there is, are, was, were, etc.** used to show that sth exists or happens: *There are many difficulties with this view.* ◇ *We might expect there to be some differences.* ◇ *In many universities there exist powerful academic departments.* **2** in, at or to that place or position: *She stayed there all day.* ◇ *It was very hot in there.* ◇ *The owner of the house continued to live there.* **3** existing or available: *The aim is to uncover what is already there.* ◇ *Existing customers will not be there forever.* **4** at that point (in a story, an argument, a situation, etc.): *But the story does not end there.* ◇ *There the fossil trail ends rather abruptly.* ◇ *She wants to get over the hurt of her failed marriage, but she is not there yet.* **5 ~ to do sth** used to show the role of a person or thing in a situation: *Safety cameras are there to save lives.* ◇ *The facilitator is there to make the learning process easier for those learning in groups.*
IDM **there and then** (*also* **then and there**) immediately: *A customer who really needs something there and then will have to go to a shop to buy it.* ➲ *more at* GET, HERE

there·after /ˌðeərˈɑːftə(r); *NAmE* ˌðerˈæftər/ *adv.* (*formal*) after the time or event mentioned: *He made his way to Kolonos in Attica and died shortly thereafter.* ◇ *Thereafter, their fortunes suffered a steep decline.* ➲ *compare* HEREAFTER (2)

there·by AWL /ˌðeəˈbaɪ; *NAmE* ˌðerˈbaɪ/ *adv.* (*formal*) used to introduce the result of the action or situation mentioned: *The agency's main objective is to help energy consumers use energy more efficiently, thereby reducing the environmental load.* ◇ *Their policy is to name key authors, and thereby allow sources to be identified from the references at the end of the book.*

there·fore /ˈðeəfɔː(r); *NAmE* ˈðerfɔːr/ *adv.* used to introduce the logical result of sth that has just been mentioned: *Social success is a matter of Destiny; Confucius therefore concludes that it is futile to pursue it.* ◇ *Overall, therefore, the early Tudor achievement in the borderlands was insubstantial.* ➲ language bank *on* page 830

there·in /ˌðeərˈɪn; *NAmE* ˌðerˈɪn/ *adv.* (*law* or *formal*) in the place, object or document mentioned: *Data subjects must have the right to access data and to secure the correction of any errors contained therein.*
IDM **therein lies...** used to emphasize the result or consequence of a particular situation: *An unexpected finding may lead a scientist in a direction that nobody imagined, and therein lies the very essence of discovery.*

there·of /ˌðeərˈɒv; *NAmE* ˌðerˈʌv/ *adv.* (*law* or *formal*) of the thing mentioned: *Is the property or any part thereof used for commercial activity?*

ther·mal /ˈθɜːml; *NAmE* ˈθɜːrml/ *adj.* [only before noun] (*technical*) connected with heat: *As the temperature is raised, the thermal energy is increased.* ◇ *Thermal*

T

LANGUAGE BANK

Ways of saying 'for this reason'

The following words and expressions can be used in academic writing for linking a statement to an earlier statement which gives a reason for it.

therefore ◆ for this/that reason ◆ this is why ◆ thus ◆ hence

- *Their study is based on only seven soil profiles and is, **therefore**, difficult to apply regionally.*
- *Left to its own devices, he argued, a capitalist economy is not likely to provide jobs all the time for all who seek them. **For this reason**, Keynes urged the adoption of policies that...*
- *Society's welfare was thought to depend on the official cults. **This is why** modern notions of separation of church and state do not fit the ancient world.*
- *She is pregnant and is **thus** reluctant to take any of the drugs recommended to her.*
- *The existing capacity of the landfill is inadequate—**hence** the need for extension of the site.*

See also the Language Bank at **cause**.

conductivity and membrane thickness determine the heat transfer resistance between two airstreams. ◇ *Complete burnout of the fuel increases the thermal efficiency of the plant.* ■ **ther·mal·ly** /ˈθɜːməli; *NAmE* ˈθɜːrməli/ *adv.*: *The very small conductivity observed is entirely due to the thermally activated motion of ions through the crystal.*

thermo·dynam·ics /ˌθɜːməʊdaɪˈnæmɪks; *NAmE* ˌθɜːrmoʊdaɪˈnæmɪks/ *noun* [U] the science that deals with the relations between heat and other forms of energy: *The first law of thermodynamics states that energy can be neither created nor destroyed.* ■ **thermo·dynam·ic** *adj.*: *The thermodynamic properties of ions can be determined with the aid of electrode potentials.*

therm·om·eter /θəˈmɒmɪtə(r); *NAmE* θərˈmɑːmɪtər/ *noun* an instrument used for measuring the temperature of the air, a person's body, etc: *Temperature was monitored using an alcohol thermometer which was checked daily.*

the·saurus /θɪˈsɔːrəs/ *noun* (*pl.* **the·sauri** /θɪˈsɔːraɪ/or **the·saur·uses** /θɪˈsɔːrəsɪz/) a work of reference that lists words in groups that have similar meanings: *You can generate synonyms using a thesaurus (either a book or one built into your software).*

T

these ➲ THIS[1], THIS[2]

thesis AWL /ˈθiːsɪs/ *noun* (*pl.* **theses** /ˈθiːsiːz/) **1** a statement or an opinion that is discussed in a logical way and presented with evidence in order to prove that it is true: *Despite some flaws, the book's central thesis is interesting and deserves more careful investigation.* ◇ *to advance/ defend a thesis* ◇ **~ that...** *The presented data do not seem to support the thesis that European industry has become more innovative.* ➲ thesaurus note *at* HYPOTHESIS **2 ~ (on sth)** a long piece of writing completed by a student as part of a university degree, based on their own research: *She is currently completing a doctoral thesis on the influence of surrealism on Carter's early fiction.*

they /ðeɪ/ *pron.* (used as the subject of a verb) **1** people, animals or things that have already been mentioned or are easily identified: *It may difficult to motivate people if they are unhappy about their working environment.* ◇ *Taylor's ideas are important because they continue to inform the production of goods and services today.* **2** used instead of *he* or *she* to refer to a person whose sex is not mentioned or not known: *As the patient eats less, they lose weight.* **3** people in authority or experts: *They say that 40% of people will die of heart attacks.* ◇ *They are threatening to scrutinize the performance of all directors more carefully.*

GRAMMAR POINT

they ◆ them ◆ their ◆ themselves ◆ he ◆ she

When you are writing in English, it is often important to use languge that includes both men and women equally. Some people may be offended if you do not.

- **He** used to be considered to refer to both men and women. This is not now generally acceptable. Instead, after *someone, somebody, anyone, anybody, everyone* and *everybody* or a general noun like *person, child* or *patient*, one of the plural pronouns **they, them, their** and **themselves** is often used: *Asking **a patient** to identify someone in **their** immediate circle of family and friends who is able to support them is crucial.*
- Some people prefer to use **he or she, his or her** and **him or her** in their writing. **S/he** or **(s)he** are also used. These uses can seem awkward when they are used a lot. One alternative used by some writers is to use **she** to refer to either a male or female subject, or to alternate **she** and **he** in a text: *Tell your child she should not be angry with a new step-parent.* However, it may often be possible to change the sentence, using a plural noun. Instead of saying *A carer may not know when he or she provides high-quality care* you can say *Carers may not know when they provide high-quality care.*

thick /θɪk/ *adj.* (**thick·er, thick·est**) **1** having a larger distance between opposite sides or surfaces than other similar objects or than normal: *The dermis is the thickest layer of the skin (3-5 mm).* ◇ *The thick wooden walls insulate the interior from warming by residual solar absorption.* ➲ *see also* THICKNESS **2** used to talk about the distance between opposite sides or surfaces: *The continental ice sheets are over 3 km thick in many places.* **3** (of hair, fur or trees) growing closely together in large numbers: *Thick fur is useful in the Arctic and harmful in the tropics.* ◇ *The thick forest, which until recently covered the islands, is disappearing rapidly.* **4** (of clouds, smoke, air, etc.) difficult to see through; difficult to breathe in: *Thick cloud cover normally shields the earth's surface from cooling through the long winter nights.*

thick·en /ˈθɪkən/ *verb* [I, T] to become thicker; to make sth thicker: *The rock formation gradually thickens to the west.* ◇ **~ sth** *The 'greenhouse effect' thickens the natural canopy of gases in the atmosphere and causes more heat to become trapped.*

thick·ness /ˈθɪknəs/ *noun* [U, C] the size of sth between opposite surfaces or sides: **in ~** *The film typically varies from 0.1 to 1 µm in thickness.* ◇ **~ (of sth)** *The upper layer of the aquifer has a thickness of 30 m.* ◇ *It uses sound waves to visualize and measure ventricular wall thickness.* ➲ *compare* WIDTH

thief /θiːf/ *noun* (*pl.* **thieves** /θiːvz/) a person who steals sth from another person or place: *Thieves broke in the day after the bank vaults were cleared.* ➲ *see also* THEFT

thin[1] /θɪn/ *adj.* (**thin·ner, thin·nest**) **1** having a smaller distance between opposite sides or surfaces than other similar objects or than normal: *Evaporation of the solvent leaves a thin film of protein molecules on the plate.* ◇ *Overbank flooding may leave thin layers of fine sand, silt and clay.* ◇ *The use of thin sections greatly aids the description of rocks and the identification of minerals.* ➲ *usage note at* NARROW[1] **2** (*sometimes disapproving*) (of a person or part of the body) not covered with much fat: *On examination, the patient appeared thin and pale.* **3** (of hair) not growing closely together or in large amounts: *His hair was going thin.* **4** (of air) containing less OXYGEN than normal: *In the* *thin air of the Swiss Alps, his condition becomes severe.* ◇ *The atmosphere of Mars is thinner than that of Venus.* **5** of poor quality; lacking an important quality: *His more recent work has been criticized for resting on rather thin sociological evidence.* ⮊ *usage note at* NARROW[1]

thin[2] /θɪn/ *verb* (-nn-) [I, T] to become less thick; to make sth become less thick: *Many sufferers do not like the fact that their hair is thinning.* ◇ **~ sth** *Lateral stretching thins the earth's crust.* ◇ *The treatment for deep vein thrombosis is medication to thin the blood.*

thing /θɪŋ/ *noun* **1** [C] a fact, an event, a situation or an action; what sb says or thinks: *The same thing has happened in other industries.* ◇ *The first thing to note about this argument is that it relies on a claim that is not necessarily true.* ◇ *The main thing is to maintain the learning focus of the class.* ◇ *Among other things, this work outlined for the first time Freud's concept of the unconscious.* **2** [C, usually sing.] what is needed or socially acceptable: *If long-term trends are improving, the best thing government can do is leave well alone.* ◇ *Ethics focuses on whether something is the right thing to do from a moral standpoint, as opposed to whether it is lawful.* **3 things** [pl.] (*rather informal*) the general situation: *To make things simpler, we show the results for just the first two groups.* ◇ **as things stand** *As things currently stand, the trend to increasing specialization looks set to continue.* ◇ **all things considered** *All things considered, however, it would seem that the first option outlined is the best.* **4** [C] an object that is not alive in the way that people and plants are: *A magnet attracts others things made of iron to it.* ◇ *The child was able to recognize the series of pictures of people and things familiar in his environment.* **5** [C] an object whose name you do not use because you do not need to or want to, or because you do not know it: *The patient's cravings are towards fruits and related sweet things.* **6** [C] (used with an adjective) a living creature: *Semipermeable membranes are essential components of nearly all living things.* **7 things** [pl.] (*formal*) (followed by an adjective) all that can be described in a particular way: *Cato sometimes expressed great hostility to all things Greek.*

IDM **A is ˈone thing, B is aˈnother | it's ˈone thing to do A, it's aˈnother thing to do B** B is very different from A, for example it is more difficult, serious or important: *It is one thing to recognize an obligation and another thing to fulfil it.* **be all things to all ˈmen/ˈpeople** (of things) to be understood or used in different ways by different people: *It is difficult for companies to admit that they are not capable of being all things to all people.* **come to/be the same ˈthing** to have the same result or meaning: *To spend more than their current incomes they will have to borrow or, what is essentially the same thing, to buy on credit.* **for ˈone thing** used to introduce one of two or more reasons for doing sth: *The sheer number of relevant texts, for one thing, makes this an impossible task.* ⮊ *more at* EQUAL[1], NATURE, SCHEME, TURN[1]

think /θɪŋk/ *verb* (**thought, thought** /θɔːt/) **1** [T, I] (not used in the progressive tenses) to have a particular idea or opinion about sth/sb; to believe sth: **~ (that)...** *Most people think that the Great Depression was a catastrophic economic event.* ◇ **it is thought that...** *It is often thought that social, economic and cultural influences inevitably make fertility research more challenging.* ◇ **~ sth (about sth)** *The study was designed to find out what people think about current issues and politics.* ◇ **~ so** *Such use of irony may be necessary to feminist writers—certainly Virginia Woolf thought so.* ◇ **~ sb/sth + adj.** *The commitee thought it important that companies stated to what extent they had followed the recommendations.* ◇ **be thought to be/do sth** *The detergent action of the bile salts is also thought to destroy many bacteria.* **2** [I, T] to use your mind to consider sth, to form connected ideas, to try to solve problems, etc: *Children must use the concrete before they are able to think in the abstract.* ◇ **~ about sth** *This model provides space for students to think critically about complex local and global problems.* ◇ *Managers may need to think more carefully about the impact of their actions.* ◇ **~ in terms of sth** *Many geographers believe that the best way to approach agricultural issues is to think in terms of ecosystems.* ◇ **~ what/how, etc...** *Try to think what types of drug might help with the patient's symptoms.* **3** [T] (usually used in the progressive tenses) **~ sth** to have ideas, words or images in your mind: *These children have an inability to judge correctly what other people are thinking.* **4** [T] **~ (that)...** to expect sth: *Many of these women never thought that they would be able to talk about their experiences so openly.* ◇ *A shared vision can lead to staff achieving more than they thought they could.*

IDM **if/when you ˈthink about it** used to draw attention to a fact that is not obvious or has not previously been mentioned: *If you think about it, for most product categories, most people are aware of more than one brand.* **ˌthink aˈgain** to consider a situation again and perhaps change your idea or intention: *These difficulties led him to think again about the mapping problem.* **think ˈtwice about sth/about/before doing sth** to think carefully before deciding to do sth: *The credit crisis is making consumers think twice about their new car purchases.* **think highly, not much, little, etc. of sb/sth** to have a very good, poor, etc. opinion of sb/sth: *Prestige cars are status symbols that gain value as more people think highly of them.* ◇ *Byron had previously not thought much of Wordsworth, finding his ruminations on Nature incomprehensible.* ⮊ *more at* FIT[3], LIKE[2]

PHR V **ˈthink about/of sb/sth** to consider sb/sth when you are doing or planning sth: *These are the benefits that people think about when they are looking for brands.* **ˌthink aˈhead (to sth)** to think about a future event or situation and plan for it: *In competition for a mate, the advantage is with those who think ahead and predict outcomes.* **ˌthink ˈback (to sth)** to think about sth that happened in the past: *Thinking back to the strategic planning process, the first four steps identified the target audience.* **ˌthink for yourˈself** to form your own opinions and make decisions without depending on others: *Philosophical questions require the student to think for her/himself.* **ˈthink of sth/sb 1** to have an image or idea of sth/sb in your mind: *For one person, thinking of Vienna may conjure up images of Strauss waltzes.* **2** to create an idea in your imagination: *Patients may also have correct ideas that doctors had not thought of.* **ˈthink of sb/sth as sb/sth** to consider sb/sth in a particular way: *The literary figures traditionally thought of as the Romantics are Wordsworth, Coleridge, Blake, Byron, Shelley and Keats.* **ˌthink sth ˈout** to consider or plan sth carefully: *For these industries, any detailed plan, no matter how well thought out, becomes obsolete within weeks or months.* **ˌthink sth ˈover** to consider sth carefully, especially before reaching a decision: *The essay gave Cohen reason to think over his position towards religion.* **ˌthink sth ˈthrough** to consider a problem or a possible course of action fully: *A particular proposal might raise further ethical issues that need to be thought through.* **ˌthink sth ˈup** (*rather informal*) to create sth in your mind SYN DEVISE, INVENT (1): *Humans are creative creatures and they are constantly thinking up new words and expressions.*

think·er /ˈθɪŋkə(r)/ *noun* **1** a person who thinks seriously, and often writes about important things, such as philosophy or science: *a liberal/Jewish/Christian/Greek thinker* ◇ *Jean-Jacques Rousseau was one of the most influential thinkers of the Enlightenment.* **2** a person who thinks in a particular way: *It is vital to encourage children to be critical thinkers.*

think·ing /ˈθɪŋkɪŋ/ *noun* [U] **1** the process of thinking about sth: *Parents can help their child develop a way of* *thinking that increases their development of healthy anger.* ➲ *see also* CRITICAL THINKING **2** ideas or opinions about sth: **~ about/on sth** *Members are kept up to date on current thinking about teaching through our newsletter.* ◇ **~ (behind sth)** *Interviewees were asked to explain the thinking behind their decisions.* ◇ *The First World War shifted liberal thinking towards a recognition that peace is not a natural condition but is one that must be constructed.*

third[1] /θɜːd; *NAmE* θɜːrd/ *det., ordinal number* happening or coming 3rd in a series or list: *There was another important development between the third and sixth centuries.* ◇ *It is the third largest grocery retailer in the world.* ◇ *This analysis is the third in a series of reviews.* ◇ *He became the king's astronomer and moved to Windsor where George III could visit him.* HELP In this example, **George III** is pronounced 'George the third'.

third[2] /θɜːd; *NAmE* θɜːrd/ *noun* each of three equal parts of sth: *The Black Death cut European populations by one third.* ◇ *Average R&D expenditures are around $3 million, and roughly two thirds are spent on development.* ◇ **~ of sb/sth** *A third of patients presenting with arterial disease have severe coronary artery disease.* ➲ language bank *at* PROPORTION

third·ly /ˈθɜːdli; *NAmE* ˈθɜːrdli/ *adv.* used to introduce the third of a list of points you want to make in a speech or piece of writing: *Secondly, it can provide very important information about the mechanism, and thirdly, it helps us to understand the physiological role of the enzyme.*

ˌthird ˈparty *noun* a person who is involved in a situation in addition to the two main people involved: *If data are disclosed to a third party, notification must be given.* ◇ *Mediation programmes provide a neutral third party to help adversaries sort out their differences.*

the ˌthird ˈperson *noun* [sing.] **1** (*grammar*) the form of a pronoun or verb used by a speaker to refer to other people and things: *The verb marker -s occurs only on present tense verbs with a third person singular subject like 'he'.* **2** a way of writing a report, novel, etc. using third person forms: *Like 'Clash', 'The Division Bell Mystery' uses third person narration.* ◇ **in the ~** *The report is generally written in the third person (i.e. avoiding the use of 'I', 'we', and 'you') and in the past tense.* ➲ *compare* FIRST PERSON, SECOND PERSON

T

the ˌThird ˈWorld *noun* [sing.] a way of referring to the poor or developing countries of Africa, Asia and Latin America, which is sometimes considered offensive: *In much of the Third World, the family household retains its significance as a unit of production.* ◇ **+ noun** *These policies are not restricted to poorer Third World states.* HELP The most widely used and accepted term for these countries is now **developing countries**. ➲ *see also* DEVELOPING (1)

this[1] /ðɪs/ *det.* (*pl.* **these** /ðiːz/) **1** used to refer to a particular person, thing or event that is close to you, especially compared with another: *In his poems, particularly in this one, Heschel conducts an internal dialogue.* ◇ *The major strength of this book is the author's use of primary sources.* **2** used to refer to sth/sb that has already been mentioned: *Press coverage of this incident generated significant controversy.* ◇ *These two countries have limited economic assets, which will hinder economic recovery.* **3** used with periods of time related to the present: *This year sees the bicentenary of the births of both Verdi and Wagner.* ◇ **these days** *These days, both glass- and carbon-fibre composites are used for infrastructure constructions and repairs.*

this[2] /ðɪs/ *pron.* (*pl.* **these** /ðiːz/) **1** used to refer to a particular person, thing or event that is close to you, especially compared with another: *This is the first time that these techniques have successfully been applied to medieval Chinese texts.* **2** used to refer to sth/sb that has already been mentioned: *The company was transformed and Ward had played a vital role in bringing this about.* ◇ *Several studies have shown... This is surprising, in view of the fact that...*

thorax /ˈθɔːræks/ *noun* (*pl.* **thor·axes** or **thor·aces** /ˈθɔːrəsiːz/) **1** (*anatomy*) the part of the human body between the neck and the waist: *No direct pressure may be applied to the neck, thorax, abdomen, back or pelvis.* **2** the middle section of the body of an insect or animal: *The normal fly has wings on the second segment of the thorax and balancers on the third.* ■ **thor·acic** /θɔːˈræsɪk/ *adj.* [only before noun] *The thoracic segments of Drosophila are the segments that carry the legs and wings in the adult.*

thor·ough /ˈθʌrə; *NAmE* ˈθɜːroʊ/ *adj.* **1** done completely; with great attention to detail: *A thorough clinical examination is required to determine the cause of the confusion.* ◇ *An organization must have a thorough understanding of its target buyers.* **2** [not usually before noun] (of a person) doing things very carefully and with great attention to detail: *The governors were honest, competent and thorough.* ◇ *It is important to be thorough in these experiments, and to make sure that the results are consistent.* ■ **thor·ough·ness** *noun* [U] **~ (of sb/sth)** *A statement was issued noting the thoroughness of the Commissioners' work.* ◇ *At that time, the British civil service was known for its competence and thoroughness.*

thor·ough·ly /ˈθʌrəli; *NAmE* ˈθɜːrəli/ *adv.* **1** very; very much; completely: *It is important to be thoroughly familiar with all the equipment and techniques required.* ◇ *Some ideas about language change have been thoroughly discredited.* **2** carefully and with great attention to detail: *The skin is cleaned thoroughly before the sample is taken.* ◇ *She only begins work on a campaign after the target market has been thoroughly researched.*

those ➲ THAT[1], THAT[2]

though[1] /ðəʊ; *NAmE* ðoʊ/ *conj.* **1** despite the fact that SYN ALTHOUGH: *The share of the world's Internet users in Europe and North America will fall, though absolute numbers will continue to rise in both regions.* ◇ *Though research in this field is still at an early stage, the indications are promising.* ◇ *Jim, though guilty of no crime, was imprisoned for six months.* ➲ *see also* EVEN THOUGH ➲ grammar note *at* DESPITE **2** used to add a fact or an opinion that makes the previous statement less strong or less important SYN BUT[1] (1): *Any of these elements can be read without the others, though they will make most sense when read together.* IDM *see* AS[3]

though[2] /ðəʊ; *NAmE* ðoʊ/ *adv.* however; used to add a fact or an opinion that contrasts with a statement that has been made or makes it less true or important: *The price of progress, though, can be high.* ◇ *Feelings have been notoriously hard to study in psychology. Now, though, we can investigate how brain activity changes with feelings.* HELP In spoken English, **though** as an adverb is often used at the end of a sentence: *The price of progress can be high, though.* However, this can sound very informal and is best avoided in academic writing. Unlike 'however', **though** cannot be used as an adverb at the beginning of a sentence: ~~*Though, the price of progress can be high.*~~

thought[1] /θɔːt/ *noun* **1** [C] something that you think of or remember: **~ of (sb/sth) doing sth** *The thought of people suffering famine or natural disasters will generally arouse people's sympathy.* ◇ **~ of sth** *Diagnosis also requires loss of interest or pleasure and recurrent thoughts of death.* ◇ **~ on/about sth** *Opinion polls frequently ask the public to provide their thoughts on this issue.* ◇ **~ that...** *It is a sobering thought that the human race could have been wiped out by several of these technical* *developments in the past.* **2 thoughts** [pl.] a person's mind and all the ideas that they have in it when they are thinking: *Patients should be encouraged to discuss their feelings and thoughts with others.* **3** [U] the power or process of thinking: *The authors demonstrate Madison's own significance and his independence of thought.* ◇ *For Descartes, thought is a transaction with 'ideas', which are supposed to be intrinsically full of content.* **4** [U] the act of thinking seriously and carefully about sth SYN CONSIDERATION (2): *A little more thought soon leads one to a number of other conclusions.* ◇ *Not enough thought was given to the long-term effects of building the bridge.* **5** [U, C] **~ (of sth/doing sth)** an intention or a hope of doing sth: *Many researchers contributed directly and indirectly to the book, with no thought of reward or recognition.* ◇ *As soon as the financial crisis hit in the autumn of 2008, all thoughts of displacing Brown as leader were dropped.* **6** [U] ideas in politics, science, etc. connected with a particular person, group or period of history: *Tacitus was present at the origin and evolution of modern political thought.* ◇ **a line of ~** *At least since the 1960s, another line of thought has been gradually gaining ground.*

IDM **have ˌsecond ˈthoughts** to change your opinion after thinking about sth again: *After his initial confrontation with Molotov, Truman appeared to have second thoughts.* ➲ *more at* FOOD, SCHOOL, TRAIN[2]

thought[2] *past tense, past part. of* THINK

ˈthought experiment *noun* an experiment that involves thinking through what would happen in an imaginary situation rather than actually performing a real experiment: *Most thought experiments are impossible to carry out, although some end up turning into real experiments as technology changes.*

thought·ful /ˈθɔːtfl/ *adj.* showing signs of careful thought: *The book's analyses of the international drugs trade are thoughtful and provocative.* ◇ *Teachers have begun to use historical simulations, in a sensitive and thoughtful way, to teach about the Holocaust.* ■ **thought·ful·ly** /ˈθɔːtfəli/ *adv.*: *They are inclined to act too quickly, rather than thoughtfully evaluate ways of responding.*

ˈthought-provok·ing *adj.* making people think seriously about a particular subject or issue: *Sivakumaran's analysis is fresh and thought-provoking.* ◇ *The article raises thought-provoking questions about the film's 'documentary aesthetics'.*

thou·sand /ˈθaʊznd/ *number* (*abbr.* K) **1** 1 000: **a ~ (sth)** *The project took more than a thousand statements.* ◇ *Only a tiny percentage of transactions are fraudulent—perhaps around one in a thousand.* **thousands (of...)** *These changes typically happen over a long period (thousands of years).* HELP You say **a, one, two, etc. thousand** without a final 's' on 'thousand'. **Thousands (of...)** can be used if there is no number or quantity before it. Always use a plural verb with **thousand** or **thousands**, except when an amount of money is mentioned: *Four thousand (people) are expected to attend.* ◇ *Two thousand (pounds) was withdrawn from the account.* **2 the thousands** the numbers from 1 000 to 9 999: **in the thousands** *The insects in a nest may number in the thousands.*

thread /θred/ *noun* **1** [C] an idea or a feature that is part of sth greater; an idea that connects the different parts of sth: *Stimulating the market for quality food products is a central thread running through the whole strategy.* ◇ **~ of sth** *I shall attempt to pull the threads of the discussion together.* **2** [U, C] a thin string of cotton or other material, used for sewing or making cloth: *By changing the colour of the thread, a particular pattern can be woven.* ◇ *The Japanese began exporting silk thread in great quantities after the late 1860s.* **3** [C] a long thin line of sth: *It is visible in the electron microscope as a tangled fine thread called a nucleoid.* ◇ **~ of sth** *Discrete threads of water join to form streams.* **4** [C] a series of connected messages in an Internet discussion that have been sent by different people: *'Views' refer to the number of times that Internet surfers clicked on a thread to read it.* ◇ *Content analysis was used to classify the range of topics reflected in the threads.*

threat /θret/ *noun* **1** [C] a statement in which you tell sb that you will punish or harm them, especially if they do not do what you want: *Death threats were made against him and his wife.* ◇ **~ to do sth** *A five-year-old hitting her brother and making serious threats to harm him should be viewed with much concern.* ◇ **~ of sth** *Threats of violence made by the patient should be taken seriously.* **2** [U, C, usually sing.] the possibility of trouble, danger or disaster: *In conclusion, the global terrorist threat calls for a reappraisal of risk assessment methods.* ◇ **be/come under ~** *The USA resorted to protectionism when its steel industry came under threat from cheap imports.* ◇ **~ of sth** *In the early 1990s, the threat of superpower nuclear war faded.* **3** [C] a person or thing that is likely to cause trouble, danger, etc: *Transfer of an animal virus through an infected vaccine is a serious threat that requires strict safeguards.* ◇ **~ to sb/sth** *Conflicts pose serious threats to economic recovery and sustainability.*

▸ ADJECTIVE + THREAT **serious • real • great • major • significant • perceived • new • potential • imminent • immediate • constant • external • global** *He was dealing effectively with the potential threat of further attacks.*

▸ NOUN + THREAT **terrorist • security** *Bird flu came to be perceived as a pressing global security threat.*

▸ VERB + THREAT **make • issue • use • receive • respond to** *He accuses religion of using threats and promises to influence people.* | **pose, present • constitute, represent • remain • be perceived as, be seen as • face • identify • meet • address • respond to • deal with • counter • reduce • eliminate** *Chafe argues that Russia at no time constituted a military threat to the United States.*

▸ THREAT TO + NOUN **peace • security • life • health • freedom • democracy • stability** *At no time was there any threat to international peace and security.*

▸ THREAT OF + NOUN **terrorism • violence • attack • war** *She was terrified by her brother's threats of physical violence.*

threat·en /ˈθretn/ *verb* **1** [T] to say that you will cause trouble, hurt sb, etc. if you do not get what you want: **~ sb** *An ex-policeman claimed that his chief constable had threatened him during an investigation.* ◇ **~ sb with sth** *The applicant has already been directly threatened with serious harm in his country of origin.* ◇ **~ sth** *The youths had not threatened violence towards the police officers.* ◇ *He was elected to deal with a threatened German invasion.* ◇ **~ to do sth** *Gangsters threatened to destroy his business unless he made a payment of $10 000.* ◇ **~ that...** *The President threatened that the US would intervene militarily to keep the oil pipelines flowing.* **2** [T] to be a danger to sth; to be likely to harm sth SYN ENDANGER: **~ sth** *The proposals threatened their job security.* ◇ *Computer viruses endlessly threaten the survival of computer networks.* ◇ **be threatened with sth** *Many more species are threatened with extinction.* **3** [I] to seem likely to happen or cause sth unpleasant: *Unless war threatened, national politics remained the focus of attention.* ◇ **~ to do sth** *The movement threatened to undermine the social order.*

threat·en·ing /ˈθretnɪŋ/ *adj.* expressing a threat of harm or violence: *They received threatening letters and were victims of acts of vandalism.* ◇ *He became loud and physically threatening.* HELP In law, **threatening** behaviour is behaviour that shows that a person intends to harm sb.

three /θriː/ *number* 3 HELP There are examples of how to use numbers at the entry for **five**.

ˌthree-diˈmension·al *adj.* (*abbr.* 3D, 3-D) having, or appearing to have, length, width and depth: *Computer graphics programs make it easy to visualize the three-*

T

dimensional arrangement of atoms. ◇ *The two cameras produce a three-dimensional image which the surgeon views through an eyepiece.*

thresh·old /ˈθreʃhəʊld; *NAmE* ˈθreʃhoʊld/ *noun* **1** [C] the level at which sth starts to happen or have an effect: **~ (of sth)** *A threshold of 70 dB was used in the analysis.* ◇ **~ for sth** *The estimates do not cross the conventional thresholds for statistical significance.* ◇ **a high/low ~** *Many survivors have a low threshold for stress.* ◇ **below/under a... ~** *Management will only intervene if performance falls below a certain threshold.* ◇ **above/beyond/over a... ~** *Multiple cases might prove to be beyond the threshold of human tolerance.* ◇ **+ noun** *97% had match rates that exceeded the threshold value.* **2** [sing.] the point just before a new situation or period begins: **on the ~ of sth** *The country stands on the threshold of a grave economic crisis.* ◇ **at the ~ of sth** *He seeks to convince them that they stand at the threshold of faith.*

threw *past tense of* THROW

thrive /θraɪv/ *verb* [I] to become, and continue to be, successful, strong or healthy SYN FLOURISH: *Successful schools will thrive in a competitive environment.* ◇ **failure to ~** *Neglect of a child's emotional needs and nutrition may lead to failure to thrive physically.* ■ **thriv·ing** *adj.*: *A thriving new enterprise producing tomatoes was ruined when the power supply was cut off.*

PHR V ˈ**thrive on sth** to be successful in a particular situation, or enjoy sth, especially sth that other people would not like: *Science thrives on the free exchange of ideas and on intellectual competition.* ◇ *While people who like working in a team tend to be uncomfortable with uncertainty, individualists thrive on it.*

throat /θrəʊt; *NAmE* θroʊt/ *noun* a passage in the neck through which food and air pass on their way into the body; the front part of the neck: *A sore throat and fever kept him off work for several days.*

through¹ /θruː/ *prep.* HELP For the special uses of **through** in phrasal verbs, look at the entries for the verbs. For example **get through sth** is in the phrasal verb section at **get**. **1** from one end or side of sth/sb to the other: *Water was then pumped through the vessel.* ◇ *Access to the disk is through a sliding metal window.* ◇ *Sidney portrayed the poet as a mouthpiece for the breath of God flowing through him.* **2** past a barrier, stage or test: *The steroid molecule passes straight through the cell membrane.* ◇ *Few errors got through the preliminary tests and final checks.* ◇ *The Family Law Act had a difficult passage through Parliament.* **3** from the beginning to the end of an activity or a period of time: *The central event of the plot occurs halfway through the film.* ◇ *Hardy flora such as these were able to live through the glacial period.* ◇ *Outward and inward foreign investment ratios varied significantly through time.* **4** by means of; because of: *The emperor asserted his authority through an elite class of public administrators.* ◇ *The estimated loss through all forms of fraud was over 12 billion dollars per annum.* ◇ *These elderly individuals, through no fault of their own, were no longer able to look after themselves.* **5** (*NAmE*) until, and including: *This is a long-term study of development from infancy through adulthood.* **6** used to describe how far sth turns from one angle to another: *The detector is fixed and the crystal is rotated through a series of angles in order to collect a complete data set.*

T

through² /θruː/ *adv.* HELP For the special uses of **through** in phrasal verbs, look at the entries for the verbs. For example **carry sth through** is in the phrasal verb section at **carry**. **1** from one end or side of sth to the other: *Pressure regulators maintain the desired pressure as the water flows through.* ◇ *On an ordinary day at the temple, 20 000 to 25 000 visitors may pass through.* **2** from the beginning to the end of an activity, thing or period of time: *First, we analysed the stages the customer goes through in making a purchase decision.* ◇ *It is hard to realize the significance of the global crisis we are living through.* **3** past a barrier, stage or test: *The local neural network acts as a gate, deciding which signals to let through to the brain.* ◇ *Pelvic size must be sufficient to allow the infant's head to pass through during birth.*

IDM ˌ**through and** ˈ**through** completely; in every way: *The author insists he is a Darwinian through and through.*

through·out /θruːˈaʊt/ *prep.* **1** in or into every part of sth: *A number of studies have been conducted throughout Europe and North America.* ◇ *The challenge was to redistribute resources throughout society rather than concentrating them among elites.* **2** during the whole period of time of sth: *Income fell throughout the 1970s.* ◇ *Truman was a loyal supporter of Roosevelt throughout his years in the Senate.* ■ **through·out** *adv.*: *After the meeting, she noted that Calgar had remained silent throughout.*

throw /θrəʊ; *NAmE* θroʊ/ *verb* (**threw** /θruː/, **thrown** /θrəʊn; *NAmE* θroʊn/) **1** [T, I] to send sth from your hand through the air by moving your hand or arm quickly: **~ sth (at sb/sth)** *The defendant admitted throwing a stone at a group of people.* ◇ **~ (sth to sb)** *Each participant throws the ball to the next person to speak.* ◇ *Gamblers have been observed to throw hard when they require a high number on a dice.* **2** [T] **~ sth/sb/yourself + adv./prep.** to move sth/sb suddenly and with force: *He was thrown to his death from the city walls.* ◇ *She tried to throw herself out of the window.* ◇ *The fracture occurs when the upper body is thrown forward while the pelvis is held stable.* **3** [T] **~ sth + adv./prep.** to put sth in a particular place quickly and carelessly: *She refused to work and threw her books on the floor.* **4** [T, usually passive] to make sb/sth be in a particular bad state: **~ sb/sth + adv./prep.** *The crisis is a human crisis, with millions of people thrown out of work.* ◇ **~ sb/sth into doubt, question, confusion, etc.** *If excuses for theft were allowed, human society would be thrown into confusion.* **5** [T] **~ sth on/at sb/sth** to direct sth at sb/sth: *Recent events have thrown some doubt on the correctness of this approach.* ◇ *She is able to apply her understanding and knowledge to every question that is thrown at her.*

IDM Idioms containing **throw** are at the entries for the nouns and adjectives in the idioms, for example **throw light on sth** is at **light** *noun*.

PHR V ˌ**throw sth a**ˈ**way** **1** (*also* ˌ**throw sth** ˈ**out**) to get rid of sth that you no longer want: *Of all direct mail, 33% is thrown away unopened.* **2** to fail to make use of sth; to waste sth: *After a good start, King John threw away a strong position in France, and lost all the lands north of the Loire.* ˌ**throw sth** ˈ**in** to include sth with what you are selling or offering, without increasing the price: *Many opportunities will be unpaid, but accommodation and food may be thrown in.* ˌ**throw yourself/sth** ˈ**into sth** to begin to do sth with energy and enthusiasm: *She left Germany to throw herself into the revolutionary movement in Poland.* ˌ**throw sth/sb** ˈ**off** to manage to get rid of sth/sb that is making you suffer: *The Americans had thrown off the yoke of British rule and founded a new republic.* ˌ**throw sb** ˈ**out (of...)** to force sb to leave a place: *The police found nothing but a group of drunken teenagers, who had been thrown out of a pub.* ˌ**throw sth** ˈ**out** **1** to say sth in a way that suggests you have not given it a lot of thought: *The teacher did not wait long for the answers from the students, and instead she kept throwing out questions.* **2** to not to accept a proposal, an idea, etc: *He was an inspiration for all those who wished to throw out the old politics of compromise and bring in a new politics of principle.* **3** = THROW STH AWAY ˌ**throw sth** ˈ**up** **1** to produce sth, so that people notice it: *The observations throw up an important contradiction.* **2** to build sth suddenly or quickly: *Workers* *and students threw up barricades and the National Guard refused to fire on them.*

thrust[1] /θrʌst/ *noun* **1 the thrust** [sing.] **~ (of sth)** the main point of an argument, a policy, etc: *The main thrust of the argument is that bureaucratic structures work well in stable environments but they are not innovative and cannot cope with novelty or change.* **2** [C] **~ (of sth)** a sudden big effort to do or achieve sth: *Two main thrusts of expansion began at the end of the fifteenth century.* **3** [U, sing.] (*physics*) a force that pushes sth in a particular direction: *An aeroplane propeller is designed to produce a large thrust.* ◇ *The inward pull on the chains counteracts the outward thrust from the arch.*

thrust[2] /θrʌst/ *verb* (**thrust, thrust**) **1 ~ sth/sb + adv/prep.** to push sth/sb suddenly or violently in a particular direction: *People were thrusting their hands through the taxi window, begging.* ◇ *During this time, rocks in the southern part of the belt were thrust onto the Kalahari block.* **2 ~ sb/sth + adv./prep.** to force sb/sth to do sth or to be in a particular situation: *She was thrust into the role of caring for a parent.* ◇ *The country was thrust into deep recession.*

thumb /θʌm/ *noun* the short thick finger at the side of the hand, slightly apart from the other four: *The wrist brace should allow full movement of fingers and thumb.* IDM *see* RULE[1]

thun·der /ˈθʌndə(r)/ *noun* [U] the loud noise that you hear after a flash of LIGHTNING, during a storm: *The days became very hot, and the nights constantly brought on tremendous thunder, lightning and rain.*

thus /ðʌs/ *adv.* **1** in this way; like this: *Other countries' higher incomes will increase the demand for the home country's exports, thus creating jobs in the home country.* ◇ *There were sound reasons for thinking thus.* ◇ **~, for example** *Sometimes this geographic and social mobility was associated with particular groups. Thus, for example, Scots entrepreneurs and settlers were notably prominent...* **2** as a result of sth just mentioned SYN HENCE, THEREFORE: *The ploughs are not produced domestically and thus have to be acquired from another country.* ◇ *Socio-economic status has a direct bearing on health status. Thus, the promotion of positive health requires a lessening of inequality.* ➲ language bank *at* THEREFORE IDM *see* FAR[1]

thwart /θwɔːt; *NAmE* θwɔːrt/ *verb* to prevent sb from doing what they want to do SYN FRUSTRATE: **~ sth** *There were claims that the governor had used his influence to thwart her political ambitions.* ◇ **~ sb in sth** *The party was thwarted in its attempt to regain control of the local council.*

thy·roid /ˈθaɪrɔɪd/ (*also* ˈ**thyroid gland**) *noun* (*anatomy*) a small organ at the front of the neck that produces HORMONES that control the way in which the body grows and functions: *Patients with an underactive thyroid have a decreased metabolic rate.* ◇ **+ noun** *It has been shown that changes in thyroid hormone levels can also be caused by a number of environmental factors.*

tick[1] /tɪk/ *verb* **1** [T] (*BrE*) (*NAmE* **check**) to put a mark (✔) next to an item on a list, an answer, etc: **~ sth** *Customers who do not tick the box are considered to have given their consent.* ◇ **~ sb/sth off** *She ticked the figures off in pencil to make sure they were not counted twice.* **2** [I] (of a clock, etc.) to make short, light, regular repeated sounds to mark time passing: *Let us say a cheap watch ticks on average once a second.*

tick[2] /tɪk/ *noun* **1** (*BrE*) (*NAmE* ˈ**check mark, check**) a mark (✔) put beside a sum or an item on a list, usually to show that it has been checked or done or is correct: *They are supposed to place a tick next to the appropriate answer.* ➲ *compare* CROSS[2](1) **2** a small insect that bites humans and animals and SUCKS their blood. There are several types of tick, some of which can carry diseases: *Ranchers were concerned about Texas fever, a disease spread by ticks carried on Texas cattle.*

ticket /ˈtɪkɪt/ *noun* **1** a printed piece of paper that gives you the right to travel on a particular bus, train, etc. or to go into a theatre, etc: *Train tickets were increasingly sold online.* ◇ **~ for sth** *A ticket for the Jazz Festival cost $130.* ◇ **~ to sth** *She purchased a return ticket to England.* ◇ **+ noun** *Three football clubs were accused of artifically inflating ticket prices.* **2** a printed piece of paper with a number or numbers on it, that you buy in order to have the chance of winning a prize if the number or numbers are later chosen: *There are a huge number of outlets where National Lottery tickets may be bought.* **3** [usually sing.] (*especially NAmE*) a list of candidates that are supported by a particular political party in an election: **on a... ~** *He was elected to the New York City Council in 1947 on a Communist Party ticket.*

tidal /ˈtaɪdl/ *adj.* connected with, or affected by tides: *The tidal flow from the deep ocean not only gives rise to an enhanced tidal range but also is accompanied by strong tidal currents.*

tide /taɪd/ *noun* **1** [C, U] a regular rise and fall in the level of the sea, caused by the pull of the moon and sun; the flow of water that happens as the sea rises and falls: *The tide ebbs more slowly than normal, and may never fall as low as previously.* ◇ **high/low ~** *The floods in the delta are augmented by the arrival of high tides in the middle of the wet season.* ◇ **at high/low ~** *At low tide, these areas can support vast densities of wading birds.* ◇ **+ noun** *This article has reviewed tide and wave energy resources and technologies that exploit them.* **2** [C, usually sing.] **~ of sth** a large amount of sth unpleasant that is increasing and is difficult to control: *Politicians seemed powerless to stem the tide of violence.* ◇ *Their ambition is to be the first major nation to reverse the rising tide of obesity in the population.* **3** [C, usually sing.] **~ of sth** the direction in which the opinion of a large number of people seems to be moving: *Between April and July, there was a rising tide of protest.* IDM **go, swim, etc. with/against the** ˈ**tide** to agree with/oppose the attitudes or opinions that most other people have: *In this election, two seats went against the general tide.* ◇ *The minister was moving with the tide of public and judicial opinion in seeking to reduce the jail population.* **the** ˈ**tide turns** used to say that there is a change in how lucky or successful sb/sth is being: *Unemployment topped 10%, and Americans still waited for a signal that the tide had turned and things were getting better.* **turn the** ˈ**tide** to change a situation, so that sth is more successful than it was previously: *Social conservatives would like to turn the tide, by encouraging the government to play a more assertive role in preserving marriage.*

tie[1] /taɪ/ *verb* (**ties, tying, tied, tied**) **1** to use string, rope, etc. to attach or hold two or more things together; to make a join using string, rope, etc: **~ sth + adv./prep.** *These are the ropes used to tie boats together.* ◇ *The letters were bundled together and tied with a ribbon.* ◇ **~ sth** *The scouts learned to tie knots.* **2** [often passive] to connect or link sth closely with sth else: **~ sth to sth** *A person's self-esteem is closely tied to the holding of a job.* ◇ *These problems are intimately tied to economic questions.* ◇ *People may also wish to retain benefits tied to employment, such as health insurance.* ◇ **~ sb/sth together** *The great noble families were tied together by marriage.* ◇ *Her findings enable her to tie together some of the elements outlined above.* ◇ **~ sth into sth** *Their self-image was tied into heroics and risk-taking.* **3** [often passive] to limit sb's freedom or choices: **~ sb to sb/sth** *Buyers in a market may be tied to suppliers by long-term supply contracts.* ◇ **~ sb into (doing) sth**

Technology is tying farmers into buying seed and pesticide from the same company. ◇ **~ sb in** *Supermarkets tie in their petrol customers by bundling product benefits together.* ◇ **~ sb down** *They should not be tied down with domestic responsibilities.*

PHR V **tie sth down** to decide or state what exactly sth is: *These are more difficult concepts to tie down.* **ˌtie ˈin (with sth) | be ˌtied ˈin (with sth)** to match sth; to be linked to sth: *Such studies tie in well with simulations of the glacial climate across Europe.* ◇ *The choice of source of supply is tied in with the relative transaction costs.* **ˌtie sth ˈup (in sth)** [often passive] to invest money so that it is not easily available for use: *Their wealth is tied up in the assets of established firms.* **ˌtie sth ˈup to/with sth** [usually passive] to connect or link sth to sth else: *The argument is tied up to a more general criticism.* ◇ *The politics of choosing emperors became tied up with the persecution of Christians.*

tie² /taɪ/ *noun* [usually pl.] a strong connection between people or organizations: *Kinship ties were stronger than they are now.* ◇ *social/family ties* ◇ **~ between/among A and B** *The close ties between the two countries may be one of the reasons for this situation.* ◇ **~ with sb/sth** *The child maintained ties with his family of origin.* ◇ **~ to sb/sth** *The programme has made a major impact in strengthening ties to industry.* ◇ **~ within sth** *Religious conversion tended to sever ties within the community.* ◇ **~ of sth** *Many people never break free of the influence and ties of social background.*

tight /taɪt/ *adj.* (**tight·er, tight·est**) **1** held, fixed or closed firmly; difficult to move or open: *The valves feature a set of teeth and sockets, which ensures a tight fit when the valves close.* ◇ *The threads are held tight in a thin bamboo frame.* **2** (of a rule or a form of control) very strict and firm: *Most authoritarian regimes keep tight control over the main television channels.* ◇ *The policy may be too lax in areas of high economic growth and too tight in areas of slow growth.* ◇ *The East Asian tiger economies have generally maintained a tight grip on inflation.* **3** (of clothes, etc.) fitting closely to the body and sometimes uncomfortable: *Excessively tight bandages or plaster casts may cause a problem.* OPP LOOSE (5) **4** stretched or pulled so that it cannot stretch much further: *The skin over the fingers and face is smooth, shiny and tight.* **5** [usually before noun] with things or people packed closely together, leaving little space between them: *A fierce battle followed, with two hundred ships rammed together in a tight space.* ◇ *It took a great deal of training to hold together such an extremely tight formation in battle.* **6** (of a piece of writing, an argument, etc.) well organized, giving only the information that is important SYN CONCISE: *The author does a good job of presenting the entire drama in a tight narrative.* ◇ *Tighter editing would have reduced repetition.* **7** (of time, money, etc.) difficult to manage with because there is not enough: *There are now tighter deadlines for preparing and filing accounts.* ◇ *When budgets are tight, consumers pay close attention to their spending habits.* **8** (of part of the body) feeling painful or uncomfortable because of illness or emotion: *His chest feels tight and he is unable to take long, slow breaths in.* ◇ *She was aware of muscle tension and a tight feeling in her stomach.* **9** having a close relationship with sb else or with other people SYN CLOSE³ (5): *This view assumes a tight connection between community and individuals.* **10** curving suddenly or in a small circle rather than gradually SYN SHARP (6): *The bundle of cables must have a small diameter for flexibility in bending around tight corners.* ■ **tight·ness** *noun* [U] **~ (of sth)** *The lids were checked for tightness prior to placing the containers into ice chests for storage at reduced temperatures.* ◇ *The ever-increasing size of ships and the tightness of their schedules has led to changes in the shipping industry.* ◇ *Levels of reported chest tightness were similar in each study group*

tight·en /ˈtaɪtn/ *verb* **1 ~ sth (up)** to make sth become stricter: *After the mutiny, discipline was tightened.* ◇ *The government was forced to tighten monetary controls.* ◇ *The French solution to the problem was to tighten up state regulation.* OPP LOOSEN (3) **2 ~ sth** to make sth become tight or tighter: *She tightened her grip on his arm.* OPP LOOSEN (1)

tight·ly /ˈtaɪtli/ *adv.* **1** closely or firmly: *These metal ions are typically tightly bound to the enzyme.* ◇ *The container was sealed tightly and sent to the laboratory as quickly as possible.* ◇ **~ knit** *He lives in a very traditional Turkish home within a tightly knit Turkish community.* ◇ **~ packed** *The loosely packed unsaturated fatty acids are more fluid at room temperature than the tightly packed saturated fatty acids.* **2** in a strict way: *Retail outlets have become larger and less tightly regulated by governments.* ◇ *At this time, Jews were excluded from public office and their access to the professions was tightly controlled.* **3** using clear standards or principles; using or mentioning only the information that is important: *Questioning was restricted to fairly tightly defined topics.* ◇ *Stronger editorial control might have produced a more tightly argued book.*

till /tɪl/ *conj., prep.* (*informal*) = UNTIL

time¹ /taɪm/ *noun* ➲ *see also* TIMES **1** [U] what is measured in minutes, hours, days, etc: *As time went on, workers found employment in huge factories and mills.* ◇ *Plato's thinking evolved with the passing of time.* ◇ **over ~** *There have been many changes over time in patterns of migration.* ◇ **back in ~** *The history of landslide activity in southeast Brazil has been traced much further back in time.* ◇ **+ noun** *Over the same time period, the per capita GDP of the twenty wealthiest nations doubled relative to the twenty poorest.* **2** [U] the amount of time available to work, rest, etc; an amount of time: *The study showed that boys spent significantly more time (20 minutes) than girls at the computer.* ◇ *It takes time to make changes in the law.* ◇ *Teleconferencing can save significant amounts of time and energy.* ◇ *Doctors commented that a lot of time was wasted with unnecessary reporting.* ◇ **~ for sth** *More effective managers tended to allow sufficient time for decision-making.* ◇ **~ to do sth** *Participants were given time to reflect on their feelings about the course and their results.* ➲ *see also* REAL TIME (1), TIME-CONSUMING **3** [U, C] the particular time when sth happens or when sth should happen: **at the ~** *Businesses pay this tax at the same time as they pay VAT.* ◇ **on ~** *The new Terminal 5 was opened on time on 27 March 2008.* ◇ **by the ~ (that)...** *By the time that the decade ended, the reforms were well under way.* ◇ **~ for sth** *Many commentators argued that the time had come for greater banking regulation.* ◇ **it is ~ to do sth** *It is surely time to widen the scope of research into such ancient Mexican religions.* ◇ *Data were gathered from widely separated places and times.* ➲ *see also* REAL TIME (2) **4** [U, pl.] a period of history connected with particular events or experiences in people's lives: *Schleier analyses the films within the context of the sexual and financial politics of the time.* ◇ *Recent times have seen attempts to further develop cooperative teaching methods.* ◇ **at the ~ (of sth)** *The novel tells the story of the fighting at the time of Indian Independence.* **5 a time** [sing.] a period of time, either long or short, during which sth happens or when sb does sth: *The entire process took a very long time to complete.* ◇ **at one, that, etc. ~** *At one time, the building was used as a research centre.* ◇ **for a ~** *As a young man, he studied for a time in India.* **6** [C] an occasion when sth happens or when sb does sth: *Every time a customer accesses the website, they see the message.* ◇ *The annual global catch of inland fish passed 10 million tonnes for the first time in 2008.* ◇ *However, at the time of writing, the Health and Social Care Act 2008 is yet to come fully into force.* HELP To talk about the first or the last time that sb/sth does sth, use **the first/last**

time (that)...: *This is the first time that Roth has written at length on the subject.* ◇ ~~*This is the first time for Roth to write at length on the subject.*~~ **7** [U] the time measured in a particular part of the world: *The series of photographs was taken between 01:30 and 03:00 local time.* **8** [U] the time shown on a clock in minutes and hours: *Different prices are charged depending on what time of the evening a customer enters the bar.*

IDM **at all ˈtimes** always: *Hall argues that at all times 'the press performs a significant role as a social educator' (1975: 11).* **at the same ˈtime 1** at one time; together: *Two students began to speak at the same time.* **2** used to introduce contrasting facts: *The potential for trade union activity markedly increased, while at the same time the unions became endangered in new ways.* **at a ˈtime** separately or in groups of two, three, etc. on each occasion: *The variables were analysed one at a time.* **at ˈtimes** sometimes: *Protest, at times, becomes the only available means for socially marginalized groups to express their political demands.* **in time (for sth/to do sth)** not late; with enough time to be able to do sth: *The product was launched in time for Christmas.* **keep up/move with the ˈtimes** to change and develop your ideas, way of working, etc. so that you do what is modern and what is expected: *Trying to keep up with the times, they created an interactive website.* **of all ˈtime** that has ever existed: *'Man with a Movie Camera' is considered by many critics to be one of the most original films of all time.* **only time will ˈtell** used to say that you will have to wait for some time to find out the result of a situation: *Only time will tell if these precautions will be successful in preventing the spread of disease.* ➲ more at MATTER[1], SIGN[1], TEST[1]

LANGUAGE BANK

Time expressions

In academic writing, time expressions are important for specifying when an event or change took place; for saying how long a process lasted; or for comparing quantities over time.

- **over (a period of)** 5 years/months/decades/centuries
- **over a** long/short/10-year, etc. **period**
- **over the past** 10 years/3 decades/few months
- **over time/the years**
- **for (a period of)** 5 years/months/decades/centuries
- **for many/several** years/decades/months
- **since** 1935/last year/March
- **in the** medieval/Victorian/post-war **period**
- **in the past** 10 years/3 decades/few months
- **in recent** years/months/decades
- **during the past/last** 10 years/3 decades/few months
- **during this** time/period

- *__Over__ several __days__, their performance improved significantly.*
- *The interviews were conducted __over__ a seven-month __period__ in 2006.*
- *__Over the past__ 100 years, the cost of transporting goods over long distances has dramatically fallen.*
- *__Over time__, entire cities, tribes, kingdoms and the Roman Empire itself accepted the new religion.*
- *Daniel (409–493) joined a monastery at age twelve and stayed __for__ 25 __years__.*
- *Tree-ring properties have been used __for many years__ to reconstruct past climates.*
- *__Since__ 1995, there have been more deaths from cancer than from ischaemic heart disease.*
- *Phillips and Hardy (2002: 75–8) analysed 127 cartoons that appeared in Canadian newspapers __in the__ 1987–9 __period__.*
- *There has been a huge increase in general practice workload __in the past__ three decades.*
- *School dropout rates have remained fairly stable __in recent years__.*
- *13 major lava dams were formed and subsequently destroyed in the Grand Canyon __during the last__ one to two million years.*
- *__During this__ 30-year __period__, per capita consumption increased from less than 2 lb to 6.6 lb.*

time[2] /taɪm/ *verb* **1** [often passive] to arrange to do sth or arrange for sth to happen at a particular time: *Philip's planned invasion of the Persian Empire was well timed, as the 330s were a time of severe crisis for Persia.* ◇ **~ sth to do sth** *Male birds timed their fights to coincide with the fertile period of females.* ◇ *The bomb was placed on a passenger aircraft and timed to go off in mid-flight.* **2** to measure how long it takes for sth to happen or for sb to do sth: **~ sth** *Each part of the job was timed and retimed and then averaged.* ◇ **~ how long...** *Researchers timed how long it took the eye to become tired.*

ˈtime-consum·ing *adj.* taking or needing a lot of time: *Measuring the temperature at each stage was very time-consuming.*

ˈtime frame *noun* the length of time that is used or available for sth: **over a... ~** *The data were collected over a 10-year time frame.* ◇ **within a... ~** *We aimed to develop a method that could be administered within a limited time frame and with limited resources.*

ˈtime lag *noun* = LAG[2]

time·less /ˈtaɪmləs/ *adj.* not affected by the passing of time or by changes in fashion: *The Romantic ideology values art that is transcendent, timeless and universal.* ■ **time·less·ness** *noun* [U] **~ (of sth)** *the timelessness of great art*

ˈtime limit *noun* the length of time within which you must do or complete sth: **~ (of sth) (for sth)** *The Act sets a time limit of six weeks for applications to the High Court.* ◇ **within a... ~** *Students worked together on tasks within given time limits.*

time·line /ˈtaɪmlaɪn/ *noun* a horizontal line that is used to represent time, with the past towards the left and the future towards the right: **~ for sth** *A timeline for the completion of each objective was constructed.* ◇ **~ of sth** *The site provides a timeline of Nelson's life.*

time·ly /ˈtaɪmli/ *adj.* happening at exactly the right time: *It was vital that the data were produced in a timely and accurate manner.* ◇ *Clarke's findings are significant and timely.* ■ **time·li·ness** *noun* [U] **~ (of sth)** *Suppliers competed on price, product quality and timeliness of delivery.*

times /taɪmz/ *noun* [pl.] used in comparisons to show how much more, better, etc. sth is than sth else: **~ as many/long, etc.** *Table 22.1 shows that China had six times as many university students as the UK in 2001.* ◇ **~ greater/longer, etc.** *In fact, Livy's history of the Roman Republic is six times longer than Tacitus's Annals.* ◇ **~ the size/length, etc.** *The cell measures up to 1 000 times the length of a bacterium and can be seen under low magnification.* ➲ language bank *at* PROPORTION

time·scale /ˈtaɪmskeɪl/ *noun* the period of time that it takes for sth to happen or be completed: *A timescale should be set for completing the assessment.* ◇ **at/on/over a ~** *Over timescales of thousands to millions of years, the temperature of the sun and the earth's orbital patterns have varied.*

ˈtime span *noun* a period of time: **~ of sth** *This study will cover a time span of 55 years.* ◇ **over a... ~** *Comparisons made over a longer time span have produced more convincing data.*

time·table /ˈtaɪmteɪbl/ *noun* **1** a plan of when you expect or hope particular events to happen SYN SCHEDULE[1] (2): *The euro was introduced exactly according to the timetable drawn up at the time of the Maastricht Treaty negotiations in 1991.* ◇ **~ for sth** *The Clinton* *administration was forced to announce a timetable for the withdrawal of all US forces.* **2** (*especially BrE*) (*NAmE usually* **sched·ule**) a list showing the times at which particular events will happen: *The school timetable required 40-minute lessons.*

tim·ing /ˈtaɪmɪŋ/ *noun* **1** [U, C] the act of choosing when sth happens; a particular point or period of time when sth happens or is planned: **~ (of sth)** *The correct timing of surgery is important to decrease patient risk.* ◇ *Environmental effects could alter the timing of hatching.* ◇ *These reports set out the details, together with the timings of each stage and a brief description of what occurred.* ◇ **+ noun** *In modern engines, an electronic circuit sends a timing signal to the ignition system.* **2** [U] the skill of doing sth at exactly the right time: *Success was a combination of good luck, good judgement and good timing.*

tin /tɪn/ *noun* **1** [U] (*symb.* **Sn**) the chemical element of ATOMIC NUMBER 50. Tin is a soft silver-white metal that is often mixed with other metals: *Obstructing sea trade in the Aegean would have cut off the supply of tin and copper for bronze production.* **2** (*BrE*) **~ (of sth)** = CAN[2]

tiny /ˈtaɪni/ *adj.* (**tini·er**, **tini·est**) very small in size or amount: *Jinmen is a tiny island situated 2 km off the coast of China.* ◇ *The tiny amount of fuel that is needed is one of the attractions of fusion.* ◇ *Those who were refused entry into the country represent only a tiny fraction (0.8%) of all visitors.* ◇ *It seems that the health risks associated with minimal exposure to asbestos are tiny.*

tip[1] /tɪp/ *noun* **1** the thin pointed end of sth: **~ (of sth)** *the tips of your fingers* ◇ **at the ~ of sth** *Singapore is situated at the southern tip of the Malay peninsula.* ◇ **on the ~ of sth** *Some of the insects have a spot of dark pigment on the tip of the wing.* **2** a small piece of advice about sth practical SYN HINT[1] (4): *GPs can make an assessment of diet and offer practical tips.* ◇ **~ on sth** *Most tips on exam technique are fairly basic.* ◇ **~ for (doing) sth** *They present some tips for effective data recording and for using computer technology.* **3** a small amount of extra money that you give to sb, for example sb who serves you in a restaurant: *Only a small number of customers will leave a tip in addition to service charges.*

IDM **the tip of the ˈiceberg** only a small part of a much larger problem: *Reported cases of corruption in business are probably just the tip of the iceberg, since most financial crime is invisible.*

T

tip[2] /tɪp/ *verb* (**-pp-**) **1** [I, T] to move so that one end or side is higher than the other; to move sth into this position: **+ adv./prep.** *The weight makes you feel as though you are tipping forward.* ◇ **~ sth + adv./prep.** *The force is sufficient to tip the train sideways off the track.* **2** [T] **~ sth + adv./prep.** to make sth come out of a container by holding the container at an angle: *The juice from the crushed sugar cane is tipped into the cauldrons.* **3** [I, T] to develop in a particular direction; to make sth develop in a particular direction: **+ adv./prep.** *In some cases, sadness and grief tips over into depression.* ◇ **~ sth + adv./prep.** *Constant talk of catastrophe is in danger of tipping society onto a negative, depressive and reactionary path.*

IDM **tip the ˈbalance/ˈscales (in favour of, against, etc. sb/sth)** to give sb/sth enough of an advantage or disadvantage, so that the result of sth is affected: *He remained confident that French intervention would tip the military balance.*

PHRV **ˌtip ˈup/ˈover | ˌtip sth ˈup/ˈover** to fall or turn over; to make sth do this: *Each stone cannot project out very far; otherwise it would tip over and fall.* ◇ *The initial approach of the massive wave tipped the boat over.*

tired /ˈtaɪəd; *NAmE* ˈtaɪərd/ *adj.* **1** feeling that you would like to sleep or rest; needing rest: *More than half of the respondents reported feeling tired or lacking in energy.* ◇ *The study found that tired doctors took significantly longer to complete clinical tasks.* **2 ~ of (doing) sth** feeling that you have had enough of sth because you no longer find it interesting or because it makes you angry or unhappy: *In Europe, armies grew tired of fighting.* ◇ *The younger Japanese were tired of hearing about foreign superiority.*
■ **tired·ness** *noun* [U] *Many experience no symptoms at all while others experience extreme tiredness and can feel very unwell.*

tis·sue /ˈtɪʃuː; *BrE also* ˈtɪsjuː/ *noun* [U] (*also* **tissues**) [pl.] a collection of cells that form the different parts of humans, animals and plants: *These data correlate with a study of tissue from breast cancer patients, including malignant lymph tissue.* ◇ *Five per cent of the bats tested positive, and viruses were isolated from their tissues.* ◇ **+ noun** *A recent review suggests that the drug effectively reduces pain in soft tissue injuries.* ➲ *see also* SOFT TISSUE

▸ ADJECTIVE + TISSUE **normal • healthy • human • adult • surrounding, adjacent • peripheral • soft • fibrous • connective • adipose • neural • vascular • ovarian • somatic** *The tumour was benign, and relatively separated from surrounding tissue.*

▸ NOUN + TISSUE **animal • plant • muscle • lung • breast • brain • scar** *The concentration of nitrogen in plant tissue averages about 1.5% by mass.*

▸ TISSUE + NOUN **type • sample • culture • section • growth • disease • damage, injury • engineering** *The amount of tissue damage is not an accurate predictor of pain intensity.*

title[1] /ˈtaɪtl/ *noun* **1** [C] the name of a book, poem, film, piece of music, etc: *Arnold's best-known essay, 'Culture and Anarchy', expressed the fear of revolt in its very title.* ◇ **~ of sth** *Unfortunately, the title of the book is entirely misleading.* ◇ **under the ~ (of)...** *The essays were collected and published under the title 'Moses and Monotheism'.* ◇ **~ page** *The title page should include: a date; the name of the study; and the name of the author.* **2** [C] a particular book or magazine: *In terms of magazines, Bertelsmann owns 18 titles.* **3** [C] a word in front of a person's name to show their rank or profession, whether or not they are married, etc: *He inherited the title Earl of Lovelace.* ◇ *The database contains postal address, postcode, name and title (Mr, Ms, Mrs, etc.).* ◇ **~ of sth** *Sir Martin J. Rees holds the honorary title of Astronomer Royal.* **4** [U, C] **~ (to sth/to do sth)** (*law*) the legal right to own sth, especially land or property; the document that shows you have this right: *After the Russian Revolution, the Church lost legal title to its property.* ◇ *The new Act preserves the register of titles.* **5** [C] a name that describes a job: *After rationalization, the firm had fewer job titles and broader responsibilities within each title.*

title[2] /ˈtaɪtl/ *verb* [usually passive] **~ sth + noun** to give a book, piece of music, etc. a particular name: *Rancière published his research in the evocatively titled 'Nights of Labour'.* ◇ *The designers of the experiment titled their report 'A Fine Is a Price'.*

to[1] /*before consonants* tə; *before vowels* tu; *strong form* tuː/ *prep.* HELP For the special uses of **to** in phrasal verbs, look at the entries for the verbs. For example **see to sth** is in the phrasal verb section at **see**. **1** used to say where sb/sth arrives, or where they are going: *This was his first trip to Africa.* ◇ *More children are driven to school than walk or cycle.* ◇ **from A ~ B** *Coaches travelled from London to Manchester.* **2** used to state a position or direction: *The external magnetic field was applied parallel and perpendicular to the tube axis.* ◇ **be ~ the sth (of sth)** *The energy plant is 325 km to the south.* ◇ *The islands lie to the west of the mainland.* **3** used to show that two things are attached or connected: *The tongue is attached to the lower jaw.* ◇ *Movement is tracked by a device glued to the insect's back.* ◇ *Most lakes are connected to river systems.* **4** used to say that sb/sth reaches or approaches a particular state, situation or amount: *This instability could lead to a major war.* ◇ *The agenda changed to the study of DNA.* ◇ *These young people have limited access to adult support.* ◇ *The price of these goods has fallen to half their original price.* ◇ *Its numerical value increases to approximately 6.7.* ◇ **~ doing sth** *The young man is well on the way to becoming a mature thinker.* ◇ **from sth ~ sth** *The crisis appears to have gone from bad to worse.* **5** used to show the end of a range or period of time: **from sth ~ sth** *The amount of variance was small to moderate, ranging from 2% to 25%.* ◇ *The occupation lasted from 1945 to 1952.* ◇ **up ~** *It may be necessary to continue this treatment for up to 3 days.* **6** used to state who receives sth: *She wrote to her mother in December 1962.* ◇ *No one knew who owed money to whom.* ◇ *This greater professionalization is a positive signal to investors.* **7** used to state who or what is affected by sth: *He was unfaithful to her.* ◇ *It was a threat to regional peace and security.* ◇ *They made significant improvements to this crucial area of work.* ◇ *Both perspectives have contributed greatly to the contemporary understanding of religion.* **8** used to state what causes sth: *This was simply a short-term reaction to political and economic uncertainties.* ◇ *Movement of the fetus in response to external stimuli occurs at 8 weeks.* **9** used to say who or what is involved: *There were few references to previous studies.* ◇ *He alludes to the fact that...* **10** used to introduce the second part of a comparison or RATIO: *These results are similar to those found in previous studies.* ◇ *Responses were compared to those of control subjects.* ◇ *The ratio of females to males is 102 to 100.* **11** used to show a relationship between one person or thing and another: *She had been married to her husband for 15 years.* ◇ *She remained close to her brother.* ◇ *They maintained their close ties to the United States.* ◇ *He was science adviser to the World Energy Council.* ◇ *Cohabitation was typically a prelude to marriage.* ◇ *This tension is connected to violence and aggression.* ◇ *Contrary to these expectations, the level increased.* **12** used to show a reaction, attitude or effect: *The newly restored theatre was opened to great acclaim.* ◇ *Many girls were already participating in domestic labour, to the detriment of their schoolwork.* ◇ *The jury acquitted them, much to the delight of those attending the trial.* **13** used to show what sb's opinion or feeling about sth is: *It was clear to her parents that she was unhappy.* **14** (after a verb of movement) used to show that sb offers help: *Two fellow workers went to his aid.* ◇ *States cannot assume that other states will come to their defence.* **15** (*mathematics*) indicating the POWER to which a number is raised: *ten to the minus thirty-three*

to² /*before consonants* tə; *before vowels* tu; *strong form* tuː/ *infinitive marker* HELP **To** is often used before the base form of a verb to show that the verb is in the infinitive. **1** used to say what happens or may happen, or what sb does or may do: *This statement seems to suggest two things.* ◇ *The party failed to make progress in the polls.* ◇ *Only one key variable—distance from market—was allowed to vary.* ◇ *He has tried to answer this question in his recent work.* ◇ *They want people who are able to work without close supervision.* **2** used to show purpose or intention: *These laws are designed to prevent abuse.* ◇ *He used his influence to protect the arts.* ◇ *To avoid errors of this kind, the researcher can adopt one of the following methods.* HELP After a verb or verb group, you can also use **in order to**: *Many new programmes were created in order to achieve the stated goals.* Note that *were used to* often means 'were used in order to': *Minor ambiguities or discrepancies were used to discredit the applicants.* ➲ grammar note *at* SO² **3** used to say what/who sth/sb is: *The next step is to outline the critical flow of the activities.* ◇ *A creative way to improve profitability involves strategic partnering.* ◇ *The best person to bring up a child is the natural parent.* ◇ **where/what, etc. ~...** *The firm must decide where to invest.* **4** used to show what is known, believed or said about sb/sth: *Both effects are known to occur frequently.* ◇ *Most cases of reinfection are thought to be asymptomatic.* ◇ *The drugs are reported to lessen the severity of the attacks.* **5** used to show an action that you want or are advised to do: *Respondents were asked whether they would be willing to pay more.* ◇ *More than 90% of the parents agreed to participate.* ◇ *They do not wish to be involved in further testing.* ◇ *This chapter explains how to write up a medical history.* HELP **To** is sometimes used without a following verb, if the missing verb is easy to understand: *People had an opportunity to ask questions about the project if they wished to.* Depending on the vocabulary used, this can make the sentence rather informal; using **to do so** or **to do this** will make the sentence more formal: *She had worked at that location in the past and wanted to do so again.* ◇ *If the patient was unable to complete the questionnaire, the carer was asked to do this on their behalf.* **6** used after an adjective to give the action described by the adjective: *It is interesting to note that...* ◇ *It seems reasonable to assume that this would happen.* ◇ *It would be fair to say that this report was received unenthusiastically.* ◇ *Such behaviours are extremely difficult to interpret.* **7** if sb/sth **is to** do sth, they must or should do it: *The author is to be commended for making this subject accessible.* ◇ *Collectivization was to be voluntary.* HELP If sth **was to** happen from a particular point in the past, it often happened from that point onwards: *This text was to influence Gandhi deeply throughout his life.* **8** used to introduce sth, for example sb else's words or ideas: *They were, to quote Langton, 'a remarkably sophisticated... programme of behaviour modifications'.* ◇ *To paraphrase George Orwell's 'Animal Farm': all states remained equal, but some became more equal than others.* ➲ *see also* BE GOING TO DO STH, HAVE TO

to·bacco /təˈbækəʊ; *NAmE* təˈbækoʊ/ *noun* [U] the dried leaves of the tobacco plant that are used for making cigarettes, smoking in a pipe, etc: *In most developed countries, tobacco accounts for up to 30 per cent of all malignant tumours (Doll and Peto, 2003).* ◇ **+ noun** *The major risk factors for oral cancer are tobacco use and alcohol consumption (Macfarlane et al., 1995).* ◇ *Many studies show that environmental tobacco smoke is hazardous to the respiratory health of children.*

today¹ /təˈdeɪ/ *adv.* **1** on this day: *He will appear in court today.* **2** at the present period SYN NOWADAYS: *Teachers today have to deal with a much wider range of abilities and behaviours than many once had.* ◇ *A patient diagnosed today has around an 80% chance of surviving five years. In 1970 that figure was 50%.*

today² /təˈdeɪ/ *noun* [U] **1** this day: *Today is the 200th anniversary of Jane Austen's 'Pride and Prejudice'.* **2** the present period of time: *Today's world is very different.* ◇ **of ~** *The economic world of today bears little resemblance to that of 1960.*

toe /təʊ; *NAmE* toʊ/ *noun* one of the five small parts that stick out from the foot: *the big/little toe*

to·gether /təˈgeðə(r)/ *adv.* HELP For the special uses of **together** in phrasal verbs, look at the entries for the verbs. For example **pull sth together** is in the phrasal verb section at **pull**. **1** with or near to sb/sth else; with each other: *Engineers and suppliers worked closely together on the project.* ◇ *These locations are grouped together because they exhibit similar histories.* ◇ *Together, Tylor and Morgan established the comparative method of ethnographic inquiry.* **2** so that two or more things touch or are joined to or combined with each other: *A series of photographs of the canyon were taken, enlarged and fitted together.* ◇ *These categories together constitute around 45% of migrants in each census.* ◇ **taken ~** *Taken together, these three factors accounted for a significant proportion of the variance.*

IDM **together with** in addition to; as well as: *Advertising, together with the other tools of the communications mix, is a means of managing demand.*

token[1] /'təʊkən; *NAmE* 'toʊkən/ *noun* **1** **~ (of sth)** something that is a symbol of a feeling, a fact, an event, etc. **SYN** EXPRESSION (1), MARK[2] (1): *Participants were given R50 (approx $7) as a token of appreciation.* ◇ *The ring was given as token of trust.* **2** a round piece of metal or plastic used instead of money to operate some machines or as a form of payment: *She placed the token into the machine.* ◇ *The Sumerians made small tokens out of clay to represent the items being traded.* **3** (*computing, linguistics*) an individual OCCURRENCE of a symbol or string of characters: *The search yielded 20 221 word tokens, which consisted of 4 885 different word types.*

IDM **by the same 'token** for the same reasons: *There is little evidence to substantiate this theory though, by the same token, there is little to disprove it.*

token[2] /'təʊkən; *NAmE* 'toʊkən/ *adj.* [only before noun] **1** done, employed or invited only in order to give the appearance of being sincere or correct: *There was one token male in the room.* ◇ *The cities of Flanders opened their gates after little more than token resistance.* **2** done as a symbol to show that you are serious about sth and will keep a promise or an agreement or do more later: *One advantage in the token agreement is that it provides concrete evidence of intention.*

told *past tense, past part. of* TELL

tol·er·ance /'tɒlərəns; *NAmE* 'tɑːlərəns/ *noun* **1** [U] willingness to accept or tolerate sb/sth, especially opinions or behaviour that you may not agree with, or people who are not like you: *Religious tolerance did not necessarily mean the end of tensions.* ◇ **~ of/for sb/sth** *The tolerance of the slave trade ended with the passage of the 13th Amendment.* ◇ **~ towards sb/sth** *As Procurator, Golitsyn showed great tolerance towards the many minor religions of Russia.* **2** [C, U] the ability to suffer sth, especially pain, difficult conditions, etc. without being harmed: **~ to sth** *Sea stars are known to have low tolerance to low oxygen levels.* ◇ *Tolerance to morphine may lead to dependence.* ◇ **~ for sth** *Women were considered to have greater tolerance for cold, heat, pain and loneliness.* **3** [C, U] **~ (of sth)** (*technical*) the amount by which the measurements of a MANUFACTURED object may be allowed to vary without causing problems: *Improved machine tools meant that a craftsman could manufacture components to a tolerance of 0.001%.*

tol·er·ant /'tɒlərənt; *NAmE* 'tɑːlərənt/ *adj.* **1** able to accept what other people say or do even if you do not agree with it: *The data suggest that the French have a relatively relaxed and tolerant attitude towards the sexual behaviour of public figures.* ◇ **~ of sb/sth** *The authors conclude that women tend to be more tolerant of homosexuality (ibid.: 260).* **2** (of plants, animals, machines or systems) able to survive or operate in difficult conditions: *These were the least cold tolerant and most heat tolerant species.* ◇ **~ of sth** *Adaptive companies build corporate cultures that are tolerant of change and risk.*

tol·er·ate /'tɒləreɪt; *NAmE* 'tɑːləreɪt/ *verb* **1** **~ sth/sb** to allow the existence of sth that you do not agree with or do not like, and not take action against it **SYN** PUT UP WITH SB/STH: *Tolerating racism would be incompatible with Kant's basic principle of respect for humanity in each person.* ◇ *Americans appear willing to tolerate a surprising degree of restriction on their liberty.* **2** **~ sth/sb** to accept sth/sb that is unpleasant without complaining **SYN** PUT UP WITH SB/STH: *By 11 o'clock, the heat is hard to tolerate.* **3** **~ sth** to be able to be affected by a drug, difficult conditions, etc. without being harmed: *The patient was unable to tolerate morphine.* ◇ *The cannabis plant tolerates a wide range of growing conditions.*

tol·er·ation /ˌtɒlə'reɪʃn; *NAmE* ˌtɑːlə'reɪʃn/ *noun* [U] a willingness to allow sth to happen or continue, even if you do not like or agree with it **SYN** TOLERANCE (1): *In 1789, the National Assembly granted complete religious toleration in France.* ◇ **~ of sth** *The main reason for these accidents was the toleration of unsafe working practices by management and workers.*

to·mor·row[1] /tə'mɒrəʊ; *NAmE* tə'mɔːroʊ; tə'mɑːroʊ/ *adv.* on or during the day after today: *The first question was: 'If there were a general election tomorrow, who would you like to be Prime Minister?'*

to·mor·row[2] /tə'mɒrəʊ; *NAmE* tə'mɔːroʊ; tə'mɑːroʊ/ *noun* [U] **1** the day after today: *By tomorrow at the same time, the earth's population will have risen by almost 100 000.* **2** the future: **of ~** *It will be interesting to see how this research is adapted to the workplaces of tomorrow.*

ton /tʌn/ *noun* (*pl.* **tons** or **ton**) a unit for measuring weight, in Britain 2 240 POUNDS (1016.05 kg) **(long ton)** and in the US 2 000 POUNDS (907.19 kg) **(short ton)**: *An Indian elephant weighs about 2–5 tons.* ➲ *compare* TONNE

tone /təʊn; *NAmE* toʊn/ *noun* **1** [sing.] the general character and attitude of sth such as a piece of writing; the atmosphere of an event: *The letters were written in a warm and candid tone.* ◇ **~ of sth** *The tone of the poem is clearly not comic.* ◇ *The elder Cato used his position to attempt to raise the moral tone of Roman life.* ◇ **set the ~ for/of sth** *The first decree of the Provisional Government set the tone for the new regime.* **2** [C] the quality of sb's voice, especially expressing a particular emotion: *His tone was deadly serious.* ◇ **~ of voice** *The teacher provided advice on developing effective eye contact, tone of voice and body language.* **3** [C] the quality of a sound, especially the sound of a musical instrument or one produced by electronic equipment: *The acoustic coupler converts the local computer data into audible tones.* ◇ *The low tones produced by large earthquakes are not generally within the audible range for humans.* **4** [C] **~ (of sth)** the extent to which a particular form of a colour is light or dark: *The design of the advertisement uses subtle tones of blue and green.* **5** [U] how strong and firm your muscles or skin are: *Common symptoms of PNS include difficulty in walking and loss of muscle tone.*

tongue /tʌŋ/ *noun* **1** the soft part in the mouth that moves around, used for tasting, swallowing, speaking, etc: *Symptoms include shortness of breath with pale tongue and slow pulse.* **2** (*formal* or *literary*) a language: *Whitley et al. found that ethnic minorities would prefer services delivered in their native tongue.* ➲ *see also* MOTHER TONGUE

tonne /tʌn/ (*pl.* **tonnes** or **tonne**) (*also* ˌ**metric 'ton**) *noun* a unit for measuring weight, equal to 1 000 kilograms: *Global cocoa production is over 3 million tonnes per year.* ➲ *compare* TON

too /tuː/ *adv.* **1** used before adjectives and adverbs to say that sth is more than is good, necessary, possible, etc: *Some argue that mothers now spend too much time at work rather than with their children.* ◇ *Attempts to halt the conflict were too few and came too late.* ◇ **(far) ~... to do sth** *This question is far too complex to permit full treatment here.* ◇ **~... for sth/sb** *Firewood is too expensive for most villagers.* **2** (usually placed at the end of a clause) also; as well: *Business must be responsive, but charities need to listen to the market too.* ◇ *Policy varies enormously in the EU, and so too does the policymaking process.*

took *past tense of* TAKE

tool /tuːl/ *noun* **1** a thing that helps sb to do a job or to achieve sth: *Authoritarian regimes have long used radio and television as propaganda tools.* ◇ *Planned*

T

organizational change is a powerful management tool. ◇ **~ for (doing) sth** *In these cases, the Internet acts as a networking tool for contacting family and friends.* ◇ **~ to do sth** *Wilson et al. (1994) describe the life cycle concept as a useful tool to assess an organization's marketing activity.* ◇ **~ kit** *Video recordings were used to supplement the traditional tool kit of research methods.* **2** a piece of equipment held in the hand, that is used for making things or repairing things: *In 1500 goods were made almost entirely by hand, using simple tools.* ◇ *Increased yields encouraged the development of more efficient agricultural tools such as the large scythe.*

▸ ADJECTIVE + TOOL **simple • basic • standard • new • sophisticated • powerful, effective • important, essential, vital • valuable • useful • practical • appropriate** *The use of telephone hotlines proved to be an effective information dissemination tool during the SARS outbreak.* | **mathematical • statistical • analytical • conceptual • modelling • methodological • software • online, web-based • diagnostic** *Hierarchy theory (Allen, 1996) was the main analytical tool employed in this research.*

▸ NOUN + TOOL **screening • assessment • measurement • communication • marketing • management** *The limitations of Body Mass Index as a risk assessment tool are increasingly recognized.* | **hand • stone • cutting** *The main industrial uses of diamonds include cutting tools, abrasives, and powder for grinding and polishing.*

▸ VERB + TOOL **use • utilize, employ • apply • provide • develop • design • offer • become • be used as, serve as** *Humans using hand tools were replaced by complex machines powered by steam.*

▸ PHRASE **tools of the trade, tools of their/his, etc. trade** *Social scientists, equipped with surveys and other tools of their trade, began to research the issue.*

tooth /tu:θ/ *noun* (*pl.* **teeth** /ti:θ/) **1** any of the hard white structures in the mouth used for biting: *Acanthodians had small sharp teeth and fed on small invertebrates and fish.* **2** a narrow pointed part that sticks out of an object: *Generally, as gear wheels get bigger, the size of the teeth on the gear wheel gets bigger too.*

top¹ /tɒp; *NAmE* tɑ:p/ *noun* **1** [C] the highest part or point of sth: **at the ~ (of sth)** *The search bar is placed at the very top of the web page.* ◇ **on the ~ (of sth)** *Vast amounts of marine sediment were deposited on the top of the Kaibab Formation (Hintze, 1988).* ◇ **from ~ to bottom** *In Figure 3, the timeline runs from top to bottom, each row representing one recording.* OPP BOTTOM¹ (1) **2** [sing.] the highest or most important rank or position: **at the ~ (of sth)** *Headquarter cities are at the top of the global hierarchy.* ◇ *At the top of the list of disadvantages is the threat of legal action.* ◇ **reach/rise to the ~** *Women were not badly represented in middle management but few reached the top.* ◇ **from the ~ down** *The Frankish people were converted from the top down, with the king and his family being baptized first.* OPP BOTTOM¹ (2) ➲ *see also* TOP-DOWN **3** [C] the upper flat surface of sth: *Space does not lie flat and true like the top of a table.*

IDM **on ˈtop 1** on the highest point or surface: *The six free-standing units each had a lamp on top.* **2** in a leading position; in control: *The group on top, in any given society, will not necessarily be happier than other groups.* ◇ *In the presidential debates, most commentators agreed that Obama came out on top.* **on top of sth/sb 1** on, over or covering sth/sb: *'The Prelude' ends with the poet standing on top of a mountain, looking down on nature.* ◇ *Metal is deposited on top of the oxide layer to form the gate electrode.* **2** in addition to sth: *Parlin, on top of his many other roles, thus became an expert salesman.* ◇ *The final film won a Best Picture Oscar on top of a multitude of other prizes.* **3** in control of a situation: *Banking regulators failed to keep on top of fast-paced financial developments.*

top² /tɒp; *NAmE* tɑ:p/ *adj.* [usually before noun] highest in position, rank or degree: *The most recent increases are shown on the chart (Figure 1a, top right).* ◇ *It is widely accepted that the top 500 multinational enterprises are driving globalization.* ◇ *Wailerdsak and Suehiro (2004) conducted a study of top executives of listed firms.* ◇ *The company had given top priority to quality improvement.*

ˌtop-ˈdown *adj.* **1** starting from or involving the people who have higher positions in an organization: *Politicians need to cease their top-down approach and genuinely engage with local communities.* OPP BOTTOM-UP (2) **2** (of a plan, project, etc.) starting with a general idea to which details are added later: *In this top-down approach, a view of the whole system is used to try and understand the significance of the individual components.* OPP BOTTOM-UP (1)

topic AWL /ˈtɒpɪk; *NAmE* ˈtɑ:pɪk/ *noun* a particular subject that is studied, written about or discussed: *Remote-sensing techniques have become an important research topic in this field.* ◇ **~ of sth** *The topic of human effects on soils and landscapes is discussed in Chapter 11.* ◇ **on this ~** | **on the ~ of sth** *Clearly, further research is needed on this topic.* ◇ **~ area** *Weber's 'Sociology of Religion' covers four general topic areas.*

▸ ADJECTIVE + TOPIC **specific, particular, certain • general • related • important, major • main, key, central • relevant • popular • controversial, hot • sensitive • interesting** *Earlier reviews focused on more specific topics such as river basin planning.*

▸ VERB + TOPIC **cover, discuss, deal with, focus on, be devoted to • address • explore, pursue • approach • choose • study, research • return to** *This book deals with the topic of child soldiers.* ◇ *Arid lands (Friend et al., 2000) and rock glaciers (Barsch, 1996) are among the many geomorphic topics addressed in the literature.*

▸ NOUN + OF + TOPIC(S) **range, variety • aspect • discussion • understanding • teaching • treatment** *These articles cover a wide range of topics.* ◇ *A detailed treatment of the topic is given by van Holde et al. (1998).*

top·ic·al AWL /ˈtɒpɪkl; *NAmE* ˈtɑ:pɪkl/ *adj.* **1** connected with sth that is happening or of interest at the present time: *The Council reacts to topical issues of the day but also attempts to have an overall coverage.* ◇ *Some contributions to the collection are not merely interesting but also highly topical.* **2** (*medical*) connected with, or put directly on, a part of the body: *When the condition is localized, topical treatment is sufficient.* ■ **top·ic·al·ity** /ˌtɒpɪˈkæləti; *NAmE* ˌtɑ:pɪˈkæləti/ *noun* [U] *Britain's acquisition of an eastern Mediterranean empire explains the topicality of Byron's 'Turkish Tales'.*

top·og·raphy /təˈpɒgrəfi; *NAmE* təˈpɑ:grəfi/ *noun* [U, C] (*technical*) the physical features of an area of land, especially the position of its rivers, mountains, etc: *Local topography makes railway construction expensive.* ◇ **~ of sth** *The gradient is influenced by the topography of the estuary.* ■ **topo·graph·ic·al** /ˌtɒpəˈgræfɪkl; *NAmE* ˌtɑ:pəˈgræfɪkl/ (*also* **topo·graph·ic** /ˌtɒpəˈgræfɪk; *NAmE* ˌtɑ:pəˈgræfɪk/) *adj.* [usually before noun] *Topographical maps and radar images are available.* ◇ *Similar topographic features have also been recorded in Malawi.* **topo·graph·ic·al·ly** /ˌtɒpəˈgræfɪkli; *NAmE* ˌtɑ:pəˈgræfɪkli/ *adv.*: *This is a topographically complex area.*

top·ology /təˈpɒlədʒi; *NAmE* təˈpɑ:lədʒi/ *noun* [U, C] (*technical*) the way in which the parts of sth are arranged and related: *The Canadian banking topology is relatively flat, with a few large banks controlling the entire market.* ◇ **~ of sth** *The three-level topology of the phone network is designed to exploit the fact that most calls are local.*

tore *past tense of* TEAR¹

torn *past part. of* TEAR¹

tort /tɔːt; *NAmE* tɔːrt/ *noun* [C, U] (*law*) an action that harms sb and for which the person responsible can be taken to court, although it is not a crime; the law in relation to this: *The employee committed a tort.* ◇ *It was held that A was liable in tort to C for the financial loss caused.*

tor·ture¹ /ˈtɔːtʃə(r); *NAmE* ˈtɔːrtʃər/ *noun* [U] the act of causing sb severe pain or suffering, usually in order to punish them or make them tell you sth: *He was at risk of being subjected to torture.* ◇ *Physical and mental torture had been used to obtain confessions.* ◇ **~ of sb** *the torture of political prisoners*

tor·ture² /ˈtɔːtʃə(r); *NAmE* ˈtɔːrtʃər/ *verb* [often passive] **~ sb** to hurt sb physically or mentally, usually in order to punish them or make them tell you sth: *Those who defied the authorities were imprisoned, tortured or killed.*

total¹ /ˈtəʊtl; *NAmE* ˈtoʊtl/ *adj.* [usually before noun] **1** being the amount or number after everyone or everything is counted or added together: *Historians are still arguing about the total number of victims.* ◇ *Estimates of the total amount of carbon in the crust, ocean and atmosphere of Earth are similar to those for Venus.* ◇ *Total costs increased by 13%.* **2** used when you are emphasizing sth, to mean 'to the greatest degree possible' SYN COMPLETE¹ (2): *Because of the total darkness in winter, most growth occurs in the summer.* ◇ *There is an almost total lack of written sources for the early history of north Britain.*
▸ TOTAL + NOUN **number • amount • quantity • sample • volume • concentration • mass • area • length • score • variance** *The total volume of water passing along the Comite River had not changed.* | **cost • expenditure, spending • budget • output • sales • income • assets • population • consumption • energy • pressure • momentum • emissions** *Total annual water consumption in Singapore was only about 120 million m³ in the mid-1960s.*

total² /ˈtəʊtl; *NAmE* ˈtoʊtl/ *noun* the amount you get when you add several numbers or amounts together; the final number of people or things when they have all been counted: *In Europe, annual rainfall totals have increased steadily since the middle of the nineteenth century.* ◇ **~ of sth** *The combined total of the Conservative and UKIP votes was greater than that of the winning Labour candidate.* ◇ *Out of a total of some 70 000 species of fungi, about 300 are parasites of animals.* ◇ **in ~** *In total, 53 interviews were recorded.*

total³ /ˈtəʊtl; *NAmE* ˈtoʊtl/ *verb* (-ll-, *US also* -l-) **1 ~ sth** to reach a particular total: *In 2002 the World Bank provided loans totalling $11.5 billion in support of 96 projects.* **2 ~ sth/sb (up)** to add up the numbers of sth/sb and get a total: *The volume of material moved as solutes, suspended sediment or bedload was totalled for each year.*

to·tal·ity /təʊˈtæləti; *NAmE* toʊˈtæləti/ *noun* [C, U] the state of being complete or whole; the whole amount or number: **in its ~** *The Appeal Body held that the Panel had falied to consider the evidence in its totality.* ◇ **~ of sth** *There is nothing outside the universe for it to expand into, since it is the totality of all that exists.*

to·tal·ly /ˈtəʊtəli; *NAmE* ˈtoʊtəli/ *adv.* (used to emphasize the following word or phrase) completely: *The two organisms are totally different in structure and physiology.* ◇ *The refugees are almost totally dependent on agencies to provide for their basic needs.*

touch¹ /tʌtʃ/ *verb* **1** [T] **~ sb/sth** to bring your hand or another part of your body into contact with sb/sth: *Everything King Midas touched changed into gold.* **2** [I, T] (of two or more things or surfaces) to be or come so close together that there is no space between them: *It is important that the wires do not touch.* ◇ **~ sth** *The weights are hanging freely and not touching the floor.* ◇ **~ each other** *View B shows how the spheres within each layer do not touch each other.* **3** [T] to affect or concern sb/sth: **~ sb/sth** *This is a law that touches the lives of every American.* ◇ **be touched by sth** *Far more people are touched by poverty than was previously thought.* **4** [T] **~ sb/sth** to make sb feel grateful, sympathetic or upset: *The accounts of their lives are presented in such a way as to touch the heart.* ◇ *The author explores how far paintings should and could touch individuals.* **5** [T] (often in negative sentences) **~ sth/sb** to move sth, especially in such a way that you damage it; to hit or harm sb: *The children need to understand which pieces of equipment they must not touch.* ◇ *The women's resistance to the Census of 1911 was on so large a scale that the government was unable to touch them.* **6** [T] (usually in negative sentences) **~ sth** to eat, drink or use sth: *He has never touched alcohol in his life.* IDM *see* NERVE
PHR V ˌ**touch sth ˈoff** to make sth begin, especially a difficult or violent situation: *His speech touched off a new wave of democratic demands.* ˈ**touch on/upon sth** to mention or deal with a subject in only a few words, without going into detail: *Marx touches on religion in his many books, letters and articles on other subjects.*

touch² /tʌtʃ/ *noun* **1** [U] the sense that makes you aware of things and what they are like when you put your hands and fingers on them: *Touch is the most basic form of communication.* ◇ **sense of ~** *In this syndrome, patients develop impairment in their sense of touch.* ◇ **by ~** *The screen can be operated by touch.* **2** [C, usually sing.] an act of bringing your hand or another part of your body into contact with sb/sth: **~ (of sth)** *He claimed to have the power to cure cancer completely with only the touch of his hand.* ◇ **at the ~ of a button** *At the touch of a button, email messages go to hundreds of respondents simultaneously.* **3** [sing.] the way that sth feels when you put your hand or fingers on it or when it comes into contact with your body: **(at the) ~ of sth** *Some children will scream with fear at the touch of fur.* ◇ **to the ~** *The reddened skin is warm to the touch.* **4** [C] a small detail that is added to sth in order to improve it or make it complete: *The online component of the course is also a nice touch.* ◇ **finishing touches** *All that remains to do is to put the finishing touches to the report.* **5** [sing., U] a way or style of doing sth: *It is just one of the ways in which companies can bring a personal touch to doing business.* ◇ *The book is written with a lightness of touch that makes it highly accessible.* **6** [C, usually sing.] **~ of sth** a very small amount of sth SYN TRACE² (2): *There is more than a touch of romanticism in this view.*
IDM **be, get, keep, etc. in ˈtouch (with sb)** to communicate with sb, for example by writing to them or by telephone or email: *Bishops kept in touch with one another through letters and messengers.* **be, keep, etc. in ˈtouch (with sth)** to continue to know what is happening in a particular subject or area: *He kept in touch with events in his homeland.* **be, become, etc. out of ˈtouch (with sth)** to not know or understand what is happening in a particular subject or area: *The position taken by the leadership highlighted how out of touch with contemporary society the party had become.* **lose ˈtouch (with sb/sth)** to no longer understand sb/sth, especially how ordinary people feel: *He was concerned with defending economics against the charge that it had lost touch with ethics.* ➲ *more at* LIGHT²

tough /tʌf/ *adj.* (**tough·er, tough·est**) **1** (of a thing) not easily damaged; strong: *Yeast cells have a tough cell wall.* ◇ *Silicon carbide is a tough, wear-resistant material with a hardness close to that of diamond.* ➲ *compare* RESILIENT (2) **2** (*rather informal*) having or causing problems SYN DIFFICULT (2): *Times are increasingly tough for a large number of families.* ◇ *They were going to have some tough decisions to make.* ◇ *This is a tough question for governments.* ◇ **it is ~ to do sth** *Refugees are finding it tough to land a job.*

3 (*rather informal*) demanding that laws be obeyed, and not accepting any reasons for not obeying them: *Manufacturers faced tougher regulation.* ◇ **~ on sb/sth** *They promised to be tough on crime.* OPP SOFT (5) **4** (*rather informal*) (of a person) strong enough to deal successfully with difficult conditions or situations: *They were tough, pioneering hill farmers.* ◇ *He was concerned to appear 'tough' and manly.* HELP **Tough** can sometimes suggest that sb may be violent. The more formal word **resilient** does not suggest this: *The vision was to create strong and resilient youth, families and community.* ■ **tough·ness** *noun* [U] **~ (of sth)** *Methods for increasing toughness of composite structures are discussed.* ◇ *This depends greatly on the toughness of environmental restrictions.* ◇ *He earned a reputation for fairness and toughness.*

tour[1] /tʊə(r); tɔː(r); *NAmE* tʊr/ *noun* **1** a visit or journey in which you are shown or see several different things or places: *The museum offers guided tours.* ◇ *The online virtual tour is helpful.* ◇ **~ of sth** *He embarked on a walking tour of the region in the summer of 1802.* ◇ *A 'grand tour' of Europe was considered essential for the sons of wealthy families.* **2** a series of visits that, for example, a speaker, singer or sports team makes to different places: **~ (of sth)** *She undertook an extensive speaking tour of Europe.* ◇ **on ~** *Music societies provide concert opportunities for musicians on tour.* **3** (*also* **tour of duty**) a period when a soldier or other worker is working away from home: *He returned after two tours of duty with the Marines.*

tour[2] /tʊə(r); tɔː(r); *NAmE* tʊr/ *verb* [T, I] to go on a visit or a series of visits, in order to see different things or to take part in a series of events: **~ sth** *The research team toured the facilities and observed staff members carrying out interventions.* ◇ *They were invited to tour South Africa with the England rugby team.* ◇ **+ adv./prep.** *He toured throughout the United States lecturing.* HELP To **tour** a display or show is to let it be seen in a series of different places: *They toured the exhibition around schools.*

tour·ism /ˈtʊərɪzəm; ˈtɔːrɪzəm; *NAmE* ˈtʊrɪzəm/ *noun* [U] the business activities involving accommodation, services and entertainment for people who are visiting a place for pleasure: *The organization works with tourism businesses to promote sustainable tourism.* ◇ **+ noun** *The tourism industry has experienced dramatic growth since about 1960.*

tour·ist /ˈtʊərɪst; ˈtɔːrɪst; *NAmE* ˈtʊrɪst/ *noun* a person who is travelling or visiting a place for pleasure: *The region attracts numerous tourists for its combination of natural and cultural features.* ◇ **+ noun** *They had entered the country on tourist visas.* ◇ *the tourist industry/trade* ◇ *tourist attractions/destinations/resorts*

to·wards /təˈwɔːdz; *NAmE* tɔːrdz/ (*also* **to·ward** /təˈwɔːd; *NAmE* tɔːrd/ *especially in NAmE*) *prep.* **1** in the direction of sb/sth: *Warm air from the equator rises and moves towards the poles.* ◇ *The ritual prayers are said five times a day while facing towards Mecca.* **2** aiming to achieve sth; moving closer to achieving sth: *Their work was largely directed towards the search for mineral resources.* ◇ *We are reorienting health services towards health promotion and disease prevention.* **3** close or closer to a point in time: *Some of the detainees were released towards the end of the war.* **4** in relation to sb/sth: *Language has a powerful influence in shaping our attitudes towards disability.* ◇ *He frequently expresses anger towards his mother and stepfather.*

tower /ˈtaʊə(r)/ *noun* a tall narrow building or part of a building: *A taller control tower was erected to give better oversight of the airfield.* ◇ *Evaporated water rises from the cooling tower.* ◇ *She calculated the height of the cathedral tower.*

town /taʊn/ *noun* [C, U] a place with many houses, shops, etc. where people live and work. It is larger than a village but smaller than a city: *Towns and cities continued to grow across Europe.* ◇ **in a ~** *Many live in outlying provincial towns.* ◇ **in ~** *They established offices in town.* ◇ **the ~ of sth** *The goods were produced in the nearby town of Banbury.* ◇ **+ noun** *The towns were administered by the town councils.*

toxic /ˈtɒksɪk; *NAmE* ˈtɑːksɪk/ *adj.* **1** containing poison; poisonous: *In Malaysia, it is estimated that industries generate some 380 000 m^3 of toxic wastes yearly.* ◇ *The company had no experience of disposing of highly toxic materials.* ◇ *Research has focused on the potential toxic effects of nanoparticles (Hoet et al., 2004).* **2** used to describe a level of debt that has a high risk of not being paid back: *Toxic debts rapidly infected the global financial system.* ◇ *The 2008 government bailouts aimed to replace the worthless toxic assets on the banks' balance sheets.*

tox·icity /tɒkˈsɪsəti; *NAmE* tɑːkˈsɪsəti/ *noun* (*pl.* **-ies**) **1** [U] **~ (of sth)** the quality of being poisonous; the extent to which sth is poisonous: *Because of their high toxicity, detergents and dispersants are today only used as a last resort.* **2** [C] **~ (of sth)** the effect that a poisonous substance has: *There is a need for further research into the potential long-term toxicities of carbon nanotubes.*

toxin /ˈtɒksɪn; *NAmE* ˈtɑːksɪn/ *noun* a poisonous substance, especially one that is produced by bacteria in plants and animals: *Certain microbial species produce toxins that can severely damage or kill the host.*

toy /tɔɪ/ *noun* an object for children to play with: *The children were playing happily with their toys.*

trace[1] AWL /treɪs/ *verb* **1** [often passive] **~ sth (back) (to sth)** to discover or describe when or how sth began: *The families could trace their ancestry back to Rurik, the reputed founder of the Russian state.* ◇ *It is not always possible to trace the origin of a particular creole feature to a unique source.* ◇ *This change in attitude could be traced back to ideas emerging in the 1960s among economists.* **2 ~ sth (from sth) (to sth)** to describe a process or the development of sth: *The book traces the history of Somaliland from the nineteenth century to the present day.* **3** [often passive] to find or discover sb/sth by looking carefully for them/it: **~ sb/sth** *Early Quaternary volcanoes that have lost most of their volcanic landform characteristics can be traced in western Bali.* ◇ **~ sb/sth to sth** *Of the 1 191 respondents, 94 had moved and were traced to their new location.* **4 ~ sth (out)** to draw a line or lines on a surface: *The line traced out on the diagram depicts the path of an object or light pulse.* **5 ~ sth** to take a particular path or route: *The read/write head traces a circular path around the disk.* **6 ~ sth** to follow the shape or outline of sth: *The children can see the edges of the triangle and trace them with their finger.*

trace[2] AWL /treɪs/ *noun* **1** [C, U] a mark, object or sign that shows that sb/sth existed or was present: *Plant roots leave distinctive traces in sediments.* ◇ **no ~** *Most internment camps were dismantled and documents destroyed so that little to no trace remained.* ◇ **~ of sb/sth** *Soil analysis may be an appropriate tool for detecting traces of human activity.* ◇ **without (a) ~** *These earlier written sources have not disappeared without trace.* HELP A **trace fossil** is the evidence of animal activity preserved in a rock: *Information about the behaviour of dinosaurs has been gleaned from trace fossils, mainly footprints.* **2** [C] a very small amount of sth: **~ of sth** *The water may contain traces of mildly radioactive isotopes of hydrogen and nitrogen.* ◇ **+ noun** *Additional elements (including metals) are present in rain in trace amounts.* ➲ *see also* TRACE ELEMENT **3** [C] a line or pattern displayed by a machine to show information about sth that is being recorded or measured: *The top trace shows the velocity.* **4** [C] **~ (of sth)** a line following the path of sth: *We tested how an ant's behaviour is adapted to the topographical features of the beach by comparing a trace of the ant's path with a trace of the contour of the beach.*

trace·able AWL /ˈtreɪsəbl/ *adj.* if sth is **traceable**, you can find out where it came from, where it has gone, when it began or what its cause was: *The bones have changed shape over the generations, but the common ancestry is still traceable.* ◇ *Retailers need meat from farm-assured producers who can satisfy the consumer's desire for a fully traceable product.* ◇ **~ to sb/sth** *If they neglect their duty, they will be held responsible for the consequences traceable to that neglect.*

ˈtrace element *noun* **1** a chemical substance that is found in very small amounts: *The medium contains inorganic salts of nitrogen, sulfate, phosphate, calcium and various trace elements.* **2** a chemical substance that living things need only in very small amounts to be able to grow well: *Manganese is an essential trace element, although deficiency is rare.*

tra·cing /ˈtreɪsɪŋ/ *noun* a line or pattern that shows information about sth that is being recorded or measured: *Electrodes are placed on the patient's scalp and a tracing is made in the form of wavy lines.*

track[1] /træk/ *noun* **1** [C, usually pl.] a mark or line of marks left by a person, animal or moving vehicle: *Only the largest animals were able to make tracks in wet sand.* ◇ **~ of sb/sth** *This is one of three major locations in central Australia where the tracks of several ancestral groups cross.* **2** [C] the course or route that sb/sth is following: *People had no idea what life would have been like if history had followed a different track.* ◇ *Maps of storm tracks compiled by month by the National Weather Service are available for the years 1885–1996.* ◇ **~ of sb/sth** *Once contact with the ground is made, the track of a tornado at ground level may extend for only a few kilometres.* ◇ **fast ~** *The minister may use a special 'fast track' procedure for introducing the new legislation.* **3** [C, U] a continuous line of rails that a train moves along: *Towns sprang up along the tracks with names like Yuma, Akron, Burlington and Cheyenne Wells.* ◇ *A breakdown of one train could tie up traffic over hundreds of miles of track.* **4** [C] a rough path or road, usually one that has not been built but that has been made by people walking there: *Local roads were no more than muddy tracks.* **5** [C] a piece of music or song that has been recorded: *He recorded some of the tracks for his latest album in Los Angeles.* **6** [C] part of a tape, CD or computer disk that music or data can be recorded on: *Several parallel tracks are recorded simultaneously across the width of the tape.*

IDM **ˌback on ˈtrack** (*rather informal*) once again following a course that is likely to achieve what is required, after a mistake or failure: *Krugman has described the strategy necessary to put Japan's economy back on track.* **keep/lose track of sb/sth** to be aware of what is happening or where sb/sth is: *Educators in large schools commonly lament that they cannot keep track of hundreds or thousands of young people.* ◇ *In this section, the author seems to lose track of his argument.* **on the right/wrong ˈtrack** (*rather informal*) following a course that is likely to result in success/failure: *Voters who thought the country was on the right track voted almost two to one for the existing leader.* **on ˈtrack (to do sth)** following a course that is likely to achieve what is required: *Such reviews are necessary to determine whether or not the project is on track.* **stop/halt sb in their ˈtracks | stop/halt in your ˈtracks** (*rather informal*) to make sb stop suddenly; to stop suddenly: *A threat from Austria to intervene in support of Milan stopped the Bulgarian army in its tracks.*

track[2] /træk/ *verb* **1** [T] to follow the progress or development of sb/sth: **~ sb/sth** *Exporters must continue to track changes in consumers' tastes as they become more used to a product.* ◇ **~ how/what, etc...** *Historical methods can be used to track how those processes unfold over time in various domains.* ◇ **tracking system** *Furthermore, the supplier can provide online tracking systems so that the customer can check at any one time where her product is.* **2** [T] to follow the movements of sb/sth, especially by using special electronic equipment: **~ sb/sth** *The radar is used to track a target 10 km away.* ◇ *Terrorists have been able to move rapidly within and between borders, and this complicates efforts to track them.* ◇ **tracking system** *Two mobile automatic data recorders worked in conjunction with a radar tracking system.* **3** [T] to follow sb/sth, or to find sb/sth by following the marks, information, etc, that they have left behind them: *Wildlife can be tracked by means of radio collars.* ◇ **~ (from...) (to...)** *There are now improved supply chain systems, for example for tracking food from farm to shop.* **4** [I] **+ adv./prep.** to follow a particular course or route: *In June 1972, Hurricane Agnes tracked up the eastern seaboard of the USA.* **5** [I] **+ adv./prep.** (of a camera) to move in relation to the thing that is being filmed: *The camera tracks backwards as the creatures run past on either side.*

PHR V **ˌtrack sb/sth ˈdown** to find sb/sth after a thorough or difficult search SYN TRACE[1] (3): *It would be extremely costly tracking down each person.* ◇ *Holmes then tracked down many previous experiments and found that most showed the same results.*

tract /trækt/ *noun* **1** (*biology*) a system of connected organs or TISSUES along which materials or messages pass: *Olive oil is protective to the digestive tract.* ◇ **+ noun** *There was no evidence of a urinary tract infection.* **2 ~ (of sth)** an area of land, especially a large one: *Substantial tracts of land were set aside for parks.* **3** a short piece of writing, especially on a religious, moral or political subject, that is intended to influence people's ideas: *Several political tracts written after the Act of Union reflect on the new political alignment.*

trade[1] /treɪd/ *noun* **1** [U] the activity of buying and selling or of exchanging goods or services between people or countries: *US foreign trade declined once the depression began.* ◇ *Food is an important component of world trade.* ◇ **~ in sth** *The aim is to protect endangered species by imposing controls on international trade in those species.* ◇ **~ between A and B** *Such conduct is liable to affect trade between Member States.* ◇ **~ with sb/sth** *China is increasing trade with Canada.* ◇ **+ noun** *In a free trade area, barriers to trade are removed.* HELP **Fair trade** is trade between companies in developed countries and producers in developing countries in which fair prices are paid to the producers: *The idea behind fair trade is that consumers pay a guaranteed price plus a small premium to groups of small producers supplying commodity goods such as coffee, tea, chocolate and fruit.* ⊃ *see also* FREE TRADE, TERMS OF TRADE, TRADE BALANCE **2** [C] a particular type of business: *The follow-up study was of employees aged 15–64 years in the retail trade.* ◇ *Technological developments have transformed the book trade.* ◇ **+ noun** *Trade associations are expected to take the lead when an issue affects everyone in an industry.* **3 the trade** [sing.+ sing./pl. v.] the people or companies that are connected with a particular area of business: *Soon there will be only minimal spending on promotion to the trade.* **4** [C, U] a job, especially one that involves working with your hands and that requires special training and skills: *He had not been able to pursue his trade for nine months.* ◇ *He was sent to Baltimore to learn a trade.* ◇ **by ~** *Spencer was an engineer by trade.* ◇ **the tools of the/your ~** *Workers who owned the tools of their trade were thus able to work for themselves.* **5** [U, sing.] the amount of goods or services that are sold SYN BUSINESS (4): *They said that trade was difficult.* ◇ *Figure 6.4 illustrates the development in total trade (exports*

T

plus imports) in services. ◇ **~ in sth** *The US government supported the commercial hunting of the bison, to exploit a growing trade in buffalo hides.*

▸ ADJECTIVE + TRADE **international • global • foreign, overseas • external • regional • bilateral • multilateral • long-distance** *Russian-South Korean bilateral trade collapsed because of the Asian financial crisis.*

▸ NOUN + TRADE **retail • book • fur • drug • slave** *The authors maintain that European demand was a key driver of the North American fur trade.*

▸ VERB + TRADE **promote, encourage • facilitate • regulate • restrict • prevent • liberalize • conduct, engage in • dominate • affect • distort** *It is Commission policy to promote cross-border trade.* ◇ *These reforms had increased the state's power to regulate trade.*

▸ TRADE + NOUN **policy • agreement • negotiations • liberalization • barriers • restrictions • balance • costs • deficit • surplus • flow • theory • law • dispute • relations • route • rule • reform** *They argue that the best way to address global inequality is through trade liberalization.*

▸ NOUN + OF + TRADE **share • pattern • growth, expansion • impact • centre** *The company reportedly had the largest share of the Australia-Japan beef trade.* | **terms • volume • importance • liberalization • regulation • pattern • benefit** *Powerful Western interests continue to dictate the terms of trade to their own advantage*

trade² /treɪd/ *verb* **1** [I, T] to buy and sell goods and services HELP In economics, **trade** is usually used to refer to one country or economy exchanging goods or services with another: **~ (in sth) (with sb)** *The group started in the 1960s, trading in textiles and yarn.* ◇ *Greece trades with its European neighbours, especially Germany.* ◇ **~ sth (with sb)** *They were given permission to trade their rum and syrup with the northern colonies.* **2** [I] to exist and operate as a business or company: *In 2008, the furniture retailer ceased trading, with the loss of 1 400 jobs.* ◇ **~ as sb/sth** *A partnership may also trade as a limited partnership under the Limited Partnerships Act 1907.* **3** [I, T] to be bought and sold, or to buy and sell sth, on a STOCK EXCHANGE or other financial institution: **~ (sth) at sth** *By its first birthday, the euro was trading at around 1 euro to 1 US dollar.* ◇ **~ sth** *The shares cannot be traded for a period of time before the company's annual general meeting.* ◇ **~ sth on sth** *These securities were traded on global bond markets.* **4** [T] to exchange sth that you have for sth else: **~ sth** *They develop their own networks where they trade information about key skills and employment opportunities.* ◇ **~ sth for sth** *Prisoners trade various items in jail for cigarettes.* ◇ **~ sth with sb** *At the next level up, children will bargain or trade favours with others.*

PHR V **ˌtrade ˈdown** to spend less money on things than you used to: *Discount stores found that their sales grew relatively quickly as customers traded down.* **ˌtrade sth ˈin** to give sth used as part of the payment for sth new: *They are offered extremely favourable terms when trading in their car for a new model.* **ˌtrade sth ˈoff (against/for sth)** to balance two things or situations that are opposed to each other: *Organisms have to trade off the quality of their offspring against the quantity.* ◇ *Consumers are increasingly keen to trade off shopping time for leisure time.* ➲ *related noun* TRADE-OFF **ˈtrade on sth** to use sth to get an advantage for yourself SYN EXPLOIT (3): *Swart focuses on the growing number of workers who trade on their knowledge and work in knowledge-intensive firms.* **ˌtrade ˈup (to sth)** to sell sth in order to buy sth more expensive: *If the cost of running their vehicle comes down, they may trade up to the larger luxury vehicle.*

ˈtrade balance (*also* **ˌbalance of ˈtrade**) *noun* [sing.] the difference in value between imports and exports: *Imports slowed down in response to the falling lira and the trade balance improved significantly.*

trade·mark /ˈtreɪdmɑːk; *NAmE* ˈtreɪdmɑːrk/ *noun* (*abbr.* TM) a name, symbol or design that a company uses for its products and that cannot be used by anyone else: *The company claimed this was an unauthorized use of their registered trademark.*

ˈtrade-off *noun* the act of balancing two things that are opposed to each other: *This can often mean making trade-offs in order to meet the collective concerns of the group.* ◇ **~ between A and B** *Reproduction involves a trade-off between number of offspring and the energy invested in each one.*

trader /ˈtreɪdə(r)/ *noun* a person or organization that buys and sells things as a job or business: *Financial markets consist of networks of banks and other traders that buy and sell currencies, options and other securities.* ◇ *With the opening of ocean routes to the East by European traders during the 15th to 17th centuries, commercial cultivation expanded.* HELP A **sole trader** is a person who runs a business on their own: *A sole trader is the simplest business organization due to the ease of establishing and dissolving the business.*

ˌtrade ˈunion (*BrE also* **ˌtrades ˈunion**) *noun* = UNION (1)

trad·ing /ˈtreɪdɪŋ/ *noun* [U] the activity of buying and selling things: *Trading is made more difficult by numerous taxes charged if you move goods between states and even within some states.* ◇ **~ of sth** *A ban on the trading of many goods on a Sunday used to exist in the UK.* ◇ **+ noun** *The next section examines the strategies of British trading companies from the late eighteenth century into the twenty-first.* ◇ *The members of the group are the main aid donors as well as the major trading nations.* ◇ *a trading bloc/sector*

trad·ition AWL /trəˈdɪʃn/ *noun* [C, U] a belief, custom, story or way of doing sth that has existed for a long time among a particular group of people; a set of these beliefs, etc: **~ (of sth)** *Russia had no tradition of constitutional government.* ◇ *There was no dramatic break with tradition, and in some regions the old style continued for some time.* ◇ **by ~** *By tradition, the provision of education and health care was left to charity.* ◇ **in/within a... ~** *Many of these sociologists had formerly worked within a Marxist tradition.* ◇ **in/within the ~ of sb/sth** *Aron was a French liberal social theorist in the tradition of Alexis de Tocqueville.* ◇ **according to (a) ~** *Tens of thousands of Indonesian villages are organized according to the tradition of mutual assistance.*

▸ ADJECTIVE + TRADITION **long • old • early • different • strong • liberal • classical • national • local • oral • literary • religious • cultural • legal • intellectual • political • philosophical** *There is a long tradition of travel to other countries in pursuit of learning and education.*

▸ VERB + TRADITION **follow • continue, preserve, perpetuate, carry on, maintain • be rooted in • draw on • break with • invent • initiate, introduce • represent • reflect • challenge** *Rimsky-Korsakov had initially followed family tradition by becoming a naval officer.*

▸ TRADITION OF + NOUN **thought • scholarship • inquiry • criticism • writing • philosophy • poetry** *Such ideas reflect a tradition of thought that goes back to the Enlightenment.*

trad·ition·al AWL /trəˈdɪʃənl/ *adj.* **1** following older methods and ideas rather than modern or different ones SYN CONVENTIONAL (1): *Such issues may have been overlooked in more traditional approaches to data collection.* ◇ *Despite technological improvements, traditional methods remain of utmost importance.* **2** being part of the beliefs, customs or way of life that have existed for a long time among a particular group of people: *Some churches find same-sex marriage incompatible with their traditional beliefs.* ◇ **it is ~ (for sb) to do sth** *It is*

T

traditional for an opposition MP to be chairman of the Public Accounts Committee.

▸ TRADITIONAL + NOUN **method • technique • system • way • form • pattern • structure • practice** *The committee decided that traditional methods of making Camembert cheese, using raw milk, had to be maintained.* | **approach • model • view • notion • concern • theory • analysis • role • factor • marketing • advertising • media** *The national curriculum is more and more dominated by traditional models of testing.* | **belief • value • culture • religion • family • society** *The exiles retain many aspects of their traditional culture.*

trad·ition·al·ist AWL /trəˈdɪʃənəlɪst/ *noun* a person who prefers traditional ideas or methods to modern ones: *The proposed changes were firmly rejected by traditionalists.* ■ **trad·ition·al·ist** AWL *adj.*: *Traditionalist support for the death penalty far outweighs progressive opposition in most American states.*

trad·ition·al·ly AWL /trəˈdɪʃənəli/ *adv.* **1** according to what has always or usually happened in the past: *The states of the Midwest, and especially Wisconsin, are traditionally regarded as the 'dairy states'.* ◇ *Traditionally, British capitalism has been among the least regulated of capitalist patterns.* **2** according to the beliefs, customs or way of life that have existed for a long time among a particular group of people; according to what is believed: *Processions are traditionally held on 1 May to celebrate May Day.* ◇ *Tarquinius Priscus, the fifth king of Rome (traditionally 616–579 BC), was believed to be the son of Demaratus of Corinth.*

traf·fic¹ /ˈtræfɪk/ *noun* [U] **1** the vehicles that are on a road at a particular time: *In cities, heavy traffic can be a serious problem at almost any time of the day or night.* ◇ **+ noun** *The lower back pain initially developed after a road traffic accident.* ◇ *Thirdly, traffic congestion generates excessive pollution of many kinds:...* **2** the movement of ships, trains, aircraft, etc. along a particular route: *Pilots should keep right and yield to traffic on their left or below them.* **3** the movement of people or goods from one place to another: *The very large increase in passenger traffic illustrates the success of deregulation in the airline industry.* **4** the movement of messages and signals through an electronic communication system: *By 2006, video downloads occupied perhaps half the total traffic on the Internet.* **5 ~ (in sb/sth)** illegal trade in sb/sth: *Traffic in human beings is the third most lucrative in the world today, after drugs and arms.*

T

traf·fic² /ˈtræfɪk/ *verb* **(-ck-)** to buy and sell things or people illegally: **~ sb/sth** *This article considers a protection framework that could assist women who have been trafficked.* ◇ **~ in sb/sth** *He was convicted of conspiracy to traffic in drugs.* ■ **traf·fick·er** *noun*: *Women and girls are especially targeted by traffickers.*

traf·fick·ing /ˈtræfɪkɪŋ/ *noun* [U] the practice of conducting an illegal trade in sb/sth: *Australia and Canada have implemented assistance programmes for victims of human trafficking.* ◇ **~ (in sb/sth)** *There was to be increased cooperation between customs and police authorities in combating trafficking in drugs and arms.*

tra·gedy /ˈtrædʒədi/ *noun* (*pl.* **-ies**) [C, U] **1** a very sad event or situation, especially one that involves death: *This type of conflict leads to enormous human tragedies.* ◇ *The voyage ended in tragedy.* ◇ **~ of sth** *Both experienced the tragedy of the Great War.* **2** a serious play with a sad ending, especially one in which the main character dies; plays of this type: *He wrote two tragedies.* ◇ *He discusses his interest in Greek tragedy.* ➲ *compare* COMEDY

tra·gic /ˈtrædʒɪk/ *adj.* **1** making you feel very sad, usually because sb has died or suffered a lot: *This course of action proved to have tragic consequences.* ◇ *His death was a tragic event.* ◇ *He suffered the tragic loss of one of his children.* ◇ *Her life was tragic.* **2** [usually before noun] connected with tragedy (= the style of literature): *Hamlet's end contrasts with the more resolute deaths of Shakespeare's other tragic heroes.* ◇ *Like other tragic poets, Sophocles reworked the familiar plots of Greek mythology.* ■ **tra·gic·al·ly** /ˈtrædʒɪkli/ *adv.*: *Tragically, she died in March 2007, aged just 42.*

train¹ /treɪn/ *verb* **1** [T, I] to teach a person or an animal the skills for a particular job or activity; to be taught in this way: **~ sb/sth (to do sth)** *Teachers are trained to understand the principles of conflict resolution.* ◇ *Simmons initially trained bats to discriminate targets placed at different distances.* ◇ *Cost has a knock-on effect on the use of highly trained personnel.* ◇ **~ (sb) (as/in/for sth)** *Employers must also train staff in how to perform activities safely.* ◇ *Taylor originally trained as a lawyer.* ◇ *They trained for careers in the navy.* ◇ **~ to do/be sth** *He trained to be a navy pilot, then went off to serve in the Vietnam war.* **2** [I, T] to prepare yourself/sb for a particular activity, especially a sport, by doing a lot of exercise; to prepare a person or an animal in this way: *At the time of interview, he was training in the gym every other day.* ◇ **~ for sth** *These militias trained for guerrilla war.* ◇ **~ sb/sth (for sth)** *The state paid and trained a team of runners for the torch races at festivals within Athens.* **3** [T] **~ sth (to do sth)** to develop a natural ability or quality so that it improves: *An expert with a trained eye will spot the difference immediately.* ◇ *It is a question of training your mind to think positively.*

train² /treɪn/ *noun* **1** a railway engine pulling a number of COACHES or TRUCKS, taking people and goods from one place to another: *to take/catch/board a train* ◇ *a passenger/freight train* ◇ **by ~** *Travelling to Strasbourg from Brussels is a five-hour journey by train.* ◇ **+ noun** *Being near a main train station may be crucial for attracting a target market of urban professionals.* **2** a number of people or animals moving in a line: **+ noun** *Roman merchants improved camel train routes across the desert to the Nile.* **3** [usually sing.] **~ (of sth)** a series of events or actions that are connected: *This might lead to the melting of the ice cap, which might in turn set a train of events in motion.* ◇ *The oscillogram reveals that each syllable is comprised of an uninterrupted train of sound waves.*

IDM **set sth in ˈtrain** (*formal*) to prepare or start sth: *It was part of the broader geopolitical transformations set in train by the Second World War.* **a train of ˈthought** the connected series of thoughts that are in your head at a particular time: *It is interesting to consider how this train of thought might be developed.*

train·ee /ˌtreɪˈniː/ *noun* a person who is being taught how to do a particular job: *Some trainees require greater support than is currently provided.* ◇ **+ noun** *a trainee doctor/teacher/pilot*

train·er /ˈtreɪnə(r)/ *noun* a person who teaches people or animals to perform a particular job or skill well: *a teacher trainer*

train·ing /ˈtreɪnɪŋ/ *noun* [U] the process of learning the skills that you need to do a job: **~ (in sth/in doing sth)** *Students had received formal training in search strategies.* ◇ *Matsuda investigates how World Englishes are incorporated into ELT teacher training in Japan.* ◇ *professional/vocational/military training* ◇ **+ noun** *a training programme/course/session*

trait /treɪt/ *noun* a particular quality or characteristic, especially in sb's personality: *The four cases share several traits.* ◇ *Europeans often adopted selected Aboriginal cultural traits judged to be advantageous in the new environmental setting.* ◇ *Testosterone is a hormone involved in the development of male secondary sexual traits.* HELP In biology, a **trait** is a characteristic in a person or animal that depends on the GENES passed down from the parents: *An individual may inherit certain traits, although these are undoubtedly influenced by social relationships.* ◇ *Complex genetic traits influence our health and life span.* ➲ thesaurus note *at* FEATURE[1]

▸ ADJECTIVE + TRAIT **certain, particular ♦ selected ♦ distinctive ♦ desirable ♦ negative ♦ complex ♦ personal ♦ human ♦ male ♦ female ♦ genetic, heritable, inherited ♦ phenotypic ♦ adaptive ♦ biological ♦ physiological ♦ sexual ♦ behavioural ♦ cognitive ♦ morphological ♦ cultural** *The Greek idea of character included both the personal traits and the ethics of an individual.*

▸ NOUN + TRAIT **personality, character ♦ life history** *The study shows that to get good grades one also has to develop certain personality traits.*

▸ VERB + TRAIT **possess ♦ exhibit ♦ share ♦ inherit ♦ acquire** *Some individuals possess behavioural traits that allow them to be more reproductively successful than others.*

tra·jec·tory /trəˈdʒektəri/ (*pl.* **-ies**) *noun* (*technical*) **1** the curved path of sth that has been fired, hit or thrown into the air: *From this observation, we would thus expect light rays to follow curved trajectories in gravitational fields.* ◇ **along a/the ~** *Ions with similar mass-to-charge ratios will travel along the same trajectory.* **2** the way in which a person, an event or a process develops over a period of time, often leading to a particular result: *Sylvestre believed that males and females have different developmental trajectories.* ◇ *The transitions to democracy in Southern Europe in the 1970s followed greatly different trajectories.* ◇ *a/an technological/evolutionary/narrative trajectory*

trans·act /trænˈzækt/ *verb* [T, I] **~ (sth) (with sb)** to do business with a person or an organization: *The prime source of customer satisfaction was the speed with which customers could transact business with the bank.* ◇ *The dealer must know the price at which he is prepared to transact.*

trans·ac·tion /trænˈzækʃn/ *noun* **1** [C] a piece of business that is done between people, especially an act of buying or selling **SYN** DEAL[2] (1): *UK financial markets attracted a significant share of global financial transactions.* ◇ *business/commercial/market/economic transactions* ◇ **~ between A and B** *27 per cent of this figure represented transactions between business and consumers.* ◇ **+ noun** *Business groups can bypass high transaction costs through a variety of strategies.* **2** [U] **~ of sth** (*formal*) the process of doing sth: *The administrative unit ensures the transaction of Council business according to the rules of procedure.*

tran·scend /trænˈsend/ *verb* **~ sth** to be or go beyond the usual limits of sth: *The need to protect fundamental human rights transcended national boundaries.* ◇ *Transhumanism is the belief that science can be used to transcend the limitations of the human body and brain.*

tran·scend·ent /trænˈsendənt/ *adj.* going beyond the usual limits; extremely great: *The Bible sees human beings as created by a transcendent God in His own image.* ■ **tran·scend·ence** /trænˈsendəns/ *noun* [U] **~ (of sth)** *Schopenhauer believed transcendence of the will was the only path to liberation.*

tran·scen·den·tal /ˌtrænsenˈdentl/ *adj.* [usually before noun] going beyond the limits of human knowledge, experience or reason, especially in a religious or spiritual way: *They believe specific conditions exist because of transcendental forces, such as divine will.*

tran·scribe /trænˈskraɪb/ *verb* **1 ~ sth (from sth) (into sth)** to record thoughts, speech or data in a written form, or in a different written form from the original: *Qualitative data were transcribed verbatim from digital recordings or other formats.* ◇ *All interviews were recorded on tape and then transcribed into written form.* **2 ~ sth** (*biochemistry*) to produce RNA from existing DNA, so that GENETIC information is copied: *The virus is then released and conveyed to the host cell nucleus where the therapeutic gene is transcribed.*

tran·script /ˈtrænskrɪpt/ *noun* **1** (*also* **tran·scrip·tion**) a written or printed copy of words that have been spoken: *The survey yielded more than 80 interview transcripts.* **2** (*biochemistry*) a length of RNA or DNA that has been transcribed from a DNA or RNA TEMPLATE: *Elongation of the RNA transcript continues until RNA polymerase encounters a DNA sequence known as a terminator.* ◇ **~ of sth** *cDNA transcripts of mature mRNA, contain only exons.* **3** (*especially NAmE*) an official record of a student's work that shows the courses they have taken and the grades they have achieved: **+ noun** *In addition to demographic and transcript information, students were asked to write about their future college aspirations.*

tran·scrip·tion /trænˈskrɪpʃn/ *noun* **1** [U] the act or process of representing sth in a written or printed form: *The transcription of answers to tape-recorded open questions is immensely time-consuming.* **2** [C] **~ (of sth)** = TRANSCRIPT (1): *The summary and transcription of each interview were sent to him for approval.* **3** [C] something that is represented in writing: *A number of glossaries helpfully provide phonetic transcriptions alongside definitions.* **4** [U] **~ (of sth)** (*biochemistry*) the process of transcribing RNA from DNA: *RNA polymerase must bind to the promoter before transcription of the gene can begin.* **HELP** **Reverse transcription** happens when a virus with an RNA GENOME makes a STRAND of DNA from RNA, using a special ENZYME.

trans·ducer /trænzˈdjuːsə(r); trænsˈdjuːsə(r); *NAmE* trænzˈduːsər; trænsˈduːsər/ *noun* a device for producing an electrical signal from changes in a physical quantity such as pressure, or for producing changes in a physical quantity from an electrical signal: *The water level of a stream can be measured by a pressure transducer.*

trans·fer[1] **AWL** /ˈtrænsfɜː(r)/ *noun* [U, C] the act of moving sb/sth from one place, group or job to another; an occasion when this happens: **~ (of sb/sth) (between A and B)** *The integrated circuit is designed to facilitate the transfer of data between a computer and external peripherals such as modems and printers.* ◇ **~ (of sb/sth) (from...) (to...)** *The impact of an oil price rise involves a transfer of income from oil importers to oil exporters.* ◇ *The combustion chamber is designed to enhance the efficiency of heat transfer and therefore to minimize fuel use.* ◇ **+ noun** *As the Internet evolves, page download speeds and data transfer rates will increase.*

trans·fer[2] **AWL** /trænsˈfɜː(r)/ *verb* (**-rr-**) **1** [I, T] to move from one place to another; to move sth/sb from one place to another: **~ (from...) (to...)** *Production transferred to Germany in 2011.* ◇ **~ sth/sb (from...) (to...)** *Waves are transient phenomena which transfer energy but not mass.* ◇ *The surroundings remain at a constant pressure when heat is transferred to or from the system.* ◇ *There are mechanisms for transferring funds to the regional hospitals.* ◇ *The patient was transferred to hospital for further assessment.* **2** [I, T] to move from one job, school, situation, etc. to another; to arrange for sb to move: **~ (from...) (to...)** *A worker's refusal to transfer from full-time to part-time work should not constitute a valid reason for termination of employment.* ◇ **~ sb (from...) (to...)** *The boy was transferred to a school with facilities for children with special disabilities.* **3** [T] **~ sth (from...) (to...)** to copy information, music, an idea, etc. from one method of recording or presenting it to another: *The data were transferred to a secure database.* ◇ *The same ideas can be transferred to the work of classical scholars.* **4** [T, I] **~ (sth) (from...) (to...)** if you **transfer** a feeling, a disease or a power, or if it **transfers** from one person to another, the second person has it, often instead of the first: *Many of Trotsky's adherents*

T

transferred their loyalties to Stalin. ◇ *Infection may be transferred from one area of the body to another by scratching or contact.* ◇ *In June 2001, responsibility for work permit applications transferred from the Department of Education and Employment to the Home Office.* **5** [T] **~ sth (to sb)** to officially arrange for sth to belong to sb else: *There are certain circumstances under which one party can reclaim property transferred to another party under an illegal contract.*

trans·fer·able AWL /træns'fɜːrəbl/ *adj.* that can be moved from one place, person or use to another: *Workers wish to develop transferable skills that will make them attractive to prospective employers.* ◇ **~ between A and B** *Individual or family health care savings accounts are transferable between family members.* ◇ **~ from A to B** *Property rights should be transferable from one owner to another through a voluntary exchange.* ■ **trans·fer·abil·ity** /ˌtrænsˌfɜːrə'bɪləti/ *noun* [U] **~ (of sth)** *Consultants hold different views on the transferability of practices between organizations within one industry.*

trans·form AWL /træns'fɔːm; *NAmE* træns'fɔːrm/ *verb* **1 ~ sth/sb (from sth) (into/to sth)** to change the form of sth/sb SYN CONVERT[1] (1): *Energy can neither be created nor destroyed but is just transformed from one form into another.* ◇ *Neptune granted Mestra the power to transform herself from a woman to a man or animal and back.* **2 ~ sth/sb** to completely change the appearance or character of sth/sb, especially so that it is better: *Khrushchev transformed Soviet society, even though many of his innovations failed.* ◇ *The rural landscape was dramatically transformed by the process of enclosure.* **3 ~ sth (into/to sth)** (*mathematics*) to change a shape, expression or function by transformation: *Not every matrix can be transformed to the identity by performing elementary row operations on it.*

trans·form·ation AWL /ˌtrænsfə'meɪʃn; *NAmE* ˌtrænsfər'meɪʃn/ *noun* **1** [C] a complete change in sb/sth: *Food shopping underwent a dramatic transformation during the first half of the twentieth century in the United States.* ◇ *Cities are both the cause and the consequence of larger economic and social transformations.* ◇ **~ (from sth) (to/into sth)** *Pakistan's 1971 civil war resulted in the transformation of East Pakistan into independent Bangladesh.* ◇ **+ noun** *Throughout the 1990s, Argentina underwent a broad transformation process.* HELP In ecology, **transformation** is the process of changing INORGANIC matter into ORGANIC matter and the other way round: *The organic components' subsequent transformation back into the inorganic form by decomposition processes completes the cycle.* **2** [C] (*mathematics*) a process by which an expression is changed by replacing one set of VARIABLES with another or a shape is changed following a particular rule: *A transformation was performed on the quadratic equation in order that it should pass through the origin.* ◇ *Tetris allows the player to perform a transformation by rotation on the shapes.* **3** [U] (*biology*) the GENETIC alteration of a cell, by introducing DNA not naturally found in the cell: *Transformation is one of the key mechanisms in which bacteria are capable of DNA transfer.* ■ **trans·form·ation·al** /ˌtrænsfə'meɪʃənl; *NAmE* ˌtrænsfər'meɪʃənl/ *adj.*: *The fundamental challenge is to drive transformational change at the speed and scale required.* ◇ *The authors believe Internet communication can have transformational effects.*

trans·fu·sion /træns'fjuːʒn/ *noun* [C, U] = BLOOD TRANSFUSION ■ **trans·fuse** /træns'fjuz/ *verb* **~ sb (with sth)| ~ sth (into sb/sth)** *The medical team caring for her feel that if she is not transfused with blood now, she will not survive.*

trans·gen·der /trænz'dʒendə(r); træns'dʒendə(r)/ *adj.* describing or connected with a person whose personal sense of identity does not easily fit in with the CONVENTIONAL division between male and female GENDER: *Historian Susan Stryker defines transgender people as 'those... who move away from the gender they were assigned at birth, people who cross over the boundaries constructed by their culture to define and contain that gender'.* ■ **trans·gen·dered** *adj.*: *Transgendered persons will also benefit from this change in the law.*

trans·gen·ic /ˌtrænz'dʒenɪk; 'træns'dʒenɪk/ *adj.* (*biology*) (of a plant or an animal) having GENETIC material introduced from another type of plant or animal: *The first use of transgenic mice was to study gene function in the whole animal.* ➲ *compare* GENETICALLY MODIFIED

trans·gress /trænz'gres; træns'gres/ *verb* **~ sth** (*formal*) to go beyond the limit of what is morally or legally acceptable: *According to the Bible, Adam and Eve, by transgressing God's law, brought death into the world.* ◇ *Young people enjoy using the Internet to transgress boundaries that are perhaps better policed in the offline world.* ■ **trans·gres·sor** *noun*: *The court ordered the transgressor to stop infringing the copyright.*

trans·gres·sion /trænz'greʃn; træns'greʃn/ *noun* [C, U] **1** (*formal*) an action that goes beyond the limit of what is morally or legally acceptable: *They were severely punished for alleged moral and sexual transgressions.* ◇ **~ of sth** *Extreme transgression of human rights could itself be a justification for intervention by the international community.* **2** (*earth science*) a **marine transgression** occurs when the sea level rises and leaves behind evidence in GEOLOGICAL DEPOSITS: *As the shoreline migrates landward, the successive deposits in a marine transgression are commonly of greater area than those beneath.*

tran·si·ent /'trænziənt; *NAmE* 'trænʃnt/ *adj.* **1** continuing for only a short time: *When the circuit was broken, the needle registered a transient current in the opposite direction.* ◇ *The rash is usually transient and can disappear within hours.* ◇ *These experiences impressed upon him above all the transient nature of human existence.* ➲ *compare* TEMPORARY **2** staying or working in a place for only a short time, before moving on: *The records from Liverpool and Southampton illuminate the particular problems of large, growing, busy port centres with transient populations.* ■ **tran·si·ence** /'trænziəns; *NAmE* 'trænʃəns/ *noun* [U] **~ (of sth)** *The frailty and transience of human life preoccupies baroque culture.*

tran·sis·tor /træn'zɪstə(r); træn'sɪstə(r)/ *noun* a small electronic device used in computers, radios, televisions, etc. for controlling an electric current as it passes along a CIRCUIT: *Such circuits will vary in complexity from those using a single transistor to those with 20 or more devices.*

tran·sit AWL /'trænzɪt; 'trænsɪt/ *noun* [U] **1** the process of being moved or carried from one place to another: **during ~** *Packaging has a functional role to protect and preserve products during transit.* ◇ **in ~** *The question of responsibility when asylum seekers are in transit has life and death implications.* **2** the act of going through a place on the way to somewhere else: **+ noun** *Transit visas are available to those who are entering the UK en route to another destination.* ◇ *The timing of the peak daily flow largely depends on the transit time for water to flow through the glacier system.* **3** (*NAmE*) the system of buses, trains, etc. which people use to travel from one place to another: *A number of middle-class parents perceived public transit to be unsafe.*

tran·si·tion AWL /træn'zɪʃn; træn'sɪʃn/ *noun* [U, C] the process or a period of changing from one state or condition to another: **~ between A and B** *Europe stood at the point of transition between the pre-modern and the modern worlds.* ◇ **in ~** *The programme aims to accelerate the process of emissions reduction in developing countries and economies in transition.* ◇ **~ (from sth) (to sth)** *Recent urban growth has accompanied an economic transition from agriculture to industry.* ◇ *to undergo/experience a*

T

transition ◇ *Such demographic transitions are taking place with increasing rapidity in most parts of the world.* ◇ **~ into sth** *Young people show a growing dependence on their peers for support and guidance as they make the transition into adolescence.* HELP In physics and chemistry, a **phase transition** is a change from one state (solid, liquid or gas) to another without any change in chemical COMPOSITION: *For both Antarctic ecosystems, the ice-to-water phase transition is, therefore, a critical temperature threshold.* A **transition** may also be a change of an atom, ELECTRON, etc. from one QUANTUM state to another, releasing or taking in RADIATION: *These transitions depend on the solar electron density and the neutrino energy.*

tran·si·tion·al AWL /træn'zɪʃənl; træn'sɪʃənl/ *adj.* connected with the process or a period of changing from one state or condition to another: *The agreement set a transitional period to allow European manufacturers to adapt to the changes.* ◇ *This research also sheds light on poverty as one of the common social factors in transitional economies.*

tran'sition metal (*also* **tran'sition element**) *noun* (*chemistry*) one of the group of metals in the centre of the PERIODIC TABLE which form coloured COMPOUNDS and often act as CATALYSTS: *Transition metals show a wide range of oxidation states in their compounds.* ◇ *Transition metals make good catalysts as they can bring reacting atoms close together by adsorbing them on their surface.*

tran·si·tive /'trænsətɪv/ *adj.* **1** (*grammar*) (of verbs) used with a DIRECT OBJECT: *Samoan has verbs that appear in both intransitive and transitive forms.* OPP INTRANSITIVE **2** (*mathematics*) a **transitive** relation is one that, if it applies between one member of a series and the next, it must also apply between any two members taken in order: *If the relation among the values A, B and C is transitive, then the following must hold: if A is as good as B, and C is better than A, then C is better than B.*

tran·si·tiv·ity /ˌtrænsə'tɪvəti; ˌtrænzə'tɪvəti/ *noun* [U] **1** (*grammar*) the fact of whether a verb is transitive or INTRANSITIVE: *Transitivity relates to the number of objects a verb requires or takes in a given instance.* **2** (*mathematics*) the fact that a relation is transitive: *Transitivity requires that if a voting rule ranks candidate A over B and B over C, then A should be ranked over C.*

trans·late /træns'leɪt; trænz'leɪt/ *verb* **1** [T, I] to express the meaning of speech or writing in a different language: **~ sth (from sth) (into sth)** *Her books have been translated into 21 languages.* ◇ *The earliest text was translated from Greek.* ◇ **~ sth (as sth)** *The Hebrew word translated as 'spirit', 'ruach', also means 'wind' or 'breath'.* ◇ **~ (from sth) (into sth)** *Using a questionnaire in more than one country is not a simple case of translating from one language to another.* **2** [I] to be changed from one language to another: *Rolls Royce found that the name of its Silver Cloud model did not translate well into German.* ◇ **~ as sth** *The Latin word 'poena' translates as 'pain'.* **3** [T, I] to change sth into a different form; to be changed into a different form: **~ sth (into sth)** *Some countries are more successful than others in translating economic success into better lives for people.* ◇ **~ into sth** *A larger scale of operations will not directly translate into higher profits.* **4** [T, I] **~ (sth) (as sth)** to understand sth in a particular way; to give sth a particular meaning SYN INTERPRET (2): *Problems can arise if a long reply from a patient is translated as a simple 'yes' or 'no'.* **5** [T] **~ sth (into sth)** (*biochemistry*) to change a SEQUENCE of NUCLEOTIDES in MESSENGER RNA to a sequence of AMINO ACIDS in a POLYPEPTIDE by using the GENETIC CODE: *First the DNA is transcribed into messenger RNA by the enzyme RNA polymerase; then the messenger RNA is translated into polypeptide by enzymes on the ribosomes.*

trans·la·tion /træns'leɪʃn; trænz'leɪʃn/ *noun* **1** [U] the process of changing sth that is written or spoken into another language: **~ (of sth) (into sth)** *Free translation of English lexical items into Chinese often fails.* ◇ **~ (from sth) (into sth)** *The book will help Danish users with translation from English into Danish.* ◇ **in ~** *Unlike poetry, which gets lost in translation, plot can be preserved in translation.* **2** [C, U] a text or work that has been changed from one language into another: *The movie titles were generally literal translations and many in fact did not present well the themes of the movies.* ◇ **~ of sth** *In 1484 he published his Latin translation of Plato's collected works.* ◇ **in ~** *The winning article will be published in translation in the 'Journal of American History'.* **3** [U] **~ (of sth) into sth** the process of changing sth into a different form: *The partnership was set up to promote the translation of public health research into practice.* ◇ *The translation of votes into seats affects the political fortunes of parties.* **4** [U] (*biochemistry*) the process by which a SEQUENCE of NUCLEOTIDE TRIPLETS in a MESSENGER RNA MOLECULE results in a particular sequence of AMINO ACIDS during SYNTHESIS of a POLYPEPTIDE: *Translation is the second step of gene expression.* ◇ *These amino acids are the raw ingredients of the polypeptide that is synthesized during translation.*

trans·la·tor /træns'leɪtə(r); trænz'leɪtə(r)/ *noun* a person who translates writing or speech into a different language, especially as a job: *The 'purist' view has been that professional translators should only translate into their first language.* ◇ **~ of sth** *Some of the early translators of the Bible, such as William Tyndale, were even burned by the church authorities.* ➲ *compare* INTERPRETER (1)

trans·mis·sion AWL /træns'mɪʃn; trænz'mɪʃn/ *noun* **1** [U] the act or process of passing sth from one person, place or thing to another: *The risks of infectious disease transmission are higher in prisons than in the community.* ◇ *Traditional knowledge is handed down through generations by cultural transmission.* ◇ **~ of sth (to sb)** *The drug reduces mother-to-child transmission of HIV/AIDS.* ➲ *compare* TRANSFER¹ (1) **2** [U] the act or process of sending out an electronic signal or message or of broadcasting a radio or television programme: *3G wireless systems are capable of supporting high-speed data transmission and Internet connection.* ◇ **+ noun** *The transmission bandwidth of AM systems cannot be changed.* **3** [C] a radio or television message or broadcast: *'Jamming' refers to CB radio slang for the illegal electronic disruption of radio or TV transmissions.* **4** [U, C] the system in a vehicle by which power is passed from the engine to the wheels: *The drive shaft connecting the transmission to the wheels utilizes a differential gear.* ◇ *The car is available in three basic body forms, with the choice of automatic or manual transmission.*

trans·mit AWL /træns'mɪt; trænz'mɪt/ *verb* (-tt-) **1** [T, I] to send an electronic signal, radio or television broadcast, etc: **~ sth** *Each connector can transmit many electrical signals concurrently.* ◇ *Traditional television channels now transmit their programmes online.* ◇ **~ (sth) (from...) (to...)** *Each transmit antenna can transmit to all receive antennas.* ◇ *A satellite can be used to transmit messages from one point on the earth's surface to another point up to approximately 12 000 km away.* **2** [T] to pass sth from one person to another: **~ sth to sb** *Graphic illustrations may be used to transmit information to existing and potential customers.* ◇ *Of most concern here is the source of infections transmitted to humans.* ◇ **~ sth (through sth)** *HIV can be transmitted through sexual intercourse.* ◇ *people at risk of sexually transmitted diseases* ➲ *compare* TRANSFER² (4) **3** [T] **~ sth** (*technical*) to allow heat, light, sound, etc. to pass through: *The amount of light transmitted is measured to give the absorbance of the solution.* ➲ *compare* CONDUCT¹ (2)

trans·mit·ter /træns'mɪtə(r); trænz'mɪtə(r)/ *noun* **1** a piece of equipment used for sending electronic signals, especially radio or television signals: *The use of radio*

T

transmitters allows the animals to be located within their natural environment at any time. ➲ *compare* RECEIVER (1) **2 ~ of sth** (*formal*) a person or thing that transmits sth from one person or thing to another: *Current approaches point to a return to the idea of the teacher as the transmitter of knowledge.* **3** = NEUROTRANSMITTER

trans·nation·al /ˌtrænzˈnæʃnəl; ˌtrænsˈnæʃnəl/ *adj.* (*business, politics*) existing in or involving many different countries: *Total investment abroad by transnational corporations was less than $50 billion in the early 1970s.* ◇ *Transnational networks engaged in smuggling and drug-running pose daily challenges to the control of borders by states.* ◇ *A higher level of transnational relations between countries means a higher level of interdependence.*

trans·par·ency /trænsˈpærənsi/ *noun* [U] **1** a situation in which it is easy to understand sth or to know whether sth is true or right: *Transparency, accountability and fairness are the pillars of corporate governance.* ◇ **~ of sth** *The report identifies 'grave shortcomings' in the transparency of decision-making processes.* ◇ **~ in sth** *The lack of transparency in the present system means that voters are unclear about whom to hold responsible.* **2** the quality of sth, such as glass, that allows you to see through it: *These proteins give the eye lens its transparency.*

trans·par·ent /trænsˈpærənt/ *adj.* **1** easy to understand; easy to see whether sth is true or right: *These principles foster public confidence in a transparent justice system.* ◇ *The procedures were perceived as rigid, complex and insufficiently transparent.* OPP OPAQUE (2) **2** (of glass, plastic, etc.) allowing you to see through it: *The grid was printed on a transparent plastic sheet.* OPP OPAQUE (1) ■ **trans·par·ent·ly** *adv.*: *Effective boards act transparently to ensure full accountability to shareholders.*

trans·plant¹ /trænsˈplɑːnt; trænzˈplɑːnt; *NAmE* trænsˈplænt; trænzˈplænt/ *verb* **1** [often passive] **~ sth (from sb/sth) (into/to sb/sth)** to take an organ, skin, etc. from one person, animal, part of the body, etc. and put it into or onto another: *In the first study, cells were transplanted into female adult rats.* ◇ *The goal of immunosuppressive therapy is to prevent rejection of the transplanted organ.* **2 ~ sth** to move a growing plant and plant it somewhere else: *They transplant rice seedlings in spring and then cut the rice in autumn.* **3 ~ sb/sth (from sb/sth) (into/to sb/sth)** to move sb/sth to a different place or environment: *Cultural differences often limit the possibility of transplanting political institutions from one country to another.* ■ **trans·plan·ta·tion** /ˌtrænsplɑːnˈteɪʃn; ˌtrænzplɑːnˈteɪʃn; *NAmE* ˌtrænsplænˈteɪʃn; ˌtrænzplænˈteɪʃn/ *noun* [U] *liver/stem cell/bone marrow transplantation* ◇ **~ of sth** *This showed a strong negative influence on survival one year after transplantation of seedlings.* ◇ *the transplantation of entire communities overseas*

trans·plant² /ˈtrænsplɑːnt; ˈtrænzplɑːnt; *NAmE* ˈtrænsplænt; ˈtrænzplænt/ *noun* **1** [C, U] a medical operation in which a damaged organ, etc. is replaced with one from another person: *The patient had had a renal transplant.* ◇ *a liver/bone marrow/heart transplant* ◇ *The stem cells are usually cryopreserved until required for transplant.* **2** [C] an organ, etc. that is used in a transplant operation: *This explains why tissue transplants may be rejected.*

trans·port¹ AWL /ˈtrænspɔːt; *NAmE* ˈtrænspɔːrt/ *noun* [U] **1** (*especially BrE*) (*NAmE usually* **trans·por·ta·tion**) a system for carrying people or goods from one place to another using vehicles, roads, etc: *Britain's economy relies heavily on road transport.* ◇ *air/freight/rail transport* ◇ **+ noun** *Both fresh vegetables and dairy products have high transport costs.* ◇ *Less fuel is used for the transport sector in Cuba as a percentage of total energy use.* ➲ *see also* PUBLIC TRANSPORT **2** (*BrE*) (*NAmE* **trans·por·ta·tion**) a vehicle or method of travel: *Faster modes of transport, such as high-speed rail and air transport, continue to grow as incomes rise.* ◇ *On discharge, patients without their own transport will have this provided.* ◇ **~ to...** *Helicopter transport to critical sites was provided by the US Geological Survey.* ◇ **a mode/means of ~** *Urban transport also relies on more modes of transport than transport in non-urban areas.* **3** (*especially BrE*) (*also* **trans·por·ta·tion** *NAmE, BrE*) the activity or business of carrying goods from one place to another using TRUCKS, trains, etc: *Common sources of groundwater contamination include spills or leaks of fuel during transport.* ◇ **~ of sth** *La Rance was an important route for the transport of goods inland from the port of St Malo.*

trans·port² AWL /trænˈspɔːt; *NAmE* trænˈspɔːrt/ *verb* **1 ~ sth/sb (+ adv./prep.)** to take sth/sb from one place to another in a vehicle: *Over the past 100 years, the cost of transporting goods over long distances has dramatically fallen.* ◇ *The primary purpose of the London Underground is to transport passengers into and around the capital city.* **2 ~ sth (+ adv./prep.)** to move sth somewhere by means of a natural process SYN CARRY (1): *Oxygen is transported to cells across arterial capillary walls.* ◇ *Passive dispersal involves seeds being transported by wind or by animals.* **3 ~ sb (+ adv./prep.)** to make sb feel that they are in a different place, time or situation: *Students who participated in the living history programme said they felt transported back in time.* **4 ~ sb (+ adv./prep.)** (in the past) to send sb to a far away place as a punishment: *British convicts were transported to Australia for life.*

trans·por·ta·tion AWL /ˌtrænspɔːˈteɪʃn; *NAmE* ˌtrænspɔːrˈteɪʃn/ *noun* [U] **1** (*especially NAmE*) = TRANSPORT¹: *urban/road transportation* ◇ **~ of sth** *The containers provided for the safe storage and transportation of the fruit.* ◇ **+ noun** *a transportation network* ◇ *In many cities, public transportation systems have not been adequately modernized.* ◇ *Transportation costs for heavier products were very high.* **2 ~ (to...)** (in the past) the act of sending criminals to a place that is far away as a form of punishment: *In France, transportation to the French colonies only ended in 1938.*

trans·verse /ˈtrænzvɜːs; ˈtrænsvɜːs; *NAmE* ˈtrænzvɜːrs; ˈtrænsvɜːrs/ *adj.* [usually before noun] (*technical*) placed across sth: *A simple fracture is a single transverse fracture of bone with only two main fragments.* ◇ *Longitudinal and transverse sections of the root apex show intracellular connections.* ➲ *compare* DIAGONAL¹

trap¹ /træp/ *noun* **1** a piece of equipment for catching animals: *Traps were deliberately placed in positions that would be favoured by small mammals.* **2** a container or device used to collect sth; a place where sth collects: *An ion trap is a device in which ions may be formed and then stored for some period of time.* **3** a mistake or problem that is not obvious, and may seem at first to be a good idea: **~ for sb** *A major trap for those proposing to import new organisms is that most species are normally not considered invasive in their home range.* ◇ **~ of doing sth** *Many parents fall into the trap of attending to kids when they misbehave and leaving children alone when they behave well.* **4** [usually sing.] an unpleasant situation from which it is hard to escape: *We can define the unemployment trap as the situation where a move into paid employment leads to no significant increase in overall income.* ◇ *He was caught in a trap of his own making.* **5 ~ (for sb)** a plan designed to deceive sb, either by capturing them or by making them do or say sth that they did not mean to do or say: *Detectives laid a cunning trap for the killer.*

trap² /træp/ *verb* (**-pp-**) **1** [often passive] **~ sb (in sth)** to keep sb in a dangerous place or bad situation that they want to get out of but cannot: *Impaired cognitive development in early childhood traps people in a negative cycle of poor educational achievement.* ◇ *His plays revealed a* *profound sympathy with women trapped in political or emotional situations over which they had little control.* ◇ *Nine miners were trapped underground for over 78 hours.* **2** [often passive] to catch or keep sth in a place and prevent it from escaping, especially so that you can use it: **~ sth** *Environment Africa holds training workshops on soil conservation and how to use an 'A' frame to trap rainwater.* ◇ **~ sth + adv./prep.** *Methane is trapped in permafrost through the annual cycle of summer thawing and winter freezing.* **3** [often passive] **~ sb/sth (+ adv./prep.)** to force sb/sth into a place or situation that they cannot escape from, especially in order to catch them: *The car had been specially adapted by the police to trap any person who attempted to steal it.* ◇ *She became, in effect, a prisoner trapped in her own home.* **4 ~ sth** to catch an animal in a trap: *Mesolithic rock paintings depict people hunting game, gathering plant resources and trapping animals.* **5 ~ sb (into sth/into doing sth)** to deceive sb into doing sth: *Poorly educated prisoners were trapped into making false confessions.*

trauma /ˈtrɔːmə; *NAmE* ˈtraʊmə/ *noun* **1** [U] a mental condition caused by severe shock, especially when the harmful effects last for a long time: *This is an account of the long-term effects of psychological trauma in childhood.* ◇ *People experience trauma during a period of change.* **2** [C] **~ (of sth)** an unpleasant experience that makes you feel upset and/or anxious: *The agonizing trauma of the war led some Europeans to look for new understandings of life and death.* ◇ *It is very difficult for the child to speak about traumas in the past.* **3** [U, C] (*medical*) a physical injury: *Inflammation due to trauma is the most common cause of compartment syndrome.* ◇ **~ to sth** *These fractures are caused by a significant trauma to the skull.*

trau·mat·ic /trɔːˈmætɪk; *NAmE* traʊˈmætɪk/ *adj.* **1** extremely unpleasant and causing you to feel upset and/or anxious: *Scars may serve as a permanent reminder of a traumatic event.* ◇ *His time in prison was traumatic and he suffered psychiatric illness as a consequence.* **2** [only before noun] connected with or caused by a traumatic experience: *While most children achieve full recovery over time, many experience acute traumatic stress reactions.* **3** [only before noun] (*medical*) connected with or caused by physical injury: *Traumatic injuries require urgent treatment necessitating smooth, timely referral between facilities.*

trau·ma·tize (*BrE also* **-ise**) /ˈtrɔːmətaɪz; *NAmE* ˈtraʊmətaɪz/ *verb* [usually passive] to shock and upset sb very much, often making them unable to think or work normally: **be traumatized (by sth)** *Parents are often traumatized by their child's injury.* ◇ **traumatized + noun** *As traumatized victims of war and conflict, refugees are dependent on external aid.*

travel[1] /ˈtrævl/ *verb* (**-ll-**, *US* **-l-**) **1** [I, T] to go from one place to another, especially over a long distance: *For many, retirement is a period of great freedom, presenting opportunities to travel.* ◇ **+ adv./prep.** *Increasingly, patients are travelling abroad in search of health care.* ◇ **~ to sth** *Relief teams travel to disaster areas around the world.* ◇ **~ sth** *The cost of a telephone interview is much less than the cost involved in travelling long distances.* **2** [I, T] **(+ adv./prep.)** to go or move at a particular speed, in a particular direction, or a particular distance: *Because radio waves travel at a fixed speed, radar can be used to measure the bearing and distance of each aircraft.* ◇ *As the tsunami travelled away from the shore, it encountered rapidly deepening ocean water.* ◇ **~ sth** *The time it takes light to travel a particular distance is equal to the distance divided by the velocity.*

travel[2] /ˈtrævl/ *noun* **1** [U] the act or activity of travelling: *The rapid economic growth in China is likely to be accompanied by growth in air travel.* ◇ **+ adv./prep.** *Poor public transport meant that, for many workers, the day included hours of uncomfortable travel to and from work.* ◇ **+ noun** *Some companies have successfully offset a portion of these increased travel costs by using telesales.* **2 travels** [pl.] time spent travelling, especially in foreign countries, for pleasure or to discover new places: *In 128 BCE, Chang Chi'en discovered the Mediterranean region and described his travels.*

trav·el·ler (*US* **trav·el·er**) /ˈtrævələ(r)/ *noun* a person who is travelling or who often travels: *Demand for hotel accommodation is higher during the week than weekends due to business travellers.* ◇ **~ to...** *Many vaccines and immunizations are available for travellers to countries where serious diseases remain endemic.*

trav·el·ling (*US* **trav·el·ing**) /ˈtrævəlɪŋ/ *noun* [U] the act of travelling: *The Internet can save you the expense of travelling.*

treat /triːt/ *verb* **1** to behave in a particular way when dealing with sb/sth: **~ sb + adv.** *We judge our society by how we treat the young and the old.* ◇ *He argues that we should not treat animals differently simply because they are 'less intelligent' than us.* ◇ **~ sb/sth with sth** *Blood cultures should be treated with care: breakages can occur and glass bottles can cause cuts.* ◇ **~ sb/sth as sth** *This section provides an overview of women's struggles to be treated as equals in medical practice.* ◇ **~ sb/sth like sth** *A child may want to be treated like an adult and also have the privileges of being a child.* **2** to consider sth in a particular way: **~ sth as sth** *Scientific theorists of human nature such as E.O. Wilson have treated humans as a product of evolution.* ◇ *The accounts provided by Europeans are not to be treated as objective, factual and truthful.* ◇ **~ sth with sth** *We should treat such general conclusions with caution.* **3** [often passive] to deal with or discuss a subject in a piece of writing or speech: **~ sth** *Martin Klein's chapter treats the entire period from emancipation to the present.* ◇ **~ sth + adv./prep.** *This last subject is treated separately below at 12.7.4.* ◇ *The longstanding rivalry between these two groups is extensively treated by the author.* **4** [often passive] to give medical care or attention to a person, an illness or an injury: **~ sb/sth** *Before a doctor or other health care professional treats a patient, they need to obtain their consent.* ◇ *Of all pulmonary diseases, these are the most difficult to treat successfully.* ◇ **~ sb/sth with sth** *These trials demonstrated a 16% higher incidence of stroke among patients treated with beta blockers.* ◇ **~ sb for sth** *1 408 men had received screening and 48 were diagnosed and treated for prostate cancer.* **5** to use a chemical substance or process to clean, protect, preserve, etc. sth: **~ sth** *By chemically treating the eggs, scientists have been able to induce them to divide and develop into embryos.* ◇ **~ sth with sth** *Previously drained soils can be treated with lime if the acidity is not too great.*

▸ TREAT + NOUN **patient** • **disease**, **illness** • **condition**, **disorder**, **problem** • **case** • **infection** • **symptom** • **cause** • **pain** • **cancer** *By understanding why we age, we can better appreciate the consequences of treating the symptoms of ageing.*

▸ NOUN + TREAT **court**, **law** • **government**, **state** • **authorities** *Human rights set minimal standards on how people should be treated by their governments.* | **doctor**, **clinician**, **physician** • **specialist** • **hospital** *Hospitals treating a high proportion of uninsured people cannot recover enough of their costs to stay afloat.*

▸ ADVERB + TREAT **often**, **usually**, **generally**, **normally** • **sometimes** • **always** *An aesthetic point of view always treats works of art as individual and unique.* | **effectively**, **successfully** • **surgically** *This explains why warfarin overdose is effectively treated by intravenous vitamin K.*

▸ TREAT + ADVERB **differently** • **equally**, **fairly** • **unfairly**, **unequally** • **well** *He felt that he had been treated unfairly and wrote a formal letter of complaint to the company.* |

T

cautiously *This comparison should be treated cautiously since some of these studies used different assays.* | **early, promptly, immediately** • **surgically** • **conservatively** • **appropriately** • **successfully** *Most fractures heal with no complications whether treated conservatively or surgically.*

▸ TREAT SB/STH WITH + NOUN **respect** • **care** • **dignity** • **suspicion** • **contempt** *A healthy organizational culture in which all staff treat each other with respect and dignity should be promoted.* | **caution, suspicion, scepticism** *These predictions should be treated with considerable scepticism.*

treat·able /'tri:təbl/ *adj.* possible to cure using medicine or other medical treatment: *HIV is now a treatable medical condition and is increasingly managed as a chronic disease.* ◇ **~ with sth** *These infections are treatable with a short course of antibiotics.*

trea·tise /'tri:tɪs; 'tri:tɪz/ *noun* **~ (on sth)** a long and serious piece of writing on a particular subject: *Published in 1838, this was the first American treatise on women's rights.*

treat·ment /'tri:tmənt/ *noun* **1** [U, C] something that is done to cure an illness or injury, or to help sb with a physical or mental problem: **~ (of sth)** *Digoxin is a drug used for long-term treatment of heart failure.* ◇ *New treatments, such as gene therapy, are currently being trialled.* ◇ **~ for sth** *40% of respondents had received no medical treatment for their condition.* ◇ *She had previously had treatment for atopic asthma.* ◇ **in ~** *A significant proportion of patients will be in treatment primarily because of a personality disorder.* ◇ **+ noun** *The treatment options for breast cancer depend on the stage of the cancer.* **2** [U] **~ (of sb/sth)** a way of behaving towards or dealing with a person or thing: *Discrimination is defined as unfair treatment of a person or group of persons on the basis of prejudice.* ◇ *The government can promote exports by persuading other countries to give favourable treatment to its exports.* **3** [U, C] **~ (of sth)** a way of dealing with or discussing a subject in a piece of writing or speech: *Extensive treatment of this topic can be found in Chapter 13.* ◇ *Conrad was drawn to Stevenson's treatment of colonial themes.* ◇ *A more detailed treatment of this research can be found in Hodson (1990).* **4** [U, C] (*biology*) a process or set of conditions that is made to affect a group of people, animals or things as part of an experiment: *Such a study might include a series of experimental treatments where either predators or wave action or both were removed.* ◇ **+ noun** *This study uses a quasi-experimental design, in which a control group is compared with two treatment groups.* **5** [U, C] a process by which sth is cleaned or protected against sth: **~ for sth** *Chemical soil treatment for the prevention of termite infestation in structures has been practised since at least the late 1920s.* ◇ **+ noun** *Wastewater treatment plants are one of the most common types of chemical plants in the world.*

▸ ADJECTIVE + TREATMENT **medical** • **effective** • **appropriate** • **early** • **long-term** • **new** • **pharmacological** • **antibiotic** • **surgical** • **psychological** *The appropriate treatment for a person with depressive disorder depends on the severity of the disorder.* | **equal** • **special** • **different** • **differential** • **preferential, favourable** • **degrading** *Feminist theorists emphasize that the differential treatment of boys and girls is a nearly universal, cross-cultural circumstance.*

▸ NOUN + TREATMENT **drug** • **cancer** *Almost all patients with a manic episode will need drug treatment.*

▸ VERB + TREATMENT **receive, get** • **undergo, have** • **start** • **require, need** • **provide, give** • **seek** • **refuse** • **offer** • **access** *Undergoing cancer treatment can be emotionally and physically demanding for patients and their families.*

▸ TREATMENT + VERB **include, involve, consist of** • **affect** • **cause, induce** • **fail** *Treatment includes analgesia, rest and supportive measures.*

▸ TREATMENT + NOUN **option** • **effect, outcome** • **plan, strategy, programme** • **regimen, regime** • **planning** • **decision** • **centre, service** *Diabetes treatment regimens are complicated, encompassing lifestyle changes and medication intake.*

treaty /'tri:ti/ *noun* (*pl.* **-ies**) a formal agreement between two or more countries: *Countries that have ratified the treaty are required to implement effective tobacco control policies.* ◇ *The terms of the Paris peace treaty concluded in April 1856 dealt a series of heavy blows to Russian power.* ◇ *Asylum-seeking children are better protected when international human rights treaties are applied.* ◇ *to draft/negotiate/sign a treaty*

tree /tri:/ *noun* **1** a tall plant that can live a long time. Trees have a thick central wooden TRUNK from which branches grow, usually with leaves on them: *Most tropical forests are dominated by broad-leaved trees that maintain a canopy throughout the year.* ◇ **+ noun** *Hemlocks are the third most prevalent tree species in the New England forests.* **2** something that has a structure of branches like a tree: *Family historians worked backwards to construct their family trees.* ◇ *By comparing the similarities and differences in the DNA sequences of different species, it is possible to reconstruct their history as an evolutionary tree.* ◇ **~ diagram** *One way of representing a sentence is in the form of a tree diagram.*

trend AWL /trend/ *noun* a general direction in which a situation is changing or developing: *If current trends continue, China's population will begin to decline about the year 2042.* ◇ **~ in sth** *The report identifies two major trends in global alliances, increased breadth and increased cooperation.* ◇ *The exact reasons for this change are unknown, but they are likely related to long-term trends in climate.* ◇ **~ towards sth** *Data on dietary intake in the US population show a clear trend towards increased dietary energy intake.* ◇ **+ noun** *Trend analysis showed a marked and statistically significant increase in reported cases.*

▸ ADJECTIVE + TREND **general, overall, broad** • **recent, current** • **long-term** • **similar** • **downward** • **increasing, upward** • **linear** • **significant, clear, evident** • **future** • **historical** • **global, national** • **demographic** *Supporters of globalization remain convinced that the general trend is one of trade liberalization.* ◇ *Fifty years of data (1949–1998) show a downward trend.*

▸ VERB + TREND **show, exhibit** • **indicate** • **follow** • **reflect** • **reverse** • **identify, observe, see, find, note** • **examine, analyse** • **monitor** • **describe** • **discuss** • **explain** • **understand** *The empirical evidence does not indicate a long-run trend of increasing prices.* ◇ *The NHS North West figures follow the national trend closely at all times.*

▸ TREND + VERB **continue** • **emerge** *The use of violence for political purposes had failed in its purpose and a new trend was emerging.*

trial[1] /'traɪəl/ *noun* [C, U] **1** the process of testing sth/sb to find out whether they are effective, successful, suitable, etc: *One could conduct a randomized trial in which there are two groups—one randomly assigned to use a new technology and the other not.* ◇ *Many individuals self-medicate with vitamin C to 'prevent colds', but clinical trials have not shown any objective benefit.* ◇ **~ period** *You could consider implementing the procedure within your department for a trial period and auditing the results.* **2** a formal examination of evidence in court by a judge and often a JURY, to decide if sb accused of a crime is guilty or not: *The Magna Carta embodied the principle that everyone is entitled to a fair trial held before a jury of their peers.* ◇ **~ of sb** *Conservative writers exploited the trial and execution of Charles I to proclaim the king's 'martyrdom'.* ◇ **~ for sth** *The defendant argued that he was unfit to stand trial for murder due to amnesia.* ◇ **on ~** *When the grand jury completed its work on March 1, seven close Nixon aides were placed on trial.*

T

LANGUAGE BANK

Describing trends

A number of nouns and verbs are used to describe a change in sth over time. To describe the size or speed of the change, you can use an adjective (with the noun) or an adverb (with the verb).

increase • growth/grow • rise • decrease • decline • drop • fall

- (a/an) increase/growth/rise/decrease/decline/drop/fall in sth
- (a) **dramatic/rapid/significant/substantial** increase/growth/rise/decrease/decline/fall
- (a) **substantial/steady** increase/growth/rise/decrease/decline
- a **sharp** increase/rise/decrease/decline/fall
- a **gradual/slight** increase/rise/decrease/decline
- (a) **50%** increase/growth/rise/decrease/decline/drop/fall
- a **tenfold** increase/decrease
- to increase/grow/rise/decrease/decline/drop/fall **steadily/rapidly**
- to increase/grow/rise/decrease/decline/fall **significantly/substantially/dramatically**
- to increase/grow/rise/decrease/drop **considerably**
- to increase/rise/decrease/decline/drop/fall **sharply**
- to increase/decrease **markedly**

– *The **steady increase** in seabird numbers has been attributed to...*
– *The last 30 years have seen **a tenfold increase** in the number of people with access to high caloric diets.*
– *Life expectancy **increased dramatically** as a result of improvements in health and living conditions.*

• You can also use the preposition *of* following the noun, or the preposition *by* following the verb, to describe the **size** of the change:

- (a/an) increase/growth/rise/decrease/declein/drop/fall **of** 10%/6 dB/1 million
- to increase/grow/rise/decrease/decline/drop/fall **by** 50%/>5 mm/500 g

– *A 3% drop in air pressure is associated with **a fall of just under 1%** in absolute air temperature.*
– *Oil demand **declined by 0.6 per cent**, driven by the recession and the oil price spike.*

IDM ˌ**trial and ˈerror** the process of solving a problem by trying various methods, amounts, etc. until you find one that is successful: *Using this value as a starting point, a more exact value can be found by trial and error.* ◇ *Students engaged in trial and error strategies, through guessing and checking.*

trial² /ˈtraɪəl/ *verb* (**-ll-**, *NAmE* **-l-**) **~ sth** to test sth/sb to find out whether they are effective, successful, suitable, etc: *Live voice or click-to-call technologies are increasingly being trialled and adopted.*

tri·angle /ˈtraɪæŋgl/ *noun* **1** a flat shape with three straight sides and three angles; a thing in the shape of a triangle: *The three points form a triangle.* ◇ *An equilateral triangle has sides of equal length and angles of 60 degrees.* ◇ (*BrE*) *a right-angled triangle* ◇ (*NAmE*) *a right triangle* **2** a situation involving three places, things or people, sometimes represented as a triangle: *By 1993 this area had evolved into the Indonesia-Malaysia-Singapore growth triangle.* ◇ *Competitive advantage is shown at the corner of the triangle where resources and businesses meet.*

tri·angu·lar /traɪˈæŋgjələ(r)/ *adj.* **1** shaped like a triangle: *The age structure is triangular, because relatively few survive to older ages.* ◇ *The input signal is assumed to have a triangular waveform.* **2** [usually before noun] involving three places, things or people: *There is evidence of a new and difficult triangular relationship between postmodernism, globalization and democracy.*

tri·bal /ˈtraɪbl/ *adj.* [usually before noun] connected with a tribe or tribes: *The bridewealth is the price given by the groom to the bride's family in tribal societies.* ◇ *Totem use was a practice associated with the tribal custom of dividing into different clans, or kinship groups.*

tribe /traɪb/ *noun* **1** a social group in a traditional society consisting of families or communities with the same culture, language, religion, etc. and usually with a particular leader: *The Huns, a federation of nomadic tribes, migrated westward out of the central Asian grasslands.* ◇ *The chief leads his tribe into battle.* **2** (*biology*) a group of related animals or plants that is larger than a GENUS and smaller than a family: *In an analysis of relationships within a family, biologists will often try to include exemplars of all tribes or all genera.*

tri·bu·nal /traɪˈbjuːnl/ *noun* [C+sing./pl. v.] a type of court with the authority to deal with a particular problem or disagreement: *Cases that go to court or to an employment tribunal are frequently won or lost on procedural issues.*

trib·ute /ˈtrɪbjuːt/ *noun* **1** [U, C] an act, a statement or a gift that is intended to show your respect or admiration, especially for a dead person: **pay ~ to sb** *Both Mill and Schumpeter paid tribute to the French tradition in this field.* ◇ **as a ~ to sb** *As a tribute to Sidney Hillman, the union's executive board appointed his wife one of the ACWA's 22 vice presidents.* **2** [sing.] **~ to sth/sb (that...)** a sign of the good effects or influence of sth/sb: *It is certainly a tribute to Athenian democracy that it produced its own most astute critics.* **3** [U, C] (especially in the past) money given by one country or ruler to another, especially in return for protection or for not being attacked: *Alexander retained much of the Persian organization of Egypt, including the requirement that Egyptians pay tribute.* ◇ *In the Roman empire this took the form of the payment of tributes by the outlying provinces back to the Roman heartland.*

tried¹ /traɪd/ *adj.*
IDM ˌ**tried and ˈtested/ˈtrusted** (*BrE*) (*NAmE* ˌ**tried and ˈtrue**) that you have used or relied on in the past successfully: *Interviews are a well tried and tested method for identifying ways to improve patient care (Siriwardena et al., 2008).*

tried² *past tense, past part. of* TRY

trig·ger¹ AWL /ˈtrɪgə(r)/ *verb* **1** to make sth start to happen SYN SET STH OFF (1): **~ sth** *The election of Barack Obama in 2008 triggered substantial changes in perceptions of racial discrimination in America.* ◇ *Cellulose is biocompatible and does not trigger an immune response when embedded in bodily tissue.* ◇ **~ sth off** *It was this act that triggered off the Spanish War of Independence.* **2 ~ sth** to cause a device to start functioning SYN SET STH OFF: *A degree of technical competence would be required to determine how to trigger the device.*

trig·ger² AWL /ˈtrɪgə(r)/ *noun* **1** something that is the cause of a particular reaction or development, especially a bad one: **~ for sth** *Both of these factors suggest an environmental trigger for the disease.* ◇ **~ to sth/to do sth** *The trigger to activate a vote of no confidence in the party leader was increased from 10 to 15 per cent of MPs.* ◇ **+ noun** *There has to be some kind of a trigger mechanism for a crisis to occur.* **2** the part of a gun that you press in order to fire it: *The defendant did pull the trigger and killed his friend.*

trip /trɪp/ *noun* **~ (to...)** a journey to a place and back again, especially a short one for pleasure or a particular purpose: *In September 1909, Freud made his only trip to America, where he and Jung lectured at Clark University.* ◇ *Students went on a field trip to a local nature reserve as* *part of a module on contemporary poetry and the environment.* ◇ *a business/shopping/hunting trip*

triple /ˈtrɪpl/ *adj.* [only before noun] **1** having three parts; involving three people or groups: *Class tension was evident in the national coal strike of 1912 and the formation of a triple alliance of miners, railwaymen and transport workers in 1914.* HELP In chemistry, a **triple bond** is a chemical bond in which three pairs of ELECTRONS are shared between two atoms: *Hydrocarbon molecules with a double or triple bond are very reactive.* **2** three times as much or as many as sth: *Their jobs pay triple the minimum wage.*

trip·let /ˈtrɪplət/ *noun* **1** one of three children born at the same time to the same mother: *She was expecting triplets.* **2** (*also* ˈ**triplet code**) (*biochemistry*) the standard version of the GENETIC CODE, in which a particular AMINO ACID is SPECIFIED by a SEQUENCE of three NUCLEOTIDES: *This review addresses the question of why particular nucleotide triplets correspond to specific amino acids.*

tri·umph[1] /ˈtraɪʌmf/ *noun* **1** [C, U] a great success, achievement or victory: *Jefferson's single greatest triumph was the Louisiana Purchase.* ◇ **~ of sth** *The role proved to be one of the triumphs of a long and distinguished acting career.* ◇ **~ over sb/sth** *This book also has a message of hope and triumph over illness.* **2** [U] the state of having achieved a great success or victory; the feeling of happiness that you get from this: **in ~** *The king returned home in triumph.*

tri·umph[2] /ˈtraɪʌmf/ *verb* [I] to defeat sb/sth; to be successful: *In academia, too, nationalist ideologies triumphed.* ◇ **~ over sb/sth** *Liberal democracy had triumphed over the one-party model.*

tri·umph·ant /traɪˈʌmfənt/ *adj.* very successful; showing great happiness about a victory or success: *The veteran conservatives made a triumphant return to power.* ◇ *The party could emerge triumphant.* ■ **tri·umph·ant·ly** *adv.*: *The victorious armies triumphantly entered Paris.*

triv·ial /ˈtrɪviəl/ *adj.* **1** not important, serious or valuable; not worth considering: *Failing to consult even on trivial matters can provoke rebellion against a change which would otherwise have been accepted.* HELP **Trivial** is often used with a negative, to show that sth is important, serious or valuable, and needs attention: *The sums of money are not trivial.* ◇ *Evaluating an eLearning platform is not a trivial task; there are many aspects to consider.* OPP NON-TRIVIAL (1) **2** (*mathematics*) used to describe the solution given when the value of each VARIABLE in the EQUATION is zero or their sum equals an IDENTITY: *Solve this quadratic equation, including trivial solutions in your answer.* OPP NON-TRIVIAL (2) ■ **trivi·al·ly** /ˈtrɪviəli/ *adv.*: *Many other examples will differ only trivially from each other.*

troop /truːp/ *noun* **1 troops** [pl.] soldiers or other armed forces: *France and Britain sent troops to aid the Ottomans and prevent Russian expansion.* ◇ *Britain had troops stationed in Germany.* ◇ *In these cases, troops might be deployed.* ◇ *All combat troops were withdrawn.* HELP Before another noun, the form **troop** is used: *Troop movements are carefully detailed.* **2** [C] **~ of sth** a group of people or animals of a particular kind: *Carlson and Isbell (2001) studied a troop of patas monkeys in Kenya.*

trop·ic /ˈtrɒpɪk; *NAmE* ˈtrɑːpɪk/ *noun* **1** [C, usually sing.] one of the two imaginary lines drawn around the world 23° 26′ north (**the Tropic of Cancer**) or south (**the Tropic of Capricorn**) of the EQUATOR: *The zenith sun moves from the Tropic of Capricorn in late December to the Tropic of Cancer in late June.* **2 the tropics** [pl.] the area between the two tropics, which is the hottest part of the world: *Disease species diversity is higher in the tropics than in temperate areas (Guernier et al., 2004).*

trop·ic·al /ˈtrɒpɪkl; *NAmE* ˈtrɑːpɪkl/ *adj.* coming from, found in or typical of the tropics: *A study of a Puerto Rican tropical rainforest provides dramatic contrast to the arid south-western United States.* ◇ *Acacia mangium is a leguminous tree that can grow quickly in the acidic soils of tropical regions.* ◇ *Global warming could result in the spread of tropical diseases, such as malaria, to currently temperate zones.* ➲ *see also* SUBTROPICAL

trouble[1] /ˈtrʌbl/ *noun* **1** [U, C] a problem, worry, difficulty, etc; a situation causing this: *Nitrate levels in many rivers and groundwater do not reach high enough levels to cause trouble.* ◇ *They faced significant financial troubles with the onset of the 1994 and 2001 economic crises.* ◇ **~ with sb/sth** *She said she was having trouble with the task.* ◇ **~ doing sth** *Subjects had no trouble following these instructions.* **2** [U] something that is wrong with a part of the body, machine, vehicle, etc: *Among the 1 457 respondents, 77 reported heart trouble and 33 reported cancer.* ◇ *The plane developed engine trouble and a crash seemed imminent.* **3** [U] a situation that is difficult or dangerous; a situation in which you can be criticized or punished: **in/into ~** *Many African-American mothers do not feel they can turn to the police to help them if their children are in trouble.* ◇ **(in/into) ~ with sb/sth** *Low scorers are apt to flout society's rules and get into trouble with the law.* **4** [U] an angry or violent situation: *They banned the export of live animals, ostensibly to prevent trouble from animal rights demonstrators.* **5** [U] extra effort or work: *It is possible nowadays to move almost anything if you go to enough trouble and expense.*
IDM **take trouble over/with sth | take trouble doing/to do sth** to try hard to do sth well: *It is so important that it is worth taking some trouble to grasp the ideas.* **take the trouble to do sth** to do sth even though it involves effort or difficulty: *A relatively low proportion of customers will actually take the trouble to complain.* **the trouble (with sth/sb) is...** used when saying what is difficult about or wrong with an idea, solution, person, etc: *Orwell mocked the ethics of the competitive society by remarking that 'the trouble with competitions is that someone has to win'.*

trouble[2] /ˈtrʌbl/ *verb* [often passive] **1 ~ sb** to make sb worried or unhappy: *She is unorthodox and her style has troubled some critics.* ◇ *Socrates was troubled by the notion of amateur government.* **2 ~ sb** (of a medical problem) to cause pain or problems: *A 74-year-old man has been troubled by pain in his calves for many years.*

troubled /ˈtrʌbld/ *adj.* having a lot of problems, especially when these lead to violence: *It is a nation with a deeply troubled history.* ◇ *There were efforts to get troubled youths to engage with their communities through volunteering.*

trouble·some /ˈtrʌblsəm/ *adj.* causing trouble, pain or difficulties: *Patients with troublesome recurrent symptoms may require surgery.* ◇ **~ for sb/sth** *Group liability may be particularly troublesome for small business owners.*

trough /trɒf; *NAmE* trɔːf/ *noun* **1** a low point in the level of sth that rises and falls: *Job creation declines, reaching a trough in the fourth quarter.* OPP PEAK[1] (1) **2** a period of time when sth is not growing or improving, especially a business or the economy: *From the trough in 1933, heavy industry saw the fastest growth in employment.* **3** a long low area between hills or in the earth's surface: *On average, the troughs are a few metres deep and a few tens of metres wide.*

truck /trʌk/ *noun* **1** (*especially NAmE*) (*BrE also* **lorry**) a large vehicle for carrying heavy loads by road: *The company has a staff of 2 500 and a fleet of 800 trucks with 1 700 trailers, making it the tenth largest haulier in the UK.* **2** a vehicle that is open at the back, used for carrying goods, soldiers, animals, etc: *A drunken soldier fell off the back of a truck.* **3** (*BrE*) (*NAmE* **car**) an open railway vehicle for carrying goods or animals: *After a brief journey in open railway trucks, they had to march the rest of the way.*

true /tru:/ *adj.* (**truer**, **tru·est**) **1** connected with facts rather than things that have been invented or guessed: *Page after page of photographs tells the true story of the disaster: a city reduced to rubble and ash.* ◇ **~ of sth** *The laws of physics are intended to be true of all objects in space and time.* ◇ **this/the same/the opposite, etc. is ~ (for sth)** *Among those born in Western Europe, women significantly outnumber men. The reverse is true for those from Eastern Europe.* ◇ **it is ~ to say...** *It is true to say that some languages change more than others, but all languages change.* ◇ **it is ~ (that...)** *It is true that Speransky had codified Russian laws, but the way those laws were applied was inconsistent.* ◇ **~ or false** *Statements about how the economy works are either true or false, however difficult it may be to determine which.* OPP FALSE (1), UNTRUE **2** [only before noun] real or actual, especially when this is different from how sth seems: *Aristotle's ideal goal is not a feeling of happiness but true happiness or having a good life.* ◇ *The social context has changed so much that the words 'equity' and 'justice' have lost their true meaning.* **3** [only before noun] (especially in the results of scientific tests) accurate or exact: *Accuracy is the sum of true positives and true negatives over the entire population.* **4** showing respect and support for a particular person or belief in a way that does not change: *For true believers, the introduction of God into human government would improve the protection of human dignity.* ◇ **~ to sb/sth** *Mrs Thatcher, true to free-market principles, opposed entry on the grounds that it was futile to try and 'fix' the exchange rate.* **5** [only before noun] being a genuine example of the thing mentioned: *The poem's theme is the poet's discovery that he is a true poet.*

IDM **come 'true** (of sth that sb predicts, expects, hopes for sth, etc.) to happen or become real: *The predictions of great losses to the economy of the people have not come true.* ➲ *more at* HOLD[1]

▸ TRUE + NOUN **statement** • **proposition** • **sentence** • **premise** • **story** • **belief** *Scientific theories are potentially true statements about reality, rather than merely convenient fictions.* | **nature** • **identity** • **meaning** • **sense** • **value** • **cost** • **incidence, prevalence** • **essence** • **self** • **intention** • **cause** • **reality** • **feelings** • **owner** • **heir** *External agencies are sometimes accused of losing sight of the true nature of a product and its target customers.* | **positive** • **negative** • **picture** • **reflection** *Recent research indicates that the true picture is more complex.* | **love** • **happiness** • **loyalty** • **democracy** • **faith, belief** *We distinguish between mere belief (which might be false) and true belief or belief that is right.*

▸ ADVERB + TRUE **especially, particularly** • **certainly, undoubtedly, definitely, always** • **partially, partly** • **approximately** • **(not) necessarily** • **(not) strictly** • **not entirely** • **equally** • **literally** • **obviously, clearly** • **universally** • **generally** • **possibly** • **probably** • **actually** • **perfectly** *It is certainly true that 'acting like a machine' has become synonymous with lack of adaptability.*

truly /'tru:li/ *adv.* **1** used to emphasize a particular quality: *What was truly remarkable about the invention of the transistor was its short timescale.* **2** to the fullest degree; in the most complete way: *The naturalist approach truly took off with Georges-Louis Leclerc, Comte de Buffon.* **3** in a way that is honest or genuine: *According to Kennan, the Russians truly believed the world to be divided permanently into capitalist and socialist camps.* **4** used to emphasize that a particular description is accurate or correct: *Many non-profits are now truly global in scope.*

trunk /trʌŋk/ *noun* **1** [C] the thick main STEM of a tree, that the branches grow from: *The quantity of coal burned resulted in pollution that darkened the tree trunks.* **2** [C, usually sing.] the main part of the human body apart from the head, arms and legs: *The blisters are painless and usually form on the trunk, arms and legs.*

trust[1] /trʌst/ *noun* **1** [U] the belief that sb is good, honest, etc. and will not try to harm or deceive you: *Doctors should try to build trust with these patients.* ◇ *The more an individual perceives their own ethnic group is in a minority in an area, the lower their reported levels of trust.* ◇ *The patterns of social trust are an important predictor of political participation.* ◇ **~ in sb** *This 'top-down approach', which relies heavily on public trust in scientists, has lost much credibility.* **2** [U] **~ (in sth)** the belief that sth is true or correct or that you can rely on it: *Many people feel so let down that they are placing their trust in alternatives to modern technologies.* ◇ *She argues that unless standards of reporting are improved, we cannot expect any increase in public trust in medicine, science and biotechnology.* **3** [C, U] an arrangement by which an organization or a group of people has legal control of money or property that has been given to sb: *One risk is that people will use trusts for unlawful purposes, such as hiding assets from tax authorities.* ◇ **in ~** *Almost any right can be held in trust, including money, company shares, interests in land and lottery tickets.* **4** [C] an organization or a group of people that invests money that is given or lent to it and uses the profits to help a charity: *The museum was constituted a charitable trust in 1989 and is run by a board of trustees.*

IDM **take sth on 'trust** to believe what sb says even though you do not have any proof or evidence to show that it is true: *In fact, none of these supposed 'facts' could be taken on trust*

trust[2] /trʌst/ *verb* **1** to have confidence in sb because you believe that they are good, honest, etc: **~ sb** *From October 1989 to June 1991, the number who fully trusted Gorbachev fell from 52 to 10 per cent.* ◇ **~ sb to do sth** *One widespread perception was that you could never trust people to repay a favour.* ◇ **trusted + noun** *Poll research suggests that doctors still occupy first place among 'trusted professions'.* **2 ~ sth** to believe that sth is true or correct or that you can rely on it: *As Lawrence aptly reminded us, 'trust the tale, not the teller'.* ◇ *Where he could, Herodotus preferred to trust what he could see for himself.* **3 ~ (that)...** to hope and expect that sth is true: *When buying online, customers have to trust that their payment details will be safe.*

IDM *see* TRIED[1]

PHR V **'trust in sb/sth** to have confidence in sb/sth; to believe that sb/sth is good and can be relied on: *It took decades for consumers to trust in industrially canned foods.* **'trust sb with sth/sb** to allow sb to have, use or take care of sb/sth because you have confidence in them: *Employers trust employees with significant access to information that could be of great value to a rival.*

trust·ee /trʌ'sti:/ *noun* **1** a person or an organization that has control of money or property that has been put into a trust for sb: *There is a duty to transfer the assets to trustees properly appointed and willing to carry out the trust.* **2** a member of a group of people that controls the financial affairs of a charity or other organization: *The senior staff and board of trustees wholeheartedly committed themselves to creating community schools.*

trust·ing /'trʌstɪŋ/ *adj.* tending to believe that other people are good, honest, etc; showing this: *In some new markets, it may take time to build up a trusting relationship before any purchase commitment is secured.*

trust·worthy /'trʌstwɜ:ði; *NAmE* 'trʌstwɜ:rði/ *adj.* **1** (of a person, business, organization, etc.) that you can rely on to be good, honest, etc. SYN RELIABLE (2): *People of this type are reliable, trustworthy and attentive to their duties and obligations.* **2** (of research, reports, information, etc.) that you can rely on as true and accurate SYN RELIABLE (1): *There is a need for focused and trustworthy qualitative research into the patients' perspective on care.* ◇ *States have difficulties in obtaining trustworthy information about the motives and intentions of other states.* ■ **trust·worthi·ness** *noun* [U] **~ (of sb/sth)** *It is important to establish what factors influence patient perceptions of the trustworthiness of health care professionals.* ◇ *Of the 100 or so studies available, hardly one exactly repeats the previous studies, so we do not have a check on the trustworthiness of the findings.*

truth /tru:θ/ *noun* (*pl.* **truths** /tru:ðz/) **1** [U] the quality or state of being true: *He maintains that there is no such thing as 'truth', only different perspectives.* ◇ **there is some/no/a good deal of ~ in sth** *There is some truth in the notion that consumer behaviour was an important part of the post-1997 growth phase.* ◇ **the ~ of sth** *The risk is that they will not be able to prove the truth of the allegations that they make.* **2 the truth** [sing.] the true facts about sth, rather than the things that have been invented or guessed: *A religious leader might regard his or her actions as simply based on revealing the truth to their followers.* ◇ **the ~ about sth** *Gradually the pioneer myth supplanted the truth about the island's origins as a penal colony.* **3** [C] a fact that is believed by most people to be true: *Many metaphors are so commonplace that we forget they are metaphors and treat them as literal truths.* ◇ **~ about sth** *These stories all seek to express basic truths about the world and the human condition.*
IDM **in 'truth** used to emphasize the true facts about a situation: *There is, in truth, no ideal outcome waiting to be discovered.* **to tell/speak the 'truth** to say things that are true: *Telling the truth is right, Kant argued, because to claim the opposite is irrational.*

truth·ful /'tru:θfl/ *adj.* **1** (of a statement) giving the true facts about sth: *The historian claims to offer a fair-minded, truthful interpretation of historical documents.* **2** (of a person) saying only what is true SYN HONEST (1): *What people self-report is affected by how inclined they are to be open and truthful.* ■ **truth·ful·ly** /'tru:θfəli/ *adv.*: *If the patient has questions, these should be answered truthfully and openly.* **truth·ful·ness** *noun* [U] *Documentaries have been valuable to governments precisely because of their claims to truthfulness.*

'truth value *noun* whether a PROPOSITION (= a statement) is true or false is called its **truth value**: *Strictly speaking, these relations hold between propositions, not between sentences, because sentences do not have truth values.*

try /traɪ/ *verb* (**tries, try·ing, tried, tried**) **1** [I, T] to make an attempt or effort to do or get sth: *They assume that if parents just cared enough and tried hard, their children would do well.* ◇ **~ to do sth** *In 1997 the group tried unsuccessfully to get Fairtrade products used in local cafes and restaurants.* ◇ **~ your best/hardest (to do sth)** *Participants said they tried their best to earn more money, given the uncertainty of a future retirement pension.* ◇ **~ and do sth** *Because the courts are important, politicians work hard to try and get their favoured candidates nominated.* **2** [T] to use, do or test sth in order to see if it is good, suitable, etc: **~ sth** *Over 50% of the first group wanted to try the brand.* ◇ *Having exhausted the possibilities of his first strategy, Stokes tried another approach.* ◇ **~ doing sth** *He tried living as a hermit in the Syrian desert but could not endure it.* **3** [T, often passive] to examine evidence in court and decide whether sb is guilty or not guilty of a crime: **~ sb (for sth)** *The doctor involved was tried for murder but was acquitted.* ◇ **~ sth** *The constitutional function of the Chinese courts is solely to try cases in accordance with the law.*
IDM **try your 'hand (at sth)** (*rather informal*) to do sth such as an activity or a sport for the first time: *All the major Romantic poets tried their hand at drama.*
PHR V **,try sth 'out** to test or use sth in order to see how good or effective it is: *Time is important, particularly when trying out new ideas in the classroom.*

tube /tju:b; *NAmE* tu:b/ *noun* **1** a long pipe made of metal, plastic, glass, etc, used for holding or transporting liquids or gases: *Samples are prepared in glass tubes.* ◇ *The capillary tubes are made of fused silica and coated externally with a polymer.* **2** a part inside a human or animal body or a plant that is shaped like a tube: *The oesophagus is the tube leading from the throat to the stomach.* ◇ *The growth rates of pollen tubes from self- and cross-pollinations were roughly the same.*

tu·ition /tju'ɪʃn; *NAmE* tu'ɪʃn/ *noun* [U] **1** the act of teaching sth, especially to one person or to people in small groups: *Participants receive 300 hours' language tuition as well as information about Norwegian society.* ◇ **~ in sth** *He gave private tuition in philosophy and other subjects.* **2** (*also* **tu'ition fees** [pl.]) the money that you pay to be taught, especially in a college or university: *Higher tuition fees may deter some students from going to university.*

tu·mour (*US* **tu·mor**) /'tju:mə(r); *NAmE* 'tu:mər/ *noun* a mass of cells growing in or on a part of the body where they should not, usually causing medical problems: *She was diagnosed with a brain tumour.* ◇ *Some viruses may lie dormant, or they may transform the host cell into a benign or malignant tumour.*

tun·nel /'tʌnl/ *noun* a passage under the ground, through rock or ice, or under water: *The city has extensive underground tunnels.* ◇ *The tunnels excavated by ragworms make oxygen available to microbes in the sediment.* ◇ *The Channel Tunnel is the longest underwater rail tunnel in Europe.* HELP A similar passage that is not underground may also be called a **tunnel**: *Field mice tend to move through tunnels in grass or snow, rather than across open areas.*

tur·bine /'tɜ:baɪn; *NAmE* 'tɜ:rbaɪn/ *noun* a machine or an engine that receives its power from a wheel that is turned by the pressure of water, air or gas: *This steam drives the low-pressure turbine.* ➲ *see also* WIND TURBINE

turn¹ /tɜ:n; *NAmE* tɜ:rn/ *verb* **1** [I, T] to move or make sth move around a central point: **(+ adv./prep.)** *The wheels of the combination lock turn through a number of discrete positions.* ◇ **~ sth (+ adv./prep.)** *The motor turns the wheels from position to position.* **2** [I, T] to move your body or part of your body so as to face or start moving in a different direction: *The Trojans turned and fled.* ◇ **~ to do sth** *The figure is caught in close-up as he turns to look into the hallway.* ◇ **~ (sth) (+ adv./prep.)** *The natural response of hunting owls when hearing a noise is for the bird to turn its head towards the source of sound.* **3** [T] **~ sb/sth + adv./prep.** to move sb/sth into a different position or to face a different direction: *Turn the patient on their side, if possible.* ◇ (*figurative*) *Unethical practices may turn away many more potential customers.* **4** [I, T] to change the direction you are moving or travelling in; to make sth change the direction it is moving in: **+ adv./prep.** *To turn left, the swimming turtles extend the left rear flipper.* ◇ **~ sth** *When the car turns a sharp corner, once again the passengers will feel themselves thrust into motion.* **5** [I] **+ adv./prep.** to curve in a particular direction: *The Danube flows east from the Black Forest and then turns south.* **6** [I, T] to direct your interest or attention in a particular direction: **+ adv./prep.** *US petroleum companies have increasingly turned to foreign sources of crude oil.* ◇ *By graduation, his interests had already begun to turn in the direction of anthropology.* ◇ *Voters were turning away from Labour and flocking to the Conservatives.* ◇ **~ sth + adv./prep.** *In 1789, Coulomb turned his attention* *to physics and published seven memoirs on electricity and magnetism.* **7** linking verb to change into a particular state or condition; to make sth do this: **+ adj.** *Blue litmus paper turns red in acid solution.* ◇ *Street demonstrations turned violent after some marchers were injured in confrontations with the police.* ◇ **~ sth + adj.** *The disease stimulates melanin production, thus turning the skin brown.* ◇ **+ noun** *In late sixteenth-century London, James Burbage, a joiner turned actor turned entrepreneur, established a permanent playhouse in Shoreditch.* **8** linking verb (not used in the progressive tenses) **+ noun** to reach or pass a particular age: *Most MPs have turned 40 by the time they first enter Parliament.* **9** [T, I] to move the page of a book or magazine so that you can read the next page: **~ sth** *Print advertisements must arrest the reader's attention so that they do not continue turning the page before the message can register.* ◇ **~ to sth** *This interactive book requires the readers to turn to different pages depending on their answers to certain questions.*

IDM Most idioms containing **turn** are at the entries for the nouns and adjectives in the idioms, for example **turn your back on sb/sth** is at **back** noun. **as it/things turned ˈout** as was shown or proved by later events: *In many cases it was suspected, rightly as it turned out, that these officials were obtaining the capital by fraud.*

PHR V **ˌturn aˈgainst sb/sth | ˌturn sb aˈgainst sb/sth** to stop or make sb stop being friendly towards or suppporting sb/sth: *Castro had turned against the United States and had allied with the Soviet Union.*

ˌturn aˈround/ˈround | ˌturn sb/sth aˈround/ˈround to change position or direction so as to face the other way; to make sb/sth do this: *In the closing shot of the sequence, her face is out of focus before she turns around to face forward.*

ˌturn aˈround/ˈround | ˌturn sth aˈround/ˈround (of a business or an economy) to start being successful after it has been unsuccessful for a time; to make a business or an economy do this: *By 1984, the economy had turned around and many Americans were better off than they had been four years previously.* ◇ *The campaign helped turn the company around and changed the face of the athletic shoe industry.*

ˌturn sb ˈaway (from sth) to refuse to allow sb to enter a place: *Asylum seekers, by reason of their situation, may lack proper documents and be turned away from a flight.*

ˌturn sth ˈback to make sth return the way it has come: *Emperor Julian rallied supporters who wanted to halt or turn back the advance of Christianity.*

ˌturn sb/sth ˈdown to reject or refuse to consider an offer, a proposal, a request, etc. or the person who makes it: *She was forced to leave the practice after her request for part-time working was turned down.* **ˌturn sth ˈdown** to reduce the noise, heat, etc. produced by a piece of equipment by moving its controls: *Governments are encouraging people to reduce their energy consumption by driving less and turning down the thermostat.*

ˌturn sth ˈin (especially NAmE) to give sth to sb in authority: *Around 36 000 questionnaires were turned in and opinions could also be submitted via a website.* **ˌturn ˈin on itself/yourself** to become too concerned with your own problems and stop communicating with others: *After the Second War, Judaism generally turned in on itself in order to survive.*

ˌturn (from sth) ˈinto sth to become sth: *Sweden has turned into a multi-ethnic society with a large proportion born abroad.* **ˌturn sb/sth (from sth) ˈinto sth** to make sb/sth become sth: *His imprisonment for seditious libel in 1768 turned him into a martyr for liberty.*

ˌturn ˈoff (of the flow of electricity, gas, water, etc.) to stop: *When the building reaches the desired temperature, the furnace turns off.* **ˌturn sb ˈoff** to make sb feel bored or not interested: *Many philosophers will be turned off by Brewer's radical rhetoric.* **ˌturn sth ˈoff** to stop the flow of electricity, gas, water, etc. by moving a switch, button, etc: *The temperature of the room rises and eventually the heater is turned off.*

ˌturn ˈon (of the flow of electricity, gas, water, etc.) to begin: *When the system runs, you will see the LEDs turn on and off.* **ˈturn on sth** [no passive] to have sth as its main topic: *The case turned on whether the airspace formed part of the claimant's land.* **ˌturn sth ˈon** to start the flow of electricity, gas, water, etc. by moving a switch, button, etc: *As the power supply is turned on, oscillations will grow in amplitude.*

ˌturn ˈout **1** to be present at an event: *Only 38 per cent of eligible voters turned out at the polls.* ➲ related noun TURNOUT **2** (used with an adverb or adjective, or in questions with *how*) to happen in a particular way; to develop or end in a particular way: *How a particular approach will turn out cannot be foreseen with certainty.* ◇ **~ out + adv.** *In this play, all turns out well in the end.* ◇ **~ out + adj.** *The two sets of results turned out almost identical.* **3** to be discovered to be; to prove to be: **~ out that...** *It turns out that any unit can be expressed in terms of these dimensions.* ◇ **~ out to be/have sth** *The legislation turned out to be a great success.* **ˌturn sb/sth ˈout** to produce sb/sth: *The typical automobile assembly line in the US turns out 60 cars per hour*

ˌturn ˈover sth to do business worth a particular amount of money in a particular period of time: *From a small mobile-phone shop, they created a business that turned over around £4 billion in 2007.* ➲ related noun TURNOVER (2)

ˌturn sth ˈover **1** to make sth change position so that the other side is facing towards the outside or the top: *Turning the soil over either after a harvest or prior to planting is typically seen as beneficial.* **2** (of a shop or business) to sell goods and replace them: *The company turns over inventory every six days on average, keeping related costs low.* ➲ related noun TURNOVER (2) **ˌturn sb ˈover to sb** to deliver sb to the control or care of sb else, especially sb in authority: *Alexander turned Bessus over to his Persian supporters for trial and execution.* **ˌturn sth ˈover to sb** to give the control of sth to sb: *After some negotiations, he agreed to turn the property over to Hawks for development.* **ˌturn sth ˈover to sth** to change the use or function of sth: *Existing arable land was turned over to biofuels crop production.*

ˈturn to sb/sth (for sth/to do sth) to go to sb/sth for help, advice, information, etc: *Rehabilitation care teams advise patients on who to turn to for advice.*

turn to sth to go on to consider sth next: *I shall now turn to the question of the impact of outsourcing activity on public sector employment relations.* ◇ **~ to do sth** *Decaux then turns to consider a number of cases where states were found in breach of international law.*

ˌturn ˈup **1** to appear or be found, especially by chance, after being lost: *In central and southern Greece, major deposits of armour have turned up, not in graves, but in sanctuaries.* **2** (of a person) to arrive or attend an event: *So biased was the new system that no Hungarian, Czech or Croatian representatives turned up to the meeting.* **ˌturn sth ˈup** **1** to increase the sound, heat, etc. of a piece of equipment: *As the jet is gradually turned up, a definite series of changes occurs.* **2** to find sth: *A re-examination of their results turns up nothing that really supports this claim.*

turn² /tɜːn; NAmE tɜːrn/ noun [C] **1 ~ to/towards sth** a change in direction: *The lava then moved due south where the river makes an abrupt turn to the south.* **2** a time when the way that people think about sth or do sth changes a lot: *Their words marked a decisive turn that affected not just Jewish history but the entire world.* ◇ **~ towards sth** *For US historians, the mid-century turn towards consensus thinking further eroded the concept of terrorism.* **3** the time when sb in a group of people should or is allowed to do sth: *These activities were mostly cooperative games, during which participants were often required to wait their turn.* ◇ **~ to do sth** *Both players are*

T

rational whenever it is their turn to move; this includes assuming that the other player will also behave rationally. IDM **at every ˈturn** everywhere or every time you try and do sth: *Baudry's central argument is beset by problems at every turn.* **in its, his, their, etc. ˈturn** as the result of a previous action, process or situation: *Competition also takes place among the buyers, which in its turn causes the commodities offered to rise in price.* **in ˈturn 1** as a result of sth in a series of events: *One photon stimulates the emission of another photon, which in turn stimulates more (Fig. 13.30).* **2** one after the other in a particular order: *In turn, all the factions pledged to support the adoption of the legal reforms envisioned under the agreement.* **take a new, different, etc. ˈturn** to change in the way stated: *During the 1990s, competition in the petrol retail industry took a new turn.* **take ˈturns (in sth/to do sth)** if people **take turns** to do sth, they do it one after the other to make sure it is done fairly: *Students were asked to take turns in their group reading statements aloud.* **the ˌturn of the ˈcentury/ˈyear** the time when a new century/year starts: *Just before the turn of the century, a new common currency, the euro, was born.* **a ˌturn of eˈvents** a development or change in a situation: *Angered by this turn of events, he refused to repay the loan.* **a ˌturn of ˈphrase** a particular way of describing sth: *In a wonderful turn of phrase, Sommers (2008) suggests that to taste wine is to 'taste geography'.*

ˈturning point *noun* **~ (in sth)** the time when an important change takes place, usually with the result that a situation improves: *The conference marked a turning point in the development of international environmental politics.*

turn·out /ˈtɜːnaʊt; *NAmE* ˈtɜːrnaʊt/ *noun* [C, U] the number of people who vote in a particular election: *Elections in which a close outcome is predicted usually have higher turnouts.* ◇ *There have been other proposed reforms to increase voter turnout.*

turn·over /ˈtɜːnəʊvə(r); *NAmE* ˈtɜːrnoʊvər/ *noun* **1** [sing., U] the rate at which employees leave a company and are replaced by other people: **~ (of sb)** *A high turnover of staff in an organization may be symptomatic of a deeper problem.* ◇ *We also asked about staff turnover and retention.* ◇ **+ noun** *The sales force had a high turnover rate (40 per cent per year).* **2** [C, usually sing., U] **~ (of sth)** the total amount of goods or services sold by a company during a particular period of time: *Taken together, these companies have an annual turnover of £9.1 billion.*

tutor /ˈtjuːtə(r); *NAmE* ˈtuːtər/ *noun* **1** (*especially BrE*) a teacher in a college or university, especially one who is responsible for teaching or advising a student or a group of students: *Learners in medical education tend to rate their tutors higher than those tutors rate themselves.* **2** a private teacher, especially one who teaches an individual student or a very small group: *One person who took advantage of the new political climate was the philosopher Aristotle, the former tutor of Alexander.*

tu·tor·ial /tjuːˈtɔːriəl; *NAmE* tuːˈtɔːriəl/ *noun* **1** a period of teaching in a university that involves discussion between an individual student or a small group of students and a tutor: *Seminars and tutorials depend to a large extent upon student preparation and participation for their success.* **2** a short piece of writing or computer program that gives information on a particular subject or explains how sth is done: *Appendix C provides a short tutorial.*

TV /ˌtiː ˈviː/ *noun* [U, C] (*rather informal*) television: *Films, TV, the Internet, etc. may all reinforce this message.* ◇ *A TV may keep children occupied without active parental involvement.* ◇ **+ noun** *a TV set/show/channel*

twice /twaɪs/ *adv.* **1** two times; on two occasions: *The process was repeated twice.* ◇ *He was twice deported from the United Kingdom.* ◇ *Teeth should be brushed twice daily.* ◇ *The Senior Leadership Team meets once or twice a month.* **2** double in quantity, rate, etc: **~ the...** *This amount is twice the original cost.* ◇ **~ as... (as...)** *Humans live at least twice as long as expected for a primate of their body size.* ◇ *Patients with the disease are twice as likely to die prematurely.*
IDM **twice ˈover** not just once but twice: *Global wave energy is sufficient to satisfy the world's electricity consumption twice over.* IDM *see* THINK

twin¹ /twɪn/ *noun* one of two children born at the same time to the same mother: *Identical twins, on average, resemble each other more than fraternal twins.* ◇ **+ noun** *Twin studies can provide useful insight into the relative contributions of genetic and environmental factors.*

twin² /twɪn/ *adj.* [only before noun] **1** born at the same time to the same mother: *She is close to her twin sister.* **2** used to describe two things that are connected, or present or happening at the same time: *The twin goals of greater efficiency and greater effectiveness have underpinned the new business structure.* ◇ *These twin processes are considered vital for successful organizational transformation.*

twist¹ /twɪst/ *verb* [I, T] to bend or turn into a particular shape or in a particular direction; to bend or turn sth in this way: *The lumbar region is under continuous pressure from bending, twisting and lifting.* ◇ *A leaf can twist and turn to follow the sun.* ◇ **~ sth** *A strip of metal is twisted to form a hollow tube.*

twist² /twɪst/ *noun* **1** [C] an unexpected change or development in a story or situation: *Then the campaign took an interesting twist.* ◇ *These developments added a surprising twist to the debates.* **2** [C] **~ (of sth)** an act of turning sth; the shape that this makes: *An eel seizes the prey with its jaws and then performs a single twist of its body.* ◇ *You now have a loop with a twist in it.* **3** [U] (*technical*) the action of turning sth; the amount by which sth is turned; the force that produces this: *Twist should be taken into account whenever one seeks to describe the shape of an elastic rod.*

two /tuː/ *number* 2: *They have two children.* ◇ *Two of the three main uses of the Internet by teenagers involved private communication.* ◇ *27% regularly spent two or more hours at home alone after school.* ◇ *Lions hunting in twos and groups had a greater success rate than lions hunting singly by daylight.* ◇ *The family lives in a two-room mud hut.*
IDM **a ˈday, ˈmoment, ˈword, etc. or two** one or a few days, moments, words, etc: *It is a simple virus infection which will resolve spontaneously in a day or two.* **in ˈtwo** in or into two pieces or halves: *The country has been split in two since rebel forces took control of the northern half of the country.*

ˌtwo-diˈmension·al *adj.* flat; having no depth; appearing to have only two DIMENSIONS: *Cinema, like painting, is a two-dimensional art which creates the illusion of a third dimension.* ◇ *Figure 3.1 shows a two-dimensional representation of the structure.*

two·fold /ˈtuːfəʊld; *NAmE* ˈtuːfoʊld/ *adj.* **1** twice as much or as many: *These numbers show that, at the earth's centre, compression causes nearly a twofold increase in the density of core material.* **2** consisting of two parts: *The leaders' task is twofold: to ensure that organizational objectives are accomplished while sustaining the people charged with accomplishing those objectives.*

ˌtwo-ˈway *adj.* [usually before noun] **1** (of communication or relationships) involving equal effort from both people or groups involved: *There is a two-way interaction between the business community and the media.* **2** moving in two different directions: *Intra-industry trade is of*

T

large and increasing importance, consisting to a large extent of two-way flows of similar goods.

type[1] /taɪp/ *noun* **1** [C] **~ (of sth)** a class or group of things or people that share particular qualities or features: *Freshwater mussels show three different types of life cycle.* ◇ *John Ford's 'Young Mr Lincoln' is a film of this type.* ◇ *Membrane proteins crystals can be classified in two types, defined as type I and type II (Fig. 9.21).* HELP In linguistics, a **type** is a category or class of linguistic item or unit, as distinct from actual examples of words in speech or writing: *The search yielded 20 221 word tokens, which consisted of 4 885 different word types.* ➲ *compare* TOKEN[1] (3) ➲ language bank *at* DEFINE **2** [U] letters that are printed or typed: *Key terms and concepts are highlighted in bold type.*
▸ ADJECTIVE + TYPE **different** ◆ **various** ◆ **certain**, **particular**, **specific** ◆ **distinct**, **distinctive** ◆ **specialized** ◆ **similar** ◆ **main**, **major**, **principal** ◆ **basic** ◆ **common** ◆ **new** ◆ **ideal** ◆ **multiple** ◆ **numerous** *Recent research suggests that individuals with certain types of personality are more likely to experience anger.*
▸ NOUN + TYPE **personality** ◆ **cell** ◆ **tissue** ◆ **tumour** ◆ **habitat** ◆ **forest** ◆ **vegetation** ◆ **food** ◆ **soil** ◆ **sediment** ◆ **rock** *First, the genomic DNA from the two cell types is isolated.*
▸ VERB + TYPE **distinguish**, **differentiate** ◆ **recognize** ◆ **identify**, **determine** ◆ **specify** ◆ **classify**, **categorize** ◆ **define** ◆ **describe**, **outline**, **characterize** ◆ **show** ◆ **indicate** ◆ **consider** ◆ **discuss** ◆ **cover** ◆ **illustrate** ◆ **represent** ◆ **investigate**, **examine**, **explore**, **study**, **analyse** *The noted American geographer Whittlesey identified nine major regional types of agriculture.*

type[2] /taɪp/ *verb* **1** [I, T] **~ sth (out/in/up)** to write sth using a computer, etc. by pressing the keys: *I took notes during the interview and then typed up my notes.* **2** [T] **~ sb/sth** (*medical*) to find out the group or class that a person, their blood or TISSUE belongs to: *Blood samples were taken from the samples for typing.*

typ·ical /ˈtɪpɪkl/ *adj.* **1** having the usual qualities or features of a particular type of person, thing or group: *Kineton, in Warwickshire, is considered to be a typical example of a medieval urban failure.* ◇ *The pattern by which transport systems evolved in Britain is fairly typical.* ◇ **~ of sb/sth** *The Hubbard family was typical of most families of European descent then living in North America.* OPP ATYPICAL ➲ *compare* REPRESENTATIVE[2] (1) **2** happening in the usual way; showing what sth is usually like: *On a typical night, at least two thirds of the news coverage was from inside Greece.* ◇ **~ for sb/sth** *Chromosomal instability is typical for almost any cells maintained for a long time in vitro.* ◇ **~ for sb/sth to do sth** *In the factories, it was typical for bureaucrats to outnumber production workers.* ➲ *compare* NORMAL[1] (1) **3** behaving in the way that you expect: *Kipling made the case with typical epigrammatic economy: 'And what should they know of England who only England know?'* ◇ **~ of sb/sth** *This behaviour is typical of African lions (Panthera leo; Bertram, 1975; Packer et al., 1988).*
▸ TYPICAL + NOUN **example** ◆ **pattern** ◆ **feature** ◆ **element** ◆ **appearance** ◆ **experiment** *Disturbance of colour vision is a typical feature of optic nerve disorders.* | **day** ◆ **night** ◆ **scenario** ◆ **situation** ◆ **case**, **instance** ◆ **reaction** ◆ **configuration** ◆ **value** ◆ **shape** ◆ **length** ◆ **radius** ◆ **profile** *Typical values are in the range 1.5–2.0, but many polymerizations yield considerably larger values.*

typ·ic·al·ly /ˈtɪpɪkli/ *adv.* **1** used to say that sth usually happens in the way that you are stating: *Most measuring systems typically involve some standard unit such as the kilometre.* ◇ *Tropical deciduous forests typically occur in regions with a three- to seven-month dry season.* ◇ *Typically, both copies of a duplicated gene in a genome can generate the corresponding protein.* **2** in a way that shows the usual qualities or features of a particular type of person, thing or group: *Production units were typically small, but there were exceptions.* ◇ *These people are typically socially anxious and shy around others.*

typ·ify /ˈtɪpɪfaɪ/ *verb* (**typi·fies**, **typi·fy·ing**, **typi·fied**, **typi·fied**) (not usually used in the progressive tenses) [often passive] **1 ~ sth** to be a typical example of sth: *Mass production, typified by Henry Ford, is based on assembly lines producing standardized products.* **2 ~ sth** to be a typical feature of sth: *High tension typified the period before the Korean War.*

typ·ology /taɪˈpɒlədʒi; *NAmE* taɪˈpɑːlədʒi/ *noun* (*pl.* **-ies**) **~ (of sth)** (*technical*) a system of dividing things into different types: *They developed a typology of electoral systems.*

U u

ubi·qui·tous /juːˈbɪkwɪtəs/ *adj.* present, appearing or found everywhere: *Vitamin B_6 is so ubiquitous in foodstuffs that deficiency is rare.* ◇ *Danger is a ubiquitous concern.* ◇ *Given the ubiquitous nature of mobile email, there are few legitimate excuses for not responding.* ■ **ubi·qui·tous·ly** *adv.*: *Lipids serve many biological functions and are found almost ubiquitously in nature.* **ubi·quity** /juːˈbɪkwəti/ *noun* [U] *Yet despite its ubiquity in democracies, voting is not necessarily the most effective means of exercising influence on political decision-making.*

ul·tim·ate AWL /ˈʌltɪmət/ *adj.* [only before noun] **1** happening at the end of a process SYN FINAL (1): *The ultimate goal of the project is to decrease maternal mortality among poor socio-economic groups.* ◇ *the ultimate aim/objective of sth* ◇ *The ultimate destinations of these immigrants, however, tend to be global cities.* ◇ *The new committee would have ultimate responsibility for all university marketing activity.* **2** most extreme; best, worst, greatest, most important, etc: *The ultimate test of any concept is its usefulness.* ◇ *The Civil War was widely viewed throughout America as a struggle between ultimate good and ultimate evil.* **3** from which sth originally comes SYN FUNDAMENTAL (2): *The ultimate source of most energy available on earth is the sun.* ◇ *A postmodern scholar might argue that there is no ultimate reality, only multiple versions of reality.*

ul·tim·ate·ly AWL /ˈʌltɪmətli/ *adv.* **1** in the end; finally: *Change in one's personal life can produce stress and ultimately lead to illness.* ◇ *This programme was ultimately unsuccessful, but once it was one of the biggest hopes of theoretical physics.* ◇ *Ultimately, however, all organic material is broken down to inorganic forms.* ◇ *This, he argued, gave rise to a curious state of affairs in which no sector of Japanese society was ultimately responsible for political decisions.* **2** at the most basic and important level SYN BASICALLY, ESSENTIALLY: *Energy from wind ultimately depends on the heating of the atmosphere by solar radiation.* ◇ *All the cellular components of the immune system are derived ultimately from the bone marrow.*

ultra·sound /ˈʌltrəsaʊnd/ *noun* **1** [U, C] a medical process that produces an image of what is inside your body: *Women generally report attending the clinics to confirm a pregnancy through ultrasound.* ◇ **~ of sth** *The diagnosis is confirmed by an ultrasound of the abdomen.* ◇ **+ noun** *An ultrasound scan of the liver will be necessary to determine the diagnosis.* **2** [U] sound that is higher than humans can hear: *Bats scan their surroundings with their own generated ultrasound.*

ultra·vio·let /ˌʌltrəˈvaɪələt/ (*abbr.* **UV**) *adj.* [usually before noun] having or using ELECTROMAGNETIC waves that are just shorter than those in the normal visible SPECTRUM, but longer than X-RAYS: *The ozone layer filters out harmful ultraviolet radiation from the sun.* ◇ *Photographs were taken under ultraviolet light.* ➲ *compare* INFRARED

um·brella /ʌmˈbrelə/ *noun* **1** a thing that contains or includes many different parts or elements: **(under) the ~ of sth** *It could be argued that after-sales service falls under the general umbrella of customer service.* ◇ **+ noun** *'Coal' is an umbrella term encompassing a wide range of fuels.* **2** a country or system that protects people: **(under) the ~ of sth** *Some would argue that society can only succeed under the umbrella of a strong social order.*

un·able /ʌnˈeɪbl/ *adj.* [not before noun] not having the skill, strength, time, knowledge, etc. to do sth: **~ to do sth** *Firms found themselves unable to pay for the rising costs of raw materials.* ◇ *She feels unable to cope, and she is frightened that she may hurt her children.* ◇ **~ to do so** *Although teachers are constantly encouraged to 'reflect' on their teaching, they are unable to do so effectively unless they are specifically trained in how to reflect.* ◇ **~ or unwilling/unwilling or ~** *The company was unable or unwilling to solve the most significant problem: the dependence on one field of business only.* OPP ABLE (1) ➲ grammar note *at* CAN[1]

un·accept·able /ˌʌnəkˈseptəbl/ *adj.* that you cannot accept, allow or approve of: *Workers in the bars continue to face a significant and unacceptable health risk.* ◇ *A vegan might consider all forms of dairy farming to be ethically unacceptable.* ◇ **~ to sb** *Such an outcome may be unacceptable to those involved.* OPP ACCEPTABLE ■ **un·accept·ably** /ˌʌnəkˈseptəbli/ *adv.*: *Maternal mortality levels remain unacceptably high across the developing world.*

un·adjust·ed /ˌʌnəˈdʒʌstɪd/ *adj.* (*statistics*) (of figures or models) not adjusted according to particular facts or circumstances: *We examined these associations in both unadjusted models and in models adjusted for sex, age, race/ethnicity and education.*

un·affect·ed AWL /ˌʌnəˈfektɪd/ *adj.* not changed or influenced by sth; not affected by sth: *If hospital waiting lists fall, it does not follow that demand remains unaffected.* ◇ **~ by sth** *Many people work in government or in services so they are largely unaffected by globalization as workers, but benefit as consumers.*

un·altered AWL /ʌnˈɔːltəd; *NAmE* ʌnˈɔːltərd/ *adj.* that has not changed or been changed: *The first and second processes remain unaltered as the pH of the solution is lowered from the initial value of 5.2 (Fig. 3.2).*

un·am·bigu·ous AWL /ˌʌnæmˈbɪɡjuəs/ *adj.* clear in meaning; that can only be understood in one way: *The buyer must be able to present his argument in a clear and unambiguous way.* ◇ *Tree ring analysis by Briffa et al. (1990) failed to find any unambiguous evidence for this warm phase.* OPP AMBIGUOUS ■ **un·am·bigu·ous·ly** AWL *adv.*: *DNA sequences provide the means to unambiguously identify a biological sample.*

un·answered /ʌnˈɑːnsəd; *NAmE* ʌnˈænsərd/ *adj.* (of a question or problem) that has not been answered: *Many questions still remain unanswered, mostly due to a lack of empirical data.*

un·antici·pated AWL /ˌʌnænˈtɪsɪpeɪtɪd/ *adj.* that you have not expected or predicted; that you have not ANTICIPATED: *There were two important and unanticipated consequences that flowed from this development.* ◇ *Countries had to confront debt-repayment problems that were entirely unanticipated.*

un·attract·ive /ˌʌnəˈtræktɪv/ *adj.* **1 ~ (to sb)** not good, interesting or pleasant: *Those who had been out of work for long periods became increasingly unattractive to employers.* OPP ATTRACTIVE (3) **2** not attractive or pleasant to look at: *Several studies have shown that men with hair loss perceive themselves to be physically unattractive.* OPP ATTRACTIVE (1)

un·author·ized (*BrE also* **-ised**) /ʌnˈɔːθəraɪzd/ *adj.* without official permission: *The defendant was a computer hacker who gained unauthorized access to a computer network.* ➲ *see also* AUTHORIZE

un·avail·able AWL /ˌʌnəˈveɪləbl/ *adj.* [not usually before noun] **1** that cannot be obtained: *When funding was unavailable, some health facilities temporarily reinstated user fees.* ◇ **~ to sb/sth** *The employer had access to information that was unavailable to the employees.* ◇ **~ for sth** *In some fields, the recording of data is either insufficient, absent or unavailable for use.* OPP AVAILABLE (1) **2 ~ (for sth)** (of a person) not free or not willing to do sth: *Eight patients could not be contacted or were unavailable for interview within the time frame available.* OPP AVAILABLE (2) ■ **un·avail·abil·ity** /ˌʌnəveɪləˈbɪləti/ *noun* [U] **~ (of sth)** *The unavailability of resources was a recurrent theme of the study.*

un·avoid·able /ˌʌnəˈvɔɪdəbl/ *adj.* impossible to avoid or prevent SYN INEVITABLE (1): *Limitations in human knowledge had unavoidable negative consequences.* ◇ **it is ~ that...** *It is unavoidable that individuals will have to change attitudes towards planning for retirement.* OPP AVOIDABLE ■ **un·avoid·ably** /ˌʌnəˈvɔɪdəbli/ *adv.*: *These long delays unavoidably create uncertainty.* ◇ *The networking between different firms is unavoidably fluid and loose.*

un·aware AWL /ˌʌnəˈweə(r); *NAmE* ˌʌnəˈwer/ *adj.* [not before noun] not knowing or realizing that sth is happening or that sth exists: **~ (of sth)** *To avoid participant bias, all participants were unaware of the specific nature of the experimental manipulation.* ◇ **~ that...** *Some patients are unaware that their physical symptoms may have a psychological cause.* OPP AWARE (1)

un·bal·anced /ˌʌnˈbælənst/ *adj.* **1** not fair because too much or too little importance has been given to one side or one aspect of sth: *The concessions are considered to have been entirely unbalanced in favour of foreign private interests.* **2** [usually before noun] not having the correct or equal amounts of all that is needed: *Highly unbalanced sample sizes lower the statistical power in longitudinal models.* **3** [not usually before noun] (of a person) slightly mentally ill: *Violent women were considered mentally unbalanced or possessed by unimaginable evil (Ward, 2004).*

un·biased AWL /ʌnˈbaɪəst/ *adj.* fair and not influenced by your own or sb else's opinions or wishes SYN IMPARTIAL: *This approach produces an unbiased estimate of the HIV rate.* ◇ *What was so remarkable about this data set is that the information in it was extraordinarily unbiased.* OPP BIASED (2)

un·born /ˌʌnˈbɔːn; *NAmE* ˌʌnˈbɔːrn/ *adj.* [usually before noun] not yet born: *Infection during pregnancy can have adverse effects on the unborn child, as well as the mother.*

un·cer·tain /ʌnˈsɜːtn; *NAmE* ʌnˈsɜːrtn/ *adj.* **1** [not before noun] feeling doubt about sth; not sure: *This situation leaves many young people feeling uncertain and confused.* ◇ **~ about/of sth** *Most organizations were uncertain about the financial impact of work-related illness.* OPP CERTAIN[1] (2) **2** likely to change, especially in a negative or unpleasant way: *The organization faced a highly uncertain future.* ◇ *Secure work becomes uncertain in the global economy.* **3** not definite or decided; not known exactly SYN UNCLEAR (1): *The original reason for covering bridges is uncertain, although it does provide shelter and a location for market stalls.* ◇ **it is ~ if/whether...** *It is uncertain whether these results would differ if the study were to be repeated at a later age.* ◇ **remain ~** *Political, economic and cultural circumstances also change at the global scale, the precise consequences of which remain uncertain.* **4** not confident: *He had an uncertain grasp of media*

U

presentation. ◇ *The EU remains an often uncertain and hesitant global power.*

IDM **in ˌno unˌcertain ˈterms** clearly and strongly: *He told the president in no uncertain terms that the operation would be a disaster.*

un·cer·tainty /ʌnˈsɜːtnti; *NAmE* ʌnˈsɜːrtnti/ *noun* (*pl.* **-ies**) **1** [U] the state of not knowing or of not being known exactly; the state of being uncertain: *As the uncertainty associated with the business declines, the amount of cash invested rises.* ◇ *There remains considerable uncertainty surrounding the effects of the drug.* ◇ *All data contain some degree of uncertainty, inaccuracy and associated errors.* ◇ **~ of sth** *The uncertainty of the result should be clearly quantified, if any reliable judgements are to be made from the data.* ◇ **~ about sth** *There are several good reasons for the continuing uncertainty about the meaning of this basic term.* ◇ **~ in sth** *One of the most important caveats relates to the uncertainty in the rate of greenhouse gas emissions over the next 100 years.* **2** [C, usually pl.] something that you cannot be sure about; a situation that causes you to be uncertain: *The only way these uncertainties can be resolved is through continued careful analysis of all data.* ◇ *The negative human consequences of unemployment will be magnified by the uncertainties associated with the business cycle.*

▸ ADJECTIVE + UNCERTAINTY **considerable** • **great** • **increasing** • **environmental** • **political** • **legal** • **scientific** *The search for profitable new markets takes place in an environment of great uncertainty.*

▸ VERB + UNCERTAINTY **reduce** • **create** • **increase** • **introduce** • **lead to** • **deal with** *Many organizations provide teams to work with the client in an attempt to generate trust and reduce uncertainty.*

▸ NOUN + OF UNCERTAINTY **degree** • **level** • **measure** • **source** *High levels of uncertainty favour the selection of flexible strategies, since mistakes are easier to put right.*

un·chal·lenged /ʌnˈtʃælɪndʒd/ *adj.* **1** not doubted; accepted without question; not challenged: *The risk society thesis has not gone unchallenged.* ◇ *Many violations of human rights appear to go unchallenged at the international level.* **2** (of a ruler or leader, or their position) not opposed by anyone: *The recent re-elections mean that the Prime Minister will be unchallenged over the next five-year period.*

un·changed /ʌnˈtʃeɪndʒd/ *adj.* [not usually before noun] that has stayed the same and not changed SYN UNALTERED: *The proportion of poor working-age adults was unchanged at 17 per cent.* ◇ **remain ~** *Soil temperature remained unchanged and soil moisture increased only slightly.* ◇ **leave sth ~** *This policy leaves the wage rate of middle-skilled workers essentially unchanged.*

un·chan·ging /ʌnˈtʃeɪndʒɪŋ/ *adj.* that always stays the same and does not change: *These concerns reflect a belief in the need for an essentially unchanging national culture.* ◇ *It was impossible for him to construct a model of a cosmos that is static and unchanging with time.*

un·clear /ˌʌnˈklɪə(r); *NAmE* ˌʌnˈklɪr/ *adj.* [not usually before noun] **1** not clear or definite; difficult to understand or be sure about: *The impact of these two changes is still unclear.* ◇ *This case highlights the importance of assessing a patient if the diagnosis is unclear.* ◇ **it is ~ whether/how, etc...** *It is unclear whether similar problems occur in other ethnic groups.* ◇ **remain ~** *The extent to which genetic factors influence successful ageing remains unclear.* OPP CLEAR[1] (1) **2 ~ (about sth)** not fully understanding sth SYN UNCERTAIN (1): *The lack of transparency in the present system means that voters are unclear about whom to hold responsible for spending and taxing.* OPP CLEAR[1] (3)

un·com·fort·able /ʌnˈkʌmftəbl; ʌnˈkʌmfətəbl; *NAmE* ʌnˈkʌmfərtəbl/ *adj.* **1** anxious, embarrassed or afraid and unable to relax; making you feel like this: *Patients felt uncomfortable when doctors asked them questions about their personal life.* ◇ **~ with sth** *It was evident that the president was uncomfortable with press criticism.* ◇ **~ about sth** *Some people were uncomfortable about calling others by their first name.* OPP COMFORTABLE (1) **2** not feeling physically relaxed, warm, etc: *Although medication helps, he feels uncomfortable when moving around and lifting things.* OPP COMFORTABLE (2) **3** not letting you feel physically comfortable; unpleasant to wear, sit on, etc: *For many workers, the day included hours of uncomfortable travel to and from work.* OPP COMFORTABLE (3) **4** unpleasant or difficult to deal with: *The financial crisis should not hide the uncomfortable reality that governments are imposing more financial responsibility on individuals.* ◇ *He is attempting to distract himself from uncomfortable emotions such as anger and hurt.*

un·com·mon /ʌnˈkɒmən; *NAmE* ʌnˈkɑːmən/ *adj.* **1** not happening very often; not existing in large numbers or in many places SYN UNUSUAL, RARE: *Historically, obesity was a relatively uncommon problem.* ◇ **not ~ (for sb/sth) (to do sth)** *It is not uncommon for patients to drop out of clinical trials of medicines.* OPP COMMON[1] (1) **2** unusually large in degree or amount; great SYN REMARKABLE: *The business has grown partly because of its uncommon commitment to delivering high-quality service.*

un·com·pli·cated /ʌnˈkɒmplɪkeɪtɪd; *NAmE* ʌnˈkɑːmplɪkeɪtɪd/ *adj.* **1** simple; without any difficulty or confusion SYN STRAIGHTFORWARD: *The structured interview approach is a standardized procedure, which enables accurate data collection and uncomplicated quantitative analysis.* OPP COMPLICATED (1) **2** (of a medical condition) free from any extra problems: *Women can have a delivery at home if they continue to have an uncomplicated pregnancy.* OPP COMPLICATED (2)

un·con·di·tion·al /ˌʌnkənˈdɪʃənl/ *adj.* without any conditions or limits: *There would be no unconditional surrender and no decisive victory.* OPP CONDITIONAL (1) ■ **un·con·di·tion·al·ly** /ˌʌnkənˈdɪʃənəli/ *adv.*: *The government agreed unconditionally to these terms.*

un·con·nect·ed /ˌʌnkəˈnektɪd/ *adj.* not related or connected in any way SYN UNRELATED (1): *The novel is actually a collection of unconnected short stories.* ◇ **~ with sth** *Each officer was transferred to duties unconnected with criminal investigation.* ◇ **~ to sth** *Few issues in human geography are unconnected to values and justice.*

un·con·scious[1] /ʌnˈkɒnʃəs; *NAmE* ʌnˈkɑːnʃəs/ *adj.* **1** in a state like sleep because of an injury or illness, and not able to use your senses: *The patient may get restless and agitated and become unconscious.* OPP CONSCIOUS (2) **2** (of feelings, thoughts, etc.) existing or happening without you realizing or being aware; not deliberate or controlled: *The argument is that humans have an unconscious desire to establish order in their world.* OPP CONSCIOUS (3) **3 ~ of sb/sth** not aware of sb/sth; not noticing sth; not conscious: *You may be conscious of someone entering the room, but unconscious of the hardness of your chair or the hum of distant traffic.* OPP CONSCIOUS (1)

the un·con·scious[2] /ʌnˈkɒnʃəs; *NAmE* ʌnˈkɑːnʃəs/ *noun* [sing.] (*psychology*) the part of a person's mind with thoughts and feelings that they are not aware of and cannot control but which can sometimes be understood by studying their behaviour or dreams: *Unaccepted feelings and desires, which are repressed into the unconscious, return in other forms.*

un·con·scious·ly /ʌnˈkɒnʃəsli; *NAmE* ʌnˈkɑːnʃəsli/ *adv.* without being aware: *By their behaviour, consciously and unconsciously, parents greatly influence how their child handles anger.* OPP CONSCIOUSLY

U

un·con·sti·tu·tion·al AWL /ˌʌnˌkɒnstɪˈtjuːʃənl; *NAmE* ˌʌnkɑːnstəˈtuːʃənl/ *adj.* not allowed by the CONSTITUTION of a country, a political system or an organization: *Part of the National Industrial Recovery Act had been declared unconstitutional by the Supreme Court.* OPP CONSTITUTIONAL

un·con·strained AWL /ˌʌnkənˈstreɪnd/ *adj.* not limited: *Human interactions are never completely unconstrained; instead they are always guided by social norms.* ◇ **~ by sth** *Unconstrained by government bureaucracy or the profit needs of shareholders, voluntary organizations have been able to take immediate action.* ➲ *see also* CONSTRAIN (1)

un·con·trol·lable /ˌʌnkənˈtrəʊləbl; *NAmE* ˌʌnkənˈtroʊləbl/ *adj.* that you cannot control or prevent: *Crises may happen due to uncontrollable events such as climate change.* ■ **un·con·trol·lably** /ˌʌnkənˈtrəʊləbli; *NAmE* ˌʌnkənˈtroʊləbli/ *adv.*: *The patient has vomited several times and is shivering uncontrollably.*

un·con·trolled /ˌʌnkənˈtrəʊld; *NAmE* ˌʌnkənˈtroʊld/ *adj.* **1** that is not limited or managed: *Regional overconsumption and uncontrolled population growth present a serious problem to the health of our planet.* HELP In medicine, an **uncontrolled** disease or medical condition is one that is given no medical treatment: *Uncontrolled hypertension leads to an increased risk of stroke.* ➲ *compare* CONTROLLED (3) **2** (of a research method) that does not use a control group for comparison of results: *Evidence from uncontrolled studies in this field may need to be treated with particular caution.* ◇ *One should bear in mind the possibility of uncontrolled experimental bias in the results.* OPP CONTROLLED (1) **3** (of emotions or behaviour) that sb cannot control or stop: *The first symptoms are usually mental disturbances and mild uncontrolled movements.* ◇ *The system of legal trials replaced private, uncontrolled vengeance with a measured process.*

un·con·tro·ver·sial AWL /ˌʌnˌkɒntrəˈvɜːʃl; *NAmE* ˌʌnkɑːntrəˈvɜːrʃl/ *adj.* not causing, or not likely to cause, any disagreement; accepted by most people as right: *The abolition of the tax was relatively uncontroversial.* OPP CONTROVERSIAL

un·con·ven·tion·al AWL /ˌʌnkənˈvenʃənl/ *adj.* different from what is usually done or used; not considered to be normal by most people: *This section examines the global distribution of unconventional gas resources.* ◇ *The presentation of Chapter 5 is somewhat unconventional as it mixes two branches of economic geography generally treated apart.* OPP CONVENTIONAL (2)

U

un·count·able /ʌnˈkaʊntəbl/ *adj.* (*grammar*) a noun that is **uncountable** cannot be made plural or used with *a* or *an*, for example *water*, *bread* and *information*: *Some nouns, such as 'information' and 'equipment' are uncountable in English, although their equivalents are countable in some other languages.* OPP COUNTABLE ➲ *compare* COUNTLESS

un·cover /ʌnˈkʌvə(r)/ *verb* **1 ~ sth** to discover sth that was previously hidden or secret: *The fieldwork had uncovered evidence of organizational malpractice.* ◇ *The journalist used his investigative skills to uncover the truth behind the plot.* **2 ~ sth** to remove sth that is covering sth: *On the holy journey to Mecca, the Hajj, you have to uncover your face.* ◇ *The excavations have uncovered remains of Roman buildings that had been built there many years previously.*

un·crit·ic·al /ˌʌnˈkrɪtɪkl/ *adj.* (*usually disapproving*) not willing or able to criticize sb/sth or to judge whether sb/sth is right or wrong: *Children were considered vulnerable, on account of their uncritical acceptance of advertising claims.* ◇ *Their approach is more emotive, but all too often uncritical and unquestioning.* OPP CRITICAL (2) ■ **un·crit·ic·al·ly** /ˌʌnˈkrɪtɪkli/ *adv.*: *His views have been widely and uncritically accepted.*

un·defined AWL /ˌʌndɪˈfaɪnd/ *adj.* not made clear or definite: *Although the actual boundaries of 'Europe' remain undefined, in theory any 'European' state can apply for membership.*

un·deni·able AWL /ˌʌndɪˈnaɪəbl/ *adj.* true or certain; that cannot be denied: *The examination of resource use is based on the undeniable fact that resources are overstretched and cannot meet all needs.* ◇ **it is ~ that...** *It is undeniable that chronic medical conditions affect many children.* ■ **un·deni·ably** /ˌʌndɪˈnaɪəbli/ *adv.*: *Environmental concerns have undeniably become a worldwide challenge.*

under[1] /ˈʌndə(r)/ *prep.* **1** in, to or through a position that is below sth: *The details of the study are presented in the caption under the figure.* ◇ *The area under the curve represents the heat absorbed in the process.* **2** below the surface of sth; covered by sth: *Groundwater can be found everywhere under the earth's surface, even under the driest deserts.* **3** less than; younger than: *More than two thirds of all Americans earned under $10 000 a year by the end of the sixties.* ◇ *In 2008, women occupied just under 10% of the board seats available on the top 300 European companies.* ◇ *As early as 1995, the Hong Kong government prohibited tobacco sales to youths under 18 years of age.* **4** used to say who or what controls, governs or manages sb/sth: *Five of the companies still remain under government control.* ◇ *In 1949, the thirty-year-long Chinese civil war ended in victory for the communists under Mao Zedong.* ◇ *Under communism, individuals were not permitted to accumulate financial assets.* **5** according to an agreement, a law or a system: *The government loyally fulfilled its obligations under the agreement.* ◇ *Identical packaging for tobacco and non-tobacco products is banned under existing legislation.* **6** experiencing a particular process: *By 2001 there were ten high-rise buildings still under construction.* ◇ *The period under study is 1970–2000.* ◇ *The nature of the processes is currently under investigation.* **7** affected by sth: *Driving under the influence of alcohol can have potentially fatal consequences.* ◇ *Under conditions of exceptionally heavy labour, both male and female workers need an additional 450 calories.* ◇ *The government finds itself under increasing pressure to demonstrate progress in the provision of educational services.* **8** using a particular name: *Mary Ann Evans published her novels under the name 'George Eliot' precisely in order to conceal her true identity.* **9** found in a particular part of a book, list, etc: *The forces involved can be described under the following categories:...* ◇ *The report includes several different items under the heading 'Standards of Care'.*

under[2] /ˈʌndə(r)/ *adv.* **1** below sth: *A clear height of 41 m was specified for the bridge to allow ships to pass under.* **2** less; younger: *Over 50% of current smokers in the survey had started smoking at age 13 or under.*

under·devel·oped /ˌʌndədɪˈveləpt; *NAmE* ˌʌndərdɪˈveləpt/ *adj.* **1** (of a country, society, etc.) having few industries and a low standard of living: *Parasites remain major causes of mortality, particularly in underdeveloped regions of the world.* ◇ *There are many examples of countries that remain underdeveloped in spite of natural advantages.* HELP **Developing** country is now the usual expression. ➲ *compare* DEVELOPED (1), DEVELOPING (1) **2** not fully developed: *The community services are underfunded and underdeveloped.* ➲ *compare* DEVELOPED (2), DEVELOPING (2) ■ **under·devel·op·ment** *noun* [U] *The causes of conflict are often related to poverty and underdevelopment.*

under·esti·mate AWL /ˌʌndərˈestɪmeɪt/ *verb* **1** to think or guess that the amount, cost, size or importance of sth is smaller or less than it really is: **~ sth** *The table* *seriously underestimates the actual transport costs of international trade.* ◇ *Emergency care staff often underestimate the importance of wound cleansing.* ◇ **~ how/what, etc...** *They underestimated how difficult it would be to create the necessary institutions for the effective functioning of a market economy.* OPP OVERESTIMATE **2 ~ sb/sth** to not realize how good, strong, determined, etc. sb/sth really is: *The resources of the local library and its librarians should not be underestimated.* OPP OVERESTIMATE ■ **under·esti·mate** /ˌʌndərˈestɪmət/ *noun* **~ (of sth)** *This figure is likely to be a considerable underestimate of current costs.* **under·esti·ma·tion** /ˌʌndərˈestɪˈmeɪʃn/ *noun* [U, C] **~ (of sth)** *This led to serious underestimation of costs.*

under·go AWL /ˌʌndəˈɡəʊ; *NAmE* ˌʌndərˈɡoʊ/ *verb* (**under·goes** /ˌʌndəˈɡəʊz; *NAmE* ˌʌndərˈɡoʊz/, **under·went** /ˌʌndəˈwent; *NAmE* ˌʌndərˈwent/, **under·gone** /ˌʌndəˈɡɒn; *NAmE* ˌʌndərˈɡɔːn; ˌʌndərˈɡɑːn/) **~ sth** to experience sth, especially a change or sth unpleasant: *Any economic system will undergo further change in the future.* ◇ *Soon after its creation, the organization underwent a process of rapid expansion.* ◇ *Children undergoing eye surgery will nearly always require general anaesthesia.*

under·gradu·ate /ˌʌndəˈɡrædʒuət; *NAmE* ˌʌndərˈɡrædʒuət/ *noun* a university or college student who is studying for their first degree: *She read the book as an undergraduate at Oxford.* ◇ **+ noun** *All participants were first-year undergraduate students.* ➲ *compare* GRADUATE[1]

under·ground *adj.* /ˌʌndəˈɡraʊnd; *NAmE* ˌʌndərˈɡraʊnd/ [only before noun] **1** under the surface of the ground: *Acid producers can cause considerable damage to underground concrete pipes.* ◇ *Crowding increased in underground trains but fell in commuter trains.* **2** operating secretly and often illegally, especially against a government: *The explosion was carried out by a group of underground anarchists.* ◇ *An underground counterculture flourished, challenging traditional social and moral values.* ■ **under·ground** *adv.*: *The carbon dioxide may be stored underground as waste material.* ◇ *Tens of thousands were arrested, with thousands more fleeing the country or going underground.*

under·lie AWL /ˌʌndəˈlaɪ; *NAmE* ˌʌndərˈlaɪ/ *verb* (**under·lying**, **under·lay** /ˌʌndəˈleɪ; *NAmE* ˌʌndərˈleɪ/, **under·lain** /ˌʌndəˈleɪn; *NAmE* ˌʌndərˈleɪn/) **1** [no passive] **~ sth** to be the basis or cause of sth: *Similar approaches and assumptions underlie most of the methods.* ◇ *It is now possible to investigate the protein changes that may underlie many diseases.* **2** [usually passive] (of a layer of rock or soil) to lie under sth: **be underlain (by sth)** *About one quarter of the earth's land surface is underlain by permafrost, including over half of Canada and Alaska.* ➲ *see also* UNDERLYING

under·line /ˌʌndəˈlaɪn; *NAmE* ˌʌndərˈlaɪn/ (*also* **under·score** *especially in NAmE*) *verb* **1** (of results or evidence) to show that sth is important or true: **~ sth** *The findings underline the importance of more intensive and coordinated research.* ◇ **~ the fact that...** *Our findings underline the fact that disadvantaged populations may be particularly at risk of depressive symptoms.* ◇ **~ how/what, etc...** *The continuing evidence of weak management underlines just how chronic the problems are.* ◇ **~ that...** *The financial crisis underlined that some states suffer the impact of globalization more than others.* **2** (of a person) to emphasize that sth is important or true: **~ sth** *Williams (2001) underlines the importance of emotional and personal closeness at times of vulnerability such as bereavement.* ◇ **be underlined that...** *It must be underlined that the data set was lacking in cultural variables.* **3 ~ sth** to put a line under a word, sentence, etc, especially in order to emphasize it: *Respondents should underline the answer that comes closest to how they have felt in the past 7 days.* ◇ *Segments of the text are underlined and marked with numbers.*

under·lying AWL /ˌʌndəˈlaɪɪŋ; *NAmE* ˌʌndərˈlaɪɪŋ/ *adj.* [only before noun] **1** important in a situation but not always easily noticed or stated clearly: *The analysis is political in that it focuses on the underlying causes of poverty.* ◇ *There was an underlying assumption that all children have friends in their immediate neighbourhood.* **2** forming the basis of sth: *The cost of the treatment generally reflects the costliness of the underlying health care system.* ◇ *The metre is the basic underlying pattern of stressed and unstressed syllables in a line of poetry.* **3** existing under the surface of sth else: *Little attention was paid to the details of the underlying rocks.* ◇ *Ice sheets can protect the underlying land surface from erosion.* ➲ *see also* UNDERLIE

▸ UNDERLYING + NOUN **cause • reason • assumption • principle • idea • motivation • mechanism • problem • disease • condition** *It is important to understand whether the underlying motivation driving behaviour is positive or negative.* | **pattern • system • model** *The ranking of the alternative policy regimes depends on the structure of the underlying analytic model.* | **rock • surface • mantle • structure** *The crust is a thin layer of rocks that have been derived from the underlying mantle.*

under·mine /ˌʌndəˈmaɪn; *NAmE* ˌʌndərˈmaɪn/ *verb* **1 ~ sth** to make sth, especially sb's confidence or authority, gradually weaker or less effective: *An ineffective police response during a disaster can undermine public confidence in the police.* ◇ *Governments also have little incentive to introduce any reforms which might undermine their own authority in office* ◇ *The possibility of bias will undermine the credibility of the study.* ◇ *Market failures may prevent poorer households from contributing to the economy, thereby undermining growth.* **2 ~ sth** to make sth weaker at the base, for example by digging under it: *Seepage of water through foundation rocks beneath a dam can undermine the stability of the dam.*

under·pin /ˌʌndəˈpɪn; *NAmE* ˌʌndərˈpɪn/ *verb* (**-nn-**) to support or form the basis of sth: **~ sth** *The assumptions underpinning this approach have been criticized.* ◇ *Policy was underpinned by a belief in the desirability of free markets.* ◇ *The 'growth ethic' underpins modern capitalist societies.* ◇ **(be) underpinned by sth** *These topics each cover a vast array of practices, underpinned by an extensive body of research.*

under·pin·ning /ˌʌndəˈpɪnɪŋ; *NAmE* ˌʌndərˈpɪnɪŋ/ *noun* [C, U] something, for example a set of ideas, that allows sth to exist or that forms the basis for sth; support for sth: *Much of the research discussed earlier is well done but lacking in strong theoretical underpinnings.* ◇ **~ of sth** *Investigation of the socio-cultural underpinnings of the Nordic economies remains an important focus of current research.* ◇ **~ for sth** *They have invested heavily in education and research—providing the underpinning for industrial innovation.*

under·score /ˌʌndəˈskɔː(r); *NAmE* ˌʌndərˈskɔːr/ *verb* (*especially NAmE*) = UNDERLINE: *Technological advances underscore the importance of lifelong learning, as mastery of technology will never be finite.*

under·stand /ˌʌndəˈstænd; *NAmE* ˌʌndərˈstænd/ *verb* (**under·stood**, **under·stood** /ˌʌndəˈstʊd; *NAmE* ˌʌndərˈstʊd/) (not usually used in the progressive tenses) **1** [T] to know or realize sth, for example what sb/sth is like, how or why people do things, how sth happens or why sth is important: **~ sth** *It is important to understand the nature of existing work practices.* ◇ **~ sb** *A basic knowledge of theories of personality will help health professionals to understand individual patients.* ◇ **~ sth + adv./prep.** *The underlying mechanism is not fully understood.* ◇ **~ sth about sth** *More needs to be understood about the exact role of such proteins.* ◇ **~ what/how, etc...** *Employees need to understand*

U

what constitutes a mistake. ◇ **~ that...** *The company understood that having high visibility for its brand was crucial to its success.* ◇ **be understood as sth** *Strategic management is increasingly understood as the task of the top management team.* ◇ **it is understood that...** *It is understood that these classifications should not be too rigidly applied.* ◇ **it is not understood what/why, etc...** *It is not fully understood what causes this imbalance.* **2** [T, I] to know or realize the meaning of words, a language, what sb says, etc: *The students did not understand, and so the teacher gave them the translation.* ◇ **~ sth** *Most of them did not understand the meaning of the word.* ◇ **~ sb** *Many participants complained that they could not understand him.* ◇ **~ what...** *Although most people have heard these terms, they may not really understand what the words mean.* ◇ **be understood to do sth** *'Ideal' in this sense is understood to mean 'most efficient'.*

under·stand·able /ˌʌndəˈstændəbl; *NAmE* ˌʌndərˈstændəbl/ *adj.* **1** (of behaviour, feelings or reactions) seeming normal and reasonable in a particular situation SYN NATURAL (2): *Her concerns—while understandable in the light of earlier failures—proved unfounded.* ◇ *The justice system, for understandable reasons, had difficulties processing the numbers involved.* ◇ **it is ~ that...** *It is understandable that most people reach the end of the training with a feeling of relief.* **2** (of language, documents, etc.) easy to understand SYN COMPREHENSIBLE: *The authors tried to generate applicable and understandable guidelines.* ◇ **~ to sb** *The resources are accessibly written and easily understandable to non-economists.*

under·stand·ably /ˌʌndəˈstændəbli; *NAmE* ˌʌndərˈstændəbli/ *adv.* in a way that seems normal and reasonable in a particular situation SYN NATURALLY: *People are understandably reluctant to talk about sensitive personal matters.* ◇ *Most biographies have understandably focused on his eventful political life.* ◇ *Understandably, these emotional reactions are more common in the young than in the old.*

under·stand·ing /ˌʌndəˈstændɪŋ; *NAmE* ˌʌndərˈstændɪŋ/ *noun* **1** [U, C, usually sing.] the fact or state of knowing or realizing sth, for example what sb/sth is like, how or why people do things, how sth happens or why sth is important: *Establishing common ground between the two communicators will aid mutual understanding.* ◇ **~ of sth** *This would allow a better understanding of other flowering plants.* ◇ **~ about sth** *Many partners lack any understanding about their rights in their family home.* ◇ **~ between A and B** *Increased agreement and understanding between patient and provider can lead to better clinical outcomes.* ◇ **towards ... ~ (of sth)** *This is another step towards greater understanding of the process.* ◇ **beyond ~** *Before these techniques became available, these phenomena were beyond understanding.* ◇ **without... ~ (of sth)** *Without an understanding of electromagnetics, there would be no televisions, telephones or computers.* **2** [U] kindness and sympathy, often towards sb who has different views or who has behaved badly: *These students need extra support, empathy and understanding.* **3** [C, usually sing.] an agreement, often not written in a contract, that people will help each other or that sth will happen in a particular way: **~ (of sth)** *They seemed to be coming to a tacit understanding of the rules of the game.* ◇ **~ between A and B** *There was a fundamental understanding between the shareholders which formed the basis of their association.* ◇ **on the ~ that...** *The family house was put in the father's name on the understanding that it would be held for the daughter's benefit.* **4** [U, C] **~ (of sth) (is that...)** the particular way in which sb understands sth: *The current understanding is that academic investigation does not fall within the provisions of the Act.* ◇ *Each of these approaches has different understandings of power.*

U

▸ ADJECTIVE + UNDERSTANDING **good • better, improved • greater • clear • sound, proper • accurate • thorough, full, comprehensive, complete • detailed, in-depth • deep • nuanced, sophisticated • limited, poor • sufficient, adequate • basic, fundamental, broad • intuitive • shared, mutual, common** *There was a clear understanding of the need for a given individual to support the needs of others.* | **popular • general • theoretical • conceptual • critical • conventional • contextual • contemporary, current • historical • sociological • scientific • mechanistic** *Both acknowledged the need for a more sophisticated theoretical understanding of regimes.*

▸ VERB + UNDERSTANDING **require, need • have • lack • gain, achieve, reach, arrive at, get, acquire • demonstrate, convey • share • aid, facilitate, promote, foster, enable, build, provide, yield, allow, lead to • enrich, deepen, enhance, improve, develop, broaden • reinforce, expand, extend, increase, add to, contribute to, further, advance • inform, shape, refine, clarify, illuminate • check • challenge • revolutionize, transform** *Gaining some understanding of these factors helps clients to recognize why treatment is not progressing as they would like.* ◇ *Other societies do not share this understanding of justice.*

under·stood *past tense, past part. of* UNDERSTAND

under·take AWL /ˌʌndəˈteɪk; *NAmE* ˌʌndərˈteɪk/ *verb* (**under·took** /ˌʌndəˈtʊk; *NAmE* ˌʌndərˈtʊk/, **under·taken** /ˌʌndəˈteɪkən; *NAmE* ˌʌndərˈteɪkən/) **1 ~ sth** to make yourself responsible for sth and start doing it: *Morris (2001) undertook an analysis of research trends during the 1990s.* ◇ *A research study was undertaken to understand better the role of the imagination in thinking.* ◇ *The buyer actually undertakes the task of buying a product by going into the shop or ordering online.* ➲ thesaurus note *at* CARRY **2** to agree or promise that you will do sth: **~ to do sth** *A gas supply agreement is a purchase agreement under which a customer undertakes to pay the purchase price.* ◇ **~ that...** *They undertook that the company should be compensated.*

▸ UNDERTAKE + NOUN **study • research • investigation • experiment • work • task • project, initiative • programme • analysis • assessment, evaluation • review • survey • activity • action • effort • training • investment • reform** *Geological collections are capable of saying much about how geological investigations were undertaken in the past.*

under·tak·ing AWL /ˌʌndəˈteɪkɪŋ; *NAmE* ˌʌndərˈteɪkɪŋ/ *noun* **1** a task or project, especially one that is important and/or difficult: *Diabetes screening will be a huge undertaking for most health care systems.* ◇ *Lobbying is a complex undertaking that often requires the right connections to people in high places.* **2** an agreement or promise to do sth: *The case was resolved by accepting undertakings from the doctor concerned.* ◇ **~ to do sth** *The Romanian government made an undertaking not to increase royalties again until 2014.* ◇ **~ that...** *The government gave an undertaking that no one would be convicted retroactively under the legislation.* **3** (*law*) a company or business: *A trademark is defined as any sign that can be represented graphically and that is capable of distinguishing goods or services of one undertaking from those of other undertakings.*

under·value /ˌʌndəˈvæljuː; *NAmE* ˌʌndərˈvæljuː/ *verb* [usually passive] to not recognize how good, valuable or important sb/sth really is: **be undervalued** *The currency was undervalued by nearly 54 per cent.*

under·weight /ˌʌndəˈweɪt; *NAmE* ˌʌndərˈweɪt/ *adj.* (especially of a person) weighing less than the normal or expected weight: *The prevalence of underweight children below 5 years of age was 27% for all developing countries.* OPP OVERWEIGHT ■ **under·weight** *noun*: *It was suggested that low birth weight and subsequent underweight in* *infancy are related to an increased risk of a number of chronic diseases in adulthood.*

under·went *past tense of* UNDERGO

un·desir·able /ˌʌndɪˈzaɪərəbl/ *adj.* not wanted or approved of; likely to cause trouble or problems: *Two policy recommendations are proposed to avoid or reduce undesirable social consequences.* ◇ *One of the objections against increased aspirin use is the undesirable effects of the medicine.* OPP DESIRABLE

un·dif·fer·en·ti·ated /ˌʌndɪfəˈrenʃieɪtɪd/ *adj.* having parts that you cannot distinguish between; not split into different parts or sections: *Blastomas are rare cancers of immature undifferentiated cells.*

un·dis·turbed /ˌʌndɪˈstɜːbd; *NAmE* ˌʌndɪˈstɜːrbd/ *adj.* **1** (of a place) not having been changed in the way that other places have been changed: *Red squirrel densities in undisturbed habitats, away from the trails, are higher than those in disturbed habitats.* ◇ **~ by sb** *The field has been largely undisturbed by humans.* OPP DISTURBED (2) **2** [not usually before noun] not moved or touched by anyone or anything SYN UNTOUCHED: *Nestor's palace had lain undisturbed since its destruction around 1200 BCE.* **3** not interrupted by anyone: *During each interview, the researcher tried to create an environment that was as calm and undisturbed as possible.* **4** [not usually before noun] **~ (by sth)** not affected or upset by sth: *He was undisturbed by the rejection of his theory.*

un·docu·ment·ed /ˌʌnˈdɒkjumentɪd; *NAmE* ˌʌnˈdɑːkjumentɪd/ *adj.* **1** not having the necessary documents, especially permission to live and work in a foreign country: *Undocumented migrants have access to only basic medical services.* **2** not supported by written evidence: *Unfortunately, many of these initiatives have gone undocumented.*

undue /ˌʌnˈdjuː; *NAmE* ˌʌnˈduː/ *adj.* [only before noun] more than is reasonable or necessary SYN EXCESSIVE (1): *The court held that there had not been undue delay.* ◇ *Private citizens should be allowed to lead their lives without undue interference from the state.* ⊃ *compare* DUE[1] (2)

un·duly /ˌʌnˈdjuːli; *NAmE* ˌʌnˈduːli/ *adv.* more than is reasonable or necessary SYN EXCESSIVELY, UNNECESSARILY: *Such a view appears unduly restrictive.* ◇ *The court held that she was unduly influenced by her mother.* ⊃ *compare* DULY (1)

un·ease /ʌnˈiːz/ (*also* **un·easi·ness** /ʌnˈiːzinəs/) *noun* [U, sing.] the feeling of being worried or unhappy about sth, especially because of a fear that sth bad may happen or that sth is wrong SYN ANXIETY (1): *They were left with a sense of unease.* ◇ **~ about sth** *These cases prompted unease about the ability of the judicial process to protect individual liberties.* ◇ **~ at/with sth** *Twenty-nine per cent expressed unease at their financial situation.*

un·easy /ʌnˈiːzi/ *adj.* **1** (of a situation or relationship) not settled or relaxed and so likely to change; involving worry or difficulties: *An uneasy compromise has been reached.* ◇ *His relationship with the government was uneasy.* **2** [only before noun] used to describe a mixture of things that do not go well together: *The result is an uneasy mixture of reminiscence and comment.* **3** [not usually before noun] **~ (about sth/about doing sth)** feeling worried or unhappy about sth, especially because of a fear that sth bad may happen or that sth is wrong SYN ANXIOUS (1): *He was clearly uneasy about such new developments.* ■ **un·eas·ily** /ʌnˈiːzɪli/ *adv.*: *A separate north and south coexisted uneasily.* ◇ *His personal life uneasily combined classical aesthetic values and idiosyncratic independence of vision.*

un·employed /ˌʌnɪmˈplɔɪd/ *adj.* without a job, although able to work and actively looking for work: *Unemployed workers and their families often blame political leaders for their distress.* ◇ *50 million are unemployed.* ■ **the un·employed** *noun* [pl.] *The government initiated training programmes for the long-term unemployed.*

un·employ·ment /ˌʌnɪmˈplɔɪmənt/ *noun* [U] **1** the situation in which people do not have jobs but are actively looking for jobs; the number of people who are unemployed in a country or area: *Families move from their country of origin because of unemployment, war and famine.* ◇ *The government wants to try to reduce unemployment further.* ◇ *Unemployment had fallen to less than 2%.* ◇ *These changes coincided with rising unemployment.* ⊃ *compare* EMPLOYMENT (2) **2** the situation of a person not having a job but actively looking for one: *Many young people only experienced unemployment for a short period before going into further education.* ◇ **+ noun** *Some workers were covered by unemployment insurance.* ⊃ *compare* EMPLOYMENT (1)

un·equal /ʌnˈiːkwəl/ *adj.* **1** in which people are treated in different ways or have different advantages in a way that seems unfair: *There has been an unequal distribution of property, privilege and power.* ◇ *Unequal access to childcare is unlikely to be overcome.* ◇ *The distribution of income remains highly unequal.* **2** different in size, amount or degree: *This is not just a problem caused by unequal sample sizes.* ◇ **~ in sth** *The two valves are unequal in size.* ■ **un·equal·ly** /ʌnˈiːkwəli/ *adv.*: *Income is very unequally distributed in these countries.* ◇ *The electron pair is shared unequally by the two atoms.*

un·equivo·cal /ˌʌnɪˈkwɪvəkl/ *adj.* showing or expressing sth very clearly and firmly; leaving no doubt SYN UNAMBIGUOUS: *The warning was clear and unequivocal.* ◇ *There is no unequivocal archaeological evidence for Caesar's invasions.* ■ **un·equivo·cal·ly** /ˌʌnɪˈkwɪvəkəli/ *adv.*: *They stated unequivocally that 'lean production is a superior way for humans to make things'.*

un·eth·ic·al AWL /ʌnˈeθɪkl/ *adj.* not morally acceptable: *Employees must be able to communicate their concerns about illegal or unethical practices.* ◇ *There is a danger that scientists might unwittingly promote technologies that turn out to be unethical.* OPP ETHICAL (2)

un·even /ʌnˈiːvn/ *adj.* **1** not following a regular pattern; not happening at the same rate or having the same quality in all parts SYN IRREGULAR (1): *One should note the uneven pattern of change across developed countries.* ◇ *Economic restructuring continues to contribute to uneven development.* ◇ *Progress was geographically uneven, with some provinces seeing far more rapid reduction in poverty than others.* ◇ *Across the south of England, the Liberal Democrats' performance was uneven.* OPP EVEN[2] (1) **2** organized in a way that is not regular and/or fair SYN UNEQUAL: *Social tension from uneven income distribution is expected to become even more serious with large-scale unemployment.* **3** not level, smooth or flat: *Most ankle injuries occur during sports activities or when walking or running on an uneven surface.* ■ **un·even·ly** *adv.*: *All data indicate that violent crime is unevenly distributed and affects the poor especially.* ◇ *Postmodernism emerged slowly and unevenly in several different places around the world.* **un·even·ness** *noun* [U] *The car tyre bends and distorts to absorb shocks and unevenness on road surfaces.*

un·ex·pect·ed /ˌʌnɪkˈspektɪd/ *adj.* surprising; not expected: *There are several possible explanations for this unexpected finding.* ◇ *Unexpected events can create new opportunities.* ◇ *Often, the results are quite unexpected.* ■ **the un·ex·pect·ed** *noun* [sing.] *The challenge for global marketers is to be ready for the unexpected.* **un·ex·pec·ted·ly** *adv.*: *Inflation is unexpectedly low.* ◇ *Heart attacks occur unexpectedly in most patients.* ⊃ *compare* EXPECT, EXPECTED

un·ex·plained /ˌʌnɪkˈspleɪnd/ *adj.* for which the reason or cause is not known; that has not been explained: *The*

U

reasons for this variation remain unexplained. ◇ *Of course, medically unexplained symptoms may have an organic cause that just has not yet been identified.*

un·ex·plored /ˌʌnɪk'splɔːd; *NAmE* ˌʌnɪk'splɔːrd/ *adj.* **1** (of a country or an area of land) that no one has investigated or put on a map; that has not been EXPLORED: *Large areas of the globe remained unexplored.* ◇ *Forests, especially tropical forests, are major, and largely unexplored, reserves of biodiversity.* **2** (of an area of activity or thought) that has not yet been examined or discussed thoroughly: *Such themes remain unexplored.* ◇ *This is an important contribution to the still relatively unexplored field of Islamic natural philosophy.*

un·fair /ˌʌn'feə(r); *NAmE* ˌʌn'fer/ *adj.* not right or fair according to a set of rules or principles; not treating people equally: *The law was changed to deal with unfair dismissal.* ◇ *The committee found the applicant guilty of attempting to secure an unfair advantage.* ◇ **~ to sb** *This is bad news for the firm and very unfair to the managers concerned.* OPP FAIR[1] ➲ *compare* UNJUST ■ **un·fair·ly** *adv.*: *He had been unfairly dismissed.* ◇ *They felt they were treated unfairly by their bosses.* **un·fair·ness** *noun* [U] **~ (of sth)** *The reform was supposed to address the perceived unfairness of the current system.*

un·famil·iar /ˌʌnfə'mɪliə(r)/ *adj.* **1** that you do not know or recognize: *Some young people resist engaging in unfamiliar social situations.* ◇ **~ to sb** *The target words were unfamiliar to all of the students.* OPP FAMILIAR (2) **2 ~ with sth** not having any knowledge or experience of sth: *Some users were unfamiliar with these concepts.* OPP FAMILIAR (1) ■ **un·famili·ar·ity** /ˌʌnfəˌmɪli'ærəti/ *noun* [U] **~ (with sth)** *Stress is often caused by unfamiliarity with the surroundings.*

un·favour·able (*US* **un·favor·able**) /ʌn'feɪvərəbl/ *adj.* **1** (of conditions or a situation) not good and likely to cause problems or make sth more difficult: *Unfavourable environmental conditions have a major impact on health.* ◇ **~ to sth** *Any delay would be very unfavourable to their relationship.* ◇ **~ for sth** *The initial conditions are unfavourable for communication.* OPP FAVOURABLE (1) **2** showing or causing a bad opinion of sth: *These projects might attract unfavourable media comment.* ◇ *The comparisons cast an unfavourable light on the industry's performance.* OPP FAVOURABLE (2) ■ **un·favour·ably** (*BrE*) (*US* **un·favor·ably**) *adv.*: *Imports are treated unfavourably in comparison with domestic products.* ◇ *The owners reacted unfavourably because of the costs involved.* ◇ *Health and life expectancy compare unfavourably with the rest of the UK.*

U

un·fin·ished /ʌn'fɪnɪʃt/ *adj.* not complete; not finished SYN INCOMPLETE (2): *Many projects remained unfinished when he died in 1962.* ◇ *There is unfinished business in areas such as devolution and the reform of the House of Lords.*

unfit /ʌn'fɪt/ *adj.* **1** not of the necessary standard; not suitable for sth: **~ for sth** *His house was declared unfit for human habitation.* ◇ *The fresh water will become contaminated with salt and will be unfit for drinking.* ◇ **~ to do sth** *The bacteria will make the milk unfit to drink.* OPP FIT[3] (2) **2** (of a person) not capable or suitable, for example because of illness or because of not having the appropriate skills or character: *She was considered by the court to be an unfit mother.* ◇ **~ for sth** *This may provide relief for patients who are unfit for surgery.* ◇ **~ to do sth** *He was subject to a condition rendering him unfit to drive.* OPP FIT[3] (2) **3** (of a person) not in good condition, usually because of lack of exercise: *There is a small group of very elderly or unfit patients who cannot be treated surgically.* OPP FIT[3] (1)

un·fold /ʌn'fəʊld; *NAmE* ʌn'foʊld/ *verb* **1** [I] to gradually happen or be made known: *It is hard to predict how events will unfold.* ◇ *Rather than being told in flashback, the story unfolds entirely in the present.* **2** [I, T] to become open and flat; to spread open or flat sth that has previously been folded: *New leaves unfold in April when 2- or 3-year-old leaves are shed in about 1 month.* ◇ **~ sth** *Subjects then drew one of the pieces of paper from the box and unfolded it.* OPP FOLD[1]

un·fore·seen /ˌʌnfɔː'siːn; *NAmE* ˌʌnfɔːr'siːn/ *adj.* [usually before noun] that you did not expect to happen SYN UNEXPECTED: *This had unforeseen consequences.* ◇ *Similarly, unforeseen events can affect responses.* ➲ *compare* FORESEE

un·for·tu·nate /ʌn'fɔːtʃənət; *NAmE* ʌn'fɔːrtʃənət/ *adj.* **1** if you say that a situation is **unfortunate**, you wish that it had not happened or that it had been different: *The often unfortunate social consequences of economic restructuring are not evident only in more developed world cities.* ◇ **it is ~ that...** *It is unfortunate that some countries with large reserves of oil have not benefited significantly from this resource.* **2** caused by bad luck; having bad luck: *The case involved an unfortunate accident which occurred during a practical joke.* ◇ **~ enough to be/do sth** *You are four times more likely to die if you are unfortunate enough to be the driver of the car colliding with a truck.* OPP FORTUNATE

un·for·tu·nate·ly /ʌn'fɔːtʃənətli; *NAmE* ʌn'fɔːrtʃənətli/ *adv.* used to say that a particular situation or fact makes you sad or disappointed SYN SADLY (1): *Engineers on site checked the stresses but unfortunately made some basic errors.* ◇ *Unfortunately, however, hard empirical evidence to substantiate these claims is still lacking.* OPP FORTUNATELY

un·found·ed AWL /ʌn'faʊndɪd/ *adj.* not based on reason or fact: *They based their predictions on unfounded assumptions.* ◇ *The claim is clearly unfounded.*

un·friend·ly /ʌn'frendli/ *adj.* not kind or pleasant to sb: *Reformers were faced with an increasingly unfriendly political environment.* OPP FRIENDLY

un·happy /ʌn'hæpi/ *adj.* (**un·hap·pier**, **un·happi·est**) (You can also use **more unhappy** and **most unhappy**.) **1** not happy; sad: *Most people feel unhappy from time to time.* ◇ *His early life was largely unhappy.* ◇ *Many individuals were trapped in unhappy marriages.* **2** not pleased or satisfied with sth: *Many unhappy customers do not switch banks because of the perceived costs of doing so.* ◇ **~ with sth** *Many fans were unhappy with the way in which the club was being run.* ◇ **~ about sth** *Some members of the public are unhappy about this arrangement.* **3** [only before noun] unfortunate or not suitable: *Marx asserts that belief in a god is an unhappy by-product of the class struggle.* ■ **un·hap·pi·ness** *noun* [U] *The child shows mounting signs of unhappiness and anxiety.* ◇ **~ with sth** *Many stakeholders expressed their unhappiness with the system.*

un·healthy /ʌn'helθi/ *adj.* **1** harmful to your health; likely to make you ill: *An unhealthy lifestyle has been shown to be related to poorer health status.* ◇ *unhealthy foods/diets/eating* OPP HEALTHY (2) **2** not having good health; showing a lack of good health: *Some families did not feel that their children were obese or unhealthy, and did not feel they needed to change.* ◇ *Her skin looked pale and unhealthy.* OPP HEALTHY (1) **3** (of sb's attitude or behaviour) not normal and likely to be harmful: *They have a rather unhealthy focus on the short-term share price of the company.* OPP HEALTHY (4)

un·help·ful /ʌn'helpfl/ *adj.* not helpful or useful: *While this is factually correct, it is an unhelpful way of framing the issue.* ◇ **~ in (doing) sth** *Plain X-rays are unhelpful in diagnosis of this condition.* OPP HELPFUL ■ **un·help·ful·ly** AWL /ʌn'helpfəli/ *adv.*: *The cause of death was unhelpfully defined as 'convulsions'.*

uni·cel·lu·lar /ˌjuːnɪˈseljələ(r)/ *adj.* [usually before noun] (*biology*) (of a living thing) consisting of only one cell: *These unicellular organisms occur at abundances of 102–104 per ml in the surface waters.* ➲ *compare* MULTICELLULAR

un·iden·ti·fied /ˌʌnaɪˈdentɪfaɪd/ *adj.* not recognized or known; not identified: *One of the aides was shot and killed by two unidentified assailants.*

uni·fi·ca·tion /ˌjuːnɪfɪˈkeɪʃn/ *noun* [U] **1** the act of joining people or countries together: *German unification had macroeconomic implications well beyond its borders.* ◇ **~ of sth** *They are likely to support further unification of the EU.* **2 ~ (of sth)** the fact or process of putting things, especially ideas, together in a good or helpful way: *Strength lies in diversification of activities coupled with unification of values.*

uni·form[1] AWL /ˈjuːnɪfɔːm; *NAmE* ˈjuːnɪfɔːrm/ *adj.* not varying; the same in all parts and at all times: *A uniform distribution would not adequately represent the relationships being modelled.* ◇ *The size and density are fairly uniform.* ◇ **~ throughout/across/over sth** *Culture may not be uniform throughout a large organization.* ◇ **~ in sth** *These agents are not uniform in character.*

uni·form[2] /ˈjuːnɪfɔːm; *NAmE* ˈjuːnɪfɔːrm/ *noun* [C, U] the special set of clothes worn by members of an organization: *He was required to wear a uniform.* ◇ **in (...) ~** *The men were dressed in military uniform.*

uni·form·ity AWL /ˌjuːnɪˈfɔːməti; *NAmE* ˌjuːnɪˈfɔːrməti/ *noun* (*pl.* **-ies**) [U, C] the fact or state of not varying; an example of this: **~ of sth** *Some uniformity of cultural practice is evident.* ◇ **~ (in sth)** *Cooperation is required to ensure uniformity in the application of EU law.* ◇ *These uniformities must be explained primarily in terms of social organization.*

uni·form·ly AWL /ˈjuːnɪfɔːmli; *NAmE* ˈjuːnɪfɔːrmli/ *adv.* in a way that does not vary; in all parts and at all times: *The components are not uniformly distributed.* ◇ *The soil is uniformly poor.*

unify AWL /ˈjuːnɪfaɪ/ *verb* (**uni·fies, uni·fy·ing, uni·fied, uni·fied**) **1 ~ sth** to join people or countries together so that they form a single unit: *He was determined to unify the country by force.* ◇ *This was a means to unify a society divided by ideology, religion and class.* **2 ~ sth (into sth)** to put things, especially ideas, together in a good or helpful way: *The contributors unify the text into a readable, interesting volume.* ◇ *These approaches do have similarities, but are far from constituting a unified field of study.* ◇ *These ideas have no unifying thread binding them together.*

uni·lat·eral /ˌjuːnɪˈlætrəl/ *adj.* **1** [usually before noun] done by one member of a group or organization without the agreement of the other members: *The regime's unilateral declaration of independence was not recognized by the United Nations.* ➲ *compare* BILATERAL (1), MULTILATERAL **2** (*medical*) involving only one side of an organ or the body: *Unilateral headache is more common.* ➲ *compare* BILATERAL (2) ■ **uni·lat·eral·ly** /ˌjuːnɪˈlætrəli/ *adv.*: *Member states cannot act unilaterally.*

un·im·port·ant /ˌʌnɪmˈpɔːtnt; *NAmE* ˌʌnɪmˈpɔːrtnt/ *adj.* not important: *Content validity would be compromised if unimportant variables were included.* ◇ **~ to sb** *Price was relatively unimportant to them as long as they found the right product.* ◇ **~ for sth** *Many psychologists considered personality testing to be unimportant for employment decisions.*

un·in·sured /ˌʌnɪnˈʃʊəd; ˌʌnɪnˈʃɔːd; *NAmE* ˌʌnɪnˈʃʊrd/ *adj.* not having insurance; not covered by insurance: *Hospitalization results in large medical costs for uninsured households.* ◇ *In 2003, 70.3% of the population was still uninsured.*

un·in·tend·ed /ˌʌnɪnˈtendɪd/ *adj.* an **unintended** effect, result or meaning is one that you did not plan or intend to happen: *Another, largely unintended, consequence has been the movement of workers to the private sector.*

un·in·ten·tion·al /ˌʌnɪnˈtenʃənl/ *adj.* [usually before noun] not done deliberately, but happening by accident: *Data for unintentional injuries are limited.* ◇ *Unforeseen or unintentional factors may influence the outcome.* OPP INTENTIONAL ■ **un·in·ten·tion·al·ly** /ˌʌnɪnˈtenʃənəli/ *adv.*: *In many cases, preventative measures are intentionally or unintentionally ignored.*

un·inter·rupt·ed /ˌʌnˌɪntəˈrʌptɪd/ *adj.* not stopped or blocked by anything; continuous and not interrupted: *The power system provides uninterrupted power supply.*

union /ˈjuːniən/ *noun* **1** (*also* ˌ**trade** ˈ**union**) (*BrE also* ˌ**trades** ˈ**union**) (*NAmE also* ˈ**labor union**) [C] an organization of workers, usually in a particular industry, that exists to protect their interests, improve conditions of work, etc: *Some employers have paid relatively high wages in order to dissuade their employees from joining unions.* ◇ *Wherever a majority of a workforce want to be represented by a trade union, management must formally recognize the union.* ◇ **+ noun** *The decline in union membership in the US was especially rapid during the 1980s and 1990s.* ◇ *union members/leaders* **2** [C] a group of states or countries that have the same central government or that agree to work together: *Many countries create a written constitution when several countries unite to form a new union.* ◇ *the countries of the former Soviet Union* ◇ *member countries of the European Union* ➲ *see also* CUSTOMS UNION **3** [U, sing.] the state of being joined together; the act of joining two or more things together: *There is no firm empirical evidence available on how monetary union has affected unemployment in Europe.* ◇ **~ with sth** *He was opposed to closer political or economic union with Europe.* ➲ *see also* MONETARY UNION **4** [C, U] **~ (of A and B)** (*mathematics*) the set that consists of all the elements (and no others) of two or more particular sets; the operation of forming a union: *The set of all humans is the union of the set of all men, the set of all women and the set of all children.*

union·ize (*BrE also* **-ise**) /ˈjuːniənaɪz/ *verb* [T, I] **~ (sth)** to organize people to become members of a trade union; to become a member of a trade union: *Only a portion of the labour force was unionized.* ◇ *South Korean women began to organize labour unions and fight for their rights to unionize.* ■ **union·iza·tion, -isa·tion** /ˌjuːniənaɪˈzeɪʃn; *NAmE* ˌjuːniənəˈzeɪʃn/ *noun* [U] *This chapter will focus on contemporary developments in British industrial relations, such as the decline of unionization.*

unique AWL /juˈniːk/ *adj.* **1** being the only one of their/its kind; different from everyone or everything else: *Each patient is unique and care must be tailored to the individual.* ◇ *Business groups in China have their own unique characteristics, reflecting the socio-economic context of the country.* ◇ **~ among sb/sth** *Birds are unique among vertebrates in that biparental care is the norm.* HELP In general English, **unique** is sometimes used after a word such as 'very' or 'rather', to suggest that sth is very or rather unusual or special: *This is a very unique case.* This use is best avoided in academic writing. **2 ~ to sb/sth** involving one particular person, place or thing: *It was claimed that tool use was unique to humans.* ◇ *Such methods were hardly unique to Africa.* ■ **unique·ly** AWL *adv.*: *He sees human beings as one kind of animal, uniquely capable of rational thought.* ◇ *She is uniquely positioned to tell this story.* ◇ *This was not a uniquely American experience, but a wider phenomenon.* **unique·ness** AWL *noun* [U] **~ (of sth)** *Many families have their own traditions which mark the uniqueness of their way of life and their identity.*

▸ UNIQUE + NOUN **position, situation • circumstances • opportunity • advantage • challenge • solution • insight, perspective • capabilities • contribution • characteristics • character • feature • properties • identity • identifier • data set • set • sequence • combination, mix** *A unique opportunity to test this hypothesis came from the Ariaal of Kenya.*
▸ ADVERB + UNIQUE **not necessarily • hardly • almost • quite, truly** *Wolsey was almost unique in the kingdom as a non-monk heading a monastery (the wealthy St Albans Abbey).*

unit /ˈjuːnɪt/ *noun* **1** a single thing, person or group that is complete by itself but can also form part of sth larger: *A crystal is made up of repeating units called unit cells.* ◇ *Twins may be treated as a unit by their parents.* ◇ **~ of sth** *Sinclair proposed that the basic units of meaning were 'lexical items'.* **2** (*business*) a single item of the type of product that a company sells: *A lower price will mean more units sold.* ◇ **per ~** *The goods were priced at 40p per unit.* ◇ **~ cost** *Investment can be spread over high volumes to reduce the unit cost.* **3** a group of people who work or live together, especially for a particular purpose: *Police and military units were placed on high alert.* **4** a department, especially in a hospital, that provides a particular type of care or treatment: *The patient may need urgent referral to a specialized drug unit.* ◇ *the intensive care/maternity unit* **5** a fixed quantity that is used as a standard measurement: *The signal-to-noise ratio (SNR) of a system is expressed in units called decibels.* ◇ **~ of sth** *He drinks 15 units of alcohol per week.* ◇ *China's unit of currency is the yuan.* **6** a small machine that has a particular purpose or is part of a larger machine: *As an experiment, gas cooking units were activated until high levels of carbon monoxide were produced.* **7** one of the parts into which a TEXTBOOK or a series of lessons is divided: *Each module is divided into four two-page units.*

uni·tary /ˈjuːnətri; *NAmE* ˈjuːnəteri/ *adj.* **1** (of a country or an organization) consisting of a number of areas or groups that are joined together and are controlled by one government or group: *Although the United Kingdom is composed of four nations, it is a unitary state.* **2** single; forming one unit: *Memory is not a unitary phenomenon.*

unite /juˈnaɪt/ *verb* **1** [I] to join together with other people in order to do sth as a group: **~ in (doing) sth** *The provinces united in applying political pressure on the federal government.* ◇ **~ behind sb/sth** *All members should unite behind a common purpose or strategy.* ◇ **~ against sb/sth** *The Athenians and the Spartans united against him.* **2** [T, I] **~ (sb/sth) (with sb/sth)** to make people or things join together to form a unit; to join together: *The EU was intended to unite the peoples of Europe.* ◇ *Britain's borders were consolidated as England absorbed Wales in 1536 and united with Scotland in 1707.* ◇ *Platelets unite to form clots and arrest bleeding.*

U

united /juˈnaɪtɪd/ *adj.* **1** (of countries) joined together as a political unit or by shared aims: *Unlike the United States, however, a united Europe would be multinational.* ◇ **~ by sth** *For centuries, Wales was a country consisting of a number of minor kingdoms united by a common language and culture.* **2** (of people or groups) in agreement and working together: *Participants are united in opposition to the political power of large corporations.* ◇ *The desire for a united church was still strong.*
IDM **a united ˈfront** an appearance of being in agreement: *The EU has some way to go before it can present a united front on these policy areas.*

unity /ˈjuːnəti/ *noun* (*pl.* **-ies**) **1** [U, sing.] the state of being joined together to form one unit; the state of being in agreement and working together: *These nationalist minorities were perceived as a real threat to national unity.* ◇ **~ of sth** *Consistent success generally requires an organizational culture which motivates and creates unity of purpose.* **2** [sing.] a single thing that may consist of a number of different parts: *If society is to exist as a unity, its members must have shared values.* **3** [U] (in art, literature, etc.) the state of looking or being complete in a natural and pleasing way: *The repeated phrase gives the piece unity and cohesion.* ◇ **~ of sth** *By the 1770s, the visual arts had lost the stylistic unity of the baroque period.* **4** [U] (*mathematics*) the number one: *The slope of each dotted line is less than unity.*

uni·vari·ate /juːnɪˈveəriət; *NAmE* juːnɪˈveriət/ *adj.* (*statistics*) involving or depending on only one VARIABLE: *Additional univariate analyses were conducted to summarize demographic characteristics of hospitals and respondents.* ➲ *compare* BIVARIATE, MULTIVARIATE

uni·ver·sal /juːnɪˈvɜːsl; *NAmE* juːnɪˈvɜːrsl/ *adj.* **1** done by or involving all the people in the world or in a particular group: *Universal vaccination programmes are the best way of reducing disease.* ◇ *Fast food has become an almost universal feature of the busy American lifestyle.* ◇ *In the UN system, a set of universal human rights has been legally instituted.* **2** true or right at all times and in all places: *There are few universal truths about business.* ◇ *Realists are sceptical of the idea that universal moral principles exist.* ■ **uni·ver·sal·ity** /juːnɪvɜːˈsæləti; *NAmE* juːnɪvɜːrˈsæləti/ *noun* **~ (of sth)** *The universality of religion suggests that it serves a basic human need.* ◇ *Newton demonstrates the universality of his laws of motion.*

uni·ver·sal·ly /juːnɪˈvɜːsəli; *NAmE* juːnɪˈvɜːrsəli/ *adv.* **1** by everyone: *There is no universally accepted definition of terrorism.* ◇ *It is universally recognized that humans process speech and language in chunks.* **2** everywhere; in every situation: *Information is now universally available.* ◇ *Kant insisted that there is no moral law that is not universally valid.*

uni·verse /ˈjuːnɪvɜːs; *NAmE* ˈjuːnɪvɜːrs/ *noun* **1 the universe** [sing.] the whole of space and everything in it, including the earth, the planets and the stars SYN COSMOS (1): *He believed in a God who created the universe.* **2** [C] a system of stars, planets, etc. in space outside our own: *Our particular universe may be just one of an enormous number of parallel universes.* **3** [sing.] a set of experiences of a particular type: *Ireland and England inhabited different economic universes.*

uni·ver·sity /juːnɪˈvɜːsəti; *NAmE* juːnɪˈvɜːrsəti/ *noun* (*pl.* **-ies**) [C, U] (*abbr.* **Univ.**) an institution at the highest level of education where you can study for a degree or do research: *At many of the leading research universities, the best researchers are also the most dedicated teachers.* ◇ **at ~** (*BrE*) *She recently finished a history degree at university.* ◇ **+ noun** *A university education is considered very important.* ◇ *a university student/graduate/professor/lecturer*

un·just /ˌʌnˈdʒʌst/ *adj.* not deserved or fair SYN UNFAIR: *Discrimination against women is fundamentally unjust.* ◇ *Locke argued that waging an unjust war was a violation of natural law.* OPP JUST[2] (1) ■ **un·just·ly** *adv.*: *The parental right not to be unjustly accused competes with the child's right to protection.*

un·jus·ti·fied AWL /ʌnˈdʒʌstɪfaɪd/ *adj.* not fair or reasonable SYN UNWARRANTED: *National measures should not be used as unjustified barriers to international trade.* ◇ *This view is not entirely unjustified.* OPP JUSTIFIED (2)

un·known[1] /ˌʌnˈnəʊn; *NAmE* ˌʌnˈnoʊn/ *adj.* **1** not known or identified: *The efficacy of the drugs is largely unknown.* ◇ *It is a rare disorder with an unknown cause.* ◇ **~ to sb** *He made collections of flora and fauna previously unknown to science.* **2** (of people) not famous or well known: *He translated a novel by an almost entirely unknown author.* **3** never happening or existing: **(+ adv./prep.)** *The disease was unknown in Europe before the fifteenth century.* ◇ **it is**

~ for sb/sth to do sth *It is almost unknown for a lion to kill one of his own cubs.*
IDM **unknown to sb** without the person mentioned being aware of it: *Unknown to her husband, she gave birth to a girl.*

un·known² /ˌʌnˈnəʊn; *NAmE* ˌʌnˈnoʊn/ *noun* **1 the unknown** [sing.] places or things that are not known about: *The strongest kind of fear is fear of the unknown.* ◇ *Each publisher has its own known readership and few are willing to venture into the unknown.* **2** [C] a person who is not well known: *Without the enormous influence of American culture, Steinbeck would be an unknown.* **3** [C] a fact or an influence that is not known: *There are numerous unknowns that could increase the risk.* **4** [C] (*mathematics*) a quantity that does not have a known value: *In the equation, there are two unknowns, x and y.*

un·law·ful /ʌnˈlɔːfl/ *adj.* not allowed by the law: *The difficulty lies in identifying the unlawful act which causes the death of the victim.* ◇ **it is ~ to do sth** *It is unlawful to be in possession of a controlled drug.* HELP **Unlawful** is usually used when talking about whether a particular act is allowed according to the law, when this might not be immediately obvious. To talk more generally about acts that are not allowed by law, use **illegal**. OPP LAWFUL ■ **un·law·ful·ly** /ʌnˈlɔːfəli/ *adv.*: *She complained of being unlawfully detained.*

un·leash /ʌnˈliːʃ/ *verb* to suddenly let a strong force be felt or have an effect SYN RELEASE¹ (3): **~ sth** *A wave of emigration to central Europe was unleashed.* ◇ **~ sth on/upon sb/sth** *The Education Act of 1988 unleashed the power of market forces on the management of schools.*

un·less /ənˈles/ *conj.* except if (used to give the only situation in which sth will not happen or be true): *These steps are ineffective unless students are inspired and highly motivated to learn.* ◇ *Unless stated otherwise, the source of all data in this chapter is the World Bank Development Indicators CD-ROM 2005.* HELP **Unless** is used to talk about a situation that could happen, or sth that could be true, in the future. If you know that sth has not happened or that sth is not true, use **if... not**: *The accident would not have occurred if the employer had not been negligent.* ➲ *compare* EXCEPT²

un·like /ˌʌnˈlaɪk/ *prep.* **1** in contrast to sb/sth: *Unlike other children, she was rarely allowed to play unsupervised.* ◇ *Nicholas stood firm, unlike his fellow rulers in Austria and Prussia.* **2** different from sb/sth; not similar to sb/sth: *Insects have compound eyes quite unlike our own.* ◇ *Recent scientific findings suggest that fast food creates an addictive effect not unlike that of tobacco.*

un·like·ly /ʌnˈlaɪkli/ *adj.* (**un·like·lier**, **un·likeli·est**) (**more unlikely** and **most unlikely** are the usual forms.) **1** not likely to happen: *The establishment of a European welfare state remains an unlikely prospect.* ◇ *She was advised to return to her GP in the unlikely event that she should experience any further problems.* ◇ **it is ~ that...** *It was unlikely that he would escape prosecution.* ◇ **~ to do sth** *These changes are unlikely to affect who wins at the next election.* OPP LIKELY¹ (1) ➲ *compare* IMPROBABLE **2** [only before noun] not the person, thing or place that you would normally think of or expect: *Coalitions sometimes bring together some unlikely partners.* ◇ *Ideas can come from the most unlikely places.* **3** [only before noun] not likely to be true SYN IMPLAUSIBLE: *Genetic differences seem an unlikely explanation.* ◇ *They state that all craters less than 10 million years old have been found—an unlikely assumption.*

un·lim·it·ed /ʌnˈlɪmɪtɪd/ *adj.* as much or as many as is possible; not limited in any way: *The maximum penalty for the offence is 10 years' imprisonment or an unlimited fine.* ◇ *Markets behave as if fossil fuel resources are unlimited.*

un·load /ˌʌnˈləʊd; *NAmE* ˌʌnˈloʊd/ *verb* [T, I] to remove things from a vehicle or ship after it has taken them somewhere: **~ sth from sth** *Workers refused to unload the cargo from a ship that had just arrived.* ◇ **~ (sth)** *Of course it takes time to load and unload the vehicles.* OPP LOAD² (1)

un·mar·ried /ˌʌnˈmærid/ *adj.* not married SYN SINGLE¹ (3): *A young unmarried couple wanted to rent a flat together.* ◇ *Children could not obtain British citizenship from their father if their parents were unmarried.*

unmet /ˌʌnˈmet/ *adj.* (of needs, demands, etc.) not satisfied: *Nearly 50 per cent of respondents defined innovation as delivering unmet customer needs or finding better ways of doing something.* ◇ *When basic needs such as adequate food and safe water are unmet, earthquake safety can seem like a luxury.*

un·nat·ural /ʌnˈnætʃrəl/ *adj.* **1** different from what is normal or expected, or from what is generally accepted as being right: *These word combinations sound unnatural to native speakers of English.* OPP NATURAL (2), NORMAL¹ (1) **2** different from anything in nature: *This observation task is limited by factors that may create an unnatural environment, such as the video camera.* OPP NATURAL ➲ *compare* ABNORMAL (1), ARTIFICIAL ■ **un·nat·ur·al·ly** /ʌnˈnætʃrəli/ *adv.*: *Typical images produced with 3-D computer graphics still appear unnaturally clean and sharp.*

un·neces·sary /ʌnˈnesəsəri; *NAmE* ʌnˈnesəseri/ *adj.* **1** not needed: *Recent trials have suggested that this practice is unnecessary.* ◇ **it is ~ (for sb) to do sth** *Fast food makes it unnecessary for members of a family to sit down to a meal together.* ◇ **~ for sb/sth** *Special equipment was unnecessary for the tasks we were performing.* OPP NECESSARY (1) **2** more than is needed SYN EXCESSIVE (1), UNJUSTIFIED: *They wanted to avoid causing unnecessary suffering to the animals.* ◇ *Arbitration seeks to resolve disputes without unnecessary delay or expense.* ■ **un·neces·sar·ily** /ˌʌnˈnesəsərəli; *NAmE* ˌʌnˌnesəˈserəli/ *adv.*: *Countries should not implement measures that unnecessarily restrict trade.* ◇ *The approach makes a relatively simple problem unnecessarily complicated.*

un·noticed /ˌʌnˈnəʊtɪst; *NAmE* ˌʌnˈnoʊtɪst/ *adj.* [not before noun] not seen or noticed: *Screening can highlight problems that would otherwise remain unnoticed.* ◇ **go ~** *These subtle expressions of anger may go unnoticed.*

un·ob·served /ˌʌnəbˈzɜːvd; *NAmE* ˌʌnəbˈzɜːrvd/ *adj.* not seen; without being seen: *Several growers stated that monitoring found previously unobserved pests.* ◇ *The later deaths went unobserved and unrecorded.*

un·occu·pied /ˌʌnˈɒkjupaɪd; *NAmE* ˌʌnˈɑːkjupaɪd/ *adj.* (of a building, seat, area, etc.) empty, with no one living there or using it: *The housing units include both occupied and unoccupied dwellings.* ◇ *The birds' territories are grouped in only one part of the habitat, and a large portion of the habitat remains unoccupied.* OPP OCCUPIED (2)

un·offi·cial /ˌʌnəˈfɪʃl/ *adj.* **1** that does not have permission or approval from sb in authority: *The government's claims that it could count on the loyalty of the unions were shattered by the official and unofficial strikes that broke out.* OPP OFFICIAL² (2) **2** that is not part of sb's official business: *It is simplistic to draw sharp lines dividing official and unofficial diplomacy.* OPP OFFICIAL² (1)

un·paid /ˌʌnˈpeɪd/ *adj.* **1** done or taken without payment: *The company offered staff the option of taking unpaid leave or working part-time.* ◇ *Women still undertake the bulk of unpaid domestic work.* OPP PAID¹ (1) **2** not yet paid: *She becomes angry when she finds the electricity stopped because of unpaid bills.* ◇ *Rich investors did not want to have their names associated with unpaid debts.* **3** (of people) not receiving payment for work that they do: *It is argued that voluntary agencies are cheaper, because they use unpaid volunteers.* OPP PAID[1] (2)

un·par·al·leled AWL /ʌn'pærəleld/ *adj.* used to emphasize that sth is bigger, better or worse than anything else like it SYN EXCEPTIONAL (2): *The dawn of the Soviet period offered unparalleled opportunities.* ◇ **~ in sth** *The global oil industry is unparalleled in its geopolitical impact.* ➲ *compare* PARALLEL[3] (1)

un·planned /ˌʌn'plænd/ *adj.* not planned in advance: *Preventing teenage unplanned pregnancies is more complex than simply providing sex education.* ◇ *Groundwater utilization in cities is commonly unplanned and uncontrolled.*

un·pleas·ant /ʌn'pleznt/ *adj.* **1** not pleasant or comfortable: *This drug is expensive and has unpleasant side effects.* ◇ *Employers sometimes 'coerce' employees to resign by making their working lives very unpleasant.* OPP PLEASANT **2** not kind, friendly or polite: *There was some rather unpleasant name-calling.* ◇ *Some fairly unpleasant selfish people seem to suffer no guilt.* ➲ *compare* RUDE (1)

un·popu·lar /ʌn'pɒpjələ(r); *NAmE* ʌn'pɑːpjələr/ *adj.* not liked or enjoyed by a person, a group or people in general: *It is not unusual for politicians to adopt unpopular policies, ignoring community objections.* ◇ *Raising taxes may be politically unpopular and further borrowing may be prohibitively expensive.* ◇ **~ with/among sb** *The idea of water privatization was extraordinarily unpopular with all sections of the public.* OPP POPULAR ■ **un·popu·lar·ity** /ˌʌnˌpɒpju'lærəti; *NAmE* ʌnˌpɑːpju'lærəti/ *noun* [U] *His international image as a flexible, enlightened leader stood in sharp contrast to his growing unpopularity at home.*

un·pre·ced·ent·ed AWL /ʌn'presɪdentɪd/ *adj.* that has never happened, been done or been known before: *The era was one of unprecedented economic growth.* ◇ *The government started to print money on an unprecedented scale.* ■ **un·pre·ced·ent·ed·ly** *adv.*: *London's population swelled to unprecedentedly large numbers.*

un·pre·dict·able AWL /ˌʌnprɪ'dɪktəbl/ *adj.* that cannot be predicted because it changes a lot or depends on too many different things: *Changes in tastes and habits can be totally unpredictable.* ◇ *During these episodes, his behaviour became unpredictable and irrational.* ◇ *Due to unpredictable weather variations, spring was unusually late in 2010.* OPP PREDICTABLE ■ **un·pre·dict·abil·ity** AWL /ˌʌnprɪˌdɪktə'bɪləti/ *noun* [U] **~ (of sth)** *The unpredictability of war requires a quick and relevant response.* **un·pre·dict·ably** *adv.*: *Everything is changing quickly and unpredictably.*

U

un·prob·lem·at·ic /ˌʌnˌprɒblə'mætɪk; *NAmE* ˌʌnˌprɑːblə'mætɪk/ *adj.* not having or causing problems: *The process of incorporating new technologies is regarded as relatively unproblematic.* OPP PROBLEMATIC ■ **un·prob·lem·at·ic·al·ly** /ˌʌnˌprɒblə'mætɪkli; *NAmE* ˌʌnˌprɑːblə'mætɪkli/ *adv.*: *Under this model, the market is treated unproblematically as the mechanism by which to respond both to rights and needs.*

un·pro·duct·ive /ˌʌnprə'dʌktɪv/ *adj.* not producing very much; not producing good results: *Vegetation clearance can quickly turn large areas into unproductive wasteland.* ◇ *The financial crisis was due to excessive investments, many of which turned out to be too optimistic and too unproductive.* OPP PRODUCTIVE

un·pub·lished AWL /ʌn'pʌblɪʃt/ *adj.* (of a piece of writing or information) not made available to the public: *Many unpublished manuscripts were taken from their hiding places and printed.* ◇ *Extrapair males often sired young in nests situated a long way from their own nest (Eikenaar C, unpublished data).* ➲ *compare* PUBLISH

un·quali·fied /ˌʌn'kwɒlɪfaɪd; *NAmE* ˌʌn'kwɑːlɪfaɪd/ *adj.* **1** not having the right knowledge, experience or qualifications to do sth: *Further research should focus on effective methods of working with the traditional healers and unqualified doctors relied upon by so many.* ◇ **~ to do sth** *Candidates who might end up as governors could really be unqualified or unsuitable to head the region.* OPP QUALIFIED (1) **2** /ʌn'kwɒlɪfaɪd; *NAmE* ʌn'kwɑːlɪfaɪd/ [usually before noun] complete; not limited by any negative qualities: *The unqualified enthusiasm that initially greeted the transition to democracy gave way to a more sober appreciation of the problems.* OPP QUALIFIED (3)

un·real·is·tic /ˌʌnrɪə'lɪstɪk; *NAmE* ˌʌnriːə'lɪstɪk/ *adj.* not showing or accepting things as they are: *The authors argue that the claims are highly misleading and give rise to unrealistic public expectations.* ◇ **it is ~ to do sth** *It is unrealistic to assume that national views regarding nuclear weapons will change anytime soon.* OPP REALISTIC ■ **un·real·is·tic·al·ly** *adv.*: *Values over 20 000 were recorded as 20 000 to limit unrealistically high averages.*

un·rea·son·able /ʌn'riːznəbl/ *adj.* not fair, practical or sensible; expecting too much: *There had been unreasonable delays in the appeals process.* ◇ *It is difficult to sit and listen to a child who appears totally unreasonable.* ◇ **it is ~ (for sb) to do sth** *It is not unreasonable to suggest that most European airlines will have a market or markets where they will be dominant.* OPP REASONABLE (1) ■ **un·rea·son·able·ness** *noun* [U] **~ (of sth)** *The unreasonableness of their demands frustrated the government.* **un·rea·son·ably** /ʌn'riːznəbli/ *adv.*: *The Court held that he was not acting unreasonably in refusing to sell his shares.*

un·rec·og·nized (*BrE also* **-ised**) /ʌn'rekəgnaɪzd/ *adj.* **1** that people are not aware of or do not realize is important SYN UNNOTICED: *A previously unrecognized fungal disease has appeared in many different countries around the world and is devastating rice crops.* ◇ **go ~** *The condition is extremely dangerous and can lead to permanent brain damage if symptoms go unrecognized.* **2** (of a person) not having received the admiration they deserve for sth that they have done or achieved: *He was a gifted journalist and unconventional genius whose role has been unrecognized until now.*

un·regu·lated AWL /ˌʌn'regjuleɪtɪd/ *adj.* not controlled by laws or official rules: *The aquarium industry is largely unregulated.* ◇ *We can contrast buyer behaviour in areas with strict licensing with areas where a relatively unregulated market exists.* ➲ *compare* FREE[1] (1), REGULATE (2)

un·re·lated /ˌʌnrɪ'leɪtɪd/ *adj.* **1** not connected; not related to sth else SYN UNCONNECTED: *Drugs may be used for several, sometimes seemingly unrelated, purposes.* ◇ **~ to sth** *The volume of agricultural production is often unrelated to population density.* OPP RELATED (1) **2** (of people, animals, etc.) not belonging to the same family: *Many apparently unrelated people have common ancestors.* OPP RELATED (3)

un·re·li·able AWL /ˌʌnrɪ'laɪəbl/ *adj.* that cannot be trusted or depended on: *This procedure is notoriously unreliable.* ◇ *Decision-makers often rely on inaccurate or unreliable data.* OPP RELIABLE ■ **un·re·li·abil·ity** /ˌʌnrɪˌlaɪə'bɪləti/ *noun* [U] *Oral storytelling is notorious for its unreliability.*

un·re·mark·able /ˌʌnrɪ'mɑːkəbl; *NAmE* ˌʌnrɪ'mɑːrkəbl/ *adj.* ordinary; not special in any way: *The European Court of Justice is located in an unremarkable building in Luxembourg.* OPP REMARKABLE

un·re·solved AWL /ˌʌnrɪ'zɒlvd; *NAmE* ˌʌnrɪ'zɑːlvd; ˌʌnrɪ'zɔːlvd/ *adj.* (of a problem or question) not yet solved or answered; not having been RESOLVED: *Many issues remained unresolved.* ◇ *These unresolved tensions in society reinforce radicalism, violence and dissent.*

un·re·spon·sive AWL /ˌʌnrɪˈspɒnsɪv; *NAmE* ˌʌnrɪˈspɑːnsɪv/ *adj.* not reacting to sb/sth; not giving the response that you would expect or hope for SYN INSENSITIVE (2): *She described him as being 'emotionally unresponsive'.* ◇ **~ to sth** *Personality disorders are generally unresponsive to treatment.* OPP RESPONSIVE

un·rest /ʌnˈrest/ *noun* [U] a situation in which people are angry and likely to protest against the government or their employers SYN DISORDER (2): *Those in power did not want to provoke civil unrest.* ◇ *social/political/industrial/popular unrest*

un·re·strict·ed AWL /ˌʌnrɪˈstrɪktɪd/ *adj.* not controlled or limited in any way SYN UNLIMITED: *Local buyers have unrestricted access to the international market.* OPP RESTRICTED

un·safe /ʌnˈseɪf/ *adj.* **1** (of a thing, a place or an activity) not safe; dangerous: *The fact that a bridge is 'deficient' does not imply that it is likely to collapse or that it is unsafe.* ◇ *Most key actors recognize that widespread unsafe abortion is a serious problem.* OPP SAFE (2) **2** (of people) in danger of being harmed: *The chart shows the share of population feeling unsafe or very unsafe walking alone in their area after dark.* OPP SAFE (1)

un·sat·is·fac·tory /ˌʌnˌsætɪsˈfæktəri/ *adj.* not good enough SYN INADEQUATE (1), UNACCEPTABLE: *Eight schools in the district had low or unsatisfactory performance.* ◇ **it is ~ that...** *It is unsatisfactory that after ten years this conflict remains unresolved.* OPP SATISFACTORY

un·seen /ˌʌnˈsiːn/ *adj.* **1** not previously seen: *The president's popularity plummeted to previously unseen lows.* ◇ *The book contains many hitherto unseen photographs.* **2** that cannot be seen: *The man was shot by an unseen assailant.*

un·skilled /ˌʌnˈskɪld/ *adj.* not having or needing special skills or training: *Food canning was primarily the job of unskilled workers.* ◇ *unskilled labour/jobs/work* OPP SKILLED (2)

un·speci·fied AWL /ˌʌnˈspesɪfaɪd/ *adj.* not stated clearly or exactly; not having been SPECIFIED SYN UNDEFINED (1), UNKNOWN[1] (1): *Donated blood is used for unspecified research purposes.* ◇ *This would take place at some unspecified date in the future.*

un·stable AWL /ʌnˈsteɪbl/ *adj.* **1** likely to change or fail suddenly SYN VOLATILE (2): *The country has continued to be politically unstable.* ◇ *The slopes and cliffs reflect a highly unstable and dynamic landscape.* OPP STABLE (1) **2** (*technical*) (of a substance) not staying in the same chemical or ATOMIC state: *An unstable nucleus with an excess of protons or neutrons emits radiation until a stable ratio occurs.* OPP STABLE (2) **3** (of a person or their behaviour) often having mental problems or sudden changes of mood: *They try to mitigate guilt by claiming to be mentally unstable.* **4** likely to move or fall: *The rear-engined design made the car unstable.* OPP STABLE (3) ⊃ *see also* INSTABILITY

un·struc·tured AWL /ʌnˈstrʌktʃəd; *NAmE* ʌnˈstrʌktʃərd/ *adj.* without structure or organization: *Researchers carried out 73 relatively unstructured interviews.*

un·suc·cess·ful /ˌʌnsəkˈsesfl/ *adj.* not successful; not achieving what you wanted to: *However, the strategy proved unsuccessful.* ◇ *The country has seen a series of unsuccessful coup attempts.* ◇ **~ in (doing) sth** *The USA was unsuccessful in persuading her allies to take a strong line on trade.* OPP SUCCESSFUL (1) ■ **un·suc·cess·ful·ly** /ˌʌnsəkˈsesfəli/ *adv.*: *At least 63% had unsuccessfully tried to quit smoking one or more times.*

un·suit·able /ʌnˈsuːtəbl; *BrE also* ʌnˈsjuːtəbl/ *adj.* not right or appropriate for a particular person, purpose or occasion SYN INAPPROPRIATE: *The school setting may be an unsuitable environment for healthy eating interventions.* ◇ **~ for sb/sth** *This factor makes such soils completely unsuitable for agriculture.* OPP SUITABLE

un·sure /ˌʌnˈʃʊə(r); ˌʌnˈʃɔː(r); *NAmE* ˌʌnˈʃʊr/ *adj.* [not before noun] not certain of sth; having doubts: *The president appeared unsure and indecisive.* ◇ **~ about (doing) sth** *Teachers are often still unsure about using up so much class time on the project.* ◇ **~ of sth** *Students might feel unsure of the arguments Wright is trying to put forward.* ◇ **~ whether/what, etc...** *He became unsure whether what he was doing was legally correct.* ◇ **~ of/as to whether/what, etc...** *They remain unsure of whether they should adopt this controversial technology.*

un·sur·pris·ing /ˌʌnsəˈpraɪzɪŋ; *NAmE* ˌʌnsərˈpraɪzɪŋ/ *adj.* not causing surprise: *This is an unsurprising finding and is due to a number of factors.* ◇ **it is ~ that...** *It is unsurprising that technology is one of the prominent elements associated with globalization.* OPP SURPRISING ■ **un·sur·pris·ing·ly** *adv.*: *Perhaps unsurprisingly, the two methods came up with slightly different conclusions about population structure.*

un·sus·tain·able AWL /ˌʌnsəˈsteɪnəbl/ *adj.* **1** that cannot be continued at the same level or rate: *Government debt reached an unsustainable level.* ◇ *Any improvements have been unsustainable in the long term.* OPP SUSTAINABLE (2) **2** damaging the environment by using up natural resources: *Some unsustainable farming practices were actively encouraged.* OPP SUSTAINABLE (1)

un·think·able /ʌnˈθɪŋkəbl/ *adj.* impossible to imagine or accept SYN INCONCEIVABLE: *War between Member States would be truly unthinkable today.* ◇ **it is ~ (for sb) to do sth** *In some organizations, it is unthinkable for employees to use their full leave entitlement.* ◇ **it is ~ that...** *It was unthinkable that the couple would travel to the UK to stay with his parents.* ■ **the un·think·able** *noun* [sing.] *He believes in having the courage to think the unthinkable.*

until /ənˈtɪl/ *conj., prep.* up to the point in time or the event mentioned: *She remained in hospital for two more days until she had no breathing difficulties.* ◇ *Survey data were not reported until 12–18 months after data collection was complete.* ◇ *The evidence suggests that until 1993 the pace of privatization was more rapid in the service sector.* ◇ *Until now, public sector expenditure on crime and justice has increased in real terms.* ◇ *I shall leave discussion of the details until the next chapter.* HELP In spoken English and informal written English, **till** is sometimes used instead of **until**. However, it is best avoided in more formal academic writing. It is never used at the beginning of a sentence.

U

un·touched /ʌnˈtʌtʃt/ *adj.* [not usually before noun] not affected or changed by sth, especially sth bad or unpleasant; not damaged: *Population settlement left few landscapes untouched.* ◇ *The Management Board was not unhappy, since their power base remained largely untouched.* ◇ **~ by sth** *Few people and places are today completely untouched by economic globalization.*

un·treat·ed /ˌʌnˈtriːtɪd/ *adj.* **1** (of a patient, a disease or a medical condition) not receiving medical treatment: *The poor may resort to self-treatment or may go untreated.* ◇ *The patient's blood pressure is checked, as untreated hypertension will accelerate the course of the disease.* **2** (of substances) not made safe by chemical or other treatment: *The contamination is mainly due to the infiltration of untreated domestic sewage.*

un·true /ʌnˈtruː/ *adj.* not true; not based on facts SYN INCORRECT: *To suggest that a firm conclusion has been reached would be misleading and untrue.*

un·used /ˌʌnˈjuːzd/ *adj.* not being used at the moment; never having been used: *He set up a workshop in an* *unused room of the house.* ◇ *This company can then sell its unused pollution rights to another company.*

un·usual /ʌnˈjuːʒuəl; ʌnˈjuːʒəl/ *adj.* different from what is usual or normal SYN UNCOMMON (1): *There is some evidence to suggest that animals show unusual behaviour before an earthquake.* ◇ *Carbonates have the unusual property of having a solubility which decreases with increasing temperature.* ◇ **it is ~ (for sb/sth) to do sth** *In Denmark, for example, it is unusual for a woman not to work outside the home.* ◇ *Previously, it was not unusual for junior doctors to work a 70-hour week.*

un·usual·ly /ʌnˈjuːʒuəli; ʌnˈjuːʒəli/ *adv.* **1** used before adjectives to emphasize that a particular quality is greater than normal: *Levels of atmospheric CO_2 were unusually high.* ◇ *Unusually hot weather is now recognized as a serious public health threat.* ➲ language bank *at* EXCEPTIONALLY **2** used to say that a particular situation is not normal or expected: *Unusually, the school had not been cleaned that weekend.* ◇ **~ for sb/sth** *The novel was serialized weekly and then, unusually for Dickens, published in three unillustrated volumes.*

un·want·ed /ˌʌnˈwɒntɪd; *NAmE* ˌʌnˈwɑːntɪd; ˌʌnˈwɔːntɪd/ *adj.* that you do not want: *All of the problems mentioned have unwanted effects on the economy.* ◇ *Unwanted pregnancies are associated with anxiety and depression.* ➲ *compare* UNDESIRABLE

un·war·rant·ed /ʌnˈwɒrəntɪd; *NAmE* ʌnˈwɔːrəntɪd; ʌnˈwɑːrəntɪd/ *adj.* not reasonable or necessary; not appropriate SYN UNJUSTIFIED: *There are two main reasons why this assumption may be unwarranted.* ◇ *The press should not make unwarranted intrusions into people's private lives.*

un·wel·come /ʌnˈwelkəm/ *adj.* not wanted: *The consequences, in terms of cutbacks in the future, could be extremely unwelcome and unpopular.* OPP WELCOME[2] (1)

un·well /ʌnˈwel/ *adj.* [not before noun] ill: *Patients who are acutely unwell require immediate hospital admission.* ◇ *She has felt unwell for 5 days and is concerned that her symptoms have not improved.* OPP WELL[2] (1)

un·will·ing /ʌnˈwɪlɪŋ/ *adj.* **1** [not usually before noun] not wanting to do sth and refusing to do it: *A patient may need to be admitted to hospital but be unwilling.* ◇ **~ to do sth** *Workers were unwilling to accept the higher taxes imposed on them.* OPP WILLING **2** [only before noun] not wanting to do or be sth, but forced to by other people SYN RELUCTANT: *She maintained that she was an unwilling partner in the deception.* OPP WILLING ■ **un·will·ing·ly** *adv.*: *Willingly or unwillingly, presidents often find themselves standing at the centre of political storms.* **un·will·ing·ness** *noun* [U, sing.] **~ (of sb) to do sth** *The impact of these measures was limited by the unwillingness of consumers to spend.* ◇ *An unwillingness to use computers might reduce an individual's scope for employment.*

un·wise /ˌʌnˈwaɪz/ *adj.* showing a lack of good judgement: *This proved to be an unwise decision.* ◇ **it is ~ to do sth** *It may be unwise to overstate the role of the monarchy in the UK constitution.* OPP WISE (2) ■ **un·wise·ly** *adv.*: *Unwisely, Bukharin turned to his former opponent Kamenev for support.*

un·writ·ten /ˌʌnˈrɪtn/ *adj.* [usually before noun] **1 ~ rule, law, etc.** known about and accepted even though it has not been made official: *Slaves did not have any legal rights, but there were unwritten rules about how they should be treated.* **2** (*law*) based on past legal decisions and practices rather than on a written document: *The British have taken pride in the flexibility provided by their unwritten constitution.*

up[1] /ʌp/ *adv.* HELP For the special uses of **up** in phrasal verbs, look at the entries for the verbs. For example **break up** is in the phrasal verb section at **break**. **1** towards or in a higher position: *People climbed up on the roofs of buildings to watch.* ◇ *Snowfall increases with altitude and is greatest high up on the glacier.* **2** to or at a higher level: *As the wage rate goes up, employees will put more effort into what they are doing and output per hour will rise.* **3** to the place where sb/sth is: *Campers could drive up to the trunk of a giant redwood, park at will and pitch a tent.* **4** completely or to a large degree: *Long lengths of railway track had been torn up.* ◇ *Not all migrants who arrived in Vienna finished up at the bottom of the pile.* ◇ *Far from blogs being a cheap strategy, they are a very expensive one, in that they eat up time.* **5** (of a period of time) finished; over: *When the year was up, Li Xiucheng again approached the city and attacked.*

IDM **be up to sb** to be sb's duty or responsibility; to be for sb to decide: *Living a healthy lifestyle is not necessarily up to the individual.* **up against sth** (*rather informal*) facing problems or opposition: *Public systems of water supply were up against droughts and scarcities.* ˌ**up and ˈdown 1** in one direction and then in the opposite direction: *There was some movement up and down in both sets of data.* **2** moving upwards and downwards: *In this vertical position, the rib cage has to move up and down.* **up for sth** (*rather informal*) that can be be discussed, sold or considered: *Some procedures and routines are not up for negotiation, however.* ◇ *The authors conclude that market access is up for sale and foreign lobbies are buying it.* **up to sth 1** as far as a particular number, level, etc: *The pain comes on 2–3 hours after a meal and lasts for up to 6–8 hours.* **2** (*also* **up until sth**) not further or later than sth; until sth: *Up to now, however, no studies have addressed this precise question.* ◇ *Because of methodological limitations, we could only use data up until 2002 for North Karelia.* **3** as high or as good as sth: *The 'workers' faculties' (Rabfaks) were intended to bring workers up to the level at which they could enter higher education.* **4** (*also* **up to doing sth**) capable of doing sth: *The realities prove that politics clearly is out of touch and not up to dealing with challenges adequately.* ➲ *more at* POINT[1]

up[2] /ʌp/ *prep.* **1** to or in a higher position somewhere: *The moth climbs up the stigma and applies some pollen.* ◇ *The gods told the old couple to follow them on foot up a nearby mountain.* **2** along or further along a road or path: *They ran for safety as a 'wall of water' advanced up the street.*

IDM **up and down sth 1** in one direction and then in the opposite direction along sth: *Tidal currents are significant, so that the whole water body moves up and down the estuary with the tide.* **2** to a higher level and then to a lower level: *Power and influence were traded up and down the hierarchy at all levels.*

up·bring·ing /ˈʌpbrɪŋɪŋ/ *noun* [sing., U] the way in which a child is cared for and taught how to behave while it is growing up: *Her novels describe a world very different from her own suburban upbringing.*

up·date[1] /ˌʌpˈdeɪt/ *verb* **~ sth** to get or give sb the most recent information about sth; to add the most recent information to sth: *It is important for GPs to regularly update their knowledge and skills.* ◇ *The guidelines had recently been updated to reflect these changes.* ◇ *to update records/information/data* ◇ *an updated version/edition*

up·date[2] /ˈʌpdeɪt/ *noun* **~ (on sth)** a report that gives the most recent information about sth; a new version of sth containing the most recent information: *Relevant information should include an update on the situation of the available drugs, supplies, staff and future plans.* ◇ *It is a challenge to issue regular updates in a field as fast-moving as this.*

up·grade[1] /ˌʌpˈɡreɪd/ *verb* **1** [T, I] to make a piece of machinery, computer system, etc. more powerful and

U

efficient; to buy a better version of a piece of machinery, computer system, etc: **~ sth** *Energy service companies help customers upgrade their facilities and reduce energy costs.* ◇ **~ to sth** *A $700 rebate encouraged more than half of customers to upgrade to the higher-priced model.* **2** [T, I] **~ (sth) (to sth)** to improve sb's skills, qualifications, position, etc: *They offered a range of specialized training programmes designed to allow employees to upgrade their skills.* ◇ *Over time, a number of ship captains upgraded their status to that of merchant.* **3** [T] **~ sth (to sth)** to change an organization or institution to a higher level: *In some countries, three- or four-year colleges have been upgraded to universities.* **4** [T, I] **~ (sth)** to improve the condition of a building, etc. in order to provide a better service: *As important as upgrading the building itself is improving the environmental performance of its heating, lighting and appliances.*

up·grade² /ˈʌpgreɪd/ *noun* [C, U] **1** equipment or software that makes a computer, machine, etc. more efficient, easier to use, etc: *Recent upgrades have made the system much more user-friendly and adaptable.* **2** the act or process of starting to use a new and better piece of equipment, machinery, etc: *The strategy encourages potential motorcycle owners and those ready for an upgrade to purchase pre-owned Honda models.* ◇ *Tsunami warning systems in the Caribbean were planned for upgrade.* **3** a better seat on a plane, room in a hotel, etc. than sb has paid for: *Customers are offered added-value benefits such as quick check-ins, upgrades, discount car hire and hotels, etc.*

up·hold /ʌpˈhəʊld; *NAmE* ʌpˈhoʊld/ *verb* (**up·held, up·held** /ʌpˈheld/) **1 ~ sth** to support sth that you think is right and make sure that it continues to exist: *States are also expected to uphold human rights.* ◇ *The board of trustees should set the organization's strategic direction and uphold its values.* **2 ~ sth** (especially of a court of law) to agree that a previous decision was correct or that a request is reasonable: *The convictions were upheld by the Court of Appeal.* ◇ *The court upheld 12 complaints concerning illegal waste.*

up·land /ˈʌplənd/ *noun* [U] (*also* **uplands** [pl.]) an area of high land that is not near the coast: *Parts of the hilly uplands include fertile soils and provided ideal situations for farming communities.* ■ **up·land** *adj.* [only before noun] *Large tracts of unspoiled upland prairie were turned into pastures for a growing cattle business.* ◇ *upland areas/farms*

up·lift¹ /ˈʌplɪft/ *noun* [U, sing.] **1** an increase or improvement in sth: *With its renewed investment in advertising, the brand saw an immediate uplift in sales.* ◇ *Party membership gave a social uplift that increased men's opportunities.* **2** (*earth science*) an upward movement of part of the earth's surface: *With time, uplift and erosion brought the roof of the chamber closer to the surface.*

up·lift² /ˌʌpˈlɪft/ *verb* [often passive] **~ sth** (*earth science*) to make part of the earth's surface move upwards: *The areas to the east were uplifted along faults.* ◇ *An earthquake in Chile noticeably uplifted the earth.*

up·load /ˌʌpˈləʊd; *NAmE* ˌʌpˈloʊd/ *verb* **~ sth (to/onto sth)** (*computing*) to move data to a larger computer system from a smaller one: *All data were time- and date-stamped and uploaded to a database at the end of the study.* OPP DOWNLOAD¹

upon /əˈpɒn; *NAmE* əˈpɑːn; əˈpɔːn/ *prep.* (*formal*) used in formal contexts instead of 'on': *This decision was based upon two considerations.* ◇ *More than any other country, Japan is dependent upon a liberal world trade order.*

upper /ˈʌpə(r)/ *adj.* [only before noun] **1** located above sth else, especially sth of the same type or the other of a pair: *Figure 13.16 (a) shows the upper part of the body of the robot and figure 13.16 (b) shows the lower part.* ◇ *Soil covers the upper surface of much of the earth and supports plant life.* OPP LOWER¹ (1) **2** at or near the top of sth: *In 1998, the upper age limit for the screening programme was extended to women aged 70–74 years.* ◇ *Seas remaining at the upper end of their temperature range are one cause of coral bleaching.* OPP LOWER¹ (2) ➲ *see also* UPPER CLASS **3** (of a place) located away from the coast, on high ground or towards the north of an area: *This may partially explain the lack of fish in the upper reaches of the river.* ◇ *An occasional narrow sand or shingle beach is found in the upper tidal zone.* OPP LOWER¹ (3)

IDM **gain, get, have, etc. the ˌupper ˈhand** to get an advantage over sb so that you are in control of a particular situation: *Employers generally have the upper hand, but they do not always get what they want.*

the ˌupper ˈclass *noun* [sing.] (*also* **the ˌupper ˈclasses** [pl.]) the groups of people that are considered to have the highest social position and that have more money and/or power than other people in society: *The literature of the Greeks and Romans was generally produced by and for the upper classes.* ➲ *compare* LOWER CLASSES, MIDDLE CLASS, WORKING CLASS ■ **ˌupper ˈclass** *adj.*: *Bourdieu wrote specifically about French middle- and upper-class society.*

up·ris·ing /ˈʌpraɪzɪŋ/ *noun* **~ (against sth)** a situation in which a group of people join together in order to fight against the people who are in power SYN REBELLION (1), REVOLT: *It was the first widespread popular uprising against British rule in colonial America.*

upset¹ /ʌpˈset/ *verb* (**up·set·ting, upset, upset**) **1 ~ sth** to make sth stop working or continuing in the normal way SYN DISRUPT (1): *There is often a reluctance to upset the established order.* ◇ *Ecosystems can be finely balanced and upset by an apparently small change.* **2 ~ sb** to make sb feel unhappy, anxious or angry: *She says she does not like school but cannot identify anything in particular that upsets her while there.*

upset² /ˌʌpˈset/ *adj.* [not before noun] unhappy or disappointed because of sth unpleasant that has happened: **~ about/by sth** *She is upset about the impact of the disease on her life.* ◇ **~ that...** *Ms Baldwin was upset that it had taken them so long to notify her.*

ˌupside ˈdown *adv.* in or into a position in which the top of sth is where the bottom is normally found and the bottom is where the top is normally found: *The test tube is then turned upside down and placed in an open container of mercury.* ■ **ˌupside ˈdown** *adj.*: *It reflects light in such a way that you get an upside-down image.*

IDM **turn sth ˌupside ˈdown** to cause large changes and confusion in a person's life or in society*The world of the seventeenth century had been turned upside down.*

U

upstream /ˌʌpˈstriːm/ *adv.* /ˈʌpstriːm/ *adj.* **1** in or towards a position along a river that is further away from the sea: *As the fish migrate upstream, they develop hooked upper jaws.* ◇ *A pipe connected to the upstream reservoir conducts high-pressure water to the inlet of a hydroturbine.* ◇ **~ of/from sth** *Their usual habitat is upstream of waterfalls.* OPP DOWNSTREAM (1) **2** at an earlier point in a process or series: *Each gene has a promoter and control sites immediately upstream of the transcription starting point.* HELP In economics, **upstream** markets contribute to your supplies and **downstream** markets are the people who use your goods: *Firms have been driven to develop closer relationships with upstream suppliers and downstream customers.* OPP DOWNSTREAM (2)

up·take /ˈʌpteɪk/ *noun* [U, sing.] **1** the process by which sth is taken into a body or system; the rate at which this happens: *Plants can avoid drought stress by maximizing water uptake or minimizing water loss.* ◇ **~ of sth** *Once released, insulin stimulates the uptake of glucose by muscle* *and fat cells.* **2 ~ (of sth)** the use that is made of sth that has become available: *Targeted health promotion in a local area could potentially have a large impact on the uptake of screening.*

ˌup to ˈdate *adj.* **1** having or including the most recent information: *For the first time, any number of staff could access customer data that were completely up to date.* ◇ *It is crucial that all people involved in the strategy process are well informed with accurate and up-to-date information.* ◇ **keep ~ (with sth)** *All scientists are required to keep up to date with advancements in their profession.* ◇ **bring sth/sb ~** *The bibliography has been brought up to date.* **2** modern; including the most recent developments: *Workers are given a programme of continuous training to assist them in adapting to new production processes using up-to-date technology.*

up·ward /ˈʌpwəd; *NAmE* ˈʌpwərd/ *adj.* [only before noun] **1** increasing in amount or price: *In recent years, there has been a clear upward shift in public expenditure.* ◇ *Extracting oil reserves will eventually become more difficult, putting upward pressure on prices.* OPP DOWNWARD **2** pointing towards or facing a higher place or position: *The contaminated soil acted as a waterproof barrier, effectively preventing the upward movement of water.* ◇ *The prospects for upward social mobility through higher education will increase.* OPP DOWNWARD

up·wards /ˈʌpwədz; *NAmE* ˈʌpwərdz/ (*especially BrE*) (*also* **up·ward** *especially in NAmE*) *adv.* **1** towards a higher place or position: *The air and fuel mixture is compressed within the cylinder as the piston moves upwards.* ◇ *The glaciers left behind a terrain that slopes upwards gradually from the lakeshore to a ridge about 50 km inland.* OPP DOWNWARDS **2** towards a higher amount or price: *After a sharp decline between 1947 and 1968, the Gini index has crept steadily upwards.* OPP DOWNWARDS **3 ~ of sth** more than the amount or number mentioned: *There are probably upwards of 10 million species, most not even recorded.*

urban /ˈɜːbən; *NAmE* ˈɜːrbən/ *adj.* [usually before noun] connected with a town or city: *Practical distinctions between rural and urban areas have blurred as they have become more interdependent.* ◇ *China's urban population has grown by 300 million since 1990.* ◇ *Recent urban growth has accompanied an economic transition from agriculture to industry.* ➲ *compare* RURAL

▸ URBAN + NOUN **area • centre • population • resident, dweller • household • community • neighbourhood • space • environment • landscape • setting • life • development • growth • settlement • agglomeration • planning • infrastructure • slum • economy • geography** *These events clearly indicated the vital importance of urban space to political control.* ◇ *Urban development typically requires substantial public investment.*

ur·ban·iza·tion (*BrE also* **-isa·tion**) /ˌɜːbənaɪˈzeɪʃn; *NAmE* ˌɜːrbənəˈzeɪʃn/ *noun* [U] the process by which people move from the country to live and work in towns and cities: *These countries are currently undergoing rapid urbanization.*

ur·ban·ized (*BrE also* **-ised**) /ˈɜːbənaɪzd; *NAmE* ˈɜːrbənaɪzd/ *adj.* **1** (of a country or an area) having a lot of towns and cities rather than countryside: *In the less developed world, Latin America and the Caribbean were already highly urbanized in 2008.* **2** (of people) living and working in towns and cities rather than in the country: *Obesity has increased more dramatically in urbanized populations.*

urge[1] /ɜːdʒ; *NAmE* ɜːrdʒ/ *verb* **1** to advise or try hard to persuade sb to do sth: **~ sb to do sth** *Businesses will urge the government to adopt policies that will raise their own profit rates.* ◇ **~ that...** *Molotov urged that each country present its own needs independently to the United States.* **2 ~ sth (on/upon sb)** to recommend sth strongly: *The researchers urge caution in interpreting these results.* ◇ *On 27 February 1861, the radicals planned a huge demonstration to urge their strategy on the landowners.*

urge[2] /ɜːdʒ; *NAmE* ɜːrdʒ/ *noun* **~ (to do sth)** a strong desire to do sth: *Education is one area where the urge to 'deliver' has led to a culture of targeting.* ◇ *sexual urges*

ur·gent /ˈɜːdʒənt; *NAmE* ˈɜːrdʒənt/ *adj.* **1** that needs to be dealt with or to happen immediately: *Urgent action is needed in all of these areas.* ◇ *There is an urgent need to find new agents to combat disease caused by resistant bacteria.* ◇ *Mrs Harrison will need urgent referral to a neurosurgical unit.* **2** showing that you think that sth needs to be dealt with immediately: *The tone of discussions became more urgent.* ◇ *The poem is both a celebration and a cry of urgent desire.* ■ **ur·gen·cy** /ˈɜːdʒənsi; *NAmE* ˈɜːrdʒənsi/ *noun* [U, sing.] *This research agenda should be approached with urgency.* ◇ *As hostilities resumed in Europe, a renewed sense of urgency gripped military planners.* **ur·gent·ly** /ˈɜːdʒəntli; *NAmE* ˈɜːrdʒəntli/ *adv.*: *An international ban on the mining and use of asbestos is urgently needed.* ◇ *Patients with these signs and symptoms should be referred urgently to cancer specialists.*

urin·ary /ˈjʊərɪnəri; *NAmE* ˈjʊrəneri/ *adj.* [usually before noun] (*medical*) connected with urine or the parts of the body through which it passes: *Most urinary tract infections are easily treated and result in few complications.*

urine /ˈjʊərɪn; ˈjʊəraɪn; *NAmE* ˈjʊrən/ *noun* [U] the waste liquid that collects in the BLADDER and that you pass from your body: *She has not been able to pass any urine for 12 hours.* ◇ **+ noun** *Urine samples may be highly contaminated if they are not collected properly.*

us /əs; *strong form* ʌs/ *pron.* (the object form of *we*) used when the speaker or writer and another or others are the object of a verb or preposition: *They would not tell us who they were.* ◇ *Let us consider the following example:...* ◇ *Most of us get headaches from time to time.*

us·able /ˈjuːzəbl/ *adj.* that can be used; good enough to be used: *All usable data were analysed.* ◇ *A questionnaire was sent to the chairman/CEO of 67 business groups, of which 20 provided usable responses.*

usage /ˈjuːsɪdʒ; ˈjuːzɪdʒ/ *noun* **1** [U] the fact of sth being used; how much sth is used: *Total energy usage was estimated for each farm.* ◇ **~ of sth** *Studies conducted in Denmark and Germany confirmed that the rate of usage of GP services increases with declining social class.* **2** [U, C] the way in which words are used in a language: *In modern common usage an 'entrepreneur' is 'a person who undertakes an enterprise, especially a commercial one'.* ◇ *Usages that are characteristic of a particular dialect have the power of evoking their home contexts.* **3** [C] a custom, practice or habit that people have: *All office holders were required to conform to Anglican usages and beliefs.*

use[1] /juːz/ *verb* (**used, used** /juːzd/) **1** [T] to perform an activity or a task with sth such as an object, a method or particular information: **~ sth** *The methods used by WHO to measure these objectives are detailed in the report (WHO, 2000).* ◇ *Finally, using data from an empirical survey, the relationship between financial and non-financial outcomes is examined.* ◇ **~ sth for (doing) sth** *Conductivity sensors are widely used for monitoring the quality of laboratory water purification systems.* ◇ **~ sth to do sth** *Numerous kinds of statistics are used to measure the effectiveness of evidence-based treatment.* ◇ **~ sth as sth** *Propaganda is used as a tool by leaders to foster the institutions of war.* **2** [T] **~ sth** to say or write particular words or a particular type of language: *There are dozens of studies that have shown that using familiar words in familiar ways helps learning.* ◇ *The two terms are often used interchangeably.* **3** [T] **~ sth** to take a particular amount of sth such as a liquid or substance in order to achieve or make sth: *Major industrial sectors in Japan started to use more energy after 1990.* ◇ *The Boeing 737-800 series aircraft uses much less fuel than the original Boeing 737 of 20 years ago.* **4** [T, I] **~ (sth)** to take illegal drugs: *Almost one third of teens report that they have used illicit drugs.* **5** [T] **~ sb** (*disapproving*) to be kind or friendly to sb with the intention of getting an advantage for yourself from them SYN EXPLOIT (3): *He lacked the education and experience to see through those who, protesting friendship, were merely using him.*

PHR V **ˌuse sth ˈup** to use all of sth so that there is none left: *The bacteria quickly use up the available oxygen to break down the organic material.*

▸ USE + NOUN **method, technique, procedure • approach, strategy • data, information • model • system • test • analysis • measure • tool • technology • criterion • material** *The specific strategies used will be described in the relevant sections below.* | **term, word • name • language** *Arthritis is the name used to describe inflammation of a joint.*

▸ ADVERB + USE | USE + ADVERB **extensively, widely • commonly, frequently • regularly • increasingly • mainly, primarily** *The electron microscope is used extensively in tumour diagnosis.* | **successfully, effectively • routinely** *This approach has been used effectively to perform reverse genetics in mice.*

▸ ADVERB + USE **currently • previously • originally • rarely, seldom • generally • usually, normally** *This Greek term is rarely used today.* | **actually • traditionally • typically** *Calcareous grasslands were traditionally used in agriculture as grazing land, typically for sheep and cows.*

▸ USE + ADVERB **exclusively • repeatedly • correctly, appropriately • instead • elsewhere** *This indicator tends to be used exclusively in economics.* | **interchangeably, synonymously • metaphorically • loosely • correctly** *The two words are often used synonymously.*

THESAURUS

use • employ • draw on/upon • utilize • deploy *verb*
These words all mean to use sth for a particular purpose.

- to use/employ/utilize/deploy sth **in/for/as** sth
- to use/employ/utilize sth **to do** sth
- to use/employ/utilize/deploy a **method/technique/strategy/technology**
- to use/employ/utilize/draw on a **model/approach**
- to use/utilize/draw on (a) **source/data/information**
- to use/utilize/draw on/deploy **resources/skills**
- to **widely/commonly/frequently** use/employ/utilize sth
- to **successfully/effectively** use/deploy sth
- to draw **heavily** on/upon sth

- Of all these words, **use** can be used to talk about the widest range of things, including physical objects, language, methods, information and resources: *Researchers can use computers in order to create models.* ◇ *In open questions, the respondent is allowed to use their own words.*
- **Employ** and **utilize** are more formal words; **employ** is used especially about using particular methods and skills; **utilize** can also be used to talk about making use of resources: *Later sections focus on the methods employed in analysis and research.* ◇ *They need to find ways of utilizing scarce human resources to meet quality standards.*
- **Draw on/upon** is especially used to talk about people using their own experience and knowledge, or the work or results of others: *This chapter draws heavily on the author's personal experience.* ◇ *He draws on the work of several Latin and African philosophers to develop this paradigm...*
- **Deploy** is used to talk about using the resources you have available in the most effective way: *One of the striking things is how differently countries deploy resources.*

use[2] /juːs/ *noun* **1** [U, sing.] the act of using sth; the state of being used: **in ~** *There are many different kinds of mass spectrometry in use in the modern laboratory.* ◇ **~ of sth** *The use of military force was always an option in the case of conflict between national leaders.* ◇ **for ~** *The test is available for general use in clinical situations.* ◇ *Only a limited number of antiviral drugs are suitable for human use.* **2** [C, U] a purpose for which sth is used; a way in which sth is or can be used: *Every word in the dictionary has a use.* ◇ *The range of uses to which animals are put has increased substantially in recent years.* ◇ **~ for sth** *Using computational methods to find new uses for drugs is an important step towards reducing the burden of disease.* ◇ **~ of sth (to do sth)** *The use of rewards to increase student motivation may in effect work against developing intrinsic motivation.* **3** [U] **~ (of sth)** the right or opportunity to use sth, for example sth that belongs to sb else: *The new treaty stated that the Kansa tribe would have use of the Council Grove site forever.* ◇ *A registered trademark provides its owner with exclusive use of the mark.*

IDM **be (of) no ˈuse (to sb)** to be USELESS: *Antibiotics are no use in combating viral infections.* **be of ˈuse (to sb)** to be useful: *The results could be of use in discovering new, positive ways of using interactive and software technologies for children.* **come into ˈuse** to start being used: *The term 'gentrification' only came into use in the early 1960s.* **make ˈuse of sth/sb** to use sth/sb, especially in order to get an advantage: *This initiative led to promising innovations in education that made use of advanced technology.* ◇ *The work makes use of a considerable number of primary sources, both printed and archival.* ◇ *Institutions will want to ensure that they are making an efficient use of their resources.* **put sth to good ˈuse** to be able to use sth for a purpose, and get an advantage from doing so: *Sometimes volunteers simply want a chance to put their talents to good use.*

▸ ADJECTIVE + USE **increasing • widespread, great, extensive • good, effective, efficient** *There are many reasons to favour increasing use of renewable energy (Goodall, 2008).* ◇ *Today, there is greater use of these techniques.* | **common • practical • clinical** *Measurements made under real life conditions are so variable that they have little practical use.*

▸ NOUN + USE **land • water • resource • energy • drug, substance • alcohol • tobacco • Internet • computer • language** *Scientists have expressed growing interest in understanding the effect of historical land use on ecosystem dynamics.*

▸ VERB + USE **include • involve • allow, permit • require • support • limit • increase • promote, encourage • recommend • reduce, restrict** *Prevention of lung cancer will be achieved by reducing tobacco use.*

U

used to[1] /ˈjuːst tə; *before vowels and finally* ˈjuːst tu/ *modal verb* used to say that sth happened continuously or frequently during a period in the past: *Diplomacy used to be called statecraft to emphasize the traditional dominance of states as international actors.* ◇ *In the light of recent evidence, the gulf between ourselves and primates or dolphins may be less absolute than we used to think.*

used to[2] /ˈjuːst tə; *before vowels* ˈjuːst tu/ *adj.* [not before noun] familiar with sth because you do it or experience it often: **~ sth** *During wartime, women had become used to higher wages and greater social freedom.* ◇ **~ doing sth** *Local business customs may present an obstacle to western companies used to doing business along traditional lines.*

use·ful /ˈjuːsfl/ *adj.* helping sb/sth to do or achieve sth: *Further investigations may provide useful information in this case.* ◇ *Comparative studies have proven particularly useful in the south-western United States.* ◇ **~ to do sth** *I found it useful to consider the strengths and weaknesses of the existing strategy.* ◇ **~ to sb** *For education to be valid*

and useful to the learner, it needs to be relevant. ◇ **~ for (doing) sth** *Positron emission tomography is particularly useful for producing images of the brain.*
▸ USEFUL + NOUN **information, data • tool • way • insights • purpose • guide • framework • model • measure, indicator • summary, overview • point • concept • example • source • resource** *This framework offers useful insights which help to explain the sharp rise in oil prices in 2008.*

use·ful·ly /ˈjuːsfəli/ *adv.* in a way that helps sb/sth to do or achieve sth: *Qualitative research methods can be usefully applied in economic analyses.* ◇ *Future research could usefully explore these issues more deeply or more broadly.*

use·ful·ness /ˈjuːsfəlnəs/ *noun* [U] **~ (of sth)** the fact of being useful or possible to use: *There are several factors that limit the usefulness of current results.* ◇ *Karl Marx considered nationalism a characteristic of bourgeois society which had outlived its usefulness.*

use·less /ˈjuːsləs/ *adj.* not useful; not doing or achieving what is needed or wanted: **~ as sth** *For many scientists, the old notion of race had become useless as a classificatory concept.* ◇ **~ for (doing) sth** *Miege, a teacher of French, considered Cotgrave's dictionary useless for pedagogical purposes.* ◇ **it is ~ to do sth** *It is useless, he argued, to attempt to eradicate opinions by means of repression.*

user /ˈjuːzə(r)/ *noun* **1** a person or thing that uses sth: *In 1991, the decision was taken in the United States to allow commercial users to access the Internet.* ◇ *The NHS Constitution sets out rights and responsibilities for staff and health service users (DH, 2009b)* ◇ *Internet/dictionary/language users* ◇ *Most experts now agree that dictionaries should be compiled with the users' needs foremost in mind.* ◇ **~ of sth** *Children and young people are usually among the most enthusiastic users of information and communication technologies.* ◇ **+ noun** *Once the appropriate user groups have been determined, the manager must build a profile of them.* ➲ *see also* END-USER **2** a person who uses illegal drugs: *Drug use has a huge impact on the users' medical, social and economic lives.* ◇ *Intravenous drug users are at high risk of blood-borne infections, for example HIV and hepatitis.*

ˌuser-ˈfriend·ly *adj.* easy for people who are not experts to use or understand: *The service provides its subscribers with a convenient and user-friendly interface for uploading and sharing videos.* ■ **ˌuser-ˈfriendli·ness** *noun* [U] **~ (of sth)** *The user-friendliness of the tool not only depends on structure, layout and language, but also on the support given to users.*

U

usual /ˈjuːʒuəl; ˈjuːʒəl/ *adj.* that happens or is done most of the time or in most cases SYN NORMAL[1] (1): *Patients were asked whether asthma had interfered with their usual daily activities.* ◇ *The usual way in which organizations attempt to manage their relationships with governments is through lobbying.* ◇ **it is ~ (for sb/sth) to do sth** *It was usual for the entire firm to meet once a year for sessions lasting two or three days.* ➲ *compare* UNUSUAL (1)
IDM **as usual** in the same way as what happens most of the time or in most cases: *Thus, as usual in engineering design, a compromise becomes necessary.* ◇ *The USA has largely continued to do business as usual in the other countries of the Middle East.* ◇ *As usual, efforts made by a character to thwart a fated outcome are in vain.*

usu·al·ly /ˈjuːʒuəli; ˈjuːʒəli/ *adv.* in the way that is usual or normal; most often: *Metals in fresh water are usually present in small concentrations.* ◇ *In the Arab world, globalization is usually associated with American economic and cultural dominance.*

uterus /ˈjuːtərəs/ *noun* (*anatomy*) the organ in women and female animals in which babies develop before they are born: *The uterus contracts and the baby positions itself for birth.* ■ **uter·ine** /ˈjuːtəraɪn/ *adj.* [only before noun] *The commonest cause of IVF failure is the inability of the embryo to implant in the uterine wall.*

utili·tar·ian /ˌjuːtɪlɪˈteəriən; *NAmE* ˌjuːtɪlɪˈteriən/ *adj.* **1** (*philosophy*) based on or supporting the ideas of utilitarianism: *Education should not be rushed, Nietsche says, and should not have pragmatic or utilitarian goals.* ◇ *utilitarian reasoning/principles* **2** designed to be useful and practical rather than attractive: *According to Etzioni, a factory is a more extreme example of a utilitarian organization than, say, an architects' firm.*

utili·tar·ian·ism /ˌjuːtɪlɪˈteəriənɪzəm; *NAmE* ˌjuːtɪlɪˈteriənɪzəm/ *noun* [U] (*philosophy*) the belief that the right course of action is the one that will produce the greatest happiness of the greatest number of people: *Utilitarianism is widely used to justify aspects of science and technology where risks are involved.*

util·ity AWL /juːˈtɪləti/ *noun* (*pl.* **-ies**) **1** [U] the quality of being useful SYN USEFULNESS: *The technique has potential diagnostic utility.* ◇ **~ in (doing) sth** *These scales appear to have utility in identifying individuals who may be at risk.* ◇ **~ of (doing) sth** *This work demonstrated the utility of considering specific issues within a general policy area.* **2** [U, C] (*economics, psychology*) a measure of the PREFERENCES of sb between different OUTCOMES, usually used as a MOTIVATION to make choices: *Decisions are based upon the principle of maximizing utility.* ◇ *Individuals will try to choose an alternative that yields them the highest utility.* ◇ **~ of (doing) sth** *The marginal utility of having more children goes from positive to negative.* **3** [C] a service provided for the public, for example an electricity, water or gas supply: *The privatization of public utilities called for a transformation from a bureaucratic to a task-oriented culture.* **4** [C] (*computing*) a piece of computer software that performs a particular task: *This software contains third-party utilities, simulators and documentation.*

util·iza·tion (*BrE also* **-isa·tion**) AWL /ˌjuːtəlaɪˈzeɪʃn; *NAmE* ˌjuːtələˈzeɪʃn/ *noun* [U] the act of making use of sth, especially for a practical purpose: *No significant differences were found between the groups on health care utilization.* ◇ **~ of sth** *The continual increases in global energy demand call for greater utilization of sustainable energy sources.*

util·ize (*BrE also* **-ise**) AWL /ˈjuːtəlaɪz/ *verb* to use sth, especially for a practical purpose: **~ sth** *The present study utilizes data from 18 countries.* ◇ *The economy was not fully utilizing its resources.* ◇ **~ sth in sth** *Wood chips are mainly utilized in the furniture industry and in interior panelling for ceilings, walls and floors.* ◇ **~ sth as sth** *Several centres have initiated clinical trials utilizing stem cells as a treatment for this disease.* ➲ thesaurus note *at* USE[1]

ut·most /ˈʌtməʊst; *NAmE* ˈʌtmoʊst/ *adj.* [only before noun] greatest; most extreme: *Clarity and precision in the law are clearly of the utmost importance.*

utter[1] /ˈʌtə(r)/ *adj.* [only before noun] used to emphasize how complete sth is SYN TOTAL[1] (2): *After the earthquake, he found himself in the midst of utter confusion.* ■ **ut·ter·ly** *adv.*: *Category 5 tornadoes are very rare but utterly devastating.*

utter[2] /ˈʌtə(r)/ *verb* **~ sth** to make a sound with your voice; to say sth: *Before we even utter a word, other people think they know something about us.* ◇ *He never uttered a sound all the time he sat there.*

ut·ter·ance /ˈʌtərəns/ *noun* (*formal*) **1** [C] something that you say: *The early utterances of children growing up bilingually will often contain lexical items from both languages.* **2** [U] **~ (of sth)** the act of expressing sth in words:

The act of promising and the utterance of the promise are one and the same thing.

UV /ˌjuː ˈviː/ *abbr.* ULTRAVIOLET: *Most birds can detect UV light.* ◇ *These detectors were easily damaged by exposure to UV radiation.*

V v

va·cancy /ˈveɪkənsi/ *noun* (*pl.* **-ies**) **1** [C] a job that is available for sb to do: *Finding people to fill vacancies has become a major challenge in some industries.* **2** [C, U] (an) empty space: *The high-energy electron immediately falls back into the vacancy it left behind.*

va·cant /ˈveɪkənt/ *adj.* **1** (of a seat, piece of land, etc.) empty; not being used SYN UNOCCUPIED: *She found a vacant seat and sat down.* ◇ *There is no vacant land in the city.* OPP OCCUPIED (2) **2** (of a job in a company) available for sb to take; not filled: *They provide information on vacant job positions.* ◇ *When the Chair in the Philosophy Department became vacant, the Appointments Committee did nothing for six months.*

vac·ation /vəˈkeɪʃn; veɪˈkeɪʃn/ *noun* **1** [C] (in the UK) one of the periods of time when universities or courts of law are closed; (in the US) one of the periods of time when schools, colleges, universities or courts of law are closed: *The students had a 2-month summer vacation.* **2** [C, U] (*NAmE*) = HOLIDAY (1): *They take a vacation together every summer.* ◇ **on ~** *They are on vacation.*

vac·cin·ate /ˈvæksɪneɪt/ *verb* [often passive] **~ sb (against sth)** to give a person or an animal a vaccine, especially by INJECTING it, in order to protect them against a disease: *US service members were routinely vaccinated against smallpox until 1984.* ➲ *compare* IMMUNIZE ■ **vac·cin·ation** /ˌvæksɪˈneɪʃn/ *noun* [C, U] *Eighty-seven per cent of respondents had received a smallpox vaccination in their lifetime.* ◇ *In 1998, most of the world's population still lived in countries without universal infant vaccination.*

vac·cine /ˈvæksiːn; *NAmE* vækˈsiːn/ *noun* [C, U] a substance that is put into the blood and that protects the body from a disease: *Chen et al. reported that 87% of the children had received three doses of hepatitis B vaccine.* ◇ *to administer/give a vaccine to sb* ◇ **~ against sth** *In Denmark, the live vaccine against smallpox was phased out in the 1970s.*

vac·uum /ˈvækjuəm/ *noun* **1** a space that is completely empty of all substances, including all air or other gas: *In the seventeenth century, it was shown that magnetic effects and light could transmit through a vacuum.* **2** [usually sing.] a situation in which sb/sth is missing or lacking: *The fall of the regime in October 2001 created a governmental and security vacuum.* ◇ *Community organizations evolved to fill the vacuum arising from the failure of the state to fulfil its basic functions.*

IDM **in a ˈvacuum** existing separately from other people, events, etc. when there should be a connection: *Children's education does not take place in a vacuum, and attention must be paid to their medical, emotional and social needs.*

vague /veɪɡ/ *adj.* (**vaguer**, **vaguest**) not having or giving enough information or details about sth: *At the moment, the details of the project remain vague.* ◇ *We have only a vague notion of the numbers of London infants who were involved.* ◇ **~ about sth** *The report was rather vague about what reconciliation might mean in practice.* ■ **vague·ness** *noun* [U] *Dicey considered that the concept remained full of 'vagueness and ambiguity'.* ◇ **~ of sth** *The vagueness of Miller's critical vocabulary can be frustrating.*

vague·ly /ˈveɪɡli/ *adv.* **1** in a way that is not detailed or exact: *The powers of the European Council are only vaguely defined.* ◇ *Early on in the book, the child becomes vaguely aware that something is wrong.* **2** slightly: *The symptoms vaguely resembled those of myocardial infarction.*

valid AWL /ˈvælɪd/ *adj.* **1** based on what is logical or true: *Each party had its own quite valid reasons for its policies.* ◇ *These two options seem equally valid.* ◇ **it is ~ to do sth** *It may not be valid to compare directly the absolute scores of such different groups.* OPP INVALID (1) **2** that is legally or officially acceptable: *The court refused to accept the marriage as valid.* ◇ *In law, such an agreement was never a valid contract.* OPP INVALID (2) ■ **val·id·ly** AWL *adv.*: *The literature shows that Rorschach scales validly identify psychotic diagnoses (Garb, 2000; Archer, 2001).* ◇ *The court found that the couple were validly married.*

> **WORD FAMILY**
> valid *adj.*
> validate *verb*
> validation *noun*
> validity *noun*
> invalid *adj.*
> invalidate *verb*
> invalidation *noun*

val·id·ate AWL /ˈvælɪdeɪt/ *verb* **1 ~ sth** to prove that sth is true or accurate: *In this study, we develop and validate a medication-based risk assessment score.* ◇ **~ sth against sth** *The model predictions were validated against two sets of experimental results.* OPP INVALIDATE (1) ➲ thesaurus note *at* CONFIRM **2 ~ sth** to support or show the value of sth: *The aim of the interviews was to validate female workers' experiences.*

val·id·ation AWL /ˌvælɪˈdeɪʃn/ *noun* [U, C] **1** an act of proving that sth is true or accurate: **~ (of sth)** *Validation of survey data is critical for the methodology to yield sensible results.* ◇ *Another limitation of the study was that analysis was solely from the client perspective, with no independent validations.* ◇ **+ noun** *Both internal and external validation methods were employed.* **2 ~ (of sth)** an act of supporting or showing the value of sth: *Helping children discuss their feelings offers them validation of their feelings.*

val·id·ity AWL /vəˈlɪdəti/ *noun* [U] **1** the state of being logical and true: *Such retrospective reports of injury severity have doubtful validity.* ◇ **~ of sth** *The reliability and validity of this measure were confirmed by later studies.* ◇ *Criteria for assessing the validity of these more uncertain models have been proposed.* ◇ *to examine/challenge/demonstrate/establish the validity of sth* ◇ **~ of doing sth** *Much recent cultural history has questioned the validity of dividing history into well-defined 'periods'.* ◇ **+ noun** *Finally, external validity analyses were conducted on several existing databases.* **2** the state of being legally or officially acceptable: *The regulations had no legal validity in Sweden.* ◇ **~ of sth** *There was a lengthy dispute about the validity of the contract.*

val·ley /ˈvæli/ *noun* an area of low land between hills or mountains, often with a river flowing through it: *The high summer temperatures discouraged settlement in the lowland river valley.* ◇ **+ noun** *Some rift valley floors may fall below sea level, as in the Dead Sea.*

valu·able /ˈvæljuəbl/ *adj.* **1** very useful or important: *Herodotus and Thucydides provide much valuable information on early Athens.* ◇ *Several valuable insights were gained in this rigorous analysis:...* ◇ *The Internet is a valuable resource that has transformed the way in which we conduct business, education and social activities.* ◇ *a valuable tool/asset* ◇ *a valuable contribution to the debate* ◇ **~ for sth** *Museum specimens have proved particularly valuable for DNA analysis.* ◇ **~ to sb/sth** *Both these concepts are valuable to geographers.* ◇ **it is ~ to do sth** *It would be valuable to have more systematic investigation in these areas.* **2** worth a lot of money: *In 1500, only very valuable* *and lightweight goods such as spices and silks were profitable to transport.* OPP WORTHLESS (1) ➲ *compare* INVALUABLE

valu·ation /ˌvæljuˈeɪʃn/ *noun* **1** [C, U] a professional judgement about how much money sth is worth; its estimated value: *Increasingly, managers are replacing their own judgements about likely outcomes with market valuations.* ◇ *Keller (1999) suggests taking a long-term perspective in terms of brand valuation.* ◇ **~ of sth** *The Greek State sold the Cassandra Mines without any independent valuation of the mines' assets.* **2** [U, C] **~ (of sth)** a judgement about how useful or important sth is; its estimated importance: *Fetherstonhaugh et al. (1997) found evidence that our valuation of human lives obeys Weber's Law.* ◇ *Many scholars have challenged traditional valuations of topics suitable for religious study.*

value¹ /ˈvæljuː/ *noun* **1** [U, C] how much sth is worth in money or other goods for which it can be exchanged: **~ (of sth)** *The dollar value of global trade was US$11.8 trillion in 2006.* ◇ *The value of assets began to fall.* ◇ *It seems that such projects increase local property values (Lewis et al., 1999).* ◇ **+ noun** *Increasingly, the service priorities of the highest value customers take precedence.* ➲ *see also* EXPECTED VALUE, FACE VALUE, MARKET VALUE **2** [U] how much sth is worth compared with its price: *Malaysian cars are relatively good value compared with Japanese makes.* **3** [U, sing.] the quality of being useful or important: *This model has some value in terms of predicting the price and output outcome in a given market situation.* ◇ *Relationship development can be the key to delivering superior value to customers.* ◇ *Government statistical agencies place a high value on their independence from any political ideology.* ◇ **~ of sth** *Even these more pessimistic students did not completely dismiss the value of education.* ◇ **of (great/little/no) ~ (to sb)** *It is to be hoped that this work will be of value to future resarchers.* **4** [C] the amount represented by a letter or symbol; a size, number or quantity: *Improvements can be made by increasing the k value.* ◇ *We found that a value equal to 0.3 was optimal.* ◇ *The radial expansion has a minimum value between 20 mm and 40 mm.* ◇ **~ of sth** *Equations for estimating the values of the four indices were developed from empirical data.* ➲ *see also* TRUTH VALUE **5 values** [pl.] beliefs about what is right and wrong and what is important in life: *The partnership was based on shared values.* ◇ *Durkheim considers instruction in moral values essential to the health of any society.* ◇ *Anti-government values, beliefs and rhetoric play a significant role in American politics.* ➲ *see also* VALUE JUDGEMENT
IDM **value for ˈmoney** (*BrE*) used to describe sth that is worth what you pay for it: *There is scope to cut spending on services which do not provide value for money.* ➲ *more at* FACE VALUE

V

▸ ADJECTIVE + VALUE **actual, true, real • high • low** *Russia's rapid privatization programmes sold assets at a small fraction of their actual value.* | **great • intrinsic • added** *Such ethical theories assert that some aspects of Nature have intrinsic value.* ◇ *Efficient service represents added value for the customer.* | **total • average • maximum • minimum • nominal • present** *The total value of world exports in 2007 was US$13 619 billion.* | **economic • commercial** *Women's labour in the household has a genuine economic value.* | **moral • cultural • social • aesthetic** *Many teachers are ill-informed about the family or cultural values of their students' parents.* | **numerical • mean • absolute • large • small • corresponding • expected • possible • typical • missing • predictive • negative • positive** *All parameters were calculated using the mean values from three independent experiments.* | **shared • traditional • core • absolute** *Culturally, East Asia is a region infused with the core values of Confucianism.*

▸ VERB + VALUE **have • reflect • be based on • depend on • derive from • compare** *European maps of the period clearly reflect medieval Christian values.* | **maximize • reduce** *Dyer (1997) examined how firms in a production network could maximize production value.* | **add • enhance • create • generate • give • assess** *The income was used to enhance the recreational value of the park.* ◇ *A number of titrations gave a mean titre value of 20.42 cm³.* | **place • ascribe • attach • demonstrate • recognize • deliver** *A 'Citizen's Income' (Fitzpatrick, 1999) would recognize the value of unpaid work.* | **calculate, determine, find, compute • measure • estimate • assume • specify • assign • choose • obtain • represent • correspond to • exceed • take • substitute • yield** *Kepler took values of planetary radii from the data of Copernicus.*

▸ VALUE + VERB **depend • lie • range, vary • exceed • indicate** *All ratings were scored so that higher values indicated higher ratings of self-worth.*

value² /ˈvæljuː/ *verb* **1** (not used in the progressive tenses) to think that sb/sth is important because of their positive qualities: *Although individuals may claim to value privacy, they frequently appear to do little to protect themselves.* ◇ *The after-sales service was highly valued by customers.* ◇ **~ sb/sth as sth** *For many adolescent males, fighting is valued as a sign of strength and manhood.* ◇ **~ sb/sth for sth** *Deposits of halloysite are valued for use in high-quality ceramics.* **2** [usually passive] **~ sth (at sth)** to decide that sth is worth a particular amount of money: *The trust fund was valued at £100 000.*

ˈvalue judgement (*also* ˈ**value judgment** *especially in NAmE*) *noun* a judgement about how good or important sth is, based on sb's standards, or what they think is important: *Care is needed when making value judgements about the quality of life of older patients.*

ˈvalue system *noun* the ideas about what is morally right or wrong that an individual or group holds: *The world is composed of a multitude of cultures, each with its unique value system.*

valve /vælv/ *noun* **1** a device for controlling the flow of a liquid or gas, letting it move in one direction only: *Current begins to flow through the valve once the grid voltage reaches a certain level.* **2** (*biology*) a structure in the heart or in a VEIN that lets blood flow in one direction only: *The heart valves may become thickened and fail to work properly.*

van·ish /ˈvænɪʃ/ *verb* **1** [I] to stop existing: *Half of all routine steel-making jobs in America vanished between 1974 and 1988.* ◇ *There is a fear that these indigenous languages will vanish.* **2** [I] to disappear suddenly: *Major monasteries of the pre-Viking era vanish from the records in the ninth century.* **3** [I] (*mathematics*) to become zero: *If the force vanishes, so does the acceleration, and the body continues on its way at the same velocity.*

vant·age point /ˈvɑːntɪdʒ pɔɪnt; *NAmE* ˈvæntɪdʒ pɔɪnt/ *noun* [usually sing.] **1** a point in time or a situation from which you consider sth, especially the past: *All writing reflects a particular vantage point and is inevitably marked by its origins.* ◇ **from the ~ of sb/sth** *He analysed Japan's long post-war period from the vantage point of the late 1990s.* **2** a position from which you watch or look at sth: *From a vantage point far above its north pole, the earth would be seen to rotate on its axis in an anti-clockwise fashion.*

va·pour (*US* **vapor**) /ˈveɪpə(r)/ *noun* [U, C] a mass of very small drops of liquid in the air, for example steam: *The amount of warming depends on how much water vapour condenses.* ◇ *Gases and vapours are produced by heating liquids or when working in higher temperatures.*

vari·abil·ity AWL /ˌveəriəˈbɪləti; *NAmE* ˌveriəˈbɪləti; ˌværiəˈbɪləti/ *noun* [U] the fact of sth being likely to vary:

The data show considerable variability. ◇ *We consider the effects of climate variability on ecosystems.* ◇ **~ in sth** *There is wide variability in public preferences across the different policies.* ◇ **~ of sth** *In these areas, the variability of the rainfall is set to increase.*

vari·able[1] AWL /ˈveəriəbl; *NAmE* ˈveriəbl; ˈværiəbl/ *noun* **1** an element or a feature that is likely to vary or change: *It is virtually impossible for any one model to take into account all of the many variables involved.* **2** a property that is measured or observed in an experiment or a study; a property that is adjusted in an experiment: *The key variables in this study are weight, cholesterol measurements and height.* ◇ *The following basic demographic variables were included in the model: gender, age and occupation.* ◇ **~ of sth** *Age is an important explanatory variable of diverse consumption patterns and is expected to be a strong predictor of ICT ownership and use.* OPP CONSTANT[2] (2) ➲ *see also* CATEGORICAL VARIABLE, CONTINUOUS VARIABLE, CONTROL VARIABLE, DEPENDENT VARIABLE, DUMMY VARIABLE, INDEPENDENT VARIABLE, LATENT VARIABLE, OUTCOME VARIABLE, PREDICTOR VARIABLE, RANDOM VARIABLE **3** (*mathematics*) a quantity in a calculation that can take any of a set of different NUMERICAL values, represented by a symbol such as *x*: *The formulae show how the values of the variables x and y are calculated.*

vari·able[2] AWL /ˈveəriəbl; *NAmE* ˈveriəbl; ˈværiəbl/ *adj.* **1** often changing; likely to change SYN FLUCTUATING: *Variable costs vary according to the number of units of goods made or services sold.* ◇ *While rainfall is highly variable, it is generally distributed across two rainy seasons.* ◇ **~ over sth** *In addition, soil moisture is influenced by precipitation, which is variable over time and space.* OPP CONSTANT[1] (2) **2** not the same in all parts or cases; not having a fixed pattern SYN DIVERSE: *Studies demonstrate variable rates of nitrogen fixation in microbial communities.* ◇ **~ in sth** *Eggs are large and variable in size, depending on the species.* ◇ **~ between/across/among sth** *Preferred habitats are variable between members of the family and range from temporary ponds to large rivers to swamps.* HELP When **variable** is used to describe the quality of sth, the tone is slightly disapproving, meaning that some parts of it are good and some are bad SYN INCONSISTENT (3), MIXED (1): *The quality of the pictures is variable, and some images might better have been omitted.* OPP CONSISTENT (3), UNIFORM[1] **3** that can be changed to meet different needs or suit different conditions: *A variable timer allows for close control of the final concrete temperature.* ◇ *Variable pay is associated with one economic outcome, change in productivity.* OPP FIXED (1) ➲ *compare* INVARIABLE **4** (*mathematics*) (of a quantity) that can take any of a set of different NUMERICAL values, represented by a symbol such as *x*: *In this paper, we study linear fractional differential equations with variable coefficients.*

▸ VARIABLE + NOUN **amount** • **degree** • **rate** • **cost** • **thickness** • **quality** • **environment** *Although of variable quality, the group teaching sessions have been largely relevant and useful.* ◇ *Populations of all sizes may suffer in variable environments, but the implications are far more serious when numbers are low.*

▸ ADVERB + VARIABLE **highly**, **extremely** • **quite** • **continuously** *Mineral waters are extremely variable in composition.* ◇ *Lacking indisputable natural frontiers, the shape and the size of Poland have been continuously variable.*

vari·ably AWL /ˈveəriəbli; *NAmE* ˈveriəbli; ˈværiəbli/ *adv.* **1** in a variety of ways: *The term has been defined and used variably in several disciplines, namely community psychology, health promotion and social planning.* **2** varying in strength or quality: *There are medical treatments and surgical treatments for the condition, which are variably effective.* ➲ *compare* INVARIABLY

vari·ance AWL /ˈveəriəns; *NAmE* ˈveriəns; ˈværiəns/ *noun* [U, C] (*statistics*) a measure of how much variation there is among the values in a set of data, defined as a quantity equal to the square of the STANDARD DEVIATION HELP In statistics, **variance** is one way of describing a **distribution**. It describes how far values lie from the **mean**: **~ (of sth)** *The mean and variance of both distributions are changing through time and are affected by factors such as region and acres planted.* ◇ **~ in sth** *The predictor variables accounted for 11% of the variance in academic achievement (see Table 7.1).* ◇ **~ between/across/among sth** *Analysis of variance was utilized to assess variance between the groups in terms of age and duration of symptoms.* ➲ *see also* ANOVA HELP In non-technical language, **variance** is sometimes used to mean 'the amount by which sth changes or is different from sth else'; this use is best avoided in academic writing: use **variation** instead: *All categories showed significant variation between regions.*

IDM **at ˈvariance (with sb/sth)** disagreeing with or opposing sb/sth: *These findings are at variance with previous research among children in this age group.*

vari·ant AWL /ˈveəriənt; *NAmE* ˈveriənt; ˈværiənt/ *noun* a thing that is a slightly different form or type of sth else SYN VARIATION (3): *A common genetic variant is associated with adult and childhood obesity.* ◇ **~ of sth** *In ancient Rome, a variant of Greek was spoken by many of the occupants.* ◇ **~ on sth** *The film is a variant on the mad scientist genre.* ■ **vari·ant** *adj.*: *Names in Arabic have a number of variant spellings.*

vari·ation AWL /ˌveəriˈeɪʃn; *NAmE* ˌveriˈeɪʃn/ *noun* **1** [C, U] a change or difference, especially in the amount or level of sth, usually within particular limits: **~ (in sth)** *There is a wide variation in the price range between different pharmaceutical brands.* ◇ *The sites were sampled every five days over two separate months to measure seasonal variation.* ◇ **~ of sth** *There is clear evidence emerging that the variation of drug concentration among subjects can be very high.* ◇ **~ between/among sth** *These differences highlight the existence of variations between countries.* **2** [U] (*biology*) the fact of a living thing occurring in more than one different colour or form: *Mutation is the primary source of genetic variation upon which natural selection can act.* ◇ **~ within sth** *Darwin's theory of evolutionary selection holds that variation within species occurs randomly.* ◇ **~ between/among sth** *Preliminary data suggest that there is low variation between individuals.* **3** [C] **~ (on sth)** a thing that is different from other things in the same general group: *The artist's genre scenes are variations on rustic themes first popularized by Pieter Bruegel the elder.*

▸ ADJECTIVE + VARIATION **slight**, **minor** • **subtle** *A slight variation on this approach can be seen in Kitzinger's (1994) study.* | **considerable**, **substantial**, **great** • **significant** • **random** • **natural** *The natural climatic variations make quantitative calculations even more difficult.* | **wide** • **local** • **regional** • **geographical** • **environmental** • **seasonal** • **spatial** • **temporal** • **diurnal** • **climatic** • **cultural** • **systematic** *Regional variations in raw material supply led to rich varieties of papers.* | **genetic** • **phenotypic** • **morphological** • **adaptive** • **heritable** *Random phenotypic variation can protect genotypes from elimination by selection during cycles of environmental change.*

▸ VERB + VARIATION **introduce** *McDonald (2012) introduces a variation on this method.* | **exhibit**, **show**, **display** • **reveal**, **indicate** • **reflect** • **observe**, **find** • **detect** • **measure** • **cause** • **minimize** *Many countries exhibit significant internal variations in mortality patterns.* | **explain** • **examine**, **study** • **ignore** *Our analysis seeks to identify some of the important factors that explain these regional variations.*

▸ VARIATION IN + NOUN **temperature** • **frequency** • **intensity** • **rate** • **ratio** • **size** • **density** • **concentration** •

composition • **pattern** • **quality** • **behaviour** • **climate** *For the oak species, variation in rates of mortality was considerable (Table 3.3).* | **trait** • **phenotype** • **size** • **colour** • **behaviour** *The amount of variation in some critical trait may allow a species to adapt and evolve quickly.*

var·ied AWL /ˈveərid; *NAmE* ˈverid; ˈværid/ *adj.* **1** of many different types; consisting of many different types of sth: *The geology of the island is immensely varied for such a small area.* ◇ *She eats a healthy and varied diet that is rich in vegetables and fruit.* **2** not staying the same, but changing often: *Broadcasting in France had a varied history from the 1920s to the 1970s.*

var·iety /vəˈraɪəti/ *noun* (*pl.* **-ies**) **1** [sing.] **~ (of sth)** a number or range of different things of the same general type: *A single higher organism contains a huge variety of cell types.* ◇ *The authors draw from a wide variety of sources.* ◇ *Vibrations occur for a whole variety of reasons.* **2** [U] the quality of not being the same in all parts or not doing the same thing all the time SYN DIVERSITY: **~ in sth** *There is little variety in their diet and they live mainly on rice.* ◇ *Before 1753 there existed much confusion and variety in practices.* ◇ **~ among sth** *Powell found great variety among the workers he studied.* **3** [C] a type of a thing, for example a plant or language, that is different from others in the same general group: *grape/rice/soybean varieties* ◇ **~ of sth** *Many varieties of English are spoken worldwide.* ◇ *There are more than 100 different varieties of cancer.* HELP In biology, a **variety** is a category below a **species** and **subspecies**, used especially to describe plants.

▸ ADJECTIVE + VARIETY **great** • **considerable** • **infinite**, **endless** • **extraordinary** *The infinite variety of the human condition never ceased to surprise her.* | **wide**, **broad** • **enormous**, **huge** • **bewildering** • **whole** *The word 'normal' can convey a bewildering variety of meanings.*

▸ VERB + VARIETY **cover** • **contain** • **encompass** • **offer** • **produce** • **exhibit** • **employ**, **use** *Greenland et al. (1994) cover a wide variety of potential ecosystem responses.*

▸ VARIETY OF + NOUN **reasons** • **factors** • **ways** • **forms** • **types** • **perspectives** • **disciplines** • **topics** • **settings** • **sources** • **techniques** • **methods** *Behaviour management programmes have been used to help children in a variety of settings.*

vari·ous /ˈveəriəs; *NAmE* ˈveriəs; ˈværiəs/ *adj.* several different: *These events had a profound impact on various aspects of contemporary life.* ◇ *Companies have to implement various types of advertising and promotion strategies.* ◇ *However, the estimates in Table 5.2 may be criticized for various reasons. First,...* ➲ *compare* DIVERSE

V

WHICH WORD?

various • **different**

- **Various** and **different** both mean 'separate and individual': *various/different forms/kinds/parts/types/ways* ◇ *various/different social contexts*
- With **various**, the focus is more on the range of people or things; with **different**, the focus is more on the differences between them: *To date, more than 200 individuals have participated in various aspects of the project.* ◇ *It is obvious that these different aspects of transparency are interrelated.*
- The main meaning of **different** is 'not the same'; **various** is not used with this meaning: *Interacting online produced significantly different results.* ◇ ~~*significantly various results*~~

vari·ous·ly /ˈveəriəsli; *NAmE* ˈveriəsli; ˈværiəsli/ *adv.* in several different ways, usually by several different people: *The flower colour has been variously described as scarlet, red and crimson.* ◇ *Historians have variously interpreted the treaty's importance.*

vary AWL /ˈveəri; *NAmE* ˈveri; ˈværi/ *verb* (**vary·ing**, **var·ied**, **var·ied**) **1** [I] (of a group of similar things) to be different from each other in size, shape, etc: **~ in sth** *These fluid particles can vary greatly in size.* ◇ **~ from... to...** *The age of the participants varied from 18 to 82.* ◇ **~ (in sth) (from... to...)** *There were 150 participants, who varied in age from 18 to 52.* ◇ **~ between/across sb/sth** *We compared how interest rates and investment varied across countries.* ➲ *compare* DIFFER (1), RANGE² (1) **2** [I] to change or be different according to the situation: *Estimates vary because measurement techniques differ from study to study.* ◇ **~ with sth** *The viscosity varies considerably with temperature.* ◇ **~ according to sth** *Treatment varies according to the severity of the disease.* ◇ **~ from A to B** *Pulse rates vary slightly from one person to another.* ◇ **~ between... and...** *The crystal sizes seem to vary between 72 and 278 microns in length.* ◇ **~ over sth** *The growth rates of their populations have varied greatly over time (Figure 2.3).* ◇ **varying degrees of sth** *Different strategies have been tried, with varying degrees of success.* **3** [T] **~ sth** to make changes to sth to make it slightly different: *A wide range of colours can be generated by varying the intensity of the electronic beam.*

WORD FAMILY
vary *verb*
varied *adj.*
variable *adj., noun*
variability *noun*
variation *noun*
various *adj.*
variety *noun*
variant *noun, adj.*
variance *noun*
invariable *adj.*
invariably *adv.*

▸ NOUN + VARY **estimate** • **opinion** • **ratio** • **size** • **rate** • **frequency** • **temperature** *Opinions vary as to the reasons for this increase.* ◇ *Infection rates vary substantially according to geographic region.*

▸ VARY + ADVERB **considerably**, **substantially** • **greatly**, **enormously** • **widely** • **significantly** • **markedly** • **dramatically** • **somewhat** • **slightly** *Countries vary widely in the health of their populations.* | **inversely** • **continuously** • **systematically** • **seasonally** *The cost varies inversely with supply.*

vas·cu·lar /ˈvæskjələ(r)/ *adj.* [usually before noun] (*medical*) connected with or containing VEINS: *90% of patients with vascular disease are smokers.*

vast /vɑːst; *NAmE* væst/ *adj.* extremely large in area, size or amount SYN HUGE: *Vast areas of the world—entire continents—are nuclear-weapon free.* ◇ *The vast majority of Americans believe themselves to be members of the middle class.* ◇ *Many plants produce vast numbers of seeds but only a small fraction will grow to maturity.* ◇ *There is a vast amount of information available on the topic.* ◇ *Yet the problem of poverty was too vast for eighteenth-century governments to solve.* ■ **vast·ness** *noun* [U] **~ (of sth)** *The Sun seems to lead the Earth and other planets in a cosmic dance around the vastness of space.*

vast·ly /ˈvɑːstli; *NAmE* ˈvæstli/ *adv.* very much: *EU member states have vastly different foreign policy capabilities.* ◇ *The invaders were vastly outnumbered by the people they ruled.*

vec·tor /ˈvektə(r)/ *noun* **1** (*mathematics*) a quantity that has both size and direction: *We also calculated the angle between the two vectors.* ➲ *compare* SCALAR **2 ~ (for sth)** (*biology*) an insect or other animal that carries a particular disease from one living thing to another: *Anopheles mosquitoes are vectors for malaria.* **3 ~ (for sth)** (*biology*) a means of carrying a living thing from one environment to another: *Aquaculture is another important vector for the transport of alien marine species.*

vege·table /ˈvedʒtəbl/ *noun* a plant or part of a plant that is eaten as food: *The research focused on leafy green vegetables, in particular lettuce and spinach.* ◇ **+ noun** *Fruit and vegetable consumption in the United States varies among the population partly according to income.* ➲ *compare* ANIMAL, FRUIT (1), MINERAL

vege·ta·tion /ˌvedʒəˈteɪʃn/ *noun* [U] plants in general, especially the plants that are found in a particular area or environment: *Figure A1.6 maps the global distribution of natural vegetation.* ◇ **+ noun** *Industrialization has dramatically reduced vegetation cover and accelerated erosion.*

ve·hicle AWL /ˈviːəkl; *NAmE also* ˈviːhɪkl/ *noun* **1** a thing that is used for transporting people or goods from one place to another, such as a car or TRUCK: *The effects of such drugs can be hazardous for people who drive motor vehicles or operate machines.* ◇ **+ noun** *Vehicle exhaust emissions are an important contributor to photochemical air pollution.* **2** something that can be used to express your ideas or feelings or as a way of achieving sth: *Television became the primary vehicle by which people learned about the world beyond their own experience.* ◇ **~ for (doing) sth** *The arts have often been seen as an important vehicle for facilitating social change.* ◇ **~ of sth** *All three groups of students profiled here viewed schooling as the vehicle of mobility from poverty to success.* **3** a privately controlled company through which an individual or organization conducts a particular kind of business, especially investment: *Most companies offer investment vehicles, such as mutual funds, that are already managed by experienced and qualified money managers.*

vein /veɪn/ *noun* **1** [C] any of the tubes that carry blood from all parts of the body towards the heart: *The stem cells are given back to the patient by infusion into a vein.* ➲ *compare* ARTERY (1) **2** [sing., U] a particular style, manner or point of view: *Subsequent research in this vein has provided mixed findings.* ◇ **in a similar ~** *A landmark study by Kraut et al. (1998) linked heavy Internet use with depression and isolation. In a similar vein, Nie (2000) worried that time spent online undermines social life.* **3** [sing.] **~ (of sth)** an amount of a particular quality or feature in sth: *The poetry of the period provides a rich vein of material for sociological analysis.* **4** [C] a thin layer of minerals or metal contained in rock: *Quartz is the dominant mineral in veins in siliceous rocks.*

vel·ocity /vəˈlɒsəti; *NAmE* vəˈlɑːsəti/ *noun* (*pl.* **-ies**) [U, C] **1** (*technical*) the speed of sth in a particular direction: *Since the car moves with constant velocity, the acceleration over any time interval should be zero.* ◇ *To measure the water velocity, a combined Pitot tube was used.* ◇ *Penetration occurred more often for small masses travelling at high velocities.* **2** (*also* **veˌlocity of circuˈlation**) (*economics*) the rate at which money passes between people, companies, etc. within an economy: *He assumed no international trade effects, an unchanged money supply and a constant velocity of circulation.*

ven·ous /ˈviːnəs/ *adj.* (*medical*) connected with or contained in veins: *If venous pressure is elevated, then look for signs of pulmonary hypertension.*

ven·ti·late /ˈventɪleɪt/ *verb* **1 ~ sth** to allow fresh air to enter and move around a room, building, etc: *The dangers are higher when cooking devices release gases inside poorly ventilated rooms.* **2 ~ sb** (*medical*) to help sb to breathe by sending air in and out of their lungs, especially by using a machine: *Delirium in critically ill patients is a common occurrence (between 60% and 80% of ventilated patients).*

ven·ti·lation /ˌventɪˈleɪʃn/ *noun* [U] **1** the movement of fresh air around a room, building, etc: **+ noun** *Many of the traditional buildings exhibit the use of ventilation shafts to increase air circulation.* **2** (*medical*) the supply of air to sb's lungs, usually by using a machine: *Ventilation is required for patients with airway burns, pulmonary injury or hypoxia.*

ven·tral /ˈventrəl/ *adj.* [only before noun] (*biology*) on or connected with the part of a fish or an animal that is under the fish/animal: *The mouth is always on the ventral side.* ➲ *compare* DORSAL

ven·ture¹ /ˈventʃə(r)/ *noun* a business project or activity, especially one that involves taking risks SYN UNDERTAKING (1): *Hoffmann (2007) analyses how people start new ventures and develop them into high-growth firms.* ➲ *see also* JOINT VENTURE

ven·ture² /ˈventʃə(r)/ *verb* **1** [I] **+ adv./prep.** to go somewhere or do sth even though it involves risks: *During the first half of the fifteenth century, Spanish conquistadors ventured across the Atlantic in search of wealth and glory.* ◇ *After 2005, the company decided to venture into developing countries and emerging markets.* **2** [T, I] (*formal*) to say or do sth in a careful way, especially because it might upset or offend sb: **~ sth** *We would like to venture a few additional thoughts on two controversies in the literature.* ◇ **~ to do sth** *I venture to claim that such a phenomenon is not unique to China.*

ˈventure capital *noun* [U] (*business*) money that is invested in a new company to help it develop, which may involve a lot of risk: *The recipients of venture capital are usually small innovative companies unable to obtain mainstream finance.*

verb /vɜːb; *NAmE* vɜːrb/ *noun* (*grammar*) a word or group of words that expresses an action (such as *eat*), an event (such as *happen*) or a state (such as *exist*): *An English clause containing a transitive verb also contains an object and a subject.* ➲ *see also* PHRASAL VERB

ver·bal /ˈvɜːbl; *NAmE* ˈvɜːrbl/ *adj.* **1** involving words: *Players are taught how to stay calm under physical and verbal abuse.* OPP NON-VERBAL **2** spoken, not written: *Participants were given verbal instructions in addition to the written information.* ◇ *The procedure must be explained to the patients and verbal consent gained.* ➲ *compare* ORAL (1)

ver·bal·ly /ˈvɜːbəli; *NAmE* ˈvɜːrbəli/ *adv.* in spoken words and not in writing or actions: *A project employee gave written information to those who verbally agreed to be included in the study.* ◇ *It is important to demonstrate empathy and understanding verbally and non-verbally.*

ver·ba·tim /vɜːˈbeɪtɪm; *NAmE* vɜːrˈbeɪtɪm/ *adj., adv.* exactly as spoken or written SYN WORD FOR WORD: *Verbatim transcripts of each interview were produced.* ◇ *Copying material verbatim is plagiarism.*

ver·dict /ˈvɜːdɪkt; *NAmE* ˈvɜːrdɪkt/ *noun* **1** a decision that is made in court, stating if sb is considered guilty of a crime or not: *When the magistrates or jury reach their verdict, they will deliver it in open court.* ◇ **~ of sth** *The jury returned a special verdict of not guilty by reason of insanity.* **2 ~ (on sth/sb)** a decision that you make or an opinion that you give about sth, after you have tested it or considered it carefully: *By and large, the international community has delivered a favourable verdict on recent developments in the country.*

ver·ify /ˈverɪfaɪ/ *verb* (**veri·fies**, **veri·fy·ing**, **veri·fied**, **veri·fied**) **1** to check that sth is true or accurate by careful investigation: **~ sth** *The court ruled the council had been negligent in failing to verify the identity of the three men.* ◇ **~ that...** *First, we verified that all participants understood the risks involved.* ◇ **~ whether/what, etc...** *The aim was to verify whether it is really the poorest who benefit from abolition of user fees.* **2** to show or say that sth is true or accurate SYN CONFIRM (1): **~ sth** *The results were verified by later research.* ◇ *His friend was present during the interview and verified Robbie's version of events.* ◇ **~ that...** *The pharmacist verified that none of the medicines contained caffeine.* ➲ thesaurus note *at* CONFIRM ■ **veri·fi·able** /ˈverɪfaɪəbl/ *adj.*: *We analysed the results to see which characteristics were most significant and verifiable.* **veri·fi·ca·tion** /ˌverɪfɪˈkeɪʃn/ *noun* [U, sing.] *Before the 1960s, in the absence*

V

of empirical verification, the study of conflict remained speculative. ◇ *The formula provided an early verification of Einstein's general theory of relativity.*

ver·nacu·lar /vəˈnækjələ(r); *NAmE* vərˈnækjələr/ *noun* (*usually* **the vernacular**) the language spoken in a particular area or by a particular group, especially one that is not the official or written language: *Stevenson used the Scots vernacular to reinforce a sense of Scottish place within the novel.* ■ **ver·nacu·lar** *adj.*: *Nationalist musicians played songs from the vernacular tradition and played local instruments.*

verse /vɜːs; *NAmE* vɜːrs/ *noun* **1** [U] writing that is arranged in lines, often with a regular rhythm or pattern of RHYME: *He also wrote light verse in a variety of metres.* ◇ **in ~** *Byron's 'Don Juan' is a kind of serial novel in verse.* ➲ *compare* POETRY, PROSE **2** [C] **~ (of sth)** a group of lines that form a unit in a poem or song: *The first verse of the poem describes a landscape made up of 'A host of dancing Daffodils'.* **3** [C] **~ (of sth)** any one of the short numbered divisions of a chapter in the Bible, the Qur'an, etc: *The first four verses of Luke's gospel are taken up with one Greek sentence.*

ver·sion AWL /ˈvɜːʃn; ˈvɜːʒn; *NAmE* ˈvɜːrʒn/ *noun* **1** a form of sth that is slightly different from an earlier form or from other forms of the same thing: *The original version was published in 1798.* ◇ *an early/a different/a modified/a revised version* ◇ **~ of sth** *This argument is a version of Bernard Williams's argument from his 'Internal and External Reasons'.* **2 ~ (of sth)** a film, play, piece of music, etc. that is based on a particular piece of work but is in a different form, style or language: *A Spanish-language version of 'Dracula' was released in 1931.* **3 ~ (of sth)** a description of an event from the position of a particular person or group of people: *When Boswell published his own version of the same trip, he included more conversational detail.*

ver·sus /ˈvɜːsəs; *NAmE* ˈvɜːrsəs/ *prep.* (*abbr.* **v**, **vs**) **1** used to compare two different numbers, ideas, choices, etc: *Figure 9.8 shows the vehicle speed versus time for each cycle.* ◇ *The acceptance rate was significantly higher in the first experiment (77.1% versus 59.0%).* ◇ *The issue of market versus non-market allocation is complex (Pitelis, 2003).* **2** (*law*) used to show that two sides are against each other: *She refers to the case of Edwards versus the National Coal Board.*

ver·te·brate /ˈvɜːtɪbrət; *NAmE* ˈvɜːrtɪbrət/ *noun* any animal with a BACKBONE, including all MAMMALS, birds, fish and REPTILES: *Insect legs have a quite different structure from those of vertebrates.* ➲ *compare* INVERTEBRATE ■ **ver·te·brate** *adj.* [usually before noun] *Formation of the lens is a crucial step in vertebrate eye development.*

V

ver·tex /ˈvɜːteks; *NAmE* ˈvɜːrteks/ *noun* (*pl.* **ver·ti·ces** /ˈvɜːtɪsiːz; *NAmE* ˈvɜːrtɪsiːz/ or **ver·texes**) (*geometry*) **1** a point where two lines meet to form an angle, especially the point of a triangle or CONE opposite the base: *A polygonal network is visible in the picture, with straight edges connecting vertices.* **2** the point where a curve is most extreme; the point where the GRADIENT is zero: *A parabola has only one vertex, whereas an ellipse has two vertices.*

ver·ti·cal /ˈvɜːtɪkl; *NAmE* ˈvɜːrtɪkl/ *adj.* **1** (of a line, etc.) going straight up or down from a level surface or from top to bottom in a picture, etc. SYN PERPENDICULAR: *The vertical axis represents the expected return from the investment.* ◇ *The Redwall Limestone consistently forms massive vertical cliffs 150 to 250 m high about midway up the canyon wall.* OPP HORIZONTAL (1) **2** having a structure in which there are top, middle and bottom levels: *Chinese business groups typically maintain a vertical structure.* HELP In business, **vertical integration** is the combination in one company of two or more stages of production normally operated by separate companies: *Finally, size of firm, vertical integration, diversification, and form of organization were found to be important direct influences.* OPP HORIZONTAL (2) **3** passed from one generation to the next: *HIV-positive pregnant women were given treatment to reduce the likelihood of vertical transmission of HIV.* OPP HORIZONTAL (2)

ver·ti·cal·ly /ˈvɜːtɪkli; *NAmE* ˈvɜːrtɪkli/ *adv.* **1** straight up or down from a level surface or from top to bottom in a picture, etc: *A chimney ran vertically from the ceiling level right through the pitched roof.* OPP HORIZONTALLY (1) **2** between members of an organization, system, etc. that are on different levels: *For culture to be transmittable, cultural variation must also be transmitted vertically down generations.* OPP HORIZONTALLY (2)

very[1] /ˈveri/ *adv.* **1** used before adjectives, adverbs and determiners to mean 'to a high degree' or 'extremely': *Members of a social class may be very different from one another.* ◇ *Cultures change very slowly over a period of centuries.* ◇ *Very few items cost less today than they did 20 years ago.* ◇ **~ much + adj.** *In many ways, the Korean and the US higher education systems are very much alike.* ◇ **not ~** *At that time, the gap between the richest and the poorest in the world was not very large.* ◇ *The findings are not very encouraging.* **2** used to emphasize a superlative adjective or before *own*: *There was provision for sending the very best students abroad for postgraduate study.* ◇ *The Lowlands contained their very own problem area in the form of the Borders.* **3 the ~ same** exactly the same: *Shakespeare uses the very same phrase in 'Troilus and Cressida'.*

very[2] /ˈveri/ *adj.* [only before noun] **1** used to emphasize that you are talking about a particular thing or person and not about another SYN ACTUAL (2): *These are the very questions that we are seeking answers to.* ◇ *By its very nature, much of this type of information is personal and private.* ◇ *A close textual reading helps us to grasp the actual intentions of these writers at the very moment when their texts were written.* **2** used to emphasize an extreme place or time: *In 1936, Inge Lehmann was able to show that there was a solid inner core at the very centre of the Earth.* ◇ *From the very beginning, economic integration was always seen as a means to achieving political union.* **3** without the addition of anything else SYN MERE (1): *Sometimes, the very presence of the nurse is sufficient to bring this comfort.* IDM *see* EYE

▸ VERY + NOUN **nature, essence • existence • possibility • fact • thing • idea, notion, concept • reason • foundation • act • process • moment** *At its most fundamental level, the very existence of the state depends on the economy and its performance.* | **beginning • end • top • centre • heart** *There seems to be a contradiction at the very heart of Marxist social theory.*

ves·sel /ˈvesl/ *noun* **1** a tube that carries blood through the body of a person or an animal, or liquid through the parts of a plant: *The disease causes the red blood cells to change shape and block smaller vessels.* ➲ *see also* BLOOD VESSEL **2** (*formal*) a large ship or boat: *Data are collected on board a commercial fishing vessel.* **3** (*formal*) a container used for holding liquids, such as a bowl or cup: *One or two ceramic vessels were common in both women's and men's graves.*

vest /vest/ *verb*
PHRV **ˈvest sth in sb** | **ˈvest sb with sth** [often passive] (*formal*) **1** to give sb the legal right or power to do sth: *The Spanish court had specifically vested interim custody in the father.* **2** to make sb the legal owner of land or property: *In Europe, mineral rights are vested with the state rather than the landowner.*

ˌvested ˈinterest *noun* **1 ~ (in sth/in doing sth)** a personal reason for wanting sth to happen, especially because you get some advantage from it: *Firms which fund research frequently have a vested interest in the outcomes of the research.* **2** [usually pl.] a person or group that has reasons for wanting sth to happen, because they will get some advantage from it: *Governments will have to resist pressure from powerful industries and other vested interests.*

vet·eran /ˈvetərən/ *noun* **1** a person who has served in the army, navy, etc, especially during a war: *'Patriotism' has different meanings for war veterans and war protesters.* ◇ **~ of sth** *Veterans of the war had major roles in the new conflict.* **2 ~ (of sth)** a person who has a lot of experience in a particular area or activity: *Peter is a veteran of marketing in Asia.*

via AWL /ˈvaɪə; ˈviːə/ *prep.* **1** going through one place on the way to another: *A large volume of trade passed to and from Europe via the Cape of Good Hope.* ◇ *The patient is fed with a fine tube that is passed via the nose to the first part of the jejunum.* **2** by means of a particular person, system, etc: *Papal policy might also be conveyed via bishops who visited Rome to attend synods.* ◇ *Teams mostly communicate via email.* ◇ *Many of these compounds may be made artificially via industrial processes.*

via·bil·ity /ˌvaɪəˈbɪləti/ *noun* [U] **1** how possible or likely sth is to be achieved or successful SYN FEASIBILITY: *Financial and economic viability includes corporate growth, national growth and investors' expectations.* ◇ **~ of sth** *Doubt was expressed regarding the viability of the approach.* **2** the ability to develop and survive independently: *It was concluded that milk-based substrates could prolong cell viability.* ◇ **~ of sth** *Females may search for males with 'good genes' because these increase the viability of their offspring.*

vi·able /ˈvaɪəbl/ *adj.* **1** that can be done; that will be successful SYN FEASIBLE: *Spending more on marketing did not seem to be a viable option.* ◇ *Italians emigrated when declining grain prices made farming no longer a viable way of life.* ◇ **commercially/financially/economically ~** *In Britain, discoveries of commercially viable natural gas were made later than in the US.* **2** capable of developing and surviving independently: *The percentage of viable cells increased to 82.37%.* ◇ *In some species, the female produces viable eggs that develop without fertilization.*

vi·brate /vaɪˈbreɪt; *NAmE* ˈvaɪbreɪt; vaɪˈbreɪt/ *verb* [I, T] to move from side to side continuously with very quick, small movements; to make sth move in this way: *The molecule is vibrating and rotating at the same time.* ◇ **~ sth** *Swallowed air must be expelled in short gulps to vibrate the pharynx.*

vi·bra·tion /vaɪˈbreɪʃn/ *noun* [C, U] **1 ~ (of sth)** a continuous shaking movement: *The fish have sense organs for detecting vibrations in the water.* ◇ *Excessive noise and vibration from heavy goods vehicles passing along the highway could amount to a public nuisance.* **2 ~ (of sth)** (*physics*) OSCILLATION in a substance about its EQUILIBRIUM state: *The vibrations of larger molecules can be analysed by studying the normal modes.*

vice versa /ˌvaɪs ˈvɜːsə; ˌvaɪsi ˈvɜːsə; *NAmE* ˌvaɪs ˈvɜːrsə; ˌvaɪsi ˈvɜːrsə/ *adv.* with the main items of the previous statement the other way round: *High inflation occurred when the unemployment rate was low, and vice versa.*

vicin·ity /vəˈsɪnəti/ *noun* [sing.] the area near or around a particular place, person or thing: *Researchers assembled a range of biophysical information for the High Plains of north-eastern Colorado and vicinity.* ◇ **the ~ of sth** *Gulls remove empty eggshells from the vicinity of their nests because they attract predators.* ◇ **in the ~ (of sth/sb)** *The earthquake occurred somewhere in the vicinity of the San Andreas fault.* ◇ **the immediate ~** *The DNA in the immediate vicinity of genes can be in a highly dynamic state.*

IDM **in the vicinity of sth** used to say that the number given is not exact: *These very large eruptions occur with a frequency in the vicinity of 1.4–2 events per million years (Mason et al., 2004).*

vi·cious /ˈvɪʃəs/ *adj.* **1** violent and cruel SYN BRUTAL: *The uprising turned into a vicious and bloody conflict.* **2** (of an attack, criticism, etc.) full of hate and anger: *Aristophanes' comedies regularly include vicious attacks on politicians.*

ˌvicious ˈcircle (*also* **ˌvicious ˈcycle**) *noun* [sing.] **~ (of sth)** a situation in which one problem causes another problem which then makes the first problem worse: *With growing markets and increased investment, the poor countries might be able to break out of the vicious circle of poverty.*

vic·tim /ˈvɪktɪm/ *noun* **1** a person who has been injured or killed as the result of a crime, disease, accident, etc: *They have devised new rules for compensating accident victims.* ◇ **~ of sb/sth** *Victims of crime may suffer immediate and long-term psychological consequences.* **2** a person, organization, etc. that has suffered because of a difficult situation, or because of the attitudes or actions of other people: *It is important to see these women not only as victims, but as people in their own right.* ◇ **~ of sb/sth** *It was assumed that only a human being, and not a machine, could be the victim of deception.* ◇ *This bank was Britain's first big victim of the financial crisis.* **3** an animal or person that is killed and offered to a god: *Athens was considered exceptional for the number of festivals and the quantity of sacrificial victims.*

IDM **fall ˈvictim (to sth)** to be injured, killed, damaged or destroyed by sth: *The plan immediately fell victim to Cold War politics.*

vic·tim·ize (*BrE also* **-ise**) /ˈvɪktɪmaɪz/ *verb* [often passive] **~ sb** to make sb suffer unfairly because you do not like them, their opinions or sth that they have done: *As Van der Kolk states, 'Once people have been traumatized, they are vulnerable to being victimized on future occasions.'* ■ **vic·tim·iza·tion, -isa·tion** /ˌvɪktɪmaɪˈzeɪʃn; *NAmE* ˌvɪktɪməˈzeɪʃn/ *noun* [U] *Peer victimization has been recognized as a serious and growing problem for youth throughout the world.*

vic·tor /ˈvɪktə(r)/ *noun* the winner of a battle, competition, game, etc: *His supporters were convinced that they would be the victors on election day.*

vic·tori·ous /vɪkˈtɔːriəs/ *adj.* having won a victory; that ends in victory SYN SUCCESSFUL (1), TRIUMPHANT: *In all his campaigns he emerged victorious.* ◇ *After the fight, the victorious male defends the females from subordinate males.* ◇ *The burdens even of victorious warfare were becoming unsustainable.*

vic·tory /ˈvɪktəri/ *noun* (*pl.* **-ies**) [C, U] success in a war, an election or other competition: *The Democrats won a resounding victory in that year's presidential election.* ◇ *He achieved two notable military victories.* ◇ *In spite of victory in battle, they were forced once again to a humiliating peace.* ◇ **~ over/against sb/sth** *The bridge was named to commemorate Napoleon's victory over the Prussians in 1806.*

video /ˈvɪdiəʊ; *NAmE* ˈvɪdioʊ/ *noun* (*pl.* **-os**) **1** [U] a system of recording and broadcasting moving pictures and sound: *The use of video and film in theatre can still have a powerful impact.* ◇ **on ~** *The incident was recorded on video by a girl in a passing car.* ◇ **+ noun** *A video camera monitors activity and transmits that information for observation.* **2** (*also* **ˈvideo clip**) [C] a short film or recording of an event, that can be viewed on a computer or mobile phone, especially over the Internet: *They found the site to be more user-friendly because it allowed them to upload* *videos.* **3** [C] a recorded copy of a film, programme, etc: *Andrew spends long periods of time in his room watching videos and playing computer games.*

view[1] /vjuː/ *noun* **1** [C] a personal opinion about sth; an attitude towards sth: *They have strongly held political views.* ◇ **~ on/about sth** *Keynes's views on this issue evolved during the 1930s.* ◇ **~ that...** *Darwin did not at first make explicit his view that human beings are descended from apelike ancestors.* ◇ **in sb's ~** *In their view, the application of reason and science to society necessarily meant progress.* ➲ *see also* POINT OF VIEW (1) ➲ language bank *at* ACCORDING TO **2** [sing.] a way of understanding or thinking about sth: **~ of sth** *Hobbes had a more pessimistic view of human nature.* ◇ **according to this, etc. ~** *According to this view, there is no one correct way of writing cultural geography or of representing the world.* ◇ **contrary to the... ~** *His finding was that, contrary to the popular view, hooligans are not a highly organized group with easily identifiable leaders.* ➲ *see also* WORLD VIEW **3** [U, sing.] used when you are talking about whether sb/sth can be seen from a particular place : **~ of sb/sth** *Four satellites are always visible to an observer anywhere on earth with a good view of the sky.* ◇ **be in ~** *Objects that are currently in view are compared with descriptions of objects seen previously.* ◇ **come into ~** *The group dispersed when the police car came into view.* ◇ **disappear from ~** *These massive stars have long since disappeared from view.* **4** [C] what you can see from a particular place, especially beautiful countryside: *Customers may make explicit requests, for example for a room with a sea view.* ◇ **~ of sth** *He owned an exquisite estate, complete with a breathtaking view of Washington, DC.* ◇ **~ from sth** *She has a spectacular view from her window to the north-west.*

IDM **have, etc. sth in ˈview** to have a particular aim, plan, etc. in your mind: *Mao was determined to gain certain ends which he had in view.* **in full ˈview (of sb/sth)** completely visible, directly in front of sb/sth: *The attack on a peaceful march took place in full view of the global media.* **in view of sth** because of sth; as a result of sth: *In view of its urgency, the case had been scheduled for immediate examination.* ◇ *This finding is particularly worrying in view of the high HIV-prevalence rates in the country.* **on ˈview** being shown in a public place so that people can look at it: *The new space was designed primarily to get more of the museum's collection on view.* **with a view to (doing) sth** with the intention, aim or hope of doing sth: *Negotiations were in progress between France, Britain and the USSR with a view to an alliance.* ➲ *more at* BIRD, LONG[1]

▸ ADJECTIVE + VIEW **different • alternative • similar • own • personal • prevailing, dominant • common, general • popular • traditional • orthodox, conventional, standard • new • liberal • particular • negative • positive • opposing • critical** *There are different views about the importance of regulating global economic processes.* | **strong • political • religious** *Strong views have been expressed on both sides of the debate.* | **optimistic • pessimistic • narrow • broad** *Campbell takes a broader view of what foreign policy is.*

▸ VERB + VIEW **have, hold • take, adopt • accept • express • share • support • reinforce • endorse • defend • promote • reject • challenge • reflect • represent • present, provide, offer, give • form • develop • change • consider, discuss** *For psychological reasons, most people like to gather with people who share their view of the world.*

view[2] /vjuː/ *verb* **1 ~ sb/sth +adv./prep.** to think about sb/sth in a particular way: *Women who have previously been married tend to view marriage more realistically, based on their own experience.* ◇ *Virtually nothing is known about how Spartans viewed the world during this period.* ◇ **~ sb/sth as sth** *European integration needs to be viewed as a continuous process.* ◇ **~ sb/sth with sth** *In this political climate, radical groups were viewed with great suspicion.* **2** to look at sth: **~ sth (from sth)** *Large remnants of lava flows can be seen when the area is viewed from the air.* **3 ~ sth** to watch television, a film, etc: *Many more will view the film outside cinemas on their televisions or computer screens.*

view·er /ˈvjuːə(r)/ *noun* **1** a person watching television or a film: *Frequent television viewers are more inclined to hold beliefs that reflect television's dominant and recurrent messages.* ◇ **~ of sth** *27.5 per cent of regular viewers of Fox News thought that the programme was biased in favour of Republicans.* **2 ~ (of sth)** a person who looks at or considers sth: *A viewer of contemporary art must be prepared for media that include foodstuffs, bodily fluids and industrial materials.* **3** a device for examining sth: *This type of viewer has been used for many years by scientists to analyse 3D structures of molecules and generate high-quality images.*

view·point /ˈvjuːpɔɪnt/ *noun* **1** a way of thinking about a subject SYN POINT OF VIEW: *The coal companies, however, have a different viewpoint.* ◇ **~ on sth** *Tagore presents a striking new viewpoint on some of India's most cherished literature.* ◇ **from a ... ~** *From a scientific viewpoint, the opportunity to understand the workings of such a system is unique.* ◇ **from sb's ~/the ~ of sb** *One quality control procedure is to imagine reading the report from the viewpoint of many different readers.* ◇ **from the ~ of sth** *It is interesting to examine the properties of individual atoms from the viewpoint of quantum mechanics.* **2** a direction or place from which you look at sth: *They climbed farther up the mountain to reach a higher viewpoint.* ◇ **from a.../sb's ~** *From his elevated viewpoint, the poet looks down on the fields of Runnymede.* ◇ *Figure 3.17 is a diagram drawn from the viewpoint of observer A.*

vig·or·ous /ˈvɪɡərəs/ *adj.* **1** involving physical strength, effort or energy: *Respondents were asked how many minutes of vigorous physical activity they engaged in on each of the last 7 days.* **2** done with determination, energy or enthusiasm: *The issue was the subject of vigorous debate throughout the 18th century.* **3** strong and healthy: *Mothers may kill and eat the smallest newborn, thereby allowing the most vigorous offspring to obtain more resources.*

vig·or·ous·ly /ˈvɪɡərəsli/ *adv.* **1** with determination, energy or enthusiasm: *Clinton vigorously promoted reconciliation and peace in Northern Ireland.* **2** in a way that involves physical strength, effort or energy: *The patient had exercised vigorously in the previous 48 hours.* ◇ *Sodium reacts vigorously with cold water.*

vig·our (*US* vigor) /ˈvɪɡə(r)/ *noun* [U] **1** effort, energy and enthusiasm: **~ (of sth)** *Firms facing the intensity and vigour of domestic competition will only be successful by continually reducing costs.* ◇ **with ~** *Marx defended this view with vigour.* **2 ~ (of sth)** physical strength; good health: *A high level of genetic variation may contribute to the vigour of a species.*

vil·lage /ˈvɪlɪdʒ/ *noun* **1** [C] a very small town in a country area: *In this part of the country, people live in small villages along the coast and in the interior.* ◇ **~ of...** *The Russian army stopped retreating and formed up in a defensive position on high ground near the village of Borodino.* ◇ **+ noun** *This form of human association was assumed to be characteristic of traditional village communities.* ◇ **global ~** *We now live in a global village, buying products from, and selling products to, countries all over the world.* HELP **Village** is not used to talk about small towns in the US. In American English, **village** is used for a very small town in a country area outside the United States. **2 the village** [sing.] (*especially BrE*) the people who live in a village: *The village would then arm itself and fight the bandits.*

vio·late AWL /ˈvaɪəleɪt/ *verb* **1 ~ sth** to go against or refuse to obey a law, an agreement, etc: *The company was found guilty in 1999 of violating the antitrust laws of the United States.* ◇ *This decree was said to violate a fundamental principle of justice.* **2 ~ sth** to not treat sth with respect: *The return of the applicant to Greece would violate his rights under Article 3 of the Convention.* ◇ *When buying online, consumers often have to give a lot of personal information and may feel that their privacy is being violated.* ■ **vio·la·tor** *noun* **~ (of sth)** *They are unable to take any real action against the violators of the law.*

vio·la·tion AWL /ˌvaɪəˈleɪʃn/ *noun* [C, U] **1** the action of going against or refusing to obey a law, agreement, etc: **~ (of sth)** *The Court found that there had been a violation of Article 13 of the Convention.* ◇ **in ~ of sth** *It is claimed that the actions of the government are in violation of WTO rules.* **2** the action of disturbing or not respecting sb's rights, peace, PRIVACY, etc: *The country has a record of human rights violations.* ◇ **~ of sth** *The fight against terrorism is used to justify continued violation of personal privacy.*

vio·lence /ˈvaɪələns/ *noun* [U] **1** behaviour involving physical force that is intended to hurt, damage or kill sb/sth: *In many countries, the violence committed by youths in public places is one of the main topics in the crime policy debate.* ◇ **~ of sb/sth** *The violence of the Normans and French is a regular theme in the contemporary sources.* ◇ **~ against sb** *She tries to raise public awareness about violence against women.* ◇ **domestic ~** *Women who suffer domestic violence are often unwilling to talk to anyone about their problems as a result of fear of further violence.* ◇ **an act of ~** *Riots were common, as were other isolated acts of violence.* **2 ~ (of sth)** great force or strength: *The violence of the eruptions poses a threat to human settlements near the volcanoes.*

IDM **do violence to sth** to damage or have a harmful effect on sth; to go against sth: *Even if real democracy does not exist, we cannot afford to do violence to democratic principles.*

vio·lent /ˈvaɪələnt/ *adj.* **1** using or involving physical force intended to hurt, damage or kill sb/sth: *Violent conflict nowadays takes place mainly inside states, especially inside weak states.* ◇ *The overall rate of violent crime in US schools has actually decreased.* ◇ *The woman's boyfriend was a drug dealer and a violent man.* ◇ *A march of 2 000 protesters turned violent, causing dozens of injuries and significant property damage.* **2** involving great force: *The last years of the century were characterized by some of the most violent storms on record.* **3** showing or involving very strong emotion: *A number of his postings were intended to provoke a violent response from other posters.*

vio·lent·ly /ˈvaɪələntli/ *adv.* **1** in a way that involves physical violence: *These personality characteristics are commonly found in people who behave violently.* **2** in a way that shows or involves very strong emotion: *The socialist party was violently opposed to the law.* **3** with great force: *The flames spread, aided by the wind which at that time was blowing violently.*

viral /ˈvaɪrəl/ *adj.* **1** connected with, like or caused by a virus: *Influenza is a viral infection that can be fatal in very young and elderly people.* ◇ *Hershey and Chase labelled viral proteins with radioactive sulfur, and labelled viral DNA with radioactive phosphorous.* HELP In medicine, the **viral load** is a measure of the number of viral PARTICLES present in a person, animal, place, etc, for example the number of HIV viruses in the blood. **2** (of an image, video, piece of information, etc.) spread quickly from one Internet user to another: *With blogs, viral campaigns and other tools, you can spread information faster and to a larger audience than ever before.* ◇ **~ marketing** *Viral marketing is a strategy based on consumers being motivated to pass along marketing messages to friends or colleagues.*

vir·tual AWL /ˈvɜːtʃuəl; *NAmE* ˈvɜːrtʃuəl/ *adj.* [only before noun] **1** done, stored or connected by means of computers, especially over a network: *Reviews often involve authors from multiple settings, disciplines and countries, working in virtual teams.* ◇ *All of these resources can be incorporated into an institution's existing virtual learning environment.* **2** made to appear to exist by the use of computer software: *The team is experimenting with virtual 3D images of museum artefacts.* ◇ **~ reality** *Virtual reality systems are allowing customers to get a feel of the final product at a very early stage.* **3** almost or very nearly the thing described, so that any slight difference is not important: *There is a virtual absence of research into reading in African languages.* **4** (*physics*) connected with PARTICLES that exist for an extremely short time, that are not actually seen but are thought to take part in a process: *Neutral metal plates attract each other due to the existence of virtual particles.*

vir·tu·al·ly AWL /ˈvɜːtʃuəli; *NAmE* ˈvɜːrtʃuəli/ *adv.* **1** almost or very nearly, so that any slight difference is not important: *Affordable housing was virtually impossible to find.* ◇ *A highly contagious disease could spread to virtually all parts of the world within a matter of days.* ◇ *By the next century, Buddhism in India had virtually disappeared.* **2** by the use of computer software that makes sth appear to exist: *Individual plants are reconstructed virtually.* **3** by means of computers and computer networks: *Instead of travelling to a meeting, people can meet virtually from the comfort of their desks.*

vir·tue /ˈvɜːtʃuː; *NAmE* ˈvɜːrtʃuː/ *noun* **1** [C, U] **~ (of sth)** an attractive or useful quality SYN ADVANTAGE[1]: *Socialist realism sought to convince viewers of the virtues of the existing political order.* ◇ *The genetic approach has the virtue of simplicity, as the initial experiments are easy to do.* **2** [C] a particular good quality or habit: *When students are taught socialization skills and the importance of civic virtues, social cohesion may be enhanced.* **3** [U] behaviour or attitudes that show high moral standards: *It is painfully obvious that virtue is not always rewarded with happiness in the world as we know it.*

IDM **by/in virtue of (doing) sth** (*formal*) because or as a result of sth: *Human beings have rights only by virtue of being citizens of states.*

vir·tu·ous /ˈvɜːtʃuəs; *NAmE* ˈvɜːrtʃuəs/ *adj.* behaving in a very good and moral way: *Although Aristotle assumed that happiness is the reward of a virtuous life, this is not necessarily the case.*

viru·lent /ˈvɪrələnt; ˈvɪrjələnt/ *adj.* (of a disease or sth that causes a disease) extremely dangerous or harmful and quick to have an effect: *Similar outbreaks of highly virulent flu strains have been reported previously, forcing the destruction of entire chicken farms.* ■ **viru·lence** /ˈvɪrələns; ˈvɪrjələns/ *noun* [U] *High virulence can impede total transmission because it kills the current host too quickly.*

virus /ˈvaɪrəs/ *noun* **1** a small thing made of NUCLEIC ACID surrounded by a PROTEIN coat, which is too small to be seen with a normal light MICROSCOPE and can only REPRODUCE inside a living cell: *Most throat infections are caused by a virus.* ◇ *Viruses are not really living organisms—or are they?* ◇ *Different viruses infect specific animal and plant cells.* ◇ *A pregnant woman can transmit the virus to her unborn child.* ◇ **+ noun** *Only one in 200 polio virus infections leads to irreversible paralysis (WHO Factsheets, 2003).* **2** an infection or disease caused by a virus: *In the UK, approximately one in 1 000 people is thought to have the virus.* **3** a set of instructions hidden within a computer program and designed to cause faults or destroy

V

data: *Some viruses search address books for the addresses of new victims to infect.* ➲ *see also* VIRAL

vis-à-vis /ˌviːz ɑː ˈviː/ *prep.* (*from French*) **1** in relation to: *The government has failed to realize its broader policy goals vis-à-vis society and the economy.* **2** in comparison with: *Devaluation is the reduction in the value of one currency vis-à-vis another country's currency.*

vis·cos·ity /vɪˈskɒsəti; *NAmE* vɪˈskɑːsəti/ *noun* (*pl.* **-ies**) [U, C] (of a FLUID) the state of being thick and sticky, and so not flowing freely; the degree to which sth is thick and sticky: *The decreased blood flow may be due to increased blood viscosity.* ◇ **~ of sth** *Carbon dioxide can be used to reduce the viscosity of the solutions.* ◇ **high/low ~** *Polymer solutions of organic liquids often possess high viscosities.*

vis·cous /ˈvɪskəs/ *adj.* (of a FLUID) thick and sticky; not flowing freely: *Moisture then transforms the sliding mass of soil into a viscous fluid.*

visi·bil·ity AWL /ˌvɪzəˈbɪləti/ *noun* [U] **1** how far or well you can see, especially as affected by the light or the weather: *During winter, there is increased visibility due to the lack of vegetation on deciduous trees.* **2** the degree to which sth attracts attention; the fact or state of being easy to see: *Foreign policy expertise has high visibility and prestige.* ◇ **~ of sth** *The strategies should increase the visibility of the website in search engine results.*

vis·ible AWL /ˈvɪzəbl/ *adj.* **1** that can be seen: *Visible light is a term used to describe the wavelengths of light that human eyes can sense.* ◇ **~ to sb/sth** *The Andromeda Galaxy is the most distant object that is visible to the naked eye.* ◇ **~ for/from...** *Lightning is clearly visible for many tens of kilometres at night if there are no intervening clouds.* OPP INVISIBLE (1) **2** that is obvious enough to attract attention easily SYN OBVIOUS (1): *Sleeping rough is the most visible sign of being homeless.* ◇ *Humour had a fairly visible presence in many of the blogs surveyed.* ◇ *The debate about authenticity has become more visible in recent years.* OPP INVISIBLE (2)

vis·ibly AWL /ˈvɪzəbli/ *adv.* in a way that is easily noticed: *Paine was among the first American men to actively and visibly support women's equality.* ◇ *Most visibly, the rising demand for biofuels has sparked a debate over the threat that energy security poses to food security.*

vi·sion AWL /ˈvɪʒn/ *noun* **1** [U] the ability to see; the area that you can see from a particular position: *Symptoms include mildly blurred vision and a dislike of bright lights.* ◇ *Patients with reduced visual acuity will have reduced colour vision.* ◇ **field of ~** *Glaucoma results in permanent reduction in the field of vision.* **2** [C] an idea or a picture in your imagination, especially of what the future will or could be like: *He argues that Schumpeter and Marx shared a common vision.* ◇ **~ of (doing) sth** *Noble reframed the familiar events within an alternative vision of American history.* ◇ **~ for sth** *Businesses need a long-term vision for industrial growth.* **3** [U] the ability to think about or plan the future with great imagination and intelligence: *Decision-makers should be people of vision who create ambitious plans.* ◇ *The organization had lost its vision and direction.*

visit¹ /ˈvɪzɪt/ *verb* **1** [T] **~ sb/sth** to go to see sb/sth for a particular purpose, for example to give or receive professional advice: *Inspectors had visited the detention centre in May 2010 and found the conditions there unacceptable.* ◇ *Males who had a higher education were more likely to have visited a GP.* **2** [T] **~ sb** to go to see and spend time with sb socially: *The security situation prevented them from visiting their families.* **3** [I, T] to stay somewhere for a short time as a guest or tourist: *He was just visiting, with no intention of staying long-term.* ◇ **~ sth** *The total number of people around the world who visited foreign countries in 2007 was over 900 million.* HELP A **visiting professor/scholar, etc.** is a professor, etc. who is working for a fixed period of time at a different university from their own: *She is currently a visiting scholar at the Max Planck Institute for the Study of Societies in Cologne, Germany.* **4** [T] **~ sth** to go to and look at a website on the Internet: *Respondents are invited to visit the site to complete the questionnaire.*
PHR V **ˈvisit sth on/upon sb/sth** (*formal*) to make sb/sth suffer sth unpleasant: *Henriot portrayed them as foreign bandits and communists who visited misery on good French citizens.* **ˈvisit with sb** (*NAmE*) to spend time with sb, especially talking socially: *A small group of Marines came to the facility each week to visit with other veterans.*

visit² /ˈvɪzɪt/ *noun* **1** an occasion or period of time when sb goes to see sb/sth for a particular purpose, for example to give or receive professional advice: *Doctors complain of lack of time for their patient visits.* ◇ *The research team made four visits over a period of 1–2 months, resulting in 114 interviews/observations.* ◇ **~ to sb/sth** *The concern might not be sufficient to warrant a visit to the doctor.* ◇ **~ from sb** *His firm was subject to a visit from members of the Security Exchange Commission.* ◇ **home ~** *The under-fives have more home visits than any other group except the elderly.* **2** an occasion or period of time when sb goes or stays somewhere for a short time as a guest or tourist: **~ to sth** *Her visit to America in the late 1940s proved a turning point in her life.* ◇ **on a ~ to sth** *He had been convicted of a criminal offence whilst on a visit to the UK.* **3** an occasion when sb goes to and looks at a website on the Internet: *Our website handles around 150 million visits a year.* ◇ **~ to sth** *By the end of 2008, there were over 100 million individual visits to the site.* **4 ~ (with sb)** (*NAmE*) an occasion when two or more people meet to talk in an informal way: *Data show that visits with friends and family decrease more for Internet users than for non-Internet users.*

vis·it·or /ˈvɪzɪtə(r)/ *noun* **1** a person who visits a person or place, especially socially or as a tourist: *Sporting events, especially, attract both visitors and television viewing audiences.* ◇ **~ to sb/sth** *This approach was employed in my study of visitors to Disney theme parks.* ◇ *Visitors to Malaysia get the added bonus of the strong euro or pound exchange rate.* **2** a person who goes to and looks at a website on the Internet: *Their website receives around 74 000 unique visitors every month.* ◇ **~ to sth** *Simple records of visitors to a website are prone to many errors.* **3** a bird, animal, etc. that is only present in an area at particular times: *The shearwaters are seasonal visitors that migrate to higher latitudes.* ◇ **~ to sth** *The nearest mainland relative of the beetle is capable of flight and is a regular visitor to the island.*

vis·ual¹ AWL /ˈvɪʒuəl/ *adj.* of or connected with seeing or sight: *Most advertising uses visual images as well as, or instead of, language.* ◇ *Many modern films rely for a great deal of their visual impact upon computer-generated images.* ◇ *The Arts Council supports music, drama and the visual arts with government funds.* ◇ *visual disturbance/impairment/loss* ■ **visu·al·ly** AWL *adv.*: *Advertisers attempt to create visually appealing scenarios of society.* ◇ *Visually impaired people may lack confidence out of their normal environment.*

vis·ual² AWL /ˈvɪʒuəl/ *noun* a picture, piece of film, map, etc. used to make sth easier to understand or more interesting: *The message and the visual must work together to stimulate quickly a positive brand attitude.* ➲ language bank *at* TABLE

visu·al·ize (*BrE also* **-ise**) AWL /ˈvɪʒuəlaɪz/ *verb* **1** to form a picture of sb/sth in your mind SYN IMAGINE (1): **~ sb/sth/yourself (as sth)** *In the Graeco-Roman world, the universe was visualized as having a heaven, an earth and an underworld.* ◇ **~ what/how, etc...** *The diagram is* *helpful in visualizing what is going on.* **2** to make sth visible to the eye: *Small cysts in the ovaries can be visualized by ultrasound examination.* ◇ *Fluorescent cells are subsequently visualized under the microscope.* ■ **visu·al·iza·tion, -isa·tion** AWL /ˌvɪʒuəlaɪˈzeɪʃn; *NAmE* ˌvɪʒuələˈzeɪʃn/ *noun* [U, C] **~ (of sth)** *Colonoscopy allows visualization and biopsy of the entire colon.* ◇ *Browne's visualizations of Dickens's characters have become fixed in the visual imaginations of generations of readers.*

vital /ˈvaɪtl/ *adj.* **1** necessary or essential in order for sth to succeed or exist: *These industries are of vital importance to Italy's economy.* ◇ *The courts play a vital role in interpreting the Constitution.* ◇ **~ for sth** *Grammatical accuracy is vital for successful written communication.* ◇ **~ to (doing) sth** *Practice is vital to developing fluency in any language.* ◇ **it is ~ that...** *For an accurate reading, it is vital that the correct probe is used.* ◇ **it is ~ to do sth** *It is vital to have sufficient resources to push projects through.* ➲ thesaurus note *at* ESSENTIAL[1] **2** [only before noun] connected with or necessary for staying alive: *It is important to support the vital organs in patients with severe sepsis.* ◇ **~ signs** *It is essential that the patient's vital signs (pulse, blood pressure, temperature and respiratory rate) are assessed quickly.*

vi·tal·ity /vaɪˈtæləti/ *noun* [U] the state of being strong and active; energy SYN VIGOUR (2): *These facts support the use of city growth as an indicator of economic vitality.* ◇ **~ of sth** *These developments attest to the continuing vitality of Freud's revolutionary work in contemporary thought.*

vi·tal·ly /ˈvaɪtəli/ *adv.* extremely; in an essential way: *Understanding what drives trade is vitally important to managers.*

vita·min /ˈvɪtəmɪn; *NAmE* ˈvaɪtəmɪn/ *noun* a natural substance found in food that is an essential part of what humans and animals eat to help them grow and stay healthy. There are many different vitamins: *The fat-soluble vitamins include vitamins A, D, E and K.* ◇ **+ noun** *Vitamin supplements are advised until children are 4 years old.* ◇ *Osteomalacia is a softening of the bones in adults due to vitamin D deficiency.*

vitro ➲ IN VITRO

vivid /ˈvɪvɪd/ *adj.* **1** (of memories, a description, etc.) producing very clear pictures in your mind SYN GRAPHIC (1): *His letters give us a vivid picture of the society he lived in.* ◇ *Many of the interviewees recounted vivid memories of the migration experience.* **2** (of light, colours, etc.) very bright: *Many chemical reactions generate vivid colours which often provide sufficient information to perform an analysis.* ■ **viv·id·ly** *adv.*: *This example vividly illustrates that mortality can decline rapidly in response to political, social and economic change.* **viv·id·ness** *noun* [U] **~ (of sth)** *The vividness of Dickens's imaginative account of urban violence was intended both to shock and to inform his readers.*

vivo ➲ IN VIVO

vo·cabu·lary /vəˈkæbjələri; *NAmE* vəˈkæbjəleri/ *noun* (*pl.* **-ies**) [U, C] **1** all the words that a person knows or uses: *Diagnosis can be difficult if the child cannot give a clear history due to limited vocabulary.* ◇ *A child begins by learning a minimal vocabulary and a few elementary syntactic rules.* ◇ **+ noun** *Vocabulary acquisition is pivotal to reading and language learning.* ➲ *see also* DEFINING VOCABULARY **2** all the words in a particular language: *The study views the development of the Sanskrit vocabulary.* **3** the words that people use when they are talking about a particular subject: *EU legislation is full of technical vocabulary and concepts.* ◇ **~ of sth** *The contemporary vocabulary of political debate is increasingly about markets, competition, choice and consumer rights.*

vocal /ˈvəʊkl; *NAmE* ˈvoʊkl/ *adj.* **1** [only before noun] connected with the voice: *Syllables can be short or long depending on the position of the human vocal organs.* ◇ *In North Africa, genres of strictly vocal music are greeted with greater favour than are genres employing instruments.* HELP The **vocal cords** are thin pieces of TISSUE in the throat that are moved by the flow of air to produce the voice. **2** telling people your opinions or protesting about sth loudly and with confidence: *It is not difficult to find vocal critics of the current system.*

vo·ca·tion /vəʊˈkeɪʃn; *NAmE* voʊˈkeɪʃn/ *noun* **1** [C] **~ (as sth)** a type of work or way of life that you believe is especially suitable for you SYN CALLING (2): *Gurney treated poetry as a relief from his vocation as a composer.* ◇ *Nursing as a vocation has been evident for many centuries.* **2** [C, U] a belief that a particular type of work or way of life is especially suitable for you; a belief that you have been chosen by God to be a priest or NUN SYN CALLING (1): **~ to sth** *Gerard Manley Hopkins had twin vocations to the Jesuit priesthood and to poetry.* ◇ **~ to do sth** *Thomas More determined that his vocation to serve God lay in the sphere of public life.* ◇ **sense of ~** *Little is made of the sense of vocation within the service nor the acknowledgement of policing for the public good.*

vo·ca·tion·al /vəʊˈkeɪʃənl; *NAmE* voʊˈkeɪʃənl/ *adj.* connected with the skills, knowledge, etc. that you need to have in order to do a particular job: *Young workers pursue lengthy vocational training programmes to develop skills that are highly specific to their industries.* ◇ *Many other countries want to develop stronger forms of vocational education and apprenticeship.*

voice[1] /vɔɪs/ *noun* **1** [C, U] the sound or sounds produced through the mouth by a person speaking or singing: *His is the first voice heard in the recorded interview.* ◇ *Behaviours associated with emotion include raising your voice when you are angry.* ◇ **tone of ~** *Two thirds of the meaning we ascribe to social interaction comes from non-verbal emotional cues like facial expression, tone of voice and gestures.* **2** [C, U] the individual, personal style of an author or piece of writing: *The female narrative voice and point of view within Austen's 'Pride and Prejudice' give a strong sense of Elizabeth as subject, not as object.* **3** [sing.] **~ (in sth)** the right to express your opinion and influence decisions: *Individuals and communities should have a voice in plans, strategies and decisions affecting their futures.* **4** [C] a particular attitude, opinion or feeling that is expressed; a feeling or an opinion that you become aware of inside yourself: *The bill passed both Houses without a dissenting voice.* ◇ **~ (of sb/sth)** *Napoleon was an emperor astute enough to listen to the voice of the people through referenda.* ◇ *Optimistic or pessimistic beliefs form the basis of the inner voice that offers meaning, makes appraisals and explains events.* **5** [sing.] **~ (of sb/sth)** a person, organization, newspaper, etc. that expresses the opinions of a particular group of people: *As the voice of organized labour, the TUC has to speak on various issues to the government of the day.* **6** [sing.] **the active/passive ~** the form of a verb that shows whether the subject of a sentence performs the action (*the active voice*) or is affected by it (*the passive voice*): *The pictures were designed so that they could be described in either the passive or active voice.*

IDM **give voice to sth/sb** to express your feelings, worries, etc; to allow sb's feelings, worries, etc. to be expressed: *The authors are strongly committed to giving voice to the suffering of Slovenians forced to leave their country.* **have/make your ˈvoice heard** to express your feelings, opinions, etc. in a way that makes people notice and consider them: *Shareholder pressure groups are increasingly making their voices heard in the boardroom.* **with ˌone ˈvoice** as a group; with everyone agreeing: *The*

EU speaks with one voice represented by the Commission in world trade talks. ➲ *more at* FIND[1], RAISE[1]

voice² /vɔɪs/ *verb* **~ sth** to tell people your feelings or opinions about sth: *From the inception of the National Lottery, concern was voiced about its impact upon charitable giving.* ◇ *The Athenians were committed to a political set-up in which anyone was entitled to voice their opinion.*

void¹ /vɔɪd/ *noun* a large empty space: *The voids between the rock are filled with dark grey or black ash.* ◇ *Her characters often inhabit a void: they are vagrants, lacking a social and cultural background.*

void² /vɔɪd/ *adj.* **1** (*law*) (of a contract, an agreement, etc.) not valid or legal: *The consequence of this is that any agreement made which purports to be a contract will be void.* **2 ~ of sth** (*formal*) completely lacking sth SYN DEVOID: *Lack of proper habitat management leaves some ditches completely void of all vegetation.* **3** (*technical*) empty: *The rate of water movement is again controlled by the number and size of the void spaces within the soil.* IDM *see* NULL

vol. AWL *abbr.* VOLUME

vola·tile /ˈvɒlətaɪl; *NAmE* ˈvɑːlətl/ *adj.* **1** (*chemistry*) (of a substance) that changes easily into a gas: *The molecules are volatile at temperatures below 200–400°C.* ◇ *cleaning aids that contain volatile solvents* **2** (of a situation) likely to change suddenly; easily becoming dangerous SYN UNSTABLE: *Recently, stock prices have been highly volatile.* ◇ *Oil imports will come increasingly from politically volatile areas in the Middle East and Asia.* **3** (*computing*) (of a computer's memory) keeping data only as long as there is power supplied: *Volatile memory loses its stored data when the power is removed.* ■ **vola·til·ity** /ˌvɒləˈtɪləti; *NAmE* ˌvɑːləˈtɪləti/ *noun* [U] *Many of these organic compounds have low volatility and extremely low water solubility.* ◇ *The combination of these effects makes for natural price volatility.*

vol·can·ic /vɒlˈkænɪk; *NAmE* vɑːlˈkænɪk; vɔːlˈkænɪk/ *adj.* caused or produced by a volcano: *Fallout from volcanic eruptions causes airborne pollution.* ◇ *Pumice is volcanic rock with a light mass.* ◇ *The cascades represent some of the most recent volcanic activity within the canyon.*

vol·cano /vɒlˈkeɪnəʊ; *NAmE* vɑːlˈkeɪnoʊ; vɔːlˈkeɪnoʊ/ *noun* (*pl.* **-oes** or **-os**) a mountain with a large opening at the top through which gases and LAVA are forced out into the air, or have been in the past: *When volcanoes erupt, they send gases into the atmosphere which can alter the global climate.* ◇ *Mount Kelud is a highly active volcano with a long record of eruptions.* ◇ *a dormant/an extinct volcano*

V

volt /vəʊlt; vɒlt; *NAmE* voʊlt/ *noun* (*abbr.* **V**) a unit for measuring voltage: *For residential use, a further reduction to 120-240 volts is required.*

volt·age /ˈvəʊltɪdʒ; *NAmE* ˈvoʊltɪdʒ/ *noun* [C, U] the difference in electrical POTENTIAL ENERGY between two points, measured in volts, which can cause an electrical current to flow: *When a voltage was applied to the device, a current started to flow.* ◇ *a high/low voltage* ◇ **+ noun** *With a 1-V AC input, the resulting AC output corresponds to the voltage gain of the circuit.*

vol·ume AWL /ˈvɒljuːm; *NAmE* ˈvɑːljuːm; ˈvɑːljəm/ *noun* **1** [U, C] **~ (of sth)** the amount of space that an object or a substance fills; the amount of space that a container has: *The amount of material needed depends upon both the concentration and the total volume of the solution to be prepared.* ◇ *Gases undergo large changes in volume as they are heated in vessels that are able to expand.* ◇ *Water vapour is much less dense than liquid, and occupies a volume about a thousand times greater than liquid.* ◇ *The experiment is carried out with a mixture of gases, in a container of a particular volume and at a given temperature.* **2** [U, C] **~ (of sth)** the amount of sth: *The difficulty lies in the sheer volume of work involved.* ◇ *The high-powered computers can handle large volumes of data.* ◇ *Migration increases in volume as industries and commerce develop and transport improves.* **3** [U] the amount of sound that is produced by a television, radio, etc: *Listeners with impaired hearing cannot hear soft passages without turning the volume up so far that loud passages are distorted.* **4** [C] (*abbr.* **vol.**) a book that is part of a series of books: *Cultural geographers regularly publish in geography education journals or edited volumes.* ◇ **~ of sth** *Among 19 volumes of 'Studies in Business History' was a life of John Jacob Astor of real-estate fame (Porter, 1931).* **5** [C] **~ (of sth)** (*formal*) a book: *John Clare published four volumes of poetry during his lifetime.* ◇ *By 1959 there were about 135 000 libraries in the country holding 800 million volumes.* **6** (*abbr.* **vol.**) **~ (of sth)** a series of different issues of the same magazine, especially all the issues for one year: *He has overseen publication of 16 issues (four volumes) of the journal.* IDM *see* SPEAK

vol·un·tar·ily AWL /ˈvɒləntrəli; *NAmE* ˌvɑːlənˈterəli/ *adv.* willingly; without being forced: *Refugees tend to be a vulnerable population, in that they have not voluntarily chosen to leave their country of origin.*

vol·un·tary AWL /ˈvɒləntri; *NAmE* ˈvɑːlənteri/ *adj.* **1** done willingly, not because you are forced: *Participation in the study was entirely voluntary.* ◇ *They argue that the alcohol industry, on a voluntary basis, should be encouraged to market alcohol in a responsible fashion.* OPP COMPULSORY ➲ *compare* INVOLUNTARY (1) **2** [usually before noun] connected with work done by people who choose to do it without being paid: *Many over-65s contribute to the economy through voluntary work.* ◇ *These care homes are run by not-for-profit voluntary organizations.* ◇ *She describes a range of the current issues facing non-profit and voluntary sector managers.* ◇ *In determining the membership of the labour force, the numbers of unpaid and voluntary workers may also be relevant.* **3** (*technical*) (of movements of the body) that you can control: *In REM sleep, the voluntary muscles are paralysed.* OPP INVOLUNTARY (2)

vol·un·teer¹ AWL /ˌvɒlənˈtɪə(r); *NAmE* ˌvɑːlənˈtɪr/ *noun* **1** a person who does a job without being paid for it: *These organizations rely mainly on unpaid volunteers.* **2** a person who offers to do sth without being forced to do it: *Nine volunteers were recruited to take part in the study.* **3** a person who chooses to join the armed forces without being forced to join: **+ noun** *As Taylor noted, volunteer armies are relatively more expensive than those raised by conscription.* ➲ *compare* CONSCRIPT²

vol·un·teer² AWL /ˌvɒlənˈtɪə(r); *NAmE* ˌvɑːlənˈtɪr/ *verb* **1** [I, T] to offer to do sth without being forced to do it or without getting paid for it: **~ to do sth** *Five hospitals volunteered to participate in the study.* ◇ **~ for sth** *Plenty of people volunteered for the clinical trials between 1993 and 1996.* ◇ **~ as sth** *Many female artists were involved in war work or volunteered as nurses.* ◇ **~ (sth) (for/as sth)** *The regulations only protect those agents who are paid rather than volunteer their services.* ◇ *Volunteering has been shown to facilitate a route into work and to increase volunteers' confidence.* **2** [T] **~ sth** to suggest sth or tell sb sth without being asked: *The applicant is under a duty to volunteer information, not just to answer questions.* **3** [I] to join the army, etc. without being forced to: **~ for sth** *Among all groups, volunteering for the military rose again in 2008.* ◇ **~ to do sth** *After the successful suppression of the uprising, Kurt volunteered to command a unit on the German-Polish border.*

vomit /ˈvɒmɪt; *NAmE* ˈvɑːmɪt/ *verb* [I, T] to bring food from the stomach back out through the mouth SYN BE SICK:

The pain returned after his lunch and he has vomited twice. ◇ **~ sth** *She began to vomit blood.*

vote¹ /vəʊt; *NAmE* voʊt/ *noun* **1** [C] a formal choice that you make in an election or at a meeting in order to choose sb or decide sth: *The government lost votes on a number of important issues.* ◇ *The motion was carried by 50 votes to 29.* ◇ *Most matters are decided by a simple majority of total number of votes cast by individual delegates.* ◇ **~ for sb/sth** *The votes for each of the seven candidates are detailed in the table.* ◇ **~ against sb/sth** *Unhappiness over this initiative was evidenced in the vote against it in the European Parliament.* **2** [C, usually sing.] an occasion when a group of people vote on sth: *All decisions had to be by unanimous vote.* ◇ **(take a) ~ on sth** *When a vote was taken on the issue, the new scheme was approved by five states to four.* ◇ **put sth to the ~** *The new constitution was being put to the vote on the same day.* **3 the vote** [sing.] the total number of votes in an election: *In the 1992 presidential election, Ross Perot received 19 per cent of the popular vote.* ◇ *The party won its third highest share of the vote since 1929.* ◇ **+ noun** *The party's average vote share declined by 0.36%.* **4 the vote** [sing.] the vote given by a particular group of people, or for a particular party, etc: *Scarborough was courted for his ability to sway the black vote.* ◇ *In England, the Liberal Democrat vote was up by 1.3%.* **5 the vote** [sing.] the right to vote, especially in political elections: *The main reason why children are not given the vote is that they are thought to lack political competence.*

IDM **a vote of ˈconfidence/no ˈconfidence** a formal vote to show that people support/do not support a leader, a political party, an idea, etc: *In the Duma, Chernomyrdin lost a vote of confidence tabled by the communists.*

vote² /vəʊt; *NAmE* voʊt/ *verb* **1** [I, T] to show formally by marking a paper or raising your hand which person you want to win an election, or which plan or idea you support: *Voter turnout is defined as the percentage of the adult population that voted in elections.* ◇ **~ for sb/sth** *A majority of Americans voted for a Republican candidate for president in 1968 and 1972.* ◇ **~ against sb/sth** *As many as twelve Commissioners could vote against a motion but then have to support it publicly.* ◇ **~ in favour of sth** *283 MPs voted in favour of the bill.* ◇ **~ on sth** *Uncontroversial resolutions are normally voted on by a show of hands only.* ◇ **+ noun** *35.1% of men stated that they intended to vote Conservative.* ◇ **~ to do sth** *In the summer of 395, the Athenians voted overwhelmingly to join the Thebans in war.* **2** [T, usually passive] to choose sb/sth for a position or an award by voting: **be voted + noun** *His work was voted the most influential modern art work of the twentieth century.* **3** [T] **~ sb/yourself sth** to agree to give sb/yourself sth by voting: *In order to cope with these volumes of inquiries, members have voted themselves generous allowances.*

IDM **ˌvote with your ˈfeet** to show what you think about sth by going or not going somewhere: *Reduced confidence in public institutions increases people's desire to vote with their feet through emigration.*

PHR V **ˌvote sb/sth ˈdown** to reject or defeat sb/sth by voting for sb/sth else: *The Bill was voted down by the Lords on three occasions.* **ˌvote sb ˈin** | **ˌvote sb ˈinto/ˈonto sth** to choose sb for a position by voting: *The first meeting set out to vote in the club's officers.* **ˌvote sb ˈout** | **ˌvote sb ˈout of/ˈoff sth** to DISMISS sb from a position by voting: *The fundamentalists were voted off the board the following year.*

voter /ˈvəʊtə(r); *NAmE* ˈvoʊtər/ *noun* a person who votes or has the right to vote, especially in a political election: *These were key concerns for many traditional Labour voters.* ◇ **+ noun** *Voter turnout in European Parliament elections has fallen with each election.*

vot·ing /ˈvəʊtɪŋ; *NAmE* ˈvoʊtɪŋ/ *noun* [U] the action of choosing sb/sth in an election or at a meeting: *In relation to annual general meetings, companies should offer facilities for electronic voting.* ◇ **+ noun** *New Zealand (1893), Australia (1902) and Finland (1904) were the first countries to introduce full women's voting rights.*

vowel /ˈvaʊəl/ *noun* (*phonetics*) **1** a speech sound in which the mouth is open and the tongue is not touching the top of the mouth, the teeth, etc, for example /ɑː, e, ɔː/: *There is more socially significant variation in the pronunciation of English vowels than in consonants.* **2** a letter that represents a vowel sound. In English the vowels are a, e, i, o and u. ➲ *compare* CONSONANT, DIPHTHONG

vul·ner·able /ˈvʌlnərəbl/ *adj.* **~ (to sb/sth)** weak and easily hurt physically or emotionally: *Infants are particularly vulnerable to influenza infections.* ◇ *The scheme will help charities working with vulnerable adults and young people.* ◇ *These bodies provide expert service to vulnerable groups in society, who are most likely to be victims of human rights violations.* ■ **vul·ner·abil·ity** /ˌvʌlnərəˈbɪləti/ *noun* [U] **~ (of sb/sth) (to sth)** *The findings of other studies have highlighted the vulnerability of this group to economic exploitation.* ◇ *In infancy, there is greatest vulnerability to infectious diseases.*

W w

wage¹ /weɪdʒ/ *noun* [sing.] (*also* **wages** [pl.]) a regular amount of money that you earn, usually every week, for work or services: *Unionized firms paid wages that were on average 10–20% higher than those in the non-union sector.* ◇ **high/low ~** *Workers who were already working for low wages saw their real wages decline even further.* ◇ **~ of sth** *Part-time male workers receive an hourly wage of $12.06.* ◇ **~ of sb** *The wages of computer specialists and engineers actually fell relative to those of high school graduates.* ◇ **wages rise/fall** *In the Netherlands, wages rose by a third to a half from 1650 to 1700.* ◇ **+ noun** *By agreeing to restrain wage increases, unions helped maintain competitiveness in export markets.* ◇ *Most adult family caretakers are also wage earners.* **HELP** In economics, **wages** are the price of providing labour, paid to the labourer. Wages are one part of **income** which also includes other sources of payments, such as interest on money that has been invested. ➲ *compare* SALARY ➲ *see also* MINIMUM WAGE

wage² /weɪdʒ/ *verb* to begin and continue a war or struggle: **~ sth** *By this time, the anti-slave trade campaign had been waged inside and outside Parliament for 19 years.* ◇ **~ sth against/on sb/sth** *Fruit growers wage constant battles against insects and disease.* ◇ **~ (a) war** *The 'end of history' thesis is based on the idea that liberal democracies do not wage war against one another (Fukuyama, 1992).*

wait¹ /weɪt/ *verb* **1** [I, T] to stay where you are or delay doing sth until sb/sth comes or sth happens: **+ adv./prep.** *Wealth tends to get older in ageing societies because individuals wait longer before they inherit.* ◇ *The system must wait until the circuit has had time to settle down before the next operation is started.* ◇ **~ for sb/sth** *An asylum seeker may wait many months or even years for a decision on their application for leave to enter.* ◇ **~ for sb/sth to do sth** *The United States believed that the costs of waiting for sanctions to work increasingly exceeded the benefits.* ◇ **~ to do sth** *You have to wait to get refugee status before you can train or teach.* **2** [I] **~ (for sth)** to hope or watch for sth to happen, especially for a long time: *There is a difference between listening and simply waiting for an opportunity to speak.* **3 be waiting** [I] (of things) to be ready for sb to have or use: **~ for sb** *The most respected members had chairs in the front row waiting for them.* ◇ **~ to do sth** *There are a couple of questions on this point that are* *waiting to be addressed.* **4** [I] to be left to be dealt with at a later time because it is not urgent: *English overseas colonization would have to wait for the end of hostilities.*

IDM **keep sb/sth ˈwaiting** to make sb/sth have to wait or be delayed: *Unless an order for sale is made, the bank will be kept waiting indefinitely for any payment.* ➲ *more at* WING

wait² /weɪt/ *noun* **~ (for sb/sth)** a period of waiting: *Long waits for medical care are a source of dissatisfaction for patients.*

ˈwaiting list (*NAmE also* **ˈwait list**) *noun* a list of people who are waiting for sth such as a service, school place or medical treatment that is not yet available: *The final decision is based on the time patients have spent on the waiting list.* ◇ **~ for sth** *There is a long waiting list for these jobs.*

waive /weɪv/ *verb* **~ sth** to choose not to demand sth in a particular case, even though you have a legal or official right to do so: *She was willing to waive her right to confidentiality.* ◇ *The law contains provision for waiving the language requirement if it would be unreasonable to expect the applicant to fulfil it.*

waiver /ˈweɪvə(r)/ *noun* (*law*) a situation in which sb gives up a legal right or claim; an official document stating this: *When the visa waiver granted to Ecuadorians was terminated, the inflow of Ecuadorians to Spain halted almost immediately.*

wake¹ /weɪk/ *noun*

IDM **in the wake of sth | in sth's wake** coming after or following sb/sth: *In the wake of the crisis, the United States and many other countries considered legislation to respond to these flaws in the financial system.*

wake² /weɪk/ *verb* (**woke** /wəʊk; *NAmE* woʊk/, **woken** /ˈwəʊkən; *NAmE* ˈwoʊkən/) [I, T] to stop sleeping; to make sb stop sleeping: **~ (up)** *Sleep is often reduced, but the patient wakes up feeling lively and energetic.* ◇ **~ to sth** *Many people have the experience of dreaming about a bell ringing, only to wake to the sound of their alarm clock.* ◇ **~ from sth** *About a quarter of patients experience episodes of paralysis on waking from sleep.* ◇ **~ to do sth** *She was brought into the Emergency Department by her husband who woke to find her shivering.* ◇ **~ sb (up) (from sth)** *The patient had a sudden onset of chest pain that woke him up.*

PHR V **ˌwake ˈup to sth** (*rather informal*) to become aware of sth; to realize sth: *Eventually, Clinton's campaign team woke up to the possibility that they might lose.*

walk¹ /wɔːk/ *verb* [I] to move or go somewhere by putting one foot in front of the other on the ground, but without running: **(+ adv./prep.)** *Classroom behaviour was poor with students walking around during seat work.* ◇ *Many people switched from motorized transport to more sustainable modes such as walking and cycling.* ◇ **walking distance** *Most children live within walking distance of their school.* ◇ **+ noun** *Gandhi and his followers walked 240 miles to the sea at Dandi to break the Salt Laws.*

IDM **walk the streets** to walk around the streets of a town or city: *Residents complained that it was no longer safe to walk the streets at night.*

PHR V **ˌwalk aˈway (from sb/sth)** to leave a difficult situation or relationship, etc. instead of staying and trying to deal with it: *In May 2009, Chinalco walked away from the proposed deal.* **ˌwalk ˈout (of sth)** to leave a meeting, performance, etc. suddenly, especially in order to show your disapproval: *The Bolshevik delegates walked out after failing to get their resolutions passed.*

walk² /wɔːk/ *noun* **1** [C] a journey on foot, usually for pleasure or exercise: **go for/take a ~** *Nowadays, you do not really have to leave the inner city to go for a walk in the English countryside.* **2** [sing.] used to show the time that it will take to reach a place on foot or the distance to be travelled: *Every single dwelling is within a 7-minute walk of a public transport stop.*

IDM **walk of life** (*rather informal*) a person's job or position in society: *The ideal behind the common school was that it enabled students from all walks of life to mix.*

wall /wɔːl/ *noun* **1** a long vertical solid structure, made of stone, brick, etc. that surrounds, divides or protects an area of land or water: *The Ho prepared for another invasion by building a twelve-mile-long defensive wall.* ◇ *a stone/brick wall* ◇ **~ of sth** *Burials took place within the walls of the lower town as early as the middle of the fourth century.* **2** any of the vertical sides of a building or room: *135 of 216 residences (62.5%) had cement block walls with corrugated iron roofing.* ◇ **on the ~** *The classroom was bright and stimulating, with colourful posters and charts on the walls.* ◇ **~ of sth** *Archaeologists have uncovered evidence of advertising from ancient Rome and Pompeii in the form of painted signs on the walls of buildings.* **3** any high vertical surface: *Canyons cut in hard, resistant rocks have steep walls and narrow, V-shaped or vertical profiles.* ◇ **~ of sth** *Photographs show a wall of water advancing rapidly towards the shore.* **4** the outer layer of sth hollow such as an organ of the body or a cell of an animal or a plant: *The bacterial cell has a rigid cell wall around it.* ◇ *the chest/abdominal/bowel wall* ◇ **~ of sth** *As the cardiac muscles relax, the muscular walls of the ventricles begin their contraction.* **5** something that forms a barrier or stops you from making progress: *The revolutionaries built ideological walls around themselves and engaged in feuds against other revolutionary groups.*

want¹ /wɒnt; *NAmE* wɑːnt; wɔːnt/ *verb* (not usually used in the progressive tenses) to have a desire or a wish for sth: **~ sth** *Their customers wanted high-quality products, customized features and on-time delivery.* ◇ *Patients want information about their condition and their outlook, even when the news is bad.* ◇ **~ to do sth** *Organizations must have a clear vision of what they want to do and be realistic about their goals.* ◇ **~ sb/sth to do sth** *The mother may want the children to live with her; the father may want the children to live with him.* ◇ **~ sb/sth + adj.** *A number of those who had wanted him acquitted had a change of heart and voted for the death penalty.*

PHR V **want sth from sth/sb** to hope to get sth from a particular experience or person: *Different employees want different things from their careers.*

want² /wɒnt; *NAmE* wɑːnt; wɔːnt/ *noun* **1** [C, usually pl.] something that you want: *Politics always involves conflict, based on disagreement between rival opinions and different wants.* ◇ **wants and needs/needs and wants** *The basic aim of any business activity is to satisfy human wants and needs.* **2** [U, sing.] **~ of sth** (*formal*) a situation in which there is not enough of sth SYN LACK¹: *Malthus stated that the greatest check to the increase of plants and animals is want of room and nourishment.* ◇ *They approved the removal of officers whose acts showed 'a want of honesty'.* **3** [U] (*formal*) the state of being poor, not having food, etc: *The famous four freedoms announced by President Roosevelt in 1941 were freedom of speech and expression, freedom of religion, freedom from want and freedom from fear.*

IDM **for want of sth** because of a lack of sth; because sth is not available: *The danger of this policy, however, was that native industries would fail for want of outlets for their products.*

war /wɔː(r)/ *noun* **1** [U, C] a situation in which two or more countries or groups of people fight against each other over a period of time: *When, in September 1939, Hitler invaded Poland, the western allies declared war on Germany.* ◇ *Parliament refused to support the government's decision to go to war.* ◇ **at ~** *Even countries not at war are heavily committed to military expenditure.* ◇ **~ between A and B** *This was one of the significant episodes* *in the war between Athens and Sparta.* ◇ *In Manchuria, at this time, a war was fought between China and Russia.* ◇ **~ with/against sb/sth** *The war with France began in 1793 and culminated at Waterloo in 1815.* ◇ **~ of sth** *Baroody refers specifically to the Crusades and other wars of religion that justified political expansion through the 'right' to convert others.* ◇ **+ noun** *Bristol lost ground to its north-western rival in the war years of the 1740s.* ➲ *see also* CIVIL WAR, COLD WAR, POST-WAR, WARRING **2** [C, U] a situation in which there is aggressive competition between groups, companies, countries, etc: *The problem with price-based competition is that it reduces overall profitability and can lead to price wars.* ◇ *In the essay 'Chartism', he confronted the growing threat of class war posed by the new political articulacy of industrial workers.* **3** [U, sing.] **~ (on/against sb/sth)** a fight or an effort over a long period of time to get rid of or stop sth unpleasant: *Many observers see this as key to winning the war on global poverty.* ◇ *He has also analysed the war against illegal drugs waged by the United States.*

▸ ADJECTIVE + WAR **global** • **major** • **total** • **great** • **just** • **unjust** • **holy, religious** • **revolutionary** • **civil** • **nuclear** *Can there be such a thing as a just war?*

▸ NOUN + WAR **world** • **guerrilla** *War has grown more and more destructive, culminating in the two world wars of the twentieth century.*

▸ VERB + WAR **fight, wage** • **declare** • **go to** • **start, launch** • **end** • **continue** • **enter** • **prevent, avoid** • **win** • **lose** • **oppose** • **fight in** • **survive** *On the diplomatic front, there was the danger that Sweden and even Austria would enter the war.*

▸ WAR + VERB **break out, begin, start** • **continue** • **rage** • **end** *When war broke out between Athens and Sparta, few Greeks foresaw that it would be different from any war they had ever experienced.*

▸ WAR + NOUN **effort** • **years** • **period** • **ministry** • **zone** • **veteran** • **memorial** • **crime** *American geographers assisted the war effort by providing descriptions of the physical landscapes surrounding major training camps.*

▸ NOUN + OF + WAR **threat** • **cause** • **outbreak** • **beginning** • **end** • **conduct** • **course** • **time** • **aftermath** • **impact, effect, consequences** *The strike was finally suppressed less than a week before the outbreak of war.*

ˈwar crime *noun* a cruel act that is committed during a war and that is against the international rules of war: *Many of the actions perpetrated by the armed factions could be considered war crimes under customary international humanitarian law.* ◇ **+ noun** *A war crimes tribunal was set up.*

ward /wɔːd; *NAmE* wɔːrd/ *noun* **1** a separate room or area in a hospital for people with the same type of medical condition: *A 59-year-old man was admitted to the medical ward with acute chest pain.* ◇ **on a ~** *Mrs Robson has been a patient on the ward for three days.* ◇ **+ noun** *Nurses should also attend the ward round in order to understand the medical management plan.* **2 ~ (of sb/sth)** (*law*) a person, especially a child, who is under the legal protection of a court or another person (called a GUARDIAN): *If a child is a ward of court, the court has parental responsibility until further order.*

war·fare /ˈwɔːfeə(r); *NAmE* ˈwɔːrfer/ *noun* [U] **1** the activity of fighting a war, especially using particular weapons or methods: *The rebels marched south, gathered recruits and engaged in guerrilla warfare.* ◇ *In nuclear, chemical and biological warfare, technical change has been rapid.* **2** the activity of competing in an aggressive way with another group, company, etc: *The regime also engaged in open warfare with other international players.* ◇ *There was class warfare at different points in the early republic.*

warm¹ /wɔːm; *NAmE* wɔːrm/ *adj.* (**warm·er**, **warm·est**) **1** at a fairly high temperature that is not very hot and not cold: *The greatest impacts result from hurricanes that travel northward over the warm waters of the Gulf Stream.* ◇ *Each time the door is opened, cold air inside the refrigerator is replaced by warm outside air, thus wasting energy.* ◇ *Climate models indicate that, between about 9 000 and 6 850 years before present (b.p.), the climate was warmer and drier than it is today.* **2** keeping you warm; staying warm in cold weather: *Some 6.5 million adults go without essential clothing, such as a warm waterproof coat, because of a lack of money.* ◇ **keep ~** *Without access to either peat or wood, it was impossible to cook meals and keep warm.* **3** showing or feeling enthusiasm and/or affection: *Many airlines require cabin staff to greet passengers with a warm welcome.* ◇ *Once inside the school, you get a warm feeling of being welcomed into the space.* ➲ *see also* WARMTH ■ **warm·ly** *adv.*: *He was advised to dress warmly whenever exposed to cold ambient conditions.* ◇ *Lord Byron warmly embraced Greek culture, both ancient and modern.*

warm² /wɔːm; *NAmE* wɔːrm/ *verb* [T, I] to make sth/sb warm or warmer; to become warm or warmer: **~ sth/sb/yourself (up)** *Condensing 1 g of vapour in 1 kg of air warms the air by 2.5°C.* ◇ **~ (up)** *The groundwater that has warmed up during the heat exchange process is returned to the aquifer.* ◇ **~ (sth) to sth** *The tube is warmed to 37°C and slowly rotated in a machine.*

PHR V **ˈwarm to sth/sb** to like or start to like sth/sb: *A nation obsessed with success does not warm to tales of failure.*

warm·ing /ˈwɔːmɪŋ; *NAmE* ˈwɔːrmɪŋ/ *noun* [U] the process of becoming warm or warmer: *In north-west Europe, the end of the Ice Age saw rapid warming.* ➲ *see also* GLOBAL WARMING

warmth /wɔːmθ; *NAmE* wɔːrmθ/ *noun* [U] **1** the state or quality of being warm, rather than hot or cold: *Fire, clothing and the building of shelters provided protection and warmth to early humans.* **2** enthusiasm, affection or kindness: *The film communicated human warmth rather than delivering political information.*

warn /wɔːn; *NAmE* wɔːrn/ *verb* **1** [T, I] to tell sb about sth, especially sth dangerous or unpleasant that is likely to happen, so that they can avoid it: **~ (sb) about/against sb/sth** *Patients should be warned about the effects of taking alcohol.* ◇ **~ (sb) of sth** *They warned of the dangers of too much state intervention.* ◇ **~ (sb) that...** *Levitt (1960) warned that many companies fail to recognize the competitive threat from newly developing products and services.* **2** [I, T] to strongly advise sb to do or not to do sth in order to avoid danger or punishment SYN ADVISE (1): **~ (sb) against/about sth** *He warns against accepting any particular economic opinion as true without careful scrutiny.* ◇ **~ sb (to do sth)** *The fire happened immediately after they had been warned to leave.*

warn·ing /ˈwɔːnɪŋ; *NAmE* ˈwɔːrnɪŋ/ *noun* **1** [C, U] a statement, an event, etc. telling sb that sth bad or unpleasant may happen in the future so that they can try to avoid it: *It is a legal obligation for tobacco companies to print a health warning on cigarette packets.* ◇ **~ against sth** *Doctors issued a warning against eating any fish caught in the river.* ◇ **~ of sth** *Pilots may receive no advance warning of when the manoeuvre will be needed.* ◇ **~ that...** *Many couples ignore warnings that future children will be at high risk.* ◇ **without ~** *The earthquake struck without warning on October 29.* ◇ **+ noun** *This led the Russian early warning system to conclude initially that Russia was under nuclear attack (Forden, 2001).* ◇ **a word of ~** *A word of warning might perhaps be in order at this point.* **2** [C] a statement telling sb that they will be punished if they continue to behave in a particular way SYN CAUTION¹ (2): *Transport Canada issued warnings to the airline but did not take further action.* ◇ *Disciplinary procedures commonly involve a system of spoken and written warnings.*

W

war·rant[1] /ˈwɒrənt; *NAmE* ˈwɔːrənt; ˈwɑːrənt/ *verb* to make sth necessary or appropriate in a particular situation SYN JUSTIFY: **~ sth** *This is a key issue that warrants further investigation.* ◇ **~ (sb/sth) doing sth** *The individual benefit to a patient may be small enough to warrant doing nothing.* ◇ **not ~ sth** *Many doctors prescribed antibiotics, even though they were fairly sure that the condition did not warrant antibiotic therapy.* ➲ *see also* UNWARRANTED

war·rant[2] /ˈwɒrənt; *NAmE* ˈwɔːrənt; ˈwɑːrənt/ *noun* **1** [C] a legal document that is signed by a judge and gives the police authority to do sth: *The police may not, unless invited, enter a person's premises without a search warrant.* ◇ **~ for sth** *In 1997 Austrian authorities issued a warrant for his arrest.* ◇ **~ to do sth** *They obtained warrants to search the premises under section 20C of the Taxes Management Act 1970.* **2** [C] **~ (for sth)** a document that gives you the right to receive money, services, etc: *In total, 1 140 warrants for free passage were issued in 1919.* **3** [sing., U] a reason that makes it acceptable to do sth SYN JUSTIFICATION: *The success of the theory gives some reason, though not a conclusive warrant, to believe it.* ◇ **~ for (doing) sth** *These were deep factional conflicts driven by goups claiming divine warrant for their actions.*

war·ring /ˈwɔːrɪŋ/ *adj.* [only before noun] involved in a war or argument: *A US-brokered peace deal was signed by the warring parties at Dayton.* ◇ *At that time, the Spanish Left was divided into several warring factions.*

war·rior /ˈwɒriə(r); *NAmE* ˈwɔːriər/ *noun* (*formal*) (especially in the past) a brave or experienced solider or fighter: *Bands of warriors from the north suddenly appeared to terrorize the peoples of the Mediterranean world.*

war·time /ˈwɔːtaɪm; *NAmE* ˈwɔːrtaɪm/ *noun* [U] the period during which a country is fighting a war: **during/in ~** *Different rules applied in wartime.* ◇ **+ noun** *These women were profoundly changed by their wartime experiences.* ➲ *compare* PEACETIME

was /wəz; *strong form* wɒz; *NAmE* wʌz/ ➲ BE[1], BE[2]

wash[1] /wɒʃ; *NAmE* wɑːʃ; wɔːʃ/ *verb* **1** [T] to make sth clean using water or another liquid: **~ sth** *Remove your coat and wash your hands before leaving the laboratory.* ◇ **~ sth with sth** *Next, the cells were washed three times with phosphate-buffered saline (PBS).* ◇ **~ sth from sth** *Saliva washes food from the mouth, reducing the time that food is in contact with the teeth.* **2** [T, I] (of water) to flow or carry sth in a particular direction; to be carried in a particular direction by water: **~ sth/sb + adv./prep.** *Wind and rain eroded the hills, and the sediments were washed into the sea.* ◇ **+ adv./prep.** *The weed dries in winter, breaks off and washes downstream.*

PHR V **ˌwash sb/sth aˈway** (of water) to remove or carry sb/sth away to another place: *When the weathered granite is washed away, the formations are exposed as boulders.* **ˌwash sth ˈoff (sth)** to remove sth from the surface of sth by washing: *The cream is left for 12–24 hours (depending on the preparation) and then washed off.* **ˌwash sth ˈout** to wash the inside of sth to remove dirt, etc: *The eyes must be washed out continuously with clean water for 10–15 minutes.* **wash up** to be carried onto land by water: **+ adv./prep.** *Strange gelatinous material occasionally washes up on beaches around the world.* **ˌwash sb/sth ˈup** (of water) to carry sb/sth onto land: *Equiano and the crew are washed up on one of the many Bahama islands.*

wash[2] /wɒʃ; *NAmE* wɑːʃ; wɔːʃ/ *noun* **1** [C] **~ (with sth)** (*especially BrE*) an act of cleaning sth using water or another liquid: *After three washes with the calcium chloride solution, the roots were observed with a microscope.* **2** [C, U] a liquid used for cleaning part of your body: *The use of an antibacterial wash may be all that is required in uncomplicated cases.*

wash·ing /ˈwɒʃɪŋ; *NAmE* ˈwɑːʃɪŋ; ˈwɔːʃɪŋ/ *noun* [U] the act of cleaning sth using water or another liquid: *Encourage hand washing and general infection control at all times.*

waste[1] /weɪst/ *noun* **1** [U] (*also* **wastes**) [pl.] materials that are no longer needed and are thrown away: *The amount of waste produced in the two cities and the way the waste is managed are compared.* ◇ *The company plans to identify all the potentially usable industrial wastes within 350 km of its production facilities.* ◇ *The major sources of these toxic and hazardous wastes are metal-finishing industries, textile industries, gas processing and metal works.* ◇ *radioactive/nuclear waste* ◇ *The aim is to educate and make people more aware of the need to reduce and recycle household waste.* ◇ **+ noun** *The site had been used as a chemical and municipal waste disposal site until 1953.* **2** [U] material that the body gets rid of as solid or liquid material: *Much of the city's human waste is disposed of by the drainage of rainwater through open ditches.* **3** [U, sing.] the act of using sth in a careless or unnecessary way, causing it to be lost or destroyed: *His remit was to reduce costs and eliminate waste.* ◇ *Car manufacturers cut steel to make vehicle bodywork, and in the process, a proportion of this material goes to waste.* ◇ **~ of sth** *This prevents waste of a relatively scarce resource and also reduces lab costs.* ◇ *It would be a waste of resources not to leverage their skills.* **4** [sing.] **~ of sth** a situation in which it is not worth spending time, money, etc. on sth: *It seemed as if the interview process, as a selection device, was a complete waste of time.* ◇ *If the campaign does not achieve its targets, the advertiser may feel that continuing to run it would be a waste of money.*

waste[2] /weɪst/ *verb* **1** to use more of sth than is necessary or useful: **~ sth** *The study design was too inflexible and we ended up wasting time and resources.* ◇ *Large energy systems can be inefficient, often wasting excess thermal energy.* ◇ **~ sth on sth** *The desk research phase ensures that the company is not wasting its money on research that has already been conducted.* ◇ **~ sth (in) doing sth** *He did not want to waste time building a reduced prototype, too small for the kind of computing that he envisaged.* **2** to give, say, use, etc. sth where it is not valued or used to its full or best effect: **~ sth** *It was widely accepted that Perot had no realistic chance of winning the White House, so to support him was to waste a vote.* ◇ **~ sth on sb/sth** *She portrays Burke as a man of sensibility wasting his talents on an absurdity.*

waste[3] /weɪst/ *adj.* [usually before noun] **1** no longer needed for a particular process or remaining after a process has finished, and therefore thrown away: *Discharge of untreated waste water degrades the quality of the rivers and canals.* ◇ *Plants produce oxygen as a waste product.* **2** (of land) not suitable for building or growing things on and therefore not used: *The orchid is capable of colonizing waste ground and abandoned industrial sites.*

IDM **lay sth ˈwaste | lay ˈwaste (to) sth** to destroy a place completely: *Vesuvius was the volcano whose lava laid waste to ancient Pompeii.*

waste·ful /ˈweɪstfl/ *adj.* using more of sth than is necessary; not saving or keeping sth that could be used: *In 1994, the PAC issued a damning report criticizing corruption and wasteful expenditure within the public sector.* ◇ **~ of sth** *Health systems which allow direct access may be more wasteful of resources and costly to maintain.*

watch[1] /wɒtʃ; *NAmE* wɑːtʃ/ *verb* **1** [I, T] to look at sb/sth for a time, paying attention to what happens: *A pilot study could mean going to the study site and watching for a few hours or days.* ◇ **~ sb/sth** *Most research shows that people strongly prefer visiting and conversing with friends to watching television.* ◇ **~ (sth/sb) for sth** *Watch closely for any cues that they are giving you and respond to those cues.* ◇ **~ what/how, etc...** *Keep your eyes fixated on the central dot and watch what happens.* ◇ **~ sb/sth doing sth**

W

Watching people eating and enjoying themselves is often more compelling than a static shot of the food. ◇ **~ sb/sth do sth** *They might stand on the playground in the morning to watch a child interact with her parent.* **2** [I, T] to pay attention to a situation so that you notice any changes: *The general practitioner is in a good position to watch patiently, waiting for opportunities to help.* ◇ **~ sth/sb** *A rise in the level of external debt relative to reserves or exports is likely to be closely watched by investors.* ◇ **~ (sb/sth) for sth** *Road haulage companies should watch for any changes that impact on transport development.*

PHR V **ˌwatch ˈout for sb/sth** to make an effort to be aware of what is happening, so that you will notice if anything bad or unusual happens: *For a wildebeest, living in a large group affords protection and reduces the costs of watching out for predators.* **ˌwatch ˈover sb/sth** to take care of sb/sth; to guard and protect sb/sth: *Parental care, provided by the female alone, consists essentially of watching over the young and defending the family feeding territory.*

watch² /wɒtʃ; *NAmE* wɑːtʃ/ *noun* **1** [C] a type of small clock that you usually wear on your wrist: *The digital watch contains a substantially different sort of mechanism from mechanical watches with their springs and gears.* **2** [sing., U] the act of watching sb/sth carefully in case of possible danger or problems: **keep (a) ~ on sb/sth** *Seismic monitoring is a very effective way of keeping watch on a volcano.* IDM *see* CLOSE³

water¹ /ˈwɔːtə(r); *NAmE also* ˈwɑːtər/ *noun* **1** [U] a liquid without colour, smell or taste that falls as rain, is in lakes, rivers and seas, and is used for drinking, washing, etc. HELP **Water** is a COMPOUND of HYDROGEN and OXYGEN, chemical formula **H_2O:** *Today, many people in the world still do not have clean drinking water.* ◇ *There is a growing pressure to limit the wasteful use of water by irrigation.* ◇ **+ noun** *The GM tomatoes had lower water content than traditional varieties.* ◇ *water quality/pollution* **2** [U] an area of water, especially a lake, river, sea or ocean: *Each of the workers throws his or her net into the water five times each hour.* ◇ *Ice containing large pieces of glacial debris floats over deep water and drops its load when the ice melts.* ➲ *see also* FRESHWATER **3 waters** [pl.] the water in a particular lake, river, sea or ocean: *Fogs form in summer in the coastal waters round the British Isles.* ◇ **~ of sth** *The canyon was formed by swiftly flowing waters of the Colorado River cutting into rock layers of the south-western Colorado Plateau.* **4** [U] the surface of a mass of water: **on the ~** *We might expect light to behave like the ripples on the water.* ◇ **under ~** *Many invertebrates rise to the surface to breathe or transport and store bubbles of air under water.* **5 waters** [pl.] an area of sea or ocean belonging to a particular country: *An unarmed spy plane was shot down over international waters in April 1969.*

water² /ˈwɔːtə(r); *NAmE also* ˈwɑːtər/ *verb* **1 ~ sth** to pour water on plants, etc: *Plants were hand watered as required.* **2 ~ sth** (of a river, etc.) to provide an area of land with water: *The Severn is the river that waters the western marches of England.*

PHR V **ˌwater sth ˈdown** [often passive] to change a statement, suggestion, agreement, etc. in order to make it less strong or extreme SYN DILUTE¹ (2): *The original plan had to be watered down to placate France and its allies.*

water·shed /ˈwɔːtəʃed; *NAmE* ˈwɔːtərʃed; ˈwɑːtərʃed/ *noun* **1** an event or a period of time that marks an important change: **~ in sth** *Godwin's book certainly marks a watershed in the development of literary biography.* ◇ **~ moment** *This proved to be a watershed moment in post-war history.* **2** a line of high land where streams on one side flow into one river, and streams on the other side flow into a different river: *Large watersheds tend to have extensive flatland areas.*

ˈwater supply *noun* [C, U] the water provided for a town, an area or a building; the act of or system for supplying water to a town, etc: *a clean/contaminated water supply* ◇ *They dug wells to maintain the water supply.*

ˈwater table *noun* [usually sing.] (*technical*) the level at and below which water is found in the ground: *These characteristics are indicative of a permanently high water table.*

wave¹ /weɪv/ *noun* **1** the form that some types of energy such as sound, light, etc. take as they move, characterized by a regular OSCILLATION: *Earthquakes can sometimes generate sound waves in the audible frequency range.* ◇ *The overall reach of an earthquake depends on the type of rocks through which the waves travel.* ◇ *The higher the amplitude of the wave, the brighter the light will be.* ◇ *This proved IR radiation to be a wave like visible light which allowed accurate measurement of its wavelength.* ➲ *see also* MICROWAVE, SHOCK WAVE, WAVELENGTH **2** a raised line of water that moves across the surface of the sea, ocean, etc: *Hatchlings are unable to leave their hatching site on the beach until washed out by waves high enough to release them.* ◇ *If the wind grows, the height of the waves increases.* ◇ **+ noun** *Seawater spray forms when the wind rips small droplets off wave crests.* **3** a sudden increase in a particular activity or feeling: **~ of sth** *A strike for higher wages triggered a wave of labour unrest across the country.* ◇ *Hunter's conclusions helped begin a great wave of fossil research.* ◇ **in waves** *The pandemic is likely to strike in waves of around 15 weeks.* **4 ~ (of sb/sth)** a large number of people or things suddenly moving or appearing somewhere: *It is unlikely that another massive wave of immigrants will arrive in Israel, short of an unforeseen event.* ◇ *The gold rush drew waves of new Portuguese migrants to Brazil.*

▸ ADJECTIVE + WAVE **electromagnetic** • **seismic** • **gravitational** • **acoustic** *The velocity of seismic waves generally increases with depth in the upper mantle.*

▸ NOUN + WAVE **light** • **sound** • **radio** • **gravity** • **earthquake** *Microwaves behave more like rays of light than ordinary radio waves.* | **ocean** • **storm** • **surface** *A tsunami is classified as a surface wave.*

▸ VERB + WAVE **produce** • **cause** • **initiate** *The onset of the economic crisis caused a wave of corporate downsizing and outsourcing.* | **emit** • **generate** • **send** • **transmit** • **diffract** • **propagate** • **radiate** • **record** • **detect** *Generally speaking, shock waves are transmitted faster through denser material.* | **unleash** • **prompt** • **experience** *Ecuador experienced an unprecedented wave of emigration following the severe economic crisis of the late 1990s.* | **trigger** • **provoke** *The budgetary reductions provoked a new wave of public protests.*

▸ WAVE + VERB **propagate** • **travel, move** • **spread** *The vector vibrates perpendicular to the direction in which the light wave is propagating.* | **wash** • **break** *The emergent tidal zone is washed by waves at high tide and subject to desiccation at low tide.*

▸ WAVE + NOUN **propagation** • **crest** • **velocity** • **speed** • **height** • **motion** • **amplitude** • **shape** *Below the crust, seismic wave speeds increase uniformly down to the core.* | **erosion** • **attack** • **action** • **energy** *Mangroves have been drastically reduced leading to further coastal erosion by wave attack.*

wave² /weɪv/ *verb* **1** [I, T] to move your hand or arm from side to side in the air in order to attract sb's attention, greet them, etc: **~ at/to sb** *They just waved to each other and carried on.* ◇ **~ sth** *Male fiddler crabs wave their one enormous claw rhythmically during courtship.* **2** [T] **~ sb/sth + adv./prep.** to show where sth is, show sb where to go, etc. by moving your hand in a particular direction: *The immigration officer glanced at his British passport and waved him through.* **3** [T] to hold sth in your hand and move it from side to side: **~ sth** *They distributed leaflets* and waved placards and banners. ◇ **~ sth + adv./prep.** *The gunman screamed at her and waved a rifle in her face.*

wave·form /ˈweɪvfɔːm; *NAmE* ˈweɪvfɔːrm/ *noun* **~ (of sth)** (*physics*) a curve showing the shape of a wave at a particular time: *The oscilloscope recorded the waveform of the sound waves from the microphone.*

wave·length /ˈweɪvleŋθ/ *noun* the distance between two similar points in a wave, especially points in a sound wave or ELECTROMAGNETIC wave, such as light: *The light with these longer wavelengths will be perceived as yellowish orange.* ◇ *Microwaves are electromagnetic waves of very short wavelengths.* ◇ **~ of sth** *The human eye is constructed so that it is able to discriminate the different wavelengths of light.*

way /weɪ/ *noun* **1** [C] a method, style or manner of doing sth: **~ to do sth** *Companies need to find new ways to sustain the loyalty of their employees.* ◇ **~ of doing sth** *There are two different ways of approaching this debate.* ◇ **~ (that)...** *The Web and email have changed the way individuals interact with one another.* ◇ **in a ~ (that)...** *Economic factors can influence health in many ways.* ◇ *The directors may have been acting in a way that was detrimental to the shareholders.* **2** [C, usually sing.] the route along which sb/sth is moving; the route that sb/sth would take if there was nothing stopping them/it: **on your/its ~** *The spaces between galaxies increase while light is on its way from one galaxy to another.* ◇ **along the ~** (*figurative*) *The project may develop problems along the way.* ◇ **in/out of your/its ~** *The water ahead of you when swimming needs to move out of your way, so you have to apply a force to it to get it to do this.* ◇ **find your/its ~** *Scavenging leads to condemned food from the landfill finding its way into poor households.* ◇ **fight your/its ~** (*figurative*) *Antidemocratic revolutionary forces fought their way to power.* **3** [C, usually sing.] a particular direction; in a particular direction: **which, this, that, etc. ~** *The network has an arrow on each edge indicating which way it runs.* ◇ (*figurative*) *Regardless which way the Supreme Court rules in these cases, the outcomes could be important indicators.* ◇ **the other ~** *If a pipe is full of fluid flowing one way, then there is no room for fluid flowing the other way too.* ➲ *see also* ONE-WAY, TWO-WAY **4** [sing.] a distance or period of time between two points: **all the ~ (+ adv./prep.)** *Prospect Lake extended all the way up through the Grand Canyon.* ◇ **a long ~ (+ adv./prep.)** *Experiments are in progress but a long way from clinical use.* **5** [C] a particular aspect of sth SYN RESPECT[1] (1): **in this, that, every, etc. ~** *Unless different markets are identical in every way, profit-maximizing firms will generally set different prices in different markets.* ◇ **in the same ~** *Herbivore numbers may be limited by their consumers. In the same way, predators may themselves be limited by the numbers of predators or parasites consuming them.* ◇ **one ~ or another** *Clearly, the value systems of the different players exert a powerful influence, one way or another, over public attitudes.*

IDM **cut both/two ˈways** (of an action, argument, etc.) to have two opposite effects or results: *It cuts both ways of course, because highly educated people, while they can achieve more for the economy, do not like being told what to think or do.* **either way | one way or the other** used to say that it does not matter which one of two possibilities happens, is chosen or is true: *Not enough is known about this topic to make any categorical statements one way or the other.* **get in the way of sth** to prevent sb from doing sth; to prevent sth from happening: *Such attitudes can get in the way of learning if students avoid any instruction that seems to be 'academic'.* **give ˈway** to break or fall down: *River bed disturbances caused banks to give way.* **give way to sth** **1** to be replaced by sth: *Sea transportation gave way to air travel after the Second World War.* **2** to stop resisting sth; to agree to do sth that you do not want to do: *Modern industrial strength in the US began to give way to the pressures of global capital flight.* **go a long/some way towards/to doing sth** to help very much/a little in achieving sth: *Two further developments go some way to filling this gap.* **go out of your way (to do sth)** to make a special effort to do sth: *In his November speech, Gorbachev went out of his way to praise Khrushchev.* **go your own ˈway** to do as you choose, especially when sb has advised you against it: *In December 1991, an election and a referendum showed that the Ukraine was as determined as Russia to go its own way.* **have it ˈboth ways** to have the advantages of two different situations or ways of behaving that are impossible to combine: *The government was able to have it both ways, presenting itself as nobly pursuing the same economic policy while in fact relaxing it.* **in a big/small way** on a large/small scale: *During the 1990s, the process of internationalization took off in a big way among the Argentinian business groups.* **in her, his, its, etc. (own) ˈway** in a manner that is appropriate to or typical of a person or thing but that may seem unusual to other people: *The construction of these suburbs was an enterprise as socially significant in its way as the building of the medieval cathedrals.* **in a ˈway | in ˈone way | in ˈsome way(s)** to some extent; not completely: *Cells are, in a way, more complex than the embryo itself.* **in no way** not at all: *The examples given here in no way cover all possible approaches.* **(in) one way or another | (in) one way or the other** used to show that sth is true for various reasons that are not mentioned: *In one way or another, national culture can influence the competitive environment.* **in the way of sth** used in questions and negative sentences to talk about the types of sth that are available: *Most schools offer little if anything in the way of Middle Eastern studies.* **look the other ˈway** to deliberately avoid seeing sth bad that is happening instead of trying to stop it: *Some politicians prefer to look the other way during the election contest, in the interest of a smooth election.* **lose your ˈway** to forget or move away from the purpose or reason for sth: *Some concerns still exist within the profession that nursing has lost its way.* **make ˈway for sb/sth** to allow sb/sth to take the place of sb/sth: *Fifty per cent of the forest in the district has been removed to make way for coffee cultivation.* **on your/the/its ˈway** **1** going or coming: *The banking sector crisis was well on the way to becoming a sovereign debt crisis.* **2** during the journey: *The kinetic energy of a rock crashing to the ground is converted into heat by friction on the way down.* **the ˌother way ˈround** the opposite situation: *Science advances by making theories conform to facts rather than the other way round.* **(not) stand in sb's ˈway/stand in the way of sth** to (not) prevent sb from doing sth/prevent sth from happening or progressing: *Liberals argued that Russia should not stand in the way of independence movements.* **under ˈway** (*also* **under·way**) having started: *Pilot schemes are already under way in Scotland and Denmark.* ◇ *Plans are under way to extend screening to older age groups.* **a/the/sb's way of ˈlife** the typical pattern of behaviour of a person or group: *Eisenhower recognized that the American way of life relied on underlying American prosperity.* **ˌways and ˈmeans** the methods and materials available for doing sth: *Health scares have resulted in an enhanced consumer sensitivity to the ways and means of food production and processing.* **a way ˈinto sth** (*also* **a way ˈin to sth**) something that allows you to join a group of people, an industry, etc. that it is difficult to join, or to understand sth that it is difficult to understand: *Government strategy on refugee employment encouraged volunteering as a way into the labour market.* ◇ *Other kinds of non-literary texts might profitably offer a way into the Renaissance.* **ˌwork your ˈway through college, round the world, etc.** to have a job or series of jobs while studying, travelling, etc. in order to pay for your education, etc: *Chekhov qualified as a doctor after working his way through university.* **ˌwork your way ˈthrough sth** to do sth from beginning to end, especially when it takes a lot of time or effort: *Reviews*

W

have been prioritized to enable the reader to work their way through the vast amount of literature on the topic. ˌ**work your way ˈup** to move regularly to a more senior position in a company: *Byrd worked his way up the administrative ladder, becoming vice president in 1932.* ➲ *more at* CLEAR², ERROR, EXAMPLE, FIND¹, HARD¹, LONG¹, MIDDLE¹, OPEN², PAVE, PAY¹, SEPARATE¹

we /wi; *strong form* wiː/ *pron.* (used as the subject of a verb) **1** I and another person or other people; I and you: *We studied a sample from Kenya collected in 2001.* ◇ *We would like to thank students and staff for their cooperation.* HELP In academic language, **we** meaning 'I and you' is used especially by experts writing for students, for example in a TEXTBOOK: *Earlier, we considered the example of a plane taking off.* ◇ *In this chapter, we shall see...* However, **we** is rarely used in this way by experts writing for other experts, for example in a research article; and it is best avoided by students writing for a tutor or examiner. However, students can use it, for example, in a spoken presentation, where the fact of standing up in front of an audience to deliver a talk gives a kind of temporary 'expert' status. **2** people in general: *We often react with anger when anger is directed towards us.*

weak /wiːk/ *adj.* (**weaker**, **weakest**) **1** (of people or animals) not physically strong: *This morning he felt too weak to get out of bed.* ◇ *In bad years, food is so scarce that they all grow weaker, the younger children especially so.* ◇ *She presented to her GP complaining of a weak left leg.* OPP STRONG (9) **2** (of objects or materials) that can be easily broken, damaged or destroyed: *The molecules are held together by relatively weak bonds.* ◇ *Muds and mudstones give rise to many problems in civil engineering because they are weak and shrink or swell on being dried or wetted.* OPP STRONG (10) **3** lacking power or influence: *No government wants to appear weak in the eyes of its voters.* ◇ *Many people feel weak and inadequate when they do not achieve their goals.* ◇ *Employees in the UK would therefore be in a weaker position than their German counterparts.* OPP STRONG (3) **4 the weak** *noun* [pl.] people or animals who are sick, lack strength or have little power or influence: *The knight swore a binding oath of loyalty to his lord and pledged himself to protect the weak.* ◇ *Predators often take the weak and the infirm.* OPP STRONG (17) **5** (of relationships) not close or firmly established: *Cities locate separately from one another and have only weak links to rural areas.* ◇ *The study documents only a weak correlation between overall patient satisfaction and overall job satisfaction.* OPP STRONG (2) **6** producing only a small force or a small amount of energy: *This weak signal had to be separated from the radio 'noise' produced by the universe.* ◇ *Many fish are able to detect weak magnetic fields.* OPP STRONG (11) **7** of a low standard; not performing or performed well: *Newspapers reported that job growth had been unexpectedly weak in January.* ◇ *Climate change research is still relatively weak in this region.* ◇ *Weaker students may need additional support.* ◇ **~ in sth** *He was not deranged or even weak in reasoning power as they had thought at first.* OPP STRONG (5) **8** (of an argument, evidence, etc.) that people are not likely to believe or be persuaded by; easy to attack or criticize: *Evidence is weaker that employment growth is sustained through new enterprise formation.* ◇ *The arguments seem so weak that they can amount to nothing better than excuses.* ◇ **~ point/spot** *The theory, at least in its present form, has two serious weak points.* OPP STRONG (1) **9** (of prices, an economy, etc.) having a value that is low or falling: *The weaker pound also contributed to rising costs, as fuel is bought in US dollars.* OPP STRONG (15) **10** (*chemistry*) only slightly broken down into its IONS when dissolved in water: *The weak base will cause the pH of the solution typically to be approximately 8.0–9.0.* HELP In non-scientific language, a **weak** liquid is one that contains a lot of water: *a cup of weak tea.* In scientific terms, the word for this is **dilute**: *a dilute solution of potassium permanganate in water* and its opposite is **concentrated**. OPP STRONG (14)

IDM **the weak link (in the ˈchain)** the point at which a system or an organization is most likely to fail: *Manufacturing capability might be the weakest link in the company's move towards improving their competitiveness.*

weak·en /ˈwiːkən/ *verb* **1** [T, I] **~ (sb/sth)** to make sb/sth less strong or powerful; to become less strong or powerful: *These changes weakened trade unions, making it more difficult for them to organize industrial action.* ◇ *The growth of suburban shopping malls and industrial parks began to weaken the link between suburbs and the city centre.* ◇ *Ptolemaic authority in Egypt weakened significantly in the third century BC.* OPP STRENGTHEN (2) **2** [T, I] **~ (sth)** to make sth less physically strong; to become less physically strong: *Faults usually weaken rocks by shattering them to some extent.* ◇ *The immune system of an individual infected by HIV weakens over time, leaving the body less and less able to combat infection.* OPP STRENGTHEN (1) **3** [I, T] to become less determined or certain about sth; to make sb less determined or certain: *In the past decade, this enthusiasm for public opinion polls may have weakened.* ◇ **~ sth** *Behind this continued suppression was the view that Buddhism weakens the military resolve of the nation.* OPP STRENGTHEN (3)

weak·ly /ˈwiːkli/ *adv.* in a way that lacks strength or force: *Brown's conclusions are only weakly supported by the evidence.* ◇ *Over land, winds flatten crops, uproot trees, and severely damage or destroy weakly constructed buildings.* OPP STRONGLY

weak·ness /ˈwiːknəs/ *noun* **1** [U] **~ (of sb/sth)** lack of strength, power or determination: *Over the next year, Jane's muscle weakness worsened and she was unable to continue with her work.* ◇ *This apparent weakness of American political parties has been accounted for in a number of ways:...* ◇ *He may well have resented his father's weakness in converting to Christianity just to save his law practice.* OPP STRENGTH **2** [C] a weak point in an object, a system, sb's character, etc: *Each approach has its strengths and weaknesses.* ◇ *Johnson knew every senator intimately, his likes and dislikes, his weaknesses and his strengths.* ◇ *Rock falls happen when inherent weaknesses in the rock or soil allow a block of the material to detach and fall to the ground.* ◇ **~ of sth** *One of the major weaknesses of such an approach was that the guilds stifled innovation.* OPP STRENGTH (3) ➲ language bank *at* CRITICAL

wealth /welθ/ *noun* **1** [U] a large amount of money, property, etc. that a person or country owns: *The ownership of private wealth gives the individual power.* ◇ *personal/household wealth* ◇ *This school of thought argued for the involvement of the state in economic life so as to increase national wealth and power.* ◇ *Duke left the industry and gave much of his wealth to found Duke University.* ◇ *Unequal distribution of wealth has increased within the region.* ➲ thesaurus note *at* MONEY **2** [U] the state of being rich SYN PROSPERITY: *Knowledge is a key factor in creating economic wealth.* ◇ *By introducing commercial activity and the profit motive on a large scale, capitalism produces great wealth for some.* **3** [U] (in compounds) large supplies of a particular resource: *One reason for the conflict is to gain access to the country's vast mineral wealth.* **4** [sing.] **~ of sth** a large amount of sth: *For the Mycenaean Age (c.1600–1200 BC), we have a wealth of material evidence that permits a fairly detailed picture of the society.* ➲ *compare* RICHNESS

wealthy /ˈwelθi/ *adj.* (**wealth·ier**, **wealthi·est**) **1** having a lot of money, possessions or resources SYN AFFLUENT, RICH (1): *The likely result is that children from wealthy families will use the educational marketplace to greater advantage.* ◇ *Traditionally, Denmark, the Netherlands and*

W

Germany are among the relatively wealthy EU countries. ◇ *The elderly may be wealthier on average than the rest of the population.* **2 the wealthy** *noun* [pl.] people who are rich: *Chinese porcelain was much prized by the wealthy.*

weapon /ˈwepən/ *noun* **1** an object such as a knife, gun, bomb, etc. that is used for fighting or attacking sb: *He was convicted in 2006 of burglary and possessing an offensive weapon.* ◇ **weapons + noun** *Global efforts to constrain nuclear weapons acquisition began soon after 1945.* **2** something such as knowledge, words, actions, etc. that can be used to attack or fight against sb/sth: *The threat of firing continues to be a powerful weapon in the hands of an employer.* ◇ **~ against sb/sth** *The only weapons against plague were quarantine, isolation of patients and burial of corpses.*

wear[1] /weə(r); *NAmE* wer/ *verb* (**wore** /wɔː(r)/, **worn** /wɔːn; *NAmE* wɔːrn/) [T] **~ sth** to have sth on your body as a piece of clothing, a decoration, etc: *Clinical laboratory personnel rarely wear a uniform.* ◇ *Lawrence, who was not wearing a helmet, suffered serious head injuries.*
PHR V ˌ**wear sth ˈaway/down** to make sth become gradually smaller or smoother by continuously using it or putting pressure on it: *Some rocks that are compact and hard resist being worn down, even by the action of glaciers.* ˌ**wear sb/sth ˈdown** to make sb/sth weaker or less determined, especially by continuously attacking or putting pressure on them/it over a period of time: *Gradually, the opposition was worn down.* ˌ**wear ˈoff** to gradually disappear or stop: *Normally, the effects of the drug wear off within a few hours.* ˌ**wear ˈon** (of time) to pass, especially in a way that seems slow: *As the eighteenth century wore on, other groups began forming in English society.* ˌ**wear ˈout** | ˌ**wear sth ˈout** to become, or make sth become, thin or no longer able to be used, usually because it has been used too much: *Unprocessed rubber is rather soft and quickly wears out.* ◇ *There was a need to rebuild and refurbish worn out plant.*

wear[2] /weə(r); *NAmE* wer/ *noun* [U] the damage or loss of quality that is caused when sth has been used a lot: *The pressure on each pad should be as small as possible to minimize wear.*
IDM ˌ**wear and ˈtear** the damage to objects, furniture, property, etc. that is the result of normal use: *It may be impossible to reduce the amount of wear and tear on machines per labour hour.*

wea·ther[1] /ˈweðə(r)/ *noun* [U] the condition of the atmosphere at a particular place and time, such as the temperature, and if there is wind, rain, sun, etc: *An automatic landing system is commonly used in bad weather.* ◇ *cold/hot/warm/dry/wet/severe weather* ◇ *A restaurant may need the flexibility to take on or lay off staff at very short notice, depending on the weather.* ◇ **+ noun** *More extreme weather events are becoming a feature of the changing climate in the UK.* ◇ *High pressure weather systems can result in the trapping of air pollution at ground level.* ◇ *Under good weather conditions, an electric field of the order 100 V/m exists near the earth's surface.* ➲ *compare* CLIMATE (1)

W

wea·ther[2] /ˈweðə(r)/ *verb* **1** [I, T] to change, or make sth change, colour or shape because of the effect of sun, rain, wind, etc: *Typically, the upper part of the main cliff weathers back into a series of ledges.* ◇ **~ sth** *High rainfall and consistently high temperatures have caused the granite to be deeply weathered.* ◇ *weathered rock/granite/material* **2** [T] **~ sth** to come safely through a difficult period or experience: *By the early 1980s, the EC had weathered the storm of recession.*

wea·ther·ing /ˈweðərɪŋ/ *noun* [U] the action of sun, rain, wind, etc. on rocks, making them change shape or colour: *Vegetation increases chemical weathering by supplying CO_2 and organic acids to soil waters.*

weave /wiːv/ *verb* (**wove** /wəʊv; *NAmE* woʊv/, **woven** /ˈwəʊvn; *NAmE* ˈwoʊvn/) **1** [T, I] to make cloth by crossing threads or strips across, over and under each other by hand or by machine: **~ (sth)** *Women habitually baked bread, spun yarn and wove cloth.* ◇ *Specialist female workers gathered in collective workshops to spin, weave and make clothes.* ◇ **~ A from B** *A number of Italian towns revived their luxury industries, notably of fabrics woven from silk and gold thread.* ◇ **~ B into A** *The strands can be twisted to form yarn for weaving into glass-fibre cloth.* **2** [T] to put facts, events, details, etc. together to make a story or a closely connected whole: **~ sth (out of sth)** *Sources are the raw material of history out of which historians weave their stories.* ◇ **~ sth into sth** *These ceremonies are tightly woven into the social fabric.* ◇ **~ sth together** *Both traditions weave together different elements of Buddhist thought and practice.*

web /web/ *noun* **1** [C] a complicated pattern of things that are closely connected to each other: *The smaller and more abundant species tend to be prey to other species higher up the food web.* ◇ **~ of sth** *The analysis indicates that a complex web of cultural, religious and political factors is at work.* ➲ *see also* FOOD WEB **2 the Web, the web** [sing.] a system for finding information on the Internet, in which documents are connected to other documents: *Men mostly use home PCs for games, work and surfing the Web.* ◇ *Further information can be obtained from the web.* ◇ **+ noun** *Each chapter provides specific references to relevant web links.*

web·log /ˈweblɒɡ; *NAmE* ˈweblɔːɡ; ˈweblɑːɡ/ *noun* = BLOG

ˈ**web page** *noun* a document that is connected to the Web and that anyone with an Internet connection can see, usually forming part of a website: *This web page is automatically updated every 15 minutes.* ◇ **on a ~** *Details of these facilities are available on the web page.*

web·site /ˈwebsaɪt/ *noun* a place connected to the Internet, where a company or an organization, or an individual person, puts information: *A virus may be transmitted when an unsuspecting individual visits a website.* ◇ **on a ~** *On the website, the links are arranged according to chapter.*

week /wiːk/ *noun* **1** a period of seven days, either from Monday to Sunday or from Sunday to Saturday: *Work filled up six days of the week.* ◇ *Respondents were asked how many hours a week they spent using the Internet.* **2** any period of seven days: *Radiotherapy may last several weeks.* ◇ *A 77-year-old man has been increasingly short of breath for the past three weeks.* **3** the five days other than Saturday and Sunday: *James lives with his mother during the week and spends the weekends with his father.* ◇ *Her parents are frustrated by the fact that Jody has now missed three weeks of school.* **4** the part of the week when you go to work: *After the birth of the second child, the father started full-time work in another town and spent his working week away.* ◇ *Studies show that even unemployed husbands do much less housework than wives who work a forty-hour week.*

week·ly /ˈwiːkli/ *adj.* happening, done or published once a week or every week: *My primary sources were the five most widely read women's weekly magazines.* ◇ *He also has a regular weekly meeting with the Prime Minister on Monday mornings.* ◇ *The average weekly alcohol consumption was 4.3 drinks in women and 13.7 drinks in men.* ■ **week·ly** *adv.*: *Precipitation chemistry has been measured weekly at each station since 1971.* ◇ *The Joint Intelligence Committee meets weekly.*

weigh /weɪ/ *verb* **1** *linking verb* **+ noun** to have a particular weight: *The turbine rotor for this plant weighed 7.5 tons.* ◇ *After only 18 months in the ocean, the salmon reach* *a length of up to 90 cm and weigh up to 7 kg.* **2** [T] **~ sb/sth/yourself** to measure how heavy sb/sth is: *Patients were weighed throughout the test.* ◇ *It is important that the sample is weighed in thermal equilibrium with its surroundings.* **3** [T] to consider sth carefully before making a decision: **~ sth (up)** *There are not enough data to weigh up the social costs and benefits of this kind of finance.* ◇ *The court should give the director the benefit of any doubt when weighing the evidence of his misconduct.* ◇ **~ (up) sth against sth** *The dangers must be weighed against the benefits.* **4** [I] **~ (with sb) (against sb/sth)** to have an influence on sb's opinion or the result of sth: *Two factors weighed against any widespread acceptance of this theory.* ◇ *The obvious reasons to stop behaving in this way do not weigh with him as decisively as one might expect.*

PHR V **ˌweigh sb ˈdown** to make sb feel worried or anxious SYN BURDEN²: *Her grief and sadness, rather than weighing her down, turned to rage.* **ˌweigh sb/sth ˈdown** **1** to make sb/sth heavier so that they are not able to move easily: *As a pollutant, oil physically obstructs living organisms, smothering and weighing them down.* **2** to prevent sb/sth from working or doing sth as well or as easily as they should: *Weighed down by a deficit more than four times the EU's limit, Greece has initiated a number of austerity measures.* **ˌweigh ˈin (on sth) (with sth)** (*rather informal*) to join in a discussion, an argument, an activity, etc. in a strong, confident way and try to influence it: *A number of authors have weighed in on the subject of including test scores in reports.* **ˈweigh on sb/sth** **1** to make sb anxious or worried: *Her friend's absence is weighing on her mind.* **2** to have a great or negative influence on sb/sth: *The global impact of HIV weighs heavily on medical resources worldwide.* **ˌweigh sth ˈout** to measure and take an amount of a particular weight from a larger quantity of a substance: *Weighing out fine powders is hazardous and requires the use of a weighing station.*

weight¹ /weɪt/ *noun* **1** [U, C] how heavy sb/sth is, which can be measured in, for example, kilograms: *These patients should be encouraged to lose weight.* ◇ *He has lost a stone in weight.* ◇ *Low birth weight and premature delivery can result from infection during pregnancy.* ◇ *In the coastal region, soil moisture averages about 1% by weight.* ◇ **+ noun** *Approved drug therapy may also have a role in weight loss.* ➲ *see also* OVERWEIGHT, UNDERWEIGHT HELP In physics, **weight** is defined as the force applied to a body by a GRAVITATIONAL field. It contrasts with **mass**, which is the quantity of matter that a body contains, independent of GRAVITY: *An object of the same mass weighs a different amount on the earth and the moon.* **2** [U] the quality of being heavy: **~ (of sth)** *Rafters, trusses and beams bear the weight of the roof.* ◇ **under the ~ of sth** *Roofs of houses and buildings collapse under the weight of accumulating ash, especially when wet.* **3** [U] importance, influence or strength: *Others argue that we should attach greater weight to the interests of the less well off.* ◇ *In the novel, the two narratives are given roughly equal weight.* ◇ **~ of sth** *The weight of evidence for the existence of supermassive black holes at the centre of galaxies is considered to be overwhelming.* **4** [C] (*statistics*) a number or quantity that is given to each item in a set to represent its importance relative to the other members of the set: *A larger weight is assigned to the lowest ranked group as compared with the higher ranked groups.* ◇ *The different factors carry different weights.* **5** [sing.] **~ (of sth)** a great responsibility or worry SYN BURDEN¹: *Although handsome and talented, he was simply unable to carry the weight of expectation.* ◇ *She is too young to have to bear the weight of responsibility for a parent who lacks authority.* **6** [C] an object that is heavy or that weighs a known amount: *Patients should avoid bending down and lifting heavy weights.* ◇ *Big arches with big stones may have small stresses but carry very large weights.* **7** [C] an object used to keep sth in position or as part of a machine: *The lighter of the pair of weights will be pulled up as the heavier weight falls down.* **8** [C] a unit or system of units by which weight is measured: *By revising Athenian weights and measures, he facilitated trade with other states.*

IDM **throw/put your weight behind sth** to use all your influence and power to support sth: *The French President and German Chancellor threw their combined political weight behind the idea.* ➲ *more at* PULL¹

▸ ADJECTIVE + WEIGHT **normal • average • low • high • equal • minimum • excess • great • total • relative • equivalent • healthy • ideal • dry • molecular • atomic** *Half the dry weight of a tree is carbon.*

▸ NOUN + WEIGHT **birth • body** *Excess body weight is now the most common childhood disorder in Europe.*

▸ VERB + WEIGHT **lose • gain, put on • watch • measure • calculate • estimate • maintain • reduce** *Height and weight were measured and a clinical history taken.* | **attach, assign, place, put, give • lend • accord • add • carry** *This solution puts too much weight on a rather uncertain hypothesis.* ◇ *Their opinions carried great weight in the highest circles of society.*

▸ WEIGHT + NOUN **loss • gain • reduction • management • control** *Stair climbing could be useful in terms of weight control.*

weight² /weɪt/ *verb* **1** [often passive] **~ sth** to give different values to things to show how important you think each of them is compared with the others: *The data were weighted on age and gender.* ◇ **~ sth by sth** *This component is weighted by a factor of 1.5 in the computation of the total index.* **2 ~ sth** to give importance or value to sth: *Certain words are weighted further by repetition.* **3 ~ sth (down) (with sth)** to attach a weight to sth in order to keep it in the right position or make it heavier: *His body was wrapped in furs, weighted with sand and sunk in the river.*

weight·ed /ˈweɪtɪd/ *adj.* [not usually before noun] arranged in such a way that a particular person or thing has an advantage or a disadvantage SYN BIASED: **~ towards sb/sth** *Business regulatory systems in the UK were historically weighted towards voluntary self-regulation.* ◇ **~ against sb/sth** *The balance of the debate is no longer as heavily weighted against change as it once was.* ◇ **~ in favour of sb/sth** *Ordinary citizens in court found that the whole system was weighted in favour of the prosecution.*

weight·ing /ˈweɪtɪŋ/ *noun* [C, U] a value that you give to each of a number of things to show how important it is compared with the others: *Policymakers give a rather low weighting to the criterion of efficiency.* ◇ **+ noun** *Other weighting schemes may provide different interpretations.*

wel·come¹ /ˈwelkəm/ *verb* **1 ~ sb (to sth)** to greet sb in a friendly way when they arrive somewhere: *He was warmly welcomed on his return to Rome.* **2 ~ sb (+ adv./prep.)** to be pleased that sb has come or has joined an organization, activity, etc: *They welcomed women into their ranks more than previous armies of the world had.* **3 ~ sth** to be pleased to receive or accept sth: *Although supervisors might actively welcome suggestions from their teams, workers may find their ideas are not implemented.* ◇ *Most governments in the region welcome foreign investment.*

wel·come² /ˈwelkəm/ *adj.* **1** that you are pleased to have or receive: *This collection of conference papers is a welcome addition to the research literature on early language learning.* ◇ *This elevated political priority is a welcome development for proponents of global health.* **2** (of people) accepted or wanted somewhere: *Effective teachers have the capacity to make students feel welcome in class.*

wel·fare AWL /ˈwelfeə(r); *NAmE* ˈwelfer/ *noun* [U] **1 ~ (of sb/sth)** the general health and happiness of a person, an animal or a group SYN WELL-BEING: *Adoption now* *places the welfare of the child as paramount.* ◇ *She was not convinced that her husband was sufficiently attentive to her welfare.* **2** practical or financial help, care or protection that is provided, often by the government or other organizations, for people, animals or groups that need it: *Meat produced under circumstances which promote better animal welfare is often better in quality.* ◇ **+ noun** *The new government soon proposed a series of major welfare reforms to try to get more people back to work.* ➲ *see also* WELFARE STATE **3** (*especially NAmE*) (*BrE also* ˌ**social seˈcurity**) money that the government pays regularly to people who are poor, unemployed, sick, etc: **on ~** *She ended up on welfare, making a few extra dollars by working as a cleaning woman.* **4** (*economics*) a measure that reflects the PREFERENCES of the economy overall, which allows for the TRADE-OFF between the UTILITY (= preferences and benefit) of different people in the economy HELP A **welfare gain** happens when a person is made better off without making anyone worse off; a **welfare loss** happpens when a person is made worse off without making anyone better off: *Countries increase their own economic welfare by trading with each other.* ◇ *International trade leads to welfare gains irrespective of absolute costs.* ◇ *A monopoly may create a welfare loss in society.*

▸ ADJECTIVE + WELFARE **national** • **public** • **social** *In an increasingly interdependent world, isolation is not good for national welfare.* | **collective** • **general** • **overall** • **economic** • **material** • **human** *The Court must uphold individual rights, not consider collective welfare.*

▸ NOUN + WELFARE **animal** • **child** • **consumer** *Competition rules have become more directed towards enhancing consumer welfare.*

▸ VERB + WELFARE **maximize** • **improve** • **enhance** • **increase, raise** • **reduce** *In 2002, the company committed itself to minimizing ecological damage and improving animal welfare.* | **promote** • **ensure** • **protect** • **affect** • **consider** *The Workplace Regulations ensure the welfare of employees.*

▸ WELFARE + NOUN **provision** • **reform** • **benefit** • **spending** • **programme** • **services** • **policy** • **officer** • **system** *Policymakers are concerned about the burden that old people place upon the welfare system.* | **recipient** • **payment** *The Food Stamp Plan limited the amount of money welfare recipients could spend on alcohol, tobacco or luxuries.*

ˌwelfare ˈstate *noun* **1** (*often* **the Welfare State**) [usually sing.] a system by which the government provides a range of free services to people who need them, for example medical care, money for people without work, and care for old people: *The ideas informing the development of the welfare state had a strong social, democratic influence.* ◇ **+ noun** *Implementing labour market and welfare state reforms may not solve the country's unemployment problem.* **2** [C] a country that has such a system: *Many conservatives supported the development of European welfare states.*

W

well[1] /wel/ *adv.* (**bet·ter** /ˈbetə(r)/, **best** /best/) **1** in a good or satisfactory way: *He had not performed well on recent tests.* ◇ *The traditional model generally works well.* ◇ *It is unrealistic to expect a patient to come with a well thought-out definition of health.* ◇ **however/no matter how ~** *No matter how well one plans for these events, unexpected things happen.* OPP BADLY (5) **2** thoroughly and completely: *They must know each other well by now.* ◇ *Few investigators have used the soils to better understand archaeological landscapes.* **3** very; very much: *He is well aware that power can be misused.* ◇ *The Industrial Revolution in Europe was well under way.* **4** far in time or distance: **~ away (from sth)** *The bears are found in the far north, well away from most humans.* ◇ **~ after/before (sth)** *His work was not appreciated until well after his death.* ◇ **~ into sth** *This pattern persisted well into the 1970s.* **5 can/could well** easily: *They never bought luxury items, although they could well afford it.* **6 can/could/may/might well** probably: *People may well be confronted with price increases.* ◇ *This could well take as long as a week.*

IDM **as well (as sb/sth)** in addition to sb/sth SYN ALSO (1), IN ADDITION (TO SB/STH): *Time is set aside for counselling and relaxation as well.* ◇ *As well as water, electrolytes are needed.* ◇ *Many businesses as well as consumers may be fearful of the risks involved.* **do ˈwell** to be successful: *Many corporations did not do well in that year.* ◇ *Chinstrap penguin populations are increasing because they do better in open-water conditions (Fraser et al., 1992).* **sb would do ˈwell to do sth** used for saying you think sb would be sensible or wise to do sth: *Researchers would do well to familiarize themselves with some of the useful literature.* **sb might (just) as well do sth** used for saying that sb should do sth, not because they want to do it but because there is no benefit in doing anything else: *He felt as though he might as well give up.*

well[2] /wel/ *adj.* (**bet·ter** /ˈbetə(r)/, **best** /best/) [not usually before noun] in good health: *He is otherwise fit and well and does not take any regular medications.* ◇ *Sunita started taking the tablets and felt better after a couple of days.* IDM **all is (not) well (with sb/sth)** everything is (not) in a good state or position: *At the beginning of a relationship, when all is well, a couple is often optimistic about life.* ◇ *However, even in this happy state, there are worrying signs that all is not well with the nation.* **it is/would be as well to do sth** it is/would be sensible or a good idea to do sth: *Before proceeding further, it is as well to answer various questions that suggest themselves.* ➲ *more at* ALIVE

well[3] /wel/ *noun* **1** a deep hole made in the ground to obtain oil or gas: *Pipes have been laid to offshore oil wells in the Gulf of Mexico.* ◇ *Modern petroleum exploitation in Romania began in 1857 when the first commercial well was drilled.* **2** a deep hole in the ground from which people obtain water. The sides of wells are usually covered with brick or stone and there is usually some covering or a small wall at the top of the well: *In much of Niger, hand-dug wells have been used as water sources for generations.*

ˈwell-being *noun* [U] general health and happiness: *Physical activity can improve emotional well-being for all age groups.* ◇ **~ of sb** *There is a range of effective interventions to promote the psychological well-being of adults.* ◇ *Evidently, the economic well-being of populations is closely tied to their energy consumption.*

ˌwell deˈfined *adj.* easy to see or understand: *Growth after birth follows a well-defined pattern.* ◇ *These categories are not well defined.*

ˌwell ˈdocumented *adj.* having a lot of written evidence to prove, support or explain it: *Citizen participation in policy development has had a rich and well-documented history.* ◇ **it is ~ that...** *It is well documented that chronic illnesses are associated with greater incidence of mental health concerns.*

ˌwell eˈstablished *adj.* **1** having existed or been used for a long time: *Nuclear power is a well-established technology for generating electricity.* ◇ *There is a well-established tradition of using personality questionnaires in making personnel decisions.* **2 it is ~ that...** used for saying that sth is accepted as true or right because it has been proven over time: *It is well established that sales and service activities require quite different skills.*

ˌwell ˈfounded (*also less frequent* ˌ**well ˈgrounded**) *adj.* having good reasons or evidence to cause or support it: *They claimed that they were refugees since they had a well-founded fear of persecution.* ◇ *McLean's call for more robust empirical evidence is well founded.*

well 'known *adj.* **1** known about by a lot of people SYN FAMOUS: *Chanel No. 5 perfume is a well-known brand and most buyers will already know what it smells like.* ◇ *They conducted interviews with well-known figures from the movement.* ◇ *The Rhine rift is another well-known example of an intracontinental rift.* ◇ **~ for sth** *These writers are well known for their achievements in fiction.* **2** (of a fact) generally known and accepted: *It is a well-known fact that at a depth of about 3–6 m, the earth provides a very stable thermal environment.* ◇ *The circumstances surrounding the case are well known.*

well 'off *adj.* **1** (*comparative* **better 'off**) having a lot of money SYN RICH (1): *For families that are less well off, a car may represent more responsibility than freedom.* ◇ *There are often large inequalities in health between poor and better-off households.* **2** (*comparative* **better 'off**, *superlative* **best 'off**) in a good situation: *Car producers are better off focusing on a narrower range of activities that more specifically address the core values of the product.*

went *past tense of* GO

were /wə(r); *strong form* wɜː(r)/ ➲ BE[1], BE[2]

west[1] /west/ *noun* [U, sing.] (*abbr.* **W**) **1** (*usually* **the west**) the direction that you look towards to see the sun go down; one of the four main points of the COMPASS: *Rain is spreading from the west.* ◇ **to the ~ (of...)** *a town to the west of London* ➲ *compare* EAST[1], NORTH[1], SOUTH[1] **2 the West** Europe, N America and Canada, contrasted with Eastern countries: *He was born in Japan, but has lived in the West for some years now.* **3 the West** (*NAmE*) the western side of the US: *the history of the American West* **4 the West** (in the past) Western Europe and N America, when contrasted with the Communist countries of Eastern Europe: *East-West relations*

west[2] /west/ *adj.* [only before noun] (*abbr.* **W**) in or towards the west: *West Africa* ◇ *the west coast of Scotland* ■ **west** *adv.*: *The house faces west.*

west·ern /ˈwestən; *NAmE* ˈwestərn/ *adj.* **1** [only before noun] (*abbr.* **W**) (*also* **Western**) located in the west or facing west: *western Spain* ◇ *Western Europe* ◇ *the western slopes of the mountain* **2** (*usually* **Western**) connected with the west part of the world, especially Europe and N America: *Western art*

wet /wet/ *adj.* (**wet·ter**, **wet·test**) **1** covered with or containing liquid, especially water: *The wet surface of the fibre sheet is completely saturated.* ◇ *These soils are difficult to work when they are either too wet or too dry.* **2** (of weather) with rain: *Floods are common in the wet season.* ◇ *Cool and wet conditions predominated from January 1788 to winter 1790.* ◇ *Despite its wet climate, grain yields in Ireland were similar to those for England.*

wet·land /ˈwetlənd/ *noun* [C, U] (*also* **wetlands** [pl.]) an area of wet land: *The loss of some coastal wetlands has been blamed on rising water levels.* ◇ **+ noun** *Aquatic species have benefited at the expense of wetland species.*

what /wɒt; *NAmE* wɑːt; wʌt/ *pron., det.* **1** used in questions to ask for particular information about sb/sth: *What are the benefits of this marketing approach?* ◇ *What do employees want from their jobs?* ◇ *What changes have taken place in the external environment?* ◇ *John is worried about how he and his wife will cope and what resources they can draw upon.* ➲ *compare* WHICH (1) **2** the thing or things that; whatever: *What follows is essentially a personal view.* ◇ *She has been trying to find out what has happened to a memorial plaque for the men who were killed on the Island.* ◇ *Linguistic evidence indicates that Ancient Macedonian was in fact separate from what later became Greek.* **3** used to emphasize sth that is surprising or remarkable: *What a difference a hundred years makes.* ◇ *The interview had made her realize 'what a waste' she had made of her life.*

IDM **'what about...?** (*rather informal*) **1** used to make a suggestion: *What about doing something with the stream behind the school?* **2** used to introduce sb/sth into a conversation or discussion: *But what about other animals? Are cats or dogs or dolphins aware of themselves?* **what if...?** what would happen if?: *What if the damage done to the company's image is serious?* ◇ *If you can meet all the requirements, all well and good, but what if you cannot?*

what·ever /wɒtˈevə(r); *NAmE* wətˈevər; wɑːtˈevər/ *det., pron.* **1** any or every; anything or everything: *It is a monopoly and it can charge whatever price brings it the most profit.* ◇ *For whatever reason, Jonson was charged with treason.* ◇ *Good parents do whatever is necessary for their children to reach their goals.* ◇ *Despite leading a life of poverty, she would share whatever she had with others.* **2** used when you are saying that it does not matter what sb does or what happens, because the result will be the same: *Whatever decision is reached today, it is unlikely to lead to an enduring and effective solution.* ◇ *They believed that all people were equal in the eyes of God, whatever their skin colour and worldly status.*

IDM **or what'ever** (*informal*) or sth of a similar type: *Interviewers might be asked to collect scraps of information about the home, school, firm, or whatever.*

wheat /wiːt/ *noun* [U] a plant grown for its grain that is used to produce the flour for bread, etc; the grain of this plant: *The major grain crops such as wheat and maize are now grown on every continent.*

wheel /wiːl/ *noun* **1** [C] one of the round objects under a vehicle that turns when it moves: *The wheels of a car enable it to move smoothly over the ground.* ◇ *Most magnesium was used in alloys for a variety of aircraft parts, including wheels, engine casings and doors.* **2** [C] a flat round part in a machine: *The motor turns the wheels from position to position.* ◇ *Just as water pushes the blades of a water wheel, steam pushes the blades of a steam turbine.* **3 wheels** [pl.] an organization or a system that seems to work like a complicated machine that is difficult to understand: *The wheels had been set in motion for a change in government.* ◇ **~ of sth** *In these cases, inequality throws sand in the wheels of progress.* **4** [C, usually sing.] the round object used to control the direction of a car or ship: *Fractures to the sternum are usually caused from either the seatbelt or steering wheel.* **5 -wheeled** (in adjectives) having the number or type of wheels mentioned: *These engines are mostly used to power two-wheeled vehicles, such as motorcycles and mopeds.*

wheel·chair /ˈwiːltʃeə(r); *NAmE* ˈwiːltʃer/ *noun* a special chair with wheels that sb who cannot walk uses for moving around: *Only about 4% of disabled people use a wheelchair.* ◇ **+ noun** *Heumann was a polio survivor and wheelchair user.* ◇ *A ramp was fitted to provide wheelchair access into the town hall.*

when[1] /wen/ *adv.* **1** (used in questions) at what time; how soon; in what circumstances: *When did the Big Bang happen?* ◇ *So we know what a search order does, but when will it be granted?* ◇ *When would such a rule be justifiable?* **2** used after an expression of time to mean 'at which' or 'on which': *There was a time when governments did not exist.* ◇ *There may come a day when the situation will change.* **3** at which time; in which circumstances: *The first known decline in fertility rates occurred in the 17th century, when the rate fell from about 7 to 4.*

when[2] /wen/ *conj.* **1** at or during the time that: *When he was interviewed, Stephen had been a stepfather for almost ten years.* ◇ *When electrons are at an equilibrium state, they may be identified as a particle.* **2** after: *It was only when they were able to understand the other's position that they were able to achieve change.* ◇ *When she had* recovered, Molly's boss insisted that she have a medical assessment. **3** at any time that; whenever: *When possible, a specialist opinion should be obtained before prescribing.* ◇ *People took medical practice into their own hands when it was convenient.* **4** in the case that: *Analysis of variance is the correct test to use when all the groups have a normal distribution.* **5** just after which: *The exchange in Tokyo opens just when New York's closes.* IDM *see* AS[3]

when·ever /wen'evə(r)/ *conj.* **1** every time that: *He returned whenever he could.* ◇ *A glacier will form whenever a body of snow accumulates, compacts and turns to ice.* ◇ *Whenever possible, patients returning to the clinic see the same physician.* **2** at any time that; on any occasion that: *It is possible to listen to high-quality music whenever we like.*

where[1] /weə(r); *NAmE* wer/ *adv.* **1** in or to what place or situation: *Where did they meet?* ◇ *She began to wonder where the real danger actually lay.* ◇ *If we accept this viewpoint, where does it lead?* **2** used after words or phrases that refer to a place or situation to mean 'at, in or to which': *The situation is worse in countries where governments are unwilling to meet the cost of controlling pollution.* ◇ *Continued growth eventually led to a situation where growth was no longer possible.* **3** the place or situation in which: *Marx settled in London, where he and his family suffered in grinding poverty.*

where[2] /weə(r); *NAmE* wer/ *conj.* (in) the place or situation in which: *This is where things get more complicated.* ◇ *The most intense social problems will be especially likely to occur where the inequalities are greatest.* ◇ *Where graphs are concerned, one is free to plot any variable one chooses against any other.*

where·as AWL /ˌweər'æz; *NAmE* ˌwer'æz/ *conj.* used to compare or contrast two facts: *Life expectancy at birth in rich countries is now 78 years, whereas it is about 58 years in poor countries.* ◇ *Whereas an organism carries the same genome in each of its cells, the proteome will vary from cell to cell.* ➲ language bank *at* COMPARE

where·by AWL /weə'baɪ; *NAmE* wer'baɪ/ *adv.* by which; because of which: *The process whereby shareholders may dispose of their holdings is now more efficient.* ◇ *There are three principal mechanisms whereby bacteria cause intestinal disease.*

where·in /weər'ɪn; *NAmE* wer'ɪn/ *adv., conj.* (*formal*) in which place, situation or thing; in what way: *This is an issue wherein I wholeheartedly agree with his thesis.* ◇ *an organization wherein each employee is valued and respected*

wher·ever /weər'evə(r); *NAmE* wer'evər/ *conj.* **1** in any place: *Peasants were not free to live wherever they wished.* ◇ *Wedgwood sought the best quality raw materials from wherever he could find them.* **2** in all places that SYN EVERYWHERE: *Southern white men carry the violent history of the region with them wherever they go.* **3** in all cases that SYN WHENEVER: *Organizations work, wherever possible, to reduce uncertainty and risk.*

whether /'weðə(r)/ *conj.* **1** used to express a doubt or choice between two possibilities: *The question of whether a machine can ever be said to 'think' has a long and controversial history.* ◇ **~ ... or...** *This protein regulates whether a gene is on or off.* ◇ **~ ... or ~ ...** *Economists cannot agree on whether the economy is headed for a recession or whether the business cycle expansion will soon peak.* ◇ **~ or not...** *The most important decision is whether or not to weight nations according to their population size.* **2** used to show that sth is true in either of two cases: **~ or not...** *They should be paid something whether or not they are successful.* ◇ **~ ... or not...** *Whether we like it or not, human beings are different from atoms and insects.*

GRAMMAR POINT

whether ♦ if

- **Whether** and **if** are each used to introduce possibilities. Either word may be used after verbs such as *ask, know, find out* and *wonder*: *The first question* ***asked if*** *respondents had been contacted by a political party, candidate or other political group.* ◇ *During a public discussion in Moscow, Tarkovsky* ***was asked whether*** *he was interested in making abstract films.*
- **Whether** is usually used with verbs such as *analyse* and *investigate*, which express an action that is done in a piece of research: *Schroder (2007)* ***analysed whether*** *stock indices that represent socially responsible investments exhibit a different performance to conventional indices.* ◇ *We* ***investigated whether*** *birth order is associated with the risk of childhood diabetes.* ◇ *We* ***studied whether*** *the scheme increased access to hospital care.*

which /wɪtʃ/ *pron., det.* **1** used in questions to ask sb to be exact about one or more people or things from a limited number: *Which is the best method to use?* ◇ *In which direction do these lines seem to run?* ◇ **~ of sth** *Participants were asked to identify which of the two voices they found the most attractive.* ➲ *compare* WHAT (1) **2** used to be exact about the thing or things that you mean: *The ships which sailed for America were packed with emigrants.* ◇ *It is important to understand the situation in which doctors work.* HELP **That** can be used instead of **which** in this meaning, but it is not used immediately after a preposition: *It is important to understand the situation that doctors work in.* **3** used to give more information about sth: *The main symptom of the disease is chest pain, which can often be intense.* ◇ **in ~ case...** *The material may have been obtained commercially, in which case details of the supplier should be given.* HELP **That** cannot be used instead of **which** in this meaning.
IDM **ˌwhich is 'which** used to talk about distinguishing one person or thing from another: *The samples are labelled to keep track of which is which.*

which·ever /wɪtʃ'evə(r)/ *det., pron.* **1** used to say what feature or quality is important in deciding sth: *Customers will choose whichever brand they prefer.* ◇ *The pension should be increased annually in line with earnings or prices, whichever is the higher.* **2** used to say that it does not matter which, as the result will be the same: *Most cases would be decided in the same way whichever approach is adopted.* ◇ *Whichever they choose, we must accept their decision.*

while[1] /waɪl/ *conj.* (*also* **whilst** /waɪlst/ *especially in BrE*) **1** during the time that sth is happening; at the same time that sth is happening: *While writing up his notes, he recorded the following observations:...* ◇ *Carefully watch both arms while the patient walks across the room.* **2** used to contrast two things SYN WHEREAS: *Some children are born into privileged circumstances, while others are born into poverty.* ◇ *Phobias that began in childhood often continue for many years, while those starting in adult life may improve with time.* ➲ language bank *at* COMPARE **3** (used at the beginning of a sentence) although; despite the fact that...: *While her findings are based on a small sample, they are very interesting.*

while[2] /waɪl/ *noun* [sing.] a period of time: *It takes a while to prepare a mould for another casting.* ◇ **for a ~** *For a while, the business enjoyed good profitability.* ◇ **all the ~** *He spent almost two years with them, all the while writing his doctoral dissertation.* ◇ **once in a ~** *83.1% of employed respondents reported taking medications once in a while.*
IDM *see* WORTH[1]

W

white[1] /waɪt/ *adj.* (**whiter**, **whit·est**) **1** having the colour of fresh snow or of milk: *The flowers appear white, without any distinct pattern.* ◇ *A white object looks white because it reflects essentially all of the visible spectrum.* ◇ *A heated metal bar glowing red hot becomes white hot when heated further.* **2** belonging to or connected with a race of people who have pale skin: *The sample was predominantly white (87%) with 8% black, 2% Asian and 1% multiracial parents.* ◇ *The earliest historians of slavery relied on sources generated by white people.* ◇ *The disorder occurs almost exclusively in the white population.* **3** (of the skin) pale because of illness or emotion: *Frostbite makes the skin white and numb.* ■ **white·ness** *noun* [U, sing.] *There are obvious connections between discourses of whiteness and those of imperial mastery.*

white[2] /waɪt/ *noun* **1** [U] the colour of fresh snow or of milk: *Most opaque minerals have colours in reflected light that range from nearly pure white to various shades of grey.* **2** [C, usually pl.] a member of a race or people who have pale skin: *Whites were a minority in all of the Caribbean islands; they comprised less than 10 per cent of the population.* ◇ *The success of the civil rights movement alienated many southern whites from the Democratic Party, but helped to win black support.* **3** [C, U] the outer, liquid part of an egg that surrounds the yellow part in the middle: *When the egg white is heated, it changes irreversibly from liquid to solid.* IDM *see* BLACK[2]

ˌwhite-ˈcollar *adj.* [usually before noun] working in an office, rather than in a factory, etc; connected with work in offices: *There are now large numbers of white-collar workers such as office staff, government employees, medical staff, teachers and lawyers.* ◇ *white-collar jobs/work/crime* ➲ *compare* BLUE-COLLAR

who /huː/ *pron.* **1** what or which person: *Who will benefit from the research?* ◇ *Individuals have a right to know who holds data on them.* **2** used to show which person or people you mean: *The man who first landed on the moon was born in the USA.* ◇ *It is a no-go area for those who live outside it.* **3** used to give more information about a person or people who have been previously mentioned: *They are a group of people who share common goals.* ◇ *After Thomas Arne, who wrote principally for the theatre, English music declined.* ➲ *compare* WHOM

who·ever /huːˈevə(r)/ *pron.* **1** the person or people who; any person who: *Whoever sets the agenda enjoys an advantage.* **2** used to say that it does not matter who, since the result will be the same: *Whoever said 'the best things in life are free' was wrong—very little in life is free.*

whole[1] /həʊl; *NAmE* hoʊl/ *adj.* **1** [only before noun] full; complete: *Cells were progressively organized into tissues, organs, systems and, finally, the whole body.* ◇ *But this is not the whole story.* ◇ *Coding the data is one of the key phases in the whole process of qualitative data analysis.* ◇ *He considered Rome to have won control of the whole world.* **2 a ~ range/series/host/spectrum, etc. (of sth)** used to emphasize that there are many different things: *A simple word may encompass a whole range of ideas.* ◇ *A whole series of reforms have been implemented.* ◇ *People have developed a whole host of new ways to spend their leisure time.* **3 ~ blood/milk** blood or milk with no part taken away: *Serum is obtained from whole blood that has been allowed to form a clot.* ➲ *see also* WHOLLY ■ **whole·ness** *noun* [U] *Critics look at how a book's constituent parts contribute to its wholeness.*

whole[2] /həʊl; *NAmE* hoʊl/ *noun* **1** [C] a thing that is complete in itself: *All of the genes within an organism operate together as a unified whole.* ◇ *A framework can be used to organize the different parts of the story into a coherent whole.* **2** [sing.] **the ~ of sth** all that there is of sth: *The city and surrounding area have been recognized as one of the poorest regions within the whole of Europe.* ◇ *Kant spent almost the whole of his life in Königsberg, East Prussia.*

IDM **as a ˈwhole** as one thing or piece and not as separate parts: *Taken as a whole, the earth's water is referred to as the hydrosphere.* ◇ *The pursuit of self-interest does not always benefit society as a whole.* **on the whole** considering everything; in general: *The capitalist economic system has on the whole become more stable.*

whole·sale /ˈhəʊlseɪl; *NAmE* ˈhoʊlseɪl/ *adj.* [only before noun] **1** connected with goods that are bought and sold in large quantities, especially so they can be sold again to make a profit: *Wholesale and retail trade now accounts for about two thirds of Thailand's GDP.* ◇ *The wholesale price of lettuce has increased.* ◇ *The biggest wholesale market for flowers is in the Netherlands.* ➲ *compare* RETAIL **2** (especially of sth bad) happening or done to a very large number of people or things: *The wholesale destruction of the rainforest continues.* ◇ *Sharsar advocates an openness to new ideas without a wholesale rejection of tradition.* ■ **whole·sale** *adv.*: *Wheat flour sold wholesale for about $10 per 100 pounds.* ◇ *American traditionalists reject the gun control case wholesale.*

whol·ly /ˈhəʊlli; *NAmE* ˈhoʊlli/ *adv.* completely SYN TOTALLY: *The supervisory board consists wholly of non-executives.* ◇ *Despite wholly inadequate resources, the army remained in the war.* ◇ *The company is a wholly owned subsidiary of Motorola.* OPP PARTLY, PARTIALLY

whom /huːm/ *pron.* used instead of 'who' as the object of a verb or preposition: *Hasler was mostly inspired by the work of Karl von Frisch, whom he met for the first time in 1945.* ◇ *The Soviet managers with whom they were dealing had to consult the Moscow ministries about quite minor details.* ◇ *To whom should they look for guidance?*

whose /huːz/ *det., pron.* **1** belonging to or coming from which person: *The question is, whose city is it?* ◇ *The number could have been anything between 14 000 and 170 000, depending on whose estimates one follows.* **2** used to say which person or thing you mean: *A patient whose BMI is <20 is underweight.* ◇ *Firms are institutions whose sole purpose is to produce goods and services for the market.* **3** used to give more information about a person or thing: *The Colorado River, whose name in Spanish means 'coloured red', now often runs clear.*

why /waɪ/ *adv.* **1** used to talk about a reason for sth: *There are many reasons why patients travel overseas for medical care.* ◇ *These are very demanding qualities and this is why leadership is hard.* ◇ *It was not difficult to understand why change was necessary.* ◇ *Equally important is why and how some people resist becoming smokers.* **2** used in questions to ask the reason for sth: *In one of his most influential works, Sen asked the question: why do famines occur?* ◇ *Epidemiology is poorly equipped to answer such questions as 'Why do people smoke?'.* ◇ *What went wrong, where and why?* ◇ *Why did they do that? They did it because...* ◇ *Why is this?*

wide /waɪd/ *adj.* (**wider**, **wid·est**) **1** including or affecting a large number or variety of different people or things: *A wide range of equipment is available.* ◇ *The database comprises newspaper articles from a wide variety of newspapers.* ◇ *His books brought his learning to a wide audience in France and abroad.* ◇ *This procedure has wider application.* OPP NARROW[1] (2) ➲ *compare* BROAD (2) **2** very big: *The results show wide variation across the region.* ◇ *Winters are extremely harsh over a wide area.* ➲ *compare* BROAD (5) **3** (mainly used in the comparative and superlative) considering or dealing with the more general aspects of a situation or issue, rather than the details: *This political argument was part of a wider debate on state intervention into economic issues.* ◇ *There is always need for education in the widest sense.* ➲ *compare* BROAD (3) **4 the wider community/public/society/world, etc.** the

W

community, general public, etc. as compared with an individual, family, organization or other smaller group: *How students feel about themselves, both in the classroom and in the wider community, is vital to their learning.* ◇ *The banking crisis spilled over into the wider economy.* **5 -wide** (in adjectives and adverbs) happening or existing in the whole of a country, etc: *There are industry-wide targets for cutting greenhouse gas emissions.* ◇ *a country-wide survey* ◇ *a nationwide search* **6** measuring a lot from one side to the other: *The river is wide and relatively deep.* ◇ *Doorways must be wide enough for wheelchairs to pass through.* OPP NARROW[1] (1) ➲ *compare* BROAD (1) **7** measuring a particular distance from one side to the other: *The huge caverns are many metres wide.* ➲ *see also* WIDTH

IDM **wide of the ˈmark** not accurate: *Some predictions have proved wide of the mark.* ➲ *more at* FAR[1]

▸ WIDE + NOUN **range, array, variety, spectrum • scope • audience • readership • interest • appeal • acceptance • use • application** *Animal biotechnologies raise a very wide spectrum of concerns.*

▸ WIDER + NOUN **context • issue • debate • network • group • set • sense • implications** *Emphasis is placed on the wider economic context in which company law operates.*

WHICH WORD?

wide • broad

- Both **wide** and **broad** are used to describe sth that includes a large variety of different people or things: *a wide/broad range/array/spectrum/scope* ◇ *a wide/broad audience/coalition/community/public/readership*. Both **wide** and **broad** can be used with *variety*, but **wide** is very much more frequent.
- Both **wide** and **broad** can be used to mean 'general'. However, in this meaning, both words, but especially **wide**, are most often used in the comparative form (**wider**, **broader**): *a wider/broader perspective/ interpretation* ◇ *the wider/broader implications*
- **Broad**, but not **wide**, can be used to mean 'not detailed': *a broad outline/overview*
- Both **wide** and **broad** mean 'large', especially when referring to the distance from one side to another: *wide streets* ◇ *a broad band of territory*
- **Wide** is used after the measurement when saying how big sth is from one side to the other: *a giant cube 7 feet tall by 7 feet wide by 10 feet long*

wide·ly /ˈwaɪdli/ *adv.* **1** by a lot of people; in or to many places HELP In this meaning, **widely** often comes before a past participle: *There are a number of widely used techniques for sampling.* ◇ *This argument is now widely accepted.* ◇ *VCRs became widely available in the mid-1980s.* **2** to a large degree; a lot HELP This meaning is used to describe big differences or variations in sth: *Countries vary widely in the health of their populations.* ◇ *They come from widely different social backgrounds.* **3 ~ spaced/separated** with large spaces or periods between: *This part of the forest consists of a few widely spaced trees.* ◇ *The events leading to early death may be widely separated in time from the event.* **4** over a large area or range SYN EXTENSIVELY (2): *He travelled widely throughout the Greek world.*

▸ WIDELY + VERB **accepted, recognized, acknowledged • believed, held • regarded, perceived • known • distributed, dispersed, disseminated • spread • circulated • shared • publicized, reported • used, employed • adopted • practised • cited • studied • read • discussed • criticized** *The report was widely distributed both in the United States and England.*

▸ VERB + WIDELY **vary, differ • range • fluctuate** *Countries differ widely in how their labour markets are organized.*

▸ WIDELY + ADJECTIVE **available • applicable • influential** *The system is simple and widely applicable.* | **divergent, disparate, different** *Initially, the two industries had widely divergent rates of return.*

widen /ˈwaɪdn/ *verb* **1** [I, T] to become larger in degree or range; to make sth larger in degree or range SYN EXPAND (1), INCREASE[1]: *The gap between rich and poor continues to widen.* ◇ **~ sth** *It will be necessary to widen the scope of attention.* OPP NARROW[2] (1) **2** [I, T] to become wider; to make sth wider: *In females, the pelvis widens and the body gets rounder.* ◇ **~ sth** *Eventually, erosion may widen the channel.* OPP NARROW[2] (2)

ˌwide-ˈranging *adj.* including or dealing with a large number of different subjects or areas: *A wide-ranging study found no evidence that foreign aid promotes democracy in these countries.* ◇ *The past decade has seen the beginnings of wide-ranging reforms in the health care system.*

wide·spread AWL /ˈwaɪdspred/ *adj.* existing or happening over a large area or among many people SYN EXTENSIVE (2): *The widespread use of pesticides in agriculture is of great environmental concern.* ◇ *There was widespread support for the war.* ◇ *By 2005, there was a fairly widespread agreement amongst the parties that health and education spending should remain priorities.* ◇ *widespread concern/interest* ◇ *Gentzkow and Shapiro (2008a) challenge the widespread belief that television is detrimental to cognitive development and academic achievement.* ◇ *a widespread perception/recognition* ◇ **~ in/among sth** *Bribery was widespread in the USSR.*

width /wɪdθ; wɪtθ/ *noun* [U, C] the distance from one side of sth to the other; how wide sth is: **~ of sth** *They measured the width of the lake at its narrowest point.* ◇ **in ~** *The channel had narrowed to 9 m in width.* ◇ **of ~** *The two discs were of different widths.* ➲ *compare* BREADTH, LENGTH (1)

wield /wiːld/ *verb* **1 ~ sth** to have and use power or control: *Numerous European countries have brought in legislation to stop supermarkets from wielding excessive power.* ◇ *Business groups tend to wield more influence than smaller firms.* **2 ~ sth** to hold sth, ready to use it as a weapon or tool: *Instead of wielding a spear or sword, each soldier used both hands to hold a long pike steady in front of him.*

wife /waɪf/ *noun* (*pl.* **wives** /waɪvz/) **~ (of sb)** the woman that a man is married to; a married woman: *In 1830 Mill met Harriet Taylor, the wife of a London merchant.* ◇ *The contribution many farmers' wives still made to agricultural production was downplayed.* ◇ *She ultimately rejects her role as a wife and mother.* ➲ *see also* HOUSEWIFE

wild[1] /waɪld/ *adj.* (**wild·er**, **wild·est**) [usually before noun] **1** (of an animal or plant) living or growing in natural conditions; not kept in a house or on a farm: *Limited data are available on wild animals.* ◇ *A large number of wild flower species have been endangered.* **2** (of land) in its natural state; not changed by people: *The success of civilization seemed to mandate the destruction of wild places.* ◇ *The area had a wild, almost savage character.* **3** lacking control; done or happening freely: *There were wild celebrations.* **4** not sensible or accurate; not based on careful thought: *Such wild speculations are well beyond the scope of the current discussion.* ➲ *see also* WILDLY ■ **wild·ness** *noun* [U] *Nature's wildness should be appreciated for itself, beyond human control or utility.* ◇ *His imaginative wildness and emotional excess seemed offensive to good taste.*

wild[2] /waɪld/ *noun* **the wild** [sing.] a natural environment that is not controlled by people: **in the ~** *Animals in the wild are likely to die before the symptoms of ageing become manifest.* ◇ **into the ~** *They can be released back into the wild.* HELP **The wilds (of sth)** refers to an area that is far away from towns or people: *There was an underground tunnel running out into the wilds of the marshes.*

W

wil·der·ness /ˈwɪldənəs; *NAmE* ˈwɪldərnəs/ *noun* [usually sing.] a large area of land that has never been developed or used for growing crops because it is difficult to live there: *Once a pair of gibbons are deemed fit to survive on their own, they are released back into the remaining protected wilderness on the island.* ◇ (*figurative*) *Without kindness, human society would be a barren wilderness devoid of compassion and warmth.* ◇ **+ noun** *Oil extraction in Alaska's last wilderness areas will disrupt the ecosystem and break up the habitat of large animals such as bears and wolves.*

wild·life /ˈwaɪldlaɪf/ *noun* [U] animals, birds, insects, etc. that are wild and live in a natural environment: *All dam and reservoir projects will have to consider their impacts on communities and wildlife.* ◇ **+ noun** *Land use practices should be compatible with wildlife conservation.*

wild·ly /ˈwaɪldli/ *adv.* **1** extremely; to a very great degree: *He was wildly popular.* ◇ *Prices tend to fluctuate wildly.* **2** in a way that is not controlled: *They were torn to shreds in front of 50 000 wildly cheering spectators.*

will[1] /wɪl/ *modal verb* (*short form* **'ll** /l/, *negative* **will not**, *short form* **won't** /wəʊnt; *NAmE* woʊnt/, *pt* **would** /wəd; *strong form* wʊd/, *short form* **'d** /d/, *negative* **would not**, *short form* **wouldn't** /ˈwʊdnt/) HELP Unless you are quoting, the short form **'d** should not be used in academic writing. The forms **'ll**, **won't** and **wouldn't** should also be avoided, unless you are quoting or deliberately using a less formal style. **1** used when talking about what is going to happen in the future: *The impacts of climate change will fall disproportionately upon developing countries.* ◇ *It is still possible that success will be achieved at a future date.* ◇ *Of course, the matter may—and often will—become more complex.* ◇ *Governor John Lynch said he would oppose such a step.* ➲ *compare* SHALL **2** used to show what you are going to write about: *Finally, I will explore whether the social citizenship model has a wider relevance.* ◇ *This paper will report on the broad themes and sub-themes that emerged from the case studies.* **3** used when describing what usually happens in a particular situation or process: *The majority of patients will lose weight due to the inability to eat comfortably.* ◇ *Once collected, the data will normally contain replicate measurements for each data point.* ◇ *Over time, the cement will absorb CO_2 from the air.* **4** used when stating what always happens in a particular situation: *If he is negligent, he will be responsible for the foreseeable loss.* ◇ *A firm will reinvest profits only if it expects to earn more profits.* **5** used when stating what you expect to be true: *Historians will be interested in his perspectives on the Great Depression and World War II.* ◇ *The coming years will no doubt see a greater involvement of researchers with different expertise.* **6** used for showing that sb is willing to do sth: *These children have parents who cannot or will not help them with their homework.* ➲ grammar note *at* MODAL[1]

GRAMMAR POINT

will • would

- To express what may happen or what is expected to happen in future, use **will**: *It remains to be seen whether external funding* ***will*** *have a future effect for TB.* ◇ *Between 2014 and 2020, the company* ***will*** *integrate 3 800 MW of wind energy onto the grid.*
- **Would** is used as the past form of *will*, especially in reported speech: *Eighty-four per cent of respondents reported that it* ***would*** *be very difficult for them to use public transport for their work.*

will[2] /wɪl/ *noun* **1** [U, sing.] the ability to control your thoughts and actions in order to achieve what you want to do; a feeling of strong determination to do sth that you want to do: *The offence was an act of will rather than a product of social circumstances.* ◇ **~ for sth** *There was a lack of political will for reform.* ◇ **~ to do sth** *Leadership requires the will to act as a mentor to others.* ➲ *see also* FREE WILL **2** [C, usually sing.] what sb wants to happen in a particular situation: *They are prepared to resort to violence in order to impose their will on others.* ◇ **~ of sb/sth** *All of this, of course, was in harmony with the will and design of God.* ◇ **against sb's ~** *They were sent home against their will.* **3** [C] a legal document that says what is to happen to sb's money and property after they die: *Divorce does not automatically revoke a will.* ◇ **under sb's ~** *She was a beneficiary under his will.* ◇ **in sb's ~** *She made no provision for him in her will.*

IDM **at ˈwill** used to say that sb can do sth at any time, for any reason: *They could expel students at will.*

will[3] /wɪl/ *verb* **1** to use the power of your mind to do sth or to make sth happen: **~ sth** *People felt as though they had willed the movements themselves.* ◇ **~ sb/sth/yourself to do sth** *People cannot simply will themselves to believe in obvious fabrications just because they want to believe in them.* ◇ **~ sth into (doing) sth** *These positive environments cannot be willed into being.* **2** [T, usually passive] to intend or want sth to happen: **(be) willed (by sb)** *Under this view, moral evil is a consequence of free will, permitted but not willed by God.*

will[4] /wɪl/ *verb* (*third person sing. pres. t.* **will**) [I] (only used in the simple present tense, mainly in phrases such as **as he will** and **what they will**) (*literary*) to want or like: *No society lets each do exactly as he or she will.* ◇ *The Act removed these restrictions, leaving operators free to charge subscribers what they will.*

IDM **if you will** (*rather informal*) used when expressing sth in a new or different way HELP This phrase is best avoided in more formal academic writing: *The problem, a paradox if you will, is that...* ◇ *The workers, if you will, vote with their feet.*

will·ing /ˈwɪlɪŋ/ *adj.* **1** happy or ready to do sth, without needing to be persuaded; not objecting to sth: *They proved willing allies.* ◇ **~ to do sth** *Many were quite willing to fight.* ◇ *Some households may be willing and able to pay higher rents.* OPP UNWILLING **2** done or given freely: *The reader engages through what Coleridge called 'the willing suspension of disbelief'.* ■ **will·ing·ly** *adv.*: *She willingly accepts his proposal.*

will·ing·ness /ˈwɪlɪŋnəs/ *noun* [U, sing.] **~ (of sb) to do sth** the fact of being willing to do sth: *Employment protection legislation may affect the willingness of employers to hire workers.* ◇ *All parties showed a willingness to cooperate.*

win /wɪn/ *verb* (**win·ning**, **won**, **won** /wʌn/) **1** [T, I] **~ (sth)** to be the person or group that is successful in an election, contest or battle: *The party has won two consecutive elections.* ◇ *Their naval strength had been instrumental in winning the war.* ◇ *In the eyes of cosmopolitan America, the evolutionists won the argument.* ◇ *Labrador went on to win, defeating Minnick after just one term in the US House.* **2** [T] **~ sth** to get sth as the result of success in an election, contest or battle: *The party won only two seats.* ◇ *Other parties are more likely to win votes in Scotland and Wales.* ◇ *Shirakawa, MacDiarmid and Heeger won the Nobel prize for chemistry in 2000.* ◇ *He engaged in battle and won a resounding victory.* **3** [T] to achieve or get sth: **~ sth** *He won the praise of prominent economists.* ◇ *His rival opposed the plan and won popular support.* ◇ *Sales shot up once she won a contract with the supermarket.* ◇ **~ sth from sb** *Only the ability to win approval from one's peers could assure success.* ➲ *see also* WINNER

IDM *see* DAY

PHRV **ˌwin sth/sb ˈback** to get or have again sth/sb that you had before: *They provide a four-step process for* *winning back lost customers.* **ˌwin ˈout (over sth/sb)** to be more successful than sth/sb else: *The big chains won out, and large firms came to dominate food retailing.* **ˌwin sb ˈover (to sth)** to get sb's support or approval by persuading them that you are right: *Officials sought to win him over to the 'departmental view'.*

wind[1] /wɪnd/ *noun* [C, U] (*also* **the wind**) [sing.] air that moves quickly as a result of natural forces: *Dry winds blow salt-laden deposits over vast areas.* ◇ *The prevailing winds come from the south-west.* ◇ *The strong westerly winds brought large supplies of rainfall.* ◇ *Seeds are easily carried by the wind.* ◇ **+ noun** *With a sustained wind speed of about 200 km/h, Hurricane Katrina passed directly through New Orleans.* ◇ *wind velocity/direction* ◇ *wind energy/power*

IDM **a wind/the winds of ˈchange** events that will cause change; a feeling that things are about to change: *The winds of change were clearly blowing.*

wind[2] /waɪnd/ *verb* (**wound, wound** /waʊnd/) **1** [I] **+ adv./prep.** (of a road, river, etc.) to have many bends and twists: *Surface drainage is accomplished by streams winding between the hills.* **2** [T] **~ sth + adv./prep.** to wrap or twist sth around itself or sth else: *The DNA is wound around proteins called histones.* **3** [T] **~ sth (up)** to make a piece of machinery work by turning a handle, key, etc: *When the weights reach the floor, the clock has to be wound, hoisting the weights back up.*

PHR V **ˌwind ˈdown | ˌwind sth ˈdown** (of an activity) to end gradually over a period of time; to bring a business, an activity, etc. to an end gradually over a period of time: *By early 1953, the conflict in Korea was winding down.* ◇ *British mercantile interests in Chile were wound down during the 1970s.* **ˌwind ˈup** (*rather informal*) (of a person) to arrive or find yourself in a particular place or situation: *A large percentage of the immigrants eventually wound up in New York.* **ˌwind sth ˈup** to stop running a company, business, etc. and close it completely: *If a decision is made to wind up the company, the court will order the appointment of a liquidator.*

ˈwind farm *noun* an area of land or water on which there are a lot of wind turbines: *Other offshore wind farms have been built or proposed in the Irish Sea.*

win·dow /ˈwɪndəʊ; *NAmE* ˈwɪndoʊ/ *noun* **1** an opening in the wall or roof of a building, car, etc, usually covered with glass, that allows light and air to come in and people to see out; the glass in a window: *The heat loss through windows accounts for approximately half the total heat loss in the building.* **2** [sing.] a way of seeing and learning about sth: **~ on/onto sth** *The Peace Corps website provides a window on different peoples and cultures across the globe.* ◇ **~ into sth** *Superhero comics offer a suprisingly valuable window into twentieth-century US history.* **3 ~ (of opportunity)** a time when there is an opportunity to do sth, although it may not last long: *The recent financial crisis has provided a window of opportunity for Asia to capitalize on.* **4** an area within a frame on a computer screen, in which a particular program is operating or in which data of a particular type are shown: *Received information was presented in red in the data display window.*

ˈwind turbine *noun* a tall structure with parts that turn round, used for changing the power of the wind into electricity: *In addition to becoming much larger, wind turbines have become more efficient.*

wine /waɪn/ *noun* [U, C] a common alcoholic drink made from the juice of GRAPES: *She drinks approximately two bottles of wine per week.* ◇ *Some vineyards have been able to produce wines of consistently higher quality.*

wing /wɪŋ/ *noun* **1** one of the body parts that a bird or insect uses to fly: *The variety of colour markings on butterfly wings is remarkable.* ◇ **+ noun** *In birds, the fingers have become fused and act only as supports for the wing feathers.* **2** one of the large flat parts that stick out from the side of a plane and help to keep it in the air when it is flying: *A wing generates lift but it also creates drag.* **3 ~ (of sth)** one of the parts of a large building that sticks out from the main part: *Glazebrook took the second floor of the north wing of Bushy House as a private residence.* **4 ~ (of sth)** a group within a political party or other organization, whose members share particular opinions: *Subsequently, a militant wing of the movement emerged.* ◇ *He finally broke with the moderate wing of the party.* ◇ *on the left/right wing of the party* ➲ *see also* LEFT-WING, RIGHT-WING

IDM **(waiting) in the ˈwings** ready to do sth or to be used when possible or necessary: *There were over twenty reality shows on TV and several waiting in the wings.*

win·ner /ˈwɪnə(r)/ *noun* a person, team, animal, etc. that wins sth: *Many politicians still believe that success in war is beneficial for the winner.* ◇ **~ of sth** *The total number of electoral college votes decides the winner of the US presidential election.* ◇ *Other distinguished figures, including the future Nobel Prize winner Bunin, were deported in 1922.* IDM *see* PICK

win·ter /ˈwɪntə(r)/ *noun* [U, C] the coldest season of the year, between autumn and spring: *During the Antarctic winter, this region is in darkness and cools to temperatures as low as -85°C.* ◇ *Beijing's climate is temperate continental, with hot rainy summers and cold dry winters.* ◇ **in (the) ~** *Females lay their eggs in winter and early spring at 500–3 000 m depth.* ◇ **in the ~ of...** *In the winter of 1990–91, the situation became critical.* ◇ **+ noun** *During the winter months, these rivers and reservoirs are prone to flooding.*

wire /ˈwaɪə(r)/ *noun* **1** [U, C] metal in the form of thin thread; a piece of this: *Stems were secured with wire.* ◇ *One common technique is to use many thin wires in ducts along the length of the concrete beam.* ◇ **+ noun** *The enclosures were constructed of 10 mm wire mesh.* **2** [C, U] a piece of wire that is used to carry an electric current or signal: *The rod is connected to a copper or aluminium wire.* ◇ *A coil of electric wire carries the current around the cylinder.* ➲ *see also* WIRING

wire·less /ˈwaɪələs; *NAmE* ˈwaɪərləs/ *adj.* [usually before noun] not using wires: *Wireless communication was expanding at an incredible pace.*

wir·ing /ˈwaɪərɪŋ/ *noun* [U] **~ (of sth)** the system of wires that is used for supplying electricity to a building or machine: *Converting the buildings for modern office use is very expensive because it involves new wiring, the construction of car parks, etc.* ◇ *It was necessary to modify some of the machine's wiring.*

wis·dom /ˈwɪzdəm/ *noun* **1** [U, sing.] the ability to make sensible decisions and give good advice, because of the experience and knowledge that you have: *Buddhists meditate in order to cultivate wisdom and compassion.* **2** [U, C] the knowledge and experience that develops within a particular society or group of people: *The language was regarded as a key to a storehouse of ancient wisdom.* ◇ *Success relies on applying wisdoms from alternative disciplines.* ◇ **~ of sb/sth** *The book has been informed by the collective wisdom of the education research community.* HELP **(The) conventional/received wisdom** is what most people believe to be true: *Contrary to conventional wisdom, this is not particularly unusual.* ◇ *At that time, the received wisdom was that the universe was static.* **Common, popular** and **traditional** are also used in this way: *Some of these studies challenge common wisdom.* **3** [sing.] **the ~ of (doing) sth** how sensible sth is: *The wisdom of this strategy was doubtful.* ◇ *Stuckler et al. (2009) question the wisdom of cutting public spending.*

W

wise /waɪz/ *adj.* (**wiser**, **wis·est**) **1** able to make sensible decisions and give good advice because of the experience and knowledge that you have: *He was portrayed as a monarch who was wise, peaceful and generous.* **2** (of actions, behaviour and advice) sensible; based on good judgement SYN PRUDENT: *Land values and rents rose, making it a wise investment.* ◇ *Breaking up the company might not be a wise decision.* ◇ **it is ~ to do sth** *It is generally wise to plan ahead.* ■ **wise·ly** *adv.*: *The government wisely refrained from intervention.* ◇ *The company must choose wisely.*

wish[1] /wɪʃ/ *verb* [T, I] (not usually used in the progressive tenses) to want to do or have sth; to want sth to happen or be true: *He may, if he so wishes, take into account other relevant experience.* ◇ *She would be permitted to reside there for as long as she wished.* ◇ *The decision supports the view that people should be free to do as they wish with their money and property.* ◇ **~ to do sth** *I also wish to thank my supervisor, Dr Diane Wood, for her advice and support throughout the project.* ◇ **~ sb/sth to do sth** *Some of these groups wish their work to remain an apolitical issue.* ◇ **~ (that)...** *Some moralists might wish it were otherwise.* ◇ *Young doctors especially wished they had more support.* ◇ **~ for sth** *He wishes vainly for something exciting to break his monotony.*

wish[2] /wɪʃ/ *noun* a feeling that you want to do or have sth, or that you want sth to happen; the thing that you want: *These people feel entitled to be treated in a way that always fulfils their wishes and needs.* ◇ *The gods granted her wish.* ◇ **~ of sb** *It is necessary to respect the wishes of the parents.* ◇ **~ to do sth** *Fathers express a wish to become closer to their children.* ◇ **~ for sth** *The government had no wish for war.* HELP In children's or traditional stories, to *make a wish* is to attempt to make sth happen by magic, by thinking about it really hard. If this thing happens, your *wish comes true*.

with /wɪð; wɪθ/ *prep.* HELP For the special uses of **with** in phrasal verbs, look at the entries for the verbs. For example **deal with sb/sth** is in the phrasal verb section at **deal**. **1** in the company of sb/sth: *The young rats usually remain with their mothers until they are at least two months old.* ◇ *It has long been known that bananas should not be stored with other fruit.* ◇ *It was not necessary to prove that the defendant had the weapon with him at the time of entry.* **2** having or owning sth: *Then, as now, many people imagined God as an elderly, fatherly figure with a flowing beard.* ◇ *By 1935, Oxford was one of a handful of British cities with a booming industry.* **3** affected by a particular fact or condition: *Pain is the symptom most feared by patients with cancer.* **4** using sth: *With this device, people could walk about, read signs and even identify faces.* ◇ *She shot and killed them with her bow and arrows.* ◇ *Chest infections are treated with IV antibiotics.* **5** used to say what fills, covers, etc. sth: *The lake behind the Prospect Dam required 22 years to fill with water.* ◇ *Most if not all of the earth was covered with permanent ice.* ◇ *Seeds were germinated in a Petri dish lined with moist filter paper.* **6** wearing or carrying sth: *Men with suits and walkie-talkies were moving people towards the exits.* **7** in opposition to sb/sth; against sb/sth: *Within a 25-year period, Britain had fought two wars with Germany.* ◇ *In a focus group, individuals will often argue with each other and challenge each other's views.* **8** concerning sb/sth; in the case of sb/sth: *He became intensely angry with himself when he did not fulfil his own expectations.* ◇ *Over 87% of respondents reported that they were satisfied or very satisfied with the service that they received.* ◇ *With these models, a given set of inputs produces a small number of possible outputs.* **9** used when considering one fact in relation to another: *A national system of mass schooling developed relatively late in England in comparison with other European countries.* **10** used to show the way in which sb does sth, or the way in which sth happens: *Students are taught skills for behaving with compassion and empathy towards one another.* ◇ *These technologies evolved with astonishing speed.* **11** because of sth and as it happens: *Reported happiness was found on average to have increased with rising incomes.* **12** in the same direction as sth: *A small leaf will rotate in a clockwise direction as it is carried along with the stream.* **13** used to show who has charge of or responsibility for sth: *An investor in one country may leave assets with a fund manager in a second country.* **14** employed by sb/sth: *The majority had been with their employer for more than two years.* **15** using the services of sb/sth: *Building societies are owned by the people who save with them.* **16** showing separation from sth/sb: *In many cases, the company will be made to part with its funds on inadequate security.* **17** despite sth: *With all its positive aspects, the Internet has also made it possible for hate groups to reach large numbers of people.*

with·draw /wɪðˈdrɔː; wɪθˈdrɔː/ *verb* (**with·drew** /wɪðˈdruː; wɪθˈdruː/, **with·drawn** /wɪðˈdrɔːn; wɪθˈdrɔːn/) **1** [T, I] (used especially about armed forces) to make people leave a place; to leave a place: **~ sb/sth** *Russia agreed to withdraw her troops by the end of 1903.* ◇ **~ sb/sth from sth** *They declared their intention to withdraw their military forces from the region.* ◇ *Foreign workers were temporarily withdrawn from projects in the north of the country.* ◇ **~ (from sth)** *Although forced to withdraw, he remained a menace.* **2** [I] **~ (to sth)** to leave a room; to go away from other people: *When strangers were in the house, women and girls would withdraw to the secluded parts of the home.* **3** [T] to move sth back, out or away from sth: **~ sth** *After the samples are obtained, the needle is withdrawn.* ◇ **~ sth from sth** *Participants in the experiment could withdraw their hand from the cold water at any time.* **4** [T] to take money out of a bank account or financial institution: **~ sth** *There were queues at the banks as people withdrew their savings.* ◇ **~ sth from sth** *Investors withdrew their money from the domestic banking system.* **5** [I] to stop taking part in sth: *There is the problem of subjects choosing to withdraw at later stages of the research.* ◇ **~ from sth** *The defendant withdrew from the negotiations and sold the business to a third party.* **6** [I] to stop wanting to speak to, or be with, other people: **~ from sb/sth** *Some old people gradually withdraw from society.* ◇ **~ into sth** *A distressed child may withdraw into fantasy for extended periods.* **7** [T] to no longer provide or offer sth; to no longer make sth available: **~ sth** *Withdrawal symptoms are less likely if the drug is withdrawn gradually over several weeks.* ◇ *After much controversy and protest, many financial institutions withdrew support.* ◇ **~ sth from sth** *The book was subsequently withdrawn from sale.* **8** [T] **~ sth** to say that you no longer agree with what you said before: *The allegations had been withdrawn.* ◇ *The mother later withdrew her consent.*

with·draw·al /wɪðˈdrɔːəl; wɪθˈdrɔːəl/ *noun* **1** [U, C] the act of moving back, out or away; the act of taking sb/sth back, out or away: **~ of sth (from sth)** *The UN monitored the withdrawal of foreign troops from the country.* ◇ **~ from sth** *Water withdrawals from rivers for irrigation and industrial use have doubled.* **2** [C] **~ (of sth) (from sth)** the act of taking money out of a bank account or financial institution: *Only one withdrawal was ever made from the account.* ◇ *The banks experienced large withdrawals of foreign deposits.* **3** [U, C] **~ (from sth)** the act of no longer taking part in sth: *The party called for outright British withdrawal from the EU.* ◇ *The number of withdrawals from each group of study participants was recorded.* **4** [U] the behaviour of sb who stops wanting to speak to, or be with, other people: *Withdrawal can be a coping strategy, intended to control anger by avoiding the situation.* ◇ **~ from sb/sth** *Symptoms include crying,* *withdrawal from others and difficulty concentrating.* **5** [U, sing.] **~ of sth** the fact of no longer providing or offering sth or of no longer making sth available: *The withdrawal of government subsidies had drastic economic effects.* **6** [U, C] the process of stopping taking a drug, especially an ADDICTIVE one; the unpleasant effects experienced by sb doing this: *Withdrawal is achieved by reducing the dose progressively over a period of 1–3 weeks.* ◇ *Clinically significant withdrawals may be seen in alcohol and cocaine.* ◇ **~ from sth** *Seizures may be due to withdrawal from drugs.* ◇ **+ noun** *Up to a third of patients experience withdrawal symptoms when the drug is stopped.* **7** [U] **~ of sth** the act of saying that you no longer agree with what you said or asked for before: *She needs to show that withdrawal of her consent is reasonable.*

with·hold /wɪð'həʊld; wɪθ'həʊld; *NAmE* wɪð'hoʊld; wɪθ'hoʊld/ *verb* (**with·held**, **with·held** /wɪð'held; wɪθ'held/) to refuse to give sth to sb: **~ sth** *The House has no powers to withhold consent.* ◇ **~ sth from sb/sth** *The company had a right to withhold information from competitors.*

with·in¹ /wɪ'ðɪn/ *prep.* **1** inside sth/sb: *The largest magnitude earthquakes found on earth occur within subduction zones.* ◇ *Six of the clinics fall within the Africa Centre Demographic Surveillance Area.* ◇ *Class, gender and ethnic differences can multiply within a supposedly equal community (Lewis, 2004).* ◇ *Films such as 'The Defector' (1966) clearly demand wider appreciation within film studies.* **2** not further than a particular distance from sth: *The law prohibits marches within a mile of Parliament when it is in session.* ◇ *The Family Health Centre is within walking distance of the school.* **3** before a particular period of time has passed; during a particular period of time: *Newly diagnosed HIV patients should be seen by a specialist, preferably within 48 hours and certainly within two weeks.* **4** inside the range or limits of sth: *Most of the lower Tanner Canyon fan lies within the range of prehistoric floods.* ◇ *The court held that the product in question did not come within the scope of the legislation.* ◇ *Her blood glucose level was within normal limits.*

with·in² /wɪ'ðɪn/ *adv.* inside: *Crayfish enter the aperture of the shell to extract the body within.* ◇ **from ~** *Democratic states frequently experience challenges from within, especially from ethnic or regional groups that feel marginalized.*

with·out /wɪ'ðaʊt/ *prep.* **1** not doing the action mentioned: **~ doing sth** *The X-rays were taken without informing the patient.* ◇ **~ sb doing sth** *The challenge lies in enabling the poor to escape poverty without the rich being unduly penalized.* **2** not having, experiencing or showing sth: *The performance improvement programme was repeated without much success.* ◇ *The establishment of biobanks has not been without controversy.* ◇ *The best example of complicated clocks was without doubt marine chronometers.* **3** not using or taking sth: *He was the first person to make the ascent without oxygen.*

with·stand /wɪð'stænd; wɪθ'stænd/ *verb* (**with·stood**, **with·stood** /wɪð'stʊd; wɪθ'stʊd/) **~ sth** to be strong enough not to be affected, hurt or damaged by sth SYN RESIST (2), STAND UP TO STH: *The vessel is able to withstand high pressures.* ◇ *This claim does not withstand scrutiny.*

wit·ness¹ /'wɪtnəs/ *noun* **1** (*also* **eye·wit·ness**) a person who sees sth happen and is able to describe it to other people: *Witnesses had seen company representatives attempting to bribe members of the community.* ◇ **~ to sth** *The project includes interviews with witnesses to the brutal civil rights struggle of the 1960s.* **2** a person who gives evidence in court: *The court accepted the evidence of the expert witnesses.* **3** a person who is present when an official document is signed and who also signs it to prove that they saw this happen: *Two witnesses must be present to sign the contract.*

IDM **be 'witness to sth** **1** to see sth take place: *The children have been witness to the strains and problems in the marriage.* ◇ *The new century was also witness to unprecedented shifts in social and technological experience.* **2** to show that sth is true; to provide evidence for sth: *The continued process of economic reform is witness to the ability of the state to evolve its stance towards the regulation of business.* ➲ *more at* BEAR

wit·ness² /'wɪtnəs/ *verb* **1** **~ sth** to see sth happen (typically a crime or an accident): *26.7% of respondents had witnessed serious violence in their neighbourhood.* ◇ *Many commentators argue that we are witnessing the rise of an increasingly homogenized global popular culture.* **2** **~ sth** to be the period, place, organization, etc. in which particular events take place: *The 1940s and 1950s also witnessed the emergence of a new form of jazz.* ◇ *The holiday resort of Matalascanas witnesses a seasonal population increase of 200 000.* **3** **~ sth** to be present when an official document is signed and sign it yourself to prove that you saw this happen: *The consent form was signed and witnessed.* **4** [often passive] to be a sign or proof of sth: **~ sth** *The political agonies of 1968 witnessed the cresting of progressive forces that had been building since the late 1950s.* ◇ **as witnessed by sth** *The mid-1980s saw an intensification of interest in community care, as witnessed by the publication of four major reports.* **5** **~ sth** used when giving an example that proves sth you have just said: *The nuclear family is a vulnerable institution—witness the rates of marital breakdown.*

wives *pl. of* WIFE

woke *past tense of* WAKE²

woken *past part. of* WAKE²

woman /'wʊmən/ *noun* (*pl.* **women** /'wɪmɪn/) **1** an adult female human: *As a young woman, she had travelled and lived in Asia.* ◇ *Uptake was higher among women than among men* ◇ **+ noun** *Numerous women writers joined the movement.* **2** (in compounds) a woman who is connected with a particular activity or job: *Congresswoman Molinari delivered the keynote address.* ◇ *She was the highest-ranking British policewoman.* ◇ *People engaged with her as a saleswoman.* HELP It is now more common to use terms such as 'police officer' or 'salesperson', which do not show whether you are talking about a man or a woman: *The role of the salesperson has changed.* IDM *see* MAN

won *past tense, past part. of* WIN

won·der¹ /'wʌndə(r)/ *verb* [T, I] to think about sth and try to decide what is true, what will happen, what you should do, etc: **~ how/where, etc...** *The reader is left wondering just how to react.* ◇ **~ if/whether...** *A similar decline is occurring elsewhere, leading some observers to wonder if the age of mass political parties is over.* ◇ **~ about sth** *Castaneda forces us to wonder about the nature of hallucinations.*

won·der² /'wʌndə(r)/ *noun* **1** [U] a feeling of surprise and admiration that you have when you see or experience sth beautiful, unusual or unexpected: *The sense of wonder that Coleridge felt before nature was not unshakeable, though.* ◇ *The abundance and variety of marine life surrounding the ship was a source of wonder and amazement for many British explorers.* **2** [C] **~ (of sth)** something that fills you with surprise and admiration: *The Grand Canyon of the Colorado River is one of the most frequently visited natural wonders of the world.*

IDM **(it is) no/little/small 'wonder (that)...** it is not surprising: *Coal production had fallen from 29 million to 9 million tons. Small wonder that the attitude towards the government changed from apathy to resentment.* ◇ *The clinician often does not tell a patient anything. It is no*

W

wonder that many patients fail to return to the second session.

won·der·ful /ˈwʌndəfl; *NAmE* ˈwʌndərfl/ *adj.* very good, pleasant or enjoyable: *A museum visit is a wonderful opportunity for students to explore primary sources and hone analytical skills.* ◇ *Zieger provides a wonderful example of how he uses song to explore themes of race and power.*

wood /wʊd/ *noun* **1** [U, C] the hard material that the TRUNK and branches of a tree are made of; this material when it is used to build or make things with, or when it is used as a fuel: *Deforestation was driven by the strong market for firewood and other wood products.* ◇ *Hard woods are exported from the forests of Thailand and Indonesia.* ◇ **of ~** *Before the earthquake, Tokyo was like a large village in which most houses were built of wood.* **2** [C] (*also* **woods** [pl.]) an area of trees, smaller than a forest: *Forests and woods remained a vital resource, particularly for fuel and building material.*

wood·en /ˈwʊdn/ *adj.* [usually before noun] made of wood: *Stone bridges were safer and more durable than the wooden bridges they replaced.*

wood·land /ˈwʊdlənd/ *noun* [U, C] (*also* **wood·lands** [pl.]) an area of land that is covered with trees: *Areas of woodland may provide habitats for pollinating insects vital to crop production.* ◇ *The woodlands lay along the frontier with Czechoslovakia.* ◇ **+ noun** *These patches would support a range of woodland species.*

wool /wʊl/ *noun* [U] **1** the soft fine hair that covers the body of sheep and some other animals: *Some breeds of sheep have naturally itchy, rough, thick wool.* **2** long thick thread made from animal's wool, used for KNITTING: *That was where the local women gathered to spin wool.* **3** cloth made from animal's wool, used for making clothes, etc: **+ noun** *The town was an important commercial centre, vital in the English wool trade.*

word[1] /wɜːd; *NAmE* wɜːrd/ *noun* **1** [C] a single unit of language which means sth and can be spoken or written: *Clearly, understanding what is meant by the word 'culture' is not a simple task.* ◇ *I shall use the word 'Christianization' to describe the social changes that followed conversion.* ◇ **a/the ~ for sth** *The Romans did not have a word for democracy.* ◇ **in your own words** *For the interviews, patients were encouraged to express their problems in their own words.* ◇ **in the… sense of the ~** *The report noted that some voluntary statements made in court were not actually 'voluntary' in the strict sense of the word.* **2** [C] a thing that you say; a remark or statement: *Donatus uttered the famous words: 'What has the Emperor to do with the Church?'* ◇ **a ~ of sth** *A word of warning, however: always follow the manufacturer's instructions.* ◇ **in the words of sb** *In the words of one interviewee, 'Love is what's left after the excitement's gone.'* **3** [sing.] a promise that you will do sth or that sth will happen or is true: **keep/break your ~** *Agreement was hard to reach since neither side trusted the other to keep their word.* ◇ **~ of sb** *Too often, social workers took the word of parents at face value without considering the effects on the child.* **4** [sing.] a piece of information or news: **send ~** *Alcibiades sent word to Athens that he was negotiating with the Persians.* ◇ **spread the ~** *The association relies on members to spread the word about the benefits and encourage others to join.*

IDM **ˌword of ˈmouth** the process by which people hear about sth because they are told about it by other people and not because they read about it or watch it on television: *Word of mouth is a particularly strong means of marketing communication, as it effectively legitimizes a message.* ◇ *Participants were recruited by word of mouth.* **in ˈother words** used to introduce an explanation of sth: *The variables are regarded as factors common to all the countries. In other words, the 149 countries are treated as parallel economies.* ➲ language bank *at* I.E. **in a ˈword** used for giving a very short comment or description: *Thus, environmental problems tend to be interconnected and multidimensional; they are, in a word, complex.* **the last/final word (on sth)** the last comment or decision about sth: *The RPC model is not the last word on this subject.* **ˌword for ˈword** in exactly the same words or (when translated) exactly EQUIVALENT words: *In some cases, Miege copied almost word for word what he found in Pomey's dictionary.* ➲ *more at* PLAY[2], PRINT[1], WRITTEN[1]

word[2] /wɜːd; *NAmE* wɜːrd/ *verb* [often passive] **~ sth** to write or say sth using particular words: *It was suggested that the decision be worded so that there would be some room for negotiations.* ■ **word·ed** *adj.*: *Campaign sponsors sent a strongly worded letter to the World Bank president.*

word·ing /ˈwɜːdɪŋ; *NAmE* ˈwɜːrdɪŋ/ *noun* [U, C, usually sing.] the words that are used in a piece of writing or speech, especially when they have been carefully chosen: *The new regulations use similar wording to the old ones.* ◇ **~ of sth** *The wording of Question 5 was rather unclear.*

wore *past tense of* WEAR[1]

work[1] /wɜːk; *NAmE* wɜːrk/ *noun* **1** [U] the job that a person does, especially in order to earn money SYN EMPLOYMENT (1): *The aim of the policy was to get the long-term unemployed back into work.* ◇ *In those currently employed, 20% were in manual work and 1% in unskilled work.* ◇ *Several of the patients do voluntary work in local education.* ◇ *Respondents were interviewed at their place of work.* **2** [U] (used without *the*) the place where you do your job: *Only 2.5% of the population who travelled to work used a bicycle in 2006.* ◇ **at ~** *It is widely acknowledged that men incline more to technology than do women, both at work and at home.* **3** [U] tasks that need to be done: *Supervisors were responsible for ensuring that all necessary work was completed to schedule.* ◇ **~ of (doing) sth** *Gradually, much of the work of rearing children and other tasks in the home has been entrusted to outside professionals.* ◇ **+ noun** *High levels of productivity were maintained through a strong work ethic among members.* **4** [U] the use of physical strength or mental power in order to do or make sth: *In 1759 work was started on a canal to carry coal to Manchester.* ◇ *Learners gave their views about the relationship between talent, hard work and achievement.* ➲ *see also* FIELDWORK, SOCIAL WORK **5** [U] a thing or things that are produced by doing an activity or by doing your job: *Deming argues that people are motivated by a desire to produce good work.* ◇ *Fred Wiseman, whose work was primarily shown on TV, produced films that feature the victims of impersonal social systems.* ◇ *Workers were paid $0.50 for each piece of work completed, in this case, sewing a collar on a shirt.* **6** [U, C] the process of academic research; an academic article, book, etc: *A large body of empirical work has shown that freeing trade enables economies to grow faster.* ◇ *Much of the information presented here is a refinement of earlier works by pioneer researchers.* ◇ **~ of sb** *Since the early work of Resser (1946), there has been virtually no work done on the taxonomy of the Cambrian strata.* ◇ **~ on sth** *The author's own work on the Labour Party suggests that there is a strong continuity in the party's thinking.* ◇ **~ of sth** *'Empire of Sacrifice' is a provocative and engaging work of cultural criticism.* **7** [C] a book, piece of music, painting, etc: *Before the Internet, methods of disseminating a work widely involved physical transfer of copies.* ◇ *Seneca's most important poetical works are his tragedies.* ◇ *The Berne Convention provides copyright protection to literary, dramatic and musical works.* ➲ *compare* WORK OF ART **8** [U] (*physics*) the use of force to produce movement: *We do work when we raise a weight against the opposing force of gravity.* ◇ *Exercise requires the delivery of more oxygen as the muscle fibres perform more work.* **9** [U] **~ of sb/sth**

the result of an action; what is done by sb: *The uprising was initially the work of artisans and fishermen.* **10 works** (*pl.* **works**) [C+sing./pl. v.] (often in compounds) a place where things are made or industrial processes take place: *The steelworks closed in the 1980s, leaving a desolate wasteland.* **11 works** [pl.] (often in compounds) activities involving building or repairing sth: *The only way of removing the hazard was to carry out drainage works on Rochdale's land.* ➲ *see also* PUBLIC WORKS

IDM **at 'work 1** having an effect on sth: *Seismologists do not fully understand the processes that are at work when a major fault approaches failure.* **2** busy doing sth: *Evidence suggests that there were many missionaries at work at this time.* ◇ **~ on sth** *She is at work on a new book.* **off 'work** not at the place where you do your job, usually because of illness or a holiday: *Of those people who are off work for 6 months, 80% will remain off work for 5 years.* ◇ *The company had failed to allow its employees their statutory time off work.* **out of 'work** without a job: *The number of people out of work for more than a year increased by 85 000.* ➲ *more at* DIRTY

▸ ADJECTIVE + WORK **paid • unpaid • voluntary • part-time • full-time • domestic • manual • skilled • unskilled** *Students are increasingly financing their education with part-time work (Lucas, 1997).* | **recent • previous • later, subsequent • future • further • own** *These exploratory studies suggest a need for further experimental work.* | **early • original • creative • experimental • published • seminal, major, classic** *Avant-garde and original works congratulate the audience by implying it has the capacity to understand them.* ◇ *Bourdieu's seminal work on cultural capital was built on Marxist frameworks.* | **scholarly, academic • empirical • theoretical • critical • pioneering** *Scholem's scholarly work had the effect of encouraging a renewed interest in the kabbalistic tradition.* | **literary • musical • artistic** *Literary works characteristically represent individuals struggling with their sense of identity.*

▸ VERB + WORK **do • begin, start • continue • organize, coordinate** *How human work is organized differs from one economic system to another.* | **seek • find • need, require • provide • create** *A basic principle of a full-employment economy is that everyone seeking work has a right to find it.* | **undertake, perform, carry out, conduct • need, require • support** *The work of harvesting was largely carried out by women.* ◇ *Two examples will be given of the uses of technology to support the work of teachers.* | **create • complete • describe • discuss** *Aboriginal artists such as Tracey Moffatt created work that not only documented experience but used experimental and fictional approaches to do so.* | **produce • write • publish • read • review • present • mention • cite • translate • inform • extend** *Descartes published his major philosophical work, 'Meditations on First Philosophy', in 1641.*

▸ WORK + VERB **demonstrate, show, reveal • emphasize • focus • address • deal with • suggest • influence • inspire • provide** *Our new work suggests that basin deepening took place in three locations.*

▸ WORK + NOUN **schedule • team • practices • process • performance • environment, setting • situation • colleague • ethic** *Safe work practices are implemented to help minimize the risk of accident.*

work² /wɜːk; *NAmE* wɜːrk/ *verb* **1** [I] to do sth that involves physical or mental effort in order to achieve a result, especially as part of a job: *The other students continued working.* ◇ **~ at sth** *The monks worked at the tasks needed to manage a farm.* ◇ **~ on sth** *He was one of the scientists who worked on the Manhattan project.* ◇ **+ noun** *US workers in 2000 actually worked more hours than they did 20 years earlier.* **2** [I] to have a job: *From 1945 to 1970, relatively few women worked.* ◇ **~ for sb/sth** *He no longer works for the company.* ◇ **~ in sth** *In 2005 in Haiti, there were only 730 doctors working in the public sector.* ◇ **~ with sb/sth** *Help is available from teachers skilled in working with children with emotional or behavioural problems.* ◇ **~ as sth** *In West Kingston, most men worked as labourers or artisans.* **3** [I] to function; to operate: *Waltz and Mearsheimer make a number of assumptions about the way the international system works.* ◇ **~ by (doing) sth** *Natural selection works by modifying existing forms, not by creating new ones from scratch.* **4** [I] to have the result or effect that you want: *While this strategy can work, it is extremely risky.* ◇ **~ on sb/sth** *Drugs that calm anxious people also work on anxious mice.* **5** [I] to make efforts to achieve sth: **~ for sth** *She founded a number of activist political groups working for peace.* ◇ **~ to do sth** *The organization works to ensure a minimum price for farmers' produce.* **6** [T] **~ sth** to manage or operate sth to gain benefit from it: *Serfs worked the land in medieval Europe.* **7** [T] **~ sth** to make a machine or device operate: *The younger, unmarried women were drafted into the factories to work the spinning machines.* **8** [I] to have a particular effect: **~ against sb** *Increased competition and technological change have generally worked against less skilled workers.* ◇ **~ in sb's favour** *International events, meanwhile, worked in Reagan's favour.* **9** [T] **~ sth** to cause or produce sth as a result of effort: *By 1983, there was a widespread belief that his economic policies had indeed finally worked their magic.* ◇ *to work wonders/miracles* **10** [T] to make a material into a particular shape or form by pressing, stretching, hitting it, etc: **~ sth** *The artist had used material which was difficult to work.* ◇ **~ sth into sth** *Our ancestors had learned to work these metals into useful and ornamental objects by at least seven to eight thousand years ago.* **11** [I] **~ in/with sth** (of an artist, etc.) to use a particular material to produce a picture or other item: *Praxiteles, the Athenian sculptor, worked in both bronze and marble.* **12** [T] **~ your way + adv./prep.** to move or pass to a particular place or state, usually gradually: *Many large charities now have fair-trade operations that allow poor communities to work their way out of poverty.*

IDM Idioms containing **work** are at the entries for the nouns and adjectives in the idioms, for example **work your way through sth** is at **way**.

PHR V **'work at sth** to make great efforts to achieve sth or do sth well: *For all his inspiration, the artist still had to work at his art and find people to buy it.* ◇ **~ at doing sth** *He works at developing a nurturing and intimate relationship with his son.* **'work on sth** to try hard to improve or achieve sth: *She is working on her language skills to improve her employability.* **ˌwork 'out 1** to develop in a successful way: *This plan, however, did not work out.* **2** to train the body by physical exercise: *Women can work out, build muscle and perform challenging physical tasks in the same manner as men.* **ˌwork 'out (at sth)** if sth **works out** at sth, you calculate that it will be a particular amount: *In 1997, the average allowance worked out at around £6 000 per candidate for the main parties.* ◇ **+ adj.** *Arbitration is popular because it often works out cheaper.* **ˌwork sth 'out 1** to calculate sth: *Working out the value of x is not entirely straightforward.* **2** (*especially BrE*) to find the answer to sth SYN SOLVE (2): *Two questions remained to be worked out.* ◇ **~ how/what, etc...** *Chimpanzees can work out how to pile up boxes to reach a suspended banana.* **3** to plan or think of sth: *A compromise was worked out.* **'work to sth** to follow a plan, system, etc: *Call centre employees work to targets which require them to deal with a specific number of inquiries per hour.* **'work towards sth** to try to reach or achieve a goal: *All parties concerned are working towards the same goals.*

work·able /ˈwɜːkəbl; *NAmE* ˈwɜːrkəbl/ *adj.* (of a system, an idea, etc.) that can be used successfully and effectively SYN PRACTICAL (2): *The Director's role was to ensure that the new system was clear, coherent and workable.* ◇

Management and staff worked together to find a workable solution.

work·day /ˈwɜːkdeɪ; *NAmE* ˈwɜːrkdeɪ/ *noun* **1** (*NAmE*) = WORKING DAY (1) **2** = WORKING DAY (2)

work·er /ˈwɜːkə(r); *NAmE* ˈwɜːrkər/ *noun* **1** (often in compounds) a person who works, especially one who does a particular kind of work: *Between 1983 and 1987, 4.6 million US workers lost their jobs.* ◇ *The report announced a global shortfall of some 4.3 million health care workers.* ➲ *see also* CO-WORKER, KNOWLEDGE WORKER, SOCIAL WORKER **2** [usually pl.] a person who is employed in a company or industry, especially sb who does physical work rather than organizing things or managing people: *Many of the new workers were peasants unfamiliar with factory discipline.* ◇ *Workers and employers occupy different positions in the production process.* ◇ *The union hierarchy imposed itself between workers and management.*

▸ ADJECTIVE + WORKER **female** ◆ **male** ◆ **young** ◆ **older** ◆ **individual** ◆ **employed** ◆ **unemployed** ◆ **part-time** ◆ **full-time** ◆ **temporary** ◆ **skilled, trained** ◆ **unskilled** ◆ **low-skilled** ◆ **manual** ◆ **industrial, blue-collar** ◆ **white-collar, clerical** ◆ **agricultural** ◆ **domestic** ◆ **migrant** *Table 14.1 shows that mortality rates for unskilled manual workers are two and a half times higher than for professional workers.*

▸ NOUN + WORKER **factory, manufacturing** ◆ **office** ◆ **knowledge** ◆ **farm** ◆ **health care** ◆ **sex** *Advanced information technologies have increased the demand for highly skilled technical and knowledge workers.*

▸ VERB + WORKER **employ, hire, recruit, engage** ◆ **attract** ◆ **fire** ◆ **pay** ◆ **treat** ◆ **encourage** ◆ **train** ◆ **protect** ◆ **organize** ◆ **exploit** *All workers employed in an industry, whether skilled or unskilled, could now join a single industry-wide union.*

▸ WORKER + VERB **work** ◆ **produce** ◆ **face, experience** ◆ **receive** ◆ **report** *Part-time male workers received an hourly wage of $12.06.*

ˈwork experience *noun* [U] **1** the work or jobs that you have done in your life so far: *Estimates made by managers with significant work experience were as inaccurate as those of their less experienced colleagues.* **2** (*BrE*) a period of time that a young person, especially a student, spends working in a company as a form of training: *Trainees alternate periods in a formal education institution with periods of work experience in a firm.*

work·force /ˈwɜːkfɔːs; *NAmE* ˈwɜːrkfɔːrs/ *noun* [C+sing./pl. v.] **1** all the people who work for a particular company or organization SYN STAFF[1] (1): *In 1790, nearly one quarter of Wedgwood's workforce were apprentices.* ◇ *Despite their skilled workforces and modern machinery, the Philadelphia mills were badly hit by the slump.* **2** all the people in a country or an area who are available for work: *Nearly 30 per cent of the total workforce are employed by central and local government.* ◇ *Women then began to enter the workforce in greater numbers.*

work·ing[1] /ˈwɜːkɪŋ; *NAmE* ˈwɜːrkɪŋ/ *adj.* [only before noun] **1** connected with your job and the time you spend doing it: *Employers agreed to a reduction in working hours.* ◇ *The Constitution guarantees equality at work in relation to working conditions.* ◇ *Performance improvements generally require a positive working relationship between employers and employees.* ◇ *Most top bureaucrats had been in the civil service all their working life.* **2** having a job for which you are paid: *Unemployment in the UK in 2009 reached 2.261 million, which represented 7.2% of the working population.* ◇ *In 1985, 63 per cent of all children in the United States had working mothers.* **3** (used especially when talking about the past) having a job that involves hard physical work rather than office work, studying, etc: *Through popular lectures to working men, Huxley bought evolution to ordinary people.* **4** functioning or able to function: *Babbage exhibited a small working model of his 'Difference Engine' in 1822.* **5** being used in order to do work: *There are 23 official working languages in the EU.* ◇ *The working fluid flows through the engine and is not recycled.* **6** used as a basis for work, discussion, etc. but likely to be changed or improved in the future: *The working title during most of the novel's years of composition was 'The Strike'.* ◇ *Kaplan's working assumption was that economic and human collapse in parts of Africa would threaten world stability.* **7** if you have a **working** knowledge of sth, you can use it at a basic level: *After a year in the city, most of the group had acquired a working knowledge of the local language.* IDM *see* ORDER[1]

work·ing[2] /ˈwɜːkɪŋ; *NAmE* ˈwɜːrkɪŋ/ *noun* [usually pl.] **~ (of sth)** the way in which a machine, a system, an organization, etc. works: *In this way, all the workings of a cell are viewed as a single system.* ◇ *The staff meetings were an opportunity to learn about the inner workings of a high school.*

the ˌworking ˈclass *noun* [sing.+ sing./pl. v.] (*also* **the ˌworking ˈclasses** [pl.]) the social class whose members do not have much money or power and are usually employed to do MANUAL work (= physical work using their hands): *Until the interwar years, the working class had little power in British society.* ◇ *Wilkinson was appalled by the plight of the working classes at this time of mass unemployment.* ➲ *compare* MIDDLE CLASS, UPPER CLASS

ˌworking-ˈclass *adj.* connected with or belonging to the working class: *Some but not all the women come from working-class backgrounds.* ➲ *compare* MIDDLE-CLASS, UPPER CLASS

ˌworking ˈday *noun* (*BrE*) **1** (*NAmE* **work·day**) the part of a day during which you work: *Wages rose, an eight-hour working day was agreed and workers' committees were formed in the factories.* **2** (*also less frequent* **work·day**) a day on which you usually work or on which most people usually work: *Obtaining test results often takes at least seven working days.*

ˈworking group (*BrE also* **ˈworking party**) *noun* [C+sing./pl. v.] **~ (on sth)** a group of people chosen to study a particular problem or situation in order to suggest ways of dealing with it: *In 1981, a UN working group was established to draft a Declaration on the Right to Development.*

work·load /ˈwɜːkləʊd; *NAmE* ˈwɜːrkloʊd/ *noun* the amount of work that has to be done by a particular person or organization: *The changes resulted in a heavy workload for staff.* ◇ *The employer had not taken any steps to reduce the employee's workload or provide him with support.*

ˌwork of ˈart *noun* (*pl.* **ˌworks of ˈart**) a painting, statue, etc: *Many important works of art went missing during the war years.*

work·place /ˈwɜːkpleɪs; *NAmE* ˈwɜːrkpleɪs/ *noun* (*often* **the workplace**) [sing.] a place where people work, such as an office or factory: *Many workplaces have a clothing and personal appearance policy.* ◇ **in the ~** *Women still face barriers to equality in the workplace.*

works *noun* ➲ WORK[1]

work·shop /ˈwɜːkʃɒp; *NAmE* ˈwɜːrkʃɑːp/ *noun* **1** a period of discussion and practical work on a particular subject, in which a group of people share their knowledge and experience: *A second one-day workshop was held in Lisbon in December 2009.* ◇ **~ on sth** *Monthly workshops on topics concerning adolescent development issues are also offered to parents.* **2** a room or building in which things are made or repaired using tools or machinery: *Before the emergence of capitalism, most production took place within families, in small workshops, on farms, etc.*

world /wɜːld; *NAmE* wɜːrld/ *noun* **1 the world** [sing.] the earth, with all its countries, peoples and natural features: *Asia has almost 61% of the world's population.* ◇ **around the ~** *Relief teams travel to disaster areas around the world.* ◇ **all over the ~** *Such infections are common all over the world.* ◇ **in the ~** *It was the largest company in the world in 2002.* ◇ **+ noun** *The EU now has a central role in world politics.* **2** (*often* **the world**) [sing.] our society and the way people live and behave; the people in the world: *The world is changing at a rapid pace.* ◇ *They are living in a world vastly different from that of their grandparents.* ◇ *The world was duly impressed by the company's reaction to the situation.* **3** [C, usually sing.] a particular part of the earth; a particular group of countries or people: *Heart disease is the leading cause of death in the Western world.* ◇ *Wood has become increasingly scarce in the developing world.* ➲ *see also* THIRD WORLD **4** [C, usually sing.] a particular period of history and the people of that period: *Alexandria was one of the great cities of the ancient world.* ◇ *She examines numerous assumptions concerning the place of religion in the modern world.* **5** [usually sing.] (usually used with an adjective) everything that exists of a particular kind; a particular kind of life or existence: *They proposed considering the natural world in scientific terms rather than in a context of religion or superstition.* ◇ **in the... ~** *Rarely do we find such a clear-cut situation in the real world.* ◇ **~ of sth** *Angela Carter's fiction presents its readers with a world of magic.* ◇ *The book is a means of entering the imaginative world of ancient myth.* **6** [C] **~ (of sth)** the people belonging to a particular group; the people or things connected with a particular interest, job, etc: *Machiavelli insisted that he wrote about the world of politics as it was, not as it should be.* ◇ *The authors were familiar with the new world of popular journalism.* ◇ *Teenagers decided to delay entering the world of work and stay on for sixth form and university.* **7** [sing.] **sb's ~** a person's environment, experiences, friends and family, etc: *School is a major aspect of a child's world.* **8** [C] a particular group of living things: **the animal/plant/insect ~** *Our understanding of the animal world and its evolution has greatly increased in recent years.* **9** [C] a planet like the earth: *Mathematical entities could be used as a language with which to communicate with alien beings from other worlds.* **10 the world** [sing.] a way of life where possessions and physical pleasures are important, rather than spiritual values: *The Taoists urged a life of self-denial and escape from the world.*

IDM **the best of 'both worlds** the benefits of two completely different situations that you can enjoy at the same time: *However, some farmers have discovered ways to have the best of both worlds.* **in an ideal/a perfect 'world** used to say that sth is what you would like to happen or what should happen, but you know it cannot: *In an ideal world, all children would grow up in intact, cohesive, nuclear families.* **in the world** (*informal*) used to emphasize sth: *It should be the easiest thing in the world to achieve.* **a 'world away (from sth)** used to emphasize how different two things are: *What these veterans underwent is a world away from the experience of average undergraduates.* **a 'world of difference (between A and B)** used to emphasize how much difference there is between two people or things: *There is a world of difference between the two playwrights.* **the world 'over** everywhere in the world: *In 2000, the G8 countries announced that 'IT empowers, benefits and links people the world over'.* ➲ *more at* BRAVE

▸ ADJECTIVE + WORLD **whole, entire • new** *Literacy has the potential to open up a whole world of ideas.* ◇ *An infectious biological agent can spread across the entire world.* | **real, actual • possible • natural • social • outside • external • physical • material** *Flaherty believed Inuit culture was polluted by contact with the outside world.*

▸ VERB + WORLD **see, view • create • describe • dominate • inhabit • study • consider • divide** *Another type of medieval map divided the world into climatic zones.* | **understand • experience • imagine • perceive • construct • shape • explain • characterize • change • transform • represent • present** *Knowledge is crucial to how students come to understand the world.*

▸ WORLD + NOUN **politics • affairs • economy • market • trade • production • demand • price • order • system • population • city • history • government • leader • society • religion • peace** *Most of the great world religions trace their origin to a transforming prophetic figure.*

▸ NOUN + OF THE WORLD **image • state • nature • description • representation** *They produced several predictions for the state of the world up to 2100.* | **part • region • area • rest • country, nation • language • people • history • end** *In many parts of the world, the job one does is determined by one's sex.* | **view • picture • conception • knowledge • experience • understanding • aspect, feature • structure** *War was breaking out between two very different states with opposing views of the world.*

world·ly /ˈwɜːldli; *NAmE* ˈwɜːrldli/ *adj.* **1** [only before noun] connected with the world in which we live rather than with spiritual things: *He was persuaded to give up his spiritual quest and return to the worldly life.* OPP SPIRITUAL **2** having a lot of experience of life and therefore not easily shocked: *Pacelli was a worldly, shrewd and experienced diplomat.*

ˌworld ˈview *noun* a person's way of thinking about and understanding life, which depends on their beliefs and attitudes: *All three concepts were central parts of the Christian world view of the later eighteenth century.*

world·wide[1] /ˈwɜːldwaɪd; *NAmE* ˈwɜːrldwaɪd/ *adj.* [usually before noun] affecting all parts of the world: *The group has a worldwide network of over 116 branch offices.* ◇ *Obama initiated a worldwide effort to control nuclear proliferation.*

world·wide[2] /ˌwɜːldˈwaɪd; *NAmE* ˌwɜːrldˈwaɪd/ *adv.* in or to all parts of the world: *The virus occurs worldwide.* ◇ *He describes the doctrine as a system that spread worldwide.*

worn *past part. of* WEAR[1]

wor·ried /ˈwʌrid; *NAmE* ˈwɜːrid/ *adj.* thinking about unpleasant things that have happened or that might happen and therefore feeling unhappy and afraid: **~ about sb/sth** *His neighbours were becoming increasingly worried about his safety.* ◇ **~ by sth** *Other Spartans were worried by the implications of this policy.* ◇ **~ (that)...** *Her father suffered from Parkinson's disease and she is worried that she may have it.*

worry[1] /ˈwʌri; *NAmE* ˈwɜːri/ *verb* (**wor·ries, worry·ing, wor·ried, wor·ried**) **1** [I] to keep thinking about unpleasant things that might happen or about problems that you have: **~ about sb/sth** *Some conservation biologists worry about the genetic effects of inbreeding in small populations.* ◇ **~ (that)...** *Mothers worry that because their teenage children have not had a lot of experience, they are not in a good position to assess danger.* **2** [T] to make sb/yourself anxious about sb/sth: *Initially, he decided not to tell Monique because he did not want to worry her.* ◇ *Ask them what is worrying them or why they have come to hospital.*

worry[2] /ˈwʌri; *NAmE* ˈwɜːri/ *noun* (*pl.* **-ies**) **1** [C] something that worries you: *Encourage patients to express any worries or concerns.* ◇ *Care home fees are a worry for a lot of people.* ◇ **~ about/over sth** *Mothers were interviewed about their worries about child underweight and undereating.* **2** [U] the state of worrying about sth SYN ANXIETY (1): *The feeling of worry appears to be very low in the general population.*

worry·ing /ˈwʌriɪŋ; *NAmE* ˈwɜːriɪŋ/ *adj.* that makes you worry: *The literature has already revealed worrying trends in students' motivation and attitudes towards learning.*

■ **worry·ing·ly** *adv.*: *Worryingly, the effects of social inequalities appear to be influencing childhood obesity.*

worse¹ /wɜːs; *NAmE* wɜːrs/ *adj.* (comparative of *bad*) **1** more serious or severe: **~ than sth** *In many developing countries, pollution levels are worse than in European cities.* ◇ **~ than doing sth** *Believing in false gods was considered worse than being a simple non-believer.* ◇ **get ~** *The world food crisis can only get worse.* ◇ **far ~** *This situation is likely to be far worse in low-income countries.* ◇ **make things ~** *Subsequent action may make things worse.* **2** of poorer quality or lower standard; less good or more unpleasant: *The practical argument is that the alternative is worse.* ◇ **~ than sth** *Ten months after the earthquake, the country's public health system is worse than ever.* ◇ **~ than doing sth** *There is nothing worse than having a law and not enforcing it, since that promotes disrespect for the law.* ◇ **even ~** *Poor conditions for refugees generally can often mean even worse conditions for women specifically.* **3** [not before noun] **~ (than sth)** more ill or unhappy: *One typical symptom of depressive disorder is feeling worse in the morning than in the evening.* ◇ **much ~** *Her mother was much worse than when she had last seen her three days previously.*

worse² /wɜːs; *NAmE* wɜːrs/ *adv.* (comparative of *badly*) **1 ~ (than sb/sth)** less well: *Divorced men would fare, on average, worse than divorced women.* ◇ *The party did worse than predicted on polling day.* **2** used to introduce a statement about sth that is more serious or unpleasant than things already mentioned: *The Confederacy did not have enough men to defend its territory. Worse, Jefferson Davis started the war too soon.* ◇ **even ~** *Many other countries had experienced slow growth, or even worse, stagnation and decline.* ◇ **~ still/yet** *Sales of houses are down 30%. Worse still, property prices are down 8% on last year.*

IDM **be ˌworse ˈoff (than sb/sth)** to be poorer, unhappier, etc. than before or than sb else: *Factory workers are even worse off, suggests Deming.* ◇ *Indigenous people continue to be worse off than other Australians.* ◇ *With these tax rates, an increase in earnings could mean that the low paid would actually be worse off than before.*

worse³ /wɜːs; *NAmE* wɜːrs/ *noun* [U] more problems or bad news: *As it turned out, there was worse to come.*

IDM **for the ˈworse** into a less good or pleasant state or condition: *In 1949, things took a turn for the worse.*

worsen /ˈwɜːsn; *NAmE* ˈwɜːrsn/ *verb* [I, T] to become or make sth worse than it was before: *As the demand for motor vehicles rises, pollution is likely to worsen.* ◇ **~ sth** *Problems with oil supply in the Middle East have worsened the situation.* ➲ *compare* DETERIORATE ■ **worsen·ing** *adj.*: *It is plausible to assume that increasing age is generally related to worsening health.* **worsen·ing** *noun* [sing.] **~ (of sth)** *This contributed to a general worsening of relations between the two countries.*

wor·ship¹ /ˈwɜːʃɪp; *NAmE* ˈwɜːrʃɪp/ *noun* [U] the practice of showing respect for God or a god, by saying prayers, singing with others, etc; a ceremony for this: *The mosque is not solely a place of worship but also one of socialization.* ◇ *The basilica was ideally suited for Christian worship.*

wor·ship² /ˈwɜːʃɪp; *NAmE* ˈwɜːrʃɪp/ *verb* (**-pp-**, *NAmE also* **-p-**) **1** [T] **~ sb/sth** to show respect for God or a god, especially by saying prayers, singing, etc. with other people in a religious building: *The pagan religions of the empire worshipped many gods in ways that seemed appropriate to them.* **2** [I] to go to a service in a religious building: *Globalization is not simply economic: it concerns languages, political rights, how people worship, and the arts.*

worst¹ /wɜːst; *NAmE* wɜːrst/ *adj.* (superlative of *bad*) **1** most serious or severe: *The 1995 Oklahoma City bombing was recognized at the time as the worst act of terrorism committed on American soil.* ◇ **the ~ excesses of sb/sth** *An attempt was made to address some of the worst excesses of the tabloid press.* **2** of the poorest quality or lowest standard; least good or most unpleasant: *India does significantly better than the worst performers in terms of life expectancy.* ◇ *Sixty per cent of residents considered violent crime to be the worst aspect of living in the city.*

worst² /wɜːst; *NAmE* wɜːrst/ *adv.* (superlative of *badly*) **1** most seriously or severely: *Four of the economies worst affected by the Asian financial crisis are among this group.* **2** least well: *These children do worst at school.*

IDM **ˌworst of ˈall** used to introduce a statement about sth that is the most serious or unpleasant of a series of bad things already mentioned: *Only 2.2% of the forests were in satisfactory condition; all advice given by foresters had been ignored. Worst of all, millions of roubles would be needed to repair the damage.*

worst³ /wɜːst; *NAmE* wɜːrst/ *noun* [sing.] **1 the worst** the most serious or unpleasant thing that could happen: *Every expert in government was predicting the worst.* ◇ **fear the ~** *The Emperor, fearing the worst, left for Innsbruck.* **2** the part, situation or possibility that is worse than any other: **the ~ of sth** *Investors seemed to think that the worst of the recession might be over.* ◇ **at sth's ~** *At their worst, these winds pose a hazard to large vehicles.*

IDM **at (the) ˈworst** used for saying what is the worst thing that can happen: *At the worst, half of older people will suffer from dementia.*

ˈworst-case *adj.* [only before noun] involving the worst situation that could happen: *The worst-case scenario is that the single currency will collapse.*

worth¹ /wɜːθ; *NAmE* wɜːrθ/ *adj.* [not before noun] (used like a preposition, followed by a noun, pronoun or number, or by the *-ing* form of a verb) **1 ~ sth** having a value equal to the amount of money or thing mentioned: *The world travel and tourism industry was worth $685 billion in 2005.* ◇ *The objective is to generate a final product that is worth more than the costs of providing it.* **2** used to recommend the action mentioned because you think it may be useful, enjoyable, etc: **~ sth** *Both websites give a valuable insight into mental health in the recent past and are worth a visit.* ◇ **~ doing sth** *For these reasons, it is worth looking at the raw data to see whether anything unusual appears to be happening.* ◇ **be well ~ (doing) sth** *In the author's opinion, it is also well worth consulting information sources such as market reports.* **3** important, good or enjoyable enough to make sb feel satisfied, especially when difficulty or effort is involved: **~ sth** *Continuing with this approach is probably not worth the effort.* ◇ **~ doing sth** *The Emperor Constantine believed that the Christian God was a mighty god whose patronage was worth having.* ◇ **it is ~ it** *They have lost many old customers but they think it is worth it because they will attract higher-spending new customers.* ➲ *see also* WORTHWHILE

IDM **ˌworth sb's ˈwhile (to do sth/doing sth)** interesting or useful for sb to do: *They could rely on making enough profit for it to be worth their while incurring the costs and risks of experimenting.*

worth² /wɜːθ; *NAmE* wɜːrθ/ *noun* [U] **1 ten dollars', £40, etc. ~ of sth** an amount of sth that has the value mentioned: *Approximately $3.6 trillion worth of goods were produced in that year.* **2 a week's, month's, etc. ~ of sth** an amount of sth that lasts or covers a period of a week, etc: *The conclusions are based on decades' worth of data.* **3 ~ (of sth)** the financial value of sth: *The total worth of the private security business in the US had increased to $52 billion by 1991.* **4** the level at which sb/sth deserves to be valued or rated: *The French Revolution gave the common people a sense of their own worth.* ◇ **prove your/its ~** *The*

W

British system had proved its worth by surviving for so long.

worth·less /ˈwɜːθləs; *NAmE* ˈwɜːrθləs/ *adj.* **1** having no practical or financial value: *The company's shares became worthless and its employees all lost their jobs.* ◇ *Legislation restricted the rights of some British subjects to the extent that these rights became practically worthless.* OPP VALUABLE **2** (of a person) having no good qualities or useful skills: *He was accused of giving diplomas to worthless students whom he happened to like.*

worth·while /ˌwɜːθˈwaɪl; *NAmE* ˌwɜːrθˈwaɪl/ *adj.* important, enjoyable, interesting, etc; worth spending time, money or effort on: *They decided to pool their experience in order to make a really worthwhile contribution on a national scale.* ◇ **it is ~ (for sb) to do sth** *This makes it worthwhile for Australian universities to increase the number of international students they take.* ◇ **it is ~ doing sth** *It would probably be worthwhile extending the test to include more patients.* HELP This word can also be written **worth while**, except when it is used before a noun.

worthy /ˈwɜːði; *NAmE* ˈwɜːrði/ *adj.* (**wor·thier**, **wor·thi·est**) **1 ~ (of sb/sth)** having the qualities that deserve sb/sth: *There are other factors worthy of consideration.* ◇ *She was worthy of a better husband than Connolly.* **2** [usually before noun] having qualities that deserve respect, attention or admiration SYN DESERVING: *His radicalism led him to espouse a whole range of worthy causes.* **3 ~ of sb/sth** typical of what a particular person or thing might do, give, etc: *The article was a parable, worthy of Wu Han himself.* **4** having good qualities but not very interesting or exciting: *There is no point in being worthy but ineffectual.* **5 -worthy** (in compounds) deserving, or suitable for, the thing mentioned: *Those who are least creditworthy pay most for mortgages.* ➲ *see also* TRUSTWORTHY

would / *strong form* wʊd; *weak form* wəd; əd/ *modal verb* (*short form* **'d** /d/, *negative* **would not**, *short form* **wouldn't** /ˈwʊdnt/) HELP The short form **wouldn't** should not be used in academic writing, unless you are quoting or deliberately using a less formal style. **1** used as the past form of *will*, especially when reporting what sb has said or thought: *Respondents were asked whether they would be prepared to be interviewed by telephone.* ◇ *The next 5 years would see the population of the Kansas Territory grow from 8 500 to almost 100 000 (Unrau, 1971).* ➲ grammar note *at* WILL[1] **2** used for talking about the result of an event that you imagine: *In order to achieve this, wages would have to rise.* ◇ *I am convinced that the educational problems I have discussed would benefit from multidisciplinary solutions.* **3** used for describing a possible action or event that did not in fact happen, because sth else did not happen first: *Without the colonies, economic expansion would have driven up the price of cotton, sugar and other raw materials.* ◇ *At first, it seemed that these plants would never operate at their rated capacity and produce profit.* **4 so that/in order that sb/sth ~ ...** used for saying why sb does sth: *Warring states encouraged national solidarity so that citizens would remain loyal in moments of crisis.* **5** used to show that sb/sth was not willing or refused to do sth: *Many philosophers today would not accept scripture as a reliable source of truth.* **6** used to say what sb likes or prefers: **~ like, love, hate, prefer, etc. sth/(sb) to do sth** *Claire would like to be a great writer like Katherine Paterson one day.* ◇ **~ rather do sth/sb did sth** *Hannah would rather sit and chat with her friends than do schoolwork.* **7 ~ imagine, say, think, etc. (that)...** used to give opinions that you are not certain about: *I would imagine that Heschel had this concept in mind when he wrote this poem.* **8** used for talking about things that often happened in the past SYN USED TO[1]: *The couple stated that Frank would often lock himself in his room after being shouted at.* **9 I would...** used to give advice: *I would recommend this book to all occupational health professionals working in health care.* ◇ *I would say addressing poverty is the number one priority health need.* **10 wish (that) sb/sth ~ ...** used for saying what you want to happen: *I wish economists would take more responsibility for delivering what they promise.* ➲ grammar note *at* MODAL[1]

ˈwould-be *adj.* [only before noun] used to describe sb who is hoping to become the type of person mentioned: *Disagreement among would-be reformers has prevented change of a fundamental nature.*

wound[1] /wuːnd/ *noun* **1** an injury to part of the body, especially one in which a hole is made in the skin: *Clips and stitches are removed after 7–10 days when the wound has healed.* ◇ *The infection of a surgical wound is a relatively common event.* **2** mental or emotional pain caused by sth unpleasant that has been said or done to you: *Heaney seems to be arguing that independent-minded, imaginative literature can heal wounds.*

wound[2] /wuːnd/ *verb* [often passive] **1 ~ sb/sth** to injure part of the body, especially by making a hole in the skin using a weapon: *Bagration was mortally wounded, and died some weeks later.* **2 ~ sb/sth** to hurt sb's feelings: *When Americans demanded a greater voice in the French military effort, French pride was wounded.*

wound[3] /waʊnd/ *past tense, past part. of* WIND[2]

wound·ed /ˈwuːndɪd/ *adj.* **1** injured by a weapon, for example in a war: *After the battle of Solferino, Dunant dedicated himself to easing the suffering of wounded soldiers.* **2 the wounded** *noun* [pl.] people who are wounded, for example in a war: *The treaty contained provisions on the treatment of the wounded and sick.*

wove *past tense of* WEAVE

woven *past part. of* WEAVE

wrap /ræp/ *verb* (**-pp-**) **1 ~ sth (in sth)** to cover sth completely in paper or material: *Never apply ice directly on to the skin: wrap it in a cloth or towel before applying.* **2 ~ sth around/round sth/sb** to put sth firmly around sb/sth: *Steel bands were wrapped around the concrete posts.*

wrist /rɪst/ *noun* the joint between the hand and the arm: *She complained of pain in her left wrist and hand.*

write /raɪt/ *verb* (**wrote** /rəʊt; *NAmE* roʊt/, **writ·ten** /ˈrɪtn/) **1** [I, T] to make letters or numbers on a surface, especially using a pen or pencil: *From the sixth century, more and more children learned to read and write.* ◇ **~ sth** *He wrote the literal meaning in pencil above each Latin word.* **2** [T, I] to produce sth in written form so that people can read, perform or use it: **~ sth** *She has written five books and more than 100 articles.* ◇ *Bach wrote the greatest music ever composed for the organ.* ◇ **~ sth about/on sb/sth** *A great deal has been written about the distinction between data, information and knowledge.* ◇ **~ about sb/sth** *McLaren writes about his experience of teaching for five years in schools in America.* ◇ **~ for sth** *Marx began writing for a liberal daily the authorities closed down in 1843.* ◇ **at the time of writing** *At the time of writing, this matter was still unresolved.* ◇ **~ sb sth** *An unknown poet wrote his mother the 'Consolation to Livia'.* **3** [I, T] to put information, a message of good wishes, etc. in a letter and send it to sb: *The Secretary of State wrote to say that he had decided not to grant the request.* ◇ **~ (sth) (to sb)** *The members of the group were encouraged to write to the Prime Minister to say what he should do about the country.* ◇ **~ sb sth** *His mother used to write him letters in English.* ◇ **~ that...** *In his resignation letter, Bevan wrote that it was wrong to impose national health charges.* ◇ **~ doing sth** *Later, L'Estrange wrote requesting that Graucob remove the machine.* **4** [T, I] to state the information or the words mentioned: **~ that...** *In his autobiography, he writes that he did not see Plath much at this time.* ◇ **~ of sth** *Modern* *scholars increasingly write of a 'transformation' of Graeco-Roman society.* ◇ **+ speech** *'The present century', he wrote, 'has been marked by a prodigious increase in wealth-producing power.'* **5** [T] to put information in the appropriate places on a printed form: **~ sth (out)** *The junior doctor had been asked to write out the prescription.* ◇ **~ sb (out) sth** *They wrote him a cheque for two hundred euros.* **6** [T, I] **~ (sth) to/onto sth** to record data in the memory of a computer: *The processor may either read data from a memory location or write data to a memory location.* ◇ *True read/write optical storage systems write data onto the disk, read it and then erase it.*

PHR V **ˌwrite ˈback (to sb)** to write sb a letter replying to their letter SYN REPLY[1] (1): *He wrote back to his colleague immediately.* **ˌwrite sth ˈdown 1** to write sth on paper, especially in order to remember or record it: *It is useful to write down the essential points for the patient to study at home.* **2** to reduce the value of an ASSET when stating it in a company's accounts: *This approach involves closing insolvent financial institutions and writing down shareholders' capital.* **ˌwrite ˈin (to sb/sth)** to write a letter to an organization or a company, for example to ask about sth or to express an opinion: *People often write in to newspapers and magazines to complain about new usages.* **ˌwrite sth ˈinto sth** to include a rule or condition in a contract or an agreement when it is made: *Holiday entitlement is usually written into a contract of employment.* **ˌwrite sth ˈoff** to cancel a debt; to recognize that sth is a failure or has no value: *The creditors were only willing to write off less than 2% of the group's debt.* ◇ *Their fixed assets have already been written off.* **ˌwrite sb/sth ˈoff (as sth)** to decide that sb/sth is a failure or not worth paying any attention to SYN DISMISS (2): *In the mid-1970s, commentators tended to write off Mrs Thatcher as a prospective Prime Minister.* **ˌwrite sth ˈout** to write sth on paper, including all the details, especially a piece of work or an account of sth: *It was assumed that Elizabeth I delivered her speeches from a text written out in advance.* ➲ *see also* WRITE (5) **ˌwrite sth ˈup** to record sth in writing in a full and complete form, often using notes that you made earlier: *Darwin hurriedly wrote up his research in his book, 'The Origin of Species'.*

writer /ˈraɪtə(r)/ *noun* **1** a person whose job is writing books, stories, articles, etc: *John Galsworthy was a very prolific writer.* ◇ **~ of sth** *He abandoned a promising career as a writer of fiction.* ◇ **~ on sth** *Other writers on the subject have expressed similar views.* **2** **~ (of sth)** a person who has written a particular thing: *The writer of the letter wished to keep his name secret.*

▸ ADJECTIVE + WRITER **great • prolific • young • male • feminist • early • later • contemporary • modern • ancient • Romantic** *This largely pessimistic view of international relations is shared by many contemporary writers.*

▸ VERB + WRITER **become • influence • discuss • read** *Shelley and Keats influenced American writers as diverse as Wallace Stevens and F. Scott Fitzgerald.*

▸ WRITER + VERB **use, employ • argue • suggest • write • work • describe** *Many writers have argued that schooling reinforces social divisions.*

writ·ing /ˈraɪtɪŋ/ *noun* **1 writings** [pl.] books, stories or other written works, especially by a particular person or on a particular subject: **writings of sb** *Her second novel was heavily influenced by the writings of Jean-Jacques Rousseau.* ◇ **sb's writings** *In his writings, he occasionally referred to his own life and times.* ◇ **writings on sth** *Aristotle's writings on science provided scholars with a wealth of new insights.* **2** [U] written work, especially with regard to its style or quality: *She emphasizes that good writing is a product of effort, time and multiple drafts.* **3** [U] the activity of writing, in contrast to reading, speaking, etc: *The National Literacy Strategy was designed to raise standards in reading and writing.* **4** [U] the activity of writing books, articles, etc, especially as a job: *Chekhov qualified as a doctor after university, but soon devoted himself entirely to writing.* **5** [U] **~ (on sth)** letters, words or symbols marked on a surface: *The Vietnamese government required advertisers to reduce the amount of writing on signs in English.* **6** [U] the particular way in which sb forms letters when they write: *Her writing is neat and legible.*

IDM **in ˈwriting** in the form of a letter, document, etc, and therefore official: *The consent of the patient should be obtained in writing.* ◇ *Concerns about staffing levels should be put in writing and sent to managers.*

writ·ten[1] /ˈrɪtn/ *adj.* **1** [only before noun] in the form of a letter, document, etc. and therefore official: *All participants gave written consent.* **2** [usually before noun] expressed in writing rather than in speech: *The situation with regard to the written language is somewhat different.* **3** [usually before noun] (of an exam, piece of work, etc.) involving writing rather than speaking or practical skills: *The first stage of the selection process consists of written tests.*

IDM **the ˌwritten ˈword** language expressed in writing rather than in speech: *It is important not to underestimate the authority of the written word in early medieval Europe.*

writ·ten[2] *past part. of* WRITE

wrong[1] /rɒŋ; *NAmE* rɔːŋ/ *adj.* **1** [not before noun] (of a person) not right about sth/sb SYN MISTAKEN (2): *We now know that Hubble was wrong.* ◇ *Duhem pointed out that Arago was wrong on two counts.* ◇ **~ about sth/sb** *He was right about the problem, but wrong about the solution.* ◇ **~ to do sth** *He is wrong to think that this is always the case.* OPP RIGHT[2] (2) **2** not right or correct: *Sometimes students will get the answer wrong or only partially correct.* ◇ *Experimental results showed that the underlying reasoning was seriously wrong.* ◇ *This is a legitimate point, but Rawls overstates it and draws the wrong conclusion from it.* ◇ **~ with sth** *Gaunilo has not shown what is wrong with the argument's logic.* ◇ **it is ~ to do sth** *It would be wrong to claim that all of these changes were supported enthusiastically by all member states.* OPP RIGHT[2] (5) **3** [usually before noun] not suitable, right or what you need: *The report made no impact simply because it was published at the wrong time.* ◇ *If poor data cause the wrong decision to be made, the result may be very costly indeed.* ◇ **~ (sth) (for sth)** *Too much focus on cost may be the wrong business model for this market.* ◇ *The pumps were the wrong voltage for the United Kingdom electricity supply.* OPP RIGHT[2] (1) **4** [not before noun] **~ with sb/sth** causing problems or difficulties; not as it should be: *Before you close the interview, you will need to give the patient information about what is wrong with them.* ◇ *D. Lane, in 'The Rise and Fall of State Socialism', interprets what went wrong with the communist system as a whole.* OPP RIGHT[2] (4) **5** [not usually before noun] not morally right or honest: **~ (for sb) (to do sth)** *Kant wrote that it is wrong for a person to be cruel to animals.* ◇ **~ with (doing) sth** *Roman society saw nothing wrong with cruel public punishments.* ◇ **morally ~** *It must be proved that the defendant did not know that the act was legally wrong, rather than merely morally wrong.* OPP RIGHT[2] (3) ■ **wrong·ness** *noun* [U] *The very concept of murder seems to include the idea of wrongness.* IDM *see* TRACK[1]

wrong[2] /rɒŋ; *NAmE* rɔːŋ/ *adv.* (used after verbs) in a way that produces a result that is not correct or that you do not want: *Others in the marketing department are forced to guess what the strategy is and they may guess wrong.* OPP RIGHT[3] (3)

IDM **get sth ˈwrong** to make a mistake with sth: *Getting a brand name wrong can cost a company dearly.* ◇ *Predicting inflation each year over the next 15 years is extremely difficult—even the Treasury experts get it wrong.* **go**

ˈ**wrong** **1** to experience problems or difficulties: *Everything started to go wrong for Nixon during the fall of 1973.* **2** to make a mistake: *Webster makes it plain where the council went wrong.*

wrong³ /rɒŋ; *NAmE* rɔːŋ/ *noun* **1** [U] behaviour that is not honest or morally acceptable: *Sanity involves the ability to know the difference between right and wrong.* **2** [C] (*formal*) an act that is not legal, honest or morally acceptable: *Where a wrong has been done against a company, the proper claimant is the company itself.* ◇ *These individuals have committed a public wrong.* OPP RIGHT¹ (3)

IDM **in the ˈwrong** deserving the blame for sth such as an accident or a mistake; not being correct in an argument: *A review of the evidence can usually reveal who is in the wrong and thereby establish agreement.* ◇ *Although technically in the wrong, he felt that he had been treated unfairly.*

wrong·doing /ˈrɒŋduːɪŋ; *NAmE* ˈrɔːŋduːɪŋ/ *noun* [U, C] (*formal*) illegal or dishonest behaviour SYN CRIME, OFFENCE (1): *The Belgium criminal courts had cleared Cresson of any criminal wrongdoing.* ◇ *Perpetrators need a forum for acknowledging their wrongdoings.*

wrong·ful /ˈrɒŋfl; *NAmE* ˈrɔːŋfl/ *adj.* [usually before noun] (*law*) not fair, morally right or legal: *The prosecution carries a heavy burden of proof so as to minimize the risk of wrongful conviction.* ■ **wrong·ful·ly** /ˈrɒŋfəli; *NAmE* ˈrɔːŋfəli/ *adv.*: *It was further claimed that the defendant had acted wrongfully in terminating the contract.*

wrong·ly /ˈrɒŋli; *NAmE* ˈrɔːŋli/ *adv.* in a way that is unfair, immoral or not correct: *He was wrongly convicted of the offence and sent to prison.* ◇ *The local authority accepted that it had acted wrongly.* ◇ **rightly or ~** *Most of us feel, rightly or wrongly, that it is our conscious thoughts that form our personalities and inspire our actions.*

wrote *past tense of* WRITE

Xx

X-ray /ˈeks reɪ/ *noun* **1** [C, usually pl.] a type of RADIATION that can pass through objects that are not transparent and make it possible to see inside them HELP **X-rays** are ELECTROMAGNETIC waves of high energy and very short WAVELENGTH: *The densities of the structures inside the body affect the penetration of X-rays and therefore their appearance on the image.* ◇ **+ noun** *These structures have been determined by X-ray diffraction of crystalline materials.* **2** [C, U] a medical examination using X-rays: *The condition is diagnosed from chest X-ray, CT scan and lung biopsy.* **3** [C] a photograph made by X-rays, especially one showing bones or organs in the body: *Typical appearance on X-rays and scans indicates localized enlargement of bone.*

Yy

yard /jɑːd; *NAmE* jɑːrd/ *noun* **1** (*abbr.* **yd**) **~ (of sth)** a unit for measuring length, equal to 3 feet (36 inches) or 0.9144 of a metre: *Fifty yards of cloth was needed for the sail.* **2** (*NAmE*) the garden of a house: *There was a beautiful tree growing in the yard.* **3** (*BrE*) an area outside a building, usually with a hard surface and a surrounding wall: *a factory/prison yard*

year /jɪə(r); jɜː(r); *NAmE* jɪr/ *noun* (*abbr.* **yr**) **1** (*also technical* ˌ**calendar** ˈ**year**) [C] the period from 1 January to 31 December, that is 365 or 366 days, divided into 12 months: *By the year 2025, about 5 billion people will live in cities.* ◇ *Capital-intensive industries required the presence of workers all the year round.* ◇ **in a ~** *In an average year, a breeding pair of barn owls may consume as many as 5 000 small mammals.* ◇ *In Britain, public-sector net borrowing in the 2009 calendar year reached 159.2 billion.* **2** [C] a period of 12 months, measured from any particular time: *It took 20 years for the Aral Sea to show signs of ecological decline.* ◇ *Schaffer spent seven years in Berlin, eventually earning a doctorate.* ◇ **for... years** *Iraq and its people have suffered the destruction of war for the past 30 years.* ◇ **-year + noun** *The latest available figures cover the 25-year period from 2006 to 2031.* ➲ language bank *at* TIME¹ **3** [C] a period of 12 months connected with a particular activity: *A tax year runs from 6th April one year to 5th April the next.* ◇ *Data collection took place during the 2007–08 academic year.* ◇ *Parental support for physical activity may differ in the summer compared with the school year.* **4** [C, usually pl.] age; time of life: *Paul is 21 years old.* ◇ *A total of 1 449 respondents aged 16 years and over were interviewed.* ◇ *More than 60% of UK 15–19 year-olds were in either part-time technical or full-time general education.* ◇ *In his later years, Bohr became very concerned with philosophical issues.* **5 years** [pl.] a long time: *Online videoconferencing has been around for years.* ◇ *The growth of knowledge in the airline industry over the years has been extremely productive.* ◇ *He began to remember classmates he had not thought about in years.* **6** [C] (*especially BrE*) (at a school, etc.) a level that you stay in for one year; a student at a particular level: *Most students begin their GCSE courses in year 10.* ◇ *We interviewed 167 year-seven pupils.* ◇ *Although Luke is fairly bright, his grades have declined to the point that he may fail the academic year.*

IDM ˌ**year after** ˈ**year** every year for many years: *The average energy of the sun reaching earth remains constant, and crops can be grown and harvested year after year.* ˌ**year by** ˈ**year** as the years pass; each year: *The environmental lobby is gaining strength year by year.* ˌ**year on** ˈ**year** (used especially when talking about figures, prices or quantities) each year, compared with the last year: *Ethical shopping for everything from energy-efficient fridges to organic food is rising steadily year on year.* ◇ *Year-on-year volume sales are 25.7 per cent ahead.* ➲ *more at* ADVANCED, TURN²

year·ly /ˈjɪəli; ˈjɜːli; *NAmE* ˈjɪrli/ *adj.* **1** paid, valid or calculated for one year: *Residential investment grew at an average yearly rate of 7.45% between 2002 and 2005.* ◇ *High variability is common in yearly rainfall totals and seasonal distribution (Hayden, 1998).* **2** happening once a year or every year: *Nursing facilities are inspected on a yearly basis.* ◇ *Samples were collected at yearly intervals.* ◇ *The Committee on Trade and Investment publishes a yearly progress report.* ■ **year·ly** *adv.*: *Flight simulator performance and cognition were tested yearly.* ◇ *The risk of property damage from storms has increased yearly.*

yeast /jiːst/ *noun* [U, C] any of a group of FUNGI in which the body consists of individual cells, which may occur separately, in groups of two or three, or in chains HELP One species of **yeast** can turn sugar into alcohol and CARBON DIOXIDE and is used in making beer and bread; other species can cause disease: *As an organism, yeast is amenable to molecular and genetic experimentation.* ◇ *The use of broad-spectrum antibiotics can lead to overgrowth of yeasts at various body sites.* ◇ **+ noun** *Folate is found in liver, yeast extract and green vegetables.*

yel·low /ˈjeləʊ; *NAmE* ˈjeloʊ/ *adj.* (**yel·lower, yel·lowest**) having the colour of butter: *The plant has a single shoot with bright yellow flowers.* ■ **yel·low** *noun* [U, C] *The colour changes from pale yellow to dark brown as iodine doping progresses.*

yes /jes/ *exclamation* **1** used to answer a question and say that sth is correct or true: *'Do you understand?' 'Yes.'* **2** used to show that you agree with what has been said:

'I enjoyed her latest novel.' 'Yes, so did I.' **3** used to disagree with sth negative that sb has just said: *'I've never met her before.' 'Yes, you have.'* **4** used to agree to a request or to give permission: *We are hoping that they will say yes to our proposals.* **5** used to accept an offer or invitation: *'Would you like a drink?' 'Yes, please/thanks.'* **6** used for replying politely when sb calls you: *Yes? How can I help you?* ◇ *Yes, sir.*

yes·ter·day /ˈjestədeɪ; ˈjestədi; *NAmE* ˈjestərdeɪ; ˈjestərdi/ *adv.* on the day before today: *Yesterday, he openly refused to work and threw his books on the floor.* ◇ *Yesterday morning, her flatmates noticed that her eyes were a bit yellow.* ■ **yes·ter·day** *noun*: *Salespeople cannot presume that yesterday's answers and solutions are applicable today.*

yet[1] /jet/ *adv.* **1** used in negative sentences and questions to talk about sth that has not happened but that you expect to happen: *There are still a number of important challenges that have yet to be properly addressed.* ◇ *The control mechanisms are not yet known, but several of the genes involved have been identified.* ◇ *Studies in which the individuals included had not yet reached adulthood are excluded from the analysis.* **2 could, might, may, etc. do sth ~** used to say that sth could, might, etc. happen in the future, even though it seems unlikely: *Ketamine may yet prove to have a place in neurosurgery.* ◇ *The cause of New Deal liberalism could yet be salvaged within the Democratic Party.* **3** used to emphasize an increase in number or amount or the number of times sth happens: **~ another** *Adolescents often will view the clinician as yet another authority figure.* ◇ **~ more** *With the establishment of the EEC, the project of European integration became yet more ambitious in its objectives.* ◇ **~ again** *Yet again, there is no mention of these advances in the book.* **4 ~ worse, more importantly, etc.** used to emphasize an increase in how bad, important, etc. sth is SYN EVEN[1] (2), STILL[1] (3): *These difficulties became yet greater following the international economic crises of 1973–4 and 1978–9.* ◇ *The Corinthian ships were forced to retreat in turn upon the arrival of a yet larger Athenian force.* **5 the best, longest, etc. sth ~ (done)** the best, longest, etc. thing of its kind made, produced, written, etc. until now/then: *The creation of the Social Democratic Party posed the most formidable challenge yet to the two-party system.* **6** from now until the period of time mentioned has passed: *The general consensus is that the Internet's advertising growth will continue for many years yet.* **7** (used in negative sentences) now; as soon as this: *She may not be able to return to front line practice just yet.* **8** despite sth that has just been mentioned SYN NEVERTHELESS: *And yet, once again, there seems to be a significant gap between the facts that Tacitus provides and the overall impression of this dark time.*
IDM **as ˈyet** until now; until a particular time in the past: *None of these cases has as yet been heard before the court.* ◇ *The reasons for this behaviour are, as yet, unknown.*

yet[2] /jet/ *conj.* despite what has just been said SYN NEVERTHELESS: *Each rapid is unique, yet all are similar.* ◇ *Women helped to keep the movement running on a day-to-day basis, yet were excluded from power.* ◇ *Much of this chapter's discussion paints a grim picture. Yet there are also promising signs.* ➲ language bank *at* HOWEVER

yield[1] /jiːld/ *verb* **1** [T] **~ sth** to produce or provide sth, for example a result, information or a profit: *This analysis yielded several insights.* ◇ *The study suggests that this methodology yields promising results.* ◇ *Non-timber products tend to yield higher net returns per hectare than timber.* ➲ thesaurus note *at* SUPPLY[2] **2** [I] to stop resisting sth/sb; to agree to do sth that you do not want to do SYN GIVE WAY TO STH (2): *The Western powers now yielded when they should have resisted.* ◇ **~ to sth/sb** *Councils sometimes yielded to the emperor's pressure to reach a consensus.* **3** [T] **~ sth/sb (to sb)** to allow sb to win, have or take control of sth that has been yours until now SYN SURRENDER[1] (2): *Magnus yielded control over the Scandinavian settlements to the king of Scots.*
▸ YIELD + NOUN **result, finding • insight • information • conclusion • value • figure • total • score • estimate • benefit • gain • return, profit • solution • equation** *His approach would continue to yield vital information for decades.* ◇ *Typical values are in the range 1.5–2.0, but many polymerizations yield considerably larger values.*

yield[2] /jiːld/ *noun* [C, U] the total amount of sth that is grown or produced: *Loss of soil leads to lower crop yields.* ◇ **~ on sth** *These purchasers took advantage of the higher yields on this risky debt.* ◇ **~ of sth** *It has been found that this technique increases the yield of juice from fruits and vegetables over that of simple mechanical pressing.*

you /ju; *NAmE* jə *strong form* juː/ *pron.* **1** used as the subject or object of a verb or after a preposition to refer to the person or people being spoken or written to: *It happened when you and I were still boys.* ◇ *Who told you the story?* ◇ *Obviously, it is important for you to win.* **2** used for referring to people in general: *When you first learn to read, every word is difficult.* ◇ *Your anger gives you information about your core motivations.*

young[1] /jʌŋ/ *adj.* (**young·er** /ˈjʌŋgə(r)/, **young·est** /ˈjʌŋgɪst/) **1** not yet old; not as old as others: *A notable feature of unemployment is that it particularly affects young people.* ◇ *Rossini was 22 years younger than Beethoven.* ◇ *His own death came in 1917 at the relatively young age of 59.* OPP OLD (2) **2** having lived or existed for only a short time; not fully developed: *These caterpillars seek out the young leaves of the black cherry (Prunus serotina).* ◇ *The food offered was unsuitable for very young babies.* ◇ *The Juan Fernandez Islands are very young, the oldest being only 4 million years old.* OPP OLD (4) **3** consisting of young people or young children; with a low average age: *The vast majority of commercial stations are aimed at young audiences.* ◇ *The younger age groups, namely those of primary-school children, continued to show an increase in mean body weight.*

young[2] /jʌŋ/ *noun* [pl.] **1** (*usually* **the young**) young people considered as a group: *Both the young and the old are vulnerable to discrimination on the grounds of age alone.* ◇ *The interview group included both old and young.* **2** young animals of a particular type or that belong to a particular mother: *Mammals devote long periods to feeding and caring for their young.*

your /jɔː(r); *NAmE* jʊr *weak form* jə(r)/ *det.* (the possessive form of *you*) **1** of or belonging to the person or people being spoken or written to: *Do you use your car a lot?* ◇ *The doctor will review your medical history.* ◇ *Watch your breath as it flows in and out.* **2** of or belonging to people in general: *The younger you are, the more romantic your view tends to be.* ◇ *Being noticed and having your presence appreciated is powerful.*

yours /jɔːz; *NAmE* jərz; jɔːrz; jʊrz/ *pron.* **1** of or belonging to you: *Our duties are different from yours.* ◇ *These experiences are yours alone.* ◇ *The more your competitors promote their work, the more you will find it necessary to promote yours.* **2** (*usually* **Yours**) used at the end of a letter before signing your name: (*BrE*) *Yours sincerely/faithfully* ◇ (*NAmE*) *Sincerely Yours/Yours Truly*

your·self /jɔːˈself; *NAmE* jɔːrˈself; jʊrˈself *weak form* jəˈself/ (*pl.* **your·selves** /jɔːˈselvz; *NAmE* jɔːrˈselvz; jʊrˈselvz *weak form* jəˈselvz/) *pron.* **1** (the reflexive form of *you*) used when the person or people being spoken to both cause and are affected by an action: *There is no need to blame yourself.* ◇ *Take a few breaths and calm yourself down.* ◇ *You must no longer allow yourselves to feel locked out from the decision-making process.* **2** used to emphasize the fact that the person who is being spoken to is doing sth: *You yourself*

may have stong feelings about an issue. ◇ *It is for you to decide for yourself.* ◇ *Would you like me to explain this to your family or do you want to talk to them yourself?*
IDM **by your'self/your'selves** **1** alone; without anyone else: *Meditation can be done by yourself or in a group.* **2** without help: *You are left to deal with everything all by yourself.*

youth /juːθ/ *noun* (*pl.* **youths** /juːðz/) **1** [pl.] young people considered as a group: *Many African American youth in poor, urban areas construct group identities.* ◇ **+ noun** *Serious concerns about youth violence are not unique to the US.* ◇ *Dance music significantly impacted 1990s British youth culture.* **2** [C] a young person, especially a young man: *Through college, Japanese youths have less private space compared with their US counterparts.* **3** [U] the time of life when a person is young, especially the time before a child becomes an adult: *In his youth, Heschel wrote many poems.* ◇ *The story that he spent his youth in exile is probably invented.* **4** [U] the quality or state of being young: *These conflicting and changing ideas of youth developed over a long period.* ◇ *Some older people say they feel alienated from a society so preoccupied by health, youth and beauty.*

youth·ful /ˈjuːθfl/ *adj.* **1** young; appearing or seeming younger than they are: *This is a very youthful population, with over 11 million children aged 12 years or younger.* ◇ *Negativity towards older women leads to pressure to maintain a youthful appearance.* **2** typical of young people: *Many novels are the story of youthful illusions crushed.*

Zz

zero[1] /ˈzɪərəʊ; *NAmE* ˈzɪroʊ; ˈziːroʊ/ *number* **1** (*pl.* **-os**) (*BrE also* **nought**) 0: *In this case, x is almost equal to zero.* **2** a temperature, pressure, etc. that is equal to zero on a scale: *At temperatures above absolute zero, electrons can be excited by the thermal motion of the atoms.* ◇ **+ noun** *These energies are measured on a scale whose zero point corresponds to the electron being infinitely removed from the nucleus.* **3** the lowest possible amount or level; nothing at all: **+ noun** *The given birth and death rates ultimately result in zero growth.*

zero[2] /ˈzɪərəʊ; *NAmE* ˈzɪroʊ; ˈziːroʊ/ *verb* (**zer·oes, zero·ing, zer·oed, zer·oed**) **~ sth** to turn or set an instrument or control to zero: *Zeroing is performed by opening the transducer to atmospheric pressure and electronically zeroing the system.*
PHR V **ˌzero ˈin on sb/sth** to fix all your attention on the person or thing mentioned: *Time Warner has zeroed in on global television as the most lucrative area for growth.*

zinc /zɪŋk/ *noun* [U] (*symb.* **Zn**) the chemical element of ATOMIC NUMBER 30. Zinc is a blue-white metal that is used to cover and protect other metals such as iron and steel: *Lead and zinc are commonly found together in many types of ore deposit.* ◇ **+ noun** *Electrons leave the cell from the zinc electrode and enter it again through the copper electrode.*

Z

zone /zəʊn; *NAmE* zoʊn/ *noun* **1** an area or a region with a particular feature or use: *Many states have created special economic zones in order to attract so-called global factories.* ◇ **~ of sth** *The major terrestrial ecosystems form broad bands that trace the climatic zones of the planet.* ◇ **in a ~** *Within the region, 143 million live in the coastal zone, and the number is increasing.* **2** an area or a part of an object, especially one that is different from its surroundings: *The downward motion of the piston has created a reduced pressure zone within the mixing cylinder.* ◇ **~ of sth** *Epidermal cells were counted in four zones of the leaf: one at the tip, one at the base and two intermediary zones.* **3** one of the parts that the earth's surface is divided into by imaginary lines that are PARALLEL to the EQUATOR: *True hurricanes can occur only in tropical zones.* ◇ *Today's poor countries lie mainly in the tropics, whereas the rich countries are mostly in temperate zones.* **4** one of the areas that a larger area is divided into for the purpose of organization: *The whole country is divided into three zones: zone 1 is Bangkok and neighbouring provinces, zone 2 is the central provinces, and zone 3 is all outlying provinces.* HELP A **time zone** is one of the 24 areas that the world is divided into, each with its own time that is one hour earlier than that of the time zone immediately to the east: *Variations in cultural practices can cause errors in the communications between partners, who may speak different languages and operate in different time zones.*

zy·gote /ˈzaɪɡəʊt; *NAmE* ˈzaɪɡoʊt/ *noun* (*biology*) a single cell that develops into a person, animal or plant, formed by the joining together of a male and a female GAMETE: *Gametes from two parents fuse to form a diploid zygote, which develops into an embryo.* ■ **zy·gotic** /zaɪˈɡɒtɪk; *NAmE* zaɪˈɡɑːtɪk/ *adj.*: *Zygotic genes are those required during the development of the embryo.*

Oxford Academic Writing Tutor

Using the Oxford Learner's Dictionary of Academic English to improve your writing

Whether you are writing an academic email or your dissertation, your dictionary can be a powerful tool to assist you in becoming a better writer in English.

Using the main part of the dictionary

You can use the A–Z of the dictionary to help you:

- **Choose your words carefully.** Many words in English have similar or related meanings, but are used in different contexts or situations.

Look carefully at the example sentences provided in the entries. Look for the SYN symbol and also at any THESAURUS notes to help you choose alternative words.

- **Combine words naturally and effectively.** In English, certain pairs of words go together and sound natural to native speakers (for example, *a broad approach*), and others do not (~~*a wide approach*~~). This is called **collocation**. Information on which words collocate with each other can be found in many of the dictionary entries.

Look up the key nouns you have used in your writing to check which adjectives and verbs are usually used with them. At many entries, you will find lists of adjectives, verbs, nouns, etc. that collocate with the word, illustrated with examples.

Look at the LANGUAGE BANK notes and WORD FAMILY boxes for help with expressing your ideas in different ways.

- **Edit and check your work.** You can use your dictionary to check any problem areas such as spelling, parts of speech, irregular forms, grammar and prepositions.

Look at the GRAMMAR POINT notes, WHICH WORD? notes and HELP notes for extra help with grammar and usage.

Using the Academic Writing Tutor

In the following pages, you will find examples of different types of academic writing that you can use as models for your own work. You will also find advice about planning, organizing and writing each type of text, and help with using sources appropriately.

- **Examples of written texts**

Look carefully at:
- the structure and organization of the text
- the way ideas and paragraphs are linked
- the language and style
- the notes on particular points

- **Tips** These are quick reminders and advice to help while you are writing.
- **Language Banks** give you some useful phrases that you can use in each type of writing.
- **Grammar Focus** gives you help with tenses, etc. for specific types of writing.

Contents

The Writing Process

Whether you are writing an essay, a case study or a dissertation, the process of writing is basically the same.

1. Preliminary Phase

Understand the question or task

Think about the question and ensure that you understand exactly what you are being asked to do.

- What is the topic and which aspect of it am I being asked to write about?
- How can I define the subject so it is not too wide in scope?
- What is the purpose of the piece of writing?

➲ See pages AWT4–5 Answering the Question.

Who is my audience?

For example:

- your tutor or other experts in your field
- an examiner
- fellow students or colleagues

Plan your time

Work backwards from the deadline date and plan when you will do each task. Allow time to review and edit your work.

2. Research Phase

Find relevant information

- Use a variety of sources such as books and journal articles.
- Secondary sources such as bibliographies may help you find relevant sources.

Evaluate and select sources

Is the content relevant?

- Read the abstract, or the introduction and the conclusion.

Is the source reliable?

- Is the author an expert in the field?
- Is it a respected journal?

Read critically

Before you read, think of questions you would like the text to answer. While you read, identify any assumptions the author makes–are they valid? Are the arguments supported by sufficient evidence?

Take notes

- Record bibliographic data (title, author, date, publisher and page numbers) for every source you read.
- Use your own words to take notes on what you read.

Organize and plan

- Organize your notes into logical sections depending on your purpose.
- Plan your essay by writing an outline of the main points.

3. Writing Phase

Academic writing is a recursive process in which you draft, review and revise your work several times.

Draft

- Start with your outline.
- Synthesize your ideas into paragraphs, clearly linking them.
- Focus on ensuring that your ideas are clear and your arguments are logically structured.
- Use your own words, except when using a direct quotation.
- Use sources to support the points you are making.
- Keep referring back to your purpose.

Review and revise

Read your writing with a critical eye. In early drafts, ask yourself:

- Have I answered the question/achieved my purpose?
- Have I introduced my subject, developed it logically, and come to a conclusion?
- Is my supporting evidence adequate? Do I need further examples, statistics or quotations?
- Have I used headings to help the reader, if appropriate?

In later drafts, ask yourself:

- Are the grammar, punctuation and spelling correct?
- Have I used the citation style recommended by my tutor or department? ➲ See pages AWT 46–47 Citations and Bibliography.
- Have I met the word count requirements?
- Have I presented my work in the correct style and format?

After each review, return to the drafting step, revising and editing your writing as necessary.

Academic Language

Different academic disciplines and text types typically use slightly different styles of language. When you read, notice the kind of language that is used in the type of writing you need to do.

Some features of academic language are common to most academic writing. It is always important to express ideas clearly, in a way your readers can easily understand. Academic writing tends to be:

Concise

Write concisely by using noun phrases:
adjective + **noun**

strong empirical ***evidence***

noun + **noun**

water purification ***methods***

You can add detail by using a noun with a **prepositional phrase** or a **clause**:
noun + prepositional phrase

In this study, we promote a promising ***method*** *for producing porous membranes* …

noun + clause

The ***results*** *shown in Table 1 indicate that* …

We present in Table 1 the ***occupations*** *that have experienced the largest expansion* …

➲ See pages R15–16 Noun phrases.

Formal and precise

Use words that have a precise meaning to avoid vague or ambiguous statements. Use more specific **synonyms** for common or informal words with general meanings:

We ***performed*** *two field experiments.* (not *did*)

The results ***obtained*** *are shown below.* (not *got*)

Analyses were performed using 100 g of protein in ***each instance****.* (not *every time*)

Notice and use words that have a specific academic usage:

The legislation contains ***express*** *limits.* (express = clearly stated)

The material may crack under tensile ***stress****.* (stress = physical pressure put on sth)

Avoid contracted forms (e.g. *weren't*); use the full form:

Electricity and water still ***were not*** *available.*

Impersonal

Focus on the topic, not the writer, by making the thing you are studying the subject of the sentence:

impersonal subject + passive verb

Physical activity *was assessed at the beginning of the programme.*

impersonal subject + active verb

This paper *presents new evidence for* …

The most recent data *show that* …

Use an impersonal '**It**' structure to express evaluation:
It is + adjective

It is *important to note that* …

It is *clear that the X-ray beam will* …

In some types of writing, **personal pronouns** are used to make the writer or researcher more visible. Check when and how this is used in your discipline.

In this study, ***we*** *explore* …

Our *study focuses on* …

Tentative

In academic writing, it is important to use tentative language when making claims. This does not mean you are uncertain about your claims, but shows you are aware that claims are based on limited data. You can do this by using **hedging language**:
Modal verbs such as *could*, *may* and *might*:

These results ***could*** *indicate* …

Teamwork ***may*** *be associated with better performance in the workplace.*

Other tentative language:

It is ***possible*** *that* …

Our findings ***suggest*** *that* …

➲ See also the Language Bank at **hedge**.

Carefully structured

Clearly link ideas and show the progression of your argument using **cohesion markers**; however, be careful not to overuse these:

More recently, ***however****, reports suggest* …
Thus*, it is important to evaluate* …

Fuel cell technologies may … ***In addition****, fuel cell vehicles offer the potential for* …

First*, we explore* … ***Secondly****, we focus on* …

Link back to previous ideas in your text using **synonyms** or **general nouns**:

Some researchers have examined …
One study linked … ***These arguments*** *all suggest that* …

Answering the Question

When you are asked to give in a piece of writing for assessment, you are usually given questions or a topic to write about. You may need to write a long answer–for example, a 2,000-word coursework essay or an exam essay that you could write in 2 hours–or give short answers (50–100 words) to a series of questions. Either way, it is essential that you fulfil the requirements of the question (even if it is not exactly a question).

A question usually has the following components:

- Topic
- Focus
- Scope
- Angle
- Viewpoint (in some questions)

Topic

The **topic** is likely to be something that you have studied on the course. It may be the object of the instruction verb in the question:

> Evaluate the effectiveness of any two **development theories** ...

The **topic** may follow a question word as subject of the verb:

> How did **textile manufacturers** respond to the economic crisis of the Great Depression?

The **topic** may follow an abstract word + 'of', especially in a 'What?' question:

> What are the definitions of a **'knowledge economy'**?

Focus and Scope

You will probably be asked to write about a particular aspect of the topic (this is your **focus**), and to expand or limit the context in which the topic is considered (this is the **scope**). You can find the focus and scope by asking questions about the topic:

- (Focus) Does the question focus on a particular aspect of the topic? Look for ways that the topic is modified, either before the topic with phrases with 'of', e.g. 'the distribution of....'; or after it using prepositions such as 'by', 'within' or 'as', e.g. '*as* developed by'.
- (Scope) Does the question specify a particular time period or context? Look for phrases with 'in', 'during' or 'for', e.g. '*in* the 1930s'.

Consider this example:

> Evaluate *the effectiveness of* any two development theories studied on the course.

The focus words are in italics: write only about how effective the theories have been.
The scope is underlined: limit your answer to two theories that you have already studied.

The focus may also be in the question word + verb:

> *How can* being born deaf *impair* the acquisition of a natural language?

The focus words are in italics: write about how the condition may impair language acquisition, rather than only about the condition itself.

Key words

The following **abstract nouns**, commonly used in questions, often point to the focus of the question:

(singular) concept, contrast, definition, difference, extent, factor, function, idea, importance, issue, problem, purpose, relationship, role, structure, value, view

(plural) achievements, advantages, causes, characteristics, concerns, disadvantages, effects, factors, goals, issues, limitations, origins, perspectives, principles, weaknesses

Adjectives may also be used:

central, effective, key, overall, significant

Phrases that direct the focus of the question:

in relation to; in the context of; with respect to.

Angle

The type of answer or the **angle** you are expected to give can be found in the **verb** or **question structure**:

Verb	Question structure	
Account for	What are the reasons for …?	Give reasons for the focus of the topic.
Analyse	How and why …? In what ways …?	Write about a number of aspects of the focus of the topic, organizing your points clearly.
Assess	To what extent …?	Write evaluatively about the focus of the topic you are given.
Compare	How does x differ from y?	Write about two or more aspects of the topic, giving both similarities and differences.
Consider	What is the significance of …? In what context …? What impact did … have?	Think about the topic in relation to the focus and write about what seems to be important.
Contrast (often used with 'compare')		Write about two or more aspects of the topic, showing how different they are.
Define	What does … mean? What constitutes …? What do you understand by …?	Give the meaning of the words or phrases given.
Discuss	What are the implications of …? What role does … play?	Write about a number of aspects of the topic or a given statement, evaluating one against another.
Evaluate (often used with 'critically')	How successful was …? What can you conclude from …?	Write about the qualities of the topic or the focus, showing how you reached your opinion.
Examine	What factors affect …? What evidence is there of …?	Write about the topic in detail, paying attention to the scope of the question.
Explain	Why …? What caused …?	Describe the topic and give reasons according to the focus of the question.

A question often has two or more of these verbs, or it may include a question structure:

> **Describe and distinguish between** ice caps, glaciers, icebergs and sea ice.

> **Assess** the impact of … **How might** outcomes be improved?

Viewpoint

A question may start with a statement which you are asked to discuss:

> Trade unions in the workplace can only have a negative impact on productivity. **Discuss.**

Here, you need to write about the arguments that support the statement *and* those which contrast with it. You are not required to take a particular stance.

You may be asked to give your own opinion:

> The War on Poverty was a failure. **Would you agree?**

Here, you need to give a balanced discussion of both sides of the argument *and* show which one you prefer.

Exam Question Tips

- Read the instructions before starting the exam–be very clear how many questions you need to answer from each section.
- Analyse the questions carefully, identifying the topic, focus, scope, angle and viewpoint. (Use a highlighter pen.)
- Once you have understood the questions, choose which you will answer and give each a difficulty rating. Answer the easiest question first–if you run out of time, it is better to lose marks on your weakest answer.
- Divide your time according to the marks given per question.
- Do not write a rough draft–make notes and write your essay straight away.
- Use the words of the question in your opening paragraph–it will help you to be sure you are answering it accurately.

Writing from Sources

Academic writing is not only about the writer's own ideas; it builds on what is already known about a topic, and so writers usually have to find and read various sources of information and include part of what they learned from their sources in their texts. Learning the right ways to use sources is important.

Writers use sources for many different reasons, including:

- proving that facts are true;
- explaining what is known about a topic;
- giving credit for ideas, discoveries, etc.;
- showing that experts agree or disagree;
- convincing readers that the writer is knowledgeable.

Appropriate references to sources make your writing stronger, but only if readers understand how sources have been used.

Show your reader:

- which ideas come from sources;
- which sources you have used;
- whether you have used the source's language.

The most common way to show that an idea, a fact, etc. comes from a source is to give a **reference** (also called a **citation**). If you do not give a reference, readers will assume that the idea is yours.

Think about:

- positioning references carefully to show what material they cover;
- reporting ideas carefully, so that they are not changed or distorted.

Sources are identified in two places:

- the reference in the body of the text;
- a reference list (also called a works cited list) at the end.

Secondary citation is when writers refer to sources they have seen mentioned but have not read. Try to avoid secondary citation by going to the original source, but if that is not possible, then signal a secondary citation clearly.

Material from sources can be reported in several ways, including:

Quoting This means repeating the language from the source exactly.

- Use **quotation marks** (also called inverted commas) at the beginning and the end of the quotation.
- If any words have been left out, replace them with an **ellipsis** (three dots separated by spaces).
- If any words are changed, put the new word in **square brackets** [ ].

Be sure that changes and omissions do not change the basic meaning of the quotation.

Quotation is very uncommon in the natural sciences and technical fields and more common in the humanities and the social sciences. Use quotations when they can support your own ideas, for instance when the exact wording is important. Do not let quotations replace your own ideas.

Paraphrasing This means taking an idea from a source and expressing it in your own words. This is an essential skill in academic writing, because stepping away from the source's language allows you to move your text in the direction you want it to go. Some inexperienced writers copy from a source and make small changes (replacing some words with synonyms, changing the word order, etc.). This is not paraphrasing. It makes a text harder to read and can appear to be **plagiarism** (see below).

Steps to a good paraphrase:

- Clearly understand the idea you want to report.
- Read your source several times.
- Use a dictionary to check important words.
- Put the source away, and write what you understand, on your own.
- Check whether the details are right.

Plagiarism and how to avoid it

By using sources to support your ideas and by showing your reader what role sources play in your writing, you can produce texts which are both effective and appropriate.

Plagiarism means using sources in a way which is intended to deceive the reader. One example of plagiarism is turning in an assignment which someone else wrote. Many teachers would consider a copy-and-change strategy to be plagiarism.

Plagiarism is taken extremely seriously in the English-speaking world and universities punish it severely, often by requiring students to leave the university.

Students on a sociolinguistics module were asked to write a short reflection on a variety of English they found personally important.

Student A used sources more successfully than Student B.

Student A

The writer has a point to make, so it is easier to use sources to support that point.

An important variety of English for me is Australian English (henceforth AusE), for three reasons. First, Australia is the nearest inner circle English-speaking country (Kachru, 1985) to my own, and as a result has political and economic importance for us.

The reference shows who originated this term.

Paraphrase

The second is that AusE resembles British English in many respects (Smith, 2012), probably because it is a former British colony. While it is true that these similarities are greater in some varieties of AusE than others (Mitchell & Delbridge, 1965, cited in Smith, 2012), their existence makes AusE easier for those of us who learned British English at school.

The writer knows that this is common knowledge; no reference needed.

The position of the reference shows that the first half of the sentence comes from the source, but not the second.

Secondary citation

Finally, AusE is distinctive in several ways. One is the use of shortened forms like 'barbie' for barbecue and 'arvo' for afternoon (Smith, 2012). Indeed, Simpson, 2001, identifies 346 Australian hypocorisms for place names alone. There are also a number of Aboriginal terms, such as 'kookaburra' and 'wallaby' (Melchers & Shaw, 2011). This combination of 'borrowed' and 'native' features creates an interesting effect, or, as Smith enthusiastically puts it, 'an exciting, twenty-first century mélange of ... the old and new world' (2001, p. 45). My shared fascination for this mixture helps explain my liking for this variety of English.

'Enthusiastically' gives the writer's interpretation of Smith; the enthusiastic wording may be why the writer felt a quotation was needed.

This writer uses several sources and relates them to each other. In the second paragraph, Smith's general statement is limited by Mitchell and Delbridge.

Quotation marks show where the quotation begins and ends. An ellipsis (...) shows omitted words.

By citing a range of sources, the writer gives a more thorough view of the topic.

References

Kachru B. B. (1985) Standards ...

Reference list

Student B

A less clear focus leads the writer into the trap of simply listing facts from sources, rather than using them for a purpose.

I have chosen to write about Australian English, which is very similar to British English, especially in its phonology and ...

But some parts of Australian English are different, too, including some words like the pervasive Australian hypocorisms, which are shortened word forms. Smith (2012) gives examples such as 'barbie' (barbecue), 'brekky' (breakfast) and 'addy' (address).

It is unclear from the position of the reference that this and the preceding sentence both come from Smith.

Copying with changes is not a good paraphrase.

So, because of these similarities and differences, Australian English is an important variety.

From Smith, chapter four: Australian English

Australian English (AusE) presents an interesting case for the sociolinguistic observer. Its description usually takes British English as a reference variety, and many similarities exist. Indeed, what has been termed 'cultivated' AusE is extremely close to RP (Mitchell & Delbridge, 1965). Phonologically, AusE is non-rhotic, and its long vowels . . .

However, it would be wrong to disregard the many features which make this variety unique. One of the most typical examples is the pervasive Australian hypocorisms: shortened word forms such as 'barbie' (barbecue), 'brekky' (breakfast) and 'addy' (address). Other lexical features of note include . . .

Australia is commonly perceived around the world as a vibrant, dynamic young country. It is possible that the unique variety of English which has emerged there—an exciting, twenty-first century mélange of the European and the antipodal, the old and new world—is in part responsible for that view.

Writing Essays 1: an explanation essay

The explanation essay allows you to demonstrate your understanding of a particular subject area without having to analyse, interpret, criticize or provide an opinion. Prompts may include 'Discuss …' or 'Consider the advantages and disadvantages …'.

The extract below is from an essay in the area of psychology. Note that the essay prompt is a three-part prompt: 1) describe the two approaches; 2) explain how they are different; and 3) contrast them in one specific context.

Essay prompt	**Describe and distinguish between Pavlovian (classical) and instrumental conditioning. Discuss how performance in an omission schedule can distinguish between these two types of conditioning.**
Paragraph 1 **Introduction** Places the two approaches in context and relates them to one another.	Associative learning is the process of linking the onset of a particular stimulus with that of another, subsequent event. Animals can be conditioned to acquire such associative links, and the behaviour that goes with them, by two means: Pavlovian conditioning and instrumental conditioning.
Paragraph 2 **Description of the first approach** Includes definitions of key vocabulary related to this approach.	Pavlovian conditioning was noted by Pavlov in 1927. While conducting various digestive experiments on dogs, he found that they began salivating at the sight of the experimenter who brought their food. Thus, the stimulus of the experimenter's presence predicted the arrival of food: an association was formed. In such cases, the experimenter is termed the conditioned stimulus (CS), due to its capacity to elicit the conditioned response (CR)–salivation–depending on the learning experience. The food is the unconditioned stimulus (US), as it would provoke the unconditioned response (also salivation) even without any learning. The US is also termed the reinforcer because it strengthens the CR. Inversely, in the absence of a reinforcer, the CR will extinguish over time. [A paragraph follows (omitted) giving further description of the first approach, explaining two types of Pavlovian conditioning: appetitive and aversive.]
Paragraph 4 **Description of the second approach and contrast with the first approach**	Instrumental conditioning involves a more voluntary kind of response. The original experiment by Thorndike showed that, over time, cats learned to press a lever in order to access food. Again, we have a reinforcer, the food, responsible for strengthening the instrumental behaviour. In this case, however, a behavioural change is produced as a result of the causal relationship between the subject's behaviour and the reinforcer. This is in comparison to Pavlovian conditioning, in which the behavioural change is produced by the predictive relationship between a signal (CS) and the reinforcer. [Three paragraphs follow giving further description of the second approach, namely two kinds of instrumental responses: habitual and goal-directed.]
Paragraph 8 **Definition and applications of omission training** Includes a discussion of the effects of omission training within a Pavlovian approach.	In omission training, the reinforcer is given when the action is not performed. In Pavlovian conditioning, the association between the CS and the reinforcer tends to persist. For example, the dog cannot control its salivation, nor can a human prevent sweating before receiving an expected shock. Thus, omission scheduling will not bring about a change in the innate behaviour displayed after Pavlovian conditioning.

Paragraph 9
Further applications of omission training
Discussion of the contrasting effects of omission training within an instrumental approach.

On the other hand, instrumental behaviour can be suppressed in such a schedule. If a pleasant reward is given only when an action is not performed, and nothing is given when it is, the action will be extinguished. If, by contrast, subjects are initially trained that an instrumental response leads to an aversive 'punisher', they will not perform that behaviour. In the omission schedule, the punishment is delivered only if the response is not performed. This will again lead to a reversal of behaviour in an attempt to avoid the punishment.

Paragraph 10
Conclusion
A final summary of the two contradictory effects of omission scheduling in the two approaches captures the essay's main point.

Pavlovian conditioning involves the pairing of an unrelated stimulus with a biologically relevant reinforcer. Instrumental conditioning involves the pairing of an action with a resulting reinforcer. These two approaches may be distinguished by the effect omission scheduling has on them. In the former case, behaviour is not modified by omission, as the response is autonomic. In only the latter case, behaviour is modified to suit the omission schedule. Thus, the behaviour is extinguished in instrumental but not in Pavlovian conditioning.

Words and phrases to highlight differences between two elements.

Words and phrases to show cause and effect.

Defining language to describe theories and processes. Use the present tense, unless providing a historical perspective.

The passive voice is often used in academic and scientific writing, especially in cases where the agent or actor is unknown, unimportant or obvious.

Preparing to Write

- As in most academic writing, explanation essays begin with an introduction and end with a conclusion. The structure and ordering of the body paragraphs will vary depending on the prompt or assignment.
- The example essay above uses the following structure:

Introduction
Concept 1 (Pavlovian)
Concept 2 (Instrumental)
Context (Omission training)
Application of context to concept 1
(Contrasting) application of context to concept 2
Conclusion
References (not present here, but usually obligatory)

Tips

- Remember that explanation essays should not include your opinion or any criticism unless the prompt specifically asks for it.
- In an essay prompt, 'compare' asks you to explain how two elements are similar; 'contrast' and 'distinguish' ask how they are different.

Language Bank

Defining
X is/seems to be/is assumed to be Y.
X is a kind/category/variety/form of Y.
X contains/consists of/is related to Y.
X is (also) termed/referred to as/known as Y.
X involves/requires/concerns/is relevant to Y.
X is affected by/is influenced by Y.
X affects/necessitates Y.
X coincides with/correlates with/is linked to/is associated with Y.

Providing historical background
X was first noted/observed/identified/recognized/reported by …
X was first studied/demonstrated by …
X was first established/used/proposed by …
Pavlov first noted/identified/recognized/reported X.
… first studied/demonstrated X.
… first established/used/proposed X.

Cause and effect
X results in/leads to/causes/brings about/produces Y.
Y results from/is caused by/is brought about by/is produced by X.

➲ For useful language for comparing and contrasting, see the Language Bank on page AWT13. See also the Language Bank at **example**.

Writing Essays 2: an argument essay

The argument essay is one of the most common types of essay you will encounter at school or university. In this type of essay, you need to display your ability to weigh up different viewpoints and arrive at an informed conclusion. These viewpoints are a result of reading and evaluating research on the topic. In most cases, the essay will require you to state what your opinion is, but in some cases it might only be a presentation of a series of arguments and counterarguments.

The extract below is from an essay about language acquisition by deaf children. It is divided into four parts–introduction, spoken language acquisition, sign language acquisition and conclusion.

Introduction
This introduction features three key things:
1. background information on the topic
2. a specific introduction to the topic
3. the scope and aim of the essay

Introduction

[1]There are approximately 688,000 people who are severely or profoundly deaf in the United Kingdom, and 840 children who are born deaf each year (RNID, 2011a). It is clear from these figures that there is a large community of people who are deaf in the United Kingdom alone. [2]Consequently, it must be considered how deafness may affect language acquisition and what steps caregivers can take to overcome any difficulties. [3]There are different levels of deafness and hearing loss (RNID, 2011b); however, it is not within the scope of this essay to consider all of these levels. [3]Therefore, this essay will mainly focus on people who are born with severe or profound deafness (RNID, 2011b).

Spoken language acquisition
This section explores research around the issue of how deaf children acquire spoken language and lists the different methods available. It points out the difficulties with these methods.
All the points are supported by research studies.

Spoken language acquisition

Ninety per cent of children who are deaf are born into hearing families ... [Statistics are presented.] ...

Researchers have argued that deaf people are less proficient in speechreading than hearing people as the auditory aspect of language enables more competence in speech recognition (Bernstein *et al.*, 1998: 212). ... [Evidence is provided through research studies.] Therefore, speechreading will not be an effective means of communication for all people who are deaf.

Cued Speech is another method used by some people to help children who are deaf to communicate. ... [Elaboration on benefits and drawbacks is provided through citing research studies.] However, Bavelier *et al.* (2003: 3) reason that this form of communication is not a natural language ... This method could therefore impact negatively on the deaf child's language development (*ibid.*).

Lewis (1987: 74) suggests that the acquisition of a spoken language can depend on many factors. [Elaboration on these factors follows.] ... However, regardless of the level of assistance ... it is advisable that another approach to language could be sought to enable a child who is deaf to communicate.

Sign language acquisition
This section promotes the use of sign language as the solution to the problem highlighted in the previous section. It presents an alternative combined system as the most useful solution.
All the points are supported by research studies.

Sign language acquisition

Sign language appears to be a more natural language of people who are deaf (Sacks, 1989: 27–28). A way of teaching deaf children to communicate, using both signed and spoken language, was through simultaneous communication (Dodd *et al.*, 1998: 229). [Elaboration on this method follows.] ...

Nevertheless, the majority of children who were educated with the simultaneous communication method had poor spoken and signed English ... [Evidence is cited from research.]

Sign languages, such as British Sign Language, are naturally occurring languages. Each one is a unique system of communication

Phrases which express the writer's viewpoints more objectively.	Words which show the connection and progression of the argument.	Hedging language is useful for putting your view across less assertively.	Appropriate reporting verbs show how the cited source fits in with your argument.

... Bavelier *et al.* (2003: 6–7) support this notion by highlighting research ... [Related issues around the learning of sign language, including an example of a case study, are highlighted.]

Conclusion
The conclusion presents opposing views to the use of sign language, promoted in the previous paragraph. It addresses the opposing views by promoting a bilingual approach.

Conclusion

In conclusion, this essay has ... [Evaluation of the approaches suggested in the essay follows.] ... Thus, it seems that sign language is a more natural choice of communication. This has implications ... [Elaboration on the implications follows.] ...

Although some parents may be concerned that learning a sign language will isolate their child from the community of hearing people, Mayberry *et al.* (2002, cited in Bavelier *et al.*, 2003: 12) suggest that the acquisition of a sign language could facilitate the acquisition of a spoken language. ... Thus, to reduce the risk of this happening, Bavelier *et al.* (2003: 15) propose that there should be a bilingual approach ... This approach may help children who are deaf to reach their full potential. [A full list of references follows.]

Preparing to write

- Read widely around your topic and note the different points that emerge.
- Focus on the question and decide what your stance is going to be.
- Select two or three arguments and identify suitable supporting evidence.
- Explain each argument in terms of how it supports your viewpoint or provides an opposing argument, for which you then present a counterargument (i.e. present evidence which questions the validity of the opposing argument).
- Decide on a suitable organization of your ideas. Here are two suggestions:

Option 1 (structure adopted here)
Introduction: background information, specific explanation of the topic, aims and/or scope of the essay.
Paragraph/s presenting the arguments against your case, including evidence.
Paragraph/s presenting arguments for your case, including evidence.
Conclusion

Option 2
Introduction (as Option 1)
Argument 1: explanation of a point and supporting evidence and/or counterarguments.
Argument 2 (as above)
Argument 3 (as above)
Conclusion

Tips (presenting a valid argument)

- **Use counterarguments** This involves presenting a viewpoint that opposes yours and suggesting why this viewpoint is not valid. This shows that you have weighed up the different viewpoints before arriving at your position.
- **Provide good evidence** This is crucial for any argument. Draw on statistics, the results of research studies, or case studies.
- **Use hedging language** This shows a degree of caution around your views and presents you as an objective writer.

Language Bank

Showing your position
Use the **first person pronoun**.
Based on these points, ***I suggest*** *that ...*
I would like *to put forward that ...*

Use an **'It'** or a **'There'** phrase.
It is *clear/obvious/important ...*
There is *sufficient evidence to prove/show ...*

Showing progression in your argument
To introduce **a counterargument**:
However, *Charles (2006) argues that ...*

To add **additional points**:
Furthermore, *... /**Additionally,** ...*

To signal **a conclusion**:
Thus, *it is obvious that ... /**Therefore,** it seems reasonable to suggest that ...*

Writing Essays 3: a compare and contrast essay

The compare and contrast essay is used when you need to point out similarities (compare) or differences (contrast) between two or more theories, arguments or ideas. In many essays, you will need to focus on both similarities and differences. The essay will need to show your understanding of the two or more things you are comparing and/or contrasting by referring to research.

Occasionally, you will be asked to write a critique instead of an essay, in which you compare or contrast two or more issues. This is similar to the essay, but in addition to showing your understanding of the similarities and differences between the issues, you will need to display an element of critical evaluation. This means you need to question the information you read and assess its validity.

The extract below is an example of a compare and contrast critique from the area of development economics.

Essay prompt

Examine any two development theories, evaluating their effectiveness.

Paragraph 1 Introduction
The introduction begins with an overall statement on the topic and then articulates the two theories to be compared and contrasted. It also states the aims of the essay.

The concept of development as a means to alleviate poverty and improve the lives of people is an extremely complex, problematic thesis … This essay will focus on two development theories: firstly, Rostow's 1960 … modernization theory, and secondly dependency theory. Both of these theories will be examined critically by placing them in a wider temporal context, and their effectiveness evaluated in relation to their practical application.

Paragraph 2
This paragraph introduces the first theory. It provides a definition and explains the theory in the light of some reading.

Modernization theory is a concept explicated … by American economist Walt Rostow in 1960. Rostow outlines five stages … [Description of the five stages follows.] … This conceptualization of development can therefore be seen to offer an optimistic pathway for countries to follow and ultimately achieve modernization.

Paragraph 3
Highlights problems with the first theory. Points out the limitations of the theory.

The thematic, structured approach by Rostow presents value for examination … [Evaluation of the theory follows.] ... Three further fundamental problems undermine Rostow's model … [Three problems are stated.] These criticisms are echoed by Kothari and Minogue (2002) … It is clear that there are a variety of limitations …

Paragraph 4 Differences
This paragraph introduces the second theory as a solution to the problems of the first theory. It highlights the different focus that dependency theory has.

These critiques were contemporarily recognized, and led to the emergence of dependency theory as a development thesis. This chronological development arguably represents that only a few years hindsight was sufficient to discredit Rostow and modernization as a practical means of development. The dependency school is most commonly associated with the work of Andre Gunder Frank in 1967… [Reference to other research follows.] … It is therefore more realistic to view the global economic system not as a potentially cooperative one as implied by Rostow and modernization, but as an exploitative system, reliant on inequality that fundamentally benefits the core and stifles any notion of significant development for the periphery. This contextual approach offers an insight into development issues that modernization fails to capture and, in this respect, dependency theory offers a more plausible framework of how development strategies should be considered.

Dependency theory is a valuable geographical concept … However, it has continued to receive extensive criticism within the field of development studies. Gulalp (1998) argues that …

Phrases which express the notion of comparison and contrast.

Negative evaluative words which help with comparison.

Phrases which reflect the writer's position.

Paragraph 5
Highlights the limitations of this theory. Refers to research to explain the limitations.

These critiques pose several questions ... Although it offers some rational explanation as to the situation of many developing countries, it fails to offer enough reason and clarity in formulating a holistic development strategy.

Paragraph 6 Similarities
This paragraph assesses the research presented thus far and evaluates both theories. The conclusion is that both theories are limited. This is the author's evaluation and interpretation of the research.

The final point of comment with regard to both of the development theories is how they relate to a wider development paradigm. Both theories emerged chronologically ... They both, however, strongly represent what development at that time meant ... In this context, the dynamic nature of the entire development thesis renders both modernization and dependency theory of little realistic value and arguably ineffective as development theories.

Paragraph 7 Conclusion
This paragraph summarizes the information in the essay, highlights its value, and mentions the limitations of both theories.

In conclusion, it is clear that both Rostow's modernization model and dependency theory have attempted to address the complex notion of development in different ways. ... The two theories, however, have received extensive criticism ... The overall contribution of modernization theory and dependency theory cannot be entirely disregarded, as they have each helped contemporary development theories realize their present form, but their effectiveness in their own right holds little practical value within the current field of development.

Preparing to write

- The starting point of this essay is research. You need to read about each issue/idea/theory you wish to compare and make notes on them.
- Decide on an organizational structure for your essay or critique. You can focus on the characteristics of each issue/idea/theory and compare or contrast these, or select categories for comparison and contrast and organize your essay or critique around these.
- Several options are presented below:

Option 1
Introduction
Similarities between X and Y: explain and provide supporting evidence.
Differences between X and Y: explain and provide supporting evidence.
A discussion of whether X and Y are more similar or more different from each other.
Conclusion

Option 2
Introduction
A description and explanation of X: use research and provide supporting evidence.
A description and explanation of Y: use research and provide supporting evidence.
A discussion evaluating the similarities and differences between X and Y.
Conclusion

Option 3
Introduction
Compare and contrast X and Y according to criterion 1; refer to research.
Compare and contrast X and Y according to criterion 2 (and so on); refer to research.
Conclusion

Language Bank

Contrast structures
I have shown that theory X is ***potentially more*** *powerful* ***than*** *Y because ...*
X is ***clearly*** *a* ***better*** *way of viewing the issue* ***than*** *Y is because ...*
Y is a ***less effective*** *argument* ***than*** *X, as ...*

Comparison structures
I have shown that theory X is ***exactly the same as*** *theory Y since ...*
X and Y have ***virtually the same*** *premises, hence ...*
The argument put forward by X is ***as persuasive as*** *Y's, because ....*

Tips

- Write a good introduction which clearly states what you are comparing/contrasting and how your essay will be organized.
- Ensure all the points you are discussing are given equal treatment in the essay.
- Conclude your essay by addressing the outcome of the comparison or contrast.

Critical Evaluation

Almost all student writing in any discipline will involve an element of critical evaluation. The purpose of critical evaluation is to show your ability to assess the merits of, for example, a policy document, the results of an experimental study, a legal case report, a business environment or a company, a teaching observation or whatever the central topic of your writing is. Evaluation involves highlighting the positive and negative aspects of the focus of your discussion, as well as the arguments presented in favour of these aspects. It is part of constructing a viewpoint or an argument which is objective and informed by further reading or experimental study.

The annotated text below is from the discipline of engineering. The text contains three parts of a longer research report– the introduction, a discussion of results, and recommendations. All of these sections display critical evaluation.

Introduction
Introduces the topic. (L2–3)
States the aim of the study. (L4–5)
Introduces the methodology and provides an evaluation of the method. (L6–21)

Introduction

This assignment deals with the analysis of one aspect of the suspension set-up of the formula student single-seater race car. The aim of the assignment is to determine how the suspension performance will change if the suspension geometry is altered. By modelling one area of the suspension … [describes the methodology and provides a rationale for the method], I chose to investigate the front suspension set-up of the car and, in particular, decided to investigate:

How changing the vertical position of the upper pickup points would affect camber compensation and the lateral position of the roll centre during roll.

I chose to change position of the upper pickup points of the suspension by:

+20 mm, +10 mm, -20 mm, -10 mm from the original position, as I consider this to be a fairly realistic range of changes that would be possible to make.

I also decided to plot my results for roll in 0.5 degree increments from 0 to 3 degrees. I believe this to be a realistic representation of the vehicle's actual roll as it is a fairly stiff set-up and would therefore not roll a huge amount.

The results I obtained and their graphical representations can be seen on the following pages.

Analysis and evaluation of the results
Begins with an introductory evaluation about the results being 'interesting'. (L25–28)
Presents and evaluates the results in two sections. (L29–45)
Discusses and evaluates the main point on 'conflict'. (L46–51)

Analysis and evaluation of results

The results I obtained from the Mitchell analysis show some interesting results in the relationship between the vertical position of the upper pickup points and the performance indicators.

Relationship with camber

The results I obtained show that … [discussion of results] I do not have any data for the tyres used on the formula student, and cannot therefore make any definite decisions. With regard to camber compensation, I can, however, suggest that raising the position of the upper pickup points would be detrimental to the car's performance … This is definitely not what is required as it would reduce the contact patch between the road and tyre, therefore reducing grip. I would therefore suggest that the lower

Phrases which express the writer's opinion/ evaluation.

Evaluative adjectives.

Phrases which indicate the writer is providing a recommendation, sometimes with the pronoun 'I'.

the position of the pickup, the better the camber compensation. This is not the definitive answer, however, as this may conflict with other performance indicators (discussed later).

Relationship with lateral roll centre position

The results I obtained show that … This would suggest that the higher the position of the pickup, the better the suspension will work. This is the complete opposite to the relationship between the pickup point and camber.

Conflicts between results

The results I obtained for the performance indicators conflict completely with each other. … [More detail about the conflict is provided.] This makes it very difficult to recommend any changes that could be made. This would be easier to achieve with some tyre data to work with.

Recommended modifications

Discusses recommendations. (L52–62)

Provides an evaluation on the methodology used in the study. (L63–64)

Recommended modifications

I would recommend that ... I say this because … I believe that the improvements in camber compensation would outweigh the loss of grip caused by the movement of the RC. … I would suggest … I believe this to be the optimum position as it will improve the camber compensation without moving the RC out too far. Any more than this would, in my opinion, lead to too much loss in grip … This would mean that … Any further than this would provide excessive camber compensation and may lead to ... However, as I suggested earlier, this would depend entirely on the application, tyres and other unknown variables. More data and further investigation would be required to give a more definitive answer to the best modifications.

Language Bank

Critical Evaluation

Evaluating theories/arguments/ideas:

*A particular **strength/weakness** of this theory is …*
*What Jacobson **fails** to account for is …*
***A counterargument** to this might be …*
*There is **an inconsistency** in this argument.*
*This theory does **not** account for …*

Evaluating methods:

*This method was **particularly useful** because …*
*There are **a number of benefits** to using this data collection method.*
*This appears to be **successful** because …*
*This approach has its **disadvantages**.*
*The **drawback** with this method is …*

Making recommendations on ideas/ theories, methods or results:

***A better approach** could have been …*
***A more systematic study** of this aspect is needed.*
***I would suggest** making the following changes to the study …*
*Theory X might have been **more relevant** because …*
*Further research **is recommended**.*
***The wider implications** of this are likely to be ...*

Tips

- Critical evaluation does not only address the negative or weak points of a theory, method or result, but points out the positive aspects too.
- Evaluation needs to be accompanied by a rationale or justification, so ensure you provide evidence for your evaluations.
- Use a wide range of adjectives which show your positive (e.g. *interesting*) or negative (e.g. *difficult*) evaluation.
- Do not overuse the pronoun 'I'; achieve a balance with phrases such as *This might be because* … instead of *I think this might be because* ...

Case Studies 1: business

A business case study explores, in detail, a specific company or business situation. The main purpose of writing a case study is to demonstrate your ability to apply the analytical techniques learned on your course to a specific business case. The following extract from a business case report about the retailer Marks and Spencer plc applies two such techniques: PESTEL and SWOT.

Introduction
Introduces the company/the situation. States the focus and aims of the text.

Introduction

Since the late 1990s, Marks and Spencer plc has been through some turbulent times. The giant of the British high street has seen its share price fluctuate from a worrying low of less than 200 pence per share in 2000 to a comfortable high of around 750 pence in 2007 (Johnson, Scholes and Whittington, 2008: 839). This aside, M&S has long been regarded as one of the most spectacular corporate successes in the UK (Tse, 1985).

Using a 2011 report by Johnson and Collier, this paper will look at some of the strategic decisions which might have led M&S to the problems of 2008. I will also offer some recommendations for the long-term strategic development of the organization using corporate strategy frameworks.

Context
Here, PESTEL is used to evaluate the company's position within the business environment.

Strategic Position

Firstly, let us look at the strategic position and analyse the macro environment ... using the PESTEL framework (Johnson, Scholes and Whittington, 2008: 55). Johnson and Collier (2011) point to several social and technological factors that may have had an effect on the business. For instance, M&S always sold clothing under their own 'St Michael' label; this line offered good value for money but failed to keep up with current fashions. Meanwhile, consumer requirements were changing, and other high street retail outlets were popping up and offering alternatives to the basics at M&S. [Two paragraphs follow (omitted) stating the company's reluctance to enter the online marketplace and to set out an effective long-term strategy.] ...

Description and analysis
Applies an analytical tool–SWOT analysis–to the business case.

Future Development

It would appear that the company was slow to react to the changing social and technological environment. ... Let us now use a SWOT analysis to examine M&S's strengths, weaknesses, opportunities and threats (as described in Kew and Stredwick, 2008: 11), focusing on what is most important for the future success of the company.

Strengths:
- Largest UK retailer
- Strong balance sheet/Stakeholder investment
- Product diversity (clothes, food, home furnishings, financial products, flowers, wine)

Weaknesses:
- Premium retailer with premium prices
- Unsure of target market
- Internal politics with board members, CEO and Chairman engaged in power struggles

Opportunities:
- Diversify into other markets
- Invite more brand names into store
- Acquisitions of smaller retail organizations to increase market share

Threats:
- Economic recession

Words and phrases to give recommendations.

Words and phrases to introduce examples.

Words and phrases to guide the reader through the document.

Transitions and connecting words and phrases.

Lower-cost retailers/market competition
Takeover bids (e.g. Philip Green–Arcadia group)

Recommendations
Suggests actions to be taken.

Recommendations

For long-term success, M&S will need to rebuild its reputation and its brand. The company must also make some important strategic choices which take into account both internal and external factors. The organization has diversified into finance and possibly should consider other ways to break into emerging markets, particularly those with strong e-commerce potential. [Further recommendations and discussion follow (three paragraphs omitted).] ...

Conclusion
Generalizes out from the recommendations to the wider context.

Conclusion

Going forward, perhaps the company would be better served with a more diverse and transparent management structure, such as one based on the approach of a 'learning organization', defined by Johnson, Scholes and Whittington as one which is 'capable of continual regeneration from the variety of knowledge, experience and skills of individuals within a culture which encourages mutual questioning and challenge around a shared purpose or vision' (Johnson, Scholes and Whittington, 2008: 421).

In 2008, CEO Sir Stuart Rose introduced the necessary changes and implemented the short-term strategies that helped M&S recover. However, for the long-term success of M&S, current and future CEOs must continue on this path, or else they will risk destroying this icon of British retailing.

Preparing to Write

- A case study often looks at a problem and suggests possible solutions.
- You can use the following outline to help you structure your case study:

Introduction Give background information and state the focus of your case.
Context Explain how this case fits within its greater environment.
Description and analysis of the case Details of the case, including how theory applies to it (omitted in this case extract).
Recommendations Suggest actions to be taken/give possible solutions.
Conclusion Generalize out to the wider context.

Language Bank

Making Recommendations
Use the **modal verbs** *must, need to* and *should.*
*The company **must** make some important choices.*
*The business will **need to** rebuild its reputation.*
*The company **should** be careful not to ...*

Use a **first person pronoun**.
***I** would (strongly) advise that caution be used.*
***My** main recommendation is for the company to implement ...*

Use an '**It**' or a '**There**' phrase.
***There is** a need to ...*
***It is** generally best to/**It is** a good idea to ...*

Use the **modal verbs** *could* and *might*, or the **adverbs** *perhaps* and *possibly*, to hedge your recommendations and sound objective.
*The organization **could/might** consider reorganizing.*
***Perhaps** the company would be better served with ...*

➲ For more hedging language, see the Language Bank at **hedge**.

Case Studies 2: health sciences

Case studies are widely used in the health sciences, where they generally have the following main features: (1) **introduction**: identifying a problem or describing an issue relating to a patient; (2) **presentation of the case**, e.g. a patient's case from the medical, social and family perspectives; (3) **evaluation**, using criteria such as legislation and/or professional guidelines; (4) **recommendations**, addressing any failings/ problems you identified; and (5) **conclusion** (may come before recommendations): summarizing the achievements of your assignment and generalizing your findings.

The extracts below are taken from a case study relating to a patient suffering from Parkinson's Disease, written by a student nurse.

Section 1
Introduction of the case study (omitted)
Identifies the patient under study and the framework and criteria for assessment.

Section 2
The case presentation (omitted)
Presents the patient's case. Explains that the patient suffers from a long-term condition and is cared for by her husband. States that the patient was admitted to hospital following a fall in her home. Identifies a problem: failure in the care provided at discharge.

Section 3
Evaluation of the case from legal and policy perspectives
Background information (omitted) outlines long-term conditions, supported by statistics and references to official and professional sources. These points are related to the case, leading to questions about the management of the case. (L1–10)

The legal guidelines are set out. (L11–18)

The particulars of the case are assessed, leading to criticism of the shortcomings. (L19–28)

As seen in the above case study, Mr Jones suggested he was unable to manage the sole care of his wife. Many authors have suggested anxiety and depression to be high amongst full-time carers (Playfer *et al.*, 2001; Twigg *et al.*, 1994). So, what acts, policies, recommendations and frameworks have been set in place to ensure that Mr Jones is able not only to provide a good quality of life to his wife, but to expect a quality of life he was unable to have without outside input? Furthermore, was the discharge planning in hospital of clinical governance standard, or did the multi-disciplinary team overlook Mr Jones's needs?

Supporting the carer through clinical governance and policies

Ensuring patients and carers receive the gold standard of care is the responsibility of clinical governance. Implemented in the 1998 Health Act ..., it set out to provide a quality service and clear lines for accountability, the management of risks and addressing poor performance (National Audit Office, 2007) ... [Further paragraphs (omitted here) discuss the legal guidelines and clinical best practice in more detail.] ...

Applying the National Service Framework for Long-term Conditions (2005) to the case study leads to the conclusion that health care professionals did not comply with the necessary requirements of the framework. The key requirements of this framework state that the care provided must be patient- and carer-centred so that they can make their own informed decisions on the care that will be installed.

When these guidelines are applied to Mrs Jones and compared with the actions taken by the MDT, those actions appear inadequate. ...

Due to the failure to recognize other falls prevention plans, clinical governance has not been applied at an optimal level.

Section 4
Recommendations
Contains recommendations for learning points for future care.

Recommendations

If the planning of Mrs Jones's discharge were to occur again, then the following steps should be taken so that it was carried out in accordance with the Local Discharge Policy (2007) as well as the NICE falls assessment (2004), the Community Care Act (1990), the NSF for Long-term Conditions (2005) and the New Deal for Carers (2008) policy.

The most important point is identified first.

First and foremost, admission through to discharge must be personalized to the individual patient (NSF, 2005). This ensures that the patient receives the best standard of care tailored to their needs, in accordance with clinical governance (McSherry, 2007). To ensure this personalized care is put into action, individual care plans must be drawn up so that they include, in Mrs Jones's case, mobility, dignity, falls and hygiene (NSF, 2005; NICE, 2004; Lee, 2008). [Two further paragraphs (omitted here) identify more learning points.]

Section 5 Conclusion
Contains more general reflections on what can be learnt from this case study about managing patients' care.

Conclusion

This assignment has revealed a gap in providing support for informal carers ... Patients with long-term conditions, and their carers, are not being provided with the appropriate knowledge needed to live independently, because of poor communication with members of the MDT. As well as this, an increase in funding and therefore availability of services needs to be addressed so that those who need the services can access them easily. To conclude, patients and their carers are the best people to inform health care professionals of their needs, not the other way around.

Evaluation (negative and positive).

Modal verbs used to make recommendations.

Words and phrases to state purpose.

Preparing to Write

- Check the expected structure of the case study required by your supervisor/tutor.
- There may be variation in the aims, the amount of reflection that is expected, and the type of analysis, depending on the discipline and/or institution. Check what is required in your department.
- Consider the audience for your case study: your supervisor and/or other health professionals in your field.
- Consider your reasons for choosing a particular case, the criteria for analysing it, how realistic and achievable your recommendations are, and what can be learnt from the study.

Language Bank

Describing the case
You can use **the active form** of the verb.
*… as a result, **she fractured** her left arm.*

You can also use **the passive form** of the verb.
*Mrs Jones **was admitted** to hospital following …*
*Informal care **is provided** by …*

Evaluating the case
*One of the main **areas of concern** was …*
*Due to **the failure** to recognize …,*
*Staff **overlooked** the carer's needs.*
*Staff **failed** to provide quality care.*

Use **positive and negative adjectives**.
*Upon reflection, **good** aspects which emerged were …*
*These actions appear **inadequate**.*
*However, the assessment tool assesses only **limited** aspects …*

Use words such as *no, not, only, even.*
*Staff did **not** provide a holistic approach.*
*Even the local policies were **not** adhered to.*
*It assesses **only** limited aspects …*

Making recommendations
Use the **modal verbs** *should* and *must*, + **the passive form** of the verb.
*The following steps **should be taken** ...*
*Individual care plans **must be drawn up**.*

Stating why the recommendations are made (purpose)
You can use the *to* form of the verb + **clause**.
***To ensure personalized care is put into action**, …*

You also have the option of using *so that* + **clause**.
*Individual care plans must be drawn up **so that they include** …*

Reflective Writing

Academic learning is not simply acquiring new knowledge; it also involves developing skills and new ways of thinking. Reflective writing asks students to think critically about the course and themselves as learners.

You may be asked to reflect on an experience, such as a field trip, on specific aspects of a task, such as how you chose a topic, or on your course as a whole. The writing may be a task on its own or a final section to an assignment such as a research report. You will need to show evidence that you are developing relevant skills and attitudes, that you can question your initial assumptions, and that you can connect theory and practice. You do this by reflecting on how a particular theory relates to your personal experience of an event or a situation.

Connecting theory to practice
Give a reference to a key academic related to your course. This demonstrates an awareness of the important writers/researchers in your field. (L3–6)
Connect what you have read to what you have personally experienced. (L6–12)

The three abstract nouns listed preview the structure of the text. (L7–9)

Internal changes
The writer admits a previous mistaken belief–if you feel you have changed your thinking about a topic, include this. (L13–17)
Give concrete examples–if you generalize, have some examples for clarification.

The writer summarizes the lesson learnt by making a generalization. (L21–23)

External evidence
Give specific examples to back up your claims. Even if this event is negative, it is effective to show how you have learnt from the problem. (L29–36)

Learning from failure
This paragraph shows self-awareness. You do not need to have completely gained a skill –it is usually enough to reflect on how you are changing, and admit to weaknesses that you are working on.

The Impact of the Introduction to Stage Two Counselling Skills on my Personal Development

Carl Rogers argued that becoming a counsellor is not just the acquiring of a set of skills, but is a way of being; utilizing the three core conditions is a key aspect of this (Sanders, 2002: 67). Since embarking on the Introduction to Counselling Skills course, I have been made aware of Rogers' core conditions of genuineness, empathy and acceptance. I believe I possessed elements of these unknowingly; however, becoming conscious of them has enabled me to incorporate them into my being and to develop personally.

The Counselling Skills course has taught me the importance of listening to others attentively. I thought that this was a skill I always held. However, on reflection, I noticed that I would often be preoccupied with other endeavours, such as watching television or sending a text. Recently, I have made a conscious effort to give my full attention to conversations and I have begun to notice when others do not offer me the same courtesy. This is sometimes hurtful. Listening to people and showing my interest and genuineness is a valuable skill to have and one that makes other people feel appreciated.

This course has also taught me the difference between 'knowing' how people feel and understanding how people may feel from their perspective. I have learnt that it is impossible to know exactly how someone else feels and to say that one does may distract attention away from their problem. For example, my course friends and I have found the first term back at university stressful and we frequently share our feelings about this. I am often tempted to tell them 'I know exactly how you feel'. However, I am now more considered in my response and rephrase this to something like 'I understand how you must be feeling'. This validates what the others have said whilst letting them know I appreciate their views.

I have also learnt the difference between empathizing and sympathizing; this is extremely beneficial to me. I am a person that can get caught up in other people's difficulties; this is neither helpful nor supportive. Much better is to empathize and remain objective as this is both helpful and supportive and may enable the other person to progress.

Comparing past with present
Compare present feelings/skills with earlier ones.
Show awareness of relevant literature. Reflective writing that is assessed should have a balance of academic rigour and personal reflection. (L45–47)
Make reference to the words of your assignment task in your conclusion. (L60–63)
Look to the future too–what changes in yourself or the situation do you expect to see?

During the course, I have learnt that before you can understand others you must first understand yourself. Sutton and Stewart (2002: 20) argue that by gaining self-awareness our chances of becoming genuine and empathic increase. This course has provided me with an opportunity to reflect on my own thoughts and my belief system. As a result of this, I am becoming more aware of my prejudices and values and have learnt that, in order to develop an empathic understanding, I need to try to suspend these so I can give a non-judgemental and respectful response. I am much more aware of how this challenges me personally. I would find it difficult to deal with racist, sexist or prejudiced people as this opposes how I have been brought up to think. However, I now understand that other people may have been brought up with a different belief system. As a result of the course, I feel more capable of being less judgemental. Looking inward is the biggest and perhaps most difficult element of the Counselling Skills module, but the one which has been most beneficial to my personal development.

Use the personal pronouns 'I' and 'me' to make personal claims.

The present perfect tense and the present continuous tense express an unfinished, ongoing process.

Words and phrases to compare and contrast.

Preparing to write

- Read the assignment brief carefully. What exactly do you need to reflect on?
- Make notes on academic sources that might be useful–choose a good quotation or write a summarizing statement.
- List events, key incidents, or examples that will support your case.
- Compose a draft, writing freely. Start by describing events, problems and outcomes, but aim at giving reasons and interpreting, eventually putting these events, problems and outcomes into a broader perspective. Can you identify where learning has taken place? Can you see these issues from another perspective?
- Look for themes in your draft and rearrange your writing around topics. Can you link these topics back to literature in the field? How would you do things differently in future?
- Give your writing an introduction that previews your themes and shows awareness of the academic context. You may find it easiest to write your introduction last.
- You can use the following outline to structure your reflective writing. Use this sequence or vary it as necessary.

Connecting theory to practice
1. Set out the general framework, using a quotation if relevant.
2. Connect the theory to your experience.

External evidence
1. Describe the specific event or aspect you wish to focus on.
2. Connect specific events or aspects to your course or a given theory.

Internal changes
1. Explore the reasons for your feelings and behaviour, or for those of others.
2. Describe any changes that have taken place in your thinking.

Learning from failure
1. Admit to problems, if appropriate.
2. Interpret the situation in the light of your given framework.

Comparing past with present and future
1. Compare your past thinking with your present thinking.
2. Consider the implications for the future.
3. Conclude your reflection with reference to the task brief and your future plans.

➲ For useful language for reflective writing, see the Language Bank at **reflective**.

Writing a Research Proposal

The aim of the research proposal is to present your proposed research clearly and concisely so that institutions can assess whether they will be able to supervise your research, or–for undergraduates–to show that you have carefully planned the research project for your dissertation.

It is essential for you to show that you understand the field and the focus of your research. The core sections of the research proposal are: (1) the literature review; (2) the aims or research questions; and (3) the data and methodology. You will also need to include (4) limitations and (5) contribution of the study. Each of these sections will shed light on how your research will make an original contribution to the field.

The following annotated text from the field of Human Resources Management shows the structure and aims of each section of a research proposal.

Introduction
Introduces the reader to the current state of knowledge in the field.
Provides definitions, summarizes key research and links these to the purposes of the research.
The present tense is used to introduce the general field of research and any definitions (*provides, refers*).

Literature Review
Demonstrates an understanding of the current literature.
Displays the ability to critically evaluate the cited sources.
Shows that the proposed research will be an original contribution to the field.
The past tense is used to refer to cited research, e.g. *conducted, revealed*.

Phrases with 'this study' or 'this research' identify and link different aspects of the discussion to the current study.

Phrases using words such as 'lack' show the research gap and point to the originality of 'this study'.

Use of the personal pronoun 'I' to take ownership of the study.

The research proposal uses a combination of tenses and modal verbs.

TABLE OF CONTENTS (omitted)

INTRODUCTION

Learning and development provides opportunities ... Organisational Learning (OL) is a term which refers to ... (Sadler-Smith, 2006). The literature has shown that ...

This research project will therefore seek to explore and investigate the potential connection between Organisational Learning and competitive advantage.

LITERATURE REVIEW

[The Literature Review moves from the more general field to the specific focus. The first section (omitted here) deals with the concept of Organisational Learning.] ...

Competitive Advantage

Competitive advantage is the term used to ... Despite the fact that there is a vast amount of literature on Organisational Learning and development, there is not a great deal of empirical evidence relating it to competitive advantage. Nevertheless, it is widely recognized that ...

The link between OL and Competitive Advantage

A study conducted by Longnecker and Ariss (2002) revealed that ... Chakravarthy *et al.* (2006) argue that ...

However, a recent survey ... shows that ...

In their study ... Harvey and Denton (1999) suggested that ... Their findings indicated that ...

Achieving Competitive Advantage through Firm Performance

Prior studies have shown that ... For instance, Huselid *et al.* (1997) conducted a study ... Their findings revealed that ... These findings were also reflected in a study carried out ... (Yeo, 2003). ... Tippins and Sohi (2003) conducted a study ... Their results proved that ...

In sum, although there is a great deal of rhetoric on OL and its link to competitive advantage, there appears to be a lack of empirical evidence to back it up. I wish to address this gap in the research by investigating the effect Organisational Learning can have on competitive advantage.

Purpose of the study
Lists the aims of the study, using numbers and research verbs (*find out, identify*).

PURPOSE OF THE STUDY

The purpose of this study is to investigate whether there is a relationship between Organisational Learning (OL) and Competitive Advantage (CA).

Objectives:
1. Find out to what extent HR managers use OL.
2. Identify the OL methods which potentially improve a company's performance.
3. Identify differences between organisations that use OL in contrast to companies that do not use OL, in relation to performance.

Methodology
Clarifies the proposed methodological approach and the data collection procedures. Situates the proposed methodology within other research.
The future tense is used to refer to the proposed method, e.g. *will use.*

METHODOLOGY

Type of Investigation

This cross-sectional study will take an exploratory approach since there appears to be a lack of empirical research ... This study will seek to explore whether ...

Sampling Design

The companies that I will use ... Once a general questionnaire has been sent out ... I will ... interview their managers.

Data Collection Method

In this research, I will be looking at two variables. Firstly ... Secondly ... The study conducted by Lee *et al.* (2000) provided a framework ... They used an audit tool ... Similarly, I will propose ... and ask related questions. Throughout the interview procedure, notes will be taken ...

Limitations
Highlights limitations, showing awareness of the challenges of the research. Proposes possible solutions.
Modal verbs are used to suggest limitations, e.g. *should.*

LIMITATIONS

One could identify a few limitations to this study. Perhaps the study should be longitudinal in order to determine more accurate results and allow for a larger and more valid sample size. Furthermore, the study could prove to be more expensive and require more resources than are available ... Finally, there may be biased information from some managers ...

Contributions
Emphasizes the originality of the research. Lists possible contributions of the research.
Modal verbs are used to hedge contributions, e.g. *should.*

CONTRIBUTION OF THE STUDY

The aim of this investigation is to reaffirm that ... there is a relationship between Organisational Learning and competitive advantage. ... The results of this research will contribute to the minimization of the literature gap in this area.

In addition, it will help HR managers become more aware ...
The results should help managers detect where their weaknesses lie ...
This could be done using companies that have high performance as a benchmark.

Bibliography
Shows breadth of reading.

BIBLIOGRAPHY (omitted)

Tips

- Write concisely and avoid repetition.
- Organize your writing using headings and subheadings.
- Be critical in your Literature Review by choosing appropriate reporting verbs/phrases.
- Introduce the steps in your method with words such as *firstly, then, the next stage.*
- Point out the originality of your research by identifying the gap in the research.
- Provide a statement of how you will access resources and acquire skills, such as using statistical software, if asked to do so.

Writing a Dissertation, Research Report or Long Essay

You may have to write a long assignment as part of your course assessment. This may be a dissertation, long essay, project, research report, etc. The purpose of these assignments is to show the examiner that you:

- have gained research skills, knowledge and understanding from your course;
- can apply the methods of your field to a topic of your own choice;
- can complete an extended, in-depth piece of work.

Requirements and conventions vary in different fields, departments and institutions. Always consult your tutor/supervisor and departmental guidelines for specific details.

Each section of a typical dissertation is explained with examples in a following *Academic Writing Tutor* section. Select and combine sections for detailed information, tips and language suggestions for the whole of your dissertation.

A dissertation may have all or only some of the following parts, usually presented in the following order:

- **Title page** Contains the dissertation title, your name, department, degree and date of submission. There may be a specific form of words required, e.g. 'A dissertation submitted for the degree of …'.
- **Abstract** A short summary of the whole text; usually 100–200 words.
- **Acknowledgements** Optional. Thanks are often given in the following order:
  1. your tutor/supervisor
  2. other academic help
  3. technical and financial support; participants in your study
  4. friends and relations.
- **Table of contents** List all the parts of your dissertation with page numbers. Include chapter titles, headings and subheadings, if used.
- **List of figures, tables or other graphic matter** Each graphic element should have a title and a number, e.g. Table 2.4 is the fourth table in Chapter 2.
- **Chapters 1, 2,** etc.
- **References/Bibliography** Include all the works mentioned in your dissertation. Do not include references to works that you do not mention. ➲ See pages AWT46–47 Citations and Bibliography.
- **Appendix 1, 2,** etc. Appendices are for extra matter which supports your dissertation but is not part of it, e.g. a survey questionnaire in social science.

Tip

- Choose titles and headings that are short but informative. The examiner needs to know the content of each chapter and section clearly.

Long texts consist of several shorter sections which you may also have to write as separate assignments, e.g. Introduction, Methods.

Structure 1 for empirical studies which report data and findings

Abstract

Introduction

Literature Review may be a separate chapter or may be included in the Introduction.

Methods may be called, for example, Methodology, Materials and Methods, Methods and Data.

Results may be combined with the Discussion.

Discussion may be combined with the Conclusion.

Conclusion

Structure 2 for discursive studies which discuss themes, theories, texts, etc.

Abstract (optional)

Introduction

Literature Review may be a separate chapter, or the relevant literature may be discussed within each body chapter.

Chapters (2–4) with titles based on their content.

Conclusion

- In the arts and humanities, body chapters may analyse/interpret texts, art works, etc.
- In the natural and social sciences, body chapters may describe and evaluate theories, approaches, models, etc.

Carrying out a research study

Preparing for your study

Consult your departmental guidelines and regulations so that you know exactly:

- what is required (e.g. formatting, the submission date and the procedure);
- how the study will be assessed (the criteria used and their relative importance).

Look at past assignments to see the scope and standard of successful work.

Finding your topic

- Start thinking about a possible topic at an early date.
- Note possible topics from lectures, assignments, readings, departmental lists.
- Are there issues arising from your own experience that you could investigate?

Narrowing down your topic

When you have decided on a general area, focus your reading more specifically.

- What is already known about the topic? What could you find out?
- What methods are used? Could you use these methods?

Discuss your proposed topic with a potential tutor/supervisor. Is it:

- too wide/difficult: cannot be done with the time and resources available?
- too narrow/easy: cannot show an adequate level of knowledge and skill?
- not relevant: cannot show your knowledge of course material?

Define your research question(s)/hypotheses/problem(s).

- What information do you aim to find out?
- What hypotheses do you aim to test?
- What problem do you aim to solve?

Formulate the statements/questions as clearly as you can and check them with your tutor/supervisor.

- Can your proposed methods provide the necessary data?

Carrying out your research

- Design your study/experiment using the methods that you learned on the course.
- Carry out a pilot study if necessary.
- Collect your data.
- Analyse the data, using statistical tests if necessary.
- Relate the data to your questions/hypotheses/problems. What conclusions can you draw?
- Make full notes or write up the sections.

Writing up

Write up individual sections as you carry out your research or write up the whole assignment after you have finished the research.

- Divide your material into chapters and plan roughly how many words in each.
- The introduction and conclusion are usually shorter than the body chapters.

Order of writing

You do not have to write the chapters in order.

- Writers often begin with the Literature Review or Methods.
- The Introduction is often the last chapter to be written.
- Write the Abstract after you have finished the whole assignment.

Revising

As you write, you may need to revise your plan, so be flexible.

- Re-read and revise each section as you write.
- When you have a first draft of all the chapters, edit and revise the whole assignment to make sure it is clear and consistent.

Final checks

Allow plenty of time for proofreading, checking, formatting, printing and binding. Allow some extra time for computer or printer failure.

Have you:

- proofread (for completeness, accuracy, repetition, grammar) and spell-checked?
- formatted your references consistently using a suitable convention for your field?
- followed all the requirements for submission?

➲ See also page AWT2 The Writing Process.

Tips

- Chapters do not have to be the same length. Each chapter should be as long as necessary to cover the material.
- Do not be worried by the total number of words. Individual sections are often the same length as assignments you have written already.
- Divide the assignment into manageable sections and build up your writing section by section.
- Get someone else to proofread your text. They often notice problems more easily.

Writing an Abstract

The abstract occurs at the beginning of your dissertation or thesis. The main aim of the abstract is to provide the reader with a summary of your research.

Abstracts in most disciplines have a combination of four moves: providing background information, presenting the aims of the research, describing the methodology and summarizing the results. In some disciplines, other moves are present. The most common additional move is highlighting implications of the research.

Three short abstracts are presented from different fields, showing differences in structure and language. The following is an abstract from the field of physical/life sciences. The article is from the journal *Mathematical Medicine and Biology* and is about tear film deposition and draining.

Presenting the aims	This paper investigates the deposition of the tear film on the cornea of the human eye. The tear film is laid down by the motion of the upper eyelid and then subsequently flows and thins. Of particular interest is the stability of the tear layer and the development of dry patches on the cornea.
Providing background information	While there has been significant research on the behaviour of tear films between blinks, this paper focuses on understanding the mechanisms which control the shape and thickness of the deposited film and how this affects the subsequent film behaviour.
Explaining the methods	Numerical and analytical methods are applied to a lubrication model which includes the effects of surface tension, viscosity, gravity and evaporation.
Summarizing the results	The model reveals the importance of the eyelid velocity, motion of the surface lipid layer and the storage of tear film between blinks. (Jones *et al.*, 2005)

Use of the present tense, the present perfect tense or the past tense for presenting background information and presenting aims.

Use of the passive voice when explaining the method.

Use of the present tense or the past tense when summarizing results.

The next example is from a social science field and appears in the journal *Applied Linguistics*. The research is on the use of language within a family and considers the impact of this on language fluency and school performance. The abstract has only three moves and the order of the moves is different from the example above.

Explaining the methods	Working-class and middle-class mothers of Cuban heritage were questioned about their modes of accommodation to America in terms of language proficiencies. Specifically, they were asked about their own language fluency, in both Spanish and English, and that of their children.
Presenting the aims	The focus was on the within-family dynamics of the accommodation process, and the links between mothers' and children's language fluencies and children's school performance.
Summarizing the results	Two distinct patterns emerged. For working-class mothers, the emphasis was more on encouraging their children to learn English in order to 'succeed' in America, especially in school–a 'subtractive' form of bilingualism and biculturalism where advances in English appear to be at the expense of Spanish fluency and heritage culture maintenance. In contrast, for middle-class mothers, success was associated more with the encouragement of Spanish competence, not English–a form of 'additive' bilingualism where the heritage language and culture are protected as the process of Americanization runs its course. (Lambert and Taylor, 1996)

The following extract is from an abstract in the field of medicine, from the *European Journal of Public Health*. It is common in this discipline to structure the abstract with headings. Note the inclusion of the 'highlighting implications' move.

Providing background information	**Background:** The Netherlands Nutrition Centre (NNC) recommends eating a daily breakfast, preferably including products from five food groups.
Presenting the aims	The aims of this study were to examine to what extent breakfast consumption ...
Explaining the methods	**Methods:** A cross-sectional study was conducted ...
Summarizing the results	**Results:** The percentage of participants who reported consuming breakfast every day varied between 62.9 and 95.5 in different subgroups ...
Highlighting implications	**Conclusion:** Health promotion efforts should aim to stimulate breakfast consumption ... Future research should investigate ... (Adapted from Raaijmakers *et al.*, 2010.)

Grammar Focus

Providing background information

To highlight the current state of knowledge in the field, use the **present progressive tense** or a combination of the **present perfect tense** and the **present tense.**

Anthropogenic disturbances of wildlife, such as noise and motor vehicles, ***are becoming*** *an increasing concern in conservation biology.*

While language aptitude ***has been investigated*** *actively,* ***there is a current dearth*** *of research on ...*

Presenting the aims

To summarize the aims of your text, i.e. this essay or dissertation, use the **present tense**; to summarize your research (its aims, methods, findings), use the **past tense**.

This paper ***estimates*** *the effects on earnings of 'gap years' between school and university.*

The aim of the present investigation ***was to explore*** *the role of language for ...*

Explaining the methods

The usual tense is the **past tense**, although some disciplines in the sciences use the **present tense**. You also have the option of using the **passive voice** or a **personal pronoun**, depending on how visible you would like to be in the writing as the researcher of the study.

Clinical and lifestyle factors ***were assessed*** *using standard questionnaires and procedures.*

Using an operational weather radar, ***we quantified*** *the reaction of birds to fireworks in 3 consecutive years.*

Summarizing the results

Use either the **past tense** (most disciplines) or the **present tense** (typical in physical/social science disciplines). You may also use a **personal pronoun** or an **it-structure**.

Current smoking significantly ***declined*** *in males as age increased ($P < 0.001$).*

We find *a strong and significant effect of birth order on IQ, and* ***our*** *results* ***suggest*** *...*

It was also seen that *GJT scores were ...*

After Swales and Feak (2004)

Language Bank

Highlighting implications

Use the **modal verbs** *should* and *may*.

Future research ***should*** *further evaluate .../* ***should*** *investigate whether ...*
... studies investigating ... ***should*** *take into account .../**should*** *be informed by ...*
... ***may*** *contribute to our understanding of ...*
... ***may*** *be especially useful to teaching ...*
... the principles proposed ***may*** *also be ...*

Tips

- The abstract is usually written at the end of the research process, and after writing the rest of the dissertation.
- The abstract is a summary of *key* information: include only key findings.
- It is best to avoid too many technical terms and lengthy references.

Writing an Introduction 1: physical and life sciences

The main purpose of an introduction is to situate research within its context, showing how it relates to other research in the field and/or to circumstances in the world. The introduction to a dissertation is important because it gives the examiners their first impression of your study and shows your knowledge of the research area. This helps them know what to expect and makes it easier for them to follow the rest of your work.

Introductions in all disciplines often consist of a sequence of three moves (Swales and Feak, 2004): (1) **Establishing a territory** gives the general background to your study; (2) **Establishing a niche** shows that there is a need for your study, often by establishing that there is a gap or problem in previous research; (3) **Occupying the niche** gives details of your study, showing how it fills the gap or deals with the problem. There are differences between disciplines in the way the moves are typically carried out, so look at dissertations in your field to see exactly how it is done.

This is an extract from an introduction to a research article published in the *Journal of Electron Microscopy*. It describes a new form of water purification.

Move 1: Establishing a territory

Gives background information. Describes an important world problem. (L1–4)

Claims that the general study area (water purification methods) is important and relevant to the problem. Refers to the literature to support the claim. (L4–7)

Makes a generalization about the study area. Gives examples. (L7–11)

Narrows down the general area to a specific topic (filtration). Claims that filtration is the best method (implies that it is worth studying). Refers to the literature to support the claim. (L12–14)

Makes generalizations about the topic. Gives examples and details. (L14–18)

Narrows down the topic to a specific subtopic (MF membranes). Claims that these membranes are effective in some cases. (L23–29)

Move 2: Establishing a niche

Indicates a problem related to the subtopic. Refers to the literature to support the claim. (L26–31)

More than one billion people currently lack access to low-cost drinking water and more than 2.3 billion people live in water-stressed areas. Thus, it is of paramount importance to develop efficient and cost-effective water purification methods especially for the removal of bacteria and viruses [1–10]. There are many water purification methods, including filtration (size separation), adsorption, chemical coagulation, photodegradation, biodegradation, distillation and active sludge, but filtration is the most versatile chemical-free method, and it is extremely cost-effective, time- and energy-saving [11,12]. Filtration systems have considerably improved in the past decade and many of them possess complex structures, mechanisms and materials such as porous media, polymer membranes … The filtration processes are categorized mainly by the average size of the pores in the membranes, which include microfiltration (MF), ultrafiltration (UF), nanofiltration and reverse osmosis. MF filters have relatively large pores and thus yield a high flux rate compared with UF filters with smaller pores (10–100 nm) [13,14]. An MF membrane with a pore size ranging from 0.1 to 10 μm nominally is capable of retaining microbe-like bacteria larger than 0.2 μm in diameter, but this is not suitable for removing viruses, which are often smaller in size by a factor of 10 [15].

The present tense is often used in all three moves of the introduction.

The past tense is used for describing the work carried out.

Presenting your research using reporting verbs.

Move 3: Occupying the niche

Presents the research. Claims that it addresses the problem. (L32–36)

Work carried out (L36–38)

Method (L39–42)

Results and product of research (L43–46)

Results and significance of the research (L47–49)

Significance of the research (L49–53)

In this study, we report a promising method for producing porous membranes that are based on MF but have capabilities for retaining viruses. The membranes are composed of ultra-fine cellulose nanofibers (UFCNs) (5–10 nm in diameter) derived from safe, inexpensive and sustainable nanomaterials such as wood pulp. The cellulose nanofibers were infused into the submicron-sized fibrous scaffolds (100–300 nm in diameter) fabricated by electrospinning. By controlling the processing parameters and material ingredients, we were able to create a composite fibrous membrane structure that has an appropriate pore size to sieve bacteria and a suitable static charge to adsorb viruses.

Measurements of the filtration properties indicate that these membranes have a high retention rate in removing bacteria (*Escherichia coli*, hereafter referred to as *E. coli*) and viruses (MS2 bacteriophage) in water, while maintaining high flux permeation. High-resolution electron microscopy investigations revealed, for the first time, the detailed nanoscale fibrous networks in membranes that are responsible for these superior filtration properties. The demonstrated membrane system opens a door to the further development of other nanostructured biomaterials to adsorb water pathogens and contaminants and increases the realization of the much needed inexpensive MF membranes. (Sato *et al.*, 2011)

Preparing to write

- Think about the needs of your readers. You have to show that you know the research context and that your study is a valid and useful piece of research. Consider what information you need to give them.
- Use the three-move structure (right) to help you write your introduction. Note that:
  - the three moves usually occur in sequence;
  - each move narrows down the focus of the text;
  - each move is made up of several possible steps. Choose only those that are appropriate for your study. Use the sequence of steps given or vary it as necessary.
- **Specific disciplines**
  - **Engineering** often defines its terms in move 1 and describes the product of the research, its application and evaluation in move 3.
  - **Medicine** often uses step 3 in move 2: Continuing the work of other researchers.
  - **Computer science** usually describes and evaluates the solution to a problem in move 3.

➲ Look at the Tips on page AWT31.

Move 1: Establishing a territory

Steps

1. Describe why your general study area is relevant or important in the field and/or the world. ➲ See the Language Bank at **research**.
2. Make generalizations about your area; give background information or examples. Each generalization becomes narrower until you focus on your own specific topic.
3. Review previous research.

Move 2: Establishing a niche

Steps

1. Indicate a gap, problem or need in previous research. ➲ See the Language Bank at **research**.
2. Indicate a problem or need in the world.
3. Continue or extend the work of other researchers.

Move 3: Occupying the niche

Steps

1. Present your research, state its purposes, aims or objectives.
2. State your research questions or hypotheses.
3. Describe briefly the work you carried out.
4. Describe briefly the methods, materials or subjects you used.
5. Give brief details of your findings or results.
6. Justify your research by showing the significance or contribution of your study.
7. Describe briefly the organization of your dissertation.

Writing an Introduction 2: social sciences and humanities

Social science and humanities introductions often have a similar three-move structure to that of the natural sciences. However, the introduction is likely to be more discursive, with extended descriptions and examples to establish the context of the research. There is more flexibility in the sequence of moves, and moves may overlap or be performed simultaneously. A wider range of steps is also found.

This is an extract from an introduction to a research article in the *Journal of African Economies*. The study estimates the benefits and costs of improving the road network in Africa.

Paragraph 1
Move 3: Occupying the niche
Presents the contribution of the research (attracts attention). (L1–3)

Move 1: Establishing a territory
Gives background information. (L3–5)
Describes an important world problem. (L5–7)

This paper presents evidence on the trade expansion potential of improvements in Sub-Saharan Africa's road network. At present, overland transport is so difficult and costly that Africa's diverse regions remain largely isolated from one another. Overland trade between the large urban centres of West Africa and South Africa is almost non-existent. ...

Paragraph 2
Reviews the literature
Makes a summary statement about the literature so far. (L8–10)
Cites individual studies. Gives details of their findings. (L10–17)

Generalizes from the literature.
Claims that the area is important.
Quotes the literature for support. (L17–24)

Numerous empirical studies have examined the economic impact of poor road conditions (see, e.g., Henderson *et al.*, 2001, for a review). Amjadi and Yeats (1995) find that the relatively low level of Sub-Saharan African exports is essentially due to high transport costs. In a study of transport costs and trade, Limao and Venables (2001) find that poor infrastructure accounts for 60% of transport costs for landlocked countries, as opposed to 40% for coastal countries. Improving cross-border infrastructure is therefore an important part of the development agenda in Africa: '*The vision and ultimate objective for Africa should be to create a single market of 750 million people that is competitive within itself and within the global economy. A critical pre-requisite to this is regional infrastructure integration across Africa.*' (Simuyemba, 2000, p. 3).

Paragraph 3
Reviews the situation in the world
Makes a generalization about programmes for addressing the problem. Gives examples. (L25–30)

Generalizes about the programmes.
Claims that they are important.
Refers to the literature to support the claim. (L30–32)

The World Bank and the African Development Bank (ADB) have both launched initiatives to encourage more integrated infrastructure development. The [World] Bank's Sub-Saharan Africa Transport Policy Program (SSATP) has focused on ... The ADB has proposed ... Such programmes could give a significant boost to regional integration efforts on the continent (Deichmann and Gill, 2008; Naudé, 2009).

Paragraph 4
Situates the research in relation to previous work

Move 2: Establishing a niche
Raises a new question. (L33–35)

Moves 2 and 3: Establishing and occupying the niche
Presents the research as a continuation of previous work. Gives the method ('by developing...'). (L35–38) Indicates how this study differs from previous research approaches. (L38–48)

How much difference would an integrated, functional road network make for African development? This paper extends the previously cited work by developing an analytical framework for quantifying the benefits and costs of continental road network upgrading. In contrast to the trade literature on the topic discussed in what follows, we estimate the costs as well as trade benefits of transport improvements and we base our analysis on geographically explicit modelling of a realistic trans-African transport network.

Paragraph 5
Organization of the paper

Move 3: Occupying the niche
Gives details of the contents of each section in turn. (L49–61)

The present tense is often used in the introduction.

The present perfect tense is used to look back over a recent time period and to summarize what has been done so far in the literature or in the world.

Different ways of describing the organization and contents of your dissertation.

Different ways of referring to the literature.

In contrast to project cost-benefit analysis or engineering studies, we estimate the continent-wide economic benefits from transport improvements, rather than focusing on local benefits alone, which are often measured as traffic volume increases or imputed time savings.

The remainder of the paper is organised as follows. Section 2 reviews the theoretical and empirical literature on gravity models, highlighting evidence on overland trade flows in developing countries. In Section 3, we identify a network of primary roads connecting all 42 mainland Sub-Saharan capitals ... Section 4 estimates a gravity model for Sub-Saharan Africa ... We use the results to estimate current trade flows in the inter-city network and to simulate the impact of a major improvement in road network quality. We then explore the implications of our results for trade expansion at the regional, country and city levels. In Section 5, we estimate the costs of network improvement, using a World Bank database ... Section 6 concludes the paper. (Buys *et al.*, 2010)

Preparing to write

- You can use the three-move structure below to help you write your introduction.
- You will not need all the steps; e.g. a discursive study would outline the argument, but not include methods or results.

Move 1: Establishing a territory
Steps
1. Attract the reader's attention and interest, e.g. with a relevant example or quotation.
2. Describe why your general study area is relevant/important in research/the world.
3. Make generalizations about your area; give background information or examples. Each generalization becomes narrower until you focus on your own specific topic.
4. Define terms, especially when there is no agreement in the field.
5. Review previous research.

Move 2: Establishing a niche
Steps
1. Indicate a gap, problem or need in previous research.
2. Indicate a problem or need in the world.
3. Raise a new question to be answered.
4. Continue or extend the work of other researchers.

Move 3: Occupying the niche
Steps
1. Present your research and state its purposes, aims or objectives.
2. State your research questions or hypotheses.
3. State your theoretical position.
4. Set out the parameters of your research.
5. Describe briefly your methods and participants in survey research.
6. Outline your argument.
7. Give brief details of your findings or a model you propose.
8. Justify your research by showing the significance or contribution of your study.
9. Describe the organization of your dissertation.

After Swales and Feak (2004)

Tips
- In a long dissertation, you may need to situate your research in relation to several different areas. To do this, repeat the cycle of moves and steps as often as necessary.
- Many research articles have several authors, while a dissertation is written by a single author. Instead of using 'We' to present your work, you can use:
  – a passive verb form with a prepositional phrase (*In this study, it is shown that …*);
  – an active verb form with a noun phrase referring to your study (*This dissertation investigates …*).
- In many social science and humanities disciplines you can use *I* (*I argue that …*). Check whether this is possible in your discipline.

Writing a Literature Review 1: physical and life sciences

A literature review is a section in a piece of research writing which describes the existing work that has been done on the writer's research topic. By describing the research already done, the writer can point out what has not been done, and demonstrate the need for the new research. In this sense, the review helps accomplish the objectives ('moves' and 'steps') in the introduction. In fact, the literature review may be part of the introduction, although in some research texts–particularly dissertations–it may occupy a separate section. Literature reviews are often organized according to a general-to-specific pattern, starting with claims about the research area in broad terms and moving on to specific areas, problems or unanswered questions within it.

The following extract from a research article published in the *ICES Journal of Marine Science* uses a review of the literature to establish the need for a genetic study of farmed and wild Atlantic cod. As is common in the sciences, it makes great use of non-integral references (see also the *Academic Writing Tutor* pages on Citations and Bibliography).

The literature review begins with a general statement about the broad topic. (L1–4)

The reference to Myers helps establish that the research topic is important and has real-life implications. (L4–5)

The Atlantic cod, *Gadus morhua*, is both ecologically and economically important, and it has sustained commercial fisheries on both the east and west sides of the North Atlantic. However, overexploitation has led to declines and stock collapses (Myers *et al.*, 1996), and in many regions, cod are regarded as threatened (Jonzen *et al.*, 2002; Svedang and Bardon, 2003; Trzcinski *et al.*, 2006; Arnason *et al.*, 2009). Declines in abundance, along with an established consumer market, have provided a catalyst stimulating widespread interest in the production of this species by aquaculture.

As it develops, the review covers more specific aspects of the research topic. (L11–12)

Language showing time relationships (*in recent years*) and changing trends in a research area is common. (L11–16)

Important advances in cod aquaculture have been made in recent years (Rosenlund and Halldorsson, 2007). For example, heritability estimates of production-related traits have been published (Gjerde *et al.*, 2004; Kolstad *et al.*, 2006; Odegard *et al.*, 2009), and commercial broodstocks have been established from wild captured fish. ... [Two sentences omitted.] Genetic gains through selective breeding programmes will generate fish capable of enhanced productivity in the aquaculture environment (Glover *et al.*, 2009a), but it is very likely that domestication will be at the expense of fitness in the natural environment, as has been observed in the Atlantic salmon (*Salmo salar*; McGinnity *et al.*, 1997, 2003; Fleming *et al.*, 2000).

By moving to problems with aquaculture, the review becomes more specific still. (L24–34)

A big challenge with most forms of aquaculture is containment .... [Two sentences omitted.] Cod have a greater frequency of escaping from fish farms than salmonids (Moe *et al.*, 2007), and behavioural studies have indicated that escapees may mix with wild cod (Uglem *et al.*, 2008), providing opportunity for a range of ecological and genetic interactions (Bekkevold *et al.*, 2006). Moreover, farmed cod may be able to interact with wild populations without physically escaping, when spawning in their cages (Jørstad *et al.*, 2008). Consequently, potential ecological and genetic interactions between wild and farmed cod are of concern.

By showing a gap in the existing research, i.e. a question which little or no research has addressed, the authors can demonstrate the need for their study. (L35–36)

Knowledge of the genetic interactions between wild and farmed marine fish is sparse, but several attempts at quantifying interactions between farmed and wild Atlantic salmon have been published (Crozier, 1993, 2000; Clifford *et al.*, 1998a, b; Skaala *et al.*, 2006). These studies range from the quantification of gene flow from single escapement events affecting specific wild populations, to more ambitious investigations quantifying genetic changes in historical and contemporary samples of wild populations that have been subject to differing numbers of farmed escapees over time. Both approaches have demonstrated genetic changes in wild populations, although the full extent of introgression and the long-term implications for conservation remain open to debate.

To show that an idea is widely accepted or clearly demonstrated, it can be useful to cite several sources. (L48–53)

Genetic studies of wild cod have revealed considerable differentiation among populations over varying geographic ranges (Frydenberg *et al.*, 1965; Dahle and Jørstad, 1993; Knutsen *et al.*, 2003; Pampoulie *et al.*, 2006; Jorde *et al.*, 2007; O'Leary *et al.*, 2007; Westgaard and Fevolden, 2007; Nielsen *et al.*, 2009). However, except for a study of genetic diversity within and among farmed cod reared in sea cages (Glover *et al.*, 2010a), and a study of spawning in sea cages (Jørstad *et al.*, 2008), no genetic studies have addressed the identification of farmed-escaped cod in the wild. Consequently, the aim here was to evaluate the potential for identifying farmed-escaped cod in the wild … (Glover, Dahle and Jørstad, 2011)

A further gap in the research is identified; the aim of the current study is stated. (L56–59)

Non-integral references make passive verb forms especially likely.

The present tense emphasizes sources cited as currently available and currently relevant.

The present perfect tense shows that studies have taken place over a period of time, and may suggest that they are still relevant today.

Sometimes no verbs are used to introduce a reference; an idea is simply stated, together with a reference to the work which shows that the idea is correct.

The purpose of citations

References to the existing literature can serve a range of functions; for example:

- providing support for a fact or an idea;
- showing that there is agreement or disagreement among experts on a topic;
- showing whether a research tradition is established or new;
- showing the development in knowledge about a topic.

Try to understand what function or purpose a reference to a source can serve, and use each reference selectively and to that purpose.

Tips

- Read widely, so that you are familiar with the existing research related to your topic.
- It is appropriate to use a literature review to show your teachers, examiners, etc. that you have read widely. However, do not cite works which are not relevant.
- Have a clear idea of how each area you raise in your literature review is connected to your own research.
- Show the relationships between works, e.g. that one builds upon another or identifies problems with an earlier work.
- Use the review to highlight a gap in the existing literature which your work will fill.

Language Bank

Research verbs describe the research which was done, its aims, processes and results.

Important advances have been ***made*** *in recent years.*
…, as has been ***observed*** *in the Atlantic salmon.*
Both approaches have ***demonstrated*** *…*
Commercial broodstocks have been ***established****.*
Several studies have ***examined*** *the use of …*

Reporting verbs emphasize the research article, book, etc. as a text which communicates, and what it says, shows, reveals, etc.

Behavioural studies have ***indicated*** *that …*
Genetic studies of wild cod have ***revealed*** *…*
Studies of dune systems have ***shown*** *that …*
Recent work has ***suggested*** *that …*
Prior research has ***documented*** *…*
Previous research has ***noted*** *that …*

Writing a Literature Review 2: social sciences

The literature review in the social sciences serves the same basic function as in the natural sciences, namely to set the new work in the context of what has already been done on the topic. However, there are a number of differences in the way reviews are written in the two subject areas. Integral citations, where the name of the researcher or study is mentioned within the sentence, are relatively common in the social sciences. Because of this, a wider range of verbs is used to report on what earlier works said and did. Verbs may also occur in a wider range of grammatical forms. Because the ideas dealt with in the social sciences may be more subject to disagreement or questioning, writers often need to express some sort of evaluation of earlier work. For example, *Shaw notes …* suggests that the writer believes that Shaw was correct, while *Shaw states …* does not indicate the writer's view about whether Shaw was correct or not.

Here are the opening paragraphs from a literature review included in a study of the relationship between income and happiness, published in the *Cambridge Journal of Regions, Economy and Society*.

The writers relate earlier works to each other. Older views are contrasted with the findings of more recent researchers. (L1–10)

Verbs appear in various forms: the past, the present perfect and the present are very common.

While it was initially found that the relationship between income and happiness only holds within and not across countries– the so-called 'Easterlin effect'–more recent econometric studies by Deaton (2008) and Stevenson and Wolfers (2008) based on new data collected worldwide by the Gallup Organization have challenged this view, finding that income exerts strong effects on happiness across the board. Sacks *et al.* (2010) suggest that there is a close relationship between material living standards and life satisfaction and that countries that experience a rapid economic growth also get an equivalent increase in life satisfaction levels.

Graham's argument is briefly summarized, using the present tense. (L12–22)

A range of verbs is used to report what other researchers have said, done or concluded. (L22–32)

While income levels matter for happiness, work by Graham (2008) finds the relationship between the two is relative. Noting the paradox of the 'happy peasant and the miserable millionaire', Graham contends that although people can adapt to be happy at low levels of income, they are far less happy when there is uncertainty over their future wealth. Thus, the income effect on happiness is not only based on individual perceptions but also on the social and economic context in which individuals are embedded. The effects of unemployment on happiness tend to be larger in places where unemployment is generally low, while the effect is weaker if the individual lives in a place with high unemployment and thus the future is more uncertain. Helliwell (2003) suggests that happiness is affected by institutional factors such as governmental stability or effectiveness more so than economic ones. Helliwell and Putnam (2004) note [a] strong connection between social capital and happiness, beyond income effects. Deaton (2008) examines the relationship between income and life satisfaction and concludes that there is a strong relationship between the two. Deaton does, however, question the usefulness of health or health satisfaction as happiness measures, as he finds such measures have little relation with life satisfaction as a whole.

The writers identify a solid body of existing work. (L33–43)

References can be integral (L41–43) or non-integral (see pages AWT32–33).

There is a substantial literature documenting the transformation from industrial to post-industrial economies and societies. Nearly a half-century ago, Machlup (1962) identified the rise of the knowledge economy. Drucker (1967) coined the term 'knowledge worker' to refer to the emerging social group of workers who understand how to apply knowledge to productive use. This construct was later expanded to one of a 'knowledge society' (Drucker, 1993) where the traditional means of production are replaced by human capital and new institutional structures. Bell (1973) predicted the rise of a 'post-industrial society' led by a class of highly educated scientists and technocrats. ... [Two paragraphs follow.] (Mellander, Florida and Rentfrow, 2012)

Reporting verbs relate to what the source said.

Thinking verbs place the focus on the author's thought processes.

Research verbs relate to the research that was done, including its aims, processes and results.

Evaluative verbs indicate agreement with the researcher's findings.

Grammar Focus

The **present tense** shifts the emphasis from the research which was done to the research article, book, etc. which reports on it. It may also be used to show that ideas from earlier works are still current/relevant.

*Irvine (2001) **provides** ...*
*As Charles (2006) **shows**, ...*

The **past tense** puts the emphasis on the research processes carried out, rather than their current existence in literature. It may also be used to position research as belonging to an older tradition, allowing the writer to introduce challenges to it.

*Becher (1997) **surveyed** registered voters in the 21–30 age group ...*
*It was once **believed** that ... (Martin, 1985). However, more recent research suggests that ...*
*Brewer's (1967) classic text **established** the importance of investigations of this nature.*

The **present perfect tense** can be used to show cumulative trends in earlier work.

*A considerable volume of research **has** consistently **demonstrated** that ...*
*Beginning with Danielson's (2004) study, numerous scholars **have employed** ...*

The subject of the verb may be:

The research (e.g. the study or investigation). This places the emphasis on the work that was done or the conclusions that must be drawn from it, which are not really open to debate. This is common in both the natural and the social sciences.

__Studies__ have shown that work-life policies have a positive influence on staff retention (Almer and Kaplan, 2002).

The text(s) in which the research is reported. Here, the focus is on the arguments or findings that the work contains, but the implication is that these arguments or findings have been generally accepted. This is more common in the social sciences.

__Literature__ indicates that evidence from research is underutilized (Innvær et al., 2002).

The researcher. This places the emphasis on the researcher's thoughts, views and arguments, with which other researchers (and you) may agree or which you may wish to challenge. This is probably the most common way of introducing an integral citation in the social sciences (but is not very common in the natural sciences).

__Porter (2008)__ suggested that the configuration of the five forces ...

Language Bank

Referring to the collected work on a topic

The literature on ...
The body of research/literature on ...

Describing how much research has been done

There is a large/small/substantial/sizeable body of research ...
There is little/some/considerable evidence to suggest that ...
... has received scant/a great deal of attention.

Describing the development of research

It was initially/traditionally believed that ...; however, recent research suggests that ...
Early research on the topic addressed ...
Recent studies, by contrast, have investigated ...
An initial focus of investigation for researchers on this topic was ...

➲ For language to indicate a gap in pevious research, see the Language Bank at **research**.

Writing up Methods 1: an experimental method

Reporting on the method used in undertaking your research is a crucial part of the research writing process. Method sections in dissertations in any discipline will usually have a combination of the following three purposes. A method section aims to:

1. **describe** the data and method used;
2. **explain** how the data were collected and how the method(s) were employed in the research; and
3. **justify** why the data were selected and why particular method(s) were chosen.

Method sections in different disciplines differ in terms of the emphasis they place on the different purposes. Science disciplines tend to favour a more concise description and explanation of the data and method used. Humanities and social science disciplines tend to favour a more extended discussion of the explanations and justifications of how and why things were done. Whatever the discipline, the primary goal of the method section is to convey to the readers the validity of the research you have undertaken.

A key feature of the method section in the sciences is the need for a description of the experiment, i.e. the procedures followed and how the results were calculated. This is a method section from a research article published in the journal *Behavioral Ecology*, investigating the feeding preferences of hummingbirds.

Paragraph 1
Description of the data
Describes the data in terms of size and location.

Twelve male rufous hummingbirds (6 in 2007 and 6 in 2008), which had been defending territories containing a 250-ml inverted bottle feeder (filled with 14% sucrose) for at least a week, were trapped, color-marked, banded for individual identification, and released. The field site was the Westcastle river valley in the Rocky Mountains, Alberta, Canada (lat: 49.349024, long: –114.410902).

Paragraph 2
Explanation of the design of the experiment
Explains the set-up of the experiment. Information on the materials used, how they were prepared for the study, and the duration of the experiment is included here.

Not less than 3 days after trapping, birds were trained to feed from an artificial flower containing 14% sucrose during the course of a day (6–9 h). The "flower" was a red cardboard disk (diameter 4.5 cm) with a syringe cap inserted through its center to act as a well. The flower was taped with red tape to the top of a cane (1 m), which was pushed into the ground within 5 m of the usual position of the feeder. Observers sat at least 10 m from the flower.

Paragraph 3
Description of the experiment
Describes the list of procedures followed in carrying out the experiment.

Following training, there were 2 experimental days: Treatment 1 and Treatment 2, which weather permitting immediately followed the training day. As on the training day, the feeder was removed and replaced with the artificial flower. In Treatment 1 (low, high, and low), the flower contained 14% sucrose for the first 3 h, 25% sucrose for the next 3 h, and 14% sucrose for the final 3 h. In Treatment 2 (high, low, and high), the flower contained 25% sucrose for the first 3 h, 14% sucrose for the next 3 h, and 25% sucrose for the final 3 h. Half the birds received Treatment 1 first and the other half Treatment 2 first.

Paragraph 4
Explanation of the method
Explains how the results were calculated. This includes information on how the calculations were obtained.

The volume drunk and the timing and duration of each of a bird's visit[s] to the flower were recorded during both training and treatment days. Volumes were measured by refilling the syringe cap using a repeating pipette accurate to 10 µl. Duration of a feeding bout was the interval between the first insertion of the bird's bill into the flower and the last withdrawal from the flower before flying away. (Bacon *et al.*, 2011)

Complex noun phrases are used for concise description.

A series of verbs describes actions that follow one after the other.

Additional information, such as measurements or timing, is provided in parentheses.

Preparing to write

- Consider who is going to read your dissertation and what they will need to know about your research.
- An examiner will want to see the rationale behind your choices, especially with the experimental design.
- You can use the outline below to help you structure your experimental method section.

Data and data collection

1. **Description of the chosen data**
   Describe the size, location and characteristics of your data.
2. **Explanation of the technique used to collect your data**
   Explain how you chose your data. Include information on how your data were restricted or whether there were any conditions which limited the collection of your data.

Method

1. **Description of the design of the experiment**
   Describe how your experiment was set up, including any information on materials used.
   Describe the experiment step by step and in a chronological order.
2. **Explanation of the method**
   Explain how you arrived at your results. Usually, this might be how your results were calculated; for example, this might involve the use of statistics or other types of measurements.
3. **Justification of the method**
   Justify the experimental design and method by providing reasons why this is the best method for your research.

After Lim (2006)

Grammar Focus

How it was done:

The passive voice + by ...ing

Volumes ***were measured by refilling*** *the syringe cap.*

Water content ***was calculated by subtracting*** *dry weight from fresh weight.*

Red squirrel densities ***were estimated by counting*** *squirrels along visual line transects.*

The test chemical ***was prepared by dissolving*** *CAF in distilled water.*

The test ***was carried out by using*** *saturated solution of sodium sulphate.*

The passive voice + by + noun

The cells ***were collected by centrifugation****.*

DNA ***was prepared by the method of*** *Sherman et al. (1982).*

IISV lesions ***were induced by means of*** *exposure to ultraviolet radiation.*

Why it was done:

The passive voice + to + verb

The QBR index ***was used to measure*** *the quality of riparian habitat.*

to + verb, + the passive voice

To improve *the separation of phases, a centrifuge* ***was used*** *for 20 min.*

In order to control for *any confounding effects of familiarity, domestic animals* ***were excluded****.*

Tips

- In an experimental method section, use the **passive voice** to describe what *was done* (rather than the active voice to describe what *you did*): the focus is not on you as the researcher but on the experiment.
- You can use **relational processes** ('X is Y' structures) to describe the location, materials, tools and parameters of your experiment: *The field site was the Westcastle river valley ...; The "flower" was a red cardboard disk ...; Duration of the feeding bout was the interval between ...*
- A detailed step-by-step explanation is crucial as it allows other researchers to replicate your experiment.

Writing up Methods 2: a survey method

In social science disciplines, readers are likely to be as interested in your method as in your findings. This is particularly true of methods that involve a survey as there are a number of issues which need to be taken into account– for example, the sampling technique, the representativeness of the sample, the variables involved, and the questions posed in the survey. The method section may therefore be a detailed account of the steps undertaken in the research. Almost all method sections using a non-experimental approach are likely to have the three main components of description, explanation, and justification of data and method.

This is an extract from a method section in a research article published in *Social Science Japan Journal*, describing a survey of parental attitudes towards public school education in Tokyo.

Target profiling: Description and explanation of method
Explains the data collection method. (L7–15)

Describes the method used (target profiling) by relating it to an existing method in the field. (L17–22)

Explains how the method was used (target profiling in two stages). (L23–28)

2. Analytical Framework

2.1. Target Profiling

Our study differs significantly from previous research in its approach to categorizing parents. The typical approach is to group parents by a single characteristic, such as age or employment status, and then cross-tabulate with other variables. We forgo this method in order to create multidimensional profiles of parents that more closely approximate reality by taking several factors into account to develop a comprehensive and more true-to-life view of parents. For example, we do not lump all young parents into one group based on the single characteristic of age. Instead, we simultaneously consider several other factors such as parents' degree of cooperativeness, the strength of their sense of responsibility and whether their children attend cram schools. In short, we present a comprehensive narrative of parenting in Japan. ...

When considering which methodology to apply, we were drawn to target profiling, a method used primarily in fields such as marketing science and psychology. In target profiling,[7] members of a sample are classified into several groups based on shared characteristics. The degree of divergence between groups is revealed by comparing their responses to a set of questions.[8]

We conducted our target profiling in two main stages. First, using cluster analysis and attribute data compiled from parents, we categorized parents into several groups and uncovered the distinct characteristics of each group. Second, we assessed how much these groups differed from one another in their responses to questions on school education.

Subjects of analysis: Description and justification of data
Describes the data (who they are, where they are located and how many there are). (L29–33; 44–46)

Justifies the data (providing reasons for the exclusion of fathers and restriction to the Tokyo area). (L33–44)

2.2. Subjects of Analysis

For our sample, we selected mothers of second grade students attending public elementary schools in Tokyo, who had participated in the 2003 Benesse/Asahi Shinbun survey mentioned above. Although fathers and other legal guardians also sent in responses, roughly 90% of survey participants were mothers, so we focus solely on them. Given that younger mothers have been blamed for the burgeoning number of complaints filed against schools and teachers, we chose mothers of second graders in the expectation that they would be younger on average than the other mothers in the survey. Under the assumption that parents' concerns about middle school admission tests may further heighten their concerns regarding elementary school performance,[9] we further narrowed our focus

Variables: Explanation and justification of method
Explains each variable and provides reasons for its inclusion. (L47–56)

Explains how the results were calculated (the selection of responses to particular questions). (L59–62)

Listing steps, variables or categories using numbers or letters is a useful way of presenting information.

Verbs used to describe the research process.

Use **by + verb-ing** to show how a particular result was achieved.

Different ways of connecting your research to other research in the field.

to residents of Tokyo proper, where such admission tests are more prevalent, to control for this variation. After filtering out participants by these criteria and eliminating missing values, 116 mothers remained in our study.

2.3. Variables

We used eleven variables in our cluster analysis: age, employment ... access to information, tendency to worry, and cultural capital, for the following reasons[10]:

1 Age. Included to test whether younger mothers are more likely to file complaints against schools.
2 Employment. The amount of time a mother can spend with her child depends on her working status, and dual income (full-time) families presumably have higher incomes than those with mothers working part-time or not at all. [Nine further variables are presented with reasons for their inclusion.]

To test the extent to which different types of parents have different attitudes toward schools, we selected responses to survey questions that focused on parents' expectations and level of satisfaction with their children's elementary schools. These questions generally fall into five categories (see Table 4 below for a detailed list of survey questions): (a) general expectations of schooling (e.g. what type of education and guidance should all schools provide?); (b) expectations of one's own child's school; ... [Three further categories are listed]. (Yamashita and Okada, 2011)

Preparing to write

- You can use the outline below to help you structure your survey method section.
- Note the justification step: this occurs when you discuss your data collection procedures and provide reasons for the method you have chosen to use.

Data and data collection

1. **Description of the data**
   Describe the size, location and characteristics of the data.
2. **Explanation of the data collection procedures**
   Explain the steps in the data collection. Include information on restrictions and other limiting factors.
3. **Justification of the data collection procedure**
   Provide reasons for the advantages of using the chosen procedure of data collection. You may compare your approach with others in the field.

Method

1. **Description of the method**
   Describe the chosen method. You may wish to refer to other research in the field.
2. **Explanation of the method**
   Explain how the method was employed in the research. Specify any items in questionnaires or other research instruments that were used. Define variables and explain the ways in which you arrived at your findings.
   If you used any kind of measurement, e.g. statistics, you will need to explain this here.
3. **Justification of the method**
   Justify the method you have used by highlighting its advantages. You may wish to do so by illustrating its use in other research in your field.

After Lim (2006)

Grammar Focus

In social science survey methods, it is usual to use the **first person pronoun + past tense verb** to describe/explain your research. You do not have to use the passive.
***We conducted** our target profiling in two main stages.*
*For our sample, **we selected** mothers ...*
Use the **first person pronoun + present tense verb** to justify your research decisions.
***Our study differs** significantly from previous research ...*
*For example, **we do not** group ...*

Presenting Data

One of the main ways you can present your data effectively is to use visuals. Visuals summarize your data and make it easy for readers to understand what has been found in your research. There are many different visuals you can choose from to present your data. Two options will be presented here: **tables** and **bar charts**.

This is an extract from a findings section in a research article published in the *Socio-Economic Review*. The study looked at occupational change in Britain, Germany, Spain and Switzerland from 1990–2008. The writers have chosen tables to present their findings. Tables are used when the data contain relatively few numbers and there are only one or two categories of information that need to be displayed.

Section heading

4. Findings for the pattern of occupational change, 1990–2008

Statements before the tables summarize what the tables are going to be about. (L2–7)

Before examining changes in quintiles' sizes, we present in Tables 1 and 2 the three occupations that have experienced the largest expansion or decline over the last two decades in each country. To convey a sense of quintiles' occupational compositions, the last columns of Tables 1 and 2 report the job quality quintile in which each occupation falls.

Title for the table

Table 1 The three occupations with the largest increase in their relative share of employment.

Country	Occupation	Change in relative employment share (in percentage points)	Job quality quintile[a]
GB, 1991–2008	Care assistants and attendants	1.26	1
	Treasurers and financial managers	1.12	5
	Educational assistants	1.09	1
DE, 1990–2007	Legal professional, not specified	2.57	5
	Nursing associate professionals	1.01	3
	Social workers	1.01	3

[More data follow.]

Commentary based on the table

This interprets the findings for the reader by:

- pointing out a trend in the data (L12–14);
- contrasting the findings with other findings (usually from this study but it can sometimes be from other studies too). (L22–25)

Strongly *growing* occupations can be divided into two groups: the first comprises highly qualified occupations such as financial managers, legal and computer professionals set in (private) business services; the second includes (public) social service occupations such as health care employees, teachers and social workers. It is noteworthy that computer professionals and (assistant) nurses have expanded very strongly in all four countries. In contrast, we can distinguish three groups of strongly *declining* occupations. A first group comprises the victims of de-industrialization and includes production workers such as mechanics, maintenance fitters and assemblers. These manufacturing jobs are not particularly low-paid, spreading across the middle Quintiles 2 to 4. The same observation applies to a second group of shrinking occupations–office clerks and secretaries–which represent typical mid-range jobs set in the intermediary Quintile 3. Finally, the fall in employment has also been strong among agricultural workers and farmers. Yet unlike jobs in production or the secretariat, these jobs are unequivocally associated with low earnings and set in Quintile 1.
[Further discussion follows.]
(Oesch and Rodríguez Menés, 2011)

Use numbers or ordering to list findings.

Use passives to report findings.

Words and phrases that highlight trends.

The following extract is from the *European Journal of Public Health*. It reports on a study of how Swedish children travel to school. The results are reported using a bar chart. Bar charts are useful for showing differences between discrete groups or categories.

Commentary on the bar chart
This interprets the findings for the reader by:
- summarizing the overall finding (L1–2);
- pointing out a trend. (L3–5)

Active commuting was reported by 62.9% of the whole national sample (37.8% walking and 25.6% cycling at least one way). However, it decreased with age (figure 1): 76.4% of fifth graders (~11 years old), 61.9% of seventh graders (~13 years old) and 50.0% of ninth graders (~15 years old). Public transport on the other hand increased with age: 18.8% of fifth graders, 36.3% of seventh graders and 42.6% of ninth graders. Only around 10% in any age group got to school by car or moped, though significantly fewer in the seventh grade, compared with both grades five and nine.

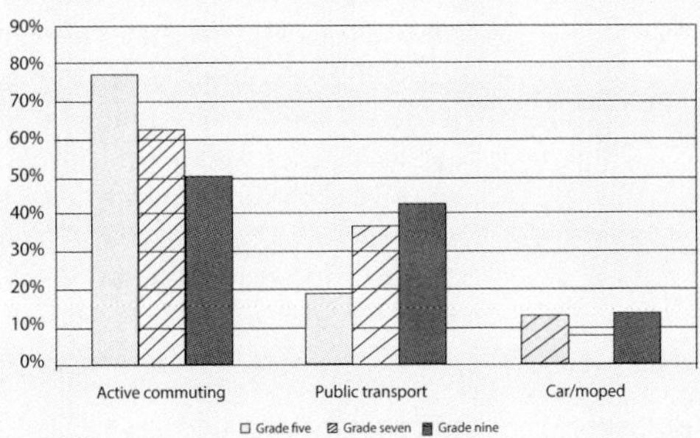

Caption for the bar chart

Figure 1 Active commuting, public transport and car/moped/motorcycle use to or from school in grades five, seven and nine in Sweden. Data from HBSC 2005/06.

(Johansson, Laflamme and Hasselberg, 2012)

Preparing to write

You must know and understand your data well and then use visuals carefully to ensure that they efficiently display your data in a meaningful way.

All visuals need to be accompanied by two elements. These are:

1. Statements that summarize what your visual is about. These usually occur before your visual within the text or as a title for your visual.
2. A commentary that interprets your findings for the reader. This interpretation may include the following items:
   - highlighting a trend you want the reader to notice;
   - commenting on unexpected findings;
   - explaining your findings in relation to other findings in your research;
   - drawing some preliminary conclusions based on the data.

Tips

- The commentary on your findings will include some discussion of the significance of your findings. This should not be confused with your discussion section. The commentary on the findings only interprets the data for your reader. In your discussion section, you will widen the discussion by linking it to literature on the topic and discussing the implications of your findings.
- Other common forms of visual are **line graphs** and **pie charts**. Line graphs show developments over time. Pie charts are used for comparing percentages of parts of a set of data.

➲ For useful language for referring to visuals, see the Language Bank at **table**. For language for describing statistics, see the Language Bank at **statistic**. For language for describing trends, see the Language Bank at **trend**.

Discussing Results

In the previous 'Presenting Data' section, the focus was on the findings of the study and the interpretation of the findings for the reader. In the discussion section of the dissertation, your aim is to persuade the reader to accept the findings you have previously highlighted. It therefore primarily involves an explanation of your findings.

This is an extract from the discussion section of a research article published in *Health Education Research*. The topic is on the eating habits of children. Several different paragraphs have been extracted to show you the different ways in which you can explain your findings.

Paragraph 1
Move 1: Background information on the study
Step 1: Restating the purpose of the study (L1–3)

Step 2: Summarizing the main finding of the study (L3–6)

Step 3: Pointing out the value of the study (L6–12)

The purpose of the current study was to explore the family and environmental factors underlying resilience to unhealthy eating. Individual interview discussions with mothers from disadvantaged neighbourhoods and their children revealed the presence of parental strategies and external barriers and supports to promoting healthy eating behaviours. This is one of the first studies to include both mother and child reports and focus exclusively on low SEP families of children who eat well. Our study underscores the importance of focussing specifically on 'resilient' children (i.e. those eating relatively well) to further elucidate potentially effective parent–child attitudes and behaviours in preventing unhealthy eating.

Paragraph 2
Move 3: Discussing the finding
Step 1: Comparing the finding with other studies (L13–17)

Move 2: Stating the finding (L15–17)

Move 3: Discussing the finding
Step 2: Explaining the finding by providing an example (L17–22)

Compared with previous studies that have predominantly focussed on the barriers to healthy eating and a healthy weight status, our results highlighted the active role mothers from disadvantaged neighbourhoods played in promoting healthy eating. For instance, almost all the mothers in the current study believed that parents were the main vehicle for influencing healthy eating and as a result, they exercised significant control over their child's food by implementing 'food rules', providing access to fruit and vegetables and restricting unhealthy food items.

Paragraph 3 repeats the cycle of moves and steps in Paragraph 2.

Although there is some evidence to suggest that excessive control over access to certain foods and implementing food rules has a negative effect on eating and weight [18, 19, 21], the children did not report their mothers to be too strict or controlling. Perhaps, this was because mothers also offered education and explanations about unhealthy food items and promoted the importance of being healthy. It is also possible that the children in the current study, particularly those who were younger, were also accustomed to this parenting style (or unaware of anything different) and shared similar attitudes about food and eating. [Two paragraphs follow with a further discussion on parental attributes and style.]

Paragraph 6
Move 2: Stating the finding (L35–38)

Move 3: Discussing the finding
Step 1: Comparing with previous studies (L38–45)

Step 2: Explaining the finding by using an example (L45–48)

The results from our study also highlighted some environmental influences as both barriers and supports to healthy eating among families residing in disadvantaged neighbourhoods. Previous research has indicated the negative impact on eating of advertising and poorer access and availability of healthy food options [40, 41]. Some mothers from our study reported instances of poor availability and quality of healthy produce yet many had developed strategies to overcome these barriers, namely, through responding to and creating more sustainable access to fruit and vegetables and

Step 3: Hypothesizing on the specific findings (L48–54)

other healthy food options. For instance, many families had their own fruit and vegetable garden, a practice consistently associated with increased fruit and vegetable consumption [23, 42]. Although a number of families in the current study benefited from residing in rural or provincial areas where fruit and vegetables were the town's primary industry and accessibility to larger garden space was more available, it is possible that provision of skills and resources for home-grown produce is a potential avenue for increasing fruit and vegetable consumption among low SEP families.

Paragraph 7 repeats the cycle of moves and steps in Paragraph 2.

Here, Move 3, Step 2 is: Explaining the finding by giving possible reasons (L60–61)

Previous research has consistently highlighted the negative impact advertising has on children's eating, yet our results indicated that although some children reported an awareness of the negative influence of food advertising, most children did not feel negatively influenced by televised food advertisements. There are three plausible explanations for this finding. Firstly ... Secondly ... Thirdly ... [Three reasons are provided and explained.] (Williams, Veitch and Ball, 2011)

Use the past tense when stating the findings of the study.

Refer to previous research to compare and contrast your own findings.

Use hedging language when giving reasons for, or hypothesizing from, the findings.

Preparing to write

- You will not be able to discuss all the findings of your research, so in your discussion section you will need to focus on a few of the core findings.
- Your findings will need to be made relevant to the wider academic community, so it is essential that your discussion is rooted in other relevant research.
- Use the following move and step structure to organize your discussion. Your discussion section will typically include several **cycles** of Moves 2 and 3, with each cycle focusing on a different finding from your study.

Move 1: Background information on the study
Step 1: Restating the purpose of the study
Step 2: Summarizing the main findings of the study
Step 3: Pointing out the value of the study
Step 3 is optional, as pointing out the value of your study may take place in the 'Conclusion' section.

Move 2: Stating the finding
Move 2 may occur as an independent move (as in Paragraph 6 of the model text) or it may be embedded within Move 3 (as in Paragraphs 2 and 3). In either case, it is an important move as it contextualizes the discussion which follows. There are several ways in which Move 2 can be used. In addition to reminding your reader of the finding, this move can also mark a finding as expected or unexpected.

Move 3: Discussing the finding
Step 1: Comparing with previous studies
Step 2: Explaining the finding by using an example or providing reasons
Step 3: Hypothesizing on the specific findings
There are several possible steps in Move 3. A very common step is to compare your study with previous studies. This may include pointing out similarities/differences between your study and the ones you are referring to.

Tips

- The discussion section is where you can show yourself more visibly as the researcher of the study by using pronouns (*Consistent with our hypothesis, we found ...*).
- In certain fields, the discussion section may be integrated with the findings section or with the conclusion section. The move structure would still be the same but you will need to incorporate your discussion with the findings or extend your discussion by evaluating it, highlighting the limitations, or suggesting future research.

➲ For hedging language, see the Language Bank at **hedge**.

Writing a Conclusion

In the conclusion, writers stand back from their work in order to view it in the wider context of the discipline as a whole or the real-world situation. Thus, the purpose of the conclusion is in direct contrast to that of the introduction: it leads out from the narrow topic of the dissertation to more general issues.

In some disciplines, there may be some overlap between the Conclusion and the Discussion. For example, the final chapter may be called 'General Discussion'. In this case, the conclusion may be a section of the final chapter. It is still important to include a conclusion, however, because it gives you the opportunity to highlight the most important points in your dissertation. It is the final impression that the examiners take away from your work, so it should finish on a positive note.

This is an extract from a conclusion to a research article published in *Applied Linguistics.* The study analysed the language of academic weblogs (blogs).

Paragraph 1
Move 1: Summary of the findings

This study has explored the manner in which academic blog participants define group relationships and create social meaning through interaction. The findings reveal that the academic weblogs in this study are social forums for self-presentation, networking, discussion, and idea testing, in many ways more similar to face-to-face academic discussions ... than to written academic genres. The affective indicators ... help to compensate for face-to-face affordances such as body language, facial expression or intonation. However, the specific features of weblogs (e.g. written medium, potential anonymity) also allow for the use of anti-social features more typical of some written genres in various disciplines.

[Paragraph 2, Move 1: Summary (omitted).]

Paragraph 3
Move 2: Evaluation of the study (limitations) (L12–16; 23–26)
Move 3: Suggestions for future research (L16–19; 26–31)

Negative evaluation, signalling the limitations of the writer's research.

Positive evaluation of the future research.

This study was intended to analyse some aspects of relational communication in academic blogs, but I am aware that it is limited in several key respects. First, although academic bloggers are quite a heterogeneous group, this study has treated them as a homogeneous group. Categorizing weblogs along several dimensions (e.g. participants' status, gender, motivation or discipline) could reveal significant results about relational communication. ... Additionally, since previous research on academic discourse has revealed disciplinary differences in the use of some discourse strategies, a cross-disciplinary study of markers of relational behaviour in academic blogs could yield interesting results. Another limitation stems from the fact that data sampling procedures (restricting the number of comments taken from each posting) interfered with the collection of whole message threads. Since there are online discussions where disagreement escalates and exchanges get more heated, the analysis of whole discussions could yield a higher frequency of anti-social indicators. Future research could examine whole message threads in order to provide a more accurate picture of interaction patterns.

Paragraph 4
Move 4: Implications of the study, with Move 2: Evaluation of the study (achievements) (L32–35)
Move 5: Applications of the research, with Move 2: Evaluation of the study (achievements) (L35–48)

Despite the limitations, findings from the present study can help in understanding online academic literacy practices and developing research-informed pedagogical approaches to teaching such emerging practices. The results of this study may be useful in the preparation of materials intended to help postgraduate students and scholars participate effectively in online academic settings and make them aware of strategies to construct their authorial identity in such settings. The potential of academic blogs to engender solidarity and interaction revealed by this study

Positive evaluation of the applications of the writer's research.

Modal verbs are used to signal the future research and potential applications of the writer's research.

could also be tapped in academic writing courses to help students discuss and revise a paper and foster in them a sense of community. In addition, ... the results can help EAP students become familiar with the discursive features of informal scholarly genres, both digital (e.g. informal e-mails) and face-to-face. Finally, academic blogs can be used together with other genres ... to help students acquire a repertoire of linguistic practices and associate these practices with specific genres. (Adapted from Luzón, 2011.)

Preparing to write

- Think about what your dissertation has achieved: the most important ideas or findings that you want the examiners to know.
- All studies have limitations, so think also about what your dissertation has not been able to cover. Mentioning its limitations shows that you are able to evaluate your own work objectively and according to the standards of the discipline.
- Use the four-move structure below to help you write your conclusion. Note that:
  - The sequence of Moves 2, 3 and 4 may vary. They may also be combined or incorporated into Move 1.
  - Each move widens the focus of the conclusion, moving from more specific to more general statements.

Move 1: Summary

- Restate briefly the work carried out, the aims, hypotheses or research questions.
- Highlight the most important findings or results.

Move 2: Evaluation of the study

- State what you consider to be the achievements and limitations of your work. ➲ See the Language Bank at **evaluation**.
- Assess how far the aims of your study have been satisfied.
- Include a personal assessment of what you have learned from doing the dissertation, if you are asked to provide this.

Move 3: Suggestions for future research

- Suggest how the work reported in the dissertation can lead to new research possibilities. These suggestions often follow from the limitations of the study. ➲ See the Language Bank at **suggestion**.

Move 4: Implications of the study

- Place the study in the wider context of research in the discipline and/or a situation in the real world, e.g. 'Theoretical implications' or 'Pedagogical implications'.

Applied fields may also use move 5 and/or move 6.

Move 5: Applications of the research

- Indicate how the research may be practically useful in real-world situations. This may appear within Moves 1 or 3.

Move 6: Recommendations

- Give specific suggestions for real-world actions to be taken on the basis of the research.

Grammar Focus

Use the **present perfect tense** to sum up/ evaluate the whole study or previous research.

*This study **has explored** ...*
*It **has attempted** to show ...*

Use the **past tense** to state what your aim was and to refer to the actions you carried out.

*This study **was intended** to analyse ...*
*The aim of this study **was** to ...*
*We **used** target profiling ...*

Use the **present tense** to evaluate your study and to state the generalizations and implications that you draw from your findings.

*The results **add** to knowledge of ...*
*These findings **suggest** that ...*

You can use either the **present tense** or the **past tense** to summarize your results. Check which tense is used in your discipline.

*The findings **reveal** that ...*
*Densities **are** much lower ...*
*It **was found** that ...*
*We **identified** four types ...*

Citations and Bibliography

In academic writing, it is necessary to support your points by referring to or citing other authors. This is done in your text through a citation. Any in-text citation must be accompanied by a full reference in the bibliography. The bibliography provides all the additional details (the title, author, publisher, etc.) a reader would need if they wished to read the source for themselves.

A citation is useful to the reader for several reasons:

- It provides information on the location of your source.
- It assures the reader that you have read around your topic.
- It gives evidence that you are not plagiarizing the information, but giving credit to the original source of the information.

The format of an in-text citation and the bibliography is determined by the citation style. There are different styles and these vary between and within disciplines. It is important to check the citation style used in your discipline or department and to follow it consistently and precisely.

The citation style determines the referencing system you will adopt. There are two systems– the author-date system and the footnote/ endnote system. These systems determine a number of different referencing styles (for example, APA Style or Chicago Style).

The author-date system

This system is used in the physical and social science fields. The author's surname and the year of publication of the cited source appear in the text. Other details of the source are provided in the bibliography at the end of the text.

There are different ways in which citations may appear in the text. You could be referring to them in-text or quoting them directly.

In-text citation: referring to sources

Diets rich in fruit and vegetables have ... cancers and type 2 diabetes (Faller and Fialho, 2009).

There is a great amount of literature ... in raw fruit and vegetables (Sun *et al.*, 2007; Gawlik-Dziki, 2008; Roy *et al.*, 2009; Lemoine, Chaves and Martinez, 2010).

In the text, sources in a list are cited according to year of publication, separated by semi-colons.

In-text citation: quoting

Organizational environments are systems of ... '... negotiated political interactions' (Kostova *et al.*, 2008, p. 1002).

In the text, a comma is used between author surname and date of publication.

The Bibliography in the author-date system is presented in alphabetical order.

Bibliography: books

Rothstein S. *Structuring Events*. Oxford: Blackwell Publishing; 2004.
Schein B. *Plurals and Events*. Cambridge, MA: MIT Press; 1993.

an article/a chapter in an edited book

Hoepelman J., Rohrer C. 'On the mass count distinction and the French imparfait and passé simple'. In: Rohrer C., editor. *Time, Tense and Aspect*. Niemeyer. Tuebingen. 1980. p. 629–45.

conference proceedings

Nakanishi K. 'On comparative quantification in the verbal domain'. In: Young Robert B., editor. *Proceedings of SALT XIV. CLC Publications*. Ithaca, NY: Cornell University; 2004. pp. 179–96.

a dissertation

Hackl M., 2000. *Comparative Quantifiers. Dissertation, Massachusetts Institute of Technology*.

a journal article

Kostova T., Roth K., and Dacin M. T., Institutional Theory in the Study of Multinational Corporations: A Critique and New Directions. Academy of Management Review, 2008, 33:994–1006.

Note the different uses of punctuation, italics and abbreviations in the Bibliography. There is variation between disciplines, so it is important to check the preferred format. The most important point is consistency.

Use of punctuation. | Ordering of citations/references. | Use of italics. | Use of abbreviations/suffixes.

The footnote/endnote system

This system is used especially in the arts and humanities, but also in some science fields. References are numbered in-text and these correspond to a full reference which appears either at the end of the page in a footnote or at the end of the text in an endnote. Here are some examples:

In-text citation: number in brackets (endnote)

The first demonstration of ... was reported by Uchida and Tonomura [3].

In-text citation: number in superscript (footnote)

For his part, Neville Chamberlain ... among the working classes,[14]and ...

At the end of the page or at the end of the document, you need to refer to your sources according to the numbers you have used. In the examples (right), there is variation in terms of punctuation, italics and abbreviations. Please check for the preferred format in your department.

[3] Uchida M. and Tonomura A., Generation of electron beams carrying orbital angular momentum. *Nature 2010*;464:737–739.

14 Self, *Neville Chamberlain*: *A Biography*. Vermont: Ashgate; 2006: 75–7, 91.

40 S. Eskilson, *Graphic Design: A New History*. Yale University Press, New Haven, CT, 2007.

43 S. Yavuz, 'Mediating Messages: Cultural Reproduction Through Advertising' in A. Bennett, *Design Studies: Theory and Research in Graphic Design*, Princeton Architectural Press, New York, 2006, pp. 273–290.

An important difference between the systems is that in the **footnote/endnote system** the references are presented numerically, whereas in the **author-date system** the references are alphabetical.

Other points to note

You might find it helpful to use the following abbreviations.

(1) Use of *et al.*

Use *et al.* in your in-text citations when a source has more than two authors:

In text:

Civic leaders ... (Karpyn *et al.*, 2010).

Bibliography:

Karpyn A., Manon M., Treuhaft S., Giang T., Harries C. and McCoubrey K. 'Policy solutions to the 'grocery gap' '. *Health Affairs*, 2010; 29: 473–480.

(2) Use of ibid.

This abbreviation avoids repetition of the full reference: 'ibid.' is used when the source cited is the same as the one immediately before.

In-text:

Designers ... tend to be practical, pragmatic and goal-oriented (Dodgson *et al.*, 2005). Design relies heavily on rules-of-thumb ... and experience with real-world problems (*ibid.*).

(3) Use of suffixes

You might also need to refer to two *different* pieces of work by the same author. This is achieved through the use of suffixes.

In text:

Yet, as pointed out by Ulrich Beck, not everybody ... same extent (Beck, 2002a).

First, as several studies ... local change (Beck, 2002a, 2002b; Vertovec and Cohen, 2002; Wimmer and Glick Schiller, 2002, 2003).

Bibliography:

Beck U., 'The cosmopolitan society and its enemies', *Theory, Culture and Society*, 2002a, 19: 1–2. 17–44.

Beck U., 'The cosmopolitan perspective ...', in ... 2002b: 61–84.

In the footnote/endnote system, each reference will have a different number and be referenced accordingly in the footnotes/ endnotes.

Other citation styles

The website owl.english.purdue.edu/owl (Purdue University Online Writing Lab (OWL)) provides information on the formatting styles used by the American Psychological Association (APA style) and the Modern Language Association (MLA Style).

Detailed information can be found in:

www.apastyle.org
www.mla.org
www.chicagomanualofstyle.org

The OSCOLA style for the discipline of law:

www.law.ox.ac.uk/publications/oscola.php

Writing Academic Emails

- It is always better to make a good impression as a student, whether in face-to-face communication or by email.
- Academic emails are usually **personal**, not official. You are writing to a specific, named individual, not to somebody in their official role.
- If you need to request something, it is particularly important to be polite. You do this by reducing the impact of what you are asking, giving options, and showing that you have made an effort to help yourself before writing your request.
- The level of **politeness** you need will vary. If you are asking a favour of an academic outside your university, you need to express a higher level of politeness than if you are asking your own teacher for a meeting.
- If in doubt, be more polite and formal than informal. It is more effective to acknowledge the trouble you may be giving than to flatter the person you are writing to.
- If you know the person you are writing to well, you can be much less formal. Remember to use a level of formality and politeness to achieve an appropriate **tone**.

After Robbins (2011)

Formal – A request from a student to an academic from a different department

Low-status writer to high-status reader whom he does not know

Tone: *Personal, very formal, very polite*

Use a clear, brief subject line.

Introduce yourself by giving your position in the university.

Say why you are writing, giving brief supporting/ background information. Mention any academic contact.

Ending: very polite Or: *I would really appreciate your help.* (not ~~*Thank you for your time/attention*~~. –used only in spoken English.) Do not repeat your request.

> Subject: Request for statistical help
>
> Dear Dr Barr
>
> I am a first year PhD student in the department of linguistics and my research topic is a quantitative study of verb forms in academic writing.
>
> As I need to use advanced statistical tools for processing the data, my supervisor, Dr John Pugh, suggested I contact you for advice.
>
> Would it be possible for me to come to see you to discuss what I need? Or if you are too busy to meet, perhaps we could talk on the phone? I attach a copy of my draft research proposal to give you an idea of the scope of my study.
>
> I would be very grateful indeed for any help you could give me.
>
> Best wishes
>
> David Brown
> 024 7654 3210

Greeting: Use *Dear* + academic title and family name or Mr, Ms, etc. and family name.

Would it be possible (very polite)
Or: *Could I possibly* (not ~~I kindly request~~)

Give an option– remember the person you are writing to may be busy. Only ask for something that is relatively easy for them to do.

Show that you have been working hard, as far as you are able.

Close: polite Or: *Regards*
Give your full name. Add position and contact details if necessary.

Less formal – A request from a student to their own supervisor

Lower-status writer to higher-status reader whom she knows well

Tone: *Personal, polite, less formal*

Subject: you can use '?' to show a request.

A way of introducing a polite indirect request. Use it to remind somebody of higher status about something.

Acknowledge the possibility that your supervisor is busy.

Abbreviations may be used in less formal emails.

> Subject: Meeting this week?
>
> Dear Ruth
>
> I was wondering if you've had a chance to look at my paper yet. If so, could we have a meeting sometime this week? The best day for me would be Tues. I start my fieldwork at the end of the week and it would be very useful to have some feedback before then.
>
> Many thanks
>
> Nicole

Greeting: first name, as they know each other well.

Could, would: These are less abrupt/direct forms.

Justify the need for your request. Reasons that are out of your control or that are institutional are more effective than personal preference.

Close: informal–Nicole has the right to ask for a meeting.

Reference section contents

Irregular verbs

This appendix lists all the verbs with irregular forms that are included in the dictionary, except for those formed with a hyphenated prefix and the modal verbs (e.g. can, must). Irregular forms that are only used in certain senses are marked with an asterisk (e.g. *been). Full information on usage, pronunciation, etc. is given at the entry.

Infinitive	Past tense	Past participle
arise	arose	arisen
bear	bore	borne
beat	beat	beaten
become	became	become
begin	began	begun
bend	bent	bent
bid	bid	bid
bind	bound	bound
bite	bit	bitten
bleed	bled	bled
blow	blew	blown
break	broke	broken
breastfeed	breastfed	breastfed
breed	bred	bred
bring	brought	brought
broadcast	broadcast	broadcast, broadcasted
build	built	built
burn	burnt, burned	burnt, burned
burst	burst	burst
buy	bought	bought
cast	cast	cast
catch	caught	caught
choose	chose	chosen
come	came	come
cost	cost, *costed	cost, *costed
cut	cut	cut
deal	dealt	dealt
dig	dug	dug
draw	drew	drawn
dream	dreamt, dreamed	dreamt, dreamed
drink	drank	drunk
drive	drove	driven
dwell	dwelt, dwelled	dwelt, dwelled
eat	ate	eaten
fall	fell	fallen
feed	fed	fed
feel	felt	felt
fight	fought	fought
find	found	found
fit	fitted (*NAmE usually* fit)	fitted (*NAmE usually* fit)
flee	fled	fled
fly	flew	flown
forbid	forbade	forbidden
forecast	forecast, forecasted	forecast, forecasted

Infinitive	Past tense	Past participle
foresee	foresaw	foreseen
forget	forgot	forgotten
forgive	forgave	forgiven
forgo	forwent	forgone
freeze	froze	frozen
get	got	got (*NAmE spoken* gotten)
give	gave	given
go	went	gone, *been
grow	grew	grown
hang	hung, *hanged	hung, *hanged
hear	heard	heard
hide	hid	hidden
hit	hit	hit
hold	held	held
hurt	hurt	hurt
input	input, inputted	input, inputted
keep	kept	kept
knit	knitted, *knit	knitted, *knit
know	knew	known
lay	laid	laid
lead	led	led
lean	leaned (*BrE also* leant)	leaned (*BrE also* leant)
learn	learnt, learned	learnt, learned
leave	left	left
lend	lent	lent
let	let	let
lie[1]	lay	lain
light	lit, *lighted	lit, *lighted
lose	lost	lost
make	made	made
mean	meant	meant
meet	met	met
mislead	misled	misled
mistake	mistook	mistaken
misunderstand	misunderstood	misunderstood
offset	offset	offset
output	output	output
overcome	overcame	overcome
override	overrode	overridden
oversee	oversaw	overseen
overtake	overtook	overtaken
overthrow	overthrew	overthrown
pay	paid	paid

Infinitive	Past tense	Past participle
plead	pleaded (*NAmE also* pled)	pleaded (*NAmE also* pled)
prove	proved	proved (*also* proven *especially in NAmE*)
put	put	put
quit	quit (*BrE also* quitted)	quit (*BrE also* quitted)
read /riːd/	read /red/	read /red/
rebuild	rebuilt	rebuilt
redraw	redrew	redrawn
rethink	rethought	rethought
rewrite	rewrote	rewritten
rid	rid	rid
ring[3]	rang	rung
rise	rose	risen
run	ran	run
say	said	said
see	saw	seen
seek	sought	sought
sell	sold	sold
send	sent	sent
set	set	set
sew	sewed	sewn, sewed
shake	shook	shaken
shed	shed	shed
shine	shone, *shined	shone, *shined
shoot	shot	shot
show	showed	shown, *showed
shrink	shrank, shrunk	shrunk
shut	shut	shut
sing	sang	sung
sit	sat	sat
sleep	slept	slept
slide	slid	slid
smell	smelled (*BrE also* smelt)	smelled (*BrE also* smelt)
speak	spoke	spoken
spell	spelt, spelled	spelt, spelled
spend	spent	spent

Infinitive	Past tense	Past participle
spill	spilled (*BrE also* spilt)	spilled (*BrE also* spilt)
spin	spun	spun
split	split	split
spoil	spoiled (*BrE also* spoilt)	spoiled (*BrE also* spoilt)
spread	spread	spread
spring	sprang (*NAmE also* sprung)	sprung
stand	stood	stood
steal	stole	stolen
stick	stuck	stuck
strike	struck	struck
strive	strove, *strived	striven, *strived
sweep	swept	swept
swell	swelled	swollen, swelled
swim	swam	swum
swing	swung	swung
take	took	taken
teach	taught	taught
tear	tore	torn
tell	told	told
think	thought	thought
throw	threw	thrown
thrust	thrust	thrust
undergo	underwent	undergone
underlie	underlay	underlain
understand	understood	understood
undertake	undertook	undertaken
uphold	upheld	upheld
upset	upset	upset
wake	woke	woken
wear	wore	worn
weave	wove	woven
win	won	won
wind[2] /waɪnd/	wound /waʊnd/	wound /waʊnd/
withdraw	withdrew	withdrawn
withhold	withheld	withheld
withstand	withstood	withstood
write	wrote	written

Be, do, have

Full forms	Short forms	Negative short forms
***be* present tense**		
I am	I'm	I'm not
you are	you're	you aren't/you're not
he is	he's	he isn't/he's not
she is	she's	she isn't/she's not
it is	it's	it isn't/it's not
we are	we're	we aren't/we're not
you are	you're	you aren't/you're not
they are	they're	they aren't/they're not
***be* past tense**		
I was	—	I wasn't
you were	—	you weren't
he was	—	he wasn't
she was	—	she wasn't
it was	—	it wasn't
we were	—	we weren't
you were	—	you weren't
they were	—	they weren't
***have* present tense**		
I have	I've	I haven't/I've not
you have	you've	you haven't/you've not
he has	he's	he hasn't/he's not
she has	she's	she hasn't/she's not
it has	it's	it hasn't/it's not
we have	we've	we haven't/we've not
you have	you've	you haven't/you've not
they have	they've	they haven't/they've not
***have* past tense** (all persons)		
had	I'd you'd etc.	hadn't
***do* present tense**		
I do	—	I don't
you do	—	you don't
he does	—	he doesn't
she does	—	she doesn't
it does	—	it doesn't
we do	—	we don't
you do	—	you don't
they do	—	they don't
***do* past tense** (all persons)		
did	—	didn't

	be	*do*	*have*
present participle	being	doing	having
past participle	been	done	had

The negative full forms are formed by adding **not**.

- Questions in the present and past are formed by placing the verb before the subject:
  - *am I?* *isn't he?* *was I?* *weren't we?* *do I?* *don't you?* *did I?* *didn't I?* *have I?* *hadn't they?* etc.
- Questions using the negative full form are more formal. Notice the change in word order:
  - *has he not? do you not? am I not? etc.*
- The short negative question form for **I am** is **aren't**:
  - *aren't I?*

  But note that all short forms are rather informal and are best avoided in academic and formal writing.
- When **do** or **have** is used as a main verb, questions and negative statements can be formed with **do/does/do not/does not** and **did/did not**:
  - *Did she do much for nursing research?*
  - *The product does not do what it is supposed to do.*
  - *What image do residents have of the cities they inhabit?*
  - *These two changes did not have an immediate effect.*
- The short forms *'ve*, *'s* and *'d* are not usually used when **have** is a main verb:
  - *I have a shower every morning.* NOT ~~*I've a shower every morning.*~~
- The short form *'s* can be added to other subjects in informal writing:
  - *Sally's ill.*
  - *The car's been damaged.*
- The **other tenses** of **be**, **do** and **have** are formed in the same way as those of other verbs:
  - *will be* *would be* *has been* *will do* *would do* *has done* *will have* *would have* *have had*; etc.
- The **pronunciation** of each form of **be**, **do** and **have** is given at its entry in the dictionary.

Verbs

Transitive and intransitive

- *The economy grew.*
- *She studied radioactivity.*
- *These data look very different.*

Each of these sentences has a subject *(the economy, she, these data*) and a verb (*grow, study, look*).

In the first sentence, *grow* stands alone. Verbs like this are called **intransitive.**

In the second sentence, *study* is **transitive** because it is used with an object (*radioactivity*).

In the third sentence, *look* has no object but it cannot be used alone without an adjective. An adjective like *different* that gives more information about the subject of a verb is called a **complement**. Verbs that take complements are called **linking verbs.**

Verb codes

In the dictionary, grammatical codes at the start of each meaning show you whether a verb is always transitive or always intransitive, or whether it can be sometimes transitive and sometimes intransitive.

The code [T] shows you that, in this meaning, **change** is always transitive.

change[2] /tʃeɪndʒ/ *verb* **1** [T] **~ sth** to make sth different SYN ALTER (1): *Technology is changing the way children learn.* ◇ *Difficulties arise when research participants change their behaviour because they know they are being studied.* ◇ *The operating speed of the engine can be changed by altering the air/fuel ratio.* **2** [I] to become different SYN ALTER (1): *The political balance has changed substantially.* ◇ *And, of course, the existing technologies are constantly changing.* **3** [T] to make sth pass from one

The code [I] shows you that, in this meaning, **change** is always intransitive.

The code [T, I] shows you that, in this meaning, **change** is sometimes transitive and sometimes intransitive.

scarce resource. **6** [T, I] to replace sth with sth else: **~ sth (to sth)** *We changed the name of the zoo to ZSL in order to reflect the conservation work of the Zoological Society of London.* ◇ **~ to sth** *There is no doubt that changing to new, simpler architectures made many more developments possible.* ➲ *see also* UNCHANGING

Transitive verbs are the most common type of verb. A verb that is always transitive in all its meanings is just marked *verb*, and no other verb code is given.

Verb frames

Transitive verbs can take different types of object —a noun, a phrase or a clause. Both transitive and intransitive verbs can combine with different prepositions or adverbs. Different linking verbs can take either adjectives or nouns as complements.

In the dictionary, the different patterns (or 'verb frames') in which a verb can be used are shown in **bold type,** usually just before an example showing that pattern in context.

pro·vide /prəˈvaɪd/ *verb* **1** to give sth to sb or make it available for them to use SYN SUPPLY²: **~ sth** *The state must enforce the rule of law and provide essential public services.* ◇ *Their results provide insight into the geographic effects of climate variability.* ◇ *Arid lands tend to be more sparsely populated, providing opportunities for comparing cultivated and uncultivated soils.* ◇ **~ sth for sb** *Special day centres have been developed to provide care for older people.* ◇ **~ sb with sth** *The International Monetary Fund and the World Bank provided Brazil with about $50 billion in loans during the 1990s.* ➲ thesaurus note *at* SUPPLY² **2 ~ that...** (*formal*) (of a law or rule) to state that sth will or must happen SYN STIPULATE: *If there is evidence of mental disorder, mental health laws provide that the patient can be held in hospital for a brief period.* ➲ *see also* PROVISION

If a particular verb, or one particular meaning of a verb, is always used in the same pattern, this pattern is shown in **bold type** before the definition.

Intransitive verbs [I]

Intransitive verbs do not take an object. When they are used alone after a subject, there is no verb frame.

The example showing this use will usually appear first, before any other patterns and examples.

res·on·ate /ˈrezəneɪt/ *verb* **1** [I] to remind sb of sth; to be similar to what sb thinks or believes: *Many of the problems the women discuss continue to resonate, including patriarchy, motherhood and childcare.* ◇ **~ with sb/sth** *These word choices were intended to resonate with readers.* ◇ *Their platform resonated strongly with the aims of regional and local governments elsewhere.* **2** [I] (of a voice, an

Some intransitive verbs are often used with a particular preposition or adverb. This pattern will be shown in **bold type,** usually before an example.

Some intransitive verbs are always or usually used with a preposition or adverb, but not always the same one. These are often verbs showing movement in a particular direction:

- *North America is slowly* ***drifting away from*** *Africa and Europe.*
- *As the army* ***marched farther eastward,*** *morale dropped steadily.*

In the dictionary, this use will be shown by the frame + **adv./prep.** If a preposition or an adverb is often used, but not always, there will be brackets round the frame: (+ **adv./prep.**)

float /fləʊt; *NAmE* floʊt/ *verb* **1** [I] **+ adv./prep.** to move slowly on or in water or in the air: *These planktonic species float freely in the upper 50 m of ocean.* ◇ *There are abundant salt particles floating in the air above the ocean.* ◇ *Icebergs break off and float away in ocean currents.* ◇ *In solution, ions do not float around free, but instead have strong interactions with the solvent.* **2** [I] to stay on or near

Transitive verbs [T]

Transitive verbs must have an object. The object can be a noun or pronoun, a noun phrase or a clause.

For information on verbs that take a clause as the object, see page R7.

The frames used to show a transitive verb with a noun, pronoun or noun phrase as object are **~ sb**, **~ sth** and **~ sb/sth**.

~ sth is used when the object is a thing.

dis·turb /dɪˈstɜːb; *NAmE* dɪˈstɜːrb/ *verb* **1** **~ sth** to change the arrangement of sth, or affect how sth functions: *When the price level changes, it disturbs the equilibrium in the money markets.* ◇ *Such plants mostly occupy habitats that have been disturbed, such as roadsides.* **2** **~ sb/sth** to interrupt sb and prevent them from continuing with what they are doing: *Caller ID may be used by an individual to avoid being disturbed by unwanted calls.* **3** **~ sb** to make sb feel anxious or upset: *The racism they encountered disturbed them but they did not feel that they were in danger.* ◇ *People in affluent areas are often disturbed by images of suffering in poorer regions.*

~ sb/sth is used when the object can be a person or a thing.

~ sb is used when the object is a person.

As with intransitive verbs, some transitive verbs are often used with a preposition or an adverb.

If a particular preposition or adverb is used, then it is given in the frame.

wave[2] /weɪv/ *verb* **1** [I, T] to move your hand or arm from side to side in the air in order to attract sb's attention, greet them, etc: **~ at/to sb** *They just waved to each other and carried on.* ◇ **~ sth** *Male fiddler crabs wave their one enormous claw rhythmically during courtship.* **2** [T] **~ sb/sth + adv./prep.** to show where sth is, show sb where to go, etc. by moving your hand in a particular direction: *The immigration officer glanced at his British passport and waved him through.* **3** [T] to hold sth in your hand and

If there is a wide range of possible prepositions or adverbs, a frame such as **sb/sth + adv./prep.** is used.

Transitive verbs with two objects

Some verbs, like *sell* and *buy*, can be used with two objects. This is shown by the frame **~ sb sth**:

- *She sold them the rights to the story.*
- *Mike's parents bought him a car.*

You can often express the same idea by using the verb as an ordinary transitive verb and adding a prepositional phrase starting with *to* or *for*:

- *She sold the rights to them.*
- *They bought a car for him.*

These will be shown by the frames **~ sth to sb** and **~ sth for sb**.

Two separate examples illustrate the two different frames **~ sb sth** and **~ sth to sb**:

grant[1] AWL /ɡrɑːnt; *NAmE* ɡrænt/ *verb* **1** [often passive] to agree to give sb what they ask for, especially formal or legal permission to do sth: **~ sth** *He had expected that his application would be granted.* ◇ **~ sb sth** *Over 98 per cent of countries in the world have granted women the right to vote.* ◇ **~ sth to sb/sth** *Aid granted to the company by the German government was found to be unlawful by the court.* **2** **~ (that)...** to admit that sth is true, although

Linking verbs

- *This explanation sounds likely.*
- *She became an MP.*

In these sentences, the linking verb (*sound, become*) is followed by a complement—an adjective (*likely*) or a noun phrase (*an MP*)—that tells you more about the subject.

Verbs that have an adjective as the complement have the frame **+ adj.**, and verbs with a noun phrase as the complement have the frame **+ noun**. Verbs that can take either an adjective or a noun phrase as the complement may have the frame **+ adj./noun**, or the two frames may be shown separately with an example for each.

prove /pruːv/ *verb* (**proved**, **proved** or **proved**, **proven**

DENCE[1] **2** *linking verb* if sth **proves** dangerous, expensive, etc. or if it **proves to be** dangerous, etc, you discover that it is dangerous, etc. over a period of time: **+ adj.** *Achieving these aims has proved very difficult.* ◇ **+ noun** *Jackson's election in 1828 proved a turning point in American history.* ◇ **~ to be sth** *As Bishop of Alexandria, he proved to be a man of energy and bravery.* **3** [T] **~ yourself (to sb)** to

The linking verb **prove** can be used with either an adjective or a noun phrase.

There are also verbs that take both an object and a complement:

- *The political system makes reform difficult.*
- *They elected him president.*

The complement (*difficult, president*) tells you more about the object of the verb (*reform, him*). The frames for these verbs are **~ sb/sth + adj.**, **sb/sth + noun** or **sb/sth + adj./noun**.

Verbs used with 'that clauses'

The frame **~ that...** shows that a verb is followed by a clause beginning with *that*:

- *He **replied that** this would be impossible.*

However, it is not always necessary to use the word *that* itself:

- *Environmentalists **say that** tougher measures are needed.*
- *Environmentalists **say** tougher measures are needed.*

These two sentences mean the same. In the dictionary, they are shown by the frame ~ **(that)...**

Some verbs can be used with both a noun phrase and a 'that clause'. The frame for verbs used like this is ~ **sb that...** or ~ **sb (that)...**:

- *Frazer reminds us that cultures evolve slowly through time.*
- *His teacher told him (that) he was making good progress.*

Verbs used with 'wh- clauses'

A 'wh- clause' (or phrase) is a clause or phrase beginning with one of the following words: **wh**ich, **wh**at, **wh**ose, **wh**y, **wh**ere, **wh**en, **wh**o, **wh**om, how, if, **wh**ether:

- *No one else **saw what** happened.*
- *The reader is left **wondering how** to react.*
- *Predators do not **care whether** it is sunny or not.*

In the dictionary, verbs used like this have a frame such as ~ **how/what, etc...** or ~ **why/where, etc...**

The particular 'wh- words' given in each frame will be words that are typical for that verb, but the 'etc.' shows that other 'wh- clauses' are possible.

won·der¹ /ˈwʌndə(r)/ *verb* [T, I] to think about sth and try to decide what is true, what will happen, what you should do, etc: **~ how/where, etc...** *The reader is left wondering just how to react.* ◇ **~ if/whether...** *A similar decline is occurring elsewhere, leading some observers to wonder if the age of mass political parties is over.* ◇ **~ about sth** *Castaneda forces us to wonder about the nature of hallucinations.*

If there is no 'etc.' in the frame, then this verb, meaning or use can only take the particular 'wh- words' that are listed.

Some verbs can be used with both a noun phrase and a 'wh- clause'. Verbs used like this have a frame such as ~ **sb where, when, etc...**

- *She **asked him why** he was crying.*
- *He **teaches his students how** to research a subject thoroughly.*

Verbs with infinitive phrases

Eat and *to eat* are both the infinitive form of the verb. *Eat* is called a **bare infinitive** and *to eat* is called a **to-infinitive**. Most verbs that take an infinitive are used with the to-infinitive. The frame for these verbs is ~ **to do sth**:

- *She never **learned to read**.*
- *Businesses **need to meet** customer demands more effectively.*

Some verbs can be used with both a noun phrase and a to-infinitive. The frame for these is ~ **sb to do sth**, ~ **sth to do sth** or ~ **sb/sth to do sth**. The noun phrase can be the object of the main verb:

- *They failed to persuade **voters** to trust them.*

or the noun phrase and the infinitive phrase together can be the object:

- *Experts expect **this figure to rise** substantially.*

Only two groups of verbs are used with a bare infinitive (without *to*). One is the group of **modal verbs** (or **modal auxiliaries**). These are the special verbs like *can, must* and *will* that go before a main verb and show that an action is possible, necessary, etc. These verbs have special treatment in the dictionary and are labelled *modal verb*. There is more information about the use of modal verbs in academic writing on page R12.

A small group of ordinary verbs, for example *see* and *hear*, can be used with a noun phrase and a bare infinitive. The frame for these is ~ **sb do sth**, ~ **sth do sth** or ~ **sb/sth do sth**:

- *They **watched the children play**.*

Verbs with '-ing phrases'

An '-ing phrase' is a phrase containing a **present participle**. The present participle is the form of the verb that ends in **-ing**, for example **doing**, **eating** or **catching**. Sometimes the '-ing phrase' consists of a present participle on its own. The frame for a verb that takes an '-ing phrase' is ~ **doing sth**:

- *Her doctor advised her to stop smoking.*
- *He started looking for a job two years ago.*

Some verbs can be used with both a noun phrase and an '-ing phrase'. The frame for this is ~ **sb doing sth**, ~ **sth doing sth** or ~ **sb/sth doing sth**. The noun phrase can be the object of the main verb:

- *Her comments **set me thinking**.*

or the noun phrase and the '-ing phrase' together can be the object:

- *Nothing would prevent **him speaking out** against injustice.*

In this pattern, you can replace *him* with the possessive pronoun *his*:

- *Nothing would prevent **his speaking out** against injustice.*

However, sentences with a possessive pronoun sound very formal and the object pronoun is more common, especially in American English.

Verbs with direct speech

Verbs like *say, answer* and *demand* can be used either to report what somebody has said using a 'that clause' or to give their exact words in **direct speech**, using quotation marks (' '). Verbs that can be used with direct speech have the frame **+ speech**. Compare these two sentences:

- **+ speech** *'All of us were afraid', she recalled.*
- **~ that...** *She recalled that they had all been afraid.*

Some verbs can be used with both direct speech and a noun phrase, to show who is being spoken to. The frame for this is **~ sb + speech**:

- *I asked him, 'What would you like to do now?'*

Verbs in the passive

Most transitive verbs can be used in the passive:

- *The idea* ***attracted*** *me.*
- *I* ***was attracted*** *by the idea.*

If a verb can be active or passive, the same verb frame is used. If the verb is often passive, there will be examples in the passive.

ac·cept /ək'sept/ *verb* **1** to take sth that is offered: **~ sth** *review are accepted for publication.* OPP REJECT (3) **2** to believe or recognize that an idea is true or valid: **~ sth** *Lacan accepted the key ideas of Saussure's structural linguistics.* ◇ *This argument was accepted by the court.* ◇ **~ sth as sth** *Genocide is now accepted as an international war crime.* ◇ **~ that...** *Most scholars accept that Mark's gospel was the first to be written down.* ◇ **it is accepted that...** *It is generally accepted that early humans were genetically very similar to humans today.* OPP REJECT (1) **3** to

If a pattern is *only* used in the passive, then the frame is put in the passive. This happens especially with verbs that take 'it' and a 'that clause'.

If a transitive verb cannot be used in the passive, the label [no passive] appears before the definition.

For more information about the use of the passive in academic writing, see page R9.

Verbs in different patterns

Many verbs, for example *watch*, can be used in a number of different ways:

- **~ sb/sth do sth** *I watched him eat.*
- **~ sb/sth doing sth** *I watched him eating.*
- **~ sb/sth** *I watched the pianist's left hand.*
- **~ what/how, etc...** *I watched how the pianist used her left hand.*

The dictionary entry for each verb shows the different ways in which it can be used by giving a range of example sentences. The frame before each example shows what type of grammatical pattern is being used. When an example follows another one illustrating the same pattern, the frame is not repeated.

Sometimes, patterns can combine with each other to form a longer pattern. This happens epecially with patterns involving particular prepositions or adverbs; and sometimes there is a choice of two or three different prepositions or adverbs:

- **~ sth** *We shared the tasks.*
- **~ sth out** *We shared out the tasks.*
- **~ sth among sb** *We shared the tasks among the four of us.*
- **~ sth between sb** *We shared the tasks between the four of us.*
- **~ sth out among sb** *We shared the tasks out among the four of us.*
- **~ sth out between sb** *We shared the tasks out between the four of us.*

In cases like this, the dictionary does not always give a separate frame and example for each different combination. It may use brackets to show where part of a long frame can be left out, and slashes to show where there is a choice between two or three different words in the frame:

share[1] /ʃeə(r); *NAmE* ʃer/ *verb* **1** [T, I] to have the same

new friends insisted on sharing their food with me. **6** [T] **~ sth (out) (among/between sb)** to divide sth between two or more people: *Food is shared equally among all group members.* ◇ *In the two smaller doctors' practices, staff shared out tasks flexibly.*

The frame ~ **(sb)**, ~ **(sth)** or ~ **(sb/sth)** may also be used, where a verb can be used without an object (that is, it can be intransitive) but is more commonly used with a noun phrase as object. In these cases, the more common, transitive, use is given in the first example(s), and any intransitive examples are placed after that:

com·mence AWL /kə'mens/ *verb* [T, I] (*formal*) to begin sth; to begin to happen: **~ (sth)** *The bank commenced proceedings to sell the property.* ◇ *A public inquiry is due to commence on the 16th.* ◇ **~ with sth** *The chapter commences with a brief consideration of communication theory.* ◇ **~ doing sth** *She commenced working on the project in 1980.*

Sb and **sth** may also appear within brackets within longer frames, for example to show a verb that can take a preposition, an adverb or a 'that clause', either with or without a noun phrase as another object:

warn /wɔːn; *NAmE* wɔːrn/ *verb* **1** [T, I] to tell sb about sth, especially sth dangerous or unpleasant that is likely to happen, so that they can avoid it: **~ (sb) about/against sb/sth** *Patients should be warned about the effects of taking alcohol.* ◇ **~ (sb) of sth** *They warned of the dangers of too much state intervention.* ◇ **~ (sb) that...** *Levitt (1960) warned that many companies fail to recognize the competitive threat from newly developing products and services.* **2** [I, T] to strongly advise sb to do or not to do sth

The passive

In an active sentence, the subject is the person or thing that performs the **action**:

- *We* ***assessed*** *physical activity at the start of the programme.*

When you make this into a passive sentence, the object of the verb becomes the subject. Making the topic the subject of the sentence focuses on the topic rather than the writer:

- *Physical activity* ***was assessed*** *at the start of the programme.*

The passive is formed with the auxiliary verb ***be*** + **the past participle** of the verb:

- *A sample of the pooled data* ***is shown*** *in Table 1.*
- *Similar findings* ***are reported*** *by Jones (2000).*
- *Interviews* ***were conducted*** *with long-term members of the orchestra.*

In negative sentences, the verb *be* comes before *not*:

- *This treatment* ***is not recommended*** *for children.*

The passive may be used with a modal verb. The modal verb comes before the verb *be*:

- *It can* ***be seen*** *that the rate of output increases ...*
- *Several important issues must* ***be considered*** *...*

The passive may be followed by a to-infinitive or the -ing form of the verb:

- *A tungsten light source* ***was used*** *to measure photosynthesis ...*
- *Volumes* ***were measured*** *by refilling the syringe ...*

In the dictionary

Some verbs are used *only* in the passive:

born /bɔːn; *NAmE* bɔːrn/ *verb* **be born** (used only in the passive, without *by*) **1** (*abbr.* **b.**) to come out of your mother's body at the beginning of your life: *Frederic Chopin was born in Poland in 1810.* ◇ *Human babies are born with relatively underdeveloped brains.* ◇ **~ into sth** *Max Weber*

Some meanings are *usually* used in the passive:

The label [usually passive] is given before the definition.

charge² /tʃɑːdʒ; *NAmE* tʃɑːrdʒ/ *verb* **1** [T, I] to ask an

duty. **3** [T, usually passive] to give sb a responsibility or task: **be charged with sth** *The NGO is charged with the task of identifying and cleaning contaminated water sources.* ◇ **be charged with doing sth** *Overseers were charged with disciplining the field workers.* **4** [T] **~ sth**

The verb frames may be shown in the passive.

Some meanings are *not usually* used in the passive; others have *no passive form*:

enter /ˈentə(r)/ *verb* **1** [I, T] (not usually used in the passive) **~ sth** to come or go into sth: *He had entered the UK, but did not find work.* ◇ *A judge entered the room and was seated.* ◇ *The earth had entered a new phase in its history.* ◇ *This image repeatedly enters the patient's mind.* **2** [T, no passive] **~ sth** to start taking part in an activity or start working in an organization or profession; to become part of sth: *Students had been learning English for about six years before entering university.* ◇ *Both men became suc-*

Using the passive in your academic writing

- **Describing methods and processes** of a study or an experiment, where the focus is on the method rather than the researcher.
  - *A pilot study* ***was conducted*** *with nine learners.*
  - *Temperature* ***is measured and controlled*** *with an automatic control system.*

  To say *how* something was done, use **the passive** + *by* + a noun or the -ing form of the verb:

  - *Primary outcomes* ***were obtained*** *by questionnaire.*
  - *Discrepancies* ***were calculated*** *by subtracting self-reported from measured values.*

  To say *why* something was done, use **the passive** + a to-infinitive:

  - *A GPS* ***was used*** *to gain site coordinates.*

- **Reporting** what someone did or said, or the findings of research. Use reporting verbs such as *report, believe, think, estimate* and *predict*:
  - *This effect* ***was reported*** *by Cryer et. al. (1986).*
  - *It* ***is estimated*** *that, by 2050, ten countries will have a median age above 50.*

- Making **factual statements**. A modal verb may also be used:
  - *Informal care* ***is provided*** *by ...*
  - *Strongly growing occupations can* ***be divided*** *into two groups.*

- **Signposting** (= stating how your writing is organized) and referring to visuals.
  - *This paper* ***is organized*** *as follows ...*
  - *A summary of the results* ***is presented*** *in Table 27.*

- Using **defining language.**
  - *Any population with no inward or outward migration* ***is termed*** *a closed population.*

- *Making* **recommendations and suggestions.**
  - *Further research* ***is recommended.***

Use of tenses

Writing about the present

The **present simple** is used:

- to refer to a permanent situation or something that is always true:
  - ▸ *Typically, the metal atoms **are** copper, nickel and cobalt.*
  - ▸ *Most aquatic insects **have** a terrestrial adult phase.*
- to refer to something that happens regularly:
  - ▸ *Among those people who **use** the Web regularly …*
- to give a definition:
  - ▸ *This stage **is** known as diffusion.*
  - ▸ *We **define** firms as institutions that …*
  - ▸ *In this study, resolution **is** defined as …*
- to provide background information to your study (the present perfect and the past simple may also be used):
  - ▸ *The French National Public Health Council **recommends** that adults receive vaccinations against …*
- to present the aims of your study (the past simple may also be used):
  - ▸ *This paper **investigates** the French response to the Brunswick Manifesto of July 1792.*
- to review the literature on a topic, especially to show it is relevant:
  - ▸ *Belcher and Belcher (2000) **suggest** that …*
  - ▸ *Putnam (2000) **argues** that television viewing is one cause of the lack of civic participation …*
- to describe the methods of your study, especially to justify your methods (otherwise, the past is often used):
  - ▸ *We **group** the sentences according to their length. The first group …*
- to refer to visuals:
  - ▸ *Figure 2 **illustrates** the sequence of events.*
  - ▸ *Table 6 **shows** the process times …*
- to present the findings of your study (the past is also used):
  - ▸ *Our findings **reveal** that an association exists between …*
- to evaluate your study and to state the implications of your findings. This may be done in your conclusion:
  - ▸ *Our findings **support** both research hypotheses.*
  - ▸ *The results **add** to knowledge of these plants.*

The **present progressive** *am/is/are* + present participle (*-ing* form) is used:

- to describe an action that is currently in progress or that is temporary:
  - ▸ *At the same time, we **are improving and increasing** our services to health professionals.*
  - ▸ *The Loiza watershed **is currently experiencing** substantial land clearing …*
  - ▸ *As a result of this course, I **am becoming** more aware of my values.*
- to describe a current trend
  - ▸ *The need for fast and reliable transportation **is increasing** throughout the world.*
  - ▸ *Surveillance technology **is improving** rapidly.*
- to describe an action that is not yet finished, even if you are not doing it at the present time:
  - ▸ *Our research **is investigating** how the Internet can enhance involvement in the local community.*

> NOTE Some verbs are not used in the progressive tenses, for example *believe, know, realize* and *seem.* These verbs typically refer to a state rather than an action. This information is given in the entries.

Writing about the past

The **past simple** is used:

- to describe an action that happened in the past:
  - ▸ *As a result, she **fractured** her left arm.*
- to describe the methods used in your study/an earlier study:
  - ▸ *Butcher, Rouse and Perry (2000) **surveyed** 64 psychotherapists.*
  - ▸ *To measure these variables, we **used** two scales ...*
- to present the findings of your study:
  - ▸ *The results **indicated** that sun protection for young children is a priority.*
  - ▸ *All participants **reported** a substantial intake of fruits, meeting and surpassing recommendations.*
- to highlight a trend in your data:
  - ▸ *Patient satisfaction **decreased** with level of education and household income.*
- in your conclusion, to state what your aim was and to refer to actions you carried out in the study:
  - ▸ *This study **aimed** to determine the nature and extent of food and beverage sponsorship of children's sport.*
  - ▸ *We **used** three sampling methods ...*

- to make an evaluation of a study or case:
  - ▸ *Staff **overlooked** the carer's needs.*
  - ▸ *Good aspects which **emerged** from the case were …*

The **present perfect** *have/has* + past participle is used:

- to summarize research already done; to show developments over time:
  - ▸ *There **has been** little research on … Therefore, in this study, we aim to develop …*
  - ▸ *Quality **has been defined** as 'conforming to requirements' (Crosby, 1984). However, …*
  - ▸ *Recently, several new techniques **have emerged** for studying past hurricanes.*
- with *for* and *since* to show the duration of an action or a state until the present time:
  - ▸ *Five events of magnitude 5.0 or greater on the Richter scale **have occurred** in the region **since** 1900.*
  - ▸ *She **has felt** unwell **for** the last 24 hours.*
- to refer to the result of an ongoing action, for example in a piece of reflective writing:
  - ▸ *I **have also learnt** the difference between empathizing and sympathizing.*
- in your conclusion, to summarize the present study and to state its achievements:
  - ▸ *This study **has identified** three main assumptions surrounding barriers to higher education.*
  - ▸ *This study **has shown** that working long hours consecutively has significant negative effects …*
  - ▸ *This research **has contributed** to improved information on safety procedures.*

The **present perfect progressive** *have/has been* + present participle is used:

- with *for* and *since* to describe an activity that started in the past and is still happening:
  - ▸ *In this case, the patient **has been vomiting** for 48 hours …*
  - ▸ *She **has been practising** Zen since the early 1980s.*

The **past progressive** *was/were* + present participle is used:

- to describe an action that was in progress at a particular time in the past:
  - ▸ *By the year 1000, English elites **were consuming** more beef and pork than did their ancestors.*

The **present progressive** *am/is/are* + present participle is used:

- to refer to an action that is unfinished at a particular point in the past:
  - ▸ *In the reign of Trajan, when he **is writing**, Tacitus …*

Writing about the future

The **future simple** *will* + bare infinitive is used:

- to make a prediction:
  - ▸ *The NAST (2000) report predicts that higher evaporation rates **will result** in decreased water availability.*
  - ▸ *It is predicted that by 2024, 40% of the UK population **will be** over 50.*

The **future progressive** *will be* + present participle is used:

- to predict a trend:
  - ▸ *This means that total output **will be increasing** as more variable factors of production are added.*

The **future perfect** *will have* + past participle is used:

- to state what is typical in a situation:
  - ▸ *Typically, patients undergoing a hip replacement **will have lived** with their arthritis for many years.*

In the dictionary

Some verbs or meanings are *not used* or *not usually used* in the progressive tenses:

> **be·lieve** /bɪˈliːv/ *verb* (not used in the progressive tenses) **1** [often passive] to think that sth is true or possible, although you are not completely certain: **~ (that)…** *Seventy per cent of biologists today believe the world is experiencing the fastest extinction of living species in the history of the planet.* ◇ **it is believed (that)…** *It is believed that the*

Some meanings are used *only* or *especially* in the progressive tenses:

> **burn**[1] /bɜːn; *NAmE* bɜːrn/ *verb* (**burnt, burnt** /bɜːnt; *NAmE* bɜːrnt/or, **burned, burned** /bɜːnd; *NAmE* bɜːrnd/) **1** [I] to produce flames and heat while using a fuel such as wood or coal: *There may be a rise in 'copy-cat' arson incidents once large fires are already burning.* ◇ *Low-mass stars will burn for trillions of years.* **2** [I] (used especially in the progressive tenses) to be on fire: *By nightfall the whole city was burning.* ◇ *Patients who have jumped from a burning*

Modal verbs

Modal verbs express stance (= the opinion that someone has about something). The modal verbs in English are:

can could may might must
shall should will would

There are also a number of **semi-modal verbs:**

be able to have to need (to)
ought to used to

Modal verbs

- are followed by the infinitive without 'to'
- have only one form
- are used before *not* in negatives:
  - ▸ *The company **must** make some important choices.*
  - ▸ *Organizations **must** work within strict data protection laws when storing customer data.*
  - ▸ *Russia had to divide her ships between two fleets which **could not** be united.*

Semi-modal verbs

- are followed by the infinitive with 'to' (which, however, is considered to be part of the semi-modal verb: *have to, need to, used to,* etc.)
  - ▸ *This is a skill that **has to** be practised regularly.*
- **need** is a special case as it also occurs as a modal verb without 'to', followed by a bare infinitive:
  - ▸ *With electronic ticketing, the customer **need** only quote the booking number.*
- **have to** and **need to** have forms ending in *-s* and *-d/-ed*:
  - ▸ *The heart **needs to** contract and relax 100 000 times a day.*
  - ▸ *The ground **needed to** be tilled regularly until harvest.*

In the dictionary

Modal and semi-modal verbs are labelled *modal verb* in the dictionary entries. HELP notes at some entries give information on usage:

> **may** /meɪ/ *modal verb* (*negative* **may not**, *pt* **might** /maɪt/, *negative* **might not**) HELP Note that **might** is used as the past form for **may**, especially in indirect speech: *If he had requested consent to send her an email, she would have said that of course he might.* **may have** + past participle is also used to talk about past possibilities: *There may have been other factors that contributed to this result.* **1** used to say that sth is possible: *Free trade may lead to a deterioration of labour conditions in developed countries.* ◇ The

Using modal verbs in your academic writing

obligation and necessity

must should need to have to ought to

Must and **have to** are stronger than **should** and **ought to**. Use **had to** to refer to the past.

- Expressing responsibility:
  - ▸ *Today, firms **must** comply with environmental regulations.*
- Stating the limitations of your study or findings:
  - ▸ *Several limitations **should** be noted.*

permission

can could may

Use **could** to refer to the past.

- Stating what is/is not permitted:
  - ▸ *Formerly, employers **could** insist that ...*
  - ▸ *A representative of the European Commission **may** attend meetings but **may not** vote.*

ability and probability

can could may might should would

You can use **could** or **could/may/might/should/would have** to refer to the past.

- Stating the implications/contributions of your research; making suggestions for future research:
  - ▸ *These findings **can** help to ...*
  - ▸ *Future research **could** examine ...*
- Making factual statements:
  - ▸ *Occupations **can** be divided into two groups.*

being tentative

can could may

- Hedging your claims so you sound **objective**:
  - ▸ *Teamwork **may** be associated with better performance in the workplace.*

stating intentions

will shall

- Signposting (= stating how your writing is organized):
  - ▸ *The purpose of this chapter **will** be to examine ...*

prediction

will would

- ▸ *The model predicts that there **will** not be ...*

Phrasal verbs

What are phrasal verbs?

- *Congress* ***turned down*** *Kennedy's tax reform proposals.*
- *There are alternative ways of* ***dealing with*** *these situations.*
- *Customers will not* ***put up with*** *poor service.*

Phrasal verbs are verbs that consist of two, or sometimes three, words. The first word is a verb and it is followed by an adverb (turn *down*) or a preposition (deal *with*) or both (put *up with*). These adverbs or prepositions are sometimes called **particles**.

Phrasal verbs are very frequently used in spoken English. They are less frequent in academic and written English, where one-word verbs are more often preferred. However, some phrasal verbs are also used in academic English and these verbs are included in this dictionary.

In this dictionary, phrasal verbs are listed at the end of the entry for the main verb in a section marked PHR V. They are listed in alphabetical order of the particles following them:

PHR V **ˌfight ˈback (against sb/sth)** to protect yourself with actions or words by attacking sb who has attacked you: *Female chimpanzees routinely fight back against bullying behaviour by group males.* **ˌfight sb/sth ˈoff** to resist sb/sth by fighting against them/it: *Her body was unable to fight off a disease that she contracted.* ◇ *Clinton successfully fought off efforts to impose a budget that, in his view, would have destroyed many essential programmes.* **ˌfight ˈout sth** | **ˌfight it ˈout** to fight or argue until an agreement or result has been achieved: *The matter was fought out in the courts for months.*

Meaning of phrasal verbs

- *He sat down on the bed.*

The meaning of some phrasal verbs, such as *sit down*, is easy to guess because the verb and the particle keep their usual meaning. However, many phrasal verbs have idiomatic meanings that you need to learn. The separate meanings of *put*, *up* and *with*, for example, do not add up to the meaning of *put up with* (= tolerate).

Some particles have particular meanings that are the same when they are used with a number of different verbs:

- *Most of the carbon in the product would eventually burn up.*
- *Piloting the questionnaire may clear up problems in question formulation.*

Up adds the meaning of 'completely; until there is/are none left' and is also used in a similar way with many other verbs, such as *break*, *dry* and *finish*.

Grammar of phrasal verbs

Phrasal verbs can be **transitive** (they take an object) or **intransitive** (they have no object). Some phrasal verbs can be used in both ways:

- *We broke down the costs into two distinct categories.* (transitive)
- *The costs break down into two distinct categories.* (intransitive)

Intransitive phrasal verbs are written in the dictionary without **sb** (somebody) or **sth** (something) after them. This shows that they do not have an object:

this time, the apostles themselves had begun to die off. **ˌdie ˈout** to stop existing: *Towards the end of the period, the dinosaurs and giant marine reptiles died out.*

Die out is intransitive, and the two parts of the verb cannot be separated by any other word. You can say:

- *The language eventually died out.*

BUT NOT ~~*The language died eventually out.*~~

In order to use **transitive** phrasal verbs correctly, you need to know where to put the object. With some phrasal verbs (often called **separable** verbs), the object can go either between the verb and the particle or after the particle:

- *They* ***called*** *the deal* ***off****.*
- *They* ***called off*** *the deal.*

When the object is a long phrase, it usually comes after the particle:

- *They* ***called off*** *all the deals that had provisionally been agreed.*

When the object is a pronoun (for example, 'it' standing for 'the deal'), it must always go between the verb and the particle:

- *They reviewed the terms of the deal and then* ***called*** *it* ***off****.*

In the dictionary, verbs that are separable are written like this: **call sth off**

The object is shown between the two parts of the verb.

With other phrasal verbs (sometimes called **inseparable** verbs), the two parts of the verb cannot be separated by an object:

- *She* ***cares for*** *her elderly parents.*

NOT ~~*She cares her elderly parents for.*~~

In the dictionary, verbs that are inseparable are written like this: **care for sb**

Nouns

The two biggest groups of nouns are **countable** nouns and **uncountable** nouns. Most countable nouns are words for separate things that can be counted, like *books*, *students* or *questions*. Uncountable nouns are usually words for things that are thought of as a quantity or mass, like *water* or *time*.

However, there are some nouns in English that you might expect to be countable but which are not. For example, *advice*, *information* and *equipment* are all uncountable nouns in English, although they are countable in some other languages.

Countable nouns [C]

A countable noun has a singular form and a plural form. When it is singular, it must always have a **determiner** (a word such as *a*, *the*, *both*, *each*) in front of it. In the plural, it can be used with or without a determiner:

- *Morris et al. (1977) conducted **an experiment** …*
- ***Several experiments** demonstrate the framework.*
- ***Experiments** were carried out under …*

Countable nouns are the most common type of noun. If they have only one meaning, or if all the meanings are countable, they are just marked *noun*. For nouns that have a number of meanings, some of which are not countable, each meaning that is countable is marked [C].

Uncountable nouns [U]

An uncountable noun has only one form, not separate singular and plural forms. It can be used with or without a determiner:

- ***Wealth** has become more unequally held.*
- *Many of the immigrants possessed **little wealth**.*

If an uncountable noun is the subject of a verb, the verb is singular:

- *Extra **money has** been found for this project.*

With nouns such as *advice*, *information* and *equipment*, as with many other uncountable nouns, you can talk about amounts of the thing or separate parts of the thing by using phrases like *a piece of* or *two items of*:

- ***Three pieces of information** are required …*
- ***Items of equipment** were electronically monitored.*

Plural nouns [pl.]

Some nouns are always plural and have no singular form. Nouns that refer to things that have two parts joined together, for example *glasses*, are often plural nouns. You can usually also talk about *a pair of glasses*, etc.

- *A substantial number of people wear **glasses** or contact lenses.*
- *A very fine **pair of scissors** is required.*

An example is given in the entry for the noun to show that it can be used in this way. Some plural nouns, such as *police*, look as if they are singular. Nouns like this usually refer to a group of people or animals of a particular type, when they are considered together as one unit. They take a plural verb:

- *The **police are** often put under competing pressures.*

Singular nouns [sing.]

Some nouns are always singular and have no plural form. Many nouns like this can be used in only a limited number of ways:

Nouns with singular or plural verbs

Cosmos is always used in the phrase **the cosmos.**

cos·mos /ˈkɒzmɒs; *NAmE* ˈkɑːzmoʊs; ˈkɑːzməs/ *noun* **the cosmos** [sing.] the universe, especially when it is thought of as an ordered system: *The Buddha taught that the cosmos is uncreated and dynamic.* ◇ *He sought to exploit this*

[sing.+sing./pl. v.][C+sing./pl. v.][U+sing./pl. v.]

In British English, some singular nouns (or countable nouns in their singular form) can be used with a plural verb as well as a singular one. Nouns like this usually refer to a group of people, an organization or a place and can be thought of either as the organization, place or group (singular) or as many individual people (plural):

- *The **company has/have** created a significant global presence.*
- *The **government has/have** decided to raise taxes.*

These nouns are marked [sing.+sing./pl. v.] if they are always singular in form, and [C+sing./ pl. v.] if they also have a plural form. The plural form always agrees with a plural verb.

> NOTE In American English, the singular form of these nouns must take a singular verb:

- *The government **says it is** committed to tax reform.*

Some uncountable nouns can be used with a plural verb as well as a singular one. These include some nouns that end in **-s** and therefore look as though they are plural:

- *Early modern imperial **politics were** …*
- *Moreover, **politics was** …*

Noun phrases

The purpose of using a **noun phrase** is to give more information about the noun itself, so that your meaning is more precise. This is important in academic writing, in which the ideas you are writing about are often complex. Using a noun phrase also helps you to communicate your ideas concisely. A noun phrase consists of a noun plus a **pre-modifier** and/or a **postmodifier**.

Pre-modifiers

A **pre-modifier** comes *before the noun*. It may be a determiner, an adjective or another noun:

- *the conflict* (determiner + **noun**)
- *scientific* methods (adj. + **noun**)
- *field* research (noun + **noun**)

determiner + noun

Determiners define the noun. They include the articles *a, an* and *the,* and words such as *this, those* and *his*:

- *One of the earliest examples of* ***a study*** *of a transportation network is* ***the study*** *by Pitts [268].*
- ***This approach*** *seeks to encourage individuals to adopt healthy lifestyles by ...*

See also page R18 Articles.

adjective + noun

The noun may be modified by a compound adjective. These are often hyphenated before the noun:

- *a web-based longitudinal* ***study*** (noun-past participle + adj. + **noun**)

See page R19 for compound adjectives.

noun + noun

The term **head noun** is used for a noun that is pre-modified by another noun. In the example *field research* (above), *research* is the head noun (= the topic of the phrase), and *field* is the pre-modifier, giving information about the *type* of research. Sometimes, a head noun may have more than one noun pre-modifier:

- *government assistance* ***programmes*** (= programmes providing assistance from the government) (noun + noun + **noun**)

Post-modifiers

A **post-modifier** comes *after the noun*. It may be a prepositional phrase (starting with *of, with, for,* etc.), an infinitive phrase or a clause:

- *a process of erosion* (prep. phrase)
- *patients with diabetes* (prep. phrase)
- *the need to improve productivity* (infinitive phrase)
- *cells that form the bones of the face* (*that-* clause)

Complex noun phrases

In grammatical terms, a noun phrase is **complex** if it has more than one modifier. In the following examples, the **noun** is bold and each modifier is underlined.

The first examples each have *two* pre-modifiers:

- *recent historical* ***research*** (adj. + adj. + **noun**)
- *global business* ***activity*** (adj. + noun + **noun**)

The next examples each have *two* post-modifiers:

- *the* ***study*** *of philosophy in the Roman Empire* (**noun** + prep. phrase + prep. phrase)
- *an* ***increase*** *in spending of 1 million dollars* (**noun** + prep. phrase + prep. phrase)

The following examples each have one or more pre-modifiers and post-modifiers:

- *alternative technical* ***methods*** *for recording interviews* (adj. + adj. + **noun** + prep. phrase)
- *an important* ***tool*** *for assessing crop performance in the post-rainy cropping systems* (adj. + **noun** + prep. phrase + prep. phrase)

Patterns with nouns in the dictionary

When a noun is often followed by a particular preposition or a particular type of phrase or clause, it is shown in the dictionary by a frame in **bold type**. Where part of the frame is optional, it is shown in brackets. The frame usually appears directly before an example sentence:

> **pro·cess[1]** AWL /ˈprəʊses; *NAmE* ˈprɑːses; ˈproʊses/ *noun* **1** a series of actions that are taken in order to achieve a particular result: *Data from the market research informed the decision-making process.* ◇ **~ of (doing) sth** *The term 'remote sensing' describes the process of obtaining data using both photographic and non-photographic sensor systems.* **2** a series of things that happen, especially ones

However, for patterns that are always used with a particular meaning of a word, the frame may appear before the definition:

> **pre·ser·va·tion** /ˌprezəˈveɪʃn; *NAmE* ˌprezərˈveɪʃn/ *noun* [U] **1 ~ of sth** the fact or process of making sure that a particular quality or feature is kept: *It is clear that one such duty is the preservation of the peace.* ◇ *She is interested in conservation biology and the preservation of biodiversity.*

noun + prepositional phrase

Nouns that are formed from a verb, such as *analysis* (from the verb *analyse*) and *examination* (from the verb *examine*), are often followed by the preposition **of**:

an·aly·sis AWL /əˈnæləsɪs/ *noun* (*pl.* **an·aly·ses** /əˈnæləsiːz/) **1** [U, C] the detailed study or examination of sth in order to understand more about it; the result of the study: *Statistical analysis reveals an interaction between all three factors.* ◇ **~ of sth** *Detailed analysis of earthquake data suggested a subduction zone event.* ◇ *This*

Nouns that show judgement or an estimate, such as **likelihood, possibility** and **importance**, are often followed by the preposition **of**:

like·li·hood /ˈlaɪklihʊd/ *noun* [U, sing.] the chance of sth happening; how likely sth is to happen SYN PROBABILITY (1): *Most of the risks classified as severe were considered of low likelihood (<1%).* ◇ **~ of sth** *This principle applies where there is a likelihood of environmental damage.* ◇ **~**

Other patterns have to be learned. These include **~ about sth, ~ over sth, ~ as to sth, ~ on/upon sb/sth, ~ in doing sth** and others.

Where two or more alternative prepositions can perform the same function, they may be given within a single frame, separated by a slash.

con·fu·sion /kənˈfjuːʒn/ *noun* **1** [U] a state of not being certain about what is happening, what you should do, what sth means, etc: **~ about/over sth** *Employees may feel confusion over their roles and responsibilities.* ◇ **~ as to sth** *This led to some confusion as to the nature of the disease.* **2** [U, C] the fact of making a mistake about who

ef·fect[1] /ɪˈfekt/ *noun* **1** [C, U] a change that sb/sth causes

scheduled elections took place as planned in October. ◇ **~ on/upon sb/sth** *Wind turbines can have an adverse effect on communication systems through electromagnetic interference.* ◇ *The Second World War had a very significant*

suc·cess /səkˈses/ *noun* **1** [U] the fact that sth/sb

students attribute both success and failure in education to luck. ◇ **~ in doing sth** *Mexico has had remarkable success in using the soap opera format to encourage family planning and literacy.* ◇ **~ in sth** *The presence of educational*

noun + infinitive phrase

Nouns that are followed by an infinitive phrase are shown in the dictionary by the frame **~ to do sth**

abil·ity /əˈbɪləti/ *noun* (*pl.* **-ies**) **1** [sing.] the fact that sb/sth is able to do sth: **~ to do sth** *Many animals possess the ability to distinguish light of different wavelengths.* ◇ *Some of these children acquired an increased ability to cope with*

noun + *that*- clause

Nouns that may be followed by a *that*- clause are shown in the dictionary by the frame **~ that...**

as·sump·tion AWL /əˈsʌmpʃn/ *noun* **1** [C] a belief

tions behind these labels. ◇ **~ that...** *Democracy is based on the assumption that all citizens participate equally in political affairs.* ◇ **under the ~ that...** *Information and*

In some cases, the word *that* itself may be omitted. In these cases, it appears in the frame in brackets as **~ (that)...**

In academic writing, nouns are often followed by two (or more) patterns. Where patterns can be combined, they are shown together, with brackets around any sections that are optional:

method AWL /ˈmeθəd/ *noun* [C] a particular way of doing sth: *Managers are frequently not familiar with scientific methods.* ◇ **~ of sth** *Our results with these two methods of analysis are mutually supportive.* ◇ **~ (of sth) (that...)** *Firms will tend to introduce the methods of production that are most profitable.* ◇ **~ of doing sth** *There are several methods of delivering nursing care.* ◇ **~ for doing sth** *There*

WORD FAMILY
method *noun*
methodical *adj.*
methodically *adv.*
methodology *noun*
methodological *adj.*
methodologically *adv.*

noun + noun

Where a noun is frequently used as a pre-modifier of other nouns, this is shown in the entry by the frame **+ noun**

re·search[1] AWL /rɪˈsɜːtʃ; ˈriːsɜːtʃ; *NAmE* rɪˈsɜːrtʃ; ˈriːsɜːrtʃ/ *noun* [U] careful study of a subject, especially in order to discover new facts or information about it: *There is a need*

behaviour. ◇ **+ noun** *Some interesting research questions are raised by these data.* HELP The plural form **researches**

nouns with different patterns

Some nouns may be followed by a number of different prepositional phrases and other patterns. Each frame is shown in the entry before an example that illustrates the pattern:

study[1] /ˈstʌdi/ *noun* (*pl.* **-ies**) **1** [C] a piece of research that examines a subject or question in detail: *A recent study calculated the effect of globalization on union bargaining power.* ◇ *One study found that having a home computer was associated with higher test scores in reading.* ◇ **~ of sth** *In the 1980s, the political scientist James Flynn conducted a study of IQ test results from 14 nations.* ◇ **~ on sth** *Their studies on spontaneous mutation appeared in 1943.* ◇ **~ into sth** *In a major study into the US retail banking sector, Schneider (1980) noted...* ◇ **+ noun**

Adjectives

Many adjectives can be used both before a noun and after a **linking verb** such as *be, appear, look* and *seem*:

- *a significant increase*
- *The difference is significant.*

For more information about linking verbs, see page R7. See also pages R15–16 for information about noun phrases.

However, some adjectives, or particular meanings of adjectives, are used only before a noun, and cannot be used after a linking verb. These adjectives are called **attributive** adjectives:

- *cardiac surgery*
- *economic development*

Other adjectives are only used after a linking verb. They are called **predicative** adjectives:

- *We are aware that ...*
- *Some people are afraid of ...*

Adjectives in the dictionary

[only before noun] [usually before noun]

Attributive adjectives are labelled [only before noun]. The label [usually before noun] is used when it is rare but possible to use the adjective after a verb.

Sense 1 has no grammar label because it can be used both before a noun and after a linking verb.

popu·lar /ˈpɒpjələ(r); *NAmE* ˈpɑːpjələr/ *adj.* **1** liked or admired by many people or by a particular person or group: *Email is a popular method of communication.* ◇ *Organic farming is becoming increasingly popular in many Western countries.* ◇ **~ with sb** *If changes take place, these may be popular with some employees, but not others.* OPP UNPOPULAR **2** [only before noun] (*sometimes disapproving*) made for the tastes and knowledge of ordinary people: *No other environmental issue receives quite as much attention in the popular press.* **3** [only before noun]

Sense 2 can only be used before a noun.

[not before noun] [not usually before noun]

Predicative adjectives are labelled [not before noun]. The label [not usually before noun] is used when it is rare but possible to use the adjective before a noun.

The grammar label straight after the adj. label shows that all the meanings must be used after a linking verb.

afraid /əˈfreɪd/ *adj.* [not before noun] **1** worried about what might happen; unwilling to do sth because of this: **~ of doing sth** *Some of the participants were afraid of appearing racist.* ◇ **~ to do sth** *The students were not afraid to express their opinions.* ◇ **~ (that)...** *Some Western countries were afraid that their economies would suffer from China's fast growth.* **2** feeling fear; frightened

[after noun]

A small number of adjectives, or particular meanings of adjectives, always follow the noun they describe. This is shown in the dictionary by the label [after noun]:

proper /ˈprɒpə(r); *NAmE* ˈprɑːpər/ *adj.* **1** [only before noun]

use environments as they saw fit. OPP IMPROPER (1) **4** [after noun] according to the most exact meaning of the word: *Urban authorities are making efforts to integrate squatter settlements into the city proper.* **5 ~ to sb/sth** belonging

Order of adjectives

Many adjectives that describe size, colour, age, etc. may be modified by an adverb of degree such as *fairly* or *very*:

- *a fairly recent development*
- *a very small study*

If you are using two or more of these adjectives, put them in the following order:

opinion size quality age shape colour origin material purpose

- ***rare native** species* (quality, origin)
- *The Korean economy is **large and diverse**.* (size, quality)

Adjectives which cannot be modified with an adverb are usually put first:

- ***unique** chemical properties*

Adjectives ending in *-ed* or *-ing*, that are formed from a verb, usually follow adjectives of size, colour, age, etc:

- *a **leading** academic*
- *a white, wooden **ventilated** box*

Adjectives that describe nationality, and those that are formed from a noun, such as *technological* (from the noun *technology*), are usually put next to the noun:

- *two leading **English** philosophers*
- *increasingly complex **technological** developments*

Compound adjectives

Compound adjectives are formed from two words joined together, and are often hyphenated when they appear before a noun:

- ***long-term** strategy* (adjective + noun)
- *a **tax-free** benefit* (noun + adjective)
- ***left-over** electrons* (past participle + adverb)
- ***community-based** organizations* (noun + past participle)

Articles

Use the definite article *the*

with **singular**, **uncountable** or **plural nouns**

- when the person or thing you are referring to has already been mentioned in the text, when it is obvious which person or thing is meant, or when it is the only person or thing of that kind:
  - ▸ *The archipelago consists of 140 islands. Some of **the islands** ...*
  - ▸ *In total, 20 members of the community were interviewed. **The information** was recorded ...*
  - ▸ *He is employed as **the chief pilot** in the company.*

See also Relative clauses on page R20.

with **singular** or **plural** nouns

- with the names of oceans, rivers, deserts, groups of islands and chains of mountains:
  - ▸ *the Pacific*
  - ▸ *the Mekong*
  - ▸ *the Sahara*
  - ▸ *the Seychelles*
  - ▸ *the Dolomites*
- when talking about playing a musical instrument:
  - ▸ *Playing the piano involves ...*

  However, **the** is not usually used when referring to modern music such as jazz, rock, etc.:
  - ▸ *He plays guitar in a band.*

Use the indefinite article *a/an*

only with **singular** nouns

- when talking about an individual example of a type or class of person or thing:
  - ▸ *Gerald Mast's work as **a film historian** helped to establish the field.*
  - ▸ *Gypsum, **a mineral** that is soluble in water, is not commonly found in sand form.*
- in phrases describing frequency and speed:
  - ▸ *Oily fish is recommended **twice a week**.*
  - ▸ *Heads of government meet **three times a year**.*
  - ▸ *If the display is updated at **60 frames a second** ...*

> NOTE *Per* is often used instead of *a/an*, especially with the nouns *frequency* and *speed*: *The frequency of Internet use **per week** ... ◇ a wind speed of one nautical mile **per hour***

- sometimes with *hundred, thousand, million*, etc.:
  - ▸ ***a hundred** acres*
  - ▸ *a temperature of about **a trillion** degrees*

Use no article

with **uncountable** or **plural** nouns

- when you are talking in general about people or things:
  - ▸ ***Money** is supplied by the banking system.*
  - ▸ ***Plants** use photosynthesis to grow.*
- with most names of countries, states, counties, cities, towns, streets and lakes:
  - ▸ *In **Italy**, there are almost 40 000 worker cooperatives.*
  - ▸ *With the exception of **Vermont**, US states ...*
  - ▸ *Pottery production in **Staffordshire** developed rapidly.*
  - ▸ *Among the other rich streets are **Fifth Avenue** in **New York City** ...*
  - ▸ ***Lake Victoria** had a large number of fish species.*
- with the names of religions:
  - ▸ ***Christianity** has its roots in **Judaism**.*
- with a person's title when the person's *name* is mentioned:
  - ▸ *President Obama*

> NOTE Use **the** when the person's title is used without their name: *the President of the United States*

- with the words for meals, months and days of the week:
  - ▸ *Compared with boys, girls ate **breakfast** less regularly at age 15.*
  - ▸ *A peace treaty was signed in **October** 1646.*
  - ▸ *On **Monday** May 1, 2006, over a million people poured into the streets in protest.*

BUT *Trading on **a Sunday** was prohibited.* (= every Sunday)

> NOTE Articles are used when an adjective is used: ***A light breakfast** is recommended. ◇ War broke out on **the following Sunday**.*

- when a place such as a school, university, hospital, court or prison is being referred to as an institution:
  - ▸ *At **school**, Colin had been a star athlete.*
  - ▸ *Today, more children are driven to **school** than walk or cycle.*

> NOTE Use **the** when you are referring to the building or using the name of a particular institution: *We were conducting a project at **the school**. ◇ Lederberg became an assistant professor in **the School of Agriculture** at **the University of Wisconsin**.*

Use a possessive (not an article)

- when talking about possessions or parts of a person's body:
  - ▸ *She finds that shaking **her arm** vigorously relieves the symptoms.*

> NOTE **the** is often used in a medical context to refer to parts of the body, especially when not talking about a particular person: *Refer all fractures within **the knee** to ...*

Pronouns

Personal pronouns

subject	object	subject	object
I	me	it	it
you	you	we	us
he	him	you	you
she	her	they	them

Personal pronouns include **subject pronouns** and **object pronouns**. They replace nouns:

- *Anna is a 30-year-old woman ... **She** may have an early appendicitis. The decision is taken to re-examine **her**.*
- *Stromboli is the northernmost volcano of ... **It** is an exceptionally well-studied volcano.*

Subject pronouns are used mainly as subjects before verbs:

- *When Caesar dominated Rome, **he** made his peace with Cicero.*

See page AWT39 for further tips on using personal pronouns in academic writing.

Object pronouns are used in most other cases:

- in comparisons: in the following example, the object pronoun *them* agrees with the noun *people*:
  - *People often choose those who know more than **them** to join their networks (Dwyer, 2007).*
- after prepositions: in the following example, the object pronoun *it* agrees with the noun *the bridge*:
  - *In tests on the bridge, there was no sway with 156 people on **it**.*

Reflexive pronouns

reflexive pronouns

myself	itself
yourself	ourselves
himself	yourselves
herself	themselves

Reflexive pronouns are used:

- when the person or thing doing the action is also the person or thing affected by it:
  - *Gauss taught **himself** reading and arithmetic.*
  - *The river extended **itself** southward.*
- for emphasis:
  - *Coase **himself** made the implications of his work clear.* (= Coase, not someone else.)
- following a preposition:
  - *Sharing information **about ourselves** is one way of increasing the level of intimacy in a friendship.*

Possessive adjectives and possessive pronouns

adjectives		pronouns	
my	its	mine	
your	our	yours	ours
his	your	his	yours
her	their	hers	theirs

Possessive adjectives are used only *before a noun*. A possessive adjective agrees with the owner, not the possession:

- *She wrote to **her** son.*
- *We plotted **our** original data on photographs.*

Possessive pronouns are used only *without a following noun*. No article is used with them:

- *The island is **theirs**.*
- *The primary decision is **his**.*

Demonstrative adjectives and demonstrative pronouns

Demonstrative adjectives are a form of **determiner**. They are used only *before a noun*.

Use **this** with singular or uncountable nouns, and **these** with plural nouns:

- to introduce something in your text:
  - ***This study** examines ...*
- to refer to something previously mentioned:
  - *The samples were cooled. We then observed **these samples** using polarized microscopy.*

Often, a synonym or a more general noun is used with **this** or **these** to refer back to something that has already been mentioned in greater detail:

- *Government debt fell ... A significant contribution to **this achievement** was ...*

Use **that** with singular or uncountable nouns, and **those** with plural nouns:

- to express your distance from a particular theory, approach, point of view, etc.:
  - *A conventional explanation is ... However, **that argument** makes no attempt to ...*
- to compare your study with an earlier study:
  - *In a recent paper, Gray and Fu (2004) studied the use of ... In **that study**, subjects were ...*

Demonstrative pronouns are used *without a following noun*:

- to refer to something previously mentioned in the text:
  - *Most people want to be healthy. For some people, **this** is an important driver in their life.*

Relative clauses

Relative clauses are formed using either a **relative pronoun** *who, whom, whose, which* or *that* or a **relative adverb** *why, when* or *where*.

Defining relative clauses

Defining relative clauses define or identify which person or thing you are referring to. They are formed with a **relative pronoun**. There is no comma before a defining relative clause.

Use **who** or **that** when the subject is a person. In academic writing, the use of **who** is more common in this context than **that**:

- *This research targets **children who** speak languages other than English.*
- *We analysed data from a sample of **girls who** attended school in urban southern California.*

Use **that** or **which** when the subject is a thing. In academic writing, the use of **that** is more common in this context than **which**:

- ***cells that** respond to hormones*
- ***enzymes which** digest starch and disaccharides*

> NOTE If the person or thing is the subject of a verb in the passive, **who, that** or **which** may be left out. Note that the auxiliary verb **be** is also left out: *Children (who were) born at home ...*

Use **that, whom** or **who**, or **no relative pronoun**, when the object is a person. **Whom** is more formal; **who** may be considered incorrect in very formal contexts:

- *The **people (that/whom/who)** we interviewed ...*

Use **that** or **which**, or no relative pronoun, when the object is a thing:

- *The **research (that/which)** we carried out ...*

Use **whose** to show that something belongs to someone:

- ***A patient whose** BMI is <20 is underweight.*

Whose may also be used to refer to things, especially collective nouns such as an organization, a company or a society:

- ***Organizations whose** pollution can be readily seen will attract attention.*

It is sometimes possible to replace **whose** with **of which** when referring to things. This sounds more formal. Notice the use of **the** with **of which**:

- *A soil chronosequence is a group of soils **whose** properties vary primarily as a function of age variability.*
- *A soil chronosequence is a group of soils, **the** properties **of which** vary primarily as a function of age variability.*

Non-defining relative clauses

Non-defining relative clauses add extra information about a person or thing, which could be left out and the sentence would still make sense. This extra information is separated from the main clause by commas:

- *The leading partner, who might hold a share in the voyage, was known as the ship's husband.*
- *The copper wire, which conducts electrical current, is in contact with ...*

A non-defining relative clause is formed using a **relative pronoun** *who, whom, whose* or *which*:

Use **who** when the subject is a person:

- *Mothers and fathers, **who** must let teenage children have more freedom, face great challenges.*

Use **which** when the subject—or object—is a thing:

- *The Tanner Member, **which** overlooks the Tanner Rapids of the Colorado River, consists of ...*
- *Special observations, **which** I performed with glass tubes, show the two kinds of motion very clearly.*

Use **who** or **whom** when the object is a person. **Whom** is more formal; **who** may be considered incorrect in very formal contexts:

- *The Apache in central Kansas, **who/whom** the French referred to as the Padoucas, were ...*

Use **whose** when something belongs to someone:

- *Lower-level employees, **whose** need may be greatest, often lack access to paid leave.*

Use of the relative adverbs **why, when** or **where**:

- *In certain cases, **when** no formation of petals takes place, each of the pairs of long stamens may take the position of a petal.*
- *In Desta's world, **where** the extended family influnces household decisions, grandparents ...*

Relative clauses and prepositions

In formal written English, a preposition in a relative clause is usually put *before* the relative pronoun. However, in spoken English and less formal written English, it can sound more natural to put the preposition at the end of the sentence.

- when the object is a person:
  - *The majority of the women **with whom** I spoke were ...*
  - *Most of the women I spoke with were ...*
- when the object is a thing
  - *the house **in which** the soldiers were billeted*
  - *the house the soldiers were billeted in*

Word formation

When you are reading a text that contains unfamiliar words, it can help to identify what **part of speech** or **word class** each word is. You can often do this by looking at how the word is formed.

Word class may often be identified by the word ending:

verb -ate -ify -ize
adjective -able -al -ent -ful -ive -less -ous
adverb -ally -ly
noun -age -al -ent -er -ery -ism -ity -ment -ness -ship -tion

Some **verbs** are formed from a noun by adding a *suffix*:

- *exemplify* (example + -ify)
- *strengthen* (strength + -en)

Verbs may be formed from another verb by adding a *prefix*:

- *coexist* (co- + exist)
- *overestimate* (over- + estimate)
- *recalculate* (re- + calculate)

Some **adjectives** are formed from a noun or verb by adding a *suffix*:

- *different* (differ + -ent)
- *regional* (region + -al)

Adjectives may be formed from another adjective by adding a *prefix*:

- *unmotivated* (un- + motivated)
- *disproportionate* (dis- + proportionate)
- *antisocial* (anti- + social)

Some **adverbs** are formed from an adjective by adding a *suffix*:

- *clearly* (clear + -ly)
- *enthusiastically* (enthusiastic + -ally)

Some **abstract nouns** are formed from a verb or an adjective by adding a *suffix*:

- *development* (develop + -ment)
- *intervention* (intervene + -tion)
- *implementation* (implement + a + -tion)
- *difficulty* (difficult + -y)
- *completeness* (complete + -ness)

See pages R38–41 for a full list of prefixes and suffixes.

In the dictionary

Look at the Word Family boxes at some entries to find related nouns, verbs, adjectives and adverbs:

dif·fer·ent /ˈdɪfrənt/ *adj.* **1** not the same as sb/sth; not like sb/sth else: *In Switzerland, he discovered a different type of industrial organization.* ◇ **~ from sth** *Islamic banking systems are quite different from those of the West.* ◇ *Reported intentions are different from actual behaviour.* ◇ **~ from each other/ one another** *These explanations are all so different from each other that it is hard to assess their relative merit.* HELP In British English, **different to** is sometimes used instead of **different from**; in American English, **different than** is sometimes used. However, these expressions are slightly more informal; in academic writing it is better to use **different from.** OPP SIMILAR **2** [only before noun] (of

WORD FAMILY
different *adj.*
differently *adv.*
difference *noun*
differ *verb*
differentiate *verb*
differentiation *noun*

Developing your academic writing

You can build your vocabulary by learning families of words with different parts of speech. This may enable you to express the same idea in two or three different ways and choose the one that is most appropriate. Academic writing uses nouns more than verbs (whereas general English uses more verbs). Consider the following examples:

- *There were significant **variations** in soil pH levels at both sites.*

  Compare: *The soil pH levels **varied** significantly at both sites.*

- *Early **intervention** may prevent the **development** of this disease.*

  Compare: ***Intervening** early may prevent the patient from **developing** this disease.*

- *The prairie has been one of the key elements in the **development** of the region.*

  Compare: *The prairie has been one of the key elements in how the region has **developed**.*

TIP Look at the Word Family boxes. Try using the noun in place of the related verb in your own writing.

Academic vocabulary and collocations

What is 'academic' vocabulary?

The vocabulary of academic writing can be divided into three broad categories. First, there is ordinary general English vocabulary. This includes all the function words such as *the, and, because, for, about*, as well as common verbs and adjectives and nouns for everyday things. At the other extreme, there is specialist subject vocabulary. This differs between different academic disciplines and can be highly technical; typically, students will need to learn these words as part of their subject studies, whether or not they are also learners of English. In between these two extremes, there is so-called 'subtechnical' or 'general academic' vocabulary. These are words that tend to be used across most, or all, academic disciplines; most are also used in general English. However, the way they are used in academic writing is often rather different, which is why these words deserve special study by the student of academic English. It is these 'general academic' words that are the main focus of this dictionary.

Word lists

In recent years, researchers have turned their attention to identifying the core vocabulary of academic English. Averil Coxhead (2000) analysed a corpus of academic English to identify 570 word families that are particularly important for academic writing. The words were selected on the basis of their frequency across the range of academic disciplines. The 2000 most frequent words in general English were excluded, as being already known to students at this level. The 570 word families cover roughly 10% of most written academic texts and together form the Academic Word List (AWL). Words from this list are labelled **AWL** in this dictionary. You can find out more about the AWL on this website: www.victoria.ac.nz/lals/staff/averil-coxhead.aspx

The Academic Word List has established itself with teachers and students as a useful means of building students' vocabulary resources and enhancing their ability to write fluently and precisely about their chosen subject. However, it has also been criticized on a number of counts. One criticism is that the vocabulary and conventions of academic writing do vary significantly across disciplines, and a single word list for all disciplines may not capture all the important words, even at a subtechnical level; this may be particularly true in the sciences.

In this dictionary, we have attempted to address this point by creating four new lists of 200–400 words each to supplement the AWL. These can be found on the CD-ROM dictionary under the 'Word lists' tab, along with the AWL itself. The lists have been developed using the Oxford Corpus of Academic English, an 85-million-word database of written academic language taken from student textbooks and academic journals and handbooks. There is a list for each of the four main subject areas of physical sciences, life sciences, social sciences, and arts and humanities. Within each list, words were chosen for their range and frequency across the disciplines in that subject area. For example, words on the physical sciences list include *atom* and *density*; whilst life sciences includes *cell* and *gene*; social sciences *gender* and *growth*; and arts and humanities *discourse* and *era*. In addition, the 'Word lists' tab also includes a list of the 2300-word defining vocabulary used in the dictionary. These are mostly general English words that students at this level will already be familiar with; but you may wish to check that you know them all, in order to get the most out of your dictionary.

What does it mean to 'know' a word?

The first thing you need to know about a new word, obviously, is what it means. For some words this will be relatively easy, because they carry roughly the same meaning in most contexts, for example *achieve*. Other words have a number of different meanings; many of these may be related to each other, but used in slightly different ways (e.g. *capital*). Yet other words have a quite specific meaning in a particular area of study, for example *significant*, which you may know as a synonym of *important*, but which has a much more precise meaning in statistics.

However, there is more to knowing a word than just knowing what it means. If you are to use a word correctly and effectively in your writing, you need to know how it behaves in context and how it combines with other words. This includes knowing its grammar—if a verb, whether it is transitive or intransitive (= does/does not take an object); if a noun, whether it is countable or uncountable; and if an adjective, whether it is used before a noun or after a linking verb. You also need to know what grammatical structures and complementation patterns a word may take: whether it is followed by a *that*- clause, for example, or needs to be followed by a particular preposition. The dictionary entries give detailed information on all these points; and the other pages in this reference section explain clearly how these features of the entries work for verbs, nouns and adjectives.

Academic writing tends to be rather formal and the normal register of most of the words in this dictionary is formal or neutral (neither formal nor informal). Some expressions are common in certain, more informal types of academic language—talks, lectures, some textbooks, and some types of more personal, reflective writing—but are not suitable in more formal academic writing. An example of this would be *quote* used as a noun instead of the more formal *quotation*. Expressions like this are labelled *rather informal* in the dictionary. Words and expressions that are marked *formal* are very formal, even by the standards of academic writing.

What is collocation?

Collocation is the way in which particular words tend to occur or belong together. For example, you can say:

▸ *The typhoon brought heavy rain and strong winds.*
But not: ~~*The typhoon brought strong rain and heavy winds.*~~

Both these sentences seem to mean the same thing, but in English, *heavy* **collocates** with *rain* and not with *wind*; whilst *strong* collocates with *wind* but not with *rain*. Getting collocations 'wrong' may not prevent people from understanding your text, but it can often make the meaning less precise, and may sound odd. Choosing the right collocation will enable you to express yourself more precisely and will focus attention where it should be, on the content of what you have to say, not on how you are saying it.

Types of collocation

In order to write natural and correct English, you need to know, for example:

- which adjectives are used with a particular noun
- which nouns a particular adjective is used with
- which verbs are used with a particular noun
- which adverbs are used to intensify a particular adjective

Collocation in the dictionary

Collocations are shown in **the example sentences** at the dictionary entries:

re·search¹ AWL /rɪˈsɜːtʃ; ˈriːsɜːtʃ; *NAmE* rɪˈsɜːrtʃ; ˈriːsɜːrtʃ/ *noun* [U] careful study of a subject, especially in order to discover new facts or information about it: *There is a need for further qualitative research in this area.* ◇ *Linguists*

Strong collocations are sometimes also shown in **bold type** before the example sentence at some dictionary entries:

con·no·ta·tion /ˌkɒnəˈteɪʃn; *NAmE* ˌkɑːnəˈteɪʃn/ *noun* [usually pl.] an idea suggested by a word in addition to its main meaning: **~ (of sth)** *Describing migrants as 'illegal' carries connotations of criminality that are often quite inappropriate.* ◇ **negative/positive connotations** *The term 'cartel' has negative connotations, as in drug or economic cartels.* ➲ *compare* DENOTATION

Many of the **key academic words** in the dictionary include a **collocations section**. The collocations are presented at the end of the entry and are organized by part of speech:

This section shows adjectives that typically describe the noun **theory**.

▸ ADJECTIVE + THEORY **modern, contemporary • international • traditional • conventional • standard • basic • general • liberal • critical • scientific • evolutionary • political • economic • legal • moral, ethical • philosophical • mathematical • physical • psychological • normative** *Publicly verifiable evidence is the ultimate test of scientific theories.* | **current, existing • recent • early • competing • alternative • underlying • successful • adequate • explanatory • grand** *Current theories seek to link these ideas to recent advances in molecular genetics.* | **social • feminist • democratic • literary • classical • neoclassical • multicultural • cognitive • psychoanalytic • ecological • behavioural • linguistic • sociological** *Social theory is closely related to the discipline of sociology.*

This section shows verbs that typically take **theory** as an object.

▸ VERB + THEORY **develop, formulate, construct, build • test • propose, advance, present, outline • apply • criticize • challenge • reject • abandon • accept • defend • support • discuss • summarize • review** *I will look briefly at how this theory can be applied, its successes and its limitations.*

▸ THEORY + VERB **suggest, postulate • inform • explain • guide • imply • emphasize • predict • assume • account for • be based on • be grounded in** *Globalization theory predicts the end of the national economy.*

This section shows verbs that have **theory** as the subject.

On the CD-ROM dictionary, there is an additional option of seeing the collocations that apply only to each particular meaning of a word. Click on the 'collocations' button at each sense to see the collocations that are associated with it.

Usage notes in the dictionary

The dictionary provides further help with academic vocabulary in the form of usage notes. These give help with synonyms, easily confused words and particular points of grammar, and also provide useful expressions for performing particular functions in academic writing.

For a full list of usage notes in the dictionary, see pages xi–xii at the front of the dictionary.

Idioms

What are idioms?

An idiom is a phrase whose meaning is difficult or sometimes impossible to guess by looking at the meanings of the individual words it contains. For example, the phrase **bread and butter** has a literal meaning that is easy to understand, but it also has a common idiomatic meaning:

- *Academic targets have become the bread and butter of school management.*

Here, **bread and butter** means 'the main work or business'.

Some idioms are imaginative expressions that draw a comparison with another area of activity:

- *Freeborg (2011)* ***casts his net widely*** *and includes a wide range of sources.* (= He considers a wide range of possibilities.)
- *Gorbachev* ***broke the mould*** *of Soviet politics.* (= He changed what people expected from it.)

However, imaginative idioms like this are actually very rare in academic English, so very few are included in this dictionary. Most idioms used in academic writing are not vivid in this way. They are considered as idioms because their form is fixed:

- **for certain**
- **in any case**

Idioms in the dictionary

Idioms are defined at the entry for the first 'full' word (a noun, a verb, an adjective or an adverb) that they contain. This means ignoring any grammatical words such as articles and prepositions. Idioms follow the main meanings of a word, in a section marked IDM:

> IDM **after the eˈvent** (*BrE*) after sth has happened: *Most accounts of the revolution were collected long after the event and could not be directly verified.* **in ˈany event | at ˈall events** used to emphasize or show that sth is true or will happen despite other circumstances SYN IN ANY CASE: *Contesting a petition is costly and, in any event, is unlikely to succeed.* **in the eˈvent** when a situation actually happened: *The ACE computer had serious problems in development but in the event it proved to be a commercial success.* **in the event of sth | in the event that sth happens** if sth happens: *The father stated he did not want resuscitation in the event of heart failure.* ➲ more at TURN²

The words **after, in** and **any** in these idioms do not count as 'full' words, and so the idioms are not listed at the entries for these words.

Deciding where idioms start and stop is not always easy. If you hear the expression:

- *The design process gets short shrift in this account.*

you might think that **shrift** is the only word you do not know and look that up. In fact, **give sth** or **get short shrift** is an idiomatic expression and it is defined at **short**. At **shrift** you will find a cross-reference directing you to **short**:

> **shrift** /ʃrɪft/ *noun* IDM *see* SHORT¹

Sometimes, one 'full' word of an idiom can be replaced by another. For example, in the idiom **cast light on sth, cast** can be replaced by **shed** or **throw**. This is shown as **cast/shed/throw light on sth** and the idiom is defined at the first full fixed word, **light**. If you try to look the phrase, up at **cast, shed** or **throw**, you will find a cross-reference to **light** at the end of the idioms section.

> **shed** /ʃed/ *verb* (**shed·ding, shed, shed**) **1 ~ sth** if an ani-
> *political leaders do not have the moral right to shed the blood of their own citizens on behalf of suffering foreigners.*
> IDM *see* LIGHT¹

A few very common verbs and the adjectives **bad** and **good** have so many idioms that they cannot all be listed in the entry. Instead, there is a note telling you to look at the entry for the next noun, verb, adjective, etc. in the idiom:

> IDM Most idioms containing **go** are at the entries for the nouns or adjectives in the idioms. For example, **go it alone** is at **alone**. **anything goes** (*informal*) used to say that any-

In some idioms, many alternatives are possible. In the expression **see the error of your ways**, you could replace **see** with **realize, admit** or **acknowledge**. In the dictionary this is shown as **see, realize, etc. the error of your ways**, showing that you can use other words with a similar meaning to 'see' in the idiom. Since the first 'full' word of the idiom is not fixed, the expression is defined at **error** with a cross-reference only at **way**.

If you cannot find an idiom in the dictionary, look it up at the entry for one of the other main words in the expression.

Some idioms only contain grammatical words such as **all, it**, or **one**. These idioms are defined at the first word that appears in them. For example, the idiom **all but** is defined at the entry for **all**.

Idioms are given in alphabetical order within the idioms sections. Grammatical words such as **a/an** or **the, sb/sth** and the possessive forms **your, sb's, his, her**, etc., as well as words in brackets ( ) or after a slash (/), are ignored.

Punctuation

. full stop (*BrE*) period (*NAmE*)

- at the end of a sentence that is not a question or an exclamation:
  - ▸ *There are two main factors to consider. The first of these is funding.*
- sometimes in abbreviations:
  - ▸ *Jan. e.g. a.m. etc.*
- in Internet and email addresses (said 'dot')
  - ▸ *www.oup.com*

, comma

- to separate words in a list, though it is often omitted before *and*:
  - ▸ *a number of economic, social and political issues*
  - ▸ *meat, fish, milk or eggs*
- to separate phrases or clauses:
  - ▸ *If war was declared, Prussia would ally with France.*
  - ▸ *She has four children, all of whom are in their thirties.*
- before and after a clause or phrase that gives additional, but not essential, information about the noun it follows:
  - ▸ *People with fair skin, which tends to burn easily, are at greatest risk.*

  Do not use commas before and after a clause that **defines** the noun it follows:
  - ▸ *The hills that separate Lancashire from Yorkshire are called the Pennines.*
- to separate main clauses, especially long ones, linked by a conjunction such as *and, as, but, for, or*:
  - ▸ *California is not only famous for its earthquakes, but also for its summer fog.*
- to separate an introductory word or phrase, or an adverb or adverbial phrase that applies to the whole sentence, from the rest of the sentence:
  - ▸ *Firstly, the sample was heated to evaporate off the solvent.*
  - ▸ *However, as it happens, studies have proved this wrong.*
  - ▸ *Nevertheless, most people in the city still rely on public transport to get to work.*
- before a short quotation:
  - ▸ *Byron famously remarked, 'I awoke one morning and found myself famous.'*
- before or after 'he said', etc. when writing down conversation:
  - ▸ *'Come back soon,' she said.*
- to separate a tag question from the rest of the sentence:
  - ▸ *It's quite expensive, isn't it?*
  - ▸ *You've seen the nurse, haven't you?*

  Question tags are not often used in academic or formal writing.

: colon

- to introduce a list of items:
  - ▸ *Corrective action includes these options: replacing the school staff; implementing a new curriculum; or reorganizing the school.*
- before a clause or phrase that gives more information about the main clause. (You can use a semicolon or a full stop, but not a comma, instead of a colon here.)
  - ▸ *Shale gas has been known about for a long time: what is new is the technology needed to extract it at relatively low cost.*
- to introduce a quotation, which may be indented:
  - ▸ *As Kenneth Morgan writes:*

    The truth was, perhaps, that Britain in the years from 1914 to 1983 had not changed all that fundamentally.

    Others, however, have challenged this view ...
- to introduce a subtitle after the title of a work:
  - ▸ *The Romans: From Village to Empire*

; semicolon

- instead of a comma to separate parts of a sentence that already contain commas:
  - ▸ *Frequently, the same overall choice is presented, whatever the specific context; either to drive forward economic development, or to protect the environment.*
- to separate two main clauses, especially those not joined by a conjunction:
  - ▸ *These are the facts as we know them; the rest is all guesswork.*

? question mark

- at the end of a direct question:
  - ▸ *Can you identify this quotation?*
  - ▸ *Are organic foods really better for consumers?*

Do not use a question mark at the end of an indirect question:

- *I asked if he could identify the quotation.*
- *Some observers are questioning whether organic foods really are better for consumers.*

- especially with a date, to express doubt:
  - *John Marston (?1575–1634)*

! exclamation mark (*BrE*) exclamation point (*NAmE*)

- at the end of a sentence expressing surprise, joy, anger, shock or another strong emotion:
  - *The plan was a success!*
  - *'Never!' she cried.*

An exclamation mark is not often used in academic or formal writing.

’ apostrophe

- with *s* to indicate that a thing or person belongs to someone or something:
  - *the government's advisers*
  - *the actress's career*
  - *King James's crown/King James' crown*
  - *the student's books*
  - *the students' books*
  - *the women's jobs*
- sometimes, with *s* to form the plural of a letter, a figure or an abbreviation:
  - *roll your r's*
  - *during the 1990's*
- in short forms, to indicate that letters or figures have been omitted:
  - *I'm (I am)*
  - *they'd (they had/they would)*
  - *the summer of '89 (1989)*

Short forms are not usually used in academic or formal writing.

- hyphen

- to form a compound from two or more other words:
  - *cost-effective*
  - *decision-maker*
  - *mother-to-be*
  - *Marxist-Leninist theory*
- to form a compound from a prefix and a proper name:
  - *pre-Raphaelite*
  - *pro-European*
  - *Franco-German*
- when writing compound numbers between 21 and 99 in words:
  - *seventy-three*
  - *thirty-one*
- sometimes, in British English, to separate a prefix ending in a vowel from a word beginning with the same vowel:
  - *co-operate*
  - *pre-eminent*
- after the first section of a word that is divided between one line and the next:
  - *We must decide what to do in order to avoid mis-takes of this kind in the future.*

– dash

- to express a connection or relation between words:
  - *the Dover–Calais crossing*
  - *the Permian–Carboniferous boundary*

In this case a short dash is used.

- in pairs or singly to separate additional details or comment from the rest of the sentence:
  - *When these ten countries were accepted for membership, three others—Romania, Bulgaria and Turkey—were not considered ready to join.*
  - *No damage had been done—or so it was claimed.*

In this case a long dash is used.

- in informal English, instead of a colon or semicolon, to indicate that what follows is a summary or conclusion of what has gone before:
  - *Men were shouting, women were screaming, children were crying—it was chaos.*

This is also a long dash, but this style is not usually used in academic or formal writing.

... dots/ellipsis

- to indicate that words have been omitted, especially from a quotation or at the end of a conversation:
  - *... challenging the view that Britain ... had not changed all that fundamentally.*

/ slash/oblique

- to separate alternative words or phrases:
  - *single/married/widowed/divorced*
  - *In these myths, women are very often portrayed as victims and/or deadly avengers.*

- in Internet and email addresses to separate the different elements (often said 'forward slash'):
  - ▸ *www.oup.com/elt/*

' ' " " quotation marks

- to enclose words and punctuation in direct speech:
  - ▸ *'All of us were afraid,' another demonstrator recalled.*
  - ▸ *I asked him, 'What would you like to do now?'*
- to draw attention to a word that is unusual for the context, for example a slang expression, or to a word that is being used for special effect, such as irony:
  - ▸ *He told me in no uncertain terms to 'get lost'.*
  - ▸ *Thousands were imprisoned in the name of 'national security'.*
- around the titles of articles, books, poems, plays, etc:
  - ▸ *Keats's 'Ode to Autumn'*
  - ▸ *The poet Brodsky translated 'Yellow Submarine' into Russian.*
- around short quotations or sayings:
  - ▸ *It was Alexander Pope who originated the saying: 'A little learning is a dangerous thing.'*
  - ▸ *Money, in Marx's phrase, is 'an objectified relation between persons'.*
- in American English, double quotation marks are used:
  - ▸ *"All of us were afraid," she said.*

( ) brackets (*BrE*) parentheses (*NAmE or formal*)

- to separate extra information or a comment from the rest of a sentence:
  - ▸ *Mount Robson (12 972 feet) is the highest mountain in the Canadian Rockies.*
  - ▸ *Modern music (i.e. anything written after 1900) was not mentioned in the lecture.*
- to enclose cross-references:
  - ▸ *This moral ambiguity is a feature of Shakespeare's later works (see Chapter Eight).*
- around numbers or letters in text:
  - ▸ *Our objectives are (1) to increase output, (2) to improve quality and (3) to maximize profits.*
  - ▸ *An upper respiratory infection (URI) was diagnosed.*

[ ] square brackets (*BrE*) brackets (*NAmE*)

- around words inserted to make a quotation grammatically correct:
  - ▸ *Britain in [these] years was without ...*

italics

- to show emphasis:
  - ▸ I'm not going to do it—*you* are.
  - ▸ ... proposals which we cannot accept *under any circumstances*
- to indicate the titles of books, plays, etc:
  - ▸ Joyce's *Ulysses*
  - ▸ the title role in Puccini's *Tosca*
  - ▸ a letter in *The Times*
- for foreign words or phrases:
  - ▸ the English oak *(Quercus robur)*
  - ▸ I had to renew my *permesso di soggiorno* (residence permit).

Quoting conversation

- When you write down a conversation, you normally begin a new paragraph for each new speaker.
- Quotation marks enclose the words spoken:
  - ▸ *'You're sure of this?' I asked.*
    He nodded grimly.
    'I'm certain.'
- Verbs used to indicate direct speech, for example *he said, she complained*, are separated by commas from the words spoken, unless a question mark or an exclamation mark is used:
  - ▸ *'That's all I know,' said Nick.*
  - ▸ *Nick said, 'That's all I know.'*
  - ▸ *'Why?' asked Nick.*
- When *he said* or *said Nick* follows the words spoken, the comma is placed inside the quotation marks, as in the first example above. If, however, the writer puts the words *said Nick* within the actual words Nick speaks, the comma is outside the quotation marks:
  - ▸ *'That', said Nick, 'is all I know.'*
- Double quotation marks are used to indicate direct speech being quoted by somebody else within direct speech:
  - ▸ *'You told the defendant you loved her. "I'll never leave you, Sue, as long as I live." That's what you said, isn't it?'*

Numbers

Writing and saying numbers

Numbers over 20

- are written with a hyphen:
  - ▸ 35 *thirty-five*
  - ▸ 67 *sixty-seven*

Numbers over 100

329 *three hundred and twenty-nine*

- The **and** is pronounced /n/ and the stress is on the final number.
- In American English the **and** is sometimes left out.

Numbers over 1 000

1 100 *one thousand one hundred*
2 500 *two thousand five hundred*

- A comma or (in *BrE*) a space is often used to divide large numbers into groups of 3 figures:
  - ▸ *33,423 or 33 423 (thirty-three thousand four hundred and twenty-three)*
  - ▸ *2,768,941 or 2 768 941 (two million seven hundred and sixty-eight thousand nine hundred and forty-one)*

A or one?

130 *a/one hundred and thirty*
1 000 000 *a/one million*

- **one** is more formal and more precise and can be used for emphasis:
  - ▸ *The total cost was one hundred and sixty-three pounds exactly.*
  - ▸ *It cost about a hundred and fifty pounds.*
- **a** can only be used at the beginning of a number:
  - ▸ 1 000 *a/one thousand*
  - ▸ 2 100 *two thousand one hundred*
    ~~*two thousand a hundred*~~
- **a** is not usually used between 1 100 and 1 999:
  - ▸ 1 099 *a/one thousand and ninety-nine*
  - ▸ 1 100 *one thousand one hundred*
  - ▸ 1 340 *one thousand three hundred and forty*
    ~~*a thousand three hundred and forty*~~

Ordinal numbers

1st	*first*	5th	*fifth*
2nd	*second*	9th	*ninth*
3rd	*third*	12th	*twelfth*
4th	*fourth*	21st	*twenty-first*
			etc.

Fractions

½ *a/one half*
⅓ *a/one third*
¼ *a/one quarter (NAmE also a/one fourth)*

(for emphasis use **one** instead of **a**)

1/12 *one twelfth*
1/16 *one sixteenth*
⅔ *two thirds*
¾ *three quarters (NAmE also three fourths)*
9/10 *nine tenths*

More complex fractions

- use **over**:
  - ▸ 19/56 *nineteen* **over** *fifty-six*
  - ▸ 31/144 *thirty-one* **over** *one four four*

Whole numbers and fractions

- link with **and:**
  - ▸ 2 ½ *two* **and** *a half*
  - ▸ 5 ⅔ *five* **and** *two thirds*
- **one** plus a fraction is followed by a plural noun:
  - ▸ *one and a half* **kilometres** *per second*

Fractions/percentages and noun phrases

- use **of**:
  - ▸ ***a*** *fifth* ***of*** *the women questioned*
  - ▸ *three quarters* ***of*** *the population*
  - ▸ *75%* ***of*** *the population*
- with **half** do not use **a**, and **of** can sometimes be omitted:
  - ▸ *Only half (of) the respondents made comments.*
- with expressions of measurement or quantity use **half**, not **half of**:
  - ▸ *A spoken word typically lasts about half a second.*
  - ▸ *The patient lost half a stone in six months.*
- use **of** before pronouns:
  - ▸ *Of the 45 included studies, half* ***of*** *them were published in the period 2005–06.*

Fractions/percentages and verbs

- If a fraction/percentage is used with an uncountable or a singular noun, the verb is generally singular:
  - ▸ *Fifty per cent of the land is cultivated.*
  - ▸ *Half (of) the land is cultivated.*
- If the noun is singular but represents a group of people, the verb is singular in American English but in British English it may be singular or plural:
  - ▸ *Almost 40% of the population is/are poor.*

- If the noun is plural, the verb is plural:
  - ▸ *Approximately 10% of the children were classified as overweight/obese.*

Decimals

- write and say with a point (.) (not a comma):
  - ▸ 79.3 *seventy-nine point three*
- say each figure after the point separately:
  - ▸ 3.142 *three point one four two*
  - ▸ 0.67 *(zero) point six seven*
    (BrE also) nought point six seven

Mathematical expressions

+	plus
-	minus
×	times/multiplied by
÷	divided by
=	equals/is
%	per cent (*NAmE usually* percent)
3^2	three squared
5^3	five cubed
6^{10}	six to the power of ten
√	square root of

The figure '0'

- The figure 0 has several different names in English, although in American English **zero** is commonly used in all cases:

Zero

- used in precise scientific, medical and economic contexts and to talk about temperature:
  - ▸ *zero inflation/growth/profit*
  - ▸ *The temperature decreased to below zero degrees centigrade.*

Nought

- used in British English to talk about a number, age, etc:
  - ▸ *To write $2.1 trillion requires the addition of eleven noughts after the '2' and the '1'.*
  - ▸ *the nought to six age bracket*

'o' /əʊ/ *NAmE* /oʊ/

- used when saying a telephone number, etc.

Nil

- used to mean 'nothing at all':
  - ▸ *The chances of controlling any infectious disease would be practically nil.*

Temperature

- The Celsius or centigrade (°C) scale is officially used in Britain and for scientific purposes in the US:
  - ▸ *The average temperature is 25.3 degrees Celsius.*
  - ▸ *Once the temperature reaches 0°C, the liquid becomes more stable.*
- The Fahrenheit (°F) scale is used in all other contexts in the US and is also still commonly used in Britain:
  - ▸ *Global temperatures soared by about 14°F in about a decade (Mithin, 2003).*

Writing and saying dates

British English

- ▸ *14 October 1998 or 14th October 1998 (14/10/98)*
- ▸ *The policy was launched on **the** eighteenth **of** May.*
- ▸ *The policy was launched on May **the** eighteenth.*

American English

- ▸ *October 14, 1998 (10/14/98)*
- ▸ *The policy was launched May 18th.*

Years

1999	*nineteen ninety-nine*
1608	*sixteen o eight* (or, less commonly, *nineteen <u>hundred</u> and ninety-nine and sixteen <u>hundred</u> and eight)*
1700	*seventeen hundred*
2000	*(the year) two thousand*
2002	*two thousand and two*
2015	*twenty fifteen*

AD 76 / A.D. 76	*AD seventy-six*
76 CE / 76 C.E.	*seventy-six CE*

(Both these expressions mean '76 years after the beginning of the Christian calendar'.)

1000 BC / 1000 B.C.	one thousand BC
1000 BCE / 1000 B.C.E	one thousand BCE

(Both these expressions mean '1000 years before the beginning of the Christian calendar'.)

Age

- when saying a person's age, use only numbers:
  - ▸ *In the UK, one in five Internet users is over 55.*
  - ▸ *He was eighteen at the time of the offence.*
- a man/woman/boy/girl, etc. of ...
  - ▸ *At his coronation Henry II was a formidable young man of 21.*

- in writing, in descriptions or to emphasize sb's age use … **years old**:
  - ▸ *Most of the respondents are aged 20–29 years old (54.5%).*
  - ▸ *He was tall and lean and appeared only about 25 years old.*
  - ▸ *Alexander III was only twenty years old at the time of his father's death.*
- … **years old** is also used for things:
  - ▸ *The caves are at least 2 million years old.*
- You can also say **a … year-old/month-old/ week-old**, etc:
  - ▸ *One in ten 6-year-olds were classed as obese.*
  - ▸ *They had an 11-month-old child.*
- You can also use … **years of age**:
  - ▸ *The legal age of cigarette purchase increased from 16 to 18 years of age.*
- Use **the … age group** to talk about people between certain ages:
  - ▸ *78.4% of all injuries were in the 14–17 age group.*
- To give the approximate age of a person:
  - ▸ 13–19 *in his/her teens*
  - ▸ 21–29 *in his/her twenties*
  - ▸ 31–33 *in his/her early thirties*
  - ▸ 34–36 *in his/her mid thirties*
  - ▸ 37–39 *in his/her late thirties*
- To refer to a particular event you can use **at/by/ before**, etc. **the age of …**
  - ▸ *Most people affected die before the age of 50.*
  - ▸ *Most secondary teeth are usually present by the age of 14 years.*

Numbers in time

- There is often more than one way of telling the time:

Half hours

6:30 *six thirty*
half past six (*BrE*)

Other times

5:45	*five forty-five*	*(a) quarter to six* (*BrE*) *(a) quarter to/of six* (*NAmE*)
2:15	*two fifteen*	*(a) quarter past two* (*BrE*) *(a) quarter after two* (*NAmE*)
1:10	*one ten*	*ten past one* (*BrE*) *ten after one* (*NAmE*)
3:05	*three o five*	*five past three* (*BrE*) *five after three* (*NAmE*)
1:55	*one fifty-five*	*five to two* (*BrE*) *five to/of two* (*NAmE*)

- with 5, 10, 20 and 25 the word **minutes** is not necessary with **past/after** or **to/of**, but it is used with other numbers:
  - ▸ *10.25 twenty-five past/after ten*
  - ▸ *10.17 seventeen* ***minutes*** *past/after ten*
- use **o'clock** only for whole hours:
  - ▸ *It's three o'clock.*
- If it is necessary to specify the time of day, use **in the morning, in the afternoon, in the evening** or **at night**.
- **a.m.** = in the morning or after midnight
  p.m. = in the afternoon, in the evening or before midnight
  - ▸ *Significant numbers of students at all schools left home before 7 a.m.*

Do not use **o'clock** with **a.m.** or **p.m.**:

- ▸ ~~*The website was mostly viewed between 10 o'clock a.m. and 6 o'clock p.m.*~~
- ▸ *The website was mostly viewed between 10 o'clock in the morning and 6 o'clock in the evening.*

Twenty-four hour clock

- used for military purposes and in some other particular contexts, for example on train timetables in Britain:
  - ▸ 13:52 *thirteen fifty-two* (*1:52 p.m.*)
  - ▸ 22:30 *twenty-two thirty* (*10:30 p.m.*)
- for military purposes whole hours are said as **hundred hours**:
  - ▸ 0400 *(o) four hundred hours* (*4 a.m.*)
  - ▸ 2400 *twenty four hundred hours* (*midnight*)

Expressing time

- When referring to days, weeks, etc. in the past, present and future, the following expressions are used, speaking from a point of view in the present:

	past	present	future
morning	*yesterday morning*	*this morning*	*tomorrow morning*
afternoon	*yesterday afternoon*	*this afternoon*	*tomorrow afternoon*
evening	*yesterday evening*	*this evening*	*tomorrow evening*
night	*last night*	*tonight*	*tomorrow night*
day	*yesterday*	*today*	*tomorrow*
week	*last week*	*this week*	*next week*
month	*last month*	*this month*	*next month*
year	*last year*	*this year*	*next year*

- To talk about a time further back in the past or further forward in the future use:

past	future
the day before yesterday	*the day after tomorrow*
the week/month/year before last	*the week/month/year after next*
two days/weeks, etc. ago	*in two days/weeks, etc. time*

- To talk about sth that happens regularly use expressions with **every**:
  - ▸ *Bad harvests occurred on average **every third** year.*
  - ▸ *He trained in the gym **every other** day (= every second day).*
- In British English a period of two weeks is a **fortnight**:
  - ▸ *The patient was seen by the surgeons within a **fortnight**.*

Prepositions of time

in (the)

parts of the day (not night)	*in the morning(s), in the evening(s), etc.*
months	*in February*
seasons	*in (the) summer*
years	*in 1995*
decades	*in the 1920s*
centuries	*in the 20th century*

at (the)

clock time	*at 5 o'clock* *at 7.45 p.m.*
night	*at night*
holiday periods	*at Christmas*
	at the weekend (BrE)

on (the)

days of the week	*on Saturdays*
dates	*on (the) 20th (of) May (NAmE also on May 20th)*
particular days	*on Good Friday*
	on New Year's Day
	on her birthday
	on the following day

Numbers in measurement in Britain and America

Both metric and non-metric systems of measurement are used in many cases, especially in the UK. Often the choice depends on the speaker or the situation. In the UK, the metric system is used on packaging and for displaying prices by weight or measurement in shops. In the US, in many contexts, non-metric measures are more commonly used. However, in a scientific context, SI units are always used (see below).

Item being measured	Unit of measurement	Examples
length of time	**hours (hrs)**	*The interviews lasted approximately 1 hour.*
	minutes (mins)	*Within 10 minutes the blood pressure had returned to normal.*
	seconds (secs)	*Total collecting time was 3 minutes, 20 seconds.*
	milliseconds	*Each set of operations lasted less than 4 milliseconds.*
height	**feet and inches**	*The marble statue is twenty feet high.*
	metres and centimetres	*The dam is more than two kilometres wide and 185 metres high.* *The individual is 120 kg and 180 cm tall.*
distance	**miles**	*100 students were selected from within 15 miles of Pittsburgh.* *The vehicle was shown to have travelled for 11 kilometres.*
	kilometres	*The light has to travel a distance of 3 metres.*
	metres	

Item being measured	Unit of measurement	Examples
length	**miles**	*The camera was on a cable two and a half miles long.*
	feet and **inches**	*Rats of up to four inches in length were found.*
	kilometres	*The Austrian stretch of the Danube is 351 km in length.*
	metres and **centimetres**	*The total length of the bridge is 414 m.*
speed	**miles per hour (mph)**	*Wind speeds reached over 150 miles per hour.*
	kilometres / metres per hour, second, etc.	*Most of the vehicles were at speeds in the range 90–110 kph.* *The velocity is about one and a half kilometres per second.*
distance in sport	**metres**	*a 100-metre sprint*
area of land	**acres / hectares**	*The area under cultivation increased from 5 to 9 million acres.* *Few farms in the area had more than two hectares of land.*
	square metres	*The office buildings will take up 11 000 square metres of land.*
regions or areas of a country	**square miles**	*The flooding spanned over nine square miles of the city.*
	square kilometres	*The state covered 108 808 square kilometres of land.*
area of a room / garden, etc.	**square yards / feet**	*The cooperative opened a new store of 8 000 square feet.*
	square metres	*A manager typically has an office of 20 to 30 square metres.*
	... by ... (... × ...)	*The wound was 6 cm by 4 cm in size.*
volume	**cubic metres**	*The volume of gas imported into the EU in 2007 was 312 billion cubic metres.*
	cubic centimetres	*Concentrations are often expressed in molecules per cubic centimetre.*
	cubic feet	*Gas production reached 1.8 trillion cubic feet per year.*
weight	**tons / tonnes**	*Global cocoa production is over 3 million tonnes per year.*
	pounds and **ounces**	*The device weighs just over 4 ounces.*
	kilograms and **grams**	*Density is expressed in kilograms per cubic metre.* *Ten grams of the solute is dissolved in 50 cm³ of water.*
weight of a person	**stones** and **pounds** (UK)	*She weighs 8 st 10 lb.* *He feels lethargic and has lost about half a stone in weight.*
	pounds only (US)	*He is six feet, five inches tall and weighs over 300 pounds.*
	pounds and **ounces** (for a baby)	*Each baby weighed between 3 pounds 7 ounces and 3 pounds 15 ounces.*
	kilograms	*The boy weighs 13.5 kg and is 90 cm tall.* *The baby weighs 8 kg and is 68 cm long.*
drinks	**litres / centilitres**	*The world market for soft drinks is about 500 billion litres.*
other liquids	**litres**	*Water is charged at a fixed price per litre.*
	gallons	*The plant was designed to process 30 million gallons of seawater a day.*
	millilitres	*Fifteen millilitres of blood was collected from each subject.*
petrol (*BrE*) (*NAmE* gasoline) / diesel	**litres** (UK)	*The average price of a litre of petrol has risen by 21%.*
	gallons (US)	*A new sports utility vehicle averages 22 miles per gallon.*

SI units

In scientific contexts, the **International System of Units** (**SI units**) is used in both the US and the UK. It is a metric system consisting of seven **base units**. These **base units** are then used to form **derived units**. So, for example, *the metre* and *the second* are two base units, and can be used to create the **derived unit** *metres per second*. There are also a number of **derived units** that have their own special names, such as *joule*, which is the unit of energy. This system also includes a set of prefixes that indicate multiplication by different factors of ten.

Units

Base units	Physical Quantity	Name	Symbol
	length	**metre** / ˈmiːtə(r); *NAmE* ˈmiːtər/	m
	mass	**kilogram** / ˈkɪləɡræm/	kg
	time	**second** / ˈsekənd/	s
	electric current	**ampere** / ˈæmpeə(r); *NAmE* ˈæmpɪr; -per/	A
	thermodynamic temperature	**kelvin** / ˈkelvɪn /	K
	luminous intensity	**candela** / kænˈdelə; kænˈdiːlə; ˈkændɪlə/	cd
	amount of substance	**mole** /məʊl; *NAmE* moʊl/	mol
Derived units	**Physical Quantity**	**Name**	**Symbol**
	frequency	**hertz** /hɜːts; *NAmE* hɜːrts/	Hz
	force, weight	**newton** /ˈnjuːtən; *NAmE* ˈnuːtən/	N
	energy, work, heat	**joule** /dʒuːl/	J
	electrical power	**watt** / wɒt; *NAmE* wɑːt/	W
	force of an electric current	**volt** /vəʊlt; vɒlt; *NAmE* voʊlt/	V
	electrical resistance	**ohm** /əʊm; *NAmE* oʊm/	Ω
	temperature	**degree Celsius** /dɪˌɡri ˈselsiəs/	°C

Prefixes

Multiple	Prefix	Symbol
10	**deca**- /ˈdekə/	da
10^{2}	**hecto**- /ˈhektəʊ; *NAmE* -toʊ/	h
10^{3}	**kilo**- /ˈkɪləʊ; *NAmE* -loʊ/	k
10^{6}	**mega**- /ˈmeɡə/	M
10^{9}	**giga**- /ˈɡɪɡə; ˈdʒɪɡə/	G
10^{12}	**tera**- /ˈterə/	T
10^{15}	**peta**- /ˈpetə/	P
10^{18}	**exa**- /ˈeksə/	E
10^{21}	**zetta**- /ˈzetə/	Z
10^{24}	**yotta**- /ˈjɒtə; *NAmE* ˈjɑːtə/	Y

Sub-multiple	Prefix	Symbol
10^{-1}	**deci**- /ˈdesɪ/	d
10^{-2}	**centi**- /ˈsentɪ/	c
10^{-3}	**milli**- /ˈmɪli/	m
10^{-6}	**micro**- /ˈmaɪkrəʊ; *NAmE* -kroʊ/	μ
10^{-9}	**nano**- /ˈnænəʊ; *NAmE* -noʊ/	n
10^{-12}	**pico**- /ˈpiːkəʊ; ˈpaɪkəʊ-; *NAmE* -koʊ/	p
10^{-15}	**femto**- /ˈfemtəʊ; *NAmE* -toʊ/	f
10^{-18}	**atto**- /ˈætəʊ; *NAmE* -toʊ/	a
10^{-21}	**zepto**- /ˈzeptəʊ; *NAmE* -toʊ/	z
10^{-24}	**yocto**- /ˈjɒktəʊ; *NAmE* ˈjɑːktoʊ/	y

Geographical names

These lists show the spelling and pronunciation of geographical names.

If a country has different words for the country, adjective and person, all are given, (e.g. **Denmark**; Danish, **a Dane**). To make the plural of a word for a person from a particular country, add -s, except for Swiss and for words ending in **-ese** (e.g. Japanese), which stay the same, and for words that end in **-man** or **-woman**, which change to **-men** or **-women**.

(Inclusion in this list does not imply status as a sovereign state.)

Noun	Adjective, Person
Afghanistan /æfˈɡænɪstɑːn; -stæn/	Afghan /ˈæfɡæn/
Africa /ˈæfrɪkə/	African /ˈæfrɪkən/
Albania /ælˈbeɪniə/	Albanian /ælˈbeɪniən/
Algeria /ælˈdʒɪəriə; *NAmE* -ˈdʒɪr-/	Algerian /ælˈdʒɪəriən; *NAmE* -ˈdʒɪr-/
America /əˈmerɪkə/	American /əˈmerɪkən/
Andorra /ænˈdɔːrə/	Andorran /ænˈdɔːrən/
Angola /æŋˈɡəʊlə; *NAmE* -ˈɡoʊ-/	Angolan /æŋˈɡəʊlən; *NAmE* -ˈɡoʊ-/
Antarctica /ænˈtɑːktɪkə; *NAmE* -ˈtɑːrk-/	Antarctic /ænˈtɑːktɪk; *NAmE* -ˈtɑːrk-/
Antigua and Barbuda /ænˌtiːɡə ən bɑːˈbjuːdə; *NAmE* bɑːrˈb-/	Antiguan /ænˈtiːɡən/ Barbudan /bɑːˈbjuːdən; *NAmE* bɑːrˈb-/
(the) Arctic /ˌɑːktɪk; *NAmE* ˌɑːrktɪk/	Arctic /ˈɑːktɪk; *NAmE* ˈɑːrk-/
Argentina /ˌɑːdʒənˈtiːnə; *NAmE* ˌɑːrdʒ-/	Argentinian /ˌɑːdʒənˈtɪniən; *NAmE* ˌɑːrdʒ-/ Argentine /ˈɑːdʒəntaɪn; *NAmE* ˈɑːrdʒ-/
Armenia /ɑːˈmiːniə; *NAmE* ɑːrˈm-/	Armenian /ɑːˈmiːniən; *NAmE* ɑːrˈm-/
Asia /ˈeɪʒə; ˈeɪʃə/	Asian /ˈeɪʒn; ˈeɪʃn/
Australia /ɒˈstreɪliə; *NAmE* ɔːˈs-/	Australian /ɒˈstreɪliən; *NAmE* ɔːˈs-/
Austria /ˈɒstriə; *NAmE* ˈɔːs-/	Austrian /ˈɒstriən; *NAmE* ˈɔːs-/
Azerbaijan /ˌæzəbaɪˈdʒɑːn; *NAmE* -zərb-/	Azerbaijani /ˌæzəbaɪˈdʒɑːni; *NAmE* -zərb-/ Azeri /əˈzeəri; *NAmE* əˈzeri/
(the) Bahamas /bəˈhɑːməz/	Bahamian /bəˈheɪmiən/
Bahrain /bɑːˈreɪn/	Bahraini /bɑːˈreɪni/
Bangladesh /ˌbæŋɡləˈdeʃ/	Bangladeshi /ˌbæŋɡləˈdeʃi/
Barbados /bɑːˈbeɪdɒs; *NAmE* bɑːrˈbeɪdoʊs/	Barbadian /bɑːˈbeɪdiən; *NAmE* bɑːrˈb-/
Belarus /ˌbeləˈruːs/	Belarusian /ˌbeləˈruːsiən/ Belorussian /ˌbeləˈrʌʃn/
Belgium /ˈbeldʒəm/	Belgian /ˈbeldʒən/
Belize /bəˈliːz; beˈl-/	Belizean /bəˈliːziən; beˈl-/
Benin /beˈniːn/	Beninese /ˌbenɪˈniːz/
Bhutan /buːˈtɑːn/	Bhutanese /ˌbuːtəˈniːz/
Bolivia /bəˈlɪviə/	Bolivian /bəˈlɪviən/
Bosnia and Herzegovina /ˌbɒzniə ən ˌhɜːtsəɡəˈviːnə; *NAmE* ˌbɑːzniə ən ˌhɜːrts-; ˌbɔːz-/	Bosnian /ˈbɒzniən; *NAmE* ˈbɑːz-; ˈbɔːz-/ Herzegovinian /ˌhɜːtsəɡəˈvɪniən; *NAmE* ˌhɜːrts-/
Botswana /bɒtˈswɑːnə; *NAmE* bɑːt-/	Botswanan /bɒtˈswɑːnən; *NAmE* bɑːt-/ *person* **a Motswana** /mɒtˈswɑːnə; *NAmE* mɑːt-/ *people* **Batswana** /bætˈswɑːnə/
Brazil /brəˈzɪl/	Brazilian /brəˈzɪliən/
Brunei /bruːˈnaɪ/	Bruneian /bruːˈnaɪən/
Bulgaria /bʌlˈɡeəriə; *NAmE* -ˈɡer-/	Bulgarian /bʌlˈɡeəriən; *NAmE* -ˈɡer-/
Burkina /bɜːˈkiːnə; *NAmE* bɜːrˈk-/	Burkinan /ˌbɜːˈkiːnən; *NAmE* ˌbɜːrˈk-/ Burkinabe /bɜːˌkiːnəˈbeɪ; *NAmE* bɜːrˌk-/
Burma /ˈbɜːmə; *NAmE* ˈbɜːrmə/ see also ***Myanmar***	Burmese /bɜːˈmiːz; *NAmE* bɜːrˈm-/
Burundi /bʊˈrʊndi/	Burundian /bʊˈrʊndiən/
Cambodia /kæmˈbəʊdiə; *NAmE* -ˈboʊ-/	Cambodian /kæmˈbəʊdiən; *NAmE* -ˈboʊ-/
Cameroon /ˌkæməˈruːn/	Cameroonian /ˌkæməˈruːniən/

Noun	Adjective, Person
Canada /ˈkænədə/	Canadian /kəˈneɪdiən/
Cape Verde /ˌkeɪp ˈvɜːd; *NAmE* ˈvɜːrd/	Cape Verdean /ˌkeɪp ˈvɜːdiən; *NAmE* ˈvɜːrd-/
Central African Republic /ˌsentrəl ˌæfrɪkən rɪˈpʌblɪk/	Central African /ˌsentrəl ˈæfrɪkən/
Chad /tʃæd/	Chadian /ˈtʃædiən/
Chile /ˈtʃɪli/	Chilean /ˈtʃɪliən/
China /ˈtʃaɪnə/	Chinese /tʃaɪˈniːz/
Colombia /kəˈlɒmbiə; -ˈlʌm-; *NAmE* -ˈlʌm-/	Colombian /kəˈlɒmbiən; -ˈlʌm-; *NAmE* -ˈlʌm-/
Comoros /ˈkɒmərəʊz; *NAmE* ˈkɑːməroʊz/	Comoran /kəˈmɔːrən/
Congo /ˈkɒŋgəʊ; *NAmE* ˈkɑːŋgoʊ/	Congolese /ˌkɒŋgəˈliːz; *NAmE* ˌkɑːŋ-/
(the) Democratic Republic of the Congo (DR Congo) /ˌdeməˌkrætɪk rɪˌpʌblɪk əv ðə ˈkɒŋgəʊ; *NAmE* ˈkɑːŋgoʊ/	Congolese /ˌkɒŋgəˈliːz; *NAmE* ˌkɑːŋ-/
Costa Rica /ˌkɒstə ˈriːkə; *NAmE* ˌkɑːstə; ˌkoʊstə/	Costa Rican /ˌkɒstə ˈriːkən; *NAmE* ˌkɑːstə; ˌkoʊstə/
Côte d'Ivoire /ˌkəʊt diːˈvwɑː; *NAmE* ˌkoʊt diːˈvwɑːr/ see also ***Ivory Coast***	Ivorian /aɪˈvɔːriən/
Croatia /krəʊˈeɪʃə; *NAmE* kroʊ-/	Croatian /krəʊˈeɪʃn; *NAmE* kroʊ-/
Cuba /ˈkjuːbə/	Cuban /ˈkjuːbən/
Cyprus /ˈsaɪprəs/	Cypriot /ˈsɪpriət/
(the) Czech Republic /ˌtʃek rɪˈpʌblɪk/	Czech /tʃek/
Denmark /ˈdenmɑːk; *NAmE* -mɑːrk/	Danish /ˈdeɪnɪʃ/ **a Dane** /deɪn/
Djibouti /dʒɪˈbuːti/	Djiboutian /dʒɪˈbuːtiən/
Dominica /ˌdɒmɪˈniːkə; *NAmE* ˌdɑːməˈn-/	Dominican /ˌdɒmɪˈniːkən; *NAmE* ˌdɑːməˈn-/
(the) Dominican Republic /dəˌmɪnɪkən rɪˈpʌblɪk/	Dominican /dəˈmɪnɪkən/
East Timor /ˌiːst ˈtiːmɔː(r)/	East Timorese /ˌiːst tɪməˈriːz/
Ecuador /ˈekwədɔː(r)/	Ecuadorian, Ecuadorean /ˌekwəˈdɔːriən/
Egypt /ˈiːdʒɪpt/	Egyptian /iˈdʒɪpʃn/
El Salvador /ˌel ˈsælvədɔː(r)/	Salvadorean /ˌsælvəˈdɔːriən/
Equatorial Guinea /ˌekwətɔːriəl ˈgɪni/	Equatorial Guinean /ˌekwətɔːriəl ˈgɪniən/
Eritrea /ˌerɪˈtreɪə; *NAmE* -ˈtriːə/	Eritrean /ˌerɪˈtreɪən; *NAmE* -ˈtriːən/
Estonia /eˈstəʊniə; *NAmE* eˈstoʊ-/	Estonian /eˈstəʊniən; *NAmE* eˈstoʊ-/
Ethiopia /ˌiːθiˈəʊpiə; *NAmE* -ˈoʊ-/	Ethiopian /ˌiːθiˈəʊpiən; *NAmE* -ˈoʊ-/
Europe /ˈjʊərəp; *NAmE* ˈjʊrəp/	European /ˌjʊərəˈpiːən; *NAmE* ˌjʊrə-/
Fiji /ˈfiːdʒiː/	Fijian /fiːˈdʒiːən; *NAmE also* ˈfiːdʒiːən/
Finland /ˈfɪnlənd/	Finnish /ˈfɪnɪʃ/ **a Finn** /fɪn/
France /frɑːns; *NAmE* fræns/	French /frentʃ/ **a Frenchman** /ˈfrentʃmən/ **a Frenchwoman** /ˈfrentʃwʊmən/
FYROM /ˈfaɪrɒm; *NAmE* -rɑːm/ see also ***Former Yugoslav Republic of Macedonia***	
Gabon /gæˈbɒn; *NAmE* gæˈboʊn/	Gabonese /ˌgæbəˈniːz/
(the) Gambia /ˈgæmbiə/	Gambian /ˈgæmbiən/
Georgia /ˈdʒɔːdʒə; *NAmE* ˈdʒɔːrdʒə/	Georgian /ˈdʒɔːdʒən; *NAmE* ˈdʒɔːrdʒən/
Germany /ˈdʒɜːməni; *NAmE* ˈdʒɜːrm-/	German /ˈdʒɜːmən; *NAmE* ˈdʒɜːrm-/
Ghana /ˈgɑːnə/	Ghanaian /gɑːˈneɪən/
Greece /griːs/	Greek /griːk/
Grenada /grəˈneɪdə/	Grenadian /grəˈneɪdiən/
Guatemala /ˌgwɑːtəˈmɑːlə; *BrE also* ˌgwæt-/	Guatemalan /ˌgwɑːtəˈmɑːlən; *BrE also* ˌgwæt-/
Guinea /ˈgɪni/	Guinean /ˈgɪniən/
Guinea-Bissau /ˌgɪni bɪˈsaʊ/	Guinean /ˈgɪniən/
Guyana /gaɪˈænə/	Guyanese /ˌgaɪəˈniːz/
Haiti /ˈheɪti/	Haitian /ˈheɪʃn/
Honduras /hɒnˈdjʊərəs; *NAmE* hɑːnˈdʊrəs/	Honduran /hɒnˈdjʊərən; *NAmE* hɑːnˈdʊrən/
Hungary /ˈhʌŋgəri/	Hungarian /hʌŋˈgeəriən; *NAmE* -ˈger-/

Noun	Adjective, Person
Iceland /ˈaɪslənd/	Icelandic /aɪsˈlændɪk/ **an Icelander** /ˈaɪsləndə(r)/
India /ˈɪndiə/	Indian /ˈɪndiən/
Indonesia /ˌɪndəˈniːʒə; *BrE also* -ˈniːziə/	Indonesian /ˌɪndəˈniːʒn; *BrE also* -ˈniːziən/
Iran /ɪˈrɑːn; ɪˈræn/	Iranian /ɪˈreɪniən/
Iraq /ɪˈrɑːk; ɪˈræk/	Iraqi /ɪˈrɑːki; ɪˈræki/
Israel /ˈɪzreɪl/	Israeli /ɪzˈreɪli/
Italy /ˈɪtəli/	Italian /ɪˈtæliən/
(the) Ivory Coast /ˌaɪvəri ˈkəʊst; *NAmE* ˈkoʊst/ see also ***Côte d'Ivoire***	Ivorian /aɪˈvɔːriən/
Jamaica /dʒəˈmeɪkə/	Jamaican /dʒəˈmeɪkən/
Japan /dʒəˈpæn/	Japanese /ˌdʒæpəˈniːz/
Jordan /ˈdʒɔːdn; *NAmE* ˈdʒɔːrdn/	Jordanian /dʒɔːˈdeɪniən; *NAmE* dʒɔːrˈd-/
Kazakhstan /ˌkæzækˈstɑːn; -ˈstæn/	Kazakh /kəˈzæk; ˈkæzæk/
Kenya /ˈkenjə; *NAmE also* ˈkiːnjə/	Kenyan /ˈkenjən; *NAmE also* ˈkiːnjən/
Kiribati /ˌkɪrɪˈbɑːti; -ˈbæs; *NAmE* ˈkɪrəbæs/	Kiribati
Kuwait /kʊˈweɪt/	Kuwaiti /kʊˈweɪti/
Kyrgyzstan /ˌkɜːgɪˈstɑːn; ˌkɪəgɪˈs-; -ˈstæn; *NAmE* ˌkɪrg-/	Kyrgyz /ˈkɜːgɪz; ˈkɪəgɪz; *NAmE* ˈkɪrg-/
Laos /laʊs/	Laotian /ˈlaʊʃn; *NAmE also* leɪˈoʊʃn/ Lao /laʊ/
Latvia /ˈlætviə/	Latvian /ˈlætviən/
Lebanon /ˈlebənən; *NAmE also* -nɑːn/	Lebanese /ˌlebəˈniːz/
Lesotho /ləˈsuːtuː/	*person* **a Mosotho** /məˈsuːtuː/ *people* **Basotho** /bəˈsuːtuː/
Liberia /laɪˈbɪəriə; *NAmE* -ˈbɪr-/	Liberian /laɪˈbɪəriən; *NAmE* -ˈbɪr-/
Libya /ˈlɪbiə/	Libyan /ˈlɪbiən/
Liechtenstein /ˈlɪktənstaɪn; ˈlɪxt-/	Liechtenstein /ˈlɪktənstaɪn; ˈlɪxt-/ **a Liechtensteiner** /ˈlɪktenstaɪnə(r); ˈlɪxt-/
Lithuania /ˌlɪθjuˈeɪniə; *NAmE* ˌlɪθu-/	Lithuanian /ˌlɪθjuˈeɪniən; *NAmE* ˌlɪθu-/
Luxembourg /ˈlʌksəmbɜːg; *NAmE* -bɜːrg/	Luxembourg /ˈlʌksəmbɜːg; *NAmE* -bɜːrg/ **a Luxembourger** /ˈlʌksəmbɜːgə(r); *NAmE* -bɜːrgər/
(the) Former Yugoslav Republic of Macedonia /ˌfɔːmə ˌjuːgəslɑːv rɪˌpʌblɪk əv ˌmæsəˈdəʊniə; *NAmE* ˌfɔːrmər ˌjuːgəslɑːv rɪˌpʌblɪk əv ˌmæsəˈdoʊniə; *NAmE also* -goʊ-/	Macedonian /ˌmæsəˈdəʊniən; *NAmE* -ˈdoʊ-/
Madagascar /ˌmædəˈgæskə(r)/	Madagascan /ˌmædəˈgæskən/ Malagasy /ˌmæləˈgæsi/
Malawi /məˈlɑːwi/	Malawian /məˈlɑːwiən/
Malaysia /məˈleɪʒə; *BrE also* -ˈleɪziə/	Malaysian /məˈleɪʒn; *BrE also* -ˈleɪziən/
(the) Maldives /ˈmɔːldiːvz/	Maldivian /mɔːlˈdɪviən/
Mali /ˈmɑːli/	Malian /ˈmɑːliən/
Malta /ˈmɔːltə/	Maltese /mɔːlˈtiːz/
Mauritania /ˌmɒrɪˈteɪniə; *NAmE* ˌmɔːr-/	Mauritanian /ˌmɒrɪˈteɪniən; *NAmE* ˌmɔːr-/
Mauritius /məˈrɪʃəs; *NAmE* mɔːˈr-/	Mauritian /məˈrɪʃn; *NAmE* mɔːˈr-/
Mexico /ˈmeksɪkəʊ; *NAmE* -koʊ/	Mexican /ˈmeksɪkən/
Moldova /mɒlˈdəʊvə; *NAmE* mɑːlˈdoʊvə; mɔːl-/	Moldovan /mɒlˈdəʊvn; *NAmE* mɑːlˈdoʊvn; mɔːl-/
Monaco /ˈmɒnəkəʊ; *NAmE* ˈmɑːnəkoʊ/	Monégasque /ˌmɒnɪˈgæsk; ˌmɒneɪˈg-; *NAmE* ˌmɑːn-/
Mongolia /mɒŋˈgəʊliə; *NAmE* mɑːŋˈgoʊ-/	Mongolian /mɒŋˈgəʊliən; *NAmE* mɑːŋˈgoʊ-/ Mongol /ˈmɒŋgl; *NAmE* ˈmɑːŋ-/
Montenegro /ˌmɒntɪˈniːgrəʊ; *NAmE* ˌmɑːntəˈneɪgroʊ; -ˈneg-/	Montenegrin /ˌmɒntɪˈniːgrɪn; *NAmE* ˌmɑːntəˈneɪgrɪn; -ˈneg-/
Morocco /məˈrɒkəʊ; *NAmE* məˈrɑːkoʊ/	Moroccan /məˈrɒkən; *NAmE* -ˈrɑːk-/

Noun	Adjective, Person
Mozambique /ˌməʊzæmˈbiːk; *NAmE* ˌmoʊ-/	Mozambican /ˌməʊzæmˈbiːkən; *NAmE* ˌmoʊ-/
Myanmar /miˌænˈmɑː(r)/ **see also *Burma***	
Namibia /nəˈmɪbiə/	Namibian /nəˈmɪbiən/
Nauru /ˈnaʊruː/	Nauruan /naʊˈruːən/
Nepal /nəˈpɔːl/	Nepalese /ˌnepəˈliːz/
(the) Netherlands /ˈneðələndz; *NAmE* -ðərl-/	Dutch /dʌtʃ/ **a Dutchman** /ˈdʌtʃmən/ **a Dutchwoman** /ˈdʌtʃwʊmən/
New Zealand (NZ) /ˌnjuː ˈziːlənd; *NAmE* ˌnuː/	New Zealand **a New Zealander** /ˌnjuː ˈziːləndə(r); *NAmE* ˌnuː/
Nicaragua /ˌnɪkəˈrægjuə; *NAmE* -gwə/	Nicaraguan /ˌnɪkəˈrægjuən; *NAmE* -gwən/
Niger /niːˈʒeə(r)/	Nigerien /niːˈʒeəriən/
Nigeria /naɪˈdʒɪəriə; *NAmE* -ˈdʒɪr-/	Nigerian /naɪˈdʒɪəriən; *NAmE* -ˈdʒɪr-/
North Korea /ˌnɔːθ kəˈriə; *NAmE* ˌnɔːrθ/	North Korean /ˌnɔːθ kəˈriən; *NAmE* ˌnɔːrθ/
Norway /ˈnɔːweɪ; *NAmE* ˈnɔːrweɪ/	Norwegian /nɔːˈwiːdʒən; *NAmE* nɔːrˈw-/
Oman /əʊˈmɑːn; *BrE also* -ˈmæn; *NAmE* oʊˈmɑːn/	Omani /əʊˈmɑːni; *BrE also* -ˈmæni; *NAmE* oʊˈmɑːni/
Pakistan /ˌpɑːkɪˈstɑːn; ˌpækɪ-; -ˈstæn/	Pakistani /ˌpɑːkɪˈstɑːni; ˌpækɪ-; -ˈstæni/
Panama /ˈpænəmɑː/	Panamanian /ˌpænəˈmeɪniən/
Papua New Guinea (PNG) /ˌpæpjuə ˌnjuː ˈgɪni; *BrE also* ˌpæpuə; *NAmE* ˌpæpuə ˌnuː ˈgɪni/	Papua New Guinean /ˌpæpjuə ˌnjuː ˈgɪniən; *BrE also* ˌpæpuə; *NAmE* ˌpæpuə ˌnuː ˈgɪniən/
Paraguay /ˈpærəgwaɪ/	Paraguayan /ˌpærəˈgwaɪən/
Peru /pəˈru/	Peruvian /pəˈruːviən/
(the) Philippines /ˈfɪlɪpiːnz/	Philippine /ˈfɪlɪpiːn/ **a Filipino** /ˌfɪlɪˈpiːnəʊ; *NAmE* -noʊ/ **a Filipina** /ˌfɪlɪˈpiːnə/
Poland /ˈpəʊlənd; *NAmE* ˈpoʊ-/	Polish /ˈpəʊlɪʃ; *NAmE* ˈpoʊ-/ **a Pole** /pəʊl; *NAmE* poʊl/
Portugal /ˈpɔːtʃʊgl; *NAmE* ˈpɔːrtʃ-/	Portuguese /ˌpɔːtʃʊˈgiːz; *NAmE* ˌpɔːrtʃ-/
Qatar /ˈkʌtɑː(r); ˈkæt-; *NAmE* ˈkɑːtɑːr; kəˈtɑːr/	Qatari /kʌˈtɑːri; kæˈt-; *NAmE* ˈkɑːtɑːri; kəˈtɑːri/
Romania /ruˈmeɪniə/	Romanian /ruˈmeɪniən/
Russia /ˈrʌʃə/	Russian /ˈrʌʃn/
Rwanda /ruˈændə/	Rwandan /ruˈændən/
Samoa /səˈməʊə; *NAmE* səˈmoʊə/	Samoan /səˈməʊən; *NAmE* səˈmoʊən/
San Marino /ˌsæn məˈriːnəʊ; *NAmE* -noʊ/	
São Tomé and Príncipe /ˌsaʊ təˌmeɪ ən ˈprɪnsɪpeɪ/	
Saudi Arabia /ˌsaʊdi əˈreɪbiə/	Saudi /ˈsaʊdi/ Saudi Arabian /ˌsaʊdi əˈreɪbiən/
Senegal /ˌsenɪˈgɔːl/	Senegalese /ˌsenɪgəˈliːz/
Serbia /ˈsɜːbiə; *NAmE* ˈsɜːrb-/	Serbian /ˈsɜːbiən; *NAmE* ˈsɜːrb-/ **a Serb** /sɜːb; *NAmE* sɜːrb/
(the) Seychelles /seɪˈʃelz/	Seychellois /ˌseɪʃelˈwɑː/
Sierra Leone /siˌerə liˈəʊn; *NAmE* liˈoʊn/	Sierra Leonean /siˌerə liˈəʊniən; *NAmE* liˈoʊniən/
Singapore /ˌsɪŋəˈpɔː(r)/	Singaporean /ˌsɪŋəˈpɔːriən/
Slovakia /sləˈvækiə; *NAmE* sloʊˈv-/	Slovak /ˈsləʊvæk; *NAmE* ˈsloʊ-/ Slovakian /sləˈvækiən; *NAmE* sloʊˈv-/
Slovenia /sləˈviːniə; *NAmE* sloʊˈv-/	Slovene /ˈsləʊviːn; *NAmE* ˈsloʊ-/ Slovenian /sləˈviːniən; *NAmE* sloʊˈv-/
(the) Solomon Islands /ˈsɒləmən aɪləndz; *NAmE* ˈsɑːl-/	**a Solomon Islander** /ˈsɒləmən aɪləndə(r); *NAmE* ˈsɑːl-/
Somalia /səˈmɑːliə/	Somali /səˈmɑːli/
South Africa /ˌsaʊθ ˈæfrɪkə/	South African /ˌsaʊθ ˈæfrɪkən/
South Korea /ˌsaʊθ kəˈriə/	South Korean /ˌsaʊθ kəˈriən/
South Sudan /ˌsaʊθ suˈdɑːn; -ˈdæn/	South Sudanese /ˌsaʊθ suːdəˈniːz/
Spain /speɪn/	Spanish /ˈspænɪʃ/ **a Spaniard** /ˈspænɪəd; *NAmE* -njərd/

Noun	Adjective, Person
Sri Lanka /ˌsri ˈlæŋkə; *NAmE also* ˈlɑːŋkə/	Sri Lankan /ˌsri ˈlæŋkən; *NAmE also* ˈlɑːŋ-/
St Kitts and Nevis /snt ˌkɪts ən ˈniːvɪs; *NAmE also* seɪnt/	Kittitian /kɪˈtɪʃn/ Nevisian /niːˈvɪsiən; *NAmE* nəˈvɪʒn/
St Lucia /ˌsnt ˈluːʃə; *NAmE also* ˌseɪnt/	St Lucian /ˌsnt ˈluːʃən; *NAmE also* ˌseɪnt/
St Vincent and the Grenadines /snt ˌvɪnsnt ən ðə ˈgrenədiːnz; *NAmE also* seɪnt/	Vincentian /vɪnˈsenʃn/
Sudan /suˈdɑːn; -ˈdæn/	Sudanese /ˌsuːdəˈniːz/
Suriname /ˌsʊərɪˈnɑːm; -ˈnæm; *NAmE* ˌsʊr-/	Surinamese /ˌsʊərɪnəˈmiːz; *NAmE* ˌsʊr-/
Swaziland /ˈswɑːzilænd/	Swazi /ˈswɑːzi/
Sweden /ˈswiːdn/	Swedish /ˈswiːdɪʃ/ **a Swede** /swiːd/
Switzerland /ˈswɪtsələnd; *NAmE* -ərl-/	Swiss /swɪs/
Syria /ˈsɪriə/	Syrian /ˈsɪriən/
Tajikistan /tæˌdʒiːkɪˈstɑːn; -ˈstæn/	Tajik /tæˈdʒiːk/
Tanzania /ˌtænzəˈniːə/	Tanzanian /ˌtænzəˈniːən/
Thailand /ˈtaɪlænd/	Thai /taɪ/
Togo /ˈtəʊgəʊ; *NAmE* ˈtoʊgoʊ/	Togolese /ˌtəʊgəˈliːz; *NAmE* ˌtoʊ-/
Tonga /ˈtɒŋə; ˈtɒŋgə; *NAmE* ˈtɑːŋgə/	Tongan /ˈtɒŋən; ˈtɒŋgən; *NAmE* ˈtɑːŋgən/
Trinidad and Tobago /ˌtrɪnɪdæd ən təˈbeɪgəʊ; *NAmE* -goʊ/	Trinidadian /ˌtrɪnɪˈdædiən/ Tobagan /təˈbeɪgən/ Tobagonian /ˌtəʊbəˈgəʊniən; *NAmE* ˌtoʊbəˈgoʊ-/
Tunisia /tjuˈnɪziə; *NAmE usually* tuˈniːʒə/	Tunisian /tjuˈnɪziən; *NAmE usually* tuˈniːʒən/
Turkey /ˈtɜːki; *NAmE* ˈtɜːrki/	Turkish /ˈtɜːkɪʃ; *NAmE* ˈtɜːrkɪʃ/ **a Turk** /tɜːk; *NAmE* tɜːrk/
Turkmenistan /tɜːkˌmenɪˈstɑːn; -ˈstæn; *NAmE* tɜːrk-/	Turkmen /ˈtɜːkmen; *NAmE* ˈtɜːrk-/
Tuvalu /tuːˈvɑːluː/	Tuvaluan /ˌtuːvɑːˈluːən/
Uganda /juːˈgændə/	Ugandan /juːˈgændən/
Ukraine /juːˈkreɪn/	Ukrainian /juːˈkreɪniən/
(the) United Arab Emirates (UAE) /juˌnaɪtɪd ˌærəb ˈemɪrəts/	Emirati /emɪˈrɑːti/
(the) United States of America (USA) /juˌnaɪtɪd ˌsteɪts əv əˈmerɪkə/	American /əˈmerɪkən/
Uruguay /ˈjʊərəgwaɪ; *NAmE* ˈjʊr-/	Uruguayan /ˌjʊərəˈgwaɪən; *NAmE* ˌjʊr-/
Uzbekistan /ʊzˌbekɪˈstɑːn; -ˈstæn/	Uzbek /ˈʊzbek/
Vanuatu /ˌvænuːˈɑːtuː; ˌvænwɑːˈtuː/	Vanuatuan /ˌvænwɑːˈtuːən/
Venezuela /ˌvenəˈzweɪlə/	Venezuelan /ˌvenəˈzweɪlən/
Vietnam /ˌvjetˈnæm; ˌviːet-; -ˈnɑːm/	Vietnamese /ˌvjetnəˈmiːz; viːˌetnə-/
Yemen /ˈjemən/	Yemeni /ˈjeməni/
Zambia /ˈzæmbiə/	Zambian /ˈzæmbiən/
Zimbabwe /zɪmˈbɑːbwi; -ˈbɑːbweɪ/	Zimbabwean /zɪmˈbɑːbwiən/

The British Isles /ðə ˌbrɪtɪʃ ˈaɪlz/

Noun	Adjective, Person
(the) United Kingdom (UK) /juˌnaɪtɪd ˈkɪŋdəm/	British /ˈbrɪtɪʃ/ **a Briton** /ˈbrɪtn/
Great Britain /ˌgreɪt ˈbrɪtn/	
England /ˈɪŋglənd/	English /ˈɪŋglɪʃ/
Scotland /ˈskɒtlənd; *NAmE* ˈskɑːt-/	Scottish /ˈskɒtɪʃ; *NAmE* ˈskɑːt-/ **a Scot** /skɒt; *NAmE* skɑːt/
Wales /weɪlz/	Welsh /welʃ/
Northern Ireland /ˌnɔːðən ˈaɪələnd; *NAmE* ˌnɔːrðərn ˈaɪərlənd/	Northern Irish /ˌnɔːðən ˈaɪərɪʃ; *NAmE* ˌnɔːrðərn ˈaɪərɪʃ/
(the Republic of) Ireland /rɪˌpʌblɪk əv ˈaɪələnd; *NAmE* ˈaɪərlənd/	Irish /ˈaɪərɪʃ/

Prefixes and suffixes

Often long words are made from shorter words combined with a few letters at the beginning (a prefix), or a few letters at the end (a suffix).
Prefixes generally alter the meaning of a word and suffixes change its part of speech. Below is a list of prefixes and suffixes with their meaning and use.

Prefixes

a- not: without: *atypical*
aero- connected with air or aircraft: *aeroplane*
agri-, agro- connected with farming: *agriculture*
ambi- referring to both of two: *ambivalent*
ante- before; in front of: *antenatal* ◇ *antecedent* —compare POST-, PRE-
anthropo- connected with human beings: *anthropology*
anti- **1** opposed to; against: *antisocial* **2** preventing: *antidepressant* ◇ *anti-inflammatory*
astro- connected with the stars or outer space: *astronomy*
audio- connected with hearing or sound: *audiotape*
auto- **1** about or by yourself: *autonomy* **2** by itself, without a person to operate it: *automation*
bi- two; twice; double: *bilateral* ◇ *bilingual*
biblio- connected with books: *bibliography*
bio- connected with living things or human life: *biodiversity* ◇ *biotechnology*
by- less important: *by-product*
cardio- connected with the heart: *cardiovascular*
chrono- connected with time: *chronological*
circum- around: *circumference*
co- together with: *coexist* ◇ *co-worker*
con- with; together: *concurrent*
contra- against; opposite: *contradict*
counter- **1** against; opposite: *counterproductive* **2** CORRESPONDING: *counterpart*
cross- involving movement or action from one thing to another or between two things: *cross-cultural*
crypto- secret: *crypto-Christian*
cyber- connected with electronic communication networks, especially the Internet: *cyberspace*
de- **1** the opposite of: *deform* ◇ *destabilization* **2** taking sth away: *deregulation*
deca- ten; having ten: *decade*
deci- one tenth: *decimal*
demi- half; partly: *demigod*
demo- connected with people or population: *democracy*
di- (*chemistry*) containing two atoms of the type mentioned: *dioxide*
dis- not; the opposite of: *discontinue* ◇ *disobedience*
e- connected with the use of electronic communication, especially the Internet, for sending information, doing business, etc.: *email*
eco- connected with the environment: *ecosystem*
electro- connected with electricity: *electromagnetism*
en- (also **em-** before *b*, *m* or *p*) **1** to put into the thing or condition mentioned: *endanger* ◇ *empower* **2** to cause to be: *enlarge*
equi- equal; equally: *equivalent*
extra- outside; beyond: *extracellular*
fore- **1** before; in advance: *foresee* **2** in front of: *foreground*
geo- of the earth: *geothermal*
haemo- (*BrE*) (*NAmE* **hemo-**) connected with blood: *haemotology*
hetero- other; different: *heterogeneous*—compare HOMO-
hexa-, hex- six; having six: *hexagonal*
homo- the same: *homogeneous*—compare HETERO-
hydr(o)- **1** connected with water: *hydrolysis* **2** (*chemistry*) connected with or mixed with HYDROGEN: *hydrocarbon*
hyper- more than normal; too much: *hypersensitive*
hypo-, hyp- under; below normal: *hypodermic* ◇ *hypoglycaemia*
in- **1** (**il-, im-, ir-**) not; the opposite of: *inactive* ◇ *illegal* ◇ *immobile* ◇ *irresponsible* **2** (**im-**) to put into the condition mentioned: *imprison*
infra- below a particular limit: *infrared*— compare ULTRA-
inter- between; from one to another: *interface* ◇ *international*
intra- inside; within: *intravenous*
iso- equal: *isotope*
kilo- one thousand: *kilometre*
macro- large; on a large scale: *macroeconomic* OPP MICRO-
mal- bad or badly; not correct or correctly: *malnutrition*
mega- **1** very large or great: *mega-city* **2** one million: *megaton*
meta- **1** connected with a change of position or state: *metabolic* **2** higher; beyond: *metaphysics*

micro- small; on a small scale: *microbiology* OPP MACRO-

mid- in the middle of: *mid-century* ◇ *midwinter*

mini- small: *mini-radar*

mis- bad or wrong; badly or wrongly: *misconduct* ◇ *misunderstand*

mono-, mon- one; single: *monograph* ◇ *monopoly*

multi- many; more than one: *multicultural* ◇ *multimedia*

neo- new; in a later form: *neonatal* ◇ *neoclassical*

neuro- connected with the nerves: *neuroscience*

non- not: *non-human* ◇ *nonsense*
HELP Most compounds with **non** are written with a hyphen in British English but are written as one word with no hyphen in American English.

oct-, octo- eight; having eight: *octagonal*

off- not on; away from: *offline*

omni- of all things; in all ways or places: *omnipotence*

ortho- correct; standard: *orthodox*

osteo- connected with bones: *osteoarthritis*

out- 1 greater, better, further, longer, etc.: *outperfom* 2 outside; OUTWARD; away from *outpatient*

over- more than normal; too much: *overdose* ◇ *overestimate*

paed-, ped- connected with children: *paediatrician*

palaeo- (especially *BrE*) (*NAmE* usually **paleo-**): connected with ancient times: *palaeomagnetic*

pan- including all of sth; connected with the whole of sth: *pandemic*

para- similar to but not official or not fully qualified: *paramilitary*

patho- connected with disease: *pathology*

penta- five; having five: *pentagon*

petro- connected with petrol: *petrochemical*

phono- connected with sound or sounds: *phonetic*

photo- connected with light: *photosynthesis*

physio- connected with PHYSIOLOGY: *physiotherapy*

poly- many: *polymer*

post- after: *post-war*—compare ANTE-, PRE-

pre- before: *presuppose* ◇ *pre-war*—compare ANTE-, POST-

pro- in favour of; supporting: *pro-reform*

proto- original; from which others develop: *prototype*

psycho-, pysch- connected with the mind: *psychology*

quad-, quadri- four; having four: *quadrant*

quasi- partly; almost: *quasi-spherical*

radio- connected with RADIOACTIVITY: *radiographer*

re- again: *recurrence*

retro- back or backwards: *retrospective*

self- of, to or by yourself or itself: *self-control*

semi- half; partly: *semi-structured*

socio- connected with society or the study of society: *sociolinguistics*

step- related to as a result of one parent marrying again: *stepmother*

sub- 1 below; less than: *subtropical* 2 under: *substratum* 3 making a smaller part of sth: *subdivide* ◇ *subgroup*

super- 1 extremely; more or better than normal: *superpower* 2 above; over: *superimpose*

techno- connected with technology: *technophobia*

tele- over a long distance; far: *telecommunications* ◇ *telescope*

theo- connected with God or a god: *theology*

thermo- connected with heat: *thermodynamics*

trans- 1 across; beyond: *transatlantic* 2 into another place or state: *transplant*

tri- three; having three: *triangle*

ultra- extremely; beyond a certain limit: *ultra-pure*

un- 1 not; the opposite of: *unclear* 2 (in verbs that describe the opposite of a process): *unfold*

under- 1 below: *underground* 2 lower in age, level or position: *undergraduate* 3 not enough: *underweight*

uni- one; having one: *unicellular*

up- higher; upwards; towards the top of sth: *upstream*

vice- next in rank to sb and able to represent them or act for them: *vice-president*

Suffixes

-able, -ible (to make adjectives) 1 possible to: *adaptable* ◇ *flexible* 2 having the quality of: *changeable* ◇ *comfortable* ▶ **-ability, -ibility** (to make nouns): *availability* ◇ *responsibility* **-ably, -ibly** (to make adverbs): *reliably* ◇ *visibly*

-age (to make nouns) 1 the action or result of: *breakage* 2 a process or state: *drainage* ◇ *shortage* 3 a set or group of: *assemblage* 4 an amount of: *dosage* 5 a place where: *storage*

-al 1 (to make adjectives) connected with: *behavioural* ◇ *coastal* 2 (to make nouns) process or state of: *survival* ▶ **-ally** (to make adverbs): *textually*

-ance, -ence (to make nouns) an action, process or state: *appearance* ◇ *dependence*

-ancy, -ency (to make nouns) the state or quality of: *pregnancy* ◇ *transparency*

-ant, -ent 1 (to make adjectives) that is or does sth: *tolerant* ◇ *violent* 2 (to make nouns) a person or thing that: *assistant* ◇ *deterrent*

-arian (to make nouns) believing in; practising: *authoritarian* ◇ *humanitarian*

-ary (to make adjectives) connected with: *budgetary* ◇ *disciplinary*

-ate **1** (to make adjectives) full of or having the quality of: *passionate* **2** (to make verbs) to give the thing or quality mentioned to: *automate* **3** (to make nouns) the status or function of: *doctorate* **4** (to make nouns) a group with the status or function of: *electorate* **5** (to make nouns) (chemistry) a salt formed by the action of a particular acid: *sulphate*

-ative (to make adjectives) doing or tending to do sth: *argumentative* ▶ **-atively** (to make adverbs): *alternatively*

-ator (to make nouns) a person or thing that does sth: *administrator* ◇ *creator*

-ble ➲ -ABLE

-built (to make adjectives) made in the particular way that is mentioned: *purpose-built*

-centric (to make adjectives) (*often disapproving*) based on a particular way of thinking: *ethnocentric*

-cide (to make nouns) **1** the act of killing: *homicide* **2** a person or thing that kills: *insecticide* ▶ **-cidal** (to make adjectives): *suicidal*

-cracy (to make nouns) the government or rule of: *democracy*

-crat (to make nouns) a member or supporter of a particular type of government or system: *democrat* ▶ **-cratic** (to make adjectives): *bureaucratic*

-cy (to make nouns) **1** the state or quality of: *bankruptcy* ◇ efficiency **2** the status or position of: *primacy*

-dimensional (to make adjectives) having the number of dimensions mentioned: *multidimensional* ◇ *three-dimensional*

-dom (to make nouns) **1** the condition or state of: *freedom* **2** the rank of; an area ruled by: *kingdom*

-ectomy (to make nouns) a medical operation in which part of the body is removed: *laryngectomy*

-ed, -d **1** (to make adjectives) having a particular state or quality: *alarmed* ◇ *disorganized* **2** (to make the past tense and past participle of regular verbs): *acted* ◇ *decreased* ◇ *identified*

-ee (to make nouns) **1** a person affected by an action: *employee* ◇ *trainee*—compare -ER, -OR **2** a person described as or concerned with: *refugee*

-eer (to make nouns) a person concerned with: *volunteer*

-en **1** (to make verbs) to give sth a particular quality: *broaden* ◇ *flatten* (but note: *lengthen*) **2** (to make adjectives) made of; looking like: *golden* ◇ *wooden*

-ence ➲ -ANCE

-ency ➲ -ANCY

-ent ➲ -ANT

-er **1** (to make nouns) a person or thing that: *computer* ◇ *consumer*—compare -EE, -OR **2** (to make nouns) a person or thing that has the quality mentioned: *foreigner* **3** (to make nouns) a person concerned with: *astronomer* **4** (to make comparative adjectives and adverbs): *bigger* ◇ *closer* ◇ *darker* ◇ *drier*

-ery, -ry (to make nouns) **1** the group or class of: *machinery* **2** the state or character of: *mastery* **3** a place where sth is made, grows, lives, etc.: *fishery*

-ese (to make adjectives) from a place: *Chinese* ◇ *Japanese*

-esque (to make adjectives) in the style of: *Kafkaesque*

-ess (to make nouns) a woman who does sth as a job: *actress*

-est (to make superlative adjectives and adverbs): *biggest* ◇ *closest* ◇ *darkest* ◇ *driest*

-ette (to make nouns) small: *statuette*

-fold (to make adjectives and adverbs) multiplied by; having the number of parts mentioned: *twofold*

-ful (to make adjectives) **1** having a particular quality: *beautiful* ◇ *powerful* ◇ *useful* **2** an amount that fills sth: *handful*

-graphy (to make nouns) **1** a type of art or science: *geography* **2** a form of writing or drawing: *biography*

-hood (to make nouns) **1** a state, often during a particular period of time: *childhood* ◇ *motherhood* **2** a group with sth in common: *neighbourhood*

-ial (to make adjectives) typical of: *managerial* ▶ **-ially** (to make adverbs): *potentially*

-ian, -an (to make nouns) a person who does sth as a job or hobby: *musician* ◇ *statistician*

-ible ➲ -ABLE

-ic **1** (to make adjectives and nouns) connected with: *economic* ◇ *scientific* **2** (to make adjectives) that performs the action mentioned: *specific* ▶ **-ical** (to make adjectives): *geographical* **-ically** (to make adverbs): *specifically*

-ics (to make nouns) the science, art or activity of: *mechanics* ◇ *physics*

-ide (to make nouns) (in chemistry) a COMPOUND of: *oxide*

-ify (to make verbs) to make or become: *modify* ◇ *simplify*

-ing **1** (to make adjectives) producing a particular state or effect: *encouraging* **2** (to make the present participle of verbs): *acting* ◇ *decreasing* ◇ *identifying*

-ion, -ation, -ition, -sion, -tion, -xion (to make nouns) the action or state of: *addition* ◇ *circulation*

-ish (to make adjectives) describing nationality or language: *English* ◇ *Polish*

-ism (to make nouns) **1** the action or result of: *criticism* **2** the state or quality of: *heroism* ◇ *patriotism* **3** the teaching, system or movement of: *capitalism* ◇ *feminism* **4** unfair treatment or hatred for the reason mentioned: *racism* ◇ *sexism* **5** a medical condition or disease: *alcoholism*

-ist (to make nouns) **1** a person who has studied sth or does sth as a job: *archaeologist* ◇ *scientist* **2** a person who believes in sth or belongs to a particular group: *anarchist* ◇ *capitalist*

-ite (to make nouns) (*often disapproving*) a person who follows or supports: *Thatcherite*

-itis (to make nouns) a disease of: *bronchitis*

-ity (to make nouns) the quality or state of: *clarity* ◇ *purity*

-ive (to make adjectives) having a particular quality: *effective* ◇ *reflective*

-ize, -ise (to make verbs) **1** to become, make or make like: *industrialize* ◇ *standardize* **2** to place in: *hospitalize* ▶ **-ization, -isation** (to make nouns): *individualization* **-izationally, -isationally** (to make adverbs) *organizationally*

-less (to make adjectives) not having sth: *childless* ◇ *useless* ▶ **-lessly** (to make adverbs) *carelessly* **-lessness** (to make nouns): *meaninglessness*

-let (to make nouns) small; not very important: *droplet*

-like (to make adjectives) similar to; typical of: *wave-like*

-ling (to make nouns) (*sometimes disapproving*) small; not important: *seedling*

-logue (*NAmE* also **-log**) (to make nouns) talk or speech: *dialogue*

-ly 1 (to make adverbs) in a particular way: *badly* ◇ *seriously* **2** (to make adjectives) having the qualities of: *scholarly* **3** (to make adjectives or adverbs) at intervals of: *hourly*

-ment (to make nouns) a state, action or quality: *arrangement* ◇ *development* ◇ *measurement* ▶ **-mental** (to make adjectives): *departmental*

-most (to make adjectives) the furthest: *foremost*

-ness (to make nouns) a state or quality: *illness* ◇ *responsiveness*

-oid (to make adjectives and nouns) similar to: *humanoid*

-ology (to make nouns) the study of a subject: *psychology* ◇ *sociology* ▶ **-ological, -ologic** (to make adjectives): *methodological* **-ologist** ▶ (to make nouns): *neurologist*

-or (to make nouns) a person who does sth, often as a job: *auditor* ◇ *negotiator*—compare -EE, -ER

-ory 1 (to make adjectives) that does: *explanatory* **2** (to make nouns) a place for: *repository*

-ous (to make adjectives) having a particular quality: *ambitious* ◇ *victorious* ▶ **-ously** (to make adverbs): *continuously* **-ousness** (to make nouns): *conscientiousness*

-phobia (to make nouns) a strong unreasonable fear or hatred of a particular things: *technophobia*

-scape (to make nouns) a view or scene of: *landscape*

-ship (to make nouns) **1** the state or quality of: *friendship* ◇ *ownership* **2** showing status: *citizenship* ◇ *leadership* **3** the group of: *membership* ◇ *readership*

-some (to make adjectives) producing; likely to: *troublesome*

-th 1 (to make ordinal numbers): *fifteenth* **2** (to make nouns) the action or process of: *growth*

-ure (to make nouns) the action, process or result of: *closure* ◇ *failure*

-ward (to make adverbs), **-wards** (to make adjectives) in a particular direction: *backward* ◇ *downwards*

-ways (to make adjectives and adverbs) in the direction of: *sideways*

-wise (to make adjectives and adverbs) in the manner or direction of: *stepwise*

-y, -ey (to make adjectives) **1** having the quality of the thing mentioned: *guilty* ◇ *healthy* ◇ *rocky* **2** tending to: *sticky*

Abbreviations

This is a list of abbreviations that are used in this dictionary in entries and example sentences, and what they stand for. More information about many of them can be found at the entries in the A–Z of the dictionary.

a/c account

AD, A.D. Anno Domini (Latin for 'in the year of our Lord')

A & E accident and emergency

AI artificial intelligence

AIDS, Aids Acquired Immune Deficiency Syndrome

AM amplitude modulation

a.m., A.M. between midnight and midday (from Latin 'ante meridiem')

anon. anonymous

ANOVA analysis of variance
approx. approximate; approximately
Assoc. association
Asst assistant
Ave., Av. avenue
b. born
B2B business-to-business
BA, B.A. Bachelor of Arts
BBC British Broadcasting Corporation
BC, B.C. before Christ
BCE, B.C.E. before the Common Era
BMI body mass index
BSc, B.Sc. Bachelor of Science
c, cent. century
CCTV closed-circuit television
CD compact disc
CD-ROM compact disc read-only memory
CEO chief executive officer
cert. certificate
cf. compare
chap. chapter
CIA Central Intelligence Agency
cm centimetre
CNN Cable News Network
Co. company; county
col. column
Con. conservative
Corp. corporation
cos cosine
cu cubic
D, Dem. democrat; democratic
deg. degree
Dept department
Div. division
DNA deoxyribonucleic acid
D.O.B. date of birth
Dr doctor
DVD digital versatile disc
EAP English for Academic Purposes
ed. edited (by); edition; editor
EFL English as a foreign language
e.g. for example (from Latin 'exempli gratia')
ELT English Language Teaching
ER emergency room
ESL English as a second language
esp. especially
et al. and other people or things (from Latin 'et alii/alia')
etc. and so on (from Latin 'et cetera')
EU European Union
FAQ frequently asked questions
FBI Federal Bureau of Investigation
fig. figure
FM frequency modulation
ft foot
g gravity
g, gm gram
GB gigabyte
GDP gross domestic product
GHz gigahertz
GM genetically modified
GNP gross national product
govt government
GP general practitioner
GPA grade point average
GPS global positioning system
HE higher education
HIV human immunodeficiency virus
Hon honorary
Hons honours
HQ headquarters
HR human resources
hr, hr. hour
I, I. , Is. island
ibid., ib. in the same source (from Latin 'in the same place')
ICU intensive care unit
ID identification; identity
i.e. that is (from Latin 'id est')
IMF International Monetary Fund
in. inch
incl. including
Insp inspector
IPA International Phonetic Alphabet
IQ intelligence quotient
IT information technology
IV intravenous
J joule
K thousand; kelvin(s)
k, km kilometre
kg kilogram
kHz kilohertz
kJ kilojoule(s)

kph kilometres per hour
L. lake
l line
Lab. Labour
lat. latitude
lb pound
Lib. Liberal
Lib. Dem. Liberal Democrat
long. longitude
Ltd Limited
M medium
m male; metre; million
MA, M.A. Master of Arts
max maximum
M.C. Member of Congress
MD managing director
MHz megahertz
min. minimum; minute
mm millimetre
MP member of parliament
mph miles per hour
MRI magnetic resonance imaging
MS manuscript
MSc, M.Sc. Master of Science
N neutral
n. noun
n/a not applicable
NASA National Aeronautics and Space Administration
NATO North Atlantic Treaty Organization
NB, N.B. take note (from Latin 'nota bene')
neg. negative
NGO non-governmental organization
NHS National Health Service
No. number
OECD Organisation for Economic Co-operation and Development
OPEC Organization of Petroleum Exporting Countries
p page
p.a. per year (from Latin 'per annum')
par., para. paragraph
PC personal computer
PhD, Ph.D. Doctor of Philosophy (from Latin 'philosophiae doctor')
pl. plural
plc, PLC public company; public limited company
PM prime minister
p.m., P.M. after midday (from Latin 'post meridiem')
pop. population
Pt. port
PR public relations
Prof. professor
R. river
R & D research and development
ref. reference
R, Rep. republican
S, St saint
sec. second
Sen. senator
SI International System (from French 'Système International')
sin sine
sq square
St street
St. state
st stone
tan tangent
temp temperature
TM trademark
TV television
UK United Kingdom
UN, U.N. United Nations
UNESCO, Unesco United Nations Educational, Scientific and Cultural Organization
UNHCR United Nations High Commission for Refugees
UNICEF United Nations Children's Fund
Univ. university
URL uniform/universal resource locator
US, USA United States, United States of America
USB universal serial bus
UV ultraviolet
V volt
v, vs versus
VAT value added tax
vol. volume
WHO World Health Organization
WTO World Trade Organization
WWW World Wide Web
yd yard
yr year

Pronunciation and phonetic symbols

The British pronunciations given are those of younger speakers of British English. They are the most general and are not strongly regional. Where two pronunciations for one word are given, both are acceptable. The first one is considered to be the more common. The American pronunciations chosen are also the most general. If there is a difference between British and American pronunciations of a word, the British one is given first, with *NAmE* before the American pronunciation.

Consonants

p	pen	/pen/	s	see	/siː/
b	bad	/bæd/	z	zero	/ˈzɪərəʊ/
t	team	/tiːm/	ʃ	shop	/ʃɒp/
d	did	/dɪd/	ʒ	vision	/ˈvɪʒn/
k	cap	/kæp/	h	hand	/hænd/
g	get	/get/	m	man	/mæn/
tʃ	chain	/tʃeɪn/	n	now	/naʊ/
dʒ	jet	/dʒet/	ŋ	sing	/sɪŋ/
f	fall	/fɔːl/	l	leg	/leg/
v	vote	/vəʊt/	r	red	/red/
θ	thin	/θɪn/	j	yes	/jes/
ð	this	/ðɪs/	w	wet	/wet/

Vowels and diphthongs

iː	see	/siː/	ɜː	fur	/fɜː(r)/
i	happy	/ˈhæpi/	ə	about	/əˈbaʊt/
ɪ	sit	/sɪt/	eɪ	say	/seɪ/
e	pen	/pen/	əʊ	go	/gəʊ/ (*BrE*)
æ	sat	/sæt/	oʊ	go	/goʊ/ (*NAmE*)
ɑː	father	/ˈfɑːðə(r)/			
ɒ	got	/gɒt/	aɪ	my	/maɪ/
ɔː	saw	/sɔː/	ɔɪ	boy	/bɔɪ/
ʊ	put	/pʊt/	aʊ	now	/naʊ/
u	actual	/ˈæktʃuəl/	ɪə	near	/nɪə(r)/
uː	too	/tuː/	eə	hair	/heə(r)/
ʌ	cut	/kʌt/	ʊə	pure	/pjʊə(r)/

- The symbol (r) indicates that British pronunciation will have /r/ only if a vowel sound follows directly at the beginning of the next word, as in **far away**; otherwise the /r/ is omitted. For American English, all the /r/ sounds should be pronounced.

- Nasalized vowels, marked with /˜/ may be retained in certain words taken from French, as in **genre** /ˈʒɒ̃rə/.

Syllabic consonants

- The sounds /l/ and /n/ can often be 'syllabic' - that is, they can form a syllable by themselves without a vowel. There is a syllabic /l/ in the usual pronunciation of **middle** /ˈmɪdl/, and a syllabic /n/ in **sudden** /ˈsʌdn/.

Weak vowels /i/ and /u/

- The sounds represented by /iː/ and /ɪ/ must always be made different, as in **heat** /hiːt/ compared with **hit** /hɪt/. The symbol /i/ represents a vowel that can be sounded as either /iː/ or /ɪ/, or as a sound which is a compromise between them, as in **happy** /ˈhæpi/.

- In the same way, the two vowels represented /uː/ and /ʊ/ must be kept distinct, but /u/ represents a weak vowel that varies between them, as in **stimulate** /ˈstɪmjuleɪt/.

Weak forms and strong forms

- Certain very common words, for example **at, and, for, can**, have two pronunciations. We give the usual (weak) pronunciation first. The second pronunciation (strong) must be used if the word is stressed, and also generally when the word is at the end of a sentence. For example:
  - ▸ *Can /kən/ you come to the seminar?*
  - ▸ *I'll come if I can /kæn/.*

Stress

- The mark /ˈ/ shows the main (primary) stress in a word. Compare **able** /ˈeɪbl/, stressed on the first syllable, with **ability** /əˈbɪləti/, stressed on the second.

- Longer words may have one or more secondary stresses coming before the main stress. These are marked with /ˌ/ as in **abbreviation** /əˌbriːviˈeɪʃn/, **agricultural** /ˌægrɪˈkʌltʃərəl/. They feel like beats in a rhythm leading up to the main stress.

- Weak stresses coming after the main stress in a word are not marked in this dictionary.

References

Model texts and extracts:

Al Najdi K. and McCrea R. S., 'The History of Advertising Design in Kuwait: Post-Oil Cultural Shifts 1947–1959', *Journal of Design History*, 2012, 25(1): 55–87.

Bacon I., Hurly T. A. and Healy S. D., 'Hummingbirds choose not to rely on good taste: information use during foraging', *Behavioral Ecology*, 2011, 22(3): 471–477.

Buys P., Deichmann U. and Wheeler D., 'Road Network Upgrading and Overland Trade Expansion in Sub-Saharan Africa', *Journal of African Economies*, 2010, 19(3): 399–432.

Clarke P., O'Malley P. M., Johnston L. D. and Schulenberg J. E., 'Social disparities in BMI trajectories across adulthood by gender, race/ethnicity and lifetime socio-economic position: 1986-2004', *International Journal of Epidemiology*, 2009, 38(2): 499–509.

Donald B., 'Food retail and access after the crash: rethinking the food desert problem', *Journal of Economic Geography*, 2008, 8(5): 231–237.

Francis M., ''A Crusade to Enfranchise the Many': Thatcherism and the 'Property-Owning Democracy'', *Twentieth Century British History*, 2012, 23(2): 275–297.

Glover K. A., Dahle G. and Jørstad K. E., 'Genetic identification of farmed and wild Atlantic cod, *Gadus morhua*, in coastal Norway', *ICES Journal of Marine Science: Journal du Conseil*, 2011, 68(5): 901–910.

Heidenreich M., 'The social embeddedness of multinational companies: a literature review', *Socio-Economic Review*, 2012, 10(3): 549–579.

Johansson K., Laflamme L. and Hasselberg M., 'Active commuting to and from school among Swedish children—a national and regional study', *The European Journal of Public Health*, 2012, 22(2): 209–214.

Jones M. B., Please C. P., McElwain D. L. S., Fulford G. R., Roberts A. P. and Collins M. J., 'Dynamics of tear film deposition and draining', *Mathematical Medicine and Biology: A Journal of the IMA*, September 2005, 22(3): 265–288.

Lambert W. E. and Taylor D. M., 'Language in the Lives of Ethnic Minorities: Cuban American Families in Miami', *Applied Linguistics*, 1996, 17(4): 477–500.

Luzón M. J., ''Interesting Post, But I Disagree': Social Presence and Antisocial Behaviour in Academic Weblogs', *Applied Linguistics*, 2011, 32(5): 517–540.

Mellander C., Florida R. and Rentfrow J., 'The creative class, post-industrialism and the happiness of nations', *Cambridge Journal of Regions, Economy and Society*, 2012, 5(1): 31–43.

Oesch D. and Rodríguez Menés J., 'Upgrading or polarization? Occupational change in Britain, Germany, Spain and Switzerland, 1990–2008', *Socio-Economic Review*, 2011, 9(3): 503–531.

Porter Y., 'Antioxidant properties of green broccoli and purple-sprouting broccoli under different cooking conditions', *Bioscience Horizons*, 2012, 5.

Raaijmakers L. G. M., Bessems K. M. H. H., Kremers S. P. J. and van Assema P., 'Breakfast consumption among children and adolescents in the Netherlands', *The European Journal of Public Health*, 2010, 20(3): 318–324.

Saitoh K., Hasegawa Y., Tanaka N. and Uchida M., 'Production of electron vortex beams carrying large orbital angular momentum using spiral zone plates', *Journal of Electron Microscopy* (Tokyo), 2012, 61(3): 171–177.

Sato A., Wang R., Ma H., Hsiao B. S. and Chu B., 'Novel nanofibrous scaffolds for water filtration with bacteria and virus removal capability', *Journal of Electron Microscopy* (Tokyo), 2011, 60(3): 201–209.

Schmoll C., 'The making of a transnational marketplace. Naples and the impact of the Mediterranean cross-border trade on regional economies', *Cambridge Journal of Regions, Economy and Society*, 2012, 5(2): 221–238.

Sunley P., Pinch S., Reimer S. and Macmillen J., 'Innovation in a creative production system: the case of design', *Journal of Economic Geography*, 2008, 8(5): 675–698.

Wellwood A., Hacquard V. and Pancheva R., 'Measuring and Comparing Individuals and Events', *Journal of Semantics*, 2012, 29(2): 207–228.

Williams L. K., Veitch J. and Ball K., 'What helps children eat well? A qualitative exploration of resilience among disadvantaged families', *Health Education Research*, 2011, 26(2): 296–307.

Yamashita J. and Okada S., 'Parental Attitudes Toward Public School Education in Tokyo', *Social Science Japan Journal*, Winter 2011, 14(1): 39–54.

The model text on pages AWT8–9 was written by Alastair Ward.

The texts on pages AWT10–23 were written by British university students and were collected by Dr Sheena Gardner and Professor Hilary Nesi at Coventry University.

Research that contributed to the Academic Writing Tutor and reference pages:

Biber D. and Gray B., 2010, 'Challenging stereotypes about academic writing: Complexity, elaboration, explicitness', *Journal of English for Academic Purposes*, 9(1): 2-20.

Bruce I., 2008, 'Cognitive genre structures in Methods sections of research articles: A corpus study', *Journal of English for Academic Purposes*, 7: 38-54.

Bunton D., 2005, 'The structure of PhD conclusion chapters', *Journal of English for Academic Purposes*, 4: 207–224.

Coxhead A., 'A New Academic Word List', *TESOL Quarterly*, 2000, 34(2): 213–238.

Dudley-Evans T., 1986, 'Genre Analysis: An Investigation of the Introduction and Discussion Sections of MSc Dissertations'. In M. Coulthard (Ed.), *Talking About Text* (Discourse Monograph, 13). English Language Research, University of Birmingham: 128–145.

ESRC: Writing your abstract, downloaded 4 August 2011 at: http://www.esrc.ac.uk/funding-and-guidance/guidance/grant-holders/submitting-abstract.aspx

ESRC and EPSRC Grant Proposal Guidelines, in Koutsantoni D., 'Persuading Sponsors and Securing Funding: Rhetorical Patterns in Grant Proposals', in *Academic Writing: At the Interface of Corpus and Discourse*, Charles M., Pecorari D. and Hunston S. (Eds), London, New York: Continuum; 2009: 42.

Gillett A., Using English for Academic Purposes: A Guide for Students in Higher Education: Academic Writing, accessed on 23 June 2011 at: http://www.uefap.com/writing/writfram.htm

Harwood N., 2005, ''I hoped to counteract the memory problem, but I made no impact whatsoever': Discussing methods in computing science using *I*', *English for Specific Purposes* 24: 243-267.

Hopkins A. and Dudley-Evans T., 1988, 'A Genre-based Investigation of the Discussion Sections in Articles and Dissertations', *English for Special Purposes*, 7: 113–121.

Koutsantoni D., 'Persuading Sponsors and Securing Funding: Rhetorical Patterns in Grant Proposals', in *Academic Writing: At the Interface of Corpus and Discourse*, Charles M., Pecorari D. and Hunston S. (Eds), London, New York: Continuum; 2009: 43ff.

Kwan B. S. C., 2006, 'The schematic structure of literature reviews in doctoral theses of applied linguistics', *English for Specific Purposes*, 25(1): 30-55.

Lim J. M. H., 2006, 'Method sections of management research articles: A pedagogically motivated qualitative study', *English for Specific Purposes*, 25(3): 282-309.

Nesi H. and Gardner S., *Genres across the Disciplines: Student writing in higher education*, Cambridge University Press; 2012: 38, 188ff.

Paquot M., *Academic Vocabulary in Learner Writing: From Extraction to Analysis*, London, New York: Continuum; 2010: 5ff.

Robbins J., 2011, *What works in academic email: A genre analysis with teacher and student perspectives.* Masters dissertation, Department of Language and Linguistics, University of Essex. Available at http://essex.academia.edu/JoyRobbins/Papers

Ruiying Y. and Allison D., 2003, 'Research articles in linguistics: moving from results to conclusions', *English for Specific Purposes*, 22: 365–385.

Swales J. M., *Research Genres: Explorations and Applications*, Cambridge University Press, 2004: 226-232.

Swales J. M. and Feak C. B., *Academic Writing for Graduate Students: Essential Tasks and Skills*, Ann Arbor: The University of Michigan Press; 2004: 227, 244, 254 f., 268-277.

Toulmin S. E., *The Uses of Argument*, Cambridge University Press; 2003: 94ff.

University of Oxford, School of Geography and the Environment, *Guidelines to writing a research proposal*, accessed 19 October 2012 at: http://www.geog.ox.ac.uk/graduate/apply/research_proposal.html

University of Reading: *Answering exam questions*, accessed 24 October 2012 at: http://www.reading.ac.uk/studyadvice/StudyResources/exams/sta-answering.aspx